A CONCORDANCE TO MILTON'S ENGLISH POETRY

A CONCORDANCE TO MILTON'S ENGLISH POETRY

EDITED BY

WILLIAM INGRAM

AND

KATHLEEN SWAIM

OXFORD
AT THE CLARENDON PRESS
1972

Oxford University Press, Ely House, London W. I

GLASGOW NEW YORK TORONTO MELBOURNE WELLINGTON
CAPE TOWN IBADAN NAIROBI DAR ES SALAAM LUSAKA ADDIS ABABA
DELHI BOMBAY CALCUTTA MADRAS KARACHI LAHORE DACCA
KUALA LUMPUR SINGAPORE HONG KONG TOKYO

FILMSET BY COMPUTAPRINT LIMITED
AND PRINTED IN GREAT BRITAIN
AT THE UNIVERSITY PRESS, OXFORD
BY VIVIAN RIDLER
PRINTER TO THE UNIVERSITY

INTRODUCTION

BY now we have all grown weary of being told how quickly and effortlessly concordances are produced by computer. This concordance was generated by an IBM 360/67 at the University of Michigan, and while it is true that the computer expanded the prepared text of Milton's English poetry into separate entries and arranged those entries in alphabetical order in a matter of minutes, it is equally true that the editorial preparation of the text, as the necessary preliminary to this dazzling performance, took several years.

This concordance is based on the texts of Milton's poems that were published in his lifetime, on certain authoritative manuscripts of the same period, and in a few instances on later-seventeenth-century texts as well. It is not based on any modern edition of the poems. An editor's task is to make judgements about textual problems, to interpret conflicting evidence, and to produce a readable final text. The task of the concordance-maker, by contrast, is to point out the sources of the problems which the editor has tried to resolve, and to record the ambiguities and conflicts in the data; that is, to serve as an index to the editor's evidence and not to his conclusions.

All of the texts that were used in this concordance have been newly collated, and all the manuscript material read afresh. Decisions about difficult manuscript readings are eclectic, but hopefully never whimsical. For each poem we selected one text as a base text, to be used as a source for citation lines whenever a word from that poem was concorded. Each poem has its own base text, not selected by formula (e.g. 'the latest version published during Milton's lifetime', or 'the first edition in every case'), but by individual consideration. Whenever the readings of an alternative text depart from the reading of the base text, these readings are listed as variants. Agreements with the base text are not noted. A list of the chosen base text and the available variant texts for each poem is given below.

Milton's vagaries of spelling provide no basis for orderly organization of the concordance entries; accordingly, all head-words are spelled in conformity with modern usage, and second entries are provided where required. *Azza* will be found under that spelling as well as under *Gaza*, but *intyre* will be found only under *entire*. In some cases we attempted to discriminate homographs, such as *will*, *well*, *even*, and the like, but our list is far from exhaustive. A more precise statement of our editorial principles follows.

EDITORIAL PRINCIPLES

Punctuation

The punctuation of the citation line is reproduced as it appears in the base text. Differences of punctuation in other texts are not recorded as variants except as they may appear in an entry recording verbal variants. Where the errata notes to the base-text edition call for changes only in punctuation, those changes have been incorporated into the citation line silently.

Italics

Words printed in italic fount are by virtue of this distinction alone considered as variants if they appear in roman in other texts, even though no other difference appears. The final *s* in italicized possessives was conventionally set in roman type: where the only difference between two italicized possessives is the fount of the final *s*, no note is made. In those cases where entire passages (such as the songs in *Mask*) or entire poems (like the 1637 edition of *Lycidas*) were set in italic, we have treated the material as though it were in roman, recording the occasional word in roman fount as being in italic. Except for certain proper names in the manuscript of Book One of *Paradise Lost*, no attempt has been made to record the presence or absence of italic hand in the various manuscripts, or to note that a word written in secretary hand appears in print as italic.

Capitalization

Capitalization in the manuscripts, especially in the Trinity manuscript, is erratic. The first words of lines and of sentences are usually not capitalized. Where this is the only variation from the base text, no note is made. Sometimes manuscript readings are repunctuated in print, with the resultant capitalization of certain words. For example, *Mask* 583 in the 1645 edition reads 'Alone, and helpless! Is this the confidence', while the same line in the Trinity manuscript reads 'alone, & helplesse, is this the confidence'. The uncapitalized *is* in the manuscript has not been noted as a variant, since the capital in the printed version is the result only of altered punctuation. All occasions where a capital or its lack suggests authorial choice are recorded, and all uncapitalized words in manuscript where one might reasonably expect to find capitals, such as proper nouns, are entered as variants.

Misprints

Certain vagaries of the printing shop are reproduced but not noticed. For example, *dislolutest* in *Paradise Regained* 2. 150 is concorded under *dissolutest* and there reproduced in its maimed form, but has no note calling attention to it as a misprint. In the case of common errors like turned *u*, as in *snch* for *such* in *Mask* 15 in 1645, the citation line is corrected to read *such*, and an explanatory note added.

Transpositions

No note is taken of the transpositions of lines in different texts. For example, lines 7 and 8 of *Mask* 1645 occur in reverse order in the Trinity manuscript, as do lines 546 and 547. Likewise, no note is taken of word transpositions; for example, line 90 in *Mask* 1645 has 'likeliest, and neerest' where the Trinity manuscript has 'neerest & likliest'. Though the different forms of *likeliest* are noted, no account is taken of its changed position. Similarly, *Mask* 404 'it recks me not' in 1645, 'it recks not me' in the Trinity manuscript, or *Mask* 656 'Yet will they' in 1645, 'yet they will' in the Trinity manuscript.

Contractions

Manuscript contractions are silently expanded. They are of interest primarily to students of handwriting, since they reflect no firm convictions about spelling practices. We have expanded wch to which, wth to with, $w^{th}out$ to without, y^{e} to the, y^{t} to that, yor to your, ꝑ to either per or par depending on the context, *-cōn* to -cion, *m̄* to mm, $-m^{t}$ to -ment, *frō* to from, initial *ff* to F, and so on. Manuscript *i* and *j* are normalized, but *u* and *v* have been kept distinct. When a manuscript contraction contains a spelling variant—as in *Lycidas* 1645 *perfet*, Trinity manuscript *ꝑfect*—the variant word is expanded and entered as a variant, in this case as *perfect*.

Elisions

The special headings *in the*, *of the*, and *I'll* have been entered to accommodate such forms as *i'th*, *ith'*, *ith*, *o'th*, *oth'*, *oth*, *Ile*, and the like.

Accents and special forms

Lower-case accented *ô* as a variant of *O* is recorded as a lower-case letter with no accent indication given. Diaereses, as in *Faëry* (*Mask* 436) or *aëreal* (*Mask* 3), have been omitted. The ligature *Æ* is recorded as *Ae*, *æ* as *ae*, and *œ* as *oe*. The exigencies of machine typesetting made retention of these forms impossible.

Multiple manuscript readings

One feature of this concordance which may cause the user some confusion if not properly understood is the manner of recording multiple readings from manuscript, especially from the Trinity manuscript. Several poems exist in working drafts, in which earlier readings are superseded by later ones, and in all such instances our endeavour has been to ascertain as closely as possible, and to record as clearly as possible, the sequence of changes leading to the final manuscript reading. For example, in the Trinity manuscript draft of *Arcades* Milton first wrote line 12 as 'lesse then halfe she hath express't', and then in the margin he emended the line to 'wee find express't'. The latter reading corresponds, except for spelling variants, to the reading of the 1645 edition. A user looking under *find* will encounter the following entry:

Less then half we find exprest — Arcades 12
Trinity ms 'wee find' ← 'she hath'

That is, in the Trinity manuscript 'wee find' is the final reading, and supersedes an earlier reading, 'she hath'. A user looking under *we* or *she* or *hath* will encounter the same entry.

Line 10 of *Arcades* shows a larger change, but follows the same principle. A user looking under *justly* will encounter the following entry:

We may justly now accuse — Arcades 10
Trinity ms 'wee may justly now accuse' ←
'now seemes guiltie of abuse'

In this instance the entire line has replaced an earlier line. The entry is repeated for each of the words concerned. All multiple readings are entered according to this principle. An example of a complex entry may be found under *lecherous* in the concordance.

Such a system, because of its simplicity, may be inadvertently misleading in several ways, and the user ought to be cautioned against over-interpretation of the data. Some forms of manuscript correction have not been recorded: for example, when a word has been excised and then restored without any intervening changes, no note is made. In *Mask* 318, Milton wrote *rowse* four times and deleted it three times. No indication of these changes is given in the concordance. Alternatively, some kinds of variants, though recorded, are of minimal significance. For example, in the eighth line of Sonnet Eleven an amanuensis miscopied *then* as *the* in the Trinity manuscript. This change is recorded, but no indication given that it is merely a copying error, or that it is the error of an amanuensis and not a change by the author. Similarly, in the seventh line of Sonnet Twelve a multiple entry may be misleading. Milton wrote *Fee* in his draft of this sonnet, but when his amanuensis copied the poem on to another page he miscopied the word as *fee*, which he then scratched out and rewrote as *Fee*. A user will therefore encounter the following entry:

Trinity ms 'Fee' ← 'fee' ← 'Fee'

No indication is given that these changes are accidents, or that they differ in any way from Milton's own deliberate changes of capitalization as recorded elsewhere. For a proper understanding of these and other changes, the user must of course refer to the texts themselves.

Omissions

We have omitted certain high-frequency words from the concordance, with reluctance to be sure, but with an awareness of the practicalities involved. The user may calculate for himself how many pages were saved merely by not including the nearly six thousand occurrences of *and*. Such omitted words have been held to a minimum: they are *a, and, by, for, in, of, on, the, to*, and *with*. The entries are preserved on magnetic tape at the University of Michigan, however, and scholars who require listings of these omitted words are invited to write the Chairman, English Department, University of Michigan, Ann Arbor 48104, for details.

Passages in prose, such as the stage directions in *Mask* or *Arcades*, or the Arguments prefixed to the various Books of *Paradise Lost*, have been omitted. The speech headings in the dramatic works, such as *Eld. Bro.* or *La.* or *Cho.* or *Sams.*, have been omitted from the concordance as entries, though they appear in the citation line where appropriate. Conversely, fragments of verse found in the prose works have been concorded; see under 'Proses' in the table of individual works.

Not all items of textual interest have been included in the concordance. One example will suffice: there are some marginal corrections, presumably in Milton's hand, in a copy of the 1637 edition of *Mask* in the Pforzheimer Library. These entries correct certain readings in the 1637 text, so that they conform to the readings which later appeared in the 1645 edition (the base text for that poem). These marginalia from 1637 are not entered in the concordance. It seems unfortunate not to draw attention to such items, but since the readings they offer are not variants (though the 1637 readings they correct are, and are listed as such), it seemed illogical to note them.

CATALOGUE OF THE TEXTS USED FOR EACH POEM, ARRANGED ALPHABETICALLY BY SHORT-FORM IDENTIFIER

(A useful source for these texts is the four-volume facsimile edition of Milton's complete poetical works edited by H. F. Fletcher. There are also facsimiles of the Trinity manuscript, transcribed by W. Aldis Wright, and of the manuscript to Book One of *Paradise Lost*, transcribed by Helen Darbishire.)

Allegro
L'Allegro. The base text is the edition of 1645, with variants recorded from the edition of 1673.

Another
Another on the Same (the second Hobson poem). The base text is the edition of 1645, with variants recorded from the versions of 1640, 1657, and 1658, and from the edition of 1673. Italics are reversed in the 1640 and 1657 texts. No collation was made with the manuscript versions of this poem in the Bodleian or the Huntington, as they are of questionable authority: for a discussion of these texts, see *MLN* 57: 192–4.

Arcades
Arcades. The base text is the edition of 1645, with variants recorded from the edition of 1673 and from the draft in Milton's hand in the Trinity manuscript.

Carrier
On the University Carrier. The base text is the edition of 1645, with variants recorded from the version of 1658 and from the edition of 1673. No collation was made with the manuscript version of this poem in the Folger Shakespeare Library, as it is of questionable authority: for a discussion of this text, see *MLN* 57: 192–4.

Circum
Upon the circumcision. The base text is the edition of 1645, with variants recorded from the edition of 1673 and from the draft in Milton's hand in the Trinity manuscript.

Fair Inf
On the Death of a Fair Infant Dying of a Cough. The text is the edition of 1673.

Forcers
On the New Forcers of Conscience Under the Long Parliament. The base text is the edition of 1673, with variants recorded from the draft by an amanuensis in the Trinity manuscript. For an explanation of references like 'Forcers Tr. ms 45.17', s.v. Mask.

Horace
The Fifth Ode of Horace. The text is the edition of 1673.

Lycidas
Lycidas. The base text is the edition of 1645, with variants recorded from the editions of 1638 and 1673, and from the draft in Milton's hand in the Trinity manuscript. Italics are reversed in the 1637 edition. For an explanation of references like 'Lycidas Tr. ms 28.18', s.v. Mask.

Mask
A Mask (Comus). The base text is the edition of 1645, with variants recorded from the editions of 1637 and 1673, and from the Bridgewater manuscript, the drafts in Milton's hand in the Trinity manuscript, the British Museum manuscript of the five songs, and the Milton autograph in the autograph album of Camillus Cardoyn, now in the Harvard Library. Some lines in the Trinity and Bridgewater manuscripts do not appear in any printed version; these lines are marked 'Mask Tr. ms' and 'Mask Br. ms'. Conventional line numbers cannot, of course, apply to these entries; the user should interpret a reference like 'Mask Tr. ms 16.22' as referring to page 16 of the Trinity manuscript, line 22. Fletcher's transcription of the Bridgewater manuscript is not to be trusted.

May Morn
Song: On May Morning. The base text is the edition of 1645, with variants recorded from the edition of 1673.

Musick

At a Solemn Musick. The base text is the edition of 1645, with variants recorded from the edition of 1673 and from the two rough drafts and the fair copy, all in Milton's hand, in the Trinity manuscript. For an explanation of references like 'Musick Tr. ms 4.21', s.v. Mask.

Nativity

On the Morning of Christ's Nativity. The base text is the edition of 1645, with variants recorded from the edition of 1673.

On Time

On Time. The base text is the edition of 1645, with variants recorded from the edition of 1673 and from the draft in Milton's hand in the Trinity manuscript.

Par Lost

Paradise Lost. The base text is the edition of 1674, with variants recorded from the edition of 1667, including those issues of that edition whose title-pages are dated 1668 and 1669, and from the manuscript version of Book One.

Par Reg

Paradise Regained. The text is the edition of 1671.

Passion

The Passion. The base text is the edition of 1645, with variants recorded from the edition of 1673.

Penseroso

Il Penseroso. The base text is the edition of 1645, with variants recorded from the edition of 1673.

Prose 1

Two lines from Dante, *Inferno* xix: 115 ff., in *Of Reformation Touching Church Discipline*, 1641, p. 30.

Prose 2

Four lines from Petrarch, Sonnet 108, in *Of Reformation Touching Church Discipline*, 1641, p. 30.

Prose 3

Five lines from Ariosto, *Orlando Furioso* xxxiv: 73 ff., in *Of Reformation Touching Church Discipline*, 1641, p. 31.

Prose 4

Four lines from Ariosto, *Orlando Furioso* xxxiv: 80 ff., in *Of Reformation Touching Church Discipline*, 1641, p. 31.

Prose 5
A line attributed to Tiberius, in *The Reason of Church Government*, 1641/2, p. 15.

Prose 6
Three lines from Horace, *Satires* I. i. 24 ff., in *An Apology [for] Smectymnuus*, 1642, p. 26.

Prose 7
Two lines from Horace, *Satires* I. x. 14 ff., in *An Apology [for] Smectymnuus*, 1642, p. 26.

Prose 8
Two lines from Sophocles, *Electra* 624, in *An Apology [for] Smectymnuus*, 1642, p. 27.

Prose 9
Five lines from Euripides, *Supplices* 438 ff., in *Areopagitica*, 1644, title-page.

Prose 10
Six lines from Horace, *Epistles* I. xvi. 40 ff., in *Tetrachordon*, 1645, p. 39.

Prose 11
Three lines from Seneca, *Hercules Furens* 922 ff., in *Tenure of Kings and Magistrates*, first edition 1649, p. 18, and second edition 1650, p. 20.

Prose 12
Fourteen lines from Geoffrey of Monmouth, in sonnet form, from *The History of Britain*, 1670, p. 11.

Prose 13
Two lines from Matthew of Westminster, from *The History of Britain*, 1670, p. 186.

Psalms 1 to 8 and 80 to 88
Psalms 1 to 8 and 80 to 88. The text is the edition of 1673.

Psalm 114
A paraphrase on Psalm 114. The base text is the edition of 1645, with variants recorded from the edition of 1673.

Psalm 136
Psalm 136. The base text is the edition of 1645, with variants recorded from the edition of 1673.

Samson
Samson Agonistes. The text is the edition of 1671.

Shakespear

On Shakespear. The base text is the edition of 1645, with variants recorded from the versions of 1632 (three states), 1640, and 1663–4, and from the edition of 1673. Italics are reversed in all three states of 1632.

Sonnet 1

Sonnet 1 ('O Nightingale . . .'). The base text is the edition of 1645, with variants recorded from the edition of 1673.

Sonnet 7

Sonnet 7 ('How soon hath time . . .'). The base text is the edition of 1645, with variants recorded from the edition of 1673 and from the draft in Milton's hand in the Trinity manuscript.

Sonnet 8

Sonnet 8: When the Assault was Intended to the City ('Captain or Colonel . . .'). The base text is the edition of 1645, with variants recorded from the edition of 1673 and from the draft by an amanuensis in the Trinity manuscript.

Sonnet 9

Sonnet 9 ('Lady that in the prime . . .'). The base text is the edition of 1645, with variants recorded from the edition of 1673 and from the draft in Milton's hand in the Trinity manuscript.

Sonnet 10

Sonnet 10 ('Daughter to that good Earl . . .'). The base text is the edition of 1645, with variants recorded from the edition of 1673 and from the draft in Milton's hand in the Trinity manuscript.

Sonnet 11

Sonnet 11 ('A book was writ . . .'). The base text is the edition of 1673, with variants recorded from the rough draft in Milton's hand and the later fair copy by an amanuensis in the Trinity manuscript.

Sonnet 12

Sonnet 12 ('I did but prompt . . .'). The base text is the edition of 1673, with variants recorded from the draft in Milton's hand and the fair copy by an amanuensis in the Trinity manuscript.

Sonnet 13

Sonnet 13: To Mr. H. Lawes, on his Aires ('Harry, whose tuneful . . .'). The base text is the edition of 1673, with variants recorded from the edition of 1648 and from the rough draft and fair copy in Milton's hand and the second fair copy by an amanuensis in the Trinity manuscript. For an explanation of references like 'Sonnet 13, Tr. ms 40.03', s.v. Mask.

Sonnet 14

Sonnet 14 ('When faith and love . . .'). The base text is the edition of 1673, with variants recorded from the draft and fair copy in Milton's hand and the second fair copy by an amanuensis in the Trinity manuscript. For an explanation of references like 'Sonnet 14, Tr. ms 41.06', s.v. Mask.

Sonnet 15

Sonnet 15: On the Lord General Fairfax at the Siege of Colchester ('Fairfax, whose name . . .'). The base text is the draft in Milton's hand in the Trinity manuscript, with variants recorded from the text printed in 1694.

Sonnet 16

Sonnet 16: To the Lord General Cromwell, May 1652 ('Cromwell, our chief . . .'). The base text is the draft by an amanuensis in the Trinity manuscript, with variants recorded from the text printed in 1694.

Sonnet 17

Sonnet 17 ('Vane, young in years . . .'). The base text is the draft by an amanuensis in the Trinity manuscript, with variants recorded from the texts printed in 1662 and 1694. For an explanation of references like 'Sonnet 17, Tr. ms 45.11', s.v. Mask.

Sonnet 18

Sonnet 18: On the Late Massacher in Piemont ('Avenge, O Lord . . .'). The text is the edition of 1673, where it is numbered XV.

Sonnet 19

Sonnet 19 ('When I consider . . .'). The text is the edition of 1673, where it is numbered XVI.

Sonnet 20

Sonnet 20 ('Lawrence of vertuous Father . . .'). The text is the edition of 1673, where it is numbered XVII.

Sonnet 21

Sonnet 21 ('Cyriack, whose grandsire . . .'). The base text is the edition of 1673, where it is numbered XVIII, with variants recorded from the fragment (lines 5–14) by an amanuensis in the Trinity manuscript.

Sonnet 22

Sonnet 22 ('Cyriack, this three years . . .'). The base text is the draft by an amanuensis in the Trinity manuscript, with variants recorded from the text printed in 1694.

Sonnet 23

Sonnet 23 ('Methought I saw . . .'). The base text is the edition of 1673, where it is numbered XIX, with variants recorded from the draft by an amanuensis in the Trinity manuscript.

Vacation
At a Vacation Exercise in the College. The text is the edition of 1673.

Winchester
An Epitaph on the Marchioness of Winchester. The base text is the edition of 1645, with variants recorded from the edition of 1673.

LIST OF THE TEXTS REFERRED TO IN THE ENTRIES OF VARIANTS

1632
The Second Folio of Shakespeare's plays, containing a version of *On Shakespear*.

1637
A Maske Presented at Ludlow Castle, 1634. London, 1637. The first edition of *A Mask*.

1638
Justa Edvardo King naufrago &c., Cambridge, 1638. The final poem in this collection is *Lycidas*.

1640
A Banquet of Jests, London, 1640. Contains a version of the second Hobson poem.

1640
Shakespeare, *Poems*, London, 1640. Contains a version of *On Shakespear*.

1645
Poems of Mr. John Milton, Both English and Latin, Composed at Several Times, London, 1645. Contains Nativity, Psalm 114, Psalm 136, Passion, On Time, Circum, Musick, Winchester, May Morn, Shakespear, Carrier, Another, Allegro, Penseroso, Sonnets 1–10, Arcades, Lycidas, Mask.

1648
Henry Lawes, *Choice Psalms Put into Music for Three Voices*, London, 1648. Contains a version of Sonnet 13.

1657
A Banquet of Jests, London, 1657. Contains a version of the second Hobson poem.

1658
Wit Restored, London, 1658. Contains versions of both Hobson poems.

1662
The Life and Death of Sir Henry Vane, [n.p.] 1662. Contains a version of Sonnet 17.

1663–4
The Third Folio of Shakespeare's plays, containing a version of *On Shakespear*.

1667
Paradise Lost, London, 1667. The first edition.

1668
Another issue of the first edition of *Paradise Lost.*

1669
Another issue of the first edition of *Paradise Lost.*

1671
Paradise Regained [and] *Samson Agonistes*, London, 1671. The first edition of both poems.

1673
Poems, &c. Upon Several Occasions, by Mr. John Milton, London, 1673. Contains Nativity, Psalm 114, Psalm 136, Fair Inf, Passion, On Time, Circum, Musick, Winchester, May Morn, Shakespear, Carrier, Another, Allegro, Penseroso, Sonnets 1–19, Horace, Vacation, Forcers, Arcades, Lycidas, Mask, Psalms 1–8 and 80–8.

1674
Paradise Lost, London, 1674. The second edition.

1694
Edward Phillips, *Letters of State*, London, 1694. Contains versions of Sonnets 15, 16, and 22.

ms
A manuscript copy of the first book of *Paradise Lost*, now in the Pierpont Morgan library in New York.

Bridgewater ms
A manuscript copy of *A Mask*, the property of the Earl of Ellesmere and preserved at Bridgewater House.

B.M. ms
A manuscript in the British Museum (Ms. Add. 11518) containing five songs from *A Mask.*

Trinity ms
A manuscript in the library of Trinity College, Cambridge, containing among other things the following poems, in one or more states, mostly in Milton's hand: Arcades, Musick, On Time, Circum, Mask, Lycidas, Forcers, and Sonnets 7–17 and 21–3.

Cardoyn
Camillus Cardoyn's autograph album, now in the Harvard Library; Milton's autograph includes the closing lines of *Mask.*

This project was supported in its initial stages by Drexel Institute of Technology in Philadelphia, and later by the University of Michigan; we are indebted to various members of the computing staff at both these institutions. Miss Patricia Hibbs, formerly of Drexel Institute, and Professor L. K. Flanigan of the University of Michigan have earned our special gratitude for time and energy expended on our behalf. For sharing advice and counsel (though in no way implicating themselves in the result), and for their encouragement, we are obliged to Merritt Y. Hughes, Allan H. Gilbert, John T. Shawcross, and Trevor Howard-Hill. We are also grateful for the warm support and reassurance of many friends and colleagues in Ann Arbor, Philadelphia, Amherst, and New York, and to the Delegates of the Oxford University Press for undertaking to publish the completed work. In the division of editorial labours, Kathleen Swaim took responsibility for *Paradise Lost*; I did the remainder, and most of the programming. The editors would be grateful if users would communicate to them any errors or omissions in the concordance, for which the editors take full responsibility. Our computer must be held blameless; it did, by and large, as it was told. Like most computers, it was at times temperamental, but otherwise it was obedient to a fault.

WILLIAM INGRAM

Ann Arbor

ADDENDA

All
And mix no more with goodness, when at last — Mask 594
Trinity ms '& mixe no more' ←'till all to place'

Art
With wond'rous Art found out the massie Ore, — Par Lost 1.703
ms 'art'

Battles
No War, or Battails sound — Nativity 53
1673 'Battels'

Bear
With those just Spirits that wear victorious Palms, — Musick 14
Trinity ms 'weare' ←'beare' ←'weare'

Beshrew
I could be willing though now i' th darke to trie — Mask Tr. ms 16.38
'I could be willing' ←'beshrew me but I would' ←'beshew me'

But
I could be willing though now i' th darke to trie — Mask Tr. ms 16.38
'I could be willing' ←'beshrew me but I would' ←'beshew me'

Ever
The soothest Shepherd that ere pip't on plains. — Mask 823
Trinity ms 'e're'

Heaven
Toward Heav'ns descent had slop'd his westering wheel. — Lycidas 31
Trinity ms 'heavens'

Liberty
In libertyes defence, my noble task, — Sonnet 22, 11
1694 'Liberties'

Me
2. *Bro*. Me thought so too; what should it be? *Eld. Bro*. For certain — Mask 482
Trinity ms 'mee'
I could be willing though now i' th darke to trie — Mask Tr. ms 16.38
'I could be willing' ←'beshrew me but I would' ←'beshew me'

Natheless
Nathless he so endur'd, till on the Beach — Par Lost 1.299
ms 'Nathlesse'

Place
And mix no more with goodness, when at last — Mask 594
Trinity ms '& mixe no more' ←'till all to place'

Than
End Green. Why is it harder Sirs then Gordon, — Sonnet 11,8
Trinity ms 'then' ←'the' ←'then'

Till
And mix no more with goodness, when at last — Mask 594
Trinity ms '& mixe no more' ←'till all to place'

Were
He di'd for heavines that his Cart went light, — Another 22
1640, 1657 'were light'

Wind
Wind me into the easie-hearted man, — Mask 163
Bridgewater ms 'winde'

Would
I could be willing though now i' th darke to trie — Mask Tr. ms 16.38
'I could be willing' ←'beshrew me but I would' ←'beshew me'

A	
Listings of this word are omitted; see the Introduction.	
Aaron	
In *Aarons* Brest-plate, and a stone besides	Par Lost 3.598
Moses and *Aaron*) sent from God to claime	Par Lost 12.170
On *Aaron*'s breast: or tongue of Seers old	Par Reg 3.15
Abaddon	
No triumph; in all her gates *Abaddon* rues	Par Reg 4.624
Abana	
Of *Abbana* and *Pharphar*, lucid streams.	Par Lost 1.469
ms 'Abbana'	
Abandon	
Abandon fear; to strength and counsel joind	Par Lost 6.494
Abandoned	
Abandond at the terror of thy Power	Par Lost 6.134
To sorrow abandond, but worse felt within,	Par Lost 10.717
As one past hope, abandon'd,	Samson 120
Abarim	
Of Southmost *Abarim;* in *Hesebon*	Par Lost 1.408
ms 'Abarim'	
Abashed	
They heard, and were abasht, and up they sprung	Par Lost 1.331
ms 'abash'd'	
Invincible: abasht the Devil stood,	Par Lost 4.846
To whom thus half abash't *Adam* repli'd.	Par Lost 8.595
Till *Adam*, though not less then *Eve* abash't,	Par Lost 9.1065
1667 'abasht'	
Bold or loquacious, thus abasht repli'd.	Par Lost 10.161
At every sudden slighting quite abasht:	Par Reg 2.224
To whom the Fiend with fear abasht reply'd.	Par Reg 4.195
And in a moment shall be quite abash't.	Psalm 6, 24
Abassin	
Nor where *Abassin* Kings thir issue Guard,	Par Lost 4.280
Abate	
To slacken Virtue, and abate her edge,	Par Reg 2.455
Abated	
Which now abated, for the Clouds were fled,	Par Lost 11.841
Abbana	
Of *Abbana* and *Pharphar*, lucid streams.	Par Lost 1.469
ms 'Abbana'	
Abdiel	
Abdiel, then whom none with more zeale ador'd	Par Lost 5.805
So spake the Seraph *Abdiel* faithful found,	Par Lost 5.896
Abdiel that sight endur'd not, where he stood	Par Lost 6.111
To whom in brief thus *Abdiel* stern repli'd.	Par Lost 6.171
Nor stood unmindful *Abdiel* to annoy	Par Lost 6.369
Abhor	
To do what else though damnd I should abhorre.	Par Lost 4.392
That what in sleep thou didst abhorr to dream,	Par Lost 5.120
Abhor to joyn; and by imprudence mixt,	Par Lost 11.686
Now both abhor, since thou hast dar'd to utter	Par Reg 4.172
Abhorred	
In this abhorred deep to utter woe;	Par Lost 2.87
Abhorred *Styx* the flood of deadly hate,	Par Lost 2.577
Within unseen. Farr less abhorrd than these	Par Lost 2.659
They worse abhorr'd. *Satan* beheld thir plight,	Par Lost 6.607
To me my own, on such abhorred pact,	Par Reg 4.191
Doing abhorred rites to *Hecate*	Mask 535
Comes the blind *Fury* with th' abhorred shears,	Lycidas 75
From them whose sin ye envi'd, not abhor'd,	Forcers 4
Trinity ms 'abhorr'd'	
Of men abhor'd	Psalm 3, 22
Abhorrest	
To whom thus *Michael*. Justly thou abhorr'st	Par Lost 12.79
Abide	
Among the Nations round, and durst abide	Par Lost 1.385
How dearly I abide that boast so vaine,	Par Lost 4.87
Under his great Vice-gerent Reign abide	Par Lost 5.609
From forth this loathsom prison-house, to abide	Samson 922
Where strength can least abide, though all thy hairs	Samson 1136
All the Swains that there abide,	Mask 951
Longer dare abide,	Nativity 225
Yet more; the stroke of death he must abide,	Passion 20
In judgment, or abide their tryal then,	Psalm 1, 13
Abides	
Impresst the effulgence of his Glorie abides,	Par Lost 3.388
Where he abides, think there thy native soile.	Par Lost 11.292
Ability	
If aught in my ability may serve	Samson 743
Abject	
Abject and lost lay these, covering the Flood,	Par Lost 1.312
Or in this abject posture have ye sworn	Par Lost 1.322
The trodden Herb, of abject thoughts and low,	Par Lost 9.572
Therefore so abject is thir punishment,	Par Lost 11.520
To lowest pitch of abject fortune thou art fall'n.	Samson 169
Abjure	
Her loss, and other pleasures all abjure:	Par Lost 8.480
Say and unsay, feign, flatter, or abjure?	Par Reg 1.474
Able	
Som other able, and as willing, pay	Par Lost 3.211
Vernal delight and joy, able to drive	Par Lost 4.155
For God's, yet able to make Gods of Men:	Par Lost 5.70
That I must leave ye, Sons; O were I able	Par Lost 10.819
Beare thine own first, ill able to sustaine	Par Lost 10.950
With spiritual Armour, able to resist	Par Lost 12.491
Found able by invasion to annoy	Par Reg 3.365
Dead things with inbreath'd sense able to pierce,	Musick 4
Abler	
Of female Seed, far abler to resist	Par Reg 1.151
Abode	
Adams abode, those loftie shades his Bowre.	Par Lost 3.734
Better abode, and my afflicted Powers	Par Lost 4.939
Up to the Heav'n of Heav'ns his high abode,	Par Lost 7.553
Was this the cottage, and the safe abode	Mask 693
Bridgewater ms 'aboade'	
To welcom him to this his new abode,	Nativity 18
And after short abode flie back with speed,	Fair Inf 60
when as they journey'd from this dark abode	Sonnet 14, Tr. ms 41.07
Through out the land of thy abode	Psalm 81, 37
They find their safe abode,	Psalm 84, 14
Then dwell in Tents, *and rich abode*	Psalm 84, 39
Abolish	
Abolish his own works. This would surpass	Par Lost 2.370
Abolish thy Creation, and unmake,	Par Lost 3.163
Us to abolish, least the Adversary	Par Lost 9.947
Abolished	
We should be quite abolisht and expire.	Par Lost 2.93
Abominable	
Abominable, inutterable, and worse	Par Lost 2.626
Abominable, accurst, the house of woe,	Par Lost 10.465
The abominable terms, impious condition;	Par Reg 4.173
A *Nazarite* in place abominable	Samson 1359
Abominations	
Abominations; and with cursed things	Par Lost 1.389
Abominations rather, as did once	Par Reg 3.162
Abortive	
Threatens him, plung'd in that abortive gulf.	Par Lost 2.441
Abortive, monstrous, or unkindly mixt,	Par Lost 3.456
Abortive, to torment me ere thir being,	Par Lost 11.769
From many a horrid rift abortive pour'd	Par Reg 4.411
Abortive as the first-born bloom of spring	Samson 1576
Abound	
In future dayes, if Malice should abound,	Par Lost 6.502
From God, and over wrauth grace shall abound.	Par Lost 12.478
Where Springs and Showrs abound.	Psalm 84, 24
Abounded	
Love hath abounded more then Glory abounds,	Par Lost 3.312
Abounds	
Love hath abounded more then Glory abounds,	Par Lost 3.312
With vast increase their corn and wine abounds	Psalm 4, 36
About	
Pour forth thir populous youth about the Hive	Par Lost 1.770
Of some new Race call'd *Man*, about this time	Par Lost 2.348
With mortal sting: about her middle round	Par Lost 2.653
About him all the Sanctities of Heaven	Par Lost 3.60
Drawn round about thee like a radiant Shrine,	Par Lost 3.379
He brings, and round about him, nor from Hell	Par Lost 4.21
Alone as they. About them frisking playd	Par Lost 4.340
By word or action markt: about them round	Par Lost 4.401
About him exercis'd Heroic Games	Par Lost 4.551
To wed her Elm; she spous'd about him twines	Par Lost 5.216
In song and dance about the sacred Hill,	Par Lost 5.619
Melodious Hymns about the sovran Throne	Par Lost 5.656
About the great reception of thir King,	Par Lost 5.769
Against us from about his Throne, and judg'd	Par Lost 6.426
And from about him fierce Effusion rowld	Par Lost 6.765
About his Chariot numberless were pour'd	Par Lost 7.197
And from about her shot Darts of desire	Par Lost 8.62
Incited, dance about him various rounds?	Par Lost 8.125
Stood on my feet; about me round I saw	Par Lost 8.261
Above, or round about thee or beneath.	Par Lost 8.318
About her, as a guard Angelic plac't.	Par Lost 8.559
Thrice Fugitive about *Troy* Wall; or rage	Par Lost 9.16
Pleasures about me, so much more I feel	Par Lost 9.120
About her glowd, oft stooping to support	Par Lost 9.427
About the mossie Trunk I wound me soon,	Par Lost 9.589
About him. But to *Adam* in what sort	Par Lost 9.816
About thir spirits had plaid, and inmost powers	Par Lost 9.1048
And honour from about them, naked left	Par Lost 9.1057
About the Mother Tree, a Pillard shade	Par Lost 9.1106
About the new-arriv'd, in multitudes	Par Lost 10.26

About(*cont*)
And all about found desolate; for those — Par Lost 10.420
Farr to the inland retir'd, about the walls — Par Lost 10.423
He sate, and round about him saw unseen: — Par Lost 10.448
Pitcht about *Sechem*, and the neighbouring Plaine — Par Lost 12.136
About the world, at that assembly fam'd — Par Reg 1.34
About his Altar, handling holy things, — Par Reg 1.489
He could not lose himself; but went about — Par Reg 2.98
About the wine-press where sweet moust is powr'd, — Par Reg 4.16
About thy ransom: well they may by this — Samson 483
I walk'd about admir'd of all and dreaded — Samson 530
That wandring loose about — Samson 675
About t' have spoke, but now, with head declin'd — Samson 727
May ever tend about thee to old age — Samson 925
Hath walk'd about, and each limb to survey, — Samson 1089
Garrison'd round about him like a Camp — Samson 1497
Useless, and thence ridiculous about him. — Samson 1501
Of highest wisdom brings about, — Samson 1747
Of som chast footing neer about this ground. — Mask 146
About my Mother *Circe*. Thus I hurl — Mask 153
Bridgewater ms 'abouts'
Whom thrift keeps up about his Country gear, — Mask 167
And yet came off: if you have this about you — Mask 647
That sing about the golden tree: — Mask 983
About the cedar'n alleys fling — Mask 990
Ay round about *Joves* Altar sing. — Penseroso 48
Above, about, or underneath, — Penseroso 152
Shakes the high thicket, haste I all about, — Arcades 58
In dismall dance about the furnace blue, — Nativity 210
And all about the Courtly Stable, — Nativity 243
I have some naked thoughts that rove about — Vacation 23
Then quick about thy purpos'd business come, — Vacation 57
And sweetly singing round about thy Bed — Vacation 63
About the supreme Throne — On Time 17
The Subject new: it walk'd the Town a while, — Sonnet 11, 3
Trinity ms 'walk'd' ←'It went off well about'
I fear not though incamping round about — Psalm 3, 17
All day they round about me go, — Psalm 88, 67

Above
Above th' *Aonian* Mount, while it pursues — Par Lost 1.15
To set himself in Glory above his Peers, — Par Lost 1.39
With Head up-lift above the wave, and Eyes — Par Lost 1.193
Above his equals. Farewel happy Fields — Par Lost 1.249
Of riot ascends above thir loftiest Towrs, — Par Lost 1.499
ms 'aboue'
Thir dread commander: he above the rest — Par Lost 1.589
Above them all th' Arch Angel: but his face — Par Lost 1.600
ms 'Aboue'
And plunge us in the flames? or from above — Par Lost 2.172
Of him who rules above; so was his will — Par Lost 2.351
Above his fellows, with Monarchal pride — Par Lost 2.428
Of hazard more, as he above the rest — Par Lost 2.455
For him who sits above and laughs the while — Par Lost 2.731
Save he who reigns above, none can resist. — Par Lost 2.814
But what ow I to his commands above — Par Lost 2.856
Now had the Almighty Father from above, — Par Lost 3.56
High Thron'd above all highth, bent down his eye, — Par Lost 3.58
Elect above the rest; so is my will: — Par Lost 3.184
To mortal men, above which only shon — Par Lost 3.268
Thus they in Heav'n, above the starry Sphear, — Par Lost 3.416
So high above the circling Canopie — Par Lost 3.556
He stayd not to enquire: above them all — Par Lost 3.571
I fell, how glorious once above thy Spheare; — Par Lost 4.39
Shade above shade, a woodie Theatre — Par Lost 4.141
He held it vain; awe from above had quelld — Par Lost 4.860
Unspeakable, who sitst above these Heavens — Par Lost 5.156
Above all Hills. As when by night the Glass — Par Lost 5.261
Wilde above Rule or Art; enormous bliss. — Par Lost 5.297
Since by descending from the Thrones above, — Par Lost 5.363
Of things above his World, and of thir being — Par Lost 5.455
In place thy self so high above thy Peeres. — Par Lost 5.812
Thir perfet ranks; for high above the ground — Par Lost 6.71
Gave them above thir foes, not to have sinnd, — Par Lost 6.402
In Heav'n and Hell thy Power above compare, — Par Lost 6.705
Following, above th' *Olympian* Hill I soare, — Par Lost 7.3
Above the flight of *Pegasean* wing. — Par Lost 7.4
Standing on Earth, not rapt above the Pole, — Par Lost 7.23
Things above Earthly thought, which yet concernd — Par Lost 7.82
Thy hearing, such Commission from above — Par Lost 7.118
The Waters underneath from those above — Par Lost 7.268
And let Fowle flie above the Earth, with wings — Par Lost 7.389
Rising, the crumbl'd Earth above them threw — Par Lost 7.468
Invisible else above all Starrs, the Wheele — Par Lost 8.135
Leave them to God above, him serve and feare; — Par Lost 8.168
Above, or round about thee or beneath. — Par Lost 8.318
O by what Name, for thou above all these, — Par Lost 8.357
Above mankinde, or aught then mankinde higher, — Par Lost 8.358
Light above Light, for thee alone, as seems, — Par Lost 9.105
Compare above all living Creatures deare, — Par Lost 9.228
Fould above fould a surging Maze, his Head — Par Lost 9.499
To me so friendly grown above the rest — Par Lost 9.564
Wherein God set thee above her made of thee, — Par Lost 10.149
Above all Cattle, each Beast of the Field; — Par Lost 10.176
Above the rest still to retain; they all — Par Lost 10.532
His will who reigns above, to aggravate — Par Lost 10.549
Praying, for from the Mercie-seat above — Par Lost 11.2
Strength added from above, new hope to spring — Par Lost 11.138
Or of the Thrones above, such Majestie — Par Lost 11.232

Above(*cont*)
Prince above Princes, gently hast thou tould — Par Lost 11.298
And Judgment from above: him old and young — Par Lost 11.668
Above the highest Hills: then shall this Mount — Par Lost 11.829
Above his Brethren, to himself assuming — Par Lost 12.65
Above the Clouds will pine his entrails gross, — Par Lost 12.77
Above all names in Heav'n; and thence shall come, — Par Lost 12.458
Above Heroic, though in secret done, — Par Reg 1.15
Out of the water, Heav'n above the Clouds — Par Reg 1.81
All righteous things: therefore above my years, — Par Reg 1.206
Can raise them, though above example high; — Par Reg 1.232
Which I believ'd was from above; but he — Par Reg 1.274
But thou art plac't above me, thou art Lord; — Par Reg 1.475
Permission from above; thou canst not more. — Par Reg 1.496
And fears as eminent, above the lot — Par Reg 2.70
Above all Sacrifice, or hallow'd gift — Par Reg 3.116
Above the highth of Mountains interpos'd. — Par Reg 4.39
Above the rest lifting his stately head — Par Reg 4.48
Light from above, from the fountain of light, — Par Reg 4.289
Happ'ly had ends above my reach to know: — Samson 62
My Vessel trusted to me from above, — Samson 199
His mighty Champion, strong above compare, — Samson 556
Above the nerve of mortal arm — Samson 639
Some sourse of consolation from above; — Samson 664
Above the faith of wedlock-bands, my tomb — Samson 986
Most shines and most is acceptable above. — Samson 1052
Above the Sons of men; but sight bereav'd — Samson 1294
Above the smoak and stirr of this dim spot, — Mask 5
The Sea o'refraught would swell, & th' unsought diamonds — Mask 732
Trinity ms 'swell' ←'heave her waters up above the shoare'
But farr above in spangled sheen — Mask 1003
line not in Bridgewater ms
To set her beauties praise above — Penseroso 20
Above, about, or underneath, — Penseroso 152
There entertain him all the Saints above, — Lycidas 178
Our great redemption from above did bring; — Nativity 4
To rise above the watry plain. — Psalm 136, 22
Above the reach of mortall ey. — Psalm 136, 94
Above mortalitie that shew'd thou wast divine. — Fair Inf 35
Whether above that high first-moving Spheare — Fair Inf 39
Above the wheeling poles, and at Heav'ns dore — Vacation 34
Yet being above them, he shall be below them; — Vacation 80
Were lost in death, till he that dwelt above — Circum 18
and gives thee praise above the pipe of Pan; — Sonnet 13, Tr. ms 40.06
So as above the Heavens thy praise to set — Psalm 8, 3

Abraham
Whom *faithful Abraham* due time shall call, — Par Lost 12.152
Promisd to *Abraham* and his Seed: the rest — Par Lost 12.260
From *Abraham*, Son of *Isaac*, and from him — Par Lost 12.268
Just *Abraham* and his Seed: now first I finde — Par Lost 12.273
Foretold to *Abraham*, as in whom shall trust — Par Lost 12.328
Not onely to the Sons of *Abrahams* Loines — Par Lost 12.447
Of *Abrahams* Faith wherever through the world; — Par Lost 12.449
Remembring *Abraham* by some wond'rous call — Par Reg 3.434
Or benefit reveal'd to *Abraham*'s race? — Samson 29
Before the God of *Abraham*. He, be sure, — Samson 465

Abroad
Against a wakeful Foe, while I abroad — Par Lost 2.463
Within thir stony caves, but rush'd abroad — Par Reg 4.414
Whole to my self, unhazarded abroad, — Samson 809
Eye-sight exposes daily men abroad. — Samson 919
When all abroad was rumour'd that this day — Samson 1600
Let us blaze his Name abroad, — Psalm 136, 5
With my whole heart, and blaze abroad — Psalm 86, 43
Of thee *abroad* are spoke; — Psalm 87, 10

Abrupt
Over the vast abrupt, ere he arrive — Par Lost 2.409

Abruptly
So lately found, and so abruptly gone, — Par Reg 2.10

Absence
Oft in her absence mimic Fansie wakes — Par Lost 5.110
Or we can bid his absence, till thy Song — Par Lost 7.107
Thee satiate, to short absence I could yield. — Par Lost 9.248
Thy absence from my sight, but to avoid — Par Lost 9.294
The pain of absence from thy sight. But strange — Par Lost 9.861
Since understand; much more his absence now — Par Reg 2.100
Wailing thy absence in my widow'd bed; — Samson 806

Absent
Shall enter Heaven long absent, and returne, — Par Lost 3.261
For I that Day was absent, as befell, — Par Lost 8.229
Those two; the third best absent is condemn'd, — Par Lost 10.82
Privation meer of light and absent day. — Par Reg 4.400
Was absent, after all his mischief done, — Par Reg 4.440
Not to be absent at that spectacle. — Samson 1604
From the glad sound would not be absent long, — Lycidas 35

Absents
Go; for thy stay, not free, absents thee more; — Par Lost 9.372
Absents thee, or what chance detains? Come forth. — Par Lost 10.108

Absolute
Fixt Fate, free will, foreknowledg absolute, — Par Lost 2.560
Thir will, dispos'd by absolute Decree — Par Lost 3.115
Absolute rule; and Hyacinthin Locks — Par Lost 4.301
And through all numbers absolute, though One; — Par Lost 8.421
Her loveliness, so absolute she seems — Par Lost 8.547
Of absolute perfection, therein Man — Par Lost 10.483
But prayer against his absolute Decree — Par Lost 11.311
Dominion absolute; that right we hold — Par Lost 12.68
Perfections absolute, Graces divine, — Par Reg 2.138

Absolute(*cont*)
To such as owe them absolute subjection; Samson 1405
Absolutely
Command me absolutely not to go, Par Lost 9.1156
Absolve
Imputed shall absolve them who renounce Par Lost 3.291
Forc't I absolve: all my evasions vain, Par Lost 10.829
Absolved
Absolv'd, if unforbid thou maist unfould Par Lost 7.94
Abstain
Our Maker bids increase, who bids abstain Par Lost 4.748
Of knowledge within bounds; beyond abstain Par Lost 7.120
Though to delude them sent, could not abstain, Par Lost 10.557
Conversing, looking, loving, to abstain Par Lost 10.993
Though ravenous, taught to abstain from what they brought: Par Reg 2.269
Abstained
Much pleasure we have lost, while we abstain'd Par Lost 9.1022
Abstaining
Suffering, abstaining, quietly expecting Par Reg 3.192
Abstemious
Abstemious I grew up and thriv'd amain; Samson 637
Abstinence
That sacred Fruit, sacred to abstinence, Par Lost 9.924
Praising the lean and sallow Abstinence. Mask 709
Bridgewater ms 'abstinence'
Trinity ms 'abstinence'
Abstract
Abstract as in a transe methought I saw, Par Lost 8.462
Abstracted
That space the Evil one abstracted stood Par Lost 9.463
Abstruse
Entring on studious thoughts abstruse, which *Eve* Par Lost 8.40
Sam. Be less abstruse, my riddling days are past. Samson 1064
Abstrusest
Abstrusest thoughts, from forth his holy Mount Par Lost 5.712
Absurd
Will condescend to such absurd commands? Samson 1337
Abundance
For us too large, where thy abundance wants Par Lost 4.730
Abundance, fit to honour and receive Par Lost 5.315
To us, in such aboundance lies our choice, Par Lost 9.620
1667 'abundance'
With her abundance, she good cateress Mask 764
Abundant
Communicated, more abundant growes, Par Lost 5.72
Reptil with Spawn abundant, living Soule: Par Lost 7.388
Abundantly
Abundantly his gifts hath also pour'd Par Lost 8.220
Abuse
To worst abuse, or to thir meanest use. Par Lost 4.204
And look for adoration to th' abuse Par Lost 5.800
No more shalt thou by oracling abuse Par Reg 1.455
To daily fraud, contempt, abuse and wrong, Samson 76
Sam. Shall I abuse this Consecrated gift Samson 1354
We may justly now accuse Arcades 10
Trinity ms 'wee may justly now accuse' ←'now seemes guiltie of abuse'
Abused
With monstrous shapes and sorceries abus'd Par Lost 1.479
Things that on earth were lost, or were abus'd. Prose 2, 4
Abyss
Dove-like satst brooding on the vast Abyss Par Lost 1.21
ms 'Abysse'
Caelestial Spirits in Bondage, nor th' Abyss Par Lost 1.658
ms 'Abysse'
1667 'Abysse'
The dark unbottom'd infinite Abyss Par Lost 2.405
By Haralds voice explain'd: the hollow Abyss Par Lost 2.518
Chance governs all. Into this wilde Abyss, Par Lost 2.910
Into this wild Abyss the warie fiend Par Lost 2.917
Or Spirit of the nethermost Abyss Par Lost 2.956
And Spirits of this nethermost Abyss, Par Lost 2.969
Over the dark Abyss, whose boiling Gulf Par Lost 2.1027
Heapt on him there, nor yet the main Abyss Par Lost 3.83
To wing the desolate Abyss, and spie Par Lost 4.936
They view'd the vast immeasurable Abyss Par Lost 7.211
Cover'd th' Abyss: but on the watrie calme Par Lost 7.234
Over the vext Abyss, following the track Par Lost 10.314
With this portentous Bridge the dark Abyss. Par Lost 10.371
Th' untractable Abysse, plung'd in the womb Par Lost 10.476
O Conscience, into what Abyss of fears Par Lost 10.842
Till time stand fixt: beyond is all abyss, Par Lost 12.555
To thir abyss and horrid pains confin'd. Samson 501
Abyssinian
Nor where *Abassin* Kings thir issue Guard, Par Lost 4.280
Academe
See there the Olive Grove of *Academe*, Par Reg 4.244
Academics
Of Academics old and new, with those Par Reg 4.278
Acanthus
Acanthus, and each odorous bushie shrub Par Lost 4.696
Accaron
And *Accaron* and *Gaza*'s frontier bounds. Par Lost 1.466
ms 'Accaron'
Accent
And with perswasive accent thus began. Par Lost 2.118
Thus her reply with accent sweet renewd. Par Lost 9.321
Words with just note and accent, not to scan Sonnet 13, 3

Accept
Accept this dark opprobrious Den of shame, Par Lost 2.58
So hardie as to proffer or accept Par Lost 2.425
Refusing to accept as great a share Par Lost 2.452
In those who, when they may, accept not grace. Par Lost 3.302
Accept your Makers work; he gave it me, Par Lost 4.380
Of blowing Myrrh and Balme; if thou accept Par Lost 9.629
Thou didst accept them; wilt thou enjoy the good, Par Lost 10.758
Accept me, and in mee from these receave Par Lost 11.37
What we receive, would either not accept Par Lost 11.505
Why shouldst thou not accept it? but I see Par Reg 2.398
He will accept thee to defend his cause, Samson 1179
Whether he durst accept the offer or not, Samson 1255
To accept of ransom for my Son thir pris'ner, Samson 1460
Acceptable
So fit, so acceptable, so Divine, Par Lost 10.139
Said hee, with one thrice acceptable stroke Par Lost 10.855
Most shines and most is acceptable above. Samson 1052
No sacrifice to God more acceptable Prose 11, 2
Acceptance
Findes no acceptance, nor can find, for how Par Lost 5.531
Permissive, and acceptance found, which gain'd Par Lost 8.435
Of new acceptance, hopeful to regaine Par Lost 10.972
From Heav'n acceptance; but the bloodie Fact Par Lost 11.457
Acceptance of large Grace, from servil fear Par Lost 12.305
In vain, where no acceptance it can find, Par Reg 2.388
My supplication with acceptance fair Psalm 6, 19
Accepted
Food not of Angels, yet accepted so, Par Lost 5.465
Accepted, fearless in his righteous Cause, Par Lost 6.804
All thy request for Man, accepted Son, Par Lost 11.46
Accepting
Obtrud'st thy offer'd aid, that I accepting Par Reg 4.493
Accepts
Who evermore approves and more accepts Samson 510
Access
Attended: all access was throng'd, the Gates Par Lost 1.761
ms 'accesse'
With Armed watch, that render all access Par Lost 2.130
Access deni'd; and over head up grew Par Lost 4.137
Access in every Vertue, in thy sight Par Lost 9.310
At first, as one who sought access, but feard Par Lost 9.511
And giv'st access, though secret she retire. Par Lost 9.810
Instructed that to God is no access Par Lost 12.239
Inspir'd; disdain not such access to me. Par Reg 1.492
For thou wilt *grant* me *free access* Psalm 86, 23
Accessible
Accessible from Earth, one entrance high; Par Lost 4.546
Accessories
Alike, to Serpents all as accessories Par Lost 10.520
Accident
For whither is he gone, what accident Par Reg 2.39
Man. Some dismal accident it needs must be; Samson 1519
Man. The accident was loud, & here before thee Samson 1552
& may upon any needfull accident Mask Tr. ms 16.55
Shall subject be to many an Accident. Vacation 74
Accidents
There exercise all his fierce accidents, Samson 612
Acclaim
With deafning shout, return'd them loud acclaim. Par Lost 2.520
Back from pursuit thy Powers with loud acclaime Par Lost 3.397
Thir mighty Chief returnd: loud was th' acclaime: Par Lost 10.455
He ceas'd, and heard thir grant in loud acclaim; Par Reg 2.235
Acclamation
Followd with acclamation and the sound Par Lost 7.558
Acclamations
With joy and acclamations loud, that one Par Lost 6.23
Loud acclamations ring. Psalm 81, 4
Accompanied
Silence accompanied, for Beast and Bird, Par Lost 4.600
Accompani'd then with his own compleat Par Lost 5.352
Best with thy self accompanied, seek'st not Par Lost 8.428
Accompanied to Heaven Gate, from whence Par Lost 10.88
Accompanied, with damps and dreadful gloom, Par Lost 10.848
Accompanied of things past and to come Par Reg 1.300
Accomplish
How to begin, how to accomplish best Par Reg 2.113
Accomplish what they did, perhaps and more? Par Reg 2.452
Accomplished
Yet with revenge accomplish't and to Hell Par Lost 3.160
Daughter of God and Man, accomplisht *Eve*, Par Lost 4.660
So Ev'n and Morn accomplish'd the Sixt day: Par Lost 7.550
That specious Monster, my accomplisht snare. Samson 230
Accomplishing
Accomplishing great things, by things deemd weak Par Lost 12.567
Accomplishment
Made and set wholly on the accomplishment Par Reg 2.207
Accord
To union, and firm Faith, and firm accord, Par Lost 2.36
As if (which might induce us to accord) Par Lost 2.503
Thy actions to thy words accord, thy words Par Reg 3.9
Now of my own accord such other tryal Samson 1643
According
Hath honourd me according to his will. Par Lost 6.816
According to his doom: he would have spoke, Par Lost 10.517
By which all Causes else according still Par Lost 10.806
That live according to her sober laws, Mask 766
Bridgewater ms 'accordinge'

According(*cont*)
According to my righteousness Psalm 7, 32
According to his justice raise Psalm 7, 62
Accost
Yet thus, unmovd with fear, accost him soon. Par Lost 4.822
Accosts
O're Sea and Land: him *Satan* thus accostes; Par Lost 3.653
With soothing words renew'd, him thus accosts. Par Reg 3.6
Account
Account mee man; I for his sake will leave Par Lost 3.238
And Country whereof here needs no account, Par Lost 4.235
And of thir doings God takes no account. Par Lost 4.622
But come, for thou, besure, shalt give account Par Lost 4.841
As is most just; this I my Glorie account, Par Lost 6.726
Or much more grievous pain? Ye have th' account Par Lost 10.501
How many have with a smile made small account Par Reg 2.193
My true account, least he returning chide, Sonnet 19, 6
Accountable
Free, and to none accountable, preferring Par Lost 2.255
Accountable made haste to make appear Par Lost 10.29
Accursed
Accurst, and in a cursed hour he hies. Par Lost 2.1055
Be then his Love accurst, since love or hate, Par Lost 4.69
O alienate from God, O spirit accurst, Par Lost 5.877
Among th' accurst, that witherd all thir strength, Par Lost 6.850
Of his Creation; justly then accurst, Par Lost 10.168
Because thou hast done this, thou art accurst Par Lost 10.175
Abominable, accurst, the house of woe, Par Lost 10.465
Accurst of blessed, hide me from the face Par Lost 10.723
A shameful and accurst, naild to the Cross Par Lost 12.413
To worship thee accurst, now more accurst Par Reg 4.179
Nor think me so unwary or accurst Samson 930
Accusation
Thus they in mutual accusation spent Par Lost 9.1187
Accuse
So were created, nor can justly accuse Par Lost 3.112
Thou hadst: whom hast thou then or what to accuse, Par Lost 4.67
Accuse not Nature, she hath don her part; Par Lost 8.561
Shee first his weak indulgence will accuse. Par Lost 9.1186
My self the total Crime, or to accuse Par Lost 10.127
Though of Rebellion others he accuse. Par Lost 12.37
Rather accuse him under usual names, Par Reg 4.316
We may justly now accuse Arcades 10
Trinity ms 'wee may justly now accuse' ←'now seemes guiltie of abuse'
Accused
To Judgement he proceeded on th' accus'd Par Lost 10.164
Curs'd his Creation, Death as oft accus'd Par Lost 10.852
Accuser
The Tempter ere th' Accuser of man-kind, Par Lost 4.10
And thou th' accuser. Thus it shall befall Par Lost 9.1182
Accustomed
Forth issuing at th' accustomd hour stood armd Par Lost 4.779
Less pure, accustomd to immortal Fruits? Par Lost 11.285
Gently o're th' accustom'd Oke; Penseroso 60
Ache
For all my bones, that even with anguish ake, Psalm 6, 5
Acheron
Sad *Acheron* of sorrow, black and deep; Par Lost 2.578
Under the sooty flag of *Acheron*, Mask 604
Achieve
The Serpent, by what means he shall achieve Par Lost 12.234
All vertue, grace and wisdom to atchieve Par Reg 1.68
Achieved
Hath bin achievd of merit, yet this loss Par Lost 2.21
Som advantagious act may be achiev'd Par Lost 2.363
Had been achiev'd, whereof all Hell had rung, Par Lost 2.723
Thou hast atchiev'd our libertie, confin'd Par Lost 10.368
With peril great atchiev'd. Long were to tell Par Lost 10.469
Thus Fame shall be atchiev'd, renown on Earth, Par Lost 11.698
1667 'achiev'd'
Subduing Nations, and achievd thereby Par Lost 11.792
High actions; but wherewith to be atchiev'd? Par Reg 2.411
With all those high exploits by him atchiev'd, Samson 1492
Achieving
Deterrd not from atchieving what might leade Par Lost 9.696
Achilles
Of stern *Achilles* on his Foe pursu'd Par Lost 9.15
Acknowledge
Acknowledge him thy Greater, sound his praise Par Lost 5.172
But grateful to acknowledge whence his good Par Lost 7.512
The more she will acknowledge thee her Head, Par Lost 8.574
Acknowledge my Redeemer ever blest. Par Lost 12.573
Thee homage, and acknowledge thee thir Lord: Par Reg 2.376
Sam. Father, I do acknowledge and confess Samson 448
I cannot but acknowledge; yet if tears Samson 735
Acknowledge them from God inflicted on me Samson 1170
Acknowledged
Allegeance to th' acknowldg'd Power supream? Par Lost 4.956
1667 'acknowledg'd'
Acknowledg'd and deplor'd, in *Adam* wraught Par Lost 10.939
Taught them, but they his gifts acknowledg'd none. Par Lost 11.612
Full grown to Man, acknowledg'd, as I hear, Par Reg 2.83
Acknowledg'd not, or not at all consider'd Samson 245
Acquaint
To my associate Powers, them to acquaint Par Lost 10.395
Like fortunes may her soul acquaint, Winchester 72
Acquainted
Nearer acquainted, now I feel by proof, Par Reg 1.400
Acquist
His servants he with new acquist Samson 1755
Acquit
To acquit themselves and prosecute their foes Samson 897
Acquittance
Forbearance no acquittance ere day end. Par Lost 10.53
Acquitted
With me? how can they then acquitted stand Par Lost 10.827
Act
Belial, in act more graceful and humane; Par Lost 2.109
Som advantagious act may be achiev'd Par Lost 2.363
By Act of Grace my former state; how soon Par Lost 4.94
To act or not, Necessitie and Chance Par Lost 7.172
With act intelligential; but his sleep Par Lost 9.190
Fluctuats disturbd, yet comely and in act Par Lost 9.668
Motion, each act won audience ere the tongue, Par Lost 9.674
Meanwhile the hainous and despightfull act Par Lost 10.1
To observe the sequel, saw his guileful act Par Lost 10.334
Triumphal with triumphal act have met, Par Lost 10.390
To the reception of thir matter act, Par Lost 10.807
And one bad act with many deeds well done Par Lost 11.256
By Faith not void of workes: this God-like act Par Lost 12.427
In sin for ever lost from life; this act Par Lost 12.429
Secular power, though feigning still to act Par Lost 12.517
The time and means: each act is rightliest done, Par Reg 4.475
His Godlike presence, and from some great act Samson 28
I thought it lawful from my former act, Samson 231
But act not in thy own affliction, Son, Samson 503
What act more execrably unclean, prophane? Samson 1362
By some great act, or of my days the last. Samson 1389
But most by leud and lavish act of sin, Mask 465
Action
By word or action markt: about them round Par Lost 4.401
Of gesture or lest action overawd Par Lost 9.460
As by that early action may be judg'd, Par Reg 4.215
Actions
From all her words and actions mixt with Love Par Lost 8.602
Much reason, and in thir actions oft appeers. Par Lost 9.559
His thoughts, his looks, words, actions all infect, Par Lost 10.608
High actions; but wherewith to be atchiev'd? Par Reg 2.411
Thy actions to thy words accord, thy words Par Reg 3.9
In all things that to greatest actions lead. Par Reg 3.239
High actions, and high passions best describing: Par Reg 4.266
As in thy wond'rous actions hath been seen. Samson 1440
Active
Each in thir several active Sphears assignd, Par Lost 5.477
Active within beyond the sense of brute. Par Lost 9.96
If cause were to unfold some active Scene Par Reg 2.239
Or active, tended on by glory, or fame, Par Reg 4.371
Activity
To make them sport with blind activity? Samson 1328
Acts
Holy Memorials, acts of Zeale and Love Par Lost 5.593
These Acts of hateful strife, hateful to all, Par Lost 6.264
In might though wondrous and in Acts of Warr, Par Lost 6.377
Eye witnesses of his Almightie Acts, Par Lost 6.883
Immediate are the Acts of God, more swift Par Lost 7.176
Creation and the Six dayes acts they sung, Par Lost 7.601
So much delights me as those graceful acts, Par Lost 8.600
We are by doom to pay; rather such acts Par Lost 10.1026
First seen in acts of prowess eminent Par Lost 11.789
Flam'd in my heart, heroic acts, one while Par Reg 1.216
Great acts require great means of enterprise, Par Reg 2.412
All Earth her wonder at thy acts, thy self Par Reg 3.24
Who seeing those great acts which God had done Samson 243
Of acts indeed heroic, far beyond Samson 527
The highest name for valiant Acts, that honour Samson 1101
Single Rebellion and did Hostile Acts. Samson 1210
Chor. Where the heart joins not, outward acts defile not. Samson 1368
With all his Trophies hung, and Acts enroll'd Samson 1736
His Godlike acts, and his temptations fierce, Passion 24
That call Fame on such gentle acts as these, Sonnet 8, 6
For what can Warr, but endless warr still breed, Sonnet 15, 10
1694 'but Acts of War'
Or wondrous acts be known, Psalm 88, 50
Actual
Once actual, now in body, and to dwell Par Lost 10.587
Adam
By wondrous birth: Be thou in *Adams* room Par Lost 3.285
The Head of all mankind, though *Adams* Son. Par Lost 3.286
Adams abode, those loftie shades his Bowre. Par Lost 3.734
Adam the goodliest man of men since borne Par Lost 4.323
Grip't in each paw: When *Adam* first of men Par Lost 4.408
When *Adam* thus to *Eve*: Fair Consort, th' hour Par Lost 4.610
Adam from his fair Spouse, nor *Eve* the Rites Par Lost 4.742
When *Adam* wak't, so customd, for his sleep Par Lost 5.3
On *Adam*, whom imbracing, thus she spake. Par Lost 5.27
Related, and thus *Adam* answerd sad. Par Lost 5.94
Converse with *Adam*, in what Bowre or shade Par Lost 5.230
Adam discernd, as in the dore he sat Par Lost 5.299
Earths inmost womb, more warmth then *Adam* needs; Par Lost 5.302
Berrie or Grape: to whom thus *Adam* call'd. Par Lost 5.307
To whom thus *Eve*. *Adam*, earths hallowd mould, Par Lost 5.321
Neerer his presence *Adam* though not awd, Par Lost 5.358
Adam, I therefore came, nor art thou such Par Lost 5.372
In *Adam*, not to let th' occasion pass Par Lost 5.453

Adam(*cont*)
O *Adam*, one Almightie is, from whom Par Lost 5.469
Thus *Adam* made request, and *Raphael* Par Lost 5.561
All thy Dominion, *Adam*, is no more Par Lost 5.751
Adam by dire example to beware Par Lost 7.42
In Paradise to *Adam* or his Race, Par Lost 7.45
With Blessedness. Whence *Adam* soon repeal'd Par Lost 7.59
Thus *Adam* his illustrious Guest besought: Par Lost 7.109
This said, he formd thee, *Adam*, thee O Man Par Lost 7.524
The Angel ended, and in *Adams* Eare Par Lost 8.1
line not in 1667 edition
Adam relating, she sole Auditress; Par Lost 8.51
And *Raphael* now to *Adam*'s doubt propos'd Par Lost 8.64
To whom thus *Adam* cleerd of doubt, repli'd. Par Lost 8.179
And said, thy Mansion wants thee, *Adam*, rise, Par Lost 8.296
Of thy Associates, *Adam*, and wilt taste Par Lost 8.401
Thus farr to try thee, *Adam*, I was pleas'd, Par Lost 8.437
To whom thus half abash't *Adam* repli'd. Par Lost 8.595
So saying, he arose; whom *Adam* thus Par Lost 8.644
From the thick shade, and *Adam* to his Bowre. Par Lost 8.653
Adam, well may we labour still to dress Par Lost 9.205
To whom mild answer *Adam* thus return'd. Par Lost 9.226
Adam, missthought of her to thee so dear? Par Lost 9.289
To whom with healing words *Adam* replyd. Par Lost 9.290
So spake domestick *Adam* in his care Par Lost 9.318
To whom thus *Adam* fervently repli'd. Par Lost 9.342
Thy utmost reach or *Adams:* Round the Tree Par Lost 9.591
About him. But to *Adam* in what sort Par Lost 9.816
And *Adam* wedded to another *Eve*, Par Lost 9.828
Adam shall share with me in bliss or woe: Par Lost 9.831
From Nectar, drink of Gods. *Adam* the while Par Lost 9.838
Hast thou not wonderd, *Adam*, at my stay? Par Lost 9.856
On th' other side, *Adam*, soon as he heard Par Lost 9.888
So *Adam*, and thus *Eve* to him repli'd. Par Lost 9.960
Adam, from whose deare side I boast me sprung, Par Lost 9.965
On my experience, *Adam*, freely taste, Par Lost 9.988
Original; while *Adam* took no thought, Par Lost 9.1004
Till *Adam* thus 'gan *Eve* to dalliance move, Par Lost 9.1016
Till *Adam*, though not less then *Eve* abash't, Par Lost 9.1065
Adam, estrang'd in look and alterd stile, Par Lost 9.1132
What words have past thy Lips, *Adam* severe, Par Lost 9.1144
To whom then first incenst *Adam* repli'd, Par Lost 9.1162
Approaching, thus to *Adam* call'd aloud. Par Lost 10.102
Where art thou *Adam*, wont with joy to meet Par Lost 10.103
Whence *Adam* faultring long, thus answer'd brief. Par Lost 10.115
To whom thus *Adam* sore beset repli'd. Par Lost 10.124
On *Adam* last thus judgement he pronounc'd. Par Lost 10.197
The growing miseries, which *Adam* saw Par Lost 10.715
For this we may thank *Adam;* but his thanks Par Lost 10.736
Thus *Adam* to himself lamented loud Par Lost 10.845
Forsake me not thus, *Adam*, witness Heav'n Par Lost 10.914
Acknowledg'd and deplor'd, in *Adam* wraught Par Lost 10.939
Adam, by sad experiment I know Par Lost 10.967
But *Adam* with such counsel nothing sway'd, Par Lost 10.1010
To *Adam* what shall come in future dayes, Par Lost 11.114
The Earth, when *Adam* and first Matron *Eve* Par Lost 11.136
Adam observ'd, and with his Eye the chase Par Lost 11.191
And carnal fear that day dimm'd *Adams* eye. Par Lost 11.212
To find where *Adam* shelterd, took his way, Par Lost 11.223
Not unperceav'd of *Adam*, who to *Eve*, Par Lost 11.224
Adam bowd low, hee Kingly from his State Par Lost 11.249
Adam, Heav'ns high behest no Preface needs: Par Lost 11.251
He added not, for *Adam* at the newes Par Lost 11.263
Adam by this from the cold sudden damp Par Lost 11.293
Adam, thou know'st Heav'n his, and all the Earth. Par Lost 11.335
To whom thus *Adam* gratefully repli'd. Par Lost 11.370
Our second *Adam* in the Wilderness, Par Lost 11.383
Michael from *Adams* eyes the Filme remov'd Par Lost 11.412
That *Adam* now enforc't to close his eyes, Par Lost 11.419
Adam, now ope thine eyes, and first behold Par Lost 11.423
Much at that sight was *Adam* in his heart Par Lost 11.448
These two are Brethren, *Adam*, and to come Par Lost 11.454
Drie-ey'd behold? *Adam* could not, but wept, Par Lost 11.495
I yield it just, said *Adam*, and submit. Par Lost 11.526
Of *Adam*, soon enclin'd to admit delight, Par Lost 11.596
To whom thus *Adam* of short joy bereft. Par Lost 11.628
Adam was all in tears, and to his guide Par Lost 11.674
How didst thou grieve then, *Adam*, to behold Par Lost 11.754
Whereat the heart of *Adam* erst so sad Par Lost 11.868
If *Adam* aught perhaps might interpose; Par Lost 12.4
line not in 1667 edition
Whereto thus *Adam* fatherly displeas'd. Par Lost 12.63
Here *Adam* interpos'd. O sent from Heav'n, Par Lost 12.270
He ceas'd, discerning *Adam* with such joy Par Lost 12.372
He ended; and thus *Adam* last reply'd. Par Lost 12.552
Descended, *Adam* to the Bowre where *Eve* Par Lost 12.607
So spake our Mother *Eve*, and *Adam* heard Par Lost 12.624
Since *Adam* and his facil consort *Eve* Par Reg 1.51
And ruine *Adam*, and the exploit perform'd Par Reg 1.102
In *Adam*'s overthrow, and led thir march Par Reg 1.115
Then when I dealt with *Adam* first of Men, Par Reg 2.133
Though *Adam* by his Wives allurement fell, Par Reg 2.134
Supplanted *Adam*, and by vanquishing Par Reg 4.607
For *Adam* and his chosen Sons, whom thou Par Reg 4.614

Adamant
Ninefold, and gates of burning Adamant Par Lost 2.436
Came towring, armd in Adamant and Gold; Par Lost 6.110
Of tenfold Adamant, his ample Shield Par Lost 6.255

Adamant(*cont*)
Of this round World: with Pinns of Adamant Par Lost 10.318
Of Adamant, and as a Center, firm Par Reg 4.534

Adamantean
Adamantean Proof; Samson 134

Adamantine
In Adamantine Chains and penal Fire, Par Lost 1.48
ms 'adamantine'
Three Iron, three of Adamantine Rock, Par Lost 2.646
These Adamantine Gates; against all force Par Lost 2.853
His Adamantine coat gird well, and each Par Lost 6.542
And turn the Adamantine spindle round, Arcades 66
Trinity ms 'adamantine'

Add
False fugitive, and to thy speed add wings, Par Lost 2.700
But with no friendly voice, and add thy name Par Lost 4.36
Satan, and couldst thou faithful add? O name, Par Lost 4.950
To add more sweetness, and they thus began. Par Lost 5.152
Embattell'd in her field: and the humble Shrub, Par Lost 7.322
1667 'add'
That to corporeal substances could adde Par Lost 8.109
Without Copartner? so to add what wants Par Lost 9.821
And all the rule, one Empire; onely add Par Lost 12.581
Deeds to thy knowledge answerable, add Faith, Par Lost 12.582
Add vertue, Patience, Temperance, add Love, Par Lost 12.583
Much less my mind; though thou should'st add to tell Par Reg 4.113
Sam. Of such examples adde mee to the roul, Samson 290
Vant-brass and Greves, and Gauntlet, add thy Spear Samson 1121
Favour renew'd, and add a greater sin Samson 1357
Vertue could see to do what vertue would Mask 373
Trinity ms 'see' ← 'ad all her'
And adde the power of som adjuring verse. Mask 858
Bridgewater ms 'add'
And adde to these retired leasure, Penseroso 49
next adde Narcissus that still weeps in vaine Lycidas Tr. ms 28.19

Added
Severe in youthful beautie, added grace Par Lost 4.845
Thir Snakie foulds, and added wings. First crept Par Lost 7.484
Sufficient penaltie, why hast thou added Par Lost 10.753
He added not, and from her turn'd, but *Eve* Par Lost 10.909
Strength added from above, new hope to spring Par Lost 11.138
He added not, for *Adam* at the newes Par Lost 11.263
He added not; and Satan bowing low Par Reg 1.497
The Son of God; and added thus in scorn: Par Reg 4.550
Added to her noble birth, Winchester 5

Adder
To whom the wilie Adder, blithe and glad. Par Lost 9.625
So much of Adders wisdom I have learn't Samson 936

Addicted
Then to a worldly Crown, addicted more Par Reg 4.213

Adding
Thy words by adding fuel to the flame? Samson 1351

Addition
But with addition strange; yet be not sad. Par Lost 5.116
Th' addition of his Empire, how it shew'd Par Lost 7.555

Address
Address, and to begirt th' Almighty Throne Par Lost 5.868
But now again she makes address to speak. Samson 731

Addressed
They ended parle, and both addrest for fight Par Lost 6.296
Address'd his way, not with indented wave, Par Lost 9.496
Flourishd, since mute, to som great cause addrest, Par Lost 9.672
Which with bland words at will she thus addrest. Par Lost 9.855
To *Michael* thus his humble words addressd. Par Lost 11.295
And with fair speech these words to him address'd. Par Reg 2.301
And words addrest seem into tears dissolv'd, Samson 729
That is addrest to unattending Ears, Mask 272

Ades
Orcus and *Ades*, and the dreaded name Par Lost 2.964

Adhere
Thir lighter wings. To whom these most adhere, Par Lost 2.906
Father and Mother, and to his Wife adhere; Par Lost 8.498

Adherents
And thy adherents: how hast thou disturb'd Par Lost 6.266
And his Adherents, that with so much ease Par Lost 10.622

Adiabene
Of *Adiabene*, *Media*, and the South Par Reg 3.320

Adjoined
Adjoynd, from each thing met conceaves delight, Par Lost 9.449
Small consolation then, were Man adjoyn'd: Par Reg 1.403

Adjourn
A day entire, and Nights due course adjourne, Par Lost 12.264

Adjudged
Must have bin lost, adjudg'd to Death and Hell Par Lost 3.223
Which of those rebell Spirits adjudg'd to Hell Par Lost 4.823
As Battel hath adjudg'd, from this new World Par Lost 10.377
Without Reprieve adjudg'd to death, Samson 288

Adjure
Dare ye for this adjure the Civill Sword Forcers 5

Adjured
Adjur'd by all the bonds of civil Duty Samson 853

Adjuring
And adde the power of som adjuring verse. Mask 858
Trinity ms 'adjuring' ← 'strong'
Bridgewater ms 'adiuringe'

Admiral
Of some great Ammiral, were but a wand, Par Lost 1.294
ms 'Ammirall'

Admiration
Of his great Father. Admiration seis'd — Par Lost 3.271
Or open admiration him behold — Par Lost 3.672
With admiration, and deep Muse to heare — Par Lost 7.52
Reasoning to admiration, and with mee — Par Lost 9.872
In the admiration only of weak minds — Par Reg 2.221
To admiration, led by Natures light; — Par Reg 4.228

Admire
And dig'd out ribs of Gold. Let none admire — Par Lost 1.690
Useless besides, reasoning I oft admire, — Par Lost 8.25
Rather admire; or if they list to try — Par Lost 8.75
I ask the rather, and the more admire, — Par Reg 1.326
To love, at least comtemplate and admire — Par Reg 1.380
Her dictates from thy mouth? most men admire — Par Reg 1.482
Led captive; cease to admire, and all her Plumes — Par Reg 2.222
They praise and they admire they know not what; — Par Reg 3.52
Unwonted shall admire: — Horace 8

Admired
Th' undaunted Fiend what this might be admir'd, — Par Lost 2.677
Admir'd, not fear'd; God and his Son except, — Par Lost 2.678
Th' invention all admir'd, and each, how hee — Par Lost 6.498
Much hee the Place admir'd, the Person more. — Par Lost 9.444
Where universally admir'd; but here — Par Lost 9.542
Though kept from Man, and worthy to be admir'd, — Par Lost 9.746
For in those dayes Might onely shall be admir'd, — Par Lost 11.689
And was admir'd by all, yet this not all — Par Reg 1.214
I walk'd about admir'd of all and dreaded — Samson 530

Admires
Great *Julius*, whom now all the world admires — Par Reg 3.39

Admirest
For what admir'st thou, what transports thee so, — Par Lost 8.567

Admiring
Were always downward bent, admiring more — Par Lost 1.681
Admiring enter'd, and the work some praise — Par Lost 1.731
But as in gaze admiring: Oft he bowd — Par Lost 9.524
I also err'd in overmuch admiring — Par Lost 9.1178
Long hee admiring stood, till Sin, his faire — Par Lost 10.352
Admiring stood a space, then into Hymns — Par Reg 1.169
Thou thy self doat'st on womankind, admiring — Par Reg 2.175

Admit
Would not admit; thine and of all thy Sons — Par Lost 8.637
Wouldst thou admit for his contempt of thee — Par Lost 10.763
Eve, easily may Faith admit, that all — Par Lost 11.141
Of *Adam*, soon enclin'd to admit delight, — Par Lost 11.596
And healing words from these thy friends admit. — Samson 605
Gracious to re-admit the suppliant; — Samson 1173
Mirth, admit me of thy crue — Allegro 38

Admits
Of hazard, which admits no long debate, — Par Reg 1.95

Admitting
Admitting Motion in the Heav'ns, to shew — Par Lost 8.115

Admonish
Shall them admonish, and before them set — Par Lost 11.813

Admonished
Admonisht by his ear, and strait was known — Par Lost 3.647
I warn'd thee, I admonish'd thee, foretold — Par Lost 9.1171

Admonishment
Immortal thanks, and his admonishment — Par Lost 7.77

Adonis
While smooth *Adonis* from his native Rock — Par Lost 1.450
ms 'Adonis'
Or of reviv'd *Adonis*, or renownd — Par Lost 9.440
Where young *Adonis* oft reposes, — Mask 999
Bridgewater ms 'many a Cherub soft'
Trinity ms 'young Adonis oft' ←'many a cherub soft'
B.M. ms 'many'a Cherub soft'

Adopted
Her dowr th' adopted Clusters, to adorn — Par Lost 5.218

Adoration
With solemn adoration down they cast — Par Lost 3.351
Observing none, but adoration pure — Par Lost 4.737
And look for adoration to th' abuse — Par Lost 5.800
In adoration at his feet I fell — Par Lost 8.315
With sudden adoration, and blank aw. — Mask 452
Bridgewater ms 'adoracion'

Adore
To adore the Conquerour? who now beholds — Par Lost 1.323
And Devils to adore for Deities: — Par Lost 1.373
His odious offrings, and adore the Gods — Par Lost 1.475
Adore him, who to compass all this dies, — Par Lost 3.342
Adore the Son, and honour him as mee. — Par Lost 3.343
While they adore me on the Throne of Hell, — Par Lost 4.89
Directed in Devotion, to adore — Par Lost 7.514
Tell me, how may I know him, how adore, — Par Lost 8.280
Adore thee, Author of this Universe, — Par Lost 8.360
Sent from whose sovran goodness I adore. — Par Lost 8.647
By gift, and thy Celestial Beautie adore — Par Lost 9.540
Of glory, and farr off his steps adore. — Par Lost 11.333
Thine or whom I with *Israel*'s Sons adore. — Samson 1177
In wanton dance they praise the bounteous *Pan*, — Mask 176
Trinity ms 'they praise' ←'adore' ←'they praise'
Whom with low reverence I adore as mine, — Arcades 37
Trinity ms defective here
Thee honour, and adore — Psalm 86, 42

Adored
Thir Altars by his Altar, Gods ador'd — Par Lost 1.384
Both turnd, and under op'n Skie ador'd — Par Lost 4.721
Once fawn'd, and cring'd, and servilly ador'd — Par Lost 4.959

Adored(*cont*)
Abdiel, then whom none with more zeale ador'd — Par Lost 5.805
A Goddess among Gods, ador'd and serv'd — Par Lost 9.547
Too long, then lay'st thy scapes on names ador'd, — Par Reg 2.189
As sitting Queen ador'd on Beauties Throne, — Par Reg 2.212

Adorers
Of his adorers: hee to be aveng'd, — Par Lost 9.143
To thy Adorers; thou with trembling fear, — Par Reg 1.451

Adoring
Lowly they bow'd adoring, and began — Par Lost 5.144

Adorn
Her dowr th' adopted Clusters, to adorn — Par Lost 5.218
Made so adorn for thy delight the more, — Par Lost 8.576
Of choicest Flours a Garland to adorne — Par Lost 9.840
To deck her Sons, and that no corner might — Mask 717
Trinity ms 'deck' ←'adorne' ←'deck'

Adorned
Oft to the Image of a Brute, adorn'd — Par Lost 1.371
And this Imperial Sov'ranty, adorn'd — Par Lost 2.446
With Opal Towrs and Battlements adorn'd — Par Lost 2.1049
With glistering Spires and Pinnacles adornd, — Par Lost 3.550
To whom thus *Eve* with perfet beauty adornd. — Par Lost 4.634
Brought her in naked beauty more adorn'd, — Par Lost 4.713
This continent of spacious Heav'n, adornd — Par Lost 6.474
Distant so high, with moving Fires adornd — Par Lost 7.87
Spangling the Hemisphere: then first adornd — Par Lost 7.384
Such as I saw her in my dream, adornd — Par Lost 8.482
To *Pales*, or *Pomona* thus adornd, — Par Lost 9.393
I saw thee first and wedded thee, adorn'd — Par Lost 9.1030
Hers in all real dignitie: Adornd — Par Lost 10.151
Thee lastly nuptial Bowre, by mee adornd — Par Lost 11.280
With more then humane gifts from Heaven adorn'd, — Par Reg 2.137
On seven small Hills, with Palaces adorn'd, — Par Reg 4.35
And as a blessing with such pomp adorn'd? — Samson 357
With gifts and graces eminently adorn'd, — Samson 679

Adorns
Adorns him, colour'd with the Florid hue — Par Lost 7.445

Adramelech
Vanquish'd *Adramelec*, and *Asmadai*, — Par Lost 6.365

Adria
Fled over *Adria* to th' *Hesperian* Fields, — Par Lost 1.520
ms 'Adria'

Adrift
With all his verdure spoil'd, and Trees adrift — Par Lost 11.832

Adulterers
In thy Adulterers, or thy ill got wealth? — Prose 3, 4

Adulterous
By thee adulterous lust was driv'n from men — Par Lost 4.753

Adultery
Rape or Adulterie, where passing faire — Par Lost 11.717

Adust
And vapour as the *Libyan* Air adust, — Par Lost 12.635

Adusted
Concocted and adusted they reduc'd — Par Lost 6.514

Advance
That dar'st, though grim and terrible, advance — Par Lost 2.682
Rising or falling still advance his praise. — Par Lost 5.191
When to advance, or stand, or turn the sway — Par Lost 6.234
Or Shee from West her silent course advance — Par Lost 8.163
Determin'd to advance into our room — Par Lost 9.148
See with what heat these Dogs of Hell advance — Par Lost 10.616
Safe towards *Canaan* from the shoar advance — Par Lost 12.215
And what will he not do to advance his Son? — Par Reg 1.88
That who advance his glory, not thir own, — Par Reg 3.143
Them he himself to glory will advance. — Par Reg 3.144

Advanced
In Arms not worse, in foresight much advanc't, — Par Lost 1.119
Th' Imperial Ensign, which full high advanc't — Par Lost 1.536
Advanc't in view, they stand, a horrid Front — Par Lost 1.563
With Diadem and Scepter high advanc'd — Par Lost 4.90
1667 'advanc't' in some copies
Into our room of bliss thus high advanc't — Par Lost 4.359
Ten thousand thousand Ensignes high advanc'd, — Par Lost 5.588
Far was advanc't on winged speed, an Host — Par Lost 5.744
Satan with vast and haughtie strides advanc't, — Par Lost 6.109
In Cubic Phalanx firm advanc't entire, — Par Lost 6.399
With Jubilie advanc'd; and as they went, — Par Lost 6.884
And sons of men, whom God hath thus advanc't, — Par Lost 7.626
Homeward returning. High in Front advanc't, — Par Lost 12.632
While I to sorrows am no less advanc't, — Par Reg 2.69
When insupportably his foot advanc't, — Samson 136
To *Dagon*, and advanc'd his praises high — Samson 450
Celestial *Cupid* her fam'd Son advanc't, — Mask 1004
line not in Bridgewater ms
Advanc'd their lofty head. — Psalm 80, 44

Advancing
Advancing, sow'd the earth with Orient Pearle, — Par Lost 5.2

Advantage
Th' advantage, and descending tread us down — Par Lost 1.327
Will covet more. With this advantage then — Par Lost 2.35
Yours be th' advantage all, mine the revenge. — Par Lost 2.987
And no advantage gaine. What if the Sun — Par Lost 8.122
His wish and best advantage, us asunder, — Par Lost 9.258
The Gods are first, and that advantage use — Par Lost 9.718
No advantage, and his strength as oft assay. — Par Reg 2.234
Or rather flight, no great advantage on me; — Samson 1118
If they intend advantage of my labours — Samson 1259

Advantaged
Me naught advantag'd, missing what I aim'd. — Par Reg 4.208
To set upon them, what advantag'd best; — Samson 255

Advantageous
Som advantagious act may be achiev'd — Par Lost 2.363

Advantages
Such high advantages thir innocence — Par Lost 6.401
To thir own vile advantages shall turne — Par Lost 12.510
Yet knowing thir advantages too many, — Samson 1401

Adventure
Dreaded not more th' adventure then his voice — Par Lost 2.474
On bold adventure to discover wide — Par Lost 2.571
Little inferiour, by my adventure hard — Par Lost 10.468

Adventurer
Each hour their great adventurer from the search — Par Lost 10.440

Adventures
To matchless valour, and adventures high: — Samson 1740

Adventurous
Invoke thy aid to my adventrous Song, — Par Lost 1.13
In confus'd march forlorn, th' adventrous Bands — Par Lost 2.615
Heroic Ardor to advent'rous deeds — Par Lost 6.66
Bold deed thou hast presum'd, adventrous *Eve*, — Par Lost 9.921
Adventrous work, yet to thy power and mine — Par Lost 10.255
Chances to passe through this adventrous glade, — Mask 79
Trinity ms 'advent'rous' ←'adventurous'
Bridgewater ms 'advent'rous'

Adversary
Mean while the Adversary of God and Man, — Par Lost 2.629
Transports our adversarie, whom no bounds — Par Lost 3.81
Or shall the Adversarie thus obtain — Par Lost 3.156
The Adversarie. Nor think thou with wind — Par Lost 6.282
Us to abolish, least the Adversary — Par Lost 9.947
To a fell Adversarie, his hate or shame: — Par Lost 10.906
The adversarie Serpent, and bring back — Par Lost 12.312
That heard the Adversary, who roving still — Par Reg 1.33
To understand my Adversary, who — Par Reg 4.527

Adverse
His utmost power with adverse power oppos'd — Par Lost 1.103
To us is adverse. Who but felt of late — Par Lost 2.77
Useful of hurtful, prosperous of adverse — Par Lost 2.259
The adverse Legions, nor less hideous joyn'd — Par Lost 6.206
Adverse, that they shall fear we have disarmd — Par Lost 6.490
Adverse to life: then founded, then conglob'd — Par Lost 7.239
As when two Polar Winds blowing adverse — Par Lost 10.289
With adverse blast up-turns them from the South — Par Lost 10.701
Prosperous or adverse: so shalt thou lead — Par Lost 11.364
Be try'd in humble state, and things adverse, — Par Reg 3.189
They swarm, but in adverse withdraw their head — Samson 192
Adverse and turbulent, or by her charms — Samson 1040

Adversities
Of dangers, and adversities and pains, — Par Reg 4.479

Advice
By my advice; since fate inevitable — Par Lost 2.197
Yet not for thy advise or threats I fly — Par Lost 5.889
Oft my advice by presages and signs, — Par Reg 1.394
By my advice, as nearer and of late — Par Reg 3.364
And Advice with scrupulous head, — Mask 108
Bridgewater ms 'advice'
Trinity ms 'Advice' ←'nice tom', ms defective

Advise
We now debate; who can advise, may speak. — Par Lost 2.42
All thoughts of warr: ye have what I advise. — Par Lost 2.283
Faded so soon. Advise if this be worth — Par Lost 2.376
As may advise him of his happie state, — Par Lost 5.234
Let us advise, and to this hazard draw — Par Lost 5.729
Thy disobedience. Well thou didst advise, — Par Lost 5.888
Tending to wilde. Thou therefore now advise — Par Lost 9.212
For God is also in sleep, and Dreams advise, — Par Lost 12.611
Advise thee, gain them as thou canst, or not. — Par Reg 4.211
Old *Manoah:* advise — Samson 328
Then to advise how warr may best, upheld, — Sonnet 17, 7
And O that Israel would *advise* — Psalm 81, 55
Having to advise the public may speak free, — Prose 9, 2

Advised
This was that caution giv'n thee; be advis'd. — Par Lost 5.523
This tumult, and permitted all, advis'd: — Par Lost 6.674
The fleshliest Incubus, and thus advis'd. — Par Reg 2.152
Think what, and be adviz'd, you are but young yet. — Mask 755
line not in Bridgewater ms
Trinity ms 'advis'd'

Advising
Advising peace: for such another Field — Par Lost 2.292

Advocate
Interpret for him, mee his Advocate — Par Lost 11.33

Aegean
On *Lemnos* th' *Aegaean* Ile: thus they relate, — Par Lost 1.746
ms 'Aegaean'
Where on the *Aegean* shore a City stands — Par Reg 4.238

Aemilian
Or on the *Aemilian*, some from farthest South, — Par Reg 4.69

Aenon
The City of Palms, *Aenon*, and *Salem* Old, — Par Reg 2.21

Aeolian
Aeolian charms and *Dorian Lyric* Odes, — Par Reg 4.257

Aerial
Up hither like Aereal vapours flew — Par Lost 3.445
Aereal Music send: nor knew I not — Par Lost 5.548
The mid Aereal Skie: Others on ground — Par Lost 7.442

Aerial(*cont*)
With terror through the dark Aereal Hall. — Par Lost 10.667
Of bright aereal Spirits live insphear'd — Mask 3
Bridgewater ms 'aereall'
1637 'aereall'
Trinity ms 'aereall'

Aery
Thir State affairs. So thick the aerie crowd — Par Lost 1.775
The Bird of *Jove*, stoopt from his aerie tour, — Par Lost 11.185

Aetna
Of thundring *Aetna*, whose combustible — Par Lost 1.233
ms 'Etna'
A God, leap'd fondly into *Aetna* flames, — Par Lost 3.470

Afer
Notus and *Afer* black with thundrous Clouds — Par Lost 10.702

Affable
The affable Arch-Angel, had forewarn'd — Par Lost 7.41
Gentle to me and affable hath been — Par Lost 8.648

Affairs
Thir State affairs. So thick the aerie crowd — Par Lost 1.775
If your joynt power prevailes, th' affaires of Hell — Par Lost 10.408
In manner at our will th' affairs of Earth, — Par Reg 1.50
With man or mens affairs, how I begin — Par Reg 1.132
Like turbulencies in the affairs of men, — Par Reg 4.462

Affect
Too mean pretense, but what we more affect, — Par Lost 6.421
As might affect the Earth with cold and heat — Par Lost 10.653
For Empires sake, nor Empire to affect — Par Reg 3.45
In choice, but oftest to affect the wrong? — Samson 1030

Affecting
Affecting God-head, and so loosing all, — Par Lost 3.206
Affecting all equality with God, — Par Lost 5.763
Such trouble brought, affecting to subdue — Par Lost 12.81
Affecting private life, or more obscure — Par Reg 3.22

Affection
No way assur'd. But conjugal affection — Samson 739

Affects
Affects me equally; nor can I like — Par Lost 5.97
That musing meditation most affects — Mask 386

Affirm
All what we affirm or what deny, and call — Par Lost 5.107
Not that I so affirm, though so it seem — Par Lost 8.117
Nor were it contradiction to affirm — Another 13
1640 'affirme'
line not in 1658 text

Affirming
Affirming it thy Star new grav'n in Heaven, — Par Reg 1.253

Afflict
Of righteous *Job*, then cruelly to afflict him — Par Reg 1.425
Thir daily practice to afflict me more. — Samson 114
To afflict thy self in vain: though sight be lost, — Samson 914
Some way or other yet further to afflict thee. — Samson 1252

Afflicted
And reassembling our afflicted Powers, — Par Lost 1.186
Better abode, and my afflicted Powers — Par Lost 4.939
Exhausted, spiritless, afflicted, fall'n. — Par Lost 6.852
Whom thus afflicted when sad *Eve* beheld, — Par Lost 10.863
Afflicted I may be, it seems, and blest; — Par Reg 2.93
But with th' afflicted in his pangs thir sound — Samson 660
Bruz'd, and afflicted and *so low* — Psalm 88, 61

Afflicting
With Heav'ns afflicting Thunder, and besought — Par Lost 2.166

Affliction
That witness'd huge affliction and dismay — Par Lost 1.57
At my affliction, and perhaps to insult, — Samson 113
Which is my chief affliction, shame and sorrow, — Samson 457
But act not in thy own affliction, Son, — Samson 503
Much more affliction then already felt — Samson 1257
Through sorrow, and affliction great — Psalm 88, 37

Afflictions
My Exaltation to Afflictions high; — Par Reg 2.92

Afflicts
This most afflicts me, that departing hence, — Par Lost 11.315
Yet that which was the worst now least afflicts me, — Samson 195

Afford
What could be less then to afford him praise, — Par Lost 4.46
Our Heav'nly stranger; well we may afford — Par Lost 5.316
Another Rib afford, yet loss of thee — Par Lost 9.912
Be wanting, but afford thee equal aid, — Par Lost 10.271
Afford me place to shew what recompence — Samson 910
Afford me assassinated and betray'd, — Samson 1109
Afford a present to the Infant God? — Nativity 16
Thy saving health to us afford — Psalm 85, 27
Of my *incessant* praiers afford — Psalm 86, 19
Some sign of good to me afford, — Psalm 86, 61

Affords
This day affords, declaring thee resolvd, — Par Lost 9.968

Affright
Our number may affright: Som Virgin sure — Mask 148
What if in wild amazement, and affright, — Mask 356

Affrighted
Affrighted; but strict Fate had cast too deep — Par Lost 6.869

Affrights
Affrights the *Flamins* at their service quaint; — Nativity 194

Affront
And with thir darkness durst affront his light. — Par Lost 1.391
If such affront I labour to avert — Par Lost 9.302
Rather by this his last affront resolv'd, — Par Reg 4.444

Affront(*cont*)
On hostile ground, none daring my affront. Samson 531
Affronts
Tempting affronts us with his foul esteem Par Lost 9.328
The Temple, oft the Law with foul affronts, Par Reg 3.161
Afield
We drove a field, and both together heard Lycidas 27
1638 'a-field'
Trinity ms 'afeild'
Afloat
Afloat, when with fierce Winds *Orion* arm'd Par Lost 1.305
Afraid
All th' Host of Heav'n; back they recoild affraid Par Lost 2.759
Affraid, being naked, hid my self. To whom Par Lost 10.117
What man can do against them, not affraid, Par Lost 12.493
Afresh
A fresh with conscious terrours vex me round, Par Lost 2.801
1667 'Afresh'
Afric
Or whom *Biserta* sent from *Afric* shore Par Lost 1.585
ms 'Afric'
Pontus and *Lucrine* Bay, and *Afric* Coast. Par Reg 2.347
Africa
How hee sirnam'd of *Africa* dismiss'd Par Reg 2.199
'Twixt *Africa* and *Inde*, Ile find him out, Mask 606
African
Aught suffer'd; if young *African* for fame Par Reg 3.101
The feirce Epeirot and the African bold, Sonnet 17, 4
1662, 1694 '*African*'
After
Long after known in *Palestine*, and nam'd Par Lost 1.80
Shot after us in storm, oreblown hath laid Par Lost 1.172
After the toyl of Battel to repose Par Lost 1.319
Thir Seats long after next the Seat of God, Par Lost 1.383
Whom he had vanquisht. After these appear'd Par Lost 1.476
For who can yet beleeve, though after loss, Par Lost 1.631
Frequent and full. After short silence then Par Lost 1.797
Of all his aim, after some dire revenge. Par Lost 2.128
Not peace: and after him thus *Mammon* spake. Par Lost 2.228
After the Tempest: Such applause was heard Par Lost 2.290
Drew after him the third part of Heav'ns Sons Par Lost 2.692
But hee once past, soon after when man fell, Par Lost 2.1023
Pav'd after him a broad and beat'n way Par Lost 2.1026
Draw after him the whole Race of mankind, Par Lost 3.161
Light after light well us'd they shall attain, Par Lost 3.196
And after all thir tribulations long Par Lost 3.336
Long after, now unpeopl'd, and untrod; Par Lost 3.497
Who after came from Earth, sayling arriv'd, Par Lost 3.520
Such wonder seis'd, though after Heaven seen, Par Lost 3.552
They sat them down, and after no more toil Par Lost 4.327
After soft showers; and sweet the coming on Par Lost 4.646
Glistring with dew, nor fragrance after showers, Par Lost 4.653
After his charge receivd; but from among Par Lost 5.248
Taste after taste upheld with kindliest change, Par Lost 5.336
Long after to blest *Marie*, second *Eve*. Par Lost 5.387
After short pause assenting, thus began. Par Lost 5.562
Drew after him the third part of Heav'ns Host: Par Lost 5.710
Interpreted) which not long after, he Par Lost 5.762
Burnt after them to the bottomless pit. Par Lost 6.866
Know then, that after *Lucifer* from Heav'n Par Lost 7.131
Wave rowling after Wave, where way they found, Par Lost 7.298
And Fruit Tree yielding Fruit after her kind; Par Lost 7.311
And every Bird of wing after his kinde; Par Lost 7.394
After thir kindes; I bring them to receave Par Lost 8.343
As one intended first, not after made Par Lost 8.555
The Sun was sunk, and after him the Starr Par Lost 9.48
Him after long debate, irresolute Par Lost 9.87
For what God after better worse would build? Par Lost 9.102
Recomforted, and after thoughts disturbd Par Lost 9.918
As meet is, after such delicious Fare; Par Lost 9.1028
Hee after *Eve* seduc't, unminded slunk Par Lost 10.332
That I must after thee with this thy Son; Par Lost 10.363
In sight of God? Him after all Disputes Par Lost 10.828
That after wretched Life must be at last Par Lost 10.985
His final remedie, and after Life Par Lost 11.62
Though after sleepless Night; for see the Morn, Par Lost 11.173
After short blush of Morn; nigh in her sight Par Lost 11.184
Fusil or grav'n in mettle. After these, Par Lost 11.573
As after thirst, which made thir flowing shrink Par Lost 11.846
And after him, the surer messenger, Par Lost 11.856
To *Haran*, after him a cumbrous Train Par Lost 12.131
More hard'nd after thaw, till in his rage Par Lost 12.194
Nor after resurrection shall he stay Par Lost 12.436
Andrew and *Simon*, famous after known Par Reg 2.7
After appearance, and again prolong Par Reg 2.41
The sensuallest, and after *Asmodai* Par Reg 2.151
Hearts after them tangl'd in Amorous Nets. Par Reg 2.162
After forty days fasting had remain'd, Par Reg 2.243
And eat the second time after repose, Par Reg 2.275
Mules after these, Camels and Dromedaries, Par Reg 3.335
After his aerie jaunt, though hurried sore, Par Reg 4.402
After a night of storm so ruinous, Par Reg 4.436
Was absent, after all his mischief done, Par Reg 4.440
After a dismal night; I heard the rack Par Reg 4.452
So after many a foil the Tempter proud, Par Reg 4.569
Came lagging after; say if he be here. Samson 337
Full of divine instinct, after some proof Samson 526
After the brunt of battel, can as easie Samson 583

After(*cont*)
After offence returning, to regain Samson 1004
After my great transgression, so requite Samson 1356
Rode up in flames after his message told Samson 1433
The whole roof after them, with burst of thunder Samson 1651
After this mortal change, to her true Servants Mask 10
After the *Tuscan* Mariners transform'd Mask 48
Refreshment after toil, ease after pain, Mask 687
line not in Bridgewater ms
After her wandring labours long, Mask 1006
line not in Bridgewater ms
After the heavenly tune, which none can hear Arcades 72
Fly after the Night-steeds, leaving their Moon-lov'd maze. Nativity 236
After long toil their liberty had won, Psalm 114, 2
And after short abode flie back with speed, Fair Inf 60
After so short time of breath, Winchester 9
After this thy travail sore Winchester 49
Who after yeers of barrennes, Winchester 64
Which after held the Sun and Moon in fee. Sonnet 12, 7
To after age thou shalt be writ the man, Sonnet 13, 7
Trinity ms 'after-age' ← 'after age'
In mirth, that after no repenting drawes; Sonnet 21, 6
After-bands
Bind us with after-bands, what profits then Par Lost 9.761
Afternoon
Noontide repast, or Afternoons repose. Par Lost 9.403
After-times
Wider by farr then that of after-times Par Lost 3.529
Again
Th' event is fear'd; should we again provoke Par Lost 2.82
Should intermitted vengeance arm again Par Lost 2.173
Then Crown'd again thir gold'n Harps they took, Par Lost 3.365
If our proposals once again were heard Par Lost 6.618
That wisht the Mountains now might be again Par Lost 6.842
Again, God said, let ther be Firmament Par Lost 7.261
Again th' Almightie spake: Let there be Lights Par Lost 7.339
To live again in these wilde Woods forlorn? Par Lost 9.910
Earth trembl'd from her entrails, as again Par Lost 9.1000
A Dove sent forth once and agen to spie Par Lost 11.857
Least it again dissolve and showr the Earth? Par Lost 11.883
The Earth again by flood, nor let the Sea Par Lost 11.893
This having heard, strait I again revolv'd Par Reg 1.259
Rode up to Heaven, yet once again to come. Par Reg 2.17
After appearance, and again prolong Par Reg 2.41
So spake the Son of God; and here again Par Reg 3.145
Have been before contemn'd, and may agen: Par Reg 4.537
And shall again, pretend they ne're so wise. Samson 212
Cause light again within thy eies to spring, Samson 584
But now again she makes address to speak. Samson 731
Again transgresses, and again submits; Samson 758
To bring my feet again into the snare Samson 931
In perfet thraldom, how again betray me, Samson 946
Again in safety what thou wouldst have done Samson 1128
In confidence whereof I once again Samson 1174
Of strength, again returning with my hair Samson 1355
His strength again to grow up with his hair Samson 1496
2. *Bro*. Heav'n keep my sister, agen agen and neer, Mask 486
Trinity ms 'agen, agen' ← 'yet agen, agen'
Spir. What voice is that, my young Lord? speak agen. Mask 492
And wouldst thou seek again to trap me here Mask 699
1637 'againe'
Trinity ms 'againe'
line not in Bridgewater ms
And cam'st again to visit us once more? Fair Inf 52
O may we soon again renew that Song, Musick 25
Trinity ms 'againe'
I lay and slept, I wak'd again, Psalm 3, 13
Turn us again, *thy grace divine* Psalm 80, 13
And us again revive, Psalm 85, 22
Against
Against the Throne and Monarchy of God Par Lost 1.42
His Temple right against the Temple of God Par Lost 1.402
He also against the house of God was bold: Par Lost 1.470
Against the Highest, and fierce with grasped Arms Par Lost 1.667
Formost to stand against the Thunderers aim Par Lost 2.28
Against the Torturer; when to meet the noise Par Lost 2.64
With upright wing against a higher foe. Par Lost 2.72
If we were wise, against so great a foe Par Lost 2.202
Banded against his Throne, but to remaine Par Lost 2.320
Against a wakeful Foe, while I abroad Par Lost 2.463
Conjur'd against the highest, for which both Thou Par Lost 2.693
Against thy only Son? What fury O Son, Par Lost 2.728
Against thy Fathers head? and know'st for whom; Par Lost 2.730
In bold conspiracy against Heav'ns King, Par Lost 2.751
These Adamantine Gates; against all force Par Lost 2.853
Made head against Heav'ns King, though overthrown. Par Lost 2.992
On even ground against his mortal foe, Par Lost 3.179
Against the high Supremacie of Heav'n, Par Lost 3.205
Direct against which op'nd from beneath, Par Lost 3.526
Warring in Heav'n against Heav'ns matchless King: Par Lost 4.41
Nay curs'd be thou; since against his thy will Par Lost 4.71
Against the eastern Gate of Paradise Par Lost 4.542
Against a rumord Warr, the Smuttie graine Par Lost 4.817
Single against thee wicked, and thence weak. Par Lost 4.856
What thou and thy gay Legions dare against; Par Lost 4.942
With envie against the Son of God, that day Par Lost 5.662
Against thee are gon forth without recall; Par Lost 5.885
Against revolted multitudes the Cause Par Lost 6.31

Against(*cont*)
Against th' Omnipotent to rise in Arms; Par Lost 6.136
Against his worthier, as thine now serve thee, Par Lost 6.180
Armie against Armie numberless to raise Par Lost 6.224
Against us from about his Throne, and judg'd Par Lost 6.426
Against unequal armes to fight in paine, Par Lost 6.454
Against unpaind, impassive; from which evil Par Lost 6.455
Against such hellish mischief fit to oppose. Par Lost 6.636
Against God and *Messiah*, or to fall Par Lost 6.796
Yet envied; against mee is all thir rage, Par Lost 6.813
Or I alone against them, since by strength Par Lost 6.820
As a despite don against the most High, Par Lost 6.906
Against a solemn day, harnest at hand, Par Lost 7.202
To lessen thee, against his purpose serves Par Lost 7.614
Against the charm of Beauties powerful glance. Par Lost 8.533
Against temptation: thou thy self with scorne Par Lost 9.299
Against his will he can receave no harme. Par Lost 9.350
Impart against his will if all be his? Par Lost 9.728
Against his better knowledge, not deceav'd, Par Lost 9.998
Against his Maker; no Decree of mine Par Lost 10.43
Against the day of Battel, to a Field, Par Lost 10.275
Constant, mature, proof against all assaults, Par Lost 10.882
Against a Foe by doom express assign'd us, Par Lost 10.926
Against God onely, I against God and thee, Par Lost 10.931
Against us this deceit: to crush his head Par Lost 10.1035
Against our selves, and wilful barrenness, Par Lost 10.1042
Reluctance against God and his just yoke Par Lost 10.1045
Against the *Syrian* King, who to surprize Par Lost 11.218
But prayer against his absolute Decree Par Lost 11.311
No more availes then breath against the winde, Par Lost 11.312
And testifi'd against thir wayes; hee oft Par Lost 11.721
Against invaders; therefore coold in zeale Par Lost 11.801
In a dark Age, against example good, Par Lost 11.809
Against allurement, custom, and a World Par Lost 11.810
Sin against Law to fight; that when they see Par Lost 12.289
The Law that is against thee, and the sins Par Lost 12.416
What man can do against them, not affraid, Par Lost 12.493
Though to the death, against such cruelties Par Lost 12.494
Who against Faith and Conscience can be heard Par Lost 12.529
Against the Spiritual Foe, and broughtst him thence Par Reg 1.10
At first against mankind so well had thriv'd Par Reg 1.114
Against whate're may tempt, whate're seduce, Par Reg 1.178
Against a Winters day when winds blow keen, Par Reg 1.317
Spoken against, that through my very Soul Par Reg 2.90
In battel, though against thy few in arms. Par Reg 3.20
Against the *Scythian*, whose incursions wild Par Reg 3.301
Sharp sleet of arrowie showers against the face Par Reg 3.324
Or surging waves against a solid rock, Par Reg 4.18
Proof against all temptation as a rock Par Reg 4.533
Thou chance to dash thy foot against a stone. Par Reg 4.559
Against th' Attempter of thy Fathers Throne, Par Reg 4.603
Singly by me against their Conquerours Samson 244
Against his vow of strictest purity, Samson 319
To save himself against a coward arm'd Samson 347
Her spurious first-born; Treason against me? Samson 391
Against all competition, nor will long Samson 476
Against the Eastern ray, translucent, pure. Samson 548
Against another object more enticing? Samson 559
Against the uncircumcis'd, our enemies. Samson 640
Against thee but safe custody, and hold: Samson 802
To oppose against such powerful arguments? Samson 862
Thou mine, not theirs: if aught against my life Samson 888
Against the law of nature, law of nations, Samson 890
To fence my ear against thy sorceries. Samson 937
Man. O lastly over-strong against thy self! Samson 1590
Shoots against the dusky Pole, Mask 99
Which must not be, for that's against my course; Mask 159
Or 'gainst the rugged bark of som broad Elm Mask 354
  Bridgewater ms 'gainst'
Against th' unarmed weakness of one Virgin Mask 582
Shall be unsaid for me: against the threats Mask 586
Against th' opposing will and arm of Heav'n Mask 600
'Gainst all inchantments, mildew blast, or damp Mask 640
  Trinity ms 'gainst'
  Bridgewater ms 'gainst'
Against the Sun-clad power of Chastity, Mask 782
  line not in Trinity ms
  line not in Bridgewater ms
Against the canon laws of our foundation; Mask 808
I throw it on the ground Mask Tr. ms 22.22
  'on' ←'against'
Right against the Eastern gate, Allegro 59
And ever against eating Cares, Allegro 135
Jarr'd against natures chime, and with harsh din Musick 20
  Trinity ms 'jarr'd against' ←'drown'd'
'Gainst old truth) motion number'd out his time; Another 8
Lift not thy spear against the Muses Bowre Sonnet 8, 9
Against heavns hand or will, nor bate a jot Sonnet 22, 7
Against the Lord and his Messiah dear Psalm 2, 5
That in arms against me rise Psalm 3, 3
They pitch against me their Pavillions. Psalm 3, 18
Still on; for against thee they have rebell'd; Psalm 5, 32
Against thy peoples praire. Psalm 80, 20
And turn my hand against *all those* Psalm 81, 59
Against thy people they contrive Psalm 83, 9
Themselves against thee they unite Psalm 83, 19
O God the proud against me rise Psalm 86, 49
'Gainst them that rais'd thee dost thou lift thy horn, Prose 3, 2

Agape
Dazles the croud, and sets them all agape. Par Lost 5.357

Agate
Thick set with Agat, and the azurn sheen Mask 893
  1637 'agat'
  Bridgewater ms 'Agate'

Age
What in an age they with incessant toyle Par Lost 1.698
That name, unless an age too late, or cold Par Lost 9.44
This is old age; but then thou must outlive Par Lost 11.538
Of middle Age one rising, eminent Par Lost 11.665
In a dark Age, against example good, Par Lost 11.809
And all the Prophets in thir Age the times Par Lost 12.243
And unrecorded left through many an Age, Par Reg 1.16
To such perfection, that e're yet my age Par Reg 1.209
Though of this Age the wonder and the fame, Par Reg 2.209
Now at full age, fulness of time, thy season, Par Reg 4.380
Dungeon, or beggery, or decrepit age! Samson 69
Your younger feet, while mine cast back with age Samson 336
To a contemptible old age obscure. Samson 572
Inglorious, unimploy'd, with age out-worn. Samson 580
In crude old age; Samson 700
May ever tend about thee to old age Samson 925
Sons wont to nurse thir Parents in old age, Samson 1487
Thou in old age car'st how to nurse thy Son. Samson 1488
Made older then thy age through eye-sight lost. Samson 1489
And here their tender age might suffer perill, Mask 40
Who ripe, and frolick of his full grown age, Mask 59
Strict Age, and sowre Severity, Mask 109
  Trinity ms 'age'
  Bridgewater ms 'age'
Or what (though rare) of later age, Penseroso 101
And may at last my weary age Penseroso 167
Time will run back, and fetch the age of gold, Nativity 135
A *Sybil* old, bow-bent with crooked age, Vacation 69
The labour of an age in piled Stones, Shakespear 2
  1663-4 'Age'
  1632 'Age'
Thy age, like ours, O Soul of Sir *John Cheek*, Sonnet 11, 12
I did but prompt the age to quit their cloggs Sonnet 12, 1
To after age thou shalt be writ the man, Sonnet 13, 7
  Trinity ms 'after-age' ←'after age'
From age to age on us? Psalm 85, 20

Aged
But now an aged man in Rural weeds, Par Reg 1.314
Hitting thy aged ear should pierce too deep. Samson 1568
Bearing her straight to aged *Nereus* Hall, Mask 835
From betwixt two aged Okes, Allegro 82
The aged Earth agast Nativity 160
As *when* an *aged* wood takes fire Psalm 83, 53

Agents
Of highest Agents, deemd however wise. Par Lost 9.683

Ages
Ages of hopeless end; this would be worse. Par Lost 2.186
Of all past Ages to the general Doom Par Lost 3.328
His good to Worlds and Ages infinite. Par Lost 7.191
New Heav'n and Earth shall to the Ages rise, Par Lost 10.647
Who of all Ages to succeed, but feeling Par Lost 10.733
Or monument to Ages, and thereon Par Lost 11.326
The burd'n of many Ages, on me light Par Lost 11.767
New Heav'ns, new Earth, Ages of endless date Par Lost 12.549
How many Ages, as the years of men, Par Reg 1.48
So many Ages, and shall yet regain Par Reg 2.441
All these the *Parthian*, now some Ages past, Par Reg 3.294
As I by thee, to Ages an example. Samson 765
A secular bird ages of lives. Samson 1707

Aggravate
The Fiend by easie ascent, or aggravate Par Lost 3.524
His will who reigns above, to aggravate Par Lost 10.549
Rather then aggravate my evil state, Par Reg 3.218
And aggravate my folly who committed Samson 1000

Aggravations
By it self, with aggravations not surcharg'd, Samson 769

Aggregated
Cathaian Coast. The aggregated Soyle Par Lost 10.293

Aghast
With shuddring horror pale, and eyes agast Par Lost 2.616
With looks agast and sad he thus bespake. Par Reg 1.43
The aged Earth agast Nativity 160
Shake earth, and at the presence be agast Psalm 114, 15

Agitation
Kindl'd through agitation to a Flame, Par Lost 9.637

Agony
Here in perpetual agonie and pain, Par Lost 2.861
Thy presence, agonie of love till now Par Lost 9.858
Of heart-sick Agonie, all feavorous kinds, Par Lost 11.482

Agra
To *Agra* and *Lahor* of great *Mogul* Par Lost 11.391

Agreeable
Conceiv'd, agreeable to a Fathers love, Samson 1506

Agrican
When *Agrican* with all his Northern powers Par Reg 3.338

Ah
Ah wherefore! he deservd no such return Par Lost 4.42
Ah gentle pair, yee little think how nigh Par Lost 4.366
Me now your curse! Ah, why should all mankind Par Lost 10.822
Mess. Ah *Manoa* I refrain, too suddenly Samson 1565
Ay me, I fondly dream! Lycidas 56

Ah(*cont*)
1638 'Ah me'
Ah! Who hath reft (quoth he) my dearest pledge? Lycidas 107
Ah *Constantine*, of how much ill was cause Prose 1, 1
Ahab
To draw the proud King *Ahab* into fraud Par Reg 1.372
Ahaz
Ahaz his sottish Conquerour, whom he drew Par Lost 1.472
ms 'Ahaz'
Aialon
And thou Moon in the vale of *Aialon*, Par Lost 12.266
Aid
Invoke thy aid to my adventrous Song, Par Lost 1.13
ms 'aide'
Of Rebel Angels, by whose aid aspiring Par Lost 1.38
ms 'aide'
Sublim'd with Mineral fury, aid the Winds, Par Lost 1.235
Happie for man, so coming; he her aide Par Lost 3.232
(So call that opposite fair Starr) her aide Par Lost 3.727
Thy fiercest, when in Battel to thy aide Par Lost 4.927
His puissance, trusting in th' Almightie's aide, Par Lost 6.119
And join him nam'd *Almighty* to thy aid, Par Lost 6.294
Forthwith on all sides to his aide was run Par Lost 6.335
All like himself rebellious, by whose aid Par Lost 7.140
By Nature as in aide, and clos'd mine eyes. Par Lost 8.459
Perfet within, no outward aid require; Par Lost 8.642
Aid us, the work under our labour grows, Par Lost 9.208
To other speedie aide might lend at need; Par Lost 9.260
Angels, nor think superfluous others aid. Par Lost 9.308
Be wanting, but afford thee equal aid, Par Lost 10.271
Whereon I live, thy gentle looks, thy aid, Par Lost 10.919
His counsel whom she had displeas'd, his aide; Par Lost 10.944
But call in aide, which makes a bloody Fray; Par Lost 11.651
In sharp contest of Battel found no aide Par Lost 11.800
Of him so lately promiss'd to thy aid Par Lost 12.542
If not disposer; lend them oft my aid, Par Reg 1.393
With clamour was assur'd thir utmost aid Par Reg 2.148
Have wasted *Sogdiana;* to her aid Par Reg 3.302
Nicely or cautiously my offer'd aid, Par Reg 4.377
The perfet season offer'd with my aid Par Reg 4.468
Obtrud'st thy offer'd aid, that I accepting Par Reg 4.493
Go to his Temple, invocate his aid Samson 1146
Likeliest, and neerest to the present ayd Mask 90
Trinity ms 'aide' ←'chance' ←'aide'
Bridgewater ms 'ayde'
1637 'aide'
To aid a Virgin, such as was her self Mask 856
Bridgewater ms 'ayde'
Trinity ms 'aide'
I pray thee then deny me not thy aide Vacation 15
To aid the Sons of Lot. Psalm 83, 32
Will call on thee *for aid;* Psalm 86, 22
Aided
Remains thee, aided by this host of friends, Par Lost 6.38
Aidless
The aidless innocent Lady his wish't prey, Mask 574
Trinity ms 'aidlesse' ←'helplesse'
1637 'aidlesse'
Bridgewater ms 'aideless'
Aids
Of enemies, of aids, battels and leagues, Par Reg 3.392
Aim
If he oppos'd; and with ambitious aim Par Lost 1.41
His inmost counsels from thir destind aim. Par Lost 1.168
Formost to stand against the Thunderers aim Par Lost 2.28
1667 'aime'
Of all his aim, after some dire revenge. Par Lost 2.128
Leveld his deadly aime; thir fatall hands Par Lost 2.712
Aim therefore at no less then all the world, Par Reg 4.105
Aim at the highest, without the highest attain'd Par Reg 4.106
Others more moderate seeming, but thir aim Samson 1464
Aimed
Uplifted imminent one stroke they aim'd Par Lost 6.317
Let it; I reck not, so it light well aim'd, Par Lost 9.173
Of honour, wealth, high fare, aim'd not beyond Par Reg 2.202
Me naught advantag'd, missing what I aim'd. Par Reg 4.208
Aimest
To whom th' Archangel. Dextrously thou aim'st; Par Lost 11.884
Aims
Vaine hopes, vaine aimes, inordinate desires Par Lost 4.808
Air
Aloft, incumbent on the dusky Air Par Lost 1.226
ms 'air'
Of cold *Olympus* rul'd the middle Air Par Lost 1.516
ms 'air'
Ten thousand Banners rise into the Air Par Lost 1.545
ms 'air'
Looks through the Horizontal misty Air Par Lost 1.595
ms 'air'
Thick swarm'd, both on the ground and in the air, Par Lost 1.767
Or Summers Noon-tide air, while thus he spake. Par Lost 2.309
Purge off this gloom; the soft delicious Air, Par Lost 2.400
Part on the Plain, or in the Air sublime Par Lost 2.528
Rend up both Rocks and Hills, and ride the Air Par Lost 2.540
Where Armies whole have sunk: the parching Air Par Lost 2.594
In secret, riding through the Air she comes Par Lost 2.663
To joyn thir dark Encounter in mid air: Par Lost 2.718
Wing silently the buxom Air, imbalm'd Par Lost 2.842

Air(*cont*)
Of neither Sea, nor Shore, nor Air, nor Fire, Par Lost 2.912
Or in the emptier waste, resembling Air, Par Lost 2.1045
In the dun Air sublime, and ready now Par Lost 3.72
Uncertain which, in Ocean or in Air. Par Lost 3.76
I through the ample Air in Triumph high Par Lost 3.254
Of glimmering air less vext with tempest loud: Par Lost 3.429
Into the devious Air; then might ye see Par Lost 3.489
Through the pure marble Air his oblique way Par Lost 3.564
Shadow from body opaque can fall, and the Aire, Par Lost 3.619
The cumbrous Elements, Earth, Flood, Aire, Fire, Par Lost 3.715
That Lantskip: And of pure now purer aire Par Lost 4.153
Earth, Aire, and Sea. Then let us not think hard Par Lost 4.432
Impress the Air, and shews the Mariner Par Lost 4.558
Celestial voices to the midnight air, Par Lost 4.682
The God that made both Skie, Air, Earth and Heav'n Par Lost 4.722
With sudden blaze diffus'd, inflames the Aire: Par Lost 4.818
To settle here on Earth, or in mid Aire; Par Lost 4.940
The pendulous round Earth with ballanc't Aire Par Lost 4.1000
But somtimes in the Air, as wee, somtimes Par Lost 5.79
Aire, and ye Elements the eldest birth Par Lost 5.180
Winnows the buxom Air; till within soare Par Lost 5.270
Earth and the Sea feed Air, the Air those Fires Par Lost 5.417
Streame in the Aire, and for distinction serve Par Lost 5.590
Thir march was, and the passive Air upbore Par Lost 6.72
Tormented all the Air; all Air seemd then Par Lost 6.244
Now wav'd thir fierie Swords, and in the Aire Par Lost 6.304
Receive, no more then can the fluid Aire: Par Lost 6.349
Came flying, and in mid Aire aloud thus cri'd. Par Lost 6.536
Emboweld with outragious noise the Air, Par Lost 6.587
Main Promontories flung, which in the Air Par Lost 6.654
So Hills amid the Air encounterd Hills Par Lost 6.664
An Earthlie Guest, and drawn Empyreal Aire, Par Lost 7.14
All space, the ambient Aire wide interfus'd Par Lost 7.89
1669 'Air'
Disparted, and between spun out the Air, Par Lost 7.241
Transparent, Elemental Air, diffus'd Par Lost 7.265
They summ'd thir Penns, and soaring th' air sublime Par Lost 7.421
Her annual Voiage, born on Windes; the Aire Par Lost 7.431
With Fish replenisht, and the Aire with Fowle, Par Lost 7.447
Consummate lovly smil'd; Aire, Water, Earth, Par Lost 7.502
Over the Fish and Fowle of Sea and Aire, Par Lost 7.521
Over Fish of the Sea, and Fowle of the Aire, Par Lost 7.533
Angelic harmonies: the Earth, the Aire Par Lost 7.560
Over his Works, on Earth, in Sea, or Air, Par Lost 7.629
Sent from her through the wide transpicuous aire, Par Lost 8.141
And beares thee soft with the smooth Air along, Par Lost 8.166
From where I first drew Aire, and first beheld Par Lost 8.284
And over Fields and Waters, as in Aire Par Lost 8.301
Or live in Sea, or Aire, Beast, Fish, and Fowle. Par Lost 8.341
Thir Element to draw the thinner Aire. Par Lost 8.348
With various living creatures, and the Aire Par Lost 8.370
And into all things from her Aire inspir'd Par Lost 8.476
Easier then Air with Air, if Spirits embrace, Par Lost 8.626
Where Houses thick and Sewers annoy the Aire, Par Lost 9.446
Her graceful Innocence, her every Aire Par Lost 9.459
Organic, or impulse of vocal Air, Par Lost 9.530
Yet Lords declar'd of all in Earth or Aire? Par Lost 9.658
Prince of the Aire; then rising from his Grave Par Lost 10.185
Captivity led captive through the Aire, Par Lost 10.188
Before him naked to the aire, that now Par Lost 10.212
His Nostril wide into the murkie Air, Par Lost 10.280
Dominion exercise and in the Aire, Par Lost 10.400
Sea, Aire, and Shoar, the Thunder when to rowle Par Lost 10.666
Wholsom and cool, and mild, but with black Air Par Lost 10.847
The Air attrite to Fire, as late the Clouds Par Lost 10.1073
Watering the ground, and with our sighs the Air Par Lost 10.1090
Watering the ground, and with thir sighs the Air Par Lost 10.1102
As a distemper, gross to aire as gross, Par Lost 11.53
On Bird, Beast, Aire, Aire suddenly eclips'd Par Lost 11.183
Of flight pursu'd in th' Air and ore the ground Par Lost 11.202
And wilde, how shall we breath in other Aire Par Lost 11.284
Land, Sea, and Aire, and every kinde that lives, Par Lost 11.337
To what thou hast, and for the Aire of youth Par Lost 11.542
Himself and his rash Armie, where thin Aire Par Lost 12.76
With victory, triumphing through the aire Par Lost 12.452
The Serpent, Prince of aire, and drag in Chaines Par Lost 12.454
Or works of God in Heav'n, Aire, Earth, or Sea, Par Lost 12.579
1667 'Air'
And vapour as the *Libyan* Air adust, Par Lost 12.635
Flies to his place, nor rests, but in mid air Par Reg 1.39
O ancient Powers of Air and this wide world, Par Reg 1.44
For much more willingly I mention Air, Par Reg 1.45
In this fair Empire won of Earth and Air; Par Reg 1.63
Or range in th' Air, nor from the Heav'n of Heav'ns Par Reg 1.366
Into thin Air diffus'd: for now began Par Reg 1.499
From the bleak air; a Stable was our warmth, Par Reg 2.74
Up to the middle Region of thick Air, Par Reg 2.117
Powers of Fire, Air, Water, and Earth beneath, Par Reg 2.124
All these are Spirits of Air, and Woods, and Springs, Par Reg 2.374
Of vision multiplyed through air, or glass Par Reg 4.41
Tetrarchs of fire, air, flood, and on the earth Par Reg 4.201
Built nobly, pure the air, and light the soil, Par Reg 4.239
Of *Hippogrif* bore through the Air sublime Par Reg 4.542
Throttl'd at length in the Air, expir'd and fell; Par Reg 4.568
As on a floating couch through the blithe Air, Par Reg 4.585
The air imprison'd also, close and damp, Samson 8
Sam. I hear the sound of words, thir sense the air Samson 176

Air(*cont*)
Nor breath of Vernal Air from snowy *Alp*. Samson 628
Or swing thee in the Air, then dash thee down Samson 1240
Rifted the Air clamouring thir god with praise, Samson 1621
In Regions milde of calm and serene Ayr, Mask 4
Trinity ms 'aire'
Bridgewater ms 'ayre'
And makes one blot of all the ayr, Mask 133
Trinity ms 'all the aire' ←'nature'
Bridgewater ms 'aire'
My dazling Spells into the spungy ayr, Mask 154
Bridgewater ms 'aire'
1637 'air'
Trinity ms 'aire'
And with these raptures moves the vocal air Mask 247
Bridgewater ms 'ayre'
1637 'aire'
Trinity ms 'aire'
Som far off hallow break the silent Air. Mask 481
Trinity ms 'aire'
1637 'aire'
Bridgewater ms 'ayre'
And fill'd the Air with barbarous dissonance, Mask 550
Trinity ms 'aire'
1637 'aire'
Bridgewater ms 'aire'
And stole upon the Air, that even Silence Mask 557
1637 'aire'
Trinity ms 'aire'
Bridgewater ms 'aire'
Th' earth cumber'd, and the wing'd air dark't with plumes, Mask 730
Trinity ms 'aire'
Bridgewater ms 'ayre'
1637 'aire'
In this unhallow'd air, but that this Jugler Mask 757
Bridgewater ms 'ayre'
1637 'aire'
Trinity ms 'aire'
Summer drouth, or singed air Mask 928
Trinity ms 'aire'
1637 'aire'
Bridgewater ms 'aire'
There I suck the liquid ayr Mask 980
1673 'air'
1637 'ayre'
Trinity ms 'aire'
Bridgewater ms 'ayre'
B.M. ms 'Air'
the feilds with cattell & the aire with fowle Mask Tr. ms 21.57
Or if the Ayr will not permit, Penseroso 77
In fire, air, flood, or under ground, Penseroso 94
The Ayr was calm, and on the level brine, Lycidas 98
Trinity ms 'aire'
1673 'Air'
1638 'aire'
She woo's the gentle Air Nativity 38
The Air such pleasure loth to lose, Nativity 99
The dreadfull Judge in middle Air shall spread his throne. Nativity 164
Through middle empire of the freezing aire Fair Inf 16
And mistie Regions of wide air next under, Vacation 41
Wherwith the stage of Ayr and Earth did ring, Passion 2
Went to the ground: And the repeated air Sonnet 8, 12
Trinity ms 'aire'
That with smooth aire couldst humor best our tongue. Sonnet 13, 8
Trinity ms 'aire' ←'aires'
1648 'Aire'
Warble immortal Notes and *Tuskan* Ayre? Sonnet 20, 12

Airs
The Birds thir quire apply; aires, vernal aires, Par Lost 4.264
Joyous the Birds; fresh Gales and gentle Aires Par Lost 8.515
The season, prime for sweetest Sents and Aires: Par Lost 9.200
From Noon, and gentle Aires due at thir hour Par Lost 10.93
And all the while Harmonious Airs were heard Par Reg 2.362
Lap me in soft *Lydian* Aires, Allegro 136
Me softer airs befit, and softer strings Passion 27

Airy
Can execute thir aerie purposes, Par Lost 1.430
Thir State affairs. So thick the aerie crowd Par Lost 1.775
His uncouth way, or spread his aerie flight Par Lost 2.407
Prick forth the Aerie Knights, and couch thir Spears Par Lost 2.536
Throws his steep flight in many an Aerie wheele, Par Lost 3.741
Bent all on speed, and markt his Aerie Gate; Par Lost 4.568
Was Aerie light from pure digestion bred, Par Lost 5.4
She forms Imaginations, Aerie shapes, Par Lost 5.105
More aerie, last the bright consummate floure Par Lost 5.481
Of airie threats to aw whom yet with deeds Par Lost 6.283
To journie through the airie gloom began, Par Lost 7.246
Thir Aierie Caravan high over Sea's Par Lost 7.428
The Bird of *Jove*, stoopt from his aerie tour, Par Lost 11.185
My Aerie Microscope) thou may'st behold Par Reg 4.57
After his aerie jaunt, though hurried sore, Par Reg 4.402
Bears greatest names in his wild aerie flight. Samson 974
And airy tongues, that syllable mens names Mask 208
1637 'ayrie'
line not in Bridgewater ms
Trinity ms 'ayrie'
Within thy airy shell Mask 231
B.M. ms 'Airy'

Airy(*cont*)
1637 'ayrie'
Trinity ms 'ayrie'
Bridgewater ms 'ayrie'
Wave at his Wings in Airy stream, Penseroso 148
Of *Cynthia*'s seat, the Airy region thrilling, Nativity 103

Alabaster
Of Alablaster, pil'd up to the Clouds, Par Lost 4.544
Of Alabaster, top't with Golden Spires: Par Reg 4.548
Your nervs are all chain'd up in Alablaster, Mask 660
1637 'alablaster'
Trinity ms 'alablaster'
Bridgewater ms 'alablaster'

Alack
Alack that so to change thee winter had no power. Fair Inf 28

Alacrity
With fresh alacritie and force renew'd Par Lost 2.1012

Aladule
The Realm of *Aladule*, in his retreate Par Lost 10.435

Alarm
And with perpetual inrodes to Allarme, Par Lost 2.103
Instant without disturb they took Allarm, Par Lost 6.549
Without our hazard, labour, or allarme, Par Lost 10.491

Alarmed
Prove chaff. On th' other side *Satan* allarm'd Par Lost 4.985
Least entring on the *Canaanite* allarmd Par Lost 12.217

Alarms
Or if they be but false alarms of Fear, Mask 364
line not in Trinity ms
line not in Bridgewater ms

Alas
The punishment all on thy self; alas, Par Lost 10.949
Alas, both for the deed and for the cause! Par Lost 11.461
Alas, from what high hope to what relapse Par Reg 2.30
Alas how simple, to these Cates compar'd, Par Reg 2.348
Alas what can they teach, and not mislead; Par Reg 4.309
For inward light alas Samson 162
Alas methinks whom God hath chosen once Samson 368
Curs'd as his life. *Spir*. Alas good ventrous youth, Mask 609
Trinity ms 'alas'
Alas! What boots it with uncessant care Lycidas 64
But kill'd alas, and then bewayl'd his fatal bliss. Fair Inf 7
Alas, how soon our sin Circum 12
She had told, alas too soon, Winchester 8
1673 'alass'
A here alas, hath laid him in the dirt, Carrier 2
1658 'alasse'
I am a man, but weak alas Psalm 88, 15

Albracca
Besieg'd *Albracca*, as Romances tell; Par Reg 3.339

Alcairo
Nor great *Alcairo* such magnificence Par Lost 1.718
ms 'Alcairo'

Alcestis
Brought to me like *Alcestis* from the grave, Sonnet 23, 2

Alchemist
Of sooty coal the Empiric Alchimist Par Lost 5.440

Alchemy
Put to thir mouths the sounding Alchymie Par Lost 2.517

Alcides
As when *Alcides* from *Oechalia* Crown'd Par Lost 2.542
With *Joves Alcides*, and oft foil'd still rose, Par Reg 4.565

Alcinous
Alcinous reign'd, fruit of all kindes, in coate, Par Lost 5.341
Alcinous, host of old *Laertes* Son, Par Lost 9.441
In solemn Songs at King *Alcinous* feast, Vacation 49

Ale
Then to the Spicy Nut-brown Ale, Allegro 100
Fainted, and died, nor would with Ale be quickn'd; Another 16
line not in 1640, 1657, 1658 texts

Aleian
Dismounted, on th' *Aleian* Field I fall Par Lost 7.19

Alexander
Great *Alexander* to subdue the world, Par Reg 4.252

Algarsife
Of *Camball*, and of *Algarsife*, Penseroso 111

Algiers
Marocco and *Algiers*, and *Tremisen;* Par Lost 11.404

Alien
Alien from Heav'n, with passions foul obscur'd: Par Lost 4.571
No alien God shall be Psalm 81, 38

Alienate
O alienate from God, O spirit accurst, Par Lost 5.877

Alienated
Of alienated *Judah*. Next came one Par Lost 1.457
Now alienated, distance and distaste, Par Lost 9.9
Retiring, by his own doom alienated, Par Lost 10.378

Alighted
Satan alighted walks: a Globe farr off Par Lost 3.422

Alights
Down he alights among the sportful Herd Par Lost 4.396

Alike
Warr therefore, open or conceal'd, alike Par Lost 2.187
Of hazard as of honour, due alike Par Lost 2.453
Not all parts like, but all alike informd Par Lost 3.593
To me alike, it deals eternal woe. Par Lost 4.70
All seasons and thir change, all please alike. Par Lost 4.640
No ingrateful food: and food alike those pure Par Lost 5.407

Alike(*cont*)
Should win in Arms, in both disputes alike — Par Lost 6.123
Distinct alike with multitude of eyes, — Par Lost 6.847
Tedious alike: Of fellowship I speak — Par Lost 8.389
Alike, to Serpents all as accessories — Par Lost 10.520
Alike is Hell, or Paradise, or Heaven, — Par Lost 10.598
And what thou fearst, alike destroyes all hope — Par Lost 10.838
God is as here, and will be found alike — Par Lost 11.350
The Spirit of God, promisd alike and giv'n — Par Lost 12.519
And will alike be punish'd; whether thou — Par Reg 3.214
Just or unjust, alike seem miserable, — Samson 703
For oft alike, both come to evil end. — Samson 704
Sam. Or peace or not, alike to me he comes. — Samson 1074

Alimental
From all his alimental recompence — Par Lost 5.424

Alive
The one just Man alive; by his command — Par Lost 11.818
Of sight, reserv'd alive to be repeated — Samson 645
By thee preserv'd alive. — Psalm 85, 24

All
Brought Death into the World, and all our woe, — Par Lost 1.3
Before all Temples th' upright heart and pure, — Par Lost 1.18
Had cast him out from Heav'n, with all his Host — Par Lost 1.37
A Dungeon horrible, on all sides round — Par Lost 1.61
That comes to all; but torture without end — Par Lost 1.67
All is not lost; the unconquerable Will, — Par Lost 1.106
Hath lost us Heav'n, and all this mighty Host — Par Lost 1.136
Though all our Glory extinct, and happy state — Par Lost 1.141
Leviathan, which God of all his works — Par Lost 1.201
How all his malice serv'd but to bring forth — Par Lost 1.217
And leave a singed bottom all involv'd — Par Lost 1.236
And what I should be, all but less then he — Par Lost 1.257
Of battel when it rag'd, in all assaults — Par Lost 1.277
He call'd so loud, that all the hollow Deep — Par Lost 1.314
Like Night, and darken'd all the Land of *Nile:* — Par Lost 1.343
On the firm brimstone, and fill all the Plain; — Par Lost 1.350
In amorous dittyes all a Summers day, — Par Lost 1.449
Both her first born and all her bleating Gods. — Par Lost 1.489
Or in *Dodona*, and through all the bounds — Par Lost 1.518
All these and more came flocking; but with looks — Par Lost 1.522
Seraphic arms and Trophies: all the while — Par Lost 1.539
All in a moment through the gloom were seen — Par Lost 1.544
Warr'd on by Cranes: though all the Giant brood — Par Lost 1.576
And all who since, Baptiz'd or Infidel — Par Lost 1.582
When *Charlemain* with all his Peerage fell — Par Lost 1.586
All her Original brightness, nor appear'd — Par Lost 1.592
Above them all th' Arch Angel: but his face — Par Lost 1.600
With all his Peers: attention held them mute. — Par Lost 1.618
That all these puissant Legions, whose exile — Par Lost 1.632
For mee be witness all the Host of Heav'n, — Par Lost 1.635
Equal'd in all thir glories, to inshrine — Par Lost 1.719
By all his Engins, but was headlong sent — Par Lost 1.750
Attended: all access was throng'd, the Gates — Par Lost 1.761
Car'd not to be at all; with that care lost — Par Lost 2.48
Went all his fear: of God, or Hell, or worse — Par Lost 2.49
Arm'd with Hell flames and fury all at once — Par Lost 2.61
But all was false and hollow; though his Tongue — Par Lost 2.112
Of all his aim, after some dire revenge. — Par Lost 2.128
With Armed watch, that render all access — Par Lost 2.130
By force, and at our heels all Hell should rise — Par Lost 2.135
All incorruptible would on his Throne — Par Lost 2.138
Th' Almighty Victor to spend all his rage, — Par Lost 2.144
His red right hand to plague us? what if all — Par Lost 2.174
Views all things at one view? he from heav'ns highth — Par Lost 2.190
All these our motions vain, sees and derides; — Par Lost 2.191
Then wise to frustrate all our plots and wiles. — Par Lost 2.193
And publish Grace to all, on promise made — Par Lost 2.238
The sensible of pain. All things invite — Par Lost 2.278
All thoughts of warr: ye have what I advise. — Par Lost 2.283
The sound of blustring winds, which all night long — Par Lost 2.286
Thither let us bend all our thoughts, to learn — Par Lost 2.354
All as our own, and drive as we were driven, — Par Lost 2.366
But from the Author of all ill could Spring — Par Lost 2.381
To mingle and involve, done all to spite — Par Lost 2.384
Sparkl'd in all thir eyes; with full assent — Par Lost 2.388
All circumspection, and we now no less — Par Lost 2.414
The weight of all and our last hope relies. — Par Lost 2.416
The perilous attempt: but all sat mute, — Par Lost 2.420
Barr'd over us prohibit all egress. — Par Lost 2.437
Through all the Coasts of dark destruction seek — Par Lost 2.464
Deliverance for us all: this enterprize — Par Lost 2.465
The Monarch, and prevented all reply, — Par Lost 2.467
Thir rising all at once was as the sound — Par Lost 2.476
Loose all her virtue; least bad men should boast — Par Lost 2.483
Heard farr and wide, and all the host of Hell — Par Lost 2.519
Vain wisdom all, and false Philosophie: — Par Lost 2.565
Of ancient pile; all else deep snow and ice, — Par Lost 2.591
At certain revolutions all the damn'd — Par Lost 2.597
In sweet forgetfulness all pain and woe, — Par Lost 2.608
All in one moment, and so neer the brink; — Par Lost 2.609
All taste of living wight, as once it fled — Par Lost 2.613
Where all life dies, death lives, and Nature breeds, — Par Lost 2.624
Perverse, all monstrous, all prodigious things, — Par Lost 2.625
Had been achiev'd, whereof all Hell had rung, — Par Lost 2.723
Of all the Seraphim with thee combin'd — Par Lost 2.750
All on a sudden miserable pain — Par Lost 2.752
All th' Host of Heav'n; back they recoild affraid — Par Lost 2.759
Through all the Empyrean: down they fell — Par Lost 2.771

All(*cont*)
Distorted, all my nether shape thus grew — Par Lost 2.784
From all her Caves, and back resounded *Death*. — Par Lost 2.789
Mee overtook his mother all dismaid, — Par Lost 2.792
Both him and thee, and all the heav'nly Host — Par Lost 2.824
This uncouth errand sole, and one for all — Par Lost 2.827
Immeasurably, all things shall be your prey. — Par Lost 2.844
These Adamantine Gates; against all force — Par Lost 2.853
Sad instrument of all our woe, she took; — Par Lost 2.872
Which but her self not all the *Stygian* powers — Par Lost 2.875
Chance governs all. Into this wilde Abyss, — Par Lost 2.910
But all these in thir pregnant causes mixt — Par Lost 2.913
With all her battering Engines bent to rase — Par Lost 2.923
A vast vacuitie: all unawares — Par Lost 2.932
Of stunning sounds and voices all confus'd — Par Lost 2.952
And *Tumult* and *Confusion* all imbroild, — Par Lost 2.966
All usurpation thence expell'd, reduce — Par Lost 2.983
Yours be th' advantage all, mine the revenge. — Par Lost 2.987
Keep residence; if all I can will serve, — Par Lost 2.999
Of fighting Elements, on all sides round — Par Lost 2.1015
Shine inward, and the mind through all her powers — Par Lost 3.52
Irradiate, there plant eyes, all mist from thence — Par Lost 3.53
High Thron'd above all highth, bent down his eye, — Par Lost 3.58
About him all the Sanctities of Heaven — Par Lost 3.60
Prescrib'd, no barrs of Hell, nor all the chains — Par Lost 3.82
Through all restraint broke loose he wings his way — Par Lost 3.87
All he could have; I made him just and right, — Par Lost 3.98
Such I created all th' Ethereal Powers — Par Lost 3.100
They trespass, Authors to themselves in all — Par Lost 3.122
All Heav'n, and in the blessed Spirits elect — Par Lost 3.136
Most glorious, in him all his Father shon — Par Lost 3.139
Of all things made, and judgest onely right. — Par Lost 3.155
All hast thou spok'n as my thoughts are, all — Par Lost 3.171
All his deliv'rance, and to none but me. — Par Lost 3.182
But yet all is not don; Man disobeying, — Par Lost 3.203
Affecting God-head, and so loosing all, — Par Lost 3.206
Dwels in all Heaven charitie so deare? — Par Lost 3.216
He ask'd, but all the Heav'nly Quire stood mute, — Par Lost 3.217
And now without redemption all mankind — Par Lost 3.222
To visit all thy creatures, and to all — Par Lost 3.230
Well pleas'd, on me let Death wreck all his rage; — Par Lost 3.241
All that of me can die, yet that debt paid, — Par Lost 3.246
While by thee rais'd I ruin all my Foes, — Par Lost 3.258
All Heav'n, what this might mean, and whither tend — Par Lost 3.272
To me are all my works, nor Man the least — Par Lost 3.277
The Head of all mankind, though *Adams* Son. — Par Lost 3.286
As in him perish all men, so in thee — Par Lost 3.287
His crime makes guiltie all his Sons, thy merit — Par Lost 3.290
God-like fruition, quitted all to save — Par Lost 3.307
Anointed universal King; all Power — Par Lost 3.317
All knees to thee shall bow, of them that bide — Par Lost 3.321
Thy dread Tribunal: forthwith from all Windes — Par Lost 3.326
Of all past Ages to the general Doom — Par Lost 3.328
Then all thy Saints assembl'd, thou shalt judge — Par Lost 3.330
And after all thir tribulations long — Par Lost 3.336
God shall be All in All. But all ye Gods, — Par Lost 3.341
Adore him, who to compass all this dies, — Par Lost 3.342
No sooner had th' Almighty ceas't, but all — Par Lost 3.344
Eternal King; thee Author of all being, — Par Lost 3.374
Thee next they sang of all Creation first, — Par Lost 3.383
Hee Heav'n of Heavens and all the Powers therein — Par Lost 3.390
Of all things transitorie and vain, when Sin — Par Lost 3.446
Both all things vain, and all who in vain things — Par Lost 3.448
All who have thir reward on Earth, the fruits — Par Lost 3.451
All th' unaccomplisht works of Natures hand, — Par Lost 3.455
White, Black and Grey, with all thir trumperie. — Par Lost 3.475
The sport of Winds: all these upwhirld aloft — Par Lost 3.493
All this dark Globe the Fiend found as he pass'd, — Par Lost 3.498
Of all this World at once. As when a Scout — Par Lost 3.543
All night; at last by break of chearful dawne — Par Lost 3.545
At sight of all this World beheld so faire. — Par Lost 3.554
He stayd not to enquire: above them all — Par Lost 3.571
Not all parts like, but all alike informd — Par Lost 3.593
But all Sun-shine, as when his Beams at Noon — Par Lost 3.616
That run through all the Heav'ns, or down to th' Earth — Par Lost 3.651
Where all his Sons thy Embassie attend; — Par Lost 3.658
All these his wondrous works, but chiefly Man, — Par Lost 3.663
All these his works so wondrous he ordaind, — Par Lost 3.665
In which of all these shining Orbes hath Man — Par Lost 3.668
But all these shining Orbes his choice to dwell; — Par Lost 3.670
Worlds, and on whom hath all these graces powrd; — Par Lost 3.674
That both in him and all things, as is meet, — Par Lost 3.675
To serve him better: wise are all his wayes. — Par Lost 3.680
The sharpest sighted Spirit of all in Heav'n; — Par Lost 3.691
For wonderful indeed are all his works, — Par Lost 3.702
Pleasant to know, and worthiest to be all — Par Lost 3.703
Of this new World; at whose sight all the Starrs — Par Lost 4.34
How due! yet all his good prov'd ill in me, — Par Lost 4.48
Or from without, to all temptations arm'd. — Par Lost 4.65
But Heav'ns free Love dealt equally to all? — Par Lost 4.68
All hope excluded thus, behold in stead — Par Lost 4.105
Farwel Remorse: all Good to me is lost; — Par Lost 4.109
As he suppos'd, all unobserv'd, unseen. — Par Lost 4.130
All sadness but despair: now gentle gales — Par Lost 4.156
All path of Man or Beast that past that way: — Par Lost 4.177
At one slight bound high over leap'd all bound — Par Lost 4.181
To all delight of human sense expos'd — Par Lost 4.206
All Trees of noblest kind for sight, smell, taste; — Par Lost 4.217

All(*cont*)

And all amid them stood the Tree of Life,	Par Lost 4.218
Flours of all hue, and without Thorn the Rose:	Par Lost 4.256
Was gatherd, which cost *Ceres* all that pain	Par Lost 4.271
Saw undelighted all delight, all kind	Par Lost 4.286
In naked Majestie seemd Lords of all,	Par Lost 4.290
Sin-bred, how have ye troubl'd all mankind	Par Lost 4.315
All Beasts of th' Earth, since wilde, and of all chase	Par Lost 4.341
To make them mirth us'd all his might, and wreathd	Par Lost 4.346
Your change approaches, when all these delights	Par Lost 4.367
And send forth all her Kings; there will be room,	Par Lost 4.383
Turnd him all eare to hear new utterance flow.	Par Lost 4.410
Sole partner and sole part of all these joyes,	Par Lost 4.411
Dearer thy self then all; needs must the power	Par Lost 4.412
In all this happiness, who at his hand	Par Lost 4.417
This one, this easie charge, of all the Trees	Par Lost 4.421
Over all other Creatures that possess	Par Lost 4.431
Free leave so large to all things else, and choice	Par Lost 4.434
For wee to him indeed all praises owe,	Par Lost 4.444
From thir own mouths; all is not theirs it seems:	Par Lost 4.513
Bent all on speed, and markt his Aerie Gate;	Par Lost 4.568
Had in her sober Liverie all things clad;	Par Lost 4.599
Were slunk, all but the wakeful Nightingale;	Par Lost 4.602
She all night long her amorous descant sung;	Par Lost 4.603
Of night, and all things now retir'd to rest	Par Lost 4.611
Our eye-lids; other Creatures all day long	Par Lost 4.616
And the regard of Heav'n on all his waies;	Par Lost 4.620
With thee conversing I forget all time,	Par Lost 4.639
All seasons and thir change, all please alike.	Par Lost 4.640
But wherfore all night long shine these, for whom	Par Lost 4.657
This glorious sight, when sleep hath shut all eyes?	Par Lost 4.658
In Nature and all things, which these soft fires	Par Lost 4.667
Thir stellar vertue on all kinds that grow	Par Lost 4.671
All these with ceasless praise his works behold	Par Lost 4.679
All things to mans delightful use; the roofe	Par Lost 4.692
Iris all hues, Roses, and Gessamin	Par Lost 4.698
Endowd with all thir gifts, and O too like	Par Lost 4.715
And mutual love, the Crown of all our bliss	Par Lost 4.728
Pure, and commands to som, leaves free to all.	Par Lost 4.747
In Paradise of all things common else.	Par Lost 4.752
Relations dear, and all the Charities	Par Lost 4.756
Or all at once; more glorie will be wonn,	Par Lost 4.853
Came not all Hell broke loose? is pain to them	Par Lost 4.918
Thy blasting vollied Thunder made all speed	Par Lost 4.928
A faithful Leader, not to hazard all	Par Lost 4.933
Collecting all his might dilated stood,	Par Lost 4.986
Of Heav'n perhaps, or all the Elements	Par Lost 4.993
Wherein all things created first he weighd,	Par Lost 4.999
In counterpoise, now ponders all events,	Par Lost 4.1001
O Sole in whom my thoughts find all repose,	Par Lost 5.28
If none regard; Heav'n wakes with all his eyes,	Par Lost 5.44
In whose sight all things joy, with ravishment	Par Lost 5.46
Her office holds; of all external things,	Par Lost 5.103
All what we affirm or what deny, and call	Par Lost 5.107
So all was cleard, and to the Field they haste.	Par Lost 5.136
Discovering in wide Lantskip all the East	Par Lost 5.142
On Earth joyn all ye Creatures to extoll	Par Lost 5.164
And nourish all things, let your ceasless change	Par Lost 5.183
Joyn voices all ye living Souls, ye Birds,	Par Lost 5.197
In them at once to ruin all mankind.	Par Lost 5.228
All Justice: nor delaid the winged Saint	Par Lost 5.247
Through all th' Empyreal road; till at the Gate	Par Lost 5.253
Above all Hills. As when by night the Glass	Par Lost 5.261
Of Towring Eagles, to all the Fowles he seems	Par Lost 5.271
A *Phaenix*, gaz'd by all, as that sole Bird	Par Lost 5.272
The circuit wide. Strait knew him all the Bands	Par Lost 5.287
All seasons, ripe for use hangs on the stalk;	Par Lost 5.323
Alcinous reign'd, fruit of all kindes, in coate,	Par Lost 5.341
Perfections, in himself was all his state,	Par Lost 5.353
Dazles the croud, and sets them all agape.	Par Lost 5.357
All *Autumn* pil'd, though *Spring* and *Autumn* here	Par Lost 5.394
All perfet good unmeasur'd out, descends,	Par Lost 5.399
That one Celestial Father gives to all.	Par Lost 5.403
The Sun that light imparts to all, receives	Par Lost 5.423
From all his alimental recompence	Par Lost 5.424
All things proceed, and up to him return,	Par Lost 5.470
If not deprav'd from good, created all	Par Lost 5.471
Such to perfection, one first matter all,	Par Lost 5.472
Your bodies may at last turn all to Spirit,	Par Lost 5.497
My self and all th' Angelic Host that stand	Par Lost 5.535
To motion, measures all things durable	Par Lost 5.581
Forthwith from all the ends of Heav'n appeerd	Par Lost 5.586
Hear all ye Angels, Progenie of Light,	Par Lost 5.600
All knees in Heav'n, and shall confess him Lord:	Par Lost 5.608
All seemd well pleas'd, all seem'd, but were not all	Par Lost 5.617
Of Planets and of fixt in all her Wheeles	Par Lost 5.621
Desirous; all in Circles as they stood,	Par Lost 5.631
Excess, before th' all bounteous King, who showrd 1667 'all-bounteous'	Par Lost 5.640
All but the unsleeping eyes of God to rest,	Par Lost 5.647
Wide over all the Plain, and wider farr	Par Lost 5.648
Then all this globous Earth in Plain out spred,	Par Lost 5.649
Alternate all night long: but not so wak'd	Par Lost 5.657
With all his Legions to dislodge, and leave	Par Lost 5.669
Of all those Myriads which we lead the chief;	Par Lost 5.684
And all who under me thir Banners wave,	Par Lost 5.687
Who speedily through all the Hierarchies	Par Lost 5.692
Or taint integritie; but all obey'd	Par Lost 5.704

All(*cont*)

In full resplendence, Heir of all my might,	Par Lost 5.720
With speed what force is left, and all imploy	Par Lost 5.730
Illustrates, when they see all Regal Power	Par Lost 5.739
All thy Dominion, *Adam*, is no more	Par Lost 5.751
Then what this Garden is to all the Earth,	Par Lost 5.752
And all the Sea, from one entire globose	Par Lost 5.753
Affecting all equality with God,	Par Lost 5.763
For thither he assembl'd all his Train,	Par Lost 5.767
All Power, and us eclipst under the name	Par Lost 5.776
Of King anointed, for whom all this haste	Par Lost 5.777
By none, and if not equal all, yet free,	Par Lost 5.791
Expected, least of all from thee, ingrate	Par Lost 5.811
One over all with unsucceeded power.	Par Lost 5.821
Or all Angelic Nature joind in one,	Par Lost 5.834
All things, ev'n thee, and all the Spirits of Heav'n	Par Lost 5.837
His Laws our Laws, all honour to him done	Par Lost 5.844
Forsak'n of all good; I see thy fall	Par Lost 5.878
All night the dreadless Angel unpursu'd	Par Lost 6.1
Shot through with orient Beams: when all the Plain	Par Lost 6.15
Then violence: for this was all thy care	Par Lost 6.35
To darken all the Hill, and smoak to rowl	Par Lost 6.57
Reaching beyond all limit at one blow	Par Lost 6.140
All are not of thy Train; there be who Faith	Par Lost 6.143
From all: my Sect thou seest, now learn too late	Par Lost 6.147
To heav'nly Soules had bin all one; but now	Par Lost 6.165
Half sunk with all his Pines. Amazement seis'd	Par Lost 6.198
And inextinguishable rage; all Heav'n	Par Lost 6.217
Resounded, and had Earth bin then, all Earth	Par Lost 6.218
Of all thir Regions: how much more of Power	Par Lost 6.223
Tormented all the Air; all Air seemd then	Par Lost 6.244
And visage all enflam'd first thus began.	Par Lost 6.261
These Acts of hateful strife, hateful to all,	Par Lost 6.264
From all her Confines. Heav'n the seat of bliss	Par Lost 6.273
All his right side; then *Satan* first knew pain,	Par Lost 6.327
And all his Armour staind ere while so bright.	Par Lost 6.334
Forthwith on all sides to his aide was run	Par Lost 6.335
All Heart they live, all Head, all Eye, all Eare,	Par Lost 6.350
All Intellect, all Sense, and as they please,	Par Lost 6.351
Enter'd, and foul disorder; all the ground	Par Lost 6.388
Which all subdues, and makes remiss the hands	Par Lost 6.458
All patience. He who therefore can invent	Par Lost 6.464
Th' invention all admir'd, and each, how hee	Par Lost 6.498
So all ere day-spring, under conscious Night	Par Lost 6.521
In order, quit of all impediment;	Par Lost 6.548
That all may see who hate us, how we seek	Par Lost 6.559
What we propound, and loud that all may hear.	Par Lost 6.567
Not long, for sudden all at once thir Reeds	Par Lost 6.582
But soon obscur'd with smoak, all Heav'n appeerd,	Par Lost 6.585
And all her entrails tore, disgorging foule	Par Lost 6.588
Such as we might perceive amus'd them all,	Par Lost 6.623
All doubt of Victorie, eternal might	Par Lost 6.630
And all his Host derided, while they stood	Par Lost 6.633
They pluckt the seated Hills with all thir load,	Par Lost 6.644
They saw them whelm'd, and all thir confidence	Par Lost 6.651
Upon confusion rose: and now all Heav'n	Par Lost 6.669
This tumult, and permitted all, advis'd:	Par Lost 6.674
All power on him transferr'd: whence to his Son	Par Lost 6.678
Immense I have transfus'd, that all may know	Par Lost 6.704
Of all things, to be Heir and to be King	Par Lost 6.708
That shake Heav'ns basis, bring forth all my Warr,	Par Lost 6.712
From all Heav'ns bounds into the utter Deep:	Par Lost 6.716
Shon full, he all his Father full exprest	Par Lost 6.720
Fulfill'd, which to fulfil is all my bliss.	Par Lost 6.729
Thou shalt be All in All, and I in thee	Par Lost 6.732
For ever, and in mee all whom thou lov'st:	Par Lost 6.733
Image of thee in all things; and shall soon,	Par Lost 6.736
Had wondrous, as with Starrs thir bodies all	Par Lost 6.754
Hee in Celestial Panoplie all armd	Par Lost 6.760
Under thir Head imbodied all in one.	Par Lost 6.779
To all his Host on either hand thus spake.	Par Lost 6.800
Yet envied; against mee is all thir rage,	Par Lost 6.813
In Battel which the stronger proves, they all,	Par Lost 6.819
They measure all, of other excellence	Par Lost 6.821
All but the Throne it self of God. Full soon	Par Lost 6.834
Plagues; they astonisht all resistance lost,	Par Lost 6.838
All courage; down thir idle weapons drop'd;	Par Lost 6.839
Among th' accurst, that witherd all thir strength,	Par Lost 6.850
To meet him all his Saints, who silent stood	Par Lost 6.882
Which would be all his solace and revenge,	Par Lost 6.905
Of all tastes else to please thir appetite,	Par Lost 7.49
All space, the ambient Aire wide interfus'd	Par Lost 7.89
Through all Eternitie so late to build	Par Lost 7.92
All like himself rebellious, by whose aid	Par Lost 7.140
Immense, and all his Father in him shon.	Par Lost 7.196
For *Chaos* heard his voice: him all his Traine	Par Lost 7.221
This Universe, and all created things:	Par Lost 7.227
Appeer'd not: over all the face of Earth	Par Lost 7.278
Prolific humour soft'ning all her Globe,	Par Lost 7.280
All but within those banks, where Rivers now	Par Lost 7.305
Went up and waterd all the ground, and each	Par Lost 7.334
Regent of Day, and all th' Horizon round	Par Lost 7.371
Ceas'd warbling, but all night tun'd her soft layes:	Par Lost 7.436
In all the Liveries dect of Summers pride	Par Lost 7.478
Streaking the ground with sinuous trace; not all	Par Lost 7.481
The Serpent suttl'st Beast of all the field,	Par Lost 7.495
Now Heav'n in all her Glorie shon, and rowld	Par Lost 7.499
Of all yet don; a Creature who not prone	Par Lost 7.506

All(*cont*)

Of all his works: therefore the Omnipotent	Par Lost 7.516
Beast of the Field, and over all the Earth,	Par Lost 7.522
And freely all thir pleasant fruit for food	Par Lost 7.540
Gave thee, all sorts are here that all th' Earth yields,	Par Lost 7.541
Here finish'd hee, and all that he had made	Par Lost 7.548
View'd, and behold all was entirely good;	Par Lost 7.549
The Heav'ns and all the Constellations rung,	Par Lost 7.562
Author and end of all things, and from work	Par Lost 7.591
As resting on that day from all his work,	Par Lost 7.593
And Dulcimer, all Organs of sweet stop,	Par Lost 7.596
All sounds on Fret by String or Golden Wire	Par Lost 7.597
And all her numberd Starrs, that seem to rowle	Par Lost 8.19
One day and night; in all thir vast survey	Par Lost 8.24
Into all Eyes to wish her still in sight.	Par Lost 8.63
Invisible else above all Starrs, the Wheele	Par Lost 8.135
God hath bid dwell farr off all anxious cares,	Par Lost 8.185
Speaking or mute all comliness and grace	Par Lost 8.222
Birds on the branches warbling; all things smil'd,	Par Lost 8.265
Before mine Eyes all real, as the dream	Par Lost 8.310
Said mildely, Author of all this thou seest	Par Lost 8.317
Not onely these fair bounds, but all the Earth	Par Lost 8.338
Possess it, and all things that therein live,	Par Lost 8.340
O by what Name, for thou above all these,	Par Lost 8.357
And all this good to man, for whose well being	Par Lost 8.361
Thou hast provided all things: but with mee	Par Lost 8.363
Or all enjoying, what contentment find?	Par Lost 8.366
Replenisht, and all these at thy command	Par Lost 8.371
All rational delight, wherein the brute	Par Lost 8.391
Wors then can Man with Beast, and least of all.	Par Lost 8.397
From all Eternitie, for none I know	Par Lost 8.406
All human thoughts come short, Supream of things;	Par Lost 8.414
And through all numbers absolute, though One;	Par Lost 8.421
That what seemd fair in all the World, seemd now	Par Lost 8.472
And into all things from her Aire inspir'd	Par Lost 8.476
Her loss, and other pleasures all abjure:	Par Lost 8.480
With what all Earth or Heaven could bestow	Par Lost 8.483
Grace was in all her steps, Heav'n in her Eye,	Par Lost 8.488
Giver of all things faire, but fairest this	Par Lost 8.493
Of all thy gifts, nor enviest. I now see	Par Lost 8.494
The more desirable, or to say all,	Par Lost 8.505
I led her blushing like the Morn: all Heav'n,	Par Lost 8.511
Thus I have told thee all my State, and brought	Par Lost 8.521
In all things else delight indeed, but such	Par Lost 8.524
Commotion strange, in all enjoyments else	Par Lost 8.531
All higher knowledge in her presence falls	Par Lost 8.551
Occasionally; and to consummate all,	Par Lost 8.556
And to realities yield all her shows:	Par Lost 8.575
Beyond all other, think the same voutsaf't	Par Lost 8.581
In procreation common to all kindes	Par Lost 8.597
From all her words and actions mixt with Love	Par Lost 8.602
Be strong, live happie, and love, but first of all	Par Lost 8.633
Would not admit; thine and of all thy Sons	Par Lost 8.637
And all the Blest: stand fast; to stand or fall	Par Lost 8.640
And all temptation to transgress repel.	Par Lost 8.643
Deprest, and much they may, if all be mine,	Par Lost 9.46
Consider'd every Creature, which of all	Par Lost 9.84
The Serpent suttlest Beast of all the Field.	Par Lost 9.86
In thee concentring all thir precious beams	Par Lost 9.106
Is Center, yet extends to all, so thou	Par Lost 9.108
Centring receav'st from all those Orbs; in thee,	Par Lost 9.109
Not in themselves, all thir known vertue appeers	Par Lost 9.110
Of Growth, Sense, Reason, all summ'd up in Man.	Par Lost 9.113
Of contraries; all good to me becomes	Par Lost 9.122
For whom all this was made, all this will soon	Par Lost 9.132
Thir morning incense, when all things that breath,	Par Lost 9.194
For while so near each other thus all day	Par Lost 9.220
Compare above all living Creatures deare,	Par Lost 9.228
Ofspring of Heav'n and Earth, and all Earths Lord,	Par Lost 9.273
O Woman, best are all things as the will	Par Lost 9.343
Of all that he Created, much less Man,	Par Lost 9.346
On what thou hast of vertue, summon all,	Par Lost 9.374
And all things in best order to invite	Par Lost 9.402
She most, and in her look summs all Delight.	Par Lost 9.454
Fierce hate he recollects, and all his thoughts	Par Lost 9.471
Of pleasure, but all pleasure to destroy,	Par Lost 9.477
The Woman, opportune to all attempts,	Par Lost 9.481
Thee all things living gaze on, all things thine	Par Lost 9.539
Created mute to all articulat sound;	Par Lost 9.557
Thee, Serpent, suttlest beast of all the field	Par Lost 9.560
Easie to mee it is to tell thee all	Par Lost 9.569
All other Beasts that saw, with like desire	Par Lost 9.592
Considerd all things visible in Heav'n,	Par Lost 9.604
Or Earth, or Middle, all things fair and good;	Par Lost 9.605
But all that fair and good in thy Divine	Par Lost 9.606
Of prohibition, root of all our woe;	Par Lost 9.645
Of all these Garden Trees ye shall not eate,	Par Lost 9.657
Yet Lords declar'd of all in Earth or Aire?	Par Lost 9.658
The Tempter all impassiond thus began.	Par Lost 9.678
On our belief, that all from them proceeds;	Par Lost 9.719
Them nothing: If they all things, who enclos'd	Par Lost 9.722
Impart against his will if all be his?	Par Lost 9.728
And yet unknown, is as not had at all.	Par Lost 9.757
Here grows the Cure of all, this Fruit Divine,	Par Lost 9.776
Sighing through all her Works gave signs of woe,	Par Lost 9.783
That all was lost. Back to the Thicket slunk	Par Lost 9.784
O Sovran, vertuous, precious of all Trees	Par Lost 9.795
Of thy full branches offer'd free to all;	Par Lost 9.802

All(*cont*)

In knowledge, as the Gods who all things know;	Par Lost 9.804
Our great Forbidder, safe with all his Spies	Par Lost 9.815
So dear I love him, that with him all deaths	Par Lost 9.832
Ran through his veins, and all his joynts relax'd;	Par Lost 9.891
Down drop'd, and all the faded Roses shed:	Par Lost 9.893
Of all Gods works, Creature in whom excell'd	Par Lost 9.897
Set over all his Works, which in our Fall,	Par Lost 9.941
With all perfections, so enflame my sense	Par Lost 9.1031
Of all thir vertue: silent, and in face	Par Lost 9.1063
Of all our good, sham'd, naked, miserable.	Par Lost 9.1139
Omniscient, who in all things wise and just,	Par Lost 10.7
All were who heard, dim sadness did not spare	Par Lost 10.23
How all befell: they towards the Throne Supream	Par Lost 10.28
And flatter'd out of all, believing lies	Par Lost 10.42
All Judgement, whether in Heav'n, or Earth, or Hell.	Par Lost 10.57
Resplendent all his Father manifest	Par Lost 10.66
Convict by flight, and Rebel to all Law	Par Lost 10.83
Eden and all the Coast in prospect lay.	Par Lost 10.89
However insupportable, be all	Par Lost 10.134
Hers in all real dignitie: Adornd	Par Lost 10.151
Above all Cattle, each Beast of the Field;	Par Lost 10.176
And dust shalt eat all the dayes of thy Life.	Par Lost 10.178
Shalt eate thereof all the days of thy Life;	Par Lost 10.202
All, though all-knowing, what had past with Man	Par Lost 10.227
Of merit high to all th' infernal Host,	Par Lost 10.259
The savour of Death from all things there that live:	Par Lost 10.269
And Chains they made all fast, too fast they made	Par Lost 10.319
By *Eve*, though all unweeting, seconded	Par Lost 10.335
Thine now is all this World, thy vertue hath won	Par Lost 10.372
Of all things parted by th' Empyreal bounds,	Par Lost 10.380
Amply have merited of me, of all	Par Lost 10.388
All yours, right down to Paradise descend;	Par Lost 10.398
Chiefly on Man, sole Lord of all declar'd,	Par Lost 10.401
My hold of this new Kingdom all depends,	Par Lost 10.406
And all about found desolate; for those	Par Lost 10.420
Flown to the upper World; the rest were all	Par Lost 10.422
Of *Turkish* Crescent, leaves all waste beyond	Par Lost 10.434
Was left him, or false glitter: All amaz'd	Par Lost 10.452
Both his beloved Man and all his World,	Par Lost 10.489
To rule, as over all he should have rul'd.	Par Lost 10.493
On all sides, from innumerable tongues	Par Lost 10.507
To forked tongue, for now were all transform'd	Par Lost 10.519
Alike, to Serpents all as accessories	Par Lost 10.520
Above the rest still to retain; they all	Par Lost 10.532
Where all yet left of that revolted Rout	Par Lost 10.534
Second of *Satan* sprung, all conquering *Death*,	Par Lost 10.591
Which here, though plenteous, all too little seems	Par Lost 10.600
His thoughts, his looks, words, actions all infect,	Par Lost 10.608
All kinds, and for destruction to mature	Par Lost 10.612
Of Passion, I to them had quitted all,	Par Lost 10.627
Righteous are thy Decrees on all thy Works;	Par Lost 10.644
And Fish with Fish; to graze the Herb all leaving,	Par Lost 10.711
All that I eat or drink, or shall beget,	Par Lost 10.728
Who of all Ages to succeed, but feeling	Par Lost 10.733
Mine own that bide upon me, all from mee	Par Lost 10.738
All I receav'd, unable to performe	Par Lost 10.750
Pursues me still, least all I cannot die,	Par Lost 10.783
All of me then shall die: let this appease	Par Lost 10.792
For though the Lord of all be infinite,	Par Lost 10.794
By which all Causes else according still	Par Lost 10.806
Nor I on my part single, in mee all	Par Lost 10.817
To waste it all my self, and leave ye none!	Par Lost 10.820
Me now your curse! Ah, why should all mankind	Par Lost 10.822
But all corrupt, both Mind and Will deprav'd,	Par Lost 10.825
In sight of God? Him after all Disputes	Par Lost 10.828
Forc't I absolve: all my evasions vain,	Par Lost 10.829
Of all corruption, all the blame lights due;	Par Lost 10.833
Then all the World much heavier, though divided	Par Lost 10.836
And what thou fearst, alike destroyes all hope	Par Lost 10.838
Beyond all past example and future,	Par Lost 10.840
All things with double terror: On the Ground	Par Lost 10.850
Thy inward fraud, to warn all Creatures from thee	Par Lost 10.871
Constant, mature, proof against all assaults,	Par Lost 10.882
And understood not all was but a shew	Par Lost 10.883
Rather then solid vertu, all but a Rib	Par Lost 10.884
And tresses all disorderd, at his feet	Par Lost 10.911
There with my cries importune Heaven, that all	Par Lost 10.933
On me, sole cause to thee of all this woe,	Par Lost 10.935
As one disarm'd, his anger all he lost,	Par Lost 10.945
The punishment all on thy self; alas,	Par Lost 10.949
That on my head all might be visited,	Par Lost 10.955
Which his own hand manuring all the Trees	Par Lost 11.28
And propitiation, all his works on mee	Par Lost 11.34
All my redeemd may dwell in joy and bliss,	Par Lost 11.43
All thy request for Man, accepted Son,	Par Lost 11.46
Obtain, all thy request was my Decree:	Par Lost 11.47
Distemperd all things, and of incorrupt	Par Lost 11.56
But let us call to Synod all the Blest	Par Lost 11.67
Filld all the Regions: from thir blissful Bowrs	Par Lost 11.77
Good by it self, and Evil not at all.	Par Lost 11.89
Bewailing thir excess, all terror hide.	Par Lost 11.111
Wide waving, all approach farr off to fright,	Par Lost 11.121
And guard all passage to the Tree of Life:	Par Lost 11.122
To Spirits foule, and all my Trees thir prey,	Par Lost 11.124
Had, like a double *Janus*, all thir shape	Par Lost 11.129
Eve, easily may Faith admit, that all	Par Lost 11.141
Kneel'd and before him humbl'd all my heart,	Par Lost 11.150

All(*cont*)

Eve rightly call'd, Mother of all Mankind,	Par Lost 11.159
Mother of all things living, since by thee	Par Lost 11.160
Man is to live, and all things live for Man.	Par Lost 11.161
Rather belongs, distrust and all dispraise:	Par Lost 11.166
That I who first brought Death on all, am grac't	Par Lost 11.168
All unconcern'd with our unrest, begins	Par Lost 11.174
Goodliest of all the Forrest, Hart and Hinde;	Par Lost 11.189
That all his senses bound; *Eve*, who unseen	Par Lost 11.265
Yet all had heard, with audible lament	Par Lost 11.266
Familiar to our eyes, all places else	Par Lost 11.305
Of him who all things can, I would not cease	Par Lost 11.309
Adam, thou know'st Heav'n his, and all the Earth.	Par Lost 11.335
All th' Earth he gave thee to possess and rule,	Par Lost 11.339
All generations, and had hither come	Par Lost 11.344
From all the ends of th' Earth, to celebrate	Par Lost 11.345
To shew him all Earths Kingdomes and thir Glory.	Par Lost 11.384
Sunk down and all his Spirits became intranst:	Par Lost 11.420
On the cleft Wood, and all due Rites perform'd.	Par Lost 11.440
To his grim Cave, all dismal; yet to sense	Par Lost 11.469
Numbers of all diseas'd, all maladies	Par Lost 11.480
Of heart-sick Agonie, all feavorous kinds,	Par Lost 11.482
Obtuse, all taste of pleasure must forgoe,	Par Lost 11.541
Instinct through all proportions low and high	Par Lost 11.562
Just men they seemd, and all thir study bent	Par Lost 11.577
Loves Harbinger appeerd; then all in heat	Par Lost 11.589
With Feast and Musick all the Tents resound.	Par Lost 11.592
Here Nature seems fulfilld in all her ends.	Par Lost 11.602
Yet empty of all good wherein consists	Par Lost 11.616
Shall yield up all thir vertue, all thir fame	Par Lost 11.623
Through all the Plain, and refuge none was found.	Par Lost 11.673
Adam was all in tears, and to his guide	Par Lost 11.674
All now was turn'd to jollitie and game,	Par Lost 11.714
But all in vain: which when he saw, he ceas'd	Par Lost 11.726
Wide hovering, all the Clouds together drove	Par Lost 11.739
Rode tilting o're the Waves, all dwellings else	Par Lost 11.747
Flood overwhelmd, and them with all thir pomp	Par Lost 11.748
All left, in one small bottom swum imbark't.	Par Lost 11.753
The end of all thy Ofspring, end so sad,	Par Lost 11.755
His Children, all in view destroyd at once;	Par Lost 11.761
All would have then gon well, peace would have crownd	Par Lost 11.781
Shall with thir freedom lost all vertu loose	Par Lost 11.798
So all shall turn degenerate, all deprav'd,	Par Lost 11.806
And shelterd round, but all the Cataracts	Par Lost 11.824
Raine day and night, all fountains of the Deep	Par Lost 11.826
Beyond all bounds, till inundation rise	Par Lost 11.828
With all his verdure spoil'd, and Trees adrift	Par Lost 11.832
The ancient Sire descends with all his Train;	Par Lost 11.862
With all the Creatures, and thir seed preserve.	Par Lost 11.873
From him, and all his anger to forget.	Par Lost 11.878
The whole Earth fill'd with violence, and all flesh	Par Lost 11.888
Shall hold thir course, till fire purge all things new,	Par Lost 11.900
Not understood, till hoarse, and all in rage,	Par Lost 12.58
From all the rest, of whom to be invok'd,	Par Lost 12.112
All Nations shall be blest; he straight obeys,	Par Lost 12.126
Not wandring poor, but trusting all his wealth	Par Lost 12.133
Gift to his Progenie of all that Land;	Par Lost 12.138
This ponder, that all Nations of the Earth	Par Lost 12.147
Frogs, Lice and Flies must all his Palace fill	Par Lost 12.177
With loath'd intrusion, and fill all the land;	Par Lost 12.178
Botches and blaines must all his flesh imboss,	Par Lost 12.180
And all his people; Thunder mixt with Haile,	Par Lost 12.181
Darkness must overshadow all his bounds,	Par Lost 12.187
Last with one midnight stroke all the first-born	Par Lost 12.189
All night he will pursue, but his approach	Par Lost 12.206
God looking forth will trouble all his Host	Par Lost 12.209
And all the Prophets in thir Age the times	Par Lost 12.243
Of mee and all Mankind; but now I see	Par Lost 12.276
His day, in whom all Nations shall be blest,	Par Lost 12.277
All Prophecie, That of the Royal Stock	Par Lost 12.325
All Nations, and to Kings foretold, of Kings	Par Lost 12.329
With all his sacred things, a scorn and prey	Par Lost 12.341
Proclaiming Life to all who shall believe	Par Lost 12.407
Of all mankinde, with him there crucifi'd,	Par Lost 12.417
To teach all nations what of him they learn'd	Par Lost 12.440
All Nations they shall teach; for from that day	Par Lost 12.446
So in his seed all Nations shall be blest.	Par Lost 12.450
Through all his Realme, and there confounded leave;	Par Lost 12.455
Above all names in Heav'n; and thence shall come,	Par Lost 12.458
Shall all be Paradise, far happier place	Par Lost 12.464
That all this good of evil shall produce,	Par Lost 12.470
To guide them in all truth, and also arme	Par Lost 12.490
To evangelize the Nations, then on all	Par Lost 12.499
To speak all Tongues, and do all Miracles,	Par Lost 12.501
Who all the sacred mysteries of Heav'n	Par Lost 12.509
To all Beleevers; and from that pretense,	Par Lost 12.520
On all who in the worship persevere	Par Lost 12.532
Till time stand fixt: beyond is all abyss,	Par Lost 12.555
Mercifull over all his works, with good	Par Lost 12.565
Of wisdome; hope no higher, though all the Starrs	Par Lost 12.576
Thou knewst by name, and all th' ethereal Powers,	Par Lost 12.577
All secrets of the deep, all Natures works,	Par Lost 12.578
And all the riches of this World enjoydst,	Par Lost 12.580
And all the rule, one Empire; onely add	Par Lost 12.581
Of all the rest: then wilt thou not be loath	Par Lost 12.585
Portending good, and all her spirits compos'd	Par Lost 12.596
(For by the Womans Seed) on all Mankind.	Par Lost 12.601
Art all things under Heav'n, all places thou,	Par Lost 12.618

All(*cont*)

I carry hence; though all by mee is lost,	Par Lost 12.621
By mee the Promis'd Seed shall all restore.	Par Lost 12.623
To thir fixt Station, all in bright array	Par Lost 12.627
They looking back, all th' Eastern side beheld	Par Lost 12.641
The World was all before them, where to choose	Par Lost 12.646
Recover'd Paradise to all mankind,	Par Reg 1.3
Through all temptation, and the Tempter foil'd	Par Reg 1.5
In all his wiles, defeated and repuls't,	Par Reg 1.6
To all Baptiz'd: to his great Baptism flock'd	Par Reg 1.21
To Councel summons all his mighty Peers,	Par Reg 1.40
Broken be not intended all our power	Par Reg 1.61
All vertue, grace and wisdom to atchieve	Par Reg 1.68
His coming, is sent Harbinger, who all	Par Reg 1.71
To do him honour as their King; all come,	Par Reg 1.75
In all his lineaments, though in his face	Par Reg 1.92
Unanimous they all commit the care	Par Reg 1.111
Temptation and all guile on him to try;	Par Reg 1.123
Thou and all Angels conversant on Earth	Par Reg 1.131
All his sollicitations, and at length	Par Reg 1.152
All his vast force, and drive him back to Hell,	Par Reg 1.153
And all the world, and mass of sinful flesh;	Par Reg 1.162
That all the Angels and Aetherial Powers,	Par Reg 1.163
So spake the Eternal Father, and all Heaven	Par Reg 1.168
Be frustrate all ye stratagems of Hell,	Par Reg 1.180
To me was pleasing, all my mind was set	Par Reg 1.202
Born to that end, born to promote all truth,	Par Reg 1.205
All righteous things: therefore above my years,	Par Reg 1.206
And was admir'd by all, yet this not all	Par Reg 1.214
Then to subdue and quell o're all the earth	Par Reg 1.218
All Heaven and Earth, Angels and Sons of men,	Par Reg 1.237
Like things of thee to all that present stood.	Par Reg 1.258
I as all others to his Baptism came,	Par Reg 1.273
And last the sum of all, my Father's voice,	Par Reg 1.283
And when to all his Angels he propos'd	Par Reg 1.371
Of all his flattering Prophets glibb'd with lyes	Par Reg 1.375
Or vertuous, I should so have lost all sense.	Par Reg 1.382
To all mankind: why should I? they to me	Par Reg 1.388
To all the Host of Heaven; the happy place	Par Reg 1.416
With all inflictions, but his patience won?	Par Reg 1.426
Yet thou pretend'st to truth; all Oracles	Par Reg 1.430
To all truth requisite for men to know.	Par Reg 1.464
All fear of thee, arise and vindicate	Par Reg 2.47
Let us be glad of this, and all our fears	Par Reg 2.53
All his great work to come before him set;	Par Reg 2.112
Where all his Potentates in Council sate;	Par Reg 2.118
Of like succeeding here; I summon all	Par Reg 2.143
So spake the old Serpent doubting, and from all	Par Reg 2.147
All others by thy self; because of old	Par Reg 2.174
Delight not all; among the Sons of Men,	Par Reg 2.192
All her assaults, on worthier things intent?	Par Reg 2.195
A youth, how all the Beauties of the East	Par Reg 2.197
Descend with all her winning charms begirt	Par Reg 2.213
All her array; her female pride deject,	Par Reg 2.219
Led captive; cease to admire, and all her Plumes	Par Reg 2.222
Our Saviour, and found all was but a dream,	Par Reg 2.283
Of all things destitute, and well I know,	Par Reg 2.305
By a providing Angel; all the race	Par Reg 2.310
They all had need, I as thou seest have none.	Par Reg 2.318
Hast thou not right to all Created things,	Par Reg 2.324
Owe not all Creatures by just right to thee	Par Reg 2.325
But tender all their power? nor mention I	Par Reg 2.327
From all the Elements her choicest store	Par Reg 2.334
Gris-amber-steam'd; all Fish from Sea or Shore,	Par Reg 2.344
And all the while Harmonious Airs were heard	Par Reg 2.362
All these are Spirits of Air, and Woods, and Springs,	Par Reg 2.374
Said'st thou not that to all things I had right?	Par Reg 2.379
And all thy heart is set on high designs,	Par Reg 2.410
In highth of all thir flowing wealth dissolv'd:	Par Reg 2.436
That for the Publick all this weight he bears.	Par Reg 2.465
At length collecting all his Serpent wiles,	Par Reg 3.5
Of conduct would be such, that all the world	Par Reg 3.18
All Earth her wonder at thy acts, thy self	Par Reg 3.24
Aetherial, who all pleasures else despise,	Par Reg 3.28
All treasures and all gain esteem as dross,	Par Reg 3.29
And dignities and powers all but the highest?	Par Reg 3.30
Great *Julius*, whom now all the world admires	Par Reg 3.39
For glories sake by all thy argument.	Par Reg 3.46
To all his Angels, who with true applause	Par Reg 3.63
And all the flourishing works of peace destroy,	Par Reg 3.80
And for his glory all things made, all things	Par Reg 3.111
By all his Angels glorifi'd, requires	Par Reg 3.113
Glory from men, from all men good or bad,	Par Reg 3.114
Above all Sacrifice, or hallow'd gift	Par Reg 3.116
Promiscuous from all Nations, Jew, or Greek,	Par Reg 3.118
And reason; since his word all things produc'd,	Par Reg 3.122
And so of all true good himself despoil'd,	Par Reg 3.139
Insatiable of glory had lost all,	Par Reg 3.148
Judaea now and all the promis'd land	Par Reg 3.157
All things are best fullfil'd in their due time,	Par Reg 3.182
And time there is for all things, Truth hath said:	Par Reg 3.183
He in whose hand all times and seasons roul.	Par Reg 3.187
Let that come when it comes; all hope is lost	Par Reg 3.204
Happiest both to thy self and all the world,	Par Reg 3.225
In all things that to greatest actions lead.	Par Reg 3.239
There *Babylon* the wonder of all tongues,	Par Reg 3.280
Judah and all thy Father *David*'s house	Par Reg 3.282
All these the *Parthian*, now some Ages past,	Par Reg 3.294

All(*cont*)

In *Ctesiphon* hath gather'd all his Host	Par Reg 3.300
All Horsemen, in which fight they most excel;	Par Reg 3.307
The field all iron cast a gleaming brown,	Par Reg 3.326
Cuirassiers all in steel for standing fight;	Par Reg 3.328
When *Agrican* with all his Northern powers	Par Reg 3.338
All this fair sight; thy Kingdom though foretold	Par Reg 3.351
In all things, and all men, supposes means,	Par Reg 3.355
By free consent of all, none opposite,	Par Reg 3.358
To just extent over all *Israel*'s Sons;	Par Reg 3.406
And all the Idolatries of Heathen round,	Par Reg 3.418
Made answer meet, that made void all his wiles.	Par Reg 3.442
Though all to shivers dash't, the assault renew,	Par Reg 4.19
All Nations now to *Rome* obedience pay,	Par Reg 4.80
These having shewn thee, I have shewn thee all	Par Reg 4.88
The Kingdoms of the world, and all thir glory.	Par Reg 4.89
All publick cares, and yet of him suspicious,	Par Reg 4.96
Hated of all, and hating; with what ease	Par Reg 4.97
Aim therefore at no less then all the world,	Par Reg 4.105
Peeling thir Provinces, exhausted all	Par Reg 4.136
Spreading and over-shadowing all the Earth,	Par Reg 4.148
All Monarchies besides throughout the world,	Par Reg 4.150
I see all offers made by me how slight	Par Reg 4.155
All these which in a moment thou behold'st,	Par Reg 4.162
Easily done, and hold them all of me;	Par Reg 4.168
The first of all Commandments, Thou shalt worship	Par Reg 4.176
God over all supreme? if giv'n to thee,	Par Reg 4.186
Nations besides from all the quarter'd winds,	Par Reg 4.202
So let extend thy mind o're all the world,	Par Reg 4.223
In knowledge, all things in it comprehend,	Par Reg 4.224
All knowledge is not couch't in *Moses* Law,	Par Reg 4.225
Mellifluous streams that water'd all the schools	Par Reg 4.277
The first and wisest of them all profess'd	Par Reg 4.293
A third sort doubted all things, though plain sence;	Par Reg 4.296
Wise, perfect in himself, and all possessing	Par Reg 4.302
As fearing God nor man, contemning all	Par Reg 4.304
For all his tedious talk is but vain boast,	Par Reg 4.307
Much of the Soul they talk, but all awrie,	Par Reg 4.313
All glory arrogate, to God give none,	Par Reg 4.315
That solace? All our Law and Story strew'd	Par Reg 4.334
With *Sion*'s songs, to all true tasts excelling,	Par Reg 4.347
By light of Nature not in all quite lost.	Par Reg 4.352
Then all the Oratory of *Greece* and *Rome*.	Par Reg 4.360
Quite at a loss, for all his darts were spent,	Par Reg 4.366
On *David*'s Throne; or Throne of all the world,	Par Reg 4.379
Who all things now behold more fresh and green,	Par Reg 4.435
Was absent, after all his mischief done,	Par Reg 4.440
Yet with no new device, they all were spent,	Par Reg 4.443
All to the push of Fate, persue thy way	Par Reg 4.470
At least might seem to hold all power of thee,	Par Reg 4.494
By all the Prophets; of thy birth at length	Par Reg 4.503
Till at the Ford of *Jordan* whither all	Par Reg 4.510
All men are Sons of God; yet thee I thought	Par Reg 4.520
Where by all best conjectures I collect	Par Reg 4.524
Proof against all temptation as a rock	Par Reg 4.533
With all his Army, now thou hast aveng'd	Par Reg 4.606
No triumph; in all her gates *Abaddon* rues	Par Reg 4.624
To dread the Son of God: he all unarm'd	Par Reg 4.626
Of both my Parents all in flames ascended	Samson 25
Divine Prediction; what if all foretold	Samson 44
And proves the sourse of all my miseries;	Samson 64
Would ask a life to wail, but chief of all,	Samson 66
And all her various objects of delight	Samson 71
Without all hope of day!	Samson 82
Let there be light, and light was over all;	Samson 84
She all in every part; why was the sight	Samson 93
And not as feeling through all parts diffus'd,	Samson 96
To all the miseries of life,	Samson 107
Yet *Israel* still serves with all his Sons.	Samson 240
Acknowledg'd not, or not at all consider'd	Samson 245
Unless there be who think not God at all,	Samson 295
And such a Son as all Men hail'd me happy;	Samson 354
Nothing of all these evils hath befall'n me	Samson 374
This well I knew, nor was at all surpris'd,	Samson 381
Yet the fourth time, when mustring all her wiles,	Samson 402
I yielded, and unlock'd her all my heart,	Samson 407
Might easily have shook off all her snares:	Samson 409
Samson, of all thy sufferings think the heaviest,	Samson 445
Of all reproach the most with shame that ever	Samson 446
With me hath end; all the contest is now	Samson 461
Of all these boasted Trophies won on me,	Samson 470
Against all competition, nor will long	Samson 476
Contempt, and scorn of all, to be excluded	Samson 494
All friendship, and avoided as a blab,	Samson 495
God will relent, and quit thee all his debt;	Samson 509
All mortals I excell'd, and great in hopes	Samson 523
I walk'd about admir'd of all and dreaded	Samson 530
Of all my strength in the lascivious lap	Samson 536
Like a tame Weather, all my precious fleece,	Samson 538
Chor. Desire of wine and all delicious drinks,	Samson 541
Hast'n the welcom end of all my pains.	Samson 576
Sam. All otherwise to me my thoughts portend,	Samson 590
My hopes all flat, nature within me seems	Samson 595
In all her functions weary of her self;	Samson 596
There exercise all his fierce accidents,	Samson 612
Left me all helpless with th' irreparable loss	Samson 644
Hopeless are all my evils, all remediless;	Samson 648
The close of all my miseries, and the balm.	Samson 651

All(*cont*)

And to the bearing well of all calamities,	Samson 655
All chances incident to mans frail life	Samson 656
With all her bravery on, and tackle trim,	Samson 717
Courted by all the winds that hold them play,	Samson 719
To break all faith, all vows, deceive, betray,	Samson 750
In me, but incident to all our sex,	Samson 774
Wherein consisted all thy strength and safety?	Samson 780
As her at *Timna*, sought by all means therefore	Samson 795
Be not unlike all others, not austere	Samson 815
If thou in strength all mortals dost exceed,	Samson 817
All wickedness is weakness: that plea therefore	Samson 834
Adjur'd by all the bonds of civil Duty	Samson 853
And combated in silence all these reasons	Samson 864
Sam. I thought where all thy circling wiles would end;	Samson 871
I before all the daughters of my Tribe	Samson 876
Too well, unbosom'd all my secrets to thee,	Samson 879
With all things grateful chear'd, and so suppli'd,	Samson 926
If in my flower of youth and strength, when all men	Samson 938
To all posterity may stand defam'd,	Samson 977
If any of these or all, the *Timnian* bride	Samson 1018
Seeming at first all heavenly under virgin veil,	Samson 1035
But vertue which breaks through all opposition,	Samson 1050
And all temptation can remove,	Samson 1051
If thou at all art known. Much I have heard	Samson 1082
Then put on all thy gorgeous arms, thy Helmet	Samson 1119
Where strength can least abide, though all thy hairs	Samson 1136
No less through all my sinews, joints and bones,	Samson 1142
Sam. All these indignities, for such they are	Samson 1168
When I perceiv'd all set on enmity,	Samson 1201
Had not disabl'd me, not all your force:	Samson 1219
Sam. I dread him not, nor all his Giant-brood,	Samson 1247
All of Gigantic size, *Goliah* chief.	Samson 1249
The righteous and all such as honour Truth;	Samson 1276
He all thir Ammunition	Samson 1277
And Victor over all	Samson 1290
Rise therefore with all speed and come along,	Samson 1316
The worst of all indignities, yet on me	Samson 1341
(So mutable are all the ways of men)	Samson 1407
I heard all as I came, the City rings	Samson 1449
For his redemption all my Patrimony,	Samson 1482
Thou for thy Son art bent to lay out all;	Samson 1486
With all those high exploits by him atchiev'd,	Samson 1492
Mess. *Gaza* yet stands, but all her Sons are fall'n,	Samson 1558
All in a moment overwhelm'd and fall'n.	Samson 1559
Man. The worst indeed, O all my hope's defeated	Samson 1571
To free him hence! but death who sets all free	Samson 1572
All by him fell thou say'st, by whom fell he,	Samson 1580
The Edifice where all were met to see him	Samson 1588
When all abroad was rumour'd that this day	Samson 1600
With seats where all the Lords and each degree	Samson 1607
All with incredible, stupendious force,	Samson 1627
As with amaze shall strike all who behold.	Samson 1645
This utter'd, straining all his nerves he bow'd,	Samson 1646
Upon the heads of all who sate beneath,	Samson 1652
Met from all parts to solemnize this Feast.	Samson 1656
Then all thy life had slain before.	Samson 1668
Through all *Philistian* bounds. To *Israel*	Samson 1714
And which is best and happiest yet, all this	Samson 1718
Will send for all my kindred, all my friends	Samson 1730
With all his Trophies hung, and Acts enroll'd	Samson 1736
Thither shall all the valiant youth resort,	Samson 1738
Chor. All is best, though we oft doubt,	Samson 1745
And all that band them to resist	Samson 1753
And calm of mind all passion spent.	Samson 1758
Imperial rule of all the Sea-girt Iles	Mask 21
Trinity ms 'all the' ←'each'	
The greatest, and the best of all the main	Mask 28
And all this tract that fronts the falling Sun	Mask 30
All other parts remaining as they were,	Mask 72
And all their friends, and native home forget	Mask 76
The Sounds, and Seas with all their finny drove	Mask 115
And makes one blot of all the ayr,	Mask 133
Of all thy dues be done, and none left out,	Mask 137
That he, the Supreme good, t' whom all things ill	Mask 217
line not in Bridgewater ms	
And give resounding grace to all Heav'ns Harmonies.	Mask 243
Co. And left your fair side all unguarded Lady?	Mask 283
Vertue could see to do what vertue would	Mask 373
Trinity ms 'see' ←'ad all her'	
Were all to ruffl'd, and somtimes impair'd.	Mask 380
Secure without all doubt, or controversie:	Mask 409
Till all be made immortal: but when lust	Mask 463
Of pilfering Woolf, not all the fleecy wealth	Mask 504
Deep skill'd in all his mothers witcheries,	Mask 523
Still to be so displac't. I was all eare,	Mask 560
With all the greisly legions that troop	Mask 603
Harpyies and *Hydra's*, or all the monstrous forms	Mask 605
And crumble all thy sinews. *Eld*. *Bro*. Why prethee Shepherd	Mask 615
Trinity ms 'all thy' ←'every'	
'Gainst all inchantments, mildew blast, or damp	Mask 640
Your nervs are all chain'd up in Alablaster,	Mask 660
Withall thy charms, although this corporal rinde	Mask 664
Trinity ms 'with all'	
1673 'With all'	
Bridgewater ms 'with all'	
Sorrow flies farr: See here be all the pleasures	Mask 668
By which all mortal frailty must subsist,	Mask 686

All(*cont*)
line not in Bridgewater ms
That have been tir'd all day without repast, Mask 688
Bridgewater ms 'aldaye'
This will restore all soon. *La*. 'Twill not false traitor, Mask 690
But all to please, and sate the curious taste? Mask 714
To store her children with; if all the world Mask 720
Till all thy magick structures rear'd so high, Mask 798
line not in Trinity ms
line not in Bridgewater ms
Dips me all o're, as when the wrath of *Jove* Mask 803
line not in Bridgewater ms
line not in Trinity ms
But this will cure all streight, one sip of this Mask 811
Helping all urchin blasts, and ill luck signes Mask 845
By all the *Nymphs* that nightly dance Mask 883
All the Swains that there abide, Mask 951
Will double all their mirth and chere; Mask 955
All amidst the Gardens fair Mask 981
Thither all their bounties bring, Mask 987
line not in Bridgewater ms
And stretch'd out all the Chimney's length, Allegro 111
To win her Grace, whom all commend. Allegro 124
Untwisting all the chains that ty Allegro 143
Or fill the fixed mind with all your toyes; Penseroso 4
All in a robe of darkest grain, Penseroso 33
Far from all resort of mirth, Penseroso 81
And bring all Heav'n before mine eyes. Penseroso 166
Was all in honour and devotion ment Arcades 35
And with all helpful service will comply Arcades 38
And all my Plants I save from nightly ill, Arcades 48
Over the mount, and all this hallow'd ground, Arcades 55
Shakes the high thicket, haste I all about, Arcades 58
Where ye may all that are of noble stemm Arcades 82
All *Arcadia* hath not seen. Arcades 95
All *Arcadia* hath not seen. Arcades 109
Trinity ms 'All' ←'As'
And all their echoes mourn. Lycidas 41
Sleek *Panope* with all her sisters play'd. Lycidas 99
Throw hither all your quaint enameld eyes, Lycidas 139
And purple all the ground with vernal flowres. Lycidas 141
Bid *Amaranthus* all his beauty shed, Lycidas 149
There entertain him all the Saints above, Lycidas 178
To all that wander in that perilous flood. Lycidas 185
And now the Sun had stretch'd out all the hills, Lycidas 190
And all the spangled host keep watch in squadrons bright? Nativity 21
All meanly wrapt in the rude manger lies; Nativity 31
For all the morning light, Nativity 73
Was all that did their silly thoughts so busie keep. Nativity 92
As all their souls in blisfull rapture took: Nativity 98
Could hold all Heav'n and Earth in happier union. Nativity 108
His burning Idol all of blackest hue, Nativity 207
Nor all the gods beside, Nativity 224
And all about the Courtly Stable, Nativity 243
All the day long his cours to run. Psalm 136, 30
The Tawny King with all his power. Psalm 136, 54
With all his over-hardy crew. Psalm 136, 70
All living creatures he doth feed, Psalm 136, 85
But all unwares with his cold-kind embrace Fair Inf 20
In Heav'ns defiance mustering all his waves; Vacation 44
While sad *Ulisses* soul and all the rest Vacation 50
Strew all their blessings on thy sleeping Head. Vacation 64
O're all his Brethren he shall Reign as King, Vacation 75
The leaves should all be black wheron I write, Passion 34
Would soon unboosom all thir Echoes milde, Passion 53
And last of all, thy greedy self consum'd, On Time 10
Then all this Earthy grosnes quit, On Time 20
He who with all Heav'ns heraldry whileare Circum 10
Broke the fair musick that all creatures made Musick 21
while all the starrie rounds & arches blue Musick Tr. ms 4.21
'while all the starrie rounds' ←'starrie frame' ←'whilst then' ←'whilst the whole frame of' ←'while all the' ←'that all'
of clamourous sin that all our musick marres Musick Tr. ms 5.04
Time numbers motion, yet (without a crime Another 7
1640, 1657 'all'
Rest that gives all men life, gave him his death, Another 11
But vow though the cross Doctors all stood hearers, Another 19
line not in 1640, 1657, 1658 texts
His Letters are deliver'd all and gon, Another 33
line not in 1658 text
Warbl'st at eeve, when all the Woods are still, Sonnet 1, 2
All is, if I have grace to use it so, Sonnet 7, 13
That all both judge you to relate them true, Sonnet 10, 13
For all this wast of wealth, and loss of blood. Sonnet 12, 14
Thy Works and Alms and all thy good Endeavour Sonnet 14, 5
Filling each mouth with envy, or with praise, Sonnet 15, 2
1694 'all'
And all her jealous monarchs with amaze, Sonnet 15, 3
In all her equipage; besides to know Sonnet 17, 9
When all our Fathers worship't Stocks and Stones, Sonnet 18, 4
O're all th' *Italian* fields where still doth sway Sonnet 18, 11
Of which all Europe talks from side to side. Sonnet 22, 12
Came vested all in white, pure as her mind: Sonnet 23, 9
But we do hope to find out all your tricks, Forcers 13
Who now enjoyes thee credulous, all Gold, Horace 9
And what he takes in hand shall prosper all. Psalm 1, 10
Happy all those who have in him their stay. Psalm 2, 28

All(*cont*)
On the cheek-bone all my foes, Psalm 3, 21
All workers of iniquity Psalm 5, 13
Push them in their rebellions all Psalm 5, 31
Then all who trust in thee shall bring Psalm 5, 33
For all my bones, that even with anguish ake, Psalm 6, 5
Ith' mid'st of all mine enemies that mark. Psalm 6, 15
Depart all ye that work iniquitie. Psalm 6, 16
Mine enemies shall all be blank and dash't Psalm 6, 21
All people from the worlds foundation. Psalm 7, 30
And glorious is thy name through all the earth? Psalm 8, 2
Hast founded strength because of all thy foes Psalm 8, 6
Thou hast put all under his lordly feet, Psalm 8, 18
All Flocks, and Herds, by thy commanding word, Psalm 8, 19
All beasts that in the field or forrest meet, Psalm 8, 20
And glorious is thy name through all the earth. Psalm 8, 24
With her *green* shade *that* cover'd *all*, Psalm 80, 41
That all may pluck her, as they go, Psalm 80, 51
To Jacobs God, *that all may hear* Psalm 81, 3
To serve me *all their daies*, Psalm 81, 54
And turn my hand against *all those* Psalm 81, 59
The Earths foundations all are mov'd Psalm 82, 19
I said that ye were Gods, yea all Psalm 82, 21
The Nations all possess. Psalm 82, 28
For they consult with all their might, Psalm 83, 17
And all as one in mind Psalm 83, 18
All these have lent their armed hands Psalm 83, 31
That wasted all the Coast Psalm 83, 34
Till all the mountains blaze, Psalm 83, 56
O're all the earth *art one*. Psalm 83, 68
Till all before *our* God *at length* Psalm 84, 27
And all their Sin, *that did thee grieve* Psalm 85, 7
Thine anger all thou hadst remov'd, Psalm 85, 9
To pardon, thou to all Psalm 86, 14
Of all that other gods have done Psalm 86, 27
The Nations all whom thou hast made Psalm 86, 29
Shall come, *and all shall frame* Psalm 86, 30
Then all the dwellings *faire* Psalm 87, 6
And all within his care. Psalm 87, 8
And all my fountains *clear*. Psalm 87, 28
All day to thee I cry; Psalm 88, 2
And all night long, before thee *weep* Psalm 88, 3
Hast set me *all forlorn*, Psalm 88, 26
Thou break'st upon me all thy waves, Psalm 88, 31
And all thy waves break me. Psalm 88, 32
Lord all the day I thee entreat, Psalm 88, 39
All day they round about me go, Psalm 88, 67

Allay
Deceav'd; they fondly thinking to allay Par Lost 10.564
From the dry ground to spring, thy thirst to allay Samson 582
His glowing Axle doth allay Mask 96
Bridgewater ms 'allaye'

Allayed
Yet scarce allay'd still eyes the current streame, Par Lost 7.67
Hystorian, who thus largely hast allayd Par Lost 8.7
And sweet allay'd, yet terrible to approach, Par Reg 2.160

Allaying
I drank, from the clear milkie juice allaying Samson 550

All-bearing
Whatever Earth all-bearing Mother yields Par Lost 5.338

All-bounteous
Excess, before th' all bounteous King, who showrd Par Lost 5.640
1667 'all-bounteous'

All-cheering
Days, months, & years, towards his all-chearing Lamp Par Lost 3.581

All-commanding
That by his all-commanding might, Psalm 136, 25

Allege
Sam. He must allege some cause, and offer'd fight Samson 1253

Alleged
The first in flight from pain, had'st thou alledg'd Par Lost 4.921
1667 'alleg'd'

Allegiance
Of true allegiance, constant Faith or Love, Par Lost 3.104
Allegeance to th' acknowldg'd Power supream? Par Lost 4.956

Allegoric
Real or Allegoric I discern not, Par Reg 4.390

Alley
Co. I know each lane, and every alley green Mask 311
Bridgewater ms 'Alley'

Alleys
Yon flourie Arbors, yonder Allies green, Par Lost 4.626
High rooft and walks beneath, and alleys brown Par Reg 2.293
In the blind mazes of this tangl'd Wood? Mask 181
Trinity ms 'mazes' ←'alleys'
About the cedar'n alleys fling Mask 990
Bridgewater ms 'allyes'

All-giver
Th' all-giver would be unthank't, would be unprais'd, Mask 723
Trinity ms 'all giver'
Bridgewater ms 'allgiver'

All-judging
And perfet witnes of all-judging *Jove;* Lycidas 82

All-knowing
All, though all-knowing, what had past with Man Par Lost 10.227

Allotted
Allotted there; and other Suns perhaps Par Lost 8.148
Each of his reign allotted, rightlier call'd, Par Reg 2.123

Allow
Vigour Divine within them, can allow Par Lost 6.158
Allowance
Or else with just allowance counterpois'd, Samson 770
In such a scant allowance of Star-light, Mask 308
All-powerful
And by command of Heav'ns all-powerful King Par Lost 2.851
All-ruling
And high permission of all-ruling Heaven Par Lost 1.212
ms 'all-ruleing'
Thick clouds and dark doth Heav'ns all-ruling Sire Par Lost 2.264
All-seeing
Of God All-seeing, or deceave his Heart Par Lost 10.6
Allure
Allure, or terrifie, or undermine. Par Reg 1.179
More then of arms before, allure mine eye, Par Reg 4.112
Allure thee from the cool Crystalline stream. Samson 546
Allured
Whose annual wound in *Lebanon* allur'd Par Lost 1.447
Allur'd his eye: Thither his course he bends Par Lost 3.573
The starrie flock, allur'd them, and with lyes Par Lost 5.709
Allurd them; thence from Cups to civil Broiles. Par Lost 11.718
Allurement
Against allurement, custom, and a World Par Lost 11.810
Though *Adam* by his Wives allurement fell, Par Reg 2.134
For no allurement yields to appetite, Par Reg 2.409
Alluring
Of that alluring fruit, urg'd me so keene. Par Lost 9.588
Sleeking her soft alluring locks, Mask 882
Bridgewater ms 'alluringe'
Allusion
Of *Lucifer*, so by allusion calld, Par Lost 10.425
All-worshipped
She hutch't th' all-worshipt ore, and precious gems Mask 719
Bridgewater ms 'all worshipt'
1637 'all worshipt'
Trinity ms 'all-worship't'
Almansor
The Kingdoms of *Almansor*, *Fez* and *Sus*, Par Lost 11.403
Almighty
With vain attempt. Him the Almighty Power Par Lost 1.44
Of force believe Almighty, since no less Par Lost 1.144
We shall be free; th' Almighty hath not built Par Lost 1.259
ms 'Almightie'
Matchless, but with th' Almighty, and that strife Par Lost 1.623
Of his Almighty Engin he shall hear Par Lost 2.65
Th' Almighty Victor to spend all his rage, Par Lost 2.144
Not more Almighty to resist our might Par Lost 2.192
(For what could else) to our Almighty Foe Par Lost 2.769
Unless th' Almighty Maker them ordain Par Lost 2.915
Now had the Almighty Father from above, Par Lost 3.56
Wondring; but soon th' Almighty thus reply'd: Par Lost 3.273
No sooner had th' Almighty ceas't, but all Par Lost 3.344
Made visible, th' Almighty Father shines, Par Lost 3.386
More of th' Almighties works, and chiefly Man Par Lost 4.566
Almightie, thine this universal Frame, Par Lost 5.154
O *Adam*, one Almightie is, from whom Par Lost 5.469
Innumerable before th' Almighties Throne Par Lost 5.585
Of Heav'ns Almightie. Thou to me thy thoughts Par Lost 5.676
Address, and to begirt th' Almighty Throne Par Lost 5.868
His puissance, trusting in th' Almightie's aide, Par Lost 6.119
And join him nam'd *Almighty* to thy aid, Par Lost 6.294
1667 '*Almightie*'
Together both with next to Almightie Arme, Par Lost 6.316
Had not th' Almightie Father where he sits Par Lost 6.671
My Bow and Thunder, my Almightie Arms Par Lost 6.713
Eye witnesses of his Almightie Acts, Par Lost 6.883
In presence of th' Almightie Father, pleas'd Par Lost 7.11
1669 'Almighty'
Obtaine: though to recount Almightie works Par Lost 7.112
So spake th' Almightie, and to what he spake Par Lost 7.174
When such was heard declar'd th' Almightie's will; Par Lost 7.181
Again th' Almightie spake: Let there be Lights Par Lost 7.339
Wherto th' Almighty answer'd, not displeas'd. Par Lost 8.398
What he *Almightie* styl'd, six Nights and Days Par Lost 9.137
Antagonist of Heav'ns Almightie King) Par Lost 10.387
Sooner or later; which th' Almightie seeing, Par Lost 10.613
Th' Almighty thus pronouncd his sovran Will. Par Lost 11.83
Led by the strength of the Almighties hand, Psalm 114, 4
Almost
Of amplitude almost immense, with Starr's Par Lost 7.620
Speed almost Spiritual; mee thou thinkst not slow, Par Lost 8.110
And almost life it self, if it be true Samson 91
Now was almost won Nativity 104
My Soul doth long and almost die Psalm 84, 5
For I am poor, and almost pine Psalm 86, 3
Alms
Thy Works and Alms and all thy good Endeavour Sonnet 14, 5
Trinity ms 'Almes'
Aloft
Aloft, incumbent on the dusky Air Par Lost 1.226
As many miles aloft: that furie stay'd, Par Lost 2.938
And flours aloft shading the Fount of Life, Par Lost 3.357
The sport of Winds: all these upwhirld aloft Par Lost 3.493
His mounted scale aloft: nor more; but fled Par Lost 4.1014
Brandisht aloft the horrid edge came down Par Lost 6.252
Aloft by Angels born, his Sign in Heav'n: Par Lost 6.776
Crested aloft, and Carbuncle his Eyes; Par Lost 9.500

Aloft(*cont*)
But lives and spreds aloft by those pure eyes, Lycidas 81
Alone
Alone the dreadful voyage; till at last Par Lost 2.426
Alone th' Antagonist of Heav'n, nor less Par Lost 2.509
Alone, but long I sat not, till my womb Par Lost 2.778
Alone, and without guide, half lost, I seek Par Lost 2.975
Son of my bosom, Son who art alone Par Lost 3.169
Walk'd up and down alone bent on his prey, Par Lost 3.441
Alone, for other Creature in this place Par Lost 3.442
Alone thus wandring. Brightest Seraph tell Par Lost 3.667
Invisible, except to God alone, Par Lost 3.684
From thy Empyreal Mansion thus alone, Par Lost 3.699
He markd and mad demeanour, then alone, Par Lost 4.129
Any, but God alone, to value right Par Lost 4.202
Alone as they. About them frisking playd Par Lost 4.340
And wisdom, which alone is truly fair. Par Lost 4.491
Thus talking hand in hand alone they pass'd Par Lost 4.689
But wherefore thou alone? wherefore with thee Par Lost 4.917
I therefore, I alone first undertook Par Lost 4.935
And on, methought, alone I pass'd through ways Par Lost 5.50
The flaming Seraph fearless, though alone Par Lost 5.875
To thee not visible, when I alone Par Lost 6.145
Found worthy not of Libertie alone, Par Lost 6.420
Or I alone against them, since by strength Par Lost 6.820
And solitude; yet not alone, while thou Par Lost 7.28
Not Words alone pleas'd her. O when meet now Par Lost 8.57
Earth sitting still, when she alone receaves Par Lost 8.89
What happiness, who can enjoy alone, Par Lost 8.365
Of happiness, or not? who am alone Par Lost 8.405
Thou in thy secresie although alone, Par Lost 8.427
And finde thee knowing not of Beasts alone, Par Lost 8.438
Knew it not good for Man to be alone, Par Lost 8.445
Light above Light, for thee alone, as seems, Par Lost 9.105
From thee alone, which on us both at once Par Lost 9.303
Alone, without exterior help sustaind? Par Lost 9.336
Thus earlie, thus alone; her Heav'nly forme Par Lost 9.457
Occasion which now smiles, behold alone Par Lost 9.480
Might tempt alone, and in her ears the sound Par Lost 9.736
Irrational till then. For us alone Par Lost 9.766
This my attempt, I would sustain alone Par Lost 9.978
Possession of the Garden; hee alone, Par Lost 11.222
Alone fulfill the Law; thy punishment Par Lost 12.404
One day forth walk'd alone, the Spirit leading; Par Reg 1.189
Me his beloved Son, in whom alone Par Reg 1.285
That which to God alone of right belongs; Par Reg 3.141
That which alone can truly reinstall thee Par Reg 3.372
Alone into the Temple; there was found Par Reg 4.217
Of Hornets arm'd, no sooner found alone, Samson 20
Lov'd, honour'd, fear'd me, thou alone could hate me Samson 939
Alone, and helpless! Is this the confidence Mask 583
Love vertue, she alone is free, Mask 1019
This this is she alone, Arcades 17
Which I full oft amidst these shades alone Arcades 42
She knew such harmony alone Nativity 107
Of him, t' whose happy-making sight alone, On Time 18
Speak to your hearts alone, Psalm 4, 20
For thou alone dost keep Psalm 4, 39
Thou Lord alone in safety mak'st me dwell. Psalm 4, 42
Jehova is alone, Psalm 83, 66
Art full of mercy, thou *alone* Psalm 86, 15
Remainest God alone. Psalm 86, 36
Along
And to the fierce contention brought along Par Lost 1.100
Four ways thir flying March, along the Banks Par Lost 2.574
Hence then, and evil go with thee along Par Lost 6.275
I send along, ride forth, and bid the Deep Par Lost 7.166
And beares thee soft with the smooth Air along, Par Lost 8.166
Inseparable must with mee along: Par Lost 10.250
Rise therefore with all speed and come along, Samson 1316
I with this Messenger will go along, Samson 1384
Sam. Brethren farewel, your company along Samson 1413
That crawls along the side of yon small hill, Mask 295
Bridgewater ms 'alonge'
Visits the herds along the twilight meadows, Mask 844
Bridgewater ms 'alonge'
Along the crisped shades and bowres Mask 984
line not in Bridgewater ms
And the mute Silence hist along, Penseroso 55
Where other groves, and other streams along, Lycidas 174
His thirty Armes along the indented Meads, Vacation 94
So sweetly sung your Joy the Clouds along Circum 4
The *cheerfull* Psaltry bring along Psalm 81, 7
Aloof
While the promiscuous croud stood yet aloof? Par Lost 1.380
Alooff the vulgar Constellations thick, Par Lost 3.577
The Lion and fierce Tiger glar'd aloof. Par Reg 1.313
But safest he who stood aloof, Samson 135
I among these aloof obscurely stood. Samson 1611
Aloud
Vaunting aloud, but rackt with deep despare: Par Lost 1.126
Th' *Apocalyps*, heard cry in Heaven aloud, Par Lost 4.2
Thou following cryd'st aloud, Return faire *Eve;* Par Lost 4.481
Gabriel from the Front thus calld aloud. Par Lost 4.865
Came flying, and in mid Aire aloud thus cri'd. Par Lost 6.536
I overjoyd could not forbear aloud. Par Lost 8.490
Approaching, thus to *Adam* call'd aloud. Par Lost 10.102
At last with head erect thus cryed aloud, Samson 1639

Aloud(*cont*)
Aloud I cry'd Psalm 3, 10
My heart and flesh aloud do crie, Psalm 84, 7
Alp
O're many a Frozen, many a fierie Alpe, Par Lost 2.620
Nor breath of Vernal Air from snowy *Alp*. Samson 628
Alpheus
Divine *Alpheus*, who by secret sluse, Arcades 30
Return *Alpheus*, the dread voice is past, Lycidas 132
Alpine
Lie scatter'd on the Alpine mountains cold, Sonnet 18, 2
Already
Already known what he for news had thought Par Lost 6.20
Already done, to have dispeopl'd Heav'n Par Lost 7.151
Alreadie by thy reasoning this I guess, Par Lost 8.85
Shouldst propagat, already infinite; Par Lost 8.420
Which he presumes already vain and void, Par Lost 10.50
Alreadie in part, though hid in gloomiest shade, Par Lost 10.716
Shall meet, alreadie linkt and Wedlock-bound Par Lost 10.905
On me alreadie lost, mee then thy self Par Lost 10.929
1667 'already'
Neglected. I already have made way Samson 481
What do I beg? how hast thou dealt already? Samson 707
Har. Dost thou already single me; I thought Samson 1092
Much more affliction then already felt Samson 1257
Already, ere my best speed could praevent, Mask 573
Trinity ms 'alreadie'
Bridgewater ms 'alreadie'
1637 'Alreadie'
Already, and for him intended Psalm 7, 47
That am already bruis'd, and shake Psalm 88, 59
Also
In *Sion* also not unsung, where stood Par Lost 1.442
He also against the house of God was bold: Par Lost 1.470
In Courts and Palaces he also Reigns Par Lost 1.497
Men also, and by his suggestion taught, Par Lost 1.685
Our torments also may in length of time Par Lost 2.274
I also; at which time this powerful Key Par Lost 2.774
When Will and Reason (Reason also is choice) Par Lost 3.108
Thir Nature also to thy Nature joyn; Par Lost 3.282
With thee thy Manhood also to this Throne; Par Lost 3.314
The same whom *John* saw also in the Sun: Par Lost 3.623
Those Blossoms also, and those dropping Gumms, Par Lost 4.630
And starrie Pole: Thou also mad'st the Night, Par Lost 4.724
Ambrosia; on that Tree he also gaz'd; Par Lost 5.57
Partake thou also; happie though thou art, Par Lost 5.75
(For wee have also our Eevning and our Morn, Par Lost 5.628
Thee also from obedience, that with him Par Lost 6.902
This also thy request with caution askt Par Lost 7.111
Thee also happier, shall not be withheld Par Lost 7.117
With his great Father (for he also went Par Lost 7.588
Abundantly his gifts hath also pour'd Par Lost 8.220
Thir language and thir wayes, they also know, Par Lost 8.373
In outward also her resembling less Par Lost 8.543
Thy praise hee also who forbids thy use, Par Lost 9.750
Have also tasted, and have also found Par Lost 9.874
Thou therefore also taste, that equal Lot Par Lost 9.881
I also err'd in overmuch admiring Par Lost 9.1178
Thorns also and Thistles it shall bring thee forth Par Lost 10.203
Now also evidence, but straight I felt Par Lost 10.361
True is, mee also he hath judg'd, or rather Par Lost 10.494
Is his wrauth also? be it, man is not so, Par Lost 10.795
Reach also of the Tree of Life, and eat, Par Lost 11.94
The World: in Spirit perhaps he also saw Par Lost 11.406
T' whom *Michael* thus, hee also mov'd, repli'd. Par Lost 11.453
Of tears and sorrow a Floud thee also drown'd, Par Lost 11.757
The conquerd also, and enslav'd by Warr Par Lost 11.797
This also shall they gain by thir delay Par Lost 12.223
To guide them in all truth, and also arme Par Lost 12.490
To whom thus also th' Angel last repli'd: Par Lost 12.574
Her also I with gentle Dreams have calm'd Par Lost 12.595
For God is also in sleep, and Dreams advise, Par Lost 12.611
What happ'ns new; Fame also finds us out. Par Reg 1.334
He saw the Prophet also how he fled Par Reg 2.270
That I have also power to give thou seest, Par Reg 2.393
May also in this poverty as soon Par Reg 2.451
(For I have also heard, perhaps have read) Par Reg 4.116
On the other side know also thou, that I Par Reg 4.159
The *Gentiles* also know, and write, and teach Par Reg 4.227
The Prince of darkness, glad would also seem Par Reg 4.441
The Son of God I also am, or was, Par Reg 4.518
To whom thus Jesus: also it is written, Par Reg 4.560
The air imprison'd also, close and damp, Samson 8
More Faith? who also in her prime of love, Samson 388
Was it not weakness also to make known Samson 778
The Virgins also shall on feastful days Samson 1741
They also serve who only stand and waite. Sonnet 19, 14
With them *great* Asshur also bands Psalm 83, 29
The Lord will also then bestow Psalm 85, 49
Alt
In motion or in alt: him soon they met Par Lost 6.532
In Paradise, and on a Hill made alt, Par Lost 11.210
Altar
Thir Altars by his Altar, Gods ador'd Par Lost 1.384
ms 'altar'
His righteous Altar, bowing lowly down Par Lost 1.434
Gods Altar to disparage and displace Par Lost 1.473
ms 'altar'

Altar(*cont*)
Or Altar smoak'd; yet who more oft then hee Par Lost 1.493
ms 'altar'
Our envied Sovran, and his Altar breathes Par Lost 2.244
From th' Earths great Altar send up silent praise Par Lost 9.195
With incense, where the Golden Altar fum'd, Par Lost 11.18
Ith' midst an Altar as the Land-mark stood Par Lost 11.432
Men who attend the Altar, and should most Par Lost 12.354
Before the Altar and the vested Priest, Par Reg 1.257
About his Altar, handling holy things, Par Reg 1.489
From off the Altar, where an Off'ring burn'd, Samson 26
Ay round about *Joves* Altar sing. Penseroso 48
From out his secret Altar toucht with hallow'd fire. Nativity 28
Altars
Thir Altars by his Altar, Gods ador'd Par Lost 1.384
ms 'altars'
In Temples and at Altars, when the Priest Par Lost 1.494
So many grateful Altars I would reare Par Lost 11.323
In Urns, and Altars round, Nativity 192
Ev'n *by* thy Altars Lord of Hoasts Psalm 84, 13
Alter
Could alter high Decrees, I to that place Par Lost 10.953
Alteration
Strange alteration! Sin and Death amain Par Lost 2.1024
Strange alteration in me, to degree Par Lost 9.599
Altered
Alterd her cheek. On whom the Angel *Haile* Par Lost 5.385
Adam, estrang'd in look and alterd stile, Par Lost 9.1132
Nor alter'd his offence; yet God at last Par Lost 10.171
Altern
The less by Night alterne: and made the Starrs, Par Lost 7.348
Alternate
Alternate all night long: but not so wak'd Par Lost 5.657
Although
Thou in thy secresie although alone, Par Lost 8.427
Although thir drudge, to be thir fool or jester, Samson 1338
Withall thy charms, although this corporal rinde Mask 664
Always
Were always downward bent, admiring more Par Lost 1.681
ms 'alwayes'
There alwayes, but drawn up to Heav'n somtimes Par Lost 3.517
1667 'alwaies'
Had in remembrance alwayes with delight; Par Lost 3.704
First, Highest, Holiest, Best, thou alwayes seekst Par Lost 6.724
To glorifie thy Son, I alwayes thee, Par Lost 6.725
But the hot Hell that alwayes in him burnes, Par Lost 9.467
Is lost, which alwayes with right Reason dwells Par Lost 12.84
The peoples praise, if always praise unmixt? Par Reg 3.48
Obeys *Tiberius;* nor is always rul'd Par Reg 3.159
Yet always pity or pardon hath obtain'd. Samson 814
Who alwayes vacant alwayes amiable Horace 10
Am
Though now to Death I yield, and am his due Par Lost 3.245
Which way I flie is Hell; my self am Hell; Par Lost 4.75
And without whom am to no end, my Guide Par Lost 4.442
Of bliss on bliss, while I to Hell am thrust, Par Lost 4.508
Then when I am thy captive talk of chaines, Par Lost 4.970
If dream'd, not as I oft am wont, of thee, Par Lost 5.32
Her shadowie Cloud withdraws, I am to haste, Par Lost 5.686
Visibly, what by Deitie I am, Par Lost 6.682
Boundless the Deep, because I am who fill Par Lost 7.168
And feel that I am happier then I know, Par Lost 8.282
Submiss: he rear'd me, and Whom thou soughtst I am, Par Lost 8.316
Of happiness, or not? who am alone Par Lost 8.405
With Gods to sit the highest, am now constraind Par Lost 9.164
When I am present, and thy trial choose Par Lost 9.316
And I perhaps am secret; Heav'n is high, Par Lost 9.811
Being as I am, why didst not thou the Head Par Lost 9.1155
And am I now upbraided, as the cause Par Lost 9.1168
Mee and Mankinde; I am to bruise his heel; Par Lost 10.498
That dust I am, and shall to dust returne: Par Lost 10.770
Why am I mockt with death, and length'nd out Par Lost 10.774
Am found Eternal, and incorporate both, Par Lost 10.816
Restor'd by thee, vile as I am, to place Par Lost 10.971
Made one with me as I with thee am one. Par Lost 11.44
That I who first brought Death on all, am grac't Par Lost 11.168
Permits not; to remove thee I am come, Par Lost 11.260
Ere thou from hence depart, know I am sent Par Lost 11.356
Such favour I unworthie am voutsaft, Par Lost 12.622
This is my Son belov'd, in him am pleas'd. Par Reg 1.85
I am; this chiefly, that my way must lie Par Reg 1.263
And now by some strong motion I am led Par Reg 1.290
Knowing who I am, as I know who thou art? Par Reg 1.356
'Tis true, I am that Spirit unfortunate, Par Reg 1.358
While I to sorrows am no less advanc't, Par Reg 2.69
But I to wait with patience am inur'd; Par Reg 2.102
Therefore I am return'd, lest confidence Par Reg 2.140
Who sent me, and thereby witness whence I am. Par Reg 3.107
I know them not; not therefore am I short Par Reg 4.287
The Son of God I also am, or was, Par Reg 4.518
And if I was, I am; relation stands; Par Reg 4.519
There I am wont to sit, when any chance Samson 4
Times past, what once I was, and what am now. Samson 22
Why am I thus bereav'd thy prime decree? Samson 85
Am I not sung and proverbd for a Fool Samson 203
The base degree to which I now am fall'n, Samson 414
I state not that; this I am sure; our Foes Samson 424
Nor am I in the list of them that hope; Samson 647

Am(*cont*)
Yet now am judg'd an enemy. Why then — Samson 882
Though for no friendly intent. I am of *Gath*, — Samson 1078
And now am come to see of whom such noise — Samson 1088
Sam. Thou knowst I am an *Ebrew*, therefore tell them, — Samson 1319
Off. I am sorry what this stoutness will produce. — Samson 1346
To thee I am bid say. Art thou our Slave, — Samson 1392
Like a wild Beast, I am content to go. — Samson 1403
No, I am fixt not to part hence without him. — Samson 1481
If need be, I am ready to forgo — Samson 1483
I am here. — Mask 901
For know by lot from *Jove* I am the powr — Arcades 44
Trinity ms defective here
Both them I serve, and of their train am I. — Sonnet 1, 14
That I to manhood am arriv'd so near, — Sonnet 7, 6
Pity me Lord for I am much deject — Psalm 6, 3
Am very weak and faint; heal and amend me, — Psalm 6, 4
Wearied I am with sighing out my dayes, — Psalm 6, 11
I am the Lord thy God which brought — Psalm 81, 41
For I am poor, and almost pine — Psalm 86, 3
Reck'n'd I am with them that pass — Psalm 88, 13
I am a man, but weak alas — Psalm 88, 15
That am already bruis'd, and shake — Psalm 88, 59

Amain
What when we fled amain, pursu'd and strook — Par Lost 2.165
Strange alteration! Sin and Death amain — Par Lost 2.1024
Up to the *Tropic* Crab; thence down amaine — Par Lost 10.675
Sent up amain; and now the thick'nd Skie — Par Lost 11.742
They whom I favour thrive in wealth amain, — Par Reg 2.430
Abstemious I grew up and thriv'd amain; — Samson 637
Comes on amain, speed in his look. — Samson 1304
(The Golden opes, the Iron shuts amain) — Lycidas 111
Trinity ms 'amaine'

Amalek
And *hateful* Amalec, — Psalm 83, 26

Amalthea
Hid *Amalthea* and her Florid Son — Par Lost 4.278
With fruits and flowers from *Amalthea*'s horn, — Par Reg 2.356

Amara
Mount *Amara*, though this by som suppos'd — Par Lost 4.281

Amarant
Thir Crowns inwove with Amarant and Gold, — Par Lost 3.352
Immortal Amarant, a Flour which once — Par Lost 3.353

Amaranthus
Bid *Amaranthus* all his beauty shed, — Lycidas 149
1673 '*Amarantus*'

Amarantine
Of *Amarantin* Shade, Fountain or Spring, — Par Lost 11.78

Amaryllis
To sport with *Amaryllis* in the shade, — Lycidas 68

A-maying
As he met her once a Maying, — Allegro 20

Amaze
Up lifting bore them in thir hands: Amaze, — Par Lost 6.646
And oft supported so as shall amaze — Par Lost 12.496
Into perplexity and new amaze: — Par Reg 2.38
As with amaze shall strike all who behold. — Samson 1645
The Stars with deep amaze — Nativity 69
And all her jealous monarchs with amaze, — Sonnet 15, 3
1694 'Amaze'

Amazed
As we erewhile, astounded and amaz'd, — Par Lost 1.281
Back stept those two faire Angels half amaz'd — Par Lost 4.820
Yet more amaz'd unwarie thus reply'd. — Par Lost 9.614
Misleads th' amaz'd Night-wanderer from his way — Par Lost 9.640
The fatal Trespass don by *Eve*, amaz'd, — Par Lost 9.889
Was left him, or false glitter: All amaz'd — Par Lost 10.452
Lose thir defence distracted and amaz'd. — Samson 1286
Amaz'd I stood, harrow'd with grief and fear, — Mask 565
Amazed Heav'n and Earth to shake. — Psalm 136, 14

Amazement
Under amazement of thir hideous change. — Par Lost 1.313
ms 'amazment'
Out of thy head I sprung: amazement seis'd — Par Lost 2.758
Half sunk with all his Pines. Amazement seis'd — Par Lost 6.198
Of much amazement to th' infernal Crew, — Par Reg 1.107
But Satan smitten with amazement fell — Par Reg 4.562
What if in wild amazement, and affright, — Mask 356
Trinity ms 'amazment'

Amazonian
They gatherd, broad as *Amazonian* Targe, — Par Lost 9.1111

Amber
Rowls o're *Elisian* Flours her Amber stream; — Par Lost 3.359
Amber, and colours of the showrie Arch. — Par Lost 6.759
Gris-amber-steam'd; all Fish from Sea or Shore, — Par Reg 2.344
There *Susa* by *Choaspes*, amber stream, — Par Reg 3.288
An Amber sent of odorous perfume — Samson 720
Stoop thy pale visage through an amber cloud, — Mask 333
Rob'd in flames, and Amber light, — Allegro 61

Amber-dropping
The loose train of thy amber-dropping hair, — Mask 863
B.M. ms 'Amber dropping'
Bridgewater ms 'Amber-droppinge'

Ambient
So beauteous, op'ning to the ambient light. — Par Lost 6.481
All space, the ambient Aire wide interfus'd — Par Lost 7.89

Ambiguous
Ambiguous words and jealousies, to sound — Par Lost 5.703

Ambiguous(*cont*)
So scoffing in ambiguous words he scarce, — Par Lost 6.568
As Plants: ambiguous between Sea and Land — Par Lost 7.473
Ambiguous and with double sense deluding, — Par Reg 1.435

Ambition
To reign is worth ambition though in Hell: — Par Lost 1.262
Or clos ambition varnisht o're with zeal. — Par Lost 2.485
Till Pride and worse Ambition threw me down — Par Lost 4.40
Ambition. Yet why not? som other Power — Par Lost 4.61
In miserie; such joy Ambition findes. — Par Lost 4.92
But what will not Ambition and Revenge — Par Lost 9.168
Hee with a crew, whom like Ambition joyns — Par Lost 12.38
Of lucre and ambition, and the truth — Par Lost 12.511
Without ambition, war, or violence; — Par Reg 3.90
Us'd no ambition to commend my deeds, — Samson 247

Ambitious
If he oppos'd; and with ambitious aim — Par Lost 1.41
Of present pain, that with ambitious mind — Par Lost 2.34
Before thy fellows, ambitious to win — Par Lost 6.160
Of proud ambitious heart, who not content — Par Lost 12.25
By lust and rapine; first ambitious grown — Par Reg 4.137
Ambitious spirit, and wouldst be thought my God, — Par Reg 4.495
Thou needst not be ambitious to be first, — Vacation 11

Ambrosia
Ambrosia; on that Tree he also gaz'd; — Par Lost 5.57
1667 'Ambrosia'

Ambrosial
Ambrosial Odours and Ambrosial Flowers, — Par Lost 2.245
Thus while God spake, ambrosial fragrance fill'd — Par Lost 3.135
High eminent, blooming Ambrosial Fruit — Par Lost 4.219
Of life ambrosial frutage bear, and vines — Par Lost 5.427
Now when ambrosial Night with Clouds exhal'd — Par Lost 5.642
With Plant, Fruit, Flour Ambrosial, Gemms & Gold, — Par Lost 6.475
New gatherd, and ambrosial smell diffus'd. — Par Lost 9.852
Your Tribes, and water from th' ambrosial Fount? — Par Lost 11.279
Ambrosial, Fruits fetcht from the tree of life, — Par Reg 4.589
And from the fount of life Ambrosial drink, — Par Reg 4.590
I would not soil these pure Ambrosial weeds, — Mask 16
1637 'ambrosial'
Trinity ms 'ambrosiall'
Bridgewater ms 'ambrosiall'
Dropt in Ambrosial Oils till she reviv'd, — Mask 840
Trinity ms 'ambrosiall'
1637 'ambrosial'
Bridgewater ms 'abrosiall'

Ambush
Or ambush from the Deep. What if we find — Par Lost 2.344
Such ambush hid among sweet Flours and Shades — Par Lost 9.408

Ambushes
Nor in the house with chamber Ambushes — Samson 1112

Amend
Am very weak and faint; heal and amend me, — Psalm 6, 4

Amends
This turn hath made amends; thou hast fulfill'd — Par Lost 8.491
The Serpents head; piteous amends, unless — Par Lost 10.1032
Unwholsom draught: but here I feel amends, — Samson 9
Thy mind with what amends is in my power, — Samson 745

Amerced
Millions of Spirits for his fault amerc't — Par Lost 1.609
ms 'amerc'd'

American
Columbus found th' *American* so girt — Par Lost 9.1116

Amiable
Hung amiable, *Hesperian* Fables true, — Par Lost 4.250
To make her amiable: On she came, — Par Lost 8.484
Holy, divine, good, amiable, or sweet! — Par Lost 9.899
Who alwayes vacant alwayes amiable — Horace 10

Amiably
Less winning soft, less amiablie milde, — Par Lost 4.479

Amice
Came forth with Pilgrim steps in amice gray; — Par Reg 4.427

Amid
In hurdl'd Cotes amid the field secure, — Par Lost 4.186
And all amid them stood the Tree of Life, — Par Lost 4.218
Amid the Suns bright circle where thou sitst, — Par Lost 4.578
So Hills amid the Air encounterd Hills — Par Lost 6.664
So easily obeyd amid the choice — Par Lost 7.48
Amid the Waters, and let it divide — Par Lost 7.262
Amid the Garden by the Tree of Life, — Par Lost 8.326
To be returnd by Noon amid the Bowre, — Par Lost 9.401
Amid the Tree now got, where plenty hung — Par Lost 9.594
Unseen amid the throng: so violence — Par Lost 11.671
O dark, dark, dark, amid the blaze of noon, — Samson 80

Amidst
Though without number still amidst the Hall — Par Lost 1.791
Of darkness do we dread? How oft amidst — Par Lost 2.263
Eternal *Anarchie*, amidst the noise — Par Lost 2.896
Amidst the glorious brightness where thou sit'st — Par Lost 3.376
Or Pilot from amidst the *Cyclades* — Par Lost 5.264
Amidst as from a flaming Mount, whose top — Par Lost 5.598
1667 'A midst'
Though single. From amidst them forth he passd, — Par Lost 5.903
From midst a Golden Cloud thus milde was heard. — Par Lost 6.28
(So call him, brighter once amidst the Host — Par Lost 7.132
Amidst his circling Spires, that on the grass — Par Lost 9.502
But of the Fruit of this fair Tree amidst — Par Lost 9.661
Amidst in Thunder utter'd thus his voice. — Par Lost 10.33
To save himself and houshold from amidst — Par Lost 11.820

Amidst(*cont*)
A gloomy Consistory; and them amidst — Par Reg 1.42
At his command; when from amidst them rose — Par Reg 2.149
Nor yet amidst this joy and brightest morn — Par Reg 4.439
Renewing fresh assaults, amidst his pride — Par Reg 4.570
By th' Idolatrous rout amidst thir wine; — Samson 443
Amidst thir highth of noon, — Samson 683
Amidst the flowry-kirtl'd *Naiades* — Mask 254
Trinity ms 'amidst' ←'sitting amidst'
1673 'Amid'st'
The wonted roar was up amidst the Woods, — Mask 549
Ne're looks to Heav'n amidst his gorgeous feast, — Mask 777
All amidst the Gardens fair — Mask 981
amidst the Hesperian gardens, on whose bancks — Mask Tr. ms 10.05
Which I full oft amidst these shades alone — Arcades 42
Rouze thy self amidst the rage — Psalm 7, 20
For they amidst their pride have said — Psalm 83, 45

Amiss
And thank the gods amiss. I should be loath — Mask 177
1637 'amisse'
Trinity ms 'amisse'
Bridgewater ms 'amisse'
And their power that do amiss. — Psalm 7, 36

Amity
And mutual amitie so streight, so close, — Par Lost 4.376
Collateral love, and deerest amitie. — Par Lost 8.426
With secret amity things of like kinde — Par Lost 10.248

Ammon
Whom Gentiles *Ammon* call and *Lybian Jove*, — Par Lost 4.277
Gebal and Ammon *there conspire*, — Psalm 83, 25

Ammonian
Ammonian Jove, or *Capitoline* was seen, — Par Lost 9.508

Ammonite
To his grim Idol. Him the *Ammonite* — Par Lost 1.396
ms 'Ammonite'
Defended *Israel* from the *Ammonite*, — Samson 285

Ammunition
He all thir Ammunition — Samson 1277

Among
Nor had they yet among the Sons of *Eve* — Par Lost 1.364
Among the Nations round, and durst abide — Par Lost 1.385
In clusters; they among fresh dews and flowers — Par Lost 1.771
Among his Angels; and his Throne it self — Par Lost 2.68
Pronounc'd among the Gods, and by an Oath, — Par Lost 2.352
Astonisht: none among the choice and prime — Par Lost 2.423
Others among the chief might offer now — Par Lost 2.469
Among themselves, and levie cruel warres, — Par Lost 2.501
To that new world of light and bliss, among — Par Lost 2.867
And be thy self Man among men on Earth, — Par Lost 3.283
Among the spirits beneath, whom I seduc'd — Par Lost 4.83
Down he alights among the sportful Herd — Par Lost 4.396
Among so many signes of power and rule — Par Lost 4.429
Among our other torments not the least, — Par Lost 4.510
Among the bestial herds to raunge, by thee — Par Lost 4.754
Taste this, and be henceforth among the Gods — Par Lost 5.77
Reason as chief; among these Fansie next — Par Lost 5.102
Among the Groves, the Fountains, and the Flours — Par Lost 5.126
Among sweet dewes and flours; where any row — Par Lost 5.212
After his charge receivd; but from among — Par Lost 5.248
Eastward among those Trees, what glorious shape — Par Lost 5.309
By living Streams among the Trees of Life, — Par Lost 5.652
Among the sons of Morn, what multitudes — Par Lost 5.716
Had audience, when among the Seraphim — Par Lost 5.804
Among the faithless, faithful only hee; — Par Lost 5.897
Among innumerable false, unmov'd, — Par Lost 5.898
Among those friendly Powers, who him receav'd — Par Lost 6.22
Among the mightiest, bent on highest deeds, — Par Lost 6.112
Among the Constellations warr were sprung, — Par Lost 6.312
From far with thundring noise among our foes — Par Lost 6.487
So they among themselves in pleasant veine — Par Lost 6.628
Hymns of high praise, and I among them chief. — Par Lost 6.745
Among them he arriv'd; in his right hand — Par Lost 6.835
Among th' accurst, that witherd all thir strength, — Par Lost 6.850
Among th' Angelic Powers, and the deep fall — Par Lost 6.898
Of Angels, then that Starr the Starrs among) — Par Lost 7.133
Among the Trees in Pairs they rose, they walk'd: — Par Lost 7.459
Thir seasons: among these the seat of men, — Par Lost 7.623
Rose, and went forth among her Fruits and Flours, — Par Lost 8.44
Up hither, from among the Trees appeer'd — Par Lost 8.313
Among unequals what societie — Par Lost 8.383
Among the Beasts no Mate for thee was found. — Par Lost 8.594
To mee shall be the glorie sole among — Par Lost 9.135
Such ambush hid among sweet Flours and Shades — Par Lost 9.408
Among thick-wov'n Arborets and Flours — Par Lost 9.437
Among the pleasant Villages and Farmes — Par Lost 9.448
In this enclosure wild, these Beasts among, — Par Lost 9.543
A Goddess among Gods, ador'd and serv'd — Par Lost 9.547
Among the Trees on Iles and woodie Shores. — Par Lost 9.1118
And from his presence hid themselves among — Par Lost 10.100
You two this way, among these numerous Orbs — Par Lost 10.397
Among the Heathen of thir purchase got, — Par Lost 10.579
From his transcendent Seat the Saints among, — Par Lost 10.614
Daughter of Sin, among th' irrational, — Par Lost 10.708
Take to thee from among the Cherubim — Par Lost 11.100
Celestial, whether among the Thrones, or nam'd — Par Lost 11.296
Stood visible, among these Pines his voice — Par Lost 11.321
At length a Reverend Sire among them came, — Par Lost 11.719
Among the Builders; each to other calls — Par Lost 12.57

Among(*cont*)
His presence from among them, and avert — Par Lost 12.108
Among them to set up his Tabernacle, — Par Lost 12.247
Among whom God will deigne to dwell on Earth — Par Lost 12.281
Among them; how can God with such reside? — Par Lost 12.284
Will reign among them, as of thee begot; — Par Lost 12.286
But first among the Priests dissension springs, — Par Lost 12.353
His faithful, left among th' unfaithful herd, — Par Lost 12.481
And he himself among them was baptiz'd, — Par Reg 1.76
Among wild Beasts: they at his sight grew mild, — Par Reg 1.310
I came among the Sons of God, when he — Par Reg 1.368
Among the Prime in Splendour, now depos'd, — Par Reg 1.413
Among the Nations? that hath been thy craft, — Par Reg 1.432
Among them to declare his Providence — Par Reg 1.445
Hale highly favour'd, among women blest; — Par Reg 2.68
Among daughters of men the fairest found; — Par Reg 2.154
Delight not all; among the Sons of Men, — Par Reg 2.192
Among the Heathen, (for throughout the World — Par Reg 2.443
Th' intelligent among them and the wise — Par Reg 3.58
In *Habor*, and among the *Medes* dispers't, — Par Reg 3.376
From the *Asian* Kings and *Parthian* among these, — Par Reg 4.73
Shar'd among petty Kings too far remov'd; — Par Reg 4.87
Among the gravest Rabbies disputant — Par Reg 4.218
Flock'd to the Baptist, I among the rest, — Par Reg 4.511
Blind among enemies, O worse then chains, — Samson 68
Among inhuman foes. — Samson 109
Among the Heathen round; to God have brought — Samson 451
Shav'n, and disarm'd among my enemies. — Samson 540
And of my Nation chose thee from among — Samson 877
Among illustrious women, faithful wives: — Samson 957
My name perhaps among the Circumcis'd — Samson 975
I shall be nam'd among the famousest — Samson 982
Among the Slaves and Asses thy comrades, — Samson 1162
Sam. Among the Daughters of the *Philistines* — Samson 1192
Great among the Heathen round: — Samson 1430
He now be dealing dole among his foes, — Samson 1529
Among his foes? *Mess*. Inevitable cause — Samson 1586
I among these aloof obscurely stood. — Samson 1611
Among thy slain self-kill'd — Samson 1664
Among them he a spirit of phrenzie sent, — Samson 1675
Stirs up among the loose unleter'd Hinds, — Mask 174
Trinity ms 'amoungst'
Bridgewater ms 'amonge'
Till free consent the gods among — Mask 1007
line not in Bridgewater ms
Thee Chauntress oft the Woods among, — Penseroso 63
that didst reform thy art, the cheif among — Sonnet 13, Tr. ms 40.08
Among themselves they laugh, they play, — Psalm 80, 27
Among the gods on both his hands — Psalm 82, 3
Like thee among the gods is none — Psalm 86, 25
Among the holy Mountains *high* — Psalm 87, 1
Among the dead *to sleep*, — Psalm 88, 18

Amongst
Amongst innumerable Starrs, that shon — Par Lost 3.565
Amongst the enthron'd gods on Sainted seats. — Mask 11
Trinity ms 'amoungst'
From the chill dew, amongst rude burrs and thistles? — Mask 352
Trinity ms 'amoungst rude burrs & thistles' ←'in this surrounding wilde' ←'in this dead solitude'
Amongst the rest a small unsightly root, — Mask 629
These oughly-headed Monsters? Mercy guard me! — Mask 695
Trinity ms 'amoung'st these'
'Mongst horrid shapes, and shreiks, and sights unholy, — Allegro 4
Amongst their Ews, the little Hills like Lambs. — Psalm 114, 12
Amongst her spangled sisters bright. — Psalm 136, 34
Which 'mongst the wanton gods a foul reproach was held. — Fair Inf 14
Amongst us here below to hide thy nectar'd head. — Fair Inf 49

Amorous
In amorous dittyes all a Summers day, — Par Lost 1.449
And sweet reluctant amorous delay. — Par Lost 4.311
She all night long her amorous descant sung; — Par Lost 4.603
The spirit of love and amorous delight. — Par Lost 8.477
Disporting, till the amorous Bird of Night — Par Lost 8.518
Of amorous intent, well understood — Par Lost 9.1035
Oppress'd them, wearied with thir amorous play. — Par Lost 9.1045
Soft amorous Ditties, and in dance came on: — Par Lost 11.584
Rove without rein, till in the amorous Net — Par Lost 11.586
Expert in amorous Arts, enchanting tongues — Par Reg 2.158
Hearts after them tangl'd in Amorous Nets. — Par Reg 2.162
And amorous reproaches to win from me — Samson 393
And secret sting of amorous remorse. — Samson 1007
With Turtle wing the amorous clouds dividing, — Nativity 50
For he being amorous on that lovely die — Fair Inf 5
Have linkt that amorous power to thy soft lay, — Sonnet 1, 8

Amorrean
That rul'd the *Amorrean* coast. — Psalm 136, 66

Amours
Casual fruition, nor in Court Amours — Par Lost 4.767

Amphisbaena
Scorpion and Asp, and *Amphisbaena* dire, — Par Lost 10.524

Amphitrite
To wait in *Amphitrite*'s bowr. — Mask 921
Bridgewater ms 'Amphitrites'
Trinity ms 'in Amphitrites' ←'on amphitrite in her'

Ample
Within, her ample spaces, o're the smooth — Par Lost 1.725
I through the ample Air in Triumph high — Par Lost 3.254
Transfus'd on thee his ample Spirit rests. — Par Lost 3.389

Ample(*cont*)
That made us, and for us this ample World Par Lost 4.413
And on her ample Square from side to side Par Lost 5.393
Of tenfold Adamant, his ample Shield Par Lost 6.255
A broad and ample rode, whose dust is Gold Par Lost 7.577
And gaz'd a while the ample Skie, till rais'd Par Lost 8.258
In ample space under the broadest shade Par Reg 2.339
In ample Territory, wealth and power, Par Reg 4.82
Ampler
Dimm erst, dilated Spirits, ampler Heart, Par Lost 9.876
Amplest
Stretcht out to the amplest reach of prospect lay. Par Lost 11.380
Strength, comliness of shape, or amplest merit Samson 1011
Amplier
Now amplier known thy Saviour and thy Lord, Par Lost 12.544
Amplitude
Of amplitude almost immense, with Starr's Par Lost 7.620
And amplitude of mind to greatest Deeds. Par Reg 2.139
Amply
So amply, and with hands so liberal Par Lost 8.362
Amply have merited of me, of all Par Lost 10.388
Amram
Of *Amrams* Son in *Egypts* evill day Par Lost 1.339
ms 'Amrams'
Amused
Collected stood within our thoughts amus'd, Par Lost 6.581
Such as we might perceive amus'd them all, Par Lost 6.623
Amymone
Or *Amymone*, *Syrinx*, many more Par Reg 2.188
An
That were an ignominy and shame beneath Par Lost 1.115
By Spirits reprobate, and in an hour Par Lost 1.697
What in an age they with incessant toyle Par Lost 1.698
As in an Organ from one blast of wind Par Lost 1.708
Rose like an Exhalation, with the sound Par Lost 1.711
Pronounc'd among the Gods, and by an Oath, Par Lost 2.352
Throws his steep flight in many an Aerie wheele, Par Lost 3.741
Henceforth an individual solace dear; Par Lost 4.486
Why satst thou like an enemie in waite Par Lost 4.825
Far was advanc't on winged speed, an Host Par Lost 5.744
Is now an Iron Rod to bruise and breake Par Lost 5.887
With many an inrode gor'd; deformed rout Par Lost 6.387
An Earthlie Guest, and drawn Empyreal Aire, Par Lost 7.14
For thou art Heav'nlie, shee an empty dreame. Par Lost 7.39
An Atom, with the Firmament compar'd Par Lost 8.18
An Edifice too large for him to fill, Par Lost 8.104
As with an object that excels the sense, Par Lost 8.456
Build in her loveliest, and create an awe Par Lost 8.558
An outside? fair no doubt, and worthy well Par Lost 8.568
That name, unless an age too late, or cold Par Lost 9.44
That such an Enemie we have, who seeks Par Lost 9.274
An eager appetite, rais'd by the smell Par Lost 9.740
Satan in likeness of an Angel bright Par Lost 10.327
Your wonder, with an Apple; he thereat Par Lost 10.487
Ith' midst an Altar as the Land-mark stood Par Lost 11.432
And there take root an Iland salt and bare, Par Lost 11.834
An Olive leafe he brings, pacific signe: Par Lost 11.860
An Ark, and in the Ark his Testimony, Par Lost 12.251
And unrecorded left through many an Age, Par Reg 1.16
But now an aged man in Rural weeds, Par Reg 1.314
In pious Hearts, an inward Oracle Par Reg 1.463
Without new trouble; such an Enemy Par Reg 2.126
On whom his leisure will vouchsafe an eye Par Reg 2.210
Nor proffer'd by an Enemy, though who Par Reg 2.330
On each side an Imperial City stood, Par Reg 4.33
To *Capreae* an Island small but strong Par Reg 4.92
An empty cloud. However many books Par Reg 4.321
Rule in the Clouds; like an Autumnal Star Par Reg 4.619
Twice by an Angel, who at last in sight Samson 24
From off the Altar, where an Off'ring burn'd, Samson 26
The daughter of an Infidel: they knew not Samson 221
Himself an Army, now unequal match Samson 346
The miracle of men: then in an hour Samson 364
An Amber sent of odorous perfume Samson 720
As I by thee, to Ages an example. Samson 765
It would be to ensnare an irreligious Samson 860
Yet now am judg'd an enemy. Why then Samson 882
No more thy countrey, but an impious crew Samson 891
Nor from that right to part an hour, Samson 1056
To have wrought such wonders with an Asses Jaw; Samson 1095
I only with an Oak'n staff will meet thee, Samson 1123
Sam. Thou knowst I am an *Ebrew*, therefore tell them, Samson 1319
An *Ebrew*, as I guess, and of our Tribe. Samson 1540
And as an ev'ning Dragon came, Samson 1692
Of tame villatic Fowl; but as an Eagle Samson 1695
An old, and haughty Nation proud in Arms: Mask 33
Stoop thy pale visage through an amber cloud, Mask 333
For who would rob a Hermit of his Weeds, Mask 390
Bridgewater ms 'an hermitt'
1637 'an Hermit'
Of Misers treasure by an out-laws den, Mask 399
Yet where an equall poise of hope and fear Mask 410
Till an unusuall stop of sudden silence Mask 552
And harshly deal like an ill borrower Mask 683
line not in Bridgewater ms
If you let slip time, like a neglected rose Mask 743
Trinity ms 'like an'
Pillows his chin upon an Orient wave, Nativity 231

An(*cont*)
This if thou do he will an off-spring give, Fair Inf 76
Shall subject be to many an Accident. Vacation 74
With an individual kiss; On Time 12
A Vicounts daughter, an Earls heir, Winchester 3
The labour of an age in piled Stones, Shakespear 2
And like an Engin mov'd with wheel and waight, Another 9
1658 'some Engine'
1640, 1657 'some engine'
He had bin an immortall Carrier. Another 28
An open grave their throat, their tongue they smooth. Psalm 5, 28
As *when* an *aged* wood takes fire Psalm 83, 53
Then an unjust and wicked King Prose 11, 3
Anak
The Sons of *Anac*, famous now and blaz'd, Samson 528
As *Og* or *Anak* and the *Emims* old Samson 1080
Anarch
Thus *Satan;* and him thus the Anarch old Par Lost 2.988
Anarchy
Eternal *Anarchie*, amidst the noise Par Lost 2.896
Through his wilde Anarchie, so huge a rout Par Lost 6.873
Wide Anarchie of *Chaos* damp and dark Par Lost 10.283
Subject himself to Anarchy within, Par Reg 2.471
Ancestor
To whom our general Ancestor repli'd. Par Lost 4.659
My Head, Ill fare our Ancestor impure, Par Lost 10.735
The Balme of Life. To whom our Ancestor. Par Lost 11.546
Ancestors
And *Chaos*, Ancestors of Nature, hold Par Lost 2.895
Anchises
Sprung of old *Anchises* line, Mask 923
Anchor
With fixed Anchor in his skaly rind Par Lost 1.206
Anchors
Or Pinnace anchors in a craggy Bay Par Lost 2.289
Ancient
By ancient *Tarsus* held, or that Sea-beast Par Lost 1.200
In ancient *Greece;* and in *Ausonian* land Par Lost 1.739
(if ancient and prophetic fame in Heav'n Par Lost 2.346
Neerer our ancient Seat; perhaps in view Par Lost 2.394
Of ancient pile; all else deep snow and ice, Par Lost 2.591
Chaos and *ancient Night*, I come no Spy, Par Lost 2.970
Erect the Standard there of *ancient Night;* Par Lost 2.986
First from the ancient World those Giants came Par Lost 3.464
Seem'd thir Petition, then when th' ancient Pair Par Lost 11.10
In Fables old, less ancient yet then these, Par Lost 11.11
The ancient Sire descends with all his Train; Par Lost 11.862
O ancient Powers of Air and this wide world, Par Reg 1.44
Under the covert of some ancient Oak, Par Reg 1.305
Princes, Heavens antient Sons, Aethereal Thrones, Par Reg 2.121
Witness those antient Empires of the Earth, Par Reg 2.435
Assyria and her Empires antient bounds, Par Reg 3.270
As antient, but rebuilt by him who twice Par Reg 3.281
Who freed, as to thir antient Patrimony, Par Reg 3.428
The schools of antient Sages; his who bred Par Reg 4.251
Those antient, whose resistless eloquence Par Reg 4.268
In antient and in modern books enroll'd; Samson 653
My daily walks and ancient neighbourhood, Mask 314
Bridgewater ms 'antient'
And yet more med'cinal is it then that *Moly* Mask 636
Trinity ms 'Moly' ← 'ancient Moly'
Or Coaly *Tine*, or antient hollowed *Dee*, Vacation 98
By the known rules of antient libertie, Sonnet 12, 2
Trinity ms 'ancient'
Who were thy Sheep and in their antient Fold Sonnet 18, 6
Thou antient stock of Israel, Psalm 81, 35
Anciently
We mean to hold what anciently we claim Par Lost 5.723
And
Listings of this word are omitted; see the Introduction.
Andrew
Andrew and *Simon*, famous after known Par Reg 2.7
Andromeda
Andromeda farr off *Atlantic* Seas Par Lost 3.559
Angel
So spake th' Apostate Angel, though in pain, Par Lost 1.125
ms 'Angell'
Said then the lost Arch-Angel, this the seat Par Lost 1.243
1667 'ArchAngel'
ms 'Archangell'
His Legions, Angel Forms, who lay intrans't Par Lost 1.301
ms 'Angell'
Less then Arch Angel ruind, and th' excess Par Lost 1.593
ms 'Archangel'
Above them all th' Arch Angel: but his face Par Lost 1.600
ms 'Archangel'
Art thou that Traitor Angel, art thou hee, Par Lost 2.689
That mighty leading Angel, who of late Par Lost 2.991
Saw within kenn a glorious Angel stand, Par Lost 3.622
He drew not nigh unheard, the Angel bright, Par Lost 3.645
Th' Arch-Angel *Uriel*, one of the seav'n Par Lost 3.648
For neither Man nor Angel can discern Par Lost 3.682
Fair Angel, thy desire which tends to know Par Lost 3.694
Me some inferiour Angel, I had stood Par Lost 4.59
Of God or Angel, for they thought no ill: Par Lost 4.320
What day the genial Angel to our Sire Par Lost 4.712
Thus he in scorn. The warlike Angel mov'd, Par Lost 4.902
Insulting Angel, well thou knowst I stood Par Lost 4.926

Angel(*cont*)
To whom the warriour Angel, soon repli'd. Par Lost 4.946
To entertain our Angel guest, as hee Par Lost 5.328
Alterd her cheek. On whom the Angel *Haile* Par Lost 5.385
To whom the Angel. Therefore what he gives Par Lost 5.404
The Angel, nor in mist, the common gloss Par Lost 5.435
To whom the Angel. Son of Heav'n and Earth, Par Lost 5.519
If not the first Arch-Angel, great in Power, Par Lost 5.660
So spake the false Arch-Angel, and infus'd Par Lost 5.694
So spake the fervent Angel, but his zeale Par Lost 5.849
All night the dreadless Angel unpursu'd Par Lost 6.1
At first, that Angel should with Angel warr, Par Lost 6.92
From flight, seditious Angel, to receave Par Lost 6.152
Th' Arch-Angel trumpet; through the vast of Heaven Par Lost 6.203
1667 'Arch-angel'
The great Arch-Angel from his warlike toile Par Lost 6.257
By thousands, Angel on Arch-Angel rowl'd; Par Lost 6.594
The affable Arch-Angel, had forewarn'd Par Lost 7.41
1667 'Arch-angel'
1669 'Arch-Angel'
And thus the Godlike Angel answerd milde. Par Lost 7.110
The Angel ended, and in *Adams* Eare Par Lost 8.1
line not in 1667 edition
Before the Angel, and of him to ask Par Lost 8.53
From Man or Angel the great Architect Par Lost 8.72
Intelligence of Heav'n, Angel serene, Par Lost 8.181
To whom the Angel with contracted brow. Par Lost 8.560
To whom the Angel with a smile that glow'd Par Lost 8.618
So parted they, the Angel up to Heav'n Par Lost 8.652
No more of talk where God or Angel Guest Par Lost 9.1
Subjected to his service Angel wings, Par Lost 9.155
And from the parting Angel over-heard Par Lost 9.276
Henceforth of God or Angel, earst with joy Par Lost 9.1081
Satan in likeness of an Angel bright Par Lost 10.327
In shew Plebeian Angel militant Par Lost 10.442
He ended; and th' Arch-Angel soon drew nigh, Par Lost 11.238
Whom thus the Angel interrupted milde. Par Lost 11.286
But him the gentle Angel by the hand Par Lost 11.421
Dismai'd, and thus in haste to th' Angel cri'd. Par Lost 11.449
True opener of mine eyes, prime Angel blest, Par Lost 11.598
Said th' Angel, who should better hold his place Par Lost 11.635
By th' Angel, on thy feet thou stoodst at last, Par Lost 11.759
And scarce to th' Angel utterdst thus thy plaint. Par Lost 11.762
To whom th' Archangel. Dextrously thou aim'st; Par Lost 11.884
Though bent on speed, so heer th' Arch-angel paus'd Par Lost 12.2
line not in 1667 edition
Though present in his Angel, who shall goe Par Lost 12.201
Conducted by his Angel to the Land Par Lost 12.259
His place of birth a solemn Angel tells Par Lost 12.364
So spake th' Archangel *Michael*, then paus'd, Par Lost 12.466
Be sure they will, said th' Angel; but from Heav'n Par Lost 12.485
To whom thus also th' Angel last repli'd: Par Lost 12.574
Th' Archangel stood, and from the other Hill Par Lost 12.626
1669 'ArchAngel'
In either hand the hastning Angel caught Par Lost 12.637
And by the Angel was bid rise and eat, Par Reg 2.274
By a providing Angel; all the race Par Reg 2.310
By Prophet or by Angel, unless thou Par Reg 3.352
Twice by an Angel, who at last in sight Samson 24
For this did the Angel twice descend? for this Samson 361
Send thee the Angel of thy Birth, to stand Samson 1431
Thou hovering Angel girt with golden wings, Mask 214
Trinity ms 'angell'
line not in Bridgewater ms
And som good angel bear a sheild before us. Mask 658
Bridgewater ms 'Angell'
1637 'angell'
Trinity ms 'angell'
Look homeward Angel now, and melt with ruth. Lycidas 163
And joyn thy voice unto the Angel Quire, Nativity 27
Their loud up-lifted Angel trumpets blow, Musick 11
Trinity ms 'angell' ←'arch-angell' ←'symphonie of silver'

Angelic
Chief of th' Angelic Guards, awaiting night; Par Lost 4.550
While thus he spake, th' Angelic Squadron bright Par Lost 4.977
Here, happie Creature, fair Angelic *Eve*, Par Lost 5.74
Flew through the midst of Heav'n; th' angelic Quires Par Lost 5.251
Whom thus th' Angelic Vertue answerd milde. Par Lost 5.371
My self and all th' Angelic Host that stand Par Lost 5.535
(Such are the Courts of God) Th' Angelic throng Par Lost 5.650
Or all Angelic Nature joind in one, Par Lost 5.834
Where erst was thickest fight, th' Angelic throng, Par Lost 6.308
Among th' Angelic Powers, and the deep fall Par Lost 6.898
Angelic harmonies: the Earth, the Aire Par Lost 7.560
About her, as a guard Angelic plac't. Par Lost 8.559
Th' Angelic Name, and thinner left the throng Par Lost 9.142
Angelic, but more soft, and Feminine, Par Lost 9.458
Th' Angelic Guards ascended, mute and sad Par Lost 10.18
To sound at general Doom. Th' Angelic blast Par Lost 11.76
He ceas'd; and th' Archangelic Power prepar'd Par Lost 11.126
And of the Angelic Song in *Bethlehem* field, Par Reg 4.505
Or thirst, and as he fed, Angelic Quires Par Reg 4.593
The Angelic orders and inferiour creatures mute, Samson 672
Make up full consort to th' Angelike symphony. Nativity 132

Angelica
The fairest of her Sex *Angelica* Par Reg 3.341

Angelical
With notes Angelical to many a Harp Par Lost 2.548

Angelical(*cont*)
Betwixt th' Angelical and Human kinde: Par Lost 3.462

Angels
Of Rebel Angels, by whose aid aspiring Par Lost 1.38
ms 'Angells'
At once as far as Angels kenn he views Par Lost 1.59
ms 'Angells'
So numberless were those bad Angels seen Par Lost 1.344
ms 'Angells'
Tears such as Angels weep, burst forth: at last Par Lost 1.620
ms 'angels'
Where Scepter'd Angels held thir residence, Par Lost 1.734
Among his Angels; and his Throne it self Par Lost 2.68
Of Angels watching round? Here he had need Par Lost 2.413
God and good Angels guard by special grace. Par Lost 2.1033
The summoning Arch-Angels to proclaime Par Lost 3.325
Bad men and Angels, they arraignd shall sink Par Lost 3.331
The multitude of Angels with a shout Par Lost 3.345
Thou drov'st of warring Angels disarraid. Par Lost 3.396
Angels ascending and descending, bands Par Lost 3.511
Wafted by Angels, or flew o're the Lake Par Lost 3.521
On high behests his Angels to and fro Par Lost 3.533
Back stept those two faire Angels half amaz'd Par Lost 4.820
Angels, for yee behold him, and with songs Par Lost 5.161
Of Angels under watch; and to his state, Par Lost 5.288
Food not of Angels, yet accepted so, Par Lost 5.465
With Angels may participate, and find Par Lost 5.494
Of Angels by Imperial summons call'd, Par Lost 5.584
Hear all ye Angels, Progenie of Light, Par Lost 5.600
With Angels Food, and rubied Nectar flows Par Lost 5.633
Millions of fierce encountring Angels fought Par Lost 6.220
So spake the Prince of Angels; to whom thus Par Lost 6.281
Of Angels, can relate, or to what things Par Lost 6.298
By Angels many and strong, who interpos'd Par Lost 6.336
Angels contented with thir fame in Heav'n Par Lost 6.375
Michael and his Angels prevalent Par Lost 6.411
Up rose the Victor Angels, and to Arms Par Lost 6.525
Which God hath in his mighty Angels plac'd) Par Lost 6.638
Aloft by Angels born, his Sign in Heav'n: Par Lost 6.776
Ye Angels arm'd, this day from Battel rest; Par Lost 6.802
Of Angels, then that Starr the Starrs among) Par Lost 7.133
Then from the Giant Angels; thee that day Par Lost 7.605
More Angels to Create, if they at least Par Lost 9.146
Angels, nor think superfluous others aid. Par Lost 9.308
Guiltless of fire had formd, or Angels brought. Par Lost 9.392
By Angels numberless, thy daily Train. Par Lost 9.548
But to be Gods, or Angels Demi-gods. Par Lost 9.937
Assembl'd Angels, and ye Powers return'd Par Lost 10.34
His mightie Angels gave them several charge, Par Lost 10.650
Some say he bid his Angels turne ascanse Par Lost 10.668
With Men as Angels without Feminine, Par Lost 10.893
As how with peccant Angels late they saw; Par Lost 11.70
Not that more glorious, when the Angels met Par Lost 11.213
Of squadrond Angels hear his Carol sung. Par Lost 12.367
Of Angels, thus to *Gabriel* smiling spake. Par Reg 1.129
Thou and all Angels conversant on Earth Par Reg 1.131
That all the Angels and Aetherial Powers, Par Reg 1.163
All Heaven and Earth, Angels and Sons of men, Par Reg 1.237
Of Angels in the fields of *Bethlehem* sung Par Reg 1.243
And when to all his Angels he propos'd Par Reg 1.371
But from him or his Angels President Par Reg 1.447
And call swift flights of Angels ministrant Par Reg 2.385
To all his Angels, who with true applause Par Reg 3.63
By all his Angels glorifi'd, requires Par Reg 3.113
Though Sons of God both Angels are and Men, Par Reg 4.197
What both from Men and Angels I receive, Par Reg 4.200
For Angels have proclaim'd it, but concealing Par Reg 4.474
Concerning thee to his Angels, in thir hands Par Reg 4.557
Of Angels on full sail of wing flew nigh, Par Reg 4.582
Equivalent to Angels walk'd thir streets, Samson 343
A thousand liveried Angels lacky her, Mask 455
Trinity ms 'angells'
1637 'angels'
Bridgewater ms 'Angells'
Bright-harnest Angels sit in order serviceable. Nativity 244
My muse with Angels did divide to sing; Passion 4

Anger
The Vassals of his anger, when the Scourge Par Lost 2.90
Them in his anger, whom his anger saves Par Lost 2.158
His anger, and perhaps thus farr remov'd Par Lost 2.211
I offer, on mee let thine anger fall; Par Lost 3.237
Of anger shall remain, but peace assur'd, Par Lost 3.263
Can equal anger infinite provok't. Par Lost 4.916
Anger and just rebuke, and judgement giv'n, Par Lost 9.10
And anger wouldst resent the offer'd wrong, Par Lost 9.300
Began to rise, high Passions, Anger, Hate, Par Lost 9.1123
Anger, and obstinacie, and hate, and guile. Par Lost 10.114
For angers sake, finite to infinite Par Lost 10.802
As one disarm'd, his anger all he lost, Par Lost 10.945
From him, and all his anger to forget. Par Lost 11.878
Though inly stung with anger and disdain, Par Reg 1.466
In uncompassionate anger do not so. Samson 818
Thy anger, unappeasable, still rages, Samson 963
Here dwel no frowns, nor anger, from these gates Mask 667
No anger find in thee, but pity and ruth. Sonnet 9, 8
In anger and ye perish in the way Psalm 2, 26
Lord in thine anger do not reprehend me Psalm 6, 1
Thine anger all thou hadst remov'd, Psalm 85, 9

Angola
Of *Congo*, and *Angola* fardest South; Par Lost 11.401
Angry
But see the angry Victor hath recall'd Par Lost 1.169
ms 'Angry'
From Heav'n, they fabl'd, thrown by angry *Jove* Par Lost 1.741
Let this be good, whether our angry Foe Par Lost 2.152
When angry most he seem'd and most severe, Par Lost 10.1095
For though I fled him angrie, yet recall'd Par Lost 11.330
Thy smoaking wrath, *and angry brow* Psalm 80, 19
Wilt thou be angry without end, Psalm 85, 17
For ever angry thus Psalm 85, 18
Slow to be angry, and *art stil'd* Psalm 86, 55
Anguish
Anguish and doubt and fear and sorrow and pain Par Lost 1.558
Pain for a while or anguish, and excite Par Lost 2.567
Gnashing for anguish and despite and shame Par Lost 6.340
That kept thir watch; thence full of anguish driv'n, Par Lost 9.62
Not thy contempt, but anguish and regret Par Lost 10.1018
Famin and anguish will at last consume Par Lost 11.778
So strook with dread and anguish fell the Fiend, Par Reg 4.576
The anguish of my Soul, that suffers not Samson 458
From anguish of the mind and humours black, Samson 600
In pensive trance, and anguish, and ecstatick fit. Passion 42
For all my bones, that even with anguish ake, Psalm 6, 5
Animal
Th' animal Spirits that from pure blood arise Par Lost 4.805
To vital Spirits aspire, to animal, Par Lost 5.484
Animals
While other Animals unactive range, Par Lost 4.621
Animate
Which two great Sexes animate the World, Par Lost 8.151
Of Creatures animate with gradual life Par Lost 9.112
Anna
Just *Simeon* and Prophetic *Anna*, warn'd Par Reg 1.255
Annexed
But Justice, and some fatal curse annext Par Lost 12.99
Annihilating
Cannot but by annihilating die; Par Lost 6.347
Announced
Announc't by *Gabriel* with the first I knew, Par Reg 4.504
Annoy
Nor stood unmindful *Abdiel* to annoy Par Lost 6.369
Where Houses thick and Sewers annoy the Aire, Par Lost 9.446
Found able by invasion to annoy Par Reg 3.365
Which was expresly giv'n thee to annoy them? Samson 578
Annual
Whose annual wound in *Lebanon* allur'd Par Lost 1.447
ms 'annuall'
Her annual Voiage, born on Windes; the Aire Par Lost 7.431
This annual humbling certain number'd days, Par Lost 10.576
With odours visited and annual flowers. Samson 987
Annulled
Annull'd, which might in part my grief have eas'd, Samson 72
Annuls
Annuls thy doom, the death thou shouldst have dy'd, Par Lost 12.428
Anointed
Anointed universal King; all Power Par Lost 3.317
Him have anointed, whom ye now behold Par Lost 5.605
Messiah King anointed, could not beare Par Lost 5.664
Of King anointed, for whom all this haste Par Lost 5.777
These tidings carrie to th' anointed King; Par Lost 5.870
To honour his Anointed Son aveng'd Par Lost 6.676
God and *Messiah* his anointed King. Par Lost 6.718
Anointed King *Messiah* might be born Par Lost 12.359
Sent his Anointed, and to us reveal'd him, Par Reg 2.50
anointed have my King (though ye rebell) Psalm 2, 12
Of thy anointed *dear*. Psalm 84, 32
Anon
With scatter'd Arms and Ensigns, till anon Par Lost 1.325
Of depth immeasurable: Anon they move Par Lost 1.549
ms 'anon'
Anon out of the earth a Fabrick huge Par Lost 1.710
1667 'A non'
By place or choice the worthiest; they anon Par Lost 1.759
Refrein'd his tongue blasphemous; but anon Par Lost 6.360
Heav'n witness thou anon, while we discharge Par Lost 6.564
Rustic, of grassie sord; thither anon Par Lost 11.433
To Council in the Citie Gates: anon Par Lost 11.661
Anon drie ground appeers, and from his Arke Par Lost 11.861
The Serpents head; whereof to thee anon Par Lost 12.150
Sometimes, anon in shady vale, each night Par Reg 1.304
Up to a hill anon his steps he rear'd, Par Reg 2.285
Then to the well-trod stage anon, Allegro 131
And yet anon repairs his drooping head, Lycidas 169
Another
Advising peace: for such another Field Par Lost 2.292
Err not) another World, the happy seat Par Lost 2.347
Another part in Squadrons and gross Bands, Par Lost 2.570
Now lately Heaven and Earth, another World Par Lost 2.1004
Another side, umbrageous Grots and Caves Par Lost 4.257
Smooth Lake, that to me seemd another Skie. Par Lost 4.459
Imparadis't in one anothers arms Par Lost 4.506
Comes this way moving; seems another Morn Par Lost 5.310
The secrets of another world, perhaps Par Lost 5.569
Another now hath to himself ingross't Par Lost 5.775
Stood rankt of Seraphim another row Par Lost 6.604
Another World, out of one man a Race Par Lost 7.155

Another(*cont*)
Witness this new-made World, another Heav'n Par Lost 7.617
And *Adam* wedded to another *Eve*, Par Lost 9.828
Should God create another *Eve*, and I Par Lost 9.911
Another Rib afford, yet loss of thee Par Lost 9.912
And now prepare thee for another sight. Par Lost 11.555
But now prepare thee for another Scene. Par Lost 11.637
Depopulation; thee another Floud, Par Lost 11.756
That God voutsafes to raise another World Par Lost 11.877
Thir own Faith not anothers: for on Earth Par Lost 12.528
Yet of another Plea bethought him soon. Par Reg 3.149
Another plain, long but in bredth not wide; Par Reg 4.27
Another method I must now begin. Par Reg 4.540
Sam. Ay me, another inward grief awak't, Samson 330
And let another hand, not thine, exact Samson 507
Against another object more enticing? Samson 559
And at another to let in the foe Samson 561
Chor. But this another kind of tempest brings. Samson 1063
Expect another message more imperious, Samson 1352
But in another Countrey, as he said, Mask 632
Trinity ms 'an other'
line not in Bridgewater ms
There was another meaning in these gifts, Mask 754
line not in Bridgewater ms
Trinity ms 'a nother'
Som other means I have which may be us'd, Mask 821
Trinity ms 'some other meanes I have' ←'there is another way'
Expectance calls thee now another way, Vacation 54
Another *Constantine* comes not in hast. Prose 3, 5
There to thy Sons another *Troy* shall rise, Prose 12, 12
Anow
Man had not hellish foes anow besides, Par Lost 2.504
Anow of such as for their bellies sake, Lycidas 114
1638 'Enough'
Trinity ms 'anough'
Answer
In his uprightness answer thus returnd. Par Lost 3.693
Made answer. Mightie Father, thou thy foes Par Lost 5.735
I have receav'd, to answer thy desire Par Lost 7.119
This happie Light, when answer none return'd, Par Lost 8.285
This answer from the gratious voice Divine. Par Lost 8.436
To whom mild answer *Adam* thus return'd. Par Lost 9.226
Not unamaz'd she thus in answer spake. Par Lost 9.552
To answer, and resound farr other Song. Par Lost 10.862
Dissembl'd, and this Answer smooth return'd. Par Reg 1.467
To whom quick answer Satan thus return'd. Par Reg 2.172
Satan had not to answer, but stood struck Par Reg 3.146
To whom our Saviour answer thus return'd. Par Reg 3.181
Made answer meet, that made void all his wiles. Par Reg 3.442
If thy appearance answer loud report. Samson 1090
These shifts refuted, answer thy appellant Samson 1220
Har. This insolence other kind of answer fits. Samson 1236
Off. This answer, be assur'd, will not content them. Samson 1322
To give me answer from her mossie Couch. Mask 276
Trinity ms 'answere'
And sage *Hippotades* their answer brings, Lycidas 96
May rightly answer that melodious noise; Musick 18
Trinity ms 'answere'
Answer me when I call Psalm 4, 1
And answer, *what I pray'd*. Psalm 86, 24
Answerable
If answerable style I can obtaine Par Lost 9.20
Deeds to thy knowledge answerable, add Faith, Par Lost 12.582
With answerable pains, but more intense, Samson 615
Answered
And him thus answer'd soon his bold Compeer. Par Lost 1.127
Thus answer'd. Leader of those Armies bright, Par Lost 1.272
Soon learnd, now milder, and thus answerd smooth. Par Lost 2.816
Answer'd. I know thee, stranger, who thou art, Par Lost 2.990
To which the Fiend thus answerd frowning stern. Par Lost 4.924
Related, and thus *Adam* answerd sad. Par Lost 5.94
Whom thus th' Angelic Vertue answerd milde. Par Lost 5.371
Encompass'd round with foes, thus answerd bold. Par Lost 5.876
Thus answerd. Ill for thee, but in wisht houre Par Lost 6.150
And thus the Godlike Angel answerd milde. Par Lost 7.110
1669 'answered'
To whom thus *Raphael* answer'd heav'nly meek. Par Lost 8.217
Wherto th' Almighty answer'd, not displeas'd. Par Lost 8.398
He ceas'd, I lowly answer'd. To attaine Par Lost 8.412
Answer'd. Let it suffice thee that thou know'st Par Lost 8.620
Express'd, and thus divinely answer'd milde. Par Lost 10.67
Whence *Adam* faultring long, thus answer'd brief. Par Lost 10.115
Whom thus the meager Shadow answerd soon. Par Lost 10.264
Whom thus the Prince of Darkness answerd glad. Par Lost 10.383
Whom thus the Sin-born Monster answerd soon. Par Lost 10.596
Thir Makers Image, answerd *Michael*, then Par Lost 11.515
Well pleas'd, but answer'd not; for now too nigh Par Lost 12.625
Whom thus answer'd th' Arch Fiend now undisguis'd. Par Reg 1.357
The giver, answer'd Jesus. Why should that Par Reg 2.322
To whom thus answer'd Satan malecontent: Par Reg 2.392
To whom our Saviour answer'd thus unmov'd. Par Reg 3.386
Whom thus our Saviour answer'd with disdain. Par Reg 4.170
And staid not, but in brief him answer'd thus. Par Reg 4.485
Till thou our summons answer'd have. Mask 888
Bridgewater ms 'answered'
Trinity ms 'answerd'
I answer'd thee in thunder deep Psalm 81, 29

Answering
Pleas'd it returnd as soon with answering looks Par Lost 4.464
To whom thus *Zephon*, answering scorn with scorn. Par Lost 4.834
And cloudie in aspect thus answering spake. Par Lost 6.450
And thus the filial Godhead answering spake. Par Lost 6.722
Answering his great Idea. Up he rode Par Lost 7.557
Answering the stringed noise, Nativity 97
Answers
And answers, oracles, portents and dreams, Par Reg 1.395
But what have been thy answers, what but dark Par Reg 1.434
Antaeus
As when Earths Son *Antaeus* (to compare Par Reg 4.563
Antagonist
Alone th' Antagonist of Heav'n, nor less Par Lost 2.509
Antagonist of Heav'ns Almightie King) Par Lost 10.387
None daring to appear Antagonist. Samson 1628
Antarctic
Downward as farr Antartic; and in length Par Lost 9.79
Anthems
Sung Heavenly Anthems of his victory Par Reg 4.594
In Service high, and Anthems cleer, Penseroso 163
In vain with Timbrel'd Anthems dark Nativity 219
Antics
Juglers and Dancers, Antics, Mummers, Mimics, Samson 1325
Antigonus
Antigonus, and old *Hyrcanus* bound, Par Reg 3.367
Antioch
From the luxurious Kings of *Antioch* won. Par Reg 3.297
Antiochus
Antiochus: and think'st thou to regain Par Reg 3.163
Antiopa
Daphne, or *Semele*, *Antiopa*, Par Reg 2.187
Antipater
What rais'd *Antipater* the *Edomite*, Par Reg 2.423
Antipathy
Death introduc'd through fierce antipathie: Par Lost 10.709
Antique
With mask, and antique Pageantry, Allegro 128
With antick Pillars massy proof, Penseroso 158
Antiquity
Antiquity from the old Schools of Greece Mask 439
Trinity ms 'antiquity'
Bridgewater ms 'antiquitie'
Anubis
Isis and *Orus*, and the Dog *Anubis* hast. Nativity 212
Anxious
God hath bid dwell farr off all anxious cares, Par Lost 8.185
Lenient of grief and anxious thought, Samson 659
Any
There rest, if any rest can harbour there, Par Lost 1.185
These past, if any pass, the void profound Par Lost 2.438
That dismal world, if any Clime perhaps Par Lost 2.572
Him counterfet, if any eye beheld. Par Lost 4.117
Any, but God alone, to value right Par Lost 4.202
Among sweet dewes and flours; where any row Par Lost 5.212
In Bowre and Field he sought, where any tuft Par Lost 9.417
If any be, of tasting this fair Fruit, Par Lost 9.972
Little suspicious to any King; but now Par Reg 2.82
They shall up lift thee, lest at any time Par Reg 4.558
There I am wont to sit, when any chance Samson 4
If any be, they walk obscure; Samson 296
If any of these or all, the *Timnian* bride Samson 1018
Therfore when any favour'd of high *Jove*, Mask 78
Com. Can any mortal mixture of Earths mould Mask 244
Not any boast of skill, but extreme shift Mask 273
Or do his gray hairs any violence? Mask 392
How cam'st thou here good Swain? hath any ram Mask 497
& may upon any needfull accident Mask Tr. ms 16.55
Or any other of that heav'nly brood Fair Inf 55
For he had any time this ten yeers full, Carrier 7
If any ask for him, it shall be sed, Carrier 17
O Lord, nor any works Psalm 86, 26
Aonian
Above th' *Aonian* Mount, while it pursues Par Lost 1.15
Apace
Shall lead thir lives, and multiplie apace, Par Lost 12.17
Eld. Bro. Thyrsis lead on apace, Ile follow thee, Mask 657
Daily devours apace, and nothing sed, Lycidas 129
That it *began to grow apace*, Psalm 80, 39
Iunkets and knacks, that they may learne apace. Prose 6, 3
Apart
Others apart sat on a Hill retir'd, Par Lost 2.557
And said to me apart, high are thy thoughts Par Reg 1.229
So many, and so huge, that each apart Samson 65
Apathy
Passion and Apathie, and glory and shame, Par Lost 2.564
Ape
So well converse, nor with the Ox the Ape; Par Lost 8.396
Apes
Of Owles and Cuckoes, Asses, Apes and Doggs. Sonnet 12, 4
Trinity ms 'apes'
Apocalypse
Th' *Apocalyps*, heard cry in Heaven aloud, Par Lost 4.2
Apollo
Apollo, *Neptune*, *Jupiter*, or *Pan*, Par Reg 2.190
But musical as is *Apollo*'s lute, Mask 478
Bridgewater ms 'Apolloes'
Root-bound, that fled *Apollo*, *La*. Fool do not boast, Mask 662
Apollo(*cont*)
Apollo from his shrine Nativity 176
For so *Apollo*, with unweeting hand Fair Inf 23
Listening to what unshorn *Apollo* sings Vacation 37
Apology
Came Prologue, and Apologie to prompt, Par Lost 9.854
Apostasy
Apostasie, by what befell in Heaven Par Lost 7.43
Of his Apostasie; he might have learnt Par Reg 1.146
Apostate
So spake th' Apostate Angel, though in pain, Par Lost 1.125
Th' Apostat, and more haughty thus repli'd. Par Lost 5.852
Th' Apostat in his Sun-bright Chariot sate Par Lost 6.100
Apostat, still thou errst, nor end wilt find Par Lost 6.172
Of Spirits apostat and thir Counsels vaine Par Lost 7.610
Apostates
To those Apostates, least the like befall Par Lost 7.44
Apostles
Powrd first on his Apostles, whom he sends Par Lost 12.498
Appaid
So onely can high Justice rest appaid. Par Lost 12.401
Apparent
Apparent Queen unvaild her peerless light, Par Lost 4.608
Or to each other, but apparent guilt, Par Lost 10.112
Chose to impart to thy apparent need, Par Reg 2.397
Apparition
Whose inward apparition gently mov'd Par Lost 8.293
A glorious Apparition, had not doubt Par Lost 11.211
Or gastly furies apparition; Mask 641
Appear
Celestial vertues rising, will appear Par Lost 2.15
1667 'appeer' in some copies
Dropt Manna, and could make the worse appear Par Lost 2.113
Of servile Pomp. Our greatness will appeer Par Lost 2.257
1667 'appear'
Farr off the flying Fiend: at last appear Par Lost 2.643
Before thir eyes in sudden view appear Par Lost 2.890
Shalt in the Sky appeer, and from thee send Par Lost 3.324
Dark with excessive bright thy skirts appeer, Par Lost 3.380
Within these hallowd limits thou appeer, Par Lost 4.964
Into one place, and let dry Land appeer. Par Lost 7.284
Immediately the Mountains huge appeer Par Lost 7.285
And pavement Starrs, as Starrs to thee appeer, Par Lost 7.578
Shall I appeer? shall I to him make known Par Lost 9.817
Accountable made haste to make appear Par Lost 10.29
Inhospitable appeer and desolate, Par Lost 11.306
Before thee shall appear; that thou mayst know Par Lost 11.475
Who slew his Brother; studious they appere Par Lost 11.609
And now the tops of Hills as Rocks appeer; Par Lost 11.852
Longer on Earth then certaine times to appeer Par Lost 12.437
Appeer of respiration to the just, Par Lost 12.540
E're in the head of Nations he appear Par Reg 1.98
To be at hand, and at his beck appear, Par Reg 2.238
See how in warlike muster they appear, Par Reg 3.308
Bare in thy guilt how foul must thou appear? Samson 902
To appear as fits before th' illustrious Lords. Samson 1318
None daring to appear Antagonist. Samson 1628
I shall appear som harmles Villager Mask 166
1637 'appeare'
Trinity ms 'appeare'
Bridgewater ms 'appere'
Listen and appear to us Mask 867
Trinity ms 'appeare'
Bridgewater ms 'appere'
1637 'appeare'
There let *Hymen* oft appear Allegro 125
Till civil-suited Morn appeer, Penseroso 122
He saw a greater Sun appear Nativity 83
And inward ripenes doth much less appear, Sonnet 7, 7
Trinity ms 'appeare'
Nor to thir idle orbs doth sight appear Sonnet 22, 4
With trembling; kiss the Son least he appear Psalm 2, 25
Will rank my Prayers, and watch till thou appear. Psalm 5, 8
In Sion do appear. Psalm 84, 28
And glory shall *ere long appear* Psalm 85, 39
Appearance
Meer Serpent in appearance, forth was come, Par Lost 9.413
After appearance, and again prolong Par Reg 2.41
If thy appearance answer loud report. Samson 1090
Appearances
To save appeerances, how gird the Sphear Par Lost 8.82
His bright appearances, or foot step-trace? Par Lost 11.329
Appeared
And such appear'd in hue, as when the force Par Lost 1.230
Whom he had vanquisht. After these appear'd Par Lost 1.476
Down cast and damp, yet such wherein appear'd Par Lost 1.523
Appear'd, and serried Shields in thick array Par Lost 1.548
All her Original brightness, nor appear'd Par Lost 1.592
His look suspence, awaiting who appeer'd Par Lost 2.418
Where onely what they needs must do, appeard, Par Lost 3.105
Divine compassion visibly appeerd, Par Lost 3.141
Patron or Intercessor none appeerd, Par Lost 3.219
At top whereof, but farr more rich appeerd Par Lost 3.504
Appeerd, with gay enameld colours mixt: Par Lost 4.149
A Shape within the watry gleam appeerd Par Lost 4.461
Forthwith from all the ends of Heav'n appeerd Par Lost 5.586
Farr in th' Horizon to the North appeer'd Par Lost 6.79
As not of power, at once; nor odds appeerd Par Lost 6.319

Appeared(*cont*)
Now when fair Morn Orient in Heav'n appeerd — Par Lost 6.524
A while, but suddenly at head appeerd — Par Lost 6.556
But soon obscur'd with smoak, all Heav'n appeerd, — Par Lost 6.585
Before the Hills appeerd, or Fountain flow'd, — Par Lost 7.8
On his great Expedition now appeer'd, — Par Lost 7.193
Appeer'd not: over all the face of Earth — Par Lost 7.278
With thousand thousand Starres, that then appeer'd — Par Lost 7.383
The grassie Clods now Calv'd, now half appeer'd — Par Lost 7.463
Of Commonaltie: swarming next appeer'd — Par Lost 7.489
Up hither, from among the Trees appeer'd — Par Lost 8.313
And of thir vain contest appeer'd no end. — Par Lost 9.1189
Where obvious dutie erewhile appear'd unsaught: — Par Lost 10.106
And shape Starr bright appeer'd, or brighter, clad — Par Lost 10.450
Nor that which on the flaming Mount appeerd — Par Lost 11.216
On this Mount he appeerd, under this Tree — Par Lost 11.320
Before his eyes appeard, sad, noysom, dark, — Par Lost 11.478
Loves Harbinger appeerd; then all in heat — Par Lost 11.589
And that he durst not plain enough appear'd. — Samson 1256
Together both, ere the high Lawns appear'd — Lycidas 25

Appearest
Get thee behind me; plain thou now appear'st — Par Reg 4.193

Appearing
Delos or *Samos* first appeering kenns — Par Lost 5.265
Least by some faire appeering good surpris'd — Par Lost 9.354
A Star, not seen before in Heaven appearing — Par Reg 1.249
Appearing, and beginning noble deeds, — Par Reg 4.99
Her pile, far off appearing like a Mount — Par Reg 4.547

Appears
Worth waiting, since our present lot appeers — Par Lost 2.223
As when to warn proud Cities warr appears — Par Lost 2.533
Of light appears, and from the walls of Heav'n — Par Lost 2.1035
And now a stripling Cherube he appeers, — Par Lost 3.636
Which from his darksom passage now appeers, — Par Lost 4.232
For aught appeers, and on thir Orbs impose — Par Lost 8.30
Not in themselves, all thir known vertue appeers — Par Lost 9.110
Much reason, and in thir actions oft appeers. — Par Lost 9.559
Crooked by nature, bent, as now appears, — Par Lost 10.885
Anon drie ground appeers, and from his Arke — Par Lost 11.861
So law appears imperfet, and but giv'n — Par Lost 12.300
By this appears: I gave, thou say'st, th' example, — Samson 822

Appease
Thir sinful state, and to appease betimes — Par Lost 3.186
He to appease thy wrauth, and end the strife — Par Lost 3.406
And tempt not these; but hast'n to appease — Par Lost 5.846
Them fully satisfied, and thee appease. — Par Lost 10.79
All of me then shall die: let this appease — Par Lost 10.792
By Prayer th' offended Deitie to appease, — Par Lost 11.149
Cannot appease, nor Man the moral part — Par Lost 12.298
To light'n what thou suffer'st, and appease — Samson 744

Appeased
In glory as of old, to him appeas'd — Par Lost 10.226
Mayst cover: well may then thy Lord appeas'd — Par Lost 11.257
Distended as the Brow of God appeas'd, — Par Lost 11.880

Appellant
These shifts refuted, answer thy appellant — Samson 1220

Appertain
Ordaine them Lawes; part such as appertaine — Par Lost 12.230

Appertains
Kingdom and Power and Glorie appertains, — Par Lost 6.815

Appetence
Of lustful appetence, to sing, to dance, — Par Lost 11.619

Appetite
More easie, wholsom thirst and appetite — Par Lost 4.330
So quick'nd appetite, that I, methought, — Par Lost 5.85
True appetite, and not disrelish thirst — Par Lost 5.305
Of all tastes else to please thir appetite, — Par Lost 7.49
Her Temperance over Appetite, to know — Par Lost 7.127
And govern well thy appetite, least sin — Par Lost 7.546
Tempting, stirr'd in me sudden appetite — Par Lost 8.308
Grateful to appetite, more pleas'd my sense — Par Lost 9.580
An eager appetite, rais'd by the smell — Par Lost 9.740
To sensual Appetite, who from beneathe — Par Lost 9.1129
Thir appetite with gust, instead of Fruit — Par Lost 10.565
To serve ungovern'd appetite, and took — Par Lost 11.517
Nor tasted, nor had appetite; that Fast — Par Reg 2.247
And dream'd, as appetite is wont to dream, — Par Reg 2.264
For no allurement yields to appetite, — Par Reg 2.409
To a wel-govern'd and wise appetite. — Mask 705

Appian
In various habits on the *Appian* road, — Par Reg 4.68

Applauded
They led him high applauded, and present — Par Lost 6.26

Applause
After the Tempest: Such applause was heard — Par Lost 2.290
Hoarce murmur echo'd to his words applause — Par Lost 5.873
Thir universal shout and high applause — Par Lost 10.505
As in thir crime. Thus was th' applause they meant, — Par Lost 10.545
To all his Angels, who with true applause — Par Reg 3.63
And fell *Charybdis* murmur'd soft applause: — Mask 259
Of Brittish *Themis*, with no mean applause — Sonnet 21, 2
line not in Trinity ms

Apple
Your wonder, with an Apple; he thereat — Par Lost 10.487
Was that crude Apple that diverted *Eve!* — Par Reg 2.349

Apples
Of tasting those fair Apples, I resolv'd — Par Lost 9.585

Applied
(For time, though in Eternitie, appli'd — Par Lost 5.580
Put forth, and to a narrow vent appli'd — Par Lost 6.583
To *Satan* first in sin his doom apply'd, — Par Lost 10.172

Apply
The Birds thir quire apply; aires, vernal aires, — Par Lost 4.264
Since to each meaning savour me apply, — Par Lost 9.1019

Appoint
At my right hand; your Head I him appoint; — Par Lost 5.606
Sam. Appoint not heavenly disposition, Father, — Samson 373

Appointed
Each had his place appointed, each his course, — Par Lost 3.720
Appointed, which declares his Dignitie, — Par Lost 4.619
Which we in our appointed work imployd — Par Lost 4.726
Freely our part; yee who appointed stand — Par Lost 6.565
Within appointed bounds be Heav'n and Earth, — Par Lost 7.167
Appointed to sit there, had left thir charge, — Par Lost 10.421
Which I must keep till my appointed day — Par Lost 11.550
Appointed to await me thirty spies, — Samson 1197
Th' appointed time, the day wheron — Psalm 81, 11

Appointment
Whom I by his appointment had provok't, — Samson 643

Appoints
Vengeance is his, or whose he sole appoints; — Par Lost 6.808

Apprehend
Human desires can seek or apprehend? — Par Lost 5.518
This yet I apprehend not, why to those — Par Lost 12.280
Capacity not rais'd to apprehend — Samson 1028
Thou hast nor Eare, nor Soul to apprehend — Mask 784
line not in Trinity ms
line not in Bridgewater ms

Apprehended
Or Sex, and apprehended nothing high: — Par Lost 9.574

Apprehension
My sudden apprehension: but in these — Par Lost 8.354
In apprehension then in substance feel — Par Lost 11.775

Apprehensive
Mangle my apprehensive tenderest parts, — Samson 624

Approach
Day, or the sweet approach of Ev'n or Morn, — Par Lost 3.42
Approach not, but with both wings veil thir eyes. — Par Lost 3.382
Meets his approach, and to the heart inspires — Par Lost 4.154
No evil thing approach or enter in; — Par Lost 4.563
With first approach of light, we must be ris'n, — Par Lost 4.624
Yet with submiss approach and reverence meek, — Par Lost 5.359
A vast circumference: At his approach — Par Lost 6.256
Approach not mee, and what I will is Fate. — Par Lost 7.173
O're other Creatures; yet when I approach — Par Lost 8.546
Disturbd not, waiting close th' approach of Morn. — Par Lost 9.191
Displeas'd that I approach thee thus, and gaze — Par Lost 9.535
Wide waving, all approach farr off to fright, — Par Lost 11.121
All night he will pursue, but his approach — Par Lost 12.206
He saw approach, who first with curious eye — Par Reg 1.319
To see thee and approach thee, whom I know — Par Reg 1.384
To approach thy Temples, give thee in command — Par Reg 1.449
And sweet allay'd, yet terrible to approach, — Par Reg 2.160
The morns approach, and greet her with his Song: — Par Reg 2.281
Dal. Let me approach at least, and touch thy hand. — Samson 951
How durst thou then thy self approach so neer — Mask 616
Approach, and kiss her sacred vestures hemm. — Arcades 83

Approached
He scarce had ended, when those two approachd — Par Lost 4.874
Listens delighted. Eevning now approach'd — Par Lost 5.627
1667 'approachd'
And beautie, not approacht by stronger hate, — Par Lost 9.491
Congratulant approach'd him, who with hand — Par Lost 10.458
While the great Visitant approachd, thus spake. — Par Lost 11.225

Approaches
Your change approaches, when all these delights — Par Lost 4.367

Approaching
Approaching gross and huge; in hollow Cube — Par Lost 6.552
But long ere our approaching heard within — Par Lost 8.242
Approaching two and two, These cowring low — Par Lost 8.350
Approaching, thus to *Adam* call'd aloud. — Par Lost 10.102
Desolate where she sate, approaching nigh, — Par Lost 10.864
Hath took no print of the approching light, — Nativity 20
1673 'approaching'

Approbation
Looking on the Earth, with approbation marks — Par Reg 3.61

Appropriating
By spiritual, to themselves appropriating — Par Lost 12.518

Approve
Of others, who approve not to transgress — Par Lost 4.880
Approve the best, and follow what I approve. — Par Lost 8.611
Wouldst thou approve thy constancie, approve — Par Lost 9.367
Let none henceforth seek needless cause to approve — Par Lost 9.1140
Nay didst permit, approve, and fair dismiss. — Par Lost 9.1159

Approved
To stand approv'd in sight of God, though Worlds — Par Lost 6.36
And with obsequious Majestie approv'd — Par Lost 8.509
And easily approv'd; when the most High — Par Lost 10.31
Will be aveng'd, and th' others Faith approv'd — Par Lost 11.458
Rather approv'd them not; but thou didst plead — Samson 421

Approves
Who evermore approves and more accepts — Samson 510

April
Brisk as the *April* buds in Primrose-season. — Mask 671
Trinity ms 'Aprill' ←'Aprills'

April(*cont*)	
Bridgewater ms 'Aprill'	
Apt	
But apt the Mind or Fancie is to roave	Par Lost 8.188
The wise mans cumbrance if not snare, more apt	Par Reg 2.454
Thee, of thy self so apt, in regal Arts,	Par Reg 3.248
Salve to thy Sores, apt words have power to swage	Samson 184
Of Lute, or Viol still, more apt for mournful things.	Passion 28
Apter	
On Earth, made hereby apter to receive	Par Lost 4.672
Aqueducts	
Porches and Theatres, Baths, Aqueducts,	Par Reg 4.36
Aquilo	
For since grim Aquilo his charioter	Fair Inf 8
Arabia	
Of *Arabie* the blest, with such delay	Par Lost 4.163
Arabian	
Borders on *Aegypt* and the *Arabian* shoare;	Par Lost 3.537
Of gentlest gale *Arabian* odors fann'd	Par Reg 2.364
And inaccessible the *Arabian* drouth:	Par Reg 3.274
In the *Arabian* woods embost,	Samson 1700
Arable	
Part arable and tilth, whereon were Sheaves	Par Lost 11.430
Araby	
Of *Arabie* the blest, with such delay	Par Lost 4.163
Arachosia	
From *Arachosia*, from *Candaor* East,	Par Reg 3.316
Araxes	
Araxes and the *Caspian* lake, thence on	Par Reg 3.271
Arbiter	
By which he Reigns: next him high Arbiter	Par Lost 2.909
Twilight upon the Earth, short Arbiter	Par Lost 9.50
Arbitrary	
And stripes, and arbitrary punishment	Par Lost 2.334
Arbitrate	
Does arbitrate th' event, my nature is	Mask 411
Arbitrator	
And Heav'ns high Arbitrator sit secure	Par Lost 2.359
Arbitrement	
Free in thine own Arbitrement it lies.	Par Lost 8.641
Arbitress	
Sits Arbitress, and neerer to the Earth	Par Lost 1.785
ms 'arbitress'	
Arbor	
They came, that like *Pomona*'s Arbour smil'd	Par Lost 5.378
The Woodbine round this Arbour, or direct	Par Lost 9.216
Arborets	
Among thick-wov'n Arborets and Flours	Par Lost 9.437
Arborous	
But first from under shadie arborous roof,	Par Lost 5.137
Arbors	
Yon flourie Arbors, yonder Allies green,	Par Lost 4.626
Arcadia	
All *Arcadia* hath not seen.	Arcades 95
Trinity ms 'Ar', ms defective	
All *Arcadia* hath not seen.	Arcades 109
Arcadian	
Charm'd with *Arcadian* Pipe, the Pastoral Reed	Par Lost 11.132
Arcady	
And thou shalt be our star of *Arcady*,	Mask 341
1637 '*Arcadie*'	
Trinity ms 'Arcadie'	
Of famous *Arcady* ye are, and sprung	Arcades 28
Arch	
Intestine War in Heav'n, the arch foe subdu'd	Par Lost 6.259
Amber, and colours of the showrie Arch.	Par Lost 6.759
Archangel	
Said then the lost Arch-Angel, this the seat	Par Lost 1.243
1667 'ArchAngel'	
ms 'Archangell'	
Less then Arch Angel ruind, and th' excess	Par Lost 1.593
ms 'Archangel'	
Above them all th' Arch Angel: but his face	Par Lost 1.600
ms 'Archangel'	
Th' Arch-Angel *Uriel*, one of the seav'n	Par Lost 3.648
If not the first Arch-Angel, great in Power,	Par Lost 5.660
So spake the false Arch-Angel, and infus'd	Par Lost 5.694
Th' Arch-Angel trumpet; through the vast of Heaven	Par Lost 6.203
1667 'Arch-angel'	
The great Arch-Angel from his warlike toile	Par Lost 6.257
By thousands, Angel on Arch-Angel rowl'd;	Par Lost 6.594
The affable Arch-Angel, had forewarn'd	Par Lost 7.41
1669 'Arch-Angel'	
1667 'Arch-angel'	
He ended; and th' Arch-Angel soon drew nigh,	Par Lost 11.238
To whom th' Archangel. Dextrously thou aim'st;	Par Lost 11.884
Though bent on speed, so heer th' Arch-angel paus'd	Par Lost 12.2
line not in 1667 edition	
So spake th' Archangel *Michael*, then paus'd,	Par Lost 12.466
Th' Archangel stood, and from the other Hill	Par Lost 12.626
1669 'ArchAngel'	
Their loud up-lifted Angel trumpets blow,	Musick 11
Trinity ms 'angell' ←'arch-angell' ←'symphonie of silver'	
Archangelic	
He ceas'd; and th' Archangelic Power prepar'd	Par Lost 11.126
Archangels	
The summoning Arch-Angels to proclaime	Par Lost 3.325
Arch-chemic	
Th' Arch-chimic Sun so farr from us remote	Par Lost 3.609
Arched	
And level pavement: from the arched roof	Par Lost 1.726
Thir downie Brest; the Swan with Arched neck	Par Lost 7.438
Over the foaming deep high Archt, a Bridge	Par Lost 10.301
That to the arched roof gave main support.	Samson 1634
In the blind mazes of this tangl'd Wood?	Mask 181
Trinity ms 'tangled' ←'arched'	
To arched walks of twilight groves,	Penseroso 133
Runs through the arched roof in words deceiving.	Nativity 175
Arch-enemy	
Beelzebub. To whom th' Arch-Enemy,	Par Lost 1.81
ms 'Arch-enemy'	
Archers	
Of Archers, nor of labouring Pioners	Par Reg 3.330
Archers, and Slingers, Cataphracts and Spears.	Samson 1619
Arches	
while all the starrie rounds & arches blue	Musick Tr. ms 4.21
Arch-felon	
On th' other side: which when th' arch-fellon saw	Par Lost 4.179
Arch-fiend	
Whereto with speedy words th' Arch-fiend reply'd.	Par Lost 1.156
So stretcht out huge in length the Arch-fiend lay	Par Lost 1.209
Whom thus answer'd th' Arch Fiend now undisguis'd.	Par Reg 1.357
Arch-foe	
Intestine War in Heav'n, the arch foe subdu'd	Par Lost 6.259
Archimedes	
Let *Euclid* rest and *Archimedes* pause,	Sonnet 21, 7
Architect	
And some the Architect: his hand was known	Par Lost 1.732
Divine the sov'ran Architect had fram'd.	Par Lost 5.256
From Man or Angel the great Architect	Par Lost 8.72
Thou art thir Author and prime Architect:	Par Lost 10.356
Architects	
The Structure, skill of noblest Architects,	Par Reg 4.52
Architrave	
With Golden Architrave; nor did there want	Par Lost 1.715
Arcs	
Statues and Trophees, and Triumphal Arcs,	Par Reg 4.37
Arctic	
In th' Artick Sky, and from his horrid hair	Par Lost 2.710
Ardent	
Her long with ardent look his Eye pursu'd	Par Lost 9.397
Ardour	
Heroic Ardor to advent'rous deeds	Par Lost 6.66
With ardor to enjoy thee, fairer now	Par Lost 9.1032
Ardours	
Thousand Celestial Ardors, where he stood	Par Lost 5.249
Are	
And Strength and Art are easily out-done	Par Lost 1.696
And cannot cease to be, we are at worst	Par Lost 2.100
First, what Revenge? the Towrs of Heav'n are fill'd	Par Lost 2.129
Say they who counsel Warr, we are decreed,	Par Lost 2.160
I laugh, when those who at the Spear are bold	Par Lost 2.204
Of what we are and were, dismissing quite	Par Lost 2.282
Synod of Gods, and like to what ye are,	Par Lost 2.391
Are brought: and feel by turns the bitter change	Par Lost 2.598
And they outcast from God, are here condemn'd	Par Lost 2.694
And time and place are lost; where eldest Night	Par Lost 2.894
Havock and spoil and ruin are my gain.	Par Lost 2.1009
All hast thou spok'n as my thoughts are, all	Par Lost 3.171
To me are all my works, nor Man the least	Par Lost 3.277
As many as are restor'd, without thee none.	Par Lost 3.289
On Hills where Flocks are fed, flies toward the Springs	Par Lost 3.435
Turn swift thir various motions, or are turnd	Par Lost 3.582
Stand ready at command, and are his Eyes	Par Lost 3.650
To serve him better: wise are all his wayes.	Par Lost 3.680
For wonderful indeed are all his works,	Par Lost 3.702
Are ever cleer. Whereof hee soon aware,	Par Lost 4.119
Beyond the *Cape of Hope*, and now are past	Par Lost 4.160
Short pleasures, for long woes are to succeed.	Par Lost 4.535
Are many lesser Faculties that serve	Par Lost 5.101
These are thy glorious works, Parent of good,	Par Lost 5.153
Whose progenie you are. Mean while enjoy	Par Lost 5.503
And som are fall'n, to disobedience fall'n,	Par Lost 5.541
Tables are set, and on a sudden pil'd	Par Lost 5.632
Excess, before th' all bounteous King, who showrd	Par Lost 5.640
1667 'Are fill'd'	
(Such are the Courts of God) Th' Angelic throng	Par Lost 5.650
Against thee are gon forth without recall;	Par Lost 5.885
All are not of thy Train; there be who Faith	Par Lost 6.143
Second Omnipotence, two dayes are past,	Par Lost 6.684
Two dayes are therefore past, the third is thine;	Par Lost 6.699
Of what we are. But since thou hast voutsaf't	Par Lost 7.80
Immediate are the Acts of God, more swift	Par Lost 7.176
With Honey stor'd: the rest are numberless,	Par Lost 7.492
Gave thee, all sorts are here that all th' Earth yields,	Par Lost 7.541
Great are thy works, *Jehovah*, infinite	Par Lost 7.602
Yet not to Earth are those bright Luminaries	Par Lost 8.98
Nor are thy lips ungraceful, Sire of men,	Par Lost 8.218
Beneath what other Creatures are to thee?	Par Lost 8.411
Are his Created, or to spite us more,	Par Lost 9.147
To brute deni'd, and are of Love the food,	Par Lost 9.240
How are we happie, still in fear of harm?	Par Lost 9.326
O Woman, best are all things as the will	Par Lost 9.343
Of brutal kind, that daily are in sight?	Par Lost 9.565
For many are the Trees of God that grow	Par Lost 9.618

Are(*cont*)	
Yet are but dim, shall perfetly be then	Par Lost 9.707
And what are Gods that Man may not become	Par Lost 9.716
The Gods are first, and that advantage use	Par Lost 9.718
Great are thy Vertues, doubtless, best of Fruits.	Par Lost 9.745
As Reapers oft are wont thir Harvest Queen.	Par Lost 9.842
This Tree is not as we are told, a Tree	Par Lost 9.863
Not dead, as we are threatn'd, but thenceforth	Par Lost 9.870
Our State cannot be severd, we are one,	Par Lost 9.958
Are to behold the Judgment, but the judg'd,	Par Lost 10.81
O Parent, these are thy magnific deeds,	Par Lost 10.354
Through multitude that sung: Just are thy ways,	Par Lost 10.643
Righteous are thy Decrees on all thy Works;	Par Lost 10.644
What thoughts in my unquiet brest are ris'n,	Par Lost 10.975
We are by doom to pay; rather such acts	Par Lost 10.1026
See Father, what first fruits on Earth are sprung	Par Lost 11.22
Who knows, or more then this, that we are dust,	Par Lost 11.199
Sufficient that thy Prayers are heard, and Death,	Par Lost 11.252
These two are Brethren, *Adam*, and to come	Par Lost 11.454
Of Death, and many are the wayes that lead	Par Lost 11.468
Assemble, and Harangues are heard, but soon	Par Lost 11.663
Lamenting turnd full sad; O what are these,	Par Lost 11.675
To whom thus *Michael*. These are the product	Par Lost 11.683
In Triumph and luxurious wealth, are they	Par Lost 11.788
So many and so various Laws are giv'n;	Par Lost 12.282
And said to me apart, high are thy thoughts	Par Reg 1.229
Where ought we hear, and curious are to hear,	Par Reg 1.333
By thee are giv'n, and what confest more true	Par Reg 1.431
The Gentiles; henceforth Oracles are ceast,	Par Reg 1.456
Hard are the ways of truth, and rough to walk,	Par Reg 1.478
Unlook'd for are we fall'n, our eyes beheld	Par Reg 2.31
Many are in each Region passing fair	Par Reg 2.155
None are, thou think'st, but taken with such toys.	Par Reg 2.177
These are not Fruits forbidden, no interdict	Par Reg 2.369
All these are Spirits of Air, and Woods, and Springs,	Par Reg 2.374
Riches are mine, Fortune is in my hand;	Par Reg 2.429
Riches are needless then, both for themselves,	Par Reg 2.484
Thy years are ripe, and over-ripe, the Son	Par Reg 3.31
Are few, and glory scarce of few is rais'd.	Par Reg 3.59
And Duty; Zeal and Duty are not slow;	Par Reg 3.172
They themselves rather are occasion best,	Par Reg 3.174
All things are best fullfil'd in their due time,	Par Reg 3.182
The rest are barbarous, and scarce worth the sight,	Par Reg 4.86
Though Sons of God both Angels are and Men,	Par Reg 4.197
Therefore let pass, as they are transitory,	Par Reg 4.209
But these are false, or little else but dreams,	Par Reg 4.291
Wise men have said are wearisom; who reads	Par Reg 4.322
Such are from God inspir'd, not such from thee;	Par Reg 4.350
When Prophesies of thee are best fullfill'd.	Par Reg 4.381
Are to the main as inconsiderable,	Par Reg 4.457
To mans less universe, and soon are gone;	Par Reg 4.459
All men are Sons of God; yet thee I thought	Par Reg 4.520
In Paradise to tempt; his snares are broke:	Par Reg 4.611
But who are these? for with joint pace I hear	Samson 110
And are as Balm to fester'd wounds.	Samson 186
How counterfeit a coin they are who friends	Samson 189
Are come upon him his deserts? yet why?	Samson 205
Chor. Just are the ways of God,	Samson 293
Why are his gifts desirable, to tempt	Samson 358
Hopeless are all my evils, all remediless;	Samson 648
Chor. Many are the sayings of the wise	Samson 652
Sam. Out, out *Hyaena;* these are thy wonted arts,	Samson 748
Are drawn to wear out miserable days,	Samson 762
It fits not; thou and I long since are twain;	Samson 929
Are reconcil'd at length, and Sea to Shore:	Samson 962
Sam. Be less abstruse, my riddling days are past.	Samson 1064
Sam. All these indignities, for such they are	Samson 1168
My heels are fetter'd, but my fist is free.	Samson 1235
Chor. Consider, *Samson;* matters now are strain'd	Samson 1348
Commands are no constraints. If I obey them,	Samson 1372
(So mutable are all the ways of men)	Samson 1407
I know not. Lords are Lordliest in thir wine;	Samson 1418
Chor. Fathers are wont to lay up for thir Sons,	Samson 1485
Chor. Thy hopes are not ill founded nor seem vain	Samson 1504
Blood, death, and deathful deeds are in that noise,	Samson 1513
Mess. *Gaza* yet stands, but all her Sons are fall'n,	Samson 1558
Are in confusion, give us if thou canst,	Samson 1593
So fond are mortal men	Samson 1682
Are coming to attend their Fathers state,	Mask 35
We that are of purer fire	Mask 111
But where they are, and why they came not back,	Mask 191
Are but as slavish officers of vengeance,	Mask 218
line not in Bridgewater ms	
Prompt me; and they perhaps are not far off.	Mask 229
That likest thy *Narcissus* are?	Mask 237
Were all to ruffl'd, and somtimes impair'd.	Mask 380
Trinity ms 'were' ←'are'	
Such are those thick and gloomy shadows damp	Mask 470
That hallow I should know, what are you? speak;	Mask 490
Spir. Ay me unhappy then my fears are true.	Mask 511
He and his monstrous rout are heard to howl	Mask 533
How are ye joyn'd with hell in triple knot	Mask 581
Your nervs are all chain'd up in Alablaster,	Mask 660
Co. Why are you vext Lady? why do you frown?	Mask 666
Thou told'st me of? What grim aspects are these,	Mask 694
But such as are good men can give good things,	Mask 703
Think what, and be adviz'd, you are but young yet.	Mask 755
line not in Bridgewater ms	
Are(*cont*)	
And try her yet more strongly. Com, no more,	Mask 806
Trinity ms 'no more' ←'y'are too morall'	
Where this night are met in state	Mask 948
Com let us haste, the Stars grow high,	Mask 956
Bridgewater ms 'are high'	
1637 'are high'	
Trinity ms 'grow' ←'are'	
Two blissful twins are to be born,	Mask 1010
line not in Bridgewater ms	
O my simplicity what sights are these? with darke disguises	Mask Tr. ms 22.19
Are at their savory dinner set	Allegro 84
And of those *Daemons* that are found	Penseroso 93
While rocking Winds are Piping loud,	Penseroso 126
Of famous *Arcady* ye are, and sprung	Arcades 28
Where ye may all that are of noble stemm	Arcades 82
What recks it them? What need they? They are sped;	Lycidas 122
The hungry Sheep look up, and are not fed,	Lycidas 125
Wash far away, where ere thy bones are hurld,	Lycidas 155
Are seen in glittering ranks with wings displaid,	Nativity 114
The Oracles are dumm,	Nativity 173
Are held with his melodious harmonie	Vacation 51
To harbour those that are at enmity.	Vacation 88
And former sufferings other where are found;	Passion 25
That Heav'n and Earth are colour'd with my wo;	Passion 32
My sorrows are too dark for day to know:	Passion 33
For sure so well instructed are my tears,	Passion 48
Woods and Groves, are of thy dressing,	May Morn 7
His Letters are deliver'd all and gon,	Another 33
line not in 1658 text	
Warbl'st at eeve, when all the Woods are still,	Sonnet 1, 2
Now that the Fields are dank, and ways are mire,	Sonnet 20, 2
Lord how many are my foes	Psalm 3, 1
Many are they	Psalm 3, 4
Are troubled, yea my soul is troubled sore	Psalm 6, 6
Wherwith their cheeks are wet.	Psalm 80, 24
That are their enemies.	Psalm 81, 60
The Earths foundations all are mov'd	Psalm 82, 19
How lovely are thy dwellings fair!	Psalm 84, 1
The *pleasant* Tabernacles are!	Psalm 84, 3
Whose waies are just and right.	Psalm 84, 44
Now *joyfully* are met	Psalm 85, 42
And hand in hand are set.	Psalm 85, 44
By thy strong hand are done,	Psalm 86, 34
And violent men are met	Psalm 86, 50
Of thee *abroad* are spoke;	Psalm 87, 10
With sacred Songs are there,	Psalm 87, 26
And to my cries, that *ceaseless are*,	Psalm 88, 7
And as in darkness are.	Psalm 88, 72
Aread	
But mark what I arreede thee now, avant;	Par Lost 4.962
Arethuse	
Stole under Seas to meet his *Arethuse;*	Arcades 31
O Fountain *Arethuse*, and thou honour'd floud,	Lycidas 85
Argent	
Those argent Fields more likely habitants,	Par Lost 3.460
Argestes	
Boreas and *Caecias* and *Argestes* loud	Par Lost 10.699
Argo	
And more endanger'd, then when *Argo* pass'd	Par Lost 2.1017
Argob	
In *Argob* and in *Basan*, to the stream	Par Lost 1.398
ms 'Argob'	
Argue	
Argue thy inexperience what behooves	Par Lost 4.931
To argue in thee somthing more sublime	Par Lost 10.1014
So many Laws argue so many sins	Par Lost 12.283
I will not argue that, nor will repine.	Par Reg 2.94
Or man or woman. Yet I argue not	Sonnet 22, 6
Argued	
Of good and evil much they argu'd then,	Par Lost 2.562
That argu'd fear; each on himself reli'd,	Par Lost 6.238
I chose a Wife, which argu'd me no foe;	Samson 1193
Argues	
The former vain to hope argues as vain	Par Lost 2.234
Not to know mee argues your selves unknown,	Par Lost 4.830
Argues no Leader but a lyar trac't,	Par Lost 4.949
Thir distance argues and thir swift return	Par Lost 8.21
Which argues over-just, and self-displeas'd	Samson 514
Arguing	
None arguing stood, innumerable hands	Par Lost 6.508
Of his weak arguing, and fallacious drift;	Par Reg 3.4
Argument	
That to the highth of this great Argument	Par Lost 1.24
ms 'argument'	
O argument blasphemous, false and proud!	Par Lost 5.809
Various, with boastful Argument portraid,	Par Lost 6.84
Deaths Harbinger: Sad task, yet argument	Par Lost 9.13
Warrs, hitherto the onely Argument	Par Lost 9.28
Nor skilld nor studious, higher Argument	Par Lost 9.42
Impossible is held, as Argument	Par Lost 10.800
Sung with the voice, and this the argument.	Par Reg 1.172
For glories sake by all thy argument.	Par Reg 3.46
Luggage of war there shewn me, argument	Par Reg 3.401
Had dealt with *Jephtha*, who by argument,	Samson 283
With studied argument, and much perswasion sought	Samson 658
Dal. In argument with men a woman ever	Samson 903

Arguments
To oppose against such powerful arguments? Samson 862
I hate when vice can bolt her arguments, Mask 760
Argus
Of *Argus*, and more wakeful then to drouze, Par Lost 11.131
Ariel
Ariel and *Arioc*, and the violence Par Lost 6.371
Aries
His *Zenith*, while the Sun in *Aries* rose: Par Lost 10.329
Aright
Not uninvented that, which thou aright Par Lost 6.470
And person, had'st thou known thy self aright. Par Lost 10.156
To worship God aright, and know his works Par Lost 11.578
To know, and knowing worship God aright, Par Reg 2.475
Where God is prais'd aright, and Godlike men, Par Reg 4.348
To have guided me aright, I know not how, Samson 1547
Arimaspian
Pursues the *Arimaspian*, who by stelth Par Lost 2.945
Arioch
Ariel and *Arioc*, and the violence Par Lost 6.371
Arise
Awake, arise, or be for ever fall'n. Par Lost 1.330
Th' animal Spirits that from pure blood arise Par Lost 4.805
Useful, whence haply mention may arise Par Lost 8.200
Whence heavie persecution shall arise Par Lost 12.531
All fear of thee, arise and vindicate Par Reg 2.47
But will arise and his great name assert: Samson 467
Rivers arise; whether thou be the Son, Vacation 91
No less renownd then warr, new foes arise Sonnet 16, 11
Trinity ms 'aries'
Shall the deceas'd arise Psalm 88, 42
Arises
While day arises, that sweet hour of Prime. Par Lost 5.170
Ark
Who mourn'd in earnest, when the Captive Ark Par Lost 1.458
Shall build a wondrous Ark, as thou beheldst, Par Lost 11.819
Select for life shall in the Ark be lodg'd, Par Lost 11.823
He lookd, and saw the Ark hull on the floud, Par Lost 11.840
The Ark no more now flotes, but seems on ground Par Lost 11.850
Forthwith from out the Arke a Raven flies, Par Lost 11.855
Anon drie ground appeers, and from his Arke Par Lost 11.861
Of him who built the Ark, who for the shame Par Lost 12.102
An Ark, and in the Ark his Testimony, Par Lost 12.251
The clouded Ark of God till then in Tents Par Lost 12.333
Thir Citie, his Temple, and his holy Ark Par Lost 12.340
The sable-stoled Sorcerers bear his worshipt Ark. Nativity 220
Arm
Who from the terrour of this Arm so late Par Lost 1.113
ms 'arm'
Should intermitted vengeance arm again Par Lost 2.173
1667 'Arme'
Beyond his Potent arm, to live exempt Par Lost 2.318
Fallacious hope, or arm th' obdured brest Par Lost 2.568
From my prevailing arme, though Heavens King Par Lost 4.973
This said he paus'd not, but with ventrous Arme Par Lost 5.64
These Elements, and arm him with the force Par Lost 6.222
As onely in his arm the moment lay Par Lost 6.239
Together both with next to Almightie Arme, Par Lost 6.316
Our yet unwounded Enemies, or arme Par Lost 6.466
Arme, Warriours, Arme for fight, the foe at hand, Par Lost 6.537
Thou canst, who art sole Wonder, much less arm Par Lost 9.533
Of thy victorious Arm, well-pleasing Son, Par Lost 10.634
To guide them in all truth, and also arme Par Lost 12.490
Much ostentation vain of fleshly arm, Par Reg 3.387
Above the nerve of mortal arm Samson 639
Against th' opposing will and arm of Heav'n Mask 600
Trinity ms 'arme'
1637 'arme'
Bridgewater ms 'arme'
Arm his profane tongue with contemptuous words Mask 781
line not in Bridgewater ms
1637 'Arme'
line not in Trinity ms
Armed
Innumerable force of Spirits arm'd Par Lost 1.101
Afloat, when with fierce Winds *Orion* arm'd Par Lost 1.305
Had to impose: He through the armed Files Par Lost 1.567
Of Pioners with Spade and Pickax arm'd Par Lost 1.676
Wont ride in arm'd, and at the Soldans chair Par Lost 1.764
Arm'd with Hell flames and fury all at once Par Lost 2.61
With Armed watch, that render all access Par Lost 2.130
With splendor, arm'd with power, if aught propos'd Par Lost 2.447
Voluminous and vast, a Serpent arm'd Par Lost 2.652
Then shining heav'nly fair, a Goddess arm'd Par Lost 2.757
Of Spirits that in our just pretenses arm'd Par Lost 2.825
Light-arm'd or heavy, sharp, smooth, swift or slow, Par Lost 2.902
Or from without, to all temptations arm'd. Par Lost 4.65
Forth issuing at th' accustomd hour stood armd Par Lost 4.779
Invincible, lead forth my armed Saints Par Lost 6.47
Came towring, armd in Adamant and Gold; Par Lost 6.110
So pondering, and from his armed Peers Par Lost 6.127
Such hast thou arm'd, the Minstrelsie of Heav'n, Par Lost 6.168
A numerous Host, in strength each armed hand Par Lost 6.231
Though huge, and in a Rock of Diamond Armd, Par Lost 6.364
Invulnerable, impenitrably arm'd: Par Lost 6.400
Omniscient thought. True is, less firmly arm'd, Par Lost 6.430
Lookd round, and Scouts each Coast light-armed scoure, Par Lost 6.529
Came shadowing, and opprest whole Legions arm'd, Par Lost 6.655
Armed(*cont*)
As likeliest was, when two such Foes met arm'd; Par Lost 6.688
With Mountains as with Weapons arm'd, which makes Par Lost 6.697
Armd with thy might, rid Heav'n of these rebell'd, Par Lost 6.737
Hee in Celestial Panoplie all armd Par Lost 6.760
Ye Angels arm'd, this day from Battel rest; Par Lost 6.802
Though not as shee with Bow and Quiver armd, Par Lost 9.390
Of Man, with strength entire, and free will arm'd, Par Lost 10.9
Bursting thir brazen Dungeon, armd with ice Par Lost 10.697
Hath wiselier arm'd his vengeful ire then so Par Lost 10.1023
The City gates out powr'd, light armed Troops Par Reg 3.311
A multitude with Spades and Axes arm'd Par Reg 3.331
Of Hornets arm'd, no sooner found alone, Samson 20
To save himself against a coward arm'd Samson 347
Thoughts my Tormenters arm'd with deadly stings Samson 623
Arm'd thee or charm'd thee strong, which thou from Heaven Samson 1134
Went up with armed powers thee only seeking, Samson 1190
And celestial vigour arm'd, Samson 1280
That of a Nation arm'd the strength contain'd: Samson 1494
And Timbrels, on each side went armed guards, Samson 1617
The Trumpet spake not to the armed throng, Nativity 58
All these have lent their armed hands Psalm 83, 31
Armies
Thus answer'd. Leader of those Armies bright, Par Lost 1.272
ms 'armies'
Wag'd in the troubl'd Skie, and Armies rush Par Lost 2.534
Where Armies whole have sunk: the parching Air Par Lost 2.594
Go *Michael* of Celestial Armies Prince, Par Lost 6.44
Have rais'd incessant Armies to defeat Par Lost 6.138
It sounded, and the faithful Armies rung Par Lost 6.204
On the swift flouds: as Armies at the call Par Lost 7.295
Of Trumpet (for of Armies thou hast heard) Par Lost 7.296
Where Armies lie encampt, come flying, lur'd Par Lost 10.276
Ran on embattelld Armies clad in Iron, Samson 129
Duell'd thir Armies rank't in proud array, Samson 345
Arming
Arming to Battel, and in stead of rage Par Lost 1.553
My obvious breast, arming to overcom Par Lost 11.374
Armoric
Begirt with *British* and *Armoric* Knights; Par Lost 1.581
ms 'Armoric'
Armour
Was never, Arms on Armour clashing bray'd Par Lost 6.209
And all his Armour staind ere while so bright. Par Lost 6.334
With shiverd armour strow'n, and on a heap Par Lost 6.389
Thir armor help'd thir harm, crush't in and bruis'd Par Lost 6.656
In jointed Armour watch: on smooth the Seale, Par Lost 7.409
With spiritual Armour, able to resist Par Lost 12.491
Armouries
Thir Armories and Magazins contemns, Samson 1281
Armoury
Celestial Armourie, Shields, Helmes, and Speares, Par Lost 4.553
Of *Michael* from the Armorie of God Par Lost 6.321
From the Armoury of God, where stand of old Par Lost 7.200
Arms
Who durst defie th' Omnipotent to Arms. Par Lost 1.49
ms 'armes'
The force of those dire Arms? yet not for those, Par Lost 1.94
ms 'arm's'
In Arms not worse, in foresight much advanc't, Par Lost 1.119
ms 'arms'
With rallied Arms to try what may be yet Par Lost 1.269
ms 'arms'
With scatter'd Arms and Ensigns, till anon Par Lost 1.325
ms 'arms'
Seraphic arms and Trophies: all the while Par Lost 1.539
Of dreadful length and dazling Arms, in guise Par Lost 1.564
ms 'arms'
Against the Highest, and fierce with grasped Arms Par Lost 1.667
1667 'arm's'
ms 'arm's'
Millions that stand in Arms, and longing wait Par Lost 2.55
Turning our Tortures into horrid Arms Par Lost 2.63
When he who most excels in fact of Arms, Par Lost 2.124
Thus sitting, thus consulting, thus in Arms? Par Lost 2.164
Of those bright confines, whence with neighbouring Arms Par Lost 2.395
With bright imblazonrie, and horrent Arms. Par Lost 2.513
Till thickest Legions close; with feats of Arms Par Lost 2.537
Unbrok'n, and in proud rebellious Arms Par Lost 2.691
To be invulnerable in those bright Arms, Par Lost 2.812
Imparadis't in one anothers arms Par Lost 4.506
To boast what Arms can doe, since thine no more Par Lost 4.1008
Her mariageable arms, and with her brings Par Lost 5.217
Of our Omnipotence, and with what Arms Par Lost 5.722
Chariots and flaming Armes, and fierie Steeds Par Lost 6.17
Of Truth, in word mightier then they in Armes; Par Lost 6.32
Rebellious, them with Fire and hostile Arms Par Lost 6.50
Should win in Arms, in both disputes alike Par Lost 6.123
Against th' Omnipotent to rise in Arms; Par Lost 6.136
Was never, Arms on Armour clashing bray'd Par Lost 6.209
Prodigious power had shewn, and met in Armes Par Lost 6.247
Stood they or mov'd, in stature, motion, arms Par Lost 6.302
Down clov'n to the waste, with shatterd Armes Par Lost 6.361
O now in danger tri'd, now known in Armes Par Lost 6.418
The remedie; perhaps more valid Armes, Par Lost 6.438
Sore toild, his riv'n Armes to havoc hewn, Par Lost 6.449
Against unequal armes to fight in paine, Par Lost 6.454
Up rose the Victor Angels, and to Arms Par Lost 6.525

Arms(*cont*)
The matin Trumpet Sung: in Arms they stood — Par Lost 6.526
The sooner for thir Arms, unarm'd they might — Par Lost 6.595
Rage prompted them at length, and found them arms — Par Lost 6.635
Thir Arms away they threw, and to the Hills — Par Lost 6.639
The rest in imitation to like Armes — Par Lost 6.662
My Bow and Thunder, my Almightie Arms — Par Lost 6.713
In *Malabar* or *Decan* spreds her Armes — Par Lost 9.1103
His Armes clung to his Ribs, his Leggs entwining — Par Lost 10.512
They felt themselves now changing; down thir arms, — Par Lost 10.541
Clad to meet Man; over his lucid Armes — Par Lost 11.240
Concours in Arms, fierce Faces threatning Warr, — Par Lost 11.641
Part wield thir Arms, part courb the foaming Steed, — Par Lost 11.643
With Carcasses and Arms th' ensanguind Field — Par Lost 11.654
Untraind in Armes, where rashness leads not on. — Par Lost 12.222
Defeating Sin and Death, his two maine armes, — Par Lost 12.431
With dreadful Faces throng'd and fierie Armes: — Par Lost 12.644
Now entring his great duel, not of arms, — Par Reg 1.174
In battel, though against thy few in arms. — Par Reg 3.20
Easily from possession won with arms; — Par Reg 3.156
Retir'd unto the Desert, but with arms; — Par Reg 3.166
They issue forth, Steel Bows, and Shafts their arms — Par Reg 3.305
And fragile arms, much instrument of war — Par Reg 3.388
Civility of Manners, Arts, and Arms, — Par Reg 4.83
More then of arms before, allure mine eye, — Par Reg 4.112
Error by his own arms is best evinc't. — Par Reg 4.235
Since neither wealth, nor honour, arms nor arts, — Par Reg 4.368
Whose branching arms thick intertwind might shield — Par Reg 4.405
Made Arms ridiculous, useless the forgery — Samson 131
In scorn of thir proud arms and warlike tools, — Samson 137
Intestin, far within defensive arms — Samson 1038
I should have forc'd thee soon wish other arms, — Samson 1096
Then put on all thy gorgeous arms, thy Helmet — Samson 1119
Har. Thou durst not thus disparage glorious arms — Samson 1130
To fight with thee no man of arms will deign. — Samson 1226
With both his arms on those two massie Pillars — Samson 1633
Felt in his arms, with head a while enclin'd, — Samson 1636
An old, and haughty Nation proud in Arms: — Mask 33
Trinity ms 'armes'
1637 'Armes'
Bridgewater ms 'armes'
To testifie the arms of Chastity? — Mask 440
1637 'armes'
Bridgewater ms 'armes'
Farr other arms, and other weapons must — Mask 612
Bridgewater ms 'armes'
his farre-extended armes till with steepe fall — Mask Tr. ms 10.13
Of Wit, or Arms, while both contend — Allegro 123
His thirty Armes along the indented Meads, — Vacation 94
Captain or Colonel, or Knight in Arms, — Sonnet 8, 1
Trinity ms 'armes'
Fairfax, whose name in armes through Europe rings — Sonnet 15, 1
1694 'Arms'
The helme of Rome, when gownes not armes repelld — Sonnet 17, 3
1662, 1694 'Arms'
That in arms against me rise — Psalm 3, 3

Army
Armie of Fiends, fit body to fit head; — Par Lost 4.953
Armie against Armie numberless to raise — Par Lost 6.224
His Armie, circumfus'd on either Wing, — Par Lost 6.778
Himself and his rash Armie, where thin Aire — Par Lost 12.76
With all his Army, now thou hast aveng'd — Par Reg 4.606
Himself an Army, now unequal match — Samson 346

Arnon
Of utmost *Arnon*. Nor content with such — Par Lost 1.399
ms 'Arnon'

Aroar
From *Aroar* to *Nebo*, and the wild — Par Lost 1.407
1667 '*Aroer*'
ms 'Aroer'

Arose
A growing burden. Mean while Warr arose, — Par Lost 2.767
Not burd'nd Nature, sudden mind arose — Par Lost 5.452
The doubts that in his heart arose: and now — Par Lost 7.60
The Sixt, and of Creation last arose — Par Lost 7.449
Eev'ning arose in *Eden*, for the Sun — Par Lost 7.582
So saying, he arose; whom *Adam* thus — Par Lost 8.644

Around
Thir embryon Atoms; they around the flag — Par Lost 2.900
Was heard the World around: — Nativity 54

Arraigned
Bad men and Angels, they arraignd shall sink — Par Lost 3.331

Arras
Th' enameld *Arras* of the Rainbow wearing, — Nativity 143
1673 'Orb'd in a Rain-bow and like glories wearing'

Array
Appear'd, and serried Shields in thick array — Par Lost 1.548
With Horse and Chariots rankt in loose array; — Par Lost 2.887
Of Birds in orderly array on wing — Par Lost 6.74
Presented stood in terrible array — Par Lost 6.106
And with fierce Ensignes pierc'd the deep array — Par Lost 6.356
Stand still in bright array ye Saints, here stand — Par Lost 6.801
Heav'n-fall'n, in station stood or just array, — Par Lost 10.535
Single or in Array of Battel rang'd — Par Lost 11.644
To thir fixt Station, all in bright array — Par Lost 12.627
All her array; her female pride deject, — Par Reg 2.219
That might require th' array of war, thy skill — Par Reg 3.17
Duell'd thir Armies rank't in proud array, — Samson 345

Array(*cont*)
Till thou hast deck't them in thy best aray; — Vacation 26

Arrayed
Such as in highest Heav'n, arrayd in Gold — Par Lost 6.13
Array'd in Glory on my cup to attend: — Par Reg 2.386
That with long beams the shame-fac't night array'd, — Nativity 111

Arraying
Arraying with reflected Purple and Gold — Par Lost 4.596
Araying cover'd from his Fathers sight. — Par Lost 10.223

Arrive
Over the vast abrupt, ere he arrive — Par Lost 2.409
Possesses lately, thither to arrive — Par Lost 2.979
And to the end persisting, safe arrive. — Par Lost 3.197
Therefore, if at great things thou wouldst arrive, — Par Reg 2.426

Arrived
Who after came from Earth, sayling arriv'd, — Par Lost 3.520
Thus at thir shadie Lodge arriv'd, both stood — Par Lost 4.720
This Eevning from the Sun's decline arriv'd — Par Lost 4.792
Of Heav'n arriv'd, the gate self-opend wide — Par Lost 5.254
Among them he arriv'd; in his right hand — Par Lost 6.835
The Filial Power arriv'd, and sate him down — Par Lost 7.587
Where God resides, and ere mid-day arriv'd — Par Lost 8.112
From Earth arriv'd at Heaven Gate, displeas'd — Par Lost 10.22
About the new-arriv'd, in multitudes — Par Lost 10.26
Too soon arriv'd, *Sin* there in power before, — Par Lost 10.586
That I to manhood am arriv'd so near, — Sonnet 7, 6

Arrives
Chor. His fraught we soon shall know, he now arrives. — Samson 1075

Arrogate
Will arrogate Dominion undeserv'd — Par Lost 12.27
All glory arrogate, to God give none, — Par Reg 4.315

Arrow
His deadly arrow; neither vainly hope — Par Lost 2.811

Arrows
But ratling storm of Arrows barbd with fire. — Par Lost 6.546
His arrows, from the fourfold-visag'd Foure, — Par Lost 6.845
And like a quiver'd Nymph with Arrows keen — Mask 422
Trinity ms 'arrows'
Bridgewater ms 'arrowes'
1637 'arrowes'
(His arrows purposely made he — Psalm 7, 49

Arrowy
Sharp sleet of arrowie showers against the face — Par Reg 3.324

Arsaces
By great *Arsaces* led, who founded first — Par Reg 3.295

Arsenal
Shook the Arsenal and fulmin'd over *Greece*, — Par Reg 4.270

Art
Whence and what art thou, execrable shape, — Par Lost 2.681
Art thou that Traitor Angel, art thou hee, — Par Lost 2.689
What thing thou art, thus double-form'd, and why — Par Lost 2.741
Thou art my Father, thou my Author, thou — Par Lost 2.864
Answer'd. I know thee, stranger, who thou art, — Par Lost 2.990
That farr be from thee, Father, who art Judg — Par Lost 3.154
Son of my bosom, Son who art alone — Par Lost 3.169
The first art wont his great authentic will — Par Lost 3.656
And here art likeliest by supream decree — Par Lost 3.659
Whose image thou art, him thou shalt enjoy — Par Lost 4.472
Whom fli'st thou? whom thou fli'st, of him thou art, — Par Lost 4.482
Where thou art weigh'd, and shown how light, how weak, — Par Lost 4.1012
Partake thou also; happie though thou art, — Par Lost 5.75
Adam, I therefore came, nor art thou such — Par Lost 5.372
Attend: That thou art happie, owe to God; — Par Lost 5.520
Thee what thou art, and formd the Pow'rs of Heav'n — Par Lost 5.824
Proud, art thou met? thy hope was to have reacht — Par Lost 6.131
If rightly thou art call'd, whose Voice divine — Par Lost 7.2
For thou art Heav'nlie, shee an empty dreame. — Par Lost 7.39
Who art to lead thy ofspring, and supposest — Par Lost 8.86
Thou in thy self art perfet, and in thee — Par Lost 8.415
Thy mate, who sees when thou art seen least wise. — Par Lost 8.578
For such thou art, from sin and blame entire: — Par Lost 9.292
Thou canst, who art sole Wonder, much less arm — Par Lost 9.533
How art thou lost, how on a sudden lost, — Par Lost 9.900
Bone of my Bone thou art, and from thy State — Par Lost 9.915
My own in thee, for what thou art is mine; — Par Lost 9.957
Eve, now I see thou art exact of taste, — Par Lost 9.1017
Where art thou *Adam*, wont with joy to meet — Par Lost 10.103
So dreadful to thee? that thou art naked, who — Par Lost 10.121
Because thou hast done this, thou art accurst — Par Lost 10.175
For dust thou art, and shalt to dust returne. — Par Lost 10.208
Thou art thir Author and prime Architect: — Par Lost 10.356
Childless thou art, Childless remaine: — Par Lost 10.989
Thy Husband, him to follow thou art bound; — Par Lost 11.291
Created, as thou art, to nobler end — Par Lost 11.605
Art all things under Heav'n, all places thou, — Par Lost 12.618
Who for my wilful crime art banisht hence. — Par Lost 12.619
As thou art wont, my prompted Song else mute, — Par Reg 1.12
For know, thou art no Son of mortal man, — Par Reg 1.234
Knowing who I am, as I know who thou art? — Par Reg 1.356
But thou art serviceable to Heaven's King. — Par Reg 1.421
But thou art plac't above me, thou art Lord; — Par Reg 1.475
Natures own work it seem'd (Nature taught Art) — Par Reg 2.295
Thou art not to be harm'd, therefore not mov'd; — Par Reg 2.407
Thou art unknown, unfriended, low of birth, — Par Reg 2.413
Inglorious: but thou yet art not too late. — Par Reg 3.42
But to a Kingdom thou art born, ordain'd — Par Reg 3.152
My everlasting Kingdom, why art thou — Par Reg 3.199
That thou who worthiest art should'st be thir King? — Par Reg 3.226

Art(*cont*)
Indu'd with Regal Vertues as thou art, — Par Reg 4.98
Who then thou art, whose coming is foretold — Par Reg 4.204
Thou shalt be what thou art ordain'd, no doubt; — Par Reg 4.473
Mee to thy will; desist, thou art discern'd — Par Reg 4.497
In what degree or meaning thou art call'd — Par Reg 4.516
Thou art to be my fatal enemy. — Par Reg 4.525
Therefore to know what more thou art then man, — Par Reg 4.538
A Saviour art come down to re-install. — Par Reg 4.615
Thou art become (O worst imprisonment!) — Samson 155
To lowest pitch of abject fortune thou art fall'n. — Samson 169
Bitterly hast thou paid, and still art paying — Samson 432
As thou art strong, inflexible as steel. — Samson 816
Dal. I see thou art implacable, more deaf — Samson 960
If thou at all art known. Much I have heard — Samson 1082
Had brought me to the field where thou art fam'd — Samson 1094
And black enchantments, some Magicians Art — Samson 1133
To thee I am bid say. Art thou our Slave, — Samson 1392
Sam. I could be well content to try thir Art, — Samson 1399
Thou for thy Son art bent to lay out all; — Samson 1486
Excells his Mother at her mighty Art, — Mask 63
Trinity ms 'art'
Bridgewater ms 'arte'
That ne're art call'd, but when the Dragon woom — Mask 131
1637 'at'
(For so I can distinguish by mine Art) — Mask 149
Trinity ms 'art'
Bridgewater ms 'arte'
Would overtask the best Land-Pilots art, — Mask 309
Bridgewater ms 'arte'
Root-bound, that fled *Apollo*, *La*. Fool do not boast, — Mask 662
Trinity ms 'doe not boast' ←'thou art over proud'
And thou art worthy that thou shouldst not know — Mask 788
line not in Trinity ms
line not in Bridgewater ms
Thou art not fit to hear thy self convinc't; — Mask 792
line not in Trinity ms
line not in Bridgewater ms
And bound him fast; without his rod revers't, — Mask 816
Trinity ms 'rod' ←'art'
Listen where thou art sitting — Mask 860
Trinity ms 'art sitting' ←'sit'st'
Yet thou art higher far descended, — Penseroso 22
But O the heavy change, now thou art gon, — Lycidas 37
Now thou art gon, and never must return! — Lycidas 38
That to the faithfull Herdmans art belongs! — Lycidas 121
Hence forth thou art the Genius of the shore, — Lycidas 183
Yet art thou not inglorious in thy fate; — Fair Inf 22
Yet can I not perswade me thou art dead — Fair Inf 29
But thou canst best perform that office where thou art. — Fair Inf 70
For whilst to th' shame of slow-endeavouring art, — Shakespear 9
1640 'Art'
1663-4 'Art'
1632 'Art'
And with those few art eminently seen, — Sonnet 9, 3
that didst reform thy art, the cheif among — Sonnet 13, Tr. ms 40.08
Thou art my Son I have begotten thee — Psalm 2, 15
But thou Lord art my shield my glory, — Psalm 3, 7
For thou art not a God that takes — Psalm 5, 9
Since thou art the just God that tries — Psalm 7, 38
When I behold thy Heavens, thy Fingers art, — Psalm 8, 9
That him thou visit'st and of him art found; — Psalm 8, 14
For thou art he who shalt by right — Psalm 82, 27
Art the most high, *and thou the same* — Psalm 83, 67
O're all the earth *art one*. — Psalm 83, 68
For thou art good, thou Lord art prone — Psalm 86, 13
Art full of mercy, thou *alone* — Psalm 86, 15
For great thou art, and wonders great — Psalm 86, 33
But thou Lord art the God most mild — Psalm 86, 53
Slow to be angry, and *art stil'd* — Psalm 86, 55

Art
And Strength and Art are easily out-done — Par Lost 1.696
ms 'art'
With wond'rous Art found out the massie Ore, — Par Lost 1.703
ms 'art'
Nor want we skill or Art, from whence to raise — Par Lost 2.272
1674 'art' in some copies
1667 'art'
The happy Ile; what strength, what art can then — Par Lost 2.410
In vain, though by thir powerful Art they binde — Par Lost 3.602
But rather to tell how, if Art could tell, — Par Lost 4.236
Flours worthy of Paradise which not nice Art — Par Lost 4.241
Assaying by his Devilish art to reach — Par Lost 4.801
Wilde above Rule or Art; enormous bliss. — Par Lost 5.297
1667 'art' in some copies
Thither to come, and with calumnious Art — Par Lost 5.770
They found, they mingl'd, and with suttle Art, — Par Lost 6.513
But with such Gardning Tools as Art yet rude, — Par Lost 9.391
Now had they brought the work by wondrous Art — Par Lost 10.312

Artaxata
Artaxata, *Teredon*, *Tesiphon*, — Par Reg 3.292

Artaxerxes
To *Macedon*, and *Artaxerxes* Throne; — Par Reg 4.271

Artful
With Hymns, our Psalms with artful terms inscrib'd, — Par Reg 4.335
El. *Bro*. *Thyrsis?* Whose artful strains have oft delaid — Mask 494
Bridgewater ms 'art full'
Trinity ms 'artfull'

Artful(*cont*)
1637 'artfull'
To hear the Lute well toucht, or artfull voice — Sonnet 20, 11

Articulate
Created mute to all articulat sound; — Par Lost 9.557

Artifice
The skill of Artifice or Office mean, — Par Lost 9.39

Artificer
Artificer of fraud; and was the first — Par Lost 4.121

Artificers
Carv'd work, the hand of fam'd Artificers — Par Reg 4.59

Artillery
With Heav'ns Artillery fraught, come rattling on — Par Lost 2.715

Artist
Through Optic Glass the *Tuscan* Artist views — Par Lost 1.288

Artists
Of Gymnic Artists, Wrestlers, Riders, Runners, — Samson 1324

Arts
Of Arts that polish Life, Inventers rare, — Par Lost 11.610
Expert in amorous Arts, enchanting tongues — Par Reg 2.158
Thee, of thy self so apt, in regal Arts, — Par Reg 3.248
Civility of Manners, Arts, and Arms, — Par Reg 4.83
Athens the eye of *Greece*, Mother of Arts — Par Reg 4.240
That rather *Greece* from us these Arts deriv'd; — Par Reg 4.338
Since neither wealth, nor honour, arms nor arts, — Par Reg 4.368
Sam. Out, out *Hyaena;* these are thy wonted arts, — Samson 748
And arts of every woman false like thee, — Samson 749
Sam. I know no Spells, use no forbidden Arts; — Samson 1139

As
At once as far as Angels kenn he views — Par Lost 1.59
As one great Furnace flam'd, yet from those flames — Par Lost 1.62
As far remov'd from God and light of Heav'n — Par Lost 1.73
As from the Center thrice to th' utmost Pole. — Par Lost 1.74
As far as Gods and Heav'nly Essences — Par Lost 1.138
Then such could hav orepow'rd such force as ours) — Par Lost 1.145
Or do him mightier service as his thralls — Par Lost 1.149
As being the contrary to his high will — Par Lost 1.161
Which oft times may succeed, so as perhaps — Par Lost 1.166
Lay floating many a rood, in bulk as huge — Par Lost 1.196
As whom the Fables name of monstrous size, — Par Lost 1.197
Deeming some Island, oft, as Sea-men tell, — Par Lost 1.205
With solid, as the Lake with liquid fire; — Par Lost 1.229
And such appear'd in hue, as when the force — Par Lost 1.230
As Gods, and by thir own recover'd strength, — Par Lost 1.240
As we erewhile, astounded and amaz'd, — Par Lost 1.281
Thick as Autumnal Leaves that strow the Brooks — Par Lost 1.302
If such astonishment as this can sieze — Par Lost 1.317
To slumber here, as in the Vales of Heav'n? — Par Lost 1.321
Upon the wing, as when men wont to watch — Par Lost 1.332
Innumerable. As when the potent Rod — Par Lost 1.338
Till, as a signal giv'n, th' uplifted Spear — Par Lost 1.347
At thir great Emperors call, as next in worth — Par Lost 1.378
To bestial Gods; for which thir heads as low — Par Lost 1.435
Turns Atheist, as did *Ely*'s Sons, who fill'd — Par Lost 1.495
Azazel as his right, a Cherube tall: — Par Lost 1.534
Of Flutes and soft Recorders; such as rais'd — Par Lost 1.551
Thir visages and stature as of Gods, — Par Lost 1.570
Met such imbodied force, as nam'd with these — Par Lost 1.574
Of Glory obscur'd: As when the Sun new ris'n — Par Lost 1.594
Thir Glory witherd. As when Heavens Fire — Par Lost 1.612
Tears such as Angels weep, burst forth: at last — Par Lost 1.620
As this place testifies, and this dire change — Par Lost 1.625
As stood like these, could ever know repulse? — Par Lost 1.630
Monarch in Heav'n, till then as one secure — Par Lost 1.638
So as not either to provoke, or dread — Par Lost 1.644
A numerous Brigad hasten'd. As when Bands — Par Lost 1.675
A third as soon had form'd within the ground — Par Lost 1.705
As in an Organ from one blast of wind — Par Lost 1.708
As from a sky. The hasty multitude — Par Lost 1.730
And sat as Princes, whom the supreme King — Par Lost 1.735
Brusht with the hiss of russling wings. As Bees — Par Lost 1.768
As not behind in hate; if what was urg'd — Par Lost 2.120
And utter dissolution, as the scope — Par Lost 2.127
The Victors will. To suffer, as to doe, — Par Lost 2.199
The former vain to hope argues as vain — Par Lost 2.234
As he our darkness, cannot we his Light — Par Lost 2.269
As soft as now severe, our temper chang'd — Par Lost 2.276
Th' Assembly, as when hollow Rocks retain — Par Lost 2.285
As *Mammon* ended, and his Sentence pleas'd, — Par Lost 2.291
Drew audience and attention still as Night — Par Lost 2.308
Us here, as with his Golden those in Heav'n. — Par Lost 2.328
All as our own, and drive as we were driven, — Par Lost 2.366
So hardie as to proffer or accept — Par Lost 2.425
Then unknown dangers and as hard escape. — Par Lost 2.444
Refusing to accept as great a share — Par Lost 2.452
Of hazard as of honour, due alike — Par Lost 2.453
Of hazard more, as he above the rest — Par Lost 2.455
Thir rising all at once was as the sound — Par Lost 2.476
With awful reverence prone; and as a God — Par Lost 2.478
As when from mountain tops the dusky clouds — Par Lost 2.488
As if (which might induce us to accord) — Par Lost 2.503
Pursues, as inclination or sad choice — Par Lost 2.524
As at th' Olympian Games or *Pythian* fields; — Par Lost 2.530
As when to warn proud Cities warr appears — Par Lost 2.533
As when *Alcides* from *Oechalia* Crown'd — Par Lost 2.542
With stubborn patience as with triple steel. — Par Lost 2.569
A gulf profound as that *Serbonian* Bog — Par Lost 2.592
And wish and struggle, as they pass, to reach — Par Lost 2.606

As(*cont*)

All taste of living wight, as once it fled	Par Lost 2.613
As when farr off at Sea a Fleet descri'd	Par Lost 2.636
For each seem'd either; black it stood as Night,	Par Lost 2.670
Fierce as ten Furies, terrible as Hell,	Par Lost 2.671
The Monster moving onward came as fast	Par Lost 2.675
With horrid strides, Hell trembled as he strode.	Par Lost 2.676
Each cast at th' other, as when two black Clouds	Par Lost 2.714
Surround me, as thou sawst, hourly conceiv'd	Par Lost 2.796
At thy right hand voluptuous, as beseems	Par Lost 2.869
Swarm populous, unnumber'd as the Sands	Par Lost 2.903
As in a cloudy Chair ascending rides	Par Lost 2.930
As many miles aloft: that furie stay'd,	Par Lost 2.938
As when a Gryfon through the Wilderness	Par Lost 2.943
Wandring this darksome Desart, as my way,	Par Lost 2.973
As from her outmost works a brok'd foe	Par Lost 2.1039
This pendant world, in bigness as a Starr	Par Lost 2.1052
Of God, as with a Mantle didst invest	Par Lost 3.10
Harmonious numbers; as the wakeful Bird	Par Lost 3.38
Stood thick as Starrs, and from his sight receiv'd	Par Lost 3.61
Not mee. They therefore as to right belongd,	Par Lost 3.111
As if predestination over-rul'd	Par Lost 3.114
All hast thou spok'n as my thoughts are, all	Par Lost 3.171
As my Eternal purpose hath decreed:	Par Lost 3.172
And I will place within them as a guide	Par Lost 3.194
Som other able, and as willing, pay	Par Lost 3.211
Filial obedience: as a sacrifice	Par Lost 3.269
As in him perish all men, so in thee	Par Lost 3.287
As from a second root shall be restor'd,	Par Lost 3.288
As many as are restor'd, without thee none.	Par Lost 3.289
Receive new life. So Man, as is most just,	Par Lost 3.294
Thy Merits; under thee as Head Supream	Par Lost 3.319
Adore the Son, and honour him as mee.	Par Lost 3.343
Loud as from numbers without number, sweet	Par Lost 3.346
As from blest voices, uttering joy, Heav'n rung	Par Lost 3.347
As when a Vultur on *Imaus* bred,	Par Lost 3.431
Fit retribution, emptie as thir deeds;	Par Lost 3.454
Not in the neighbouring Moon, as some have dreamd;	Par Lost 3.459
All this dark Globe the Fiend found as he pass'd,	Par Lost 3.498
The work as of a Kingly Palace Gate	Par Lost 3.505
The Stairs were such as whereon *Jacob* saw	Par Lost 3.510
To darkness, such as bound the Ocean wave.	Par Lost 3.539
Of all this World at once. As when a Scout	Par Lost 3.543
Dispenses Light from farr; they as they move	Par Lost 3.579
With radiant light, as glowing Iron with fire;	Par Lost 3.594
But all Sun-shine, as when his Beams at Noon	Par Lost 3.616
Culminate from th' *Aequator*, as they now	Par Lost 3.617
Glad was the Spirit impure as now in hope	Par Lost 3.630
Not of the prime, yet such as in his face	Par Lost 3.637
Like honour to obtain, and as his Eye	Par Lost 3.660
That both in him and all things, as is meet,	Par Lost 3.675
Numberless, as thou seest, and how they move;	Par Lost 3.719
His day, which else as th' other Hemisphere	Par Lost 3.725
As to superior Spirits is wont in Heaven,	Par Lost 3.737
As great might have aspir'd, and me though mean	Par Lost 4.62
Drawn to his part; but other Powers as great	Par Lost 4.63
Vows made in pain, as violent and void.	Par Lost 4.97
This knows my punisher; therefore as farr	Par Lost 4.103
From granting hee, as I from begging peace:	Par Lost 4.104
As Man ere long, and this new World shall know.	Par Lost 4.113
As he suppos'd, all unobserv'd, unseen.	Par Lost 4.130
As with a rural mound the champain head	Par Lost 4.134
A Silvan Scene, and as the ranks ascend	Par Lost 4.140
Those balmie spoiles. As when to them who saile	Par Lost 4.159
As one continu'd brake, the undergrowth	Par Lost 4.175
Lights on his feet. As when a prowling Wolfe,	Par Lost 4.183
Or as a Thief bent to unhoord the cash	Par Lost 4.188
That Mountain as his Garden mould high rais'd	Par Lost 4.226
Not equal, as thir sex not equal seemd;	Par Lost 4.296
Shee as a vail down to the slender waste	Par Lost 4.304
As the Vine curles her tendrils, which impli'd	Par Lost 4.307
Yielded them, side-long as they sat recline	Par Lost 4.333
Still as they thirsted scoop the brimming stream;	Par Lost 4.336
Wanted, nor youthful dalliance as beseems	Par Lost 4.338
Alone as they. About them frisking playd	Par Lost 4.340
When *Satan* still in gaze, as first he stood,	Par Lost 4.356
As now is enterd; yet no purpos'd foe	Par Lost 4.373
Which I as freely give; Hell shall unfold,	Par Lost 4.381
Melt, as I doe, yet public reason just,	Par Lost 4.389
Now other, as thir shape servd best his end	Par Lost 4.398
Then as a Tyger, who by chance hath spi'd	Par Lost 4.403
His couchant watch, as one who chose his ground	Par Lost 4.406
As liberal and free as infinite,	Par Lost 4.415
Pure as th' expanse of Heav'n; I thither went	Par Lost 4.456
As I bent down to look, just opposite,	Par Lost 4.460
Pleas'd it returnd as soon with answering looks	Par Lost 4.464
Smil'd with superior Love, as *Jupiter*	Par Lost 4.499
Still as it rose, impossible to climbe.	Par Lost 4.548
On a Sun beam, swift as a shooting Starr	Par Lost 4.556
A Spirit, zealous, as he seem'd, to know	Par Lost 4.565
The vigilance here plac't, but such as come	Par Lost 4.580
Labour and rest, as day and night to men	Par Lost 4.613
Mean while, as Nature wills, Night bids us rest.	Par Lost 4.633
And when we seek, as now, thy gift of sleep.	Par Lost 4.735
Defaming as impure what God declares	Par Lost 4.746
Present, or past, as Saints and Patriarchs us'd.	Par Lost 4.762
Our circuit meets full West. As flame they part	Par Lost 4.784
Illusions as he list, Phantasms and Dreams,	Par Lost 4.803

As(*cont*)

Discoverd and surpriz'd. As when a spark	Par Lost 4.814
Your message, like to end as much in vain?	Par Lost 4.833
As when thou stoodst in Heav'n upright and pure;	Par Lost 4.837
But still thy words at random, as before,	Par Lost 4.930
And Seale thee so, as henceforth not to scorne	Par Lost 4.966
With ported Spears, as thick as when a field	Par Lost 4.980
To trample thee as mire: for proof look up,	Par Lost 4.1010
As through unquiet rest: he on his side	Par Lost 5.11
Milde, as when *Zephyrus* on *Flora* breathes,	Par Lost 5.16
If dream'd, not as I oft am wont, of thee,	Par Lost 5.32
I rose as at thy call, but found thee not;	Par Lost 5.48
And as I wondring lookt, beside it stood	Par Lost 5.54
Forbidd'n here, it seems, as onely fit	Par Lost 5.69
But somtimes in the Air, as wee, somtimes	Par Lost 5.79
Reason as chief; among these Fansie next	Par Lost 5.102
Kiss'd as the gracious signs of sweet remorse	Par Lost 5.134
Soon as they forth were come to open sight	Par Lost 5.138
Fountains and yee, that warble, as ye flow,	Par Lost 5.195
Disperse it, as now light dispels the dark.	Par Lost 5.208
Go therefore, half this day as friend with friend	Par Lost 5.229
As may advise him of his happie state,	Par Lost 5.234
On golden Hinges turning, as by work	Par Lost 5.255
Above all Hills. As when by night the Glass	Par Lost 5.261
A *Phaenix*, gaz'd by all, as that sole Bird	Par Lost 5.272
Wantond as in her prime, and plaid at will	Par Lost 5.295
Adam discernd, as in the dore he sat	Par Lost 5.299
To entertain our Angel guest, as hee	Par Lost 5.328
God hath dispenst his bounties as in Heav'n.	Par Lost 5.330
What order, so contriv'd as not to mix	Par Lost 5.334
As to a superior Nature, bowing low,	Par Lost 5.360
As may not oft invite, though Spirits of Heav'n	Par Lost 5.374
As doth your Rational; and both contain	Par Lost 5.409
Ethereal, and as lowest first the Moon;	Par Lost 5.418
As may compare with Heaven; and to taste	Par Lost 5.432
As from the Mine. Mean while at Table *Eve*	Par Lost 5.443
As that more willingly thou couldst not seem	Par Lost 5.466
As neerer to him plac't or neerer tending	Par Lost 5.476
If I refuse not, but convert, as you,	Par Lost 5.492
Ethereal, as wee, or may at choice	Par Lost 5.499
Hold, as you yours, while our obedience holds;	Par Lost 5.537
Because wee freely love, as in our will	Par Lost 5.539
As may express them best, though what if Earth	Par Lost 5.574
As yet this world was not, and *Chaos* wilde	Par Lost 5.577
As Heav'ns great Year brings forth, th' Empyreal Host	Par Lost 5.583
Amidst as from a flaming Mount, whose top	Par Lost 5.598
United as one individual Soule	Par Lost 5.610
That day, as other solemn dayes, they spent	Par Lost 5.618
Desirous; all in Circles as they stood,	Par Lost 5.631
Soon as midnight brought on the duskie houre	Par Lost 5.667
Under him Regent, tells, as he was taught,	Par Lost 5.698
His count'nance, as the Morning Starr that guides	Par Lost 5.708
Innumerable as the Starrs of Night,	Par Lost 5.745
High on a Hill, far blazing, as a Mount	Par Lost 5.757
Monarchie over such as live by right	Par Lost 5.795
Such as he pleasd, and circumscrib'd thir being?	Par Lost 5.825
As by his Word the mighty Father made	Par Lost 5.836
None seconded, as out of season judg'd,	Par Lost 5.850
We know no time when we were not as now;	Par Lost 5.859
He said, and as the sound of waters deep	Par Lost 5.872
Such as in highest Heav'n, arrayd in Gold	Par Lost 6.13
Thir nimble tread, as when the total kind	Par Lost 6.73
Unanimous, as sons of one great Sire	Par Lost 6.95
High in the midst exalted as a God	Par Lost 6.99
As both thir deeds compar'd this day shall prove.	Par Lost 6.170
Against his worthier, as thine now serve thee,	Par Lost 6.180
From mee returnd, as erst thou saidst, from flight,	Par Lost 6.187
His massie Spear upstaid; as if on Earth	Par Lost 6.195
And clamour such as heard in Heav'n till now	Par Lost 6.208
As each divided Legion might have seemd	Par Lost 6.230
Each Warriour single as in Chief, expert	Par Lost 6.233
As onely in his arm the moment lay	Par Lost 6.239
Surceas'd, and glad as hoping here to end	Par Lost 6.258
Unnam'd in Heav'n, now plenteous, as thou seest	Par Lost 6.263
Of such commotion, such as to set forth	Par Lost 6.310
As not of power, at once; nor odds appeerd	Par Lost 6.319
Sanguin, such as Celestial Spirits may bleed,	Par Lost 6.333
Vital in every part, not as frail man	Par Lost 6.345
All Intellect, all Sense, and as they please,	Par Lost 6.351
Assume, as likes them best, condense or rare.	Par Lost 6.353
Till now not known, but known as soon contemnd,	Par Lost 6.432
Of evil then so small as easie think	Par Lost 6.437
As one he stood escap't from cruel fight,	Par Lost 6.448
Enjoyment of our right as Gods; yet hard	Par Lost 6.452
These things, as not to mind from whence they grow	Par Lost 6.477
Such implements of mischief as shall dash	Par Lost 6.488
Do as you have in charge, and briefly touch	Par Lost 6.566
Though standing else as Rocks, but down they fell	Par Lost 6.593
Have easily as Spirits evaded swift	Par Lost 6.596
As they would dance, yet for a dance they seemd	Par Lost 6.615
Such as we might perceive amus'd them all,	Par Lost 6.623
Light as the Lightning glimps they ran, they flew,	Par Lost 6.642
Two dayes, as we compute the dayes of Heav'n,	Par Lost 6.685
As likeliest was, when two such Foes met arm'd;	Par Lost 6.688
With Mountains as with Weapons arm'd, which makes	Par Lost 6.697
There let them learn, as likes them, to despise	Par Lost 6.717
As is most just; this I my Glorie account,	Par Lost 6.726
Thy terrors, as I put thy mildness on,	Par Lost 6.735

As(*cont*)

Had wondrous, as with Starrs thir bodies all	Par Lost 6.754
And as ye have receivd, so have ye don	Par Lost 6.805
Of his fierce Chariot rowld, as with the sound	Par Lost 6.829
Gloomie as Night; under his burning Wheeles	Par Lost 6.832
Before him, such as in thir Soules infix'd	Par Lost 6.837
Thrown on them as a shelter from his ire.	Par Lost 6.843
The overthrown he rais'd, and as a Heard	Par Lost 6.856
With Jubilie advanc'd; and as they went,	Par Lost 6.884
As a despite don against the most High,	Par Lost 6.906
Least from this flying Steed unrein'd, (as once	Par Lost 7.17
So unimaginable as hate in Heav'n,	Par Lost 7.54
Driv'n back redounded as a flood on those	Par Lost 7.57
Before his memorie, as one whose drouth	Par Lost 7.66
Our knowing, as to highest wisdom seemd,	Par Lost 7.83
But Knowledge is as food, and needs no less	Par Lost 7.126
1669 'a food'	
Wisdom to Folly, as Nourishment to Winde.	Par Lost 7.130
So told as earthly notion can receave.	Par Lost 7.179
Outrageous as a Sea, dark, wasteful, wilde,	Par Lost 7.212
And surging waves, as Mountains to assault	Par Lost 7.214
Dividing: for as Earth, so he the World	Par Lost 7.269
The Earth was form'd, but in the Womb as yet	Par Lost 7.276
So high as heav'd the tumid Hills, so low	Par Lost 7.288
As drops on dust conglobing from the drie;	Par Lost 7.292
On the swift flouds: as Armies at the call	Par Lost 7.295
Rose as in Dance the stately Trees, and spred	Par Lost 7.324
And let them be for Lights as I ordaine	Par Lost 7.343
And sowd with Starrs the Heav'n thick as a field:	Par Lost 7.358
Hither as to thir Fountain other Starrs	Par Lost 7.364
Thir Brood as numerous hatch, from the Egg that soon	Par Lost 7.418
Floats, as they pass, fann'd with unnumber'd plumes:	Par Lost 7.432
As from his Laire the wilde Beast where he wonns	Par Lost 7.457
His hinder parts, then springs as broke from Bonds,	Par Lost 7.465
The Libbard, and the Tyger, as the Moale	Par Lost 7.467
As Plants: ambiguous between Sea and Land	Par Lost 7.473
These as a line thir long dimension drew,	Par Lost 7.480
Her motions, as the great first-Movers hand	Par Lost 7.500
And Brute as other Creatures, but endu'd	Par Lost 7.507
Is yet distinct by name, thence, as thou know'st	Par Lost 7.536
And pavement Starrs, as Starrs to thee appeer,	Par Lost 7.578
Which nightly as a circling Zone thou seest	Par Lost 7.580
As resting on that day from all his work,	Par Lost 7.593
Then as new wak't thus gratefully repli'd.	Par Lost 8.4
1667 'To whom thus *Adam*'	
With wonder, but delight, and, as is due,	Par Lost 8.11
As Tribute such a sumless journey brought	Par Lost 8.36
Yet went she not, as not with such discourse	Par Lost 8.48
Not unattended, for on her as Queen	Par Lost 8.60
Is as the Book of God before thee set,	Par Lost 8.67
To the terrestrial Moon be as a Starr	Par Lost 8.142
Enlightning her by Day, as she by Night	Par Lost 8.143
As Clouds, and Clouds may rain, and Rain produce	Par Lost 8.146
Of other Creatures, as him pleases best,	Par Lost 8.169
For I that Day was absent, as befell,	Par Lost 8.229
For state, as Sovran King, and to enure	Par Lost 8.239
Induc'd me. As new wak't from soundest sleep	Par Lost 8.253
As thitherward endevoring, and upright	Par Lost 8.260
With supple joints, and lively vigour led:	Par Lost 8.269
1667 'as'	
And over Fields and Waters, as in Aire	Par Lost 8.301
Before mine Eyes all real, as the dream	Par Lost 8.310
To thee and to thy Race I give; as Lords	Par Lost 8.339
As thus he spake, each Bird and Beast behold	Par Lost 8.349
I nam'd them, as they pass'd, and understood	Par Lost 8.352
As with a smile more bright'nd, thus repli'd.	Par Lost 8.368
Such as I seek, fit to participate	Par Lost 8.390
And no such companie as then thou saw'st	Par Lost 8.446
As with an object that excels the sense,	Par Lost 8.456
By Nature as in aide, and clos'd mine eyes.	Par Lost 8.459
Abstract as in a transe methought I saw,	Par Lost 8.462
Such as I saw her in my dream, adornd	Par Lost 8.482
As us'd or not, works in the mind no change,	Par Lost 8.525
As one intended first, not after made	Par Lost 8.555
About her, as a guard Angelic plac't.	Par Lost 8.559
Less excellent, as thou thy self perceav'st.	Par Lost 8.566
So much delights me as those graceful acts,	Par Lost 8.600
As Flesh to mix with Flesh, or Soul with Soul.	Par Lost 8.629
With Man, as with his Friend, familiar us'd	Par Lost 9.2
Downward as farr Antartic; and in length	Par Lost 9.79
As from his wit and native suttletie	Par Lost 9.93
More justly, Seat worthier of Gods, as built	Par Lost 9.100
Light above Light, for thee alone, as seems,	Par Lost 9.105
Of sacred influence: As God in Heav'n	Par Lost 9.107
Torment within me, as from the hateful siege	Par Lost 9.121
As I, though thereby worse to me redound:	Par Lost 9.128
Follow, as to him linkt in weal or woe,	Par Lost 9.133
Descend to? who aspires must down as low	Par Lost 9.169
As high he soard, obnoxious first or last	Par Lost 9.170
Now when as sacred Light began to dawne	Par Lost 9.192
1667 'whenas'	
Labour, as to debarr us when we need	Par Lost 9.236
Will keep from Wilderness with ease, as wide	Par Lost 9.245
As we need walk, till younger hands ere long	Par Lost 9.246
As one who loves, and some unkindness meets,	Par Lost 9.271
As in a shadie nook I stood behind,	Par Lost 9.277
As wee, not capable of death or paine,	Par Lost 9.283
As not secure to single or combin'd.	Par Lost 9.339

As(*cont*)

O Woman, best are all things as the will	Par Lost 9.343
Not keeping strictest watch, as she was warnd.	Par Lost 9.363
Though not as shee with Bow and Quiver armd,	Par Lost 9.390
But with such Gardning Tools as Art yet rude,	Par Lost 9.391
Repeated, shee to him as oft engag'd	Par Lost 9.400
As one who long in populous City pent,	Par Lost 9.445
Prone on the ground, as since, but on his reare,	Par Lost 9.497
At first, as one who sought access, but feard	Par Lost 9.511
As when a Ship by skilful Stearsman wrought	Par Lost 9.513
Veres oft, as oft so steers, and shifts her Saile;	Par Lost 9.515
Of rusling Leaves, but minded not, as us'd	Par Lost 9.519
But as in gaze admiring: Oft he bowd	Par Lost 9.524
I was at first as other Beasts that graze	Par Lost 9.571
As was my food, nor aught but food discern'd	Par Lost 9.573
As leaves a greater store of Fruit untoucht,	Par Lost 9.621
Bright'ns his Crest, as when a wandring Fire,	Par Lost 9.634
New part puts on, and as to passion mov'd,	Par Lost 9.667
Rais'd, as of som great matter to begin.	Par Lost 9.669
As when of old som Orator renound	Par Lost 9.670
Somtimes in highth began, as no delay	Par Lost 9.675
Op'nd and cleerd, and ye shall be as Gods,	Par Lost 9.708
Knowing both Good and Evil as they know.	Par Lost 9.709
That ye should be as Gods, since I as Man,	Par Lost 9.710
As they, participating God-like food?	Par Lost 9.717
And yet unknown, is as not had at all.	Par Lost 9.757
Regarded, such delight till then, as seemd,	Par Lost 9.787
And hight'nd as with Wine, jocond and boon,	Par Lost 9.793
And thy fair Fruit let hang, as to no end	Par Lost 9.798
In knowledge, as the Gods who all things know;	Par Lost 9.804
As yet my change, and give him to partake	Par Lost 9.818
But first low Reverence don, as to the power	Par Lost 9.835
As Reapers oft are wont thir Harvest Queen.	Par Lost 9.842
This Tree is not as we are told, a Tree	Par Lost 9.863
Or not restraind as wee, or not obeying,	Par Lost 9.868
Not dead, as we are threatn'd, but thenceforth	Par Lost 9.870
For bliss, as thou hast part, to me is bliss,	Par Lost 9.879
May joyne us, equal Joy, as equal Love;	Par Lost 9.882
On th' other side, *Adam*, soon as he heard	Par Lost 9.888
So having said, as one from sad dismay	Par Lost 9.917
Lives, as thou saidst, and gaines to live as Man	Par Lost 9.933
To us, as likely tasting to attaine	Par Lost 9.935
Consort with thee, Death is to mee as Life;	Par Lost 9.954
Had so enobl'd, as of choice to incurr	Par Lost 9.992
Earth trembl'd from her entrails, as again	Par Lost 9.1000
As with new Wine intoxicated both	Par Lost 9.1008
As wantonly repaid; in Lust they burne:	Par Lost 9.1015
As meet is, after such delicious Fare;	Par Lost 9.1028
Soon as the force of that fallacious Fruit,	Par Lost 9.1046
As from unrest, and each the other viewing,	Par Lost 9.1052
How dark'nd; innocence, that as a veile	Par Lost 9.1054
Confounded long they sate, as struck'n mute,	Par Lost 9.1064
And brown as Evening: Cover me ye Pines,	Par Lost 9.1088
But let us now, as in bad plight, devise	Par Lost 9.1091
There sit not, and reproach us as unclean,	Par Lost 9.1098
But such as at this day to *Indians* known	Par Lost 9.1102
They gatherd, broad as *Amazonian* Targe,	Par Lost 9.1111
Thus fenc't, and as they thought, thir shame in part	Par Lost 9.1119
With me, as I besought thee, when that strange	Par Lost 9.1135
Remaind still happie, not as now, despoild	Par Lost 9.1138
Of wandring, as thou call'st it, which who knows	Par Lost 9.1146
But might as ill have happ'nd thou being by,	Par Lost 9.1147
Fraud in the Serpent, speaking as he spake;	Par Lost 9.1150
As good have grown there still a liveless Rib.	Par Lost 9.1154
Being as I am, why didst not thou the Head	Par Lost 9.1155
Going into such danger as thou saidst?	Par Lost 9.1157
And am I now upbraided, as the cause	Par Lost 9.1168
Entrance unseen. Soon as th' unwelcome news	Par Lost 10.21
Because not yet inflicted, as he fear'd,	Par Lost 10.51
Justice shall not return as bountie scorn'd.	Par Lost 10.54
Justice with Mercie, as may illustrate most	Par Lost 10.78
And gav'st me as thy perfet gift, so good,	Par Lost 10.138
Were such as under Government well seem'd,	Par Lost 10.154
As vitiated in Nature: more to know	Par Lost 10.169
Though in mysterious terms, judg'd as then best:	Par Lost 10.173
As when he wash'd his servants feet so now	Par Lost 10.215
As Father of his Familie he clad	Par Lost 10.216
Or as the Snake with youthful Coate repaid;	Par Lost 10.218
In glory as of old, to him appeas'd	Par Lost 10.226
Or transmigration, as thir lot shall lead.	Par Lost 10.261
Of mortal change on Earth. As when a flock	Par Lost 10.273
Solid or slimie, as in raging Sea	Par Lost 10.286
As when two Polar Winds blowing adverse	Par Lost 10.289
As with a Trident smote, and fix't as firm	Par Lost 10.295
As *Delos* floating once; the rest his look	Par Lost 10.296
And with *Asphaltic* slime; broad as the Gate,	Par Lost 10.298
Thy Trophies, which thou view'st as not thine own,	Par Lost 10.355
As Battel hath adjudg'd, from this new World	Par Lost 10.377
As when the *Tartar* from his *Russian* Foe	Par Lost 10.431
At last as from a Cloud his fulgent head	Par Lost 10.449
As Lords, a spacious World, to our native Heaven	Par Lost 10.467
To rule, as over all he should have rul'd.	Par Lost 10.493
Alike, to Serpents all as accessories	Par Lost 10.520
Down fell both Spear and Shield, down they as fast,	Par Lost 10.542
As in thir crime. Thus was th' applause they meant,	Par Lost 10.545
Hunger and thirst constraining, drugd as oft,	Par Lost 10.568
Into the same illusion, not as Man	Par Lost 10.571
That laugh, as if transported with some fit	Par Lost 10.626

As*(cont)*

Sung *Halleluia*, as the sound of Seas,	Par Lost 10.642
As sorted best with present things. The Sun	Par Lost 10.651
As might affect the Earth with cold and heat	Par Lost 10.653
As deep as *Capricorne*, to bring in change	Par Lost 10.677
From cold *Estotiland*, and South as farr	Par Lost 10.686
The Sun, as from *Thyestean* Banquet, turn'd	Par Lost 10.688
From *Serraliona;* thwart of these as fierce	Par Lost 10.703
On mee as on thir natural center light	Par Lost 10.740
In this delicious Garden? as my Will	Par Lost 10.746
As in my Mothers lap? there I should rest	Par Lost 10.778
Impossible is held, as Argument	Par Lost 10.800
That Death be not one stroak, as I suppos'd,	Par Lost 10.809
On mee, mee onely, as the sourse and spring	Par Lost 10.832
Through the still Night, not now, as ere man fell,	Par Lost 10.846
Curs'd his Creation, Death as oft accus'd	Par Lost 10.852
Befits thee with him leagu'd, thy self as false	Par Lost 10.868
Crooked by nature, bent, as now appears,	Par Lost 10.885
Well if thrown out, as supernumerarie	Par Lost 10.887
With Men as Angels without Feminine,	Par Lost 10.893
As some misfortune brings him, or mistake,	Par Lost 10.900
As joyn'd in injuries, one enmitie	Par Lost 10.925
As one disarm'd, his anger all he lost,	Par Lost 10.945
Unwarie, and too desirous, as before,	Par Lost 10.947
His full wrauth whose thou feelst as yet lest part,	Par Lost 10.951
Restor'd by thee, vile as I am, to place	Par Lost 10.971
As in our evils, and of easier choice.	Par Lost 10.978
Had entertaind, as di'd her Cheeks with pale.	Par Lost 10.1009
Or if thou covet death, as utmost end	Par Lost 10.1020
Resolv'd, as thou proposest; so our Foe	Par Lost 10.1038
The Air attrite to Fire, as late the Clouds	Par Lost 10.1073
Beseeching him, so as we need not fear	Par Lost 10.1082
Made one with me as I with thee am one.	Par Lost 11.44
As a distemper, gross to aire as gross,	Par Lost 11.53
And mortal food, as may dispose him best	Par Lost 11.54
As how with peccant Angels late they saw;	Par Lost 11.70
As I shall thee enlighten, intermix	Par Lost 11.115
So prevalent as to concerne the mind	Par Lost 11.144
As *Raphael*, that I should much confide,	Par Lost 11.235
Not in his shape Celestial, but as Man	Par Lost 11.239
As in a glistering *Zodiac* hung the Sword,	Par Lost 11.247
As from his face I shall be hid, deprivd	Par Lost 11.316
God is as here, and will be found alike	Par Lost 11.350
As once thou slepst, while Shee to life was formd.	Par Lost 11.369
Ith' midst an Altar as the Land-mark stood	Par Lost 11.432
Uncull'd, as came to hand; a Shepherd next	Par Lost 11.436
Whereat hee inlie rag'd, and as they talk'd,	Par Lost 11.444
Some, as thou saw'st, by violent stroke shall die,	Par Lost 11.471
With vows, as thir chief good, and final hope.	Par Lost 11.493
Created, as thou art, to nobler end	Par Lost 11.605
Did, as thou sawst, receave, to walk with God	Par Lost 11.707
Marrying or prostituting, as befell,	Par Lost 11.716
Conversion and Repentance, as to Souls	Par Lost 11.724
Came seavens, and pairs, and enterd in, as taught	Par Lost 11.735
And sunk thee as thy Sons; till gently reard	Par Lost 11.758
Though comfortless, as when a Father mourns	Par Lost 11.760
Shall build a wondrous Ark, as thou beheldst,	Par Lost 11.819
Wrinkl'd the face of Deluge, as decai'd;	Par Lost 11.843
As after thirst, which made thir flowing shrink	Par Lost 11.846
His Sluces, as the Heav'n his windows shut.	Par Lost 11.849
And now the tops of Hills as Rocks appeer;	Par Lost 11.852
As present, Heav'nly instructer, I revive	Par Lost 11.871
Distended as the Brow of God appeas'd,	Par Lost 11.880
Or serve they as a flourie verge to binde	Par Lost 11.881
As one who in his journey bates at Noone, line not in 1667 edition	Par Lost 12.1
And Man as from a second stock proceed.	Par Lost 12.7
With Warr and hostile snare such as refuse	Par Lost 12.31
Before the Lord, as in despite of Heav'n,	Par Lost 12.34
As mockt they storm; great laughter was in Heav'n	Par Lost 12.59
Who oft as undeservedly enthrall	Par Lost 12.94
Thus will this latter, as the former World,	Par Lost 12.105
As to forsake the living God, and fall	Par Lost 12.118
In prospect, as I point them; on the shoare	Par Lost 12.143
To stop thir overgrowth, as inmate guests	Par Lost 12.166
Humbles his stubborn heart, but still as Ice	Par Lost 12.193
As on drie land between two christal walls,	Par Lost 12.197
Ordaine them Lawes; part such as appertaine	Par Lost 12.230
Seaven Lamps as in a Zodiac representing	Par Lost 12.255
Will reign among them, as of thee begot;	Par Lost 12.286
From whom as oft he saves them penitent	Par Lost 12.319
Foretold to *Abraham*, as in whom shall trust	Par Lost 12.328
Such follow him, as shall be registerd	Par Lost 12.335
God, as to leave them, and expose thir Land,	Par Lost 12.339
To *David*, stablisht as the dayes of Heav'n.	Par Lost 12.347
Surcharg'd, as had like grief bin dew'd in tears,	Par Lost 12.373
As of a Duel, or the local wounds	Par Lost 12.387
Out of his grave, fresh as the dawning light,	Par Lost 12.423
His death for Man, as many as offerd Life	Par Lost 12.425
As at the Worlds great period; and our Sire	Par Lost 12.467
And oft supported so as shall amaze	Par Lost 12.496
As did thir Lord before them. Thus they win	Par Lost 12.502
They die; but in thir room, as they forewarne,	Par Lost 12.507
As in his presence, ever to observe	Par Lost 12.563
Gliding meteorous, as Ev'ning Mist	Par Lost 12.629
Fierce as a Comet; which with torrid heat,	Par Lost 12.634
And vapour as the *Libyan* Air adust,	Par Lost 12.635
Led them direct, and down the Cliff as fast	Par Lost 12.639

As*(cont)*

As thou art wont, my prompted Song else mute,	Par Reg 1.12
To the flood *Jordan*, came as then obscure,	Par Reg 1.24
As to his worthier, and would have resign'd	Par Reg 1.27
How many Ages, as the years of men,	Par Reg 1.48
To do him honour as their King; all come,	Par Reg 1.75
I as all others to his Baptism came,	Par Reg 1.273
As much his greater, and was hardly won;	Par Reg 1.279
But as I rose out of the laving stream,	Par Reg 1.280
But openly begin, as best becomes	Par Reg 1.288
Lodg'd in his brest, as well might recommend	Par Reg 1.301
Following, as seem'd, the quest of some stray Ewe,	Par Reg 1.315
Knowing who I am, as I know who thou art?	Par Reg 1.356
To his destruction, as I had in charge.	Par Reg 1.376
As a poor miserable captive thrall,	Par Reg 1.411
And not well understood as good not known?	Par Reg 1.437
And tuneable as Silvan Pipe or Song;	Par Reg 1.480
I bid not or forbid; do as thou find'st	Par Reg 1.495
And as the days increas'd, increas'd thir doubt:	Par Reg 2.12
And for a time caught up to God, as once	Par Reg 2.14
Therefore as those young Prophets then with care	Par Reg 2.18
And fears as eminent, above the lot	Par Reg 2.70
Full grown to Man, acknowledg'd, as I hear,	Par Reg 2.83
But trouble, as old *Simeon* plain fore-told,	Par Reg 2.87
I lost him, but so found, as well I saw	Par Reg 2.97
I, as I undertook, and with the vote	Par Reg 2.129
As the noon Skie; more like to Goddesses	Par Reg 2.156
As the Magnetic hardest Iron draws.	Par Reg 2.168
As sitting Queen ador'd on Beauties Throne,	Par Reg 2.212
To enamour, as the Zone of *Venus* once	Par Reg 2.214
Seated as on the top of Vertues hill,	Par Reg 2.217
His constancy, with such as have more shew	Par Reg 2.226
No advantage, and his strength as oft assay.	Par Reg 2.234
And dream'd, as appetite is wont to dream,	Par Reg 2.264
Or as a guest with *Daniel* at his pulse.	Par Reg 2.278
As lightly from his grassy Couch up rose	Par Reg 2.282
Not rustic as before, but seemlier clad,	Par Reg 2.299
As one in City, or Court, or Palace bred,	Par Reg 2.300
As story tells, have trod this Wilderness;	Par Reg 2.307
They all had need, I as thou seest have none.	Par Reg 2.318
Would'st thou not eat? Thereafter as I like	Par Reg 2.321
To treat thee as beseems, and as her Lord	Par Reg 2.335
He spake no dream, for as his words had end,	Par Reg 2.337
I can at will, doubt not, as soon as thou,	Par Reg 2.383
May also in this poverty as soon	Par Reg 2.451
A while as mute confounded what to say,	Par Reg 3.2
Thy Counsel would be as the Oracle	Par Reg 3.13
All treasures and all gain esteem as dross,	Par Reg 3.29
And know not whom, but as one leads the other;	Par Reg 3.53
As thou to thy reproach mayst well remember,	Par Reg 3.66
Shall I seek glory then, as vain men seek	Par Reg 3.105
Though chiefly not for glory as prime end,	Par Reg 3.123
Of glory as thou wilt, said he, so deem,	Par Reg 3.150
Abominations rather, as did once	Par Reg 3.162
Interposition, as a summers cloud.	Par Reg 3.222
(As he who seeking Asses found a Kingdom)	Par Reg 3.242
As far as *Indus* East, *Euphrates* West,	Par Reg 3.272
As antient, but rebuilt by him who twice	Par Reg 3.281
With bridges rivers proud, as with a yoke;	Par Reg 3.334
Besieg'd *Albracca*, as Romances tell;	Par Reg 3.339
Endeavour, as thy Father *David* did,	Par Reg 3.353
By my advice, as nearer and of late	Par Reg 3.364
Thus long from *Israel;* serving as of old	Par Reg 3.378
My brethren, as thou call'st them; those Ten Tribes	Par Reg 3.403
As for those captive Tribes, themselves were they	Par Reg 3.414
Who freed, as to thir antient Patrimony,	Par Reg 3.428
As the Red Sea and *Jordan* once he cleft,	Par Reg 3.438
But as a man who had been matchless held	Par Reg 4.10
Or as a swarm of flies in vintage time,	Par Reg 4.15
Beat off, returns as oft with humming sound;	Par Reg 4.17
Indu'd with Regal Vertues as thou art,	Par Reg 4.98
Or as a stone that shall to pieces dash	Par Reg 4.149
On what I offer set as high esteem,	Par Reg 4.160
And worship me as thy superior Lord,	Par Reg 4.167
As offer them to me the Son of God,	Par Reg 4.190
That I fall down and worship thee as God?	Par Reg 4.192
Therefore let pass, as they are transitory,	Par Reg 4.209
Advise thee, gain them as thou canst, or not.	Par Reg 4.211
As by that early action may be judg'd,	Par Reg 4.215
As morning shews the day. Be famous then	Par Reg 4.221
By wisdom; as thy Empire must extend,	Par Reg 4.222
Ruling them by perswasion as thou mean'st,	Par Reg 4.230
These here revolve, or, as thou lik'st, at home,	Par Reg 4.281
As fearing God nor man, contemning all	Par Reg 4.304
Fortune and Fate, as one regardless quite	Par Reg 4.317
As Children gathering pibles on the shore.	Par Reg 4.330
As in our native Language can I find	Par Reg 4.333
As varnish on a Harlots cheek, the rest,	Par Reg 4.344
Thir Orators thou then extoll'st, as those	Par Reg 4.353
And lovers of thir Country, as may seem;	Par Reg 4.355
As men divinely taught, and better teaching	Par Reg 4.357
Nor when, eternal sure, as without end,	Par Reg 4.391
As day-light sunk, and brought in lowring night	Par Reg 4.398
Though rooted deep as high, and sturdiest Oaks	Par Reg 4.417
As Earth and Skie would mingle; but my self	Par Reg 4.453
As dangerous to the pillard frame of Heaven,	Par Reg 4.455
Are to the main as inconsiderable,	Par Reg 4.457
And harmless, if not wholsom, as a sneeze	Par Reg 4.458

As(*cont*)

Yet as being oft times noxious where they light	Par Reg 4.460
May warn thee, as a sure fore-going sign.	Par Reg 4.483
And threatning nigh; what they can do as signs	Par Reg 4.489
As false portents, not sent from God, but thee;	Par Reg 4.491
Proof against all temptation as a rock	Par Reg 4.533
Of Adamant, and as a Center, firm	Par Reg 4.534
As when Earths Son *Antaeus* (to compare	Par Reg 4.563
And as that *Theban* Monster that propos'd	Par Reg 4.572
As on a floating couch through the blithe Air,	Par Reg 4.585
Or thirst, and as he fed, Angelic Quires	Par Reg 4.593
As in a fiery column charioting	Samson 27
As of a person separate to God,	Samson 31
Within doors, or without, still as a fool,	Samson 77
And silent as the Moon,	Samson 87
To such a tender ball as th' eye confin'd?	Samson 94
And not as feeling through all parts diffus'd,	Samson 96
As in the land of darkness yet in light,	Samson 99
As one past hope, abandon'd,	Samson 120
Who tore the Lion, as the Lion tears the Kid,	Samson 128
And are as Balm to fester'd wounds.	Samson 186
Then of thine own Tribe fairer, or as fair,	Samson 217
At least of thy own Nation, and as noble.	Samson 218
Into their hands, and they as gladly yield me	Samson 259
As thir Deliverer; if he aught begin,	Samson 274
As to his own edicts, found contradicting,	Samson 301
As if they would confine th' interminable,	Samson 307
With careful step, Locks white as doune,	Samson 327
As I suppose, towards your once gloried friend,	Samson 334
Chor. As signal now in low dejected state,	Samson 338
As earst in highest, behold him where he lies.	Samson 339
And such a Son as all Men hail'd me happy;	Samson 354
And as a blessing with such pomp adorn'd?	Samson 357
As Graces, draw a Scorpions tail behind?	Samson 360
Ordain'd thy nurture holy, as of a Plant;	Samson 362
He should not so o'rewhelm, and as a thrall	Samson 370
As vile hath been my folly, who have profan'd	Samson 377
As was my former servitude, ignoble,	Samson 416
To *Dagon*, as their God who hath deliver'd	Samson 437
Such a discomfit, as shall quite despoil him	Samson 469
I as a Prophecy receive: for God,	Samson 473
As I deserve, pay on my punishment;	Samson 489
All friendship, and avoided as a blab,	Samson 495
Then who self-rigorous chooses death as due;	Samson 513
Sam. His pardon I implore; but as for life,	Samson 521
After the brunt of battel, can as easie	Samson 583
As on entrails, joints, and limbs,	Samson 614
As a lingring disease,	Samson 618
To deaths benumming Opium as my only cure.	Samson 630
But now hath cast me off as never known,	Samson 641
Extolling Patience as the truest fortitude;	Samson 654
Not evenly, as thou rul'st	Samson 671
Grow up and perish, as the summer flie,	Samson 676
But such as thou hast solemnly elected,	Samson 678
Then as repentant to submit, beseech,	Samson 751
As I by thee, to Ages an example.	Samson 765
First granting, as I do, it was a weakness	Samson 773
As her at *Timna*, sought by all means therefore	Samson 795
As thou art strong, inflexible as steel.	Samson 816
Such pardon therefore as I give my folly,	Samson 825
Knowing, as needs I must, by thee betray'd?	Samson 840
It was not gold, as to my charge thou lay'st,	Samson 849
Vertue, as I thought, truth, duty so enjoyning.	Samson 870
Bin, as it ought, sincere, it would have taught thee	Samson 874
My enemies, lov'd thee, as too well thou knew'st,	Samson 878
Then, as since then, thy countries foe profest:	Samson 884
Deceiveable, in most things as a child	Samson 942
Haughty as is his pile high-built and proud.	Samson 1069
As these perhaps, yet wish it had not been,	Samson 1077
As *Og* or *Anak* and the *Emims* old	Samson 1080
Sam. Such usage as your honourable Lords	Samson 1108
As good for nothing else, no better service	Samson 1163
As a League-breaker and deliver'd bound	Samson 1184
As on my enemies, where ever chanc'd,	Samson 1202
As a league-breaker gave up bound, presum'd	Samson 1209
As a petty enterprise of small enforce.	Samson 1223
The righteous and all such as honour Truth;	Samson 1276
Swift as the lightning glance he executes	Samson 1284
To appear as fits before th' illustrious Lords.	Samson 1318
And hamper thee, as thou shalt come of force,	Samson 1397
To such as owe them absolute subjection;	Samson 1405
Of me as of a common Enemy,	Samson 1416
As in thy wond'rous actions hath been seen.	Samson 1440
I heard all as I came, the City rings	Samson 1449
In both which we, as next participate.	Samson 1507
As if the whole inhabitation perish'd,	Samson 1512
Chor. Yet God hath wrought things as incredible	Samson 1532
An *Ebrew*, as I guess, and of our Tribe.	Samson 1540
As at some distance from the place of horrour,	Samson 1550
Abortive as the first-born bloom of spring	Samson 1576
And as the gates I enter'd with Sun-rise,	Samson 1597
Was *Samson* as a public servant brought,	Samson 1615
(For so from such as nearer stood we heard)	Samson 1631
As over-tir'd to let him lean a while	Samson 1632
And eyes fast fixt he stood, as one who pray'd,	Samson 1637
I have perform'd, as reason was, obeying,	Samson 1641
As with amaze shall strike all who behold.	Samson 1645
As with the force of winds and waters pent,	Samson 1647

As(*cont*)

As thir own ruin on themselves to invite,	Samson 1684
And as an ev'ning Dragon came,	Samson 1692
Of tame villatic Fowl; but as an Eagle	Samson 1695
Deprest, and overthrown, as seem'd,	Samson 1698
With God not parted from him, as was feard,	Samson 1719
Coasting the *Tyrrhene* shore, as the winds listed,	Mask 49
To quench the drouth of *Phoebus*, which as they taste	Mask 66
Soon as the Potion works, their human count'nance,	Mask 68
All other parts remaining as they were,	Mask 72
Swift as the Sparkle of a glancing Star,	Mask 80
As now I do: But first I must put off	Mask 82
Be well stock't with as fair a herd as graz'd	Mask 152
Such as the jocond Flute, or gamesom Pipe	Mask 173
Stept as they se'd to the next Thicket side	Mask 185
As the kind hospitable Woods provide.	Mask 187
This is the place, as well as I may guess,	Mask 201
line not in Bridgewater ms	
Are but as slavish officers of vengeance,	Mask 218
line not in Bridgewater ms	
Such noise as I can make to be heard farthest	Mask 227
Who as they sung, would take the prison'd soul,	Mask 256
Bridgewater ms 'whoe when'	
La. As smooth as *Hebe*'s their unrazor'd lips.	Mask 290
Their port was more then human, as they stood;	Mask 297
And as I past, I worshipt; if those you seek	Mask 302
As that the single want of light and noise	Mask 369
(Not being in danger, as I trust she is not)	Mask 370
And sits as safe as in a Senat house,	Mask 389
You may as well spred out the unsun'd heaps	Mask 398
And tell me it is safe, as bid me hope	Mask 400
Inferr, as if I thought my sisters state	Mask 408
As you imagine, she has a hidden strength	Mask 415
As loath to leave the body that it lov'd,	Mask 473
Not harsh, and crabbed as dull fools suppose,	Mask 477
But musical as is *Apollo*'s lute,	Mask 478
As a stray'd Ewe, or to pursue the stealth	Mask 503
Or our neglect, we lost her as we came.	Mask 510
Curs'd as his life. *Spir*. Alas good ventrous youth,	Mask 609
Trinity ms 'downe to the hips' ←'lowest hips' ←'hipps'	
Bridgewater ms 'downe to the hipps'	
1637 'Downe to the hipps'	
As to make this relation? *Spir*. Care and utmost shifts	Mask 617
But in another Countrey, as he said,	Mask 632
line not in Bridgewater ms	
And bad me keep it as of sovran use	Mask 639
(As I will give you when we go) you may	Mask 648
Trinity ms 'when we goe' ←'on the way' ←'as wee goe'	
And you a statue; or as *Daphne* was	Mask 661
Brisk as the *April* buds in Primrose-season.	Mask 671
Is of such power to stir up joy as this,	Mask 677
But such as are good men can give good things,	Mask 703
And we should serve him as a grudging master,	Mask 725
As a penurious niggard of his wealth,	Mask 726
And live like Natures bastards, not her sons,	Mask 727
Trinity ms 'like' ←'for' ←'as'	
Would think to charm my judgement, as mine eyes	Mask 758
As if she would her children should be riotous	Mask 763
Dips me all o're, as when the wrath of *Jove*	Mask 803
line not in Bridgewater ms	
line not in Trinity ms	
And, as the old Swain said, she can unlock	Mask 852
To aid a Virgin, such as was her self	Mask 856
That bends not as I tread,	Mask 899
As *Mercury* did first devise	Mask 963
Trinity ms 'as' ←'such as'	
And from thence can soar as soon	Mask 1016
so fares as did forsaken Proserpine	Mask Tr. ms 15.52
soe fares as did forsaken Proserpine	Mask Br. ms 344
As ragged as thy Locks,	Allegro 9
Or whether (as som Sager sing)	Allegro 17
As he met her once a Maying,	Allegro 20
Such as hang on *Hebe*'s cheek,	Allegro 29
Com, and trip it as ye go	Allegro 33
Such sights as youthfull Poets dream	Allegro 129
Such as the meeting soul may pierce	Allegro 138
Such streins as would have won the ear	Allegro 148
As thick and numberless	Penseroso 7
As the gay motes that people the Sun Beams,	Penseroso 8
Black, but such as in esteem,	Penseroso 17
Thou fix them on the earth as fast.	Penseroso 44
And oft, as if her head she bow'd,	Penseroso 71
Such notes as warbled to the string,	Penseroso 106
Not trickt and frounc't as she was wont,	Penseroso 123
With such consort as they keep,	Penseroso 145
And as I wake, sweet musick breath	Penseroso 151
As may with sweetnes, through mine ear,	Penseroso 164
Fair silver-buskind Nymphs as great and good,	Arcades 33
Whom with low reverence I adore as mine,	Arcades 37
Inimitable sounds, yet as we go,	Arcades 78
Follow me as I sing,	Arcades 86
Clad in splendor as befits	Arcades 92
All *Arcadia* hath not seen.	Arcades 109
Trinity ms 'All' ←'As'	
And as he passes turn,	Lycidas 21
As killing as the Canker to the Rose,	Lycidas 45
Were it not better don as others use,	Lycidas 67
As he pronounces lastly on each deed,	Lycidas 83

As(*cont*)
Anow of such as for their bellies sake, Lycidas 114
As if they surely knew their sovran Lord was by. Nativity 60
As his inferiour flame, Nativity 81
As never was by mortall finger strook, Nativity 95
As all their souls in blisfull rapture took: Nativity 98
Such Musick (as 'tis said) Nativity 117
And Heav'n as at som festivall, Nativity 147
As on mount *Sinai* rang Nativity 158
The brutish gods of *Nile* as fast, Nativity 211
As a faint host that hath receiv'd the foil. Psalm 114, 10
As if to shew what creatures Heav'n doth breed, Fair Inf 61
And, if it happen as I did forecast, Vacation 13
Such as may make thee search thy coffers round, Vacation 31
Such as the wise *Demodocus* once told Vacation 48
O're all his Brethren he shall Reign as King, Vacation 75
My plaining vers as lively as before; Passion 47
For when as each thing bad thou hast entomb'd, On Time 9
And Joy shall overtake us as a flood, On Time 13
As once we did, till disproportion'd sin Musick 19
and as your equall raptures temper'd sweet Musick Tr. ms 4.05
'as' ←'whilst'
Bin as compleat as was her praise, Winchester 12
And in his Garland as he stood, Winchester 21
Side-ways as on a dying bed, Winchester 42
As he were prest to death, he cry'd more waight; Another 26
line not in 1640, 1657, 1658 texts
But had his doings lasted as they were, Another 27
As thou from yeer to yeer hast sung too late Sonnet 1, 11
As ever in my great task Masters eye. Sonnet 7, 14
That call Fame on such gentle acts as these, Sonnet 8, 6
Broke him, as that dishonest victory Sonnet 10, 6
As when those Hinds that were transform'd to Froggs Sonnet 12, 5
But as Faith pointed with her golden rod, Sonnet 14, 7
when as they journey'd from this dark abode Sonnet 14, Tr. ms 41.07
Mine as whom washt from spot of child-bed taint, Sonnet 23, 5
And such, as yet once more I trust to have Sonnet 23, 7
Came vested all in white, pure as her mind: Sonnet 23, 9
So clear, as in no face with more delight. Sonnet 23, 12
But O as to embrace me she enclin'd, Sonnet 23, 13
Cropp yee as close as marginall P---s eares Forcers Tr. ms 45.17
He shall be as a tree which planted grows Psalm 1, 7
Not so the wicked, but as chaff which fann'd Psalm 1, 11
As thy possession I on thee bestow Psalm 2, 17
Th' Heathen, and as thy conquest to be sway'd Psalm 2, 18
As in a rocky Cell Psalm 4, 41
As with a shield thou wilt surround Psalm 5, 39
Least as a Lion (and no wonder) Psalm 7, 4
As in a womb, and from that mould Psalm 7, 53
So as above the Heavens thy praise to set Psalm 8, 3
Her Bows as *high as* Cedars tall Psalm 80, 43
That all may pluck her, as they go, Psalm 80, 51
Blow, *as is wont*, in the new Moon Psalm 81, 9
When as he pass'd through Aegypt land; Psalm 81, 19
As other Princes *die*. Psalm 82, 24
And all as one in mind Psalm 83, 18
Do to them as to Midian *bold* Psalm 83, 33
To Sisera, and as *is told* Psalm 83, 35
As dung upon the plain. Psalm 83, 40
As Zeb and Oreb evil sped Psalm 83, 41
As Zeba, and Zalmunna *bled* Psalm 83, 43
My God, oh make them as a wheel Psalm 83, 49
As *when* an *aged* wood takes fire Psalm 83, 53
As through a fruitfull watry Dale Psalm 84, 23
To trespass as before. Psalm 85, 36
Surely to such as do him fear Psalm 85, 37
As ready to expire, Psalm 88, 62
And as in darkness are. Psalm 88, 72
Which once smelt sweet, now stinks as odiously; Prose 4, 2
What hinders? as some teachers give to Boyes Prose 6, 2

Ascalon
Of *Palestine*, in *Gath* and *Ascalon* Par Lost 1.465
ms 'Ascalon'
At *Askalon*, who never did thee harm, Samson 1187

Ascalonite
Spurn'd them to death by Troops. The bold *Ascalonite* Samson 138

Ascend
Hath emptied Heav'n, shall fail to re-ascend Par Lost 1.633
ms 'reascend'
The Signal to ascend, sit lingring here Par Lost 2.56
That in our proper motion we ascend Par Lost 2.75
A Silvan Scene, and as the ranks ascend Par Lost 4.140
Ascend to Heav'n, by merit thine, and see Par Lost 5.80
That singing up to Heaven Gate ascend, Par Lost 5.198
Improv'd by tract of time, and wingd ascend Par Lost 5.498
By steps we may ascend to God. But say, Par Lost 5.512
Ascend my Chariot, guide the rapid Wheeles Par Lost 6.711
Into the Clouds, thir tops ascend the Skie: Par Lost 7.287
By which to heav'nly Love thou maist ascend, Par Lost 8.592
But that from us ought should ascend to Heav'n Par Lost 11.143
Thy mortal passage when it comes. Ascend Par Lost 11.366
Ascend, I follow thee, safe Guide, the path Par Lost 11.371
If so I may attain. So both ascend Par Lost 11.376
The Power of the most High; he shall ascend Par Lost 12.369
Then to the Heav'n of Heav'ns he shall ascend Par Lost 12.451
From slaughter of one foe could not ascend. Samson 1518
With sighs devout ascend Psalm 88, 6

Ascended
Ascended, at his right hand Victorie Par Lost 6.762
While the bright Pomp ascended jubilant. Par Lost 7.564
Th' Angelic Guards ascended, mute and sad Par Lost 10.18
Ascended his high Throne, which under state Par Lost 10.445
Of both my Parents all in flames ascended Samson 25

Ascending
In wealth and luxurie. Th' ascending pile Par Lost 1.722
Ascending, while the North wind sleeps, o'respread Par Lost 2.489
As in a cloudy Chair ascending rides Par Lost 2.930
Ascending by degrees magnificent Par Lost 3.502
Angels ascending and descending, bands Par Lost 3.511
To th' Ocean Iles, and in th' ascending Scale Par Lost 4.354
The glorious Train ascending: He through Heav'n, Par Lost 7.574
Now made a stye, and in his place ascending Par Reg 4.101

Ascends
Of riot ascends above thir loftiest Towrs, Par Lost 1.499
But neither breath of Morn when she ascends Par Lost 4.650

Ascension
In open shew, and with ascention bright Par Lost 10.187

Ascent
We sunk thus low? Th' ascent is easie then; Par Lost 2.81
Of Heav'ns ascent they lift thir Feet, when loe Par Lost 3.486
The Fiend by easie ascent, or aggravate Par Lost 3.524
Now to th' ascent of that steep savage Hill Par Lost 4.172
Conspicuous farr, winding with one ascent Par Lost 4.545
Proportional ascent, which cannot be Par Lost 9.936
To him with swift ascent he up returnd, Par Lost 10.224

Ascribe
Which else to several Sphears thou must ascribe, Par Lost 8.131

Ascribest
Then to thy self ascrib'st the truth fore-told. Par Reg 1.453

Ashamed
Nature asham'd, or better to express, Par Reg 2.332
Asham'd and troubl'd let them be, Psalm 83, 61
And be asham'd, because thou Lord Psalm 86, 63

Ashdod
Rear'd in *Azotus*, dreaded through the Coast Par Lost 1.464
ms 'Azotus'
In *Ecron*, *Gaza*, *Asdod*, and in *Gath* Samson 981

Ashes
The World shall burn, and from her ashes spring Par Lost 3.334
Chewd bitter Ashes, which th' offended taste Par Lost 10.566
From under ashes into sudden flame, Samson 1691
To Heav'n. Their martyr'd blood and ashes sow Sonnet 18, 10

Ashkelon
At *Askalon*, who never did thee harm, Samson 1187

Ashkelonite
Spurn'd them to death by Troops. The bold *Ascalonite* Samson 138

Ashore
May thy billows rowl ashoar Mask 932
Trinity ms 'a shore'
Bridgewater ms 'a shoare'
1637 'a shoare'

Ashtaroth
Of *Baalim* and *Ashtaroth*, those male, Par Lost 1.422
ms 'Ashtaroth'
Came *Astoreth*, whom the *Phoenicians* call'd Par Lost 1.438
ms 'Astoreth'
Of *Egypt*, *Baal* next and *Ashtaroth*, Par Reg 3.417
Har. By *Astaroth* e're long thou shalt lament Samson 1242
And mooned *Ashtaroth*, Nativity 200

Ashy
From out her ashie womb now teem'd, Samson 1703

Asia
Bridging his way, *Europe* with *Asia* joyn'd, Par Lost 10.310
Won *Asia* and the Throne of *Cyrus* held Par Reg 3.33

Asian
From the *Asian* Kings and *Parthian* among these, Par Reg 4.73

Aside
With kisses pure: aside the Devil turnd Par Lost 4.502
Enterd so faire, should turn aside to tread Par Lost 11.630
But here she comes, I fairly step aside Mask 168
He laid aside; and here with us to be, Nativity 12

Ask
Might in that noise reside, of whom to ask Par Lost 2.957
Ask riddance, if we mean to tread with ease; Par Lost 4.632
Why ask ye, and superfluous begin Par Lost 4.832
Or not, who ask what boldness brought him hither Par Lost 4.908
Proceeded thus to ask his Heav'nly Guest. Par Lost 7.69
What wee, not to explore the secrets aske Par Lost 7.95
To ask, nor let thine own inventions hope Par Lost 7.121
Before the Angel, and of him to ask Par Lost 8.53
To ask or search I blame thee not, for Heav'n Par Lost 8.66
Of somthing not unseasonable to ask Par Lost 8.201
Bear with me then, if lawful what I ask; Par Lost 8.614
I ask the rather, and the more admire, Par Reg 1.326
Will ask thee skill; I to thy Fathers house Par Reg 4.552
Ask for this great Deliverer now, and find him Samson 40
Would ask a life to wail, but chief of all, Samson 66
Here I salute thee and thy pardon ask, Vacation 7
If any ask for him, it shall be sed, Carrier 17
I fondly ask; But patience to prevent Sonnet 19, 8
Right onward. What supports me dost thou ask? Sonnet 22, 9
This day; ask of me, and the grant is made; Psalm 2, 16
Ask large enough, and I, *besought*, Psalm 81, 43

Askance
Ey'd them askance, and to himself thus plaind. Par Lost 4.504

Askance*(cont)*
Whom the grand foe with scornful eye askance Par Lost 6.149
Some say he bid his Angels turne ascanse Par Lost 10.668
Asked
That be assur'd, without leave askt of thee: Par Lost 2.685
He ask'd, but all the Heav'nly Quire stood mute, Par Lost 3.217
And such I held thee; but this question askt Par Lost 4.887
In that dark durance: thus much what was askt. Par Lost 4.899
This also thy request with caution askt Par Lost 7.111
And thy request think now fulfill'd, that ask'd Par Lost 7.635
Which they who ask'd have seldom understood, Par Reg 1.436
He ask'd thee, hast thou seen my servant *Job?* Par Reg 3.67
Who gently ask't if he had seen such two, Mask 575
Trinity ms 'askt'
Bridgewater ms 'askt'
He ask'd the Waves, and ask'd the Fellon winds, Lycidas 91
Trinity ms both 'askt'
Asks
Nature hath need of what she asks; yet God Par Reg 2.253
Asleep
Now laid perhaps asleep secure of harme. Par Lost 4.791
Beautie, which whether waking or asleep, Par Lost 5.14
And fell asleep; but O how glad I wak'd Par Lost 5.92
Wearied I fell asleep: but now lead on; Par Lost 12.614
By whispering Windes soon lull'd asleep. Allegro 116
Aslope
Fruit of thy Womb: On mee the Curse aslope Par Lost 10.1053
Asmadai
Then *Asmodeus* with the fishie fume, Par Lost 4.168
Vanquish'd *Adramelec*, and *Asmadai*, Par Lost 6.365
Asmodai
The sensuallest, and after *Asmodai* Par Reg 2.151
Asmodeus
Then *Asmodeus* with the fishie fume, Par Lost 4.168
Vanquish'd *Adramelec*, and *Asmadai*, Par Lost 6.365
The sensuallest, and after *Asmodai* Par Reg 2.151
Asp
Scorpion and Asp, and *Amphisbaena* dire, Par Lost 10.524
Hated not Learning wors then Toad or Asp; Sonnet 11, 13
Aspect
Aspect he rose, and in his rising seem'd Par Lost 2.301
His words here ended, but his meek aspect Par Lost 3.266
Slowly descended, and with right aspect Par Lost 4.541
To whom the Son with calm aspect and cleer Par Lost 5.733
In battailous aspect, and neerer view Par Lost 6.81
Two Planets rushing from aspect maligne Par Lost 6.313
And cloudie in aspect thus answering spake. Par Lost 6.450
In that aspect, and still that distance keepes Par Lost 7.379
Not to incur; but soon his cleer aspect Par Lost 8.336
Bent thir aspect, and whom they wish'd beheld, Par Lost 10.454
From that placid aspect and meek regard, Par Reg 3.217
Aspects
Thir planetarie motions and aspects Par Lost 10.658
Thou told'st me of? What grim aspects are these, Mask 694
Asperses
For hee who tempts, though in vain, at least asperses Par Lost 9.296
Asphaltic
And *Eleale* to th' *Asphaltick* Pool. Par Lost 1.411
ms 'Asphaltick'
And with *Asphaltic* slime; broad as the Gate, Par Lost 10.298
Asphaltus
With *Naphtha* and *Asphaltus* yeilded light Par Lost 1.729
ms 'Asphaltus'
Asphodel
Pansies, and Violets, and Asphodel, Par Lost 9.1040
In nectar'd lavers strew'd with Asphodil, Mask 838
1637 'asphodil'
Trinity ms 'Asphodil' ←'Asphodel'
Bridgewater ms 'Asphodill' ←'Asphodell'
Aspire
To vital Spirits aspire, to animal, Par Lost 5.484
O execrable Son so to aspire Par Lost 12.64
Beyond which was my folly to aspire. Par Lost 12.560
Which way or from what hope dost thou aspire Par Reg 2.417
Yet som there be that by due steps aspire Mask 12
To scorn the sordid world, and unto Heav'n aspire. Fair Inf 63
Aspired
As great might have aspir'd, and me though mean Par Lost 4.62
That to the hight of Deitie aspir'd; Par Lost 9.167
To which my Spirit aspir'd, victorious deeds Par Reg 1.215
Aspirer
Aspirer, but thir thoughts prov'd fond and vain Par Lost 6.90
Aspires
Thus high uplifted beyond hope, aspires Par Lost 2.7
And ignominie, yet to glorie aspires Par Lost 6.383
Descend to? who aspires must down as low Par Lost 9.169
And who attains not, ill aspires to rule Par Reg 2.469
Aspiring
Of Rebel Angels, by whose aid aspiring Par Lost 1.38
Th' aspiring Dominations: thou that day Par Lost 3.392
Equal with Gods; aspiring to be such, Par Lost 4.526
The highth of thy aspiring unoppos'd, Par Lost 6.132
Took envie, and aspiring to his highth, Par Lost 6.793
Of those too high aspiring, who rebelld Par Lost 6.899
Aspramont
Jousted in *Aspramont* or *Montalban*, Par Lost 1.583
ms 'Aspramont'

Ass
The Jaw of a dead Ass, his sword of bone, Samson 143
To have wrought such wonders with an Asses Jaw; Samson 1095
Or left thy carkass where the Ass lay thrown: Samson 1097
Assail
His vertue or weakness which way to assail: Samson 756
For valour to assail, nor by the sword Samson 1165
Or we shall find such Engines to assail Samson 1396
When trouble did thee sore assaile, Psalm 81, 25
Assailant
Assailant on the perched roosts, Samson 1693
Assailed
And with rebounding surge the barrs assaild, Par Lost 10.417
Vertue may be assail'd, but never hurt, Mask 589
Trinity ms 'assayl'd'
Assassinated
Afford me assassinated and betray'd, Samson 1109
Assassin-like
One man, Assassin-like had levied Warr, Par Lost 11.219
Assault
Heav'n, whose high walls fear no assault or Siege, Par Lost 2.343
Cross-barrd and bolted fast, fear no assault, Par Lost 4.190
Fearless assault, and to the brow of Heav'n Par Lost 6.51
Both Battels maine, with ruinous assault Par Lost 6.216
And surging waves, as Mountains to assault Par Lost 7.214
By sly assault; and somwhere nigh at hand Par Lost 9.256
Or daring, first on mee th' assault shall light. Par Lost 9.305
Great Cities by assault: what do these Worthies, Par Reg 3.74
Though all to shivers dash't, the assault renew, Par Reg 4.19
With mention of that name renews th' assault. Samson 331
Boldly assault the necromancers hall; Mask 649
Bridgewater ms 'assaulte'
Assaulted
Ensnar'd, assaulted, overcome, led bound, Samson 365
Assaulting
Assaulting; others from the wall defend Par Lost 11.657
Assaults
Of battel when it rag'd, in all assaults Par Lost 1.277
Born through the hollow dark assaults his eare Par Lost 2.953
Constant, mature, proof against all assaults, Par Lost 10.882
Satans assaults, and quench his fierie darts, Par Lost 12.492
All her assaults, on worthier things intent? Par Reg 2.195
Renewing fresh assaults, amidst his pride Par Reg 4.570
With blandisht parlies, feminine assaults, Samson 403
Hear what assaults I had, what snares besides, Samson 845
Assay
And Man there plac't, with purpose to assay Par Lost 3.90
Thy merited reward, the first assay Par Lost 6.153
Whose taste, too long forborn, at first assay Par Lost 9.747
To Satan; let him tempt and now assay Par Reg 1.143
Through many a hard assay even to the death, Par Reg 1.264
No advantage, and his strength as oft assay. Par Reg 2.234
What I foretold thee, many a hard assay Par Reg 4.478
I will assay, her worth to celebrate, Arcades 80
Assayed
Thrice he assayd, and thrice in spight of scorn, Par Lost 1.619
ms 'assay'd'
With spattering noise rejected: oft they assayd, Par Lost 10.567
Soft words to his fierce passion she assay'd: Par Lost 10.865
Thrice she assay'd with flattering prayers and sighs, Samson 392
Which without help of eye, might be assay'd, Samson 1625
Assaying
Assaying by his Devilish art to reach Par Lost 4.801
Assays
From hard assaies and ill successes past Par Lost 4.932
And sent them here through hard assays Mask 972
Bridgewater ms 'assaies'
Trinity ms 'assayes'
B.M. ms 'Assays'
Assemble
To utter is not safe. Assemble thou Par Lost 5.683
Assemble, and Harangues are heard, but soon Par Lost 11.663
Assembled
Then all thy Saints assembl'd, thou shalt judge Par Lost 3.330
For thither he assembl'd all his Train, Par Lost 5.767
Assembl'd Angels, and ye Powers return'd Par Lost 10.34
Assemblies
Frequented thir Assemblies, whereso met, Par Lost 11.722
So th' assemblies of each Nation Psalm 7, 25
Assembly
Th' Assembly, as when hollow Rocks retain Par Lost 2.285
In Heav'n, when at th' Assembly, and in sight Par Lost 2.749
He sat; and in th' assembly next upstood Par Lost 6.446
About the world, at that assembly fam'd Par Reg 1.34
To honour this great Feast, and great Assembly; Samson 1315
Fly swiftly to this fair Assembly's ears; Vacation 28
Nor sinners in th' assembly of just men. Psalm 1, 14
God in the great assembly stands Psalm 82, 1
Assent
Sparkl'd in all thir eyes; with full assent Par Lost 2.388
Assenting
After short pause assenting, thus began. Par Lost 5.562
Assert
I may assert Eternal Providence, Par Lost 1.25
Of those Imperial Titles which assert Par Lost 5.801
Thir Deities to assert, who while they feel Par Lost 6.157
But will arise and his great name assert: Samson 467

Asses	
(As he who seeking Asses found a Kingdom)	Par Reg 3.242
Among the Slaves and Asses thy comrades,	Samson 1162
Of Owles and Cuckoes, Asses, Apes and Doggs.	Sonnet 12, 4
Trinity ms 'asses'	
Assessor	
Th' Assessor of his Throne he thus began.	Par Lost 6.679
Asshur	
With them *great* Asshur also bands	Psalm 83, 29
Assiduous	
To wearie him with my assiduous cries:	Par Lost 11.310
Assigned	
Each in thir several active Sphears assignd,	Par Lost 5.477
Therefore to mee thir doom he hath assig'n'd;	Par Lost 6.817
God hath assign'd us, nor of me shalt pass	Par Lost 9.231
Against a Foe by doom express assign'd us,	Par Lost 10.926
Therefore without feign'd shifts let be assign'd	Samson 1116
I was to do my part from Heav'n assign'd,	Samson 1217
Assimilate	
Tasting concoct, digest, assimilate,	Par Lost 5.412
Assist	
Assist us: But if much converse perhaps	Par Lost 9.247
Or counsel to assist; lest I who erst	Par Reg 2.145
Assisting	
But favouring and assisting to the end.	Samson 1720
Associate	
Of his Associate; hee together calls,	Par Lost 5.696
Sole *Eve*, Associate sole, to me beyond	Par Lost 9.227
To my associate Powers, them to acquaint	Par Lost 10.395
Associates	
Th' associates and copartners of our loss	Par Lost 1.265
ms 'Associates'	
Of thy Associates, *Adam*, and wilt taste	Par Lost 8.401
Assuage	
Nor wanting power to mitigate and swage	Par Lost 1.556
Salve to thy Sores, apt words have power to swage	Samson 184
Or medcinal liquor can asswage,	Samson 627
And wake for me, their furi' asswage;	Psalm 7, 22
Assume	
Can either Sex assume, or both; so soft	Par Lost 1.424
Mee from attempting. Wherefore do I assume	Par Lost 2.450
Nor shalt thou by descending to assume	Par Lost 3.303
I give thee, reign for ever, and assume	Par Lost 3.318
Who can in reason then or right assume	Par Lost 5.794
Assume, as likes them best, condense or rare.	Par Lost 6.353
Scepter and Power, thy giving, I assume,	Par Lost 6.730
Thenceforth the form of servant to assume,	Par Lost 10.214
Far more magnanimous, then to assume.	Par Reg 2.483
Assuming	
Above his Brethren, to himself assuming	Par Lost 12.65
Assure	
Assur'd me, and still assure: though what thou tellst	Par Lost 5.553
Assured	
Could have assur'd us; and by what best way,	Par Lost 2.40
That be assur'd, without leave askt of thee:	Par Lost 2.685
Of anger shall remain, but peace assur'd,	Par Lost 3.263
Of *Galileo*, less assur'd, observes	Par Lost 5.262
Assur'd me, and still assure: though what thou tellst	Par Lost 5.553
What next I bring shall please thee, be assur'd,	Par Lost 8.449
Pernicious to thy Peace, chiefly assur'd	Par Lost 9.981
At this last sight, assur'd that Man shall live	Par Lost 11.872
With clamour was assur'd thir utmost aid	Par Reg 2.148
No way assur'd. But conjugal affection	Samson 739
Why then reveal'd? I was assur'd by those	Samson 800
Off. This answer, be assur'd, will not content them.	Samson 1322
Assures	
Assures me that the bitterness of death	Par Lost 11.157
Assyria	
Thir Kings, when *Aegypt* with *Assyria* strove	Par Lost 1.721
ms 'Assyria'	
Assyria and her Empires antient bounds,	Par Reg 3.270
Assyrian	
The way he went, and on th' *Assyrian* mount	Par Lost 4.126
From this *Assyrian* Garden, where the Fiend	Par Lost 4.285
And at their passing cleave the *Assyrian* flood,	Par Reg 3.436
Sadly sits th' *Assyrian* Queen;	Mask 1002
line not in Bridgewater ms	
Astarte	
Astarte, Queen of Heav'n, with crescent Horns;	Par Lost 1.439
ms 'Astarte'	
Asthmas	
Dropsies, and Asthma's, and Joint-racking Rheums.	Par Lost 11.488
Astonied	
Astonied stood and Blank, while horror chill	Par Lost 9.890
Astonished	
Lye thus astonisht on th' oblivious Pool,	Par Lost 1.266
Astonisht: none among the choice and prime	Par Lost 2.423
Plagues; they astonisht all resistance lost,	Par Lost 6.838
Astonish'd with thine ire.	Psalm 88, 64
Astonishment	
If such astonishment as this can sieze	Par Lost 1.317
And my quaint habits breed astonishment,	Mask 157
Thou in our wonder and astonishment	Shakespear 7
1640 'astoneshment'	
Astoreth	
Of *Baalim* and *Ashtaroth*, those male,	Par Lost 1.422
ms 'Ashtaroth'	
Came *Astoreth*, whom the *Phoenicians* call'd	Par Lost 1.438
Astoreth(*cont*)	
ms 'Astoreth'	
Har. By *Astaroth* e're long thou shalt lament	Samson 1242
And mooned *Ashtaroth*,	Nativity 200
Astound	
These thoughts may startle well, but not astound	Mask 210
line not in Bridgewater ms	
Astounded	
As we erewhile, astounded and amaz'd,	Par Lost 1.281
Astracan	
By *Astracan* over the Snowie Plaines	Par Lost 10.432
Astray	
Like one that had bin led astray	Penseroso 69
Bless'd is the man who hath not walk'd astray	Psalm 1, 1
Astrea	
Betwixt *Astrea* and the *Scorpion* signe,	Par Lost 4.998
Astronomer	
Astronomer in the Sun's lucent Orbe	Par Lost 3.589
Asunder	
His wish and best advantage, us asunder,	Par Lost 9.258
And those that cannot live from him asunder	Vacation 77
He hast to tear my Soul asunder	Psalm 7, 5
At	
At once as far as Angels kenn he views	Par Lost 1.59
Left him at large to his own dark designs,	Par Lost 1.213
Whom Thunder hath made greater? Here at least	Par Lost 1.258
At Ev'ning from the top of *Fesole*,	Par Lost 1.289
At thir great Emperors call, as next in worth	Par Lost 1.378
In Temples and at Altars, when the Priest	Par Lost 1.494
Then strait commands that at the warlike sound	Par Lost 1.531
At which the universal Host upsent	Par Lost 1.541
That fought at *Theb*'s and *Ilium*, on each side	Par Lost 1.578
Tears such as Angels weep, burst forth: at last	Par Lost 1.620
Put forth at full, but still his strength conceal'd,	Par Lost 1.641
At length from us may find, who overcomes	Par Lost 1.648
At *Pandaemonium*, the high Capital	Par Lost 1.756
ms defective here	
Wont ride in arm'd, and at the Soldans chair	Par Lost 1.764
At once with joy and fear his heart rebounds.	Par Lost 1.788
Reduc'd thir shapes immense, and were at large,	Par Lost 1.790
Thus farr at least recover'd, hath much more	Par Lost 2.22
Car'd not to be at all; with that care lost	Par Lost 2.48
Arm'd with Hell flames and fury all at once	Par Lost 2.61
And cannot cease to be, we are at worst	Par Lost 2.100
By force, and at our heels all Hell should rise	Par Lost 2.135
Will he, so wise, let loose at once his ire,	Par Lost 2.155
Views all things at one view? he from heav'ns highth	Par Lost 2.190
That so ordains: this was at first resolv'd,	Par Lost 2.201
I laugh, when those who at the Spear are bold	Par Lost 2.204
Or chang'd at length, and to the place conformd	Par Lost 2.217
Secure, and at the brightning Orient beam	Par Lost 2.399
Alone the dreadful voyage; till at last	Par Lost 2.426
Terror of Heav'n, though fall'n; intend at home,	Par Lost 2.457
Forbidding; and at once with him they rose;	Par Lost 2.475
Thir rising all at once was as the sound	Par Lost 2.476
Thence more at ease thir minds and somwhat rais'd	Par Lost 2.521
As at th' Olympian Games or *Pythian* fields;	Par Lost 2.530
At certain revolutions all the damn'd	Par Lost 2.597
As when farr off at Sea a Fleet descri'd	Par Lost 2.636
Farr off the flying Fiend: at last appeer	Par Lost 2.643
Eclipses at thir charms. The other shape,	Par Lost 2.666
Satan was now at hand, and from his seat	Par Lost 2.674
Shakes Pestilence and Warr. Each at the Head	Par Lost 2.711
Each cast at th' other, as when two black Clouds	Par Lost 2.714
Grew darker at thir frown, so matcht they stood;	Par Lost 2.720
At thee ordain'd his drudge, to execute	Par Lost 2.732
She spake, and at her words the hellish Pest	Par Lost 2.735
In Heav'n, when at th' Assembly, and in sight	Par Lost 2.749
At first, and call'd me *Sin*, and for a Sign	Par Lost 2.760
I also; at which time this powerful Key	Par Lost 2.774
At last this odious offspring whom thou seest	Par Lost 2.781
Hell trembl'd at the hideous Name, and sigh'd	Par Lost 2.788
Shall dwell at ease, and up and down unseen	Par Lost 2.841
The Gods who live at ease, where I shall Reign	Par Lost 2.868
At thy right hand voluptuous, as beseems	Par Lost 2.869
The stedfast Earth. At last his Sail-broad Vannes	Par Lost 2.927
At length a universal hubbub wilde	Par Lost 2.951
But now at last the sacred influence	Par Lost 2.1034
Weighs his spread wings, at leasure to behold	Par Lost 2.1046
Before the Heavens thou wert, and at the voice	Par Lost 3.9
And wisdome at one entrance quite shut out.	Par Lost 3.50
His own works and their works at once to view:	Par Lost 3.59
The powers of darkness bound. Thou at the sight	Par Lost 3.256
Here walk'd the Fiend at large in spacious field.	Par Lost 3.430
And now Saint *Peter* at Heav'ns Wicket seems	Par Lost 3.484
To wait them with his Keys, and now at foot	Par Lost 3.485
And long he wanderd, till at last a gleame	Par Lost 3.499
At top whereof, but farr more rich appeerd	Par Lost 3.504
Looks down with wonder at the sudden view	Par Lost 3.542
Of all this World at once. As when a Scout	Par Lost 3.543
All night; at last by break of chearful dawne	Par Lost 3.545
At sight of all this World beheld so faire.	Par Lost 3.554
But all Sun-shine, as when his Beams at Noon	Par Lost 3.616
Stand ready at command, and are his Eyes	Par Lost 3.650
At wisdoms Gate, and to simplicitie	Par Lost 3.687
I saw when at his Word the formless Mass,	Par Lost 3.708
Till at his second bidding darkness fled,	Par Lost 3.712
Of this new World; at whose sight all the Starrs	Par Lost 4.34

At(*cont*)

By owing owes not, but still pays, at once	Par Lost 4.56
O then at last relent: is there no place	Par Lost 4.79
Evil be thou my Good; by thee at least	Par Lost 4.110
Blossoms and Fruits at once of golden hue	Par Lost 4.148
Mozambic, off at Sea North-East windes blow	Par Lost 4.161
At one slight bound high over leap'd all bound	Par Lost 4.181
Watching where Shepherds pen thir Flocks at eeve	Par Lost 4.185
In at the window climbs, or o're the tiles;	Par Lost 4.191
Scarce thus at length faild speech recoverd sad.	Par Lost 4.357
And should I at your harmless innocence	Par Lost 4.388
In some Purlieu two gentle Fawnes at play,	Par Lost 4.404
In all this happiness, who at his hand	Par Lost 4.417
Th' unarmed Youth of Heav'n, but nigh at hand	Par Lost 4.552
This day at highth of Noon came to my Spheare	Par Lost 4.564
See farr and wide: in at this Gate none pass	Par Lost 4.579
Rising in clouded Majestie, at length	Par Lost 4.607
And at our pleasant labour, to reform	Par Lost 4.625
Our walk at noon, with branches overgrown,	Par Lost 4.627
Thus at thir shadie Lodge arriv'd, both stood	Par Lost 4.720
Forth issuing at th' accustomd hour stood armd	Par Lost 4.779
Squat like a Toad, close at the eare of *Eve;*	Par Lost 4.800
At least distemperd, discontented thoughts,	Par Lost 4.807
Here watching at the head of these that sleep?	Par Lost 4.826
Or all at once; more glorie will be wonn,	Par Lost 4.853
But still thy words at random, as before,	Par Lost 4.930
At least had gon to rack, disturbd and torne	Par Lost 4.994
Close at mine ear one call'd me forth to walk	Par Lost 5.36
I rose as at thy call, but found thee not;	Par Lost 5.48
At such bold words voucht with a deed so bold:	Par Lost 5.66
And various: wondring at my flight and change	Par Lost 5.89
In them at once to ruin all mankind.	Par Lost 5.228
Through all th' Empyreal road; till at the Gate	Par Lost 5.253
At once on th' Eastern cliff of Paradise	Par Lost 5.275
Wantond as in her prime, and plaid at will	Par Lost 5.295
And *Eve* within, due at her hour prepar'd	Par Lost 5.303
I have at will. So to the Silvan Lodge	Par Lost 5.377
In humid exhalations, and at Even	Par Lost 5.425
As from the Mine. Mean while at Table *Eve*	Par Lost 5.443
Enamour'd at that sight; but in those hearts	Par Lost 5.448
At Heav'ns high feasts to have fed: yet what compare?	Par Lost 5.467
Your bodies may at last turn all to Spirit,	Par Lost 5.497
Ethereal, as wee, or may at choice	Par Lost 5.499
At my right hand; your Head I him appoint;	Par Lost 5.606
Laugh'st at thir vain designes and tumults vain,	Par Lost 5.737
At length into the limits of the North	Par Lost 5.755
Light issues forth, and at the other dore	Par Lost 6.9
At which command the Powers Militant,	Par Lost 6.61
Tenfold the length of this terrene: at last	Par Lost 6.78
At first, that Angel should with Angel warr,	Par Lost 6.92
His daring foe, at this prevention more	Par Lost 6.129
Abandond at the terror of thy Power	Par Lost 6.134
Reaching beyond all limit at one blow	Par Lost 6.140
At first I thought that Libertie and Heav'n	Par Lost 6.164
Hosanna to the Highest: nor stood at gaze	Par Lost 6.205
Of fighting Seraphim confus'd, at length	Par Lost 6.249
Squadrons at once, with huge two-handed sway	Par Lost 6.251
A vast circumference: At his approach	Par Lost 6.256
As not of power, at once; nor odds appeerd	Par Lost 6.319
And at his Chariot wheeles to drag him bound	Par Lost 6.358
Thick-rammd, at th' other bore with touch of fire	Par Lost 6.485
Arme, Warriours, Arme for fight, the foe at hand,	Par Lost 6.537
To hide the fraud. At interview both stood	Par Lost 6.555
A while, but suddenly at head appeerd	Par Lost 6.556
Portending hollow truce; at each behind	Par Lost 6.578
Not long, for sudden all at once thir Reeds	Par Lost 6.582
Rage prompted them at length, and found them arms	Par Lost 6.635
Purest at first, now gross by sinning grown.	Par Lost 6.661
Ascended, at his right hand Victorie	Par Lost 6.762
At his command the uprooted Hills retir'd	Par Lost 6.781
Grieving to see his Glorie, at the sight	Par Lost 6.792
Weening to prosper, and at length prevaile	Par Lost 6.795
At once the Four spred out thir Starrie wings	Par Lost 6.827
Incumberd him with ruin: Hell at last	Par Lost 6.874
Where now he sits at the right hand of bliss.	Par Lost 6.892
At thy request, and that thou maist beware	Par Lost 6.894
At least our envious Foe hath fail'd, who thought	Par Lost 7.139
They open to themselves at length the way	Par Lost 7.158
Against a solemn day, harnest at hand,	Par Lost 7.202
On the swift flouds: as Armies at the call	Par Lost 7.295
Or in thir Pearlie shells at ease, attend	Par Lost 7.407
And seems a moving Land, and at his Gilles	Par Lost 7.415
Draws in, and at his Trunck spouts out a Sea.	Par Lost 7.416
Op'ning her fertil Woomb teem'd at a Birth	Par Lost 7.454
Pasturing at once, and in broad Herds upsprung.	Par Lost 7.462
At once came forth whatever creeps the ground,	Par Lost 7.475
Not noxious, but obedient at thy call.	Par Lost 7.498
Forerunning Night; when at the holy mount	Par Lost 7.584
Her Nurserie; they at her coming sprung	Par Lost 8.46
His laughter at thir quaint Opinions wide	Par Lost 8.78
That not to know at large of things remote	Par Lost 8.191
A lower flight, and speak of things at hand	Par Lost 8.199
And hunger both, from labour, at the houre	Par Lost 8.213
Least hee incenst at such eruption bold,	Par Lost 8.235
When suddenly stood at my Head a dream,	Par Lost 8.292
In adoration at his feet I fell	Par Lost 8.315
Replenisht, and all these at thy command	Par Lost 8.371
More then enough; at least on her bestow'd	Par Lost 8.537

At(*cont*)

At Joust and Torneament; then marshal'd Feast	Par Lost 9.37
By Night he fled, and at Midnight return'd	Par Lost 9.58
Where *Tigris* at the foot of Paradise	Par Lost 9.71
At *Darien*, thence to the Land where flowes	Par Lost 9.81
More Angels to Create, if they at least	Par Lost 9.146
To basest things. Revenge, at first though sweet,	Par Lost 9.171
Fearless unfeard he slept: in at his Mouth	Par Lost 9.187
By sly assault; and somwhere nigh at hand	Par Lost 9.256
To other speedie aide might lend at need;	Par Lost 9.260
Just then returnd at shut of Evening Flours.	Par Lost 9.278
For hee who tempts, though in vain, at least asperses	Par Lost 9.296
From thee alone, which on us both at once	Par Lost 9.303
At first, as one who sought access, but feard	Par Lost 9.511
From every Beast, more duteous at her call,	Par Lost 9.521
Then at *Circean* call the Herd disguis'd.	Par Lost 9.522
His gentle dumb expression turnd at length	Par Lost 9.527
Though at the voice much marveling; at length	Par Lost 9.551
The first at lest of these I thought denid	Par Lost 9.555
I was at first as other Beasts that graze	Par Lost 9.571
Of Ewe or Goat dropping with Milk at Eevn,	Par Lost 9.582
Not to deferr; hunger and thirst at once,	Par Lost 9.586
Powerful perswaders, quick'nd at the scent	Par Lost 9.587
At Feed or Fountain never had I found.	Par Lost 9.597
Sated at length, ere long I might perceave	Par Lost 9.598
To Man, and indignation at his wrong,	Par Lost 9.666
Whose taste, too long forborn, at first assay	Par Lost 9.747
And yet unknown, is as not had at all.	Par Lost 9.757
To reach, and feed at once both Bodie and Mind?	Par Lost 9.779
And knew not eating Death: Satiate at length,	Par Lost 9.792
Which with bland words at will she thus addrest.	Par Lost 9.855
Hast thou not wonderd, *Adam*, at my stay?	Par Lost 9.856
Speechless he stood and pale, till thus at length	Par Lost 9.894
Wept at compleating of the mortal Sin	Par Lost 9.1003
At length gave utterance to these words constraind.	Par Lost 9.1066
But such as at this day to *Indians* known	Par Lost 9.1102
At Loopholes cut through thickest shade: Those Leaves	Par Lost 9.1110
Coverd, but not at rest or ease of Mind,	Par Lost 9.1120
Raind at thir Eyes, but high Winds worse within	Par Lost 9.1122
From Earth arriv'd at Heaven Gate, displeas'd	Par Lost 10.22
Nor troubl'd at these tidings from the Earth,	Par Lost 10.36
From Noon, and gentle Aires due at thir hour	Par Lost 10.93
Nor alter'd his offence; yet God at last	Par Lost 10.171
Whom he shall tread at last under our feet;	Par Lost 10.190
Powerful at greatest distance to unite	Par Lost 10.247
And at the brink of *Chaos*, neer the foot	Par Lost 10.347
Great joy was at thir meeting, and at sight	Par Lost 10.350
Of richest texture spred, at th' upper end	Par Lost 10.446
At last as from a Cloud his fulgent head	Par Lost 10.449
At that so sudden blaze the *Stygian* throng	Par Lost 10.453
Had leasure, wondring at himself now more;	Par Lost 10.510
Then stil at Hels dark threshold to have sate watch,	Par Lost 10.594
At random yielded up to their misrule;	Par Lost 10.628
With suckt and glutted offal, at one sling	Par Lost 10.633
Both *Sin*, and *Death*, and yawning *Grave* at last	Par Lost 10.635
Beneath *Magellan*. At that tasted Fruit	Par Lost 10.687
Thy punishment then justly is at his Will.	Par Lost 10.768
But Death comes not at call, Justice Divine	Par Lost 10.858
With Spirits Masculine, create at last	Par Lost 10.890
Of Nature, and not fill the World at once	Par Lost 10.892
And tresses all disorderd, at his feet	Par Lost 10.911
Now at his feet submissive in distress,	Par Lost 10.942
By Death at last, and miserable it is	Par Lost 10.981
That after wretched Life must be at last	Par Lost 10.985
Then both our selves and Seed at once to free	Par Lost 10.999
Before thee reconcil'd, at least his days	Par Lost 11.39
Corrupted. I at first with two fair gifts	Par Lost 11.57
To sound at general Doom. Th' Angelic blast	Par Lost 11.76
Good by it self, and Evil not at all.	Par Lost 11.89
And live for ever, dream at least to live	Par Lost 11.95
At the sad Sentence rigorously urg'd,	Par Lost 11.109
He added not, for *Adam* at the newes	Par Lost 11.263
At Eev'n, which I bred up with tender hand	Par Lost 11.276
I heard, here with him at this Fountain talk'd:	Par Lost 11.322
Much at that sight was *Adam* in his heart	Par Lost 11.448
More terrible at th' entrance then within.	Par Lost 11.470
In other part stood one who at the Forge	Par Lost 11.564
(Erelong to swim at large) and laugh; for which	Par Lost 11.626
In factious opposition, till at last	Par Lost 11.664
At length a Reverend Sire among them came,	Par Lost 11.719
By th' Angel, on thy feet thou stoodst at last,	Par Lost 11.759
His Children, all in view destroyd at once;	Par Lost 11.761
At once, by my foreknowledge gaining Birth	Par Lost 11.768
Famin and anguish will at last consume	Par Lost 11.778
At this last sight, assur'd that Man shall live	Par Lost 11.872
Griev'd at his heart, when looking down he saw	Par Lost 11.887
As one who in his journey bates at Noone, line not in 1667 edition	Par Lost 12.1
Still tend from bad to worse, till God at last	Par Lost 12.106
See where it flows, disgorging at seaven mouthes	Par Lost 12.158
The River-dragon tam'd at length submits	Par Lost 12.191
Save when they journie, and at length they come,	Par Lost 12.258
Upon the Temple it self: at last they seise	Par Lost 12.356
Barr'd of his right; yet at his Birth a Starr	Par Lost 12.360
His Seat at Gods right hand, exalted high	Par Lost 12.457
As at the Worlds great period; and our Sire	Par Lost 12.467
With joy the tidings brought from Heav'n: at length	Par Lost 12.504
And vengeance to the wicked, at return	Par Lost 12.541

At(*cont*)
Thir motion, at whose Front a flaming Sword, Par Lost 12.592
To meek submission: thou at season fit Par Lost 12.597
And gathers ground fast at the Labourers heel Par Lost 12.631
Repentance, and Heavens Kingdom nigh at hand Par Reg 1.20
About the world, at that assembly fam'd Par Reg 1.34
In manner at our will th' affairs of Earth, Par Reg 1.50
At least if so we can, and by the head Par Reg 1.60
At these sad tidings; but no time was then Par Reg 1.109
At first against mankind so well had thriv'd Par Reg 1.114
All his sollicitations, and at length Par Reg 1.152
O what a multitude of thoughts at once Par Reg 1.196
Had measur'd twice six years, at our great Feast Par Reg 1.210
At least to try, and teach the erring Soul Par Reg 1.224
By words at times cast forth inly rejoyc'd, Par Reg 1.228
At thy Nativity a glorious Quire Par Reg 1.242
To Shepherds watching at their folds by night, Par Reg 1.244
Till those days ended, hunger'd then at last Par Reg 1.309
Among wild Beasts: they at his sight grew mild, Par Reg 1.310
To warm him wet return'd from field at Eve, Par Reg 1.318
Our new baptizing Prophet at the Ford Par Reg 1.328
To love, at least comtemplate and admire Par Reg 1.380
At first it may be; but long since with wo Par Reg 1.399
Who ever by consulting at thy shrine Par Reg 1.438
Shalt be enquir'd at *Delphos* or elsewhere, Par Reg 1.458
At least in vain, for they shall find thee mute. Par Reg 1.459
And talk at least, though I despair to attain. Par Reg 1.485
At *Jordan* with the Baptist, and had seen Par Reg 2.2
Now, now, for sure, deliverance is at hand, Par Reg 2.35
By his great Prophet, pointed at and shown, Par Reg 2.51
To find whom at the first they found unsought: Par Reg 2.59
Nor left at *Jordan*, tydings of him none; Par Reg 2.62
Into himself descended, and at once Par Reg 2.111
If he be Man by Mothers side at least, Par Reg 2.136
At his command; when from amidst them rose Par Reg 2.149
At will the manliest, resolutest brest, Par Reg 2.167
For *Solomon* he liv'd at ease, and full Par Reg 2.201
At every sudden slighting quite abasht: Par Reg 2.224
To be at hand, and at his beck appear, Par Reg 2.238
Or as a guest with *Daniel* at his pulse. Par Reg 2.278
To rest at noon, and entr'd soon the shade Par Reg 2.292
And at a stately side-board by the wine Par Reg 2.350
Thir taste no knowledge works, at least of evil, Par Reg 2.371
I can at will, doubt not, as soon as thou, Par Reg 2.383
Bred up in poverty and streights at home; Par Reg 2.415
Or at thy heels the dizzy Multitude, Par Reg 2.420
Therefore, if at great things thou wouldst arrive, Par Reg 2.426
At length collecting all his Serpent wiles, Par Reg 3.5
All Earth her wonder at thy acts, thy self Par Reg 3.24
At his dispose, young *Scipio* had brought down Par Reg 3.34
The deed becomes unprais'd, the man at least, Par Reg 3.103
I would be at the worst; worst is my Port, Par Reg 3.209
At home, scarce view'd the *Gallilean* Towns, Par Reg 3.233
It was a Mountain at whose verdant feet Par Reg 3.253
At sight whereof the Fiend yet more presum'd, Par Reg 3.345
To render thee the *Parthian* at dispose; Par Reg 3.369
Yet he at length, time to himself best known, Par Reg 3.433
And at their passing cleave the *Assyrian* flood, Par Reg 3.436
Perplex'd and troubl'd at his bad success Par Reg 4.1
Aim therefore at no less then all the world, Par Reg 4.105
Aim at the highest, without the highest attain'd Par Reg 4.106
Wielded at will that fierce Democratie, Par Reg 4.269
These here revolve, or, as thou lik'st, at home, Par Reg 4.281
Quite at a loss, for all his darts were spent, Par Reg 4.366
Now at full age, fulness of time, thy season, Par Reg 4.380
But shelter'd slept in vain, for at his head Par Reg 4.407
Some bent at thee thir fiery darts, while thou Par Reg 4.424
This Tempest at this Desert most was bent; Par Reg 4.465
Of men at thee, for only thou here dwell'st. Par Reg 4.466
At least might seem to hold all power of thee, Par Reg 4.494
By all the Prophets; of thy birth at length Par Reg 4.503
Till at the Ford of *Jordan* whither all Par Reg 4.510
They shall up lift thee, lest at any time Par Reg 4.558
Throttl'd at length in the Air, expir'd and fell; Par Reg 4.568
Twice by an Angel, who at last in sight Samson 24
Eyeless in *Gaza* at the Mill with slaves, Samson 41
That she might look at will through every pore? Samson 97
At my affliction, and perhaps to insult, Samson 113
See how he lies at random, carelesly diffus'd, Samson 118
This with the other should, at least, have paird, Samson 208
At least of thy own Nation, and as noble. Samson 218
Sam. The first I saw at *Timna*, and she pleas'd Samson 219
Acknowledg'd not, or not at all consider'd Samson 245
To count them things worth notice, till at length Samson 250
How frequent to desert him, and at last Samson 275
Unless there be who think not God at all, Samson 295
Down Reason then, at least vain reasonings down, Samson 322
At one spears length. O ever failing trust Samson 348
This well I knew, nor was at all surpris'd, Samson 381
At times when men seek most repose and rest, Samson 406
Weakly at least, and shamefully: A sin Samson 499
At length to lay my head and hallow'd pledge Samson 535
What boots it at one gate to make defence, Samson 560
And at another to let in the foe Samson 561
Better at home lie bed-rid, not only idle, Samson 579
But God who caus'd a fountain at thy prayer Samson 581
But yield to double darkness nigh at hand: Samson 593
And now at nearer view, no other certain Samson 723

At(*cont*)
As her at *Timna*, sought by all means therefore Samson 795
While I at home sate full of cares and fears Samson 805
Fearless at home of partners in my love. Samson 810
Was not behind, but ever at my ear, Samson 858
With hard contest: at length that grounded maxim Samson 865
Didst thou at first receive me for thy husband? Samson 883
At home in leisure and domestic ease, Samson 917
Dal. Let me approach at least, and touch thy hand. Samson 951
At distance I forgive thee, go with that; Samson 954
Are reconcil'd at length, and Sea to Shore: Samson 962
Of Women, sung at solemn festivals, Samson 983
At this who ever envies or repines Samson 995
Seeming at first all heavenly under virgin veil, Samson 1035
Embarqu'd with such a Stears-mate at the Helm? Samson 1045
If thou at all art known. Much I have heard Samson 1082
Thou oft shalt wish thy self at *Gath* to boast Samson 1127
Feignst at thy birth was giv'n thee in thy hair, Samson 1135
At my Nativity this strength, diffus'd Samson 1141
At *Askalon*, who never did thee harm, Samson 1187
A Public Officer, and now at hand. Samson 1306
Our Law forbids at thir Religious Rites Samson 1320
And over-labour'd at thir publick Mill, Samson 1327
Present in Temples at Idolatrous Rites Samson 1378
Our Captive, at the public Mill our drudge, Samson 1393
And dar'st thou at our sending and command Samson 1394
Be efficacious in thee now at need. Samson 1437
Was not at present here to find my Son, Samson 1446
To come and play before them at thir Feast. Samson 1448
Either at home, or through the high street passing, Samson 1458
Or at some proof of strength before them shown. Samson 1475
Ruin, destruction at the utmost point. Samson 1514
As at some distance from the place of horrour, Samson 1550
To utter what will come at last too soon; Samson 1566
Brought him so soon at variance with himself Samson 1585
At once both to destroy and be destroy'd; Samson 1587
I sorrow'd at his captive state, but minded Samson 1603
Not to be absent at that spectacle. Samson 1604
At sight of him the people with a shout Samson 1620
At length for intermission sake they led him Samson 1629
At last with head erect thus cryed aloud, Samson 1639
At last betakes him to this ominous Wood, Mask 61
Excells his Mother at her mighty Art, Mask 63
At every fall smoothing the Raven doune Mask 251
And the swink't hedger at his Supper sate; Mask 293
Leans her unpillow'd head fraught with sad fears. Mask 355
Trinity ms 'fraught with sad feares' ←'musing at our unkindnesse'
Danger will wink on Opportunity, Mask 401
Bridgewater ms 'winke at'
That breaks his magick chains at *curfeu* time, Mask 435
And spotted mountain pard, but set at nought Mask 444
Or els som neighbour Wood-man, or at worst, Mask 484
Like stabl'd wolves, or tigers at their prey, Mask 534
At which I ceas't, and listen'd them a while, Mask 551
At last a soft and solemn breathing sound Mask 555
And mix no more with goodness, when at last Mask 594
Would grow inur'd to light, and com at last Mask 735
In courts, at feasts, and high solemnities Mask 746
line not in Bridgewater ms
Where most may wonder at the workmanship; Mask 747
line not in Bridgewater ms
Her maid'n gentlenes, and oft at Eeve Mask 843
For which the Shepherds at their festivals Mask 848
Gentle swain at thy request Mask 900
We shall catch them at their sport, Mask 953
Whom lovely *Venus* at a birth Allegro 14
And at my window bid good morrow, Allegro 46
While the Plowman neer at hand, Allegro 63
Are at their savory dinner set Allegro 84
Basks at the fire his hairy strength; Allegro 112
Or let my Lamp at midnight hour, Penseroso 85
That at her flowry work doth sing, Penseroso 143
Wave at his Wings in Airy stream, Penseroso 148
And may at last my weary age Penseroso 167
Have sate to wonder at, and gaze upon: Arcades 43
Oft till the Star that rose, at Ev'ning, bright Lycidas 30
Trinity ms 'in Evning'
1638 'Oft till the ev'n-starre bright'
Then how to scramble at the shearers feast, Lycidas 117
But that two-handed engine at the door, Lycidas 130
At last he rose, and twitch'd his Mantle blew: Lycidas 192
Wherwith he wont at Heav'ns high Councel-Table, Nativity 10
And lay it lowly at his blessed feet; Nativity 25
At last surrounds their sight Nativity 109
And Heav'n as at som festivall, Nativity 147
When at the worlds last session, Nativity 163
And then at last our bliss Nativity 165
Affrights the *Flamins* at their service quaint; Nativity 194
Nor can he be at rest Nativity 216
Shake earth, and at the presence be agast Psalm 114, 15
Above the wheeling poles, and at Heav'ns dore Vacation 34
May tell at length how green-ey'd *Neptune* raves, Vacation 43
In solemn Songs at King *Alcinous* feast, Vacation 49
Good luck befriend thee Son; for at thy birth Vacation 59
Yet shall he live in strife, and at his dore Vacation 85
To harbour those that are at enmity. Vacation 88
That whirl'd the Prophet up at *Chebar* flood, Passion 37

At(*cont*)	
The God that sits at marriage feast;	Winchester 18
He at their invoking came	Winchester 19
Spoil'd at once both fruit and tree:	Winchester 30
And at her next birth much like thee,	Winchester 67
But lately finding him so long at home,	Carrier 11
Untill his revolution was at stay.	Another 6
1658 'made of stay'	
Warbl'st at eeve, when all the Woods are still,	Sonnet 1, 2
And at thy growing vertues fret their spleen,	Sonnet 9, 7
Passes to bliss at the mid hour of night,	Sonnet 9, 13
At *Chaeronea*, fatal to liberty	Sonnet 10, 7
Raild at *Latona*'s twin-born progenie	Sonnet 12, 6
Is Kingly. Thousands at his bidding speed	Sonnet 19, 12
Which others at their Barr so often wrench;	Sonnet 21, 4
line not in Trinity ms	
New Presbyter is but *Old Priest* writ Large.	Forcers 20
Trinity ms 'large' ←'at large'	
And now be wise at length ye Kings averse	Psalm 2, 22
And set at large; now spare,	Psalm 4, 5
And be at peace within.	Psalm 4, 22
In peace at once will I	Psalm 4, 37
Upon me: cause at length to cease	Psalm 7, 34
Saves th' upright of Heart at last.	Psalm 7, 42
Hath at length brought forth a Lie.	Psalm 7, 54
And flouts at us they throw	Psalm 80, 28
And fill'd the land *at last*.	Psalm 80, 40
They perish at thy dreadfull ire,	Psalm 80, 67
At thy rebuke and frown.	Psalm 80, 68
I tri'd thee at the water *steep*	Psalm 81, 31
Be not thou silent *now at length*	Psalm 83, 1
When at the brook of Kishon *old*	Psalm 83, 37
At Endor quite cut off, and rowl'd	Psalm 83, 39
Till all before *our* God *at length*	Psalm 84, 27
A thousand daies *at best*.	Psalm 84, 36
Salvation is at hand	Psalm 85, 38
O turn to me *thy face at length*,	Psalm 86, 57
My life *at deaths uncherful dore*	Psalm 88, 11
And to be short, at last his guid him brings	Prose 2, 1
Goddess of Shades, and Huntress, who at will	Prose 12, 1
Atabalipa	
Of *Atabalipa*, and yet unspoil'd	Par Lost 11.409
Atahualpa	
Of *Atabalipa*, and yet unspoil'd	Par Lost 11.409
Atheist	
Turns Atheist, as did *Ely*'s Sons, who fill'd	Par Lost 1.495
The Atheist crew, but with redoubl'd blow	Par Lost 6.370
Atheists	
Of these fair Atheists, and now swim in joy,	Par Lost 11.625
Of Idolists, and Atheists; have brought scandal	Samson 453
Athenian	
By boistrous rape th' Athenian damsel got,	Fair Inf 9
To save th' *Athenian* Walls from ruine bare.	Sonnet 8, 14
Athens	
In *Athens* or free *Rome*, where Eloquence	Par Lost 9.671
Athens the eye of *Greece*, Mother of Arts	Par Reg 4.240
Atheous	
Suffers the Hypocrite or Atheous Priest	Par Reg 1.487
Athwart	
Thy miscreated Front athwart my way	Par Lost 2.683
Atlantean	
With *Atlantean* shoulders fit to bear	Par Lost 2.306
Atlantic	
Andromeda farr off *Atlantic* Seas	Par Lost 3.559
1667 '*Atlantick*'	
Atlantick Sisters, and the *Spartan* Twins	Par Lost 10.674
On *Cittron* tables or *Atlantic* stone;	Par Reg 4.115
In the steep *Atlantick* stream,	Mask 97
1637 '*Atlantik*'	
Trinity ms 'Atlantick' ←'Tartessian'	
Bridgewater ms 'Atlantique'	
halfe his wast flood the wide Atlantique fills	Mask Tr. ms 10.14
Atlas	
Like *Teneriff* or *Atlas* unremov'd:	Par Lost 4.987
Or thence from *Niger* Flood to *Atlas* Mount	Par Lost 11.402
Of *Hesperus*, and his daughters three	Mask 982
Trinity ms 'Hesperus' ←'Atlas'	
Atom	
An Atom, with the Firmament compar'd	Par Lost 8.18
Atoms	
Thir embryon Atoms; they around the flag	Par Lost 2.900
Atonement	
Attonement for himself or offering meet,	Par Lost 3.234
Atropatia	
From *Atropatia* and the neighbouring plains	Par Reg 3.319
Atrophy	
And Moon-struck madness, pining Atrophie,	Par Lost 11.486
line not in 1667 edition	
Atropos	
Atropos for *Lucina* came;	Winchester 28
Attached	
And charming Symphonies attach'd the heart	Par Lost 11.595
Attack	
No equal, raunging through the dire attack	Par Lost 6.248
Close-banded durst attaque me, no not sleeping,	Samson 1113
Attain	
Light after light well us'd they shall attain,	Par Lost 3.196
Yet what thou canst attain, which best may serve	Par Lost 7.115
Attain(*cont*)	
This to attain, whether Heav'n move or Earth,	Par Lost 8.70
He ceas'd, I lowly answer'd. To attaine	Par Lost 8.412
Th' offence, that Man should thus attain to know?	Par Lost 9.726
To us, as likely tasting to attaine	Par Lost 9.935
Of thy perfection, how shall I attaine,	Par Lost 9.964
If so I may attain. So both ascend	Par Lost 11.376
E're I the promis'd Kingdom can attain,	Par Reg 1.265
And talk at least, though I despair to attain.	Par Reg 1.485
The end I would attain, my final good.	Par Reg 3.211
Till old experience do attain	Penseroso 173
Attained	
And life more perfet have attaind then Fate	Par Lost 9.689
This having learnt, thou hast attaind the summe	Par Lost 12.575
But men endu'd with these have oft attain'd	Par Reg 2.437
It may by means far different be attain'd	Par Reg 3.89
Aim at the highest, without the highest attain'd	Par Reg 4.106
Attains	
Serv'd by more noble then her self, attaines	Par Lost 8.34
That whoso eats thereof, forthwith attains	Par Lost 9.724
Canaan he now attains, I see his Tents	Par Lost 12.135
Which every wise and vertuous man attains:	Par Reg 2.468
And who attains not, ill aspires to rule	Par Reg 2.469
Attempt	
With vain attempt. Him the Almighty Power	Par Lost 1.44
Which tempted our attempt, and wrought our fall.	Par Lost 1.642
The perilous attempt: but all sat mute,	Par Lost 2.420
But Fate withstands, and to oppose th' attempt	Par Lost 2.610
Begins his dire attempt, which nigh the birth	Par Lost 4.15
Thy Empire? easily the proud attempt	Par Lost 7.609
Not that they durst without his leave attempt,	Par Lost 8.237
Th' attempt it self, intended by our Foe.	Par Lost 9.295
This my attempt, I would sustain alone	Par Lost 9.978
Or here th' attempt, thou couldst not have discernd	Par Lost 9.1149
No evil durst attempt thee, but I rue	Par Lost 9.1180
Hinder'd not *Satan* to attempt the minde	Par Lost 10.8
To him their great Dictator, whose attempt	Par Reg 1.113
But he whom we attempt is wiser far	Par Reg 2.205
For this attempt bolder then that on *Eve*,	Par Reg 4.180
Thy bold attempt; hereafter learn with awe	Par Reg 4.625
Draw thir own ruin who attempt the deed.	Samson 1267
Lest som ill greeting touch attempt the person	Mask 406
Attempted	
And where thir weakness, how attempted best,	Par Lost 2.357
Not seeing thee attempted, who attest?	Par Lost 9.369
Man. I have attempted one by one the Lords	Samson 1457
Attempter	
Against th' Attempter of thy Fathers Throne,	Par Reg 4.603
Attempting	
Attempting, or to sit in darkness here	Par Lost 2.377
Mee from attempting. Wherefore do I assume	Par Lost 2.450
Attempts	
The Woman, opportune to all attempts,	Par Lost 9.481
That sole excites to high attempts the flame	Par Reg 3.26
Though by his blindness maim'd for high attempts,	Samson 1221
Attend	
Where all his Sons thy Embassie attend;	Par Lost 3.658
The Clouds that on his Western Throne attend:	Par Lost 4.597
Attend: That thou art happie, owe to God;	Par Lost 5.520
Or in thir Pearlie shells at ease, attend	Par Lost 7.407
But thy relation now; for I attend,	Par Lost 8.247
Of rendring up, and patiently attend	Par Lost 11.551
phrase not in 1667 edition	
Thou therefore give due audience, and attend.	Par Lost 12.12
Men who attend the Altar, and should most	Par Lost 12.354
Array'd in Glory on my cup to attend:	Par Reg 2.386
To fetch him hence and solemnly attend	Samson 1731
Are coming to attend their Fathers state,	Mask 35
And so attend ye toward her glittering state;	Arcades 81
Of heart or hope; but still bear vp and steer	Sonnet 22, 8
Trinity ms 'bear vp and' ←'attend to'	
Attendance	
Attendance none shall need, nor Train, where none	Par Lost 10.80
And if your stray attendance be yet lodg'd,	Mask 315
Attendant	
Attendant on thir Lord: Heav'n op'nd wide	Par Lost 7.205
Surprise thee, and her black attendant Death.	Par Lost 7.547
With thir attendant Moons thou wilt descrie	Par Lost 8.149
Attended	
Attended: all access was throng'd, the Gates	Par Lost 1.761
When thou attended gloriously from Heav'n	Par Lost 3.323
Attended with ten thousand thousand Saints,	Par Lost 6.767
The vertuous mind, that ever walks attended	Mask 211
line not in Bridgewater ms	
Attending	
With dread attending when that fatal wound	Par Reg 1.53
Her sleeping Lord with Handmaid Lamp attending.	Nativity 242
Attends	
Glad to be offer'd, he attends the will	Par Lost 3.270
Attends thee, and each word, each motion formes,	Par Lost 8.223
Which oft, they say, some evil Spirit attends	Par Lost 9.638
But that success attends him; if mishap,	Par Lost 10.239
Attends thee, scorns, reproaches, injuries,	Par Reg 4.387
Thy care is fixt and zealously attends	Sonnet 9, 9
Attent	
Declar'd the Son of God, to hear attent	Par Reg 1.385
Attention	
With all his Peers: attention held them mute.	Par Lost 1.618

Attention(*cont*)
Drew audience and attention still as Night Par Lost 2.308
Of her attention gaind, with Serpent Tongue Par Lost 9.529
Say, for such wonder claims attention due. Par Lost 9.566
Silence, and with these words attention won. Par Lost 10.459
Soon rais'd, and his attention thus recall'd. Par Lost 11.422
And chid her barking waves into attention, Mask 258

Attentive
Attentive, and with more delighted eare, Par Lost 5.545
The storie heard attentive, and was fill'd Par Lost 7.51
To better hopes his more attentive minde Par Lost 10.1011

Attest
Attest thir joy, that hill and valley rings. Par Lost 2.495
Not seeing thee attempted, who attest? Par Lost 9.369
Such high attest was giv'n, a while survey'd Par Reg 1.37

Attested
This man of men, attested Son of God, Par Reg 1.122

Attic
Plato's retirement, where the *Attic* Bird Par Reg 4.245
With the Attick Boy to hunt, Penseroso 124
Of Attick tast, with Wine, whence we may rise Sonnet 20, 10

Attire
First wheeld thir course; Earth in her rich attire Par Lost 7.501
But cull those richest Robes, and gay'st attire Vacation 21
The frozen earth; and cloth in fresh attire Sonnet 20, 7

Attired
The Musk-rose, and the well attir'd Woodbine, Lycidas 146
Trinity ms 'well-attir'd woodbine' ←'garish columbine'
1638 'well-attir'd'
Attir'd with Stars, we shall for ever sit, On Time 21

Attract
Shee was indeed, and lovely to attract Par Lost 10.152

Attracted
Attracted by thy beauty still to gaze. Par Lost 5.47

Attraction
Of conjugal attraction unreprov'd, Par Lost 4.493
By this new felt attraction and instinct. Par Lost 10.263

Attractive
I pleas'd, and with attractive graces won Par Lost 2.762
For softness shee and sweet attractive Grace, Par Lost 4.298
By his attractive vertue and thir own Par Lost 8.124
Attractive, human, rational, love still; Par Lost 8.587
Thir shape, thir colour, and attractive grace, Par Reg 2.176

Attracts
Is yet more Kingly, this attracts the Soul, Par Reg 2.476

Attribute
The swiftness of those Circles attribute, Par Lost 8.107

Attributed
With glorie attributed to the high Par Lost 8.12
Less attributed to her Faith sincere, Par Lost 9.320
Where glory is false glory, attributed Par Reg 3.69

Attributes
To teach thee that God attributes to place Par Lost 11.836

Attributing
By attributing overmuch to things Par Lost 8.565

Attrite
The Air attrite to Fire, as late the Clouds Par Lost 10.1073

Attune
Breathing the smell of field and grove, attune Par Lost 4.265

Audacious
Audacious neighbourhood, the wisest heart Par Lost 1.400
Audacious, but that seat soon failing, meets Par Lost 2.931

Audible
Yet all had heard, with audible lament Par Lost 11.266

Audibly
Present) thus to his Son audibly spake. Par Lost 7.518
Audibly heard from Heav'n, pronounc'd me his, Par Reg 1.284

Audience
Drew audience and attention still as Night Par Lost 2.308
The thronging audience. In discourse more sweet Par Lost 2.555
Had audience, when among the Seraphim Par Lost 5.804
Urania, and fit audience find, though few. Par Lost 7.31
Haste to thy audience, Night with her will bring Par Lost 7.105
Motion, each act won audience ere the tongue, Par Lost 9.674
He ended, and the heav'nly Audience loud Par Lost 10.641
Thou therefore give due audience, and attend. Par Lost 12.12

Auditress
Adam relating, she sole Auditress; Par Lost 8.51

Aught
To do ought good never will be our task, Par Lost 1.159
ms 'aught'
Then aught divine or holy else enjoy'd Par Lost 1.683
Fell long before; nor aught avail'd him now Par Lost 1.748
With splendor, arm'd with power, if aught propos'd Par Lost 2.447
If aught disturb'd thir noyse, into her woomb, Par Lost 2.657
Might hap to move new broiles: Be this or aught Par Lost 2.837
Or aught by me immutablie foreseen, Par Lost 3.121
Compar'd with aught on Earth, Medal or Stone; Par Lost 3.592
Aught whereof hee hath need, hee who requires Par Lost 4.419
Have gathered aught of evil or conceald, Par Lost 5.207
Superior, nor of violence fear'd aught; Par Lost 5.905
Unsound and false; nor is it aught but just, Par Lost 6.121
If I conjecture aught, no drizling showr, Par Lost 6.545
Aught, not surpassing human measure, say. Par Lost 7.640
For aught appeers, and on thir Orbs impose Par Lost 8.30
Above mankinde, or aught then mankinde higher, Par Lost 8.358
To them made common and divulg'd, if aught Par Lost 8.583
Neither her out-side formd so fair, nor aught Par Lost 8.596

Aught(*cont*)
Thy Judgement to do aught, which else free Will Par Lost 8.636
If I could joy in aught, sweet interchange Par Lost 9.115
Or aught that might his happie State secure, Par Lost 9.347
1667 'ought'
As was my food, nor aught but food discern'd Par Lost 9.573
Rather then Death or aught then Death more dread Par Lost 9.969
Since this days Death denounc't, if ought I see, Par Lost 10.962
But that from us ought should ascend to Heav'n Par Lost 11.143
If *Adam* aught perhaps might interpose; Par Lost 12.4
line not in 1667 edition
Where ought we hear, and curious are to hear, Par Reg 1.333
Nor lightens aught each mans peculiar load. Par Reg 1.402
Then prompt her to do aught may merit praise. Par Reg 2.456
But if there be in glory aught of good, Par Reg 3.88
Yet if for fame and glory aught be done, Par Reg 3.100
Aught suffer'd; if young *African* for fame Par Reg 3.101
On my part aught endeavouring, or to need Par Reg 3.399
Thin sown with aught of profit or delight, Par Reg 4.345
Kingdom nor Empire pleases thee, nor aught Par Reg 4.369
Now contrary, if I read aught in Heaven, Par Reg 4.382
Or Heav'n write aught of Fate, by what the Stars Par Reg 4.383
What hunger, if aught hunger had impair'd, Par Reg 4.592
As thir Deliverer; if he aught begin, Samson 274
Sole Author I, sole cause: if aught seem vile, Samson 376
If aught in my ability may serve Samson 743
Thou mine, not theirs: if aught against my life Samson 888
If there be aught of presage in the mind, Samson 1387
With zeal, if aught Religion seem concern'd: Samson 1420
And if ought els, great *Bards* beside, Penseroso 116
A Sheep-hook, or have learn'd ought els the least Lycidas 120

Augment
His glory to augment. The bold design Par Lost 2.386
Both to and fro, thir sorrow to augment, Par Lost 2.605
By tincture or reflection they augment Par Lost 7.367
A long days dying to augment our paine, Par Lost 10.964
Quench not the thirst of glory, but augment. Par Reg 3.38

Augmented
Precipitate thee with augmented paine. Par Lost 6.280
Augmented, op'nd Eyes, new Hopes, new Joyes, Par Lost 9.985

Auran
From *Auran* Eastward to the Royal Towrs Par Lost 4.211
To *Haran*, after him a cumbrous Train Par Lost 12.131

Aurora
Of leaves and fuming rills, *Aurora*'s fan, Par Lost 5.6
Zephir with *Aurora* playing, Allegro 19

Ausonian
In ancient *Greece;* and in *Ausonian* land Par Lost 1.739
ms 'Ausonian'

Austere
With sweet austeer composure thus reply'd, Par Lost 9.272
Be not unlike all others, not austere Samson 815

Austerely
Whatever Hypocrites austerely talk Par Lost 4.744

Austerity
But rigid looks of Chast austerity, Mask 450
1637 'austeritie'
Bridgewater ms 'awsteritie'

Authentic
The first art wont his great authentic will Par Lost 3.656
On him who had stole *Joves* authentic fire. Par Lost 4.719

Author
But from the Author of all ill could Spring Par Lost 2.381
Thou art my Father, thou my Author, thou Par Lost 2.864
Eternal King; thee Author of all being, Par Lost 3.374
My Author and Disposer, what thou bidst Par Lost 4.635
The Author not impair'd, but honourd more? Par Lost 5.73
In honour to the Worlds great Author rise, Par Lost 5.188
Our Authour. Heav'nly stranger, please to taste Par Lost 5.397
Author of evil, unknown till thy revolt, Par Lost 6.262
Author and end of all things, and from work Par Lost 7.591
Said mildely, Author of all this thou seest Par Lost 8.317
Adore thee, Author of this Universe, Par Lost 8.360
The good befall'n him, Author unsuspect, Par Lost 9.771
Idlely, while Satan our great Author thrives Par Lost 10.236
Thou art thir Author and prime Architect: Par Lost 10.356
Sole Author I, sole cause: if aught seem vile, Samson 376

Authority
Whence true autoritie in men; though both Par Lost 4.295
Authority and Reason on her waite, Par Lost 8.554
1667 'Authoritie'
Authoritie usurpt, from God not giv'n: Par Lost 12.66
The Authority which I deriv'd from Heaven. Par Reg 1.289
And on that high Authority had believ'd, Par Reg 2.5
To greatness? whence Authority deriv'st, Par Reg 2.418
Private respects must yield; with grave authority Samson 868

Authors
They trespass, Authors to themselves in all Par Lost 3.122

Autumn
In *Autumn* thwarts the night, when vapors fir'd Par Lost 4.557
All *Autumn* pil'd, though *Spring* and *Autumn* here Par Lost 5.394

Autumnal
Thick as Autumnal Leaves that strow the Brooks Par Lost 1.302
ms 'Autumnall'
Rule in the Clouds; like an Autumnal Star Par Reg 4.619

Auxiliar
Mixt with auxiliar Gods; and what resounds Par Lost 1.579

Avail
What can it then avail though yet we feel Par Lost 1.153
ms 'availe'
But to convince the proud what Signs availe, Par Lost 6.789
What may no less perhaps availe us known, Par Lost 7.85
1669 'avail'
Then shall they seek to avail themselves of names, Par Lost 12.515
But here thy sword can do thee little stead, Mask 611
Trinity ms 'little stead' ←'small availe' ←'little stead'
Availed
Fell long before; nor aught avail'd him now Par Lost 1.748
Sam. But what avail'd this temperance, not compleat Samson 558
Avails
Ruin must needs ensue; for what availes Par Lost 6.456
No more availes then breath against the winde, Par Lost 11.312
O what avails me now that honour high Par Reg 2.66
Avarice
While Avarice, and Rapine share the land. Sonnet 15, 14
Avaunt
But mark what I arreede thee now, avant; Par Lost 4.962
Avenge
Avenge O Lord thy slaughter'd Saints, whose bones Sonnet 18, 1
Avenged
Mankind with her faire looks, to be aveng'd Par Lost 4.718
To honour his Anointed Son aveng'd Par Lost 6.676
Of his adorers: hee to be aveng'd, Par Lost 9.143
With odds what Warr hath lost, and fully aveng'd Par Lost 10.374
Will be aveng'd, and th' others Faith approv'd Par Lost 11.458
With all his Army, now thou hast aveng'd Par Reg 4.606
Avenger
By his Avengers, since no place like this Par Lost 10.241
1667 'Avenger'
To stint th' enemy, and slack th' avengers brow Psalm 8, 7
Avengers
By his Avengers, since no place like this Par Lost 10.241
1667 'Avenger'
Avenging
Ere this avenging Sword begin thy doome, Par Lost 6.278
Glorie to him whose just avenging ire Par Lost 7.184
Aver
Though Reason here aver Samson 323
Averse
The most averse, thee chiefly, who full oft Par Lost 2.763
Travelling East, and with her part averse Par Lost 8.138
On the eighth return'd, and on the Coast averse Par Lost 9.67
Some much averse I found and wondrous harsh, Samson 1461
And now be wise at length ye Kings averse Psalm 2, 22
Aversion
What if with like aversion I reject Par Reg 2.457
Avert
If such affront I labour to avert Par Lost 9.302
His presence from among them, and avert Par Lost 12.108
Where thou mayst bring thy off'rings, to avert Samson 519
Avoid
Expos'd a Matron to avoid worse rape. Par Lost 1.505
1667 'prevent'
Thy absence from my sight, but to avoid Par Lost 9.294
Seek not temptation then, which to avoide Par Lost 9.364
Thou canst avoid, self-preservation bids; Samson 505
And run to meet what he would most avoid? Mask 363
line not in Bridgewater ms
line not in Trinity ms
Avoided
Avoided pinching cold and scorching heate? Par Lost 10.691
All friendship, and avoided as a blab, Samson 495
Avon
Or Rockie *Avon*, or of Sedgie *Lee*, Vacation 97
Avow
Avow, and challenge *Dagon* to the test, Samson 1151
Await
Appointed to await me thirty spies, Samson 1197
Awaited
Meekly compos'd awaited the fulfilling: Par Reg 2.108
Awaiting
Awaiting what command thir mighty Chief Par Lost 1.566
ms 'A-waiting'
His look suspence, awaiting who appeer'd Par Lost 2.418
Chief of th' Angelic Guards, awaiting night; Par Lost 4.550
Awaiting next command. To whom thir Chief Par Lost 4.864
Awaits
O *Eve*, some furder change awaits us nigh, Par Lost 11.193
Awaits the good, the rest what punishment? Par Lost 11.710
O yet a nobler task awaites thy hand; Sonnet 15, 9
1694 'awaits'
Awake
Awake, arise, or be for ever fall'n. Par Lost 1.330
Rouse and bestir themselves ere well awake. Par Lost 1.334
Her hand soft touching, whisperd thus. Awake Par Lost 5.17
Awake, the morning shines, and the fresh field Par Lost 5.20
To the night-warbling Bird, that now awake Par Lost 5.40
Still glorious before whom awake I stood; Par Lost 8.464
Compell'd me to awake the courteous Echo Mask 275
Awake thy strength, come, and *be seen* Psalm 80, 11
Awaked
Awak'd should blow them into sevenfold rage Par Lost 2.171
I first awak't, and found my self repos'd Par Lost 4.450
Of wrauth awak't: nor with less dread the loud Par Lost 6.59
Under a Juniper; then how awakt, Par Reg 2.272

Awaked(*cont*)
Sam. Ay me, another inward grief awak't, Samson 330
Awakened
Awakn'd in me swarm, while I consider Par Reg 1.197
Awakening
Awak'ning, thus to him in secret spake. Par Lost 5.672
Awakes
Awakes the slumbring leaves, or tasseld horn Arcades 57
Aware
Are ever cleer. Whereof hee soon aware, Par Lost 4.119
So warnd he them aware themselves, and soon Par Lost 6.547
Was took e're she was ware, and wish't she might Mask 558
Away
Thir Arms away they threw, and to the Hills Par Lost 6.639
Thy country, and captive lead away her Kings Par Reg 3.366
It withers on the stalk with languish't head. Mask 744
Trinity ms 'with languish't head' ←'and fades away'
And shove away the worthy bidden guest. Lycidas 118
Wash far away, where ere thy bones are hurld, Lycidas 155
And Hell it self will pass away, Nativity 139
Thereby to wipe away th' infamous blot, Fair Inf 12
Or drive away the slaughtering pestilence, Fair Inf 68
Pull'd off his Boots, and took away the light: Carrier 16
Meerly to drive the time away he sickn'd, Another 15
line not in 1640, 1657, 1658 texts
Awe
Such was thir awe of Man. In shadie Bower Par Lost 4.705
He held it vain; awe from above had quelld Par Lost 4.860
And pious awe, that feard to have offended. Par Lost 5.135
Of airie threats to aw whom yet with deeds Par Lost 6.283
Presence Divine. Rejoycing, but with aw Par Lost 8.314
Build in her loveliest, and create an awe Par Lost 8.558
Why then was this forbid? Why but to awe, Par Lost 9.703
Devourd each other; nor stood much in awe Par Lost 10.712
With aw the Regions round, and with them came Par Reg 1.22
Or turn to reverent awe? for Beauty stands Par Reg 2.220
Thy bold attempt; hereafter learn with awe Par Reg 4.625
Over his female in due awe, Samson 1055
Has in his charge, with temper'd awe to guide Mask 32
Trinity ms 'aw'
Where through the sacred rayes of Chastity, Mask 425
Trinity ms 'rays' ←'aw'
With sudden adoration, and blank aw. Mask 452
Trinity ms 'and blank aw' ←'of bright rays' ←'of her puerenesse'
Bridgewater ms 'awe'
Nature in aw to him Nativity 32
1673 'awe'
Shall aw the World, and Conquer Nations bold. Prose 12, 14
Awed
Neerer his presence *Adam* though not awd, Par Lost 5.358
Aw'd by the rod of *Moses* so to stand Par Lost 12.198
Which might have aw'd the best resolv'd of men, Samson 847
Be aw'd, and do not sin, Psalm 4, 19
Awe-struck
And play i' th plighted clouds. I was aw-strook, Mask 301
Bridgewater ms 'awe-strooke'
Trinity ms 'aw strooke'
1637 'aw-strooke'
Awful
Of Sovran power, with awful Ceremony Par Lost 1.753
ms 'awfull'
With awful reverence prone; and as a God Par Lost 2.478
And felt how awful goodness is, and saw Par Lost 4.847
Heav'ns awful Monarch? wherefore but in hope Par Lost 4.960
So awful, that with honour thou maist love Par Lost 8.577
Thy awful brow, more awful thus retir'd. Par Lost 9.537
More awful then the sound of Trumpet, cri'd Par Reg 1.19
And Kings sate still with awfull eye, Nativity 59
Awhile
Pain for a while or anguish, and excite Par Lost 2.567
Stood on the brink of Hell and look'd a while, Par Lost 2.918
By loosing thee a while, the whole Race lost. Par Lost 3.280
Those happie places thou hast deignd a while Par Lost 5.364
Danc'd hand in hand. A while discourse they hold; Par Lost 5.395
A while, but suddenly at head appeerd Par Lost 6.556
A while in trouble; but they stood not long, Par Lost 6.634
So Charming left his voice, that he a while Par Lost 8.2
line not in 1667 edition
And gaz'd a while the ample Skie, till rais'd Par Lost 8.258
Pausing a while, thus to her self she mus'd. Par Lost 9.744
Was plac't in regal lustre. Down a while Par Lost 10.447
So having said, a while he stood, expecting Par Lost 10.504
They first re-edifie, and for a while Par Lost 12.350
Such high attest was giv'n, a while survey'd Par Reg 1.37
A while as mute confounded what to say, Par Reg 3.2
As over-tir'd to let him lean a while Samson 1632
Felt in his arms, with head a while enclin'd, Samson 1636
At which I ceas't, and listen'd them a while, Mask 551
Trinity ms 'awhile'
snatch us from earth a while Musick Tr. ms 4.07
The Subject new: it walk'd the Town a while, Sonnet 11, 3
Awry
Blows them transverse ten thousand Leagues awry Par Lost 3.488
Much of the Soul they talk, but all awrie, Par Reg 4.313
Draws him awry enslav'd Samson 1041
Axe
Of Pioners with Spade and Pickax arm'd Par Lost 1.676

Axe(*cont*)
ms 'pick axe'
1667 'Pickaxe'
Where the rude Ax with heaved stroke, Penseroso 136
Axes
A multitude with Spades and Axes arm'd Par Reg 3.331
And cut *with Axes* down, Psalm 80, 66
Axle
In mutinie had from her Axle torn Par Lost 2.926
Revolvd on Heav'ns great Axle, and her Reign Par Lost 7.381
On her soft Axle, while she paces Eev'n, Par Lost 8.165
From the Suns Axle; they with labour push'd Par Lost 10.670
His glowing Axle doth allay Mask 96
Bridgewater ms 'axle'
Trinity ms 'axle'
Axletree
Then his bright Throne, or burning Axletree could bear. Nativity 84
Ay
Th' Omnipotent. Ay me, they little know Par Lost 4.86
To perpetuitie; Ay me, that fear Par Lost 10.813
Sam. Ay me, another inward grief awak't, Samson 330
Spir. Ay me unhappy then my fears are true. Mask 511
1637 'Aye'
Ay me, I fondly dream! Lycidas 56
1638 'Ah me'
Ay me! Whilst thee the shores, and sounding Seas Lycidas 154
For his mercies ay endure, Psalm 136, 3 etc.
Aye
Ay round about *Joves* Altar sing. Penseroso 48
Of him that ever was, and ay shall last, Psalm 114, 16
Ay sung before the saphire-colour'd throne Musick 7
For aye, with Temples vow'd, and Virgin quires. Prose 12, 6
Azazel
Azazel as his right, a Cherube tall: Par Lost 1.534
ms 'Azazel'
Azores
Beneath th' *Azores;* whither the prime Orb, Par Lost 4.592
Azotus
Rear'd in *Azotus*, dreaded through the Coast Par Lost 1.464
ms 'Azotus'
Azure
On Heavens Azure, and the torrid Clime Par Lost 1.297
ms 'azure'
With spots of Gold and Purple, azure and green: Par Lost 7.479
Carnation, Purple, Azure, or spect with Gold, Par Lost 9.429
And azure wings, that up they flew so drest, Sonnet 14, 11
Azurn
Thick set with Agat, and the azurn sheen Mask 893
1637 'azurne'
Trinity ms 'azurne'
Bridgewater ms 'Azur'd'
Azza
The Gates of *Azza*, Post, and massie Bar Samson 147
Baal
Of *Egypt*, *Baal* next and *Ashtaroth*, Par Reg 3.417
Baalim
Of *Baalim* and *Ashtaroth*, those male, Par Lost 1.422
ms 'Baalim'
Peor, and *Baalim*, Nativity 197
Babble
This is meer moral babble, and direct Mask 807
Trinity ms 'meere moral bable' ←'your morall stuffe' ←'meere morall stuffe'
Babe
The Babe lies yet in smiling Infancy, Nativity 151
Our Babe to shew his Godhead true, Nativity 227
Hath laid her Babe to rest. Nativity 238
The haples Babe before his birth Winchester 31
Babel
Of *Babel*, and the works of *Memphian* Kings Par Lost 1.694
ms 'Babell'
The builders next of *Babel* on the Plain Par Lost 3.466
I mention Babel to my friends, Psalm 87, 13
Babels
New *Babels*, had they wherewithall, would build: Par Lost 3.468
Babes
Out of the mouths of babes and sucklings thou Psalm 8, 5
Babylon
The Roof was fretted Gold. Not *Babilon*, Par Lost 1.717
ms 'Babilon'
Left in confusion, *Babylon* thence call'd. Par Lost 12.343
Returnd from *Babylon* by leave of Kings Par Lost 12.348
There *Babylon* the wonder of all tongues, Par Reg 3.280
Our Hebrew Songs and Harps in *Babylon*, Par Reg 4.336
Babylonian
Early may fly the *Babylonian* wo. Sonnet 18, 14
Baca
They pass through Baca's *thirstie* Vale, Psalm 84, 21
Bacchus
Young *Bacchus* from his Stepdame *Rhea*'s eye; Par Lost 4.279
Of *Bacchus* and his revellers, the Race Par Lost 7.33
Bacchus that first from out the purple Grape, Mask 46
Of *Bacchus*, and of *Circe* born, great *Comus*, Mask 522
To Ivy-crowned *Bacchus* bore; Allegro 16
Back
Back to the Gates of Heav'n: the Sulphurous Hail Par Lost 1.171
Periods of time, thence hurried back to fire. Par Lost 2.603
Thy King and Lord? Back to thy punishment, Par Lost 2.699

Back(*cont*)
All th' Host of Heav'n; back they recoild affraid Par Lost 2.759
From all her Caves, and back resounded *Death*. Par Lost 2.789
Back from pursuit thy Powers with loud acclaime Par Lost 3.397
His back was turnd, but not his brightness hid; Par Lost 3.624
And like a devillish Engine back recoiles Par Lost 4.17
Bending to look on me, I started back, Par Lost 4.462
It started back, but pleas'd I soon returnd, Par Lost 4.463
Then that smooth watry image; back I turnd, Par Lost 4.480
Back stept those two faire Angels half amaz'd Par Lost 4.820
Seavenfold, and scourge that wisdom back to Hell, Par Lost 4.914
Back to th' infernal pit I drag thee chaind, Par Lost 4.965
And with retorted scorn his back he turn'd Par Lost 5.906
Back on thy foes more glorious to return Par Lost 6.39
He back recoild; the tenth on bended knee Par Lost 6.194
Back to his Chariot; where it stood retir'd Par Lost 6.338
But firm Battalion; back with speediest Sail Par Lost 6.534
Our overture, and turn not back perverse; Par Lost 6.562
Of Thunder: back defeated to return Par Lost 6.606
Driv'n back redounded as a flood on those Par Lost 7.57
Light back to them, is obvious to dispute. Par Lost 8.158
Bitter ere long back on it self recoiles; Par Lost 9.172
To intercept thy way, or send thee back Par Lost 9.410
That all was lost. Back to the Thicket slunk Par Lost 9.784
But least the difficultie of passing back Par Lost 10.252
Desirous to resigne, and render back Par Lost 10.749
Comes thundring back with dreadful revolution Par Lost 10.814
Blown stifling back on him that breaths it forth: Par Lost 11.313
With glory and spoile back to thir promis'd Land. Par Lost 12.172
Return them back to *Egypt*, choosing rather Par Lost 12.219
The adversarie Serpent, and bring back Par Lost 12.312
The space of seventie years, then brings them back, Par Lost 12.345
They looking back, all th' Eastern side beheld Par Lost 12.641
All his vast force, and drive him back to Hell, Par Reg 1.153
May bring them back repentant and sincere, Par Reg 3.435
Brought back the Son of God, and left him there, Par Reg 4.396
Your younger feet, while mine cast back with age Samson 336
Were bristles rang'd like those that ridge the back Samson 1137
But where they are, and why they came not back, Mask 191
But evil on it self shall back recoyl, Mask 593
1637 'backe'
And force him to restore his purchase back, Mask 607
1637 'backe'
Trinity ms 'purchase back' ←'new got prey'
This will restore all soon. *La.* 'Twill not false traitor, Mask 690
Trinity ms 't'will not' ←'stand back'
Spir. Back Shepherds, back, anough your play, Mask 958
B.M. ms 'Back enough'
Time will run back, and fetch the age of gold, Nativity 135
And after short abode flie back with speed, Fair Inf 60
I wak'd, she fled, and day brought back my night. Sonnet 23, 14
So shall we not go back from thee Psalm 80, 73
Returned Jacob back. Psalm 85, 4
Backed
To equal length back'd with a ridge of hills Par Reg 4.29
Back'd on the North and West by a thick wood, Par Reg 4.448
Backs
Emergent, and thir broad bare backs upheave Par Lost 7.286
Thir plated backs under his heel; Samson 140
Backside
Fly o're the backside of the World farr off Par Lost 3.494
Backward
Drivn backward slope thir pointing spires, and rowld Par Lost 1.223
Strook them with horror backward, but far worse Par Lost 6.863
And backward mutters of dissevering power, Mask 817
Bactra
His City there thou seest, and *Bactra* there; Par Reg 3.285
Bactrian
Retires, or *Bactrian* Sophi from the hornes Par Lost 10.433
Bad
So numberless were those bad Angels seen Par Lost 1.344
To that bad eminence; and from despair Par Lost 2.6
Loose all her virtue; least bad men should boast Par Lost 2.483
His mother bad, and thus bespake her Sire. Par Lost 2.849
Bad men and Angels, they arraignd shall sink Par Lost 3.331
The barrs of Hell, on errand bad no doubt: Par Lost 4.795
Bad influence into th' unwarie brest Par Lost 5.695
In Serpent, Inmate bad, and toward *Eve* Par Lost 9.495
In recompence (for such compliance bad Par Lost 9.994
Bad Fruit of Knowledge, if this be to know, Par Lost 9.1073
But let us now, as in bad plight, devise Par Lost 9.1091
On his bad Errand, Man should be seduc't Par Lost 10.41
With that bad Woman? Thus what thou desir'st Par Lost 10.837
And one bad act with many deeds well done Par Lost 11.256
To thee and to thy Ofspring; good with bad Par Lost 11.358
Where good with bad were matcht, who of themselves Par Lost 11.685
Still tend from bad to worse, till God at last Par Lost 12.106
Part good, part bad, of bad the longer scrowle, Par Lost 12.336
To good malignant, to bad men benigne, Par Lost 12.538
Glory from men, from all men good or bad, Par Reg 3.114
Perplex'd and troubl'd at his bad success Par Reg 4.1
Have err'd, and by bad Women been deceiv'd; Samson 211
Chor. Of good or bad so great, of bad the sooner; Samson 1537
For when as each thing bad thou hast entomb'd, On Time 9
And the way of bad men to ruine must. Psalm 1, 16
Bade
And bad me keep it as of sovran use Mask 639

Baffled
Sams. Go baffl'd coward, lest I run upon thee, Samson 1237
Bait
Which grew in Paradise, the bait of *Eve* Par Lost 10.551
Thence to the bait of Women lay expos'd; Par Reg 2.204
The bait of honied words; a rougher tongue Samson 1066
Baited
Baited with reasons not unplausible Mask 162
Bridgewater ms 'bayted'
Baits
For evil news rides post, while good news baits. Samson 1538
Yet have they many baits, and guilefull spells Mask 537
Bridgewater ms 'baites'
With lickerish baits fit to ensnare a brute? Mask 700
line not in Bridgewater ms
Trinity ms 'baites'
Balaam
To *Balaam* Reprobate, a Prophet yet Par Reg 1.491
Balance
Thir course, in even ballance down they light Par Lost 1.349
And that Crystalline Sphear whose ballance weighs Par Lost 3.482
Balanced
The pendulous round Earth with ballanc't Aire Par Lost 4.1000
And Earth self ballanc't on her Center hung. Par Lost 7.242
1667 'self-ballanc't'
And the well-ballanc't world on hinges hung, Nativity 122
Baleful
Torments him; round he throws his baleful eyes Par Lost 1.56
ms 'balefull'
Into the burning Lake thir baleful streams; Par Lost 2.576
Culling their Potent hearbs, and balefull drugs, Mask 255
Ball
Mixt Dance, or wanton Mask, or Midnight Bal, Par Lost 4.768
To such a tender ball as th' eye confin'd? Samson 94
Balls
Whereof to found thir Engins and thir Balls Par Lost 6.518
Balm
New rub'd with Baum, expatiate and confer Par Lost 1.774
1667 'Baume'
ms 'baume'
Shall breathe her balme. But first whom shall we send Par Lost 2.402
Groves whose rich Trees wept odorous Gumms and Balme, Par Lost 4.248
And flouring Odours, Cassia, Nard, and Balme; Par Lost 5.293
Of blowing Myrrh and Balme; if thou accept Par Lost 9.629
The Balme of Life. To whom our Ancestor. Par Lost 11.546
And are as Balm to fester'd wounds. Samson 186
The close of all my miseries, and the balm. Samson 651
With spirits of balm, and fragrant Syrops mixt. Mask 674
1637 'balme'
Trinity ms 'baulme' ←'balme'
Bridgewater ms 'baulme'
Nard, and *Cassia*'s balmy smels. Mask 991
Trinity ms 'Nard' ←'nard' ←'balme'
Balmy
Those balmie spoiles. As when to them who saile Par Lost 4.159
What drops the Myrrhe, and what the balmie Reed, Par Lost 5.23
In Balmie Sweat, which with his Beames the Sun Par Lost 8.255
Rapt in a balmie Cloud with winged Steeds Par Lost 11.706
Nard, and *Cassia*'s balmy smels. Mask 991
1637 'balmie'
Bridgewater ms 'balmie'
Trinity ms 'baulmie' ←'balmy' ←'fragrant'
Balsara
Of *Susiana* to *Balsara*'s hav'n. Par Reg 3.321
Ban
Much more to taste it under banne to touch. Par Lost 9.925
Band
Forthwith from every Squadron and each Band Par Lost 1.356
ms 'band'
From every Band and squared Regiment Par Lost 1.758
ms 'band'
1667 'and Band', 1668 errata 'Band and'
Gently with Mirtle band, mindless the while, Par Lost 9.431
One way a Band select from forage drives Par Lost 11.646
Then forthwith to him takes a chosen band Par Reg 2.236
And all that band them to resist Samson 1753
To undoe the charmed band Mask 904
Banded
Banded against his Throne, but to remaine Par Lost 2.320
Were banded to oppose his high Decree; Par Lost 5.717
The banded Powers of *Satan* hasting on Par Lost 6.85
Soon banded; others from the dawning Hills Par Lost 6.528
Close-banded durst attaque me, no not sleeping, Samson 1113
Bandit
No savage fierce, Bandite, or mountaneer Mask 426
Bridgewater ms 'bandite'
1637 'bandite'
Trinity ms 'bandite'
Bands
A numerous Brigad hasten'd. As when Bands Par Lost 1.675
ms 'bands'
1667 'bands'
Another part in Squadrons and gross Bands, Par Lost 2.570
In confus'd march forlorn, th' adventrous Bands Par Lost 2.615
Pourd out by millions her victorious Bands Par Lost 2.997
Angels ascending and descending, bands Par Lost 3.511
Singing thir great Creator: oft in bands Par Lost 4.684
The circuit wide. Strait knew him all the Bands Par Lost 5.287

Bands(*cont*)
1667 'bands' in some copies
Disperst in Bands and Files thir Camp extend Par Lost 5.651
Bind us with after-bands, what profits then Par Lost 9.761
He err'd not, for by this the heav'nly Bands Par Lost 11.208
Above the faith of wedlock-bands, my tomb Samson 986
Can in his swadling bands controul the damned crew. Nativity 228
While the Hebrew Bands did pass. Psalm 136, 50
With them *great* Asshur also bands Psalm 83, 29
Bane
Deserve the precious bane. And here let those Par Lost 1.692
Should prove a bitter Morsel, and his bane, Par Lost 2.808
Who came thir bane, though with them better pleas'd Par Lost 4.167
Bane, and in Heav'n much worse would be my state. Par Lost 9.123
Spreading thir bane; the blasted Starrs lookt wan, Par Lost 10.412
Suffices that to me strength is my bane, Samson 63
Pray'd for, but often proves our woe, our bane? Samson 351
Baneful
By sly enticement gives his banefull cup, Mask 525
1673 'baneful'
Banias
From *Paneas* the fount of *Jordans* flood Par Lost 3.535
Banish
And gladly banish squint suspicion. Mask 413
Banished
And banisht from mans life his happiest life, Par Lost 4.317
Lost sight of him; one of the banisht crew Par Lost 4.573
Heav'n-banisht Host, left desert utmost Hell Par Lost 10.437
Who for my wilful crime art banisht hence. Par Lost 12.619
1669 'banish't'
That thou hast banish't from thy tongue with lies, Mask 692
Trinity ms 'banisht'
Bridgewater ms 'banisht'
Banishment
Perpetual banishment. Yet least they faint Par Lost 11.108
Bank
That to the fringed Bank with Myrtle crownd, Par Lost 4.262
On the soft downie Bank damaskt with flours: Par Lost 4.334
On the green bank, to look into the cleer Par Lost 4.458
Bank the mid Sea: part single or with mate Par Lost 7.403
On a green shadie Bank profuse of Flours Par Lost 8.286
Imborderd on each Bank, the hand of *Eve:* Par Lost 9.438
Her hand he seis'd, and to a shadie bank, Par Lost 9.1037
Then on the bank of *Jordan*, by a Creek: Par Reg 2.25
On a green bank, and set before him spred Par Reg 4.587
For yonder bank hath choice of Sun or shade, Samson 3
Perhaps som cold bank is her boulster now Mask 353
1637 'banke'
Bridgewater ms 'banke'
Trinity ms 'bank' ←'bancke', 'banke' in margin
I sate me down to watch upon a bank Mask 543
Bridgewater ms 'banke'
Trinity ms 'banke'
By the rushy-fringed bank, Mask 890
Bridgewater ms 'banke'
Trinity ms 'banck'
1637 'banke'
Banks
Was fair *Damascus*, on the fertil Banks Par Lost 1.468
ms 'banks'
Four ways thir flying March, along the Banks Par Lost 2.574
All but within those banks, where Rivers now Par Lost 7.305
Divided by a river, of whose banks Par Reg 4.32
On banks and scaffolds under Skie might stand; Samson 1610
And here and there thy banks upon Mask 936
Trinity ms 'bancks'
Bridgewater ms 'bankes'
Waters the odorous banks that blow Mask 993
Bridgewater ms 'bankes'
B.M. ms 'Banks'
amidst the Hesperian gardens, on whose bancks Mask Tr. ms 10.05
'on whose bancks' ←'where the banks' ←'on whose bancks'
By sandy *Ladons* Lillied banks. Arcades 97
Trinity ms 'bancks'
Sent thee from the banks of *Came*, Winchester 59
Bannered
That with extended wings a Bannerd Host Par Lost 2.885
Banners
Ten thousand Banners rise into the Air Par Lost 1.545
ms 'banners'
And all who under me thir Banners wave, Par Lost 5.687
Banquet
The Sun, as from *Thyestean* Banquet, turn'd Par Lost 10.688
Banquets
Were it a draft for *Juno* when she banquets, Mask 701
Bridgewater ms 'banquetts'
Baptism
To all Baptiz'd: to his great Baptism flock'd Par Reg 1.21
I as all others to his Baptism came, Par Reg 1.273
Refus'd on me his Baptism to confer, Par Reg 1.278
Others return'd from Baptism, not her Son, Par Reg 2.61
Baptist
Unmarkt, unknown; but him the Baptist soon Par Reg 1.25
The Baptist, (of whose birth I oft had heard, Par Reg 1.270
At *Jordan* with the Baptist, and had seen Par Reg 2.2
By *John* the Baptist, and in publick shown, Par Reg 2.84
Flock'd to the Baptist, I among the rest, Par Reg 4.511

Baptized
And all who since, Baptiz'd or Infidel — Par Lost 1.582
ms 'baptiz'd'
Baptiz'd, shall them with wondrous gifts endue — Par Lost 12.500
To all Baptiz'd: to his great Baptism flock'd — Par Reg 1.21
His witness unconfirm'd: on him baptiz'd — Par Reg 1.29
And he himself among them was baptiz'd, — Par Reg 1.76
Lodg'd in *Bethabara* where *John* baptiz'd, — Par Reg 1.184
Mean while the new-baptiz'd, who yet remain'd — Par Reg 2.1
Though not to be Baptiz'd, by voice from Heav'n — Par Reg 4.512

Baptizing
Baptizing in the profluent stream, the signe — Par Lost 12.442
Our new baptizing Prophet at the Ford — Par Reg 1.328

Bar
Th' intricate wards, and every Bolt and Bar — Par Lost 2.877
Spiritual substance with corporeal barr. — Par Lost 4.585
His will who bound us? let him surer barr — Par Lost 4.897
The Gates of *Azza*, Post, and massie Bar — Samson 147
Which others at their Barr so often wrench; — Sonnet 21, 4
line not in Trinity ms

Barbaric
Showrs on her Kings *Barbaric* Pearl and Gold, — Par Lost 2.4
1667 'Barbaric' in some copies

Barbarous
Rhene or the *Danaw*, when her barbarous Sons — Par Lost 1.353
But drive farr off the barbarous dissonance — Par Lost 7.32
Or Barbarous, nor exception hath declar'd; — Par Reg 3.119
The rest are barbarous, and scarce worth the sight, — Par Reg 4.86
And fill'd the Air with barbarous dissonance, — Mask 550
Those rugged names to our like mouths grow sleek — Sonnet 11, 10
Trinity ms 'rugged' ←'rough hewn' ←'barbarous'
When strait a barbarous noise environs me — Sonnet 12, 3

Barbed
But ratling storm of Arrows barbd with fire. — Par Lost 6.546

Barber
But by the Barbers razor best subdu'd. — Samson 1167

Barca
Of *Barca* or *Cyrene*'s torrid soil, — Par Lost 2.904

Bard
Of that wilde Rout that tore the *Thracian* Bard — Par Lost 7.34
From old, or modern Bard in Hall, or Bowr. — Mask 45
Bridgewater ms 'bard'

Bards
And if ought els, great *Bards* beside, — Penseroso 116
Where your old *Bards*, the famous *Druids* ly, — Lycidas 53
Trinity ms 'bards'

Bare
Came singly where he stood on the bare strand, — Par Lost 1.379
With singed top thir stately growth though bare — Par Lost 1.614
On the bare outside of this World, that seem'd — Par Lost 3.74
Emergent, and thir broad bare backs upheave — Par Lost 7.286
He scarce had said, when the bare Earth, till then — Par Lost 7.313
Desert and bare, unsightly, unadornd, — Par Lost 7.314
Shorn of his strength, They destitute and bare — Par Lost 9.1062
From out of *Chaos* to the out side bare — Par Lost 10.317
And there take root an Iland salt and bare, — Par Lost 11.834
Bare in thy guilt how foul must thou appear? — Samson 902
He with his bare wand can unthred thy joynts, — Mask 614
To save th' *Athenian* Walls from ruine bare. — Sonnet 8, 14

Bark
Sea-faring men orewatcht, whose Bark by chance — Par Lost 2.288
Kindles the gummie bark of Firr or Pine, — Par Lost 10.1076
Or 'gainst the rugged bark of som broad Elm — Mask 354
Trinity ms 'barke'
1637 'barke'
Bridgewater ms 'barke'
It was that fatall and perfidious Bark — Lycidas 100
1638 'bark'
Trinity ms 'barke'

Barked
A cry of Hell Hounds never ceasing bark'd — Par Lost 2.654
And kennel there, yet there still bark'd and howl'd, — Par Lost 2.658

Barking
And chid her barking waves into attention, — Mask 258
Bridgewater ms 'barkinge'

Barn
And to the stack, or the Barn dore, — Allegro 51

Barons
Where throngs of Knights and Barons bold, — Allegro 119

Barred
Barr'd over us prohibit all egress. — Par Lost 2.437
Cross-barrd and bolted fast, fear no assault, — Par Lost 4.190
The facil gates of hell too slightly barrd. — Par Lost 4.967
West from *Orontes* to the Ocean barr'd — Par Lost 9.80
Barr'd of his right; yet at his Birth a Starr — Par Lost 12.360
Be barr'd that happines, might we but hear — Mask 343
Deaths hideous house hath barr'd. — Psalm 88, 24

Barren
But in his way lights on the barren Plaines — Par Lost 3.437
His barren leaves. Them thus imploid beheld — Par Lost 5.219
More plenty then the Sun that barren shines, — Par Lost 8.94
Wandred this barren waste, the same I now: — Par Reg 1.354
For barren desert fountainless and dry. — Par Reg 3.264
Mountains on whose barren brest — Allegro 73
That dry and barren ground — Psalm 84, 22

Barrenness
Against our selves, and wilful barrenness, — Par Lost 10.1042
I pray'd for Children, and thought barrenness — Samson 352

Barrenness(*cont*)
Who after yeers of barrennes, — Winchester 64
1673 'barrenness'

Barricadoed
The dismal Gates, and barricado'd strong; — Par Lost 8.241

Bars
Prescrib'd, no barrs of Hell, nor all the chains — Par Lost 3.82
The barrs of Hell, on errand bad no doubt: — Par Lost 4.795
Of membrane, joynt, or limb, exclusive barrs: — Par Lost 8.625
And with rebounding surge the barrs assaild, — Par Lost 10.417

Basan
In *Argob* and in *Basan*, to the stream — Par Lost 1.398
ms 'Basan'

Base
Exalted from so base original, — Par Lost 9.150
Circular base of rising foulds, that tour'd — Par Lost 9.498
That people victor once, now vile and base, — Par Reg 4.132
The base degree to which I now am fall'n, — Samson 414
These rags, this grinding, is not yet so base — Samson 415
And earths base built on stubble. But com let's on. — Mask 599
With visor'd falshood, and base forgery, — Mask 698
line not in Bridgewater ms
But with besotted base ingratitude — Mask 778

Baser
Her mischief, and purge off the baser fire — Par Lost 2.141

Bases
Bases and tinsel Trappings, gorgious Knights — Par Lost 9.36

Basest
To basest things. Revenge, at first though sweet, — Par Lost 9.171

Bashan
In *Argob* and in *Basan*, to the stream — Par Lost 1.398
ms 'Basan'

Basis
That shake Heav'ns basis, bring forth all my Warr, — Par Lost 6.712
Or to the Earths dark basis underneath, — Par Reg 4.456

Basks
Basks at the fire his hairy strength; — Allegro 112

Bass
And let the Base of Heav'ns deep Organ blow, — Nativity 130

Bastards
And live like Natures bastards, not her sons, — Mask 727

Bate
Against heavns hand or will, nor bate a jot — Sonnet 22, 7

Bates
As one who in his journey bates at Noone, — Par Lost 12.1
line not in 1667 edition

Bathe
Will bathe the drooping spirits in delight — Mask 812
Trinity ms 'bath'
Bridgewater ms 'bath'

Bathed
Others on Silver Lakes and Rivers Bath'd — Par Lost 7.437

Bathing
Vex'd *Scylla* bathing in the Sea that parts — Par Lost 2.660

Baths
Porches and Theatres, Baths, Aqueducts, — Par Reg 4.36

Battailous
In battailous aspect, and neerer view — Par Lost 6.81

Battalion
The whole Battalion views, thir order due, — Par Lost 1.569
ms 'battalion'
But firm Battalion; back with speediest Sail — Par Lost 6.534

Battening
Batt'ning our flocks with the fresh dews of night, — Lycidas 29
Trinity ms 'batning'

Battered
With that twise batter'd god of *Palestine*, — Nativity 199

Batteries
Tongue-batteries, she surceas'd not day nor night — Samson 404

Battering
With all her battering Engines bent to rase — Par Lost 2.923

Battery
Lay Seige, encampt; by Batterie, Scale, and Mine, — Par Lost 11.656
Vain battry, and in froth or bubbles end; — Par Reg 4.20

Battle
Rais'd impious War in Heav'n and Battel proud — Par Lost 1.43
ms 'battell'
In dubious Battel on the Plains of Heav'n, — Par Lost 1.104
ms 'battell'
Of battel when it rag'd, in all assaults — Par Lost 1.277
ms 'battell'
After the toyl of Battel to repose — Par Lost 1.319
ms 'battell'
Bow'd down in Battel, sunk before the Spear — Par Lost 1.436
ms 'battell'
Arming to Battel, and in stead of rage — Par Lost 1.553
ms 'battell'
Desperate revenge, and Battel dangerous — Par Lost 2.107
To Battel in the Clouds, before each Van — Par Lost 2.535
By doom of Battel; and complain that Fate — Par Lost 2.550
Strive here for Maistrie, and to Battel bring — Par Lost 2.899
Of that first Battel, and his flight to Hell: — Par Lost 4.12
Thy fiercest, when in Battel to thy aide — Par Lost 4.927
In battel, what our Power is, or our right. — Par Lost 5.728
Gabriel, lead forth to Battel these my Sons — Par Lost 6.46
Of Battel now began, and rushing sound — Par Lost 6.97
On the rough edge of battel ere it joyn'd, — Par Lost 6.108
Of Battel: whereat *Michael* bid sound — Par Lost 6.202

Battle(*cont*)
Of Battel, open when, and when to close — Par Lost 6.235
The Battel hung; till *Satan*, who that day — Par Lost 6.246
And now thir Mightiest quelld, the battel swerv'd, — Par Lost 6.386
To final Battel drew, disdaining flight, — Par Lost 6.798
Ye Angels arm'd, this day from Battel rest; — Par Lost 6.802
In Battel which the stronger proves, they all, — Par Lost 6.819
Against the day of Battel, to a Field, — Par Lost 10.275
As Battel hath adjudg'd, from this new World — Par Lost 10.377
Single or in Array of Battel rang'd — Par Lost 11.644
To overcome in Battle, and subdue — Par Lost 11.691
1667 'Battel'
In sharp contest of Battel found no aide — Par Lost 11.800
In battel, though against thy few in arms. — Par Reg 3.20
He saw them in thir forms of battell rang'd, — Par Reg 3.322
In that sore battel when so many dy'd — Samson 287
After the brunt of battel, can as easie — Samson 583
Which greatest Heroes have in battel worn, — Samson 1131
Feirce signe of battail make, and menace high, — Mask 654
1637 'battaile'
Trinity ms 'battaile'
Bridgewater ms 'battaile'
No War, or Battails sound — Nativity 53
In bloody battail he brought down — Psalm 136, 61
1673 'battel'

Battlements
Sheer o're the Chrystal Battlements; from Morn — Par Lost 1.742
ms 'battlements'
With Opal Towrs and Battlements adorn'd — Par Lost 2.1049
With gilded battlements, conspicuous far, — Par Reg 4.53
Towers, and Battlements it sees — Allegro 77

Battles
Battels and Realms: in these he put two weights — Par Lost 4.1002
Both Battels maine, with ruinous assault — Par Lost 6.216
In Battels feign'd; the better fortitude — Par Lost 9.31
Were long to tell, how many Battels fought, — Par Lost 12.261
Large Countries, and in field great Battels win, — Par Reg 3.73
Of enemies, of aids, battels and leagues, — Par Reg 3.392
Hast reard Gods Trophies and his work pursu'd. — Sonnet 16, 6
1694 'And Fought God's Battels'
And Worsters laureat wreath; yet much remaines — Sonnet 16, 9

Baulk
Clip your Phylacteries, though bauk your Ears, — Forcers 17
Trinity ms 'bauke'
1673 'bank', errata 'bauk'

Bawl
That bawle for freedom in their senceless mood, — Sonnet 12, 9
Trinity ms 'bawl'

Bay
Or Pinnace anchors in a craggy Bay — Par Lost 2.289
Forthwith the Sounds and Seas, each Creek and Bay — Par Lost 7.399
Pontus and *Lucrine* Bay, and *Afric* Coast. — Par Reg 2.347
And oft beyond; to South the *Persian* Bay, — Par Reg 3.273
And now was dropt into the Western bay; — Lycidas 191
1673 'Bay'

Bayona
Looks toward *Namancos* and *Bayona*'s hold; — Lycidas 162

Bays
With a crown of deathless Praise, — Mask 973
Trinity ms 'praise' ←'bays'
And som Flowers, and som Bays, — Winchester 57

Be
And shook his throne. What though the field be lost? — Par Lost 1.105
And what is else not to be overcome? — Par Lost 1.109
By right of Warr, what e're his business be — Par Lost 1.150
ms 'bee'
Fall'n Cherube, to be weak is miserable — Par Lost 1.157
ms 'bee'
Doing or Suffering: but of this be sure, — Par Lost 1.158
To do ought good never will be our task, — Par Lost 1.159
ms 'bee'
Our labour must be to pervert that end, — Par Lost 1.164
For that celestial light? Be it so, since he — Par Lost 1.245
What shall be right: fardest from him is best — Par Lost 1.247
A mind not to be chang'd by Place or Time. — Par Lost 1.253
What matter where, if I be still the same, — Par Lost 1.256
And what I should be, all but less then he — Par Lost 1.257
We shall be free; th' Almighty hath not built — Par Lost 1.259
With rallied Arms to try what may be yet — Par Lost 1.269
Hewn on *Norwegian* hills, to be the Mast — Par Lost 1.293
Awake, arise, or be for ever fall'n. — Par Lost 1.330
ms 'bee'
Be no memorial blotted out and ras'd — Par Lost 1.362
Of Trumpets loud and Clarions be upreard — Par Lost 1.532
For mee be witness all the Host of Heav'n, — Par Lost 1.635
Thither, if but to pry, shall be perhaps — Par Lost 1.655
Open or understood must be resolv'd. — Par Lost 1.662
A solemn Councel forthwith to be held — Par Lost 1.755
More then can be in Heav'n, we now return — Par Lost 2.37
His trust was with th' Eternal to be deem'd — Par Lost 2.46
Equal in strength, and rather then be less — Par Lost 2.47
Car'd not to be at all; with that care lost — Par Lost 2.48
To our destruction: if there be in Hell — Par Lost 2.84
Fear to be worse destroy'd: what can be worse — Par Lost 2.85
We should be quite abolisht and expire. — Par Lost 2.93
Or if our substance be indeed Divine, — Par Lost 2.99
And cannot cease to be, we are at worst — Par Lost 2.100
I should be much for open Warr, O Peers, — Par Lost 2.119

Be(*cont*)
And that must end us, that must be our cure, — Par Lost 2.145
To be no more; sad cure; for who would loose, — Par Lost 2.146
Let this be good, whether our angry Foe — Par Lost 2.152
Caught in a fierie Tempest shall be hurl'd — Par Lost 2.180
Ages of hopeless end; this would be worse. — Par Lost 2.186
We warr, if warr be best, or to regain — Par Lost 2.230
The latter: for what place can be for us — Par Lost 2.235
Our servile offerings. This must be our task — Par Lost 2.246
Must we renounce, and changing stile be call'd — Par Lost 2.312
His captive multitude: For he, be sure — Par Lost 2.323
Voutsaf't or sought; for what peace will be giv'n — Par Lost 2.332
To be created like to us, though less — Par Lost 2.349
By force or suttlety: Though Heav'n be shut, — Par Lost 2.358
Som advantagious act may be achiev'd — Par Lost 2.363
Faded so soon. Advise if this be worth — Par Lost 2.376
Of those Heav'n-warring Champions could be found — Par Lost 2.424
While here shall be our home, what best may ease — Par Lost 2.458
More tollerable; if there be cure or charm — Par Lost 2.460
(Certain to be refus'd) what erst they feard; — Par Lost 2.470
If shape it might be call'd that shape had none — Par Lost 2.667
Or substance might be call'd that shadow seem'd, — Par Lost 2.669
Th' undaunted Fiend what this might be admir'd, — Par Lost 2.677
That be assur'd, without leave askt of thee: — Par Lost 2.685
When ever that shall be; so Fate pronounc'd. — Par Lost 2.809
To be invulnerable in those bright Arms, — Par Lost 2.812
Should be, and, by concurring signs, ere now — Par Lost 2.831
Might hap to move new broiles: Be this or aught — Par Lost 2.837
With odours; there ye shall be fed and fill'd — Par Lost 2.843
Immeasurably, all things shall be your prey. — Par Lost 2.844
His famine should be fill'd, and blest his mawe — Par Lost 2.847
Fearless to be o'rmatcht by living might. — Par Lost 2.855
Yours be th' advantage all, mine the revenge. — Par Lost 2.987
If that way be your walk, you have not farr; — Par Lost 2.1007
For should Man finally be lost, should Man — Par Lost 3.150
With his own folly? that be from thee farr, — Par Lost 3.153
That farr be from thee, Father, who art Judg — Par Lost 3.154
Be questiond and blaspheam'd without defence. — Par Lost 3.166
Man shall not quite be lost, but sav'd who will, — Par Lost 3.173
The rest shall hear me call, and oft be warnd — Par Lost 3.185
Mine ear shall not be slow, mine eye not shut. — Par Lost 3.193
But hard be hard'nd, blind be blinded more, — Par Lost 3.200
Which of ye will be mortal to redeem — Par Lost 3.214
And reconcilement; wrauth shall be no more — Par Lost 3.264
Glad to be offer'd, he attends the will — Par Lost 3.270
And be thy self Man among men on Earth, — Par Lost 3.283
Made flesh, when time shall be, of Virgin seed, — Par Lost 3.284
By wondrous birth: Be thou in *Adams* room — Par Lost 3.285
As from a second root shall be restor'd, — Par Lost 3.288
Shall satisfie for Man, be judg'd and die, — Par Lost 3.295
Found worthiest to be so by being Good, — Par Lost 3.310
Thenceforth shall be for ever shut. Mean while — Par Lost 3.333
God shall be All in All. But all ye Gods, — Par Lost 3.341
Love no where to be found less then Divine! — Par Lost 3.411
Shall be the copious matter of my Song — Par Lost 3.413
Living or liveless to be found was none, — Par Lost 3.443
Others came single; he who to be deemd — Par Lost 3.469
And they who to be sure of Paradise — Par Lost 3.478
Pleasant to know, and worthiest to be all — Par Lost 3.703
Came furious down to be reveng'd on men, — Par Lost 4.4
Of what he was, what is, and what must be — Par Lost 4.25
What could be less then to afford him praise, — Par Lost 4.46
Be then his Love accurst, since love or hate, — Par Lost 4.69
Nay curs'd be thou; since against his thy will — Par Lost 4.71
Evil be thou my Good; by thee at least — Par Lost 4.110
And send forth all her Kings; there will be room, — Par Lost 4.383
Be infinitly good, and of his good — Par Lost 4.414
Multitudes like thy self, and thence be call'd — Par Lost 4.474
Envie them that? can it be sin to know, — Par Lost 4.517
Can it be death? and do they onely stand — Par Lost 4.518
Equal with Gods; aspiring to be such, — Par Lost 4.526
What further would be learnt. Live while ye may, — Par Lost 4.533
New troubles; him thy care must be to find. — Par Lost 4.575
With first approach of light, we must be ris'n, — Par Lost 4.624
Mankind with her faire looks, to be aveng'd — Par Lost 4.718
Farr be it, that I should write thee sin or blame, — Par Lost 4.758
Or undiminisht brightness, to be known — Par Lost 4.836
But come, for thou, besure, shalt give account — Par Lost 4.841
Or all at once; more glorie will be wonn, — Par Lost 4.853
Or less be lost. Thy fear, said *Zephon* bold, — Par Lost 4.854
Less pain, less to be fled, or thou then they — Par Lost 4.919
Happier thou mayst be, worthier canst not be: — Par Lost 5.76
Taste this, and be henceforth among the Gods — Par Lost 5.77
But with addition strange; yet be not sad. — Par Lost 5.116
Be not disheart'nd then, nor cloud those looks — Par Lost 5.122
That wont to be more chearful and serene — Par Lost 5.123
Witness if I be silent, Morn or Eeven, — Par Lost 5.202
Hail universal Lord, be bounteous still — Par Lost 5.205
By violence, no, for that shall be withstood, — Par Lost 5.242
This day to be our Guest. But goe with speed, — Par Lost 5.313
Be over, and the Sun more coole decline. — Par Lost 5.370
(Whose praise be ever sung) to man in part — Par Lost 5.405
Spiritual, may of purest Spirits be found — Par Lost 5.406
To be sustaind and fed; of Elements — Par Lost 5.415
Think not I shall be nice. So down they sat, — Par Lost 5.433
If ye be found obedient, and retain — Par Lost 5.501
What meant that caution joind, *if ye be found* — Par Lost 5.513
This was that caution giv'n thee; be advis'd. — Par Lost 5.523

Be(*cont*)

Can hearts, not free, be tri'd whether they serve	Par Lost 5.532
To be both will and deed created free;	Par Lost 5.549
The full relation, which must needs be strange,	Par Lost 5.556
Worthy of Sacred silence to be heard;	Par Lost 5.557
Be but the shaddow of Heav'n, and things therein	Par Lost 5.575
Neerly it now concernes us to be sure	Par Lost 5.721
Know whether I be dextrous to subdue	Par Lost 5.741
Thy Rebels, or be found the worst in Heav'n.	Par Lost 5.742
With what may be devis'd of honours new	Par Lost 5.780
Erre not, much less for this to be our Lord,	Par Lost 5.799
While Pardon may be found in time besought.	Par Lost 5.848
No more be troubl'd how to quit the yoke	Par Lost 5.882
Will not be now voutsaf't, other Decrees	Par Lost 5.884
All are not of thy Train; there be who Faith	Par Lost 6.143
Behests obey, worthiest to be obey'd,	Par Lost 6.185
Two potent Thrones, that to be less then Gods	Par Lost 6.366
Therfore Eternal silence be thir doome.	Par Lost 6.385
Unwearied, unobnoxious to be pain'd	Par Lost 6.404
Not to be overpowerd, Companions deare,	Par Lost 6.419
Nor long shall be our labour, yet ere dawne,	Par Lost 6.492
Think nothing hard, much less to be despaird.	Par Lost 6.495
To be th' inventer miss'd, so easie it seemd	Par Lost 6.499
Be sure, and terrour seis'd the rebel Host,	Par Lost 6.647
Endless, and no solution will be found:	Par Lost 6.694
Have sufferd, that the Glorie may be thine	Par Lost 6.701
To manifest thee worthiest to be Heir	Par Lost 6.707
Of all things, to be Heir and to be King	Par Lost 6.708
Thou shalt be All in All, and I in thee	Par Lost 6.732
His count'nance too severe to be beheld	Par Lost 6.825
That wisht the Mountains now might be again	Par Lost 6.842
Which would be all his solace and revenge,	Par Lost 6.905
Thee also happier, shall not be withheld	Par Lost 7.117
That detriment, if such it be to lose	Par Lost 7.153
And Earth be chang'd to Heav'n, & Heav'n to Earth,	Par Lost 7.160
This I perform, speak thou, and be it don:	Par Lost 7.164
Within appointed bounds be Heav'n and Earth,	Par Lost 7.167
Cannot without process of speech be told,	Par Lost 7.178
This be thy just Circumference, O World.	Par Lost 7.231
Let ther be Light, said God, and forthwith Light	Par Lost 7.243
Again, God said, let ther be Firmament	Par Lost 7.261
Be gather'd now ye Waters under Heav'n	Par Lost 7.283
Easie, e're God had bid the ground be drie,	Par Lost 7.304
Again th' Almightie spake: Let there be Lights	Par Lost 7.339
The Day from Night; and let them be for Signes,	Par Lost 7.341
And let them be for Lights as I ordaine	Par Lost 7.343
Be fruitful, multiply, and in the Seas	Par Lost 7.396
And let the Fowle be multiply'd on the Earth.	Par Lost 7.398
Be fruitful, multiplie, and fill the Earth,	Par Lost 7.531
His secrets to be scann'd by them who ought	Par Lost 8.74
Be Center to the World, and other Starrs	Par Lost 8.123
To the terrestrial Moon be as a Starr	Par Lost 8.142
This Earth? reciprocal, if Land be there,	Par Lost 8.144
To know what passes there; be lowlie wise:	Par Lost 8.173
My Maker, be propitious while I speak.	Par Lost 8.380
Which must be mutual, in proportion due	Par Lost 8.385
Cannot be human consort; they rejoyce	Par Lost 8.392
And be so minded still; I, ere thou spak'st,	Par Lost 8.444
Knew it not good for Man to be alone,	Par Lost 8.445
What next I bring shall please thee, be assur'd,	Par Lost 8.449
And they shall be one Flesh, one Heart, one Soule.	Par Lost 8.499
That would be woo'd, and not unsought be won,	Par Lost 8.503
Do thou but thine, and be not diffident	Par Lost 8.562
To Cattel and each Beast; which would not be	Par Lost 8.582
Be strong, live happie, and love, but first of all	Par Lost 8.633
Thy condescension, and shall be honour'd ever	Par Lost 8.649
Be good and friendly still, and oft return.	Par Lost 8.651
Deprest, and much they may, if all be mine,	Par Lost 9.46
Bane, and in Heav'n much worse would be my state.	Par Lost 9.123
Nor hope to be my self less miserable	Par Lost 9.126
To mee shall be the glorie sole among	Par Lost 9.135
Of his adorers: hee to be aveng'd,	Par Lost 9.143
Unprais'd: for nothing lovelier can be found	Par Lost 9.232
Whether his first design be to withdraw	Par Lost 9.261
Can by his fraud be shak'n or seduc't;	Par Lost 9.287
Suttle he needs must be, who could seduce	Par Lost 9.307
Shame to be overcome or over-reacht	Par Lost 9.313
If this be our condition, thus to dwell	Par Lost 9.322
Fraile is our happiness, if this be so,	Par Lost 9.340
To be returnd by Noon amid the Bowre,	Par Lost 9.401
Not terrible, though terrour be in Love	Par Lost 9.490
Who sees thee? (and what is one2) who shouldst be seen	Par Lost 9.546
What thou commandst, and right thou shouldst be obeyd:	Par Lost 9.570
Fruitless to mee, though Fruit be here to excess,	Par Lost 9.648
Shall that be shut to Man, which to the Beast	Par Lost 9.691
Of Death denounc't, whatever thing Death be,	Par Lost 9.695
Be real, why not known, since easier shunnd?	Par Lost 9.699
God therefore cannot hurt ye, and be just;	Par Lost 9.700
Yet are but dim, shall perfetly be then	Par Lost 9.707
Op'nd and cleerd, and ye shall be as Gods,	Par Lost 9.708
That ye should be as Gods, since I as Man,	Par Lost 9.710
Human, to put on Gods, death to be wisht,	Par Lost 9.714
Impart against his will if all be his?	Par Lost 9.728
Though kept from Man, and worthy to be admir'd,	Par Lost 9.746
Forbids us good, forbids us to be wise?	Par Lost 9.759
This may be well: but what if God have seen,	Par Lost 9.826
And Death ensue? then I shall be no more,	Par Lost 9.827
Not felt, nor shall be twice, for never more	Par Lost 9.859

Be(*cont*)

Whatever can to sight or thought be formd,	Par Lost 9.898
Mine never shall be parted, bliss or woe.	Par Lost 9.916
Proportional ascent, which cannot be	Par Lost 9.936
But to be Gods, or Angels Demi-gods.	Par Lost 9.937
Be frustrate, do, undo, and labour loose,	Par Lost 9.944
Creation could repeate, yet would be loath	Par Lost 9.946
Matter of scorne, not to be given the Foe,	Par Lost 9.951
Our State cannot be severd, we are one,	Par Lost 9.958
If any be, of tasting this fair Fruit,	Par Lost 9.972
True relish, tasting; if such pleasure be	Par Lost 9.1024
In things to us forbidden, it might be wish'd,	Par Lost 9.1025
Bad Fruit of Knowledge, if this be to know,	Par Lost 9.1073
Be sure then. How shall I behold the face	Par Lost 9.1080
From unsuccessful charge, be not dismaid,	Par Lost 10.35
On his bad Errand, Man should be seduc't	Par Lost 10.41
Easie it might be seen that I intend	Par Lost 10.58
When time shall be, for so I undertook	Par Lost 10.74
However insupportable, be all	Par Lost 10.134
This Woman whom thou mad'st to be my help,	Par Lost 10.137
For us his ofspring deare? It cannot be	Par Lost 10.238
Be wanting, but afford thee equal aid,	Par Lost 10.271
So, if great things to small may be compar'd,	Par Lost 10.306
High proof ye now have giv'n to be the Race	Par Lost 10.385
No detriment need feare, goe and be strong.	Par Lost 10.409
Then Heav'n and Earth renewd shall be made pure	Par Lost 10.638
Shall be the execration; so besides	Par Lost 10.737
Be it so, for I submit, his doom is fair,	Par Lost 10.769
Mortalitie my sentence, and be Earth	Par Lost 10.776
For though the Lord of all be infinite,	Par Lost 10.794
Is his wrauth also? be it, man is not so,	Par Lost 10.795
That Death be not one stroak, as I suppos'd,	Par Lost 10.809
For one mans fault thus guiltless be condemn'd,	Par Lost 10.823
Justice Divine not hast'n to be just?	Par Lost 10.857
Not to be trusted, longing to be seen	Par Lost 10.877
Between us two let there be peace, both joyning,	Par Lost 10.924
Would speed before thee, and be louder heard,	Par Lost 10.954
That on my head all might be visited,	Par Lost 10.955
Which must be born to certain woe, devourd	Par Lost 10.980
To be to others cause of misery,	Par Lost 10.982
That after wretched Life must be at last	Par Lost 10.985
So Death shall be deceav'd his glut, and with us two	Par Lost 10.990
Be forc'd to satisfie his Rav'nous Maw.	Par Lost 10.991
With like desire, which would be meserie	Par Lost 10.997
To be forestall'd; much more I fear least Death	Par Lost 10.1024
Be meant, whom I conjecture, our grand Foe	Par Lost 10.1033
Would be revenge indeed; which will be lost	Par Lost 10.1036
No more be mention'd then of violence	Par Lost 10.1041
Be open, and his heart to pitie incline,	Par Lost 10.1061
And what may else be remedie or cure	Par Lost 10.1079
What can be toilsom in these pleasant Walkes?	Par Lost 11.179
And thither must return and be no more.	Par Lost 11.200
New Laws to be observ'd; for I descrie	Par Lost 11.228
That must be mortal to us both. O flours,	Par Lost 11.273
As from his face I shall be hid, deprivd	Par Lost 11.316
God is as here, and will be found alike	Par Lost 11.350
Which that thou mayst beleeve, and be confirmd	Par Lost 11.355
Will be aveng'd, and th' others Faith approv'd	Par Lost 11.458
To be thus wrested from us? rather why	Par Lost 11.503
Glad to be so dismist in peace. Can thus	Par Lost 11.507
To such unsightly sufferings be debas't	Par Lost 11.510
In part, from such deformities be free,	Par Lost 11.513
Into thy Mothers lap, or be with ease	Par Lost 11.536
Life much, bent rather how I may be quit	Par Lost 11.548
First his own Tooles; then, what might else be wrought	Par Lost 11.572
For in those dayes Might onely shall be admir'd,	Par Lost 11.689
Man-slaughter, shall be held the highest pitch	Par Lost 11.693
Of triumph, to be styl'd great Conquerours,	Par Lost 11.695
Thus Fame shall be atchiev'd, renown on Earth,	Par Lost 11.698
With Foes for daring single to be just,	Par Lost 11.703
With thought that they must be. Let no man seek	Par Lost 11.770
Henceforth to be foretold what shall befall	Par Lost 11.771
Him or his Childern, evil he may be sure,	Par Lost 11.772
More then anough, that temperance may be tri'd:	Par Lost 11.805
Select for life shall in the Ark be lodg'd,	Par Lost 11.823
Of Paradise by might of Waves be moovd	Par Lost 11.830
No sanctitie, if none be thither brought	Par Lost 11.837
Hunting (and Men not Beasts shall be his game)	Par Lost 12.30
A mightie Hunter thence he shall be styl'd	Par Lost 12.33
In foraign Lands thir memorie be lost	Par Lost 12.46
His outward freedom: Tyrannie must be,	Par Lost 12.95
From all the rest, of whom to be invok'd,	Par Lost 12.112
(Canst thou believe2) should be so stupid grown,	Par Lost 12.116
All Nations shall be blest; he straight obeys,	Par Lost 12.126
Shall in his Seed be blessed; by that Seed	Par Lost 12.148
Plainlier shall be reveald. This Patriarch blest,	Par Lost 12.151
Raise him to be the second in that Realme	Par Lost 12.162
Must be compelld by Signes and Judgements dire;	Par Lost 12.175
To blood unshed the Rivers must be turnd,	Par Lost 12.176
His day, in whom all Nations shall be blest,	Par Lost 12.277
Some bloud more precious must be paid for Man,	Par Lost 12.293
The last, for of his Reign shall be no end.	Par Lost 12.330
Such follow him, as shall be registerd	Par Lost 12.335
Anointed King *Messiah* might be born	Par Lost 12.359
Why our great expectation should be call'd	Par Lost 12.378
In thee and in thy Seed: nor can this be,	Par Lost 12.395
For this he shall live hated, be blasphem'd,	Par Lost 12.411
Salvation shall be Preacht, but to the Sons	Par Lost 12.448

Be(*cont*)

So in his seed all Nations shall be blest.	Par Lost 12.450
When this worlds disolution shall be ripe,	Par Lost 12.459
Shall all be Paradise, far happier place	Par Lost 12.464
Be sure they will, said th' Angel; but from Heav'n	Par Lost 12.485
Who against Faith and Conscience can be heard	Par Lost 12.529
Rarely be found: so shall the World goe on,	Par Lost 12.537
Last in the Clouds from Heav'n to be reveald	Par Lost 12.545
Of all the rest: then wilt thou not be loath	Par Lost 12.585
That ye may live, which will be many dayes,	Par Lost 12.602
Would not be last, and with the voice divine	Par Reg 1.35
Shall be inflicted by the Seed of *Eve*	Par Reg 1.54
Broken be not intended all our power	Par Reg 1.61
To be infring'd, our freedom and our being	Par Reg 1.62
Not thence to be more pure, but to receive	Par Reg 1.77
But must with something sudden be oppos'd,	Par Reg 1.96
Then toldst her doubting how these things could be	Par Reg 1.137
Be frustrate all ye stratagems of Hell,	Par Reg 1.180
What might be publick good; my self I thought	Par Reg 1.204
Thou shouldst be great and sit on *David*'s Throne,	Par Reg 1.240
And of thy Kingdom there should be no end.	Par Reg 1.241
Full weight must be transferr'd upon my head.	Par Reg 1.267
But if thou be the Son of God, Command	Par Reg 1.342
That out of these hard stones be made thee bread;	Par Reg 1.343
To be belov'd of God, I have not lost	Par Reg 1.379
What can be then less in me then desire	Par Reg 1.383
At first it may be; but long since with wo	Par Reg 1.399
Man fall'n shall be restor'd, I never more.	Par Reg 1.405
To be a lyer in four hundred mouths;	Par Reg 1.428
But this thy glory shall be soon retrench'd;	Par Reg 1.454
Shalt be enquir'd at *Delphos* or elsewhere,	Par Reg 1.458
Sometimes they thought he might be only shewn,	Par Reg 2.13
The Kingdom shall to *Israel* be restor'd:	Par Reg 2.36
Let us be glad of this, and all our fears	Par Reg 2.53
Could be obtain'd to shelter him or me	Par Reg 2.73
That to the fall and rising he should be	Par Reg 2.88
Afflicted I may be, it seems, and blest;	Par Reg 2.93
Far other labour to be undergon	Par Reg 2.132
If he be Man by Mothers side at least,	Par Reg 2.136
Rather to be in readiness, with hand	Par Reg 2.144
Thought none my equal, now be over-match'd.	Par Reg 2.146
Is to be found, in the wide Wilderness;	Par Reg 2.232
To be at hand, and at his beck appear,	Par Reg 2.238
Thou art not to be harm'd, therefore not mov'd;	Par Reg 2.407
High actions; but wherewith to be atchiev'd?	Par Reg 2.411
So reigning can be no sincere delight.	Par Reg 2.480
And for thy reason why they should be sought,	Par Reg 2.485
Thy Counsel would be as the Oracle	Par Reg 3.13
Of conduct would be such, that all the world	Par Reg 3.18
And what delight to be by such extoll'd,	Par Reg 3.54
To live upon thir tongues and be thir talk,	Par Reg 3.55
Of whom to be disprais'd were no small praise?	Par Reg 3.56
His lot who dares be singularly good.	Par Reg 3.57
Then swell with pride, and must be titl'd Gods,	Par Reg 3.81
But if there be in glory aught of good,	Par Reg 3.88
It may by means far different be attain'd	Par Reg 3.89
Yet if for fame and glory aught be done,	Par Reg 3.100
Be now in powerful hands, that will not part	Par Reg 3.155
Be try'd in humble state, and things adverse,	Par Reg 3.189
And my promotion will be thy destruction?	Par Reg 3.202
If there be worse, the expectation more	Par Reg 3.207
I would be at the worst; worst is my Port,	Par Reg 3.209
And will alike be punish'd; whether thou	Par Reg 3.214
If I then to the worst that can be hast,	Par Reg 3.223
That thou who worthiest art should'st be thir King?	Par Reg 3.226
No wonder, for though in thee be united	Par Reg 3.229
What of perfection can in man be found,	Par Reg 3.230
The wisest, unexperienc't, will be ever	Par Reg 3.240
Maugre the *Roman:* it shall be my task	Par Reg 3.368
Still will be tempting him who foyls him still,	Par Reg 4.13
Will be for thee no sitting, or not long	Par Reg 4.107
On *David*'s Throne, be propheci'd what will.	Par Reg 4.108
On *David*'s Throne, it shall be like a tree	Par Reg 4.147
And of my Kingdom there shall be no end:	Par Reg 4.151
Means there shall be to this, but what the means,	Par Reg 4.152
Be not so sore offended, Son of God;	Par Reg 4.196
As by that early action may be judg'd,	Par Reg 4.215
As morning shews the day. Be famous then	Par Reg 4.221
Will far be found unworthy to compare	Par Reg 4.346
And mad despight to be so oft repell'd.	Par Reg 4.446
Thou shalt be what thou art ordain'd, no doubt;	Par Reg 4.473
Not when it must, but when it may be best.	Par Reg 4.476
If thou observe not this, be sure to find,	Par Reg 4.477
Ambitious spirit, and wouldst be thought my God,	Par Reg 4.495
Though not to be Baptiz'd, by voice from Heav'n	Par Reg 4.512
Thou art to be my fatal enemy.	Par Reg 4.525
For though that seat of earthly bliss be fail'd,	Par Reg 4.612
Where they shall dwell secure, when time shall be	Par Reg 4.616
Let there be light, and light was over all;	Samson 84
And almost life it self, if it be true	Samson 91
So obvious and so easie to be quench't,	Samson 95
Or do my eyes misrepresent? Can this be hee,	Samson 124
I would be understood) in prosperous days	Samson 191
Not to be found, though sought. Yee see, O friends,	Samson 193
Unless there be who think not God at all,	Samson 295
If any be, they walk obscure;	Samson 296
Yet more there be who doubt his ways not just,	Samson 300
Came lagging after; say if he be here.	Samson 337

Be(*cont*)

Who would be now a Father in my stead?	Samson 355
Be it but for honours sake of former deeds.	Samson 372
So *Dagon* shall be magnifi'd, and God,	Samson 440
Before the God of *Abraham*. He, be sure,	Samson 465
Endure it, doubtful whether God be Lord,	Samson 477
Or *Dagon*. But for thee what shall be done?	Samson 478
Contempt, and scorn of all, to be excluded	Samson 494
Man. Be penitent and for thy fault contrite,	Samson 502
To what can I be useful, wherein serve	Samson 564
Nor shall his wondrous gifts be frustrate thus.	Samson 589
And I shall shortly be with them that rest.	Samson 598
By ransom or how else: mean while be calm,	Samson 604
Sam. O that torment should not be confin'd	Samson 606
Of sight, reserv'd alive to be repeated	Samson 645
This one prayer yet remains, might I be heard,	Samson 649
But that on th' other side if it be weigh'd	Samson 768
Be not unlike all others, not austere	Samson 815
It would be to ensnare an irreligious	Samson 860
Not therefore to be obey'd. But zeal mov'd thee;	Samson 895
Of their own deity, Gods cannot be:	Samson 899
Less therefore to be pleas'd, obey'd, or fear'd,	Samson 900
Goes by the worse, whatever be her cause.	Samson 904
To afflict thy self in vain: though sight be lost,	Samson 914
Eternal tempest never to be calm'd.	Samson 964
I shall be nam'd among the famousest	Samson 982
Love once possest, nor can be easily	Samson 1005
What e're it be, to wisest men and best	Samson 1034
Sam. Be less abstruse, my riddling days are past.	Samson 1064
And thou hast need much washing to be toucht.	Samson 1107
Therefore without feign'd shifts let be assign'd	Samson 1116
For proof hereof, if *Dagon* be thy god,	Samson 1145
Which I to be the power of *Israel*'s God	Samson 1150
Har. Presume not on thy God, what e're he be,	Samson 1156
His message will be short and voluble.	Samson 1307
Off. This answer, be assur'd, will not content them.	Samson 1322
Although thir drudge, to be thir fool or jester,	Samson 1338
Sam. Be of good courage, I begin to feel	Samson 1381
Nothing to do, be sure, that may dishonour	Samson 1385
If there be aught of presage in the mind,	Samson 1387
This day will be remarkable in my life	Samson 1388
Sam. I could be well content to try thir Art,	Samson 1399
Yet this be sure, in nothing to comply	Samson 1408
Of *Israel* be thy guide	Samson 1428
Of thy conception, and be now a shield	Samson 1434
Be efficacious in thee now at need.	Samson 1437
May compass it, shall willingly be paid	Samson 1477
If need be, I am ready to forgo	Samson 1483
Man. It shall be my delight to tend his eyes,	Samson 1490
Man. Some dismal accident it needs must be;	Samson 1519
From whom could else a general cry be heard?	Samson 1524
He now be dealing dole among his foes,	Samson 1529
Man. That were a joy presumptuous to be thought.	Samson 1531
Mess. Feed on that first, there may in grief be surfet.	Samson 1562
At once both to destroy and be destroy'd;	Samson 1587
Samson should be brought forth to shew the people	Samson 1601
Not to be absent at that spectacle.	Samson 1604
Which without help of eye, might be assay'd,	Samson 1625
Yet som there be that by due steps aspire	Mask 12
Of hatefull steps, I must be viewles now.	Mask 92
Of all thy dues be done, and none left out,	Mask 137
Trinity ms 'bee'	
Be well stock't with as fair a herd as graz'd	Mask 152
Which must not be, for that's against my course;	Mask 159
This way the noise was, if mine ear be true,	Mask 170
And thank the gods amiss. I should be loath	Mask 177
What might this be? A thousand fantasies	Mask 205
line not in Bridgewater ms	
Such noise as I can make to be heard farthest	Mask 227
So maist thou be translated to the skies,	Mask 242
And she shall be my Queen. Hail forren wonder	Mask 265
Bridgewater ms 'shalbe'	
And if your stray attendance be yet lodg'd,	Mask 315
But loyal cottage, where you may be safe	Mask 320
Till further quest'. *La*. Shepherd I take thy word,	Mask 321
Trinity ms 'quest' ←'quest be made'	
I cannot be, that I should fear to change it.	Mask 328
Or if your influence be quite damm'd up	Mask 336
And thou shalt be our star of *Arcady*,	Mask 341
Be barr'd that happines, might we but hear	Mask 343
T'would be som solace yet, som little chearing	Mask 348
Eld. *Bro*. Peace brother, be not over-exquisite	Mask 359
line not in Bridgewater ms	
line not in Trinity ms	
For grant they be so, while they rest unknown,	Mask 361
line not in Bridgewater ms	
line not in Trinity ms	
Or if they be but false alarms of Fear,	Mask 364
line not in Trinity ms	
line not in Bridgewater ms	
Which if Heav'n gave it, may be term'd her own:	Mask 419
Be it not don in pride, or in presumption.	Mask 431
Trinity ms 'bee'	
Till all be made immortal: but when lust	Mask 463
1637 'bee'	
2. *Bro*. Me thought so too; what should it be? *Eld*. *Bro*. For certain	Mask 482
If he be friendly he comes well, if not,	Mask 488
Defence is a good cause, and Heav'n be for us.	Mask 489

Be(*cont*)
For such there be, but unbelief is blind. Mask 519
Deny her nature, and be never more Mask 559
Still to be so displac't. I was all eare, Mask 560
Shall be unsaid for me: against the threats Mask 586
Bridgewater ms 'shalbe'
Vertue may be assail'd, but never hurt, Mask 589
It shall be in eternal restless change Mask 596
1637 'bee'
Bridgewater ms 'shalbe'
May never this just sword be lifted up, Mask 601
But for that damn'd magician, let him be girt Mask 602
Be those that quell the might of hellish charms, Mask 613
Where if he be, with dauntless hardihood, Mask 650
Sorrow flies farr: See here be all the pleasures Mask 668
Why should you be so cruel to your self, Mask 679
line not in Bridgewater ms
Be vacant of her plenty, in her own loyns Mask 718
Th' all-giver would be unthank't, would be unprais'd, Mask 723
Trinity ms 'be''
Who would be quite surcharg'd with her own weight, Mask 728
List Lady be not coy, and be not cosen'd Mask 737
line not in Bridgewater ms
Beauty is natures coyn, must not be hoorded, Mask 739
line not in Bridgewater ms
But must be currant, and the good thereof Mask 740
line not in Bridgewater ms
Beauty is natures brag, and must be shown Mask 745
line not in Bridgewater ms
Think what, and be adviz'd, you are but young yet. Mask 755
line not in Bridgewater ms
As if she would her children should be riotous Mask 763
Natures full blessings would be well dispenc't Mask 772
And then the giver would be better thank't, Mask 775
That must be utter'd to unfold the sage Mask 786
line not in Trinity ms
line not in Bridgewater ms
That dumb things would be mov'd to sympathize, Mask 796
line not in Trinity ms
line not in Bridgewater ms
Beyond the bliss of dreams. Be wise, and taste.---- Mask 813
Trinity ms 'be'
Yet stay, be not disturb'd, now I bethink me, Mask 820
Som other means I have which may be us'd, Mask 821
If she be right invok't in warbled Song, Mask 854
For maid'nhood she loves, and will be swift Mask 855
Bridgewater ms 'wilbe'
May thy lofty head be crown'd Mask 934
I shall be your faithfull guide Mask 944
Bridgewater ms 'shalbe'
Here be without duck or nod Mask 960
Other trippings to be trod Mask 961
(List mortals, if your ears be true) Mask 997
line not in Bridgewater ms
Two blissful twins are to be born, Mask 1010
line not in Bridgewater ms
I could be willing though now i'th darke to trie Mask Tr. ms 16.38
'I could be willing' ←'beshrew me but I would' ←'beshew me'
she might be free from perill where she is Mask Tr. ms 16.42
be it not don in pride or in praesumption Mask Tr. ms 16.56
'be' ←'may be' ←'be'
he may scratch his forehead. heere be brambles Mask Tr. ms 17.57
I could be willinge though now i'th darke to trie Mask Br. ms 391
she might be free from perill where she is, Mask Br. ms 395
If *Jonsons* learned Sock be on, Allegro 132
Be seen in som high lonely Towr, Penseroso 86
Too divine to be mistook: Arcades 4
Might she the wise *Latona* be, Arcades 20
And bid fair peace be to my sable shrowd. Lycidas 22
From the glad sound would not be absent long, Lycidas 35
Shall now no more be seen, Lycidas 43
Sunk though he be beneath the watry floar, Lycidas 167
In thy large recompense, and shalt be good Lycidas 184
when she beheld (the gods farre sighted bee) Lycidas Tr. ms 29.60
He laid aside; and here with us to be, Nativity 12
This must not yet be so, Nativity 150
Nor can he be at rest Nativity 216
Naught but profoundest Hell can be his shroud, Nativity 218
Shake earth, and at the presence be agast Psalm 114, 15
(If so it be that thou these plaints dost hear) Fair Inf 37
Thou needst not be ambitious to be first, Vacation 11
The daintest dishes shall be serv'd up last. Vacation 14
Thou know'st it must be now thy only bent Vacation 55
Shall subject be to many an Accident. Vacation 74
Yet being above them, he shall be below them; Vacation 80
To find a Foe it shall not be his hap, Vacation 83
Yea it shall be his natural property Vacation 87
Rivers arise; whether thou be the Son, Vacation 91
The leaves should all be black wheron I write, Passion 34
Prove to be presaging tears Winchester 44
Here be tears of perfect moan Winchester 55
Or that his hallow'd reliques should be hid Shakespear 3
If any ask for him, it shall be sed, Carrier 17
Fainted, and died, nor would with Ale be quickn'd; Another 16
line not in 1640, 1657, 1658 texts
If I may not carry, sure Ile ne're be fetch'd, Another 18
line not in 1640, 1657, 1658 texts

Be(*cont*)
That even to his last breath (ther be that say't) Another 25
line not in 1640, 1657, 1658 texts
Yet be it less or more, or soon or slow, Sonnet 7, 9
It shall be still in strictest measure eev'n, Sonnet 7, 10
And Hope that reaps not shame. Therefore be sure Sonnet 9, 11
And still revolt when truth would set them free. Sonnet 12, 10
Trinity ms 'still revolt when Truth would sett them' ←'make them' ←'set them' ←'hate the truth wherby they should be'
For who loves that, must first be wise and good; Sonnet 12, 12
To after age thou shalt be writ the man, Sonnet 13, 7
Till Truth, and Right from Violence be freed, Sonnet 15, 11
And Public Faith cleard from the shamefull brand Sonnet 15, 12
1694 'be rescu'd'
The drift of hollow states hard to be spelld, Sonnet 17, 6
Help wast a sullen day; what may be won Sonnet 20, 4
Must now be nam'd and printed Hereticks Forcers 11
He shall be as a tree which planted grows Psalm 1, 7
Th' Heathen, and as thy conquest to be sway'd Psalm 2, 18
And now be wise at length ye Kings averse Psalm 2, 22
Be taught ye Judges of the earth; with fear Psalm 2, 23
How long be thus forborn Psalm 4, 9
Be aw'd, and do not sin, Psalm 4, 19
And be at peace within. Psalm 4, 22
Many there be that say Psalm 4, 25
For thou Jehovah wilt be found Psalm 5, 37
Mine enemies shall all be blank and dash't Psalm 6, 21
And in a moment shall be quite abash't. Psalm 6, 24
Be in my hands, if I have wrought Psalm 7, 9
Judge me Lord, be judge in this Psalm 7, 31
Scarce to be less then Gods, thou mad'st his lot, Psalm 8, 15
Awake thy strength, come, and *be seen* Psalm 80, 11
And then we shall be safe. Psalm 80, 16
And then we shall be safe. Psalm 80, 32
Let thy *good* hand be *laid*, Psalm 80, 70
And then we shall be safe. Psalm 80, 80
No alien God shall be Psalm 81, 38
O that my people would *be wise* Psalm 81, 53
Who hate the Lord should *then be fain* Psalm 81, 61
Be not thou silent *now at length* Psalm 83, 1
Till they no Nation be Psalm 83, 14
Be lost in memory. Psalm 83, 16
Asham'd and troubl'd let them be, Psalm 83, 61
For one day in thy Courts *to be* Psalm 84, 33
No good from them shall be with-held Psalm 84, 43
Wilt thou be angry without end, Psalm 85, 17
Her fruits *to be our food*. Psalm 85, 52
Then will he come, and not be slow Psalm 85, 55
Slow to be angry, and *art stil'd* Psalm 86, 55
And be asham'd, because thou Lord Psalm 86, 63
Of Jacobs *Land, though there be store*, Psalm 87, 7
Be said of Sion *last* Psalm 87, 18
That ne're shall be out-worn Psalm 87, 22
Or wondrous acts be known, Psalm 88, 50
E're yet my life be spent, Psalm 88, 54
And to be short, at last his guid him brings Prose 2, 1
When I dye, let the earth be roul'd in flames. Prose 5, 1
What can be juster in a State then this? Prose 9, 5
There can be slaine Prose 11, 1
And *Kings* be born of thee, whose dredded might Prose 12, 13

Beach
Nathless he so endur'd, till on the Beach Par Lost 1.299
ms 'beach'
Deep to the Roots of Hell the gather'd beach Par Lost 10.299

Beads
And flutterd into Raggs, then Reliques, Beads, Par Lost 3.491
For who would rob a Hermit of his Weeds, Mask 390
Trinity ms 'weeds' ←'beads' ←'gowne' ←'beads'
His few Books, or his Beads, or Maple Dish, Mask 391
1637 'beades'
Trinity ms 'beads' ←'hairie gowne'
Bridgewater ms 'beads'

Beaked
Uplifted; and secure with beaked prow Par Lost 11.746
That blows from off each beaked Promontory, Lycidas 94

Beaks
And saw the Ravens with their horny beaks Par Reg 2.267

Beam
Secure, and at the brightning Orient beam Par Lost 2.399
Extend his ev'ning beam, the fields revive, Par Lost 2.493
Or of th' Eternal Coeternal beam Par Lost 3.2
By his Magnetic beam, that gently warms Par Lost 3.583
On a Sun beam, swift as a shooting Starr Par Lost 4.556
Returnd on that bright beam, whose point now raisd Par Lost 4.590
The latter quick up flew, and kickt the beam; Par Lost 4.1004
From the Suns beam meet Night, her other part Par Lost 8.139
O first created Beam, and thou great Word, Samson 83
Puts forth no visual beam. Samson 163
A Weavers beam, and seven-times-folded shield, Samson 1122
And the slope Sun his upward beam Mask 98
1637 'beame'
Trinity ms 'beame'
Bridgewater ms 'beame'
Begin to cast a beam on th' outward shape, Mask 460
Trinity ms 'beame'
1637 'beame'
Bridgewater ms 'beame'

Beaming
Of beaming sunnie Raies, a golden tiar Par Lost 3.625
And that far-beaming blaze of Majesty, Nativity 9
Beams
Shorn of his Beams, or from behind the Moon Par Lost 1.596
ms 'beames'
Bind thir resplendent locks inwreath'd with beams, Par Lost 3.361
The full blaze of thy beams, and through a cloud Par Lost 3.378
Which now the Rising Sun guilds with his beams. Par Lost 3.551
But all Sun-shine, as when his Beams at Noon Par Lost 3.616
O Sun, to tell thee how I hate thy beams Par Lost 4.37
On which the Sun more glad impress'd his beams Par Lost 4.150
His orient Beams, on herb, tree, fruit, and flour, Par Lost 4.644
Shot through with orient Beams: when all the Plain Par Lost 6.15
Bristl'd with upright beams innumerable Par Lost 6.82
Her gather'd beams, great Palace now of Light. Par Lost 7.363
His beams, unactive else, thir vigour find. Par Lost 8.97
In Balmie Sweat, which with his Beames the Sun Par Lost 8.255
In thee concentring all thir precious beams Par Lost 9.106
Leave cold the Night, how we his gather'd beams Par Lost 10.1070
And now the Sun with more effectual beams Par Reg 4.432
As the gay motes that people the Sun Beams, Penseroso 8
His flaring beams, me Goddes bring Penseroso 132
Shooting her beams like silver threds, Arcades 16
And tricks his beams, and with new spangled Ore, Lycidas 170
That with long beams the shame-fac't night array'd, Nativity 111
Thy hand-maids, clad them o're with purple beams Sonnet 14, 10
Trinity ms 'beames'
Bear
Our doom; which if we can sustain and bear, Par Lost 2.209
With *Atlantean* shoulders fit to bear Par Lost 2.306
Suffice, or what evasion bear him safe Par Lost 2.411
Bear his swift errands over moist and dry, Par Lost 3.652
In Paradise that bear delicious fruit Par Lost 4.422
1667 'beare'
Inseparablie thine, to him shalt beare Par Lost 4.473
Bear on your wings and in your notes his praise; Par Lost 5.199
Of life ambrosial frutage bear, and vines Par Lost 5.427
Or in thir glittering Tissues bear imblaz'd Par Lost 5.592
Messiah King anointed, could not beare Par Lost 5.664
Universal reproach, far worse to beare Par Lost 6.34
Find pastime, and beare rule; thy Realm is large. Par Lost 8.375
Bear with me then, if lawful what I ask; Par Lost 8.614
That shine, yet bear thir bright officious Lamps, Par Lost 9.104
Or bear what to my minde first thoughts present, Par Lost 9.213
1667 'hear'
Unseemly to beare rule, which was thy part Par Lost 10.155
The miserie, I deserv'd it, and would beare Par Lost 10.726
That burden heavier then the Earth to bear Par Lost 10.835
I beare thee, and unweeting have offended, Par Lost 10.916
Beare thine own first, ill able to sustaine Par Lost 10.950
By moderation either state to beare, Par Lost 11.363
Anough to beare; those now, that were dispenst Par Lost 11.766
1667 'bear'
Grievous to bear: but that care now is past, Par Lost 11.776
Shall leave them to enjoy; for th' Earth shall bear Par Lost 11.804
And bear through highth or depth of natures bounds Par Reg 1.13
In *Galilee*, that she should bear a Son Par Reg 1.135
Like whom the Gentiles feign to bear up Heav'n. Samson 150
Bear in their Superscription (of the most Samson 190
Thou never wast remiss, I bear thee witness: Samson 239
Bear not too sensibly, nor still insist Samson 913
More Lordly thund'ring then thou well wilt bear. Samson 1353
Into som brutish form of Woolf, or Bear, Mask 70
Bridgewater ms 'Beare'
Trinity ms 'beare'
1637 'Beare'
And som good angel bear a sheild before us. Mask 658
1637 'beare'
Bridgewater ms 'beare'
Trinity ms 'beare'
Where I may oft out-watch the *Bear*, Penseroso 87
Or Frost to Flowers, that their gay wardrop wear, Lycidas 47
Trinity ms 'weare' ←'beare' ←'weare'
Then his bright Throne, or burning Axletree could bear. Nativity 84
The sable-stoled Sorcerers bear his worshipt Ark. Nativity 220
To bear me where the Towers of *Salem* stood, Passion 39
Now mourn, and if sad share with us to bear Circum 6
Trinity ms 'beare'
Bear his milde yoak, they serve him best, his State Sonnet 19, 11
Of heart or hope; but still bear vp and steer Sonnet 22, 8
Trinity ms 'bear vp and' ←'attend to'
Bearded
Her bearded Grove of ears, which way the wind Par Lost 4.982
Rough, or smooth rin'd, or bearded husk, or shell Par Lost 5.342
Or Ounce, or Tiger, Hog, or bearded Goat, Mask 71
Bearers
For one Carrier put down to make six bearers. Another 20
line not in 1640, 1657, 1658 texts
Bearest
And my displeasure bearst so ill. If Prayers Par Lost 10.952
Then these thou bear'st that title, have propos'd Par Reg 4.199
Tacit, was in thy power; true; and thou bear'st Samson 430
From the unforeskinn'd race, of whom thou bear'st Samson 1100
Bearing
Whatever Earth all-bearing Mother yields Par Lost 5.338
Pains onely in Child-bearing were foretold, Par Lost 10.1051
His Name and Office bearing, who shall quell Par Lost 12.311
Bearing(*cont*)
And to the bearing well of all calamities, Samson 655
Bearing my words and doings to the Lords Samson 947
Bearing her straight to aged *Nereus* Hall, Mask 835
Bridgewater ms 'bearinge'
Trinity ms 'bearing' ←'and bore'
Bears
Of *Libra* to the fleecie Starr that bears Par Lost 3.558
Dandl'd the Kid; Bears, Tygers, Ounces, Pards, Par Lost 4.344
To rest, and what the Garden choicest bears Par Lost 5.368
And beares thee soft with the smooth Air along, Par Lost 8.166
1667 'bears'
Moses in figure beares, to introduce Par Lost 12.241
That for the Publick all this weight he bears. Par Reg 2.465
The Son of God, which bears no single sence; Par Reg 4.517
But to subserve where wisdom bears command. Samson 57
Her husband, how far urg'd his patience bears, Samson 755
Bears greatest names in his wild aerie flight. Samson 974
A Scepter or quaint staff he bears, Samson 1303
And every flower that sad embroidery wears: Lycidas 148
Trinity ms 'weares' ←'beares' ←'weare' ←'beares' ←'weares'
Bearth
Help to disburden Nature of her Bearth. Par Lost 9.624
Beast
By ancient *Tarsus* held, or that Sea-beast Par Lost 1.200
All path of Man or Beast that past that way: Par Lost 4.177
Silence accompanied, for Beast and Bird, Par Lost 4.600
Beast, Bird, Insect, or Worm durst enter none; Par Lost 4.704
Cattel and Creeping things, and Beast of the Earth, Par Lost 7.452
As from his Laire the wilde Beast where he wonns Par Lost 7.457
The Serpent suttl'st Beast of all the field, Par Lost 7.495
By Fowl, Fish, Beast, was flown, was swum, was walkt Par Lost 7.503
Beast of the Field, and over all the Earth, Par Lost 7.522
Or live in Sea, or Aire, Beast, Fish, and Fowle. Par Lost 8.341
In signe whereof each Bird and Beast behold Par Lost 8.342
As thus he spake, each Bird and Beast behold Par Lost 8.349
Much less can Bird with Beast, or Fish with Fowle Par Lost 8.395
Wors then can Man with Beast, and least of all. Par Lost 8.397
To Cattel and each Beast; which would not be Par Lost 8.582
The Serpent suttlest Beast of all the Field. Par Lost 9.86
Into a Beast, and mixt with bestial slime, Par Lost 9.165
From every Beast, more duteous at her call, Par Lost 9.521
Thee, Serpent, suttlest beast of all the field Par Lost 9.560
Shall that be shut to Man, which to the Beast Par Lost 9.691
For Beasts it seems: yet that one Beast which first Par Lost 9.769
Above all Cattle, each Beast of the Field; Par Lost 10.176
Feed first, on each Beast next, and Fish, and Fowle, Par Lost 10.604
Beast now with Beast gan war, and Fowle with Fowle, Par Lost 10.710
On Bird, Beast, Aire, Aire suddenly eclips'd Par Lost 11.183
Down from a Hill the Beast that reigns in Woods, Par Lost 11.187
For Man and Beast: when loe a wonder strange! Par Lost 11.733
Of every Beast, and Bird, and Insect small Par Lost 11.734
No sooner hee with them of Man and Beast Par Lost 11.822
With Man therein or Beast; but when he brings Par Lost 11.895
He gave us onely over Beast, Fish, Fowl Par Lost 12.67
On man, beast, plant, wastful and turbulent, Par Reg 4.461
Put to the labour of a Beast, debas't Samson 37
No strength of man, or fiercest wild beast could withstand; Samson 127
Like a wild Beast, I am content to go. Samson 1403
And the inglorious likenes of a beast Mask 528
Beasts
All Beasts of th' Earth, since wilde, and of all chase Par Lost 4.341
And finde thee knowing not of Beasts alone, Par Lost 8.438
Among the Beasts no Mate for thee was found. Par Lost 8.594
Proceeding, which in other Beasts observ'd Par Lost 9.94
In this enclosure wild, these Beasts among, Par Lost 9.543
To Beasts, whom God on thir Creation-Day Par Lost 9.556
I was at first as other Beasts that graze Par Lost 9.571
All other Beasts that saw, with like desire Par Lost 9.592
This intellectual food, for beasts reserv'd? Par Lost 9.768
For Beasts it seems: yet that one Beast which first Par Lost 9.769
Thir nakedness with Skins of Beasts, or slain, Par Lost 10.217
Of Beasts, but inward nakedness, much more Par Lost 10.221
Hunting (and Men not Beasts shall be his game) Par Lost 12.30
Among wild Beasts: they at his sight grew mild, Par Reg 1.310
And now wild Beasts came forth the woods to roam. Par Reg 1.502
And savour, Beasts of chase, or Fowl of game, Par Reg 2.342
Of fighting beasts, and men to beasts expos'd, Par Reg 4.140
All beasts that in the field or forrest meet, Psalm 8, 20
Wild Beasts there brouze, and make their food Psalm 80, 55
Beat
Lies dark and wilde, beat with perpetual storms Par Lost 2.588
That beat out life; he fell, and deadly pale Par Lost 11.446
Beat off, returns as oft with humming sound; Par Reg 4.17
Com, knit hands, and beat the ground, Mask 143
Trinity ms 'beate'
1637 'beate'
Bridgewater ms 'beate'
Beaten
Pav'd after him a broad and beat'n way Par Lost 2.1026
And like a weather-beaten Vessel holds Par Lost 2.1043
Beatific
In vision beatific: by him first Par Lost 1.684
Beatitude
Beatitude past utterance; on his right Par Lost 3.62
Beauteous
Fenc'd up the verdant wall; each beauteous flour, Par Lost 4.697

Beauteous(*cont*)
So beauteous, op'ning to the ambient light. — Par Lost 6.481
Yet they a beauteous ofspring shall beget; — Par Lost 11.613

Beauties
A youth, how all the Beauties of the East — Par Reg 2.197
Or that thy beauties lie in wormie bed, — Fair Inf 31

Beauty
How beauty is excelld by manly grace — Par Lost 4.490
Both of her Beauty and submissive Charms — Par Lost 4.498
To whom thus *Eve* with perfet beauty adornd. — Par Lost 4.634
Brought her in naked beauty more adorn'd, — Par Lost 4.713
Severe in youthful beautie, added grace — Par Lost 4.845
Beautie, which whether waking or asleep, — Par Lost 5.14
Attracted by thy beauty still to gaze. — Par Lost 5.47
Against the charm of Beauties powerful glance. — Par Lost 8.533
And beautie, not approacht by stronger hate, — Par Lost 9.491
By gift, and thy Celestial Beautie adore — Par Lost 9.540
Semblance, and in thy Beauties heav'nly Ray — Par Lost 9.607
For never did thy Beautie since the day — Par Lost 9.1029
Thy youth, thy strength, thy beauty, which will change — Par Lost 11.539
Some beauty rare, *Calisto*, *Clymene*, — Par Reg 2.186
Of beauty and her lures, easily scorn'd — Par Reg 2.194
As sitting Queen ador'd on Beauties Throne, — Par Reg 2.212
Or turn to reverent awe? for Beauty stands — Par Reg 2.220
Chor. Yet beauty, though injurious, hath strange power, — Samson 1003
But beauty like the fair Hesperian Tree — Mask 393
1637 'beautie'
Trinity ms 'beautie'
Bridgewater ms 'bewtie'
Beauty is natures coyn, must not be hoorded, — Mask 739
Trinity ms 'beautie'
1637 'Beautie'
line not in Bridgewater ms
Beauty is natures brag, and must be shown — Mask 745
line not in Bridgewater ms
Trinity ms 'beautie'
1637 'Beautie'
Wher perhaps som beauty lies, — Allegro 79
To set her beauties praise above — Penseroso 20
Bid *Amaranthus* all his beauty shed, — Lycidas 149
Trinity ms 'beauties' ←'beautie'

Became
A help, became thy snare; to mee reproach — Par Lost 11.165
Sunk down and all his Spirits became intranst: — Par Lost 11.420

Becamest
Becam'st enamour'd, and such joy thou took'st — Par Lost 2.765
Express, and thou becam'st a living Soul. — Par Lost 7.528

Because
Because thou hast, though Thron'd in highest bliss — Par Lost 3.305
Farr more then Great or High; because in thee — Par Lost 3.311
Because wee freely love, as in our will — Par Lost 5.539
Because the Father, t' whom in Heav'n supream — Par Lost 6.814
Boundless the Deep, because I am who fill — Par Lost 7.168
To God or thee, because we have a foe — Par Lost 9.280
Because not yet inflicted, as he fear'd, — Par Lost 10.51
Because thou hast done this, thou art accurst — Par Lost 10.175
Because thou hast heark'nd to the voice of thy Wife, — Par Lost 10.198
From penaltie, because from death releast — Par Lost 11.197
His utmost subtilty, because he boasts — Par Reg 1.144
All others by thy self; because of old — Par Reg 2.174
Thou valu'st, because offer'd, and reject'st: — Par Reg 4.156
Yet so it may fall out, because thir end — Samson 1265
Because they shall not trail me through thir streets — Samson 1402
Because you have thrown of your Prelate Lord, — Forcers 1
Lead me because of those — Psalm 5, 22
Hast founded strength because of all thy foes — Psalm 8, 6
And be asham'd, because thou Lord — Psalm 86, 63

Beck
To be at hand, and at his beck appear, — Par Reg 2.238

Beckoning
Of calling shapes, and beckning shadows dire, — Mask 207
line not in Bridgewater ms

Becks
Nods, and Becks, and Wreathed Smiles, — Allegro 28

Become
Become our Elements, these piercing Fires — Par Lost 2.275
But I should ill become this Throne, O Peers, — Par Lost 2.445
And what are Gods that Man may not become — Par Lost 9.716
Hath eat'n of the fruit, and is become, — Par Lost 9.869
That errour now, which is become my crime, — Par Lost 9.1181
But still rejoyc't, how is it now become — Par Lost 10.120
The Glory of that Glory, who now becom — Par Lost 10.722
O Sons, like one of us Man is become — Par Lost 11.84
Erwhile perplext with thoughts what would becom — Par Lost 12.275
Inferiour to the vilest now become — Samson 73
Thou art become (O worst imprisonment!) — Samson 155

Becomes
One of our number thus reduc't becomes, — Par Lost 5.843
Of contraries; all good to me becomes — Par Lost 9.122
Till I provided Death; so Death becomes — Par Lost 11.61
Imputed becomes theirs by Faith, his merits — Par Lost 12.409
But openly begin, as best becomes — Par Reg 1.288
The deed becomes unprais'd, the man at least, — Par Reg 3.103

Becoming
And put them into mis-becoming plight. — Mask 372
1637 'mis-becomming'
Trinity ms 'misbecomming'
Bridgewater ms 'misbecomminge'

Becurled
And sought to hide his froth-becurled head — Psalm 114, 8

Bed
Espoused *Eve* deckt first her nuptial Bed, — Par Lost 4.710
Whose bed is undefil'd and chaste pronounc't, — Par Lost 4.761
1667 'Bed'
Capacious bed of Waters: thither they — Par Lost 7.290
(Though higher of the genial Bed by far, — Par Lost 8.598
Wailing thy absence in my widow'd bed; — Samson 806
Successour in thy bed, — Samson 1021
Rigor now is gon to bed, — Mask 107
From thy coral-pav'n bed, — Mask 886
Thus don the Tales, to bed they creep, — Allegro 115
From golden slumber on a bed — Allegro 146
So sinks the day-star in the Ocean bed, — Lycidas 168
So when the Sun in bed, — Nativity 229
Of long-uncoupled bed, and childless eld, — Fair Inf 13
Or that thy beauties lie in wormie bed, — Fair Inf 31
And sweetly singing round about thy Bed — Vacation 63
Side-ways as on a dying bed, — Winchester 42
Hobson has supt, and's newly gon to bed. — Carrier 18
Nay, quoth he, on his swooning bed outstretch'd, — Another 17
line not in 1640, 1657, 1658 texts
Mine as whom washt from spot of child-bed taint, — Sonnet 23, 5
Trinity ms 'childe-bed'
My Bed I water with my tears; mine Eie — Psalm 6, 13
And praise thee *from their loathsom bed* — Psalm 88, 43

Bedecked
That so bedeckt, ornate, and gay, — Samson 712

Bedewed
bedew'd with nectar, & celestiall songs — Mask Tr. ms 10.06
What slender Youth bedew'd with liquid odours — Horace 1

Bedrid
Better at home lie bed-rid, not only idle, — Samson 579

Bedropped
Bedropt with blood of *Gorgon*, or the Isle — Par Lost 10.527

Beds
From Beds of raging Fire to starve in Ice — Par Lost 2.600
In Beds and curious Knots, but Nature boon — Par Lost 4.242
Beds of *Hyacinth*, and roses — Mask 998
There on Beds of Violets blew, — Allegro 21
Upon your beds, each one, — Psalm 4, 21

Bedward
Or Bedward ruminating: for the Sun — Par Lost 4.352

Bee
How Nature paints her colours, how the Bee — Par Lost 5.24
The Female Bee that feeds her Husband Drone — Par Lost 7.490
While the Bee with Honied thie, — Penseroso 142

Beelzebub
Beelzebub. To whom th' Arch-Enemy, — Par Lost 1.81
ms 'Beelzebub'
So *Satan* spake, and him *Beelzebub* — Par Lost 1.271
ms 'Beelzebub'
Which when *Beelzebub* perceiv'd, then whom, — Par Lost 2.299
Hatching vain Empires. Thus *Beelzebub* — Par Lost 2.378
Har. O *Baal-zebub!* can my ears unus'd — Samson 1231

Been
Hath bin achievd of merit, yet this loss — Par Lost 2.21
Had been achiev'd, whereof all Hell had rung, — Par Lost 2.723
Down had been falling, had not by ill chance — Par Lost 2.935
Must have bin lost, adjudg'd to Death and Hell — Par Lost 3.223
A World from utter loss, and hast been found — Par Lost 3.308
While time was, our first-Parents had bin warnd — Par Lost 4.6
For prospect, what well us'd had bin the pledge — Par Lost 4.200
Then had the Sons of God excuse to have bin — Par Lost 5.447
To heav'nly Soules had bin all one; but now — Par Lost 6.165
Resounded, and had Earth bin then, all Earth — Par Lost 6.218
These disobedient; sore hath been thir fight, — Par Lost 6.687
Faithful hath been your warfare, and of God — Par Lost 6.803
What might have else to human Race bin hid; — Par Lost 6.896
Us timely of what might else have bin our loss, — Par Lost 7.74
Contented that thus farr hath been reveal'd — Par Lost 8.177
Gentle to me and affable hath been — Par Lost 8.648
Before had bin contriving, though perhaps — Par Lost 9.139
What hath bin warn'd us, what malicious Foe — Par Lost 9.253
For had the gift bin theirs, it had not here — Par Lost 9.806
Hath bin the cause, and wonderful to heare: — Par Lost 9.862
And hath bin tasted such: the Serpent wise. — Par Lost 9.867
Had it been onely coveting to Eye — Par Lost 9.923
1667 'bin'
So eminently never had bin known. — Par Lost 9.976
For this one Tree had bin forbidden ten. — Par Lost 9.1026
Or to thy self perhaps: hadst thou been there, — Par Lost 9.1148
1667 'bin'
Hadst thou bin firm and fixt in thy dissent, — Par Lost 9.1160
That lay in wait; beyond this had bin force, — Par Lost 9.1173
I thus contest; then should have been refusd — Par Lost 10.756
My bread; what harm? Idleness had bin worse; — Par Lost 10.1055
Of Paradise or *Eden:* this had been — Par Lost 11.342
Rescu'd, had in his Righteousness bin lost? — Par Lost 11.682
Surcharg'd, as had like grief bin dew'd in tears, — Par Lost 12.373
Among the Nations? that hath been thy craft, — Par Reg 1.432
But what have been thy answers, what but dark — Par Reg 1.434
Hath been our dwelling many years, his life — Par Reg 2.80
My heart hath been a store-house long of things — Par Reg 2.103
To me is not unknown what hath been done — Par Reg 2.444
Besides to give a Kingdom hath been thought — Par Reg 2.481
Thy life hath yet been private, most part spent — Par Reg 3.232

Been(*cont*)
But as a man who had been matchless held Par Reg 4.10
Have been before contemn'd, and may agen: Par Reg 4.537
Had been fulfilld but through mine own default, Samson 45
Then had I not been thus exil'd from light; Samson 98
Have err'd, and by bad Women been deceiv'd; Samson 211
As vile hath been my folly, who have profan'd Samson 377
How hainous had the fact been, how deserving Samson 493
Bin, as it ought, sincere, it would have taught thee Samson 874
Where once I have been caught; I know thy trains Samson 932
As these perhaps, yet wish it had not been, Samson 1077
So had the glory of Prowess been recover'd Samson 1098
This Idols day hath bin to thee no day of rest, Samson 1297
As in thy wond'rous actions hath been seen. Samson 1440
That have been tir'd all day without repast, Mask 688
Trinity ms 'bin'
That hath so well been taught her dazling fence, Mask 791
1637 'beene'
line not in Bridgewater ms
line not in Trinity ms
how have I bin betrai'd Mask Tr. ms 22.18
Like one that had bin led astray Penseroso 69
Where no print of step hath been, Arcades 85
Had ye bin there---for what could that have don? Lycidas 57
1638 'been'
Bin as compleat as was her praise, Winchester 12
He had bin an immortall Carrier. Another 28
1640 'beene'
1657, 1658 'been'
1673 'been'
Would have been held in high esteem with *Paul* Forces 10
Trinity ms 'bin'
Thou hast not Lord been slack, Psalm 85, 2

Beersaba
To *Beersaba*, where the *Holy Land* Par Lost 3.536

Beersheba
To *Beersaba*, where the *Holy Land* Par Lost 3.536

Bees
Brusht with the hiss of russling wings. As Bees Par Lost 1.768
ms 'bees'
Of Bees industrious murmur oft invites Par Reg 4.248

Beest
If thou beest he; But O how fall'n! how chang'd Par Lost 1.84

Beetle
They had their name thence; course complexions Mask 749
Trinity ms 'complexions' ←'beetle brows'

Beeves
A herd of Beeves, faire Oxen and faire Kine Par Lost 11.647

Befall
Saw him disfigur'd, more then could befall Par Lost 4.127
To those Apostates, least the like befall Par Lost 7.44
Befall thee sever'd from me; for thou knowst Par Lost 9.252
And thou th' accuser. Thus it shall befall Par Lost 9.1182
And more that shall befall, innumerable Par Lost 10.896
Henceforth to be foretold what shall befall Par Lost 11.771
Pure, and in mind prepar'd, if so befall, Par Lost 12.444

Befallen
Befalln us unforeseen, unthought of, know Par Lost 2.821
The good befall'n him, Author unsuspect, Par Lost 9.771
Mankind? this mischief had not then befall'n, Par Lost 10.895
Thy hatred for this miserie befall'n, Par Lost 10.928
O Teacher, some great mischief hath befall'n Par Lost 11.450
Nothing of all these evils hath befall'n me Samson 374
Could have befall'n thee and thy Fathers house. Samson 447

Befell
The discord which befel, and Warr in Heav'n Par Lost 6.897
Apostasie, by what befell in Heaven Par Lost 7.43
For I that Day was absent, as befell, Par Lost 8.229
How all befell: they towards the Throne Supream Par Lost 10.28
Marrying or prostituting, as befell, Par Lost 11.716

Befit
Me softer airs befit, and softer strings Passion 27

Befits
Befits thee with him leagu'd, thy self as false Par Lost 10.868
Clad in splendor as befits Arcades 92
Trinity ms 'befitts'

Before
Before all Temples th' upright heart and pure, Par Lost 1.18
Bow'd down in Battel, sunk before the Spear Par Lost 1.436
Fell long before; nor aught avail'd him now Par Lost 1.748
Hard liberty before the easie yoke Par Lost 2.256
To Battel in the Clouds, before each Van Par Lost 2.535
Yet unconsum'd. Before the Gates there sat Par Lost 2.648
Strange horror seise thee, and pangs unfelt before. Par Lost 2.703
Before mine eyes in opposition sits Par Lost 2.803
Before thir eyes in sudden view appear Par Lost 2.890
Whose Fountain who shall tell? before the Sun, Par Lost 3.8
Before the Heavens thou wert, and at the voice Par Lost 3.9
Before his decent steps a Silver wand. Par Lost 3.644
The good before him, but perverts best things Par Lost 4.203
Or where the Sons of *Eden* long before Par Lost 4.213
Gambold before them, th' unwieldy Elephant Par Lost 4.345
But still thy words at random, as before, Par Lost 4.930
Innumerable before th' Almighties Throne Par Lost 5.585
Excess, before th' all bounteous King, who showrd Par Lost 5.640
Nightly before him, saw without thir light Par Lost 5.714
Natives and Sons of Heav'n possest before Par Lost 5.790
Know none before us, self-begot, self-rais'd Par Lost 5.860

Before(*cont*)
Empyreal, from before her vanisht Night, Par Lost 6.14
Before the seat supream; from whence a voice Par Lost 6.27
Of hideous length: before the cloudie Van, Par Lost 6.107
Before thy fellows, ambitious to win Par Lost 6.160
Before him Power Divine his way prepar'd; Par Lost 6.780
Before him, such as in thir Soules infix'd Par Lost 6.837
Drove them before him Thunder-struck, pursu'd Par Lost 6.858
Before the Hills appeerd, or Fountain flow'd, Par Lost 7.8
Before his memorie, as one whose drouth Par Lost 7.66
God made, and every Herb, before it grew Par Lost 7.336
Dawn, and the *Pleiades* before him danc'd Par Lost 7.374
And what before thy memorie was don Par Lost 7.637
Before the Angel, and of him to ask Par Lost 8.53
Is as the Book of God before thee set, Par Lost 8.67
That which before us lies in daily life, Par Lost 8.193
Of Earth before scarce pleasant seemd. Each Tree Par Lost 8.306
Before mine Eyes all real, as the dream Par Lost 8.310
To come and play before thee, know'st thou not Par Lost 8.372
Still glorious before whom awake I stood; Par Lost 8.464
Sweetness into my heart, unfelt before, Par Lost 8.475
Before me; Woman is her Name, of Man Par Lost 8.496
When *Satan* who late fled before the threats Par Lost 9.53
Before had bin contriving, though perhaps Par Lost 9.139
To such disport before her through the Field, Par Lost 9.520
Hee boulder now, uncall'd before her stood; Par Lost 9.523
Taste so Divine, that what of sweet before Par Lost 9.986
Before thee; and not repenting, this obtaine Par Lost 10.75
Before my Judge, either to undergoe Par Lost 10.126
Before his voice, or was shee made thy guide, Par Lost 10.146
Confessing soon, yet not before her Judge Par Lost 10.160
Before him naked to the aire, that now Par Lost 10.212
Too soon arriv'd, *Sin* there in power before, Par Lost 10.586
Unwarie, and too desirous, as before, Par Lost 10.947
Would speed before thee, and be louder heard, Par Lost 10.954
Before the present object languishing Par Lost 10.996
Before him reverent, and there confess Par Lost 10.1088
Before him reverent, and both confess'd Par Lost 10.1100
The Race of Mankind drownd, before the Shrine Par Lost 11.13
Before the Fathers Throne: Them the glad Son Par Lost 11.20
With Incense, I thy Priest before thee bring, Par Lost 11.25
Before thee reconcil'd, at least his days Par Lost 11.39
Kneel'd and before him humbl'd all my heart, Par Lost 11.150
Two Birds of gayest plume before him drove: Par Lost 11.186
Before thee shall appear; that thou mayst know Par Lost 11.475
Before his eyes appeard, sad, noysom, dark, Par Lost 11.478
Before him, Towns, and rural works between, Par Lost 11.639
Shall them admonish, and before them set Par Lost 11.813
Before the Lord, as in despite of Heav'n, Par Lost 12.34
Before them in a Cloud, and Pillar of Fire, Par Lost 12.202
Of two bright Cherubim, before him burn Par Lost 12.254
Unseen before in Heav'n proclaims him com, Par Lost 12.361
As did thir Lord before them. Thus they win Par Lost 12.502
Lay sleeping ran before, but found her wak't; Par Lost 12.608
The brandisht Sword of God before them blaz'd Par Lost 12.633
The World was all before them, where to choose Par Lost 12.646
Before him a great Prophet, to proclaim Par Reg 1.70
A Star, not seen before in Heaven appearing Par Reg 1.249
Before the Altar and the vested Priest, Par Reg 1.257
Before Messiah and his way prepare. Par Reg 1.272
Such Solitude before choicest Society. Par Reg 1.302
Comes to the place where he before had sat Par Reg 1.412
All his great work to come before him set; Par Reg 2.112
Before the Flood thou with thy lusty Crew, Par Reg 2.178
When suddenly a man before him stood, Par Reg 2.298
Not rustic as before, but seemlier clad, Par Reg 2.299
Tell me if Food were now before thee set, Par Reg 2.320
Those rudiments, and see before thine eyes Par Reg 3.245
This offer sets before thee to deliver. Par Reg 3.380
Before mine eyes thou hast set; and in my ear Par Reg 3.390
Before the *Parthian;* these two Thrones except, Par Reg 4.85
More then of arms before, allure mine eye, Par Reg 4.112
Have been before contemn'd, and may agen: Par Reg 4.537
On a green bank, and set before him spred Par Reg 4.587
Bound, and to torment sent before thir time. Par Reg 4.632
In feeble hearts, propense anough before Samson 455
Before the God of *Abraham*. He, be sure, Samson 465
But God hath set before us, to return thee Samson 517
I before all the daughters of my Tribe Samson 876
With solemnest devotion, spread before him Samson 1147
To appear as fits before th' illustrious Lords. Samson 1318
To shew them feats, and play before thir god, Samson 1340
To come and play before them at thir Feast. Samson 1448
Thir once great dread, captive, & blind before them, Samson 1474
Or at some proof of strength before them shown. Samson 1475
Man. The accident was loud, & here before thee Samson 1552
In thir state Livery clad; before him Pipes Samson 1616
Both horse and foot before him and behind Samson 1618
Came to the place, and what was set before him Samson 1624
Then all thy life had slain before. Samson 1668
Before our living Dread who dwells Samson 1673
Before the starry threshold of *Joves* Court Mask 1
All other parts remaining as they were, Mask 72
Trinity ms 'they were' ← 'before'
But boast themselves more comely then before Mask 75
And som good angel bear a sheild before us. Mask 658
Stoutly struts his Dames before, Allegro 52
And bring all Heav'n before mine eyes. Penseroso 166

Before*(cont)*
Shatter your leaves before the mellowing year. Lycidas 5
Before was never made, Nativity 118
Or wert thou that just Maid who once before Fair Inf 50
Where he had mutely sate two years before: Vacation 6
Before thou cloath my fancy in fit sound: Vacation 32
How he before the thunderous throne doth lie, Vacation 36
My plaining vers as lively as before; Passion 47
Ay sung before the saphire-colour'd throne Musick 7
The haples Babe before his birth Winchester 31
To him that serv'd for her before, Winchester 66
First heard before the shallow Cuccoo's bill Sonnet 1, 6
Before the Judge, who thenceforth bid thee rest Sonnet 14, 13
Set thy wayes right before, where my step goes. Psalm 5, 24
Till all before *our* God *at length* Psalm 84, 27
To trespass as before. Psalm 85, 36
Before him Righteousness shall go Psalm 85, 53
To bow them low before thee Lord, Psalm 86, 31
And all night long, before thee *weep* Psalm 88, 3
Before thee *prostrate lie*. Psalm 88, 4

Beforehand
And rash, before-hand had no better weigh'd Par Reg 4.8
Good reason then, if I before-hand seek Par Reg 4.526

Befriend
Wherin thou rid'st with *Hecat'*, and befriend Mask 135
Trinity ms 'befreind'
Good luck befriend thee Son; for at thy birth Vacation 59
Befriend me night best Patroness of grief, Passion 29

Beg
I beg, and clasp thy knees; bereave me not, Par Lost 10.918
Humbly our faults, and pardon beg, with tears Par Lost 10.1089
Life offer'd, or soon beg to lay it down, Par Lost 11.506
And beg to hide them in a herd of Swine, Par Reg 4.630
What do I beg? how hast thou dealt already? Samson 707
He lov'd me well, and oft would beg me sing, Mask 623
Bridgewater ms 'begg'

Began
Breaking the horrid silence thus began. Par Lost 1.83
And summons read, the great consult began. Par Lost 1.798
And with perswasive accent thus began. Par Lost 2.118
And with disdainful look thus first began. Par Lost 2.680
Began to bloom, but soon for mans offence Par Lost 3.355
Then much revolving, thus in sighs began. Par Lost 4.31
But with sly circumspection, and began Par Lost 4.537
Impetuous winds: he thus began in haste. Par Lost 4.560
Thir Phalanx, and began to hemm him round Par Lost 4.979
Lowly they bow'd adoring, and began Par Lost 5.144
To add more sweetness, and they thus began. Par Lost 5.152
No fear lest Dinner coole; when thus began Par Lost 5.396
After short pause assenting, thus began. Par Lost 5.562
So spake the Sovran voice, and Clouds began Par Lost 6.56
Ethereal Trumpet from on high gan blow: Par Lost 6.60
Of Battel now began, and rushing sound Par Lost 6.97
And visage all enflam'd first thus began. Par Lost 6.261
Now Night her course began, and over Heav'n Par Lost 6.406
And in the midst thus undismai'd began. Par Lost 6.417
Th' Assessor of his Throne he thus began. Par Lost 6.679
And the third sacred Morn began to shine Par Lost 6.748
Of Heav'n and Earth conspicious first began, Par Lost 7.63
How first began this Heav'n which we behold Par Lost 7.86
To journie through the airie gloom began, Par Lost 7.246
How first this World and face of things began, Par Lost 7.636
For Man to tell how human Life began Par Lost 8.250
Now when as sacred Light began to dawne Par Lost 9.192
And *Eve* first to her Husband thus began. Par Lost 9.204
His fraudulent temptation thus began. Par Lost 9.531
Somtimes in highth began, as no delay Par Lost 9.675
The Tempter all impassiond thus began. Par Lost 9.678
Thus to her self she pleasingly began. Par Lost 9.794
Began to cast lascivious Eyes, she him Par Lost 9.1014
Till *Adam* thus 'gan *Eve* to dalliance move, Par Lost 9.1016
Began to rise, high Passions, Anger, Hate, Par Lost 9.1123
Sin opening, who thus now to Death began. Par Lost 10.234
On his pale Horse: to whom *Sin* thus began. Par Lost 10.590
Sirocco, and *Libecchio*, Thus began Par Lost 10.706
Beast now with Beast gan war, and Fowle with Fowle, Par Lost 10.710
Presenting, thus to intercede began. Par Lost 11.21
Began to build a Vessel of huge bulk, Par Lost 11.729
Began to parch that temperate Clime; whereat Par Lost 12.636
Into thin Air diffus'd: for now began Par Reg 1.499
Began to doubt, and doubted many days, Par Reg 2.11
Sollicitous and blank he thus began. Par Reg 2.120
Our Saviour, and new train of words began. Par Reg 3.266
And how the world began, and how man fell Par Reg 4.311
Gan thunder, and both ends of Heav'n, the Clouds Par Reg 4.410
With flaunting Hony-suckle, and began Mask 545
His raign of peace upon the earth began: Nativity 63
That it *began to grow apace*, Psalm 80, 39

Beget
His single imperfection, and beget Par Lost 8.423
Doubt might beget of Diabolic pow'r Par Lost 9.95
All that I eat or drink, or shall beget, Par Lost 10.728
Wherefore didst thou beget me? I sought it not Par Lost 10.762
Yet they a beauteous ofspring shall beget; Par Lost 11.613
That fancy can beget on youthfull thoughts, Mask 669
Trinity ms 'beget on' ←'invent in' ←'beget on'
Bridgewater ms 'begett'

Beggary
Dungeon, or beggery, or decrepit age! Samson 69

Begged
Humbly thir faults, and pardon beg'd, with tears Par Lost 10.1101

Begging
From granting hee, as I from begging peace: Par Lost 4.104

Begin
Why ask ye, and superfluous begin Par Lost 4.832
Ere this avenging Sword begin thy doome, Par Lost 6.278
Hee from the East his flaming rode begin, Par Lost 8.162
Rais'd, as of som great matter to begin. Par Lost 9.669
Such proof, conclude, they then begin to faile. Par Lost 9.1142
Must suffer change, disdain'd not to begin Par Lost 10.213
Holds on the same, from Woman to begin. Par Lost 11.633
Thus thou hast seen one World begin and end; Par Lost 12.6
With man or mens affairs, how I begin Par Reg 1.132
How best the mighty work he might begin Par Reg 1.186
But openly begin, as best becomes Par Reg 1.288
How to begin, how to accomplish best Par Reg 2.113
That it shall never end, so when begin Par Reg 3.185
But what concerns it thee when I begin Par Reg 3.198
Another method I must now begin. Par Reg 4.540
Now enter, and begin to save mankind. Par Reg 4.635
I might begin *Israel's* Deliverance, Samson 225
As thir Deliverer; if he aught begin, Samson 274
Sam. Be of good courage, I begin to feel Samson 1381
Com let us our rights begin, Mask 125
Bridgewater ms 'begyn'
Begin to throng into my memory Mask 206
line not in Bridgewater ms
Begin to cast a beam on th' outward shape, Mask 460
Bridgewater ms 'begins'
Trinity ms 'begin' ←'begins'
To hear the Lark begin his flight, Allegro 41
Begin then, Sisters of the sacred well, Lycidas 15
Begin, and somwhat loudly sweep the string. Lycidas 17
Sore doth begin Circum 13

Beginning
In the Beginning how the Heav'ns and Earth Par Lost 1.9
ms 'beginning'
His journies end and our beginning woe. Par Lost 3.633
From the beginning, that posteritie Par Lost 7.638
Is hard; for who himself beginning knew? Par Lost 8.251
Pleas'd me long choosing, and beginning late; Par Lost 9.26
From the beginning, and in lies wilt end; Par Reg 1.408
Appearing, and beginning noble deeds, Par Reg 4.99
Without beginning; for no date prefixt Par Reg 4.392

Begins
A glimmering dawn; here Nature first begins Par Lost 2.1037
Begins his dire attempt, which nigh the birth Par Lost 4.15
Hath finisht half his journey, and scarce begins Par Lost 5.559
Which now the Skie with various Face begins Par Lost 10.1064
All unconcern'd with our unrest, begins Par Lost 11.174
From Mans effeminate slackness it begins, Par Lost 11.634
The happier raign the sooner it begins, Par Reg 3.179
Wher the great Sun begins his state, Allegro 60
And when the Sun begins to fling Penseroso 131
But now begins; for from this happy day Nativity 167

Begirt
Begirt with *British* and *Armoric* Knights; Par Lost 1.581
Address, and to begirt th' Almighty Throne Par Lost 5.868
Descend with all her winning charms begirt Par Reg 2.213

Begot
Ingendring with me, of that rape begot Par Lost 2.794
This day I have begot whom I declare Par Lost 5.603
Know none before us, self-begot, self-rais'd Par Lost 5.860
But Natural necessity begot. Par Lost 10.765
Will reign among them, as of thee begot; Par Lost 12.286
His first-begot we know, and sore have felt, Par Reg 1.89
And coupl'd with them, and begot a race. Par Reg 2.181
And think'st upon him; or of man begot Psalm 8, 13

Begotten
Thine own begotten, breaking violent way Par Lost 2.782
Onely begotten Son, seest thou what rage Par Lost 3.80
Begotten Son, Divine Similitude, Par Lost 3.384
Equal to him begotten Son, by whom Par Lost 5.835
And thou my Word, begotten Son, by thee Par Lost 7.163
Our own begotten, and of our Loines to bring Par Lost 10.983
Like that self-begott'n bird Samson 1699
Thou art my Son I have begotten thee Psalm 2, 15

Beguile
us of our selves & native woes beguile Musick Tr. ms 4.08

Beguiled
Beguil'd by fair Idolatresses, fell Par Lost 1.445
Where no ill seems: Which now for once beguil'd Par Lost 3.689
Of Enemie hath beguil'd thee, yet unknown, Par Lost 9.905
The Serpent me beguil'd and I did eate. Par Lost 10.162
Fool'd and beguil'd, by him thou, I by thee, Par Lost 10.880
Women, when nothing else, beguil'd the heart Par Reg 2.169
That wisest and best men full oft beguil'd Samson 759
And I (for grief is easily beguild) Passion 54

Begun
In *Chaos*, and the work begun, how soon Par Lost 7.93
Had lively shadowd: Here had new begun Par Lost 8.311
Our dayes work brought to little, though begun Par Lost 9.224
From this day onward, which I feel begun Par Lost 10.811

Behalf
And silence was in Heav'n: on mans behalf Par Lost 3.218

Behalf(*cont*)
Or in behalf of Man, or to invade Par Lost 11.102
Beheld
The Sojourners of *Goshen*, who beheld Par Lost 1.309
(Far other once beheld in bliss) condemn'd Par Lost 1.607
His onely Son; On Earth he first beheld Par Lost 3.64
At sight of all this World beheld so faire. Par Lost 3.554
Him counterfet, if any eye beheld. Par Lost 4.117
Which they beheld, the Moons resplendent Globe Par Lost 4.723
Hung over her enamour'd, and beheld Par Lost 5.13
With him I flew, and underneath beheld Par Lost 5.87
His barren leaves. Them thus imploid beheld Par Lost 5.219
They worse abhorr'd. *Satan* beheld thir plight, Par Lost 6.607
Son in whose face invisible is beheld Par Lost 6.681
His count'nance too severe to be beheld Par Lost 6.825
Eternal Father from his Throne beheld Par Lost 7.137
Exhaling first from Darkness they beheld; Par Lost 7.255
From where I first drew Aire, and first beheld Par Lost 8.284
With ravishment beheld, there best beheld Par Lost 9.541
United I beheld; no Fair to thine Par Lost 9.608
And rapture so oft beheld? those heav'nly shapes Par Lost 9.1082
Bent thir aspect, and whom they wish'd beheld, Par Lost 10.454
Whom thus afflicted when sad *Eve* beheld, Par Lost 10.863
His eyes he op'nd, and beheld a field, Par Lost 11.429
They looking back, all th' Eastern side beheld Par Lost 12.641
And looking round on every side beheld Par Reg 1.295
Unlook'd for are we fall'n, our eyes beheld Par Reg 2.31
Our Saviour lifting up his eyes beheld Par Reg 2.338
Which earst my eyes beheld and yet behold; Samson 1543
Not without wonder or delight beheld. Samson 1642
when she beheld (the gods farre sighted bee) Lycidas Tr. ms 29.60
Beheld us in our misery. Psalm 136, 78
Beheldest
But hee the seventh from thee, whom thou beheldst Par Lost 11.700
Shall build a wondrous Ark, as thou beheldst, Par Lost 11.819
Behemoth
Behemoth biggest born of Earth upheav'd Par Lost 7.471
Behest
Ris'n on mid-noon; som great behest from Heav'n Par Lost 5.311
Michael, this my behest have thou in charge, Par Lost 11.99
Adam, Heav'ns high behest no Preface needs: Par Lost 11.251
Gentle swain at thy request Mask 900
Trinity ms 'request' ←'behe'
Behests
On high behests his Angels to and fro Par Lost 3.533
Behests obey, worthiest to be obey'd, Par Lost 6.185
But us he sends upon his high behests Par Lost 8.238
Behind
Behind him cast; the broad circumference Par Lost 1.286
To Idols foul. *Thammuz* came next behind, Par Lost 1.446
Shorn of his Beams, or from behind the Moon Par Lost 1.596
As not behind in hate; if what was urg'd Par Lost 2.120
Circl'd his Head, nor less his Locks behind Par Lost 3.626
No spot or blame behind: Which gives me hope Par Lost 5.119
Portending hollow truce; at each behind Par Lost 6.578
Urg'd them behind; headlong themselves they threw Par Lost 6.864
As in a shadie nook I stood behind, Par Lost 9.277
Leads thee, I shall not lag behinde, nor erre Par Lost 10.266
Habitual habitant; behind her *Death* Par Lost 10.588
Behinde them, while th' obdurat King pursues: Par Lost 12.205
They have exalted, and behind them cast Par Reg 2.46
Then those thir Conquerours, who leave behind Par Reg 3.78
How quick they wheel'd, and flying behind them shot Par Reg 3.323
Impenitent, and left a race behind Par Reg 3.423
Get thee behind me; plain thou now appear'st Par Reg 4.193
As Graces, draw a Scorpions tail behind? Samson 360
Her harbinger, a damsel train behind; Samson 721
Was not behind, but ever at my ear, Samson 858
And yet perhaps more trouble is behind. Samson 1300
Set God behind: which in his jealousie Samson 1375
Both horse and foot before him and behind Samson 1618
Staid not behind, nor in the grave were trod; Sonnet 14, 6
Trinity ms 'behind' ←'behinde'
Behold
Signs of remorse and passion to behold Par Lost 1.605
Behold a wonder! they but now who seemd Par Lost 1.777
Bordering on light; when strait behold the Throne Par Lost 2.959
Weighs his spread wings, at leasure to behold Par Lost 2.1046
Behold mee then, mee for him, life for life Par Lost 3.236
Whom else no Creature can behold; on thee Par Lost 3.387
Or open admiration him behold Par Lost 3.672
All hope excluded thus, behold in stead Par Lost 4.105
O Hell! what doe mine eyes with grief behold, Par Lost 4.358
All these with ceasless praise his works behold Par Lost 4.679
So sudden to behold the grieslie King; Par Lost 4.821
Whom to behold but thee, Natures desire, Par Lost 5.45
Angels, for yee behold him, and with songs Par Lost 5.161
Haste hither *Eve*, and worth thy sight behold Par Lost 5.308
Him have anointed, whom ye now behold Par Lost 5.605
Son, thou in whom my glory I behold Par Lost 5.719
Who is our equal: then thou shalt behold Par Lost 5.866
And onward move Embattelld; when behold Par Lost 6.550
Forthwith (behold the excellence, the power Par Lost 6.637
Nor multitude, stand onely and behold Par Lost 6.810
How first began this Heav'n which we behold Par Lost 7.86
Follow'd in bright procession to behold Par Lost 7.222
Delectable both to behold and taste; Par Lost 7.539
View'd, and behold all was entirely good; Par Lost 7.549
Behold(*cont*)
Thence to behold this new created World Par Lost 7.554
When I behold this goodly Frame, this World Par Lost 8.15
In signe whereof each Bird and Beast behold Par Lost 8.342
As thus he spake, each Bird and Beast behold Par Lost 8.349
When out of hope, behold her, not farr off, Par Lost 8.481
Farr otherwise, transported I behold, Par Lost 8.529
Harmonie to behold in wedded pair Par Lost 8.605
Such Pleasure took the Serpent to behold Par Lost 9.455
Occasion which now smiles, behold alone Par Lost 9.480
A goodly Tree farr distant to behold Par Lost 9.576
Fixt on the Fruit she gaz'd, which to behold Par Lost 9.735
Be sure then. How shall I behold the face Par Lost 9.1080
Are to behold the Judgment, but the judg'd, Par Lost 10.81
To Paradise first tending, when behold Par Lost 10.326
Of God, whom to behold was then my highth Par Lost 10.724
For I behold them softn'd and with tears Par Lost 11.110
Gladly behold though but his utmost skirts Par Lost 11.332
Adam, now ope thine eyes, and first behold Par Lost 11.423
Of terrour, foul and ugly to behold, Par Lost 11.464
Drie-ey'd behold? *Adam* could not, but wept, Par Lost 11.495
Long had not walkt, when from the Tents behold Par Lost 11.581
Which now direct thine eyes and soon behold. Par Lost 11.711
How didst thou grieve then, *Adam*, to behold Par Lost 11.754
And now what further shall ensue, behold. Par Lost 11.839
Mount *Hermon*, yonder Sea, each place behold Par Lost 12.142
Gabriel this day by proof thou shalt behold, Par Reg 1.130
The time prefixt I waited, when behold Par Reg 1.269
Thy wisdom, and behold thy God-like deeds? Par Reg 1.386
Behold the Kings of the Earth how they oppress Par Reg 2.44
Would scruple that, with want opprest? behold Par Reg 2.331
Turning with easie eye thou may'st behold. Par Reg 3.293
Of that high mountain, whence he might behold Par Reg 4.26
My Aerie Microscope) thou may'st behold Par Reg 4.57
Westward, much nearer by Southwest, behold Par Reg 4.237
Who all things now behold more fresh and green, Par Reg 4.435
Immeasurable strength they might behold Samson 206
As earst in highest, behold him where he lies. Samson 339
Behold him in this state calamitous, and turn Samson 708
Hath led me on desirous to behold Samson 741
Chor. Doubtless the people shouting to behold Samson 1473
Which earst my eyes beheld and yet behold; Samson 1543
Of sort, might sit in order to behold, Samson 1608
As with amaze shall strike all who behold. Samson 1645
And first behold this cordial Julep here Mask 672
Trinity ms 'first behold' ←'looke upon'
Bridgewater ms 'behould'
Here behold so goodly grown Mask 968
Bridgewater ms 'behould'
yet thence I come and oft from thence behold Mask Tr. ms 10.18
To behold the wandring Moon, Penseroso 67
And lead ye where ye may more neer behold Arcades 40
For them that persecute.) Behold Psalm 7, 50
When I behold thy Heavens, thy Fingers art, Psalm 8, 9
Behold *us, but without a frown,* Psalm 80, 59
Beholders
Beholders rude, and shallow to discerne Par Lost 9.544
Beholdest
Cut shorter many a league; here thou behold'st Par Reg 3.269
All these which in a moment thou behold'st, Par Reg 4.162
Beholding
Him God beholding from his prospect high, Par Lost 3.77
Beholding shall confess that here on Earth Par Lost 5.329
To mark thir doings, them beholding soon, Par Lost 12.50
Beholds
To adore the Conquerour? who now beholds Par Lost 1.323
Wherein past, present, future he beholds, Par Lost 3.78
Which of us who beholds the bright surface Par Lost 6.472
Grateful to Heav'n, over his head beholds Par Lost 11.864
Behoof
To your behoof, if I that Region lost, Par Lost 2.982
Which carefull *Jove* in natures true behoofe Fair Inf 45
Behoves
Half flying; behoves him now both Oare and Saile. Par Lost 2.942
Argue thy inexperience what behooves Par Lost 4.931
Being
Strength undiminisht, or eternal being Par Lost 1.154
As being the contrary to his high will Par Lost 1.161
Then miserable to have eternal being: Par Lost 2.98
Though full of pain, this intellectual being, Par Lost 2.147
Wide gaping, and with utter loss of being Par Lost 2.440
Forthwith his former state and being forgets, Par Lost 2.585
My being gav'st me; whom should I obey Par Lost 2.865
Found worthiest to be so by being Good, Par Lost 3.310
Eternal King; thee Author of all being, Par Lost 3.374
His flesh, his bone; to give thee being I lent Par Lost 4.483
Of things above his World, and of thir being Par Lost 5.455
Reason receives, and reason is her being, Par Lost 5.487
Our being ordain'd to govern, not to serve? Par Lost 5.802
Such as he pleasd, and circumscrib'd thir being? Par Lost 5.825
Thy making, while the Maker gave thee being? Par Lost 5.858
Think onely what concernes thee and thy being; Par Lost 8.174
My fancy to believe I yet had being, Par Lost 8.294
And all this good to man, for whose well being Par Lost 8.361
That gave thee being, still shades thee and protects. Par Lost 9.266
His violence thou fearst not, being such, Par Lost 9.282
But might as ill have happ'nd thou being by, Par Lost 9.1147
Being as I am, why didst not thou the Head Par Lost 9.1155

Being(*cont*)
Affraid, being naked, hid my self. To whom   Par Lost 10.117
Concurd not to my being, it were but right   Par Lost 10.747
The Race unblest, to being yet unbegot.   Par Lost 10.988
Abortive, to torment me ere thir being,   Par Lost 11.769
Twinn'd, and from her hath no dividual being: Par Lost 12.85
Highly belov'd, being but the Minister   Par Lost 12.308
To be infring'd, our freedom and our being   Par Reg 1.62
His end of being on Earth, and mission high: Par Reg 2.114
Yet as being oft times noxious where they light   Par Reg 4.460
Being once a wife, for me thou wast to leave   Samson 885
Strive to keep up a frail, and Feaverish being   Mask 8
Bridgewater ms 'beeinge'
Trinity ms 'beeing'
(Not being in danger, as I trust she is not)   Mask 370
Trinity ms 'beeing'
Bridgewater ms 'beinge'
The divine property of her first being.   Mask 469
Trinity ms 'beeing'
Bridgewater ms 'beeinge'
For he being amorous on that lovely die   Fair Inf 5
Yet being above them, he shall be below them;   Vacation 80
Or els the ways being foul, twenty to one,   Carrier 3
His principles being ceast, he ended strait.   Another 10
1658 'once'

Belated
Or Fountain some belated Peasant sees,   Par Lost 1.783

Belched
Belch'd fire and rowling smoak; the rest entire   Par Lost 1.671
From those deep throated Engins belcht, whose roar   Par Lost 6.586

Belching
Stood open wide, belching outrageous flame   Par Lost 10.232

Beldam
When Beldam Nature in her cradle was;   Vacation 46

Belial
Belial came last, then whom a Spirit more lewd   Par Lost 1.490
ms 'Belial'
Of *Belial*, flown with insolence and wine.   Par Lost 1.502
ms 'Belial'
Belial, in act more graceful and humane;   Par Lost 2.109
Thus *Belial* with words cloath'd in reasons garb   Par Lost 2.226
To whom thus *Belial* in like gamesom mood,   Par Lost 6.620
Belial the dislolutest Spirit that fell,   Par Reg 2.150
Belial, in much uneven scale thou weigh'st   Par Reg 2.173

Belief
Of Day and Night; which needs not thy beleefe,   Par Lost 8.136
On our belief, that all from them proceeds;   Par Lost 9.719
Hard to belief may seem; yet this will Prayer,   Par Lost 11.146
O change beyond report, thought, or belief!   Samson 117
Yet Hope would fain subscribe, and tempts Belief.   Samson 1535
And work my flatter'd fancy to belief,   Passion 31

Believe
Of force believe Almighty, since no less   Par Lost 1.144
ms 'beleive'
For who can yet beleeve, though after loss,   Par Lost 1.631
ms 'beleive'
My fancy to believe I yet had being,   Par Lost 8.294
Queen of this Universe, doe not believe   Par Lost 9.684
Which that thou mayst beleeve, and be confirmd   Par Lost 11.355
(Canst thou believe2) should be so stupid grown,   Par Lost 12.116
Proclaiming Life to all who shall believe   Par Lost 12.407
And his Salvation, them who shall beleeve   Par Lost 12.441
Man. Believe not these suggestions which proceed   Samson 599
And I believe it, weakness to resist   Samson 830
I see ye visibly, and now beleeve   Mask 216
line not in Bridgewater ms
Trinity ms '& now beleeve' ←'now I beleeve' ←'& while I see yee'
1673 'believe'
Do ye beleeve me yet, or shall I call   Mask 438
1673 'believe'
Believe me I have thither packt the worst: Vacation 12

Believed
Which I believ'd was from above; but he   Par Reg 1.274
And on that high Authority had believ'd,   Par Reg 2.5

Believers
To all Beleevers; and from that pretense,   Par Lost 12.520

Believes
Not knowing to what Land, yet firm believes: Par Lost 12.127

Believest
Believst so main to our success, I bring;   Par Lost 6.471
1667 'Beleivst'

Believing
And flatter'd out of all, believing lies   Par Lost 10.42

Belike
Belike through impotence, or unaware,   Par Lost 2.156

Bellerophon
Bellerophon, though from a lower Clime)   Par Lost 7.18

Bellerus
Sleep'st by the fable of *Bellerus* old,   Lycidas 160
Trinity ms 'Bellerus' ←'Corineus'

Bellied
The high, huge-bellied Mountains skip like Rams   Psalm 114, 11

Bellies
Anow of such as for their bellies sake,   Lycidas 114

Bellman
Or the Belmans drousie charm,   Penseroso 83

Bellona
Great things with small) then when *Bellona* storms,   Par Lost 2.922

Bellow
To bellow through the vast and boundless Deep.   Par Lost 1.177

Bellowing
And uncouth paine fled bellowing. On each wing   Par Lost 6.362

Bells
When the merry Bells ring round,   Allegro 93
Their Bels, and Flourets of a thousand hues.   Lycidas 135
1673 'Bells'
1638 'bells'
Trinity ms 'bells'

Belly
Upon thy Belly groveling thou shalt goe,   Par Lost 10.177
A monstrous Serpent on his Belly prone,   Par Lost 10.514

Belong
If better thou belong not to the dawn,   Par Lost 5.167
Ill worthie I such title should belong   Par Lost 11.163

Belonged
Not mee. They therefore as to right belongd,   Par Lost 3.111

Belongs
The punishment to other hand belongs,   Par Lost 6.807
Conviction to the Serpent none belongs.   Par Lost 10.84
Man I deceav'd: that which to mee belongs,   Par Lost 10.496
Rather belongs, distrust and all dispraise: Par Lost 11.166
Hath nothing, and to whom nothing belongs   Par Reg 3.135
That which to God alone of right belongs;   Par Reg 3.141
That to the service of this house belongs,   Mask 85
That to the faithfull Herdmans art belongs!   Lycidas 121

Beloved
Effulgence of my Glorie, Son belov'd,   Par Lost 6.680
Supream, that thou in mee thy Son belov'd   Par Lost 10.70
Both his beloved Man and all his World,   Par Lost 10.489
Highly belov'd, being but the Minister   Par Lost 12.308
From Heav'n pronounc'd him his beloved Son.   Par Reg 1.32
This is my Son belov'd, in him am pleas'd.   Par Reg 1.85
Me his beloved Son, in whom alone   Par Reg 1.285
To be belov'd of God, I have not lost   Par Reg 1.379
Heard thee pronounc'd the Son of God belov'd.   Par Reg 4.513

Below
That stone, or like to that which here below   Par Lost 3.600
Here sleep below while thou to foresight wak'st,   Par Lost 11.368
And so bestudd with Stars, that they below   Mask 734
Bridgewater ms 'belowe'
To the full voic'd Quire below,   Penseroso 162
Was kindly com to live with them below;   Nativity 90
Amongst us here below to hide thy nectar'd head.   Fair Inf 49
But oh why didst thou not stay here below   Fair Inf 64
Yet being above them, he shall be below them;   Vacation 80
That we on Earth with undiscording voice   Musick 17
Trinity ms 'on earth' ←'below may learne'

Belus
Belus or *Serapis* thir Gods, or seat   Par Lost 1.720
ms 'Belus'

Bench
Cyriack, whose Grandsire on the Royal Bench   Sonnet 21, 1
line not in Trinity ms

Bend
To speak; whereat thir doubl'd Ranks they bend   Par Lost 1.616
Thither let us bend all our thoughts, to learn   Par Lost 2.354
Of Thunder heard remote. Towards him they bend   Par Lost 2.477
Might yield them easier habitation, bend   Par Lost 2.573
Possesses thee to bend that mortal Dart   Par Lost 2.729
Will ye submit your necks, and chuse to bend   Par Lost 5.787
Shall bend the knee, and in that honour due   Par Lost 5.817
From innocence. Now therefore bend thine eare   Par Lost 11.30
Where the bow'd welkin slow doth bend,   Mask 1015
To whom our vows and wishes bend,   Arcades 6
In honour bend thy knee.   Psalm 81, 40
To bow to him and bend,   Psalm 81, 62
Thine ear with favour bend.   Psalm 88, 8
Now void, it fitts thy people; thether bend   Prose 12, 10

Bended
He back recoild; the tenth on bended knee   Par Lost 6.194
And bended Dolphins play: part huge of bulk   Par Lost 7.410
The bended Twigs take root, and Daughters grow   Par Lost 9.1105
His Sword he whets, his Bow hath bended   Psalm 7, 46

Bending
Bending to look on me, I started back,   Par Lost 4.462
Bending his eare; perswasion in me grew   Par Lost 11.152
Bending one way their pretious influence,   Nativity 71

Bends
Allur'd his eye: Thither his course he bends   Par Lost 3.573
Of *Ceres* ripe for harvest waving bends   Par Lost 4.981
That bends not as I tread,   Mask 899
That bends his rage thy providence to oppose   Psalm 8, 8

Beneath
That were an ignominy and shame beneath   Par Lost 1.115
Beneath *Gibralter* to the *Lybian* sands.   Par Lost 1.355
Your dungeon stretching far and wide beneath;   Par Lost 2.1003
Thee *Sion* and the flowrie Brooks beneath   Par Lost 3.30
Beneath thy Sentence; Hell her numbers full,   Par Lost 3.332
Direct against which op'nd from beneath,   Par Lost 3.526
Took leave, and toward the coast of Earth beneath,   Par Lost 3.739
Among the spirits beneath, whom I seduc'd   Par Lost 4.83
Beneath him with new wonder now he views   Par Lost 4.205
Clustring, but not beneath his shoulders broad: Par Lost 4.303
Beneath th' *Azores;* whither the prime Orb,   Par Lost 4.592

Beneath(*cont*)
Humbl'd by such rebuke, so farr beneath Par Lost 6.342
Wide the Celestial soile, and saw beneath Par Lost 6.510
Above, or round about thee or beneath. Par Lost 8.318
And these inferiour farr beneath me set? Par Lost 8.382
Beneath what other Creatures are to thee? Par Lost 8.411
To sensual Appetite, who from beneathe Par Lost 9.1129
Beneath *Magellan*. At that tasted Fruit Par Lost 10.687
Powers of Fire, Air, Water, and Earth beneath, Par Reg 2.124
High rooft and walks beneath, and alleys brown Par Reg 2.293
God of this world invok't and world beneath; Par Reg 4.203
But herein to our Prophets far beneath, Par Reg 4.356
Thir foe to misery beneath thir fears, Samson 1469
Upon the heads of all who sate beneath, Samson 1652
That from beneath the seat of *Jove* doth spring, Lycidas 16
Sunk though he be beneath the watry floar, Lycidas 167
Beneath the hollow round Nativity 102
His starry front low-rooft beneath the skies; Passion 18

Benediction
Follow'd with benediction. Since to part, Par Lost 8.645
His benediction so, that in his Seed Par Lost 12.125
Then glory and benediction, that is thanks, Par Reg 3.127

Benefactors
Great Benefactors of mankind, Deliverers, Par Reg 3.82

Beneficence
For so much good, so much beneficence. Par Reg 3.133

Benefit
The benefit: consider first, that Great Par Lost 8.90
Neglect not, and the benefit imbrace Par Lost 12.426
Or benefit reveal'd to *Abraham*'s race? Samson 29

Benefits
Who for so many benefits receiv'd Par Reg 3.137

Benevolent
Benevolent and facil thus repli'd. Par Lost 8.65

Bengal
Close sailing from *Bengala*, or the Iles Par Lost 2.638

Bengala
Close sailing from *Bengala*, or the Iles Par Lost 2.638

Benighted
Benighted in these Woods. Now to my charms, Mask 150
Benighted walks under the mid-day Sun; Mask 384
Trinity ms 'benighted walks under the midday sun' ←'walks in black vapours though the noontyde brand'
Bridgewater ms 'walks in black vapours though the noone tyde brand'

Benign
Thy words, Creator bounteous and benigne, Par Lost 8.492
To whom thus *Michael* with regard benigne. Par Lost 11.334
To good malignant, to bad men benigne, Par Lost 12.538

Benison
That wontst to love the travailers benizon, Mask 332

Benjamin
In Ephraims view and Benjamins, Psalm 80, 9

Bent
Were always downward bent, admiring more Par Lost 1.681
With all her battering Engines bent to rase Par Lost 2.923
High Thron'd above all highth, bent down his eye, Par Lost 3.58
Wide interrupt can hold; so bent he seems Par Lost 3.84
Walk'd up and down alone bent on his prey, Par Lost 3.441
Or as a Thief bent to unhoord the cash Par Lost 4.188
As I bent down to look, just opposite, Par Lost 4.460
Bent all on speed, and markt his Aerie Gate; Par Lost 4.568
Hitherward bent (who could have thought?) escap'd Par Lost 4.794
To make us less, bent rather to exalt Par Lost 5.829
Among the mightiest, bent on highest deeds, Par Lost 6.112
For sin, on warr and mutual slaughter bent. Par Lost 6.506
And full of wrauth bent on his Enemies. Par Lost 6.826
In meditated fraud and malice, bent Par Lost 9.55
So bent, the more shall shame him his repulse. Par Lost 9.384
Bent thir aspect, and whom they wish'd beheld, Par Lost 10.454
Crooked by nature, bent, as now appears, Par Lost 10.885
Direct to th' Eastern Gate was bent thir flight. Par Lost 11.190
Life much, bent rather how I may be quit Par Lost 11.548
Just men they seemd, and all thir study bent Par Lost 11.577
The bent of Nature; which he thus express'd. Par Lost 11.597
Though bent on speed, so heer th' Arch-angel paus'd Par Lost 12.2
line not in 1667 edition
Thither he bent his way, determin'd there Par Reg 2.291
Some bent at thee thir fiery darts, while thou Par Reg 4.424
This Tempest at this Desert most was bent; Par Reg 4.465
Thou for thy Son art bent to lay out all; Samson 1486
Thou know'st it must be now thy only bent Vacation 55
A *Sybil* old, bow-bent with crooked age, Vacation 69
Lodg'd with me useless, though my Soul more bent Sonnet 19, 4

Benumb
Of that forgetful Lake benumm not still, Par Lost 2.74
1667 'benumme'

Benumbed
Our Limbs benumm'd, ere this diurnal Starr Par Lost 10.1069

Benumbing
To deaths benumming Opium as my only cure. Samson 630

Bereave
I beg, and clasp thy knees; bereave me not, Par Lost 10.918

Bereaved
Bereavd of happiness thou maist partake Par Lost 6.903
His Malice, and with rapine sweet bereav'd Par Lost 9.461
Why am I thus bereav'd thy prime decree? Samson 85
Above the Sons of men; but sight bereav'd Samson 1294

Bereaving
Bereaving sense, but endless miserie Par Lost 10.810
Then thou our fancy of it self bereaving, Shakespear 13

Bereft
To whom thus *Adam* of short joy bereft. Par Lost 11.628
In what part lodg'd, how easily bereft me, Samson 48
Co. What chance good Lady hath bereft you thus? Mask 277
Bereft of light thir seeing have forgot, Sonnet 22, 3
Of head bereft li'th poor *Kenelm* King-born. Prose 13, 2

Berries
With Ivy berries wreath'd, and his blithe youth, Mask 55
To bring me Berries, or such cooling fruit Mask 186
Bridgewater ms 'berries'
Trinity ms 'berries'
I com to pluck your Berries harsh and crude, Lycidas 3
1638 'berries'
Trinity ms 'berries'

Berry
Berrie or Grape: to whom thus *Adam* call'd. Par Lost 5.307
From many a berrie, and from sweet kernels prest Par Lost 5.346

Beryl
Of Beril, and careering Fires between; Par Lost 6.756
The beryl, and the golden ore, Mask 933
1637 'beryll'
Trinity ms 'beryll'
Bridgewater ms 'beryll'

Beseech
To mortal eare is dreadful; they beseech Par Lost 12.236
Then as repentant to submit, beseech, Samson 751

Beseeching
Beseeching or besieging. This report, Par Lost 5.869
Beseeching him, so as we need not fear Par Lost 10.1082

Beseem
Prince *Memnons* sister might beseem, Penseroso 18

Beseeming
Had but a moderate and beseeming share Mask 769
Bridgewater ms 'beseeminge'

Beseems
At thy right hand voluptuous, as beseems Par Lost 2.869
Wanted, nor youthful dalliance as beseems Par Lost 4.338
To treat thee as beseems, and as her Lord Par Reg 2.335

Beset
Environ'd wins his way; harder beset Par Lost 2.1016
To whom thus *Adam* sore beset repli'd. Par Lost 10.124
And therefore hated, therefore so beset Par Lost 11.702
The harrass of thir Land, beset me round; Samson 257

Besetting
In hard besetting need, this will I try Mask 857
Bridgewater ms 'besettinge'
Trinity ms 'distressed' ←'in honourd vertues cause'

Beside
And as I wondring lookt, beside it stood Par Lost 5.54
Sate Eagle-wing'd, beside him hung his Bow Par Lost 6.763
Co. Imports their loss, beside the present need? Mask 287
His wish't presence, and beside Mask 950
And if ought els, great *Bards* beside, Penseroso 116
Nor all the gods beside, Nativity 224
And the full wrath beside Circum 23

Besides
For one restraint, Lords of the World besides? Par Lost 1.32
That sparkling blaz'd, his other Parts besides Par Lost 1.194
Smote on him sore besides, vaulted with Fire; Par Lost 1.298
With what besides, in Counsel or in Fight, Par Lost 2.20
Besides what hope the never-ending flight Par Lost 2.221
Man had not hellish foes anow besides, Par Lost 2.504
In *Aarons* Brest-plate, and a stone besides Par Lost 3.598
Not understood, this gift they have besides, Par Lost 6.626
Anough is left besides to search and know. Par Lost 7.125
Useless besides, reasoning I oft admire, Par Lost 8.25
Shall be the execration; so besides Par Lost 10.737
And in performing end us; what besides Par Lost 11.300
But is there yet no other way, besides Par Lost 11.527
Thy temperance invincible besides, Par Reg 2.408
Besides to give a Kingdom hath been thought Par Reg 2.481
Besides thir other worse then heathenish crimes; Par Reg 3.419
Many a fair Edifice besides, more like Par Reg 4.55
All Monarchies besides throughout the world, Par Reg 4.150
Nations besides from all the quarter'd winds, Par Reg 4.202
Who hast of sorrow thy full load besides; Samson 214
Besides whom is no God, compar'd with Idols, Samson 441
Hear what assaults I had, what snares besides, Samson 845
Besides, how vile, contemptible, ridiculous, Samson 1361
But to my task. *Neptune* besides the sway Mask 18
Trinity ms 'besids' ←'whose'
Besides what the grim Woolf with privy paw Lycidas 128
Besides what her vertues fair Winchester 4
Here besides the sorrowing Winchester 53
In all her equipage; besides to know Sonnet 17, 9
1694 'Besides'

Besiege
Or did of late earths Sonnes besiege the wall Fair Inf 47

Besieged
Besieg'd *Albracca*, as Romances tell; Par Reg 3.339

Besieging
Beseeching or besieging. This report, Par Lost 5.869

Besmeared
First *Moloch*, horrid King besmear'd with blood Par Lost 1.392
Of Horses led, and Grooms besmeard with Gold Par Lost 5.356

Besotted
But with besotted base ingratitude — Mask 778
Trinity ms 'besotted' ← 'a sottish'
Bridgewater ms 'beesotted'

Besought
With Heav'ns afflicting Thunder, and besought — Par Lost 2.166
While Pardon may be found in time besought. — Par Lost 5.848
Thus *Adam* his illustrious Guest besought: — Par Lost 7.109
With me, as I besought thee, when that strange — Par Lost 9.1135
Fell humble, and imbracing them, besaught — Par Lost 10.912
And terror cease; he grants what they besaught — Par Lost 12.238
1667 'them thir desire'
Humbled themselves, or penitent besought — Par Reg 3.421
Ask large enough, and I, *besought*, — Psalm 81, 43

Bespake
His mother bad, and thus bespake her Sire. — Par Lost 2.849
Which *Gabriel* spying, thus bespake the Fiend. — Par Lost 4.1005
With looks agast and sad he thus bespake. — Par Reg 1.43
He shook his Miter'd locks, and stern bespake, — Lycidas 112
Untill their Lord himself bespake, and bid them go. — Nativity 76

Besprent
Of Knot-grass dew-besprent, and were in fold, — Mask 542
Trinity ms 'dew besprent'

Best
What shall be right: fardest from him is best — Par Lost 1.247
That riches grow in Hell; that soyle may best — Par Lost 1.691
Defi'd the best of *Panim* chivalry — Par Lost 1.765
Could have assur'd us; and by what best way, — Par Lost 2.40
We warr, if warr be best, or to regain — Par Lost 2.230
Of order, how in safety best we may — Par Lost 2.280
And where thir weakness, how attempted best, — Par Lost 2.357
While here shall be our home, what best may ease — Par Lost 2.458
The good before him, but perverts best things — Par Lost 4.203
And by her yielded, by him best receivd, — Par Lost 4.309
Now other, as thir shape servd best his end — Par Lost 4.398
Which God likes best, into thir inmost bowre — Par Lost 4.738
To his proud fair, best quitted with disdain. — Par Lost 4.770
Best with the best, the Sender not the sent, — Par Lost 4.852
Heav'ns last best gift, my ever new delight, — Par Lost 5.19
Best Image of my self and dearer half, — Par Lost 5.95
Speak yee who best can tell, ye Sons of light, — Par Lost 5.160
What choice to chuse for delicacie best, — Par Lost 5.333
As may express them best, though what if Earth — Par Lost 5.574
This onely to consult how we may best — Par Lost 5.779
Assume, as likes them best, condense or rare. — Par Lost 6.353
First, Highest, Holiest, Best, thou alwayes seekst — Par Lost 6.724
Yet what thou canst attain, which best may serve — Par Lost 7.115
Ordain'd for uses to his Lord best known. — Par Lost 8.106
Of other Creatures, as him pleases best, — Par Lost 8.169
Best with thy self accompanied, seek'st not — Par Lost 8.428
Seems wisest, vertuousest, discreetest, best; — Par Lost 8.550
Approve the best, and follow what I approve. — Par Lost 8.611
From dust: spite then with spite is best repaid. — Par Lost 9.178
Then commune how that day they best may ply — Par Lost 9.201
How we might best fulfill the work which here — Par Lost 9.230
For solitude somtimes is best societie, — Par Lost 9.249
His wish and best advantage, us asunder, — Par Lost 9.258
With me, best witness of thy Vertue tri'd. — Par Lost 9.317
O Woman, best are all things as the will — Par Lost 9.343
And all things in best order to invite — Par Lost 9.402
From her best prop so farr, and storm so nigh. — Par Lost 9.433
With ravishment beheld, there best beheld — Par Lost 9.541
Great are thy Vertues, doubtless, best of Fruits. — Par Lost 9.745
Best guide; not following thee, I had remaind — Par Lost 9.808
O fairest of Creation, last and best — Par Lost 9.896
Such recompence best merits) from the bough — Par Lost 9.995
What best may from the present serve to hide — Par Lost 9.1092
Those two; the third best absent is condemn'd, — Par Lost 10.82
Though in mysterious terms, judg'd as then best: — Par Lost 10.173
There best, where most with ravin I may meet; — Par Lost 10.599
As sorted best with present things. The Sun — Par Lost 10.651
Out of my sight, thou Serpent, that name best — Par Lost 10.867
And mortal food, as may dispose him best — Par Lost 11.54
Safest thy life, and best prepar'd endure — Par Lost 11.365
Choicest and best; then sacrificing, laid — Par Lost 11.438
His best of Man, and gave him up to tears — Par Lost 11.497
To whom thus *Michael*. Judg not what is best — Par Lost 11.603
Henceforth I learne, that to obey is best, — Par Lost 12.561
Induces best to hope of like success. — Par Reg 1.105
How best the mighty work he might begin — Par Reg 1.186
But openly begin, as best becomes — Par Reg 1.288
How to begin, how to accomplish best — Par Reg 2.113
When and where likes me best, I can command? — Par Reg 2.382
What best to say canst say, to do canst do; — Par Reg 3.8
They themselves rather are occasion best, — Par Reg 3.174
So shalt thou best fullfil, best verifie — Par Reg 3.177
All things are best fullfil'd in their due time, — Par Reg 3.182
What I can suffer, how obey? who best — Par Reg 3.194
Can suffer, best can do; best reign, who first — Par Reg 3.195
Why move thy feet so slow to what is best, — Par Reg 3.224
Best school of best experience, quickest in sight — Par Reg 3.238
How best their opposition to withstand. — Par Reg 3.250
Yet he at length, time to himself best known, — Par Reg 3.433
Error by his own arms is best evinc't. — Par Reg 4.235
In *Chorus* or *Iambic*, teachers best — Par Reg 4.262
High actions, and high passions best describing: — Par Reg 4.266
These only with our Law best form a King. — Par Reg 4.364
When Prophesies of thee are best fullfill'd. — Par Reg 4.381

Best(*cont*)
Not when it must, but when it may be best. — Par Reg 4.476
Where by all best conjectures I collect — Par Reg 4.524
Have brought thee, and highest plac't, highest is best, — Par Reg 4.553
To set upon them, what advantag'd best; — Samson 255
For with his own Laws he can best dispence. — Samson 314
(Best pleas'd with humble and filial submission) — Samson 511
That wisest and best men full oft beguil'd — Samson 759
Which might have aw'd the best resolv'd of men, — Samson 847
In what I thought would have succeeded best. — Samson 908
Or value what is best — Samson 1029
What e're it be, to wisest men and best — Samson 1034
But had we best retire, I see a storm? — Samson 1061
But by the Barbers razor best subdu'd. — Samson 1167
The worst that he can give, to me the best. — Samson 1264
To what may serve his glory best, & spread his name — Samson 1429
Chor. Best keep together here, lest running thither — Samson 1521
And which is best and happiest yet, all this — Samson 1718
Chor. All is best, though we oft doubt, — Samson 1745
And ever best found in the close. — Samson 1748
The greatest, and the best of all the main — Mask 28
My best guide now, me thought it was the sound — Mask 171
Would overtask the best Land-Pilots art, — Mask 309
Where with her best nurse Contemplation — Mask 377
Best draw, and stand upon our guard. *Eld. Bro*. Ile hallow, — Mask 487
Already, ere my best speed could praevent, — Mask 573
Sab. Shepherd 'tis my office best — Mask 908
he may scratch his forehead. heere be brambles — Mask Tr. ms 17.57
'he may scratch' ← 'he may chaunce' ← 'chance' ← 'had best look to'
& good heaven cast his best regard upon us — Mask Tr. ms 21.32
But thou canst best perform that office where thou art. — Fair Inf 70
Till thou hast deck't them in thy best aray; — Vacation 26
Befriend me night best Patroness of grief, — Passion 29
That with smooth aire couldst humor best our tongue. — Sonnet 13, 8
Love led them on, and Faith who knew them best — Sonnet 14, 9
Then to advise how warr may best, upheld, — Sonnet 17, 7
What severs each thou 'hast learnt, which few hav don. — Sonnet 17, 11
Either man's work or his own gifts, who best — Sonnet 19, 10
Bear his milde yoak, they serve him best, his State — Sonnet 19, 11
A thousand daies *at best*. — Psalm 84, 36

Bestead
How little you bested, — Penseroso 3

Bestial
To bestial Gods; for which thir heads as low — Par Lost 1.435
ms 'bestiall'
And towards the Gate rouling her bestial train, — Par Lost 2.873
Among the bestial herds to raunge, by thee — Par Lost 4.754
Into a Beast, and mixt with bestial slime, — Par Lost 9.165

Bestir
Rouse and bestir themselves ere well awake. — Par Lost 1.334
ms 'bestirr'

Bestirs
Bestirs her then, and from each tender stalk — Par Lost 5.337

Bestow
Our givers thir own gifts, and large bestow — Par Lost 5.317
With what all Earth or Heaven could bestow — Par Lost 8.483
As thy possession I on thee bestow — Psalm 2, 17
The Lord will also then bestow — Psalm 85, 49

Bestowed
On whom the great Creator hath bestowd — Par Lost 3.673
From large bestowd, where Nature multiplies — Par Lost 5.318
Bestowd, the holy salutation us'd — Par Lost 5.386
More then enough; at least on her bestow'd — Par Lost 8.537
What I might have bestow'd on whom I pleas'd, — Par Reg 2.395

Bestrewn
And broken Chariot Wheels, so thick bestrown — Par Lost 1.311
That lie bestrowne unsightly and unsmooth, — Par Lost 4.631

Bestuck
Bestuck with slandrous darts, and works of Faith — Par Lost 12.536

Bestud
And so bestudd with Stars, that they below — Mask 734
1637 'bestudde'
Bridgewater ms 'would soe emblaze with starrs that they belowe'
Trinity ms 'and so bestudde with starres' ← 'would so be studde the center with thire starre light'

Besure
But come, for thou, besure, shalt give account — Par Lost 4.841

Betake
Whither shall I betake me, where subsist? — Par Lost 10.922
Where may she wander now, whether betake her — Mask 351

Betakes
At last betakes him to this ominous Wood, — Mask 61
Trinity ms 'betaks'

Bethabara
Lodg'd in *Bethabara* where *John* baptiz'd, — Par Reg 1.184
Nigh to *Bethabara;* in *Jerico* — Par Reg 2.20

Bethel
Doubl'd that sin in *Bethel* and in *Dan*, — Par Lost 1.485
ms 'Bethel'
Of *Bethel* and of *Dan?* no, let them serve — Par Reg 3.431

Bethink
Let such bethink them, if the sleepy drench — Par Lost 2.73
Yet stay, be not disturb'd, now I bethink me, — Mask 820
1637 'bethinke'
Trinity ms 'bethinke'
Bridgewater ms 'bethinke'

Bethlehem	
Of Angels in the fields of *Bethlehem* sung	Par Reg 1.243
With Infant blood the streets of *Bethlehem;*	Par Reg 2.78
And of the Angelic Song in *Bethlehem* field,	Par Reg 4.505
The rayes of *Bethlehem* blind his dusky eyn;	Nativity 223
Bethought	
Yet of another Plea bethought him soon.	Par Reg 3.149
Betide	
Must reascend, what will betide the few	Par Lost 12.480
Betides	
Fair morning yet betides thee Son of God,	Par Reg 4.451
Betimes	
Thir sinful state, and to appease betimes	Par Lost 3.186
To measure life, learn thou betimes, and know	Sonnet 21, 9
Betokening	
Betok'ning peace from God, and Cov'nant new.	Par Lost 11.867
Betok'ning, or ill boding, I contemn	Par Reg 4.490
Betook	
Betook them, and the neighbouring Hills uptore;	Par Lost 6.663
Betook her to the Groves, but *Delia*'s self	Par Lost 9.388
This said, they both betook them several wayes,	Par Lost 10.610
Hungry and cold betook him to his rest,	Par Reg 4.403
Betray	
Of *Timna* first betray me, and reveal	Samson 383
She purpos'd to betray me, and (which was worse	Samson 399
To break all faith, all vows, deceive, betray,	Samson 750
In perfet thraldom, how again betray me,	Samson 946
Betrayed	
Which marrd his borrow'd visage, and betraid	Par Lost 4.116
Betray'd, Captiv'd, and both my Eyes put out,	Samson 33
Of vow, and have betray'd it to a woman,	Samson 379
Knowing, as needs I must, by thee betray'd?	Samson 840
Afford me assassinated and betray'd,	Samson 1109
Hast thou betrai'd my credulous innocence	Mask 697
1637 'betray'd'	
line not in Bridgewater ms	
Trinity ms 'betrayd'	
how have I bin betrai'd	Mask Tr. ms 22.18
Better	
Better to reign in Hell, then serve in Heav'n.	Par Lost 1.263
New warr, provok't; our better part remains	Par Lost 1.645
For Treasures better hid. Soon had his crew	Par Lost 1.688
The better reason, to perplex and dash	Par Lost 2.114
Chains and these Torments? better these then worse	Par Lost 2.196
To serve him better: wise are all his wayes.	Par Lost 3.680
Who came thir bane, though with them better pleas'd	Par Lost 4.167
Your numerous ofspring; if no better place,	Par Lost 4.385
Which taught thee yet no better, that no pain	Par Lost 4.915
Better abode, and my afflicted Powers	Par Lost 4.939
If better thou belong not to the dawn,	Par Lost 5.167
But what if better counsels might erect	Par Lost 5.785
The better fight, who single hast maintaind	Par Lost 6.30
May serve to better us, and worse our foes,	Par Lost 6.440
Of Spirits maligne a better Race to bring	Par Lost 7.189
That better might with farr less compass move,	Par Lost 8.33
In Battels feign'd; the better fortitude	Par Lost 9.31
For what God after better worse would build?	Par Lost 9.102
Were better, and most likelie if from mee	Par Lost 9.365
Against his better knowledge, not deceav'd,	Par Lost 9.998
With travail difficult, not better farr	Par Lost 10.593
To better hopes his more attentive minde	Par Lost 10.1011
Som better shroud, som better warmth to cherish	Par Lost 10.1068
What better can we do, then to the place	Par Lost 10.1086
To better life shall yeeld him, where with mee	Par Lost 11.42
Better end heer unborn. Why is life giv'n	Par Lost 11.502
Much better seems this Vision, and more hope	Par Lost 11.599
Said th' Angel, who should better hold his place	Par Lost 11.635
O Visions ill foreseen! better had I	Par Lost 11.763
Up to a better Cov'nant, disciplin'd	Par Lost 12.302
And his deep thoughts, the better to converse	Par Reg 1.190
For in the Inn was left no better room:	Par Reg 1.248
Nor mind it, fed with better thoughts that feed	Par Reg 2.258
Nature asham'd, or better to express,	Par Reg 2.332
To gain a Scepter, oftest better miss't.	Par Reg 2.486
Raign then; what canst thou better do the while?	Par Reg 3.180
Were better farthest off) is not yet come;	Par Reg 3.397
And rash, before-hand had no better weigh'd	Par Reg 4.8
As men divinely taught, and better teaching	Par Reg 4.357
Desperate of better course, to vent his rage,	Par Reg 4.445
To visit or bewail thee, or if better,	Samson 182
Better at home lie bed-rid, not only idle,	Samson 579
Wherewith to serve him better then thou hast;	Samson 585
No better way I saw then by importuning	Samson 797
As good for nothing else, no better service	Samson 1163
Night hath better sweets to prove,	Mask 123
And then the giver would be better thank't,	Mask 775
A better soyl shall give ye thanks.	Arcades 101
Were it not better don as others use,	Lycidas 67
The better part with *Mary*, and the *Ruth*,	Sonnet 9, 5
Then whome a better Senatour nere held	Sonnet 17, 2
Content though blind, had I no better guide.	Sonnet 22, 14
Is better, *and more blest*	Psalm 84, 34
Stronglier, and better oft then earnest can.	Prose 7, 2
Between	
Between the Cherubim; yea, often plac'd	Par Lost 1.387
Ris'n, and with hideous outcry rush'd between.	Par Lost 2.726
Hell and the Gulf between, and *Satan* there	Par Lost 3.70
Rear'd high thir flourish heads between, and wrought	Par Lost 4.699
Between(*cont*)	
Sailes between worlds and worlds, with steddie wing	Par Lost 5.268
Of nectarous draughts between, from milkie stream,	Par Lost 5.306
Tells the suggested cause, and casts between	Par Lost 5.702
Destruction to the rest: this pause between	Par Lost 6.162
Or equal what between us made the odds,	Par Lost 6.441
Of Beril, and careering Fires between;	Par Lost 6.756
Myriads between two brazen Mountains lodg'd	Par Lost 7.201
Disparted, and between spun out the Air,	Par Lost 7.241
Between her white wings mantling proudly, Rowes	Par Lost 7.439
As Plants: ambiguous between Sea and Land	Par Lost 7.473
Refreshment, whether food, or talk between,	Par Lost 9.237
High overarch't, and echoing Walks between;	Par Lost 9.1107
No ground of enmitie between us known,	Par Lost 9.1151
Between Thee and the Woman I will put	Par Lost 10.179
Enmitie, and between thine and her Seed;	Par Lost 10.180
Though distant from thee Worlds between, yet felt	Par Lost 10.362
Is enmity, which he will put between	Par Lost 10.497
Between us two let there be peace, both joyning,	Par Lost 10.924
Before him, Towns, and rural works between,	Par Lost 11.639
As on drie land between two christal walls,	Par Lost 12.197
Darkness defends between till morning Watch;	Par Lost 12.207
A Mercie-seat of Gold between the wings	Par Lost 12.253
Would stand between me and thy Fathers ire,	Par Reg 3.219
Th' one winding, the other strait and left between	Par Reg 3.256
Between two such enclosing enemies	Par Reg 3.361
Between the pillars; he his guide requested	Samson 1630
And Mercy set between,	Nativity 144
1673 'Mercy will sit between'	
That sitt'st between the Cherubs *bright*	Psalm 80, 5
Between their wings out-spread,	Psalm 80, 6
Betwixt	
'Twixt upper, nether, and surrounding Fires;	Par Lost 1.346
ms 'T'wixt'	
Betwixt *Damiata* and mount *Casius* old,	Par Lost 2.593
Through *Bosporus* betwixt the justling Rocks:	Par Lost 2.1018
Betwixt th' Angelical and Human kinde:	Par Lost 3.462
Betwixt them Lawns, or level Downs, and Flocks	Par Lost 4.252
Betwixt these rockie Pillars *Gabriel* sat	Par Lost 4.549
Betwixt *Astrea* and the *Scorpion* signe,	Par Lost 4.998
Standards, and Gonfalons twixt Van and Reare	Par Lost 5.589
'Twixt Host and Host but narrow space was left,	Par Lost 6.104
Twixt Day and Night, and now from end to end	Par Lost 9.51
Betwixt the *Centaure* and the *Scorpion* stearing	Par Lost 10.328
Betwixt the world destroy'd and world restor'd,	Par Lost 12.3
line not in 1667 edition	
Took in by lot 'twixt high, and neather *Jove*,	Mask 20
Trinity ms 'twixt'	
Bridgewater ms 'twixt'	
'Twixt *Africa* and *Inde*, Ile find him out,	Mask 606
Trinity ms 'twixt'	
Bridgewater ms 'twixt'	
From betwixt two aged Okes,	Allegro 82
To stand 'twixt us and our deserved smart	Fair Inf 69
Dodg'd with him, betwixt *Cambridge* and the Bull.	Carrier 8
1658 ''twixt'	
Bevy	
A Beavie of fair Women, richly gay	Par Lost 11.582
Bewail	
Which shall I first bewail,	Samson 151
To visit or bewail thee, or if better,	Samson 182
Bewail thy falshood, and the pious works	Samson 955
Bewailed	
But kill'd alas, and then bewayl'd his fatal bliss.	Fair Inf 7
Bewailing	
Bewailing thir excess, all terror hide.	Par Lost 11.111
Visit his Tomb with flowers, only bewailing	Samson 1742
Beware	
From what point of his Compass to beware	Par Lost 4.559
Yet mutable; whence warne him to beware	Par Lost 5.237
At thy request, and that thou maist beware	Par Lost 6.894
Adam by dire example to beware	Par Lost 7.42
Death is the penaltie impos'd, beware,	Par Lost 7.545
The weal or woe in thee is plac't; beware.	Par Lost 8.638
But bid her well beware, and still erect,	Par Lost 9.353
Beyond	
And *Horonaim*, *Seons* Realm, beyond	Par Lost 1.409
A shout that tore Hells Concave, and beyond	Par Lost 1.542
By *Fontarabbia*. Thus far these beyond	Par Lost 1.587
Beyond the *Indian* Mount, or Faerie Elves,	Par Lost 1.781
Thus high uplifted beyond hope, aspires	Par Lost 2.7
Beyond thus high, insatiate to pursue	Par Lost 2.8
Beyond his Potent arm, to live exempt	Par Lost 2.318
Beyond this flood a frozen Continent	Par Lost 2.587
Beyond compare the Son of God was seen	Par Lost 3.138
Beyond th' *Horizon;* then from Pole to Pole	Par Lost 3.560
The place he found beyond expression bright,	Par Lost 3.591
Beyond the *Cape of Hope*, and now are past	Par Lost 4.160
Thy goodness beyond thought, and Power Divine:	Par Lost 5.159
Reaching beyond all limit at one blow	Par Lost 6.140
Stood scoffing, highthn'd in thir thoughts beyond	Par Lost 6.629
Of knowledge within bounds; beyond abstain	Par Lost 7.120
Beyond all other, think the same voutsaf't	Par Lost 8.581
Beyond the Earths green Cape and verdant Isles	Par Lost 8.631
Maeotis, up beyond the River *Ob;*	Par Lost 9.78
Active within beyond the sense of brute.	Par Lost 9.96
Sole *Eve*, Associate sole, to me beyond	Par Lost 9.227
Beyond his hope, *Eve* separate he spies,	Par Lost 9.424

Beyond(*cont*)
Beyond a row of Myrtles, on a Flat, Par Lost 9.627
That lay in wait; beyond this had bin force, Par Lost 9.1173
Beyond this Deep; whatever drawes me on, Par Lost 10.245
Beyond *Petsora* Eastward, to the rich Par Lost 10.292
Of *Turkish* Crescent, leaves all waste beyond Par Lost 10.434
Successful beyond hope, to lead ye forth Par Lost 10.463
Beyond the Polar Circles; to them Day Par Lost 10.681
His Sentence beyond dust and Natures Law, Par Lost 10.805
Beyond all past example and future, Par Lost 10.840
Beyond all bounds, till inundation rise Par Lost 11.828
Till time stand fixt: beyond is all abyss, Par Lost 12.555
Beyond which was my folly to aspire. Par Lost 12.560
Of honour, wealth, high fare, aim'd not beyond Par Reg 2.202
Lawful desires of Nature, not beyond; Par Reg 2.230
And oft beyond; to South the *Persian* Bay, Par Reg 3.273
From *Egypt* to *Euphrates* and beyond Par Reg 3.384
Beyond *Danubius* to the *Tauric* Pool. Par Reg 4.79
O change beyond report, thought, or belief! Samson 117
Of acts indeed heroic, far beyond Samson 527
Beyond the bliss of dreams. Be wise, and taste.---- Mask 813
Quickly to the green earths end, Mask 1014
Trinity ms 'quickly to' ←'farre beyond'
beyond the written date of mortall change Mask Tr. ms 10.22
Whether beyond the stormy *Hebrides*, Lycidas 156
Beyond the Realm of *Gaul*, a Land there lies, Prose 12, 8

Bickering
Of smoak and bickering flame, and sparkles dire; Par Lost 6.766

Bid
Who now is Sovran can dispose and bid Par Lost 1.246
Then of thir Session ended they bid cry Par Lost 2.514
Or Nature; God and Nature bid the same, Par Lost 6.176
Of Battel: whereat *Michael* bid sound Par Lost 6.202
Or we can bid his absence, till thy Song Par Lost 7.107
I send along, ride forth, and bid the Deep Par Lost 7.166
Easie, e're God had bid the ground be drie, Par Lost 7.304
God hath bid dwell farr off all anxious cares, Par Lost 8.185
Sung Spousal, and bid haste the Eevning Starr Par Lost 8.519
But bid her well beware, and still erect, Par Lost 9.353
Some say he bid his Angels turne ascanse Par Lost 10.668
Was bid turn Reines from th' Equinoctial Rode Par Lost 10.672
They light the Nuptial Torch, and bid invoke Par Lost 11.590
I bid not or forbid; do as thou find'st Par Reg 1.495
And by the Angel was bid rise and eat, Par Reg 2.274
Duty and Service, nor to stay till bid, Par Reg 2.326
Bid go with evil omen and the brand Samson 967
Off. Samson, to thee our Lords thus bid me say; Samson 1310
To thee I am bid say. Art thou our Slave, Samson 1392
And tell me it is safe, as bid me hope Mask 400
And at my window bid good morrow, Allegro 46
Or bid the soul of *Orpheus* sing Penseroso 105
Envy bid conceal the rest. Arcades 13
And bid fair peace be to my sable shrowd. Lycidas 22
And call the Vales, and bid them hither cast Lycidas 134
Bid *Amaranthus* all his beauty shed, Lycidas 149
Untill their Lord himself bespake, and bid them go. Nativity 76
And bid the weltring waves their oozy channel keep. Nativity 124
The great *Emathian* Conqueror bid spare Sonnet 8, 10
Trinity ms 'bidd'
Before the Judge, who thenceforth bid thee rest Sonnet 14, 13
Trinity ms 'bid' ←'bidd'

Bidden
And shove away the worthy bidden guest. Lycidas 118

Biddest
My Author and Disposer, what thou bidst Par Lost 4.635
What Land, what Seat of rest thou bidst me seek, Prose 12, 4

Bidding
Till at his second bidding darkness fled, Par Lost 3.712
If patiently thy bidding they obey, Par Lost 11.112
Therefore to his great bidding I submit. Par Lost 11.314
Is Kingly. Thousands at his bidding speed Sonnet 19, 12

Bide
All knees to thee shall bow, of them that bide Par Lost 3.321
Mine own that bide upon me, all from mee Par Lost 10.738
Must bide the stroak of that long threatn'd wound, Par Reg 1.59
In this wild solitude so long should bide Par Reg 2.304
Happy, whose strength in thee doth bide, Psalm 84, 19
I in thy truth will bide, Psalm 86, 38

Biding
Unhous'd thy Virgin Soul from her fair biding place. Fair Inf 21
Evil with thee no biding makes Psalm 5, 11

Bids
What e're his wrath, which he calls Justice, bids, Par Lost 2.733
Mean while, as Nature wills, Night bids us rest. Par Lost 4.633
Our Maker bids increase, who bids abstain Par Lost 4.748
Of these fair spreading Trees; which bids us seek Par Lost 10.1067
For what he bids I do; though I have lost Par Reg 1.377
Thou canst avoid, self-preservation bids; Samson 505
Comus. The Star that bids the Shepherd fold, Mask 93

Bier
He must not flote upon his watry bear Lycidas 12
Trinity ms 'beare'
1638 'biere'

Big
when the big rowling flakes of pitchie clowds Mask Tr. ms 15.52
when the bigg rowling flakes of pitchie clouds Mask Br. ms 345
He travels big with vanitie, Psalm 7, 51

Biggest
Behemoth biggest born of Earth upheav'd Par Lost 7.471

Bigness
In bigness to surpass Earths Giant Sons Par Lost 1.778
ms defective here
This pendant world, in bigness as a Starr Par Lost 2.1052

Bill
The second time returning, in his Bill Par Lost 11.859
First heard before the shallow Cuccoo's bill Sonnet 1, 6

Billows
In billows, leave i' th' midst a horrid Vale. Par Lost 1.224
May thy billows rowl ashoar Mask 932
Trinity ms 'billowes'
1637 'billowes'
Bridgewater ms 'billowes'

Bind
Bind thir resplendent locks inwreath'd with beams, Par Lost 3.361
In vain, though by thir powerful Art they binde Par Lost 3.602
Flatly unjust, to binde with Laws the free, Par Lost 5.819
Lop overgrown, or prune, or prop, or bind, Par Lost 9.210
Such prohibitions binde not. But if Death Par Lost 9.760
Bind us with after-bands, what profits then Par Lost 9.761
Or serve they as a flourie verge to binde Par Lost 11.881
But force the Spirit of Grace it self, and binde Par Lost 12.525
Who made our Laws to bind us, not himself, Samson 309
With *Thestylis* to bind the Sheaves; Allegro 88
Threatning to bind our soules with secular chaines: Sonnet 16, 12
And in firm union bind. Psalm 83, 20

Bindest
Pyrrha for whom bindst thou Horace 3

Bird
Harmonious numbers; as the wakeful Bird Par Lost 3.38
Silence accompanied, for Beast and Bird, Par Lost 4.600
With this her solemn Bird and this fair Moon, Par Lost 4.648
With this her solemn Bird, nor walk by Moon, Par Lost 4.655
Beast, Bird, Insect, or Worm durst enter none; Par Lost 4.704
To the night-warbling Bird, that now awake Par Lost 5.40
A *Phaenix*, gaz'd by all, as that sole Bird Par Lost 5.272
And every Bird of wing after his kinde; Par Lost 7.394
In signe whereof each Bird and Beast behold Par Lost 8.342
As thus he spake, each Bird and Beast behold Par Lost 8.349
With blandishment, each Bird stoop'd on his wing. Par Lost 8.351
Much less can Bird with Beast, or Fish with Fowle Par Lost 8.395
Disporting, till the amorous Bird of Night Par Lost 8.518
On Bird, Beast, Aire, Aire suddenly eclips'd Par Lost 11.183
The Bird of *Jove*, stoopt from his aerie tour, Par Lost 11.185
Of every Beast, and Bird, and Insect small Par Lost 11.734
Plato's retirement, where the *Attic* Bird Par Reg 4.245
Like that self-begott'n bird Samson 1699
A secular bird ages of lives. Samson 1707
Sweet Bird that shunn'st the noise of folly, Penseroso 61
Now timely sing, ere the rude Bird of Hate Sonnet 1, 9

Birds
The birds thir notes renew, and bleating herds Par Lost 2.494
The Birds thir quire apply; aires, vernal aires, Par Lost 4.264
With charm of earliest Birds; pleasant the Sun Par Lost 4.642
With charm of earliest Birds, nor rising Sun Par Lost 4.651
Of Birds on every bough; so much the more Par Lost 5.8
Joyn voices all ye living Souls, ye Birds, Par Lost 5.197
Of Birds in orderly array on wing Par Lost 6.74
From Branch to Branch the smaller Birds with song Par Lost 7.433
Birds on the branches warbling; all things smil'd, Par Lost 8.265
Joyous the Birds; fresh Gales and gentle Aires Par Lost 8.515
Walks, and the melodie of Birds; but here Par Lost 8.528
Two Birds of gayest plume before him drove: Par Lost 11.186
With chaunt of tuneful Birds resounding loud; Par Reg 2.290
From drooping plant, or dropping tree; the birds Par Reg 4.434
While Birds of Calm sit brooding on the charmed wave. Nativity 68

Birth
By wondrous birth: Be thou in *Adams* room Par Lost 3.285
Begins his dire attempt, which nigh the birth Par Lost 4.15
Aire, and ye Elements the eldest birth Par Lost 5.180
Had circl'd his full Orbe, the birth mature Par Lost 5.862
His Generation, and the rising Birth Par Lost 7.102
Birth-day of Heav'n and Earth; with joy and shout Par Lost 7.256
Op'ning her fertil Woomb teem'd at a Birth Par Lost 7.454
Productive in Herb, Plant, and nobler birth Par Lost 9.111
Help to disburden Nature of her Bearth. Par Lost 9.624
Out of the ground wast taken, know thy Birth, Par Lost 10.207
At once, by my foreknowledge gaining Birth Par Lost 11.768
Barr'd of his right; yet at his Birth a Starr Par Lost 12.360
His place of birth a solemn Angel tells Par Lost 12.364
His birth to our just fear gave no small cause, Par Reg 1.66
To shew him worthy of his birth divine Par Reg 1.141
A messenger from God fore-told thy birth Par Reg 1.238
The Baptist, (of whose birth I oft had heard, Par Reg 1.270
Of other women, by the birth I bore, Par Reg 2.71
Thou art unknown, unfriended, low of birth, Par Reg 2.413
By all the Prophets; of thy birth at length Par Reg 4.503
O wherefore was my birth from Heaven foretold Samson 23
Whom long descent of birth Samson 171
Of birth from Heav'n foretold and high exploits, Samson 525
Feigndst at thy birth was giv'n thee in thy hair, Samson 1135
Send thee the Angel of thy Birth, to stand Samson 1431
Whom lovely *Venus* at a birth Allegro 14
Good luck befriend thee Son; for at thy birth Vacation 59
And joyous news of heav'nly Infants birth, Passion 3
To live with him, and sing in endles morn of light. Musick 28

Birth(*cont*)
Trinity ms 'morne' ←'birth'
Added to her noble birth, Winchester 5
Her high birth, and her graces sweet, Winchester 15
The haples Babe before his birth Winchester 31
And at her next birth much like thee, Winchester 67
Out of the tender mouths of latest bearth, Psalm 8, 4
Birthday
Birth-day of Heav'n and Earth; with joy and shout Par Lost 7.256
Birthnight
On thy birth-night, that sung thee Saviour born. Par Reg 4.506
Birthright
With his enormous brood, and birthright seis'd Par Lost 1.511
By Merit more then Birthright Son of God, Par Lost 3.309
Births
Produce prodigious Births of bodie or mind. Par Lost 11.687
Biserta
Or whom *Biserta* sent from *Afric* shore Par Lost 1.585
ms 'Biserta'
Bit
Lost in a Desert here and hunger-bit: Par Reg 2.416
Bites
Or hurtfull Worm with canker'd venom bites. Arcades 53
Bitter
Are brought: and feel by turns the bitter change Par Lost 2.598
Should prove a bitter Morsel, and his bane, Par Lost 2.808
That slumberd, wakes the bitter memorie Par Lost 4.24
And shun the bitter consequence: for know, Par Lost 8.328
Bitter ere long back on it self recoiles; Par Lost 9.172
Chewd bitter Ashes, which th' offended taste Par Lost 10.566
I led the way; bitter reproach, but true, Samson 823
How bitter is such self-delusion? Mask 365
line not in Bridgewater ms
line not in Trinity ms
Bitter constraint, and sad occasion dear, Lycidas 6
That on the bitter cross Nativity 152
Bitterly
Bitterly hast thou paid, and still art paying Samson 432
Bitterness
Assures me that the bitterness of death Par Lost 11.157
Bituminous
Neer that bituminous Lake where *Sodom* flam'd; Par Lost 10.562
The Plain, wherein a black bituminous gurge Par Lost 12.41
Bizance
In *Mosco*, or the Sultan in *Bizance*, Par Lost 11.395
Blab
All friendship, and avoided as a blab, Samson 495
Blabbing
Ere the blabbing Eastern scout, Mask 138
Bridgewater ms 'blabbinge'
Black
And black *Gehenna* call'd, the Type of Hell. Par Lost 1.405
Black fire and horror shot with equal rage Par Lost 2.67
Sad *Acheron* of sorrow, black and deep; Par Lost 2.578
For each seem'd either; black it stood as Night, Par Lost 2.670
Each cast at th' other, as when two black Clouds Par Lost 2.714
White, Black and Grey, with all thir trumperie. Par Lost 3.475
The black tartareous cold Infernal dregs Par Lost 7.238
Surprise thee, and her black attendant Death. Par Lost 7.547
Like a black mist low creeping, he held on Par Lost 9.180
Notus and *Afer* black with thundrous Clouds Par Lost 10.702
Wholsom and cool, and mild, but with black Air Par Lost 10.847
Meanwhile the Southwind rose, and with black wings Par Lost 11.738
The Plain, wherein a black bituminous gurge Par Lost 12.41
From anguish of the mind and humours black, Samson 600
To black mortification. Samson 622
On both his wings, one black, th' other white, Samson 973
And black enchantments, some Magicians Art Samson 1133
And in thick shelter of black shades imbowr'd, Mask 62
With black usurping mists, som gentle taper Mask 337
Benighted walks under the mid-day Sun; Mask 384
Bridgewater ms 'walks in black vapours though the noone tyde brand'
Trinity ms 'benighted walks under the midday sun' ←'walks in black vapours though the noontyde brand'
Ore laid with black staid Wisdoms hue. Penseroso 16
Black, but such as in esteem, Penseroso 17
To turn Swift-rushing black perdition hence, Fair Inf 67
The leaves should all be black wheron I write, Passion 34
Rough with black winds and storms Horace 7
Blackamoor
The Realm of *Bocchus* to the Black-moor Sea; Par Reg 4.72
Blackest
With blackest Insurrection, to confound Par Lost 2.136
To blackest grain, and into store convey'd: Par Lost 6.515
Of *Cerberus*, and blackest midnight born, Allegro 2
His burning Idol all of blackest hue, Nativity 207
Blade
And brandish't blade rush on him, break his glass, Mask 651
Trinity ms 'blade' ←'blades'
Blains
Botches and blaines must all his flesh imboss, Par Lost 12.180
Blame
That reaches blame, but rather merits praise Par Lost 3.697
Farr be it, that I should write thee sin or blame, Par Lost 4.758
No spot or blame behind: Which gives me hope Par Lost 5.119
To ask or search I blame thee not, for Heav'n Par Lost 8.66
For such thou art, from sin and blame entire: Par Lost 9.292

Blame(*cont*)
To whom soon mov'd with touch of blame thus *Eve*. Par Lost 9.1143
I should conceal, and not expose to blame Par Lost 10.130
Of all corruption, all the blame lights due; Par Lost 10.833
But rise, let us no more contend, nor blame Par Lost 10.958
The constantest to have yielded without blame. Samson 848
Dispraise, or blame, nothing but well and fair, Samson 1723
Eld. Bro. To tell thee sadly Shepherd, without blame, Mask 509
Pollute with sinfull blame, Nativity 41
But whether by mischance or blame Winchester 27
Their joy, while thou from blame Psalm 5, 34
Blamed
Each other, blam'd enough elsewhere, but strive Par Lost 10.959
Blamest
To love thou blam'st me not, for love thou saist Par Lost 8.612
Bland
And temperat vapors bland, which th' only sound Par Lost 5.5
Which with bland words at will she thus addrest. Par Lost 9.855
That with exhilerating vapour bland Par Lost 9.1047
Blandished
With blandisht parlies, feminine assaults, Samson 403
Blandishment
With blandishment, each Bird stoop'd on his wing. Par Lost 8.351
Blank
Presented with a Universal blanc Par Lost 3.48
Astonied stood and Blank, while horror chill Par Lost 9.890
Solstitial summers heat. To the blanc Moone Par Lost 10.656
Sollicitous and blank he thus began. Par Reg 2.120
And with confusion blank his Worshippers. Samson 471
With sudden adoration, and blank aw. Mask 452
Bridgewater ms 'blanke'
Trinity ms 'and blank aw' ←'of bright rays' ←'of her purenesse'
1637 'blancke'
Mine enemies shall all be blank and dash't Psalm 6, 21
Blasphemed
Be questiond and blaspheam'd without defence. Par Lost 3.166
For this he shall live hated, be blasphem'd, Par Lost 12.411
Disglorifi'd, blasphem'd, and had in scorn Samson 442
Blasphemes
Cramms, and blasphemes his feeder. Shall I go on? Mask 779
Trinity ms 'blasphems'
Bridgewater ms 'blaspheames'
Blasphemous
O argument blasphemous, false and proud! Par Lost 5.809
Refrein'd his tongue blasphemous; but anon Par Lost 6.360
And more blasphemous? which expect to rue. Par Reg 4.181
Blast
As in an Organ from one blast of wind Par Lost 1.708
Like change on Sea and Land, sideral blast, Par Lost 10.693
With adverse blast up-turns them from the South Par Lost 10.701
To sound at general Doom. Th' Angelic blast Par Lost 11.76
And with contrary blast proclaims most deeds, Samson 972
'Gainst all inchantments, mildew blast, or damp Mask 640
That not a blast was from his dungeon stray'd, Lycidas 97
With terrour of that blast, Nativity 161
Blasted
Stands on the blasted Heath. He now prepar'd Par Lost 1.615
Of *Ramiel* scorcht and blasted overthrew. Par Lost 6.372
Spreading thir bane; the blasted Starrs lookt wan, Par Lost 10.412
O Fairest flower no sooner blown but blasted, Fair Inf 1
Blasting
Thy blasting volied Thunder made all speed Par Lost 4.928
Of noisom winds, and blasting vapours chill. Arcades 49
Blasts
From cold *Septentrion* blasts, thence in the midst Par Reg 4.31
Bow'd their Stiff necks, loaden with stormy blasts, Par Reg 4.418
Helping all urchin blasts, and ill luck signes Mask 845
Blaze
Of mighty Cherubim; the sudden blaze Par Lost 1.665
The full blaze of thy beams, and through a cloud Par Lost 3.378
With sudden blaze diffus'd, inflames the Aire: Par Lost 4.818
Reflecting blaze on blaze, first met his view: Par Lost 6.18
Will dazle now this earthly, with thir blaze Par Lost 9.1083
At that so sudden blaze the *Stygian* throng Par Lost 10.453
For what is glory but the blaze of fame, Par Reg 3.47
O dark, dark, dark, amid the blaze of noon, Samson 80
Himself is his own dungeon. 2. *Bro*. Tis most true Mask 385
Trinity ms 'himselfe is his owne dungeon' ←'blaze in the summer solstice'
Bridgewater ms 'blaze in the summer solstice'
What sudden blaze of majesty Arcades 2
And yet such musick worthiest were to blaze Arcades 74
And think to burst out into sudden blaze, Lycidas 74
And that far-beaming blaze of Majesty, Nativity 9
Let us blaze his Name abroad, Psalm 136, 5
Till all the mountains blaze, Psalm 83, 56
With my whole heart, and blaze abroad Psalm 86, 43
Blazed
That sparkling blaz'd, his other Parts besides Par Lost 1.194
Blaz'd opposite, while expectation stood Par Lost 6.306
When the great Ensign of *Messiah* blaz'd Par Lost 6.775
Blaz'd forth unclouded Deitie; he full Par Lost 10.65
The brandisht Sword of God before them blaz'd Par Lost 12.633
The Sons of *Anac*, famous now and blaz'd, Samson 528
Blazing
Of Starry Lamps and blazing Cressets fed Par Lost 1.728
ms 'blazeing'

Blazing(*cont*)
Sometimes towards Heav'n and the full-blazing Sun, — Par Lost 4.29
High on a Hill, far blazing, as a Mount — Par Lost 5.757
That open'd wide her blazing Portals, led — Par Lost 7.575
Hovering and blazing with delusive Light, — Par Lost 9.639
From yonder blazing Cloud that veils the Hill — Par Lost 11.229
Of blazing Majesty and Light, — Winchester 70

Bleak
From the bleak air; a Stable was our warmth, — Par Reg 2.74
Forbidding every bleak unkindly Fog — Mask 269
1637 'bleake'
Trinity ms 'bleake'
Bridgewater ms 'bleake'
Bleak winters force that made thy blossome drie; — Fair Inf 4

Blear
Of power to cheat the eye with blear illusion, — Mask 155
1637 'bleare'
Trinity ms 'bleare' ←'blind' ←'sleight'
Bridgewater ms 'bleare'

Bleating
Both her first born and all her bleating Gods. — Par Lost 1.489
The birds thir notes renew, and bleating herds — Par Lost 2.494
His vastness: Fleec't the Flocks and bleating rose, — Par Lost 7.472
Ewes and thir bleating Lambs over the Plaine, — Par Lost 11.649

Bled
As Zeba, and Zalmunna *bled* — Psalm 83, 43

Bleed
Sanguin, such as Celestial Spirits may bleed, — Par Lost 6.333
Of Public Fraud. In vain doth Valour bleed — Sonnet 15, 13
So let their Princes *bleed*. — Psalm 83, 44

Bleeds
Enter'd the world, now bleeds to give us ease; — Circum 11

Blemish
To outward view, of blemish or of spot; — Sonnet 22, 2

Bless
So disinherited how would ye bless — Par Lost 10.821
To bless the dores from nightly harm: — Penseroso 84
With puissant words, and murmurs made to bless, — Arcades 60
Trinity ms 'blesse'
Once bless our human ears, — Nativity 126
His chosen people he did bless — Psalm 136, 57
To bless us with thy heav'n-lov'd innocence, — Fair Inf 65
Cries the stall-reader, bless us! what a word on — Sonnet 11, 5
To bless the just man still, — Psalm 5, 38

Blessed
His famine should be fill'd, and blest his mawe — Par Lost 2.847
All Heav'n, and in the blessed Spirits elect — Par Lost 3.136
Encompass'd shall resound thee ever blest. — Par Lost 3.149
As from blest voices, uttering joy, Heav'n rung — Par Lost 3.347
Of *Arabie* the blest, with such delay — Par Lost 4.163
Blest pair; and O yet happiest if ye seek — Par Lost 4.774
Long after to blest *Marie*, second *Eve*. — Par Lost 5.387
Cast out from God and blessed vision, falls — Par Lost 5.613
In Heav'n God ever blest, and his Divine — Par Lost 6.184
1667 'blessed', 1668 errata 'blest'
Heav'ns blessed peace, and into Nature brought — Par Lost 6.267
And saw that it was good, and bless'd them, saying, — Par Lost 7.395
Female for Race; then bless'd Mankinde, and said, — Par Lost 7.530
Now resting, bless'd and hallowd the Seav'nth day, — Par Lost 7.592
And all the Blest: stand fast; to stand or fall — Par Lost 8.640
In Paradise, of operation blest — Par Lost 9.796
Accurst of blessed, hide me from the face — Par Lost 10.723
But let us call to Synod all the Blest — Par Lost 11.67
Of God high-blest, or to incline his will, — Par Lost 11.145
His blessed count'nance; here I could frequent, — Par Lost 11.317
True opener of mine eyes, prime Angel blest, — Par Lost 11.598
All Nations shall be blest; he straight obeys, — Par Lost 12.126
Shall in his Seed be blessed; by that Seed — Par Lost 12.148
Plainlier shall be reveald. This Patriarch blest, — Par Lost 12.151
His day, in whom all Nations shall be blest, — Par Lost 12.277
So in his seed all Nations shall be blest. — Par Lost 12.450
How soon hath thy prediction, Seer blest, — Par Lost 12.553
Acknowledge my Redeemer ever blest. — Par Lost 12.573
Hale highly favour'd, among women blest; — Par Reg 2.68
Afflicted I may be, it seems, and blest; — Par Reg 2.93
Dwell'st here with *Pan*, or *Silvan*, by blest Song — Mask 268
Eie me blest Providence, and square my triall — Mask 329
In the blest Kingdoms meek of joy and love. — Lycidas 177
line not in 1638 edition
And lay it lowly at his blessed feet; — Nativity 25
But see the Virgin blest, — Nativity 237
Resolve me then oh Soul most surely blest — Fair Inf 36
Blest pair of *Sirens*, pledges of Heav'ns joy, — Musick 1
Bless'd is the man who hath not walk'd astray — Psalm 1, 1
Is better, *and more blest* — Psalm 84, 34
That man is *truly* blest, — Psalm 84, 46

Blessedness
With Blessedness. Whence *Adam* soon repeal'd — Par Lost 7.59

Blessing
And as a blessing with such pomp adorn'd? — Samson 357
Hill and Dale, doth boast thy blessing. — May Morn 8
Thy blessing on thy people flows. — Psalm 3, 24

Blessings
Natures full blessings would be well dispenc't — Mask 772
Bridgewater ms 'blessinge'
Strew all their blessings on thy sleeping Head. — Vacation 64

Blest
Mock us with his blest sight, then snatch him hence, — Par Reg 2.56

Blest(*cont*)
When the blest seed of *Terah*'s faithfull Son, — Psalm 114, 1

Blew
To the bright Minister that watchd, hee blew — Par Lost 11.73

Blind
Blind *Thamyris* and blind *Maeonides*, — Par Lost 3.35
But hard be hard'nd, blind be blinded more, — Par Lost 3.200
Of painful Superstition and blind Zeal, — Par Lost 3.452
Blind *Melesigenes* thence *Homer* call'd, — Par Reg 4.259
Blind among enemies, O worse then chains, — Samson 68
Thy Foes derision, Captive, Poor, and Blind — Samson 366
Thee *Samson* bound and blind into thir hands, — Samson 438
Now blind, disheartn'd, sham'd, dishonour'd, quell'd, — Samson 563
How wouldst thou use me now, blind, and thereby — Samson 941
Har. To combat with a blind man I disdain, — Samson 1106
To make them sport with blind activity? — Samson 1328
Thir once great dread, captive, & blind before them, — Samson 1474
Semichor. But he though blind of sight, — Samson 1687
Of power to cheat the eye with blear illusion, — Mask 155
Trinity ms 'bleare' ←'blind' ←'sleight'
In the blind mazes of this tangl'd Wood? — Mask 181
Bridgewater ms 'blinde'
For such there be, but unbelief is blind. — Mask 519
Bridgewater ms 'blinde'
Comes the blind *Fury* with th' abhorred shears, — Lycidas 75
Blind mouthes! that scarce themselves know how to hold — Lycidas 119
The rayes of *Bethlehem* blind his dusky eyn; — Nativity 223
Content though blind, had I no better guide. — Sonnet 22, 14
Their own devises blind. — Psalm 81, 52

Blinded
But hard be hard'nd, blind be blinded more, — Par Lost 3.200

Blindness
Blindness, for had I sight, confus'd with shame, — Samson 196
True slavery, and that blindness worse then this, — Samson 418
Though by his blindness maim'd for high attempts, — Samson 1221
And with blindness internal struck. — Samson 1686

Bliss
(Far other once beheld in bliss) condemn'd — Par Lost 1.607
Then to dwell here, driv'n out from bliss, condemn'd — Par Lost 2.86
Thir frail Original, and faded bliss, — Par Lost 2.375
Created vast and round, a place of bliss — Par Lost 2.832
To that new world of light and bliss, among — Par Lost 2.867
Because thou hast, though Thron'd in highest bliss — Par Lost 3.305
And where the river of Bliss through midst of Heavn — Par Lost 3.358
Regardless of the Bliss wherein hee sat — Par Lost 3.408
His sad exclusion from the dores of Bliss. — Par Lost 3.525
Into our room of bliss thus high advanc't — Par Lost 4.359
Of bliss on bliss, while I to Hell am thrust, — Par Lost 4.508
And mutual love, the Crown of all our bliss — Par Lost 4.728
Whose dwelling God hath planted here in bliss? — Par Lost 4.884
The fall of others from like state of bliss; — Par Lost 5.241
Wilde above Rule or Art; enormous bliss. — Par Lost 5.297
1667 'blisse' in some copies
Full to the utmost measure of what bliss — Par Lost 5.517
From what high state of bliss into what woe! — Par Lost 5.543
By whom in bliss imbosom'd sat the Son, — Par Lost 5.597
Pursuing drive them out from God and bliss, — Par Lost 6.52
From all her Confines. Heav'n the seat of bliss — Par Lost 6.273
Fulfill'd, which to fulfil is all my bliss. — Par Lost 6.729
Where now he sits at the right hand of bliss. — Par Lost 6.892
And Warr so neer the Peace of God in bliss — Par Lost 7.55
To the Garden of bliss, thy seat prepar'd. — Par Lost 8.299
My Storie to the sum of earthly bliss — Par Lost 8.522
Conjugal Love, then which perhaps no bliss — Par Lost 9.263
Despoild of Innocence, of Faith, of Bliss. — Par Lost 9.411
Adam shall share with me in bliss or woe: — Par Lost 9.831
For bliss, as thou hast part, to me is bliss, — Par Lost 9.879
Mine never shall be parted, bliss or woe. — Par Lost 9.916
Who might have liv'd and joyd immortal bliss, — Par Lost 9.1166
With pitie, violated not thir bliss. — Par Lost 10.25
There dwell and Reign in bliss, thence on the Earth — Par Lost 10.399
But up and enter now into full bliss. — Par Lost 10.503
All my redeemd may dwell in joy and bliss, — Par Lost 11.43
High in Salvation and the Climes of bliss, — Par Lost 11.708
His faithful, and receave them into bliss, — Par Lost 12.462
To bring forth fruits Joy and eternal Bliss. — Par Lost 12.551
1669 'Blis' in some copies
With them from bliss to the bottomless deep, — Par Reg 1.361
Lost bliss, to thee no more communicable, — Par Reg 1.419
In the bosom of bliss, and light of light — Par Reg 4.597
For though that seat of earthly bliss be fail'd, — Par Reg 4.612
Such sober certainty of waking bliss — Mask 263
Trinity ms 'blisse'
1637 'blisse'
Consists in mutual and partak'n bliss, — Mask 741
Trinity ms 'blisse'
line not in Bridgewater ms
1637 'blisse'
Beyond the bliss of dreams. Be wise, and taste.---- — Mask 813
1637 'blisse'
Trinity ms 'blisse'
Bridgewater ms 'blisse'
And then at last our bliss — Nativity 165
But kill'd alas, and then bewayl'd his fatal bliss. — Fair Inf 7
Then long Eternity shall greet our bliss — On Time 11
Trinity ms 'blisse'
High thron'd in secret bliss, for us frail dust — Circum 19
Trinity ms 'blisse'

Bliss(*cont*)
Passes to bliss at the mid hour of night, Sonnet 9, 13
Trinity ms 'bliss' ←'Bliss'
Of Death, call'd Life; which us from Life doth sever. Sonnet 14, 4
Trinity ms 'from life' ←'from blis' ←'from life' ←'from heavn'
Follow'd thee up to joy and bliss for ever. Sonnet 14, 8
Trinity ms 'blis' ←'bliss'

Blissful
Restore us, and regain the blissful Seat, Par Lost 1.5
ms 'blisfull'
In blissful solitude; he then survey'd Par Lost 3.69
Just o're the blissful seat of Paradise, Par Lost 3.527
A Heav'n on Earth, for blissful Paradise Par Lost 4.208
On to thir blissful Bower; it was a place Par Lost 4.690
Into the blissful field, through Groves of Myrrhe, Par Lost 5.292
1667 'blisul' in some copies
Into his blissful bosom reassum'd Par Lost 10.225
Filld all the Regions: from thir blissful Bowrs Par Lost 11.77
Two blissful twins are to be born, Mask 1010
1637 'blissfull'
line not in Bridgewater ms
Trinity ms 'blissfull'
& sacred limits of this blisfull Isle Mask Tr. ms 10.11
'blisfull' ←'blissfull' ←'happie'
As all their souls in blisfull rapture took: Nativity 98
1673 'blissfull'
Look in, and see each blissful Deitie Vacation 35

Blithe
To whom the wilie Adder, blithe and glad. Par Lost 9.625
Thus *Eve* with Countnance blithe her storie told; Par Lost 9.886
Of Goddesses, so blithe, so smooth, so gay, Par Lost 11.615
As on a floating couch through the blithe Air, Par Reg 4.585
With Ivy berries wreath'd, and his blithe youth, Mask 55
1637 'blith'
Trinity ms 'blith'
Bridgewater ms 'blith'
So bucksom, blith, and debonair. Allegro 24
And the Milkmaid singeth blithe, Allegro 65

Blood
First *Moloch*, horrid King besmear'd with blood Par Lost 1.392
Ran purple to the Sea, suppos'd with blood Par Lost 1.451
Lur'd with the smell of infant blood, to dance Par Lost 2.664
Th' animal Spirits that from pure blood arise Par Lost 4.805
And Life-blood streaming fresh; wide was the wound, Par Lost 8.467
Bedropt with blood of *Gorgon*, or the Isle Par Lost 10.527
Groand out his Soul with gushing bloud effus'd. Par Lost 11.447
Hopeful and cheerful, in thy blood will reigne Par Lost 11.543
Who having spilt much blood, and don much waste Par Lost 11.791
To blood unshed the Rivers must be turnd, Par Lost 12.176
The bloud of Bulls and Goats, they may conclude Par Lost 12.292
Some bloud more precious must be paid for Man, Par Lost 12.293
With Infant blood the streets of *Bethlehem;* Par Reg 2.78
Then cruel, by thir sports to blood enur'd Par Reg 4.139
Blood, death, and deathful deeds are in that noise, Samson 1513
Sok't in his enemies blood, and from the stream Samson 1726
When the fresh blood grows lively, and returns Mask 670
And setlings of a melancholy blood; Mask 810
Bridgewater ms 'bloud'
Unstain'd with hostile blood, Nativity 57
Once glorious Towers, now sunk in guiltles blood; Passion 40
For all this wast of wealth, and loss of blood. Sonnet 12, 14
While Darwen stream with blood of Scotts imbru'd, Sonnet 16, 7
1694 'Blood'
To Heav'n. Their martyr'd blood and ashes sow Sonnet 18, 10
Moab, with them of Hagars blood Psalm 83, 23

Bloody
For death, the following day, in bloodie fight. Par Lost 10.278
From Heav'n acceptance; but the bloodie Fact Par Lost 11.457
But call in aide, which makes a bloody Fray; Par Lost 11.651
In bloody battail he brought down Psalm 136, 61
1673 'bloudy'
Slayn by the bloody *Piemontese* that roll'd Sonnet 18, 7
The bloodi' and guileful man God doth detest. Psalm 5, 16
And like the slain *in bloody fight* Psalm 88, 19

Bloom
Or sight of vernal bloom, or Summers Rose, Par Lost 3.43
Began to bloom, but soon for mans offence Par Lost 3.355
Sits on the Bloom extracting liquid sweet. Par Lost 5.25
To visit how they prosper'd, bud and bloom, Par Lost 8.45
Abortive as the first-born bloom of spring Samson 1576
Co. Were they of manly prime, or youthful bloom? Mask 289
Bridgewater ms 'bloome'
Trinity ms 'bloome' ←'blome'

Blooming
High eminent, blooming Ambrosial Fruit Par Lost 4.219
Laden with blooming gold, had need the guard Mask 394
Bridgewater ms 'bloominge'
With those just Spirits that wear victorious Palms, Musick 14
Trinity ms 'victorious' ←'blooming' ←'victorious' ←'blooming' ←'fresh greene'
And at thy growing vertues fret their spleen, Sonnet 9, 7
Trinity ms 'growing' ←'prospering' ←'blooming'

Bloomy
O Nightingale, that on yon bloomy Spray Sonnet 1, 1

Blossom
aeternall roses grow & hyacinth Mask Tr. ms 10.07
'grow' ←'blosme' ←'grow' ←'blow' ←'yeeld' ←'grow'

Blossom(*cont*)
Bleak winters force that made thy blossome drie; Fair Inf 4
But the fair blossom hangs the head Winchester 41
But my late spring no bud or blossom shew'th. Sonnet 7, 4
Trinity ms 'blossome'
Shall bud and blossom *then*, Psalm 85, 46

Blossoms
Blossoms and Fruits at once of golden hue Par Lost 4.148
Those Blossoms also, and those dropping Gumms, Par Lost 4.630
Thir blossoms: with high woods the hills were crownd, Par Lost 7.326
1667 'Blossoms'
To save her blossoms, and defend her fruit Mask 396

Blot
That he relents, not to blot out mankind, Par Lost 11.891
Palpable darkness, and blot out three dayes; Par Lost 12.188
Her Bond-slave; O indignity, O blot Samson 411
With malediction mention'd, and the blot Samson 978
And makes one blot of all the ayr, Mask 133
Thereby to wipe away th' infamous blot, Fair Inf 12

Blotted
Be no memorial blotted out and ras'd Par Lost 1.362

Blow
Awak'd should blow them into sevenfold rage Par Lost 2.171
Hov'ring a space, till Winds the signal blow Par Lost 2.717
Mozambic, off at Sea North-East windes blow Par Lost 4.161
His praise ye Winds, that from four Quarters blow, Par Lost 5.192
Ethereal Trumpet from on high gan blow: Par Lost 6.60
Reaching beyond all limit at one blow Par Lost 6.140
The Atheist crew, but with redoubl'd blow Par Lost 6.370
Blow moist and keen, shattering the graceful locks Par Lost 10.1066
Against a Winters day when winds blow keen, Par Reg 1.317
Waters the odorous banks that blow Mask 993
Bridgewater ms 'blowe'
aeternall roses grow & hyacinth Mask Tr. ms 10.07
'grow' ←'blosme' ←'grow' ←'blow' ←'yeeld' ←'grow'
There let the pealing Organ blow, Penseroso 161
And let the Base of Heav'ns deep Organ blow, Nativity 130
Their loud up-lifted Angel trumpets blow, Musick 11
Blow, *as is wont*, in the new Moon Psalm 81, 9

Blowing
Sonorous mettal blowing Martial sounds: Par Lost 1.540
Of blowing Myrrh and Balme; if thou accept Par Lost 9.629
As when two Polar Winds blowing adverse Par Lost 10.289
Drivn by a keen North-winde, that blowing drie Par Lost 11.842
The breath of Heav'n fresh-blowing, pure and sweet, Samson 10
With flaunting Hony-suckle, and began Mask 545
Trinity ms 'flaunting' ←'blowing' ←'suckling'

Blown
Blown up with high conceits ingendring pride. Par Lost 4.809
Her bosom smelling sweet: and these scarce blown, Par Lost 7.319
When from the boughes a savorie odour blow'n, Par Lost 9.579
Blow'n vagabond or frustrate: in they passd Par Lost 11.16
Blown stifling back on him that breaths it forth: Par Lost 11.313
Comes he in peace? what wind hath blown him hither Samson 1070
And fresh-blown Roses washt in dew, Allegro 22
When the gust hath blown his fill, Penseroso 128
O Fairest flower no sooner blown but blasted, Fair Inf 1

Blows
Blows them transverse ten thousand Leagues awry Par Lost 3.488
Our tended Plants, how blows the Citron Grove, Par Lost 5.22
When first the White thorn blows; Lycidas 48
1638 'blowes'
That blows from off each beaked Promontory, Lycidas 94
1638 'blowes'

Blue
O're the blew Firmament a radiant white, Par Lost 11.206
Blew meager Hag, or stubborn unlaid ghost, Mask 434
Trinity ms 'Blue'
Of Turkis blew, and Emrauld green Mask 894
yellow, watchet, greene, & blew Mask Tr. ms 26.21
yellow, watchett, greene and blew Mask Br. ms 17
There on Beds of Violets blew, Allegro 21
And heal the harms of thwarting thunder blew, Arcades 51
At last he rose, and twitch'd his Mantle blew: Lycidas 192
In dismall dance about the furnace blue, Nativity 210
while all the starrie rounds & arches blue Musick Tr. ms 4.21

Blue-haired
He quarters to his blu-hair'd deities, Mask 29
Bridgewater ms 'blew haired'

Blush
After short blush of Morn; nigh in her sight Par Lost 11.184

Blushing
I led her blushing like the Morn: all Heav'n, Par Lost 8.511

Bluster
Thir corners, when with bluster to confound Par Lost 10.665

Blustering
The sound of blustring winds, which all night long Par Lost 2.286
Of *Chaos* blustring round, inclement skie; Par Lost 3.426

Boar
The *tusked* Boar out of the wood Psalm 80, 53

Board
To many a row of Pipes the sound-board breaths. Par Lost 1.709
ms 'sound-bord'
She gathers, Tribute large, and on the board Par Lost 5.343
And at a stately side-board by the wine Par Reg 2.350

Boars
Of chaf't wild Boars, or ruffl'd Porcupines. Samson 1138

Boast
Who boast in mortal things, and wond'ring tell — Par Lost 1.693
More unexpert, I boast not: them let those — Par Lost 2.52
Loose all her virtue; least bad men should boast — Par Lost 2.483
Far off and fearless, nor with cause to boast, — Par Lost 4.14
How dearly I abide that boast so vaine, — Par Lost 4.87
To boast what Arms can doe, since thine no more — Par Lost 4.1008
(Unanswerd least thou boast) to let thee know; — Par Lost 6.163
Adam, from whose deare side I boast me sprung, — Par Lost 9.965
Of that defended Fruit; but let him boast — Par Lost 11.86
There without sign of boast, or sign of joy, — Par Reg 2.119
For all his tedious talk is but vain boast, — Par Reg 4.307
Sam. Boast not of what thou wouldst have done, but do — Samson 1104
Thou oft shalt wish thy self at *Gath* to boast — Samson 1127
But boast themselves more comely then before — Mask 75
Not any boast of skill, but extreme shift — Mask 273
Root-bound, that fled *Apollo*, *La*. Fool do not boast, — Mask 662
Trinity ms 'doe not boast' ←'thou art over proud'
Hill and Dale, doth boast thy blessing. — May Morn 8

Boasted
Thir boasted Parents; *Titan* Heav'ns first born — Par Lost 1.510
Of all these boasted Trophies won on me, — Samson 470

Boaster
Sam. Cam'st thou for this, vain boaster, to survey me, — Samson 1227

Boastest
Who boast'st release from Hell, and leave to come — Par Reg 1.409

Boastful
Various, with boastful Argument portraid, — Par Lost 6.84

Boasting
Then to submit, boasting I could subdue — Par Lost 4.85

Boasts
His utmost subtilty, because he boasts — Par Reg 1.144
Which when he lists, he leaves, or boasts he can, — Par Reg 4.306

Bocchus
The Realm of *Bocchus* to the Black-moor Sea; — Par Reg 4.72

Bodies
Your bodies may at last turn all to Spirit, — Par Lost 5.497
Or hollow'd bodies made of Oak or Firr — Par Lost 6.574
Had wondrous, as with Starrs thir bodies all — Par Lost 6.754
For of Celestial Bodies first the Sun — Par Lost 7.354
So many nobler Bodies to create, — Par Lost 8.28
That bodies bright and greater should not serve — Par Lost 8.87
1667 'Bodies'
Or by collision of two bodies grinde — Par Lost 10.1072

Boding
Betok'ning, or ill boding, I contemn — Par Reg 4.490

Body
Shadow from body opaque can fall, and the Aire, — Par Lost 3.619
Man hath his daily work of body or mind — Par Lost 4.618
Armie of Fiends, fit body to fit head; — Par Lost 4.953
Till body up to spirit work, in bounds — Par Lost 5.478
Whatever pure thou in the body enjoy'st — Par Lost 8.622
To reach, and feed at once both Bodie and Mind? — Par Lost 9.779
Once actual, now in body, and to dwell — Par Lost 10.587
And sin? the Bodie properly hath neither. — Par Lost 10.791
Produce prodigious Births of bodie or mind. — Par Lost 11.687
Without this bodies wasting, I content me, — Par Reg 2.256
That other o're the body only reigns, — Par Reg 2.478
Ease to the body some, none to the mind — Samson 18
O impotence of mind, in body strong! — Samson 52
In real darkness of the body dwells, — Samson 159
To the bodies wounds and sores — Samson 607
And though her body die, her fame survives, — Samson 1706
Let us go find the body where it lies — Samson 1725
As loath to leave the body that it lov'd, — Mask 473
Trinity ms 'bodie'
Bridgewater ms 'bodye'
1673 'Body'

Bog
A gulf profound as that *Serbonian* Bog — Par Lost 2.592
Ore bog or steep, through strait, rough, dense, or rare, — Par Lost 2.948

Boggy
Quencht in a Boggie *Syrtis*, neither Sea, — Par Lost 2.939

Bogs
Rocks, Caves, Lakes, Fens, Bogs, Dens, and shades of death, — Par Lost 2.621
To Boggs and Mires, and oft through Pond or Poole, — Par Lost 9.641

Boiled
In pastry built, or from the spit, or boyl'd, — Par Reg 2.343

Boiling
A various mould, and from the boyling cells — Par Lost 1.706
ms 'boyleing'
Under yon boyling Ocean, wrapt in Chains; — Par Lost 2.183
Over the dark Abyss, whose boiling Gulf — Par Lost 2.1027

Boils
Now rowling, boiles in his tumultuous brest, — Par Lost 4.16
Boiles out from under ground, the mouth of Hell; — Par Lost 12.42

Boisterous
With those thy boyst'rous locks, no worthy match — Samson 1164
The brute and boist'rous force of violent men — Samson 1273
By boistrous rape th' Athenian damsel got, — Fair Inf 9

Bold
And thence in Heav'n call'd Satan, with bold words — Par Lost 1.82
And him thus answer'd soon his bold Compeer. — Par Lost 1.127
He also against the house of God was bold: — Par Lost 1.470
(Though like a cover'd field, where Champions bold — Par Lost 1.763
I laugh, when those who at the Spear are bold — Par Lost 2.204
His glory to augment. The bold design — Par Lost 2.386
On bold adventure to discover wide — Par Lost 2.571

Bold*(cont)*
In bold conspiracy against Heav'ns King, — Par Lost 2.751
Yet not rejoycing in his speed, though bold, — Par Lost 4.13
Or less be lost. Thy fear, said *Zephon* bold, — Par Lost 4.854
To question thy bold entrance on this place; — Par Lost 4.882
At such bold words voucht with a deed so bold: — Par Lost 5.66
Thus farr his bold discourse without controule — Par Lost 5.803
Encompass'd round with foes, thus answerd bold. — Par Lost 5.876
Least hee incenst at such eruption bold, — Par Lost 8.235
The Enemie, though bold, will hardly dare, — Par Lost 9.304
Then voluble and bold, now hid, now seen — Par Lost 9.436
She scarse had said, though brief, when now more bold — Par Lost 9.664
Bold deed thou hast presum'd, adventrous *Eve*, — Par Lost 9.921
Bold or loquacious, thus abasht repli'd. — Par Lost 10.161
To his bold Riot: dreadful was the din — Par Lost 10.521
Giants of mightie Bone, and bould emprise; — Par Lost 11.642
Rain'd from Heaven Manna, and that Prophet bold — Par Reg 2.312
Thy bold attempt; hereafter learn with awe — Par Reg 4.625
Spurn'd them to death by Troops. The bold *Ascalonite* — Samson 138
Offering to combat thee his Champion bold, — Samson 1152
From the rash hand of bold Incontinence. — Mask 397
I love thy courage yet, and bold Emprise, — Mask 610
Where throngs of Knights and Barons bold, — Allegro 119
The story of *Cambuscan* bold, — Penseroso 110
He foild bold *Seon* and his host, — Psalm 136, 65
The feirce Epeirot and the African bold, — Sonnet 17, 4
Who thence grow bold and strong — Psalm 82, 8
Do to them as to Midian *bold* — Psalm 83, 33
Shall aw the World, and Conquer Nations bold. — Prose 12, 14

Bolder
Thee I re-visit now with bolder wing, — Par Lost 3.13
Hee boulder now, uncall'd before her stood; — Par Lost 9.523
Self-left. Least therefore his now bolder hand — Par Lost 11.93
For this attempt bolder then that on *Eve*, — Par Reg 4.180

Boldest
Where boldest; though to sight unconquerable? — Par Lost 6.118

Boldly
T' whom *Satan* turning boldly, thus. Ye Powers — Par Lost 2.968
And boldly venture to whatever place — Par Lost 4.891
Boldly assault the necromancers hall; — Mask 649

Boldness
Or not, who ask what boldness brought him hither — Par Lost 4.908

Bolster
Perhaps som cold bank is her boulster now — Mask 353

Bolt
Th' intricate wards, and every Bolt and Bar — Par Lost 2.877
The Thunderer of his only dreaded bolt. — Par Lost 6.491
The frivolous bolt of *Cupid*, gods and men — Mask 445
I hate when vice can bolt her arguments, — Mask 760
Bridgewater ms 'boult'
Trinity ms 'bolt' ←'boult'

Bolted
Cross-barrd and bolted fast, fear no assault, — Par Lost 4.190
And Quiver with three-bolted Thunder stor'd, — Par Lost 6.764
His cloudless thunder bolted on thir heads. — Samson 1696

Bond
The Bond of Nature draw me to my owne, — Par Lost 9.956

Bondage
Caelestial Spirits in Bondage, nor th' Abyss — Par Lost 1.658
ms 'bondage'
In strictest bondage, though thus far remov'd, — Par Lost 2.321
Thy Bondage or lost Sight, — Samson 152
Then to love Bondage more then Liberty, — Samson 270
Bondage with ease then strenuous liberty; — Samson 271

Bonds
Exile, or ignominy, or bonds, or pain, — Par Lost 2.207
His hinder parts, then springs as broke from Bonds, — Par Lost 7.465
Himself in bonds under *Philistian* yoke; — Samson 42
Adjur'd by all the bonds of civil Duty — Samson 853
Their bonds, and cast from us, no more to wear, — Psalm 2, 7

Bondslave
Lower then bondslave! Promise was that I — Samson 38
Her Bond-slave; O indignity, O blot — Samson 411

Bondwoman
The Fugitive Bond-woman with her Son — Par Reg 2.308

Bone
His flesh, his bone; to give thee being I lent — Par Lost 4.483
Bone of my Bone, Flesh of my Flesh, my Self — Par Lost 8.495
Bone of my Bone thou art, and from thy State — Par Lost 9.915
Giants of mightie Bone, and bould emprise; — Par Lost 11.642
The Jaw of a dead Ass, his sword of bone, — Samson 143
On the cheek-bone all my foes, — Psalm 3, 21

Bones
Nor founded on the brittle strength of bones, — Par Lost 1.427
No less through all my sinews, joints and bones, — Samson 1142
Wash far away, where ere thy bones are hurld, — Lycidas 155
What needs my *Shakespear* for his honour'd Bones, — Shakespear 1
1640 'bones'
1663-4 'bones'
1632 'bones'
Avenge O Lord thy slaughter'd Saints, whose bones — Sonnet 18, 1
For all my bones, that even with anguish ake, — Psalm 6, 5

Bonnet
His Mantle hairy, and his Bonnet sedge, — Lycidas 104
Trinity ms 'bonnet'
1638 'bonnet'

Bonny
Of pancies, pinks, and gaudy Daffadils. — Mask 851

Bonny(*cont*)
Trinity ms 'gaudie' ←'bonnie'
Book
Cut off, and for the Book of knowledg fair — Par Lost 3.47
Is as the Book of God before thee set, — Par Lost 8.67
Or so unprincipl'd in vertues book, — Mask 367
Bridgewater ms 'booke'
Trinity ms 'booke'
Hath from the leaves of thy unvalu'd Book, — Shakespear 11
1632 'Booke'
1640 'Booke'
A Book was writ of late call'd *Tetrachordon;* — Sonnet 11, 1
Trinity ms 'booke' ←'book'
Forget not: in thy book record their groanes — Sonnet 18, 5
Books
By thir Rebellion, from the Books of Life. — Par Lost 1.363
ms 'books'
An empty cloud. However many books — Par Reg 4.321
Deep verst in books and shallow in himself, — Par Reg 4.327
In antient and in modern books enroll'd; — Samson 653
His few Books, or his Beads, or Maple Dish, — Mask 391
Trinity ms 'books'
Bridgewater ms 'bookes'
1637 'books'
Boon
In Beds and curious Knots, but Nature boon — Par Lost 4.242
And hight'nd as with Wine, jocond and boon, — Par Lost 9.793
Boots
What boots it at one gate to make defence, — Samson 560
Alas! What boots it with uncessant care — Lycidas 64
Pull'd off his Boots, and took away the light: — Carrier 16
1658 'boots'
Booty
Thir Bootie; scarce with Life the Shepherds flye, — Par Lost 11.650
Border
The utmost border of his Kingdom, left — Par Lost 2.361
So on he fares, and to the border comes, — Par Lost 4.131
Bordering
With these came they, who from the bordring flood — Par Lost 1.419
ms 'bord'ring'
Impregnable; oft on the bordering Deep — Par Lost 2.131
Bordering on light; when strait behold the Throne — Par Lost 2.959
He entred now the bordering Desert wild, — Par Reg 1.193
In *Dan*, in *Judah*, and the bordering Tribes, — Samson 976
Borders
Borders on *Aegypt* and the *Arabian* shoare; — Par Lost 3.537
With borders long the Rivers. That Earth now — Par Lost 7.328
Wetting the borders of her silk'n veil: — Samson 730
Bore
Soon recollecting, with high words, that bore — Par Lost 1.528
Bore him slope downward to the Sun now fall'n — Par Lost 4.591
Defence, while others bore him on thir Shields — Par Lost 6.337
Thick-rammd, at th' other bore with touch of fire — Par Lost 6.485
Up lifting bore them in thir hands: Amaze, — Par Lost 6.646
Bore up his branching head: scarse from his mould — Par Lost 7.470
Hee with *Olympias*, this with her who bore — Par Lost 9.509
But confidence then bore thee on, secure — Par Lost 9.1175
Descri'd, divinely warn'd, and witness bore — Par Reg 1.26
Of other women, by the birth I bore, — Par Reg 2.71
Prauncing their riders bore, the flower and choice — Par Reg 3.314
Of *Hippogrif* bore through the Air sublime — Par Reg 4.542
Then by main force pull'd up, and on his shoulders bore — Samson 146
Bore witness gloriously; whence *Gaza* mourns — Samson 1752
Bore a bright golden flowre, but not in this soyl: — Mask 633
line not in Bridgewater ms
Bearing her straight to aged *Nereus* Hall, — Mask 835
Trinity ms 'bearing' ←'and bore'
To Ivy-crowned *Bacchus* bore; — Allegro 16
To solitary *Saturn* bore; — Penseroso 24
What could the Muse her self that *Orpheus* bore, — Lycidas 58
Two massy Keyes he bore of metals twain, — Lycidas 110
Of vengeful Justice bore for our excess, — Circum 24
The highly favour'd *Joseph* bore — Winchester 65
Boreas
Boreas and *Caecias* and *Argestes* loud — Par Lost 10.699
Born
Titanian, or *Earth-born*, that warr'd on *Jove*, — Par Lost 1.198
ms 'earth-born'
Both her first born and all her bleating Gods. — Par Lost 1.489
Thir boasted Parents; *Titan* Heav'ns first born — Par Lost 1.510
Hell-born, not to contend with Spirits of Heav'n. — Par Lost 2.687
And hourly born, with sorrow infinite — Par Lost 2.797
Inhabitant of Heav'n, and heav'nlie-born, — Par Lost 2.860
Hail holy Light, ofspring of Heav'n first-born, — Par Lost 3.1
Hither of ill-joynd Sons and Daughters born — Par Lost 3.463
Adam the goodliest man of men since borne — Par Lost 4.323
Creatures of other mould, earth-born perhaps, — Par Lost 4.360
Of old *Olympus* dwell'st, but Heav'nlie borne, — Par Lost 7.7
1669 'Heav'nly born'
Behemoth biggest born of Earth upheav'd — Par Lost 7.471
And *Ops*, ere yet *Dictaean Jove* was born. — Par Lost 10.584
Whom thus the Sin-born Monster answerd soon. — Par Lost 10.596
Which must be born to certain woe, devourd — Par Lost 10.980
Turchestan-born; nor could his eye not ken — Par Lost 11.396
Though not of Woman born; compassion quell'd — Par Lost 11.496
Last with one midnight stroke all the first-born — Par Lost 12.189
Anointed King *Messiah* might be born — Par Lost 12.359
Destin'd to this, is late of woman born, — Par Reg 1.65

Born(*cont*)
O're-shadow her: this man born and now up-grown, — Par Reg 1.140
Born to that end, born to promote all truth, — Par Reg 1.205
And told them the Messiah now was born, — Par Reg 1.245
By which they knew thee King of *Israel* born. — Par Reg 1.254
Men to much misery and hardship born; — Par Reg 1.341
In such a season born when scarce a Shed — Par Reg 2.72
But to a Kingdom thou art born, ordain'd — Par Reg 3.152
Then hear, O Son of *David*, Virgin-born; — Par Reg 4.500
On thy birth-night, that sung thee Saviour born. — Par Reg 4.506
With day-spring born; here leave me to respire. — Samson 11
Her spurious first-born; Treason against me? — Samson 391
Abortive as the first-born bloom of spring — Samson 1576
Of *Bacchus*, and of *Circe* born, great *Comus*, — Mask 522
Trinity ms 'borne'
1637 'borne'
Bridgewater ms 'bòrne'
In *Egypt* gave to *Jove*-born *Helena* — Mask 676
Bridgewater ms 'Jove-borne'
1637 '*Iove*-borne'
Trinity ms 'Jove borne'
Two blissful twins are to be born, — Mask 1010
1637 'borne'
line not in Bridgewater ms
Trinity ms 'borne'
Of *Cerberus*, and blackest midnight born, — Allegro 2
Of wedded Maid, and Virgin Mother born, — Nativity 3
While the Heav'n-born-childe, — Nativity 30
With unexpressive notes to Heav'ns new-born Heir. — Nativity 116
Smote the first-born of *Egypt* Land. — Psalm 136, 38
Young *Hyacinth* born on *Eurota*'s strand — Fair Inf 25
Or *Trent*, who like some earth-born Giant spreads — Vacation 93
Sphear-born harmonious Sisters, Voice, and Vers, — Musick 2
Trinity ms 'Spheare borne' ←'Spheare-borne'
Though later born, then to have known the dayes — Sonnet 10, 9
Raild at *Latona*'s twin-born progenie — Sonnet 12, 6
Lo this man there was born: — Psalm 87, 16
This and this man was born in her, — Psalm 87, 19
That this man there was born. — Psalm 87, 24
This is true Liberty when free born men — Prose 9, 1
And *Kings* be born of thee, whose dredded might — Prose 12, 13
Of head bereft li'th poor *Kenelm* King-born. — Prose 13, 2
Borne
Born through the hollow dark assaults his eare — Par Lost 2.953
Through utter and through middle darkness borne — Par Lost 3.16
And for the testimonie of Truth hast born — Par Lost 6.33
Born eevn or high, for this day will pour down, — Par Lost 6.544
Aloft by Angels born, his Sign in Heav'n: — Par Lost 6.776
Her annual Voiage, born on Windes; the Aire — Par Lost 7.431
Or one short sigh of humane breath, up-borne — Par Lost 11.147
Liv'd ignorant of future, so had borne — Par Lost 11.764
Him whom thy wrongs with Saintly patience born, — Par Reg 3.93
where grows the right-borne gold upon his native tree — Mask Tr. ms 27.08
Borrow
Burn in your sighs, and borrow — Circum 8
Borrowed
Th' infection when thir borrow'd Gold compos'd — Par Lost 1.483
With borrowd light her countenance triform — Par Lost 3.730
Which marrd his borrow'd visage, and betraid — Par Lost 4.116
Borrower
And harshly deal like an ill borrower — Mask 683
line not in Bridgewater ms
Borrowing
His mirror, with full face borrowing her Light — Par Lost 7.377
Bosky
And every bosky bourn from side to side — Mask 313
Bridgewater ms 'boskie'
1637 'boskie'
Bosom
Shoots farr into the bosom of dim Night — Par Lost 2.1036
Son of my bosom, Son who art alone — Par Lost 3.169
Thy bosom, and this glorie next to thee — Par Lost 3.239
Thee from my bosom and right hand, to save, — Par Lost 3.279
Her bosom smelling sweet: and these scarce blown, — Par Lost 7.319
Into his blissful bosom reassum'd — Par Lost 10.225
In the bosom of bliss, and light of light — Par Reg 4.597
Entangl'd with a poysnous bosom snake, — Samson 763
The unadorned boosom of the Deep, — Mask 23
Trinity ms 'bosome'
1637 'bosome'
Bridgewater ms 'bosom'
Far within the boosom bright — Winchester 69
Bosomed
That open now thir choicest bosom'd smells — Par Lost 5.127
The Graces, and the rosie-boosom'd Howres, — Mask 986
Trinity ms 'rosie-bosom'd'
line not in Bridgewater ms
1637 'rosie-bosom'd'
Boosom'd high in tufted Trees, — Allegro 78
Bosoms
And the sweet peace that goodnes boosoms ever, — Mask 368
Trinity ms 'bosomes'
1637 'bosoms'
Bridgewater ms 'bosoms'
Bosporus
Through *Bosporus* betwixt the justling Rocks: — Par Lost 2.1018
Bossy
Cornice or Freeze, with bossy Sculptures grav'n, — Par Lost 1.716

Botches
Botches and blaines must all his flesh imboss, Par Lost 12.180
Both
Both of lost happiness and lasting pain Par Lost 1.55
Both glorying to have scap't the *Stygian* flood Par Lost 1.239
Can either Sex assume, or both; so soft Par Lost 1.424
Both her first born and all her bleating Gods. Par Lost 1.489
Thick swarm'd, both on the ground and in the air, Par Lost 1.767
Rend up both Rocks and Hills, and ride the Air Par Lost 2.540
Forgets both joy and grief, pleasure and pain. Par Lost 2.586
Both to and fro, thir sorrow to augment, Par Lost 2.605
Conjur'd against the highest, for which both Thou Par Lost 2.693
His wrath which one day will destroy ye both. Par Lost 2.734
Both him and thee, and all the heav'nly Host Par Lost 2.824
He ceas'd, for both seemd highly pleasd, and Death Par Lost 2.845
Half flying; behoves him now both Oare and Saile. Par Lost 2.942
And Spirits, both them who stood and them who faild; Par Lost 3.101
Useless and vain, of freedom both despoild, Par Lost 3.109
Made passive both, had servd necessitie, Par Lost 3.110
Both what they judge and what they choose; for so Par Lost 3.123
The other none: in Mercy and Justice both, Par Lost 3.132
For which both Heav'n and Earth shall high extoll Par Lost 3.146
So should thy goodness and thy greatness both Par Lost 3.165
Thir own both righteous and unrighteous deeds, Par Lost 3.292
Both God and Man, Son both of God and Man, Par Lost 3.316
Approach not, but with both wings veil thir eyes. Par Lost 3.382
Both all things vain, and all who in vain things Par Lost 3.448
That both in him and all things, as is meet, Par Lost 3.675
Both where the morning Sun first warmly smote Par Lost 4.244
Whence true autoritie in men; though both Par Lost 4.295
Whence rushing he might surest seize them both Par Lost 4.407
Both of her Beauty and submissive Charms Par Lost 4.498
Unseen, both when we wake, and when we sleep: Par Lost 4.678
Both day and night: how often from the steep Par Lost 4.680
Thus at thir shadie Lodge arriv'd, both stood Par Lost 4.720
Both turnd, and under op'n Skie ador'd Par Lost 4.721
The God that made both Skie, Air, Earth and Heav'n Par Lost 4.722
Thy goodness infinite, both when we wake, Par Lost 4.734
What seemd both Spear and Shield: now dreadful deeds Par Lost 4.990
Thou Sun, of this great World both Eye and Soule, Par Lost 5.171
In thy eternal course, both when thou climbst, Par Lost 5.173
As doth your Rational; and both contain Par Lost 5.409
To intellectual, give both life and sense, Par Lost 5.485
To be both will and deed created free; Par Lost 5.549
Spring both, the face of brightest Heav'n had changd Par Lost 5.644
Both waking we were one; how then can now Par Lost 5.678
Both of thy crime and punishment: henceforth Par Lost 5.881
Should win in Arms, in both disputes alike Par Lost 6.123
As both thir deeds compar'd this day shall prove. Par Lost 6.170
Both Battels maine, with ruinous assault Par Lost 6.216
They ended parle, and both addrest for fight Par Lost 6.296
Together both with next to Almightie Arme, Par Lost 6.316
Under her Cloudie covert both retir'd, Par Lost 6.409
To hide the fraud. At interview both stood Par Lost 6.555
Both Harp and Voice; nor could the Muse defend Par Lost 7.37
Both when first Eevning was, and when first Morn. Par Lost 7.260
Delectable both to behold and taste; Par Lost 7.539
And hunger both, from labour, at the houre Par Lost 8.213
Inward and outward both, his image faire: Par Lost 8.221
His Image who made both, and less expressing Par Lost 8.544
Union of Mind, or in us both one Soule; Par Lost 8.604
Leads up to Heav'n, is both the way and guide; Par Lost 8.613
Our ruin, both by thee informd I learne, Par Lost 9.275
From thee alone, which on us both at once Par Lost 9.303
Us both securer then thus warnd thou seemst, Par Lost 9.371
May finde us both perhaps farr less prepar'd, Par Lost 9.381
He sought them both, but wish'd his hap might find Par Lost 9.421
Mee who have touch'd and tasted, yet both live, Par Lost 9.688
Knowing both Good and Evil as they know. Par Lost 9.709
Of Knowledge, knowledge both of good and evil; Par Lost 9.752
To reach, and feed at once both Bodie and Mind? Par Lost 9.779
One Heart, one Soul in both; whereof good prooff Par Lost 9.967
As with new Wine intoxicated both Par Lost 9.1008
Both Good and Evil, Good lost, and Evil got, Par Lost 9.1072
So counsel'd hee, and both together went Par Lost 9.1099
Heard not her lore, both in subjection now Par Lost 9.1128
Both Ransom and Redeemer voluntarie, Par Lost 10.61
Mine both in Heav'n and Earth to do thy will Par Lost 10.69
Came the mild Judge and Intercessor both Par Lost 10.96
The thickest Trees, both Man and Wife, till God Par Lost 10.101
To offend, discount'nanc't both, and discompos'd; Par Lost 10.110
Least on my head both sin and punishment, Par Lost 10.133
So judg'd he Man, both Judge and Saviour sent, Par Lost 10.209
Then Both from out Hell Gates into the waste Par Lost 10.282
Fair Daughter, and thou Son and Grandchild both, Par Lost 10.384
Both his beloved Man and all his World, Par Lost 10.489
Down fell both Spear and Shield, down they as fast, Par Lost 10.542
This said, they both betook them several wayes, Par Lost 10.610
Both to destroy, or unimmortal make Par Lost 10.611
Both *Sin*, and *Death*, and yawning *Grave* at last Par Lost 10.635
Till then the Curse pronounc't on both precedes. Par Lost 10.640
Both in me, and without me, and so last Par Lost 10.812
On my defensless head; both Death and I Par Lost 10.815
Am found Eternal, and incorporate both, Par Lost 10.816
But all corrupt, both Mind and Will deprav'd, Par Lost 10.825
To *Satan* only like both crime and doom. Par Lost 10.841
Between us two let there be peace, both joyning, Par Lost 10.924
More miserable; both have sin'd, but thou Par Lost 10.930
Both*(cont)*
Then both our selves and Seed at once to free Par Lost 10.999
From what we fear for both, let us make short, Par Lost 10.1000
And gracious temper he both heard and judg'd Par Lost 10.1047
Before him reverent, and both confess'd Par Lost 10.1100
To know both Good and Evil, since his taste Par Lost 11.85
That must be mortal to us both. O flours, Par Lost 11.273
If so I may attain. So both ascend Par Lost 11.376
Alas, both for the deed and for the cause! Par Lost 11.461
Both Horse and Foot, nor idely mustring stood; Par Lost 11.645
Both Heav'n and Earth, wherein the just shall dwell. Par Lost 11.901
The second, both for pietie renownd Par Lost 12.321
Both by obedience and by love, though love Par Lost 12.403
With glory and power to judge both quick and dead, Par Lost 12.460
Both in one Faith unanimous though sad, Par Lost 12.603
He ended, and they both descend the Hill; Par Lost 12.606
Both Table and Provision vanish'd quite Par Reg 2.402
Riches are needless then, both for themselves, Par Reg 2.484
Happiest both to thy self and all the world, Par Reg 3.225
Both *Paynim*, and the Peers of *Charlemane*. Par Reg 3.343
Outside and inside both, pillars and roofs Par Reg 4.58
Syene, and where the shadow both way falls, Par Reg 4.70
Now both abhor, since thou hast dar'd to utter Par Reg 4.172
Though Sons of God both Angels are and Men, Par Reg 4.197
What both from Men and Angels I receive, Par Reg 4.200
Her shadowy off-spring unsubstantial both, Par Reg 4.399
Gan thunder, and both ends of Heav'n, the Clouds Par Reg 4.410
For both the when and how is no where told, Par Reg 4.472
To the utmost of meer man both wise and good, Par Reg 4.535
Hail Son of the most High, heir of both worlds, Par Reg 4.633
Of both my Parents all in flames ascended Samson 25
Betray'd, Captiv'd, and both my Eyes put out, Samson 33
For oft alike, both come to evil end. Samson 704
To publish them, both common female faults: Samson 777
On both his wings, one black, th' other white, Samson 973
Nor both so loosly disally'd Samson 1022
To put out both thine eyes, and fetter'd send thee Samson 1160
Private reward, for which both God and State Samson 1465
In both which we, as next participate. Samson 1507
At once both to destroy and be destroy'd; Samson 1587
Both horse and foot before him and behind Samson 1618
With both his arms on those two massie Pillars Samson 1633
I fear the dred events that dog them both, Mask 405
And Laughter holding both his sides. Allegro 32
Of Wit, or Arms, while both contend Allegro 123
Together both, ere the high Lawns appear'd Lycidas 25
We drove a field, and both together heard Lycidas 27
So both himself and us to glorifie: Nativity 154
Heav'ns Queen and Mother both, Nativity 201
Spoil'd at once both fruit and tree: Winchester 30
Both them I serve, and of their train am I. Sonnet 1, 14
Who liv'd in both, unstain'd with gold or fee, Sonnet 10, 3
And left them both, more in himself content, Sonnet 10, 4
That all both judge you to relate them true, Sonnet 10, 13
And wov'n close, both matter, form and stile; Sonnet 11, 2
Both spirituall powre and civill, what each meanes Sonnet 17, 10
Both lay me down and sleep Psalm 4, 38
In him who both just and wise Psalm 7, 41
Among the gods on both his hands Psalm 82, 3
For God the Lord both Sun and Shield Psalm 84, 41
Both they who sing, and they who dance Psalm 87, 25
Bottom
And leave a singed bottom all involv'd Par Lost 1.236
Transfix us to the bottom of this Gulfe. Par Lost 1.329
Harsh Thunder, that the lowest bottom shook Par Lost 2.882
His troubl'd thoughts, and from the bottom stirr Par Lost 4.19
The bottom of the Mountains upward turn'd, Par Lost 6.649
Up from the bottom turn'd by furious windes Par Lost 7.213
Down sunk a hollow bottom broad and deep, Par Lost 7.289
All left, in one small bottom swum imbark't. Par Lost 11.753
Only in a bottom saw a pleasant Grove, Par Reg 2.289
That brow this bottom glade, whence night by night Mask 532
Bridgewater ms 'bottome'
1637 'bottome'
Trinity ms 'bottome'
The water Nymphs that in the bottom plaid, Mask 833
1637 'bottome'
Trinity ms 'bottome'
Visit'st the bottom of the monstrous world; Lycidas 158
Trinity ms 'bottome'
Bottomless
To bottomless perdition, there to dwell Par Lost 1.47
ms 'bottomles'
Burnt after them to the bottomless pit. Par Lost 6.866
With them from bliss to the bottomless deep, Par Reg 1.361
Bough
Of Birds on every bough; so much the more Par Lost 5.8
But I will haste and from each bough and break, Par Lost 5.326
A bough of fairest fruit that downie smil'd, Par Lost 9.851
Such recompence best merits) from the bough Par Lost 9.995
Boughs
Nectarine Fruits which the compliant boughes Par Lost 4.332
Thir pamperd boughes, and needed hands to check Par Lost 5.214
Yield Nectar, though from off the boughs each Morn Par Lost 5.428
When from the boughes a savorie odour blow'n, Par Lost 9.579
Ye Cedars, with innumerable boughs Par Lost 9.1089
In this close dungeon of innumerous bowes. Mask 349
Bridgewater ms 'bows'

Boughs(*cont*)
And from the Boughs brush off the evil dew, — Arcades 50
Trinity ms 'bowes' ← 'leaves'
Bought
Short intermission bought with double smart. — Par Lost 4.102
Knowledge of Good bought dear by knowing ill. — Par Lost 4.222
Reigns here and revels; not in the bought smile — Par Lost 4.765
Of Paradise, deare bought with lasting woes! — Par Lost 10.742
Chor. O dearly-bought revenge, yet glorious! — Samson 1660
Bound
Within Heav'ns bound, unless Heav'ns Lord supream — Par Lost 2.236
Illimitable Ocean without bound, — Par Lost 2.892
The powers of darkness bound. Thou at the sight — Par Lost 3.256
To darkness, such as bound the Ocean wave. — Par Lost 3.539
From *Media* post to *Aegypt*, there fast bound. — Par Lost 4.171
At one slight bound high over leap'd all bound — Par Lost 4.181
His will who bound us? let him surer barr — Par Lost 4.897
And at his Chariot wheeles to drag him bound — Par Lost 6.358
Her dark foundations, and too fast had bound. — Par Lost 6.870
Half yet remaines unsung, but narrower bound — Par Lost 7.21
Who can impair thee, mighty King, or bound — Par Lost 7.608
Bound with *Gorgonian* rigor not to move, — Par Lost 10.297
To stuff this Maw, this vast unhide-bound Corps. — Par Lost 10.601
Shall meet, alreadie linkt and Wedlock-bound — Par Lost 10.905
That all his senses bound; *Eve*, who unseen — Par Lost 11.265
Thy Husband, him to follow thou art bound; — Par Lost 11.291
The Throne hereditarie, and bound his Reign — Par Lost 12.370
Of many Provinces from bound to bound; — Par Reg 3.315
Antigonus, and old *Hyrcanus* bound, — Par Reg 3.367
Bound, and to torment sent before thir time. — Par Reg 4.632
Bound with two cords; but cords to me were threds — Samson 261
Ensnar'd, assaulted, overcome, led bound, — Samson 365
Thee *Samson* bound and blind into thir hands, — Samson 438
Of *Tarsus*, bound for th' Isles — Samson 715
As a League-breaker and deliver'd bound — Samson 1184
As a league-breaker gave up bound, presum'd — Samson 1209
Root-bound, that fled *Apollo*, *La*. Fool do not boast, — Mask 662
Bridgewater ms 'roote bound'
1637 'Root bound'
Trinity ms 'root-bound'
And bound him fast; without his rod revers't, — Mask 816
In straiter limits bound, — Nativity 169
To this Horizon is my *Phoebus* bound, — Passion 23
Bound
At one slight bound high over leap'd all bound — Par Lost 4.181
For on som message high they guessd him bound. — Par Lost 5.290
Bound on a voyage uncouth and obscure, — Par Lost 8.230
Boundless
To bellow through the vast and boundless Deep. — Par Lost 1.177
ms 'boundlesse'
It seem'd, now seems a boundless Continent — Par Lost 3.423
Boundless the Deep, because I am who fill — Par Lost 7.168
Bounds
And *Accaron* and *Gaza*'s frontier bounds. — Par Lost 1.466
Or in *Dodona*, and through all the bounds — Par Lost 1.518
Hell bounds high reaching to the horrid Roof, — Par Lost 2.644
What readiest path leads where your gloomie bounds — Par Lost 2.976
Transports our adversarie, whom no bounds — Par Lost 3.81
Whose snowie ridge the roving *Tartar* bounds, — Par Lost 3.432
So wide the op'ning seemd, where bounds were set — Par Lost 3.538
So minded, have oreleapt these earthie bounds — Par Lost 4.583
Why hast thou, *Satan*, broke the bounds prescrib'd — Par Lost 4.878
Unlicenc't from his bounds in Hell prescrib'd; — Par Lost 4.909
Till body up to spirit work, in bounds — Par Lost 5.478
Of surfet where full measure onely bounds — Par Lost 5.639
line not in 1667 edition
From all Heav'ns bounds into the utter Deep: — Par Lost 6.716
With terrors and with furies to the bounds — Par Lost 6.859
Of knowledge within bounds; beyond abstain — Par Lost 7.120
Within appointed bounds be Heav'n and Earth, — Par Lost 7.167
And said, thus farr extend, thus farr thy bounds, — Par Lost 7.230
Not onely these fair bounds, but all the Earth — Par Lost 8.338
Hell could no longer hold us in her bounds, — Par Lost 10.365
Of all things parted by th' Empyreal bounds, — Par Lost 10.380
Through Heav'ns wide bounds; from them I will not hide — Par Lost 11.68
His presence to these narrow bounds confin'd — Par Lost 11.341
Beyond all bounds, till inundation rise — Par Lost 11.828
Surpass his bounds, nor Rain to drown the World — Par Lost 11.894
Darkness must overshadow all his bounds, — Par Lost 12.187
With earths wide bounds, his glory with the Heav'ns. — Par Lost 12.371
And bear through highth or depth of natures bounds — Par Reg 1.13
Assyria and her Empires antient bounds, — Par Reg 3.270
Through all *Philistian* bounds. To *Israel* — Samson 1714
That flames, and dances in his crystal bounds — Mask 673
The bounds of either sword to thee wee ow. — Sonnet 17, 12
Earths utmost bounds: them shalt thou bring full low — Psalm 2, 19
Whose bounds the Sea doth check. — Psalm 83, 28
Bounteous
Hail universal Lord, be bounteous still — Par Lost 5.205
Excess, before th' all bounteous King, who showrd — Par Lost 5.640
1667 'all-bounteous'
Thy words, Creator bounteous and benigne, — Par Lost 8.492
In wanton dance they praise the bounteous *Pan*, — Mask 176
Bridgewater ms 'bounteus'
Hail bounteous *May* that dost inspire — May Morn 5
Bounties
God hath dispenst his bounties as in Heav'n. — Par Lost 5.330
These bounties which our Nourisher, from whom — Par Lost 5.398

Bounties(*cont*)
Wherefore did Nature powre her bounties forth, — Mask 710
Thither all their bounties bring, — Mask 987
line not in Bridgewater ms
Bounty
His bountie, following our delightful task — Par Lost 4.437
Varied his bounty so with new delights, — Par Lost 5.431
Then ever, bountie of this vertuous Tree. — Par Lost 9.1033
Justice shall not return as bountie scorn'd. — Par Lost 10.54
Yet so much bounty is in God, such grace, — Par Reg 3.142
Bourn
And every bosky bourn from side to side — Mask 313
1637 'bourne'
Trinity ms 'bourne'
Bridgewater ms 'bourne'
Bout
In notes, with many a winding bout — Allegro 139
Bow
Extort from me. To bow and sue for grace — Par Lost 1.111
All knees to thee shall bow, of them that bide — Par Lost 3.321
Towards either Throne they bow, and to the ground — Par Lost 3.350
Then in fair Evening Cloud, or humid Bow, — Par Lost 4.151
And by my Self have sworn to him shall bow — Par Lost 5.607
My Bow and Thunder, my Almightie Arms — Par Lost 6.713
Sate Eagle-wing'd, beside him hung his Bow — Par Lost 6.763
Though not as shee with Bow and Quiver armd, — Par Lost 9.390
A dewie Cloud, and in the Cloud a Bow — Par Lost 11.865
His triple-colour'd Bow, whereon to look — Par Lost 11.897
And made him bow to the Gods of his Wives. — Par Reg 2.171
Hence had the huntress *Dian* her dred bow — Mask 441
Iris there with humid bow, — Mask 992
B.M. ms 'Bow'
Bridgewater ms 'bowe'
Heav'n it self would stoop to her. — Mask 1023
Trinity ms 'stoope' ← 'bow'
His Sword he whets, his Bow hath bended — Psalm 7, 46
To bow to him and bend, — Psalm 81, 62
To bow them low before thee Lord, — Psalm 86, 31
Bow-bent
A *Sybil* old, bow-bent with crooked age, — Vacation 69
Bowed
Bow'd down in Battel, sunk before the Spear — Par Lost 1.436
Lowly they bow'd adoring, and began — Par Lost 5.144
But as in gaze admiring: Oft he bowd — Par Lost 9.524
Adam bowd low, hee Kingly from his State — Par Lost 11.249
Bow'd their Stiff necks, loaden with stormy blasts, — Par Reg 4.418
This utter'd, straining all his nerves he bow'd, — Samson 1646
Where the bow'd welkin slow doth bend, — Mask 1015
Trinity ms 'the bow'd welkin' ← 'the welkin'
And oft, as if her head she bow'd, — Penseroso 71
Bowels
Rifl'd the bowels of thir mother Earth — Par Lost 1.687
ms 'bowells'
My Bowels, thir repast; then bursting forth — Par Lost 2.800
Of mine own brood, that on my bowels feed: — Par Lost 2.863
Bower
Adams abode, those loftie shades his Bowre. — Par Lost 3.734
On to thir blissful Bower; it was a place — Par Lost 4.690
Such was thir awe of Man. In shadie Bower — Par Lost 4.705
Which God likes best, into thir inmost bowre — Par Lost 4.738
1667 'bower'
Daz'ling the Moon; these to the Bower direct — Par Lost 4.798
Converse with *Adam*, in what Bowre or shade — Par Lost 5.230
Of his coole Bowre, while now the mounted Sun — Par Lost 5.300
This spacious ground, in yonder shadie Bowre — Par Lost 5.367
To visit thee; lead on then where thy Bowre — Par Lost 5.375
My pleaded reason. To the Nuptial Bowre — Par Lost 8.510
From the thick shade, and *Adam* to his Bowre. — Par Lost 8.653
To be returnd by Noon amid the Bowre, — Par Lost 9.401
In Bowre and Field he sought, where any tuft — Par Lost 9.417
Thee lastly nuptial Bowre, by mee adornd — Par Lost 11.280
Descended, *Adam* to the Bowre where *Eve* — Par Lost 12.607
1669 'Bower'
From old, or modern Bard in Hall, or Bowr. — Mask 45
Trinity ms 'bowre'
1637 'bowre'
Bridgewater ms 'bowre'
To wait in *Amphitrite*'s bowr. — Mask 921
Bridgewater ms 'bower'
1637 'bowre'
Trinity ms 'bowre'
And then in haste her Bowre she leaves, — Allegro 87
Might raise *Musaeus* from his bower, — Penseroso 104
Of this fair Wood, and live in Oak'n bowr, — Arcades 45
Trinity ms 'er', ms defective
Lift not thy spear against the Muses Bowre, — Sonnet 8, 9
Trinity ms 'bowre'
And Justice from her heavenly bowr — Psalm 85, 47
Bowers
Imbround the noontide Bowrs: Thus was this place, — Par Lost 4.246
Planted, with Walks, and Bowers, that what I saw — Par Lost 8.305
These paths & Bowers doubt not but our joynt hands — Par Lost 9.244
O Woods, O Fountains, Hillocks, Dales and Bowrs, — Par Lost 10.860
Filld all the Regions: from thir blissful Bowrs — Par Lost 11.77
In their obscured haunts of inmost bowres. — Mask 536
Trinity ms 'bowers'
Bridgewater ms 'bowers'
Along the crisped shades and bowres — Mask 984

Bowers(*cont*)
line not in Bridgewater ms
Trinity ms 'bowrs'
Oft in glimmering Bowres, and glades Penseroso 27
Bowest
With sickness and disease thou bow'st them down, Samson 698
Bowing
His righteous Altar, bowing lowly down Par Lost 1.434
Thus said, he turnd, and *Satan* bowing low, Par Lost 3.736
As to a superior Nature, bowing low, Par Lost 5.360
So said, he o're his Scepter bowing, rose Par Lost 6.746
He added not; and Satan bowing low Par Reg 1.497
Bowl
To ern his Cream-bowle duly set, Allegro 106
Bows
They issue forth, Steel Bows, and Shafts their arms Par Reg 3.305
Her Bows as *high as* Cedars tall Psalm 80, 43
Boy
With the Attick Boy to hunt, Penseroso 124
Boys
What hinders? as some teachers give to Boyes Prose 6, 2
Brace
First hunter then, pursu'd a gentle brace, Par Lost 11.188
Vant-brass and Greves, and Gauntlet, add thy Spear Samson 1121
Brag
Beauty is natures brag, and must be shown Mask 745
line not in Bridgewater ms
Braid
Braid your Locks with rosie Twine Mask 105
Bridgewater ms 'braide'
Braided
His breaded train, and of his fatal guile Par Lost 4.349
Braids
In twisted braids of Lillies knitting Mask 862
Bridgewater ms 'braides'
Brain
Dwell in som idle brain, Penseroso 5
Brained
By shallow *Edwards* and Scotch what d' ye call: Forcers 12
Trinity ms 'shallow' ←'hare braind' ←'haire braind'
Brains
To the hazard of thy brains and shatter'd sides. Samson 1241
Brake
As one continu'd brake, the undergrowth Par Lost 4.175
But I will haste and from each bough and break, Par Lost 5.326
In Forrest wilde, in Thicket, Brake, or Den; Par Lost 7.458
In every Bush and Brake, where hap may finde Par Lost 9.160
While the red fire, and smouldring clouds out brake: Nativity 159
Brakes
Run to your shrouds, within these Brakes and Trees, Mask 147
Trinity ms 'braks'
Bridgewater ms 'brakes'
Brambles
he may scratch his forehead. heere be brambles Mask Tr. ms 17.57
Branch
From Branch to Branch the smaller Birds with song Par Lost 7.433
And the young branch, that for thy self Psalm 80, 63
Branches
Our walk at noon, with branches overgrown, Par Lost 4.627
With branches lopt, in Wood or Mountain fell'd) Par Lost 6.575
Thir branches hung with copious Fruit; or gemm'd Par Lost 7.325
Birds on the branches warbling; all things smil'd, Par Lost 8.265
For high from ground the branches would require Par Lost 9.590
Of thy full branches offer'd free to all; Par Lost 9.802
Three fair branches of your own, Mask 969
B.M. ms 'Branches'
Her branches *on the western side* Psalm 80, 45
Her other branches *went*. Psalm 80, 48
Branching
Cedar, and Pine, and Firr, and branching Palm, Par Lost 4.139
Shaded with branching Palme, each order bright, Par Lost 6.885
Bore up his branching head: scarse from his mould Par Lost 7.470
Braunching so broad and long, that in the ground Par Lost 9.1104
Whose branching arms thick intertwind might shield Par Reg 4.405
Of Laurel ever green, and branching Palm, Samson 1735
Of branching Elm Star-proof, Arcades 89
Brand
Wav'd over by that flaming Brand, the Gate Par Lost 12.643
Bid go with evil omen and the brand Samson 967
Benighted walks under the mid-day Sun; Mask 384
Trinity ms 'benighted walks under the midday sun' ←'walks in black vapours though the noontyde brand'
Bridgewater ms 'walks in black vapours though the noone tyde brand'
And Public Faith cleard from the shamefull brand Sonnet 15, 12
Brandished
Brandisht aloft the horrid edge came down Par Lost 6.252
The brandisht Sword of God before them blaz'd Par Lost 12.633
1669 'brandish't'
And brandish't blade rush on him, break his glass, Mask 651
Bridgewater ms 'brandisht'
Brandishing
Forth issu'd, brandishing his fatal Dart Par Lost 2.786
Brass
And thrice threefold the Gates; three folds were Brass, Par Lost 2.645
Brass, Iron, Stonie mould, had not thir mouthes Par Lost 6.576
Labouring, two massie clods of Iron and Brass Par Lost 11.565
And Brigandine of brass, thy broad Habergeon, Samson 1120

Brass(*cont*)
And of the wondrous Hors of Brass, Penseroso 114
Braveries
These braveries in Irons loaden on thee. Samson 1243
Bravery
With all her bravery on, and tackle trim, Samson 717
Brayed
Was never, Arms on Armour clashing bray'd Par Lost 6.209
Brazen
Op'ning thir brazen foulds discover wide Par Lost 1.724
ms 'brasen'
Of brazen Chariots rag'd; dire was the noise Par Lost 6.211
Myriads between two brazen Mountains lodg'd Par Lost 7.201
1669 'Brazen'
Of huge extent somtimes, with brazen Eyes Par Lost 7.496
Bursting thir brazen Dungeon, armd with ice Par Lost 10.697
The brazen Throat of Warr had ceast to roar, Par Lost 11.713
To grind in Brazen Fetters under task Samson 35
Of brazen shield and spear, the hammer'd Cuirass, Samson 132
Breach
Her mural breach, returning whence it rowld. Par Lost 6.879
Those Notes to Tragic; foul distrust, and breach Par Lost 9.6
Bread
In the sweat of thy Face shalt thou eat Bread, Par Lost 10.205
My bread; what harm? Idleness had bin worse; Par Lost 10.1055
And famish him of Breath, if not of Bread? Par Lost 12.78
That out of these hard stones be made thee bread; Par Reg 1.343
Think'st thou such force in Bread? is it not written Par Reg 1.347
Man lives not by Bread only, but each Word Par Reg 1.349
Here rather let me drudge and earn my bread, Samson 573
Thou feed'st them with the bread of tears, Psalm 80, 21
Their bread with tears they eat, Psalm 80, 22
Breadth
Without dimension, where length, breadth, & highth, Par Lost 2.893
He views in bredth, and without longer pause Par Lost 3.561
Like distant breadth to *Taurus* with the Seav'n Par Lost 10.673
Measur'd by Cubit, length, and breadth, and highth, Par Lost 11.730
Another plain, long but in bredth not wide; Par Reg 4.27
Break
Scorning surprize. Or could we break our way Par Lost 2.134
All night; at last by break of chearful dawne Par Lost 3.545
Who would not, finding way, break loose from Hell, Par Lost 4.889
Is now an Iron Rod to bruise and breake Par Lost 5.887
For now, and since first break of dawne the Fiend, Par Lost 9.412
Let us not break in upon him; Samson 116
To break all faith, all vows, deceive, betray, Samson 750
Up to the highth, whether to hold or break; Samson 1349
To heave, pull, draw, or break, he still perform'd Samson 1626
Break off, break off, I feel the different pace, Mask 145
Bridgewater ms 'Breake'
Bridgewater ms 'breake'
Trinity ms both 'breake'
Som far off hallow break the silent Air. Mask 481
1637 'breake'
Trinity ms 'breake'
And brandish't blade rush on him, break his glass, Mask 651
Bridgewater ms 'breake'
Trinity ms 'breake'
1637 'breake'
Let us break off, say they, by strength of hand Psalm 2, 6
And all thy waves break me. Psalm 88, 32
Breaker
As a League-breaker and deliver'd bound Samson 1184
As a league-breaker gave up bound, presum'd Samson 1209
Breakest
Thou break'st upon me all thy waves, Psalm 88, 31
Breaking
Breaking the horrid silence thus began. Par Lost 1.83
Thine own begotten, breaking violent way Par Lost 2.782
Breaking her Marriage Faith to circumvent me. Samson 1115
Till the sad breaking of that Parlament Sonnet 10, 5
Breaks
Disloyal breaks his fealtie, and sinns Par Lost 3.204
Mee disobeyes, breaks union, and that day Par Lost 5.612
But vertue which breaks through all opposition, Samson 1050
That breaks his magick chains at *curfeu* time, Mask 435
Breast
Fallacious hope, or arm th' obdured brest Par Lost 2.568
Now rowling, boiles in his tumultuous brest, Par Lost 4.16
On our first Father, half her swelling Breast Par Lost 4.495
Each shoulder broad, came mantling o're his brest Par Lost 5.279
Bad influence into th' unwarie brest Par Lost 5.695
Peace and composure, and with open brest Par Lost 6.560
And Brest, (what could we more2) propounded terms Par Lost 6.612
Thir downie Brest; the Swan with Arched neck Par Lost 7.438
Thoughts, which how found they harbour in thy brest Par Lost 9.288
Superior sway: from thus distemperd brest, Par Lost 9.1131
What thoughts in my unquiet brest are ris'n, Par Lost 10.975
Home to my Brest, and to my memorie Par Lost 11.154
1667 'brest'
My obvious breast, arming to overcom Par Lost 11.374
Musing and much revolving in his brest, Par Reg 1.185
Lodg'd in his brest, as well might recommend Par Reg 1.301
Within her brest, though calm; her brest though pure, Par Reg 2.63
At will the manliest, resolutest brest, Par Reg 2.167
On *Aaron*'s breast: or tongue of Seers old Par Reg 3.15
In heart, head, brest, and reins; Samson 609
Or knock the breast, no weakness, no contempt, Samson 1722

Breast(*cont*)
Sure somthing holy lodges in that brest, Mask 246
He that has light within his own cleer brest Mask 381
Thus I sprinkle on thy brest Mask 911
Trinity ms 'brest' ←'best'
Mountains on whose barren brest Allegro 73

Breast-plate
In *Aarons* Brest-plate, and a stone besides Par Lost 3.598

Breasts
In heav'nly brests? these, these and many more Par Lost 9.730
And from his memory inflame thir breasts Samson 1739

Breath
What if the breath that kindl'd those grim fires Par Lost 2.170
Will slack'n, if his breath stir not thir flames. Par Lost 2.214
Sweet is the breath of morn, her rising sweet, Par Lost 4.641
But neither breath of Morn when she ascends Par Lost 4.650
The breath of Life; in his own Image hee Par Lost 7.526
Least that pure breath of Life, the Spirit of Man Par Lost 10.784
Horrid, if true! yet why? it was but breath Par Lost 10.789
Or one short sigh of humane breath, up-borne Par Lost 11.147
No more availes then breath against the winde, Par Lost 11.312
And famish him of Breath, if not of Bread? Par Lost 12.78
And his who gave them breath, but higher sung, Par Reg 4.258
The breath of Heav'n fresh-blowing, pure and sweet, Samson 10
Nor breath of Vernal Air from snowy *Alp*. Samson 628
Sam. For want of words no doubt, or lack of breath, Samson 905
That in a little time while breath remains thee, Samson 1126
Mess. It would burst forth, but I recover breath Samson 1555
And early ere the odorous breath of morn Arcades 56
After so short time of breath, Winchester 9
And too much breathing put him out of breath; Another 12
That even to his last breath (ther be that say't) Another 25
line not in 1640, 1657, 1658 texts

Breathe
Shall breathe her balme. But first whom shall we send Par Lost 2.402
1667 'breath'
Breathe forth *Elixir* pure, and Rivers run Par Lost 3.607
Breathe soft or loud; and wave your tops, ye Pines, Par Lost 5.193
1667 'Breath', 1668 errata 'Breathe'
Thir morning incense, when all things that breath, Par Lost 9.194
Forth issuing on a Summers Morn to breathe Par Lost 9.447
And wilde, how shall we breath in other Aire Par Lost 11.284
Breath such Divine inchanting ravishment? Mask 245
And as I wake, sweet musick breath Penseroso 151

Breathed
Deliberate valour breath'd, firm and unmov'd Par Lost 1.554
Silent yet spake, and breath'd immortal love Par Lost 3.267
Of instrumental Harmonie that breath'd Par Lost 6.65
Dust of the ground, and in thy nostrils breath'd Par Lost 7.525
In *Eden* on the humid Flours, that breathd Par Lost 9.193
Regenerate grow instead, that sighs now breath'd Par Lost 11.5
Without the vent of words, which these he breathd. Par Lost 12.374
Thir unexpected loss and plaints out breath'd. Par Reg 2.29
No nightly trance, or breathed spell, Nativity 179

Breathes
To many a row of Pipes the sound-board breaths. Par Lost 1.709
Our envied Sovran, and his Altar breathes Par Lost 2.244
Milde, as when *Zephyrus* on *Flora* breathes, Par Lost 5.16
Spirits odorous breathes: flours and thir fruit Par Lost 5.482
Blown stifling back on him that breaths it forth: Par Lost 11.313
The frolick Wind that breathes the Spring, Allegro 18

Breathest
Hell-doom'd, and breath'st defiance here and scorn Par Lost 2.697

Breathing
Breathing united force with fixed thought Par Lost 1.560
Breathing the smell of field and grove, attune Par Lost 4.265
At last a soft and solemn breathing sound Mask 555
Bridgewater ms 'breathinge'
And ye the breathing Roses of the Wood, Arcades 32
And too much breathing put him out of breath; Another 12

Breaths
Like gentle breaths from Rivers pure, thence raise Par Lost 4.806

Bred
That bred them they return, and howle and gnaw Par Lost 2.799
As when a Vultur on *Imaus* bred, Par Lost 3.431
Sin-bred, how have ye troubl'd all mankind Par Lost 4.315
Was Aerie light from pure digestion bred, Par Lost 5.4
Bred of unkindly fumes, with conscious dreams Par Lost 9.1050
At Eev'n, which I bred up with tender hand Par Lost 11.276
Had bred; then purg'd with Euphrasie and Rue Par Lost 11.414
Bred onely and completed to the taste Par Lost 11.618
Bred up in Idol-worship; O that men Par Lost 12.115
As one in City, or Court, or Palace bred, Par Reg 2.300
Bred up in poverty and streights at home; Par Reg 2.415
The schools of antient Sages; his who bred Par Reg 4.251
Thy manhood last, though yet in private bred; Par Reg 4.509
The brood of folly without father bred, Penseroso 2
us of our selves & native woes beguile Musick Tr. ms 4.08
'native' ←'home bred' ←'home-bred'

Breed
And my quaint habits breed astonishment, Mask 157
Bridgewater ms 'breede'
Whom certain these rough shades did never breed Mask 266
Bridgewater ms 'breede'
As if to shew what creatures Heav'n doth breed, Fair Inf 61
For what can Warr, but endless warr still breed, Sonnet 15, 10

Breeding
Divinitie within them breeding wings Par Lost 9.1010

Breeding(*cont*)
Why was my breeding order'd and prescrib'd Samson 30

Breeds
Where all life dies, death lives, and Nature breeds, Par Lost 2.624

Brethren
His Brethren, ransomd with his own dear life. Par Lost 3.297
These two are Brethren, *Adam*, and to come Par Lost 11.454
Make they but of thir Brethren, men of men? Par Lost 11.680
Over his brethren, and quite dispossess Par Lost 12.28
Above his Brethren, to himself assuming Par Lost 12.65
Till by two brethren (those two brethren call Par Lost 12.169
Deliverance of thy brethren, those ten Tribes Par Reg 3.374
My brethren, as thou call'st them; those Ten Tribes Par Reg 3.403
Man. Brethren and men of *Dan*, for such ye seem, Samson 332
Sam. Brethren farewel, your company along Samson 1413
Man. Peace with you brethren; my inducement hither Samson 1445
O're all his Brethren he shall Reign as King, Vacation 75
Then lies him meekly down fast by his Brethrens side. Passion 21

Brewage
Hence with thy brew'd inchantments, foul deceiver, Mask 696
Trinity ms 'brewd enchauntments' ←'foule brud' ←'hel brewd opiate' ←'hel bru'd liquor' ←'bru'd sorcerie' ←'teacherous (leacherous?) bruage' ←'teacherous kindnesse'

Brewed
Hence with thy brew'd inchantments, foul deceiver, Mask 696
Bridgewater ms 'brewd'
1637 'brewd'
Trinity ms 'brewd enchauntments' ←'foule brud' ←'hel brewd opiate' ←'hel bru'd liquor' ←'bru'd sorcerie' ←'teacherous (leacherous?) bruage' ←'teacherous kindnesse'

Briar
Through the Sweet-Briar, or the Vine, Allegro 47

Briareos
Briareos or *Typhon*, whom the Den Par Lost 1.199
1667 '*Briarios*'
ms 'Briareos'

Brick
Of Brick, and of that stuff they cast to build Par Lost 12.43

Bridal
On his Hill top, to light the bridal Lamp. Par Lost 8.520
Under pretence of Bridal friends and guests, Samson 1196

Bride
To seek in marriage that fallacious Bride, Samson 320
If any of these or all, the *Timnian* bride Samson 1018
Who threatning cruel death constrain'd the bride Samson 1198
Make her his eternal Bride, Mask 1008
Trinity ms 'bride'
line not in Bridgewater ms

Bridegroom
Thou, when the Bridegroom with his feastfull friends Sonnet 9, 12

Bridge
Tamely endur'd a Bridge of wondrous length Par Lost 2.1028
Over the foaming deep high Archt, a Bridge Par Lost 10.301
Of that stupendious Bridge his joy encreas'd. Par Lost 10.351
With this portentous Bridge the dark Abyss. Par Lost 10.371

Bridges
With bridges rivers proud, as with a yoke; Par Reg 3.334

Bridging
Bridging his way, *Europe* with *Asia* joyn'd, Par Lost 10.310

Bridle
And bridle in thy headlong wave, Mask 887

Brief
And brief related whom they brought, where found, Par Lost 4.875
To whom in brief thus *Abdiel* stern repli'd. Par Lost 6.171
She scarse had said, though brief, when now more bold Par Lost 9.664
Whence *Adam* faultring long, thus answer'd brief. Par Lost 10.115
In brief sententious precepts, while they treat Par Reg 4.264
And staid not, but in brief him answer'd thus. Par Reg 4.485
Mess. Then take the worst in brief, *Samson* is dead. Samson 1570

Briefly
Do as you have in charge, and briefly touch Par Lost 6.566
El. Bro. What fears good *Thyrsis*? Prethee briefly shew. Mask 512
Trinity ms 'breifly'

Brigade
A numerous Brigad hasten'd. As when Bands Par Lost 1.675
ms 'brigad'

Brigades
With rapid wheels, or fronted Brigads form. Par Lost 2.532

Brigandine
And Brigandine of brass, thy broad Habergeon, Samson 1120

Bright
Myriads though bright: If he whom mutual league, Par Lost 1.87
Thus answer'd. Leader of those Armies bright, Par Lost 1.272
Dilated or condens't, bright or obscure, Par Lost 1.429
To whose bright Image nightly by the Moon Par Lost 1.440
Each in his Hierarchie, the Orders bright. Par Lost 1.737
Of those bright confines, whence with neighbouring Arms Par Lost 2.395
With bright imblazonrie, and horrent Arms. Par Lost 2.513
Likest to thee in shape and count'nance bright, Par Lost 2.756
To be invulnerable in those bright Arms, Par Lost 2.812
Bright effluence of bright essence increate. Par Lost 3.6
Now in loose Garlands thick thrown off, the bright Par Lost 3.362
Dark with excessive bright thy skirts appeer, Par Lost 3.380
Of Guardians bright, when he from *Esau* fled Par Lost 3.512
Viewless, and underneath a bright Sea flow'd Par Lost 3.518
So wondrously was set his Station bright. Par Lost 3.587

Bright(*cont*)
The place he found beyond expression bright, Par Lost 3.591
He drew not nigh unheard, the Angel bright, Par Lost 3.645
In sight of God's high Throne, gloriously bright, Par Lost 3.655
In that bright eminence, and with his good Par Lost 4.44
Not Spirits, yet to heav'nly Spirits bright Par Lost 4.361
Amid the Suns bright circle where thou sitst, Par Lost 4.578
Returnd on that bright beam, whose point now raisd Par Lost 4.590
While thus he spake, th' Angelic Squadron bright Par Lost 4.977
With thy bright Circlet, praise him in thy Spheare Par Lost 5.169
Bright Temple, to *Aegyptian Theb*'s he flies. Par Lost 5.274
More aerie, last the bright consummate floure Par Lost 5.481
Under thir Hierarchs in orders bright Par Lost 5.587
By him created in thir bright degrees, Par Lost 5.838
Coverd with thick embatteld Squadrons bright, Par Lost 6.16
In silence thir bright Legions, to the sound Par Lost 6.64
Th' Apostat in his Sun-bright Chariot sate Par Lost 6.100
And all his Armour staind ere while so bright. Par Lost 6.334
Which of us who beholds the bright surface Par Lost 6.472
Stand still in bright array ye Saints, here stand Par Lost 6.801
Shaded with branching Palme, each order bright, Par Lost 6.885
Follow'd in bright procession to behold Par Lost 7.222
Invested with bright Rayes, jocond to run Par Lost 7.372
Shedding sweet influence: less bright the Moon, Par Lost 7.375
With thir bright Luminaries that Set and Rose, Par Lost 7.385
While the bright Pomp ascended jubilant. Par Lost 7.564
That bodies bright and greater should not serve Par Lost 8.87
The less not bright, nor Heav'n such journies run, Par Lost 8.88
Or Bright inferrs not Excellence: the Earth Par Lost 8.91
Yet not to Earth are those bright Luminaries Par Lost 8.98
Thus I presumptuous; and the vision bright, Par Lost 8.367
That shine, yet bear thir bright officious Lamps, Par Lost 9.104
Insufferably bright. O might I here Par Lost 9.1084
So spake the Father, and unfoulding bright Par Lost 10.63
In open shew, and with ascention bright Par Lost 10.187
Satan in likeness of an Angel bright Par Lost 10.327
Of that bright Starr to *Satan* paragond. Par Lost 10.426
And shape Starr bright appeer'd, or brighter, clad Par Lost 10.450
1667 'Starr-bright'
To those bright Orders utterd thus his voice. Par Lost 10.615
To the bright Minister that watchd, hee blew Par Lost 11.73
For swift descent, with him the Cohort bright Par Lost 11.127
The field Pavilion'd with his Guardians bright; Par Lost 11.215
In thir bright stand, there left his Powers to seise Par Lost 11.221
His bright appearances, or foot step-trace? Par Lost 11.329
Of two bright Cherubim, before him burn Par Lost 12.254
To thir fixt Station, all in bright array Par Lost 12.627
Of the most High, who in full frequence bright Par Reg 1.128
By whose bright course led on they found the place, Par Reg 1.252
In *Silo* his bright Sanctuary: Samson 1674
Of bright aereal Spirits live insphear'd Mask 3
May sit i' th center, and enjoy bright day, Mask 382
With sudden adoration, and blank aw. Mask 452
Trinity ms 'and blank aw' ←'of bright rays' ←'of her purenesse'
Bore a bright golden flowre, but not in this soyl: Mask 633
line not in Bridgewater ms
Noble Lord, and Lady bright, Mask 966
With store of Ladies, whose bright eies Allegro 121
Whose Saintly visage is too bright Penseroso 13
Sitting like a Goddes bright, Arcades 18
I see bright honour sparkle through your eyes, Arcades 27
Oft till the Star that rose, at Ev'ning, bright Lycidas 30
1638 'Oft till the ev'n-starre bright'
Trinity ms 'starre that rose' ←'ev'n starre bright'
And all the spangled host keep watch in squadrons bright? Nativity 21
Then his bright Throne, or burning Axletree could bear. Nativity 84
Amongst her spangled sisters bright. Psalm 136, 34
Tell me bright Spirit where e're thou hoverest Fair Inf 38
Ye flaming Powers, and winged Warriours bright, Circum 1
Where the bright Seraphim in burning row Musick 10
Whilst thou bright Saint high sit'st in glory, Winchester 61
Far within the boosom bright Winchester 69
Now the bright morning Star, Dayes harbinger, May Morn 1
What ever clime the Suns bright circle warms. Sonnet 8, 8
Lift up the favour of thy count'nance bright. Psalm 4, 30
The Moon and Starrs which thou so bright hast set, Psalm 8, 10
That sitt'st between the Cherubs *bright* Psalm 80, 5
Gives grace and glory *bright*, Psalm 84, 42

Brightened
As with a smile more bright'nd, thus repli'd. Par Lost 8.368

Brightening
Secure, and at the brightning Orient beam Par Lost 2.399

Brightens
Bright'ns his Crest, as when a wandring Fire, Par Lost 9.634

Brighter
(So call him, brighter once amidst the Host Par Lost 7.132
And shape Starr bright appeer'd, or brighter, clad Par Lost 10.450

Brightest
But Mercy first and last shall brightest shine. Par Lost 3.134
Yet dazle Heav'n, that brightest Seraphim Par Lost 3.381
Alone thus wandring. Brightest Seraph tell Par Lost 3.667
The starrie Host, rode brightest, till the Moon Par Lost 4.606
Spring both, the face of brightest Heav'n had changd Par Lost 5.644
Nor yet amidst this joy and brightest morn Par Reg 4.439
Brightest Lady look on me, Mask 910
Trinity ms 'Brightest' ←'vertuous'

Bright-haired
Thee bright-hair'd *Vesta* long of yore, Penseroso 23

Bright-harnessed
Bright-harnest Angels sit in order serviceable. Nativity 244

Brightness
Cloth'd with transcendent brightness didst out-shine Par Lost 1.86
ms 'brightnesse'
1667 'brightnes'
All her Original brightness, nor appear'd Par Lost 1.592
ms 'brightnesse'
Amidst the glorious brightness where thou sit'st Par Lost 3.376
His back was turnd, but not his brightness hid; Par Lost 3.624
Or undiminisht brightness, to be known Par Lost 4.836
Brightness had made invisible, thus spake. Par Lost 5.599
Much lustre of my native brightness, lost Par Reg 1.378

Brim
With wheels yet hov'ring o're the Ocean brim, Par Lost 5.140
By dimpled Brook, and Fountain brim, Mask 119

Brimmed
May thy brimmed waves for this Mask 924
Trinity ms 'brimmed' ←'crystall'

Brimming
Still as they thirsted scoop the brimming stream; Par Lost 4.336

Brimstone
On the firm brimstone, and fill all the Plain; Par Lost 1.350

Brinded
And Rampant shakes his Brinded main; the Ounce, Par Lost 7.466
Wherwith she tam'd the brinded lioness Mask 443

Brine
The Ayr was calm, and on the level brine, Lycidas 98

Bring
Out of our evil seek to bring forth good, Par Lost 1.163
How all his malice serv'd but to bring forth Par Lost 1.217
Of future dayes may bring, what chance, what change Par Lost 2.222
Of *Ternate* and *Tidore*, whence Merchants bring Par Lost 2.639
And bring ye to the place where Thou and Death Par Lost 2.840
But thee, whom follow? thou wilt bring me soon Par Lost 2.866
Strive here for Maistrie, and to Battel bring Par Lost 2.899
His malice, and thy goodness bring to naught, Par Lost 3.158
To pray, repent, and bring obedience due. Par Lost 3.190
Indebted and undon, hath none to bring: Par Lost 3.235
Interpreter through highest Heav'n to bring, Par Lost 3.657
That bring to my remembrance from what state Par Lost 4.38
And I will bring thee where no shadow staies Par Lost 4.470
Such where ye find, seise fast, and hither bring. Par Lost 4.796
Or with repose; and such discourse bring on, Par Lost 5.233
And what thy stores contain, bring forth and poure Par Lost 5.314
Tastes, not well joynd, inelegant, but bring Par Lost 5.335
Believst so main to our success, I bring; Par Lost 6.471
That shake Heav'ns basis, bring forth all my Warr, Par Lost 6.712
Haste to thy audience, Night with her will bring Par Lost 7.105
Of Spirits maligne a better Race to bring Par Lost 7.189
Let th' Earth bring forth Foul living in her kinde, Par Lost 7.451
Imbu'd, bring to thir sweetness no satietie. Par Lost 8.216
After thir kindes; I bring them to receave Par Lost 8.343
What next I bring shall please thee, be assur'd, Par Lost 8.449
Of *Hesperus*, whose Office is to bring Par Lost 9.49
To hide me, and the dark intent I bring. Par Lost 9.162
My conduct, I can bring thee thither soon. Par Lost 9.630
Though threat'nd, which no worse then this can bring. Par Lost 9.715
By thy Conception; Children thou shalt bring Par Lost 10.194
Thorns also and Thistles it shall bring thee forth Par Lost 10.203
Decrepit Winter, from the South to bring Par Lost 10.655
As deep as *Capricorne*, to bring in change Par Lost 10.677
Our own begotten, and of our Loines to bring Par Lost 10.983
With Incense, I thy Priest before thee bring, Par Lost 11.25
Our frailtie can sustain, thy tidings bring, Par Lost 11.302
Corruption to bring forth more violent deeds. Par Lost 11.428
In Meats and Drinks, which on the Earth shall bring Par Lost 11.473
Shall bring on men. Immediately a place Par Lost 11.477
Nations, and bring home spoils with infinite Par Lost 11.692
The adversarie Serpent, and bring back Par Lost 12.312
To bring forth fruits Joy and eternal Bliss. Par Lost 12.551
For this ill news I bring, the Womans seed Par Reg 1.64
Will bring me hence, no other Guide I seek. Par Reg 1.336
If of that pow'r I bring thee voluntary Par Reg 2.394
But I will bring thee where thou soon shalt quit Par Reg 3.244
May bring them back repentant and sincere, Par Reg 3.435
Counsel or Consolation we may bring, Samson 183
Cho. Thy words to my remembrance bring Samson 277
Where thou mayst bring thy off'rings, to avert Samson 519
To bring my feet again into the snare Samson 931
Fear I incurable; bring up thy van, Samson 1234
A little stay will bring some notice hither, Samson 1536
To bring me Berries, or such cooling fruit Mask 186
Bridgewater ms 'bringe'
What readiest way would bring me to that place? Mask 305
Bridgewater ms 'bringe'
Thither all their bounties bring, Mask 987
line not in Bridgewater ms
Haste thee nymph, and bring with thee Allegro 25
But first, and chiefest, with thee bring, Penseroso 51
His flaring beams, me Goddes bring Penseroso 132
And bring all Heav'n before mine eyes. Penseroso 166
I will bring you where she sits, Arcades 91
Bring your Flocks, and live with us, Arcades 103
Throw hither all your quaint enameld eyes, Lycidas 139
Trinity ms 'throw' ←'bring'

Bring(*cont*)
Bring the rathe Primrose that forsaken dies. Lycidas 142
Our great redemption from above did bring; Nativity 4
And from thy wardrope bring thy chiefest treasure; Vacation 18
Fore-saw what future dayes should bring to pass, Vacation 72
That thy noble House doth bring, Winchester 54
Earths utmost bounds: them shalt thou bring full low Psalm 2, 19
Then all who trust in thee shall bring Psalm 5, 33
The Timbrel hither bring Psalm 81, 6
The *cheerfull* Psaltry bring along Psalm 81, 7
Then would I soon bring down their foes Psalm 81, 57

Bringing
And bringing forth, soon recompenc't with joy, Par Lost 10.1052
By his own Nation, slaine for bringing Life; Par Lost 12.414
Food to *Elijah* bringing Even and Morn, Par Reg 2.268
Or of him bringing to us some glad news? Samson 1444

Brings
Receive thy new Possessor: One who brings Par Lost 1.252
Directed, no mean recompence it brings Par Lost 2.981
He brings, and round about him, nor from Hell Par Lost 4.21
Her mariageable arms, and with her brings Par Lost 5.217
To us perhaps he brings, and will voutsafe Par Lost 5.312
As Heav'ns great Year brings forth, th' Empyreal Host Par Lost 5.583
But of the Tree whose operation brings Par Lost 8.323
Not Hers who brings it nightly to my Ear. Par Lost 9.47
Hath tasted, envies not, but brings with joy Par Lost 9.770
As some misfortune brings him, or mistake, Par Lost 10.900
An Olive leafe he brings, pacific signe: Par Lost 11.860
With Man therein or Beast; but when he brings Par Lost 11.895
The space of seventie years, then brings them back, Par Lost 12.345
Endeavour Peace: thir strife pollution brings Par Lost 12.355
Money brings Honour, Friends, Conquest, and Realms; Par Reg 2.422
Brings dangers, troubles, cares, and sleepless nights Par Reg 2.460
Incessantly, and to his reading brings not Par Reg 4.323
(And what he brings, what needs he elsewhere seek) Par Reg 4.325
Chor. But this another kind of tempest brings. Samson 1063
Of highest wisdom brings about, Samson 1747
And sage *Hippotades* their answer brings, Lycidas 96
To th' touch of golden wires, while *Hebe* brings Vacation 38
Thy firm unshak'n vertue ever brings Sonnet 15, 5
And to be short, at last his guid him brings Prose 2, 1

Brink
All in one moment, and so neer the brink; Par Lost 2.609
Stood on the brink of Hell and look'd a while, Par Lost 2.918
And at the brink of *Chaos*, neer the foot Par Lost 10.347

Brisk
When the fresh blood grows lively, and returns Mask 670
Trinity ms 'fresh' ←'briske'
Brisk as the *April* buds in Primrose-season. Mask 671
Bridgewater ms 'briske'

Bristled
Bristl'd with upright beams innumerable Par Lost 6.82

Bristles
Were bristles rang'd like those that ridge the back Samson 1137

British
Begirt with *British* and *Armoric* Knights; Par Lost 1.581
ms 'Brittish'
From *Gallia*, *Gades*, and the *Brittish* West, Par Reg 4.77
Of Brittish *Themis*, with no mean applause Sonnet 21, 2
line not in Trinity ms

Brittle
Nor founded on the brittle strength of bones, Par Lost 1.427

Broad
Behind him cast; the broad circumference Par Lost 1.286
The stedfast Earth. At last his Sail-broad Vannes Par Lost 2.927
Pav'd after him a broad and beat'n way Par Lost 2.1026
Into a *Limbo* large and broad, since calld Par Lost 3.495
Clustring, but not beneath his shoulders broad: Par Lost 4.303
Each shoulder broad, came mantling o're his brest Par Lost 5.279
Made horrid Circles; two broad Suns thir Shields Par Lost 6.305
Emergent, and thir broad bare backs upheave Par Lost 7.286
Down sunk a hollow bottom broad and deep, Par Lost 7.289
Pasturing at once, and in broad Herds upsprung. Par Lost 7.462
A broad and ample rode, whose dust is Gold Par Lost 7.577
To Starr or Sun-light, spread thir umbrage broad Par Lost 9.1087
Some Tree whose broad smooth Leaves together sowd, Par Lost 9.1095
Braunching so broad and long, that in the ground Par Lost 9.1104
They gatherd, broad as *Amazonian* Targe, Par Lost 9.1111
And with *Asphaltic* slime; broad as the Gate, Par Lost 10.298
Forfeit to Death; from hence a passage broad, Par Lost 10.304
By Sin and Death a broad way now is pav'd Par Lost 10.473
On this side the broad lake *Genezaret*, Par Reg 2.23
And Brigandine of brass, thy broad Habergeon, Samson 1120
Or 'gainst the rugged bark of som broad Elm Mask 354
Bridgewater ms 'broade'
Up in the broad fields of the sky: Mask 979
Trinity ms 'broad' ←'plaine'
Set off to th' world, nor in broad rumour lies, Lycidas 80
Wisely hast shun'd the broad way and the green, Sonnet 9, 2

Broadest
In ample space under the broadest shade Par Reg 2.339

Broidered
Broiderd the ground, more colour'd then with stone Par Lost 4.702

Broils
Might hap to move new broiles: Be this or aught Par Lost 2.837
Encroacht on still through our intestine broiles Par Lost 2.1001
Thou and thy wicked crew; there mingle broiles, Par Lost 6.277
Allurd them; thence from Cups to civil Broiles. Par Lost 11.718

Broke
Who first broke peace in Heav'n and Faith, till then Par Lost 2.690
Through all restraint broke loose he wings his way Par Lost 3.87
Why hast thou, *Satan*, broke the bounds prescrib'd Par Lost 4.878
Came not all Hell broke loose? is pain to them Par Lost 4.918
Great things by small, If Natures concord broke, Par Lost 6.311
His hinder parts, then springs as broke from Bonds, Par Lost 7.465
First to himself he inward silence broke. Par Lost 9.895
Inchanting Daughter, thus the silence broke. Par Lost 10.353
Broke off the rest; so much of Death her thoughts Par Lost 10.1008
Broke up, shall heave the Ocean to usurp Par Lost 11.827
Greatly rejoyc'd, and thus his joy broke forth. Par Lost 11.869
And now the Tempter thus his silence broke. Par Reg 4.43
In Paradise to tempt; his snares are broke: Par Reg 4.611
The *Philistines*, when thou hadst broke the league, Samson 1189
Broke the fair musick that all creatures made Musick 21
Here lies old *Hobson*, Death hath broke his girt, Carrier 1
1658 'hath his desire'
Broke him, as that dishonest victory Sonnet 10, 6
Hast broke the teeth. This help was from the Lord Psalm 3, 23

Broked
As from her outmost works a brok'd foe Par Lost 2.1039
1667 'brok'n'

Broken
And broken Chariot Wheels, so thick bestrown Par Lost 1.311
When the fierce Foe hung on our brok'n Rear Par Lost 2.78
As from her outmost works a brok'd foe Par Lost 2.1039
1667 'brok'n'
Broken be not intended all our power Par Reg 1.61
Can they think me so broken, so debas'd Samson 1335
her brok'n league, to impe their serpent wings, Sonnet 15, 8
1694 'broken'
And brok'n down her Fence, Psalm 80, 50

Brood
With his enormous brood, and birthright seis'd Par Lost 1.511
Warr'd on by Cranes: though all the Giant brood Par Lost 1.576
Of mine own brood, that on my bowels feed: Par Lost 2.863
Thir Brood as numerous hatch, from the Egg that soon Par Lost 7.418
Sam. I dread him not, nor all his Giant-brood, Samson 1247
The brood of folly without father bred, Penseroso 2
Or any other of that heav'nly brood Fair Inf 55
Talking like this worlds brood; Psalm 4, 27
The tents of Edom, and the brood Psalm 83, 21

Brooding
Dove-like satst brooding on the vast Abyss Par Lost 1.21
His brooding wings the Spirit of God outspred, Par Lost 7.235
Wher brooding darknes spreads his jealous wings, Allegro 6
While Birds of Calm sit brooding on the charmed wave. Nativity 68
Hath built her *brooding* nest, Psalm 84, 12

Brook
Delight thee more, and *Siloa*'s Brook that flow'd Par Lost 1.11
ms 'brooke'
Of old *Euphrates* to the Brook that parts Par Lost 1.420
ms 'brook'
Lets her will rule; restraint she will not brook, Par Lost 9.1184
Of lustre from the brook, in memorie, Par Lost 11.325
Him thought, he by the Brook of *Cherith* stood Par Reg 2.266
Freshet, or purling Brook, of shell or fin, Par Reg 2.345
Whose drink was only from the liquid brook. Samson 557
By dimpled Brook, and Fountain brim, Mask 119
Bridgewater ms 'brooke'
Trinity ms 'brooke'
1637 'Brooke'
The huddling brook to hear his madrigal, Mask 495
Bridgewater ms 'brooke'
Trinity ms 'brooke'
There in close covert by som Brook, Penseroso 139
When at the brook of Kishon *old* Psalm 83, 37

Brooking
Of Preface brooking through his Zeal of Right. Par Lost 9.676

Brooks
Thick as Autumnal Leaves that strow the Brooks Par Lost 1.302
ms 'brooks'
Thee *Sion* and the flowrie Brooks beneath Par Lost 3.30
How from that Saphire Fount the crisped Brooks, Par Lost 4.237
Brooks not the works of violence and Warr. Par Lost 6.274
Brooks no delay: is this thy resolution? Samson 1344
Shallow Brooks, and Rivers wide. Allegro 76
Of shades and wanton winds, and gushing brooks, Lycidas 137
In thee *fresh brooks, and soft streams glance* Psalm 87, 27

Brother
Of Father, Son, and Brother first were known. Par Lost 4.757
For envie that his Brothers Offering found Par Lost 11.456
Who slew his Brother; studious they appere Par Lost 11.609
His Brother; for of whom such massacher Par Lost 11.679
Eld. Bro. Peace brother, be not over-exquisite Mask 359
line not in Bridgewater ms
1673 'Brother'
line not in Trinity ms
Of our unowned sister. *Eld. Bro*. I do not, brother, Mask 407
1673 'Brother'
As you imagine, she has a hidden strength Mask 415
Trinity ms 'imagine brother'
Bridgewater ms 'immagine brother'
'Tis chastity, my brother, chastity: Mask 420
Where no crude surfet raigns. *Eld. Bro*. List, list, I hear Mask 480
Trinity ms 'list list' ←'list bro. list'
2. *Bro*. O brother, 'tis my father Shepherd sure. Mask 493

Brother(*cont*)
You gave me Brother? *Eld. Bro*. Yes, and keep it still, Mask 584
1637 'brother'
Bridgewater ms 'brother'
Trinity ms 'brother'
& darknesse wound her in. I Bro. Peace, brother peace Mask Tr. ms 15.53
Brothers
My Brothers when they saw me wearied out Mask 182
Trinity ms 'brothers'
Bridgewater ms 'brothers'
I cannot hallow to my Brothers, but Mask 226
Bridgewater ms 'brothers'
Trinity ms 'brothers'
La. No less then if I should my brothers loose. Mask 288
Yet on his Brothers shall depend for Cloathing. Vacation 82
Brought
Brought Death into the World, and all our woe, Par Lost 1.3
And to the fierce contention brought along Par Lost 1.100
Are brought: and feel by turns the bitter change Par Lost 2.598
Hath brought me from the Quires of Cherubim Par Lost 3.666
That brought them forth, but hid thir causes deep. Par Lost 3.707
And what I was, whence thither brought, and how. Par Lost 4.452
Brought her in naked beauty more adorn'd, Par Lost 4.713
Of *Japhet* brought by *Hermes*, she ensnar'd Par Lost 4.717
And brief related whom they brought, where found, Par Lost 4.875
Or not, who ask what boldness brought him hither Par Lost 4.908
That brought me on a sudden to the Tree Par Lost 5.51
Soon as midnight brought on the duskie houre Par Lost 5.667
Heav'ns blessed peace, and into Nature brought Par Lost 6.267
Fled ignominious, to such evil brought Par Lost 6.395
Brought forth the tender Grass, whose verdure clad Par Lost 7.315
He brought thee into this delicious Grove, Par Lost 7.537
As Tribute such a sumless journey brought Par Lost 8.36
Intended thee, for trial onely brought, Par Lost 8.447
She heard me thus, and though divinely brought, Par Lost 8.500
Thus I have told thee all my State, and brought Par Lost 8.521
That brought into this World a world of woe, Par Lost 9.11
Our dayes work brought to little, though begun Par Lost 9.224
Guiltless of fire had formd, or Angels brought. Par Lost 9.392
His fierceness of the fierce intent it brought: Par Lost 9.462
What hither brought us, hate, not love, nor hope Par Lost 9.475
Brought to thir Ears, while day declin'd, they heard, Par Lost 10.99
Now had they brought the work by wondrous Art Par Lost 10.312
The evil on him brought by me, will curse Par Lost 10.734
By death brought on our selves, or childless days Par Lost 10.1037
That I who first brought Death on all, am grac't Par Lost 11.168
But this praeeminence thou hast lost, brought down Par Lost 11.347
A sweatie Reaper from his Tillage brought Par Lost 11.434
No sanctitie, if none be thither brought Par Lost 11.837
Such trouble brought, affecting to subdue Par Lost 12.81
Then that which by creation first brought forth Par Lost 12.472
With joy the tidings brought from Heav'n: at length Par Lost 12.504
Sir, what ill chance hath brought thee to this place Par Reg 1.321
To whom the Son of God. Who brought me hither Par Reg 1.335
Though ravenous, taught to abstain from what they brought: Par Reg 2.269
At his dispose, young *Scipio* had brought down Par Reg 3.34
To this high mountain top the Tempter brought Par Reg 3.265
To what end I have brought thee hither and shewn Par Reg 3.350
Long in preparing, soon to nothing brought, Par Reg 3.389
Met ever; and to shameful silence brought, Par Reg 4.22
He brought our Saviour to the western side Par Reg 4.25
Brought back the Son of God, and left him there, Par Reg 4.396
As day-light sunk, and brought in lowring night Par Reg 4.398
Have brought thee, and highest plac't, highest is best, Par Reg 4.553
And to his crew, that sat consulting, brought Par Reg 4.577
Brought on his way with joy; hee unobserv'd Par Reg 4.638
And by thir vices brought to servitude, Samson 269
But justly; I my self have brought them on, Samson 375
That I this honour, I this pomp have brought Samson 449
Among the Heathen round; to God have brought Samson 451
Of Idolists, and Atheists; have brought scandal Samson 453
That malice not repentance brought thee hither, Samson 821
Far other reasonings, brought forth other deeds. Samson 875
It hath brought forth to make thee memorable Samson 956
Had brought me to the field where thou art fam'd Samson 1094
Brought him so soon at variance with himself Samson 1585
Samson should be brought forth to shew the people Samson 1601
Was *Samson* as a public servant brought, Samson 1615
Whom therfore she brought up and *Comus* nam'd, Mask 58
To this my errand, and the care it brought. Mask 506
Brought to my mind a certain Shepherd Lad Mask 619
I have brought ye new delight, Mask 967
He brought from thence his *Israel*. Psalm 136, 42
In bloody battail he brought down Psalm 136, 61
Brought to me like *Alcestis* from the grave, Sonnet 23, 2
I wak'd, she fled, and day brought back my night. Sonnet 23, 14
Hath at length brought forth a Lie. Psalm 7, 54
A Vine from Aegypt thou hast brought, Psalm 80, 33
I am the Lord thy God which brought Psalm 81, 41
Broughtest
Against the Spiritual Foe, and broughtst him thence Par Reg 1.10
Brow
Obtains the brow of some high-climbing Hill, Par Lost 3.546
To whom thus *Satan*, with contemptuous brow. Par Lost 4.885
Fearless assault, and to the brow of Heav'n Par Lost 6.51
To whom the Angel with contracted brow. Par Lost 8.560
Thy awful brow, more awful thus retir'd. Par Lost 9.537
Distended as the Brow of God appeas'd, Par Lost 11.880

Brow(*cont*)
To whom our Saviour with unalter'd brow. Par Reg 1.493
Severest temper, smooth the rugged'st brow, Par Reg 2.164
How would one look from his Majestick brow Par Reg 2.216
Raign or raign not; though to that gentle brow Par Reg 3.215
Thus to our Saviour with stern brow reply'd. Par Reg 4.367
His habit carries peace, his brow defiance. Samson 1073
That brow this bottom glade, whence night by night Mask 532
Trinity ms 'brow' ←'brows'
Bridgewater ms 'browe'
Smoothing the rugged brow of night, Penseroso 58
To stint th' enemy, and slack th' avengers brow Psalm 8, 7
Thy smoaking wrath, *and angry brow* Psalm 80, 19
Browed
There under *Ebon* shades, and low-brow'd Rocks, Allegro 8
Brown
And brown as Evening: Cover me ye Pines, Par Lost 9.1088
High rooft and walks beneath, and alleys brown Par Reg 2.293
The field all iron cast a gleaming brown, Par Reg 3.326
Then to the Spicy Nut-brown Ale, Allegro 100
And shadows brown that *Sylvan* loves Penseroso 134
Ye Myrtles brown, with Ivy never-sear, Lycidas 2
Trinity ms 'browne'
Brows
Sat on his faded cheek, but under Browes Par Lost 1.602
ms 'browes'
The nodding horror of whose shady brows Mask 38
Bridgewater ms 'browes'
To gaze upon the Sun with shameless brows. Mask 736
Bridgewater ms 'browes'
Trinity ms 'browes'
They had their name thence; course complexions Mask 749
Trinity ms 'complexions' ←'beetle brows'
Browse
Wild Beasts there brouze, and make their food Psalm 80, 55
Bruise
Is now an Iron Rod to bruise and breake Par Lost 5.887
Her Seed shall bruse thy head, thou bruise his heel. Par Lost 10.181
1667 'bruise thy'
Eevn hee who now foretold his fatal bruise, Par Lost 10.191
Mee and Mankinde; I am to bruise his heel; Par Lost 10.498
His Seed, when is not set, shall bruise my head: Par Lost 10.499
A World who would not purchase with a bruise, Par Lost 10.500
Part of our Sentence, that thy Seed shall bruise Par Lost 10.1031
His promise, that thy Seed shall bruise our Foe; Par Lost 11.155
Is meant thy great deliverer, who shall bruise Par Lost 12.149
And shadows, of that destind Seed to bruise Par Lost 12.233
Needs must the Serpent now his capital bruise Par Lost 12.383
Thir fight, what stroke shall bruise the Victors heel. Par Lost 12.385
Satan, whose fall from Heav'n, a deadlier bruise, Par Lost 12.391
Shall bruise the head of *Satan*, crush his strength Par Lost 12.430
Then temporal death shall bruise the Victors heel, Par Lost 12.433
Bruised
Thir armor help'd thir harm, crush't in and bruis'd Par Lost 6.656
1667 'brus'd'
With Iron Scepter bruis'd, and them disperse Psalm 2, 20
That am already bruis'd, and shake Psalm 88, 59
Bruz'd, and afflicted and *so low* Psalm 88, 61
Brunt
After the brunt of battel, can as easie Samson 583
Brush
We brush mellifluous Dewes, and find the ground Par Lost 5.429
And from the Boughs brush off the evil dew, Arcades 50
Brushed
Brusht with the hiss of russling wings. As Bees Par Lost 1.768
Brutal
The Devil enterd, and his brutal sense, Par Lost 9.188
Of brutal kind, that daily are in sight? Par Lost 9.565
Brute
Oft to the Image of a Brute, adorn'd Par Lost 1.371
ms 'brute'
Maim'd his brute Image, head and hands lopt off Par Lost 1.459
And Brute as other Creatures, but endu'd Par Lost 7.507
All rational delight, wherein the brute Par Lost 8.391
My Image, not imparted to the Brute, Par Lost 8.441
Active within beyond the sense of brute. Par Lost 9.96
To brute deni'd, and are of Love the food, Par Lost 9.240
By Tongue of Brute, and human sense exprest? Par Lost 9.554
I of brute human, yee of human Gods. Par Lost 9.712
Serpent though brute, unable to transferre Par Lost 10.165
Mee not, but the brute Serpent in whose shape Par Lost 10.495
Brute violence and proud Tyrannick pow'r, Par Reg 1.219
Irrational and brute. Samson 673
The brute and boist'rous force of violent men Samson 1273
And noble grace that dash't brute violence Mask 451
With lickerish baits fit to ensnare a brute? Mask 700
line not in Bridgewater ms
And the brute Earth would lend her nerves, and shake, Mask 797
line not in Bridgewater ms
line not in Trinity ms
That had the Scepter from his father *Brute*. Mask 828
Brutish
Thir wandring Gods disguis'd in brutish forms Par Lost 1.481
Victor; though brutish that contest and foule, Par Lost 6.124
His Image whom they serv'd, a brutish vice, Par Lost 11.518
Rowling in brutish vices, and deform'd, Par Reg 3.86
A brutish monster: what if I withal Par Reg 4.128
Into som brutish form of Woolf, or Bear, Mask 70

Brutish(*cont*)
The brutish gods of *Nile* as fast, Nativity 211
Brutus
That had the Scepter from his father *Brute*. Mask 828
Brutus far to the West, in th' Ocean wide Prose 12, 7
Bubbles
Vain battry, and in froth or bubbles end; Par Reg 4.20
Bud
To visit how they prosper'd, bud and bloom, Par Lost 8.45
From the first op'ning bud, and gave ye Names, Par Lost 11.277
And every flower that sad embroidery wears: Lycidas 148
Trinity ms 'flower' ←'bud'
Ye might discern a Cipress bud. Winchester 22
But my late spring no bud or blossom shew'th. Sonnet 7, 4
Shall bud and blossom *then*, Psalm 85, 46
Budge
To those budge doctors of the *Stoick* Furr, Mask 707
Buds
Brisk as the *April* buds in Primrose-season. Mask 671
Trinity ms 'budds'
Bridgewater ms 'budds'
Buffet
And with one buffet lay thy structure low, Samson 1239
Bugs
Harpyies and *Hydra's*, or all the monstrous forms Mask 605
Bridgewater ms 'monstrous buggs'
Trinity ms 'monstrous buggs'
1637 'monstrous bugs'
Build
Of *Solomon* he led by fraud to build Par Lost 1.401
With his industrious crew to build in hell. Par Lost 1.751
Inclines, here to continue; and build up here Par Lost 2.314
New *Babels*, had they wherewithall, would build: Par Lost 3.468
O fair foundation laid whereon to build Par Lost 4.521
Through all Eternitie so late to build Par Lost 7.92
On Cliffs and Cedar tops thir Eyries build: Par Lost 7.424
The mightie frame, how build, unbuild, contrive Par Lost 8.81
Build in her loveliest, and create an awe Par Lost 8.558
For what God after better worse would build? Par Lost 9.102
Began to build a Vessel of huge bulk, Par Lost 11.729
Shall build a wondrous Ark, as thou beheldst, Par Lost 11.819
Of Brick, and of that stuff they cast to build Par Lost 12.43
Of wisest *Solomon*, and made him build, Par Reg 2.170
Home to his Fathers house: there will I build him Samson 1733
Himself to sing, and build the lofty rhyme. Lycidas 11
Builded
What thy hands builded not, thy Wisdom gain'd Par Lost 10.373
Builders
The builders next of *Babel* on the Plain Par Lost 3.466
Among the Builders; each to other calls Par Lost 12.57
Building
And hear the din; thus was the building left Par Lost 12.61
The building was a spacious Theatre Samson 1605
Builds
Deliciously, and builds her waxen Cells Par Lost 7.491
Built
We shall be free; th' Almighty hath not built Par Lost 1.259
Her Temple on th' offensive Mountain, built Par Lost 1.443
Built like a Temple, where *Pilasters* round Par Lost 1.713
To have built in Heav'n high Towrs; nor did he scape Par Lost 1.749
The suburb of thir Straw-built Cittadel, Par Lost 1.773
ms 'straw-built'
Built thir fond hopes of Glorie or lasting fame, Par Lost 3.449
Of great *Seleucia*, built by *Grecian* Kings, Par Lost 4.212
Built on circumfluous Waters calme, in wide Par Lost 7.270
The Makers high magnificence, who built Par Lost 8.101
More justly, Seat worthier of Gods, as built Par Lost 9.100
He effected; Man he made, and for him built Par Lost 9.152
Heroic built, though of terrestrial mould, Par Lost 9.485
Of him who built the Ark, who for the shame Par Lost 12.102
His living Temples, built by Faith to stand, Par Lost 12.527
In pastry built, or from the spit, or boyl'd, Par Reg 2.343
Several days journey, built by *Ninus* old, Par Reg 3.276
Built by *Emathian*, or by *Parthian* hands, Par Reg 3.290
Built nobly, pure the air, and light the soil, Par Reg 4.239
Conjectures, fancies, built on nothing firm. Par Reg 4.292
Haughty as is his pile high-built and proud. Samson 1069
And earths base built on stubble. But com let's on. Mask 599
Built in th' eclipse, and rigg'd with curses dark, Lycidas 101
Hast built thy self a live-long Monument. Shakespear 8
Hath built her *brooding* nest, Psalm 84, 12
Bulk
Lay floating many a rood, in bulk as huge Par Lost 1.196
And bended Dolphins play: part huge of bulk Par Lost 7.410
Began to build a Vessel of huge bulk, Par Lost 11.729
Though in these chains, bulk without spirit vast, Samson 1238
Bull
Dodg'd with him, betwixt *Cambridge* and the Bull. Carrier 8
1658 '*London-Bull*'
Bullion
Severing each kind, and scum'd the Bullion dross: Par Lost 1.704
ms 'bullion'
Bullock
Oft sacrificing Bullock, Lamb, or Kid, Par Lost 12.20
Bulls
Indulgences, Dispenses, Pardons, Bulls, Par Lost 3.492
The bloud of Bulls and Goats, they may conclude Par Lost 12.292
And fat regorg'd of Bulls and Goats, Samson 1671

Bulwark
Your bulwark, and condemns to greatest share Par Lost 2.29
Burden
A growing burden. Mean while Warr arose, Par Lost 2.767
Indebted and dischargd; what burden then? Par Lost 4.57
Shall tend thee, and the fertil burden ease Par Lost 9.801
That burden heavier then the Earth to bear Par Lost 10.835
Each others burden in our share of woe; Par Lost 10.961
The burd'n of many Ages, on me light Par Lost 11.767
When on his shoulders each mans burden lies; Par Reg 2.462
Enough, and more the burden of that fault; Samson 431
That with superfluous burden loads the day, Sonnet 21, 13
From burden, *and from slavish toyle* Psalm 81, 21
Burdened
Not burd'nd Nature, sudden mind arose Par Lost 5.452
Burdenous
A burdenous drone; to visitants a gaze, Samson 567
Burdensome
So burthensome still paying, still to ow; Par Lost 4.53
Of wisdom, vast, unwieldy, burdensom, Samson 54
And lack of load, made his life burdensom, Another 24
line not in 1658 text
1640, 1657 'burdensome'
Burgher
Of some rich Burgher, whose substantial dores, Par Lost 4.189
Burial
By priviledge of death and burial Samson 104
Had burial, yet not laid in earth, Winchester 32
Buried
Under the weight of Mountains buried deep, Par Lost 6.652
And buried; but O yet more miserable! Samson 101
Buried, yet not exempt Samson 103
Burn
For one of *Syrian* mode, whereon to burn Par Lost 1.474
The World shall burn, and from her ashes spring Par Lost 3.334
And from within the golden Lamps that burne Par Lost 5.713
As wantonly repaid; in Lust they burne: Par Lost 9.1015
Of two bright Cherubim, before him burn Par Lost 12.254
But rob and spoil, burn, slaughter, and enslave Par Reg 3.75
Burn in your sighs, and borrow Circum 8
Trinity ms 'burne'
Far worse then fire to burn. Psalm 85, 12
Burned
He lights, if it were Land that ever burn'd Par Lost 1.228
Thir painful steps o're the burnt soyle; and now Par Lost 1.562
Unterrifi'd, and like a Comet burn'd, Par Lost 2.708
Burnt after them to the bottomless pit. Par Lost 6.866
From off the Altar, where an Off'ring burn'd, Samson 26
Burning
With ever-burning Sulphur unconsum'd: Par Lost 1.69
Chain'd on the burning Lake, nor ever thence Par Lost 1.210
Over the burning Marle, not like those steps Par Lost 1.296
Chain'd on the burning Lake? that sure was worse. Par Lost 2.169
Ninefold, and gates of burning Adamant Par Lost 2.436
Into the burning Lake thir baleful streams; Par Lost 2.576
Gloomie as Night; under his burning Wheeles Par Lost 6.832
Then his bright Throne, or burning Axletree could bear. Nativity 84
His burning Idol all of blackest hue, Nativity 207
Where the bright Seraphim in burning row Musick 10
Trinity ms 'burning' ←'triple' ←'tripled' ←'princely' ←'princly'
Burnished
Others whose fruit burnisht with Golden Rinde Par Lost 4.249
With burnisht Neck of verdant Gold, erect Par Lost 9.501
Toward Heav'ns descent had slop'd his westering wheel. Lycidas 31
Trinity ms 'westring' ←'burnisht'
1638 'burnisht wheel'
Burns
From either end of Heav'n the welkin burns. Par Lost 2.538
Burns frore, and cold performs th' effect of Fire. Par Lost 2.595
But the hot Hell that alwayes in him burnes, Par Lost 9.467
Of mid-night Torches burns; mysterious Dame Mask 130
Trinity ms 'burnes'
Bridgewater ms 'burne'
Burs
From the chill dew, amongst rude burrs and thistles? Mask 352
Trinity ms 'amoungst rude burrs & thistles' ←'in this surrounding wilde' ←'in this dead solitude'
1637 'burs'
Burst
Tears such as Angels weep, burst forth: at last Par Lost 1.620
On what was pure, till cramm'd and gorg'd, nigh burst Par Lost 10.632
Burst forth, and in Celestial measures mov'd, Par Reg 1.170
Mess. It would burst forth, but I recover breath Samson 1555
The whole roof after them, with burst of thunder Samson 1651
And think to burst out into sudden blaze, Lycidas 74
Bursting
My Bowels, thir repast; then bursting forth Par Lost 2.800
Bursting with kindly rupture forth disclos'd Par Lost 7.419
His bursting passion into plaints thus pour'd: Par Lost 9.98
Bursting thir brazen Dungeon, armd with ice Par Lost 10.697
Bush
And Bush with frizl'd hair implicit: last Par Lost 7.323
In every Bush and Brake, where hap may finde Par Lost 9.160
Clear'd up their choicest notes in bush and spray Par Reg 4.437
Bushes
Of shrubs and tangling bushes had perplext Par Lost 4.176

Bushing	
Half spi'd, so thick the Roses bushing round	Par Lost 9.426
Bushy	
Acanthus, and each odorous bushie shrub	Par Lost 4.696
Dingle, or bushy dell of this wilde Wood,	Mask 312
Trinity ms 'bushie'	
Bridgewater ms 'bushie'	
1637 'bushie'	
Busied	
How busied, in what form and posture coucht.	Par Lost 4.876
To lure her Eye; shee busied heard the sound	Par Lost 9.518
Busiest	
Tended the sick busiest from Couch to Couch;	Par Lost 11.490
Business	
By right of Warr, what e're his business be	Par Lost 1.150
ms 'buis'nesse'	
Whose easier business were to serve thir Lord	Par Lost 4.943
His Father's business; what he meant I mus'd,	Par Reg 2.99
But to my task. *Neptune* besides the sway	Mask 18
Trinity ms 'taske' ←'buisnesse now'	
And hearken, if I may, her busines here.	Mask 169
Bridgewater ms 'businesse'	
1637 'buisnesse'	
Trinity ms 'buisnesse'	
But now my task is smoothly don,	Mask 1012
Trinity ms 'taske' ←'buisnesse' ←'message'	
Then quick about thy purpos'd business come,	Vacation 57
Busiris	
Busiris and his *Memphian* Chivalry,	Par Lost 1.307
ms 'Busiris'	
Buskined	
Ennobled hath the Buskind stage.	Penseroso 102
Fair silver-buskind Nymphs as great and good,	Arcades 33
1673 'silver-buskin'd'	
Trinity ms 'silver-buskin'd'	
Bustle	
That in the various bussle of resort	Mask 379
1637 'bustle'	
Trinity ms 'bustle'	
Busy	
And the busie humm of men,	Allegro 118
Was all that did their silly thoughts so busie keep.	Nativity 92
But	
Confounded though immortal: But his doom	Par Lost 1.53
No light, but rather darkness visible	Par Lost 1.63
That comes to all; but torture without end	Par Lost 1.67
If thou beest he; But O how fall'n! how chang'd	Par Lost 1.84
Vaunting aloud, but rackt with deep despare:	Par Lost 1.126
But what if he our Conquerour, (whom I now	Par Lost 1.143
Doing or Suffering: but of this be sure,	Par Lost 1.158
But ever to do ill our sole delight,	Par Lost 1.160
But see the angry Victor hath recall'd	Par Lost 1.169
Had ris'n or heav'd his head, but that the will	Par Lost 1.211
How all his malice serv'd but to bring forth	Par Lost 1.217
On Man by him seduc't, but on himself	Par Lost 1.219
And what I should be, all but less then he	Par Lost 1.257
But wherefore let we then our faithful friends,	Par Lost 1.264
Which but th' Omnipotent none could have foyld,	Par Lost 1.273
Of some great Ammiral, were but a wand,	Par Lost 1.294
Like cumbrous flesh; but in what shape they choose	Par Lost 1.428
All these and more came flocking; but with looks	Par Lost 1.522
Like doubtful hue: but he his wonted pride	Par Lost 1.527
Above them all th' Arch Angel: but his face	Par Lost 1.600
Sat on his faded cheek, but under Browes	Par Lost 1.602
Waiting revenge: cruel his eye, but cast	Par Lost 1.604
Matchless, but with th' Almighty, and that strife	Par Lost 1.623
Hateful to utter: but what power of mind	Par Lost 1.626
By mee, have lost our hopes. But he who reigns	Par Lost 1.637
Put forth at full, but still his strength conceal'd,	Par Lost 1.641
By force, hath overcome but half his foe.	Par Lost 1.649
Thither, if but to pry, shall be perhaps	Par Lost 1.655
Long under darkness cover. But these thoughts	Par Lost 1.659
By all his Engins, but was headlong sent	Par Lost 1.750
And Porches wide, but chief the spacious Hall	Par Lost 1.762
Behold a wonder! they but now who seemd	Par Lost 1.777
Of that infernal Court. But far within	Par Lost 1.792
Envy from each inferior; but who here	Par Lost 2.26
His own invented Torments. But perhaps	Par Lost 2.70
To us is adverse. Who but felt of late	Par Lost 2.77
But all was false and hollow; though his Tongue	Par Lost 2.112
To vice industrious, but to Nobler deeds	Par Lost 2.116
For happy though but ill, for ill not worst,	Par Lost 2.224
Of splendid vassalage, but rather seek	Par Lost 2.252
Banded against his Throne, but to remaine	Par Lost 2.320
By our revolt, but over Hell extend	Par Lost 2.326
To us enslav'd, but custody severe,	Par Lost 2.333
But to our power hostility and hate,	Par Lost 2.336
In power and excellence, but favour'd more	Par Lost 2.350
But from the Author of all ill could Spring	Par Lost 2.381
The great Creatour? But thir spite still serves	Par Lost 2.385
Shall breathe her balme. But first whom shall we send	Par Lost 2.402
The perilous attempt: but all sat mute,	Par Lost 2.420
But I should ill become this Throne, O Peers,	Par Lost 2.445
Which he through hazard huge must earn. But they	Par Lost 2.473
Thir Song was partial, but the harmony	Par Lost 2.552
Thaws not, but gathers heap, and ruin seems	Par Lost 2.590
But Fate withstands, and to oppose th' attempt	Par Lost 2.610
But ended foul in many a scaly fould	Par Lost 2.651

But(*cont*)	
For never but once more was either like	Par Lost 2.721
Portentous held me; but familiar grown,	Par Lost 2.761
Alone, but long I sat not, till my womb	Par Lost 2.778
Transform'd: but he my inbred enemie	Par Lost 2.785
I fled, but he pursu'd (though more, it seems,	Par Lost 2.790
For want of other prey, but that he knows	Par Lost 2.806
But thou O Father, I forewarn thee, shun	Par Lost 2.810
I come no enemie, but to set free	Par Lost 2.822
But what ow I to his commands above	Par Lost 2.856
But thee, whom follow? thou wilt bring me soon	Par Lost 2.866
Which but her self not all the *Stygian* powers	Par Lost 2.875
Of *Erebus*. She op'nd, but to shut	Par Lost 2.883
But all these in thir pregnant causes mixt	Par Lost 2.913
Audacious, but that seat soon failing, meets	Par Lost 2.931
The secrets of your Realm, but by constraint	Par Lost 2.972
But glad that now his Sea should find a shore,	Par Lost 2.1011
But hee once past, soon after when man fell,	Par Lost 2.1023
But now at last the sacred influence	Par Lost 2.1034
And never but in unapproached light	Par Lost 3.4
And feel thy sovran vital Lamp; but thou	Par Lost 3.22
Smit with the love of sacred Song; but chief	Par Lost 3.29
Seasons return, but not to me returns	Par Lost 3.41
But cloud in stead, and ever-during dark	Par Lost 3.45
Whose but his own? ingrate, he had of mee	Par Lost 3.97
But Mercy first and last shall brightest shine.	Par Lost 3.134
Man shall not quite be lost, but sav'd who will,	Par Lost 3.173
Yet not of will in him, but grace in me	Par Lost 3.174
All his deliv'rance, and to none but me.	Par Lost 3.182
Though but endevord with sincere intent,	Par Lost 3.192
But hard be hard'nd, blind be blinded more,	Par Lost 3.200
And none but such from mercy I exclude.	Par Lost 3.202
But yet all is not don; Man disobeying,	Par Lost 3.203
But to destruction sacred and devote,	Par Lost 3.208
He ask'd, but all the Heav'nly Quire stood mute,	Par Lost 3.217
But I shall rise Victorious, and subdue	Par Lost 3.250
Of anger shall remain, but peace assur'd,	Par Lost 3.263
Thenceforth, but in thy presence Joy entire.	Par Lost 3.265
His words here ended, but his meek aspect	Par Lost 3.266
Wondring; but soon th' Almighty thus reply'd:	Par Lost 3.273
God shall be All in All. But all ye Gods,	Par Lost 3.341
No sooner had th' Almighty ceas't, but all	Par Lost 3.344
Began to bloom, but soon for mans offence	Par Lost 3.355
No voice exempt, no voice but well could joine	Par Lost 3.370
Thron'd inaccessible, but when thou shad'st	Par Lost 3.377
Approach not, but with both wings veil thir eyes.	Par Lost 3.382
So strictly, but much more to pitie encline:	Par Lost 3.402
So strictly, but much more to pitie enclin'd,	Par Lost 3.405
But in his way lights on the barren Plaines	Par Lost 3.437
None yet, but store hereafter from the earth	Par Lost 3.444
Naught seeking but the praise of men, here find	Par Lost 3.453
At top whereof, but farr more rich appeerd	Par Lost 3.504
There alwayes, but drawn up to Heav'n somtimes	Par Lost 3.517
The Spirit maligne, but much more envy seis'd	Par Lost 3.553
Stars distant, but nigh hand seemd other Worlds,	Par Lost 3.566
Thrice happy Iles, but who dwelt happy there	Par Lost 3.570
Through the calm Firmament; but up or downe	Par Lost 3.574
Not all parts like, but all alike informd	Par Lost 3.593
But all Sun-shine, as when his Beams at Noon	Par Lost 3.616
His back was turnd, but not his brightness hid;	Par Lost 3.624
But first he casts to change his proper shape,	Par Lost 3.634
All these his wondrous works, but chiefly Man,	Par Lost 3.663
But all these shining Orbes his choice to dwell;	Par Lost 3.670
That reaches blame, but rather merits praise	Par Lost 3.697
But what created mind can comprehend	Par Lost 3.705
That brought them forth, but hid thir causes deep.	Par Lost 3.707
With light from hence, though but reflected, shines;	Par Lost 3.723
Night would invade, but there the neighbouring Moon	Par Lost 3.726
But with no friendly voice, and add thy name	Par Lost 4.36
And wrought but malice; lifted up so high	Par Lost 4.49
By owing owes not, but still pays, at once	Par Lost 4.56
Drawn to his part; but other Powers as great	Par Lost 4.63
Fell not, but stand unshak'n, from within	Par Lost 4.64
But Heav'ns free Love dealt equally to all?	Par Lost 4.68
None left but by submission; and that word	Par Lost 4.81
But say I could repent and could obtaine	Par Lost 4.93
Which would but lead me to a worse relapse	Par Lost 4.100
All sadness but despair: now gentle gales	Par Lost 4.156
But further way found none, so thick entwin'd,	Par Lost 4.174
Thereby regaind, but sat devising Death	Par Lost 4.197
Of that life-giving Plant, but only us'd	Par Lost 4.199
Any, but God alone, to value right	Par Lost 4.202
The good before him, but perverts best things	Par Lost 4.203
Nor chang'd his course, but through the shaggie hill	Par Lost 4.224
But rather to tell how, if Art could tell,	Par Lost 4.236
In Beds and curious Knots, but Nature boon	Par Lost 4.242
A whole days journy high, but wide remote	Par Lost 4.284
Severe but in true filial freedom plac't;	Par Lost 4.294
Clustring, but not beneath his shoulders broad:	Par Lost 4.303
Dissheveld, but in wanton ringlets wav'd	Par Lost 4.306
Subjection, but requir'd with gentle sway,	Par Lost 4.308
Happie, but for so happie ill secur'd	Par Lost 4.370
But let us ever praise him, and extoll	Par Lost 4.436
It started back, but pleas'd I soon returnd,	Par Lost 4.463
With thee it came and goes: but follow me,	Par Lost 4.469
But follow strait, invisibly thus led?	Par Lost 4.476
Where neither joy nor love, but fierce desire,	Par Lost 4.509
But first with narrow search I must walk round	Par Lost 4.528

But(*cont*)

A chance but chance may lead where I may meet	Par Lost 4.530
But with sly circumspection, and began	Par Lost 4.537
Th' unarmed Youth of Heav'n, but nigh at hand	Par Lost 4.552
But in the Mount that lies from *Eden* North,	Par Lost 4.569
Mine eye pursu'd him still, but under shade	Par Lost 4.572
The vigilance here plac't, but such as come	Par Lost 4.580
But if within the circuit of these walks,	Par Lost 4.586
Were slunk, all but the wakeful Nightingale;	Par Lost 4.602
But neither breath of Morn when she ascends	Par Lost 4.650
But wherfore all night long shine these, for whom	Par Lost 4.657
Not only enlighten, but with kindly heate	Par Lost 4.668
More sacred and sequesterd, though but feignd,	Par Lost 4.706
But thou hast promis'd from us two a Race	Par Lost 4.732
Observing none, but adoration pure	Par Lost 4.737
But our destroyer, foe to God and Man?	Par Lost 4.749
But chiefly where those two fair Creatures Lodge,	Par Lost 4.790
Touch of Celestial temper, but returns	Par Lost 4.812
But come, for thou, besure, shalt give account	Par Lost 4.841
His loss; but chiefly to find here observd	Par Lost 4.849
But like a proud Steed reind, went hautie on,	Par Lost 4.858
But faded splendor wan; who by his gate	Par Lost 4.870
By thy example, but have power and right	Par Lost 4.881
And such I held thee; but this question askt	Par Lost 4.887
But evil hast not tri'd: and wilt object	Par Lost 4.896
But that implies not violence or harme.	Par Lost 4.901
But wherefore thou alone? wherefore with thee	Par Lost 4.917
But still thy words at random, as before,	Par Lost 4.930
Argues no Leader but a lyar trac't,	Par Lost 4.949
Heav'ns awful Monarch? wherefore but in hope	Par Lost 4.960
But mark what I arreede thee now, avant;	Par Lost 4.962
So threatn'd hee, but *Satan* to no threats	Par Lost 4.968
Gave heed, but waxing more in rage repli'd.	Par Lost 4.969
Proud limitarie Cherube, but ere then	Par Lost 4.971
In this commotion, but the Starrie Cope	Par Lost 4.992
Neither our own but giv'n; what follie then	Par Lost 4.1007
His mounted scale aloft: nor more; but fled	Par Lost 4.1014
Such whispering wak'd her, but with startl'd eye	Par Lost 5.26
But of offence and trouble, which my mind	Par Lost 5.34
Whom to behold but thee, Natures desire,	Par Lost 5.45
I rose as at thy call, but found thee not;	Par Lost 5.48
This said he paus'd not, but with ventrous Arme	Par Lost 5.64
But he thus overjoy'd, O Fruit Divine,	Par Lost 5.67
Sweet of thy self, but much more sweet thus cropt,	Par Lost 5.68
The Author not impair'd, but honourd more?	Par Lost 5.73
But somtimes in the Air, as wee, somtimes	Par Lost 5.79
Could not but taste. Forthwith up to the Clouds	Par Lost 5.86
And fell asleep; but O how glad I wak'd	Par Lost 5.92
To find this but a dream! Thus *Eve* her Night	Par Lost 5.93
Created pure. But know that in the Soule	Par Lost 5.100
To imitate her; but misjoyning shapes,	Par Lost 5.111
But with addition strange; yet be not sad.	Par Lost 5.116
But silently a gentle tear let fall	Par Lost 5.130
But first from under shadie arborous roof,	Par Lost 5.137
But by deceit and lies; this let him know,	Par Lost 5.243
After his charge receivd; but from among	Par Lost 5.248
This day to be our Guest. But goe with speed,	Par Lost 5.313
But I will haste and from each bough and break,	Par Lost 5.326
Tastes, not well joynd, inelegant, but bring	Par Lost 5.335
With flourets deck't and fragrant smells; but *Eve*	Par Lost 5.379
Of Theologians, but with keen dispatch	Par Lost 5.436
Enamour'd at that sight; but in those hearts	Par Lost 5.448
But more refin'd, more spiritous, and pure,	Par Lost 5.475
Differing but in degree, of kind the same.	Par Lost 5.490
If I refuse not, but convert, as you,	Par Lost 5.492
By steps we may ascend to God. But say,	Par Lost 5.512
And good he made thee, but to persevere	Par Lost 5.525
Willing or no, who will but what they must	Par Lost 5.533
But more desire to hear, if thou consent,	Par Lost 5.555
Be but the shaddow of Heav'n, and things therein	Par Lost 5.575
All seemd well pleas'd, all seem'd, but were not all	Par Lost 5.617
All but the unsleeping eyes of God to rest,	Par Lost 5.647
Alternate all night long: but not so wak'd	Par Lost 5.657
Or taint integritie; but all obey'd	Par Lost 5.704
So spake the Son, but *Satan* with his Powers	Par Lost 5.743
Too much to one, but double how endur'd,	Par Lost 5.783
But what if better counsels might erect	Par Lost 5.785
Jarr not with liberty, but well consist.	Par Lost 5.793
United. But to grant it thee unjust,	Par Lost 5.831
But more illustrious made, since he the Head	Par Lost 5.842
And tempt not these; but hast'n to appease	Par Lost 5.846
So spake the fervent Angel, but his zeale	Par Lost 5.849
Aspirer, but thir thoughts prov'd fond and vain	Par Lost 6.90
Hymning th' Eternal Father: but the shout	Par Lost 6.96
'Twixt Host and Host but narrow space was left,	Par Lost 6.104
Unsound and false; nor is it aught but just,	Par Lost 6.121
Thy Legions under darkness; but thou seest	Par Lost 6.142
Thus answerd. Ill for thee, but in wisht houre	Par Lost 6.150
Omnipotence to none. But well thou comst	Par Lost 6.159
To heav'nly Soules had bin all one; but now	Par Lost 6.165
Thy self not free, but to thy self enthrall'd;	Par Lost 6.181
Which hung not, but so swift with tempest fell	Par Lost 6.190
The Rebel Thrones, but greater rage to see	Par Lost 6.199
Were don, but infinite: for wide was spred	Par Lost 6.241
And faithful, now prov'd false. But think not here	Par Lost 6.271
To flight, or if to fall, but that they rise	Par Lost 6.285
The strife which thou call'st evil, but wee style	Par Lost 6.289
I flie not, but have sought thee farr and nigh.	Par Lost 6.295

But(*cont*)

In might or swift prevention; but the sword	Par Lost 6.320
But with swift wheele reverse, deep entring shar'd	Par Lost 6.326
Pass'd through him, but th' Ethereal substance clos'd	Par Lost 6.330
Cannot but by annihilating die;	Par Lost 6.347
Refrein'd his tongue blasphemous; but anon	Par Lost 6.360
Disdain'd, but meaner thoughts learnd in thir flight,	Par Lost 6.367
The Atheist crew, but with redoubl'd blow	Par Lost 6.370
Eternize here on Earth; but those elect	Par Lost 6.374
Illaudable, naught merits but dispraise	Par Lost 6.382
Too mean pretense, but what we more affect,	Par Lost 6.421
But proves not so: then fallible, it seems,	Par Lost 6.428
Till now not known, but known as soon contemnd,	Par Lost 6.432
But live content, which is the calmest life:	Par Lost 6.461
But pain is perfet miserie, the worst	Par Lost 6.462
But firm Battalion; back with speediest Sail	Par Lost 6.534
But ratling storm of Arrows barbd with fire.	Par Lost 6.546
A while, but suddenly at head appeerd	Par Lost 6.556
But that I doubt, however witness Heaven,	Par Lost 6.563
But soon obscur'd with smoak, all Heav'n appeerd,	Par Lost 6.585
Though standing else as Rocks, but down they fell	Par Lost 6.593
By quick contraction or remove; but now	Par Lost 6.597
For joy of offerd peace: but I suppose	Par Lost 6.617
A while in trouble; but they stood not long,	Par Lost 6.634
Of ending this great Warr, since none but Thou	Par Lost 6.702
But whom thou hat'st, I hate, and can put on	Par Lost 6.734
It self instinct with Spirit, but convoyd	Par Lost 6.752
Illustrious farr and wide, but by his own	Par Lost 6.773
This saw his hapless Foes but stood obdur'd,	Par Lost 6.785
But to convince the proud what Signs availe,	Par Lost 6.789
Invincibly; but of this cursed crew	Par Lost 6.806
By mee, not you but mee they have despis'd,	Par Lost 6.812
All but the Throne it self of God. Full soon	Par Lost 6.834
Yet half his strength he put not forth, but check'd	Par Lost 6.853
Not to destroy, but root them out of Heav'n:	Par Lost 6.855
Strook them with horror backward, but far worse	Par Lost 6.863
Affrighted; but strict Fate had cast too deep	Par Lost 6.869
But list'n not to his Temptations, warne	Par Lost 6.908
Of old *Olympus* dwell'st, but Heav'nlie borne,	Par Lost 7.7
Half yet remaines unsung, but narrower bound	Par Lost 7.21
But drive farr off the barbarous dissonance	Par Lost 7.32
With such confusion: but the evil soon	Par Lost 7.56
Of what we are. But since thou hast voutsaf't	Par Lost 7.80
Of his Eternal Empire, but the more	Par Lost 7.96
But Knowledge is as food, and needs no less	Par Lost 7.126
But least his heart exalt him in the harme	Par Lost 7.150
Then time or motion, but to human ears	Par Lost 7.177
Nor staid, but on the Wings of Cherubim	Par Lost 7.218
Cover'd th' Abyss: but on the watrie calme	Par Lost 7.234
Throughout the fluid Mass, but downward purg'd	Par Lost 7.237
The Earth was form'd, but in the Womb as yet	Par Lost 7.276
Main Ocean flow'd, not idle, but with warme	Par Lost 7.279
But they, or under ground, or circuit wide	Par Lost 7.301
All but within those banks, where Rivers now	Par Lost 7.305
None was, but from the Earth a dewie Mist	Par Lost 7.333
But opposite in leveld West was set	Par Lost 7.376
Thir callow young, but featherd soon and fledge	Par Lost 7.420
Ceas'd warbling, but all night tun'd her soft layes:	Par Lost 7.436
Not noxious, but obedient at thy call.	Par Lost 7.498
And Brute as other Creatures, but endu'd	Par Lost 7.507
But grateful to acknowledge whence his good	Par Lost 7.512
Male he created thee, but thy consort	Par Lost 7.529
Varietie without end; but of the Tree	Par Lost 7.542
But not in silence holy kept; the Harp	Par Lost 7.594
Thy Thunders magnifi'd; but to create	Par Lost 7.606
Of destind habitation; but thou know'st	Par Lost 7.622
With wonder, but delight, and, as is due,	Par Lost 8.11
But in the fruitful Earth; there first receavd	Par Lost 8.96
Officious, but to thee Earths habitant.	Par Lost 8.99
By Numbers that have name. But this I urge,	Par Lost 8.114
But whether thus these things, or whether not,	Par Lost 8.159
Not of Earth onely but of highest Heav'n.	Par Lost 8.178
But apt the Mind or Fancie is to roave	Par Lost 8.188
From use, obscure and suttle, but to know	Par Lost 8.192
Though pleasant, but thy words with Grace Divine	Par Lost 8.215
But us he sends upon his high behests	Par Lost 8.238
But long ere our approaching heard within	Par Lost 8.242
But thy relation now; for I attend,	Par Lost 8.247
But who I was, or where, or from what cause,	Par Lost 8.270
Presence Divine. Rejoycing, but with aw	Par Lost 8.314
But of the Tree whose operation brings	Par Lost 8.323
Not to incur; but soon his cleer aspect	Par Lost 8.336
Not onely these fair bounds, but all the Earth	Par Lost 8.338
My sudden apprehension: but in these	Par Lost 8.354
Thou hast provided all things: but with mee	Par Lost 8.363
Giv'n and receiv'd; but in disparitie	Par Lost 8.386
Cannot well suite with either, but soon prove	Par Lost 8.388
But in degree, the cause of his desire	Par Lost 8.417
But Man by number is to manifest	Par Lost 8.422
Which thou hast rightly nam'd, but of thy self,	Par Lost 8.439
Mine eyes he clos'd, but op'n left the Cell	Par Lost 8.460
But suddenly with flesh fill'd up and heal'd:	Par Lost 8.468
Manlike, but different Sex, so lovly faire,	Par Lost 8.471
Giver of all things faire, but fairest this	Par Lost 8.493
Not obvious, not obtrusive, but retir'd,	Par Lost 8.504
In all things else delight indeed, but such	Par Lost 8.524
Walks, and the melodie of Birds; but here	Par Lost 8.528
Do thou but thine, and be not diffident	Par Lost 8.562

But(*cont*)

But if the sense of touch whereby mankind	Par Lost 8.579
But I can now no more; the parting Sun	Par Lost 8.630
Be strong, live happie, and love, but first of all	Par Lost 8.633
Not less but more Heroic then the wrauth	Par Lost 9.14
Thus he resolv'd, but first from inward griefe	Par Lost 9.97
Rocks, Dens, and Caves; but I in none of these	Par Lost 9.118
But neither here seek I, no nor in Heav'n	Par Lost 9.124
By what I seek, but others to make such	Par Lost 9.127
But what will not Ambition and Revenge	Par Lost 9.168
Nor nocent yet, but on the grassie Herbe	Par Lost 9.186
With act intelligential; but his sleep	Par Lost 9.190
Our pleasant task enjoyn'd, but till more hands	Par Lost 9.207
For not to irksom toile, but to delight	Par Lost 9.242
These paths & Bowers doubt not but our joynt hands	Par Lost 9.244
Assist us: But if much converse perhaps	Par Lost 9.247
But other doubt possesses me, least harm	Par Lost 9.251
But that thou shouldst my firmness therfore doubt	Par Lost 9.279
Thy absence from my sight, but to avoid	Par Lost 9.294
And Matrimonial Love; but *Eve*, who thought	Par Lost 9.319
But harm precedes not sin: onely our Foe	Par Lost 9.327
Sticks no dishonor on our Front, but turns	Par Lost 9.330
But God left free the Will, for what obeyes	Par Lost 9.351
But bid her well beware, and still erect,	Par Lost 9.353
Not then mistrust, but tender love enjoynes,	Par Lost 9.357
But if thou think, trial unsought may finde	Par Lost 9.370
So spake the Patriarch of Mankinde, but *Eve*	Par Lost 9.376
Betook her to the Groves, but *Delia*'s self	Par Lost 9.388
But with such Gardning Tools as Art yet rude,	Par Lost 9.391
Delighted, but desiring more her stay.	Par Lost 9.398
The onely two of Mankinde, but in them	Par Lost 9.415
He sought them both, but wish'd his hap might find	Par Lost 9.421
Eve separate, he wish'd, but not with hope	Par Lost 9.422
Angelic, but more soft, and Feminine,	Par Lost 9.458
But the hot Hell that alwayes in him burnes,	Par Lost 9.467
Of pleasure, but all pleasure to destroy,	Par Lost 9.477
Prone on the ground, as since, but on his reare,	Par Lost 9.497
At first, as one who sought access, but feard	Par Lost 9.511
Of rusling Leaves, but minded not, as us'd	Par Lost 9.519
But as in gaze admiring: Oft he bowd	Par Lost 9.524
Where universally admir'd; but here	Par Lost 9.542
I knew, but not with human voice endu'd;	Par Lost 9.561
As was my food, nor aught but food discern'd	Par Lost 9.573
Longing and envying stood, but could not reach.	Par Lost 9.593
But all that fair and good in thy Divine	Par Lost 9.606
But say, where grows the Tree, from hence how far?	Par Lost 9.617
But of this Tree we may not taste nor touch;	Par Lost 9.651
But of the Fruit of this fair Tree amidst	Par Lost 9.661
The Tempter, but with shew of Zeale and Love	Par Lost 9.665
Things in thir Causes, but to trace the wayes	Par Lost 9.682
Why then was this forbid? Why but to awe,	Par Lost 9.703
Why but to keep ye low and ignorant,	Par Lost 9.704
Yet are but dim, shall perfetly be then	Par Lost 9.707
Internal Man, is but proportion meet,	Par Lost 9.711
Forbids us then to taste, but his forbidding	Par Lost 9.753
In plain then, what forbids he but to know,	Par Lost 9.758
Such prohibitions binde not. But if Death	Par Lost 9.760
Hath tasted, envies not, but brings with joy	Par Lost 9.770
Created; but henceforth my early care,	Par Lost 9.799
About him. But to *Adam* in what sort	Par Lost 9.816
But keep the odds of Knowledge in my power	Par Lost 9.820
This may be well: but what if God have seen,	Par Lost 9.826
But first low Reverence don, as to the power	Par Lost 9.835
The pain of absence from thy sight. But strange	Par Lost 9.861
Op'ning the way, but of Divine effect	Par Lost 9.865
Not dead, as we are threatn'd, but thenceforth	Par Lost 9.870
But in her Cheek distemper flushing glowd.	Par Lost 9.887
But past who can recall, or don undoe?	Par Lost 9.926
But to be Gods, or Angels Demi-gods.	Par Lost 9.937
Ingaging me to emulate, but short	Par Lost 9.963
So faithful Love unequald; but I feel	Par Lost 9.983
Farr otherwise th' event, not Death, but Life	Par Lost 9.984
But fondly overcome with Femal charm.	Par Lost 9.999
Wherewith to scorne the Earth: but that false Fruit	Par Lost 9.1011
But come, so well refresh't, now let us play,	Par Lost 9.1027
To guiltie shame hee cover'd, but his Robe	Par Lost 9.1058
But let us now, as in bad plight, devise	Par Lost 9.1091
But such as at this day to *Indians* known	Par Lost 9.1102
Coverd, but not at rest or ease of Mind,	Par Lost 9.1120
Raind at thir Eyes, but high Winds worse within	Par Lost 9.1122
But might as ill have happ'nd thou being by,	Par Lost 9.1147
But confidence then bore thee on, secure	Par Lost 9.1175
No evil durst attempt thee, but I rue	Par Lost 9.1180
The fruitless hours, but neither self-condemning,	Par Lost 9.1188
In eevn scale. But fall'n he is, and now	Par Lost 10.47
What rests but that the mortal Sentence pass	Par Lost 10.48
By some immediate stroak; but soon shall find	Par Lost 10.52
But whom send I to judge them? whom but thee	Par Lost 10.55
On Earth these thy transgressors, but thou knowst	Par Lost 10.72
Are to behold the Judgment, but the judg'd,	Par Lost 10.81
Or to each other, but apparent guilt,	Par Lost 10.112
But still rejoyc't, how is it now become	Par Lost 10.120
By my complaint; but strict necessitie	Par Lost 10.131
Superior, or but equal, that to her	Par Lost 10.147
Of Beasts, but inward nakedness, much more	Par Lost 10.221
But that success attends him; if mishap,	Par Lost 10.239
But least the difficultie of passing back	Par Lost 10.252
Be wanting, but afford thee equal aid,	Par Lost 10.271

But(*cont*)

Disguis'd he came, but those his Children dear	Par Lost 10.330
Vain covertures; but when he saw descend	Par Lost 10.337
Hee fled, not hoping to escape, but shun	Par Lost 10.339
Not instant, but of future time. With joy	Par Lost 10.345
Now also evidence, but straight I felt	Par Lost 10.361
To expedite your glorious march; but I	Par Lost 10.474
Mee not, but the brute Serpent in whose shape	Par Lost 10.495
But up and enter now into full bliss.	Par Lost 10.503
Of public scorn; he wonderd, but not long	Par Lost 10.509
Reluctant, but in vaine, a greater power	Par Lost 10.515
But hiss for hiss returnd with forked tongue	Par Lost 10.518
Ophiusa) but still greatest hee the midst,	Par Lost 10.528
They saw, but other sight instead, a crowd	Par Lost 10.538
But on thy rould in heaps, and up the Trees	Par Lost 10.558
This more delusive, not the touch, but taste	Par Lost 10.563
Outrage from liveless things; but Discord first	Par Lost 10.707
Of Man, but fled him, or with count'nance grim	Par Lost 10.713
To sorrow abandond, but worse felt within,	Par Lost 10.717
My own deservings; but this will not serve;	Par Lost 10.727
Or multiplie, but curses on my head?	Par Lost 10.732
Who of all Ages to succeed, but feeling	Par Lost 10.733
For this we may thank *Adam;* but his thanks	Par Lost 10.736
Concurd not to my being, it were but right	Par Lost 10.747
But Natural necessity begot.	Par Lost 10.765
But I shall die a living Death? O thought	Par Lost 10.788
Horrid, if true! yet why? it was but breath	Par Lost 10.789
Of Life that sinn'd; what dies but what had life	Par Lost 10.790
But mortal doom'd. How can he exercise	Par Lost 10.796
Not to th' extent of thir own Spheare. But say	Par Lost 10.808
Bereaving sense, but endless miserie	Par Lost 10.810
If guiltless? But from me what can proceed,	Par Lost 10.824
But all corrupt, both Mind and Will deprav'd,	Par Lost 10.825
Not to do onely, but to will the same	Par Lost 10.826
But to my own conviction: first and last	Par Lost 10.831
Wholsom and cool, and mild, but with black Air	Par Lost 10.847
But Death comes not at call, Justice Divine	Par Lost 10.858
But her with stern regard he thus repell'd.	Par Lost 10.866
And hateful; nothing wants, but that thy shape,	Par Lost 10.869
To hellish falshood, snare them. But for thee	Par Lost 10.873
To over-reach, but with the Serpent meeting	Par Lost 10.879
And understood not all was but a shew	Par Lost 10.883
Rather then solid vertu, all but a Rib	Par Lost 10.884
He never shall find out fit Mate, but such	Par Lost 10.899
Through her perversness, but shall see her gaind	Par Lost 10.902
He added not, and from her turn'd, but *Eve*	Par Lost 10.909
More miserable; both have sin'd, but thou	Par Lost 10.930
But rise, let us no more contend, nor blame	Par Lost 10.958
Each other, blam'd enough elsewhere, but strive	Par Lost 10.959
Will prove no sudden, but a slow-pac't evill,	Par Lost 10.963
But if thou judge it hard and difficult,	Par Lost 10.992
That shew no end but Death, and have the power,	Par Lost 10.1004
But *Adam* with such counsel nothing sway'd,	Par Lost 10.1010
But self-destruction therefore saught, refutes	Par Lost 10.1016
Not thy contempt, but anguish and regret	Par Lost 10.1018
The penaltie pronounc't, doubt not but God	Par Lost 10.1022
What else but favor, grace, and mercie shon?	Par Lost 10.1096
But longer in that Paradise to dwell,	Par Lost 11.48
This other serv'd but to eternize woe;	Par Lost 11.60
But let us call to Synod all the Blest	Par Lost 11.67
Of that defended Fruit; but let him boast	Par Lost 11.86
Out of despaire, joy, but with fear yet linkt;	Par Lost 11.139
But that from us ought should ascend to Heav'n	Par Lost 11.143
But infinite in pardon was my Judge,	Par Lost 11.167
Farr other name deserving. But the Field	Par Lost 11.171
So spake, so wish'd much-humbl'd *Eve*, but Fate	Par Lost 11.181
But solemn and sublime, whom not to offend,	Par Lost 11.236
Not in his shape Celestial, but as Man	Par Lost 11.239
Inclin'd not, but his coming thus declar'd.	Par Lost 11.250
But longer in this Paradise to dwell	Par Lost 11.259
Lament not *Eve*, but patiently resigne	Par Lost 11.287
But prayer against his absolute Decree	Par Lost 11.311
Gladly behold though but his utmost skirts	Par Lost 11.332
But this praeeminence thou hast lost, brought down	Par Lost 11.347
Yet doubt not but in Vallie and in plaine	Par Lost 11.349
Call *El Dorado:* but to nobler sights	Par Lost 11.411
But him the gentle Angel by the hand	Par Lost 11.421
From Heav'n acceptance; but the bloodie Fact	Par Lost 11.457
But have I now seen Death? Is this the way	Par Lost 11.462
In his first shape on man; but many shapes	Par Lost 11.467
Shook, but delaid to strike, though oft invok't	Par Lost 11.492
Drie-ey'd behold? *Adam* could not, but wept,	Par Lost 11.495
Disfiguring not Gods likeness, but thir own,	Par Lost 11.521
But is there yet no other way, besides	Par Lost 11.527
This is old age; but then thou must outlive	Par Lost 11.538
Nor love thy Life, nor hate; but what thou livst	Par Lost 11.553
But on the hether side a different sort	Par Lost 11.574
Taught them, but they his gifts acknowledg'd none.	Par Lost 11.612
But still I see the tenor of Mans woe	Par Lost 11.632
But now prepare thee for another Scene.	Par Lost 11.637
But call in aide, which makes a bloody Fray;	Par Lost 11.651
Assemble, and Harangues are heard, but soon	Par Lost 11.663
Make they but of thir Brethren, men of men?	Par Lost 11.680
But who was that Just Man, whom had not Heav'n	Par Lost 11.681
But hee the seventh from thee, whom thou beheldst	Par Lost 11.700
But all in vain: which when he saw, he ceas'd	Par Lost 11.726
Grievous to bear: but that care now is past,	Par Lost 11.776
But I was farr deceav'd; for now I see	Par Lost 11.783

But(*cont*)

And great exploits, but of true vertu void;	Par Lost 11.790
Of them derided, but of God observd	Par Lost 11.817
And shelterd round, but all the Cataracts	Par Lost 11.824
The Ark no more now flotes, but seems on ground	Par Lost 11.850
But say, what mean those colourd streaks in Heavn,	Par Lost 11.879
With Man therein or Beast; but when he brings	Par Lost 11.895
Much thou hast yet to see, but I perceave	Par Lost 12.8
This second sours of Men, while yet but few;	Par Lost 12.13
But God who oft descends to visit men	Par Lost 12.48
By his donation; but Man over men	Par Lost 12.69
But this Usurper his encroachment proud	Par Lost 12.72
But Justice, and some fatal curse annext	Par Lost 12.99
I see him, but thou canst not, with what Faith	Par Lost 12.128
Not wandring poor, but trusting all his wealth	Par Lost 12.133
Jordan, true limit Eastward; but his Sons	Par Lost 12.145
But first the lawless Tyrant, who denies	Par Lost 12.173
Humbles his stubborn heart, but still as Ice	Par Lost 12.193
Swallows him with his Host, but them lets pass	Par Lost 12.196
All night he will pursue, but his approach	Par Lost 12.206
Mankinds deliverance. But the voice of God	Par Lost 12.235
Of mee and all Mankind; but now I see	Par Lost 12.276
To whom thus *Michael*. Doubt not but that sin	Par Lost 12.285
Law can discover sin, but not remove,	Par Lost 12.290
So law appears imperfet, and but giv'n	Par Lost 12.300
Highly belov'd, being but the Minister	Par Lost 12.308
But *Joshua* whom the Gentiles *Jesus* call,	Par Lost 12.310
Long time shall dwell and prosper, but when sins	Par Lost 12.316
But first a long succession must ensue,	Par Lost 12.331
But first among the Priests dissension springs,	Par Lost 12.353
A Virgin is his Mother, but his Sire	Par Lost 12.368
Not by destroying *Satan*, but his works	Par Lost 12.394
But by fulfilling that which thou didst want,	Par Lost 12.396
But to the Cross he nailes thy Enemies,	Par Lost 12.415
But soon revives, Death over him no power	Par Lost 12.420
Salvation shall be Preacht, but to the Sons	Par Lost 12.448
To judge th' unfaithful dead, but to reward	Par Lost 12.461
But say, if our deliverer up to Heav'n	Par Lost 12.479
Be sure they will, said th' Angel; but from Heav'n	Par Lost 12.485
They die; but in thir room, as they forewarne,	Par Lost 12.507
Though not but by the Spirit understood.	Par Lost 12.514
But force the Spirit of Grace it self, and binde	Par Lost 12.525
His consort Libertie; what, but unbuild	Par Lost 12.526
To leave this Paradise, but shalt possess	Par Lost 12.586
Lay sleeping ran before, but found her wak't;	Par Lost 12.608
Wearied I fell asleep: but now lead on;	Par Lost 12.614
Well pleas'd, but answer'd not; for now too nigh	Par Lost 12.625
Som natural tears they drop'd, but wip'd them soon;	Par Lost 12.645
Unmarkt, unknown; but him the Baptist soon	Par Reg 1.25
Flies to his place, nor rests, but in mid air	Par Reg 1.39
But his growth now to youths full flowr, displaying	Par Reg 1.67
Not thence to be more pure, but to receive	Par Reg 1.77
His Mother then is mortal, but his Sire,	Par Reg 1.86
But must with something sudden be oppos'd,	Par Reg 1.96
Not force, but well couch't fraud, well woven snares,	Par Reg 1.97
At these sad tidings; but no time was then	Par Reg 1.109
But contrary unweeting he fulfill'd	Par Reg 1.126
By fallacy surpriz'd. But first I mean	Par Reg 1.155
But to vanquish by wisdom hellish wiles.	Par Reg 1.175
Not wilfully mis-doing, but unware	Par Reg 1.225
O Son, but nourish them and let them soar	Par Reg 1.230
Which I believ'd was from above; but he	Par Reg 1.274
But as I rose out of the laving stream,	Par Reg 1.280
But openly begin, as best becomes	Par Reg 1.288
And he still on was led, but with such thoughts	Par Reg 1.299
But now an aged man in Rural weeds,	Par Reg 1.314
But if thou be the Son of God, Command	Par Reg 1.342
Man lives not by Bread only, but each Word	Par Reg 1.349
Kept not my happy Station, but was driv'n	Par Reg 1.360
By rigour unconniving, but that oft	Par Reg 1.363
At first it may be; but long since with wo	Par Reg 1.399
But thou art serviceable to Heaven's King.	Par Reg 1.421
What but thy malice mov'd thee to misdeem	Par Reg 1.424
With all inflictions, but his patience won?	Par Reg 1.426
But what have been thy answers, what but dark	Par Reg 1.434
Idolatrous, but when his purpose is	Par Reg 1.444
But from him or his Angels President	Par Reg 1.447
But this thy glory shall be soon retrench'd;	Par Reg 1.454
So spake our Saviour; but the subtle Fiend,	Par Reg 1.465
But misery hath rested from me; where	Par Reg 1.470
But thou art plac't above me, thou art Lord;	Par Reg 1.475
Or in *Perea*, but return'd in vain.	Par Reg 2.24
Thus we rejoyc'd, but soon our joy is turn'd	Par Reg 2.37
But let us wait; thus far he hath perform'd,	Par Reg 2.49
But to his Mother *Mary*, when she saw	Par Reg 2.60
Little suspicious to any King; but now	Par Reg 2.82
But trouble, as old *Simeon* plain fore-told,	Par Reg 2.87
But where delays he now? some great intent	Par Reg 2.95
I lost him, but so found, as well I saw	Par Reg 2.97
He could not lose himself; but went about	Par Reg 2.98
But I to wait with patience am inur'd;	Par Reg 2.102
Sole but with holiest Meditations fed,	Par Reg 2.110
Have found him, view'd him, tasted him, but find	Par Reg 2.131
None are, thou think'st, but taken with such toys.	Par Reg 2.177
Satyr, or Fawn, or Silvan? But these haunts	Par Reg 2.191
But he whom we attempt is wiser far	Par Reg 2.205
But now I feel I hunger, which declares,	Par Reg 2.252
Our Saviour, and found all was but a dream,	Par Reg 2.283

But(*cont*)

But Cottage, Herd or Sheep-cote none he saw,	Par Reg 2.288
Not rustic as before, but seemlier clad,	Par Reg 2.299
But much more wonder that the Son of God	Par Reg 2.303
But tender all their power? nor mention I	Par Reg 2.327
But life preserves, destroys life's enemy,	Par Reg 2.372
And count thy specious gifts no gifts but guiles.	Par Reg 2.391
Why shouldst thou not accept it? but I see	Par Reg 2.398
High actions; but wherewith to be atchiev'd?	Par Reg 2.411
(Thy throne) but gold that got him puissant friends?	Par Reg 2.425
But men endu'd with these have oft attain'd	Par Reg 2.437
And what in me seems wanting, but that I	Par Reg 2.450
Golden in shew, is but a wreath of thorns,	Par Reg 2.459
But to guide Nations in the way of truth	Par Reg 2.473
And dignities and powers all but the highest?	Par Reg 3.30
Quench not the thirst of glory, but augment.	Par Reg 3.38
Inglorious: but thou yet art not too late.	Par Reg 3.42
For what is glory but the blaze of fame,	Par Reg 3.47
And what the people but a herd confus'd,	Par Reg 3.49
And know not whom, but as one leads the other;	Par Reg 3.53
But rob and spoil, burn, slaughter, and enslave	Par Reg 3.75
Nothing but ruin wheresoe're they rove,	Par Reg 3.79
But if there be in glory aught of good,	Par Reg 3.88
And loses, though but verbal, his reward.	Par Reg 3.104
Oft not deserv'd? I seek not mine, but his	Par Reg 3.106
But to shew forth his goodness, and impart	Par Reg 3.124
But why should man seek glory? who of his own	Par Reg 3.134
But condemnation, ignominy, and shame?	Par Reg 3.136
Satan had not to answer, but stood struck	Par Reg 3.146
But to a Kingdom thou art born, ordain'd	Par Reg 3.152
Retir'd unto the Desert, but with arms;	Par Reg 3.166
But on Occasions forelock watchful wait.	Par Reg 3.173
But what concerns it thee when I begin	Par Reg 3.198
But I will bring thee where thou soon shalt quit	Par Reg 3.244
As antient, but rebuilt by him who twice	Par Reg 3.281
The drink of none but Kings; of later fame	Par Reg 3.289
But say thou wer't possess'd of *David*'s Throne	Par Reg 3.357
But whence to thee this zeal, where was it then	Par Reg 3.407
The God of their fore-fathers; but so dy'd	Par Reg 3.422
From Gentils, but by Circumcision vain,	Par Reg 3.425
So little here, nay lost; but *Eve* was *Eve*,	Par Reg 4.6
But as a man who had been matchless held	Par Reg 4.10
Another plain, long but in bredth not wide;	Par Reg 4.27
To *Capreae* an Island small but strong	Par Reg 4.92
But tedious wast of time to sit and hear	Par Reg 4.123
But govern ill the Nations under yoke,	Par Reg 4.135
Means there shall be to this, but what the means,	Par Reg 4.152
But I endure the time, till which expir'd,	Par Reg 4.174
If given, by whom but by the King of Kings,	Par Reg 4.185
Repaid? But gratitude in thee is lost	Par Reg 4.188
And his who gave them breath, but higher sung,	Par Reg 4.258
Think not but that I know these things, or think	Par Reg 4.286
But these are false, or little else but dreams,	Par Reg 4.291
But vertue joyn'd with riches and long life,	Par Reg 4.298
For all his tedious talk is but vain boast,	Par Reg 4.307
Much of the Soul they talk, but all awrie,	Par Reg 4.313
But herein to our Prophets far beneath,	Par Reg 4.356
So spake the Son of God; but Satan now	Par Reg 4.365
A Kingdom they portend thee, but what Kingdom,	Par Reg 4.389
But shelter'd slept in vain, for at his head	Par Reg 4.407
Within thir stony caves, but rush'd abroad	Par Reg 4.414
As Earth and Skie would mingle; but my self	Par Reg 4.453
To win thy destin'd seat, but wilt prolong	Par Reg 4.469
For Angels have proclaim'd it, but concealing	Par Reg 4.474
Not when it must, but when it may be best.	Par Reg 4.476
And staid not, but in brief him answer'd thus.	Par Reg 4.485
As false portents, not sent from God, but thee;	Par Reg 4.491
But Satan smitten with amazement fell	Par Reg 4.562
But thou, Infernal Serpent, shalt not long	Par Reg 4.618
Unwholsom draught: but here I feel amends,	Samson 9
But rush upon me thronging, and present	Samson 21
Had been fulfilld but through mine own default,	Samson 45
Whom have I to complain of but my self?	Samson 46
But weakly to a woman must reveal it,	Samson 50
But what is strength without a double share	Samson 53
But to subserve where wisdom bears command.	Samson 57
But peace, I must not quarrel with the will	Samson 60
Would ask a life to wail, but chief of all,	Samson 66
And buried; but O yet more miserable!	Samson 101
But made hereby obnoxious more	Samson 106
But who are these? for with joint pace I hear	Samson 110
But safest he who stood aloof,	Samson 135
But thee whose strength, while vertue was her mate,	Samson 173
They swarm, but in adverse withdraw their head	Samson 192
She was not the prime cause, but I my self,	Samson 234
Sam. That fault I take not on me, but transfer	Samson 241
But they persisted deaf, and would not seem	Samson 249
Not flying, but fore-casting in what place	Samson 254
Bound with two cords; but cords to me were threds	Samson 261
But what more oft in Nations grown corrupt,	Samson 268
But Gods propos'd deliverance not so.	Samson 292
But the heart of the Fool,	Samson 298
And no man therein Doctor but himself.	Samson 299
But never find self-satisfying solution.	Samson 306
But see here comes thy reverend Sire	Samson 326
Pray'd for, but often proves our woe, our bane?	Samson 351
Be it but for honours sake of former deeds.	Samson 372
But justly; I my self have brought them on,	Samson 375

But(*cont*)
But warn'd by oft experience: did not she Samson 382
But foul effeminacy held me yok't Samson 410
Rather approv'd them not; but thou didst plead Samson 421
But will arise and his great name assert: Samson 467
Or *Dagon*. But for thee what shall be done? Samson 478
But I Gods counsel have not kept, his holy secret Samson 497
But act not in thy own affliction, Son, Samson 503
Repent the sin, but if the punishment Samson 504
But God hath set before us, to return thee Samson 517
Sam. His pardon I implore; but as for life, Samson 521
Sam. But what avail'd this temperance, not compleat Samson 558
But to sit idle on the houshold hearth, Samson 566
But God who caus'd a fountain at thy prayer Samson 581
But yield to double darkness nigh at hand: Samson 593
But must secret passage find Samson 610
With answerable pains, but more intense, Samson 615
But finding no redress, ferment and rage, Samson 619
But now hath cast me off as never known, Samson 641
But with th' afflicted in his pangs thir sound Samson 660
But such as thou hast solemnly elected, Samson 678
But throw'st them lower then thou didst exalt them high, Samson 689
But who is this, what thing of Sea or Land? Samson 710
About t' have spoke, but now, with head declin'd Samson 727
But now again she makes address to speak. Samson 731
I cannot but acknowledge; yet if tears Samson 735
No way assur'd. But conjugal affection Samson 739
My rash but more unfortunate misdeed. Samson 747
Not truly penitent, but chief to try Samson 754
The penitent, but ever to forgive, Samson 761
But that on th' other side if it be weigh'd Samson 768
In me, but incident to all our sex, Samson 774
But I to enemies reveal'd, and should not. Samson 782
Against thee but safe custody, and hold: Samson 802
I led the way; bitter reproach, but true, Samson 823
Incestuous, Sacrilegious, but may plead it? Samson 833
But Love constrain'd thee; call it furious rage Samson 836
Was not behind, but ever at my ear, Samson 858
But had thy love, still odiously pretended, Samson 873
Not out of levity, but over-powr'd Samson 880
Nor under their protection but my own, Samson 887
No more thy countrey, but an impious crew Samson 891
Not therefore to be obey'd. But zeal mov'd thee; Samson 895
But by ungodly deeds, the contradiction Samson 898
For peace, reap nothing but repulse and hate? Samson 966
But in my countrey where I most desire, Samson 980
But what it is, hard is to say, Samson 1013
In choice, but oftest to affect the wrong? Samson 1030
What Pilot so expert but needs must wreck Samson 1044
But vertue which breaks through all opposition, Samson 1050
But had we best retire, I see a storm? Samson 1061
Chor. But this another kind of tempest brings. Samson 1063
Sam. The way to know were not to see but taste. Samson 1091
Sam. Boast not of what thou wouldst have done, but do Samson 1104
To *Samson*, but shalt never see *Gath* more. Samson 1129
But by the Barbers razor best subdu'd. Samson 1167
But your ill-meaning Politician Lords, Samson 1195
But I a private person, whom my Countrey Samson 1208
I was no private but a person rais'd Samson 1211
But to thir Masters gave me up for nought, Samson 1215
But take good heed my hand survey not thee. Samson 1230
My heels are fetter'd, but my fist is free. Samson 1235
And lower looks, but in a sultrie chafe. Samson 1246
But come what will, my deadliest foe will prove Samson 1262
Tyrannic power, but raging to pursue Samson 1275
But patience is more oft the exercise Samson 1287
Above the Sons of men; but sight bereav'd Samson 1294
But they must pick me out with shackles tir'd, Samson 1326
Sam. Not in thir Idol-worship, but by labour Samson 1365
But who constrains me to the Temple of *Dagon*, Samson 1370
But wherefore comes old *Manoa* in such hast Samson 1441
But that which mov'd my coming now, was chiefly Samson 1452
Others more moderate seeming, but thir aim Samson 1464
Man. He can I know, but doubt to think he will; Samson 1534
But providence or instinct of nature seems, Samson 1545
Mess. It would burst forth, but I recover breath Samson 1555
Mess. *Gaza* yet stands, but all her Sons are fall'n, Samson 1558
Man. Sad, but thou knowst to *Israelites* not saddest Samson 1560
To free him hence! but death who sets all free Samson 1572
More then anough we know; but while things yet Samson 1592
I sorrow'd at his captive state, but minded Samson 1603
He patient but undaunted where they led him, Samson 1623
Of this but each *Philistian* City round Samson 1655
Not willingly, but tangl'd in the fold, Samson 1665
Semichor. But he though blind of sight, Samson 1687
Of tame villatic Fowl; but as an Eagle Samson 1695
Honour hath left, and freedom, let but them Samson 1715
But favouring and assisting to the end. Samson 1720
Dispraise, or blame, nothing but well and fair, Samson 1723
But unexpectedly returns Samson 1750
To such my errand is, and but for such, Mask 15
But to my task. *Neptune* besides the sway Mask 18
And weild their little tridents, but this Ile Mask 27
And new-entrusted Scepter, but their way Mask 36
But that by quick command from Soveran *Jove* Mask 41
Much like his Father, but his Mother more, Mask 57
But boast themselves more comely then before Mask 75
As now I do: But first I must put off Mask 82

But(*cont*)
1637 'but'
Trinity ms 'but'
Of this occasion. But I hear the tread Mask 91
Trinity ms 'but'
Bridgewater ms 'but'
That ne're art call'd, but when the Dragon woom Mask 131
But here she comes, I fairly step aside Mask 168
But where they are, and why they came not back, Mask 191
Why shouldst thou, but for som fellonious end, Mask 196
line not in Bridgewater ms
Yet nought but single darknes do I find. Mask 204
line not in Bridgewater ms
These thoughts may startle well, but not astound Mask 210
line not in Bridgewater ms
Are but as slavish officers of vengeance, Mask 218
line not in Bridgewater ms
I cannot hallow to my Brothers, but Mask 226
Tell me but where Mask 240
But such a sacred, and home-felt delight, Mask 262
Not any boast of skill, but extreme shift Mask 273
La. They were but twain, and purpos'd quick return. Mask 284
But loyal cottage, where you may be safe Mask 320
Be barr'd that happines, might we but hear Mask 343
But O that haples virgin our lost sister Mask 350
Or if they be but false alarms of Fear, Mask 364
line not in Trinity ms
line not in Bridgewater ms
But he that hides a dark soul, and foul thoughts Mask 383
But beauty like the fair Hesperian Tree Mask 393
Yet where an equall poise of hope and fear Mask 410
Trinity ms 'but where'
Bridgewater ms 'but where'
Eld. Bro. I mean that too, but yet a hidden strength Mask 418
And spotted mountain pard, but set at nought Mask 444
But rigid looks of Chast austerity, Mask 450
Till all be made immortal: but when lust Mask 463
But most by leud and lavish act of sin, Mask 465
Bridgewater ms 'and'
Trinity ms 'and'
But musical as is *Apollo*'s lute, Mask 478
But O my Virgin Lady, where is she? Mask 507
For such there be, but unbelief is blind. Mask 519
Till fancy had her fill, but ere a close Mask 548
Under the ribs of Death, but O ere long Mask 562
Longer I durst not stay, but soon I guess't Mask 577
But furder know I not. 2. *Bro*. O night and shades, Mask 580
Trinity ms 'but' ←'and this'
Vertue may be assail'd, but never hurt, Mask 589
Surpriz'd by unjust force, but not enthrall'd, Mask 590
But evil on it self shall back recoyl, Mask 593
And earths base built on stubble. But com let's on. Mask 599
Bridgewater ms 'but'
Trinity ms 'but'
But for that damn'd magician, let him be girt Mask 602
But here thy sword can do thee little stead, Mask 611
But of divine effect, he cull'd me out; Mask 630
But in another Countrey, as he said, Mask 632
line not in Bridgewater ms
Bore a bright golden flowre, but not in this soyl: Mask 633
line not in Bridgewater ms
I purs't it up, but little reck'ning made, Mask 642
But now I find it true; for by this means Mask 644
But sease his wand, though he and his curst crew Mask 653
Trinity ms 'but' ←'and'
Yet will they soon retire, if he but shrink. Mask 656
Comus. Nay Lady sit; if I but wave this wand, Mask 659
But you invert the cov'nants of her trust, Mask 682
line not in Bridgewater ms
And timely rest have wanted, but fair Virgin Mask 689
Bridgewater ms 'heere'
Trinity ms 'but' ←'heere'
But such as are good men can give good things, Mask 703
But all to please, and sate the curious taste? Mask 714
Drink the clear stream, and nothing wear but Freize, Mask 722
But must be currant, and the good thereof Mask 740
line not in Bridgewater ms
Think what, and be adviz'd, you are but young yet. Mask 755
line not in Bridgewater ms
In this unhallow'd air, but that this Jugler Mask 757
Had but a moderate and beseeming share Mask 769
But with besotted base ingratitude Mask 778
I must not suffer this, yet 'tis but the lees Mask 809
Trinity ms 'but the lees' ←'the tilted lees' ←'the very lees'
But this will cure all streight, one sip of this Mask 811
But night sits monarch yet in the mid sky. Mask 957
But farr above in spangled sheen Mask 1003
line not in Bridgewater ms
But now my task is smoothly don, Mask 1012
word not in Bridgewater ms
word not in B.M. ms
but soft I was not sent to court your wonder Mask Tr. ms 10.16
But com thou Goddes fair and free, Allegro 11
But hail thou Goddes, sage and holy, Penseroso 11
Black, but such as in esteem, Penseroso 17
Com, but keep thy wonted state, Penseroso 37
But first, and chiefest, with thee bring, Penseroso 51
But, O sad Virgin, that thy power Penseroso 103

But(*cont*)
But Cherchef't in a comly Cloud, Penseroso 125
But let my due feet never fail, Penseroso 155
But els in deep of night when drowsines Arcades 61
But O the heavy change, now thou art gon, Lycidas 37
But the fair Guerdon when we hope to find, Lycidas 73
And slits the thin spun life. But not the praise, Lycidas 76
But lives and spreds aloft by those pure eyes, Lycidas 81
But now my Oat proceeds, Lycidas 88
But swoln with wind, and the rank mist they draw, Lycidas 126
But that two-handed engine at the door, Lycidas 130
So *Lycidas* sunk low, but mounted high, Lycidas 172
But he her fears to cease, Nativity 45
But peacefull was the night Nativity 61
But in their glimmering Orbs did glow, Nativity 75
But when of old the sons of morning sung, Nativity 119
But wisest Fate sayes no, Nativity 149
But now begins; for from this happy day Nativity 167
Naught but profoundest Hell can be his shroud, Nativity 218
But see the Virgin blest, Nativity 237
But full soon they did devour Psalm 136, 53
O Fairest flower no sooner blown but blasted, Fair Inf 1
But kill'd alas, and then bewayl'd his fatal bliss. Fair Inf 7
But all unwares with his cold-kind embrace Fair Inf 20
But then transform'd him to a purple flower Fair Inf 27
But oh why didst thou not stay here below Fair Inf 64
But thou canst best perform that office where thou art. Fair Inf 70
I know my tongue but little Grace can do thee Vacation 10
But haste thee strait to do me once a Pleasure, Vacation 17
But cull those richest Robes, and gay'st attire Vacation 21
But fie my wandring Muse how thou dost stray! Vacation 53
But headlong joy is ever on the wing, Passion 5
Whose speed is but the heavy Plummets pace; On Time 3
Just law indeed, but more exceeding love! Circum 16
This day, but O ere long Circum 26
But with a scarce-wel-lighted flame; Winchester 20
But whether by mischance or blame Winchester 27
But the fair blossom hangs the head Winchester 41
No Marchioness, but now a Queen. Winchester 74
But lately finding him so long at home, Carrier 11
While he might still jogg on, and keep his trot, Another 4
1658 'he could but'
But vow though the cross Doctors all stood hearers, Another 19
line not in 1640, 1657, 1658 texts
But had his doings lasted as they were, Another 27
1640, 1657, 1658 'For'
But my late spring no bud or blossom shew'th. Sonnet 7, 4
No anger find in thee, but pity and ruth. Sonnet 9, 8
Numbring good intellects; now seldom por'd on. Sonnet 11, 4
Trinity ms 'now' ←'but now is'
I did but prompt the age to quit their cloggs Sonnet 12, 1
But this is got by casting Pearl to Hoggs; Sonnet 12, 8
But from that mark how far they roave we see Sonnet 12, 13
But as Faith pointed with her golden rod, Sonnet 14, 7
For what can Warr, but endless warr still breed, Sonnet 15, 10
Not of warr onely, but detractions rude, Sonnet 16, 2
Vane, young in yeares, but in sage counsell old, Sonnet 17, 1
I fondly ask; But patience to prevent Sonnet 19, 8
Of heart or hope; but still bear vp and steer Sonnet 22, 8
But O as to embrace me she enclin'd, Sonnet 23, 13
But we do hope to find out all your tricks, Forcers 13
New Presbyter is but *Old Priest* writ Large. Forcers 20
Of scorners hath not sate. But in the great Psalm 1, 4
Not so the wicked, but as chaff which fann'd Psalm 1, 11
And fierce ire trouble them; but I saith hee Psalm 2, 11
But thou Lord art my shield my glory, Psalm 3, 7
Things false and vain and nothing else but lies? Psalm 4, 12
But Lord, thus let me pray, Psalm 4, 28
But I will in thy mercies dear Psalm 5, 17
But the just establish fast, Psalm 7, 37
Behold *us, but without a frown,* Psalm 80, 59
But now it is consum'd with fire, Psalm 80, 65
But *they, his People, should remain,* Psalm 81, 63
But ye shall die like men, and fall Psalm 82, 23
But let them never more Psalm 85, 34
Return to folly, *but surcease* Psalm 85, 35
But thou Lord art the God most mild Psalm 86, 53
But *twise that praise shall in our ear* Psalm 87, 17
I am a man, but weak alas Psalm 88, 15
But I to thee O Lord do cry Psalm 88, 53
Not thy Conversion, but those rich demaines Prose 1, 2
Whom doe we count a good man, whom but he Prose 10, 1
But his owne house, and the whole neighbourhood Prose 10, 5

Buttons
Or Frost to Flowers, that their gay wardrop wear, Lycidas 47
Trinity ms 'wardrope' ←'buttons'

Buxom
Wing silently the buxom Air, imbalm'd Par Lost 2.842
Winnows the buxom Air; till within soare Par Lost 5.270
So bucksom, blith, and debonair. Allegro 24

Buzzards
Of Owles and Cuckoes, Asses, Apes and Doggs. Sonnet 12, 4
Trinity ms 'Cuckoes' ←'buzzards'

By
Listings of this word are omitted; see the Introduction.

Byzantium
In *Mosco*, or the Sultan in *Bizance*, Par Lost 11.395

Cabined
From her cabin'd loop hole peep, Mask 140
Bridgewater ms 'Cabin'd'

Cache
Or as a Thief bent to unhoord the cash Par Lost 4.188

Cadence
Had rous'd the Sea, now with hoarse cadence lull Par Lost 2.287
Now was the Sun in Western cadence low Par Lost 10.92

Cadmus
Hermione and *Cadmus*, or the God Par Lost 9.506

Caecias
Boreas and *Caecias* and *Argestes* loud Par Lost 10.699

Caesar
Shalt raign, and *Rome* or *Caesar* not need fear. Par Reg 3.385

Cairo
Nor great *Alcairo* such magnificence Par Lost 1.718
ms 'Alcairo'

Calabria
Calabria from the hoarce *Trinacrian* shore: Par Lost 2.661

Calamities
And to the bearing well of all calamities, Samson 655
Or make a game of my calamities? Samson 1331

Calamitous
Subdues me, and calamitous constraint Par Lost 10.132
Behold him in this state calamitous, and turn Samson 708
And he in that calamitous prison left. Samson 1480

Calamity
How overcome this dire Calamity, Par Lost 1.189
ms 'calamity'
Which infinite calamitie shall cause Par Lost 10.907

Calculate
And calculate the Starrs, how they will weild Par Lost 8.80

Cales
Their wines of *Setia*, *Cales*, and *Falerne*, Par Reg 4.117

Calf
The Calf in *Oreb:* and the Rebel King Par Lost 1.484
ms 'Calfe'

Call
And call them not to share with us their part Par Lost 1.267
At thir great Emperors call, as next in worth Par Lost 1.378
The rest shall hear me call, and oft be warnd Par Lost 3.185
Volatil *Hermes*, and call up unbound Par Lost 3.603
(So call that opposite fair Starr) her aide Par Lost 3.727
Hide thir diminisht heads; to thee I call, Par Lost 4.35
Whom Gentiles *Ammon* call and *Lybian Jove*, Par Lost 4.277
I rose as at thy call, but found thee not; Par Lost 5.48
All what we affirm or what deny, and call Par Lost 5.107
Satan, so call him now, his former name Par Lost 5.658
The Palace of great *Lucifer*, (so call Par Lost 5.760
The meaning, not the Name I call: for thou Par Lost 7.5
(So call him, brighter once amidst the Host Par Lost 7.132
On the swift flouds: as Armies at the call Par Lost 7.295
Not noxious, but obedient at thy call. Par Lost 7.498
From every Beast, more duteous at her call, Par Lost 9.521
Then at *Circean* call the Herd disguis'd. Par Lost 9.522
And Palate call judicious; I the praise Par Lost 9.1020
I call ye and declare ye now, returnd Par Lost 10.462
Scarce tollerable, and from the North to call Par Lost 10.654
But Death comes not at call, Justice Divine Par Lost 10.858
But let us call to Synod all the Blest Par Lost 11.67
Call *El Dorado:* but to nobler sights Par Lost 11.411
But call in aide, which makes a bloody Fray; Par Lost 11.651
In other part the scepter'd Haralds call Par Lost 11.660
And call to mind his Cov'nant: Day and Night, Par Lost 11.898
To call by Vision from his Fathers house, Par Lost 12.121
(Things by thir names I call, though yet unnam'd) Par Lost 12.140
Whom *faithful Abraham* due time shall call, Par Lost 12.152
Till by two brethren (those two brethren call Par Lost 12.169
Till *Israel* overcome; so call the third Par Lost 12.267
But *Joshua* whom the Gentiles *Jesus* call, Par Lost 12.310
Plain Fishermen, no greater men them call, Par Reg 2.27
And call swift flights of Angels ministrant Par Reg 2.385
Remembring *Abraham* by some wond'rous call Par Reg 3.434
Yet stay, let me not rashly call in doubt Samson 43
But Love constrain'd thee; call it furious rage Samson 836
Men call me *Harapha*, of stock renown'd Samson 1079
Chor. Noise call you it or universal groan Samson 1511
To call in hast for thir destroyer; Samson 1678
Which men call Earth, and with low-thoughted care Mask 6
Do ye beleeve me yet, or shall I call Mask 438
Which erring men call Chance, this I hold firm, Mask 588
And adde the power of som adjuring verse. Mask 858
Trinity ms 'power' ←'call' ←'power'
Or call up him that left half told Penseroso 109
And call the Vales, and bid them hither cast Lycidas 134
They call the grisly king, Nativity 209
Call on the lazy leaden-stepping hours, On Time 2
Whether the Muse, or Love call thee his mate, Sonnet 1, 13
That call Fame on such gentle acts as these, Sonnet 8, 6
By shallow *Edwards* and Scotch what d' ye call: Forcers 12
Answer me when I call Psalm 4, 1
Shall call upon thy Name. Psalm 80, 76
On me then didst thou call, Psalm 81, 26
I call; O make rejoyce Psalm 86, 10
To them that on thee call. Psalm 86, 16
Will call on thee *for aid;* Psalm 86, 22

Called
And thence in Heav'n call'd Satan, with bold words Par Lost 1.82

Called(*cont*)
Of that inflamed Sea, he stood and call'd Par Lost 1.300
ms 'calld'
He call'd so loud, that all the hollow Deep Par Lost 1.314
ms 'calld'
Wav'd round the Coast, up call'd a pitchy cloud Par Lost 1.340
And black *Gehenna* call'd, the Type of Hell. Par Lost 1.405
Came *Astoreth*, whom the *Phoenicians* call'd Par Lost 1.438
Men call'd him *Mulciber;* and how he fell Par Lost 1.740
Of Satan and his Peers: thir summons call'd Par Lost 1.757
Must we renounce, and changing stile be call'd Par Lost 2.312
Of some new Race call'd *Man*, about this time Par Lost 2.348
Nor uglier follow the Night-Hag, when call'd Par Lost 2.662
If shape it might be call'd that shape had none Par Lost 2.667
Or substance might be call'd that shadow seem'd, Par Lost 2.669
At first, and call'd me *Sin*, and for a Sign Par Lost 2.760
Into a *Limbo* large and broad, since calld Par Lost 3.495
Multitudes like thy self, and thence be call'd Par Lost 4.474
One fatal Tree there stands of Knowledge call'd, Par Lost 4.514
From these, two strong and suttle Spirits he calld Par Lost 4.786
Gabriel from the Front thus calld aloud. Par Lost 4.865
Close at mine ear one call'd me forth to walk Par Lost 5.36
His praise, who out of Darkness call'd up Light. Par Lost 5.179
With pittie Heav'ns high King, and to him call'd Par Lost 5.220
Berrie or Grape: to whom thus *Adam* call'd. Par Lost 5.307
Of Angels by Imperial summons call'd, Par Lost 5.584
The Mountain of the Congregation call'd; Par Lost 5.766
His Potentates to Councel call'd by night; Par Lost 6.416
And to his Mates thus in derision call'd. Par Lost 6.608
If rightly thou art call'd, whose Voice divine Par Lost 7.2
Of congregated Waters he call'd Seas: Par Lost 7.308
While thus I call'd, and stray'd I knew not whither, Par Lost 8.283
First Father, call'd by thee I come thy Guide Par Lost 8.298
Of sleep, which instantly fell on me, call'd Par Lost 8.458
Approaching, thus to *Adam* call'd aloud. Par Lost 10.102
Of *Lucifer*, so by allusion calld, Par Lost 10.425
And Fabl'd how the Serpent, whom they calld Par Lost 10.580
And know not that I call'd and drew them thither Par Lost 10.629
Eve rightly call'd, Mother of all Mankind, Par Lost 11.159
And Valour and Heroic Vertu call'd; Par Lost 11.690
Destroyers rightlier call'd and Plagues of men. Par Lost 11.697
With God, who call'd him, in a land unknown. Par Lost 12.134
From *Canaan*, to a Land hereafter call'd Par Lost 12.156
Left in confusion, *Babylon* thence call'd. Par Lost 12.343
Why our great expectation should be call'd Par Lost 12.378
By name to come call'd Charitie, the soul Par Lost 12.584
Great in Renown, and call'd the Son of God; Par Reg 1.136
This perfect Man, by merit call'd my Son, Par Reg 1.166
Of *Jordan* honour'd so, and call'd thee Son Par Reg 1.329
Him whom they heard so late expresly call'd Par Reg 2.3
Each of his reign allotted, rightlier call'd, Par Reg 2.123
Of luxury, though call'd magnificence, Par Reg 4.111
Blind *Melesigenes* thence *Homer* call'd, Par Reg 4.259
By him call'd vertue; and his vertuous man, Par Reg 4.301
In what degree or meaning thou art call'd Par Reg 4.516
The work to which I was divinely call'd; Samson 226
That ne're art call'd, but when the Dragon woom Mask 131
He call'd it *Haemony*, and gave it me, Mask 638
A Book was writ of late call'd *Tetrachordon;* Sonnet 11, 1
Of Death, call'd Life; which us from Life doth sever. Sonnet 14, 4

Callest
In this infernal Vaile first met thou call'st Par Lost 2.742
Me Father, and that Fantasm call'st my Son? Par Lost 2.743
The strife which thou call'st evil, but wee style Par Lost 6.289
What call'st thou solitude, is not the Earth Par Lost 8.369
Of wandring, as thou call'st it, which who knows Par Lost 9.1146
My brethren, as thou call'st them; those Ten Tribes Par Reg 3.403

Calling
While the Creator calling forth by name Par Lost 10.649
I have in view, calling to minde with heed Par Lost 10.1030
Of calling shapes, and beckning shadows dire, Mask 207
line not in Bridgewater ms
Som roaving Robber calling to his fellows. Mask 485
Bridgewater ms 'callinge'

Calliope
What could the Muse her self that *Orpheus* bore, Lycidas 58
Trinity ms 'muse her selfe' ←'golden hayrd Calliope'

Callisto
Some beauty rare, *Calisto*, *Clymene*, Par Reg 2.186

Callow
Thir callow young, but featherd soon and fledge Par Lost 7.420

Calls
Calls us to Penance? More destroy'd then thus Par Lost 2.92
What e're his wrath, which he calls Justice, bids, Par Lost 2.733
Calls us, we lose the prime, to mark how spring Par Lost 5.21
Of his Associate; hee together calls, Par Lost 5.696
To labour calls us now with sweat impos'd, Par Lost 11.172
Among the Builders; each to other calls Par Lost 12.57
Expectance calls thee now another way, Vacation 54
And calls *Lucina* to her throws; Winchester 26

Calm
Through the calm Firmament; but up or downe Par Lost 3.574
Each perturbation smooth'd with outward calme, Par Lost 4.120
Firm peace recoverd soon and wonted calm. Par Lost 5.210
To whom the Son with calm aspect and cleer Par Lost 5.733
Cover'd th' Abyss: but on the watrie calme Par Lost 7.234
Built on circumfluous Waters calme, in wide Par Lost 7.270
Thus in calm mood his Words to *Eve* he turnd. Par Lost 9.920

Calm(*cont*)
1667 'calme'
Thir inward State of Mind, calm Region once Par Lost 9.1125
1667 'calme'
Within her brest, though calm; her brest though pure, Par Reg 2.63
Private, unactive, calm, contemplative, Par Reg 2.81
Sat'st unappall'd in calm and sinless peace. Par Reg 4.425
By ransom or how else: mean while be calm, Samson 604
And calm of mind all passion spent. Samson 1758
In Regions milde of calm and serene Ayr, Mask 4
1637 'calme'
Trinity ms 'calme'
Bridgewater ms 'Calme'
Could stir the constant mood of her calm thoughts, Mask 371
1637 'calme'
Trinity ms 'calme'
Bridgewater ms 'calme'
And joyn with thee calm Peace, and Quiet, Penseroso 45
The Ayr was calm, and on the level brine, Lycidas 98
Trinity ms 'calme'
While Birds of Calm sit brooding on the charmed wave. Nativity 68

Calmed
Her also I with gentle Dreams have calm'd Par Lost 12.595
Eternal tempest never to be calm'd. Samson 964

Calmer
Wafts on the calmer wave by dubious light Par Lost 2.1042
Successfully; a calmer voyage now Par Reg 1.103

Calmest
But live content, which is the calmest life: Par Lost 6.461

Calmly
To whom our Saviour calmly thus reply'd. Par Reg 3.43
And *calmly* didst return Psalm 85, 10

Calumnious
Thither to come, and with calumnious Art Par Lost 5.770

Calved
The grassie Clods now Calv'd, now half appeer'd Par Lost 7.463

Calves
From God to worship Calves, the Deities Par Reg 3.416

Cam
Sent thee from the banks of *Came*, Winchester 59

Camball
Of *Camball*, and of *Algarsife*, Penseroso 111

Cambalu
Of *Cambalu*, seat of *Cathaian Can* Par Lost 11.388

Cambridge
Dodg'd with him, betwixt *Cambridge* and the Bull. Carrier 8
When thou taught'st *Cambridge*, and King *Edward* Greek. Sonnet 11, 14

Cambuscan
The story of *Cambuscan* bold, Penseroso 110

Came
Came like a Deluge on the South, and spread Par Lost 1.354
Came singly where he stood on the bare strand, Par Lost 1.379
With these came they, who from the bordring flood Par Lost 1.419
Came *Astoreth*, whom the *Phoenicians* call'd Par Lost 1.438
To Idols foul. *Thammuz* came next behind, Par Lost 1.446
Of alienated *Judah*. Next came one Par Lost 1.457
Belial came last, then whom a Spirit more lewd Par Lost 1.490
All these and more came flocking; but with looks Par Lost 1.522
With hunderds and with thousands trooping came Par Lost 1.760
In order came the grand infernal Peers, Par Lost 2.507
Midst came thir mighty Paramount, and seemd Par Lost 2.508
The Monster moving onward came as fast Par Lost 2.675
First from the ancient World those Giants came Par Lost 3.464
Others came single; he who to be deemd Par Lost 3.469
Who after came from Earth, sayling arriv'd, Par Lost 3.520
This worlds material mould, came to a heap: Par Lost 3.709
Came furious down to be reveng'd on men, Par Lost 4.4
Satan, now first inflam'd with rage, came down, Par Lost 4.9
Who came thir bane, though with them better pleas'd Par Lost 4.167
With thee it came and goes: but follow me, Par Lost 4.469
Thither came *Uriel*, gliding through the Eeven Par Lost 4.555
This day at highth of Noon came to my Spheare Par Lost 4.564
Now came still Eevning on, and Twilight gray Par Lost 4.598
Came not all Hell broke loose? is pain to them Par Lost 4.918
Each shoulder broad, came mantling o're his brest Par Lost 5.279
Adam, I therefore came, nor art thou such Par Lost 5.372
They came, that like *Pomona*'s Arbour smil'd Par Lost 5.378
They came, and *Satan* to his Royal seat Par Lost 5.756
Came summond over *Eden* to receive Par Lost 6.75
Came towring, armd in Adamant and Gold; Par Lost 6.110
Brandisht aloft the horrid edge came down Par Lost 6.252
Came flying, and in mid Aire aloud thus cri'd. Par Lost 6.536
Came shadowing, and opprest whole Legions arm'd, Par Lost 6.655
He onward came, farr off his coming shon, Par Lost 6.768
Celestial Equipage; and now came forth Par Lost 7.203
At once came forth whatever creeps the ground, Par Lost 7.475
Was set, and twilight from the East came on, Par Lost 7.583
Tell, if ye saw, how came I thus, how here? Par Lost 8.277
And livd: One came, methought, of shape Divine, Par Lost 8.295
To make her amiable: On she came, Par Lost 8.484
With grateful Smell, forth came the human pair Par Lost 9.197
Came Prologue, and Apologie to prompt, Par Lost 9.854
Came the mild Judge and Intercessor both Par Lost 10.96
He came, and with him *Eve*, more loth, though first Par Lost 10.109
Came to the Sea, and over *Hellespont* Par Lost 10.309
Disguis'd he came, but those his Children dear Par Lost 10.330
Met who to meet him came, his Ofspring dear. Par Lost 10.349
By thir great Intercessor, came in sight Par Lost 11.19

Came(*cont*)
Uncull'd, as came to hand; a Shepherd next Par Lost 11.436
More meek came with the Firstlings of his Flock Par Lost 11.437
Soft amorous Ditties, and in dance came on: Par Lost 11.584
At length a Reverend Sire among them came, Par Lost 11.719
Came seavens, and pairs, and enterd in, as taught Par Lost 11.735
With aw the Regions round, and with them came Par Reg 1.22
To the flood *Jordan*, came as then obscure, Par Reg 1.24
Where they might see him, and to thee they came; Par Reg 1.246
I as all others to his Baptism came, Par Reg 1.273
The way he came not having mark'd, return Par Reg 1.297
I came among the Sons of God, when he Par Reg 1.368
And now wild Beasts came forth the woods to roam. Par Reg 1.502
Came forth with Pilgrim steps in amice gray; Par Reg 4.427
Of this fair change, and to our Saviour came, Par Reg 4.442
Then with what trivial weapon came to hand, Samson 142
I willingly on some conditions came Samson 258
Came lagging after; say if he be here. Samson 337
I came, still dreading thy displeasure, *Samson*, Samson 733
And Princes of my countrey came in person, Samson 851
I heard all as I came, the City rings Samson 1449
Came to the place, and what was set before him Samson 1624
He tugg'd, he shook, till down they came and drew Samson 1650
And as an ev'ning Dragon came, Samson 1692
But where they are, and why they came not back, Mask 191
Bridgewater ms 'come'
In his loose traces from the furrow came, Mask 292
I came not here on such a trivial toy Mask 502
Or our neglect, we lost her as we came. Mask 510
And yet came off: if you have this about you Mask 647
That came in *Neptune*'s plea, Lycidas 90
Last came, and last did go, Lycidas 108
She crown'd with Olive green, came softly sliding Nativity 47
Then sing of secret things that came to pass Vacation 45
He at their invoking came Winchester 19
Atropos for *Lucina* came; Winchester 28
Came vested all in white, pure as her mind: Sonnet 23, 9
They shall return in hast the way they came Psalm 6, 23

Camel
More then the Camel, and to drink go far, Par Reg 1.340

Camels
Mules after these, Camels and Dromedaries, Par Reg 3.335

Camest
How cam'st thou speakable of mute, and how Par Lost 9.563
Sam. Cam'st thou for this, vain boaster, to survey me, Samson 1227
Return the way thou cam'st, I will not come. Samson 1332
How cam'st thou here good Swain? hath any ram Mask 497
Bridgewater ms 'camst'
And cam'st again to visit us once more? Fair Inf 52

Camp
Forerun the Royal Camp, to trench a Field, Par Lost 1.677
ms 'camp'
Disperst in Bands and Files thir Camp extend Par Lost 5.651
In *Dothan*, cover'd with a Camp of Fire, Par Lost 11.217
Such forces met not, nor so wide a camp, Par Reg 3.337
Each others force in camp or listed field: Samson 1087
In the camp of *Dan* Samson 1436
Garrison'd round about him like a Camp Samson 1497

Campanian
On the *Campanian* shore, with purpose there Par Reg 4.93

Camus
Next *Camus*, reverend Sire, went footing slow, Lycidas 103
1638 'Chamus'

Can
And rest can never dwell, hope never comes Par Lost 1.66
Can else inflict, do I repent or change, Par Lost 1.96
Can perish: for the mind and spirit remains Par Lost 1.139
What can it then avail though yet we feel Par Lost 1.153
There rest, if any rest can harbour there, Par Lost 1.185
Who now is Sovran can dispose and bid Par Lost 1.246
Can make a Heav'n of Hell, a Hell of Heav'n. Par Lost 1.255
If such astonishment as this can sieze Par Lost 1.317
Can either Sex assume, or both; so soft Par Lost 1.424
Can execute thir aerie purposes, Par Lost 1.430
For who can yet beleeve, though after loss, Par Lost 1.631
For who can think Submission? Warr then, Warr Par Lost 1.661
For since no deep within her gulf can hold Par Lost 2.12
For which to strive, no strife can grow up there Par Lost 2.31
More then can be in Heav'n, we now return Par Lost 2.37
We now debate; who can advise, may speak. Par Lost 2.42
Fear to be worse destroy'd: what can be worse Par Lost 2.85
Can give it, or will ever? how he can Par Lost 2.153
Whatever doing, what can we suffer more, Par Lost 2.162
What can we suffer worse? is this then worst, Par Lost 2.163
My voice disswades; for what can force or guile Par Lost 2.188
Our doom; which if we can sustain and bear, Par Lost 2.209
The latter: for what place can be for us Par Lost 2.235
We can create, and in what place so e're Par Lost 2.260
Magnificence; and what can Heav'n shew more? Par Lost 2.273
Inflicted? and what peace can we return, Par Lost 2.335
The happy Ile; what strength, what art can then Par Lost 2.410
These Gates for ever shut, which none can pass Par Lost 2.776
Save he who reigns above, none can resist. Par Lost 2.814
Keep residence; if all I can will serve, Par Lost 2.999
Wide interrupt can hold; so bent he seems Par Lost 3.84
If him by force he can destroy, or worse, Par Lost 3.91
So were created, nor can justly accuse Par Lost 3.112
Can never seek, once dead in sins and lost; Par Lost 3.233

Can(*cont*)
All that of me can die, yet that debt paid, Par Lost 3.246
Whom else no Creature can behold; on thee Par Lost 3.387
Shadow from body opaque can fall, and the Aire, Par Lost 3.619
For neither Man nor Angel can discern Par Lost 3.682
But what created mind can comprehend Par Lost 3.705
One step no more then from himself can fly Par Lost 4.22
For never can true reconcilement grow Par Lost 4.98
Have nothing merited, nor can performe Par Lost 4.418
Envie them that? can it be sin to know, Par Lost 4.517
Can it be death? and do they onely stand Par Lost 4.518
They taste and die: what likelier can ensue? Par Lost 4.527
Touch'd lightly; for no falshood can endure Par Lost 4.811
Will save us trial what the least can doe Par Lost 4.855
Can equal anger infinite provok't. Par Lost 4.916
To boast what Arms can doe, since thine no more Par Lost 4.1008
Affects me equally; nor can I like Par Lost 5.97
Yet evil whence? in thee can harbour none, Par Lost 5.99
Speak yee who best can tell, ye Sons of light, Par Lost 5.160
None can then Heav'n such glorious shape contain; Par Lost 5.362
Can turn, or holds it possible to turn Par Lost 5.441
Can comprehend, incapable of more. Par Lost 5.505
Obedient? can we want obedience then Par Lost 5.514
Human desires can seek or apprehend? Par Lost 5.518
Findes no acceptance, nor can find, for how Par Lost 5.531
Can hearts, not free, be tri'd whether they serve Par Lost 5.532
By Destinie, and can no other choose? Par Lost 5.534
Sleepst thou Companion dear, what sleep can close Par Lost 5.673
Both waking we were one; how then can now Par Lost 5.678
Who can in reason then or right assume Par Lost 5.794
In freedome equal? or can introduce Par Lost 5.797
When who can uncreate thee thou shalt know. Par Lost 5.895
Vigour Divine within them, can allow Par Lost 6.158
Of Angels, can relate, or to what things Par Lost 6.298
Receive, no more then can the fluid Aire: Par Lost 6.349
Left them Superiour, while we can preserve Par Lost 6.443
All patience. He who therefore can invent Par Lost 6.464
Warr wearied hath perform'd what Warr can do, Par Lost 6.695
Can end it. Into thee such Vertue and Grace Par Lost 6.703
But whom thou hat'st, I hate, and can put on Par Lost 6.734
Or we can bid his absence, till thy Song Par Lost 7.107
What words or tongue of Seraph can suffice, Par Lost 7.113
My damage fondly deem'd, I can repaire Par Lost 7.152
So told as earthly notion can receave. Par Lost 7.179
Thy power; what thought can measure thee or tongue Par Lost 7.603
Who can impair thee, mighty King, or bound Par Lost 7.608
Which onely thy solution can resolve. Par Lost 8.14
What happiness, who can enjoy alone, Par Lost 8.365
Can sort, what harmonie or true delight? Par Lost 8.384
Much less can Bird with Beast, or Fish with Fowle Par Lost 8.395
Wors then can Man with Beast, and least of all. Par Lost 8.397
But I can now no more; the parting Sun Par Lost 8.630
If answerable style I can obtaine Par Lost 9.20
Unprais'd: for nothing lovelier can be found Par Lost 9.232
Can either not receave, or can repell. Par Lost 9.284
Can by his fraud be shak'n or seduc't; Par Lost 9.287
Against his will he can receave no harme. Par Lost 9.350
First thy obedience; th' other who can know, Par Lost 9.368
My conduct, I can bring thee thither soon. Par Lost 9.630
Though threat'nd, which no worse then this can bring. Par Lost 9.715
What can your knowledge hurt him, or this Tree Par Lost 9.727
Or is it envie, and can envie dwell Par Lost 9.729
Chiefly I sought, without thee can despise. Par Lost 9.878
Whatever can to sight or thought be formd, Par Lost 9.898
How can I live without thee, how forgoe Par Lost 9.908
But past who can recall, or don undoe? Par Lost 9.926
Nor can I think that God, Creator wise, Par Lost 9.938
Most Favors, who can please him long; Mee first Par Lost 9.949
Was known in Heav'n; for what can scape the Eye Par Lost 10.5
Can fit his punishment, or their revenge. Par Lost 10.242
For Death from Sin no power can separate. Par Lost 10.251
Nor can I miss the way, so strongly drawn Par Lost 10.262
Who can extenuate thee? Next, to the Son, Par Lost 10.645
Now death to heare! for what can I encrease Par Lost 10.731
But mortal doom'd. How can he exercise Par Lost 10.796
Can he make deathless Death? that were to make Par Lost 10.798
If guiltless? But from me what can proceed, Par Lost 10.824
With me? how can they then acquitted stand Par Lost 10.827
How little weight my words with thee can finde, Par Lost 10.968
What better can we do, then to the place Par Lost 10.1086
What can be toilsom in these pleasant Walkes? Par Lost 11.179
Our frailtie can sustain, thy tidings bring, Par Lost 11.302
Of him who all things can, I would not cease Par Lost 11.309
Of *Cambalu*, seat of *Cathaian Can* Par Lost 11.388
Glad to be so dismist in peace. Can thus Par Lost 11.507
Which neither his foreknowing can prevent, Par Lost 11.773
Among them; how can God with such reside? Par Lost 12.284
Law can discover sin, but not remove, Par Lost 12.290
In thee and in thy Seed: nor can this be, Par Lost 12.395
So onely can high Justice rest appaid. Par Lost 12.401
What man can do against them, not affraid, Par Lost 12.493
Who against Faith and Conscience can be heard Par Lost 12.529
Eternitie, whose end no eye can reach. Par Lost 12.556
Of knowledge, what this Vessel can containe; Par Lost 12.559
At least if so we can, and by the head Par Reg 1.60
He now shall know I can produce a man Par Reg 1.150
Can raise them, though above example high; Par Reg 1.232
E're I the promis'd Kingdom can attain, Par Reg 1.265

Can(*cont*)
What can be then less in me then desire Par Reg 1.383
This wounds me most (what can it less) that Man, Par Reg 1.404
From thee I can and must submiss endure Par Reg 1.476
Can satisfie that need some other way, Par Reg 2.254
When and where likes me best, I can command? Par Reg 2.382
I can at will, doubt not, as soon as thou, Par Reg 2.383
In vain, where no acceptance it can find, Par Reg 2.388
What I can do or offer is suspect; Par Reg 2.399
So reigning can be no sincere delight. Par Reg 2.480
What I can suffer, how obey? who best Par Reg 3.194
Can suffer, best can do; best reign, who first Par Reg 3.195
Of worse torments me then the feeling can. Par Reg 3.208
If I then to the worst that can be hast, Par Reg 3.223
What of perfection can in man be found, Par Reg 3.230
Or human nature can receive, consider Par Reg 3.231
That which alone can truly reinstall thee Par Reg 3.372
For what can less so great a gift deserve? Par Reg 4.169
Which when he lists, he leaves, or boasts he can, Par Reg 4.306
Alas what can they teach, and not mislead; Par Reg 4.309
As in our native Language can I find Par Reg 4.333
And threatning nigh; what they can do as signs Par Reg 4.489
To win him, or win from him what I can. Par Reg 4.530
Or do my eyes misrepresent? Can this be hee, Samson 124
For with his own Laws he can best dispence. Samson 314
To what can I be useful, wherein serve Samson 564
After the brunt of battel, can as easie Samson 583
Or medcinal liquor can asswage, Samson 627
Love once possest, nor can be easily Samson 1005
That womans love can win or long inherit; Samson 1012
And all temptation can remove, Samson 1051
Where strength can least abide, though all thy hairs Samson 1136
Is well ejected when the Conquer'd can. Samson 1207
Har. O *Baal-zebub!* can my ears unus'd Samson 1231
The worst that he can give, to me the best. Samson 1264
That tyrannie or fortune can inflict, Samson 1291
Can they think me so broken, so debas'd Samson 1335
Man. He can I know, but doubt to think he will; Samson 1534
(For so I can distinguish by mine Art) Mask 149
Such noise as I can make to be heard farthest Mask 227
Com. Can any mortal mixture of Earths mould Mask 244
I can conduct you Lady to a low Mask 319
Tell her of things that no gross ear can hear, Mask 458
But here thy sword can do thee little stead, Mask 611
He with his bare wand can unthred thy joynts, Mask 614
That fancy can beget on youthfull thoughts, Mask 669
But such as are good men can give good things, Mask 703
I hate when vice can bolt her arguments, Mask 760
And, as the old Swain said, she can unlock Mask 852
Then her purfl'd scarf can shew, Mask 995
I can fly, or I can run Mask 1013
And from thence can soar as soon Mask 1016
She can teach ye how to clime Mask 1020
After the heavenly tune, which none can hear Arcades 72
What ere the skill of lesser gods can show, Arcades 79
Can no more divine, Nativity 177
Nor can he be at rest Nativity 216
Naught but profoundest Hell can be his shroud, Nativity 218
Can in his swadling bands controul the damned crew. Nativity 228
That glassy flouds from rugged rocks can crush, Psalm 114, 17
Yet can I not perswade me thou art dead Fair Inf 29
Small loss it is that thence can come unto thee, Vacation 9
I know my tongue but little Grace can do thee Vacation 10
Your Son, said she, (nor can you it prevent) Vacation 73
Your learned hands, can loose this Gordian knot? Vacation 90
Your fiery essence can distill no tear, Circum 7
He can requite thee, for he knows the charms Sonnet 8, 5
And he can spred thy Name o're Lands and Seas, Sonnet 8, 7
For what can Warr, but endless warr still breed, Sonnet 15, 10
He who of those delights can judge, And spare Sonnet 20, 13
Who in the grave can celebrate thy praise? Psalm 6, 10
In darkness can thy mighty *hand* Psalm 88, 49
Stronglier, and better oft then earnest can. Prose 7, 2
Which he who can, and will, deserv's high praise, Prose 9, 3
Who neither can nor will, may hold his peace; Prose 9, 4
What can be juster in a State then this? Prose 9, 5
There can be slaine Prose 11, 1

Canaan
Canaan he now attains, I see his Tents Par Lost 12.135
From *Canaan*, to a Land hereafter call'd Par Lost 12.156
Safe towards *Canaan* from the shoar advance Par Lost 12.215
His whole descent, who thus shall *Canaan* win. Par Lost 12.269
Of Law, his people into *Canaan* lead; Par Lost 12.309
Meanwhile they in thir earthly *Canaan* plac't Par Lost 12.315
And past from *Pharian* fields to *Canaan* Land, Psalm 114, 3

Canaanite
Least entring on the *Canaanite* allarmd Par Lost 12.217
A *Canaanite*, my faithless enemy. Samson 380

Canace
And who had *Canace* to wife, Penseroso 112

Cancelled
Canceld from Heav'n and sacred memorie, Par Lost 6.379

Candaor
From *Arachosia*, from *Candaor* East, Par Reg 3.316

Candle
Though a rush Candle from the wicker hole Mask 338
Trinity ms 'candle'
1637 'candle'

Candle(*cont*)
Bridgewater ms 'candle'

Canker
As killing as the Canker to the Rose, Lycidas 45
1638 'canker'
Trinity ms 'canker'

Cankered
Or hurtfull Worm with canker'd venom bites. Arcades 53
Trinity ms 'cankered'

Cannot
And this Empyreal substance cannot fail, Par Lost 1.117
And cannot cease to be, we are at worst Par Lost 2.100
As he our darkness, cannot we his Light Par Lost 2.269
Cannot but by annihilating die; Par Lost 6.347
Cannot without process of speech be told, Par Lost 7.178
Not hither summond, since they cannot change Par Lost 8.347
Cannot well suite with either, but soon prove Par Lost 8.388
Cannot be human consort; they rejoyce Par Lost 8.392
I by conversing cannot these erect Par Lost 8.432
God therefore cannot hurt ye, and be just; Par Lost 9.700
Though others envie what they cannot give; Par Lost 9.805
Proportional ascent, which cannot be Par Lost 9.936
Our State cannot be severd, we are one, Par Lost 9.958
For us his ofspring deare? It cannot be Par Lost 10.238
Pursues me still, least all I cannot die, Par Lost 10.783
Which God inspir'd, cannot together perish Par Lost 10.785
Cannot appease, nor Man the moral part Par Lost 12.298
Perform, and not performing cannot live. Par Lost 12.299
Man. I cannot praise thy Marriage choises, Son, Samson 420
I cannot but acknowledge; yet if tears Samson 735
Of their own deity, Gods cannot be: Samson 899
They cannot well impose, nor I sustain; Samson 1258
My presence; for that cause I cannot come. Samson 1321
The last of me or no I cannot warrant. Samson 1426
I cannot hallow to my Brothers, but Mask 226
I cannot be, that I should fear to change it. Mask 328
Bridgewater ms 'cannott'
We cannot free the Lady that sits here Mask 818
And those that cannot live from him asunder Vacation 77
His footsteps cannot err. Psalm 85, 56

Canon
Against the canon laws of our foundation; Mask 808
Bridgewater ms 'Canon'

Canopied
With Ivy canopied, and interwove Mask 544
Bridgewater ms 'Cannopied'

Canopy
So high above the circling Canopie Par Lost 3.556

Canst
Thou therefore whom thou only canst redeem, Par Lost 3.281
Thy way thou canst not miss, me mine requires. Par Lost 3.735
Like consort to thy self canst no where find. Par Lost 4.448
Happier thou mayst be, worthier canst not be: Par Lost 5.76
Canst thou with impious obloquie condemne Par Lost 5.813
Thou canst not. Hast thou turnd the least of these Par Lost 6.284
Yet what thou canst attain, which best may serve Par Lost 7.115
Canst raise thy Creature to what highth thou wilt Par Lost 8.430
Thou canst, who art sole Wonder, much less arm Par Lost 9.533
O thou who future things canst represent Par Lost 11.870
(Canst thou believe2) should be so stupid grown, Par Lost 12.116
I see him, but thou canst not, with what Faith Par Lost 12.128
Easily canst thou find one miserable, Par Reg 1.471
Permission from above; thou canst not more. Par Reg 1.496
What Followers, what Retinue canst thou gain, Par Reg 2.419
Longer then thou canst feed them on thy cost? Par Reg 2.421
Worthy of Memorial) canst thou not remember Par Reg 2.445
What best to say canst say, to do canst do; Par Reg 3.8
Raign then; what canst thou better do the while? Par Reg 3.180
Other donation none thou canst produce: Par Reg 4.184
Advise thee, gain them as thou canst, or not. Par Reg 4.211
On thee, who now no more canst do them harm. Samson 486
Thou canst avoid, self-preservation bids; Samson 505
His labours, for thou canst, to peaceful end. Samson 709
Are in confusion, give us if thou canst, Samson 1593
Canst thou not tell me of a gentle Pair Mask 236
Thou canst not touch the freedom of my minde Mask 663
Trinity ms 'canst' ←'can'st'
These delights, if thou canst give, Allegro 151
But thou canst best perform that office where thou art. Fair Inf 70

Cany
With Sails and Wind thir canie Waggons light: Par Lost 3.439

Capable
Delighted, or not capable her eare Par Lost 8.49
As wee, not capable of death or paine, Par Lost 9.283

Capacious
Capacious bed of Waters: thither they Par Lost 7.290
I turnd my thoughts, and with capacious mind Par Lost 9.603

Capacity
Capacity not rais'd to apprehend Samson 1028

Caparisons
Impreses quaint, Caparisons and Steeds; Par Lost 9.35

Cape
Through the wide *Ethiopian* to the Cape Par Lost 2.641
Beyond the *Cape of Hope*, and now are past Par Lost 4.160
Beyond the Earths green Cape and verdant Isles Par Lost 8.631

Caphtor
And lamentation to the Sons of *Caphtor* Samson 1713

Capital
At *Pandaemonium*, the high Capital Par Lost 1.756
ms 'Capitall'
Som Capital City; or less then if this frame Par Lost 2.924
Perhaps thy Capital Seate, from whence had spred Par Lost 11.343
Needs must the Serpent now his capital bruise Par Lost 12.383
My capital secret, in what part my strength Samson 394
Due by the Law to capital punishment? Samson 1225
Capitol
Of Nations; there the Capitol thou seest Par Reg 4.47
Capitoline
Ammonian Jove, or *Capitoline* was seen, Par Lost 9.508
Capreae
To *Capreae* an Island small but strong Par Reg 4.92
Capricorn
As deep as *Capricorne*, to bring in change Par Lost 10.677
Captain
Captain or Colonel, or Knight in Arms, Sonnet 8, 1
Trinity ms 'Captaine'
Captains
Lords, Ladies, Captains, Councellors, or Priests, Samson 1653
Captive
Who mourn'd in earnest, when the Captive Ark Par Lost 1.458
ms 'captive'
His captive multitude: For he, be sure Par Lost 2.323
Shall lead Hell Captive maugre Hell, and show Par Lost 3.255
Then when I am thy captive talk of chaines, Par Lost 4.970
Or Captive drag'd in Chains, with hostile frown Par Lost 6.260
Captivity led captive through the Aire, Par Lost 10.188
As a poor miserable captive thrall, Par Reg 1.411
Led captive; cease to admire, and all her Plumes Par Reg 2.222
Made Captive, yet deserving freedom more Par Reg 3.77
Led captive, and *Jerusalem* laid waste, Par Reg 3.283
Thy country, and captive lead away her Kings Par Reg 3.366
As for those captive Tribes, themselves were they Par Reg 3.414
My Son now Captive, hither hath inform'd Samson 335
Thy Foes derision, Captive, Poor, and Blind Samson 366
Thir Captive, and thir triumph; thou the sooner Samson 426
Our Captive, at the public Mill our drudge, Samson 1393
Thir once great dread, captive, & blind before them, Samson 1474
I sorrow'd at his captive state, but minded Samson 1603
Captived
Betray'd, Captiv'd, and both my Eyes put out, Samson 33
To dogs and fowls a prey, or else captiv'd: Samson 694
Captivity
Captivity led captive through the Aire, Par Lost 10.188
There in captivitie he lets them dwell Par Lost 12.344
Israel in long captivity still mourns; Par Reg 3.279
Who wrought their own captivity, fell off Par Reg 3.415
Nor in the land of their captivity Par Reg 3.420
Life in captivity Samson 108
From whence captivity and loss of eyes. Samson 1744
In willing chains and sweet captivitie. Vacation 52
Thou hast from *hard* Captivity Psalm 85, 3
Car
He circl'd, four times cross'd the Carr of Night Par Lost 9.65
And the gilded Car of Day, Mask 95
1637 'Carre'
Bridgewater ms 'Carr'
Trinity ms 'carre'
Hath fixt her polisht Car. Nativity 241
So mounting up in ycie-pearled carr, Fair Inf 15
Caravan
Thir Aierie Caravan high over Sea's Par Lost 7.428
In Troop or Caravan, for single none Par Reg 1.323
Carbuncle
If stone, Carbuncle most or Chrysolite, Par Lost 3.596
Crested aloft, and Carbuncle his Eyes; Par Lost 9.500
Carcases
From the safe shore thir floating Carkases Par Lost 1.310
ms 'carcasses'
With Carcasses and Arms th' ensanguind Field Par Lost 11.654
Carcass
Death last, and with his Carcass glut the Grave: Par Lost 3.259
His Carcass, pin'd with hunger and with droughth? Par Reg 1.325
Or left thy carkass where the Ass lay thrown: Samson 1097
Carcasses
With sent of living Carcasses design'd Par Lost 10.277
Of Heathen and prophane, thir carkasses Samson 693
Care
Deep scars of Thunder had intrencht, and care Par Lost 1.601
Car'd not to be at all; with that care lost Par Lost 2.48
Deliberation sat and public care; Par Lost 2.303
New troubles; him thy care must be to find. Par Lost 4.575
Then violence: for this was all thy care Par Lost 6.35
Not emulous, nor care who them excells; Par Lost 6.822
So spake domestick *Adam* in his care Par Lost 9.318
Created; but henceforth my early care, Par Lost 9.799
Each thing on Earth; and other care perhaps Par Lost 9.813
Which your sincerest care could not prevent, Par Lost 10.37
If care of our descent perplex us most, Par Lost 10.979
Or Heat should injure us, his timely care Par Lost 10.1057
Grievous to bear: but that care now is past, Par Lost 11.776
Unanimous they all commit the care Par Reg 1.111
Therefore as those young Prophets then with care Par Reg 2.18
Must not omit a Fathers timely care Samson 602
Exempt from many a care and chance to which Samson 918
With me, where my redoubl'd love and care Samson 923

Care*(cont)*
Sams. No, no, of my condition take no care; Samson 928
Which men call Earth, and with low-thoughted care Mask 6
Bridgewater ms 'Care'
To this my errand, and the care it brought. Mask 506
Bridgewater ms 'Care'
As to make this relation? *Spir*. Care and utmost shifts Mask 617
Sport that wrincled Care derides, Allegro 31
Alas! What boots it with uncessant care Lycidas 64
Of other care they little reck'ning make, Lycidas 116
There ended was his quest, there ceast his care. Fair Inf 18
Sav'd with care from Winters nip, Winchester 36
Thy care is fixt and zealously attends Sonnet 9, 9
And disapproves that care, though wise in show, Sonnet 21, 12
And all within his care. Psalm 87, 8
Cared
Car'd not to be at all; with that care lost Par Lost 2.48
Career
To mortal combat or carreer with Lance) Par Lost 1.766
Declin'd was hasting now with prone carreer Par Lost 4.353
Thus night oft see me in thy pale career, Penseroso 121
My hasting dayes flie on with full career, Sonnet 7, 3
Trinity ms 'careere'
Careering
Of Beril, and careering Fires between; Par Lost 6.756
Careful
Swayes them; the careful Plowman doubting stands Par Lost 4.983
Many a dark League, reduc't in careful Watch Par Lost 10.438
With careful step, Locks white as doune, Samson 327
Which carefull *Jove* in natures true behoofe Fair Inf 45
Careless
In corporal pleasure he, and careless ease; Par Reg 4.299
And in a careless mood thus to him said. Par Reg 4.450
Carelessly
See how he lies at random, carelesly diffus'd, Samson 118
Cares
God hath bid dwell farr off all anxious cares, Par Lost 8.185
Motherly cares and fears got head, and rais'd Par Reg 2.64
Brings dangers, troubles, cares, and sleepless nights Par Reg 2.460
All publick cares, and yet of him suspicious, Par Reg 4.96
While I at home sate full of cares and fears Samson 805
And ever against eating Cares, Allegro 135
Caresses
With conjugal Caresses, from his Lip Par Lost 8.56
Carest
Thou in old age car'st how to nurse thy Son. Samson 1488
Carmel
Mount *Carmel;* here the double-founted stream Par Lost 12.144
Carnage
Of carnage, prey innumerable, and taste Par Lost 10.268
Carnal
Not sunk in carnal pleasure, for which cause Par Lost 8.593
Carnal desire enflaming, hee on *Eve* Par Lost 9.1013
And carnal fear that day dimm'd *Adams* eye. Par Lost 11.212
Spiritual Lawes by carnal power shall force Par Lost 12.521
And link't it self by carnal sensualty Mask 474
Trinity ms 'carnall'
Bridgewater ms 'carnall'
1637 'carnall'
Carnation
Carnation, Purple, Azure, or spect with Gold, Par Lost 9.429
The pride of her carnation train, Winchester 37
Carol
Of squadrond Angels hear his Carol sung. Par Lost 12.367
Carrol her goodnes lowd in rustick layes, Mask 849
Bridgewater ms 'Carroll'
1637 'Carroll'
Trinity ms 'carroll'
Carpathian
And the *Carpathian* wisards hook, Mask 872
Carpenter
A Carpenter thy Father known, thy self Par Reg 2.414
Carriage
Had not his weekly cours of carriage fail'd; Carrier 10
Carrier
For one Carrier put down to make six bearers. Another 20
line not in 1640, 1657, 1658 texts
He had bin an immortall Carrier. Another 28
1640, 1657 'carrier'
Carries
His habit carries peace, his brow defiance. Samson 1073
Carry
These tidings carrie to th' anointed King; Par Lost 5.870
I carry hence; though all by mee is lost, Par Lost 12.621
Held up their pearled wrists and took her in, Mask 834
Trinity ms '& took' ← 'to take' ← 'carie' ← 'receave'
If I may not carry, sure Ile ne're be fetch'd, Another 18
line not in 1640, 1657, 1658 texts
Carrying
Of Nuptial Love profest, carrying it strait Samson 385
Cart
He di'd for heavines that his Cart went light, Another 22
1640, 1657 'Carts'
line not in 1658 text
Carthaginian
The *Carthaginian* pride, young *Pompey* quell'd Par Reg 3.35
Carved
Carv'd work, the hand of fam'd Artificers Par Reg 4.59

Casbeen	
To *Tauris* or *Casbeen*. So these the late	Par Lost 10.436
Casella	
Then his *Casella*, whom he woo'd to sing,	Sonnet 13, 13
Trinity ms 'Casella' ←'Casell"	
Cash	
Or as a Thief bent to unhoord the cash	Par Lost 4.188
Casius	
Betwixt *Damiata* and mount *Casius* old,	Par Lost 2.593
Casket	
That was the Casket of Heav'ns richest store,	Passion 44
Caspian	
Over the *Caspian*, then stand front to front	Par Lost 2.716
To *Tauris* or *Casbeen*. So these the late	Par Lost 10.436
Araxes and the *Caspian* lake, thence on	Par Reg 3.271
Cassia	
And flouring Odours, Cassia, Nard, and Balme;	Par Lost 5.293
Nard, and *Cassia*'s balmy smels.	Mask 991
Trinity ms 'Cassia's' ←'casia's'	
Bridgewater ms 'Casias'	
Cast	
Had cast him out from Heav'n, with all his Host	Par Lost 1.37
Behind him cast; the broad circumference	Par Lost 1.286
Down cast and damp, yet such wherein appear'd	Par Lost 1.523
In loss it self; which on his count'nance cast	Par Lost 1.526
Waiting revenge: cruel his eye, but cast	Par Lost 1.604
Or cast a Rampart. *Mammon* led them on,	Par Lost 1.678
Did not disswade me most, and seem to cast	Par Lost 2.122
Each cast at th' other, as when two black Clouds	Par Lost 2.714
Cast forth redounding smoak and ruddy flame.	Par Lost 2.889
With solemn adoration down they cast	Par Lost 3.351
Of us out-cast, exil'd, his new delight,	Par Lost 4.106
Cast out from God and blessed vision, falls	Par Lost 5.613
Our minds and teach us to cast off this Yoke?	Par Lost 5.786
Affrighted; but strict Fate had cast too deep	Par Lost 6.869
Began to cast lascivious Eyes, she him	Par Lost 9.1014
Cast on themselves from thir own mouths. There stood	Par Lost 10.547
Of Brick, and of that stuff they cast to build	Par Lost 12.43
By words at times cast forth inly rejoyc'd,	Par Reg 1.228
They have exalted, and behind them cast	Par Reg 2.46
Cast wanton eyes on the daughters of men,	Par Reg 2.180
The field all iron cast a gleaming brown,	Par Reg 3.326
Thence to the gates cast round thine eye, and see	Par Reg 4.61
Cast thy self down; safely if Son of God:	Par Reg 4.555
Cast her self headlong from th' *Ismenian* steep,	Par Reg 4.575
Thou didst debel, and down from Heav'n cast	Par Reg 4.605
Your younger feet, while mine cast back with age	Samson 336
But now hath cast me off as never known,	Samson 641
To cast the fashion of uncertain evils;	Mask 360
line not in Trinity ms	
line not in Bridgewater ms	
Begin to cast a beam on th' outward shape,	Mask 460
& good heaven cast his best regard upon us	Mask Tr. ms 21.32
With a sad Leaden downward cast,	Penseroso 43
And call the Vales, and bid them hither cast	Lycidas 134
And cast the dark foundations deep,	Nativity 123
Their bonds, and cast from us, no more to wear,	Psalm 2, 7
Hearts and reins. On God is cast	Psalm 7, 39
Castalian	
Castalian Spring, might with this Paradise	Par Lost 4.274
Casting	
Not flying, but fore-casting in what place	Samson 254
Casting a dimm religious light.	Penseroso 160
But this is got by casting Pearl to Hoggs;	Sonnet 12, 8
Casts	
Casts pale and dreadful? Thither let us tend	Par Lost 1.183
But first he casts to change his proper shape,	Par Lost 3.634
Tells the suggested cause, and casts between	Par Lost 5.702
To trouble Holy Rest; Heav'n casts thee out	Par Lost 6.272
And casts a gleam over this tufted Grove.	Mask 225
line not in Bridgewater ms	
Not half so far casts his usurped sway,	Nativity 170
Casual	
Casual fruition, nor in Court Amours	Par Lost 4.767
Casual discourse draw on, which intermits	Par Lost 9.223
Had melted (whether found where casual fire	Par Lost 11.566
Cataphracts	
Archers, and Slingers, Cataphracts and Spears.	Samson 1619
Cataracts	
Of Hell should spout her Cataracts of Fire,	Par Lost 2.176
And shelterd round, but all the Cataracts	Par Lost 11.824
Catarrhs	
Convulsions, Epilepsies, fierce Catarrhs,	Par Lost 11.483
Catch	
And upstart Passions catch the Government	Par Lost 12.88
We shall catch them at their sport,	Mask 953
Catched	
Catcht by Contagion, like in punishment,	Par Lost 10.544
Cateress	
With her abundance, she good cateress	Mask 764
Bridgewater ms 'Chateresse'	
Trinity ms 'cateresse'	
1637 'cateresse'	
1673 'cateres'	
Cates	
Alas how simple, to these Cates compar'd,	Par Reg 2.348
Cathaian	
Cathaian Coast. The aggregated Soyle	Par Lost 10.293

Cathaian*(cont)*	
Of *Cambalu*, seat of *Cathaian Can*	Par Lost 11.388
Cattle	
Cattel and Creeping things, and Beast of the Earth,	Par Lost 7.452
The Cattel in the Fields and Meddowes green:	Par Lost 7.460
To Cattel and each Beast; which would not be	Par Lost 8.582
Above all Cattle, each Beast of the Field;	Par Lost 10.176
1667 'Cattel'	
Of Cattel grazing: others, whence the sound	Par Lost 11.558
Where Cattle pastur'd late, now scatterd lies	Par Lost 11.653
1667 'Cattel'	
His Cattel must of Rot and Murren die,	Par Lost 12.179
the feilds with cattell & the aire with fowle	Mask Tr. ms 21.57
and often takes our cattell with strange pinches	Mask Tr. ms 23.51
Caucasus	
Of *Caucasus*, and dark *Iberian* dales,	Par Reg 3.318
Caught	
Caught in a fierie Tempest shall be hurl'd	Par Lost 2.180
Fast caught, they lik'd, and each his liking chose;	Par Lost 11.587
In either hand the hastning Angel caught	Par Lost 12.637
And for a time caught up to God, as once	Par Reg 2.14
So saying he caught him up, and without wing	Par Reg 4.541
Where once I have been caught; I know thy trains	Samson 932
Streit mine eye hath caught new pleasures	Allegro 69
Cause	
Nor the deep Tract of Hell, say first what cause	Par Lost 1.28
Far off and fearless, nor with cause to boast,	Par Lost 4.14
To thy deserted host this cause of flight,	Par Lost 4.922
Tells the suggested cause, and casts between	Par Lost 5.702
Against revolted multitudes the Cause	Par Lost 6.31
Under thir God-like Leaders, in the Cause	Par Lost 6.67
In Nature none: if other hidden cause	Par Lost 6.442
Accepted, fearless in his righteous Cause,	Par Lost 6.804
When, and whereof created, for what cause,	Par Lost 7.64
Imbracing round this florid Earth, what cause	Par Lost 7.90
But who I was, or where, or from what cause,	Par Lost 8.270
But in degree, the cause of his desire	Par Lost 8.417
Extracted; for this cause he shall forgoe	Par Lost 8.497
Not sunk in carnal pleasure, for which cause	Par Lost 8.593
Wondrous indeed, if cause of such effects.	Par Lost 9.650
Flourishd, since mute, to som great cause addrest,	Par Lost 9.672
Hath bin the cause, and wonderful to heare:	Par Lost 9.862
Let none henceforth seek needless cause to approve	Par Lost 9.1140
And am I now upbraided, as the cause	Par Lost 9.1168
Which infinite calamitie shall cause	Par Lost 10.907
On me, sole cause to thee of all this woe,	Par Lost 10.935
To be to others cause of misery,	Par Lost 10.982
Whereon for different cause the Tempter set	Par Lost 11.382
Alas, both for the deed and for the cause!	Par Lost 11.461
With cause for evils past, yet much more cheer'd	Par Lost 12.604
His birth to our just fear gave no small cause,	Par Reg 1.66
If cause were to unfold some active Scene	Par Reg 2.239
Cause thy refusal, said the subtle Fiend,	Par Reg 2.323
What I foretell thee, soon thou shalt have cause	Par Reg 4.375
(Which Men enjoying sight oft without cause complain)	Samson 157
She was not the prime cause, but I my self,	Samson 234
Nor in respect of the enemy just cause	Samson 316
Sole Author I, sole cause: if aught seem vile,	Samson 376
Man. With cause this hope relieves thee, and these words	Samson 472
Cause light again within thy eies to spring,	Samson 584
Goes by the worse, whatever be her cause.	Samson 904
He will accept thee to defend his cause,	Samson 1179
Sam. He must allege some cause, and offer'd fight	Samson 1253
My presence; for that cause I cannot come.	Samson 1321
Sa. Perhaps thou shalt have cause to sorrow indeed.	Samson 1347
For some important cause, thou needst not doubt.	Samson 1379
Mess. By his own hands. *Man*. Self-violence? what cause	Samson 1584
Among his foes? *Mess*. Inevitable cause	Samson 1586
Nor much more cause, *Samson* hath quit himself	Samson 1709
Defence is a good cause, and Heav'n be for us.	Mask 489
Bridgewater ms 'Cause'	
Of this pure cause would kindle my rap't spirits	Mask 794
line not in Bridgewater ms	
line not in Trinity ms	
In hard besetting need, this will I try	Mask 857
Upon me: cause at length to cease	Psalm 7, 34
Cause thou thy face on us to shine	Psalm 80, 15
Cause thou thy face on us to shine,	Psalm 80, 31
Cause thou thy face on us to shine,	Psalm 80, 79
Dispatch the poor mans cause,	Psalm 82, 10
Thine indignation cause to cease	Psalm 85, 15
Cause us to see thy goodness Lord,	Psalm 85, 25
Ah *Constantine*, of how much ill was cause	Prose 1, 1
Whose witnesse and opinion winnes the cause;	Prose 10, 4
Caused	
Out of the fertil ground he caus'd to grow	Par Lost 4.216
To us for food and for delight hath caus'd	Par Lost 5.400
But God who caus'd a fountain at thy prayer	Samson 581
Caus'd what I did? I saw thee mutable	Samson 793
And caus'd the Golden-tressed Sun,	Psalm 136, 29
Causeless	
Though not disordinate, yet causless suffring	Samson 701
Causes	
But all these in thir pregnant causes mixt	Par Lost 2.913
That brought them forth, but hid thir causes deep.	Par Lost 3.707
Things in thir Causes, but to trace the wayes	Par Lost 9.682
Causes import your need of this fair Fruit.	Par Lost 9.731
By which all Causes else according still	Par Lost 10.806

Causey
The Causey to Hell Gate; on either side Par Lost 10.415
Caution
What meant that caution joind, *if ye be found* Par Lost 5.513
This was that caution giv'n thee; be advis'd. Par Lost 5.523
This also thy request with caution askt Par Lost 7.111
Cautious
From compassing the Earth, cautious of day, Par Lost 9.59
Then with more cautious and instructed skill Samson 757
Cautiously
Nicely or cautiously my offer'd aid, Par Reg 4.377
Cave
Of waters issu'd from a Cave and spread Par Lost 4.454
Unbarr'd the gates of Light. There is a Cave Par Lost 6.4
To his grim Cave, all dismal; yet to sense Par Lost 11.469
To som Caves mouth, or whether washt by stream Par Lost 11.569
Or harbour'd in one Cave, is not reveal'd; Par Reg 1.307
Hid in her vacant interlunar cave. Samson 89
Hid them in som flowry Cave, Mask 239
  Trinity ms 'cave'
In *Stygian* Cave forlorn Allegro 3
Courts thee on Roses in some pleasant Cave, Horace 2
Caverns
By grots, and caverns shag'd with horrid shades, Mask 429
  Trinity ms 'cavern's'
  Bridgewater ms 'Caverns'
Caves
Rocks, Caves, Lakes, Fens, Bogs, Dens, and shades of death, Par Lost 2.621
From all her Caves, and back resounded *Death*. Par Lost 2.789
Another side, umbrageous Grots and Caves Par Lost 4.257
Mean while the tepid Caves, and Fens and shoares Par Lost 7.417
Rocks, Dens, and Caves; but I in none of these Par Lost 9.118
Within thir stony caves, but rush'd abroad Par Reg 4.414
Thee Shepherd, thee the Woods, and desert Caves, Lycidas 39
  1638 'caves'
  Trinity ms 'caves'
Cavil
Then cavil the conditions? and though God Par Lost 10.759
Cease
And cannot cease to be, we are at worst Par Lost 2.100
To punish endless? wherefore cease we then? Par Lost 2.159
Cease I to wander where the Muses haunt Par Lost 3.27
Returns our own. Cease then this impious rage, Par Lost 5.845
Of him who all things can, I would not cease Par Lost 11.309
And terror cease; he grants what they besaught Par Lost 12.238
Led captive; cease to admire, and all her Plumes Par Reg 2.222
And never cease, though to his shame the more; Par Reg 4.14
But he her fears to cease, Nativity 45
Her false imagin'd loss cease to lament, Fair Inf 72
Devouring war shall never cease to roare: Vacation 86
Upon me: cause at length to cease Psalm 7, 34
We cry and do not cease. Psalm 83, 4
Thine indignation cause to cease Psalm 85, 15
Ceased
He scarce had ceas't when the superiour Fiend Par Lost 1.283
He ceas'd, and next him *Moloc*, Scepter'd King Par Lost 2.43
He ceas'd, for both seemd highly pleasd, and Death Par Lost 2.845
He ceas'd; and *Satan* staid not to reply, Par Lost 2.1010
No sooner had th' Almighty ceas't, but all Par Lost 3.344
Ceas'd warbling, but all night tun'd her soft layes: Par Lost 7.436
He ceas'd, I lowly answer'd. To attaine Par Lost 8.412
Not so repulst, with Tears that ceas'd not flowing, Par Lost 10.910
He ceas'd; and th' Archangelic Power prepar'd Par Lost 11.126
The brazen Throat of Warr had ceast to roar, Par Lost 11.713
But all in vain: which when he saw, he ceas'd Par Lost 11.726
When violence was ceas't, and Warr on Earth, Par Lost 11.780
He ceas'd, discerning *Adam* with such joy Par Lost 12.372
The Gentiles; henceforth Oracles are ceast, Par Reg 1.456
He ceas'd, and heard thir grant in loud acclaim; Par Reg 2.235
From that time seldom have I ceas'd to eye Par Reg 4.507
At which I ceas't, and listen'd them a while, Mask 551
  Trinity ms 'ceas'd' ←'ceased'
  Bridgewater ms 'ceast'
There ended was his quest, there ceast his care. Fair Inf 18
His principles being ceast, he ended strait. Another 10
  1657, 1658 'ceas'd'
  1640 'seasd'
Ceaseless
These yelling Monsters that with ceasless cry Par Lost 2.795
All these with ceasless praise his works behold Par Lost 4.679
And nourish all things, let your ceasless change Par Lost 5.183
And worn with Famin, long and ceasless hiss, Par Lost 10.573
And to my cries, that *ceaseless are*, Psalm 88, 7
Ceases
Perhaps hath spent his shafts, and ceases now Par Lost 1.176
Ceasing
A cry of Hell Hounds never ceasing bark'd Par Lost 2.654
Cedar
Cedar, and Pine, and Firr, and branching Palm, Par Lost 4.139
On Cliffs and Cedar tops thir Eyries build: Par Lost 7.424
Of stateliest Covert, Cedar, Pine, or Palme, Par Lost 9.435
Of Cedar, overlaid with Gold, therein Par Lost 12.250
Or Cedar, to defend him from the dew, Par Reg 1.306
In Cedar, Marble, Ivory or Gold. Par Reg 4.60
Cedarn
About the cedar'n alleys fling Mask 990
  Bridgewater ms 'Cederne'
  Trinity ms 'cedar'ne' ←'myrtle'
Cedars
Earth and the Gard'n of God, with Cedars crownd Par Lost 5.260
Ye Cedars, with innumerable boughs Par Lost 9.1089
Her Bows as *high as* Cedars tall Psalm 80, 43
Ceiling
Like a dark Ceeling stood; down rush'd the Rain Par Lost 11.743
Celebrate
Strict Laws impos'd, to celebrate his Throne Par Lost 2.241
From all the ends of th' Earth, to celebrate Par Lost 11.345
Here celebrate in *Gaza;* and proclaim Samson 435
I will assay, her worth to celebrate, Arcades 80
Who in the grave can celebrate thy praise? Psalm 6, 10
Celebrated
Worthiest to Reign: he celebrated rode Par Lost 6.888
So rife and celebrated in the mouths Samson 866
Celestial
For that celestial light? Be it so, since he Par Lost 1.245
Caelestial Spirits in Bondage, nor th' Abyss Par Lost 1.658
  ms 'celestial'
Celestial vertues rising, will appear Par Lost 2.15
So much the rather thou Celestial light Par Lost 3.51
Impurpl'd with Celestial Roses smil'd. Par Lost 3.364
Youth smil'd Celestial, and to every Limb Par Lost 3.638
Celestial Armourie, Shields, Helmes, and Speares, Par Lost 4.553
Celestial voices to the midnight air, Par Lost 4.682
Touch of Celestial temper, but returns Par Lost 4.812
And read thy Lot in yon celestial Sign Par Lost 4.1011
Thousand Celestial Ardors, where he stood Par Lost 5.249
That one Celestial Father gives to all. Par Lost 5.403
Celestial Tabernacles, where they slept Par Lost 5.654
Go *Michael* of Celestial Armies Prince, Par Lost 6.44
Sanguin, such as Celestial Spirits may bleed, Par Lost 6.333
Wide the Celestial soile, and saw beneath Par Lost 6.510
Hee in Celestial Panoplie all armd Par Lost 6.760
With thy Celestial Song. Up led by thee Par Lost 7.12
Celestial Equipage; and now came forth Par Lost 7.203
By the Celestial Quires, when Orient Light Par Lost 7.254
For of Celestial Bodies first the Sun Par Lost 7.354
In that celestial Colloquie sublime, Par Lost 8.455
Celestial rosie red, Loves proper hue, Par Lost 8.619
Of my Celestial Patroness, who deignes Par Lost 9.21
By gift, and thy Celestial Beautie adore Par Lost 9.540
That time Celestial visages, yet mixt Par Lost 10.24
Not in his shape Celestial, but as Man Par Lost 11.239
Celestial, whether among the Thrones, or nam'd Par Lost 11.296
How comes it thus? unfould, Celestial Guide, Par Lost 11.785
Burst forth, and in Celestial measures mov'd, Par Reg 1.170
A table of Celestial Food, Divine, Par Reg 4.588
And celestial vigour arm'd, Samson 1280
Celestial *Cupid* her fam'd Son advanc't, Mask 1004
  Trinity ms 'celestiall'
  line not in Bridgewater ms
  1637 'Celestiall'
bedew'd with nectar, & celestiall songs Mask Tr. ms 10.06
To the celestial *Sirens* harmony, Arcades 63
  Trinity ms 'caelestiall'
Thron'd in Celestiall sheen, Nativity 145
  1673 'Celestial'
To his celestial consort us unite, Musick 27
  Trinity ms 'celestiall'
Cell
Into her private Cell when Nature rests. Par Lost 5.109
Mine eyes he clos'd, but op'n left the Cell Par Lost 8.460
Within thy airy shell Mask 231
  Trinity ms 'shell', 'cell' written in margin
The Pensive secrecy of desert cell, Mask 387
  Bridgewater ms 'Cell'
Find out som uncouth cell, Allegro 5
The Hairy Gown and Mossy Cell, Penseroso 169
Inspire's the pale-ey'd Priest from the prophetic cell. Nativity 180
As in a rocky Cell Psalm 4, 41
Cells
Nigh on the Plain in many cells prepar'd, Par Lost 1.700
A various mould, and from the boyling cells Par Lost 1.706
Deliciously, and builds her waxen Cells Par Lost 7.491
Celtic
And ore the *Celtic* roam'd the utmost Isles. Par Lost 1.521
  ms 'Celtic'
Roaving the *Celtick*, and *Iberian* fields, Mask 60
Censer
And Prayers, which in this Golden Censer, mixt Par Lost 11.24
Censers
Fuming from Golden Censers hid the Mount. Par Lost 7.600
Censure
Thine forgive mine; that men may censure thine Samson 787
Censuring
To gloss upon, and censuring, frown or smile? Samson 948
Centaur
Betwixt the *Centaure* and the *Scorpion* stearing Par Lost 10.328
Centre
Of Adamant, and as a Center, firm Par Reg 4.534
As from the Center thrice to th' utmost Pole. Par Lost 1.74
Ransack'd the Center, and with impious hands Par Lost 1.686
  ms 'center'
By center, or eccentric, hard to tell, Par Lost 3.575
From center to circumference, whereon Par Lost 5.510
Upon her Center pois'd, when on a day Par Lost 5.579
Had to her Center shook. What wonder? when Par Lost 6.219

Centre(*cont*)
Heav'ns highth, and with the Center mix the Pole. Par Lost 7.215
And Earth self ballanc't on her Center hung. Par Lost 7.242
Be Center to the World, and other Starrs Par Lost 8.123
Is Center, yet extends to all, so thou Par Lost 9.108
On mee as on thir natural center light Par Lost 10.740
May sit i' th center, and enjoy bright day, Mask 382
Bridgewater ms 'Center'
And so bestudd with Stars, that they below Mask 734
Trinity ms 'and so bestudde with starres' ←'would so be studde the center with thire starre light'
In the center of her light. Arcades 19
Shall from the surface to the center shake; Nativity 162
Centred
One foot he center'd, and the other turn'd Par Lost 7.228
Centric
With Centric and Eccentric scribl'd o're, Par Lost 8.83
Oblique the Centric Globe: Som say the Sun Par Lost 10.671
Centring
Centring receav'st from all those Orbs; in thee, Par Lost 9.109
Cerastes
Cerastes hornd, *Hydrus*, and *Ellops* drear, Par Lost 10.525
Cerberean
With wide *Cerberian* mouths full loud, and rung Par Lost 2.655
1667 '*Cerberean*'
Cerberus
Of *Cerberus*, and blackest midnight born, Allegro 2
Ceremonies
Of Conscience, which the Law by Ceremonies Par Lost 12.297
Ceremony
Of Sovran power, with awful Ceremony Par Lost 1.753
ms 'ceremony'
Ceres
Was gatherd, which cost *Ceres* all that pain Par Lost 4.271
Of *Ceres* ripe for harvest waving bends Par Lost 4.981
Vertumnus, or to *Ceres* in her Prime, Par Lost 9.395
Juno dare's not give her odds; Arcades 23
Trinity ms 'Juno' ←'Ceres' ←'Juno'
Certain
(Certain to be refus'd) what erst they feard; Par Lost 2.470
At certain revolutions all the damn'd Par Lost 2.597
Which had no less prov'd certain unforeknown. Par Lost 3.119
Certain my resolution is to Die; Par Lost 9.907
Certain to undergoe like doom, if Death Par Lost 9.953
This annual humbling certain number'd days, Par Lost 10.576
Which must be born to certain woe, devourd Par Lost 10.980
Longer on Earth then certaine times to appeer Par Lost 12.437
Nothing more certain, will not long defer Samson 474
And now at nearer view, no other certain Samson 723
Certain to have won by mortal duel from thee, Samson 1102
Whom certain these rough shades did never breed Mask 266
Bridgewater ms 'certaine'
Trinity ms 'certaine'
1637 'certaine'
2. *Bro*. Me thought so too; what should it be? *Eld. Bro*. For certain Mask 482
Trinity ms 'certaine'
1637 'certaine'
Bridgewater ms 'certaine'
(For so by certain signes I knew) had met Mask 572
Trinity ms 'certaine'
Bridgewater ms 'certaine'
Brought to my mind a certain Shepherd Lad Mask 619
Trinity ms 'certaine'
Bridgewater ms 'certaine'
1637 'certaine'
What certain Seat, where I may worship thee Prose 12, 5
Certainly
Messiah certainly now come, so long Par Reg 2.32
Certainty
Such sober certainty of waking bliss Mask 263
Bridgewater ms 'certentie'
Chaeronea
At *Chaeronea*, fatal to liberty Sonnet 10, 7
Chafe
And lower looks, but in a sultrie chafe. Samson 1246
Chafed
Of chaf't wild Boars, or ruffl'd Porcupines. Samson 1138
Chaff
Prove chaff. On th' other side *Satan* allarm'd Par Lost 4.985
Not so the wicked, but as chaff which fann'd Psalm 1, 11
Chain
Hung ore my Realm, link'd in a golden Chain Par Lost 2.1005
And fast by hanging in a golden Chain Par Lost 2.1051
Chained
Chain'd on the burning Lake, nor ever thence Par Lost 1.210
Chain'd on the burning Lake? that sure was worse. Par Lost 2.169
Back to th' infernal pit I drag thee chaind, Par Lost 4.965
Thir devilish glut, chaind Thunderbolts and Hail Par Lost 6.589
Where I a Prisoner chain'd, scarce freely draw Samson 7
Your nervs are all chain'd up in Alablaster, Mask 660
Hath lockt up mortal sense, then listen I Arcades 62
Trinity ms 'lockt up' ←'chain'd'
Yet first to those ychain'd in sleep, Nativity 155
Chains
In Adamantine Chains and penal Fire, Par Lost 1.48
ms 'chaines'
Under yon boyling Ocean, wrapt in Chains; Par Lost 2.183
Chains and these Torments? better these then worse Par Lost 2.196

Chains(*cont*)
Prescrib'd, no barrs of Hell, nor all the chains Par Lost 3.82
Then when I am thy captive talk of chaines, Par Lost 4.970
Yet Chains in Hell, not Realms expect: mean while Par Lost 6.186
Or Captive drag'd in Chains, with hostile frown Par Lost 6.260
To chains of darkness, and th' undying Worm, Par Lost 6.739
And Chains they made all fast, too fast they made Par Lost 10.319
The Serpent, Prince of aire, and drag in Chaines Par Lost 12.454
Blind among enemies, O worse then chains, Samson 68
Though in these chains, bulk without spirit vast, Samson 1238
That breaks his magick chains at *curfeu* time, Mask 435
1637 'chaines'
Bridgewater ms 'chaines'
Speaks thunder, and the chains of *Erebus* Mask 804
line not in Trinity ms
line not in Bridgewater ms
1637 'chaines'
Untwisting all the chains that ty Allegro 143
In willing chains and sweet captivitie. Vacation 52
Threatning to bind our soules with secular chaines: Sonnet 16, 12
1694 'Chains'
Chair
Wont ride in arm'd, and at the Soldans chair Par Lost 1.764
As in a cloudy Chair ascending rides Par Lost 2.930
On points and questions fitting *Moses* Chair, Par Reg 4.219
Stay thy cloudy Ebon chair, Mask 134
Trinity ms 'chaire'
1637 'chaire'
Bridgewater ms 'chaire'
Rose from the hindmost wheels of *Phoebus* wain. Mask 190
Trinity ms 'waine' ←'chaire'
Down he descended from his Snow-soft chaire, Fair Inf 19
Chaldaea
Ur of *Chaldaea*, passing now the Ford Par Lost 12.130
Challenge
Avow, and challenge *Dagon* to the test, Samson 1151
Challenged
Whose Poem *Phoebus* challeng'd for his own. Par Reg 4.260
Chalybean
Chalybean temper'd steel, and frock of mail Samson 133
Cham
Girt with the River *Triton*, where old *Cham*, Par Lost 4.276
Chamber
Nor in the house with chamber Ambushes Samson 1112
Of his Chamber in the East. Mask 101
Trinity ms 'chamber'
Chamberlain
In the kind office of a Chamberlin Carrier 14
Chambers
In Courts and Regal Chambers how thou lurk'st, Par Reg 2.183
Champaign
As with a rural mound the champain head Par Lost 4.134
Through Heav'ns wide Champain held his way, till Morn, Par Lost 6.2
Fair Champain with less rivers interveind, Par Reg 3.257
Champing
Chaumping his iron curb: to strive or flie Par Lost 4.859
Champion
His mighty Champion, strong above compare, Samson 556
So deal not with this once thy glorious Champion, Samson 705
Offering to combat thee his Champion bold, Samson 1152
And to his faithful Champion hath in place Samson 1751
By a strong siding champion Conscience.------ Mask 212
line not in Bridgewater ms
Champions
(Though like a cover'd field, where Champions bold Par Lost 1.763
ms 'champions'
Of those Heav'n-warring Champions could be found Par Lost 2.424
For hot, cold, moist, and dry, four Champions fierce Par Lost 2.898
Chance
Whether upheld by strength, or Chance, or Fate, Par Lost 1.133
ms 'chance'
Of future dayes may bring, what chance, what change Par Lost 2.222
To fickle Chance, and *Chaos* judge the strife: Par Lost 2.233
Sea-faring men orewatcht, whose Bark by chance Par Lost 2.288
And opportune excursion we may chance Par Lost 2.396
If chance the radiant Sun with farewell sweet Par Lost 2.492
Free Vertue should enthrall to Force or Chance. Par Lost 2.551
Chance governs all. Into this wilde Abyss, Par Lost 2.910
Down had been falling, had not by ill chance Par Lost 2.935
Of *Demogorgon; Rumor* next and *Chance*, Par Lost 2.965
1667 'Chance'
Then as a Tyger, who by chance hath spi'd Par Lost 4.403
A chance but chance may lead where I may meet Par Lost 4.530
To act or not, Necessitie and Chance Par Lost 7.172
If chance with Nymphlike step fair Virgin pass, Par Lost 9.452
Absents thee, or what chance detains? Come forth. Par Lost 10.108
In Council sate, sollicitous what chance Par Lost 10.428
Sir, what ill chance hath brought thee to this place Par Reg 1.321
Of fate, and chance, and change in human life; Par Reg 4.265
Thou chance to dash thy foot against a stone. Par Reg 4.559
There I am wont to sit, when any chance Samson 4
Exempt from many a care and chance to which Samson 918
Har. I come not *Samson*, to condole thy chance, Samson 1076
May chance to number thee with those Samson 1295
Likeliest, and neerest to the present ayd Mask 90
Trinity ms 'aide' ←'chance' ←'aide'
Co. What chance good Lady hath bereft you thus? Mask 277
Bridgewater ms 'Chaunce'

Chance(*cont*)
How chance she is not in your company? Mask 508
Bridgewater ms 'chaunce'
Which erring men call Chance, this I hold firm, Mask 588
Trinity ms 'chance'
Bridgewater ms 'chaunce'
he may scratch his forehead. heere be brambles Mask Tr. ms 17.57
'he may scratch' ←'he may chaunce' ←'chance' ←'had best look to'
Triumphing over Death, and Chance, and thee O Time. On Time 22
Whose chance on these defenceless dores may sease, Sonnet 8, 2

Chanced
Of what so seldom chanc'd, when to his wish, Par Lost 9.423
Till on a day roaving the field, I chanc'd Par Lost 9.575
As on my enemies, where ever chanc'd, Samson 1202

Chances
All chances incident to mans frail life Samson 656
Chances to passe through this adventrous glade, Mask 79
Bridgewater ms 'chaunces'

Change
Can else inflict, do I repent or change, Par Lost 1.96
That we must change for Heav'n, this mournful gloom Par Lost 1.244
Under amazement of thir hideous change. Par Lost 1.313
On half the Nations, and with fear of change Par Lost 1.598
As this place testifies, and this dire change Par Lost 1.625
Of future dayes may bring, what chance, what change Par Lost 2.222
Are brought: and feel by turns the bitter change Par Lost 2.598
Of fierce extreams, extreams by change more fierce, Par Lost 2.599
Then sweet, now sad to mention, through dire change Par Lost 2.820
Till they enthrall themselves: I else must change Par Lost 3.125
But first he casts to change his proper shape, Par Lost 3.634
By change of place: Now conscience wakes despair Par Lost 4.23
Your change approaches, when all these delights Par Lost 4.367
All seasons and thir change, all please alike. Par Lost 4.640
Farthest from pain, where thou mightst hope to change Par Lost 4.892
And various: wondring at my flight and change Par Lost 5.89
And nourish all things, let your ceasless change Par Lost 5.183
Taste after taste upheld with kindliest change, Par Lost 5.336
Wee ours for change delectable, not need) Par Lost 5.629
To swerve from truth, or change his constant mind Par Lost 5.902
Not hither summond, since they cannot change Par Lost 8.347
As us'd or not, works in the mind no change, Par Lost 8.525
Venial discourse unblam'd: I now must change Par Lost 9.5
Now not, though Sin, not Time, first wraught the change, Par Lost 9.70
As yet my change, and give him to partake Par Lost 9.818
Or come I less conspicuous, or what change Par Lost 10.107
Must suffer change, disdain'd not to begin Par Lost 10.213
Of mortal change on Earth. As when a flock Par Lost 10.273
A Grove hard by, sprung up with this thir change, Par Lost 10.548
As deep as *Capricorne*, to bring in change Par Lost 10.677
Like change on Sea and Land, sideral blast, Par Lost 10.693
O *Eve*, some furder change awaits us nigh, Par Lost 11.193
Incessant I could hope to change the will Par Lost 11.308
Thy youth, thy strength, thy beauty, which will change Par Lost 11.539
Shall change thir course to pleasure, ease, and sloth, Par Lost 11.794
I look't for some great change; to Honour? no, Par Reg 2.86
My exaltation without change or end. Par Reg 3.197
Of fate, and chance, and change in human life; Par Reg 4.265
Of this fair change, and to our Saviour came, Par Reg 4.442
O change beyond report, thought, or belief! Samson 117
Man. O miserable change! is this the man, Samson 340
Or to the unjust tribunals, under change of times, Samson 695
Confess, and promise wonders in her change, Samson 753
And for a life who will not change his purpose? Samson 1406
After this mortal change, to her true Servants Mask 10
I cannot be, that I should fear to change it. Mask 328
It shall be in eternal restless change Mask 596
And underwent a quick immortal change Mask 841
beyond the written date of mortall change Mask Tr. ms 10.22
But O the heavy change, now thou art gon, Lycidas 37
Alack that so to change thee winter had no power. Fair Inf 28
In Joseph, *not to change*, Psalm 81, 18
Me to them odious, *for they change*, Psalm 88, 35

Changed
If thou beest he; But O how fall'n! how chang'd Par Lost 1.84
Though chang'd in outward lustre; that fixt mind Par Lost 1.97
A mind not to be chang'd by Place or Time. Par Lost 1.253
Or chang'd at length, and to the place conformd Par Lost 2.217
As soft as now severe, our temper chang'd Par Lost 2.276
Thrice chang'd with pale, ire, envie and despair, Par Lost 4.115
Nor chang'd his course, but through the shaggie hill Par Lost 4.224
Spring both, the face of brightest Heav'n had changd Par Lost 5.644
Of composition, strait they chang'd thir minds, Par Lost 6.613
So spake the Son, and into terrour chang'd Par Lost 6.824
And Earth be chang'd to Heav'n, & Heav'n to Earth, Par Lost 7.160
Lovelier, not those that in *Illyria* chang'd Par Lost 9.505
He look'd, and saw the face of things quite chang'd, Par Lost 11.712
Th' express resemblance of the gods, is chang'd Mask 69
On Faith and changed Gods complain: and Seas Horace 6

Changes
Strait couches close, then rising changes oft Par Lost 4.405
These changes in the Heav'ns, though slow, produc'd Par Lost 10.692

Changest
Changest thy countenance, and thy hand with no regard Samson 684

Changing
Must we renounce, and changing stile be call'd Par Lost 2.312
Into the Wood fast by, and changing shape Par Lost 10.333
They felt themselves now changing; down thir arms, Par Lost 10.541

Channel
That in the channell strayes, Mask 895
Bridgewater ms 'Channell'
Trinity ms 'in the channell straies' ←'my rich wheeles inlayes'
1673 'channel'
And bid the weltring waves their oozy channel keep. Nativity 124

Channels
And on the washie Oose deep Channels wore; Par Lost 7.303

Chant
With chaunt of tuneful Birds resounding loud; Par Reg 2.290

Chanting
Chaunting thir Idol, and preferring Samson 1672

Chantress
Thee Chauntress oft the Woods among, Penseroso 63

Chaos
Rose out of *Chaos*: Or if *Sion* Hill Par Lost 1.10
ms 'Chaos'
Frighted the Reign of *Chaos* and old Night. Par Lost 1.543
ms 'Chaos'
To fickle Chance, and *Chaos* judge the strife: Par Lost 2.233
And *Chaos*, Ancestors of Nature, hold Par Lost 2.895
Hee rules a moment; *Chaos* Umpire sits, Par Lost 2.907
Of *Chaos*, and his dark Pavilion spread Par Lost 2.960
Chaos and *ancient Night*, I come no Spy, Par Lost 2.970
Her fardest verge, and *Chaos* to retire Par Lost 2.1038
I sung of *Chaos* and *Eternal Night*, Par Lost 3.18
From *Chaos* and th' inroad of Darkness old, Par Lost 3.421
Of *Chaos* blustring round, inclement skie; Par Lost 3.426
As yet this world was not, and *Chaos* wilde Par Lost 5.577
His fiery *Chaos* to receave thir fall. Par Lost 6.55
Nine dayes they fell; confounded *Chaos* roard, Par Lost 6.871
In *Chaos*, and the work begun, how soon Par Lost 7.93
Farr into *Chaos*, and the World unborn; Par Lost 7.220
For *Chaos* heard his voice: him all his Traine Par Lost 7.221
Of *Chaos* farr remov'd, least fierce extreames Par Lost 7.272
Farr into *Chaos*, since the Fiend pass'd through, Par Lost 10.233
Wide Anarchie of *Chaos* damp and dark Par Lost 10.283
From out of *Chaos* to the out side bare Par Lost 10.317
And at the brink of *Chaos*, neer the foot Par Lost 10.347
Disparted *Chaos* over built exclaimd, Par Lost 10.416
Of unoriginal *Night* and *Chaos* wilde, Par Lost 10.477
Through *Chaos* hurld, obstruct the mouth of Hell Par Lost 10.636
And disinherit *Chaos*, that raigns here Mask 334

Character
The character of that Dominion giv'n Par Lost 8.545

Charactered
Character'd in the face; this have I learn't Mask 530
Trinity ms 'characterd'
Bridgewater ms 'charactred'

Characters
Voluminous, or single characters, Par Reg 4.384
That they would fitly fall in order'd Characters. Passion 49

Charge
Into my hand was giv'n, with charge to keep Par Lost 2.775
Lay waving round; on som great charge imploy'd Par Lost 3.628
Resigns her charge, while goodness thinks no ill Par Lost 3.688
This one, this easie charge, of all the Trees Par Lost 4.421
Charge and strict watch that to this happie Place Par Lost 4.562
So promis'd hee, and *Uriel* to his charge Par Lost 4.589
That neer him stood, and gave them thus in charge. Par Lost 4.787
To him who sent us, whose charge is to keep Par Lost 4.842
To thy transgressions, and disturbd the charge Par Lost 4.879
After his charge receivd; but from among Par Lost 5.248
Do as you have in charge, and briefly touch Par Lost 6.566
Ere Sabbath Eev'ning: so we had in charge. Par Lost 8.246
Thir earthy Charge: Of these the vigilance Par Lost 9.157
Oft he to her his charge of quick returne Par Lost 9.399
From unsuccessful charge, be not dismaid, Par Lost 10.35
Whereof I gave thee charge thou shouldst not eat? Par Lost 10.123
Appointed to sit there, had left thir charge, Par Lost 10.421
His mightie Angels gave them several charge, Par Lost 10.650
Michael, this my behest have thou in charge, Par Lost 11.99
Fairest and easiest of this combrous charge, Par Lost 11.549
Still follow'd him; to them shall leave in charge Par Lost 12.439
To his destruction, as I had in charge. Par Reg 1.376
It was not gold, as to my charge thou lay'st, Samson 849
Has in his charge, with temper'd awe to guide Mask 32
Bridgewater ms 'Chardge'
Impostor do not charge most innocent nature, Mask 762
Of this fair Wood, and live in Oak'n bowr, Arcades 45
Trinity ms '& charge of'
When they shall read this clearly in your charge Forcers 19

Charged
Charg'd not to touch the interdicted Tree, Par Lost 7.46
I charg'd thee, saying: Thou shalt not eate thereof, Par Lost 10.200

Chariot
And broken Chariot Wheels, so thick bestrown Par Lost 1.311
ms 'chariot'
Nor stop thy flaming Chariot wheels, that shook Par Lost 3.394
Rapt in a Chariot drawn by fiery Steeds. Par Lost 3.522
Th' Apostat in his Sun-bright Chariot sate Par Lost 6.100
Back to his Chariot; where it stood retir'd Par Lost 6.338
And at his Chariot wheeles to drag him bound Par Lost 6.358
Chariot and Charioter lay overturnd Par Lost 6.390
Ascend my Chariot, guide the rapid Wheeles Par Lost 6.711
The Chariot of Paternal Deitie, Par Lost 6.750
Of his fierce Chariot rowld, as with the sound Par Lost 6.829

Chariot(*cont*)	
Messiah his triumphal Chariot turnd:	Par Lost 6.881
About his Chariot numberless were pour'd	Par Lost 7.197
And craze thir Chariot wheels: when by command	Par Lost 12.210
My sliding Chariot stayes,	Mask 892
Trinity ms 'chariot'	
Bridgewater ms 'Charriott'	
1637 'chariot'	
The hooked Chariot stood	Nativity 56
See see the Chariot, and those rushing wheels,	Passion 36
Charioteer	
Chariot and Charioter lay overturnd	Par Lost 6.390
For since grim Aquilo his charioter	Fair Inf 8
Charioting	
As in a fiery column charioting	Samson 27
Chariots	
With Horse and Chariots rankt in loose array;	Par Lost 2.887
Chariots and flaming Armes, and fierie Steeds	Par Lost 6.17
Of brazen Chariots rag'd; dire was the noise	Par Lost 6.211
Chariots of God, half on each hand were seen:	Par Lost 6.770
And Vertues, winged Spirits, and Chariots wing'd,	Par Lost 7.199
Chariots or Elephants endorst with Towers	Par Reg 3.329
Charities	
Relations dear, and all the Charities	Par Lost 4.756
Charity	
Dwels in all Heaven charitie so deare?	Par Lost 3.216
By name to come call'd Charitie, the soul	Par Lost 12.584
Charlemagne	
When *Charlemain* with all his Peerage fell	Par Lost 1.586
ms 'Charlemain'	
Both *Paynim*, and the Peers of *Charlemane*.	Par Reg 3.343
Charm	
Intent, with jocond Music charm his ear;	Par Lost 1.787
ms 'charme'	
More tollerable; if there be cure or charm	Par Lost 2.460
Yet with a pleasing sorcerie could charm	Par Lost 2.566
With charm of earliest Birds; pleasant the Sun	Par Lost 4.642
With charm of earliest Birds, nor rising Sun	Par Lost 4.651
Against the charm of Beauties powerful glance.	Par Lost 8.533
But fondly overcome with Femal charm.	Par Lost 9.999
Would think to charm my judgement, as mine eyes	Mask 758
1637 'charme'	
Bridgewater ms 'charme'	
Trinity ms 'charme'	
The clasping charm, and thaw the numming spell,	Mask 853
1637 'charme'	
Trinity ms 'charme' ←'chame'	
Bridgewater ms 'Charme'	
Or the Belmans drousie charm,	Penseroso 83
Charmed	
Mov'd on in silence to soft Pipes that charm'd	Par Lost 1.561
Charm'd with *Arcadian* Pipe, the Pastoral Reed	Par Lost 11.132
Arm'd thee or charm'd thee strong, which thou from Heaven	Samson 1134
The daughter of the Sun? Whose charmed Cup	Mask 51
To undoe the charmed band	Mask 904
Trinity ms 'charmed' ←'mag'	
Bridgewater ms 'Charmed'	
his uninchanted eye, & round the verge	Mask Tr. ms 10.10
'uninchanted' ←'never charmed'	
While Birds of Calm sit brooding on the charmed wave.	Nativity 68
Charming	
Of charming symphonie they introduce	Par Lost 3.368
So smooths her charming tones, that Gods own ear	Par Lost 5.626
So Charming left his voice, that he a while	Par Lost 8.2
line not in 1667 edition	
And charming Symphonies attach'd the heart	Par Lost 11.595
Of chiming strings, or charming pipes and winds	Par Reg 2.363
2. *Bro*. How charming is divine Philosophy!	Mask 476
Bridgewater ms 'charminge'	
Charms	
(For Eloquence the Soul, Song charms the Sense,)	Par Lost 2.556
Eclipses at thir charms. The other shape,	Par Lost 2.666
Both of her Beauty and submissive Charms	Par Lost 4.498
Descend with all her winning charms begirt	Par Reg 2.213
Aeolian charms and *Dorian Lyric* Odes,	Par Reg 4.257
Temptation found'st, or over-potent charms	Samson 427
Thy fair enchanted cup, and warbling charms	Samson 934
Adverse and turbulent, or by her charms	Samson 1040
Benighted in these Woods. Now to my charms,	Mask 150
Bridgewater ms 'Charms'	
1637 'charmes'	
Trinity ms 'charmes' ←'traines'	
And to my wily trains, I shall e're long	Mask 151
Trinity ms 'trains' ←'charmes'	
Be those that quell the might of hellish charms,	Mask 613
Bridgewater ms 'Charmes'	
Withall thy charms, although this corporal rinde	Mask 664
Trinity ms 'charmes'	
Bridgewater ms 'charmes'	
He can requite thee, for he knows the charms	Sonnet 8, 5
Trinity ms 'charmes'	
Charnel	
Oft seen in Charnell vaults, and Sepulchers	Mask 471
1673 'Charnel'	
Trinity ms 'charnel'	
Charybdis	
Charybdis, and by th' other whirlpool steard.	Par Lost 2.1020
And fell *Charybdis* murmur'd soft applause:	Mask 259

Charybdis(*cont*)	
Bridgewater ms 'Caribdis'	
Chase	
With solemn touches, troubl'd thoughts, and chase	Par Lost 1.557
All Beasts of th' Earth, since wilde, and of all chase	Par Lost 4.341
To chase me hence? erre not that so shall end	Par Lost 6.288
Adam observ'd, and with his Eye the chase	Par Lost 11.191
And savour, Beasts of chase, or Fowl of game,	Par Reg 2.342
Shall chase thee with the terror of his voice	Par Reg 4.627
And with thy tempest chase;	Psalm 83, 58
Chased	
Of thunder, chas'd the clouds, and laid the winds,	Par Reg 4.429
Chaste	
Whose bed is undefil'd and chaste pronounc't,	Par Lost 4.761
1667 'chast'	
Deucalion and chaste *Pyrrha* to restore	Par Lost 11.12
Of som chast footing neer about this ground.	Mask 146
Fair silver-shafted Queen for ever chaste,	Mask 442
Bridgewater ms 'chast'	
Trinity ms 'chast'	
1637 'chast'	
But rigid looks of Chast austerity,	Mask 450
Trinity ms 'chast'	
Bridgewater ms 'chast'	
Sabrina is her name, a Virgin pure,	Mask 826
Trinity ms 'pure' ←'chast' ←'goddesse'	
I touch with chaste palms moist and cold,	Mask 918
Trinity ms 'chast'	
Bridgewater ms 'chast'	
1637 'chast'	
Founded in chast and humble Povertie,	Prose 3, 1
Chastening	
However chast'ning, to the evil turne	Par Lost 11.373
Chastity	
And thou unblemish't form of Chastity,	Mask 215
1637 'Chastitie'	
Trinity ms 'chastity'	
line not in Bridgewater ms	
'Tis chastity, my brother, chastity:	Mask 420
Bridgewater ms both 'Chastitie'	
Trinity ms both 'chastitie'	
Where through the sacred rayes of Chastity,	Mask 425
Bridgewater ms 'Chastitie'	
1637 'chastitie'	
Trinity ms 'chastitie'	
To testifie the arms of Chastity?	Mask 440
1637 'Chastitie'	
Trinity ms 'chastitie'	
Bridgewater ms 'Chastitie'	
So dear to Heav'n is Saintly chastity,	Mask 453
Bridgewater ms 'Chastitie'	
Trinity ms 'chastitie'	
1637 'chastitie'	
Against the Sun-clad power of Chastity,	Mask 782
line not in Bridgewater ms	
line not in Trinity ms	
1637 'Chastitie'	
To help insnared chastity;	Mask 909
1637 'chastitie'	
Trinity ms 'chastitie'	
Bridgewater ms 'Chastitie'	
Chatting	
Sate simply chatting in a rustick row;	Nativity 87
Cheap	
His Rivals, winning cheap the high repute	Par Lost 2.472
Cheat	
Of power to cheat the eye with blear illusion,	Mask 155
1637 'cheate'	
Trinity ms 'cheate'	
Bridgewater ms 'cheate'	
Chebar	
That whirl'd the Prophet up at *Chebar* flood,	Passion 37
Check	
Thir pamperd boughes, and needed hands to check	Par Lost 5.214
Check or reproof, and glad to scape so quit.	Par Reg 1.477
And vertue has no tongue to check her pride:	Mask 761
Whose bounds the Sea doth check.	Psalm 83, 28
Checked	
Yet half his strength he put not forth, but check'd	Par Lost 6.853
Checks	
And in her pale dominion checks the night.	Par Lost 3.732
While *Cynthia* checks her Dragon yoke,	Penseroso 59
Cheek	
Sat on his faded cheek, but under Browes	Par Lost 1.602
ms 'cheeke'	
In curles on either cheek plaid, wings he wore	Par Lost 3.641
With Tresses discompos'd, and glowing Cheek,	Par Lost 5.10
Alterd her cheek. On whom the Angel *Haile*	Par Lost 5.385
But in her Cheek distemper flushing glowd.	Par Lost 9.887
As varnish on a Harlots cheek, the rest,	Par Reg 4.344
Such as hang on *Hebe*'s cheek,	Allegro 29
Drew Iron tears down *Pluto*'s cheek,	Penseroso 107
colouring the pale cheeke of uninjoyd love	Lycidas Tr. ms 28.16
That did thy cheek envermeil, thought to kiss	Fair Inf 6
Cheek-bone	
On the cheek-bone all my foes,	Psalm 3, 21
Cheeks	
Had entertaind, as di'd her Cheeks with pale.	Par Lost 10.1009

Cheeks(*cont*)
And cheeks of sorry grain will serve to ply   Mask 750
line not in Bridgewater ms
Wherwith their cheeks are wet.   Psalm 80, 24

Cheer
He ended, and his words thir drooping chere   Par Lost 6.496
Had fill'd thir hearts with mirth, high chear, & wine,   Samson 1613
Will double all their mirth and chere;   Mask 955
Bridgewater ms 'cheere'
Trinity ms 'chere' ←'cheere'
With joy and gladsom cheer   Psalm 84, 26

Cheered
Chear'd with the grateful smell old Ocean smiles.   Par Lost 4.165
1667 'Cheard'
So cheard he his fair Spouse, and she was cheard,   Par Lost 5.129
With cause for evils past, yet much more cheer'd   Par Lost 12.604
Had chear'd the face of Earth, and dry'd the wet   Par Reg 4.433
With all things grateful chear'd, and so suppli'd,   Samson 926

Cheerful
Heav'ns chearful face, the lowring Element   Par Lost 2.490
Surrounds me, from the chearful wayes of men   Par Lost 3.46
All night; at last by break of chearful dawne   Par Lost 3.545
That wont to be more chearful and serene   Par Lost 5.123
Hopeful and cheerful, in thy blood will reigne   Par Lost 11.543
Far from the cheerfull haunt of men, and herds,   Mask 388
1637 'cheerefull'
Trinity ms 'cheerfull' ←'cherfull'
Bridgewater ms 'cheerefull'
And when God sends a cheerful hour, refrains.   Sonnet 21, 14
Trinity ms 'cheerfull'
The *cheerfull* Psaltry bring along   Psalm 81, 7

Cheering
Days, months, & years, towards his all-chearing Lamp   Par Lost 3.581
T'would be som solace yet, som little chearing   Mask 348
Bridgewater ms 'cheeringe'
Trinity ms 'cheering'

Cheerly
Chearly rouse the slumbring morn,   Allegro 54

Cheers
Or taste that cheers the heart of Gods and men,   Samson 545

Cheke
Thy age, like ours, O Soul of Sir *John Cheek*,   Sonnet 11, 12
Trinity ms 'Cheek' ←'Cheeke' ←'Cheek'

Chemic
Th' Arch-chimic Sun so farr from us remote   Par Lost 3.609

Chemos
Next *Chemos*, th' obscene dread of *Moabs* Sons,   Par Lost 1.406
ms 'Chemos'

Chemosh
Next *Chemos*, th' obscene dread of *Moabs* Sons,   Par Lost 1.406
ms 'Chemos'

Chequered
Dancing in the Chequer'd shade;   Allegro 96

Cherish
Som better shroud, som better warmth to cherish   Par Lost 10.1068
Cherish thy hast'n'd widowhood with the gold   Samson 958

Cherishing
Thy cherishing, thy honouring, and thy love,   Par Lost 8.569

Cherith
Him thought, he by the Brook of *Cherith* stood   Par Reg 2.266

Chersonese
Down to the golden *Chersonese*, or where   Par Lost 11.392
From *India* and the golden *Chersoness*,   Par Reg 4.74

Cherub
Fall'n Cherube, to be weak is miserable   Par Lost 1.157
Cherube and Seraph rowling in the Flood   Par Lost 1.324
Azazel as his right, a Cherube tall: Par Lost 1.534
ms 'Cherub'
And now a stripling Cherube he appeers,   Par Lost 3.636
So spake the Cherube, and his grave rebuke   Par Lost 4.844
Proud limitarie Cherube, but ere then   Par Lost 4.971
Hee on the wings of Cherub rode sublime   Par Lost 6.771
Cherub and Seraph, Potentates and Thrones,   Par Lost 7.198
Would send a glistring Guardian if need were   Mask 219
Trinity ms 'guardian' ←'cherub'
Where young *Adonis* oft reposes,   Mask 999
Trinity ms 'young Adonis oft' ←'many a cherub soft'
Bridgewater ms 'many a Cherub soft'
B.M. ms 'many'a Cherub soft'
The Cherub Contemplation,   Penseroso 54
My spirit som transporting *Cherub* feels,   Passion 38

Cherubic
Cherubic Songs by night from neighbouring Hills   Par Lost 5.547
Cherubic waving fires: on th' other part   Par Lost 6.413
By four Cherubic shapes, four Faces each   Par Lost 6.753
From entrance or Cherubic Watch, by stealth   Par Lost 9.68
Cherubic watch, and of a Sword the flame   Par Lost 11.120
And the Cherubick host in thousand quires   Musick 12

Cherubim
Between the Cherubim; yea, often plac'd   Par Lost 1.387
Of mighty Cherubim; the sudden blaze   Par Lost 1.665
The great Seraphic Lords and Cherubim   Par Lost 1.794
Toward the four winds four speedy Cherubim   Par Lost 2.516
Hath brought me from the Quires of Cherubim   Par Lost 3.666
And from thir Ivorie Port the Cherubim   Par Lost 4.778
With Flaming Cherubim, and golden Shields;   Par Lost 6.102
Zophiel, of Cherubim the swiftest wing,   Par Lost 6.535
Nor staid, but on the Wings of Cherubim   Par Lost 7.218

Cherubim(*cont*)
His entrance, and forewarnd the Cherubim   Par Lost 9.61
Take to thee from among the Cherubim   Par Lost 11.100
Of watchful Cherubim; four faces each   Par Lost 11.128
Of two bright Cherubim, before him burn   Par Lost 12.254
The Cherubim descended; on the ground   Par Lost 12.628
The helmed Cherubim   Nativity 112

Cherubs
That sitt'st between the Cherubs *bright*   Psalm 80, 5

Chest
Within his sacred chest,   Nativity 217

Chew
The savourie pulp they chew, and in the rinde   Par Lost 4.335

Chewed
Chewd bitter Ashes, which th' offended taste   Par Lost 10.566

Chewing
This evening late by then the chewing flocks   Mask 540
Bridgewater ms 'chewinge'

Chid
And chid her barking waves into attention,   Mask 258
Trinity ms 'chid' ←'chiding' ←'chide'

Chide
My true account, least he returning chide,   Sonnet 19, 6
Toward us, *and chide no more*.   Psalm 85, 16

Chiding
And chid her barking waves into attention,   Mask 258
Trinity ms 'chid' ←'chiding' ←'chide'

Chief
O Prince, O Chief of many Throned Powers,   Par Lost 1.128
ms 'Cheife'
The chief were those who from the Pit of Hell   Par Lost 1.381
ms 'cheife'
Obscure some glimps of joy, to have found thir chief   Par Lost 1.524
ms 'cheife'
Awaiting what command thir mighty Chief   Par Lost 1.566
ms 'Chiefe'
And Porches wide, but chief the spacious Hall   Par Lost 1.762
ms 'chiefe'
Others among the chief might offer now   Par Lost 2.469
Ended rejoycing in thir matchless Chief: Par Lost 2.487
The irksom hours, till this great Chief return.   Par Lost 2.527
Smit with the love of sacred Song; but chief   Par Lost 3.29
O Son, in whom my Soul hath chief delight,   Par Lost 3.168
His chief delight and favour, him for whom   Par Lost 3.664
Chief of th' Angelic Guards, awaiting night;   Par Lost 4.550
Awaiting next command. To whom thir Chief   Par Lost 4.864
Less hardie to endure? courageous Chief,   Par Lost 4.920
Reason as chief; among these Fansie next   Par Lost 5.102
Of all those Myriads which we lead the chief;   Par Lost 5.684
Each Warriour single as in Chief, expert   Par Lost 6.233
Hymns of high praise, and I among them chief.   Par Lost 6.745
And worship God Supream, who made him chief   Par Lost 7.515
Heroic deem'd, chief maistrie to dissect   Par Lost 9.29
Thir mighty Chief returnd: loud was th' acclaime: Par Lost 10.455
In Triumph issuing forth thir glorious Chief;   Par Lost 10.537
With vows, as thir chief good, and final hope.   Par Lost 11.493
Womans domestic honour and chief praise;   Par Lost 11.617
His Honour, Vertue, Merit and chief Praise,   Par Reg 2.464
Would ask a life to wail, but chief of all,   Samson 66
Which is my chief affliction, shame and sorrow,   Samson 457
And strongest drinks our chief support of health,   Samson 554
Not truly penitent, but chief to try   Samson 754
All of Gigantic size, *Goliah* chief.   Samson 1249
Summers chief honour if thou hadst out-lasted,   Fair Inf 3
Ease was his chief disease, and to judge right,   Another 21
line not in 1658 text
1640, 1657 'chiefe'
that didst reform thy art, the cheif among   Sonnet 13, Tr. ms 40.08
Cromwell, our cheif of men, who through a cloud   Sonnet 16, 1
1694 'Chief'
In peace, and reck'ns thee her eldest son.   Sonnet 17, 14
1694 'thee in chief'

Chiefest
But first, and chiefest, with thee bring,   Penseroso 51
And from thy wardrope bring thy chiefest treasure;   Vacation 18

Chiefly
And chiefly Thou O Spirit, that dost prefer   Par Lost 1.17
ms 'cheifly'
The most averse, thee chiefly, who full oft   Par Lost 2.763
All these his wondrous works, but chiefly Man,   Par Lost 3.663
And daily thanks, I chiefly who enjoy   Par Lost 4.445
More of th' Almighties works, and chiefly Man   Par Lost 4.566
But chiefly where those two fair Creatures Lodge,   Par Lost 4.790
His loss; but chiefly to find here observd   Par Lost 4.849
Chiefly by what thy own last reasoning words   Par Lost 9.379
Chiefly I sought, without thee can despise.   Par Lost 9.878
Pernicious to thy Peace, chiefly assur'd   Par Lost 9.981
Chiefly on Man, sole Lord of all declar'd,   Par Lost 10.401
Thou hast reveald, those chiefly which concerne   Par Lost 12.272
Chiefly what may concern her Faith to know,   Par Lost 12.599
1669 'Cheifly'
I am; this chiefly, that my way must lie   Par Reg 1.263
Though chiefly not for glory as prime end,   Par Reg 3.123
But that which mov'd my coming now, was chiefly   Samson 1452
Them to ensnare they chiefly strive   Psalm 83, 11

Child
Fair Daughter, and thou Son and Grandchild both,   Par Lost 10.384
A Son, and of his Son a Grand-childe leaves,   Par Lost 12.153

Child(*cont*)
The Grandchilde with twelve Sons increast, departs Par Lost 12.155
When I was yet a child, no childish play Par Reg 1.201
Deceiveable, in most things as a child Samson 942
Or sweetest *Shakespear* fancies childe, Allegro 133
While the Heav'n-born-childe, Nativity 30
Then thou the mother of so sweet a child Fair Inf 71

Child-bearing
Pains onely in Child-bearing were foretold, Par Lost 10.1051

Childbed
Mine as whom washt from spot of child-bed taint, Sonnet 23, 5
Trinity ms 'childe-bed'

Childhood
Teaching not taught; the childhood shews the man, Par Reg 4.220
Thy infancy, thy childhood, and thy youth, Par Reg 4.508

Childish
When I was yet a child, no childish play Par Reg 1.201
And mad'st imperfect words with childish tripps, Vacation 3

Childless
Childless thou art, Childless remaine: Par Lost 10.989
By death brought on our selves, or childless days Par Lost 10.1037
Of long-uncoupled bed, and childless eld, Fair Inf 13

Children
Thir childrens cries unheard, that past through fire Par Lost 1.395
By thy Conception; Children thou shalt bring Par Lost 10.194
1667 'Childern'
Disguis'd he came, but those his Children dear Par Lost 10.330
1667 'Childern'
His Children, all in view destroyd at once; Par Lost 11.761
1667 'Childern'
Him or his Childern, evil he may be sure, Par Lost 11.772
As Children gathering pibles on the shore. Par Reg 4.330
I pray'd for Children, and thought barrenness Samson 352
To store her children with; if all the world Mask 720
Bridgewater ms 'childeren'
As if she would her children should be riotous Mask 763

Chill
Astonied stood and Blank, while horror chill Par Lost 9.890
From the chill dew, amongst rude burrs and thistles? Mask 352
Of noisom winds, and blasting vapours chill. Arcades 49
And the chill Marble seems to sweat, Nativity 195

Chilled
He pluckt, he tasted; mee damp horror chil'd Par Lost 5.65

Chilling
Heart-strook with chilling gripe of sorrow stood, Par Lost 11.264

Chime
Of Instruments that made melodious chime Par Lost 11.559
Higher then the Spheary chime; Mask 1021
And let your silver chime Nativity 128
Jarr'd against natures chime, and with harsh din Musick 20

Chimeras
Gorgons and *Hydra's*, and *Chimera's* dire. Par Lost 2.628
Of dire *Chimera's* and inchanted Iles, Mask 517
Trinity ms 'chimaera's'
Bridgewater ms 'Chimeras'

Chiming
Of chiming strings, or charming pipes and winds Par Reg 2.363

Chimney
Hard by, a Cottage chimney smokes, Allegro 81
And stretch'd out all the Chimney's length, Allegro 111

Chin
Pillows his chin upon an Orient wave, Nativity 231

Chineses
Of *Sericana*, where *Chineses* drive Par Lost 3.438

Chios
Chios and *Creet*, and how they quaff in Gold, Par Reg 4.118

Chivalry
Busiris and his *Memphian* Chivalry, Par Lost 1.307
ms 'chivalry'
1667 'Chivalrie'
Defi'd the best of *Panim* chivalry Par Lost 1.765
Such and so numerous was thir Chivalrie; Par Reg 3.344

Choaspes
There *Susa* by *Choaspes*, amber stream, Par Reg 3.288

Choice
Here we may reign secure, and in my choyce Par Lost 1.261
A generation, whom his choice regard Par Lost 1.653
By place or choice the worthiest; they anon Par Lost 1.759
Did first create your Leader, next free choice, Par Lost 2.19
Choice in our suffrage; for on whom we send, Par Lost 2.415
Astonisht: none among the choice and prime Par Lost 2.423
Pursues, as inclination or sad choice Par Lost 2.524
When Will and Reason (Reason also is choice) Par Lost 3.108
Pass'd frequent, and his eye with choice regard Par Lost 3.534
But all these shining Orbes his choice to dwell; Par Lost 3.670
Free leave so large to all things else, and choice Par Lost 4.434
Each Plant and juciest Gourd will pluck such choice Par Lost 5.327
What choice to chuse for delicacie best, Par Lost 5.333
Ethereal, as wee, or may at choice Par Lost 5.499
So easily obeyd amid the choice Par Lost 7.48
Yet dreadful in mine eare, though in my choice Par Lost 8.335
Thou to thy self proposest, in the choice Par Lost 8.400
Let us divide our labours, thou where choice Par Lost 9.214
To us, in such aboundance lies our choice, Par Lost 9.620
Had so enobl'd, as of choice to incurr Par Lost 9.992
God made thee of choice his own, and of his own Par Lost 10.766
By Parents, or his happiest choice too late Par Lost 10.904
As in our evils, and of easier choice. Par Lost 10.978

Choice(*cont*)
Thy choice of flaming Warriours, least the Fiend Par Lost 11.101
Prauncing their riders bore, the flower and choice Par Reg 3.314
And trifles for choice matters, worth a spunge; Par Reg 4.329
For yonder bank hath choice of Sun or shade, Samson 3
Whom so it pleases him by choice Samson 311
When God with these forbid'n made choice to rear Samson 555
I was his nursling once and choice delight, Samson 633
In choice, but oftest to affect the wrong? Samson 1030
Thir choice nobility and flower, not only Samson 1654
His lot unfortunate in nuptial choice, Samson 1743
Wed your divine sounds, and mixt power employ Musick 3
Trinity ms 'divine sounds' ←'choise chords' ←'divine power'
What neat repast shall feast us, light and choice, Sonnet 20, 9
Ith' morning I to thee with choyce Psalm 5, 7
Mislik'd me for his choice. Psalm 81, 48

Choices
Man. I cannot praise thy Marriage choises, Son, Samson 420

Choicest
That open now thir choicest bosom'd smells Par Lost 5.127
To rest, and what the Garden choicest bears Par Lost 5.368
Of choicest Flours a Garland to adorne Par Lost 9.840
Choicest and best; then sacrificing, laid Par Lost 11.438
Such Solitude before choicest Society. Par Reg 1.302
From all the Elements her choicest store Par Reg 2.334
Clear'd up their choicest notes in bush and spray Par Reg 4.437
Their choicest youth; they only liv'd who fled. Samson 264
Which deepest Spirits, and choicest Wits desire: Vacation 22

Choir
He ask'd, but all the Heav'nly Quire stood mute, Par Lost 3.217
The Birds thir quire apply; aires, vernal aires, Par Lost 4.264
And joind thir vocal Worship to the Quire Par Lost 9.198
They gladly thither haste, and by a Quire Par Lost 12.366
At thy Nativity a glorious Quire Par Reg 1.242
Imitate the Starry Quire, Mask 112
1637 'quire'
Trinity ms 'quire'
Bridgewater ms 'quire'
To the full voic'd Quire below, Penseroso 162
And joyn thy voice unto the Angel Quire, Nativity 27
Harping in loud and solemn quire, Nativity 115
The Virgin quire for her request Winchester 17
To honour thee, the Priest of *Phoebus* Quire Sonnet 13, 10
Trinity ms 'quire'

Choirs
Hath brought me from the Quires of Cherubim Par Lost 3.666
And heav'nly Quires the Hymenaean sung, Par Lost 4.711
Flew through the midst of Heav'n; th' angelic Quires Par Lost 5.251
1667 'quires' in some copies
By the Celestial Quires, when Orient Light Par Lost 7.254
Or thirst, and as he fed, Angelic Quires Par Reg 4.593
And the Cherubick host in thousand quires Musick 12
Trinity ms 'in thousand quires' ←'sweet-winged squires'
For aye, with Temples vow'd, and Virgin quires. Prose 12, 6

Choose
Like cumbrous flesh; but in what shape they choose Par Lost 1.428
ms 'chuse'
By our delay? no, let us rather choose Par Lost 2.60
Choose to reside, his Glory unobscur'd, Par Lost 2.265
Both what they judge and what they choose; for so Par Lost 3.123
What choice to chuse for delicacie best, Par Lost 5.333
By Destinie, and can no other choose? Par Lost 5.534
Will ye submit your necks, and chuse to bend Par Lost 5.787
Our taske we choose, what wonder if so near Par Lost 9.221
When I am present, and thy trial choose Par Lost 9.316
Thir government, and thir great Senate choose Par Lost 12.225
The World was all before them, where to choose Par Lost 12.646
Chuse which thou wilt by conquest or by league. Par Reg 3.370
And numberd down: much rather I shall chuse Samson 1478
And I with thee will choose to live. Penseroso 176
Yet I had rather if I were to chuse, Vacation 29
(For whom to chuse he knows) Psalm 4, 16

Chooses
Then who self-rigorous chooses death as due; Samson 513

Choosing
Pleas'd me long choosing, and beginning late; Par Lost 9.26
Of many ways to die the shortest choosing, Par Lost 10.1005
Return them back to *Egypt*, choosing rather Par Lost 12.219

Choral
And choral symphonies, Day without Night, Par Lost 5.162
Choral or Unison: of incense Clouds Par Lost 7.599

Chords
Thir stops and chords was seen: his volant touch Par Lost 11.561
Wed your divine sounds, and mixt power employ Musick 3
Trinity ms 'divine sounds' ←'choise chords' ←'divine power'

Chorus
And Morning *Chorus* sung the second Day. Par Lost 7.275
In *Chorus* or *Iambic*, teachers best Par Reg 4.262

Chose
Chose freely what it now so justly rues. Par Lost 4.72
His couchant watch, as one who chose his ground Par Lost 4.406
Chose rather; hee, she knew would intermix Par Lost 8.54
Of thoughts revolv'd, his final sentence chose Par Lost 9.88
Into the thickest Wood, there soon they chose Par Lost 9.1100
Yet willingly chose rather Death with thee: Par Lost 9.1167
Fast caught, they lik'd, and each his liking chose; Par Lost 11.587

Chose*(cont)*
From what consummate vertue I have chose Par Reg 1.165
Chose to impart to thy apparent need, Par Reg 2.397
And of my Nation chose thee from among Samson 877
Her countrey from a fierce destroyer, chose Samson 985
I chose a Wife, which argu'd me no foe; Samson 1193
And chose with us a darksom House of mortal Clay. Nativity 14
Yet know the Lord hath chose Psalm 4, 13
Chose to himself a part Psalm 4, 14

Chosen
That Shepherd, who first taught the chosen Seed, Par Lost 1.8
Eternal spirits; or have ye chos'n this place Par Lost 1.318
Some I have chosen of peculiar grace Par Lost 3.183
Chos'n by the sovran Planter, when he fram'd Par Lost 4.691
The other service was thy chosen task, Par Reg 1.427
Thy chosen, to what highth thir pow'r unjust Par Reg 2.45
Then forthwith to him takes a chosen band Par Reg 2.236
For *Adam* and his chosen Sons, whom thou Par Reg 4.614
Alas methinks whom God hath chosen once Samson 368
His chosen people he did bless Psalm 136, 57
Chosen thou hast, and they that overween, Sonnet 9, 6

Christ
To force our Consciences that Christ set free, Forcers 6

Chromatic
by leaving out those harsh ill sounding jarres Musick Tr. ms 5.03
'ill sounding' ←'chromatick'

Chrysolite
If stone, Carbuncle most or Chrysolite, Par Lost 3.596

Church
So since into his Church lewd Hirelings climbe. Par Lost 4.193
What powre the Church & what the civill meanes Sonnet 17, Tr. ms 45.11

Cimmerian
In dark *Cimmerian* desert ever dwell. Allegro 10

Cincture
With featherd Cincture, naked else and wilde Par Lost 9.1117

Cinders
With soot and cinders fill'd; so oft they fell Par Lost 10.570

Cinnamon
With Groves of myrrhe, and cinnamon. Mask 937
Bridgewater ms 'Cynamon'

Circe
On *Circes* Iland fell (who knows not *Circe* Mask 50
Trinity ms 'Circe's'
About my Mother *Circe*. Thus I hurl Mask 153
My Mother *Circe* with the Sirens three, Mask 253
Of *Bacchus*, and of *Circe* born, great *Comus*, Mask 522

Circean
Then at *Circean* call the Herd disguis'd. Par Lost 9.522

Circle
Amid the Suns bright circle where thou sitst, Par Lost 4.578
Circle his Throne rejoycing, yee in Heav'n, Par Lost 5.163
Perpetual Circle, multiform; and mix Par Lost 5.182
In circle round her shining throne, Arcades 15
What ever clime the Suns bright circle warms. Sonnet 8, 8

Circled
Circl'd his Head, nor less his Locks behind Par Lost 3.626
Had circl'd his full Orbe, the birth mature Par Lost 5.862
He circl'd, four times cross'd the Carr of Night Par Lost 9.65

Circles
Desirous; all in Circles as they stood, Par Lost 5.631
Made horrid Circles; two broad Suns thir Shields Par Lost 6.305
The swiftness of those Circles attribute, Par Lost 8.107
Beyond the Polar Circles; to them Day Par Lost 10.681

Circlet
With thy bright Circlet, praise him in thy Spheare Par Lost 5.169

Circling
Impenetrable, impal'd with circling fire, Par Lost 2.647
So high above the circling Canopie Par Lost 3.556
And higher then that Wall a circling row Par Lost 4.146
Wak't by the circling Hours, with rosie hand Par Lost 6.3
Farr separate, circling thy holy Mount Par Lost 6.743
For Seasons, and for Dayes, and circling Years, Par Lost 7.342
Which nightly as a circling Zone thou seest Par Lost 7.580
Amidst his circling Spires, that on the grass Par Lost 9.502
And now too soon for us the circling hours Par Reg 1.57
Circling the Throne and Singing, while the hand Par Reg 1.171
Sam. I thought where all thy circling wiles would end; Samson 871

Circuit
In circuit, undetermind square or round, Par Lost 2.1048
The rest in circuit walles this Universe. Par Lost 3.721
But if within the circuit of these walks, Par Lost 4.586
Our circuit meets full West. As flame they part Par Lost 4.784
The circuit wide. Strait knew him all the Bands Par Lost 5.287
Of circuit inexpressible they stood, Par Lost 5.595
In circuit to the uttermost convex Par Lost 7.266
But they, or under ground, or circuit wide Par Lost 7.301
And for the Heav'ns wide Circuit, let it speak Par Lost 8.100
A Circuit wide, enclos'd, with goodliest Trees Par Lost 8.304
In narrow circuit strait'nd by a Foe, Par Lost 9.323
A spatious plain out stretch't in circuit wide Par Reg 3.254
that lurks by hedge or lane of this dead circuit Mask Tr. ms 16.40
that lurks by hedge or lane, of this dead circuit Mask Br. ms 393

Circular
Circular base of rising foulds, that tour'd Par Lost 9.498
A Globe of circular light, Nativity 110

Circumcised
My name perhaps among the Circumcis'd Samson 975

Circumcision
From Gentils, but by Circumcision vain, Par Reg 3.425

Circumference
Behind him cast; the broad circumference Par Lost 1.286
That shook Heav'ns whol circumference, confirm'd. Par Lost 2.353
From center to circumference, whereon Par Lost 5.510
A vast circumference: At his approach Par Lost 6.256
This be thy just Circumference, O World. Par Lost 7.231

Circumfluous
Built on circumfluous Waters calme, in wide Par Lost 7.270

Circumfused
His Armie, circumfus'd on either Wing, Par Lost 6.778
Earth with her nether Ocean circumfus'd, Par Lost 7.624

Circumscribe
In Gods Eternal store, to circumscribe Par Lost 7.226

Circumscribed
Such as he pleasd, and circumscrib'd thir being? Par Lost 5.825

Circumspection
All circumspection, and we now no less Par Lost 2.414
But with sly circumspection, and began Par Lost 4.537
With silent circumspection unespi'd. Par Lost 6.523

Circumstance
Man. Tell us the sum, the circumstance defer. Samson 1557

Circumvent
Hopeless to circumvent us joynd, where each Par Lost 9.259
Breaking her Marriage Faith to circumvent me. Samson 1115

Circumvented
Fall circumvented thus by fraud, though joynd Par Lost 3.152

Citadel
The suburb of thir Straw-built Cittadel, Par Lost 1.773
ms 'cittadell'
On the *Tarpeian* rock, her Cittadel Par Reg 4.49

Cited
The living, and forthwith the cited dead Par Lost 3.327

Cities
And in luxurious Cities, where the noyse Par Lost 1.498
ms 'cities'
As when to warn proud Cities warr appears Par Lost 2.533
Cities of Men with lofty Gates and Towrs, Par Lost 11.640
Cities of men, or head-strong Multitudes, Par Reg 2.470
Great Cities by assault: what do these Worthies, Par Reg 3.74
Huge Cities and high towr'd, that well might seem Par Reg 3.261
What ruins Kingdoms, and lays Cities flat; Par Reg 4.363
Towred Cities please us then, Allegro 117

Citron
Our tended Plants, how blows the Citron Grove, Par Lost 5.22
On *Cittron* tables or *Atlantic* stone; Par Reg 4.115

City
Som Capital City; or less then if this frame Par Lost 2.924
As one who long in populous City pent, Par Lost 9.445
Of *Pandaemonium*, Citie and proud seate Par Lost 10.424
City of old or modern Fame, the Seat Par Lost 11.386
Guiana, whose great Citie *Geryons* Sons Par Lost 11.410
Deserted: Others to a Citie strong Par Lost 11.655
To Council in the Citie Gates: anon Par Lost 11.661
A Citie and Towre, whose top may reach to Heav'n; Par Lost 12.44
Comes down to see thir Citie, ere the Tower Par Lost 12.51
Thir Citie, his Temple, and his holy Ark Par Lost 12.340
To that proud Citie, whose high Walls thou saw'st Par Lost 12.342
The City of Palms, *Aenon*, and *Salem* Old, Par Reg 2.21
Machaerus and each Town or City wall'd Par Reg 2.22
As one in City, or Court, or Palace bred, Par Reg 2.300
His City there thou seest, and *Bactra* there; Par Reg 3.285
The City gates out powr'd, light armed Troops Par Reg 3.311
The City of *Gallaphrone*, from thence to win Par Reg 3.340
On each side an Imperial City stood, Par Reg 4.33
The City which thou seest no other deem Par Reg 4.44
Where on the *Aegean* shore a City stands Par Reg 4.238
City or Suburban, studious walks and shades; Par Reg 4.243
The holy City lifted high her Towers, Par Reg 4.545
And in your City held my Nuptial Feast: Samson 1194
I heard all as I came, the City rings Samson 1449
The desolation of a Hostile City. Samson 1561
Mess. Occasions drew me early to this City, Samson 1596
Of this but each *Philistian* City round Samson 1655
City of God, most glorious things Psalm 87, 9

Civil
Infernal noise; Warr seem'd a civil Game Par Lost 6.667
Allurd them; thence from Cups to civil Broiles. Par Lost 11.718
To civil Justice, part religious Rites Par Lost 12.231
The solid rules of Civil Government Par Reg 4.358
Adjur'd by all the bonds of civil Duty Samson 853
Of those who have me in thir civil power. Samson 1367
More generous far and civil, who confess'd Samson 1467
Till civil-suited Morn appeer, Penseroso 122
Both spirituall powre and civill, what each meanes Sonnet 17, 10
1662 'civil'
1694 'Civil'
What powre the Church & what the civill meanes Sonnet 17, Tr. ms 45.11
Dare ye for this adjure the Civill Sword Forcers 5
Trinity ms 'civill'

Civility
Civility of Manners, Arts, and Arms, Par Reg 4.83

Clad
The flowry Dale of *Sibma* clad with Vines, Par Lost 1.410
Godlike erect, with native Honour clad Par Lost 4.289
Had in her sober Liverie all things clad; Par Lost 4.599
His lineaments Divine; the pair that clad Par Lost 5.278

Clad(*cont*)	
Brought forth the tender Grass, whose verdure clad	Par Lost 7.315
As Father of his Familie he clad	Par Lost 10.216
And shape Starr bright appeer'd, or brighter, clad	Par Lost 10.450
Dimentionless through Heav'nly dores; then clad	Par Lost 11.17
Clad to meet Man; over his lucid Armes	Par Lost 11.240
Some troubl'd thoughts, which she in sighs thus clad.	Par Reg 2.65
Not rustic as before, but seemlier clad,	Par Reg 2.299
Tall stripling youths rich clad, of fairer hew	Par Reg 2.352
In Mail thir horses clad, yet fleet and strong,	Par Reg 3.313
Ran on embattelld Armies clad in Iron,	Samson 129
Where I will see thee heartn'd and fresh clad	Samson 1317
In thir state Livery clad; before him Pipes	Samson 1616
She that has that, is clad in compleat steel,	Mask 421
Against the Sun-clad power of Chastity,	Mask 782
line not in Bridgewater ms	
line not in Trinity ms	
Clad in splendor as befits	Arcades 92
Who having clad thy self in humane weed,	Fair Inf 58
With thee there clad in radiant sheen,	Winchester 73
Thy hand-maids, clad them o're with purple beams	Sonnet 14, 10
Claim	
From Faction; for none sure will claim in Hell	Par Lost 2.32
To claim our just inheritance of old,	Par Lost 2.38
Part of my Soul I seek thee, and thee claim	Par Lost 4.487
We mean to hold what anciently we claim	Par Lost 5.723
Redeem thee quite from Deaths rapacious claime;	Par Lost 11.258
Moses and *Aaron*) sent from God to claime	Par Lost 12.170
Claimed	
His mighty Standard; that proud honour claim'd	Par Lost 1.533
Usurping over sovran Reason claimd	Par Lost 9.1130
Claimest	
Dear Daughter, since thou claim'st me for thy Sire,	Par Lost 2.817
Claiming	
Or from Heav'n claming second Sovrantie;	Par Lost 12.35
Claims	
Say, for such wonder claims attention due.	Par Lost 9.566
Clamorous	
My journey strange, with clamorous uproare	Par Lost 10.479
of clamourous sin that all our musick marres	Musick Tr. ms 5.04
'of clamourous sin' ←'of sin'	
Clamour	
And clamour such as heard in Heav'n till now	Par Lost 6.208
To rapture, till the savage clamor dround	Par Lost 7.36
1669 'clamour'	
With clamor thence the rapid Currents drive	Par Lost 11.853
With clamour was assur'd thir utmost aid	Par Reg 2.148
Clamouring	
Rifted the Air clamouring thir god with praise,	Samson 1621
Clamours	
With terrors and with clamors compasst round	Par Lost 2.862
Clang	
With clang despis'd the ground, under a cloud	Par Lost 7.422
The haunt of Seales and Orcs, and Sea-mews clang.	Par Lost 11.835
With such a horrid clang	Nativity 157
Clans	
Of each his Faction, in thir several Clanns,	Par Lost 2.901
Clarion	
Walk'd firm; the crested Cock whose clarion sounds	Par Lost 7.443
Clarions	
Of Trumpets loud and Clarions be upreard	Par Lost 1.532
ms 'clarions'	
Clashed	
Clash'd on thir sounding Shields the din of war,	Par Lost 1.668
Clashing	
Was never, Arms on Armour clashing bray'd	Par Lost 6.209
Clasp	
I beg, and clasp thy knees; bereave me not,	Par Lost 10.918
Clasping	
The clasping Ivie where to climb, while I	Par Lost 9.217
The clasping charm, and thaw the numming spell,	Mask 853
Bridgewater ms 'claspinge'	
He with his thunder-clasping hand,	Psalm 136, 37
Classic	
And ride us with a classic Hierarchy	Forcers 7
Clattered	
And raise such out-cries on thy clatter'd Iron,	Samson 1124
Clay	
Of Heav'n, this Man of Clay, Son of despite,	Par Lost 9.176
Did I request thee, Maker, from my Clay	Par Lost 10.743
The Desert, Fowls in thir clay nests were couch't;	Par Reg 1.501
Of som clay habitation visit us	Mask 339
Bridgewater ms 'claye'	
And chose with us a darksom House of mortal Clay.	Nativity 14
Cleansing	
With lavers pure and cleansing herbs wash off	Samson 1727
Clear	
Cleer Victory, to our part loss and rout	Par Lost 2.770
Cleer Spring, or shadie Grove, or Sunnie Hill,	Par Lost 3.28
Invites; for I will cleer thir senses dark,	Par Lost 3.188
If mettal, part seemd Gold, part Silver cleer;	Par Lost 3.595
No where so cleer, sharp'nd his visual ray	Par Lost 3.620
Are ever cleer. Whereof hee soon aware,	Par Lost 4.119
On the green bank, to look into the cleer	Par Lost 4.458
To whom the Son with calm aspect and cleer	Par Lost 5.733
On the cleer *Hyaline*, the Glassie Sea;	Par Lost 7.619
Not to incur; but soon his cleer aspect	Par Lost 8.336
Within me cleere, not onely to discerne	Par Lost 9.681
Clear(*cont*)	
Ye Eate thereof, your Eyes that seem so cleere,	Par Lost 9.706
And the cleer Sun on his wide watrie Glass	Par Lost 11.844
Of utmost hope! now clear I understand	Par Lost 12.376
I drank, from the clear milkie juice allaying	Samson 550
He that has light within his own cleer brest	Mask 381
1637 'cleere'	
Trinity ms 'cleere'	
Bridgewater ms 'cleere'	
And in cleer dream, and solemn vision	Mask 457
1637 'cleere'	
Trinity ms 'cleere'	
Drink the clear stream, and nothing wear but Freize,	Mask 722
Trinity ms 'cleere'	
Bridgewater ms 'cleere'	
Where the bow'd welkin slow doth bend,	Mask 1015
Trinity ms 'slow' ←'low' ←'cleere'	
In Saffron robe, with Taper clear,	Allegro 126
In Service high, and Anthems cleer,	Penseroso 163
Fame is the spur that the clear spirit doth raise	Lycidas 70
Trinity ms 'cleere'	
Low in the earth, *Jordans* clear streams recoil,	Psalm 114, 9
Cyriack, this three years day these eys, though clear	Sonnet 22, 1
So clear, as in no face with more delight.	Sonnet 23, 12
Trinity ms 'cleare'	
To God our strength sing loud, *and clear*	Psalm 81, 1
And all my fountains *clear*.	Psalm 87, 28
Cleared	
So all was cleard, and to the Field they haste.	Par Lost 5.136
To whom thus *Adam* cleerd of doubt, repli'd.	Par Lost 8.179
Op'nd and cleerd, and ye shall be as Gods,	Par Lost 9.708
Clear'd up their choicest notes in bush and spray	Par Reg 4.437
And Public Faith cleard from the shamefull brand	Sonnet 15, 12
1694 'be rescu'd'	
Clearer	
Which that false Fruit that promis'd clearer sight	Par Lost 11.413
Clearest	
The Hemisphere of Earth in cleerest Ken	Par Lost 11.379
Clearly	
When they shall read this clearly in your charge	Forcers 19
Trinity ms 'cleerly'	
Cleave	
And at their passing cleave the *Assyrian* flood,	Par Reg 3.436
Or drag him by the curls, to a foul death,	Mask 608
1637 'and cleave his scalpe'	
Bridgewater ms 'and cleave his scalpe'	
Trinity ms 'or drag him by the curls & cleave his scalpe'	
Cleaving	
A cleaving mischief, in his way to vertue	Samson 1039
Cleft	
On the cleft Wood, and all due Rites perform'd.	Par Lost 11.440
As the Red Sea and *Jordan* once he cleft,	Par Reg 3.438
The ruddy waves he cleft in twain,	Psalm 136, 45
Cleombrotus	
Cleombrotus, and many more too long,	Par Lost 3.473
Cliff	
Thir highest Heav'n; or on the *Delphian* Cliff,	Par Lost 1.517
ms 'cliff'	
The rest was craggie cliff, that overhung	Par Lost 4.547
At once on th' Eastern cliff of Paradise	Par Lost 5.275
Led them direct, and down the Cliff as fast	Par Lost 12.639
Cliffs	
On Cliffs and Cedar tops thir Eyries build:	Par Lost 7.424
And *Margiana* to the *Hyrcanian* cliffs	Par Reg 3.317
Climate	
Climat, or Years damp my intended wing	Par Lost 9.45
That never will in other Climate grow,	Par Lost 11.274
Climb	
So since into his Church lewd Hirelings climbe.	Par Lost 4.193
Still as it rose, impossible to climbe.	Par Lost 4.548
The clasping Ivie where to climb, while I	Par Lost 9.217
She can teach ye how to clime	Mask 1020
Bridgewater ms 'clyme'	
B.M. ms 'climb'	
Creep and intrude, and climb into the fold?	Lycidas 115
Trinity ms 'clime'	
1638 'climbe'	
When once our heav'nly-guided soul shall clime,	On Time 19
Climbest	
In thy eternal course, both when thou climbst,	Par Lost 5.173
1674 printed 'climb st'	
Climbing	
Obtains the brow of some high-climbing Hill,	Par Lost 3.546
Climbing, sat thicker then the snakie locks	Par Lost 10.559
Climbs	
In at the window climbs, or o're the tiles;	Par Lost 4.191
1667 'climbes'	
Where entrance up from *Eden* easiest climbes,	Par Lost 11.119
Clime	
Is this the Region, this the Soil, the Clime,	Par Lost 1.242
ms 'clime'	
On Heavens Azure, and the torrid Clime	Par Lost 1.297
ms 'clime'	
That dismal world, if any Clime perhaps	Par Lost 2.572
Now Morn her rosie steps in th' Eastern Clime	Par Lost 5.1
Bellerophon, though from a lower Clime)	Par Lost 7.18
Of Seasons to each Clime; else had the Spring	Par Lost 10.678
Began to parch that temperate Clime; whereat	Par Lost 12.636

Clime(*cont*)
with distant worlds, & strange removed clim — Mask Tr. ms 10.17
Who had thought this clime had held — Arcades 24
What ever clime the Suns bright circle warms. — Sonnet 8, 8

Climes
High in Salvation and the Climes of bliss, — Par Lost 11.708
And those happy climes that ly — Mask 977
Bridgewater ms 'Clymes'
B.M. ms 'Climes'
strange distances to heare & unknowne climes — Mask Tr. ms 10.17
'clim ', ms frayed at edge

Clip
Clip your Phylacteries, though bauk your Ears, — Forcers 17
Trinity ms 'lip', ms defective

Clod
With this corporeal Clod; then in the Grave, — Par Lost 10.786
Meekly thou didst resign this earthy load — Sonnet 14, 3
Trinity ms 'load' ←'clod'

Clods
The grassie Clods now Calv'd, now half appeer'd — Par Lost 7.463
Labouring, two massie clods of Iron and Brass — Par Lost 11.565

Clogs
I did but prompt the age to quit their cloggs — Sonnet 12, 1
Trinity ms 'clogs'

Cloister
To walk the studious Cloysters pale, — Penseroso 156

Clomb
So clomb this first grand Thief into Gods Fould: — Par Lost 4.192

Close
To work in close design, by fraud or guile — Par Lost 1.646
In close recess and secret conclave sat — Par Lost 1.795
Or clos ambition varnisht o're with zeal. — Par Lost 2.485
1667 'close'
Till thickest Legions close; with feats of Arms — Par Lost 2.537
Close sailing from *Bengala*, or the Iles — Par Lost 2.638
Of smallest Magnitude close by the Moon. — Par Lost 2.1053
His Lithe Proboscis; close the Serpent sly — Par Lost 4.347
And mutual amitie so streight, so close, — Par Lost 4.376
Strait couches close, then rising changes oft — Par Lost 4.405
Nor *Faunus* haunted. Here in close recess — Par Lost 4.708
Squat like a Toad, close at the eare of *Eve;* — Par Lost 4.800
Close at mine ear one call'd me forth to walk — Par Lost 5.36
Sleepst thou Companion dear, what sleep can close — Par Lost 5.673
Of Battel, open when, and when to close — Par Lost 6.235
Disturbd not, waiting close th' approach of Morn. — Par Lost 9.191
Close following pace for pace, not mounted yet — Par Lost 10.589
That *Adam* now enforc't to close his eyes, — Par Lost 11.419
Close in a Cottage low together got — Par Reg 2.28
The air imprison'd also, close and damp, — Samson 8
The close of all my miseries, and the balm. — Samson 651
And ever best found in the close. — Samson 1748
In thy dark lantern thus close up the Stars, — Mask 197
line not in Bridgewater ms
In this close dungeon of innumerous bowes. — Mask 349
Trinity ms 'close' ←'sad' ←'lone'
Bridgewater ms 'lone'
Till fancy had her fill, but ere a close — Mask 548
& favour our close jocondrie — Mask Tr. ms 12.29
There in close covert by som Brook, — Penseroso 139
With thousand echo's still prolongs each heav'nly close. — Nativity 100
Thy liquid notes that close the eye of Day, — Sonnet 1, 5
And wov'n close, both matter, form and stile; — Sonnet 11, 2
Cropp yee as close as marginall P---s eares — Forcers Tr. ms 45.17

Close-banded
Close-banded durst attaque me, no not sleeping, — Samson 1113

Close-curtained
That draw the litter of close-curtain'd sleep. — Mask 554
1673 'close curtain'd'

Closed
O Father, gracious was that word which clos'd — Par Lost 3.144
Pass'd through him, but th' Ethereal substance clos'd — Par Lost 6.330
Yawning receavd them whole, and on them clos'd, — Par Lost 6.875
By Nature as in aide, and clos'd mine eyes. — Par Lost 8.459
Mine eyes he clos'd, but op'n left the Cell — Par Lost 8.460
Whereof this ominous night that clos'd thee round, — Par Reg 4.481
Clos'd o're the head of your lov'd *Lycidas?* — Lycidas 51

Closing
Just met, and closing stood in squadron joind — Par Lost 4.863
Soon closing, and by native vigour heal'd. — Par Lost 6.436

Clothe
And thought not much to cloath his Enemies: — Par Lost 10.219
Before thou cloath my fancy in fit sound: — Vacation 32
The frozen earth; and cloth in fresh attire — Sonnet 20, 7

Clothed
Cloth'd with transcendent brightness didst out-shine — Par Lost 1.86
Thus *Belial* with words cloath'd in reasons garb — Par Lost 2.226
Cloath'd us unworthie, pitying while he judg'd; — Par Lost 10.1059

Clothing
Yet on his Brothers shall depend for Cloathing. — Vacation 82

Clotted
The clotted gore. I with what speed the while — Samson 1728
The soul grows clotted by contagion, — Mask 467

Cloud
Wav'd round the Coast, up call'd a pitchy cloud — Par Lost 1.340
The strong rebuff of som tumultuous cloud — Par Lost 2.936
But cloud in stead, and ever-during dark — Par Lost 3.45
Father, to see thy face, wherein no cloud — Par Lost 3.262
The full blaze of thy beams, and through a cloud — Par Lost 3.378

Cloud(*cont*)
In whose conspicuous count'nance, without cloud — Par Lost 3.385
Then in fair Evening Cloud, or humid Bow, — Par Lost 4.151
Be not disheart'nd then, nor cloud those looks — Par Lost 5.122
From hence, no cloud, or, to obstruct his sight, — Par Lost 5.257
Her shadowie Cloud withdraws, I am to haste, — Par Lost 5.686
From midst a Golden Cloud thus milde was heard. — Par Lost 6.28
This day, fear not his flight; so thick a Cloud — Par Lost 6.539
Sphear'd in a radiant Cloud, for yet the Sun — Par Lost 7.247
With clang despis'd the ground, under a cloud — Par Lost 7.422
Veild in a Cloud of Fragrance, where she stood, — Par Lost 9.425
Eternal Father from his secret Cloud, — Par Lost 10.32
At last as from a Cloud his fulgent head — Par Lost 10.449
To whom the Father, without Cloud, serene. — Par Lost 11.45
More orient in yon Western Cloud that draws — Par Lost 11.205
From yonder blazing Cloud that veils the Hill — Par Lost 11.229
Had not a Cloud descending snatch'd him thence — Par Lost 11.670
Rapt in a balmie Cloud with winged Steeds — Par Lost 11.706
A dewie Cloud, and in the Cloud a Bow — Par Lost 11.865
The fluid skirts of that same watrie Cloud, — Par Lost 11.882
Over the Earth a Cloud, will therein set — Par Lost 11.896
A darksom Cloud of Locusts swarming down — Par Lost 12.185
Before them in a Cloud, and Pillar of Fire, — Par Lost 12.202
By day a Cloud, by night a Pillar of Fire, — Par Lost 12.203
Then through the Firey Pillar and the Cloud — Par Lost 12.208
The Heav'nly fires; over the Tent a Cloud — Par Lost 12.256
Interposition, as a summers cloud. — Par Reg 3.222
An empty cloud. However many books — Par Reg 4.321
Was I deceiv'd, or did a sable cloud — Mask 221
line not in Bridgewater ms
I did not err, there does a sable cloud — Mask 223
line not in Bridgewater ms
Stoop thy pale visage through an amber cloud, — Mask 333
Bridgewater ms 'cloude'
Stooping through a fleecy cloud. — Penseroso 72
But Cherchef't in a comly Cloud, — Penseroso 125
Had got a race of mourners on som pregnant cloud. — Passion 56
Cromwell, our cheif of men, who through a cloud — Sonnet 16, 1
1694 'Croud'
Shine forth, *and from thy cloud give light,* — Psalm 80, 7

Clouded
Rising in clouded Majestie, at length — Par Lost 4.607
The clouded Ark of God till then in Tents — Par Lost 12.333

Cloudless
His cloudless thunder bolted on thir heads. — Samson 1696
To live with him, and sing in endles morn of light. — Musick 28
Trinity ms 'endlesse' ←'never-parting' ←'cloudlesse' ←'endlesse' ←'uneclipsed' ←'ever-glorious' ←'ever-endlesse'

Clouds
Thick clouds and dark doth Heav'ns all-ruling Sire — Par Lost 2.264
As when from mountain tops the dusky clouds — Par Lost 2.488
To Battel in the Clouds, before each Van — Par Lost 2.535
Hangs in the Clouds, by *Aequinoctial* Winds — Par Lost 2.637
Each cast at th' other, as when two black Clouds — Par Lost 2.714
On *Juno* smiles, when he impregns the Clouds — Par Lost 4.500
Of Alablaster, pil'd up to the Clouds, — Par Lost 4.544
The Clouds that on his Western Throne attend: — Par Lost 4.597
Could not but taste. Forthwith up to the Clouds — Par Lost 5.86
Whether to deck with Clouds the uncolourd skie, — Par Lost 5.189
Now when ambrosial Night with Clouds exhal'd — Par Lost 5.642
So spake the Sovran voice, and Clouds began — Par Lost 6.56
Into the Clouds, thir tops ascend the Skie: — Par Lost 7.287
Choral or Unison: of incense Clouds — Par Lost 7.599
As Clouds, and Clouds may rain, and Rain produce — Par Lost 8.146
Notus and *Afer* black with thundrous Clouds — Par Lost 10.702
The Air attrite to Fire, as late the Clouds — Par Lost 10.1073
Wide hovering, all the Clouds together drove — Par Lost 11.739
Which now abated, for the Clouds were fled, — Par Lost 11.841
Above the Clouds will pine his entrails gross, — Par Lost 12.77
Last in the Clouds from Heav'n to be reveald — Par Lost 12.545
Within thick Clouds and dark ten-fold involv'd, — Par Reg 1.41
Out of the water, Heav'n above the Clouds — Par Reg 1.81
Nor wanted clouds of foot, nor on each horn, — Par Reg 3.327
Gan thunder, and both ends of Heav'n, the Clouds — Par Reg 4.410
Of thunder, chas'd the clouds, and laid the winds, — Par Reg 4.429
Rule in the Clouds; like an Autumnal Star — Par Reg 4.619
And play i' th plighted clouds. I was aw-strook, — Mask 301
Trinity ms 'clowds'
when the big rowling flakes of pitchie clowds — Mask Tr. ms 15.52
when the bigg rowling flakes of pitchie clouds — Mask Br. ms 345
The clouds in thousand Liveries dight, — Allegro 62
The labouring clouds do often rest: — Allegro 74
With Turtle wing the amorous clouds dividing, — Nativity 50
With radiant feet the tissued clouds down stearing, — Nativity 146
While the red fire, and smouldring clouds out brake: — Nativity 159
So sweetly sung your Joy the Clouds along — Circum 4
Trinity ms 'clouds'
With clouds encompass'd round; — Psalm 81, 30

Cloudy
As in a cloudy Chair ascending rides — Par Lost 2.930
A cloudy spot. Down thither prone in flight — Par Lost 5.266
Of hideous length: before the cloudie Van, — Par Lost 6.107
Under her Cloudie covert both retir'd, — Par Lost 6.409
And cloudie in aspect thus answering spake. — Par Lost 6.450
Was not; shee in a cloudie Tabernacle — Par Lost 7.248
Transplanted from her cloudie Shrine, and plac'd — Par Lost 7.360
Stay thy cloudy Ebon chair, — Mask 134
Trinity ms 'clowdie' ←'polisht'

Cloudy(*cont*)
Bridgewater ms 'cloudie'
1637 'clowdie'
Curtain'd with cloudy red, Nativity 230
Let down in clowdie throne to do the world some good. Fair Inf 56
Clouted
Treads on it daily with his clouted shoon, Mask 635
line not in Bridgewater ms
Cloven
Down clov'n to the waste, with shatterd Armes Par Lost 6.361
Rough *Satyrs* danc'd, and *Fauns* with clov'n heel, Lycidas 34
1638 'cloven'
Trinity ms 'clov'en'
Cloy
Their stores doth over-cloy Psalm 4, 34
Cloyed
For cloy'd with woes and trouble store Psalm 88, 9
Clung
His Armes clung to his Ribs, his Leggs entwining Par Lost 10.512
Clustering
Clustring, but not beneath his shoulders broad: Par Lost 4.303
Forth flourish't thick the clustring Vine, forth crept Par Lost 7.320
Robustious to no purpose clustring down, Samson 569
This Nymph that gaz'd upon his clustring locks, Mask 54
Bridgewater ms 'clustringe'
Clusters
In clusters; they among fresh dews and flowers Par Lost 1.771
Her dowr th' adopted Clusters, to adorn Par Lost 5.218
Plucking ripe clusters from the tender shoots, Mask 296
Clymene
Some beauty rare, *Calisto*, *Clymene*, Par Reg 2.186
Coal
Of sooty coal the Empiric Alchimist Par Lost 5.440
Coals
He found his Supper on the coals prepar'd, Par Reg 2.273
Coaly
Or Coaly *Tine*, or antient hollowed *Dee*, Vacation 98
Coarse
They had their name thence; course complexions Mask 749
line not in Bridgewater ms
Trinity ms 'coarse'
Coast
Hath vext the Red-Sea Coast, whose waves orethrew Par Lost 1.306
ms 'coast'
Wav'd round the Coast, up call'd a pitchy cloud Par Lost 1.340
ms 'coast'
Rear'd in *Azotus*, dreaded through the Coast Par Lost 1.464
ms 'coast'
He scours the right hand coast, som times the left, Par Lost 2.633
Which way the neerest coast of darkness lyes Par Lost 2.958
A violent cross wind from either Coast Par Lost 3.487
Took leave, and toward the coast of Earth beneath, Par Lost 3.739
Uzziel, half these draw off, and coast the South Par Lost 4.782
In *Pontus* or the *Punic* Coast, or where Par Lost 5.340
Lookd round, and Scouts each Coast light-armed scoure, Par Lost 6.529
On the eighth return'd, and on the Coast averse Par Lost 9.67
Eden and all the Coast in prospect lay. Par Lost 10.89
Cathaian Coast. The aggregated Soyle Par Lost 10.293
So to the Coast of *Jordan* he directs Par Reg 1.119
Pontus and *Lucrine* Bay, and *Afric* Coast. Par Reg 2.347
That rul'd the *Amorrean* coast. Psalm 136, 66
That wasted all the Coast Psalm 83, 34
Coasting
Coasting the wall of Heav'n on this side Night Par Lost 3.71
Coasting the *Tyrrhene* shore, as the winds listed, Mask 49
Bridgewater ms 'coastinge'
Coasts
Through all the Coasts of dark destruction seek Par Lost 2.464
1667 'coasts'
Glad we return'd up to the coasts of Light Par Lost 8.245
And home they fly from round the Coasts Psalm 84, 15
Coat
Alcinous reign'd, fruit of all kindes, in coate, Par Lost 5.341
His Adamantine coat gird well, and each Par Lost 6.542
Or as the Snake with youthful Coate repaid; Par Lost 10.218
Coats
Show to the Sun thir wav'd coats dropt with Gold, Par Lost 7.406
In coats of Mail and military pride; Par Reg 3.312
Cock
Walk'd firm; the crested Cock whose clarion sounds Par Lost 7.443
Or whistle from the Lodge, or village cock Mask 346
1673 'Cock'
Bridgewater ms 'Cock'
While the Cock with lively din, Allegro 49
Ere the first Cock his Mattin rings. Allegro 114
Cocytus
Cocytus, nam'd of lamentation loud Par Lost 2.579
Coeternal
Or of th' Eternal Coeternal beam Par Lost 3.2
Coffers
Such as may make thee search thy coffers round, Vacation 31
Cogitation
He seemd, or fixt in cogitation deep. Par Lost 3.629
Cohort
For swift descent, with him the Cohort bright Par Lost 11.127
Cohorts
Legions and Cohorts, turmes of horse and wings: Par Reg 4.66

Coin
How counterfeit a coin they are who friends Samson 189
To pay my underminers in thir coin. Samson 1204
Beauty is natures coyn, must not be hoorded, Mask 739
1637 'coine'
line not in Bridgewater ms
Trinity ms 'coine'
Cold
Of cold *Olympus* rul'd the middle Air Par Lost 1.516
Burns frore, and cold performs th' effect of Fire. Par Lost 2.595
For hot, cold, moist, and dry, four Champions fierce Par Lost 2.898
The black tartareous cold Infernal dregs Par Lost 7.238
That name, unless an age too late, or cold Par Lost 9.44
Condenses, and the cold invirons round, Par Lost 9.636
Death with his Mace petrific, cold and dry, Par Lost 10.294
As might affect the Earth with cold and heat Par Lost 10.653
From cold *Estotiland*, and South as farr Par Lost 10.686
Avoided pinching cold and scorching heate? Par Lost 10.691
Outstretcht he lay, on the cold ground, and oft Par Lost 10.851
My labour will sustain me; and least Cold Par Lost 10.1056
Leave cold the Night, how we his gather'd beams Par Lost 10.1070
Adam by this from the cold sudden damp Par Lost 11.293
A melancholly damp of cold and dry Par Lost 11.544
From cold *Septentrion* blasts, thence in the midst Par Reg 4.31
Hungry and cold betook him to his rest, Par Reg 4.403
Perhaps som cold bank is her boulster now Mask 353
Bridgewater ms 'could'
Trinity ms 'cold' ←'cold hard'
And though not mortal, yet a cold shuddring dew Mask 802
line not in Trinity ms
line not in Bridgewater ms
I touch with chaste palms moist and cold, Mask 918
Bridgewater ms 'could'
Lie scatter'd on the Alpine mountains cold, Sonnet 18, 2
Cold-kind
But all unwares with his cold-kind embrace Fair Inf 20
Colic
Intestin Stone and Ulcer, Colic pangs, Par Lost 11.484
Colkitto
Colkitto, or Macdonnel, or Galasp? Sonnet 11, 9
1673 printed 'Coliktto', errata 'Colkitto'
Collateral
Collateral love, and deerest amitie. Par Lost 8.426
Of high collateral glorie: him Thrones and Powers, Par Lost 10.86
Colleague
Mercie collegue with Justice, sending thee Par Lost 10.59
Collect
Where by all best conjectures I collect Par Reg 4.524
Collected
Collected stood within our thoughts amus'd, Par Lost 6.581
Stood in himself collected, while each part, Par Lost 9.673
Collecting
Collecting all his might dilated stood, Par Lost 4.986
At length collecting all his Serpent wiles, Par Reg 3.5
Crude or intoxicate, collecting toys, Par Reg 4.328
Collision
Or by collision of two bodies grinde Par Lost 10.1072
Colloquy
In that celestial Colloquie sublime, Par Lost 8.455
Colonel
Captain or Colonel, or Knight in Arms, Sonnet 8, 1
Trinity ms 'Collonell'
Colour
Of colour glorious and effect so rare? Par Lost 3.612
They Limb themselves, and colour, shape or size Par Lost 6.352
Like his, and colour Serpentine may shew Par Lost 10.870
Thir shape, thir colour, and attractive grace, Par Reg 2.176
Coloured
Of many a colourd plume sprinkl'd with Gold, Par Lost 3.642
Broiderd the ground, more colour'd then with stone Par Lost 4.702
Adorns him, colour'd with the Florid hue Par Lost 7.445
But say, what mean those colourd streaks in Heavn, Par Lost 11.879
His triple-colour'd Bow, whereon to look Par Lost 11.897
That Heav'n and Earth are colour'd with my wo; Passion 32
Ay sung before the saphire-colour'd throne Musick 7
Trinity ms 'sapphire-colour'd' ←'saphire-colour'd'
←'saphire-colourd' ←'soveraigne'
Colouring
colouring the pale cheeke of uninjoyd love Lycidas Tr. ms 28.16
'colouring' ←'collu'
Colours
With Orient Colours waving: with them rose Par Lost 1.546
ms 'colours'
Appeerd, with gay enameld colours mixt: Par Lost 4.149
How Nature paints her colours, how the Bee Par Lost 5.24
And colours dipt in Heav'n; the third his feet Par Lost 5.283
Amber, and colours of the showrie Arch. Par Lost 6.759
Op'ning thir various colours, and made gay Par Lost 7.318
Loaden with fruit of fairest colours mixt, Par Lost 9.577
Conspicuous with three listed colours gay, Par Lost 11.866
These false pretexts and varnish'd colours failing, Samson 901
That in the colours of the Rainbow live Mask 300
Bridgewater ms 'cooleness'
Columbine
The Musk-rose, and the well attir'd Woodbine, Lycidas 146
Trinity ms 'well-attir'd woodbine' ←'garish columbine'
Columbus
Columbus found th' *American* so girt Par Lost 9.1116

Column
As in a fiery column charioting Samson 27
Colure
From Pole to Pole, traversing each Colure; Par Lost 9.66
Comb
And fair *Ligea*'s golden comb, Mask 880
Bridgewater ms 'Combe'
Trinity ms 'combe', but line deleted
Combat
To mortal combat or carreer with Lance) Par Lost 1.766
Should combat, and thir jarring Sphears confound. Par Lost 6.315
Har. To combat with a blind man I disdain, Samson 1106
Offering to combat thee his Champion bold, Samson 1152
By combat to decide whose god is God, Samson 1176
Combatant
None offering fight; who single combatant Samson 344
Combatants
So frownd the mighty Combatants, that Hell Par Lost 2.719
Combated
And combated in silence all these reasons Samson 864
Combined
Of all the Seraphim with thee combin'd Par Lost 2.750
So fitly them in pairs thou hast combin'd; Par Lost 8.394
As not secure to single or combin'd. Par Lost 9.339
Combines
That in domestic good combines: Samson 1048
Combustible
Of thundring *Aetna*, whose combustible Par Lost 1.233
Combustion
With hideous ruine and combustion down Par Lost 1.46
Dreadful combustion warring, and disturb, Par Lost 6.225
Come
With Heav'ns Artillery fraught, come rattling on Par Lost 2.715
I come no enemie, but to set free Par Lost 2.822
Chaos and *ancient Night*, I come no Spy, Par Lost 2.970
The vigilance here plac't, but such as come Par Lost 4.580
But come, for thou, besure, shalt give account Par Lost 4.841
Thou surely hadst not come sole fugitive. Par Lost 4.923
May come and go, so unapprov'd, and leave Par Lost 5.118
Soon as they forth were come to open sight Par Lost 5.138
Thir glittering Tents he passd, and now is come Par Lost 5.291
Him through the spicie Forrest onward com Par Lost 5.298
To proper substance; time may come when men Par Lost 5.493
Thither to come, and with calumnious Art Par Lost 5.770
O Friends, why come not on these Victors proud? Par Lost 6.609
Hereafter, when they come to model Heav'n Par Lost 8.79
First Father, call'd by thee I come thy Guide Par Lost 8.298
To come and play before thee, know'st thou not Par Lost 8.372
All human thoughts come short, Supream of things; Par Lost 8.414
Thou sever not: Trial will come unsought. Par Lost 9.366
Meer Serpent in appearance, forth was come, Par Lost 9.413
Mee thus, though importune perhaps, to come Par Lost 9.610
But come, so well refresh't, now let us play, Par Lost 9.1027
Foretold so lately what would come to pass, Par Lost 10.38
Or come I less conspicuous, or what change Par Lost 10.107
Absents thee, or what chance detains? Come forth. Par Lost 10.108
Where Armies lie encampt, come flying, lur'd Par Lost 10.276
To *Adam* what shall come in future dayes, Par Lost 11.114
Permits not; to remove thee I am come, Par Lost 11.260
All generations, and had hither come Par Lost 11.344
To shew thee what shall come in future dayes Par Lost 11.357
These two are Brethren, *Adam*, and to come Par Lost 11.454
These painful passages, how we may come Par Lost 11.528
And utter odious Truth, that God would come Par Lost 11.704
And full of peace, denouncing wrauth to come Par Lost 11.815
Henceforth what is to com I will relate, Par Lost 12.11
Save when they journie, and at length they come, Par Lost 12.258
Unseen before in Heav'n proclaims him com, Par Lost 12.361
Above all names in Heav'n; and thence shall come, Par Lost 12.458
By name to come call'd Charitie, the soul Par Lost 12.584
The great deliverance by her Seed to come Par Lost 12.600
To do him honour as their King; all come, Par Reg 1.75
To her a Virgin, that on her should come Par Reg 1.138
And devilish machinations come to nought. Par Reg 1.181
Not knew by sight) now come, who was to come Par Reg 1.271
Accompanied of things past and to come Par Reg 1.300
Who dwell this wild, constrain'd by want, come forth Par Reg 1.331
Who boast'st release from Hell, and leave to come Par Reg 1.409
To hear thee when I come (since no man comes) Par Reg 1.484
Rode up to Heaven, yet once again to come. Par Reg 2.17
Messiah certainly now come, so long Par Reg 2.32
Send thy Messiah forth, the time is come; Par Reg 2.43
All his great work to come before him set; Par Reg 2.112
Thy gentle Ministers, who come to pay Par Reg 2.375
Let that come when it comes; all hope is lost Par Reg 3.204
Were better farthest off) is not yet come; Par Reg 3.397
A Saviour art come down to re-install. Par Reg 4.615
Perhaps my enemies who come to stare Samson 112
We come thy friends and neighbours not unknown Samson 180
Are come upon him his deserts? yet why? Samson 205
Which to have come to pass by means of thee, Samson 444
For oft alike, both come to evil end. Samson 704
Sam. My Wife, my Traytress, let her not come near me. Samson 725
Let weakness then with weakness come to parl Samson 785
Har. I come not *Samson*, to condole thy chance, Samson 1076
And now am come to see of whom such noise Samson 1088
Come nearer, part not hence so slight inform'd; Samson 1229
But come what will, my deadliest foe will prove Samson 1262

Come(*cont*)
Rise therefore with all speed and come along, Samson 1316
My presence; for that cause I cannot come. Samson 1321
Return the way thou cam'st, I will not come. Samson 1332
Joyn'd with extream contempt? I will not come. Samson 1342
Chor. How thou wilt here come off surmounts my reach. Samson 1380
Dispute thy coming? come without delay; Samson 1395
And hamper thee, as thou shalt come of force, Samson 1397
Masters commands come with a power resistless Samson 1404
To come and play before them at thir Feast. Samson 1448
To utter what will come at last too soon; Samson 1566
Thir own destruction to come speedy upon them. Samson 1681
Man. Come, come, no time for lamentation now, Samson 1708
Com let us our rights begin, Mask 125
1637 'Come'
Trinity ms 'Come'
Bridgewater ms 'come'
Com, knit hands, and beat the ground, Mask 143
1637 'Come'
Trinity ms 'Come'
But where they are, and why they came not back, Mask 191
Bridgewater ms 'come not back'
Com not too neer, you fall on iron stakes else. Mask 491
Bridgewater ms 'come'
Trinity ms 'Come'
1637 'Come'
And earths base built on stubble. But com let's on. Mask 599
Bridgewater ms 'come'
1637 'come'
Trinity ms 'come'
Would grow inur'd to light, and com at last Mask 735
Trinity ms 'come'
1637 'come'
Bridgewater ms 'come'
And try her yet more strongly. Com, no more, Mask 806
Trinity ms 'Come'
Bridgewater ms 'Come'
1637 'come'
Com Lady while Heaven lends us grace, Mask 938
Trinity ms 'Come'
Bridgewater ms 'come'
1637 'Come'
Till we com to holier ground, Mask 943
Trinity ms 'come'
Bridgewater ms 'come'
1637 'come'
Where this night are met in state Mask 948
Trinity ms 'met' ←'come'
Com let us haste, the Stars grow high, Mask 956
Bridgewater ms 'come'
Trinity ms 'come'
1637 'Come'
yet thence I come and oft from thence behold Mask Tr. ms 10.18
But com thou Goddes fair and free, Allegro 11
Com, and trip it as ye go Allegro 33
Then to com in spight of sorrow, Allegro 45
And young and old com forth to play Allegro 97
Com pensive Nun, devout and pure, Penseroso 31
Com, but keep thy wonted state, Penseroso 37
In Scepter'd Pall com sweeping by, Penseroso 98
I com to pluck your Berries harsh and crude, Lycidas 3
1638 'come'
Trinity ms 'come'
Was kindly com to live with them below; Nativity 90
1673 'come'
Small loss it is that thence can come unto thee, Vacation 9
Then quick about thy purpos'd business come, Vacation 57
Come tripping to the Room where thou didst lie; Vacation 62
And thinking now his journeys end was come, Carrier 12
His leasure told him that his time was com, Another 23
line not in 1658 text
1640, 1657 'come'
Awake thy strength, come, and *be seen* Psalm 80, 11
Come let us cut them off say they, Psalm 83, 13
Then will he come, and not be slow Psalm 85, 55
Shall come, *and all shall frame* Psalm 86, 30
Comeliness
Speaking or mute all comliness and grace Par Lost 8.222
Strength, comliness of shape, or amplest merit Samson 1011
Comely
Fluctuats disturbd, yet comely and in act Par Lost 9.668
Chor. Oh how comely it is and how reviving Samson 1268
But boast themselves more comely then before Mask 75
Bridgewater ms 'comly'
But Cherchef't in a comly Cloud, Penseroso 125
1673 'comely'
Comer
Those middle parts, that this new commer, Shame, Par Lost 9.1097
Comes
And rest can never dwell, hope never comes Par Lost 1.66
That comes to all; but torture without end Par Lost 1.67
In secret, riding through the Air she comes Par Lost 2.663
Comes unprevented, unimplor'd, unsought, Par Lost 3.231
So on he fares, and to the border comes, Par Lost 4.131
And with them comes a third of Regal port, Par Lost 4.869
Comes this way moving; seems another Morn Par Lost 5.310
To grateful Twilight (for Night comes not there Par Lost 5.645
He comes, and settl'd in his face I see Par Lost 6.540

Comes*(cont)*
Early, and th' hour of Supper comes unearn'd. Par Lost 9.225
Comes thundring back with dreadful revolution Par Lost 10.814
The day of his offence. Why comes not Death, Par Lost 10.854
But Death comes not at call, Justice Divine Par Lost 10.858
Thy mortal passage when it comes. Ascend Par Lost 11.366
How comes it thus? unfould, Celestial Guide, Par Lost 11.785
Comes down to see thir Citie, ere the Tower Par Lost 12.51
He comes invited by a yonger Son Par Lost 12.160
Which hee, who comes thy Saviour, shall recure, Par Lost 12.393
What from without comes often to my ears, Par Reg 1.199
Comes to the place where he before had sat Par Reg 1.412
To hear thee when I come (since no man comes) Par Reg 1.484
Let that come when it comes; all hope is lost Par Reg 3.204
When that comes think not thou to find me slack Par Reg 3.398
Know therefore when my season comes to sit Par Reg 4.146
But see here comes thy reverend Sire Samson 326
Comes this way sailing Samson 713
Comes he in peace? what wind hath blown him hither Samson 1070
Sam. Or peace or not, alike to me he comes. Samson 1074
Comes on amain, speed in his look. Samson 1304
But wherefore comes old *Manoa* in such hast Samson 1441
But here she comes, I fairly step aside Mask 168
If he be friendly he comes well, if not, Mask 488
Comes the blind *Fury* with th' abhorred shears, Lycidas 75
Comes dancing from the East, and leads with her May Morn 2
Our solemn Feast *comes round*. Psalm 81, 12
Another *Constantine* comes not in hast. Prose 3, 5

Comest
Com'st thou, escap'd thy prison, and transform'd, Par Lost 4.824
Omnipotence to none. But well thou comst Par Lost 6.159
Into the Heav'n of Heavens; thou com'st indeed, Par Reg 1.410
And just in time thou com'st to have a view Par Reg 3.298

Comet
Unterrifi'd, and like a Comet burn'd, Par Lost 2.708
Fierce as a Comet; which with torrid heat, Par Lost 12.634

Comfort
Do'st help and comfort me. Psalm 86, 64

Comfortable
And sends a comfortable heat from farr, Par Lost 10.1077

Comforter
Hee to his own a Comforter will send, Par Lost 12.486

Comfortless
Though comfortless, as when a Father mourns Par Lost 11.760

Comforts
By him with many comforts, till we end Par Lost 10.1084

Coming
Happie for man, so coming; he her aide Par Lost 3.232
The coming of thir secret foe, and scap'd Par Lost 4.7
Thy coming, and thy soft imbraces, hee Par Lost 4.471
After soft showers; and sweet the coming on Par Lost 4.646
Receive him coming to receive from us Par Lost 5.781
Ere while they fierce were coming, and when wee, Par Lost 6.610
When coming towards them so dread they saw Par Lost 6.648
He onward came, farr off his coming shon, Par Lost 6.768
And Spirit coming to create new Worlds. Par Lost 7.209
Her Nurserie; they at her coming sprung Par Lost 8.46
Serpent, we might have spar'd our coming hither, Par Lost 9.647
My coming seen far off? I miss thee here, Par Lost 10.104
Invests him coming? yet not terrible, Par Lost 11.233
Inclin'd not, but his coming thus declar'd. Par Lost 11.250
He shall endure by coming in the Flesh Par Lost 12.405
His coming, is sent Harbinger, who all Par Reg 1.71
Thy coming hither, though I know thy scope, Par Reg 1.494
Who then thou art, whose coming is foretold Par Reg 4.204
Sam. Your coming, Friends, revives me, for I learn Samson 187
Dispute thy coming? come without delay; Samson 1395
But that which mov'd my coming now, was chiefly Samson 1452
Are coming to attend their Fathers state, Mask 35
Trinity ms 'comming'
Bridgewater ms 'cominge'
And our sudden coming there Mask 954
Trinity ms 'comming'
Bridgewater ms 'Cominge'
1637 'comming'

Command
Awaiting what command thir mighty Chief Par Lost 1.566
Mean while the winged Haralds by command Par Lost 1.752
And by command of Heav'ns all-powerful King Par Lost 2.851
And easily transgress the sole Command, Par Lost 3.94
Stand ready at command, and are his Eyes Par Lost 3.650
Awaiting next command. To whom thir Chief Par Lost 4.864
Our maker, and obey him whose command Par Lost 5.551
Tell them that by command, ere yet dim Night Par Lost 5.685
At which command the Powers Militant, Par Lost 6.61
At his command the uprooted Hills retir'd Par Lost 6.781
If they transgress, and slight that sole command, Par Lost 7.47
For haste; such flight the great command impress'd Par Lost 7.294
Squar'd in full Legion (such command we had) Par Lost 8.232
The day thou eat'st thereof, my sole command Par Lost 8.329
Replenisht, and all these at thy command Par Lost 8.371
His great command; take heed least Passion sway Par Lost 8.635
God so commanded, and left that Command Par Lost 9.652
Command me absolutely not to go, Par Lost 9.1156
Departing gave command, and they observ'd. Par Lost 10.430
His Eye might there command wherever stood Par Lost 11.385
The one just Man alive; by his command Par Lost 11.818
And craze thir Chariot wheels: when by command Par Lost 12.210

Command*(cont)*
But if thou be the Son of God, Command Par Reg 1.342
To approach thy Temples, give thee in command Par Reg 1.449
At his command; when from amidst them rose Par Reg 2.149
When and where likes me best, I can command? Par Reg 2.382
Command a Table in this Wilderness, Par Reg 2.384
For it is written, He will give command Par Reg 4.556
Lest he command them down into the deep Par Reg 4.631
But to subserve where wisdom bears command. Samson 57
With strength sufficient and command from Heav'n Samson 1212
Not dragging? the *Philistian* Lords command. Samson 1371
And dar'st thou at our sending and command Samson 1394
But that by quick command from Soveran *Jove* Mask 41
Bridgewater ms 'commaund'
And command which I desire. Psalm 7, 24

Commanded
Pretending so commanded to consult Par Lost 5.768
God so commanded, and left that Command Par Lost 9.652
Sollicited, commanded, threatn'd, urg'd, Samson 852

Commander
Thir great Commander; Godlike shapes and forms Par Lost 1.358
Thir dread commander: he above the rest Par Lost 1.589
ms 'Commander'
1667 'Commander'

Commandest
What thou commandst, and right thou shouldst be obeyd: Par Lost 9.570

Commanding
That the most High commanding, now ere Night, Par Lost 5.699
Satan: And thus was heard Commanding loud. Par Lost 6.557
Mans voice commanding, Sun in *Gibeon* stand, Par Lost 12.265
That by his all-commanding might, Psalm 136, 25
All Flocks, and Herds, by thy commanding word, Psalm 8, 19

Commandments
The first of all Commandments, Thou shalt worship Par Reg 4.176

Commands
Then strait commands that at the warlike sound Par Lost 1.531
But what ow I to his commands above Par Lost 2.856
Undazl'd, farr and wide his eye commands, Par Lost 3.614
Envious commands, invented with designe Par Lost 4.524
Pure, and commands to som, leaves free to all. Par Lost 4.747
The great *Messiah*, and his new commands, Par Lost 5.691
The Deitie, and divine commands obei'd, Par Lost 5.806
Will condescend to such absurd commands? Samson 1337
1671 'commands.' in some copies
Commands are no constraints. If I obey them, Samson 1372
Masters commands come with a power resistless Samson 1404
Hitherto, Lords, what your commands impos'd Samson 1640

Commend
Us'd no ambition to commend my deeds, Samson 247
To win her Grace, whom all commend. Allegro 124

Commended
Commended her fair innocence to the flood Mask 831

Commends
Commends thee more, while it inferrs the good Par Lost 9.754

Commercing
And looks commercing with the skies, Penseroso 39

Commiseration
Commiseration; soon his heart relented Par Lost 10.940

Commission
Thy hearing, such Commission from above Par Lost 7.118

Commit
How Nature wise and frugal could commit Par Lost 8.26
Unanimous they all commit the care Par Reg 1.111
The rest commit to me, I shall let pass Par Reg 2.233

Commits
By course commits to severall goverment, Mask 25
Bridgewater ms 'committs'
Trinity ms 'commits'

Committed
To me committed and by me expos'd. Par Lost 10.957
Who this high gift of strength committed to me, Samson 47
And aggravate my folly who committed Samson 1000
Into our hands: for hadst thou not committed Samson 1185

Committing
Committing to a wicked Favourite Par Reg 4.95
With *Midas* Ears, committing short and long; Sonnet 13, 4
Trinity ms 'committing' ←'misjoyning' ←'committing'

Commodiously
To pass commodiously this life, sustain'd Par Lost 10.1083

Common
Common revenge, and interrupt his joy Par Lost 2.371
In Paradise of all things common else. Par Lost 4.752
The Angel, nor in mist, the common gloss Par Lost 5.435
In common, rang'd in figure wedge thir way, Par Lost 7.426
To them made common and divulg'd, if aught Par Lost 8.583
In procreation common to all kindes Par Lost 8.597
Made common and unhallowd ere our taste; Par Lost 9.931
Daily in the common Prison else enjoyn'd me, Samson 6
Nor do I name of men the common rout, Samson 674
To publish them, both common female faults: Samson 777
A common enemy, who had destroy'd Samson 856
Into the common Prison, there to grind Samson 1161
Of me as of a common Enemy, Samson 1416

Commonalty
Of Commonaltie: swarming next appeer'd Par Lost 7.489

Commotion
In this commotion, but the Starrie Cope Par Lost 4.992
Of such commotion, such as to set forth Par Lost 6.310

Commotion(*cont*)
And this perverse Commotion governd thus, Par Lost 6.706
Commotion strange, in all enjoyments else Par Lost 8.531
Commune
Then commune how that day they best may ply Par Lost 9.201
Communed
Commun'd in silent walk, then laid him down Par Reg 2.261
Communicable
To none communicable in Earth or Heaven: Par Lost 7.124
Lost bliss, to thee no more communicable, Par Reg 1.419
His good communicable to every soul Par Reg 3.125
Communicated
Communicated, more abundant growes, Par Lost 5.72
By thee communicated, and our want: Par Lost 9.755
Communicating
Communicating Male and Femal Light, Par Lost 8.150
Communication
Social communication, yet so pleas'd, Par Lost 8.429
Communion
They eate, they drink, and in communion sweet Par Lost 5.637
1667 'with refection'
Of Union or Communion, deifi'd; Par Lost 8.431
Compact
Compact of unctuous vapor, which the Night Par Lost 9.635
Companion
Sleepst thou Companion dear, what sleep can close Par Lost 5.673
Thee once to gaine Companion of his woe. Par Lost 6.907
Companions
There the companions of his fall, o'rewhelm'd Par Lost 1.76
Not to be overpowerd, Companions deare, Par Lost 6.419
Companions of my misery and wo. Par Reg 1.398
Company
And no such companie as then thou saw'st Par Lost 8.446
Sam. Brethren farewel, your company along Samson 1413
How to regain my sever'd company Mask 274
How chance she is not in your company? Mask 508
Bridgewater ms 'Companie'
Trinity ms 'companie'
1637 'companie'
Compare
Compare of mortal prowess, yet observ'd Par Lost 1.588
With noises loud and ruinous (to compare Par Lost 2.921
Beyond compare the Son of God was seen Par Lost 3.138
As may compare with Heaven; and to taste Par Lost 5.432
At Heav'ns high feasts to have fed: yet what compare? Par Lost 5.467
In Heav'n and Hell thy Power above compare, Par Lost 6.705
Compare above all living Creatures deare, Par Lost 9.228
Will far be found unworthy to compare Par Reg 4.346
As when Earths Son *Antaeus* (to compare Par Reg 4.563
His mighty Champion, strong above compare, Samson 556
Compared
Compar'd with aught on Earth, Medal or Stone; Par Lost 3.592
As both thir deeds compar'd this day shall prove. Par Lost 6.170
An Atom, with the Firmament compar'd Par Lost 8.18
So, if great things to small may be compar'd, Par Lost 10.306
Ill sorting with my present state compar'd. Par Reg 1.200
Alas how simple, to these Cates compar'd, Par Reg 2.348
Besides whom is no God, compar'd with Idols, Samson 441
Thy Paranymph, worthless to thee compar'd, Samson 1020
Comparing
His Deity comparing and preferring Samson 464
Comparison
Though, in comparison of Heav'n, so small, Par Lost 8.92
Compass
Adore him, who to compass all this dies, Par Lost 3.342
From what point of his Compass to beware Par Lost 4.559
That better might with farr less compass move, Par Lost 8.33
The Imperial Palace, compass huge, and high Par Reg 4.51
May compass it, shall willingly be paid Samson 1477
To keep in compass of thy Predicament: Vacation 56
Compassed
With terrors and with clamors compasst round Par Lost 2.862
In darkness, and with dangers compast round, Par Lost 7.27
This dreaded time have compast, wherein we Par Reg 1.58
Compasses
He took the golden Compasses, prepar'd Par Lost 7.225
Compassing
From compassing the Earth, cautious of day, Par Lost 9.59
Still following thee, still compassing thee round Par Lost 11.352
Compassion
Divine compassion visibly appeerd, Par Lost 3.141
Though not of Woman born; compassion quell'd Par Lost 11.496
Compeer
And him thus answer'd soon his bold Compeer. Par Lost 1.127
Compeers
Ride on thy wings, and thou with thy Compeers, Par Lost 4.974
Compel
We should compel them to a quick result. Par Lost 6.619
Compelled
Equivalent or second, which compel'd Par Lost 9.609
Must be compelld by Signes and Judgements dire; Par Lost 12.175
Compell'd me to awake the courteous Echo Mask 275
Bridgewater ms 'Compeld'
Till now that this extremity compell'd, Mask 643
Compels
By conquering this new World, compels me now Par Lost 4.391
Compels me to disturb your season due: Lycidas 7
1638, 1673 'Compells'

Compels(*cont*)
Trinity ms 'compells'
Competition
Against all competition, nor will long Samson 476
Complacence
My sole complacence! well thou know'st how dear, Par Lost 3.276
From prone, nor in thir wayes complacence find. Par Lost 8.433
Complain
By doom of Battel; and complain that Fate Par Lost 2.550
Whom have I to complain of but my self? Samson 46
O loss of sight, of thee I most complain! Samson 67
(Which Men enjoying sight oft without cause complain) Samson 157
1671 printed 'complain'd', errata 'complain'
On Faith and changed Gods complain: and Seas Horace 6
Complained
Ey'd them askance, and to himself thus plaind. Par Lost 4.504
Complaining
The voyce of my complaining hear Psalm 5, 3
Complaint
By my complaint; but strict necessitie Par Lost 10.131
Thus to disburd'n sought with sad complaint. Par Lost 10.719
Harsh, and of dissonant mood from his complaint, Samson 662
Complete
Accompani'd then with his own compleat Par Lost 5.352
And in her self compleat, so well to know Par Lost 8.548
Complete to have discover'd and repulst Par Lost 10.10
These rules will render thee a King compleat Par Reg 4.283
Sam. But what avail'd this temperance, not compleat Samson 558
She that has that, is clad in compleat steel, Mask 421
Trinity ms 'compleate'
Bridgewater ms 'compleate'
Bin as compleat as was her praise, Winchester 12
Completed
Bred onely and completed to the taste Par Lost 11.618
Completing
Wept at compleating of the mortal Sin Par Lost 9.1003
Complexions
They had their name thence; course complexions Mask 749
Trinity ms 'complexions' ←'beetle brows'
line not in Bridgewater ms
Compliance
And sweet compliance, which declare unfeign'd Par Lost 8.603
In recompence (for such compliance bad Par Lost 9.994
By this compliance thou wilt win the Lords Samson 1411
Compliant
Nectarine Fruits which the compliant boughes Par Lost 4.332
Complicated
With complicated monsters head and taile, Par Lost 10.523
Compliments
So many hollow complements and lies, Par Reg 4.124
Comply
Yet this be sure, in nothing to comply Samson 1408
And with all helpful service will comply Arcades 38
Compose
Compose our present evils, with regard Par Lost 2.281
Composed
Th' infection when thir borrow'd Gold compos'd Par Lost 1.483
For dignity compos'd and high exploit: Par Lost 2.111
Whereto with look compos'd *Satan* repli'd. Par Lost 6.469
Portending good, and all her spirits compos'd Par Lost 12.596
Deservedly thou griev'st, compos'd of lyes Par Reg 1.407
Meekly compos'd awaited the fulfilling: Par Reg 2.108
Composition
Of composition, strait they chang'd thir minds, Par Lost 6.613
By parl, or composition, truce, or league Par Reg 4.529
Composure
Peace and composure, and with open brest Par Lost 6.560
With sweet austeer composure thus reply'd, Par Lost 9.272
Comprehend
But what created mind can comprehend Par Lost 3.705
Can comprehend, incapable of more. Par Lost 5.505
Or heart of man suffice to comprehend? Par Lost 7.114
In knowledge, all things in it comprehend, Par Reg 4.224
Compulsion
With what compulsion and laborious flight Par Lost 2.80
Compulsion thus transported to forget Par Lost 9.474
Such sweet compulsion doth in musick ly, Arcades 68
Compute
Thir Starry dance in numbers that compute Par Lost 3.580
Two dayes, as we compute the dayes of Heav'n, Par Lost 6.685
Of Heav'n and Earth consisting, and compute, Par Lost 8.16
Comrades
Among the Slaves and Asses thy comrades, Samson 1162
Comus
Whom therfore she brought up and *Comus* nam'd, Mask 58
Of *Bacchus*, and of *Circe* born, great *Comus*, Mask 522
Concave
A shout that tore Hells Concave, and beyond Par Lost 1.542
ms 'concave'
Up to the fiery Concave touring high. Par Lost 2.635
1667 'concave'
Conceal
Deep malice to conceale, couch't with revenge: Par Lost 4.123
Did wisely to conceal, and not divulge Par Lost 8.73
I should conceal, and not expose to blame Par Lost 10.130
Wouldst easily detect what I conceale. Par Lost 10.136
Envy bid conceal the rest. Arcades 13
Trinity ms 'conceale' ←'her hide'

Concealed
Put forth at full, but still his strength conceal'd, Par Lost 1.641
Warr therefore, open or conceal'd, alike Par Lost 2.187
Nor those mysterious parts were then conceald, Par Lost 4.312
Have gathered aught of evil or conceald, Par Lost 5.207
Discover'd in the end, till now conceal'd. Samson 998
Our conceal'd Solemnity. Mask 142
Bridgewater ms 'Conceal'd'
Concealing
For Angels have proclaim'd it, but concealing Par Reg 4.474
Conceals
Conceales not from us, naming thee the Tree Par Lost 9.751
Conceals him: when twelve years he scarce had seen, Par Reg 2.96
Conceits
Blown up with high conceits ingendring pride. Par Lost 4.809
The next to fabling fell and smooth conceits, Par Reg 4.295
Their own conceits they follow'd still Psalm 81, 51
Conceive
Fermented the great Mother to conceave, Par Lost 7.281
Conceived
Than Fables yet have feign'd, or fear conceiv'd, Par Lost 2.627
With me in secret, that my womb conceiv'd Par Lost 2.766
Surround me, as thou sawst, hourly conceiv'd Par Lost 2.796
Not well conceav'd of God, who though his Power Par Lost 9.945
Conceiv'd in me a Virgin, he fore-told Par Reg 1.239
To have conceiv'd of God, or that salute Par Reg 2.67
Though offer'd only, by the sent conceiv'd Samson 390
Conceiv'd, agreeable to a Fathers love, Samson 1506
What windy joy this day had I conceiv'd Samson 1574
Trouble he hath conceav'd of old Psalm 7, 52
Conceives
Adjoynd, from each thing met conceaves delight, Par Lost 9.449
Conceiving
And fewel'd entrals thence conceiving Fire, Par Lost 1.234
Deep malice thence conceiving and disdain, Par Lost 5.666
Insensate, hope conceiving from despair. Par Lost 6.787
Conceiving, or remote from Heaven, enshrin'd Par Reg 4.598
Dost make us Marble with too much conceaving; Shakespear 14
1632 'conceiving'
1663-4 'conceiving'
1640 'conceiving'
Concent
That undisturbed Song of pure content, Musick 6
Trinity ms 'pure concent'
1673 'pure concent'
Concentring
In thee concentring all thir precious beams Par Lost 9.106
Conception
Conception; Sulphurous and Nitrous Foame Par Lost 6.512
By thy Conception; Children thou shalt bring Par Lost 10.194
It lies, yet ere Conception to prevent Par Lost 10.987
Of thy conception, and be now a shield Samson 1434
Concern
What neerer might concern him, how this World Par Lost 7.62
And renders us in things that most concerne Par Lost 8.196
So prevalent as to concerne the mind Par Lost 11.144
Thou hast reveald, those chiefly which concerne Par Lost 12.272
Chiefly what may concern her Faith to know, Par Lost 12.599
Concerned
Things above Earthly thought, which yet concernd Par Lost 7.82
Concern'd not Man (since he no further knew) Par Lost 10.170
To flye or follow what concern'd him most, Par Reg 1.440
With zeal, if aught Religion seem concern'd: Samson 1420
So in the sad event too much concern'd. Samson 1551
Concerning
And eaten of the Tree concerning which Par Lost 10.199
Concerning the Messiah, to our Scribes Par Reg 1.261
Concerning thee to his Angels, in thir hands Par Reg 4.557
Concernments
To mix with thy concernments I desist Samson 969
Concerns
Neerly it now concernes us to be sure Par Lost 5.721
Think onely what concernes thee and thy being; Par Lost 8.174
For what concerns my knowledge God reveals. Par Reg 1.293
But what concerns it thee when I begin Par Reg 3.198
To me so fatal, me it most concerns. Par Reg 4.205
How highly it concerns his glory now Samson 1148
Conclave
In close recess and secret conclave sat Par Lost 1.795
Conclude
Such proof, conclude, they then begin to faile. Par Lost 9.1142
The bloud of Bulls and Goats, they may conclude Par Lost 12.292
Concludes
Of refuge, and concludes thee miserable Par Lost 10.839
Concludest
To whom thus Jesus; what conclud'st thou hence? Par Reg 2.317
Concoct
Tasting concoct, digest, assimilate, Par Lost 5.412
Concocted
Concocted and adusted they reduc'd Par Lost 6.514
Concoctive
Of real hunger, and concoctive heate Par Lost 5.437
Concord
Firm concord holds, men onely disagree Par Lost 2.497
Melodious part, such concord is in Heav'n. Par Lost 3.371
Great things by small, If Natures concord broke, Par Lost 6.311
Concord and law of Nature from the Earth, Par Lost 12.29
Sam. Love-quarrels oft in pleasing concord end, Samson 1008
Concourse
Concours in Arms, fierce Faces threatning Warr, Par Lost 11.641
Wherever, under some concourse of shades Par Reg 4.404
Concubine
Of a deceitful Concubine who shore me Samson 537
Concupiscence
Of foul concupiscence; whence evil store; Par Lost 9.1078
Concurred
Concurd not to my being, it were but right Par Lost 10.747
Concurring
Should be, and, by concurring signs, ere now Par Lost 2.831
Concurring to necessitate his Fall, Par Lost 10.44
Condemn
Canst thou with impious obloquie condemne Par Lost 5.813
That Gentiles in thir Parables condemn Samson 500
Condemnation
But condemnation, ignominy, and shame? Par Reg 3.136
And condemnation of the ingrateful multitude. Samson 696
Condemned
(Far other once beheld in bliss) condemn'd Par Lost 1.607
Then to dwell here, driv'n out from bliss, condemn'd Par Lost 2.86
And they outcast from God, are here condemn'd Par Lost 2.694
Till now not known, but known as soon contemnd, Par Lost 6.432
Those two; the third best absent is condemn'd, Par Lost 10.82
For one mans fault thus guiltless be condemn'd, Par Lost 10.823
Seis'd on by force, judg'd, and to death condemnd Par Lost 12.412
My crime; whatever for it self condemn'd, Par Reg 3.213
Har. With thee a Man condemn'd, a Slave enrol'd, Samson 1224
Condemning
The fruitless hours, but neither self-condemning, Par Lost 9.1188
In man or woman, though to thy own condemning, Samson 844
Condemns
Your bulwark, and condemns to greatest share Par Lost 2.29
Condense
Assume, as likes them best, condense or rare. Par Lost 6.353
Condensed
Dilated or condens't, bright or obscure, Par Lost 1.429
ms 'condens'd'
Condenses
Condenses, and the cold invirons round, Par Lost 9.636
Condescend
Will condescend to such absurd commands? Samson 1337
Condescension
This friendly condescention to relate Par Lost 8.9
Thy condescension, and shall be honour'd ever Par Lost 8.649
Condition
His fall'n condition is, and to me ow Par Lost 3.181
Live, in what state, condition or degree, Par Lost 8.176
If this be our condition, thus to dwell Par Lost 9.322
On this condition, if thou wilt fall down, Par Reg 4.166
The abominable terms, impious condition; Par Reg 4.173
Sams. No, no, of my condition take no care; Samson 928
Scorning the unexempt condition Mask 685
line not in Bridgewater ms
Conditions
Then cavil the conditions? and though God Par Lost 10.759
I willingly on some conditions came Samson 258
Condole
Har. I come not *Samson*, to condole thy chance, Samson 1076
Conduct
Under thy conduct, and in dreadful deeds Par Lost 1.130
ms 'Conduct'
Under whose conduct *Michael* soon reduc'd Par Lost 6.777
1667 'Conduct'
My conduct, I can bring thee thither soon. Par Lost 9.630
Of conduct would be such, that all the world Par Reg 3.18
I can conduct you Lady to a low Mask 319
Conducted
Conducted by his Angel to the Land Par Lost 12.259
Cone
Now had night measur'd with her shaddowie Cone Par Lost 4.776
Confer
New rub'd with Baum, expatiate and confer Par Lost 1.774
ms 'conferr'
Refus'd on me his Baptism to confer, Par Reg 1.278
Conference
Given him by this great Conference to know Par Lost 5.454
Conferred
Conferrd upon us, and Dominion giv'n Par Lost 4.430
Conferr'd upon me, for the piety Samson 993
Confess
Beholding shall confess that here on Earth Par Lost 5.329
All knees in Heav'n, and shall confess him Lord: Par Lost 5.608
Confess him rightful King? unjust thou saist Par Lost 5.818
Which I enjoy, and must confess to find Par Lost 8.523
Before him reverent, and there confess Par Lost 10.1088
To try thee, sift thee, and confess have found thee Par Reg 4.532
Sam. Father, I do acknowledge and confess Samson 448
Confess, and promise wonders in her change, Samson 753
Confess it feign'd, weakness is thy excuse, Samson 829
Confessed
Gods, yet confest later then Heav'n and Earth Par Lost 1.509
Before him reverent, and both confess'd Par Lost 10.1100
By thee are giv'n, and what confest more true Par Reg 1.431
Thir Magistrates confest it, when they took thee Samson 1183
More generous far and civil, who confess'd Samson 1467
Confessing
Confessing soon, yet not before her Judge Par Lost 10.160

Confide
As *Raphael*, that I should much confide, Par Lost 11.235
Confidence
His confidence to equal God in power. Par Lost 6.343
They saw them whelm'd, and all thir confidence Par Lost 6.651
Just confidence, and native righteousness Par Lost 9.1056
But confidence then bore thee on, secure Par Lost 9.1175
Therefore I am return'd, lest confidence Par Reg 2.140
In confidence whereof I once again Samson 1174
Alone, and helpless! Is this the confidence Mask 583
Confident
Of fond desire? or should she confident, Par Reg 2.211
Confine
Confine with Heav'n; or if som other place Par Lost 2.977
As if they would confine th' interminable, Samson 307
These latter scenes confine my roving vers, Passion 22
Confined
To sit in hateful Office here confin'd, Par Lost 2.859
Stood rul'd, stood vast infinitude confin'd; Par Lost 3.711
Thy self a Goddess, not to Earth confind, Par Lost 5.78
Thou hast atchiev'd our libertie, confin'd Par Lost 10.368
His presence to these narrow bounds confin'd Par Lost 11.341
Yet to that hideous place not so confin'd Par Reg 1.362
To such a tender ball as th' eye confin'd? Samson 94
To thir abyss and horrid pains confin'd. Samson 501
Sam. O that torment should not be confin'd Samson 606
Confin'd, and pester'd in this pin-fold here, Mask 7
Bridgewater ms 'Confinde'
Confines
Of those bright confines, whence with neighbouring Arms Par Lost 2.395
From all her Confines. Heav'n the seat of bliss Par Lost 6.273
The confines met of Empyrean Heav'n Par Lost 10.321
1667 'Confines'
Confirm
He spake: and to confirm his words, out-flew Par Lost 1.663
And doth confirm the knot, Psalm 83, 30
Confirmed
That shook Heav'ns whol circumference, confirm'd. Par Lost 2.353
A death to think. Confirm'd then I resolve, Par Lost 9.830
And in thir state, though firm, stood more confirmd. Par Lost 11.71
Which that thou mayst beleeve, and be confirmd Par Lost 11.355
Conflagrant
From the conflagrant mass, purg'd and refin'd, Par Lost 12.548
Conflict
With violence of this conflict, had not soon Par Lost 4.995
Of conflict; over head the dismal hiss Par Lost 6.212
Conflicting
Conflicting Fire: long time in eeven scale Par Lost 6.245
Conflux
What conflux issuing forth, or entring in, Par Reg 4.62
Conformed
Or chang'd at length, and to the place conformd Par Lost 2.217
Conformity
Holie and pure, conformitie divine. Par Lost 11.606
Confound
With blackest Insurrection, to confound Par Lost 2.136
So deep a malice, to confound the race Par Lost 2.382
Should combat, and thir jarring Sphears confound. Par Lost 6.315
Thir corners, when with bluster to confound Par Lost 10.665
To Humane life, and houshold peace confound. Par Lost 10.908
Confounded
Confounded though immortal: But his doom Par Lost 1.53
Confusion worse confounded; and Heav'n Gates Par Lost 2.996
Nine dayes they fell; confounded *Chaos* roard, Par Lost 6.871
Confounded long they sate, as struck'n mute, Par Lost 9.1064
Through all his Realme, and there confounded leave; Par Lost 12.455
A while as mute confounded what to say, Par Reg 3.2
Confounded, that her Makers eyes Nativity 43
Ever confounded, and so die Psalm 83, 63
Confused
In confus'd march forlorn, th' adventrous Bands Par Lost 2.615
Of stunning sounds and voices all confus'd Par Lost 2.952
Of fighting Seraphim confus'd, at length Par Lost 6.249
And what the people but a herd confus'd, Par Reg 3.49
Blindness, for had I sight, confus'd with shame, Samson 196
A mighty masse of things strangely confus'd, Prose 2, 3
Confusedly
Confus'dly, and which thus must ever fight, Par Lost 2.914
Confusion
Treble confusion, wrath and vengeance pour'd. Par Lost 1.220
In our Confusion, and our Joy upraise Par Lost 2.372
Of endless Warrs, and by confusion stand. Par Lost 2.897
And *Tumult* and *Confusion* all imbroild, Par Lost 2.966
1667 'Confusion'
Confusion worse confounded; and Heav'n Gates Par Lost 2.996
Confusion heard his voice, and wilde uproar Par Lost 3.710
1667 'Confusion'
To this uproar; horrid confusion heapt Par Lost 6.668
Upon confusion rose: and now all Heav'n Par Lost 6.669
And felt tenfold confusion in thir fall Par Lost 6.872
With such confusion: but the evil soon Par Lost 7.56
Of horrible confusion, over which Par Lost 10.472
Ridiculous, and the work Confusion nam'd. Par Lost 12.62
Left in confusion, *Babylon* thence call'd. Par Lost 12.343
And with confusion blank his Worshippers. Samson 471
So shall he least confusion draw Samson 1058
Are in confusion, give us if thou canst, Samson 1593
With much confusion; then grow red with shame, Psalm 6, 22

Confuted
What to reply, confuted and convinc't Par Reg 3.3
Congealed
Wherwith she freez'd her foes to congeal'd stone? Mask 449
Bridgewater ms 'congeald'
Conglobed
Adverse to life: then founded, then conglob'd Par Lost 7.239
Conglobing
As drops on dust conglobing from the drie; Par Lost 7.292
Congo
Of *Congo*, and *Angola* fardest South; Par Lost 11.401
Congratulant
Congratulant approach'd him, who with hand Par Lost 10.458
Congratulate
To gratulate the sweet return of morn; Par Reg 4.438
Many a friend to gratulate Mask 949
Congregated
Of congregated Waters he call'd Seas: Par Lost 7.308
Congregation
The Mountain of the Congregation call'd; Par Lost 5.766
Congregations
With power, and Princes in their Congregations Psalm 2, 3
Conjecture
Ominous conjecture on the whole success: Par Lost 2.123
If I conjecture aught, no drizling showr, Par Lost 6.545
Conjecture, he his Fabric of the Heav'ns Par Lost 8.76
Be meant, whom I conjecture, our grand Foe Par Lost 10.1033
I less conjecture then when first I saw Samson 1071
Conjectures
Conjectures, fancies, built on nothing firm. Par Reg 4.292
Where by all best conjectures I collect Par Reg 4.524
Conjoined
Of dire necessity, whose law in death conjoin'd Samson 1666
Conjugal
Of conjugal attraction unreprov'd, Par Lost 4.493
With conjugal Caresses, from his Lip Par Lost 8.56
Conjugal Love, then which perhaps no bliss Par Lost 9.263
No way assur'd. But conjugal affection Samson 739
Conjunction
And straight conjunction with this Sex: for either Par Lost 10.898
In their conjunction met, give me to spell, Par Reg 4.385
Conjured
Conjur'd against the highest, for which both Thou Par Lost 2.693
Connatural
Or sympathie, or som connatural force Par Lost 10.246
To Death, and mix with our connatural dust? Par Lost 11.529
Connexion
Still moves with thine, join'd in connexion sweet, Par Lost 10.359
Connive
Will not connive, or linger, thus provok'd, Samson 466
Conniving
A place so heav'nly, and conniving seem Par Lost 10.624
Connubial
Mysterious of connubial Love refus'd: Par Lost 4.743
Conquer
To conquer Sin and Death the two grand foes, Par Reg 1.159
By winning words to conquer willing hearts, Par Reg 1.222
To conquer still; peace hath her victories Sonnet 16, 10
1694 'Conquer'
Shall aw the World, and Conquer Nations bold. Prose 12, 14
Conquered
The conquerd also, and enslav'd by Warr Par Lost 11.797
Frugal, and mild, and temperate, conquer'd well, Par Reg 4.134
Is well ejected when the Conquer'd can. Samson 1207
Conquering
By conquering this new World, compels me now Par Lost 4.391
Second of *Satan* sprung, all conquering *Death*, Par Lost 10.591
Conqueror
But what if he our Conquerour, (whom I now Par Lost 1.143
ms 'conquerour'
To adore the Conquerour? who now beholds Par Lost 1.323
Ahaz his sottish Conquerour, whom he drew Par Lost 1.472
ms 'conquerour'
The sentence of thir Conquerour: This is now Par Lost 2.208
Yet ever plotting how the Conqueror least Par Lost 2.338
1667 'Conquerour'
Remember that *Pellean* Conquerour, Par Reg 2.196
Till Conquerour Death discover them scarce men, Par Reg 3.85
The great *Emathian* Conqueror bid spare Sonnet 8, 10
Trinity ms 'conquerour'
Conquerors
Of triumph, to be styl'd great Conquerours, Par Lost 11.695
Then those thir Conquerours, who leave behind Par Reg 3.78
Equal in fame to proudest Conquerours. Par Reg 3.99
Singly by me against their Conquerours Samson 244
Conquest
May reap his conquest, and may least rejoyce Par Lost 2.339
With conquest, felt th' envenom'd robe, and tore Par Lost 2.543
Judg'd thee perverse: the easier conquest now Par Lost 6.37
This our old Conquest, then remember Hell Par Reg 1.46
Winning by Conquest what the first man lost Par Reg 1.154
Money brings Honour, Friends, Conquest, and Realms; Par Reg 2.422
By Conquest far and wide, to over-run Par Reg 3.72
Chuse which thou wilt by conquest or by league. Par Reg 3.370
And frustrated the conquest fraudulent: Par Reg 4.609
It was the force of Conquest; force with force Samson 1206
Th' Heathen, and as thy conquest to be sway'd Psalm 2, 18

Conscience
My Umpire *Conscience*, whom if they will hear, Par Lost 3.195
By change of place: Now conscience wakes despair Par Lost 4.23
Her vertue and the conscience of her worth, Par Lost 8.502
O Conscience, into what Abyss of fears Par Lost 10.842
Which to his evil Conscience represented Par Lost 10.849
Of Conscience, which the Law by Ceremonies Par Lost 12.297
On every conscience; Laws which none shall finde Par Lost 12.522
Who against Faith and Conscience can be heard Par Lost 12.529
Let his tormenter Conscience find him out, Par Reg 4.130
Sam. My self? my conscience and internal peace. Samson 1334
By a strong siding champion Conscience.------ Mask 212
line not in Bridgewater ms
Trinity ms 'conscience'
Helpe us to save free Conscience from the paw Sonnet 16, 13
The conscience, Friend, to have lost them overply'd Sonnet 22, 10
1694 'Consçience'
Consciences
To force our Consciences that Christ set free, Forcers 6
Conscious
Conscious of highest worth, unmov'd thus spake. Par Lost 2.429
A fresh with conscious terrours vex me round, Par Lost 2.801
So all ere day-spring, under conscious Night Par Lost 6.521
Bred of unkindly fumes, with conscious dreams Par Lost 9.1050
Consecrated
Invites, and in the Consecrated stream Par Reg 1.72
Sam. Shall I abuse this Consecrated gift Samson 1354
In consecrated Earth, Nativity 189
Consent
Consent or custome, and his Regal State Par Lost 1.640
Yielded with full consent. The happier state Par Lost 2.24
Waking thou never wilt consent to do. Par Lost 5.121
But more desire to hear, if thou consent, Par Lost 5.555
By free consent of all, none opposite, Par Reg 3.358
Till free consent the gods among Mask 1007
line not in Bridgewater ms
Whose power hath a true consent Penseroso 95
Consented
What sieges girt me round, e're I consented; Samson 846
Consenting
Consenting in full frequence was impowr'd, Par Reg 2.130
Consequence
And shun the bitter consequence: for know, Par Lost 8.328
Such fatal consequence unites us three: Par Lost 10.364
Consider
The benefit: consider first, that Great Par Lost 8.90
Awakn'd in me swarm, while I consider Par Reg 1.197
Or human nature can receive, consider Par Reg 3.231
Chor. Consider, *Samson;* matters now are strain'd Samson 1348
When I consider how my light is spent, Sonnet 19, 1
Considerate
Of dauntless courage, and considerate Pride Par Lost 1.603
Considered
Consider'd every Creature, which of all Par Lost 9.84
Considerd all things visible in Heav'n, Par Lost 9.604
Acknowledg'd not, or not at all consider'd Samson 245
Consist
Jarr not with liberty, but well consist. Par Lost 5.793
Consisted
Wherein consisted all thy strength and safety? Samson 780
Consistence
Treading the crude consistence, half on foot, Par Lost 2.941
Consisting
Of Heav'n and Earth consisting, and compute, Par Lost 8.16
Consistory
A gloomy Consistory; and them amidst Par Reg 1.42
Consists
Wherein true Love consists not; love refines Par Lost 8.589
Yet empty of all good wherein consists Par Lost 11.616
Consists in mutual and partak'n bliss, Mask 741
line not in Bridgewater ms
Consolation
Recess, and onely consolation left Par Lost 11.304
This further consolation yet secure Par Lost 12.620
Small consolation then, were Man adjoyn'd: Par Reg 1.403
Counsel or Consolation we may bring, Samson 183
Some sourse of consolation from above; Samson 664
With peace and consolation hath dismist, Samson 1757
Consolations
With inward consolations recompenc't, Par Lost 12.495
Consolatories
Consolatories writ Samson 657
Consort
The Consort of his Reign; and by them stood Par Lost 2.963
1667 'consort'
Like consort to thy self canst no where find. Par Lost 4.448
When *Adam* thus to *Eve:* Fair Consort, th' hour Par Lost 4.610
Male he created thee, but thy consort Par Lost 7.529
Cannot be human consort; they rejoyce Par Lost 8.392
Consort with thee, Death is to mee as Life; Par Lost 9.954
His consort Libertie; what, but unbuild Par Lost 12.526
Since *Adam* and his facil consort *Eve* Par Reg 1.51
With such consort as they keep, Penseroso 145
Make up full consort to th' Angelike symphony. Nativity 132
To his celestial consort us unite, Musick 27
Consorted
Though wandring. He with his consorted *Eve* Par Lost 7.50

Conspicuous
Then most conspicuous, when great things of small, Par Lost 2.258
In whose conspicuous count'nance, without cloud Par Lost 3.385
Conspicuous farr, winding with one ascent Par Lost 4.545
Liken on Earth conspicuous, that may lift Par Lost 6.299
Of Heav'n and Earth conspicious first began, Par Lost 7.63
1667 'conspicuous'
Or come I less conspicuous, or what change Par Lost 10.107
Conspicuous with three listed colours gay, Par Lost 11.866
With gilded battlements, conspicuous far, Par Reg 4.53
Conspiracy
In bold conspiracy against Heav'ns King, Par Lost 2.751
Conspire
Gebal and Ammon *there conspire*, Psalm 83, 25
Conspired
Th' excepted Tree, nor with the Snake conspir'd, Par Lost 11.426
Conspiring
Of men conspiring to uphold thir state Samson 892
Constancy
Wouldst thou approve thy constancie, approve Par Lost 9.367
His constancy, with such as have more shew Par Reg 2.226
Of constancy no root infixt, Samson 1032
Constant
Of true allegiance, constant Faith or Love, Par Lost 3.104
His constant Lamp, and waves his purple wings, Par Lost 4.764
Single, is yet so just, my constant thoughts Par Lost 5.552
To swerve from truth, or change his constant mind Par Lost 5.902
Constant, mature, proof against all assaults, Par Lost 10.882
Whose constant perseverance overcame Par Reg 1.148
Could stir the constant mood of her calm thoughts, Mask 371
Trinity ms 'constant' ←'steadie'
Constantest
The constantest to have yielded without blame. Samson 848
Constantine
Ah *Constantine*, of how much ill was cause Prose 1, 1
Another *Constantine* comes not in hast. Prose 3, 5
That *Constantine* to good *Sylvestro* gave. Prose 4, 4
Constellations
Alooff the vulgar Constellations thick, Par Lost 3.577
Among the Constellations warr were sprung, Par Lost 6.312
The Heav'ns and all the Constellations rung, Par Lost 7.562
And happie Constellations on that houre Par Lost 8.512
Thir course through thickest Constellations held Par Lost 10.411
His constellations set, Nativity 121
1673 'Constellations'
Constrained
With Gods to sit the highest, am now constraind Par Lost 9.164
At length gave utterance to these words constraind. Par Lost 9.1066
Who dwell this wild, constrain'd by want, come forth Par Reg 1.331
But Love constrain'd thee; call it furious rage Samson 836
Who threatning cruel death constrain'd the bride Samson 1198
Constraining
Hunger and thirst constraining, drugd as oft, Par Lost 10.568
Constrains
Sam. Where outward force constrains, the sentence holds Samson 1369
But who constrains me to the Temple of *Dagon*, Samson 1370
Constraint
The secrets of your Realm, but by constraint Par Lost 2.972
Subdues me, and calamitous constraint Par Lost 10.132
Bitter constraint, and sad occasion dear, Lycidas 6
Constraints
Commands are no constraints. If I obey them, Samson 1372
Consult
Consult how we may henceforth most offend Par Lost 1.187
And summons read, the great consult began. Par Lost 1.798
Pretending so commanded to consult Par Lost 5.768
This onely to consult how we may best Par Lost 5.779
Should Kings and Nations from thy mouth consult, Par Reg 3.12
For they consult with all their might, Psalm 83, 17
Consultation
Due search and consultation will disclose. Par Lost 6.445
Consultations
Thus they thir doubtful consultations dark Par Lost 2.486
Consulted
Or reason though disturb'd, and scarse consulted Samson 1546
Consulting
Thus sitting, thus consulting, thus in Arms? Par Lost 2.164
Consulting on the sum of things, foreseen Par Lost 6.673
Forth rush'd in haste the great consulting Peers, Par Lost 10.456
Who ever by consulting at thy shrine Par Reg 1.438
And to his crew, that sat consulting, brought Par Reg 4.577
Consume
Will either quite consume us, and reduce Par Lost 2.96
To weigh thy Spirits down, and last consume Par Lost 11.545
Famin and anguish will at last consume Par Lost 11.778
Consume me, and oft-invocated death Samson 575
Consumed
Consum'd with nimble glance, and grateful steame; Par Lost 11.442
Self-fed, and self-consum'd, if this fail, Mask 597
Bridgewater ms 'selfe consum'd'
Trinity ms 'selfe consum'd'
1637 'selfe consum'd'
And last of all, thy greedy self consum'd, On Time 10
But now it is consum'd with fire, Psalm 80, 65
Consumes
To nourish, and superfluous moist consumes: Par Lost 5.325
Through grief consumes, is waxen old and dark Psalm 6, 14

Consummate
More aerie, last the bright consummate floure Par Lost 5.481
Consummate lovly smil'd; Aire, Water, Earth, Par Lost 7.502
Occasionally; and to consummate all, Par Lost 8.556
From what consummate vertue I have chose Par Reg 1.165
Contagion
In this perfidious fraud, contagion spred Par Lost 5.880
Catcht by Contagion, like in punishment, Par Lost 10.544
The soul grows clotted by contagion, Mask 467
Rot inwardly, and foul contagion spread: Lycidas 127
Contagious
Of *Eve*, whose Eye darted contagious Fire. Par Lost 9.1036
Contain
And what thy stores contain, bring forth and poure Par Lost 5.314
None can then Heav'n such glorious shape contain; Par Lost 5.362
As doth your Rational; and both contain Par Lost 5.409
In measure what the mind may well contain, Par Lost 7.128
Nor glistering, may of solid good containe Par Lost 8.93
Of knowledge, what this Vessel can containe; Par Lost 12.559
1669 'contain'
Contained
Mean, or in her summd up, in her containd Par Lost 8.473
That of a Nation arm'd the strength contain'd: Samson 1494
Contains
Conteins of good, wise, just, the perfect shape. Par Reg 3.11
Contemn
Canst thou with impious obloquie condemne Par Lost 5.813
Nor thou his malice and false guile contemn; Par Lost 9.306
Thy pompous Delicacies I contemn, Par Reg 2.390
Who could do mighty things, and could contemn Par Reg 2.448
Betok'ning, or ill boding, I contemn Par Reg 4.490
Contemned
Till now not known, but known as soon contemnd, Par Lost 6.432
Have been before contemn'd, and may agen: Par Reg 4.537
Thir great Deliverer contemn'd, Samson 279
Helpless, thence easily contemn'd, and scorn'd, Samson 943
Contemning
As fearing God nor man, contemning all Par Reg 4.304
Contemns
And excellent then what thy minde contemnes; Par Lost 10.1015
Thir Armories and Magazins contemns, Samson 1281
Contemplate
To love, at least comtemplate and admire Par Reg 1.380
Contemplation
For contemplation hee and valour formd, Par Lost 4.297
In contemplation of created things Par Lost 5.511
To contemplation and profound dispute, Par Reg 4.214
Where with her best nurse Contemplation Mask 377
Bridgewater ms 'contemplacion'
The Cherub Contemplation, Penseroso 54
Contemplative
Private, unactive, calm, contemplative, Par Reg 2.81
By me propos'd in life contemplative, Par Reg 4.370
Contempt
Due entrance he disdaind, and in contempt, Par Lost 4.180
Wouldst thou admit for his contempt of thee Par Lost 10.763
Eve, thy contempt of life and pleasure seems Par Lost 10.1013
Not thy contempt, but anguish and regret Par Lost 10.1018
Contempt instead, dishonour, obloquy? Par Reg 3.131
To daily fraud, contempt, abuse and wrong, Samson 76
Then undissembl'd hate) with what contempt Samson 400
Contempt, and scorn of all, to be excluded Samson 494
Joyn'd with extream contempt? I will not come. Samson 1342
Or knock the breast, no weakness, no contempt, Samson 1722
Contemptible
To a contemptible old age obscure. Samson 572
Besides, how vile, contemptible, ridiculous, Samson 1361
Contemptibly
And reason not contemptibly; with these Par Lost 8.374
Contempts
Contempts, and scorns, and snares, and violence, Par Reg 3.191
Contemptuous
To whom thus *Satan*, with contemptuous brow. Par Lost 4.885
Contemptuous, and his next subordinate Par Lost 5.671
Contemptuous, proud, set on revenge and spite; Samson 1462
Arm his profane tongue with contemptuous words Mask 781
line not in Bridgewater ms
line not in Trinity ms
1637 'reproachfull'
Contend
That with the mightiest rais'd me to contend, Par Lost 1.99
Upon the wing, or in swift Race contend, Par Lost 2.529
Hell-born, not to contend with Spirits of Heav'n. Par Lost 2.687
Undaunted. If I must contend, said he, Par Lost 4.851
Servilitie with freedom to contend, Par Lost 6.169
But rise, let us no more contend, nor blame Par Lost 10.958
Of Wit, or Arms, while both contend Allegro 123
Contended
O foul descent! that I who erst contended Par Lost 9.163
Contending
Contending, and so doubtful what might fall. Par Lost 2.203
Expect to hear, supernal Grace contending Par Lost 11.359
Contending, and remov'd his Tents farr off; Par Lost 11.727
Contends
So fares it when with truth falshood contends. Par Reg 3.443
Content
Of utmost *Arnon*. Nor content with such Par Lost 1.399
Nor so content, hath in his thought to try Par Lost 5.727
Content(*cont*)
But live content, which is the calmest life: Par Lost 6.461
Here let us live, though in fall'n state, content. Par Lost 11.180
Of proud ambitious heart, who not content Par Lost 12.25
Without this bodies wasting, I content me, Par Reg 2.256
Orders and governs, nor content in Heaven Par Reg 3.112
With *Modin* and her Suburbs once content. Par Reg 3.170
Off. This answer, be assur'd, will not content them. Samson 1322
Sam. I could be well content to try thir Art, Samson 1399
Like a wild Beast, I am content to go. Samson 1403
That undisturbed Song of pure content, Musick 6
Trinity ms 'pure concent'
1673 'pure concent'
And left them both, more in himself content, Sonnet 10, 4
Content though blind, had I no better guide. Sonnet 22, 14
Contented
Contented with report hear onely in heav'n: Par Lost 3.701
Angels contented with thir fame in Heav'n Par Lost 6.375
Contented that thus farr hath been reveal'd Par Lost 8.177
Contention
And to the fierce contention brought along Par Lost 1.100
Contentment
Or all enjoying, what contentment find? Par Lost 8.366
Thy Love, the sole contentment of my heart Par Lost 10.973
Contents
Of hard contents, and full of force urg'd home, Par Lost 6.622
Contest
Not likely to part hence without contest; Par Lost 4.872
Victor; though brutish that contest and foule, Par Lost 6.124
And of thir vain contest appeer'd no end. Par Lost 9.1189
I thus contest; then should have been refusd Par Lost 10.756
In sharp contest of Battel found no aide Par Lost 11.800
With me hath end; all the contest is now Samson 461
With hard contest: at length that grounded maxim Samson 865
Contiguous
With dreadful shade contiguous, and the Orbes Par Lost 6.828
Contiguous might distemper the whole frame: Par Lost 7.273
Continent
Beyond this flood a frozen Continent Par Lost 2.587
It seem'd, now seems a boundless Continent Par Lost 3.423
From her moist Continent to higher Orbes. Par Lost 5.422
This continent of spacious Heav'n, adornd Par Lost 6.474
Hell and this World, one Realm, one Continent Par Lost 10.392
Continual
May have diverted from continual watch Par Lost 9.814
Continue
Inclines, here to continue; and build up here Par Lost 2.314
Long to continue, and this high seat your Heav'n Par Lost 4.371
Nor th' other light of life continue long, Samson 592
Continued
From Hell continu'd reaching th' utmost Orbe Par Lost 2.1029
As one continu'd brake, the undergrowth Par Lost 4.175
The space of seven continu'd Nights he rode Par Lost 9.63
Continu'd making, and who knows how long Par Lost 9.138
Impetuous, and continu'd till the Earth Par Lost 11.744
Continues
His might continues in thee not for naught, Samson 588
Oh it continues, they have slain my Son. Samson 1516
Continuest
That thou continu'st such, owe to thy self, Par Lost 5.521
Contracted
To whom the Angel with contracted brow. Par Lost 8.560
Sam. Fair days have oft contracted wind and rain. Samson 1062
Contraction
By quick contraction or remove; but now Par Lost 6.597
Contradict
Or nothing more then still to contradict: Par Reg 4.158
Contradicting
As to his own edicts, found contradicting, Samson 301
Contradiction
Inspir'd with contradiction durst oppose Par Lost 6.155
Strange contradiction, which to God himself Par Lost 10.799
But by ungodly deeds, the contradiction Samson 898
Nor were it contradiction to affirm Another 13
Contraries
Of contraries; all good to me becomes Par Lost 9.122
Contrarious
Or might I say contrarious, Samson 669
Contrary
As being the contrary to his high will Par Lost 1.161
Mov'd contrarie with thwart obliquities, Par Lost 8.132
To fill his eare, when contrary he hears Par Lost 10.506
But contrary unweeting he fulfill'd Par Reg 1.126
Now contrary, if I read aught in Heaven, Par Reg 4.382
And with contrary blast proclaims most deeds, Samson 972
Once join'd, the contrary she proves, a thorn Samson 1037
Contribute
Onely to shine, yet scarce to contribute Par Lost 8.155
Contrite
Frequenting, sent from hearts contrite, in sign Par Lost 10.1091
Frequenting, sent from hearts contrite, in sign Par Lost 10.1103
He sorrows now, repents, and prayes contrite, Par Lost 11.90
Man. Be penitent and for thy fault contrite, Samson 502
Contrition
Sow'n with contrition in his heart, then those Par Lost 11.27
Contrive
Contrive who need, or when they need, not now Par Lost 2.53
The mightie frame, how build, unbuild, contrive Par Lost 8.81

Contrive*(cont)*	
Against thy people they contrive	Psalm 83, 9
Contrived	
What order, so contriv'd as not to mix	Par Lost 5.334
Satan, who in the Serpent hath contriv'd	Par Lost 10.1034
Contriv'd, and of provisions laid in large	Par Lost 11.732
Contriving	
For while they sit contriving, shall the rest,	Par Lost 2.54
Before had bin contriving, though perhaps	Par Lost 9.139
Control	
Thus farr his bold discourse without controule	Par Lost 5.803
Can in his swadling bands controul the damned crew.	Nativity 228
Controversies	
Who judges in great suits and controversies,	Prose 10, 3
Controversy	
Secure without all doubt, or controversie:	Mask 409
Trinity ms 'doubt or question, no'	
Bridgewater ms 'doubt or question, no'	
Contumacy	
Of contumacie will provoke the highest	Par Lost 10.1027
Convenient	
If some convenient ransom were propos'd.	Samson 1471
Conversant	
Thou and all Angels conversant on Earth	Par Reg 1.131
Conversation	
By conversation with his like to help,	Par Lost 8.418
Or they with thee hold conversation meet?	Par Reg 4.232
Converse	
There to converse with everlasting groans,	Par Lost 2.184
Converse with *Adam*, in what Bowre or shade	Par Lost 5.230
Thou with Eternal wisdom didst converse,	Par Lost 7.9
Desire with thee still longer to converse	Par Lost 8.252
So well converse, nor with the Ox the Ape;	Par Lost 8.396
How have I then with whom to hold converse	Par Lost 8.408
Assist us: But if much converse perhaps	Par Lost 9.247
Thy sweet Converse and Love so dearly joyn'd,	Par Lost 9.909
And his deep thoughts, the better to converse	Par Reg 1.190
And with the *Gentiles* much thou must converse,	Par Reg 4.229
Till oft convers with heav'nly habitants	Mask 459
Trinity ms 'converse'	
1637 'converse'	
Bridgewater ms 'converse'	
Jehovah serve, and let your joy converse	Psalm 2, 24
Conversed	
In publick, and with him we have convers'd;	Par Reg 2.52
Conversing	
With thee conversing I forget all time,	Par Lost 4.639
I by conversing cannot these erect	Par Lost 8.432
Conversing, looking, loving, to abstain	Par Lost 10.993
Conversion	
Conversion and Repentance, as to Souls	Par Lost 11.724
Not thy Conversion, but those rich demaines	Prose 1, 2
Convert	
If I refuse not, but convert, as you,	Par Lost 5.492
Converts	
The sorrow, and converts it nigh to joy.	Samson 1564
Convex	
Our prison strong, this huge convex of Fire,	Par Lost 2.434
Of this round World, whose first convex divides	Par Lost 3.419
In circuit to the uttermost convex	Par Lost 7.266
Convey	
Will he convey up thither to sustain	Par Lost 12.75
Conveyance	
By strange conveyance fill'd each hollow nook,	Par Lost 1.707
ms 'conveiance'	
Desiring; nor restrain'd conveyance need	Par Lost 8.628
By secretest conveyance. Thou my Shade	Par Lost 10.249
Conveyed	
To blackest grain, and into store convey'd:	Par Lost 6.515
1667 'conveyd'	
Each Orb a glimps of Light, conveyd so farr	Par Lost 8.156
Convict	
Convict by flight, and Rebel to all Law	Par Lost 10.83
Conviction	
Conviction to the Serpent none belongs.	Par Lost 10.84
But to my own conviction: first and last	Par Lost 10.831
Or subtle shifts conviction to evade.	Par Reg 4.308
Convince	
But to convince the proud what Signs availe,	Par Lost 6.789
Convinced	
What to reply, confuted and convinc't	Par Reg 3.3
Thou art not fit to hear thy self convinc't;	Mask 792
line not in Trinity ms	
line not in Bridgewater ms	
Convolved	
And writh'd him to and fro convolv'd; so sore	Par Lost 6.328
Convoy	
I shoot from Heav'n to give him safe convoy,	Mask 81
Convoyed	
It self instinct with Spirit, but convoyd	Par Lost 6.752
Convulsion	
With horrible convulsion to and fro,	Samson 1649
Convulsions	
Convulsions, Epilepsies, fierce Catarrhs,	Par Lost 11.483
Cool	
Of coole recess, o're which the mantling vine	Par Lost 4.258
To recommend coole *Zephyr*, and made ease	Par Lost 4.329
The cool, the silent, save where silence yields	Par Lost 5.39

Cool*(cont)*	
Of his coole Bowre, while now the mounted Sun	Par Lost 5.300
Be over, and the Sun more coole decline.	Par Lost 5.370
No fear lest Dinner coole; when thus began	Par Lost 5.396
Fannd with coole Winds, save those who in thir course	Par Lost 5.655
Shelters in coole, and tends his pasturing Herds	Par Lost 9.1109
The Eevning coole when he from wrauth more coole	Par Lost 10.95
Wholsom and cool, and mild, but with black Air	Par Lost 10.847
A shelter and a kind of shading cool	Par Reg 3.221
Allure thee from the cool Crystalline stream.	Samson 546
La. To seek i' th vally som cool friendly Spring.	Mask 282
Trinity ms 'coole'	
1637 'coole'	
Bridgewater ms 'coole'	
To life so friendly, or so cool to thirst.	Mask 678
Trinity ms 'coole'	
Bridgewater ms 'coole'	
1637 'coole'	
Under the glassie, cool, translucent wave,	Mask 861
Trinity ms 'coole'	
Bridgewater ms 'coole'	
1637 'coole'	
Cooled	
Against invaders; therefore coold in zeale	Par Lost 11.801
Cooling	
Dire inflammation which no cooling herb	Samson 626
To bring me Berries, or such cooling fruit	Mask 186
Bridgewater ms 'coolinge'	
Coolness	
That in the colours of the Rainbow live	Mask 300
Bridgewater ms 'cooleness of'	
Copartner	
Without Copartner? so to add what wants	Par Lost 9.821
Copartner in these Regions of the World,	Par Reg 1.392
Copartners	
Th' associates and copartners of our loss	Par Lost 1.265
Cope	
Hovering on wing under the Cope of Hell	Par Lost 1.345
ms 'cope'	
In this commotion, but the Starrie Cope	Par Lost 4.992
So under fierie Cope together rush'd	Par Lost 6.215
The strength he was to cope with, or his own:	Par Reg 4.9
Copious	
Shall be the copious matter of my Song	Par Lost 3.413
With copious hand, rejoycing in thir joy.	Par Lost 5.641
Thir branches hung with copious Fruit; or gemm'd	Par Lost 7.325
In copious Legend, or sweet Lyric Song.	Samson 1737
Copses	
The Willows, and the Hazle Copses green,	Lycidas 42
1638 'hasil-copses'	
Trinity ms 'copses'	
Coral	
Of Coral stray, or sporting with quick glance	Par Lost 7.405
Coral-paven	
From thy coral-pav'n bed,	Mask 886
1637 'coral-paven'	
Trinity ms 'corall-paven' ←'corall-paved'	
Bridgewater ms 'Corall paven'	
Cordial	
Leaning half-rais'd, with looks of cordial Love	Par Lost 5.12
From thence a Rib, with cordial spirits warme;	Par Lost 8.466
And first behold this cordial Julep here	Mask 672
Bridgewater ms 'cordiall'	
Trinity ms 'cordiall'	
Cords	
Bound with two cords; but cords to me were threds	Samson 261
Their twisted cords: he who in Heaven doth dwell	Psalm 2, 8
Corineus	
Sleep'st by the fable of *Bellerus* old,	Lycidas 160
Trinity ms 'Bellerus' ←'Corineus'	
Cormorant	
Sat like a Cormorant; yet not true Life	Par Lost 4.196
Corn	
Corn wine and oyle; and from the herd or flock,	Par Lost 12.19
Fertil of corn the glebe, of oyl and wine,	Par Reg 3.259
His shadowy Flale hath thresh'd the Corn	Allegro 108
With vast increase their corn and wine abounds	Psalm 4, 36
Corner	
This Garden, and no corner leave unspi'd;	Par Lost 4.529
To deck her Sons, and that no corner might	Mask 717
Corners	
Thir corners, when with bluster to confound	Par Lost 10.665
To the corners of the Moon.	Mask 1017
Bridgewater ms 'Corners'	
Cornice	
Cornice or Freeze, with bossy Sculptures grav'n,	Par Lost 1.716
Corny	
The swelling Gourd, up stood the cornie Reed	Par Lost 7.321
Coronet	
Under a Coronet his flowing haire	Par Lost 3.640
Corporal	
And from these corporal nutriments perhaps	Par Lost 5.496
By lik'ning spiritual to corporal forms,	Par Lost 5.573
In corporal pleasure he, and careless ease;	Par Reg 4.299
Though void of corporal sense.	Samson 616
With corporal servitude, that my mind ever	Samson 1336
Withall thy charms, although this corporal rinde	Mask 664
Bridgewater ms 'corporall'	

Corporal(*cont*)
Trinity ms 'corporall'
1637 'corporall'
Corporeal
Spiritual substance with corporeal barr. Par Lost 4.585
And corporeal to incorporeal turn. Par Lost 5.413
That to corporeal substances could adde Par Lost 8.109
With this corporeal Clod; then in the Grave, Par Lost 10.786
Corpse
To stuff this Maw, this vast unhide-bound Corps. Par Lost 10.601
Or that thy coarse corrupts in earths dark wombe, Fair Inf 30
Corpulence
Wondrous in length and corpulence involv'd Par Lost 7.483
Correct
Nor in thy hot displeasure me correct; Psalm 6, 2
Correspond
Magnanimous to correspond with Heav'n, Par Lost 7.511
Th' effects to correspond, opener mine Eyes, Par Lost 9.875
Corrosive
To heal the scarr of these corrosive Fires Par Lost 2.401
Corrupt
Corrupt and Pestilent: Now from the North Par Lost 10.695
But all corrupt, both Mind and Will deprav'd, Par Lost 10.825
Peace to corrupt no less then Warr to waste. Par Lost 11.784
But what more oft in Nations grown corrupt, Samson 268
Corrupted
Of Mankind they corrupted to forsake Par Lost 1.368
By him corrupted? or wilt thou thy self Par Lost 3.162
Corrupted. I at first with two fair gifts Par Lost 11.57
To them who had corrupted her, my Spies, Samson 386
Corrupting
Corrupting each thir way; yet those remoov'd, Par Lost 11.889
Corruption
For ever with corruption there to dwell; Par Lost 3.249
Of all corruption, all the blame lights due; Par Lost 10.833
Corruption to bring forth more violent deeds. Par Lost 11.428
Corrupts
Or that thy coarse corrupts in earths dark wombe, Fair Inf 30
Corydon
Where *Corydon* and *Thyrsis* met, Allegro 83
Cost
To do him wanton rites, which cost them woe. Par Lost 1.414
Was gatherd, which cost *Ceres* all that pain Par Lost 4.271
Longer then thou canst feed them on thy cost? Par Reg 2.421
Of numbring *Israel*, which cost the lives Par Reg 3.410
Though dearly to my cost, thy ginns, and toyls; Samson 933
Costliest
Of costliest Emblem: other Creature here Par Lost 4.703
Cote
If Cottage were in view, Sheep-cote or Herd; Par Reg 2.287
But Cottage, Herd or Sheep-cote none he saw, Par Reg 2.288
Cotes
In hurdl'd Cotes amid the field secure, Par Lost 4.186
The folded flocks pen'd in their watled cotes, Mask 344
Cottage
Close in a Cottage low together got Par Reg 2.28
If Cottage were in view, Sheep-cote or Herd; Par Reg 2.287
But Cottage, Herd or Sheep-cote none he saw, Par Reg 2.288
But loyal cottage, where you may be safe Mask 320
Was this the cottage, and the safe abode Mask 693
Bridgewater ms 'Cottage'
Hard by, a Cottage chimney smokes, Allegro 81
Cotytto
Dark vaild *Cotytto*, t' whom the secret flame Mask 129
Bridgewater ms 'Cotitto'
Couch
Rous'd from the slumber, on that fiery Couch, Par Lost 1.377
ms 'couch'
Prick forth the Aerie Knights, and couch thir Spears Par Lost 2.536
They to thir grassie Couch, these to thir Nests Par Lost 4.601
He led her nothing loath; Flours were the Couch, Par Lost 9.1039
Tended the sick busiest from Couch to Couch; Par Lost 11.490
As lightly from his grassy Couch up rose Par Reg 2.282
As on a floating couch through the blithe Air, Par Reg 4.585
To give me answer from her mossie Couch. Mask 276
Trinity ms 'coutch' ← 'couch'
Nightly my Couch I make a kind of Sea; Psalm 6, 12
Couchant
His couchant watch, as one who chose his ground Par Lost 4.406
Couched
Deep malice to conceale, couch't with revenge: Par Lost 4.123
Coucht, and now fild with pasture gazing sat, Par Lost 4.351
How busied, in what form and posture coucht. Par Lost 4.876
Not force, but well couch't fraud, well woven snares, Par Reg 1.97
The Desert, Fowls in thir clay nests were couch't; Par Reg 1.501
All knowledge is not couch't in *Moses* Law, Par Reg 4.225
Couches
Strait couches close, then rising changes oft Par Lost 4.405
Could
Then such could hav orepow'rd such force as ours) Par Lost 1.145
Which but th' Omnipotent none could have foyld, Par Lost 1.273
Could merit more then that small infantry Par Lost 1.575
Of knowledge past or present, could have fear'd, Par Lost 1.628
As stood like these, could ever know repulse? Par Lost 1.630
Could have assur'd us; and by what best way, Par Lost 2.40
Dropt Manna, and could make the worse appear Par Lost 2.113
Scorning surprize. Or could we break our way Par Lost 2.134
Of new Subjection; with what eyes could we Par Lost 2.239

Could(*cont*)
But from the Author of all ill could Spring Par Lost 2.381
Of those Heav'n-warring Champions could be found Par Lost 2.424
Of difficulty or danger could deterr Par Lost 2.449
(What could it less when Spirits immortal sing2) Par Lost 2.553
Yet with a pleasing sorcerie could charm Par Lost 2.566
(For what could else) to our Almighty Foe Par Lost 2.769
Could once have mov'd; then in the key-hole turns Par Lost 2.876
All he could have; I made him just and right, Par Lost 3.98
Not free, what proof could they have givn sincere Par Lost 3.103
Not what they would? what praise could they receive? Par Lost 3.106
No voice exempt, no voice but well could joine Par Lost 3.370
What could be less then to afford him praise, Par Lost 4.46
Then to submit, boasting I could subdue Par Lost 4.85
But say I could repent and could obtaine Par Lost 4.93
Saw him disfigur'd, more then could befall Par Lost 4.127
But rather to tell how, if Art could tell, Par Lost 4.236
With wonder, and could love, so lively shines Par Lost 4.363
To you whom I could pittie thus forlorne Par Lost 4.374
Mother of human Race: what could I doe, Par Lost 4.475
Hitherward bent (who could have thought2) escap'd Par Lost 4.794
Could not but taste. Forthwith up to the Clouds Par Lost 5.86
Messiah King anointed, could not beare Par Lost 5.664
Who out of smallest things could without end Par Lost 6.137
Unaided could have finisht thee, and whelmd Par Lost 6.141
Nor motion of swift thought, less could his Shield Par Lost 6.192
On either side, the least of whom could weild Par Lost 6.221
And Brest, (what could we more2) propounded terms Par Lost 6.612
Long strugling underneath, ere they could wind Par Lost 6.659
That from thy just obedience could revolt, Par Lost 6.740
In heav'nly Spirits could such perverseness dwell? Par Lost 6.788
Both Harp and Voice; nor could the Muse defend Par Lost 7.37
Unknown, which human knowledg could not reach: Par Lost 7.75
How Nature wise and frugal could commit Par Lost 8.26
That to corporeal substances could adde Par Lost 8.109
My Tongue obey'd and readily could name Par Lost 8.272
With what all Earth or Heaven could bestow Par Lost 8.483
I overjoyd could not forbear aloud. Par Lost 8.490
With what delight could I have walkt thee round, Par Lost 9.114
If I could joy in aught, sweet interchange Par Lost 9.115
Thee satiate, to short absence I could yield. Par Lost 9.248
Suttle he needs must be, who could seduce Par Lost 9.307
Longing and envying stood, but could not reach. Par Lost 9.593
I could endure, without him live no life. Par Lost 9.833
Creation could repeate, yet would be loath Par Lost 9.946
It seems, in thy restraint: what could I more? Par Lost 9.1170
Incurr'd, what could they less, the penaltie, Par Lost 10.15
Which your sincerest care could not prevent, Par Lost 10.37
That from her hand I could suspect no ill, Par Lost 10.140
Hell could no longer hold us in her bounds, Par Lost 10.365
Though to delude them sent, could not abstain, Par Lost 10.557
Could alter high Decrees, I to that place Par Lost 10.953
Of Paradise could have produc't, ere fall'n Par Lost 11.29
Incessant I could hope to change the will Par Lost 11.308
His blessed count'nance; here I could frequent, Par Lost 11.317
Turchestan-born; nor could his eye not ken Par Lost 11.396
Sight so deform what heart of Rock could long Par Lost 11.494
Drie-ey'd behold? *Adam* could not, but wept, Par Lost 11.495
Then toldst her doubting how these things could be Par Reg 1.137
Whate're his cruel malice could invent. Par Reg 1.149
Could be obtain'd to shelter him or me Par Reg 2.73
He could not lose himself; but went about Par Reg 2.98
To Idols, those young *Daniel* could refuse; Par Reg 2.329
Who could do mighty things, and could contemn Par Reg 2.448
Could not sustain thy Prowess, or subsist Par Reg 3.19
Freely; of whom what could he less expect Par Reg 3.126
From them who could return him nothing else, Par Reg 3.129
Willingly I could flye, and hope thy raign, Par Reg 3.216
Or could of inward slaves make outward free? Par Reg 4.145
I never fear'd they could, though noising loud Par Reg 4.488
Under the Seal of silence could not keep, Samson 49
No strength of man, or fiercest wild beast could withstand; Samson 127
How could I once look up, or heave the head, Samson 197
Could have befall'n thee and thy Fathers house. Samson 447
By thy request, who could deny thee nothing; Samson 881
Lov'd, honour'd, fear'd me, thou alone could hate me Samson 939
Sam. I could be well content to try thir Art, Samson 1399
From slaughter of one foe could not ascend. Samson 1518
From whom could else a general cry be heard? Samson 1524
And envious darknes, e're they could return, Mask 194
Co. Could that divide you from neer-ushering guides? Mask 279
Could stir the constant mood of her calm thoughts, Mask 371
Vertue could see to do what vertue would Mask 373
Already, ere my best speed could praevent, Mask 573
I could be willing though now i' th darke to trie Mask Tr. ms 16.38
'I could be willing' ← 'beshrew me but I would' ← 'beshew me'
I could be willinge though now i' th darke to trie Mask Br. ms 391
That ten day-labourers could not end, Allegro 109
If my inferior hand or voice could hit Arcades 77
Had ye bin there---for what could that have don? Lycidas 57
What could the Muse her self that *Orpheus* bore, Lycidas 58
How well could I have spar'd for thee young swain, Lycidas 113
Then his bright Throne, or burning Axletree could bear. Nativity 84
Could hold all Heav'n and Earth in happier union. Nativity 108
Could Heav'n for pittie thee so strictly doom? Fair Inf 33
That far events full wisely could presage, Vacation 70
As once we did, till disproportion'd sin Musick 19

Could(*cont*)
Trinity ms 'did' ←'could'
More then she could own from Earth. Winchester 6
And surely, Death could never have prevail'd, Carrier 9
That he could never die while he could move, Another 2
1640, 1657 'did'
While he might still jogg on, and keep his trot, Another 4
1658 'he could but'
Couldst
Satan, and couldst thou faithful add? O name, Par Lost 4.950
As that more willingly thou couldst not seem Par Lost 5.466
To see how thou could'st judge of fit and meet: Par Lost 8.448
Or here th' attempt, thou couldst not have discernd Par Lost 9.1149
So might the wrauth. Fond wish! couldst thou support Par Lost 10.834
Short sojourn; and what thence could'st thou observe? Par Reg 3.235
Samaritan or *Jew*; how could'st thou hope Par Reg 3.359
Thou couldst repress, nor did the dancing Rubie Samson 543
My love how couldst thou hope, who tookst the way Samson 838
How couldst thou find this dark sequester'd nook? Mask 500
That with smooth aire couldst humor best our tongue. Sonnet 13, 8
Trinity ms 'could'st' ←'cou'dst' ←'couldst'
Council
A solemn Councel forthwith to be held Par Lost 1.755
ms 'councell'
With what besides, in Counsel or in Fight, Par Lost 2.20
The *Stygian* Counsel thus dissolv'd; and forth Par Lost 2.506
1667 'Councel'
His Potentates to Councel call'd by night; Par Lost 6.416
Forthwith from Councel to the work they flew, Par Lost 6.507
In Council sate, sollicitous what chance Par Lost 10.428
To Council in the Citie Gates: anon Par Lost 11.661
To Councel summons all his mighty Peers, Par Reg 1.40
Where all his Potentates in Council sate; Par Reg 2.118
Of *Englands* Counsel, and her Treasury, Sonnet 10, 2
Council-table
Wherwith he wont at Heav'ns high Councel-Table, Nativity 10
Counsel
Full Counsel must mature: Peace is despaird, Par Lost 1.660
ms 'counsell'
With what besides, in Counsel or in Fight, Par Lost 2.20
Say they who counsel Warr, we are decreed, Par Lost 2.160
And Princely counsel in his face yet shon, Par Lost 2.304
Pleaded his devilish Counsel, first devis'd Par Lost 2.379
Abandon fear; to strength and counsel joind Par Lost 6.494
Thy counsel in this uttermost distress, Par Lost 10.920
His counsel whom she had displeas'd, his aide; Par Lost 10.944
But *Adam* with such counsel nothing sway'd, Par Lost 10.1010
The purpos'd Counsel pre-ordain'd and fixt Par Reg 1.127
Or counsel to assist; lest I who erst Par Reg 2.145
Thy Counsel would be as the Oracle Par Reg 3.13
Counsel or Consolation we may bring, Samson 183
But I Gods counsel have not kept, his holy secret Samson 497
And with malitious counsel stir them up Samson 1251
Vane, young in yeares, but in sage counsell old, Sonnet 17, 1
1694 'Councels'
1662 'counsel'
Trinity ms 'counsell' ←'counsells'
In counsel of the wicked, and ith' way Psalm 1, 2
Counselled
Counsel'd ignoble ease, and peaceful sloath, Par Lost 2.227
So counsel'd hee, and both together went Par Lost 9.1099
Counsellors
Lords, Ladies, Captains, Councellors, or Priests, Samson 1653
Counsels
United thoughts and counsels, equal hope Par Lost 1.88
ms 'counsells'
His inmost counsels from thir destind aim. Par Lost 1.168
ms 'counsells'
If counsels different, or danger shun'd Par Lost 1.636
ms 'counsells'
Maturest Counsels: for his thoughts were low; Par Lost 2.115
In what he counsels and in what excels Par Lost 2.125
To peaceful Counsels, and the settl'd State Par Lost 2.279
In us who serve, new Counsels, to debate Par Lost 5.681
But what if better counsels might erect Par Lost 5.785
Of Spirits apostat and thir Counsels vaine Par Lost 7.610
By their own counsels quell'd; Psalm 5, 30
Their Plots and Counsels deep, Psalm 83, 10
Count
Thy self though great and glorious dost thou count, Par Lost 5.833
This Paradise I give thee, count it thine Par Lost 8.319
To Vertue I impute not, or count part Par Reg 2.248
And count thy specious gifts no gifts but guiles. Par Reg 2.391
They err who count it glorious to subdue Par Reg 3.71
To count them things worth notice, till at length Samson 250
This Gaol I count the house of Liberty Samson 949
Nor shall I count it hainous to enjoy Samson 991
Count the night watches to his feathery Dames, Mask 347
Th' exalter of my head I count Psalm 3, 9
Whom doe we count a good man, whom but he Prose 10, 1
Countenance
In loss it self; which on his count'nance cast Par Lost 1.526
In others count'nance read his own dismay Par Lost 2.422
Likest to thee in shape and count'nance bright, Par Lost 2.756
In whose conspicuous count'nance, without cloud Par Lost 3.385
With borrowd light her countenance triform Par Lost 3.730
His count'nance, as the Morning Starr that guides Par Lost 5.708
His count'nance too severe to be beheld Par Lost 6.825

Countenance(*cont*)
So spake our Sire, and by his count'nance seemd Par Lost 8.39
Thus *Eve* with Countnance blithe her storie told; Par Lost 9.886
Of Man, but fled him, or with count'nance grim Par Lost 10.713
His blessed count'nance; here I could frequent, Par Lost 11.317
Changest thy countenance, and thy hand with no regard Samson 684
Soon as the Potion works, their human count'nance, Mask 68
Bridgewater ms 'Countenance'
Trinity ms 'countnance'
Lift up the favour of thy count'nance bright. Psalm 4, 30
Counterfeit
Him counterfet, if any eye beheld. Par Lost 4.117
To counterfet Mans voice, true in our Fall, Par Lost 9.1069
How counterfeit a coin they are who friends Samson 189
Teach light to counterfeit a gloom, Penseroso 80
Counterfeited
Of counterfeted truth thus held thir ears. Par Lost 5.771
Counterpoint
And give resounding grace to all Heav'ns Harmonies. Mask 243
B.M. ms 'hold a Counter point'
Trinity ms 'give resounding grace' ←'hold a counterpoint'
Bridgewater ms 'hould a Counterpointe'
Counterpoise
In counterpoise, now ponders all events, Par Lost 4.1001
Counterpoised
Or else with just allowance counterpois'd, Samson 770
Counterview
In counterview within the Gates, that now Par Lost 10.231
Countries
Large Countries, and in field great Battels win, Par Reg 3.73
Country
And Country whereof here needs no account, Par Lost 4.235
His wasted Country freed from *Punic* rage, Par Reg 3.102
Thy Country from her Heathen servitude; Par Reg 3.176
Thy country, and captive lead away her Kings Par Reg 3.366
And lovers of thir Country, as may seem; Par Reg 4.355
The *Philistine*, thy Countries Enemy, Samson 238
Home to thy country and his sacred house, Samson 518
And Princes of my countrey came in person, Samson 851
Then, as since then, thy countries foe profest: Samson 884
Parents and country; nor was I their subject, Samson 886
Thy countrey sought of thee, it sought unjustly, Samson 889
No more thy countrey, but an impious crew Samson 891
For which our countrey is a name so dear; Samson 894
But in my countrey where I most desire, Samson 980
Her countrey from a fierce destroyer, chose Samson 985
Which to my countrey I was judg'd to have shewn. Samson 994
But I a private person, whom my Countrey Samson 1208
To free my Countrey; if their servile minds Samson 1213
Whom thrift keeps up about his Country gear, Mask 167
Trinity ms 'countrie'
Bridgewater ms 'Countrie'
But in another Countrey, as he said, Mask 632
Trinity ms 'countrie'
line not in Bridgewater ms
1637 'Countrie'
Of Hearbs, and other Country Messes, Allegro 85
Countrymen
My Countreymen, whom here I knew remaining, Samson 1549
Counts
Time counts not, though with swiftest minutes wing'd. Par Lost 10.91
Couple
Fair couple, linkt in happie nuptial League, Par Lost 4.339
Coupled
And coupl'd with them, and begot a race. Par Reg 2.181
Courage
And courage never to submit or yield: Par Lost 1.108
New courage and revive, though now they lye Par Lost 1.279
Thir fanting courage, and dispel'd thir fears. Par Lost 1.530
Of dauntless courage, and considerate Pride Par Lost 1.603
ms 'valour'
Mistrustful, grounds his courage on despair Par Lost 2.126
All courage; down thir idle weapons drop'd; Par Lost 6.839
And strength, of courage hautie, and of limb Par Lost 9.484
With youthful courage and magnanimous thoughts Samson 524
Sam. Be of good courage, I begin to feel Samson 1381
Find courage to lay hold on this occasion, Samson 1716
I love thy courage yet, and bold Emprise, Mask 610
Bridgewater ms 'Courage'
Courageous
Less hardie to endure? courageous Chief, Par Lost 4.920
Course
Thir course, in even ballance down they light Par Lost 1.349
Wheels her pale course, they on thir mirth and dance Par Lost 1.786
With winged course ore Hill or moarie Dale, Par Lost 2.944
I travel this profound, direct my course; Par Lost 2.980
Allur'd his eye: Thither his course he bends Par Lost 3.573
Each had his place appointed, each his course, Par Lost 3.720
Well pleas'd they slack thir course, and many a League Par Lost 4.164
Nor chang'd his course, but through the shaggie hill Par Lost 4.224
Gabriel, to thee thy course by Lot hath giv'n Par Lost 4.561
1667 'cours'
Those have thir course to finish, round the Earth, Par Lost 4.661
In thy eternal course, both when thou climbst, Par Lost 5.173
Fannd with coole Winds, save those who in thir course Par Lost 5.655
By our own quick'ning power, when fatal course Par Lost 5.861
Now Night her course began, and over Heav'n Par Lost 6.406
First wheeld thir course; Earth in her rich attire Par Lost 7.501

Course*(cont)*
Thir wandring course now high, now low, then hid, Par Lost 8.126
Or Shee from West her silent course advance Par Lost 8.163
Thir course through thickest Constellations held Par Lost 10.411
His course intended; else how had the World Par Lost 10.689
Darkness ere Dayes mid-course, and Morning light Par Lost 11.204
Shall change thir course to pleasure, ease, and sloth, Par Lost 11.794
Shall hold thir course, till fire purge all things new, Par Lost 11.900
A day entire, and Nights due course adjourne, Par Lost 12.264
By whose bright course led on they found the place, Par Reg 1.252
Desperate of better course, to vent his rage, Par Reg 4.445
Temperst thy providence through his short course, Samson 670
By course commits to severall goverment, Mask 25
Bridgewater ms 'Course'
Which must not be, for that's against my course; Mask 159
That stay'd her flight with his cross-flowing course, Mask 832
All the day long his cours to run. Psalm 136, 30
1673 'course'
Had not his weekly cours of carriage fail'd; Carrier 10
1673 'course'
1658 'course'
In cours reciprocal, and had his fate Another 30
line not in 1658 text
1640, 1657 'course'
His mischief that due course doth keep, Psalm 7, 57
Thy course, there shalt thou find a lasting seat, Prose 12, 11

Court
Of that infernal Court. But far within Par Lost 1.792
ms 'court'
Casual fruition, nor in Court Amours Par Lost 4.767
As one in City, or Court, or Palace bred, Par Reg 2.300
Before the starry threshold of *Joves* Court Mask 1
Trinity ms 'court'
Bridgewater ms 'Courte'
Of lighter toes, and such Court guise Mask 962
Bridgewater ms 'court'
Trinity ms 'such court guise' ←'such neate guise' ←'courtly guise'
but soft I was not sent to court your wonder Mask Tr. ms 10.16

Courted
Courted by all the winds that hold them play, Samson 719

Courteous
Compell'd me to awake the courteous Echo Mask 275
Bridgewater ms 'Curteus'

Courtesy
And well plac't words of glozing courtesie Mask 161
Bridgewater ms 'Curtesie'
And trust thy honest offer'd courtesie, Mask 322
Bridgewater ms 'Curtesie'

Courtly
Of lighter toes, and such Court guise Mask 962
Trinity ms 'such court guise' ←'such neate guise' ←'courtly guise'
And all about the Courtly Stable, Nativity 243

Courts
In Courts and Palaces he also Reigns Par Lost 1.497
(Such are the Courts of God) Th' Angelic throng Par Lost 5.650
Triumphant through mid Heav'n, into the Courts Par Lost 6.889
To tread his Sacred Courts, and minister Par Reg 1.488
In Courts and Regal Chambers how thou lurk'st, Par Reg 2.183
Empires, and Monarchs, and thir radiant Courts, Par Reg 3.237
And Courts of Princes, where it first was nam'd, Mask 325
1637 'courts'
Trinity ms 'courts'
In courts, at feasts, and high solemnities Mask 746
line not in Bridgewater ms
Forsook the Courts of everlasting Day, Nativity 13
Courts thee on Roses in some pleasant Cave, Horace 2
Thy Courts O Lord to see, Psalm 84, 6
For one day in thy Courts *to be* Psalm 84, 33

Covenant
My Cov'nant in the womans seed renewd; Par Lost 11.116
Betok'ning peace from God, and Cov'nant new. Par Lost 11.867
And makes a Covenant never to destroy Par Lost 11.892
And call to mind his Cov'nant: Day and Night, Par Lost 11.898
The Records of his Cov'nant, over these Par Lost 12.252
Up to a better Cov'nant, disciplin'd Par Lost 12.302
Remembring mercie, and his Cov'nant sworn Par Lost 12.346
And that great Cov'nant which we still transgress Circum 21
Trinity ms 'cov'nant'

Covenants
But you invert the cov'nants of her trust, Mask 682
line not in Bridgewater ms

Cover
Long under darkness cover. But these thoughts Par Lost 1.659
And brown as Evening: Cover me ye Pines, Par Lost 9.1088
And girded on our loyns, may cover round Par Lost 9.1096
Mayst cover: well may then thy Lord appeas'd Par Lost 11.257
In vain thou striv'st to cover shame with shame, Samson 841

Covered
(Though like a cover'd field, where Champions bold Par Lost 1.763
Cover'd with pearly grain: yet God hath here Par Lost 5.430
Coverd with thick embatteld Squadrons bright, Par Lost 6.16
Cover'd th' Abyss: but on the watrie calme Par Lost 7.234
To guiltie shame hee cover'd, but his Robe Par Lost 9.1058
Coverd, but not at rest or ease of Mind, Par Lost 9.1120
Araying cover'd from his Fathers sight. Par Lost 10.223
In *Dothan*, cover'd with a Camp of Fire, Par Lost 11.217

Covered*(cont)*
Deep under water rould; Sea cover'd Sea, Par Lost 11.749
With her *green* shade *that* cover'd *all*, Psalm 80, 41

Covering
Abject and lost lay these, covering the Flood, Par Lost 1.312
To gird thir waste, vain Covering if to hide Par Lost 9.1113
Covering the earth with odours, fruits, and flocks, Mask 712
Bridgewater ms 'coveringe'

Covers
Covers his Throne; from whence deep thunders roar Par Lost 2.267

Covert
Whether of open Warr or covert guile, Par Lost 2.41
Sings darkling, and in shadiest Covert hid Par Lost 3.39
Of thickest covert was inwoven shade Par Lost 4.693
Under her Cloudie covert both retir'd, Par Lost 6.409
Of stateliest Covert, Cedar, Pine, or Palme, Par Lost 9.435
Under the covert of some ancient Oak, Par Reg 1.305
Under the hospitable covert nigh Par Reg 2.262
And in thick shelter of black shades imbowr'd, Mask 62
Trinity ms 'shelter' ←'covert'
Through this gloomy covert wide, Mask 945
Bridgewater ms 'Covert'
There in close covert by som Brook, Penseroso 139

Covertures
Vain covertures; but when he saw descend Par Lost 10.337

Covet
Will covet more. With this advantage then Par Lost 2.35
Or if thou covet death, as utmost end Par Lost 10.1020

Coveting
Had it been onely coveting to Eye Par Lost 9.923

Coward
To save himself against a coward arm'd Samson 347
Sams. Go baffl'd coward, lest I run upon thee, Samson 1237

Cowering
Approaching two and two, These cowring low Par Lost 8.350

Cowls
Cowles, Hoods and Habits with thir wearers tost Par Lost 3.490

Cowslip
O're the Cowslips Velvet head, Mask 898
Trinity ms 'couslips'
Bridgewater ms 'Couslips'
1637 'cowslips'
The yellow Cowslip, and the pale Primrose. May Morn 4

Cowslips
With Cowslips wan that hang the pensive hed, Lycidas 147
Trinity ms 'cowslips' ←'the cowslip'
1638 'cowslips'

Coy
Yielded with coy submission, modest pride, Par Lost 4.310
List Lady be not coy, and be not cosen'd Mask 737
line not in Bridgewater ms
Hence with denial vain, and coy excuse, Lycidas 18

Cozened
List Lady be not coy, and be not cosen'd Mask 737
Trinity ms 'cozen'd'
line not in Bridgewater ms

Crab
Up to the *Tropic* Crab; thence down amaine Par Lost 10.675

Crabbed
Not harsh, and crabbed as dull fools suppose, Mask 477

Cradle
When Beldam Nature in her cradle was; Vacation 46

Craft
Among the Nations? that hath been thy craft, Par Reg 1.432

Craggy
Or Pinnace anchors in a craggy Bay Par Lost 2.289
The rest was craggie cliff, that overhung Par Lost 4.547

Crammed
On what was pure, till cramm'd and gorg'd, nigh burst Par Lost 10.632

Cramming
Thronging the Seas with spawn innumerable, Mask 713
Trinity ms 'thronging' ←'cramming'

Crams
Cramms, and blasphemes his feeder. Shall I go on? Mask 779
Bridgewater ms 'crams'

Crane
Easing thir flight; so stears the prudent Crane Par Lost 7.430

Cranes
Warr'd on by Cranes: though all the Giant brood Par Lost 1.576

Cranks
Quips and Cranks, and wanton Wiles, Allegro 27

Crawls
That crawls along the side of yon small hill, Mask 295
Bridgewater ms 'crawles'

Craze
And craze thir Chariot wheels: when by command Par Lost 12.210
And sedentary numness craze my limbs Samson 571

Cream-bowl
To ern his Cream-bowle duly set, Allegro 106

Creams
She tempers dulcet creams, nor these to hold Par Lost 5.347

Create
Intended to create, and therein plant Par Lost 1.652
Did first create your Leader, next free choice, Par Lost 2.19
We can create, and in what place so e're Par Lost 2.260
His dark materials to create more Worlds, Par Lost 2.916
Self-lost, and in a moment will create Par Lost 7.154
Good out of evil to create, in stead Par Lost 7.188

Create(*cont*)
And Spirit coming to create new Worlds. Par Lost 7.209
Thy Thunders magnifi'd; but to create Par Lost 7.606
So many nobler Bodies to create, Par Lost 8.28
Build in her loveliest, and create an awe Par Lost 8.558
More Angels to Create, if they at least Par Lost 9.146
Should God create another *Eve*, and I Par Lost 9.911
My Substitutes I send ye, and Create Par Lost 10.403
With Spirits Masculine, create at last Par Lost 10.890
And took in strains that might create a soul Mask 561
That by his wisdom did create Psalm 136, 17

Created
Created hugest that swim th' Ocean stream: Par Lost 1.202
Glories: For never since created man, Par Lost 1.573
To be created like to us, though less Par Lost 2.349
Created evil, for evil only good, Par Lost 2.623
Created thing naught valu'd he nor shun'd; Par Lost 2.679
Created vast and round, a place of bliss Par Lost 2.832
Directly towards the new created World, Par Lost 3.89
Such I created all th' Ethereal Powers Par Lost 3.100
So were created, nor can justly accuse Par Lost 3.112
Though last created, that for him I spare Par Lost 3.278
By thee created, and by thee threw down Par Lost 3.391
Created this new happie Race of Men Par Lost 3.679
But what created mind can comprehend Par Lost 3.705
From me, whom he created what I was Par Lost 4.43
Mankind created, and for him this World. Par Lost 4.107
This new created World, whereof in Hell Par Lost 4.937
Wherein all things created first he weighd, Par Lost 4.999
Created pure. But know that in the Soule Par Lost 5.100
Created, or such place hast here to dwell, Par Lost 5.373
For know, whatever was created, needs Par Lost 5.414
If not deprav'd from good, created all Par Lost 5.471
In contemplation of created things Par Lost 5.511
To be both will and deed created free; Par Lost 5.549
By him created in thir bright degrees, Par Lost 5.838
Then who created thee lamenting learne, Par Lost 5.894
When, and whereof created, for what cause, Par Lost 7.64
This Universe, and all created things: Par Lost 7.227
Thus God the Heav'n created, thus the Earth, Par Lost 7.232
And God created the great Whales, and each Par Lost 7.391
Created thee, in the Image of God Par Lost 7.527
Male he created thee, but thy consort Par Lost 7.529
Wherever thus created, for no place Par Lost 7.535
Thence to behold this new created World Par Lost 7.554
Is greater then created to destroy. Par Lost 7.607
Created in his Image, there to dwell Par Lost 7.627
(And pure thou wert created) we enjoy Par Lost 8.623
Are his Created, or to spite us more, Par Lost 9.147
Of all that he Created, much less Man, Par Lost 9.346
Created mute to all articulat sound; Par Lost 9.557
Created; but henceforth my early care, Par Lost 9.799
For us created, needs with us must faile, Par Lost 9.942
The new created World, which fame in Heav'n Par Lost 10.481
So fair and good created, and had still Par Lost 10.618
Created him endowd, with Happiness Par Lost 11.58
Th' Image of God in man created once Par Lost 11.508
Created, as thou art, to nobler end Par Lost 11.605
Hast thou not right to all Created things, Par Reg 2.324
O first created Beam, and thou great Word, Samson 83

Createst
Thou usest, and from thence creat'st more good. Par Lost 7.616

Creating
Of God ordain'd them, his creating hand Par Lost 9.344

Creation
To waste his whole Creation, or possess Par Lost 2.365
Abolish thy Creation, and unmake, Par Lost 3.163
Thee next they sang of all Creation first, Par Lost 3.383
To visit oft this new Creation round; Par Lost 3.661
When this creation was? rememberst thou Par Lost 5.857
Equal in their Creation they were form'd, Par Lost 6.690
Creation, and the wonders of his might. Par Lost 7.223
The Sixt, and of Creation last arose Par Lost 7.449
Creation and the Six dayes acts they sung, Par Lost 7.601
Destruction with Creation might have mixt. Par Lost 8.236
O fairest of Creation, last and best Par Lost 9.896
Creation could repeate, yet would be loath Par Lost 9.946
Of his Creation; justly then accurst, Par Lost 10.168
Curs'd his Creation, Death as oft accus'd Par Lost 10.852
Then that which by creation first brought forth Par Lost 12.472

Creation-day
To Beasts, whom God on thir Creation-Day Par Lost 9.556

Creator
From thir Creator, and transgress his Will Par Lost 1.31
God thir Creator, and th' invisible Par Lost 1.369
The great Creatour? But thir spite still serves Par Lost 2.385
To whom the great Creatour thus reply'd. Par Lost 3.167
On whom the great Creator hath bestowd Par Lost 3.673
Singing thir great Creator: oft in bands Par Lost 4.684
Mov'd the Creator in his holy Rest Par Lost 7.91
God and his works, Creatour him they sung, Par Lost 7.259
Yet not till the Creator from his work Par Lost 7.551
The great Creator from his work returnd Par Lost 7.567
Creator; something yet of doubt remaines, Par Lost 8.13
Thy words, Creator bounteous and benigne, Par Lost 8.492
To the Creator, and his Nostrils fill Par Lost 9.196
Nor can I think that God, Creator wise, Par Lost 9.938
From his Creator, and the more to increase Par Lost 10.486

Creator(*cont*)
While the Creator calling forth by name Par Lost 10.649
Creator wise, that peopl'd highest Heav'n Par Lost 10.889
While the Creator Great Nativity 120

Creature
Thy creature late so lov'd, thy youngest Son Par Lost 3.151
Whom else no Creature can behold; on thee Par Lost 3.387
Alone, for other Creature in this place Par Lost 3.442
What there thou seest fair Creature is thy self, Par Lost 4.468
No Creature thence: if Spirit of other sort, Par Lost 4.582
Of costliest Emblem: other Creature here Par Lost 4.703
Here, happie Creature, fair Angelic *Eve*, Par Lost 5.74
Of all yet don; a Creature who not prone Par Lost 7.506
Canst raise thy Creature to what highth thou wilt Par Lost 8.430
Under his forming hands a Creature grew, Par Lost 8.470
Consider'd every Creature, which of all Par Lost 9.84
A Creature form'd of Earth, and him endow, Par Lost 9.149
Of all Gods works, Creature in whom excell'd Par Lost 9.897
Creature so faire his reconcilement seeking, Par Lost 10.943
By hunger, that each other Creature tames, Par Reg 2.406

Creatures
What creatures there inhabit, of what mould, Par Lost 2.355
Of Creatures rational, though under hope Par Lost 2.498
A race of upstart Creatures, to supply Par Lost 2.834
To visit all thy creatures, and to all Par Lost 3.230
Of living Creatures new to sight and strange: Par Lost 4.287
Creatures of other mould, earth-born perhaps, Par Lost 4.360
Over all other Creatures that possess Par Lost 4.431
Our eye-lids; other Creatures all day long Par Lost 4.616
Millions of spiritual Creatures walk the Earth Par Lost 4.677
But chiefly where those two fair Creatures Lodge, Par Lost 4.790
On Earth joyn all ye Creatures to extoll Par Lost 5.164
Hugest of living Creatures, on the Deep Par Lost 7.413
Innumerous living Creatures, perfet formes, Par Lost 7.455
And Brute as other Creatures, but endu'd Par Lost 7.507
Of other Creatures, as him pleases best, Par Lost 8.169
Dream not of other Worlds, what Creatures there Par Lost 8.175
Creatures that livd, and movd, and walk'd, or flew, Par Lost 8.264
And ye that live and move, fair Creatures, tell, Par Lost 8.276
With various living creatures, and the Aire Par Lost 8.370
Save with the Creatures which I made, and those Par Lost 8.409
Beneath what other Creatures are to thee? Par Lost 8.411
O're other Creatures; yet when I approach Par Lost 8.546
Of Creatures animate with gradual life Par Lost 9.112
Of Creatures wanting voice, that done, partake Par Lost 9.199
Compare above all living Creatures deare, Par Lost 9.228
Sovran of Creatures, universal Dame. Par Lost 9.612
Us his prime Creatures, dignifi'd so high, Par Lost 9.940
Thy inward fraud, to warn all Creatures from thee Par Lost 10.871
With all the Creatures, and thir seed preserve. Par Lost 11.873
Then Mortal Creatures, graceful and discreet, Par Reg 2.157
Owe not all Creatures by just right to thee Par Reg 2.325
The Angelic orders and inferiour creatures mute, Samson 672
Of som gay creatures of the element Mask 299
All living creatures he doth feed, Psalm 136, 85
As if to shew what creatures Heav'n doth breed, Fair Inf 61
Broke the fair musick that all creatures made Musick 21

Credit
The credit of whose vertue rest with thee, Par Lost 9.649
To salve his credit, and for very spight Par Reg 4.12

Credulous
Led *Eve* our credulous Mother, to the Tree Par Lost 9.644
Draw out with credulous desire, and lead Par Reg 2.166
Hast thou betrai'd my credulous innocence Mask 697
line not in Bridgewater ms
Who now enjoyes thee credulous, all Gold, Horace 9

Creek
Forthwith the Sounds and Seas, each Creek and Bay Par Lost 7.399
Then on the bank of *Jordan*, by a Creek: Par Reg 2.25

Creep
A hideous Peal: yet, when they list, would creep, Par Lost 2.656
The Earth, and stately tread, or lowly creep; Par Lost 5.201
They creep, yet see, I dark in light expos'd Samson 75
Thus don the Tales, to bed they creep, Allegro 115
Creep and intrude, and climb into the fold? Lycidas 115
Trinity ms 'creepe'

Creeping
Cattel and Creeping things, and Beast of the Earth, Par Lost 7.452
And every creeping thing that creeps the ground. Par Lost 7.523
Like a black mist low creeping, he held on Par Lost 9.180

Creeps
And swims or sinks, or wades, or creeps, or flyes: Par Lost 2.950
Layes forth her purple Grape, and gently creeps Par Lost 4.259
At once came forth whatever creeps the ground, Par Lost 7.475
And every creeping thing that creeps the ground. Par Lost 7.523

Cremona
Loud o're the rest *Cremona*'s Trump doth sound; Passion 26

Crept
Forth flourish't thick the clustring Vine, forth crept Par Lost 7.320
Soul living, each that crept, which plenteously Par Lost 7.392
Thir Snakie foulds, and added wings. First crept Par Lost 7.484

Crescent
Astarte, Queen of Heav'n, with crescent Horns; Par Lost 1.439
Of *Turkish* Crescent, leaves all waste beyond Par Lost 10.434

Cressets
Of Starry Lamps and blazing Cressets fed Par Lost 1.728

Crest
His stature reacht the Skie, and on his Crest Par Lost 4.988

Crest(*cont*)
This greeting on thy impious Crest receive. Par Lost 6.188
On the proud Crest of *Satan*, that no sight, Par Lost 6.191
His turret Crest, and sleek enamel'd Neck, Par Lost 9.525
Bright'ns his Crest, as when a wandring Fire, Par Lost 9.634

Crested
Walk'd firm; the crested Cock whose clarion sounds Par Lost 7.443
Crested aloft, and Carbuncle his Eyes; Par Lost 9.500
Or grovling soild thir crested helmets in the dust. Samson 141

Crest-fallen
Chor. His Giantship is gone somewhat crest-fall'n, Samson 1244

Crete
So *Jove* usurping reign'd: these first in *Creet* Par Lost 1.514
ms 'Creet'
Chios and *Creet*, and how they quaff in Gold, Par Reg 4.118

Crew
To mortal men, he with his horrid crew Par Lost 1.51
ms 'crue'
A crew who under Names of old Renown, Par Lost 1.477
For Treasures better hid. Soon had his crew Par Lost 1.688
With his industrious crew to build in hell. Par Lost 1.751
Lost sight of him; one of the banisht crew Par Lost 4.573
Faithful to whom? to thy rebellious crew? Par Lost 4.952
Determind, and thy hapless crew involv'd Par Lost 5.879
Equal in number to that Godless crew Par Lost 6.49
Thou and thy wicked crew; there mingle broiles, Par Lost 6.277
The Atheist crew, but with redoubl'd blow Par Lost 6.370
Invincibly; but of this cursed crew Par Lost 6.806
Diseases dire, of which a monstrous crew Par Lost 11.474
Hee with a crew, whom like Ambition joyns Par Lost 12.38
Of much amazement to th' infernal Crew, Par Reg 1.107
Before the Flood thou with thy lusty Crew, Par Reg 2.178
And to his crew, that sat consulting, brought Par Reg 4.577
No more thy countrey, but an impious crew Samson 891
But sease his wand, though he and his curst crew Mask 653
To som of *Saturns* crew. I must dissemble, Mask 805
line not in Bridgewater ms
line not in Trinity ms
Mirth, admit me of thy crue Allegro 38
Can in his swadling bands controul the damned crew. Nativity 228
With all his over-hardy crew. Psalm 136, 70

Cricket
Save the Cricket on the hearth, Penseroso 82

Cried
O Father, what intends thy hand, she cry'd, Par Lost 2.727
Made to destroy: I fled, and cry'd out *Death;* Par Lost 2.787
And waking cri'd, *This is the Gate of Heav'n* Par Lost 3.515
Came flying, and in mid Aire aloud thus cri'd. Par Lost 6.536
Dismai'd, and thus in haste to th' Angel cri'd. Par Lost 11.449
More awful then the sound of Trumpet, cri'd Par Reg 1.19
At last with head erect thus cryed aloud, Samson 1639
As he were prest to death, he cry'd more waight; Another 26
line not in 1640, 1657, 1658 texts
Aloud I cry'd Psalm 3, 10

Criedest
Thou following cryd'st aloud, Return faire *Eve;* Par Lost 4.481

Cries
Thir childrens cries unheard, that past through fire Par Lost 1.395
Mends not her slowest pace for prayers or cries. Par Lost 10.859
There with my cries importune Heaven, that all Par Lost 10.933
To wearie him with my assiduous cries: Par Lost 11.310
And raise such out-cries on thy clatter'd Iron, Samson 1124
Cries the stall-reader, bless us! what a word on Sonnet 11, 5
And to my cries, that *ceaseless are*, Psalm 88, 7

Crime
One next himself in power, and next in crime, Par Lost 1.79
The fellows of his crime, the followers rather Par Lost 1.606
Mans mortal crime, and just th' unjust to save, Par Lost 3.215
His crime makes guiltie all his Sons, thy merit Par Lost 3.290
Both of thy crime and punishment: henceforth Par Lost 5.881
Miserie, uncreated till the crime Par Lost 6.268
To undergoe with mee one Guilt, one Crime, Par Lost 9.971
That errour now, which is become my crime, Par Lost 9.1181
My self the total Crime, or to accuse Par Lost 10.127
As in thir crime. Thus was th' applause they meant, Par Lost 10.545
To *Satan* only like both crime and doom. Par Lost 10.841
Th' effects which thy original crime hath wrought Par Lost 11.424
Who for my wilful crime art banisht hence. Par Lost 12.619
My error was my error, and my crime Par Reg 3.212
My crime; whatever for it self condemn'd, Par Reg 3.213
And expiate, if possible, my crime, Samson 490
Or by evasions thy crime uncoverst more. Samson 842
Time numbers motion, yet (without a crime Another 7

Crimes
That with reiterated crimes he might Par Lost 1.214
Besides thir other worse then heathenish crimes; Par Reg 3.419

Cringe
And practis'd distances to cringe, not fight. Par Lost 4.945

Cringed
Once fawn'd, and cring'd, and servilly ador'd Par Lost 4.959

Crisped
How from that Saphire Fount the crisped Brooks, Par Lost 4.237
Along the crisped shades and bowres Mask 984
line not in Bridgewater ms

Crocodile
The River Horse and scalie Crocodile. Par Lost 7.474

Crocus
Crocus, and Hyacinth with rich inlay Par Lost 4.701

Crofts
Tending my flocks hard by i' th hilly crofts, Mask 531
Trinity ms 'crofts' ← 'lawns'
Bridgewater ms 'Crofts'

Cromwell
Cromwell, our cheif of men, who through a cloud Sonnet 16, 1

Cronian
Upon the *Cronian* Sea, together drive Par Lost 10.290

Crooked
Crooked by nature, bent, as now appears, Par Lost 10.885
A *Sybil* old, bow-bent with crooked age, Vacation 69

Crop
Labouring the soile, and reaping plenteous crop, Par Lost 12.18
Shatter your leaves before the mellowing year. Lycidas 5
Trinity ms 'shatter' ← 'and crop your young'
Who onely thought to crop the flowr Winchester 39
Cropp yee as close as marginall P---s eares Forcers Tr. ms 45.17

Crop-full
And Crop-full out of dores he flings, Allegro 113

Cropped
Sweet of thy self, but much more sweet thus cropt, Par Lost 5.68

Cross
He had to cross. Nor was his eare less peal'd Par Lost 2.920
A violent cross wind from either Coast Par Lost 3.487
A shameful and accurst, naild to the Cross Par Lost 12.413
But to the Cross he nailes thy Enemies, Par Lost 12.415
Or what the cross dire-looking Planet smites, Arcades 52
Trinity ms 'crosse'
That on the bitter cross Nativity 152
But vow though the cross Doctors all stood hearers, Another 19
line not in 1640, 1657, 1658 texts

Cross-barred
Cross-barrd and bolted fast, fear no assault, Par Lost 4.190

Crossed
He circl'd, four times cross'd the Carr of Night Par Lost 9.65
When first this Tempter cross'd the Gulf from Hell. Par Lost 10.39

Cross-flowing
That stay'd her flight with his cross-flowing course, Mask 832
Bridgewater ms 'Crosse floweinge'
1637 'crosse-flowing'
Trinity ms 'crosse flowing'

Crowd
While the promiscuous croud stood yet aloof? Par Lost 1.380
Thir State affairs. So thick the aerie crowd Par Lost 1.775
Dazles the croud, and sets them all agape. Par Lost 5.357
They saw, but other sight instead, a crowd Par Lost 10.538
Cromwell, our cheif of men, who through a cloud Sonnet 16, 1
1694 'a Croud'

Crowded
Tost up and down, together crowded drove Par Lost 10.287

Crown
The likeness of a Kingly Crown had on. Par Lost 2.673
And mutual love, the Crown of all our bliss Par Lost 4.728
Her Tresses, and her rural labours crown, Par Lost 9.841
Riches and Realms; yet not for that a Crown, Par Reg 2.458
Though Priests, the Crown, and *David*'s Throne usurp'd, Par Reg 3.169
Then to a worldly Crown, addicted more Par Reg 4.213
Whom Patience finally must crown. Samson 1296
How dy'd he? death to life is crown or shame. Samson 1579
Unmindfull of the crown that Vertue gives Mask 9
Trinity ms 'crowne'
1637 'crowne'
Bridgewater ms 'Crowne'
With a crown of deathless Praise, Mask 973
Bridgewater ms 'Crowne'
1637 'crowne'
Trinity ms 'crowne'
B.M. ms 'Crown'
Fall on his crown with ruine steep. Psalm 7, 60

Crowned
As when *Alcides* from *Oechalia* Crown'd Par Lost 2.542
Then Crown'd again thir gold'n Harps they took, Par Lost 3.365
O thou that with surpassing Glory crownd, Par Lost 4.32
That to the fringed Bank with Myrtle crownd, Par Lost 4.262
Earth and the Gard'n of God, with Cedars crownd Par Lost 5.260
With pleasant liquors crown'd: O innocence Par Lost 5.445
On flours repos'd, and with fresh flourets crownd, Par Lost 5.636
line not in 1667 edition
Crownd them with Glory, and to thir Glory nam'd Par Lost 5.839
Girt with Omnipotence, with Radiance crown'd Par Lost 7.194
Thir blossoms: with high woods the hills were crownd, Par Lost 7.326
Glad Eevning and glad Morn crownd the fourth day. Par Lost 7.386
Now Land, now Sea, and Shores with Forrest crownd, Par Lost 9.117
All would have then gon well, peace would have crownd Par Lost 11.781
Universally crown'd with highest praises. Samson 175
May thy lofty head be crown'd Mask 934
Bridgewater ms 'Crownd'
Trinity ms 'crownd'
To Ivy-crowned *Bacchus* bore; Allegro 16
Smooth-sliding *Mincius*, crown'd with vocall reeds, Lycidas 86
She crown'd with Olive green, came softly sliding Nativity 47
Or that crown'd Matron sage white-robed truth? Fair Inf 54
1673 printed 'cown'd'
And on the neck of crowned Fortune proud Sonnet 16, 5
line not in 1694 text
With honour and with state thou hast him crown'd. Psalm 8, 16

Crownest
Sure pledge of day, that crownst the smiling Morn Par Lost 5.168

Crowns
Thir Crowns inwove with Amarant and Gold, Par Lost 3.352
Now nearer, Crowns with her enclosure green, Par Lost 4.133
And gives them leave to wear their Saphire crowns, Mask 26
Bridgewater ms 'Crownes'
Crow-toe
The tufted Crow-toe, and pale Gessamine, Lycidas 143
1638 'crow-toe'
Trinity ms 'crowtoe'
Crucified
Of all mankinde, with him there crucifi'd, Par Lost 12.417
Crude
Treading the crude consistence, half on foot, Par Lost 2.941
Deep under ground, materials dark and crude, Par Lost 6.478
Th' originals of Nature in thir crude Par Lost 6.511
Was that crude Apple that diverted *Eve!* Par Reg 2.349
Crude or intoxicate, collecting toys, Par Reg 4.328
In crude old age; Samson 700
Where no crude surfet raigns. *Eld. Bro*. List, list, I hear Mask 480
I com to pluck your Berries harsh and crude, Lycidas 3
Cruel
Waiting revenge: cruel his eye, but cast Par Lost 1.604
ms 'cruell'
Among themselves, and levie cruel warres, Par Lost 2.501
As one he stood escap't from cruel fight, Par Lost 6.448
With cruel expectation. Yet one doubt Par Lost 10.782
That cruel Serpent: On me exercise not Par Lost 10.927
With cruel Tournament the Squadrons joine; Par Lost 11.652
Whate're his cruel malice could invent. Par Reg 1.149
Then cruel, by thir sports to blood enur'd Par Reg 4.139
Violence and stripes, and lastly cruel death, Par Reg 4.388
And to those cruel enemies, Samson 642
E're I to thee, thou to thy self wast cruel. Samson 784
Who threatning cruel death constrain'd the bride Samson 1198
Why should you be so cruel to your self, Mask 679
line not in Bridgewater ms
1637 'cruell'
Trinity ms 'cruell'
Cruelly
Of righteous *Job*, then cruelly to afflict him Par Reg 1.425
Cruelties
Though to the death, against such cruelties Par Lost 12.494
Cruelty
The subject of thir cruelty, or scorn. Samson 646
And with remorsles cruelty, Winchester 29
Crumble
And crumble all thy sinews. *Eld. Bro*. Why prethee Shepherd Mask 615
Crumbled
Rising, the crumbl'd Earth above them threw Par Lost 7.468
Crush
Against us this deceit: to crush his head Par Lost 10.1035
Shall bruise the head of *Satan*, crush his strength Par Lost 12.430
That glassy floods from rugged rocks can crush, Psalm 114, 17
Crushed
Thir armor help'd thir harm, crush't in and bruis'd Par Lost 6.656
Crush't the sweet poyson of mis-used Wine Mask 47
Bridgewater ms 'crusht'
Crushes
She crushes, inoffensive moust, and meathes Par Lost 5.345
Cry
Then of thir Session ended they bid cry Par Lost 2.514
A cry of Hell Hounds never ceasing bark'd Par Lost 2.654
These yelling Monsters that with ceasless cry Par Lost 2.795
Th' *Apocalyps*, heard cry in Heaven aloud, Par Lost 4.2
From whom could else a general cry be heard? Samson 1524
With rueful cry, yet what it was we hear not, Samson 1553
With Saintly shout, and solemn Jubily, Musick 9
Trinity ms 'jubilie' ←'crie'
Licence they mean when they cry libertie; Sonnet 12, 11
Will hear my voyce what time to him I crie. Psalm 4, 18
Thy protection while I crie, Psalm 7, 3
We cry and do not cease. Psalm 83, 4
My heart and flesh aloud do crie, Psalm 84, 7
give ear, and to the crie Psalm 86, 18
All day to thee I cry; Psalm 88, 2
But I to thee O Lord do cry Psalm 88, 53
Crystal
Sheer o're the Chrystal Battlements: from Morn Par Lost 1.742
ms 'chrystall'
Her chrystal mirror holds, unite thir streams. Par Lost 4.263
1667 'chrystall'
Each in thir Chrystal sluce, hee ere they fell Par Lost 5.133
1667 'chrystal'
Over thir heads a chrystal Firmament, Par Lost 6.757
And Chrystal wall of Heav'n, which op'ning wide, Par Lost 6.860
1667 'Chrystall'
Part rise in crystal Wall, or ridge direct, Par Lost 7.293
As on drie land between two christal walls, Par Lost 12.197
Unfold her Crystal Dores, thence on his head Par Reg 1.82
Crystal and Myrrhine cups imboss'd with Gems Par Reg 4.119
His orient liquor in a Crystal Glasse, Mask 65
1637 'Chrystall'
Bridgewater ms 'Christall'
Trinity ms 'crystall'
That flames, and dances in his crystal bounds Mask 673
Trinity ms 'crystall' ←'ch'
Bridgewater ms 'christall'
1637 'crystall'

Crystal(*cont*)
May thy brimmed waves for this Mask 924
Trinity ms 'brimmed' ←'crystall'
Thy molten crystal fill with mudd, Mask 931
1637 'crystall'
Bridgewater ms 'Cristall'
Trinity ms 'crystall'
Ring out ye Crystall spheares, Nativity 125
Why turned *Jordan* toward his Crystall Fountains? Psalm 114, 14
1673 'Chrystal'
Crystalline
And that Crystalline Sphear whose ballance weighs Par Lost 3.482
On the Chrystallin Skie, in Saphir Thron'd. Par Lost 6.772
1667 'Crystallin'
Crystallin Ocean, and the loud misrule Par Lost 7.271
Allure thee from the cool Crystalline stream. Samson 546
Ctesiphon
Artaxata, *Teredon*, *Tesiphon*, Par Reg 3.292
In *Ctesiphon* hath gather'd all his Host Par Reg 3.300
Cube
Approaching gross and huge; in hollow Cube Par Lost 6.552
Cubic
In Cubic Phalanx firm advanc't entire, Par Lost 6.399
Cubit
Measur'd by Cubit, length, and breadth, and highth, Par Lost 11.730
Cuckoo
First heard before the shallow Cuccoo's bill Sonnet 1, 6
Cuckoos
Of Owles and Cuckoes, Asses, Apes and Doggs. Sonnet 12, 4
Trinity ms 'Cuckoes' ←'buzzards'
Cuirass
Of brazen shield and spear, the hammer'd Cuirass, Samson 132
Cuirassiers
Cuirassiers all in steel for standing fight; Par Reg 3.328
Cull
But cull those richest Robes, and gay'st attire Vacation 21
Culled
But of divine effect, he cull'd me out; Mask 630
Trinity ms 'culld'
Culling
Culling their Potent hearbs, and balefull drugs, Mask 255
Bridgewater ms 'cullinge'
Culminate
Culminate from th' *Aequator*, as they now Par Lost 3.617
Cumbered
Th' earth cumber'd, and the wing'd air dark't with plumes, Mask 730
Bridgewater ms 'cumberd'
Cumbersome
Thy politic maxims, or that cumbersome Par Reg 3.400
Cumbrance
The wise mans cumbrance if not snare, more apt Par Reg 2.454
Cumbrous
Like cumbrous flesh; but in what shape they choose Par Lost 1.428
The cumbrous Elements, Earth, Flood, Aire, Fire, Par Lost 3.715
Fairest and easiest of this combrous charge, Par Lost 11.549
To *Haran*, after him a cumbrous Train Par Lost 12.131
Cunning
And vaunts of his great cunning to the throng Par Reg 1.145
In cunning, over-reach't where least he thought, Par Reg 4.11
With wanton heed, and giddy cunning, Allegro 141
Cunningly
Sam. How cunningly the sorceress displays Samson 819
Cup
Array'd in Glory on my cup to attend: Par Reg 2.386
Thy fair enchanted cup, and warbling charms Samson 934
The daughter of the Sun? Whose charmed Cup Mask 51
Trinity ms 'cup'
By sly enticement gives his banefull cup, Mask 525
Bridgewater ms 'Cup'
Cupid
The frivolous bolt of *Cupid*, gods and men Mask 445
Celestial *Cupid* her fam'd Son advanc't, Mask 1004
line not in Bridgewater ms
Cups
Ministerd naked, and thir flowing cups Par Lost 5.444
Allurd them; thence from Cups to civil Broiles. Par Lost 11.718
Crystal and Myrrhine cups imboss'd with Gems Par Reg 4.119
And Daffadillies fill their cups with tears, Lycidas 150
Curb
Under th' inevitable curb, reserv'd Par Lost 2.322
Part curb thir fierie Steeds, or shun the Goal Par Lost 2.531
Chaumping his iron curb: to strive or flie Par Lost 4.859
Part wield thir Arms, part courb the foaming Steed, Par Lost 11.643
That with moist curb sways the smooth Severn stream, Mask 825
Bridgewater ms 'Curbe'
Trinity ms 'curbe'
And wisely learn to curb thy sorrows wild; Fair Inf 73
Cure
And that must end us, that must be our cure, Par Lost 2.145
To be no more; sad cure; for who would loose, Par Lost 2.146
More tollerable; if there be cure or charm Par Lost 2.460
Here grows the Cure of all, this Fruit Divine, Par Lost 9.776
And what may else be remedie or cure Par Lost 10.1079
To deaths benumming Opium as my only cure. Samson 630
Misguided; only what remains past cure Samson 912
But this will cure all streight, one sip of this Mask 811
I have kept of pretious cure, Mask 913
Bridgewater ms 'Cure'

Curfew
That breaks his magick chains at *curfeu* time, Mask 435
Trinity ms 'curfew'
Bridgewater ms 'Curfew'
1637 'curfeu'
I hear the far-off *Curfeu* sound, Penseroso 74
Curiosity
Curiosity, inquisitive, importune Samson 775
Curious
In Beds and curious Knots, but Nature boon Par Lost 4.242
He saw approach, who first with curious eye Par Reg 1.319
Where ought we hear, and curious are to hear, Par Reg 1.333
Of Telescope, were curious to enquire: Par Reg 4.42
But all to please, and sate the curious taste? Mask 714
Bridgewater ms 'Curious'
Curius
Quintius, Fabricius, Curius, Regulus? Par Reg 2.446
Curl
To nurse the Saplings tall, and curl the grove Arcades 46
Trinity ms 'curle'
Curled
Curld many a wanton wreath in sight of *Eve*, Par Lost 9.517
That curld *Megaera:* greedily they pluck'd Par Lost 10.560
Som roaving Robber calling to his fellows. Mask 485
Trinity ms 'robber' ←'hedge man' ←'curl'd man of the swoord'
Curls
In curles on either cheek plaid, wings he wore Par Lost 3.641
As the Vine curles her tendrils, which impli'd Par Lost 4.307
Or drag him by the curls, to a foul death, Mask 608
Bridgewater ms 'Curles'
1637 'curles'
Current
Upon the rapid current, which through veins Par Lost 4.227
The current of his fury thus oppos'd. Par Lost 5.808
Yet scarce allay'd still eyes the current streame, Par Lost 7.67
Sam. Where ever fountain or fresh current flow'd Samson 547
But must be currant, and the good thereof Mask 740
line not in Bridgewater ms
Trinity ms 'currant' ←'current'
Currents
With clamor thence the rapid Currents drive Par Lost 11.853
Curse
Hurl'd headlong to partake with us, shall curse Par Lost 2.374
A Universe of death, which God by curse Par Lost 2.622
And on the Serpent thus his curse let fall. Par Lost 10.174
Till then the Curse pronounc't on both precedes. Par Lost 10.640
Is propagated curse. O voice once heard Par Lost 10.729
The evil on him brought by me, will curse Par Lost 10.734
Me now your curse! Ah, why should all mankind Par Lost 10.822
Fruit of thy Womb: On mee the Curse aslope Par Lost 10.1053
But Justice, and some fatal curse annext Par Lost 12.99
Don to his Father, heard this heavie curse, Par Lost 12.103
Cursed
Abominations; and with cursed things Par Lost 1.389
Accurst, and in a cursed hour he hies. Par Lost 2.1055
Nay curs'd be thou; since against his thy will Par Lost 4.71
Till on those cursed Engins triple-row Par Lost 6.650
Invincibly; but of this cursed crew Par Lost 6.806
The sacred Fruit forbidd'n? som cursed fraud Par Lost 9.904
Curs'd is the ground for thy sake, thou in sorrow Par Lost 10.201
Posteritie stands curst: Fair Patrimonie Par Lost 10.818
Curs'd his Creation, Death as oft accus'd Par Lost 10.852
Into this cursed World a woful Race, Par Lost 10.984
To a reproachful life and cursed death, Par Lost 12.406
Curs'd as his life. *Spir.* Alas good ventrous youth, Mask 609
1637 'Downe to the hipps'
Bridgewater ms 'downe to the hipps'
Trinity ms 'downe to the hips' ←'lowest hips' ←'hipps'
But sease his wand, though he and his curst crew Mask 653
Trinity ms 'curs't'
Let us fly this cursed place, Mask 939
Curses
Or multiplie, but curses on my head? Par Lost 10.732
Built in th' eclipse, and rigg'd with curses dark, Lycidas 101
Curtained
That draw the litter of close-curtain'd sleep. Mask 554
1673 'close curtain'd'
Curtain'd with cloudy red, Nativity 230
Cusco
And *Cusco* in *Peru*, the richer seat Par Lost 11.408
Custody
To us enslav'd, but custody severe, Par Lost 2.333
Had from his wakeful custody purloind Par Lost 2.946
Against thee but safe custody, and hold: Samson 802
Custom
Consent or custome, and his Regal State Par Lost 1.640
Against allurement, custom, and a World Par Lost 11.810
Customed
When *Adam* wak't, so customd, for his sleep Par Lost 5.3
Cut
Cut off, and for the Book of knowledg fair Par Lost 3.47
Descending, and in half cut sheere, nor staid, Par Lost 6.325
At Loopholes cut through thickest shade: Those Leaves Par Lost 9.1110
Cut shorter many a league; here thou behold'st Par Reg 3.269
If not by quick destruction soon cut off Samson 764
Thee he regards not, owns not, hath cut off Samson 1157
And cut *with Axes* down, Psalm 80, 66
Cut(*cont*)
Come let us cut them off say they, Psalm 83, 13
At Endor quite cut off, and rowl'd Psalm 83, 39
Thy threatnings cut me through. Psalm 88, 66
Cuts
That cuts us off from hope, and savours onely Par Lost 10.1043
Cuzco
And *Cusco* in *Peru*, the richer seat Par Lost 11.408
Cybele
Or the towred *Cybele*, Arcades 21
Cyclades
Or Pilot from amidst the *Cyclades* Par Lost 5.264
Cycle
Cycle and Epicycle, Orb in Orb: Par Lost 8.84
Cyllene
On old *Lycaeus* or *Cyllene* hoar, Arcades 98
Cymbals
In vain with Cymbals ring, Nativity 208
Cynic
And fetch their precepts from the *Cynick* Tub, Mask 708
Bridgewater ms 'Cinick'
Cynosure
Or *Tyrian* Cynosure. 2. *Bro*. Or if our eyes Mask 342
The Cynosure of neighbouring eyes. Allegro 80
Cynthia
While *Cynthia* checks her Dragon yoke, Penseroso 59
Of *Cynthia*'s seat, the Airy region thrilling, Nativity 103
Cypress
Immur'd in cypress shades a Sorcerer dwels Mask 521
Bridgewater ms 'Cipress'
1637 'cypresse'
Trinity ms 'cipresse'
And sable stole of *Cipres* Lawn, Penseroso 35
Ye might discern a Cipress bud. Winchester 22
1673 'Cypress'
Cyrene
Of *Barca* or *Cyrene*'s torrid soil, Par Lost 2.904
Cyriack
Cyriack, whose Grandsire on the Royal Bench Sonnet 21, 1
line not in Trinity ms
Cyriack, this three years day these eys, though clear Sonnet 22, 1
1694 *'Cyriac'*
Cyrus
Won *Asia* and the Throne of *Cyrus* held Par Reg 3.33
Till *Cyrus* set them free; *Persepolis* Par Reg 3.284
Cytherea
Perplex'd the *Greek* and *Cytherea*'s Son; Par Lost 9.19
Czar
In *Hispahan*, or where the *Russian Ksar* Par Lost 11.394
Daemons
And of those *Daemons* that are found Penseroso 93
Daffadillies
And Daffadillies fill their cups with tears, Lycidas 150
1638 'daffadillies'
Trinity ms 'daffadillies' ←'Daffadillies'
Daffodils
Of pancies, pinks, and gaudy Daffadils. Mask 851
Trinity ms 'daffadils'
Bridgewater ms 'daffadils'
1637 'daffadills'
And Daffadillies fill their cups with tears, Lycidas 150
Trinity ms 'daffadillies' ←'Daffadillies'
1638 'daffadillies'
Dagon
Dagon his Name, Sea Monster, upward Man Par Lost 1.462
ms 'Dagon'
To *Dagon* thir Sea-Idol, and forbid Samson 13
To *Dagon*, as their God who hath deliver'd Samson 437
So *Dagon* shall be magnifi'd, and God, Samson 440
To *Dagon*, and advanc'd his praises high Samson 450
'Twixt God and *Dagon; Dagon* hath presum'd, Samson 462
Dagon must stoop, and shall e're long receive Samson 468
Or *Dagon*. But for thee what shall be done? Samson 478
Dishonourer of *Dagon:* what had I Samson 861
For proof hereof, if *Dagon* be thy god, Samson 1145
Avow, and challenge *Dagon* to the test, Samson 1151
This day to *Dagon* is a solemn Feast, Samson 1311
Vaunting my strength in honour to thir *Dagon?* Samson 1360
But who constrains me to the Temple of *Dagon*, Samson 1370
That part most reverenc'd *Dagon* and his Priests, Samson 1463
Daily
And daily thanks, I chiefly who enjoy Par Lost 4.445
Man hath his daily work of body or mind Par Lost 4.618
That which before us lies in daily life, Par Lost 8.193
Those thousand decencies that daily flow Par Lost 8.601
By Angels numberless, thy daily Train. Par Lost 9.548
Of brutal kind, that daily are in sight? Par Lost 9.565
And from the daily Scene effeminate. Par Reg 4.142
Daily in the common Prison else enjoyn'd me, Samson 6
To daily fraud, contempt, abuse and wrong, Samson 76
Thir daily practice to afflict me more. Samson 114
Eye-sight exposes daily men abroad. Samson 919
With no small profit daily to my owners. Samson 1261
My daily walks and ancient neighbourhood, Mask 314
Bridgewater ms 'daylie'
Trinity ms 'dayly'
1637 'daylie'
Treads on it daily with his clouted shoon, Mask 635

Daily(*cont*)
line not in Bridgewater ms
1637 'dayly'
Trinity ms 'dayly'
Daily devours apace, and nothing sed, Lycidas 129
Trinity ms 'dayly'
Pitty me Lord for daily thee Psalm 86, 9
Daintiest
The daintest dishes shall be serv'd up last. Vacation 14
Dainty
And to those dainty limms which nature lent Mask 680
1637 'daintie'
line not in Bridgewater ms
Trinity ms 'daintie'
Dairy
Or Dairie, each rural sight, each rural sound; Par Lost 9.451
Daisies
The Wood-Nymphs deckt with Daisies trim, Mask 120
Trinity ms 'daysies'
1637 'daisies'
Bridgewater ms 'daisies'
Meadows trim with Daisies pide, Allegro 75
Dale
The flowry Dale of *Sibma* clad with Vines, Par Lost 1.410
ms 'dale'
With winged course ore Hill or moarie Dale, Par Lost 2.944
Powrd forth profuse on Hill and Dale and Plaine, Par Lost 4.243
Through wood, through waste, o're hill, o're dale his roam. Par Lost 4.538
Of pleasure situate in Hill and Dale) Par Lost 6.641
Hill, Dale, and shadie Woods, and sunnie Plaines, Par Lost 8.262
Well have we speeded, and o're hill and dale, Par Reg 3.267
And sweeten'd every muskrose of the dale, Mask 496
Trinity ms 'dale' ←'valley'
Under the Hawthorn in the dale. Allegro 68
From haunted spring, and dale Nativity 184
Hill and Dale, doth boast thy blessing. May Morn 8
As through a fruitfull watry Dale Psalm 84, 23
Dales
Ye Hills and Dales, ye Rivers, Woods, and Plaines, Par Lost 8.275
O Woods, O Fountains, Hillocks, Dales and Bowrs, Par Lost 10.860
Of *Caucasus*, and dark *Iberian* dales, Par Reg 3.318
Dalila
Was in the Vale of *Sorec*, *Dalila*, Samson 229
Then *Dalila* thy wife. Samson 724
The sumptuous *Dalila* floating this way: Samson 1072
Of *Philstean Dalilah*, and wak'd Par Lost 9.1061
Dalliance
Of dalliance had with thee in Heav'n, and joys Par Lost 2.819
Wanted, nor youthful dalliance as beseems Par Lost 4.338
Held dalliance with his faire *Egyptian* Spouse. Par Lost 9.443
Till *Adam* thus 'gan *Eve* to dalliance move, Par Lost 9.1016
Dally
Let our frail thoughts dally with false surmise. Lycidas 153
Dam
Slip't from the fold, or young Kid lost his dam, Mask 498
Trinity ms 'damme'
Damage
My damage fondly deem'd, I can repaire Par Lost 7.152
Damasco
Damasco, or *Marocco*, or *Trebisond*, Par Lost 1.584
ms 'Damasco'
Damascus
Was fair *Damascus*, on the fertil Banks Par Lost 1.468
ms 'Damascus'
Damasco, or *Marocco*, or *Trebisond*, Par Lost 1.584
ms 'Damasco'
Damasked
On the soft downie Bank damaskt with flours: Par Lost 4.334
Dame
Sovran of Creatures, universal Dame. Par Lost 9.612
Of mid-night Torches burns; mysterious Dame Mask 130
Bridgewater ms 'dame'
Dames
Count the night watches to his feathery Dames, Mask 347
Trinity ms 'dames'
Bridgewater ms 'dames'
Stoutly struts his Dames before, Allegro 52
Damiata
Betwixt *Damiata* and mount *Casius* old, Par Lost 2.593
Damietta
Betwixt *Damiata* and mount *Casius* old, Par Lost 2.593
Dammed
Or if your influence be quite damm'd up Mask 336
Trinity ms 'dam'd'
Damnation
Heap on himself damnation, while he sought Par Lost 1.215
Damned
His own: for neither do the Spirits damn'd Par Lost 2.482
O shame to men! Devil with Devil damn'd Par Lost 2.496
At certain revolutions all the damn'd Par Lost 2.597
To do what else though damnd I should abhorre. Par Lost 4.392
That Evil one, Satan for ever damn'd. Par Reg 4.194
Where that damn'd wisard hid in sly disguise Mask 571
1637 'dam'd'
But for that damn'd magician, let him be girt Mask 602
Can in his swadling bands controul the damned crew. Nativity 228
Damoetas
And old *Damoetas* lov'd to hear our song. Lycidas 36

Damoetas(*cont*)
1638 'Dametas'
1673 '*Damaetas*'
Damp
Down cast and damp, yet such wherein appear'd Par Lost 1.523
He pluckt, he tasted; mee damp horror chil'd Par Lost 5.65
Climat, or Years damp my intended wing Par Lost 9.45
Wide Anarchie of *Chaos* damp and dark Par Lost 10.283
Adam by this from the cold sudden damp Par Lost 11.293
A melancholly damp of cold and dry Par Lost 11.544
The air imprison'd also, close and damp, Samson 8
Such are those thick and gloomy shadows damp Mask 470
Trinity ms 'dampe'
Bridgewater ms 'dampe'
'Gainst all inchantments, mildew blast, or damp Mask 640
Trinity ms 'dampe'
Bridgewater ms 'dampe'
Damps
Accompanied, with damps and dreadful gloom, Par Lost 10.848
From dews and damps of night his shelter'd head, Par Reg 4.406
Damsel
Her harbinger, a damsel train behind; Samson 721
And put the Damsel to suspicious flight, Mask 158
Trinity ms 'damsel'
Bridgewater ms 'damsell'
She guiltless damsell flying the mad pursuit Mask 829
1673 'damsel'
Bridgewater ms 'dam'sell'
By boistrous rape th' Athenian damsel got, Fair Inf 9
Damsels
The *Syrian* Damsels to lament his fate Par Lost 1.448
ms 'damsells'
Of Fairy Damsels met in Forest wide Par Reg 2.359
Dan
Doubl'd that sin in *Bethel* and in *Dan*, Par Lost 1.485
ms 'Dan'
Of *Bethel* and of *Dan*? no, let them serve Par Reg 3.431
Man. Brethren and men of *Dan*, for such ye seem, Samson 332
In *Dan*, in *Judah*, and the bordering Tribes, Samson 976
In the camp of *Dan* Samson 1436
Danaw
Rhene or the *Danaw*, when her barbarous Sons Par Lost 1.353
ms 'Danaw'
Dance
Wheels her pale course, they on thir mirth and dance Par Lost 1.786
ms defective here
Lur'd with the smell of infant blood, to dance Par Lost 2.664
Thir Starry dance in numbers that compute Par Lost 3.580
Knit with the *Graces* and the *Hours* in dance Par Lost 4.267
Mixt Dance, or wanton Mask, or Midnight Bal, Par Lost 4.768
In mystic Dance not without Song, resound Par Lost 5.178
In song and dance about the sacred Hill, Par Lost 5.619
Mystical dance, which yonder starrie Spheare Par Lost 5.620
Forthwith from dance to sweet repast they turn Par Lost 5.630
As they would dance, yet for a dance they seemd Par Lost 6.615
Rose as in Dance the stately Trees, and spred Par Lost 7.324
Incited, dance about him various rounds? Par Lost 8.125
Noise, other then the sound of Dance or Song, Par Lost 8.243
Soft amorous Ditties, and in dance came on: Par Lost 11.584
Of lustful appetence, to sing, to dance, Par Lost 11.619
To luxurie and riot, feast and dance, Par Lost 11.715
Tipsie dance, and Jollity. Mask 104
Bridgewater ms 'daunce'
In wanton dance they praise the bounteous *Pan*, Mask 176
Bridgewater ms 'daunce'
By all the *Nymphs* that nightly dance Mask 883
Bridgewater ms 'daunce'
With Jiggs, and rural dance resort, Mask 952
Bridgewater ms 'daunce'
To triumph in victorious dance Mask 974
B.M. ms 'Dance'
Bridgewater ms 'Daunce'
Nymphs and Shepherds dance no more Arcades 96
In dismall dance about the furnace blue, Nativity 210
Both they who sing, and they who dance Psalm 87, 25
Danced
Danc'd hand in hand. A while discourse they hold; Par Lost 5.395
Dawn, and the *Pleiades* before him danc'd Par Lost 7.374
Terrestrial Heav'n, danc't round by other Heav'ns Par Lost 9.103
Rough *Satyrs* danc'd, and *Fauns* with clov'n heel, Lycidas 34
Trinity ms 'danc't'
The Faiery Ladies daunc't upon the hearth; Vacation 60
Dancers
Juglers and Dancers, Antics, Mummers, Mimics, Samson 1325
Dances
That flames, and dances in his crystal bounds Mask 673
Dancing
Thou couldst repress, nor did the dancing Rubie Samson 543
Dancing in the Chequer'd shade; Allegro 96
Comes dancing from the East, and leads with her May Morn 2
Dandled
Dandl'd the Kid; Bears, Tygers, Ounces, Pards, Par Lost 4.344
Danger
If counsels different, or danger shun'd Par Lost 1.636
Pondering the danger with deep thoughts; and each Par Lost 2.421
Of difficulty or danger could deterr Par Lost 2.449
So much the neerer danger; go and speed; Par Lost 2.1008
Which else might work him danger or delay: Par Lost 3.635

Danger(*cont*)
Through wayes of danger by himself untri'd, — Par Lost 4.934
His danger, and from whom, what enemie — Par Lost 5.239
O now in danger tri'd, now known in Armes — Par Lost 6.418
The Wife, where danger or dishonour lurks, — Par Lost 9.267
The danger lies, yet lies within his power: — Par Lost 9.349
Of danger tasted, nor to evil unknown — Par Lost 9.864
Going into such danger as thou saidst? — Par Lost 9.1157
The danger, and the lurking Enemie — Par Lost 9.1172
Either to meet no danger, or to finde — Par Lost 9.1176
Ye see our danger on the utmost edge — Par Reg 1.94
Fearless of danger, like a petty God — Samson 529
We unawares run into dangers mouth. — Samson 1522
(Not being in danger, as I trust she is not) — Mask 370
Danger will wink on Opportunity, — Mask 401
  Bridgewater ms 'dainger'

Dangerous
Desperate revenge, and Battel dangerous — Par Lost 2.107
With dangerous expedition to invade — Par Lost 2.342
Wild work in Heav'n, and dangerous to the maine. — Par Lost 6.698
Or trie thee now more dang'rous to his Throne. — Par Lost 10.382
As dangerous to the pillard frame of Heaven, — Par Reg 4.455

Dangers
Of hope in fears and dangers, heard so oft — Par Lost 1.275
Then unknown dangers and as hard escape. — Par Lost 2.444
In darkness, and with dangers compast round, — Par Lost 7.27
Brings dangers, troubles, cares, and sleepless nights — Par Reg 2.460
Of dangers, and adversities and pains, — Par Reg 4.479
Dangers, and snares, and wrongs, and worse then so, — Passion 11

Daniel
Or as a guest with *Daniel* at his pulse. — Par Reg 2.278
To Idols, those young *Daniel* could refuse; — Par Reg 2.329

Danite
Uncover'd more, so rose the *Danite* strong — Par Lost 9.1059

Dank
The Dank, and rising on stiff Pennons, towre — Par Lost 7.441
So saying, through each Thicket Danck or Drie, — Par Lost 9.179
Where grows the Willow and the Osier dank, — Mask 891
  Bridgewater ms 'danke'
  Trinity ms 'danck'
  1637 'dancke'
Now that the Fields are dank, and ways are mire, — Sonnet 20, 2
My dank and dropping weeds — Horace 15

Dante
Dante shall give Fame leave to set thee higher — Sonnet 13, 12
  Trinity ms 'Dante shall give Fame leave to' ←'Fame by the Tuscan's leav shall'
Then his *Casella*, whom he woo'd to sing, — Sonnet 13, 13
  Trinity ms 'he' ←'Dante'

Danube
Rhene or the *Danaw*, when her barbarous Sons — Par Lost 1.353
  ms 'Danaw'

Danubius
Beyond *Danubius* to the *Tauric* Pool. — Par Reg 4.79

Daphne
Of *Daphne* by *Orontes*, and th' inspir'd — Par Lost 4.273
Daphne, or *Semele*, *Antiopa*, — Par Reg 2.187
And you a statue; or as *Daphne* was — Mask 661

Dapper
Trip the pert Fairies and the dapper Elves; — Mask 118

Dappled
Till the dappled dawn doth rise; — Allegro 44

Dare
The Stairs were then let down, whether to dare — Par Lost 3.523
What thou and thy gay Legions dare against; — Par Lost 4.942
The Enemie, though bold, will hardly dare, — Par Lost 9.304
He never more henceforth will dare set foot — Par Reg 4.610
Will not dare mention, lest a question rise — Samson 1254
Will dare to soyl her Virgin purity, — Mask 427
Longer dare abide, — Nativity 225
Dare ye for this adjure the Civill Sword — Forcers 5

Dared
And peril great provok't, who thus hath dar'd — Par Lost 9.922
Now both abhor, since thou hast dar'd to utter — Par Reg 4.172

Dares
His lot who dares be singularly good. — Par Reg 3.57
Or have I said anough? To him that dares — Mask 780
  line not in Bridgewater ms
  line not in Trinity ms
Juno dare's not give her odds; — Arcades 23
  Trinity ms 'dares'

Darest
That dar'st, though grim and terrible, advance — Par Lost 2.682
Yet leudly dar'st our ministring upbraid. — Par Lost 6.182
And dar'st thou to the Son of God propound — Par Reg 4.178
And dar'st thou at our sending and command — Samson 1394

Darien
At *Darien*, thence to the Land where flowes — Par Lost 9.81

Daring
His daring foe, at this prevention more — Par Lost 6.129
Or daring, first on mee th' assault shall light. — Par Lost 9.305
With Foes for daring single to be just, — Par Lost 11.703
On hostile ground, none daring my affront. — Samson 531
None daring to appear Antagonist. — Samson 1628

Dark
And mad'st it pregnant: What in me is dark — Par Lost 1.22
  ms 'darke'
Left him at large to his own dark designs, — Par Lost 1.213

Dark(*cont*)
His eye survay'd the dark Idolatries — Par Lost 1.456
Accept this dark opprobrious Den of shame, — Par Lost 2.58
Thick clouds and dark doth Heav'ns all-ruling Sire — Par Lost 2.264
The dark unbottom'd infinite Abyss — Par Lost 2.405
Through all the Coasts of dark destruction seek — Par Lost 2.464
Thus they thir doubtful consultations dark — Par Lost 2.486
Lies dark and wilde, beat with perpetual storms — Par Lost 2.588
No rest: through many a dark and drearie Vaile — Par Lost 2.618
To joyn thir dark Encounter in mid air: — Par Lost 2.718
From out this dark and dismal house of pain, — Par Lost 2.823
The secrets of the hoarie deep, a dark — Par Lost 2.891
His dark materials to create more Worlds, — Par Lost 2.916
Born through the hollow dark assaults his eare — Par Lost 2.953
Of *Chaos*, and his dark Pavilion spread — Par Lost 2.960
Over the dark Abyss, whose boiling Gulf — Par Lost 2.1027
The rising world of waters dark and deep, — Par Lost 3.11
The dark descent, and up to reascend, — Par Lost 3.20
But cloud in stead, and ever-during dark — Par Lost 3.45
Invites; for I will cleer thir senses dark, — Par Lost 3.188
Dark with excessive bright thy skirts appeer, — Par Lost 3.380
Dark, waste, and wild, under the frown of Night — Par Lost 3.424
All this dark Globe the Fiend found as he pass'd, — Par Lost 3.498
Through dark and desart wayes with peril gone — Par Lost 3.544
Here in the dark so many precious things — Par Lost 3.611
And o're the dark her Silver Mantle threw. — Par Lost 4.609
In that dark durance: thus much what was askt. — Par Lost 4.899
Disperse it, as now light dispels the dark. — Par Lost 5.208
Nameless in dark oblivion let them dwell. — Par Lost 6.380
Far in the dark dislodg'd, and void of rest, — Par Lost 6.415
Deep under ground, materials dark and crude, — Par Lost 6.478
These in thir dark Nativitie the Deep — Par Lost 6.482
Her dark foundations, and too fast had bound. — Par Lost 6.870
Outrageous as a Sea, dark, wasteful, wilde, — Par Lost 7.212
Shee disappeerd, and left me dark, I wak'd — Par Lost 8.478
To enter, and his dark suggestions hide — Par Lost 9.90
To hide me, and the dark intent I bring. — Par Lost 9.162
Wide Anarchie of *Chaos* damp and dark — Par Lost 10.283
With this portentous Bridge the dark Abyss. — Par Lost 10.371
Many a dark League, reduc't in careful Watch — Par Lost 10.438
Rais'd from thir Dark *Divan*, and with like joy — Par Lost 10.457
  1667 'dark'
Then stil at Hels dark threshold to have sate watch, — Par Lost 10.594
With terror through the dark Aereal Hall. — Par Lost 10.667
Before his eyes appeard, sad, noysom, dark, — Par Lost 11.478
Like a dark Ceeling stood; down rush'd the Rain — Par Lost 11.743
In a dark Age, against example good, — Par Lost 11.809
Within thick Clouds and dark ten-fold involv'd, — Par Reg 1.41
And with dark shades and rocks environ'd round, — Par Reg 1.194
But what have been thy answers, what but dark — Par Reg 1.434
Of *Caucasus*, and dark *Iberian* dales, — Par Reg 3.318
Or to the Earths dark basis underneath, — Par Reg 4.456
To these dark steps, a little further on; — Samson 2
They creep, yet see, I dark in light expos'd — Samson 75
O dark, dark, dark, amid the blaze of noon, — Samson 80
Irrecoverably dark, total Eclipse — Samson 81
The Sun to me is dark — Samson 86
Inseparably dark? — Samson 154
That these dark orbs no more shall treat with light, — Samson 591
Dark vaild *Cotytto*, t' whom the secret flame — Mask 129
  Trinity ms 'Dark-vaild'
  1637 'Dark-vaild'
  Bridgewater ms 'Darke-vayld'
In thy dark lantern thus close up the Stars, — Mask 197
  1637 'darke'
  Trinity ms 'darke'
  line not in Bridgewater ms
But he that hides a dark soul, and foul thoughts — Mask 383
  Trinity ms 'darke'
  Bridgewater ms 'darke'
  1637 'darke'
How couldst thou find this dark sequester'd nook? — Mask 500
  Bridgewater ms 'darke'
  Trinity ms 'darke'
  1637 'darke'
I could be willing though now i' th darke to trie — Mask Tr. ms 16.38
O my simplicity what sights are these? with darke disguises — Mask Tr. ms 22.19
I could be willinge though now i' th darke to trie — Mask Br. ms 391
In dark *Cimmerian* desert ever dwell. — Allegro 10
Built in th' eclipse, and rigg'd with curses dark, — Lycidas 101
And cast the dark foundations deep, — Nativity 123
In vain with Timbrel'd Anthems dark — Nativity 219
Or that thy coarse corrupts in earths dark wombe, — Fair Inf 30
And in times long and dark Prospective Glass — Vacation 71
Soon swallow'd up in dark and long out-living night. — Passion 7
My sorrows are too dark for day to know: — Passion 33
when as they journey'd from this dark abode — Sonnet 14, Tr. ms 41.07
E're half my days, in this dark world and wide, — Sonnet 19, 2
Through grief consumes, is waxen old and dark — Psalm 6, 14
Of *dark* oblivion? — Psalm 88, 52

Darked
Th' earth cumber'd, and the wing'd air dark't with plumes, — Mask 730
  Bridgewater ms 'dark'd'

Darken
To darken all the Hill, and smoak to rowl — Par Lost 6.57

Darkened
Like Night, and darken'd all the Land of *Nile:* — Par Lost 1.343
  ms 'dark'n'd'

Darkened(*cont*)
Perplexes Monarchs. Dark'n'd so, yet shon — Par Lost 1.599
Scowls ore the dark'nd lantskip Snow, or showre; — Par Lost 2.491
How dark'nd; innocence, that as a veile — Par Lost 9.1054
Darkens
Darkens the Streets, then wander forth the Sons — Par Lost 1.501
Darker
Grew darker at thir frown, so matcht they stood; — Par Lost 2.720
In darker veile) and roseat Dews dispos'd — Par Lost 5.646
Darkest
All in a robe of darkest grain, — Penseroso 33
Darkish
The leaf was darkish, and had prickles on it, — Mask 631
Darkling
Sings darkling, and in shadiest Covert hid — Par Lost 3.39
Darkness
No light, but rather darkness visible — Par Lost 1.63
ms 'darknes'
In utter darkness, and thir portion set — Par Lost 1.72
ms 'darknes'
And with thir darkness durst affront his light. — Par Lost 1.391
ms 'darknesse'
Long under darkness cover. But these thoughts — Par Lost 1.659
This horror will grow milde, this darkness light, — Par Lost 2.220
Of darkness do we dread? How oft amidst — Par Lost 2.263
And with the Majesty of darkness round — Par Lost 2.266
As he our darkness, cannot we his Light — Par Lost 2.269
1667 'Darkness'
Attempting, or to sit in darkness here — Par Lost 2.377
In darkness, while thy head flames thick and fast — Par Lost 2.754
Which way the neerest coast of darkness lyes — Par Lost 2.958
To her original darkness and your sway — Par Lost 2.984
Through utter and through middle darkness borne — Par Lost 3.16
The powers of darkness bound. Thou at the sight — Par Lost 3.256
From *Chaos* and th' inroad of Darkness old, — Par Lost 3.421
To darkness, such as bound the Ocean wave. — Par Lost 3.539
Till at his second bidding darkness fled, — Par Lost 3.712
Least total darkness should by Night regaine — Par Lost 4.665
His praise, who out of Darkness call'd up Light. — Par Lost 5.179
Into utter darkness, deep ingulft, his place — Par Lost 5.614
Where light and darkness in perpetual round — Par Lost 6.6
Obsequious darkness enters, till her houre — Par Lost 6.10
To veile the Heav'n, though darkness there might well — Par Lost 6.11
Thy Legions under darkness; but thou seest — Par Lost 6.142
Inducing darkness, grateful truce impos'd, — Par Lost 6.407
Pursue these sons of Darkness, drive them out — Par Lost 6.715
To chains of darkness, and th' undying Worm, — Par Lost 6.739
1667 'Darkness'
In darkness, and with dangers compast round, — Par Lost 7.27
Matter unform'd and void: Darkness profound — Par Lost 7.233
And light from darkness by the Hemisphere — Par Lost 7.250
Divided: Light the Day, and Darkness Night — Par Lost 7.251
Exhaling first from Darkness they beheld; — Par Lost 7.255
And Light from Darkness to divide. God saw, — Par Lost 7.352
With darkness, thrice the Equinoctial Line — Par Lost 9.64
Whom thus the Prince of Darkness answerd glad. — Par Lost 10.383
Descend through Darkness, on your Rode with ease — Par Lost 10.394
From darkness to promote me, or here place — Par Lost 10.745
Darkness ere Dayes mid-course, and Morning light — Par Lost 11.204
Darkness must overshadow all his bounds, — Par Lost 12.187
Palpable darkness, and blot out three dayes; — Par Lost 12.188
Darkness defends between till morning Watch; — Par Lost 12.207
Enlightner of my darkness, gracious things — Par Lost 12.271
Light out of darkness! full of doubt I stand, — Par Lost 12.473
Feigning to disappear. Darkness now rose, — Par Reg 4.397
The Prince of darkness, glad would also seem — Par Reg 4.441
As in the land of darkness yet in light, — Samson 99
In real darkness of the body dwells, — Samson 159
But yield to double darkness nigh at hand: — Samson 593
Of Stygian darknes spets her thickest gloom, — Mask 132
Trinity ms 'darknesse'
1637 'darknesse'
1673 'darkness'
Bridgewater ms 'Darknes'
And envious darknes, e're they could return, — Mask 194
1637 'darknesse'
Trinity ms 'and envious darknesse' ←'to the soone parting light'
Bridgewater ms 'darknesse'
Yet nought but single darknes do I find. — Mask 204
Trinity ms 'darknesse'
line not in Bridgewater ms
1637 'darknesse'
Of darknes till it smil'd: I have oft heard — Mask 252
Trinity ms 'darknesse'
1637 'darknesse'
Bridgewater ms 'darkness'
La. Dim darknes, and this leavy Labyrinth. — Mask 278
Bridgewater ms 'darknesse'
1637 'darknesse'
Trinity ms 'darknesse'
In double night of darknes, and of shades; — Mask 335
1673 'darkness'
Bridgewater ms 'darkness'
Trinity ms 'darknesse'
1637 'darknesse'
& darknesse wound her in. I Bro. Peace, brother peace — Mask Tr. ms 15.53
Wher brooding darknes spreads his jealous wings, — Allegro 6

Darkness(*cont*)
1673 'darkness'
Scatters the rear of darknes thin, — Allegro 50
To house with darknes, and with death. — Winchester 10
1673 'darkness'
In darkness they walk on — Psalm 82, 18
From deepest darkness foul. — Psalm 86, 48
Where thickest darkness *hovers round*, — Psalm 88, 27
In darkness can thy mighty *hand* — Psalm 88, 49
And as in darkness are. — Psalm 88, 72
Darksome
Wandring this darksome Desart, as my way, — Par Lost 2.973
Which from his darksom passage now appeers, — Par Lost 4.232
Satan from Hell scap't through the darksom Gulf — Par Lost 5.225
A darksom Cloud of Locusts swarming down — Par Lost 12.185
And chose with us a darksom House of mortal Clay. — Nativity 14
Darling
In his disturbance; when his darling Sons — Par Lost 2.373
Thy daughter and thy darling, without end. — Par Lost 2.870
Dart
And shook a dreadful Dart; what seem'd his head — Par Lost 2.672
Thy lingring, or with one stroke of this Dart — Par Lost 2.702
Possesses thee to bend that mortal Dart — Par Lost 2.729
Forth issu'd, brandishing his fatal Dart — Par Lost 2.786
Death ready stands to interpose his dart, — Par Lost 2.854
And over them triumphant Death his Dart — Par Lost 11.491
With Dart and Jav'lin, Stones and sulfurous Fire; — Par Lost 11.658
Darted
Of *Eve*, whose Eye darted contagious Fire. — Par Lost 9.1036
Darting
Love-darting eyes, or tresses like the Morn? — Mask 753
line not in Bridgewater ms
Trinity ms 'love-darting'
Darts
Darts his experienc't eye, and soon traverse — Par Lost 1.568
Of fiery Darts in flaming volies flew, — Par Lost 6.213
And from about her shot Darts of desire — Par Lost 8.62
Satans assaults, and quench his fierie darts, — Par Lost 12.492
Bestuck with slandrous darts, and works of Faith — Par Lost 12.536
Quite at a loss, for all his darts were spent, — Par Reg 4.366
Some bent at thee thir fiery darts, while thou — Par Reg 4.424
Darwen
While Darwen stream with blood of Scotts imbru'd, — Sonnet 16, 7
1694 '*Darwent*'
Dash
The better reason, to perplex and dash — Par Lost 2.114
Such implements of mischief as shall dash — Par Lost 6.488
To dash thir pride, and joy for Man seduc't. — Par Lost 10.577
Or as a stone that shall to pieces dash — Par Reg 4.149
Thou chance to dash thy foot against a stone. — Par Reg 4.559
Or swing thee in the Air, then dash thee down — Samson 1240
Dashed
Though all to shivers dash't, the assault renew, — Par Reg 4.19
And noble grace that dash't brute violence — Mask 451
Trinity ms 'dasht'
Bridgewater ms 'dasht'
Mine enemies shall all be blank and dash't — Psalm 6, 21
Date
New Heav'ns, new Earth, Ages of endless date — Par Lost 12.549
Without beginning; for no date prefixt — Par Reg 4.392
What need a man forestall his date of grief, — Mask 362
line not in Trinity ms
line not in Bridgewater ms
beyond the written date of mortall change — Mask Tr. ms 10.22
Obedient to the Moon he spent his date — Another 29
line not in 1658 text
Daughter
Dear Daughter, since thou claim'st me for thy Sire, — Par Lost 2.817
Thy daughter and thy darling, without end. — Par Lost 2.870
Daughter of God and Man, accomplisht *Eve*, — Par Lost 4.660
Daughter of God and Man, immortal *Eve*, — Par Lost 9.291
Sole Daughter of his voice; the rest, we live — Par Lost 9.653
Inchanting Daughter, thus the silence broke. — Par Lost 10.353
Fair Daughter, and thou Son and Grandchild both, — Par Lost 10.384
Daughter of Sin, among th' irrational, — Par Lost 10.708
His daughter, sought by many Prowest Knights, — Par Reg 3.342
The daughter of an Infidel: they knew not — Samson 221
The daughter of the Sun? Whose charmed Cup — Mask 51
Trinity ms 'Daughter'
Sweet Queen of Parly, Daughter of the Sphear, — Mask 241
Trinity ms 'daughter'
Bridgewater ms 'daughter'
Whilom she was the daughter of *Locrine*, — Mask 827
Spir. Virgin, daughter of *Locrine* — Mask 922
Fill'd her with thee a daughter fair, — Allegro 23
His daughter she (in *Saturns* raign, — Penseroso 25
A Vicounts daughter, an Earls heir, — Winchester 3
Daughter to that good Earl, once President — Sonnet 10, 1
Daughters
Infected *Sions* daughters with like heat, — Par Lost 1.453
Hither of ill-joynd Sons and Daughters born — Par Lost 3.463
His Sons, the fairest of her Daughters *Eve*. — Par Lost 4.324
The bended Twigs take root, and Daughters grow — Par Lost 9.1105
Among daughters of men the fairest found; — Par Reg 2.154
Cast wanton eyes on the daughters of men, — Par Reg 2.180
I before all the daughters of my Tribe — Samson 876
Sam. Among the Daughters of the *Philistines* — Samson 1192
And gave her to his daughters to imbathe — Mask 837

Daughters(*cont*)
Of *Hesperus*, and his daughters three Mask 982
Trinity ms 'daughters' ←'neeces' ←'daughters'
To lull the daughters of *Necessity*, Arcades 69
Daunt
Was never heard the Nymphs to daunt, Penseroso 137
And rumors loud, that daunt remotest kings, Sonnet 15, 4
Dauntless
Of dauntless courage, and considerate Pride Par Lost 1.603
Rather your dauntless vertue, whom the pain Par Lost 9.694
Where if he be, with dauntless hardihood, Mask 650
1637 'dauntlesse'
Trinity ms 'dauntless hardyhood' ←'suddaine violence'
Bridgewater ms 'dauntlesse'
David
Of *David* (so I name this King) shall rise Par Lost 12.326
To *David*, stablisht as the dayes of Heav'n. Par Lost 12.347
The Scepter, and regard not *Davids* Sons, Par Lost 12.357
Thou shouldst be great and sit on *David*'s Throne, Par Reg 1.240
To sit upon thy Father *David*'s Throne; Par Reg 3.153
Though Priests, the Crown, and *David*'s Throne usurp'd, Par Reg 3.169
Judah and all thy Father *David*'s house Par Reg 3.282
Endeavour, as thy Father *David* did, Par Reg 3.353
But say thou wer't possess'd of *David*'s Throne Par Reg 3.357
In *David*'s royal seat, his true Successour, Par Reg 3.373
Thou on the Throne of *David* in full glory, Par Reg 3.383
David's true heir, and his full Scepter sway Par Reg 3.405
For *Israel*, or for *David*, or his Throne, Par Reg 3.408
On *David*'s Throne, be propheci'd what will. Par Reg 4.108
On *David*'s Throne, it shall be like a tree Par Reg 4.147
On *David*'s Throne; or Throne of all the world, Par Reg 4.379
Of gaining *David*'s Throne no man knows when, Par Reg 4.471
Then hear, O Son of *David*, Virgin-born; Par Reg 4.500
Dawn
A glimmering dawn; here Nature first begins Par Lost 2.1037
To find thy piercing ray, and find no dawn; Par Lost 3.24
All night; at last by break of chearful dawne Par Lost 3.545
If better thou belong not to the dawn, Par Lost 5.167
Nor long shall be our labour, yet ere dawne, Par Lost 6.492
Dawn, and the *Pleiades* before him danc'd Par Lost 7.374
Now when as sacred Light began to dawne Par Lost 9.192
For now, and since first break of dawne the Fiend, Par Lost 9.412
Till the dappled dawn doth rise; Allegro 44
Or ere the point of dawn, Nativity 86
Dawning
Of dawning light turnd thither-ward in haste Par Lost 3.500
Thou tellst, by morrow dawning I shall know. Par Lost 4.588
Soon banded; others from the dawning Hills Par Lost 6.528
Dawning through Heav'n: forth rush'd with whirlwind sound Par Lost 6.749
Shall long usurp; ere the third dawning light Par Lost 12.421
Out of his grave, fresh as the dawning light, Par Lost 12.423
Day
Nine times the Space that measures Day and Night Par Lost 1.50
ms 'day'
Of *Amrams* Son in *Egypts* evill day Par Lost 1.339
In amorous dittyes all a Summers day, Par Lost 1.449
A Summers day; and with the setting Sun Par Lost 1.744
One day upon our heads; while we perhaps Par Lost 2.178
That day and night for his destruction waite. Par Lost 2.505
His wrath which one day will destroy ye both. Par Lost 2.734
Day, or the sweet approach of Ev'n or Morn, Par Lost 3.42
This my long sufferance and my day of grace Par Lost 3.198
Th' aspiring Dominations: thou that day Par Lost 3.392
His day, which else as th' other Hemisphere Par Lost 3.725
A whole days journy high, but wide remote Par Lost 4.284
1667 'dayes'
That day I oft remember, when from sleep Par Lost 4.449
This day at highth of Noon came to my Spheare Par Lost 4.564
Labour and rest, as day and night to men Par Lost 4.613
Our eye-lids; other Creatures all day long Par Lost 4.616
Both day and night: how often from the steep Par Lost 4.680
What day the genial Angel to our Sire Par Lost 4.712
Maker Omnipotent, and thou the Day, Par Lost 4.725
Works of day pass't, or morrows next designe, Par Lost 5.33
Much fairer to my Fancie then by day: Par Lost 5.53
And choral symphonies, Day without Night, Par Lost 5.162
Sure pledge of day, that crownst the smiling Morn Par Lost 5.168
While day arises, that sweet hour of Prime. Par Lost 5.170
Go therefore, half this day as friend with friend Par Lost 5.229
This day to be our Guest. But goe with speed, Par Lost 5.313
And we have yet large day, for scarce the Sun Par Lost 5.558
Upon her Center pois'd, when on a day Par Lost 5.579
By present, past, and future) on such day Par Lost 5.582
This day I have begot whom I declare Par Lost 5.603
Mee disobeyes, breaks union, and that day Par Lost 5.612
That day, as other solemn dayes, they spent Par Lost 5.618
With envie against the Son of God, that day Par Lost 5.662
Grateful vicissitude, like Day and Night; Par Lost 6.8
That self same day by fight, or by surprize Par Lost 6.87
As both thir deeds compar'd this day shall prove. Par Lost 6.170
The Battel hung; till *Satan*, who that day Par Lost 6.246
Who have sustaind one day in doubtful fight Par Lost 6.423
(And if one day, why not Eternal dayes2) Par Lost 6.424
So all ere day-spring, under conscious Night Par Lost 6.521
1667 'day spring' in some copies
This day, fear not his flight; so thick a Cloud Par Lost 6.539
Born eevn or high, for this day will pour down, Par Lost 6.544
Ye Angels arm'd, this day from Battel rest; Par Lost 6.802

Day(*cont*)
Number to this dayes work is not ordain'd Par Lost 6.809
And the great Light of Day yet wants to run Par Lost 7.98
Against a solemn day, harnest at hand, Par Lost 7.202
Divided: Light the Day, and Darkness Night Par Lost 7.251
He nam'd. Thus was the first Day Eev'n and Morn: Par Lost 7.252
Birth-day of Heav'n and Earth; with joy and shout Par Lost 7.256
And Morning *Chorus* sung the second Day. Par Lost 7.275
So Eev'n and Morn recorded the Third Day. Par Lost 7.338
The Day from Night; and let them be for Signes, Par Lost 7.341
To Man, the greater to have rule by Day, Par Lost 7.347
To illuminate the Earth, and rule the Day Par Lost 7.350
Regent of Day, and all th' Horizon round Par Lost 7.371
Glad Eevning and glad Morn crownd the fourth day. Par Lost 7.386
Ev'ning and Morn solemniz'd the Fift day. Par Lost 7.448
Frequent; and of the Sixt day yet remain'd; Par Lost 7.504
Thou mai'st not; in the day thou eat'st, thou di'st; Par Lost 7.544
So Ev'n and Morn accomplish'd the Sixt day: Par Lost 7.550
Now resting, bless'd and hallowd the Seav'nth day, Par Lost 7.592
As resting on that day from all his work, Par Lost 7.593
Then from the Giant Angels; thee that day Par Lost 7.605
One day and night; in all thir vast survey Par Lost 8.24
Such restless revolution day by day Par Lost 8.31
Where God resides, and ere mid-day arriv'd Par Lost 8.112
Of Day and Night; which needs not thy beleefe, Par Lost 8.136
If Earth industrious of her self fetch Day Par Lost 8.137
Enlightning her by Day, as she by Night Par Lost 8.143
And Day is yet not spent; till then thou seest Par Lost 8.206
For I that Day was absent, as befell, Par Lost 8.229
The day thou eat'st thereof, my sole command Par Lost 8.329
From that day mortal, and this happie State Par Lost 8.331
Twixt Day and Night, and now from end to end Par Lost 9.51
From compassing the Earth, cautious of day, Par Lost 9.59
The infernal Powers, in one day to have marr'd Par Lost 9.136
Then commune how that day they best may ply Par Lost 9.201
Luxurious by restraint; what we by day Par Lost 9.209
For while so near each other thus all day Par Lost 9.220
Our dayes work brought to little, though begun Par Lost 9.224
To Beasts, whom God on thir Creation-Day Par Lost 9.556
Till on a day roaving the field, I chanc'd Par Lost 9.575
His worshippers; he knows that in the day Par Lost 9.705
Our inward freedom? In the day we eate Par Lost 9.762
This day affords, declaring thee resolvd, Par Lost 9.968
Yeild thee, so well this day thou hast purvey'd. Par Lost 9.1021
For never did thy Beautie since the day Par Lost 9.1029
But such as at this day to *Indians* known Par Lost 9.1102
On his transgression, Death denounc't that day, Par Lost 10.49
Forbearance no acquittance ere day end. Par Lost 10.53
Brought to thir Ears, while day declin'd, they heard, Par Lost 10.99
O Heav'n! in evil strait this day I stand Par Lost 10.125
And th' instant stroke of Death denounc't that day Par Lost 10.210
Against the day of Battel, to a Field, Par Lost 10.275
For death, the following day, in bloodie fight. Par Lost 10.278
Beyond the Polar Circles; to them Day Par Lost 10.681
Fixd on this day? why do I overlive, Par Lost 10.773
From this day onward, which I feel begun Par Lost 10.811
The day of his offence. Why comes not Death, Par Lost 10.854
Since this days Death denounc't, if ought I see, Par Lost 10.962
A long days dying to augment our paine, Par Lost 10.964
Was meant by Death that day, when lo, to thee Par Lost 10.1050
Wherere our days work lies, though now enjoind Par Lost 11.177
Laborious, till day droop; while here we dwell, Par Lost 11.178
Darkness ere Dayes mid-course, and Morning light Par Lost 11.204
And carnal fear that day dimm'd *Adams* eye. Par Lost 11.212
Quiet though sad, the respit of that day Par Lost 11.272
Which I must keep till my appointed day Par Lost 11.550
My part of evil onely, each dayes lot Par Lost 11.765
Raine day and night, all fountains of the Deep Par Lost 11.826
And call to mind his Cov'nant: Day and Night, Par Lost 11.898
By day a Cloud, by night a Pillar of Fire, Par Lost 12.203
One greater, of whose day he shall foretell, Par Lost 12.242
Shall rest by Day, a fiery gleame by Night, Par Lost 12.257
A day entire, and Nights due course adjourne, Par Lost 12.264
His day, in whom all Nations shall be blest, Par Lost 12.277
All Nations they shall teach; for from that day Par Lost 12.446
Under her own waight groaning till the day Par Lost 12.539
Gabriel this day by proof thou shalt behold, Par Reg 1.130
One day forth walk'd alone, the Spirit leading; Par Reg 1.189
Against a Winters day when winds blow keen, Par Reg 1.317
As morning shews the day. Be famous then Par Reg 4.221
Privation meer of light and absent day. Par Reg 4.400
This day a solemn Feast the people hold Samson 12
Without all hope of day! Samson 82
In *Ramath-lechi* famous to this day: Samson 145
No journey of a Sabbath day, and loaded so; Samson 149
Had *Judah* that day join'd, or one whole Tribe, Samson 265
Tongue-batteries, she surceas'd not day nor night Samson 404
This day the *Philistines* a popular Feast Samson 434
Of fancy, feard lest one day thou wouldst leave me Samson 794
Here I should still enjoy thee day and night Samson 807
Much like thy riddle, *Samson*, in one day Samson 1016
Th' unworthier they; whence to this day they serve. Samson 1216
This Idols day hath bin to thee no day of rest, Samson 1297
More then the working day thy hands, Samson 1299
This day to *Dagon* is a solemn Feast, Samson 1311
What windy joy this day had I conceiv'd Samson 1574
When all abroad was rumour'd that this day Samson 1600
And the gilded Car of Day, Mask 95

Day(*cont*)
Trinity ms 'day'
Bridgewater ms 'daye'
May sit i' th center, and enjoy bright day, Mask 382
Bridgewater ms 'daye'
Benighted walks under the mid-day Sun; Mask 384
Trinity ms 'benighted walks under the midday sun' ←'walks in black vapours though the noontyde brand'
Bridgewater ms 'walks in black vapours though the noone tyde brand'
Through paths, and turnings oft'n trod by day, Mask 569
Bridgewater ms 'daye'
That have been tir'd all day without repast, Mask 688
Bridgewater ms 'aldaye'
Would grow inur'd to light, and com at last Mask 735
Trinity ms 'light' ←'day'
Till next Sun-shine holiday, Mask 959
Trinity ms 'Holyday'
Bridgewater ms 'holy daye'
Where day never shuts his eye, Mask 978
Bridgewater ms 'daye'
Hide me from Day's garish eie, Penseroso 141
Forsook the Courts of everlasting Day, Nativity 13
Had given day her room, Nativity 78
And leave her dolorous mansions to the peering day. Nativity 140
But now begins; for from this happy day Nativity 167
All the day long his cours to run. Psalm 136, 30
My sorrows are too dark for day to know: Passion 33
This day, but O ere long Circum 26
where day dwells without night Musick Tr. ms 4.29
Now the bright morning Star, Dayes harbinger, May Morn 1
Thy liquid notes that close the eye of Day, Sonnet 1, 5
Doth God exact day labour, light deny'd, Sonnet 19, 7
Help wast a sullen day; what may be won Sonnet 20, 4
To day deep thoughts resolve with me to drench Sonnet 21, 5
That with superfluous burden loads the day, Sonnet 21, 13
Cyriack, this three years day these eys, though clear Sonnet 22, 1
Nor to thir idle orbs doth sight appear Sonnet 22, 4
1694 'doth day'
I wak'd, she fled, and day brought back my night. Sonnet 23, 14
And in his Law he studies day and night. Psalm 1, 6
This day; ask of me, and the grant is made; Psalm 2, 16
And God is every day offended; Psalm 7, 44
Th' appointed time, the day wheron Psalm 81, 11
For one day in thy Courts *to be* Psalm 84, 33
I in the day of my distress Psalm 86, 21
All day to thee I cry; Psalm 88, 2
Lord all the day I thee entreat, Psalm 88, 39
All day they round about me go, Psalm 88, 67

Day-labour
To respit his day-labour with repast, Par Lost 5.232

Day-labourers
That ten day-labourers could not end, Allegro 109

Daylight
As day-light sunk, and brought in lowring night Par Reg 4.398
Tis onely day-light that makes Sin Mask 126
Trinity ms 'daylight'
Bridgewater ms 'day light'
Till the live-long day-light fail, Allegro 99

Days
Of future dayes may bring, what chance, what change Par Lost 2.222
1667 'days'
To waste Eternal dayes in woe and pain? Par Lost 2.695
1667 'daies'
1674 'daies' in some copies
See golden days, fruitful of golden deeds, Par Lost 3.337
Days, months, & years, towards his all-chearing Lamp Par Lost 3.581
That day, as other solemn dayes, they spent Par Lost 5.618
(And if one day, why not Eternal dayes2) Par Lost 6.424
In future dayes, if Malice should abound, Par Lost 6.502
Second Omnipotence, two dayes are past, Par Lost 6.684
Two dayes, as we compute the dayes of Heav'n, Par Lost 6.685
Two dayes are therefore past, the third is thine; Par Lost 6.699
Nine dayes they fell; confounded *Chaos* roard, Par Lost 6.871
To hoarce or mute, though fall'n on evil dayes, Par Lost 7.25
1669 'tongues'
On evil dayes though fall'n, and evil tongues; Par Lost 7.26
For Seasons, and for Dayes, and circling Years, Par Lost 7.342
Magnificent, his Six days work, a World; Par Lost 7.568
Creation and the Six dayes acts they sung, Par Lost 7.601
His Seasons, Hours, or Dayes, or Months, or Yeares: Par Lost 8.69
1667 'Days'
What he *Almightie* styl'd, six Nights and Days Par Lost 9.137
And dust shalt eat all the dayes of thy Life. Par Lost 10.178
1667 'days'
Shalt eate thereof all the days of thy Life; Par Lost 10.202
This annual humbling certain number'd days, Par Lost 10.576
Equal in Days and Nights, except to those Par Lost 10.680
By death brought on our selves, or childless days Par Lost 10.1037
Before thee reconcil'd, at least his days Par Lost 11.39
To *Adam* what shall come in future dayes, Par Lost 11.114
Some days; how long, and what till then our life, Par Lost 11.198
Defeated of his seisure many dayes Par Lost 11.254
To shew thee what shall come in future dayes Par Lost 11.357
Of peaceful dayes portends, then those two past; Par Lost 11.600
For in those dayes Might onely shall be admir'd, Par Lost 11.689
With length of happy dayes the race of man; Par Lost 11.782
1667 'days'

Days(*cont*)
Shal spend thir dayes in joy unblam'd, and dwell Par Lost 12.22
Palpable darkness, and blot out three dayes; Par Lost 12.188
To *David*, stablisht as the dayes of Heav'n. Par Lost 12.347
Then this of *Eden*, and far happier daies. Par Lost 12.465
That ye may live, which will be many dayes, Par Lost 12.602
Mean while the Son of God, who yet some days Par Reg 1.183
Full forty days he pass'd, whether on hill Par Reg 1.303
Till those days ended, hunger'd then at last Par Reg 1.309
Moses was forty days, nor eat nor drank, Par Reg 1.352
And forty days *Eliah* without food Par Reg 1.353
Began to doubt, and doubted many days, Par Reg 2.11
And as the days increas'd, increas'd thir doubt: Par Reg 2.12
After forty days fasting had remain'd, Par Reg 2.243
Where will this end? four times ten days I have pass'd Par Reg 2.245
The strength whereof suffic'd him forty days; Par Reg 2.276
Of thee these forty days none hath regard, Par Reg 2.315
And once a year *Jerusalem*, few days Par Reg 3.234
Several days journey, built by *Ninus* old, Par Reg 3.276
By three days Pestilence? such was thy zeal Par Reg 3.412
I would be understood) in prosperous days Samson 191
The punishment of dissolute days, in fine, Samson 702
Are drawn to wear out miserable days, Samson 762
Sam. Fair days have oft contracted wind and rain. Samson 1062
Sam. Be less abstruse, my riddling days are past. Samson 1064
By some great act, or of my days the last. Samson 1389
No less the people on thir Holy-days Samson 1421
The Virgins also shall on feastful days Samson 1741
To scorn delights, and live laborious dayes; Lycidas 72
Trinity ms 'days'
Fore-saw what future dayes should bring to pass, Vacation 72
Yet had the number of her days Winchester 11
My hasting dayes flie on with full career, Sonnet 7, 3
Trinity ms 'days'
Though later born, then to have known the dayes Sonnet 10, 9
Trinity ms 'daies'
E're half my days, in this dark world and wide, Sonnet 19, 2
Wearied I am with sighing out my dayes, Psalm 6, 11
To serve me *all their daies*, Psalm 81, 54
A thousand daies *at best*. Psalm 84, 36

Day-spring
Of day-spring, and the Sun, who scarce up risen Par Lost 5.139
So all ere day-spring, under conscious Night Par Lost 6.521
1667 'day spring' in some copies
With day-spring born; here leave me to respire. Samson 11

Day-star
So sinks the day-star in the Ocean bed, Lycidas 168
1638 'day-starre'
Trinity ms 'day starre'

Dazzle
Yet dazle Heav'n, that brightest Seraphim Par Lost 3.381
Will dazle now this earthly, with thir blaze Par Lost 9.1083

Dazzled
Dazl'd and spent, sunk down, and sought repair Par Lost 8.457

Dazzles
Dazles the croud, and sets them all agape. Par Lost 5.357

Dazzling
Of dreadful length and dazling Arms, in guise Par Lost 1.564
Daz'ling the Moon; these to the Bower direct Par Lost 4.798
My dazling Spells into the spungy ayr, Mask 154
Trinity ms 'dazling' ←'powder'd'
Bridgewater ms 'dazlinge'
That hath so well been taught her dazling fence, Mask 791
line not in Trinity ms
line not in Bridgewater ms

Dead
Can never seek, once dead in sins and lost; Par Lost 3.233
The living, and forthwith the cited dead Par Lost 3.327
In *Golgotha* him dead, who lives in Heav'n; Par Lost 3.477
Not dead, as we are threatn'd, but thenceforth Par Lost 9.870
Of *Egypt* must lie dead. Thus with ten wounds Par Lost 12.190
With glory and power to judge both quick and dead, Par Lost 12.460
To judge th' unfaithful dead, but to reward Par Lost 12.461
Were dead, who sought his life, and missing fill'd Par Reg 2.77
Scarce half I seem to live, dead more then half. Samson 79
To live a life half dead, a living death, Samson 100
The Jaw of a dead Ass, his sword of bone, Samson 143
Living and dead recorded, who to save Samson 984
Mess. Then take the worst in brief, *Samson* is dead. Samson 1570
From the chill dew, amongst rude burrs and thistles? Mask 352
Trinity ms 'amoungst rude burrs & thistles' ←'in this surrounding wilde' ←'in this dead solitude'
By dead *Parthenope*'s dear tomb, Mask 879
that lurks by hedge or lane of this dead circuit Mask Tr. ms 16.40
that lurks by hedge or lane, of this dead circuit Mask Br. ms 393
For *Lycidas* is dead, dead ere his prime Lycidas 8
For *Lycidas* your sorrow is not dead, Lycidas 166
Yet can I not perswade me thou art dead Fair Inf 29
Dead things with inbreath'd sense able to pierce, Musick 4
In the dust my glory dead, Psalm 7, 16
Among the dead *to sleep*, Psalm 88, 18
Mine eye grows dim and dead, Psalm 88, 38
Wilt thou do wonders on the dead, Psalm 88, 41

Deadlier
Satan, whose fall from Heav'n, a deadlier bruise, Par Lost 12.391

Deadliest
Thy wound, yet not thy last and deadliest wound Par Reg 4.622
But come what will, my deadliest foe will prove Samson 1262

Deadly	
Abhorred *Styx* the flood of deadly hate,	Par Lost 2.577
Leveld his deadly aime; thir fatall hands	Par Lost 2.712
His deadly arrow; neither vainly hope	Par Lost 2.811
The deadly forfeiture, and ransom set.	Par Lost 3.221
Where wounds of deadly hate have peirc'd so deep:	Par Lost 4.99
Nor yet on him found deadly, he yet lives,	Par Lost 9.932
That beat out life; he fell, and deadly pale	Par Lost 11.446
From restless thoughts, that like a deadly swarm	Samson 19
Thoughts my Tormenters arm'd with deadly stings	Samson 623
How sweet thou sing'st, how neer the deadly snare!	Mask 567
That he our deadly forfeit should release,	Nativity 6
Deaf	
But they persisted deaf, and would not seem	Samson 249
Dal. I see thou art implacable, more deaf	Samson 960
Deafening	
With deafning shout, return'd them loud acclaim.	Par Lost 2.520
Deal	
When Reason hath to deal with force, yet so	Par Lost 6.125
Deaths Ministers, not Men, who thus deal Death	Par Lost 11.676
His people, who defend? will they not deale	Par Lost 12.483
So deal not with this once thy glorious Champion,	Samson 705
And harshly deal like an ill borrower	Mask 683
Trinity ms 'deale'	
1637 'deale'	
line not in Bridgewater ms	
Dealing	
He now be dealing dole among his foes,	Samson 1529
Deals	
To me alike, it deals eternal woe.	Par Lost 4.70
Dealt	
But Heav'ns free Love dealt equally to all?	Par Lost 4.68
Wors with his followers then with him they dealt?	Par Lost 12.484
Then when I dealt with *Adam* first of Men,	Par Reg 2.133
Had dealt with *Jephtha*, who by argument,	Samson 283
What do I beg? how hast thou dealt already?	Samson 707
Dear	
Dear Daughter, since thou claim'st me for thy Sire,	Par Lost 2.817
And my fair Son here showst me, the dear pledge	Par Lost 2.818
Dwels in all Heaven charitie so deare?	Par Lost 3.216
My sole complacence! well thou know'st how dear,	Par Lost 3.276
His Brethren, ransomd with his own dear life.	Par Lost 3.297
No sooner did thy dear and onely Son	Par Lost 3.403
Over the *Promis'd Land* to God so dear,	Par Lost 3.531
Henceforth an individual solace dear;	Par Lost 4.486
Relations dear, and all the Charities	Par Lost 4.756
Sleepst thou Companion dear, what sleep can close	Par Lost 5.673
Not to be overpowerd, Companions deare,	Par Lost 6.419
Is propagated seem such dear delight	Par Lost 8.580
Compare above all living Creatures deare,	Par Lost 9.228
Adam, missthought of her to thee so dear?	Par Lost 9.289
So dear I love him, that with him all deaths	Par Lost 9.832
Adam, from whose deare side I boast me sprung,	Par Lost 9.965
Shall separate us, linkt in Love so deare,	Par Lost 9.970
For us his ofspring deare? It cannot be	Par Lost 10.238
Disguis'd he came, but those his Children dear	Par Lost 10.330
Met who to meet him came, his Ofspring dear.	Par Lost 10.349
For which our countrey is a name so dear;	Samson 894
So dear to Heav'n is Saintly chastity,	Mask 453
Trinity ms 'deare'	
1637 'deare'	
Bridgewater ms 'deere'	
Of my most honour'd Lady, your dear sister.	Mask 564
Bridgewater ms 'deere'	
1637 'deare'	
Trinity ms 'deare'	
Enjoy your deer Wit, and gay Rhetorick	Mask 790
1673 'dear'	
line not in Trinity ms	
line not in Bridgewater ms	
1637 'deere'	
Listen for dear honours sake,	Mask 864
Trinity ms 'deare'	
Bridgewater ms 'deere'	
1637 'deare'	
By dead *Parthenope*'s dear tomb,	Mask 879
1637 'deare'	
Bridgewater ms 'deare'	
Trinity ms 'deare', but line deleted	
Spir. Goddess dear	Mask 902
Bridgewater ms 'deere'	
1637 'deare'	
Trinity ms 'deere'	
Holds his dear *Psyche* sweet intranc't	Mask 1005
Trinity ms 'deare'	
1637 'deare'	
line not in Bridgewater ms	
Bitter constraint, and sad occasion dear,	Lycidas 6
1638 'deare'	
Trinity ms 'deare'	
Through the dear might of him that walk'd the waves;	Lycidas 173
Trinity ms 'deare'	
Dear son of memory, great heir of Fame,	Shakespear 5
1640 'Deare'	
1632 'Deare'	
Against the Lord and his Messiah dear	Psalm 2, 5
But I will in thy mercies dear	Psalm 5, 17
And Israel *whom I lov'd so dear*	Psalm 81, 47
Dear*(cont)*	
O Lord of Hoasts, how dear	Psalm 84, 2
Of thy anointed *dear*.	Psalm 84, 32
And to his Saints *full dear*,	Psalm 85, 32
To his dear Saints he will speak peace,	Psalm 85, 33
Dear	
His Brethren, ransomd with his own dear life.	Par Lost 3.297
And heavier fall: so should I purchase deare	Par Lost 4.101
Knowledge of Good bought dear by knowing ill.	Par Lost 4.222
Of Paradise, deare bought with lasting woes!	Par Lost 10.742
Dearer	
Dearer thy self then all; needs must the power	Par Lost 4.412
Best Image of my self and dearer half,	Par Lost 5.95
Dearest	
His dearest mediation thus renewd.	Par Lost 3.226
Collateral love, and deerest amitie.	Par Lost 8.426
Ah! Who hath reft (quoth he) my dearest pledge?	Lycidas 107
Trinity ms 'deerest'	
Which on our dearest Lord did sease er'e long,	Passion 10
Dearly	
So dearly to redeem what Hellish hate	Par Lost 3.300
How dearly I abide that boast so vaine,	Par Lost 4.87
Thy sweet Converse and Love so dearly joyn'd,	Par Lost 9.909
Though dearly to my cost, thy ginns, and toyls;	Samson 933
Dearly-bought	
Chor. O dearly-bought revenge, yet glorious!	Samson 1660
Dearly-loved	
Whilome did slay his dearly-loved mate	Fair Inf 24
Dearth	
Eate freely with glad heart; fear here no dearth:	Par Lost 8.322
In time of dearth, a Son whose worthy deeds	Par Lost 12.161
Sea-paths in shoals do slide. And know no dearth.	Psalm 8, 22
Death	
Brought Death into the World, and all our woe,	Par Lost 1.3
ms 'death'	
With dread of death to flight or foul retreat,	Par Lost 1.555
Rocks, Caves, Lakes, Fens, Bogs, Dens, and shades of death,	Par Lost 2.621
A Universe of death, which God by curse	Par Lost 2.622
Where all life dies, death lives, and Nature breeds,	Par Lost 2.624
Made to destroy: I fled, and cry'd out *Death;*	Par Lost 2.787
From all her Caves, and back resounded *Death*.	Par Lost 2.789
Grim *Death* my Son and foe, who sets them on,	Par Lost 2.804
And bring ye to the place where Thou and Death	Par Lost 2.840
He ceas'd, for both seemd highly pleasd, and Death	Par Lost 2.845
Death ready stands to interpose his dart,	Par Lost 2.854
Strange alteration! Sin and Death amain	Par Lost 2.1024
The rigid satisfaction, death for death.	Par Lost 3.212
Must have bin lost, adjudg'd to Death and Hell	Par Lost 3.223
Well pleas'd, on me let Death wreck all his rage;	Par Lost 3.241
Though now to Death I yield, and am his due	Par Lost 3.245
Death his deaths wound shall then receive, and stoop	Par Lost 3.252
Death last, and with his Carcass glut the Grave:	Par Lost 3.259
Giving to death, and dying to redeeme,	Par Lost 3.299
Thereby regaind, but sat devising Death	Par Lost 4.197
Our Death the Tree of knowledge grew fast by,	Par Lost 4.221
So neer grows Death to Life, what ere Death is,	Par Lost 4.425
God hath pronounc't it death to taste that Tree,	Par Lost 4.427
Can it be death? and do they onely stand	Par Lost 4.518
Death is the penaltie impos'd, beware,	Par Lost 7.545
Surprise thee, and her black attendant Death.	Par Lost 7.547
Sinne and her shadow Death, and Miserie	Par Lost 9.12
Deaths Harbinger: Sad task, yet argument	Par Lost 9.13
As wee, not capable of death or paine,	Par Lost 9.283
Those rigid threats of Death; ye shall not Die:	Par Lost 9.685
Of Death denounc't, whatever thing Death be,	Par Lost 9.695
Your feare it self of Death removes the feare.	Par Lost 9.702
Human, to put on Gods, death to be wisht,	Par Lost 9.714
Such prohibitions binde not. But if Death	Par Lost 9.760
Was death invented? or to us deni'd	Par Lost 9.767
Of God or Death, of Law or Penaltie?	Par Lost 9.775
And knew not eating Death: Satiate at length,	Par Lost 9.792
And Death ensue? then I shall be no more,	Par Lost 9.827
A death to think. Confirm'd then I resolve,	Par Lost 9.830
Defac't, deflourd, and now to Death devote?	Par Lost 9.901
Certain to undergoe like doom, if Death	Par Lost 9.953
Consort with thee, Death is to mee as Life;	Par Lost 9.954
Rather then Death or aught then Death more dread	Par Lost 9.969
Were it I thought Death menac't would ensue	Par Lost 9.977
Farr otherwise th' event, not Death, but Life	Par Lost 9.984
And fear of Death deliver to the Windes.	Par Lost 9.989
Divine displeasure for her sake, or Death.	Par Lost 9.993
Yet willingly chose rather Death with thee:	Par Lost 9.1167
On his transgression, Death denounc't that day,	Par Lost 10.49
And th' instant stroke of Death denounc't that day	Par Lost 10.210
Within the Gates of Hell sate Sin and Death,	Par Lost 10.230
Sin opening, who thus now to Death began.	Par Lost 10.234
For Death from Sin no power can separate.	Par Lost 10.251
The savour of Death from all things there that live:	Par Lost 10.269
For death, the following day, in bloodie fight.	Par Lost 10.278
Death with his Mace petrific, cold and dry,	Par Lost 10.294
Forfeit to Death; from hence a passage broad,	Par Lost 10.304
Through Sin to Death expos'd by my exploit.	Par Lost 10.407
By Sin and Death a broad way now is pav'd	Par Lost 10.473
To Sin and Death a prey, and so to us,	Par Lost 10.490
Habitual habitant; behind her *Death*	Par Lost 10.588
Second of *Satan* sprung, all conquering *Death*,	Par Lost 10.591
Both *Sin*, and *Death*, and yawning *Grave* at last	Par Lost 10.635
Death introduc'd through fierce antipathie:	Par Lost 10.709

Death(*cont*)
Now death to heare! for what can I encrease Par Lost 10.731
Why am I mockt with death, and length'nd out Par Lost 10.774
But I shall die a living Death? O thought Par Lost 10.788
Wrath without end on Man whom Death must end? Par Lost 10.797
Can he make deathless Death? that were to make Par Lost 10.798
That Death be not one stroak, as I suppos'd, Par Lost 10.809
On my defensless head; both Death and I Par Lost 10.815
Curs'd his Creation, Death as oft accus'd Par Lost 10.852
The day of his offence. Why comes not Death, Par Lost 10.854
But Death comes not at call, Justice Divine Par Lost 10.858
Since this days Death denounc't, if ought I see, Par Lost 10.962
By Death at last, and miserable it is Par Lost 10.981
So Death shall be deceav'd his glut, and with us two Par Lost 10.990
Let us seek Death, or he not found, supply Par Lost 10.1001
That shew no end but Death, and have the power, Par Lost 10.1004
Broke off the rest; so much of Death her thoughts Par Lost 10.1008
Or if thou covet death, as utmost end Par Lost 10.1020
To be forestall'd; much more I fear least Death Par Lost 10.1024
To make death in us live: Then let us seek Par Lost 10.1028
By death brought on our selves, or childless days Par Lost 10.1037
Was meant by Death that day, when lo, to thee Par Lost 10.1050
Shall perfet, and for these my Death shall pay. Par Lost 11.36
Numberd, though sad, till Death, his doom (which I Par Lost 11.40
Till I provided Death; so Death becomes Par Lost 11.61
Assures me that the bitterness of death Par Lost 11.157
That I who first brought Death on all, am grac't Par Lost 11.168
From penaltie, because from death releast Par Lost 11.197
Sufficient that thy Prayers are heard, and Death, Par Lost 11.252
Redeem thee quite from Deaths rapacious claime; Par Lost 11.258
O unexpected stroke, worse then of Death! Par Lost 11.268
But have I now seen Death? Is this the way Par Lost 11.462
To whom thus *Michael*. Death thou hast seen Par Lost 11.466
Of Death, and many are the wayes that lead Par Lost 11.468
And over them triumphant Death his Dart Par Lost 11.491
To Death, and mix with our connatural dust? Par Lost 11.529
Gatherd, not harshly pluckt, for death mature: Par Lost 11.537
Henceforth I flie not Death, nor would prolong Par Lost 11.547
Those were of hate and death, or pain much worse, Par Lost 11.601
Deaths Ministers, not Men, who thus deal Death Par Lost 11.676
Exempt from Death; to shew thee what reward Par Lost 11.709
Disabl'd not to give thee thy deaths wound: Par Lost 12.392
On penaltie of death, and suffering death, Par Lost 12.398
To a reproachful life and cursed death, Par Lost 12.406
Seis'd on by force, judg'd, and to death condemnd Par Lost 12.412
But soon revives, Death over him no power Par Lost 12.420
Thy ransom paid, which Man from death redeems, Par Lost 12.424
His death for Man, as many as offerd Life Par Lost 12.425
Annuls thy doom, the death thou shouldst have dy'd, Par Lost 12.428
Defeating Sin and Death, his two maine armes, Par Lost 12.431
Then temporal death shall bruise the Victors heel, Par Lost 12.433
Or theirs whom he redeems, a death like sleep, Par Lost 12.434
For death, like that which the redeemer dy'd. Par Lost 12.445
Though to the death, against such cruelties Par Lost 12.494
And to the faithful Death the Gate of Life; Par Lost 12.571
To conquer Sin and Death the two grand foes, Par Reg 1.159
Through many a hard assay even to the death, Par Reg 1.264
Till Conquerour Death discover them scarce men, Par Reg 3.85
Violent or shameful death thir due reward. Par Reg 3.87
For truths sake suffering death unjust, lives now Par Reg 3.98
Wealth, pleasure, pain or torment, death and life, Par Reg 4.305
Violence and stripes, and lastly cruel death, Par Reg 4.388
To live a life half dead, a living death, Samson 100
By priviledge of death and burial Samson 104
Spurn'd them to death by Troops. The bold *Ascalonite* Samson 138
Without Reprieve adjudg'd to death, Samson 288
By pains and slaveries, worse then death inflicted Samson 485
Then who self-rigorous chooses death as due; Samson 513
Consume me, and oft-invocated death Samson 575
To deaths benumming Opium as my only cure. Samson 630
No long petition, speedy death, Samson 650
Who threatning cruel death constrain'd the bride Samson 1198
Hear these dishonours, and not render death? Samson 1232
My speediest friend, by death to rid me hence, Samson 1263
Blood, death, and deathful deeds are in that noise, Samson 1513
To free him hence! but death who sets all free Samson 1572
How dy'd he? death to life is crown or shame. Samson 1579
What glorious hand gave *Samson* his deaths wound? Samson 1581
Of dire necessity, whose law in death conjoin'd Samson 1666
And what may quiet us in a death so noble. Samson 1724
Under the ribs of Death, but O ere long Mask 562
  Bridgewater ms 'death'
Or drag him by the curls, to a foul death, Mask 608
  1637 'and cleave his scalpe'
  Bridgewater ms 'and cleave his scalpe'
  Trinity ms 'or drag him by the curls & cleave his scalpe'
Or *Severn* swift, guilty of Maidens death, Vacation 96
Yet more; the stroke of death he must abide, Passion 20
Triumphing over Death, and Chance, and thee O Time. On Time 22
Were lost in death, till he that dwelt above Circum 18
To house with darknes, and with death. Winchester 10
Here lies old *Hobson*, Death hath broke his girt, Carrier 1
Death was half glad when he had got him down; Carrier 6
And surely, Death could never have prevail'd, Carrier 9
  1658 'death'
In the kind office of a Chamberlin Carrier 14
  1658 'Death in the likenesse'
Rest that gives all men life, gave him his death, Another 11

Death(*cont*)
As he were prest to death, he cry'd more waight; Another 26
  line not in 1640, 1657, 1658 texts
Of Death, call'd Life; which us from Life doth sever. Sonnet 14, 4
  Trinity ms 'death' ← 'Flesh and sin'
And that one Talent which is death to hide, Sonnet 19, 3
Rescu'd from death by force though pale and faint. Sonnet 23, 4
For in death no remembrance is of thee; Psalm 6, 9
The tools of death, that waits him near. Psalm 7, 48
My life *at deaths uncherful dore* Psalm 88, 11
Deaths hideous house hath barr'd. Psalm 88, 24
Deathful
Blood, death, and deathful deeds are in that noise, Samson 1513
Deathless
To deathless pain? how gladly would I meet Par Lost 10.775
Can he make deathless Death? that were to make Par Lost 10.798
With a crown of deathless Praise, Mask 973
  B.M. ms 'Deathless'
  Bridgewater ms 'death lesse'
  Trinity ms 'Deathlesse'
  1637 'deathlesse'
Deaths
So dear I love him, that with him all deaths Par Lost 9.832
Debar
Labour, as to debarr us when we need Par Lost 9.236
Debase
Sam. So let her go, God sent her to debase me, Samson 999
Debased
I not; so much hath Hell debas'd, and paine Par Lost 9.487
To such unsightly sufferings be debas't Par Lost 11.510
Put to the labour of a Beast, debas't Samson 37
Can they think me so broken, so debas'd Samson 1335
Debate
We now debate; who can advise, may speak. Par Lost 2.42
Well have ye judg'd, well ended long debate, Par Lost 2.390
In us who serve, new Counsels, to debate Par Lost 5.681
That he who in debate of Truth hath won, Par Lost 6.122
Him after long debate, irresolute Par Lost 9.87
Of hazard, which admits no long debate, Par Reg 1.95
Only my love of thee held long debate; Samson 863
Debates
He judges and debates. Psalm 82, 4
Debel
Thou didst debel, and down from Heav'n cast Par Reg 4.605
Debonair
So bucksom, blith, and debonair. Allegro 24
Debt
All that of me can die, yet that debt paid, Par Lost 3.246
The debt immense of endless gratitude, Par Lost 4.52
Of sin, or legal debt; Samson 313
God will relent, and quit thee all his debt; Samson 509
Decan
In *Malabar* or *Decan* spreds her Armes Par Lost 9.1103
Decay
Made of sphear-metal, never to decay Another 5
with need, *and sad decay*. Psalm 86, 4
Decayed
Wrinkl'd the face of Deluge, as decai'd; Par Lost 11.843
Deccan
In *Malabar* or *Decan* spreds her Armes Par Lost 9.1103
Deceased
Shall the deceas'd arise Psalm 88, 42
Deceit
But by deceit and lies; this let him know, Par Lost 5.243
Friendly to man, farr from deceit or guile. Par Lost 9.772
Against us this deceit: to crush his head Par Lost 10.1035
Deceitful
To a deceitful Woman: tell me Friends, Samson 202
Of a deceitful Concubine who shore me Samson 537
Deceivable
Deceivable and vain! Nay what thing good Samson 350
Deceiveable, in most things as a child Samson 942
Deceive
With him, or who deceive his mind, whose eye Par Lost 2.189
To respite or deceive, or slack the pain Par Lost 2.461
Yet not anough had practisd to deceive Par Lost 4.124
Of God All-seeing, or deceave his Heart Par Lost 10.6
Deceive ye to perswasion over-sure Par Reg 2.142
To break all faith, all vows, deceive, betray, Samson 750
Perhaps my semblance might deceive the truth, Sonnet 7, 5
  Trinity ms 'deceave'
Deceived
Stird up with Envy and Revenge, deceiv'd Par Lost 1.35
  ms 'deceav'd'
Self-tempted, self-deprav'd: Man falls deceiv'd Par Lost 3.130
O much deceav'd, much failing, hapless *Eve*, Par Lost 9.404
Against his better knowledge, not deceav'd, Par Lost 9.998
Man I deceav'd: that which to mee belongs, Par Lost 10.496
Deceav'd; they fondly thinking to allay Par Lost 10.564
Unhappilie deceav'd; thy suppliant Par Lost 10.917
So Death shall be deceav'd his glut, and with us two Par Lost 10.990
But I was farr deceav'd; for now I see Par Lost 11.783
Lost Paradise deceiv'd by me, though since Par Reg 1.52
This far his over-match, who self deceiv'd Par Reg 4.7
Have err'd, and by bad Women been deceiv'd; Samson 211
Was I deceiv'd, or did a sable cloud Mask 221
  Trinity ms 'deceav'd'
  line not in Bridgewater ms

Deceiver
Hence with thy brew'd inchantments, foul deceiver, Mask 696
Trinity ms 'deceaver'
Bridgewater ms 'deceaver'
Deceiving
Runs through the arched roof in words deceiving. Nativity 175
Decencies
Those thousand decencies that daily flow Par Lost 8.601
Decent
Before his decent steps a Silver wand. Par Lost 3.644
Over thy decent shoulders drawn. Penseroso 36
Deception
And fall into deception unaware, Par Lost 9.362
Decide
Fit to decide the Empire of great Heav'n. Par Lost 6.303
By combat to decide whose god is God, Samson 1176
Decides
Jesting decides great things Prose 7, 1
Decision
And by decision more imbroiles the fray Par Lost 2.908
Deck
Whether to deck with Clouds the uncolourd skie, Par Lost 5.189
To deck her Sons, and that no corner might Mask 717
Trinity ms 'deck' ←'adorne' ←'deck'
Decked
Espoused *Eve* deckt first her nuptial Bed, Par Lost 4.710
With flourets deck't and fragrant smells; but *Eve* Par Lost 5.379
In all the Liveries dect of Summers pride Par Lost 7.478
The Wood-Nymphs deckt with Daisies trim, Mask 120
Trinity ms 'deck't'
Bridgewater ms 'decte'
Till thou hast deck't them in thy best aray; Vacation 26
Declare
In these thy lowest works, yet these declare Par Lost 5.158
This day I have begot whom I declare Par Lost 5.603
Upon his enemies, and to declare Par Lost 6.677
And sweet compliance, which declare unfeign'd Par Lost 8.603
I call ye and declare ye now, returnd Par Lost 10.462
Among them to declare his Providence Par Reg 1.445
That pleas'd so well our Victors ear, declare Par Reg 4.337
I will declare; the Lord to me hath say'd Psalm 2, 14
How long wilt thou declare Psalm 80, 18
Declared
His fair large Front and Eye sublime declar'd Par Lost 4.300
Messiah was declar'd in sight of Heav'n, Par Lost 5.765
When such was heard declar'd th' Almightie's will; Par Lost 7.181
And gaze, and worship thee of right declar'd Par Lost 9.611
Yet Lords declar'd of all in Earth or Aire? Par Lost 9.658
Chiefly on Man, sole Lord of all declar'd, Par Lost 10.401
Inclin'd not, but his coming thus declar'd. Par Lost 11.250
And of thir doings great dislike declar'd, Par Lost 11.720
Where he might likeliest find this new-declar'd, Par Reg 1.121
Declar'd the Son of God, to hear attent Par Reg 1.385
Jesus Messiah Son of God declar'd, Par Reg 2.4
Or Barbarous, nor exception hath declar'd; Par Reg 3.119
In some respect far higher so declar'd. Par Reg 4.521
Declares
Appointed, which declares his Dignitie, Par Lost 4.619
Defaming as impure what God declares Par Lost 4.746
But now I feel I hunger, which declares, Par Reg 2.252
Picture the sacred wall declares t' have hung Horace 14
Declarest
That thou in me well pleas'd, declarst thy will Par Lost 6.728
Declaring
This day affords, declaring thee resolvd, Par Lost 9.968
Decline
This Eevning from the Sun's decline arriv'd Par Lost 4.792
Be over, and the Sun more coole decline. Par Lost 5.370
Yet somtimes Nations will decline so low Par Lost 12.97
Declined
Declin'd was hasting now with prone carreer Par Lost 4.353
Brought to thir Ears, while day declin'd, they heard, Par Lost 10.99
About t' have spoke, but now, with head declin'd Samson 727
Decree
Subdues us, and Omnipotent Decree, Par Lost 2.198
Thir will, dispos'd by absolute Decree Par Lost 3.115
Thir nature, and revoke the high Decree Par Lost 3.126
And here art likeliest by supream decree Par Lost 3.659
Hear my Decree, which unrevok't shall stand. Par Lost 5.602
Thy eye-lids? and remembrest what Decree Par Lost 5.674
Were banded to oppose his high Decree; Par Lost 5.717
Not meerly titular, since by Decree Par Lost 5.774
The just Decree of God, pronounc't and sworn, Par Lost 5.814
And in whose hand what by Decree I doe, Par Lost 6.683
Against his Maker; no Decree of mine Par Lost 10.43
Father Eternal, thine is to decree, Par Lost 10.68
His hand to execute what his Decree Par Lost 10.772
Obtain, all thy request was my Decree: Par Lost 11.47
For ever, to remove him I decree, Par Lost 11.96
But prayer against his absolute Decree Par Lost 11.311
Why am I thus bereav'd thy prime decree? Samson 85
On *Sion* my holi' hill. A firm decree Psalm 2, 13
Decreed
Say they who counsel Warr, we are decreed, Par Lost 2.160
Or high foreknowledge; they themselves decreed Par Lost 3.116
As my Eternal purpose hath decreed: Par Lost 3.172
With Heav'nly spoils, our spoils: What he decreed Par Lost 9.151
The Father in his purpose hath decreed, Par Reg 3.186
Decreed(*cont*)
What if he hath decreed that I shall first Par Reg 3.188
Decrees
Will not be now voutsaf't, other Decrees Par Lost 5.884
Righteous are thy Decrees on all thy Works; Par Lost 10.644
Could alter high Decrees, I to that place Par Lost 10.953
Upon my head, long the decrees of Heav'n Par Reg 1.55
Decrepit
Decrepit Winter, from the South to bring Par Lost 10.655
Dungeon, or beggery, or decrepit age! Samson 69
Dee
Or Coaly *Tine*, or antient hollowed *Dee*, Vacation 98
Deed
At such bold words voucht with a deed so bold: Par Lost 5.66
To be both will and deed created free; Par Lost 5.549
None of retreat, no unbecoming deed Par Lost 6.237
Bold deed thou hast presum'd, adventrous *Eve*, Par Lost 9.921
Her doing seem'd to justifie the deed; Par Lost 10.142
Alas, both for the deed and for the cause! Par Lost 11.461
The deed becomes unprais'd, the man at least, Par Reg 3.103
Take to thy wicked deed: which when thou seest Samson 826
Draw thir own ruin who attempt the deed. Samson 1267
As he pronounces lastly on each deed, Lycidas 83
If ever deed of honour did thee please, Sonnet 8, 3
Deeds
Under thy conduct, and in dreadful deeds Par Lost 1.130
To vice industrious, but to Nobler deeds Par Lost 2.116
Thir specious deeds on earth, which glory excites, Par Lost 2.484
Thir own Heroic deeds and hapless fall Par Lost 2.549
To meet so great a foe: and now great deeds Par Lost 2.722
Prevented spares to tell thee yet by deeds Par Lost 2.739
Thir own both righteous and unrighteous deeds, Par Lost 3.292
See golden days, fruitful of golden deeds, Par Lost 3.337
Fit retribution, emptie as thir deeds; Par Lost 3.454
Worse; of worse deeds worse sufferings must ensue. Par Lost 4.26
The Tyrants plea, excus'd his devilish deeds. Par Lost 4.394
What seemd both Spear and Shield: now dreadful deeds Par Lost 4.990
Ill matching words and deeds long past or late. Par Lost 5.113
Shall teach us highest deeds, by proof to try Par Lost 5.865
Heroic Ardor to advent'rous deeds Par Lost 6.66
Among the mightiest, bent on highest deeds, Par Lost 6.112
As both thir deeds compar'd this day shall prove. Par Lost 6.170
Of victorie; deeds of eternal fame Par Lost 6.240
Of airie threats to aw whom yet with deeds Par Lost 6.283
Mean while in other parts like deeds deservd Par Lost 6.354
O Parent, these are thy magnific deeds, Par Lost 10.354
And one bad act with many deeds well done Par Lost 11.256
Corruption to bring forth more violent deeds. Par Lost 11.428
On each hand slaughter and gigantic deeds. Par Lost 11.659
Raise out of friendship hostil deeds in Peace. Par Lost 11.796
In time of dearth, a Son whose worthy deeds Par Lost 12.161
And puissant deeds, a promise shall receive Par Lost 12.322
Deeds to thy knowledge answerable, add Faith, Par Lost 12.582
With prosperous wing full summ'd to tell of deeds Par Reg 1.14
To which my Spirit aspir'd, victorious deeds Par Reg 1.215
By matchless Deeds express thy matchless Sire. Par Reg 1.233
Thy wisdom, and behold thy God-like deeds? Par Reg 1.386
And amplitude of mind to greatest Deeds. Par Reg 2.139
In lowest poverty to highest deeds; Par Reg 2.438
Infallible; or wert thou sought to deeds Par Reg 3.16
By deeds of peace, by wisdom eminent, Par Reg 3.91
Appearing, and beginning noble deeds, Par Reg 4.99
Us'd no ambition to commend my deeds, Samson 247
The deeds themselves, though mute, spoke loud the dooer; Samson 248
To heap ingratitude on worthiest deeds? Samson 276
To worthiest deeds, if he through frailty err, Samson 369
Be it but for honours sake of former deeds. Samson 372
He led me on to mightiest deeds Samson 638
Far other reasonings, brought forth other deeds. Samson 875
By worse then hostile deeds, violating the ends Samson 893
But by ungodly deeds, the contradiction Samson 898
And with contrary blast proclaims most deeds, Samson 972
To folly and shameful deeds which ruin ends. Samson 1043
Blood, death, and deathful deeds are in that noise, Samson 1513
To fill thy odorous Lamp with deeds of light, Sonnet 9, 10
Tis you that say it, not I, you do the deeds, Prose 8, 1
And your ungodly deeds finde me the words. Prose 8, 2
Deem
Of future we may deem him, though till now Par Lost 6.429
And with mysterious reverence I deem) Par Lost 8.599
Well deem in outward Rites and specious formes Par Lost 12.534
Of glory as thou wilt, said he, so deem, Par Reg 3.150
The City which thou seest no other deem Par Reg 4.44
Deemed
His trust was with th' Eternal to be deem'd Par Lost 2.46
Now in thine eye so foul, once deemd so fair Par Lost 2.748
Others came single; he who to be deemd Par Lost 3.469
My damage fondly deem'd, I can repaire Par Lost 7.152
Heroic deem'd, chief maistrie to dissect Par Lost 9.29
Of highest Agents, deemd however wise. Par Lost 9.683
Accomplishing great things, by things deemd weak Par Lost 12.567
From *Nazareth* the Son of *Joseph* deem'd Par Reg 1.23
When most unactive deem'd, Samson 1705
Deeming
Deeming some Island, oft, as Sea-men tell, Par Lost 1.205
Deep
Nor the deep Tract of Hell, say first what cause Par Lost 1.28
Vaunting aloud, but rackt with deep despare: Par Lost 1.126

Deep(*cont*)
Or do his Errands in the gloomy Deep; Par Lost 1.152
ms 'deep'
To bellow through the vast and boundless Deep. Par Lost 1.177
ms 'deep'
He call'd so loud, that all the hollow Deep Par Lost 1.314
ms 'deeps'
Deep scars of Thunder had intrencht, and care Par Lost 1.601
For since no deep within her gulf can hold Par Lost 2.12
Insulting, and pursu'd us through the Deep, Par Lost 2.79
In this abhorred deep to utter woe; Par Lost 2.87
Impregnable; oft on the bordering Deep Par Lost 2.131
The Deep to shelter us? this Hell then seem'd Par Lost 2.167
Through labour and indurance. This deep world Par Lost 2.262
Covers his Throne; from whence deep thunders roar Par Lost 2.267
A Pillar of State; deep on his Front engraven Par Lost 2.302
Or ambush from the Deep. What if we find Par Lost 2.344
So deep a malice, to confound the race Par Lost 2.382
Great things resolv'd, which from the lowest deep Par Lost 2.392
Pondering the danger with deep thoughts; and each Par Lost 2.421
With reason hath deep silence and demurr Par Lost 2.431
Sad *Acheron* of sorrow, black and deep; Par Lost 2.578
Of ancient pile; all else deep snow and ice, Par Lost 2.591
Now shaves with level wing the Deep, then soares Par Lost 2.634
Into this Deep, and in the general fall Par Lost 2.773
Th' unfounded deep, and through the void immense Par Lost 2.829
The secrets of the hoarie deep, a dark Par Lost 2.891
Ten thousand fadom deep, and to this hour Par Lost 2.934
Wide on the wasteful Deep; with him Enthron'd Par Lost 2.961
Fled not in silence through the frighted deep Par Lost 2.994
The rising world of waters dark and deep, Par Lost 3.11
Shoots invisible vertue even to the deep: Par Lost 3.586
He seemd, or fixt in cogitation deep. Par Lost 3.629
That brought them forth, but hid thir causes deep. Par Lost 3.707
And in the lowest deep a lower deep Par Lost 4.76
Where wounds of deadly hate have peirc'd so deep: Par Lost 4.99
Deep malice to conceale, couch't with revenge: Par Lost 4.123
I fear, hath ventur'd from the deep, to raise Par Lost 4.574
These then, though unbeheld in deep of night, Par Lost 4.674
Into utter darkness, deep ingulft, his place Par Lost 5.614
Deep malice thence conceiving and disdain, Par Lost 5.666
He said, and as the sound of waters deep Par Lost 5.872
But with swift wheele reverse, deep entring shar'd Par Lost 6.326
And with fierce Ensignes pierc'd the deep array Par Lost 6.356
Deep under ground, materials dark and crude, Par Lost 6.478
These in thir dark Nativitie the Deep Par Lost 6.482
On every side with shaddowing Squadrons Deep, Par Lost 6.554
From those deep throated Engins belcht, whose roar Par Lost 6.586
1667 'deep-throated'
Under the weight of Mountains buried deep, Par Lost 6.652
From all Heav'ns bounds into the utter Deep: Par Lost 6.716
Into the wastful Deep; the monstrous sight Par Lost 6.862
Affrighted; but strict Fate had cast too deep Par Lost 6.869
Among th' Angelic Powers, and the deep fall Par Lost 6.898
With admiration, and deep Muse to heare Par Lost 7.52
Of Nature from the unapparent Deep: Par Lost 7.103
Fell with his flaming Legions through the Deep Par Lost 7.134
I send along, ride forth, and bid the Deep Par Lost 7.166
Boundless the Deep, because I am who fill Par Lost 7.168
Silence, ye troubl'd waves, and thou Deep, peace, Par Lost 7.216
Sprung from the Deep, and from her Native East Par Lost 7.245
Down sunk a hollow bottom broad and deep, Par Lost 7.289
And on the washie Oose deep Channels wore; Par Lost 7.303
Hugest of living Creatures, on the Deep Par Lost 7.413
With narrow search; and with inspection deep Par Lost 9.83
Thenceforth to Speculations high or deep Par Lost 9.602
Beyond this Deep; whatever drawes me on, Par Lost 10.245
Deep to the Roots of Hell the gather'd beach Par Lost 10.299
Over the foaming deep high Archt, a Bridge Par Lost 10.301
Voyag'd th' unreal, vast, unbounded deep Par Lost 10.471
As deep as *Capricorne*, to bring in change Par Lost 10.677
I find no way, from deep to deeper plung'd! Par Lost 10.844
So deep the power of these Ingredients pierc'd, Par Lost 11.417
Dire was the tossing, deep the groans, despair Par Lost 11.489
Deep under water rould; Sea cover'd Sea, Par Lost 11.749
Raine day and night, all fountains of the Deep Par Lost 11.826
With soft foot towards the deep, who now had stopt Par Lost 11.848
All secrets of the deep, all Natures works, Par Lost 12.578
When his fierce thunder drove us to the deep; Par Reg 1.90
Distracted and surpriz'd with deep dismay Par Reg 1.108
And his deep thoughts, the better to converse Par Reg 1.190
With them from bliss to the bottomless deep, Par Reg 1.361
Perhaps thou linger'st in deep thoughts detain'd Par Reg 3.227
Vented much policy, and projects deep Par Reg 3.391
Deep verst in books and shallow in himself, Par Reg 4.327
Though rooted deep as high, and sturdiest Oaks Par Reg 4.417
Lest he command them down into the deep Par Reg 4.631
Hitting thy aged ear should pierce too deep. Samson 1568
The unadorned boosom of the Deep, Mask 23
Trinity ms 'deepe'
1637 'Deepe'
Deep skill'd in all his mothers witcheries, Mask 523
1637 'Deepe'
Trinity ms 'deepe skill'd' ← 'deepe learnt' ← 'enur'd'
Bridgewater ms 'deepe'
Would so emblaze the forhead of the Deep, Mask 733
Bridgewater ms 'would soe emblaze with starrs that they belowe'

Deep(*cont*)
Trinity ms 'deepe'
Waxing well of his deep wound Mask 1000
Trinity ms 'deepe'
1637 'deepe'
line not in Bridgewater ms
But els in deep of night when drowsines Arcades 61
Trinity ms 'deepe'
Where were ye Nymphs when the remorseless deep Lycidas 50
Trinity ms 'deepe'
The Stars with deep amaze Nativity 69
And cast the dark foundations deep, Nativity 123
And let the Base of Heav'ns deep Organ blow, Nativity 130
The wakefull trump of doom must thunder through the deep, Nativity 156
Such where the deep transported mind may soare Vacation 33
Seas wept from our deep sorrow, Circum 9
Trinity ms 'deepe'
Those Delphick lines with deep impression took, Shakespear 12
1632 'deepe'
1640 'deepe'
To day deep thoughts resolve with me to drench Sonnet 21, 5
Lay deep their plots together through each Land, Psalm 2, 4
He dig'd a pit, and delv'd it deep, Psalm 7, 55
And root it deep and fast Psalm 80, 38
I answer'd thee in thunder deep Psalm 81, 29
And raise the man in deep distress Psalm 82, 11
Their Plots and Counsels deep, Psalm 83, 10
That in the grave lie *deep*. Psalm 88, 20
Walk'st on the rowling Sphear, and through the deep, Prose 12, 2

Deeper
That they may stumble on, and deeper fall; Par Lost 3.201
I find no way, from deep to deeper plung'd! Par Lost 10.844
And fix farr deeper in his head thir stings Par Lost 12.432

Deepest
To deepest Hell, and to repair that loss Par Lost 3.678
And so from Heav'n to deepest Hell; O fall Par Lost 5.542
Which deepest Spirits, and choicest Wits desire: Vacation 22
From deepest darkness foul. Psalm 86, 48

Deeps
He call'd so loud, that all the hollow Deep Par Lost 1.314
ms 'deeps'
In horrid deeps *to mourn*. Psalm 88, 28

Deep-throated
From those deep throated Engins belcht, whose roar Par Lost 6.586
1667 'deep-throated'

Deep-vaulted
From Hell's deep-vaulted Den to dwell in light, Par Reg 1.116

Defaced
Defac't, deflourd, and now to Death devote? Par Lost 9.901
Or if his likeness, by themselves defac't Par Lost 11.522

Defamed
To all posterity may stand defam'd, Samson 977

Defaming
Defaming as impure what God declares Par Lost 4.746

Default
Imput'st thou that to my default, or will Par Lost 9.1145
Had been fulfilld but through mine own default, Samson 45

Defeat
That with sad overthrow and foul defeat Par Lost 1.135
Have rais'd incessant Armies to defeat Par Lost 6.138

Defeated
Of Thunder: back defeated to return Par Lost 6.606
Defeated of his seisure many dayes Par Lost 11.254
In all his wiles, defeated and repuls't, Par Reg 1.6
Man. The worst indeed, O all my hope's defeated Samson 1571

Defeating
Defeating Sin and Death, his two maine armes, Par Lost 12.431

Defeats
And feats of War defeats Samson 1278

Defect
This noveltie on Earth, this fair defect Par Lost 10.891

Defective
In unitie defective, which requires Par Lost 8.425

Defects
Or solace his defects. No need that thou Par Lost 8.419

Defence
To their defence who hold it: here perhaps Par Lost 2.362
Be questiond and blaspheam'd without defence. Par Lost 3.166
In our defence, lest unawares we lose Par Lost 5.731
Defence, while others bore him on thir Shields Par Lost 6.337
Our selves with like defence, to me deserves Par Lost 6.467
Single with like defence, wherever met, Par Lost 9.325
What boots it at one gate to make defence, Samson 560
Lose thir defence distracted and amaz'd. Samson 1286
I was dispatcht for their defence, and guard; Mask 42
Defence is a good cause, and Heav'n be for us. Mask 489
Trinity ms 'defence' ← 'a just Defence'
Bridgewater ms 'defence'
In libertyes defence, my noble task, Sonnet 22, 11
1694 'Defence'
My defence, and in him lies Psalm 7, 40

Defenceless
On my defensless head; both Death and I Par Lost 10.815
My sister is not so defenceless left Mask 414
Trinity ms 'defencelesse'
1637 'defencelesse'
Bridgewater ms 'defencelesse'
Whose chance on these defenceless dores may sease, Sonnet 8, 2

Defenceless(*cont*)
Trinity ms 'defenslesse'
Defend
That little which is left so to defend, Par Lost 2.1000
Both Harp and Voice; nor could the Muse defend Par Lost 7.37
Assaulting; others from the wall defend Par Lost 11.657
His people, who defend? will they not deale Par Lost 12.483
Or Cedar, to defend him from the dew, Par Reg 1.306
He will accept thee to defend his cause, Samson 1179
To save her blossoms, and defend her fruit Mask 396
Defend the poor and desolate, Psalm 82, 13
Defended
Of that defended Fruit; but let him boast Par Lost 11.86
Defended *Israel* from the *Ammonite*, Samson 285
Defendest
Defend'st them, they shall ever sing Psalm 5, 35
Defends
Darkness defends between till morning Watch; Par Lost 12.207
Defends the touching of these viands pure, Par Reg 2.370
Defensive
Defensive scarse, or with pale fear surpris'd, Par Lost 6.393
Intestin, far within defensive arms Samson 1038
Defer
Not to deferr; hunger and thirst at once, Par Lost 9.586
Nothing more certain, will not long defer Samson 474
Man. Tell us the sum, the circumstance defer. Samson 1557
Defiance
Hurling defiance toward the Vault of Heav'n. Par Lost 1.669
Hell-doom'd, and breath'st defiance here and scorn Par Lost 2.697
Stand firm, for in his look defiance lours. Par Lost 4.873
Siege and defiance: Wretched man! what food Par Lost 12.74
His habit carries peace, his brow defiance. Samson 1073
In Heav'ns defiance mustering all his waves; Vacation 44
Deficience
Is no deficience found; not so is Man, Par Lost 8.416
Deficient
Nothing imperfet or deficient left Par Lost 9.345
Defied
Defi'd the best of *Panim* chivalry Par Lost 1.765
ms 'Defy'd'
Incens't, and thus securely him defi'd. Par Lost 6.130
Of *Moloc* furious King, who him defi'd, Par Lost 6.357
Defies
Who now defies thee thrice to single fight, Samson 1222
Defile
Chor. Where the heart joins not, outward acts defile not. Samson 1368
Defilement
Lets in defilement to the inward parts, Mask 466
Deflowered
Defac't, deflourd, and now to Death devote? Par Lost 9.901
Deform
More dreadful and deform: on th' other side Par Lost 2.706
Sight so deform what heart of Rock could long Par Lost 11.494
Deformed
With many an inrode gor'd; deformed rout Par Lost 6.387
Rowling in brutish vices, and deform'd, Par Reg 3.86
Painful diseases and deform'd, Samson 699
Deformities
In part, from such deformities be free, Par Lost 11.513
Should look so neer upon her foul deformities. Nativity 44
Defy
Who durst defie th' Omnipotent to Arms. Par Lost 1.49
Defie thee to the trial of mortal fight, Samson 1175
Degenerate
So all shall turn degenerate, all deprav'd, Par Lost 11.806
These thus degenerate, by themselves enslav'd, Par Reg 4.144
To a degenerate and degraded state. Mask 475
Degenerately
That saw not how degenerately I serv'd. Samson 419
Degrade
Mans Nature, less'n or degrade thine owne. Par Lost 3.304
Nor only dost degrade them, or remit Samson 687
Degraded
Degraded, Wisdom in discourse with her Par Lost 8.552
Degraded, to what wretched state reserv'd! Par Lost 11.501
Degraded by himself, on grace depending? Par Reg 4.312
To a degenerate and degraded state. Mask 475
Degree
Differing but in degree, of kind the same. Par Lost 5.490
His name, and high was his degree in Heav'n; Par Lost 5.707
Live, in what state, condition or degree, Par Lost 8.176
But in degree, the cause of his desire Par Lost 8.417
Strange alteration in me, to degree Par Lost 9.599
Least thou not tasting, different degree Par Lost 9.883
Higher degree of Life, inducement strong Par Lost 9.934
In what degree or meaning thou art call'd Par Reg 4.516
The base degree to which I now am fall'n, Samson 414
With seats where all the Lords and each degree Samson 1607
Degrees
Ascending by degrees magnificent Par Lost 3.502
Indu'd with various forms various degrees Par Lost 5.473
Of Hierarchies, of Orders, and Degrees; Par Lost 5.591
In thir triple Degrees, Regions to which Par Lost 5.750
Equally free; for Orders and Degrees Par Lost 5.792
By him created in thir bright degrees, Par Lost 5.838
Not here, till by degrees of merit rais'd Par Lost 7.157
The Poles of Earth twice ten degrees and more Par Lost 10.669
And turns it by degrees to the souls essence, Mask 462

Deified
Of Union or Communion, deifi'd; Par Lost 8.431
Deify
With suppliant knee, and deifie his power, Par Lost 1.112
Deign
Deign to descend now lower, and relate Par Lost 7.84
Open, and henceforth oft; for God will deigne Par Lost 7.569
Among whom God will deigne to dwell on Earth Par Lost 12.281
With honour, only deign to sit and eat. Par Reg 2.336
To fight with thee no man of arms will deign. Samson 1226
'Less *Philomel* will daign a Song, Penseroso 56
1673 'deign'
Deigned
Raphael, the sociable Spirit, that deign'd Par Lost 5.221
Those happie places thou hast deignd a while Par Lost 5.364
By sufferance, and thy wonted favour deign'd. Par Lost 8.202
Deigns
Deigns none to ease thy load and taste thy sweet, Par Lost 5.59
Of my Celestial Patroness, who deignes Par Lost 9.21
Deities
And Devils to adore for Deities: Par Lost 1.373
ms 'deities'
Powers and Dominions, Deities of Heav'n, Par Lost 2.11
Thir Deities to assert, who while they feel Par Lost 6.157
From God to worship Calves, the Deities Par Reg 3.416
The vices of thir Deities, and thir own Par Reg 4.340
He quarters to his blu-hair'd deities, Mask 29
Trinity ms 'dieties'
Bridgewater ms 'dieties'
Deity
Th' incensed Deitie, while offerd grace Par Lost 3.187
Of Deitie or Empire, such a foe Par Lost 5.724
The Deitie, and divine commands obei'd, Par Lost 5.806
Visibly, what by Deitie I am, Par Lost 6.682
The Chariot of Paternal Deitie, Par Lost 6.750
Of Deitie supream, us dispossest, Par Lost 7.142
1669 'Deity'
That to the hight of Deitie aspir'd; Par Lost 9.167
Deitie for thee, when Fate will not permit. Par Lost 9.885
Blaz'd forth unclouded Deitie; he full Par Lost 10.65
By Prayer th' offended Deitie to appease, Par Lost 11.149
Fresh in thir mindes, fearing the Deitie, Par Lost 12.15
His Deity comparing and preferring Samson 464
Of their own deity, Gods cannot be: Samson 899
A deity so unparalel'd? Arcades 25
Her deity. Arcades 93
Trinity ms 'deitie'
He thought it toucht his Deitie full neer, Fair Inf 10
Look in, and see each blissful Deitie Vacation 35
And sing the Name and Deitie Psalm 7, 63
Deject
All her array; her female pride deject, Par Reg 2.219
Deject not then so overmuch thy self, Samson 213
Pity me Lord for I am much deject Psalm 6, 3
Dejected
Chor. As signal now in low dejected state, Samson 338
Dejection
Of sorrow and dejection and despair Par Lost 11.301
Delay
By our delay? no, let us rather choose Par Lost 2.60
Which else might work him danger or delay: Par Lost 3.635
Of *Arabie* the blest, with such delay Par Lost 4.163
And sweet reluctant amorous delay. Par Lost 4.311
And longer will delay to heare thee tell Par Lost 7.101
Somtimes in highth began, as no delay Par Lost 9.675
Which when the Lord God heard, without delay Par Lost 10.163
This also shall they gain by thir delay Par Lost 12.223
In mee is no delay; with thee to goe, Par Lost 12.615
Delay, for longest time to him is short; Par Reg 1.56
Brooks no delay: is this thy resolution? Samson 1344
Dispute thy coming? come without delay; Samson 1395
Delayed
All Justice: nor delaid the winged Saint Par Lost 5.247
Solace in her return, so long delay'd; Par Lost 9.844
Shook, but delaid to strike, though oft invok't Par Lost 11.492
El. Bro. Thyrsis? Whose artful strains have oft delaid Mask 494
Trinity ms 'delay'd'
Bridgewater ms 'delayed'
1637 'delayd'
Delays
Invests the Sea, and wished Morn delayes: Par Lost 1.208
O welcom hour whenever! why delayes Par Lost 10.771
But where delays he now? some great intent Par Reg 2.95
Delectable
Wee ours for change delectable, not need) Par Lost 5.629
Delectable both to behold and taste; Par Lost 7.539
Delia
Oread or *Dryad*, or of *Delia*'s Traine, Par Lost 9.387
Betook her to the Groves, but *Delia*'s self Par Lost 9.388
Deliberate
Deliberate valour breath'd, firm and unmov'd Par Lost 1.554
Deliberation
Deliberation sat and public care; Par Lost 2.303
Delicacies
Nor vehement desire, these delicacies Par Lost 8.526
Thy pompous Delicacies I contemn, Par Reg 2.390
Delicacy
What choice to chuse for delicacie best, Par Lost 5.333

Delicacy(*cont*)
For gentle usage, and soft delicacy? Mask 681
1637 'delicacie'
Trinity ms 'delicacie'
line not in Bridgewater ms
Delicious
Purge off this gloom; the soft delicious Air, Par Lost 2.400
Of *Eden*, where delicious Paradise, Par Lost 4.132
If true, here only, and of delicious taste: Par Lost 4.251
In Paradise that bear delicious fruit Par Lost 4.422
Ordaind by thee, and this delicious place Par Lost 4.729
Fruit of delicious Vines, the growth of Heav'n. Par Lost 5.635
He brought thee into this delicious Grove, Par Lost 7.537
Spot more delicious then those Gardens feign'd Par Lost 9.439
As meet is, after such delicious Fare; Par Lost 9.1028
In this delicious Garden? as my Will Par Lost 10.746
Chor. Desire of wine and all delicious drinks, Samson 541
And that which is not good, is not delicious Mask 704
Bridgewater ms 'delitious'
Deliciously
Deliciously, and builds her waxen Cells Par Lost 7.491
Delight
Delight thee more, and *Siloa*'s Brook that flow'd Par Lost 1.11
But ever to do ill our sole delight, Par Lost 1.160
In Heav'n this our delight; how wearisom Par Lost 2.247
O Son, in whom my Soul hath chief delight, Par Lost 3.168
His chief delight and favour, him for whom Par Lost 3.664
Had in remembrance alwayes with delight; Par Lost 3.704
Of us out-cast, exil'd, his new delight, Par Lost 4.106
Vernal delight and joy, able to drive Par Lost 4.155
To all delight of human sense expos'd Par Lost 4.206
Saw undelighted all delight, all kind Par Lost 4.286
Of her loose tresses hid: he in delight Par Lost 4.497
Dole with delight, which in this place I sought; Par Lost 4.894
Heav'ns last best gift, my ever new delight, Par Lost 5.19
To us for food and for delight hath caus'd Par Lost 5.400
My exaltation, and my whole delight, Par Lost 6.727
Or wander with delight, and love to haunt Par Lost 7.330
With wonder, but delight, and, as is due, Par Lost 8.11
Can sort, what harmonie or true delight? Par Lost 8.384
All rational delight, wherein the brute Par Lost 8.391
The spirit of love and amorous delight. Par Lost 8.477
In all things else delight indeed, but such Par Lost 8.524
Made so adorn for thy delight the more, Par Lost 8.576
Is propagated seem such dear delight Par Lost 8.580
With what delight could I have walkt thee round, Par Lost 9.114
For not to irksom toile, but to delight Par Lost 9.242
He made us, and delight to Reason joyn'd. Par Lost 9.243
Thir tendance or Plantation for delight Par Lost 9.419
Adjoynd, from each thing met conceaves delight, Par Lost 9.449
She most, and in her look summs all Delight. Par Lost 9.454
Though in mid Heav'n, soon ended his delight, Par Lost 9.468
Regarded, such delight till then, as seemd, Par Lost 9.787
So saying, with delight he snuff'd the smell Par Lost 10.272
Towards her, his life so late and sole delight, Par Lost 10.941
Due nourishment, not gluttonous delight, Par Lost 11.533
Of *Adam*, soon enclin'd to admit delight, Par Lost 11.596
Establisht, such delight hath God in Men Par Lost 12.245
Made it my whole delight, and in it grew Par Reg 1.208
What wonder then if I delight to hear Par Reg 1.481
Delight not all; among the Sons of Men, Par Reg 2.192
Hunger, with sweet restorative delight. Par Reg 2.373
So reigning can be no sincere delight. Par Reg 2.480
And what delight to be by such extoll'd, Par Reg 3.54
Of moral prudence, with delight receiv'd Par Reg 4.263
Or if I would delight my private hours Par Reg 4.331
Thin sown with aught of profit or delight, Par Reg 4.345
And all her various objects of delight Samson 71
I was his nursling once and choice delight, Samson 633
Man. It shall be my delight to tend his eyes, Samson 1490
Not without wonder or delight beheld. Samson 1642
But such a sacred, and home-felt delight, Mask 262
Will bathe the drooping spirits in delight Mask 812
I have brought ye new delight, Mask 967
Som times with secure delight Allegro 91
Which takes our late fantasticks with delight, Vacation 20
So clear, as in no face with more delight. Sonnet 23, 12
Jehovahs Law is ever his delight, Psalm 1, 5
In wickedness delight Psalm 5, 10
Delighted
Attentive, and with more delighted eare, Par Lost 5.545
Listens delighted. Eevning now approach'd Par Lost 5.627
Delighted, and with frequent intercourse Par Lost 7.571
Delighted, or not capable her eare Par Lost 8.49
Delighted, but desiring more her stay. Par Lost 9.398
Delightful
Him follow'd *Rimmon*, whose delightful Seat Par Lost 1.467
ms 'delightfull'
His bountie, following our delightful task Par Lost 4.437
When first on this delightful Land he spreads Par Lost 4.643
On this delightful land, nor herb, fruit, floure, Par Lost 4.652
All things to mans delightful use; the roofe Par Lost 4.692
From this delightful Fruit, nor known till now Par Lost 9.1023
Delightfully
Delightfully, *Encrease and multiply*, Par Lost 10.730
Delights
Your change approaches, when all these delights Par Lost 4.367
Unlimited of manifold delights: Par Lost 4.435

Delights(*cont*)
Varied his bounty so with new delights, Par Lost 5.431
So much delights me as those graceful acts, Par Lost 8.600
Where other senses want not their delights Samson 916
That the shrewd medling Elfe delights to make, Mask 846
These delights, if thou canst give, Allegro 151
To scorn delights, and live laborious dayes; Lycidas 72
He who of those delights can judge, And spare Sonnet 20, 13
Delilah
Was in the Vale of *Sorec*, *Dalila*, Samson 229
Then *Dalila* thy wife. Samson 724
The sumptuous *Dalila* floating this way: Samson 1072
Delineate
Of human sense, I shall delineate so, Par Lost 5.572
Deliver
Will vanish and deliver ye to woe, Par Lost 4.368
And fear of Death deliver to the Windes. Par Lost 9.989
This offer sets before thee to deliver. Par Reg 3.380
I must deliver, if I mean to raign Par Reg 3.404
Should *Israel* from *Philistian* yoke deliver; Samson 39
Deliverance
Deliverance for us all: this enterprize Par Lost 2.465
All his deliv'rance, and to none but me. Par Lost 3.182
No less then for deliverance what we owe. Par Lost 6.468
Mankinds deliverance. But the voice of God Par Lost 12.235
The great deliverance by her Seed to come Par Lost 12.600
Now, now, for sure, deliverance is at hand, Par Reg 2.35
Deliverance of thy brethren, those ten Tribes Par Reg 3.374
I might begin *Israel*'s Deliverance, Samson 225
Deliverance offerd: I on th' other side Samson 246
But Gods propos'd deliverance not so. Samson 292
To prosecute the means of thy deliverance Samson 603
Delivered
To *Dagon*, as their God who hath deliver'd Samson 437
Quite from his people, and delivered up Samson 1158
As a League-breaker and deliver'd bound Samson 1184
His Letters are deliver'd all and gon, Another 33
line not in 1658 text
Deliver'd were *by me*. Psalm 81, 24
Them from thy hand deliver'd o're Psalm 88, 23
Deliverer
Deliverer from new Lords, leader to free Par Lost 6.451
Is meant thy great deliverer, who shall bruise Par Lost 12.149
But say, if our deliverer up to Heav'n Par Lost 12.479
Ask for this great Deliverer now, and find him Samson 40
As thir Deliverer; if he aught begin, Samson 274
Thir great Deliverer contemn'd, Samson 279
Me their Deliverer sent would not receive, Samson 1214
When God into the hands of thir deliverer Samson 1270
Making them each his own Deliverer, Samson 1289
Deliverers
Great Benefactors of mankind, Deliverers, Par Reg 3.82
Delivery
Of his delivery, and thy joy thereon Samson 1505
Hopeful of his Delivery, which now proves Samson 1575
Dell
Dingle, or bushy dell of this wilde Wood, Mask 312
Delos
Delos or *Samos* first appeering kenns Par Lost 5.265
As *Delos* floating once; the rest his look Par Lost 10.296
Delphian
Thir highest Heav'n; or on the *Delphian* Cliff, Par Lost 1.517
ms 'Delphian'
Delphic
Those Delphick lines with deep impression took, Shakespear 12
1640 'Delphicke'
1632 'Delphicke'
1663-4 '*Delphick*'
Delphos
Shalt be enquir'd at *Delphos* or elsewhere, Par Reg 1.458
With hollow shreik the steep of *Delphos* leaving. Nativity 178
Delude
Though to delude them sent, could not abstain, Par Lost 10.557
With whose stol'n Fruit Man once more to delude. Par Lost 11.125
Deluded
Thrice I deluded her, and turn'd to sport Samson 396
whether deluded and soothing lies & soothing flatteries. Mask Tr. ms 22.20
Deluding
Ambiguous and with double sense deluding, Par Reg 1.435
Hence vain deluding joyes, Penseroso 1
Deluge
Still urges, and a fiery Deluge, fed Par Lost 1.68
ms 'deluge'
Came like a Deluge on the South, and spread Par Lost 1.354
ms 'deluge'
Wrinkl'd the face of Deluge, as decai'd; Par Lost 11.843
Delusion
True wisdom, finds her not, or by delusion Par Reg 4.319
How bitter is such self-delusion? Mask 365
1637 'selfe-delusion'
line not in Bridgewater ms
line not in Trinity ms
Delusions
To thy Delusions; justly, since they fell Par Reg 1.443
Delusive
Hovering and blazing with delusive Light, Par Lost 9.639
This more delusive, not the touch, but taste Par Lost 10.563

Delved	
Hid from the world in a low delved tombe;	Fair Inf 32
He dig'd a pit, and delv'd it deep,	Psalm 7, 55
Demains	
Not thy Conversion, but those rich demaines	Prose 1, 2
Demand	
Will grant thy full demand.	Psalm 81, 44
Demands	
Of him *that help demands*.	Psalm 82, 16
Demeanour	
He markd and mad demeanour, then alone,	Par Lost 4.129
And fierce demeanour seems the Prince of Hell,	Par Lost 4.871
With Goddess-like demeanour forth she went;	Par Lost 8.59
To whom thus *Eve* with sad demeanour meek.	Par Lost 11.162
Demigods	
A thousand Demy-Gods on golden seat's,	Par Lost 1.796
ms 'Demy-gods'	
But to be Gods, or Angels Demi-gods.	Par Lost 9.937
Democraty	
Wielded at will that fierce Democratie,	Par Reg 4.269
Demodocus	
Such as the wise *Demodocus* once told	Vacation 48
Demogorgon	
Of *Demogorgon; Rumor* next and *Chance*,	Par Lost 2.965
Demoniac	
Daemoniac Phrenzie, moaping Melancholie	Par Lost 11.485
line not in 1667 edition	
From thy Demoniac holds, possession foul,	Par Reg 4.628
Demonian	
Demonian Spirits now, from the Element	Par Reg 2.122
Demur	
With reason hath deep silence and demurr	Par Lost 2.431
The latter I demurre, for in thir looks	Par Lost 9.558
Demure	
Soft, modest, meek, demure,	Samson 1036
Sober, stedfast, and demure,	Penseroso 32
Demurring	
That he might fall in *Ramoth*, they demurring,	Par Reg 1.373
1671 printed 'demuring', errata 'demurring'	
Den	
Briareos or *Typhon*, whom the Den	Par Lost 1.199
Accept this dark opprobrious Den of shame,	Par Lost 2.58
In Wood or Wilderness, Forrest or Den;	Par Lost 4.342
In Forrest wilde, in Thicket, Brake, or Den;	Par Lost 7.458
Not yet in horrid Shade or dismal Den,	Par Lost 9.185
From Hell's deep-vaulted Den to dwell in light,	Par Reg 1.116
Of Misers treasure by an out-laws den,	Mask 399
Denial	
Hence with denial vain, and coy excuse,	Lycidas 18
1638 'deniall'	
Denied	
Access deni'd; and over head up grew	Par Lost 4.137
To brute deni'd, and are of Love the food,	Par Lost 9.240
The first at lest of these I thought denid	Par Lost 9.555
1674 printed 'deni d'	
Was death invented? or to us deni'd	Par Lost 9.767
Or whether thou to our moist vows deny'd,	Lycidas 159
Trinity ms 'deni'd'	
1638 'deni'd'	
Doth God exact day labour, light deny'd,	Sonnet 19, 7
Denies	
But first the lawless Tyrant, who denies	Par Lost 12.173
Denounce	
From hallowd ground th' unholie, and denounce	Par Lost 11.106
Denounced	
He ended frowning, and his look denounc'd	Par Lost 2.106
Of Death denounc't, whatever thing Death be,	Par Lost 9.695
On his transgression, Death denounc't that day,	Par Lost 10.49
And th' instant stroke of Death denounc't that day	Par Lost 10.210
Of tardie execution, since denounc't	Par Lost 10.853
Since this days Death denounc't, if ought I see,	Par Lost 10.962
Of infamy upon my name denounc't?	Samson 968
Denouncing	
And full of peace, denouncing wrauth to come	Par Lost 11.815
Dens	
Rocks, Caves, Lakes, Fens, Bogs, Dens, and shades of death,	Par Lost 2.621
Rocks, Dens, and Caves; but I in none of these	Par Lost 9.118
& yawning dens where glaring monsters house	Mask Tr. ms 16.63
and yawninge denns, where glaringe monsters house	Mask Br. ms 416
Dense	
Ore bog or steep, through strait, rough, dense, or rare,	Par Lost 2.948
Deny	
All what we affirm or what deny, and call	Par Lost 5.107
By thy request, who could deny thee nothing;	Samson 881
Deny her nature, and be never more	Mask 559
Bridgewater ms 'denye'	
I pray thee then deny me not thy aide	Vacation 15
Depart	
Then scornd thou didst depart, and to subdue	Par Lost 6.40
Hesperean sets, my Signal to depart.	Par Lost 8.632
Ere thou from hence depart, know I am sent	Par Lost 11.356
To let his sojourners depart, and oft	Par Lost 12.192
Greatly instructed I shall hence depart,	Par Lost 12.557
Depart all ye that work iniquitie.	Psalm 6, 16
Depart from me, for the voice of my weeping	Psalm 6, 17
Departed	
Departed from thee, and thou resembl'st now	Par Lost 4.839

Departing	
Departing gave command, and they observ'd.	Par Lost 10.430
This most afflicts me, that departing hence,	Par Lost 11.315
Departs	
The Grandchilde with twelve Sons increast, departs	Par Lost 12.155
Departure	
Departure from this happy place, our sweet	Par Lost 11.303
Depend	
His providence, and on him sole depend,	Par Lost 12.564
Yet on his Brothers shall depend for Cloathing.	Vacation 82
Dependent	
Dependent made; so God shall uncreate,	Par Lost 9.943
Depending	
Degraded by himself, on grace depending?	Par Reg 4.312
Depends	
My hold of this new Kingdom all depends,	Par Lost 10.406
Deplore	
To find her, or for ever to deplore	Par Lost 8.479
Though *Erymanth* your loss deplore,	Arcades 100
and heaven and hel deplore	Lycidas Tr. ms 29.59
Deplored	
Acknowledg'd and deplor'd, in *Adam* wraught	Par Lost 10.939
Depopulation	
Depopulation; thee another Floud,	Par Lost 11.756
Deport	
In gate surpass'd and Goddess-like deport,	Par Lost 9.389
In wise deport, spake much of Right and Wrong,	Par Lost 11.666
Deposed	
Among the Prime in Splendour, now depos'd,	Par Reg 1.413
Deposited	
Deposited within thee; which to have kept	Samson 429
Depraved	
Self-tempted, self-deprav'd: Man falls deceiv'd	Par Lost 3.130
If not deprav'd from good, created all	Par Lost 5.471
But all corrupt, both Mind and Will deprav'd,	Par Lost 10.825
So all shall turn degenerate, all deprav'd,	Par Lost 11.806
Though late repenting him of Man deprav'd,	Par Lost 11.886
With dotage, and his sense deprav'd	Samson 1042
Depravest	
Unjustly thou deprav'st it with the name	Par Lost 6.174
Deprecation	
And humble deprecation thus repli'd.	Par Lost 8.378
Depressed	
Deprest, and much they may, if all be mine,	Par Lost 9.46
Deprest, and overthrown, as seem'd,	Samson 1698
Deprive	
In savage Wilderness, wherefore deprive	Par Reg 3.23
Deprived	
Thee I have misst, and thought it long, depriv'd	Par Lost 9.857
As from his face I shall be hid, deprivd	Par Lost 11.316
Deprives	
Deprives them of thir outward libertie,	Par Lost 12.100
Depth	
Of depth immeasurable: Anon they move	Par Lost 1.549
Foreseeing or presaging, from the Depth	Par Lost 1.627
In heighth or depth, still first and last will Reign	Par Lost 2.324
The highth and depth of thy Eternal wayes	Par Lost 8.413
And bear through highth or depth of natures bounds	Par Reg 1.13
Derided	
And all his Host derided, while they stood	Par Lost 6.633
Of them derided, but of God observd	Par Lost 11.817
Derides	
All these our motions vain, sees and derides;	Par Lost 2.191
One night or two with wanton growth derides	Par Lost 9.211
Sport that wrincled Care derides,	Allegro 31
Derision	
Justly hast in derision, and secure	Par Lost 5.736
And to his Mates thus in derision call'd.	Par Lost 6.608
Obstruct Heav'n Towrs, and in derision sets	Par Lost 12.52
Thy Foes derision, Captive, Poor, and Blind	Samson 366
Derive	
Nor sinn'd thy sin, yet from that derive	Par Lost 11.427
1667 'that sin derive'	
And from Rebellion shall derive his name,	Par Lost 12.36
Derived	
Into the plant sciential sap, deriv'd	Par Lost 9.837
On me deriv'd, yet I shall temper so	Par Lost 10.77
And to our Seed (O hapless Seed!) deriv'd.	Par Lost 10.965
The Authority which I deriv'd from Heaven.	Par Reg 1.289
That rather *Greece* from us these Arts deriv'd;	Par Reg 4.338
Derivest	
To greatness? whence Authority deriv'st,	Par Reg 2.418
Descant	
She all night long her amorous descant sung;	Par Lost 4.603
To descant on my strength, and give thy verdit?	Samson 1228
Descend	
Descend from Heav'n *Urania*, by that name	Par Lost 7.1
Deign to descend now lower, and relate	Par Lost 7.84
Therefore from this high pitch let us descend	Par Lost 8.198
Descend to? who aspires must down as low	Par Lost 9.169
Vain covertures; but when he saw descend	Par Lost 10.337
Descend through Darkness, on your Rode with ease	Par Lost 10.394
All yours, right down to Paradise descend;	Par Lost 10.398
Or down from Heav'n descend. Such was thir song,	Par Lost 10.648
Let us descend now therefore from this top	Par Lost 12.588
He ended, and they both descend the Hill;	Par Lost 12.606
A perfect Dove descend, what e're it meant,	Par Reg 1.83
Descend with all her winning charms begirt	Par Reg 2.213

Descend(*cont*)
For this did the Angel twice descend? for this — Samson 361
Descended
Slowly descended, and with right aspect — Par Lost 4.541
Down he descended strait; the speed of Gods — Par Lost 10.90
When God descended, and perhaps once more — Par Lost 11.75
Down to the Plain descended: by thir guise — Par Lost 11.576
Descended, *Adam* to the Bowre where *Eve* — Par Lost 12.607
The Cherubim descended; on the ground — Par Lost 12.628
The Spirit descended, while the Fathers voice — Par Reg 1.31
The Spirit descended on me like a Dove, — Par Reg 1.282
Into himself descended, and at once — Par Reg 2.111
From Heaven descended to the low-rooft house — Par Reg 4.273
Yet thou art higher far descended, — Penseroso 22
Down he descended from his Snow-soft chaire, — Fair Inf 19
Descending
Th' advantage, and descending tread us down — Par Lost 1.327
Nor shalt thou by descending to assume — Par Lost 3.303
Angels ascending and descending, bands — Par Lost 3.511
Since by descending from the Thrones above, — Par Lost 5.363
Descending, and in half cut sheere, nor staid, — Par Lost 6.325
Prevenient Grace descending had remov'd — Par Lost 11.3
Had not a Cloud descending snatch'd him thence — Par Lost 11.670
Shall tremble, he descending, will himself — Par Lost 12.228
Promisd by Heavenly message twice descending. — Samson 635
Descends
All perfet good unmeasur'd out, descends, — Par Lost 5.399
Descends, thither with heart and voice and eyes — Par Lost 7.513
The good which we enjoy, from Heav'n descends; — Par Lost 11.142
And slow descends, with somthing heav'nly fraught. — Par Lost 11.207
The ancient Sire descends with all his Train; — Par Lost 11.862
But God who oft descends to visit men — Par Lost 12.48
Descent
I give not Heav'n for lost. From this descent — Par Lost 2.14
Up to our native seat: descent and fall — Par Lost 2.76
The dark descent, and up to reascend, — Par Lost 3.20
O foul descent! that I who erst contended — Par Lost 9.163
If care of our descent perplex us most, — Par Lost 10.979
For swift descent, with him the Cohort bright — Par Lost 11.127
His whole descent, who thus shall *Canaan* win. — Par Lost 12.269
Whom long descent of birth — Samson 171
Toward Heav'ns descent had slop'd his westering wheel. — Lycidas 31
Descents
To me inferiour, infinite descents — Par Lost 8.410
Describe
Speed, to describe whose swiftness Number failes. — Par Lost 8.38
Unsung; or to describe Races and Games, — Par Lost 9.33
Described
Gods latest Image: I describ'd his way — Par Lost 4.567
Describing
High actions, and high passions best describing: — Par Reg 4.266
Descried
As when farr off at Sea a Fleet descri'd — Par Lost 2.636
Since *Uriel* Regent of the Sun descri'd — Par Lost 9.60
And now thir way to Earth they had descri'd, — Par Lost 10.325
Descri'd, divinely warn'd, and witness bore — Par Reg 1.26
Descries
His travell'd steps; farr distant he descries — Par Lost 3.501
Descry
Or in *Valdarno*, to descry new Lands, — Par Lost 1.290
Each quarter, to descrie the distant foe, — Par Lost 6.530
With thir attendant Moons thou wilt descrie — Par Lost 8.149
New Laws to be observ'd; for I descrie — Par Lost 11.228
Left his ground-nest, high towring to descry — Par Reg 2.280
For I descry this way — Samson 1301
And to the tel-tale Sun discry — Mask 141
  Bridgewater ms 'descrie'
Is that which we from hence descry — Arcades 3
  Trinity ms 'descrie'
Desert
Imitate when we please? This Desart soile — Par Lost 2.270
Wandring this darksome Desart, as my way, — Par Lost 2.973
  1667 'desart'
Through dark and desart wayes with peril gone — Par Lost 3.544
To him, or possibly his love desert — Par Lost 5.515
Desert and bare, unsightly, unadornd, — Par Lost 7.314
By living Soule, desert and desolate, — Par Lost 8.154
Heav'n-banisht Host, left desert utmost Hell — Par Lost 10.437
Wandring that watrie Desert: I had hope — Par Lost 11.779
From *Hamath* Northward to the Desert South — Par Lost 12.139
Through the wilde Desert, not the readiest way, — Par Lost 12.216
Into the Desert, his Victorious Field — Par Reg 1.9
He entred now the bordering Desert wild, — Par Reg 1.193
A pathless Desert, dusk with horrid shades; — Par Reg 1.296
The Desert, Fowls in thir clay nests were couch't; — Par Reg 1.501
The while her Son tracing the Desert wild, — Par Reg 2.109
Then to the Desert takes with these his flight; — Par Reg 2.241
Into the Desert, and how there he slept — Par Reg 2.271
Lost in a Desert here and hunger-bit: — Par Reg 2.416
Retir'd unto the Desert, but with arms; — Par Reg 3.166
For barren desert fountainless and dry. — Par Reg 3.264
This Tempest at this Desert most was bent; — Par Reg 4.465
How frequent to desert him, and at last — Samson 275
On Sands, and Shoars, and desert Wildernesses. — Mask 209
  line not in Bridgewater ms
The Pensive secrecy of desert cell, — Mask 387
In dark *Cimmerian* desert ever dwell. — Allegro 10
Thee Shepherd, thee the Woods, and desert Caves, — Lycidas 39

Desert(*cont*)
That in the Desart dwell, — Psalm 83, 24
Deserted
To thy deserted host this cause of flight, — Par Lost 4.922
Deserted, then oblige thee with a fact — Par Lost 9.980
Deserted: Others to a Citie strong — Par Lost 11.655
Forty and more deserted here indeed. — Par Reg 2.316
Desertion
And sense of Heav'ns desertion. — Samson 632
Deserts
Of Wisdom, she deserts thee not, if thou — Par Lost 8.563
When she deserts the night — Samson 88
Are come upon him his deserts? yet why? — Samson 205
Deserve
Deserve the precious bane. And here let those — Par Lost 1.692
For what can less so great a gift deserve? — Par Reg 4.169
As I deserve, pay on my punishment; — Samson 489
From thine, these evils I deserve and more, — Samson 1169
Honest and lawful to deserve my food — Samson 1366
Deserved
Ah wherefore! he deservd no such return — Par Lost 4.42
Mean while in other parts like deeds deservd — Par Lost 6.354
By Sacred Unction, thy deserved right. — Par Lost 6.709
And manifold in sin, deserv'd to fall. — Par Lost 10.16
The miserie, I deserv'd it, and would beare — Par Lost 10.726
Oft not deserv'd? I seek not mine, but his — Par Reg 3.106
To stand 'twixt us and our deserved smart — Fair Inf 69
Deservedly
Deservedly thou griev'st, compos'd of lyes — Par Reg 1.407
Deservedly made vassal, who once just, — Par Reg 4.133
Deserves
Our selves with like defence, to me deserves — Par Lost 6.467
Which he who can, and will, deserv's high praise, — Prose 9, 3
Deserving
Deserving Paradise! if ever, then, — Par Lost 5.446
Farr other name deserving. But the Field — Par Lost 11.171
Made Captive, yet deserving freedom more — Par Reg 3.77
How hainous had the fact been, how deserving — Samson 493
Deservings
My own deservings; but this will not serve; — Par Lost 10.727
Design
To work in close design, by fraud or guile — Par Lost 1.646
  ms 'designe'
His glory to augment. The bold design — Par Lost 2.386
Satan with thoughts inflam'd of highest design, — Par Lost 2.630
Of *Sennaar*, and still with vain designe — Par Lost 3.467
Envious commands, invented with designe — Par Lost 4.524
Works of day pass't, or morrows next designe, — Par Lost 5.33
Whether his first design be to withdraw — Par Lost 9.261
Higher design then to enjoy his State; — Par Reg 2.203
Designed
Then this more secret now design'd, I haste — Par Lost 2.838
Mans Friend, his Mediator, his design'd — Par Lost 10.60
With sent of living Carcasses design'd — Par Lost 10.277
Design'd for great exploits; if I must dye — Samson 32
Who tempted me, that nothing was design'd — Samson 801
Designing
Designing or exhorting glorious warr, — Par Lost 2.179
Designs
Left him at large to his own dark designs, — Par Lost 1.213
This night the human pair, how he designes — Par Lost 5.227
Laugh'st at thir vain designes and tumults vain, — Par Lost 5.737
And all thy heart is set on high designs, — Par Reg 2.410
Desirable
The more desirable, or to say all, — Par Lost 8.505
Why are his gifts desirable, to tempt — Samson 358
Desire
Wrought still within them; and no less desire — Par Lost 2.295
Unspeakable desire to see, and know — Par Lost 3.662
Fair Angel, thy desire which tends to know — Par Lost 3.694
Mine eyes till now, and pin'd with vain desire, — Par Lost 4.466
Where neither joy nor love, but fierce desire, — Par Lost 4.509
With more desire to know, and to reject — Par Lost 4.523
Whom to behold but thee, Natures desire, — Par Lost 5.45
But more desire to hear, if thou consent, — Par Lost 5.555
Presage of Victorie and fierce desire — Par Lost 6.201
Led on, yet sinless, with desire to know — Par Lost 7.61
I have receav'd, to answer thy desire — Par Lost 7.119
And from about her shot Darts of desire — Par Lost 8.62
Desire with thee still longer to converse — Par Lost 8.252
But in degree, the cause of his desire — Par Lost 8.417
Thy wish exactly to thy hearts desire. — Par Lost 8.451
Nor vehement desire, these delicacies — Par Lost 8.526
To satisfie the sharp desire I had — Par Lost 9.584
All other Beasts that saw, with like desire — Par Lost 9.592
So savorie of that Fruit, which with desire, — Par Lost 9.741
Carnal desire enflaming, hee on *Eve* — Par Lost 9.1013
Desire of wandring this unhappie Morn, — Par Lost 9.1136
And with desire to languish without hope, — Par Lost 10.995
With like desire, which would be meserie — Par Lost 10.997
And terror cease; he grants what they besaught — Par Lost 12.238
  1667 'them thir desire'
What can be then less in me then desire — Par Reg 1.383
Draw out with credulous desire, and lead — Par Reg 2.166
Of fond desire? or should she confident, — Par Reg 2.211
Chor. Desire of wine and all delicious drinks, — Samson 541
But in my countrey where I most desire, — Samson 980
And urg'd them on with mad desire — Samson 1677

Desire(*cont*)
Which deepest Spirits, and choicest Wits desire: Vacation 22
Mirth and youth, and warm desire, May Morn 6
Here lies old *Hobson*, Death hath broke his girt, Carrier 1
1658 'hath his desire'
And command which I desire. Psalm 7, 24

Desires
By sin to foul exorbitant desires; Par Lost 3.177
Vaine hopes, vaine aimes, inordinate desires Par Lost 4.808
Human desires can seek or apprehend? Par Lost 5.518
Immediately inordinate desires Par Lost 12.87
Lawful desires of Nature, not beyond; Par Reg 2.230
Passions, Desires, and Fears, is more a King; Par Reg 2.467

Desirest
With that bad Woman? Thus what thou desir'st Par Lost 10.837
So now of what thou knowst not, who desir'st Par Lost 10.948

Desiring
Desiring; nor restrain'd conveyance need Par Lost 8.628
Delighted, but desiring more her stay. Par Lost 9.398

Desirous
Desirous; all in Circles as they stood, Par Lost 5.631
Waiting desirous her return, had wove Par Lost 9.839
Desirous to resigne, and render back Par Lost 10.749
Unwarie, and too desirous, as before, Par Lost 10.947
Hath led me on desirous to behold Samson 741

Desist
Mee to thy will; desist, thou art discern'd Par Reg 4.497
To mix with thy concernments I desist Samson 969

Desisting
Desisting, though unwearied, up returnd Par Lost 7.552

Desolate
To wing the desolate Abyss, and spie Par Lost 4.936
By living Soule, desert and desolate, Par Lost 8.154
And all about found desolate; for those Par Lost 10.420
Desolate where she sate, approaching nigh, Par Lost 10.864
Inhospitable appeer and desolate, Par Lost 11.306
Defend the poor and desolate, Psalm 82, 13

Desolation
The seat of desolation, voyd of light, Par Lost 1.181
The desolation of a Hostile City. Samson 1561
Yea there, where very desolation dwels Mask 428
Bridgewater ms 'desolacion'

Despair
Vaunting aloud, but rackt with deep despare: Par Lost 1.126
ms 'despair'
If not what resolution from despare. Par Lost 1.191
ms 'despair'
Not in despair, to have found themselves not lost Par Lost 1.525
ms 'despaire'
To that bad eminence; and from despair Par Lost 2.6
That fought in Heav'n; now fiercer by despair: Par Lost 2.45
Mistrustful, grounds his courage on despair Par Lost 2.126
Is flat despair: we must exasperate Par Lost 2.143
By change of place: Now conscience wakes despair Par Lost 4.23
Infinite wrauth, and infinite despaire? Par Lost 4.74
Thrice chang'd with pale, ire, envie and despair, Par Lost 4.115
All sadness but despair: now gentle gales Par Lost 4.156
Insensate, hope conceiving from despair. Par Lost 6.787
And shame, and perturbation, and despaire, Par Lost 10.113
She ended heer, or vehement despaire Par Lost 10.1007
Out of despaire, joy, but with fear yet linkt; Par Lost 11.139
Of sorrow and dejection and despair Par Lost 11.301
Dire was the tossing, deep the groans, despair Par Lost 11.489
And talk at least, though I despair to attain. Par Reg 1.485
Thence faintings, swounings of despair, Samson 631
Justly, yet despair not of his final pardon Samson 1171

Despaired
Full Counsel must mature: Peace is despaird, Par Lost 1.660
ms 'despair'd'
Think nothing hard, much less to be despaird. Par Lost 6.495

Despairing
Despairing, seeks to work us woe and shame Par Lost 9.255

Desperate
Desperate revenge, and Battel dangerous Par Lost 2.107
On desparate reveng, that shall redound Par Lost 3.85
1667 'desperat'
Yet gives not o're though desperate of success, Par Reg 4.23
Desperate of better course, to vent his rage, Par Reg 4.445

Desperation
Ruin, and desperation, and dismay, Par Reg 4.579

Despicable
Of despicable foes. With these in troop Par Lost 1.437
No despicable gift; surmise not then Par Lost 11.340

Despise
There let them learn, as likes them, to despise Par Lost 6.717
Chiefly I sought, without thee can despise. Par Lost 9.878
Aetherial, who all pleasures else despise, Par Reg 3.28
And to despise, or envy, or suspect Samson 272

Despised
That for the general safety he despis'd Par Lost 2.481
Nor God, nor Man; is Knowledge so despis'd? Par Lost 5.60
Doubl'd, would render them yet more despis'd, Par Lost 6.602
By mee, not you but mee they have despis'd, Par Lost 6.812
With clang despis'd the ground, under a cloud Par Lost 7.422
Discount'nance her despis'd, and put to rout Par Reg 2.218
Despis'd and thought extinguish't quite, Samson 1688
Not half his riches known, and yet despis'd, Mask 724
Trinity ms 'dispis'd'

Despite
Gnashing for anguish and despite and shame Par Lost 6.340
As a despite don against the most High, Par Lost 6.906
Of Heav'n, this Man of Clay, Son of despite, Par Lost 9.176
Rancor and pride, impatience and despite, Par Lost 10.1044
Before the Lord, as in despite of Heav'n, Par Lost 12.34
And mad despight to be so oft repell'd. Par Reg 4.446
And in despight of *Pharao* fell, Psalm 136, 41

Despiteful
Meanwhile the hainous and despightfull act Par Lost 10.1

Despoil
Such a discomfit, as shall quite despoil him Samson 469

Despoiled
Useless and vain, of freedom both despoild, Par Lost 3.109
Despoild of Innocence, of Faith, of Bliss. Par Lost 9.411
Remaind still happie, not as now, despoild Par Lost 9.1138
And so of all true good himself despoil'd, Par Reg 3.139
Then turn'd me out ridiculous, despoil'd, Samson 539

Despotic
Gave to the man despotic power Samson 1054

Destined
His inmost counsels from thir destind aim. Par Lost 1.168
Reserv'd and destin'd to Eternal woe; Par Lost 2.161
Destin'd to that good hour: no less rejoyc'd Par Lost 2.848
Of destind habitation; but thou know'st Par Lost 7.622
And destin'd Man himself to judge Man fall'n. Par Lost 10.62
Destin'd restorer of Mankind, by whom Par Lost 10.646
Of mightiest Empire, from the destind Walls Par Lost 11.387
And shadows, of that destind Seed to bruise Par Lost 12.233
Destin'd to this, is late of woman born, Par Reg 1.65
To win thy destin'd seat, but wilt prolong Par Reg 4.469
His destin'd from the womb, Samson 634
With lucky words favour my destin'd Urn, Lycidas 20

Destiny
O had his powerful Destiny ordaind Par Lost 4.58
By Destinie, and can no other choose? Par Lost 5.534
So hung his destiny never to rot Another 3
1640 'destinie'

Destitute
Shorn of his strength, They destitute and bare Par Lost 9.1062
Of all things destitute, and well I know, Par Reg 2.305

Destroy
Wasting the Earth, each other to destroy: Par Lost 2.502
His wrath which one day will destroy ye both. Par Lost 2.734
Made to destroy: I fled, and cry'd out *Death;* Par Lost 2.787
If him by force he can destroy, or worse, Par Lost 3.91
Though not destroy, thir happie Native seat; Par Lost 6.226
Not to destroy, but root them out of Heav'n: Par Lost 6.855
Is greater then created to destroy. Par Lost 7.607
Of pleasure, but all pleasure to destroy, Par Lost 9.477
Though threatning, will in earnest so destroy Par Lost 9.939
Both to destroy, or unimmortal make Par Lost 10.611
Destruction with destruction to destroy. Par Lost 10.1006
And makes a Covenant never to destroy Par Lost 11.892
Misled; the stubborn only to subdue. Par Reg 1.226
1671 printed 'destroy', errata 'subdue'
And all the flourishing works of peace destroy, Par Reg 3.80
At once both to destroy and be destroy'd; Samson 1587
Thou wilt destroy that speak a ly Psalm 5, 15

Destroyed
Fear to be worse destroy'd: what can be worse Par Lost 2.85
Calls us to Penance? More destroy'd then thus Par Lost 2.92
So easily destroy'd, and still destroyes Par Lost 3.301
To my relentless thoughts; and him destroyd, Par Lost 9.130
His Children, all in view destroyd at once; Par Lost 11.761
Of wicked Sons destroyd, then I rejoyce Par Lost 11.875
Betwixt the world destroy'd and world restor'd, Par Lost 12.3
line not in 1667 edition
How many Kings destroyd, and Kingdoms won, Par Lost 12.262
A common enemy, who had destroy'd Samson 856
At once both to destroy and be destroy'd; Samson 1587

Destroyer
But our destroyer, foe to God and Man? Par Lost 4.749
1667 'Destroyer'
Her countrey from a fierce destroyer, chose Samson 985
To call in hast for thir destroyer; Samson 1678

Destroyers
Destroyers rightlier call'd and Plagues of men. Par Lost 11.697

Destroying
For onely in destroying I find ease Par Lost 9.129
Save what is in destroying, other joy Par Lost 9.478
Not by destroying *Satan*, but his works Par Lost 12.394

Destroys
So easily destroy'd, and still destroyes Par Lost 3.301
And what thou fearst, alike destroyes all hope Par Lost 10.838
But life preserves, destroys life's enemy, Par Reg 2.372

Destruction
In horrible destruction laid thus low, Par Lost 1.137
To our destruction: if there be in Hell Par Lost 2.84
Through all the Coasts of dark destruction seek Par Lost 2.464
That day and night for his destruction waite. Par Lost 2.505
But to destruction sacred and devote, Par Lost 3.208
On those proud Towrs to swift destruction doom'd. Par Lost 5.907
Destruction to the rest: this pause between Par Lost 6.162
Wide wasting; such destruction to withstand Par Lost 6.253
Destruction with Creation might have mixt. Par Lost 8.236
On mans destruction, maugre what might hap Par Lost 9.56
In wo then; that destruction wide may range: Par Lost 9.134

Destruction(*cont*)
All kinds, and for destruction to mature — Par Lost 10.612
Destruction with destruction to destroy. — Par Lost 10.1006
But self-destruction therefore saught, refutes — Par Lost 10.1016
To his destruction, as I had in charge. — Par Reg 1.376
And my promotion will be thy destruction? — Par Reg 3.202
If not by quick destruction soon cut off — Samson 764
Ruin, destruction at the utmost point. — Samson 1514
Pulld down the same destruction on himself; — Samson 1658
Thir own destruction to come speedy upon them. — Samson 1681

Detain
How suttly to detaine thee I devise, — Par Lost 8.207
Detain from following thy illustrious track. — Par Lost 10.367

Detained
Escap't the *Stygian* Pool, though long detain'd — Par Lost 3.14
Perhaps thou linger'st in deep thoughts detain'd — Par Reg 3.227

Detains
Absents thee, or what chance detains? Come forth. — Par Lost 10.108

Detect
Wouldst easily detect what I conceale. — Par Lost 10.136

Deter
Of difficulty or danger could deterr — Par Lost 2.449
1667 'deterre'

Determine
That might determine, and not need repeate, — Par Lost 6.318
Of us will soon determin, or impose — Par Lost 11.227

Determined
Warr hath determin'd us, and foild with loss — Par Lost 2.330
Determind, and thy hapless crew involv'd — Par Lost 5.879
Determin'd to advance into our room — Par Lost 9.148
Thither he bent his way, determin'd there — Par Reg 2.291

Determinest
Dal. Since thou determinst weakness for no plea — Samson 843

Deterred
Deterrd not from atchieving what might leade — Par Lost 9.696

Detest
The bloodi' and guileful man God doth detest. — Psalm 5, 16

Detestable
Sight more detestable then him and thee. — Par Lost 2.745

Detraction
Of detraction from her praise, — Arcades 11

Detractions
Not of warr onely, but detractions rude, — Sonnet 16, 2
1694 'distractions'

Detriment
That detriment, if such it be to lose — Par Lost 7.153
No detriment need feare, goe and be strong. — Par Lost 10.409

Deucalion
Deucalion and chaste *Pyrrha* to restore — Par Lost 11.12

Deva
Nor yet where *Deva* spreads her wisard stream: — Lycidas 55

Device
Yet with no new device, they all were spent, — Par Reg 4.443
With som other new device. — Mask 941

Devices
Their own devises blind. — Psalm 81, 52

Devil
O shame to men! Devil with Devil damn'd — Par Lost 2.496
Here matter new to gaze the Devil met — Par Lost 3.613
With kisses pure: aside the Devil turnd — Par Lost 4.502
Invincible: abasht the Devil stood, — Par Lost 4.846
The Devil enterd, and his brutal sense, — Par Lost 9.188
Though by the Devil himself, him overweening — Par Lost 10.878
Expel a Devil who first made him such? — Par Reg 4.129

Devilish
Pleaded his devilish Counsel, first devis'd — Par Lost 2.379
And like a devillish Engine back recoiles — Par Lost 4.17
The Tyrants plea, excus'd his devilish deeds. — Par Lost 4.394
Assaying by his Devilish art to reach — Par Lost 4.801
With dev'lish machination might devise — Par Lost 6.504
Training his devilish Enginrie, impal'd — Par Lost 6.553
Thir devilish glut, chaind Thunderbolts and Hail — Par Lost 6.589
1667 'devillish'
And devilish machinations come to nought. — Par Reg 1.181

Devils
And Devils to adore for Deities: — Par Lost 1.373
ms 'divells'

Devious
Into the devious Air; then might ye see — Par Lost 3.489

Devise
With dev'lish machination might devise — Par Lost 6.504
How suttly to detaine thee I devise, — Par Lost 8.207
But let us now, as in bad plight, devise — Par Lost 9.1091
As *Mercury* did first devise — Mask 963

Devised
Pleaded his devilish Counsel, first devis'd — Par Lost 2.379
With what may be devis'd of honours new — Par Lost 5.780

Devising
Thereby regaind, but sat devising Death — Par Lost 4.197

Devoid
Devoid of sense and motion? and who knows, — Par Lost 2.151

Devolved
Devolv'd; though should I hold my peace, yet thou — Par Lost 10.135

Devote
But to destruction sacred and devote, — Par Lost 3.208
Defac't, deflourd, and now to Death devote? — Par Lost 9.901
A World devote to universal rack. — Par Lost 11.821

Devoted
These wicked Tents devoted, least the wrauth — Par Lost 5.890
Devoted to thy vertuous name; — Winchester 60

Devotion
Directed in Devotion, to adore — Par Lost 7.514
Is Pietie thus and pure Devotion paid? — Par Lost 11.452
With solemnest devotion, spread before him — Samson 1147
Was all in honour and devotion ment — Arcades 35

Devour
Outrageous to devour, immures us round — Par Lost 2.435
And me his Parent would full soon devour — Par Lost 2.805
Still threatning to devour me opens wide, — Par Lost 4.77
The Sithe of Time mowes down, devour unspar'd, — Par Lost 10.606
But full soon they did devour — Psalm 136, 53

Devoured
Devourd each other; nor stood much in awe — Par Lost 10.712
Which must be born to certain woe, devourd — Par Lost 10.980
Her riddle, and him, who solv'd it not, devour'd; — Par Reg 4.573

Devouring
His Thunder on thy head, devouring fire. — Par Lost 5.893
And wheel on th' Earth, devouring where it rouls; — Par Lost 12.183
Devouring war shall never cease to roare: — Vacation 86

Devours
What it devours not, Herb, or Fruit, or Graine, — Par Lost 12.184
Daily devours apace, and nothing sed, — Lycidas 129
1638 'devoures'
And glut thy self with what thy womb devours, — On Time 4
Trinity ms 'devoures'

Devout
Of *Themis* stood devout. To Heav'n thir prayers — Par Lost 11.14
Then with uplifted hands, and eyes devout, — Par Lost 11.863
Com pensive Nun, devout and pure, — Penseroso 31
Hymns devout and holy Psalms — Musick 15
With sighs devout ascend — Psalm 88, 6

Dew
Successive, and the timely dew of sleep — Par Lost 4.614
Glistring with dew; fragrant the fertil earth — Par Lost 4.645
Glistring with dew, nor fragrance after showers, — Par Lost 4.653
Or Cedar, to defend him from the dew, — Par Reg 1.306
Like a fair flower surcharg'd with dew, she weeps — Samson 728
From the chill dew, amongst rude burrs and thistles? — Mask 352
Bridgewater ms 'dewe'
And though not mortal, yet a cold shuddring dew — Mask 802
line not in Trinity ms
line not in Bridgewater ms
And drenches with *Elysian* dew — Mask 996
And fresh-blown Roses washt in dew, — Allegro 22
And every Herb that sips the dew; — Penseroso 172
And from the Boughs brush off the evil dew, — Arcades 50
And those Pearls of dew she wears, — Winchester 43

Dew-besprent
Of Knot-grass dew-besprent, and were in fold, — Mask 542
Trinity ms 'dew besprent'

Dewdrops
Or Starrs of Morning, Dew-drops, which the Sun — Par Lost 5.746

Dewed
Surcharg'd, as had like grief bin dew'd in tears, — Par Lost 12.373

Dews
In clusters; they among fresh dews and flowers — Par Lost 1.771
Among sweet dewes and flours; where any row — Par Lost 5.212
We brush mellifluous Dewes, and find the ground — Par Lost 5.429
In darker veile) and roseat Dews dispos'd — Par Lost 5.646
Leucothea wak'd, and with fresh dews imbalmd — Par Lost 11.135
From dews and damps of night his shelter'd head, — Par Reg 4.406
Batt'ning our flocks with the fresh dews of night, — Lycidas 29

Dewy
To Noon he fell, from Noon to dewy Eve, — Par Lost 1.743
By us oft seen; his dewie locks distill'd — Par Lost 5.56
Shot paralel to the earth his dewie ray, — Par Lost 5.141
None was, but from the Earth a dewie Mist — Par Lost 7.333
The solace of thir sin, till dewie sleep — Par Lost 9.1044
A dewie Cloud, and in the Cloud a Bow — Par Lost 11.865

Dewy-feathered
Entice the dewy-feather'd Sleep; — Penseroso 146

Dextrous
Know whether I be dextrous to subdue — Par Lost 5.741

Dextrously
To whom th' Archangel. Dextrously thou aim'st; — Par Lost 11.884

Diabolic
Doubt might beget of Diabolic pow'r — Par Lost 9.95

Diadem
With Diadem and Scepter high advanc'd — Par Lost 4.90
To him who wears the Regal Diadem, — Par Reg 2.461

Dialect
That Structure in the Dialect of men — Par Lost 5.761

Diamond
With Frontispice of Diamond and Gold — Par Lost 3.506
Hung high with Diamond flaming, and with Gold. — Par Lost 4.554
In Pearl, in Diamond, and massie Gold, — Par Lost 5.634
From Diamond Quarries hew'n, and Rocks of Gold, — Par Lost 5.759
Though huge, and in a Rock of Diamond Armd, — Par Lost 6.364
Wherwith she sits on diamond rocks — Mask 881

Diamonds
The Sea o'refraught would swell, & th' unsought diamonds — Mask 732

Diana
Nymphs of *Diana*'s train, and *Naiades* — Par Reg 2.355
Hence had the huntress *Dian* her dred bow — Mask 441

Diapason
In perfect Diapason, whilst they stood Musick 23
Trinity ms 'diapason'
Dictaean
And *Ops*, ere yet *Dictaean Jove* was born. Par Lost 10.584
Dictate
She dictate false, and missinforme the Will Par Lost 9.355
And holy dictate of spare Temperance: Mask 767
Dictates
And dictates to me slumbring, or inspires Par Lost 9.23
Her dictates from thy mouth? most men admire Par Reg 1.482
Dictator
To him their great Dictator, whose attempt Par Reg 1.113
Did
Nor did they not perceave the evil plight Par Lost 1.335
Rather then human. Nor did *Israel* scape Par Lost 1.482
Turns Atheist, as did *Ely*'s Sons, who fill'd Par Lost 1.495
With Golden Architrave; nor did there want Par Lost 1.715
To have built in Heav'n high Towrs; nor did he scape Par Lost 1.749
Did first create your Leader, next free choice, Par Lost 2.19
Did not disswade me most, and seem to cast Par Lost 2.122
No sooner did thy dear and onely Son Par Lost 3.403
Did wisely to conceal, and not divulge Par Lost 8.73
For never did thy Beautie since the day Par Lost 9.1029
All were who heard, dim sadness did not spare Par Lost 10.23
And what she did, whatever in it self, Par Lost 10.141
Shee gave me of the Tree, and I did eate. Par Lost 10.143
The Serpent me beguil'd and I did eate. Par Lost 10.162
Did I request thee, Maker, from my Clay Par Lost 10.743
To mould me Man, did I sollicite thee Par Lost 10.744
To my just number found. O why did God, Par Lost 10.888
Gods Image did not reverence in themselves. Par Lost 11.525
Did, as thou sawst, receave, to walk with God Par Lost 11.707
As did thir Lord before them. Thus they win Par Lost 12.502
Never did wrong or violence, by them Par Reg 1.389
Accomplish what they did, perhaps and more? Par Reg 2.452
Recount his praises; thus he did to *Job*, Par Reg 3.64
Abominations rather, as did once Par Reg 3.162
So did not *Machabeus:* he indeed Par Reg 3.165
Endeavour, as thy Father *David* did, Par Reg 3.353
Did I not tell thee, if thou didst reject Par Reg 4.467
Those terrors which thou speak'st of, did me none; Par Reg 4.487
O wherefore did God grant me my request, Samson 356
For this did the Angel twice descend? for this Samson 361
But warn'd by oft experience: did not she Samson 382
Thou couldst repress, nor did the dancing Rubie Samson 543
To what I did thou shewdst me first the way. Samson 781
Caus'd what I did? I saw thee mutable Samson 793
At *Askalon*, who never did thee harm, Samson 1187
To others did no violence nor spoil. Samson 1191
Single Rebellion and did Hostile Acts. Samson 1210
Was I deceiv'd, or did a sable cloud Mask 221
line not in Bridgewater ms
I did not err, there does a sable cloud Mask 223
line not in Bridgewater ms
How sweetly did they float upon the wings Mask 249
Whom certain these rough shades did never breed Mask 266
Too well I did perceive it was the voice Mask 563
Trinity ms 'might'
Bridgewater ms 'might'
Which when I did, he on the tender grass Mask 624
Wherefore did Nature powre her bounties forth, Mask 710
As *Mercury* did first devise Mask 963
so fares as did forsaken Proserpine Mask Tr. ms 15.52
soe fares as did forsaken Proserpine Mask Br. ms 344
And made Hell grant what Love did seek. Penseroso 108
On which the *Tartar* King did ride; Penseroso 115
Whom Universal nature did lament, Lycidas 60
Trinity ms 'did' ←'might'
Last came, and last did go, Lycidas 108
Our great redemption from above did bring; Nativity 4
For so the holy sages once did sing, Nativity 5
But in their glimmering Orbs did glow, Nativity 75
Was all that did their silly thoughts so busie keep. Nativity 92
Their hearts and ears did greet, Nativity 94
That by his wisdom did create Psalm 136, 17
That did the solid Earth ordain Psalm 136, 21
Did fill the new-made world with light. Psalm 136, 26
While the Hebrew Bands did pass. Psalm 136, 50
But full soon they did devour Psalm 136, 53
His chosen people he did bless Psalm 136, 57
And large-lim'd *Og* he did subdue, Psalm 136, 69
That did thy cheek envermeil, thought to kiss Fair Inf 6
Whilome did slay his dearly-loved mate Fair Inf 24
Oh no? for something in thy face did shine Fair Inf 34
Took up, and in fit place did reinstall? Fair Inf 46
Or did of late earths Sonnes besiege the wall Fair Inf 47
And, if it happen as I did forecast, Vacation 13
Thy drowsie Nurse hath sworn she did them spie Vacation 61
Wherwith the stage of Ayr and Earth did ring, Passion 2
My muse with Angels did divide to sing; Passion 4
Which on our dearest Lord did sease er'e long, Passion 10
Which he for us did freely undergo. Passion 12
As once we did, till disproportion'd sin Musick 19
Trinity ms 'did' ←'could'
Here lieth one who did most truly prove, Another 1
That he could never die while he could move, Another 2
1640, 1657 'did move'

Did*(cont)*
If ever deed of honour did thee please, Sonnet 8, 3
I did but prompt the age to quit their cloggs Sonnet 12, 1
Purification in the old Law did save, Sonnet 23, 6
When trouble did thee sore assaile, Psalm 81, 25
And I to free thee *did not faile*, Psalm 81, 27
Then did I leave them to their will Psalm 81, 49
And all their Sin, *that did thee grieve* Psalm 85, 7
Did our forefathers yoke, Psalm 87, 12
Didst
Of *Oreb*, or of *Sinai*, didst inspire Par Lost 1.7
Cloth'd with transcendent brightness didst out-shine Par Lost 1.86
Of God, as with a Mantle didst invest Par Lost 3.10
Thy Fathers dreadful Thunder didst not spare, Par Lost 3.393
Father of Mercie and Grace, thou didst not doome Par Lost 3.401
That what in sleep thou didst abhorr to dream, Par Lost 5.120
That Golden Scepter which thou didst reject Par Lost 5.886
Thy disobedience. Well thou didst advise, Par Lost 5.888
Then scornd thou didst depart, and to subdue Par Lost 6.40
Thou with Eternal wisdom didst converse, Par Lost 7.9
Wisdom thy Sister, and with her didst play Par Lost 7.10
O *Eve*, in evil hour thou didst give eare Par Lost 9.1067
Being as I am, why didst not thou the Head Par Lost 9.1155
Too facil then thou didst not much gainsay, Par Lost 9.1158
Nay didst permit, approve, and fair dismiss. Par Lost 9.1159
Was shee thy God, that her thou didst obey Par Lost 10.145
Thou did'st resigne thy Manhood, and the Place Par Lost 10.148
There didst not; there let him still Victor sway, Par Lost 10.376
Thou didst accept them; wilt thou enjoy the good, Par Lost 10.758
Wherefore didst thou beget me? I sought it not Par Lost 10.762
Then due by sentence when thou didst transgress, Par Lost 11.253
How didst thou grieve then, *Adam*, to behold Par Lost 11.754
But by fulfilling that which thou didst want, Par Lost 12.396
Did I not tell thee, if thou didst reject Par Reg 4.467
Thou didst debel, and down from Heav'n cast Par Reg 4.605
Rather approv'd them not; but thou didst plead Samson 421
But throw'st them lower then thou didst exalt them high, Samson 689
Didst thou at first receive me for thy husband? Samson 883
To please thy gods thou didst it; gods unable Samson 896
And why from us so quickly thou didst take thy flight. Fair Inf 42
Of shak't Olympus by mischance didst fall; Fair Inf 44
To earth from thy praefixed seat didst poast, Fair Inf 59
But oh why didst thou not stay here below Fair Inf 64
Didst move my first endeavouring tongue to speak, Vacation 2
Come tripping to the Room where thou didst lie; Vacation 62
that didst reform thy art, the cheif among Sonnet 13, Tr. ms 40.08
Meekly thou didst resign this earthy load Sonnet 14, 3
Trinity ms 'did'st' ←'didst'
Thou didst me disinthrall Psalm 4, 4
Judgment here thou didst ingage Psalm 7, 23
Thou did'st prepare for it a place Psalm 80, 37
On me then didst thou call, Psalm 81, 26
Thou didst to Jabins *hoast*, Psalm 83, 36
Th' iniquity thou didst forgive Psalm 85, 5
And *calmly* didst return Psalm 85, 10
Die
He with his whole posteritie must dye, Par Lost 3.209
1667 'die'
Dye hee or Justice must; unless for him Par Lost 3.210
1667 'Die'
Freely put off, and for him lastly dye Par Lost 3.240
1667 'die'
All that of me can die, yet that debt paid, Par Lost 3.246
Shall satisfie for Man, be judg'd and die, Par Lost 3.295
Second to thee, offerd himself to die Par Lost 3.409
They taste and die: what likelier can ensue? Par Lost 4.527
Cannot but by annihilating die; Par Lost 6.347
Transgrest, inevitably thou shalt dye; Par Lost 8.330
Thereof, nor shall ye touch it, least ye die. Par Lost 9.663
Those rigid threats of Death; ye shall not Die: Par Lost 9.685
So ye shall die perhaps, by putting off Par Lost 9.713
Of this fair Fruit, our doom is, we shall die. Par Lost 9.763
Certain my resolution is to Die; Par Lost 9.907
Perhaps thou shalt not Die, perhaps the Fact Par Lost 9.928
The worst, and not perswade thee rather die Par Lost 9.979
Pursues me still, least all I cannot die, Par Lost 10.783
But I shall die a living Death? O thought Par Lost 10.788
All of me then shall die: let this appease Par Lost 10.792
Of many ways to die the shortest choosing, Par Lost 10.1005
Loose no reward, though here thou see him die, Par Lost 11.459
Some, as thou saw'st, by violent stroke shall die, Par Lost 11.471
His Cattel must of Rot and Murren die, Par Lost 12.179
They die; but in thir room, as they forewarne, Par Lost 12.507
Design'd for great exploits; if I must dye Samson 32
And though her body die, her fame survives, Samson 1706
Will sicken soon and die, Nativity 137
That Kings for such a Tomb would wish to die. Shakespear 16
That he could never die while he could move, Another 2
1640, 1657 'dye'
But ye shall die like men, and fall Psalm 82, 23
As other Princes *die*. Psalm 82, 24
Ever confounded, and so die Psalm 83, 63
My Soul doth long and almost die Psalm 84, 5
When I dye, let the earth be roul'd in flames. Prose 5, 1
Died
Had entertaind, as di'd her Cheeks with pale. Par Lost 10.1009
Annuls thy doom, the death thou shouldst have dy'd, Par Lost 12.428
For death, like that which the redeemer dy'd. Par Lost 12.445

Died(*cont*)
The God of their fore-fathers; but so dy'd Par Reg 3.422
In that sore battel when so many dy'd Samson 287
How dy'd he? death to life is crown or shame. Samson 1579
Fainted, and died, nor would with Ale be quickn'd; Another 16
line not in 1640, 1657, 1658 texts
He di'd for heavines that his Cart went light, Another 22
1640, 1657 'dy'd'
line not in 1658 text

Dies
Where all life dies, death lives, and Nature breeds, Par Lost 2.624
Adore him, who to compass all this dies, Par Lost 3.342
How dies the Serpent? hee hath eat'n and lives, Par Lost 9.764
Of Life that sinn'd; what dies but what had life Par Lost 10.790
Of *Pharao:* there he dies, and leaves his Race Par Lost 12.163
In this his satisfaction; so he dies, Par Lost 12.419
Bring the rathe Primrose that forsaken dies. Lycidas 142

Diest
Thou mai'st not; in the day thou eat'st, thou di'st; Par Lost 7.544

Diet
No inconvenient Diet, nor too light Fare: Par Lost 5.495
Spare Fast, that oft with gods doth diet, Penseroso 46

Dieted
Till dieted by thee I grow mature Par Lost 9.803

Difference
Wise or unwise, no difference, no exemption; Par Reg 3.115

Different
If counsels different, or danger shun'd Par Lost 1.636
Insensibly three different Motions move? Par Lost 8.130
Manlike, but different Sex, so lovly faire, Par Lost 8.471
Least thou not tasting, different degree Par Lost 9.883
Whereon for different cause the Tempter set Par Lost 11.382
But on the hether side a different sort Par Lost 11.574
It may by means far different be attain'd Par Reg 3.89
Break off, break off, I feel the different pace, Mask 145

Differing
Differing but in degree, of kind the same. Par Lost 5.490
Farr differing from this World, thou hast reveal'd Par Lost 7.71

Difficult
The way seems difficult and steep to scale Par Lost 2.71
With travail difficult, not better farr Par Lost 10.593
But if thou judge it hard and difficult, Par Lost 10.992
Was difficult, by humane steps untrod; Par Reg 1.298
Not difficult, if thou hearken to me, Par Reg 2.428
Nothing will please the difficult and nice, Par Reg 4.157

Difficulty
Of difficulty or danger could deterr Par Lost 2.449
So he with difficulty and labour hard Par Lost 2.1021
Mov'd on, with difficulty and labour hee; Par Lost 2.1022
But least the difficultie of passing back Par Lost 10.252

Diffidence
To *Israel*, diffidence of God, and doubt Samson 454

Diffident
Do thou but thine, and be not diffident Par Lost 8.562
Not diffident of thee do I dissuade Par Lost 9.293

Diffuse
Into thir vacant room, and thence diffuse Par Lost 7.190

Diffused
Sense of new joy ineffable diffus'd: Par Lost 3.137
Sutable grace diffus'd, so well he feignd; Par Lost 3.639
With sudden blaze diffus'd, inflames the Aire: Par Lost 4.818
Transparent, Elemental Air, diffus'd Par Lost 7.265
New gatherd, and ambrosial smell diffus'd. Par Lost 9.852
Into thin Air diffus'd: for now began Par Reg 1.499
That fragrant smell diffus'd, in order stood Par Reg 2.351
And not as feeling through all parts diffus'd, Samson 96
See how he lies at random, carelesly diffus'd, Samson 118
At my Nativity this strength, diffus'd Samson 1141

Digest
Tasting concoct, digest, assimilate, Par Lost 5.412

Digestion
Was Aerie light from pure digestion bred, Par Lost 5.4

Digged
And dig'd out ribs of Gold. Let none admire Par Lost 1.690
Part hidd'n veins diggd up (nor hath this Earth Par Lost 6.516
He dig'd a pit, and delv'd it deep, Psalm 7, 55

Dight
The clouds in thousand Liveries dight, Allegro 62
And storied Windows richly dight, Penseroso 159

Dignified
Us his prime Creatures, dignifi'd so high, Par Lost 9.940
Yet toward these thus dignifi'd, thou oft Samson 682

Dignities
Excelling human, Princely Dignities, Par Lost 1.359
ms 'dignities'
And dignities and powers all but the highest? Par Reg 3.30

Dignity
In Heav'n, which follows dignity, might draw Par Lost 2.25
For dignity compos'd and high exploit: Par Lost 2.111
Appointed, which declares his Dignitie, Par Lost 4.619
And of our good, and of our dignitie Par Lost 5.827
In every gesture dignitie and love. Par Lost 8.489
Hers in all real dignitie: Adornd Par Lost 10.151

Digressions
Grateful digressions, and solve high dispute Par Lost 8.55

Dilated
Dilated or condens't, bright or obscure, Par Lost 1.429
Collecting all his might dilated stood, Par Lost 4.986

Dilated(*cont*)
Dilated and infuriate shall send forth Par Lost 6.486
Dimm erst, dilated Spirits, ampler Heart, Par Lost 9.876

Diligence
Why shouldst thou then obtrude this diligence, Par Reg 2.387
With nursing diligence, to me glad office, Samson 924

Dim
In dim Eclips disastrous twilight sheds Par Lost 1.597
ms 'dimme'
Surpris'd thee, dim thine eyes, and dizzie swumm Par Lost 2.753
Shoots farr into the bosom of dim Night Par Lost 2.1036
Or dim suffusion veild. Yet not the more Par Lost 3.26
Tell them that by command, ere yet dim Night Par Lost 5.685
Now ere dim Night had disincumberd Heav'n, Par Lost 5.700
Yet are but dim, shall perfetly be then Par Lost 9.707
Dimm erst, dilated Spirits, ampler Heart, Par Lost 9.876
All were who heard, dim sadness did not spare Par Lost 10.23
Above the smoak and stirr of this dim spot, Mask 5
Trinity ms 'dim' ← 'dim, narrow'
La. Dim darknes, and this leavy Labyrinth. Mask 278
Bridgewater ms 'dym'
Casting a dimm religious light. Penseroso 160
Inwrought with figures dim, and on the edge Lycidas 105
Forsake their Temples dim, Nativity 198
Mine eye grows dim and dead, Psalm 88, 38

Dimension
Without dimension, where length, breadth, & highth, Par Lost 2.893
These as a line thir long dimension drew, Par Lost 7.480

Dimensionless
Dimentionless through Heav'nly dores; then clad Par Lost 11.17

Dimensions
And in thir own dimensions like themselves Par Lost 1.793

Diminish
Thee to diminish, and from thee withdraw Par Lost 7.612

Diminished
Hide thir diminisht heads; to thee I call, Par Lost 4.35

Diminution
So farr remote, with diminution seen. Par Lost 7.369
Regardless of his glories diminution; Samson 303

Dimly
To us invisible or dimly seen Par Lost 5.157

Dimmed
Thus while he spake, each passion dimm'd his face Par Lost 4.114
And carnal fear that day dimm'd *Adams* eye. Par Lost 11.212

Dimple
And love to live in dimple sleek; Allegro 30

Dimpled
By dimpled Brook, and Fountain brim, Mask 119

Din
Clash'd on thir sounding Shields the din of war, Par Lost 1.668
With tumult less and with less hostile din, Par Lost 2.1040
And silence on the odious dinn of Warr: Par Lost 6.408
To his bold Riot: dreadful was the din Par Lost 10.521
And hear the din; thus was the building left Par Lost 12.61
While the Cock with lively din, Allegro 49
Jarr'd against natures chime, and with harsh din Musick 20

Dingle
Dingle, or bushy dell of this wilde Wood, Mask 312

Dinner
For dinner savourie fruits, of taste to please Par Lost 5.304
No fear lest Dinner coole; when thus began Par Lost 5.396
Are at their savory dinner set Allegro 84

Dint
Though temper'd heav'nly, for that mortal dint, Par Lost 2.813

Dipped
And colours dipt in Heav'n; the third his feet Par Lost 5.283
In time of Truce; *Iris* had dipt the wooff; Par Lost 11.244

Dips
Dips me all o're, as when the wrath of *Jove* Mask 803
line not in Bridgewater ms
line not in Trinity ms

Dipsas
And *Dipsas* (not so thick swarm'd once the Soil Par Lost 10.526

Dire
The force of those dire Arms? yet not for those, Par Lost 1.94
Too well I see and rue the dire event, Par Lost 1.134
How overcome this dire Calamity, Par Lost 1.189
Was not inglorious, though th' event was dire, Par Lost 1.624
As this place testifies, and this dire change Par Lost 1.625
Of all his aim, after some dire revenge. Par Lost 2.128
Of Whirlwind and dire Hail, which on firm land Par Lost 2.589
Gorgons and *Hydra's*, and *Chimera's* dire. Par Lost 2.628
Then sweet, now sad to mention, through dire change Par Lost 2.820
Begins his dire attempt, which nigh the birth Par Lost 4.15
Of brazen Chariots rag'd; dire was the noise Par Lost 6.211
No equal, raunging through the dire attack Par Lost 6.248
Hurl'd to and fro with jaculation dire, Par Lost 6.665
Of smoak and bickering flame, and sparkles dire; Par Lost 6.766
Adam by dire example to beware Par Lost 7.42
So glister'd the dire Snake, and into fraud Par Lost 9.643
Scorpion and Asp, and *Amphisbaena* dire, Par Lost 10.524
And the dire hiss renew'd, and the dire form Par Lost 10.543
Satans dire dread, and in his hand the Spear. Par Lost 11.248
Diseases dire, of which a monstrous crew Par Lost 11.474
Dire was the tossing, deep the groans, despair Par Lost 11.489
Must be compelld by Signes and Judgements dire; Par Lost 12.175
To tempt the Son of God with terrors dire. Par Reg 4.431
Dire inflammation which no cooling herb Samson 626

Dire(*cont*)
For dire imagination still persues me. Samson 1544
Of dire necessity, whose law in death conjoin'd Samson 1666
Of calling shapes, and beckning shadows dire, Mask 207
line not in Bridgewater ms
Of dire *Chimera's* and inchanted Iles, Mask 517
Direct
Of thir great Sultan waving to direct Par Lost 1.348
I travel this profound, direct my course; Par Lost 2.980
Direct against which op'nd from beneath, Par Lost 3.526
Shot upward still direct, whence no way round Par Lost 3.618
To find who might direct his wandring flight Par Lost 3.631
Daz'ling the Moon; these to the Bower direct Par Lost 4.798
Shot down direct his fervid Raies to warme Par Lost 5.301
Well hast thou taught the way that might direct Par Lost 5.508
He said, and on his Son with Rayes direct Par Lost 6.719
Part rise in crystal Wall, or ridge direct, Par Lost 7.293
To Gods Eternal house direct the way, Par Lost 7.576
The Woodbine round this Arbour, or direct Par Lost 9.216
Direct, or by occasion hath presented Par Lost 9.974
Direct to th' Eastern Gate was bent thir flight. Par Lost 11.190
Which now direct thine eyes and soon behold. Par Lost 11.711
Led them direct, and down the Cliff as fast Par Lost 12.639
Whereby they may direct their future life. Par Reg 1.396
This is meer moral babble, and direct Mask 807
1637 'direct''
Directed
Directed, no mean recompence it brings Par Lost 2.981
To find thee I directed then my walk; Par Lost 5.49
Directed in Devotion, to adore Par Lost 7.514
Directed to the Manger where thou lais't, Par Reg 1.247
Directly
Directly towards the new created World, Par Lost 3.89
Chor. He will directly to the Lords, I fear, Samson 1250
Directs
So to the Coast of *Jordan* he directs Par Reg 1.119
Directs me in the Starry Rubric set. Par Reg 4.393
Direful
Or while we speak within the direfull grasp Mask 357
line not in Trinity ms
line not in Bridgewater ms
1673 'direful'
Dire-looking
Or what the cross dire-looking Planet smites, Arcades 52
Dirt
A here alas, hath laid him in the dirt, Carrier 2
1658 'mire'
Dis
Her self a fairer Floure by gloomie *Dis* Par Lost 4.270
Disabled
Disabl'd not to give thee thy deaths wound: Par Lost 12.392
Had not disabl'd me, not all your force: Samson 1219
Disadvantage
Some disadvantage we endur'd and paine, Par Lost 6.431
Disagree
Firm concord holds, men onely disagree Par Lost 2.497
Disallied
Nor both so loosly disally'd Samson 1022
Disappear
Feigning to disappear. Darkness now rose, Par Reg 4.397
Disappeared
Satan with his rebellious disappeerd, Par Lost 6.414
Shee disappeerd, and left me dark, I wak'd Par Lost 8.478
To the subjected Plaine; then disappeer'd. Par Lost 12.640
His gray dissimulation, disappear'd Par Reg 1.498
Disapprove
Henceforth, nor too much disapprove my own. Samson 970
Disapproves
And disapproves that care, though wise in show, Sonnet 21, 12
Disarmed
Inglorious, of his mortall sting disarm'd. Par Lost 3.253
Adverse, that they shall fear we have disarmd Par Lost 6.490
Stupidly good, of enmitie disarm'd, Par Lost 9.465
As one disarm'd, his anger all he lost, Par Lost 10.945
Shav'n, and disarm'd among my enemies. Samson 540
Disarrayed
Thou drov'st of warring Angels disarraid. Par Lost 3.396
Disastrous
In dim Eclips disastrous twilight sheds Par Lost 1.597
Disband
Disband, and wandring, each his several way Par Lost 2.523
Disburden
Help to disburden Nature of her Bearth. Par Lost 9.624
Thus to disburd'n sought with sad complaint. Par Lost 10.719
Disburdened
Disburd'nd Heav'n rejoic'd, and soon repaird Par Lost 6.878
Disburdening
Her fertil growth, and by disburd'ning grows Par Lost 5.319
Discern
His swift pursuers from Heav'n Gates discern Par Lost 1.326
For neither Man nor Angel can discern Par Lost 3.682
Hasting this way, and now by glimps discerne Par Lost 4.867
Beholders rude, and shallow to discerne Par Lost 9.544
Within me cleere, not onely to discerne Par Lost 9.681
They now, and men hereafter may discern, Par Reg 1.164
(For I discern thee other then thou seem'st) Par Reg 1.348
Real or Allegoric I discern not, Par Reg 4.390
By his habit I discern him now Samson 1305

Discern(*cont*)
Ye might discern a Cipress bud. Winchester 22
Discerned
Of Mercy and Justice in thy face discern'd, Par Lost 3.407
Where he first lighted, soon discernd his looks Par Lost 4.570
Adam discernd, as in the dore he sat Par Lost 5.299
As was my food, nor aught but food discern'd Par Lost 9.573
Or here th' attempt, thou couldst not have discernd Par Lost 9.1149
Thir Parent soon discern'd, though in disguise. Par Lost 10.331
Mee to thy will; desist, thou art discern'd Par Reg 4.497
Discerning
He ceas'd, discerning *Adam* with such joy Par Lost 12.372
Discerns
He soon discerns, and weltring by his side Par Lost 1.78
ms 'discernes'
Mean while th' Eternal eye, whose sight discernes Par Lost 5.711
And knows, and speaks, and reasons, and discerns, Par Lost 9.765
1667 'discernes'
Discharge
Heav'n witness thou anon, while we discharge Par Lost 6.564
Us haply too secure of our discharge Par Lost 11.196
Hath paid his ransom now and full discharge. Samson 1573
Discharged
Indebted and dischargd; what burden then? Par Lost 4.57
From life discharg'd and parted quite Psalm 88, 17
Disciples
To his Disciples, Men who in his Life Par Lost 12.438
Discipline
Was this your discipline and faith ingag'd, Par Lost 4.954
Disciplined
Up to a better Cov'nant, disciplin'd Par Lost 12.302
Disclose
Due search and consultation will disclose. Par Lost 6.445
Yet these subject not; I to thee disclose Par Lost 8.607
Disclosed
Rowld inward, and a spacious Gap disclos'd Par Lost 6.861
Bursting with kindly rupture forth disclos'd Par Lost 7.419
Discomfit
Such a discomfit, as shall quite despoil him Samson 469
Discomposed
With Tresses discompos'd, and glowing Cheek, Par Lost 5.10
To offend, discount'nanc't both, and discompos'd; Par Lost 10.110
Disconsolate
Dismiss them not disconsolate; reveale Par Lost 11.113
Discontented
At least distemperd, discontented thoughts, Par Lost 4.807
Discontinuous
The griding sword with discontinuous wound Par Lost 6.329
Discord
And *Discord* with a thousand various mouths. Par Lost 2.967
1667 'Discord'
Horrible discord, and the madding Wheeles Par Lost 6.210
The discord which befel, and Warr in Heav'n Par Lost 6.897
Said then th' Omnific Word, your discord end: Par Lost 7.217
Mistrust, Suspicion, Discord, and shook sore Par Lost 9.1124
Outrage from liveless things; but Discord first Par Lost 10.707
Discountenance
Discount'nance her despis'd, and put to rout Par Reg 2.218
Discountenanced
Looses discount'nanc't, and like folly shewes; Par Lost 8.553
To offend, discount'nanc't both, and discompos'd; Par Lost 10.110
Discourse
The thronging audience. In discourse more sweet Par Lost 2.555
Or with repose; and such discourse bring on, Par Lost 5.233
Danc'd hand in hand. A while discourse they hold; Par Lost 5.395
Discursive, or Intuitive; discourse Par Lost 5.488
Thus farr his bold discourse without controule Par Lost 5.803
Yet went she not, as not with such discourse Par Lost 8.48
And sweeter thy discourse is to my eare Par Lost 8.211
Degraded, Wisdom in discourse with her Par Lost 8.552
Venial discourse unblam'd: I now must change Par Lost 9.5
Casual discourse draw on, which intermits Par Lost 9.223
Sate in thir sad discourse, and various plaint, Par Lost 10.343
Discoursed
Smooth on the tongue discourst, pleasing to th' ear, Par Reg 1.479
Discourtesy
Co. By falshood, or discourtesie, or why? Mask 281
Bridgewater ms 'discurtesie'
Discover
Serv'd onely to discover sights of woe, Par Lost 1.64
Op'ning thir brazen foulds discover wide Par Lost 1.724
On bold adventure to discover wide Par Lost 2.571
Law can discover sin, but not remove, Par Lost 12.290
Till Conquerour Death discover them scarce men, Par Reg 3.85
Discovered
Discoverd and surpriz'd. As when a spark Par Lost 4.814
Which to our eyes discoverd new and strange, Par Lost 6.571
Complete to have discover'd and repulst Par Lost 10.10
Discover'd soon the place of her retire. Par Lost 11.267
Discover'd in his fraud, thrown from his hope, Par Reg 4.3
Discover'd in the end, till now conceal'd. Samson 998
Discovering
Discovering in wide Lantskip all the East Par Lost 5.142
Discovers
Which to his eye discovers unaware Par Lost 3.547
Discreet
Then Mortal Creatures, graceful and discreet, Par Reg 2.157

Discreetest	
Seems wisest, vertuousest, discreetest, best;	Par Lost 8.550
Discursive	
Discursive, or Intuitive; discourse	Par Lost 5.488
Disdain	
And high disdain, from sence of injur'd merit,	Par Lost 1.98
ms 'disdaine'	
Disdain forbids me, and my dread of shame	Par Lost 4.82
To his proud fair, best quitted with disdain.	Par Lost 4.770
Deep malice thence conceiving and disdain,	Par Lost 5.666
Thy looks, the Heav'n of mildness, with disdain,	Par Lost 9.534
Though inly stung with anger and disdain,	Par Reg 1.466
Inspir'd; disdain not such access to me.	Par Reg 1.492
Whom thus our Saviour answer'd with disdain.	Par Reg 4.170
Har. To combat with a blind man I disdain,	Samson 1106
Disdained	
I sdeind subjection, and thought one step higher	Par Lost 4.50
Due entrance he disdaind, and in contempt,	Par Lost 4.180
Disdain'd, but meaner thoughts learnd in thir flight,	Par Lost 6.367
Must suffer change, disdain'd not to begin	Par Lost 10.213
Rejected my forewarning, and disdain'd	Par Lost 10.876
Disdainful	
And with disdainful look thus first began.	Par Lost 2.680
Disdainfully	
Disdainfully half smiling thus repli'd.	Par Lost 4.903
Disdaining	
To final Battel drew, disdaining flight,	Par Lost 6.798
In every Province, who themselves disdaining	Par Reg 1.448
Disease	
As a lingring disease,	Samson 618
With sickness and disease thou bow'st them down,	Samson 698
Ease was his chief disease, and to judge right,	Another 21
line not in 1658 text	
Yet (strange to think) his wain was his increase:	Another 32
1640, 1657 'was his disease'	
Diseased	
Numbers of all diseas'd, all maladies	Par Lost 11.480
Diseases	
Diseases dire, of which a monstrous crew	Par Lost 11.474
Painful diseases and deform'd,	Samson 699
Disencumbered	
Now ere dim Night had disincumberd Heav'n,	Par Lost 5.700
Disenthrall	
Thou didst me disinthrall	Psalm 4, 4
Disenthrone	
Either to disinthrone the King of Heav'n	Par Lost 2.229
Disespoused	
Of *Turnus* for *Lavinia* disespous'd,	Par Lost 9.17
Disfigured	
Saw him disfigur'd, more then could befall	Par Lost 4.127
Disfigurement	
Not once perceive their foul disfigurement,	Mask 74
Trinity ms 'disfigurement' ←'disfigurment'	
Disfiguring	
Disfiguring not Gods likeness, but thir own,	Par Lost 11.521
Disglorified	
Disglorifi'd, blasphem'd, and had in scorn	Samson 442
Disgorge	
Of four infernal Rivers that disgorge	Par Lost 2.575
Disgorging	
And all her entrails tore, disgorging foule	Par Lost 6.588
See where it flows, disgorging at seaven mouthes	Par Lost 12.158
Disguise	
Thir Parent soon discern'd, though in disguise.	Par Lost 10.331
Where that damn'd wisard hid in sly disguise	Mask 571
Gen. Stay gentle Swains, for though in this disguise,	Arcades 26
O what a Mask was there, what a disguise!	Passion 19
Disguised	
Thir wandring Gods disguis'd in brutish forms	Par Lost 1.481
Or in *Franciscan* think to pass disguis'd;	Par Lost 3.480
Then at *Circean* call the Herd disguis'd.	Par Lost 9.522
Disguis'd he came, but those his Children dear	Par Lost 10.330
I knew the foul inchanter though disguis'd,	Mask 645
Disguises	
These troublesom disguises which wee wear,	Par Lost 4.740
O my simplicity what sights are these? with darke disguises	Mask Tr. ms 22.19
Dish	
His few Books, or his Beads, or Maple Dish,	Mask 391
1637 'dish'	
Trinity ms 'dish'	
Bridgewater ms 'dishe'	
Disheartened	
Be not disheart'nd then, nor cloud those looks	Par Lost 5.122
Yet neither thus disheartn'd or dismay'd,	Par Reg 1.268
Now blind, disheartn'd, sham'd, dishonour'd, quell'd,	Samson 563
Dishes	
With dishes pil'd, and meats of noblest sort	Par Reg 2.341
The daintest dishes shall be serv'd up last.	Vacation 14
Dishevelled	
Dissheveld, but in wanton ringlets wav'd	Par Lost 4.306
Dishonest	
Then was not guiltie shame, dishonest shame	Par Lost 4.313
Broke him, as that dishonest victory	Sonnet 10, 6
Dishonour	
The Wife, where danger or dishonour lurks,	Par Lost 9.267
The tempted with dishonour foul, suppos'd	Par Lost 9.297
Sticks no dishonor on our Front, but turns	Par Lost 9.330
Contempt instead, dishonour, obloquy?	Par Reg 3.131
Dishonour(*cont*)	
Dishonour, obloquie, and op't the mouths	Samson 452
Nothing to do, be sure, that may dishonour	Samson 1385
Lodge it with dishonour foul.	Psalm 7, 18
Dishonourable	
Of natures works, honor dishonorable,	Par Lost 4.314
Nothing dishonourable, impure, unworthy	Samson 1424
Dishonoured	
Now blind, disheartn'd, sham'd, dishonour'd, quell'd,	Samson 563
Dishonourer	
Dishonourer of *Dagon:* what had I	Samson 861
Dishonours	
Hear these dishonours, and not render death?	Samson 1232
Disinherit	
And disinherit *Chaos*, that raigns here	Mask 334
Disinherited	
So disinherited how would ye bless	Par Lost 10.821
Disjoin	
Forget, nor from thy Fathers praise disjoine.	Par Lost 3.415
Disjoyne us, and I then too late renounce	Par Lost 9.884
Disjoining	
Which Reason joyning or disjoyning, frames	Par Lost 5.106
Dislike	
That durst dislike his reign, and me preferring,	Par Lost 1.102
Good reason was thou freely shouldst dislike,	Par Lost 8.443
And of thir doings great dislike declar'd,	Par Lost 11.720
Dislodge	
With all his Legions to dislodge, and leave	Par Lost 5.669
Lodge and dislodge by turns, which makes through Heav'n	Par Lost 6.7
Dislodged	
Far in the dark dislodg'd, and void of rest,	Par Lost 6.415
Dislodging	
Dislodging from a Region scarce of prey	Par Lost 3.433
Disloyal	
Disloyal breaks his fealtie, and sinns	Par Lost 3.204
Disloyal on the part of Man, revolt,	Par Lost 9.7
Dismal	
The dismal Situation waste and wilde,	Par Lost 1.60
That dismal world, if any Clime perhaps	Par Lost 2.572
From out this dark and dismal house of pain,	Par Lost 2.823
Of conflict; over head the dismal hiss	Par Lost 6.212
That under ground, they fought in dismal shade;	Par Lost 6.666
The dismal Gates, and barricado'd strong;	Par Lost 8.241
Not yet in horrid Shade or dismal Den,	Par Lost 9.185
A dismal universal hiss, the sound	Par Lost 10.508
Or in some other dismal place who knows	Par Lost 10.787
To his grim Cave, all dismal; yet to sense	Par Lost 11.469
The dismal expedition to find out	Par Reg 1.101
After a dismal night; I heard the rack	Par Reg 4.452
Man. Some dismal accident it needs must be;	Samson 1519
In dismall dance about the furnace blue,	Nativity 210
1673 'dismal'	
For once it was my dismal hap to hear	Vacation 68
Down to the *dismal* pit	Psalm 88, 14
Dismay	
That witness'd huge affliction and dismay	Par Lost 1.57
In others count'nance read his own dismay	Par Lost 2.422
So having said, as one from sad dismay	Par Lost 9.917
Which then not minded in dismay, yet now	Par Lost 11.156
Distracted and surpriz'd with deep dismay	Par Reg 1.108
Ruin, and desperation, and dismay,	Par Reg 4.579
Dismayed	
Mee overtook his mother all dismaid,	Par Lost 2.792
His heart, not else dismai'd. Now drew they nigh	Par Lost 4.861
From unsuccessful charge, be not dismaid,	Par Lost 10.35
Dismai'd, and thus in haste to th' Angel cri'd.	Par Lost 11.449
Yet neither thus disheartn'd or dismay'd,	Par Reg 1.268
By female usurpation, nor dismay'd.	Samson 1060
Dismiss	
End, and dismiss thee ere the Morning shine.	Par Lost 7.108
Dismiss not her, when most thou needst her nigh,	Par Lost 8.564
Nay didst permit, approve, and fair dismiss.	Par Lost 9.1159
Dismiss them not disconsolate; reveale	Par Lost 11.113
Dismissed	
So saying he dismiss'd them, they with speed	Par Lost 10.410
Glad to be so dismist in peace. Can thus	Par Lost 11.507
Pursuing whom he late dismissd, the Sea	Par Lost 12.195
How hee sirnam'd of *Africa* dismiss'd	Par Reg 2.199
With peace and consolation hath dismist,	Samson 1757
Dismissing	
Of what we are and were, dismissing quite	Par Lost 2.282
Dismission	
To life obscur'd, which were a fair dismission,	Samson 688
Dismounted	
Dismounted, on th' *Aleian* Field I fall	Par Lost 7.19
Disobedience	
Of Mans First Disobedience, and the Fruit	Par Lost 1.1
ms 'disobedience'	
And som are fall'n, to disobedience fall'n,	Par Lost 5.541
Thy disobedience. Well thou didst advise,	Par Lost 5.888
By sin of disobedience, till that hour	Par Lost 6.396
Of disobedience; firm they might have stood,	Par Lost 6.911
And disobedience: On the part of Heav'n	Par Lost 9.8
By one mans disobedience lost, now sing	Par Reg 1.2
Disobedient	
These disobedient; sore hath been thir fight,	Par Lost 6.687
Prove disobedient, and reprov'd, retort,	Par Lost 10.761

Disobeyed
Not to have disobei'd; in fight they stood Par Lost 6.403
Disobeying
But yet all is not don; Man disobeying, Par Lost 3.203
Disobeys
For ever happie: him who disobeyes Par Lost 5.611
Mee disobeyes, breaks union, and that day Par Lost 5.612
Disorder
Light shon, and order from disorder sprung: Par Lost 3.713
Enter'd, and foul disorder; all the ground Par Lost 6.388
Disordered
And to disorder'd rage let loose the reines, Par Lost 6.696
And tresses all disorderd, at his feet Par Lost 10.911
Disordinate
Though not disordinate, yet causless suffring Samson 701
Disparage
Gods Altar to disparage and displace Par Lost 1.473
Har. Thou durst not thus disparage glorious arms Samson 1130
Disparity
Giv'n and receiv'd; but in disparitie Par Lost 8.386
Disparted
Disparted, and between spun out the Air, Par Lost 7.241
Disparted *Chaos* over built exclaimd, Par Lost 10.416
Dispatch
Of Theologians, but with keen dispatch Par Lost 5.436
The hands dispatch of two Gardning so wide. Par Lost 9.203
Dispatch the poor mans cause, Psalm 82, 10
Dispatched
Through each high street: little I had dispatch't Samson 1599
I was dispatcht for their defence, and guard; Mask 42
Trinity ms 'dispatch't'
Dispatchful
So saying, with dispatchful looks in haste Par Lost 5.331
Dispelled
Thir fanting courage, and dispel'd thir fears. Par Lost 1.530
ms 'dispell'd'
Dispels
Disperse it, as now light dispels the dark. Par Lost 5.208
Dispensation
Of highest dispensation, which herein Samson 61
Dispense
Fanning thir odoriferous wings dispense Par Lost 4.157
For with his own Laws he can best dispence. Samson 314
Yet that he may dispense with me or thee Samson 1377
Dispensed
God hath dispenst his bounties as in Heav'n. Par Lost 5.330
This is dispenc't, and what surmounts the reach Par Lost 5.571
Anough to beare; those now, that were dispenst Par Lost 11.766
Natures full blessings would be well dispenc't Mask 772
Trinity ms 'dispens't'
Bridgewater ms 'dispenst'
Dispenses
Indulgences, Dispenses, Pardons, Bulls, Par Lost 3.492
Dispenses Light from farr; they as they move Par Lost 3.579
Dispeopled
Already done, to have dispeopl'd Heav'n Par Lost 7.151
Disperse
Purge and disperse, that I may see and tell Par Lost 3.54
Disperse it, as now light dispels the dark. Par Lost 5.208
With Iron Scepter bruis'd, and them disperse Psalm 2, 20
Dispersed
Down the slope hills, disperst, or in a Lake, Par Lost 4.261
Lightly dispers'd, and the shrill Matin Song Par Lost 5.7
Disperst in Bands and Files thir Camp extend Par Lost 5.651
However some tradition they dispers'd Par Lost 10.578
And get themselves a name, least far disperst Par Lost 12.45
In *Habor*, and among the *Medes* dispers't, Par Reg 3.376
Displace
Gods Altar to disparage and displace Par Lost 1.473
Displaced
Still to be so displac't. I was all eare, Mask 560
Displayed
His proud imaginations thus displaid. Par Lost 2.10
Displayd on the op'n Firmament of Heav'n. Par Lost 7.390
Farr other operation first displaid, Par Lost 9.1012
Of lively portrature display'd, Penseroso 149
Are seen in glittering ranks with wings displaid, Nativity 114
Displaying
But his growth now to youths full flowr, displaying Par Reg 1.67
Displays
Sam. How cunningly the sorceress displays Samson 819
Thir Hydra heads, and the fals North displaies Sonnet 15, 7
1694 'displays'
Displease
I do it freely; venturing to displease Samson 1373
Displeased
Wherto th' Almighty answer'd, not displeas'd. Par Lost 8.398
Displeas'd that I approach thee thus, and gaze Par Lost 9.535
From Earth arriv'd at Heaven Gate, displeas'd Par Lost 10.22
His counsel whom she had displeas'd, his aide; Par Lost 10.944
Whereto thus *Adam* fatherly displeas'd. Par Lost 12.63
Which argues over-just, and self-displeas'd Samson 514
Incredible to me, in this displeas'd, Samson 1084
Displeasure
Divine displeasure for her sake, or Death. Par Lost 9.993
And my displeasure bearst so ill. If Prayers Par Lost 10.952
From his displeasure; in whose look serene, Par Lost 10.1094
I came, still dreading thy displeasure, *Samson*, Samson 733

Displeasure*(cont)*
Nor in thy hot displeasure me correct; Psalm 6, 2
Displode
In posture to displode thir second tire Par Lost 6.605
Disport
To such disport before her through the Field, Par Lost 9.520
There they thir fill of Love and Loves disport Par Lost 9.1042
Disporting
Disporting, till the amorous Bird of Night Par Lost 8.518
Disposal
Chor. Tax not divine disposal, wisest Men Samson 210
Or th' execution leave to high disposal, Samson 506
Dispose
Who now is Sovran can dispose and bid Par Lost 1.246
Wherever plac't, let him dispose: joy thou Par Lost 8.170
And mortal food, as may dispose him best Par Lost 11.54
Of these things others quickly will dispose Par Reg 2.400
At his dispose, young *Scipio* had brought down Par Reg 3.34
To render thee the *Parthian* at dispose; Par Reg 3.369
Some rouzing motions in me which dispose Samson 1382
What th' unsearchable dispose Samson 1746
Disposed
Thir will, dispos'd by absolute Decree Par Lost 3.115
In darker veile) and roseat Dews dispos'd Par Lost 5.646
Thir Lords, whom God dispos'd, the house of God Par Lost 12.349
Houses of Gods (so well I have dispos'd Par Reg 4.56
Disposer
My Author and Disposer, what thou bidst Par Lost 4.635
If not disposer; lend them oft my aid, Par Reg 1.393
Disposition
Sam. Appoint not heavenly disposition, Father, Samson 373
Dispossess
To dispossess him, and thy self to reigne? Par Lost 4.961
Over his brethren, and quite dispossess Par Lost 12.28
Dispossessed
Of Deitie supream, us dispossest, Par Lost 7.142
Dispraise
Illaudable, naught merits but dispraise Par Lost 6.382
Rather belongs, distrust and all dispraise: Par Lost 11.166
Dispraise, or blame, nothing but well and fair, Samson 1723
Dispraised
Of whom to be disprais'd were no small praise? Par Reg 3.56
Disproportioned
As once we did, till disproportion'd sin Musick 19
Disproportions
Such disproportions, with superfluous hand Par Lost 8.27
Disputant
Among the gravest Rabbies disputant Par Reg 4.218
Dispute
Shalt thou give Law to God, shalt thou dispute Par Lost 5.822
Grateful digressions, and solve high dispute Par Lost 8.55
Light back to them, is obvious to dispute. Par Lost 8.158
To contemplation and profound dispute, Par Reg 4.214
Dispute thy coming? come without delay; Samson 1395
Disputes
Should win in Arms, in both disputes alike Par Lost 6.123
Hath left to thir disputes, perhaps to move Par Lost 8.77
In sight of God? Him after all Disputes Par Lost 10.828
Disrelish
True appetite, and not disrelish thirst Par Lost 5.305
With hatefullest disrelish writh'd thir jaws Par Lost 10.569
Dissect
Heroic deem'd, chief maistrie to dissect Par Lost 9.29
Dissemble
To som of *Saturns* crew. I must dissemble, Mask 805
line not in Trinity ms
line not in Bridgewater ms
Dissembled
Dissembl'd, and this Answer smooth return'd. Par Reg 1.467
Dissembler
So spake the false dissembler unperceivd; Par Lost 3.681
Dissension
But first among the Priests dissension springs, Par Lost 12.353
Dissent
Thy sleep dissent? new Laws thou seest impos'd; Par Lost 5.679
Seemd in thy World erroneous to dissent Par Lost 6.146
Hadst thou bin firm and fixt in thy dissent, Par Lost 9.1160
Dissevering
And backward mutters of dissevering power, Mask 817
Bridgewater ms 'disseveringe'
Dissimulation
His gray dissimulation, disappear'd Par Reg 1.498
Dissipation
Foule dissipation follow'd and forc't rout; Par Lost 6.598
Dissolute
Worldlie or dissolute, on what thir Lords Par Lost 11.803
The punishment of dissolute days, in fine, Samson 702
Dissolutest
Belial the dislolutest Spirit that fell, Par Reg 2.150
Dissolution
And utter dissolution, as the scope Par Lost 2.127
Till final dissolution, wander here, Par Lost 3.458
Immediate dissolution, which we thought Par Lost 10.1049
For dissolution wrought by Sin, that first Par Lost 11.55
My dissolution. *Michael* repli'd, Par Lost 11.552
phrase not in 1667 edition
When this worlds disolution shall be ripe, Par Lost 12.459
1667 'dissolution'

Dissolve
Your military obedience, to dissolve — Par Lost 4.955
Insensible, and forthwith to dissolve: — Par Lost 8.291
Least it again dissolve and showr the Earth? — Par Lost 11.883
In glory of the Father, to dissolve — Par Lost 12.546
Enerve, and with voluptuous hope dissolve, — Par Reg 2.165
To frustrate and dissolve these Magic spells, — Samson 1149
Dissolve me into extasies, — Penseroso 165

Dissolved
The *Stygian* Counsel thus dissolv'd; and forth — Par Lost 2.506
Dissolvd on Earth, fleet hither, and in vain, — Par Lost 3.457
In highth of all thir flowing wealth dissolv'd: — Par Reg 2.436
And words addrest seem into tears dissolv'd, — Samson 729

Dissolves
Dissolves unjointed e're it reach my ear. — Samson 177

Dissonance
But drive farr off the barbarous dissonance — Par Lost 7.32
And fill'd the Air with barbarous dissonance, — Mask 550

Dissonant
Harsh, and of dissonant mood from his complaint, — Samson 662

Dissuade
Did not disswade me most, and seem to cast — Par Lost 2.122
Not diffident of thee do I dissuade — Par Lost 9.293

Dissuades
My voice disswades; for what can force or guile — Par Lost 2.188

Distance
That from his Lordly eye keep distance due, — Par Lost 3.578
In that aspect, and still that distance keepes — Par Lost 7.379
Thir distance argues and thir swift return — Par Lost 8.21
In *Eden*, distance inexpressible — Par Lost 8.113
Now alienated, distance and distaste, — Par Lost 9.9
Powerful at greatest distance to unite — Par Lost 10.247
To recompence his distance, in thir sight — Par Lost 10.683
At distance I forgive thee, go with that; — Samson 954
As at some distance from the place of horrour, — Samson 1550

Distances
And practis'd distances to cringe, not fight. — Par Lost 4.945
strange distances to heare & unknowne climes — Mask Tr. ms 10.17

Distant
Though distant farr som small reflection gaines — Par Lost 3.428
His travell'd steps; farr distant he descries — Par Lost 3.501
Stars distant, but nigh hand seemd other Worlds, — Par Lost 3.566
To objects distant farr, whereby he soon — Par Lost 3.621
Not distant far from thence a murmuring sound — Par Lost 4.453
Each quarter, to descrie the distant foe, — Par Lost 6.530
Not distant far with heavie pace the Foe — Par Lost 6.551
Distant so high, with moving Fires adornd — Par Lost 7.87
A goodly Tree farr distant to behold — Par Lost 9.576
Though distant from thee Worlds between, yet felt — Par Lost 10.362
Like distant breadth to *Taurus* with the Seav'n — Par Lost 10.673
Then *Ganymed* or *Hylas*, distant more — Par Reg 2.353
Was distant; and these flaws, though mortals fear them — Par Reg 4.454
with distant worlds, & strange removed clim — Mask Tr. ms 10.17

Distaste
Now alienated, distance and distaste, — Par Lost 9.9

Distemper
Contiguous might distemper the whole frame: — Par Lost 7.273
But in her Cheek distemper flushing glowd. — Par Lost 9.887
As a distemper, gross to aire as gross, — Par Lost 11.53

Distempered
At least distemperd, discontented thoughts, — Par Lost 4.807
Superior sway: from thus distemperd brest, — Par Lost 9.1131
Distemperd all things, and of incorrupt — Par Lost 11.56

Distempers
For heav'nly mindes from such distempers foule — Par Lost 4.118

Distended
Distended as the Brow of God appeas'd, — Par Lost 11.880

Distends
Distends with pride, and hardning in his strength — Par Lost 1.572

Distil
Your fiery essence can distill no tear, — Circum 7

Distilled
By us oft seen; his dewie locks distill'd — Par Lost 5.56
Rose like a steam of rich distill'd Perfumes, — Mask 556

Distinct
Distinct with eyes, and from the living Wheels — Par Lost 6.846
Distinct alike with multitude of eyes, — Par Lost 6.847
Is yet distinct by name, thence, as thou know'st — Par Lost 7.536
High and remote to see from thence distinct — Par Lost 9.812
Relation more particular and distinct. — Samson 1595

Distinction
Streame in the Aire, and for distinction serve — Par Lost 5.590

Distinguish
Distinguish not: for soon expect to feel — Par Lost 5.892
(For so I can distinguish by mine Art) — Mask 149
Bridgewater ms 'distingwish'

Distinguishable
Distinguishable in member, joynt, or limb, — Par Lost 2.668
Like to themselves, distinguishable scarce — Par Reg 3.424

Distorted
Distorted, all my nether shape thus grew — Par Lost 2.784

Distract
Upon himself; horror and doubt distract — Par Lost 4.18
And sense distract, to know well what I utter. — Samson 1556

Distracted
Distracted and surpriz'd with deep dismay — Par Reg 1.108
Lose thir defence distracted and amaz'd. — Samson 1286

Distractions
Not of warr onely, but detractions rude, — Sonnet 16, 2
1694 'distractions'

Distress
Thy counsel in this uttermost distress, — Par Lost 10.920
Now at his feet submissive in distress, — Par Lost 10.942
Presaging, since with sorrow and hearts distress — Par Lost 12.613
On my refusal to distress me more, — Samson 1330
In straights and in distress — Psalm 4, 3
And raise the man in deep distress — Psalm 82, 11
I in the day of my distress — Psalm 86, 21

Distressed
Of true Virgin here distrest, — Mask 905
Trinity ms 'distres't'

Distrust
Those Notes to Tragic; foul distrust, and breach — Par Lost 9.6
Rather belongs, distrust and all dispraise: — Par Lost 11.166
Why dost thou then suggest to me distrust, — Par Reg 1.355
Without distrust or doubt, that he may know — Par Reg 3.193

Distrustfully
That of my life distrustfully thus say, — Psalm 3, 5

Disturb
Shall grieve him, if I fail not, and disturb — Par Lost 1.167
Our power sufficient to disturb his Heav'n, — Par Lost 2.102
With purpose to explore or to disturb — Par Lost 2.971
Dreadful combustion warring, and disturb, — Par Lost 6.225
Instant without disturb they took Allarm, — Par Lost 6.549
Our fealtie from God, or to disturb — Par Lost 9.262
Compels me to disturb your season due: — Lycidas 7
Trinity ms 'disturbe'

Disturbance
In his disturbance; when his darling Sons — Par Lost 2.373

Disturbances
Disturbances on Earth through Femal snares, — Par Lost 10.897

Disturbed
If aught disturb'd thir noyse, into her woomb, — Par Lost 2.657
To thy transgressions, and disturbd the charge — Par Lost 4.879
At least had gon to rack, disturbd and torne — Par Lost 4.994
Hath raisd in Paradise, and how disturbd — Par Lost 5.226
And thy adherents: how hast thou disturb'd — Par Lost 6.266
Disturbd not, waiting close th' approach of Morn. — Par Lost 9.191
Fluctuats disturbd, yet comely and in act — Par Lost 9.668
Recomforted, and after thoughts disturbd — Par Lost 9.918
Disturb'd his sleep; and either Tropic now — Par Reg 4.409
Or reason though disturb'd, and scarse consulted — Samson 1546
Yet stay, be not disturb'd, now I bethink me, — Mask 820

Dittied
Who with his soft Pipe, and smooth-dittied Song, — Mask 86
Bridgewater ms 'smooth dittied'
1673 'smooth dittied'
Trinity ms 'smoth dittied'

Ditties
In amorous dittyes all a Summers day, — Par Lost 1.449
Soft amorous Ditties, and in dance came on: — Par Lost 11.584
Mean while the Rural ditties were not mute, — Lycidas 32

Diurnal
Diurnal, or this less volubil Earth — Par Lost 4.594
Within the visible Diurnal Spheare; — Par Lost 7.22
Diurnal) meerly to officiate light — Par Lost 8.22
Nocturnal and Diurnal rhomb suppos'd, — Par Lost 8.134
Our Limbs benumm'd, ere this diurnal Starr — Par Lost 10.1069

Divan
Rais'd from thir Dark *Divan*, and with like joy — Par Lost 10.457

Diverse
Runs divers, wandring many a famous Realme — Par Lost 4.234
Flew divers, and with Power (thir Power was great) — Par Lost 10.284

Diverted
May have diverted from continual watch — Par Lost 9.814
Was that crude Apple that diverted *Eve!* — Par Reg 2.349

Divide
Divide the night, and lift our thoughts to Heaven. — Par Lost 4.688
Amid the Waters, and let it divide — Par Lost 7.262
High in th' expanse of Heaven to divide — Par Lost 7.340
And Light from Darkness to divide. God saw, — Par Lost 7.352
Let us divide our labours, thou where choice — Par Lost 9.214
And henceforth Monarchie with thee divide — Par Lost 10.379
Co. Could that divide you from neer-ushering guides? — Mask 279
Bridgewater ms 'devide'
My muse with Angels did divide to sing; — Passion 4

Divided
Divided Empire with Heav'ns King I hold — Par Lost 4.111
And now divided into four main Streams, — Par Lost 4.233
As each divided Legion might have seemd — Par Lost 6.230
For strength from Truth divided and from Just, — Par Lost 6.381
Divided, and to either Flank retir'd. — Par Lost 6.570
Divided: Light the Day, and Darkness Night — Par Lost 7.251
Then all the World much heavier, though divided — Par Lost 10.836
Egypt, divided by the River *Nile;* — Par Lost 12.157
Divided, till his rescu'd gain thir shoar: — Par Lost 12.199
Divided by a river, of whose banks — Par Reg 4.32

Divides
Of this round World, whose first convex divides — Par Lost 3.419
Nor streit'ning Vale, nor Wood, nor Stream divides — Par Lost 6.70
That fellowship in pain divides not smart, — Par Reg 1.401

Dividing
Dividing: for as Earth, so he the World — Par Lost 7.269
With Turtle wing the amorous clouds dividing, — Nativity 50

Dividual
With thousand lesser Lights dividual holds, Par Lost 7.382
Twinn'd, and from her hath no dividual being: Par Lost 12.85
Divine
Then aught divine or holy else enjoy'd Par Lost 1.683
Or if our substance be indeed Divine, Par Lost 2.99
Or flocks, or heards, or human face divine; Par Lost 3.44
Divine compassion visibly appeerd, Par Lost 3.141
In whom the fulness dwels of love divine, Par Lost 3.225
Begotten Son, Divine Similitude, Par Lost 3.384
Love no where to be found less then Divine! Par Lost 3.411
And worthie seemd, for in thir looks Divine Par Lost 4.291
In them Divine resemblance, and such grace Par Lost 4.364
But he thus overjoy'd, O Fruit Divine, Par Lost 5.67
Thy goodness beyond thought, and Power Divine: Par Lost 5.159
Divine the sov'ran Architect had fram'd. Par Lost 5.256
His lineaments Divine; the pair that clad Par Lost 5.278
Divine effulgence, whose high Power so far Par Lost 5.458
Divine instructer, I have heard, then when Par Lost 5.546
And in thir motions harmonie Divine Par Lost 5.625
Light'ning Divine, ineffable, serene, Par Lost 5.734
The Deitie, and divine commands obei'd, Par Lost 5.806
Idol of Majestie Divine, enclos'd Par Lost 6.101
Vigour Divine within them, can allow Par Lost 6.158
In Heav'n God ever blest, and his Divine Par Lost 6.184
Before him Power Divine his way prepar'd; Par Lost 6.780
If rightly thou art call'd, whose Voice divine Par Lost 7.2
Divine interpreter, by favour sent Par Lost 7.72
Of Majestie Divine, Sapience and Love Par Lost 7.195
Equal have I to render thee, Divine Par Lost 8.6
Though pleasant, but thy words with Grace Divine Par Lost 8.215
And livd: One came, methought, of shape Divine, Par Lost 8.295
Presence Divine. Rejoycing, but with aw Par Lost 8.314
This answer from the gratious voice Divine. Par Lost 8.436
But all that fair and good in thy Divine Par Lost 9.606
Here grows the Cure of all, this Fruit Divine, Par Lost 9.776
Yet oft his heart, divine of somthing ill, Par Lost 9.845
Op'ning the way, but of Divine effect Par Lost 9.865
Holy, divine, good, amiable, or sweet! Par Lost 9.899
Taste so Divine, that what of sweet before Par Lost 9.986
Divine displeasure for her sake, or Death. Par Lost 9.993
So fit, so acceptable, so Divine, Par Lost 10.139
Justice Divine not hast'n to be just? Par Lost 10.857
But Death comes not at call, Justice Divine Par Lost 10.858
Presence Divine, and to my Sons relate; Par Lost 11.319
Express, and of his steps the track Divine. Par Lost 11.354
Retaining still Divine similitude Par Lost 11.512
Holie and pure, conformitie divine. Par Lost 11.606
Thy mortal sight to faile; objects divine Par Lost 12.9
Would not be last, and with the voice divine Par Reg 1.35
To shew him worthy of his birth divine Par Reg 1.141
Perfections absolute, Graces divine, Par Reg 2.138
A table of Celestial Food, Divine, Par Reg 4.588
Divine Prediction; what if all foretold Samson 44
Chor. Tax not divine disposal, wisest Men Samson 210
Divine impulsion prompting how thou might'st Samson 422
Full of divine instinct, after some proof Samson 526
Fall'n into wrath divine, Samson 1683
Breath such Divine inchanting ravishment? Mask 245
Bridgewater ms 'divine'
Trinity ms 'divine'
The divine property of her first being. Mask 469
2. *Bro.* How charming is divine Philosophy! Mask 476
But of divine effect, he cull'd me out; Mask 630
Or the tale of *Troy* divine. Penseroso 100
Too divine to be mistook: Arcades 4
Divine *Alpheus*, who by secret sluse, Arcades 30
His goary visage down the stream was sent, Lycidas 62
Trinity ms 'goarie' ←'gorie' ←'divine'
Can no more divine, Nativity 177
Above mortalitie that shew'd thou wast divine. Fair Inf 35
And perfectly divine, On Time 15
Wed your divine sounds, and mixt power employ Musick 3
Trinity ms 'divine sounds' ←'choise chords' ←'divine power'
Turn us again, *thy grace divine* Psalm 80, 13
Return us, *and thy grace divine*, Psalm 80, 29
From Heav'n, thy Seat divine, Psalm 80, 58
Return us, *and thy grace divine* Psalm 80, 77
Divined
For I no sooner in my Heart divin'd, Par Lost 10.357
Divinely
Of radiant *Urim*, work divinely wrought, Par Lost 6.761
She heard me thus, and though divinely brought, Par Lost 8.500
Shee fair, divinely fair, fit Love for Gods, Par Lost 9.489
Express'd, and thus divinely answer'd milde. Par Lost 10.67
Descri'd, divinely warn'd, and witness bore Par Reg 1.26
As men divinely taught, and better teaching Par Reg 4.357
The work to which I was divinely call'd; Samson 226
Divinely-warbled
Divinely-warbled voice Nativity 96
1673 'Divinely-warbl'd'
Divinest
Hail divinest Melancholy, Penseroso 12
Divinity
Divinitie within them breeding wings Par Lost 9.1010
Divisible
Not long divisible, and from the gash Par Lost 6.331
Divulge
Did wisely to conceal, and not divulge Par Lost 8.73
Though Fame divulge him Father of five Sons Samson 1248
1671 printed 'divulg'd', errata 'divulge'
Divulged
To them made common and divulg'd, if aught Par Lost 8.583
Fool, have divulg'd the secret gift of God Samson 201
Divulges
The just man, and divulges him through Heaven Par Reg 3.62
Dizzy
Surpris'd thee, dim thine eyes, and dizzie swumm Par Lost 2.753
Or at thy heels the dizzy Multitude, Par Reg 2.420
Do
Can else inflict, do I repent or change, Par Lost 1.96
ms 'doe'
Or do him mightier service as his thralls Par Lost 1.149
ms 'doe'
Or do his Errands in the gloomy Deep; Par Lost 1.152
ms 'doe'
To do ought good never will be our task, Par Lost 1.159
But ever to do ill our sole delight, Par Lost 1.160
ms 'doe'
To do him wanton rites, which cost them woe. Par Lost 1.414
The Victors will. To suffer, as to doe, Par Lost 2.199
Of darkness do we dread? How oft amidst Par Lost 2.263
Mee from attempting. Wherefore do I assume Par Lost 2.450
His own: for neither do the Spirits damn'd Par Lost 2.482
Hast thou forgot me then, and do I seem Par Lost 2.747
Where onely what they needs must do, appeard, Par Lost 3.105
O Hell! what doe mine eyes with grief behold, Par Lost 4.358
Melt, as I doe, yet public reason just, Par Lost 4.389
To do what else though damnd I should abhorre. Par Lost 4.392
Mother of human Race: what could I doe, Par Lost 4.475
Can it be death? and do they onely stand Par Lost 4.518
Will save us trial what the least can doe Par Lost 4.855
To boast what Arms can doe, since thine no more Par Lost 4.1008
Waking thou never wilt consent to do. Par Lost 5.121
Do as you have in charge, and briefly touch Par Lost 6.566
What should they do? if on they rusht, repulse Par Lost 6.600
And in whose hand what by Decree I doe, Par Lost 6.683
Warr wearied hath perform'd what Warr can do, Par Lost 6.695
Nor other strife with them do I voutsafe. Par Lost 6.823
Her own, that what she wills to do or say, Par Lost 8.549
Do thou but thine, and be not diffident Par Lost 8.562
Express they, by looks onely, or do they mix Par Lost 8.616
Thy Judgement to do aught, which else free Will Par Lost 8.636
Not diffident of thee do I dissuade Par Lost 9.293
To do what God expresly hath forbid, Par Lost 9.356
For God towards thee hath done his part, do thine. Par Lost 9.375
Queen of this Universe, doe not believe Par Lost 9.684
Be frustrate, do, undo, and labour loose, Par Lost 9.944
Mine both in Heav'n and Earth to do thy will Par Lost 10.69
Fixd on this day? why do I overlive, Par Lost 10.773
Not to do onely, but to will the same Par Lost 10.826
What better can we do, then to the place Par Lost 10.1086
What man can do against them, not affraid, Par Lost 12.493
To speak all Tongues, and do all Miracles, Par Lost 12.501
To do him honour as their King; all come, Par Reg 1.75
The Prophet do him reverence, on him rising Par Reg 1.80
And what will he not do to advance his Son? Par Reg 1.88
Serious to learn and know, and thence to do Par Reg 1.203
And make perswasion do the work of fear; Par Reg 1.223
For what he bids I do; though I have lost Par Reg 1.377
Extorts, or pleasure to do ill excites? Par Reg 1.423
I bid not or forbid; do as thou find'st Par Reg 1.495
Mee hungring more to do my Fathers will. Par Reg 2.259
And with my hunger what hast thou to do? Par Reg 2.389
What I can do or offer is suspect; Par Reg 2.399
Who could do mighty things, and could contemn Par Reg 2.448
Then prompt her to do aught may merit praise. Par Reg 2.456
What best to say canst say, to do canst do; Par Reg 3.8
Great Cities by assault: what do these Worthies, Par Reg 3.74
Raign then; what canst thou better do the while? Par Reg 3.180
Can suffer, best can do; best reign, who first Par Reg 3.195
And threatning nigh; what they can do as signs Par Reg 4.489
Or do my eyes misrepresent? Can this be hee, Samson 124
In every street, do they not say, how well Samson 204
Sam. Father, I do acknowledge and confess Samson 448
On thee, who now no more canst do them harm. Samson 486
Nor do I name of men the common rout, Samson 674
What do I beg? how hast thou dealt already? Samson 707
First granting, as I do, it was a weakness Samson 773
In uncompassionate anger do not so. Samson 818
Why do I humble thus my self, and suing Samson 965
Sam. Boast not of what thou wouldst have done, but do Samson 1104
I was to do my part from Heav'n assign'd, Samson 1217
Do they not seek occasion of new quarrels Samson 1329
I do it freely; venturing to displease Samson 1373
Nothing to do, be sure, that may dishonour Samson 1385
What shall we do, stay here or run and see? Samson 1520
(For most do taste through fond intemperate thirst) Mask 67
Bridgewater ms 'doe'
Trinity ms 'doe'
1637 'doe'
As now I do: But first I must put off Mask 82
1637 'doe'
Trinity ms 'doe'
Bridgewater ms 'doe'

Do(*cont*)
What hath night to do with sleep? Mask 122
Bridgewater ms 'doe'
Trinity ms 'doe'
Yet nought but single darknes do I find. Mask 204
Trinity ms 'doe'
line not in Bridgewater ms
1637 'doe'
I do not think my sister so to seek, Mask 366
1637 'doe'
Trinity ms 'doe'
Bridgewater ms 'doe'
Vertue could see to do what vertue would Mask 373
Trinity ms 'doe'
Bridgewater ms 'doe'
1637 'doe'
Or do his gray hairs any violence? Mask 392
1637 'doe'
Trinity ms 'doe'
Bridgewater ms 'doe'
Of our unowned sister. *Eld. Bro.* I do not, brother, Mask 407
1637 'doe'
Trinity ms 'doe'
Bridgewater ms 'doe'
Do ye beleeve me yet, or shall I call Mask 438
Trinity ms 'doe'
1637 'Doe'
Bridgewater ms 'doe'
But here thy sword can do thee little stead, Mask 611
Trinity ms 'doe'
Bridgewater ms 'doe'
1637 'doe'
Root-bound, that fled *Apollo*, *La*. Fool do not boast, Mask 662
Trinity ms 'doe not boast' ←'thou art over proud'
1637 'doe'
Bridgewater ms 'doe'
Co. Why are you vext Lady? why do you frown? Mask 666
1637 'doe'
Trinity ms 'doe'
Bridgewater ms 'doe'
Impostor do not charge most innocent nature, Mask 762
Bridgewater ms 'doe'
1637 'doe'
Trinity ms 'doe'
Co. She fables not, I feel that I do fear Mask 800
1637 'doe'
line not in Trinity ms
line not in Bridgewater ms
Where the nibling flocks do stray, Allegro 72
The labouring clouds do often rest: Allegro 74
Till old experience do attain Penseroso 173
Were it not better don as others use, Lycidas 67
1638 'others do'
Let down in clowdie throne to do the world some good. Fair Inf 56
This if thou do he will an off-spring give, Fair Inf 76
I know my tongue but little Grace can do thee Vacation 10
But haste thee strait to do me once a Pleasure, Vacation 17
And wearie of their place do only stay Vacation 25
By shallow *Edwards* and Scotch what d'ye call: Forcers 12
But we do hope to find out all your tricks, Forcers 13
Trinity ms 'doe'
Why do the Gentiles tumult, and the Nations Psalm 2, 1
Be aw'd, and do not sin, Psalm 4, 19
That do observe If I transgress Psalm 5, 23
Lord in thine anger do not reprehend me Psalm 6, 1
And their power that do amiss. Psalm 7, 36
Sea-paths in shoals do slide. And know no dearth. Psalm 8, 22
We cry and do not cease. Psalm 83, 4
Do to them as to Midian *bold* Psalm 83, 33
My heart and flesh aloud do crie, Psalm 84, 7
In Sion do appear. Psalm 84, 28
Surely to such as do him fear Psalm 85, 37
Wilt thou do wonders on the dead, Psalm 88, 41
But I to thee O Lord do cry Psalm 88, 53
Tis you that say it, not I, you do the deeds, Prose 8, 1
Whom doe we count a good man, whom but he Prose 10, 1

Doctor
And no man therein Doctor but himself. Samson 299

Doctors
To those budge doctors of the *Stoick* Furr, Mask 707
1673 'Doctors'
Bridgewater ms 'Doctors'
Trinity ms 'Doctors'
But vow though the cross Doctors all stood hearers, Another 19

Doctrine
Doctrin which we would know whence learnt: who saw Par Lost 5.856
Thir doctrine and thir story written left, Par Lost 12.506
By saving Doctrine, and from errour lead Par Reg 2.474
No other doctrine needs, though granted true; Par Reg 4.290
For of such Doctrine never was there School, Samson 297
And serious doctrine of Virginity, Mask 787
line not in Trinity ms
line not in Bridgewater ms

Dodged
Dodg'd with him, betwixt *Cambridge* and the Bull. Carrier 8
1658 'dog'dd'

Dodona
Or in *Dodona*, and through all the bounds Par Lost 1.518

Dodona(*cont*)
ms 'Dodona'

Doer
The deeds themselves, though mute, spoke loud the dooer; Samson 248

Does
I did not err, there does a sable cloud Mask 223
Trinity ms 'dos'
line not in Bridgewater ms
Does arbitrate th'event, my nature is Mask 411
Trinity ms 'dos'

Doff
Off. I praise thy resolution, doff these links: Samson 1410

Doffed
Had doff't her gawdy trim, Nativity 33

Dog
I fear the dred events that dog them both, Mask 405
Isis and *Orus*, and the Dog *Anubis* hast. Nativity 212

Dogs
See with what heat these Dogs of Hell advance Par Lost 10.616
To dogs and fowls a prey, or else captiv'd: Samson 694
Of Owles and Cuckoes, Asses, Apes and Doggs. Sonnet 12, 4
Trinity ms 'dogs'

Doing
Doing or Suffering: but of this be sure, Par Lost 1.158
Whatever doing, what can we suffer more, Par Lost 2.162
In doing what we most in suffering feel? Par Lost 2.340
Her doing seem'd to justifie the deed; Par Lost 10.142
Not wilfully mis-doing, but unware Par Reg 1.225
By what he taught and suffer'd for so doing, Par Reg 3.97
Doing abhorred rites to *Hecate* Mask 535
Bridgewater ms 'doeinge'

Doings
And of thir doings God takes no account. Par Lost 4.622
And of thir doings great dislike declar'd, Par Lost 11.720
To mark thir doings, them beholding soon, Par Lost 12.50
And urg'd me hard with doings, which not will Par Reg 1.469
Bearing my words and doings to the Lords Samson 947
But had his doings lasted as they were, Another 27

Dole
Dole with delight, which in this place I sought; Par Lost 4.894
He now be dealing dole among his foes, Samson 1529

Doleful
Regions of sorrow, doleful shades, where peace Par Lost 1.65
ms 'dolefull'

Dolorous
They pass'd, and many a Region dolorous, Par Lost 2.619
Implacable, and many a dolorous groan, Par Lost 6.658
Leaving my dolorous Prison I enjoy Par Reg 1.364
And leave her dolorous mansions to the peering day. Nativity 140

Dolphins
And bended Dolphins play: part huge of bulk Par Lost 7.410
And, O ye *Dolphins*, waft the haples youth. Lycidas 164
1638 'dolphins'

Domain
To *Rome*'s great Emperour, whose wide domain Par Reg 4.81

Domains
Not thy Conversion, but those rich demaines Prose 1, 2

Domestic
Perpetual Fountain of Domestic sweets, Par Lost 4.760
So spake domestick *Adam* in his care Par Lost 9.318
Womans domestic honour and chief praise; Par Lost 11.617
At home in leisure and domestic ease, Samson 917
That in domestic good combines: Samson 1048

Dominations
Th'aspiring Dominations: thou that day Par Lost 3.392
Thrones, Dominations, Princedoms, Vertues, Powers, Par Lost 5.601
Thrones, Dominations, Princedomes, Vertues, Powers, Par Lost 5.772
Thrones, Dominations, Princedoms, Vertues, Powers, Par Lost 5.840
Princedoms, and Dominations ministrant Par Lost 10.87
Thrones, Dominations, Princedoms, Vertues, Powers, Par Lost 10.460

Dominic
Dying put on the weeds of *Dominic*, Par Lost 3.479

Dominion
From your Dominion won, th'Ethereal King Par Lost 2.978
And in her pale dominion checks the night. Par Lost 3.732
Look'st from thy sole Dominion like the God Par Lost 4.33
Conferrd upon us, and Dominion giv'n Par Lost 4.430
All thy Dominion, *Adam*, is no more Par Lost 5.751
Honour, Dominion, Glorie, and renowne, Par Lost 6.422
Son, Heir, and Lord, to him Dominion giv'n, Par Lost 6.887
Subdue it, and throughout Dominion hold Par Lost 7.532
The character of that Dominion giv'n Par Lost 8.545
Wings growing, and Dominion giv'n me large Par Lost 10.244
Dominion exercise and in the Aire, Par Lost 10.400
Will arrogate Dominion undeserv'd Par Lost 12.27
Dominion absolute; that right we hold Par Lost 12.68
To gain dominion or to keep it gain'd. Par Reg 2.434
That Empire, under his dominion holds Par Reg 3.296

Dominions
Powers and Dominions, Deities of Heav'n, Par Lost 2.11
Thrones, Princedoms, Powers, Dominions I reduce: Par Lost 3.320

Donation
By his donation; but Man over men Par Lost 12.69
Other donation none thou canst produce: Par Reg 4.184

Done
And Strength and Art are easily out-done Par Lost 1.696
ms 'outdon'
1667 'out done' in some copies, 'outdone' in others

Done(*cont*)
To mingle and involve, done all to spite Par Lost 2.384
But yet all is not don; Man disobeying, Par Lost 3.203
Thy favour, in this honour done to man, Par Lost 5.462
His Laws our Laws, all honour to him done Par Lost 5.844
Servant of God, well done, well hast thou fought Par Lost 6.29
Were don, but infinite: for wide was spred Par Lost 6.241
And as ye have receivd, so have ye don Par Lost 6.805
As a despite don against the most High, Par Lost 6.906
What within *Eden* or without was done Par Lost 7.65
Already done, to have dispeopl'd Heav'n Par Lost 7.151
This I perform, speak thou, and be it don: Par Lost 7.164
Of all yet don; a Creature who not prone Par Lost 7.506
And what before thy memorie was don Par Lost 7.637
Thee I have heard relating what was don Par Lost 8.203
Accuse not Nature, she hath don her part; Par Lost 8.561
Of Creatures wanting voice, that done, partake Par Lost 9.199
For God towards thee hath done his part, do thine. Par Lost 9.375
But first low Reverence don, as to the power Par Lost 9.835
The fatal Trespass don by *Eve*, amaz'd, Par Lost 9.889
But past who can recall, or don undoe? Par Lost 9.926
Of *Satan* done in Paradise, and how Par Lost 10.2
Say Woman, what is this which thou hast done? Par Lost 10.158
Because thou hast done this, thou art accurst Par Lost 10.175
What I have don, what sufferd, with what paine Par Lost 10.470
And one bad act with many deeds well done Par Lost 11.256
Of human Glorie, and for Glorie done Par Lost 11.694
Who having spilt much blood, and don much waste Par Lost 11.791
Don to his Father, heard this heavie curse, Par Lost 12.103
By mee done and occasiond, or rejoyce Par Lost 12.475
Above Heroic, though in secret done, Par Reg 1.15
To me is not unknown what hath been done Par Reg 2.444
Greater and nobler done, and to lay down Par Reg 2.482
Yet if for fame and glory aught be done, Par Reg 3.100
Easily done, and hold them all of me; Par Reg 4.168
Was absent, after all his mischief done, Par Reg 4.440
The time and means: each act is rightliest done, Par Reg 4.475
Who seeing those great acts which God had done Samson 243
Or *Dagon*. But for thee what shall be done? Samson 478
Sam. Boast not of what thou wouldst have done, but do Samson 1104
Again in safety what thou wouldst have done Samson 1128
Eye-witness of what first or last was done, Samson 1594
Of all thy dues be done, and none left out, Mask 137
Trinity ms 'don'
Be it not don in pride, or in presumption. Mask 431
Bridgewater ms 'done'
1637 'done'
But now my task is smoothly don, Mask 1012
Bridgewater ms 'done'
B.M. ms 'done'
1637 'done'
be it not don in pride or in praesumption Mask Tr. ms 16.56
Thus don the Tales, to bed they creep, Allegro 115
1673 'done'
Had ye bin there---for what could that have don? Lycidas 57
1638 'done'
Were it not better don as others use, Lycidas 67
1638 'done'
To think her part was don, Nativity 105
1673 'done'
What severs each thou 'hast learnt, which few hav don. Sonnet 17, 11
1662, 1694 'done'
Or done this, if wickedness Psalm 7, 8
Of all that other gods have done Psalm 86, 27
By thy strong hand are done, Psalm 86, 34

Doom
Confounded though immortal: But his doom Par Lost 1.53
ms 'doome'
Our doom; which if we can sustain and bear, Par Lost 2.209
By doom of Battel; and complain that Fate Par Lost 2.550
Or proud return though to his heavier doom, Par Lost 3.159
By doom severe, had not the Son of God, Par Lost 3.224
Of all past Ages to the general Doom Par Lost 3.328
Father of Mercie and Grace, thou didst not doome Par Lost 3.401
Perceive thee purpos'd not to doom frail Man Par Lost 3.404
Thy sin and place of doom obscure and foule. Par Lost 4.840
Ere this avenging Sword begin thy doome, Par Lost 6.278
Nor of Renown less eager, yet by doome Par Lost 6.378
Therfore Eternal silence be thir doome. Par Lost 6.385
Insensibly, for I suspend thir doom; Par Lost 6.692
Therefore to mee thir doom he hath assig'n'd; Par Lost 6.817
Of this fair Fruit, our doom is, we shall die. Par Lost 9.763
Certain to undergoe like doom, if Death Par Lost 9.953
Of right, that I may mitigate thir doom Par Lost 10.76
To *Satan* first in sin his doom apply'd, Par Lost 10.172
Thence gatherd his own doom, which understood Par Lost 10.344
Retiring, by his own doom alienated, Par Lost 10.378
According to his doom: he would have spoke, Par Lost 10.517
Be it so, for I submit, his doom is fair, Par Lost 10.769
To *Satan* only like both crime and doom. Par Lost 10.841
Against a Foe by doom express assign'd us, Par Lost 10.926
We are by doom to pay; rather such acts Par Lost 10.1026
Numberd, though sad, till Death, his doom (which I Par Lost 11.40
To sound at general Doom. Th' Angelic blast Par Lost 11.76
1667 'doom' in some copies
Annuls thy doom, the death thou shouldst have dy'd, Par Lost 12.428
The wakefull trump of doom must thunder through the deep, Nativity 156
Could Heav'n for pittie thee so strictly doom? Fair Inf 33

Doom(*cont*)
For we by rightfull doom remediles Circum 17
Trinity ms 'doome'
Foretell my hopeles doom in som Grove ny: Sonnet 1, 10

Doomed
And know not that the King of Heav'n hath doom'd Par Lost 2.316
Hell-doom'd, and breath'st defiance here and scorn Par Lost 2.697
1667 'Hell-doomd'
Though thither doomd? Thou wouldst thy self, no doubt, Par Lost 4.890
On those proud Towrs to swift destruction doom'd. Par Lost 5.907
But mortal doom'd. How can he exercise Par Lost 10.796
What hard mishap hath doom'd this gentle swain? Lycidas 92

Door
In *Gibeah*, when the hospitable door Par Lost 1.504
1667 'Dores'
ms 'doors'
Adam discernd, as in the dore he sat Par Lost 5.299
Light issues forth, and at the other dore Par Lost 6.9
Th' infernal Empire, that so neer Heav'ns dore Par Lost 10.389
Of lowest order, past; and from the dore Par Lost 10.443
Smeard round with Pitch, and in the side a dore Par Lost 11.731
With thir four Wives; and God made fast the dore. Par Lost 11.737
And to the stack, or the Barn dore, Allegro 51
But that two-handed engine at the door, Lycidas 130
1638 'doore'
Trinity ms 'dore'
Driving dum silence from the portal dore, Vacation 5
Above the wheeling poles, and at Heav'ns dore Vacation 34
Yet shall he live in strife, and at his dore Vacation 85
Passes to bliss at the mid hour of night, Sonnet 9, 13
Trinity ms 'passes to' ← 'opens the dore of'
Had rather keep a dore, Psalm 84, 38
My life *at deaths uncherful dore* Psalm 88, 11

Doors
In *Gibeah*, when the hospitable door Par Lost 1.504
1667 'Dores'
ms 'doors'
Stood fixt her stately highth, and strait the dores Par Lost 1.723
Th' infernal dores, and on thir hinges grate Par Lost 2.881
His sad exclusion from the dores of Bliss. Par Lost 3.525
Of some rich Burgher, whose substantial dores, Par Lost 4.189
Open, ye Heav'ns, your living dores; let in Par Lost 7.566
Dimentionless through Heav'nly dores; then clad Par Lost 11.17
Unfold her Crystal Dores, thence on his head Par Reg 1.82
Heaven open'd her eternal doors, from whence Par Reg 1.281
Within doors, or without, still as a fool, Samson 77
To thine whose doors my feet shall never enter. Samson 950
And Crop-full out of dores he flings, Allegro 113
To bless the dores from nightly harm: Penseroso 84
Whose chance on these defenceless dores may sease, Sonnet 8, 2

Dorian
In perfect *Phalanx* to the *Dorian* mood Par Lost 1.550
ms 'Dorian'
Aeolian charms and *Dorian Lyric* Odes, Par Reg 4.257

Doric
Of *Doric* Land; or who with *Saturn* old Par Lost 1.519
ms 'Doric'
Were set, and Doric pillars overlaid Par Lost 1.714
With eager thought warbling his *Dorick* lay: Lycidas 189

Dost
And chiefly Thou O Spirit, that dost prefer Par Lost 1.17
Thy self though great and glorious dost thou count, Par Lost 5.833
In loving thou dost well, in passion not, Par Lost 8.588
Why dost thou then suggest to me distrust, Par Reg 1.355
Which way or from what hope dost thou aspire Par Reg 2.417
These God-like Vertues wherefore dost thou hide? Par Reg 3.21
Thou neither dost perswade me to seek wealth Par Reg 3.44
What dost thou in this World? the Wilderness Par Reg 4.372
Nor only dost degrade them, or remit Samson 687
If thou in strength all mortals dost exceed, Samson 817
Har. Dost thou already single me; I thought Samson 1092
Har. Fair honour that thou dost thy God, in trusting Samson 1178
Sam. Tongue-doubtie Giant, how dost thou prove me these? Samson 1181
(If so it be that thou these plaints dost hear) Fair Inf 37
But fie my wandring Muse how thou dost stray! Vacation 53
Hail bounteous *May* that dost inspire May Morn 5
Dost make us Marble with too much conceaving; Shakespear 14
And so Sepulcher'd in such pomp dost lie, Shakespear 15
1640 'doth'
Thou with fresh hope the Lovers heart dost fill, Sonnet 1, 3
Right onward. What supports me dost thou ask? Sonnet 22, 9
For thou alone dost keep Psalm 4, 39
Thou Shepherd that dost Israel *keep* Psalm 80, 1
Whom thou dost hide and keep. Psalm 83, 12
Where thou do'st dwell so near. Psalm 84, 4
Do'st help and comfort me. Psalm 86, 64
Lord God that dost me save and keep, Psalm 88, 1
Dost never more regard, Psalm 88, 22
Thou dost my friends from me estrange, Psalm 88, 33
'Gainst them that rais'd thee dost thou lift thy horn, Prose 3, 2

Dotage
With dotage, and his sense deprav'd Samson 1042

Dotest
Thou thy self doat'st on womankind, admiring Par Reg 2.175

Doth
Thick clouds and dark doth Heav'ns all-ruling Sire Par Lost 2.264
As doth your Rational; and both contain Par Lost 5.409
Nor doth the Moon no nourishment exhale Par Lost 5.421

Doth(*cont*)
Folly to mee, so doth the Prince of Hell — Par Lost 10.621
So willingly doth God remit his Ire, — Par Lost 11.885
Nor doth this grandeur and majestic show — Par Reg 4.110
Now the top of Heav'n doth hold, — Mask 94
 Bridgewater ms 'doeth'
His glowing Axle doth allay — Mask 96
 Bridgewater ms 'doeth'
That doth enrich these Downs, is worth a thought — Mask 505
 Bridgewater ms 'doeth'
Where the bow'd welkin slow doth bend, — Mask 1015
 Bridgewater ms 'doeth'
Till the dappled dawn doth rise; — Allegro 44
Spare Fast, that oft with gods doth diet, — Penseroso 46
That at her flowry work doth sing, — Penseroso 143
Of every Star that Heav'n doth shew, — Penseroso 171
When Eev'ning gray doth rise, I fetch my round — Arcades 54
Such sweet compulsion doth in musick ly, — Arcades 68
That from beneath the seat of *Jove* doth spring, — Lycidas 16
Fame is the spur that the clear spirit doth raise — Lycidas 70
That doth the wrathfull tyrants quell. — Psalm 136, 10
That with his miracles doth make — Psalm 136, 13
All living creatures he doth feed, — Psalm 136, 85
As if to shew what creatures Heav'n doth breed, — Fair Inf 61
How he before the thunderous throne doth lie, — Vacation 36
Yet there is something that doth force my fear, — Vacation 67
Loud o're the rest *Cremona*'s Trump doth sound; — Passion 26
There doth my soul in holy vision sit — Passion 41
Sore doth begin — Circum 13
This rich Marble doth enterr — Winchester 1
That thy noble House doth bring, — Winchester 54
Hill and Dale, doth boast thy blessing. — May Morn 8
And so Sepulcher'd in such pomp dost lie, — Shakespear 15
 1640 'doth lie'
And inward ripenes doth much less appear, — Sonnet 7, 7
Of Death, call'd Life; which us from Life doth sever. — Sonnet 14, 4
Of Public Fraud. In vain doth Valour bleed — Sonnet 15, 13
O're all th' *Italian* fields where still doth sway — Sonnet 18, 11
Doth God exact day labour, light deny'd, — Sonnet 19, 7
That murmur, soon replies, God doth not need — Sonnet 19, 9
Nor to thir idle orbs doth sight appear — Sonnet 22, 4
Their twisted cords: he who in Heaven doth dwell — Psalm 2, 8
Their stores doth over-cloy — Psalm 4, 34
The bloodi' and guileful man God doth detest. — Psalm 5, 16
His mischief that due course doth keep, — Psalm 7, 57
Whose bounds the Sea doth check. — Psalm 83, 28
And doth confirm the knot, — Psalm 83, 30
My Soul doth long and almost die — Psalm 84, 5
Happy, whose strength in thee doth bide, — Psalm 84, 19
Who *only* on thee doth relie, — Psalm 84, 47
Who *still* in thee doth trust. — Psalm 86, 8
When he the Nations doth enrowle — Psalm 87, 23
Surcharg'd my Soul doth lie, — Psalm 88, 10
Full sore doth press on me; — Psalm 88, 30
And *up to thee* my praier *doth hie* — Psalm 88, 55
Thy fierce wrath over me doth flow — Psalm 88, 65

Dothan
In *Dothan*, cover'd with a Camp of Fire, — Par Lost 11.217

Double
Short intermission bought with double smart. — Par Lost 4.102
Too much to one, but double how endur'd, — Par Lost 5.783
By us? who rather double honour gaine — Par Lost 9.332
All things with double terror: On the Ground — Par Lost 10.850
Instead shall double ours upon our heads. — Par Lost 10.1040
Had, like a double *Janus*, all thir shape — Par Lost 11.129
Why else this double object in our sight — Par Lost 11.201
Ambiguous and with double sense deluding, — Par Reg 1.435
But what is strength without a double share — Samson 53
But yield to double darkness nigh at hand: — Samson 593
In double night of darknes, and of shades; — Mask 335
Will double all their mirth and chere; — Mask 955

Doubled
Doubl'd that sin in *Bethel* and in *Dan*, — Par Lost 1.485
To speak; whereat thir doubl'd Ranks they bend — Par Lost 1.616
Then Heav'n permits, nor mine, though doubld now — Par Lost 4.1009
Doubl'd, would render them yet more despis'd, — Par Lost 6.602

Double-faced
Fame if not double-fac't is double-mouth'd, — Samson 971

Double-formed
What thing thou art, thus double-form'd, and why — Par Lost 2.741

Double-founted
Mount *Carmel;* here the double-founted stream — Par Lost 12.144

Double-mouthed
Fame if not double-fac't is double-mouth'd, — Samson 971

Double-shade
Night with her sullen wing to double-shade — Par Reg 1.500

Doubt
Anguish and doubt and fear and sorrow and pain — Par Lost 1.558
What fear we then? what doubt we to incense — Par Lost 2.94
Upon himself; horror and doubt distract — Par Lost 4.18
Som dreadful thing no doubt; for well thou knowst — Par Lost 4.426
The barrs of Hell, on errand bad no doubt: — Par Lost 4.795
Puts me in doubt. Lives ther who loves his pain? — Par Lost 4.888
Though thither doomd? Thou wouldst thy self, no doubt, — Par Lost 4.890
Gravely in doubt whether to hold them wise — Par Lost 4.907
Hath past in Heav'n, som doubt within me move, — Par Lost 5.554
But that I doubt, however witness Heaven, — Par Lost 6.563
All doubt of Victorie, eternal might — Par Lost 6.630

Doubt(*cont*)
Creator; something yet of doubt remaines, — Par Lost 8.13
And *Raphael* now to *Adam*'s doubt propos'd — Par Lost 8.64
Invalid that which thee to doubt it mov'd; — Par Lost 8.116
To whom thus *Adam* cleerd of doubt, repli'd. — Par Lost 8.179
An outside? fair no doubt, and worthy well — Par Lost 8.568
Doubt might beget of Diabolic pow'r — Par Lost 9.95
These paths & Bowers doubt not but our joynt hands — Par Lost 9.244
But other doubt possesses me, least harm — Par Lost 9.251
Watches, no doubt, with greedy hope to find — Par Lost 9.257
But that thou shouldst my firmness therfore doubt — Par Lost 9.279
Serpent, thy overpraising leaves in doubt — Par Lost 9.615
With cruel expectation. Yet one doubt — Par Lost 10.782
The doubt, since humane reach no further knows. — Par Lost 10.793
The penaltie pronounc't, doubt not but God — Par Lost 10.1022
A glorious Apparition, had not doubt — Par Lost 11.211
Yet doubt not but in Vallie and in plaine — Par Lost 11.349
To whom thus *Michael*. Doubt not but that sin — Par Lost 12.285
Light out of darkness! full of doubt I stand, — Par Lost 12.473
Thenceforth the Nations may not doubt; I saw — Par Reg 1.79
Began to doubt, and doubted many days, — Par Reg 2.11
And as the days increas'd, increas'd thir doubt: — Par Reg 2.12
I can at will, doubt not, as soon as thou, — Par Reg 2.383
Without distrust or doubt, that he may know — Par Reg 3.193
Thou shalt be what thou art ordain'd, no doubt; — Par Reg 4.473
For Son of God to me is yet in doubt, — Par Reg 4.501
Yet stay, let me not rashly call in doubt — Samson 43
Yet more there be who doubt his ways not just, — Samson 300
To *Israel*, diffidence of God, and doubt — Samson 454
Prevailing over fear, and timerous doubt — Samson 740
Sam. For want of words no doubt, or lack of breath, — Samson 905
For some important cause, thou needst not doubt. — Samson 1379
Man. He can I know, but doubt to think he will; — Samson 1534
Chor. All is best, though we oft doubt, — Samson 1745
Secure without all doubt, or controversie: — Mask 409
I doubt me gentle mortalls these may seeme — Mask Tr. ms 10.16

Doubted
Doubted his Empire, that were low indeed, — Par Lost 1.114
Began to doubt, and doubted many days, — Par Reg 2.11
A third sort doubted all things, though plain sence; — Par Reg 4.296

Doubtest
What doubt'st thou Son of God? sit down and eat. — Par Reg 2.377

Doubtful
Like doubtful hue: but he his wonted pride — Par Lost 1.527
 ms 'doubtfull'
Is doubtful; that he never will is sure. — Par Lost 2.154
Contending, and so doubtful what might fall. — Par Lost 2.203
Thus they thir doubtful consultations dark — Par Lost 2.486
What doubtful may ensue, more in this place — Par Lost 5.682
Who have sustaind one day in doubtful fight — Par Lost 6.423
Endure it, doubtful whether God be Lord, — Samson 477
Dal. With doubtful feet and wavering resolution — Samson 732

Doubting
Swayes them; the careful Plowman doubting stands — Par Lost 4.983
Then toldst her doubting how these things could be — Par Reg 1.137
So spake the old Serpent doubting, and from all — Par Reg 2.147
I to the Lords will intercede, not doubting — Samson 920

Doubtless
A growing Empire; doubtless; while we dream, — Par Lost 2.315
Great are thy Vertues, doubtless, best of Fruits. — Par Lost 9.745
Chor. Doubtless the people shouting to behold — Samson 1473

Doubts
The doubts that in his heart arose: and now — Par Lost 7.60
What doubts the Son of God to sit and eat? — Par Reg 2.368

Doughty
Sam. Tongue-doubtie Giant, how dost thou prove me these? — Samson 1181

Dove
A Dove sent forth once and agen to spie — Par Lost 11.857
Heaven open'd, and in likeness of a Dove — Par Reg 1.30
A perfect Dove descend, what e're it meant, — Par Reg 1.83
The Spirit descended on me like a Dove, — Par Reg 1.282

Dovelike
Dove-like satst brooding on the vast Abyss — Par Lost 1.21

Dower
Her dowr th' adopted Clusters, to adorn — Par Lost 5.218

Down
With hideous ruine and combustion down — Par Lost 1.46
 ms 'downe'
Th' advantage, and descending tread us down — Par Lost 1.327
 ms 'downe'
Thir course, in even ballance down they light — Par Lost 1.349
His righteous Altar, bowing lowly down — Par Lost 1.434
Bow'd down in Battel, sunk before the Spear — Par Lost 1.436
Down cast and damp, yet such wherein appear'd — Par Lost 1.523
Through all the Empyrean: down they fell — Par Lost 2.771
Driv'n headlong from the Pitch of Heaven, down — Par Lost 2.772
Shall dwell at ease, and up and down unseen — Par Lost 2.841
Who hates me, and hath hither thrust me down — Par Lost 2.857
Fluttring his pennons vain plumb down he drops — Par Lost 2.933
Down had been falling, had not by ill chance — Par Lost 2.935
Taught by the heav'nly Muse to venture down — Par Lost 3.19
High Thron'd above all highth, bent down his eye, — Par Lost 3.58
Pleas'd, out of Heaven shalt look down and smile, — Par Lost 3.257
With solemn adoration down they cast — Par Lost 3.351
By thee created, and by thee threw down — Par Lost 3.391
Walk'd up and down alone bent on his prey, — Par Lost 3.441
The Stairs were then let down, whether to dare — Par Lost 3.523
A passage down to th' Earth, a passage wide, — Par Lost 3.528

Down*(cont)*
Looks down with wonder at the sudden view Par Lost 3.542
Down right into the Worlds first Region throws Par Lost 3.562
Through the calm Firmament; but up or downe Par Lost 3.574
That run through all the Heav'ns, or down to th' Earth Par Lost 3.651
Down from th' Ecliptic, sped with hop'd success, Par Lost 3.740
Came furious down to be reveng'd on men, Par Lost 4.4
Satan, now first inflam'd with rage, came down, Par Lost 4.9
Till Pride and worse Ambition threw me down Par Lost 4.40
Uriel once warnd; whose eye pursu'd him down Par Lost 4.125
Down the steep glade, and met the neather Flood, Par Lost 4.231
Down the slope hills, disperst, or in a Lake, Par Lost 4.261
Shee as a vail down to the slender waste Par Lost 4.304
They sat them down, and after no more toil Par Lost 4.327
Down he alights among the sportful Herd Par Lost 4.396
With unexperienc't thought, and laid me downe Par Lost 4.457
As I bent down to look, just opposite, Par Lost 4.460
Temper or nourish, or in part shed down Par Lost 4.670
My Guide was gon, and I, me thought, sunk down, Par Lost 5.91
A cloudy spot. Down thither prone in flight Par Lost 5.266
Shot down direct his fervid Raies to warme Par Lost 5.301
Think not I shall be nice. So down they sat, Par Lost 5.433
Brandisht aloft the horrid edge came down Par Lost 6.252
Down clov'n to the waste, with shatterd Armes Par Lost 6.361
Born eevn or high, for this day will pour down, Par Lost 6.544
Though standing else as Rocks, but down they fell Par Lost 6.593
To thir prepar'd ill Mansion driven down Par Lost 6.738
All courage; down thir idle weapons drop'd; Par Lost 6.839
Down from the verge of Heav'n, Eternal wrauth Par Lost 6.865
Thy tempring; with like safetie guided down Par Lost 7.15
Down from the Empyrean to forewarne Par Lost 7.73
Down sunk a hollow bottom broad and deep, Par Lost 7.289
The Filial Power arriv'd, and sate him down Par Lost 7.587
Down to this habitable, which returnes Par Lost 8.157
Pensive I sate me down; there gentle sleep Par Lost 8.287
Dazl'd and spent, sunk down, and sought repair Par Lost 8.457
Descend to? who aspires must down as low Par Lost 9.169
Down drop'd, and all the faded Roses shed: Par Lost 9.893
They sate them down to weep, nor onely Teares Par Lost 9.1121
Down he descended strait; the speed of Gods Par Lost 10.90
Saw Satan fall like Lightning down from Heav'n, Par Lost 10.184
Tost up and down, together crowded drove Par Lost 10.287
Smooth, easie, inoffensive down to Hell. Par Lost 10.305
All yours, right down to Paradise descend; Par Lost 10.398
Then sufferd. Th' other way *Satan* went down Par Lost 10.414
Was plac't in regal lustre. Down a while Par Lost 10.447
Each other, till supplanted down he fell Par Lost 10.513
They felt themselves now changing; down thir arms, Par Lost 10.541
Down fell both Spear and Shield, down they as fast, Par Lost 10.542
The Sithe of Time mowes down, devour unspar'd, Par Lost 10.606
Or down from Heav'n descend. Such was thir song, Par Lost 10.648
Up to the *Tropic* Crab; thence down amaine Par Lost 10.675
Insensible, how glad would lay me down Par Lost 10.777
Tine the slant Lightning, whose thwart flame driv'n down Par Lost 10.1075
Down from a Hill the Beast that reigns in Woods, Par Lost 11.187
Down from a Skie of Jasper lighted now Par Lost 11.209
How shall I part, and whither wander down Par Lost 11.282
But this praeeminence thou hast lost, brought down Par Lost 11.347
Down to the golden *Chersonese*, or where Par Lost 11.392
Sunk down and all his Spirits became intranst: Par Lost 11.420
Life offer'd, or soon beg to lay it down, Par Lost 11.506
To weigh thy Spirits down, and last consume Par Lost 11.545
Down to the veins of Earth, thence gliding hot Par Lost 11.568
Down to the Plain descended: by thir guise Par Lost 11.576
Like a dark Ceeling stood; down rush'd the Rain Par Lost 11.743
Down the great River to the op'ning Gulf, Par Lost 11.833
Griev'd at his heart, when looking down he saw Par Lost 11.887
Comes down to see thir Citie, ere the Tower Par Lost 12.51
And looking down, to see the hubbub strange Par Lost 12.60
A darksom Cloud of Locusts swarming down Par Lost 12.185
Led them direct, and down the Cliff as fast Par Lost 12.639
There he shall first lay down the rudiments Par Reg 1.157
Threat'ns then our expulsion down to Hell; Par Reg 2.128
Commun'd in silent walk, then laid him down Par Reg 2.261
What doubt'st thou Son of God? sit down and eat. Par Reg 2.377
Greater and nobler done, and to lay down Par Reg 2.482
At his dispose, young *Scipio* had brought down Par Reg 3.34
On this condition, if thou wilt fall down, Par Reg 4.166
That I fall down and worship thee as God? Par Reg 4.192
Cast thy self down; safely if Son of God: Par Reg 4.555
Then in a flowry valley set him down Par Reg 4.586
Thou didst debel, and down from Heav'n cast Par Reg 4.605
A Saviour art come down to re-install. Par Reg 4.615
Or Lightning thou shalt fall from Heav'n trod down Par Reg 4.620
Lest he command them down into the deep Par Reg 4.631
Down Reason then, at least vain reasonings down, Samson 322
Robustious to no purpose clustring down, Samson 569
With sickness and disease thou bow'st them down, Samson 698
Or swing thee in the Air, then dash thee down Samson 1240
And numberd down: much rather I shall chuse Samson 1478
And on his shoulders waving down those locks, Samson 1493
He tugg'd, he shook, till down they came and drew Samson 1650
Pulld down the same destruction on himself; Samson 1658
I sate me down to watch upon a bank Mask 543
 1637 'downe'
 Trinity ms 'downe'
 Bridgewater ms 'downe'
Then down the Lawns I ran with headlong hast Mask 568

Down*(cont)*
 Bridgewater ms 'downe'
 1637 'downe'
 Trinity ms 'downe'
Curs'd as his life. *Spir*. Alas good ventrous youth, Mask 609
 Bridgewater ms 'downe to the hipps'
 1637 'Downe to the hipps'
 Trinity ms 'downe to the hips' ← 'lowest hips' ← 'hipps'
That tumble down the snowy hills: Mask 927
 Bridgewater ms 'downe'
 1637 'downe'
 Trinity ms 'downe'
Then lies him down the Lubbar Fend, Allegro 110
Drew Iron tears down *Pluto*'s cheek, Penseroso 107
His goary visage down the stream was sent, Lycidas 62
 Trinity ms 'downe'
Down the swift *Hebrus* to the *Lesbian* shore. Lycidas 63
 Trinity ms 'downe'
his goarie scalpe rowle downe the Thracian lee Lycidas Tr. ms 29.61
Sent down the meek-eyd Peace, Nativity 46
Down through the turning sphear Nativity 48
Will down return to men, Nativity 142
With radiant feet the tissued clouds down stearing, Nativity 146
In bloody battail he brought down Psalm 136, 61
Down he descended from his Snow-soft chaire, Fair Inf 19
Let down in clowdie throne to do the world some good. Fair Inf 56
That dropt with odorous oil down his fair eyes, Passion 16
Then lies him meekly down fast by his Brethrens side. Passion 21
Death was half glad when he had got him down; Carrier 6
For one Carrier put down to make six bearers. Another 20
 line not in 1640, 1657, 1658 texts
Mother with Infant down the Rocks. Their moans Sonnet 18, 8
Both lay me down and sleep Psalm 4, 38
My life down to the earth and roul Psalm 7, 15
Down to the Sea she sent, Psalm 80, 46
And brok'n down her Fence, Psalm 80, 50
Return now, God of Hosts, look down Psalm 80, 57
And cut *with Axes* down, Psalm 80, 66
Then would I soon bring down their foes Psalm 81, 57
Look down *on mortal men*. Psalm 85, 48
Down to the *dismal* pit Psalm 88, 14

Down
With careful step, Locks white as doune, Samson 327
At every fall smoothing the Raven doune Mask 251
 1637 'downe'
 Bridgewater ms 'downe'
 Trinity ms 'downe'

Downcast
Down cast and damp, yet such wherein appear'd Par Lost 1.523

Downfall
This downfall; since by Fate the strength of Gods Par Lost 1.116

Downs
Betwixt them Lawns, or level Downs, and Flocks Par Lost 4.252
That doth enrich these Downs, is worth a thought Mask 505
 1637 'downs'
 Trinity ms 'downs'
 Bridgewater ms 'downes'

Downward
And downward Fish: yet had his Temple high Par Lost 1.463
Were always downward bent, admiring more Par Lost 1.681
Look downward on that Globe whose hither side Par Lost 3.722
Bore him slope downward to the Sun now fall'n Par Lost 4.591
Throughout the fluid Mass, but downward purg'd Par Lost 7.237
Downward as farr Antartic; and in length Par Lost 9.79
And downward fell into a groveling Swine) Mask 53
 Bridgewater ms 'downeward'
 Trinity ms 'downeward'
With a sad Leaden downward cast, Penseroso 43

Downy
On the soft downie Bank damaskt with flours: Par Lost 4.334
Skirted his loines and thighes with downie Gold Par Lost 5.282
Thir downie Brest; the Swan with Arched neck Par Lost 7.438
A bough of fairest fruit that downie smil'd, Par Lost 9.851

Draff
My Hell-hounds, to lick up the draff and filth Par Lost 10.630
Till vermin or the draff of servil food Samson 574

Drag
Back to th' infernal pit I drag thee chaind, Par Lost 4.965
And at his Chariot wheeles to drag him bound Par Lost 6.358
The Serpent, Prince of aire, and drag in Chaines Par Lost 12.454
Or drag him by the curls, to a foul death, Mask 608

Dragged
Or Captive drag'd in Chains, with hostile frown Par Lost 6.260

Dragging
Not dragging? the *Philistian* Lords command. Samson 1371

Dragon
Then when the Dragon, put to second rout, Par Lost 4.3
Now Dragon grown, larger then whom the Sun Par Lost 10.529
The River-dragon tam'd at length submits Par Lost 12.191
And as an ev'ning Dragon came, Samson 1692
That ne're art call'd, but when the Dragon woom Mask 131
 Bridgewater ms 'dragon'
 Trinity ms 'dragon'
Of dragon watch with uninchanted eye, Mask 395
the scalie-harnest dragon ever keeps Mask Tr. ms 10.09
 'dragon ever keeps' ← 'watchfull dragons keep'
While *Cynthia* checks her Dragon yoke, Penseroso 59
Th' old Dragon under ground Nativity 168

Drained
Draind through a Limbec to his Native forme. Par Lost 3.605
And of thir wonted vigour left them draind, Par Lost 6.851
From underground) the liquid Ore he dreind Par Lost 11.570
And exquisitest name, for which was drain'd Par Reg 2.346
Drank
Moses was forty days, nor eat nor drank, Par Reg 1.352
I drank, from the clear milkie juice allaying Samson 550
Draught
Unwholsom draught: but here I feel amends, Samson 9
Were it a draft for *Juno* when she banquets, Mask 701
Bridgewater ms 'drafte'
Draughts
Of nectarous draughts between, from milkie stream, Par Lost 5.306
Draw
In Heav'n, which follows dignity, might draw Par Lost 2.25
Draw after him the whole Race of mankind, Par Lost 3.161
Much less that durst upon his own head draw Par Lost 3.220
Or in thick shade retir'd, from him to draw Par Lost 4.532
Uzziel, half these draw off, and coast the South Par Lost 4.782
Let us advise, and to this hazard draw Par Lost 5.729
Stream, and perpetual draw thir humid traine. Par Lost 7.306
Repairing, in thir gold'n Urns draw Light, Par Lost 7.365
Thir Element to draw the thinner Aire. Par Lost 8.348
Casual discourse draw on, which intermits Par Lost 9.223
In Femal Sex, the more to draw his Love, Par Lost 9.822
The Link of Nature draw me: Flesh of Flesh, Par Lost 9.914
The Bond of Nature draw me to my owne, Par Lost 9.956
The way, thou leading, such a sent I draw Par Lost 10.267
Of weakness, not of Power. Will he, draw out, Par Lost 10.801
To draw the proud King *Ahab* into fraud Par Reg 1.372
Skill'd to retire, and in retiring draw Par Reg 2.161
Draw out with credulous desire, and lead Par Reg 2.166
Where I a Prisoner chain'd, scarce freely draw Samson 7
Chor. Hee speaks, let us draw nigh. Matchless in might, Samson 178
As Graces, draw a Scorpions tail behind? Samson 360
Would draw thee forth to perilous enterprises, Samson 804
So shall he least confusion draw Samson 1058
Draw thir own ruin who attempt the deed. Samson 1267
To heave, pull, draw, or break, he still perform'd Samson 1626
Best draw, and stand upon our guard. *Eld. Bro*. Ile hallow, Mask 487
Bridgewater ms 'drawe'
That draw the litter of close-curtain'd sleep. Mask 554
Bridgewater ms 'drawe'
And the low world in measur'd motion draw Arcades 71
But swoln with wind, and the rank mist they draw, Lycidas 126
Drawest
Us'd to the yoak, draw'st his triumphant wheels Par Lost 4.975
Drawn
Millions of flaming swords, drawn from the thighs Par Lost 1.664
Drawn round about thee like a radiant Shrine, Par Lost 3.379
By Model, or by shading Pencil drawn. Par Lost 3.509
There alwayes, but drawn up to Heav'n somtimes Par Lost 3.517
Rapt in a Chariot drawn by fiery Steeds. Par Lost 3.522
Drawn to his part; but other Powers as great Par Lost 4.63
Of porous Earth with kindly thirst up drawn, Par Lost 4.228
An Earthlie Guest, and drawn Empyreal Aire, Par Lost 7.14
Nor can I miss the way, so strongly drawn Par Lost 10.262
His Visage drawn he felt to sharp and spare, Par Lost 10.511
More to the part sinister from me drawn, Par Lost 10.886
Are drawn to wear out miserable days, Samson 762
Of lincked sweetnes long drawn out, Allegro 140
Over thy decent shoulders drawn. Penseroso 36
Draws
Draws in, and at his Trunck spouts out a Sea. Par Lost 7.416
Beyond this Deep; whatever drawes me on, Par Lost 10.245
More orient in yon Western Cloud that draws Par Lost 11.205
As the Magnetic hardest Iron draws. Par Reg 2.168
Draws him awry enslav'd Samson 1041
Draws hitherward, I know him by his stride, Samson 1067
In mirth, that after no repenting drawes; Sonnet 21, 6
Trinity ms 'draws'
Unto the grave draws nigh. Psalm 88, 12
Dread
On duty, sleeping found by whom they dread, Par Lost 1.333
Next *Chemos*, th' obscene dread of *Moabs* Sons, Par Lost 1.406
With dread of death to flight or foul retreat, Par Lost 1.555
Thir dread commander: he above the rest Par Lost 1.589
ms 'dred'
So as not either to provoke, or dread Par Lost 1.644
More glorious and more dread then from no fall, Par Lost 2.16
Of darkness do we dread? How oft amidst Par Lost 2.263
Than Hells dread Emperour with pomp Supream, Par Lost 2.510
Thy dread Tribunal: forthwith from all Windes Par Lost 3.326
Disdain forbids me, and my dread of shame Par Lost 4.82
Of wrauth awak't: nor with less dread the loud Par Lost 6.59
When coming towards them so dread they saw Par Lost 6.648
I dread, and to elude, thus wrapt in mist Par Lost 9.158
Rather then Death or aught then Death more dread Par Lost 9.969
And torment less then none of what we dread, Par Lost 10.998
Satans dire dread, and in his hand the Spear. Par Lost 11.248
And while the dread of judgement past remains Par Lost 12.14
With dread attending when that fatal wound Par Reg 1.53
(Whose ire I dread more then the fire of Hell) Par Reg 3.220
Of equal dread in flight, or in pursuit; Par Reg 3.306
So strook with dread and anguish fell the Fiend, Par Reg 4.576
To dread the Son of God: he all unarm'd Par Reg 4.626
The dread of *Israel*'s foes, who with a strength Samson 342

Dread*(cont)*
Sam. I dread him not, nor all his Giant-brood, Samson 1247
Thir once great dread, captive, & blind before them, Samson 1474
Before our living Dread who dwells Samson 1673
I fear the dred events that dog them both, Mask 405
Trinity ms 'dread'
Bridgewater ms 'dread'
Hence had the huntress *Dian* her dred bow Mask 441
Bridgewater ms 'dread'
Return *Alpheus*, the dread voice is past, Lycidas 132
Trinity ms 'dred'
Hath left in shadows dred, Nativity 206
And on our foes thy dread Psalm 80, 8
Dreaded
Rear'd in *Azotus*, dreaded through the Coast Par Lost 1.464
They dreaded worse then Hell: so much the fear Par Lost 2.293
Dreaded not more th' adventure then his voice Par Lost 2.474
Orcus and *Ades*, and the dreaded name Par Lost 2.964
And seconded thy else not dreaded Spear. Par Lost 4.929
The Thunderer of his only dreaded bolt. Par Lost 6.491
Thir guilt and dreaded shame; O how unlike Par Lost 9.1114
This dreaded time have compast, wherein we Par Reg 1.58
I walk'd about admir'd of all and dreaded Samson 530
So dreaded once, may now exasperate them Samson 1417
The dredded Infants hand, Nativity 222
And *Kings* be born of thee, whose dredded might Prose 12, 13
Dreadful
Under thy conduct, and in dreadful deeds Par Lost 1.130
ms 'dreadfull'
Casts pale and dreadful? Thither let us tend Par Lost 1.183
ms 'dreadfull'
Of dreadful length and dazling Arms, in guise Par Lost 1.564
ms 'dreadfull'
Alone the dreadful voyage; till at last Par Lost 2.426
And shook a dreadful Dart; what seem'd his head Par Lost 2.672
More dreadful and deform: on th' other side Par Lost 2.706
Thy Fathers dreadful Thunder didst not spare, Par Lost 3.393
Som dreadful thing no doubt; for well thou knowst Par Lost 4.426
What seemd both Spear and Shield: now dreadful deeds Par Lost 4.990
A dreadful intervall, and Front to Front Par Lost 6.105
Dreadful combustion warring, and disturb, Par Lost 6.225
With dreadful shade contiguous, and the Orbes Par Lost 6.828
Yet dreadful in mine eare, though in my choice Par Lost 8.335
So dreadful to thee? that thou art naked, who Par Lost 10.121
To his bold Riot: dreadful was the din Par Lost 10.521
And sleep secure; his dreadful voice no more Par Lost 10.779
Comes thundring back with dreadful revolution Par Lost 10.814
Accompanied, with damps and dreadful gloom, Par Lost 10.848
To mortal eare is dreadful; they beseech Par Lost 12.236
With dreadful Faces throng'd and fierie Armes: Par Lost 12.644
A dreadful way thou took'st to thy revenge. Samson 1591
Who had made thir dreadful enemy thir thrall. Samson 1622
The dreadfull Judge in middle Air shall spread his throne. Nativity 164
1673 'dreadful'
They perish at thy dreadfull ire, Psalm 80, 67
Dreading
I came, still dreading thy displeasure, *Samson*, Samson 733
Dreadless
All night the dreadless Angel unpursu'd Par Lost 6.1
Dream
A growing Empire; doubtless; while we dream, Par Lost 2.315
To find this but a dream! Thus *Eve* her Night Par Lost 5.93
This uncouth dream, of evil sprung I fear; Par Lost 5.98
Of our last Eevnings talk, in this thy dream, Par Lost 5.115
That what in sleep thou didst abhorr to dream, Par Lost 5.120
For thou art Heav'nlie, shee an empty dreame. Par Lost 7.39
Dream not of other Worlds, what Creatures there Par Lost 8.175
When suddenly stood at my Head a dream, Par Lost 8.292
Before mine Eyes all real, as the dream Par Lost 8.310
Such as I saw her in my dream, adornd Par Lost 8.482
And live for ever, dream at least to live Par Lost 11.95
To whom thus *Michael*. Dream not of thir fight, Par Lost 12.386
And dream'd, as appetite is wont to dream, Par Reg 2.264
Our Saviour, and found all was but a dream, Par Reg 2.283
He spake no dream, for as his words had end, Par Reg 2.337
And in cleer dream, and solemn vision Mask 457
Bridgewater ms 'dreame'
1637 'dreame'
Trinity ms 'dreame'
Such sights as youthfull Poets dream Allegro 129
And let som strange mysterious dream, Penseroso 147
Ay me, I fondly dream! Lycidas 56
Trinity ms 'dreame'
Dreamed
Not in the neighbouring Moon, as some have dreamd; Par Lost 3.459
Such night till this I never pass'd, have dream'd, Par Lost 5.31
If dream'd, not as I oft am wont, of thee, Par Lost 5.32
And dream'd, as appetite is wont to dream, Par Reg 2.264
Dreaming
Dreaming by night under the open Skie, Par Lost 3.514
Dreams
Or dreams he sees, while over-head the Moon Par Lost 1.784
Illusions as he list, Phantasms and Dreams, Par Lost 4.803
Wilde work produces oft, and most in dreams, Par Lost 5.112
Bred of unkindly fumes, with conscious dreams Par Lost 9.1050
Her also I with gentle Dreams have calm'd Par Lost 12.595
For God is also in sleep, and Dreams advise, Par Lost 12.611
And answers, oracles, portents and dreams, Par Reg 1.395

Dreams(*cont*)
But these are false, or little else but dreams, Par Reg 4.291
The Tempter watch'd, and soon with ugly dreams Par Reg 4.408
Beyond the bliss of dreams. Be wise, and taste.---- Mask 813
Trinity ms 'dreames'
Bridgewater ms 'dreames'
Or likest hovering dreams Penseroso 9

Drear
Cerastes hornd, *Hydrus*, and *Ellops* drear, Par Lost 10.525
Lies through the perplex't paths of this drear Wood, Mask 37
1637 'dreare'
Bridgewater ms 'dreare'
Trinity ms 'dreare'
Of Forests, and inchantments drear, Penseroso 119
A drear, and dying sound Nativity 193

Dreary
Seest thou yon dreary Plain, forlorn and wilde, Par Lost 1.180
No rest: through many a dark and drearie Vaile Par Lost 2.618

Dregs
The black tartareous cold Infernal dregs Par Lost 7.238

Drench
Let such bethink them, if the sleepy drench Par Lost 2.73
To day deep thoughts resolve with me to drench Sonnet 21, 5

Drenched
This Hill; let *Eve* (for I have drencht her eyes) Par Lost 11.367

Drenches
And drenches with *Elysian* dew Mask 996
Trinity ms 'drenches' ←'drenches oft'
Bridgewater ms 'drenches oft'

Dress
Adam, well may we labour still to dress Par Lost 9.205
In Gems and wanton dress; to the Harp they sung Par Lost 11.583
To dress, and troule the Tongue, and roule the Eye. Par Lost 11.620

Dressed
And azure wings, that up they flew so drest, Sonnet 14, 11

Dresses
Which the neat-handed *Phillis* dresses; Allegro 86

Dressing
Woods and Groves, are of thy dressing, May Morn 7

Drew
Ahaz his sottish Conquerour, whom he drew Par Lost 1.472
Drew audience and attention still as Night Par Lost 2.308
Drew after him the third part of Heav'ns Sons Par Lost 2.692
Forthwith the huge Porcullis high up drew, Par Lost 2.874
He drew not nigh unheard, the Angel bright, Par Lost 3.645
Ere he drew nigh, his radiant visage turnd, Par Lost 3.646
His heart, not else dismai'd. Now drew they nigh Par Lost 4.861
So saying, he drew nigh, and to me held, Par Lost 5.82
Drew after him the third part of Heav'ns Host: Par Lost 5.710
To final Battel drew, disdaining flight, Par Lost 6.798
Drew many, whom thir place knows here no more; Par Lost 7.144
These as a line thir long dimension drew, Par Lost 7.480
From where I first drew Aire, and first beheld Par Lost 8.284
Neerer he drew, and many a walk travers'd Par Lost 9.434
Ruddie and Gold: I nearer drew to gaze; Par Lost 9.578
Mean while the hour of Noon drew on, and wak'd Par Lost 9.739
And know not that I call'd and drew them thither Par Lost 10.629
He ended; and th' Arch-Angel soon drew nigh, Par Lost 11.238
Gaz'd hot, and of the fresh Wave largely drew, Par Lost 11.845
May expiate (though the fact more evil drew Samson 736
Mess. Occasions drew me early to this City, Samson 1596
He tugg'd, he shook, till down they came and drew Samson 1650
Drew Iron tears down *Pluto*'s cheek, Penseroso 107

Dried
Soon dri'd, and on the reaking moisture fed. Par Lost 8.256
Had chear'd the face of Earth, and dry'd the wet Par Reg 4.433

Drift
Of his weak arguing, and fallacious drift; Par Reg 3.4
The drift of hollow states hard to be spelld, Sonnet 17, 6
1694 'Drift'
Trinity ms 'drift' ←'drifts'

Drink
Heaps with unsparing hand; for drink the Grape Par Lost 5.344
They eate, they drink, and in communion sweet Par Lost 5.637
And drink the liquid Light, firm to retaine Par Lost 7.362
From Nectar, drink of Gods. *Adam* the while Par Lost 9.838
All that I eat or drink, or shall beget, Par Lost 10.728
More then the Camel, and to drink go far, Par Reg 1.340
The drink of none but Kings; of later fame Par Reg 3.289
And from the fount of life Ambrosial drink, Par Reg 4.590
Whose drink was only from the liquid brook. Samson 557
Drink the clear stream, and nothing wear but Freize, Mask 722
Trinity ms 'drinke'
Bridgewater ms 'drinke'
And drink thy fill of pure immortal streams. Sonnet 14, 14
Trinity ms 'drinke' ←'drink'
And mak'st them largely drink the tears Psalm 80, 23

Drinkest
In what thou eatst and drinkst, seeking from thence Par Lost 11.532

Drinks
Her watrie Labyrinth, whereof who drinks, Par Lost 2.584
Thus when with meats and drinks they had suffic'd, Par Lost 5.451
In Meats and Drinks, which on the Earth shall bring Par Lost 11.473
Of meats and drinks, Natures refreshment sweet; Par Reg 2.265
Chor. Desire of wine and all delicious drinks, Samson 541
And strongest drinks our chief support of health, Samson 554
The visage quite transforms of him that drinks, Mask 527
Bridgewater ms 'drinkes'

Drive
Here for his envy, will not drive us hence: Par Lost 1.260
All as our own, and drive as we were driven, Par Lost 2.366
The punie habitants, or if not drive, Par Lost 2.367
Of *Sericana*, where *Chineses* drive Par Lost 3.438
Vernal delight and joy, able to drive Par Lost 4.155
Pursuing drive them out from God and bliss, Par Lost 6.52
Pursue these sons of Darkness, drive them out Par Lost 6.715
But drive farr off the barbarous dissonance Par Lost 7.32
Upon the *Cronian* Sea, together drive Par Lost 10.290
Without remorse drive out the sinful Pair, Par Lost 11.105
With clamor thence the rapid Currents drive Par Lost 11.853
All his vast force, and drive him back to Hell, Par Reg 1.153
Or drive away the slaughtering pestilence, Fair Inf 68
Meerly to drive the time away he sickn'd, Another 15
line not in 1640, 1657, 1658 texts

Driven
Drivn backward slope thir pointing spires, and rowld Par Lost 1.223
ms 'Driv'n'
Then to dwell here, driv'n out from bliss, condemn'd Par Lost 2.86
All as our own, and drive as we were driven, Par Lost 2.366
Driv'n headlong from the Pitch of Heaven, down Par Lost 2.772
Who justly hath drivn out his Rebell Foes Par Lost 3.677
By thee adulterous lust was driv'n from men Par Lost 4.753
To thir prepar'd ill Mansion driven down Par Lost 6.738
Driv'n back redounded as a flood on those Par Lost 7.57
1669 'Driven'
Had driven out th' ungodly from his sight Par Lost 7.185
1669 'driv'n'
That kept thir watch; thence full of anguish driv'n, Par Lost 9.62
Ere this he had return'd, with fury driv'n Par Lost 10.240
Of high *Olympus*, thence by *Saturn* driv'n Par Lost 10.583
And horrors hast thou driv'n me; out of which Par Lost 10.843
Tine the slant Lightning, whose thwart flame driv'n down Par Lost 10.1075
Drivn by a keen North-winde, that blowing drie Par Lost 11.842
Kept not my happy Station, but was driv'n Par Reg 1.360

Drives
Whom hunger drives to seek new haunt for prey, Par Lost 4.184
One way a Band select from forage drives Par Lost 11.646
The wind drives, so the wicked shall not stand Psalm 1, 12

Driving
Driving far off each thing of sin and guilt, Mask 456
Bridgewater ms 'drivinge'
Driving dum silence from the portal dore, Vacation 5

Drizzling
If I conjecture aught, no drizling showr, Par Lost 6.545

Dromedaries
Mules after these, Camels and Dromedaries, Par Reg 3.335

Drone
The Female Bee that feeds her Husband Drone Par Lost 7.490
A burdenous drone; to visitants a gaze, Samson 567

Droop
Laborious, till day droop; while here we dwell, Par Lost 11.178
So much I feel my genial spirits droop, Samson 594

Drooping
Thus drooping, or with linked Thunderbolts Par Lost 1.328
He ended, and his words thir drooping chere Par Lost 6.496
Hung drooping unsustaind, them she upstaies Par Lost 9.430
From drooping plant, or dropping tree; the birds Par Reg 4.434
Will bathe the drooping spirits in delight Mask 812
Bridgewater ms 'droopinge'
And yet anon repairs his drooping head, Lycidas 169

Drop
The tempting stream, with one small drop to loose Par Lost 2.607
So thick a drop serene hath quencht thir Orbs, Par Lost 3.25
So maist thou live, till like ripe Fruit thou drop Par Lost 11.535

Dropped
Dropt from the Zenith like a falling Star, Par Lost 1.745
Dropt Manna, and could make the worse appear Par Lost 2.113
All courage; down thir idle weapons drop'd; Par Lost 6.839
Show to the Sun thir wav'd coats dropt with Gold, Par Lost 7.406
Down drop'd, and all the faded Roses shed: Par Lost 9.893
Som natural tears they drop'd, but wip'd them soon; Par Lost 12.645
Durst ever, who return'd, and dropt not here Par Reg 1.324
Dropt in Ambrosial Oils till she reviv'd, Mask 840
And now was dropt into the Western bay; Lycidas 191
That dropt with odorous oil down his fair eyes, Passion 16

Dropping
Those Blossoms also, and those dropping Gumms, Par Lost 4.630
Of Ewe or Goat dropping with Milk at Eevn, Par Lost 9.582
From drooping plant, or dropping tree; the birds Par Reg 4.434
Dropping odours, dropping Wine. Mask 106
Bridgewater ms both 'droppinge'
The loose train of thy amber-dropping hair, Mask 863
B.M. ms 'Amber dropping'
Bridgewater ms 'Amber-droppinge'
My dank and dropping weeds Horace 15

Drops
Fluttring his pennons vain plumb down he drops Par Lost 2.933
What drops the Myrrhe, and what the balmie Reed, Par Lost 5.23
Two other precious drops that ready stood, Par Lost 5.132
Or Starrs of Morning, Dew-drops, which the Sun Par Lost 5.746
As drops on dust conglobing from the drie; Par Lost 7.292
Skie lowr'd and muttering Thunder, som sad drops Par Lost 9.1002
And from the Well of Life three drops instill'd. Par Lost 11.416
Drops that from my fountain pure, Mask 912
With minute drops from off the Eaves. Penseroso 130

Dropsies
Dropsies, and Asthma's, and Joint-racking Rheums. Par Lost 11.488
Dross
Severing each kind, and scum'd the Bullion dross: Par Lost 1.704
ms 'drosse'
All treasures and all gain esteem as dross, Par Reg 3.29
And meerly mortal dross; On Time 6
Trinity ms 'drosse'
Drossiest
Metals of drossiest Ore to perfet Gold Par Lost 5.442
Drought
Before his memorie, as one whose drouth Par Lost 7.66
His Carcass, pin'd with hunger and with droughth? Par Reg 1.325
And inaccessible the *Arabian* drouth: Par Reg 3.274
To quench the drouth of *Phoebus*, which as they taste Mask 66
Summer drouth, or singed air Mask 928
Drove
Till good *Josiah* drove them thence to Hell. Par Lost 1.418
That drove him, though enamourd, from the Spouse Par Lost 4.169
Hee on his impious Foes right onward drove, Par Lost 6.831
Drove them before him Thunder-struck, pursu'd Par Lost 6.858
Tost up and down, together crowded drove Par Lost 10.287
Two Birds of gayest plume before him drove: Par Lost 11.186
Wide hovering, all the Clouds together drove Par Lost 11.739
When his fierce thunder drove us to the deep; Par Reg 1.90
These two proportiond ill drove me transverse. Samson 209
The Sounds, and Seas with all their finny drove Mask 115
We drove a field, and both together heard Lycidas 27
Drovest
Thou drov'st of warring Angels disarraid. Par Lost 3.396
And drov'st out Nations *proud and haut* Psalm 80, 35
Drown
Surpass his bounds, nor Rain to drown the World Par Lost 11.894
Drowned
To rapture, till the savage clamor dround Par Lost 7.36
The Race of Mankind drownd, before the Shrine Par Lost 11.13
Of tears and sorrow a Floud thee also drown'd, Par Lost 11.757
Jarr'd against natures chime, and with harsh din Musick 20
Trinity ms 'jarr'd against' ←'drown'd'
Drowse
Of *Argus*, and more wakeful then to drouze, Par Lost 11.131
Drowsed
My droused sense, untroubl'd, though I thought Par Lost 8.289
Drowsiness
But els in deep of night when drowsines Arcades 61
Trinity ms 'drousinesse'
Drowsy
Gave respit to the drowsie frighted steeds Mask 553
Trinity ms 'drousie'
Or the Belmans drousie charm, Penseroso 83
1673 'drowsie'
Thy drowsie Nurse hath sworn she did them spie Vacation 61
Drudge
At thee ordain'd his drudge, to execute Par Lost 2.732
Here rather let me drudge and earn my bread, Samson 573
Although thir drudge, to be thir fool or jester, Samson 1338
Our Captive, at the public Mill our drudge, Samson 1393
Drudging
Tells how the drudging *Goblin* swet, Allegro 105
Drugged
Hunger and thirst constraining, drugd as oft, Par Lost 10.568
Drugs
Thir spicie Drugs: they on the Trading Flood Par Lost 2.640
Culling their Potent hearbs, and balefull drugs, Mask 255
Bridgewater ms 'druggs'
Trinity ms 'druggs'
Druids
Where your old *Bards*, the famous *Druids* ly, Lycidas 53
Drums
Though for the noyse of Drums and Timbrels loud Par Lost 1.394
ms 'drums'
Drunk
Drunk with Idolatry, drunk with Wine, Samson 1670
Dry
That felt unusual weight, till on dry Land Par Lost 1.227
For hot, cold, moist, and dry, four Champions fierce Par Lost 2.898
Nor good dry Land: nigh founderd on he fares, Par Lost 2.940
Bear his swift errands over moist and dry, Par Lost 3.652
Into one place, and let dry Land appeer. Par Lost 7.284
As drops on dust conglobing from the drie; Par Lost 7.292
Easie, e're God had bid the ground be drie, Par Lost 7.304
The dry Land, Earth, and the great receptacle Par Lost 7.307
So saying, through each Thicket Danck or Drie, Par Lost 9.179
Death with his Mace petrific, cold and dry, Par Lost 10.294
A melancholly damp of cold and dry Par Lost 11.544
Drivn by a keen North-winde, that blowing drie Par Lost 11.842
Anon drie ground appeers, and from his Arke Par Lost 11.861
As on drie land between two christal walls, Par Lost 12.197
For barren desert fountainless and dry. Par Reg 3.264
From the dry ground to spring, thy thirst to allay Samson 582
On the dry smooth-shaven Green, Penseroso 66
Bleak winters force that made thy blossome drie; Fair Inf 4
That dry and barren ground Psalm 84, 22
Dryad
Oread or *Dryad*, or of *Delia*'s Traine, Par Lost 9.387
Dryades
With the mincing *Dryades* Mask 964
Bridgewater ms 'Driades'
Dry-eyed
Drie-ey'd behold? *Adam* could not, but wept, Par Lost 11.495
Dubious
In dubious Battel on the Plains of Heav'n, Par Lost 1.104
Wafts on the calmer wave by dubious light Par Lost 2.1042
Duck
Here be without duck or nod Mask 960
B.M. ms 'Duck'
Due
The whole Battalion views, thir order due, Par Lost 1.569
Of hazard as of honour, due alike Par Lost 2.453
To him who Reigns, and so much to him due Par Lost 2.454
The key of this infernal Pit by due, Par Lost 2.850
To pray, repent, and bring obedience due. Par Lost 3.190
To Prayer, repentance, and obedience due, Par Lost 3.191
Though now to Death I yield, and am his due Par Lost 3.245
That from his Lordly eye keep distance due, Par Lost 3.578
Where honour due and reverence none neglects, Par Lost 3.738
How due! yet all his good prov'd ill in me, Par Lost 4.48
Due entrance he disdaind, and in contempt, Par Lost 4.180
And *Eve* within, due at her hour prepar'd Par Lost 5.303
Shall bend the knee, and in that honour due Par Lost 5.817
Due search and consultation will disclose. Par Lost 6.445
With Ministeries due and solemn Rites: Par Lost 7.149
With wonder, but delight, and, as is due, Par Lost 8.11
Which must be mutual, in proportion due Par Lost 8.385
Say, for such wonder claims attention due. Par Lost 9.566
Not without Song, each Morning, and due praise Par Lost 9.800
From Noon, and gentle Aires due at thir hour Par Lost 10.93
Of all corruption, all the blame lights due; Par Lost 10.833
From Loves due Rites, Nuptial imbraces sweet, Par Lost 10.994
Then due by sentence when thou didst transgress, Par Lost 11.253
On the cleft Wood, and all due Rites perform'd. Par Lost 11.440
Due nourishment, not gluttonous delight, Par Lost 11.533
Thou therefore give due audience, and attend. Par Lost 12.12
Whom *faithful Abraham* due time shall call, Par Lost 12.152
A day entire, and Nights due course adjourne, Par Lost 12.264
The penaltie to thy transgression due, Par Lost 12.399
And due to theirs which out of thine will grow: Par Lost 12.400
To thy large heart give utterance due, thy heart Par Reg 3.10
Violent or shameful death thir due reward. Par Reg 3.87
All things are best fullfil'd in their due time, Par Reg 3.182
To his due time and providence I leave them. Par Reg 3.440
Then who self-rigorous chooses death as due; Samson 513
Over his female in due awe, Samson 1055
Due by the Law to capital punishment? Samson 1225
Yet som there be that by due steps aspire Mask 12
With everlasting oil, to give due light Mask 199
line not in Bridgewater ms
Trinity ms 'due' ←'thire'
Co. Due west it rises from this shrubby point. Mask 306
Bridgewater ms 'due'
His praise due paid, for swinish gluttony Mask 776
And if I give thee honour due, Allegro 37
But let my due feet never fail, Penseroso 155
Compels me to disturb your season due: Lycidas 7
His mischief that due course doth keep, Psalm 7, 57
And till they yield thee honour due, Psalm 83, 59
Duel
As of a Duel, or the local wounds Par Lost 12.387
Now entring his great duel, not of arms, Par Reg 1.174
Certain to have won by mortal duel from thee, Samson 1102
Duelled
Duell'd thir Armies rank't in proud array, Samson 345
Dues
Of all thy dues be done, and none left out, Mask 137
Dulcet
Of Dulcet Symphonies and voices sweet, Par Lost 1.712
ms 'dulcet'
She tempers dulcet creams, nor these to hold Par Lost 5.347
Dulcimer
And Dulcimer, all Organs of sweet stop, Par Lost 7.596
Dull
Not harsh, and crabbed as dull fools suppose, Mask 477
Unknown, and like esteem'd, and the dull swayn Mask 634
line not in Bridgewater ms
And singing startle the dull night, Allegro 42
What shallow-searching *Fame* hath left untold; Arcades 41
Trinity ms 'shallow searching' ←'vertues which dull'
What need'st thou such weak witnes of thy name? Shakespear 6
1632 'dull witnesse'
1663-4 'dull witnesse'
Duly
Thir Orisons, each Morning duly paid Par Lost 5.145
To ern his Cream-bowle duly set, Allegro 106
Dumb
His gentle dumb expression turnd at length Par Lost 9.527
That dumb things would be mov'd to sympathize, Mask 796
line not in Bridgewater ms
line not in Trinity ms
The Oracles are dumm, Nativity 173
1673 'dum'
Driving dum silence from the portal dore, Vacation 5
Dun
In the dun Air sublime, and ready now Par Lost 3.72
Which these dun shades will ne're report. Mask 127
Of utmost *Tweed*, or *Oose*, or gulphie *Dun*, Vacation 92

Dunbar
And Dunbarr feild resounds thy praises loud, Sonnet 16, 8
Trinity ms 'Worsters laureat wreath' ←'Dunbarr feild'
1694 '*Dunbarfield*'
Dung
As dung upon the plain. Psalm 83, 40
Dungeon
A Dungeon horrible, on all sides round Par Lost 1.61
ms 'dungeon'
This place our dungeon, not our safe retreat Par Lost 2.317
Your dungeon stretching far and wide beneath; Par Lost 2.1003
And Dungeon of our Tyrant: Now possess, Par Lost 10.466
Bursting thir brazen Dungeon, armd with ice Par Lost 10.697
Dungeon, or beggery, or decrepit age! Samson 69
The Dungeon of thy self; thy Soul Samson 156
Into a Dungeon thrust, to work with Slaves? Samson 367
In this close dungeon of innumerous bowes. Mask 349
Himself is his own dungeon. 2. *Bro*. Tis most true Mask 385
Trinity ms 'himselfe is his owne dungeon' ←'blaze in the summer solstice'
Bridgewater ms 'blaze in the summer solstice'
That not a blast was from his dungeon stray'd, Lycidas 97
Durable
To motion, measures all things durable Par Lost 5.581
And durable; and now in little space Par Lost 10.320
Durance
In that dark durance: thus much what was askt. Par Lost 4.899
During
But cloud in stead, and ever-during dark Par Lost 3.45
Her ever during Gates, Harmonious sound Par Lost 7.206
Durst
Who durst defie th' Omnipotent to Arms. Par Lost 1.49
That durst dislike his reign, and me preferring, Par Lost 1.102
Roaming to seek thir prey on earth, durst fix Par Lost 1.382
Among the Nations round, and durst abide Par Lost 1.385
And with thir darkness durst affront his light. Par Lost 1.391
Much less that durst upon his own head draw Par Lost 3.220
Beast, Bird, Insect, or Worm durst enter none; Par Lost 4.704
For you, there sitting where ye durst not soare; Par Lost 4.829
Inspir'd with contradiction durst oppose Par Lost 6.155
Not that they durst without his leave attempt, Par Lost 8.237
No evil durst attempt thee, but I rue Par Lost 9.1180
I, when no other durst, sole undertook Par Reg 1.100
Durst ever, who return'd, and dropt not here Par Reg 1.324
Who durst so proudly tempt the Son of God. Par Reg 4.580
Who durst not with thir whole united powers Samson 1110
Close-banded durst attaque me, no not sleeping, Samson 1113
Har. Thou durst not thus disparage glorious arms Samson 1130
Whether he durst accept the offer or not, Samson 1255
And that he durst not plain enough appear'd. Samson 1256
Longer I durst not stay, but soon I guess't Mask 577
How durst thou then thy self approach so neer Mask 616
Dusk
Vapour, and Exhalation dusk and moist, Par Lost 11.741
A pathless Desert, dusk with horrid shades; Par Reg 1.296
Dusk faces with white silken Turbants wreath'd: Par Reg 4.76
Dusky
Aloft, incumbent on the dusky Air Par Lost 1.226
As when from mountain tops the dusky clouds Par Lost 2.488
From Hill or steaming Lake, duskie or grey, Par Lost 5.186
Soon as midnight brought on the duskie houre Par Lost 5.667
In duskie wreathes, reluctant flames, the signe Par Lost 6.58
Shoots against the dusky Pole, Mask 99
Bridgewater ms 'Northerne'
Trinity ms 'dusky' ←'northren'
1637 'duskie'
this dusky hollow is a paradise & heaven gates ore my head Mask Tr. ms 13.44
The rayes of *Bethlehem* blind his dusky eyn; Nativity 223
Dust
That rais'd us from the dust and plac't us here Par Lost 4.416
Who formd us from the dust, and plac'd us here Par Lost 5.516
As drops on dust conglobing from the drie; Par Lost 7.292
Dust of the ground, and in thy nostrils breath'd Par Lost 7.525
A broad and ample rode, whose dust is Gold Par Lost 7.577
From dust: spite then with spite is best repaid. Par Lost 9.178
And dust shalt eat all the dayes of thy Life. Par Lost 10.178
For dust thou art, and shalt to dust returne. Par Lost 10.208
And equal to reduce me to my dust, Par Lost 10.748
That dust I am, and shall to dust returne: Par Lost 10.770
His Sentence beyond dust and Natures Law, Par Lost 10.805
In dust, our final rest and native home. Par Lost 10.1085
Who knows, or more then this, that we are dust, Par Lost 11.199
Rowling in dust and gore. To which our Sire. Par Lost 11.460
I must return to native dust? O sight Par Lost 11.463
To Death, and mix with our connatural dust? Par Lost 11.529
Or grovling soild thir crested helmets in the dust. Samson 141
Hath met the vertue of this Magick dust, Mask 165
High thron'd in secret bliss, for us frail dust Circum 19
In the dust my glory dead, Psalm 7, 16
In the dust and there out spread Psalm 7, 17
Duteous
From every Beast, more duteous at her call, Par Lost 9.521
Duty
On duty, sleeping found by whom they dread, Par Lost 1.333
Where obvious dutie erewhile appear'd unsaught: Par Lost 10.106
Duty and Service, nor to stay till bid, Par Reg 2.326
And Duty; Zeal and Duty are not slow; Par Reg 3.172
Zeal of thy Fathers house, Duty to free Par Reg 3.175

Duty(*cont*)
Adjur'd by all the bonds of civil Duty Samson 853
Vertue, as I thought, truth, duty so enjoyning. Samson 870
Dwarfs
Now less then smallest Dwarfs, in narrow room Par Lost 1.779
ms 'dwarfs'
Dwell
To bottomless perdition, there to dwell Par Lost 1.47
And rest can never dwell, hope never comes Par Lost 1.66
Then to dwell here, driv'n out from bliss, condemn'd Par Lost 2.86
Dwell not unvisited of Heav'ns fair Light Par Lost 2.398
Shall dwell at ease, and up and down unseen Par Lost 2.841
For ever with corruption there to dwell; Par Lost 3.249
New Heav'n and Earth, wherein the just shall dwell, Par Lost 3.335
But all these shining Orbes his choice to dwell; Par Lost 3.670
That I with you must dwell, or you with me Par Lost 4.377
Created, or such place hast here to dwell, Par Lost 5.373
Who dwell in Heav'n, whose excellence he saw Par Lost 5.456
Here or in Heav'nly Paradises dwell; Par Lost 5.500
Thou fablest, here however to dwell free, Par Lost 6.292
Nameless in dark oblivion let them dwell. Par Lost 6.380
In heav'nly Spirits could such perverseness dwell? Par Lost 6.788
Of men innumerable, there to dwell, Par Lost 7.156
Seemd like to Heav'n, a seat where Gods might dwell, Par Lost 7.329
Created in his Image, there to dwell Par Lost 7.627
God hath bid dwell farr off all anxious cares, Par Lost 8.185
To dwell, unless by maistring Heav'ns Supreame; Par Lost 9.125
If this be our condition, thus to dwell Par Lost 9.322
Or is it envie, and can envie dwell Par Lost 9.729
There dwell and Reign in bliss, thence on the Earth Par Lost 10.399
To range in, and to dwell, and over Man Par Lost 10.492
Once actual, now in body, and to dwell Par Lost 10.587
All my redeemd may dwell in joy and bliss, Par Lost 11.43
But longer in that Paradise to dwell, Par Lost 11.48
Laborious, till day droop; while here we dwell, Par Lost 11.178
But longer in this Paradise to dwell Par Lost 11.259
To dwell on eeven ground now with thy Sons: Par Lost 11.348
Of wickedness, wherein shall dwell his Race Par Lost 11.608
By Men who there frequent, or therein dwell. Par Lost 11.838
Both Heav'n and Earth, wherein the just shall dwell. Par Lost 11.901
Shal spend thir dayes in joy unblam'd, and dwell Par Lost 12.22
Shall dwell to *Senir*, that long ridge of Hills. Par Lost 12.146
The holy One with mortal Men to dwell: Par Lost 12.248
Among whom God will deigne to dwell on Earth Par Lost 12.281
Long time shall dwell and prosper, but when sins Par Lost 12.316
There in captivitie he lets them dwell Par Lost 12.344
The promise of the Father, who shall dwell Par Lost 12.487
From Hell's deep-vaulted Den to dwell in light, Par Reg 1.116
Who dwell this wild, constrain'd by want, come forth Par Reg 1.331
I gain'd what I have gain'd, and with them dwell Par Reg 1.391
And sends his Spirit of Truth henceforth to dwell Par Reg 1.462
Where they shall dwell secure, when time shall be Par Reg 4.616
Here dwel no frowns, nor anger, from these gates Mask 667
Trinity ms 'dwell'
Bridgewater ms 'dwell'
In dark *Cimmerian* desert ever dwell. Allegro 10
Dwell in som idle brain, Penseroso 5
He gave their Land therin to dwell. Psalm 136, 74
Had ripen'd thy just soul to dwell with God, Sonnet 14, 2
Their twisted cords: he who in Heaven doth dwell Psalm 2, 8
Thou Lord alone in safety mak'st me dwell. Psalm 4, 42
That in the Desart dwell, Psalm 83, 24
Where thou do'st dwell so near. Psalm 84, 4
Then dwell in Tents, *and rich abode* Psalm 84, 39
To dwell within our Land. Psalm 85, 40
Or they *who* in perdition *dwell* Psalm 88, 47
Dwellest
Of old *Olympus* dwell'st, but Heav'nlie borne, Par Lost 7.7
Of men at thee, for only thou here dwell'st. Par Reg 4.466
Dwell'st here with *Pan*, or *Silvan*, by blest Song Mask 268
Bridgewater ms 'dwel'st'
Trinity ms 'dwell'st' ←'liv'st'
Dwelling
Heav'ns fugitives, and for thir dwelling place Par Lost 2.57
Henceforth; my dwelling haply may not please Par Lost 4.378
Whose dwelling God hath planted here in bliss? Par Lost 4.884
Thir pleasant dwelling place. Thrice happie men, Par Lost 7.625
To thee who hast thy dwelling here on Earth. Par Lost 8.118
Hath been our dwelling many years, his life Par Reg 2.80
Dwellings
To future men, and in thir dwellings peace: Par Lost 7.183
To visit oft the dwellings of just Men Par Lost 7.570
Rode tilting o're the Waves, all dwellings else Par Lost 11.747
How lovely are thy dwellings fair! Psalm 84, 1
Then all the dwellings *faire* Psalm 87, 6
Dwells
Where Joy for ever dwells: Hail horrours, hail Par Lost 1.250
Dwels in all Heaven charitie so deare? Par Lost 3.216
In whom the fulness dwels of love divine, Par Lost 3.225
That Man may know he dwells not in his own; Par Lost 8.103
Is lost, which alwayes with right Reason dwells Par Lost 12.84
In real darkness of the body dwells, Samson 159
Before our living Dread who dwells Samson 1673
Yea there, where very desolation dwels Mask 428
Bridgewater ms 'dwells'
Trinity ms 'dwells'
1637 'dwells'
Immur'd in cypress shades a Sorcerer dwels Mask 521

Dwells(*cont*)	
Trinity ms 'dwells'	
Bridgewater ms 'dwells'	
1637 'dwells'	
That there eternal Summer dwels,	Mask 988
Trinity ms 'dwells'	
1637 'dwells'	
where day dwells without night	Musick Tr. ms 4.29
Dwelt	
Dwelt from Eternitie, dwelt then in thee,	Par Lost 3.5
Thrice happy Iles, but who dwelt happy there	Par Lost 3.570
Dwelt in *Telassar:* in this pleasant soile	Par Lost 4.214
That dwelt within, whose presence had infus'd	Par Lost 9.836
Were lost in death, till he that dwelt above	Circum 18
Sea-girt it lies, where Giants dwelt of old,	Prose 12, 9
Dye	
For he being amorous on that lovely die	Fair Inf 5
Dyed	
Had entertaind, as di'd her Cheeks with pale.	Par Lost 10.1009
Dying	
And dying rise, and rising with him raise	Par Lost 3.296
Giving to death, and dying to redeeme,	Par Lost 3.299
Dying put on the weeds of *Dominic*,	Par Lost 3.479
A long days dying to augment our paine,	Par Lost 10.964
Living or dying, from thee I will not hide	Par Lost 10.974
Living or dying thou hast fulfill'd	Samson 1661
A drear, and dying sound	Nativity 193
Side-ways as on a dying bed,	Winchester 42
Each	
His mighty Stature; on each hand the flames	Par Lost 1.222
Forthwith from every Squadron and each Band	Par Lost 1.356
That fought at *Theb's* and *Ilium*, on each side	Par Lost 1.578
Severing each kind, and scum'd the Bullion dross:	Par Lost 1.704
By strange conveyance fill'd each hollow nook,	Par Lost 1.707
Each in his Hierarchie, the Orders bright.	Par Lost 1.737
Envy from each inferior; but who here	Par Lost 2.26
Each on his rock transfixt, the sport and prey	Par Lost 2.181
Pondering the danger with deep thoughts; and each	Par Lost 2.421
Wasting the Earth, each other to destroy:	Par Lost 2.502
Disband, and wandring, each his several way	Par Lost 2.523
To Battel in the Clouds, before each Van	Par Lost 2.535
For each seem'd either; black it stood as Night,	Par Lost 2.670
Shakes Pestilence and Warr. Each at the Head	Par Lost 2.711
Each cast at th' other, as when two black Clouds	Par Lost 2.714
Of each his Faction, in thir several Clanns,	Par Lost 2.901
Each Stair mysteriously was meant, nor stood	Par Lost 3.516
The Univers, and to each inward part	Par Lost 3.584
Each had his place appointed, each his course,	Par Lost 3.720
Thus while he spake, each passion dimm'd his face	Par Lost 4.114
Each perturbation smooth'd with outward calme,	Par Lost 4.120
Ran Nectar, visiting each plant, and fed	Par Lost 4.240
Grip't in each paw: When *Adam* first of men	Par Lost 4.408
Sole, or responsive each to others note	Par Lost 4.683
Acanthus, and each odorous bushie shrub	Par Lost 4.696
Fenc'd up the verdant wall; each beauteous flour,	Par Lost 4.697
The sequel each of parting and of fight;	Par Lost 4.1003
Each in thir Chrystal sluce, hee ere they fell	Par Lost 5.133
Thir Orisons, each Morning duly paid	Par Lost 5.145
On each hand parting, to his speed gave way	Par Lost 5.252
Each shoulder broad, came mantling o're his brest	Par Lost 5.279
But I will haste and from each bough and break,	Par Lost 5.326
Each Plant and juciest Gourd will pluck such choice	Par Lost 5.327
Bestirs her then, and from each tender stalk	Par Lost 5.337
Yield Nectar, though from off the boughs each Morn	Par Lost 5.428
Each in thir several active Sphears assignd,	Par Lost 5.477
Proportiond to each kind. So from the root	Par Lost 5.479
Each to other like, more then on earth is thought?	Par Lost 5.576
Of onset ended soon each milder thought.	Par Lost 6.98
As each divided Legion might have seemd	Par Lost 6.230
A numerous Host, in strength each armed hand	Par Lost 6.231
Each Warriour single as in Chief, expert	Par Lost 6.233
That argu'd fear; each on himself reli'd,	Par Lost 6.238
In horror; from each hand with speed retir'd	Par Lost 6.307
And uncouth paine fled bellowing. On each wing	Par Lost 6.362
Th' invention all admir'd, and each, how hee	Par Lost 6.498
Lookd round, and Scouts each Coast light-armed scoure,	Par Lost 6.529
Each quarter, to descrie the distant foe,	Par Lost 6.530
Sad resolution and secure: let each	Par Lost 6.541
His Adamantine coat gird well, and each	Par Lost 6.542
Portending hollow truce; at each behind	Par Lost 6.578
By four Cherubic shapes, four Faces each	Par Lost 6.753
Chariots of God, half on each hand were seen:	Par Lost 6.770
Each to his place, they heard his voice and went	Par Lost 6.782
Shaded with branching Palme, each order bright,	Par Lost 6.885
With tufts the vallies and each fountain side,	Par Lost 7.327
Went up and waterd all the ground, and each	Par Lost 7.334
And God created the great Whales, and each	Par Lost 7.391
Soul living, each that crept, which plenteously	Par Lost 7.392
Forthwith the Sounds and Seas, each Creek and Bay	Par Lost 7.399
Each in their kinde. The Earth obey'd, and strait	Par Lost 7.453
Stor'd in each Orb perhaps with some that live.	Par Lost 8.152
Each Orb a glimps of Light, conveyd so farr	Par Lost 8.156
Attends thee, and each word, each motion formes,	Par Lost 8.223
Of Earth before scarce pleasant seemd. Each Tree	Par Lost 8.306
In signe whereof each Bird and Beast behold	Par Lost 8.342
As thus he spake, each Bird and Beast behold	Par Lost 8.349
With blandishment, each Bird stoop'd on his wing.	Par Lost 8.351
Each with thir kinde, Lion with Lioness;	Par Lost 8.393
Each(*cont*)	
Gave sign of gratulation, and each Hill;	Par Lost 8.514
To Cattel and each Beast; which would not be	Par Lost 8.582
From Pole to Pole, traversing each Colure;	Par Lost 9.66
So saying, through each Thicket Danck or Drie,	Par Lost 9.179
For while so near each other thus all day	Par Lost 9.220
Hopeless to circumvent us joynd, where each	Par Lost 9.259
Each Flour of slender stalk, whose head though gay	Par Lost 9.428
Imborderd on each Bank, the hand of *Eve:*	Par Lost 9.438
Adjoynd, from each thing met conceaves delight,	Par Lost 9.449
Or Dairie, each rural sight, each rural sound;	Par Lost 9.451
Of each Tree in the Garden we may eate,	Par Lost 9.660
Stood in himself collected, while each part,	Par Lost 9.673
Motion, each act won audience ere the tongue,	Par Lost 9.674
Not without Song, each Morning, and due praise	Par Lost 9.800
Each thing on Earth; and other care perhaps	Par Lost 9.813
Since to each meaning savour me apply,	Par Lost 9.1019
As from unrest, and each the other viewing,	Par Lost 9.1052
The Parts of each for other, that seem most	Par Lost 9.1093
Or to each other, but apparent guilt,	Par Lost 10.112
Above all Cattle, each Beast of the Field;	Par Lost 10.176
O Son, why sit we here each other viewing	Par Lost 10.235
From each side shoaling towards the mouth of Hell.	Par Lost 10.288
In sight, to each of these three places led.	Par Lost 10.324
Each hour their great adventurer from the search	Par Lost 10.440
Each other, till supplanted down he fell	Par Lost 10.513
Feed first, on each Beast next, and Fish, and Fowle,	Par Lost 10.604
Of Seasons to each Clime; else had the Spring	Par Lost 10.678
Devourd each other; nor stood much in awe	Par Lost 10.712
Each other, blam'd enough elsewhere, but strive	Par Lost 10.959
Each others burden in our share of woe;	Par Lost 10.961
Of watchful Cherubim; four faces each	Par Lost 11.128
Fast caught, they lik'd, and each his liking chose;	Par Lost 11.587
On each hand slaughter and gigantic deeds.	Par Lost 11.659
My part of evil onely, each dayes lot	Par Lost 11.765
Corrupting each thir way; yet those remoov'd,	Par Lost 11.889
Among the Builders; each to other calls	Par Lost 12.57
Mount *Hermon*, yonder Sea, each place behold	Par Lost 12.142
Great numbers of each Nation to receave	Par Lost 12.503
Sometimes, anon in shady vale, each night	Par Reg 1.304
Man lives not by Bread only, but each Word	Par Reg 1.349
Nor lightens aught each mans peculiar load.	Par Reg 1.402
Sought lost *Eliah*, so in each place these	Par Reg 2.19
Machaerus and each Town or City wall'd	Par Reg 2.22
Each of his reign allotted, rightlier call'd,	Par Reg 2.123
Many are in each Region passing fair	Par Reg 2.155
Of various persons each to know his part;	Par Reg 2.240
By hunger, that each other Creature tames,	Par Reg 2.406
When on his shoulders each mans burden lies;	Par Reg 2.462
Nor wanted clouds of foot, nor on each horn,	Par Reg 3.327
On each side an Imperial City stood,	Par Reg 4.33
The time and means: each act is rightliest done,	Par Reg 4.475
So many, and so huge, that each apart	Samson 65
Her importunity, each time perceiving	Samson 397
Each others force in camp or listed field:	Samson 1087
Hath walk'd about, and each limb to survey,	Samson 1089
Making them each his own Deliverer,	Samson 1289
Through each high street: little I had dispatch't	Samson 1599
With seats where all the Lords and each degree	Samson 1607
And Timbrels, on each side went armed guards,	Samson 1617
Of this but each *Philistian* City round	Samson 1655
Of every salt Flood, and each ebbing Stream,	Mask 19
Imperial rule of all the Sea-girt Iles	Mask 21
Co. I know each lane, and every alley green	Mask 311
Driving far off each thing of sin and guilt,	Mask 456
And through the porch and inlet of each sense	Mask 839
The clasping charm, and thaw the numming spell,	Mask 853
Trinity ms 'the clasping' ←'each clasping'	
Trinity ms 'thaw the numming' ←'melt each' ←'secret holding'	
As he pronounces lastly on each deed,	Lycidas 83
That blows from off each beaked Promontory,	Lycidas 94
With thousand echo's still prolongs each heav'nly close.	Nativity 100
While each peculiar power forgoes his wonted seat.	Nativity 196
Each fetter'd Ghost slips to his severall grave,	Nativity 234
Look in, and see each blissful Deitie	Vacation 35
For when as each thing bad thou hast entomb'd,	On Time 9
Thy easie numbers flow, and that each heart	Shakespear 10
Filling each mouth with envy, or with praise,	Sonnet 15, 2
1694 'all'	
Both spirituall powre and civill, what each meanes	Sonnet 17, 10
Trinity ms 'each' ←'it'	
What severs each thou 'hast learnt, which few hav don.	Sonnet 17, 11
Lay deep their plots together through each Land,	Psalm 2, 4
Upon your beds, each one,	Psalm 4, 21
So th' assemblies of each Nation	Psalm 7, 25
Each morn, and thee prevent.	Psalm 88, 56
Eager	
Nor of Renown less eager, yet by doome	Par Lost 6.378
An eager appetite, rais'd by the smell	Par Lost 9.740
With eager thought warbling his *Dorick* lay:	Lycidas 189
Eagerly	
The guarded Gold: So eagerly the fiend	Par Lost 2.947
Eagle	
In prospect; there the Eagle and the Stork	Par Lost 7.423
Of tame villatic Fowl; but as an Eagle	Samson 1695
Eagles	
Of Towring Eagles, to all the Fowles he seems	Par Lost 5.271

Eagle-winged
Sate Eagle-wing'd, beside him hung his Bow Par Lost 6.763
Ear
Intent, with jocond Music charm his ear; Par Lost 1.787
ms 'eare'
Timorous and slothful: yet he pleas'd the ear, Par Lost 2.117
1667 'eare'
He had to cross. Nor was his eare less peal'd Par Lost 2.920
Born through the hollow dark assaults his eare Par Lost 2.953
Mine ear shall not be slow, mine eye not shut. Par Lost 3.193
1667 'eare'
Admonisht by his ear, and strait was known Par Lost 3.647
1667 'eare'
Turnd him all eare to hear new utterance flow. Par Lost 4.410
Squat like a Toad, close at the eare of *Eve;* Par Lost 4.800
Close at mine ear one call'd me forth to walk Par Lost 5.36
Attentive, and with more delighted eare, Par Lost 5.545
So smooths her charming tones, that Gods own ear Par Lost 5.626
Words which no eare ever to hear in Heav'n Par Lost 5.810
All Heart they live, all Head, all Eye, all Eare, Par Lost 6.350
The Angel ended, and in *Adams* Eare Par Lost 8.1
line not in 1667 edition
Delighted, or not capable her eare Par Lost 8.49
And sweeter thy discourse is to my eare Par Lost 8.211
Yet dreadful in mine eare, though in my choice Par Lost 8.335
More grateful then harmonious sound to the eare. Par Lost 8.606
Not Hers who brings it nightly to my Ear. Par Lost 9.47
O *Eve*, in evil hour thou didst give eare Par Lost 9.1067
To fill his eare, when contrary he hears Par Lost 10.506
How much more, if we pray him, will his ear Par Lost 10.1060
From innocence. Now therefore bend thine eare Par Lost 11.30
Bending his eare; perswasion in me grew Par Lost 11.152
First Fruits, the green Eare, and the yellow Sheaf, Par Lost 11.435
To mortal eare is dreadful; they beseech Par Lost 12.236
Smooth on the tongue discourst, pleasing to th' ear, Par Reg 1.479
Before mine eyes thou hast set; and in my ear Par Reg 3.390
To sage Philosophy next lend thine ear, Par Reg 4.272
That pleas'd so well our Victors ear, declare Par Reg 4.337
Dissolves unjointed e're it reach my ear. Samson 177
Was not behind, but ever at my ear, Samson 858
Thir favourable ear, that I may fetch thee Samson 921
To fence my ear against thy sorceries. Samson 937
Whose ear is ever open; and his eye Samson 1172
Hitting thy aged ear should pierce too deep. Samson 1568
This way the noise was, if mine ear be true, Mask 170
1637 'eare'
Trinity ms 'eare'
Bridgewater ms 'eare'
Was rife, and perfet in my list'ning ear, Mask 203
line not in Bridgewater ms
Trinity ms 'eare'
1637 'eare'
Tell her of things that no gross ear can hear, Mask 458
1637 'eare'
Bridgewater ms 'eare'
Trinity ms 'eare'
Still to be so displac't. I was all eare, Mask 560
1673 'ear'
Till guided by mine ear I found the place Mask 570
Trinity ms 'eare'
1637 'eare'
Bridgewater ms 'eare'
Thou hast nor Eare, nor Soul to apprehend Mask 784
line not in Trinity ms
1673 'Ear'
line not in Bridgewater ms
Such streins as would have won the ear Allegro 148
Where more is meant then meets the ear. Penseroso 120
As may with sweetnes, through mine ear, Penseroso 164
Of human mould with grosse unpurged ear; Arcades 73
Trinity ms 'eare'
Such, *Lycidas*, thy loss to Shepherds ear. Lycidas 49
Trinity ms 'eare'
1638 'eare'
First heard by happy watchful Shepherds ear, Circum 3
Trinity ms 'eare'
Jehovah to my words give ear Psalm 5, 1
Give ear *in time of need*, Psalm 80, 2
O Jacobs God give ear, Psalm 84, 30
Thy *gracious* ear, O Lord, encline, Psalm 86, 1
give ear, and to the crie Psalm 86, 18
But *twise that praise shall in our ear* Psalm 87, 17
Thine ear with favour bend. Psalm 88, 8
Earl
A Vicounts daughter, an Earls heir, Winchester 3
1673 'Ealrs'
Daughter to that good Earl, once President Sonnet 10, 1
Trinity ms 'Earle'
Earlier
Or if the earlier season lead Allegro 89
Earliest
With charm of earliest Birds; pleasant the Sun Par Lost 4.642
With charm of earliest Birds, nor rising Sun Par Lost 4.651
From their soft wings, and *Flora*'s earliest smells. Par Reg 2.365
Lady that in the prime of earliest youth, Sonnet 9, 1
Early
Early, and th' hour of Supper comes unearn'd. Par Lost 9.225
Thus earlie, thus alone; her Heav'nly forme Par Lost 9.457
Early(*cont*)
Created; but henceforth my early care, Par Lost 9.799
My early visitation, and my last Par Lost 11.275
As by that early action may be judg'd, Par Reg 4.215
Mess. Occasions drew me early to this City, Samson 1596
And early ere the odorous breath of morn Arcades 56
Once had the early Matrons run Winchester 23
Thus we salute thee with our early Song, May Morn 9
Early may fly the *Babylonian* wo. Sonnet 18, 14
Jehovah thou my early voyce Psalm 5, 5
Earn
Which he through hazard huge must earn. But they Par Lost 2.473
Glanc'd on the ground, with labour I must earne Par Lost 10.1054
By suffering, and earne rest from labour won, Par Lost 11.375
To earn Salvation for the Sons of men. Par Reg 1.167
Here rather let me drudge and earn my bread, Samson 573
To ern his Cream-bowle duly set, Allegro 106
Earned
What thinkst thou of our Empire now, though earnd Par Lost 10.592
Whose pains have earn'd the far fet spoil. With that Par Reg 2.401
Earnest
Who mourn'd in earnest, when the Captive Ark Par Lost 1.458
Though threatning, will in earnest so destroy Par Lost 9.939
Thir earnest eyes they fix'd, imagining Par Lost 10.553
Our earnest Prayers, then giv'n with solemn hand Samson 359
Now pity me, and hear my earnest prai'r. Psalm 4, 6
Stronglier, and better oft then earnest can. Prose 7, 2
Earnestly
The Faith they owe; when earnestly they seek Par Lost 9.1141
His invitation earnestly renew'd. Par Reg 2.367
Earns
The work of many hands, which earns my keeping Samson 1260
Ears
Her bearded Grove of ears, which way the wind Par Lost 4.982
Of counterfeted truth thus held thir ears. Par Lost 5.771
In *Rhodope*, where Woods and Rocks had Eares Par Lost 7.35
Great things, and full of wonder in our eares, Par Lost 7.70
Then time or motion, but to human ears Par Lost 7.177
Might tempt alone, and in her ears the sound Par Lost 9.736
Brought to thir Ears, while day declin'd, they heard, Par Lost 10.99
Would Thunder in my ears, no fear of worse Par Lost 10.780
What from without comes often to my ears, Par Reg 1.199
Har. O *Baal-zebub!* can my ears unus'd Samson 1231
That is addrest to unattending Ears, Mask 272
1637 'Eares'
Trinity ms 'eares'
Bridgewater ms 'eares'
Co. O foolishnes of men! that lend their ears Mask 706
1637 'eares'
Trinity ms 'eares'
Bridgewater ms 'eares'
(List mortals, if your ears be true) Mask 997
line not in Bridgewater ms
Trinity ms 'eares'
1637 'eares'
Phoebus repli'd, and touch'd my trembling ears; Lycidas 77
1638 'eares'
Trinity ms 'eares'
Their hearts and ears did greet, Nativity 94
Once bless our human ears, Nativity 126
Fly swiftly to this fair Assembly's ears; Vacation 28
With *Midas* Ears, committing short and long; Sonnet 13, 4
1648 'eares'
Clip your Phylacteries, though bauk your Ears, Forcers 17
Trinity ms 'eares'
Cropp yee as close as marginall P---s eares Forcers Tr. ms 45.17
Earth
In the Beginning how the Heav'ns and Earth Par Lost 1.9
Got them new Names, till wandring ore the Earth, Par Lost 1.365
ms 'earth'
Roaming to seek thir prey on earth, durst fix Par Lost 1.382
Gods, yet confest later then Heav'n and Earth Par Lost 1.509
ms 'earth'
Rifl'd the bowels of thir mother Earth Par Lost 1.687
Anon out of the earth a Fabrick huge Par Lost 1.710
In bigness to surpass Earths Giant Sons Par Lost 1.778
ms defective here
Sits Arbitress, and neerer to the Earth Par Lost 1.785
ms 'earth'
Of mankind in one root, and Earth with Hell Par Lost 2.383
Thir specious deeds on earth, which glory excites, Par Lost 2.484
Wasting the Earth, each other to destroy: Par Lost 2.502
The stedfast Earth. At last his Sail-broad Vannes Par Lost 2.927
Now lately Heaven and Earth, another World Par Lost 2.1004
His onely Son; On Earth he first beheld Par Lost 3.64
Through Heav'n and Earth, so shall my glorie excel, Par Lost 3.133
For which both Heav'n and Earth shall high extoll Par Lost 3.146
O thou in Heav'n and Earth the only peace Par Lost 3.274
And be thy self Man among men on Earth, Par Lost 3.283
In Heaven, or Earth, or under Earth in Hell; Par Lost 3.322
New Heav'n and Earth, wherein the just shall dwell, Par Lost 3.335
None yet, but store hereafter from the earth Par Lost 3.444
All who have thir reward on Earth, the fruits Par Lost 3.451
Dissolvd on Earth, fleet hither, and in vain, Par Lost 3.457
1667 'earth'
The Portal shon, inimitable on Earth Par Lost 3.508
Who after came from Earth, sayling arriv'd, Par Lost 3.520
A passage down to th' Earth, a passage wide, Par Lost 3.528

Earth(*cont*)

Compar'd with aught on Earth, Medal or Stone;	Par Lost 3.592
That run through all the Heav'ns, or down to th' Earth	Par Lost 3.651
By his permissive will, through Heav'n and Earth:	Par Lost 3.685
The cumbrous Elements, Earth, Flood, Aire, Fire,	Par Lost 3.715
That place is Earth the seat of Man, that light	Par Lost 3.724
Hence fills and empties to enlighten th' Earth,	Par Lost 3.731
Took leave, and toward the coast of Earth beneath,	Par Lost 3.739
Wo to the inhabitants on Earth! that now,	Par Lost 4.5
When God hath showrd the earth; so lovely seemd	Par Lost 4.152
A Heav'n on Earth, for blissful Paradise	Par Lost 4.208
Of porous Earth with kindly thirst up drawn,	Par Lost 4.228
All Beasts of th' Earth, since wilde, and of all chase	Par Lost 4.341
Earth, Aire, and Sea. Then let us not think hard	Par Lost 4.432
With Earth and Ocean meets, the setting Sun	Par Lost 4.540
Accessible from Earth, one entrance high;	Par Lost 4.546
Diurnal, or this less volubil Earth	Par Lost 4.594
Glistring with dew; fragrant the fertil earth	Par Lost 4.645
Those have thir course to finish, round the Earth,	Par Lost 4.661
On Earth, made hereby apter to receive	Par Lost 4.672
Millions of spiritual Creatures walk the Earth	Par Lost 4.677
The God that made both Skie, Air, Earth and Heav'n	Par Lost 4.722
To fill the Earth, who shall with us extoll	Par Lost 4.733
To settle here on Earth, or in mid Aire;	Par Lost 4.940
The pendulous round Earth with ballanc't Aire	Par Lost 4.1000
Advancing, sow'd the earth with Orient Pearle,	Par Lost 5.2
1667 'Earth'	
Thy self a Goddess, not to Earth confind,	Par Lost 5.78
The Earth outstretcht immense, a prospect wide	Par Lost 5.88
Shot paralel to the earth his dewie ray,	Par Lost 5.141
On Earth joyn all ye Creatures to extoll	Par Lost 5.164
Or wet the thirstie Earth with falling showers,	Par Lost 5.190
The Earth, and stately tread, or lowly creep;	Par Lost 5.201
Raphael, said hee, thou hear'st what stir on Earth	Par Lost 5.224
Earth and the Gard'n of God, with Cedars crownd	Par Lost 5.260
Earths inmost womb, more warmth then *Adam* needs;	Par Lost 5.302
To whom thus *Eve*. *Adam*, earths hallowd mould,	Par Lost 5.321
Beholding shall confess that here on Earth	Par Lost 5.329
Whatever Earth all-bearing Mother yields	Par Lost 5.338
The Earth to yield; unsavourie food perhaps	Par Lost 5.401
The grosser feeds the purer, Earth the Sea,	Par Lost 5.416
1667 'earth'	
Earth and the Sea feed Air, the Air those Fires	Par Lost 5.417
To whom the Angel. Son of Heav'n and Earth,	Par Lost 5.519
As may express them best, though what if Earth	Par Lost 5.574
Each to other like, more then on earth is thought?	Par Lost 5.576
Reignd where these Heav'ns now rowl, where Earth now rests	Par Lost 5.578
Then all this globous Earth in Plain out spred,	Par Lost 5.649
Then what this Garden is to all the Earth,	Par Lost 5.752
His massie Spear upstaid; as if on Earth	Par Lost 6.195
Resounded, and had Earth bin then, all Earth	Par Lost 6.218
Liken on Earth conspicuous, that may lift	Par Lost 6.299
Eternize here on Earth; but those elect	Par Lost 6.374
Part hidd'n veins diggd up (nor hath this Earth	Par Lost 6.516
(For Earth hath this variety from Heav'n	Par Lost 6.640
Thus measuring things in Heav'n by things on Earth	Par Lost 6.893
Standing on Earth, not rapt above the Pole,	Par Lost 7.23
Of Heav'n and Earth conspicious first began,	Par Lost 7.63
Imbracing round this florid Earth, what cause	Par Lost 7.90
To none communicable in Earth or Heaven:	Par Lost 7.124
And Earth be chang'd to Heav'n, & Heav'n to Earth,	Par Lost 7.160
Within appointed bounds be Heav'n and Earth,	Par Lost 7.167
Thus God the Heav'n created, thus the Earth,	Par Lost 7.232
And Earth self ballanc't on her Center hung.	Par Lost 7.242
Birth-day of Heav'n and Earth; with joy and shout	Par Lost 7.256
Dividing: for as Earth, so he the World	Par Lost 7.269
The Earth was form'd, but in the Womb as yet	Par Lost 7.276
Appeer'd not: over all the face of Earth	Par Lost 7.278
The dry Land, Earth, and the great receptacle	Par Lost 7.307
And saw that it was good, and said, Let th' Earth	Par Lost 7.309
Whose Seed is in her self upon the Earth.	Par Lost 7.312
He scarce had said, when the bare Earth, till then	Par Lost 7.313
With borders long the Rivers. That Earth now	Par Lost 7.328
Upon the Earth, and man to till the ground	Par Lost 7.332
None was, but from the Earth a dewie Mist	Par Lost 7.333
Plant of the field, which e're it was in the Earth	Par Lost 7.335
To give Light on the Earth; and it was so.	Par Lost 7.345
To illuminate the Earth, and rule the Day	Par Lost 7.350
And let Fowle flie above the Earth, with wings	Par Lost 7.389
And let the Fowle be multiply'd on the Earth.	Par Lost 7.398
Let th' Earth bring forth Foul living in her kinde,	Par Lost 7.451
Cattel and Creeping things, and Beast of the Earth,	Par Lost 7.452
Each in their kinde. The Earth obey'd, and strait	Par Lost 7.453
Rising, the crumbl'd Earth above them threw	Par Lost 7.468
Behemoth biggest born of Earth upheav'd	Par Lost 7.471
First wheeld thir course; Earth in her rich attire	Par Lost 7.501
Consummate lovly smil'd; Aire, Water, Earth,	Par Lost 7.502
Beast of the Field, and over all the Earth,	Par Lost 7.522
Be fruitful, multiplie, and fill the Earth,	Par Lost 7.531
And every living thing that moves on the Earth.	Par Lost 7.534
Gave thee, all sorts are here that all th' Earth yields,	Par Lost 7.541
Angelic harmonies: the Earth, the Aire	Par Lost 7.560
Pouderd with Starrs. And now on Earth the Seventh	Par Lost 7.581
Earth with her nether Ocean circumfus'd,	Par Lost 7.624
Over his Works, on Earth, in Sea, or Air,	Par Lost 7.629
Of Heav'n and Earth consisting, and compute,	Par Lost 8.16
Thir magnitudes, this Earth a spot, a graine,	Par Lost 8.17
Round this opacous Earth, this punctual spot,	Par Lost 8.23

Earth(*cont*)

Repeated, while the sedentarie Earth,	Par Lost 8.32
This to attain, whether Heav'n move or Earth,	Par Lost 8.70
Earth sitting still, when she alone receaves	Par Lost 8.89
Or Bright inferrs not Excellence: the Earth	Par Lost 8.91
But in the fruitful Earth; there first receavd	Par Lost 8.96
Yet not to Earth are those bright Luminaries	Par Lost 8.98
Officious, but to thee Earths habitant.	Par Lost 8.99
To thee who hast thy dwelling here on Earth.	Par Lost 8.118
Plac'd Heav'n from Earth so farr, that earthly sight,	Par Lost 8.120
The Planet Earth, so stedfast though she seem,	Par Lost 8.129
If Earth industrious of her self fetch Day	Par Lost 8.137
This Earth? reciprocal, if Land be there,	Par Lost 8.144
Rise on the Earth, or Earth rise on the Sun,	Par Lost 8.161
Not of Earth onely but of highest Heav'n.	Par Lost 8.178
Nor less think wee in Heav'n of thee on Earth	Par Lost 8.224
And thou enlight'nd Earth, so fresh and gay,	Par Lost 8.274
Of Earth before scarce pleasant seemd. Each Tree	Par Lost 8.306
Not onely these fair bounds, but all the Earth	Par Lost 8.338
What call'st thou solitude, is not the Earth	Par Lost 8.369
With what all Earth or Heaven could bestow	Par Lost 8.483
Shed thir selectest influence; the Earth	Par Lost 8.513
Beyond the Earths green Cape and verdant Isles	Par Lost 8.631
Twilight upon the Earth, short Arbiter	Par Lost 9.50
From compassing the Earth, cautious of day,	Par Lost 9.59
O Earth, how like to Heav'n, if not preferr'd	Par Lost 9.99
A Creature form'd of Earth, and him endow,	Par Lost 9.149
Magnificent this World, and Earth his seat,	Par Lost 9.153
From th' Earths great Altar send up silent praise	Par Lost 9.195
Ofspring of Heav'n and Earth, and all Earths Lord,	Par Lost 9.273
Or Earth, or Middle, all things fair and good;	Par Lost 9.605
Yet Lords declar'd of all in Earth or Aire?	Par Lost 9.658
I question it, for this fair Earth I see,	Par Lost 9.720
Earth felt the wound, and Nature from her seat	Par Lost 9.782
Each thing on Earth; and other care perhaps	Par Lost 9.813
Earth trembl'd from her entrails, as again	Par Lost 9.1000
Wherewith to scorne the Earth: but that false Fruit	Par Lost 9.1011
And Hyacinth, Earths freshest softest lap.	Par Lost 9.1041
From Earth arriv'd at Heaven Gate, displeas'd	Par Lost 10.22
Nor troubl'd at these tidings from the Earth,	Par Lost 10.36
All Judgement, whether in Heav'n, or Earth, or Hell.	Par Lost 10.57
Mine both in Heav'n and Earth to do thy will	Par Lost 10.69
On Earth these thy transgressors, but thou knowst	Par Lost 10.72
To fan the Earth now wak'd, and usher in	Par Lost 10.94
Meanwhile ere thus was sin'd and judg'd on Earth,	Par Lost 10.229
Of mortal change on Earth. As when a flock	Par Lost 10.273
And now thir way to Earth they had descri'd,	Par Lost 10.325
That thou on Earth hadst prosper'd, which thy looks	Par Lost 10.360
There dwell and Reign in bliss, thence on the Earth	Par Lost 10.399
Plenipotent on Earth, of matchless might	Par Lost 10.404
Then Heav'n and Earth renewd shall be made pure	Par Lost 10.638
New Heav'n and Earth shall to the Ages rise,	Par Lost 10.647
As might affect the Earth with cold and heat	Par Lost 10.653
The Poles of Earth twice ten degrees and more	Par Lost 10.669
Perpetual smil'd on Earth with vernant Flours,	Par Lost 10.679
Mortalitie my sentence, and be Earth	Par Lost 10.776
That burden heavier then the Earth to bear	Par Lost 10.835
This noveltie on Earth, this fair defect	Par Lost 10.891
Disturbances on Earth through Femal snares,	Par Lost 10.897
See Father, what first fruits on Earth are sprung	Par Lost 11.22
Resignes him up with Heav'n and Earth renewd.	Par Lost 11.66
The Earth, when *Adam* and first Matron *Eve*	Par Lost 11.136
Adam, thou know'st Heav'n his, and all the Earth.	Par Lost 11.335
All th' Earth he gave thee to possess and rule,	Par Lost 11.339
From all the ends of th' Earth, to celebrate	Par Lost 11.345
The Hemisphere of Earth in cleerest Ken	Par Lost 11.379
To shew him all Earths Kingdomes and thir Glory.	Par Lost 11.384
In Meats and Drinks, which on the Earth shall bring	Par Lost 11.473
Down to the veins of Earth, thence gliding hot	Par Lost 11.568
Thus Fame shall be atchiev'd, renown on Earth,	Par Lost 11.698
Impetuous, and continu'd till the Earth	Par Lost 11.744
When violence was ceas't, and Warr on Earth,	Par Lost 11.780
Shall leave them to enjoy; for th' Earth shall bear	Par Lost 11.804
Of Heav'n set open on the Earth shall powre	Par Lost 11.825
Least it again dissolve and showr the Earth?	Par Lost 11.883
The whole Earth fill'd with violence, and all flesh	Par Lost 11.888
The Earth again by flood, nor let the Sea	Par Lost 11.893
Over the Earth a Cloud, will therein set	Par Lost 11.896
Both Heav'n and Earth, wherein the just shall dwell.	Par Lost 11.901
Concord and law of Nature from the Earth,	Par Lost 12.29
This ponder, that all Nations of the Earth	Par Lost 12.147
And wheel on th' Earth, devouring where it rouls;	Par Lost 12.183
Among whom God will deigne to dwell on Earth	Par Lost 12.281
With earths wide bounds, his glory with the Heav'ns.	Par Lost 12.371
Longer on Earth then certaine times to appeer	Par Lost 12.437
Whether in Heav'n or Earth, for then the Earth	Par Lost 12.463
Thir own Faith not anothers: for on Earth	Par Lost 12.528
New Heav'ns, new Earth, Ages of endless date	Par Lost 12.549
Or works of God in Heav'n, Aire, Earth, or Sea,	Par Lost 12.579
In manner at our will th' affairs of Earth,	Par Reg 1.50
In this fair Empire won of Earth and Air;	Par Reg 1.63
Their King, their Leader, and Supream on Earth.	Par Reg 1.99
To end his Raign on Earth so long enjoy'd:	Par Reg 1.125
Thou and all Angels conversant on Earth	Par Reg 1.131
Then to subdue and quell o're all the earth	Par Reg 1.218
All Heaven and Earth, Angels and Sons of men,	Par Reg 1.237
Large liberty to round this Globe of Earth,	Par Reg 1.365
Behold the Kings of the Earth how they oppress	Par Reg 2.44

Earth*(cont)*
His end of being on Earth, and mission high: Par Reg 2.114
Powers of Fire, Air, Water, and Earth beneath, Par Reg 2.124
False titl'd Sons of God, roaming the Earth Par Reg 2.179
Witness those antient Empires of the Earth, Par Reg 2.435
All Earth her wonder at thy acts, thy self Par Reg 3.24
Looking on the Earth, with approbation marks Par Reg 3.61
When to extend his fame through Heaven and Earth, Par Reg 3.65
Famous he was in Heaven, on Earth less known; Par Reg 3.68
The Monarchies of the Earth, thir pomp and state, Par Reg 3.246
That screen'd the fruits of the earth and seats of men Par Reg 4.30
Then great and glorious *Rome*, Queen of the Earth Par Reg 4.45
Spreading and over-shadowing all the Earth, Par Reg 4.148
Tetrarchs of fire, air, flood, and on the earth Par Reg 4.201
Had chear'd the face of Earth, and dry'd the wet Par Reg 4.433
As Earth and Skie would mingle; but my self Par Reg 4.453
Or to the Earths dark basis underneath, Par Reg 4.456
As when Earths Son *Antaeus* (to compare Par Reg 4.563
Receiving from his mother Earth new strength, Par Reg 4.566
Since man on earth unparallel'd! Samson 165
Might have subdu'd the Earth, Samson 174
To quell the mighty of the Earth, th' oppressour, Samson 1272
Which men call Earth, and with low-thoughted care Mask 6
Trinity ms 'earth'
Bridgewater ms 'earth'
Com. Can any mortal mixture of Earths mould Mask 244
Trinity ms 'earths'
And earths base built on stubble. But com let's on. Mask 599
Bridgewater ms 'earth's'
Covering the earth with odours, fruits, and flocks, Mask 712
Th' earth cumber'd, and the wing'd air dark't with plumes, Mask 730
And the brute Earth would lend her nerves, and shake, Mask 797
line not in Bridgewater ms
line not in Trinity ms
Quickly to the green earths end, Mask 1014
B.M. ms 'Earths'
Bridgewater ms 'earths greene'
Thou fix them on the earth as fast. Penseroso 44
His raign of peace upon the earth began: Nativity 63
Could hold all Heav'n and Earth in happier union. Nativity 108
The aged Earth agast Nativity 160
In consecrated Earth, Nativity 189
Low in the earth, *Jordans* clear streams recoil, Psalm 114, 9
Shake earth, and at the presence be agast Psalm 114, 15
Amazed Heav'n and Earth to shake. Psalm 136, 14
That did the solid Earth ordain Psalm 136, 21
Or that thy coarse corrupts in earths dark wombe, Fair Inf 30
Or did of late earths Sonnes besiege the wall Fair Inf 47
Forsook the hated earth, O tell me sooth Fair Inf 51
To earth from thy praefixed seat didst poast, Fair Inf 59
Wherwith the stage of Ayr and Earth did ring, Passion 2
That Heav'n and Earth are colour'd with my wo; Passion 32
That we on Earth with undiscording voice Musick 17
Trinity ms 'on earth' ← 'below may learne'
snatch us from earth a while Musick Tr. ms 4.07
More then she could own from Earth. Winchester 6
Had burial, yet not laid in earth, Winchester 32
The frozen earth; and cloth in fresh attire Sonnet 20, 7
muse a vain thing, the Kings of th' earth upstand Psalm 2, 2
Earths utmost bounds: them shalt thou bring full low Psalm 2, 19
Be taught ye Judges of the earth; with fear Psalm 2, 23
My life down to the earth and roul Psalm 7, 15
And glorious is thy name through all the earth? Psalm 8, 2
And glorious is thy name through all the earth. Psalm 8, 24
The Earths foundations all are mov'd Psalm 82, 19
Rise God, judge thou the earth *in might*, Psalm 82, 25
This *wicked* earth redress, Psalm 82, 26
O're all the earth *art one*. Psalm 83, 68
Truth from the earth *like to a flowr* Psalm 85, 45
Things that on earth were lost, or were abus'd. Prose 2, 4
When I dye, let the earth be roul'd in flames. Prose 5, 1
On thy third Reigne the Earth look now, and tell Prose 12, 3

Earth-born
Titanian, or *Earth-born*, that warr'd on *Jove*, Par Lost 1.198
ms 'earth-born'
Creatures of other mould, earth-born perhaps, Par Lost 4.360
Or *Trent*, who like some earth-born Giant spreads Vacation 93

Earthly
To enter, and these earthly fruits to taste, Par Lost 5.464
An Earthlie Guest, and drawn Empyreal Aire, Par Lost 7.14
Things above Earthly thought, which yet concernd Par Lost 7.82
So told as earthly notion can receave. Par Lost 7.179
Plac'd Heav'n from Earth so farr, that earthly sight, Par Lost 8.120
My earthly by his Heav'nly overpowerd, Par Lost 8.453
My Storie to the sum of earthly bliss Par Lost 8.522
Will dazle now this earthly, with thir blaze Par Lost 9.1083
Meanwhile they in thir earthly *Canaan* plac't Par Lost 12.315
For though that seat of earthly bliss be fail'd, Par Reg 4.612
And leprous sin will melt from earthly mould, Nativity 138

Earth-shaking
By the earth-shaking *Neptune*'s mace, Mask 869
1637 'earth shaking'
Trinity ms 'earth shaking'
Bridgewater ms 'earth-shakinge'

Earthy
So minded, have oreleapt these earthie bounds Par Lost 4.583
Thir earthy Charge: Of these the vigilance Par Lost 9.157
1667 'earthie'

Earthy*(cont)*
Then all this Earthy grosnes quit, On Time 20
Trinity ms 'earthie'
Meekly thou didst resign this earthy load Sonnet 14, 3

Ease
Your wearied vertue, for the ease you find Par Lost 1.320
Counsel'd ignoble ease, and peaceful sloath, Par Lost 2.227
Thrive under evil, and work ease out of pain Par Lost 2.261
While here shall be our home, what best may ease Par Lost 2.458
Thence more at ease thir minds and somwhat rais'd Par Lost 2.521
Shall dwell at ease, and up and down unseen Par Lost 2.841
The Gods who live at ease, where I shall Reign Par Lost 2.868
Of massie Iron or sollid Rock with ease Par Lost 2.878
That *Satan* with less toil, and now with ease Par Lost 2.1041
His flight precipitant, and windes with ease Par Lost 3.563
What feign'd submission swore: ease would recant Par Lost 4.96
Leaps o're the fence with ease into the Fould: Par Lost 4.187
To recommend coole *Zephyr*, and made ease Par Lost 4.329
Ask riddance, if we mean to tread with ease; Par Lost 4.632
Torment with ease, and soonest recompence Par Lost 4.893
Deigns none to ease thy load and taste thy sweet, Par Lost 5.59
Through Spirits with ease; nor wonder; if by fire Par Lost 5.439
Or in thir Pearlie shells at ease, attend Par Lost 7.407
For onely in destroying I find ease Par Lost 9.129
Will keep from Wilderness with ease, as wide Par Lost 9.245
Shall tend thee, and the fertil burden ease Par Lost 9.801
Coverd, but not at rest or ease of Mind, Par Lost 9.1120
Descend through Darkness, on your Rode with ease Par Lost 10.394
And his Adherents, that with so much ease Par Lost 10.622
Into thy Mothers lap, or be with ease Par Lost 11.536
Shall change thir course to pleasure, ease, and sloth, Par Lost 11.794
For *Solomon* he liv'd at ease, and full Par Reg 2.201
Hated of all, and hating; with what ease Par Reg 4.97
In corporal pleasure he, and careless ease; Par Reg 4.299
Which would have set thee in short time with ease Par Reg 4.378
This unfrequented place to find some ease, Samson 17
Ease to the body some, none to the mind Samson 18
Bondage with ease then strenuous liberty; Samson 271
At home in leisure and domestic ease, Samson 917
Refreshment after toil, ease after pain, Mask 687
line not in Bridgewater ms
For so to interpose a little ease, Lycidas 152
Enter'd the world, now bleeds to give us ease; Circum 11
Ease was his chief disease, and to judge right, Another 21
line not in 1658 text

Eased
Handed they went; and eas'd the putting off Par Lost 4.739
Mine eyes true op'ning, and my heart much eas'd, Par Lost 12.274
Annull'd, which might in part my grief have eas'd, Samson 72

Easier
Some easier enterprize? There is a place Par Lost 2.345
Might yield them easier habitation, bend Par Lost 2.573
Whose easier business were to serve thir Lord Par Lost 4.943
Judg'd thee perverse: the easier conquest now Par Lost 6.37
Unvanquisht, easier to transact with mee Par Lost 6.286
Easier then Air with Air, if Spirits embrace, Par Lost 8.626
Be real, why not known, since easier shunnd? Par Lost 9.699
As in our evils, and of easier choice. Par Lost 10.978
The easier towards me, or thy hatred less. Samson 772

Easiest
The easiest recompence, and pay him thanks, Par Lost 4.47
The easiest way, nor with perplexing thoughts Par Lost 8.183
Where entrance up from *Eden* easiest climbes, Par Lost 11.119
Fairest and easiest of this combrous charge, Par Lost 11.549
The slightest, easiest, readiest recompence Par Reg 3.128
In them is plainest taught, and easiest learnt, Par Reg 4.361

Easily
And Strength and Art are easily out-done Par Lost 1.696
And easily transgress the sole Command, Par Lost 3.94
So easily destroy'd, and still destroyes Par Lost 3.301
Have easily as Spirits evaded swift Par Lost 6.596
So easily obeyd amid the choice Par Lost 7.48
Thy Empire? easily the proud attempt Par Lost 7.609
And easily approv'd; when the most High Par Lost 10.31
Wouldst easily detect what I conceale. Par Lost 10.136
Eve, easily may Faith admit, that all Par Lost 11.141
Easily canst thou find one miserable, Par Reg 1.471
Of beauty and her lures, easily scorn'd Par Reg 2.194
Easily from possession won with arms; Par Reg 3.156
Of the Emperour, how easily subdu'd, Par Reg 4.126
Easily done, and hold them all of me; Par Reg 4.168
In what part lodg'd, how easily bereft me, Samson 48
Mee easily indeed mine may neglect, Samson 291
Might easily have shook off all her snares: Samson 409
Helpless, thence easily contemn'd, and scorn'd, Samson 943
Love once possest, nor can be easily Samson 1005
They easily would set to sale, a third Samson 1466
And I (for grief is easily beguild) Passion 54

Easing
Easing thir flight; so stears the prudent Crane Par Lost 7.430
Easing thir passage hence, for intercourse, Par Lost 10.260
And by men, heart-easing Mirth, Allegro 13

East
Or where the gorgeous East with richest hand Par Lost 2.3
Mozambic, off at Sea North-East windes blow Par Lost 4.161
One Gate there only was, and that look'd East Par Lost 4.178
Of God the Garden was, by him in the East Par Lost 4.209
By shorter flight to th' East, had left him there Par Lost 4.595

East(*cont*)
To morrow ere fresh Morning streak the East Par Lost 4.623
Discovering in wide Lantskip all the East Par Lost 5.142
In *India* East or West, or middle shoare Par Lost 5.339
Purples the East: still govern thou my Song, Par Lost 7.30
Sprung from the Deep, and from her Native East Par Lost 7.245
First in his East the glorious Lamp was seen, Par Lost 7.370
Till night, then in the East her turn she shines, Par Lost 7.380
Was set, and twilight from the East came on, Par Lost 7.583
Travelling East, and with her part averse Par Lost 8.138
Hee from the East his flaming rode begin, Par Lost 8.162
Or East or West, which had forbid the Snow Par Lost 10.685
And on the East side of the Garden place, Par Lost 11.118
One way the self-same hour? why in the East Par Lost 11.203
From *Hermon* East to the great Western Sea, Par Lost 12.141
Guided the Wise Men thither from the East, Par Reg 1.250
A youth, how all the Beauties of the East Par Reg 2.197
As far as *Indus* East, *Euphrates* West, Par Reg 3.272
From *Arachosia*, from *Candaor* East, Par Reg 3.316
Of his Chamber in the East. Mask 101
Trinity ms 'east'
Comes dancing from the East, and leads with her May Morn 2

Eastern
Of *Locusts*, warping on the Eastern Wind, Par Lost 1.341
Of Nights extended shade; from Eastern Point Par Lost 3.557
Against the eastern Gate of Paradise Par Lost 4.542
Now Morn her rosie steps in th' Eastern Clime Par Lost 5.1
At once on th' Eastern cliff of Paradise Par Lost 5.275
Direct to th' Eastern Gate was bent thir flight. Par Lost 11.190
And guides the Eastern Sages, who enquire Par Lost 12.362
Our lingring Parents, and to th' Eastern Gate Par Lost 12.638
They looking back, all th' Eastern side beheld Par Lost 12.641
Against the Eastern ray, translucent, pure. Samson 548
Ere the blabbing Eastern scout, Mask 138
Trinity ms 'eastreane'
1637 'Easterne'
Bridgewater ms 'Easterne'
Right against the Eastern gate, Allegro 59
See how from far upon the Eastern rode Nativity 22

Eastward
From *Auran* Eastward to the Royal Towrs Par Lost 4.211
Eastward among those Trees, what glorious shape Par Lost 5.309
Beyond *Petsora* Eastward, to the rich Par Lost 10.292
Jordan, true limit Eastward; but his Sons Par Lost 12.145

Easy
We sunk thus low? Th' ascent is easie then; Par Lost 2.81
Hard liberty before the easie yoke Par Lost 2.256
With easie intercourse pass to and fro Par Lost 2.1031
The Fiend by easie ascent, or aggravate Par Lost 3.524
More easie, wholsom thirst and appetite Par Lost 4.330
This one, this easie charge, of all the Trees Par Lost 4.421
One easie prohibition, who enjoy Par Lost 4.433
Of evil then so small as easie think Par Lost 6.437
To be th' inventer miss'd, so easie it seemd Par Lost 6.499
So easie, and of his Thunder made a scorn, Par Lost 6.632
Easie, e're God had bid the ground be drie, Par Lost 7.304
Easie my unpremeditated Verse: Par Lost 9.24
Easie to mee it is to tell thee all Par Lost 9.569
Into her heart too easie entrance won: Par Lost 9.734
Easie it might be seen that I intend Par Lost 10.58
Smooth, easie, inoffensive down to Hell. Par Lost 10.305
Of easie thorough-fare. Therefore while I Par Lost 10.393
His easie steps; girded with snaky wiles, Par Reg 1.120
Turning with easie eye thou may'st behold. Par Reg 3.293
So obvious and so easie to be quench't, Samson 95
After the brunt of battel, can as easie Samson 583
La. How easie my misfortune is to hit! Mask 286
Thy easie numbers flow, and that each heart Shakespear 10

Easy-hearted
Wind me into the easie-hearted man, Mask 163
Trinity ms 'easie hearted'
Bridgewater ms 'easie harted'
1637 'easie hearted'

Eat
They eate, they drink, and in communion sweet Par Lost 5.637
1667 'eat'
Fruits in her soft'nd Soile, for some to eate Par Lost 8.147
To pluck and eate; whereat I wak'd, and found Par Lost 8.309
To Till and keep, and of the Fruit to eate: Par Lost 8.320
Eate freely with glad heart; fear here no dearth: Par Lost 8.322
Tempting so nigh, to pluck and eat my fill Par Lost 9.595
Of all these Garden Trees ye shall not eate, Par Lost 9.657
Of each Tree in the Garden we may eate, Par Lost 9.660
The Garden, God hath said, Ye shall not eate Par Lost 9.662
Ye Eate thereof, your Eyes that seem so cleere, Par Lost 9.706
Our inward freedom? In the day we eate Par Lost 9.762
Forth reaching to the Fruit, she pluck'd, she eat: Par Lost 9.781
With liberal hand: he scrupl'd not to eat Par Lost 9.997
Whereof I gave thee charge thou shouldst not eat? Par Lost 10.123
Shee gave me of the Tree, and I did eate. Par Lost 10.143
The Serpent me beguil'd and I did eate. Par Lost 10.162
And dust shalt eat all the dayes of thy Life. Par Lost 10.178
I charg'd thee, saying: Thou shalt not eate thereof, Par Lost 10.200
Shalt eate thereof all the days of thy Life; Par Lost 10.202
Unbid, and thou shalt eate th' Herb of the Field, Par Lost 10.204
In the sweat of thy Face shalt thou eat Bread, Par Lost 10.205
1667 'eate'
All that I eat or drink, or shall beget, Par Lost 10.728

Eat(*cont*)
1667 'eate'
Reach also of the Tree of Life, and eat, Par Lost 11.94
Must eat, and on the ground leave nothing green: Par Lost 12.186
Moses was forty days, nor eat nor drank, Par Reg 1.352
And by the Angel was bid rise and eat, Par Reg 2.274
And eat the second time after repose, Par Reg 2.275
Twice by a voice inviting him to eat. Par Reg 2.314
Would'st thou not eat? Thereafter as I like Par Reg 2.321
With honour, only deign to sit and eat. Par Reg 2.336
What doubts the Son of God to sit and eat? Par Reg 2.368
What doubt'st thou Son of God? sit down and eat. Par Reg 2.377
How *Faery Mab* the junkets eat, Allegro 102
Their bread with tears they eat, Psalm 80, 22

Eaten
How dies the Serpent? hee hath eat'n and lives, Par Lost 9.764
Hath eat'n of the fruit, and is become, Par Lost 9.869
Hath told thee? hast thou eaten of the Tree Par Lost 10.122
And eaten of the Tree concerning which Par Lost 10.199

Eatest
Thou mai'st not; in the day thou eat'st, thou di'st; Par Lost 7.544
The day thou eat'st thereof, my sole command Par Lost 8.329
In what thou eatst and drinkst, seeking from thence Par Lost 11.532

Eating
And knew not eating Death: Satiate at length, Par Lost 9.792
Eating his fill, nor *Eve* to iterate Par Lost 9.1005
And ever against eating Cares, Allegro 135

Eats
That whoso eats thereof, forthwith attains Par Lost 9.724

Eaves
With minute drops from off the Eaves. Penseroso 130

Ebb
From standing lake to tripping ebbe, that stole Par Lost 11.847

Ebbing
Soft-ebbing; nor withstood them Rock or Hill, Par Lost 7.300
Of every salt Flood, and each ebbing Stream, Mask 19
Bridgewater ms 'ebbinge'

Ebon
Stay thy cloudy Ebon chair, Mask 134
1637 '*Ebon*'
Trinity ms 'ebon'
There under *Ebon* shades, and low-brow'd Rocks, Allegro 8

Ebrew
Sam. Thou knowst I am an *Ebrew*, therefore tell them, Samson 1319
An *Ebrew*, as I guess, and of our Tribe. Samson 1540

Ebrews
Off. *Ebrews*, the Pris'ner *Samson* here I seek. Samson 1308

Ecbatan
The *Persian* in *Ecbatan* sate, or since Par Lost 11.393

Ecbatana
Ecbatana her structure vast there shews, Par Reg 3.286

Eccentric
By center, or eccentric, hard to tell, Par Lost 3.575
Eccentric, intervolv'd, yet regular Par Lost 5.623
With Centric and Eccentric scribl'd o're, Par Lost 8.83

Echo
With other echo late I taught your Shades Par Lost 10.861
Sweet Echo, sweetest Nymph that liv'st unseen Mask 230
1637 'echo'
Trinity ms 'Echo' ←'Eccho'
Compell'd me to awake the courteous Echo Mask 275
resound and eccho Hallelu Musick Tr. ms 4.22
'eccho' ←'Eccho'

Echoed
Hoarce murmur echo'd to his words applause Par Lost 5.873

Echoes
And all their echoes mourn. Lycidas 41
Trinity ms 'Echo's' ←'Eccho'
With thousand echo's still prolongs each heav'nly close. Nativity 100
Would soon unboosom all thir Echoes milde, Passion 53

Echoing
Of echoing Hill or Thicket have we heard Par Lost 4.681
High overarch't, and echoing Walks between; Par Lost 9.1107
Through the high wood echoing shrill. Allegro 56

Eclipse
In dim Eclips disastrous twilight sheds Par Lost 1.597
ms 'eclipse'
And Planets, Planet-strook, real Eclips Par Lost 10.413
Irrecoverably dark, total Eclipse Samson 81
Built in th' eclipse, and rigg'd with curses dark, Lycidas 101

Eclipsed
All Power, and us eclipst under the name Par Lost 5.776
On Bird, Beast, Aire, Aire suddenly eclips'd Par Lost 11.183

Eclipses
Eclipses at thir charms. The other shape, Par Lost 2.666

Ecliptic
Down from th' Ecliptic, sped with hop'd success, Par Lost 3.740

Ecron
In *Ecron*, *Gaza*, *Asdod*, and in *Gath* Samson 981

Ecstasies
Dissolve me into extasies, Penseroso 165

Ecstasy
Would sit, and hearken even to extasie, Mask 625

Ecstatic
In pensive trance, and anguish, and ecstatick fit. Passion 42

Eden
With loss of *Eden*, till one greater Man Par Lost 1.4
ms 'Eden'

Eden(*cont*)
Sometimes towards *Eden* which now in his view — Par Lost 4.27
Of *Eden*, where delicious Paradise, — Par Lost 4.132
Of *Eden* planted; *Eden* stretchd her Line — Par Lost 4.210
Or where the Sons of *Eden* long before — Par Lost 4.213
Southward through *Eden* went a River large, — Par Lost 4.223
Of *Eden* strive; nor that *Nyseian* Ile — Par Lost 4.275
The happier *Eden*, shall enjoy thir fill — Par Lost 4.507
But in the Mount that lies from *Eden* North, — Par Lost 4.569
Of Paradise and *Edens* happie Plains, — Par Lost 5.143
Came summond over *Eden* to receive — Par Lost 6.75
What within *Eden* or without was done — Par Lost 7.65
Eev'ning arose in *Eden*, for the Sun — Par Lost 7.582
In *Eden*, distance inexpressible — Par Lost 8.113
Of *Gabriel* out of *Eden*, now improv'd — Par Lost 9.54
From *Eden* over *Pontus*, and the Poole — Par Lost 9.77
In *Eden* on the humid Flours, that breathd — Par Lost 9.193
And *Eden* were no *Eden* thus expos'd. — Par Lost 9.341
Eden and all the Coast in prospect lay. — Par Lost 10.89
Where entrance up from *Eden* easiest climbes, — Par Lost 11.119
Of Paradise or *Eden:* this had been — Par Lost 11.342
Marching from *Eden* towards the West, shall finde — Par Lost 12.40
Then this of *Eden*, and far happier daies. — Par Lost 12.465
Through *Eden* took thir solitarie way. — Par Lost 12.649
And *Eden* rais'd in the wast Wilderness. — Par Reg 1.7

Edge
In worst extreams, and on the perilous edge — Par Lost 1.276
In his own Temple, on the grunsel edge, — Par Lost 1.460
On the rough edge of battel ere it joyn'd, — Par Lost 6.108
Brandisht aloft the horrid edge came down — Par Lost 6.252
Nor solid might resist that edge: it met — Par Lost 6.323
Ye see our danger on the utmost edge — Par Reg 1.94
To slacken Virtue, and abate her edge, — Par Reg 2.455
Inwrought with figures dim, and on the edge — Lycidas 105

Edged
Edg'd with poplar pale. — Nativity 185

Edict
Law and Edict on us, who without law — Par Lost 5.798

Edicts
As to his own edicts, found contradicting, — Samson 301

Edifice
An Edifice too large for him to fill, — Par Lost 8.104
Many a fair Edifice besides, more like — Par Reg 4.55
The Edifice where all were met to see him — Samson 1588

Edify
They first re-edifie, and for a while — Par Lost 12.350

Edom
The tents of Edom, and the brood — Psalm 83, 21

Edomite
What rais'd *Antipater* the *Edomite*, — Par Reg 2.423

Edward
When thou taught'st *Cambridge*, and King *Edward* Greek. — Sonnet 11, 14

Edwards
By shallow *Edwards* and Scotch what d' ye call: — Forcers 12

Effect
Burns frore, and cold performs th' effect of Fire. — Par Lost 2.595
Of colour glorious and effect so rare? — Par Lost 3.612
Effect shall end our wish. Mean while revive; — Par Lost 6.493
His Word, the filial Godhead, gave effect. — Par Lost 7.175
Whose vertue on it self workes no effect, — Par Lost 8.95
Op'ning the way, but of Divine effect — Par Lost 9.865
Wrought that effect on *Jove*, so Fables tell; — Par Reg 2.215
And peoples safety, which in part they effect: — Samson 681
But of divine effect, he cull'd me out; — Mask 630

Effected
What force effected not: that he no less — Par Lost 1.647
He effected; Man he made, and for him built — Par Lost 9.152

Effects
Wondrous indeed, if cause of such effects. — Par Lost 9.650
Th' effects to correspond, opener mine Eyes, — Par Lost 9.875
Th' effects which thy original crime hath wrought — Par Lost 11.424

Effectual
My word, my wisdom, and effectual might, — Par Lost 3.170
And now the Sun with more effectual beams — Par Reg 4.432

Effeminacy
But foul effeminacy held me yok't — Samson 410

Effeminate
From Mans effeminate slackness it begins, — Par Lost 11.634
And from the daily Scene effeminate. — Par Reg 4.142

Effeminately
Effeminatly vanquish't? by which means, — Samson 562

Efficacious
Be efficacious in thee now at need. — Samson 1437

Efficacy
Of noxious efficacie, and when to joyne — Par Lost 10.660

Effluence
Bright effluence of bright essence increate. — Par Lost 3.6

Effulgence
Impresst the effulgence of his Glorie abides, — Par Lost 3.388
Divine effulgence, whose high Power so far — Par Lost 5.458
Effulgence of my Glorie, Son belov'd, — Par Lost 6.680

Effused
Groand out his Soul with gushing bloud effus'd. — Par Lost 11.447

Effusion
And from about him fierce Effusion rowld — Par Lost 6.765

Egg
Thir Brood as numerous hatch, from the Egg that soon — Par Lost 7.418

Eglantine
Or the twisted Eglantine. — Allegro 48

Egress
Barr'd over us prohibit all egress. — Par Lost 2.437

Egypt
Of *Amrams* Son in *Egypts* evill day — Par Lost 1.339
ms 'Egipts'
Egypt from *Syrian* ground, had general Names — Par Lost 1.421
ms 'Egipt'
Fanatic *Egypt* and her Priests, to seek — Par Lost 1.480
ms 'Egipt'
From *Egypt* marching, equal'd with one stroke — Par Lost 1.488
ms 'Egipt'
Thir Kings, when *Aegypt* with *Assyria* strove — Par Lost 1.721
ms 'Egipt'
Borders on *Aegypt* and the *Arabian* shoare; — Par Lost 3.537
From *Media* post to *Aegypt*, there fast bound. — Par Lost 4.171
Egypt, divided by the River *Nile;* — Par Lost 12.157
Of *Egypt* must lie dead. Thus with ten wounds — Par Lost 12.190
Return them back to *Egypt*, choosing rather — Par Lost 12.219
Thence into *Egypt*, till the Murd'rous King — Par Reg 2.76
From *Egypt* home return'd, in *Nazareth* — Par Reg 2.79
Thir Fathers in the land of *Egypt* serv'd, — Par Reg 3.379
From *Egypt* to *Euphrates* and beyond — Par Reg 3.384
Of *Egypt*, *Baal* next and *Ashtaroth*, — Par Reg 3.417
In *Egypt* gave to *Jove*-born *Helena* — Mask 676
Trinity ms 'Aegypt'
Bridgewater ms 'Egipt'
1637 '*Aegypt*'
Smote the first-born of *Egypt* Land. — Psalm 136, 38
A Vine from Aegypt thou hast brought, — Psalm 80, 33
When as he pass'd through Aegypt land; — Psalm 81, 19
Thee out of Aegypt land — Psalm 81, 42
I mention Egypt, *where proud Kings* — Psalm 87, 11

Egyptian
Bright Temple, to *Aegyptian Theb's* he flies. — Par Lost 5.274
Held dalliance with his faire *Egyptian* Spouse. — Par Lost 9.443
Haile mixt with fire must rend th' *Egyptian* Skie — Par Lost 12.182

Eight
Summers three times eight save one — Winchester 7

Eighth
On the eighth return'd, and on the Coast averse — Par Lost 9.67

Either
Can either Sex assume, or both; so soft — Par Lost 1.424
So as not either to provoke, or dread — Par Lost 1.644
Will either quite consume us, and reduce — Par Lost 2.96
Either to disinthrone the King of Heav'n — Par Lost 2.229
By sudden onset, either with Hell fire — Par Lost 2.364
From either end of Heav'n the welkin burns. — Par Lost 2.538
On either side a formidable shape; — Par Lost 2.649
For each seem'd either; black it stood as Night, — Par Lost 2.670
For never but once more was either like — Par Lost 2.721
Towards either Throne they bow, and to the ground — Par Lost 3.350
A violent cross wind from either Coast — Par Lost 3.487
In curles on either cheek plaid, wings he wore — Par Lost 3.641
Of firm and fragrant leaf; on either side — Par Lost 4.695
From either eye, and wip'd them with her haire; — Par Lost 5.131
Shaddowd from either heele with featherd maile — Par Lost 5.284
And flying vaulted either Host with fire. — Par Lost 6.214
On either side, the least of whom could weild — Par Lost 6.221
Divided, and to either Flank retir'd. — Par Lost 6.570
His Armie, circumfus'd on either Wing, — Par Lost 6.778
To all his Host on either hand thus spake. — Par Lost 6.800
Nor less on either side tempestuous fell — Par Lost 6.844
Cannot well suite with either, but soon prove — Par Lost 8.388
Can either not receave, or can repell. — Par Lost 9.284
Foundst either sweet repast, or sound repose; — Par Lost 9.407
Either to meet no danger, or to finde — Par Lost 9.1176
Love was not in thir looks, either to God — Par Lost 10.111
Before my Judge, either to undergoe — Par Lost 10.126
The Causey to Hell Gate; on either side — Par Lost 10.415
And straight conjunction with this Sex: for either — Par Lost 10.898
By moderation either state to beare, — Par Lost 11.363
What we receive, would either not accept — Par Lost 11.505
In either hand the hastning Angel caught — Par Lost 12.637
Disturb'd his sleep; and either Tropic now — Par Reg 4.409
That either they love nothing, or not long? — Samson 1033
Either of these is in thy lot, — Samson 1292
Either at home, or through the high street passing, — Samson 1458
Either som one like us night-founder'd here, — Mask 483
The bounds of either sword to thee wee ow. — Sonnet 17, 12
Either man's work or his own gifts, who best — Sonnet 19, 10

Eject
Eject him tainted now, and purge him off — Par Lost 11.52

Ejected
Ejected, emptyed, gaz'd, unpityed, shun'd, — Par Reg 1.414
Is well ejected when the Conquer'd can. — Samson 1207

Ekron
And *Accaron* and *Gaza*'s frontier bounds. — Par Lost 1.466
ms 'Accaron'
In *Ecron*, *Gaza*, *Asdod*, and in *Gath* — Samson 981

El Dorado
Call *El Dorado:* but to nobler sights — Par Lost 11.411

Elaborate
Elaborate, of inward less exact. — Par Lost 8.539

Eld
Of long-uncoupled bed, and childless eld, — Fair Inf 13

Eldest
And time and place are lost; where eldest Night Par Lost 2.894
Sat Sable-vested *Night*, eldest of things, Par Lost 2.962
Aire, and ye Elements the eldest birth Par Lost 5.180
In peace, and reck'ns thee her eldest son. Sonnet 17, 14
1694 'Eldest'
Eleale
And *Eleale* to th' *Asphaltick* Pool. Par Lost 1.411
ms 'Eleale'
Elect
All Heav'n, and in the blessed Spirits elect Par Lost 3.136
Elect above the rest; so is my will: Par Lost 3.184
With these that never fade the Spirits elect Par Lost 3.360
1667 'Elect'
Eternize here on Earth; but those elect Par Lost 6.374
And overwhelm thir Warr: the Race elect Par Lost 12.214
Elected
But such as thou hast solemnly elected, Samson 678
Election
That proud excuse? yet him not thy election, Par Lost 10.764
Electra
Of sad *Electra*'s Poet had the power Sonnet 8, 13
Elegant
And elegant, of Sapience no small part, Par Lost 9.1018
Element
Heav'ns chearful face, the lowring Element Par Lost 2.490
Return me to my Native Element: Par Lost 7.16
Thir Element to draw the thinner Aire. Par Lost 8.348
Demonian Spirits now, from the Element Par Reg 2.122
Of som gay creatures of the element Mask 299
Bridgewater ms 'Element'
With Planet, or with Element. Penseroso 96
Elemental
Transparent, Elemental Air, diffus'd Par Lost 7.265
Elements
Become our Elements, these piercing Fires Par Lost 2.275
Of Heav'n were falling, and these Elements Par Lost 2.925
Of fighting Elements, on all sides round Par Lost 2.1015
The cumbrous Elements, Earth, Flood, Aire, Fire, Par Lost 3.715
Of Heav'n perhaps, or all the Elements Par Lost 4.993
Aire, and ye Elements the eldest birth Par Lost 5.180
To be sustaind and fed; of Elements Par Lost 5.415
These Elements, and arm him with the force Par Lost 6.222
Those pure immortal Elements that know Par Lost 11.50
From all the Elements her choicest store Par Reg 2.334
Elephant
Gambold before them, th' unwieldy Elephant Par Lost 4.345
Elephants
Chariots or Elephants endorst with Towers Par Reg 3.329
Elevate
In thoughts more elevate, and reason'd high Par Lost 2.558
With Towers and Temples proudly elevate Par Reg 4.34
Elevates
To mischief swift. Hope elevates, and joy Par Lost 9.633
Elf
That the shrewd medling Elfe delights to make, Mask 846
1637 'elfe'
Eli
Turns Atheist, as did *Ely*'s Sons, who fill'd Par Lost 1.495
ms 'Ely's'
Eliah
And forty days *Eliah* without food Par Reg 1.353
Sought lost *Eliah*, so in each place these Par Reg 2.19
Elijah
And forty days *Eliah* without food Par Reg 1.353
Sought lost *Eliah*, so in each place these Par Reg 2.19
Food to *Elijah* bringing Even and Morn, Par Reg 2.268
Sometimes that with *Elijah* he partook, Par Reg 2.277
Elixir
Breathe forth *Elixir* pure, and Rivers run Par Lost 3.607
Ellops
Cerastes hornd, *Hydrus*, and *Ellops* drear, Par Lost 10.525
Elm
To wed her Elm; she spous'd about him twines Par Lost 5.216
Or 'gainst the rugged bark of som broad Elm Mask 354
Trinity ms 'elme'
1637 'Elme'
Bridgewater ms 'Elme'
Of branching Elm Star-proof, Arcades 89
Trinity ms 'elme'
1673 'Elm-Star-proof'
Elms
By Hedge-row Elms, on Hillocks green, Allegro 58
Elocution
Gave elocution to the mute, and taught Par Lost 9.748
Eloquence
(For Eloquence the Soul, Song charms the Sense,) Par Lost 2.556
Unmeditated, such prompt eloquence Par Lost 5.149
In *Athens* or free *Rome*, where Eloquence Par Lost 9.671
And Eloquence, native to famous wits Par Reg 4.241
Those antient, whose resistless eloquence Par Reg 4.268
The top of Eloquence, Statists indeed, Par Reg 4.354
Eloquent
Kil'd with report that Old man eloquent, Sonnet 10, 8
Else
Can else inflict, do I repent or change, Par Lost 1.96
And what is else not to be overcome? Par Lost 1.109
Then aught divine or holy else enjoy'd Par Lost 1.683

Else*(cont)*
Re-enter Heav'n; or else in some milde Zone Par Lost 2.397
Of ancient pile; all else deep snow and ice, Par Lost 2.591
(For what could else) to our Almighty Foe Par Lost 2.769
Till they enthrall themselves: I else must change Par Lost 3.125
Whom else no Creature can behold; on thee Par Lost 3.387
Which else might work him danger or delay: Par Lost 3.635
His day, which else as th' other Hemisphere Par Lost 3.725
To do what else though damnd I should abhorre. Par Lost 4.392
Free leave so large to all things else, and choice Par Lost 4.434
In Paradise of all things common else. Par Lost 4.752
His heart, not else dismai'd. Now drew they nigh Par Lost 4.861
And seconded thy else not dreaded Spear. Par Lost 4.929
Longer thy offerd good, why else set here? Par Lost 5.63
Though standing else as Rocks, but down they fell Par Lost 6.593
What might have else to human Race bin hid; Par Lost 6.896
Of all tastes else to please thir appetite, Par Lost 7.49
Us timely of what might else have bin our loss, Par Lost 7.74
Oppresses else with Surfet, and soon turns Par Lost 7.129
Informd by thee might know; if else thou seekst Par Lost 7.639
Things else by me unsearchable, now heard Par Lost 8.10
His beams, unactive else, thir vigour find. Par Lost 8.97
Which else to several Sphears thou must ascribe, Par Lost 8.131
Invisible else above all Starrs, the Wheele Par Lost 8.135
In all things else delight indeed, but such Par Lost 8.524
Commotion strange, in all enjoyments else Par Lost 8.531
Thy Judgement to do aught, which else free Will Par Lost 8.636
Intent now wholly on her taste, naught else Par Lost 9.786
This happie trial of thy Love, which else Par Lost 9.975
With featherd Cincture, naked else and wilde Par Lost 9.1117
Of Seasons to each Clime; else had the Spring Par Lost 10.678
His course intended; else how had the World Par Lost 10.689
By which all Causes else according still Par Lost 10.806
And what may else be remedie or cure Par Lost 10.1079
What else but favor, grace, and mercie shon? Par Lost 10.1096
Why else this double object in our sight Par Lost 11.201
Thy message, which might else in telling wound, Par Lost 11.299
Familiar to our eyes, all places else Par Lost 11.305
First his own Tooles; then, what might else be wrought Par Lost 11.572
Rode tilting o're the Waves, all dwellings else Par Lost 11.747
As thou art wont, my prompted Song else mute, Par Reg 1.12
Women, when nothing else, beguil'd the heart Par Reg 2.169
Aetherial, who all pleasures else despise, Par Reg 3.28
From them who could return him nothing else, Par Reg 3.129
Means I must use thou say'st, prediction else Par Reg 3.394
No trifle; yet with this reserve, not else, Par Reg 4.165
But these are false, or little else but dreams, Par Reg 4.291
Daily in the common Prison else enjoyn'd me, Samson 6
He would not else who never wanted means, Samson 315
And I perswade me so; why else this strength Samson 586
By ransom or how else: mean while be calm, Samson 604
To dogs and fowls a prey, or else captiv'd: Samson 694
Or else with just allowance counterpois'd, Samson 770
As good for nothing else, no better service Samson 1163
From whom could else a general cry be heard? Samson 1524
And give it false presentments, lest the place Mask 156
Trinity ms 'lest' ← 'else'
Of such late Wassailers; yet O where els Mask 179
1637 'else'
Trinity ms 'else'
Had stole them from me, els O theevish Night Mask 195
Trinity ms 'else'
word not in Bridgewater ms
1637 'else'
What if in wild amazement, and affright, Mask 356
Bridgewater ms 'or els in wild'
Trinity ms 'what if' ← 'or else'
Or els som neighbour Wood-man, or at worst, Mask 484
Trinity ms 'else'
1637 'else'
Com not too neer, you fall on iron stakes else. Mask 491
Bridgewater ms 'els'
And if ought els, great *Bards* beside, Penseroso 116
But els in deep of night when drowsines Arcades 61
Trinity ms 'else'
A Sheep-hook, or have learn'd ought els the least Lycidas 120
1638 'else'
Trinity ms 'else'
Perhaps their loves, or els their sheep, Nativity 91
1673 'else'
Or els the ways being foul, twenty to one, Carrier 3
1658 'else'
1673 'else'
Things false and vain and nothing else but lies? Psalm 4, 12
Elsewhere
Our first eruption, thither or elsewhere: Par Lost 1.656
ms 'else where'
Imagind rather oft then elsewhere seen, Par Lost 3.599
Each other, blam'd enough elsewhere, but strive Par Lost 10.959
Shalt be enquir'd at *Delphos* or elsewhere, Par Reg 1.458
(And what he brings, what needs he elsewhere seek) Par Reg 4.325
Elude
I dread, and to elude, thus wrapt in mist Par Lost 9.158
Elves
Beyond the *Indian* Mount, or Faerie Elves, Par Lost 1.781
Trip the pert Fairies and the dapper Elves; Mask 118
Bridgewater ms 'Ealves'
Trinity ms 'elves'

Ely
Turns Atheist, as did *Ely*'s Sons, who fill'd — Par Lost 1.495
ms 'Ely's'
Elysian
Rowls o're *Elisian* Flours her Amber stream; — Par Lost 3.359
And drenches with *Elysian* dew — Mask 996
Bridgewater ms 'Manna'
Trinity ms 'Elysian' ←'Sabaean' ←'manna'
Of heapt *Elysian* flowres, and hear — Allegro 147
Or in the Elisian fields (if such there were.) — Fair Inf 40
Elysium
Plato's *Elysium*, leap'd into the Sea, — Par Lost 3.472
And lap it in *Elysium*, *Scylla* wept, — Mask 257
Trinity ms 'Elizium'
Bridgewater ms 'Elisium'
Emathian
Built by *Emathian*, or by *Parthian* hands, — Par Reg 3.290
The great *Emathian* Conqueror bid spare — Sonnet 8, 10
Embalmed
Wing silently the buxom Air, imbalm'd — Par Lost 2.842
Leucothea wak'd, and with fresh dews imbalmd — Par Lost 11.135
Embarked
All left, in one small bottom swum imbark't. — Par Lost 11.753
Embarqu'd with such a Stears-mate at the Helm? — Samson 1045
Embassies
Or Embassies from Regions far remote — Par Reg 4.67
And hunger still: then Embassies thou shew'st — Par Reg 4.121
Embassy
Where all his Sons thy Embassie attend; — Par Lost 3.658
Embathe
And gave her to his daughters to imbathe — Mask 837
Trinity ms 'imbath'
Bridgewater ms 'imbath'
Embattled
That led th' imbattelld Seraphim to Warr — Par Lost 1.129
Coverd with thick embatteld Squadrons bright, — Par Lost 6.16
And onward move Embattelld; when behold — Par Lost 6.550
Stood reimbattell'd fierce, by force or fraud — Par Lost 6.794
Embattell'd in her field: and the humble Shrub, — Par Lost 7.322
On thir imbattelld ranks the Waves return, — Par Lost 12.213
Ran on embattelld Armies clad in Iron, — Samson 129
Embellished
Imbellisht, thick with sparkling orient Gemmes — Par Lost 3.507
Embers
Where glowing Embers through the room — Penseroso 79
Emblaze
Would so emblaze the forhead of the Deep, — Mask 733
Emblazed
With Gemms and Golden lustre rich imblaz'd, — Par Lost 1.538
ms 'emblaz'd'
Or in thir glittering Tissues bear imblaz'd — Par Lost 5.592
Emblazoned
Or tilting Furniture, emblazon'd Shields, — Par Lost 9.34
Emblazonry
With bright imblazonrie, and horrent Arms. — Par Lost 2.513
Emblem
Of costliest Emblem: other Creature here — Par Lost 4.703
Embodied
Met such imbodied force, as nam'd with these — Par Lost 1.574
Under thir Head imbodied all in one. — Par Lost 6.779
Embodies
Imbodies, and imbrutes, till she quite loose — Mask 468
Emboldened
Thus I embold'nd spake, and freedom us'd — Par Lost 8.434
Embordered
Imborderd on each Bank, the hand of *Eve:* — Par Lost 9.438
Embosomed
Firm land imbosom'd without Firmament, — Par Lost 3.75
By whom in bliss imbosom'd sat the Son, — Par Lost 5.597
Emboss
Botches and blaines must all his flesh imboss, — Par Lost 12.180
Embossed
Crystal and Myrrhine cups imboss'd with Gems — Par Reg 4.119
In the *Arabian* woods embost, — Samson 1700
Embowed
And love the high embowed Roof, — Penseroso 157
Embowelled
Emboweld with outragious noise the Air, — Par Lost 6.587
Embower
High overarch't imbowr; or scatterd sedge — Par Lost 1.304
ms 'imbowre'
Embowered
Thick overhead with verdant roof imbowr'd — Par Lost 9.1038
And in thick shelter of black shades imbowr'd, — Mask 62
Trinity ms 'imbour'd'
Embrace
Easier then Air with Air, if Spirits embrace, — Par Lost 8.626
Neglect not, and the benefit imbrace — Par Lost 12.426
But all unwares with his cold-kind embrace — Fair Inf 20
But O as to embrace me she enclin'd, — Sonnet 23, 13
Trinity ms 'imbrace'
Embraced
So saying, she embrac'd him, and for joy — Par Lost 9.990
Embraces
And in embraces forcible and foule — Par Lost 2.793
That ever since in loves imbraces met, — Par Lost 4.322
Thy coming, and thy soft imbraces, hee — Par Lost 4.471
Fruitless imbraces: or they led the Vine — Par Lost 5.215
Embraces(*cont*)
From Loves due Rites, Nuptial imbraces sweet, — Par Lost 10.994
1667 'embraces'
Spousal embraces, vitiated with Gold, — Samson 389
Embracing
And meek surrender, half imbracing leand — Par Lost 4.494
These lulld by Nightingales imbraceing slept, — Par Lost 4.771
On *Adam*, whom imbracing, thus she spake. — Par Lost 5.27
Imbracing round this florid Earth, what cause — Par Lost 7.90
Fell humble, and imbracing them, besaught — Par Lost 10.912
Embroidered
Broiderd the ground, more colour'd then with stone — Par Lost 4.702
And in the violet-imbroider'd vale — Mask 233
Bridgewater ms 'violett imbroderd'
1673 'violet imbroider'd'
B.M. ms 'thy violet embroiderd Vale'
Embroidery
And every flower that sad embroidery wears: — Lycidas 148
Trinity ms 'imbroidrie' ←'escutcheon' ←'liverie'
Embroiled
And *Tumult* and *Confusion* all imbroild, — Par Lost 2.966
Embroils
And by decision more imbroiles the fray — Par Lost 2.908
Embrowned
Imbround the noontide Bowrs: Thus was this place, — Par Lost 4.246
Embrutes
Imbodies, and imbrutes, till she quite loose — Mask 468
Bridgewater ms 'imbruts'
Embryon
Thir embryon Atoms; they around the flag — Par Lost 2.900
Of Waters, Embryon immature involv'd, — Par Lost 7.277
Embryos
Embryo's and Idiots, Eremits and Friers — Par Lost 3.474
Emerald
Of Turkis blew, and Emrauld green — Mask 894
Bridgewater ms 'Emerald'
1637 'Emrould'
Trinity ms 'emrauld' ←'emrald'
Emergent
Emergent, and thir broad bare backs upheave — Par Lost 7.286
Emims
As *Og* or *Anak* and the *Emims* old — Samson 1080
Eminence
To that bad eminence; and from despair — Par Lost 2.6
In that bright eminence, and with his good — Par Lost 4.44
In favour and praeeminence, yet fraught — Par Lost 5.661
In eminence, and obstacle find none — Par Lost 8.624
But this praeeminence thou hast lost, brought down — Par Lost 11.347
Eminent
In shape and gesture proudly eminent — Par Lost 1.590
High eminent, blooming Ambrosial Fruit — Par Lost 4.219
Praeeminent by so much odds, while thou — Par Lost 4.447
1667 'Preeminent'
Recorded eminent. Thus when in Orbes — Par Lost 5.594
In goodness and in power praeeminent; — Par Lost 8.279
Of middle Age one rising, eminent — Par Lost 11.665
First seen in acts of prowess eminent — Par Lost 11.789
And fears as eminent, above the lot — Par Reg 2.70
By deeds of peace, by wisdom eminent, — Par Reg 3.91
Eminently
So eminently never had bin known. — Par Lost 9.976
With gifts and graces eminently adorn'd, — Samson 679
And with those few art eminently seen, — Sonnet 9, 3
Emmet
The Parsimonious Emmet, provident — Par Lost 7.485
Empedocles
Empedocles, and hee who to enjoy — Par Lost 3.471
Emperor
At thir great Emperors call, as next in worth — Par Lost 1.378
ms 'Emperours'
Than Hells dread Emperour with pomp Supream, — Par Lost 2.510
Might intercept thir Emperour sent, so hee — Par Lost 10.429
To *Rome*'s great Emperour, whose wide domain — Par Reg 4.81
This Emperour hath no Son, and now is old, — Par Reg 4.90
Of the Emperour, how easily subdu'd, — Par Reg 4.126
Empire
Doubted his Empire, that were low indeed, — Par Lost 1.114
ms 'empire'
To found this nether Empire, which might rise — Par Lost 2.296
A growing Empire; doubtless; while we dream, — Par Lost 2.315
His Empire, and with Iron Scepter rule — Par Lost 2.327
Lies through your spacious Empire up to light, — Par Lost 2.974
Divided Empire with Heav'ns King I hold — Par Lost 4.111
Into his neather Empire neighbouring round. — Par Lost 4.145
Honour and Empire with revenge enlarg'd, — Par Lost 4.390
Of Deitie or Empire, such a foe — Par Lost 5.724
Fit to decide the Empire of great Heav'n. — Par Lost 6.303
Of his Eternal Empire, but the more — Par Lost 7.96
Th' addition of his Empire, how it shew'd — Par Lost 7.555
Thy Empire? easily the proud attempt — Par Lost 7.609
Th' infernal Empire, that so neer Heav'ns dore — Par Lost 10.389
What thinkst thou of our Empire now, though earnd — Par Lost 10.592
Of mightiest Empire, from the destind Walls — Par Lost 11.387
Th' Empire of *Negus* to his utmost Port — Par Lost 11.397
Subjection to his Empire tyrannous: — Par Lost 12.32
And all the rule, one Empire; onely add — Par Lost 12.581
In this fair Empire won of Earth and Air; — Par Reg 1.63
For Empires sake, nor Empire to affect — Par Reg 3.45

Empire(*cont*)
Assyria and her Empires antient bounds, Par Reg 3.270
That Empire, under his dominion holds Par Reg 3.296
By wisdom; as thy Empire must extend, Par Reg 4.222
Within thy self, much more with Empire joyn'd. Par Reg 4.284
Kingdom nor Empire pleases thee, nor aught Par Reg 4.369
The greatest, and the best of all the main Mask 28
Trinity ms 'maine' ←'his empire'
Through middle empire of the freezing aire Fair Inf 16
Empires
Hatching vain Empires. Thus *Beelzebub* Par Lost 2.378
Witness those antient Empires of the Earth, Par Reg 2.435
Empires, and Monarchs, and thir radiant Courts, Par Reg 3.237
Empiric
Of sooty coal the Empiric Alchimist Par Lost 5.440
Employ
With speed what force is left, and all imploy Par Lost 5.730
Wed your divine sounds, and mixt power employ Musick 3
Employed
Lay waving round; on som great charge imploy'd Par Lost 3.628
Which we in our appointed work imployd Par Lost 4.726
Imploi'd it seems to violate sleep, and those Par Lost 4.883
His barren leaves. Them thus imploid beheld Par Lost 5.219
Well hast thou motion'd, well thy thoughts imployd Par Lost 9.229
Employments
And let us to our fresh imployments rise Par Lost 5.125
Employs
Here Love his golden shafts imploies, here lights Par Lost 4.763
Empowered
Within Hell Gates till now, thou us impow'rd Par Lost 10.369
Consenting in full frequence was impowr'd, Par Reg 2.130
Empress
Empress of this fair World, resplendent *Eve*, Par Lost 9.568
Empress, the way is readie, and not long, Par Lost 9.626
Emprise
Giants of mightie Bone, and bould emprise; Par Lost 11.642
I love thy courage yet, and bold Emprise, Mask 610
Trinity ms 'emprise'
Bridgewater ms 'emprise'
Emptied
Hath emptied Heav'n, shall fail to re-ascend Par Lost 1.633
Ejected, emptyed, gaz'd, unpityed, shun'd, Par Reg 1.414
Emptied his glory, ev'n to nakednes; Circum 20
Emptier
Or in the emptier waste, resembling Air, Par Lost 2.1045
Empties
Hence fills and empties to enlighten th' Earth, Par Lost 3.731
Emptiness
Or emptiness, or fond impertinence, Par Lost 8.195
Empty
Fit retribution, emptie as thir deeds; Par Lost 3.454
For thou art Heav'nlie, shee an empty dreame. Par Lost 7.39
Yet empty of all good wherein consists Par Lost 11.616
An empty cloud. However many books Par Reg 4.321
Empty-vaulted
Of silence, through the empty-vaulted night Mask 250
1637 'emptie-vaulted'
Bridgewater ms 'empty vaulted'
Trinity ms 'empty vaulted'
Empyreal
And this Empyreal substance cannot fail, Par Lost 1.117
ms 'Empyreall'
O Progeny of Heav'n, Empyreal Thrones, Par Lost 2.430
Farr off th' Empyreal Heav'n, extended wide Par Lost 2.1047
From thy Empyreal Mansion thus alone, Par Lost 3.699
Through all th' Empyreal road; till at the Gate Par Lost 5.253
Thus to th' Empyreal Minister he fram'd. Par Lost 5.460
As Heav'ns great Year brings forth, th' Empyreal Host Par Lost 5.583
Empyreal, from before her vanisht Night, Par Lost 6.14
Since now we find this our Empyreal form Par Lost 6.433
An Earthlie Guest, and drawn Empyreal Aire, Par Lost 7.14
Of all things parted by th' Empyreal bounds, Par Lost 10.380
Empyrean
Through all the Empyrean: down they fell Par Lost 2.771
From the pure Empyrean where he sits Par Lost 3.57
The stedfast Empyrean shook throughout, Par Lost 6.833
Down from the Empyrean to forewarne Par Lost 7.73
So sung they, and the Empyrean rung, Par Lost 7.633
The confines met of Empyrean Heav'n Par Lost 10.321
Emulate
Ingaging me to emulate, but short Par Lost 9.963
Emulation
In emulation opposite to Heav'n. Par Lost 2.298
Emulous
Not emulous, nor care who them excells; Par Lost 6.822
Enamelled
Appeerd, with gay enameld colours mixt: Par Lost 4.149
His turret Crest, and sleek enamel'd Neck, Par Lost 9.525
O're the smooth enameld green Arcades 84
1673 'enamel'd'
Throw hither all your quaint enameld eyes, Lycidas 139
1638 'enammell'd'
Trinity ms 'enamel'd'
Th' enameld *Arras* of the Rainbow wearing, Nativity 143
1673 'Orb'd in a Rain-bow and like glories wearing'
Enamour
To enamour, as the Zone of *Venus* once Par Reg 2.214
Enamoured
Becam'st enamour'd, and such joy thou took'st Par Lost 2.765
That drove him, though enamourd, from the Spouse Par Lost 4.169
Hung over her enamour'd, and beheld Par Lost 5.13
Enamour'd at that sight; but in those hearts Par Lost 5.448
Encamp
Encamp thir Legions, or with obscure wing Par Lost 2.132
Encamped
Where Armies lie encampt, come flying, lur'd Par Lost 10.276
Lay Seige, encampt; by Batterie, Scale, and Mine, Par Lost 11.656
By mee encampt on yonder Hill, expect Par Lost 12.591
Encamping
Encamping, plac'd in Guard thir Watches round, Par Lost 6.412
I fear not though incamping round about Psalm 3, 17
Enchanted
Thy fair enchanted cup, and warbling charms Samson 934
Of dire *Chimera*'s and inchanted Iles, Mask 517
Trinity ms 'inchaunted'
Bridgewater ms 'enchaunted'
Enchanter
I knew the foul inchanter though disguis'd, Mask 645
Trinity ms 'enchanter'
Bridgewater ms 'Enchaunter'
Spir. What, have you let the false enchanter scape? Mask 814
Trinity ms 'enchaunter'
Bridgewater ms 'Inchaunter'
1673 'Enchanter'
Of unblest inchanter vile. Mask 907
Trinity ms 'enchanter'
Bridgewater ms 'inchaunters'
Enchanting
Inchanting Daughter, thus the silence broke. Par Lost 10.353
Expert in amorous Arts, enchanting tongues Par Reg 2.158
Chor. Look now for no inchanting voice, nor fear Samson 1065
Breath such Divine inchanting ravishment? Mask 245
Bridgewater ms 'enchauntinge'
Trinity ms 'enchaunting' ←'enchanting'
The Muse her self, for her inchanting son Lycidas 59
Trinity ms 'inchanting' ←'inchaunting'
Enchantments
And black enchantments, some Magicians Art Samson 1133
'Gainst all inchantments, mildew blast, or damp Mask 640
Bridgewater ms 'enchauntments'
Trinity ms 'enchauntments'
Hence with thy brew'd inchantments, foul deceiver, Mask 696
Trinity ms 'brewd enchauntments' ←'foule brud' ←'hel brewd opiate' ←'hel bru'd liquor' ←'bru'd sorcerie' ←'teacherous (leacherous?) bruage' ←'teacherous kindnesse'
Bridgewater ms 'enchauntments'
Of Forests, and inchantments drear, Penseroso 119
Enclose
From wing to wing, and half enclose him round Par Lost 1.617
ms 'inclose'
Enclosed
A Globe of fierie Seraphim inclos'd Par Lost 2.512
The luminous inferior Orbs, enclos'd Par Lost 3.420
By *Nilus* head, enclosd with shining Rock, Par Lost 4.283
1667 'enclos'd'
Idol of Majestie Divine, enclos'd Par Lost 6.101
Of future, in small room large heart enclos'd, Par Lost 7.486
A Circuit wide, enclos'd, with goodliest Trees Par Lost 8.304
So spake the Enemie of Mankind, enclos'd Par Lost 9.494
Them nothing: If they all things, who enclos'd Par Lost 9.722
How many evils have enclos'd me round; Samson 194
Some narrow place enclos'd, where sight may give thee, Samson 1117
Enclosing
Between two such enclosing enemies Par Reg 3.361
Enclosure
Now nearer, Crowns with her enclosure green, Par Lost 4.133
In this enclosure wild, these Beasts among, Par Lost 9.543
Encompassed
Encompass'd shall resound thee ever blest. Par Lost 3.149
Encompass'd round with foes, thus answerd bold. Par Lost 5.876
With clouds encompass'd round; Psalm 81, 30
Encounter
To joyn thir dark Encounter in mid air: Par Lost 2.718
a tough encounter with the shaggiest ruffian Mask Tr. ms 16.39
'encounter' ←'passado'
a tough encounter, with the shaggiest ruffian Mask Br. ms 392
Encountered
So Hills amid the Air encounterd Hills Par Lost 6.664
Encountering
Millions of fierce encountring Angels fought Par Lost 6.220
Encounters
Of those encounters, where we might have tri'd Samson 1086
Encroached
Encroacht on still through our intestine broiles Par Lost 2.1001
Encroaching
Ophion with *Eurynome*, the wide- Par Lost 10.581
Encroaching *Eve* perhaps, had first the rule Par Lost 10.582
Encroachment
But this Usurper his encroachment proud Par Lost 12.72
Encumbered
Incumberd him with ruin: Hell at last Par Lost 6.874
Encumberd, now had left them, up they rose Par Lost 9.1051
And she no whit encomber'd with her store, Mask 774
Bridgewater ms 'encomberd'

Encumbered(*cont*)
Trinity ms 'encumberd'
End
That comes to all; but torture without end — Par Lost 1.67
Our labour must be to pervert that end, — Par Lost 1.164
Must exercise us without hope of end — Par Lost 2.89
And that must end us, that must be our cure, — Par Lost 2.145
To give his Enemies thir wish, and end — Par Lost 2.157
Ages of hopeless end; this would be worse. — Par Lost 2.186
From either end of Heav'n the welkin burns. — Par Lost 2.538
And found no end, in wandring mazes lost. — Par Lost 2.561
His end with mine involvd; and knows that I — Par Lost 2.807
Thy daughter and thy darling, without end. — Par Lost 2.870
Love without end, and without measure Grace, — Par Lost 3.142
His end, and frustrate thine, shall he fulfill — Par Lost 3.157
And to the end persisting, safe arrive. — Par Lost 3.197
He to appease thy wrauth, and end the strife — Par Lost 3.406
His journies end and our beginning woe. — Par Lost 3.633
Now other, as thir shape servd best his end — Par Lost 4.398
And without whom am to no end, my Guide — Par Lost 4.442
Your message, like to end as much in vain? — Par Lost 4.833
Him first, him last, him midst, and without end. — Par Lost 5.165
Ordaind without redemption, without end. — Par Lost 5.615
Who out of smallest things could without end — Par Lost 6.137
Apostat, still thou errst, nor end wilt find — Par Lost 6.172
Surceas'd, and glad as hoping here to end — Par Lost 6.258
To chase me hence? erre not that so shall end — Par Lost 6.288
Effect shall end our wish. Mean while revive; — Par Lost 6.493
Can end it. Into thee such Vertue and Grace — Par Lost 6.703
And gladlier shall resign, when in the end — Par Lost 6.731
Immutably his sovran will, the end — Par Lost 7.79
End, and dismiss thee ere the Morning shine. — Par Lost 7.108
One Kingdom, Joy and Union without end. — Par Lost 7.161
Said then th' Omnific Word, your discord end: — Par Lost 7.217
There wanted yet the Master work, the end — Par Lost 7.505
Varietie without end; but of the Tree — Par Lost 7.542
Author and end of all things, and from work — Par Lost 7.591
Her end without least motion, and receaves, — Par Lost 8.35
Uncheckt, and of her roaving is no end; — Par Lost 8.189
For well I understand in the prime end — Par Lost 8.540
Twixt Day and Night, and now from end to end — Par Lost 9.51
Love not the lowest end of human life. — Par Lost 9.241
And thy fair Fruit let hang, as to no end — Par Lost 9.798
And of thir vain contest appeer'd no end. — Par Lost 9.1189
Forbearance no acquittance ere day end. — Par Lost 10.53
Of mischief, and polluted from the end — Par Lost 10.167
Of richest texture spred, at th' upper end — Par Lost 10.446
O miserable of happie! is this the end — Par Lost 10.720
Of happiness: yet well, if here would end — Par Lost 10.725
Wrath without end on Man whom Death must end? — Par Lost 10.797
To end me? Shall Truth fail to keep her word, — Par Lost 10.856
Or end, though sharp and sad, yet tolerable, — Par Lost 10.977
That shew no end but Death, and have the power, — Par Lost 10.1004
Or if thou covet death, as utmost end — Par Lost 10.1020
By him with many comforts, till we end — Par Lost 10.1084
And in performing end us; what besides — Par Lost 11.300
Better end heer unborn. Why is life giv'n — Par Lost 11.502
Created, as thou art, to nobler end — Par Lost 11.605
The end of all thy Ofspring, end so sad, — Par Lost 11.755
And whether here the Race of man will end. — Par Lost 11.786
Thus thou hast seen one World begin and end; — Par Lost 12.6
The last, for of his Reign shall be no end. — Par Lost 12.330
Eternitie, whose end no eye can reach. — Par Lost 12.556
With meditation on the happie end. — Par Lost 12.605
To end his Raign on Earth so long enjoy'd: — Par Reg 1.125
Born to that end, born to promote all truth, — Par Reg 1.205
And of thy Kingdom there should be no end. — Par Reg 1.241
From the beginning, and in lies wilt end; — Par Reg 1.408
His end of being on Earth, and mission high: — Par Reg 2.114
Where will this end? four times ten days I have pass'd — Par Reg 2.245
He spake no dream, for as his words had end, — Par Reg 2.337
That seat, and reign in *Israel* without end. — Par Reg 2.442
Though chiefly not for glory as prime end, — Par Reg 3.123
That it shall never end, so when begin — Par Reg 3.185
My exaltation without change or end. — Par Reg 3.197
The end I would attain, my final good. — Par Reg 3.211
To what end I have brought thee hither and shewn — Par Reg 3.350
Vain battry, and in froth or bubbles end; — Par Reg 4.20
And of my Kingdom there shall be no end: — Par Reg 4.151
Nor when, eternal sure, as without end, — Par Reg 4.391
And the same end; still watching to oppress — Samson 232
With me hath end; all the contest is now — Samson 461
To what end should I seek it? when in strength — Samson 522
Hast'n the welcom end of all my pains. — Samson 576
For oft alike, both come to evil end. — Samson 704
His labours, for thou canst, to peaceful end. — Samson 709
Sam. I thought where all thy circling wiles would end; — Samson 871
Discover'd in the end, till now conceal'd. — Samson 998
Sam. Love-quarrels oft in pleasing concord end, — Samson 1008
Yet so it may fall out, because thir end — Samson 1265
But favouring and assisting to the end. — Samson 1720
Us thy vow'd Priests, till utmost end — Mask 136
Why shouldst thou, but for som fellonious end, — Mask 196
line not in Bridgewater ms
Fain would I somthing say, yet to what end? — Mask 783
line not in Bridgewater ms
line not in Trinity ms
Quickly to the green earths end, — Mask 1014

End(*cont*)
That ten day-labourers could not end, — Allegro 109
Heer our solemn search hath end. — Arcades 7
That till the worlds last-end shall make thy name to live. — Fair Inf 77
And thinking now his journeys end was come, — Carrier 12
Stand spelling fals, while one might walk to Mile- — Sonnet 11, 7
End Green. Why is it harder Sirs then Gordon, — Sonnet 11, 8
Their time should have no end. — Psalm 81, 64
Wilt thou be angry without end, — Psalm 85, 17
Endamaged
The tryal hath indamag'd thee no way, — Par Reg 4.206
Endangered
Fearless, endanger'd Heav'ns perpetual King; — Par Lost 1.131
And more endanger'd, then when *Argo* pass'd — Par Lost 2.1017
Endangering
Not wedlock-trechery endangering life. — Samson 1009
Endear
How to endear, and hold thee to me firmest: — Samson 796
Endearing
Nor gentle purpose, nor endearing smiles — Par Lost 4.337
Endeavour
Endeavour Peace: thir strife pollution brings — Par Lost 12.355
Endeavour, as thy Father *David* did, — Par Reg 3.353
Dal. Yet hear me *Samson;* not that I endeavour — Samson 766
Thy Works and Alms and all thy good Endeavour — Sonnet 14, 5
Trinity ms 'Endeavour' ←'Endevor' ←'Endeavor'
Endeavoured
Though but endevord with sincere intent, — Par Lost 3.192
Endeavouring
As thitherward endevoring, and upright — Par Lost 8.260
On my part aught endeavouring, or to need — Par Reg 3.399
Didst move my first endeavouring tongue to speak, — Vacation 2
For whilst to th' shame of slow-endeavouring art, — Shakespear 9
1640 'slow-endevouring'
1632 'slow-endevouring'
Ended
He ended frowning, and his look denounc'd — Par Lost 2.106
As *Mammon* ended, and his Sentence pleas'd, — Par Lost 2.291
Well have ye judg'd, well ended long debate, — Par Lost 2.390
Ended rejoycing in thir matchless Chief: — Par Lost 2.487
Then of thir Session ended they bid cry — Par Lost 2.514
But ended foul in many a scaly fould — Par Lost 2.651
His words here ended, but his meek aspect — Par Lost 3.266
He scarce had ended, when those two approachd — Par Lost 4.874
Of onset ended soon each milder thought. — Par Lost 6.98
They ended parle, and both addrest for fight — Par Lost 6.296
He ended, and his words thir drooping chere — Par Lost 6.496
Had ended; when to Right and Left the Front — Par Lost 6.569
The Angel ended, and in *Adams* Eare — Par Lost 8.1
line not in 1667 edition
Hee ended, or I heard no more, for now — Par Lost 8.452
Though in mid Heav'n, soon ended his delight, — Par Lost 9.468
He ended, and his words replete with guile — Par Lost 9.733
He ended, and the heav'nly Audience loud — Par Lost 10.641
She ended weeping, and her lowlie plight, — Par Lost 10.937
She ended heer, or vehement despaire — Par Lost 10.1007
He ended, and the Son gave signal high — Par Lost 11.72
Had ended now thir Orisons, and found — Par Lost 11.137
He ended; and th' Arch-Angel soon drew nigh, — Par Lost 11.238
In Manhood where Youth ended; by his side — Par Lost 11.246
He ended; and thus *Adam* last reply'd. — Par Lost 12.552
He ended, and they both descend the Hill; — Par Lost 12.606
He ended, and his words impression left — Par Reg 1.106
Till those days ended, hunger'd then at last — Par Reg 1.309
He ended, and the Son of God reply'd. — Par Reg 1.346
There ended was his quest, there ceast his care. — Fair Inf 18
His principles being ceast, he ended strait. — Another 10
Ending
Besides what hope the never-ending flight — Par Lost 2.221
Still ending, still renewing, through mid Heav'n; — Par Lost 3.729
Of ending this great Warr, since none but Thou — Par Lost 6.702
Ending on the russling Leaves, — Penseroso 129
Not *Typhon* huge ending in snaky twine: — Nativity 226
Time is our tedious Song should here have ending, — Nativity 239
Endless
Here swallow'd up in endless misery. — Par Lost 1.142
ms 'endlesse'
Of endless pain? where there is then no good — Par Lost 2.30
To punish endless? wherefore cease we then? — Par Lost 2.159
Of endless Warrs, and by confusion stand. — Par Lost 2.897
The debt immense of endless gratitude, — Par Lost 4.52
Endless, and no solution will be found: — Par Lost 6.694
The sense of endless woes? inexplicable — Par Lost 10.754
Bereaving sense, but endless miserie — Par Lost 10.810
New Heav'ns, new Earth, Ages of endless date — Par Lost 12.549
The Prophets old, who sung thy endless raign, — Par Reg 3.178
To live with him, and sing in endles morn of light. — Musick 28
Trinity ms 'endlesse' ←'never-parting' ←'cloudlesse' ←'endlesse' ←'uneclipsed' ←'ever-glorious' ←'ever-endlesse'
For what can Warr, but endless warr still breed, — Sonnet 15, 10
1694 'Acts of War'
Endor
At Endor quite cut off, and rowl'd — Psalm 83, 39
Endorsed
Chariots or Elephants endorst with Towers — Par Reg 3.329
Endow
A Creature form'd of Earth, and him endow, — Par Lost 9.149

Endowed
Endowd with all thir gifts, and O too like Par Lost 4.715
Created him endowd, with Happiness Par Lost 11.58
Ends
Forthwith from all the ends of Heav'n appeerd Par Lost 5.586
From all the ends of th' Earth, to celebrate Par Lost 11.345
Here Nature seems fulfilld in all her ends. Par Lost 11.602
Gan thunder, and both ends of Heav'n, the Clouds Par Reg 4.410
Happ'ly had ends above my reach to know: Samson 62
By worse then hostile deeds, violating the ends Samson 893
To folly and shameful deeds which ruin ends. Samson 1043
I under fair pretence of friendly ends, Mask 160
And Tyre with Ethiops *utmost ends*, Psalm 87, 15
Endue
Baptiz'd, shall them with wondrous gifts endue Par Lost 12.500
Endued
Or substance, how endu'd, and what thir Power, Par Lost 2.356
Indu'd with various forms various degrees Par Lost 5.473
That to his only Son by right endu'd Par Lost 5.815
And Brute as other Creatures, but endu'd Par Lost 7.507
Thir Nature, with such knowledg God endu'd Par Lost 8.353
Suttle or violent, we not endu'd Par Lost 9.324
I knew, but not with human voice endu'd; Par Lost 9.561
Endu'd with human voice and human sense, Par Lost 9.871
But men endu'd with these have oft attain'd Par Reg 2.437
Indu'd with Regal Vertues as thou art, Par Reg 4.98
The Son of God, with Godlike force indu'd Par Reg 4.602
Samson, with might endu'd Samson 1293
Endueth
That som more timely-happy spirits indu'th. Sonnet 7, 8
Endurance
Through labour and indurance. This deep world Par Lost 2.262
1667 'endurance'
Endure
What yet they know must follow, to endure Par Lost 2.206
Touch'd lightly; for no falshood can endure Par Lost 4.811
Less hardie to endure? courageous Chief, Par Lost 4.920
Not that I less endure, or shrink from pain, Par Lost 4.925
I could endure, without him live no life. Par Lost 9.833
Safest thy life, and best prepar'd endure Par Lost 11.365
For ever shall endure; the like shall sing Par Lost 12.324
He shall endure by coming in the Flesh Par Lost 12.405
From thee I can and must submiss endure Par Reg 1.476
Though needing, what praise is it to endure? Par Reg 2.251
But I endure the time, till which expir'd, Par Reg 4.174
Endure it, doubtful whether God be Lord, Samson 477
For his mercies ay endure, Psalm 136, 3 etc.
Endured
Nathless he so endur'd, till on the Beach Par Lost 1.299
Tamely endur'd a Bridge of wondrous length Par Lost 2.1028
Too much to one, but double how endur'd, Par Lost 5.783
Abdiel that sight endur'd not, where he stood Par Lost 6.111
Some disadvantage we endur'd and paine, Par Lost 6.431
Endures
Who guards her, or with her the worst endures. Par Lost 9.269
Enemies
To give his Enemies thir wish, and end Par Lost 2.157
Our yet unwounded Enemies, or arme Par Lost 6.466
Upon his enemies, and to declare Par Lost 6.677
And full of wrauth bent on his Enemies. Par Lost 6.826
And thought not much to cloath his Enemies: Par Lost 10.219
To gratifie my scornful Enemies, Par Lost 10.625
Provoking God to raise them enemies: Par Lost 12.318
But to the Cross he nailes thy Enemies, Par Lost 12.415
The enemies of truth; who then shall guide Par Lost 12.482
Between two such enclosing enemies Par Reg 3.361
Of enemies, of aids, battels and leagues, Par Reg 3.392
Thir enemies, who serve Idols with God. Par Reg 3.432
Made of my Enemies the scorn and gaze; Samson 34
Blind among enemies, O worse then chains, Samson 68
Perhaps my enemies who come to stare Samson 112
Shav'n, and disarm'd among my enemies. Samson 540
Against the uncircumcis'd, our enemies. Samson 640
And to those cruel enemies, Samson 642
But I to enemies reveal'd, and should not. Samson 782
My enemies, lov'd thee, as too well thou knew'st, Samson 878
Into thy Enemies hand, permitted them Samson 1159
As on my enemies, where ever chanc'd, Samson 1202
Mess. Unwounded of his enemies he fell. Samson 1582
A life Heroic, on his Enemies Samson 1711
Sok't in his enemies blood, and from the stream Samson 1726
Ith' mid'st of all mine enemies that mark. Psalm 6, 15
Mine enemies shall all be blank and dash't Psalm 6, 21
That are their enemies. Psalm 81, 60
Enemy
Beelzebub. To whom th' Arch-Enemy, Par Lost 1.81
ms 'Arch-enemy'
Our Enemy, our own loss how repair, Par Lost 1.188
ms 'enemy'
Heav'ns purest Light, yet our great Enemy Par Lost 2.137
1667 'Enemie'
Transform'd: but he my inbred enemie Par Lost 2.785
I come no enemie, but to set free Par Lost 2.822
Why satst thou like an enemie in waite Par Lost 4.825
His danger, and from whom, what enemie Par Lost 5.239
Or enemie, while God was in his work, Par Lost 8.234
That such an Enemie we have, who seeks Par Lost 9.274
The Enemie, though bold, will hardly dare, Par Lost 9.304

Enemy*(cont)*
So spake the Enemie of Mankind, enclos'd Par Lost 9.494
Of Enemie hath beguil'd thee, yet unknown, Par Lost 9.905
The danger, and the lurking Enemie Par Lost 9.1172
Thy enemie; nor so is overcome Par Lost 12.390
Without new trouble; such an Enemy Par Reg 2.126
Nor proffer'd by an Enemy, though who Par Reg 2.330
But life preserves, destroys life's enemy, Par Reg 2.372
Thou art to be my fatal enemy. Par Reg 4.525
The *Philistine*, thy Countries Enemy, Samson 238
Nor in respect of the enemy just cause Samson 316
A *Canaanite*, my faithless enemy. Samson 380
A common enemy, who had destroy'd Samson 856
Yet now am judg'd an enemy. Why then Samson 882
Of me as of a common Enemy, Samson 1416
Who had made thir dreadful enemy thir thrall. Samson 1622
Of the invading enimy. Psalm 136, 82
1673 'enemy'
Let th' enemy pursue my soul Psalm 7, 13
To stint th' enemy, and slack th' avengers brow Psalm 8, 7
Enerve
Enerve, and with voluptuous hope dissolve, Par Reg 2.165
Enfeebled
Infeebl'd me, to what I was in Heav'n. Par Lost 9.488
Enfolded
That sit upon the nine enfolded Sphears, Arcades 64
Trinity ms 'enfoulded' ←'enfolded'
Enforce
As a petty enterprise of small enforce. Samson 1223
Enforced
That *Adam* now enforc't to close his eyes, Par Lost 11.419
And not inforc'd oft-times to part from truth; Par Reg 1.472
A Manger his, yet soon enforc't to flye Par Reg 2.75
Engage
That thou may'st know I seek not to engage Par Reg 3.347
Judgment here thou didst ingage Psalm 7, 23
Engaged
Was this your discipline and faith ingag'd, Par Lost 4.954
Repeated, shee to him as oft engag'd Par Lost 9.400
They had ingag'd their wandring steps too far, Mask 193
Bridgewater ms 'ingaged'
Trinity ms 'ingadg'd'
Engaging
Ingaging me to emulate, but short Par Lost 9.963
Engendered
Ingenderd in the *Pythian* Vale on slime, Par Lost 10.530
Engendering
Ingendring with me, of that rape begot Par Lost 2.794
Blown up with high conceits ingendring pride. Par Lost 4.809
Engine
Of his Almighty Engin he shall hear Par Lost 2.65
And like a devillish Engine back recoiles Par Lost 4.17
But that two-handed engine at the door, Lycidas 130
And like an Engin mov'd with wheel and waight, Another 9
1640, 1657 'some engine'
1658 'some Engine'
Engines
By all his Engins, but was headlong sent Par Lost 1.750
ms 'engins'
With all her battering Engines bent to rase Par Lost 2.923
Which into hallow Engins long and round Par Lost 6.484
Whereof to found thir Engins and thir Balls Par Lost 6.518
From those deep throated Engins belcht, whose roar Par Lost 6.586
Till on those cursed Engins triple-row Par Lost 6.650
Or we shall find such Engines to assail Samson 1396
Enginry
Training his devilish Enginrie, impal'd Par Lost 6.553
England
Of *Englands* Counsel, and her Treasury, Sonnet 10, 2
English
First taught our English Musick how to span Sonnet 13, 2
Engorged
Greedily she ingorg'd without restraint, Par Lost 9.791
Engrave
Shall on the heart engrave. What will they then Par Lost 12.524
Engraven
A Pillar of State; deep on his Front engraven Par Lost 2.302
Engrossed
Another now hath to himself ingross't Par Lost 5.775
Engulfed
Pass'd underneath ingulft, for God had thrown Par Lost 4.225
Into utter darkness, deep ingulft, his place Par Lost 5.614
Enjoined
Our pleasant task enjoyn'd, but till more hands Par Lost 9.207
Yearly enjoynd, some say, to undergo Par Lost 10.575
Wherere our days work lies, though now enjoind Par Lost 11.177
Daily in the common Prison else enjoyn'd me, Samson 6
Enjoinest
High matter thou injoinst me, O prime of men, Par Lost 5.563
Enjoining
Vertue, as I thought, truth, duty so enjoyning. Samson 870
Enjoins
Not then mistrust, but tender love enjoynes, Par Lost 9.357
Enjoy
Empedocles, and hee who to enjoy Par Lost 3.471
One easie prohibition, who enjoy Par Lost 4.433
And daily thanks, I chiefly who enjoy Par Lost 4.445
Whose image thou art, him thou shalt enjoy Par Lost 4.472

Enjoy(*cont*)
The happier *Eden*, shall enjoy thir fill — Par Lost 4.507
Yet happie pair; enjoy, till I return, — Par Lost 4.534
Whose progenie you are. Mean while enjoy — Par Lost 5.503
What happiness, who can enjoy alone, — Par Lost 8.365
Which I enjoy, and must confess to find — Par Lost 8.523
(And pure thou wert created) we enjoy — Par Lost 8.623
With ardor to enjoy thee, fairer now — Par Lost 9.1032
Thou didst accept them; wilt thou enjoy the good, — Par Lost 10.758
The good which we enjoy, from Heav'n descends; — Par Lost 11.142
Shall leave them to enjoy; for th' Earth shall bear — Par Lost 11.804
Leaving my dolorous Prison I enjoy — Par Reg 1.364
Higher design then to enjoy his State; — Par Reg 2.203
Long to enjoy it quiet and secure, — Par Reg 3.360
His horrid lusts in private to enjoy, — Par Reg 4.94
Here I should still enjoy thee day and night — Samson 807
Nor shall I count it hainous to enjoy — Samson 991
May sit i' th center, and enjoy bright day, — Mask 382
Bridgewater ms 'enioye'
Enjoy your deer Wit, and gay Rhetorick — Mask 790
line not in Bridgewater ms
line not in Trinity ms

Enjoyed
Then aught divine or holy else enjoy'd — Par Lost 1.683
Therein enjoy'd were worthy to subdue — Par Lost 8.584
Enjoy'd by us excites his envie more; — Par Lost 9.264
Who might have liv'd and joyd immortal bliss, — Par Lost 9.1166
To end his Raign on Earth so long enjoy'd: — Par Reg 1.125
Life yet hath many solaces, enjoy'd — Samson 915

Enjoyedest
And all the riches of this World enjoydst, — Par Lost 12.580

Enjoyest
Whatever pure thou in the body enjoy'st — Par Lost 8.622

Enjoying
Equal to God, and equally enjoying — Par Lost 3.306
So farr the happier Lot, enjoying thee — Par Lost 4.446
Or all enjoying, what contentment find? — Par Lost 8.366
Shall live with her enjoying, I extinct; — Par Lost 9.829
(Which Men enjoying sight oft without cause complain) — Samson 157

Enjoyment
Enjoyment of our right as Gods; yet hard — Par Lost 6.452
Unsavoury in th' injoyment of it self — Mask 742
Trinity ms 'enjoyment'
line not in Bridgewater ms

Enjoyments
Commotion strange, in all enjoyments else — Par Lost 8.531

Enjoys
Who now enjoyes thee credulous, all Gold, — Horace 9

Enlarged
Yet thence his lustful Orgies he enlarg'd — Par Lost 1.415
Honour and Empire with revenge enlarg'd, — Par Lost 4.390

Enlarges
The thoughts, and heart enlarges, hath his seat — Par Lost 8.590

Enlighten
Hence fills and empties to enlighten th' Earth, — Par Lost 3.731
Not only enlighten, but with kindly heate — Par Lost 4.668
As I shall thee enlighten, intermix — Par Lost 11.115

Enlightened
Enlightn'd, and thir languisht hope reviv'd. — Par Lost 6.497
And thou enlight'nd Earth, so fresh and gay, — Par Lost 8.274
The new-enlightn'd world no more should need; — Nativity 82
1673 'new enlightn'd'

Enlightener
Enlightner of my darkness, gracious things — Par Lost 12.271

Enlightening
Enlightning her by Day, as she by Night — Par Lost 8.143

Enlivened
Ile venter, for my new enliv'nd spirits — Mask 228
Trinity ms 'new-enliv'nd'
Bridgewater ms 'enliv'n'd'

Enmity
And works of love or enmity fulfill. — Par Lost 1.431
Yet live in hatred, enmity, and strife — Par Lost 2.500
1667 'enmitie'
Stupidly good, of enmitie disarm'd, — Par Lost 9.465
No ground of enmitie between us known, — Par Lost 9.1151
Enmitie, and between thine and her Seed; — Par Lost 10.180
Is enmity, which he will put between — Par Lost 10.497
As joyn'd in injuries, one enmitie — Par Lost 10.925
When I perceiv'd all set on enmity, — Samson 1201
To harbour those that are at enmity. — Vacation 88

Enna
Of *Enna*, where *Proserpin* gathering flours — Par Lost 4.269

Ennobled
Had so enobl'd, as of choice to incurr — Par Lost 9.992
And view him sitting in the house, enobl'd — Samson 1491
Ennobled hath the Buskind stage. — Penseroso 102

Enormous
With his enormous brood, and birthright seis'd — Par Lost 1.511
Wilde above Rule or Art; enormous bliss. — Par Lost 5.297
Wallowing unweildie, enormous in thir Gate — Par Lost 7.411

Enough
Man had not hellish foes anow besides, — Par Lost 2.504
Yet not anough had practisd to deceive — Par Lost 4.124
Anough is left besides to search and know. — Par Lost 7.125
Not proof enough such Object to sustain, — Par Lost 8.535
More then enough; at least on her bestow'd — Par Lost 8.537
Of thy transgressing? not enough severe, — Par Lost 9.1169

Enough(*cont*)
Each other, blam'd enough elsewhere, but strive — Par Lost 10.959
Anough to beare; those now, that were dispenst — Par Lost 11.766
More then anough, that temperance may be tri'd: — Par Lost 11.805
Enough, and more the burden of that fault; — Samson 431
In feeble hearts, propense anough before — Samson 455
And that he durst not plain enough appear'd. — Samson 1256
They had anough reveng'd, having reduc't — Samson 1468
More then anough we know; but while things yet — Samson 1592
Or have I said anough? To him that dares — Mask 780
line not in Bridgewater ms
line not in Trinity ms
1637 'enough'
1673 'anow'
Spir. Back Shepherds, back, anough your play, — Mask 958
Trinity ms 'enough'
Bridgewater ms 'enough'
1637 'enough'
B.M. ms 'enough'
Anow of such as for their bellies sake, — Lycidas 114
Trinity ms 'anough'
1638 'Enough'
With praise enough for Envy to look wan; — Sonnet 13, 6
Trinity ms 'anough'
Ask large enough, and I, *besought*, — Psalm 81, 43

Enrage
Where I reign King, and to enrage thee more, — Par Lost 2.698

Enraged
Evil to others, and enrag'd might see — Par Lost 1.216
His utmost ire? which to the highth enrag'd, — Par Lost 2.95
Of her enraged stepdam *Guendolen*, — Mask 830

Enrich
That doth enrich these Downs, is worth a thought — Mask 505

Enriched
So far renown'd, and with the spoils enricht — Par Reg 4.46

Enroll
When he the Nations doth enrowle — Psalm 87, 23

Enrolled
Left them inrould, or what the Spirit within — Par Lost 12.523
In antient and in modern books enroll'd; — Samson 653
Har. With thee a Man condemn'd, a Slave enrol'd, — Samson 1224
With all his Trophies hung, and Acts enroll'd — Samson 1736

Ensanguined
With Carcasses and Arms th' ensanguind Field — Par Lost 11.654

Enshrine
Equal'd in all thir glories, to inshrine — Par Lost 1.719
When to enshrine his reliques in the Sun's — Par Lost 5.273
Wandring, shall in a glorious Temple enshrine. — Par Lost 12.334

Enshrined
Conceiving, or remote from Heaven, enshrin'd — Par Reg 4.598

Ensign
Th' Imperial Ensign, which full high advanc't — Par Lost 1.536
ms 'ensign'
When the great Ensign of *Messiah* blaz'd — Par Lost 6.775

Ensigns
With scatter'd Arms and Ensigns, till anon — Par Lost 1.325
Under spread Ensigns marching might pass through — Par Lost 2.886
Ten thousand thousand Ensignes high advanc'd, — Par Lost 5.588
And with fierce Ensignes pierc'd the deep array — Par Lost 6.356
Under spred Ensignes moving nigh, in slow — Par Lost 6.533
Lictors and rods the ensigns of thir power, — Par Reg 4.65

Enslave
But rob and spoil, burn, slaughter, and enslave — Par Reg 3.75

Enslaved
To us enslav'd, but custody severe, — Par Lost 2.333
The conquerd also, and enslav'd by Warr — Par Lost 11.797
These thus degenerate, by themselves enslav'd, — Par Reg 4.144
Draws him awry enslav'd — Samson 1041

Ensnare
It would be to ensnare an irreligious — Samson 860
With lickerish baits fit to ensnare a brute? — Mask 700
line not in Bridgewater ms
Them to ensnare they chiefly strive — Psalm 83, 11

Ensnared
Of *Japhet* brought by *Hermes*, she ensnar'd — Par Lost 4.717
Ensnar'd, assaulted, overcome, led bound, — Samson 365
To help insnared chastity; — Mask 909
Bridgewater ms 'ensnared'
Trinity ms 'ensnared'

Ensue
Worse; of worse deeds worse sufferings must ensue. — Par Lost 4.26
They taste and die: what likelier can ensue? — Par Lost 4.527
What doubtful may ensue, more in this place — Par Lost 5.682
Ruin must needs ensue; for what availes — Par Lost 6.456
And Death ensue? then I shall be no more, — Par Lost 9.827
Were it I thought Death menac't would ensue — Par Lost 9.977
And left to her self, if evil thence ensue, — Par Lost 9.1185
And now what further shall ensue, behold. — Par Lost 11.839
But first a long succession must ensue, — Par Lost 12.331

Ensued
Might have ensu'd, nor onely Paradise — Par Lost 4.991
Say Goddess, what ensu'd when *Raphael*, — Par Lost 7.40

Entangled
Entangl'd with a poysnous bosom snake, — Samson 763

Enter
Re-enter Heav'n; or else in some milde Zone — Par Lost 2.397
Shall enter Heaven long absent, and returne, — Par Lost 3.261
No evil thing approach or enter in; — Par Lost 4.563

Enter(*cont*)
Beast, Bird, Insect, or Worm durst enter none; Par Lost 4.704
To enter, and these earthly fruits to taste, Par Lost 5.464
To enter, and his dark suggestions hide Par Lost 9.90
But up and enter now into full bliss. Par Lost 10.503
I suffer them to enter and possess Par Lost 10.623
Then enter into glory, and resume Par Lost 12.456
Now enter, and begin to save mankind. Par Reg 4.635
Me overthrown, to enter lists with God, Samson 463
To thine whose doors my feet shall never enter. Samson 950
Entered
Admiring enter'd, and the work some praise Par Lost 1.731
ms 'enterd'
As now is enterd; yet no purpos'd foe Par Lost 4.373
Enter'd, and foul disorder; all the ground Par Lost 6.388
The Devil enterd, and his brutal sense, Par Lost 9.188
Enterd so faire, should turn aside to tread Par Lost 11.630
Came seavens, and pairs, and enterd in, as taught Par Lost 11.735
He entred now the bordering Desert wild, Par Reg 1.193
To rest at noon, and entr'd soon the shade Par Reg 2.292
Enterd *Judea* seeking mee, who then Samson 252
And as the gates I enter'd with Sun-rise, Samson 1597
Enter'd the very lime-twigs of his spells, Mask 646
Bridgewater ms 'entered'
Poor fleshly Tabernacle entered, Passion 17
Enter'd the world, now bleeds to give us ease; Circum 11
Trinity ms 'enter'd' ← 'entred'
Entering
But with swift wheele reverse, deep entring shar'd Par Lost 6.326
Entring on studious thoughts abstruse, which *Eve* Par Lost 8.40
Least entring on the *Canaanite* allarmd Par Lost 12.217
Now entring his great duel, not of arms, Par Reg 1.174
What conflux issuing forth, or entring in, Par Reg 4.62
Enterprise
And hazard in the Glorious Enterprize, Par Lost 1.89
ms 'enterprize'
Some easier enterprize? There is a place Par Lost 2.345
Deliverance for us all: this enterprize Par Lost 2.465
And management of this main enterprize Par Reg 1.112
Great acts require great means of enterprise, Par Reg 2.412
Of the enterprize so hazardous and high; Par Reg 3.228
As a petty enterprise of small enforce. Samson 1223
Enterprises
Would draw thee forth to perilous enterprises, Samson 804
Enterprisest
Nor shall I to the work thou enterprisest Par Lost 10.270
Enters
Obsequious darkness enters, till her houre Par Lost 6.10
Entertain
Truce to his restless thoughts, and entertain Par Lost 2.526
To entertain you two, her widest Gates, Par Lost 4.382
To entertain our Angel guest, as hee Par Lost 5.328
Stood to entertain her guest from Heav'n; no vaile Par Lost 5.383
To entertain them fair with open Front Par Lost 6.611
There entertain him all the Saints above, Lycidas 178
Trinity ms 'entertaine'
Entertained
So entertaind those odorous sweets the Fiend Par Lost 4.166
Not pleas'd, thus entertaind with solitude, Par Lost 10.105
Had entertaind, as di'd her Cheeks with pale. Par Lost 10.1009
Entertainment
Fit entertainment to receive our King Par Lost 5.690
Enthral
Free Vertue should enthrall to Force or Chance. Par Lost 2.551
Till they enthrall themselves: I else must change Par Lost 3.125
Who oft as undeservedly enthrall Par Lost 12.94
Enthralled
His lapsed powers, though forfeit and enthrall'd Par Lost 3.176
Thy self not free, but to thy self enthrall'd; Par Lost 6.181
Surpriz'd by unjust force, but not enthrall'd, Mask 590
Enthralment
His people from enthralment, they return Par Lost 12.171
Enthroned
Wide on the wasteful Deep; with him Enthron'd Par Lost 2.961
In sight of God enthron'd, our happie state Par Lost 5.536
Amongst the enthron'd gods on Sainted seats. Mask 11
Bridgewater ms 'enthroned'
Entice
Lest the Sorcerer us intice Mask 940
1673 'entice'
Entice the dewy-feather'd Sleep; Penseroso 146
Enticed
Peor his other Name, when he entic'd Par Lost 1.412
Enticement
By sly enticement gives his banefull cup, Mask 525
Enticing
She gave him of that fair enticing Fruit Par Lost 9.996
Against another object more enticing? Samson 559
Entire
Have left us this our spirit and strength intire Par Lost 1.146
Belch'd fire and rowling smoak; the rest entire Par Lost 1.671
Thenceforth, but in thy presence Joy entire. Par Lost 3.265
Unalterably firm his love entire Par Lost 5.502
And all the Sea, from one entire globose Par Lost 5.753
In Cubic Phalanx firm advanc't entire, Par Lost 6.399
Whom to obey is happiness entire. Par Lost 6.741
For such thou art, from sin and blame entire: Par Lost 9.292
Of Man, with strength entire, and free will arm'd, Par Lost 10.9

Entire(*cont*)
A day entire, and Nights due course adjourne, Par Lost 12.264
Entirely
View'd, and behold all was entirely good; Par Lost 7.549
Intirely satisfi'd, Circum 22
Entitle
Who highly thus to entitle me voutsaf'st, Par Lost 11.170
Entombed
For when as each thing bad thou hast entomb'd, On Time 9
Entrails
And fewel'd entrals thence conceiving Fire, Par Lost 1.234
ms 'entrails'
Tore through my entrails, that with fear and pain Par Lost 2.783
In Entrailes, Heart or Head, Liver or Reines; Par Lost 6.346
Entrails unlike) of Mineral and Stone, Par Lost 6.517
And all her entrails tore, disgorging foule Par Lost 6.588
Earth trembl'd from her entrails, as again Par Lost 9.1000
Above the Clouds will pine his entrails gross, Par Lost 12.77
As on entrails, joints, and limbs, Samson 614
Entrance
And wisdome at one entrance quite shut out. Par Lost 3.50
Due entrance he disdaind, and in contempt, Par Lost 4.180
Accessible from Earth, one entrance high; Par Lost 4.546
To question thy bold entrance on this place; Par Lost 4.882
His entrance, and forewarnd the Cherubim Par Lost 9.61
From entrance or Cherubic Watch, by stealth Par Lost 9.68
Into her heart too easie entrance won: Par Lost 9.734
Entrance unseen. Soon as th' unwelcome news Par Lost 10.21
Where entrance up from *Eden* easiest climbes, Par Lost 11.119
More terrible at th' entrance then within. Par Lost 11.470
And rifted Rocks whose entrance leads to hell, Mask 518
Hast gain'd thy entrance, Virgin wise and pure. Sonnet 9, 14
Entranced
His Legions, Angel Forms, who lay intrans't Par Lost 1.301
Sunk down and all his Spirits became intranst: Par Lost 11.420
Holds his dear *Psyche* sweet intranc't Mask 1005
Trinity ms 'entranc't'
line not in Bridgewater ms
Entrap
How honourable, how glorious to entrap Samson 855
Entreat
Lord all the day I thee entreat, Psalm 88, 39
Entrenched
Deep scars of Thunder had intrencht, and care Par Lost 1.601
ms 'intrench't'
Entrusted
And new-entrusted Scepter, but their way Mask 36
Trinity ms 'new entrusted'
Bridgewater ms 'newe entrusted'
Entwined
But further way found none, so thick entwin'd, Par Lost 4.174
Entwining
His Armes clung to his Ribs, his Leggs entwining Par Lost 10.512
Envenomed
With conquest, felt th' envenom'd robe, and tore Par Lost 2.543
Envermeil
That did thy cheek envermeil, thought to kiss Fair Inf 6
Envied
Our envied Sovran, and his Altar breathes Par Lost 2.244
Yet envied; against mee is all thir rage, Par Lost 6.813
Thirst, and refresht; nor envy'd them the grape Samson 551
From them whose sin ye envi'd, not abhor'd, Forcers 4
Envier
To set the envier of his State, the proud Par Lost 6.89
Envies
With *Satan*, hee who envies now thy state, Par Lost 6.900
Hath tasted, envies not, but brings with joy Par Lost 9.770
At this who ever envies or repines Samson 995
Enviest
Of all thy gifts, nor enviest. I now see Par Lost 8.494
Envious
Envious commands, invented with designe Par Lost 4.524
At least our envious Foe hath fail'd, who thought Par Lost 7.139
1669 'invious'
Flew up, nor missd the way, by envious windes Par Lost 11.15
And envious darknes, e're they could return, Mask 194
Trinity ms 'and envious darknesse' ← 'to the soone parting light'
Fly envious *Time*, till thou run out thy race, On Time 1
Environed
Environ'd wins his way; harder beset Par Lost 2.1016
And with dark shades and rocks environ'd round, Par Reg 1.194
Environ'd thee, some howl'd, some yell'd, some shriek'd, Par Reg 4.423
Environs
Condenses, and the cold invirons round, Par Lost 9.636
When strait a barbarous noise environs me Sonnet 12, 3
Envy
Stird up with Envy and Revenge, deceiv'd Par Lost 1.35
ms 'envy'
Here for his envy, will not drive us hence: Par Lost 1.260
Envy from each inferior; but who here Par Lost 2.26
Will envy whom the highest place exposes Par Lost 2.27
The Spirit maligne, but much more envy seis'd Par Lost 3.553
Thrice chang'd with pale, ire, envie and despair, Par Lost 4.115
For envie, yet with jealous leer maligne Par Lost 4.503
Envie them that? can it be sin to know, Par Lost 4.517
Or envie, or what reserve forbids to taste? Par Lost 5.61
With envie against the Son of God, that day Par Lost 5.662

Envy(*cont*)
Took envie, and aspiring to his highth, Par Lost 6.793
Provokes my envie, this new Favorite Par Lost 9.175
Enjoy'd by us excites his envie more; Par Lost 9.264
Of guile, of hate, of envie, of revenge; Par Lost 9.466
Or is it envie, and can envie dwell Par Lost 9.729
Though others envie what they cannot give; Par Lost 9.805
For envie that his Brothers Offering found Par Lost 11.456
With wonder, then with envy fraught and rage Par Reg 1.38
Envy they say excites me, thus to gain Par Reg 1.397
And to despise, or envy, or suspect Samson 272
Envy bid conceal the rest. Arcades 13
Trinity ms 'Envie'
With praise enough for Envy to look wan; Sonnet 13, 6
1648 'Envie'
Filling each mouth with envy, or with praise, Sonnet 15, 2
1694 'Envy'

Envying
Envying our happiness, and of his own Par Lost 9.254
Longing and envying stood, but could not reach. Par Lost 9.593

Enwrap
Enwrap our fancy long, Nativity 134

Ephraim
And how ingrateful *Ephraim* Samson 282
Not less renown'd then in Mount *Ephraim*, Samson 988
In Ephraims view and Benjamins, Psalm 80, 9

Epicurean
Epicurean, and the *Stoic* severe; Par Reg 4.280

Epicycle
Cycle and Epicycle, Orb in Orb: Par Lost 8.84

Epidaurus
In *Epidaurus;* nor to which transformd Par Lost 9.507

Epilepsies
Convulsions, Epilepsies, fierce Catarrhs, Par Lost 11.483

Epirot
The feirce Epeirot and the African bold, Sonnet 17, 4
Trinity ms 'Epeirot' ← 'Epeirote'
1662 '*Epeirot*'
1694 '*Epirote*'

Epithets
Remove their swelling Epithetes thick laid Par Reg 4.343

Equal
United thoughts and counsels, equal hope Par Lost 1.88
ms 'equall'
In equal ruin: into what Pit thou seest Par Lost 1.91
ms 'equall'
His Spear, to equal which the tallest Pine Par Lost 1.292
ms 'equall'
Should favour equal to the Sons of Heaven: Par Lost 1.654
ms 'equall'
Equal in strength, and rather then be less Par Lost 2.47
Black fire and horror shot with equal rage Par Lost 2.67
Our strength is equal, nor the Law unjust Par Lost 2.200
Extoll him equal to the highest in Heav'n: Par Lost 2.479
Equal to God, and equally enjoying Par Lost 3.306
Not equal, as thir sex not equal seemd; Par Lost 4.296
Equal with Gods; aspiring to be such, Par Lost 4.526
Can equal anger infinite provok't. Par Lost 4.916
Equal to ours, throughout the spacious North; Par Lost 5.726
By none, and if not equal all, yet free, Par Lost 5.791
In freedome equal? or can introduce Par Lost 5.797
And equal over equals to let Reigne, Par Lost 5.820
That equal over equals Monarch Reigne: Par Lost 5.832
Equal to him begotten Son, by whom Par Lost 5.835
Who is our equal: then thou shalt behold Par Lost 5.866
Equal in number to that Godless crew Par Lost 6.49
No equal, rauhging through the dire attack Par Lost 6.248
His confidence to equal God in power. Par Lost 6.343
Or equal what between us made the odds, Par Lost 6.441
Equal in their Creation they were form'd, Par Lost 6.690
Equal have I to render thee, Divine Par Lost 8.6
On Man his Equal Love: say therefore on; Par Lost 8.228
1667 'equal'
Second to me or like, equal much less. Par Lost 8.407
Thy equal fear that my firm Faith and Love Par Lost 9.286
And render me more equal, and perhaps, Par Lost 9.823
Thou therefore also taste, that equal Lot Par Lost 9.881
May joyne us, equal Joy, as equal Love; Par Lost 9.882
Superior, or but equal, that to her Par Lost 10.147
Be wanting, but afford thee equal aid, Par Lost 10.271
Equal in Days and Nights, except to those Par Lost 10.680
And equal to reduce me to my dust, Par Lost 10.748
Thought none my equal, now be over-match'd. Par Reg 2.146
Equal in fame to proudest Conquerours. Par Reg 3.99
Of equal dread in flight, or in pursuit; Par Reg 3.306
To equal length back'd with a ridge of hills Par Reg 4.29
Equal to God, oft shames not to prefer, Par Reg 4.303
A spirit and judgment equal or superior, Par Reg 4.324
Yet where an equall poise of hope and fear Mask 410
1673 'equal'
and as your equall raptures temper'd sweet Musick Tr. ms 4.05
'your equall raptures' ← 'your raptures'
By just and equal Lawes. Psalm 82, 12

Equality
Affecting all equality with God, Par Lost 5.763
Pattern of just equalitie perhaps Par Lost 7.487
With fair equalitie, fraternal state, Par Lost 12.26

Equalled
He trusted to have equal'd the most High, Par Lost 1.40
ms 'equalld'
Whom reason hath equald, force hath made supream Par Lost 1.248
From *Egypt* marching, equal'd with one stroke Par Lost 1.488
ms 'equall'd'
Equal'd in all thir glories, to inshrine Par Lost 1.719
1667 catchword 'Equall'd' in some copies
ms 'Equall'd'
Those other two equal'd with me in Fate, Par Lost 3.33
So were I equal'd with them in renown, Par Lost 3.34

Equally
Equal to God, and equally enjoying Par Lost 3.306
But Heav'ns free Love dealt equally to all? Par Lost 4.68
Affects me equally; nor can I like Par Lost 5.97
Equally free; for Orders and Degrees Par Lost 5.792
And pious sorrow, equally enur'd Par Lost 11.362

Equals
Above his equals. Farewel happy Fields Par Lost 1.249
His equals, if in power and splendor less, Par Lost 5.796
And equal over equals to let Reigne, Par Lost 5.820
That equal over equals Monarch Reigne: Par Lost 5.832

Equator
Culminate from th' *Aequator*, as they now Par Lost 3.617

Equinoctial
Hangs in the Clouds, by *Aequinoctial* Winds Par Lost 2.637
With darkness, thrice the Equinoctial Line Par Lost 9.64
Was bid turn Reines from th' Equinoctial Rode Par Lost 10.672

Equipage
Celestial Equipage; and now came forth Par Lost 7.203
His thousands, in what martial equipage Par Reg 3.304
In all her equipage; besides to know Sonnet 17, 9
1662, 1694 'Equipage'

Equity
Till truth were freed, and equity restor'd: Par Reg 1.220

Equivalent
Equivalent or second, which compel'd Par Lost 9.609
Equivalent to Angels walk'd thir streets, Samson 343

Ercoco
Ercoco and the less Maritim Kings Par Lost 11.398

Ere
Rouse and bestir themselves ere well awake. Par Lost 1.334
There went a fame in Heav'n that he ere long Par Lost 1.651
Over the vast abrupt, ere he arrive Par Lost 2.409
Should be, and, by concurring signs, ere now Par Lost 2.831
Ere he drew nigh, his radiant visage turnd, Par Lost 3.646
The Tempter ere th' Accuser of man-kind, Par Lost 4.10
As Man ere long, and this new World shall know. Par Lost 4.113
To morrow ere fresh Morning streak the East Par Lost 4.623
Proud limitarie Cherube, but ere then Par Lost 4.971
Each in thir Chrystal sluce, hee ere they fell Par Lost 5.133
Tell them that by command, ere yet dim Night Par Lost 5.685
That the most High commanding, now ere Night, Par Lost 5.699
Now ere dim Night had disincumberd Heav'n, Par Lost 5.700
And fly, ere evil intercept thy flight. Par Lost 5.871
On the rough edge of battel ere it joyn'd, Par Lost 6.108
Ere this avenging Sword begin thy doome, Par Lost 6.278
Nor long shall be our labour, yet ere dawne, Par Lost 6.492
So all ere day-spring, under conscious Night Par Lost 6.521
Long strugling underneath, ere they could wind Par Lost 6.659
End, and dismiss thee ere the Morning shine. Par Lost 7.108
Easie, e're God had bid the ground be drie, Par Lost 7.304
Plant of the field, which e're it was in the Earth Par Lost 7.335
Where God resides, and ere mid-day arriv'd Par Lost 8.112
Ere my remembrance: now hear mee relate Par Lost 8.204
But long ere our approaching heard within Par Lost 8.242
Ere Sabbath Eev'ning: so we had in charge. Par Lost 8.246
And be so minded still; I, ere thou spak'st, Par Lost 8.444
Bitter ere long back on it self recoiles; Par Lost 9.172
As we need walk, till younger hands ere long Par Lost 9.246
Sated at length, ere long I might perceave Par Lost 9.598
Motion, each act won audience ere the tongue, Par Lost 9.674
Made common and unhallowd ere our taste; Par Lost 9.931
Forbearance no acquittance ere day end. Par Lost 10.53
Meanwhile ere thus was sin'd and judg'd on Earth, Par Lost 10.229
Ere this he had return'd, with fury driv'n Par Lost 10.240
And *Ops*, ere yet *Dictaean Jove* was born. Par Lost 10.584
Through the still Night, not now, as ere man fell, Par Lost 10.846
It lies, yet ere Conception to prevent Par Lost 10.987
Our Limbs benumm'd, ere this diurnal Starr Par Lost 10.1069
Of Paradise could have produc't, ere fall'n Par Lost 11.29
Darkness ere Dayes mid-course, and Morning light Par Lost 11.204
Ere thou from hence depart, know I am sent Par Lost 11.356
(Erelong to swim at large) and laugh; for which Par Lost 11.626
The world erelong a world of tears must weepe. Par Lost 11.627
Abortive, to torment me ere thir being, Par Lost 11.769
Comes down to see thir Citie, ere the Tower Par Lost 12.51
Shall long usurp; ere the third dawning light Par Lost 12.421
E're in the head of Nations he appear Par Reg 1.98
Of his great warfare, e're I send him forth Par Reg 1.158
To such perfection, that e're yet my age Par Reg 1.209
E're I the promis'd Kingdom can attain, Par Reg 1.265
Of *Macedonian Philip* had e're these Par Reg 3.32
Well hath obey'd; just tryal e're I merit Par Reg 3.196
Look once more e're we leave this specular Mount Par Reg 4.236
E're thou of *Israel*'s Scepter get fast hold; Par Reg 4.480
Under his feet: for proof, e're this thou feel'st Par Reg 4.621
Dissolves unjointed e're it reach my ear. Samson 177

Ere*(cont)*
Dagon must stoop, and shall e're long receive Samson 468
E're I to thee, thou to thy self wast cruel. Samson 784
I to my self was false e're thou to me, Samson 824
What sieges girt me round, e're I consented; Samson 846
Har. By *Astaroth* e're long thou shalt lament Samson 1242
Yet e're I give the rains to grief, say first, Samson 1578
Had by him, ere he parted thence, a Son Mask 56
Ere the blabbing Eastern scout, Mask 138
And to my wily trains, I shall e're long Mask 151
Trinity ms 'ere'
Bridgewater ms 'ere'
And envious darknes, e're they could return, Mask 194
Trinity ms 'ere'
Bridgewater ms 'ere'
Ere morrow wake, or the low roosted lark Mask 317
Till fancy had her fill, but ere a close Mask 548
Was took e're she was ware, and wish't she might Mask 558
Trinity ms 'ere'
Bridgewater ms 'ere'
Under the ribs of Death, but O ere long Mask 562
Already, ere my best speed could praevent, Mask 573
Bridgewater ms 'eare'
And I must haste ere morning hour Mask 920
When in one night, ere glimps of morn, Allegro 107
Ere the first Cock his Mattin rings. Allegro 114
And early ere the odorous breath of morn Arcades 56
What ere the skill of lesser gods can show, Arcades 79
For *Lycidas* is dead, dead ere his prime Lycidas 8
Together both, ere the high Lawns appear'd Lycidas 25
Wash far away, where ere thy bones are hurld, Lycidas 155
Or ere the point of dawn, Nativity 86
Which on our dearest Lord did sease er'e long, Passion 10
This day, but O ere long Circum 26
And keep in tune with Heav'n, till God ere long Musick 26
Trinity ms 'e're' ←'ere'
Now timely sing, ere the rude Bird of Hate Sonnet 1, 9
E're half my days, in this dark world and wide, Sonnet 19, 2
Hast smote ere now Psalm 3, 20
Me safe where ere I lie Psalm 4, 40
And glory shall *ere long appear* Psalm 85, 39
E're yet my life be spent, Psalm 88, 54

Erebus
Of *Erebus*. She op'nd, but to shut Par Lost 2.883
Speaks thunder, and the chains of *Erebus* Mask 804
line not in Trinity ms
line not in Bridgewater ms

Erect
Erect the Standard there of *ancient Night;* Par Lost 2.986
Two of far nobler shape erect and tall, Par Lost 4.288
Godlike erect, with native Honour clad Par Lost 4.289
Is rising, who intends to erect his Throne Par Lost 5.725
But what if better counsels might erect Par Lost 5.785
With Sanctitie of Reason, might erect Par Lost 7.508
I by conversing cannot these erect Par Lost 8.432
But bid her well beware, and still erect, Par Lost 9.353
With burnisht Neck of verdant Gold, erect Par Lost 9.501
So goodly and erect, though faultie since, Par Lost 11.509
At last with head erect thus cryed aloud, Samson 1639

Erected
Mammon, the least erected Spirit that fell Par Lost 1.679
Of most erected Spirits, most temper'd pure Par Reg 3.27

Erelong
(Erelong to swim at large) and laugh; for which Par Lost 11.626
The world erelong a world of tears must weepe. Par Lost 11.627

Eremite
Thou Spirit who ledst this glorious Eremite Par Reg 1.8

Eremites
Embryo's and Idiots, Eremits and Friers Par Lost 3.474

Erewhile
As we erewhile, astounded and amaz'd, Par Lost 1.281
ms 'ere while'
And all his Armour staind ere while so bright. Par Lost 6.334
Ere while they fierce were coming, and when wee, Par Lost 6.610
Where obvious dutie erewhile appear'd unsaught: Par Lost 10.106
Erwhile perplext with thoughts what would becom Par Lost 12.275
I Who e're while the happy Garden sung, Par Reg 1.1
With youthful steps? much livelier then e're while Samson 1442
And lay e're while a Holocaust, Samson 1702
Ere-while of Musick, and Ethereal mirth, Passion 1

Err
Err not) another World, the happy seat Par Lost 2.347
Erre not, much less for this to be our Lord, Par Lost 5.799
How few somtimes may know, when thousands err. Par Lost 6.148
To chase me hence? erre not that so shall end Par Lost 6.288
If it presume, might erre in things too high, Par Lost 8.121
Made erre, was now exhal'd, and grosser sleep Par Lost 9.1049
Leads thee, I shall not lag behinde, nor erre Par Lost 10.266
They err who count it glorious to subdue Par Reg 3.71
To worthiest deeds, if he through frailty err, Samson 369
I did not err, there does a sable cloud Mask 223
line not in Bridgewater ms
1637 'erre'
Trinity ms 'erre'
His footsteps cannot err. Psalm 85, 56

Errand
This uncouth errand sole, and one for all Par Lost 2.827
The barrs of Hell, on errand bad no doubt: Par Lost 4.795

Errand*(cont)*
On his bad Errand, Man should be seduc't Par Lost 10.41
His errand on the wicked, who surpris'd Samson 1285
To such my errand is, and but for such, Mask 15
To this my errand, and the care it brought. Mask 506

Errands
Or do his Errands in the gloomy Deep; Par Lost 1.152
ms 'errands'
Bear his swift errands over moist and dry, Par Lost 3.652
On errands of supernal Grace. So sung Par Lost 7.573

Erred
I also err'd in overmuch admiring Par Lost 9.1178
He err'd not, for by this the heav'nly Bands Par Lost 11.208
Have err'd, and by bad Women been deceiv'd; Samson 211

Errest
Apostat, still thou errst, nor end wilt find Par Lost 6.172

Erring
Erring; for he with this rebellious rout Par Lost 1.747
Of erring, from the path of truth remote: Par Lost 6.173
At least to try, and teach the erring Soul Par Reg 1.224
Which erring men call Chance, this I hold firm, Mask 588
Bridgewater ms 'erringe'

Erroneous
Seemd in thy World erroneous to dissent Par Lost 6.146
Erroneous there to wander and forlorne. Par Lost 7.20
Found so erroneous, thence by just event Par Lost 10.969

Error
With mazie error under pendant shades Par Lost 4.239
With Serpent errour wandring, found thir way, Par Lost 7.302
That errour now, which is become my crime, Par Lost 9.1181
By saving Doctrine, and from errour lead Par Reg 2.474
My error was my error, and my crime Par Reg 3.212
Error by his own arms is best evinc't. Par Reg 4.235

Erst
And Powers that earst in Heaven sat on Thrones; Par Lost 1.360
(Certain to be refus'd) what erst they feard; Par Lost 2.470
From mee returnd, as erst thou saidst, from flight, Par Lost 6.187
Where erst was thickest fight, th' Angelic throng, Par Lost 6.308
O foul descent! that I who erst contended Par Lost 9.163
Dimm erst, dilated Spirits, ampler Heart, Par Lost 9.876
Henceforth of God or Angel, earst with joy Par Lost 9.1081
Whereat the heart of *Adam* erst so sad Par Lost 11.868
Or counsel to assist; lest I who erst Par Reg 2.145
As earst in highest, behold him where he lies. Samson 339
Which earst my eyes beheld and yet behold; Samson 1543
Seem'd erst so lavish and profuse, Arcades 9
That erst with Musick, and triumphant song Circum 2

Eruption
Our first eruption, thither or elsewhere: Par Lost 1.656
Least hee incenst at such eruption bold, Par Lost 8.235

Erymanth
Though *Erymanth* your loss deplore, Arcades 100

Erythraean
Of the *Erythraean* main. Psalm 136, 46

Esau
Of Guardians bright, when he from *Esau* fled Par Lost 3.512

Escape
Rather then human. Nor did *Israel* scape Par Lost 1.482
To have built in Heav'n high Towrs; nor did he scape Par Lost 1.749
If thence he scape into whatever world, Par Lost 2.442
Then unknown dangers and as hard escape. Par Lost 2.444
However, and to scape his punishment. Par Lost 4.911
Was known in Heav'n; for what can scape the Eye Par Lost 10.5
Hee fled, not hoping to escape, but shun Par Lost 10.339
Shall scape his punishment ordain'd, and wee Par Lost 10.1039

Escaped
Both glorying to have scap't the *Stygian* flood Par Lost 1.239
Escap't the *Stygian* Pool, though long detain'd Par Lost 3.14
The coming of thir secret foe, and scap'd Par Lost 4.7
Haply so scap'd his mortal snare; for now Par Lost 4.8
Hitherward bent (who could have thought2) escap'd Par Lost 4.794
Com'st thou, escap'd thy prison, and transform'd, Par Lost 4.824
And now returns him from his prison scap't, Par Lost 4.906
Satan from Hell scap't through the darksom Gulf Par Lost 5.225
As one he stood escap't from cruel fight, Par Lost 6.448
Man is not whom to warne: those few escap't Par Lost 11.777
While yet the Patriark liv'd, who scap'd the Flood, Par Lost 12.117

Eshtaol
From *Eshtaol* and *Zora*'s fruitful Vale Samson 181

Espied
Till I espi'd thee, fair indeed and tall, Par Lost 4.477

Espoused
Espoused *Eve* deckt first her nuptial Bed, Par Lost 4.710
My fairest, my espous'd, my latest found, Par Lost 5.18
Methought I saw my late espoused Saint Sonnet 23, 1

Essence
And uncompounded is thir Essence pure, Par Lost 1.425
ms 'essence'
Our purer essence then will overcome Par Lost 2.215
Bright effluence of bright essence increate. Par Lost 3.6
This essence to incarnate and imbrute, Par Lost 9.166
And turns it by degrees to the souls essence, Mask 462
Your fiery essence can distill no tear, Circum 7

Essences
As far as Gods and Heav'nly Essences Par Lost 1.138

Essential
To nothing this essential, happier farr Par Lost 2.97
Essential Powers, nor by his Reign obscur'd, Par Lost 5.841

Establish
But the just establish fast, Psalm 7, 37
Established
Establisht in a safe unenvied Throne Par Lost 2.23
Establisht, such delight hath God in Men Par Lost 12.245
To *David*, stablisht as the dayes of Heav'n. Par Lost 12.347
Estate
In mean estate live moderate, till grown Par Lost 12.351
For him I reckon not in high estate Samson 170
Once more thy face, and know of thy estate, Samson 742
Of wicked men the low estate Psalm 82, 15
Esteem
Gabriel, thou hadst in Heav'n th' esteem of wise, Par Lost 4.886
Then self esteem, grounded on just and right Par Lost 8.572
1667 'self-esteem'
Tempting affronts us with his foul esteem Par Lost 9.328
Of our integritie: his foul esteeme Par Lost 9.329
Though men esteem thee low of Parentage, Par Reg 1.235
For I esteem those names of men so poor Par Reg 2.447
All treasures and all gain esteem as dross, Par Reg 3.29
On what I offer set as high esteem, Par Reg 4.160
Rather more honour left and more esteem; Par Reg 4.207
Black, but such as in esteem, Penseroso 17
Would have been held in high esteem with *Paul* Forcers 10
Esteemed
(Though so esteem'd by shallow ignorance) Mask 514
Unknown, and like esteem'd, and the dull swayn Mask 634
line not in Bridgewater ms
Estotiland
From cold *Estotiland*, and South as farr Par Lost 10.686
Estrange
Thou dost my friends from me estrange, Psalm 88, 33
Estranged
Adam, estrang'd in look and alterd stile, Par Lost 9.1132
Etam
Safe to the rock of *Etham* was retir'd, Samson 253
Eternal
I may assert Eternal Providence, Par Lost 1.25
1667 'th' Eternal', 1668 errata 'th" deleted
ms 'eternal'
Such place Eternal Justice had prepar'd Par Lost 1.70
ms 'eternall'
To wage by force or guile eternal Warr Par Lost 1.121
ms 'eternall'
Strength undiminisht, or eternal being Par Lost 1.154
ms 'eternall'
To undergo eternal punishment? Par Lost 1.155
ms 'eternall'
Eternal spirits; or have ye chos'n this place Par Lost 1.318
Of Heav'n, and from Eternal Splendors flung Par Lost 1.610
ms 'eternal'
His trust was with th' Eternal to be deem'd Par Lost 2.46
Then miserable to have eternal being: Par Lost 2.98
Reserv'd and destin'd to Eternal woe; Par Lost 2.161
To waste Eternal dayes in woe and pain? Par Lost 2.695
Eternal *Anarchie*, amidst the noise Par Lost 2.896
Or of th' Eternal Coeternal beam Par Lost 3.2
I sung of *Chaos* and *Eternal Night*, Par Lost 3.18
Unchangeable, Eternal, which ordain'd Par Lost 3.127
As my Eternal purpose hath decreed: Par Lost 3.172
Th' eternal Regions: lowly reverent Par Lost 3.349
Eternal King; thee Author of all being, Par Lost 3.374
To me alike, it deals eternal woe. Par Lost 4.70
Led on th' Eternal Spring. Not that faire field Par Lost 4.268
Th' Eternal to prevent such horrid fray Par Lost 4.996
In thy eternal course, both when thou climbst, Par Lost 5.173
So spake th' Eternal Father, and fulfilld Par Lost 5.246
Mean while th' Eternal eye, whose sight discernes Par Lost 5.711
Hymning th' Eternal Father: but the shout Par Lost 6.96
Had not th' Eternal King Omnipotent Par Lost 6.227
Of victorie; deeds of eternal fame Par Lost 6.240
Therfore Eternal silence be thir doome. Par Lost 6.385
(And if one day, why not Eternal dayes2) Par Lost 6.424
All doubt of Victorie, eternal might Par Lost 6.630
Down from the verge of Heav'n, Eternal wrauth Par Lost 6.865
His punishment, Eternal miserie; Par Lost 6.904
Thou with Eternal wisdom didst converse, Par Lost 7.9
1669 'eternal'
Of his Eternal Empire, but the more Par Lost 7.96
Eternal Father from his Throne beheld Par Lost 7.137
In Gods Eternal store, to circumscribe Par Lost 7.226
Eternal Father (For where is not hee Par Lost 7.517
To Gods Eternal house direct the way, Par Lost 7.576
The highth and depth of thy Eternal wayes Par Lost 8.413
Eternal Father from his secret Cloud, Par Lost 10.32
Father Eternal, thine is to decree, Par Lost 10.68
To mee, who with eternal Famin pine, Par Lost 10.597
Am found Eternal, and incorporate both, Par Lost 10.816
Safe to eternal Paradise of rest. Par Lost 12.314
To bring forth fruits Joy and eternal Bliss. Par Lost 12.551
So spake the Eternal Father, and all Heaven Par Reg 1.168
Thy Father is the Eternal King, who rules Par Reg 1.236
Heaven open'd her eternal doors, from whence Par Reg 1.281
Nor when, eternal sure, as without end, Par Reg 4.391
Eternal tempest never to be calm'd. Samson 964
To himself and Fathers house eternal fame; Samson 1717
That wise *Minerva* wore, unconquer'd Virgin, Mask 448
Trinity ms 'unconquer'd' ←'unvanquish't' ←'aeternall'

Eternal(*cont*)
It shall be in eternal restless change Mask 596
Trinity ms 'aeternall'
1637 'eternall'
Bridgewater ms 'eternall'
That there eternal Summer dwels, Mask 988
Trinity ms 'eternall' ←'aeternall'
1637 'aeternall'
Bridgewater ms 'eternall'
Make her his eternal Bride, Mask 1008
line not in Bridgewater ms
Trinity ms 'eternall'
1637 'aeternall'
aeternall roses grow & hyacinth Mask Tr. ms 10.07
Wherin the Son of Heav'ns eternal King, Nativity 2
Eternity
Those thoughts that wander through Eternity, Par Lost 2.148
Eternity so spent in worship paid Par Lost 2.248
Dwelt from Eternitie, dwelt then in thee, Par Lost 3.5
(For time, though in Eternitie, appli'd Par Lost 5.580
Through all Eternitie so late to build Par Lost 7.92
1669 'Eternity'
From all Eternitie, for none I know Par Lost 8.406
Eternitie, whose end no eye can reach. Par Lost 12.556
That ope's the Palace of Eternity: Mask 14
Bridgewater ms 'Aeternitie'
1637 'Aeternity'
Trinity ms 'aeternity'
Then long Eternity shall greet our bliss On Time 11
Trinity ms 'Aeternity'
Eternize
Eternize here on Earth; but those elect Par Lost 6.374
This other serv'd but to eternize woe; Par Lost 11.60
Etham
Safe to the rock of *Etham* was retir'd, Samson 253
Ethereal
Hurld headlong flaming from th' Ethereal Skie Par Lost 1.45
ms 'ethereal'
Ethereal temper, massy, large and round, Par Lost 1.285
Sit unpolluted, and th' Ethereal mould Par Lost 2.139
Ethereal Vertues; or these Titles now Par Lost 2.311
Thir soft Ethereal warmth, and there to pine Par Lost 2.601
From your Dominion won, th' Ethereal King Par Lost 2.978
Or hear'st thou rather pure Ethereal stream, Par Lost 3.7
Such I created all th' Ethereal Powers Par Lost 3.100
And this Ethereal quintessence of Heav'n Par Lost 3.716
He speeds, and through the vast Ethereal Skie Par Lost 5.267
Ethereal, and as lowest first the Moon; Par Lost 5.418
Ethereal, as wee, or may at choice Par Lost 5.499
Of this our native Heav'n, Ethereal Sons. Par Lost 5.863
Ethereal Trumpet from on high gan blow: Par Lost 6.60
Pass'd through him, but th' Ethereal substance clos'd Par Lost 6.330
Ethereal, first of things, quintessence pure Par Lost 7.244
Though of Ethereal Mould: then form'd the Moon Par Lost 7.356
Go heavenly Guest, Ethereal Messenger, Par Lost 8.646
Th' ethereal People ran, to hear and know Par Lost 10.27
Thou knewst by name, and all th' ethereal Powers, Par Lost 12.577
1669 'Ethereal'
That all the Angels and Aetherial Powers, Par Reg 1.163
Princes, Heavens antient Sons, Aethereal Thrones, Par Reg 2.121
Aetherial, who all pleasures else despise, Par Reg 3.28
With touch aetherial of Heav'ns fiery rod Samson 549
Ere-while of Musick, and Ethereal mirth, Passion 1
Ethereous
Of this Ethereous mould whereon we stand, Par Lost 6.473
Ethiop
True Paradise under the *Ethiop* Line Par Lost 4.282
Or that Starr'd *Ethiope* Queen that strove Penseroso 19
And Tyre with Ethiops *utmost ends*, Psalm 87, 15
Ethiopian
Through the wide *Ethiopian* to the Cape Par Lost 2.641
Etna
Of thundring *Aetna*, whose combustible Par Lost 1.233
ms 'Etna'
A God, leap'd fondly into *Aetna* flames, Par Lost 3.470
Etrurian
In *Vallombrosa*, where th' *Etrurian* shades Par Lost 1.303
ms 'Etrurian'
Euboic
Into th' *Euboic* Sea. Others more milde, Par Lost 2.546
Euclid
Let *Euclid* rest and *Archimedes* pause, Sonnet 21, 7
Euphrasy
Had bred; then purg'd with Euphrasie and Rue Par Lost 11.414
Euphrates
Of old *Euphrates* to the Brook that parts Par Lost 1.420
ms 'Euphrates'
Him on this side *Euphrates* yet residing, Par Lost 12.114
As far as *Indus* East, *Euphrates* West, Par Reg 3.272
From *Egypt* to *Euphrates* and beyond Par Reg 3.384
Euphrosyne
In Heav'n ycleap'd *Euphrosyne*, Allegro 12
Europe
Bridging his way, *Europe* with *Asia* joyn'd, Par Lost 10.310
On *Europe* thence, and where *Rome* was to sway Par Lost 11.405
Fairfax, whose name in armes through Europe rings Sonnet 15, 1
1694 '*Europe*'
Of which all Europe talks from side to side. Sonnet 22, 12

Europe(*cont*)
1694 '*Europe*'
Eurotas
Young *Hyacinth* born on *Eurota*'s strand Fair Inf 25
Eurus
Eurus and *Zephir* with thir lateral noise, Par Lost 10.705
Eurydice
His half regain'd *Eurydice*. Allegro 150
Eurynome
Ophion with *Eurynome*, the wide- Par Lost 10.581
Evade
Of miserie, so thinking to evade Par Lost 10.1021
Or subtle shifts conviction to evade. Par Reg 4.308
Evaded
Have easily as Spirits evaded swift Par Lost 6.596
Evangelize
To evangelize the Nations, then on all Par Lost 12.499
Evasion
Suffice, or what evasion bear him safe Par Lost 2.411
Evasions
Forc't I absolve: all my evasions vain, Par Lost 10.829
Or by evasions thy crime uncoverst more. Samson 842
Eve
Nor had they yet among the Sons of *Eve* Par Lost 1.364
ms 'Eve'
His Sons, the fairest of her Daughters *Eve*. Par Lost 4.324
To first of women *Eve* thus moving speech, Par Lost 4.409
To whom thus *Eve* repli'd. O thou for whom Par Lost 4.440
Thou following cryd'st aloud, Return faire *Eve;* Par Lost 4.481
When *Adam* thus to *Eve:* Fair Consort, th' hour Par Lost 4.610
To whom thus *Eve* with perfet beauty adornd. Par Lost 4.634
Daughter of God and Man, accomplisht *Eve*, Par Lost 4.660
Espoused *Eve* deckt first her nuptial Bed, Par Lost 4.710
Adam from his fair Spouse, nor *Eve* the Rites Par Lost 4.742
Squat like a Toad, close at the eare of *Eve;* Par Lost 4.800
His wonder was to find unwak'nd *Eve* Par Lost 5.9
Why sleepst thou *Eve?* now is the pleasant time, Par Lost 5.38
Here, happie Creature, fair Angelic *Eve*, Par Lost 5.74
To find this but a dream! Thus *Eve* her Night Par Lost 5.93
And *Eve* within, due at her hour prepar'd Par Lost 5.303
Haste hither *Eve*, and worth thy sight behold Par Lost 5.308
To whom thus *Eve*. *Adam*, earths hallowd mould, Par Lost 5.321
With flourets deck't and fragrant smells; but *Eve* Par Lost 5.379
Long after to blest *Marie*, second *Eve*. Par Lost 5.387
As from the Mine. Mean while at Table *Eve* Par Lost 5.443
Though wandring. He with his consorted *Eve* Par Lost 7.50
Entring on studious thoughts abstruse, which *Eve* Par Lost 8.40
And thy faire *Eve;* Heav'n is for thee too high Par Lost 8.172
And *Eve* first to her Husband thus began. Par Lost 9.204
Sole *Eve*, Associate sole, to me beyond Par Lost 9.227
To whom the Virgin Majestie of *Eve*, Par Lost 9.270
Daughter of God and Man, immortal *Eve*, Par Lost 9.291
And Matrimonial Love; but *Eve*, who thought Par Lost 9.319
So spake the Patriarch of Mankinde, but *Eve* Par Lost 9.376
O much deceav'd, much failing, hapless *Eve*, Par Lost 9.404
Eve separate, he wish'd, but not with hope Par Lost 9.422
Beyond his hope, *Eve* separate he spies, Par Lost 9.424
Imborderd on each Bank, the hand of *Eve:* Par Lost 9.438
This Flourie Plat, the sweet recess of *Eve* Par Lost 9.456
In Serpent, Inmate bad, and toward *Eve* Par Lost 9.495
Curld many a wanton wreath in sight of *Eve*, Par Lost 9.517
The Eye of *Eve* to mark his play; he glad Par Lost 9.528
Into the Heart of *Eve* his words made way, Par Lost 9.550
Empress of this fair World, resplendent *Eve*, Par Lost 9.568
So talk'd the spirited sly Snake; and *Eve* Par Lost 9.613
Lead then, said *Eve*. Hee leading swiftly rowld Par Lost 9.631
Led *Eve* our credulous Mother, to the Tree Par Lost 9.644
To whom thus *Eve* yet sinless. Of the Fruit Par Lost 9.659
The guiltie Serpent, and well might, for *Eve* Par Lost 9.785
And *Adam* wedded to another *Eve*, Par Lost 9.828
Thus *Eve* with Countnance blithe her storie told; Par Lost 9.886
The fatal Trespass don by *Eve*, amaz'd, Par Lost 9.889
From his slack hand the Garland wreath'd for *Eve* Par Lost 9.892
Should God create another *Eve*, and I Par Lost 9.911
Thus in calm mood his Words to *Eve* he turnd. Par Lost 9.920
Bold deed thou hast presum'd, adventrous *Eve*, Par Lost 9.921
So *Adam*, and thus *Eve* to him repli'd. Par Lost 9.960
Eating his fill, nor *Eve* to iterate Par Lost 9.1005
Carnal desire enflaming, hee on *Eve* Par Lost 9.1013
Till *Adam* thus 'gan *Eve* to dalliance move, Par Lost 9.1016
Eve, now I see thou art exact of taste, Par Lost 9.1017
Of *Eve*, whose Eye darted contagious Fire. Par Lost 9.1036
Till *Adam*, though not less then *Eve* abash't, Par Lost 9.1065
O *Eve*, in evil hour thou didst give eare Par Lost 9.1067
Speech intermitted thus to *Eve* renewd. Par Lost 9.1133
To whom soon mov'd with touch of blame thus *Eve*. Par Lost 9.1143
Of mine to thee, ingrateful *Eve*, exprest Par Lost 9.1164
Hee in the Serpent, had perverted *Eve*, Par Lost 10.3
He came, and with him *Eve*, more loth, though first Par Lost 10.109
So having said, he thus to *Eve* in few: Par Lost 10.157
To whom sad *Eve* with shame nigh overwhelm'd, Par Lost 10.159
When *Jesus* son of *Mary* second *Eve*, Par Lost 10.183
Hee after *Eve* seduc't, unminded slunk Par Lost 10.332
By *Eve*, though all unweeting, seconded Par Lost 10.335
Which grew in Paradise, the bait of *Eve* Par Lost 10.551
Encroaching *Eve* perhaps, had first the rule Par Lost 10.582
Whom thus afflicted when sad *Eve* beheld, Par Lost 10.863
He added not, and from her turn'd, but *Eve* Par Lost 10.909

Eve(*cont*)
To whom thus *Eve*, recovering heart, repli'd. Par Lost 10.966
Labouring had rais'd, and thus to *Eve* repli'd. Par Lost 10.1012
Eve, thy contempt of life and pleasure seems Par Lost 10.1013
So spake our Father penitent, nor *Eve* Par Lost 10.1097
The Earth, when *Adam* and first Matron *Eve* Par Lost 11.136
Which thus to *Eve* his welcome words renewd. Par Lost 11.140
Eve, easily may Faith admit, that all Par Lost 11.141
Eve rightly call'd, Mother of all Mankind, Par Lost 11.159
To whom thus *Eve* with sad demeanour meek. Par Lost 11.162
So spake, so wish'd much-humbl'd *Eve*, but Fate Par Lost 11.181
Pursuing, not unmov'd to *Eve* thus spake. Par Lost 11.192
O *Eve*, some furder change awaits us nigh, Par Lost 11.193
Not unperceav'd of *Adam*, who to *Eve*, Par Lost 11.224
Eve, now expect great tidings, which perhaps Par Lost 11.226
That all his senses bound; *Eve*, who unseen Par Lost 11.265
Lament not *Eve*, but patiently resigne Par Lost 11.287
This Hill; let *Eve* (for I have drencht her eyes) Par Lost 11.367
What miserie th' inabstinence of *Eve* Par Lost 11.476
Inductive mainly to the sin of *Eve*. Par Lost 11.519
We may no longer stay: go, waken *Eve;* Par Lost 12.594
Descended, *Adam* to the Bowre where *Eve* Par Lost 12.607
So spake our Mother *Eve*, and *Adam* heard Par Lost 12.624
Since *Adam* and his facil consort *Eve* Par Reg 1.51
Shall be inflicted by the Seed of *Eve* Par Reg 1.54
Of my success with *Eve* in Paradise Par Reg 2.141
Was that crude Apple that diverted *Eve!* Par Reg 2.349
That sleek't his tongue, and won so much on *Eve*, Par Reg 4.5
So little here, nay lost; but *Eve* was *Eve*, Par Reg 4.6
For this attempt bolder then that on *Eve*, Par Reg 4.180
Eve
To Noon he fell, from Noon to dewy Eve, Par Lost 1.743
ms 'eeve'
Watching where Shepherds pen thir Flocks at eeve Par Lost 4.185
To warm him wet return'd from field at Eve, Par Reg 1.318
Her maid'n gentlenes, and oft at Eeve Mask 843
Bridgewater ms 'Eve'
1637 'eve'
Trinity ms 'eve'
Warbl'st at eeve, when all the Woods are still, Sonnet 1, 2
Even
Thir course, in even ballance down they light Par Lost 1.349
Even to that Hill of scandal, by the Grove Par Lost 1.416
From heav'n, for ev'n in heav'n his looks and thoughts Par Lost 1.680
ms 'even'
On even ground against his mortal foe, Par Lost 3.179
Shoots invisible vertue even to the deep: Par Lost 3.586
Even to my mouth of that same fruit held part Par Lost 5.83
All things, ev'n thee, and all the Spirits of Heav'n Par Lost 5.837
Conflicting Fire: long time in eeven scale Par Lost 6.245
Born eevn or high, for this day will pour down, Par Lost 6.544
On her soft Axle, while she paces Eev'n, Par Lost 8.165
Even shame, the last of evils; of the first Par Lost 9.1079
In eevn scale. But fall'n he is, and now Par Lost 10.47
1667 'even' in some copies
Eevn hee who now foretold his fatal bruise, Par Lost 10.191
Ev'n to the Seat of God. For since I saught Par Lost 11.148
To dwell on eeven ground now with thy Sons: Par Lost 11.348
Eevn to the inmost seat of mental sight, Par Lost 11.418
Through many a hard assay even to the death, Par Reg 1.264
Whence eev'n now the tumult of loud Mirth Mask 202
Trinity ms 'even'
1637 'even'
line not in Bridgewater ms
Yea there, where very desolation dwels Mask 428
Trinity ms 'even where'
Bridgewater ms 'even where'
And stole upon the Air, that even Silence Mask 557
Yea even that which mischief meant most harm, Mask 591
Would sit, and hearken even to extasie, Mask 625
In unsuperfluous eeven proportion, Mask 773
1637 'even'
Bridgewater ms 'even'
With eev'n step, and musing gate, Penseroso 38
Emptied his glory, ev'n to nakednes; Circum 20
Trinity ms 'even'
That even to his last breath (ther be that say't) Another 25
line not in 1640, 1657, 1658 texts
It shall be still in strictest measure eev'n, Sonnet 7, 10
Trinity ms 'even'
Ev'n them who kept thy truth so pure of old Sonnet 18, 3
For all my bones, that even with anguish ake, Psalm 6, 5
There ev'n the Sparrow *freed from wrong* Psalm 84, 9
Ev'n *by* thy Altars Lord of Hoasts Psalm 84, 13
Eev'n from the lowest Hell set free Psalm 86, 47
Even
Day, or the sweet approach of Ev'n or Morn, Par Lost 3.42
Thither came *Uriel*, gliding through the Eeven Par Lost 4.555
Witness if I be silent, Morn or Eeven, Par Lost 5.202
In humid exhalations, and at Even Par Lost 5.425
He nam'd. Thus was the first Day Eev'n and Morn: Par Lost 7.252
And Heav'n he nam'd the Firmament: So Eev'n Par Lost 7.274
So Eev'n and Morn recorded the Third Day. Par Lost 7.338
Till Ev'n, nor then the solemn Nightingal Par Lost 7.435
So Ev'n and Morn accomplish'd the Sixt day: Par Lost 7.550
On her soft Axle, while she paces Eev'n, Par Lost 8.165
Of Ewe or Goat dropping with Milk at Eevn, Par Lost 9.582
At Eev'n, which I bred up with tender hand Par Lost 11.276

Even(*cont*)
Food to *Elijah* bringing Even and Morn, Par Reg 2.268
They left me then, when the gray-hooded Eev'n Mask 188
Trinity ms 'ev'n'
line not in Bridgewater ms
1637 'Ev'n'

Evening
At Ev'ning from the top of *Fesole*, Par Lost 1.289
ms 'evening'
Extend his ev'ning beam, the fields revive, Par Lost 2.493
Then in fair Evening Cloud, or humid Bow, Par Lost 4.151
Of Heav'n the Starrs that usher Evening rose: Par Lost 4.355
Leveld his eevning Rayes: it was a Rock Par Lost 4.543
Now came still Eevning on, and Twilight gray Par Lost 4.598
Of grateful Eevning milde, then silent Night Par Lost 4.647
Nor grateful Eevning mild, nor silent Night Par Lost 4.654
1667 'Evening'
By morrow Eevning, and from Land to Land Par Lost 4.662
This Eevning from the Sun's decline arriv'd Par Lost 4.792
Of our last Eevnings talk, in this thy dream, Par Lost 5.115
Oreshades; for these mid-hours, till Eevning rise Par Lost 5.376
Listens delighted. Eevning now approach'd Par Lost 5.627
(For wee have also our Eevning and our Morn, Par Lost 5.628
Or if the Starr of Eevning and the Moon Par Lost 7.104
1669 'Evening'
Both when first Eevning was, and when first Morn. Par Lost 7.260
Glad Eevning and glad Morn crownd the fourth day. Par Lost 7.386
Ev'ning and Morn solemniz'd the Fift day. Par Lost 7.448
With Eevning Harps and Mattin, when God said, Par Lost 7.450
Eev'ning arose in *Eden*, for the Sun Par Lost 7.582
Ere Sabbath Eev'ning: so we had in charge. Par Lost 8.246
Sung Spousal, and bid haste the Eevning Starr Par Lost 8.519
Just then returnd at shut of Evening Flours. Par Lost 9.278
And brown as Evening: Cover me ye Pines, Par Lost 9.1088
The Eevning coole when he from wrauth more coole Par Lost 10.95
And now of love they treat till th' Eevning Star Par Lost 11.588
Gliding meteorous, as Ev'ning Mist Par Lost 12.629
And as an ev'ning Dragon came, Samson 1692
This evening late by then the chewing flocks Mask 540
Bridgewater ms 'eveninge'
When Eev'ning gray doth rise, I fetch my round Arcades 54
1673 'Ev'ning'
Trinity ms 'evening'
Oft till the Star that rose, at Ev'ning, bright Lycidas 30
Trinity ms 'in Evning'
1638 'Oft till the ev'n-starre bright'

Evenly
Not evenly, as thou rul'st Samson 671

Evensong
I woo to hear thy eeven Song; Penseroso 64
1673 'Even-Song'

Even-star
Oft till the Star that rose, at Ev'ning, bright Lycidas 30
1638 'Oft till the ev'n-starre bright'
Trinity ms 'starre that rose' ← 'ev'n starre bright'

Event
Since through experience of this great event Par Lost 1.118
Too well I see and rue the dire event, Par Lost 1.134
Was not inglorious, though th' event was dire, Par Lost 1.624
Th' event is fear'd; should we again provoke Par Lost 2.82
In sad event, when to the unwiser Son Par Lost 4.716
Giv'n me to quell thir pride, and in event Par Lost 5.740
Favour from Heav'n, our witness from th' event. Par Lost 9.334
Of thy presum'd return! event perverse! Par Lost 9.405
Farr otherwise th' event, not Death, but Life Par Lost 9.984
Found so erroneous, thence by just event Par Lost 10.969
Such happy interview and fair event Par Lost 11.593
In the perverse event then I foresaw) Samson 737
So in the sad event too much concern'd. Samson 1551
Of true experience from this great event Samson 1756
Does arbitrate th' event, my nature is Mask 411

Events
In counterpoise, now ponders all events, Par Lost 4.1001
And sayings laid up, portending strange events. Par Reg 2.104
I fear the dred events that dog them both, Mask 405
That far events full wisely could presage, Vacation 70

Ever
By right of Warr, what e're his business be Par Lost 1.150
But ever to do ill our sole delight, Par Lost 1.160
Chain'd on the burning Lake, nor ever thence Par Lost 1.210
He lights, if it were Land that ever burn'd Par Lost 1.228
Where Joy for ever dwells: Hail horrours, hail Par Lost 1.250
Awake, arise, or be for ever fall'n. Par Lost 1.330
For ever now to have thir lot in pain, Par Lost 1.608
As stood like these, could ever know repulse? Par Lost 1.630
Can give it, or will ever? how he can Par Lost 2.153
Of racking whirlwinds, or for ever sunk Par Lost 2.182
We can create, and in what place so e're Par Lost 2.260
Yet ever plotting how the Conqueror least Par Lost 2.338
If thence he scape into whatever world, Par Lost 2.442
1667 'what ever'
1674 'what ever' in some copies
What e're his wrath, which he calls Justice, bids, Par Lost 2.733
I know thee not, nor ever saw till now Par Lost 2.744
These Gates for ever shut, which none can pass Par Lost 2.776
When ever that shall be; so Fate pronounc'd. Par Lost 2.809
Confus'dly, and which thus must ever fight, Par Lost 2.914
Undaunted to meet there what ever power Par Lost 2.955

Ever(*cont*)
Encompass'd shall resound thee ever blest. Par Lost 3.149
Life in my self for ever, by thee I live, Par Lost 3.244
For ever with corruption there to dwell; Par Lost 3.249
I give thee, reign for ever, and assume Par Lost 3.318
Thenceforth shall be for ever shut. Mean while Par Lost 3.333
Harps ever tun'd, that glittering by thir side Par Lost 3.366
Are ever cleer. Whereof hee soon aware, Par Lost 4.119
That ever since in loves imbraces met, Par Lost 4.322
So neer grows Death to Life, what ere Death is, Par Lost 4.425
But let us ever praise him, and extoll Par Lost 4.436
Heav'ns last best gift, my ever new delight, Par Lost 5.19
(Whose praise be ever sung) to man in part Par Lost 5.405
Deserving Paradise! if ever, then, Par Lost 5.446
For ever happie: him who disobeyes Par Lost 5.611
Words which no eare ever to hear in Heav'n Par Lost 5.810
In Heav'n God ever blest, and his Divine Par Lost 6.184
For ever, and in mee all whom thou lov'st: Par Lost 6.733
Her ever during Gates, Harmonious sound Par Lost 7.206
Of Godhead, fixt for ever firm and sure, Par Lost 7.586
What e're I saw. Thou Sun, said I, faire Light, Par Lost 8.273
To find her, or for ever to deplore Par Lost 8.479
Thy condescension, and shall be honour'd ever Par Lost 8.649
Then ever, bountie of this vertuous Tree. Par Lost 9.1033
Mayst ever rest well pleas'd. I go to judge Par Lost 10.71
For ever, and seal up his ravenous Jawes. Par Lost 10.637
By the waters of Life, where ere they sate Par Lost 11.79
And live for ever, dream at least to live Par Lost 11.95
For ever, to remove him I decree, Par Lost 11.96
For ever shall endure; the like shall sing Par Lost 12.324
In sin for ever lost from life; this act Par Lost 12.429
As in his presence, ever to observe Par Lost 12.563
Acknowledge my Redeemer ever blest. Par Lost 12.573
Durst ever, who return'd, and dropt not here Par Reg 1.324
Who ever by consulting at thy shrine Par Reg 1.438
The wisest, unexperienc't, will be ever Par Reg 3.240
Met ever; and to shameful silence brought, Par Reg 4.22
That Evil one, Satan for ever damn'd. Par Reg 4.194
At one spears length. O ever failing trust Samson 348
Of all reproach the most with shame that ever Samson 446
Sam. Where ever fountain or fresh current flow'd Samson 547
The penitent, but ever to forgive, Samson 761
Was not behind, but ever at my ear, Samson 858
Dal. In argument with men a woman ever Samson 903
May ever tend about thee to old age Samson 925
At this who ever envies or repines Samson 995
What e're it be, to wisest men and best Samson 1034
Har. Presume not on thy God, what e're he be, Samson 1156
Whose ear is ever open; and his eye Samson 1172
As on my enemies, where ever chanc'd, Samson 1202
With corporal servitude, that my mind ever Samson 1336
Of Laurel ever green, and branching Palm, Samson 1735
And ever best found in the close. Samson 1748
The vertuous mind, that ever walks attended Mask 211
line not in Bridgewater ms
And the sweet peace that goodnes boosoms ever, Mask 368
Fair silver-shafted Queen for ever chaste, Mask 442
The soothest Shepherd that ere pip't on plains. Mask 823
the scalie-harnest dragon ever keeps Mask Tr. ms 10.09
'dragon ever keeps' ← 'watchfull dragons keep'
In dark *Cimmerian* desert ever dwell. Allegro 10
And ever against eating Cares, Allegro 135
What ere the skill of lesser gods can show, Arcades 79
And wipe the tears for ever from his eyes. Lycidas 181
Of him that ever was, and ay shall last, Psalm 114, 16
Ever faithfull, ever sure. Psalm 136, 4 etc.
Tell me bright Spirit where e're thou hoverest Fair Inf 38
But headlong joy is ever on the wing, Passion 5
With Truth, and Peace, and Love shall ever shine On Time 16
Attir'd with Stars, we shall for ever sit, On Time 21
Peace and quiet ever have; Winchester 48
As ever in my great task Masters eye. Sonnet 7, 14
If ever deed of honour did thee please, Sonnet 8, 3
1673 'ever' follows 'thee'
What ever clime the Suns bright circle warms. Sonnet 8, 8
Follow'd thee up to joy and bliss for ever. Sonnet 14, 8
Up to the Realm of peace & Joy for ever, Sonnet 14, Tr. ms 41.08
Thy firm unshak'n vertue ever brings Sonnet 15, 5
What severs each thou 'hast learnt, which few hav don. Sonnet 17, 11
Jehovahs Law is ever his delight, Psalm 1, 5
Defend'st them, they shall ever sing Psalm 5, 35
That Israels name for ever may Psalm 83, 15
Troubl'd and sham'd for ever, Psalm 83, 62
Ever confounded, and so die Psalm 83, 63
Where thee they ever praise, Psalm 84, 18
For ever angry thus Psalm 85, 18
Thy name for ever more. Psalm 86, 44

Ever-burning
With ever-burning Sulphur unconsum'd: Par Lost 1.69

Ever-during
But cloud in stead, and ever-during dark Par Lost 3.45

Ever-endless
To live with him, and sing in endles morn of light. Musick 28
Trinity ms 'endlesse' ← 'never-parting' ← 'cloudlesse' ← 'endlesse' ← 'uneclipsed' ← 'ever-glorious' ← 'ever-endlesse'

Ever-glorious
To live with him, and sing in endles morn of light. Musick 28
Trinity ms 'endlesse' ← 'never-parting' ← 'cloudlesse'

Ever-glorious(*cont*)
←'endlesse' ←'uneclipsed' ←'ever-glorious' ←'ever-endlesse'

Everlasting
There to converse with everlasting groans, Par Lost 2.184
May hope when everlasting Fate shall yeild Par Lost 2.232
Heav'ns everlasting Frame, while o're the necks Par Lost 3.395
Open, ye everlasting Gates, they sung, Par Lost 7.565
My everlasting Kingdom, why art thou Par Reg 3.199
With everlasting oil, to give due light Mask 199
line not in Bridgewater ms
Trinity ms 'ever lasting'
Forsook the Courts of everlasting Day, Nativity 13
Thou *in thy everlasting Seat* Psalm 86, 35

Everlastingly
Singing everlastingly; Musick 16

Evermore
Who evermore approves and more accepts Samson 510
Sweet rest sease thee evermore, Winchester 50
With Sin *for evermore*. Psalm 84, 40
Thy name for ever more. Psalm 86, 44

Ever-threatening
Starless expos'd, and ever-threatning storms Par Lost 3.425

Every
Forthwith from every Squadron and each Band Par Lost 1.356
From every Band and squared Regiment Par Lost 1.758
Th' intricate wards, and every Bolt and Bar Par Lost 2.877
Youth smil'd Celestial, and to every Limb Par Lost 3.638
Of Birds on every bough; so much the more Par Lost 5.8
With every Plant, in sign of Worship wave. Par Lost 5.194
Within them every lower facultie Par Lost 5.410
Impearls on every leaf and every flouer. Par Lost 5.747
With Regal Scepter, every Soule in Heav'n Par Lost 5.816
Vital in every part, not as frail man Par Lost 6.345
On every side with shaddowing Squadrons Deep, Par Lost 6.554
One Spirit in them rul'd, and every eye Par Lost 6.848
Then Herbs of every leaf, that sudden flour'd Par Lost 7.317
God made, and every Herb, before it grew Par Lost 7.336
Globose, and every magnitude of Starrs, Par Lost 7.357
1667 'everie'
And every Bird of wing after his kinde; Par Lost 7.394
And every creeping thing that creeps the ground. Par Lost 7.523
And every living thing that moves on the Earth. Par Lost 7.534
Numerous, and every Starr perhaps a World Par Lost 7.621
Of every Tree that in the Garden growes Par Lost 8.321
In every gesture dignitie and love. Par Lost 8.489
Consider'd every Creature, which of all Par Lost 9.84
In every Bush and Brake, where hap may finde Par Lost 9.160
Access in every Vertue, in thy sight Par Lost 9.310
Her graceful Innocence, her every Aire Par Lost 9.459
From every Beast, more duteous at her call, Par Lost 9.521
Warm'd by the Sun, producing every kind, Par Lost 9.721
Of grassie Terfe, and pile up every Stone Par Lost 11.324
Land, Sea, and Aire, and every kinde that lives, Par Lost 11.337
Of every Beast, and Bird, and Insect small Par Lost 11.734
1667 'everie'
On every conscience; Laws which none shall finde Par Lost 12.522
And looking round on every side beheld Par Reg 1.295
In every Province, who themselves disdaining Par Reg 1.448
At every sudden slighting quite abasht: Par Reg 2.224
Which every wise and vertuous man attains: Par Reg 2.468
His good communicable to every soul Par Reg 3.125
Thy Vertue, and not every way secure Par Reg 3.348
She all in every part; why was the sight Samson 93
That she might look at will through every pore? Samson 97
In every street, do they not say, how well Samson 204
And arts of every woman false like thee, Samson 749
Sam. Have they not Sword-players, and ev'ry sort Samson 1323
Of every salt Flood, and each ebbing Stream, Mask 19
Bridgewater ms 'everie'
Offring to every weary Travailer, Mask 64
Bridgewater ms 'everie'
At every fall smoothing the Raven doune Mask 251
Forbidding every bleak unkindly Fog Mask 269
Co. I know each lane, and every alley green Mask 311
And every bosky bourn from side to side Mask 313
Bridgewater ms 'everie'
And sweeten'd every muskrose of the dale, Mask 496
And here to every thirsty wanderer, Mask 524
Bridgewater ms 'everie'
And crumble all thy sinews. *Eld. Bro*. Why prethee Shepherd Mask 615
Trinity ms 'all thy' ←'every'
In every vertuous plant and healing herb Mask 621
If every just man that now pines with want Mask 768
And every Shepherd tells his tale Allegro 67
Of every Star that Heav'n doth shew, Penseroso 171
And every Herb that sips the dew; Penseroso 172
Number my ranks, and visit every sprout Arcades 59
And question'd every gust of rugged wings Lycidas 93
And every flower that sad embroidery wears: Lycidas 148
Yet every one shall make him underling, Vacation 76
When every thing that is sincerely good On Time 14
And God is every day offended; Psalm 7, 44
To every neighbour foe, Psalm 80, 26

Eves
On Summer eeves by haunted stream. Allegro 130

Evidence
Illustrious evidence, example high! Par Lost 9.962
Now also evidence, but straight I felt Par Lost 10.361

Evident
And in our Faces evident the signes Par Lost 9.1077

Evil
Out of our evil seek to bring forth good, Par Lost 1.163
ms 'evill'
And out of good still to find means of evil; Par Lost 1.165
ms 'evill'
Evil to others, and enrag'd might see Par Lost 1.216
ms 'Evill'
Nor did they not perceave the evil plight Par Lost 1.335
ms 'evill'
Of *Amrams* Son in *Egypts* evill day Par Lost 1.339
Thrive under evil, and work ease out of pain Par Lost 2.261
Of good and evil much they argu'd then, Par Lost 2.562
Created evil, for evil only good, Par Lost 2.623
Hypocrisie, the onely evil that walks Par Lost 3.683
Evil be thou my Good; by thee at least Par Lost 4.110
No evil thing approach or enter in; Par Lost 4.563
But evil hast not tri'd: and wilt object Par Lost 4.896
This uncouth dream, of evil sprung I fear; Par Lost 5.98
Yet evil whence? in thee can harbour none, Par Lost 5.99
Evil into the mind of God or Man Par Lost 5.117
Have gathered aught of evil or conceald, Par Lost 5.207
And fly, ere evil intercept thy flight. Par Lost 5.871
Author of evil, unknown till thy revolt, Par Lost 6.262
Hence then, and evil go with thee along Par Lost 6.275
Thy ofspring, to the place of evil, Hell, Par Lost 6.276
The strife which thou call'st evil, but wee style Par Lost 6.289
Fled ignominious, to such evil brought Par Lost 6.395
Of evil then so small as easie think Par Lost 6.437
Against unpaind, impassive; from which evil Par Lost 6.455
To hoarce or mute, though fall'n on evil dayes, Par Lost 7.25
On evil dayes though fall'n, and evil tongues; Par Lost 7.26
With such confusion: but the evil soon Par Lost 7.56
Good out of evil to create, in stead Par Lost 7.188
Which tasted works knowledge of Good and Evil, Par Lost 7.543
To manifest the more thy might: his evil Par Lost 7.615
That space the Evil one abstracted stood Par Lost 9.463
From his own evil, and for the time remaind Par Lost 9.464
Which oft, they say, some evil Spirit attends Par Lost 9.638
To happier life, knowledge of Good and Evil; Par Lost 9.697
Of good, how just? of evil, if what is evil Par Lost 9.698
Knowing both Good and Evil as they know. Par Lost 9.709
Knowledge of Good and Evil in this Tree, Par Lost 9.723
Of Knowledge, knowledge both of good and evil; Par Lost 9.752
Under this ignorance of good and Evil, Par Lost 9.774
So saying, her rash hand in evil hour Par Lost 9.780
Of danger tasted, nor to evil unknown Par Lost 9.864
O *Eve*, in evil hour thou didst give eare Par Lost 9.1067
Both Good and Evil, Good lost, and Evil got, Par Lost 9.1072
Of foul concupiscence; whence evil store; Par Lost 9.1078
No evil durst attempt thee, but I rue Par Lost 9.1180
And left to her self, if evil thence ensue, Par Lost 9.1185
O Heav'n! in evil strait this day I stand Par Lost 10.125
The evil on him brought by me, will curse Par Lost 10.734
Which to his evil Conscience represented Par Lost 10.849
Will prove no sudden, but a slow-pac't evill, Par Lost 10.963
To know both Good and Evil, since his taste Par Lost 11.85
His knowledge of Good lost, and Evil got, Par Lost 11.87
Good by it self, and Evil not at all. Par Lost 11.89
However chast'ning, to the evil turne Par Lost 11.373
My part of evil onely, each dayes lot Par Lost 11.765
Him or his Childern, evil he may be sure, Par Lost 11.772
And hee the future evil shall no less Par Lost 11.774
Regardless whether good or evil fame. Par Lost 12.47
That all this good of evil shall produce, Par Lost 12.470
And evil turn to good; more wonderful Par Lost 12.471
Still overcoming evil, and by small Par Lost 12.566
Thir taste no knowledge works, at least of evil, Par Reg 2.371
Rather then aggravate my evil state, Par Reg 3.218
That Evil one, Satan for ever damn'd. Par Reg 4.194
For oft alike, both come to evil end. Samson 704
May expiate (though the fact more evil drew Samson 736
Bid go with evil omen and the brand Samson 967
This evil on the *Philistines* is fall'n, Samson 1523
For evil news rides post, while good news baits. Samson 1538
Lest evil tidings with too rude irruption Samson 1567
Som say no evil thing that walks by night Mask 432
Trinity ms 'evill'
1637 'evill'
Bridgewater ms 'evill'
But evil on it self shall back recoyl, Mask 593
1637 'evill'
Trinity ms 'evill'
Bridgewater ms 'evill'
And from the Boughs brush off the evil dew, Arcades 50
Trinity ms 'evill'
Evil with thee no biding makes Psalm 5, 11
Of evil men the wickedness Psalm 7, 35
As Zeb and Oreb evil sped Psalm 83, 41

Evils
Compose our present evils, with regard Par Lost 2.281
Of evils, and excessive, overturnes Par Lost 6.463
Even shame, the last of evils; of the first Par Lost 9.1079
As in our evils, and of easier choice. Par Lost 10.978
To evils which our own misdeeds have wrought, Par Lost 10.1080
With cause for evils past, yet much more cheer'd Par Lost 12.604
From worst of other evils, pains and wrongs, Samson 105

Evils(*cont*)
How many evils have enclos'd me round; Samson 194
Nothing of all these evils hath befall'n me Samson 374
Hopeless are all my evils, all remediless; Samson 648
From thine, these evils I deserve and more, Samson 1169
To cast the fashion of uncertain evils; Mask 360
line not in Trinity ms
line not in Bridgewater ms
Evince
And therefore was Law given them to evince Par Lost 12.287
Evinced
Error by his own arms is best evinc't. Par Reg 4.235
Ewe
Of Ewe or Goat dropping with Milk at Eevn, Par Lost 9.582
Following, as seem'd, the quest of some stray Ewe, Par Reg 1.315
As a stray'd Ewe, or to pursue the stealth Mask 503
Trinity ms 'ewe'
Ewes
Ewes and thir bleating Lambs over the Plaine, Par Lost 11.649
Amongst their Ews, the little Hills like Lambs. Psalm 114, 12
Exact
For wings, and smallest Lineaments exact Par Lost 7.477
Elaborate, of inward less exact. Par Lost 8.539
Eve, now I see thou art exact of taste, Par Lost 9.1017
The Law of God exact he shall fulfill Par Lost 12.402
And let another hand, not thine, exact Samson 507
The gentler, if severely thou exact not Samson 788
Doth God exact day labour, light deny'd, Sonnet 19, 7
Exactly
Thy wish exactly to thy hearts desire. Par Lost 8.451
Exacts
Exacts our parting hence; and see the Guards, Par Lost 12.590
From us his foes pronounc't glory he exacts. Par Reg 3.120
Exalt
Therefore thy Humiliation shall exalt Par Lost 3.313
To keep them low whom knowledge might exalt Par Lost 4.525
To make us less, bent rather to exalt Par Lost 5.829
But least his heart exalt him in the harme Par Lost 7.150
But throw'st them lower then thou didst exalt them high, Samson 689
Exalt their heads full hie. Psalm 83, 8
Exaltation
To this high exaltation; suddenly Par Lost 5.90
My exaltation, and my whole delight, Par Lost 6.727
My Exaltation to Afflictions high; Par Reg 2.92
My exaltation without change or end. Par Reg 3.197
Exalted
Exalted to such power, and gave to rule, Par Lost 1.736
Satan exalted sat, by merit rais'd Par Lost 2.5
High in the midst exalted as a God Par Lost 6.99
Exalted from so base original, Par Lost 9.150
His Seat at Gods right hand, exalted high Par Lost 12.457
Nigh Thunder-struck, th' exalted man, to whom Par Reg 1.36
They have exalted, and behind them cast Par Reg 2.46
Then *Solomon*, of more exalted mind, Par Reg 2.206
Exalter
Th' exalter of my head I count Psalm 3, 9
Example
By thy example, but have power and right Par Lost 4.881
Nor number, nor example with him wrought Par Lost 5.901
By terrible Example the reward Par Lost 6.910
Adam by dire example to beware Par Lost 7.42
Illustrious evidence, example high! Par Lost 9.962
Beyond all past example and future, Par Lost 10.840
In a dark Age, against example good, Par Lost 11.809
Taught this by his example whom I now Par Lost 12.572
Can raise them, though above example high; Par Reg 1.232
The rarer thy example stands, Samson 166
As I by thee, to Ages an example. Samson 765
By this appears: I gave, thou say'st, th' example, Samson 822
Examples
Sam. Of such examples adde mee to the roul, Samson 290
Exasperate
Is flat despair: we must exasperate Par Lost 2.143
1667 'exasperat' in some copies
Exasperate, exulcerate, and raise Samson 625
So dreaded once, may now exasperate them Samson 1417
Exceed
If thou in strength all mortals dost exceed, Samson 817
Exceeded
Exceeded human, and his wary speech Par Lost 5.459
Exceeding
O glorious trial of exceeding Love, Par Lost 9.961
O more exceeding love or law more just? Circum 15
Just law indeed, but more exceeding love! Circum 16
Excel
Through Heav'n and Earth, so shall my glorie excel, Par Lost 3.133
And inward Faculties, which most excell, Par Lost 8.542
All Horsemen, in which fight they most excel; Par Reg 3.307
Of man or worm; the vilest here excel me, Samson 74
Excelled
Excel'd her power; the Gates wide op'n stood, Par Lost 2.884
How beauty is excelld by manly grace Par Lost 4.490
Of all Gods works, Creature in whom excell'd Par Lost 9.897
And for thee, whose perfection farr excell'd Par Lost 10.150
All mortals I excell'd, and great in hopes Samson 523
Excellence
In power and excellence, but favour'd more Par Lost 2.350
Who dwell in Heav'n, whose excellence he saw Par Lost 5.456

Excellence(*cont*)
Forthwith (behold the excellence, the power Par Lost 6.637
They measure all, of other excellence Par Lost 6.821
Or Bright inferrs not Excellence: the Earth Par Lost 8.91
That excellence thought in thee, and implies, Par Lost 10.1017
In worth and excellence he shall out-go them, Vacation 79
Excellent
Less excellent, as thou thy self perceav'st. Par Lost 8.566
And excellent then what thy minde contemnes; Par Lost 10.1015
What I see excellent in good, or fair, Par Reg 1.381
Excelling
Excelling human, Princely Dignities, Par Lost 1.359
With *Sion*'s songs, to all true tasts excelling, Par Reg 4.347
Excels
When he who most excels in fact of Arms, Par Lost 2.124
In what he counsels and in what excels Par Lost 2.125
When he who rules is worthiest, and excells Par Lost 6.177
Not emulous, nor care who them excells; Par Lost 6.822
As with an object that excels the sense, Par Lost 8.456
Excells his Mother at her mighty Art, Mask 63
Except
Satan except, none higher sat, with grave Par Lost 2.300
Admir'd, not fear'd; God and his Son except, Par Lost 2.678
To tempt or punish mortals, except whom Par Lost 2.1032
Invisible, except to God alone, Par Lost 3.684
Half what in thee is fair, one man except, Par Lost 9.545
Equal in Days and Nights, except to those Par Lost 10.680
One Man except, the onely Son of light Par Lost 11.808
Before the *Parthian;* these two Thrones except, Par Reg 4.85
Excepted
Th' excepted Tree, nor with the Snake conspir'd, Par Lost 11.426
Exception
Or Barbarous, nor exception hath declar'd; Par Reg 3.119
Excess
Who now triumphs, and in th' excess of joy Par Lost 1.123
ms 'excesse'
Less then Arch Angel ruind, and th' excess Par Lost 1.593
The great Work-Maister, leads to no excess Par Lost 3.696
The more it seems excess, that led thee hither Par Lost 3.698
Excess, before th' all bounteous King, who showrd Par Lost 5.640
1667 'Are fill'd'
Fruitless to mee, though Fruit be here to excess, Par Lost 9.648
Bewailing thir excess, all terror hide. Par Lost 11.111
A space, till firmer thoughts restraind excess, Par Lost 11.498
Now heaps upon som few with vast excess, Mask 771
Trinity ms 'excesse'
Bridgewater ms 'excesse'
1637 'excesse'
Of vengeful Justice bore for our excess, Circum 24
Trinity ms 'excesse'
Excessive
Pregnant by thee, and now excessive grown Par Lost 2.779
Dark with excessive bright thy skirts appeer, Par Lost 3.380
Of evils, and excessive, overturnes Par Lost 6.463
Excite
Pain for a while or anguish, and excite Par Lost 2.567
Thir ruine! Hence I will excite thir minds Par Lost 4.522
Excites
Thir specious deeds on earth, which glory excites, Par Lost 2.484
Whose liquid murmur heard new thirst excites, Par Lost 7.68
Enjoy'd by us excites his envie more; Par Lost 9.264
Of mischief, gratulating, thus excites. Par Lost 9.472
Envy they say excites me, thus to gain Par Reg 1.397
Extorts, or pleasure to do ill excites? Par Reg 1.423
That sole excites to high attempts the flame Par Reg 3.26
Exclaimed
Disparted *Chaos* over built exclaimd, Par Lost 10.416
Exclude
And none but such from mercy I exclude. Par Lost 3.202
On purpose, hard thou knowst it to exclude Par Lost 4.584
Excluded
All hope excluded thus, behold in stead Par Lost 4.105
Hath he excluded my resort sometimes. Par Reg 1.367
Contempt, and scorn of all, to be excluded Samson 494
Exclusion
His sad exclusion from the dores of Bliss. Par Lost 3.525
Exclusive
Of membrane, joynt, or limb, exclusive barrs: Par Lost 8.625
Excursion
And opportune excursion we may chance Par Lost 2.396
Farr on excursion toward the Gates of Hell; Par Lost 8.231
Excuse
Then had the Sons of God excuse to have bin Par Lost 5.447
To him she hasted, in her face excuse Par Lost 9.853
That proud excuse? yet him not thy election, Par Lost 10.764
Though to the Tyrant thereby no excuse. Par Lost 12.96
Which to have merited, without excuse, Samson 734
Confess it feign'd, weakness is thy excuse, Samson 829
Philistian gold: if weakness may excuse, Samson 831
Hence with denial vain, and coy excuse, Lycidas 18
Excused
The Tyrants plea, excus'd his devilish deeds. Par Lost 4.394
Execrable
Whence and what art thou, execrable shape, Par Lost 2.681
O execrable Son so to aspire Par Lost 12.64
Execrably
What act more execrably unclean, prophane? Samson 1362

Execration
Shall be the execration; so besides Par Lost 10.737
Execute
Can execute thir aerie purposes, Par Lost 1.430
At thee ordain'd his drudge, to execute Par Lost 2.732
To execute fierce vengeance on his foes, Par Lost 3.399
His hand to execute what his Decree Par Lost 10.772
Executes
Swift as the lightning glance he executes Samson 1284
Execution
Of tardie execution, since denounc't Par Lost 10.853
Or th' execution leave to high disposal, Samson 506
Exempt
Beyond his Potent arm, to live exempt Par Lost 2.318
No voice exempt, no voice but well could joine Par Lost 3.370
Foe not informidable, exempt from wound, Par Lost 9.486
So snatcht will not exempt us from the paine Par Lost 10.1025
And for his Makers Image sake exempt? Par Lost 11.514
Exempt from Death; to shew thee what reward Par Lost 11.709
Buried, yet not exempt Samson 103
And hath full right to exempt Samson 310
Exempt from many a care and chance to which Samson 918
Exemption
Wise or unwise, no difference, no exemption; Par Reg 3.115
Exempts
Thy worth and skill exempts thee from the throng, Sonnet 13, 5
Exercise
Must exercise us without hope of end Par Lost 2.89
Dominion exercise and in the Aire, Par Lost 10.400
But mortal doom'd. How can he exercise Par Lost 10.796
That cruel Serpent: On me exercise not Par Lost 10.927
To exercise him in the Wilderness, Par Reg 1.156
There exercise all his fierce accidents, Samson 612
But patience is more oft the exercise Samson 1287
Exercised
About him exercis'd Heroic Games Par Lost 4.551
Exhalation
Rose like an Exhalation, with the sound Par Lost 1.711
ms 'exhalation'
Vapour, and Mist, and Exhalation hot, Par Lost 10.694
Vapour, and Exhalation dusk and moist, Par Lost 11.741
Exhalations
Ye Mists and Exhalations that now rise Par Lost 5.185
In humid exhalations, and at Even Par Lost 5.425
Exhale
Nor doth the Moon no nourishment exhale Par Lost 5.421
Exhaled
Now when ambrosial Night with Clouds exhal'd Par Lost 5.642
Made erre, was now exhal'd, and grosser sleep Par Lost 9.1049
Exhaling
Exhaling first from Darkness they beheld; Par Lost 7.255
Exhausted
Exhausted, spiritless, afflicted, fall'n. Par Lost 6.852
Peeling thir Provinces, exhausted all Par Reg 4.136
Exhilarating
That with exhilerating vapour bland Par Lost 9.1047
Exhorting
Designing or exhorting glorious warr, Par Lost 2.179
Exile
That all these puissant Legions, whose exile Par Lost 1.632
Exile, or ignominy, or bonds, or pain, Par Lost 2.207
Plac't in a Paradise, by our exile Par Lost 10.484
Exiled
Of us out-cast, exil'd, his new delight, Par Lost 4.106
Then had I not been thus exil'd from light; Samson 98
Exorbitant
By sin to foul exorbitant desires; Par Lost 3.177
Expanded
Then with expanded wings he stears his flight Par Lost 1.225
Expanse
Into the wilde expanse, and through the shock Par Lost 2.1014
Pure as th' expanse of Heav'n; I thither went Par Lost 4.456
The Firmament, expanse of liquid, pure, Par Lost 7.264
High in th' expanse of Heaven to divide Par Lost 7.340
Expatiate
New rub'd with Baum, expatiate and confer Par Lost 1.774
Expect
Farr heavier load thy self expect to feel Par Lost 4.972
Distinguish not: for soon expect to feel Par Lost 5.892
Yet Chains in Hell, not Realms expect: mean while Par Lost 6.186
The willinger I goe, nor much expect Par Lost 9.382
Eve, now expect great tidings, which perhaps Par Lost 11.226
Expect to hear, supernal Grace contending Par Lost 11.359
Expect with mortal paine: say where and when Par Lost 12.384
By mee encampt on yonder Hill, expect Par Lost 12.591
Freely; of whom what could he less expect Par Reg 3.126
And more blasphemous? which expect to rue. Par Reg 4.181
Expect another message more imperious, Samson 1352
Happ'n what may, of me expect to hear Samson 1423
Of so much fame in Heav'n expect thy meed. Lycidas 84
Expectance
Expectance calls thee now another way, Vacation 54
Expectation
This said, he sat; and expectation held Par Lost 2.417
Blaz'd opposite, while expectation stood Par Lost 6.306
Or fansied so, through expectation high Par Lost 9.789
Sublime with expectation when to see Par Lost 10.536
With cruel expectation. Yet one doubt Par Lost 10.782

Expectation(*cont*)
Why our great expectation should be call'd Par Lost 12.378
Our expectation? God of *Israel*, Par Reg 2.42
If there be worse, the expectation more Par Reg 3.207
Expected
Expected, least of all from thee, ingrate Par Lost 5.811
May tempt it, I expected not to hear. Par Lost 9.281
Without wrauth or reviling; wee expected Par Lost 10.1048
Expected of our Fathers; we have heard Par Reg 2.33
Expecting
Round thir Metropolis, and now expecting Par Lost 10.439
So having said, a while he stood, expecting Par Lost 10.504
Suffering, abstaining, quietly expecting Par Reg 3.192
Expedite
To expedite your glorious march; but I Par Lost 10.474
Expedition
With dangerous expedition to invade Par Lost 2.342
With furious expedition; for they weend Par Lost 6.86
On his great Expedition now appeer'd, Par Lost 7.193
The dismal expedition to find out Par Reg 1.101
With winged expedition Samson 1283
Expel
Incapable of stain would soon expel Par Lost 2.140
Might'st thou expel this monster from his Throne Par Reg 4.100
How gloriously; I shall, thou say'st, expel Par Reg 4.127
Expel a Devil who first made him such? Par Reg 4.129
Expelled
Thus trampl'd, thus expell'd to suffer here Par Lost 2.195
All usurpation thence expell'd, reduce Par Lost 2.983
Shalt loose, expell'd from hence into a World Par Lost 8.332
Experience
Since through experience of this great event Par Lost 1.118
Yet by experience taught we know how good, Par Lost 5.826
Till warn'd, or by experience taught, she learne, Par Lost 8.190
Thus grown. Experience, next to thee I owe, Par Lost 9.807
On my experience, *Adam*, freely taste, Par Lost 9.988
Best school of best experience, quickest in sight Par Reg 3.238
Now of my own experience, not by talk, Samson 188
But warn'd by oft experience: did not she Samson 382
Of true experience from this great event Samson 1756
Till old experience do attain Penseroso 173
Experienced
Darts his experienc't eye, and soon traverse Par Lost 1.568
ms 'experienc'd'
Experiment
Adam, by sad experiment I know Par Lost 10.967
Expert
Each Warriour single as in Chief, expert Par Lost 6.233
Expert in amorous Arts, enchanting tongues Par Reg 2.158
What Pilot so expert but needs must wreck Samson 1044
Expiate
To expiate his Treason hath naught left, Par Lost 3.207
And expiate, if possible, my crime, Samson 490
May expiate (though the fact more evil drew Samson 736
Expiations
Save by those shadowie expiations weak, Par Lost 12.291
Expire
We should be quite abolisht and expire. Par Lost 2.93
As ready to expire, Psalm 88, 62
Expired
But I endure the time, till which expir'd, Par Reg 4.174
Not yet expir'd) and to the Wilderness Par Reg 4.395
Throttl'd at length in the Air, expir'd and fell; Par Reg 4.568
Explain
Man. Wearied with slaughter then or how? explain. Samson 1583
Explained
By Haralds voice explain'd: the hollow Abyss Par Lost 2.518
Exploded
Exploded and had seiz'd with violent hands, Par Lost 11.669
Exploding
Turnd to exploding hiss, triumph to shame Par Lost 10.546
Exploit
For dignity compos'd and high exploit: Par Lost 2.111
With many a vain exploit, though then renownd: Par Lost 3.465
Through Sin to Death expos'd by my exploit. Par Lost 10.407
And ruine *Adam*, and the exploit perform'd Par Reg 1.102
Exploits
To human sense th' invisible exploits Par Lost 5.565
And great exploits, but of true vertu void; Par Lost 11.790
Design'd for great exploits; if I must dye Samson 32
Of birth from Heav'n foretold and high exploits, Samson 525
With all those high exploits by him atchiev'd, Samson 1492
Explore
With purpose to explore or to disturb Par Lost 2.971
What wee, not to explore the secrets aske Par Lost 7.95
Explores
Explores his solitary flight; som times Par Lost 2.632
And thus his own undaunted heart explores. Par Lost 6.113
Expose
My self expose, with lonely steps to tread Par Lost 2.828
I should conceal, and not expose to blame Par Lost 10.130
God, as to leave them, and expose thir Land, Par Lost 12.339
And high prediction, henceforth I expose Par Reg 1.142
Exposed
Expos'd a Matron to avoid worse rape. Par Lost 1.505
1667 'Yielded thir Matrons'
In his own strength, this place may lye expos'd Par Lost 2.360
Starless expos'd, and ever-threatning storms Par Lost 3.425

Exposed(*cont*)
To all delight of human sense expos'd Par Lost 4.206
And *Eden* were no *Eden* thus expos'd. Par Lost 9.341
Through Sin to Death expos'd by my exploit. Par Lost 10.407
To me committed and by me expos'd. Par Lost 10.957
Thence to the bait of Women lay expos'd; Par Reg 2.204
Of fighting beasts, and men to beasts expos'd, Par Reg 4.140
They creep, yet see, I dark in light expos'd Samson 75
Exposes
Will envy whom the highest place exposes Par Lost 2.27
Eye-sight exposes daily men abroad. Samson 919
Express
Nor fail'd they to express how much they prais'd, Par Lost 2.480
May I express thee unblam'd? since God is light, Par Lost 3.3
As may express them best, though what if Earth Par Lost 5.574
Express, and thou becam'st a living Soul. Par Lost 7.528
Express they, by looks onely, or do they mix Par Lost 8.616
Against a Foe by doom express assign'd us, Par Lost 10.926
Express, and of his steps the track Divine. Par Lost 11.354
By matchless Deeds express thy matchless Sire. Par Reg 1.233
Nature asham'd, or better to express, Par Reg 2.332
Th' express resemblance of the gods, is chang'd Mask 69
Trinity ms 'expresse'
1637 'expresse'
Bridgewater ms 'expresse'
Expressed
Substantially express'd, and in his face Par Lost 3.140
Shon full, he all his Father full exprest Par Lost 6.720
By Tongue of Brute, and human sense exprest? Par Lost 9.554
Of mine to thee, ingrateful *Eve*, exprest Par Lost 9.1164
Express'd, and thus divinely answer'd milde. Par Lost 10.67
The bent of Nature; which he thus express'd. Par Lost 11.597
Unless where moral vertue is express't Par Reg 4.351
Less then half we find exprest, Arcades 12
Trinity ms 'express't'
Expressing
Expressing well the spirit within thee free, Par Lost 8.440
His Image who made both, and less expressing Par Lost 8.544
Habit, or state, or motion, still expressing Par Reg 4.601
Expression
The place he found beyond expression bright, Par Lost 3.591
His gentle dumb expression turnd at length Par Lost 9.527
Expressly
To do what God expresly hath forbid, Par Lost 9.356
Him whom they heard so late expresly call'd Par Reg 2.3
Which was expresly giv'n thee to annoy them? Samson 578
Expulsion
Sole Victor from th' expulsion of his Foes Par Lost 6.880
Threat'ns then our expulsion down to Hell; Par Reg 2.128
Expunged
Of Natures works to mee expung'd and ras'd, Par Lost 3.49
Exquisite
Eld. Bro. Peace brother, be not over-exquisite Mask 359
line not in Bridgewater ms
1637 'over exquisite'
line not in Trinity ms
Exquisitest
And exquisitest name, for which was drain'd Par Reg 2.346
Extend
By our revolt, but over Hell extend Par Lost 2.326
Extend his ev'ning beam, the fields revive, Par Lost 2.493
Disperst in Bands and Files thir Camp extend Par Lost 5.651
And said, thus farr extend, thus farr thy bounds, Par Lost 7.230
Satisfi'd never; that were to extend Par Lost 10.804
When to extend his fame through Heaven and Earth, Par Reg 3.65
By wisdom; as thy Empire must extend, Par Reg 4.222
So let extend thy mind o're all the world, Par Reg 4.223
Wilt thou thy frowning ire extend Psalm 85, 19
Extended
Prone on the Flood, extended long and large Par Lost 1.195
That with extended wings a Bannerd Host Par Lost 2.885
Farr off th' Empyreal Heav'n, extended wide Par Lost 2.1047
Of Nights extended shade; from Eastern Point Par Lost 3.557
his farre-extended armes till with steepe fall Mask Tr. ms 10.13
Extends
Is Center, yet extends to all, so thou Par Lost 9.108
Moses once more his potent Rod extends Par Lost 12.211
Extent
Of huge extent somtimes, with brazen Eyes Par Lost 7.496
Not to th' extent of thir own Spheare. But say Par Lost 10.808
To just extent over all *Israel*'s Sons; Par Reg 3.406
Extenuate
Who can extenuate thee? Next, to the Son, Par Lost 10.645
To lessen or extenuate my offence, Samson 767
Exterior
Alone, without exterior help sustaind? Par Lost 9.336
External
Her office holds; of all external things, Par Lost 5.103
Extinct
Though all our Glory extinct, and happy state Par Lost 1.141
Shall live with her enjoying, I extinct; Par Lost 9.829
Light the prime work of God to me is extinct, Samson 70
Extinguish
Her old possession, and extinguish life Par Lost 4.666
Extinguished
Despis'd and thought extinguish't quite, Samson 1688
Extol
Extoll him equal to the highest in Heav'n: Par Lost 2.479

Extol(*cont*)
For which both Heav'n and Earth shall high extoll Par Lost 3.146
But let us ever praise him, and extoll Par Lost 4.436
To fill the Earth, who shall with us extoll Par Lost 4.733
On Earth joyn all ye Creatures to extoll Par Lost 5.164
Extol not Riches then, the toyl of Fools, Par Reg 2.453
A miscellaneous rabble, who extol Par Reg 3.50
Extolled
Thee only extoll'd, Son of thy Fathers might, Par Lost 3.398
1667 'extold'
And what delight to be by such extoll'd, Par Reg 3.54
Extollest
Thir Orators thou then extoll'st, as those Par Reg 4.353
Extolling
Extolling Patience as the truest fortitude; Samson 654
Extort
Extort from me. To bow and sue for grace Par Lost 1.111
Extorts
Extorts, or pleasure to do ill excites? Par Reg 1.423
Extracted
Extracted; for this cause he shall forgoe Par Lost 8.497
Extracting
Sits on the Bloom extracting liquid sweet. Par Lost 5.25
Extraordinary
To something extraordinary my thoughts. Samson 1383
Extravagant
Somwhat extravagant and wilde, perhaps Par Lost 6.616
Extreme
Joyn'd with extream contempt? I will not come. Samson 1342
Not any boast of skill, but extreme shift Mask 273
Bridgewater ms 'extreame'
1637 'extreame'
Extremes
In worst extreams, and on the perilous edge Par Lost 1.276
Of fierce extreams, extreams by change more fierce, Par Lost 2.599
Of *Chaos* farr remov'd, least fierce extreames Par Lost 7.272
Tending to some relief of our extremes, Par Lost 10.976
Extremity
Till now that this extremity compell'd, Mask 643
Bridgewater ms 'extremitie'
Exulcerate
Exasperate, exulcerate, and raise Samson 625
Eye
His eye survay'd the dark Idolatries Par Lost 1.456
Darts his experienc't eye, and soon traverse Par Lost 1.568
Waiting revenge: cruel his eye, but cast Par Lost 1.604
With him, or who deceive his mind, whose eye Par Lost 2.189
Now in thine eye so foul, once deemd so fair Par Lost 2.748
High Thron'd above all highth, bent down his eye, Par Lost 3.58
Mine ear shall not be slow, mine eye not shut. Par Lost 3.193
Pass'd frequent, and his eye with choice regard Par Lost 3.534
Which to his eye discovers unaware Par Lost 3.547
Allur'd his eye: Thither his course he bends Par Lost 3.573
That from his Lordly eye keep distance due, Par Lost 3.578
Undazl'd, farr and wide his eye commands, Par Lost 3.614
Like honour to obtain, and as his Eye Par Lost 3.660
Him counterfet, if any eye beheld. Par Lost 4.117
Uriel once warnd; whose eye pursu'd him down Par Lost 4.125
Young *Bacchus* from his Stepdame *Rhea*'s eye; Par Lost 4.279
His fair large Front and Eye sublime declar'd Par Lost 4.300
Mine eye pursu'd him still, but under shade Par Lost 4.572
Such whispering wak'd her, but with startl'd eye Par Lost 5.26
From either eye, and wip'd them with her haire; Par Lost 5.131
Thou Sun, of this great World both Eye and Soule, Par Lost 5.171
Mean while th' Eternal eye, whose sight discernes Par Lost 5.711
Whom the grand foe with scornful eye askance Par Lost 6.149
All Heart they live, all Head, all Eye, all Eare, Par Lost 6.350
Whose Eye so superficially surveyes Par Lost 6.476
One Spirit in them rul'd, and every eye Par Lost 6.848
Eye witnesses of his Almightie Acts, Par Lost 6.883
Load'n with fairest Fruit that hung to the Eye Par Lost 8.307
Grace was in all her steps, Heav'n in her Eye, Par Lost 8.488
Her long with ardent look his Eye pursu'd Par Lost 9.397
To lure her Eye; shee busied heard the sound Par Lost 9.518
The Eye of *Eve* to mark his play; he glad Par Lost 9.528
Sollicited her longing eye; yet first Par Lost 9.743
Fair to the Eye, inviting to the Taste, Par Lost 9.777
Had it been onely coveting to Eye Par Lost 9.923
Of *Eve*, whose Eye darted contagious Fire. Par Lost 9.1036
Was known in Heav'n; for what can scape the Eye Par Lost 10.5
Adam observ'd, and with his Eye the chase Par Lost 11.191
And carnal fear that day dimm'd *Adams* eye. Par Lost 11.212
His Eye might there command wherever stood Par Lost 11.385
Turchestan-born; nor could his eye not ken Par Lost 11.396
To dress, and troule the Tongue, and roule the Eye. Par Lost 11.620
Eternitie, whose end no eye can reach. Par Lost 12.556
He saw approach, who first with curious eye Par Reg 1.319
Set women in his eye and in his walk, Par Reg 2.153
On whom his leisure will vouchsafe an eye Par Reg 2.210
And to a Superstitious eye the haunt Par Reg 2.296
Turning with easie eye thou may'st behold. Par Reg 3.293
Thence to the gates cast round thine eye, and see Par Reg 4.61
More then of arms before, allure mine eye, Par Reg 4.112
When slipping from thy Mothers eye thou went'st Par Reg 4.216
Athens the eye of *Greece*, Mother of Arts Par Reg 4.240
From that time seldom have I ceas'd to eye Par Reg 4.507
To such a tender ball as th' eye confin'd? Samson 94
Mine eie to harbour sleep, or thoughts to rest. Samson 459

Eye(*cont*)
Under his special eie   Samson 636
Unseemly falls in human eie,   Samson 690
Whose ear is ever open; and his eye   Samson 1172
Which without help of eye, might be assay'd,   Samson 1625
Of power to cheat the eye with blear illusion,   Mask 155
And hugg him into snares. When once her eye   Mask 164
Eie me blest Providence, and square my triall   Mask 329
Bridgewater ms 'Eye'
1637 'Eye'
Trinity ms 'eye'
Of dragon watch with uninchanted eye,   Mask 395
Where day never shuts his eye,   Mask 978
B.M. ms 'Eye'
his uninchanted eye, & round the verge   Mask Tr. ms 10.10
Streit mine eye hath caught new pleasures   Allegro 69
Where no profaner eye may look,   Penseroso 140
Hide me from Day's garish eie,   Penseroso 141
And Kings sate still with awfull eye,   Nativity 59
He hath with a piteous eye   Psalm 136, 77
Above the reach of mortall ey.   Psalm 136, 94
1673 'eye'
Mine eye hath found that sad Sepulchral rock   Passion 43
Thy liquid notes that close the eye of Day,   Sonnet 1, 5
As ever in my great task Masters eye.   Sonnet 7, 14
My Bed I water with my tears; mine Eie   Psalm 6, 13
Mine eye grows dim and dead,   Psalm 88, 38

Eyed
Ey'd them askance, and to himself thus plaind.   Par Lost 4.504
Drie-ey'd behold? *Adam* could not, but wept,   Par Lost 11.495
The Men though grave, ey'd them, and let thir eyes   Par Lost 11.585
O welcom pure-ey'd Faith, white-handed Hope,   Mask 213
Trinity ms 'pure-eyd'
line not in Bridgewater ms
Sent down the meek-eyd Peace,   Nativity 46
1673 'meek-ey'd'
Inspire's the pale-ey'd Priest from the prophetic cell.   Nativity 180
May tell at length how green-ey'd *Neptune* raves,   Vacation 43

Eyeless
Eyeless in *Gaza* at the Mill with slaves,   Samson 41

Eyelids
Our eye-lids; other Creatures all day long   Par Lost 4.616
Thy eye-lids? and remembrest what Decree   Par Lost 5.674
Softly on my eye-lids laid.   Penseroso 150
Under the opening eye-lids of the morn,   Lycidas 26
Trinity ms 'eyelids'

Eyes
Torments him; round he throws his baleful eyes   Par Lost 1.56
With Head up-lift above the wave, and Eyes   Par Lost 1.193
ms 'eys'
Of new Subjection; with what eyes could we   Par Lost 2.239
Sparkl'd in all thir eyes; with full assent   Par Lost 2.388
With shuddring horror pale, and eyes agast   Par Lost 2.616
Surpris'd thee, dim thine eyes, and dizzie swumm   Par Lost 2.753
Before mine eyes in opposition sits   Par Lost 2.803
Before thir eyes in sudden view appear   Par Lost 2.890
Revisit'st not these eyes, that rowle in vain   Par Lost 3.23
Irradiate, there plant eyes, all mist from thence   Par Lost 3.53
Approach not, but with both wings veil thir eyes.   Par Lost 3.382
Stand ready at command, and are his Eyes   Par Lost 3.650
To witness with thine eyes what some perhaps   Par Lost 3.700
O Hell! what doe mine eyes with grief behold,   Par Lost 4.358
Mine eyes till now, and pin'd with vain desire,   Par Lost 4.466
So spake our general Mother, and with eyes   Par Lost 4.492
This glorious sight, when sleep hath shut all eyes?   Par Lost 4.658
If none regard; Heav'n wakes with all his eyes,   Par Lost 5.44
All but the unsleeping eyes of God to rest,   Par Lost 5.647
Which to our eyes discoverd new and strange,   Par Lost 6.571
And Wings were set with Eyes, with Eyes the wheels   Par Lost 6.755
Distinct with eyes, and from the living Wheels   Par Lost 6.846
Distinct alike with multitude of eyes,   Par Lost 6.847
Yet scarce allay'd still eyes the current streame,   Par Lost 7.67
Of Rainbows and Starrie Eyes. The Waters thus   Par Lost 7.446
Of huge extent somtimes, with brazen Eyes   Par Lost 7.496
Descends, thither with heart and voice and eyes   Par Lost 7.513
Into all Eyes to wish her still in sight.   Par Lost 8.63
Strait toward Heav'n my wondring Eyes I turnd,   Par Lost 8.257
Before mine Eyes all real, as the dream   Par Lost 8.310
By Nature as in aide, and clos'd mine eyes.   Par Lost 8.459
Mine eyes he clos'd, but op'n left the Cell   Par Lost 8.460
Crested aloft, and Carbuncle his Eyes;   Par Lost 9.500
Ye Eate thereof, your Eyes that seem so cleere,   Par Lost 9.706
To open Eyes, and make them Gods who taste;   Par Lost 9.866
Th' effects to correspond, opener mine Eyes,   Par Lost 9.875
Augmented, op'nd Eyes, new Hopes, new Joyes,   Par Lost 9.985
Began to cast lascivious Eyes, she him   Par Lost 9.1014
Soon found thir Eyes how op'nd, and thir minds   Par Lost 9.1053
False in our promis'd Rising; since our Eyes   Par Lost 9.1070
Raind at thir Eyes, but high Winds worse within   Par Lost 9.1122
Thir earnest eyes they fix'd, imagining   Par Lost 10.553
Spangl'd with eyes more numerous then those   Par Lost 11.130
Familiar to our eyes, all places else   Par Lost 11.305
This Hill; let *Eve* (for I have drencht her eyes)   Par Lost 11.367
Michael from *Adams* eyes the Filme remov'd   Par Lost 11.412
That *Adam* now enforc't to close his eyes,   Par Lost 11.419
Adam, now ope thine eyes, and first behold   Par Lost 11.423
His eyes he op'nd, and beheld a field,   Par Lost 11.429
Before his eyes appeard, sad, noysom, dark,   Par Lost 11.478

Eyes(*cont*)
The Men though grave, ey'd them, and let thir eyes   Par Lost 11.585
True opener of mine eyes, prime Angel blest,   Par Lost 11.598
Which now direct thine eyes and soon behold.   Par Lost 11.711
Then with uplifted hands, and eyes devout,   Par Lost 11.863
His holy Eyes; resolving from thenceforth   Par Lost 12.109
Mine eyes true op'ning, and my heart much eas'd,   Par Lost 12.274
Unlook'd for are we fall'n, our eyes beheld   Par Reg 2.31
Cast wanton eyes on the daughters of men,   Par Reg 2.180
Our Saviour lifting up his eyes beheld   Par Reg 2.338
Those rudiments, and see before thine eyes   Par Reg 3.245
Before mine eyes thou hast set; and in my ear   Par Reg 3.390
Gardens and Groves presented to his eyes,   Par Reg 4.38
Betray'd, Captiv'd, and both my Eyes put out,   Samson 33
Or do my eyes misrepresent? Can this be hee,   Samson 124
Cause light again within thy eies to spring,   Samson 584
Cho. Yet on she moves, now stands & eies thee fixt,   Samson 726
I lose, prevented by thy eyes put out.   Samson 1103
To put out both thine eyes, and fetter'd send thee   Samson 1160
Man. It shall be my delight to tend his eyes,   Samson 1490
Which earst my eyes beheld and yet behold;   Samson 1543
And eyes fast fixt he stood, as one who pray'd,   Samson 1637
With inward eyes illuminated   Samson 1689
From whence captivity and loss of eyes.   Samson 1744
Or *Tyrian* Cynosure. 2. *Bro*. Or if our eyes   Mask 342
Love-darting eyes, or tresses like the Morn?   Mask 753
line not in Bridgewater ms
Would think to charm my judgement, as mine eyes   Mask 758
The Cynosure of neighbouring eyes.   Allegro 80
With store of Ladies, whose bright eies   Allegro 121
Thy rapt soul sitting in thine eyes: Penseroso 40
And bring all Heav'n before mine eyes.   Penseroso 166
I see bright honour sparkle through your eyes,   Arcades 27
Hath lockt up mortal sense, then listen I   Arcades 62
Trinity ms 'mortall sense' ←'mortall eyes' ←'mortalitie'
But lives and spreds aloft by those pure eyes,   Lycidas 81
Throw hither all your quaint enameld eyes,   Lycidas 139
And wipe the tears for ever from his eyes.   Lycidas 181
Confounded, that her Makers eyes   Nativity 43
The rayes of *Bethlehem* blind his dusky eyn;   Nativity 223
From eyes of mortals walk invisible,   Vacation 66
That dropt with odorous oil down his fair eyes,   Passion 16
Cyriack, this three years day these eys, though clear   Sonnet 22, 1
1694 'Eyes'
To seek my life, and in their eyes   Psalm 86, 51
With pale and hollow eyes?   Psalm 88, 44

Eyesight
Eye-sight exposes daily men abroad.   Samson 919
Made older then thy age through eye-sight lost.   Samson 1489
And since his strength with eye-sight was not lost,   Samson 1502
God will restore him eye-sight to his strength.   Samson 1503
What if his eye-sight (for to *Israels* God   Samson 1527

Eyewitness
Eye-witness of what first or last was done,   Samson 1594

Eyn
The rayes of *Bethlehem* blind his dusky eyn;   Nativity 223

Eyries
On Cliffs and Cedar tops thir Eyries build: Par Lost 7.424

Ezekiel
Ezekiel saw, when by the Vision led   Par Lost 1.455
ms 'Ezechiel'

Fable
In Fable or *Romance* of *Uthers* Son   Par Lost 1.580
ms 'fable'
In Fable, Hymn, or Song, so personating   Par Reg 4.341
Sleep'st by the fable of *Bellerus* old,   Lycidas 160

Fabled
From Heav'n, they fabl'd, thrown by angry *Jove*   Par Lost 1.741
With long and tedious havoc fabl'd Knights   Par Lost 9.30
And Fabl'd how the Serpent, whom they calld   Par Lost 10.580
Fairer then feign'd of old, or fabl'd since   Par Reg 2.358

Fables
As whom the Fables name of monstrous size,   Par Lost 1.197
ms 'fables'
Than Fables yet have feign'd, or fear conceiv'd,   Par Lost 2.627
Hung amiable, *Hesperian* Fables true,   Par Lost 4.250
In Fables old, less ancient yet then these,   Par Lost 11.11
Wrought that effect on *Jove*, so Fables tell;   Par Reg 2.215
Co. She fables not, I feel that I do fear   Mask 800
line not in Bridgewater ms
line not in Trinity ms

Fablest
Thou fablest, here however to dwell free,   Par Lost 6.292

Fabling
The next to fabling fell and smooth conceits,   Par Reg 4.295

Fabric
Anon out of the earth a Fabrick huge   Par Lost 1.710
ms 'fabric'
Conjecture, he his Fabric of the Heav'ns   Par Lost 8.76
Long had foretold, a Fabrick wonderful   Par Lost 10.482

Fabricius
Quintius, *Fabricius*, *Curius*, *Regulus?*   Par Reg 2.446

Fabulous
Spir. Ile tell ye, 'tis not vain, or fabulous,   Mask 513

Face
Above them all th' Arch Angel: but his face   Par Lost 1.600
And Princely counsel in his face yet shon,   Par Lost 2.304
Heav'ns chearful face, the lowring Element   Par Lost 2.490

Face(*cont*)
Or flocks, or heards, or human face divine; Par Lost 3.44
Substantially express'd, and in his face Par Lost 3.140
Father, to see thy face, wherein no cloud Par Lost 3.262
Of Mercy and Justice in thy face discern'd, Par Lost 3.407
Not of the prime, yet such as in his face Par Lost 3.637
Thus while he spake, each passion dimm'd his face Par Lost 4.114
Thy face, and Morn return'd, for I this Night, Par Lost 5.30
Shadowie sets off the face of things; in vain, Par Lost 5.43
Spring both, the face of brightest Heav'n had changd Par Lost 5.644
He comes, and settl'd in his face I see Par Lost 6.540
Son in whose face invisible is beheld Par Lost 6.681
Ineffably into his face receiv'd, Par Lost 6.721
Obsequious, Heav'n his wonted face renewd, Par Lost 6.783
Appeer'd not: over all the face of Earth Par Lost 7.278
Her Universal Face with pleasant green, Par Lost 7.316
His mirror, with full face borrowing her Light Par Lost 7.377
How first this World and face of things began, Par Lost 7.636
To him she hasted, in her face excuse Par Lost 9.853
Of all thir vertue: silent, and in face Par Lost 9.1063
Be sure then. How shall I behold the face Par Lost 9.1080
In the sweat of thy Face shalt thou eat Bread, Par Lost 10.205
Accurst of blessed, hide me from the face Par Lost 10.723
Which now the Skie with various Face begins Par Lost 10.1064
As from his face I shall be hid, deprivd Par Lost 11.316
With goodness and paternal Love, his Face Par Lost 11.353
He look'd, and saw the face of things quite chang'd, Par Lost 11.712
Wrinkl'd the face of Deluge, as decai'd; Par Lost 11.843
In all his lineaments, though in his face Par Reg 1.92
Sharp sleet of arrowie showers against the face Par Reg 3.324
Had chear'd the face of Earth, and dry'd the wet Par Reg 4.433
Once more thy face, and know of thy estate, Samson 742
Oft he seems to hide his face, Samson 1749
Character'd in the face; this have I learn't Mask 530
Oh no? for something in thy face did shine Fair Inf 34
Her face was vail'd, yet to my fancied sight, Sonnet 23, 10
So clear, as in no face with more delight. Sonnet 23, 12
Cause thou thy face on us to shine Psalm 80, 15
Cause thou thy face on us to shine, Psalm 80, 31
Cause thou thy face on us to shine, Psalm 80, 79
Lord fill with shame their face. Psalm 83, 60
Thou God our shield look on the face Psalm 84, 31
O turn to me *thy face at length*, Psalm 86, 57
And hide thy face from me, Psalm 88, 58

Faced
Fame if not double-fac't is double-mouth'd, Samson 971
That with long beams the shame-fac't night array'd, Nativity 111

Faces
By four Cherubic shapes, four Faces each Par Lost 6.753
And in our Faces evident the signes Par Lost 9.1077
Of watchful Cherubim; four faces each Par Lost 11.128
Concours in Arms, fierce Faces threatning Warr, Par Lost 11.641
With dreadful Faces throng'd and fierie Armes: Par Lost 12.644
Dusk faces with white silken Turbants wreath'd: Par Reg 4.76

Facile
The facil gates of hell too slightly barrd. Par Lost 4.967
Benevolent and facil thus repli'd. Par Lost 8.65
Too facil then thou didst not much gainsay, Par Lost 9.1158
Since *Adam* and his facil consort *Eve* Par Reg 1.51

Fact
When he who most excels in fact of Arms, Par Lost 2.124
Perhaps thou shalt not Die, perhaps the Fact Par Lost 9.928
Deserted, then oblige thee with a fact Par Lost 9.980
From Heav'n acceptance; but the bloodie Fact Par Lost 11.457
How hainous had the fact been, how deserving Samson 493
May expiate (though the fact more evil drew Samson 736

Faction
From Faction; for none sure will claim in Hell Par Lost 2.32
Of each his Faction, in thir several Clanns, Par Lost 2.901
1667 'faction'

Factious
In factious opposition, till at last Par Lost 11.664
In wealth and multitude, factious they grow; Par Lost 12.352

Faculties
Are many lesser Faculties that serve Par Lost 5.101
And inward Faculties, which most excell, Par Lost 8.542
Telling their strange and vigorous faculties; Mask 628

Faculty
Within them every lower facultie Par Lost 5.410

Fade
With these that never fade the Spirits elect Par Lost 3.360

Faded
Sat on his faded cheek, but under Browes Par Lost 1.602
Thir frail Original, and faded bliss, Par Lost 2.375
Faded so soon. Advise if this be worth Par Lost 2.376
But faded splendor wan; who by his gate Par Lost 4.870
Down drop'd, and all the faded Roses shed: Par Lost 9.893

Fades
It withers on the stalk with languish't head. Mask 744
Trinity ms 'with languish't head' ← 'and fades away'

Fading
Soft silken Primrose fading timelesslie, Fair Inf 2

Faery
Beyond the *Indian* Mount, or Faerie Elves, Par Lost 1.781

Fail
And this Empyreal substance cannot fail, Par Lost 1.117
ms 'faile'
Shall grieve him, if I fail not, and disturb Par Lost 1.167

Fail(*cont*)
ms 'faile'
Hath emptied Heav'n, shall fail to re-ascend Par Lost 1.633
1667 'faile'
ms 'faile'
And vent'rous, if that fail them, shrink and fear Par Lost 2.205
There fail where Vertue fails, or weakest prove Par Lost 6.117
Her Son. So fail not thou, who thee implores: Par Lost 7.38
For us created, needs with us must faile, Par Lost 9.942
Such proof, conclude, they then begin to faile. Par Lost 9.1142
To end me? Shall Truth fail to keep her word, Par Lost 10.856
Thy mortal sight to faile; objects divine Par Lost 12.9
Lay on his Providence; he will not fail Par Reg 2.54
Will unpredict and fail me of the Throne: Par Reg 3.395
Self-fed, and self-consum'd, if this fail, Mask 597
Trinity ms 'faile'
1637 'faile'
Bridgewater ms 'fayle'
Till the live-long day-light fail, Allegro 99
But let my due feet never fail, Penseroso 155
And wrath to see his Kingdom fail, Nativity 171
And I to free thee *did not faile*, Psalm 81, 27

Failed
Nor fail'd they to express how much they prais'd, Par Lost 2.480
And Spirits, both them who stood and them who faild; Par Lost 3.101
Scarce thus at length faild speech recoverd sad. Par Lost 4.357
At least our envious Foe hath fail'd, who thought Par Lost 7.139
Or Nature faild in mee, and left some part Par Lost 8.534
Whether such vertue spent of old now faild Par Lost 9.145
Less over-weening, since he fail'd in *Job*, Par Reg 1.147
For though that seat of earthly bliss be fail'd, Par Reg 4.612
Had not his weekly cours of carriage fail'd; Carrier 10

Failing
Audacious, but that seat soon failing, meets Par Lost 2.931
O much deceav'd, much failing, hapless *Eve*, Par Lost 9.404
Whose failing, while her Faith to me remaines, Par Lost 10.129
At one spears length. O ever failing trust Samson 348
These false pretexts and varnish'd colours failing, Samson 901

Fails
There fail where Vertue fails, or weakest prove Par Lost 6.117
Speed, to describe whose swiftness Number failes. Par Lost 8.38

Fain
Yet Hope would fain subscribe, and tempts Belief. Samson 1535
Fain would I somthing say, yet to what end? Mask 783
1637 'Faine'
line not in Trinity ms
line not in Bridgewater ms
Who hate the Lord should *then be fain* Psalm 81, 61

Faint
Orewearied, through the faint Satanic Host Par Lost 6.392
Or faint retreat; when the great Son of God Par Lost 6.799
Perpetual banishment. Yet least they faint Par Lost 11.108
Paths indirect, or in the mid way faint! Par Lost 11.631
Eld. Bro. Unmuffle ye faint stars, and thou fair Moon Mask 331
Bridgewater ms 'fainte'
As a faint host that hath receiv'd the foil. Psalm 114, 10
Rescu'd from death by force though pale and faint. Sonnet 23, 4
Am very weak and faint; heal and amend me, Psalm 6, 4

Fainted
Thir fanting courage, and dispel'd thir fears. Par Lost 1.530
ms 'fainted'
1667 'fainted'
Fainted, and died, nor would with Ale be quickn'd; Another 16
line not in 1640, 1657, 1658 texts

Fainting
Thir fanting courage, and dispel'd thir fears. Par Lost 1.530
ms 'fainted'
1667 'fainted'
And fainting spirits uphold. Samson 666

Faintings
Thence faintings, swounings of despair, Samson 631

Faintly
On whose fresh lap the swart Star sparely looks, Lycidas 138
Trinity ms 'sparely' ← 'faintly' ← 'sparely'

Fair
Beguil'd by fair Idolatresses, fell Par Lost 1.445
Was fair *Damascus*, on the fertil Banks Par Lost 1.468
Dwell not unvisited of Heav'ns fair Light Par Lost 2.398
The one seem'd Woman to the waste, and fair, Par Lost 2.650
Now in thine eye so foul, once deemd so fair Par Lost 2.748
Then shining heav'nly fair, a Goddess arm'd Par Lost 2.757
And my fair Son here showst me, the dear pledge Par Lost 2.818
Cut off, and for the Book of knowledg fair Par Lost 3.47
With Joy and Love triumphing, and fair Truth. Par Lost 3.338
At sight of all this World beheld so faire. Par Lost 3.554
Fair Angel, thy desire which tends to know Par Lost 3.694
1667 'Faire'
(So call that opposite fair Starr) her aide Par Lost 3.727
Then in fair Evening Cloud, or humid Bow, Par Lost 4.151
Led on th' Eternal Spring. Not that faire field Par Lost 4.268
His fair large Front and Eye sublime declar'd Par Lost 4.300
Fair couple, linkt in happie nuptial League, Par Lost 4.339
Like this fair Paradise, your sense, yet such Par Lost 4.379
What there thou seest fair Creature is thy self, Par Lost 4.468
Till I espi'd thee, fair indeed and tall, Par Lost 4.477
Under a Platan, yet methought less faire, Par Lost 4.478
Thou following cryd'st aloud, Return faire *Eve;* Par Lost 4.481
1667 'fair'

Fair(*cont*)

And wisdom, which alone is truly fair.	Par Lost 4.491
O fair foundation laid whereon to build	Par Lost 4.521
When *Adam* thus to *Eve:* Fair Consort, th' hour	Par Lost 4.610
With this her solemn Bird and this fair Moon,	Par Lost 4.648
Mankind with her faire looks, to be aveng'd	Par Lost 4.718
Adam from his fair Spouse, nor *Eve* the Rites	Par Lost 4.742
To his proud fair, best quitted with disdain.	Par Lost 4.770
But chiefly where those two fair Creatures Lodge,	Par Lost 4.790
Back stept those two faire Angels half amaz'd	Par Lost 4.820
1667 'fair'	
Of interdicted Knowledge: fair it seem'd,	Par Lost 5.52
And O fair Plant, said he, with fruit surcharg'd,	Par Lost 5.58
Here, happie Creature, fair Angelic *Eve*,	Par Lost 5.74
Then when fair Morning first smiles on the World,	Par Lost 5.124
So cheard he his fair Spouse, and she was cheard,	Par Lost 5.129
Thus wondrous fair; thy self how wondrous then!	Par Lost 5.155
Undeckt, save with her self more lovely fair	Par Lost 5.380
Now when fair Morn Orient in Heav'n appeerd	Par Lost 6.524
To entertain them fair with open Front	Par Lost 6.611
In prospect from his Throne, how good, how faire,	Par Lost 7.556
And toucht by her fair tendance gladlier grew.	Par Lost 8.47
And thy faire *Eve;* Heav'n is for thee too high	Par Lost 8.172
Inward and outward both, his image faire:	Par Lost 8.221
What e're I saw. Thou Sun, said I, faire Light,	Par Lost 8.273
And ye that live and move, fair Creatures, tell,	Par Lost 8.276
Not onely these fair bounds, but all the Earth	Par Lost 8.338
Manlike, but different Sex, so lovly faire,	Par Lost 8.471
That what seemd fair in all the World, seemd now	Par Lost 8.472
Giver of all things faire, but fairest this	Par Lost 8.493
An outside? fair no doubt, and worthy well	Par Lost 8.568
Neither her out-side formd so fair, nor aught	Par Lost 8.596
Least by some faire appeering good surpris'd	Par Lost 9.354
Held dalliance with his faire *Egyptian* Spouse.	Par Lost 9.443
If chance with Nymphlike step fair Virgin pass,	Par Lost 9.452
Shee fair, divinely fair, fit Love for Gods,	Par Lost 9.489
Fairest resemblance of thy Maker faire,	Par Lost 9.538
Half what in thee is fair, one man except,	Par Lost 9.545
Empress of this fair World, resplendent *Eve*,	Par Lost 9.568
Of tasting those fair Apples, I resolv'd	Par Lost 9.585
Or Earth, or Middle, all things fair and good;	Par Lost 9.605
But all that fair and good in thy Divine	Par Lost 9.606
United I beheld; no Fair to thine	Par Lost 9.608
But of the Fruit of this fair Tree amidst	Par Lost 9.661
I question it, for this fair Earth I see,	Par Lost 9.720
Causes import your need of this fair Fruit.	Par Lost 9.731
Of this fair Fruit, our doom is, we shall die.	Par Lost 9.763
Fair to the Eye, inviting to the Taste,	Par Lost 9.777
And thy fair Fruit let hang, as to no end	Par Lost 9.798
If any be, of tasting this fair Fruit,	Par Lost 9.972
She gave him of that fair enticing Fruit	Par Lost 9.996
Nay didst permit, approve, and fair dismiss.	Par Lost 9.1159
Long hee admiring stood, till Sin, his faire	Par Lost 10.352
Fair Daughter, and thou Son and Grandchild both,	Par Lost 10.384
Thir penance, laden with Fruit, like that	Par Lost 10.550
1667 'fair Fruit'	
The Frutage fair to sight, like that which grew	Par Lost 10.561
So fair and good created, and had still	Par Lost 10.618
Be it so, for I submit, his doom is fair,	Par Lost 10.769
Posteritie stands curst: Fair Patrimonie	Par Lost 10.818
This noveltie on Earth, this fair defect	Par Lost 10.891
Creature so faire his reconcilement seeking,	Par Lost 10.943
Of these fair spreading Trees; which bids us seek	Par Lost 10.1067
Corrupted. I at first with two fair gifts	Par Lost 11.57
A Beavie of fair Women, richly gay	Par Lost 11.582
Such happy interview and fair event	Par Lost 11.593
For that fair femal Troop thou sawst, that seemd	Par Lost 11.614
Of these fair Atheists, and now swim in joy,	Par Lost 11.625
Enterd so faire, should turn aside to tread	Par Lost 11.630
A herd of Beeves, faire Oxen and faire Kine	Par Lost 11.647
Rape or Adulterie, where passing faire	Par Lost 11.717
With fair equalitie, fraternal state,	Par Lost 12.26
In this fair Empire won of Earth and Air;	Par Reg 1.63
What I see excellent in good, or fair,	Par Reg 1.381
Many are in each Region passing fair	Par Reg 2.155
In his prime youth the fair *Iberian* maid.	Par Reg 2.200
And with fair speech these words to him address'd.	Par Reg 2.301
Fair Champain with less rivers interveind,	Par Reg 3.257
All this fair sight; thy Kingdom though foretold	Par Reg 3.351
Many a fair Edifice besides, more like	Par Reg 4.55
Thus pass'd the night so foul till morning fair	Par Reg 4.426
Of this fair change, and to our Saviour came,	Par Reg 4.442
Fair morning yet betides thee Son of God,	Par Reg 4.451
Till underneath them fair *Jerusalem*,	Par Reg 4.544
Then of thine own Tribe fairer, or as fair,	Samson 217
Of fair fallacious looks, venereal trains,	Samson 533
To life obscur'd, which were a fair dismission,	Samson 688
Like a fair flower surcharg'd with dew, she weeps	Samson 728
Thy fair enchanted cup, and warbling charms	Samson 934
Sam. Fair days have oft contracted wind and rain.	Samson 1062
Har. Fair honour that thou dost thy God, in trusting	Samson 1178
Dispraise, or blame, nothing but well and fair,	Samson 1723
Where his fair off-spring nurs't in Princely lore,	Mask 34
Bridgewater ms 'faire'	
1637 'faire'	
Trinity ms 'faire'	
Be well stock't with as fair a herd as graz'd	Mask 152
Trinity ms 'faire'	

Fair(*cont*)

Bridgewater ms 'fayre'	
1637 'faire'	
I under fair pretence of friendly ends,	Mask 160
1637 'faire'	
Trinity ms 'faire'	
Bridgewater ms 'fayre'	
Co. And left your fair side all unguarded Lady?	Mask 283
1637 'faire'	
Bridgewater ms 'fayer'	
Bridgewater ms 'fayre'	
Eld. Bro. Unmuffle ye faint stars, and thou fair Moon	Mask 331
Trinity ms 'faire'	
Bridgewater ms 'faier'	
But beauty like the fair Hesperian Tree	Mask 393
1637 'faire'	
Trinity ms 'faire'	
Bridgewater ms 'fayre'	
Fair silver-shafted Queen for ever chaste,	Mask 442
Trinity ms 'faire'	
Bridgewater ms 'faire'	
1637 'Faire'	
And timely rest have wanted, but fair Virgin	Mask 689
1637 'faire'	
Bridgewater ms 'fayre'	
Trinity ms 'faire virgin' ←'fairest virgin' ←'sweet Ladie'	
Commended her fair innocence to the flood	Mask 831
1637 'faire'	
Trinity ms 'faire'	
Bridgewater ms 'faire'	
Sabrina fair	Mask 859
Bridgewater ms 'faire'	
1637 'faire'	
Trinity ms 'faire'	
And fair *Ligea*'s golden comb,	Mask 880
1637 'faire'	
Trinity ms 'faire', but line deleted	
Bridgewater ms 'fayer'	
Never scorch thy tresses fair,	Mask 929
Bridgewater ms 'fayer'	
1637 'faire'	
Trinity ms 'faire'	
Three fair branches of your own,	Mask 969
Trinity ms 'faire'	
Bridgewater ms 'fayer'	
1637 'faire'	
All amidst the Gardens fair	Mask 981
Trinity ms 'faire'	
1637 'faire'	
Bridgewater ms 'fayre'	
And from her fair unspotted side	Mask 1009
line not in Bridgewater ms	
1637 'faire'	
Trinity ms 'faire'	
& fruits of golden rind, on whose faire tree	Mask Tr. ms 10.08
But com thou Goddes fair and free,	Allegro 11
Fill'd her with thee a daughter fair,	Allegro 23
Fair silver-buskind Nymphs as great and good,	Arcades 33
Trinity ms 'faire'	
Of this fair Wood, and live in Oak'n bowr,	Arcades 45
And bid fair peace be to my sable shrowd.	Lycidas 22
Trinity ms 'faire'	
But the fair Guerdon when we hope to find,	Lycidas 73
Trinity ms 'faire'	
Onely with speeches fair	Nativity 37
If likewise he some fair one wedded not,	Fair Inf 11
Unhous'd thy Virgin Soul from her fair biding place.	Fair Inf 21
Fly swiftly to this fair Assembly's ears;	Vacation 28
That dropt with odorous oil down his fair eyes,	Passion 16
Broke the fair musick that all creatures made	Musick 21
Trinity ms 'faire'	
Besides what her vertues fair	Winchester 4
But the fair blossom hangs the head	Winchester 41
That fair *Syrian* Shepherdess,	Winchester 63
To whom thou untry'd seem'st fair. Me in my vow'd	Horace 13
My supplication with acceptance fair	Psalm 6, 19
How lovely are thy dwellings fair!	Psalm 84, 1
Sions *fair* Gates the Lord loves more	Psalm 87, 5
Then all the dwellings *faire*	Psalm 87, 6

Fairer

A fairer person lost not Heav'n; he seemd	Par Lost 2.110
Her self a fairer Floure by gloomie *Dis*	Par Lost 4.270
Much fairer to my Fancie then by day:	Par Lost 5.53
With ardor to enjoy thee, fairer now	Par Lost 9.1032
Tall stripling youths rich clad, of fairer hew	Par Reg 2.352
Fairer then feign'd of old, or fabl'd since	Par Reg 2.358
A fairer Paradise is founded now	Par Reg 4.613
Then of thine own Tribe fairer, or as fair,	Samson 217

Fairest

Of goodliest Trees loaden with fairest Fruit,	Par Lost 4.147
His Sons, the fairest of her Daughters *Eve*.	Par Lost 4.324
My fairest, my espous'd, my latest found,	Par Lost 5.18
Fairest of Starrs, last in the train of Night,	Par Lost 5.166
Then Wood-Nymph, or the fairest Goddess feign'd	Par Lost 5.381
Load'n with fairest Fruit that hung to the Eye	Par Lost 8.307
Giver of all things faire, but fairest this	Par Lost 8.493
Her self, though fairest unsupported Flour,	Par Lost 9.432
Fairest resemblance of thy Maker faire,	Par Lost 9.538

Fairest*(cont)*
Loaden with fruit of fairest colours mixt, Par Lost 9.577
A bough of fairest fruit that downie smil'd, Par Lost 9.851
O fairest of Creation, last and best Par Lost 9.896
Fairest and easiest of this combrous charge, Par Lost 11.549
Among daughters of men the fairest found; Par Reg 2.154
The fairest of her Sex *Angelica* Par Reg 3.341
O Fairest flower no sooner blown but blasted, Fair Inf 1
Fairfax
Fairfax, whose name in armes through Europe rings Sonnet 15, 1
1694 '*Fairfax*'
Fairies
Trip the pert Fairies and the dapper Elves; Mask 118
Bridgewater ms 'fairies'
Trinity ms 'fayries'
Fairly
By thee how fairly is the Giver now Par Reg 4.187
But here she comes, I fairly step aside Mask 168
Bridgewater ms 'fayrely'
Fairy
Beyond the *Indian* Mount, or Faerie Elves, Par Lost 1.781
Of Fairy Damsels met in Forest wide Par Reg 2.359
I took it for a faery vision Mask 298
Trinity ms 'faerie'
Bridgewater ms 'faerie'
1637 'faerie'
No goblin, or swart Faery of the mine, Mask 436
Trinity ms 'faerie'
Bridgewater ms 'fayrie'
1637 'Faerie'
How *Faery Mab* the junkets eat, Allegro 102
The Faiery Ladies daunc't upon the hearth; Vacation 60
Faith
To union, and firm Faith, and firm accord, Par Lost 2.36
Who first broke peace in Heav'n and Faith, till then Par Lost 2.690
Of true allegiance, constant Faith or Love, Par Lost 3.104
The proof of thir obedience and thir faith? Par Lost 4.520
Was this your discipline and faith ingag'd, Par Lost 4.954
Should yet remain, where faith and realtie Par Lost 6.115
All are not of thy Train; there be who Faith Par Lost 6.143
The Pledge of thy Obedience and thy Faith, Par Lost 8.325
Thy equal fear that my firm Faith and Love Par Lost 9.286
Not incorruptible of Faith, not prooff Par Lost 9.298
Less attributed to her Faith sincere, Par Lost 9.320
And what is Faith, Love, Vertue unassaid Par Lost 9.335
Despoild of Innocence, of Faith, of Bliss. Par Lost 9.411
Of Innocence, of Faith, of Puritie, Par Lost 9.1075
The Faith they owe; when earnestly they seek Par Lost 9.1141
Whose failing, while her Faith to me remaines, Par Lost 10.129
By Faith and faithful works, to second Life, Par Lost 11.64
Eve, easily may Faith admit, that all Par Lost 11.141
Will be aveng'd, and th' others Faith approv'd Par Lost 11.458
Justice and Temperance, Truth and Faith forgot; Par Lost 11.807
I see him, but thou canst not, with what Faith Par Lost 12.128
Like him in faith, in wisdom, and renown; Par Lost 12.154
To them by Faith imputed, they may finde Par Lost 12.295
To filial, works of Law to works of Faith. Par Lost 12.306
Imputed becomes theirs by Faith, his merits Par Lost 12.409
By Faith not void of workes: this God-like act Par Lost 12.427
Of *Abrahams* Faith wherever through the world; Par Lost 12.449
His Spirit within them, and the Law of Faith Par Lost 12.488
His living Temples, built by Faith to stand, Par Lost 12.527
Thir own Faith not anothers: for on Earth Par Lost 12.528
Who against Faith and Conscience can be heard Par Lost 12.529
Bestuck with slandrous darts, and works of Faith Par Lost 12.536
Deeds to thy knowledge answerable, add Faith, Par Lost 12.582
Chiefly what may concern her Faith to know, Par Lost 12.599
Both in one Faith unanimous though sad, Par Lost 12.603
More Faith? who also in her prime of love, Samson 388
To break all faith, all vows, deceive, betray, Samson 750
Above the faith of wedlock-bands, my tomb Samson 986
Breaking her Marriage Faith to circumvent me. Samson 1115
And hush the waving Woods, nor of lesse faith, Mask 88
O welcom pure-ey'd Faith, white-handed Hope, Mask 213
line not in Bridgewater ms
Their faith, their patience, and their truth. Mask 971
B.M. ms 'Faith'
When Faith and Love which parted from thee never, Sonnet 14, 1
But as Faith pointed with her golden rod, Sonnet 14, 7
Love led them on, and Faith who knew them best Sonnet 14, 9
Trinity ms 'Love led them on' ←'Faith shew'd the way' ←'Faith who led on the way'
And Public Faith cleard from the shamefull brand Sonnet 15, 12
Guided by faith and matchless Fortitude Sonnet 16, 3
1694 'Faith'
Men whose Life, Learning, Faith and pure intent Forcers 9
Trinity ms 'faith'
On Faith and changed Gods complain: and Seas Horace 6
Faithful
But wherefore let we then our faithful friends, Par Lost 1.264
ms 'faithfull'
For his revolt, yet faithfull how they stood, Par Lost 1.611
A faithful Leader, not to hazard all Par Lost 4.933
Satan, and couldst thou faithful add? O name, Par Lost 4.950
Faithful to whom? to thy rebellious crew? Par Lost 4.952
So spake the Seraph *Abdiel* faithful found, Par Lost 5.896
Among the faithless, faithful only hee; Par Lost 5.897
It sounded, and the faithful Armies rung Par Lost 6.204

Faithful*(cont)*
And faithful, now prov'd false. But think not here Par Lost 6.271
Faithful hath been your warfare, and of God Par Lost 6.803
Or this, or worse, leave not the faithful side Par Lost 9.265
So faithful Love unequald; but I feel Par Lost 9.983
By Faith and faithful works, to second Life, Par Lost 11.64
A Nation from one faithful man to spring: Par Lost 12.113
Whom *faithful Abraham* due time shall call, Par Lost 12.152
His faithful, and receave them into bliss, Par Lost 12.462
His faithful, left among th' unfaithful herd, Par Lost 12.481
And to the faithful Death the Gate of Life; Par Lost 12.571
Among illustrious women, faithful wives: Samson 957
Of faithful Souldiery, were not his purpose Samson 1498
And to his faithful Champion hath in place Samson 1751
I shall be your faithfull guide Mask 944
That to the faithfull Herdmans art belongs! Lycidas 121
When the blest seed of *Terah*'s faithfull Son, Psalm 114, 1
1673 'faithful'
Ever faithfull, ever sure. Psalm 136, 4 etc.
Faithfulness
O sacred name of faithfulness profan'd! Par Lost 4.951
Thy faithfulness *unfold?* Psalm 88, 48
Faithless
Hee and his faithless Progenie: whose fault? Par Lost 3.96
Among the faithless, faithful only hee; Par Lost 5.897
A *Canaanite*, my faithless enemy. Samson 380
Falerne
Their wines of *Setia*, *Cales*, and *Falerne*, Par Reg 4.117
Fall
Favour'd of Heav'n so highly, to fall off Par Lost 1.30
There the companions of his fall, o'rewhelm'd Par Lost 1.76
Which tempted our attempt, and wrought our fall. Par Lost 1.642
More glorious and more dread then from no fall, Par Lost 2.16
Up to our native seat: descent and fall Par Lost 2.76
Impendent horrors, threatning hideous fall Par Lost 2.177
Contending, and so doubtful what might fall. Par Lost 2.203
Thir own Heroic deeds and hapless fall Par Lost 2.549
Into this Deep, and in the general fall Par Lost 2.773
Sole pledge of his obedience: So will fall, Par Lost 3.95
Sufficient to have stood, though free to fall. Par Lost 3.99
Thir freedom, they themselves ordain'd thir fall. Par Lost 3.128
Fall circumvented thus by fraud, though joynd Par Lost 3.152
That they may stumble on, and deeper fall; Par Lost 3.201
I offer, on mee let thine anger fall; Par Lost 3.237
Shadow from body opaque can fall, and the Aire, Par Lost 3.619
The lower still I fall, onely Supream Par Lost 4.91
And heavier fall: so should I purchase deare Par Lost 4.101
Luxuriant; mean while murmuring waters fall Par Lost 4.260
But silently a gentle tear let fall Par Lost 5.130
The fall of others from like state of bliss; Par Lost 5.241
To love or not; in this we stand or fall: Par Lost 5.540
And so from Heav'n to deepest Hell; O fall Par Lost 5.542
Forsak'n of all good; I see thy fall Par Lost 5.878
His fiery *Chaos* to receave thir fall. Par Lost 6.55
To flight, or if to fall, but that they rise Par Lost 6.285
Against God and *Messiah*, or to fall Par Lost 6.796
And felt tenfold confusion in thir fall Par Lost 6.872
Among th' Angelic Powers, and the deep fall Par Lost 6.898
Dismounted, on th' *Aleian* Field I fall Par Lost 7.19
And all the Blest: stand fast; to stand or fall Par Lost 8.640
Since higher I fall short, on him who next Par Lost 9.174
And fall into deception unaware, Par Lost 9.362
Set over all his Works, which in our Fall, Par Lost 9.941
To counterfet Mans voice, true in our Fall, Par Lost 9.1069
And manifold in sin, deserv'd to fall. Par Lost 10.16
Concurring to necessitate his Fall, Par Lost 10.44
And on the Serpent thus his curse let fall. Par Lost 10.174
Saw Satan fall like Lightning down from Heav'n, Par Lost 10.184
With what permissive glory since his fall Par Lost 10.451
Repairing where he judg'd us, prostrate fall Par Lost 10.1087
O miserable Mankind, to what fall Par Lost 11.500
As to forsake the living God, and fall Par Lost 12.118
Satan, whose fall from Heav'n, a deadlier bruise, Par Lost 12.391
That he might fall in *Ramoth*, they demurring, Par Reg 1.373
That to the fall and rising he should be Par Reg 2.88
Fall flat and shrink into a trivial toy, Par Reg 2.223
Know'st thou not that my rising is thy fall, Par Reg 3.201
On this condition, if thou wilt fall down, Par Reg 4.166
That I fall down and worship thee as God? Par Reg 4.192
Fresh from his fall, and fiercer grapple joyn'd, Par Reg 4.567
Fell whence he stood to see his Victor fall. Par Reg 4.571
Or Lightning thou shalt fall from Heav'n trod down Par Reg 4.620
Proudly secure, yet liable to fall Samson 55
To waver, or fall off and joyn with Idols; Samson 456
Yet so it may fall out, because thir end Samson 1265
At every fall smoothing the Raven doune Mask 251
Com not too neer, you fall on iron stakes else. Mask 491
his farre-extended armes till with steepe fall Mask Tr. ms 10.13
Of shak't Olympus by mischance didst fall; Fair Inf 44
That they would fitly fall in order'd Characters. Passion 49
Which the sad morn had let fall Winchester 45
To yield his fruit, and his leaf shall not fall, Psalm 1, 9
God, find them guilty, let them fall Psalm 5, 29
Fall on his crown with ruine steep. Psalm 7, 60
But ye shall die like men, and fall Psalm 82, 23
Fallacious
Fallacious hope, or arm th' obdured brest Par Lost 2.568
Soon as the force of that fallacious Fruit, Par Lost 9.1046

Fallacious(*cont*)
Of his weak arguing, and fallacious drift; Par Reg 3.4
To seek in marriage that fallacious Bride, Samson 320
Of fair fallacious looks, venereal trains, Samson 533
Fallacy
By fallacy surpriz'd. But first I mean Par Reg 1.155
Fallen
If thou beest he; But O how fall'n! how chang'd Par Lost 1.84
ms 'fal'n'
From what highth fall'n, so much the stronger prov'd Par Lost 1.92
1667 'fal'n'
Fall'n Cherube, to be weak is miserable Par Lost 1.157
No wonder, fall'n such a pernicious highth. Par Lost 1.282
ms 'fal'n'
Awake, arise, or be for ever fall'n. Par Lost 1.330
ms 'fal'n'
Immortal vigor, though opprest and fall'n, Par Lost 2.13
Terror of Heav'n, though fall'n; intend at home, Par Lost 2.457
His fall'n condition is, and to me ow Par Lost 3.181
Not so on Man; him through their malice fall'n, Par Lost 3.400
Bore him slope downward to the Sun now fall'n Par Lost 4.591
Late falln himself from Heav'n, is plotting now Par Lost 5.240
1667 'fal'n' in some copies
And som are fall'n, to disobedience fall'n, Par Lost 5.541
That of so many Myriads fall'n, yet one Par Lost 6.24
Exhausted, spiritless, afflicted, fall'n. Par Lost 6.852
To hoarce or mute, though fall'n on evil dayes, Par Lost 7.25
On evil dayes though fall'n, and evil tongues; Par Lost 7.26
In eevn scale. But fall'n he is, and now Par Lost 10.47
And destin'd Man himself to judge Man fall'n. Par Lost 10.62
Heav'n-fall'n, in station stood or just array, Par Lost 10.535
Of Paradise could have produc't, ere fall'n Par Lost 11.29
Here let us live, though in fall'n state, content. Par Lost 11.180
Man fall'n shall be restor'd, I never more. Par Reg 1.405
Unlook'd for are we fall'n, our eyes beheld Par Reg 2.31
To lowest pitch of abject fortune thou art fall'n. Samson 169
The base degree to which I now am fall'n, Samson 414
Chor. His Giantship is gone somewhat crest-fall'n, Samson 1244
This evil on the *Philistines* is fall'n, Samson 1523
Mess. *Gaza* yet stands, but all her Sons are fall'n, Samson 1558
All in a moment overwhelm'd and fall'n. Samson 1559
Fall'n into wrath divine, Samson 1683
Fallest
And when high Noon hast gaind, and when thou fallst. Par Lost 5.174
Fallible
But proves not so: then fallible, it seems, Par Lost 6.428
Falling
Of Heav'n receiv'd us falling, and the Thunder, Par Lost 1.174
Dropt from the Zenith like a falling Star, Par Lost 1.745
Of Heav'n were falling, and these Elements Par Lost 2.925
Down had been falling, had not by ill chance Par Lost 2.935
Now falling with soft slumbrous weight inclines Par Lost 4.615
Or wet the thirstie Earth with falling showers, Par Lost 5.190
Rising or falling still advance his praise. Par Lost 5.191
Which of them rising with the Sun, or falling, Par Lost 10.663
And all this tract that fronts the falling Sun Mask 30
Bridgewater ms 'fallinge'
Fallows
Russet Lawns, and Fallows Gray, Allegro 71
Falls
Self-tempted, self-deprav'd: Man falls deceiv'd Par Lost 3.130
Partakers, and uncropt falls to the ground. Par Lost 4.731
Cast out from God and blessed vision, falls Par Lost 5.613
All higher knowledge in her presence falls Par Lost 8.551
Syene, and where the shadow both way falls, Par Reg 4.70
Unseemly falls in human eie, Samson 690
False
But all was false and hollow; though his Tongue Par Lost 2.112
By false presumptuous hope, the ranged powers Par Lost 2.522
Vain wisdom all, and false Philosophie: Par Lost 2.565
False fugitive, and to thy speed add wings, Par Lost 2.700
By some false guile pervert; and shall pervert Par Lost 3.92
So spake the false dissembler unperceivd; Par Lost 3.681
So spake the false Arch-Angel, and infus'd Par Lost 5.694
O argument blasphemous, false and proud! Par Lost 5.809
Among innumerable false, unmov'd, Par Lost 5.898
Unsound and false; nor is it aught but just, Par Lost 6.121
And faithful, now prov'd false. But think not here Par Lost 6.271
Nor thou his malice and false guile contemn; Par Lost 9.306
From his surmise prov'd false, find peace within, Par Lost 9.333
She dictate false, and missinforme the Will Par Lost 9.355
Wherewith to scorne the Earth: but that false Fruit Par Lost 9.1011
To that false Worm, of whomsoever taught Par Lost 9.1068
False in our promis'd Rising; since our Eyes Par Lost 9.1070
Was left him, or false glitter: All amaz'd Par Lost 10.452
Befits thee with him leagu'd, thy self as false Par Lost 10.868
Which that false Fruit that promis'd clearer sight Par Lost 11.413
His kindred and false Gods, into a Land Par Lost 12.122
False titl'd Sons of God, roaming the Earth Par Reg 2.179
Where glory is false glory, attributed Par Reg 3.69
Turn'd recreant to God, ingrate and false, Par Reg 3.138
But these are false, or little else but dreams, Par Reg 4.291
Far worse, her false resemblance only meets, Par Reg 4.320
As false portents, not sent from God, but thee; Par Reg 4.491
She proving false, the next I took to Wife Samson 227
And arts of every woman false like thee, Samson 749
I to my self was false e're thou to me, Samson 824
These false pretexts and varnish'd colours failing, Samson 901

False(*cont*)
And give it false presentments, lest the place Mask 156
Or if they be but false alarms of Fear, Mask 364
line not in Bridgewater ms
line not in Trinity ms
This will restore all soon. *La*. 'Twill not false traitor, Mask 690
Obtruding false rules pranckt in reasons garb. Mask 759
Were shatter'd into heaps o're thy false head. Mask 799
line not in Trinity ms
line not in Bridgewater ms
Spir. What, have you let the false enchanter scape? Mask 814
Let our frail thoughts dally with false surmise. Lycidas 153
Her false imagin'd loss cease to lament, Fair Inf 72
Which is no more then what is false and vain, On Time 5
Stand spelling fals, while one might walk to Mile- Sonnet 11, 7
Thir Hydra heads, and the fals North displaies Sonnet 15, 7
1694 'false'
Things false and vain and nothing else but lies? Psalm 4, 12
With judgment false and wrong Psalm 82, 6
Falsehood
That practisd falshood under saintly shew, Par Lost 4.122
Touch'd lightly; for no falshood can endure Par Lost 4.811
To hellish falshood, snare them. But for thee Par Lost 10.873
So fares it when with truth falshood contends. Par Reg 3.443
Bewail thy falshood, and the pious works Samson 955
Of falshood most unconjugal traduc't. Samson 979
Co. By falshood, or discourtesie, or why? Mask 281
Bridgewater ms 'falsehood'
With visor'd falshood, and base forgery, Mask 698
line not in Bridgewater ms
thou man of lies & falshood, if thou give me it Mask Tr. ms 22.21
'falshood' ←'fraud' ←'falshood'
Falsities
By falsities and lyes the greatest part Par Lost 1.367
Faltering
With faultring speech and visage incompos'd Par Lost 2.989
Misgave him; hee the faultring measure felt; Par Lost 9.846
Whence *Adam* faultring long, thus answer'd brief. Par Lost 10.115
For in his faltring mouth unstable Psalm 5, 25
Fame
There went a fame in Heav'n that he ere long Par Lost 1.651
Learn how thir greatest Monuments of Fame, Par Lost 1.695
ms 'fame'
(if ancient and prophetic fame in Heav'n Par Lost 2.346
Built thir fond hopes of Glorie or lasting fame, Par Lost 3.449
Fame is not silent, here in hope to find Par Lost 4.938
Of victorie; deeds of eternal fame Par Lost 6.240
Angels contented with thir fame in Heav'n Par Lost 6.375
Vain glorious, and through infamie seeks fame: Par Lost 6.384
The new created World, which fame in Heav'n Par Lost 10.481
City of old or modern Fame, the Seat Par Lost 11.386
Shall yield up all thir vertue, all thir fame Par Lost 11.623
Thus Fame shall be atchiev'd, renown on Earth, Par Lost 11.698
And what most merits fame in silence hid. Par Lost 11.699
Fame in the World, high titles, and rich prey, Par Lost 11.793
Regardless whether good or evil fame. Par Lost 12.47
What happ'ns new; Fame also finds us out. Par Reg 1.334
Though of this Age the wonder and the fame, Par Reg 2.209
The fame and glory, glory the reward Par Reg 3.25
For what is glory but the blaze of fame, Par Reg 3.47
When to extend his fame through Heaven and Earth, Par Reg 3.65
To things not glorious, men not worthy of fame. Par Reg 3.70
Equal in fame to proudest Conquerours. Par Reg 3.99
Yet if for fame and glory aught be done, Par Reg 3.100
Aught suffer'd; if young *African* for fame Par Reg 3.101
The drink of none but Kings; of later fame Par Reg 3.289
Or active, tended on by glory, or fame, Par Reg 4.371
Fame if not double-fac't is double-mouth'd, Samson 971
Though Fame divulge him Father of five Sons Samson 1248
And though her body die, her fame survives, Samson 1706
To himself and Fathers house eternal fame; Samson 1717
Fame that her high worth to raise, Arcades 8
What shallow-searching *Fame* hath left untold; Arcades 41
Fame is the spur that the clear spirit doth raise Lycidas 70
Trinity ms 'fame'
Fame is no plant that grows on mortal soil, Lycidas 78
Of so much fame in Heav'n expect thy meed. Lycidas 84
Dear son of memory, great heir of Fame, Shakespear 5
1632 '*Fame*'
1663-4 '*Fame*'
That call Fame on such gentle acts as these, Sonnet 8, 6
Dante shall give Fame leave to set thee higher Sonnet 13, 12
Trinity ms 'Dante shall give Fame leave to' ←'Fame by the Tuscan's leav shall'
Famed
Like those *Hesperian* Gardens fam'd of old, Par Lost 3.568
And his next Son for Wealth and Wisdom fam'd, Par Lost 12.332
About the world, at that assembly fam'd Par Reg 1.34
Carv'd work, the hand of fam'd Artificers Par Reg 4.59
Had brought me to the field where thou art fam'd Samson 1094
Celestial *Cupid* her fam'd Son advanc't, Mask 1004
line not in Bridgewater ms
O Fountain *Arethuse*, and thou honour'd floud, Lycidas 85
Trinity ms 'honour'd' ←'fam'd' ←'smooth'
Familiar
Familiar the fierce heat, and void of pain; Par Lost 2.219
Portentous held me; but familiar grown, Par Lost 2.761
With Man, as with his Friend, familiar us'd Par Lost 9.2

Familiar(*cont*)
Familiar to our eyes, all places else Par Lost 11.305
Families
Long time in peace by Families and Tribes Par Lost 12.23
Family
As Father of his Familie he clad Par Lost 10.216
That by strong hand his Family obtain'd, Par Reg 3.168
Famine
His famine should be fill'd, and blest his mawe Par Lost 2.847
And worn with Famin, long and ceasless hiss, Par Lost 10.573
To mee, who with eternal Famin pine, Par Lost 10.597
By Fire, Flood, Famin, by Intemperance more Par Lost 11.472
Famin and anguish will at last consume Par Lost 11.778
And from the sting of Famine fear no harm, Par Reg 2.257
Famish
And famish him of Breath, if not of Bread? Par Lost 12.78
Famished
Of *Israel* here had famish'd, had not God Par Reg 2.311
Famous
Runs divers, wandring many a famous Realme Par Lost 4.234
Andrew and *Simon*, famous after known Par Reg 2.7
Famous he was in Heaven, on Earth less known; Par Reg 3.68
Made famous in a Land and times obscure; Par Reg 3.94
As morning shews the day. Be famous then Par Reg 4.221
And Eloquence, native to famous wits Par Reg 4.241
Thence to the famous Orators repair, Par Reg 4.267
In *Ramath-lechi* famous to this day: Samson 145
The Sons of *Anac*, famous now and blaz'd, Samson 528
Which many a famous Warriour overturns, Samson 542
Of famous *Arcady* ye are, and sprung Arcades 28
Where your old *Bards*, the famous *Druids* ly, Lycidas 53
Famousest
I shall be nam'd among the famousest Samson 982
Fan
Of leaves and fuming rills, *Aurora*'s fan, Par Lost 5.6
Now on the polar windes, then with quick Fann Par Lost 5.269
1667 'Fanne' in some copies
To fan the Earth now wak'd, and usher in Par Lost 10.94
Fanatic
Fanatic *Egypt* and her Priests, to seek Par Lost 1.480
Fancied
Or fansied so, through expectation high Par Lost 9.789
Her face was vail'd, yet to my fancied sight, Sonnet 23, 10
Fancies
Her Virgin Fancies, pouring forth more sweet, Par Lost 5.296
Conjectures, fancies, built on nothing firm. Par Reg 4.292
And fancies fond with gaudy shapes possess, Penseroso 6
And to our high-rais'd phantasie present, Musick 5
Trinity ms 'phantasie' ←'Phantasie' ←'fantasie' ←'fancies then'
Fancy
The Organs of her Fancie, and with them forge Par Lost 4.802
Much fairer to my Fancie then by day: Par Lost 5.53
Reason as chief; among these Fansie next Par Lost 5.102
Oft in her absence mimic Fansie wakes Par Lost 5.110
Fansie and understanding, whence the Soule Par Lost 5.486
But apt the Mind or Fancie is to roave Par Lost 8.188
My fancy to believe I yet had being, Par Lost 8.294
1667 'Fancy'
Of Fancie my internal sight, by which Par Lost 8.461
They swim in mirth, and fansie that they feel Par Lost 9.1009
That mingle with thy fancy. I however Samson 601
Of fancy, feard lest one day thou wouldst leave me Samson 794
Till fancy had her fill, but ere a close Mask 548
Trinity ms 'fancie'
Bridgewater ms 'fansie'
1637 'fancie'
That fancy can beget on youthfull thoughts, Mask 669
Trinity ms 'fancie' ←'youth & fancie'
Bridgewater ms 'fancie'
1637 'fancie'
Or sweetest *Shakespear* fancies childe, Allegro 133
Enwrap our fancy long, Nativity 134
Before thou cloath my fancy in fit sound: Vacation 32
And work my flatter'd fancy to belief, Passion 31
Then thou our fancy of it self bereaving, Shakespear 13
Fangled
Not those new fangled toys, and triming slight Vacation 19
Fanned
Fannd with coole Winds, save those who in thir course Par Lost 5.655
Floats, as they pass, fann'd with unnumber'd plumes: Par Lost 7.432
Of gentlest gale *Arabian* odors fann'd Par Reg 2.364
Not so the wicked, but as chaff which fann'd Psalm 1, 11
Fanning
Fanning thir odoriferous wings dispense Par Lost 4.157
Fanning their joyous Leaves to thy soft layes. Lycidas 44
Fans
Insect or Worme; those wav'd thir limber fans Par Lost 7.476
Fantasies
What might this be? A thousand fantasies Mask 205
line not in Bridgewater ms
Fantastic
In a light fantastick round. Mask 144
Trinity ms 'fantastick' ←'and frolick'
On the light fantastick toe, Allegro 34
Fantastics
Which takes our late fantasticks with delight, Vacation 20

Fantasy
And to our high-rais'd phantasie present, Musick 5
Trinity ms 'phantasie' ←'Phantasie' ←'fantasie' ←'fancies then'
Far
At once as far as Angels kenn he views Par Lost 1.59
ms 'farr'
As far remov'd from God and light of Heav'n Par Lost 1.73
ms 'farr'
As far as Gods and Heav'nly Essences Par Lost 1.138
ms 'farr'
The rest were long to tell, though far renown'd, Par Lost 1.507
By *Fontarabbia*. Thus far these beyond Par Lost 1.587
ms 'farr'
(Far other once beheld in bliss) condemn'd Par Lost 1.607
ms 'Farr'
Far round illumin'd hell: highly they rag'd Par Lost 1.666
ms 'Farr'
There stood a Hill not far whose griesly top Par Lost 1.670
ms 'farr'
Of that infernal Court. But far within Par Lost 1.792
ms 'farr'
High on a Throne of Royal State, which far Par Lost 2.1
Thus farr at least recover'd, hath much more Par Lost 2.22
To nothing this essential, happier farr Par Lost 2.97
Scout farr and wide into the Realm of night, Par Lost 2.133
His anger, and perhaps thus farr remov'd Par Lost 2.211
In strictest bondage, though thus far remov'd, Par Lost 2.321
Heard farr and wide, and all the host of Hell Par Lost 2.519
Farr off from these a slow and silent stream, Par Lost 2.582
As when farr off at Sea a Fleet descri'd Par Lost 2.636
Farr off the flying Fiend: at last appeer Par Lost 2.643
Within unseen. Farr less abhorrd than these Par Lost 2.659
Inflam'd with lust then rage) and swifter far, Par Lost 2.791
Your dungeon stretching far and wide beneath; Par Lost 2.1003
If that way be your walk, you have not farr; Par Lost 2.1007
Shoots farr into the bosom of dim Night Par Lost 2.1036
Farr off th' Empyreal Heav'n, extended wide Par Lost 2.1047
Not farr off Heav'n, in the Precincts of light, Par Lost 3.88
With his own folly? that be from thee farr, Par Lost 3.153
That farr be from thee, Father, who art Judg Par Lost 3.154
Farr more then Great or High; because in thee Par Lost 3.311
Satan alighted walks: a Globe farr off Par Lost 3.422
Though distant farr som small reflection gaines Par Lost 3.428
Here Pilgrims roam, that stray'd so farr to seek Par Lost 3.476
Fly o're the backside of the World farr off Par Lost 3.494
His travell'd steps; farr distant he descries Par Lost 3.501
At top whereof, but farr more rich appeerd Par Lost 3.504
Wider by farr then that of after-times Par Lost 3.529
Andromeda farr off *Atlantic* Seas Par Lost 3.559
Dispenses Light from farr; they as they move Par Lost 3.579
Th' Arch-chimic Sun so farr from us remote Par Lost 3.609
Undazl'd, farr and wide his eye commands, Par Lost 3.614
To objects distant farr, whereby he soon Par Lost 3.621
Far off and fearless, nor with cause to boast, Par Lost 4.14
This knows my punisher; therefore as farr Par Lost 4.103
His farr more pleasant Garden God ordaind; Par Lost 4.215
Two of far nobler shape erect and tall, Par Lost 4.288
So farr the happier Lot, enjoying thee Par Lost 4.446
Not distant far from thence a murmuring sound Par Lost 4.453
Conspicuous farr, winding with one ascent Par Lost 4.545
See farr and wide: in at this Gate none pass Par Lost 4.579
Farr be it, that I should write thee sin or blame, Par Lost 4.758
Farr heavier load thy self expect to feel Par Lost 4.972
Of Fruit-trees overwoodie reachd too farr Par Lost 5.213
Transcend his own so farr, whose radiant forms Par Lost 5.457
Divine effulgence, whose high Power so far Par Lost 5.458
Wide over all the Plain, and wider farr Par Lost 5.648
Far was advanc't on winged speed, an Host Par Lost 5.744
1667 'Farr'
High on a Hill, far blazing, as a Mount Par Lost 5.757
Thus farr his bold discourse without controule Par Lost 5.803
How provident he is, how farr from thought Par Lost 5.828
Universal reproach, far worse to beare Par Lost 6.34
Farr in th' Horizon to the North appeer'd Par Lost 6.79
I flie not, but have sought thee farr and nigh. Par Lost 6.295
Humbl'd by such rebuke, so farr beneath Par Lost 6.342
Far otherwise th' inviolable Saints Par Lost 6.398
Far in the dark dislodg'd, and void of rest, Par Lost 6.415
From far with thundring noise among our foes Par Lost 6.487
Not distant far with heavie pace the Foe Par Lost 6.551
For thee I have ordain'd it, and thus farr Par Lost 6.700
Farr separate, circling thy holy Mount Par Lost 6.743
He onward came, farr off his coming shon, Par Lost 6.768
Illustrious farr and wide, but by his own Par Lost 6.773
Strook them with horror backward, but far worse Par Lost 6.863
But drive farr off the barbarous dissonance Par Lost 7.32
Farr differing from this World, thou hast reveal'd Par Lost 7.71
1669 'Far'
Yet farr the greater part have kept, I see, Par Lost 7.145
Farr into *Chaos*, and the World unborn; Par Lost 7.220
And said, thus farr extend, thus farr thy bounds, Par Lost 7.230
Of *Chaos* farr remov'd, least fierce extreames Par Lost 7.272
Of Light by farr the greater part he took, Par Lost 7.359
So farr remote, with diminution seen. Par Lost 7.369
From Heaven Gate not farr, founded in view Par Lost 7.618
That better might with farr less compass move, Par Lost 8.33
So spacious, and his Line stretcht out so farr; Par Lost 8.102

Far(*cont*)

Plac'd Heav'n from Earth so farr, that earthly sight, Par Lost 8.120
Each Orb a glimps of Light, conveyd so farr Par Lost 8.156
Contented that thus farr hath been reveal'd Par Lost 8.177
God hath bid dwell farr off all anxious cares, Par Lost 8.185
Farr on excursion toward the Gates of Hell; Par Lost 8.231
Surpassest farr my naming, how may I Par Lost 8.359
And these inferiour farr beneath me set? Par Lost 8.382
Thus farr to try thee, *Adam*, I was pleas'd, Par Lost 8.437
When out of hope, behold her, not farr off, Par Lost 8.481
Farr otherwise, transported I behold, Par Lost 8.529
(Though higher of the genial Bed by far, Par Lost 8.598
Downward as farr Antartic; and in length Par Lost 9.79
May finde us both perhaps farr less prepar'd, Par Lost 9.381
From her best prop so farr, and storm so nigh. Par Lost 9.433
Her Husband, for I view far round, not nigh, Par Lost 9.482
A goodly Tree farr distant to behold Par Lost 9.576
But say, where grows the Tree, from hence how far? Par Lost 9.617
There swallow'd up and lost, from succour farr. Par Lost 9.642
Friendly to man, farr from deceit or guile. Par Lost 9.772
Farr otherwise th' event, not Death, but Life Par Lost 9.984
Farr other operation first displaid, Par Lost 9.1012
My coming seen far off? I miss thee here, Par Lost 10.104
And for thee, whose perfection farr excell'd Par Lost 10.150
Remov'd farr off; then pittying how they stood Par Lost 10.211
Farr into *Chaos*, since the Fiend pass'd through, Par Lost 10.233
Sagacious of his Quarry from so farr. Par Lost 10.281
To fortifie thus farr, and overlay Par Lost 10.370
Farr to the inland retir'd, about the walls Par Lost 10.423
With travail difficult, not better farr Par Lost 10.593
From cold *Estotiland*, and South as farr Par Lost 10.686
To answer, and resound farr other Song. Par Lost 10.862
By a farr worse, or if she love, withheld Par Lost 10.903
And sends a comfortable heat from farr, Par Lost 10.1077
Wide waving, all approach farr off to fright, Par Lost 11.121
Farr other name deserving. But the Field Par Lost 11.171
Of glory, and farr off his steps adore. Par Lost 11.333
Contending, and remov'd his Tents farr off; Par Lost 11.727
But I was farr deceav'd; for now I see Par Lost 11.783
Farr less I now lament for one whole World Par Lost 11.874
And get themselves a name, least far disperst Par Lost 12.45
And fix farr deeper in his head thir stings Par Lost 12.432
Shall all be Paradise, far happier place Par Lost 12.464
Then this of *Eden*, and far happier daies. Par Lost 12.465
Of Spirit and Truth; the rest, farr greater part, Par Lost 12.533
1669 'far'
A paradise within thee, happier farr. Par Lost 12.587
Of female Seed, far abler to resist Par Reg 1.151
With solitude, till far from track of men, Par Reg 1.191
So far from path or road of men, who pass Par Reg 1.322
To Town or Village nigh (nighest is far) Par Reg 1.332
More then the Camel, and to drink go far, Par Reg 1.340
But let us wait; thus far he hath perform'd, Par Reg 2.49
Far other labour to be undergon Par Reg 2.132
However to this Man inferior far, Par Reg 2.135
But he whom we attempt is wiser far Par Reg 2.205
Whose pains have earn'd the far fet spoil. With that Par Reg 2.401
Far more magnanimous, then to assume. Par Reg 2.483
By Conquest far and wide, to over-run Par Reg 3.72
It may by means far different be attain'd Par Reg 3.89
As far as *Indus* East, *Euphrates* West, Par Reg 3.272
He marches now in hast; see, though from far, Par Reg 3.303
This far his over-match, who self deceiv'd Par Reg 4.7
So far renown'd, and with the spoils enricht Par Reg 4.46
With gilded battlements, conspicuous far, Par Reg 4.53
Or Embassies from Regions far remote Par Reg 4.67
Shar'd among petty Kings too far remov'd; Par Reg 4.87
From Nations far and nigh; what honour that, Par Reg 4.122
Far worse, her false resemblance only meets, Par Reg 4.320
Will far be found unworthy to compare Par Reg 4.346
But herein to our Prophets far beneath, Par Reg 4.356
In some respect far higher so declar'd. Par Reg 4.521
Her pile, far off appearing like a Mount Par Reg 4.547
That invincible *Samson*, far renown'd, Samson 341
Of acts indeed heroic, far beyond Samson 527
Her husband, how far urg'd his patience bears, Samson 755
Far other reasonings, brought forth other deeds. Samson 875
Intestin, far within defensive arms Samson 1038
More generous far and civil, who confess'd Samson 1467
They had ingag'd their wandring steps too far, Mask 193
Bridgewater ms 'farr'
Trinity ms 'farre'
Prompt me; and they perhaps are not far off. Mask 229
Trinity ms 'farre hence'
1637 'farre'
Bridgewater ms 'farr hence'
Far from the cheerfull haunt of men, and herds, Mask 388
1637 'Farre'
Bridgewater ms 'farr'
Trinity ms 'farre'
Driving far off each thing of sin and guilt, Mask 456
Trinity ms 'farre'
Bridgewater ms 'farr'
1637 'farre'
Som far off hallow break the silent Air. Mask 481
Bridgewater ms 'farr'
Trinity ms 'farre-off'
1637 'farre'

Far(*cont*)

Farr other arms, and other weapons must Mask 612
1673 'Far'
1637 'Farre'
Trinity ms 'farre'
Sorrow flies farr: See here be all the pleasures Mask 668
1673 'far'
Trinity ms 'farre'
1637 'farre'
There is a gentle Nymph not farr from hence, Mask 824
1637 'farre'
Trinity ms 'farre'
1673 'far'
But farr above in spangled sheen Mask 1003
line not in Bridgewater ms
Trinity ms 'farre'
1637 'farre'
1673 'far'
Quickly to the green earths end, Mask 1014
Trinity ms 'quickly to' ← 'farre beyond'
Yet thou art higher far descended, Penseroso 22
Far from all resort of mirth, Penseroso 81
Wash far away, where ere thy bones are hurld, Lycidas 155
Trinity ms 'farre'
1638 'farre'
See how from far upon the Eastern rode Nativity 22
Not half so far casts his usurped sway, Nativity 170
He wanderd long, till thee he spy'd from farr, Fair Inf 17
That far events full wisely could presage, Vacation 70
Far within the boosom bright Winchester 69
But from that mark how far they roave we see Sonnet 12, 13
Trinity ms 'far' ← 'farr'
Far worse then fire to burn. Psalm 85, 12
And sever'd from me far. Psalm 88, 70
Brutus far to the West, in th' Ocean wide Prose 12, 7

Far-beaming

And that far-beaming blaze of Majesty, Nativity 9

Fare

No inconvenient Diet, nor too light Fare: Par Lost 5.495
As meet is, after such delicious Fare; Par Lost 9.1028
Of easie thorough-fare. Therefore while I Par Lost 10.393
My Head, Ill fare our Ancestor impure, Par Lost 10.735
Of honour, wealth, high fare, aim'd not beyond Par Reg 2.202

Fares

Nor good dry Land: nigh founderd on he fares, Par Lost 2.940
So on he fares, and to the border comes, Par Lost 4.131
So fares it when with truth falshood contends. Par Reg 3.443
so fares as did forsaken Proserpine Mask Tr. ms 15.52
soe fares as did forsaken Proserpine Mask Br. ms 344

Farewell

Above his equals. Farewel happy Fields Par Lost 1.249
ms 'farewell'
If chance the radiant Sun with farewell sweet Par Lost 2.492
So farwel Hope, and with Hope farwel Fear, Par Lost 4.108
Farwel Remorse: all Good to me is lost; Par Lost 4.109
Of Matrimonial treason: so farewel. Samson 959
Sam. Brethren farewel, your company along Samson 1413

Far-extended

his farre-extended armes till with steepe fall Mask Tr. ms 10.13

Faring

Sea-faring men orewatcht, whose Bark by chance Par Lost 2.288

Farms

Among the pleasant Villages and Farmes Par Lost 9.448

Far-off

I hear the far-off *Curfeu* sound, Penseroso 74

Far-sighted

when she beheld (the gods farre sighted bee) Lycidas Tr. ms 29.60

Farthest

What shall be right: fardest from him is best Par Lost 1.247
Her fardest verge, and *Chaos* to retire Par Lost 2.1038
Farthest from pain, where thou mightst hope to change Par Lost 4.892
Of *Congo*, and *Angola* fardest South; Par Lost 11.401
Were better farthest off) is not yet come; Par Reg 3.397
Or on the *Aemilian*, some from farthest South, Par Reg 4.69
Such noise as I can make to be heard farthest Mask 227
Bridgewater ms 'fardest'
Trinity ms 'fardest'
1637 'fardest'

Fashion

To cast the fashion of uncertain evils; Mask 360
line not in Bridgewater ms
line not in Trinity ms

Fashioned

The Rib he formd and fashond with his hands; Par Lost 8.469

Fast

Fast by the Oracle of God; I thence Par Lost 1.12
Fast by Hell Gate, and kept the fatal Key, Par Lost 2.725
In darkness, while thy head flames thick and fast Par Lost 2.754
And fast by hanging in a golden Chain Par Lost 2.1051
In Paradise, fast by the Tree of Life Par Lost 3.354
From *Media* post to *Aegypt*, there fast bound. Par Lost 4.171
Cross-barrd and bolted fast, fear no assault, Par Lost 4.190
Our Death the Tree of knowledge grew fast by, Par Lost 4.221
Such where ye find, seise fast, and hither bring. Par Lost 4.796
Within the Mount of God, fast by his Throne, Par Lost 6.5
Fit well his Helme, gripe fast his orbed Shield, Par Lost 6.543
Her dark foundations, and too fast had bound. Par Lost 6.870
Our prompt obedience. Fast we found, fast shut Par Lost 8.240

Fast(*cont*)
And all the Blest: stand fast; to stand or fall Par Lost 8.640
The Serpent: him fast sleeping soon he found Par Lost 9.182
Fast by a Fountain, one small Thicket past Par Lost 9.628
And Chains they made all fast, too fast they made Par Lost 10.319
Into the Wood fast by, and changing shape Par Lost 10.333
Fast caught, they lik'd, and each his liking chose; Par Lost 11.587
With thir four Wives; and God made fast the dore. Par Lost 11.737
Fast on the top of som high mountain fixt. Par Lost 11.851
And gathers ground fast at the Labourers heel Par Lost 12.631
E're thou of *Israel*'s Scepter get fast hold; Par Reg 4.480
Fast by thy side, who from thy Fathers field Samson 1432
And eyes fast fixt he stood, as one who pray'd, Samson 1637
And bound him fast; without his rod revers't, Mask 816
Thou fix them on the earth as fast. Penseroso 44
The brutish gods of *Nile* as fast, Nativity 211
Then lies him meekly down fast by his Brethrens side. Passion 21
But the just establish fast, Psalm 7, 37
And root it deep and fast Psalm 80, 38
Is his foundation fast, Psalm 87, 2
High God shall fix her fast. Psalm 87, 20

Fast
The Monster moving onward came as fast Par Lost 2.675
In darkness, while thy head flames thick and fast Par Lost 2.754
Down fell both Spear and Shield, down they as fast, Par Lost 10.542
Led them direct, and down the Cliff as fast Par Lost 12.639

Fast
Nor tasted, nor had appetite; that Fast Par Reg 2.247
Spare Fast, that oft with gods doth diet, Penseroso 46

Fastened
They fasten'd, and the Mole immense wraught on Par Lost 10.300
Though thou wert firmlier fastn'd then a rock. Samson 1398

Fasting
After forty days fasting had remain'd, Par Reg 2.243
Fasting he went to sleep, and fasting wak'd. Par Reg 2.284

Fat
The Inwards and thir Fat, with Incense strew'd, Par Lost 11.439
From a fat Meddow ground; or fleecy Flock, Par Lost 11.648
And fat regorg'd of Bulls and Goats, Samson 1671

Fatal
Though inaccessible, his fatal Throne: Par Lost 2.104
Leveld his deadly aime; thir fatall hands Par Lost 2.712
Fast by Hell Gate, and kept the fatal Key, Par Lost 2.725
Forth issu'd, brandishing his fatal Dart Par Lost 2.786
Thus saying, from her side the fatal Key, Par Lost 2.871
His breaded train, and of his fatal guile Par Lost 4.349
One fatal Tree there stands of Knowledge call'd, Par Lost 4.514
By our own quick'ning power, when fatal course Par Lost 5.861
The fatal Trespass don by *Eve*, amaz'd, Par Lost 9.889
Her Husband shee, to taste the fatall fruit, Par Lost 10.4
Eevn hee who now foretold his fatal bruise, Par Lost 10.191
Such fatal consequence unites us three: Par Lost 10.364
But Justice, and some fatal curse annext Par Lost 12.99
With dread attending when that fatal wound Par Reg 1.53
And run not sooner to his fatal snare? Par Reg 1.441
To me so fatal, me it most concerns. Par Reg 4.205
Thou art to be my fatal enemy. Par Reg 4.525
Had shorn the fatal harvest of thy head. Samson 1024
It was that fatall and perfidious Bark Lycidas 100
1673 'fatal'
But kill'd alas, and then bewayl'd his fatal bliss. Fair Inf 7
At *Chaeronea*, fatal to liberty Sonnet 10, 7

Fate
This downfall; since by Fate the strength of Gods Par Lost 1.116
ms 'fate'
Whether upheld by strength, or Chance, or Fate, Par Lost 1.133
ms 'fate'
The *Syrian* Damsels to lament his fate Par Lost 1.448
And trust themselves to fear no second fate: Par Lost 2.17
By my advice; since fate inevitable Par Lost 2.197
May hope when everlasting Fate shall yeild Par Lost 2.232
Will once more lift us up, in spight of Fate, Par Lost 2.393
By doom of Battel; and complain that Fate Par Lost 2.550
Of Providence, Foreknowledge, Will and Fate, Par Lost 2.559
Fixt Fate, free will, foreknowledg absolute, Par Lost 2.560
But Fate withstands, and to oppose th' attempt Par Lost 2.610
1674 'fate' in some copies
1667 'fate'
When ever that shall be; so Fate pronounc'd. Par Lost 2.809
Those other two equal'd with me in Fate, Par Lost 3.33
Thir maker, or thir making, or thir Fate, Par Lost 3.113
So without least impulse or shadow of Fate, Par Lost 3.120
By nature free, not over-rul'd by Fate Par Lost 5.527
Affrighted; but strict Fate had cast too deep Par Lost 6.869
Approach not mee, and what I will is Fate. Par Lost 7.173
And life more perfet have attaind then Fate Par Lost 9.689
Deitie for thee, when Fate will not permit. Par Lost 9.885
Not God Omnipotent, nor Fate, yet so Par Lost 9.927
Goe whither Fate and inclination strong Par Lost 10.265
Protesting Fate supreame; thence how I found Par Lost 10.480
So spake, so wish'd much-humbl'd *Eve*, but Fate Par Lost 11.181
Of fate, and chance, and change in human life; Par Reg 4.265
Fortune and Fate, as one regardless quite Par Reg 4.317
Or Heav'n write aught of Fate, by what the Stars Par Reg 4.383
All to the push of Fate, persue thy way Par Reg 4.470
On which the fate of gods and men is wound. Arcades 67
But wisest Fate sayes no, Nativity 149
Yet art thou not inglorious in thy fate; Fair Inf 22

Fate(*cont*)
Nature and fate had had no strife Winchester 13
In cours reciprocal, and had his fate Another 30
line not in 1658 text

Father
O Father, what intends thy hand, she cry'd, Par Lost 2.727
Against thy Fathers head? and know'st for whom; Par Lost 2.730
Me Father, and that Fantasm call'st my Son? Par Lost 2.743
But thou O Father, I forewarn thee, shun Par Lost 2.810
Thou art my Father, thou my Author, thou Par Lost 2.864
Now had the Almighty Father from above, Par Lost 3.56
Most glorious, in him all his Father shon Par Lost 3.139
Which uttering thus he to his Father spake. Par Lost 3.143
O Father, gracious was that word which clos'd Par Lost 3.144
That farr be from thee, Father, who art Judg Par Lost 3.154
Father, thy word is past, man shall find grace; Par Lost 3.227
Father, to see thy face, wherein no cloud Par Lost 3.262
Of his great Father. Admiration seis'd Par Lost 3.271
Thee Father first they sung Omnipotent, Par Lost 3.372
Made visible, th' Almighty Father shines, Par Lost 3.386
Thy Fathers dreadful Thunder didst not spare, Par Lost 3.393
Thee only extoll'd, Son of thy Fathers might, Par Lost 3.398
Father of Mercie and Grace, thou didst not doome Par Lost 3.401
Forget, nor from thy Fathers praise disjoine. Par Lost 3.415
On our first Father, half her swelling Breast Par Lost 4.495
Of Father, Son, and Brother first were known. Par Lost 4.757
So spake th' Eternal Father, and fulfilld Par Lost 5.246
That one Celestial Father gives to all. Par Lost 5.403
Orb within Orb, the Father infinite, Par Lost 5.596
Honourd by his great Father, and proclaimd Par Lost 5.663
Made answer. Mightie Father, thou thy foes Par Lost 5.735
As by his Word the mighty Father made Par Lost 5.836
Th' incensed Father, and th' incensed Son, Par Lost 5.847
From Father to his Son? strange point and new! Par Lost 5.855
Hymning th' Eternal Father: but the shout Par Lost 6.96
Had not th' Almightie Father where he sits Par Lost 6.671
Go then thou Mightiest in thy Fathers might, Par Lost 6.710
Shon full, he all his Father full exprest Par Lost 6.720
O Father, O Supream of heav'nly Thrones, Par Lost 6.723
Because the Father, t' whom in Heav'n supream Par Lost 6.814
And Temple of his mightie Father Thron'd Par Lost 6.890
In presence of th' Almightie Father, pleas'd Par Lost 7.11
Eternal Father from his Throne beheld Par Lost 7.137
Immense, and all his Father in him shon. Par Lost 7.196
Eternal Father (For where is not hee Par Lost 7.517
With his great Father (for he also went Par Lost 7.588
First Father, call'd by thee I come thy Guide Par Lost 8.298
Father and Mother, and to his Wife adhere; Par Lost 8.498
Eternal Father from his secret Cloud, Par Lost 10.32
So spake the Father, and unfoulding bright Par Lost 10.63
Resplendent all his Father manifest Par Lost 10.66
Father Eternal, thine is to decree, Par Lost 10.68
As Father of his Familie he clad Par Lost 10.216
Araying cover'd from his Fathers sight. Par Lost 10.223
So spake our Father penitent, nor *Eve* Par Lost 10.1097
Before the Fathers Throne: Them the glad Son Par Lost 11.20
See Father, what first fruits on Earth are sprung Par Lost 11.22
To whom the Father, without Cloud, serene. Par Lost 11.45
Though comfortless, as when a Father mourns Par Lost 11.760
Don to his Father, heard this heavie curse, Par Lost 12.103
To call by Vision from his Fathers house, Par Lost 12.121
The promise of the Father, who shall dwell Par Lost 12.487
In glory of the Father, to dissolve Par Lost 12.546
The Spirit descended, while the Fathers voice Par Reg 1.31
The glimpses of his Fathers glory shine. Par Reg 1.93
So spake the Eternal Father, and all Heaven Par Reg 1.168
The Father knows the Son; therefore secure Par Reg 1.176
Thy Father is the Eternal King, who rules Par Reg 1.236
And last the sum of all, my Father's voice, Par Reg 1.283
Thy Father, who is holy, wise and pure, Par Reg 1.486
Son own'd from Heaven by his Father's voice; Par Reg 2.85
His Father's business; what he meant I mus'd, Par Reg 2.99
Mee hungring more to do my Fathers will. Par Reg 2.259
A Carpenter thy Father known, thy self Par Reg 2.414
Resembling thy great Father: he seeks glory, Par Reg 3.110
To sit upon thy Father *David*'s Throne; Par Reg 3.153
By Mothers side thy Father, though thy right Par Reg 3.154
Zeal of thy Fathers house, Duty to free Par Reg 3.175
The Father in his purpose hath decreed, Par Reg 3.186
Would stand between me and thy Fathers ire, Par Reg 3.219
Judah and all thy Father *David*'s house Par Reg 3.282
Endeavour, as thy Father *David* did, Par Reg 3.353
Will ask thee skill; I to thy Fathers house Par Reg 4.552
True Image of the Father whether thron'd Par Reg 4.596
Against th' Attempter of thy Fathers Throne, Par Reg 4.603
Who would be now a Father in my stead? Samson 355
Sam. Appoint not heavenly disposition, Father, Samson 373
Could have befall'n thee and thy Fathers house. Samson 447
Sam. Father, I do acknowledge and confess Samson 448
Sam. Spare that proposal, Father, spare the trouble Samson 487
Must not omit a Fathers timely care Samson 602
Though Fame divulge him Father of five Sons Samson 1248
Fast by thy side, who from thy Fathers field Samson 1432
With supplication prone and Fathers tears Samson 1459
Conceiv'd, agreeable to a Fathers love, Samson 1506
To himself and Fathers house eternal fame; Samson 1717
Home to his Fathers house: there will I build him Samson 1733
Are coming to attend their Fathers state, Mask 35

Father*(cont)*
Trinity ms 'fathers'
Bridgewater ms 'fathers'
Much like his Father, but his Mother more, Mask 57
Bridgewater ms 'father'
Trinity ms 'father'
2. *Bro*. O brother, 'tis my father Shepherd sure. Mask 493
Bridgewater ms 'fathers'

That had the Scepter from his father *Brute*. Mask 828
1673 'Father'
Is your Fathers residence, Mask 947
Trinity ms 'fathers'
Bridgewater ms 'fathers'
The brood of folly without father bred, Penseroso 2
And with his Father work us a perpetual peace. Nativity 7
Wherin your Father flourisht, yet by you Sonnet 10, 10
Lawrence of vertuous Father vertuous Son, Sonnet 20, 1
Fatherless
Regard the weak and fatherless Psalm 82, 9
Fatherly
Whereto thus *Adam* fatherly displeas'd. Par Lost 12.63
Fathers
Our Fathers here with Manna; in the Mount Par Reg 1.351
Expected of our Fathers; we have heard Par Reg 2.33
Thir Fathers in the land of *Egypt* serv'd, Par Reg 3.379
The God of their fore-fathers; but so dy'd Par Reg 3.422
When to the promis'd land thir Fathers pass'd; Par Reg 3.439
God of our Fathers, what is man! Samson 667
Chor. Fathers are wont to lay up for thir Sons, Samson 1485
When all our Fathers worship't Stocks and Stones, Sonnet 18, 4
Fathom
Ten thousand fadom deep, and to this hour Par Lost 2.934
Fault
Millions of Spirits for his fault amerc't Par Lost 1.609
Hee and his faithless Progenie: whose fault? Par Lost 3.96
Foreknowledge had no influence on their fault, Par Lost 3.118
For one mans fault thus guiltless be condemn'd, Par Lost 10.823
Immoveable till peace obtain'd from fault Par Lost 10.938
Sam. That fault I take not on me, but transfer Samson 241
Enough, and more the burden of that fault; Samson 431
Man. Be penitent and for thy fault contrite, Samson 502
Faults
Humbly our faults, and pardon beg, with tears Par Lost 10.1089
Humbly thir faults, and pardon beg'd, with tears Par Lost 10.1101
Whose foul Idolatries, and other faults Par Lost 12.337
To publish them, both common female faults: Samson 777
Faulty
So goodly and erect, though faultie since, Par Lost 11.509
Faun
Satyr, or Fawn, or Silvan? But these haunts Par Reg 2.191
Fauns
Rough *Satyrs* danc'd, and *Fauns* with clov'n heel, Lycidas 34
In some Purlieu two gentle Fawnes at play, Par Lost 4.404
Faunus
Nor *Faunus* haunted. Here in close recess Par Lost 4.708
Favonius
On smoother, till *Favonius* re-inspire Sonnet 20, 6
Favour
Should favour equal to the Sons of Heaven: Par Lost 1.654
His chief delight and favour, him for whom Par Lost 3.664
Thy favour, in this honour done to man, Par Lost 5.462
In favour and praeeminence, yet fraught Par Lost 5.661
Divine interpreter, by favour sent Par Lost 7.72
By sufferance, and thy wonted favour deign'd. Par Lost 8.202
Favour from Heav'n, our witness from th' event. Par Lost 9.334
What else but favor, grace, and mercie shon? Par Lost 10.1096
That I was heard with favour; peace returnd Par Lost 11.153
Favour unmerited by me, who sought Par Lost 12.278
Such favour I unworthie am voutsaft, Par Lost 12.622
They whom I favour thrive in wealth amain, Par Reg 2.430
Whom God hath of his special favour rais'd Samson 273
Favour renew'd, and add a greater sin Samson 1357
To favour, and perhaps to set thee free. Samson 1412
Under the spreading favour of these Pines, Mask 184
& favour our close jocondrie Mask Tr. ms 12.29
With lucky words favour my destin'd Urn, Lycidas 20
Lift up the favour of thy count'nance bright. Psalm 4, 30
Him with thy lasting favour and good will. Psalm 5, 40
Thy Land to favour graciously Psalm 85, 1
Thine ear with favour bend. Psalm 88, 8
Favourable
O favourable spirit, propitious guest, Par Lost 5.507
The sourse of life; next favourable thou, Par Lost 11.169
Thir favourable ear, that I may fetch thee Samson 921
Favoured
Favour'd of Heav'n so highly, to fall off Par Lost 1.30
In power and excellence, but favour'd more Par Lost 2.350
Hale highly favour'd, among women blest; Par Reg 2.68
A sword shall pierce, this is my favour'd lot, Par Reg 2.91
Favour'd of Heav'n who finds Samson 1046
Therfore when any favour'd of high *Jove*, Mask 78
The highly favour'd *Joseph* bore Winchester 65
Favouring
But favouring and assisting to the end. Samson 1720
Favouring the wicked *by your might*. Psalm 82, 7
Favourite
Provokes my envie, this new Favorite Par Lost 9.175

Favourite*(cont)*
Committing to a wicked Favourite Par Reg 4.95
Favours
Most Favors, who can please him long; Mee first Par Lost 9.949
Of highest favours past Samson 685
Fawned
Once fawn'd, and cring'd, and servilly ador'd Par Lost 4.959
Fawning

Or like a Fawning Parasite obey'st; Par Reg 1.452
Fays
And the yellow-skirted *Fayes*, Nativity 235
Fealty
Disloyal breaks his fealtie, and sinns Par Lost 3.204
From thee thir Names, and pay thee fealtie Par Lost 8.344
Our fealtie from God, or to disturb Par Lost 9.262
Fear
Anguish and doubt and fear and sorrow and pain Par Lost 1.558
ms 'feare'
On half the Nations, and with fear of change Par Lost 1.598
At once with joy and fear his heart rebounds. Par Lost 1.788
And trust themselves to fear no second fate: Par Lost 2.17
Went all his fear: of God, or Hell, or worse Par Lost 2.49
Fear to be worse destroy'd: what can be worse Par Lost 2.85
What fear we then? what doubt we to incense Par Lost 2.94
And vent'rous, if that fail them, shrink and fear Par Lost 2.205
They dreaded worse then Hell: so much the fear Par Lost 2.293
Heav'n, whose high walls fear no assault or Siege, Par Lost 2.343
Than Fables yet have feign'd, or fear conceiv'd, Par Lost 2.627
Tore through my entrails, that with fear and pain Par Lost 2.783
So farwel Hope, and with Hope farwel Fear, Par Lost 4.108
Cross-barrd and bolted fast, fear no assault, Par Lost 4.190
I fear, hath ventur'd from the deep, to raise Par Lost 4.574
Yet thus, unmovd with fear, accost him soon. Par Lost 4.822
Or less be lost. Thy fear, said *Zephon* bold, Par Lost 4.854
This uncouth dream, of evil sprung I fear; Par Lost 5.98
No fear lest Dinner coole; when thus began Par Lost 5.396
That argu'd fear; each on himself reli'd, Par Lost 6.238
Defensive scarse, or with pale fear surpris'd, Par Lost 6.393
Then first with fear surpris'd and sense of paine Par Lost 6.394
Not liable to fear or flight or paine. Par Lost 6.397
Adverse, that they shall fear we have disarmd Par Lost 6.490
Abandon fear; to strength and counsel joind Par Lost 6.494
This day, fear not his flight; so thick a Cloud Par Lost 6.539
Yet fell; remember, and fear to transgress. Par Lost 6.912
Leave them to God above, him serve and feare; Par Lost 8.168
Eate freely with glad heart; fear here no dearth: Par Lost 8.322
His fraud is then thy fear, which plain inferrs Par Lost 9.285
Thy equal fear that my firm Faith and Love Par Lost 9.286
How are we happie, still in fear of harm? Par Lost 9.326
Your feare it self of Death removes the feare. Par Lost 9.702
What fear I then, rather what know to feare Par Lost 9.773
And fear of Death deliver to the Windes. Par Lost 9.989
No detriment need feare, goe and be strong. Par Lost 10.409
Would Thunder in my ears, no fear of worse Par Lost 10.780
To perpetuitie; Ay me, that fear Par Lost 10.813
From what we fear for both, let us make short, Par Lost 10.1000
To be forestall'd; much more I fear least Death Par Lost 10.1024
Beseeching him, so as we need not fear Par Lost 10.1082
Out of despaire, joy, but with fear yet linkt; Par Lost 11.139
And carnal fear that day dimm'd *Adams* eye. Par Lost 11.212
That I should fear, nor sociably mild, Par Lost 11.234
True patience, and to temper joy with fear Par Lost 11.361
And fear of God, from whom thir pietie feign'd Par Lost 11.799
1667 'feare'
Warr terrifie them inexpert, and feare Par Lost 12.218
Acceptance of large Grace, from servil fear Par Lost 12.305
And love with fear the onely God, to walk Par Lost 12.562
1669 'fear'
1667 'feare'
His birth to our just fear gave no small cause, Par Reg 1.66
Things highest, greatest, multiplies my fear. Par Reg 1.69
And make perswasion do the work of fear; Par Reg 1.223
Wilt thou impute to obedience what thy fear Par Reg 1.422
To thy Adorers; thou with trembling fear, Par Reg 1.451
All fear of thee, arise and vindicate Par Reg 2.47
And from the sting of Famine fear no harm, Par Reg 2.257
For where no hope is left, is left no fear; Par Reg 3.206
Shalt raign, and *Rome* or *Caesar* not need fear. Par Reg 3.385
Long since. Wert thou so void of fear or shame, Par Reg 4.189
To whom the Fiend with fear abasht reply'd. Par Reg 4.195
Was distant; and these flaws, though mortals fear them Par Reg 4.454
Of Tempter and Temptation without fear. Par Reg 4.617
Prevailing over fear, and timerous doubt Samson 740
Chor. Look now for no inchanting voice, nor fear Samson 1065
Fear I incurable; bring up thy van, Samson 1234
Chor. He will directly to the Lords, I fear, Samson 1250
God for the fear of Man, and Man prefer, Samson 1374
From other hands we need not much to fear. Samson 1526
I cannot be, that I should fear to change it. Mask 328
Bridgewater ms 'feare'
Trinity ms 'feare'
1637 'feare'
Or if they be but false alarms of Fear, Mask 364
line not in Bridgewater ms
line not in Trinity ms
1637 'Feare'
I fear the dred events that dog them both, Mask 405

Fear(*cont*)
1637 'feare'
Bridgewater ms 'feare'
Trinity ms 'feare'
Yet where an equall poise of hope and fear — Mask 410
Trinity ms 'feare' ←'feares'
1637 'feare'
Bridgewater ms 'feare'
That I encline to hope, rather then fear, — Mask 412
Trinity ms 'feare'
Bridgewater ms 'feare'
1637 'feare'
Amaz'd I stood, harrow'd with grief and fear, — Mask 565
Trinity ms 'feare'
1637 'feare'
Bridgewater ms 'feare'
Co. She fables not, I feel that I do fear — Mask 800
line not in Trinity ms
line not in Bridgewater ms
1637 'feare'
While yet there was no fear of *Jove*. — Penseroso 30
Yet there is something that doth force my fear, — Vacation 67
Be taught ye Judges of the earth; with fear — Psalm 2, 23
I fear not though incamping round about — Psalm 3, 17
Into thy house; I in thy fear — Psalm 5, 19
Surely to such as do him fear — Psalm 85, 37
To fear thy name my heart unite — Psalm 86, 39
No fear of thee have set. — Psalm 86, 52

Feared
Of knowledge past or present, could have fear'd, — Par Lost 1.628
Th' event is fear'd; should we again provoke — Par Lost 2.82
(Certain to be refus'd) what erst they feard; — Par Lost 2.470
Admir'd, not fear'd; God and his Son except, — Par Lost 2.678
And pious awe, that feard to have offended. — Par Lost 5.135
Superior, nor of violence fear'd aught; — Par Lost 5.905
Foul on himself; then wherefore shund or feard — Par Lost 9.331
At first, as one who sought access, but feard — Par Lost 9.511
Insatiate, I thus single, nor have feard — Par Lost 9.536
Not just, not God; not feard then, nor obeyd: — Par Lost 9.701
Her former trespass fear'd, the more to soothe — Par Lost 9.1006
Because not yet inflicted, as he fear'd, — Par Lost 10.51
My voice thou oft hast heard, and hast not fear'd, — Par Lost 10.119
I never fear'd they could, though noising loud — Par Reg 4.488
Of fancy, feard lest one day thou wouldst leave me — Samson 794
Less therefore to be pleas'd, obey'd, or fear'd, — Samson 900
Lov'd, honour'd, fear'd me, thou alone could hate me — Samson 939
With God not parted from him, as was feard, — Samson 1719
Fear'd her stern frown, and she was queen oth' Woods. — Mask 446
Bridgewater ms 'feard'

Fearest
His violence thou fearst not, being such, — Par Lost 9.282
And what thou fearst, alike destroyes all hope — Par Lost 10.838

Fearing
The present, fearing guiltie what his wrauth — Par Lost 10.340
Fresh in thir mindes, fearing the Deitie, — Par Lost 12.15
As fearing God nor man, contemning all — Par Reg 4.304

Fearless
Fearless, endanger'd Heav'ns perpetual King; — Par Lost 1.131
Fearless to be o'rmatcht by living might. — Par Lost 2.855
Far off and fearless, nor with cause to boast, — Par Lost 4.14
The flaming Seraph fearless, though alone — Par Lost 5.875
Fearless assault, and to the brow of Heav'n — Par Lost 6.51
Accepted, fearless in his righteous Cause, — Par Lost 6.804
Of heavier on himself, fearless return'd. — Par Lost 9.57
Fearless unfeard he slept: in at his Mouth — Par Lost 9.187
Offended; fearless of reproach and scorn, — Par Lost 11.811
Fearless of danger, like a petty God — Samson 529
Fearless at home of partners in my love. — Samson 810

Fears
Of hope in fears and dangers, heard so oft — Par Lost 1.275
Thir fainting courage, and dispel'd thir fears. — Par Lost 1.530
ms 'feares'
O Conscience, into what Abyss of fears — Par Lost 10.842
Why stand we longer shivering under feares, — Par Lost 10.1003
For long indulgence to their fears or grief: — Par Reg 1.110
Let us be glad of this, and all our fears — Par Reg 2.53
Motherly cares and fears got head, and rais'd — Par Reg 2.64
And fears as eminent, above the lot — Par Reg 2.70
Passions, Desires, and Fears, is more a King; — Par Reg 2.467
While I at home sate full of cares and fears — Samson 805
Thir foe to misery beneath thir fears, — Samson 1469
Leans her unpillow'd head fraught with sad fears. — Mask 355
Trinity ms 'fraught with sad feares' ←'musing at our unkindnesse'
Bridgewater ms 'feares'
Spir. Ay me unhappy then my fears are true. — Mask 511
Bridgewater ms 'feares'
El. Bro. What fears good *Thyrsis?* Prethee briefly shew. — Mask 512
Trinity ms 'feares'
Bridgewater ms 'feares'
But he her fears to cease, — Nativity 45
That so they may without suspect or fears — Vacation 27
And succour our just Fears — Forcers 18
Trinity ms 'feares'

Feast
Ministring Spirits, traind up in Feast and Song; — Par Lost 6.167
At Joust and Torneament; then marshal'd Feast — Par Lost 9.37
With Feast and Musick all the Tents resound. — Par Lost 11.592

Feast(*cont*)
To luxurie and riot, feast and dance, — Par Lost 11.715
With large Wine-offerings pour'd, and sacred Feast, — Par Lost 12.21
Had measur'd twice six years, at our great Feast — Par Reg 1.210
Sung Victor, and from Heavenly Feast refresht — Par Reg 4.637
This day a solemn Feast the people hold — Samson 12
This day the *Philistines* a popular Feast — Samson 434
And in your City held my Nuptial Feast: — Samson 1194
This day to *Dagon* is a solemn Feast, — Samson 1311
To honour this great Feast, and great Assembly; — Samson 1315
To come and play before them at thir Feast. — Samson 1448
The Feast and noon grew high, and Sacrifice — Samson 1612
Met from all parts to solemnize this Feast. — Samson 1656
Mean while welcom Joy, and Feast, — Mask 102
Trinity ms 'feast'
Bridgewater ms 'feast'
And a perpetual feast of nectar'd sweets, — Mask 479
Ne're looks to Heav'n amidst his gorgeous feast, — Mask 777
Bridgewater ms 'feasts'
And pomp, and feast, and revelry, — Allegro 127
Then how to scramble at the shearers feast, — Lycidas 117
In solemn Songs at King *Alcinous* feast, — Vacation 49
The God that sits at marriage feast; — Winchester 18
What neat repast shall feast us, light and choice, — Sonnet 20, 9
Our solemn Feast *comes round*. — Psalm 81, 12

Feasted
And the well-feasted Priest then soonest fir'd — Samson 1419

Feastful
The Virgins also shall on feastful days — Samson 1741
Thou, when the Bridegroom with his feastfull friends — Sonnet 9, 12

Feasts
His holy Rites, and solemn Feasts profan'd, — Par Lost 1.390
ms 'feasts'
At Heav'ns high feasts to have fed: yet what compare? — Par Lost 5.467
Thir sumptuous gluttonies, and gorgeous feasts — Par Reg 4.114
In courts, at feasts, and high solemnities — Mask 746
line not in Bridgewater ms

Feat
With stories told of many a feat, — Allegro 101

Feathered
Shaddowd from either heele with featherd maile — Par Lost 5.284
Thir callow young, but featherd soon and fledge — Par Lost 7.420
With featherd Cincture, naked else and wilde — Par Lost 9.1117
Entice the dewy-feather'd Sleep; — Penseroso 146

Feathers
She plumes her feathers, and lets grow her wings — Mask 378

Feathery
Count the night watches to his feathery Dames, — Mask 347
Trinity ms 'featherie'
1637 'featherie'
Bridgewater ms 'featherie'

Feats
Till thickest Legions close; with feats of Arms — Par Lost 2.537
Of thy prodigious might and feats perform'd — Samson 1083
And feats of War defeats — Samson 1278
To shew them feats, and play before thir god, — Samson 1340
Proof of his mighty strength in feats and games; — Samson 1602

Feature
So sented the grim Feature, and upturn'd — Par Lost 10.279

Features
It is for homely features to keep home, — Mask 748
line not in Bridgewater ms

Fed
Still urges, and a fiery Deluge, fed — Par Lost 1.68
Of Starry Lamps and blazing Cressets fed — Par Lost 1.728
With odours; there ye shall be fed and fill'd — Par Lost 2.843
On Hills where Flocks are fed, flies toward the Springs — Par Lost 3.435
Ran Nectar, visiting each plant, and fed — Par Lost 4.240
To be sustaind and fed; of Elements — Par Lost 5.415
At Heav'ns high feasts to have fed: yet what compare? — Par Lost 5.467
Soon dri'd, and on the reaking moisture fed. — Par Lost 8.256
Proceeding from the mouth of God; who fed — Par Reg 1.350
Sole but with holiest Meditations fed, — Par Reg 2.110
Nor mind it, fed with better thoughts that feed — Par Reg 2.258
Native of *Thebez* wandring here was fed — Par Reg 2.313
Or thirst, and as he fed, Angelic Quires — Par Reg 4.593
Self-fed, and self-consum'd, if this fail, — Mask 597
Trinity ms 'selfe fed'
Bridgewater ms 'selfe fed'
1637 'Selfe fed'
Fed the same flock, by fountain, shade, and rill. — Lycidas 24
The hungry Sheep look up, and are not fed, — Lycidas 125

Fee
Who liv'd in both, unstain'd with gold or fee, — Sonnet 10, 3
Which after held the Sun and Moon in fee. — Sonnet 12, 7
Trinity ms '*fee*' ←'fee' ←'Fee'

Feeble
In feeble hearts, propense anough before — Samson 455
Or if Vertue feeble were, — Mask 1022
And here though grief my feeble hands up-lock, — Passion 45

Feed
Of mine own brood, that on my bowels feed: — Par Lost 2.863
Then feed on thoughts, that voluntarie move — Par Lost 3.37
Earth and the Sea feed Air, the Air those Fires — Par Lost 5.417
At Feed or Fountain never had I found. — Par Lost 9.597
To reach, and feed at once both Bodie and Mind? — Par Lost 9.779
Feed first, on each Beast next, and Fish, and Fowle, — Par Lost 10.604
Nor mind it, fed with better thoughts that feed — Par Reg 2.258

Feed(*cont*)
Longer then thou canst feed them on thy cost? Par Reg 2.421
Mess. Feed on that first, there may in grief be surfet. Samson 1562
Should in a pet of temperance feed on Pulse, Mask 721
Bridgewater ms 'feede'
All living creatures he doth feed, Psalm 136, 85
And we would feed them *from the shock* Psalm 81, 65

Feeder
Cramms, and blasphemes his feeder. Shall I go on? Mask 779

Feedest
Thou feed'st them with the bread of tears, Psalm 80, 21

Feeds
The grosser feeds the purer, Earth the Sea, Par Lost 5.416
The Female Bee that feeds her Husband Drone Par Lost 7.490

Feel
What can it then avail though yet we feel Par Lost 1.153
ms 'feele'
In which they were, or the fierce pains not feel; Par Lost 1.336
On this side nothing; and by proof we feel Par Lost 2.101
Thir noxious vapour, or enur'd not feel, Par Lost 2.216
In doing what we most in suffering feel? Par Lost 2.340
Are brought: and feel by turns the bitter change Par Lost 2.598
And feel thy sovran vital Lamp; but thou Par Lost 3.22
Farr heavier load thy self expect to feel Par Lost 4.972
Distinguish not: for soon expect to feel Par Lost 5.892
Thir Deities to assert, who while they feel Par Lost 6.157
And feel that I am happier then I know, Par Lost 8.282
What inward thence I feel, not therefore foild, Par Lost 8.608
Pleasures about me, so much more I feel Par Lost 9.120
Why shouldst not thou like sense within thee feel Par Lost 9.315
Mother of Science, Now I feel thy Power Par Lost 9.680
Would never from my heart; no no, I feel Par Lost 9.913
So forcible within my heart I feel Par Lost 9.955
So faithful Love unequald; but I feel Par Lost 9.983
They swim in mirth, and fansie that they feel Par Lost 9.1009
Methinks I feel new strength within me rise, Par Lost 10.243
From this day onward, which I feel begun Par Lost 10.811
Horrid to think, how horrible to feel! Par Lost 11.465
In apprehension then in substance feel Par Lost 11.775
What from within I feel my self, and hear Par Reg 1.198
Nearer acquainted, now I feel by proof, Par Reg 1.400
But now I feel I hunger, which declares, Par Reg 2.252
Unwholsom draught: but here I feel amends, Samson 9
So much I feel my genial spirits droop, Samson 594
Unless he feel within Samson 663
Soon feel, whose God is strongest, thine or mine. Samson 1155
Sam. Be of good courage, I begin to feel Samson 1381
Break off, break off, I feel the different pace, Mask 145
Trinity ms 'feele' ← 'heare'
Bridgewater ms 'feele'
1637 'feele'
Co. She fables not, I feel that I do fear Mask 800
1637 'feele'
line not in Bridgewater ms
line not in Trinity ms

Feelest
His full wrauth whose thou feelst as yet lest part, Par Lost 10.951
Under his feet: for proof, e're this thou feel'st Par Reg 4.621

Feeling
Who of all Ages to succeed, but feeling Par Lost 10.733
Of worse torments me then the feeling can. Par Reg 3.208
And not as feeling through all parts diffus'd, Samson 96

Feels
He feels from *Juda*'s Land Nativity 221
My spirit som transporting *Cherub* feels, Passion 38

Feet
Of unblest feet. Him followed his next Mate, Par Lost 1.238
Sufficient? who shall tempt with wandring feet Par Lost 2.404
With head, hands, wings or feet pursues his way, Par Lost 2.949
That wash thy hallowd feet, and warbling flow, Par Lost 3.31
To stoop with wearied wings, and willing feet Par Lost 3.73
Of Heav'ns ascent they lift thir Feet, when loe Par Lost 3.486
Lights on his feet. As when a prowling Wolfe, Par Lost 4.183
O friends, I hear the tread of nimble feet Par Lost 4.866
And colours dipt in Heav'n; the third his feet Par Lost 5.283
That whom they hit, none on thir feet might stand, Par Lost 6.592
Her state with Oarie feet: yet oft they quit Par Lost 7.440
Stood on my feet; about me round I saw Par Lost 8.261
In adoration at his feet I fell Par Lost 8.315
Whom he shall tread at last under our feet; Par Lost 10.190
As when he wash'd his servants feet so now Par Lost 10.215
And tresses all disorderd, at his feet Par Lost 10.911
Now at his feet submissive in distress, Par Lost 10.942
By th' Angel, on thy feet thou stoodst at last, Par Lost 11.759
Why move thy feet so slow to what is best, Par Reg 3.224
It was a Mountain at whose verdant feet Par Reg 3.253
Under his feet: for proof, e're this thou feel'st Par Reg 4.621
The tread of many feet stearing this way; Samson 111
Your younger feet, while mine cast back with age Samson 336
Dal. With doubtful feet and wavering resolution Samson 732
To bring my feet again into the snare Samson 931
To thine whose doors my feet shall never enter. Samson 950
Shall I inform my unacquainted feet Mask 180
Trinity ms 'feete'
Bridgewater ms 'feete'
Without the sure guess of well-practiz'd feet. Mask 310
Bridgewater ms 'feete'
By *Thetis* tinsel-slipper'd feet, Mask 877

Feet(*cont*)
Bridgewater ms 'feete'
Thus I set my printless feet Mask 897
Bridgewater ms 'feete'
But let my due feet never fail, Penseroso 155
And lay it lowly at his blessed feet; Nativity 25
With radiant feet the tissued clouds down stearing, Nativity 146
Thou hast put all under his lordly feet, Psalm 8, 18

Feign
Say and unsay, feign, flatter, or abjure? Par Reg 1.474
Like whom the Gentiles feign to bear up Heav'n. Samson 150

Feigned
Than Fables yet have feign'd, or fear conceiv'd, Par Lost 2.627
Sutable grace diffus'd, so well he feignd; Par Lost 3.639
What feign'd submission swore: ease would recant Par Lost 4.96
More sacred and sequesterd, though but feignd, Par Lost 4.706
Then Wood-Nymph, or the fairest Goddess feign'd Par Lost 5.381
In Battels feign'd; the better fortitude Par Lost 9.31
Spot more delicious then those Gardens feign'd Par Lost 9.439
Hate stronger, under shew of Love well feign'd, Par Lost 9.492
And fear of God, from whom thir pietie feign'd Par Lost 11.799
Fairer then feign'd of old, or fabl'd since Par Reg 2.358
And reconcilement move with feign'd remorse, Samson 752
Confess it feign'd, weakness is thy excuse, Samson 829
In feign'd Religion, smooth hypocrisie. Samson 872
Therefore without feign'd shifts let be assign'd Samson 1116

Feignedst
Feigndst at thy birth was giv'n thee in thy hair, Samson 1135

Feigning
Secular power, though feigning still to act Par Lost 12.517
Feigning to disappear. Darkness now rose, Par Reg 4.397

Felicity
Others in vertue plac'd felicity, Par Reg 4.297
Through pangs fled to felicity, Winchester 68

Fell
O how unlike the place from whence they fell! Par Lost 1.75
Beguil'd by fair Idolatresses, fell Par Lost 1.445
Where he fell flat, and sham'd his Worshipers: Par Lost 1.461
Fell not from Heaven, or more gross to love Par Lost 1.491
When *Charlemain* with all his Peerage fell Par Lost 1.586
Mammon, the least erected Spirit that fell Par Lost 1.679
Men call'd him *Mulciber;* and how he fell Par Lost 1.740
To Noon he fell, from Noon to dewy Eve, Par Lost 1.743
Fell long before; nor aught avail'd him now Par Lost 1.748
Through all the Empyrean: down they fell Par Lost 2.771
Fell with us from on high: from them I go Par Lost 2.826
To that side Heav'n from whence your Legions fell: Par Lost 2.1006
But hee once past, soon after when man fell, Par Lost 2.1023
Freely they stood who stood, and fell who fell. Par Lost 3.102
The first sort by thir own suggestion fell, Par Lost 3.129
I fell, how glorious once above thy Spheare; Par Lost 4.39
Fell not, but stand unshak'n, from within Par Lost 4.64
Waterd the Garden; thence united fell · Par Lost 4.230
More grateful, to thir Supper Fruits they fell, Par Lost 4.331
Since *Satan* fell, whom follie overthrew, Par Lost 4.905
And fell asleep; but O how glad I wak'd Par Lost 5.92
Each in thir Chrystal sluce, hee ere they fell Par Lost 5.133
And to thir viands fell, nor seemingly Par Lost 5.434
Which hung not, but so swift with tempest fell Par Lost 6.190
Though standing else as Rocks, but down they fell Par Lost 6.593
Flew off, and into strange vagaries fell, Par Lost 6.614
Nor less on either side tempestuous fell Par Lost 6.844
Nine dayes they fell; confounded *Chaos* roard, Par Lost 6.871
Yet fell; remember, and fear to transgress. Par Lost 6.912
Fell with his flaming Legions through the Deep Par Lost 7.134
In adoration at his feet I fell Par Lost 8.315
Of sleep, which instantly fell on me, call'd Par Lost 8.458
Each other, till supplanted down he fell Par Lost 10.513
Of ugly Serpents; horror on them fell, Par Lost 10.539
Down fell both Spear and Shield, down they as fast, Par Lost 10.542
With soot and cinders fill'd; so oft they fell Par Lost 10.570
Through the still Night, not now, as ere man fell, Par Lost 10.846
Fell humble, and imbracing them, besaught Par Lost 10.912
Repairing where he judg'd them prostrate fell Par Lost 10.1099
That beat out life; he fell, and deadly pale Par Lost 11.446
Wearied I fell asleep: but now lead on; Par Lost 12.614
To thy Delusions; justly, since they fell Par Reg 1.443
Though *Adam* by his Wives allurement fell, Par Reg 2.134
Belial the dislolutest Spirit that fell, Par Reg 2.150
To lay hills plain, fell woods, or valleys fill, Par Reg 3.332
Who wrought their own captivity, fell off Par Reg 3.415
The next to fabling fell and smooth conceits, Par Reg 4.295
And how the world began, and how man fell Par Reg 4.311
From the four hinges of the world, and fell Par Reg 4.415
But Satan smitten with amazement fell Par Reg 4.562
Throttl'd at length in the Air, expir'd and fell; Par Reg 4.568
Fell whence he stood to see his Victor fall. Par Reg 4.571
So strook with dread and anguish fell the Fiend, Par Reg 4.576
So Satan fell and strait a fiery Globe Par Reg 4.581
A thousand fore-skins fell, the flower of *Palestin* Samson 144
Then swoll'n with pride into the snare I fell Samson 532
All by him fell thou say'st, by whom fell he, Samson 1580
Mess. Unwounded of his enemies he fell. Samson 1582
On *Circes* Iland fell (who knows not *Circe* Mask 50
And downward fell into a groveling Swine) Mask 53
And fell into the pit he made, Psalm 7, 56

Fell
Others with vast *Typhoean* rage more fell Par Lost 2.539

Fell*(cont)*
To a fell Adversarie, his hate or shame: Par Lost 10.906
And fell *Charybdis* murmur'd soft applause: Mask 259
And in despight of *Pharao* fell, Psalm 136, 41
Speak to them in his wrath, and in his fell Psalm 2, 10
And they that hate thee *proud and fell* Psalm 83, 7

Felled
Saw where the Sword of *Michael* smote, and fell'd Par Lost 6.250
With branches lopt, in Wood or Mountain fell'd) Par Lost 6.575
Unarm'd, and with a trivial weapon fell'd Samson 263

Fellow
Then of our fellow servant, and inquire Par Lost 8.225

Fellows
The fellows of his crime, the followers rather Par Lost 1.606
Above his fellows, with Monarchal pride Par Lost 2.428
Before thy fellows, ambitious to win Par Lost 6.160
Som roaving Robber calling to his fellows. Mask 485
Bridgewater ms 'fellowes'

Fellowship
Tedious alike: Of fellowship I speak Par Lost 8.389
Whose fellowship therefore unmeet for thee Par Lost 8.442
That fellowship in pain divides not smart, Par Reg 1.401

Fellowships
In fellowships of joy: the Sons of Light Par Lost 11.80

Felon
On th' other side: which when th' arch-fellon saw Par Lost 4.179
He ask'd the Waves, and ask'd the Fellon winds, Lycidas 91
Trinity ms 'fellon'
1638 'felon'

Felonious
Why shouldst thou, but for som fellonious end, Mask 196
line not in Bridgewater ms

Felt
That felt unusual weight, till on dry Land Par Lost 1.227
To us is adverse. Who but felt of late Par Lost 2.77
With conquest, felt th' envenom'd robe, and tore Par Lost 2.543
Prodigious motion felt and rueful throes. Par Lost 2.780
And felt how awful goodness is, and saw Par Lost 4.847
And felt tenfold confusion in thir fall Par Lost 6.872
Transported touch; here passion first I felt, Par Lost 8.530
Earth felt the wound, and Nature from her seat Par Lost 9.782
Misgave him; hee the faultring measure felt; Par Lost 9.846
Not felt, nor shall be twice, for never more Par Lost 9.859
By this new felt attraction and instinct. Par Lost 10.263
Now also evidence, but straight I felt Par Lost 10.361
Though distant from thee Worlds between, yet felt Par Lost 10.362
His Visage drawn he felt to sharp and spare, Par Lost 10.511
They felt themselves now changing; down thir arms, Par Lost 10.541
To sorrow abandond, but worse felt within, Par Lost 10.717
Felt less remorse: they forthwith to the place Par Lost 10.1098
His first-begot we know, and sore have felt, Par Reg 1.89
Nor tasted humane food, nor hunger felt Par Reg 1.308
Repuls't, without much inward passion felt Samson 1006
Much more affliction then already felt Samson 1257
Felt in his arms, with head a while enclin'd, Samson 1636
But such a sacred, and home-felt delight, Mask 262
Trinity ms 'home felt'
Bridgewater ms 'homefelt'

Female
The Female Bee that feeds her Husband Drone Par Lost 7.490
1667 'Femal'
Female for Race; then bless'd Mankinde, and said, Par Lost 7.530
1667 'Femal'
Communicating Male and Femal Light, Par Lost 8.150
In Femal Sex, the more to draw his Love, Par Lost 9.822
But fondly overcome with Femal charm. Par Lost 9.999
Disturbances on Earth through Femal snares, Par Lost 10.897
For that fair femal Troop thou sawst, that seemd Par Lost 11.614
Of female Seed, far abler to resist Par Reg 1.151
All her array; her female pride deject, Par Reg 2.219
Femal of sex it seems, Samson 711
To publish them, both common female faults: Samson 777
Over his female in due awe, Samson 1055
By female usurpation, nor dismay'd. Samson 1060

Feminine
These Feminine. For Spirits when they please Par Lost 1.423
ms 'feminine'
Angelic, but more soft, and Feminine, Par Lost 9.458
With Men as Angels without Feminine, Par Lost 10.893
With blandisht parlies, feminine assaults, Samson 403

Fen
In fog, or fire, by lake, or moorish fen, Mask 433
Bridgewater ms 'Fen'

Fence
Leaps o're the fence with ease into the Fould: Par Lost 4.187
To fence my ear against thy sorceries. Samson 937
That hath so well been taught her dazling fence, Mask 791
line not in Trinity ms
line not in Bridgewater ms
And brok'n down her Fence, Psalm 80, 50

Fenced
Ill fenc't for Heav'n to keep out such a foe Par Lost 4.372
Fenc'd up the verdant wall; each beauteous flour, Par Lost 4.697
Thus fenc't, and as they thought, thir shame in part Par Lost 9.1119

Fenceless
Immovable of this now fenceless world Par Lost 10.303

Fennel
Then smell of sweetest Fenel or the Teats Par Lost 9.581

Fens
Rocks, Caves, Lakes, Fens, Bogs, Dens, and shades of death, Par Lost 2.621
Mean while the tepid Caves, and Fens and shoares Par Lost 7.417

Ferment
But finding no redress, ferment and rage, Samson 619

Fermented
Fermented the great Mother to conceave, Par Lost 7.281

Ferry
They ferry over this *Lethean* Sound Par Lost 2.604

Fertile
Was fair *Damascus*, on the fertil Banks Par Lost 1.468
ms 'fertile'
Out of the fertil ground he caus'd to grow Par Lost 4.216
Glistring with dew; fragrant the fertil earth Par Lost 4.645
Her fertil growth, and by disburd'ning grows Par Lost 5.319
Op'ning her fertil Woomb teem'd at a Birth Par Lost 7.454
Shall tend thee, and the fertil burden ease Par Lost 9.801
Fertil of corn the glebe, of oyl and wine, Par Reg 3.259

Fertility
And strangl'd with her waste fertility; Mask 729
1637 'fertilitie'
Trinity ms 'fertilitie'
Bridgewater ms 'fertillitie'

Fervent
So spake the fervent Angel, but his zeale Par Lost 5.849

Fervently
To whom thus *Adam* fervently repli'd. Par Lost 9.342
To whom our Saviour fervently reply'd. Par Reg 3.121

Fervid
Shot down direct his fervid Raies to warme Par Lost 5.301
Then staid the fervid Wheeles, and in his hand Par Lost 7.224

Fesole
At Ev'ning from the top of *Fesole*, Par Lost 1.289
ms 'fesole'

Fester
Rankle, and fester, and gangrene, Samson 621

Festered
And are as Balm to fester'd wounds. Samson 186

Festival
The morning Trumpets Festival proclaim'd Samson 1598
And Heav'n as at som festivall, Nativity 147
1673 'Festivall'

Festivals
So oft in Festivals of joy and love Par Lost 6.94
Triumphs or Festivals, and to them preachd Par Lost 11.723
Of Women, sung at solemn festivals, Samson 983
For which the Shepherds at their festivals Mask 848
1637 'festivalls'
Bridgewater ms 'festivalls'

Fet
Whose pains have earn'd the far fet spoil. With that Par Reg 2.401

Fetch
If Earth industrious of her self fetch Day Par Lost 8.137
Thir favourable ear, that I may fetch thee Samson 921
To fetch him hence and solemnly attend Samson 1731
And fetch their precepts from the *Cynick* Tub, Mask 708
When Eev'ning gray doth rise, I fetch my round Arcades 54
Time will run back, and fetch the age of gold, Nativity 135

Fetched
Ambrosial, Fruits fetcht from the tree of life, Par Reg 4.589
If I may not carry, sure Ile ne're be fetch'd, Another 18
line not in 1640, 1657, 1658 texts

Fetches
Should in a pet of temperance feed on Pulse, Mask 721
Trinity ms 'pulse' ← 'fetches' ← 'pulse'

Fettered
To put out both thine eyes, and fetter'd send thee Samson 1160
My heels are fetter'd, but my fist is free. Samson 1235
Each fetter'd Ghost slips to his severall grave, Nativity 234

Fetters
To grind in Brazen Fetters under task Samson 35
In stony fetters fixt, and motionless; Mask 819

Feverish
Strive to keep up a frail, and Feaverish being Mask 8
1637 'feaverish'
Trinity ms 'feavourish'
Bridgewater ms 'fevourish'

Feverous
Of heart-sick Agonie, all feavorous kinds, Par Lost 11.482

Few
The Paradise of Fools, to few unknown Par Lost 3.496
How few somtimes may know, when thousands err. Par Lost 6.148
Urania, and fit audience find, though few. Par Lost 7.31
So having said, he thus to *Eve* in few: Par Lost 10.157
Man is not whom to warne: those few escap't Par Lost 11.777
This second sours of Men, while yet but few; Par Lost 12.13
Must reascend, what will betide the few Par Lost 12.480
In battel, though against thy few in arms. Par Reg 3.20
Are few, and glory scarce of few is rais'd. Par Reg 3.59
And once a year *Jerusalem*, few days Par Reg 3.234
Which to no few of them would prove pernicious. Samson 1400
His few Books, or his Beads, or Maple Dish, Mask 391
Now heaps upon som few with vast excess, Mask 771
Bridgewater ms 'fewe'
And with those few art eminently seen, Sonnet 9, 3
What severs each thou 'hast learnt, which few hav don. Sonnet 17, 11

Fez
The Kingdoms of *Almansor*, *Fez* and *Sus*, Par Lost 11.403

Fickle
To fickle Chance, and *Chaos* judge the strife: Par Lost 2.233
Triumph and say; Fickle their State whom God Par Lost 9.948
O mirror of our fickle state, Samson 164
The fickle Pensioners of *Morpheus* train. Penseroso 10
Fie
But fie my wandring Muse how thou dost stray! Vacation 53
Field
And shook his throne. What though the field be lost? Par Lost 1.105
Forerun the Royal Camp, to trench a Field, Par Lost 1.677
ms 'field'
(Though like a cover'd field, where Champions bold Par Lost 1.763
ms 'feild'
Advising peace: for such another Field Par Lost 2.292
Here walk'd the Fiend at large in spacious field. Par Lost 3.430
To *Padan-Aram* in the field of *Luz*, Par Lost 3.513
In hurdl'd Cotes amid the field secure, Par Lost 4.186
The open field, and where the unpierc't shade Par Lost 4.245
Breathing the smell of field and grove, attune Par Lost 4.265
Led on th' Eternal Spring. Not that faire field Par Lost 4.268
With ported Spears, as thick as when a field Par Lost 4.980
Awake, the morning shines, and the fresh field Par Lost 5.20
So all was cleard, and to the Field they haste. Par Lost 5.136
Into the blissful field, through Groves of Myrrhe, Par Lost 5.292
And left large field, unsafe within the wind Par Lost 6.309
Victor and Vanquisht: on the foughten field Par Lost 6.410
Dismounted, on th' *Aleian* Field I fall Par Lost 7.19
Embattell'd in her field: and the humble Shrub, Par Lost 7.322
Plant of the field, which e're it was in the Earth Par Lost 7.335
And sowd with Starrs the Heav'n thick as a field: Par Lost 7.358
The Serpent suttl'st Beast of all the field, Par Lost 7.495
Beast of the Field, and over all the Earth, Par Lost 7.522
The Serpent suttlest Beast of all the Field. Par Lost 9.86
In Bowre and Field he sought, where any tuft Par Lost 9.417
To such disport before her through the Field, Par Lost 9.520
Thee, Serpent, suttlest beast of all the field Par Lost 9.560
Till on a day roaving the field, I chanc'd Par Lost 9.575
Above all Cattle, each Beast of the Field; Par Lost 10.176
Unbid, and thou shalt eate th' Herb of the Field, Par Lost 10.204
Against the day of Battel, to a Field, Par Lost 10.275
Him follow'd issuing forth to th' open Field, Par Lost 10.533
Farr other name deserving. But the Field Par Lost 11.171
The field Pavilion'd with his Guardians bright; Par Lost 11.215
His eyes he op'nd, and beheld a field, Par Lost 11.429
With Carcasses and Arms th' ensanguind Field Par Lost 11.654
Into the Desert, his Victorious Field Par Reg 1.9
To warm him wet return'd from field at Eve, Par Reg 1.318
Large Countries, and in field great Battels win, Par Reg 3.73
Forest and field, and flood, Temples and Towers Par Reg 3.268
The field all iron cast a gleaming brown, Par Reg 3.326
And of the Angelic Song in *Bethlehem* field, Par Reg 4.505
Each others force in camp or listed field: Samson 1087
Had brought me to the field where thou art fam'd Samson 1094
Fast by thy side, who from thy Fathers field Samson 1432
We drove a field, and both together heard Lycidas 27
1638 'a-field'
Trinity ms 'afeild'
And Dunbarr feild resounds thy praises loud, Sonnet 16, 8
Trinity ms 'Worsters laureat wreath' ← 'Dunbarr feild'
1694 '*Dunbarfield*'
All beasts that in the field or forrest meet, Psalm 8, 20
Fields
Above his equals. Farewel happy Fields Par Lost 1.249
ms 'fields'
Fled over *Adria* to th' *Hesperian* Fields, Par Lost 1.520
ms 'fields'
Extend his ev'ning beam, the fields revive, Par Lost 2.493
As at th' Olympian Games or *Pythian* fields; Par Lost 2.530
And fields were fought in Heav'n; wherein remaind Par Lost 2.768
Those argent Fields more likely habitants, Par Lost 3.460
Fortunate Fields, and Groves and flourie Vales, Par Lost 3.569
What wonder then if fields and regions here Par Lost 3.606
The Cattel in the Fields and Meddowes green: Par Lost 7.460
Feilds and Inhabitants: Her spots thou seest Par Lost 8.145
And over Fields and Waters, as in Aire Par Lost 8.301
Of Angels in the fields of *Bethlehem* sung Par Reg 1.243
Roaving the *Celtick*, and *Iberian* fields, Mask 60
Trinity ms 'feilds'
Up in the broad fields of the sky: Mask 979
Trinity ms 'feilds'
B.M. ms 'Fields'
Bridgewater ms 'field'
the feilds with cattell & the aire with fowle Mask Tr. ms 21.57
And past from *Pharian* fields to *Canaan* Land, Psalm 114, 3
1673 'Fields'
Or in the Elisian fields (if such there were.) Fair Inf 40
O're all th' *Italian* fields where still doth sway Sonnet 18, 11
Now that the Fields are dank, and ways are mire, Sonnet 20, 2
Fiend
Whereto with speedy words th' Arch-fiend reply'd. Par Lost 1.156
So stretcht out huge in length the Arch-fiend lay Par Lost 1.209
He scarce had ceas't when the superiour Fiend Par Lost 1.283
ms 'fiend'
Farr off the flying Fiend: at last appeer Par Lost 2.643
Th' undaunted Fiend what this might be admir'd, Par Lost 2.677
She finish'd, and the suttle Fiend his lore Par Lost 2.815
Into this wild Abyss the warie fiend Par Lost 2.917
The guarded Gold: So eagerly the fiend Par Lost 2.947
Fiend(*cont*)
Here walk'd the Fiend at large in spacious field. Par Lost 3.430
So on this windie Sea of Land, the Fiend Par Lost 3.440
All this dark Globe the Fiend found as he pass'd, Par Lost 3.498
The Fiend by easie ascent, or aggravate Par Lost 3.524
There lands the Fiend, a spot like which perhaps Par Lost 3.588
So entertaind those odorous sweets the Fiend Par Lost 4.166
From this *Assyrian* Garden, where the Fiend Par Lost 4.285
So spake the Fiend, and with necessitie, Par Lost 4.393
So started up in his own shape the Fiend. Par Lost 4.819
The Fiend repli'd not, overcome with rage; Par Lost 4.857
To which the Fiend thus answerd frowning stern. Par Lost 4.924
Which *Gabriel* spying, thus bespake the Fiend. Par Lost 4.1005
If thou resist. The Fiend lookt up and knew Par Lost 4.1013
For now, and since first break of dawne the Fiend, Par Lost 9.412
Much wondring how the suttle Fiend had stoln Par Lost 10.20
Farr into *Chaos*, since the Fiend pass'd through, Par Lost 10.233
Thy choice of flaming Warriours, least the Fiend Par Lost 11.101
Whom thus answer'd th' Arch Fiend now undisguis'd. Par Reg 1.357
So spake our Saviour; but the subtle Fiend, Par Reg 1.465
Cause thy refusal, said the subtle Fiend, Par Reg 2.323
At sight whereof the Fiend yet more presum'd, Par Reg 3.345
So spake *Israel*'s true King, and to the Fiend Par Reg 3.441
To whom the Fiend with fear abasht reply'd. Par Reg 4.195
And grisly Spectres, which the Fiend had rais'd Par Reg 4.430
To whom the Fiend now swoln with rage reply'd: Par Reg 4.499
So strook with dread and anguish fell the Fiend, Par Reg 4.576
Then lies him down the Lubbar Fend, Allegro 110
Fiends
Armie of Fiends, fit body to fit head; Par Lost 4.953
Fierce
And to the fierce contention brought along Par Lost 1.100
Afloat, when with fierce Winds *Orion* arm'd Par Lost 1.305
In which they were, or the fierce pains not feel; Par Lost 1.336
Against the Highest, and fierce with grasped Arms Par Lost 1.667
When the fierce Foe hung on our brok'n Rear Par Lost 2.78
Familiar the fierce heat, and void of pain; Par Lost 2.219
Heard on the ruful stream; fierce *Phlegeton* Par Lost 2.580
Of fierce extreams, extreams by change more fierce, Par Lost 2.599
Fierce as ten Furies, terrible as Hell, Par Lost 2.671
For hot, cold, moist, and dry, four Champions fierce Par Lost 2.898
To execute fierce vengeance on his foes, Par Lost 3.399
Spirit of happie sort: his gestures fierce Par Lost 4.128
Where neither joy nor love, but fierce desire, Par Lost 4.509
And fierce demeanour seems the Prince of Hell, Par Lost 4.871
And in fierce hosting meet, who wont to meet Par Lost 6.93
Presage of Victorie and fierce desire Par Lost 6.201
Millions of fierce encountring Angels fought Par Lost 6.220
And with fierce Ensignes pierc'd the deep array Par Lost 6.356
Ere while they fierce were coming, and when wee, Par Lost 6.610
And from about him fierce Effusion rowld Par Lost 6.765
Stood reimbattell'd fierce, by force or fraud Par Lost 6.794
Of his fierce Chariot rowld, as with the sound Par Lost 6.829
Of *Chaos* farr remov'd, least fierce extreames Par Lost 7.272
His fierceness of the fierce intent it brought: Par Lost 9.462
Fierce hate he recollects, and all his thoughts Par Lost 9.471
Yet parcht with scalding thurst and hunger fierce, Par Lost 10.556
From *Serraliona;* thwart of these as fierce Par Lost 10.703
Death introduc'd through fierce antipathie: Par Lost 10.709
Shall with a fierce reflux on mee redound, Par Lost 10.739
Soft words to his fierce passion she assay'd: Par Lost 10.865
Convulsions, Epilepsies, fierce Catarrhs, Par Lost 11.483
Concours in Arms, fierce Faces threatning Warr, Par Lost 11.641
Fierce as a Comet; which with torrid heat, Par Lost 12.634
When his fierce thunder drove us to the deep; Par Reg 1.90
The Lion and fierce Tiger glar'd aloof. Par Reg 1.313
Wielded at will that fierce Democratie, Par Reg 4.269
Fierce rain with lightning mixt, water with fire Par Reg 4.412
There exercise all his fierce accidents, Samson 612
Sam. Not for thy life, lest fierce remembrance wake Samson 952
Her countrey from a fierce destroyer, chose Samson 985
No savage fierce, Bandite, or mountaneer Mask 426
Bridgewater ms 'feirce'
Trinity ms 'feirce'
Feirce signe of battail make, and menace high, Mask 654
1673 'Fierce'
Bridgewater ms 'fierce'
His Godlike acts, and his temptations fierce, Passion 24
The feirce Epeirot and the African bold, Sonnet 17, 4
1662, 1694 'fierce'
And fierce ire trouble them; but I saith hee Psalm 2, 11
From thy fierce wrath which we had prov'd Psalm 85, 11
Thy fierce wrath over me doth flow Psalm 88, 65
Fiercely
That jealous of thir secrets fiercely oppos'd Par Lost 10.478
In signal of remove, waves fiercely round; Par Lost 12.593
Fierceness
His fierceness of the fierce intent it brought: Par Lost 9.462
Fiercer
That fought in Heav'n; now fiercer by despair: Par Lost 2.45
Fresh from his fall, and fiercer grapple joyn'd, Par Reg 4.567
Fiercest
Stood up, the strongest and the fiercest Spirit Par Lost 2.44
Thy fiercest, when in Battel to thy aide Par Lost 4.927
Of fiercest opposition in mid Skie, Par Lost 6.314
No strength of man, or fiercest wild beast could withstand; Samson 127
Fiery
Lay vanquisht, rowling in the fiery Gulfe Par Lost 1.52

Fiery(*cont*)
Still urges, and a fiery Deluge, fed Par Lost 1.68
The fiery Surge, that from the Precipice Par Lost 1.173
From off the tossing of these fiery waves, Par Lost 1.184
Rous'd from the slumber, on that fiery Couch, Par Lost 1.377
Caught in a fierie Tempest shall be hurl'd Par Lost 2.180
A Globe of fierie Seraphim inclos'd Par Lost 2.512
Part curb thir fierie Steeds, or shun the Goal Par Lost 2.531
O're many a Frozen, many a fierie Alpe, Par Lost 2.620
1667 'Fierie'
Up to the fiery Concave touring high. Par Lost 2.635
Rapt in a Chariot drawn by fiery Steeds. Par Lost 3.522
A Lion now he stalkes with fierie glare, Par Lost 4.402
Turnd fierie red, sharpning in mooned hornes Par Lost 4.978
Chariots and flaming Armes, and fierie Steeds Par Lost 6.17
His fiery *Chaos* to receave thir fall. Par Lost 6.55
From skirt to skirt a fierie Region, stretcht Par Lost 6.80
Of fiery Darts in flaming volies flew, Par Lost 6.213
So under fierie Cope together rush'd Par Lost 6.215
Now wav'd thir fierie Swords, and in the Aire Par Lost 6.304
And fierie foaming Steeds; what stood, recoyld Par Lost 6.391
Of spiritous and fierie spume, till toucht Par Lost 6.479
Then through the Firey Pillar and the Cloud Par Lost 12.208
Shall rest by Day, a fiery gleame by Night, Par Lost 12.257
1667 'fierie'
Satans assaults, and quench his fierie darts, Par Lost 12.492
With dreadful Faces throng'd and fierie Armes: Par Lost 12.644
The fiery Serpent fled, and noxious Worm, Par Reg 1.312
And the great *Thisbite* who on fiery wheels Par Reg 2.16
Some bent at thee thir fiery darts, while thou Par Reg 4.424
So Satan fell and strait a fiery Globe Par Reg 4.581
As in a fiery column charioting Samson 27
With touch aetherial of Heav'ns fiery rod Samson 549
His fierie vertue rouz'd Samson 1690
And make soft rills from fiery flint-stones gush. Psalm 114, 18
Your fiery essence can distill no tear, Circum 7

Fiery-wheeled
Guiding the fiery-wheeled throne, Penseroso 53

Fiesole
At Ev'ning from the top of *Fesole*, Par Lost 1.289
ms 'fesole'

Fifth
Ev'ning and Morn solemniz'd the Fift day. Par Lost 7.448

Fight
With what besides, in Counsel or in Fight, Par Lost 2.20
Confus'dly, and which thus must ever fight, Par Lost 2.914
And practis'd distances to cringe, not fight. Par Lost 4.945
The sequel each of parting and of fight; Par Lost 4.1003
The better fight, who single hast maintaind Par Lost 6.30
By Thousands and by Millions rang'd for fight; Par Lost 6.48
That self same day by fight, or by surprize Par Lost 6.87
A Legion; led in fight, yet Leader seemd Par Lost 6.232
A standing fight, then soaring on main wing Par Lost 6.243
They ended parle, and both addrest for fight Par Lost 6.296
Where erst was thickest fight, th' Angelic throng, Par Lost 6.308
Not to have disobei'd; in fight they stood Par Lost 6.403
Who have sustaind one day in doubtful fight Par Lost 6.423
As one he stood escap't from cruel fight, Par Lost 6.448
Against unequal armes to fight in paine, Par Lost 6.454
Where lodg'd, or whither fled, or if for fight, Par Lost 6.531
Arme, Warriours, Arme for fight, the foe at hand, Par Lost 6.537
These disobedient; sore hath been thir fight, Par Lost 6.687
Whence in perpetual fight they needs must last Par Lost 6.693
And to rebellious fight rallied thir Powers Par Lost 6.786
For death, the following day, in bloodie fight. Par Lost 10.278
Sin against Law to fight; that when they see Par Lost 12.289
Thir fight, what stroke shall bruise the Victors heel. Par Lost 12.385
To whom thus *Michael*. Dream not of thir fight, Par Lost 12.386
All Horsemen, in which fight they most excel; Par Reg 3.307
Cuirassiers all in steel for standing fight; Par Reg 3.328
None offering fight; who single combatant Samson 344
In fight withstand me single and unarm'd, Samson 1111
Defie thee to the trial of mortal fight, Samson 1175
Who now defies thee thrice to single fight, Samson 1222
To fight with thee no man of arms will deign. Samson 1226
Sam. He must allege some cause, and offer'd fight Samson 1253
And like the slain *in bloody fight* Psalm 88, 19

Fighting
Of fighting Elements, on all sides round Par Lost 2.1015
Of fighting Seraphim confus'd, at length Par Lost 6.249
Of fighting beasts, and men to beasts expos'd, Par Reg 4.140

Figtree
The Figtree, not that kind for Fruit renown'd, Par Lost 9.1101

Figure
In common, rang'd in figure wedge thir way, Par Lost 7.426
Moses in figure beares, to introduce Par Lost 12.241

Figures
Inwrought with figures dim, and on the edge Lycidas 105

File
A title page is this! and some in file Sonnet 11, 6

Files
Had to impose: He through the armed Files Par Lost 1.567
ms 'files'
So saying, on he led his radiant Files, Par Lost 4.797
Disperst in Bands and Files thir Camp extend Par Lost 5.651
From off the files of warr; there they him laid Par Lost 6.339
Nor serv'd it to relax thir serried files. Par Lost 6.599

Filial
Filial obedience: as a sacrifice Par Lost 3.269
Severe but in true filial freedom plac't; Par Lost 4.294
And thus the filial Godhead answering spake. Par Lost 6.722
His Word, the filial Godhead, gave effect. Par Lost 7.175
1667 'Filial'
The Filial Power arriv'd, and sate him down Par Lost 7.587
To filial, works of Law to works of Faith. Par Lost 12.306
Ventures his filial Vertue, though untri'd, Par Reg 1.177
(Best pleas'd with humble and filial submission) Samson 511

Fill
On the firm brimstone, and fill all the Plain; Par Lost 1.350
The happier *Eden*, shall enjoy thir fill Par Lost 4.507
To fill the Earth, who shall with us extoll Par Lost 4.733
Shall fill the World more numerous with thy Sons Par Lost 5.389
Your fill what happiness this happie state Par Lost 5.504
Boundless the Deep, because I am who fill Par Lost 7.168
And Lakes and running Streams the waters fill; Par Lost 7.397
Be fruitful, multiplie, and fill the Earth, Par Lost 7.531
An Edifice too large for him to fill, Par Lost 8.104
Of sweet repast; they satiate, and soon fill, Par Lost 8.214
To the Creator, and his Nostrils fill Par Lost 9.196
Tempting so nigh, to pluck and eat my fill Par Lost 9.595
Eating his fill, nor *Eve* to iterate Par Lost 9.1005
There they thir fill of Love and Loves disport Par Lost 9.1042
To fill his eare, when contrary he hears Par Lost 10.506
Of Nature, and not fill the World at once Par Lost 10.892
Frogs, Lice and Flies must all his Palace fill Par Lost 12.177
With loath'd intrusion, and fill all the land; Par Lost 12.178
Greatly in peace of thought, and have my fill Par Lost 12.558
To lay hills plain, fell woods, or valleys fill, Par Reg 3.332
Till fancy had her fill, but ere a close Mask 548
Thy molten crystal fill with mudd, Mask 931
Or fill the fixed mind with all your toyes; Penseroso 4
When the gust hath blown his fill, Penseroso 128
And Daffadillies fill their cups with tears, Lycidas 150
Did fill the new-made world with light. Psalm 136, 26
Thou with fresh hope the Lovers heart dost fill, Sonnet 1, 3
To fill thy odorous Lamp with deeds of light, Sonnet 9, 10
And drink thy fill of pure immortal streams. Sonnet 14, 14
Lord fill with shame their face. Psalm 83, 60

Filled
Turns Atheist, as did *Ely*'s Sons, who fill'd Par Lost 1.495
By strange conveyance fill'd each hollow nook, Par Lost 1.707
First, what Revenge? the Towrs of Heav'n are fill'd Par Lost 2.129
He scarce had finisht, when such murmur filld Par Lost 2.284
With odours; there ye shall be fed and fill'd Par Lost 2.843
His famine should be fill'd, and blest his mawe Par Lost 2.847
Thus while God spake, ambrosial fragrance fill'd Par Lost 3.135
With Jubilee, and loud Hosanna's filld Par Lost 3.348
1667 'fill'd'
With vanity had filld the works of men: Par Lost 3.447
Coucht, and now fild with pasture gazing sat, Par Lost 4.351
Know ye not then said *Satan*, fill'd with scorn, Par Lost 4.827
1667 'filld'
And shook his Plumes, that Heav'nly fragrance filld Par Lost 5.286
Excess, before th' all bounteous King, who showrd Par Lost 5.640
1667 'Are fill'd'
Thus foil'd thir mightiest, ours joy filld, and shout, Par Lost 6.200
The storie heard attentive, and was fill'd Par Lost 7.51
The hollow Universal Orb they fill'd, Par Lost 7.257
But suddenly with flesh fill'd up and heal'd: Par Lost 8.468
With soot and cinders fill'd; so oft they fell Par Lost 10.570
Filld all the Regions: from thir blissful Bowrs Par Lost 11.77
The whole Earth fill'd with violence, and all flesh Par Lost 11.888
Were dead, who sought his life, and missing fill'd Par Reg 2.77
Sails fill'd, and streamers waving, Samson 718
Had fill'd thir hearts with mirth, high chear, & wine, Samson 1613
That nature hung in Heav'n, and fill'd their Lamps Mask 198
line not in Bridgewater ms
And fill'd the Air with barbarous dissonance, Mask 550
Bridgewater ms 'filld'
1637 'filld'
Fill'd her with thee a daughter fair, Allegro 23
And fill'd the land *at last*. Psalm 80, 40

Filling
Filling each mouth with envy, or with praise, Sonnet 15, 2

Fills
Hence fills and empties to enlighten th' Earth, Par Lost 3.731
Innumerable, and this which yeelds or fills Par Lost 7.88
Not this Rock onely; his Omnipresence fills Par Lost 11.336
Whose heads that turbulent liquor fills with fumes. Samson 552
halfe his wast flood the wide Atlantique fills Mask Tr. ms 10.14
Filling each mouth with envy, or with praise, Sonnet 15, 2
1694 'And fills'

Film
Michael from *Adams* eyes the Filme remov'd Par Lost 11.412

Filth
My Hell-hounds, to lick up the draff and filth Par Lost 10.630

Fin
Freshet, or purling Brook, of shell or fin, Par Reg 2.345

Final
Victorious. Thus repuls'd, our final hope Par Lost 2.142
Of happiness and final misery, Par Lost 2.563
Till final dissolution, wander here, Par Lost 3.458
To final Battel drew, disdaining flight, Par Lost 6.798
Of thoughts revolv'd, his final sentence chose Par Lost 9.88
In dust, our final rest and native home. Par Lost 10.1085

Final(*cont*)
His final remedie, and after Life Par Lost 11.62
With vows, as thir chief good, and final hope. Par Lost 11.493
Into the World, to teach his final will, Par Reg 1.461
The end I would attain, my final good. Par Reg 3.211
Justly, yet despair not of his final pardon Samson 1171
Finally
For should Man finally be lost, should Man Par Lost 3.150
Whom Patience finally must crown. Samson 1296
Find
And out of good still to find means of evil; Par Lost 1.165
Your wearied vertue, for the ease you find Par Lost 1.320
At length from us may find, who overcomes Par Lost 1.648
Our stronger, some worse way his wrath may find Par Lost 2.83
Or ambush from the Deep. What if we find Par Lost 2.344
In search of this new world, whom shall we find Par Lost 2.403
And through the palpable obscure find out Par Lost 2.406
Leads him perplext, where he may likeliest find Par Lost 2.525
That rest or intermission none I find. Par Lost 2.802
But glad that now his Sea should find a shore, Par Lost 2.1011
To find thy piercing ray, and find no dawn; Par Lost 3.24
By the other first: Man therefore shall find grace, Par Lost 3.131
Thy sovran sentence, that Man should find grace; Par Lost 3.145
Say Heav'nly powers, where shall we find such love, Par Lost 3.213
Father, thy word is past, man shall find grace; Par Lost 3.227
And shall grace not find means, that finds her way, Par Lost 3.228
Naught seeking but the praise of men, here find Par Lost 3.453
To find who might direct his wandring flight Par Lost 3.631
That I may find him, and with secret gaze, Par Lost 3.671
Like consort to thy self canst no where find. Par Lost 4.448
New troubles; him thy care must be to find. Par Lost 4.575
Such where ye find, seise fast, and hither bring. Par Lost 4.796
His loss; but chiefly to find here observd Par Lost 4.849
Fame is not silent, here in hope to find Par Lost 4.938
His wonder was to find unwak'nd *Eve* Par Lost 5.9
O Sole in whom my thoughts find all repose, Par Lost 5.28
To find thee I directed then my walk; Par Lost 5.49
To find this but a dream! Thus *Eve* her Night Par Lost 5.93
Som such resemblances methinks I find Par Lost 5.114
We brush mellifluous Dewes, and find the ground Par Lost 5.429
With Angels may participate, and find Par Lost 5.494
Findes no acceptance, nor can find, for how Par Lost 5.531
Apostat, still thou errst, nor end wilt find Par Lost 6.172
To find himself not matchless, and his pride Par Lost 6.341
Since now we find this our Empyreal form Par Lost 6.433
For Gods, and too unequal work we find Par Lost 6.453
Urania, and fit audience find, though few. Par Lost 7.31
His beams, unactive else, thir vigour find. Par Lost 8.97
Or all enjoying, what contentment find? Par Lost 8.366
Find pastime, and beare rule; thy Realm is large. Par Lost 8.375
From prone, nor in thir wayes complacence find. Par Lost 8.433
And finde thee knowing not of Beasts alone, Par Lost 8.438
To find her, or for ever to deplore Par Lost 8.479
Which I enjoy, and must confess to find Par Lost 8.523
In eminence, and obstacle find none Par Lost 8.624
Find place or refuge; and the more I see Par Lost 9.119
For onely in destroying I find ease Par Lost 9.129
1667 'finde'
In every Bush and Brake, where hap may finde Par Lost 9.160
His midnight search, where soonest he might finde Par Lost 9.181
With Myrtle, find what to redress till Noon: Par Lost 9.219
Watches, no doubt, with greedy hope to find Par Lost 9.257
From his surmise prov'd false, find peace within, Par Lost 9.333
1667 'finde'
But if thou think, trial unsought may finde Par Lost 9.370
May finde us both perhaps farr less prepar'd, Par Lost 9.381
And on his Quest, where likeliest he might finde Par Lost 9.414
He sought them both, but wish'd his hap might find Par Lost 9.421
Op'nd we find indeed, and find we know Par Lost 9.1071
Either to meet no danger, or to finde Par Lost 9.1176
By some immediate stroak; but soon shall find Par Lost 10.52
I find no way, from deep to deeper plung'd! Par Lost 10.844
Or find some other way to generate Par Lost 10.894
He never shall find out fit Mate, but such Par Lost 10.899
How little weight my words with thee can finde, Par Lost 10.968
To find where *Adam* shelterd, took his way, Par Lost 11.223
1667 'finde'
Such grace shall one just Man find in his sight, Par Lost 11.890
Marching from *Eden* towards the West, shall finde Par Lost 12.40
Just *Abraham* and his Seed: now first I finde Par Lost 12.273
To them by Faith imputed, they may finde Par Lost 12.295
On every conscience; Laws which none shall finde Par Lost 12.522
The dismal expedition to find out Par Reg 1.101
Where he might likeliest find this new-declar'd, Par Reg 1.121
At least in vain, for they shall find thee mute. Par Reg 1.459
Easily canst thou find one miserable, Par Reg 1.471
To find whom at the first they found unsought: Par Reg 2.59
Have found him, view'd him, tasted him, but find Par Reg 2.131
Of greatest things; what woman will you find, Par Reg 2.208
In vain, where no acceptance it can find, Par Reg 2.388
When that comes think not thou to find me slack Par Reg 3.398
Let his tormenter Conscience find him out, Par Reg 4.130
As in our native Language can I find Par Reg 4.333
If thou observe not this, be sure to find, Par Reg 4.477
This unfrequented place to find some ease, Samson 17
Ask for this great Deliverer now, and find him Samson 40
But never find self-satisfying solution. Samson 306
Find some occasion to infest our Foes. Samson 423

Find(*cont*)
But must secret passage find Samson 610
I may, if possible, thy pardon find Samson 771
Shall never, unrepented, find forgiveness. Samson 1376
Or we shall find such Engines to assail Samson 1396
He seems: supposing here to find his Son, Samson 1443
Was not at present here to find my Son, Samson 1446
Find courage to lay hold on this occasion, Samson 1716
Let us go find the body where it lies Samson 1725
Yet nought but single darknes do I find. Mask 204
line not in Bridgewater ms
To help you find them. *La*. Gentle villager Mask 304
Bridgewater ms 'finde'
La. To find out that, good Shepherd, I suppose, Mask 307
Bridgewater ms 'finde'
How couldst thou find this dark sequester'd nook? Mask 500
Bridgewater ms 'finde'
'Twixt *Africa* and *Inde*, Ile find him out, Mask 606
Bridgewater ms 'finde'
But now I find it true; for by this means Mask 644
Bridgewater ms 'finde'
Find out som uncouth cell, Allegro 5
Find out the peacefull hermitage, Penseroso 168
Less then half we find exprest, Arcades 12
Trinity ms 'wee find' ← 'she hath'
But the fair Guerdon when we hope to find, Lycidas 73
To find a Foe it shall not be his hap, Vacation 83
No anger find in thee, but pity and ruth. Sonnet 9, 8
But we do hope to find out all your tricks, Forcers 13
God, find them guilty, let them fall Psalm 5, 29
No quiet let them find, Psalm 83, 50
They find their safe abode, Psalm 84, 14
And your ungodly deeds finde me the words. Prose 8, 2
Thy course, there shalt thou find a lasting seat, Prose 12, 11
Findest
Thou find'st him from the heat of Noon retir'd, Par Lost 5.231
What higher in her societie thou findst Par Lost 8.586
I bid not or forbid; do as thou find'st Par Reg 1.495
Mee worse then wet thou find'st not; other harm Par Reg 4.486
Finding
Who would not, finding way, break loose from Hell, Par Lost 4.889
But finding no redress, ferment and rage, Samson 619
But lately finding him so long at home, Carrier 11
Finds
And shall grace not find means, that finds her way, Par Lost 3.228
In miserie; such joy Ambition findes. Par Lost 4.92
Findes no acceptance, nor can find, for how Par Lost 5.531
What happ'ns new; Fame also finds us out. Par Reg 1.334
True wisdom, finds her not, or by delusion Par Reg 4.319
Favour'd of Heav'n who finds Samson 1046
That when a soul is found sincerely so, Mask 454
Trinity ms 'when' ← 'when it finds'
Fine
The punishment of dissolute days, in fine, Samson 702
Finest
With flowr of finest wheat, Psalm 81, 66
Finger
Who with her radiant finger still'd the roar Par Reg 4.428
Thrice upon thy fingers tip, Mask 914
As never was by mortall finger strook, Nativity 95
Fingers
And with forc'd fingers rude, Lycidas 4
When I behold thy Heavens, thy Fingers art, Psalm 8, 9
Finish
Those have thir course to finish, round the Earth, Par Lost 4.661
Finished
He scarce had finisht, when such murmur filld Par Lost 2.284
She finish'd, and the suttle Fiend his lore Par Lost 2.815
Have finisht happie in our mutual help Par Lost 4.727
Hath finisht half his journey, and scarce begins Par Lost 5.559
Unaided could have finisht thee, and whelmd Par Lost 6.141
Secret they finish'd, and in order set, Par Lost 6.522
Here finish'd hee, and all that he had made Par Lost 7.548
Like *Samson*, and heroicly hath finish'd Samson 1710
Finisher
O Prophet of glad tidings, finisher Par Lost 12.375
Finite
For angers sake, finite to infinite Par Lost 10.802
Finny
The Sounds, and Seas with all their finny drove Mask 115
1637 'finnie'
Trinity ms 'finnie'
Bridgewater ms 'finnie'
Fins
Of Fish that with thir Finns and shining Scales Par Lost 7.401
Fir
Cedar, and Pine, and Firr, and branching Palm, Par Lost 4.139
Or hollow'd bodies made of Oak or Firr Par Lost 6.574
Kindles the gummie bark of Firr or Pine, Par Lost 10.1076
Fire
In Adamantine Chains and penal Fire, Par Lost 1.48
ms 'fire'
With Floods and Whirlwinds of tempestuous fire, Par Lost 1.77
Here in the heart of Hell to work in Fire, Par Lost 1.151
ms 'fire'
With solid, as the Lake with liquid fire; Par Lost 1.229
And fewel'd entrals thence conceiving Fire, Par Lost 1.234
ms 'fire'

Fire(*cont*)	
Groveling and prostrate on yon Lake of Fire,	Par Lost 1.280
ms 'fire'	
Smote on him sore besides, vaulted with Fire;	Par Lost 1.298
ms 'fire'	
Thir childrens cries unheard, that past through fire	Par Lost 1.395
Thir Glory witherd. As when Heavens Fire	Par Lost 1.612
ms 'fire'	
Belch'd fire and rowling smoak; the rest entire	Par Lost 1.671
That underneath had veins of liquid fire	Par Lost 1.701
Black fire and horror shot with equal rage	Par Lost 2.67
Mixt with *Tartarean* Sulphur, and strange fire,	Par Lost 2.69
Where pain of unextinguishable fire	Par Lost 2.88
Her mischief, and purge off the baser fire	Par Lost 2.141
Of Hell should spout her Cataracts of Fire,	Par Lost 2.176
By sudden onset, either with Hell fire	Par Lost 2.364
Our prison strong, this huge convex of Fire,	Par Lost 2.434
Whose waves of torrent fire inflame with rage.	Par Lost 2.581
Burns frore, and cold performs th' effect of Fire.	Par Lost 2.595
From Beds of raging Fire to starve in Ice	Par Lost 2.600
Periods of time, thence hurried back to fire.	Par Lost 2.603
Impenetrable, impal'd with circling fire,	Par Lost 2.647
Of neither Sea, nor Shore, nor Air, nor Fire,	Par Lost 2.912
Instinct with Fire and Nitre hurried him	Par Lost 2.937
Springs upward like a Pyramid of fire	Par Lost 2.1013
With radiant light, as glowing Iron with fire;	Par Lost 3.594
The cumbrous Elements, Earth, Flood, Aire, Fire,	Par Lost 3.715
On him who had stole *Joves* authentic fire.	Par Lost 4.719
Through Spirits with ease; nor wonder; if by fire	Par Lost 5.439
His Thunder on thy head, devouring fire.	Par Lost 5.893
Rebellious, them with Fire and hostile Arms	Par Lost 6.50
And flying vaulted either Host with fire.	Par Lost 6.214
Conflicting Fire: long time in eeven scale	Par Lost 6.245
Thick-rammd, at th' other bore with touch of fire	Par Lost 6.485
Provide, pernicious with one touch to fire.	Par Lost 6.520
But ratling storm of Arrows barbd with fire.	Par Lost 6.546
Stood waving tipt with fire; while we suspense,	Par Lost 6.580
Glar'd lightning, and shot forth pernicious fire	Par Lost 6.849
Hell thir fit habitation fraught with fire	Par Lost 6.876
Guiltless of fire had formd, or Angels brought.	Par Lost 9.392
Bright'ns his Crest, as when a wandring Fire,	Par Lost 9.634
Of *Eve*, whose Eye darted contagious Fire.	Par Lost 9.1036
The Air attrite to Fire, as late the Clouds	Par Lost 10.1073
Which might supplie the Sun: such Fire to use,	Par Lost 10.1078
In *Dothan*, cover'd with a Camp of Fire,	Par Lost 11.217
His Offring soon propitious Fire from Heav'n	Par Lost 11.441
By Fire, Flood, Famin, by Intemperance more	Par Lost 11.472
Had melted (whether found where casual fire	Par Lost 11.566
With Dart and Jav'lin, Stones and sulfurous Fire;	Par Lost 11.658
Shall hold thir course, till fire purge all things new,	Par Lost 11.900
Haile mixt with fire must rend th' *Egyptian* Skie	Par Lost 12.182
Before them in a Cloud, and Pillar of Fire,	Par Lost 12.202
By day a Cloud, by night a Pillar of Fire,	Par Lost 12.203
Powers of Fire, Air, Water, and Earth beneath,	Par Reg 2.124
(Whose ire I dread more then the fire of Hell)	Par Reg 3.220
Tetrarchs of fire, air, flood, and on the earth	Par Reg 4.201
Fierce rain with lightning mixt, water with fire	Par Reg 4.412
Of fire; that Spirit that first rusht on thee	Samson 1435
We that are of purer fire	Mask 111
In fog, or fire, by lake, or moorish fen,	Mask 433
Basks at the fire his hairy strength;	Allegro 112
In fire, air, flood, or under ground,	Penseroso 94
From out his secret Altar toucht with hallow'd fire.	Nativity 28
While the red fire, and smouldring clouds out brake:	Nativity 159
Thereby to set the hearts of men on fire	Fair Inf 62
Then passing through the Spheres of watchful fire,	Vacation 40
Where shall we sometimes meet, and by the fire	Sonnet 20, 3
If once his wrath take fire like fuel sere.	Psalm 2, 27
Of my foes that urge like fire;	Psalm 7, 21
But now it is consum'd with fire,	Psalm 80, 65
As *when* an *aged* wood takes fire	Psalm 83, 53
Far worse then fire to burn.	Psalm 85, 12
Fired	
In *Autumn* thwarts the night, when vapors fir'd	Par Lost 4.557
And the well-feasted Priest then soonest fir'd	Samson 1419
Fires	
'Twixt upper, nether, and surrounding Fires;	Par Lost 1.346
ms 'fires'	
What if the breath that kindl'd those grim fires	Par Lost 2.170
With what is punish't; whence these raging fires	Par Lost 2.213
Become our Elements, these piercing Fires	Par Lost 2.275
To heal the scarr of these corrosive Fires	Par Lost 2.401
That fires the length of *Ophiucus* huge	Par Lost 2.709
In Nature and all things, which these soft fires	Par Lost 4.667
And yee five other wandring Fires that move	Par Lost 5.177
Earth and the Sea feed Air, the Air those Fires	Par Lost 5.417
Cherubic waving fires: on th' other part	Par Lost 6.413
Of Beril, and careering Fires between;	Par Lost 6.756
Distant so high, with moving Fires adornd	Par Lost 7.87
The Heav'nly fires; over the Tent a Cloud	Par Lost 12.256
Firm	
On the firm brimstone, and fill all the Plain;	Par Lost 1.350
Deliberate valour breath'd, firm and unmov'd	Par Lost 1.554
To union, and firm Faith, and firm accord,	Par Lost 2.36
Firm concord holds, men onely disagree	Par Lost 2.497
Of Whirlwind and dire Hail, which on firm land	Par Lost 2.589
Firm land imbosom'd without Firmament,	Par Lost 3.75
Mean while upon the firm opacous Globe	Par Lost 3.418

Firm(*cont*)	
Of firm and fragrant leaf; on either side	Par Lost 4.695
Stand firm, for in his look defiance lours.	Par Lost 4.873
Firm peace recoverd soon and wonted calm.	Par Lost 5.210
Unalterably firm his love entire	Par Lost 5.502
Indissolubly firm; nor obvious Hill,	Par Lost 6.69
That Warr and various; somtimes on firm ground	Par Lost 6.242
In Cubic Phalanx firm advanc't entire,	Par Lost 6.399
But firm Battalion; back with speediest Sail	Par Lost 6.534
Of disobedience; firm they might have stood,	Par Lost 6.911
Of this great Round: partition firm and sure,	Par Lost 7.267
And drink the liquid Light, firm to retaine	Par Lost 7.362
Walk'd firm; the crested Cock whose clarion sounds	Par Lost 7.443
Of Godhead, fixt for ever firm and sure,	Par Lost 7.586
Thy equal fear that my firm Faith and Love	Par Lost 9.286
Firm we subsist, yet possible to swerve,	Par Lost 9.359
Hadst thou bin firm and fixt in thy dissent,	Par Lost 9.1160
As with a Trident smote, and fix't as firm	Par Lost 10.295
And in thir state, though firm, stood more confirmd.	Par Lost 11.71
Not knowing to what Land, yet firm believes:	Par Lost 12.127
By one mans firm obedience fully tri'd	Par Reg 1.4
Conjectures, fancies, built on nothing firm.	Par Reg 4.292
Of Adamant, and as a Center, firm	Par Reg 4.534
Which erring men call Chance, this I hold firm,	Mask 588
1637 'firme'	
Trinity ms 'firme'	
Bridgewater ms 'firme'	
Thy firm unshak'n vertue ever brings	Sonnet 15, 5
Therfore on thy firme hand religion leanes	Sonnet 17, 13
1662 'firm'	
1694 'Right'	
Trinity ms 'firme' ← 'right'	
On *Sion* my holi' hill. A firm decree	Psalm 2, 13
No word is firm or sooth	Psalm 5, 26
Thou hast made firm and strong.	Psalm 80, 64
And in firm union bind.	Psalm 83, 20
Firmament	
Her stores were open'd, and this Firmament	Par Lost 2.175
Firm land imbosom'd without Firmament,	Par Lost 3.75
Through the calm Firmament; but up or downe	Par Lost 3.574
Silence was pleas'd: now glow'd the Firmament	Par Lost 4.604
Over thir heads a chrystal Firmament,	Par Lost 6.757
Again, God said, let ther be Firmament	Par Lost 7.261
The Firmament, expanse of liquid, pure,	Par Lost 7.264
And Heav'n he nam'd the Firmament: So Eev'n	Par Lost 7.274
Thir Office in the Firmament of Heav'n	Par Lost 7.344
And set them in the Firmament of Heav'n	Par Lost 7.349
Displayd on the op'n Firmament of Heav'n.	Par Lost 7.390
An Atom, with the Firmament compar'd	Par Lost 8.18
O're the blew Firmament a radiant white,	Par Lost 11.206
The pillar'd firmament is rott'nness,	Mask 598
In the pure firmament, then saith my heart,	Psalm 8, 11
Firmer	
A space, till firmer thoughts restraind excess,	Par Lost 11.498
Firmest	
How to endear, and hold thee to me firmest:	Samson 796
Firmlier	
Though thou wert firmlier fastn'd then a rock.	Samson 1398
Firmly	
Omniscient thought. True is, less firmly arm'd,	Par Lost 6.430
Firmness	
Save what by frugal storing firmness gains	Par Lost 5.324
But that thou shouldst my firmness therfore doubt	Par Lost 9.279
First	
Of Mans First Disobedience, and the Fruit	Par Lost 1.1
ms 'first'	
That Shepherd, who first taught the chosen Seed,	Par Lost 1.8
Instruct me, for Thou know'st; Thou from the first	Par Lost 1.19
Say first, for Heav'n hides nothing from thy view	Par Lost 1.27
Nor the deep Tract of Hell, say first what cause	Par Lost 1.28
Who first seduc'd them to that foul revolt?	Par Lost 1.33
Say, Muse, thir Names then known, who first, who last,	Par Lost 1.376
First *Moloch*, horrid King besmear'd with blood	Par Lost 1.392
Both her first born and all her bleating Gods.	Par Lost 1.489
Thir boasted Parents; *Titan* Heav'ns first born	Par Lost 1.510
So *Jove* usurping reign'd: these first in *Creet*	Par Lost 1.514
Our first eruption, thither or elsewhere:	Par Lost 1.656
In vision beatific: by him first	Par Lost 1.684
Did first create your Leader, next free choice,	Par Lost 2.19
First, what Revenge? the Towrs of Heav'n are fill'd	Par Lost 2.129
That so ordains: this was at first resolv'd,	Par Lost 2.201
In heighth or depth, still first and last will Reign	Par Lost 2.324
Pleaded his devilish Counsel, first devis'd	Par Lost 2.379
Shall breathe her balme. But first whom shall we send	Par Lost 2.402
View'd first thir lamentable lot, and found	Par Lost 2.617
And with disdainful look thus first began.	Par Lost 2.680
Who first broke peace in Heav'n and Faith, till then	Par Lost 2.690
What it intends; till first I know of thee,	Par Lost 2.740
In this infernal Vaile first met thou call'st	Par Lost 2.742
At first, and call'd me *Sin*, and for a Sign	Par Lost 2.760
Weakning the Scepter of old *Night:* first Hell	Par Lost 2.1002
A glimmering dawn; here Nature first begins	Par Lost 2.1037
His onely Son; On Earth he first beheld	Par Lost 3.64
Our two first Parents, yet the onely two	Par Lost 3.65
The first sort by thir own suggestion fell,	Par Lost 3.129
By the other first: Man therefore shall find grace,	Par Lost 3.131
But Mercy first and last shall brightest shine.	Par Lost 3.134
To Heav'n remov'd where first it grew, there grows,	Par Lost 3.356

First(*cont*)

Thee Father first they sung Omnipotent,	Par Lost 3.372
Thee next they sang of all Creation first,	Par Lost 3.383
Of this round World, whose first convex divides	Par Lost 3.419
First from the ancient World those Giants came	Par Lost 3.464
The Trepidation talkt, and that first mov'd;	Par Lost 3.483
Down right into the Worlds first Region throws	Par Lost 3.562
But first he casts to change his proper shape,	Par Lost 3.634
The first art wont his great authentic will	Par Lost 3.656
Satan, now first inflam'd with rage, came down,	Par Lost 4.9
Of that first Battel, and his flight to Hell:	Par Lost 4.12
Artificer of fraud; and was the first	Par Lost 4.121
So clomb this first grand Thief into Gods Fould:	Par Lost 4.192
Both where the morning Sun first warmly smote	Par Lost 4.244
When *Satan* still in gaze, as first he stood,	Par Lost 4.356
Grip't in each paw: When *Adam* first of men	Par Lost 4.408
To first of women *Eve* thus moving speech,	Par Lost 4.409
I first awak't, and found my self repos'd	Par Lost 4.450
On our first Father, half her swelling Breast	Par Lost 4.495
But first with narrow search I must walk round	Par Lost 4.528
Where he first lighted, soon discernd his looks	Par Lost 4.570
With first approach of light, we must be ris'n,	Par Lost 4.624
When first on this delightful Land he spreads	Par Lost 4.643
Espoused *Eve* deckt first her nuptial Bed,	Par Lost 4.710
Of Father, Son, and Brother first were known.	Par Lost 4.757
The first in flight from pain, had'st thou alledg'd	Par Lost 4.921
I therefore, I alone first undertook	Par Lost 4.935
To say and strait unsay, pretending first	Par Lost 4.947
Wherein all things created first he weighd,	Par Lost 4.999
Then when fair Morning first smiles on the World,	Par Lost 5.124
But first from under shadie arborous roof,	Par Lost 5.137
Him first, him last, him midst, and without end.	Par Lost 5.165
Delos or *Samos* first appeering kenns	Par Lost 5.265
Ethereal, and as lowest first the Moon;	Par Lost 5.418
Such to perfection, one first matter all,	Par Lost 5.472
Is heard no more in Heav'n; he of the first,	Par Lost 5.659
If not the first Arch-Angel, great in Power,	Par Lost 5.660
Reflecting blaze on blaze, first met his view:	Par Lost 6.18
At first, that Angel should with Angel warr,	Par Lost 6.92
Of my revenge, first sought for thou returnst	Par Lost 6.151
Thy merited reward, the first assay	Par Lost 6.153
Of this right hand provok't, since first that tongue	Par Lost 6.154
At first I thought that Libertie and Heav'n	Par Lost 6.164
And visage all enflam'd first thus began.	Par Lost 6.261
All his right side; then *Satan* first knew pain,	Par Lost 6.327
Then first with fear surpris'd and sense of paine	Par Lost 6.394
Purest at first, now gross by sinning grown.	Par Lost 6.661
First, Highest, Holiest, Best, thou alwayes seekst	Par Lost 6.724
First seen, them unexpected joy surpriz'd,	Par Lost 6.774
Of Heav'n and Earth conspicious first began,	Par Lost 7.63
How first began this Heav'n which we behold	Par Lost 7.86
Ethereal, first of things, quintessence pure	Par Lost 7.244
He nam'd. Thus was the first Day Eev'n and Morn:	Par Lost 7.252
Exhaling first from Darkness they beheld;	Par Lost 7.255
Both when first Eevning was, and when first Morn.	Par Lost 7.260
For of Celestial Bodies first the Sun	Par Lost 7.354
A mightie Spheare he fram'd, unlightsom first,	Par Lost 7.355
First in his East the glorious Lamp was seen,	Par Lost 7.370
Spangling the Hemisphere: then first adornd	Par Lost 7.384
Thir Snakie fouolds, and added wings. First crept	Par Lost 7.484
First wheeld thir course; Earth in her rich attire	Par Lost 7.501
How first this World and face of things began,	Par Lost 7.636
The benefit: consider first, that Great	Par Lost 8.90
But in the fruitful Earth; there first receavd	Par Lost 8.96
From where I first drew Aire, and first beheld	Par Lost 8.284
First found me, and with soft oppression seis'd	Par Lost 8.288
First Man, of Men innumerable ordain'd	Par Lost 8.297
First Father, call'd by thee I come thy Guide	Par Lost 8.298
Transported touch; here passion first I felt,	Par Lost 8.530
As one intended first, not after made	Par Lost 8.555
Be strong, live happie, and love, but first of all	Par Lost 8.633
Since first this Subject for Heroic Song	Par Lost 9.25
Now not, though Sin, not Time, first wraught the change,	Par Lost 9.70
Thus he resolv'd, but first from inward griefe	Par Lost 9.97
As high he soard, obnoxious first or last	Par Lost 9.170
To basest things. Revenge, at first though sweet,	Par Lost 9.171
And *Eve* first to her Husband thus began.	Par Lost 9.204
Or bear what to my minde first thoughts present,	Par Lost 9.213
Whether his first design be to withdraw	Par Lost 9.261
Or daring, first on mee th' assault shall light.	Par Lost 9.305
First thy obedience; th' other who can know,	Par Lost 9.368
A Foe so proud will first the weaker seek,	Par Lost 9.383
For now, and since first break of dawne the Fiend,	Par Lost 9.412
At first, as one who sought access, but feard	Par Lost 9.511
The first at lest of these I thought denid	Par Lost 9.555
I was at first as other Beasts that graze	Par Lost 9.571
The vertue of that Fruit, in thee first prov'd:	Par Lost 9.616
The Gods are first, and that advantage use	Par Lost 9.718
Sollicited her longing eye; yet first	Par Lost 9.743
Whose taste, too long forborn, at first assay	Par Lost 9.747
For Beasts it seems: yet that one Beast which first	Par Lost 9.769
But first low Reverence don, as to the power	Par Lost 9.835
That Morn when first they parted; by the Tree	Par Lost 9.848
First to himself he inward silence broke.	Par Lost 9.895
Profan'd first by the Serpent, by him first	Par Lost 9.930
Most Favors, who can please him long; Mee first	Par Lost 9.949
Farr other operation first displaid,	Par Lost 9.1012
I saw thee first and wedded thee, adorn'd	Par Lost 9.1030

First(*cont*)

Even shame, the last of evils; of the first	Par Lost 9.1079
To that first naked Glorie. Such of late	Par Lost 9.1115
To whom then first incenst *Adam* repli'd,	Par Lost 9.1162
Shee first his weak indulgence will accuse.	Par Lost 9.1186
When first this Tempter cross'd the Gulf from Hell.	Par Lost 10.39
He came, and with him *Eve*, more loth, though first	Par Lost 10.109
To *Satan* first in sin his doom apply'd,	Par Lost 10.172
First lighted from his Wing, and landed safe	Par Lost 10.316
To Paradise first tending, when behold	Par Lost 10.326
Him first make sure your thrall, and lastly kill.	Par Lost 10.402
Encroaching *Eve* perhaps, had first the rule	Par Lost 10.582
Feed first, on each Beast next, and Fish, and Fowle,	Par Lost 10.604
Had first his precept so to move, so shine,	Par Lost 10.652
Outrage from liveless things; but Discord first	Par Lost 10.707
But to my own conviction: first and last	Par Lost 10.831
Beare thine own first, ill able to sustaine	Par Lost 10.950
See Father, what first fruits on Earth are sprung	Par Lost 11.22
For dissolution wrought by Sin, that first	Par Lost 11.55
Corrupted. I at first with two fair gifts	Par Lost 11.57
The Earth, when *Adam* and first Matron *Eve*	Par Lost 11.136
That I who first brought Death on all, am grac't	Par Lost 11.168
Subscrib'd not; Nature first gave Signs, imprest	Par Lost 11.182
First hunter then, pursu'd a gentle brace,	Par Lost 11.188
From the first op'ning bud, and gave ye Names,	Par Lost 11.277
Adam, now ope thine eyes, and first behold	Par Lost 11.423
First Fruits, the green Eare, and the yellow Sheaf,	Par Lost 11.435
In his first shape on man; but many shapes	Par Lost 11.467
First his own Tooles; then, what might else be wrought	Par Lost 11.572
Hymen, then first to marriage Rites invok't;	Par Lost 11.591
First seen in acts of prowess eminent	Par Lost 11.789
But first the lawless Tyrant, who denies	Par Lost 12.173
Just *Abraham* and his Seed: now first I finde	Par Lost 12.273
By Judges first, then under Kings; of whom	Par Lost 12.320
But first a long succession must ensue,	Par Lost 12.331
They first re-edifie, and for a while	Par Lost 12.350
But first among the Priests dissension springs,	Par Lost 12.353
Then that which by creation first brought forth	Par Lost 12.472
Powrd first on his Apostles, whom he sends	Par Lost 12.498
At first against mankind so well had thriv'd	Par Reg 1.114
Winning by Conquest what the first man lost	Par Reg 1.154
By fallacy surpriz'd. But first I mean	Par Reg 1.155
There he shall first lay down the rudiments	Par Reg 1.157
Of Saviour to mankind, and which way first	Par Reg 1.187
Yet held it more humane, more heavenly first	Par Reg 1.221
Me him whose Harbinger he was; and first	Par Reg 1.277
He saw approach, who first with curious eye	Par Reg 1.319
At first it may be; but long since with wo	Par Reg 1.399
To find whom at the first they found unsought:	Par Reg 2.59
Since first her Salutation heard, with thoughts	Par Reg 2.107
Then when I dealt with *Adam* first of Men,	Par Reg 2.133
Now hungring first, and to himself thus said.	Par Reg 2.244
Meats by the Law unclean, or offer'd first	Par Reg 2.328
Get Riches first, get Wealth, and Treasure heap,	Par Reg 2.427
What if he hath decreed that I shall first	Par Reg 3.188
Can suffer, best can do; best reign, who first	Par Reg 3.195
Of that first golden Monarchy the seat,	Par Reg 3.277
By great *Arsaces* led, who founded first	Par Reg 3.295
Thou must make sure thy own, the *Parthian* first	Par Reg 3.363
Expel a Devil who first made him such?	Par Reg 4.129
By lust and rapine; first ambitious grown	Par Reg 4.137
The first of all Commandments, Thou shalt worship	Par Reg 4.176
The first and wisest of them all profess'd	Par Reg 4.293
Announc't by *Gabriel* with the first I knew,	Par Reg 4.504
O first created Beam, and thou great Word,	Samson 83
Which shall I first bewail,	Samson 151
Sam. The first I saw at *Timna*, and she pleas'd	Samson 219
Of *Timna* first betray me, and reveal	Samson 383
First granting, as I do, it was a weakness	Samson 773
To what I did thou shewdst me first the way.	Samson 781
Didst thou at first receive me for thy husband?	Samson 883
Seeming at first all heavenly under virgin veil,	Samson 1035
I less conjecture then when first I saw	Samson 1071
Of fire; that Spirit that first rusht on thee	Samson 1435
To thee first reverend *Manoa*, and to these	Samson 1548
Mess. Feed on that first, there may in grief be surfet.	Samson 1562
Yet e're I give the rains to grief, say first,	Samson 1578
Eye-witness of what first or last was done,	Samson 1594
Bacchus that first from out the purple Grape,	Mask 46
As now I do: But first I must put off	Mask 82
And Courts of Princes, where it first was nam'd,	Mask 325
The divine property of her first being.	Mask 469
And first behold this cordial Julep here	Mask 672
Trinity ms 'first behold' ←'looke upon'	
As *Mercury* did first devise	Mask 963
Ere the first Cock his Mattin rings.	Allegro 114
But first, and chiefest, with thee bring,	Penseroso 51
When first the White thorn blows;	Lycidas 48
Have thou the honour first, thy Lord to greet,	Nativity 26
Yet first to those ychain'd in sleep,	Nativity 155
Didst move my first endeavouring tongue to speak,	Vacation 2
Thou needst not be ambitious to be first,	Vacation 11
First heard by happy watchful Shepherds ear,	Circum 3
And seals obedience first with wounding smart	Circum 25
In first obedience, and their state of good;	Musick 24
First heard before the shallow Cuccoo's bill	Sonnet 1, 6
For who loves that, must first be wise and good;	Sonnet 12, 12
First taught our English Musick how to span	Sonnet 13, 2

First*(cont)*
That the first wealthy *Pope* receiv'd of thee. Prose 1, 3
First-begot
His first-begot we know, and sore have felt, Par Reg 1.89
First-born
Hail holy Light, ofspring of Heav'n first-born, Par Lost 3.1
Last with one midnight stroke all the first-born Par Lost 12.189
Her spurious first-born; Treason against me? Samson 391
Abortive as the first-born bloom of spring Samson 1576
Smote the first-born of *Egypt* Land. Psalm 136, 38
Firstlings
More meek came with the Firstlings of his Flock Par Lost 11.437
First-mover
Her motions, as the great first-Movers hand Par Lost 7.500
First-moving
Whether above that high first-moving Spheare Fair Inf 39
First-parents
While time was, our first-Parents had bin warnd Par Lost 4.6
1667 'first Parents'
First-seen
First-seen, or some renown'd Metropolis Par Lost 3.549
Fish
And downward Fish: yet had his Temple high Par Lost 1.463
ms 'fish'
Of Fish that with thir Finns and shining Scales Par Lost 7.401
With Fish replenisht, and the Aire with Fowle, Par Lost 7.447
By Fowl, Fish, Beast, was flown, was swum, was walkt Par Lost 7.503
Over the Fish and Fowle of Sea and Aire, Par Lost 7.521
Over Fish of the Sea, and Fowle of the Aire, Par Lost 7.533
Or live in Sea, or Aire, Beast, Fish, and Fowle. Par Lost 8.341
Of Fish within thir watry residence, Par Lost 8.346
Much less can Bird with Beast, or Fish with Fowle Par Lost 8.395
Feed first, on each Beast next, and Fish, and Fowle, Par Lost 10.604
And Fish with Fish; to graze the Herb all leaving, Par Lost 10.711
He gave us onely over Beast, Fish, Fowl Par Lost 12.67
Gris-amber-steam'd; all Fish from Sea or Shore, Par Reg 2.344
Fowl of the Heavens, and Fish that through the wet Psalm 8, 21
Fishermen
Plain Fishermen, no greater men them call, Par Reg 2.27
Fishy
Then *Asmodeus* with the fishie fume, Par Lost 4.168
Fist
My heels are fetter'd, but my fist is free. Samson 1235
Fit
With *Atlantean* shoulders fit to bear Par Lost 2.306
Fit retribution, emptie as thir deeds; Par Lost 3.454
His habit fit for speed succinct, and held Par Lost 3.643
Fit for the Tun som Magazin to store Par Lost 4.816
Armie of Fiends, fit body to fit head; Par Lost 4.953
Forbidd'n here, it seems, as onely fit Par Lost 5.69
Thir Maker, in fit strains pronounc't or sung Par Lost 5.148
Abundance, fit to honour and receive Par Lost 5.315
Wants her fit vessels pure, then strews the ground Par Lost 5.348
Fit entertainment to receive our King Par Lost 5.690
Fit to decide the Empire of great Heav'n. Par Lost 6.303
Fit well his Helme, gripe fast his orbed Shield, Par Lost 6.543
Against such hellish mischief fit to oppose. Par Lost 6.636
Hell thir fit habitation fraught with fire Par Lost 6.876
Urania, and fit audience find, though few. Par Lost 7.31
Such as I seek, fit to participate Par Lost 8.390
To see how thou could'st judge of fit and meet: Par Lost 8.448
Thy likeness, thy fit help, thy other self, Par Lost 8.450
Fit Vessel, fittest Imp of fraud, in whom Par Lost 9.89
Shee fair, divinely fair, fit Love for Gods, Par Lost 9.489
So fit, so acceptable, so Divine, Par Lost 10.139
Can fit his punishment, or their revenge. Par Lost 10.242
That laugh, as if transported with some fit Par Lost 10.626
He never shall find out fit Mate, but such Par Lost 10.899
Fit haunt of Gods? where I had hope to spend, Par Lost 11.271
Into fit moulds prepar'd; from which he formd Par Lost 11.571
To meek submission: thou at season fit Par Lost 12.597
Pretends to wash off sin, and fit them so Par Reg 1.73
Wrapt in a pleasing fit of melancholy Mask 546
Bridgewater ms 'fitt'
With lickerish baits fit to ensnare a brute? Mask 700
line not in Bridgewater ms
Thou art not fit to hear thy self convinc't; Mask 792
line not in Bridgewater ms
line not in Trinity ms
Som still removed place will fit, Penseroso 78
Whose lustre leads us, and for her most fit, Arcades 76
Took up, and in fit place did reinstall? Fair Inf 46
Before thou cloath my fancy in fit sound: Vacation 32
In pensive trance, and anguish, and ecstatick fit. Passion 42
Fitly
So fitly them in pairs thou hast combin'd; Par Lost 8.394
That they would fitly fall in order'd Characters. Passion 49
Fits
It fits not; thou and I long since are twain; Samson 929
Har. This insolence other kind of answer fits. Samson 1236
To appear as fits before th' illustrious Lords. Samson 1318
Now void, it fitts thy people; thether bend Prose 12, 10
Fitted
In slavish habit, ill-fitted weeds Samson 122
Fitter
The Ground whence he was taken, fitter soile. Par Lost 11.98
The ground whence thou wast tak'n, fitter Soile. Par Lost 11.262
Fittest
Fit Vessel, fittest Imp of fraud, in whom Par Lost 9.89
For thee is fittest place, I found thee there, Par Reg 4.373
Fitting
On points and questions fitting *Moses* Chair, Par Reg 4.219
Five
Which the five watchful Senses represent, Par Lost 5.104
And yee five other wandring Fires that move Par Lost 5.177
Her office they prescrib'd, to th' other five Par Lost 10.657
Though Fame divulge him Father of five Sons Samson 1248
Fix
Roaming to seek thir prey on earth, durst fix Par Lost 1.382
And fix farr deeper in his head thir stings Par Lost 12.432
Thou fix them on the earth as fast. Penseroso 44
High God shall fix her fast. Psalm 87, 20
Fixed
Though chang'd in outward lustre; that fixt mind Par Lost 1.97
With fixed Anchor in his skaly rind Par Lost 1.206
Breathing united force with fixed thought Par Lost 1.560
Stood fixt her stately highth, and strait the dores Par Lost 1.723
Mee though just right, and the fixt Laws of Heav'n Par Lost 2.18
Fixt Fate, free will, foreknowledg absolute, Par Lost 2.560
They pass the Planets seven, and pass the fixt, Par Lost 3.481
He seemd, or fixt in cogitation deep. Par Lost 3.629
His fixed seat, or fixed seat hath none, Par Lost 3.669
Of sympathie and love; there I had fixt Par Lost 4.465
With the fixt Starrs, fixt in thir Orb that flies, Par Lost 5.176
Of Planets and of fixt in all her Wheeles Par Lost 5.621
Of Godhead, fixt for ever firm and sure, Par Lost 7.586
Thought him still speaking, still stood fixt to hear; Par Lost 8.3
line not in 1667 edition
Fixt on the Fruit she gaz'd, which to behold Par Lost 9.735
However I with thee have fixt my Lot, Par Lost 9.952
Hadst thou bin firm and fixt in thy dissent, Par Lost 9.1160
As with a Trident smote, and fix't as firm Par Lost 10.295
Thir earnest eyes they fix'd, imagining Par Lost 10.553
In Synod unbenigne, and taught the fixt Par Lost 10.661
Fixd on this day? why do I overlive, Par Lost 10.773
Fast on the top of som high mountain fixt. Par Lost 11.851
Till time stand fixt: beyond is all abyss, Par Lost 12.555
To thir fixt Station, all in bright array Par Lost 12.627
The purpos'd Counsel pre-ordain'd and fixt Par Reg 1.127
Cho. Yet on she moves, now stands & eies thee fixt, Samson 726
No, I am fixt not to part hence without him. Samson 1481
And eyes fast fixt he stood, as one who pray'd, Samson 1637
And you a statue; or as *Daphne* was Mask 661
Trinity ms 'or as' ←'fixed as'
In stony fetters fixt, and motionless; Mask 819
Or fill the fixed mind with all your toyes; Penseroso 4
Stand fixt in stedfast gaze, Nativity 70
Hath fixt her polisht Car. Nativity 241
Thy care is fixt and zealously attends Sonnet 9, 9
Fixes
Lay pleasant, his grievd look he fixes sad, Par Lost 4.28
Fixes instead, unmoulding reasons mintage Mask 529
Flag
Thir embryon Atoms; they around the flag Par Lost 2.900
Under the sooty flag of *Acheron*, Mask 604
Bridgewater ms 'flagg'
Flail
His shadowy Flale hath thresh'd the Corn Allegro 108
Flakes
when the big rowling flakes of pitchie clowds Mask Tr. ms 15.52
when the bigg rowling flakes of pitchie clouds Mask Br. ms 345
Flame
Cast forth redounding smoak and ruddy flame. Par Lost 2.889
Our circuit meets full West. As flame they part Par Lost 4.784
Stood up, and in a flame of zeale severe Par Lost 5.807
Impendent, raging into sudden flame Par Lost 5.891
Shall yield us pregnant with infernal flame, Par Lost 6.483
With nicest touch. Immediate in a flame, Par Lost 6.584
Of smoak and bickering flame, and sparkles dire; Par Lost 6.766
Kindl'd through agitation to a Flame, Par Lost 9.637
Stood open wide, belching outrageous flame Par Lost 10.232
Tine the slant Lightning, whose thwart flame driv'n down Par Lost 10.1075
Cherubic watch, and of a Sword the flame Par Lost 11.120
That sole excites to high attempts the flame Par Reg 3.26
Toucht with the flame: on thir whole Host I flew Samson 262
Thy words by adding fuel to the flame? Samson 1351
From under ashes into sudden flame, Samson 1691
Dark vaild *Cotytto*, t' whom the secret flame Mask 129
To such a flame of sacred vehemence, Mask 795
line not in Bridgewater ms
line not in Trinity ms
As his inferiour flame, Nativity 81
But with a scarce-wel-lighted flame; Winchester 20
The *greedy* flame runs hier and hier Psalm 83, 55
Flamed
As one great Furnace flam'd, yet from those flames Par Lost 1.62
Neer that bituminous Lake where *Sodom* flam'd; Par Lost 10.562
Flam'd in my heart, heroic acts, one while Par Reg 1.216
Flamens
Affrights the *Flamins* at their service quaint; Nativity 194
Flames
As one great Furnace flam'd, yet from those flames Par Lost 1.62
Save what the glimmering of these livid flames Par Lost 1.182
His mighty Stature; on each hand the flames Par Lost 1.222
Arm'd with Hell flames and fury all at once Par Lost 2.61

Flames(*cont*)
And plunge us in the flames? or from above — Par Lost 2.172
1667 'Flames'
Will slack'n, if his breath stir not thir flames. — Par Lost 2.214
In darkness, while thy head flames thick and fast — Par Lost 2.754
A God, leap'd fondly into *Aetna* flames, — Par Lost 3.470
In duskie wreathes, reluctant flames, the signe — Par Lost 6.58
Flashing thick flames, Wheele within Wheele undrawn, — Par Lost 6.751
Of both my Parents all in flames ascended — Samson 25
Rode up in flames after his message told — Samson 1433
That flames, and dances in his crystal bounds — Mask 673
Trinity ms 'flams' ←'flames'
Rob'd in flames, and Amber light, — Allegro 61
Flames in the forehead of the morning sky: — Lycidas 171
Trinity ms 'flams'
When I dye, let the earth be roul'd in flames. — Prose 5, 1

Flaming
Hurld headlong flaming from th' Ethereal Skie — Par Lost 1.45
ms 'flameing'
Millions of flaming swords, drawn from the thighs — Par Lost 1.664
Nor stop thy flaming Chariot wheels, that shook — Par Lost 3.394
Hung high with Diamond flaming, and with Gold. — Par Lost 4.554
Amidst as from a flaming Mount, whose top — Par Lost 5.598
The flaming Seraph fearless, though alone — Par Lost 5.875
Chariots and flaming Armes, and fierie Steeds — Par Lost 6.17
With Flaming Cherubim, and golden Shields; — Par Lost 6.102
Of fiery Darts in flaming volies flew, — Par Lost 6.213
Fell with his flaming Legions through the Deep — Par Lost 7.134
Hee from the East his flaming rode begin, — Par Lost 8.162
And flaming Ministers to watch and tend — Par Lost 9.156
Thy choice of flaming Warriours, least the Fiend — Par Lost 11.101
Nor that which on the flaming Mount appeerd — Par Lost 11.216
Thir motion, at whose Front a flaming Sword, — Par Lost 12.592
Wav'd over by that flaming Brand, the Gate — Par Lost 12.643
Ye flaming Powers, and winged Warriours bright, — Circum 1

Flank
Divided, and to either Flank retir'd. — Par Lost 6.570

Flaring
His flaring beams, me Goddes bring — Penseroso 132

Flashing
Flashing thick flames, Wheele within Wheele undrawn, — Par Lost 6.751

Flashy
And when they list, their lean and flashy songs — Lycidas 123
Trinity ms 'flashie'
1638 'flashie'

Flat
Where he fell flat, and sham'd his Worshipers: — Par Lost 1.461
Is flat despair: we must exasperate — Par Lost 2.143
Beyond a row of Myrtles, on a Flat, — Par Lost 9.627
Hath toucht my sense, flat seems to this, and harsh. — Par Lost 9.987
Fall flat and shrink into a trivial toy, — Par Reg 2.223
What ruins Kingdoms, and lays Cities flat; — Par Reg 4.363
My hopes all flat, nature within me seems — Samson 595
Were in the flat Sea sunk. And Wisdoms self — Mask 375
Bridgewater ms 'flatt'

Flatly
Flatly unjust, to binde with Laws the free, — Par Lost 5.819

Flatter
Say and unsay, feign, flatter, or abjure? — Par Reg 1.474

Flattered
And flatter'd out of all, believing lies — Par Lost 10.42
And work my flatter'd fancy to belief, — Passion 31

Flatteries
Outlandish flatteries? then proceed'st to talk — Par Reg 4.125
whether deluded and soothing lies & soothing flatteries. — Mask Tr. ms 22.20

Flattering
Of all his flattering Prophets glibb'd with lyes — Par Reg 1.375
Thrice she assay'd with flattering prayers and sighs, — Samson 392
Hopes thee; of flattering gales — Horace 11

Flaunting
With flaunting Hony-suckle, and began — Mask 545
Bridgewater ms 'flauntinge'
Trinity ms 'flaunting' ←'blowing' ←'suckling'

Flavour
Sparkling, out-pow'rd, the flavor, or the smell, — Samson 544

Flaw
And snow and haile and stormie gust and flaw, — Par Lost 10.698

Flaws
Was distant; and these flaws, though mortals fear them — Par Reg 4.454

Fled
Fled over *Adria* to th' *Hesperian* Fields, — Par Lost 1.520
What when we fled amain, pursu'd and strook — Par Lost 2.165
All taste of living wight, as once it fled — Par Lost 2.613
Made to destroy: I fled, and cry'd out *Death;* — Par Lost 2.787
I fled, but he pursu'd (though more, it seems, — Par Lost 2.790
Fled not in silence through the frighted deep — Par Lost 2.994
Of Guardians bright, when he from *Esau* fled — Par Lost 3.512
Till at his second bidding darkness fled, — Par Lost 3.712
Less pain, less to be fled, or thou then they — Par Lost 4.919
His mounted scale aloft: nor more; but fled — Par Lost 4.1014
Murmuring, and with him fled the shades of night. — Par Lost 4.1015
And uncouth paine fled bellowing. On each wing — Par Lost 6.362
Fled ignominious, to such evil brought — Par Lost 6.395
Where lodg'd, or whither fled, or if for fight, — Par Lost 6.531
Whom fled we thought, will save us long pursuit — Par Lost 6.538
Heav'n ruining from Heav'n and would have fled — Par Lost 6.868
When *Satan* who late fled before the threats — Par Lost 9.53
By Night he fled, and at Midnight return'd — Par Lost 9.58

Fled(*cont*)
Likeliest she seemd, *Pomona* when she fled — Par Lost 9.394
Hee fled, not hoping to escape, but shun — Par Lost 10.339
Of Man, but fled him, or with count'nance grim — Par Lost 10.713
For though I fled him angrie, yet recall'd — Par Lost 11.330
Fled and pursu'd transverse the resonant fugue. — Par Lost 11.563
Which now abated, for the Clouds were fled, — Par Lost 11.841
The fiery Serpent fled, and noxious Worm, — Par Reg 1.312
He saw the Prophet also how he fled — Par Reg 2.270
Fled from his Lion ramp, old Warriors turn'd — Samson 139
Their choicest youth; they only liv'd who fled. — Samson 264
Root-bound, that fled *Apollo*, *La*. Fool do not boast, — Mask 662
And sullen *Moloch* fled, — Nativity 205
That saw the troubl'd Sea, and shivering fled, — Psalm 114, 7
Why fled the Ocean? And why skipt the Mountains? — Psalm 114, 13
Of sheenie Heav'n, and thou some goddess fled — Fair Inf 48
Through pangs fled to felicity, — Winchester 68
I wak'd, she fled, and day brought back my night. — Sonnet 23, 14

Fleddest
Flie thither whence thou fledst: if from this houre — Par Lost 4.963

Fledge
Illustrious on his Shoulders fledge with wings — Par Lost 3.627
Thir callow young, but featherd soon and fledge — Par Lost 7.420

Fleece
Like a tame Weather, all my precious fleece, — Samson 538

Fleeced
His vastness: Fleec't the Flocks and bleating rose, — Par Lost 7.472

Fleecy
Of *Libra* to the fleecie Starr that bears — Par Lost 3.558
Till the Sun paint your fleecie skirts with Gold, — Par Lost 5.187
From a fat Meddow ground; or fleecy Flock, — Par Lost 11.648
Of pilfering Woolf, not all the fleecy wealth — Mask 504
Trinity ms 'fleecie'
Bridgewater ms 'fleecie'
1637 'fleecie'
Stooping through a fleecy cloud. — Penseroso 72

Fleet
As when farr off at Sea a Fleet descri'd — Par Lost 2.636
Dissolvd on Earth, fleet hither, and in vain, — Par Lost 3.457
In Mail thir horses clad, yet fleet and strong, — Par Reg 3.313
Whilst from off the waters fleet — Mask 896
Bridgewater ms 'fleete'

Fleeting
Heavie, though in thir place. O fleeting joyes — Par Lost 10.741

Flesh
Like cumbrous flesh; but in what shape they choose — Par Lost 1.428
Made flesh, when time shall be, of Virgin seed, — Par Lost 3.284
To gorge the flesh of Lambs or yeanling Kids — Par Lost 3.434
And from whom I was formd flesh of thy flesh, — Par Lost 4.441
His flesh, his bone; to give thee being I lent — Par Lost 4.483
But suddenly with flesh fill'd up and heal'd: — Par Lost 8.468
Bone of my Bone, Flesh of my Flesh, my Self — Par Lost 8.495
And they shall be one Flesh, one Heart, one Soule. — Par Lost 8.499
As Flesh to mix with Flesh, or Soul with Soul. — Par Lost 8.629
The Link of Nature draw me: Flesh of Flesh, — Par Lost 9.914
One Flesh; to loose thee were to loose my self. — Par Lost 9.959
The stonie from thir hearts, & made new flesh — Par Lost 11.4
The whole Earth fill'd with violence, and all flesh — Par Lost 11.888
Botches and blaines must all his flesh imboss, — Par Lost 12.180
From shadowie Types to Truth, from Flesh to Spirit, — Par Lost 12.303
He shall endure by coming in the Flesh — Par Lost 12.405
And all the world, and mass of sinful flesh; — Par Reg 1.162
Of Death, call'd Life; which us from Life doth sever. — Sonnet 14, 4
Trinity ms 'death' ←'Flesh & sin'
My heart and flesh aloud do crie, — Psalm 84, 7

Fleshliest
The fleshliest Incubus, and thus advis'd. — Par Reg 2.152

Fleshly
Much ostentation vain of fleshly arm, — Par Reg 3.387
In fleshly Tabernacle, and human form, — Par Reg 4.599
Her mansion in this fleshly nook: — Penseroso 92
Poor fleshly Tabernacle entered, — Passion 17

Flew
He spake: and to confirm his words, out-flew — Par Lost 1.663
ms 'out flew'
Up hither like Aereal vapours flew — Par Lost 3.445
Wafted by Angels, or flew o're the Lake — Par Lost 3.521
Flew upward, spirited with various forms, — Par Lost 3.717
Thence up he flew, and on the Tree of Life — Par Lost 4.194
The latter quick up flew, and kickt the beam; — Par Lost 4.1004
With him I flew, and underneath beheld — Par Lost 5.87
Flew through the midst of Heav'n; th' angelic Quires — Par Lost 5.251
Of fiery Darts in flaming volies flew, — Par Lost 6.213
Forthwith from Councel to the work they flew, — Par Lost 6.507
Flew off, and into strange vagaries fell, — Par Lost 6.614
Light as the Lightning glimps they ran, they flew, — Par Lost 6.642
Creatures that livd, and movd, and walk'd, or flew, — Par Lost 8.264
Flew divers, and with Power (thir Power was great) — Par Lost 10.284
Flew up, nor missd the way, by envious windes — Par Lost 11.15
Of Angels on full sail of wing flew nigh, — Par Reg 4.582
Toucht with the flame: on thir whole Host I flew — Samson 262
And azure wings, that up they flew so drest, — Sonnet 14, 11

Flies
The Ford, and of it self the water flies — Par Lost 2.612
And swims or sinks, or wades, or creeps, or flyes: — Par Lost 2.950
On Hills where Flocks are fed, flies toward the Springs — Par Lost 3.435
With the fixt Starrs, fixt in thir Orb that flies, — Par Lost 5.176
Bright Temple, to *Aegyptian Theb*'s he flies. — Par Lost 5.274

Flies(*cont*)
Forthwith from out the Arke a Raven flies, Par Lost 11.855
Frogs, Lice and Flies must all his Palace fill Par Lost 12.177
Flies to his place, nor rests, but in mid air Par Reg 1.39
Sorrow flies farr: See here be all the pleasures Mask 668
Flies
Or as a swarm of flies in vintage time, Par Reg 4.15
Fliest
Whom fli'st thou? whom thou fli'st, of him thou art, Par Lost 4.482
Moon, that now meetst the orient Sun, now fli'st Par Lost 5.175
Flight
That with no middle flight intends to soar Par Lost 1.14
Then with expanded wings he stears his flight Par Lost 1.225
With dread of death to flight or foul retreat, Par Lost 1.555
With what compulsion and laborious flight Par Lost 2.80
Besides what hope the never-ending flight Par Lost 2.221
His uncouth way, or spread his aerie flight Par Lost 2.407
Explores his solitary flight; som times Par Lost 2.632
He spreads for flight, and in the surging smoak Par Lost 2.928
In that obscure sojourn, while in my flight Par Lost 3.15
His flight precipitant, and windes with ease Par Lost 3.563
To find who might direct his wandring flight Par Lost 3.631
Throws his steep flight in many an Aerie wheele, Par Lost 3.741
Of that first Battel, and his flight to Hell: Par Lost 4.12
By shorter flight to th' East, had left him there Par Lost 4.595
Which thou incurr'st by flying, meet thy flight Par Lost 4.913
The first in flight from pain, had'st thou alledg'd Par Lost 4.921
To thy deserted host this cause of flight, Par Lost 4.922
And various: wondring at my flight and change Par Lost 5.89
A cloudy spot. Down thither prone in flight Par Lost 5.266
And fly, ere evil intercept thy flight. Par Lost 5.871
From flight, seditious Angel, to receave Par Lost 6.152
From mee returnd, as erst thou saidst, from flight, Par Lost 6.187
The ridges of grim Warr; no thought of flight, Par Lost 6.236
To flight, or if to fall, but that they rise Par Lost 6.285
Disdain'd, but meaner thoughts learnd in thir flight, Par Lost 6.367
Not liable to fear or flight or paine. Par Lost 6.397
This day, fear not his flight; so thick a Cloud Par Lost 6.539
To final Battel drew, disdaining flight, Par Lost 6.798
Above the flight of *Pegasean* wing. Par Lost 7.4
For haste; such flight the great command impress'd Par Lost 7.294
Easing thir flight; so stears the prudent Crane Par Lost 7.430
A lower flight, and speak of things at hand Par Lost 8.199
Convict by flight, and Rebel to all Law Par Lost 10.83
Inspir'd, and wing'd for Heav'n with speedier flight Par Lost 11.7
Direct to th' Eastern Gate was bent thir flight. Par Lost 11.190
Of flight pursu'd in th' Air and ore the ground Par Lost 11.202
Then to the Desert takes with these his flight; Par Reg 2.241
Of equal dread in flight, or in pursuit; Par Reg 3.306
Of thir pursuers, and overcame by flight; Par Reg 3.325
Bears greatest names in his wild aerie flight. Samson 974
Or rather flight, no great advantage on me; Samson 1118
And put the Damsel to suspicious flight, Mask 158
Into swift flight, till I had found you here, Mask 579
That stay'd her flight with his cross-flowing course, Mask 832
To hear the Lark begin his flight, Allegro 41
And will not take their flight, Nativity 72
And why from us so quickly thou didst take thy flight. Fair Inf 42
Flights
And call swift flights of Angels ministrant Par Reg 2.385
Fling
About the cedar'n alleys fling Mask 990
Bridgewater ms 'flinge'
And when the Sun begins to fling Penseroso 131
Flings
And Crop-full out of dores he flings, Allegro 113
Flintstones
And make soft rills from fiery flint-stones gush. Psalm 114, 18
Flittering
Thou hovering Angel girt with golden wings, Mask 214
Trinity ms 'hov'ring' ←'flittering'
1637 'flittering Angel'
Float
How sweetly did they float upon the wings Mask 249
Bridgewater ms 'floate'
Trinity ms 'flote'
He must not flote upon his watry bear Lycidas 12
Floated
Floted redundant: pleasing was his shape, Par Lost 9.503
Floating
Lay floating many a rood, in bulk as huge Par Lost 1.196
From the safe shore thir floating Carkases Par Lost 1.310
As *Delos* floating once; the rest his look Par Lost 10.296
No more was seen; the floating Vessel swum Par Lost 11.745
As on a floating couch through the blithe Air, Par Reg 4.585
The sumptuous *Dalila* floating this way: Samson 1072
Floats
Floats, as they pass, fann'd with unnumber'd plumes: Par Lost 7.432
The Ark no more now flotes, but seems on ground Par Lost 11.850
Flock
The starrie flock, allur'd them, and with lyes Par Lost 5.709
Of Goats or timerous flock together throngd Par Lost 6.857
Of mortal change on Earth. As when a flock Par Lost 10.273
More meek came with the Firstlings of his Flock Par Lost 11.437
From a fat Meddow ground; or fleecy Flock, Par Lost 11.648
Corn wine and oyle; and from the herd or flock, Par Lost 12.19
And numbers thither flock, I had no will, Samson 1450
Or straggling weather the pen't flock forsook? Mask 499

Flock(*cont*)
Fed the same flock, by fountain, shade, and rill. Lycidas 24
Who leadest like a flock of sheep Psalm 80, 3
Thou antient stock of Israel, Psalm 81, 35
Flocked
To all Baptiz'd: to his great Baptism flock'd Par Reg 1.21
Flock'd to the Baptist, I among the rest, Par Reg 4.511
Flocking
All these and more came flocking; but with looks Par Lost 1.522
The flocking shadows pale, Nativity 232
Flocks
Or flocks, or heards, or human face divine; Par Lost 3.44
On Hills where Flocks are fed, flies toward the Springs Par Lost 3.435
Watching where Shepherds pen thir Flocks at eeve Par Lost 4.185
Betwixt them Lawns, or level Downs, and Flocks Par Lost 4.252
Those rare and solitarie, these in flocks Par Lost 7.461
His vastness: Fleec't the Flocks and bleating rose, Par Lost 7.472
Of Herds and Flocks, and numerous servitude; Par Lost 12.132
With herds the pastures throng'd, with flocks the hills, Par Reg 3.260
When for their teeming Flocks, and granges full Mask 175
Trinity ms 'flocks'
Bridgewater ms 'flocks'
The folded flocks pen'd in their watled cotes, Mask 344
Tending my flocks hard by i' th hilly crofts, Mask 531
This evening late by then the chewing flocks Mask 540
Covering the earth with odours, fruits, and flocks, Mask 712
Where the nibling flocks do stray, Allegro 72
Bring your Flocks, and live with us, Arcades 103
Trinity ms 'flocks'
Batt'ning our flocks with the fresh dews of night, Lycidas 29
All Flocks, and Herds, by thy commanding word, Psalm 8, 19
Flood
Prone on the Flood, extended long and large Par Lost 1.195
ms 'flood'
Both glorying to have scap't the *Stygian* flood Par Lost 1.239
Abject and lost lay these, covering the Flood, Par Lost 1.312
ms 'flood'
Cherube and Seraph rowling in the Flood Par Lost 1.324
ms 'flood'
With these came they, who from the bordring flood Par Lost 1.419
Abhorred *Styx* the flood of deadly hate, Par Lost 2.577
Beyond this flood a frozen Continent Par Lost 2.587
Thir spicie Drugs: they on the Trading Flood Par Lost 2.640
From *Paneas* the fount of *Jordans* flood Par Lost 3.535
The cumbrous Elements, Earth, Flood, Aire, Fire, Par Lost 3.715
Down the steep glade, and met the neather Flood, Par Lost 4.231
Driv'n back redounded as a flood on those Par Lost 7.57
Or thence from *Niger* Flood to *Atlas* Mount Par Lost 11.402
By Fire, Flood, Famin, by Intemperance more Par Lost 11.472
Flood overwhelmd, and them with all thir pomp Par Lost 11.748
Depopulation; thee another Floud, Par Lost 11.756
Of tears and sorrow a Floud thee also drown'd, Par Lost 11.757
Out of his place, pushd by the horned floud, Par Lost 11.831
He lookd, and saw the Ark hull on the floud, Par Lost 11.840
The Earth again by flood, nor let the Sea Par Lost 11.893
While yet the Patriark liv'd, who scap'd the Flood, Par Lost 12.117
To the flood *Jordan*, came as then obscure, Par Reg 1.24
Before the Flood thou with thy lusty Crew, Par Reg 2.178
Forest and field, and flood, Temples and Towers Par Reg 3.268
And at their passing cleave the *Assyrian* flood, Par Reg 3.436
Tetrarchs of fire, air, flood, and on the earth Par Reg 4.201
Of every salt Flood, and each ebbing Stream, Mask 19
Bridgewater ms 'flood'
Trinity ms 'flood'
Commended her fair innocence to the flood Mask 831
Nor wet *Octobers* torrent flood Mask 930
Bridgewater ms 'floud'
halfe his wast flood the wide Atlantique fills Mask Tr. ms 10.14
In fire, air, flood, or under ground, Penseroso 94
Of that renowned flood, so often sung, Arcades 29
O Fountain *Arethuse*, and thou honour'd floud, Lycidas 85
Trinity ms 'flood'
To all that wander in that perilous flood. Lycidas 185
1638 'floud'
That whirl'd the Prophet up at *Chebar* flood, Passion 37
And Joy shall overtake us as a flood, On Time 13
Floods
With Floods and Whirlwinds of tempestuous fire, Par Lost 1.77
ms 'floods'
Of torrent Floods, or of a numerous Host. Par Lost 6.830
On the swift flouds: as Armies at the call Par Lost 7.295
Ay me! Whilst thee the shores, and sounding Seas Lycidas 154
Trinity ms 'shoars' ←'floods'
That glassy flouds from rugged rocks can crush, Psalm 114, 17
The floods stood still like Walls of Glass, Psalm 136, 49
1673 'flouds'
Floor
Least on the threshing floore his hopeful sheaves Par Lost 4.984
Sunk though he be beneath the watry floar, Lycidas 167
Trinity ms 'floare'
1638 'floore'
Flora
Milde, as when *Zephyrus* on *Flora* breathes, Par Lost 5.16
From their soft wings, and *Flora*'s earliest smells. Par Reg 2.365
Florid
Hid *Amalthea* and her Florid Son Par Lost 4.278
Imbracing round this florid Earth, what cause Par Lost 7.90
Adorns him, colour'd with the Florid hue Par Lost 7.445

Flourished
Rear'd high thir flourisht heads between, and wrought Par Lost 4.699
Forth flourish't thick the clustring Vine, forth crept Par Lost 7.320
Flourishd, since mute, to som great cause addrest, Par Lost 9.672
Wherin your Father flourisht, yet by you Sonnet 10, 10
Flourishing
And all the flourishing works of peace destroy, Par Reg 3.80
Flouts
And flouts at us they throw Psalm 80, 28
Flow
That wash thy hallowd feet, and warbling flow, Par Lost 3.31
Turnd him all eare to hear new utterance flow. Par Lost 4.410
Fountains and yee, that warble, as ye flow, Par Lost 5.195
Those thousand decencies that daily flow Par Lost 8.601
Of looks and smiles, for smiles from Reason flow, Par Lost 9.239
Thy easie numbers flow, and that each heart Shakespear 10
Thy fierce wrath over me doth flow Psalm 88, 65
Flowed
Delight thee more, and *Siloa*'s Brook that flow'd Par Lost 1.11
Viewless, and underneath a bright Sea flow'd Par Lost 3.518
Flowd from thir lips, in Prose or numerous Verse, Par Lost 5.150
A stream of Nectarous humor issuing flow'd Par Lost 6.332
Before the Hills appeerd, or Fountain flow'd, Par Lost 7.8
Main Ocean flow'd, not idle, but with warme Par Lost 7.279
A militarie Vest of purple flowd Par Lost 11.241
Lay pleasant; from his side two rivers flow'd, Par Reg 3.255
Sam. Where ever fountain or fresh current flow'd Samson 547
Flower
Warriers, the Flowr of Heav'n, once yours, now lost, Par Lost 1.316
ms 'flower'
Immortal Amarant, a Flour which once Par Lost 3.353
Her self a fairer Floure by gloomie *Dis* Par Lost 4.270
His orient Beams, on herb, tree, fruit, and flour, Par Lost 4.644
On this delightful land, nor herb, fruit, floure, Par Lost 4.652
Fenc'd up the verdant wall; each beauteous flour, Par Lost 4.697
More aerie, last the bright consummate floure Par Lost 5.481
Impearls on every leaf and every flouer. Par Lost 5.747
With Plant, Fruit, Flour Ambrosial, Gemms & Gold, Par Lost 6.475
This Garden, still to tend Plant, Herb and Flour, Par Lost 9.206
Each Flour of slender stalk, whose head though gay Par Lost 9.428
Her self, though fairest unsupported Flour, Par Lost 9.432
But his growth now to youths full flowr, displaying Par Reg 1.67
Prauncing their riders bore, the flower and choice Par Reg 3.314
A thousand fore-skins fell, the flower of *Palestin* Samson 144
Like a fair flower surcharg'd with dew, she weeps Samson 728
If in my flower of youth and strength, when all men Samson 938
Thir choice nobility and flower, not only Samson 1654
Bore a bright golden flowre, but not in this soyl: Mask 633
line not in Bridgewater ms
Like to that sanguine flower inscrib'd with woe. Lycidas 106
Trinity ms 'flowre'
And every flower that sad embroidery wears: Lycidas 148
Trinity ms 'flower' ←'bud'
and that sad floure that strove Lycidas Tr. ms 28.17
O Fairest flower no sooner blown but blasted, Fair Inf 1
But then transform'd him to a purple flower Fair Inf 27
Who onely thought to crop the flowr Winchester 39
With flowr of finest wheat, Psalm 81, 66
Truth from the earth *like to a flowr* Psalm 85, 45
Flowered
Then Herbs of every leaf, that sudden flour'd Par Lost 7.317
Flowerets
With flourets deck't and fragrant smells; but *Eve* Par Lost 5.379
On flours repos'd, and with fresh flourets crownd, Par Lost 5.636
line not in 1667 edition
And with fresh Flourets Hill and Valley smil'd. Par Lost 6.784
Their Bels, and Flourets of a thousand hues. Lycidas 135
Trinity ms 'flowrets'
1638 'flowrets'
Flowering
And flouring Odours, Cassia, Nard, and Balme; Par Lost 5.293
Flower-inwoven
With flowre-inwov'n tresses torn Nativity 187
Flowers
In clusters; they among fresh dews and flowers Par Lost 1.771
Ambrosial Odours and Ambrosial Flowers, Par Lost 2.245
And flours aloft shading the Fount of Life, Par Lost 3.357
Rowls o're *Elisian* Flours her Amber stream; Par Lost 3.359
Flours worthy of Paradise which not nice Art Par Lost 4.241
Flours of all hue, and without Thorn the Rose: Par Lost 4.256
Of *Enna*, where *Proserpin* gathering flours Par Lost 4.269
On the soft downie Bank damaskt with flours: Par Lost 4.334
To prune these growing Plants, and tend these Flours, Par Lost 4.438
Under a shade of flours, much wondring where Par Lost 4.451
That shed *May* Flowers; and press'd her Matron lip Par Lost 4.501
With Flowers, Garlands, and sweet-smelling Herbs Par Lost 4.709
Among the Groves, the Fountains, and the Flours Par Lost 5.126
Among sweet dewes and flours; where any row Par Lost 5.212
Spirits odorous breathes: flours and thir fruit Par Lost 5.482
On flours repos'd, and with fresh flourets crownd, Par Lost 5.636
line not in 1667 edition
Rose, and went forth among her Fruits and Flours, Par Lost 8.44
On a green shadie Bank profuse of Flours Par Lost 8.286
I mean of Taste, Sight, Smell, Herbs, Fruits, and Flours, Par Lost 8.527
In *Eden* on the humid Flours, that breathd Par Lost 9.193
Just then returnd at shut of Evening Flours. Par Lost 9.278
Such ambush hid among sweet Flours and Shades Par Lost 9.408
Among thick-wov'n Arborets and Flours Par Lost 9.437

Flowers(*cont*)
Of choicest Flours a Garland to adorne Par Lost 9.840
He led her nothing loath; Flours were the Couch, Par Lost 9.1039
Thou therefore on these Herbs, and Fruits, and Flours Par Lost 10.603
Perpetual smil'd on Earth with vernant Flours, Par Lost 10.679
That must be mortal to us both. O flours, Par Lost 11.273
Offer sweet smelling Gumms and Fruits and Flours: Par Lost 11.327
Of love and youth not lost, Songs, Garlands, Flours, Par Lost 11.594
With fruits and flowers from *Amalthea*'s horn, Par Reg 2.356
With odours visited and annual flowers. Samson 987
Visit his Tomb with flowers, only bewailing Samson 1742
Flowers of more mingled hew Mask 994
Of heapt *Elysian* flowres, and hear Allegro 147
Or Frost to Flowers, that their gay wardrop wear, Lycidas 47
1638 'flowers'
Trinity ms 'flowrs'
And purple all the ground with vernal flowres. Lycidas 141
1638 'flowers'
Trinity ms 'flowrs'
And som Flowers, and som Bays, Winchester 57
Flowery
The flowry Dale of *Sibma* clad with Vines, Par Lost 1.410
Thee *Sion* and the flowrie Brooks beneath Par Lost 3.30
Fortunate Fields, and Groves and flourie Vales, Par Lost 3.569
Or palmie hilloc, or the flourie lap Par Lost 4.254
Yon flourie Arbors, yonder Allies green, Par Lost 4.626
And on thir naked limbs the flourie roof Par Lost 4.772
Soft on the flourie herb I found me laid Par Lost 8.254
This Flourie Plat, the sweet recess of *Eve* Par Lost 9.456
Or serve they as a flourie verge to binde Par Lost 11.881
There flowrie hill *Hymettus* with the sound Par Reg 4.247
Then in a flowry valley set him down Par Reg 4.586
Hid them in som flowry Cave, Mask 239
Bridgewater ms 'flowrie'
1637 'flowrie'
Trinity ms 'flowrie'
That at her flowry work doth sing, Penseroso 143
And peace shall lull him in her flowry lap; Vacation 84
The Flowry *May*, who from her green lap throws May Morn 3
Then past hee to a flowry Mountaine greene, Prose 4, 1
Flowery-kirtled
Amidst the flowry-kirtl'd *Naiades* Mask 254
Trinity ms 'flowrie-kirtl'd' ←'flowrie-kirtled'
Bridgewater ms 'flowrie-kyrtled'
1637 'flowrie-kirtl'd'
Flowing
Under a Coronet his flowing haire Par Lost 3.640
Naked met his under the flowing Gold Par Lost 4.496
Ministerd naked, and thir flowing cups Par Lost 5.444
Not so repulst, with Tears that ceas'd not flowing, Par Lost 10.910
As after thirst, which made thir flowing shrink Par Lost 11.846
In highth of all thir flowing wealth dissolv'd: Par Reg 2.436
That stay'd her flight with his cross-flowing course, Mask 832
Bridgewater ms 'Crosse floweinge'
1637 'crosse-flowing'
Trinity ms 'crosse flowing'
Flowing with majestick train, Penseroso 34
Linkt to the mutual flowing of the Seas, Another 31
line not in 1658 text
Flown
Of *Belial*, flown with insolence and wine. Par Lost 1.502
By Fowl, Fish, Beast, was flown, was swum, was walkt Par Lost 7.503
Flown to the upper World; the rest were all Par Lost 10.422
Flows
With Angels Food, and rubied Nectar flows Par Lost 5.633
At *Darien*, thence to the Land where flowes Par Lost 9.81
See where it flows, disgorging at seaven mouthes Par Lost 12.158
Thy blessing on thy people flows. Psalm 3, 24
Fluctuates
Fluctuats disturbd, yet comely and in act Par Lost 9.668
Fluid
Receive, no more then can the fluid Aire: Par Lost 6.349
Throughout the fluid Mass, but downward purg'd Par Lost 7.237
The fluid skirts of that same watrie Cloud, Par Lost 11.882
Flung
Of Heav'n, and from Eternal Splendors flung Par Lost 1.610
Main Promontories flung, which in the Air Par Lost 6.654
Flung Rose, flung Odours from the spicie Shrub, Par Lost 8.517
Flushing
But in her Cheek distemper flushing glowd. Par Lost 9.887
Flute
Such as the jocond Flute, or gamesom Pipe Mask 173
Trinity ms 'flute'
Bridgewater ms 'flute'
Temper'd to th' Oaten Flute, Lycidas 33
Trinity ms 'flute'
1638 'flute'
Flutes
Of Flutes and soft Recorders; such as rais'd Par Lost 1.551
ms 'flutes'
Fluttered
And flutterd into Raggs, then Reliques, Beads, Par Lost 3.491
Fluttering
Fluttring his pennons vain plumb down he drops Par Lost 2.933
Fly
Flie to and fro, or on the smoothed Plank, Par Lost 1.772
Unfast'ns: on a sudden op'n flie Par Lost 2.879
Fly o're the backside of the World farr off Par Lost 3.494

Fly(*cont*)
One step no more then from himself can fly Par Lost 4.22
Me miserable! which way shall I flie Par Lost 4.73
Which way I flie is Hell; my self am Hell; Par Lost 4.75
Chaumping his iron curb: to strive or flie Par Lost 4.859
So wise he judges it to fly from pain Par Lost 4.910
Wise to flie pain, professing next the Spie, Par Lost 4.948
Flie thither whence thou fledst: if from this houre Par Lost 4.963
And fly, ere evil intercept thy flight. Par Lost 5.871
Yet not for thy advise or threats I fly Par Lost 5.889
I flie not, but have sought thee farr and nigh. Par Lost 6.295
And let Fowle flie above the Earth, with wings Par Lost 7.389
Henceforth I flie not Death, nor would prolong Par Lost 11.547
Thir Bootie; scarce with Life the Shepherds flye, Par Lost 11.650
To flye or follow what concern'd him most, Par Reg 1.440
A Manger his, yet soon enforc't to flye Par Reg 2.75
Willingly I could flye, and hope thy raign, Par Reg 3.216
Thee and thy Legions, yelling they shall flye, Par Reg 4.629
Mess. O whither shall I run, or which way flie Samson 1541
Let us fly this cursed place, Mask 939
Spir. To the Ocean now I fly, Mask 976
Bridgewater ms 'flye'
1637 'flie'
I can fly, or I can run Mask 1013
Bridgewater ms 'flye'
What time the Gray-fly winds her sultry horn, Lycidas 28
1638 'gray-fly'
Trinity ms 'gray fly'
Fly after the Night-steeds, leaving their Moon-lov'd maze. Nativity 236
And after short abode flie back with speed, Fair Inf 60
Fly swiftly to this fair Assembly's ears; Vacation 28
Fly envious *Time*, till thou run out thy race, On Time 1
My hasting dayes flie on with full career, Sonnet 7, 3
Trinity ms 'fly'
Early may fly the *Babylonian* wo. Sonnet 18, 14
Lord my God to thee I flie Psalm 7, 1
And home they fly from round the Coasts Psalm 84, 15
They *fly me now* whom I have lov'd, Psalm 88, 71

Fly
Grow up and perish, as the summer flie, Samson 676

Flying
Four ways thir flying March, along the Banks Par Lost 2.574
Farr off the flying Fiend: at last appeer Par Lost 2.643
Half flying; behoves him now both Oare and Saile. Par Lost 2.942
Which thou incurr'st by flying, meet thy flight Par Lost 4.913
Homeward with flying march where we possess Par Lost 5.688
And flying vaulted either Host with fire. Par Lost 6.214
Came flying, and in mid Aire aloud thus cri'd. Par Lost 6.536
Least from this flying Steed unrein'd, (as once Par Lost 7.17
Flying, and over Lands with mutual wing Par Lost 7.429
Where Armies lie encampt, come flying, lur'd Par Lost 10.276
How quick they wheel'd, and flying behind them shot Par Reg 3.323
Not flying, but fore-casting in what place Samson 254
She guiltless damsell flying the mad pursuit Mask 829
Bridgewater ms 'flyinge'

Foam
Him haply slumbring on the *Norway* foam Par Lost 1.203
ms 'foame'
Conception; Sulphurous and Nitrous Foame Par Lost 6.512

Foaming
And fierie foaming Steeds; what stood, recoyld Par Lost 6.391
Over the foaming deep high Archt, a Bridge Par Lost 10.301
Part wield thir Arms, part courb the foaming Steed, Par Lost 11.643

Foe
Irreconcileable, to our grand Foe, Par Lost 1.122
Or satiate fury yield it from our Foe. Par Lost 1.179
ms 'foe'
By force, hath overcome but half his foe. Par Lost 1.649
With upright wing against a higher foe. Par Lost 2.72
When the fierce Foe hung on our brok'n Rear Par Lost 2.78
Let this be good, whether our angry Foe Par Lost 2.152
If we were wise, against so great a foe Par Lost 2.202
Our Supream Foe in time may much remit Par Lost 2.210
May prove thir foe, and with repenting hand Par Lost 2.369
Against a wakeful Foe, while I abroad Par Lost 2.463
To meet so great a foe: and now great deeds Par Lost 2.722
(For what could else) to our Almighty Foe Par Lost 2.769
Grim *Death* my Son and foe, who sets them on, Par Lost 2.804
As from her outmost works a brok'd foe Par Lost 2.1039
On even ground against his mortal foe, Par Lost 3.179
The coming of thir secret foe, and scap'd Par Lost 4.7
Ill fenc't for Heav'n to keep out such a foe Par Lost 4.372
As now is enterd; yet no purpos'd foe Par Lost 4.373
But our destroyer, foe to God and Man? Par Lost 4.749
Of Deitie or Empire, such a foe Par Lost 5.724
His daring foe, at this prevention more Par Lost 6.129
Whom the grand foe with scornful eye askance Par Lost 6.149
Intestine War in Heav'n, the arch foe subdu'd Par Lost 6.259
Uriel and *Raphael* his vaunting foe, Par Lost 6.363
Each quarter, to descrie the distant foe, Par Lost 6.530
Arme, Warriours, Arme for fight, the foe at hand, Par Lost 6.537
Not distant far with heavie pace the Foe Par Lost 6.551
At least our envious Foe hath fail'd, who thought Par Lost 7.139
1669 'foe'
Of stern *Achilles* on his Foe pursu'd Par Lost 9.15
What hath bin warn'd us, what malicious Foe Par Lost 9.253
To God or thee, because we have a foe Par Lost 9.280
Th' attempt it self, intended by our Foe. Par Lost 9.295

Foe(*cont*)
In narrow circuit strait'nd by a Foe, Par Lost 9.323
But harm precedes not sin: onely our Foe Par Lost 9.327
Some specious object by the Foe subornd, Par Lost 9.361
A Foe so proud will first the weaker seek, Par Lost 9.383
Foe not informidable, exempt from wound, Par Lost 9.486
Matter of scorne, not to be given the Foe, Par Lost 9.951
Whatever wiles of Foe or seeming Friend. Par Lost 10.11
As when the *Tartar* from his *Russian* Foe Par Lost 10.431
Against a Foe by doom express assign'd us, Par Lost 10.926
Be meant, whom I conjecture, our grand Foe Par Lost 10.1033
Resolv'd, as thou proposest; so our Foe Par Lost 10.1038
His promise, that thy Seed shall bruise our Foe; Par Lost 11.155
Against the Spiritual Foe, and broughtst him thence Par Reg 1.10
Men generally think me much a foe Par Reg 1.387
And at another to let in the foe Samson 561
Then, as since then, thy countries foe profest: Samson 884
I chose a Wife, which argu'd me no foe; Samson 1193
But come what will, my deadliest foe will prove Samson 1262
Thir foe to misery beneath thir fears, Samson 1469
From slaughter of one foe could not ascend. Samson 1518
To slake his wrath whom sin hath made our foe Fair Inf 66
To find a Foe it shall not be his hap, Vacation 83
And not fre'd my foe for naught; Psalm 7, 12
To every neighbour foe, Psalm 80, 26

Foes
Of despicable foes. With these in troop Par Lost 1.437
Man had not hellish foes anow besides, Par Lost 2.504
While by thee rais'd I ruin all my Foes, Par Lost 3.258
To execute fierce vengeance on his foes, Par Lost 3.399
Who justly hath drivn out his Rebell Foes Par Lost 3.677
Made answer. Mightie Father, thou thy foes Par Lost 5.735
Encompass'd round with foes, thus answerd bold. Par Lost 5.876
Back on thy foes more glorious to return Par Lost 6.39
Gave them above thir foes, not to have sinnd, Par Lost 6.402
May serve to better us, and worse our foes, Par Lost 6.440
From far with thundring noise among our foes Par Lost 6.487
And to thir foes a laughter; for in view Par Lost 6.603
They shew us when our foes walk not upright. Par Lost 6.627
As likeliest was, when two such Foes met arm'd; Par Lost 6.688
This saw his hapless Foes but stood obdur'd, Par Lost 6.785
Hee on his impious Foes right onward drove, Par Lost 6.831
Sole Victor from th' expulsion of his Foes Par Lost 6.880
With Foes for daring single to be just, Par Lost 11.703
Over his foes and thine; there shall surprise Par Lost 12.453
To conquer Sin and Death the two grand foes, Par Reg 1.159
From us his foes pronounc't glory he exacts. Par Reg 3.120
Among inhuman foes. Samson 109
The dread of *Israel*'s foes, who with a strength Samson 342
Thy Foes derision, Captive, Poor, and Blind Samson 366
Find some occasion to infest our Foes. Samson 423
I state not that; this I am sure; our Foes Samson 424
To acquit themselves and prosecute their foes Samson 897
He now be dealing dole among his foes, Samson 1529
Among his foes? *Mess*. Inevitable cause Samson 1586
Thee with thy slaughter'd foes in number more Samson 1667
Wherwith she freez'd her foes to congeal'd stone? Mask 449
No less renownd then warr, new foes arise Sonnet 16, 11
1694 'Foes'
Lord how many are my foes Psalm 3, 1
On the cheek-bone all my foes, Psalm 3, 21
Of my foes that urge like fire; Psalm 7, 21
Hast founded strength because of all thy foes Psalm 8, 6
And on our foes thy dread Psalm 80, 8
Then would I soon bring down their foes Psalm 81, 57
For lo thy *furious* foes *now* swell Psalm 83, 5
And let my foes *then* see Psalm 86, 62

Fog
Forbidding every bleak unkindly Fog Mask 269
Bridgewater ms 'fogg'
Trinity ms 'fogge'
In fog, or fire, by lake, or moorish fen, Mask 433
Bridgewater ms 'fogg'

Foil
Our foile in Heav'n; here thou shalt Monarch reign, Par Lost 10.375
Manhood to God-head, with more strength to foil Par Lost 12.389
So after many a foil the Tempter proud, Par Reg 4.569
Nor in the glistering foil Lycidas 79
Trinity ms 'foile'
As a faint host that hath receiv'd the foil. Psalm 114, 10

Foiled
Which but th' Omnipotent none could have foyld, Par Lost 1.273
ms 'foyl'd'
Warr hath determin'd us, and foild with loss Par Lost 2.330
Thus foil'd thir mightiest, ours joy filld, and shout, Par Lost 6.200
What inward thence I feel, not therefore foild, Par Lost 8.608
Through all temptation, and the Tempter foil'd Par Reg 1.5
With *Joves Alcides*, and oft foil'd still rose, Par Reg 4.565
He foild bold *Seon* and his host, Psalm 136, 65

Foils
Still will be tempting him who foyls him still, Par Reg 4.13

Fold
But ended foul in many a scaly fould Par Lost 2.651
So speaking and so threatning, grew tenfold Par Lost 2.705
Leaps o're the fence with ease into the Fould: Par Lost 4.187
So clomb this first grand Thief into Gods Fould: Par Lost 4.192
Fould above fould a surging Maze, his Head Par Lost 9.499
Ten thousandfould the sin of him who slew Par Lost 11.678

Fold(*cont*)
1667 'thousand fould'
Within thick Clouds and dark ten-fold involv'd, Par Reg 1.41
Not willingly, but tangl'd in the fold, Samson 1665
Confin'd, and pester'd in this pin-fold here, Mask 7
Trinity ms 'pinfold'
Bridgewater ms 'pinfold'
Comus. The Star that bids the Shepherd fold, Mask 93
Slip't from the fold, or young Kid lost his dam, Mask 498
Bridgewater ms 'fould'
Trinity ms 'fold' ←'penne'
Of Knot-grass dew-besprent, and were in fold, Mask 542
Creep and intrude, and climb into the fold? Lycidas 115
Who were thy Sheep and in their antient Fold Sonnet 18, 6
A hunder'd-fold, who having learnt thy way Sonnet 18, 13
Folded
A Weavers beam, and seven-times-folded shield, Samson 1122
The folded flocks pen'd in their watled cotes, Mask 344
Swindges the scaly Horrour of his foulded tail. Nativity 172
Folds
Op'ning thir brazen foulds discover wide Par Lost 1.724
ms 'folds'
And thrice threefold the Gates; three folds were Brass, Par Lost 2.645
Thir Snakie foulds, and added wings. First crept Par Lost 7.484
The Serpent sleeping, in whose mazie foulds Par Lost 9.161
Circular base of rising foulds, that tour'd Par Lost 9.498
New reapt, the other part sheep-walks and foulds; Par Lost 11.431
To Shepherds watching at their folds by night, Par Reg 1.244
Follow
What yet they know must follow, to endure Par Lost 2.206
Nor uglier follow the Night-Hag, when call'd Par Lost 2.662
But thee, whom follow? thou wilt bring me soon Par Lost 2.866
With thee it came and goes: but follow me, Par Lost 4.469
But follow strait, invisibly thus led? Par Lost 4.476
Approve the best, and follow what I approve. Par Lost 8.611
Follow, as to him linkt in weal or woe, Par Lost 9.133
Thy Husband, him to follow thou art bound; Par Lost 11.291
Ascend, I follow thee, safe Guide, the path Par Lost 11.371
Such follow him, as shall be registerd Par Lost 12.335
To flye or follow what concern'd him most, Par Reg 1.440
Vertue, who follow not her lore: permit me Par Reg 1.483
Headlong would follow; and to thir Gods perhaps Par Reg 3.430
Eld. Bro. Thyrsis lead on apace, Ile follow thee, Mask 657
Bridgewater ms 'followe'
Mortals that would follow me, Mask 1018
Follow me as I sing, Arcades 86
Follow me, Arcades 90
Followed
Of unblest feet. Him followed his next Mate, Par Lost 1.238
ms 'followd'
Him follow'd *Rimmon*, whose delightful Seat Par Lost 1.467
Foule dissipation follow'd and forc't rout; Par Lost 6.598
Follow'd in bright procession to behold Par Lost 7.222
Followd with acclamation and the sound Par Lost 7.558
I follow'd her, she what was Honour knew, Par Lost 8.508
Follow'd with benediction. Since to part, Par Lost 8.645
Him follow'd issuing forth to th' open Field, Par Lost 10.533
Still follow'd him; to them shall leave in charge Par Lost 12.439
And follow'd thee still on to this wast wild; Par Reg 4.523
Follow'd thee up to joy and bliss for ever. Sonnet 14, 8
Strait follow'd thee the path that Saints have trod Sonnet 14, Tr. ms 41.06
Their own conceits they follow'd still Psalm 81, 51
Followers
The fellows of his crime, the followers rather Par Lost 1.606
Wors with his followers then with him they dealt? Par Lost 12.484
What Followers, what Retinue canst thou gain, Par Reg 2.419
Following
Following his track, such was the will of Heav'n, Par Lost 2.1025
His bountie, following our delightful task Par Lost 4.437
Thou following cryd'st aloud, Return faire *Eve;* Par Lost 4.481
Following, above th' *Olympian* Hill I soare, Par Lost 7.3
Best guide; not following thee, I had remaind Par Lost 9.808
For death, the following day, in bloodie fight. Par Lost 10.278
Over the vext Abyss, following the track Par Lost 10.314
Detain from following thy illustrious track. Par Lost 10.367
Close following pace for pace, not mounted yet Par Lost 10.589
Still following thee, still compassing thee round Par Lost 11.352
Thought following thought, and step by step led on, Par Reg 1.192
Following, as seem'd, the quest of some stray Ewe, Par Reg 1.315
Follows
In Heav'n, which follows dignity, might draw Par Lost 2.25
Folly
Retire, or taste thy folly, and learn by proof, Par Lost 2.686
With his own folly? that be from thee farr, Par Lost 3.153
Since *Satan* fell, whom follie overthrew, Par Lost 4.905
Neither our own but giv'n; what follie then Par Lost 4.1007
Thy folly; or with solitarie hand Par Lost 6.139
Wisdom to Folly, as Nourishment to Winde. Par Lost 7.130
Looses discount'nanc't, and like folly shewes; Par Lost 8.553
Kept in that State, had not the folly of Man Par Lost 10.619
Folly to mee, so doth the Prince of Hell Par Lost 10.621
Beyond which was my folly to aspire. Par Lost 12.560
As vile hath been my folly, who have profan'd Samson 377
Such pardon therefore as I give my folly, Samson 825
And aggravate my folly who committed Samson 1000
To folly and shameful deeds which ruin ends. Samson 1043
O're sensual Folly, and Intemperance. Mask 975
Bridgewater ms 'folly'

Folly(*cont*)
Trinity ms 'folly'
The brood of folly without father bred, Penseroso 2
Sweet Bird that shunn'st the noise of folly, Penseroso 61
Return to folly, *but surcease* Psalm 85, 35
Foment
Of various influence foment and warme, Par Lost 4.669
Reflected, may with matter sere foment, Par Lost 10.1071
Fomented
Fomented by his virtual power and warmd: Par Lost 11.338
Fond
Built thir fond hopes of Glorie or lasting fame, Par Lost 3.449
Aspirer, but thir thoughts prov'd fond and vain Par Lost 6.90
Or emptiness, or fond impertinence, Par Lost 8.195
Fond, were it not in hope of thy reply: Par Lost 8.209
So might the wrauth. Fond wish! couldst thou support Par Lost 10.834
Thus over-fond, on that which is not thine; Par Lost 11.289
1667 'over fond'
Of fond desire? or should she confident, Par Reg 2.211
(O that I never had! fond wish too late.) Samson 228
Though fond and reasonless to some perhaps; Samson 812
So fond are mortal men Samson 1682
(For most do taste through fond intemperate thirst) Mask 67
Trinity ms 'fond' ←'weake'
And fancies fond with gaudy shapes possess, Penseroso 6
Fondly
A God, leap'd fondly into *Aetna* flames, Par Lost 3.470
My damage fondly deem'd, I can repaire Par Lost 7.152
But fondly overcome with Femal charm. Par Lost 9.999
Deceav'd; they fondly thinking to allay Par Lost 10.564
And Immortalitie: that fondly lost, Par Lost 11.59
Ay me, I fondly dream! Lycidas 56
I fondly ask; But patience to prevent Sonnet 19, 8
Fontarabbia
By *Fontarabbia*. Thus far these beyond Par Lost 1.587
ms 'fontarabbia'
Food
To us for food and for delight hath caus'd Par Lost 5.400
The Earth to yield; unsavourie food perhaps Par Lost 5.401
No ingrateful food: and food alike those pure Par Lost 5.407
Food not of Angels, yet accepted so, Par Lost 5.465
With Angels Food, and rubied Nectar flows Par Lost 5.633
But Knowledge is as food, and needs no less Par Lost 7.126
Moist nutriment, or under Rocks thir food Par Lost 7.408
And freely all thir pleasant fruit for food Par Lost 7.540
Refreshment, whether food, or talk between, Par Lost 9.237
Food of the mind, or this sweet intercourse Par Lost 9.238
To brute deni'd, and are of Love the food, Par Lost 9.240
As was my food, nor aught but food discern'd Par Lost 9.573
As they, participating God-like food? Par Lost 9.717
This intellectual food, for beasts reserv'd? Par Lost 9.768
Food for so foule a Monster, in thy power Par Lost 10.986
And mortal food, as may dispose him best Par Lost 11.54
Siege and defiance: Wretched man! what food Par Lost 12.74
Nor tasted humane food, nor hunger felt Par Reg 1.308
With Food, whereof we wretched seldom taste. Par Reg 1.345
And forty days *Eliah* without food Par Reg 1.353
For lying is thy sustenance, thy food. Par Reg 1.429
And now I know he hungers where no food Par Reg 2.231
Wandring this woody maze, and humane food Par Reg 2.246
Food to *Elijah* bringing Even and Morn, Par Reg 2.268
Tell me if Food were now before thee set, Par Reg 2.320
A table of Celestial Food, Divine, Par Reg 4.588
Till vermin or the draff of servil food Samson 574
Honest and lawful to deserve my food Samson 1366
Wild Beasts there brouze, and make their food Psalm 80, 55
Her fruits *to be our food*. Psalm 85, 52
Fool
Or potent tongue; fool, not to think how vain Par Lost 6.135
Within doors, or without, still as a fool, Samson 77
Fool, have divulg'd the secret gift of God Samson 201
Am I not sung and proverbd for a Fool Samson 203
But the heart of the Fool, Samson 298
The mark of fool set on his front? Samson 496
Dal. I was a fool, too rash, and quite mistaken Samson 907
Although thir drudge, to be thir fool or jester, Samson 1338
Root-bound, that fled *Apollo*, *La*. Fool do not boast, Mask 662
1637 'Foole'
Trinity ms 'foole'
Bridgewater ms 'foole'
Fooled
Fool'd and beguil'd, by him thou, I by thee, Par Lost 10.880
Foolish
Who like a foolish Pilot have shipwrack't, Samson 198
Foolishness
Co. O foolishnes of men! that lend their ears Mask 706
Trinity ms 'foolishnesse'
1637 'foolishnesse'
Fools
The Paradise of Fools, to few unknown Par Lost 3.496
Extol not Riches then, the toyl of Fools, Par Reg 2.453
Not harsh, and crabbed as dull fools suppose, Mask 477
Bridgewater ms 'fooles'
Trinity ms 'fooles'
Fools or mad men stand not within thy sight. Psalm 5, 12
Foot
Treading the crude consistence, half on foot, Par Lost 2.941
To wait them with his Keys, and now at foot Par Lost 3.485

Foot(*cont*)
Mosaic; underfoot the Violet, Par Lost 4.700
Had need from head to foot well understand; Par Lost 6.625
One foot he center'd, and the other turn'd Par Lost 7.228
Where *Tigris* at the foot of Paradise Par Lost 9.71
And at the brink of *Chaos*, neer the foot Par Lost 10.347
His bright appearances, or foot step-trace? Par Lost 11.329
1667 'footstep trace'
Both Horse and Foot, nor idely mustring stood; Par Lost 11.645
With soft foot towards the deep, who now had stopt Par Lost 11.848
Green Tree or ground whereon his foot may light; Par Lost 11.858
Nor wanted clouds of foot, nor on each horn, Par Reg 3.327
Thou chance to dash thy foot against a stone. Par Reg 4.559
He never more henceforth will dare set foot Par Reg 4.610
When insupportably his foot advanc't, Samson 136
Both horse and foot before him and behind Samson 1618

Footed
Thither by harpy-footed Furies hail'd, Par Lost 2.596
Of those fourfooted kindes, himself now one, Par Lost 4.397

Footing
Of som chast footing neer about this ground. Mask 146
Bridgewater ms 'footinge'
Next *Camus*, reverend Sire, went footing slow, Lycidas 103

Footstep
His bright appearances, or foot step-trace? Par Lost 11.329
1667 'footstep trace'

Footsteps
Therefore I watch'd thy footsteps from that hour, Par Reg 4.522
His footsteps cannot err. Psalm 85, 56

Footstep-trace
His bright appearances, or foot step-trace? Par Lost 11.329
1667 'footstep trace'

For
Listings of this word are omitted; see the Introduction.

Forage
One way a Band select from forage drives Par Lost 11.646

Forbear
I overjoyd could not forbear aloud. Par Lost 8.490
If th' unjust will not forbear, Psalm 7, 45

Forbearance
Forbearance no acquittance ere day end. Par Lost 10.53

Forbid
Forbid who will, none shall from me withhold Par Lost 5.62
To do what God expresly hath forbid, Par Lost 9.356
Why then was this forbid? Why but to awe, Par Lost 9.703
Or East or West, which had forbid the Snow Par Lost 10.685
I bid not or forbid; do as thou find'st Par Reg 1.495
To *Dagon* thir Sea-Idol, and forbid Samson 13

Forbiddance
The strict forbiddance, how to violate Par Lost 9.903

Forbidden
Of that Forbidden Tree, whose mortal tast Par Lost 1.2
ms 'Forbidd'n'
I keep, by him forbidden to unlock Par Lost 2.852
Forbidden them to taste: Knowledge forbidd'n? Par Lost 4.515
Forbidd'n here, it seems, as onely fit Par Lost 5.69
The sacred Fruit forbidd'n? som cursed fraud Par Lost 9.904
In things to us forbidden, it might be wish'd, Par Lost 9.1025
For this one Tree had bin forbidden ten. Par Lost 9.1026
For one forbidden Tree a multitude Par Lost 10.554
Forbidd'n knowledge by forbidd'n means. Par Lost 12.279
These are not Fruits forbidden, no interdict Par Reg 2.369
When God with these forbid'n made choice to rear Samson 555
Sam. I know no Spells, use no forbidden Arts; Samson 1139
Scandalous or forbidden in our Law. Samson 1409

Forbidder
Our great Forbidder, safe with all his Spies Par Lost 9.815

Forbidding
Forbidding; and at once with him they rose; Par Lost 2.475
Forbids us then to taste, but his forbidding Par Lost 9.753
Forbidding every bleak unkindly Fog Mask 269
Bridgewater ms 'forbiddinge'

Forbids
Disdain forbids me, and my dread of shame Par Lost 4.82
Or envie, or what reserve forbids to taste? Par Lost 5.61
Thy praise hee also who forbids thy use, Par Lost 9.750
Forbids us then to taste, but his forbidding Par Lost 9.753
In plain then, what forbids he but to know, Par Lost 9.758
Forbids us good, forbids us to be wise? Par Lost 9.759
The Law I gave to Nature him forbids: Par Lost 11.49
Our Law forbids at thir Religious Rites Samson 1320

Forbore
Forbore, then these to her *Satan* return'd: Par Lost 2.736
So said he, and forbore not glance or toy Par Lost 9.1034

Forborne
Whose taste, too long forborn, at first assay Par Lost 9.747
How long be thus forborn Psalm 4, 9

Force
The force of those dire Arms? yet not for those, Par Lost 1.94
Innumerable force of Spirits arm'd Par Lost 1.101
To wage by force or guile eternal Warr Par Lost 1.121
Of force believe Almighty, since no less Par Lost 1.144
Then such could hav orepow'rd such force as ours) Par Lost 1.145
And such appear'd in hue, as when the force Par Lost 1.230
Whom reason hath equald, force hath made supream Par Lost 1.248
Breathing united force with fixed thought Par Lost 1.560
Met such imbodied force, as nam'd with these Par Lost 1.574
How such united force of Gods, how such Par Lost 1.629

Force(*cont*)
What force effected not: that he no less Par Lost 1.647
By force, hath overcome but half his foe. Par Lost 1.649
O're Heav'ns high Towrs to force resistless way, Par Lost 2.62
By force, and at our heels all Hell should rise Par Lost 2.135
My voice disswades; for what can force or guile Par Lost 2.188
By force impossible, by leave obtain'd Par Lost 2.250
By force or suttlety: Though Heav'n be shut, Par Lost 2.358
Free Vertue should enthrall to Force or Chance. Par Lost 2.551
These Adamantine Gates; against all force Par Lost 2.853
With fresh alacritie and force renew'd Par Lost 2.1012
If him by force he can destroy, or worse, Par Lost 3.91
Of force to its own likeness: up he starts Par Lost 4.813
With speed what force is left, and all imploy Par Lost 5.730
By force, who reason for thir Law refuse, Par Lost 6.41
When Reason hath to deal with force, yet so Par Lost 6.125
These Elements, and arm him with the force Par Lost 6.222
If not to reign: mean while thy utmost force, Par Lost 6.293
The sword of *Satan* with steep force to smite Par Lost 6.324
Of hard contents, and full of force urg'd home, Par Lost 6.622
Stood reimbattell'd fierce, by force or fraud Par Lost 6.794
Secure from outward force; within himself Par Lost 9.348
Soon as the force of that fallacious Fruit, Par Lost 9.1046
That lay in wait; beyond this had bin force, Par Lost 9.1173
And force upon free will hath here no place. Par Lost 9.1174
Or sympathie, or som connatural force Par Lost 10.246
Seis'd on by force, judg'd, and to death condemnd Par Lost 12.412
Spiritual Lawes by carnal power shall force Par Lost 12.521
But force the Spirit of Grace it self, and binde Par Lost 12.525
Not force, but well couch't fraud, well woven snares, Par Reg 1.97
All his vast force, and drive him back to Hell, Par Reg 1.153
Think'st thou such force in Bread? is it not written Par Reg 1.347
And oft by force, which to a generous mind Par Reg 2.479
The Son of God, with Godlike force indu'd Par Reg 4.602
Then by main force pull'd up, and on his shoulders bore Samson 146
No more on me have power, their force is null'd, Samson 935
Each others force in camp or listed field: Samson 1087
It was the force of Conquest; force with force Samson 1206
Had not disabl'd me, not all your force: Samson 1219
The brute and boist'rous force of violent men Samson 1273
Sam. Where outward force constrains, the sentence holds Samson 1369
And hamper thee, as thou shalt come of force, Samson 1397
All with incredible, stupendious force, Samson 1627
As with the force of winds and waters pent, Samson 1647
Surpriz'd by unjust force, but not enthrall'd, Mask 590
And force him to restore his purchase back, Mask 607
Through the force, and through the wile Mask 906
Bleak winters force that made thy blossome drie; Fair Inf 4
Yet there is something that doth force my fear, Vacation 67
What power, what force, what mighty spell, if not Vacation 89
Wed your divine sounds, and mixt power employ Musick 3
Trinity ms 'mixt power' ← 'mix't' ← 'happiest sounds' ← 'joynt force'
Rescu'd from death by force though pale and faint. Sonnet 23, 4
To force our Consciences that Christ set free, Forcers 6

Forced
Forc't Halleluiah's; while he Lordly sits Par Lost 2.243
Foule dissipation follow'd and forc't rout; Par Lost 6.598
Toild out my uncouth passage, forc't to ride Par Lost 10.475
Forc't I absolve: all my evasions vain, Par Lost 10.829
Be forc'd to satisfie his Rav'nous Maw. Par Lost 10.991
I should have forc'd thee soon wish other arms, Samson 1096
Lest I should see him forc't to things unseemly. Samson 1451
And with forc'd fingers rude, Lycidas 4
Trinity ms 'forc't'

Forces
Such forces met not, nor so wide a camp, Par Reg 3.337

Forcible
And in embraces forcible and foule Par Lost 2.793
With what more forcible we may offend Par Lost 6.465
So forcible within my heart I feel Par Lost 9.955

Forcing
Winds under ground or waters forcing way Par Lost 6.196

Ford
The Ford, and of it self the water flies Par Lost 2.612
Ur of *Chaldaea*, passing now the Ford Par Lost 12.130
Our new baptizing Prophet at the Ford Par Reg 1.328
Till at the Ford of *Jordan* whither all Par Reg 4.510

Forecast
And, if it happen as I did forecast, Vacation 13

Forecasting
Not flying, but fore-casting in what place Samson 254

Forefathers
The God of their fore-fathers; but so dy'd Par Reg 3.422
Did our forefathers yoke, Psalm 87, 12

Forego
Extracted; for this cause he shall forgoe Par Lost 8.497
How can I live without thee, how forgoe Par Lost 9.908
Obtuse, all taste of pleasure must forgoe, Par Lost 11.541
Thy Husband, slight me, sell me, and forgo me; Samson 940
If need be, I am ready to forgo Samson 1483

Foregoes
While each peculiar power forgoes his wonted seat. Nativity 196

Foregoing
May warn thee, as a sure fore-going sign. Par Reg 4.483

Forehead
Would so emblaze the forhead of the Deep, Mask 733
Bridgewater ms 'would soe emblaze with starrs that they

Forehead(*cont*)
belowe'
1637 'forehead'
he may scratch his forehead. heere be brambles Mask Tr. ms 17.57
Flames in the forehead of the morning sky: Lycidas 171
Trinity ms 'forhead'

Foreign
The goodly prospect of some forein land Par Lost 3.548
Of Forrein Worlds: he through the midst unmarkt, Par Lost 10.441
In foraign Lands thir memorie be lost Par Lost 12.46
And she shall be my Queen. Hail forren wonder Mask 265
1637 'forreine'
Trinity ms 'forreine'
Bridgewater ms 'forreigne'
Nor shalt thou to a forein God Psalm 81, 39

Foreknew
Thir own revolt, not I: if I foreknew, Par Lost 3.117

Foreknowing
Which neither his foreknowing can prevent, Par Lost 11.773

Foreknowledge
Of Providence, Foreknowledge, Will and Fate, Par Lost 2.559
Fixt Fate, free will, foreknowledg absolute, Par Lost 2.560
1667 'foreknowledge'
Or high foreknowledge; they themselves decreed Par Lost 3.116
Foreknowledge had no influence on their fault, Par Lost 3.118
At once, by my foreknowledge gaining Birth Par Lost 11.768

Foreland
Nigh Rivers mouth or Foreland, where the Wind Par Lost 9.514

Forelock
Round from his parted forelock manly hung Par Lost 4.302
But on Occasions forelock watchful wait. Par Reg 3.173

Foremost
Formost to stand against the Thunderers aim Par Lost 2.28

Forerun
Forerun the Royal Camp, to trench a Field, Par Lost 1.677

Forerunners
Forerunners of his purpose, or to warn Par Lost 11.195

Forerunning
Forerunning Night; when at the holy mount Par Lost 7.584

Foresaw
In the perverse event then I foresaw) Samson 737
Fore-saw what future dayes should bring to pass, Vacation 72

Foreseeing
Foreseeing or presaging, from the Depth Par Lost 1.627
Thus to his onely Son foreseeing spake. Par Lost 3.79

Foreseen
Or aught by me immutablie foreseen, Par Lost 3.121
Consulting on the sum of things, foreseen Par Lost 6.673
O Visions ill foreseen! better had I Par Lost 11.763

Foresight
In Arms not worse, in foresight much advanc't, Par Lost 1.119
Here sleep below while thou to foresight wak'st, Par Lost 11.368

Foresignify
They oft fore-signifie and threaten ill: Par Reg 4.464

Foreskins
A thousand fore-skins fell, the flower of *Palestin* Samson 144

Forest
A Forrest huge of Spears: and thronging Helms Par Lost 1.547
ms 'forrest'
Hath scath'd the Forrest Oaks, or Mountain Pines, Par Lost 1.613
ms 'forrest'
Whose midnight Revels, by a Forrest side Par Lost 1.782
ms 'forrest'
In Wood or Wilderness, Forrest or Den; Par Lost 4.342
Him through the spicie Forrest onward com Par Lost 5.298
In Forrest wilde, in Thicket, Brake, or Den; Par Lost 7.458
Now Land, now Sea, and Shores with Forrest crownd, Par Lost 9.117
Goodliest of all the Forrest, Hart and Hinde; Par Lost 11.189
Of Fairy Damsels met in Forest wide Par Reg 2.359
Forest and field, and flood, Temples and Towers Par Reg 3.268
All beasts that in the field or forrest meet, Psalm 8, 20

Forestall
What need a man forestall his date of grief, Mask 362
line not in Trinity ms
line not in Bridgewater ms

Forestalled
To be forestall'd; much more I fear least Death Par Lost 10.1024

Forestalling
Co. Perhaps fore-stalling night prevented them. Mask 285
Trinity ms 'fore stalling'
Bridgewater ms 'forestallinge'

Forests
May trace huge Forests, and unharbour'd Heaths, Mask 423
1673 'Forrests'
Trinity ms 'forrests'
Bridgewater ms 'forrests'
1637 'forrests'
Of Forests, and inchantments drear, Penseroso 119

Foretasted
Is not so hainous now, foretasted Fruit, Par Lost 9.929

Foretell
One greater, of whose day he shall foretell, Par Lost 12.242
What I foretell thee, soon thou shalt have cause Par Reg 4.375
Foretell my hopeles doom in som Grove ny: Sonnet 1, 10

Foretold
To search with wandring quest a place foretold Par Lost 2.830
I warn'd thee, I admonish'd thee, foretold Par Lost 9.1171
Foretold so lately what would come to pass, Par Lost 10.38

Foretold(*cont*)
Eevn hee who now foretold his fatal bruise, Par Lost 10.191
Long had foretold, a Fabrick wonderful Par Lost 10.482
Pains onely in Child-bearing were foretold, Par Lost 10.1051
Henceforth to be foretold what shall befall Par Lost 11.771
A Son, the Womans Seed to thee foretold, Par Lost 12.327
Foretold to *Abraham*, as in whom shall trust Par Lost 12.328
All Nations, and to Kings foretold, of Kings Par Lost 12.329
The Womans seed, obscurely then foretold, Par Lost 12.543
A messenger from God fore-told thy birth Par Reg 1.238
Conceiv'd in me a Virgin, he fore-told Par Reg 1.239
Then to thy self ascrib'st the truth fore-told. Par Reg 1.453
But trouble, as old *Simeon* plain fore-told, Par Reg 2.87
All this fair sight; thy Kingdom though foretold Par Reg 3.351
Who then thou art, whose coming is foretold Par Reg 4.204
What I foretold thee, many a hard assay Par Reg 4.478
Of the Messiah I have heard foretold Par Reg 4.502
O wherefore was my birth from Heaven foretold Samson 23
Divine Prediction; what if all foretold Samson 44
Of birth from Heav'n foretold and high exploits, Samson 525
The work for which thou wast foretold Samson 1662

Forever
Where Joy for ever dwells: Hail horrours, hail Par Lost 1.250
Awake, arise, or be for ever fall'n. Par Lost 1.330
For ever now to have thir lot in pain, Par Lost 1.608
ms defective here
Of racking whirlwinds, or for ever sunk Par Lost 2.182
These Gates for ever shut, which none can pass Par Lost 2.776
Life in my self for ever, by thee I live, Par Lost 3.244
For ever with corruption there to dwell; Par Lost 3.249
I give thee, reign for ever, and assume Par Lost 3.318
Thenceforth shall be for ever shut. Mean while Par Lost 3.333
For ever happie: him who disobeyes Par Lost 5.611
For ever, and in mee all whom thou lov'st: Par Lost 6.733
Of Godhead, fixt for ever firm and sure, Par Lost 7.586
To find her, or for ever to deplore Par Lost 8.479
For ever, and seal up his ravenous Jawes. Par Lost 10.637
And live for ever, dream at least to live Par Lost 11.95
For ever, to remove him I decree, Par Lost 11.96
For ever shall endure; the like shall sing Par Lost 12.324
In sin for ever lost from life; this act Par Lost 12.429
That Evil one, Satan for ever damn'd. Par Reg 4.194
Fair silver-shafted Queen for ever chaste, Mask 442
And wipe the tears for ever from his eyes. Lycidas 181
Attir'd with Stars, we shall for ever sit, On Time 21
Follow'd thee up to joy and bliss for ever. Sonnet 14, 8
Up to the Realm of peace & Joy for ever, Sonnet 14, Tr. ms 41.08
That Israels name for ever may Psalm 83, 15
Troubl'd and sham'd for ever, Psalm 83, 62
With Sin *for evermore*. Psalm 84, 40
For ever angry thus Psalm 85, 18
Thy name for ever more. Psalm 86, 44

Forewarn
But thou O Father, I forewarn thee, shun Par Lost 2.810
Down from the Empyrean to forewarne Par Lost 7.73
They die; but in thir room, as they forewarne, Par Lost 12.507

Forewarned
The affable Arch-Angel, had forewarn'd Par Lost 7.41
His entrance, and forewarnd the Cherubim Par Lost 9.61
With thy permission then, and thus forewarnd Par Lost 9.378

Forewarning
Rejected my forewarning, and disdain'd Par Lost 10.876

Forfeit
His lapsed powers, though forfeit and enthrall'd Par Lost 3.176
Forfeit to Death; from hence a passage broad, Par Lost 10.304
Thy penal forfeit from thy self; perhaps Samson 508
That he our deadly forfeit should release, Nativity 6

Forfeiture
The deadly forfeiture, and ransom set. Par Lost 3.221

Forge
The Organs of her Fancie, and with them forge Par Lost 4.802
In other part stood one who at the Forge Par Lost 11.564

Forgery
Made Arms ridiculous, useless the forgery Samson 131
With visor'd falshood, and base forgery, Mask 698
Trinity ms 'forgeries'
line not in Bridgewater ms
1637 'forgerie'

Forget
Nightly I visit: nor somtimes forget Par Lost 3.32
Forget, nor from thy Fathers praise disjoine. Par Lost 3.415
Yet let me not forget what I have gain'd Par Lost 4.512
With thee conversing I forget all time, Par Lost 4.639
Yet that we never shall forget to love Par Lost 5.550
Compulsion thus transported to forget Par Lost 9.474
From him, and all his anger to forget. Par Lost 11.878
And all their friends, and native home forget Mask 76
Bridgewater ms 'forgett'
Forget thy self to Marble, till Penseroso 42
Forget not: in thy book record their groanes Sonnet 18, 5

Forgetful
Of that forgetful Lake benumm not still, Par Lost 2.74
Forgetful what from him I still receivd, Par Lost 4.54

Forgetfulness
In sweet forgetfulness all pain and woe, Par Lost 2.608

Forgets
Forthwith his former state and being forgets, Par Lost 2.585
Forgets both joy and grief, pleasure and pain. Par Lost 2.586

Forgive
The penitent, but ever to forgive, Samson 761
Thine forgive mine; that men may censure thine Samson 787
At distance I forgive thee, go with that; Samson 954
Th' iniquity thou didst forgive Psalm 85, 5
Forgiven
Thy frailtie and infirmer Sex forgiv'n, Par Lost 10.956
Forgiveness
Let me obtain forgiveness of thee, *Samson*, Samson 909
Shall never, unrepented, find forgiveness. Samson 1376
Forgot
Hast thou forgot me then, and do I seem Par Lost 2.747
Justice and Temperance, Truth and Faith forgot; Par Lost 11.807
Thou must not in the mean while here forgot Samson 479
Who now hath quite forgot to rave, Nativity 67
Bereft of light thir seeing have forgot, Sonnet 22, 3
Forked
But hiss for hiss returnd with forked tongue Par Lost 10.518
To forked tongue, for now were all transform'd Par Lost 10.519
Forlorn
Seest thou yon dreary Plain, forlorn and wilde, Par Lost 1.180
In confus'd march forlorn, th' adventrous Bands Par Lost 2.615
To you whom I could pittie thus forlorne Par Lost 4.374
Erroneous there to wander and forlorne. Par Lost 7.20
To live again in these wilde Woods forlorn? Par Lost 9.910
My onely strength and stay: forlorn of thee, Par Lost 10.921
Threats the forlorn and wandring Passinger. Mask 39
1637 'forlorne'
Bridgewater ms 'forlorne'
Trinity ms 'forlorne'
In *Stygian* Cave forlorn Allegro 3
Hast set me *all forlorn*, Psalm 88, 26
Form
Stood like a Towr; his form had yet not lost Par Lost 1.591
ms 'forme'
With rapid wheels, or fronted Brigads form. Par Lost 2.532
Draind through a Limbec to his Native forme. Par Lost 3.605
How busied, in what form and posture coucht. Par Lost 4.876
Since now we find this our Empyreal form Par Lost 6.433
1667 'forme'
Thus earlie, thus alone; her Heav'nly forme Par Lost 9.457
Thenceforth the form of servant to assume, Par Lost 10.214
1667 'forme'
And the dire hiss renew'd, and the dire form Par Lost 10.543
Henceforth; least that too heav'nly form, pretended Par Lost 10.872
These only with our Law best form a King. Par Reg 4.364
In fleshly Tabernacle, and human form, Par Reg 4.599
Into som brutish form of Woolf, or Bear, Mask 70
Bridgewater ms 'forme'
Trinity ms 'forme'
1637 'forme'
And thou unblemish't form of Chastity, Mask 215
line not in Bridgewater ms
Trinity ms 'forme'
1637 'forme'
That glorious Form, that Light unsufferable, Nativity 8
And wov'n close, both matter, form and stile; Sonnet 11, 2
Trinity ms 'forme' ←'frome' ←'form'
Formed
A third as soon had form'd within the ground Par Lost 1.705
What thing thou art, thus double-form'd, and why Par Lost 2.741
I formd them free, and free they must remain, Par Lost 3.124
For contemplation hee and valour formd, Par Lost 4.297
The hand that formd them on thir shape hath pourd. Par Lost 4.365
And from whom I was formd flesh of thy flesh, Par Lost 4.441
Who formd us from the dust, and plac'd us here Par Lost 5.516
Thee what thou art, and formd the Pow'rs of Heav'n Par Lost 5.824
That we were formd then saist thou? and the work Par Lost 5.853
Equal in their Creation they were form'd, Par Lost 6.690
The Earth was form'd, but in the Womb as yet Par Lost 7.276
Though of Ethereal Mould: then form'd the Moon Par Lost 7.356
This said, he formd thee, *Adam*, thee O Man Par Lost 7.524
The Rib he formd and fashond with his hands; Par Lost 8.469
Neither her out-side formd so fair, nor aught Par Lost 8.596
A Creature form'd of Earth, and him endow, Par Lost 9.149
Guiltless of fire had formd, or Angels brought. Par Lost 9.392
Whatever can to sight or thought be formd, Par Lost 9.898
As once thou slepst, while Shee to life was formd. Par Lost 11.369
Into fit moulds prepar'd; from which he formd Par Lost 11.571
Former
The former vain to hope argues as vain Par Lost 2.234
Forthwith his former state and being forgets, Par Lost 2.585
By Act of Grace my former state; how soon Par Lost 4.94
Satan, so call him now, his former name Par Lost 5.658
I then was passing to my former state Par Lost 8.290
Her former trespass fear'd, the more to soothe Par Lost 9.1006
Thus will this latter, as the former World, Par Lost 12.105
I thought it lawful from my former act, Samson 231
Be it but for honours sake of former deeds. Samson 372
As was my former servitude, ignoble, Samson 416
Horribly loud unlike the former shout. Samson 1510
And former sufferings other where are found; Passion 25
Formidable
On either side a formidable shape; Par Lost 2.649
Forming
Under his forming hands a Creature grew, Par Lost 8.470
Formless
Won from the void and formless infinite. Par Lost 3.12

Formless(*cont*)
I saw when at his Word the formless Mass, Par Lost 3.708
Forms
His Legions, Angel Forms, who lay intrans't Par Lost 1.301
ms 'form's'
Thir great Commander; Godlike shapes and forms Par Lost 1.358
ms 'formes'
Thir wandring Gods disguis'd in brutish forms Par Lost 1.481
Thus incorporeal Spirits to smallest forms Par Lost 1.789
Flew upward, spirited with various forms, Par Lost 3.717
She forms Imaginations, Aerie shapes, Par Lost 5.105
Transcend his own so farr, whose radiant forms Par Lost 5.457
Indu'd with various forms various degrees Par Lost 5.473
By lik'ning spiritual to corporal forms, Par Lost 5.573
Innumerous living Creatures, perfet formes, Par Lost 7.455
Attends thee, and each word, each motion formes, Par Lost 8.223
Well deem in outward Rites and specious formes Par Lost 12.534
He saw them in thir forms of battell rang'd, Par Reg 3.322
Harpyies and *Hydra's*, or all the monstrous forms Mask 605
Bridgewater ms 'buggs'
Trinity ms 'buggs'
1637 'bugs'
Forsake
Of Mankind they corrupted to forsake Par Lost 1.368
Forsake me not thus, *Adam*, witness Heav'n Par Lost 10.914
As to forsake the living God, and fall Par Lost 12.118
Forsake their Temples dim, Nativity 198
Why wilt thou Lord my soul forsake, Psalm 88, 57
Forsaken
Forsak'n of all good; I see thy fall Par Lost 5.878
so fares as did forsaken Proserpine Mask Tr. ms 15.52
soe fares as did forsaken Proserpine Mask Br. ms 344
Bring the rathe Primrose that forsaken dies. Lycidas 142
Trinity ms 'forsaken' ←'unwedded'
Forsook
For those the Race of *Israel* oft forsook Par Lost 1.432
Forsook them, when themselves they villifi'd Par Lost 11.516
Sleep hath forsook and giv'n me o're Samson 629
Or straggling weather the pen't flock forsook? Mask 499
Bridgewater ms 'forsooke'
The immortal mind that hath forsook Penseroso 91
Forsook the Courts of everlasting Day, Nativity 13
Forsook the hated earth, O tell me sooth Fair Inf 51
Fort
Gave up my fort of silence to a Woman. Samson 236
How *Succoth* and the Fort of *Penuel* Samson 278
Forth
Out of our evil seek to bring forth good, Par Lost 1.163
Consult how we may henceforth most offend Par Lost 1.187
ms 'hence forth'
How all his malice serv'd but to bring forth Par Lost 1.217
Darkens the Streets, then wander forth the Sons Par Lost 1.501
Tears such as Angels weep, burst forth: at last Par Lost 1.620
Put forth at full, but still his strength conceal'd, Par Lost 1.641
Henceforth his might we know, and know our own Par Lost 1.643
ms 'Hence forth'
Pour forth thir populous youth about the Hive Par Lost 1.770
The *Stygian* Counsel thus dissolv'd; and forth Par Lost 2.506
Prick forth the Aerie Knights, and couch thir Spears Par Lost 2.536
Threw forth, till on the left side op'ning wide, Par Lost 2.755
Forth issu'd, brandishing his fatal Dart Par Lost 2.786
My Bowels, thir repast; then bursting forth Par Lost 2.800
Cast forth redounding smoak and ruddy flame. Par Lost 2.889
Breathe forth *Elixir* pure, and Rivers run Par Lost 3.607
That brought them forth, but hid thir causes deep. Par Lost 3.707
Powrd forth profuse on Hill and Dale and Plaine, Par Lost 4.243
Layes forth her purple Grape, and gently creeps Par Lost 4.259
And send forth all her Kings; there will be room, Par Lost 4.383
Forth issuing at th' accustomd hour stood armd Par Lost 4.779
Hung forth in Heav'n his golden Scales, yet seen Par Lost 4.997
Shot forth peculiar Graces; then with voice Par Lost 5.15
Close at mine ear one call'd me forth to walk Par Lost 5.36
Soon as they forth were come to open sight Par Lost 5.138
Her Virgin Fancies, pouring forth more sweet, Par Lost 5.296
And what thy stores contain, bring forth and poure Par Lost 5.314
His god-like Guest, walks forth, without more train Par Lost 5.351
As Heav'ns great Year brings forth, th' Empyreal Host Par Lost 5.583
Abstrusest thoughts, from forth his holy Mount Par Lost 5.712
Against thee are gon forth without recall; Par Lost 5.885
Though single. From amidst them forth he passd, Par Lost 5.903
Light issues forth, and at the other dore Par Lost 6.9
Seem twilight here; and now went forth the Morn Par Lost 6.12
Gabriel, lead forth to Battel these my Sons Par Lost 6.46
Invincible, lead forth my armed Saints Par Lost 6.47
Forth stepping opposite, half way he met Par Lost 6.128
Of such commotion, such as to set forth Par Lost 6.310
With Heav'ns ray, and temperd they shoot forth Par Lost 6.480
Dilated and infuriate shall send forth Par Lost 6.486
Put forth, and to a narrow vent appli'd Par Lost 6.583
Since *Michael* and his Powers went forth to tame Par Lost 6.686
That shake Heav'ns basis, bring forth all my Warr, Par Lost 6.712
Dawning through Heav'n: forth rush'd with whirlwind sound Par Lost 6.749
Glar'd lightning, and shot forth pernicious fire Par Lost 6.849
Yet half his strength he put not forth, but check'd Par Lost 6.853
I send along, ride forth, and bid the Deep Par Lost 7.166
And put not forth my goodness, which is free Par Lost 7.171
Celestial Equipage; and now came forth Par Lost 7.203
On golden Hinges moving, to let forth Par Lost 7.207

Forth(*cont*)
Put forth the verdant Grass, Herb yielding Seed, Par Lost 7.310
Brought forth the tender Grass, whose verdure clad Par Lost 7.315
Forth flourish't thick the clustring Vine, forth crept Par Lost 7.320
Bursting with kindly rupture forth disclos'd Par Lost 7.419
Intelligent of seasons, and set forth Par Lost 7.427
Let th' Earth bring forth Foul living in her kinde, Par Lost 7.451
At once came forth whatever creeps the ground, Par Lost 7.475
Rose, and went forth among her Fruits and Flours, Par Lost 8.44
With Goddess-like demeanour forth she went; Par Lost 8.59
To see that none thence issu'd forth a spie, Par Lost 8.233
With grateful Smell, forth came the human pair Par Lost 9.197
Meer Serpent in appearance, forth was come, Par Lost 9.413
Forth issuing on a Summers Morn to breathe Par Lost 9.447
Forth reaching to the Fruit, she pluck'd, she eat: Par Lost 9.781
And forth to meet her went, the way she took Par Lost 9.847
Blaz'd forth unclouded Deitie; he full Par Lost 10.65
Absents thee, or what chance detains? Come forth. Par Lost 10.108
In sorrow forth, and to thy Husbands will Par Lost 10.195
Thorns also and Thistles it shall bring thee forth Par Lost 10.203
Forth rush'd in haste the great consulting Peers, Par Lost 10.456
Successful beyond hope, to lead ye forth Par Lost 10.463
Him follow'd issuing forth to th' open Field, Par Lost 10.533
In Triumph issuing forth thir glorious Chief; Par Lost 10.537
While the Creator calling forth by name Par Lost 10.649
Forth rush the *Levant* and the *Ponent* Windes Par Lost 10.704
And bringing forth, soon recompenc't with joy, Par Lost 10.1052
And send him from the Garden forth to Till Par Lost 11.97
So send them forth, though sorrowing, yet in peace: Par Lost 11.117
Her rosie progress smiling; let us forth, Par Lost 11.175
And send thee from the Garden forth to till Par Lost 11.261
Blown stifling back on him that breaths it forth: Par Lost 11.313
Corruption to bring forth more violent deeds. Par Lost 11.428
A Dove sent forth once and agen to spie Par Lost 11.857
Greatly rejoyc'd, and thus his joy broke forth. Par Lost 11.869
God looking forth will trouble all his Host Par Lost 12.209
Then that which by creation first brought forth Par Lost 12.472
To bring forth fruits Joy and eternal Bliss. Par Lost 12.551
Of his great warfare, e're I send him forth Par Reg 1.158
Burst forth, and in Celestial measures mov'd, Par Reg 1.170
One day forth walk'd alone, the Spirit leading; Par Reg 1.189
By words at times cast forth inly rejoyc'd, Par Reg 1.228
Who dwell this wild, constrain'd by want, come forth Par Reg 1.331
And now wild Beasts came forth the woods to roam. Par Reg 1.502
Send thy Messiah forth, the time is come; Par Reg 2.43
But to shew forth his goodness, and impart Par Reg 3.124
They issue forth, Steel Bows, and Shafts their arms Par Reg 3.305
What conflux issuing forth, or entring in, Par Reg 4.62
Wisest of men; from whose mouth issu'd forth Par Reg 4.276
Came forth with Pilgrim steps in amice gray; Par Reg 4.427
Puts forth no visual beam. Samson 163
Would draw thee forth to perilous enterprises, Samson 804
Far other reasonings, brought forth other deeds. Samson 875
From forth this loathsom prison-house, to abide Samson 922
It hath brought forth to make thee memorable Samson 956
Mess. It would burst forth, but I recover breath Samson 1555
Samson should be brought forth to shew the people Samson 1601
Turn forth her silver lining on the night? Mask 222
line not in Bridgewater ms
Turn forth her silver lining on the night, Mask 224
line not in Bridgewater ms
Wherefore did Nature powre her bounties forth, Mask 710
Bridgewater ms 'furth'
And young and old com forth to play Allegro 97
Hence forth thou art the Genius of the shore, Lycidas 183
1638 'Henceforth'
Trinity ms 'henceforth'
Let us therfore warble forth Psalm 136, 89
Hath at length brought forth a Lie. Psalm 7, 54
Shine forth, *and from thy cloud give light*, Psalm 80, 7
Our Land shall forth in plenty throw Psalm 85, 51

Forthwith
Forthwith upright he rears from off the Pool Par Lost 1.221
ms 'forth with'
Forthwith from every Squadron and each Band Par Lost 1.356
Who forthwith from the glittering Staff unfurld Par Lost 1.535
A solemn Councel forthwith to be held Par Lost 1.755
ms 'forth with'
Forthwith his former state and being forgets, Par Lost 2.585
Forthwith the huge Porcullis high up drew, Par Lost 2.874
Thy dread Tribunal: forthwith from all Windes Par Lost 3.326
The living, and forthwith the cited dead Par Lost 3.327
Could not but taste. Forthwith up to the Clouds Par Lost 5.86
Forthwith from all the ends of Heav'n appeerd Par Lost 5.586
Forthwith from dance to sweet repast they turn Par Lost 5.630
Forthwith on all sides to his aide was run Par Lost 6.335
Forthwith from Councel to the work they flew, Par Lost 6.507
Forthwith (behold the excellence, the power Par Lost 6.637
Let ther be Light, said God, and forthwith Light Par Lost 7.243
Forthwith the Sounds and Seas, each Creek and Bay Par Lost 7.399
Knew not; to speak I tri'd, and forthwith spake, Par Lost 8.271
Insensible, and forthwith to dissolve: Par Lost 8.291
That whoso eats thereof, forthwith attains Par Lost 9.724
Felt less remorse: they forthwith to the place Par Lost 10.1098
Forthwith from out the Arke a Raven flies, Par Lost 11.855
Forthwith a hideous gabble rises loud Par Lost 12.56
Then forthwith to him takes a chosen band Par Reg 2.236
Forthwith how thou oughtst to receive him. Samson 329

Fortify
To fortifie thus farr, and overlay Par Lost 10.370

Fortitude
In Battels feign'd; the better fortitude Par Lost 9.31
Is fortitude to highest victorie, Par Lost 12.570
Extolling Patience as the truest fortitude; Samson 654
Of Saints, the trial of thir fortitude, Samson 1288
Guided by faith and matchless Fortitude Sonnet 16, 3

Fortunate
Fortunate Fields, and Groves and flourie Vales, Par Lost 3.569

Fortune
Riches are mine, Fortune is in my hand; Par Reg 2.429
Fortune and Fate, as one regardless quite Par Reg 4.317
To lowest pitch of abject fortune thou art fall'n. Samson 169
Or the sphear of fortune raises; Samson 172
Gives and the Mill had tam'd thee? O that fortune Samson 1093
That tyrannie or fortune can inflict, Samson 1291
And on the neck of crowned Fortune proud Sonnet 16, 5
line not in 1694 text

Fortunes
Like fortunes may her soul acquaint, Winchester 72

Forty
Full forty days he pass'd, whether on hill Par Reg 1.303
Moses was forty days, nor eat nor drank, Par Reg 1.352
And forty days *Eliah* without food Par Reg 1.353
After forty days fasting had remain'd, Par Reg 2.243
The strength whereof suffic'd him forty days; Par Reg 2.276
Of thee these forty days none hath regard, Par Reg 2.315
Forty and more deserted here indeed. Par Reg 2.316

Fought
That fought at *Theb*'s and *Ilium*, on each side Par Lost 1.578
That fought in Heav'n; now fiercer by despair: Par Lost 2.45
And fields were fought in Heav'n; wherein remaind Par Lost 2.768
Servant of God, well done, well hast thou fought Par Lost 6.29
Millions of fierce encountring Angels fought Par Lost 6.220
Memorial, where the might of *Gabriel* fought, Par Lost 6.355
That under ground, they fought in dismal shade; Par Lost 6.666
Were long to tell, how many Battels fought, Par Lost 12.261
Hast reard Gods Trophies and his work pursu'd. Sonnet 16, 6
1694 'And Fought God's Battels'

Foughten
Victor and Vanquisht: on the foughten field Par Lost 6.410

Foul
Who first seduc'd them to that foul revolt? Par Lost 1.33
ms 'fowle'
1667 'fowl'
That with sad overthrow and foul defeat Par Lost 1.135
To Idols foul. *Thammuz* came next behind, Par Lost 1.446
ms 'foule'
With dread of death to flight or foul retreat, Par Lost 1.555
But ended foul in many a scaly fould Par Lost 2.651
Now in thine eye so foul, once deemd so fair Par Lost 2.748
And in embraces forcible and foule Par Lost 2.793
By sin to foul exorbitant desires; Par Lost 3.177
Who to the fraudulent Impostor foule Par Lost 3.692
For heav'nly mindes from such distempers foule Par Lost 4.118
Alien from Heav'n, with passions foul obscur'd: Par Lost 4.571
Thy sin and place of doom obscure and foule. Par Lost 4.840
Victor; though brutish that contest and foule, Par Lost 6.124
Enter'd, and foul disorder; all the ground Par Lost 6.388
And all her entrails tore, disgorging foule Par Lost 6.588
Foule dissipation follow'd and forc't rout; Par Lost 6.598
Those Notes to Tragic; foul distrust, and breach Par Lost 9.6
O foul descent! that I who erst contended Par Lost 9.163
The tempted with dishonour foul, suppos'd Par Lost 9.297
Tempting affronts us with his foul esteem Par Lost 9.328
Of our integritie: his foul esteeme Par Lost 9.329
Foul on himself; then wherefore shund or feard Par Lost 9.331
Of foul concupiscence; whence evil store; Par Lost 9.1078
Food for so foule a Monster, in thy power Par Lost 10.986
No gross, no unharmoneous mixture foule, Par Lost 11.51
To Spirits foule, and all my Trees thir prey, Par Lost 11.124
Of terrour, foul and ugly to behold, Par Lost 11.464
Whose foul Idolatries, and other faults Par Lost 12.337
The Temple, oft the Law with foul affronts, Par Reg 3.161
Thus pass'd the night so foul till morning fair Par Reg 4.426
From thy Demoniac holds, possession foul, Par Reg 4.628
Subject him to so foul indignities, Samson 371
But foul effeminacy held me yok't Samson 410
Bare in thy guilt how foul must thou appear? Samson 902
Not once perceive their foul disfigurement, Mask 74
1637 'foule'
Trinity ms 'foule'
Bridgewater ms 'fowle'
But he that hides a dark soul, and foul thoughts Mask 383
Bridgewater ms 'foule'
Trinity ms 'foule'
1637 'foule'
By unchaste looks, loose gestures, and foul talk, Mask 464
Bridgewater ms 'foule'
1637 'foule'
Trinity ms 'foule'
Or drag him by the curls, to a foul death, Mask 608
1637 'and cleave his scalpe'
Bridgewater ms 'and cleave his scalpe'
Trinity ms 'or drag him by the curls & cleave his scalpe'
I knew the foul inchanter though disguis'd, Mask 645
Bridgewater ms 'foule'

Foul(*cont*)
1637 'foule'
Trinity ms 'fowle'
Hence with thy brew'd inchantments, foul deceiver, Mask 696
1637 'foule'
Bridgewater ms 'fowle'
Trinity ms 'brewd enchauntments' ←'foule brud' ←'hel brewd opiate' ←'hel bru'd liquor' ←'bru'd sorcerie' ←'teacherous (leacherous?) bruage' ←'teacherous kindnesse'
Rot inwardly, and foul contagion spread: Lycidas 127
Trinity ms 'foule'
Should look so neer upon her foul deformities. Nativity 44
Which 'mongst the wanton gods a foul reproach was held. Fair Inf 14
Or els the ways being foul, twenty to one, Carrier 3
Lodge it with dishonour foul. Psalm 7, 18
From deepest darkness foul. Psalm 86, 48
Sees his foule inside through his whited skin. Prose 10, 6

Found
With stench and smoak: Such resting found the sole Par Lost 1.237
On duty, sleeping found by whom they dread, Par Lost 1.333
His own and *Rhea*'s Son like measure found; Par Lost 1.513
Obscure some glimps of joy, to have found thir chief Par Lost 1.524
Not in despair, to have found themselves not lost Par Lost 1.525
Words interwove with sighs found out thir way. Par Lost 1.621
With wond'rous Art found out the massie Ore, Par Lost 1.703
1667 'founded'
ms 'founded'
To found this nether Empire, which might rise Par Lost 2.296
Of those Heav'n-warring Champions could be found Par Lost 2.424
And found no end, in wandring mazes lost. Par Lost 2.561
View'd first thir lamentable lot, and found Par Lost 2.617
Found out for mankind under wrauth, O thou Par Lost 3.275
A World from utter loss, and hast been found Par Lost 3.308
Found worthiest to be so by being Good, Par Lost 3.310
Love no where to be found less then Divine! Par Lost 3.411
Living or liveless to be found was none, Par Lost 3.443
All this dark Globe the Fiend found as he pass'd, Par Lost 3.498
The place he found beyond expression bright, Par Lost 3.591
For sight no obstacle found here, nor shade, Par Lost 3.615
But further way found none, so thick entwin'd, Par Lost 4.174
I first awak't, and found my self repos'd Par Lost 4.450
In search of whom they sought: him there they found Par Lost 4.799
And brief related whom they brought, where found, Par Lost 4.875
The rest is true, they found me where they say; Par Lost 4.900
My fairest, my espous'd, my latest found, Par Lost 5.18
I rose as at thy call, but found thee not; Par Lost 5.48
Spiritual, may of purest Spirits be found Par Lost 5.406
If ye be found obedient, and retain Par Lost 5.501
What meant that caution joind, *if ye be found* Par Lost 5.513
Thy Rebels, or be found the worst in Heav'n. Par Lost 5.742
While Pardon may be found in time besought. Par Lost 5.848
So spake the Seraph *Abdiel* faithful found, Par Lost 5.896
Warr he perceav'd, warr in procinct, and found Par Lost 6.19
Found worthy not of Libertie alone, Par Lost 6.420
Once found, which yet unfound most would have thought Par Lost 6.500
They found, they mingl'd, and with suttle Art, Par Lost 6.513
Whereof to found thir Engins and thir Balls Par Lost 6.518
Rage prompted them at length, and found them arms Par Lost 6.635
Endless, and no solution will be found: Par Lost 6.694
Wave rowling after Wave, where way they found, Par Lost 7.298
With Serpent errour wandring, found thir way, Par Lost 7.302
Our prompt obedience. Fast we found, fast shut Par Lost 8.240
Soft on the flourie herb I found me laid Par Lost 8.254
First found me, and with soft oppression seis'd Par Lost 8.288
To pluck and eate; whereat I wak'd, and found Par Lost 8.309
I found not what me thought I wanted still; Par Lost 8.355
Is no deficience found; not so is Man, Par Lost 8.416
Permissive, and acceptance found, which gain'd Par Lost 8.435
Among the Beasts no Mate for thee was found. Par Lost 8.594
Found unsuspected way. There was a place, Par Lost 9.69
Most opportune might serve his Wiles, and found Par Lost 9.85
The Serpent: him fast sleeping soon he found Par Lost 9.182
Unprais'd: for nothing lovelier can be found Par Lost 9.232
Thoughts, which how found they harbour in thy brest Par Lost 9.288
Though ineffectual found: misdeem not then, Par Lost 9.301
At Feed or Fountain never had I found. Par Lost 9.597
Have also tasted, and have also found Par Lost 9.874
Nor yet on him found deadly, he yet lives, Par Lost 9.932
Soon found thir Eyes how op'nd, and thir minds Par Lost 9.1053
Columbus found th' *American* so girt Par Lost 9.1116
Not unagreeable, to found a path Par Lost 10.256
And all about found desolate; for those Par Lost 10.420
Protesting Fate supreame; thence how I found Par Lost 10.480
Am found Eternal, and incorporate both, Par Lost 10.816
To my just number found. O why did God, Par Lost 10.888
Found so erroneous, thence by just event Par Lost 10.969
Found so unfortunate; nevertheless, Par Lost 10.970
Let us seek Death, or he not found, supply Par Lost 10.1001
Had ended now thir Orisons, and found Par Lost 11.137
God is as here, and will be found alike Par Lost 11.350
For envie that his Brothers Offering found Par Lost 11.456
Had melted (whether found where casual fire Par Lost 11.566
Through all the Plain, and refuge none was found. Par Lost 11.673
In sharp contest of Battel found no aide Par Lost 11.800
For one Man found so perfet and so just, Par Lost 11.876
In the wide Wilderness, there they shall found Par Lost 12.224
Rarely be found: so shall the World goe on, Par Lost 12.537

Found(*cont*)
Lay sleeping ran before, but found her wak't; Par Lost 12.608
Will waft me; and the way found prosperous once Par Reg 1.104
The Law of God I read, and found it sweet, Par Reg 1.207
By whose bright course led on they found the place, Par Reg 1.252
By Vision, found thee in the Temple, and spake Par Reg 1.256
Known partly, and soon found of whom they spake Par Reg 1.262
Now missing him thir joy so lately found, Par Reg 2.9
So lately found, and so abruptly gone, Par Reg 2.10
To find whom at the first they found unsought: Par Reg 2.59
I lost him, but so found, as well I saw Par Reg 2.97
Have found him, view'd him, tasted him, but find Par Reg 2.131
Among daughters of men the fairest found; Par Reg 2.154
Is to be found, in the wide Wilderness; Par Reg 2.232
He found his Supper on the coals prepar'd, Par Reg 2.273
Our Saviour, and found all was but a dream, Par Reg 2.283
Out cast *Nebaioth*, yet found he relief Par Reg 2.309
What of perfection can in man be found, Par Reg 3.230
(As he who seeking Asses found a Kingdom) Par Reg 3.242
Found able by invasion to annoy Par Reg 3.365
Alone into the Temple; there was found Par Reg 4.217
Will far be found unworthy to compare Par Reg 4.346
For thee is fittest place, I found thee there, Par Reg 4.373
Him walking on a Sunny hill he found, Par Reg 4.447
To try thee, sift thee, and confess have found thee Par Reg 4.532
That once found out and solv'd, for grief and spight Par Reg 4.574
Of Hornets arm'd, no sooner found alone, Samson 20
Not to be found, though sought. Yee see, O friends, Samson 193
As to his own edicts, found contradicting, Samson 301
And Rivals? In this other was there found Samson 387
Found soon occasion thereby to make thee Samson 425
More strength from me, then in thy self was found. Samson 789
One vertuous rarely found, Samson 1047
Some much averse I found and wondrous harsh, Samson 1461
And ever best found in the close. Samson 1748
Which oft is sooner found in lowly sheds Mask 323
That when a soul is found sincerely so, Mask 454
Till guided by mine ear I found the place Mask 570
Into swift flight, till I had found you here, Mask 579
And of those *Daemons* that are found Penseroso 93
And former sufferings other where are found; Passion 25
Mine eye hath found that sad Sepulchral rock Passion 43
Quickly found a lover meet; Winchester 16
For thou Jehovah wilt be found Psalm 5, 37
That him thou visit'st and of him art found; Psalm 8, 14
Hath found a house of *rest*, Psalm 84, 10

Foundation
O fair foundation laid whereon to build Par Lost 4.521
Against the canon laws of our foundation; Mask 808
Bridgewater ms 'foundacion'
All people from the worlds foundation. Psalm 7, 30
Is his foundation fast, Psalm 87, 2

Foundations
From thir foundations loosning to and fro Par Lost 6.643
Her dark foundations, and too fast had bound. Par Lost 6.870
And cast the dark foundations deep, Nativity 123
The Earths foundations all are mov'd Psalm 82, 19

Founded
Nor founded on the brittle strength of bones, Par Lost 1.427
With wond'rous Art found out the massie Ore, Par Lost 1.703
ms 'founded'
1667 'founded'
Founded in Reason, Loyal, Just, and Pure, Par Lost 4.755
Adverse to life: then founded, then conglob'd Par Lost 7.239
From Heaven Gate not farr, founded in view Par Lost 7.618
Founded in righteousness and peace and love Par Lost 12.550
By great *Arsaces* led, who founded first Par Reg 3.295
A fairer Paradise is founded now Par Reg 4.613
Chor. Thy hopes are not ill founded nor seem vain Samson 1504
Hast founded strength because of all thy foes Psalm 8, 6
Founded in chast and humble Povertie, Prose 3, 1

Foundered
The Pilot of some small night-founder'd Skiff, Par Lost 1.204
ms 'night-founderd'
Nor good dry Land: nigh founderd on he fares, Par Lost 2.940
Either som one like us night-founder'd here, Mask 483
1637 'night founder'd'
Trinity ms 'night founder'd'
Bridgewater ms 'night founderd'

Foundest
Foundst either sweet repast, or sound repose; Par Lost 9.407
Temptation found'st, or over-potent charms Samson 427

Fount
And flours aloft shading the Fount of Life, Par Lost 3.357
From *Paneas* the fount of *Jordans* flood Par Lost 3.535
How from that Saphire Fount the crisped Brooks, Par Lost 4.237
Your Tribes, and water from th' ambrosial Fount? Par Lost 11.279
And from the fount of life Ambrosial drink, Par Reg 4.590

Fountain
Or Fountain some belated Peasant sees, Par Lost 1.783
ms 'fountain'
Whose Fountain who shall tell? before the Sun, Par Lost 3.8
Fountain of Light, thy self invisible Par Lost 3.375
Rose a fresh Fountain, and with many a rill Par Lost 4.229
Stood whispering soft, by a fresh Fountain side Par Lost 4.326
Some wandring Spirit of Heav'n, by Fountain side, Par Lost 4.531
Perpetual Fountain of Domestic sweets, Par Lost 4.760
To Hill, or Valley, Fountain, or fresh shade Par Lost 5.203

Fountain(*cont*)
Before the Hills appeerd, or Fountain flow'd, — Par Lost 7.8
With tufts the vallies and each fountain side, — Par Lost 7.327
Hither as to thir Fountain other Starrs — Par Lost 7.364
Rose up a Fountain by the Tree of Life; — Par Lost 9.73
By Fountain or by shadie Rivulet — Par Lost 9.420
At Feed or Fountain never had I found. — Par Lost 9.597
Fast by a Fountain, one small Thicket past — Par Lost 9.628
Of *Amarantin* Shade, Fountain or Spring, — Par Lost 11.78
I heard, here with him at this Fountain talk'd: — Par Lost 11.322
In Wood or Grove by mossie Fountain side, — Par Reg 2.184
Light from above, from the fountain of light, — Par Reg 4.289
Sam. Where ever fountain or fresh current flow'd — Samson 547
But God who caus'd a fountain at thy prayer — Samson 581
By dimpled Brook, and Fountain brim, — Mask 119
Trinity ms 'fountayne'
Bridgewater ms 'fountaine'
1637 'Fountaine'
Drops that from my fountain pure, — Mask 912
Bridgewater ms 'fountayne'
Trinity ms 'fountaine'
1637 'fountaine'
Fed the same flock, by fountain, shade, and rill. — Lycidas 24
Trinity ms 'fountaine'
O Fountain *Arethuse*, and thou honour'd floud, — Lycidas 85
Trinity ms 'Fountaine'
1638 'fountain'

Fountainless
For barren desert fountainless and dry. — Par Reg 3.264

Fountains
Among the Groves, the Fountains, and the Flours — Par Lost 5.126
Fountains and yee, that warble, as ye flow, — Par Lost 5.195
O Woods, O Fountains, Hillocks, Dales and Bowrs, — Par Lost 10.860
Raine day and night, all fountains of the Deep — Par Lost 11.826
1667 'fountaines'
Why turned *Jordan* toward his Crystall Fountains? — Psalm 114, 14
And all my fountains *clear*. — Psalm 87, 28

Founted
Mount *Carmel;* here the double-founted stream — Par Lost 12.144

Four
Toward the four winds four speedy Cherubim — Par Lost 2.516
Four ways thir flying March, along the Banks — Par Lost 2.574
Of four infernal Rivers that disgorge — Par Lost 2.575
For hot, cold, moist, and dry, four Champions fierce — Par Lost 2.898
And now divided into four main Streams, — Par Lost 4.233
Of those fourfooted kindes, himself now one, — Par Lost 4.397
His praise ye Winds, that from four Quarters blow, — Par Lost 5.192
By four Cherubic shapes, four Faces each — Par Lost 6.753
At once the Four spred out thir Starrie wings — Par Lost 6.827
His arrows, from the fourfold-visag'd Foure, — Par Lost 6.845
He circl'd, four times cross'd the Carr of Night — Par Lost 9.65
Of watchful Cherubim; four faces each — Par Lost 11.128
With thir four Wives; and God made fast the dore. — Par Lost 11.737
To be a lyer in four hundred mouths; — Par Reg 1.428
Where will this end? four times ten days I have pass'd — Par Reg 2.245
From the four hinges of the world, and fell — Par Reg 4.415

Fourfold-visaged
His arrows, from the fourfold-visag'd Foure, — Par Lost 6.845

Fourth
Glad Eevning and glad Morn crownd the fourth day. — Par Lost 7.386
Yet the fourth time, when mustring all her wiles, — Samson 402

Fowl
And let Fowle flie above the Earth, with wings — Par Lost 7.389
And let the Fowle be multiply'd on the Earth. — Par Lost 7.398
With Fish replenisht, and the Aire with Fowle, — Par Lost 7.447
Let th' Earth bring forth Foul living in her kinde, — Par Lost 7.451
1667 'Fowle'
By Fowl, Fish, Beast, was flown, was swum, was walkt — Par Lost 7.503
Over the Fish and Fowle of Sea and Aire, — Par Lost 7.521
Over Fish of the Sea, and Fowle of the Aire, — Par Lost 7.533
Or live in Sea, or Aire, Beast, Fish, and Fowle. — Par Lost 8.341
Much less can Bird with Beast, or Fish with Fowle — Par Lost 8.395
Of ravenous Fowl, though many a League remote, — Par Lost 10.274
Feed first, on each Beast next, and Fish, and Fowle, — Par Lost 10.604
Beast now with Beast gan war, and Fowle with Fowle, — Par Lost 10.710
He gave us onely over Beast, Fish, Fowl — Par Lost 12.67
And savour, Beasts of chase, or Fowl of game, — Par Reg 2.342
Of tame villatic Fowl; but as an Eagle — Samson 1695
the feilds with cattell & the aire with fowle — Mask Tr. ms 21.57
Fowl of the Heavens, and Fish that through the wet — Psalm 8, 21

Fowls
Of Towring Eagles, to all the Fowles he seems — Par Lost 5.271
1667 'fowles' in some copies
The Desert, Fowls in thir clay nests were couch't; — Par Reg 1.501
To dogs and fowls a prey, or else captiv'd: — Samson 694

Fragile
And fragile arms, much instrument of war — Par Reg 3.388

Fragrance
Thus while God spake, ambrosial fragrance fill'd — Par Lost 3.135
Glistring with dew, nor fragrance after showers, — Par Lost 4.653
And shook his Plumes, that Heav'nly fragrance filld — Par Lost 5.286
With fragrance and with joy my heart oreflow'd. — Par Lost 8.266
Veild in a Cloud of Fragrance, where she stood, — Par Lost 9.425

Fragrant
Glistring with dew; fragrant the fertil earth — Par Lost 4.645
Of firm and fragrant leaf; on either side — Par Lost 4.695
With flourets deck't and fragrant smells; but *Eve* — Par Lost 5.379
That fragrant smell diffus'd, in order stood — Par Reg 2.351

Fragrant(*cont*)
With spirits of balm, and fragrant Syrops mixt. — Mask 674
Nard, and *Cassia*'s balmy smels. — Mask 991
Trinity ms 'baulmie' ←'balmy' ←'fragrant'

Frail
Thir frail Original, and faded bliss, — Par Lost 2.375
Of this frail World; by which the Spirits perverse — Par Lost 2.1030
By me upheld, that he may know how frail — Par Lost 3.180
Perceive thee purpos'd not to doom frail Man — Par Lost 3.404
To wreck on innocent frail man his loss — Par Lost 4.11
Vital in every part, not as frail man — Par Lost 6.345
Fraile is our happiness, if this be so, — Par Lost 9.340
All chances incident to mans frail life — Samson 656
Strive to keep up a frail, and Feaverish being — Mask 8
1637 'fraile'
Trinity ms 'fraile'
Bridgewater ms 'fraile'
Let our frail thoughts dally with false surmise. — Lycidas 153
Trinity ms 'fraile' ←'sad'
High thron'd in secret bliss, for us frail dust — Circum 19
Trinity ms 'fraile'

Frailty
Thy frailtie and infirmer Sex forgiv'n, — Par Lost 10.956
Our frailtie can sustain, thy tidings bring, — Par Lost 11.302
To worthiest deeds, if he through frailty err, — Samson 369
Nor shouldst thou have trusted that to womans frailty — Samson 783
By which all mortal frailty must subsist, — Mask 686
line not in Bridgewater ms
Trinity ms 'frailtie'

Frame
Som Capital City; or less then if this frame — Par Lost 2.924
Heav'ns everlasting Frame, while o're the necks — Par Lost 3.395
Almightie, thine this universal Frame, — Par Lost 5.154
1667 'frame' in some copies
Contiguous might distemper the whole frame: — Par Lost 7.273
When I behold this goodly Frame, this World — Par Lost 8.15
The mightie frame, how build, unbuild, contrive — Par Lost 8.81
As dangerous to the pillard frame of Heaven, — Par Reg 4.455
while all the starrie rounds & arches blue — Musick Tr. ms 4.21
'while all the starrie rounds' ←'starrie frame' ←'whilst then' ←'whilst the whole frame of' ←'while all the' ←'that all'
Shall come, *and all shall frame* — Psalm 86, 30

Framed
Chos'n by the sovran Planter, when he fram'd — Par Lost 4.691
Divine the sov'ran Architect had fram'd. — Par Lost 5.256
Thus to th' Empyreal Minister he fram'd. — Par Lost 5.460
A mightie Spheare he fram'd, unlightsom first, — Par Lost 7.355
By his prescript a Sanctuary is fram'd — Par Lost 12.249

Frames
Which Reason joyning or disjoyning, frames — Par Lost 5.106

Franciscan
Or in *Franciscan* think to pass disguis'd; — Par Lost 3.480

Fraternal
With fair equalitie, fraternal state, — Par Lost 12.26

Fraud
Of *Solomon* he led by fraud to build — Par Lost 1.401
To work in close design, by fraud or guile — Par Lost 1.646
Fall circumvented thus by fraud, though joynd — Par Lost 3.152
Artificer of fraud; and was the first — Par Lost 4.121
In this perfidious fraud, contagion spred — Par Lost 5.880
To hide the fraud. At interview both stood — Par Lost 6.555
Stood reimbattell'd fierce, by force or fraud — Par Lost 6.794
He trusted to have seis'd, and into fraud — Par Lost 7.143
In meditated fraud and malice, bent — Par Lost 9.55
Fit Vessel, fittest Imp of fraud, in whom — Par Lost 9.89
His fraud is then thy fear, which plain inferrs — Par Lost 9.285
Can by his fraud be shak'n or seduc't; — Par Lost 9.287
So glister'd the dire Snake, and into fraud — Par Lost 9.643
The sacred Fruit forbidd'n? som cursed fraud — Par Lost 9.904
Fraud in the Serpent, speaking as he spake; — Par Lost 9.1150
Made happie: Him by fraud I have seduc'd — Par Lost 10.485
Thy inward fraud, to warn all Creatures from thee — Par Lost 10.871
Not force, but well couch't fraud, well woven snares, — Par Reg 1.97
To draw the proud King *Ahab* into fraud — Par Reg 1.372
Discover'd in his fraud, thrown from his hope, — Par Reg 4.3
To daily fraud, contempt, abuse and wrong, — Samson 76
thou man of lies & falshood, if thou give me it — Mask Tr. ms 22.21
'falshood' ←'fraud' ←'falshood'
Of Public Fraud. In vain doth Valour bleed — Sonnet 15, 13

Fraudulent
Who to the fraudulent Impostor foule — Par Lost 3.692
His fraudulent temptation thus began. — Par Lost 9.531
And frustrated the conquest fraudulent: — Par Reg 4.609

Fraught
With Heav'ns Artillery fraught, come rattling on — Par Lost 2.715
Thither full fraught with mischievous revenge, — Par Lost 2.1054
In favour and praeeminence, yet fraught — Par Lost 5.661
Hell thir fit habitation fraught with fire — Par Lost 6.876
And tidings fraught, to Hell he now return'd, — Par Lost 10.346
And slow descends, with somthing heav'nly fraught. — Par Lost 11.207
With wonder, then with envy fraught and rage — Par Reg 1.38
And Waggons fraught with Utensils of war. — Par Reg 3.336
Chor. His fraught we soon shall know, he now arrives. — Samson 1075
Leans her unpillow'd head fraught with sad fears. — Mask 355
Trinity ms 'fraught with sad feares' ←'musing at our unkindnesse'

Fray
And by decision more imbroiles the fray Par Lost 2.908
Th' Eternal to prevent such horrid fray Par Lost 4.996
But call in aide, which makes a bloody Fray; Par Lost 11.651
Freaked
The white Pink, and the Pansie freakt with jeat, Lycidas 144
Trinity ms 'freakt' ←'freak't'
Free
We shall be free; th' Almighty hath not built Par Lost 1.259
Did first create your Leader, next free choice, Par Lost 2.19
Free, and to none accountable, preferring Par Lost 2.255
Free Vertue should enthrall to Force or Chance. Par Lost 2.551
Fixt Fate, free will, foreknowledg absolute, Par Lost 2.560
I come no enemie, but to set free Par Lost 2.822
Sufficient to have stood, though free to fall. Par Lost 3.99
Not free, what proof could they have givn sincere Par Lost 3.103
I formd them free, and free they must remain, Par Lost 3.124
Hadst thou the same free Will and Power to stand? Par Lost 4.66
But Heav'ns free Love dealt equally to all? Par Lost 4.68
As liberal and free as infinite, Par Lost 4.415
Free leave so large to all things else, and choice Par Lost 4.434
Pure, and commands to som, leaves free to all. Par Lost 4.747
Happiness in his power left free to will, Par Lost 5.235
Left to his own free Will, his Will though free, Par Lost 5.236
By nature free, not over-rul'd by Fate Par Lost 5.527
Can hearts, not free, be tri'd whether they serve Par Lost 5.532
To be both will and deed created free; Par Lost 5.549
By none, and if not equal all, yet free, Par Lost 5.791
Equally free; for Orders and Degrees Par Lost 5.792
Flatly unjust, to binde with Laws the free, Par Lost 5.819
Thy self not free, but to thy self enthrall'd; Par Lost 6.181
Thou fablest, here however to dwell free, Par Lost 6.292
Deliverer from new Lords, leader to free, Par Lost 6.451
And put not forth my goodness, which is free Par Lost 7.171
The Tawnie Lion, pawing to get free Par Lost 7.464
Expressing well the spirit within thee free, Par Lost 8.440
Variously representing; yet still free Par Lost 8.610
Thy Judgement to do aught, which else free Will Par Lost 8.636
Free in thine own Arbitrement it lies. Par Lost 8.641
But God left free the Will, for what obeyes Par Lost 9.351
Reason, is free, and Reason he made right, Par Lost 9.352
Go; for thy stay, not free, absents thee more; Par Lost 9.372
In *Athens* or free *Rome*, where Eloquence Par Lost 9.671
Of thy full branches offer'd free to all; Par Lost 9.802
Superior; for inferior who is free? Par Lost 9.825
And force upon free will hath here no place. Par Lost 9.1174
Of Man, with strength entire, and free will arm'd, Par Lost 10.9
His free Will, to her own inclining left Par Lost 10.46
Then both our selves and Seed at once to free Par Lost 10.999
In part, from such deformities be free, Par Lost 11.513
Reserving, human left from human free. Par Lost 12.71
Man till then free. Therefore since hee permits Par Lost 12.90
Over free Reason, God in Judgement just Par Lost 12.92
From imposition of strict Laws, to free Par Lost 12.304
Thy Glory, free thy people from thir yoke, Par Reg 2.48
Zeal of thy Fathers house, Duty to free Par Reg 3.175
Till *Cyrus* set them free; *Persepolis* Par Reg 3.284
By free consent of all, none opposite, Par Reg 3.358
A victor people free from servile yoke? Par Reg 4.102
For him I was not sent, nor yet to free Par Reg 4.131
What wise and valiant man would seek to free Par Reg 4.143
Or could of inward slaves make outward free? Par Reg 4.145
To set his people free, Samson 317
To free my Countrey; if their servile minds Samson 1213
My heels are fetter'd, but my fist is free. Samson 1235
To favour, and perhaps to set thee free. Samson 1412
To free him hence! but death who sets all free Samson 1572
We cannot free the Lady that sits here Mask 818
Till free consent the gods among Mask 1007
line not in Bridgewater ms
Love vertue, she alone is free, Mask 1019
she might be free from perill where she is Mask Tr. ms 16.42
she might be free from perill where she is, Mask Br. ms 395
But com thou Goddes fair and free, Allegro 11
In unreproved pleasures free; Allegro 40
Of *Pluto*, to have quite set free Allegro 149
I know this quest of yours, and free intent Arcades 34
And still revolt when truth would set them free. Sonnet 12, 10
Helpe us to save free Conscience from the paw Sonnet 16, 13
1694 'Free'
To force our Consciences that Christ set free, Forcers 6
Thy free love made it thine, Psalm 80, 34
I set his shoulder free; Psalm 81, 22
And I to free thee *did not faile*, Psalm 81, 27
For thou wilt *grant me free access* Psalm 86, 23
Eev'n from the lowest Hell set free Psalm 86, 47
This is true Liberty when free born men Prose 9, 1
Having to advise the public may speak free, Prose 9, 2
Freed
And freed from intricacies, taught to live, Par Lost 8.182
Not longer then since I in one Night freed Par Lost 9.140
Till truth were freed, and equity restor'd: Par Reg 1.220
His wasted Country freed from *Punic* rage, Par Reg 3.102
Who freed, as to thir antient Patrimony, Par Reg 3.428
And freed us from the slavery Psalm 136, 81
Till Truth, and Right from Violence be freed, Sonnet 15, 11
And not fre'd my foe for naught; Psalm 7, 12
There ev'n the Sparrow *freed from wrong* Psalm 84, 9
Freed*(cont)*
And thou hast free'd my Soul Psalm 86, 46
Freedom
Useless and vain, of freedom both despoild, Par Lost 3.109
Thir freedom, they themselves ordain'd thir fall. Par Lost 3.128
Severe but in true filial freedom plac't; Par Lost 4.294
In freedome equal? or can introduce Par Lost 5.797
Servilitie with freedom to contend, Par Lost 6.169
Thus I embold'nd spake, and freedom us'd Par Lost 8.434
Our inward freedom? In the day we eate Par Lost 9.762
Freedom and Peace to men: they on the Plain Par Lost 11.580
Shall with thir freedom lost all vertu loose Par Lost 11.798
His outward freedom: Tyrannie must be, Par Lost 12.95
To be infring'd, our freedom and our being Par Reg 1.62
Made Captive, yet deserving freedom more Par Reg 3.77
Honour hath left, and freedom, let but them Samson 1715
Thou canst not touch the freedom of my minde Mask 663
Bridgewater ms 'freedome'
1637 'freedome'
Trinity ms 'freedome'
That bawle for freedom in their senceless mood, Sonnet 12, 9
Trinity ms 'freedome' ←'freedom'
Freely
Freely they stood who stood, and fell who fell. Par Lost 3.102
Freely voutsaft; once more I will renew Par Lost 3.175
Freely put off, and for him lastly dye Par Lost 3.240
Chose freely what it now so justly rues. Par Lost 4.72
Which I as freely give; Hell shall unfold, Par Lost 4.381
On other surety none; freely we serve, Par Lost 5.538
Because wee freely love, as in our will Par Lost 5.539
Freely our part; yee who appointed stand Par Lost 6.565
And freely all thir pleasant fruit for food Par Lost 7.540
Eate freely with glad heart; fear here no dearth: Par Lost 8.322
Good reason was thou freely shouldst dislike, Par Lost 8.443
Goddess humane, reach then, and freely taste. Par Lost 9.732
On my experience, *Adam*, freely taste, Par Lost 9.988
Freely; of whom what could he less expect Par Reg 3.126
Where I a Prisoner chain'd, scarce freely draw Samson 7
I do it freely; venturing to displease Samson 1373
Which he for us did freely undergo. Passion 12
Freezed
Wherwith she freez'd her foes to congeal'd stone? Mask 449
Bridgewater ms 'freezed'
Freezing
Wherwith she freez'd her foes to congeal'd stone? Mask 449
Trinity ms 'wherwith' ←'freezind wherwith'
Through middle empire of the freezing aire Fair Inf 16
French
And what the *Swede* intend, and what the *French*. Sonnet 21, 8
Frenzy
Daemoniac Phrenzie, moaping Melancholie Par Lost 11.485
line not in 1667 edition
Among them he a spirit of phrenzie sent, Samson 1675
Frequence
Of the most High, who in full frequence bright Par Reg 1.128
Consenting in full frequence was impowr'd, Par Reg 2.130
Frequent
Frequent and full. After short silence then Par Lost 1.797
Pass'd frequent, and his eye with choice regard Par Lost 3.534
Though wide, and this high Temple to frequent Par Lost 7.148
Frequent; and of the Sixt day yet remain'd; Par Lost 7.504
Delighted, and with frequent intercourse Par Lost 7.571
His blessed count'nance; here I could frequent, Par Lost 11.317
By Men who there frequent, or therein dwell. Par Lost 11.838
How frequent to desert him, and at last Samson 275
Frequented
Frequented thir Assemblies, whereso met, Par Lost 11.722
Frequenting
Frequenting, sent from hearts contrite, in sign Par Lost 10.1091
Frequenting, sent from hearts contrite, in sign Par Lost 10.1103
Fresh
In clusters; they among fresh dews and flowers Par Lost 1.771
A fresh with conscious terrours vex me round, Par Lost 2.801
1667 'Afresh'
With fresh alacritie and force renew'd Par Lost 2.1012
Rose a fresh Fountain, and with many a rill Par Lost 4.229
Stood whispering soft, by a fresh Fountain side Par Lost 4.326
To morrow ere fresh Morning streak the East Par Lost 4.623
Awake, the morning shines, and the fresh field Par Lost 5.20
And let us to our fresh imployments rise Par Lost 5.125
To Hill, or Valley, Fountain, or fresh shade Par Lost 5.203
On flours repos'd, and with fresh flourets crownd, Par Lost 5.636
line not in 1667 edition
And with fresh Flourets Hill and Valley smil'd. Par Lost 6.784
And thou enlight'nd Earth, so fresh and gay, Par Lost 8.274
And Life-blood streaming fresh; wide was the wound, Par Lost 8.467
Joyous the Birds; fresh Gales and gentle Aires Par Lost 8.515
Leucothea wak'd, and with fresh dews imbalmd Par Lost 11.135
Gaz'd hot, and of the fresh Wave largely drew, Par Lost 11.845
Fresh in thir mindes, fearing the Deitie, Par Lost 12.15
Out of his grave, fresh as the dawning light, Par Lost 12.423
Who all things now behold more fresh and green, Par Reg 4.435
Fresh from his fall, and fiercer grapple joyn'd, Par Reg 4.567
Renewing fresh assaults, amidst his pride Par Reg 4.570
Sam. Where ever fountain or fresh current flow'd Samson 547
Where I will see thee heartn'd and fresh clad Samson 1317
When the fresh blood grows lively, and returns Mask 670
Trinity ms 'fresh' ←'briske'

Fresh(*cont*)
Batt'ning our flocks with the fresh dews of night, Lycidas 29
On whose fresh lap the swart Star sparely looks, Lycidas 138
To morrow to fresh Woods, and Pastures new. Lycidas 193
With those just Spirits that wear victorious Palms, Musick 14
Trinity ms 'victorious' ←'blooming' ←'victorious'
←'blooming' ←'fresh greene'
Thou with fresh hope the Lovers heart dost fill, Sonnet 1, 3
The frozen earth; and cloth in fresh attire Sonnet 20, 7
In thee *fresh brooks, and soft streams glance* Psalm 87, 27

Fresh-blowing
The breath of Heav'n fresh-blowing, pure and sweet, Samson 10

Fresh-blown
And fresh-blown Roses washt in dew, Allegro 22

Freshest
And Hyacinth, Earths freshest softest lap. Par Lost 9.1041

Freshet
Freshet, or purling Brook, of shell or fin, Par Reg 2.345

Fret
All sounds on Fret by String or Golden Wire Par Lost 7.597
And at thy growing vertues fret their spleen, Sonnet 9, 7

Fretted
The Roof was fretted Gold. Not *Babilon*, Par Lost 1.717

Friar
And he by Friars Lanthorn led Allegro 104

Friars
Embryo's and Idiots, Eremits and Friers Par Lost 3.474

Friend
Go therefore, half this day as friend with friend Par Lost 5.229
With Man, as with his Friend, familiar us'd Par Lost 9.2
Whatever wiles of Foe or seeming Friend. Par Lost 10.11
Mans Friend, his Mediator, his design'd Par Lost 10.60
As I suppose, towards your once gloried friend, Samson 334
Secrets of men, the secrets of a friend, Samson 492
My speediest friend, by death to rid me hence, Samson 1263
Many a friend to gratulate Mask 949
Bridgewater ms 'freind'
1637 'freind'
Trinity ms 'freind'
The conscience, Friend, to have lost them overply'd Sonnet 22, 10
Lover and friend thou hast remov'd Psalm 88, 69

Friendliest
Friendliest to sleep and silence, he resolv'd Par Lost 5.668

Friendly
But with no friendly voice, and add thy name Par Lost 4.36
Among those friendly Powers, who him receav'd Par Lost 6.22
This friendly condescention to relate Par Lost 8.9
Be good and friendly still, and oft return. Par Lost 8.651
To me so friendly grown above the rest Par Lost 9.564
Friendly to man, farr from deceit or guile. Par Lost 9.772
Though for no friendly intent. I am of *Gath*, Samson 1078
Man. I know your friendly minds and----O what noise! Samson 1508
I under fair pretence of friendly ends, Mask 160
Trinity ms 'freindly'
Bridgewater ms 'freindly'
La. To seek i'th vally som cool friendly Spring. Mask 282
Bridgewater ms 'freindly'
Trinity ms 'freindly'
If he be friendly he comes well, if not, Mask 488
Trinity ms 'freindly'
Bridgewater ms 'freindly'
To life so friendly, or so cool to thirst. Mask 678
Trinity ms 'freindly'
Bridgewater ms 'freindly'

Friends
But wherefore let we then our faithful friends, Par Lost 1.264
ms 'freinds'
O friends, I hear the tread of nimble feet Par Lost 4.866
Remains thee, aided by this host of friends, Par Lost 6.38
O Friends, why come not on these Victors proud? Par Lost 6.609
He leaves his Gods, his Friends, and native Soile Par Lost 12.129
Money brings Honour, Friends, Conquest, and Realms; Par Reg 2.422
(Thy throne) but gold that got him puissant friends? Par Reg 2.425
We come thy friends and neighbours not unknown Samson 180
Sam. Your coming, Friends, revives me, for I learn Samson 187
How counterfeit a coin they are who friends Samson 189
Not to be found, though sought. Yee see, O friends, Samson 193
To a deceitful Woman: tell me Friends, Samson 202
And healing words from these thy friends admit. Samson 605
Under pretence of Bridal friends and guests, Samson 1196
To see me girt with Friends; and how the sight Samson 1415
Will send for all my kindred, all my friends Samson 1730
And all their friends, and native home forget Mask 76
Bridgewater ms 'freinds'
Trinity ms 'freinds'
Thou, when the Bridegroom with his feastfull friends Sonnet 9, 12
Trinity ms 'freinds'
I mention Babel to my friends, Psalm 87, 13
Thou dost my friends from me estrange, Psalm 88, 33

Friendship
Raise out of friendship hostil deeds in Peace. Par Lost 11.796
All friendship, and avoided as a blab, Samson 495

Frieze
Cornice or Freeze, with bossy Sculptures grav'n, Par Lost 1.716
ms 'freeze'
Drink the clear stream, and nothing wear but Freize, Mask 722
Bridgewater ms 'freeze'
Trinity ms 'freise'

Fright
Wide waving, all approach farr off to fright, Par Lost 11.121
Or fright them from their hallow'd haunt. Penseroso 138

Frighted
Frighted the Reign of *Chaos* and old Night. Par Lost 1.543
Fled not in silence through the frighted deep Par Lost 2.994
Gave respit to the drowsie frighted steeds Mask 553
Trinity ms 'flighted'

Fringed
That to the fringed Bank with Myrtle crownd, Par Lost 4.262
By the rushy-fringed bank, Mask 890
Bridgewater ms 'rushie fringed'
1637 'rushie fringed'
Trinity ms 'rushie-fringed'

Frisking
Alone as they. About them frisking playd Par Lost 4.340

Frith
Pondering his Voyage; for no narrow frith Par Lost 2.919

Frivolous
The frivolous bolt of *Cupid*, gods and men Mask 445

Frizzled
And Bush with frizl'd hair implicit: last Par Lost 7.323

Fro
Flie to and fro, or on the smoothed Plank, Par Lost 1.772
Both to and fro, thir sorrow to augment, Par Lost 2.605
With easie intercourse pass to and fro Par Lost 2.1031
On high behests his Angels to and fro Par Lost 3.533
And writh'd him to and fro convolv'd; so sore Par Lost 6.328
From thir foundations loosning to and fro Par Lost 6.643
Hurl'd to and fro with jaculation dire, Par Lost 6.665
With horrible convulsion to and fro, Samson 1649

Frock
Chalybean temper'd steel, and frock of mail Samson 133

Frogs
Frogs, Lice and Flies must all his Palace fill Par Lost 12.177
As when those Hinds that were transform'd to Froggs Sonnet 12, 5
Trinity ms 'frogs'

Frolic
Who ripe, and frolick of his full grown age, Mask 59
In a light fantastick round. Mask 144
Trinity ms 'fantastick' ←'and frolick'
The frolick Wind that breathes the Spring, Allegro 18

From
Instruct me, for Thou know'st; Thou from the first Par Lost 1.19
Say first, for Heav'n hides nothing from thy view Par Lost 1.27
From thir Creator, and transgress his Will Par Lost 1.31
Had cast him out from Heav'n, with all his Host Par Lost 1.37
Hurld headlong flaming from th' Ethereal Skie Par Lost 1.45
As one great Furnace flam'd, yet from those flames Par Lost 1.62
As far remov'd from God and light of Heav'n Par Lost 1.73
As from the Center thrice to th' utmost Pole. Par Lost 1.74
O how unlike the place from whence they fell! Par Lost 1.75
From him, who in the happy Realms of Light Par Lost 1.85
From what highth fall'n, so much the stronger prov'd Par Lost 1.92
And high disdain, from sence of injur'd merit, Par Lost 1.98
Extort from me. To bow and sue for grace Par Lost 1.111
Who from the terrour of this Arm so late Par Lost 1.113
His inmost counsels from thir destind aim. Par Lost 1.168
The fiery Surge, that from the Precipice Par Lost 1.173
Or satiate fury yield it from our Foe. Par Lost 1.179
From off the tossing of these fiery waves, Par Lost 1.184
What reinforcement we may gain from Hope, Par Lost 1.190
If not what resolution from despare. Par Lost 1.191
Forthwith upright he rears from off the Pool Par Lost 1.221
Torn from *Pelorus*, or the shatter'd side Par Lost 1.232
What shall be right: fardest from him is best Par Lost 1.247
At Ev'ning from the top of *Fesole*, Par Lost 1.289
From the safe shore thir floating Carkases Par Lost 1.310
His swift pursuers from Heav'n Gates discern Par Lost 1.326
Pour'd never from her frozen loyns, to pass Par Lost 1.352
Forthwith from every Squadron and each Band Par Lost 1.356
By thir Rebellion, from the Books of Life. Par Lost 1.363
Rous'd from the slumber, on that fiery Couch, Par Lost 1.377
The chief were those who from the Pit of Hell Par Lost 1.381
From *Aroar* to *Nebo*, and the wild Par Lost 1.407
Israel in *Sittim* on thir march from *Nile* Par Lost 1.413
With these came they, who from the bordring flood Par Lost 1.419
Egypt from *Syrian* ground, had general Names Par Lost 1.421
While smooth *Adonis* from his native Rock Par Lost 1.450
From *Egypt* marching, equal'd with one stroke Par Lost 1.488
Fell not from Heaven, or more gross to love Par Lost 1.491
By younger *Saturn*, he from mightier *Jove* Par Lost 1.512
Who forthwith from the glittering Staff unfurld Par Lost 1.535
From mortal or immortal minds. Thus they Par Lost 1.559
ms defective here
Or whom *Biserta* sent from *Afric* shore Par Lost 1.585
Shorn of his Beams, or from behind the Moon Par Lost 1.596
Of Heav'n, and from Eternal Splendors flung Par Lost 1.610
From wing to wing, and half enclose him round Par Lost 1.617
Foreseeing or presaging, from the Depth Par Lost 1.627
At length from us may find, who overcomes Par Lost 1.648
Millions of flaming swords, drawn from the thighs Par Lost 1.664
From heav'n, for ev'n in heav'n his looks and thoughts Par Lost 1.680
'Sluc'd from the Lake, a second multitude Par Lost 1.702
A various mould, and from the boyling cells Par Lost 1.706
As in an Organ from one blast of wind Par Lost 1.708
And level pavement: from the arched roof Par Lost 1.726
As from a sky. The hasty multitude Par Lost 1.730

From(*cont*)
From Heav'n, they fabl'd, thrown by angry *Jove* Par Lost 1.741
Sheer o're the Chrystal Battlements; from Morn Par Lost 1.742
To Noon he fell, from Noon to dewy Eve, Par Lost 1.743
Dropt from the Zenith like a falling Star, Par Lost 1.745
From every Band and squared Regiment Par Lost 1.758
ms defective here
To that bad eminence; and from despair Par Lost 2.6
I give not Heav'n for lost. From this descent Par Lost 2.14
More glorious and more dread then from no fall, Par Lost 2.16
Envy from each inferior; but who here Par Lost 2.26
From Faction; for none sure will claim in Hell Par Lost 2.32
Then to dwell here, driv'n out from bliss, condemn'd Par Lost 2.86
A refuge from those wounds: or when we lay Par Lost 2.168
And plunge us in the flames? or from above Par Lost 2.172
Views all things at one view? he from heav'ns highth Par Lost 2.190
Our own good from our selves, and from our own Par Lost 2.253
Covers his Throne; from whence deep thunders roar Par Lost 2.267
Nor want we skill or Art, from whence to raise Par Lost 2.272
From Heav'ns high jurisdiction, in new League Par Lost 2.319
Or ambush from the Deep. What if we find Par Lost 2.344
But from the Author of all ill could Spring Par Lost 2.381
Great things resolv'd, which from the lowest deep Par Lost 2.392
Mee from attempting. Wherefore do I assume Par Lost 2.450
Prudent, least from his resolution rais'd Par Lost 2.468
As when from mountain tops the dusky clouds Par Lost 2.488
From either end of Heav'n the welkin burns. Par Lost 2.538
As when *Alcides* from *Oechalia* Crown'd Par Lost 2.542
And *Lichas* from the top of *Oeta* threw Par Lost 2.545
Farr off from these a slow and silent stream, Par Lost 2.582
From Beds of raging Fire to starve in Ice Par Lost 2.600
Close sailing from *Bengala*, or the Iles Par Lost 2.638
Calabria from the hoarce *Trinacrian* shore: Par Lost 2.661
Satan was now at hand, and from his seat Par Lost 2.674
And they outcast from God, are here condemn'd Par Lost 2.694
In th' Artick Sky, and from his horrid hair Par Lost 2.710
Driv'n headlong from the Pitch of Heaven, down Par Lost 2.772
From all her Caves, and back resounded *Death*. Par Lost 2.789
From out this dark and dismal house of pain, Par Lost 2.823
Fell with us from on high: from them I go Par Lost 2.826
Thus saying, from her side the fatal Key, Par Lost 2.871
In mutinie had from her Axle torn Par Lost 2.926
Had from his wakeful custody purloind Par Lost 2.946
From your Dominion won, th' Ethereal King Par Lost 2.978
To that side Heav'n from whence your Legions fell: Par Lost 2.1006
From Hell continu'd reaching th' utmost Orbe Par Lost 2.1029
Of light appears, and from the walls of Heav'n Par Lost 2.1035
As from her outmost works a brok'd foe Par Lost 2.1039
Dwelt from Eternitie, dwelt then in thee, Par Lost 3.5
Won from the void and formless infinite. Par Lost 3.12
Surrounds me, from the chearful wayes of men Par Lost 3.46
Irradiate, there plant eyes, all mist from thence Par Lost 3.53
Now had the Almighty Father from above, Par Lost 3.56
From the pure Empyrean where he sits Par Lost 3.57
Stood thick as Starrs, and from his sight receiv'd Par Lost 3.61
Him God beholding from his prospect high, Par Lost 3.77
What pleasure I from such obedience paid, Par Lost 3.107
With his own folly? that be from thee farr, Par Lost 3.153
That farr be from thee, Father, who art Judg Par Lost 3.154
And none but such from mercy I exclude. Par Lost 3.202
Thee from my bosom and right hand, to save, Par Lost 3.279
As from a second root shall be restor'd, Par Lost 3.288
And live in thee transplanted, and from thee Par Lost 3.293
A World from utter loss, and hast been found Par Lost 3.308
When thou attended gloriously from Heav'n Par Lost 3.323
Shalt in the Sky appeer, and from thee send Par Lost 3.324
Thy dread Tribunal: forthwith from all Windes Par Lost 3.326
The World shall burn, and from her ashes spring Par Lost 3.334
Loud as from numbers without number, sweet Par Lost 3.346
As from blest voices, uttering joy, Heav'n rung Par Lost 3.347
Back from pursuit thy Powers with loud acclaime Par Lost 3.397
Forget, nor from thy Fathers praise disjoine. Par Lost 3.415
From *Chaos* and th' inroad of Darkness old, Par Lost 3.421
Save on that side which from the wall of Heav'n Par Lost 3.427
Dislodging from a Region scarce of prey Par Lost 3.433
None yet, but store hereafter from the earth Par Lost 3.444
First from the ancient World those Giants came Par Lost 3.464
A violent cross wind from either Coast Par Lost 3.487
Of Guardians bright, when he from *Esau* fled Par Lost 3.512
Who after came from Earth, sayling arriv'd, Par Lost 3.520
His sad exclusion from the dores of Bliss. Par Lost 3.525
Direct against which op'nd from beneath, Par Lost 3.526
From *Paneas* the fount of *Jordans* flood Par Lost 3.535
Satan from hence now on the lower stair Par Lost 3.540
Of Nights extended shade; from Eastern Point Par Lost 3.557
Beyond th' *Horizon;* then from Pole to Pole Par Lost 3.560
That from his Lordly eye keep distance due, Par Lost 3.578
Dispenses Light from farr; they as they move Par Lost 3.579
In various shapes old *Proteus* from the Sea, Par Lost 3.604
Th' Arch-chimic Sun so farr from us remote Par Lost 3.609
Culminate from th' *Aequator*, as they now Par Lost 3.617
Shadow from body opaque can fall, and the Aire, Par Lost 3.619
Hath brought me from the Quires of Cherubim Par Lost 3.666
From thy Empyreal Mansion thus alone, Par Lost 3.699
Light shon, and order from disorder sprung: Par Lost 3.713
With light from hence, though but reflected, shines; Par Lost 3.723
Down from th' Ecliptic, sped with hop'd success, Par Lost 3.740
His troubl'd thoughts, and from the bottom stirr Par Lost 4.19

From(*cont*)
He brings, and round about him, nor from Hell Par Lost 4.21
One step no more then from himself can fly Par Lost 4.22
Look'st from thy sole Dominion like the God Par Lost 4.33
That bring to my remembrance from what state Par Lost 4.38
From me, whom he created what I was Par Lost 4.43
Forgetful what from him I still receivd, Par Lost 4.54
Fell not, but stand unshak'n, from within Par Lost 4.64
Or from without, to all temptations arm'd. Par Lost 4.65
From granting hee, as I from begging peace: Par Lost 4.104
For heav'nly mindes from such distempers foule Par Lost 4.118
Sabean Odours from the spicie shoare Par Lost 4.162
That drove him, though enamourd, from the Spouse Par Lost 4.169
From *Media* post to *Aegypt*, there fast bound. Par Lost 4.171
From *Auran* Eastward to the Royal Towrs Par Lost 4.211
Which from his darksom passage now appeers, Par Lost 4.232
How from that Saphire Fount the crisped Brooks, Par Lost 4.237
Young *Bacchus* from his Stepdame *Rhea*'s eye; Par Lost 4.279
From this *Assyrian* Garden, where the Fiend Par Lost 4.285
Round from his parted forelock manly hung Par Lost 4.302
And banisht from mans life his happiest life, Par Lost 4.317
Then from his loftie stand on that high Tree Par Lost 4.395
That rais'd us from the dust and plac't us here Par Lost 4.416
From us no other service then to keep Par Lost 4.420
And from whom I was formd flesh of thy flesh, Par Lost 4.441
That day I oft remember, when from sleep Par Lost 4.449
Not distant far from thence a murmuring sound Par Lost 4.453
Of waters issu'd from a Cave and spread Par Lost 4.454
Seisd mine, I yielded, and from that time see Par Lost 4.489
From thir own mouths; all is not theirs it seems: Par Lost 4.513
Or in thick shade retir'd, from him to draw Par Lost 4.532
Accessible from Earth, one entrance high; Par Lost 4.546
From what point of his Compass to beware Par Lost 4.559
But in the Mount that lies from *Eden* North, Par Lost 4.569
Alien from Heav'n, with passions foul obscur'd: Par Lost 4.571
I fear, hath ventur'd from the deep, to raise Par Lost 4.574
Well known from Heav'n; and since Meridian hour Par Lost 4.581
By morrow Eevning, and from Land to Land Par Lost 4.662
Perfection from the Suns more potent Ray. Par Lost 4.673
Both day and night: how often from the steep Par Lost 4.680
But thou hast promis'd from us two a Race Par Lost 4.732
Adam from his fair Spouse, nor *Eve* the Rites Par Lost 4.742
By thee adulterous lust was driv'n from men Par Lost 4.753
And from thir Ivorie Port the Cherubim Par Lost 4.778
From these, two strong and suttle Spirits he calld Par Lost 4.786
This Eevning from the Sun's decline arriv'd Par Lost 4.792
Th' animal Spirits that from pure blood arise Par Lost 4.805
Like gentle breaths from Rivers pure, thence raise Par Lost 4.806
Departed from thee, and thou resembl'st now Par Lost 4.839
This place inviolable, and these from harm. Par Lost 4.843
He held it vain; awe from above had quelld Par Lost 4.860
Gabriel from the Front thus calld aloud. Par Lost 4.865
Who would not, finding way, break loose from Hell, Par Lost 4.889
Farthest from pain, where thou mightst hope to change Par Lost 4.892
And now returns him from his prison scap't, Par Lost 4.906
Unlicenc't from his bounds in Hell prescrib'd; Par Lost 4.909
So wise he judges it to fly from pain Par Lost 4.910
The first in flight from pain, had'st thou alledg'd Par Lost 4.921
Not that I less endure, or shrink from pain, Par Lost 4.925
From hard assaies and ill successes past Par Lost 4.932
Flie thither whence thou fledst: if from this houre Par Lost 4.963
From my prevailing arme, though Heavens King Par Lost 4.973
Was Aerie light from pure digestion bred, Par Lost 5.4
One shapd and wing'd like one of those from Heav'n Par Lost 5.55
Forbid who will, none shall from me withhold Par Lost 5.62
Reservd from night, and kept for thee in store. Par Lost 5.128
From either eye, and wip'd them with her haire; Par Lost 5.131
But first from under shadie arborous roof, Par Lost 5.137
Flowd from thir lips, in Prose or numerous Verse, Par Lost 5.150
From Hill or steaming Lake, duskie or grey, Par Lost 5.186
His praise ye Winds, that from four Quarters blow, Par Lost 5.192
Satan from Hell scap't through the darksom Gulf Par Lost 5.225
Thou find'st him from the heat of Noon retir'd, Par Lost 5.231
His danger, and from whom, what enemie Par Lost 5.239
Late falln himself from Heav'n, is plotting now Par Lost 5.240
The fall of others from like state of bliss; Par Lost 5.241
After his charge receivd; but from among Par Lost 5.248
From hence, no cloud, or, to obstruct his sight, Par Lost 5.257
Or Pilot from amidst the *Cyclades* Par Lost 5.264
Shaddowd from either heele with featherd maile Par Lost 5.284
Of nectarous draughts between, from milkie stream, Par Lost 5.306
Ris'n on mid-noon; som great behest from Heav'n Par Lost 5.311
From large bestowd, where Nature multiplies Par Lost 5.318
But I will haste and from each bough and break, Par Lost 5.326
Bestirs her then, and from each tender stalk Par Lost 5.337
From many a berrie, and from sweet kernels prest Par Lost 5.346
With Rose and Odours from the shrub unfum'd. Par Lost 5.349
Since by descending from the Thrones above, Par Lost 5.363
Stood to entertain her guest from Heav'n; no vaile Par Lost 5.383
And on her ample Square from side to side Par Lost 5.393
These bounties which our Nourisher, from whom Par Lost 5.398
From her moist Continent to higher Orbes. Par Lost 5.422
From all his alimental recompence Par Lost 5.424
Yield Nectar, though from off the boughs each Morn Par Lost 5.428
As from the Mine. Mean while at Table *Eve* Par Lost 5.443
O *Adam*, one Almightie is, from whom Par Lost 5.469
If not deprav'd from good, created all Par Lost 5.471
Proportiond to each kind. So from the root Par Lost 5.479

From(*cont*)

Springs lighter the green stalk, from thence the leaves	Par Lost 5.480
And from these corporal nutriments perhaps	Par Lost 5.496
From center to circumference, whereon	Par Lost 5.510
Who formd us from the dust, and plac'd us here	Par Lost 5.516
And so from Heav'n to deepest Hell; O fall	Par Lost 5.542
From what high state of bliss into what woe!	Par Lost 5.543
Cherubic Songs by night from neighbouring Hills	Par Lost 5.547
Forthwith from all the ends of Heav'n appeerd	Par Lost 5.586
Amidst as from a flaming Mount, whose top	Par Lost 5.598
Cast out from God and blessed vision, falls	Par Lost 5.613
Forthwith from dance to sweet repast they turn	Par Lost 5.630
From that high mount of God, whence light & shade	Par Lost 5.643
New Laws from him who reigns, new minds may raise	Par Lost 5.680
Abstrusest thoughts, from forth his holy Mount	Par Lost 5.712
And from within the golden Lamps that burne	Par Lost 5.713
And all the Sea, from one entire globose	Par Lost 5.753
From Diamond Quarries hew'n, and Rocks of Gold,	Par Lost 5.759
Receive him coming to receive from us	Par Lost 5.781
Expected, least of all from thee, ingrate	Par Lost 5.811
How provident he is, how farr from thought	Par Lost 5.828
From Father to his Son? strange point and new!	Par Lost 5.855
O alienate from God, O spirit accurst,	Par Lost 5.877
To swerve from truth, or change his constant mind	Par Lost 5.902
Though single. From amidst them forth he passd,	Par Lost 5.903
Empyreal, from before her vanisht Night,	Par Lost 6.14
Before the seat supream; from whence a voice	Par Lost 6.27
From midst a Golden Cloud thus milde was heard.	Par Lost 6.28
Pursuing drive them out from God and bliss,	Par Lost 6.52
Ethereal Trumpet from on high gan blow:	Par Lost 6.60
From skirt to skirt a fierie Region, stretcht	Par Lost 6.80
Then lighted from his gorgeous Throne, for now	Par Lost 6.103
So pondering, and from his armed Peers	Par Lost 6.127
From all: my Sect thou seest, now learn too late	Par Lost 6.147
From flight, seditious Angel, to receave	Par Lost 6.152
From me som Plume, that thy success may show	Par Lost 6.161
Of erring, from the path of truth remote:	Par Lost 6.173
From mee returnd, as erst thou saidst, from flight,	Par Lost 6.187
Sidelong, had push't a Mountain from his seat	Par Lost 6.197
From his strong hold of Heav'n high over-rul'd	Par Lost 6.228
The great Arch-Angel from his warlike toile	Par Lost 6.257
From all her Confines. Heav'n the seat of bliss	Par Lost 6.273
Or som more sudden vengeance wing'd from God	Par Lost 6.279
In horror; from each hand with speed retir'd	Par Lost 6.307
Two Planets rushing from aspect maligne	Par Lost 6.313
Of *Michael* from the Armorie of God	Par Lost 6.321
Not long divisible, and from the gash	Par Lost 6.331
From off the files of warr; there they him laid	Par Lost 6.339
Threatn'd, nor from the Holie One of Heav'n	Par Lost 6.359
Canceld from Heav'n and sacred memorie,	Par Lost 6.379
For strength from Truth divided and from Just,	Par Lost 6.381
By wound, though from thir place by violence mov'd.	Par Lost 6.405
Against us from about his Throne, and judg'd	Par Lost 6.426
As one he stood escap't from cruel fight,	Par Lost 6.448
Deliverer from new Lords, leader to free	Par Lost 6.451
Against unpaind, impassive; from which evil	Par Lost 6.455
These things, as not to mind from whence they grow	Par Lost 6.477
From far with thundring noise among our foes	Par Lost 6.487
Forthwith from Councel to the work they flew,	Par Lost 6.507
Soon banded; others from the dawning Hills	Par Lost 6.528
From those deep throated Engins belcht, whose roar	Par Lost 6.586
Had need from head to foot well understand;	Par Lost 6.625
(For Earth hath this variety from Heav'n	Par Lost 6.640
From thir foundations loosning to and fro	Par Lost 6.643
From all Heav'ns bounds into the utter Deep:	Par Lost 6.716
That from thy just obedience could revolt,	Par Lost 6.740
Then shall thy Saints unmixt, and from th' impure	Par Lost 6.742
From the right hand of Glorie where he sate,	Par Lost 6.747
And from about him fierce Effusion rowld	Par Lost 6.765
Insensate, hope conceiving from despair.	Par Lost 6.787
Ye Angels arm'd, this day from Battel rest;	Par Lost 6.802
Thrown on them as a shelter from his ire.	Par Lost 6.843
His arrows, from the fourfold-visag'd Foure,	Par Lost 6.845
Distinct with eyes, and from the living Wheels	Par Lost 6.846
Down from the verge of Heav'n, Eternal wrauth	Par Lost 6.865
Heav'n ruining from Heav'n and would have fled	Par Lost 6.868
Sole Victor from th' expulsion of his Foes	Par Lost 6.880
Thee also from obedience, that with him	Par Lost 6.902
Descend from Heav'n *Urania*, by that name	Par Lost 7.1
Least from this flying Steed unrein'd, (as once	Par Lost 7.17
Bellerophon, though from a lower Clime)	Par Lost 7.18
From whom it sprung, impossible to mix	Par Lost 7.58
Farr differing from this World, thou hast reveal'd	Par Lost 7.71
Down from the Empyrean to forewarne	Par Lost 7.73
Of Nature from the unapparent Deep:	Par Lost 7.103
Thy hearing, such Commission from above	Par Lost 7.118
Know then, that after *Lucifer* from Heav'n	Par Lost 7.131
Eternal Father from his Throne beheld	Par Lost 7.137
Had driven out th' ungodly from his sight	Par Lost 7.185
From the Armoury of God, where stand of old	Par Lost 7.200
On heav'nly ground they stood, and from the shore	Par Lost 7.210
Up from the bottom turn'd by furious windes	Par Lost 7.213
Sprung from the Deep, and from her Native East	Par Lost 7.245
And light from darkness by the Hemisphere	Par Lost 7.250
Exhaling first from Darkness they beheld;	Par Lost 7.255
The Waters from the Waters: and God made	Par Lost 7.263
The Waters underneath from those above	Par Lost 7.268
As drops on dust conglobing from the drie;	Par Lost 7.292

From(*cont*)

None was, but from the Earth a dewie Mist	Par Lost 7.333
The Day from Night; and let them be for Signes,	Par Lost 7.341
And Light from Darkness to divide. God saw,	Par Lost 7.352
Transplanted from her cloudie Shrine, and plac'd	Par Lost 7.360
Thir small peculiar, though from human sight	Par Lost 7.368
From him, for other light she needed none	Par Lost 7.378
Thir Brood as numerous hatch, from the Egg that soon	Par Lost 7.418
From Branch to Branch the smaller Birds with song	Par Lost 7.433
As from his Laire the wilde Beast where he wonns	Par Lost 7.457
His hinder parts, then springs as broke from Bonds,	Par Lost 7.465
In Hillocks; the swift Stag from under ground	Par Lost 7.469
Bore up his branching head: scarse from his mould	Par Lost 7.470
Govern the rest, self-knowing, and from thence	Par Lost 7.510
Yet not till the Creator from his work	Par Lost 7.551
In prospect from his Throne, how good, how faire,	Par Lost 7.556
The great Creator from his work returnd	Par Lost 7.567
Was set, and twilight from the East came on,	Par Lost 7.583
Author and end of all things, and from work	Par Lost 7.591
As resting on that day from all his work,	Par Lost 7.593
Fuming from Golden Censers hid the Mount.	Par Lost 7.600
Then from the Giant Angels; thee that day	Par Lost 7.605
Thee to diminish, and from thee withdraw	Par Lost 7.612
Thou usest, and from thence creat'st more good.	Par Lost 7.616
From Heaven Gate not farr, founded in view	Par Lost 7.618
From the beginning, that posteritie	Par Lost 7.638
With lowliness Majestic from her seat,	Par Lost 8.42
With conjugal Caresses, from his Lip	Par Lost 8.56
And from about her shot Darts of desire	Par Lost 8.62
From Man or Angel the great Architect	Par Lost 8.72
Who since the Morning hour set out from Heav'n	Par Lost 8.111
God to remove his wayes from human sense,	Par Lost 8.119
Plac'd Heav'n from Earth so farr, that earthly sight,	Par Lost 8.120
From the Suns beam meet Night, her other part	Par Lost 8.139
Sent from her through the wide transpicuous aire,	Par Lost 8.141
Hee from the East his flaming rode begin,	Par Lost 8.162
Or Shee from West her silent course advance	Par Lost 8.163
And freed from intricacies, taught to live,	Par Lost 8.182
To interrupt the sweet of Life, from which	Par Lost 8.184
From use, obscure and suttle, but to know	Par Lost 8.192
Therefore from this high pitch let us descend	Par Lost 8.198
And hunger both, from labour, at the houre	Par Lost 8.213
Induc'd me. As new wak't from soundest sleep	Par Lost 8.253
But who I was, or where, or from what cause,	Par Lost 8.270
From whom I have that thus I move and live,	Par Lost 8.281
From where I first drew Aire, and first beheld	Par Lost 8.284
Up hither, from among the Trees appeer'd	Par Lost 8.313
From that day mortal, and this happie State	Par Lost 8.331
Shalt loose, expell'd from hence into a World	Par Lost 8.332
From thee thir Names, and pay thee fealtie	Par Lost 8.344
From all Eternitie, for none I know	Par Lost 8.406
From prone, nor in thir wayes complacence find.	Par Lost 8.433
This answer from the gratious voice Divine.	Par Lost 8.436
From thence a Rib, with cordial spirits warme;	Par Lost 8.466
And in her looks, which from that time infus'd	Par Lost 8.474
And into all things from her Aire inspir'd	Par Lost 8.476
Whisper'd it to the Woods, and from thir wings	Par Lost 8.516
Flung Rose, flung Odours from the spicie Shrub,	Par Lost 8.517
Or from my side subducting, took perhaps	Par Lost 8.536
From all her words and actions mixt with Love	Par Lost 8.602
Who meet with various objects, from the sense	Par Lost 8.609
Sent from whose sovran goodness I adore.	Par Lost 8.647
From the thick shade, and *Adam* to his Bowre.	Par Lost 8.653
Twixt Day and Night, and now from end to end	Par Lost 9.51
From compassing the Earth, cautious of day,	Par Lost 9.59
From Pole to Pole, traversing each Colure;	Par Lost 9.66
From entrance or Cherubic Watch, by stealth	Par Lost 9.68
From *Eden* over *Pontus*, and the Poole	Par Lost 9.77
West from *Orontes* to the Ocean barr'd	Par Lost 9.80
From sharpest sight: for in the wilie Snake,	Par Lost 9.91
As from his wit and native suttletie	Par Lost 9.93
Thus he resolv'd, but first from inward griefe	Par Lost 9.97
Centring receav'st from all those Orbs; in thee,	Par Lost 9.109
Torment within me, as from the hateful siege	Par Lost 9.121
From servitude inglorious welnigh half	Par Lost 9.141
Exalted from so base original,	Par Lost 9.150
From dust: spite then with spite is best repaid.	Par Lost 9.178
From th' Earths great Altar send up silent praise	Par Lost 9.195
Of looks and smiles, for smiles from Reason flow,	Par Lost 9.239
Will keep from Wilderness with ease, as wide	Par Lost 9.245
Befall thee sever'd from me; for thou knowst	Par Lost 9.252
Our fealtie from God, or to disturb	Par Lost 9.262
And from the parting Angel over-heard	Par Lost 9.276
For such thou art, from sin and blame entire:	Par Lost 9.292
Thy absence from my sight, but to avoid	Par Lost 9.294
From thee alone, which on us both at once	Par Lost 9.303
I from the influence of thy looks receave	Par Lost 9.309
From his surmise prov'd false, find peace within,	Par Lost 9.333
Favour from Heav'n, our witness from th' event.	Par Lost 9.334
Secure from outward force; within himself	Par Lost 9.348
Were better, and most likelie if from mee	Par Lost 9.365
Thus saying, from her Husbands hand her hand	Par Lost 9.385
Yet Virgin of *Proserpina* from *Jove*.	Par Lost 9.396
Thou never from that houre in Paradise	Par Lost 9.406
From her best prop so farr, and storm so nigh.	Par Lost 9.433
Adjoynd, from each thing met conceaves delight,	Par Lost 9.449
From his own evil, and for the time remaind	Par Lost 9.464
Foe not informidable, exempt from wound,	Par Lost 9.486

From(*cont*)

From every Beast, more duteous at her call,	Par Lost 9.521
When from the boughes a savorie odour blow'n,	Par Lost 9.579
For high from ground the branches would require	Par Lost 9.590
But say, where grows the Tree, from hence how far?	Par Lost 9.617
Misleads th' amaz'd Night-wanderer from his way	Par Lost 9.640
There swallow'd up and lost, from succour farr.	Par Lost 9.642
Deterrd not from atchieving what might leade	Par Lost 9.696
On our belief, that all from them proceeds;	Par Lost 9.719
Though kept from Man, and worthy to be admir'd,	Par Lost 9.746
Conceales not from us, naming thee the Tree	Par Lost 9.751
Friendly to man, farr from deceit or guile.	Par Lost 9.772
Earth felt the wound, and Nature from her seat	Par Lost 9.782
Of knowledg, nor was God-head from her thought.	Par Lost 9.790
High and remote to see from thence distinct	Par Lost 9.812
May have diverted from continual watch	Par Lost 9.814
So saying, from the Tree her step she turnd,	Par Lost 9.834
From Nectar, drink of Gods. *Adam* the while	Par Lost 9.838
Scarse from the Tree returning; in her hand	Par Lost 9.850
The pain of absence from thy sight. But strange	Par Lost 9.861
From his slack hand the Garland wreath'd for *Eve*	Par Lost 9.892
Would never from my heart; no no, I feel	Par Lost 9.913
Bone of my Bone thou art, and from thy State	Par Lost 9.915
So having said, as one from sad dismay	Par Lost 9.917
Adam, from whose deare side I boast me sprung,	Par Lost 9.965
Such recompence best merits) from the bough	Par Lost 9.995
Earth trembl'd from her entrails, as again	Par Lost 9.1000
From this delightful Fruit, nor known till now	Par Lost 9.1023
As from unrest, and each the other viewing,	Par Lost 9.1052
Had shadow'd them from knowing ill, was gon,	Par Lost 9.1055
And honour from about them, naked left	Par Lost 9.1057
Herculean Samson from the Harlot-lap	Par Lost 9.1060
What best may from the present serve to hide	Par Lost 9.1092
The Parts of each for other, that seem most	Par Lost 9.1093
1667 'from'	
To sensual Appetite, who from beneathe	Par Lost 9.1129
Superior sway: from thus distemperd brest,	Par Lost 9.1131
1667 'From'	
Was I to have never parted from thy side?	Par Lost 9.1153
Up into Heav'n from Paradise in haste	Par Lost 10.17
From Earth arriv'd at Heaven Gate, displeas'd	Par Lost 10.22
Eternal Father from his secret Cloud,	Par Lost 10.32
From unsuccessful charge, be not dismaid,	Par Lost 10.35
Nor troubl'd at these tidings from the Earth,	Par Lost 10.36
When first this Tempter cross'd the Gulf from Hell.	Par Lost 10.39
Thus saying, from his radiant Seat he rose	Par Lost 10.85
Accompanied to Heaven Gate, from whence	Par Lost 10.88
From Noon, and gentle Aires due at thir hour	Par Lost 10.93
The Eevning coole when he from wrauth more coole	Par Lost 10.95
And from his presence hid themselves among	Par Lost 10.100
That from her hand I could suspect no ill,	Par Lost 10.140
Of mischief, and polluted from the end	Par Lost 10.167
Saw Satan fall like Lightning down from Heav'n,	Par Lost 10.184
Prince of the Aire; then rising from his Grave	Par Lost 10.185
Araying cover'd from his Fathers sight.	Par Lost 10.223
For Death from Sin no power can separate.	Par Lost 10.251
Over this Maine from Hell to that new World	Par Lost 10.257
The savour of Death from all things there that live:	Par Lost 10.269
Sagacious of his Quarry from so farr.	Par Lost 10.281
Then Both from out Hell Gates into the waste	Par Lost 10.282
From each side shoaling towards the mouth of Hell.	Par Lost 10.288
Forfeit to Death; from hence a passage broad,	Par Lost 10.304
From *Susa* his *Memnonian* Palace high	Par Lost 10.308
First lighted from his Wing, and landed safe	Par Lost 10.316
From out of *Chaos* to the out side bare	Par Lost 10.317
Though distant from thee Worlds between, yet felt	Par Lost 10.362
Detain from following thy illustrious track.	Par Lost 10.367
As Battel hath adjudg'd, from this new World	Par Lost 10.377
His Quadrature, from thy Orbicular World,	Par Lost 10.381
Issuing from mee: on your joynt vigor now	Par Lost 10.405
As when the *Tartar* from his *Russian* Foe	Par Lost 10.431
Retires, or *Bactrian* Sophi from the hornes	Par Lost 10.433
Each hour their great adventurer from the search	Par Lost 10.440
Of lowest order, past; and from the dore	Par Lost 10.443
At last as from a Cloud his fulgent head	Par Lost 10.449
Rais'd from thir Dark *Divan*, and with like joy	Par Lost 10.457
From his Creator, and the more to increase	Par Lost 10.486
On all sides, from innumerable tongues	Par Lost 10.507
Cast on themselves from thir own mouths. There stood	Par Lost 10.547
From his transcendent Seat the Saints among,	Par Lost 10.614
Or down from Heav'n descend. Such was thir song,	Par Lost 10.648
Scarce tollerable, and from the North to call	Par Lost 10.654
Decrepit Winter, from the South to bring	Par Lost 10.655
From the Suns Axle; they with labour push'd	Par Lost 10.670
Was bid turn Reines from th' Equinoctial Rode	Par Lost 10.672
From cold *Estotiland*, and South as farr	Par Lost 10.686
The Sun, as from *Thyestean* Banquet, turn'd	Par Lost 10.688
Corrupt and Pestilent: Now from the North	Par Lost 10.695
With adverse blast up-turns them from the South	Par Lost 10.701
From *Serraliona;* thwart of these as fierce	Par Lost 10.703
Outrage from liveless things; but Discord first	Par Lost 10.707
Glar'd on him passing: these were from without	Par Lost 10.714
Accurst of blessed, hide me from the face	Par Lost 10.723
Mine own that bide upon me, all from mee	Par Lost 10.738
Did I request thee, Maker, from my Clay	Par Lost 10.743
From darkness to promote me, or here place	Par Lost 10.745
From this day onward, which I feel begun	Par Lost 10.811
If guiltless? But from me what can proceed,	Par Lost 10.824

From(*cont*)

I find no way, from deep to deeper plung'd!	Par Lost 10.844
Thy inward fraud, to warn all Creatures from thee	Par Lost 10.871
To trust thee from my side, imagin'd wise,	Par Lost 10.881
More to the part sinister from me drawn,	Par Lost 10.886
He added not, and from her turn'd, but *Eve*	Par Lost 10.909
The sentence from thy head remov'd may light	Par Lost 10.934
Immoveable till peace obtain'd from fault	Par Lost 10.938
Living or dying, from thee I will not hide	Par Lost 10.974
From Loves due Rites, Nuptial imbraces sweet,	Par Lost 10.994
From what we fear for both, let us make short,	Par Lost 10.1000
So snatcht will not exempt us from the paine	Par Lost 10.1025
That cuts us off from hope, and savours onely	Par Lost 10.1043
And sends a comfortable heat from farr,	Par Lost 10.1077
Frequenting, sent from hearts contrite, in sign	Par Lost 10.1091
From his displeasure; in whose look serene,	Par Lost 10.1094
Frequenting, sent from hearts contrite, in sign	Par Lost 10.1103
Praying, for from the Mercie-seat above	Par Lost 11.2
The stonie from thir hearts, & made new flesh	Par Lost 11.4
From thy implanted Grace in Man, these Sighs	Par Lost 11.23
Fruits of more pleasing savour from thy seed	Par Lost 11.26
From innocence. Now therefore bend thine eare	Par Lost 11.30
Accept me, and in mee from these receave	Par Lost 11.37
Through Heav'ns wide bounds; from them I will not hide	Par Lost 11.68
Filld all the Regions: from thir blissful Bowrs	Par Lost 11.77
And took thir Seats; till from his Throne supream	Par Lost 11.82
And send him from the Garden forth to Till	Par Lost 11.97
Take to thee from among the Cherubim	Par Lost 11.100
Hast thee, and from the Paradise of God	Par Lost 11.104
From hallowd ground th' unholie, and denounce	Par Lost 11.106
To them and to thir Progenie from thence	Par Lost 11.107
Where entrance up from *Eden* easiest climbes,	Par Lost 11.119
Strength added from above, new hope to spring	Par Lost 11.138
The good which we enjoy, from Heav'n descends;	Par Lost 11.142
But that from us ought should ascend to Heav'n	Par Lost 11.143
I never from thy side henceforth to stray,	Par Lost 11.176
The Bird of *Jove*, stoopt from his aerie tour,	Par Lost 11.185
Down from a Hill the Beast that reigns in Woods,	Par Lost 11.187
From penaltie, because from death releast	Par Lost 11.197
Down from a Skie of Jasper lighted now	Par Lost 11.209
From yonder blazing Cloud that veils the Hill	Par Lost 11.229
Adam bowd low, hee Kingly from his State	Par Lost 11.249
Redeem thee quite from Deaths rapacious claime;	Par Lost 11.258
And send thee from the Garden forth to till	Par Lost 11.261
From the first op'ning bud, and gave ye Names,	Par Lost 11.277
Your Tribes, and water from th' ambrosial Fount?	Par Lost 11.279
With what to sight or smell was sweet; from thee	Par Lost 11.281
Adam by this from the cold sudden damp	Par Lost 11.293
Departure from this happy place, our sweet	Par Lost 11.303
As from his face I shall be hid, deprivd	Par Lost 11.316
Of lustre from the brook, in memorie,	Par Lost 11.325
Perhaps thy Capital Seate, from whence had spred	Par Lost 11.343
From all the ends of th' Earth, to celebrate	Par Lost 11.345
Ere thou from hence depart, know I am sent	Par Lost 11.356
By suffering, and earne rest from labour won,	Par Lost 11.375
Of Paradise the highest, from whose top	Par Lost 11.378
Of mightiest Empire, from the destind Walls	Par Lost 11.387
Or thence from *Niger* Flood to *Atlas* Mount	Par Lost 11.402
Michael from *Adams* eyes the Filme remov'd	Par Lost 11.412
And from the Well of Life three drops instill'd.	Par Lost 11.416
In some to spring from thee, who never touch'd	Par Lost 11.425
Nor sinn'd thy sin, yet from that derive	Par Lost 11.427
A sweatie Reaper from his Tillage brought	Par Lost 11.434
His Offring soon propitious Fire from Heav'n	Par Lost 11.441
From Heav'n acceptance; but the bloodie Fact	Par Lost 11.457
Tended the sick busiest from Couch to Couch;	Par Lost 11.490
To be thus wrested from us? rather why	Par Lost 11.503
In part, from such deformities be free,	Par Lost 11.513
In what thou eatst and drinkst, seeking from thence	Par Lost 11.532
From underground) the liquid Ore he dreind	Par Lost 11.570
Into fit moulds prepar'd; from which he formd	Par Lost 11.571
From the high neighbouring Hills, which was thir Seat,	Par Lost 11.575
Long had not walkt, when from the Tents behold	Par Lost 11.581
Holds on the same, from Woman to begin.	Par Lost 11.633
From Mans effeminate slackness it begins,	Par Lost 11.634
One way a Band select from forage drives	Par Lost 11.646
From a fat Meddow ground; or fleecy Flock,	Par Lost 11.648
Assaulting; others from the wall defend	Par Lost 11.657
And Judgment from above: him old and young	Par Lost 11.668
But hee the seventh from thee, whom thou beheldst	Par Lost 11.700
Exempt from Death; to shew thee what reward	Par Lost 11.709
Allurd them; thence from Cups to civil Broiles.	Par Lost 11.718
Then from the Mountain hewing Timber tall,	Par Lost 11.728
From under Heav'n; the Hills to their supplie	Par Lost 11.740
And fear of God, from whom thir pietie feign'd	Par Lost 11.799
To save himself and houshold from amidst	Par Lost 11.820
From standing lake to tripping ebbe, that stole	Par Lost 11.847
Forthwith from out the Arke a Raven flies,	Par Lost 11.855
Anon drie ground appeers, and from his Arke	Par Lost 11.861
Betok'ning peace from God, and Cov'nant new.	Par Lost 11.867
From him, and all his anger to forget.	Par Lost 11.878
And Man as from a second stock proceed.	Par Lost 12.7
Corn wine and oyle; and from the herd or flock,	Par Lost 12.19
Concord and law of Nature from the Earth,	Par Lost 12.29
Or from Heav'n claming second Sovrantie;	Par Lost 12.35
And from Rebellion shall derive his name,	Par Lost 12.36
Marching from *Eden* towards the West, shall finde	Par Lost 12.40
Boiles out from under ground, the mouth of Hell;	Par Lost 12.42

From(*cont*)

Authoritie usurpt, from God not giv'n:	Par Lost 12.66
Reserving, human left from human free.	Par Lost 12.71
Twinn'd, and from her hath no dividual being:	Par Lost 12.85
From Reason, and to servitude reduce	Par Lost 12.89
Subjects him from without to violent Lords;	Par Lost 12.93
From vertue, which is reason, that no wrong,	Par Lost 12.98
Still tend from bad to worse, till God at last	Par Lost 12.106
His presence from among them, and avert	Par Lost 12.108
His holy Eyes; resolving from thenceforth	Par Lost 12.109
From all the rest, of whom to be invok'd,	Par Lost 12.112
A Nation from one faithful man to spring:	Par Lost 12.113
To call by Vision from his Fathers house,	Par Lost 12.121
Which he will shew him, and from him will raise	Par Lost 12.123
From *Hamath* Northward to the Desert South	Par Lost 12.139
From *Hermon* East to the great Western Sea,	Par Lost 12.141
From *Canaan*, to a Land hereafter call'd	Par Lost 12.156
Moses and *Aaron*) sent from God to claime	Par Lost 12.170
His people from enthralment, they return	Par Lost 12.171
Safe towards *Canaan* from the shoar advance	Par Lost 12.215
God from the Mount of *Sinai*, whose gray top	Par Lost 12.227
From *Abraham*, Son of *Isaac*, and from him	Par Lost 12.268
Here *Adam* interpos'd. O sent from Heav'n,	Par Lost 12.270
From shadowie Types to Truth, from Flesh to Spirit,	Par Lost 12.303
From imposition of strict Laws, to free	Par Lost 12.304
Acceptance of large Grace, from servil fear	Par Lost 12.305
From whom as oft he saves them penitent	Par Lost 12.319
Returnd from *Babylon* by leave of Kings	Par Lost 12.348
High in the love of Heav'n, yet from my Loynes	Par Lost 12.380
Thou shalt proceed, and from thy Womb the Son	Par Lost 12.381
Satan, whose fall from Heav'n, a deadlier bruise,	Par Lost 12.391
Thy ransom paid, which Man from death redeems,	Par Lost 12.424
In sin for ever lost from life; this act	Par Lost 12.429
Of washing them from guilt of sin to Life	Par Lost 12.443
All Nations they shall teach; for from that day	Par Lost 12.446
From God, and over wrauth grace shall abound.	Par Lost 12.478
Be sure they will, said th' Angel; but from Heav'n	Par Lost 12.485
With joy the tidings brought from Heav'n: at length	Par Lost 12.504
To all Beleevers; and from that pretense,	Par Lost 12.520
Last in the Clouds from Heav'n to be reveald	Par Lost 12.545
From the conflagrant mass, purg'd and refin'd,	Par Lost 12.548
Let us descend now therefore from this top	Par Lost 12.588
Th' Archangel stood, and from the other Hill	Par Lost 12.626
Ris'n from a River o're the marish glides,	Par Lost 12.630
From *Nazareth* the Son of *Joseph* deem'd	Par Reg 1.23
From Heav'n pronounc'd him his beloved Son.	Par Reg 1.32
From Hell's deep-vaulted Den to dwell in light,	Par Reg 1.116
From what consummate vertue I have chose	Par Reg 1.165
With solitude, till far from track of men,	Par Reg 1.191
What from within I feel my self, and hear	Par Reg 1.198
What from without comes often to my ears,	Par Reg 1.199
To rescue *Israel* from the *Roman* yoke,	Par Reg 1.217
A messenger from God fore-told thy birth	Par Reg 1.238
Guided the Wise Men thither from the East,	Par Reg 1.250
Which I believ'd was from above; but he	Par Reg 1.274
Me him (for it was shew'n him so from Heaven)	Par Reg 1.276
Heaven open'd her eternal doors, from whence	Par Reg 1.281
Audibly heard from Heav'n, pronounc'd me his,	Par Reg 1.284
The Authority which I deriv'd from Heaven.	Par Reg 1.289
Or Cedar, to defend him from the dew,	Par Reg 1.306
To warm him wet return'd from field at Eve,	Par Reg 1.318
So far from path or road of men, who pass	Par Reg 1.322
Proceeding from the mouth of God; who fed	Par Reg 1.350
With them from bliss to the bottomless deep,	Par Reg 1.361
Or range in th' Air, nor from the Heav'n of Heav'ns	Par Reg 1.366
From the beginning, and in lies wilt end;	Par Reg 1.408
Who boast'st release from Hell, and leave to come	Par Reg 1.409
But from him or his Angels President	Par Reg 1.447
But misery hath rested from me; where	Par Reg 1.470
And not inforc'd oft-times to part from truth;	Par Reg 1.472
From thee I can and must submiss endure	Par Reg 1.476
Her dictates from thy mouth? most men admire	Par Reg 1.482
Permission from above; thou canst not more.	Par Reg 1.496
Alas, from what high hope to what relapse	Par Reg 2.30
Hath rapt him from us? will he now retire	Par Reg 2.40
Thy Glory, free thy people from thir yoke,	Par Reg 2.48
Others return'd from Baptism, not her Son,	Par Reg 2.61
From the bleak air; a Stable was our warmth,	Par Reg 2.74
From *Egypt* home return'd, in *Nazareth*	Par Reg 2.79
Son own'd from Heaven by his Father's voice;	Par Reg 2.85
Demonian Spirits now, from the Element	Par Reg 2.122
With more then humane gifts from Heaven adorn'd,	Par Reg 2.137
So spake the old Serpent doubting, and from all	Par Reg 2.147
At his command; when from amidst them rose	Par Reg 2.149
How would one look from his Majestick brow	Par Reg 2.216
Where still from shade to shade the Son of God	Par Reg 2.242
And from the sting of Famine fear no harm,	Par Reg 2.257
Though ravenous, taught to abstain from what they brought:	Par Reg 2.269
As lightly from his grassy Couch up rose	Par Reg 2.282
From whose high top to ken the prospect round,	Par Reg 2.286
Rain'd from Heaven Manna, and that Prophet bold	Par Reg 2.312
From all the Elements her choicest store	Par Reg 2.334
In pastry built, or from the spit, or boyl'd,	Par Reg 2.343
Gris-amber-steam'd; all Fish from Sea or Shore,	Par Reg 2.344
With fruits and flowers from *Amalthea*'s horn,	Par Reg 2.356
From their soft wings, and *Flora*'s earliest smells.	Par Reg 2.365
Which way or from what hope dost thou aspire	Par Reg 2.417
Riches though offer'd from the hand of Kings.	Par Reg 2.449

From(*cont*)

By saving Doctrine, and from errour lead	Par Reg 2.474
Should Kings and Nations from thy mouth consult,	Par Reg 3.12
His wasted Country freed from *Punic* rage,	Par Reg 3.102
Glory from men, from all men good or bad,	Par Reg 3.114
Promiscuous from all Nations, Jew, or Greek,	Par Reg 3.118
From us his foes pronounc't glory he exacts.	Par Reg 3.120
From them who could return him nothing else,	Par Reg 3.129
Easily from possession won with arms;	Par Reg 3.156
Thy Country from her Heathen servitude;	Par Reg 3.176
From that placid aspect and meek regard,	Par Reg 3.217
Lay pleasant; from his side two rivers flow'd,	Par Reg 3.255
From the luxurious Kings of *Antioch* won.	Par Reg 3.297
He marches now in hast; see, though from far,	Par Reg 3.303
Of many Provinces from bound to bound;	Par Reg 3.315
From *Arachosia*, from *Candaor* East,	Par Reg 3.316
From *Atropatia* and the neighbouring plains	Par Reg 3.319
The City of *Gallaphrone*, from thence to win	Par Reg 3.340
Thus long from *Israel;* serving as of old	Par Reg 3.378
These if from servitude thou shalt restore	Par Reg 3.381
From *Egypt* to *Euphrates* and beyond	Par Reg 3.384
From God to worship Calves, the Deities	Par Reg 3.416
From Gentils, but by Circumcision vain,	Par Reg 3.425
Discover'd in his fraud, thrown from his hope,	Par Reg 4.3
From cold *Septentrion* blasts, thence in the midst	Par Reg 4.31
Or Embassies from Regions far remote	Par Reg 4.67
Or on the *Aemilian*, some from farthest South,	Par Reg 4.69
From the *Asian* Kings and *Parthian* among these,	Par Reg 4.73
From *India* and the golden *Chersoness*,	Par Reg 4.74
From *Gallia*, *Gades*, and the *Brittish* West,	Par Reg 4.77
Old, and lascivious, and from *Rome* retir'd	Par Reg 4.91
Might'st thou expel this monster from his Throne	Par Reg 4.100
A victor people free from servile yoke?	Par Reg 4.102
From Nations far and nigh; what honour that,	Par Reg 4.122
And from the daily Scene effeminate.	Par Reg 4.142
What both from Men and Angels I receive,	Par Reg 4.200
Nations besides from all the quarter'd winds,	Par Reg 4.202
When slipping from thy Mothers eye thou went'st	Par Reg 4.216
From Heaven descended to the low-rooft house	Par Reg 4.273
Wisest of men; from whose mouth issu'd forth	Par Reg 4.276
Light from above, from the fountain of light,	Par Reg 4.289
That rather *Greece* from us these Arts deriv'd;	Par Reg 4.338
Such are from God inspir'd, not such from thee;	Par Reg 4.350
From dews and damps of night his shelter'd head,	Par Reg 4.406
From many a horrid rift abortive pour'd	Par Reg 4.411
From the four hinges of the world, and fell	Par Reg 4.415
From drooping plant, or dropping tree; the birds	Par Reg 4.434
As false portents, not sent from God, but thee;	Par Reg 4.491
From that time seldom have I ceas'd to eye	Par Reg 4.507
Though not to be Baptiz'd, by voice from Heav'n	Par Reg 4.512
Therefore I watch'd thy footsteps from that hour,	Par Reg 4.522
To win him, or win from him what I can.	Par Reg 4.530
Worth naming Son of God by voice from Heav'n,	Par Reg 4.539
Receiving from his mother Earth new strength,	Par Reg 4.566
Fresh from his fall, and fiercer grapple joyn'd,	Par Reg 4.567
Cast her self headlong from th' *Ismenian* steep,	Par Reg 4.575
From his uneasie station, and upbore	Par Reg 4.584
Ambrosial, Fruits fetcht from the tree of life,	Par Reg 4.589
And from the fount of life Ambrosial drink,	Par Reg 4.590
Conceiving, or remote from Heaven, enshrin'd	Par Reg 4.598
Thou didst debel, and down from Heav'n cast	Par Reg 4.605
Or Lightning thou shalt fall from Heav'n trod down	Par Reg 4.620
From thy Demoniac holds, possession foul,	Par Reg 4.628
Sung Victor, and from Heavenly Feast refresht	Par Reg 4.637
Relieves me from my task of servile toyl,	Samson 5
Retiring from the popular noise, I seek	Samson 16
From restless thoughts, that like a deadly swarm	Samson 19
O wherefore was my birth from Heaven foretold	Samson 23
From off the Altar, where an Off'ring burn'd,	Samson 26
His Godlike presence, and from some great act	Samson 28
Should *Israel* from *Philistian* yoke deliver;	Samson 39
Then had I not been thus exil'd from light;	Samson 98
From worst of other evils, pains and wrongs,	Samson 105
Fled from his Lion ramp, old Warriors turn'd	Samson 139
Shut up from outward light	Samson 160
By how much from the top of wondrous glory,	Samson 167
From *Eshtaol* and *Zora*'s fruitful Vale	Samson 181
My Vessel trusted to me from above,	Samson 199
From intimate impulse, and therefore urg'd	Samson 223
I thought it lawful from my former act,	Samson 231
Defended *Israel* from the *Ammonite*,	Samson 285
From National obstriction, without taint	Samson 312
The secret wrested from me in her highth	Samson 384
And amorous reproaches to win from me	Samson 393
Thy penal forfeit from thy self; perhaps	Samson 508
Of birth from Heav'n foretold and high exploits,	Samson 525
Allure thee from the cool Crystalline stream.	Samson 546
I drank, from the clear milkie juice allaying	Samson 550
Whose drink was only from the liquid brook.	Samson 557
My Nation, and the work from Heav'n impos'd,	Samson 565
From the dry ground to spring, thy thirst to allay	Samson 582
From anguish of the mind and humours black,	Samson 600
And healing words from these thy friends admit.	Samson 605
Nor breath of Vernal Air from snowy *Alp*.	Samson 628
His destin'd from the womb,	Samson 634
Harsh, and of dissonant mood from his complaint,	Samson 662
Some sourse of consolation from above;	Samson 664
From thee on them, or them to thee of service.	Samson 686

From(*cont*)

More strength from me, then in thy self was found. Samson 789
And of my Nation chose thee from among Samson 877
Exempt from many a care and chance to which Samson 918
From forth this loathsom prison-house, to abide Samson 922
Her countrey from a fierce destroyer, chose Samson 985
Nor from that right to part an hour, Samson 1056
From the unforeskinn'd race, of whom thou bear'st Samson 1100
Certain to have won by mortal duel from thee, Samson 1102
Which long shall not with-hold mee from thy head, Samson 1125
Arm'd thee or charm'd thee strong, which thou from Heaven Samson 1134
Quite from his people, and delivered up Samson 1158
From thine, these evils I deserve and more, Samson 1169
Acknowledge them from God inflicted on me Samson 1170
To wring from me and tell to them my secret, Samson 1199
With strength sufficient and command from Heav'n Samson 1212
I was to do my part from Heav'n assign'd, Samson 1217
Sam. No man with-holds thee, nothing from thy hand Samson 1233
Off. Samson, this second message from our Lords Samson 1391
Fast by thy side, who from thy Fathers field Samson 1432
For never was from Heaven imparted Samson 1438
From slaughter of one foe could not ascend. Samson 1518
From whom could else a general cry be heard? Samson 1524
From other hands we need not much to fear. Samson 1526
As at some distance from the place of horrour, Samson 1550
(For so from such as nearer stood we heard) Samson 1631
Met from all parts to solemnize this Feast. Samson 1656
From under ashes into sudden flame, Samson 1691
From out her ashie womb now teem'd, Samson 1703
With God not parted from him, as was feard, Samson 1719
Sok't in his enemies blood, and from the stream Samson 1726
And from his memory inflame thir breasts Samson 1739
From whence captivity and loss of eyes. Samson 1744
Of true experience from this great event Samson 1756
But that by quick command from Soveran *Jove* Mask 41
From old, or modern Bard in Hall, or Bowr. Mask 45
  Trinity ms 'from' ←'by'
Bacchus that first from out the purple Grape, Mask 46
I shoot from Heav'n to give him safe convoy, Mask 81
From her cabin'd loop hole peep, Mask 140
Rose from the hindmost wheels of *Phoebus* wain. Mask 190
  line not in Bridgewater ms
Had stole them from me, els O theevish Night Mask 195
To give me answer from her mossie Couch. Mask 276
Co. Could that divide you from neer-ushering guides? Mask 279
In his loose traces from the furrow came, Mask 292
Plucking ripe clusters from the tender shoots, Mask 296
Co. Due west it rises from this shrubby point. Mask 306
And every bosky bourn from side to side Mask 313
From her thach't pallat rowse, if otherwise Mask 318
Though a rush Candle from the wicker hole Mask 338
Or whistle from the Lodge, or village cock Mask 346
From the chill dew, amongst rude burrs and thistles? Mask 352
Far from the cheerfull haunt of men, and herds, Mask 388
From the rash hand of bold Incontinence. Mask 397
Antiquity from the old Schools of Greece Mask 439
Slip't from the fold, or young Kid lost his dam, Mask 498
  Trinity ms 'from' ←'ore'
How to secure the Lady from surprisal, Mask 618
Here dwel no frowns, nor anger, from these gates Mask 667
That thou hast banish't from thy tongue with lies, Mask 692
I would not taste thy treasonous offer; none Mask 702
  Trinity ms 'would not taste' ←'should reject' ←'hate it from thy hands'
And fetch their precepts from the *Cynick* Tub, Mask 708
They had their name thence; course complexions Mask 749
  Trinity ms 'thence' ←'from thence' ←'thence'
There is a gentle Nymph not farr from hence, Mask 824
That had the Scepter from his father *Brute*. Mask 828
From thy coral-pav'n bed, Mask 886
Whilst from off the waters fleet Mask 896
Drops that from my fountain pure, Mask 912
From a thousand petty rills, Mask 926
That tumble down the snowy hills: Mask 927
  Trinity ms 'the' ←'from'
Spir. To the Ocean now I fly, Mask 976
  B.M. ms 'From the Heav'ns'
  Bridgewater ms 'From the heavens'
And from her fair unspotted side Mask 1009
  line not in Bridgewater ms
And from thence can soar as soon Mask 1016
yet thence I come and oft from thence behold Mask Tr. ms 10.18
she might be free from perill where she is Mask Tr. ms 16.42
she might be free from perill where she is, Mask Br. ms 395
From his watch-towre in the skies, Allegro 43
From the side of som Hoar Hill, Allegro 55
From betwixt two aged Okes, Allegro 82
From golden slumber on a bed Allegro 146
Far from all resort of mirth, Penseroso 81
To bless the dores from nightly harm: Penseroso 84
Might raise *Musaeus* from his bower, Penseroso 104
With minute drops from off the Eaves. Penseroso 130
Or fright them from their hallow'd haunt. Penseroso 138
Hide me from Day's garish eie, Penseroso 141
Is that which we from hence descry Arcades 3
Of detraction from her praise, Arcades 11
For know by lot from *Jove* I am the powr Arcades 44
And all my Plants I save from nightly ill, Arcades 48

From(*cont*)

And from the Boughs brush off the evil dew, Arcades 50
From the stony *Maenalus*, Arcades 102
That from beneath the seat of *Jove* doth spring, Lycidas 16
From the glad sound would not be absent long, Lycidas 35
That blows from off each beaked Promontory, Lycidas 94
That not a blast was from his dungeon stray'd, Lycidas 97
And wipe the tears for ever from his eyes. Lycidas 181
Our great redemption from above did bring; Nativity 4
See how from far upon the Eastern rode Nativity 22
From out his secret Altar toucht with hallow'd fire. Nativity 28
And leprous sin will melt from earthly mould, Nativity 138
Shall from the surface to the center shake; Nativity 162
But now begins; for from this happy day Nativity 167
Apollo from his shrine Nativity 176
Inspire's the pale-ey'd Priest from the prophetic cell. Nativity 180
From haunted spring, and dale Nativity 184
He feels from *Juda's* Land Nativity 221
And past from *Pharian* fields to *Canaan* Land, Psalm 114, 3
That glassy flouds from rugged rocks can crush, Psalm 114, 17
And make soft rills from fiery flint-stones gush. Psalm 114, 18
He brought from thence his *Israel*. Psalm 136, 42
And freed us from the slavery Psalm 136, 81
He wanderd long, till thee he spy'd from farr, Fair Inf 17
Down he descended from his Snow-soft chaire, Fair Inf 19
Unhous'd thy Virgin Soul from her fair biding place. Fair Inf 21
Hid from the world in a low delved tombe; Fair Inf 32
And why from us so quickly thou didst take thy flight. Fair Inf 42
Wert thou some Starr which from the ruin'd roofe Fair Inf 43
To earth from thy praefixed seat didst poast, Fair Inf 59
Driving dum silence from the portal dore, Vacation 5
And from thy wardrope bring thy chiefest treasure; Vacation 18
From eyes of mortals walk invisible, Vacation 66
And those that cannot live from him asunder Vacation 77
From others he shall stand in need of nothing, Vacation 81
Seas wept from our deep sorrow, Circum 9
snatch us from earth a while Musick Tr. ms 4.07
More then she could own from Earth. Winchester 6
Sav'd with care from Winters nip, Winchester 36
New shot up from vernall showr; Winchester 40
Sent thee from the banks of *Came*, Winchester 59
Comes dancing from the East, and leads with her May Morn 2
The Flowry *May*, who from her green lap throws May Morn 3
Hath from the leaves of thy unvalu'd Book, Shakespear 11
As thou from yeer to yeer hast sung too late Sonnet 1, 11
Guard them, and him within protect from harms, Sonnet 8, 4
To save th'*Athenian* Walls from ruine bare. Sonnet 8, 14
But from that mark how far they roave we see Sonnet 12, 13
Thy worth and skill exempts thee from the throng, Sonnet 13, 5
When Faith and Love which parted from thee never, Sonnet 14, 1
Of Death, call'd Life; which us from Life doth sever. Sonnet 14, 4
when as they journey'd from this dark abode Sonnet 14, Tr. ms 41.07
Till Truth, and Right from Violence be freed, Sonnet 15, 11
And Public Faith cleard from the shamefull brand Sonnet 15, 12
Helpe us to save free Conscience from the paw Sonnet 16, 13
The triple Tyrant: that from these may grow Sonnet 18, 12
From the hard Season gaining: time will run Sonnet 20, 5
Of which all Europe talks from side to side. Sonnet 22, 12
Brought to me like *Alcestis* from the grave, Sonnet 23, 2
Rescu'd from death by force though pale and faint. Sonnet 23, 4
Mine as whom washt from spot of child-bed taint, Sonnet 23, 5
From them whose sin ye envi'd, not abhor'd, Forcers 4
Their bonds, and cast from us, no more to wear, Psalm 2, 7
And heard me from his holy mount. Psalm 3, 12
Hast broke the teeth. This help was from the Lord Psalm 3, 23
Jehovah from on high Psalm 4, 17
And from their plenteous grounds Psalm 4, 35
Their joy, while thou from blame Psalm 5, 34
Depart from me, for the voice of my weeping Psalm 6, 17
All people from the worlds foundation. Psalm 7, 30
As in a womb, and from that mould Psalm 7, 53
Shine forth, *and from thy cloud give light*, Psalm 80, 7
A Vine from Aegypt thou hast brought, Psalm 80, 33
From Heav'n, thy Seat divine, Psalm 80, 58
So shall we not go back from thee Psalm 80, 73
From whence they might not swerve. Psalm 81, 16
From burden, *and from slavish toyle* Psalm 81, 21
His hands from pots, *and mirie soyle* Psalm 81, 23
And we would feed them *from the shock* Psalm 81, 65
And satisfie them from the rock Psalm 81, 67
And rescue from the hands Psalm 82, 14
Like stubble from the wind. Psalm 83, 52
There ev'n the Sparrow *freed from wrong* Psalm 84, 9
And home they fly from round the Coasts Psalm 84, 15
They journey on from strength to strength Psalm 84, 25
No good from them shall be with-held Psalm 84, 43
Thou hast from *hard* Captivity Psalm 85, 3
From thy fierce wrath which we had prov'd Psalm 85, 11
From age to age on us? Psalm 85, 20
Truth from the earth *like to a flowr* Psalm 85, 45
And Justice from her heavenly bowr Psalm 85, 47
Eev'n from the lowest Hell set free Psalm 86, 47
From deepest darkness foul. Psalm 86, 48
From life discharg'd and parted quite Psalm 88, 17
Them from thy hand deliver'd o're Psalm 88, 23
Thy wrath *from which no shelter saves* Psalm 88, 29
Thou dost my friends from me estrange, Psalm 88, 33
And praise thee *from their loathsom bed* Psalm 88, 43

From(*cont*)
And hide thy face from me, Psalm 88, 58
With terror sent from thee; Psalm 88, 60
And sever'd from me far. Psalm 88, 70
Front
Advanc't in view, they stand, a horrid Front Par Lost 1.563
ms 'front'
A Pillar of State; deep on his Front engraven Par Lost 2.302
Thy miscreated Front athwart my way Par Lost 2.683
Over the *Caspian*, then stand front to front Par Lost 2.716
His fair large Front and Eye sublime declar'd Par Lost 4.300
Gabriel from the Front thus calld aloud. Par Lost 4.865
A dreadful intervall, and Front to Front Par Lost 6.105
Vanguard, to Right and Left the Front unfould; Par Lost 6.558
Had ended; when to Right and Left the Front Par Lost 6.569
To entertain them fair with open Front Par Lost 6.611
His Stature, and upright with Front serene Par Lost 7.509
Sticks no dishonor on our Front, but turns Par Lost 9.330
Thir motion, at whose Front a flaming Sword, Par Lost 12.592
Homeward returning. High in Front advanc't, Par Lost 12.632
1669 'front'
The mark of fool set on his front? Samson 496
To hide her guilty front with innocent Snow, Nativity 39
His starry front low-rooft beneath the skies; Passion 18
Fronted
With rapid wheels, or fronted Brigads form. Par Lost 2.532
Frontier
And *Accaron* and *Gaza*'s frontier bounds. Par Lost 1.466
Frontiers
Pursuing. I upon my Frontieres here Par Lost 2.998
Frontispiece
With Frontispice of Diamond and Gold Par Lost 3.506
Fronts
And all this tract that fronts the falling Sun Mask 30
Frore
Burns frore, and cold performs th' effect of Fire. Par Lost 2.595
Frost
Seed time and Harvest, Heat and hoary Frost Par Lost 11.899
Nipt with the lagging rear of winters frost. Samson 1577
Or Frost to Flowers, that their gay wardrop wear, Lycidas 47
1638 'frost'
Trinity ms 'frost'
Froth
Vain battry, and in froth or bubbles end; Par Reg 4.20
Froth-becurled
And sought to hide his froth-becurled head Psalm 114, 8
Frounced
Not trickt and frounc't as she was wont, Penseroso 123
Frown
No second stroke intend, and such a frown Par Lost 2.713
Grew darker at thir frown, so matcht they stood; Par Lost 2.720
Dark, waste, and wild, under the frown of Night Par Lost 3.424
Or Captive drag'd in Chains, with hostile frown Par Lost 6.260
To gloss upon, and censuring, frown or smile? Samson 948
Fear'd her stern frown, and she was queen oth' Woods. Mask 446
1637 'frowne'
Trinity ms 'frowne'
Bridgewater ms 'frowne'
Co. Why are you vext Lady? why do you frown? Mask 666
1637 'frowne'
Trinity ms 'frow' ←'frowne', ms defective
Bridgewater ms 'frowne'
Behold *us, but without a frown,* Psalm 80, 59
At thy rebuke and frown. Psalm 80, 68
Frowned
So frownd the mighty Combatants, that Hell Par Lost 2.719
Frowning
He ended frowning, and his look denounc'd Par Lost 2.106
To which the Fiend thus answerd frowning stern. Par Lost 4.924
Wilt thou thy frowning ire extend Psalm 85, 19
Frowns
Here dwel no frowns, nor anger, from these gates Mask 667
Bridgewater ms 'frownes'
Frozen
Pour'd never from her frozen loyns, to pass Par Lost 1.352
Beyond this flood a frozen Continent Par Lost 2.587
Immovable, infixt, and frozen round, Par Lost 2.602
O're many a Frozen, many a fierie Alpe, Par Lost 2.620
The frozen earth; and cloth in fresh attire Sonnet 20, 7
Frugal
Save what by frugal storing firmness gains Par Lost 5.324
How Nature wise and frugal could commit Par Lost 8.26
Frugal, and mild, and temperate, conquer'd well, Par Reg 4.134
Fruit
Of Mans First Disobedience, and the Fruit Par Lost 1.1
ms 'fruit'
Of goodliest Trees loaden with fairest Fruit, Par Lost 4.147
High eminent, blooming Ambrosial Fruit Par Lost 4.219
Others whose fruit burnisht with Golden Rinde Par Lost 4.249
In Paradise that bear delicious fruit Par Lost 4.422
His orient Beams, on herb, tree, fruit, and flour, Par Lost 4.644
On this delightful land, nor herb, fruit, floure, Par Lost 4.652
And O fair Plant, said he, with fruit surcharg'd, Par Lost 5.58
But he thus overjoy'd, O Fruit Divine, Par Lost 5.67
Even to my mouth of that same fruit held part Par Lost 5.83
Alcinous reign'd, fruit of all kindes, in coate, Par Lost 5.341
Spirits odorous breathes: flours and thir fruit Par Lost 5.482
Fruit of delicious Vines, the growth of Heav'n. Par Lost 5.635

Fruit(*cont*)
With Plant, Fruit, Flour Ambrosial, Gemms & Gold, Par Lost 6.475
And Fruit Tree yielding Fruit after her kind; Par Lost 7.311
Thir branches hung with copious Fruit; or gemm'd Par Lost 7.325
And freely all thir pleasant fruit for food Par Lost 7.540
Load'n with fairest Fruit that hung to the Eye Par Lost 8.307
To Till and keep, and of the Fruit to eate: Par Lost 8.320
Loaden with fruit of fairest colours mixt, Par Lost 9.577
Of that alluring fruit, urg'd me so keene. Par Lost 9.588
The vertue of that Fruit, in thee first prov'd: Par Lost 9.616
As leaves a greater store of Fruit untoucht, Par Lost 9.621
Fruitless to mee, though Fruit be here to excess, Par Lost 9.648
Indeed? hath God then said that of the Fruit Par Lost 9.656
To whom thus *Eve* yet sinless. Of the Fruit Par Lost 9.659
But of the Fruit of this fair Tree amidst Par Lost 9.661
How should ye? by the Fruit? it gives you Life Par Lost 9.686
Causes import your need of this fair Fruit. Par Lost 9.731
Fixt on the Fruit she gaz'd, which to behold Par Lost 9.735
So savorie of that Fruit, which with desire, Par Lost 9.741
Of this fair Fruit, our doom is, we shall die. Par Lost 9.763
Here grows the Cure of all, this Fruit Divine, Par Lost 9.776
Forth reaching to the Fruit, she pluck'd, she eat: Par Lost 9.781
In Fruit she never tasted, whether true Par Lost 9.788
And thy fair Fruit let hang, as to no end Par Lost 9.798
A bough of fairest fruit that downie smil'd, Par Lost 9.851
Hath eat'n of the fruit, and is become, Par Lost 9.869
The sacred Fruit forbidd'n? som cursed fraud Par Lost 9.904
That sacred Fruit, sacred to abstinence, Par Lost 9.924
Is not so hainous now, foretasted Fruit, Par Lost 9.929
If any be, of tasting this fair Fruit, Par Lost 9.972
She gave him of that fair enticing Fruit Par Lost 9.996
Wherewith to scorne the Earth: but that false Fruit Par Lost 9.1011
From this delightful Fruit, nor known till now Par Lost 9.1023
Soon as the force of that fallacious Fruit, Par Lost 9.1046
Bad Fruit of Knowledge, if this be to know, Par Lost 9.1073
The Figtree, not that kind for Fruit renown'd, Par Lost 9.1101
Her Husband shee, to taste the fatall fruit, Par Lost 10.4
The high Injunction not to taste that Fruit, Par Lost 10.13
Thir penance, laden with Fruit, like that Par Lost 10.550
1667 'fair Fruit'
Thir appetite with gust, instead of Fruit Par Lost 10.565
Beneath *Magellan*. At that tasted Fruit Par Lost 10.687
Fruit of thy Womb: On mee the Curse aslope Par Lost 10.1053
Of that defended Fruit; but let him boast Par Lost 11.86
With whose stol'n Fruit Man once more to delude. Par Lost 11.125
Which that false Fruit that promis'd clearer sight Par Lost 11.413
So maist thou live, till like ripe Fruit thou drop Par Lost 11.535
What it devours not, Herb, or Fruit, or Graine, Par Lost 12.184
To bring me Berries, or such cooling fruit Mask 186
Bridgewater ms 'fruite'
To save her blossoms, and defend her fruit Mask 396
Trinity ms 'fruite' ←'frite'
Bridgewater ms 'fruite'
Spoil'd at once both fruit and tree: Winchester 30
To yield his fruit, and his leaf shall not fall, Psalm 1, 9
Fruitage
Of life ambrosial frutage bear, and vines Par Lost 5.427
The Frutage fair to sight, like that which grew Par Lost 10.561
Fruitful
See golden days, fruitful of golden deeds, Par Lost 3.337
More fruitful, which instructs us not to spare. Par Lost 5.320
Haile Mother of Mankind, whose fruitful Womb Par Lost 5.388
Be fruitful, multiply, and in the Seas Par Lost 7.396
Be fruitful, multiplie, and fill the Earth, Par Lost 7.531
But in the fruitful Earth; there first receavd Par Lost 8.96
From *Eshtaol* and *Zora*'s fruitful Vale Samson 181
As through a fruitfull watry Dale Psalm 84, 23
Fruition
God-like fruition, quitted all to save Par Lost 3.307
Casual fruition, nor in Court Amours Par Lost 4.767
Fruitless
Fruitless imbraces: or they led the Vine Par Lost 5.215
Fruitless to mee, though Fruit be here to excess, Par Lost 9.648
The fruitless hours, but neither self-condemning, Par Lost 9.1188
Fruits
Reaping immortal fruits of joy and love, Par Lost 3.67
All who have thir reward on Earth, the fruits Par Lost 3.451
Blossoms and Fruits at once of golden hue Par Lost 4.148
More grateful, to thir Supper Fruits they fell, Par Lost 4.331
Nectarine Fruits which the compliant boughes Par Lost 4.332
For dinner savourie fruits, of taste to please Par Lost 5.304
Then with these various fruits the Trees of God Par Lost 5.390
To enter, and these earthly fruits to taste, Par Lost 5.464
Rose, and went forth among her Fruits and Flours, Par Lost 8.44
Fruits in her soft'nd Soile, for some to eate Par Lost 8.147
Then Fruits of Palm-tree pleasantest to thirst Par Lost 8.212
I mean of Taste, Sight, Smell, Herbs, Fruits, and Flours, Par Lost 8.527
Great are thy Vertues, doubtless, best of Fruits. Par Lost 9.745
Thou therefore on these Herbs, and Fruits, and Flours Par Lost 10.603
See Father, what first fruits on Earth are sprung Par Lost 11.22
Fruits of more pleasing savour from thy seed Par Lost 11.26
Less pure, accustomd to immortal Fruits? Par Lost 11.285
Offer sweet smelling Gumms and Fruits and Flours: Par Lost 11.327
First Fruits, the green Eare, and the yellow Sheaf, Par Lost 11.435
To bring forth fruits Joy and eternal Bliss. Par Lost 12.551
With fruits and flowers from *Amalthea*'s horn, Par Reg 2.356
These are not Fruits forbidden, no interdict Par Reg 2.369
That screen'd the fruits of the earth and seats of men Par Reg 4.30

Fruits*(cont)*
Ambrosial, Fruits fetcht from the tree of life, Par Reg 4.589
Covering the earth with odours, fruits, and flocks, Mask 712
Trinity ms 'fruits' ←'& with fruits'
& fruits of golden rind, on whose faire tree Mask Tr. ms 10.08
Her fruits *to be our food*. Psalm 85, 52
Fruit-trees
Of Fruit-trees overwoodie reachd too farr Par Lost 5.213
Frustrate
Then wise to frustrate all our plots and wiles. Par Lost 2.193
His end, and frustrate thine, shall he fulfill Par Lost 3.157
Be frustrate, do, undo, and labour loose, Par Lost 9.944
Blow'n vagabond or frustrate: in they passd Par Lost 11.16
Be frustrate all ye stratagems of Hell, Par Reg 1.180
Nor shall his wondrous gifts be frustrate thus. Samson 589
To frustrate and dissolve these Magic spells, Samson 1149
Frustrated
And frustrated the conquest fraudulent: Par Reg 4.609
Fry
With Frie innumerable swarme, and Shoales Par Lost 7.400
Fuel
Thy words by adding fuel to the flame? Samson 1351
If once his wrath take fire like fuel sere. Psalm 2, 27
Fuelled
And fewel'd entrals thence conceiving Fire, Par Lost 1.234
ms 'fewell'd'
Fugitive
False fugitive, and to thy speed add wings, Par Lost 2.700
Thou surely hadst not come sole fugitive. Par Lost 4.923
Thrice Fugitive about *Troy* Wall; or rage Par Lost 9.16
The Fugitive Bond-woman with her Son Par Reg 2.308
Fugitives
Heav'ns fugitives, and for thir dwelling place Par Lost 2.57
Fugue
Fled and pursu'd transverse the resonant fugue. Par Lost 11.563
Fulfil
And works of love or enmity fulfill. Par Lost 1.431
His end, and frustrate thine, shall he fulfill Par Lost 3.157
That his great purpose he might so fulfill, Par Lost 6.675
Fulfill'd, which to fulfil is all my bliss. Par Lost 6.729
How we might best fulfill the work which here Par Lost 9.230
The Law of God exact he shall fulfill Par Lost 12.402
Alone fulfill the Law; thy punishment Par Lost 12.404
So shalt thou best fullfil, best verifie Par Reg 3.177
Fulfilled
So spake th' Eternal Father, and fulfilld Par Lost 5.246
Fulfill'd, which to fulfil is all my bliss. Par Lost 6.729
And thy request think now fulfill'd, that ask'd Par Lost 7.635
This turn hath made amends; thou hast fulfill'd Par Lost 8.491
Here Nature seems fulfilld in all her ends. Par Lost 11.602
But contrary unweeting he fulfill'd Par Reg 1.126
All things are best fullfil'd in their due time, Par Reg 3.182
When Prophesies of thee are best fullfill'd. Par Reg 4.381
Had been fulfilld but through mine own default, Samson 45
Living or dying thou hast fulfill'd Samson 1661
Fulfilling
But by fulfilling that which thou didst want, Par Lost 12.396
Meekly compos'd awaited the fulfilling: Par Reg 2.108
And that her raign had here its last fulfilling; Nativity 106
Fulgent
At last as from a Cloud his fulgent head Par Lost 10.449
Full
With gay Religions full of Pomp and Gold, Par Lost 1.372
Th' Imperial Ensign, which full high advanc't Par Lost 1.536
Put forth at full, but still his strength conceal'd, Par Lost 1.641
Full Counsel must mature: Peace is despaird, Par Lost 1.660
Frequent and full. After short silence then Par Lost 1.797
Yielded with full consent. The happier state Par Lost 2.24
Though full of pain, this intellectual being, Par Lost 2.147
Sparkl'd in all thir eyes; with full assent Par Lost 2.388
With wide *Cerberian* mouths full loud, and rung Par Lost 2.655
To whom the Goblin full of wrauth reply'd, Par Lost 2.688
The most averse, thee chiefly, who full oft Par Lost 2.763
And me his Parent would full soon devour Par Lost 2.805
Thither full fraught with mischievous revenge, Par Lost 2.1054
Beneath thy Sentence; Hell her numbers full, Par Lost 3.332
The full blaze of thy beams, and through a cloud Par Lost 3.378
In full harmonic number joind, thir songs Par Lost 4.687
Our circuit meets full West. As flame they part Par Lost 4.784
Full Orb'd the Moon, and with more pleasing light Par Lost 5.42
Full to the utmost measure of what bliss Par Lost 5.517
The full relation, which must needs be strange, Par Lost 5.556
Of surfet where full measure onely bounds Par Lost 5.639
line not in 1667 edition
In full resplendence, Heir of all my might, Par Lost 5.720
Had circl'd his full Orbe, the birth mature Par Lost 5.862
Of hard contents, and full of force urg'd home, Par Lost 6.622
Shon full, he all his Father full exprest Par Lost 6.720
And full of wrauth bent on his Enemies. Par Lost 6.826
All but the Throne it self of God. Full soon Par Lost 6.834
Great things, and full of wonder in our eares, Par Lost 7.70
His mirror, with full face borrowing her Light Par Lost 7.377
Limb'd and full grown: out of the ground up rose Par Lost 7.456
Squar'd in full Legion (such command we had) Par Lost 8.232
That kept thir watch; thence full of anguish driv'n, Par Lost 9.62
Of thy full branches offer'd free to all; Par Lost 9.802
Full happiness with mee, or rather not, Par Lost 9.819
And full of Peace, now tost and turbulent: Par Lost 9.1126
Full*(cont)*
Blaz'd forth unclouded Deitie; he full Par Lost 10.65
But up and enter now into full bliss. Par Lost 10.503
His full wrauth whose thou feelst as yet lest part, Par Lost 10.951
Lamenting turnd full sad; O what are these, Par Lost 11.675
And full of peace, denouncing wrauth to come Par Lost 11.815
With purpose to resign them in full time Par Lost 12.301
Light out of darkness! full of doubt I stand, Par Lost 12.473
With prosperous wing full summ'd to tell of deeds Par Reg 1.14
But his growth now to youths full flowr, displaying Par Reg 1.67
Of the most High, who in full frequence bright Par Reg 1.128
Full weight must be transferr'd upon my head. Par Reg 1.267
Now full, that I no more should live obscure, Par Reg 1.287
Full forty days he pass'd, whether on hill Par Reg 1.303
His words, his wisdom full of grace and truth, Par Reg 2.34
Full grown to Man, acknowledg'd, as I hear, Par Reg 2.83
Consenting in full frequence was impowr'd, Par Reg 2.130
For *Solomon* he liv'd at ease, and full Par Reg 2.201
Thou on the Throne of *David* in full glory, Par Reg 3.383
David's true heir, and his full Scepter sway Par Reg 3.405
Now at full age, fulness of time, thy season, Par Reg 4.380
Of Angels on full sail of wing flew nigh, Par Reg 4.582
Who hast of sorrow thy full load besides; Samson 214
And hath full right to exempt Samson 310
Full of divine instinct, after some proof Samson 526
That wisest and best men full oft beguil'd Samson 759
While I at home sate full of cares and fears Samson 805
Took full possession of me and prevail'd; Samson 869
Hath paid his ransom now and full discharge. Samson 1573
Who ripe, and frolick of his full grown age, Mask 59
When for their teeming Flocks, and granges full Mask 175
With such a full and unwithdrawing hand, Mask 711
Natures full blessings would be well dispenc't Mask 772
Their full tribute never miss Mask 925
And Crop-full out of dores he flings, Allegro 113
To the full voic'd Quire below, Penseroso 162
Which I full oft amidst these shades alone Arcades 42
Full little thought they than, Nativity 88
Make up full consort to th' Angelike symphony. Nativity 132
Full and perfect is, Nativity 166
The painted Heav'ns so full of state. Psalm 136, 18
But full soon they did devour Psalm 136, 53
And with full hand supplies their need. Psalm 136, 86
He thought it toucht his Deitie full neer, Fair Inf 10
That far events full wisely could presage, Vacation 70
And the full wrath beside Circum 23
For he had any time this ten yeers full, Carrier 7
My hasting dayes flie on with full career, Sonnet 7, 3
Full sight of her in Heaven without restraint, Sonnet 23, 8
Earths utmost bounds: them shalt thou bring full low Psalm 2, 19
Unto Jehovah, he full soon reply'd Psalm 3, 11
Will grant thy full demand. Psalm 81, 44
Exalt their heads full hie. Psalm 83, 8
And to his Saints *full dear*, Psalm 85, 32
Art full of mercy, thou *alone* Psalm 86, 15
Philistia *full of scorn*, Psalm 87, 14
Full sore doth press on me; Psalm 88, 30
Full-blazing
Sometimes towards Heav'n and the full-blazing Sun, Par Lost 4.29
Fullness
In whom the fulness dwels of love divine, Par Lost 3.225
Now at full age, fulness of time, thy season, Par Reg 4.380
Fully
How fully hast thou satisfi'd mee, pure Par Lost 8.180
Them fully satisfied, and thee appease. Par Lost 10.79
With odds what Warr hath lost, and fully aveng'd Par Lost 10.374
By one mans firm obedience fully tri'd Par Reg 1.4
Fully reveng'd, hath left them years of mourning, Samson 1712
Fulmined
Shook the Arsenal and fulmin'd over *Greece*, Par Reg 4.270
Fume
Then *Asmodeus* with the fishie fume, Par Lost 4.168
Is the prime Wisdom, what is more, is fume, Par Lost 8.194
Fumed
With incense, where the Golden Altar fum'd, Par Lost 11.18
Fumes
Bred of unkindly fumes, with conscious dreams Par Lost 9.1050
Whose heads that turbulent liquor fills with fumes. Samson 552
Fuming
Of leaves and fuming rills, *Aurora*'s fan, Par Lost 5.6
Fuming from Golden Censers hid the Mount. Par Lost 7.600
Functions
In all her functions weary of her self; Samson 596
Funeral
With silent obsequie and funeral train Samson 1732
On her hast'ning funerall. Winchester 46
Fur
To those budge doctors of the *Stoick* Furr, Mask 707
1637 'furre'
Trinity ms 'furre' ←'gowne'
Bridgewater ms 'furr'
Furies
Thither by harpy-footed Furies hail'd, Par Lost 2.596
Fierce as ten Furies, terrible as Hell, Par Lost 2.671
With terrors and with furies to the bounds Par Lost 6.859
Let in these wastful Furies, who impute Par Lost 10.620
Infernal Ghosts, and Hellish Furies, round Par Reg 4.422
Or gastly furies apparition; Mask 641

Furies(*cont*)
Trinity ms 'Furies'
Furious
Came furious down to be reveng'd on men, Par Lost 4.4
With furious expedition; for they weend Par Lost 6.86
Of *Moloc* furious King, who him defi'd, Par Lost 6.357
Up from the bottom turn'd by furious windes Par Lost 7.213
Torment, and loud lament, and furious rage. Par Lost 8.244
Towards the retreating Sea thir furious tyde. Par Lost 11.854
But Love constrain'd thee; call it furious rage Samson 836
For lo thy *furious* foes *now* swell Psalm 83, 5
Furlongs
And not many furlongs thence Mask 946
Furnace
As one great Furnace flam'd, yet from those flames Par Lost 1.62
ms 'furnace'
So wide they stood, and like a Furnace mouth Par Lost 2.888
In dismall dance about the furnace blue, Nativity 210
Furniture
Or tilting Furniture, emblazon'd Shields, Par Lost 9.34
Furrow
In his loose traces from the furrow came, Mask 292
Bridgewater ms 'furrowe'
Furrowed
Whistles ore the Furrow'd Land, Allegro 64
Further
But further way found none, so thick entwin'd, Par Lost 4.174
What further would be learnt. Live while ye may, Par Lost 4.533
Concern'd not Man (since he no further knew) Par Lost 10.170
Now ris'n, to work them furder woe or shame; Par Lost 10.555
The doubt, since humane reach no further knows. Par Lost 10.793
And teach us further by what means to shun Par Lost 10.1062
O *Eve*, some furder change awaits us nigh, Par Lost 11.193
And now what further shall ensue, behold. Par Lost 11.839
This further consolation yet secure Par Lost 12.620
To these dark steps, a little further on; Samson 2
His further ire, with praiers and vows renew'd. Samson 520
Some way or other yet further to afflict thee. Samson 1252
To use him further yet in some great service, Samson 1499
Till further quest'. *La*. Shepherd I take thy word, Mask 321
Bridgewater ms 'furder'
Trinity ms 'furder'
But furder know I not. 2. *Bro*. O night and shades, Mask 580
1673 'further'
1637 'farther'
To further this nights glad solemnity; Arcades 39
Trinity ms 'furder'
Fury
Or satiate fury yield it from our Foe. Par Lost 1.179
Sublim'd with Mineral fury, aid the Winds, Par Lost 1.235
Arm'd with Hell flames and fury all at once Par Lost 2.61
Against thy only Son? What fury O Son, Par Lost 2.728
As many miles aloft: that furie stay'd, Par Lost 2.938
The current of his fury thus oppos'd. Par Lost 5.808
The horrid shock: now storming furie rose, Par Lost 6.207
Level'd, with such impetuous furie smote, Par Lost 6.591
Ere this he had return'd, with fury driv'n Par Lost 10.240
Comes the blind *Fury* with th' abhorred shears, Lycidas 75
1638 'Furie'
Trinity ms 'Furie'
And wake for me, their furi' asswage; Psalm 7, 22
Fusile
Fusil or grav'n in mettle. After these, Par Lost 11.573
Future
Of future dayes may bring, what chance, what change Par Lost 2.222
Wherein past, present, future he beholds, Par Lost 3.78
By present, past, and future) on such day Par Lost 5.582
Of future we may deem him, though till now Par Lost 6.429
In future dayes, if Malice should abound, Par Lost 6.502
To future men, and in thir dwellings peace: Par Lost 7.183
Of future, in small room large heart enclos'd, Par Lost 7.486
Not instant, but of future time. With joy Par Lost 10.345
Beyond all past example and future, Par Lost 10.840
To *Adam* what shall come in future dayes, Par Lost 11.114
To shew thee what shall come in future dayes Par Lost 11.357
Liv'd ignorant of future, so had borne Par Lost 11.764
And hee the future evil shall no less Par Lost 11.774
O thou who future things canst represent Par Lost 11.870
Whereby they may direct their future life. Par Reg 1.396
Fore-saw what future dayes should bring to pass, Vacation 72
Gabble
Forthwith a hideous gabble rises loud Par Lost 12.56
Gabriel
Betwixt these rockie Pillars *Gabriel* sat Par Lost 4.549
Gabriel, to thee thy course by Lot hath giv'n Par Lost 4.561
When *Gabriel* to his next in power thus spake. Par Lost 4.781
Gabriel from the Front thus calld aloud. Par Lost 4.865
To whom with stern regard thus *Gabriel* spake. Par Lost 4.877
Gabriel, thou hadst in Heav'n th' esteem of wise, Par Lost 4.886
Which *Gabriel* spying, thus bespake the Fiend. Par Lost 4.1005
Gabriel, lead forth to Battel these my Sons Par Lost 6.46
Memorial, where the might of *Gabriel* fought, Par Lost 6.355
Of *Gabriel* out of *Eden*, now improv'd Par Lost 9.54
Of Angels, thus to *Gabriel* smiling spake. Par Reg 1.129
Gabriel this day by proof thou shalt behold, Par Reg 1.130
Announc't by *Gabriel* with the first I knew, Par Reg 4.504
Gadding
With wilde Thyme and the gadding Vine o'regrown, Lycidas 40
Gades
From *Gallia*, *Gades*, and the *Brittish* West, Par Reg 4.77
Gadier
Of *Javan* or *Gadier* Samson 716
Gain
What reinforcement we may gain from Hope, Par Lost 1.190
ms 'gaine'
Havock and spoil and ruin are my gain. Par Lost 2.1009
Thee once to gaine Companion of his woe. Par Lost 6.907
And no advantage gaine. What if the Sun Par Lost 8.122
By us? who rather double honour gaine Par Lost 9.332
Or whom he wishes most shall seldom gain Par Lost 10.901
Divided, till his rescu'd gain thir shoar: Par Lost 12.199
This also shall they gain by thir delay Par Lost 12.223
Envy they say excites me, thus to gain Par Reg 1.397
What Followers, what Retinue canst thou gain, Par Reg 2.419
To gain dominion or to keep it gain'd. Par Reg 2.434
To gain a Scepter, oftest better miss't. Par Reg 2.486
All treasures and all gain esteem as dross, Par Reg 3.29
Advise thee, gain them as thou canst, or not. Par Reg 4.211
With God or Man will gain thee no remission. Samson 835
So little is thy gain. On Time 8
Trinity ms 'gaine'
Gained
A Leper once he lost and gain'd a King, Par Lost 1.471
Yet let me not forget what I have gain'd Par Lost 4.512
And when high Noon hast gaind, and when thou fallst. Par Lost 5.174
Permissive, and acceptance found, which gain'd Par Lost 8.435
Of her attention gaind, with Serpent Tongue Par Lost 9.529
What thy hands builded not, thy Wisdom gain'd Par Lost 10.373
Through her perversness, but shall see her gaind Par Lost 10.902
I gain'd what I have gain'd, and with them dwell Par Reg 1.391
To gain dominion or to keep it gain'd. Par Reg 2.434
In wedlock a reproach; I gain'd a Son, Samson 353
Hast gain'd thy entrance, Virgin wise and pure. Sonnet 9, 14
Gaining
At once, by my foreknowledge gaining Birth Par Lost 11.768
Of gaining *David*'s Throne no man knows when, Par Reg 4.471
From the hard Season gaining: time will run Sonnet 20, 5
Gains
Though distant farr som small reflection gaines Par Lost 3.428
Save what by frugal storing firmness gains Par Lost 5.324
Lives, as thou saidst, and gaines to live as Man Par Lost 9.933
Gainsay
Too facil then thou didst not much gainsay, Par Lost 9.1158
Gainst
Or 'gainst the rugged bark of som broad Elm Mask 354
Bridgewater ms 'gainst'
'Gainst all inchantments, mildew blast, or damp Mask 640
Trinity ms 'gainst'
Bridgewater ms 'gainst'
'Gainst old truth) motion number'd out his time; Another 8
'Gainst them that rais'd thee dost thou lift thy horn, Prose 3, 2
Gait
Bent all on speed, and markt his Aerie Gate; Par Lost 4.568
But faded splendor wan; who by his gate Par Lost 4.870
Wallowing unweildie, enormous in thir Gate Par Lost 7.411
In gate surpass'd and Goddess-like deport, Par Lost 9.389
One of the heav'nly Host, and by his Gate Par Lost 11.230
With eev'n step, and musing gate, Penseroso 38
Galasp
Colkitto, or Macdonnel, or Galasp? Sonnet 11, 9
Galaxy
Seen in the Galaxie, that Milkie way Par Lost 7.579
Gale
Of gentlest gale *Arabian* odors fann'd Par Reg 2.364
Gales
All sadness but despair: now gentle gales Par Lost 4.156
Joyous the Birds; fresh Gales and gentle Aires Par Lost 8.515
Hopes thee; of flattering gales Horace 11
Galilean
At home, scarce view'd the *Gallilean* Towns, Par Reg 3.233
The Pilot of the *Galilean* lake, Lycidas 109
Galilee
In *Galilee*, that she should bear a Son Par Reg 1.135
Galileo
Of *Galileo*, less assur'd, observes Par Lost 5.262
Gallaphrone
The City of *Gallaphrone*, from thence to win Par Reg 3.340
Gallia
From *Gallia*, *Gades*, and the *Brittish* West, Par Reg 4.77
Gambolled
Gambold before them, th' unwieldy Elephant Par Lost 4.345
Game
Infernal noise; Warr seem'd a civil Game Par Lost 6.667
All now was turn'd to jollitie and game, Par Lost 11.714
Hunting (and Men not Beasts shall be his game) Par Lost 12.30
And savour, Beasts of chase, or Fowl of game, Par Reg 2.342
Or make a game of my calamities? Samson 1331
Games
As at th' Olympian Games or *Pythian* fields; Par Lost 2.530
About him exercis'd Heroic Games Par Lost 4.551
Unsung; or to describe Races and Games, Par Lost 9.33
With Sacrifices, Triumph, Pomp, and Games; Samson 1312
Proof of his mighty strength in feats and games; Samson 1602
Gamesome
To whom thus *Belial* in like gamesom mood, Par Lost 6.620
Such as the jocond Flute, or gamesom Pipe Mask 173

Gamesome*(cont)*
Bridgewater ms 'gamesome'
1637 'gamesome'
Trinity ms 'gamesome'
Gan
Ethereal Trumpet from on high gan blow: Par Lost 6.60
Till *Adam* thus 'gan *Eve* to dalliance move, Par Lost 9.1016
Beast now with Beast gan war, and Fowle with Fowle, Par Lost 10.710
Gan thunder, and both ends of Heav'n, the Clouds Par Reg 4.410
Ganges
Of *Ganges* or *Hydaspes*, *Indian* streams; Par Lost 3.436
Ganges and *Indus:* thus the Orb he roam'd Par Lost 9.82
Gangrene
Ranckle, and fester, and gangrene, Samson 621
Ganymede
Then *Ganymed* or *Hylas*, distant more Par Reg 2.353
Gaol
This Gaol I count the house of Liberty Samson 949
Troop to th' infernall jail, Nativity 233
1673 'Jail'
Gap
Rowld inward, and a spacious Gap disclos'd Par Lost 6.861
Gaped
With hideous orifice gap't on us wide, Par Lost 6.577
Gaping
Wide gaping, and with utter loss of being Par Lost 2.440
Garb
Thus *Belial* with words cloath'd in reasons garb Par Lost 2.226
Obtruding false rules pranckt in reasons garb. Mask 759
Trinity ms 'garbe'
Bridgewater ms 'garbe'
1637 'garbe'
Garden
Of mankind, in the happie Garden plac't, Par Lost 3.66
Of God the Garden was, by him in the East Par Lost 4.209
His farr more pleasant Garden God ordaind; Par Lost 4.215
That Mountain as his Garden mould high rais'd Par Lost 4.226
Waterd the Garden; thence united fell Par Lost 4.230
From this *Assyrian* Garden, where the Fiend Par Lost 4.285
This Garden, and no corner leave unspi'd; Par Lost 4.529
Search through this Garden, leave unsearcht no nook, Par Lost 4.789
Earth and the Gard'n of God, with Cedars crownd Par Lost 5.260
To rest, and what the Garden choicest bears Par Lost 5.368
Then what this Garden is to all the Earth, Par Lost 5.752
This Garden, planted with the Trees of God, Par Lost 7.538
To the Garden of bliss, thy seat prepar'd. Par Lost 8.299
Of every Tree that in the Garden growes Par Lost 8.321
Amid the Garden by the Tree of Life, Par Lost 8.326
This Garden, still to tend Plant, Herb and Flour, Par Lost 9.206
Of all these Garden Trees ye shall not eate, Par Lost 9.657
Of each Tree in the Garden we may eate, Par Lost 9.660
The Garden, God hath said, Ye shall not eate Par Lost 9.662
Now walking in the Garden, by soft windes Par Lost 10.98
I heard thee in the Garden, and of thy voice Par Lost 10.116
In this delicious Garden? as my Will Par Lost 10.746
And send him from the Garden forth to Till Par Lost 11.97
And on the East side of the Garden place, Par Lost 11.118
Possession of the Garden; hee alone, Par Lost 11.222
And send thee from the Garden forth to till Par Lost 11.261
I Who e're while the happy Garden sung, Par Reg 1.1
Gardening
Of thir sweet Gardning labour then suffic'd Par Lost 4.328
The hands dispatch of two Gardning so wide. Par Lost 9.203
But with such Gardning Tools as Art yet rude, Par Lost 9.391
Garden-plot
Of Grove or Garden-Plot more pleasant lay, Par Lost 9.418
Gardens
Like those *Hesperian* Gardens fam'd of old, Par Lost 3.568
Spot more delicious then those Gardens feign'd Par Lost 9.439
Gardens and Groves presented to his eyes, Par Reg 4.38
All amidst the Gardens fair Mask 981
1637 'gardens'
Trinity ms 'gardens'
B.M. ms 'Garden'
Bridgewater ms 'gardens'
amidst the Hesperian gardens, on whose bancks Mask Tr. ms 10.05
That in trim Gardens takes his pleasure; Penseroso 50
Garish
Iris there with humid bow, Mask 992
Trinity ms 'humid' ←'garish' ←'garnish't'
Hide me from Day's garish eie, Penseroso 141
The Musk-rose, and the well attir'd Woodbine, Lycidas 146
Trinity ms 'well-attir'd woodbine' ←'garish columbine'
Garland
Of choicest Flours a Garland to adorne Par Lost 9.840
From his slack hand the Garland wreath'd for *Eve* Par Lost 9.892
And throw sweet garland wreaths into her stream Mask 850
And in his Garland as he stood, Winchester 21
Garlands
Now in loose Garlands thick thrown off, the bright Par Lost 3.362
With Flowers, Garlands, and sweet-smelling Herbs Par Lost 4.709
Of love and youth not lost, Songs, Garlands, Flours, Par Lost 11.594
Garners
When for their teeming Flocks, and granges full Mask 175
Trinity ms 'granges' ←'garners'
Garnished
Iris there with humid bow, Mask 992
Trinity ms 'humid' ←'garish' ←'garnish't'
Garrisoned
Garrison'd round about him like a Camp Samson 1497
Garrulity
Shameful garrulity. To have reveal'd Samson 491
Gash
Not long divisible, and from the gash Par Lost 6.331
Gasp
That would have made *Quintilian* stare and gasp. Sonnet 11, 11
Gate
Fast by Hell Gate, and kept the fatal Key, Par Lost 2.725
T' whom thus the Portress of Hell Gate reply'd; Par Lost 2.746
And towards the Gate rouling her bestial train, Par Lost 2.873
The work as of a Kingly Palace Gate Par Lost 3.505
And waking cri'd, *This is the Gate of Heav'n* Par Lost 3.515
1667 'Gate'
That scal'd by steps of Gold to Heav'n Gate Par Lost 3.541
At wisdoms Gate, and to simplicitie Par Lost 3.687
One Gate there only was, and that look'd East Par Lost 4.178
Against the eastern Gate of Paradise Par Lost 4.542
See farr and wide: in at this Gate none pass Par Lost 4.579
That singing up to Heaven Gate ascend, Par Lost 5.198
Through all th' Empyreal road; till at the Gate Par Lost 5.253
Of Heav'n arriv'd, the gate self-opend wide Par Lost 5.254
From Heaven Gate not farr, founded in view Par Lost 7.618
From Earth arriv'd at Heaven Gate, displeas'd Par Lost 10.22
Accompanied to Heaven Gate, from whence Par Lost 10.88
And with *Asphaltic* slime; broad as the Gate, Par Lost 10.298
The Causey to Hell Gate; on either side Par Lost 10.415
That scorn'd his indignation: through the Gate, Par Lost 10.418
Direct to th' Eastern Gate was bent thir flight. Par Lost 11.190
And to the faithful Death the Gate of Life; Par Lost 12.571
Our lingring Parents, and to th' Eastern Gate Par Lost 12.638
Wav'd over by that flaming Brand, the Gate Par Lost 12.643
What boots it at one gate to make defence, Samson 560
Right against the Eastern gate, Allegro 59
Gates
Back to the Gates of Heav'n: the Sulphurous Hail Par Lost 1.171
ms 'gates'
His swift pursuers from Heav'n Gates discern Par Lost 1.326
ms 'gates'
Attended: all access was throng'd, the Gates Par Lost 1.761
ms 'gates'
Ninefold, and gates of burning Adamant Par Lost 2.436
Puts on swift wings, and towards the Gates of Hell Par Lost 2.631
And thrice threefold the Gates; three folds were Brass, Par Lost 2.645
Yet unconsum'd. Before the Gates there sat Par Lost 2.648
To yonder Gates? through them I mean to pass, Par Lost 2.684
These Gates for ever shut, which none can pass Par Lost 2.776
These Adamantine Gates; against all force Par Lost 2.853
Excel'd her power; the Gates wide op'n stood, Par Lost 2.884
Confusion worse confounded; and Heav'n Gates Par Lost 2.996
To entertain you two, her widest Gates, Par Lost 4.382
His Iron Gates, if he intends our stay Par Lost 4.898
The facil gates of hell too slightly barrd. Par Lost 4.967
Unbarr'd the gates of Light. There is a Cave Par Lost 6.4
Her ever during Gates, Harmonious sound Par Lost 7.206
Open, ye everlasting Gates, they sung, Par Lost 7.565
Farr on excursion toward the Gates of Hell; Par Lost 8.231
The dismal Gates, and barricado'd strong; Par Lost 8.241
Within the Gates of Hell sate Sin and Death, Par Lost 10.230
In counterview within the Gates, that now Par Lost 10.231
Then Both from out Hell Gates into the waste Par Lost 10.282
Within Hell Gates till now, thou us impow'rd Par Lost 10.369
Cities of Men with lofty Gates and Towrs, Par Lost 11.640
To Council in the Citie Gates: anon Par Lost 11.661
And *Hecatompylos* her hunderd gates, Par Reg 3.287
The City gates out powr'd, light armed Troops Par Reg 3.311
Thence to the gates cast round thine eye, and see Par Reg 4.61
No triumph; in all her gates *Abaddon* rues Par Reg 4.624
The Gates of *Azza*, Post, and massie Bar Samson 147
And as the gates I enter'd with Sun-rise, Samson 1597
Here dwel no frowns, nor anger, from these gates Mask 667
this dusky hollow is a paradise & heaven gates ore my head Mask Tr. ms 13.44
Will open wide the Gates of her high Palace Hall. Nativity 148
Sions *fair* Gates the Lord loves more Psalm 87, 5
Gath
Of *Palestine*, in *Gath* and *Ascalon* Par Lost 1.465
ms 'Gath'
They had by this possess'd the Towers of *Gath*, Samson 266
In *Ecron*, *Gaza*, *Asdod*, and in *Gath* Samson 981
The Giant *Harapha* of *Gath*, his look Samson 1068
Though for no friendly intent. I am of *Gath*, Samson 1078
Thou oft shalt wish thy self at *Gath* to boast Samson 1127
To *Samson*, but shalt never see *Gath* more. Samson 1129
Gather
Or wither'd sticks to gather; which might serve Par Reg 1.316
Gathered
Was gatherd, which cost *Ceres* all that pain Par Lost 4.271
Have gathered aught of evil or conceald, Par Lost 5.207
Be gather'd now ye Waters under Heav'n Par Lost 7.283
Her gather'd beams, great Palace now of Light. Par Lost 7.363
New gatherd, and ambrosial smell diffus'd. Par Lost 9.852
They gatherd, broad as *Amazonian* Targe, Par Lost 9.1111
Deep to the Roots of Hell the gather'd beach Par Lost 10.299
Thence gatherd his own doom, which understood Par Lost 10.344
Leave cold the Night, how we his gather'd beams Par Lost 10.1070
Gatherd, not harshly pluckt, for death mature: Par Lost 11.537
In *Ctesiphon* hath gather'd all his Host Par Reg 3.300

Gathered(*cont*)
Thir Lords the *Philistines* with gather'd powers — Samson 251
Gather'd like scum, and setl'd to it self — Mask 595

Gathering
Of *Enna*, where *Proserpin* gathering flours — Par Lost 4.269
1667 'gathring'
As Children gathering pibles on the shore. — Par Reg 4.330

Gathers
Thaws not, but gathers heap, and ruin seems — Par Lost 2.590
She gathers, Tribute large, and on the board — Par Lost 5.343
And gathers ground fast at the Labourers heel — Par Lost 12.631

Gaudy
Of pancies, pinks, and gaudy Daffadils. — Mask 851
1637 'gaudie'
Trinity ms 'gaudie' ← 'bonnie'
Bridgewater ms 'guady'
And fancies fond with gaudy shapes possess, — Penseroso 6
Had doff't her gawdy trim, — Nativity 33

Gaul
Beyond the Realm of *Gaul*, a Land there lies, — Prose 12, 8

Gauntlet
Vant-brass and Greves, and Gauntlet, add thy Spear — Samson 1121

Gave
Exalted to such power, and gave to rule, — Par Lost 1.736
Which to our general Sire gave prospect large — Par Lost 4.144
Gave proof unheeded; others on the grass — Par Lost 4.350
Accept your Makers work; he gave it me, — Par Lost 4.380
That neer him stood, and gave them thus in charge. — Par Lost 4.787
Gave heed, but waxing more in rage repli'd. — Par Lost 4.969
On each hand parting, to his speed gave way — Par Lost 5.252
Thy making, while the Maker gave thee being? — Par Lost 5.858
Gave them above thir foes, not to have sinnd, — Par Lost 6.402
His Word, the filial Godhead, gave effect. — Par Lost 7.175
Gave thee, all sorts are here that all th' Earth yields, — Par Lost 7.541
Gave sign of gratulation, and each Hill; — Par Lost 8.514
That gave thee being, still shades thee and protects. — Par Lost 9.266
Gave elocution to the mute, and taught — Par Lost 9.748
Sighing through all her Works gave signs of woe, — Par Lost 9.783
She gave him of that fair enticing Fruit — Par Lost 9.996
In pangs, and Nature gave a second groan, — Par Lost 9.1001
At length gave utterance to these words constraind. — Par Lost 9.1066
Whereof I gave thee charge thou shouldst not eat? — Par Lost 10.123
Shee gave me of the Tree, and I did eate. — Par Lost 10.143
Departing gave command, and they observ'd. — Par Lost 10.430
His mightie Angels gave them several charge, — Par Lost 10.650
The Law I gave to Nature him forbids: — Par Lost 11.49
He ended, and the Son gave signal high — Par Lost 11.72
Subscrib'd not; Nature first gave Signs, imprest — Par Lost 11.182
From the first op'ning bud, and gave ye Names, — Par Lost 11.277
All th' Earth he gave thee to possess and rule, — Par Lost 11.339
His best of Man, and gave him up to tears — Par Lost 11.497
He gave us onely over Beast, Fish, Fowl — Par Lost 12.67
His birth to our just fear gave no small cause, — Par Reg 1.66
Gave up into my hands *Uzzean Job* — Par Reg 1.369
And his who gave them breath, but higher sung, — Par Reg 4.258
God, when he gave me strength, to shew withal — Samson 58
Gave up my fort of silence to a Woman. — Samson 236
By this appears: I gave, thou say'st, th' example, — Samson 822
Gave to the man despotic power — Samson 1054
My trust is in the living God who gave me — Samson 1140
As a league-breaker gave up bound, presum'd — Samson 1209
But to thir Masters gave me up for nought, — Samson 1215
What glorious hand gave *Samson* his deaths wound? — Samson 1581
That to the arched roof gave main support. — Samson 1634
Which if Heav'n gave it, may be term'd her own: — Mask 419
Gave respit to the drowsie frighted steeds — Mask 553
You gave me Brother? *Eld. Bro*. Yes, and keep it still, — Mask 584
That *Hermes* once to wise *Ulysses* gave; — Mask 637
line not in Bridgewater ms
He call'd it *Haemony*, and gave it me, — Mask 638
In *Egypt* gave to *Jove*-born *Helena* — Mask 676
And gave her to his daughters to imbathe — Mask 837
He gave their Land therin to dwell. — Psalm 136, 74
Rest that gives all men life, gave him his death, — Another 11
Whom *Joves* great Son to her glad Husband gave, — Sonnet 23, 3
That *Constantine* to good *Sylvestro* gave. — Prose 4, 4

Gavest
My being gav'st me; whom should I obey — Par Lost 2.865
And thou thir Natures know'st, & gav'st them Names, — Par Lost 7.493
And gav'st me as thy perfet gift, so good, — Par Lost 10.138

Gay
With gay Religions full of Pomp and Gold, — Par Lost 1.372
Appeerd, with gay enameld colours mixt: — Par Lost 4.149
What thou and thy gay Legions dare against; — Par Lost 4.942
Op'ning thir various colours, and made gay — Par Lost 7.318
The silent hours, and th' other whose gay Traine — Par Lost 7.444
And thou enlight'nd Earth, so fresh and gay, — Par Lost 8.274
Each Flour of slender stalk, whose head though gay — Par Lost 9.428
A Beavie of fair Women, richly gay — Par Lost 11.582
Of Goddesses, so blithe, so smooth, so gay, — Par Lost 11.615
Conspicuous with three listed colours gay, — Par Lost 11.866
That so bedeckt, ornate, and gay, — Samson 712
Of som gay creatures of the element — Mask 299
Bridgewater ms 'gaye'
Enjoy your deer Wit, and gay Rhetorick — Mask 790
line not in Bridgewater ms
line not in Trinity ms
As the gay motes that people the Sun Beams, — Penseroso 8

Gay(*cont*)
Or Frost to Flowers, that their gay wardrop wear, — Lycidas 47

Gayest
Two Birds of gayest plume before him drove: — Par Lost 11.186
But cull those richest Robes, and gay'st attire — Vacation 21

Gaza
And *Accaron* and *Gaza*'s frontier bounds. — Par Lost 1.466
ms 'Gaza's'
Eyeless in *Gaza* at the Mill with slaves, — Samson 41
The Gates of *Azza*, Post, and massie Bar — Samson 147
Here celebrate in *Gaza;* and proclaim — Samson 435
In *Ecron*, *Gaza*, *Asdod*, and in *Gath* — Samson 981
Mess. *Gaza* yet stands, but all her Sons are fall'n, — Samson 1558
(*Gaza* is not in plight to say us nay) — Samson 1729
Bore witness gloriously; whence *Gaza* mourns — Samson 1752

Gaze
Here matter new to gaze the Devil met — Par Lost 3.613
That I may find him, and with secret gaze, — Par Lost 3.671
When *Satan* still in gaze, as first he stood, — Par Lost 4.356
Attracted by thy beauty still to gaze. — Par Lost 5.47
Hosanna to the Highest: nor stood at gaze — Par Lost 6.205
But as in gaze admiring: Oft he bowd — Par Lost 9.524
Displeas'd that I approach thee thus, and gaze — Par Lost 9.535
Thee all things living gaze on, all things thine — Par Lost 9.539
Ruddie and Gold: I nearer drew to gaze; — Par Lost 9.578
And gaze, and worship thee of right declar'd — Par Lost 9.611
Made of my Enemies the scorn and gaze; — Samson 34
A burdenous drone; to visitants a gaze, — Samson 567
To gaze upon the Sun with shameless brows. — Mask 736
Bridgewater ms 'gase'
Have sate to wonder at, and gaze upon: — Arcades 43
Trinity ms defective here
Stand fixt in stedfast gaze, — Nativity 70

Gazed
Ambrosia; on that Tree he also gaz'd; — Par Lost 5.57
A *Phaenix*, gaz'd by all, as that sole Bird — Par Lost 5.272
And gaz'd a while the ample Skie, till rais'd — Par Lost 8.258
Fixt on the Fruit she gaz'd, which to behold — Par Lost 9.735
Gaz'd hot, and of the fresh Wave largely drew, — Par Lost 11.845
Ejected, emptyed, gaz'd, unpityed, shun'd, — Par Reg 1.414
This Nymph that gaz'd upon his clustring locks, — Mask 54
Bridgewater ms 'gazed'

Gazing
Coucht, and now fild with pasture gazing sat, — Par Lost 4.351

Gear
Whom thrift keeps up about his Country gear, — Mask 167
Bridgewater ms 'geare'
1637 'geare'
Trinity ms 'geare'

Gebal
Gebal and Ammon *there conspire*, — Psalm 83, 25

Gehenna
And black *Gehenna* call'd, the Type of Hell. — Par Lost 1.405
ms 'Gehenna'

Gemmed
Thir branches hung with copious Fruit; or gemm'd — Par Lost 7.325

Gems
With Gemms and Golden lustre rich imblaz'd, — Par Lost 1.538
ms 'gemms'
Wants not her hidden lustre, Gemms and Gold; — Par Lost 2.271
Imbellisht, thick with sparkling orient Gemmes — Par Lost 3.507
And these the Gemms of Heav'n, her starrie train: — Par Lost 4.649
With Plant, Fruit, Flour Ambrosial, Gemms & Gold, — Par Lost 6.475
In Gems and wanton dress; to the Harp they sung — Par Lost 11.583
Urim and *Thummim*, those oraculous gems — Par Reg 3.14
Crystal and Myrrhine cups imboss'd with Gems — Par Reg 4.119
That like to rich, and various gemms inlay — Mask 22
Trinity ms 'gems' ← 'gemms'
Bridgewater ms 'gems'
She hutch't th' all-worshipt ore, and precious gems — Mask 719
Trinity ms 'gemms'

General
Yet to thir Generals Voyce they soon obeyd — Par Lost 1.337
ms 'Generalls'
Egypt from *Syrian* ground, had general Names — Par Lost 1.421
ms 'generall'
That for the general safety he despis'd — Par Lost 2.481
Into this Deep, and in the general fall — Par Lost 2.773
Of all past Ages to the general Doom — Par Lost 3.328
Which to our general Sire gave prospect large — Par Lost 4.144
So spake our general Mother, and with eyes — Par Lost 4.492
To whom our general Ancestor repli'd. — Par Lost 4.659
To sound at general Doom. Th' Angelic blast — Par Lost 11.76
From whom could else a general cry be heard? — Samson 1524

Generally
Men generally think me much a foe — Par Reg 1.387

Generate
And God said, let the Waters generate — Par Lost 7.387
Or find some other way to generate — Par Lost 10.894

Generated
The waters generated by thir kindes, — Par Lost 7.393

Generation
A generation, whom his choice regard — Par Lost 1.653
His Generation, and the rising Birth — Par Lost 7.102

Generations
All generations, and had hither come — Par Lost 11.344

Generous
And oft by force, which to a generous mind — Par Reg 2.479

Generous(*cont*)
More generous far and civil, who confess'd Samson 1467
Genezaret
On this side the broad lake *Genezaret*, Par Reg 2.23
Genial
What day the genial Angel to our Sire Par Lost 4.712
Satiate with genial moisture, when God said Par Lost 7.282
(Though higher of the genial Bed by far, Par Lost 8.598
So much I feel my genial spirits droop, Samson 594
Genius
Or th' unseen Genius of the Wood. Penseroso 154
Hence forth thou art the Genius of the shore, Lycidas 183
The parting Genius is with sighing sent, Nativity 186
Gennesaret
On this side the broad lake *Genezaret*, Par Reg 2.23
Gentiles
Whom Gentiles *Ammon* call and *Lybian Jove*, Par Lost 4.277
But *Joshua* whom the Gentiles *Jesus* call, Par Lost 12.310
The Gentiles; henceforth Oracles are ceast, Par Reg 1.456
From Gentils, but by Circumcision vain, Par Reg 3.425
The *Gentiles* also know, and write, and teach Par Reg 4.227
And with the *Gentiles* much thou must converse, Par Reg 4.229
Like whom the Gentiles feign to bear up Heav'n. Samson 150
That Gentiles in thir Parables condemn Samson 500
Why do the Gentiles tumult, and the Nations Psalm 2, 1
Gentle
With gentle penetration, though unseen, Par Lost 3.585
All sadness but despair: now gentle gales Par Lost 4.156
Subjection, but requir'd with gentle sway, Par Lost 4.308
Nor gentle purpose, nor endearing smiles Par Lost 4.337
Ah gentle pair, yee little think how nigh Par Lost 4.366
In some Purlieu two gentle Fawnes at play, Par Lost 4.404
My other half: with that thy gentle hand Par Lost 4.488
Like gentle breaths from Rivers pure, thence raise Par Lost 4.806
With gentle voice, I thought it thine; it said, Par Lost 5.37
But silently a gentle tear let fall Par Lost 5.130
Pensive I sate me down; there gentle sleep Par Lost 8.287
Joyous the Birds; fresh Gales and gentle Aires Par Lost 8.515
Gentle to me and affable hath been Par Lost 8.648
His gentle dumb expression turnd at length Par Lost 9.527
From Noon, and gentle Aires due at thir hour Par Lost 10.93
Whereon I live, thy gentle looks, thy aid, Par Lost 10.919
First hunter then, pursu'd a gentle brace, Par Lost 11.188
But him the gentle Angel by the hand Par Lost 11.421
A gentle wafting to immortal Life. Par Lost 12.435
Her also I with gentle Dreams have calm'd Par Lost 12.595
Thy gentle Ministers, who come to pay Par Reg 2.375
Raign or raign not; though to that gentle brow Par Reg 3.215
Canst thou not tell me of a gentle Pair Mask 236
La. Nay gentle Shepherd ill is lost that praise Mask 271
To help you find them. *La*. Gentle villager Mask 304
Bridgewater ms 'gentle'
With black usurping mists, som gentle taper Mask 337
For gentle usage, and soft delicacy? Mask 681
line not in Bridgewater ms
There is a gentle Nymph not farr from hence, Mask 824
Gentle swain at thy request Mask 900
I doubt me gentle mortalls these may seeme Mask Tr. ms 10.16
Gen. Stay gentle Swains, for though in this disguise, Arcades 26
So may som gentle Muse Lycidas 19
What hard mishap hath doom'd this gentle swain? Lycidas 92
She woo's the gentle Air Nativity 38
The gentle neighbourhood of grove and spring Passion 52
Gentle Lady may thy grave Winchester 47
That call Fame on such gentle acts as these, Sonnet 8, 6
Gentleness
Her maid'n gentlenes, and oft at Eeve Mask 843
Trinity ms 'gentlenesse'
Bridgewater ms 'gentleness'
1637 'gentlenesse'
Gentler
The gentler, if severely thou exact not Samson 788
Gentlest
Of gentlest gale *Arabian* odors fann'd Par Reg 2.364
Gently
Semblance of worth, not substance, gently rais'd Par Lost 1.529
By his Magnetic beam, that gently warms Par Lost 3.583
Layes forth her purple Grape, and gently creeps Par Lost 4.259
Gently for our instruction to impart Par Lost 7.81
Whose inward apparition gently mov'd Par Lost 8.293
Gently with Mirtle band, mindless the while, Par Lost 9.431
Prince above Princes, gently hast thou tould Par Lost 11.298
And sunk thee as thy Sons; till gently reard Par Lost 11.758
Who gently ask't if he had seen such two, Mask 575
Trinity ms 'gently' ← 'tooke him'
Gently o're th' accustom'd Oke; Penseroso 60
Gerent
Under his great Vice-gerent Reign abide Par Lost 5.609
Germans
Germans and *Scythians*, and *Sarmatians* North Par Reg 4.78
Geryon
Guiana, whose great Citie *Geryons* Sons Par Lost 11.410
Gessamine
Iris all hues, Roses, and Gessamin Par Lost 4.698
The tufted Crow-toe, and pale Gessamine, Lycidas 143
1638 'gessamine'
Trinity ms 'Gessamie'
Gesture
In shape and gesture proudly eminent Par Lost 1.590
In every gesture dignitie and love. Par Lost 8.489
Of gesture or lest action overawd Par Lost 9.460
Gestures
Spirit of happie sort: his gestures fierce Par Lost 4.128
By unchaste looks, loose gestures, and foul talk, Mask 464
Bridgewater ms 'gesturs'
Get
The Tawnie Lion, pawing to get free Par Lost 7.464
And get themselves a name, least far disperst Par Lost 12.45
Get Riches first, get Wealth, and Treasure heap, Par Reg 2.427
Get thee behind me; plain thou now appear'st Par Reg 4.193
E're thou of *Israel*'s Scepter get fast hold; Par Reg 4.480
To learn thy secrets, get into my power Samson 798
Ghastly
Grinnd horrible a gastly smile, to hear Par Lost 2.846
Mangl'd with gastly wounds through Plate and Maile, Par Lost 6.368
Of gastly Spasm, or racking torture, qualmes Par Lost 11.481
Or gastly furies apparition; Mask 641
Bridgewater ms 'gastlie'
Ghost
The Holy Ghost, and the power of the highest Par Reg 1.139
Blew meager Hag, or stubborn unlaid ghost, Mask 434
Trinity ms 'Ghost'
Each fetter'd Ghost slips to his severall grave, Nativity 234
Ghosts
Infernal Ghosts, and Hellish Furies, round Par Reg 4.422
Giant
Warr'd on by Cranes: though all the Giant brood Par Lost 1.576
ms 'giant'
In bigness to surpass Earths Giant Sons Par Lost 1.778
ms 'giant-sons'
Then from the Giant Angels; thee that day Par Lost 7.605
The Giant *Harapha* of *Gath*, his look Samson 1068
Sam. Tongue-doubtie Giant, how dost thou prove me these? Samson 1181
Or *Trent*, who like some earth-born Giant spreads Vacation 93
Giant-brood
Sam. I dread him not, nor all his Giant-brood, Samson 1247
Giants
First from the ancient World those Giants came Par Lost 3.464
Giants of mightie Bone, and bould emprise; Par Lost 11.642
Such were these Giants, men of high renown; Par Lost 11.688
Up to the Hill by *Hebron*, seat of Giants old, Samson 148
Sea-girt it lies, where Giants dwelt of old, Prose 12, 9
Giantship
Chor. His Giantship is gone somewhat crest-fall'n, Samson 1244
Giant-sons
In bigness to surpass Earths Giant Sons Par Lost 1.778
ms 'giant-sons'
Gibeah
In *Gibeah*, when the hospitable door Par Lost 1.504
ms 'Gibeah'
Gibeon
Mans voice commanding, Sun in *Gibeon* stand, Par Lost 12.265
Gibraltar
Beneath *Gibralter* to the *Lybian* sands. Par Lost 1.355
ms 'Gibraltar'
1667 '*Gibraltar*'
Giddy
With wanton heed, and giddy cunning, Allegro 141
Giddy and *restless* let *them reel* Psalm 83, 51
Gideon
Gideon and *Jephtha*, and the Shepherd lad, Par Reg 2.439
The matchless *Gideon* in pursuit Samson 280
Gift
And when we seek, as now, thy gift of sleep. Par Lost 4.735
Heav'ns last best gift, my ever new delight, Par Lost 5.19
Two onely, who yet by sov'ran gift possess Par Lost 5.366
Not understood, this gift they have besides, Par Lost 6.626
By gift, and thy Celestial Beautie adore Par Lost 9.540
For had the gift bin theirs, it had not here Par Lost 9.806
And gav'st me as thy perfet gift, so good, Par Lost 10.138
No despicable gift; surmise not then Par Lost 11.340
Gift to his Progenie of all that Land; Par Lost 12.138
Shall I receive by gift what of my own, Par Reg 2.381
Above all Sacrifice, or hallow'd gift Par Reg 3.116
For what can less so great a gift deserve? Par Reg 4.169
Who this high gift of strength committed to me, Samson 47
How slight the gift was, hung it in my Hair. Samson 59
Fool, have divulg'd the secret gift of God Samson 201
Man. Wilt thou then serve the *Philistines* with that gift Samson 577
Sam. Shall I abuse this Consecrated gift Samson 1354
Not to sit idle with so great a gift Samson 1500
This was that gift (if you the truth will have) Prose 4, 3
Gifted
With this Heav'n-gifted strength? O glorious strength Samson 36
Gifts
Endowd with all thir gifts, and O too like Par Lost 4.715
Our givers thir own gifts, and large bestow Par Lost 5.317
Abundantly his gifts hath also pour'd Par Lost 8.220
Of all thy gifts, nor enviest. I now see Par Lost 8.494
Thy Love, not thy Subjection, and her Gifts Par Lost 10.153
Corrupted. I at first with two fair gifts Par Lost 11.57
Taught them, but they his gifts acknowledg'd none. Par Lost 11.612
By wisdome, and superiour gifts receav'd. Par Lost 11.636
Baptiz'd, shall them with wondrous gifts endue Par Lost 12.500
With more then humane gifts from Heaven adorn'd, Par Reg 2.137

Gifts(*cont*)
And count thy specious gifts no gifts but guiles. Par Reg 2.391
Why are his gifts desirable, to tempt Samson 358
Nor shall his wondrous gifts be frustrate thus. Samson 589
With gifts and graces eminently adorn'd, Samson 679
Was lavish't on thir Sex, that inward gifts Samson 1026
There was another meaning in these gifts, Mask 754
line not in Bridgewater ms
Trinity ms 'guifts'
Either man's work or his own gifts, who best Sonnet 19, 10
Gigantic
On each hand slaughter and gigantic deeds. Par Lost 11.659
All of Gigantic size, *Goliah* chief. Samson 1249
Gilded
With gilded battlements, conspicuous far, Par Reg 4.53
And the gilded Car of Day, Mask 95
Gilds
Which now the Rising Sun guilds with his beams. Par Lost 3.551
And hence the Morning Planet guilds her horns; Par Lost 7.366
Gills
And seems a moving Land, and at his Gilles Par Lost 7.415
Gins
Though dearly to my cost, thy ginns, and toyls; Samson 933
Gird
His Adamantine coat gird well, and each Par Lost 6.542
Gird on, and Sword upon thy puissant Thigh; Par Lost 6.714
To save appeerances, how gird the Sphear Par Lost 8.82
To gird thir waste, vain Covering if to hide Par Lost 9.1113
Girded
And girded on our loyns, may cover round Par Lost 9.1096
His easie steps; girded with snaky wiles, Par Reg 1.120
Girt
Girt with the River *Triton*, where old *Cham*, Par Lost 4.276
Girt like a Starrie Zone his waste, and round Par Lost 5.281
Girt with Omnipotence, with Radiance crown'd Par Lost 7.194
Columbus found th' *American* so girt Par Lost 9.1116
What sieges girt me round, e're I consented; Samson 846
To see me girt with Friends; and how the sight Samson 1415
Imperial rule of all the Sea-girt Iles Mask 21
Trinity ms 'sea-girt'
Thou hovering Angel girt with golden wings, Mask 214
line not in Bridgewater ms
But for that damn'd magician, let him be girt Mask 602
Now sits not girt with Tapers holy shine, Nativity 202
Here lies old *Hobson*, Death hath broke his girt, Carrier 1
1658 'hath his desire'
Sea-girt it lies, where Giants dwelt of old, Prose 12, 9
Give
I give not Heav'n for lost. From this descent Par Lost 2.14
Can give it, or will ever? how he can Par Lost 2.153
To give his Enemies thir wish, and end Par Lost 2.157
I give thee, reign for ever, and assume Par Lost 3.318
Which I as freely give; Hell shall unfold, Par Lost 4.381
His flesh, his bone; to give thee being I lent Par Lost 4.483
But come, for thou, besure, shalt give account Par Lost 4.841
To give us onely good; and if the night Par Lost 5.206
To intellectual, give both life and sense, Par Lost 5.485
Intends to pass triumphant, and give Laws. Par Lost 5.693
Shalt thou give Law to God, shalt thou dispute Par Lost 5.822
To give Light on the Earth; and it was so. Par Lost 7.345
This Paradise I give thee, count it thine Par Lost 8.319
To thee and to thy Race I give; as Lords Par Lost 8.339
Though others envie what they cannot give; Par Lost 9.805
As yet my change, and give him to partake Par Lost 9.818
O *Eve*, in evil hour thou didst give eare Par Lost 9.1067
Thou therefore give due audience, and attend. Par Lost 12.12
Disabl'd not to give thee thy deaths wound: Par Lost 12.392
To approach thy Temples, give thee in command Par Reg 1.449
That I have also power to give thou seest, Par Reg 2.393
Besides to give a Kingdom hath been thought Par Reg 2.481
To thy large heart give utterance due, thy heart Par Reg 3.10
Is given, and by that right I give it thee. Par Reg 4.104
Nor what I part with mean to give for naught; Par Reg 4.161
The Kingdoms of the world to thee I give; Par Reg 4.163
For giv'n to me, I give to whom I please, Par Reg 4.164
All glory arrogate, to God give none, Par Reg 4.315
In their conjunction met, give me to spell, Par Reg 4.385
For it is written, He will give command Par Reg 4.556
Then give the rains to wandring thought, Samson 302
Such pardon therefore as I give my folly, Samson 825
Some narrow place enclos'd, where sight may give thee, Samson 1117
To descant on my strength, and give thy verdit? Samson 1228
The worst that he can give, to me the best. Samson 1264
To give ye part with me what hope I have Samson 1453
Yet e're I give the rains to grief, say first, Samson 1578
Are in confusion, give us if thou canst, Samson 1593
I shoot from Heav'n to give him safe convoy, Mask 81
1637 'giue'
Likeliest, and neerest to the present ayd Mask 90
Trinity ms 'the' ← 'give'
And give it false presentments, lest the place Mask 156
With everlasting oil, to give due light Mask 199
line not in Bridgewater ms
And give resounding grace to all Heav'ns Harmonies. Mask 243
Bridgewater ms 'hould a Counterpointe'
Trinity ms 'give resounding grace' ← 'hold a counterpoint'
B.M. ms 'hold a Counter point'
To give me answer from her mossie Couch. Mask 276

Give(*cont*)
(As I will give you when we go) you may Mask 648
But such as are good men can give good things, Mask 703
thou man of lies & falshood, if thou give me it Mask Tr. ms 22.21
And if I give thee honour due, Allegro 37
These delights, if thou canst give, Allegro 151
These pleasures *Melancholy* give, Penseroso 175
Juno dare's not give her odds; Arcades 23
A better soyl shall give ye thanks. Arcades 101
This if thou do he will an off-spring give, Fair Inf 76
She heard them give thee this, that thou should'st still Vacation 65
Enter'd the world, now bleeds to give us ease; Circum 11
That to give the world encrease, Winchester 51
Dante shall give Fame leave to set thee higher Sonnet 13, 12
Trinity ms 'Dante shall give Fame leave to' ← 'Fame by the Tuscan's leav shall'
Jehovah to my words give ear Psalm 5, 1
Give ear *in time of need*, Psalm 80, 2
Shine forth, *and from thy cloud give light*, Psalm 80, 7
O Jacobs God give ear, Psalm 84, 30
give ear, and to the crie Psalm 86, 18
Unto thy servant give thy strength, Psalm 86, 59
What hinders? as some teachers give to Boyes Prose 6, 2
Given
Till, as a signal giv'n, th' uplifted Spear Par Lost 1.347
ms 'given'
Swarm'd and were straitn'd; till the Signal giv'n, Par Lost 1.776
Voutsaf't or sought; for what peace will be giv'n Par Lost 2.332
Into my hand was giv'n, with charge to keep Par Lost 2.775
Not free, what proof could they have givn sincere Par Lost 3.103
Lie vanquisht; thou hast givn me to possess Par Lost 3.243
Conferrd upon us, and Dominion giv'n Par Lost 4.430
Gabriel, to thee thy course by Lot hath giv'n Par Lost 4.561
Neither our own but giv'n; what follie then Par Lost 4.1007
Given him by this great Conference to know Par Lost 5.454
This was that caution giv'n thee; be advis'd. Par Lost 5.523
Giv'n me to quell thir pride, and in event Par Lost 5.740
Was giv'n him temperd so, that neither keen Par Lost 6.322
Son, Heir, and Lord, to him Dominion giv'n, Par Lost 6.887
Giv'n and receiv'd; but in disparitie Par Lost 8.386
The character of that Dominion giv'n Par Lost 8.545
Anger and just rebuke, and judgement giv'n, Par Lost 9.10
Matter of scorne, not to be given the Foe, Par Lost 9.951
Wings growing, and Dominion giv'n me large Par Lost 10.244
High proof ye now have giv'n to be the Race Par Lost 10.385
Offended, worth your laughter, hath giv'n up Par Lost 10.488
Giv'n thee of Grace, wherein thou may'st repent, Par Lost 11.255
Better end heer unborn. Why is life giv'n Par Lost 11.502
Authoritie usurpt, from God not giv'n: Par Lost 12.66
So many and so various Laws are giv'n; Par Lost 12.282
And therefore was Law given them to evince Par Lost 12.287
So law appears imperfet, and but giv'n Par Lost 12.300
The Spirit of God, promisd alike and giv'n Par Lost 12.519
Such high attest was giv'n, a while survey'd Par Reg 1.37
By thee are giv'n, and what confest more true Par Reg 1.431
For God hath justly giv'n the Nations up Par Reg 1.442
With that (such power was giv'n him then) he took Par Reg 3.251
Is given, and by that right I give it thee. Par Reg 4.104
For giv'n to me, I give to whom I please, Par Reg 4.164
The Kingdoms of the world to thee were giv'n, Par Reg 4.182
If given, by whom but by the King of Kings, Par Reg 4.185
God over all supreme? if giv'n to thee, Par Reg 4.186
And by himself given over; Samson 121
Our earnest Prayers, then giv'n with solemn hand Samson 359
The mystery of God giv'n me under pledge Samson 378
Which was expresly giv'n thee to annoy them? Samson 578
Sleep hath forsook and giv'n me o're Samson 629
Feigndst at thy birth was giv'n thee in thy hair, Samson 1135
So vertue giv'n for lost, Samson 1697
Had given day her room, Nativity 78
This was a Statute *giv'n of old* Psalm 81, 13
Giver
Giver of all things faire, but fairest this Par Lost 8.493
The giver, answer'd Jesus. Why should that Par Reg 2.322
By thee how fairly is the Giver now Par Reg 4.187
Th' all-giver would be unthank't, would be unprais'd, Mask 723
Trinity ms 'all giver'
Bridgewater ms 'allgiver'
And then the giver would be better thank't, Mask 775
Givers
Our givers thir own gifts, and large bestow Par Lost 5.317
Gives
No spot or blame behind: Which gives me hope Par Lost 5.119
That one Celestial Father gives to all. Par Lost 5.403
To whom the Angel. Therefore what he gives Par Lost 5.404
In what he gives to thee, this Paradise Par Lost 8.171
Not that which justly gives Heroic name Par Lost 9.40
How should ye? by the Fruit? it gives you Life Par Lost 9.686
Yet gives not o're though desperate of success, Par Reg 4.23
Unmindfull of the crown that Vertue gives Mask 9
And gives them leave to wear their Saphire crowns, Mask 26
Trinity ms 'give'
By sly enticement gives his banefull cup, Mask 525
Rest that gives all men life, gave him his death, Another 11
and gives thee praise above the pipe of Pan; Sonnet 13, Tr. ms 40.06
Gives grace and glory *bright*, Psalm 84, 42
Givest
And giv'st access, though secret she retire. Par Lost 9.810

Giving
Giving to death, and dying to redeeme, Par Lost 3.299
Of that life-giving Plant, but only us'd Par Lost 4.199
Scepter and Power, thy giving, I assume, Par Lost 6.730
O Sacred, Wise, and Wisdom-giving Plant, Par Lost 9.679
In giving limit to her life. Winchester 14
Glad
But glad that now his Sea should find a shore, Par Lost 2.1011
Glad to be offer'd, he attends the will Par Lost 3.270
Glad was the Spirit impure as now in hope Par Lost 3.630
On which the Sun more glad impress'd his beams Par Lost 4.150
My Glorie, my Perfection, glad I see Par Lost 5.29
And fell asleep; but O how glad I wak'd Par Lost 5.92
Surceas'd, and glad as hoping here to end Par Lost 6.258
Hasted with glad precipitance, uprowld Par Lost 7.291
Glad Eevning and glad Morn crownd the fourth day. Par Lost 7.386
1674 printed 'G!ad Eevning'
Glad we return'd up to the coasts of Light Par Lost 8.245
Eate freely with glad heart; fear here no dearth: Par Lost 8.322
The Eye of *Eve* to mark his play; he glad Par Lost 9.528
To whom the wilie Adder, blithe and glad. Par Lost 9.625
Whom thus the Prince of Darkness answerd glad. Par Lost 10.383
Insensible, how glad would lay me down Par Lost 10.777
Before the Fathers Throne: Them the glad Son Par Lost 11.20
Glad to be so dismist in peace. Can thus Par Lost 11.507
O Prophet of glad tidings, finisher Par Lost 12.375
Check or reproof, and glad to scape so quit. Par Reg 1.477
Let us be glad of this, and all our fears Par Reg 2.53
The Prince of darkness, glad would also seem Par Reg 4.441
With nursing diligence, to me glad office, Samson 924
Or of him bringing to us some glad news? Samson 1444
To further this nights glad solemnity; Arcades 39
From the glad sound would not be absent long, Lycidas 35
Death was half glad when he had got him down; Carrier 6
Whom *Joves* great Son to her glad Husband gave, Sonnet 23, 3
Glade
Down the steep glade, and met the neather Flood, Par Lost 4.231
In solitude live savage, in some glade Par Lost 9.1085
Chances to passe through this adventrous glade, Mask 79
That brow this bottom glade, whence night by night Mask 532
Glades
Oft in glimmering Bowres, and glades Penseroso 27
Gladlier
And gladlier shall resign, when in the end Par Lost 6.731
And toucht by her fair tendance gladlier grew. Par Lost 8.47
Gladly
Gladly the Port, though Shrouds and Tackle torn; Par Lost 2.1044
To have reported: gladly then he mixt Par Lost 6.21
Gladly into the wayes of God with Man: Par Lost 8.226
And gladly of our Union heare thee speak, Par Lost 9.966
To deathless pain? how gladly would I meet Par Lost 10.775
Gladly behold though but his utmost skirts Par Lost 11.332
They gladly thither haste, and by a Quire Par Lost 12.366
Into thir hands, and they as gladly yield me Samson 259
And gladly banish squint suspicion. Mask 413
Quick'n us thou, then *gladly* wee Psalm 80, 75
Gladness
And gladness thou hast put Psalm 4, 32
Gladsome
Let us with a gladsom mind Psalm 136, 1
With joy and gladsom cheer Psalm 84, 26
Glance
Of Coral stray, or sporting with quick glance Par Lost 7.405
Against the charm of Beauties powerful glance. Par Lost 8.533
So said he, and forbore not glance or toy Par Lost 9.1034
Consum'd with nimble glance, and grateful steame; Par Lost 11.442
Swift as the lightning glance he executes Samson 1284
Upon thy streams with wily glance, Mask 884
Bridgewater ms 'glaunce'
In thee *fresh brooks, and soft streams glance* Psalm 87, 27
Glanced
Glanc'd on the ground, with labour I must earne Par Lost 10.1054
Glancing
Swift as the Sparkle of a glancing Star, Mask 80
Trinity ms 'glancing' ←'glauncing'
Bridgewater ms 'glauncinge'
Glare
A Lion now he stalkes with fierie glare, Par Lost 4.402
Glared
Glar'd lightning, and shot forth pernicious fire Par Lost 6.849
Glar'd on him passing: these were from without Par Lost 10.714
The Lion and fierce Tiger glar'd aloof. Par Reg 1.313
Glaring
& yawning dens where glaring monsters house Mask Tr. ms 16.63
and yawninge denns, where glaringe monsters house Mask Br. ms 416
Glass
Through Optic Glass the *Tuscan* Artist views Par Lost 1.288
ms 'glasse'
Above all Hills. As when by night the Glass Par Lost 5.261
And the cleer Sun on his wide watrie Glass Par Lost 11.844
Of vision multiplyed through air, or glass Par Reg 4.41
His orient liquor in a Crystal Glasse, Mask 65
1673 'Glass'
Trinity ms 'glasse'
Bridgewater ms 'glasse'
1637 'glasse'
And brandish't blade rush on him, break his glass, Mask 651
Trinity ms 'glasse'

Glass(*cont*)
Bridgewater ms 'glasse'
1637 'glasse'
That own'd the vertuous Ring and Glass, Penseroso 113
The floods stood still like Walls of Glass, Psalm 136, 49
And in times long and dark Prospective Glass Vacation 71
Glassy
On the cleer *Hyaline*, the Glassie Sea; Par Lost 7.619
Under the glassie, cool, translucent wave, Mask 861
B.M. ms 'glassy'
That glassy flouds from rugged rocks can crush, Psalm 114, 17
Glaucus
And old sooth-saying *Glaucus* spell, Mask 874
Glazed
Through his glaz'd Optic Tube yet never saw. Par Lost 3.590
Gleam
And long he wanderd, till at last a gleame Par Lost 3.499
A Shape within the watry gleam appeerd Par Lost 4.461
Shall rest by Day, a fiery gleame by Night, Par Lost 12.257
And casts a gleam over this tufted Grove. Mask 225
1637 'gleame'
line not in Bridgewater ms
Trinity ms 'gleame'
Gleaming
The field all iron cast a gleaming brown, Par Reg 3.326
Glebe
Fertil of corn the glebe, of oyl and wine, Par Reg 3.259
Glibbed
Of all his flattering Prophets glibb'd with lyes Par Reg 1.375
Glide
Yee that in Waters glide, and yee that walk Par Lost 5.200
Glide under the green Wave, in Sculles that oft Par Lost 7.402
Of midnight vapor glide obscure, and prie Par Lost 9.159
Glides
Ris'n from a River o're the marish glides, Par Lost 12.630
Gliding
Thither came *Uriel*, gliding through the Eeven Par Lost 4.555
Down to the veins of Earth, thence gliding hot Par Lost 11.568
Gliding meteorous, as Ev'ning Mist Par Lost 12.629
Glimmering
Save what the glimmering of these livid flames Par Lost 1.182
A glimmering dawn; here Nature first begins Par Lost 2.1037
Of glimmering air less vext with tempest loud: Par Lost 3.429
Oft in glimmering Bowres, and glades Penseroso 27
Under the opening eye-lids of the morn, Lycidas 26
1638 'glimmering'
Trinity ms 'opening' ←'glimmering'
But in their glimmering Orbs did glow, Nativity 75
Glimpse
Obscure some glimps of joy, to have found thir chief Par Lost 1.524
ms 'glimpse'
Hasting this way, and now by glimps discerne Par Lost 4.867
Light as the Lightning glimps they ran, they flew, Par Lost 6.642
Each Orb a glimps of Light, conveyd so farr Par Lost 8.156
When in one night, ere glimps of morn, Allegro 107
Glimpses
The glimpses of his Fathers glory shine. Par Reg 1.93
Glistered
So glister'd the dire Snake, and into fraud Par Lost 9.643
Glistering
With glistering Spires and Pinnacles adornd, Par Lost 3.550
Glistring with dew; fragrant the fertil earth Par Lost 4.645
Glistring with dew, nor fragrance after showers, Par Lost 4.653
Nor glistering, may of solid good containe Par Lost 8.93
As in a glistering *Zodiac* hung the Sword, Par Lost 11.247
Would send a glistring Guardian if need were Mask 219
line not in Bridgewater ms
Nor in the glistering foil Lycidas 79
1638 'glistring'
Glitter
Was left him, or false glitter: All amaz'd Par Lost 10.452
Glittering
Who forthwith from the glittering Staff unfurld Par Lost 1.535
Harps ever tun'd, that glittering by thir side Par Lost 3.366
Or glittering Starr-light without thee is sweet. Par Lost 4.656
Thir glittering Tents he passd, and now is come Par Lost 5.291
Or in thir glittering Tissues bear imblaz'd Par Lost 5.592
Turrets and Terrases, and glittering Spires. Par Reg 4.54
And so attend ye toward her glittering state; Arcades 81
Are seen in glittering ranks with wings displaid, Nativity 114
Globe
Rivers or Mountains in her spotty Globe. Par Lost 1.291
ms 'globe'
A Globe of fierie Seraphim inclos'd Par Lost 2.512
Mean while upon the firm opacous Globe Par Lost 3.418
Satan alighted walks: a Globe farr off Par Lost 3.422
All this dark Globe the Fiend found as he pass'd, Par Lost 3.498
Look downward on that Globe whose hither side Par Lost 3.722
Which they beheld, the Moons resplendent Globe Par Lost 4.723
Prolific humour soft'ning all her Globe, Par Lost 7.280
Oblique the Centric Globe: Som say the Sun Par Lost 10.671
Large liberty to round this Globe of Earth, Par Reg 1.365
So Satan fell and strait a fiery Globe Par Reg 4.581
A Globe of circular light, Nativity 110
Globes
Not unconform to other shining Globes, Par Lost 5.259
Of Iron Globes, which on the Victor Host Par Lost 6.590

Globose
And all the Sea, from one entire globose Par Lost 5.753
Globose, and every magnitude of Starrs, Par Lost 7.357
Globous
Then all this globous Earth in Plain out spred, Par Lost 5.649
Gloom
That we must change for Heav'n, this mournful gloom Par Lost 1.244
All in a moment through the gloom were seen Par Lost 1.544
Purge off this gloom; the soft delicious Air, Par Lost 2.400
Into this gloom of *Tartarus* profound, Par Lost 2.858
To journie through the airie gloom began, Par Lost 7.246
Accompanied, with damps and dreadful gloom, Par Lost 10.848
Of Stygian darknes spets her thickest gloom, Mask 132
Bridgewater ms 'gloome'
Trinity ms 'gloome' ←'glome'
1637 'gloome'
Teach light to counterfeit a gloom, Penseroso 80
And though the shady gloom Nativity 77
Gloomiest
Alreadie in part, though hid in gloomiest shade, Par Lost 10.716
Gloomy
Or do his Errands in the gloomy Deep; Par Lost 1.152
What readiest path leads where your gloomie bounds Par Lost 2.976
Under his gloomie power I shall not long Par Lost 3.242
Her self a fairer Floure by gloomie *Dis* Par Lost 4.270
Gloomie as Night; under his burning Wheeles Par Lost 6.832
A gloomy Consistory; and them amidst Par Reg 1.42
To incorporate with gloomy night; Samson 161
Such are those thick and gloomy shadows damp Mask 470
Trinity ms 'gloomie'
Bridgewater ms 'gloomie'
1637 'gloomie'
Through this gloomy covert wide, Mask 945
1637 'gloomie'
Trinity ms 'gloomie'
Bridgewater ms 'gloomie'
Thy justice in the *gloomy* land Psalm 88, 51
Gloried
As I suppose, towards your once gloried friend, Samson 334
Glories
Glories: For never since created man, Par Lost 1.573
Equal'd in all thir glories, to inshrine Par Lost 1.719
Th'enameld *Arras* of the Rainbow wearing, Nativity 143
1673 'Orb'd in a Rain-bow and like glories wearing'
Glorified
By all his Angels glorifi'd, requires Par Reg 3.113
Glorify
The works of God, thereby to glorifie Par Lost 3.695
To glorifie thy Son, I alwayes thee, Par Lost 6.725
To glorifie the Maker, and inferr Par Lost 7.116
So both himself and us to glorifie: Nativity 154
And glorifie thy name. Psalm 86, 32
Glorious
And hazard in the Glorious Enterprize, Par Lost 1.89
ms 'glorious'
More glorious and more dread then from no fall, Par Lost 2.16
Designing or exhorting glorious warr, Par Lost 2.179
Most glorious, in him all his Father shon Par Lost 3.139
Amidst the glorious brightness where thou sit'st Par Lost 3.376
Of colour glorious and effect so rare? Par Lost 3.612
Saw within kenn a glorious Angel stand, Par Lost 3.622
I fell, how glorious once above thy Spheare; Par Lost 4.39
The image of thir glorious Maker shon, Par Lost 4.292
This glorious sight, when sleep hath shut all eyes? Par Lost 4.658
These are thy glorious works, Parent of good, Par Lost 5.153
Eastward among those Trees, what glorious shape Par Lost 5.309
None can then Heav'n such glorious shape contain; Par Lost 5.362
The ruin of so many glorious once Par Lost 5.567
Thy self though great and glorious dost thou count, Par Lost 5.833
Back on thy foes more glorious to return Par Lost 6.39
Vain glorious, and through infamie seeks fame: Par Lost 6.384
First in his East the glorious Lamp was seen, Par Lost 7.370
The glorious Train ascending: He through Heav'n, Par Lost 7.574
Still glorious before whom awake I stood; Par Lost 8.464
O glorious trial of exceeding Love, Par Lost 9.961
Matter of glorious trial; and perhaps Par Lost 9.1177
Mine with this glorious Work, and made one Realm Par Lost 10.391
To expedite your glorious march; but I Par Lost 10.474
In Triumph issuing forth thir glorious Chief; Par Lost 10.537
Of this new glorious World, and mee so late Par Lost 10.721
A glorious Apparition, had not doubt Par Lost 11.211
Not that more glorious, when the Angels met Par Lost 11.213
Wandring, shall in a glorious Temple enshrine. Par Lost 12.334
Thou Spirit who ledst this glorious Eremite Par Reg 1.8
At thy Nativity a glorious Quire Par Reg 1.242
To things not glorious, men not worthy of fame. Par Reg 3.70
They err who count it glorious to subdue Par Reg 3.71
Then great and glorious *Rome*, Queen of the Earth Par Reg 4.45
And higher yet the glorious Temple rear'd Par Reg 4.546
Queller of Satan, on thy glorious work Par Reg 4.634
With this Heav'n-gifted strength? O glorious strength Samson 36
Select, and Sacred, Glorious for a while, Samson 363
So deal not with this once thy glorious Champion, Samson 705
How honourable, how glorious to entrap Samson 855
Har. Thou durst not thus disparage glorious arms Samson 1130
What glorious hand gave *Samson* his deaths wound? Samson 1581
Chor. O dearly-bought revenge, yet glorious! Samson 1660
That glorious Form, that Light unsufferable, Nativity 8

Glorious*(cont)*
Once glorious Towers, now sunk in guiltles blood; Passion 40
To live with him, and sing in endles morn of light. Musick 28
Trinity ms 'endlesse' ←'never parting' ←'cloudlesse' ←'endlesse' ←'uneclipsed' ← 'ever-glorious'←'ever-endlesse'
And speak the truth of thee on glorious Theams Sonnet 14, 12
To peace and truth thy glorious way hast plough'd, Sonnet 16, 4
1694 'Glorious'
Thence to thy glorious habitation Psalm 7, 27
And glorious is thy name through all the earth? Psalm 8, 2
And glorious is thy name through all the earth. Psalm 8, 24
Like to thy *glorious* works. Psalm 86, 28
City of God, most glorious things Psalm 87, 9
Gloriously
When thou attended gloriously from Heav'n Par Lost 3.323
In sight of God's high Throne, gloriously bright, Par Lost 3.655
How gloriously; I shall, thou say'st, expel Par Reg 4.127
Gloriously rigg'd; and for a word, a tear, Samson 200
Bore witness gloriously; whence *Gaza* mourns Samson 1752
Glory
To set himself in Glory above his Peers, Par Lost 1.39
ms 'glory'
That Glory never shall his wrath or might Par Lost 1.110
ms 'glory'
Though all our Glory extinct, and happy state Par Lost 1.141
ms 'glory'
Glory of him that made them, to transform Par Lost 1.370
Of Glory obscur'd: As when the Sun new ris'n Par Lost 1.594
ms 'glory'
Thir Glory witherd. As when Heavens Fire Par Lost 1.612
ms 'glory'
Choose to reside, his Glory unobscur'd, Par Lost 2.265
His glory to augment. The bold design Par Lost 2.386
Satan, whom now transcendent glory rais'd Par Lost 2.427
Thir specious deeds on earth, which glory excites, Par Lost 2.484
Passion and Apathie, and glory and shame, Par Lost 2.564
The radiant image of his Glory sat, Par Lost 3.63
Through Heav'n and Earth, so shall my glorie excel, Par Lost 3.133
For him, what for thy glorie thou hast made? Par Lost 3.164
Thy bosom, and this glorie next to thee Par Lost 3.239
Love hath abounded more then Glory abounds, Par Lost 3.312
Impresst the effulgence of his Glorie abides, Par Lost 3.388
Built thir fond hopes of Glorie or lasting fame, Par Lost 3.449
O thou that with surpassing Glory crownd, Par Lost 4.32
That Glorie then, when thou no more wast good, Par Lost 4.838
Or all at once; more glorie will be wonn, Par Lost 4.853
My Glorie, my Perfection, glad I see Par Lost 5.29
Son, thou in whom my glory I behold Par Lost 5.719
Matter to mee of Glory, whom thir hate Par Lost 5.738
Crownd them with Glory, and to thir Glory nam'd Par Lost 5.839
The strife of Glorie: which we mean to win, Par Lost 6.290
And ignominie, yet to glorie aspires Par Lost 6.383
Honour, Dominion, Glorie, and renowne, Par Lost 6.422
Effulgence of my Glorie, Son belov'd, Par Lost 6.680
Have sufferd, that the Glorie may be thine Par Lost 6.701
As is most just; this I my Glorie account, Par Lost 6.726
From the right hand of Glorie where he sate, Par Lost 6.747
Grieving to see his Glorie, at the sight Par Lost 6.792
Kingdom and Power and Glorie appertains, Par Lost 6.815
On high: who into Glorie him receav'd, Par Lost 6.891
Glorie they sung to the most High, good will Par Lost 7.182
Glorie to him whose just avenging ire Par Lost 7.184
1669 'Glory'
Glorie and praise, whose wisdom had ordain'd Par Lost 7.187
The King of Glorie in his powerful Word Par Lost 7.208
Uplifted, in Paternal Glorie rode Par Lost 7.219
Now Heav'n in all her Glorie shon, and rowld Par Lost 7.499
With glorie attributed to the high Par Lost 8.12
To mee shall be the glorie sole among Par Lost 9.135
To that first naked Glorie. Such of late Par Lost 9.1115
Toward the right hand his Glorie, on the Son Par Lost 10.64
Of high collateral glorie: him Thrones and Powers, Par Lost 10.86
In glory as of old, to him appeas'd Par Lost 10.226
Of *Satan* (for I glorie in the name, Par Lost 10.386
With what permissive glory since his fall Par Lost 10.451
The Glory of that Glory, who now becom Par Lost 10.722
Of glory, and farr off his steps adore. Par Lost 11.333
To shew him all Earths Kingdomes and thir Glory. Par Lost 11.384
Of human Glorie, and for Glorie done Par Lost 11.694
With glory and spoile back to thir promis'd Land. Par Lost 12.172
With earths wide bounds, his glory with the Heav'ns. Par Lost 12.371
Then enter into glory, and resume Par Lost 12.456
With glory and power to judge both quick and dead, Par Lost 12.460
To God more glory, more good will to Men Par Lost 12.477
In glory of the Father, to dissolve Par Lost 12.546
1669 'glorie'
The glimpses of his Fathers glory shine. Par Reg 1.93
But this thy glory shall be soon retrench'd; Par Reg 1.454
Thy Glory, free thy people from thir yoke, Par Reg 2.48
Of worth, of honour, glory, and popular praise; Par Reg 2.227
Array'd in Glory on my cup to attend: Par Reg 2.386
The fame and glory, glory the reward Par Reg 3.25
Quench not the thirst of glory, but augment. Par Reg 3.38
With glory, wept that he had liv'd so long Par Reg 3.41
For glories sake by all thy argument. Par Reg 3.46
For what is glory but the blaze of fame, Par Reg 3.47
Are few, and glory scarce of few is rais'd. Par Reg 3.59
This is true glory and renown, when God Par Reg 3.60

Glory(*cont*)
Where glory is false glory, attributed Par Reg 3.69
But if there be in glory aught of good, Par Reg 3.88
Yet if for fame and glory aught be done, Par Reg 3.100
Shall I seek glory then, as vain men seek Par Reg 3.105
Think not so slight of glory; therein least Par Reg 3.109
Resembling thy great Father: he seeks glory, Par Reg 3.110
And for his glory all things made, all things Par Reg 3.111
Glory from men, from all men good or bad, Par Reg 3.114
Glory he requires, and glory he receives Par Reg 3.117
From us his foes pronounc't glory he exacts. Par Reg 3.120
Though chiefly not for glory as prime end, Par Reg 3.123
Then glory and benediction, that is thanks, Par Reg 3.127
But why should man seek glory? who of his own Par Reg 3.134
That who advance his glory, not thir own, Par Reg 3.143
Them he himself to glory will advance. Par Reg 3.144
Insatiable of glory had lost all, Par Reg 3.148
Of glory as thou wilt, said he, so deem, Par Reg 3.150
The world thou hast not seen, much less her glory, Par Reg 3.236
Thou on the Throne of *David* in full glory, Par Reg 3.383
The Kingdoms of the world, and all thir glory. Par Reg 4.89
All glory arrogate, to God give none, Par Reg 4.315
Or active, tended on by glory, or fame, Par Reg 4.371
Not more; for Honours, Riches, Kingdoms, Glory Par Reg 4.536
By how much from the top of wondrous glory, Samson 167
The glory late of *Israel*, now the grief; Samson 179
Regardless of his glories diminution; Samson 303
To vindicate the glory of his name Samson 475
My race of glory run, and race of shame, Samson 597
To some great work, thy glory, Samson 680
So had the glory of Prowess been recover'd Samson 1098
How highly it concerns his glory now Samson 1148
To what may serve his glory best, & spread his name Samson 1429
Shall in the happy trial prove most glory. Mask 592
1637 'glorie'
Bridgewater ms 'glorie'
That sing, and singing in their glory move, Lycidas 180
Trinity ms 'glorie'
His praise and glory was in *Israel* known. Psalm 114, 6
Emptied his glory, ev'n to nakednes; Circum 20
Whilst thou bright Saint high sit'st in glory, Winchester 61
But thou Lord art my shield my glory, Psalm 3, 7
My glory have in scorn Psalm 4, 8
In the dust my glory dead, Psalm 7, 16
Gives grace and glory *bright*, Psalm 84, 42
And glory shall *ere long appear* Psalm 85, 39
Glorying
Both glorying to have scap't the *Stygian* flood Par Lost 1.239
Gloss
The Angel, nor in mist, the common gloss Par Lost 5.435
To gloss upon, and censuring, frown or smile? Samson 948
Glossy
Shon with a glossie scurff, undoubted sign Par Lost 1.672
Glow
But in their glimmering Orbs did glow, Nativity 75
Glowed
Silence was pleas'd: now glow'd the Firmament Par Lost 4.604
To whom the Angel with a smile that glow'd Par Lost 8.618
About her glowd, oft stooping to support Par Lost 9.427
But in her Cheek distemper flushing glowd. Par Lost 9.887
Glowing
With radiant light, as glowing Iron with fire; Par Lost 3.594
With Tresses discompos'd, and glowing Cheek, Par Lost 5.10
His glowing Axle doth allay Mask 96
Bridgewater ms 'glowinge'
And well plac't words of glozing courtesie Mask 161
Bridgewater ms 'gloweinge Curtesie'
Where glowing Embers through the room Penseroso 79
The glowing Violet. Lycidas 145
Glozed
So gloz'd the Tempter, and his Proem tun'd; Par Lost 9.549
Glozing
For man will hark'n to his glozing lyes, Par Lost 3.93
And well plac't words of glozing courtesie Mask 161
Bridgewater ms 'gloweinge'
Glut
Death last, and with his Carcass glut the Grave: Par Lost 3.259
Thir devilish glut, chaind Thunderbolts and Hail Par Lost 6.589
So Death shall be deceav'd his glut, and with us two Par Lost 10.990
And glut thy self with what thy womb devours, On Time 4
Then when a year of glut Psalm 4, 33
Glutinous
Smear'd with gumms of glutenous heat Mask 917
Bridgewater ms 'gluttenous'
Glutted
With suckt and glutted offal, at one sling Par Lost 10.633
Gluttonies
Thir sumptuous gluttonies, and gorgeous feasts Par Reg 4.114
Gluttonous
Due nourishment, not gluttonous delight, Par Lost 11.533
Gluttony
His praise due paid, for swinish gluttony Mask 776
Bridgewater ms 'gluttonie'
Trinity ms 'gluttonie'
Gnashing
Gnashing for anguish and despite and shame Par Lost 6.340
Gnaw
That bred them they return, and howle and gnaw Par Lost 2.799

Go
High honourd sits? Go therfore mighty Powers, Par Lost 2.456
Fell with us from on high: from them I go Par Lost 2.826
So much the neerer danger; go and speed; Par Lost 2.1008
1667 'goe'
May come and go, so unapprov'd, and leave Par Lost 5.118
Go therefore, half this day as friend with friend Par Lost 5.229
This day to be our Guest. But goe with speed, Par Lost 5.313
Go *Michael* of Celestial Armies Prince, Par Lost 6.44
1667 'Goe'
Hence then, and evil go with thee along Par Lost 6.275
Go then thou Mightiest in thy Fathers might, Par Lost 6.710
Go heavenly Guest, Ethereal Messenger, Par Lost 8.646
Go; for thy stay, not free, absents thee more; Par Lost 9.372
Go in thy native innocence, relie Par Lost 9.373
The willinger I goe, nor much expect Par Lost 9.382
Command me absolutely not to go, Par Lost 9.1156
Mayst ever rest well pleas'd. I go to judge Par Lost 10.71
Upon thy Belly groveling thou shalt goe, Par Lost 10.177
Goe whither Fate and inclination strong Par Lost 10.265
No detriment need feare, goe and be strong. Par Lost 10.409
Though present in his Angel, who shall goe Par Lost 12.201
Rarely be found: so shall the World goe on, Par Lost 12.537
1669 'go'
We may no longer stay: go, waken *Eve;* Par Lost 12.594
In mee is no delay; with thee to goe, Par Lost 12.615
1669 'go'
Is to go hence unwilling; thou to mee Par Lost 12.617
More then the Camel, and to drink go far, Par Reg 1.340
At distance I forgive thee, go with that; Samson 954
Bid go with evil omen and the brand Samson 967
Sam. So let her go, God sent her to debase me, Samson 999
Go to his Temple, invocate his aid Samson 1146
Sams. Go baffl'd coward, lest I run upon thee, Samson 1237
I with this Messenger will go along, Samson 1384
Like a wild Beast, I am content to go. Samson 1403
Chor. Go, and the Holy One Samson 1427
Let us go find the body where it lies Samson 1725
(As I will give you when we go) you may Mask 648
Trinity ms 'when we goe' ←'on the way' ←'as wee goe'
Bridgewater ms 'goe'
1637 'goe'
Cramms, and blasphemes his feeder. Shall I go on? Mask 779
1637 'goe'
word not in Bridgewater ms
word not in Trinity ms
Com, and trip it as ye go Allegro 33
Inimitable sounds, yet as we go, Arcades 78
Trinity ms 'goe'
Last came, and last did go, Lycidas 108
Trinity ms 'goe'
Untill their Lord himself bespake, and bid them go. Nativity 76
In worth and excellence he shall out-go them, Vacation 79
Thy numerous mercies go Psalm 5, 18
That all may pluck her, as they go, Psalm 80, 51
So shall we not go back from thee Psalm 80, 73
I will *go strait and* hear, Psalm 85, 30
Before him Righteousness shall go Psalm 85, 53
All day they round about me go, Psalm 88, 67
Goal
Part curb thir fierie Steeds, or shun the Goal Par Lost 2.531
Pacing toward the other gole Mask 100
Bridgewater ms 'goale'
Trinity ms 'goale'
Goat
Of Ewe or Goat dropping with Milk at Eevn, Par Lost 9.582
Or Ounce, or Tiger, Hog, or bearded Goat, Mask 71
Bridgewater ms 'goate'
Trinity ms 'goate'
Goats
Of Goats or timerous flock together throngd Par Lost 6.857
The bloud of Bulls and Goats, they may conclude Par Lost 12.292
And fat regorg'd of Bulls and Goats, Samson 1671
Goblin
To whom the Goblin full of wrauth reply'd, Par Lost 2.688
No goblin, or swart Faery of the mine, Mask 436
1673 'Goblin'
Bridgewater ms 'goblinge'
Tells how the drudging *Goblin* swet, Allegro 105
God
Fast by the Oracle of God; I thence Par Lost 1.12
And justifie the wayes of God to men. Par Lost 1.26
Against the Throne and Monarchy of God Par Lost 1.42
As far remov'd from God and light of Heav'n Par Lost 1.73
Leviathan, which God of all his works Par Lost 1.201
Through Gods high sufferance for the tryal of man, Par Lost 1.366
God thir Creator, and th' invisible Par Lost 1.369
Thir Seats long after next the Seat of God, Par Lost 1.383
His Temple right against the Temple of God Par Lost 1.402
He also against the house of God was bold: Par Lost 1.470
Gods Altar to disparage and displace Par Lost 1.473
With lust and violence the house of God. Par Lost 1.496
Went all his fear: of God, or Hell, or worse Par Lost 2.49
Seduce them to our Party, that thir God Par Lost 2.368
With awful reverence prone; and as a God Par Lost 2.478
Of heavenly Grace: and God proclaiming peace, Par Lost 2.499
A Universe of death, which God by curse Par Lost 2.622
Mean while the Adversary of God and Man, Par Lost 2.629

God *(cont)*

Admir'd, not fear'd; God and his Son except,	Par Lost 2.678
And they outcast from God, are here condemn'd	Par Lost 2.694
God and good Angels guard by special grace.	Par Lost 2.1033
May I express thee unblam'd? since God is light,	Par Lost 3.3
Of God, as with a Mantle didst invest	Par Lost 3.10
Him God beholding from his prospect high,	Par Lost 3.77
Thus while God spake, ambrosial fragrance fill'd	Par Lost 3.135
Beyond compare the Son of God was seen	Par Lost 3.138
By doom severe, had not the Son of God,	Par Lost 3.224
Equal to God, and equally enjoying	Par Lost 3.306
By Merit more then Birthright Son of God,	Par Lost 3.309
Both God and Man, Son both of God and Man,	Par Lost 3.316
God shall be All in All. But all ye Gods,	Par Lost 3.341
Hail Son of God, Saviour of Men, thy Name	Par Lost 3.412
A God, leap'd fondly into *Aetna* flames,	Par Lost 3.470
Over the *Promis'd Land* to God so dear,	Par Lost 3.531
Who in Gods presence, neerest to his Throne	Par Lost 3.649
In sight of God's high Throne, gloriously bright, 1667 'Gods' in some copies	Par Lost 3.655
Invisible, except to God alone,	Par Lost 3.684
The works of God, thereby to glorifie	Par Lost 3.695
Look'st from thy sole Dominion like the God	Par Lost 4.33
When God hath showrd the earth; so lovely seemd	Par Lost 4.152
So clomb this first grand Thief into Gods Fould:	Par Lost 4.192
Any, but God alone, to value right	Par Lost 4.202
Of God the Garden was, by him in the East	Par Lost 4.209
His farr more pleasant Garden God ordaind;	Par Lost 4.215
Pass'd underneath ingulft, for God had thrown	Par Lost 4.225
Hee for God only, shee for God in him:	Par Lost 4.299
Of God or Angel, for they thought no ill:	Par Lost 4.320
God hath pronounc't it death to taste that Tree,	Par Lost 4.427
Gods latest Image: I describ'd his way	Par Lost 4.567
Mind us of like repose, since God hath set	Par Lost 4.612
And of thir doings God takes no account.	Par Lost 4.622
Unargu'd I obey; so God ordains,	Par Lost 4.636
God is thy Law, thou mine: to know no more	Par Lost 4.637
Daughter of God and Man, accomplisht *Eve*,	Par Lost 4.660
That heav'n would want spectators, God want praise;	Par Lost 4.676
The God that made both Skie, Air, Earth and Heav'n	Par Lost 4.722
Which God likes best, into thir inmost bowre	Par Lost 4.738
Defaming as impure what God declares	Par Lost 4.746
But our destroyer, foe to God and Man?	Par Lost 4.749
Whose dwelling God hath planted here in bliss?	Par Lost 4.884
Nor God, nor Man; is Knowledge so despis'd?	Par Lost 5.60
Evil into the mind of God or Man	Par Lost 5.117
Earth and the Gard'n of God, with Cedars crownd	Par Lost 5.260
Of God inspir'd, small store will serve, where store,	Par Lost 5.322
God hath dispenst his bounties as in Heav'n.	Par Lost 5.330
Then with these various fruits the Trees of God	Par Lost 5.390
Cover'd with pearly grain: yet God hath here	Par Lost 5.430
Then had the Sons of God excuse to have bin	Par Lost 5.447
Inhabitant with God, now know I well	Par Lost 5.461
Wonder not then, what God for you saw good	Par Lost 5.491
By steps we may ascend to God. But say,	Par Lost 5.512
Attend: That thou art happie, owe to God;	Par Lost 5.520
God made thee perfet, not immutable;	Par Lost 5.524
In sight of God enthron'd, our happie state	Par Lost 5.536
Cast out from God and blessed vision, falls	Par Lost 5.613
So smooths her charming tones, that Gods own ear	Par Lost 5.626
From that high mount of God, whence light & shade	Par Lost 5.643
All but the unsleeping eyes of God to rest,	Par Lost 5.647
(Such are the Courts of God) Th' Angelic throng	Par Lost 5.650
With envie against the Son of God, that day	Par Lost 5.662
Affecting all equality with God,	Par Lost 5.763
The just Decree of God, pronounc't and sworn,	Par Lost 5.814
Shalt thou give Law to God, shalt thou dispute	Par Lost 5.822
O alienate from God, O spirit accurst,	Par Lost 5.877
Of Gods *Messiah;* those indulgent Laws	Par Lost 5.883
Within the Mount of God, fast by his Throne,	Par Lost 6.5
Servant of God, well done, well hast thou fought	Par Lost 6.29
To stand approv'd in sight of God, though Worlds	Par Lost 6.36
Pursuing drive them out from God and bliss,	Par Lost 6.52
Of God and his *Messiah*. On they move	Par Lost 6.68
To win the Mount of God, and on his Throne	Par Lost 6.88
High in the midst exalted as a God	Par Lost 6.99
The Throne of God unguarded, and his side	Par Lost 6.133
Prefer, and Pietie to God, though then	Par Lost 6.144
Of *Servitude* to serve whom God ordains,	Par Lost 6.175
Or Nature; God and Nature bid the same,	Par Lost 6.176
In Heav'n God ever blest, and his Divine	Par Lost 6.184
Or som more sudden vengeance wing'd from God	Par Lost 6.279
Of *Michael* from the Armorie of God	Par Lost 6.321
His confidence to equal God in power.	Par Lost 6.343
Which God hath in his mighty Angels plac'd)	Par Lost 6.638
God and *Messiah* his anointed King.	Par Lost 6.718
Chariots of God, half on each hand were seen:	Par Lost 6.770
Against God and *Messiah*, or to fall	Par Lost 6.796
Or faint retreat; when the great Son of God	Par Lost 6.799
Faithful hath been your warfare, and of God	Par Lost 6.803
Gods indignation on these Godless pourd	Par Lost 6.811
All but the Throne it self of God. Full soon	Par Lost 6.834
And Warr so neer the Peace of God in bliss	Par Lost 7.55
Immediate are the Acts of God, more swift	Par Lost 7.176
From the Armoury of God, where stand of old	Par Lost 7.200
In Gods Eternal store, to circumscribe	Par Lost 7.226
Thus God the Heav'n created, thus the Earth,	Par Lost 7.232
His brooding wings the Spirit of God outspred,	Par Lost 7.235

God *(cont)*

Let ther be Light, said God, and forthwith Light	Par Lost 7.243
Sojourn'd the while. God saw the Light was good;	Par Lost 7.249
God and his works, Creatour him they sung,	Par Lost 7.259
Again, God said, let ther be Firmament	Par Lost 7.261
The Waters from the Waters: and God made	Par Lost 7.263
Satiate with genial moisture, when God said	Par Lost 7.282
Easie, e're God had bid the ground be drie,	Par Lost 7.304
Her sacred shades: though God had yet not rain'd	Par Lost 7.331
God made, and every Herb, before it grew	Par Lost 7.336
On the green stemm; God saw that it was good.	Par Lost 7.337
And God made two great Lights, great for thir use	Par Lost 7.346
And Light from Darkness to divide. God saw,	Par Lost 7.352
And God said, let the Waters generate	Par Lost 7.387
And God created the great Whales, and each	Par Lost 7.391
With Eevning Harps and Mattin, when God said,	Par Lost 7.450
And worship God Supream, who made him chief	Par Lost 7.515
Created thee, in the Image of God	Par Lost 7.527
This Garden, planted with the Trees of God,	Par Lost 7.538
Open, and henceforth oft; for God will deigne	Par Lost 7.569
To Gods Eternal house direct the way,	Par Lost 7.576
And sons of men, whom God hath thus advanc't,	Par Lost 7.626
Is as the Book of God before thee set,	Par Lost 8.67
Where God resides, and ere mid-day arriv'd	Par Lost 8.112
God to remove his wayes from human sense,	Par Lost 8.119
Leave them to God above, him serve and feare;	Par Lost 8.168
God hath bid dwell farr off all anxious cares,	Par Lost 8.185
Nor tongue ineloquent; for God on thee	Par Lost 8.219
Gladly into the wayes of God with Man:	Par Lost 8.226
For God we see hath honour'd thee, and set	Par Lost 8.227
Or enemie, while God was in his work,	Par Lost 8.234
Thir Nature, with such knowledg God endu'd	Par Lost 8.353
No more of talk where God or Angel Guest	Par Lost 9.1
For what God after better worse would build?	Par Lost 9.102
Of sacred influence: As God in Heav'n	Par Lost 9.107
God hath assign'd us, nor of me shalt pass	Par Lost 9.231
Our fealtie from God, or to disturb	Par Lost 9.262
To God or thee, because we have a foe	Par Lost 9.280
Daughter of God and Man, immortal *Eve*,	Par Lost 9.291
Of God ordain'd them, his creating hand	Par Lost 9.344
But God left free the Will, for what obeyes	Par Lost 9.351
To do what God expresly hath forbid,	Par Lost 9.356
For God towards thee hath done his part, do thine.	Par Lost 9.375
Hermione and *Cadmus*, or the God	Par Lost 9.506
To Beasts, whom God on thir Creation-Day	Par Lost 9.556
For many are the Trees of God that grow	Par Lost 9.618
God so commanded, and left that Command	Par Lost 9.652
Indeed? hath God then said that of the Fruit	Par Lost 9.656
The Garden, God hath said, Ye shall not eate	Par Lost 9.662
Is open? or will God incense his ire	Par Lost 9.692
God therefore cannot hurt ye, and be just;	Par Lost 9.700
Not just, not God; not feard then, nor obeyd:	Par Lost 9.701
Of God or Death, of Law or Penaltie?	Par Lost 9.775
This may be well: but what if God have seen,	Par Lost 9.826
Of all Gods works, Creature in whom excell'd	Par Lost 9.897
Should God create another *Eve*, and I	Par Lost 9.911
Not God Omnipotent, nor Fate, yet so	Par Lost 9.927
Nor can I think that God, Creator wise,	Par Lost 9.938
Dependent made; so God shall uncreate,	Par Lost 9.943
Not well conceav'd of God, who though his Power	Par Lost 9.945
Triumph and say; Fickle their State whom God	Par Lost 9.948
Henceforth of God or Angel, earst with joy	Par Lost 9.1081
Of God All-seeing, or deceave his Heart	Par Lost 10.6
To sentence Man: the voice of God they heard	Par Lost 10.97
The thickest Trees, both Man and Wife, till God	Par Lost 10.101
Love was not in thir looks, either to God	Par Lost 10.111
Was shee thy God, that her thou didst obey	Par Lost 10.145
Wherein God set thee above her made of thee,	Par Lost 10.149
Which when the Lord God heard, without delay	Par Lost 10.163
Nor alter'd his offence; yet God at last	Par Lost 10.171
The Son of God to judge them terrifi'd	Par Lost 10.338
Of God, whom to behold was then my highth	Par Lost 10.724
Then cavil the conditions? and though God	Par Lost 10.759
God made thee of choice his own, and of his own	Par Lost 10.766
Which God inspir'd, cannot together perish	Par Lost 10.785
Strange contradiction, which to God himself	Par Lost 10.799
In sight of God? Him after all Disputes	Par Lost 10.828
To my just number found. O why did God,	Par Lost 10.888
Against God onely, I against God and thee,	Par Lost 10.931
The penaltie pronounc't, doubt not but God	Par Lost 10.1022
Reluctance against God and his just yoke	Par Lost 10.1045
When God descended, and perhaps once more	Par Lost 11.75
Hast thee, and from the Paradise of God	Par Lost 11.104
Of God high-blest, or to incline his will,	Par Lost 11.145
Ev'n to the Seat of God. For since I saught	Par Lost 11.148
God is as here, and will be found alike	Par Lost 11.350
In the Visions of God: It was a Hill	Par Lost 11.377
Th' Image of God in man created once	Par Lost 11.508
Disfiguring not Gods likeness, but thir own,	Par Lost 11.521
Gods Image did not reverence in themselves.	Par Lost 11.525
To worship God aright, and know his works	Par Lost 11.578
Religious titl'd them the Sons of God,	Par Lost 11.622
And utter odious Truth, that God would come	Par Lost 11.704
Did, as thou sawst, receave, to walk with God	Par Lost 11.707
With thir four Wives; and God made fast the dore.	Par Lost 11.737
And fear of God, from whom thir pietie feign'd	Par Lost 11.799
Of them derided, but of God observd	Par Lost 11.817
To teach thee that God attributes to place	Par Lost 11.836

God(*cont*)

Betok'ning peace from God, and Cov'nant new.	Par Lost 11.867
That God voutsafes to raise another World	Par Lost 11.877
Distended as the Brow of God appeas'd,	Par Lost 11.880
So willingly doth God remit his Ire,	Par Lost 11.885
But God who oft descends to visit men	Par Lost 12.48
Authoritie usurpt, from God not giv'n:	Par Lost 12.66
Stayes not on Man; to God his Tower intends	Par Lost 12.73
Over free Reason, God in Judgement just	Par Lost 12.92
Still tend from bad to worse, till God at last	Par Lost 12.106
As to forsake the living God, and fall	Par Lost 12.118
For Gods! yet him God the most High voutsafes	Par Lost 12.120
With God, who call'd him, in a land unknown.	Par Lost 12.134
Moses and *Aaron*) sent from God to claime	Par Lost 12.170
To know thir God, or message to regard,	Par Lost 12.174
Such wondrous power God to his Saint will lend,	Par Lost 12.200
God looking forth will trouble all his Host	Par Lost 12.209
God from the Mount of *Sinai*, whose gray top	Par Lost 12.227
Mankinds deliverance. But the voice of God	Par Lost 12.235
Instructed that to God is no access	Par Lost 12.239
Establisht, such delight hath God in Men	Par Lost 12.245
Among whom God will deigne to dwell on Earth	Par Lost 12.281
Among them; how can God with such reside?	Par Lost 12.284
Justification towards God, and peace	Par Lost 12.296
And therefore shall not *Moses*, though of God	Par Lost 12.307
Provoking God to raise them enemies:	Par Lost 12.318
The clouded Ark of God till then in Tents	Par Lost 12.333
God, as to leave them, and expose thir Land,	Par Lost 12.339
Thir Lords, whom God dispos'd, the house of God	Par Lost 12.349
Of God most High; So God with Man unites.	Par Lost 12.382
Obedience to the Law of God, impos'd	Par Lost 12.397
The Law of God exact he shall fulfill	Par Lost 12.402
His Seat at Gods right hand, exalted high	Par Lost 12.457
To God more glory, more good will to Men	Par Lost 12.477
From God, and over wrauth grace shall abound.	Par Lost 12.478
The Spirit of God, promisd alike and giv'n	Par Lost 12.519
And love with fear the onely God, to walk	Par Lost 12.562
Or works of God in Heav'n, Aire, Earth, or Sea,	Par Lost 12.579
For God is also in sleep, and Dreams advise,	Par Lost 12.611
The brandisht Sword of God before them blaz'd	Par Lost 12.633
By proof the undoubted Son of God, inspire,	Par Reg 1.11
This man of men, attested Son of God,	Par Reg 1.122
Great in Renown, and call'd the Son of God;	Par Reg 1.136
Victory and Triumph to the Son of God	Par Reg 1.173
Mean while the Son of God, who yet some days	Par Reg 1.183
The Law of God I read, and found it sweet,	Par Reg 1.207
A messenger from God fore-told thy birth	Par Reg 1.238
For what concerns my knowledge God reveals.	Par Reg 1.293
Of God; I saw and heard, for we sometimes	Par Reg 1.330
To whom the Son of God. Who brought me hither	Par Reg 1.335
But if thou be the Son of God, Command	Par Reg 1.342
He ended, and the Son of God reply'd.	Par Reg 1.346
Proceeding from the mouth of God; who fed	Par Reg 1.350
I came among the Sons of God, when he	Par Reg 1.368
To be belov'd of God, I have not lost	Par Reg 1.379
Declar'd the Son of God, to hear attent	Par Reg 1.385
For God hath justly giv'n the Nations up	Par Reg 1.442
God hath now sent his living Oracle	Par Reg 1.460
Jesus Messiah Son of God declar'd,	Par Reg 2.4
And for a time caught up to God, as once	Par Reg 2.14
Our expectation? God of *Israel*,	Par Reg 2.42
To have conceiv'd of God, or that salute	Par Reg 2.67
False titl'd Sons of God, roaming the Earth	Par Reg 2.179
Where still from shade to shade the Son of God	Par Reg 2.242
Or God support Nature without repast	Par Reg 2.250
Nature hath need of what she asks; yet God	Par Reg 2.253
But much more wonder that the Son of God	Par Reg 2.303
Of *Israel* here had famish'd, had not God	Par Reg 2.311
What doubts the Son of God to sit and eat?	Par Reg 2.368
What doubt'st thou Son of God? sit down and eat.	Par Reg 2.377
To know, and knowing worship God aright,	Par Reg 2.475
So spake the Son of God, and Satan stood	Par Reg 3.1
This is true glory and renown, when God	Par Reg 3.60
Turn'd recreant to God, ingrate and false,	Par Reg 3.138
That which to God alone of right belongs;	Par Reg 3.141
Yet so much bounty is in God, such grace,	Par Reg 3.142
So spake the Son of God; and here again	Par Reg 3.145
The Son of God up to a Mountain high.	Par Reg 3.252
From God to worship Calves, the Deities	Par Reg 3.416
The God of their fore-fathers; but so dy'd	Par Reg 3.422
And God with Idols in thir worship joyn'd.	Par Reg 3.426
Thir enemies, who serve Idols with God.	Par Reg 3.432
To whom the Son of God unmov'd reply'd.	Par Reg 4.109
The Lord thy God, and only him shalt serve;	Par Reg 4.177
And dar'st thou to the Son of God propound	Par Reg 4.178
God over all supreme? if giv'n to thee,	Par Reg 4.186
As offer them to me the Son of God,	Par Reg 4.190
That I fall down and worship thee as God?	Par Reg 4.192
Be not so sore offended, Son of God;	Par Reg 4.196
Though Sons of God both Angels are and Men,	Par Reg 4.197
God of this world invok't and world beneath;	Par Reg 4.203
Equal to God, oft shames not to prefer,	Par Reg 4.303
As fearing God nor man, contemning all	Par Reg 4.304
Ignorant of themselves, of God much more,	Par Reg 4.310
All glory arrogate, to God give none,	Par Reg 4.315
Where God is prais'd aright, and Godlike men,	Par Reg 4.348
Such are from God inspir'd, not such from thee;	Par Reg 4.350
So spake the Son of God; but Satan now	Par Reg 4.365

God(*cont*)

Brought back the Son of God, and left him there,	Par Reg 4.396
O patient Son of God, yet only stoodst	Par Reg 4.420
To tempt the Son of God with terrors dire.	Par Reg 4.431
Fair morning yet betides thee Son of God,	Par Reg 4.451
So talk'd he, while the Son of God went on	Par Reg 4.484
As false portents, not sent from God, but thee;	Par Reg 4.491
Ambitious spirit, and wouldst be thought my God,	Par Reg 4.495
For Son of God to me is yet in doubt,	Par Reg 4.501
Heard thee pronounc'd the Son of God belov'd.	Par Reg 4.513
The Son of God, which bears no single sence;	Par Reg 4.517
The Son of God I also am, or was,	Par Reg 4.518
All men are Sons of God; yet thee I thought	Par Reg 4.520
Worth naming Son of God by voice from Heav'n,	Par Reg 4.539
The Son of God; and added thus in scorn:	Par Reg 4.550
Cast thy self down; safely if Son of God:	Par Reg 4.555
Tempt not the Lord thy God, he said and stood.	Par Reg 4.561
Who durst so proudly tempt the Son of God.	Par Reg 4.580
The Son of God, with Godlike force indu'd	Par Reg 4.602
To dread the Son of God: he all unarm'd	Par Reg 4.626
Thus they the Son of God our Saviour meek	Par Reg 4.636
As of a person separate to God,	Samson 31
God, when he gave me strength, to shew withal	Samson 58
Light the prime work of God to me is extinct,	Samson 70
Fool, have divulg'd the secret gift of God	Samson 201
That what I motion'd was of God; I knew	Samson 222
Who seeing those great acts which God had done	Samson 243
Whom God hath of his special favour rais'd	Samson 273
But Gods propos'd deliverance not so.	Samson 292
Chor. Just are the ways of God,	Samson 293
Unless there be who think not God at all,	Samson 295
O wherefore did God grant me my request,	Samson 356
Alas methinks whom God hath chosen once	Samson 368
The mystery of God giv'n me under pledge	Samson 378
To *Dagon*, as their God who hath deliver'd	Samson 437
So *Dagon* shall be magnifi'd, and God,	Samson 440
Besides whom is no God, compar'd with Idols,	Samson 441
Among the Heathen round; to God have brought	Samson 451
To *Israel*, diffidence of God, and doubt	Samson 454
'Twixt God and *Dagon; Dagon* hath presum'd,	Samson 462
Me overthrown, to enter lists with God,	Samson 463
Before the God of *Abraham*. He, be sure,	Samson 465
I as a Prophecy receive: for God,	Samson 473
Endure it, doubtful whether God be Lord,	Samson 477
But I Gods counsel have not kept, his holy secret	Samson 497
God will relent, and quit thee all his debt;	Samson 509
For self-offence, more then for God offended.	Samson 515
But God hath set before us, to return thee	Samson 517
Fearless of danger, like a petty God	Samson 529
When God with these forbid'n made choice to rear	Samson 555
But God who caus'd a fountain at thy prayer	Samson 581
God of our Fathers, what is man!	Samson 667
With God or Man will gain thee no remission.	Samson 835
Sam. So let her go, God sent her to debase me,	Samson 999
Therefore Gods universal Law	Samson 1053
My trust is in the living God who gave me	Samson 1140
For proof hereof, if *Dagon* be thy god,	Samson 1145
Which I to be the power of *Israel*'s God	Samson 1150
Soon feel, whose God is strongest, thine or mine.	Samson 1155
Har. Presume not on thy God, what e're he be,	Samson 1156
Acknowledge them from God inflicted on me	Samson 1170
By combat to decide whose god is God,	Samson 1176
1671 'god is god' in some copies	
Har. Fair honour that thou dost thy God, in trusting	Samson 1178
When God into the hands of thir deliverer	Samson 1270
To shew them feats, and play before thir god,	Samson 1340
God for the fear of Man, and Man prefer,	Samson 1374
Set God behind: which in his jealousie	Samson 1375
Our God, our Law, my Nation, or my self,	Samson 1425
Private reward, for which both God and State	Samson 1465
And I perswade me God had not permitted	Samson 1495
God will restore him eye-sight to his strength.	Samson 1503
What if his eye-sight (for to *Israels* God	Samson 1527
Chor. Yet God hath wrought things as incredible	Samson 1532
Rifted the Air clamouring thir god with praise,	Samson 1621
With God not parted from him, as was feard,	Samson 1719
Afford a present to the Infant God?	Nativity 16
With that twise batter'd god of *Palestine*,	Nativity 199
For of gods he is the God;	Psalm 136, 6
Think what a present thou to God hast sent,	Fair Inf 74
And keep in tune with Heav'n, till God ere long	Musick 26
The God that sits at marriage feast;	Winchester 18
Had ripen'd thy just soul to dwell with God,	Sonnet 14, 2
Hast reard Gods Trophies and his work pursu'd.	Sonnet 16, 6
1694 'And Fought God's Battels'	
Doth God exact day labour, light deny'd,	Sonnet 19, 7
That murmur, soon replies, God doth not need	Sonnet 19, 9
And when God sends a cheerful hour, refrains.	Sonnet 21, 14
Trinity ms 'God' ← 'Gods'	
Against heavns hand or will, nor bate a jot	Sonnet 22, 7
Trinity ms 'heavns' ← 'Gods'	
To the stern God of Sea.	Horace 16
No help for him in God there lies.	Psalm 3, 6
Rise Lord, save me my God for thou	Psalm 3, 19
God of my righteousness	Psalm 4, 2
My King and God for unto thee I pray.	Psalm 5, 4
For thou art not a God that takes	Psalm 5, 9
The bloodi' and guileful man God doth detest.	Psalm 5, 16

God(*cont*)
God, find them guilty, let them fall Psalm 5, 29
Lord my God to thee I flie Psalm 7, 1
Lord my God if I have thought Psalm 7, 7
Since thou art the just God that tries Psalm 7, 38
Hearts and reins. On God is cast Psalm 7, 39
God is a just Judge and severe, Psalm 7, 43
And God is every day offended; Psalm 7, 44
To us O God *vouchsafe;* Psalm 80, 14
Lord God of Hosts, how long wilt thou, Psalm 80, 17
O God of Hosts *vouchsafe* Psalm 80, 30
Return now, God of Hosts, look down Psalm 80, 57
Lord God of Hosts *voutsafe*, Psalm 80, 78
To God our strength sing loud, *and clear* Psalm 81, 1
Sing loud to God *our King*, Psalm 81, 2
To Jacobs God, *that all may hear* Psalm 81, 3
A Law of Jacobs God, *to hold* Psalm 81, 15
No alien God shall be Psalm 81, 38
Nor shalt thou to a forein God Psalm 81, 39
I am the Lord thy God which brought Psalm 81, 41
God in the great assembly stands Psalm 82, 1
The Sons of God most high Psalm 82, 22
Rise God, judge thou the earth *in might*, Psalm 82, 25
O God hold not thy peace, Psalm 83, 2
Sit not thou still O God of *strength* Psalm 83, 3
Gods houses, and *will now invade* Psalm 83, 47
My God, oh make them as a wheel Psalm 83, 49
O living God, for thee. Psalm 84, 8
Toward thee, My King, my God. Psalm 84, 16
Till all before *our* God *at length* Psalm 84, 27
Lord God of Hoasts hear *now* my praier Psalm 84, 29
O Jacobs God give ear, Psalm 84, 30
Thou God our shield look on the face Psalm 84, 31
I in the temple of my God Psalm 84, 37
For God the Lord both Sun and Shield Psalm 84, 41
Lord *God* of Hoasts *that raign'st on high*, Psalm 84, 45
God of our saving health and peace, Psalm 85, 13
And now what God the Lord will speak Psalm 85, 29
Save thou thy servant O my God Psalm 86, 7
Remainest God alone. Psalm 86, 36
Thee will I praise O Lord my God Psalm 86, 41
O God the proud against me rise Psalm 86, 49
But thou Lord art the God most mild Psalm 86, 53
City of God, most glorious things Psalm 87, 9
High God shall fix her fast. Psalm 87, 20
Lord God that dost me save and keep, Psalm 88, 1
No sacrifice to God more acceptable Prose 11, 2
Goddess
Then shining heav'nly fair, a Goddess arm'd Par Lost 2.757
Thy self a Goddess, not to Earth confind, Par Lost 5.78
Then Wood-Nymph, or the fairest Goddess feign'd Par Lost 5.381
Say Goddess, what ensu'd when *Raphael*, Par Lost 7.40
A Goddess among Gods, ador'd and serv'd Par Lost 9.547
Goddess humane, reach then, and freely taste. Par Lost 9.732
Hail Goddesse of Nocturnal sport Mask 128
Bridgewater ms 'goddess'
1673 'Goddess'
Trinity ms 'goddesse'
Unlesse the Goddes that in rurall shrine Mask 267
1637 'Goddesse'
Bridgewater ms 'goddess'
Trinity ms 'goddesse'
Sabrina is her name, a Virgin pure, Mask 826
Trinity ms 'pure' ←'chast' ←'goddesse'
Made Goddess of the River; still she retains Mask 842
1637 'goddesse'
Trinity ms 'goddesse'
Bridgewater ms 'goddess'
Goddess of the silver lake, Mask 865
Trinity ms 'Goddesse'
1637 'Goddesse'
Spir. Goddess dear Mask 902
1637 'Goddesse'
Trinity ms 'Goddesse'
But com thou Goddes fair and free, Allegro 11
1673 'Goddess'
But hail thou Goddes, sage and holy, Penseroso 11
1673 'Goddess'
His flaring beams, me Goddes bring Penseroso 132
1673 'Goddess'
Sitting like a Goddes bright, Arcades 18
Trinity ms 'goddesse'
Of sheenie Heav'n, and thou some goddess fled Fair Inf 48
Goddess of Shades, and Huntress, who at will Prose 12, 1
Goddesses
Of Goddesses, so blithe, so smooth, so gay, Par Lost 11.615
As the noon Skie; more like to Goddesses Par Reg 2.156
Goddess-like
With Goddess-like demeanour forth she went; Par Lost 8.59
In gate surpass'd and Goddess-like deport, Par Lost 9.389
Godhead
With warbl'd Hymns, and to his Godhead sing Par Lost 2.242
Affecting God-head, and so loosing all, Par Lost 3.206
And thus the filial Godhead answering spake. Par Lost 6.722
His Word, the filial Godhead, gave effect. Par Lost 7.175
Of Godhead, fixt for ever firm and sure, Par Lost 7.586
Of knowledg, nor was God-head from her thought. Par Lost 9.790
And growing up to Godhead; which for thee Par Lost 9.877

Godhead(*cont*)
Manhood to God-head, with more strength to foil Par Lost 12.389
With th' utmost of his Godhead seconded: Samson 1153
Our Babe to shew his Godhead true, Nativity 227
Godless
Equal in number to that Godless crew Par Lost 6.49
Gods indignation on these Godless pourd Par Lost 6.811
Godlike
Thir great Commander; Godlike shapes and forms Par Lost 1.358
And God-like imitated State; him round Par Lost 2.511
God-like fruition, quitted all to save Par Lost 3.307
Godlike erect, with native Honour clad Par Lost 4.289
His god-like Guest, walks forth, without more train Par Lost 5.351
Under thir God-like Leaders, in the Cause Par Lost 6.67
Of Godlike Power: for likest Gods they seemd, Par Lost 6.301
And thus the Godlike Angel answerd milde. Par Lost 7.110
So spake the Godlike Power, and thus our Sire. Par Lost 8.249
As they, participating God-like food? Par Lost 9.717
By Faith not void of workes: this God-like act Par Lost 12.427
Publish his God-like office now mature, Par Reg 1.188
Thy wisdom, and behold thy God-like deeds? Par Reg 1.386
These God-like Vertues wherefore dost thou hide? Par Reg 3.21
Where God is prais'd aright, and Godlike men, Par Reg 4.348
The Son of God, with Godlike force indu'd Par Reg 4.602
His Godlike presence, and from some great act Samson 28
His Godlike acts, and his temptations fierce, Passion 24
Gods
This downfall; since by Fate the strength of Gods Par Lost 1.116
ms 'God's'
As far as Gods and Heav'nly Essences Par Lost 1.138
As Gods, and by thir own recover'd strength, Par Lost 1.240
Thir Altars by his Altar, Gods ador'd Par Lost 1.384
ms 'gods'
To bestial Gods; for which thir heads as low Par Lost 1.435
ms 'gods'
His odious offrings, and adore the Gods Par Lost 1.475
Thir wandring Gods disguis'd in brutish forms Par Lost 1.481
Both her first born and all her bleating Gods. Par Lost 1.489
Th' *Ionian* Gods, of *Javans* Issue held Par Lost 1.508
Gods, yet confest later then Heav'n and Earth Par Lost 1.509
Thir visages and stature as of Gods, Par Lost 1.570
Mixt with auxiliar Gods; and what resounds Par Lost 1.579
How such united force of Gods, how such Par Lost 1.629
Belus or *Serapis* thir Gods, or seat Par Lost 1.720
A thousand Demy-Gods on golden seat's, Par Lost 1.796
ms 'Demy-gods'
To less then Gods. On th' other side up rose Par Lost 2.108
Pronounc'd among the Gods, and by an Oath, Par Lost 2.352
Synod of Gods, and like to what ye are, Par Lost 2.391
The Gods who live at ease, where I shall Reign Par Lost 2.868
God shall be All in All. But all ye Gods, Par Lost 3.341
Equal with Gods; aspiring to be such, Par Lost 4.526
More lovely then *Pandora*, whom the Gods Par Lost 4.714
For God's, yet able to make Gods of Men: Par Lost 5.70
1667 'Gods'
And why not Gods of Men, since good, the more Par Lost 5.71
Taste this, and be henceforth among the Gods Par Lost 5.77
What life the Gods live there, and such live thou. Par Lost 5.81
A third part of the Gods, in Synod met Par Lost 6.156
Of Godlike Power: for likest Gods they seemd, Par Lost 6.301
Two potent Thrones, that to be less then Gods Par Lost 6.366
Enjoyment of our right as Gods; yet hard Par Lost 6.452
For Gods, and too unequal work we find Par Lost 6.453
Seemd like to Heav'n, a seat where Gods might dwell, Par Lost 7.329
More justly, Seat worthier of Gods, as built Par Lost 9.100
With Gods to sit the highest, am now constraind Par Lost 9.164
Shee fair, divinely fair, fit Love for Gods, Par Lost 9.489
A Goddess among Gods, ador'd and serv'd Par Lost 9.547
Op'nd and cleerd, and ye shall be as Gods, Par Lost 9.708
That ye should be as Gods, since I as Man, Par Lost 9.710
I of brute human, yee of human Gods. Par Lost 9.712
Human, to put on Gods, death to be wisht, Par Lost 9.714
And what are Gods that Man may not become Par Lost 9.716
The Gods are first, and that advantage use Par Lost 9.718
In knowledge, as the Gods who all things know; Par Lost 9.804
From Nectar, drink of Gods. *Adam* the while Par Lost 9.838
To open Eyes, and make them Gods who taste; Par Lost 9.866
But to be Gods, or Angels Demi-gods. Par Lost 9.937
Down he descended strait; the speed of Gods Par Lost 10.90
Of my performance: What remains, ye Gods, Par Lost 10.502
Fit haunt of Gods? where I had hope to spend, Par Lost 11.271
Patrons of Mankind, Gods, and Sons of Gods, Par Lost 11.696
For Gods! yet him God the most High voutsafes Par Lost 12.120
His kindred and false Gods, into a Land Par Lost 12.122
He leaves his Gods, his Friends, and native Soile Par Lost 12.129
Regents and Potentates, and Kings, yea gods Par Reg 1.117
And made him bow to the Gods of his Wives. Par Reg 2.171
Of Wood-Gods and Wood-Nymphs; he view'd it round, Par Reg 2.297
Then swell with pride, and must be titl'd Gods, Par Reg 3.81
Headlong would follow; and to thir Gods perhaps Par Reg 3.430
Houses of Gods (so well I have dispos'd Par Reg 4.56
Thir Gods ridiculous, and themselves past shame. Par Reg 4.342
Or taste that cheers the heart of Gods and men, Samson 545
Preaching how meritorious with the gods Samson 859
To please thy gods thou didst it; gods unable Samson 896
Of their own deity, Gods cannot be: Samson 899
Amongst the enthron'd gods on Sainted seats. Mask 11
Which he to grace his tributary gods Mask 24

Gods(*cont*)
Bridgewater ms 'Gods'
Th' express resemblance of the gods, is chang'd — Mask 69
Bridgewater ms 'Gods'
And thank the gods amiss. I should be loath — Mask 177
Bridgewater ms 'Gods'
The frivolous bolt of *Cupid*, gods and men — Mask 445
Bridgewater ms 'Gods'
Till free consent the gods among — Mask 1007
line not in Bridgewater ms
Spare Fast, that oft with gods doth diet, — Penseroso 46
Mother of a hunderd gods; — Arcades 22
On which the fate of gods and men is wound. — Arcades 67
What ere the skill of lesser gods can show, — Arcades 79
when she beheld (the gods farre sighted bee) — Lycidas Tr. ms 29.60
The brutish gods of *Nile* as fast, — Nativity 211
Nor all the gods beside, — Nativity 224
1673 'Gods'
For of gods he is the God; — Psalm 136, 6
Which 'mongst the wanton gods a foul reproach was held. — Fair Inf 14
On Faith and changed Gods complain: and Seas — Horace 6
Scarce to be less then Gods, thou mad'st his lot, — Psalm 8, 15
Among the gods on both his hands — Psalm 82, 3
I said that ye were Gods, yea all — Psalm 82, 21
Like thee among the gods is none — Psalm 86, 25
Of all that other gods have done — Psalm 86, 27

Goes
With thee it came and goes: but follow me, — Par Lost 4.469
Thy going is not lonely, with thee goes — Par Lost 11.290
Goes by the worse, whatever be her cause. — Samson 904
And now with second hope she goes, — Winchester 25
Set thy wayes right before, where my step goes. — Psalm 5, 24

Going
Going into such danger as thou saidst? — Par Lost 9.1157
Thy going is not lonely, with thee goes — Par Lost 11.290
May warn thee, as a sure fore-going sign. — Par Reg 4.483

Gold
With gay Religions full of Pomp and Gold, — Par Lost 1.372
ms 'gold'
Th' infection when thir borrow'd Gold compos'd — Par Lost 1.483
ms 'gold'
The riches of Heav'ns pavement, trod'n Gold, — Par Lost 1.682
1667 'gold' in some copies
ms 'gold'
And dig'd out ribs of Gold. Let none admire — Par Lost 1.690
ms 'gold'
The Roof was fretted Gold. Not *Babilon*, — Par Lost 1.717
ms 'gold'
Showrs on her Kings *Barbaric* Pearl and Gold, — Par Lost 2.4
Wants not her hidden lustre, Gemms and Gold; — Par Lost 2.271
The guarded Gold: So eagerly the fiend — Par Lost 2.947
Thir Crowns inwove with Amarant and Gold, — Par Lost 3.352
With Frontispice of Diamond and Gold — Par Lost 3.506
That scal'd by steps of Gold to Heav'n Gate — Par Lost 3.541
If mettal, part seemd Gold, part Silver cleer; — Par Lost 3.595
Potable Gold, when with one vertuous touch — Par Lost 3.608
Of many a colourd plume sprinkl'd with Gold, — Par Lost 3.642
Of vegetable Gold; and next to Life — Par Lost 4.220
Rowling on Orient Pearl and sands of Gold, — Par Lost 4.238
Naked met his under the flowing Gold — Par Lost 4.496
Hung high with Diamond flaming, and with Gold. — Par Lost 4.554
Arraying with reflected Purple and Gold — Par Lost 4.596
Till the Sun paint your fleecie skirts with Gold, — Par Lost 5.187
Skirted his loines and thighes with downie Gold — Par Lost 5.282
Of Horses led, and Grooms besmeard with Gold — Par Lost 5.356
Metals of drossiest Ore to perfet Gold — Par Lost 5.442
In Pearl, in Diamond, and massie Gold, — Par Lost 5.634
From Diamond Quarries hew'n, and Rocks of Gold, — Par Lost 5.759
Such as in highest Heav'n, arrayd in Gold — Par Lost 6.13
Came towring, armd in Adamant and Gold; — Par Lost 6.110
With Plant, Fruit, Flour Ambrosial, Gemms & Gold, — Par Lost 6.475
Show to the Sun thir wav'd coats dropt with Gold, — Par Lost 7.406
With spots of Gold and Purple, azure and green: — Par Lost 7.479
A broad and ample rode, whose dust is Gold — Par Lost 7.577
Carnation, Purple, Azure, or spect with Gold, — Par Lost 9.429
With burnisht Neck of verdant Gold, erect — Par Lost 9.501
Ruddie and Gold: I nearer drew to gaze; — Par Lost 9.578
Of Cedar, overlaid with Gold, therein — Par Lost 12.250
A Mercie-seat of Gold between the wings — Par Lost 12.253
His place, to offer Incense, Myrrh, and Gold; — Par Lost 12.363
To honour thee with Incense, Myrrh, and Gold, — Par Reg 1.251
(Thy throne) but gold that got him puissant friends? — Par Reg 2.425
In Cedar, Marble, Ivory or Gold. — Par Reg 4.60
Chios and *Creet*, and how they quaff in Gold, — Par Reg 4.118
Spousal embraces, vitiated with Gold, — Samson 389
Philistian gold: if weakness may excuse, — Samson 831
It was not gold, as to my charge thou lay'st, — Samson 849
Cherish thy hast'n'd widowhood with the gold — Samson 958
Till they had hir'd a woman with their gold — Samson 1114
Laden with blooming gold, had need the guard — Mask 394
Bridgewater ms 'gould'
where grows the right-borne gold upon his native tree — Mask Tr. ms 27.08
Time will run back, and fetch the age of gold, — Nativity 135
Who liv'd in both, unstain'd with gold or fee, — Sonnet 10, 3
Move by her two maine nerves, Iron and Gold — Sonnet 17, 8
Who now enjoyes thee credulous, all Gold, — Horace 9

Golden
With Gemms and Golden lustre rich imblaz'd, — Par Lost 1.538
ms 'golden'
With Golden Architrave; nor did there want — Par Lost 1.715
ms 'golden'
A thousand Demy-Gods on golden seat's, — Par Lost 1.796
Us here, as with his Golden those in Heav'n. — Par Lost 2.328
Hung ore my Realm, link'd in a golden Chain — Par Lost 2.1005
And fast by hanging in a golden Chain — Par Lost 2.1051
See golden days, fruitful of golden deeds, — Par Lost 3.337
Then Crown'd again thir gold'n Harps they took, — Par Lost 3.365
The golden Sun in splendor likest Heaven — Par Lost 3.572
Of beaming sunnie Raies, a golden tiar — Par Lost 3.625
Blossoms and Fruits at once of golden hue — Par Lost 4.148
Others whose fruit burnisht with Golden Rinde — Par Lost 4.249
Her unadorned golden tresses wore — Par Lost 4.305
Here Love his golden shafts imploies, here lights — Par Lost 4.763
Hung forth in Heav'n his golden Scales, yet seen — Par Lost 4.997
On golden Hinges turning, as by work — Par Lost 5.255
And from within the golden Lamps that burne — Par Lost 5.713
That Golden Scepter which thou didst reject — Par Lost 5.886
From midst a Golden Cloud thus milde was heard. — Par Lost 6.28
With Flaming Cherubim, and golden Shields; — Par Lost 6.102
Of Golden Panoplie, refulgent Host, — Par Lost 6.527
On golden Hinges moving, to let forth — Par Lost 7.207
He took the golden Compasses, prepar'd — Par Lost 7.225
1669 'Golden'
And touch't thir Golden Harps, and hymning prais'd — Par Lost 7.258
Repairing, in thir gold'n Urns draw Light, — Par Lost 7.365
All sounds on Fret by String or Golden Wire — Par Lost 7.597
Fuming from Golden Censers hid the Mount. — Par Lost 7.600
With incense, where the Golden Altar fum'd, — Par Lost 11.18
And Prayers, which in this Golden Censer, mixt — Par Lost 11.24
Down to the golden *Chersonese*, or where — Par Lost 11.392
Golden in shew, is but a wreath of thorns, — Par Reg 2.459
Of that first golden Monarchy the seat, — Par Reg 3.277
From *India* and the golden *Chersoness*, — Par Reg 4.74
Of Alabaster, top't with Golden Spires: — Par Reg 4.548
To lay their just hands on that Golden Key — Mask 13
Trinity ms 'golden'
1637 'golden'
Bridgewater ms 'goulden'
Thou hovering Angel girt with golden wings, — Mask 214
line not in Bridgewater ms
Bore a bright golden flowre, but not in this soyl: — Mask 633
line not in Bridgewater ms
And fair *Ligea*'s golden comb, — Mask 880
The beryl, and the golden ore, — Mask 933
Bridgewater ms 'goulden'
That sing about the golden tree: — Mask 983
Bridgewater ms 'goulden'
& fruits of golden rind, on whose faire tree — Mask Tr. ms 10.08
From golden slumber on a bed — Allegro 146
Him that yon soars on golden wing, — Penseroso 52
What could the Muse her self that *Orpheus* bore, — Lycidas 58
Trinity ms 'muse her selfe' ←'golden hayrd Calliope'
(The Golden opes, the Iron shuts amain) — Lycidas 111
Trinity ms 'golden'
1638 'golden'
To th' touch of golden wires, while *Hebe* brings — Vacation 38
Touch their immortal Harps of golden wires, — Musick 13
But as Faith pointed with her golden rod, — Sonnet 14, 7
In wreaths thy golden Hair, — Horace 4

Golden-tressed
And caus'd the Golden-tressed Sun, — Psalm 136, 29

Golden-winged
Or wert thou of the golden-winged hoast, — Fair Inf 57

Golgotha
In *Golgotha* him dead, who lives in Heav'n; — Par Lost 3.477

Goliath
All of Gigantic size, *Goliah* chief. — Samson 1249

Gone
Through dark and desart wayes with peril gone — Par Lost 3.544
At least had gon to rack, disturbd and torne — Par Lost 4.994
My Guide was gon, and I, me thought, sunk down, — Par Lost 5.91
Against thee are gon forth without recall; — Par Lost 5.885
Had gon to wrack, with ruin overspred, — Par Lost 6.670
1667 'gone'
Had shadow'd them from knowing ill, was gon, — Par Lost 9.1055
All would have then gon well, peace would have crownd — Par Lost 11.781
So lately found, and so abruptly gone, — Par Reg 2.10
For whither is he gone, what accident — Par Reg 2.39
Had left him vacant, and with speed was gon — Par Reg 2.116
To mans less universe, and soon are gone; — Par Reg 4.459
Chor. She's gone, a manifest Serpent by her sting — Samson 997
Chor. His Giantship is gone somewhat crest-fall'n, — Samson 1244
He's gone, and who knows how he may report — Samson 1350
Rigor now is gon to bed, — Mask 107
1637 'gone'
Bridgewater ms 'gone'
But O the heavy change, now thou art gon, — Lycidas 37
Trinity ms 'gone'
1638 'gone'
Now thou art gon, and never must return! — Lycidas 38
1638 'gone'
Hobson has supt, and's newly gon to bed. — Carrier 18
His Letters are deliver'd all and gon, — Another 33
line not in 1658 text
1640, 1657 'gone'

Gone(*cont*)
And out of order gon. Psalm 82, 20
Gonfalons
Standards, and Gonfalons twixt Van and Reare Par Lost 5.589
Good
To do ought good never will be our task, Par Lost 1.159
Out of our evil seek to bring forth good, Par Lost 1.163
And out of good still to find means of evil; Par Lost 1.165
Till good *Josiah* drove them thence to Hell. Par Lost 1.418
Of endless pain? where there is then no good Par Lost 2.30
Let this be good, whether our angry Foe Par Lost 2.152
Our own good from our selves, and from our own Par Lost 2.253
Of good and evil much they argu'd then, Par Lost 2.562
Created evil, for evil only good, Par Lost 2.623
Destin'd to that good hour: no less rejoyc'd Par Lost 2.848
Nor good dry Land: nigh founderd on he fares, Par Lost 2.940
God and good Angels guard by special grace. Par Lost 2.1033
Found worthiest to be so by being Good, Par Lost 3.310
In that bright eminence, and with his good Par Lost 4.44
How due! yet all his good prov'd ill in me, Par Lost 4.48
Farwel Remorse: all Good to me is lost; Par Lost 4.109
Evil be thou my Good; by thee at least Par Lost 4.110
The good before him, but perverts best things Par Lost 4.203
Knowledge of Good bought dear by knowing ill. Par Lost 4.222
Be infinitly good, and of his good Par Lost 4.414
That Glorie then, when thou no more wast good, Par Lost 4.838
To thee no reason; who knowst only good, Par Lost 4.895
Longer thy offerd good, why else set here? Par Lost 5.63
And why not Gods of Men, since good, the more Par Lost 5.71
These are thy glorious works, Parent of good, Par Lost 5.153
To give us onely good; and if the night Par Lost 5.206
All perfet good unmeasur'd out, descends, Par Lost 5.399
If not deprav'd from good, created all Par Lost 5.471
Wonder not then, what God for you saw good Par Lost 5.491
And good he made thee, but to persevere Par Lost 5.525
Not lawful to reveal? yet for thy good Par Lost 5.570
Yet by experience taught we know how good, Par Lost 5.826
And of our good, and of our dignitie Par Lost 5.827
Forsak'n of all good; I see thy fall Par Lost 5.878
For which to the infinitly Good we owe Par Lost 7.76
Glorie they sung to the most High, good will Par Lost 7.182
Good out of evil to create, in stead Par Lost 7.188
His good to Worlds and Ages infinite. Par Lost 7.191
Sojourn'd the while. God saw the Light was good; Par Lost 7.249
And saw that it was good, and said, Let th' Earth Par Lost 7.309
On the green stemm; God saw that it was good. Par Lost 7.337
Surveying his great Work, that it was good: Par Lost 7.353
And saw that it was good, and bless'd them, saying, Par Lost 7.395
But grateful to acknowledge whence his good Par Lost 7.512
Which tasted works knowledge of Good and Evil, Par Lost 7.543
View'd, and behold all was entirely good; Par Lost 7.549
In prospect from his Throne, how good, how faire, Par Lost 7.556
Thou usest, and from thence creat'st more good. Par Lost 7.616
Nor glistering, may of solid good containe Par Lost 8.93
Knowledg of good and ill, which I have set Par Lost 8.324
And all this good to man, for whose well being Par Lost 8.361
Good reason was thou freely shouldst dislike, Par Lost 8.443
Knew it not good for Man to be alone, Par Lost 8.445
Be good and friendly still, and oft return. Par Lost 8.651
Of contraries; all good to me becomes Par Lost 9.122
In Woman, then to studie houshold good, Par Lost 9.233
And good workes in her Husband to promote. Par Lost 9.234
Least by some faire appeering good surpris'd Par Lost 9.354
Stupidly good, of enmitie disarm'd, Par Lost 9.465
Or Earth, or Middle, all things fair and good; Par Lost 9.605
But all that fair and good in thy Divine Par Lost 9.606
To happier life, knowledge of Good and Evil; Par Lost 9.697
Of good, how just? of evil, if what is evil Par Lost 9.698
Knowing both Good and Evil as they know. Par Lost 9.709
Knowledge of Good and Evil in this Tree, Par Lost 9.723
Of Knowledge, knowledge both of good and evil; Par Lost 9.752
Commends thee more, while it inferrs the good Par Lost 9.754
For good unknown, sure is not had, or had Par Lost 9.756
Forbids us good, forbids us to be wise? Par Lost 9.759
The good befall'n him, Author unsuspect, Par Lost 9.771
Under this ignorance of good and Evil, Par Lost 9.774
1667 'Good'
Holy, divine, good, amiable, or sweet! Par Lost 9.899
One Heart, one Soul in both; whereof good prooff Par Lost 9.967
Whose vertue, for of good still good proceeds, Par Lost 9.973
Both Good and Evil, Good lost, and Evil got, Par Lost 9.1072
Of all our good, sham'd, naked, miserable. Par Lost 9.1139
As good have grown there still a liveless Rib. Par Lost 9.1154
And gav'st me as thy perfet gift, so good, Par Lost 10.138
So fair and good created, and had still Par Lost 10.618
The good I sought not. To the loss of that, Par Lost 10.752
Thou didst accept them; wilt thou enjoy the good, Par Lost 10.758
Good or not good ingraft, my Merit those Par Lost 11.35
To know both Good and Evil, since his taste Par Lost 11.85
His knowledge of Good lost, and Evil got, Par Lost 11.87
Good by it self, and Evil not at all. Par Lost 11.89
The good which we enjoy, from Heav'n descends; Par Lost 11.142
To thee and to thy Ofspring; good with bad Par Lost 11.358
With vows, as thir chief good, and final hope. Par Lost 11.493
Yet empty of all good wherein consists Par Lost 11.616
Where good with bad were matcht, who of themselves Par Lost 11.685
Awaits the good, the rest what punishment? Par Lost 11.710
In a dark Age, against example good, Par Lost 11.809

Good(*cont*)
Regardless whether good or evil fame. Par Lost 12.47
Part good, part bad, of bad the longer scrowle, Par Lost 12.336
That all this good of evil shall produce, Par Lost 12.470
And evil turn to good; more wonderful Par Lost 12.471
Much more, that much more good thereof shall spring, Par Lost 12.476
To God more glory, more good will to Men Par Lost 12.477
To good malignant, to bad men benigne, Par Lost 12.538
Mercifull over all his works, with good Par Lost 12.565
Portending good, and all her spirits compos'd Par Lost 12.596
Which he hath sent propitious, some great good Par Lost 12.612
What might be publick good; my self I thought Par Reg 1.204
What I see excellent in good, or fair, Par Reg 1.381
And not well understood as good not known? Par Reg 1.437
Conteins of good, wise, just, the perfect shape. Par Reg 3.11
His lot who dares be singularly good. Par Reg 3.57
But if there be in glory aught of good, Par Reg 3.88
Glory from men, from all men good or bad, Par Reg 3.114
His good communicable to every soul Par Reg 3.125
For so much good, so much beneficence. Par Reg 3.133
And so of all true good himself despoil'd, Par Reg 3.139
The end I would attain, my final good. Par Reg 3.211
Good reason then, if I before-hand seek Par Reg 4.526
To the utmost of meer man both wise and good, Par Reg 4.535
Deceivable and vain! Nay what thing good Samson 350
These reasons in Loves law have past for good, Samson 811
Of wisest men; that to the public good Samson 867
That in domestic good combines: Samson 1048
As good for nothing else, no better service Samson 1163
But take good heed my hand survey not thee. Samson 1230
Sam. Be of good courage, I begin to feel Samson 1381
With good success to work his liberty. Samson 1454
Chor. Of good or bad so great, of bad the sooner; Samson 1537
For evil news rides post, while good news baits. Samson 1538
That he, the Supreme good, t' whom all things ill Mask 217
line not in Bridgewater ms
Co. What chance good Lady hath bereft you thus? Mask 277
La. To find out that, good Shepherd, I suppose, Mask 307
Defence is a good cause, and Heav'n be for us. Mask 489
How cam'st thou here good Swain? hath any ram Mask 497
El. Bro. What fears good *Thyrsis*? Prethee briefly shew. Mask 512
Curs'd as his life. *Spir*. Alas good ventrous youth, Mask 609
And som good angel bear a sheild before us. Mask 658
Thou haste immanacl'd, while Heav'n sees good. Mask 665
But such as are good men can give good things, Mask 703
And that which is not good, is not delicious Mask 704
But must be currant, and the good thereof Mask 740
line not in Bridgewater ms
With her abundance, she good cateress Mask 764
Means her provision onely to the good Mask 765
& good heaven cast his best regard upon us Mask Tr. ms 21.32
And at my window bid good morrow, Allegro 46
Sent by som spirit to mortals good, Penseroso 153
Fair silver-buskind Nymphs as great and good, Arcades 33
Trinity ms 'od', ms defective
In thy large recompense, and shalt be good Lycidas 184
Let down in clowdie throne to do the world some good. Fair Inf 56
Good luck befriend thee Son; for at thy birth Vacation 59
When every thing that is sincerely good On Time 14
In first obedience, and their state of good. Musick 24
Daughter to that good Earl, once President Sonnet 10, 1
Numbring good intellects; now seldom por'd on. Sonnet 11, 4
For who loves that, must first be wise and good; Sonnet 12, 12
Thy Works and Alms and all thy good Endeavour Sonnet 14, 5
Toward solid good what leads the nearest way; Sonnet 21, 10
The good and meek of heart Psalm 4, 15
Who yet will shew us good? Psalm 4, 26
Him with thy lasting favour and good will. Psalm 5, 40
Let thy *good* hand be *laid*, Psalm 80, 70
No good from them shall be with-held Psalm 84, 43
Whatever thing is good Psalm 85, 50
For thou art good, thou Lord art prone Psalm 86, 13
Some sign of good to me afford, Psalm 86, 61
That *Constantine* to good *Sylvestro* gave. Prose 4, 4
Whom doe we count a good man, whom but he Prose 10, 1
Goodliest
Of goodliest Trees loaden with fairest Fruit, Par Lost 4.147
Adam the goodliest man of men since borne Par Lost 4.323
A Circuit wide, enclos'd, with goodliest Trees Par Lost 8.304
Goodliest of all the Forrest, Hart and Hinde; Par Lost 11.189
Goodly
The goodly prospect of some forein land Par Lost 3.548
When I behold this goodly Frame, this World Par Lost 8.15
A goodly Tree farr distant to behold Par Lost 9.576
So goodly and erect, though faultie since, Par Lost 11.509
Here behold so goodly grown Mask 968
Into a goodly valley, where he sees Prose 2, 2
Goodness
Infinite goodness, grace and mercy shewn Par Lost 1.218
ms 'goodnesse'
His malice, and thy goodness bring to naught, Par Lost 3.158
So should thy goodness and thy greatness both Par Lost 3.165
Resigns her charge, while goodness thinks no ill Par Lost 3.688
Thy goodness infinite, both when we wake, Par Lost 4.734
And felt how awful goodness is, and saw Par Lost 4.847
Thy goodness beyond thought, and Power Divine: Par Lost 5.159
And put not forth my goodness, which is free Par Lost 7.171
In goodness and in power praeeminent; Par Lost 8.279

Goodness(*cont*)
Sent from whose sovran goodness I adore. Par Lost 8.647
With goodness and paternal Love, his Face Par Lost 11.353
O goodness infinite, goodness immense! Par Lost 12.469
But to shew forth his goodness, and impart Par Reg 3.124
With goodness principl'd not to reject Samson 760
And the sweet peace that goodnes boosoms ever, Mask 368
Bridgewater ms 'goodness'
1637 'goodnesse'
Trinity ms 'goodnesse'
And mix no more with goodness, when at last Mask 594
1637 'goodnesse'
Bridgewater ms 'goodnesse'
Trinity ms 'goodnesse'
Carrol her goodnes lowd in rustick layes, Mask 849
1637 'goodnesse'
Trinity ms 'goodnesse'
Love, sweetness, goodness, in her person shin'd Sonnet 23, 11
My soul, O save me for thy goodness sake Psalm 6, 8
Cause us to see thy goodness Lord, Psalm 85, 25
Gordian
Insinuating, wove with Gordian twine Par Lost 4.348
Your learned hands, can loose this Gordian knot? Vacation 90
Gordon
End Green. Why is it harder Sirs then Gordon, Sonnet 11, 8
Gore
Rowling in dust and gore. To which our Sire. Par Lost 11.460
The clotted gore. I with what speed the while Samson 1728
Gored
With many an inrode gor'd; deformed rout Par Lost 6.387
Gorge
To gorge the flesh of Lambs or yeanling Kids Par Lost 3.434
Gorged
On what was pure, till cramm'd and gorg'd, nigh burst Par Lost 10.632
Gorgeous
Or where the gorgeous East with richest hand Par Lost 2.3
Vaild with his gorgeous wings, up springing light Par Lost 5.250
Then lighted from his gorgeous Throne, for now Par Lost 6.103
Bases and tinsel Trappings, gorgious Knights Par Lost 9.36
Thir sumptuous gluttonies, and gorgeous feasts Par Reg 4.114
Then put on all thy gorgeous arms, thy Helmet Samson 1119
Ne're looks to Heav'n amidst his gorgeous feast, Mask 777
Som time let Gorgeous Tragedy Penseroso 97
Gorgon
Bedropt with blood of *Gorgon*, or the Isle Par Lost 10.527
What was that snaky-headed *Gorgon* sheild Mask 447
Gorgonian
Medusa with *Gorgonian* terror guards Par Lost 2.611
Bound with *Gorgonian* rigor not to move, Par Lost 10.297
Gorgons
Gorgons and *Hydra's*, and *Chimera's* dire. Par Lost 2.628
Gory
His goary visage down the stream was sent, Lycidas 62
Trinity ms 'goarie' ←'gorie' ←'divine'
his goarie scalpe rowle downe the Thracian lee Lycidas Tr. ms 29.61
Goshen
The Sojourners of *Goshen*, who beheld Par Lost 1.309
ms 'Goshen'
Gospel
Of hireling wolves whose Gospell is their maw. Sonnet 16, 14
1694 'Gospel'
Got
Got them new Names, till wandring ore the Earth, Par Lost 1.365
Amid the Tree now got, where plenty hung Par Lost 9.594
Both Good and Evil, Good lost, and Evil got, Par Lost 9.1072
Among the Heathen of thir purchase got, Par Lost 10.579
His knowledge of Good lost, and Evil got, Par Lost 11.87
Close in a Cottage low together got Par Reg 2.28
Motherly cares and fears got head, and rais'd Par Reg 2.64
(Thy throne) but gold that got him puissant friends? Par Reg 2.425
And force him to restore his purchase back, Mask 607
Trinity ms 'purchase back' ←'new got prey'
By boistrous rape th' Athenian damsel got, Fair Inf 9
Had got a race of mourners on som pregnant cloud. Passion 56
Death was half glad when he had got him down; Carrier 6
But this is got by casting Pearl to Hoggs; Sonnet 12, 8
In thy Adulterers, or thy ill got wealth? Prose 3, 4
Gourd
Each Plant and juciest Gourd will pluck such choice Par Lost 5.327
The swelling Gourd, up stood the cornie Reed Par Lost 7.321
Govern
Our being ordain'd to govern, not to serve? Par Lost 5.802
Purples the East: still govern thou my Song, Par Lost 7.30
Govern the rest, self-knowing, and from thence Par Lost 7.510
And govern well thy appetite, least sin Par Lost 7.546
But govern ill the Nations under yoke, Par Reg 4.135
Governed
And this perverse Commotion governd thus, Par Lost 6.706
To a wel-govern'd and wise appetite. Mask 705
Trinity ms 'well govern'd'
Bridgewater ms 'well govern'd'
1673 'well-govern'd'
Government
Were such as under Government well seem'd, Par Lost 10.154
And upstart Passions catch the Government Par Lost 12.88
Thir government, and thir great Senate choose Par Lost 12.225
The solid rules of Civil Government Par Reg 4.358
By course commits to severall goverment, Mask 25
Governors
On *Israel's* Governours, and Heads of Tribes, Samson 242
Governs
Chance governs all. Into this wilde Abyss, Par Lost 2.910
Them whom he governs. This is servitude, Par Lost 6.178
Governs the inner man, the nobler part, Par Reg 2.477
Orders and governs, nor content in Heaven Par Reg 3.112
Gown
For who would rob a Hermit of his Weeds, Mask 390
Trinity ms 'weeds' ←'beads' ←'gowne' ←'beads'
His few Books, or his Beads, or Maple Dish, Mask 391
Trinity ms 'beads' ←'hairie gown'
To those budge doctors of the *Stoick* Furr, Mask 707
Trinity ms 'furre' ←'gowne'
The Hairy Gown and Mossy Cell, Penseroso 169
Gowns
The helme of Rome, when gownes not armes repelld Sonnet 17, 3
1662, 1694 'Gowns'
Grace
Extort from me. To bow and sue for grace Par Lost 1.111
Infinite goodness, grace and mercy shewn Par Lost 1.218
And publish Grace to all, on promise made Par Lost 2.238
Of heavenly Grace: and God proclaiming peace, Par Lost 2.499
God and good Angels guard by special grace. Par Lost 2.1033
By the other first: Man therefore shall find grace, Par Lost 3.131
Love without end, and without measure Grace, Par Lost 3.142
Thy sovran sentence, that Man should find grace; Par Lost 3.145
Yet not of will in him, but grace in me Par Lost 3.174
Some I have chosen of peculiar grace Par Lost 3.183
Th' incensed Deitie, while offerd grace Par Lost 3.187
This my long sufferance and my day of grace Par Lost 3.198
Father, thy word is past, man shall find grace; Par Lost 3.227
And shall grace not find means, that finds her way, Par Lost 3.228
In those who, when they may, accept not grace. Par Lost 3.302
Father of Mercie and Grace, thou didst not doome Par Lost 3.401
Sutable grace diffus'd, so well he feignd; Par Lost 3.639
By Act of Grace my former state; how soon Par Lost 4.94
For softness shee and sweet attractive Grace, Par Lost 4.298
In them Divine resemblance, and such grace Par Lost 4.364
How beauty is excelld by manly grace Par Lost 4.490
Severe in youthful beautie, added grace Par Lost 4.845
Can end it. Into thee such Vertue and Grace Par Lost 6.703
On errands of supernal Grace. So sung Par Lost 7.573
And Grace that won who saw to wish her stay, Par Lost 8.43
Though pleasant, but thy words with Grace Divine Par Lost 8.215
Speaking or mute all comliness and grace Par Lost 8.222
Grace was in all her steps, Heav'n in her Eye, Par Lost 8.488
To serve him, thy reward was of his grace, Par Lost 10.767
Hee will instruct us praying, and of Grace Par Lost 10.1081
What else but favor, grace, and mercie shon? Par Lost 10.1096
Prevenient Grace descending had remov'd Par Lost 11.3
From thy implanted Grace in Man, these Sighs Par Lost 11.23
Giv'n thee of Grace, wherein thou may'st repent, Par Lost 11.255
Expect to hear, supernal Grace contending Par Lost 11.359
Such grace shall one just Man find in his sight, Par Lost 11.890
Acceptance of large Grace, from servil fear Par Lost 12.305
From God, and over wrauth grace shall abound. Par Lost 12.478
But force the Spirit of Grace it self, and binde Par Lost 12.525
All vertue, grace and wisdom to atchieve Par Reg 1.68
His words, his wisdom full of grace and truth, Par Reg 2.34
Thir shape, thir colour, and attractive grace, Par Reg 2.176
Yet so much bounty is in God, such grace, Par Reg 3.142
Of my reception into grace; what worse? Par Reg 3.205
Degraded by himself, on grace depending? Par Reg 4.312
Which he to grace his tributary gods Mask 24
And give resounding grace to all Heav'ns Harmonies. Mask 243
Trinity ms 'give resounding grace' ←'hold a counterpoint'
Bridgewater ms 'hould a Counterpointe'
B.M. ms 'hold a Counter point'
And noble grace that dash't brute violence Mask 451
Com Lady while Heaven lends us grace, Mask 938
To win her Grace, whom all commend. Allegro 124
Here ye shall have greater grace, Arcades 104
I know my tongue but little Grace can do thee Vacation 10
All is, if I have grace to use it so, Sonnet 7, 13
Turn us again, *thy grace divine* Psalm 80, 13
Return us, *and thy grace divine*, Psalm 80, 29
Return us, *and thy grace divine* Psalm 80, 77
Gives grace and glory *bright*, Psalm 84, 42
Readiest thy grace to shew, Psalm 86, 54
Graced
That I who first brought Death on all, am grac't Par Lost 11.168
Graceful
Belial, in act more graceful and humane; Par Lost 2.109
So much delights me as those graceful acts, Par Lost 8.600
Her graceful Innocence, her every Aire Par Lost 9.459
Blow moist and keen, shattering the graceful locks Par Lost 10.1066
Then Mortal Creatures, graceful and discreet, Par Reg 2.157
Graces
I pleas'd, and with attractive graces won Par Lost 2.762
Worlds, and on whom hath all these graces powrd; Par Lost 3.674
Knit with the *Graces* and the *Hours* in dance Par Lost 4.267
Shot forth peculiar Graces; then with voice Par Lost 5.15
A pomp of winning Graces waited still, Par Lost 8.61
Perfections absolute, Graces divine, Par Reg 2.138
As Graces, draw a Scorpions tail behind? Samson 360
With gifts and graces eminently adorn'd, Samson 679
The Graces, and the rosie-boosom'd Howres, Mask 986

Graces(*cont*)
line not in Bridgewater ms
With two sister Graces more — Allegro 15
Her high birth, and her graces sweet, — Winchester 15

Gracious
O Father, gracious was that word which clos'd — Par Lost 3.144
Kiss'd as the gracious signs of sweet remorse — Par Lost 5.134
Return'd and gracious purpose thus renew'd. — Par Lost 8.337
1667 'gratious'
This answer from the gratious voice Divine. — Par Lost 8.436
The gracious Judge without revile repli'd. — Par Lost 10.118
And gracious temper he both heard and judg'd — Par Lost 10.1047
Enlightner of my darkness, gracious things — Par Lost 12.271
Gracious to re-admit the suppliant; — Samson 1173
Thy *gracious* ear, O Lord, encline, — Psalm 86, 1

Graciously
Thy Land to favour graciously — Psalm 85, 1
Thy hearing graciously. — Psalm 86, 20

Gradual
Mans nourishment, by gradual scale sublim'd — Par Lost 5.483
Of Creatures animate with gradual life — Par Lost 9.112

Grain
Against a rumord Warr, the Smuttie graine — Par Lost 4.817
Skie-tinctur'd grain. Like *Maia's* son he stood, — Par Lost 5.285
Cover'd with pearly grain: yet God hath here — Par Lost 5.430
To blackest grain, and into store convey'd: — Par Lost 6.515
Thir magnitudes, this Earth a spot, a graine, — Par Lost 8.17
The smell of Grain, or tedded Grass, or Kine, — Par Lost 9.450
Livelier then *Meliboean*, or the graine — Par Lost 11.242
What it devours not, Herb, or Fruit, or Graine, — Par Lost 12.184
Who with a grain of manhood well resolv'd — Samson 408
And cheeks of sorry grain will serve to ply — Mask 750
1637 'graine'
Trinity ms 'graine'
line not in Bridgewater ms
All in a robe of darkest grain, — Penseroso 33
to write his owne woes on the vermeil graine — Lycidas Tr. ms 28.18

Grand
Mov'd our Grand Parents in that happy State, — Par Lost 1.29
ms 'grand'
Irreconcileable, to our grand Foe, — Par Lost 1.122
In order came the grand infernal Peers, — Par Lost 2.507
So clomb this first grand Thief into Gods Fould: — Par Lost 4.192
Whom the grand foe with scornful eye askance — Par Lost 6.149
There kept thir Watch the Legions, while the Grand — Par Lost 10.427
Be meant, whom I conjecture, our grand Foe — Par Lost 10.1033
To conquer Sin and Death the two grand foes, — Par Reg 1.159

Grandchild
Fair Daughter, and thou Son and Grandchild both, — Par Lost 10.384
A Son, and of his Son a Grand-childe leaves, — Par Lost 12.153
The Grandchilde with twelve Sons increast, departs — Par Lost 12.155

Grandeur
Nor doth this grandeur and majestic show — Par Reg 4.110

Grandsire
Cyriack, whose Grandsire on the Royal Bench — Sonnet 21, 1
line not in Trinity ms

Granges
When for their teeming Flocks, and granges full — Mask 175
Trinity ms 'granges' ← 'garners'

Grant
United. But to grant it thee unjust, — Par Lost 5.831
He ceas'd, and heard thir grant in loud acclaim; — Par Reg 2.235
O wherefore did God grant me my request, — Samson 356
For grant they be so, while they rest unknown, — Mask 361
line not in Bridgewater ms
line not in Trinity ms
And made Hell grant what Love did seek. — Penseroso 108
This day; ask of me, and the grant is made; — Psalm 2, 16
Will grant thy full demand. — Psalm 81, 44
For thou wilt *grant* me *free access* — Psalm 86, 23

Granted
With granted leave officious I return, — Par Reg 2.302
No other doctrine needs, though granted true; — Par Reg 4.290

Granting
From granting hee, as I from begging peace: — Par Lost 4.104
First granting, as I do, it was a weakness — Samson 773

Grants
And terror cease; he grants what they besaught — Par Lost 12.238

Grape
Layes forth her purple Grape, and gently creeps — Par Lost 4.259
Berrie or Grape: to whom thus *Adam* call'd. — Par Lost 5.307
Heaps with unsparing hand; for drink the Grape — Par Lost 5.344
Thirst, and refresht; nor envy'd them the grape — Samson 551
Bacchus that first from out the purple Grape, — Mask 46
Bridgewater ms 'grapes'
Trinity ms 'grape'

Grapes
Her Grapes and tender Shoots. — Psalm 80, 56

Grapple
Fresh from his fall, and fiercer grapple joyn'd, — Par Reg 4.567

Grasp
Sat horror Plum'd; nor wanted in his graspe — Par Lost 4.989
Or while we speak within the direfull grasp — Mask 357
1637 'graspe'
line not in Trinity ms
line not in Bridgewater ms

Grasped
Against the Highest, and fierce with grasped Arms — Par Lost 1.667

Grasping
Grasping ten thousand Thunders, which he sent — Par Lost 6.836

Grass
Gave proof unheeded; others on the grass — Par Lost 4.350
Put forth the verdant Grass, Herb yielding Seed, — Par Lost 7.310
Brought forth the tender Grass, whose verdure clad — Par Lost 7.315
The smell of Grain, or tedded Grass, or Kine, — Par Lost 9.450
Amidst his circling Spires, that on the grass — Par Lost 9.502
Of Knot-grass dew-besprent, and were in fold, — Mask 542
Trinity ms 'knot grasse'
Bridgewater ms 'knot grasse'
Which when I did, he on the tender grass — Mask 624
1637 'grasse'
Trinity ms 'grasse'
Bridgewater ms 'grasse'
Trampling the unshowr'd Grasse with lowings loud: — Nativity 215
1673 'Grass'

Grassy
They to thir grassie Couch, these to thir Nests — Par Lost 4.601
Have heap'd this Table. Rais'd of grassie terf — Par Lost 5.391
The grassie Clods now Calv'd, now half appeer'd — Par Lost 7.463
Nor nocent yet, but on the grassie Herbe — Par Lost 9.186
Of grassie Terfe, and pile up every Stone — Par Lost 11.324
Rustic, of grassie sord; thither anon — Par Lost 11.433
As lightly from his grassy Couch up rose — Par Reg 2.282
La. They left me weary on a grassie terf. — Mask 280

Grate
Th' infernal dores, and on thir hinges grate — Par Lost 2.881
1667 'great', 1668 errata 'grate'
Grate on their scrannel Pipes of wretched straw, — Lycidas 124

Grateful
And understood not that a grateful mind — Par Lost 4.55
Chear'd with the grateful smell old Ocean smiles. — Par Lost 4.165
More grateful, to thir Supper Fruits they fell, — Par Lost 4.331
Of grateful Eevning milde, then silent Night — Par Lost 4.647
Nor grateful Eevning mild, nor silent Night — Par Lost 4.654
To grateful Twilight (for Night comes not there — Par Lost 5.645
Grateful vicissitude, like Day and Night; — Par Lost 6.8
Inducing darkness, grateful truce impos'd, — Par Lost 6.407
But grateful to acknowledge whence his good — Par Lost 7.512
Grateful digressions, and solve high dispute — Par Lost 8.55
More grateful then harmonious sound to the eare. — Par Lost 8.606
With grateful Memorie: thou to mankind — Par Lost 8.650
With grateful Smell, forth came the human pair — Par Lost 9.197
1667 'gratefull'
Grateful to appetite, more pleas'd my sense — Par Lost 9.580
So many grateful Altars I would reare — Par Lost 11.323
Consum'd with nimble glance, and grateful steame; — Par Lost 11.442
Grateful to Heav'n, over his head beholds — Par Lost 11.864
With all things grateful chear'd, and so suppli'd, — Samson 926

Gratefully
Then as new wak't thus gratefully repli'd. — Par Lost 8.4
To whom thus *Adam* gratefully repli'd. — Par Lost 11.370

Gratify
To gratifie my scornful Enemies, — Par Lost 10.625

Gratitude
The debt immense of endless gratitude, — Par Lost 4.52
Repaid? But gratitude in thee is lost — Par Reg 4.188

Gratulate
To gratulate the sweet return of morn; — Par Reg 4.438
Many a friend to gratulate — Mask 949

Gratulating
Of mischief, gratulating, thus excites. — Par Lost 9.472

Gratulation
Gave sign of gratulation, and each Hill; — Par Lost 8.514

Grave
The Womb of nature and perhaps her Grave, — Par Lost 2.911
Thou wilt not leave me in the loathsom grave — Par Lost 3.247
Death last, and with his Carcass glut the Grave: — Par Lost 3.259
Prince of the Aire; then rising from his Grave — Par Lost 10.185
Both *Sin*, and *Death*, and yawning *Grave* at last — Par Lost 10.635
With this corporeal Clod; then in the Grave, — Par Lost 10.786
Out of his grave, fresh as the dawning light, — Par Lost 12.423
My self, my Sepulcher, a moving Grave, — Samson 102
Private respects must yield; with grave authority — Samson 868
With their grave Saws in slumber ly. — Mask 110
1637 'graue'
Lingering, and sitting by a new made grave, — Mask 472
And *Tethys* grave majestick pace, — Mask 870
Each fetter'd Ghost slips to his severall grave, — Nativity 234
Gentle Lady may thy grave — Winchester 47
Staid not behind, nor in the grave were trod; — Sonnet 14, 6
Brought to me like *Alcestis* from the grave, — Sonnet 23, 2
An open grave their throat, their tongue they smooth. — Psalm 5, 28
Who in the grave can celebrate thy praise? — Psalm 6, 10
Unto the grave draws nigh. — Psalm 88, 12
That in the grave lie *deep*. — Psalm 88, 20
On whom the grave *hath hold*, — Psalm 88, 46

Grave
Satan except, none higher sat, with grave — Par Lost 2.300
So spake the Cherube, and his grave rebuke — Par Lost 4.844
The Men though grave, ey'd them, and let thir eyes — Par Lost 11.585
Grey-headed men and grave, with Warriours mixt, — Par Lost 11.662
Thence what the lofty grave Tragoedians taught — Par Reg 4.261

Gravely
Gravely in doubt whether to hold them wise — Par Lost 4.907

Graven
Cornice or Freeze, with bossy Sculptures grav'n, — Par Lost 1.716

Graven(*cont*)
Fusil or grav'n in mettle. After these, Par Lost 11.573
Affirming it thy Star new grav'n in Heaven, Par Reg 1.253
Graver
Thy service in some graver subject use, Vacation 30
Gravest
Among the gravest Rabbies disputant Par Reg 4.218
Graze
Graze the Sea weed thir pasture, and through Groves Par Lost 7.404
I was at first as other Beasts that graze Par Lost 9.571
And Fish with Fish; to graze the Herb all leaving, Par Lost 10.711
Or Taint-worm to the weanling Herds that graze, Lycidas 46
Grazed
Lik'ning his Maker to the Grazed Ox, Par Lost 1.486
ms 'grazed'
Be well stock't with as fair a herd as graz'd Mask 152
Grazing
Grasing the tender herb, were interpos'd, Par Lost 4.253
Of Cattel grazing: others, whence the sound Par Lost 11.558
Great
That to the highth of this great Argument Par Lost 1.24
As one great Furnace flam'd, yet from those flames Par Lost 1.62
Since through experience of this great event Par Lost 1.118
Of some great Ammiral, were but a wand, Par Lost 1.294
Of thir great Sultan waving to direct Par Lost 1.348
Thir great Commander; Godlike shapes and forms Par Lost 1.358
At thir great Emperors call, as next in worth Par Lost 1.378
Nor great *Alcairo* such magnificence Par Lost 1.718
The great Seraphic Lords and Cherubim Par Lost 1.794
And summons read, the great consult began. Par Lost 1.798
Heav'ns purest Light, yet our great Enemy Par Lost 2.137
If we were wise, against so great a foe Par Lost 2.202
Then most conspicuous, when great things of small, Par Lost 2.258
The great Creatour? But thir spite still serves Par Lost 2.385
Great things resolv'd, which from the lowest deep Par Lost 2.392
Refusing to accept as great a share Par Lost 2.452
With Trumpets regal sound the great result: Par Lost 2.515
The irksom hours, till this great Chief return. Par Lost 2.527
To meet so great a foe: and now great deeds Par Lost 2.722
Great things with small) then when *Bellona* storms, Par Lost 2.922
To whom the great Creatour thus reply'd. Par Lost 3.167
Of his great Father. Admiration seis'd Par Lost 3.271
Farr more then Great or High; because in thee Par Lost 3.311
Or Longitude, where the great Luminarie Par Lost 3.576
Lay waving round; on som great charge imploy'd Par Lost 3.628
The first art wont his great authentic will Par Lost 3.656
On whom the great Creator hath bestowd Par Lost 3.673
The great Work-Maister, leads to no excess Par Lost 3.696
As great might have aspir'd, and me though mean Par Lost 4.62
Drawn to his part; but other Powers as great Par Lost 4.63
Of great *Seleucia*, built by *Grecian* Kings, Par Lost 4.212
Singing thir great Creator: oft in bands Par Lost 4.684
Thou Sun, of this great World both Eye and Soule, Par Lost 5.171
Varie to our great Maker still new praise. Par Lost 5.184
In honour to the Worlds great Author rise, Par Lost 5.188
Ris'n on mid-noon; som great behest from Heav'n Par Lost 5.311
Mean while our Primitive great Sire, to meet Par Lost 5.350
Given him by this great Conference to know Par Lost 5.454
To whom our great Progenitor. Thy words Par Lost 5.544
His other half in the great Zone of Heav'n. Par Lost 5.560
As Heav'ns great Year brings forth, th' Empyreal Host Par Lost 5.583
Under his great Vice-gerent Reign abide Par Lost 5.609
If not the first Arch-Angel, great in Power, Par Lost 5.660
Honourd by his great Father, and proclaimd Par Lost 5.663
The great *Messiah*, and his new commands, Par Lost 5.691
The great Hierarchal Standard was to move; Par Lost 5.701
Of thir great Potentate; for great indeed Par Lost 5.706
The Palace of great *Lucifer*, (so call Par Lost 5.760
About the great reception of thir King, Par Lost 5.769
Thy self though great and glorious dost thou count, Par Lost 5.833
Unanimous, as sons of one great Sire Par Lost 6.95
The great Arch-Angel from his warlike toile Par Lost 6.257
Fit to decide the Empire of great Heav'n. Par Lost 6.303
Great things by small, If Natures concord broke, Par Lost 6.311
That his great purpose he might so fulfill, Par Lost 6.675
Of ending this great Warr, since none but Thou Par Lost 6.702
When the great Ensign of *Messiah* blaz'd Par Lost 6.775
Or faint retreat; when the great Son of God Par Lost 6.799
Great things, and full of wonder in our eares, Par Lost 7.70
And the great Light of Day yet wants to run Par Lost 7.98
Into his place, and the great Son returnd Par Lost 7.135
Great triumph and rejoycing was in Heav'n Par Lost 7.180
On his great Expedition now appeer'd, Par Lost 7.193
Of this great Round: partition firm and sure, Par Lost 7.267
Fermented the great Mother to conceave, Par Lost 7.281
For haste; such flight the great command impress'd Par Lost 7.294
The dry Land, Earth, and the great receptacle Par Lost 7.307
And God made two great Lights, great for thir use Par Lost 7.346
Surveying his great Work, that it was good: Par Lost 7.353
Her gather'd beams, great Palace now of Light. Par Lost 7.363
Revolvd on Heav'ns great Axle, and her Reign Par Lost 7.381
And God created the great Whales, and each Par Lost 7.391
Her motions, as the great first-Movers hand Par Lost 7.500
Answering his great Idea. Up he rode Par Lost 7.557
The great Creator from his work returnd Par Lost 7.567
With his great Father (for he also went Par Lost 7.588
Great are thy works, *Jehovah*, infinite Par Lost 7.602
From Man or Angel the great Architect Par Lost 8.72

Great(*cont*)
The benefit: consider first, that Great Par Lost 8.90
Which two great Sexes animate the World, Par Lost 8.151
Not of my self; by some great Maker then, Par Lost 8.278
His great command; take heed least Passion sway Par Lost 8.635
From th' Earths great Altar send up silent praise Par Lost 9.195
Rais'd, as of som great matter to begin. Par Lost 9.669
Flourishd, since mute, to som great cause addrest, Par Lost 9.672
Great are thy Vertues, doubtless, best of Fruits. Par Lost 9.745
Our great Forbidder, safe with all his Spies Par Lost 9.815
Great joy he promis'd to his thoughts, and new Par Lost 9.843
And peril great provok't, who thus hath dar'd Par Lost 9.922
Idlely, while Satan our great Author thrives Par Lost 10.236
Flew divers, and with Power (thir Power was great) Par Lost 10.284
So, if great things to small may be compar'd, Par Lost 10.306
Great joy was at thir meeting, and at sight Par Lost 10.350
Each hour their great adventurer from the search Par Lost 10.440
Forth rush'd in haste the great consulting Peers, Par Lost 10.456
With peril great atchiev'd. Long were to tell Par Lost 10.469
By thir great Intercessor, came in sight Par Lost 11.19
While the great Visitant approachd, thus spake. Par Lost 11.225
Eve, now expect great tidings, which perhaps Par Lost 11.226
None of the meanest, some great Potentate Par Lost 11.231
Therefore to his great bidding I submit. Par Lost 11.314
And reverence thee thir great Progenitor. Par Lost 11.346
To *Agra* and *Lahor* of great *Mogul* Par Lost 11.391
Guiana, whose great Citie *Geryons* Sons Par Lost 11.410
O Teacher, some great mischief hath befall'n Par Lost 11.450
Of triumph, to be styl'd great Conquerours, Par Lost 11.695
And of thir doings great dislike declar'd, Par Lost 11.720
And great exploits, but of true vertu void; Par Lost 11.790
Down the great River to the op'ning Gulf, Par Lost 11.833
As mockt they storm; great laughter was in Heav'n Par Lost 12.59
From *Hermon* East to the great Western Sea, Par Lost 12.141
Is meant thy great deliverer, who shall bruise Par Lost 12.149
Thir government, and thir great Senate choose Par Lost 12.225
Of great *Messiah* shall sing. Thus Laws and Rites Par Lost 12.244
Why our great expectation should be call'd Par Lost 12.378
As at the Worlds great period; and our Sire Par Lost 12.467
Great numbers of each Nation to receave Par Lost 12.503
Accomplishing great things, by things deemd weak Par Lost 12.567
The great deliverance by her Seed to come Par Lost 12.600
Which he hath sent propitious, some great good Par Lost 12.612
Now had the great Proclaimer with a voice Par Reg 1.18
To all Baptiz'd: to his great Baptism flock'd Par Reg 1.21
Before him a great Prophet, to proclaim Par Reg 1.70
To him their great Dictator, whose attempt Par Reg 1.113
Great in Renown, and call'd the Son of God; Par Reg 1.136
And vaunts of his great cunning to the throng Par Reg 1.145
Of his great warfare, e're I send him forth Par Reg 1.158
Now entring his great duel, not of arms, Par Reg 1.174
Had measur'd twice six years, at our great Feast Par Reg 1.210
Thou shouldst be great and sit on *David*'s Throne, Par Reg 1.240
And the great *Thisbite* who on fiery wheels Par Reg 2.16
By his great Prophet, pointed at and shown, Par Reg 2.51
I look't for some great change; to Honour? no, Par Reg 2.86
But where delays he now? some great intent Par Reg 2.95
Thus long to some great purpose he obscures. Par Reg 2.101
All his great work to come before him set; Par Reg 2.112
Great acts require great means of enterprise, Par Reg 2.412
Therefore, if at great things thou wouldst arrive, Par Reg 2.426
Great *Julius*, whom now all the world admires Par Reg 3.39
Large Countries, and in field great Battels win, Par Reg 3.73
Great Cities by assault: what do these Worthies, Par Reg 3.74
Great Benefactors of mankind, Deliverers, Par Reg 3.82
Resembling thy great Father: he seeks glory, Par Reg 3.110
The great *Seleucia*, *Nisibis*, and there Par Reg 3.291
By great *Arsaces* led, who founded first Par Reg 3.295
Of his great power; for now the *Parthian* King Par Reg 3.299
Then great and glorious *Rome*, Queen of the Earth Par Reg 4.45
To *Rome*'s great Emperour, whose wide domain Par Reg 4.81
For what can less so great a gift deserve? Par Reg 4.169
Great *Alexander* to subdue the world, Par Reg 4.252
His Godlike presence, and from some great act Samson 28
Design'd for great exploits; if I must dye Samson 32
Ask for this great Deliverer now, and find him Samson 40
O first created Beam, and thou great Word, Samson 83
Who seeing those great acts which God had done Samson 243
Thir great Deliverer contemn'd, Samson 279
Great Pomp, and Sacrifice, and Praises loud Samson 436
But will arise and his great name assert: Samson 467
All mortals I excell'd, and great in hopes Samson 523
To some great work, thy glory, Samson 680
Or rather flight, no great advantage on me; Samson 1118
To honour this great Feast, and great Assembly; Samson 1315
After my great transgression, so requite Samson 1356
By some great act, or of my days the last. Samson 1389
Great among the Heathen round: Samson 1430
Measure of strength so great to mortal seed, Samson 1439
Thir once great dread, captive, & blind before them, Samson 1474
To use him further yet in some great service, Samson 1499
Not to sit idle with so great a gift Samson 1500
Chor. Of good or bad so great, of bad the sooner; Samson 1537
Or some great matter in his mind revolv'd. Samson 1638
Of true experience from this great event Samson 1756
Of *Bacchus*, and of *Circe* born, great *Comus*, Mask 522
Bridgewater ms 'greate'
In name of great *Oceanus*, Mask 868

Great(*cont*)
Bridgewater ms 'greate'
Wher the great Sun begins his state, Allegro 60
With thrice great *Hermes*, or unsphear Penseroso 88
And if ought els, great *Bards* beside, Penseroso 116
Fair silver-buskind Nymphs as great and good, Arcades 33
To the great Mistres of yon princely shrine, Arcades 36
Where the great vision of the guarded Mount Lycidas 161
Our great redemption from above did bring; Nativity 4
With her great Master so to sympathize: Nativity 34
While the Creator Great Nativity 120
1673 'great'
And that great Cov'nant which we still transgress Circum 21
To their great Lord, whose love their motion sway'd Musick 22
Dear son of memory, great heir of Fame, Shakespear 5
As ever in my great task Masters eye. Sonnet 7, 14
The great *Emathian* Conqueror bid spare Sonnet 8, 10
Whom *Joves* great Son to her glad Husband gave, Sonnet 23, 3
Of scorners hath not sate. But in the great Psalm 1, 4
Great ones how long will ye Psalm 4, 7
O Jehovah our Lord how wondrous great Psalm 8, 1
O Jehovah our Lord how wondrous great Psalm 8, 23
God in the great assembly stands Psalm 82, 1
With them *great* Asshur also bands Psalm 83, 29
For great thou art, and wonders great Psalm 86, 33
For great thy mercy is toward me, Psalm 86, 45
Through sorrow, and affliction great Psalm 88, 37
Jesting decides great things Prose 7, 1
Who judges in great suits and controversies, Prose 10, 3

Greater
With loss of *Eden*, till one greater Man Par Lost 1.4
Whom Thunder hath made greater? Here at least Par Lost 1.258
Acknowledge him thy Greater, sound his praise Par Lost 5.172
The Rebel Thrones, but greater rage to see Par Lost 6.199
Yet farr the greater part have kept, I see, Par Lost 7.145
To Man, the greater to have rule by Day, Par Lost 7.347
Of Light by farr the greater part he took, Par Lost 7.359
Relate thee; greater now in thy return Par Lost 7.604
Is greater then created to destroy. Par Lost 7.607
Greater so manifold to this one use, Par Lost 8.29
That bodies bright and greater should not serve Par Lost 8.87
As leaves a greater store of Fruit untoucht, Par Lost 9.621
Reluctant, but in vaine, a greater power Par Lost 10.515
One greater, of whose day he shall foretell, Par Lost 12.242
Of Spirit and Truth; the rest, farr greater part, Par Lost 12.533
As much his greater, and was hardly won; Par Reg 1.279
Plain Fishermen, no greater men them call, Par Reg 2.27
Greater and nobler done, and to lay down Par Reg 2.482
Favour renew'd, and add a greater sin Samson 1357
I mean to shew you of my strength, yet greater; Samson 1644
Here ye shall have greater grace, Arcades 104
1673 'geater'
He saw a greater Sun appear Nativity 83

Greatest
By falsities and lyes the greatest part Par Lost 1.367
Learn how thir greatest Monuments of Fame, Par Lost 1.695
Your bulwark, and condemns to greatest share Par Lost 2.29
Powerful at greatest distance to unite Par Lost 10.247
Ophiusa) but still greatest hee the midst, Par Lost 10.528
Things highest, greatest, multiplies my fear. Par Reg 1.69
And amplitude of mind to greatest Deeds. Par Reg 2.139
Of greatest things; what woman will you find, Par Reg 2.208
Rocks whereon greatest men have oftest wreck'd; Par Reg 2.228
In all things that to greatest actions lead. Par Reg 3.239
Small things with greatest) in *Irassa* strove Par Reg 4.564
Bears greatest names in his wild aerie flight. Samson 974
Which greatest Heroes have in battel worn, Samson 1131
The greatest, and the best of all the main Mask 28

Greatly
Thy sorrow I will greatly multiplie Par Lost 10.193
Greatly rejoyc'd, and thus his joy broke forth. Par Lost 11.869
Greatly instructed I shall hence depart, Par Lost 12.557
Greatly in peace of thought, and have my fill Par Lost 12.558

Greatness
Of servile Pomp. Our greatness will appeer Par Lost 2.257
So should thy goodness and thy greatness both Par Lost 3.165
Greatness of mind and nobleness thir seat Par Lost 8.557
To greatness? whence Authority deriv'st, Par Reg 2.418

Greaves
Vant-brass and Greves, and Gauntlet, add thy Spear Samson 1121

Grecian
Of great *Seleucia*, built by *Grecian* Kings, Par Lost 4.212

Greece
In ancient *Greece;* and in *Ausonian* land Par Lost 1.739
ms 'Greece'
Xerxes, the Libertie of *Greece* to yoke, Par Lost 10.307
Athens the eye of *Greece*, Mother of Arts Par Reg 4.240
Shook the Arsenal and fulmin'd over *Greece*, Par Reg 4.270
That rather *Greece* from us these Arts deriv'd; Par Reg 4.338
Then all the Oratory of *Greece* and *Rome*. Par Reg 4.360
Antiquity from the old Schools of Greece Mask 439
1673 *'Greece'*

Greedier
Luxurious by thir wealth, and greedier still, Par Reg 4.141

Greedily
Greedily she ingorg'd without restraint, Par Lost 9.791
That curld *Megaera:* greedily they pluck'd Par Lost 10.560

Greedy
Watches, no doubt, with greedy hope to find Par Lost 9.257
And last of all, thy greedy self consum'd, On Time 10
Trinity ms 'greedie'
The *greedy* flame runs hier and hier Psalm 83, 55

Greek
Perplex'd the *Greek* and *Cytherea*'s Son; Par Lost 9.19
Promiscuous from all Nations, Jew, or Greek, Par Reg 3.118
When thou taught'st *Cambridge*, and King *Edward* Greek. Sonnet 11, 14

Green
Now nearer, Crowns with her enclosure green, Par Lost 4.133
Under a tuft of shade that on a green Par Lost 4.325
On the green bank, to look into the cleer Par Lost 4.458
Yon flourie Arbors, yonder Allies green, Par Lost 4.626
Springs lighter the green stalk, from thence the leaves Par Lost 5.480
Her Universal Face with pleasant green, Par Lost 7.316
On the green stemm; God saw that it was good. Par Lost 7.337
Glide under the green Wave, in Sculles that oft Par Lost 7.402
The Cattel in the Fields and Meddowes green: Par Lost 7.460
With spots of Gold and Purple, azure and green: Par Lost 7.479
On a green shadie Bank profuse of Flours Par Lost 8.286
Beyond the Earths green Cape and verdant Isles Par Lost 8.631
First Fruits, the green Eare, and the yellow Sheaf, Par Lost 11.435
Green Tree or ground whereon his foot may light; Par Lost 11.858
Must eat, and on the ground leave nothing green: Par Lost 12.186
In Valley or Green Meadow to way-lay Par Reg 2.185
Who all things now behold more fresh and green, Par Reg 4.435
On a green bank, and set before him spred Par Reg 4.587
Of Laurel ever green, and branching Palm, Samson 1735
By slow *Meander*'s margent green, Mask 232
Bridgewater ms 'greene'
1637 'greene'
Trinity ms 'greene'
I saw them under a green mantling vine Mask 294
Bridgewater ms 'greene'
1637 'greene'
Trinity ms 'greene'
Co. I know each lane, and every alley green Mask 311
Trinity ms 'greene'
1637 'greene'
Bridgewater ms 'greene'
That in their green shops weave the smooth-hair'd silk Mask 716
Trinity ms 'greene'
Bridgewater ms 'greene'
Of Turkis blew, and Emrauld green Mask 894
Trinity ms 'greene'
Bridgewater ms 'greene'
1637 'greene'
Quickly to the green earths end, Mask 1014
Trinity ms 'greene'
1637 'greene'
Bridgewater ms 'earths greene'
yellow, watchet, greene, & blew Mask Tr. ms 26.21
yellow, watchett, greene and blew Mask Br. ms 17
By Hedge-row Elms, on Hillocks green, Allegro 58
On the dry smooth-shaven Green, Penseroso 66
O're the smooth enameld green Arcades 84
Trinity ms 'greene'
The Willows, and the Hazle Copses green, Lycidas 42
Trinity ms 'greene'
That on the green terf suck the honied showres, Lycidas 140
Trinity ms 'greene'
She crown'd with Olive green, came softly sliding Nativity 47
In *Memphian* Grove, or Green, Nativity 214
With those just Spirits that wear victorious Palms, Musick 14
Trinity ms 'victorious' ←'blooming' ←'victorious' ←'blooming' ←'freshe greene'
The Flowry *May*, who from her green lap throws May Morn 3
Wisely hast shun'd the broad way and the green, Sonnet 9, 2
End Green. Why is it harder Sirs then Gordon, Sonnet 11, 8
Trinity ms 'Greene' ←'Green'
With her *green* shade *that* cover'd *all*, Psalm 80, 41
Then past hee to a flowry Mountaine greene, Prose 4, 1

Green-eyed
May tell at length how green-ey'd *Neptune* raves, Vacation 43

Greet
The morns approach, and greet her with his Song: Par Reg 2.281
Have thou the honour first, thy Lord to greet, Nativity 26
Their hearts and ears did greet, Nativity 94
Then long Eternity shall greet our bliss On Time 11
To greet her of a lovely son, Winchester 24

Greeting
This greeting on thy impious Crest receive. Par Lost 6.188
Lest som ill greeting touch attempt the person Mask 406
Bridgewater ms 'greetinge'

Grew
So speaking and so threatning, grew tenfold Par Lost 2.705
Grew darker at thir frown, so matcht they stood; Par Lost 2.720
Distorted, all my nether shape thus grew Par Lost 2.784
To Heav'n remov'd where first it grew, there grows, Par Lost 3.356
Access deni'd; and over head up grew Par Lost 4.137
The middle Tree and highest there that grew, Par Lost 4.195
Our Death the Tree of knowledge grew fast by, Par Lost 4.221
Laurel and Mirtle, and what higher grew Par Lost 4.694
God made, and every Herb, before it grew Par Lost 7.336
And toucht by her fair tendance gladlier grew. Par Lost 8.47
Under his forming hands a Creature grew, Par Lost 8.470
Which grew in Paradise, the bait of *Eve* Par Lost 10.551

Grew(*cont*)
The Frutage fair to sight, like that which grew Par Lost 10.561
Bending his eare; perswasion in me grew Par Lost 11.152
Made it my whole delight, and in it grew Par Reg 1.208
Among wild Beasts: they at his sight grew mild, Par Reg 1.310
The more he grew in years, the more inflam'd Par Reg 3.40
Abstemious I grew up and thriv'd amain; Samson 637
The Feast and noon grew high, and Sacrifice Samson 1612
Grey
White, Black and Grey, with all thir trumperie. Par Lost 3.475
Now came still Eevning on, and Twilight gray Par Lost 4.598
From Hill or steaming Lake, duskie or grey, Par Lost 5.186
His Longitude through Heav'ns high rode: the gray Par Lost 7.373
To witherd weak and gray; thy Senses then Par Lost 11.540
God from the Mount of *Sinai*, whose gray top Par Lost 12.227
His gray dissimulation, disappear'd Par Reg 1.498
Came forth with Pilgrim steps in amice gray; Par Reg 4.427
Or do his gray hairs any violence? Mask 392
Bridgewater ms 'graye'
Russet Lawns, and Fallows Gray, Allegro 71
When Eev'ning gray doth rise, I fetch my round Arcades 54
While the still morn went out with Sandals gray, Lycidas 187
Grey-fly
What time the Gray-fly winds her sultry horn, Lycidas 28
1638 'gray-fly'
Trinity ms 'gray fly'
Grey-headed
Grey-headed men and grave, with Warriours mixt, Par Lost 11.662
Grey-hooded
They left me then, when the gray-hooded Eev'n Mask 188
line not in Bridgewater ms
Trinity ms 'gray-hoodded'
Griding
The griding sword with discontinuous wound Par Lost 6.329
Grief
Forgets both joy and grief, pleasure and pain. Par Lost 2.586
O Hell! what doe mine eyes with grief behold, Par Lost 4.358
Thus he resolv'd, but first from inward griefe Par Lost 9.97
Surcharg'd, as had like grief bin dew'd in tears, Par Lost 12.373
For long indulgence to their fears or grief: Par Reg 1.110
That once found out and solv'd, for grief and spight Par Reg 4.574
Annull'd, which might in part my grief have eas'd, Samson 72
The glory late of *Israel*, now the grief; Samson 179
Sam. Ay me, another inward grief awak't, Samson 330
Lenient of grief and anxious thought, Samson 659
And in my midst of sorrow and heart-grief Samson 1339
Mess. Feed on that first, there may in grief be surfet. Samson 1562
Yet e're I give the rains to grief, say first, Samson 1578
What need a man forestall his date of grief, Mask 362
line not in Bridgewater ms
1637 'griefe'
line not in Trinity ms
Amaz'd I stood, harrow'd with grief and fear, Mask 565
1637 'griefe'
Bridgewater ms 'greife'
Trinity ms 'greife'
Befriend me night best Patroness of grief, Passion 29
And here though grief my feeble hands up-lock, Passion 45
And I (for grief is easily beguild) Passion 54
Through grief consumes, is waxen old and dark Psalm 6, 14
Griefs
My griefs not only pain me Samson 617
Grieve
Shall grieve him, if I fail not, and disturb Par Lost 1.167
How didst thou grieve then, *Adam*, to behold Par Lost 11.754
And all their Sin, *that did thee grieve* Psalm 85, 7
Grieved
Lay pleasant, his grievd look he fixes sad, Par Lost 4.28
Griev'd at his heart, when looking down he saw Par Lost 11.887
Grievest
Deservedly thou griev'st, compos'd of lyes Par Reg 1.407
Grieving
Grieving to see his Glorie, at the sight Par Lost 6.792
Grievous
Or much more grievous pain? Ye have th' account Par Lost 10.501
Grievous to bear: but that care now is past, Par Lost 11.776
Wolves shall succeed for teachers, grievous Wolves, Par Lost 12.508
Too grievous for the trespass or omission, Samson 691
Griffon
As when a Gryfon through the Wilderness Par Lost 2.943
Grim
To his grim Idol. Him the *Ammonite* Par Lost 1.396
What if the breath that kindl'd those grim fires Par Lost 2.170
That dar'st, though grim and terrible, advance Par Lost 2.682
Grim *Death* my Son and foe, who sets them on, Par Lost 2.804
The ridges of grim Warr; no thought of flight, Par Lost 6.236
So sented the grim Feature, and upturn'd Par Lost 10.279
Of Man, but fled him, or with count'nance grim Par Lost 10.713
To his grim Cave, all dismal; yet to sense Par Lost 11.469
Thou told'st me of? What grim aspects are these, Mask 694
Besides what the grim Woolf with privy paw Lycidas 128
1638 'grimme'
For since grim Aquilo his charioter Fair Inf 8
Grind
Or by collision of two bodies grinde Par Lost 10.1072
To grind in Brazen Fetters under task Samson 35
Into the common Prison, there to grind Samson 1161
Grinding
These rags, this grinding, is not yet so base Samson 415
Grinned
Grinnd horrible a gastly smile, to hear Par Lost 2.846
Grip
Fit well his Helme, gripe fast his orbed Shield, Par Lost 6.543
Gripe
Heart-strook with chilling gripe of sorrow stood, Par Lost 11.264
Gripped
Grip't in each paw: When *Adam* first of men Par Lost 4.408
Gris-amber-steamed
Gris-amber-steam'd; all Fish from Sea or Shore, Par Reg 2.344
Grisly
There stood a Hill not far whose griesly top Par Lost 1.670
So spake the grieslie terrour, and in shape, Par Lost 2.704
So sudden to behold the grieslie King; Par Lost 4.821
And grisly Spectres, which the Fiend had rais'd Par Reg 4.430
With all the greisly legions that troop Mask 603
Bridgewater ms 'grisley'
They call the grisly king, Nativity 209
Groan
Under what torments inwardly I groane; Par Lost 4.88
Implacable, and many a dolorous groan, Par Lost 6.658
In pangs, and Nature gave a second groan, Par Lost 9.1001
Chor. Noise call you it or universal groan Samson 1511
Groaned
Groand out his Soul with gushing bloud effus'd. Par Lost 11.447
Groaning
Under her own waight groaning till the day Par Lost 12.539
Groans
There to converse with everlasting groans, Par Lost 2.184
Dire was the tossing, deep the groans, despair Par Lost 11.489
Forget not: in thy book record their groanes Sonnet 18, 5
Grooms
Of Horses led, and Grooms besmeard with Gold Par Lost 5.356
Gross
Fell not from Heaven, or more gross to love Par Lost 1.491
ms 'grosse'
Another part in Squadrons and gross Bands, Par Lost 2.570
Approaching gross and huge; in hollow Cube Par Lost 6.552
Purest at first, now gross by sinning grown. Par Lost 6.661
No gross, no unharmoneous mixture foule, Par Lost 11.51
As a distemper, gross to aire as gross, Par Lost 11.53
Above the Clouds will pine his entrails gross, Par Lost 12.77
Tell her of things that no gross ear can hear, Mask 458
1637 'grosse'
Trinity ms 'grosse'
Bridgewater ms 'grosse'
Of human mould with grosse unpurged ear; Arcades 73
1673 'gross'
Grosser
The grosser feeds the purer, Earth the Sea, Par Lost 5.416
Made erre, was now exhal'd, and grosser sleep Par Lost 9.1049
Grossness
Then all this Earthy grosnes quit, On Time 20
1673 'grosness'
Trinity ms 'grossnesse' ←'grosnesse'
Grotesque
With thicket overgrown, grottesque and wilde, Par Lost 4.136
1674 printed 'gottesque'
Grots
Another side, umbrageous Grots and Caves Par Lost 4.257
By grots, and caverns shag'd with horrid shades, Mask 429
Ground
Egypt from *Syrian* ground, had general Names Par Lost 1.421
A third as soon had form'd within the ground Par Lost 1.705
Thick swarm'd, both on the ground and in the air, Par Lost 1.767
Uplifted spurns the ground, thence many a League Par Lost 2.929
On even ground against his mortal foe, Par Lost 3.179
Towards either Throne they bow, and to the ground Par Lost 3.350
Out of the fertil ground he caus'd to grow Par Lost 4.216
His couchant watch, as one who chose his ground Par Lost 4.406
Broiderd the ground, more colour'd then with stone Par Lost 4.702
Partakers, and uncropt falls to the ground. Par Lost 4.731
Wants her fit vessels pure, then strews the ground Par Lost 5.348
This spacious ground, in yonder shadie Bowre Par Lost 5.367
We brush mellifluous Dewes, and find the ground Par Lost 5.429
Thir perfet ranks; for high above the ground Par Lost 6.71
Winds under ground or waters forcing way Par Lost 6.196
That Warr and various; somtimes on firm ground Par Lost 6.242
Enter'd, and foul disorder; all the ground Par Lost 6.388
Deep under ground, materials dark and crude, Par Lost 6.478
That under ground, they fought in dismal shade; Par Lost 6.666
On heav'nly ground they stood, and from the shore Par Lost 7.210
But they, or under ground, or circuit wide Par Lost 7.301
Easie, e're God had bid the ground be drie, Par Lost 7.304
Upon the Earth, and man to till the ground Par Lost 7.332
Went up and waterd all the ground, and each Par Lost 7.334
With clang despis'd the ground, under a cloud Par Lost 7.422
The mid Aereal Skie: Others on ground Par Lost 7.442
Limb'd and full grown: out of the ground up rose Par Lost 7.456
In Hillocks; the swift Stag from under ground Par Lost 7.469
At once came forth whatever creeps the ground, Par Lost 7.475
Streaking the ground with sinuous trace; not all Par Lost 7.481
And every creeping thing that creeps the ground. Par Lost 7.523
Dust of the ground, and in thy nostrils breath'd Par Lost 7.525
Into a Gulf shot under ground, till part Par Lost 9.72
Prone on the ground, as since, but on his reare, Par Lost 9.497

Ground(*cont*)
Fawning, and lick'd the ground whereon she trod. Par Lost 9.526
For high from ground the branches would require Par Lost 9.590
Braunching so broad and long, that in the ground Par Lost 9.1104
No ground of enmitie between us known, Par Lost 9.1151
Curs'd is the ground for thy sake, thou in sorrow Par Lost 10.201
Till thou return unto the ground, for thou Par Lost 10.206
Out of the ground wast taken, know thy Birth, Par Lost 10.207
All things with double terror: On the Ground Par Lost 10.850
1667 'ground'
Outstretcht he lay, on the cold ground, and oft Par Lost 10.851
Glanc'd on the ground, with labour I must earne Par Lost 10.1054
Watering the ground, and with our sighs the Air Par Lost 10.1090
Watering the ground, and with thir sighs the Air Par Lost 10.1102
The Ground whence he was taken, fitter soile. Par Lost 11.98
From hallowd ground th' unholie, and denounce Par Lost 11.106
Of flight pursu'd in th' Air and ore the ground Par Lost 11.202
The ground whence thou wast tak'n, fitter Soile. Par Lost 11.262
To dwell on eeven ground now with thy Sons: Par Lost 11.348
From underground) the liquid Ore he dreind Par Lost 11.570
From a fat Meddow ground; or fleecy Flock, Par Lost 11.648
The Ark no more now flotes, but seems on ground Par Lost 11.850
Green Tree or ground whereon his foot may light; Par Lost 11.858
Anon drie ground appeers, and from his Arke Par Lost 11.861
Boiles out from under ground, the mouth of Hell; Par Lost 12.42
Must eat, and on the ground leave nothing green: Par Lost 12.186
The Cherubim descended; on the ground Par Lost 12.628
And gathers ground fast at the Labourers heel Par Lost 12.631
On hostile ground, none daring my affront. Samson 531
From the dry ground to spring, thy thirst to allay Samson 582
Com, knit hands, and beat the ground, Mask 143
Of som chast footing neer about this ground. Mask 146
And shed the lushious liquor on the ground, Mask 652
Till we com to holier ground, Mask 943
In slumber soft, and on the ground Mask 1001
line not in Bridgewater ms
I throw it on the ground Mask Tr. ms 22.22
Oft on a Plat of rising ground, Penseroso 73
In fire, air, flood, or under ground, Penseroso 94
Over the mount, and all this hallow'd ground, Arcades 55
1673 'groun'd'
And purple all the ground with vernal flowres. Lycidas 141
Th' old Dragon under ground Nativity 168
Went to the ground: And the repeated air Sonnet 8, 12
That dry and barren ground Psalm 84, 22

Grounded
Then self esteem, grounded on just and right Par Lost 8.572
With hard contest: at length that grounded maxim Samson 865

Ground-nest
Left his ground-nest, high towring to descry Par Reg 2.280

Grounds
Mistrustful, grounds his courage on despair Par Lost 2.126
On no slight grounds thy safety; hear, and mark Par Reg 3.349
And from their plenteous grounds Psalm 4, 35

Grove
On that opprobrious Hill, and made his Grove Par Lost 1.403
ms 'grove'
Even to that Hill of scandal, by the Grove Par Lost 1.416
ms 'grove'
Cleer Spring, or shadie Grove, or Sunnie Hill, Par Lost 3.28
Breathing the smell of field and grove, attune Par Lost 4.265
To seek her through the world; nor that sweet Grove Par Lost 4.272
Her bearded Grove of ears, which way the wind Par Lost 4.982
Our tended Plants, how blows the Citron Grove, Par Lost 5.22
He brought thee into this delicious Grove, Par Lost 7.537
Of Grove or Garden-Plot more pleasant lay, Par Lost 9.418
A Grove hard by, sprung up with this thir change, Par Lost 10.548
In Wood or Grove by mossie Fountain side, Par Reg 2.184
Only in a bottom saw a pleasant Grove, Par Reg 2.289
See there the Olive Grove of *Academe*, Par Reg 4.244
And casts a gleam over this tufted Grove. Mask 225
line not in Bridgewater ms
Trinity ms 'grove'
Of woody *Ida*'s inmost grove, Penseroso 29
To nurse the Saplings tall, and curl the grove Arcades 46
In *Memphian* Grove, or Green, Nativity 214
The gentle neighbourhood of grove and spring Passion 52
Foretell my hopeles doom in som Grove ny: Sonnet 1, 10

Groveling
Or grovling soild thir crested helmets in the dust. Samson 141

Grovelling
Groveling and prostrate on yon Lake of Fire, Par Lost 1.280
Upon thy Belly groveling thou shalt goe, Par Lost 10.177
And downward fell into a groveling Swine) Mask 53
1637 'grovling'
Bridgewater ms 'grovelinge'

Groves
Fortunate Fields, and Groves and flourie Vales, Par Lost 3.569
Groves whose rich Trees wept odorous Gumms and Balme, Par Lost 4.248
Among the Groves, the Fountains, and the Flours Par Lost 5.126
Into the blissful field, through Groves of Myrrhe, Par Lost 5.292
Graze the Sea weed thir pasture, and through Groves Par Lost 7.404
Betook her to the Groves, but *Delia*'s self Par Lost 9.388
Gardens and Groves presented to his eyes, Par Reg 4.38
With Groves of myrrhe, and cinnamon. Mask 937
Trinity ms 'groves'
Bridgewater ms 'groves'
1637 'groves'

Groves(*cont*)
To arched walks of twilight groves, Penseroso 133
Where other groves, and other streams along, Lycidas 174
Woods and Groves, are of thy dressing, May Morn 7

Grow
That riches grow in Hell; that soyle may best Par Lost 1.691
For which to strive, no strife can grow up there Par Lost 2.31
This horror will grow milde, this darkness light, Par Lost 2.220
For never can true reconcilement grow Par Lost 4.98
Out of the fertil ground he caus'd to grow Par Lost 4.216
Thir stellar vertue on all kinds that grow Par Lost 4.671
These things, as not to mind from whence they grow Par Lost 6.477
For many are the Trees of God that grow Par Lost 9.618
Grow up to thir provision, and more hands Par Lost 9.623
Till dieted by thee I grow mature Par Lost 9.803
The bended Twigs take root, and Daughters grow Par Lost 9.1105
Regenerate grow instead, that sighs now breath'd Par Lost 11.5
That never will in other Climate grow, Par Lost 11.274
In wealth and multitude, factious they grow; Par Lost 12.352
And due to theirs which out of thine will grow: Par Lost 12.400
Grow up and perish, as the summer flie, Samson 676
His strength again to grow up with his hair Samson 1496
She plumes her feathers, and lets grow her wings Mask 378
Would grow inur'd to light, and com at last Mask 735
Bridgewater ms 'growe'
Com let us haste, the Stars grow high, Mask 956
1637 'are'
Trinity ms 'grow' ←'are'
Bridgewater ms 'are'
aeternall roses grow & hyacinth Mask Tr. ms 10.07
'grow' ←'blosme' ←'grow' ←'blow' ←'yeeld' ←'grow'
Those rugged names to our like mouths grow sleek Sonnet 11, 10
The triple Tyrant: that from these may grow Sonnet 18, 12
With much confusion; then grow red with shame, Psalm 6, 22
That it *began to grow apace*, Psalm 80, 39
Who thence grow bold and strong Psalm 82, 8

Growing
A growing Empire; doubtless; while we dream, Par Lost 2.315
A growing burden. Mean while Warr arose, Par Lost 2.767
To prune these growing Plants, and tend these Flours, Par Lost 4.438
Thir growing work: for much thir work outgrew Par Lost 9.202
And growing up to Godhead; which for thee Par Lost 9.877
Wings growing, and Dominion giv'n me large Par Lost 10.244
The growing miseries, which *Adam* saw Par Lost 10.715
Growing into a Nation, and now grown Par Lost 12.164
These growing thoughts my Mother soon perceiving Par Reg 1.227
And at thy growing vertues fret their spleen, Sonnet 9, 7
Trinity ms 'growing' ←'prospering' ←'blooming'

Grown
Portentous held me; but familiar grown, Par Lost 2.761
Pregnant by thee, and now excessive grown Par Lost 2.779
Purest at first, now gross by sinning grown. Par Lost 6.661
Limb'd and full grown: out of the ground up rose Par Lost 7.456
To me so friendly grown above the rest Par Lost 9.564
Inclinable now grown to touch or taste, Par Lost 9.742
Thus grown. Experience, next to thee I owe, Par Lost 9.807
As good have grown there still a liveless Rib. Par Lost 9.1154
Now Dragon grown, larger then whom the Sun Par Lost 10.529
(Canst thou believe2) should be so stupid grown, Par Lost 12.116
Growing into a Nation, and now grown Par Lost 12.164
In mean estate live moderate, till grown Par Lost 12.351
O're-shadow her: this man born and now up-grown, Par Reg 1.140
Full grown to Man, acknowledg'd, as I hear, Par Reg 2.83
By lust and rapine; first ambitious grown Par Reg 4.137
But what more oft in Nations grown corrupt, Samson 268
Who ripe, and frolick of his full grown age, Mask 59
1637 'growne'
Bridgewater ms 'growne'
Trinity ms 'growne'
Here behold so goodly grown Mask 968
Trinity ms 'growne'
Bridgewater ms 'growne'
1637 'growne'

Grows
To Heav'n remov'd where first it grew, there grows, Par Lost 3.356
So neer grows Death to Life, what ere Death is, Par Lost 4.425
Communicated, more abundant growes, Par Lost 5.72
Her fertil growth, and by disburd'ning grows Par Lost 5.319
Of every Tree that in the Garden growes Par Lost 8.321
Aid us, the work under our labour grows, Par Lost 9.208
But say, where grows the Tree, from hence how far? Par Lost 9.617
Here grows the Cure of all, this Fruit Divine, Par Lost 9.776
The soul grows clotted by contagion, Mask 467
1637 'growes'
Bridgewater ms 'growes'
When the fresh blood grows lively, and returns Mask 670
Where grows the Willow and the Osier dank, Mask 891
Bridgewater ms 'growes'
1637 'growes'
where grows the right-borne gold upon his native tree Mask Tr. ms 27.08
Fame is no plant that grows on mortal soil, Lycidas 78
1638 'growes'
He shall be as a tree which planted grows Psalm 1, 7
Mine eye grows dim and dead, Psalm 88, 38

Growth
With singed top thir stately growth though bare Par Lost 1.614
More hands then ours to lop thir wanton growth: Par Lost 4.629
Her fertil growth, and by disburd'ning grows Par Lost 5.319

Growth*(cont)*
Fruit of delicious Vines, the growth of Heav'n. Par Lost 5.635
Of Growth, Sense, Reason, all summ'd up in Man. Par Lost 9.113
One night or two with wanton growth derides Par Lost 9.211
But his growth now to youths full flowr, displaying Par Reg 1.67
To touch the prosperous growth of this tall Wood. Mask 270

Grudging
And we should serve him as a grudging master, Mask 725
Bridgewater ms 'grudgeinge'

Grunsel
In his own Temple, on the grunsel edge, Par Lost 1.460
ms 'grundsell'

Gryfon
As when a Gryfon through the Wilderness Par Lost 2.943

Guard
God and good Angels guard by special grace. Par Lost 2.1033
Nor where *Abassin* Kings thir issue Guard, Par Lost 4.280
Encamping, plac'd in Guard thir Watches round, Par Lost 6.412
About her, as a guard Angelic plac't. Par Lost 8.559
And guard all passage to the Tree of Life: Par Lost 11.122
I was dispatcht for their defence, and guard; Mask 42
Laden with blooming gold, had need the guard Mask 394
Best draw, and stand upon our guard. *Eld. Bro*. Ile hallow, Mask 487
These oughly-headed Monsters? Mercy guard me! Mask 695
Guard them, and him within protect from harms, Sonnet 8, 4

Guarded
The guarded Gold: So eagerly the fiend Par Lost 2.947
Where the great vision of the guarded Mount Lycidas 161

Guardian
Would send a glistring Guardian if need were Mask 219
line not in Bridgewater ms
Trinity ms 'guardian' ←'cherub'

Guardians
Of Guardians bright, when he from *Esau* fled Par Lost 3.512
The field Pavilion'd with his Guardians bright; Par Lost 11.215

Guards
Medusa with *Gorgonian* terror guards Par Lost 2.611
Chief of th' Angelic Guards, awaiting night; Par Lost 4.550
The western Point, where those half-rounding guards Par Lost 4.862
Who guards her, or with her the worst endures. Par Lost 9.269
Th' Angelic Guards ascended, mute and sad Par Lost 10.18
Exacts our parting hence; and see the Guards, Par Lost 12.590
And Timbrels, on each side went armed guards, Samson 1617

Guendolen
Of her enraged stepdam *Guendolen*, Mask 830
Bridgewater ms 'Gwendolen'

Guerdon
But the fair Guerdon when we hope to find, Lycidas 73
Trinity ms 'guerdon'
1638 'guerdon'

Guess
Alreadie by thy reasoning this I guess, Par Lost 8.85
An *Ebrew*, as I guess, and of our Tribe. Samson 1540
This is the place, as well as I may guess, Mask 201
1637 'guesse'
line not in Bridgewater ms
Trinity ms 'guesse'
Without the sure guess of well-practiz'd feet. Mask 310
Trinity ms 'guesse' ←'steerage'
Bridgewater ms 'guesse'
1637 'guesse'

Guessed
For on som message high they guessd him bound. Par Lost 5.290
Longer I durst not stay, but soon I guess't Mask 577
Bridgewater ms 'guest'
Trinity ms 'gues't'

Guest
This day to be our Guest. But goe with speed, Par Lost 5.313
To entertain our Angel guest, as hee Par Lost 5.328
His god-like Guest, walks forth, without more train Par Lost 5.351
Stood to entertain her guest from Heav'n; no vaile Par Lost 5.383
O favourable spirit, propitious guest, Par Lost 5.507
An Earthlie Guest, and drawn Empyreal Aire, Par Lost 7.14
Proceeded thus to ask his Heav'nly Guest. Par Lost 7.69
Thus *Adam* his illustrious Guest besought: Par Lost 7.109
Go heavenly Guest, Ethereal Messenger, Par Lost 8.646
No more of talk where God or Angel Guest Par Lost 9.1
Or as a guest with *Daniel* at his pulse. Par Reg 2.278
And shove away the worthy bidden guest. Lycidas 118

Guests
To stop thir overgrowth, as inmate guests Par Lost 12.166
Too numerous; whence of guests he makes them slaves Par Lost 12.167
Under pretence of Bridal friends and guests, Samson 1196

Guiana
Guiana, whose great Citie *Geryons* Sons Par Lost 11.410

Guide
Alone, and without guide, half lost, I seek Par Lost 2.975
And I will place within them as a guide Par Lost 3.194
And without whom am to no end, my Guide Par Lost 4.442
My Guide was gon, and I, me thought, sunk down, Par Lost 5.91
Ascend my Chariot, guide the rapid Wheeles Par Lost 6.711
First Father, call'd by thee I come thy Guide Par Lost 8.298
My wandring, had not hee who was my Guide Par Lost 8.312
Leads up to Heav'n, is both the way and guide; Par Lost 8.613
Which when she saw, thus to her guide she spake. Par Lost 9.646
Best guide; not following thee, I had remaind Par Lost 9.808
Before his voice, or was shee made thy guide, Par Lost 10.146
Ascend, I follow thee, safe Guide, the path Par Lost 11.371

Guide*(cont)*
Adam was all in tears, and to his guide Par Lost 11.674
How comes it thus? unfould, Celestial Guide, Par Lost 11.785
To guide them in thir journey, and remove Par Lost 12.204
The enemies of truth; who then shall guide Par Lost 12.482
To guide them in all truth, and also arme Par Lost 12.490
Thir place of rest, and Providence thir guide: Par Lost 12.647
Will bring me hence, no other Guide I seek. Par Reg 1.336
But to guide Nations in the way of truth Par Reg 2.473
Of *Israel* be thy guide Samson 1428
Between the pillars; he his guide requested Samson 1630
Has in his charge, with temper'd awe to guide Mask 32
Bridgewater ms 'guyde'
My best guide now, me thought it was the sound Mask 171
Bridgewater ms 'guyde'
I shall be your faithfull guide Mask 944
Content though blind, had I no better guide. Sonnet 22, 14
1694 'Guide'
And to be short, at last his guid him brings Prose 2, 1

Guided
Thy tempring; with like safetie guided down Par Lost 7.15
And guided by his voice, nor uninformd Par Lost 8.486
Guided the Wise Men thither from the East, Par Reg 1.250
To have guided me aright, I know not how, Samson 1547
Till guided by mine ear I found the place Mask 570
Bridgewater ms 'guyded'
When once our heav'nly-guided soul shall clime, On Time 19
Trinity ms 'heavenly-guided'
Guided by faith and matchless Fortitude Sonnet 16, 3

Guides
His count'nance, as the Morning Starr that guides Par Lost 5.708
And guides the Eastern Sages, who enquire Par Lost 12.362
Co. Could that divide you from neer-ushering guides? Mask 279
Trinity ms 'guids' ←'hands'
Bridgewater ms 'guydes'

Guiding
Sams. A Little onward lend thy guiding hand Samson 1
Guiding the fiery-wheeled throne, Penseroso 53

Guile
Th' infernal Serpent; he it was, whose guile Par Lost 1.34
To wage by force or guile eternal Warr Par Lost 1.121
To work in close design, by fraud or guile Par Lost 1.646
Whether of open Warr or covert guile, Par Lost 2.41
My voice disswades; for what can force or guile Par Lost 2.188
By some false guile pervert; and shall pervert Par Lost 3.92
His breaded train, and of his fatal guile Par Lost 4.349
Nor thou his malice and false guile contemn; Par Lost 9.306
Of guile, of hate, of envie, of revenge; Par Lost 9.466
He ended, and his words replete with guile Par Lost 9.733
Friendly to man, farr from deceit or guile. Par Lost 9.772
Anger, and obstinacie, and hate, and guile. Par Lost 10.114
Temptation and all guile on him to try; Par Reg 1.123
Of Spirits likest to himself in guile Par Reg 2.237
Jael, who with inhospitable guile Samson 989

Guileful
To whom the guileful Tempter thus reply'd. Par Lost 9.567
To observe the sequel, saw his guileful act Par Lost 10.334
Yet have they many baits, and guilefull spells Mask 537
Bridgewater ms 'guylefull'
1673 'guileful'
Trinity ms 'guilefull' ←'gil'
The bloodi' and guileful man God doth detest. Psalm 5, 16

Guilefully
To whom the Tempter guilefully repli'd. Par Lost 9.655

Guiles
And count thy specious gifts no gifts but guiles. Par Reg 2.391

Guilt
To undergoe with mee one Guilt, one Crime, Par Lost 9.971
Took largely, of thir mutual guilt the Seale, Par Lost 9.1043
Thir guilt and dreaded shame; O how unlike Par Lost 9.1114
Or to each other, but apparent guilt, Par Lost 10.112
The Guilt on him who made him instrument Par Lost 10.166
Of washing them from guilt of sin to Life Par Lost 12.443
With guilt of his own sin, for he himself Par Reg 3.147
Bare in thy guilt how foul must thou appear? Samson 902
Driving far off each thing of sin and guilt, Mask 456
Bridgewater ms 'guilte'

Guiltless
Guiltless of fire had formd, or Angels brought. Par Lost 9.392
For one mans fault thus guiltless be condemn'd, Par Lost 10.823
If guiltless? But from me what can proceed, Par Lost 10.824
She guiltless damsell flying the mad pursuit Mask 829
Trinity ms 'guiltlesse'
1637 'guiltlesse'
Once glorious Towers, now sunk in guiltles blood; Passion 40
1673 'guiltless'

Guilty
His crime makes guiltie all his Sons, thy merit Par Lost 3.290
Then was not guiltie shame, dishonest shame Par Lost 4.313
The guiltie Serpent, and well might, for *Eve* Par Lost 9.785
To guiltie shame hee cover'd, but his Robe Par Lost 9.1058
The present, fearing guiltie what his wrauth Par Lost 10.340
We may justly now accuse Arcades 10
Trinity ms 'wee may justly now accuse' ←'now seemes guiltie of abuse'
To hide her guilty front with innocent Snow, Nativity 39
Or *Severn* swift, guilty of Maidens death, Vacation 96
God, find them guilty, let them fall Psalm 5, 29

Guise
Of dreadful length and dazling Arms, in guise Par Lost 1.564
Down to the Plain descended: by thir guise Par Lost 11.576
Of lighter toes, and such Court guise Mask 962
B.M. ms 'Guise'
Gulf
Lay vanquisht, rowling in the fiery Gulfe Par Lost 1.52
ms 'gulfe'
Transfix us to the bottom of this Gulfe. Par Lost 1.329
ms 'gulfe'
For since no deep within her gulf can hold Par Lost 2.12
Threatens him, plung'd in that abortive gulf. Par Lost 2.441
A gulf profound as that *Serbonian* Bog Par Lost 2.592
Over the dark Abyss, whose boiling Gulf Par Lost 2.1027
Hell and the Gulf between, and *Satan* there Par Lost 3.70
Satan from Hell scap't through the darksom Gulf Par Lost 5.225
Into thir place of punishment, the Gulf Par Lost 6.53
Into a Gulf shot under ground, till part Par Lost 9.72
When first this Tempter cross'd the Gulf from Hell. Par Lost 10.39
Stay his return perhaps over this Gulfe Par Lost 10.253
Nor this unvoyageable Gulf obscure Par Lost 10.366
Down the great River to the op'ning Gulf, Par Lost 11.833
Gulfy
Of utmost *Tweed*, or *Oose*, or gulphie *Dun*, Vacation 92
Gummy
Kindles the gummie bark of Firr or Pine, Par Lost 10.1076
Gums
Groves whose rich Trees wept odorous Gumms and Balme, Par Lost 4.248
Those Blossoms also, and those dropping Gumms, Par Lost 4.630
Offer sweet smelling Gumms and Fruits and Flours: Par Lost 11.327
Smear'd with gumms of glutenous heat Mask 917
1637 'gummes'
Gurge
The Plain, wherein a black bituminous gurge Par Lost 12.41
Gush
And make soft rills from fiery flint-stones gush. Psalm 114, 18
Gushing
Groand out his Soul with gushing bloud effus'd. Par Lost 11.447
Of shades and wanton winds, and gushing brooks, Lycidas 137
Trinity ms 'gushing' ←'goshing'
Gust
Thir appetite with gust, instead of Fruit Par Lost 10.565
And snow and haile and stormie gust and flaw, Par Lost 10.698
When the gust hath blown his fill, Penseroso 128
And question'd every gust of rugged wings Lycidas 93
Gwendolen
Of her enraged stepdam *Guendolen*, Mask 830
Bridgewater ms 'Gwendolen'
Gymnic
Of Gymnic Artists, Wrestlers, Riders, Runners, Samson 1324
Gyves
Gives and the Mill had tam'd thee? O that fortune Samson 1093
Habergeon
And Brigandine of brass, thy broad Habergeon, Samson 1120
Habit
His habit fit for speed succinct, and held Par Lost 3.643
Habit, or state, or motion, still expressing Par Reg 4.601
In slavish habit, ill-fitted weeds Samson 122
His habit carries peace, his brow defiance. Samson 1073
By his habit I discern him now Samson 1305
Habitable
Down to this habitable, which returnes Par Lost 8.157
Habitant
Officious, but to thee Earths habitant. Par Lost 8.99
Habitual habitant; behind her *Death* Par Lost 10.588
Habitants
The punie habitants, or if not drive, Par Lost 2.367
Those argent Fields more likely habitants, Par Lost 3.460
Till oft convers with heav'nly habitants Mask 459
Habitation
Might yield them easier habitation, bend Par Lost 2.573
Hell thir fit habitation fraught with fire Par Lost 6.876
Of destind habitation; but thou know'st Par Lost 7.622
Our hated habitation; well ye know Par Reg 1.47
Of som clay habitation visit us Mask 339
Bridgewater ms 'habitacion'
Thence to thy glorious habitation Psalm 7, 27
Habitations
And th' habitations of the just; to him Par Lost 7.186
Unseen, and through thir habitations walks Par Lost 12.49
Habits
Cowles, Hoods and Habits with thir wearers tost Par Lost 3.490
In various habits on the *Appian* road, Par Reg 4.68
And my quaint habits breed astonishment, Mask 157
Bridgewater ms 'habitts'
Habitual
Habitual habitant; behind her *Death* Par Lost 10.588
Habor
In *Habor*, and among the *Medes* dispers't, Par Reg 3.376
Had
Had cast him out from Heav'n, with all his Host Par Lost 1.37
Such place Eternal Justice had prepar'd Par Lost 1.70
Had ris'n or heav'd his head, but that the will Par Lost 1.211
He scarce had ceas't when the superiour Fiend Par Lost 1.283
Nor had they yet among the Sons of *Eve* Par Lost 1.364
Egypt from *Syrian* ground, had general Names Par Lost 1.421
And downward Fish: yet had his Temple high Par Lost 1.463
Whom he had vanquisht. After these appear'd Par Lost 1.476

Had(*cont*)
Had to impose: He through the armed Files Par Lost 1.567
Stood like a Towr; his form had yet not lost Par Lost 1.591
Deep scars of Thunder had intrencht, and care Par Lost 1.601
For Treasures better hid. Soon had his crew Par Lost 1.688
That underneath had veins of liquid fire Par Lost 1.701
A third as soon had form'd within the ground Par Lost 1.705
He scarce had finisht, when such murmur filld Par Lost 2.284
Had rous'd the Sea, now with hoarse cadence lull Par Lost 2.287
Of Angels watching round? Here he had need Par Lost 2.413
Man had not hellish foes anow besides, Par Lost 2.504
If shape it might be call'd that shape had none Par Lost 2.667
The likeness of a Kingly Crown had on. Par Lost 2.673
Had been achiev'd, whereof all Hell had rung, Par Lost 2.723
Had not the Snakie Sorceress that sat Par Lost 2.724
Of dalliance had with thee in Heav'n, and joys Par Lost 2.819
He had to cross. Nor was his eare less peal'd Par Lost 2.920
In mutinie had from her Axle torn Par Lost 2.926
Down had been falling, had not by ill chance Par Lost 2.935
Had from his wakeful custody purloind Par Lost 2.946
Now had the Almighty Father from above, Par Lost 3.56
Whose but his own? ingrate, he had of mee Par Lost 3.97
Made passive both, had servd necessitie, Par Lost 3.110
Foreknowledge had no influence on their fault, Par Lost 3.118
Which had no less prov'd certain unforeknown. Par Lost 3.119
By doom severe, had not the Son of God, Par Lost 3.224
No sooner had th' Almighty ceas't, but all Par Lost 3.344
With vanity had filld the works of men: Par Lost 3.447
New *Babels*, had they wherewithall, would build: Par Lost 3.468
Had in remembrance alwayes with delight; Par Lost 3.704
Each had his place appointed, each his course, Par Lost 3.720
While time was, our first-Parents had bin warnd Par Lost 4.6
O had his powerful Destiny ordaind Par Lost 4.58
Me some inferiour Angel, I had stood Par Lost 4.59
Then happie; no unbounded hope had rais'd Par Lost 4.60
Yet not anough had practisd to deceive Par Lost 4.124
Satan had journied on, pensive and slow; Par Lost 4.173
Of shrubs and tangling bushes had perplext Par Lost 4.176
For prospect, what well us'd had bin the pledge Par Lost 4.200
Pass'd underneath ingulft, for God had thrown Par Lost 4.225
Of sympathie and love; there I had fixt Par Lost 4.465
Had not a voice thus warnd me, What thou seest, Par Lost 4.467
Incredible how swift, had thither rowl'd Par Lost 4.593
By shorter flight to th' East, had left him there Par Lost 4.595
Had in her sober Liverie all things clad; Par Lost 4.599
On him who had stole *Joves* authentic fire. Par Lost 4.719
Now had night measur'd with her shaddowie Cone Par Lost 4.776
He held it vain; awe from above had quelld Par Lost 4.860
He scarce had ended, when those two approachd Par Lost 4.874
At least had gon to rack, disturbd and torne Par Lost 4.994
With violence of this conflict, had not soon Par Lost 4.995
Which he had pluckt; the pleasant savourie smell Par Lost 5.84
Divine the sov'ran Architect had fram'd. Par Lost 5.256
Thir Table was, and mossie seats had round, Par Lost 5.392
Then had the Sons of God excuse to have bin Par Lost 5.447
Thus when with meats and drinks they had suffic'd, Par Lost 5.451
Brightness had made invisible, thus spake. Par Lost 5.599
Spring both, the face of brightest Heav'n had changd Par Lost 5.644
Now ere dim Night had disincumberd Heav'n, Par Lost 5.700
Had audience, when among the Seraphim Par Lost 5.804
Had circl'd his full Orbe, the birth mature Par Lost 5.862
Already known what he for news had thought Par Lost 6.20
To heav'nly Soules had bin all one; but now Par Lost 6.165
I see that most through sloth had rather serve, Par Lost 6.166
Sidelong, had push't a Mountain from his seat Par Lost 6.197
Resounded, and had Earth bin then, all Earth Par Lost 6.218
Had to her Center shook. What wonder? when Par Lost 6.219
Had not th' Eternal King Omnipotent Par Lost 6.227
Prodigious power had shewn, and met in Armes Par Lost 6.247
What Heavens Lord had powerfullest to send Par Lost 6.425
Had ended; when to Right and Left the Front Par Lost 6.569
Brass, Iron, Stonie mould, had not thir mouthes Par Lost 6.576
Had need from head to foot well understand; Par Lost 6.625
Had gon to wrack, with ruin overspred, Par Lost 6.670
Had not th' Almightie Father where he sits Par Lost 6.671
Had wondrous, as with Starrs thir bodies all Par Lost 6.754
Affrighted; but strict Fate had cast too deep Par Lost 6.869
Her dark foundations, and too fast had bound. Par Lost 6.870
In *Rhodope*, where Woods and Rocks had Eares Par Lost 7.35
The affable Arch-Angel, had forewarn'd Par Lost 7.41
Had driven out th' ungodly from his sight Par Lost 7.185
Glorie and praise, whose wisdom had ordain'd Par Lost 7.187
Easie, e're God had bid the ground be drie, Par Lost 7.304
He scarce had said, when the bare Earth, till then Par Lost 7.313
Her sacred shades: though God had yet not rain'd Par Lost 7.331
Here finish'd hee, and all that he had made Par Lost 7.548
Had work and rested not, the solemn Pipe, Par Lost 7.595
The thirst I had of knowledge, and voutsaf't Par Lost 8.8
Squar'd in full Legion (such command we had) Par Lost 8.232
Ere Sabbath Eev'ning: so we had in charge. Par Lost 8.246
My fancy to believe I yet had being, Par Lost 8.294
Had lively shadowd: Here had new begun Par Lost 8.311
My wandring, had not hee who was my Guide Par Lost 8.312
Which it had long stood under, streind to the highth Par Lost 8.454
Nights Hemisphere had veild the Horizon round: Par Lost 9.52
Where to lie hid; Sea he had searcht and Land Par Lost 9.76
Before had bin contriving, though perhaps Par Lost 9.139
Guiltless of fire had formd, or Angels brought. Par Lost 9.392

Had*(cont)*

To satisfie the sharp desire I had	Par Lost 9.584
At Feed or Fountain never had I found.	Par Lost 9.597
She scarse had said, though brief, when now more bold	Par Lost 9.664
For good unknown, sure is not had, or had	Par Lost 9.756
And yet unknown, is as not had at all.	Par Lost 9.757
For had the gift bin theirs, it had not here	Par Lost 9.806
Best guide; not following thee, I had remaind	Par Lost 9.808
That dwelt within, whose presence had infus'd	Par Lost 9.836
Waiting desirous her return, had wove	Par Lost 9.839
Had it been onely coveting to Eye	Par Lost 9.923
So eminently never had bin known.	Par Lost 9.976
Had so enobl'd, as of choice to incurr	Par Lost 9.992
For this one Tree had bin forbidden ten.	Par Lost 9.1026
About thir spirits had plaid, and inmost powers	Par Lost 9.1048
Encumberd, now had left them, up they rose	Par Lost 9.1051
Had shadow'd them from knowing ill, was gon,	Par Lost 9.1055
And with what skill they had, together sowd,	Par Lost 9.1112
I know not whence possessd thee; we had then	Par Lost 9.1137
Neither had I transgress'd, nor thou with mee.	Par Lost 9.1161
That lay in wait; beyond this had bin force,	Par Lost 9.1173
Hee in the Serpent, had perverted *Eve*,	Par Lost 10.3
Much wondring how the suttle Fiend had stoln	Par Lost 10.20
All, though all-knowing, what had past with Man	Par Lost 10.227
Ere this he had return'd, with fury driv'n	Par Lost 10.240
Now had they brought the work by wondrous Art	Par Lost 10.312
And now thir way to Earth they had descri'd,	Par Lost 10.325
Appointed to sit there, had left thir charge,	Par Lost 10.421
Long had foretold, a Fabrick wonderful	Par Lost 10.482
Had leasure, wondring at himself now more;	Par Lost 10.510
Encroaching *Eve* perhaps, had first the rule	Par Lost 10.582
So fair and good created, and had still	Par Lost 10.618
Kept in that State, had not the folly of Man	Par Lost 10.619
Of Passion, I to them had quitted all,	Par Lost 10.627
Had first his precept so to move, so shine,	Par Lost 10.652
Of Seasons to each Clime; else had the Spring	Par Lost 10.678
Had unbenighted shon, while the low Sun	Par Lost 10.682
Had rounded still th' *Horizon*, and not known	Par Lost 10.684
Or East or West, which had forbid the Snow	Par Lost 10.685
His course intended; else how had the World	Par Lost 10.689
Of Life that sinn'd; what dies but what had life	Par Lost 10.790
I had persisted happie, had not thy pride	Par Lost 10.874
Mankind? this mischief had not then befall'n,	Par Lost 10.895
His counsel whom she had displeas'd, his aide;	Par Lost 10.944
Had entertaind, as di'd her Cheeks with pale.	Par Lost 10.1009
Labouring had rais'd, and thus to *Eve* repli'd.	Par Lost 10.1012
My bread; what harm? Idleness had bin worse;	Par Lost 10.1055
Prevenient Grace descending had remov'd	Par Lost 11.3
Happier, had it suffic'd him to have known	Par Lost 11.88
Had, like a double *Janus*, all thir shape	Par Lost 11.129
Had ended now thir Orisons, and found	Par Lost 11.137
A glorious Apparition, had not doubt	Par Lost 11.211
One man, Assassin-like had levied Warr,	Par Lost 11.219
In time of Truce; *Iris* had dipt the wooff;	Par Lost 11.244
Yet all had heard, with audible lament	Par Lost 11.266
Fit haunt of Gods? where I had hope to spend,	Par Lost 11.271
Of Paradise or *Eden:* this had been	Par Lost 11.342
Perhaps thy Capital Seate, from whence had spred	Par Lost 11.343
All generations, and had hither come	Par Lost 11.344
Had bred; then purg'd with Euphrasie and Rue	Par Lost 11.414
The visual Nerve, for he had much to see;	Par Lost 11.415
To that meek man, who well had sacrific'd;	Par Lost 11.451
Had melted (whether found where casual fire	Par Lost 11.566
Had wasted woods on Mountain or in Vale,	Par Lost 11.567
Long had not walkt, when from the Tents behold	Par Lost 11.581
Exploded and had seiz'd with violent hands,	Par Lost 11.669
Had not a Cloud descending snatch'd him thence	Par Lost 11.670
But who was that Just Man, whom had not Heav'n	Par Lost 11.681
Rescu'd, had in his Righteousness bin lost?	Par Lost 11.682
The brazen Throat of Warr had ceast to roar,	Par Lost 11.713
O Visions ill foreseen! better had I	Par Lost 11.763
Liv'd ignorant of future, so had borne	Par Lost 11.764
Wandring that watrie Desert: I had hope	Par Lost 11.779
With soft foot towards the deep, who now had stopt	Par Lost 11.848
Surcharg'd, as had like grief bin dew'd in tears,	Par Lost 12.373
Now had the great Proclaimer with a voice	Par Reg 1.18
At first against mankind so well had thriv'd	Par Reg 1.114
Had measur'd twice six years, at our great Feast	Par Reg 1.210
The Baptist, (of whose birth I oft had heard,	Par Reg 1.270
To his destruction, as I had in charge.	Par Reg 1.376
Comes to the place where he before had sat	Par Reg 1.412
At *Jordan* with the Baptist, and had seen	Par Reg 2.2
And on that high Authority had believ'd,	Par Reg 2.5
Conceals him: when twelve years he scarce had seen,	Par Reg 2.96
Recalling what remarkably had pass'd	Par Reg 2.106
Had left him vacant, and with speed was gon	Par Reg 2.116
After forty days fasting had remain'd,	Par Reg 2.243
Nor tasted, nor had appetite; that Fast	Par Reg 2.247
Of *Israel* here had famish'd, had not God	Par Reg 2.311
They all had need, I as thou seest have none.	Par Reg 2.318
He spake no dream, for as his words had end,	Par Reg 2.337
Said'st thou not that to all things I had right?	Par Reg 2.379
Of *Macedonian Philip* had e're these	Par Reg 3.32
At his dispose, young *Scipio* had brought down	Par Reg 3.34
The *Pontic* King and in triumph had rode.	Par Reg 3.36
With glory, wept that he had liv'd so long	Par Reg 3.41
Satan had not to answer, but stood struck	Par Reg 3.146
Insatiable of glory had lost all,	Par Reg 3.148

Had*(cont)*

The Tempter stood, nor had what to reply,	Par Reg 4.2
And rash, before-hand had no better weigh'd	Par Reg 4.8
But as a man who had been matchless held	Par Reg 4.10
And grisly Spectres, which the Fiend had rais'd	Par Reg 4.430
Had chear'd the face of Earth, and dry'd the wet	Par Reg 4.433
And opportunity I here have had	Par Reg 4.531
What hunger, if aught hunger had impair'd,	Par Reg 4.592
Had been fulfilld but through mine own default,	Samson 45
Happ'ly had ends above my reach to know:	Samson 62
Then had I not been thus exil'd from light;	Samson 98
Blindness, for had I sight, confus'd with shame,	Samson 196
(O that I never had! fond wish too late.)	Samson 228
Who seeing those great acts which God had done	Samson 243
Had *Judah* that day join'd, or one whole Tribe,	Samson 265
They had by this possess'd the Towers of *Gath*,	Samson 266
Had dealt with *Jephtha*, who by argument,	Samson 283
Had not his prowess quell'd thir pride	Samson 286
To them who had corrupted her, my Spies,	Samson 386
Disglorifi'd, blasphem'd, and had in scorn	Samson 442
How hainous had the fact been, how deserving	Samson 493
Whom I by his appointment had provok't,	Samson 643
Hear what assaults I had, what snares besides,	Samson 845
A common enemy, who had destroy'd	Samson 856
Dishonourer of *Dagon:* what had I	Samson 861
But had thy love, still odiously pretended,	Samson 873
Had not so soon preferr'd	Samson 1019
Had shorn the fatal harvest of thy head.	Samson 1024
But had we best retire, I see a storm?	Samson 1061
As these perhaps, yet wish it had not been,	Samson 1077
Gives and the Mill had tam'd thee? O that fortune	Samson 1093
Had brought me to the field where thou art fam'd	Samson 1094
So had the glory of Prowess been recover'd	Samson 1098
Till they had hir'd a woman with their gold	Samson 1114
Thir ornament and safety, had not spells	Samson 1132
That solv'd the riddle which I had propos'd.	Samson 1200
And had perform'd it if my known offence	Samson 1218
Had not disabl'd me, not all your force:	Samson 1219
And numbers thither flock, I had no will,	Samson 1450
They had anough reveng'd, having reduc't	Samson 1468
And I perswade me God had not permitted	Samson 1495
What windy joy this day had I conceiv'd	Samson 1574
Through each high street: little I had dispatch't	Samson 1599
Had fill'd thir hearts with mirth, high chear, & wine,	Samson 1613
Who had made thir dreadful enemy thir thrall.	Samson 1622
Then all thy life had slain before.	Samson 1668
Had by him, ere he parted thence, a Son	Mask 56
They had ingag'd their wandring steps too far,	Mask 193
Had stole them from me, els O theevish Night	Mask 195
Laden with blooming gold, had need the guard	Mask 394
Hence had the huntress *Dian* her dred bow	Mask 441
Had ta'n their supper on the savoury Herb	Mask 541
Till fancy had her fill, but ere a close	Mask 548
(For so by certain signes I knew) had met	Mask 572
Who gently ask't if he had seen such two,	Mask 575
Into swift flight, till I had found you here,	Mask 579
The leaf was darkish, and had prickles on it,	Mask 631
They had their name thence; course complexions	Mask 749
line not in Bridgewater ms	
La. I had not thought to have unlockt my lips	Mask 756
Had but a moderate and beseeming share	Mask 769
That had the Scepter from his father *Brute*.	Mask 828
he may scratch his forehead. heere be brambles	Mask Tr. ms 17.57
'he may scratch' ←'he may chaunce' ←'chance' ←'had best look to'	
Like one that had bin led astray	Penseroso 69
And who had *Canace* to wife,	Penseroso 112
Who had thought this clime had held	Arcades 24
Trinity ms 'had' ←'would have'	
Toward Heav'ns descent had slop'd his westering wheel.	Lycidas 31
Had ye bin there---for what could that have don?	Lycidas 57
Trinity ms 'had', but word deleted	
And now the Sun had stretch'd out all the hills,	Lycidas 190
Had doff't her gawdy trim,	Nativity 33
Had given day her room,	Nativity 78
And that her raign had here its last fulfilling;	Nativity 106
After long toil their liberty had won,	Psalm 114, 2
Alack that so to change thee winter had no power.	Fair Inf 28
Where he had mutely sate two years before:	Vacation 6
Yet I had rather if I were to chuse,	Vacation 29
Had got a race of mourners on som pregnant cloud.	Passion 56
She had told, alas too soon,	Winchester 8
Yet had the number of her days	Winchester 11
Nature and fate had had no strife	Winchester 13
Once had the early Matrons run	Winchester 23
Had burial, yet not laid in earth,	Winchester 32
Which the sad morn had let fall	Winchester 45
Death was half glad when he had got him down;	Carrier 6
For he had any time this ten yeers full,	Carrier 7
1658 'hath'	
Had not his weekly cours of carriage fail'd;	Carrier 10
And that he had tane up his latest Inne,	Carrier 13
But had his doings lasted as they were,	Another 27
He had bin an immortall Carrier.	Another 28
In cours reciprocal, and had his fate	Another 30
line not in 1658 text	
Of sad *Electra*'s Poet had the power	Sonnet 8, 13
Had ripen'd thy just soul to dwell with God,	Sonnet 14, 2

Had(*cont*)
Content though blind, had I no better guide. Sonnet 22, 14
Had rather keep a dore, Psalm 84, 38
From thy fierce wrath which we had prov'd Psalm 85, 11
Hades
Orcus and *Ades*, and the dreaded name Par Lost 2.964
Hadst
Hadst thou the same free Will and Power to stand? Par Lost 4.66
Thou hadst: whom hast thou then or what to accuse, Par Lost 4.67
Gabriel, thou hadst in Heav'n th' esteem of wise, Par Lost 4.886
The first in flight from pain, had'st thou alledg'd Par Lost 4.921
Thou surely hadst not come sole fugitive. Par Lost 4.923
Would thou hadst heark'nd to my words, and stai'd Par Lost 9.1134
Or to thy self perhaps: hadst thou been there, Par Lost 9.1148
Hadst thou bin firm and fixt in thy dissent, Par Lost 9.1160
And person, had'st thou known thy self aright. Par Lost 10.156
That thou on Earth hadst prosper'd, which thy looks Par Lost 10.360
To wish thou never hadst rejected thus Par Reg 4.376
Into our hands: for hadst thou not committed Samson 1185
The *Philistines*, when thou hadst broke the league, Samson 1189
Summers chief honour if thou hadst out-lasted, Fair Inf 3
For my relief; yet hadst no reason why, Sonnet 1, 12
Thine anger all thou hadst remov'd, Psalm 85, 9
Haemony
He call'd it *Haemony*, and gave it me, Mask 638
Bridgewater ms 'Hemony'
Hag
Nor uglier follow the Night-Hag, when call'd Par Lost 2.662
Blew meager Hag, or stubborn unlaid ghost, Mask 434
1637 'hag'
Trinity ms 'hagge'
Bridgewater ms 'hag'
Hagar
Moab, with them of Hagars blood Psalm 83, 23
Hail
Back to the Gates of Heav'n: the Sulphurous Hail Par Lost 1.171
ms 'haile'
Where Joy for ever dwells: Hail horrours, hail Par Lost 1.250
ms 'Haile Horrours, Haile'
Of Whirlwind and dire Hail, which on firm land Par Lost 2.589
Hail holy Light, ofspring of Heav'n first-born, Par Lost 3.1
Hail Son of God, Saviour of Men, thy Name Par Lost 3.412
Haile wedded Love, mysterious Law, true source Par Lost 4.750
Hail universal Lord, be bounteous still Par Lost 5.205
Alterd her cheek. On whom the Angel *Haile* Par Lost 5.385
Haile Mother of Mankind, whose fruitful Womb Par Lost 5.388
Thir devilish glut, chaind Thunderbolts and Hail Par Lost 6.589
And snow and haile and stormie gust and flaw, Par Lost 10.698
Th' inclement Seasons, Rain, Ice, Hail and Snow, Par Lost 10.1063
Is past, and we shall live. Whence Haile to thee, Par Lost 11.158
And all his people; Thunder mixt with Haile, Par Lost 12.181
Haile mixt with fire must rend th' *Egyptian* Skie Par Lost 12.182
The seed of Woman: Virgin Mother, Haile, Par Lost 12.379
Hale highly favour'd, among women blest; Par Reg 2.68
Hail Son of the most High, heir of both worlds, Par Reg 4.633
Hail Goddesse of Nocturnal sport Mask 128
1637 'Haile'
Bridgewater ms 'haile'
Trinity ms 'Haile'
And she shall be my Queen. Hail forren wonder Mask 265
1637 'Haile'
Bridgewater ms 'Haile'
Trinity ms 'Haile'
But hail thou Goddes, sage and holy, Penseroso 11
Hail divinest Melancholy, Penseroso 12
Hail native Language, that by sinews weak Vacation 1
Hail bounteous *May* that dost inspire May Morn 5
Hailed
Thither by harpy-footed Furies hail'd, Par Lost 2.596
And such a Son as all Men hail'd me happy; Samson 354
Hair
In th' Artick Sky, and from his horrid hair Par Lost 2.710
Under a Coronet his flowing haire Par Lost 3.640
From either eye, and wip'd them with her haire; Par Lost 5.131
And Bush with frizl'd hair implicit: last Par Lost 7.323
How slight the gift was, hung it in my Hair. Samson 59
Feigndst at thy birth was giv'n thee in thy hair, Samson 1135
Of strength, again returning with my hair Samson 1355
His strength again to grow up with his hair Samson 1496
The loose train of thy amber-dropping hair, Mask 863
Trinity ms 'haire'
B.M. ms 'Hair'
1637 'haire'
Bridgewater ms 'haire'
Or with the tangles of *Neaera*'s hair? Lycidas 69
Trinity ms 'haire'
In wreaths thy golden Hair, Horace 4
Haired
He quarters to his blu-hair'd deities, Mask 29
Bridgewater ms 'blew haired'
That in their green shops weave the smooth-hair'd silk Mask 716
Bridgewater ms 'smoote-haired'
Trinity ms 'smooth haird'
Thee bright-hair'd *Vesta* long of yore, Penseroso 23
What could the Muse her self that *Orpheus* bore, Lycidas 58
Trinity ms 'muse her selfe' ←'golden hayrd Calliope'
Hairs
Where strength can least abide, though all thy hairs Samson 1136

Hairs(*cont*)
Or do his gray hairs any violence? Mask 392
Bridgewater ms 'haiers'
Hairy
Of a steep wilderness, whose hairie sides Par Lost 4.135
And hairie Main terrific, though to thee Par Lost 7.497
His few Books, or his Beads, or Maple Dish, Mask 391
Trinity ms 'beads' ←'hairie gown'
Basks at the fire his hairy strength; Allegro 112
The Hairy Gown and Mossy Cell, Penseroso 169
His Mantle hairy, and his Bonnet sedge, Lycidas 104
Trinity ms 'hairie'
1638 'hairie'
Haled
Thither by harpy-footed Furies hail'd, Par Lost 2.596
Half
On half the Nations, and with fear of change Par Lost 1.598
From wing to wing, and half enclose him round Par Lost 1.617
ms 'halfe'
By force, hath overcome but half his foe. Par Lost 1.649
Treading the crude consistence, half on foot, Par Lost 2.941
Half flying; behoves him now both Oare and Saile. Par Lost 2.942
Alone, and without guide, half lost, I seek Par Lost 2.975
By thee, and more then half perhaps will reigne; Par Lost 4.112
My other half: with that thy gentle hand Par Lost 4.488
And meek surrender, half imbracing leand Par Lost 4.494
On our first Father, half her swelling Breast Par Lost 4.495
Half way up Hill this vast Sublunar Vault, Par Lost 4.777
Uzziel, half these draw off, and coast the South Par Lost 4.782
Half wheeling to the Shield, half to the Spear. Par Lost 4.785
Back stept those two faire Angels half amaz'd Par Lost 4.820
Disdainfully half smiling thus repli'd. Par Lost 4.903
Best Image of my self and dearer half, Par Lost 5.95
Go therefore, half this day as friend with friend Par Lost 5.229
Hath finisht half his journey, and scarce begins Par Lost 5.559
His other half in the great Zone of Heav'n. Par Lost 5.560
Forth stepping opposite, half way he met Par Lost 6.128
Half sunk with all his Pines. Amazement seis'd Par Lost 6.198
Descending, and in half cut sheere, nor staid, Par Lost 6.325
Chariots of God, half on each hand were seen: Par Lost 6.770
Yet half his strength he put not forth, but check'd Par Lost 6.853
Half yet remaines unsung, but narrower bound Par Lost 7.21
The grassie Clods now Calv'd, now half appeer'd Par Lost 7.463
To whom thus half abash't *Adam* repli'd. Par Lost 8.595
From servitude inglorious welnigh half Par Lost 9.141
Half spi'd, so thick the Roses bushing round Par Lost 9.426
Half what in thee is fair, one man except, Par Lost 9.545
Unnam'd, undreaded, and thy self half starv'd? Par Lost 10.595
In Rhombs and wedges, and half moons, and wings. Par Reg 3.309
Scarce half I seem to live, dead more then half. Samson 79
To live a life half dead, a living death, Samson 100
Half round on two main Pillars vaulted high, Samson 1606
Not half his riches known, and yet despis'd, Mask 724
1637 'halfe'
Trinity ms 'halfe'
Bridgewater ms 'halfe'
halfe his wast flood the wide Atlantique fills Mask Tr. ms 10.14
& halfe the slow unfadom'd Stygian poole Mask Tr. ms 10.15
His half regain'd *Eurydice*. Allegro 150
Or call up him that left half told Penseroso 109
Less then half we find exprest, Arcades 12
Trinity ms 'halfe'
Not half so far casts his usurped sway, Nativity 170
Half unpronounc't, slide through my infant-lipps, Vacation 4
Death was half glad when he had got him down; Carrier 6
E're half my days, in this dark world and wide, Sonnet 19, 2
Half-raised
Leaning half-rais'd, with looks of cordial Love Par Lost 5.12
Half-rounding
The western Point, where those half-rounding guards Par Lost 4.862
Hall
And Porches wide, but chief the spacious Hall Par Lost 1.762
ms 'hall'
Though without number still amidst the Hall Par Lost 1.791
ms 'hall'
Serv'd up in Hall with Sewers, and Seneshals; Par Lost 9.38
Of that *Plutonian* Hall, invisible Par Lost 10.444
Of hissing through the Hall, thick swarming now Par Lost 10.522
With terror through the dark Aereal Hall. Par Lost 10.667
From old, or modern Bard in Hall, or Bowr. Mask 45
Bridgewater ms 'hall'
1637 'hall'
Trinity ms 'hall'
Boldly assault the necromancers hall; Mask 649
Bearing her straight to aged *Nereus* Hall, Mask 835
Bridgewater ms 'hall'
Trinity ms 'hall'
1637 'hall'
Will open wide the Gates of her high Palace Hall. Nativity 148
Hallelujah
Sung *Halleluia*, as the sound of Seas, Par Lost 10.642
resound and eccho Hallelu Musick Tr. ms 4.22
Hallelujahs
Forc't Halleluiah's; while he Lordly sits Par Lost 2.243
Unfained *Halleluiahs* to thee sing, Par Lost 6.744
With *Halleluiahs:* Thus was Sabbath kept. Par Lost 7.634
Hallo
I cannot hallow to my Brothers, but Mask 226

Hallo*(cont)*	
Bridgewater ms 'hollowe'	
Som far off hallow break the silent Air.	Mask 481
Bridgewater ms 'hollowe'	
Best draw, and stand upon our guard. *Eld. Bro.* Ile hallow,	Mask 487
Bridgewater ms 'hallowe'	
That hallow I should know, what are you? speak;	Mask 490
Bridgewater ms 'hallowe'	
Hallow	
Which into hallow Engins long and round	Par Lost 6.484
Hallowed	
That wash thy hallowd feet, and warbling flow,	Par Lost 3.31
Within these hallowd limits thou appeer,	Par Lost 4.964
To whom thus *Eve. Adam*, earths hallowd mould,	Par Lost 5.321
Now resting, bless'd and hallowd the Seav'nth day,	Par Lost 7.592
From hallowd ground th' unholie, and denounce	Par Lost 11.106
Above all Sacrifice, or hallow'd gift	Par Reg 3.116
At length to lay my head and hallow'd pledge	Samson 535
Or fright them from their hallow'd haunt.	Penseroso 138
Over the mount, and all this hallow'd ground,	Arcades 55
Trinity ms 'hallowed'	
From out his secret Altar toucht with hallow'd fire.	Nativity 28
Or Coaly *Tine*, or antient hollowed *Dee*,	Vacation 98
Or that his hallow'd reliques should be hid	Shakespear 3
Halls	
With smoaky rafters, then in tapstry Halls	Mask 324
1637 'halls'	
Trinity ms 'halls'	
Bridgewater ms 'halls'	
Halt	
In motion or in alt: him soon they met	Par Lost 6.532
In Paradise, and on a Hill made alt,	Par Lost 11.210
Ham	
Girt with the River *Triton*, where old *Cham*,	Par Lost 4.276
Hamath	
From *Hamath* Northward to the Desert South	Par Lost 12.139
Hamlets	
The up-land Hamlets will invite,	Allegro 92
Hammered	
Of brazen shield and spear, the hammer'd Cuirass,	Samson 132
Hammon	
Whom Gentiles *Ammon* call and *Lybian Jove*,	Par Lost 4.277
The Libyc *Hammon* shrinks his horn,	Nativity 203
Hamper	
And hamper thee, as thou shalt come of force,	Samson 1397
Hand	
His mighty Stature; on each hand the flames	Par Lost 1.222
And some the Architect: his hand was known	Par Lost 1.732
Or where the gorgeous East with richest hand	Par Lost 2.3
His red right hand to plague us? what if all	Par Lost 2.174
May prove thir foe, and with repenting hand	Par Lost 2.369
He scours the right hand coast, som times the left,	Par Lost 2.633
Satan was now at hand, and from his seat	Par Lost 2.674
O Father, what intends thy hand, she cry'd,	Par Lost 2.727
Thou interposest, that my sudden hand	Par Lost 2.738
Into my hand was giv'n, with charge to keep	Par Lost 2.775
At thy right hand voluptuous, as beseems	Par Lost 2.869
Thee from my bosom and right hand, to save,	Par Lost 3.279
All th' unaccomplisht works of Natures hand,	Par Lost 3.455
Stars distant, but nigh hand seemd other Worlds,	Par Lost 3.566
So hand in hand they passd, the lovliest pair	Par Lost 4.321
The hand that formd them on thir shape hath pourd.	Par Lost 4.365
In all this happiness, who at his hand	Par Lost 4.417
My other half: with that thy gentle hand	Par Lost 4.488
Th' unarmed Youth of Heav'n, but nigh at hand	Par Lost 4.552
Thus talking hand in hand alone they pass'd	Par Lost 4.689
Her hand soft touching, whisperd thus. Awake	Par Lost 5.17
On each hand parting, to his speed gave way	Par Lost 5.252
Heaps with unsparing hand; for drink the Grape	Par Lost 5.344
Danc'd hand in hand. A while discourse they hold;	Par Lost 5.395
At my right hand; your Head I him appoint;	Par Lost 5.606
With copious hand, rejoycing in thir joy.	Par Lost 5.641
Our puissance is our own, our own right hand	Par Lost 5.864
Wak't by the circling Hours, with rosie hand	Par Lost 6.3
Thy folly; or with solitarie hand	Par Lost 6.139
Of this right hand provok't, since first that tongue	Par Lost 6.154
A numerous Host, in strength each armed hand	Par Lost 6.231
In horror; from each hand with speed retir'd	Par Lost 6.307
Arme, Warriours, Arme for fight, the foe at hand,	Par Lost 6.537
A Seraph stood, and in his hand a Reed	Par Lost 6.579
And in whose hand what by Decree I doe,	Par Lost 6.683
From the right hand of Glorie where he sate,	Par Lost 6.747
Ascended, at his right hand Victorie	Par Lost 6.762
Chariots of God, half on each hand were seen:	Par Lost 6.770
To all his Host on either hand thus spake.	Par Lost 6.800
The punishment to other hand belongs,	Par Lost 6.807
Among them he arriv'd; in his right hand	Par Lost 6.835
Where now he sits at the right hand of bliss.	Par Lost 6.892
Against a solemn day, harnest at hand,	Par Lost 7.202
Then staid the fervid Wheeles, and in his hand	Par Lost 7.224
Her motions, as the great first-Movers hand	Par Lost 7.500
Such disproportions, with superfluous hand	Par Lost 8.27
A lower flight, and speak of things at hand	Par Lost 8.199
So saying, by the hand he took me rais'd,	Par Lost 8.300
By sly assault; and somwhere nigh at hand	Par Lost 9.256
Of God ordain'd them, his creating hand	Par Lost 9.344
Thus saying, from her Husbands hand her hand	Par Lost 9.385
Imborderd on each Bank, the hand of *Eve:*	Par Lost 9.438
Hand*(cont)*	
So saying, her rash hand in evil hour	Par Lost 9.780
Scarse from the Tree returning; in her hand	Par Lost 9.850
From his slack hand the Garland wreath'd for *Eve*	Par Lost 9.892
With liberal hand: he scrupl'd not to eat	Par Lost 9.997
Her hand he seis'd, and to a shadie bank,	Par Lost 9.1037
Toward the right hand his Glorie, on the Son	Par Lost 10.64
That from her hand I could suspect no ill,	Par Lost 10.140
And of this World, and on the left hand Hell	Par Lost 10.322
Congratulant approach'd him, who with hand	Par Lost 10.458
His hand to execute what his Decree	Par Lost 10.772
Which his own hand manuring all the Trees	Par Lost 11.28
Self-left. Least therefore his now bolder hand	Par Lost 11.93
Satans dire dread, and in his hand the Spear.	Par Lost 11.248
At Eev'n, which I bred up with tender hand	Par Lost 11.276
Thou lead'st me, and to the hand of Heav'n submit,	Par Lost 11.372
But him the gentle Angel by the hand	Par Lost 11.421
Uncull'd, as came to hand; a Shepherd next	Par Lost 11.436
On each hand slaughter and gigantic deeds.	Par Lost 11.659
His Seat at Gods right hand, exalted high	Par Lost 12.457
In either hand the hastning Angel caught	Par Lost 12.637
They hand in hand with wandring steps and slow,	Par Lost 12.648
Repentance, and Heavens Kingdom nigh at hand	Par Reg 1.20
Circling the Throne and Singing, while the hand	Par Reg 1.171
Now, now, for sure, deliverance is at hand,	Par Reg 2.35
Rather to be in readiness, with hand	Par Reg 2.144
To be at hand, and at his beck appear,	Par Reg 2.238
Riches are mine, Fortune is in my hand;	Par Reg 2.429
Riches though offer'd from the hand of Kings.	Par Reg 2.449
That by strong hand his Family obtain'd,	Par Reg 3.168
He in whose hand all times and seasons roul.	Par Reg 3.187
And rash, before-hand had no better weigh'd	Par Reg 4.8
Carv'd work, the hand of fam'd Artificers	Par Reg 4.59
By voice or hand, and various-measur'd verse,	Par Reg 4.256
Good reason then, if I before-hand seek	Par Reg 4.526
Sams. A Little onward lend thy guiding hand	Samson 1
Then with what trivial weapon came to hand,	Samson 142
Our earnest Prayers, then giv'n with solemn hand	Samson 359
And let another hand, not thine, exact	Samson 507
But yield to double darkness nigh at hand:	Samson 593
That thou towards him with hand so various,	Samson 668
Changest thy countenance, and thy hand with no regard	Samson 684
Dal. Let me approach at least, and touch thy hand.	Samson 951
What then thou would'st, thou seest it in thy hand.	Samson 1105
Into thy Enemies hand, permitted them	Samson 1159
But take good heed my hand survey not thee.	Samson 1230
Sam. No man with-holds thee, nothing from thy hand	Samson 1233
Some other tending, in his hand	Samson 1302
A Public Officer, and now at hand.	Samson 1306
What glorious hand gave *Samson* his deaths wound?	Samson 1581
From the rash hand of bold Incontinence.	Mask 397
With such a full and unwithdrawing hand,	Mask 711
We implore thy powerful hand	Mask 903
And in thy right hand lead with thee,	Allegro 35
While the Plowman neer at hand,	Allegro 63
If my inferior hand or voice could hit	Arcades 77
The dredded Infants hand,	Nativity 222
Led by the strength of the Almighties hand,	Psalm 114, 4
He with his thunder-clasping hand,	Psalm 136, 37
And with full hand supplies their need.	Psalm 136, 86
For so *Apollo*, with unweeting hand	Fair Inf 23
O yet a nobler task awaites thy hand;	Sonnet 15, 9
1694 'Hand'	
Therfore on thy firme hand religion leanes	Sonnet 17, 13
Against heavns hand or will, nor bate a jot	Sonnet 22, 7
1694 'Hand'	
And what he takes in hand shall prosper all.	Psalm 1, 10
Let us break off, say they, by strength of hand	Psalm 2, 6
O're the works of thy hand thou mad'st him Lord,	Psalm 8, 17
Visit this Vine, which thy right hand	Psalm 80, 61
Upon the man of thy right hand	Psalm 80, 69
Let thy *good* hand be *laid*,	Psalm 80, 70
And turn my hand against *all those*	Psalm 81, 59
Salvation is at hand	Psalm 85, 38
And hand in hand are set.	Psalm 85, 44
By thy strong hand are done,	Psalm 86, 34
Them from thy hand deliver'd o're	Psalm 88, 23
In darkness can thy mighty *hand*	Psalm 88, 49
Handed	
Handed they went; and eas'd the putting off	Par Lost 4.739
Squadrons at once, with huge two-handed sway	Par Lost 6.251
O welcom pure-ey'd Faith, white-handed Hope,	Mask 213
line not in Bridgewater ms	
Which the neat-handed *Phillis* dresses;	Allegro 86
But that two-handed engine at the door,	Lycidas 130
Trinity ms 'tow-handed'	
Handling	
About his Altar, handling holy things,	Par Reg 1.489
Handmaid	
Her sleeping Lord with Handmaid Lamp attending.	Nativity 242
And save thy hand-maids Son.	Psalm 86, 60
Handmaids	
Thy hand-maids, clad them o're with purple beams	Sonnet 14, 10
Trinity ms 'handmaides' ← 'handmaids'	
Hands	
Maim'd his brute Image, head and hands lopt off	Par Lost 1.459
Ransack'd the Center, and with impious hands	Par Lost 1.686
And hands innumerable scarce perform.	Par Lost 1.699

Hands(*cont*)
Leveld his deadly aime; thir fatall hands Par Lost 2.712
With head, hands, wings or feet pursues his way, Par Lost 2.949
More hands then ours to lop thir wanton growth: Par Lost 4.629
Thir pamperd boughes, and needed hands to check Par Lost 5.214
Of secondarie hands, by task transferd Par Lost 5.854
Which all subdues, and makes remiss the hands Par Lost 6.458
None arguing stood, innumerable hands Par Lost 6.508
Up lifting bore them in thir hands: Amaze, Par Lost 6.646
So amply, and with hands so liberal Par Lost 8.362
The Rib he formd and fashond with his hands; Par Lost 8.469
Under his forming hands a Creature grew, Par Lost 8.470
The hands dispatch of two Gardning so wide. Par Lost 9.203
Our pleasant task enjoyn'd, but till more hands Par Lost 9.207
These paths & Bowers doubt not but our joynt hands Par Lost 9.244
As we need walk, till younger hands ere long Par Lost 9.246
Grow up to thir provision, and more hands Par Lost 9.623
What thy hands builded not, thy Wisdom gain'd Par Lost 10.373
With our own hands his Office on our selves; Par Lost 10.1002
Hath unbesaught provided, and his hands Par Lost 10.1058
Exploded and had seiz'd with violent hands, Par Lost 11.669
Then with uplifted hands, and eyes devout, Par Lost 11.863
Gave up into my hands *Uzzean Job* Par Reg 1.369
Be now in powerful hands, that will not part Par Reg 3.155
Built by *Emathian*, or by *Parthian* hands, Par Reg 3.290
Concerning thee to his Angels, in thir hands Par Reg 4.557
Into thir hands, and they as gladly yield me Samson 259
Thee *Samson* bound and blind into thir hands, Samson 438
Into our hands: for hadst thou not committed Samson 1185
The work of many hands, which earns my keeping Samson 1260
When God into the hands of thir deliverer Samson 1270
More then the working day thy hands, Samson 1299
From other hands we need not much to fear. Samson 1526
Mess. By his own hands. *Man*. Self-violence? what cause Samson 1584
To lay their just hands on that Golden Key Mask 13
Com, knit hands, and beat the ground, Mask 143
Co. Could that divide you from neer-ushering guides? Mask 279
Trinity ms 'guids' ←'hands'
I would not taste thy treasonous offer; none Mask 702
Trinity ms 'would not taste' ←'should reject' ←'hate it from thy hands'
By *Leucothea*'s lovely hands, Mask 875
Your learned hands, can loose this Gordian knot? Vacation 90
And here though grief my feeble hands up-lock, Passion 45
Be in my hands, if I have wrought Psalm 7, 9
His hands from pots, *and mirie soyle* Psalm 81, 23
Among the gods on both his hands Psalm 82, 3
And rescue from the hands Psalm 82, 14
All these have lent their armed hands Psalm 83, 31
My hands to thee I spread. Psalm 88, 40

Hang
And thy fair Fruit let hang, as to no end Par Lost 9.798
Such as hang on *Hebe*'s cheek, Allegro 29
With Cowslips wan that hang the pensive hed, Lycidas 147
Trinity ms 'hang' ←'hangs his'

Hanging
And fast by hanging in a golden Chain Par Lost 2.1051
Still hanging incorruptible, till men Par Lost 9.622

Hangs
Hangs in the Clouds, by *Aequinoctial* Winds Par Lost 2.637
All seasons, ripe for use hangs on the stalk; Par Lost 5.323
But the fair blossom hangs the head Winchester 41

Hap
Might hap to move new broiles: Be this or aught Par Lost 2.837
On mans destruction, maugre what might hap Par Lost 9.56
In every Bush and Brake, where hap may finde Par Lost 9.160
He sought them both, but wish'd his hap might find Par Lost 9.421
For once it was my dismal hap to hear Vacation 68
To find a Foe it shall not be his hap, Vacation 83

Hapless
Thir own Heroic deeds and hapless fall Par Lost 2.549
Determind, and thy hapless crew involv'd Par Lost 5.879
This saw his hapless Foes but stood obdur'd, Par Lost 6.785
O much deceav'd, much failing, hapless *Eve*, Par Lost 9.404
By Night, and listening where the hapless Paire Par Lost 10.342
And to our Seed (O hapless Seed!) deriv'd. Par Lost 10.965
But O that haples virgin our lost sister Mask 350
1637 'haplesse'
Trinity ms 'haplesse'
And O poor hapless Nightingale thought I, Mask 566
1637 'haplesse'
And, O ye *Dolphins*, waft the haples youth. Lycidas 164
Trinity ms 'haplesse'
1638 'haplesse'
The haples Babe before his birth Winchester 31
Unmindfull. Hapless they Horace 12

Haply
Him haply slumbring on the *Norway* foam Par Lost 1.203
Haply so scap'd his mortal snare; for now Par Lost 4.8
Henceforth; my dwelling haply may not please Par Lost 4.378
Impossible: yet haply of thy Race Par Lost 6.501
Useful, whence haply mention may arise Par Lost 8.200
Us haply too secure of our discharge Par Lost 11.196
Happ'ly had ends above my reach to know: Samson 62

Happen
Happ'n what may, of me expect to hear Samson 1423
And, if it happen as I did forecast, Vacation 13

Happened
But might as ill have happ'nd thou being by, Par Lost 9.1147

Happens
What happ'ns new; Fame also finds us out. Par Reg 1.334

Happier
Yielded with full consent. The happier state Par Lost 2.24
To nothing this essential, happier farr Par Lost 2.97
So farr the happier Lot, enjoying thee Par Lost 4.446
The happier *Eden*, shall enjoy thir fill Par Lost 4.507
No happier state, and know to know no more. Par Lost 4.775
Happier thou mayst be, worthier canst not be: Par Lost 5.76
Thee also happier, shall not be withheld Par Lost 7.117
And feel that I am happier then I know, Par Lost 8.282
To happier life, knowledge of Good and Evil; Par Lost 9.697
In other Worlds, and happier Seat provides Par Lost 10.237
Happier, had it suffic'd him to have known Par Lost 11.88
Shall all be Paradise, far happier place Par Lost 12.464
Then this of *Eden*, and far happier daies. Par Lost 12.465
A paradise within thee, happier farr. Par Lost 12.587
The happier raign the sooner it begins, Par Reg 3.179
Could hold all Heav'n and Earth in happier union. Nativity 108

Happiest
And banisht from mans life his happiest life, Par Lost 4.317
Is womans happiest knowledge and her praise. Par Lost 4.638
Blest pair; and O yet happiest if ye seek Par Lost 4.774
By Parents, or his happiest choice too late Par Lost 10.904
Happiest both to thy self and all the world, Par Reg 3.225
And which is best and happiest yet, all this Samson 1718
Wed your divine sounds, and mixt power employ Musick 3
Trinity ms 'mixt power' ←'mix't' ←'happiest sounds' ←'joynt force'
That tun'st their happiest lines in Hymn, or Story. Sonnet 13, 11

Happiness
Both of lost happiness and lasting pain Par Lost 1.55
Of happiness and final misery, Par Lost 2.563
Or happiness in this or th' other life; Par Lost 3.450
In all this happiness, who at his hand Par Lost 4.417
Happiness in his power left free to will, Par Lost 5.235
Your fill what happiness this happie state Par Lost 5.504
Whom to obey is happiness entire. Par Lost 6.741
Bereavd of happiness thou maist partake Par Lost 6.903
Thir happiness, and persevere upright. Par Lost 7.632
What happiness, who can enjoy alone, Par Lost 8.365
A nice and suttle happiness I see Par Lost 8.399
Of happiness, or not? who am alone Par Lost 8.405
Us happie, and without Love no happiness. Par Lost 8.621
Envying our happiness, and of his own Par Lost 9.254
Fraile is our happiness, if this be so, Par Lost 9.340
Full happiness with mee, or rather not, Par Lost 9.819
Of happiness: yet well, if here would end Par Lost 10.725
Created him endowd, with Happiness Par Lost 11.58
Imparts to thee no happiness, no joy, Par Reg 1.417
Be barr'd that happines, might we but hear Mask 343
1637 'happinesse'
Trinity ms 'happinesse'
More happines then this thy present lot. Mask 789
line not in Bridgewater ms
1673 'happiness'
line not in Trinity ms
1637 'hapinesse'

Happy
Mov'd our Grand Parents in that happy State, Par Lost 1.29
ms 'happie'
From him, who in the happy Realms of Light Par Lost 1.85
ms 'happie'
Though all our Glory extinct, and happy state Par Lost 1.141
ms 'happie'
Above his equals. Farewel happy Fields Par Lost 1.249
ms 'happie'
For happy though but ill, for ill not worst, Par Lost 2.224
Err not) another World, the happy seat Par Lost 2.347
The happy Ile; what strength, what art can then Par Lost 2.410
Of mankind, in the happie Garden plac't, Par Lost 3.66
Happie for man, so coming; he her aide Par Lost 3.232
Thir happie hours in joy and hymning spent. Par Lost 3.417
By which, to visit oft those happy Tribes, Par Lost 3.532
Or other Worlds they seemd, or happy Iles, Par Lost 3.567
Thrice happy Iles, but who dwelt happy there Par Lost 3.570
To Paradise the happie seat of Man, Par Lost 3.632
Created this new happie Race of Men Par Lost 3.679
Then happie; no unbounded hope had rais'd Par Lost 4.60
Spirit of happie sort: his gestures fierce Par Lost 4.128
A happy rural seat of various view; Par Lost 4.247
Fair couple, linkt in happie nuptial League, Par Lost 4.339
Happie, but for so happie ill secur'd Par Lost 4.370
By Ignorance, is that thir happie state, Par Lost 4.519
Yet happie pair; enjoy, till I return, Par Lost 4.534
Charge and strict watch that to this happie Place Par Lost 4.562
Have finisht happie in our mutual help Par Lost 4.727
Here, happie Creature, fair Angelic *Eve*, Par Lost 5.74
Partake thou also; happie though thou art, Par Lost 5.75
Of Paradise and *Edens* happie Plains, Par Lost 5.143
As may advise him of his happie state, Par Lost 5.234
Those happie places thou hast deignd a while Par Lost 5.364
Your fill what happiness this happie state Par Lost 5.504
Attend: That thou art happie, owe to God; Par Lost 5.520
In sight of God enthron'd, our happie state Par Lost 5.536
For ever happie: him who disobeyes Par Lost 5.611

Happy(*cont*)
Our happie state under one Head more neer — Par Lost 5.830
Though not destroy, thir happie Native seat; — Par Lost 6.226
Thir pleasant dwelling place. Thrice happie men, — Par Lost 7.625
Holy and just: thrice happie if they know — Par Lost 7.631
This happie Light, when answer none return'd, — Par Lost 8.285
From that day mortal, and this happie State — Par Lost 8.331
And happie Constellations on that houre — Par Lost 8.512
Us happie, and without Love no happiness. — Par Lost 8.621
Be strong, live happie, and love, but first of all — Par Lost 8.633
How are we happie, still in fear of harm? — Par Lost 9.326
Let us not then suspect our happie State — Par Lost 9.337
Or aught that might his happie State secure, — Par Lost 9.347
This happie trial of thy Love, which else — Par Lost 9.975
Remaind still happie, not as now, despoild — Par Lost 9.1138
Made happie: Him by fraud I have seduc'd — Par Lost 10.485
O miserable of happie! is this the end — Par Lost 10.720
I had persisted happie, had not thy pride — Par Lost 10.874
Thee Native Soile, these happie Walks and Shades, — Par Lost 11.270
Departure from this happy place, our sweet — Par Lost 11.303
Such happy interview and fair event — Par Lost 11.593
With length of happy dayes the race of man; — Par Lost 11.782
With meditation on the happie end. — Par Lost 12.605
1669 'happy'
Of Paradise, so late thir happie seat, — Par Lost 12.642
I Who e're while the happy Garden sung, — Par Reg 1.1
Kept not my happy Station, but was driv'n — Par Reg 1.360
To all the Host of Heaven; the happy place — Par Reg 1.416
What makes a Nation happy, and keeps it so, — Par Reg 4.362
And such a Son as all Men hail'd me happy; — Samson 354
Happy that house! his way to peace is smooth: — Samson 1049
Shall in the happy trial prove most glory. — Mask 592
Bridgewater ms 'happie'
Trinity ms 'happie'
1637 'happie'
And those happy climes that ly — Mask 977
1637 'happie'
Trinity ms 'happie'
& sacred limits of this blisfull Isle — Mask Tr. ms 10.11
'blisfull' ← 'blissfull' ← 'happie'
This is the Month, and this the happy morn — Nativity 1
But now begins; for from this happy day — Nativity 167
First heard by happy watchful Shepherds ear, — Circum 3
Trinity ms 'happie'
in high misterious happie spousall meet — Musick Tr. ms 4.06
'happie' ← 'holie'
That som more timely-happy spirits indu'th. — Sonnet 7, 8
Trinity ms 'tymely-happie'
Happy all those who have in him their stay. — Psalm 2, 28
Happy, who in thy house reside — Psalm 84, 17
Happy, whose strength in thee doth bide, — Psalm 84, 19

Happy-making
Of him, t' whose happy-making sight alone, — On Time 18

Haran
From *Auran* Eastward to the Royal Towrs — Par Lost 4.211
To *Haran*, after him a cumbrous Train — Par Lost 12.131

Harangues
Assemble, and Harangues are heard, but soon — Par Lost 11.663

Harapha
The Giant *Harapha* of *Gath*, his look — Samson 1068
Men call me *Harapha*, of stock renown'd — Samson 1079

Harass
The harrass of thir Land, beset me round; — Samson 257

Harbinger
Deaths Harbinger: Sad task, yet argument — Par Lost 9.13
Loves Harbinger appeerd; then all in heat — Par Lost 11.589
His coming, is sent Harbinger, who all — Par Reg 1.71
Me him whose Harbinger he was; and first — Par Reg 1.277
Her harbinger, a damsel train behind; — Samson 721
His ready Harbinger, — Nativity 49
Now the bright morning Star, Dayes harbinger, — May Morn 1
His Royal Harbinger, — Psalm 85, 54

Harbour
There rest, if any rest can harbour there, — Par Lost 1.185
Yet evil whence? in thee can harbour none, — Par Lost 5.99
Thoughts, which how found they harbour in thy brest — Par Lost 9.288
My harbour and my ultimate repose, — Par Reg 3.210
Mine eie to harbour sleep, or thoughts to rest. — Samson 459
To harbour those that are at enmity. — Vacation 88

Harboured
Or harbour'd in one Cave, is not reveal'd; — Par Reg 1.307

Hard
Of *Moloch* homicide, lust hard by hate; — Par Lost 1.417
Hard liberty before the easie yoke — Par Lost 2.256
And hard, that out of Hell leads up to light; — Par Lost 2.433
Then unknown dangers and as hard escape. — Par Lost 2.444
So he with difficulty and labour hard — Par Lost 2.1021
Though hard and rare: thee I revisit safe, — Par Lost 3.21
But hard be hard'nd, blind be blinded more, — Par Lost 3.200
By center, or eccentric, hard to tell, — Par Lost 3.575
Upbraided none; nor was his service hard. — Par Lost 4.45
Earth, Aire, and Sea. Then let us not think hard — Par Lost 4.432
On purpose, hard thou knowst it to exclude — Par Lost 4.584
From hard assaies and ill successes past — Par Lost 4.932
Sad task and hard, for how shall I relate — Par Lost 5.564
Enjoyment of our right as Gods; yet hard — Par Lost 6.452
Think nothing hard, much less to be despaird. — Par Lost 6.495
Of hard contents, and full of force urg'd home, — Par Lost 6.622

Hard(*cont*)
Is hard; for who himself beginning knew? — Par Lost 8.251
Little inferiour, by my adventure hard — Par Lost 10.468
A Grove hard by, sprung up with this thir change, — Par Lost 10.548
Thy terms too hard, by which I was to hold — Par Lost 10.751
But if thou judge it hard and difficult, — Par Lost 10.992
Hard to belief may seem; yet this will Prayer, — Par Lost 11.146
Through many a hard assay even to the death, — Par Reg 1.264
That out of these hard stones be made thee bread; — Par Reg 1.343
And urg'd me hard with doings, which not will — Par Reg 1.469
Hard are the ways of truth, and rough to walk, — Par Reg 1.478
Hard recompence, unsutable return — Par Reg 3.132
What I foretold thee, many a hard assay — Par Reg 4.478
With hard contest: at length that grounded maxim — Samson 865
But what it is, hard is to say, — Samson 1013
Nothing is hard) by miracle restor'd, — Samson 1528
Perhaps som cold bank is her boulster now — Mask 353
Trinity ms 'cold' ← 'cold hard'
Tending my flocks hard by i' th hilly crofts, — Mask 531
In hard besetting need, this will I try — Mask 857
Trinity ms 'hard' ← 'in honourd vertues cause'
And sent them here through hard assays — Mask 972
Hard by, a Cottage chimney smokes, — Allegro 81
What hard mishap hath doom'd this gentle swain? — Lycidas 92
Of labours huge and hard, too hard for human wight. — Passion 14
The drift of hollow states hard to be spelld, — Sonnet 17, 6
From the hard Season gaining: time will run — Sonnet 20, 5
Thou hast from *hard* Captivity — Psalm 85, 3

Hardened
But hard be hard'nd, blind be blinded more, — Par Lost 3.200
They hard'nd more by what might most reclame, — Par Lost 6.791
More hard'nd after thaw, till in his rage — Par Lost 12.194

Hardening
Distends with pride, and hardning in his strength — Par Lost 1.572

Harder
Environ'd wins his way; harder beset — Par Lost 2.1016
Harder to hit, — Samson 1014
End Green. Why is it harder Sirs then Gordon, — Sonnet 11, 8

Hardest
As the Magnetic hardest Iron draws. — Par Reg 2.168

Hardihood
Where if he be, with dauntless hardihood, — Mask 650
Trinity ms 'dauntless hardyhood' ← 'suddaine violence'
Bridgewater ms 'hardy-hood'

Hardly
The Enemie, though bold, will hardly dare, — Par Lost 9.304
As much his greater, and was hardly won; — Par Reg 1.279

Hardship
Men to much misery and hardship born; — Par Reg 1.341

Hardy
So hardie as to proffer or accept — Par Lost 2.425
Less hardie to endure? courageous Chief, — Par Lost 4.920
Hardy and industrious to support — Samson 1274
With all his over-hardy crew. — Psalm 136, 70

Hare-brained
By shallow *Edwards* and Scotch what d' ye call: — Forcers 12
Trinity ms 'shallow' ← 'hare braind' ← 'haire braind'

Harlot
As varnish on a Harlots cheek, the rest, — Par Reg 4.344

Harlot-lap
Herculean Samson from the Harlot-lap — Par Lost 9.1060

Harlots
Of Harlots, loveless, joyless, unindeard, — Par Lost 4.766

Harm
Now laid perhaps asleep secure of harme. — Par Lost 4.791
This place inviolable, and these from harm. — Par Lost 4.843
But that implies not violence or harme. — Par Lost 4.901
Thir armor help'd thir harm, crush't in and bruis'd — Par Lost 6.656
But least his heart exalt him in the harme — Par Lost 7.150
But other doubt possesses me, least harm — Par Lost 9.251
How are we happie, still in fear of harm? — Par Lost 9.326
But harm precedes not sin: onely our Foe — Par Lost 9.327
Against his will he can receave no harme. — Par Lost 9.350
Why hee should mean me ill, or seek to harme. — Par Lost 9.1152
My bread; what harm? Idleness had bin worse; — Par Lost 10.1055
And from the sting of Famine fear no harm, — Par Reg 2.257
Mee worse then wet thou find'st not; other harm — Par Reg 4.486
On thee, who now no more canst do them harm. — Samson 486
At *Askalon*, who never did thee harm, — Samson 1187
Yea even that which mischief meant most harm, — Mask 591
Bridgewater ms 'harme'
Trinity ms 'harme'
1637 'harme'
To bless the dores from nightly harm: — Penseroso 84

Harmed
Nor sleeping him nor waking harm'd, his walk — Par Reg 1.311
Thou art not to be harm'd, therefore not mov'd; — Par Reg 2.407

Harmless
And should I at your harmless innocence — Par Lost 4.388
And harmless, if not wholsom, as a sneeze — Par Reg 4.458
I shall appear som harmles Villager — Mask 166
Trinity ms 'harmlesse'
1637 'harmlesse'

Harmonic
In full harmonic number joind, thir songs — Par Lost 4.687

Harmonies
Angelic harmonies: the Earth, the Aire — Par Lost 7.560
And give resounding grace to all Heav'ns Harmonies. — Mask 243

Harmonies*(cont)*
Bridgewater ms 'harmonies'
Trinity ms 'harmonies'
Harmonious
Harmonious numbers; as the wakeful Bird | Par Lost 3.38
Her ever during Gates, Harmonious sound | Par Lost 7.206
More grateful then harmonious sound to the eare. | Par Lost 8.606
And all the while Harmonious Airs were heard | Par Reg 2.362
Sphear-born harmonious Sisters, Voice, and Vers, | Musick 2
Harmony
Thir Song was partial, but the harmony | Par Lost 2.552
And in thir motions harmonie Divine | Par Lost 5.625
Of instrumental Harmonie that breath'd | Par Lost 6.65
Can sort, what harmonie or true delight? | Par Lost 8.384
Harmonie to behold in wedded pair | Par Lost 8.605
My Heart, which by a secret harmonie | Par Lost 10.358
Of harmony in tones and numbers hit | Par Reg 4.255
The hidden soul of harmony. | Allegro 144
To the celestial *Sirens* harmony, | Arcades 63
Trinity ms 'harmonie'
She knew such harmony alone | Nativity 107
And with your ninefold harmony | Nativity 131
Are held with his melodious harmonie | Vacation 51
Harms
And heal the harms of thwarting thunder blew, | Arcades 51
Trinity ms 'harmes'
Guard them, and him within protect from harms, | Sonnet 8, 4
Trinity ms 'harmes'
Harnessed
Against a solemn day, harnest at hand, | Par Lost 7.202
the scalie-harnest dragon ever keeps | Mask Tr. ms 10.09
Bright-harnest Angels sit in order serviceable. | Nativity 244
Harp
With notes Angelical to many a Harp | Par Lost 2.548
Henceforth, and never shall my Harp thy praise | Par Lost 3.414
More tuneable then needed Lute or Harp | Par Lost 5.151
Both Harp and Voice; nor could the Muse defend | Par Lost 7.37
But not in silence holy kept; the Harp | Par Lost 7.594
Was heard, of Harp and Organ; and who moovd | Par Lost 11.560
In Gems and wanton dress; to the Harp they sung | Par Lost 11.583
And set my Harpe to notes of saddest wo, | Passion 9
1673 'Harp'
And Harp *with* pleasant *string*, | Psalm 81, 8
Harpies
With sound of Harpies wings, and Talons heard; | Par Reg 2.403
Harpyies and *Hydra's*, or all the monstrous forms | Mask 605
Trinity ms 'harpyes'
Bridgewater ms 'Harpies'
1673 '*Harpyes*'
Harping
Harping in loud and solemn quire, | Nativity 115
Harps
Then Crown'd again thir gold'n Harps they took, | Par Lost 3.365
Harps ever tun'd, that glittering by thir side | Par Lost 3.366
And touch't thir Golden Harps, and hymning prais'd | Par Lost 7.258
With Eevning Harps and Mattin, when God said, | Par Lost 7.450
Symphonious of ten thousand Harpes that tun'd | Par Lost 7.559
Our Hebrew Songs and Harps in *Babylon*, | Par Reg 4.336
Touch their immortal Harps of golden wires, | Musick 13
Trinity ms 'harps'
Harpy-footed
Thither by harpy-footed Furies hail'd, | Par Lost 2.596
Harrowed
Amaz'd I stood, harrow'd with grief and fear, | Mask 565
Harry
Harry whose tuneful and well measur'd Song | Sonnet 13, 1
Harsh
Harsh Thunder, that the lowest bottom shook | Par Lost 2.882
Hath toucht my sense, flat seems to this, and harsh. | Par Lost 9.987
Harsh, and of dissonant mood from his complaint, | Samson 662
Some much averse I found and wondrous harsh, | Samson 1461
Not harsh, and crabbed as dull fools suppose, | Mask 477
Bridgewater ms 'harshe'
I com to pluck your Berries harsh and crude, | Lycidas 3
Jarr'd against natures chime, and with harsh din | Musick 20
Trinity ms 'harsh' ←'tumultuous'
by leaving out those harsh ill sounding jarres | Musick Tr. ms 5.03
Harshly
Gatherd, not harshly pluckt, for death mature: | Par Lost 11.537
And harshly deal like an ill borrower | Mask 683
line not in Bridgewater ms
Hart
Goodliest of all the Forrest, Hart and Hinde; | Par Lost 11.189
Harvest
Of *Ceres* ripe for harvest waving bends | Par Lost 4.981
As Reapers oft are wont thir Harvest Queen. | Par Lost 9.842
Seed time and Harvest, Heat and hoary Frost | Par Lost 11.899
Had shorn the fatal harvest of thy head. | Samson 1024
Has
Has in his charge, with temper'd awe to guide | Mask 32
He that has light within his own cleer brest | Mask 381
As you imagine, she has a hidden strength | Mask 415
She that has that, is clad in compleat steel, | Mask 421
Hath hurtfull power o're true virginity. | Mask 437
Bridgewater ms 'has'
Trinity ms 'has'
1637 'Has'
And vertue has no tongue to check her pride: | Mask 761

Has*(cont)*
Hobson has supt, and's newly gon to bed. | Carrier 18
Hast
Hast thou forgot me then, and do I seem | Par Lost 2.747
For him, what for thy glorie thou hast made? | Par Lost 3.164
All hast thou spok'n as my thoughts are, all | Par Lost 3.171
Lie vanquisht; thou hast givn me to possess | Par Lost 3.243
Because thou hast, though Thron'd in highest bliss | Par Lost 3.305
A World from utter loss, and hast been found | Par Lost 3.308
Thou hadst: whom hast thou then or what to accuse, | Par Lost 4.67
And Head, what thou hast said is just and right. | Par Lost 4.443
But thou hast promis'd from us two a Race | Par Lost 4.732
Why hast thou, *Satan*, broke the bounds prescrib'd | Par Lost 4.878
But evil hast not tri'd: and wilt object | Par Lost 4.896
And when high Noon hast gaind, and when thou fallst. | Par Lost 5.174
Those happie places thou hast deignd a while | Par Lost 5.364
Created, or such place hast here to dwell, | Par Lost 5.373
Under whose lowly roof thou hast voutsaf't | Par Lost 5.463
Well hast thou taught the way that might direct | Par Lost 5.508
Justly hast in derision, and secure | Par Lost 5.736
Servant of God, well done, well hast thou fought | Par Lost 6.29
The better fight, who single hast maintaind | Par Lost 6.30
And for the testimonie of Truth hast born | Par Lost 6.33
Such hast thou arm'd, the Minstrelsie of Heav'n, | Par Lost 6.168
And thy adherents: how hast thou disturb'd | Par Lost 6.266
Of thy Rebellion? how hast thou instill'd | Par Lost 6.269
Thou canst not. Hast thou turnd the least of these | Par Lost 6.284
Farr differing from this World, thou hast reveal'd | Par Lost 7.71
Of what we are. But since thou hast voutsaf't | Par Lost 7.80
Of Trumpet (for of Armies thou hast heard) | Par Lost 7.296
Thou hast repeld, while impiously they thought | Par Lost 7.611
Hystorian, who thus largely hast allayd | Par Lost 8.7
To thee who hast thy dwelling here on Earth. | Par Lost 8.118
How fully hast thou satisfi'd mee, pure | Par Lost 8.180
My Storie, which perhaps thou hast not heard; | Par Lost 8.205
Thou hast provided all things: but with mee | Par Lost 8.363
Hast thou not made me here thy substitute, | Par Lost 8.381
So fitly them in pairs thou hast combin'd; | Par Lost 8.394
Which thou hast rightly nam'd, but of thy self, | Par Lost 8.439
This turn hath made amends; thou hast fulfill'd | Par Lost 8.491
Well hast thou motion'd, well thy thoughts imployd | Par Lost 9.229
On what thou hast of vertue, summon all, | Par Lost 9.374
Hast thou not wonderd, *Adam*, at my stay? | Par Lost 9.856
For bliss, as thou hast part, to me is bliss, | Par Lost 9.879
Rather how hast thou yeelded to transgress | Par Lost 9.902
Bold deed thou hast presum'd, adventrous *Eve*, | Par Lost 9.921
And peril great provok't, who thus hath dar'd | Par Lost 9.922
1667 'hast'
Yeild thee, so well this day thou hast purvey'd. | Par Lost 9.1021
My voice thou oft hast heard, and hast not fear'd, | Par Lost 10.119
Hath told thee? hast thou eaten of the Tree | Par Lost 10.122
Say Woman, what is this which thou hast done? | Par Lost 10.158
Because thou hast done this, thou art accurst | Par Lost 10.175
Because thou hast heark'nd to the voice of thy Wife, | Par Lost 10.198
Thou hast atchiev'd our libertie, confin'd | Par Lost 10.368
Sufficient penaltie, why hast thou added | Par Lost 10.753
And horrors hast thou driv'n me; out of which | Par Lost 10.843
What justly thou hast lost; nor set thy heart, | Par Lost 11.288
Prince above Princes, gently hast thou tould | Par Lost 11.298
But this praeeminence thou hast lost, brought down | Par Lost 11.347
To whom thus *Michael*. Death thou hast seen | Par Lost 11.466
To what thou hast, and for the Aire of youth | Par Lost 11.542
Thus thou hast seen one World begin and end; | Par Lost 12.6
Much thou hast yet to see, but I perceave | Par Lost 12.8
Thou hast reveald, those chiefly which concerne | Par Lost 12.272
This having learnt, thou hast attaind the summe | Par Lost 12.575
Let her with thee partake what thou hast heard, | Par Lost 12.598
To thee not known, whence hast thou then thy truth, | Par Reg 1.446
Sharply thou hast insisted on rebuke, | Par Reg 1.468
How hast thou hunger then? Satan reply'd, | Par Reg 2.319
Hast thou not right to all Created things, | Par Reg 2.324
And with my hunger what hast thou to do? | Par Reg 2.389
He ask'd thee, hast thou seen my servant *Job?* | Par Reg 3.67
The world thou hast not seen, much less her glory, | Par Reg 3.236
Before mine eyes thou hast set; and in my ear | Par Reg 3.390
Now both abhor, since thou hast dar'd to utter | Par Reg 4.172
Thou hast permission on me. It is written | Par Reg 4.175
With all his Army, now thou hast aveng'd | Par Reg 4.606
Temptation, hast regain'd lost Paradise, | Par Reg 4.608
Who hast of sorrow thy full load besides; | Samson 214
Bitterly hast thou paid, and still art paying | Samson 432
Wherewith to serve him better then thou hast; | Samson 585
But such as thou hast solemnly elected, | Samson 678
What do I beg? how hast thou dealt already? | Samson 707
That what by me thou hast lost thou least shalt miss. | Samson 927
And thou hast need much washing to be toucht. | Samson 1107
Chor. In time thou hast resolv'd, the man returns. | Samson 1390
Living or dying thou hast fulfill'd | Samson 1661
Thou haste immanacl'd, while Heav'n sees good. | Mask 665
Trinity ms 'hast'
1637 'hast'
Bridgewater ms 'hast'
That have been tir'd all day without repast, | Mask 688
Bridgewater ms 'hast'
Trinity ms 'have' ←'hast'
And timely rest have wanted, but fair Virgin | Mask 689
Trinity ms 'have' ←'hast'
That thou hast banish't from thy tongue with lies, | Mask 692

Hast(*cont*)
Hast thou betrai'd my credulous innocence — Mask 697
line not in Bridgewater ms
Thou hast nor Eare, nor Soul to apprehend — Mask 784
line not in Bridgewater ms
line not in Trinity ms
poore ladie thou hast need of some refreshing — Mask Tr. ms 20.09
poore ladie thou hast neede of some refreshinge — Mask Br. ms 660
Hast thou no vers, no hymn, or solemn strein, — Nativity 17
Think what a present thou to God hast sent, — Fair Inf 74
Till thou hast deck't them in thy best aray; — Vacation 26
For when as each thing bad thou hast entomb'd, — On Time 9
Shortned hast thy own lives lease, — Winchester 52
Hast built thy self a live-long Monument. — Shakespear 8
As thou from yeer to yeer hast sung too late — Sonnet 1, 11
Wisely hast shun'd the broad way and the green, — Sonnet 9, 2
Chosen thou hast, and they that overween, — Sonnet 9, 6
Hast gain'd thy entrance, Virgin wise and pure. — Sonnet 9, 14
To peace and truth thy glorious way hast plough'd, — Sonnet 16, 4
Hast reard Gods Trophies and his work pursu'd. — Sonnet 16, 6
1694 'And Fought God's Battels'
What severs each thou 'hast learnt, which few hav don. — Sonnet 17, 11
1662, 1694 'hast'
Hast smote ere now — Psalm 3, 20
Hast broke the teeth. This help was from the Lord — Psalm 3, 23
And gladness thou hast put — Psalm 4, 32
Hast founded strength because of all thy foes — Psalm 8, 6
The Moon and Starrs which thou so bright hast set, — Psalm 8, 10
With honour and with state thou hast him crown'd. — Psalm 8, 16
Thou hast put all under his lordly feet, — Psalm 8, 18
A Vine from Aegypt thou hast brought, — Psalm 80, 33
Why hast thou laid her Hedges low — Psalm 80, 49
Thou hast made firm and strong. — Psalm 80, 64
Strong for thy self hast made. — Psalm 80, 72
Thou hast not Lord been slack, — Psalm 85, 2
Thou hast from *hard* Captivity — Psalm 85, 3
Hast hid *where none shall know*. — Psalm 85, 8
The Nations all whom thou hast made — Psalm 86, 29
And thou hast free'd my Soul — Psalm 86, 46
Hast set me *all forlorn*, — Psalm 88, 26
Lover and friend thou hast remov'd — Psalm 88, 69
Impudent whoore, where hast thou plac'd thy hope? — Prose 3, 3

Haste
The Heads and Leaders thither hast where stood — Par Lost 1.357
Then this more secret now design'd, I haste — Par Lost 2.838
Of dawning light turnd thither-ward in haste — Par Lost 3.500
Impetuous winds: he thus began in haste. — Par Lost 4.560
So all was cleard, and to the Field they haste. — Par Lost 5.136
On to thir mornings rural work they haste — Par Lost 5.211
Haste hither *Eve*, and worth thy sight behold — Par Lost 5.308
But I will haste and from each bough and break, — Par Lost 5.326
So saying, with dispatchful looks in haste — Par Lost 5.331
Her shadowie Cloud withdraws, I am to haste, — Par Lost 5.686
Of King anointed, for whom all this haste — Par Lost 5.777
Haste to thy audience, Night with her will bring — Par Lost 7.105
For haste; such flight the great command impress'd — Par Lost 7.294
Sung Spousal, and bid haste the Eevning Starr — Par Lost 8.519
Up into Heav'n from Paradise in haste — Par Lost 10.17
1667 'hast'
Accountable made haste to make appear — Par Lost 10.29
Forth rush'd in haste the great consulting Peers, — Par Lost 10.456
Hast thee, and from the Paradise of God — Par Lost 11.104
Dismai'd, and thus in haste to th' Angel cri'd. — Par Lost 11.449
They gladly thither haste, and by a Quire — Par Lost 12.366
If I then to the worst that can be hast, — Par Reg 3.223
He marches now in hast; see, though from far, — Par Reg 3.303
While to their native land with joy they hast, — Par Reg 3.437
Were left for hast unfinish't, judgment scant, — Samson 1027
But wherefore comes old *Manoa* in such hast — Samson 1441
To call in hast for thir destroyer; — Samson 1678
Then down the Lawns I ran with headlong hast — Mask 568
And I must haste ere morning hour — Mask 920
Bridgewater ms 'hast'
Trinity ms 'hast'
1637 'hast'
Com let us haste, the Stars grow high, — Mask 956
Trinity ms 'hast'
1637 'hast'
Bridgewater ms 'hast'
Haste thee nymph, and bring with thee — Allegro 25
And then in haste her Bowre she leaves, — Allegro 87
Shakes the high thicket, haste I all about, — Arcades 58
Trinity ms 'hast'
The Star-led Wisards haste with odours sweet: — Nativity 23
Isis and *Orus*, and the Dog *Anubis* hast. — Nativity 212
But haste thee strait to do me once a Pleasure, — Vacation 17
They shall return in hast the way they came — Psalm 6, 23
He hast to tear my Soul asunder — Psalm 7, 5
Another *Constantine* comes not in hast. — Prose 3, 5

Hasted
Swift to thir several Quarters hasted then — Par Lost 3.714
He hasted, and oppos'd the rockie Orb — Par Lost 6.254
Hasted with glad precipitance, uprowld — Par Lost 7.291
To him she hasted, in her face excuse — Par Lost 9.853
Hasted, resorting to the Summons high, — Par Lost 11.81

Hasten
Shall hast'n, such a peal shall rouse thir sleep. — Par Lost 3.329
And tempt not these; but hast'n to appease — Par Lost 5.846

Hasten(*cont*)
Justice Divine not hast'n to be just? — Par Lost 10.857
Hast'n the welcom end of all my pains. — Samson 576

Hastened
A numerous Brigad hasten'd. As when Bands — Par Lost 1.675
Cherish thy hast'n'd widowhood with the gold — Samson 958
Too long vacation hastned on his term. — Another 14
line not in 1658 text

Hastening
In either hand the hastning Angel caught — Par Lost 12.637
On her hast'ning funerall. — Winchester 46

Hasting
Declin'd was hasting now with prone carreer — Par Lost 4.353
Hasting this way, and now by glimps discerne — Par Lost 4.867
The banded Powers of *Satan* hasting on — Par Lost 6.85
Hasting or on return, in robes of State; — Par Reg 4.64
My hasting dayes flie on with full career, — Sonnet 7, 3

Hasty
As from a sky. The hasty multitude — Par Lost 1.730

Hatch
Thir Brood as numerous hatch, from the Egg that soon — Par Lost 7.418

Hatching
Hatching vain Empires. Thus *Beelzebub* — Par Lost 2.378

Hate
Mixt with obdurate pride and stedfast hate: — Par Lost 1.58
And study of revenge, immortal hate, — Par Lost 1.107
Of *Moloch* homicide, lust hard by hate; — Par Lost 1.417
As not behind in hate; if what was urg'd — Par Lost 2.120
To whom we hate. Let us not then pursue — Par Lost 2.249
But to our power hostility and hate, — Par Lost 2.336
Abhorred *Styx* the flood of deadly hate, — Par Lost 2.577
So Heav'nly love shall outdoo Hellish hate — Par Lost 3.298
So dearly to redeem what Hellish hate — Par Lost 3.300
O Sun, to tell thee how I hate thy beams — Par Lost 4.37
Be then his Love accurst, since love or hate, — Par Lost 4.69
Where wounds of deadly hate have peirc'd so deep: — Par Lost 4.99
Matter to mee of Glory, whom thir hate — Par Lost 5.738
That all may see who hate us, how we seek — Par Lost 6.559
But whom thou hat'st, I hate, and can put on — Par Lost 6.734
So unimaginable as hate in Heav'n, — Par Lost 7.54
Of guile, of hate, of envie, of revenge; — Par Lost 9.466
Fierce hate he recollects, and all his thoughts — Par Lost 9.471
What hither brought us, hate, not love, nor hope — Par Lost 9.475
And beautie, not approacht by stronger hate, — Par Lost 9.491
Hate stronger, under shew of Love well feign'd, — Par Lost 9.492
Began to rise, high Passions, Anger, Hate, — Par Lost 9.1123
Anger, and obstinacie, and hate, and guile. — Par Lost 10.114
To a fell Adversarie, his hate or shame: — Par Lost 10.906
Nor love thy Life, nor hate; but what thou livst — Par Lost 11.553
Those were of hate and death, or pain much worse, — Par Lost 11.601
Sorrows, and labours, opposition, hate, — Par Reg 4.386
Then undissembl'd hate) with what contempt — Samson 400
And what if Love, which thou interpret'st hate, — Samson 790
To raise in me inexpiable hate, — Samson 839
Lov'd, honour'd, fear'd me, thou alone could hate me — Samson 939
For peace, reap nothing but repulse and hate? — Samson 966
Is hate, not help to me, it may with mine — Samson 1266
I would not taste thy treasonous offer; none — Mask 702
Trinity ms 'would not taste' ←'should reject' ←'hate it from thy hands'
I hate when vice can bolt her arguments, — Mask 760
Now timely sing, ere the rude Bird of Hate — Sonnet 1, 9
And still revolt when truth would set them free. — Sonnet 12, 10
Trinity ms 'still revolt when Truth would sett them' ←'make them' ←'set them' ←'hate the truth wherby they should be'
Who hate the Lord should *then be fain* — Psalm 81, 61
And they that hate thee *proud and fell* — Psalm 83, 7

Hated
And therefore hated, therefore so beset — Par Lost 11.702
For this he shall live hated, be blasphem'd, — Par Lost 12.411
Our hated habitation; well ye know — Par Reg 1.47
Hated of all, and hating; with what ease — Par Reg 4.97
Forsook the hated earth, O tell me sooth — Fair Inf 51
Hated not Learning wors then Toad or Asp; — Sonnet 11, 13

Hateful
Hateful to utter: but what power of mind — Par Lost 1.626
ms 'Hatefull'
To sit in hateful Office here confin'd, — Par Lost 2.859
Sight hateful, sight tormenting! thus these two — Par Lost 4.505
These Acts of hateful strife, hateful to all, — Par Lost 6.264
Torment within me, as from the hateful siege — Par Lost 9.121
And hateful; nothing wants, but that thy shape, — Par Lost 10.869
Of hatefull steps, I must be viewles now. — Mask 92
Trinity ms 'hatefull' ←'virgin'
And *hateful* Amalec, — Psalm 83, 26

Hatefulest
With hatefullest disrelish writh'd thir jaws — Par Lost 10.569

Hates
Who hates me, and hath hither thrust me down — Par Lost 2.857

Hatest
But whom thou hat'st, I hate, and can put on — Par Lost 6.734
Thou hat'st; and them unblest — Psalm 5, 14

Hath
Joynd with me once, now misery hath joynd — Par Lost 1.90
Hath lost us Heav'n, and all this mighty Host — Par Lost 1.136
But see the angry Victor hath recall'd — Par Lost 1.169
Shot after us in storm, oreblown hath laid — Par Lost 1.172
Perhaps hath spent his shafts, and ceases now — Par Lost 1.176

Hath(*cont*)

Whom reason hath equald, force hath made supream	Par Lost 1.248
Whom Thunder hath made greater? Here at least	Par Lost 1.258
We shall be free; th' Almighty hath not built	Par Lost 1.259
Hath vext the Red-Sea Coast, whose waves orethrew	Par Lost 1.306
Hath scath'd the Forrest Oaks, or Mountain Pines,	Par Lost 1.613
Hath emptied Heav'n, shall fail to re-ascend	Par Lost 1.633
By force, hath overcome but half his foe.	Par Lost 1.649
Hath bin achievd of merit, yet this loss	Par Lost 2.21
Thus farr at least recover'd, hath much more	Par Lost 2.22
And know not that the King of Heav'n hath doom'd	Par Lost 2.316
Warr hath determin'd us, and foild with loss	Par Lost 2.330
With reason hath deep silence and demurr	Par Lost 2.431
Who hates me, and hath hither thrust me down	Par Lost 2.857
So thick a drop serene hath quencht thir Orbs,	Par Lost 3.25
O Son, in whom my Soul hath chief delight,	Par Lost 3.168
As my Eternal purpose hath decreed:	Par Lost 3.172
To expiate his Treason hath naught left,	Par Lost 3.207
Indebted and undon, hath none to bring:	Par Lost 3.235
Love hath abounded more then Glory abounds,	Par Lost 3.312
Hath brought me from the Quires of Cherubim	Par Lost 3.666
In which of all these shining Orbes hath Man	Par Lost 3.668
His fixed seat, or fixed seat hath none,	Par Lost 3.669
On whom the great Creator hath bestowd	Par Lost 3.673
Worlds, and on whom hath all these graces powrd;	Par Lost 3.674
Who justly hath drivn out his Rebell Foes	Par Lost 3.677
When God hath showrd the earth; so lovely seemd	Par Lost 4.152
The hand that formd them on thir shape hath pourd.	Par Lost 4.365
Then as a Tyger, who by chance hath spi'd	Par Lost 4.403
Aught whereof hee hath need, hee who requires	Par Lost 4.419
God hath pronounc't it death to taste that Tree,	Par Lost 4.427
Gabriel, to thee thy course by Lot hath giv'n	Par Lost 4.561
I fear, hath ventur'd from the deep, to raise	Par Lost 4.574
Mind us of like repose, since God hath set	Par Lost 4.612
Man hath his daily work of body or mind	Par Lost 4.618
This glorious sight, when sleep hath shut all eyes?	Par Lost 4.658
Whose dwelling God hath planted here in bliss?	Par Lost 4.884
Hath raisd in Paradise, and how disturbd	Par Lost 5.226
God hath dispenst his bounties as in Heav'n.	Par Lost 5.330
To us for food and for delight hath caus'd	Par Lost 5.400
Cover'd with pearly grain: yet God hath here	Par Lost 5.430
Hath past in Heav'n, som doubt within me move,	Par Lost 5.554
Hath finisht half his journey, and scarce begins	Par Lost 5.559
Of yesterday, so late hath past the lips	Par Lost 5.675
Nor so content, hath in his thought to try	Par Lost 5.727
Another now hath to himself ingross't	Par Lost 5.775
That he who in debate of Truth hath won,	Par Lost 6.122
When Reason hath to deal with force, yet so	Par Lost 6.125
To serve th' unwise, or him who hath rebelld	Par Lost 6.179
Part hidd'n veins diggd up (nor hath this Earth	Par Lost 6.516
Which God hath in his mighty Angels plac'd)	Par Lost 6.638
(For Earth hath this variety from Heav'n	Par Lost 6.640
These disobedient; sore hath been thir fight,	Par Lost 6.687
Save what sin hath impaird, which yet hath wrought	Par Lost 6.691
Warr wearied hath perform'd what Warr can do,	Par Lost 6.695
Faithful hath been your warfare, and of God	Par Lost 6.803
Hath honourd me according to his will.	Par Lost 6.816
Therefore to mee thir doom he hath assig'n'd;	Par Lost 6.817
Onely Omniscient, hath suppresst in Night,	Par Lost 7.123
At least our envious Foe hath fail'd, who thought	Par Lost 7.139
Hath Omnipresence) and the work ordain'd,	Par Lost 7.590
And sons of men, whom God hath thus advanc't,	Par Lost 7.626
Hath left to thir disputes, perhaps to move	Par Lost 8.77
Contented that thus farr hath been reveal'd	Par Lost 8.177
God hath bid dwell farr off all anxious cares,	Par Lost 8.185
Abundantly his gifts hath also pour'd	Par Lost 8.220
For God we see hath honour'd thee, and set	Par Lost 8.227
This turn hath made amends; thou hast fulfill'd	Par Lost 8.491
Accuse not Nature, she hath don her part;	Par Lost 8.561
The thoughts, and heart enlarges, hath his seat	Par Lost 8.590
Gentle to me and affable hath been	Par Lost 8.648
God hath assign'd us, nor of me shalt pass	Par Lost 9.231
Yet not so strictly hath our Lord impos'd	Par Lost 9.235
What hath bin warn'd us, what malicious Foe	Par Lost 9.253
To do what God expresly hath forbid,	Par Lost 9.356
For God towards thee hath done his part, do thine.	Par Lost 9.375
I not; so much hath Hell debas'd, and paine	Par Lost 9.487
Indeed? hath God then said that of the Fruit	Par Lost 9.656
The Garden, God hath said, Ye shall not eate	Par Lost 9.662
How dies the Serpent? hee hath eat'n and lives,	Par Lost 9.764
Hath tasted, envies not, but brings with joy	Par Lost 9.770
Hath bin the cause, and wonderful to heare:	Par Lost 9.862
And hath bin tasted such: the Serpent wise,	Par Lost 9.867
Hath eat'n of the fruit, and is become,	Par Lost 9.869
Perswasively hath so prevaild, that I	Par Lost 9.873
Of Enemie hath beguil'd thee, yet unknown,	Par Lost 9.905
And mee with thee hath ruind, for with thee	Par Lost 9.906
And peril great provok't, who thus hath dar'd	Par Lost 9.922
1667 'hast'	
Direct, or by occasion hath presented	Par Lost 9.974
Hath toucht my sense, flat seems to this, and harsh.	Par Lost 9.987
And force upon free will hath here no place.	Par Lost 9.1174
Hath told thee? hast thou eaten of the Tree	Par Lost 10.122
Thine now is all this World, thy vertue hath won	Par Lost 10.372
With odds what Warr hath lost, and fully aveng'd	Par Lost 10.374
As Battel hath adjudg'd, from this new World	Par Lost 10.377
Offended, worth your laughter, hath giv'n up	Par Lost 10.488
True is, mee also he hath judg'd, or rather	Par Lost 10.494

Hath(*cont*)

Which mans polluting Sin with taint hath shed	Par Lost 10.631
And sin? the Bodie properly hath neither.	Par Lost 10.791
Hath wiselier arm'd his vengeful ire then so	Par Lost 10.1023
Satan, who in the Serpent hath contriv'd	Par Lost 10.1034
Hath unbesaught provided, and his hands	Par Lost 10.1058
Th' effects which thy original crime hath wrought	Par Lost 11.424
O Teacher, some great mischief hath befall'n	Par Lost 11.450
Out of thy loyns; th' unjust the just hath slain,	Par Lost 11.455
Twinn'd, and from her hath no dividual being:	Par Lost 12.85
Establisht, such delight hath God in Men	Par Lost 12.245
How soon hath thy prediction, Seer blest,	Par Lost 12.553
Which he hath sent propitious, some great good	Par Lost 12.612
Sir, what ill chance hath brought thee to this place	Par Reg 1.321
Hath he excluded my resort sometimes.	Par Reg 1.367
Among the Nations? that hath been thy craft,	Par Reg 1.432
For God hath justly giv'n the Nations up	Par Reg 1.442
God hath now sent his living Oracle	Par Reg 1.460
But misery hath rested from me; where	Par Reg 1.470
Hath rapt him from us? will he now retire	Par Reg 2.40
But let us wait; thus far he hath perform'd,	Par Reg 2.49
Hath been our dwelling many years, his life	Par Reg 2.80
My heart hath been a store-house long of things	Par Reg 2.103
Such object hath the power to soft'n and tame	Par Reg 2.163
Nature hath need of what she asks; yet God	Par Reg 2.253
Of thee these forty days none hath regard,	Par Reg 2.315
Troubl'd that thou shouldst hunger, hath purvey'd	Par Reg 2.333
To me is not unknown what hath been done	Par Reg 2.444
Besides to give a Kingdom hath been thought	Par Reg 2.481
Or Barbarous, nor exception hath declar'd;	Par Reg 3.119
Hath nothing, and to whom nothing belongs	Par Reg 3.135
And time there is for all things, Truth hath said:	Par Reg 3.183
If of my raign Prophetic Writ hath told,	Par Reg 3.184
The Father in his purpose hath decreed,	Par Reg 3.186
What if he hath decreed that I shall first	Par Reg 3.188
Well hath obey'd; just tryal e're I merit	Par Reg 3.196
Thy life hath yet been private, most part spent	Par Reg 3.232
In *Ctesiphon* hath gather'd all his Host	Par Reg 3.300
This Emperour hath no Son, and now is old,	Par Reg 4.90
The tryal hath indamag'd thee no way,	Par Reg 4.206
For yonder bank hath choice of Sun or shade,	Samson 3
Whom God hath of his special favour rais'd	Samson 273
And hath full right to exempt	Samson 310
My Son now Captive, hither hath inform'd	Samson 335
Alas methinks whom God hath chosen once	Samson 368
Nothing of all these evils hath befall'n me	Samson 374
As vile hath been my folly, who have profan'd	Samson 377
To *Dagon*, as their God who hath deliver'd	Samson 437
With me hath end; all the contest is now	Samson 461
'Twixt God and *Dagon; Dagon* hath presum'd,	Samson 462
But God hath set before us, to return thee	Samson 517
Sleep hath forsook and giv'n me o're	Samson 629
But now hath cast me off as never known,	Samson 641
My penance hath not slack'n'd, though my pardon	Samson 738
Hath led me on desirous to behold	Samson 741
And Love hath oft, well meaning, wrought much wo,	Samson 813
Yet always pity or pardon hath obtain'd.	Samson 814
Life yet hath many solaces, enjoy'd	Samson 915
It hath brought forth to make thee memorable	Samson 956
Chor. Yet beauty, though injurious, hath strange power,	Samson 1003
Comes he in peace? what wind hath blown him hither	Samson 1070
Hath walk'd about, and each limb to survey,	Samson 1089
Thee he regards not, owns not, hath cut off	Samson 1157
This Idols day hath bin to thee no day of rest,	Samson 1297
As in thy wond'rous actions hath been seen.	Samson 1440
Chor. Yet God hath wrought things as incredible	Samson 1532
Hath paid his ransom now and full discharge.	Samson 1573
Nor much more cause, *Samson* hath quit himself	Samson 1709
Like *Samson*, and heroicly hath finish'd	Samson 1710
Fully reveng'd, hath left them years of mourning,	Samson 1712
Honour hath left, and freedom, let but them	Samson 1715
And to his faithful Champion hath in place	Samson 1751
With peace and consolation hath dismist,	Samson 1757
What hath night to do with sleep?	Mask 122
Night hath better sweets to prove,	Mask 123
Bridgewater ms 'has'	
Trinity ms 'has'	
Hath met the vertue of this Magick dust,	Mask 165
Co. What chance good Lady hath bereft you thus?	Mask 277
Hath hurtfull power o're true virginity.	Mask 437
1637 'Has'	
Bridgewater ms 'has'	
Trinity ms 'has'	
How cam'st thou here good Swain? hath any ram	Mask 497
That hath so well been taught her dazling fence,	Mask 791
line not in Bridgewater ms	
line not in Trinity ms	
Now the spell hath lost his hold;	Mask 919
Heav'n hath timely tri'd their youth,	Mask 970
Youth and Joy; so *Jove* hath sworn.	Mask 1011
line not in Bridgewater ms	
Streit mine eye hath caught new pleasures	Allegro 69
His shadowy Flale hath thresh'd the Corn	Allegro 108
The immortal mind that hath forsook	Penseroso 91
Whose power hath a true consent	Penseroso 95
Ennobled hath the Buskind stage.	Penseroso 102
When the gust hath blown his fill,	Penseroso 128
Heer our solemn search hath end.	Arcades 7

Hath*(cont)*
Less then half we find exprest, Arcades 12
Trinity ms 'wee find' ←'she hath'
What shallow-searching *Fame* hath left untold; Arcades 41
Hath lockt up mortal sense, then listen I Arcades 62
Where no print of step hath been, Arcades 85
All *Arcadia* hath not seen. Arcades 95
Trinity ms defective here
All *Arcadia* hath not seen. Arcades 109
Young *Lycidas*, and hath not left his peer: Lycidas 9
What hard mishap hath doom'd this gentle swain? Lycidas 92
Ah! Who hath reft (quoth he) my dearest pledge? Lycidas 107
Hath took no print of the approching light, Nativity 20
Who now hath quite forgot to rave, Nativity 67
Hath left in shadows dred, Nativity 206
Hath laid her Babe to rest. Nativity 238
Hath fixt her polisht Car. Nativity 241
As a faint host that hath receiv'd the foil. Psalm 114, 10
He hath with a piteous eye Psalm 136, 77
That his mansion hath on high Psalm 136, 93
To slake his wrath whom sin hath made our foe Fair Inf 66
Thy drowsie Nurse hath sworn she did them spie Vacation 61
Mine eye hath found that sad Sepulchral rock Passion 43
Hath from the leaves of thy unvalu'd Book, Shakespear 11
Here lies old *Hobson*, Death hath broke his girt, Carrier 1
A here alas, hath laid him in the dirt, Carrier 2
For he had any time this ten yeers full, Carrier 7
1658 'he hath'
How soon hath Time the suttle theef of youth, Sonnet 7, 1
To conquer still; peace hath her victories Sonnet 16, 10
Bless'd is the man who hath not walk'd astray Psalm 1, 1
Of sinners hath not stood, and in the seat Psalm 1, 3
Of scorners hath not sate. But in the great Psalm 1, 4
I will declare; the Lord to me hath say'd Psalm 2, 14
Yet know the Lord hath chose Psalm 4, 13
The Lord hath heard, the Lord hath heard my prai'r Psalm 6, 18
His Sword he whets, his Bow hath bended Psalm 7, 46
Trouble he hath conceav'd of old Psalm 7, 52
Hath at length brought forth a Lie. Psalm 7, 54
Hath set, and planted *long*, Psalm 80, 62
Hath found a house of *rest*, Psalm 84, 10
Hath built her *brooding* nest, Psalm 84, 12
Deaths hideous house hath barr'd. Psalm 88, 24
On whom the grave *hath hold*, Psalm 88, 46

Hating
Hated of all, and hating; with what ease Par Reg 4.97

Hatred
While with perfidious hatred they pursu'd Par Lost 1.308
Yet live in hatred, enmity, and strife Par Lost 2.500
Thy hatred for this miserie befall'n, Par Lost 10.928
The easier towards me, or thy hatred less. Samson 772

Haught
And drov'st out Nations *proud and haut* Psalm 80, 35

Haughty
But like a proud Steed reind, went hautie on, Par Lost 4.858
Th' Apostat, and more haughty thus repli'd. Par Lost 5.852
Satan with vast and haughtie strides advanc't, Par Lost 6.109
And strength, of courage hautie, and of limb Par Lost 9.484
Haughty as is his pile high-built and proud. Samson 1069
An old, and haughty Nation proud in Arms: Mask 33
Trinity ms 'haughtie'
1637 'haughtie'

Haunt
Cease I to wander where the Muses haunt Par Lost 3.27
Whom hunger drives to seek new haunt for prey, Par Lost 4.184
Or wander with delight, and love to haunt Par Lost 7.330
Fit haunt of Gods? where I had hope to spend, Par Lost 11.271
The haunt of Seales and Orcs, and Sea-mews clang. Par Lost 11.835
And to a Superstitious eye the haunt Par Reg 2.296
Far from the cheerfull haunt of men, and herds, Mask 388
Bridgewater ms 'haunte'
Or fright them from their hallow'd haunt. Penseroso 138

Haunted
Nor *Faunus* haunted. Here in close recess Par Lost 4.708
On Summer eeves by haunted stream. Allegro 130
From haunted spring, and dale Nativity 184

Haunts
Satyr, or Fawn, or Silvan? But these haunts Par Reg 2.191
In their obscured haunts of inmost bowres. Mask 536

Haut
And drov'st out Nations *proud and haut* Psalm 80, 35

Have
He trusted to have equal'd the most High, Par Lost 1.40
ms 'haue'
Then such could hav orepow'rd such force as ours) Par Lost 1.145
ms 'haue'
Have left us this our spirit and strength intire Par Lost 1.146
ms 'Haue'
Both glorying to have scap't the *Stygian* flood Par Lost 1.239
ms 'haue'
Which but th' Omnipotent none could have foyld, Par Lost 1.273
ms 'haue'
Eternal spirits; or have ye chos'n this place Par Lost 1.318
ms 'haue'
Or in this abject posture have ye sworn Par Lost 1.322
ms 'haue'
Obscure some glimps of joy, to have found thir chief Par Lost 1.524
ms 'haue'

Have*(cont)*
Not in despair, to have found themselves not lost Par Lost 1.525
ms 'haue'
For ever now to have thir lot in pain, Par Lost 1.608
ms 'haue'
Of knowledge past or present, could have fear'd, Par Lost 1.628
ms 'haue'
By mee, have lost our hopes. But he who reigns Par Lost 1.637
ms 'haue'
To have built in Heav'n high Towrs; nor did he scape Par Lost 1.749
ms 'haue'
Could have assur'd us; and by what best way, Par Lost 2.40
Then miserable to have eternal being: Par Lost 2.98
All thoughts of warr: ye have what I advise. Par Lost 2.283
Well have ye judg'd, well ended long debate, Par Lost 2.390
Where Armies whole have sunk: the parching Air Par Lost 2.594
Than Fables yet have feign'd, or fear conceiv'd, Par Lost 2.627
Could once have mov'd; then in the key-hole turns Par Lost 2.876
If that way be your walk, you have not farr; Par Lost 2.1007
All he could have; I made him just and right, Par Lost 3.98
Sufficient to have stood, though free to fall. Par Lost 3.99
Not free, what proof could they have givn sincere Par Lost 3.103
Some I have chosen of peculiar grace Par Lost 3.183
Must have bin lost, adjudg'd to Death and Hell Par Lost 3.223
All who have thir reward on Earth, the fruits Par Lost 3.451
Not in the neighbouring Moon, as some have dreamd; Par Lost 3.459
Philosophers in vain so long have sought, Par Lost 3.601
As great might have aspir'd, and me though mean Par Lost 4.62
Where wounds of deadly hate have peirc'd so deep: Par Lost 4.99
Sin-bred, how have ye troubl'd all mankind Par Lost 4.315
Have nothing merited, nor can performe Par Lost 4.418
Substantial Life, to have thee by my side Par Lost 4.485
Yet let me not forget what I have gain'd Par Lost 4.512
So minded, have oreleapt these earthie bounds Par Lost 4.583
Those have thir course to finish, round the Earth, Par Lost 4.661
Of echoing Hill or Thicket have we heard Par Lost 4.681
Have finisht happie in our mutual help Par Lost 4.727
Hitherward bent (who could have thought2) escap'd Par Lost 4.794
By thy example, but have power and right Par Lost 4.881
Might have ensu'd, nor onely Paradise Par Lost 4.991
Such night till this I never pass'd, have dream'd, Par Lost 5.31
And pious awe, that feard to have offended. Par Lost 5.135
Have gathered aught of evil or conceald, Par Lost 5.207
I have at will. So to the Silvan Lodge Par Lost 5.377
Have heap'd this Table. Rais'd of grassie terf Par Lost 5.391
Then had the Sons of God excuse to have bin Par Lost 5.447
At Heav'ns high feasts to have fed: yet what compare? Par Lost 5.467
Divine instructer, I have heard, then when Par Lost 5.546
And we have yet large day, for scarce the Sun Par Lost 5.558
This day I have begot whom I declare Par Lost 5.603
Him have anointed, whom ye now behold Par Lost 5.605
And by my Self have sworn to him shall bow Par Lost 5.607
(For wee have also our Eevning and our Morn, Par Lost 5.628
To have reported: gladly then he mixt Par Lost 6.21
I mean to try, whose Reason I have tri'd Par Lost 6.120
Proud, art thou met? thy hope was to have reacht Par Lost 6.131
Have rais'd incessant Armies to defeat Par Lost 6.138
Unaided could have finisht thee, and whelmd Par Lost 6.141
As each divided Legion might have seemd Par Lost 6.230
I flie not, but have sought thee farr and nigh. Par Lost 6.295
Gave them above thir foes, not to have sinnd, Par Lost 6.402
Not to have disobei'd; in fight they stood Par Lost 6.403
Who have sustaind one day in doubtful fight Par Lost 6.423
Adverse, that they shall fear we have disarmd Par Lost 6.490
Once found, which yet unfound most would have thought Par Lost 6.500
Do as you have in charge, and briefly touch Par Lost 6.566
Have easily as Spirits evaded swift Par Lost 6.596
Not understood, this gift they have besides, Par Lost 6.626
For thee I have ordain'd it, and thus farr Par Lost 6.700
Have sufferd, that the Glorie may be thine Par Lost 6.701
Immense I have transfus'd, that all may know Par Lost 6.704
And as ye have receivd, so have ye don Par Lost 6.805
By mee, not you but mee they have despis'd, Par Lost 6.812
That they may have thir wish, to trie with mee Par Lost 6.818
Heav'n ruining from Heav'n and would have fled Par Lost 6.868
By what is past, to thee I have reveal'd Par Lost 6.895
What might have else to human Race bin hid; Par Lost 6.896
Thy weaker; let it profit thee to have heard Par Lost 6.909
Of disobedience; firm they might have stood, Par Lost 6.911
Into the Heav'n of Heav'ns I have presum'd, Par Lost 7.13
Us timely of what might else have bin our loss, Par Lost 7.74
I have receav'd, to answer thy desire Par Lost 7.119
He trusted to have seis'd, and into fraud Par Lost 7.143
Yet farr the greater part have kept, I see, Par Lost 7.145
Already done, to have dispeopl'd Heav'n Par Lost 7.151
To Man, the greater to have rule by Day, Par Lost 7.347
Equal have I to render thee, Divine Par Lost 8.6
By Numbers that have name. But this I urge, Par Lost 8.114
Thee I have heard relating what was don Par Lost 8.203
Destruction with Creation might have mixt. Par Lost 8.236
From whom I have that thus I move and live, Par Lost 8.281
Knowledg of good and ill, which I have set Par Lost 8.324
How have I then with whom to hold converse Par Lost 8.408
Thus I have told thee all my State, and brought Par Lost 8.521
With what delight could I have walkt thee round, Par Lost 9.114
The infernal Powers, in one day to have marr'd Par Lost 9.136
That such an Enemie we have, who seeks Par Lost 9.274
To God or thee, because we have a foe Par Lost 9.280

Have(*cont*)

Thoughts, whither have ye led me, with what sweet	Par Lost 9.473
Insatiate, I thus single, nor have feard	Par Lost 9.536
Serpent, we might have spar'd our coming hither,	Par Lost 9.647
Mee who have touch'd and tasted, yet both live,	Par Lost 9.688
And life more perfet have attaind then Fate	Par Lost 9.689
May have diverted from continual watch	Par Lost 9.814
This may be well: but what if God have seen,	Par Lost 9.826
Thee I have misst, and thought it long, depriv'd	Par Lost 9.857
Have also tasted, and have also found	Par Lost 9.874
However I with thee have fixt my Lot,	Par Lost 9.952
Much pleasure we have lost, while we abstain'd	Par Lost 9.1022
What words have past thy Lips, *Adam* severe,	Par Lost 9.1144
But might as ill have happ'nd thou being by,	Par Lost 9.1147
Or here th' attempt, thou couldst not have discernd	Par Lost 9.1149
Was I to have never parted from thy side?	Par Lost 9.1153
As good have grown there still a liveless Rib.	Par Lost 9.1154
Who might have liv'd and joyd immortal bliss,	Par Lost 9.1166
Complete to have discover'd and repulst	Par Lost 10.10
For still they knew, and ought to have still remember'd	Par Lost 10.12
Vicegerent Son, to thee I have transferr'd	Par Lost 10.56
High proof ye now have giv'n to be the Race	Par Lost 10.385
Amply have merited of me, of all	Par Lost 10.388
Triumphal with triumphal act have met,	Par Lost 10.390
What I have don, what sufferd, with what paine	Par Lost 10.470
Made happie: Him by fraud I have seduc'd	Par Lost 10.485
To rule, as over all he should have rul'd.	Par Lost 10.493
Or much more grievous pain? Ye have th' account	Par Lost 10.501
According to his doom: he would have spoke,	Par Lost 10.517
Then stil at Hels dark threshold to have sate watch,	Par Lost 10.594
I thus contest; then should have been refusd	Par Lost 10.756
I beare thee, and unweeting have offended,	Par Lost 10.916
More miserable; both have sin'd, but thou	Par Lost 10.930
That shew no end but Death, and have the power,	Par Lost 10.1004
I have in view, calling to minde with heed	Par Lost 10.1030
To evils which our own misdeeds have wrought,	Par Lost 10.1080
Of Paradise could have produc't, ere fall'n	Par Lost 11.29
Happier, had it suffic'd him to have known	Par Lost 11.88
Michael, this my behest have thou in charge,	Par Lost 11.99
This Hill; let *Eve* (for I have drencht her eyes)	Par Lost 11.367
But have I now seen Death? Is this the way	Par Lost 11.462
All would have then gon well, peace would have crownd	Par Lost 11.781
What oft my steddiest thoughts have searcht in vain,	Par Lost 12.377
Annuls thy doom, the death thou shouldst have dy'd,	Par Lost 12.428
Greatly in peace of thought, and have my fill	Par Lost 12.558
Her also I with gentle Dreams have calm'd	Par Lost 12.595
Worthy t' have not remain'd so long unsung.	Par Reg 1.17
As to his worthier, and would have resign'd	Par Reg 1.27
This Universe we have possest, and rul'd	Par Reg 1.49
This dreaded time have compast, wherein we	Par Reg 1.58
His first-begot we know, and sore have felt,	Par Reg 1.89
Of his Apostasie; he might have learnt	Par Reg 1.146
From what consummate vertue I have chose	Par Reg 1.165
For what he bids I do; though I have lost	Par Reg 1.377
To be belov'd of God, I have not lost	Par Reg 1.379
Or vertuous, I should so have lost all sense.	Par Reg 1.382
I gain'd what I have gain'd, and with them dwell	Par Reg 1.391
But what have been thy answers, what but dark	Par Reg 1.434
Which they who ask'd have seldom understood,	Par Reg 1.436
Expected of our Fathers; we have heard	Par Reg 2.33
They have exalted, and behind them cast	Par Reg 2.46
In publick, and with him we have convers'd;	Par Reg 2.52
To have conceiv'd of God, or that salute	Par Reg 2.67
Have found him, view'd him, tasted him, but find	Par Reg 2.131
Have we not seen, or by relation heard,	Par Reg 2.182
How many have with a smile made small account	Par Reg 2.193
His constancy, with such as have more shew	Par Reg 2.226
Rocks whereon greatest men have oftest wreck'd;	Par Reg 2.228
Where will this end? four times ten days I have pass'd	Par Reg 2.245
As story tells, have trod this Wilderness;	Par Reg 2.307
They all had need, I as thou seest have none.	Par Reg 2.318
That I have also power to give thou seest,	Par Reg 2.393
What I might have bestow'd on whom I pleas'd,	Par Reg 2.395
Whose pains have earn'd the far fet spoil. With that	Par Reg 2.401
But men endu'd with these have oft attain'd	Par Reg 2.437
With temperate sway; oft have they violated	Par Reg 3.160
Well have we speeded, and o're hill and dale,	Par Reg 3.267
And just in time thou com'st to have a view	Par Reg 3.298
Have wasted *Sogdiana;* to her aid	Par Reg 3.302
To what end I have brought thee hither and shewn	Par Reg 3.350
Houses of Gods (so well I have dispos'd	Par Reg 4.56
These having shewn thee, I have shewn thee all	Par Reg 4.88
(For I have also heard, perhaps have read)	Par Reg 4.116
Then these thou bear'st that title, have propos'd	Par Reg 4.199
Wise men have said are wearisom; who reads	Par Reg 4.322
What I foretell thee, soon thou shalt have cause	Par Reg 4.375
Which would have set thee in short time with ease	Par Reg 4.378
For Angels have proclaim'd it, but concealing	Par Reg 4.474
Of the Messiah I have heard foretold	Par Reg 4.502
From that time seldom have I ceas'd to eye	Par Reg 4.507
And opportunity I here have had	Par Reg 4.531
To try thee, sift thee, and confess have found thee	Par Reg 4.532
Have been before contemn'd, and may agen:	Par Reg 4.537
Have brought thee, and highest plac't, highest is best,	Par Reg 4.553
Whom have I to complain of but my self?	Samson 46
Annull'd, which might in part my grief have eas'd,	Samson 72
Might have subdu'd the Earth,	Samson 174
Salve to thy Sores, apt words have power to swage	Samson 184

Have(*cont*)

How many evils have enclos'd me round;	Samson 194
Who like a foolish Pilot have shipwrack't,	Samson 198
Fool, have divulg'd the secret gift of God	Samson 201
This with the other should, at least, have paird,	Samson 208
Have err'd, and by bad Women been deceiv'd;	Samson 211
Yet truth to say, I oft have heard men wonder	Samson 215
Have prompted this Heroic *Nazarite*,	Samson 318
But justly; I my self have brought them on,	Samson 375
As vile hath been my folly, who have profan'd	Samson 377
Of vow, and have betray'd it to a woman,	Samson 379
Might easily have shook off all her snares:	Samson 409
Deposited within thee; which to have kept	Samson 429
Which to have come to pass by means of thee,	Samson 444
Could have befall'n thee and thy Fathers house.	Samson 447
That I this honour, I this pomp have brought	Samson 449
Among the Heathen round; to God have brought	Samson 451
Of Idolists, and Atheists; have brought scandal	Samson 453
Neglected. I already have made way	Samson 481
Have satisfi'd thir utmost of revenge	Samson 484
Shameful garrulity. To have reveal'd	Samson 491
But I Gods counsel have not kept, his holy secret	Samson 497
Presumptuously have publish'd, impiously,	Samson 498
About t' have spoke, but now, with head declin'd	Samson 727
Which to have merited, without excuse,	Samson 734
Nor shouldst thou have trusted that to womans frailty	Samson 783
These reasons in Loves law have past for good,	Samson 811
To satisfie thy lust: Love seeks to have Love;	Samson 837
Which might have aw'd the best resolv'd of men,	Samson 847
The constantest to have yielded without blame.	Samson 848
Bin, as it ought, sincere, it would have taught thee	Samson 874
In what I thought would have succeeded best.	Samson 908
Towards thee I intend for what I have misdone,	Samson 911
Where once I have been caught; I know thy trains	Samson 932
No more on me have power, their force is null'd,	Samson 935
So much of Adders wisdom I have learn't	Samson 936
Which to my countrey I was judg'd to have shewn.	Samson 994
Sam. Fair days have oft contracted wind and rain.	Samson 1062
If thou at all art known. Much I have heard	Samson 1082
Of those encounters, where we might have tri'd	Samson 1086
To have wrought such wonders with an Asses Jaw;	Samson 1095
I should have forc'd thee soon wish other arms,	Samson 1096
Certain to have won by mortal duel from thee,	Samson 1102
Sam. Boast not of what thou wouldst have done, but do	Samson 1104
Again in safety what thou wouldst have done	Samson 1128
Which greatest Heroes have in battel worn,	Samson 1131
Sam. Have they not Sword-players, and ev'ry sort	Samson 1323
Sa. Perhaps thou shalt have cause to sorrow indeed.	Samson 1347
Of those who have me in thir civil power.	Samson 1367
To give ye part with me what hope I have	Samson 1453
Man. I have attempted one by one the Lords	Samson 1457
Oh it continues, they have slain my Son.	Samson 1516
To have guided me aright, I know not how,	Samson 1547
I have perform'd, as reason was, obeying,	Samson 1641
O if thou have	Mask 238
Of darknes till it smil'd: I have oft heard	Mask 252
Bridgewater ms 'haue'	
El. Bro. Thyrsis? Whose artful strains have oft delaid	Mask 494
Bridgewater ms 'haue'	
Character'd in the face; this have I learn't	Mask 530
Yet have they many baits, and guilefull spells	Mask 537
And yet came off: if you have this about you	Mask 647
That have been tir'd all day without repast,	Mask 688
Bridgewater ms 'hast'	
Trinity ms 'have' ←'hast'	
And timely rest have wanted, but fair Virgin	Mask 689
Trinity ms 'have' ←'hast'	
Bridgewater ms 'hast'	
La. I had not thought to have unlockt my lips	Mask 756
Or have I said anough? To him that dares	Mask 780
line not in Trinity ms	
line not in Bridgewater ms	
Spir. What, have you let the false enchanter scape?	Mask 814
O ye mistook, ye should have snatcht his wand	Mask 815
Bridgewater ms 'haue'	
Som other means I have which may be us'd,	Mask 821
Bridgewater ms 'haue'	
Trinity ms 'some other meanes I have' ←'there is another way'	
Till thou our summons answer'd have.	Mask 888
I have kept of pretious cure,	Mask 913
I have brought ye new delight,	Mask 967
to have her by my side, though I were sure	Mask Tr. ms 16.41
how have I bin betrai'd	Mask Tr. ms 22.18
to have her by my side, though I were suer	Mask Br. ms 394
Such streins as would have won the ear	Allegro 148
Of *Pluto*, to have quite set free	Allegro 149
In sage and solemn tunes have sung,	Penseroso 117
Who had thought this clime had held	Arcades 24
Trinity ms 'had' ←'would have'	
Have sate to wonder at, and gaze upon:	Arcades 43
Here ye shall have greater grace,	Arcades 104
Had ye bin there---for what could that have don?	Lycidas 57
How well could I have spar'd for thee young swain,	Lycidas 113
A Sheep-hook, or have learn'd ought els the least	Lycidas 120
Have thou the honour first, thy Lord to greet,	Nativity 26
(If ye have power to touch our senses so)	Nativity 127
Time is our tedious Song should here have ending,	Nativity 239

Have(*cont*)
Believe me I have thither packt the worst: Vacation 12
For this same small neglect that I have made: Vacation 16
I have some naked thoughts that rove about Vacation 23
And loudly knock to have their passage out; Vacation 24
And letters where my tears have washt a wannish white. Passion 35
So have I seen som tender slip Winchester 35
Peace and quiet ever have; Winchester 48
And surely, Death could never have prevail'd, Carrier 9
Have linkt that amorous power to thy soft lay, Sonnet 1, 8
All is, if I have grace to use it so, Sonnet 7, 13
Though later born, then to have known the dayes Sonnet 10, 9
That would have made *Quintilian* stare and gasp. Sonnet 11, 11
Strait follow'd thee the path that Saints have trod Sonnet 14, Tr. ms 41.06
What severs each thou 'hast learnt, which few hav don. Sonnet 17, 11
1662, 1694 'have'
Bereft of light thir seeing have forgot, Sonnet 22, 3
The conscience, Friend, to have lost them overply'd Sonnet 22, 10
And such, as yet once more I trust to have Sonnet 23, 7
Because you have thrown of your Prelate Lord, Forcers 1
Would have been held in high esteem with *Paul* Forcers 10
Picture the sacred wall declares t' have hung Horace 14
anointed have my King (though ye rebell) Psalm 2, 12
Thou art my Son I have begotten thee Psalm 2, 15
Happy all those who have in him their stay. Psalm 2, 28
My glory have in scorn Psalm 4, 8
Still on; for against thee they have rebell'd; Psalm 5, 32
The Lord will own, and have me in his keeping. Psalm 6, 20
Lord my God if I have thought Psalm 7, 7
Be in my hands, if I have wrought Psalm 7, 9
Or to him have render'd less, Psalm 7, 11
Their time should have no end. Psalm 81, 64
All these have lent their armed hands Psalm 83, 31
For they amidst their pride have said Psalm 83, 45
Sweet Peace and Righteousness have kiss'd Psalm 85, 43
Preserve my soul, for I have trod Psalm 86, 5
Of all that other gods have done Psalm 86, 27
No fear of thee have set. Psalm 86, 52
And me have mercy on, Psalm 86, 58
They *fly me now* whom I have lov'd, Psalm 88, 71
This was that gift (if you the truth will have) Prose 4, 3

Haven
Of *Susiana* to *Balsara*'s hav'n. Par Reg 3.321

Having
Stretcht into Longitude; which having pass'd Par Lost 5.754
So having said, as one from sad dismay Par Lost 9.917
So having said, he thus to *Eve* in few: Par Lost 10.157
So having said, a while he stood, expecting Par Lost 10.504
Who having spilt much blood, and don much waste Par Lost 11.791
This having learnt, thou hast attaind the summe Par Lost 12.575
This having heard, strait I again revolv'd Par Reg 1.259
The way he came not having mark'd, return Par Reg 1.297
These having shewn thee, I have shewn thee all Par Reg 4.88
They had anough reveng'd, having reduc't Samson 1468
Who having clad thy self in humane weed, Fair Inf 58
A hunder'd-fold, who having learnt thy way Sonnet 18, 13
Having to advise the public may speak free, Prose 9, 2

Havoc
Havock and spoil and ruin are my gain. Par Lost 2.1009
1667 'Havook' in some copies
Sore toild, his riv'n Armes to havoc hewn, Par Lost 6.449
With long and tedious havoc fabl'd Knights Par Lost 9.30
To waste and havoc yonder World, which I Par Lost 10.617

Hawthorn
Under the Hawthorn in the dale. Allegro 68

Haycock
To the tann'd Haycock in the Mead, Allegro 90

Hazard
And hazard in the Glorious Enterprize, Par Lost 1.89
Of hazard as of honour, due alike Par Lost 2.453
Of hazard more, as he above the rest Par Lost 2.455
Which he through hazard huge must earn. But they Par Lost 2.473
A faithful Leader, not to hazard all Par Lost 4.933
Let us advise, and to this hazard draw Par Lost 5.729
Without our hazard, labour, or allarme, Par Lost 10.491
Of hazard, which admits no long debate, Par Reg 1.95
To the hazard of thy brains and shatter'd sides. Samson 1241

Hazardous
Of the enterprize so hazardous and high; Par Reg 3.228

Hazel
The Willows, and the Hazle Copses green, Lycidas 42
Trinity ms 'haze'l'
1638 'hasil-copses'

He
Th' infernal Serpent; he it was, whose guile Par Lost 1.34
ms 'hee'
He trusted to have equal'd the most High, Par Lost 1.40
ms 'Hee'
If he oppos'd; and with ambitious aim Par Lost 1.41
To mortal men, he with his horrid crew Par Lost 1.51
ms 'hee'
Torments him; round he throws his baleful eyes Par Lost 1.56
At once as far as Angels kenn he views Par Lost 1.59
He soon discerns, and weltring by his side Par Lost 1.78
ms 'Hee'
If thou beest he; But O how fall'n! how chang'd Par Lost 1.84
Myriads though bright: If he whom mutual league, Par Lost 1.87
ms 'hee'

He(*cont*)
He with his Thunder: and till then who knew Par Lost 1.93
ms 'Hee'
But what if he our Conquerour, (whom I now Par Lost 1.143
ms 'hee'
That with reiterated crimes he might Par Lost 1.214
ms 'hee'
Heap on himself damnation, while he sought Par Lost 1.215
ms 'hee'
Forthwith upright he rears from off the Pool Par Lost 1.221
Then with expanded wings he stears his flight Par Lost 1.225
He lights, if it were Land that ever burn'd Par Lost 1.228
For that celestial light? Be it so, since he Par Lost 1.245
1667 'hee'
And what I should be, all but less then he Par Lost 1.257
1667 'hee'
He scarce had ceas't when the superiour Fiend Par Lost 1.283
ms 'Hee'
He walkt with to support uneasie steps Par Lost 1.295
Nathless he so endur'd, till on the Beach Par Lost 1.299
ms 'hee'
Of that inflamed Sea, he stood and call'd Par Lost 1.300
ms 'hee'
He call'd so loud, that all the hollow Deep Par Lost 1.314
Came singly where he stood on the bare strand, Par Lost 1.379
ms 'hee'
Of *Solomon* he led by fraud to build Par Lost 1.401
ms 'hee'
Peor his other Name, when he entic'd Par Lost 1.412
Yet thence his lustful Orgies he enlarg'd Par Lost 1.415
Where he fell flat, and sham'd his Worshipers: Par Lost 1.461
He also against the house of God was bold: Par Lost 1.470
A Leper once he lost and gain'd a King, Par Lost 1.471
Ahaz his sottish Conquerour, whom he drew Par Lost 1.472
Whom he had vanquisht. After these appear'd Par Lost 1.476
Jehovah, who in one Night when he pass'd Par Lost 1.487
Or Altar smoak'd; yet who more oft then hee Par Lost 1.493
In Courts and Palaces he also Reigns Par Lost 1.497
By younger *Saturn*, he from mightier *Jove* Par Lost 1.512
ms 'hee'
Like doubtful hue: but he his wonted pride Par Lost 1.527
Had to impose: He through the armed Files Par Lost 1.567
ms 'hee'
Thir number last he summs. And now his heart Par Lost 1.571
Thir dread commander: he above the rest Par Lost 1.589
ms 'hee'
Stands on the blasted Heath. He now prepar'd Par Lost 1.615
Thrice he assayd, and thrice in spight of scorn, Par Lost 1.619
By mee, have lost our hopes. But he who reigns Par Lost 1.637
What force effected not: that he no less Par Lost 1.647
There went a fame in Heav'n that he ere long Par Lost 1.651
ms 'hee'
He spake: and to confirm his words, out-flew Par Lost 1.663
Men call'd him *Mulciber;* and how he fell Par Lost 1.740
To Noon he fell, from Noon to dewy Eve, Par Lost 1.743
Erring; for he with this rebellious rout Par Lost 1.747
To have built in Heav'n high Towrs; nor did he scape Par Lost 1.749
Or dreams he sees, while over-head the Moon Par Lost 1.784
ms 'hee'
He ceas'd, and next him *Moloc*, Scepter'd King Par Lost 2.43
He reck'd not, and these words thereafter spake. Par Lost 2.50
Of his Almighty Engin he shall hear Par Lost 2.65
He ended frowning, and his look denounc'd Par Lost 2.106
A fairer person lost not Heav'n; he seemd Par Lost 2.110
Timorous and slothful: yet he pleas'd the ear, Par Lost 2.117
When he who most excels in fact of Arms, Par Lost 2.124
In what he counsels and in what excels Par Lost 2.125
Can give it, or will ever? how he can Par Lost 2.153
Is doubtful; that he never will is sure. Par Lost 2.154
Will he, so wise, let loose at once his ire, Par Lost 2.155
Views all things at one view? he from heav'ns highth Par Lost 2.190
We overpower? Suppose he should relent Par Lost 2.237
Forc't Halleluiah's; while he Lordly sits Par Lost 2.243
As he our darkness, cannot we his Light Par Lost 2.269
He scarce had finisht, when such murmur filld Par Lost 2.284
Aspect he rose, and in his rising seem'd Par Lost 2.301
Majestic though in ruin: sage he stood Par Lost 2.305
Or Summers Noon-tide air, while thus he spake. Par Lost 2.309
His captive multitude: For he, be sure Par Lost 2.323
They vote: whereat his speech he thus renews. Par Lost 2.389
Over the vast abrupt, ere he arrive Par Lost 2.409
Of Angels watching round? Here he had need Par Lost 2.413
This said, he sat; and expectation held Par Lost 2.417
If thence he scape into whatever world, Par Lost 2.442
Of hazard more, as he above the rest Par Lost 2.455
Which he through hazard huge must earn. But they Par Lost 2.473
That for the general safety he despis'd Par Lost 2.481
Leads him perplext, where he may likeliest find Par Lost 2.525
He scours the right hand coast, som times the left, Par Lost 2.633
With horrid strides, Hell trembled as he strode. Par Lost 2.676
Created thing naught valu'd he nor shun'd; Par Lost 2.679
Art thou that Traitor Angel, art thou hee, Par Lost 2.689
What e're his wrath, which he calls Justice, bids, Par Lost 2.733
Transform'd: but he my inbred enemie Par Lost 2.785
I fled, but he pursu'd (though more, it seems, Par Lost 2.790
For want of other prey, but that he knows Par Lost 2.806
Save he who reigns above, none can resist. Par Lost 2.814
He ceas'd, for both seemd highly pleasd, and Death Par Lost 2.845

He(*cont*)

Hee rules a moment; *Chaos* Umpire sits,	Par Lost 2.907
By which he Reigns: next him high Arbiter	Par Lost 2.909
He had to cross. Nor was his eare less peal'd	Par Lost 2.920
He spreads for flight, and in the surging smoak	Par Lost 2.928
Fluttring his pennons vain plumb down he drops	Par Lost 2.933
Nor good dry Land: nigh founderd on he fares,	Par Lost 2.940
With loudest vehemence: thither he plyes,	Par Lost 2.954
He ceas'd; and *Satan* staid not to reply,	Par Lost 2.1010
So he with difficulty and labour hard	Par Lost 2.1021
Mov'd on, with difficulty and labour hee;	Par Lost 2.1022
But hee once past, soon after when man fell,	Par Lost 2.1023
Accurst, and in a cursed hour he hies.	Par Lost 2.1055
From the pure Empyrean where he sits	Par Lost 3.57
His onely Son; On Earth he first beheld	Par Lost 3.64
In blissful solitude; he then survey'd	Par Lost 3.69
Wherein past, present, future he beholds,	Par Lost 3.78
Wide interrupt can hold; so bent he seems	Par Lost 3.84
Through all restraint broke loose he wings his way	Par Lost 3.87
If him by force he can destroy, or worse,	Par Lost 3.91
Hee and his faithless Progenie: whose fault?	Par Lost 3.96
Whose but his own? ingrate, he had of mee	Par Lost 3.97
All he could have; I made him just and right,	Par Lost 3.98
Which uttering thus he to his Father spake.	Par Lost 3.143
His end, and frustrate thine, shall he fulfill	Par Lost 3.157
Upheld by me, yet once more he shall stand	Par Lost 3.178
By me upheld, that he may know how frail	Par Lost 3.180
He with his whole posteritie must dye,	Par Lost 3.209
Dye hee or Justice must; unless for him	Par Lost 3.210
He ask'd, but all the Heav'nly Quire stood mute,	Par Lost 3.217
Happie for man, so coming; he her aide	Par Lost 3.232
Glad to be offer'd, he attends the will	Par Lost 3.270
Hee Heav'n of Heavens and all the Powers therein	Par Lost 3.390
He to appease thy wrauth, and end the strife	Par Lost 3.406
Regardless of the Bliss wherein hee sat	Par Lost 3.408
Others came single; he who to be deemd	Par Lost 3.469
1667 'hee'	
Empedocles, and hee who to enjoy	Par Lost 3.471
All this dark Globe the Fiend found as he pass'd,	Par Lost 3.498
And long he wanderd, till at last a gleame	Par Lost 3.499
His travell'd steps; farr distant he descries	Par Lost 3.501
1667 'hee'	
Of Guardians bright, when he from *Esau* fled	Par Lost 3.512
Round he surveys, and well might, where he stood	Par Lost 3.555
He views in bredth, and without longer pause	Par Lost 3.561
He stayd not to enquire: above them all	Par Lost 3.571
Allur'd his eye: Thither his course he bends	Par Lost 3.573
The place he found beyond expression bright,	Par Lost 3.591
To objects distant farr, whereby he soon	Par Lost 3.621
He seemd, or fixt in cogitation deep.	Par Lost 3.629
1667 'Hee'	
But first he casts to change his proper shape,	Par Lost 3.634
And now a stripling Cherube he appeers,	Par Lost 3.636
Sutable grace diffus'd, so well he feignd;	Par Lost 3.639
In curles on either cheek plaid, wings he wore	Par Lost 3.641
He drew not nigh unheard, the Angel bright,	Par Lost 3.645
Ere he drew nigh, his radiant visage turnd,	Par Lost 3.646
All these his works so wondrous he ordaind,	Par Lost 3.665
Thus said, he turnd, and *Satan* bowing low,	Par Lost 3.736
Nor staid, till on *Niphates* top he lights.	Par Lost 3.742
O for that warning voice, which he who saw	Par Lost 4.1
He brings, and round about him, nor from Hell	Par Lost 4.21
Of what he was, what is, and what must be	Par Lost 4.25
Lay pleasant, his grievd look he fixes sad,	Par Lost 4.28
Ah wherefore! he deservd no such return	Par Lost 4.42
From me, whom he created what I was	Par Lost 4.43
From granting hee, as I from begging peace:	Par Lost 4.104
Thus while he spake, each passion dimm'd his face	Par Lost 4.114
Are ever cleer. Whereof hee soon aware,	Par Lost 4.119
The way he went, and on th' *Assyrian* mount	Par Lost 4.126
He markd and mad demeanour, then alone,	Par Lost 4.129
As he suppos'd, all unobserv'd, unseen.	Par Lost 4.130
So on he fares, and to the border comes,	Par Lost 4.131
Due entrance he disdaind, and in contempt,	Par Lost 4.180
Thence up he flew, and on the Tree of Life	Par Lost 4.194
Beneath him with new wonder now he views	Par Lost 4.205
Out of the fertil ground he caus'd to grow	Par Lost 4.216
For contemplation hee and valour formd,	Par Lost 4.297
Hee for God only, shee for God in him:	Par Lost 4.299
When *Satan* still in gaze, as first he stood,	Par Lost 4.356
Accept your Makers work; he gave it me,	Par Lost 4.380
Down he alights among the sportful Herd	Par Lost 4.396
To mark what of thir state he more might learn	Par Lost 4.400
A Lion now he stalkes with fierie glare,	Par Lost 4.402
Whence rushing he might surest seize them both	Par Lost 4.407
Aught whereof hee hath need, hee who requires	Par Lost 4.419
Thy coming, and thy soft imbraces, hee	Par Lost 4.471
Of her loose tresses hid: he in delight	Par Lost 4.497
On *Juno* smiles, when he impregns the Clouds	Par Lost 4.500
So saying, his proud step he scornful turn'd,	Par Lost 4.536
Impetuous winds: he thus began in haste.	Par Lost 4.560
A Spirit, zealous, as he seem'd, to know	Par Lost 4.565
Where he first lighted, soon discernd his looks	Par Lost 4.570
In whatsoever shape he lurk, of whom	Par Lost 4.587
So promis'd hee, and *Uriel* to his charge	Par Lost 4.589
When first on this delightful Land he spreads	Par Lost 4.643
Chos'n by the sovran Planter, when he fram'd	Par Lost 4.691
From these, two strong and suttle Spirits he calld	Par Lost 4.786

He(*cont*)

So saying, on he led his radiant Files,	Par Lost 4.797
Illusions as he list, Phantasms and Dreams,	Par Lost 4.803
Or if, inspiring venom, he might taint	Par Lost 4.804
Of force to its own likeness: up he starts	Par Lost 4.813
Undaunted. If I must contend, said he,	Par Lost 4.851
He held it vain; awe from above had quelld	Par Lost 4.860
He scarce had ended, when those two approachd	Par Lost 4.874
His Iron Gates, if he intends our stay	Par Lost 4.898
Thus he in scorn. The warlike Angel mov'd,	Par Lost 4.902
1667 'hee'	
So wise he judges it to fly from pain	Par Lost 4.910
So threatn'd hee, but *Satan* to no threats	Par Lost 4.968
While thus he spake, th' Angelic Squadron bright	Par Lost 4.977
Wherein all things created first he weighd,	Par Lost 4.999
Battels and Realms: in these he put two weights	Par Lost 4.1002
As through unquiet rest: he on his side	Par Lost 5.11
Ambrosia; on that Tree he also gaz'd;	Par Lost 5.57
And O fair Plant, said he, with fruit surcharg'd,	Par Lost 5.58
This said he paus'd not, but with ventrous Arme	Par Lost 5.64
He pluckt, he tasted; mee damp horror chil'd	Par Lost 5.65
But he thus overjoy'd, O Fruit Divine,	Par Lost 5.67
So saying, he drew nigh, and to me held,	Par Lost 5.82
Which he had pluckt; the pleasant savourie smell	Par Lost 5.84
So cheard he his fair Spouse, and she was cheard,	Par Lost 5.129
Each in thir Chrystal sluce, hee ere they fell	Par Lost 5.133
1667 'he' in some copies	
Raphael, said hee, thou hear'st what stir on Earth	Par Lost 5.224
This night the human pair, how he designes	Par Lost 5.227
He swerve not too secure: tell him withall	Par Lost 5.238
Least wilfully transgressing he pretend	Par Lost 5.244
Thousand Celestial Ardors, where he stood	Par Lost 5.249
Starr interpos'd, however small he sees,	Par Lost 5.258
He speeds, and through the vast Ethereal Skie	Par Lost 5.267
Of Towring Eagles, to all the Fowles he seems	Par Lost 5.271
Bright Temple, to *Aegyptian Theb's* he flies.	Par Lost 5.274
He lights, and to his proper shape returns	Par Lost 5.276
A Seraph wingd; six wings he wore, to shade	Par Lost 5.277
Skie-tinctur'd grain. Like *Maia's* son he stood,	Par Lost 5.285
Thir glittering Tents he passd, and now is come	Par Lost 5.291
Adam discernd, as in the dore he sat	Par Lost 5.299
To us perhaps he brings, and will voutsafe	Par Lost 5.312
To entertain our Angel guest, as hee	Par Lost 5.328
To whom the Angel. Therefore what he gives	Par Lost 5.404
Who dwell in Heav'n, whose excellence he saw	Par Lost 5.456
Thus to th' Empyreal Minister he fram'd.	Par Lost 5.460
And good he made thee, but to persevere	Par Lost 5.525
He left it in thy power, ordaind thy will	Par Lost 5.526
Our voluntarie service he requires,	Par Lost 5.529
Is heard no more in Heav'n; he of the first,	Par Lost 5.659
Friendliest to sleep and silence, he resolv'd	Par Lost 5.668
Of his Associate; hee together calls,	Par Lost 5.696
Under him Regent, tells, as he was taught,	Par Lost 5.698
Interpreted) which not long after, he	Par Lost 5.762
1667 'hee'	
For thither he assembl'd all his Train,	Par Lost 5.767
Such as he pleasd, and circumscrib'd thir being?	Par Lost 5.825
How provident he is, how farr from thought	Par Lost 5.828
But more illustrious made, since he the Head	Par Lost 5.842
He said, and as the sound of waters deep	Par Lost 5.872
Among the faithless, faithful only hee;	Par Lost 5.897
His Loyaltie he kept, his Love, his Zeale;	Par Lost 5.900
Though single. From amidst them forth he passd,	Par Lost 5.903
Long way through hostile scorn, which he susteind	Par Lost 5.904
And with retorted scorn his back he turn'd	Par Lost 5.906
Warr he perceav'd, warr in procinct, and found	Par Lost 6.19
Already known what he for news had thought	Par Lost 6.20
To have reported: gladly then he mixt	Par Lost 6.21
Abdiel that sight endur'd not, where he stood	Par Lost 6.111
That he who in debate of Truth hath won,	Par Lost 6.122
Forth stepping opposite, half way he met	Par Lost 6.128
When he who rules is worthiest, and excells	Par Lost 6.177
Them whom he governs. This is servitude,	Par Lost 6.178
So saying, a noble stroke he lifted high,	Par Lost 6.189
He back recoild; the tenth on bended knee	Par Lost 6.194
He hasted, and oppos'd the rockie Orb	Par Lost 6.254
Yet soon he heal'd; for Spirits that live throughout	Par Lost 6.344
He sat; and in th' assembly next upstood	Par Lost 6.446
As one he stood escap't from cruel fight,	Par Lost 6.448
All patience. He who therefore can invent	Par Lost 6.464
He ended, and his words thir drooping chere	Par Lost 6.496
Th' invention all admir'd, and each, how hee	Par Lost 6.498
He comes, and settl'd in his face I see	Par Lost 6.540
So warnd he them aware themselves, and soon	Par Lost 6.547
So scoffing in ambiguous words he scarce,	Par Lost 6.568
Had not th' Almightie Father where he sits	Par Lost 6.671
That his great purpose he might so fulfill,	Par Lost 6.675
Th' Assessor of his Throne he thus began.	Par Lost 6.679
He said, and on his Son with Rayes direct	Par Lost 6.719
Shon full, he all his Father full exprest	Par Lost 6.720
So said, he o're his Scepter bowing, rose	Par Lost 6.746
From the right hand of Glorie where he sate,	Par Lost 6.747
Hee in Celestial Panoplie all armd	Par Lost 6.760
He onward came, farr off his coming shon,	Par Lost 6.768
Hee on the wings of Cherub rode sublime	Par Lost 6.771
Vengeance is his, or whose he sole appoints;	Par Lost 6.808
Therefore to mee thir doom he hath assig'n'd;	Par Lost 6.817
Hee on his impious Foes right onward drove,	Par Lost 6.831

He*(cont)*

Among them he arriv'd; in his right hand	Par Lost 6.835
Grasping ten thousand Thunders, which he sent	Par Lost 6.836
O're Shields and Helmes, and helmed heads he rode	Par Lost 6.840
Yet half his strength he put not forth, but check'd	Par Lost 6.853
His Thunder in mid Volie, for he meant	Par Lost 6.854
The overthrown he rais'd, and as a Heard	Par Lost 6.856
Worthiest to Reign: he celebrated rode	Par Lost 6.888
Where now he sits at the right hand of bliss.	Par Lost 6.892
With *Satan*, hee who envies now thy state,	Par Lost 6.900
Who now is plotting how he may seduce	Par Lost 6.901
Though wandring. He with his consorted *Eve*	Par Lost 7.50
Held by thy voice, thy potent voice he heares,	Par Lost 7.100
He trusted to have seis'd, and into fraud	Par Lost 7.143
So spake th' Almightie, and to what he spake	Par Lost 7.174
He took the golden Compasses, prepar'd	Par Lost 7.225
One foot he center'd, and the other turn'd	Par Lost 7.228
He nam'd. Thus was the first Day Eev'n and Morn:	Par Lost 7.252
Dividing: for as Earth, so he the World	Par Lost 7.269
1667 'hee'	
And Heav'n he nam'd the Firmament: So Eev'n	Par Lost 7.274
Of congregated Waters he call'd Seas:	Par Lost 7.308
He scarce had said, when the bare Earth, till then	Par Lost 7.313
A mightie Spheare he fram'd, unlightsom first,	Par Lost 7.355
Of Light by farr the greater part he took,	Par Lost 7.359
As from his Laire the wilde Beast where he wonns	Par Lost 7.457
Eternal Father (For where is not hee	Par Lost 7.517
This said, he formd thee, *Adam*, thee O Man	Par Lost 7.524
The breath of Life; in his own Image hee	Par Lost 7.526
Male he created thee, but thy consort	Par Lost 7.529
He brought thee into this delicious Grove,	Par Lost 7.537
Here finish'd hee, and all that he had made	Par Lost 7.548
Answering his great Idea. Up he rode	Par Lost 7.557
The glorious Train ascending: He through Heav'n,	Par Lost 7.574
With his great Father (for he also went	Par Lost 7.588
So Charming left his voice, that he a while	Par Lost 8.2
line not in 1667 edition	
Chose rather; hee, she knew would intermix	Par Lost 8.54
Conjecture, he his Fabric of the Heav'ns	Par Lost 8.76
That Man may know he dwells not in his own;	Par Lost 8.103
Hee from the East his flaming rode begin,	Par Lost 8.162
In what he gives to thee, this Paradise	Par Lost 8.171
Least hee incenst at such eruption bold,	Par Lost 8.235
But us he sends upon his high behests	Par Lost 8.238
So saying, by the hand he took me rais'd,	Par Lost 8.300
My wandring, had not hee who was my Guide	Par Lost 8.312
Submiss: he rear'd me, and Whom thou soughtst I am,	Par Lost 8.316
Of woe and sorrow. Sternly he pronounc'd	Par Lost 8.333
As thus he spake, each Bird and Beast behold	Par Lost 8.349
He ceas'd, I lowly answer'd. To attaine	Par Lost 8.412
Hee ended, or I heard no more, for now	Par Lost 8.452
Mine eyes he clos'd, but op'n left the Cell	Par Lost 8.460
The Rib he formd and fashond with his hands;	Par Lost 8.469
Extracted; for this cause he shall forgoe	Par Lost 8.497
So saying, he arose; whom *Adam* thus	Par Lost 8.644
By Night he fled, and at Midnight return'd	Par Lost 9.58
The space of seven continu'd Nights he rode	Par Lost 9.63
He circl'd, four times cross'd the Carr of Night	Par Lost 9.65
Where to lie hid; Sea he had searcht and Land	Par Lost 9.76
Ganges and *Indus:* thus the Orb he roam'd	Par Lost 9.82
Thus he resolv'd, but first from inward griefe	Par Lost 9.97
What he *Almightie* styl'd, six Nights and Days	Par Lost 9.137
Of his adorers: hee to be aveng'd,	Par Lost 9.143
With Heav'nly spoils, our spoils: What he decreed	Par Lost 9.151
He effected; Man he made, and for him built	Par Lost 9.152
As high he soard, obnoxious first or last	Par Lost 9.170
Like a black mist low creeping, he held on	Par Lost 9.180
His midnight search, where soonest he might finde	Par Lost 9.181
The Serpent: him fast sleeping soon he found	Par Lost 9.182
Fearless unfeard he slept: in at his Mouth	Par Lost 9.187
He made us, and delight to Reason joyn'd.	Par Lost 9.243
For hee who tempts, though in vain, at least asperses	Par Lost 9.296
Suttle he needs must be, who could seduce	Par Lost 9.307
Of all that he Created, much less Man,	Par Lost 9.346
Against his will he can receave no harme.	Par Lost 9.350
Reason, is free, and Reason he made right,	Par Lost 9.352
Oft he to her his charge of quick returne	Par Lost 9.399
And on his Quest, where likeliest he might finde	Par Lost 9.414
In Bowre and Field he sought, where any tuft	Par Lost 9.417
He sought them both, but wish'd his hap might find	Par Lost 9.421
Eve separate, he wish'd, but not with hope	Par Lost 9.422
Beyond his hope, *Eve* separate he spies,	Par Lost 9.424
Neerer he drew, and many a walk travers'd	Par Lost 9.434
Much hee the Place admir'd, the Person more.	Par Lost 9.444
And tortures him now more, the more he sees	Par Lost 9.469
Fierce hate he recollects, and all his thoughts	Par Lost 9.471
Hee with *Olympias*, this with her who bore	Par Lost 9.509
To interrupt, side-long he works his way.	Par Lost 9.512
So varied hee, and of his tortuous Traine	Par Lost 9.516
Hee boulder now, uncall'd before her stood;	Par Lost 9.523
But as in gaze admiring: Oft he bowd	Par Lost 9.524
The Eye of *Eve* to mark his play; he glad	Par Lost 9.528
Lead then, said *Eve*. Hee leading swiftly rowld	Par Lost 9.631
His worshippers; he knows that in the day	Par Lost 9.705
He ended, and his words replete with guile	Par Lost 9.733
Thy praise hee also who forbids thy use,	Par Lost 9.750
In plain then, what forbids he but to know,	Par Lost 9.758
How dies the Serpent? hee hath eat'n and lives,	Par Lost 9.764

He*(cont)*

Great joy he promis'd to his thoughts, and new	Par Lost 9.843
Misgave him; hee the faultring measure felt;	Par Lost 9.846
Of Knowledge he must pass, there he her met,	Par Lost 9.849
On th' other side, *Adam*, soon as he heard	Par Lost 9.888
Speechless he stood and pale, till thus at length	Par Lost 9.894
First to himself he inward silence broke.	Par Lost 9.895
Thus in calm mood his Words to *Eve* he turnd.	Par Lost 9.920
Nor yet on him found deadly, he yet lives,	Par Lost 9.932
He ruind, now Mankind; whom will he next?	Par Lost 9.950
Tenderly wept, much won that he his Love	Par Lost 9.991
With liberal hand: he scrupl'd not to eat	Par Lost 9.997
Carnal desire enflaming, hee on *Eve*	Par Lost 9.1013
So said he, and forbore not glance or toy	Par Lost 9.1034
Her hand he seis'd, and to a shadie bank,	Par Lost 9.1037
He led her nothing loath; Flours were the Couch,	Par Lost 9.1039
To guiltie shame hee cover'd, but his Robe	Par Lost 9.1058
So counsel'd hee, and both together went	Par Lost 9.1099
Fraud in the Serpent, speaking as he spake;	Par Lost 9.1150
Why hee should mean me ill, or seek to harme.	Par Lost 9.1152
Hee in the Serpent, had perverted *Eve*,	Par Lost 10.3
I told ye then he should prevail and speed	Par Lost 10.40
In eevn scale. But fall'n he is, and now	Par Lost 10.47
Which he presumes already vain and void,	Par Lost 10.50
Because not yet inflicted, as he fear'd,	Par Lost 10.51
Blaz'd forth unclouded Deitie; he full	Par Lost 10.65
Thus saying, from his radiant Seat he rose	Par Lost 10.85
Down he descended strait; the speed of Gods	Par Lost 10.90
The Eevning coole when he from wrauth more coole	Par Lost 10.95
He came, and with him *Eve*, more loth, though first	Par Lost 10.109
So having said, he thus to *Eve* in few:	Par Lost 10.157
To Judgement he proceeded on th' accus'd	Par Lost 10.164
Concern'd not Man (since he no further knew)	Par Lost 10.170
Whom he shall tread at last under our feet;	Par Lost 10.190
Eevn hee who now foretold his fatal bruise,	Par Lost 10.191
Thine shall submit, hee over thee shall rule.	Par Lost 10.196
On *Adam* last thus judgement he pronounc'd.	Par Lost 10.197
So judg'd he Man, both Judge and Saviour sent,	Par Lost 10.209
As when he wash'd his servants feet so now	Par Lost 10.215
As Father of his Familie he clad	Par Lost 10.216
Nor hee thir outward onely with the Skins	Par Lost 10.220
To him with swift ascent he up returnd,	Par Lost 10.224
Ere this he had return'd, with fury driv'n	Par Lost 10.240
So saying, with delight he snuff'd the smell	Par Lost 10.272
Of *Satan*, to the self same place where hee	Par Lost 10.315
Disguis'd he came, but those his Children dear	Par Lost 10.330
Hee after *Eve* seduc't, unminded slunk	Par Lost 10.332
Vain covertures; but when he saw descend	Par Lost 10.337
Hee fled, not hoping to escape, but shun	Par Lost 10.339
And tidings fraught, to Hell he now return'd,	Par Lost 10.346
Long hee admiring stood, till Sin, his faire	Par Lost 10.352
So saying he dismiss'd them, they with speed	Par Lost 10.410
Might intercept thir Emperour sent, so hee	Par Lost 10.429
Of Forrein Worlds: he through the midst unmarkt,	Par Lost 10.441
He sate, and round about him saw unseen:	Par Lost 10.448
Your wonder, with an Apple; he thereat	Par Lost 10.487
To rule, as over all he should have rul'd.	Par Lost 10.493
True is, mee also he hath judg'd, or rather	Par Lost 10.494
Is enmity, which he will put between	Par Lost 10.497
So having said, a while he stood, expecting	Par Lost 10.504
To fill his eare, when contrary he hears	Par Lost 10.506
Of public scorn; he wonderd, but not long	Par Lost 10.509
His Visage drawn he felt to sharp and spare,	Par Lost 10.511
Each other, till supplanted down he fell	Par Lost 10.513
Now rul'd him, punisht in the shape he sin'd,	Par Lost 10.516
According to his doom: he would have spoke,	Par Lost 10.517
Ophiusa) but still greatest hee the midst,	Par Lost 10.528
Huge *Python*, and his Power no less he seem'd	Par Lost 10.531
He ended, and the heav'nly Audience loud	Par Lost 10.641
1667 'Hee'	
Some say he bid his Angels turne ascanse	Par Lost 10.668
But mortal doom'd. How can he exercise	Par Lost 10.796
Can he make deathless Death? that were to make	Par Lost 10.798
Of weakness, not of Power. Will he, draw out,	Par Lost 10.801
Outstretcht he lay, on the cold ground, and oft	Par Lost 10.851
Said hee, with one thrice acceptable stroke	Par Lost 10.855
But her with stern regard he thus repell'd.	Par Lost 10.866
He never shall find out fit Mate, but such	Par Lost 10.899
Or whom he wishes most shall seldom gain	Par Lost 10.901
He added not, and from her turn'd, but *Eve*	Par Lost 10.909
As one disarm'd, his anger all he lost,	Par Lost 10.945
Let us seek Death, or he not found, supply	Par Lost 10.1001
1667 'hee'	
And gracious temper he both heard and judg'd	Par Lost 10.1047
Cloath'd us unworthie, pitying while he judg'd;	Par Lost 10.1059
Hee will instruct us praying, and of Grace	Par Lost 10.1081
Repairing where he judg'd us, prostrate fall	Par Lost 10.1087
Undoubtedly he will relent and turn	Par Lost 10.1093
When angry most he seem'd and most severe,	Par Lost 10.1095
Repairing where he judg'd them prostrate fell	Par Lost 10.1099
He ended, and the Son gave signal high	Par Lost 11.72
To the bright Minister that watchd, hee blew	Par Lost 11.73
He sorrows now, repents, and prayes contrite,	Par Lost 11.90
The Ground whence he was taken, fitter soile.	Par Lost 11.98
He ceas'd; and th' Archangelic Power prepar'd	Par Lost 11.126
He err'd not, for by this the heav'nly Bands	Par Lost 11.208
Jacob in *Mahanaim*, where he saw	Par Lost 11.214
Possession of the Garden; hee alone,	Par Lost 11.222

He(*cont*)

He ended; and th' Arch-Angel soon drew nigh,	Par Lost 11.238
Adam bowd low, hee Kingly from his State	Par Lost 11.249
He added not, for *Adam* at the newes	Par Lost 11.263
Where he abides, think there thy native soile.	Par Lost 11.292
With worship, place by place where he voutsaf'd	Par Lost 11.318
On this Mount he appeerd, under this Tree	Par Lost 11.320
All th' Earth he gave thee to possess and rule,	Par Lost 11.339
The World: in Spirit perhaps he also saw	Par Lost 11.406
The visual Nerve, for he had much to see;	Par Lost 11.415
His eyes he op'nd, and beheld a field,	Par Lost 11.429
Whereat hee inlie rag'd, and as they talk'd,	Par Lost 11.444
That beat out life; he fell, and deadly pale	Par Lost 11.446
T' whom *Michael* thus, hee also mov'd, repli'd.	Par Lost 11.453
He lookd and saw a spacious Plaine, whereon	Par Lost 11.556
From underground) the liquid Ore he dreind	Par Lost 11.570
Into fit moulds prepar'd; from which he formd	Par Lost 11.571
The bent of Nature; which he thus express'd.	Par Lost 11.597
He lookd and saw wide Territorie spred	Par Lost 11.638
But hee the seventh from thee, whom thou beheldst	Par Lost 11.700
He look'd, and saw the face of things quite chang'd,	Par Lost 11.712
And testifi'd against thir wayes; hee oft	Par Lost 11.721
But all in vain: which when he saw, he ceas'd	Par Lost 11.726
Him or his Childern, evil he may be sure,	Par Lost 11.772
And hee the future evil shall no less	Par Lost 11.774
Or violence, hee of thir wicked wayes	Par Lost 11.812
No sooner hee with them of Man and Beast	Par Lost 11.822
He lookd, and saw the Ark hull on the flood,	Par Lost 11.840
An Olive leafe he brings, pacific signe:	Par Lost 11.860
Griev'd at his heart, when looking down he saw	Par Lost 11.887
That he relents, not to blot out mankind,	Par Lost 11.891
With Man therein or Beast; but when he brings	Par Lost 11.895
A mightie Hunter thence he shall be styl'd	Par Lost 12.33
Though of Rebellion others he accuse.	Par Lost 12.37
Hee with a crew, whom like Ambition joyns	Par Lost 12.38
He gave us onely over Beast, Fish, Fowl	Par Lost 12.67
He made not Lord; such title to himself	Par Lost 12.70
Will he convey up thither to sustain	Par Lost 12.75
Man till then free. Therefore since hee permits	Par Lost 12.90
Which he will shew him, and from him will raise	Par Lost 12.123
All Nations shall be blest; he straight obeys,	Par Lost 12.126
1667 'hee'	
He leaves his Gods, his Friends, and native Soile	Par Lost 12.129
Canaan he now attains, I see his Tents	Par Lost 12.135
Of *Moreh;* there by promise he receaves	Par Lost 12.137
He comes invited by a yonger Son	Par Lost 12.160
Of *Pharao:* there he dies, and leaves his Race	Par Lost 12.163
Too numerous; whence of guests he makes them slaves	Par Lost 12.167
Pursuing whom he late dismissd, the Sea	Par Lost 12.195
All night he will pursue, but his approach	Par Lost 12.206
Shall tremble, he descending, will himself	Par Lost 12.228
The Serpent, by what means he shall achieve	Par Lost 12.234
And terror cease; he grants what they besaught	Par Lost 12.238
One greater, of whose day he shall foretell,	Par Lost 12.242
Obedient to his will, that he voutsafes	Par Lost 12.246
From whom as oft he saves them penitent	Par Lost 12.319
There in captivitie he lets them dwell	Par Lost 12.344
The Power of the most High; he shall ascend	Par Lost 12.369
He ceas'd, discerning *Adam* with such joy	Par Lost 12.372
Without the vent of words, which these he breathd.	Par Lost 12.374
Which hee, who comes thy Saviour, shall recure,	Par Lost 12.393
The Law of God exact he shall fulfill	Par Lost 12.402
He shall endure by coming in the Flesh	Par Lost 12.405
For this he shall live hated, be blasphem'd,	Par Lost 12.411
But to the Cross he nailes thy Enemies,	Par Lost 12.415
In this his satisfaction; so he dies,	Par Lost 12.419
Or theirs whom he redeems, a death like sleep,	Par Lost 12.434
Nor after resurrection shall he stay	Par Lost 12.436
Then to the Heav'n of Heav'ns he shall ascend	Par Lost 12.451
Hee to his own a Comforter will send,	Par Lost 12.486
Powrd first on his Apostles, whom he sends	Par Lost 12.498
He ended; and thus *Adam* last reply'd.	Par Lost 12.552
He ended, and they both descend the Hill;	Par Lost 12.606
Which he hath sent propitious, some great good	Par Lost 12.612
With looks agast and sad he thus bespake.	Par Reg 1.43
And he himself among them was baptiz'd,	Par Reg 1.76
The testimony of Heaven, that who he is	Par Reg 1.78
He who obtains the Monarchy of Heav'n,	Par Reg 1.87
And what will he not do to advance his Son?	Par Reg 1.88
Who this is we must learn, for man he seems	Par Reg 1.91
E're in the head of Nations he appear	Par Reg 1.98
He ended, and his words impression left	Par Reg 1.106
So to the Coast of *Jordan* he directs	Par Reg 1.119
Where he might likeliest find this new-declar'd,	Par Reg 1.121
So to subvert whom he suspected rais'd	Par Reg 1.124
But contrary unweeting he fulfill'd	Par Reg 1.126
His utmost subtilty, because he boasts	Par Reg 1.144
Of his Apostasie; he might have learnt	Par Reg 1.146
Less over-weening, since he fail'd in *Job*,	Par Reg 1.147
He now shall know I can produce a man	Par Reg 1.150
There he shall first lay down the rudiments	Par Reg 1.157
How best the mighty work he might begin	Par Reg 1.186
He entred now the bordering Desert wild,	Par Reg 1.193
Conceiv'd in me a Virgin, he fore-told	Par Reg 1.239
Which I believ'd was from above; but he	Par Reg 1.274
Me him whose Harbinger he was; and first	Par Reg 1.277
He was well pleas'd; by which I knew the time	Par Reg 1.286
The way he came not having mark'd, return	Par Reg 1.297

He(*cont*)

And he still on was led, but with such thoughts	Par Reg 1.299
Full forty days he pass'd, whether on hill	Par Reg 1.303
He saw approach, who first with curious eye	Par Reg 1.319
By Miracle he may, reply'd the Swain,	Par Reg 1.337
He ended, and the Son of God reply'd.	Par Reg 1.346
Hath he excluded my resort sometimes.	Par Reg 1.367
I came among the Sons of God, when he	Par Reg 1.368
And when to all his Angels he propos'd	Par Reg 1.371
That he might fall in *Ramoth*, they demurring,	Par Reg 1.373
For what he bids I do; though I have lost	Par Reg 1.377
Comes to the place where he before had sat	Par Reg 1.412
He added not; and Satan bowing low	Par Reg 1.497
Sometimes they thought he might be only shewn,	Par Reg 2.13
For whither is he gone, what accident	Par Reg 2.39
Hath rapt him from us? will he now retire	Par Reg 2.40
But let us wait; thus far he hath perform'd,	Par Reg 2.49
Lay on his Providence; he will not fail	Par Reg 2.54
That to the fall and rising he should be	Par Reg 2.88
But where delays he now? some great intent	Par Reg 2.95
Conceals him: when twelve years he scarce had seen,	Par Reg 2.96
He could not lose himself; but went about	Par Reg 2.98
His Father's business; what he meant I mus'd,	Par Reg 2.99
Thus long to some great purpose he obscures.	Par Reg 2.101
Sollicitous and blank he thus began.	Par Reg 2.120
If he be Man by Mothers side at least,	Par Reg 2.136
He slightly view'd, and slightly over-pass'd;	Par Reg 2.198
How hee sirnam'd of *Africa* dismiss'd	Par Reg 2.199
For *Solomon* he liv'd at ease, and full	Par Reg 2.201
But he whom we attempt is wiser far	Par Reg 2.205
And now I know he hungers where no food	Par Reg 2.231
He ceas'd, and heard thir grant in loud acclaim;	Par Reg 2.235
Of Trees thick interwoven; there he slept,	Par Reg 2.263
Him thought, he by the Brook of *Cherith* stood	Par Reg 2.266
He saw the Prophet also how he fled	Par Reg 2.270
Into the Desert, and how there he slept	Par Reg 2.271
He found his Supper on the coals prepar'd,	Par Reg 2.273
Sometimes that with *Elijah* he partook,	Par Reg 2.277
Fasting he went to sleep, and fasting wak'd.	Par Reg 2.284
Up to a hill anon his steps he rear'd,	Par Reg 2.285
But Cottage, Herd or Sheep-cote none he saw,	Par Reg 2.288
Thither he bent his way, determin'd there	Par Reg 2.291
Of Wood-Gods and Wood-Nymphs; he view'd it round,	Par Reg 2.297
Out cast *Nebaioth*, yet found he relief	Par Reg 2.309
He spake no dream, for as his words had end,	Par Reg 2.337
That for the Publick all this weight he bears.	Par Reg 2.465
Yet he who reigns within himself, and rules	Par Reg 2.466
Or lawless passions in him which he serves.	Par Reg 2.472
The more he grew in years, the more inflam'd	Par Reg 3.40
With glory, wept that he had liv'd so long	Par Reg 3.41
Recount his praises; thus he did to *Job*,	Par Reg 3.64
He ask'd thee, hast thou seen my servant *Job?*	Par Reg 3.67
Famous he was in Heaven, on Earth less known;	Par Reg 3.68
By what he taught and suffer'd for so doing,	Par Reg 3.97
Resembling thy great Father: he seeks glory,	Par Reg 3.110
Glory he requires, and glory he receives	Par Reg 3.117
From us his foes pronounc't glory he exacts.	Par Reg 3.120
Freely; of whom what could he less expect	Par Reg 3.126
Them he himself to glory will advance.	Par Reg 3.144
With guilt of his own sin, for he himself	Par Reg 3.147
Of glory as thou wilt, said he, so deem,	Par Reg 3.150
So did not *Machabeus:* he indeed	Par Reg 3.165
He in whose hand all times and seasons roul.	Par Reg 3.187
What if he hath decreed that I shall first	Par Reg 3.188
Without distrust or doubt, that he may know	Par Reg 3.193
(As he who seeking Asses found a Kingdom)	Par Reg 3.242
With that (such power was giv'n him then) he took	Par Reg 3.251
He marches now in hast; see, though from far,	Par Reg 3.303
He look't and saw what numbers numberless	Par Reg 3.310
He saw them in thir forms of battell rang'd,	Par Reg 3.322
Yet he at length, time to himself best known,	Par Reg 3.433
As the Red Sea and *Jordan* once he cleft,	Par Reg 3.438
The strength he was to cope with, or his own:	Par Reg 4.9
In cunning, over-reach't where least he thought,	Par Reg 4.11
He brought our Saviour to the western side	Par Reg 4.25
Of that high mountain, whence he might behold	Par Reg 4.26
Of knowing what I aught: he who receives	Par Reg 4.288
To know this only, that he nothing knew;	Par Reg 4.294
In corporal pleasure he, and careless ease;	Par Reg 4.299
Which when he lists, he leaves, or boasts he can,	Par Reg 4.306
(And what he brings, what needs he elsewhere seek)	Par Reg 4.325
So saying he took (for still he knew his power	Par Reg 4.394
Him walking on a Sunny hill he found,	Par Reg 4.447
Out of the wood he starts in wonted shape;	Par Reg 4.449
So talk'd he, while the Son of God went on	Par Reg 4.484
And what he is; his wisdom, power, intent,	Par Reg 4.528
So saying he caught him up, and without wing	Par Reg 4.541
There on the highest Pinacle he set	Par Reg 4.549
For it is written, He will give command	Par Reg 4.556
Tempt not the Lord thy God, he said and stood.	Par Reg 4.561
Fell whence he stood to see his Victor fall.	Par Reg 4.571
Or thirst, and as he fed, Angelic Quires	Par Reg 4.593
He never more henceforth will dare set foot	Par Reg 4.610
To dread the Son of God: he all unarm'd	Par Reg 4.626
Lest he command them down into the deep	Par Reg 4.631
Brought on his way with joy; hee unobserv'd	Par Reg 4.638
God, when he gave me strength, to shew withal	Samson 58
Chor. This, this is he; softly a while,	Samson 115

He(*cont*)
See how he lies at random, carelesly diffus'd, Samson 118
Or do my eyes misrepresent? Can this be hee, Samson 124
But safest he who stood aloof, Samson 135
Chor. Hee speaks, let us draw nigh. Matchless in might, Samson 178
As thir Deliverer; if he aught begin, Samson 274
For with his own Laws he can best dispence. Samson 314
He would not else who never wanted means, Samson 315
Came lagging after; say if he be here. Samson 337
As earst in highest, behold him where he lies. Samson 339
To worthiest deeds, if he through frailty err, Samson 369
He should not so o'rewhelm, and as a thrall Samson 370
Before the God of *Abraham*. He, be sure, Samson 465
He led me on to mightiest deeds Samson 638
Unless he feel within Samson 663
So shall he least confusion draw Samson 1058
Comes he in peace? what wind hath blown him hither Samson 1070
Sam. Or peace or not, alike to me he comes. Samson 1074
Chor. His fraught we soon shall know, he now arrives. Samson 1075
Har. Presume not on thy God, what e're he be, Samson 1156
Thee he regards not, owns not, hath cut off Samson 1157
He will accept thee to defend his cause, Samson 1179
Chor. He will directly to the Lords, I fear, Samson 1250
Sam. He must allege some cause, and offer'd fight Samson 1253
Whether he durst accept the offer or not, Samson 1255
And that he durst not plain enough appear'd. Samson 1256
The worst that he can give, to me the best. Samson 1264
He all thir Ammunition Samson 1277
Swift as the lightning glance he executes Samson 1284
A Scepter or quaint staff he bears, Samson 1303
Chor. His manacles remark him, there he sits. Samson 1309
He's gone, and who knows how he may report Samson 1350
Yet that he may dispense with me or thee Samson 1377
He seems: supposing here to find his Son, Samson 1443
And he in that calamitous prison left. Samson 1480
He now be dealing dole among his foes, Samson 1529
Man. He can I know, but doubt to think he will; Samson 1534
How dy'd he? death to life is crown or shame. Samson 1579
All by him fell thou say'st, by whom fell he, Samson 1580
Mess. Unwounded of his enemies he fell. Samson 1582
Upon thir heads and on his own he pull'd. Samson 1589
He patient but undaunted where they led him, Samson 1623
To heave, pull, draw, or break, he still perform'd Samson 1626
Between the pillars; he his guide requested Samson 1630
He unsuspitious led him; which when *Samson* Samson 1635
And eyes fast fixt he stood, as one who pray'd, Samson 1637
This utter'd, straining all his nerves he bow'd, Samson 1646
He tugg'd, he shook, till down they came and drew Samson 1650
Among them he a spirit of phrenzie sent, Samson 1675
Semichor. But he though blind of sight, Samson 1687
Oft he seems to hide his face, Samson 1749
His servants he with new acquist Samson 1755
Which he to grace his tributary gods Mask 24
He quarters to his blu-hair'd deities, Mask 29
Had by him, ere he parted thence, a Son Mask 56
That he, the Supreme good, t' whom all things ill Mask 217
line not in Bridgewater ms
And run to meet what he would most avoid? Mask 363
line not in Trinity ms
line not in Bridgewater ms
He that has light within his own cleer brest Mask 381
But he that hides a dark soul, and foul thoughts Mask 383
If he be friendly he comes well, if not, Mask 488
He and his monstrous rout are heard to howl Mask 533
Who gently ask't if he had seen such two, Mask 575
He with his bare wand can unthred thy joynts, Mask 614
He lov'd me well, and oft would beg me sing, Mask 623
Which when I did, he on the tender grass Mask 624
But of divine effect, he cull'd me out; Mask 630
But in another Countrey, as he said, Mask 632
line not in Bridgewater ms
He call'd it *Haemony*, and gave it me, Mask 638
Where if he be, with dauntless hardihood, Mask 650
But sease his wand, though he and his curst crew Mask 653
Yet will they soon retire, if he but shrink. Mask 656
he may scratch his forehead. heere be brambles Mask Tr. ms 17.57
As he met her once a Maying, Allegro 20
And he by Friars Lanthorn led Allegro 104
1673 'And by the'
And Crop-full out of dores he flings, Allegro 113
He met her, and in secret shades Penseroso 28
Who would not sing for *Lycidas?* he knew Lycidas 10
He must not flote upon his watry bear Lycidas 12
And as he passes turn, Lycidas 21
As he pronounces lastly on each deed, Lycidas 83
He ask'd the Waves, and ask'd the Fellon winds, Lycidas 91
Ah! Who hath reft (quoth he) my dearest pledge? Lycidas 107
Two massy Keyes he bore of metals twain, Lycidas 110
He shook his Miter'd locks, and stern bespake, Lycidas 112
Sunk though he be beneath the watry floar, Lycidas 167
With *Nectar* pure his oozy Lock's he laves, Lycidas 175
He touch'd the tender stops of various Quills, Lycidas 188
At last he rose, and twitch'd his Mantle blew: Lycidas 192
That he our deadly forfeit should release, Nativity 6
Wherwith he wont at Heav'ns high Councel-Table, Nativity 10
He laid aside; and here with us to be, Nativity 12
But he her fears to cease, Nativity 45
He saw a greater Sun appear Nativity 83

He(*cont*)
Nor can he be at rest Nativity 216
He feels from *Juda*'s Land Nativity 221
Praise the Lord, for he is kind, Psalm 136, 2
For of gods he is the God; Psalm 136, 6
He with his thunder-clasping hand, Psalm 136, 37
He brought from thence his *Israel*. Psalm 136, 42
The ruddy waves he cleft in twain, Psalm 136, 45
His chosen people he did bless Psalm 136, 57
In bloody battail he brought down Psalm 136, 61
He foild bold *Seon* and his host, Psalm 136, 65
And large-lim'd *Og* he did subdue, Psalm 136, 69
He gave their Land therin to dwell. Psalm 136, 74
He hath with a piteous eye Psalm 136, 77
All living creatures he doth feed, Psalm 136, 85
For he being amorous on that lovely die Fair Inf 5
He thought it toucht his Deitie full neer, Fair Inf 10
If likewise he some fair one wedded not, Fair Inf 11
He wanderd long, till thee he spy'd from farr, Fair Inf 17
Down he descended from his Snow-soft chaire, Fair Inf 19
And render him with patience what he lent; Fair Inf 75
This if thou do he will an off-spring give, Fair Inf 76
Where he had mutely sate two years before: Vacation 6
How he before the thunderous throne doth lie, Vacation 36
O're all his Brethren he shall Reign as King, Vacation 75
In worth and excellence he shall out-go them, Vacation 79
Yet being above them, he shall be below them; Vacation 80
From others he shall stand in need of nothing, Vacation 81
Yet shall he live in strife, and at his dore Vacation 85
Which he for us did freely undergo. Passion 12
He sov'ran Priest stooping his regall head Passion 15
Yet more; the stroke of death he must abide, Passion 20
He who with all Heav'ns heraldry whileare Circum 10
Were lost in death, till he that dwelt above Circum 18
He at their invoking came Winchester 19
And in his Garland as he stood, Winchester 21
He's here stuck in a slough, and overthrown. Carrier 4
Death was half glad when he had got him down; Carrier 6
For he had any time this ten yeers full, Carrier 7
And that he had tane up his latest Inne, Carrier 13
Shew'd him his room where he must lodge that night, Carrier 15
That he could never die while he could move, Another 2
While he might still jogg on, and keep his trot, Another 4
His principles being ceast, he ended strait. Another 10
Meerly to drive the time away he sickn'd, Another 15
line not in 1640, 1657, 1658 texts
Nay, quoth he, on his swooning bed outstretch'd, Another 17
line not in 1640, 1657, 1658 texts
He di'd for heavines that his Cart went light, Another 22
line not in 1658 text
As he were prest to death, he cry'd more waight; Another 26
line not in 1640, 1657, 1658 texts
He had bin an immortall Carrier. Another 28
Obedient to the Moon he spent his date Another 29
line not in 1658 text
He can requite thee, for he knows the charms Sonnet 8, 5
And he can spred thy Name o're Lands and Seas, Sonnet 8, 7
Then his *Casella*, whom he woo'd to sing, Sonnet 13, 13
Trinity ms 'he' ← 'Dante'
My true account, least he returning chide, Sonnet 19, 6
He who of those delights can judge, And spare Sonnet 20, 13
Plain in thy neatness; O how oft shall he Horace 5
And in his Law he studies day and night. Psalm 1, 6
He shall be as a tree which planted grows Psalm 1, 7
And what he takes in hand shall prosper all. Psalm 1, 10
Their twisted cords: he who in Heaven doth dwell Psalm 2, 8
And fierce ire trouble them; but I saith hee Psalm 2, 11
With trembling; kiss the Son least he appear Psalm 2, 25
Unto Jehovah, he full soon reply'd Psalm 3, 11
(For whom to chuse he knows) Psalm 4, 16
He hast to tear my Soul asunder Psalm 7, 5
His Sword he whets, his Bow hath bended Psalm 7, 46
(His arrows purposely made he Psalm 7, 49
He travels big with vanitie, Psalm 7, 51
Trouble he hath conceav'd of old Psalm 7, 52
He dig'd a pit, and delv'd it deep, Psalm 7, 55
And fell into the pit he made, Psalm 7, 56
This he a Testimony ordain'd Psalm 81, 17
When as he pass'd through Aegypt land; Psalm 81, 19
And we would feed them *from the shock* Psalm 81, 65
He judges and debates. Psalm 82, 4
For thou art he who shalt by right Psalm 82, 27
For to his people he speaks peace Psalm 85, 31
To his dear Saints he will speak peace, Psalm 85, 33
Then will he come, and not be slow Psalm 85, 55
When he the Nations doth enrowle Psalm 87, 23
Into a goodly valley, where he sees Prose 2, 2
Then past hee to a flowry Mountaine greene, Prose 4, 1
Which he who can, and will, deserv's high praise, Prose 9, 3
Whom doe we count a good man, whom but he Prose 10, 1

Head
With Head up-lift above the wave, and Eyes Par Lost 1.193
ms 'head'
Had ris'n or heav'd his head, but that the will Par Lost 1.211
Maim'd his brute Image, head and hands lopt off Par Lost 1.459
Or dreams he sees, while over-head the Moon Par Lost 1.784
ms 'over head'
1667 'over head'

Head(*cont*)	
And shook a dreadful Dart; what seem'd his head	Par Lost 2.672
Shakes Pestilence and Warr. Each at the Head	Par Lost 2.711
Against thy Fathers head? and know'st for whom;	Par Lost 2.730
In darkness, while thy head flames thick and fast	Par Lost 2.754
Out of thy head I sprung: amazement seis'd	Par Lost 2.758
With head, hands, wings or feet pursues his way,	Par Lost 2.949
Made head against Heav'ns King, though overthrown.	Par Lost 2.992
Upon his own rebellious head. And now	Par Lost 3.86
Affecting God-head, and so loosing all,	Par Lost 3.206
Much less that durst upon his own head draw	Par Lost 3.220
The Head of all mankind, though *Adams* Son.	Par Lost 3.286
Thy Merits; under thee as Head Supream	Par Lost 3.319
Circl'd his Head, nor less his Locks behind	Par Lost 3.626
As with a rural mound the champain head	Par Lost 4.134
Access deni'd; and over head up grew	Par Lost 4.137
By *Nilus* head, enclosd with shining Rock,	Par Lost 4.283
And Head, what thou hast said is just and right.	Par Lost 4.443
Here watching at the head of these that sleep?	Par Lost 4.826
Armie of Fiends, fit body to fit head;	Par Lost 4.953
At my right hand; your Head I him appoint;	Par Lost 5.606
Our happie state under one Head more neer	Par Lost 5.830
But more illustrious made, since he the Head	Par Lost 5.842
His Thunder on thy head, devouring fire.	Par Lost 5.893
Of conflict; over head the dismal hiss	Par Lost 6.212
In Entrailes, Heart or Head, Liver or Reines;	Par Lost 6.346
All Heart they live, all Head, all Eye, all Eare,	Par Lost 6.350
A while, but suddenly at head appeerd	Par Lost 6.556
Had need from head to foot well understand;	Par Lost 6.625
Under thir Head imbodied all in one.	Par Lost 6.779
Bore up his branching head: scarse from his mould	Par Lost 7.470
When suddenly stood at my Head a dream,	Par Lost 8.292
The more she will acknowledge thee her Head,	Par Lost 8.574
His head the midst, well stor'd with suttle wiles:	Par Lost 9.184
In heart or head, possessing soon inspir'd	Par Lost 9.189
Each Flour of slender stalk, whose head though gay	Par Lost 9.428
Fould above fould a surging Maze, his Head	Par Lost 9.499
Of knowledg, nor was God-head from her thought.	Par Lost 9.790
Being as I am, why didst not thou the Head	Par Lost 9.1155
Least on my head both sin and punishment,	Par Lost 10.133
Her Seed shall bruse thy head, thou bruise his heel.	Par Lost 10.181
At last as from a Cloud his fulgent head	Par Lost 10.449
His Seed, when is not set, shall bruise my head:	Par Lost 10.499
With complicated monsters head and taile,	Par Lost 10.523
Or multiplie, but curses on my head?	Par Lost 10.732
My Head, Ill fare our Ancestor impure,	Par Lost 10.735
On my defensless head; both Death and I	Par Lost 10.815
The sentence from thy head remov'd may light	Par Lost 10.934
That on my head all might be visited,	Par Lost 10.955
The Serpents head; piteous amends, unless	Par Lost 10.1032
Against us this deceit: to crush his head	Par Lost 10.1035
Till many years over thy head return:	Par Lost 11.534
Grateful to Heav'n, over his head beholds	Par Lost 11.864
The Serpents head; whereof to thee anon	Par Lost 12.150
Of head or heel: not therefore joynes the Son	Par Lost 12.388
Manhood to God-head, with more strength to foil	Par Lost 12.389
Shall bruise the head of *Satan*, crush his strength	Par Lost 12.430
And fix farr deeper in his head thir stings	Par Lost 12.432
Upon my head, long the decrees of Heav'n	Par Reg 1.55
At least if so we can, and by the head	Par Reg 1.60
Unfold her Crystal Dores, thence on his head	Par Reg 1.82
E're in the head of Nations he appear	Par Reg 1.98
Full weight must be transferr'd upon my head.	Par Reg 1.267
Motherly cares and fears got head, and rais'd	Par Reg 2.64
Above the rest lifting his stately head	Par Reg 4.48
From dews and damps of night his shelter'd head,	Par Reg 4.406
But shelter'd slept in vain, for at his head	Par Reg 4.407
With languish't head unpropt,	Samson 119
They swarm, but in adverse withdraw their head	Samson 192
How could I once look up, or heave the head,	Samson 197
At length to lay my head and hallow'd pledge	Samson 535
In heart, head, brest, and reins;	Samson 609
About t' have spoke, but now, with head declin'd	Samson 727
Had shorn the fatal harvest of thy head.	Samson 1024
Which long shall not with-hold mee from thy head,	Samson 1125
Felt in his arms, with head a while enclin'd,	Samson 1636
At last with head erect thus cryed aloud,	Samson 1639
And Advice with scrupulous head,	Mask 108
Leans her unpillow'd head fraught with sad fears.	Mask 355
It withers on the stalk with languish't head.	Mask 744
Trinity ms 'with languish't head' ←'and fades away'	
line not in Bridgewater ms	
Were shatter'd into heaps o're thy false head.	Mask 799
line not in Bridgewater ms	
line not in Trinity ms	
Who piteous of her woes, rear'd her lank head,	Mask 836
Rise, rise, and heave thy rosie head	Mask 885
O're the Cowslips Velvet head,	Mask 898
May thy lofty head be crown'd	Mask 934
this dusky hollow is a paradise & heaven gates ore my head	Mask Tr. ms 13.44
That *Orpheus* self may heave his head	Allegro 145
And oft, as if her head she bow'd,	Penseroso 71
Clos'd o're the head of your lov'd *Lycidas?*	Lycidas 51
His goary visage down the stream was sent,	Lycidas 62
Trinity ms 'visage' ←'head' ←'scalpe'	
That sunk so low that sacred head of thine.	Lycidas 102
With Cowslips wan that hang the pensive hed,	Lycidas 147
1638 'head'	
Trinity ms 'head'	
And yet anon repairs his drooping head,	Lycidas 169
And hid his head for shame,	Nativity 80
And sought to hide his froth-becurled head	Psalm 114, 8
Amongst us here below to hide thy nectar'd head.	Fair Inf 49
Strew all their blessings on thy sleeping Head.	Vacation 64
He sov'ran Priest stooping his regall head	Passion 15
But the fair blossom hangs the head	Winchester 41
Th' exalter of my head I count	Psalm 3, 9
Turns on his head, and his ill trade	Psalm 7, 58
Advanc'd their lofty head.	Psalm 80, 44
Of head bereft li'th poor *Kenelm* King-born.	Prose 13, 2
Headed	
Grey-headed men and grave, with Warriours mixt,	Par Lost 11.662
What was that snaky-headed *Gorgon* sheild	Mask 447
Trinity ms 'snakie-headed'	
Bridgewater ms 'snakie headed'	
1637 'snakie headed'	
These oughly-headed Monsters? Mercy guard me!	Mask 695
Bridgewater ms 'ougley headed'	
1637 'ougly-headed'	
Trinity ms 'ougly headed' ←'ougly musl'd' ←'musl'd'	
Headlong	
Hurld headlong flaming from th' Ethereal Skie	Par Lost 1.45
ms 'head long'	
By all his Engins, but was headlong sent	Par Lost 1.750
ms 'head long'	
Hurl'd headlong to partake with us, shall curse	Par Lost 2.374
Driv'n headlong from the Pitch of Heaven, down	Par Lost 2.772
Urg'd them behind; headlong themselves they threw	Par Lost 6.864
Headlong would follow; and to thir Gods perhaps	Par Reg 3.430
Cast her self headlong from th' *Ismenian* steep,	Par Reg 4.575
Then down the Lawns I ran with headlong hast	Mask 568
Bridgewater ms 'headlonge'	
And bridle in thy headlong wave,	Mask 887
Bridgewater ms 'headlonge'	
But headlong joy is ever on the wing,	Passion 5
Heads	
The Heads and Leaders thither hast where stood	Par Lost 1.357
ms 'heads'	
To bestial Gods; for which thir heads as low	Par Lost 1.435
One day upon our heads; while we perhaps	Par Lost 2.178
Hide thir diminisht heads; to thee I call,	Par Lost 4.35
Rear'd high thir flourisht heads between, and wrought	Par Lost 4.699
Themselves invaded next, and on thir heads	Par Lost 6.653
Over thir heads a chrystal Firmament,	Par Lost 6.757
O're Shields and Helmes, and helmed heads he rode	Par Lost 6.840
Instead shall double ours upon our heads.	Par Lost 10.1040
Over whose heads they rore, and seem to point,	Par Reg 4.463
On *Israel*'s Governours, and Heads of Tribes,	Samson 242
Whose heads that turbulent liquor fills with fumes.	Samson 552
Heads without name no more rememberd,	Samson 677
Upon thir heads and on his own he pull'd.	Samson 1589
Upon the heads of all who sate beneath,	Samson 1652
His cloudless thunder bolted on thir heads.	Samson 1696
Thir Hydra heads, and the fals North displaies	Sonnet 15, 7
1694 'Hydra-heads'	
Exalt their heads full hie.	Psalm 83, 8
Headstrong	
Cities of men, or head-strong Multitudes,	Par Reg 2.470
Heal	
To heal the scarr of these corrosive Fires	Par Lost 2.401
And heal the harms of thwarting thunder blew,	Arcades 51
Trinity ms 'heale'	
Am very weak and faint; heal and amend me,	Psalm 6, 4
Healed	
Yet soon he heal'd; for Spirits that live throughout	Par Lost 6.344
Soon closing, and by native vigour heal'd.	Par Lost 6.436
But suddenly with flesh fill'd up and heal'd:	Par Lost 8.468
Healing	
To whom with healing words *Adam* replyd.	Par Lost 9.290
And healing words from these thy friends admit.	Samson 605
In every vertuous plant and healing herb	Mask 621
Bridgewater ms 'healinge'	
Heals	
Which she with pretious viold liquors heals.	Mask 847
Trinity ms 'heales'	
1637 'heales'	
line not in Bridgewater ms	
Health	
And strongest drinks our chief support of health,	Samson 554
God of our saving health and peace,	Psalm 85, 13
Thy saving health to us afford	Psalm 85, 27
Healthful	
While they pervert pure Natures healthful rules	Par Lost 11.523
Heap	
Heap on himself damnation, while he sought	Par Lost 1.215
Thaws not, but gathers heap, and ruin seems	Par Lost 2.590
This worlds material mould, came to a heap:	Par Lost 3.709
Lights on a heap of nitrous Powder, laid	Par Lost 4.815
With shiverd armour strow'n, and on a heap	Par Lost 6.389
Get Riches first, get Wealth, and Treasure heap,	Par Reg 2.427
To heap ingratitude on worthiest deeds?	Samson 276
Heaped	
Heapt on him there, nor yet the main Abyss	Par Lost 3.83
Have heap'd this Table. Rais'd of grassie terf	Par Lost 5.391
To this uproar; horrid confusion heapt	Par Lost 6.668

Heaped(*cont*)
Heapt to the popular summe, will so incense Par Lost 12.338
Of heapt *Elysian* flowres, and hear Allegro 147
Heaps
Heaps with unsparing hand; for drink the Grape Par Lost 5.344
But on thy rould in heaps, and up the Trees Par Lost 10.558
And over heaps of slaughter'd walk his way? Samson 1530
You may as well spred out the unsun'd heaps Mask 398
Bridgewater ms 'heapes'
Trinity ms 'heapes'
Now heaps upon som few with vast excess, Mask 771
Bridgewater ms 'heap's'
Trinity ms 'heapes'
Were shatter'd into heaps o're thy false head. Mask 799
line not in Trinity ms
line not in Bridgewater ms
Hear
If once they hear that voyce, thir liveliest pledge Par Lost 1.274
ms 'heare'
Of his Almighty Engin he shall hear Par Lost 2.65
Grinnd horrible a gastly smile, to hear Par Lost 2.846
The rest shall hear me call, and oft be warnd Par Lost 3.185
My Umpire *Conscience*, whom if they will hear, Par Lost 3.195
Contented with report hear onely in heav'n: Par Lost 3.701
1667 'heare'
Turnd him all eare to hear new utterance flow. Par Lost 4.410
1667 'heare'
O friends, I hear the tread of nimble feet Par Lost 4.866
Of sense, whereby they hear, see, smell, touch, taste, Par Lost 5.411
But more desire to hear, if thou consent, Par Lost 5.555
Hear all ye Angels, Progenie of Light, Par Lost 5.600
Hear my Decree, which unrevok't shall stand. Par Lost 5.602
Words which no eare ever to hear in Heav'n Par Lost 5.810
What we propound, and loud that all may hear. Par Lost 6.567
With admiration, and deep Muse to heare Par Lost 7.52
And longer will delay to heare thee tell Par Lost 7.101
1669 'hear'
Thought him still speaking, still stood fixt to hear; Par Lost 8.3
line not in 1667 edition
Ere my remembrance: now hear mee relate Par Lost 8.204
Inviting thee to hear while I relate, Par Lost 8.208
Or bear what to my minde first thoughts present, Par Lost 9.213
1667 'hear'
May tempt it, I expected not to hear. Par Lost 9.281
Hath bin the cause, and wonderful to heare: Par Lost 9.862
And gladly of our Union heare thee speak, Par Lost 9.966
Th' ethereal People ran, to hear and know Par Lost 10.27
Now death to heare! for what can I encrease Par Lost 10.731
To supplication, heare his sighs though mute; Par Lost 11.31
Expect to hear, supernal Grace contending Par Lost 11.359
And hear the din; thus was the building left Par Lost 12.61
Of squadrond Angels hear his Carol sung. Par Lost 12.367
What from within I feel my self, and hear Par Reg 1.198
I went into the Temple, there to hear Par Reg 1.211
Where ought we hear, and curious are to hear, Par Reg 1.333
Declar'd the Son of God, to hear attent Par Reg 1.385
What wonder then if I delight to hear Par Reg 1.481
To hear thee when I come (since no man comes) Par Reg 1.484
Full grown to Man, acknowledg'd, as I hear, Par Reg 2.83
On no slight grounds thy safety; hear, and mark Par Reg 3.349
But tedious wast of time to sit and hear Par Reg 4.123
There thou shalt hear and learn the secret power Par Reg 4.254
Then hear, O Son of *David*, Virgin-born; Par Reg 4.500
But who are these? for with joint pace I hear Samson 110
Sam. I hear the sound of words, thir sense the air Samson 176
Dal. Yet hear me *Samson*; not that I endeavour Samson 766
Hear what assaults I had, what snares besides, Samson 845
Hear these dishonours, and not render death? Samson 1232
Happ'n what may, of me expect to hear Samson 1423
With thee; say reverend Sire, we thirst to hear. Samson 1456
With rueful cry, yet what it was we hear not, Samson 1553
Of this occasion. But I hear the tread Mask 91
Bridgewater ms 'heare'
1637 'heare'
Trinity ms 'heare'
Break off, break off, I feel the different pace, Mask 145
Trinity ms 'feele' ←'heare'
Be barr'd that happines, might we but hear Mask 343
1637 'heare'
Bridgewater ms 'heare'
Trinity ms 'heare'
Tell her of things that no gross ear can hear, Mask 458
Trinity ms 'heare'
1637 'heare'
Bridgewater ms 'heare'
Where no crude surfet raigns. *Eld. Bro*. List, list, I hear Mask 480
Bridgewater ms 'heare'
Trinity ms 'I heare' ←'I heard' ←'me thought'
1637 'heare'
The huddling brook to hear his madrigal, Mask 495
1637 'heare'
Bridgewater ms 'heere'
Trinity ms 'heare'
Thou art not fit to hear thy self convinc't; Mask 792
1637 'heare'
line not in Bridgewater ms
line not in Trinity ms
strange distances to heare & unknowne climes Mask Tr. ms 10.17

Hear(*cont*)
To hear the Lark begin his flight, Allegro 41
Of heapt *Elysian* flowres, and hear Allegro 147
I woo to hear thy eeven Song; Penseroso 64
I hear the far-off *Curfeu* sound, Penseroso 74
After the heavenly tune, which none can hear Arcades 72
Trinity ms 'heare'
And old *Damoetas* lov'd to hear our song. Lycidas 36
1638 'heare'
Trinity ms 'heare'
(If so it be that thou these plaints dost hear) Fair Inf 37
For once it was my dismal hap to hear Vacation 68
To hear the Lute well toucht, or artfull voice Sonnet 20, 11
Now pity me, and hear my earnest prai'r. Psalm 4, 6
Will hear my voyce what time to him I crie. Psalm 4, 18
The voyce of my complaining hear Psalm 5, 3
Shalt in the morning hear Psalm 5, 6
To Jacobs God, *that all may hear* Psalm 81, 3
Hear O my people, *heark'n well*, Psalm 81, 33
And yet my people would not *hear*, Psalm 81, 45
Lord God of Hoasts hear *now* my praier Psalm 84, 29
Wilt thou not turn, and *hear our voice* Psalm 85, 21
I will *go strait and* hear, Psalm 85, 30
O hear me *I thee pray*, Psalm 86, 2
Heard
Of hope in fears and dangers, heard so oft Par Lost 1.275
They heard, and were abasht, and up they sprung Par Lost 1.331
After the Tempest: Such applause was heard Par Lost 2.290
Of Thunder heard remote. Towards him they bend Par Lost 2.477
Heard farr and wide, and all the host of Hell Par Lost 2.519
Heard on the ruful stream; fierce *Phlegeton* Par Lost 2.580
I saw and heard, for such a numerous Host Par Lost 2.993
Confusion heard his voice, and wilde uproar Par Lost 3.710
Th' *Apocalyps*, heard cry in Heaven aloud, Par Lost 4.2
Of echoing Hill or Thicket have we heard Par Lost 4.681
Divine instructer, I have heard, then when Par Lost 5.546
Worthy of Sacred silence to be heard; Par Lost 5.557
Is heard no more in Heav'n; he of the first, Par Lost 5.659
From midst a Golden Cloud thus milde was heard. Par Lost 6.28
And clamour such as heard in Heav'n till now Par Lost 6.208
Satan: And thus was heard Commanding loud. Par Lost 6.557
If our proposals once again were heard Par Lost 6.618
And twentie thousand (I thir number heard) Par Lost 6.769
Each to his place, they heard his voice and went Par Lost 6.782
Hell heard th' unsufferable noise, Hell saw Par Lost 6.867
Thy weaker; let it profit thee to have heard Par Lost 6.909
The storie heard attentive, and was fill'd Par Lost 7.51
Whose liquid murmur heard new thirst excites, Par Lost 7.68
When such was heard declar'd th' Almightie's will; Par Lost 7.181
For *Chaos* heard his voice: him all his Traine Par Lost 7.221
Of Trumpet (for of Armies thou hast heard) Par Lost 7.296
Things else by me unsearchable, now heard Par Lost 8.10
Thee I have heard relating what was don Par Lost 8.203
My Storie, which perhaps thou hast not heard; Par Lost 8.205
But long ere our approaching heard within Par Lost 8.242
Hee ended, or I heard no more, for now Par Lost 8.452
She heard me thus, and though divinely brought, Par Lost 8.500
And from the parting Angel over-heard Par Lost 9.276
To lure her Eye; shee busied heard the sound Par Lost 9.518
On th' other side, *Adam*, soon as he heard Par Lost 9.888
Heard not her lore, both in subjection now Par Lost 9.1128
All were who heard, dim sadness did not spare Par Lost 10.23
To sentence Man: the voice of God they heard Par Lost 10.97
Brought to thir Ears, while day declin'd, they heard, Par Lost 10.99
I heard thee in the Garden, and of thy voice Par Lost 10.116
My voice thou oft hast heard, and hast not fear'd, Par Lost 10.119
Which when the Lord God heard, without delay Par Lost 10.163
Is propagated curse. O voice once heard Par Lost 10.729
Would speed before thee, and be louder heard, Par Lost 10.954
And gracious temper he both heard and judg'd Par Lost 10.1047
His Trumpet, heard in *Oreb* since perhaps Par Lost 11.74
That I was heard with favour; peace returnd Par Lost 11.153
Sufficient that thy Prayers are heard, and Death, Par Lost 11.252
Yet all had heard, with audible lament Par Lost 11.266
I heard, here with him at this Fountain talk'd: Par Lost 11.322
Was heard, of Harp and Organ; and who moovd Par Lost 11.560
Assemble, and Harangues are heard, but soon Par Lost 11.663
Don to his Father, heard this heavie curse, Par Lost 12.103
Who against Faith and Conscience can be heard Par Lost 12.529
Let her with thee partake what thou hast heard, Par Lost 12.598
So spake our Mother *Eve*, and *Adam* heard Par Lost 12.624
That heard the Adversary, who roving still Par Reg 1.33
And out of Heav'n the Sov'raign voice I heard, Par Reg 1.84
This having heard, strait I again revolv'd Par Reg 1.259
The Baptist, (of whose birth I oft had heard, Par Reg 1.270
Audibly heard from Heav'n, pronounc'd me his, Par Reg 1.284
Of God; I saw and heard, for we sometimes Par Reg 1.330
Him whom they heard so late expresly call'd Par Reg 2.3
Expected of our Fathers; we have heard Par Reg 2.33
Since first her Salutation heard, with thoughts Par Reg 2.107
Have we not seen, or by relation heard, Par Reg 2.182
He ceas'd, and heard thir grant in loud acclaim; Par Reg 2.235
And all the while Harmonious Airs were heard Par Reg 2.362
With sound of Harpies wings, and Talons heard; Par Reg 2.403
(For I have also heard, perhaps have read) Par Reg 4.116
After a dismal night; I heard the rack Par Reg 4.452
Of the Messiah I have heard foretold Par Reg 4.502
Heard thee pronounc'd the Son of God belov'd. Par Reg 4.513

Heard(*cont*)
Yet truth to say, I oft have heard men wonder — Samson 215
This one prayer yet remains, might I be heard, — Samson 649
If thou at all art known. Much I have heard — Samson 1082
I heard all as I came, the City rings — Samson 1449
Man. Of ruin indeed methought I heard the noise, — Samson 1515
From whom could else a general cry be heard? — Samson 1524
Man. The accident was loud, & here before thee — Samson 1552
1671 printed 'heard', errata 'here'
(For so from such as nearer stood we heard) — Samson 1631
What never yet was heard in Tale or Song — Mask 44
Such noise as I can make to be heard farthest — Mask 227
Of darknes till it smil'd: I have oft heard — Mask 252
I never heard till now. Ile speak to her — Mask 264
Where no crude surfet raigns. *Eld. Bro*. List, list, I hear — Mask 480
Trinity ms 'I heare' ←'I heard' ←'me thought'
He and his monstrous rout are heard to howl — Mask 533
Was never heard the Nymphs to daunt, — Penseroso 137
We drove a field, and both together heard — Lycidas 27
That strain I heard was of a higher mood: — Lycidas 87
Was heard the World around: — Nativity 54
Nature that heard such sound — Nativity 101
A voice of weeping heard, and loud lament; — Nativity 183
She heard them give thee this, that thou should'st still — Vacation 65
First heard by happy watchful Shepherds ear, — Circum 3
First heard before the shallow Cuccoo's bill — Sonnet 1, 6
And heard me from his holy mount. — Psalm 3, 12
The Lord hath heard, the Lord hath heard my prai'r — Psalm 6, 18
The Tongue I heard, was strange. — Psalm 81, 20

Heardest
Resounded, (thou remember'st, for thou heardst) — Par Lost 7.561

Hearers
But vow though the cross Doctors all stood hearers, — Another 19
line not in 1640, 1657, 1658 texts

Hearest
Or hear'st thou rather pure Ethereal stream, — Par Lost 3.7
Raphael, said hee, thou hear'st what stir on Earth — Par Lost 5.224

Hearing
Thy hearing, such Commission from above — Par Lost 7.118
Thy hearing graciously. — Psalm 86, 20

Hearken
For man will hark'n to his glozing lyes, — Par Lost 3.93
1667 'heark'n'
Not difficult, if thou hearken to me, — Par Reg 2.428
And hearken, if I may, her busines here. — Mask 169
Would sit, and hearken even to extasie, — Mask 625
Hear O my people, *heark'n well*, — Psalm 81, 33
Nor hearken to my voice; — Psalm 81, 46

Hearkened
Would thou hadst heark'nd to my words, and stai'd — Par Lost 9.1134
Because thou hast heark'nd to the voice of thy Wife, — Par Lost 10.198

Hears
Held by thy voice, thy potent voice he heares, — Par Lost 7.100
1669 'hears'
To fill his eare, when contrary he hears — Par Lost 10.506
And hears the Muses in a ring, — Penseroso 47
And hears the unexpressive nuptiall Song, — Lycidas 176
Trinity ms '& heares' ←'listening'

Hearse
To strew the Laureat Herse where *Lycid* lies. — Lycidas 151
1638 'herse'
Trinity ms 'herse'
For thy Hears to strew the ways, — Winchester 58

Heart
Before all Temples th' upright heart and pure, — Par Lost 1.18
Here in the heart of Hell to work in Fire, — Par Lost 1.151
Audacious neighbourhood, the wisest heart — Par Lost 1.400
By that uxorious King, whose heart though large, — Par Lost 1.444
Thir number last he summs. And now his heart — Par Lost 1.571
At once with joy and fear his heart rebounds. — Par Lost 1.788
Meets his approach, and to the heart inspires — Par Lost 4.154
Out of my side to thee, neerest my heart — Par Lost 4.484
His heart, not else dismai'd. Now drew they nigh — Par Lost 4.861
And thus his own undaunted heart explores. — Par Lost 6.113
In Entrailes, Heart or Head, Liver or Reines; — Par Lost 6.346
All Heart they live, all Head, all Eye, all Eare, — Par Lost 6.350
The doubts that in his heart arose: and now — Par Lost 7.60
Or heart of man suffice to comprehend? — Par Lost 7.114
But least his heart exalt him in the harme — Par Lost 7.150
Of future, in small room large heart enclos'd, — Par Lost 7.486
Descends, thither with heart and voice and eyes — Par Lost 7.513
With fragrance and with joy my heart oreflow'd. — Par Lost 8.266
Eate freely with glad heart; fear here no dearth: — Par Lost 8.322
Thy wish exactly to thy hearts desire. — Par Lost 8.451
Sweetness into my heart, unfelt before, — Par Lost 8.475
And they shall be one Flesh, one Heart, one Soule. — Par Lost 8.499
The thoughts, and heart enlarges, hath his seat — Par Lost 8.590
In heart or head, possessing soon inspir'd — Par Lost 9.189
Into the Heart of *Eve* his words made way, — Par Lost 9.550
Into her heart too easie entrance won: — Par Lost 9.734
Yet oft his heart, divine of somthing ill, — Par Lost 9.845
Dimm erst, dilated Spirits, ampler Heart, — Par Lost 9.876
Would never from my heart; no no, I feel — Par Lost 9.913
So forcible within my heart I feel — Par Lost 9.955
One Heart, one Soul in both; whereof good prooff — Par Lost 9.967
Of God All-seeing, or deceave his Heart — Par Lost 10.6
For I no sooner in my Heart divin'd, — Par Lost 10.357
My Heart, which by a secret harmonie — Par Lost 10.358

Heart(*cont*)
What love sincere, and reverence in my heart — Par Lost 10.915
Commiseration; soon his heart relented — Par Lost 10.940
To whom thus *Eve*, recovering heart, repli'd. — Par Lost 10.966
Thy Love, the sole contentment of my heart — Par Lost 10.973
Be open, and his heart to pitie incline, — Par Lost 10.1061
Sow'n with contrition in his heart, then those — Par Lost 11.27
His heart I know, how variable and vain — Par Lost 11.92
Kneel'd and before him humbl'd all my heart, — Par Lost 11.150
What justly thou hast lost; nor set thy heart, — Par Lost 11.288
Much at that sight was *Adam* in his heart — Par Lost 11.448
Sight so deform what heart of Rock could long — Par Lost 11.494
And charming Symphonies attach'd the heart — Par Lost 11.595
Whereat the heart of *Adam* erst so sad — Par Lost 11.868
Griev'd at his heart, when looking down he saw — Par Lost 11.887
Of proud ambitious heart, who not content — Par Lost 12.25
Humbles his stubborn heart, but still as Ice — Par Lost 12.193
Mine eyes true op'ning, and my heart much eas'd, — Par Lost 12.274
Shall on the heart engrave. What will they then — Par Lost 12.524
Presaging, since with sorrow and hearts distress — Par Lost 12.613
Flam'd in my heart, heroic acts, one while — Par Reg 1.216
My heart hath been a store-house long of things — Par Reg 2.103
Women, when nothing else, beguil'd the heart — Par Reg 2.169
And all thy heart is set on high designs, — Par Reg 2.410
To thy large heart give utterance due, thy heart — Par Reg 3.10
But the heart of the Fool, — Samson 298
I yielded, and unlock'd her all my heart, — Samson 407
Or taste that cheers the heart of Gods and men, — Samson 545
In heart, head, brest, and reins; — Samson 609
Chor. Where the heart joins not, outward acts defile not. — Samson 1368
Will pierce more neer his heart. — Circum 28
Trinity ms 'heart' ←'hart'
That we on Earth with undiscording voice — Musick 17
Trinity ms 'voice' ←'hart & voice'
Thy easie numbers flow, and that each heart — Shakespear 10
1632 'part'
1663-4 'part'
Thou with fresh hope the Lovers heart dost fill, — Sonnet 1, 3
Of heart or hope; but still bear vp and steer — Sonnet 22, 8
1694 'Heart'
The good and meek of heart — Psalm 4, 15
Into my heart more joy — Psalm 4, 31
Saves th' upright of Heart at last. — Psalm 7, 42
In the pure firmament, then saith my heart, — Psalm 8, 11
My heart and flesh aloud do crie, — Psalm 84, 7
To fear thy name my heart unite — Psalm 86, 39
With my whole heart, and blaze abroad — Psalm 86, 43

Heart-easing
And by men, heart-easing Mirth, — Allegro 13

Hearted
Wind me into the easie-hearted man, — Mask 163
1637 'easie hearted'
Trinity ms 'easie hearted'
Bridgewater ms 'easie harted'

Heartened
Where I will see thee heartn'd and fresh clad — Samson 1317

Heart-grief
And in my midst of sorrow and heart-grief — Samson 1339

Hearth
But to sit idle on the houshold hearth, — Samson 566
Save the Cricket on the hearth, — Penseroso 82
And on the holy Hearth, — Nativity 190
The Faiery Ladies daunc't upon the hearth; — Vacation 60

Hearts
What may suffice, and soft'n stonie hearts — Par Lost 3.189
Enamour'd at that sight; but in those hearts — Par Lost 5.448
Can hearts, not free, be tri'd whether they serve — Par Lost 5.532
Frequenting, sent from hearts contrite, in sign — Par Lost 10.1091
Frequenting, sent from hearts contrite, in sign — Par Lost 10.1103
The stonie from thir hearts, & made new flesh — Par Lost 11.4
Working through love, upon thir hearts shall write, — Par Lost 12.489
By winning words to conquer willing hearts, — Par Reg 1.222
In pious Hearts, an inward Oracle — Par Reg 1.463
Hearts after them tangl'd in Amorous Nets. — Par Reg 2.162
In feeble hearts, propense anough before — Samson 455
In human hearts, nor less in mine towards thee, — Samson 792
Had fill'd thir hearts with mirth, high chear, & wine, — Samson 1613
Semichor. While thir hearts were jocund and sublime, — Samson 1669
Their hearts and ears did greet, — Nativity 94
Thereby to set the hearts of men on fire — Fair Inf 62
Speak to your hearts alone, — Psalm 4, 20
Hearts and reins. On God is cast — Psalm 7, 39
And in their hearts thy waies. — Psalm 84, 20

Heart-sick
Of heart-sick Agonie, all feavorous kinds, — Par Lost 11.482

Heart-struck
Heart-strook with chilling gripe of sorrow stood, — Par Lost 11.264

Heat
Infected *Sions* daughters with like heat, — Par Lost 1.453
ms 'heate'
Familiar the fierce heat, and void of pain; — Par Lost 2.219
Not only enlighten, but with kindly heate — Par Lost 4.668
Thou find'st him from the heat of Noon retir'd, — Par Lost 5.231
To sit and taste, till this meridian heat — Par Lost 5.369
Of real hunger, and concoctive heate — Par Lost 5.437
There oft the *Indian* Herdsman shunning heate — Par Lost 9.1108
See with what heat these Dogs of Hell advance — Par Lost 10.616
As might affect the Earth with cold and heat — Par Lost 10.653

Heat(*cont*)
Solstitial summers heat. To the blanc Moone Par Lost 10.656
Avoided pinching cold and scorching heate? Par Lost 10.691
Or Heat should injure us, his timely care Par Lost 10.1057
And sends a comfortable heat from farr, Par Lost 10.1077
Loves Harbinger appeerd; then all in heat Par Lost 11.589
Seed time and Harvest, Heat and hoary Frost Par Lost 11.899
Fierce as a Comet; which with torrid heat, Par Lost 12.634
Of Savage hunger, or of Savage heat? Mask 358
line not in Bridgewater ms
line not in Trinity ms
Smear'd with gumms of glutenous heat Mask 917
1637 'heate'
Trinity ms 'heate'
Bridgewater ms 'heate'
Heath
Stands on the blasted Heath. He now prepar'd Par Lost 1.615
ms 'heath'
Heathen
And various Idols through the Heathen World. Par Lost 1.375
ms 'heathen'
Among the Heathen of thir purchase got, Par Lost 10.579
Among the Heathen, (for throughout the World Par Reg 2.443
Thy Country from her Heathen servitude; Par Reg 3.176
And all the Idolatries of Heathen round, Par Reg 3.418
Among the Heathen round; to God have brought Samson 451
Of Heathen and prophane, thir carkasses Samson 693
Great among the Heathen round: Samson 1430
Th' Heathen, and as thy conquest to be sway'd Psalm 2, 18
Heathenish
Besides thir other worse then heathenish crimes; Par Reg 3.419
Heaths
May trace huge Forests, and unharbour'd Heaths, Mask 423
Bridgewater ms 'heaths'
1637 'heaths'
Heave
Broke up, shall heave the Ocean to usurp Par Lost 11.827
How could I once look up, or heave the head, Samson 197
To heave, pull, draw, or break, he still perform'd Samson 1626
The Sea o'refraught would swell, & th' unsought diamonds Mask 732
Trinity ms 'swell' ←'heave her waters up above the shoare'
Rise, rise, and heave thy rosie head Mask 885
That *Orpheus* self may heave his head Allegro 145
Heaved
Had ris'n or heav'd his head, but that the will Par Lost 1.211
So high as heav'd the tumid Hills, so low Par Lost 7.288
Where the rude Ax with heaved stroke, Penseroso 136
Heaven
Say first, for Heav'n hides nothing from thy view Par Lost 1.27
ms 'heav'n'
Favour'd of Heav'n so highly, to fall off Par Lost 1.30
ms 'heav'n'
Had cast him out from Heav'n, with all his Host Par Lost 1.37
ms 'heav'n'
Rais'd impious War in Heav'n and Battel proud Par Lost 1.43
ms 'heav'n'
As far remov'd from God and light of Heav'n Par Lost 1.73
And thence in Heav'n call'd Satan, with bold words Par Lost 1.82
In dubious Battel on the Plains of Heav'n, Par Lost 1.104
Sole reigning holds the Tyranny of Heav'n. Par Lost 1.124
ms 'Heaven'
Fearless, endanger'd Heav'ns perpetual King; Par Lost 1.131
ms 'Heavens'
Hath lost us Heav'n, and all this mighty Host Par Lost 1.136
ms 'Heavn'
Back to the Gates of Heav'n: the Sulphurous Hail Par Lost 1.171
ms 'Heaven'
Of Heav'n receiv'd us falling, and the Thunder, Par Lost 1.174
ms 'heaven'
And high permission of all-ruling Heaven Par Lost 1.212
ms 'heaven'
That we must change for Heav'n, this mournful gloom Par Lost 1.244
Can make a Heav'n of Hell, a Hell of Heav'n. Par Lost 1.255
Better to reign in Hell, then serve in Heav'n. Par Lost 1.263
Regaind in Heav'n, or what more lost in Hell? Par Lost 1.270
On Heavens Azure, and the torrid Clime Par Lost 1.297
Warriers, the Flowr of Heav'n, once yours, now lost, Par Lost 1.316
To slumber here, as in the Vales of Heav'n? Par Lost 1.321
His swift pursuers from Heav'n Gates discern Par Lost 1.326
And Powers that earst in Heaven sat on Thrones; Par Lost 1.360
Astarte, Queen of Heav'n, with crescent Horns; Par Lost 1.439
ms 'heav'n'
Fell not from Heaven, or more gross to love Par Lost 1.491
ms 'heaven'
Gods, yet confest later then Heav'n and Earth Par Lost 1.509
ms 'heav'n'
Thir boasted Parents; *Titan* Heav'ns first born Par Lost 1.510
ms 'heav'ns'
Thir highest Heav'n; or on the *Delphian* Cliff, Par Lost 1.517
ms 'heav'n'
Of Heav'n, and from Eternal Splendors flung Par Lost 1.610
Thir Glory witherd. As when Heavens Fire Par Lost 1.612
Hath emptied Heav'n, shall fail to re-ascend Par Lost 1.633
ms 'heav'n'
For mee be witness all the Host of Heav'n, Par Lost 1.635
ms 'heav'n'
Monarch in Heav'n, till then as one secure Par Lost 1.638
ms 'heav'n'

Heaven(*cont*)
There went a fame in Heav'n that he ere long Par Lost 1.651
Should favour equal to the Sons of Heaven: Par Lost 1.654
Hurling defiance toward the Vault of Heav'n. Par Lost 1.669
ms 'heav'n'
From heav'n, for ev'n in heav'n his looks and thoughts Par Lost 1.680
The riches of Heav'ns pavement, trod'n Gold, Par Lost 1.682
In Heav'n by many a Towred structure high, Par Lost 1.733
ms 'heav'n'
From Heav'n, they fabl'd, thrown by angry *Jove* Par Lost 1.741
ms 'heav'n'
To have built in Heav'n high Towrs; nor did he scape Par Lost 1.749
ms 'heav'n'
Vain Warr with Heav'n, and by success untaught Par Lost 2.9
Powers and Dominions, Deities of Heav'n, Par Lost 2.11
I give not Heav'n for lost. From this descent Par Lost 2.14
Mee though just right, and the fixt Laws of Heav'n Par Lost 2.18
In Heav'n, which follows dignity, might draw Par Lost 2.25
More then can be in Heav'n, we now return Par Lost 2.37
That fought in Heav'n; now fiercer by despair: Par Lost 2.45
Heav'ns fugitives, and for thir dwelling place Par Lost 2.57
O're Heav'ns high Towrs to force resistless way, Par Lost 2.62
Our power sufficient to disturb his Heav'n, Par Lost 2.102
A fairer person lost not Heav'n; he seemd Par Lost 2.110
First, what Revenge? the Towrs of Heav'n are fill'd Par Lost 2.129
Heav'ns purest Light, yet our great Enemy Par Lost 2.137
With Heav'ns afflicting Thunder, and besought Par Lost 2.166
Views all things at one view? he from heav'ns highth Par Lost 2.190
Shall we then live thus vile, the Race of Heav'n Par Lost 2.194
Either to disinthrone the King of Heav'n Par Lost 2.229
Within Heav'ns bound, unless Heav'ns Lord supream Par Lost 2.236
In Heav'n this our delight; how wearisom Par Lost 2.247
Unacceptable, though in Heav'n, our state Par Lost 2.251
Thick clouds and dark doth Heav'ns all-ruling Sire Par Lost 2.264
Must'ring thir rage, and Heav'n resembles Hell? Par Lost 2.268
Magnificence; and what can Heav'n shew more? Par Lost 2.273
In emulation opposite to Heav'n. Par Lost 2.298
Thrones and Imperial Powers, off-spring of heav'n Par Lost 2.310
And know not that the King of Heav'n hath doom'd Par Lost 2.316
From Heav'ns high jurisdiction, in new League Par Lost 2.319
Us here, as with his Golden those in Heav'n. Par Lost 2.328
Heav'n, whose high walls fear no assault or Siege, Par Lost 2.343
(if ancient and prophetic fame in Heav'n Par Lost 2.346
That shook Heav'ns whol circumference, confirm'd. Par Lost 2.353
By force or suttlety: Though Heav'n be shut, Par Lost 2.358
And Heav'ns high Arbitrator sit secure Par Lost 2.359
Re-enter Heav'n; or else in some milde Zone Par Lost 2.397
Dwell not unvisited of Heav'ns fair Light Par Lost 2.398
O Progeny of Heav'n, Empyreal Thrones, Par Lost 2.430
Terror of Heav'n, though fall'n; intend at home, Par Lost 2.457
Extoll him equal to the highest in Heav'n: Par Lost 2.479
Heav'ns chearful face, the lowring Element Par Lost 2.490
Alone th' Antagonist of Heav'n, nor less Par Lost 2.509
From either end of Heav'n the welkin burns. Par Lost 2.538
Hell-born, not to contend with Spirits of Heav'n. Par Lost 2.687
Who first broke peace in Heav'n and Faith, till then Par Lost 2.690
Drew after him the third part of Heav'ns Sons Par Lost 2.692
And reck'n'st thou thy self with Spirits of Heav'n, Par Lost 2.696
With Heav'ns Artillery fraught, come rattling on Par Lost 2.715
In Heav'n, when at th' Assembly, and in sight Par Lost 2.749
In bold conspiracy against Heav'ns King, Par Lost 2.751
All th' Host of Heav'n; back they recoild affraid Par Lost 2.759
And fields were fought in Heav'n; wherein remaind Par Lost 2.768
Driv'n headlong from the Pitch of Heaven, down Par Lost 2.772
Of dalliance had with thee in Heav'n, and joys Par Lost 2.819
1667 'Heavn'' in some copies
In the Pourlieues of Heav'n, and therein plac't Par Lost 2.833
Least Heav'n surcharg'd with potent multitude Par Lost 2.836
And by command of Heav'ns all-powerful King Par Lost 2.851
Inhabitant of Heav'n, and heav'nlie-born, Par Lost 2.860
Of Heav'n were falling, and these Elements Par Lost 2.925
Confine with Heav'n; or if som other place Par Lost 2.977
Made head against Heav'ns King, though overthrown. Par Lost 2.992
Confusion worse confounded; and Heav'n Gates Par Lost 2.996
Now lately Heaven and Earth, another World Par Lost 2.1004
To that side Heav'n from whence your Legions fell: Par Lost 2.1006
Following his track, such was the will of Heav'n, Par Lost 2.1025
Of light appears, and from the walls of Heav'n Par Lost 2.1035
Farr off th' Empyreal Heav'n, extended wide Par Lost 2.1047
Hail holy Light, ofspring of Heav'n first-born, Par Lost 3.1
About him all the Sanctities of Heaven Par Lost 3.60
Coasting the wall of Heav'n on this side Night Par Lost 3.71
Not farr off Heav'n, in the Precincts of light, Par Lost 3.88
Through Heav'n and Earth, so shall my glorie excel, Par Lost 3.133
All Heav'n, and in the blessed Spirits elect Par Lost 3.136
For which both Heav'n and Earth shall high extoll Par Lost 3.146
Against the high Supremacie of Heav'n, Par Lost 3.205
Dwels in all Heaven charitie so deare? Par Lost 3.216
And silence was in Heav'n: on mans behalf Par Lost 3.218
Pleas'd, out of Heaven shalt look down and smile, Par Lost 3.257
Shall enter Heaven long absent, and returne, Par Lost 3.261
All Heav'n, what this might mean, and whither tend Par Lost 3.272
O thou in Heav'n and Earth the only peace Par Lost 3.274
In Heaven, or Earth, or under Earth in Hell; Par Lost 3.322
When thou attended gloriously from Heav'n Par Lost 3.323
New Heav'n and Earth, wherein the just shall dwell, Par Lost 3.335
As from blest voices, uttering joy, Heav'n rung Par Lost 3.347
To Heav'n remov'd where first it grew, there grows, Par Lost 3.356

Heaven(*cont*)

And where the river of Bliss through midst of Heavn	Par Lost 3.358
Melodious part, such concord is in Heav'n.	Par Lost 3.371
Yet dazle Heav'n, that brightest Seraphim	Par Lost 3.381
Hee Heav'n of Heavens and all the Powers therein	Par Lost 3.390
Heav'ns everlasting Frame, while o're the necks	Par Lost 3.395
Thus they in Heav'n, above the starry Sphear,	Par Lost 3.416
Save on that side which from the wall of Heav'n	Par Lost 3.427
In *Golgotha* him dead, who lives in Heav'n;	Par Lost 3.477
And now Saint *Peter* at Heav'ns Wicket seems	Par Lost 3.484
Of Heav'ns ascent they lift thir Feet, when loe	Par Lost 3.486
Up to the wall of Heaven a Structure high,	Par Lost 3.503
And waking cri'd, *This is the Gate of Heav'n*	Par Lost 3.515
1667 'Heav'n'	
There alwayes, but drawn up to Heav'n somtimes	Par Lost 3.517
That scal'd by steps of Gold to Heav'n Gate	Par Lost 3.541
Such wonder seis'd, though after Heaven seen,	Par Lost 3.552
The golden Sun in splendor likest Heaven	Par Lost 3.572
Interpreter through highest Heav'n to bring,	Par Lost 3.657
By his permissive will, through Heav'n and Earth:	Par Lost 3.685
The sharpest sighted Spirit of all in Heav'n;	Par Lost 3.691
Contented with report hear onely in heav'n:	Par Lost 3.701
And this Ethereal quintessence of Heav'n	Par Lost 3.716
Still ending, still renewing, through mid Heav'n;	Par Lost 3.729
As to superior Spirits is wont in Heaven,	Par Lost 3.737
1667 'Heav'n' in some copies	
Th' *Apocalyps*, heard cry in Heaven aloud,	Par Lost 4.2
Sometimes towards Heav'n and the full-blazing Sun,	Par Lost 4.29
Warring in Heav'n against Heav'ns matchless King:	Par Lost 4.41
But Heav'ns free Love dealt equally to all?	Par Lost 4.68
To which the Hell I suffer seems a Heav'n.	Par Lost 4.78
Divided Empire with Heav'ns King I hold	Par Lost 4.111
A Heav'n on Earth, for blissful Paradise	Par Lost 4.208
Of Heav'n the Starrs that usher Evening rose:	Par Lost 4.355
Long to continue, and this high seat your Heav'n	Par Lost 4.371
Ill fenc't for Heav'n to keep out such a foe	Par Lost 4.372
Pure as th' expanse of Heav'n; I thither went	Par Lost 4.456
Some wandring Spirit of Heav'n, by Fountain side,	Par Lost 4.531
Mean while in utmost Longitude, where Heav'n	Par Lost 4.539
Th' unarmed Youth of Heav'n, but nigh at hand	Par Lost 4.552
Alien from Heav'n, with passions foul obscur'd:	Par Lost 4.571
Well known from Heav'n; and since Meridian hour	Par Lost 4.581
And the regard of Heav'n on all his waies;	Par Lost 4.620
And these the Gemms of Heav'n, her starrie train:	Par Lost 4.649
That heav'n would want spectators, God want praise;	Par Lost 4.676
Divide the night, and lift our thoughts to Heaven.	Par Lost 4.688
The God that made both Skie, Air, Earth and Heav'n	Par Lost 4.722
As when thou stoodst in Heav'n upright and pure;	Par Lost 4.837
Gabriel, thou hadst in Heav'n th' esteem of wise,	Par Lost 4.886
O loss of one in Heav'n to judge of wise,	Par Lost 4.904
High up in Heav'n, with songs to hymne his Throne,	Par Lost 4.944
Heav'ns awful Monarch? wherefore but in hope	Par Lost 4.960
From my prevailing arme, though Heavens King	Par Lost 4.973
In progress through the rode of Heav'n Star-pav'd.	Par Lost 4.976
Of Heav'n perhaps, or all the Elements	Par Lost 4.993
Hung forth in Heav'n his golden Scales, yet seen	Par Lost 4.997
Then Heav'n permits, nor mine, though doubld now	Par Lost 4.1009
Heav'ns last best gift, my ever new delight,	Par Lost 5.19
If none regard; Heav'n wakes with all his eyes,	Par Lost 5.44
One shapd and wing'd like one of those from Heav'n	Par Lost 5.55
Ascend to Heav'n, by merit thine, and see	Par Lost 5.80
Circle his Throne rejoycing, yee in Heav'n,	Par Lost 5.163
That singing up to Heaven Gate ascend,	Par Lost 5.198
With pittie Heav'ns high King, and to him call'd	Par Lost 5.220
Late falln himself from Heav'n, is plotting now	Par Lost 5.240
1667 'Heaven' in some copies	
Flew through the midst of Heav'n; th' angelic Quires	Par Lost 5.251
Of Heav'n arriv'd, the gate self-opend wide	Par Lost 5.254
And colours dipt in Heav'n; the third his feet	Par Lost 5.283
Ris'n on mid-noon; som great behest from Heav'n	Par Lost 5.311
God hath dispenst his bounties as in Heav'n.	Par Lost 5.330
Thus said. Native of Heav'n, for other place	Par Lost 5.361
None can then Heav'n such glorious shape contain;	Par Lost 5.362
As may not oft invite, though Spirits of Heav'n	Par Lost 5.374
Stood to entertain her guest from Heav'n; no vaile	Par Lost 5.383
Sups with the Ocean: though in Heav'n the Trees	Par Lost 5.426
As may compare with Heaven; and to taste	Par Lost 5.432
Who dwell in Heav'n, whose excellence he saw	Par Lost 5.456
At Heav'ns high feasts to have fed: yet what compare?	Par Lost 5.467
To whom the Angel. Son of Heav'n and Earth,	Par Lost 5.519
And so from Heav'n to deepest Hell; O fall	Par Lost 5.542
Hath past in Heav'n, som doubt within me move,	Par Lost 5.554
His other half in the great Zone of Heav'n.	Par Lost 5.560
Be but the shaddow of Heav'n, and things therein	Par Lost 5.575
As Heav'ns great Year brings forth, th' Empyreal Host	Par Lost 5.583
Forthwith from all the ends of Heav'n appeerd	Par Lost 5.586
All knees in Heav'n, and shall confess him Lord:	Par Lost 5.608
Fruit of delicious Vines, the growth of Heav'n.	Par Lost 5.635
Spring both, the face of brightest Heav'n had changd	Par Lost 5.644
Is heard no more in Heav'n; he of the first,	Par Lost 5.659
Of Heav'ns Almightie. Thou to me thy thoughts	Par Lost 5.676
Now ere dim Night had disincumberd Heav'n,	Par Lost 5.700
His name, and high was his degree in Heav'n;	Par Lost 5.707
Drew after him the third part of Heav'ns Host:	Par Lost 5.710
Thy Rebels, or be found the worst in Heav'n.	Par Lost 5.742
Messiah was declar'd in sight of Heav'n,	Par Lost 5.765
Natives and Sons of Heav'n possest before	Par Lost 5.790
Words which no eare ever to hear in Heav'n	Par Lost 5.810

Heaven(*cont*)

With Regal Scepter, every Soule in Heav'n	Par Lost 5.816
Thee what thou art, and formd the Pow'rs of Heav'n	Par Lost 5.824
All things, ev'n thee, and all the Spirits of Heav'n	Par Lost 5.837
Of this our native Heav'n, Ethereal Sons.	Par Lost 5.863
Through Heav'ns wide Champain held his way, till Morn,	Par Lost 6.2
Lodge and dislodge by turns, which makes through Heav'n	Par Lost 6.7
To veile the Heav'n, though darkness there might well	Par Lost 6.11
Such as in highest Heav'n, arrayd in Gold	Par Lost 6.13
Fearless assault, and to the brow of Heav'n	Par Lost 6.51
That stood for Heav'n, in mighty Quadrate joyn'd	Par Lost 6.62
Of Heav'n they march'd, and many a Province wide	Par Lost 6.77
O Heav'n! that such resemblance of the Highest	Par Lost 6.114
At first I thought that Libertie and Heav'n	Par Lost 6.164
Such hast thou arm'd, the Minstrelsie of Heav'n,	Par Lost 6.168
In Heav'n God ever blest, and his Divine	Par Lost 6.184
Th' Arch-Angel trumpet; through the vast of Heaven	Par Lost 6.203
1667 'Heav'n'	
And clamour such as heard in Heav'n till now	Par Lost 6.208
And inextinguishable rage; all Heav'n	Par Lost 6.217
From his strong hold of Heav'n high over-rul'd	Par Lost 6.228
Intestine War in Heav'n, the arch foe subdu'd	Par Lost 6.259
Unnam'd in Heav'n, now plenteous, as thou seest	Par Lost 6.263
Heav'ns blessed peace, and into Nature brought	Par Lost 6.267
To trouble Holy Rest; Heav'n casts thee out	Par Lost 6.272
From all her Confines. Heav'n the seat of bliss	Par Lost 6.273
Or turn this Heav'n it self into the Hell	Par Lost 6.291
Fit to decide the Empire of great Heav'n.	Par Lost 6.303
Threatn'd, nor from the Holie One of Heav'n	Par Lost 6.359
Angels contented with thir fame in Heav'n	Par Lost 6.375
Canceld from Heav'n and sacred memorie,	Par Lost 6.379
Now Night her course began, and over Heav'n	Par Lost 6.406
What Heavens Lord had powerfullest to send	Par Lost 6.425
This continent of spacious Heav'n, adornd	Par Lost 6.474
With Heav'ns ray, and temperd they shoot forth	Par Lost 6.480
Now when fair Morn Orient in Heav'n appeerd	Par Lost 6.524
But that I doubt, however witness Heaven,	Par Lost 6.563
Heav'n witness thou anon, while we discharge	Par Lost 6.564
But soon obscur'd with smoak, all Heav'n appeerd,	Par Lost 6.585
(For Earth hath this variety from Heav'n	Par Lost 6.640
Upon confusion rose: and now all Heav'n	Par Lost 6.669
Shrin'd in his Sanctuarie of Heav'n secure,	Par Lost 6.672
Two dayes, as we compute the dayes of Heav'n,	Par Lost 6.685
Wild work in Heav'n, and dangerous to the maine.	Par Lost 6.698
In Heav'n and Hell thy Power above compare,	Par Lost 6.705
That shake Heav'ns basis, bring forth all my Warr,	Par Lost 6.712
From all Heav'ns bounds into the utter Deep:	Par Lost 6.716
Armd with thy might, rid Heav'n of these rebell'd,	Par Lost 6.737
Dawning through Heav'n: forth rush'd with whirlwind sound	Par Lost 6.749
Aloft by Angels born, his Sign in Heav'n:	Par Lost 6.776
Obsequious, Heav'n his wonted face renewd,	Par Lost 6.783
Because the Father, t' whom in Heav'n supream	Par Lost 6.814
Not to destroy, but root them out of Heav'n:	Par Lost 6.855
And Chrystal wall of Heav'n, which op'ning wide,	Par Lost 6.860
Down from the verge of Heav'n, Eternal wrauth	Par Lost 6.865
Heav'n ruining from Heav'n and would have fled	Par Lost 6.868
Disburd'nd Heav'n rejoic'd, and soon repaird	Par Lost 6.878
Triumphant through mid Heav'n, into the Courts	Par Lost 6.889
Thus measuring things in Heav'n by things on Earth	Par Lost 6.893
The discord which befel, and Warr in Heav'n	Par Lost 6.897
Descend from Heav'n *Urania*, by that name	Par Lost 7.1
Into the Heav'n of Heav'ns I have presum'd,	Par Lost 7.13
Apostasie, by what befell in Heaven	Par Lost 7.43
So unimaginable as hate in Heav'n,	Par Lost 7.54
Of Heav'n and Earth conspicious first began,	Par Lost 7.63
How first began this Heav'n which we behold	Par Lost 7.86
Much of his Race though steep, suspens in Heav'n	Par Lost 7.99
To none communicable in Earth or Heaven:	Par Lost 7.124
Know then, that after *Lucifer* from Heav'n	Par Lost 7.131
Thir station, Heav'n yet populous retaines	Par Lost 7.146
Already done, to have dispeopl'd Heav'n	Par Lost 7.151
And Earth be chang'd to Heav'n, & Heav'n to Earth,	Par Lost 7.160
1669 'to Heav'n'	
1667 'to Heavn'	
Mean while inhabit laxe, ye Powers of Heav'n,	Par Lost 7.162
Within appointed bounds be Heav'n and Earth,	Par Lost 7.167
Great triumph and rejoycing was in Heav'n	Par Lost 7.180
Attendant on thir Lord: Heav'n op'nd wide	Par Lost 7.205
Heav'ns highth, and with the Center mix the Pole.	Par Lost 7.215
Thus God the Heav'n created, thus the Earth,	Par Lost 7.232
Birth-day of Heav'n and Earth; with joy and shout	Par Lost 7.256
And Heav'n he nam'd the Firmament: So Eev'n	Par Lost 7.274
Be gather'd now ye Waters under Heav'n	Par Lost 7.283
Seemd like to Heav'n, a seat where Gods might dwell,	Par Lost 7.329
High in th' expanse of Heaven to divide	Par Lost 7.340
Thir Office in the Firmament of Heav'n	Par Lost 7.344
And set them in the Firmament of Heav'n	Par Lost 7.349
And sowd with Starrs the Heav'n thick as a field:	Par Lost 7.358
His Longitude through Heav'ns high rode: the gray	Par Lost 7.373
Revolvd on Heav'ns great Axle, and her Reign	Par Lost 7.381
Displayd on the op'n Firmament of Heav'n.	Par Lost 7.390
Now Heav'n in all her Glorie shon, and rowld	Par Lost 7.499
Magnanimous to correspond with Heav'n,	Par Lost 7.511
Up to the Heav'n of Heav'ns his high abode,	Par Lost 7.553
The glorious Train ascending: He through Heav'n,	Par Lost 7.574
Of Heav'ns high-seated top, th' Impereal Throne	Par Lost 7.585
Witness this new-made World, another Heav'n	Par Lost 7.617
From Heaven Gate not farr, founded in view	Par Lost 7.618

Heaven(*cont*)
Of Heav'n and Earth consisting, and compute, Par Lost 8.16
To ask or search I blame thee not, for Heav'n Par Lost 8.66
This to attain, whether Heav'n move or Earth, Par Lost 8.70
Hereafter, when they come to model Heav'n Par Lost 8.79
The less not bright, nor Heav'n such journies run, Par Lost 8.88
Though, in comparison of Heav'n, so small, Par Lost 8.92
And for the Heav'ns wide Circuit, let it speak Par Lost 8.100
Who since the Morning hour set out from Heav'n Par Lost 8.111
Plac'd Heav'n from Earth so farr, that earthly sight, Par Lost 8.120
Whether the Sun predominant in Heav'n Par Lost 8.160
And thy faire *Eve;* Heav'n is for thee too high Par Lost 8.172
Not of Earth onely but of highest Heav'n. Par Lost 8.178
Intelligence of Heav'n, Angel serene, Par Lost 8.181
For while I sit with thee, I seem in Heav'n, Par Lost 8.210
Nor less think wee in Heav'n of thee on Earth Par Lost 8.224
Strait toward Heav'n my wondring Eyes I turnd, Par Lost 8.257
With what all Earth or Heaven could bestow Par Lost 8.483
Grace was in all her steps, Heav'n in her Eye, Par Lost 8.488
I led her blushing like the Morn: all Heav'n, Par Lost 8.511
Leads up to Heav'n, is both the way and guide; Par Lost 8.613
So parted they, the Angel up to Heav'n Par Lost 8.652
And disobedience: On the part of Heav'n Par Lost 9.8
O Earth, how like to Heav'n, if not preferr'd Par Lost 9.99
Terrestrial Heav'n, danc't round by other Heav'ns Par Lost 9.103
Of sacred influence: As God in Heav'n Par Lost 9.107
Bane, and in Heav'n much worse would be my state. Par Lost 9.123
But neither here seek I, no nor in Heav'n Par Lost 9.124
To dwell, unless by maistring Heav'ns Supreame; Par Lost 9.125
Of Heav'n, this Man of Clay, Son of despite, Par Lost 9.176
Ofspring of Heav'n and Earth, and all Earths Lord, Par Lost 9.273
Favour from Heav'n, our witness from th' event. Par Lost 9.334
Though in mid Heav'n, soon ended his delight, Par Lost 9.468
Infeebl'd me, to what I was in Heav'n. Par Lost 9.488
Thy looks, the Heav'n of mildness, with disdain, Par Lost 9.534
Considerd all things visible in Heav'n, Par Lost 9.604
And I perhaps am secret; Heav'n is high, Par Lost 9.811
Was known in Heav'n; for what can scape the Eye Par Lost 10.5
Up into Heav'n from Paradise in haste Par Lost 10.17
From Earth arriv'd at Heaven Gate, displeas'd Par Lost 10.22
All Judgement, whether in Heav'n, or Earth, or Hell. Par Lost 10.57
Mine both in Heav'n and Earth to do thy will Par Lost 10.69
Accompanied to Heaven Gate, from whence Par Lost 10.88
O Heav'n! in evil strait this day I stand Par Lost 10.125
Saw Satan fall like Lightning down from Heav'n, Par Lost 10.184
The confines met of Empyrean Heav'n Par Lost 10.321
Our foile in Heav'n; here thou shalt Monarch reign, Par Lost 10.375
Antagonist of Heav'ns Almightie King) Par Lost 10.387
Th' infernal Empire, that so neer Heav'ns dore Par Lost 10.389
As Lords, a spacious World, to our native Heaven Par Lost 10.467
The new created World, which fame in Heav'n Par Lost 10.481
Alike is Hell, or Paradise, or Heaven, Par Lost 10.598
Then Heav'n and Earth renewd shall be made pure Par Lost 10.638
New Heav'n and Earth shall to the Ages rise, Par Lost 10.647
Or down from Heav'n descend. Such was thir song, Par Lost 10.648
Creator wise, that peopl'd highest Heav'n Par Lost 10.889
Forsake me not thus, *Adam*, witness Heav'n Par Lost 10.914
There with my cries importune Heaven, that all Par Lost 10.933
Inspir'd, and wing'd for Heav'n with speedier flight Par Lost 11.7
Of *Themis* stood devout. To Heav'n thir prayers Par Lost 11.14
Resignes him up with Heav'n and Earth renewd. Par Lost 11.66
Through Heav'ns wide bounds; from them I will not hide Par Lost 11.68
The good which we enjoy, from Heav'n descends; Par Lost 11.142
But that from us ought should ascend to Heav'n Par Lost 11.143
Which Heav'n by these mute signs in Nature shews Par Lost 11.194
Adam, Heav'ns high behest no Preface needs: Par Lost 11.251
Adam, thou know'st Heav'n his, and all the Earth. Par Lost 11.335
Thou lead'st me, and to the hand of Heav'n submit, Par Lost 11.372
His Offring soon propitious Fire from Heav'n Par Lost 11.441
From Heav'n acceptance; but the bloodie Fact Par Lost 11.457
Live well, how long or short permit to Heav'n: Par Lost 11.554
But who was that Just Man, whom had not Heav'n Par Lost 11.681
From under Heav'n; the Hills to their supplie Par Lost 11.740
Of Heav'n set open on the Earth shall powre Par Lost 11.825
His Sluces, as the Heav'n his windows shut. Par Lost 11.849
Grateful to Heav'n, over his head beholds Par Lost 11.864
But say, what mean those colourd streaks in Heavn, Par Lost 11.879
Both Heav'n and Earth, wherein the just shall dwell. Par Lost 11.901
Before the Lord, as in despite of Heav'n, Par Lost 12.34
Or from Heav'n claming second Sovrantie; Par Lost 12.35
A Citie and Towre, whose top may reach to Heav'n; Par Lost 12.44
Obstruct Heav'n Towrs, and in derision sets Par Lost 12.52
As mockt they storm; great laughter was in Heav'n Par Lost 12.59
Or how the Sun shall in mid Heav'n stand still Par Lost 12.263
Here *Adam* interpos'd. O sent from Heav'n, Par Lost 12.270
To *David*, stablisht as the dayes of Heav'n. Par Lost 12.347
Unseen before in Heav'n proclaims him com, Par Lost 12.361
High in the love of Heav'n, yet from my Loynes Par Lost 12.380
Satan, whose fall from Heav'n, a deadlier bruise, Par Lost 12.391
Then to the Heav'n of Heav'ns he shall ascend Par Lost 12.451
Above all names in Heav'n; and thence shall come, Par Lost 12.458
Whether in Heav'n or Earth, for then the Earth Par Lost 12.463
But say, if our deliverer up to Heav'n Par Lost 12.479
Be sure they will, said th' Angel; but from Heav'n Par Lost 12.485
With joy the tidings brought from Heav'n: at length Par Lost 12.504
Who all the sacred mysteries of Heav'n Par Lost 12.509
Last in the Clouds from Heav'n to be reveald Par Lost 12.545
Or works of God in Heav'n, Aire, Earth, or Sea, Par Lost 12.579

Heaven(*cont*)
Art all things under Heav'n, all places thou, Par Lost 12.618
Repentance, and Heavens Kingdom nigh at hand Par Reg 1.20
Heaven open'd, and in likeness of a Dove Par Reg 1.30
From Heav'n pronounc'd him his beloved Son. Par Reg 1.32
Upon my head, long the decrees of Heav'n Par Reg 1.55
The testimony of Heaven, that who he is Par Reg 1.78
Out of the water, Heav'n above the Clouds Par Reg 1.81
And out of Heav'n the Sov'raign voice I heard, Par Reg 1.84
He who obtains the Monarchy of Heav'n, Par Reg 1.87
So spake the Eternal Father, and all Heaven Par Reg 1.168
So they in Heav'n their Odes and Vigils tun'd: Par Reg 1.182
All Heaven and Earth, Angels and Sons of men, Par Reg 1.237
A Star, not seen before in Heaven appearing Par Reg 1.249
Affirming it thy Star new grav'n in Heaven, Par Reg 1.253
Me him (for it was shew'n him so from Heaven) Par Reg 1.276
Heaven open'd her eternal doors, from whence Par Reg 1.281
Audibly heard from Heav'n, pronounc'd me his, Par Reg 1.284
The Authority which I deriv'd from Heaven. Par Reg 1.289
Or range in th' Air, nor from the Heav'n of Heav'ns Par Reg 1.366
Into the Heav'n of Heavens; thou com'st indeed, Par Reg 1.410
To all the Host of Heaven; the happy place Par Reg 1.416
So never more in Hell then when in Heaven. Par Reg 1.420
But thou art serviceable to Heaven's King. Par Reg 1.421
Rode up to Heaven, yet once again to come. Par Reg 2.17
Son own'd from Heaven by his Father's voice; Par Reg 2.85
Princes, Heavens antient Sons, Aethereal Thrones, Par Reg 2.121
With more then humane gifts from Heaven adorn'd, Par Reg 2.137
Rain'd from Heaven Manna, and that Prophet bold Par Reg 2.312
The just man, and divulges him through Heaven Par Reg 3.62
When to extend his fame through Heaven and Earth, Par Reg 3.65
Famous he was in Heaven, on Earth less known; Par Reg 3.68
Orders and governs, nor content in Heaven Par Reg 3.112
From Heaven descended to the low-rooft house Par Reg 4.273
Now contrary, if I read aught in Heaven, Par Reg 4.382
Or Heav'n write aught of Fate, by what the Stars Par Reg 4.383
Gan thunder, and both ends of Heav'n, the Clouds Par Reg 4.410
As dangerous to the pillard frame of Heaven, Par Reg 4.455
Though not to be Baptiz'd, by voice from Heav'n Par Reg 4.512
Worth naming Son of God by voice from Heav'n, Par Reg 4.539
Conceiving, or remote from Heaven, enshrin'd Par Reg 4.598
Thou didst debel, and down from Heav'n cast Par Reg 4.605
Or Lightning thou shalt fall from Heav'n trod down Par Reg 4.620
The breath of Heav'n fresh-blowing, pure and sweet, Samson 10
O wherefore was my birth from Heaven foretold Samson 23
Like whom the Gentiles feign to bear up Heav'n. Samson 150
Of birth from Heav'n foretold and high exploits, Samson 525
With touch aetherial of Heav'ns fiery rod Samson 549
My Nation, and the work from Heav'n impos'd, Samson 565
And sense of Heav'ns desertion. Samson 632
Favour'd of Heav'n who finds Samson 1046
Arm'd thee or charm'd thee strong, which thou from Heaven Samson 1134
With strength sufficient and command from Heav'n Samson 1212
I was to do my part from Heav'n assign'd, Samson 1217
For never was from Heaven imparted Samson 1438
Mercy of Heav'n what hideous noise was that! Samson 1509
I shoot from Heav'n to give him safe convoy, Mask 81
  Trinity ms 'heaven'
  Bridgewater ms 'heaven'
  1637 'heav'n'
Now the top of Heav'n doth hold, Mask 94
  Bridgewater ms 'Heaven'
  1637 'heav'n'
  Trinity ms 'heav'n'
That nature hung in Heav'n, and fill'd their Lamps Mask 198
  Trinity ms 'heaven'
  line not in Bridgewater ms
And give resounding grace to all Heav'ns Harmonies. Mask 243
  Bridgewater ms 'heavn's'
  Trinity ms 'heavns'
It were a journey like the path to Heav'n, Mask 303
  Bridgewater ms 'heav'n'
  Trinity ms 'heav'n'
  1637 'heav'n'
Unless the strength of Heav'n, if you mean that? Mask 417
  Trinity ms 'heaven'
  1637 'heav'n'
  Bridgewater ms 'heav'n'
Which if Heav'n gave it, may be term'd her own: Mask 419
  1637 'heav'n'
  Bridgewater ms 'heaven'
  Trinity ms 'heaven'
So dear to Heav'n is Saintly chastity, Mask 453
  1637 'heav'n'
  Bridgewater ms 'heav'n'
  Trinity ms 'heaven'
2. *Bro*. Heav'n keep my sister, agen agen and neer, Mask 486
  Bridgewater ms 'heav'n'
  Trinity ms 'heav'n'
Defence is a good cause, and Heav'n be for us. Mask 489
  Bridgewater ms 'heav'n'
  Trinity ms 'heav'n'
Against th' opposing will and arm of Heav'n Mask 600
  Trinity ms 'heav'n'
  1637 'heav'n'
  Bridgewater ms 'heav'n'
Thou haste immanacl'd, while Heav'n sees good. Mask 665
  Trinity ms 'heavn' ←'heaven'

Heaven(*cont*)
1637 'heav'n'
Bridgewater ms 'heav'n'
Ne're looks to Heav'n amidst his gorgeous feast, Mask 777
1637 'heav'n'
Bridgewater ms 'heav'n'
Trinity ms 'heav'n'
Com Lady while Heaven lends us grace, Mask 938
Bridgewater ms 'heav'n'
1637 'heaven'
Trinity ms 'heav'n'
Heav'n hath timely tri'd their youth, Mask 970
Heav'n it self would stoop to her. Mask 1023
Trinity ms 'heaven' ←'heav'n'
Cardoyn 'Heaven'
Bridgewater ms 'Heven'
this dusky hollow is a paradise & heaven gates ore my head Mask Tr. ms 13.44
& good heaven cast his best regard upon us Mask Tr. ms 21.32
In Heav'n ycleap'd *Euphrosyne*, Allegro 12
Through the Heav'ns wide pathles way; Penseroso 70
And bring all Heav'n before mine eyes. Penseroso 166
Of every Star that Heav'n doth shew, Penseroso 171
Toward Heav'ns descent had slop'd his westering wheel. Lycidas 31
Of so much fame in Heav'n expect thy meed. Lycidas 84
1638 'heav'n'
Trinity ms 'heav'n'
and heaven and hel deplore Lycidas Tr. ms 29.59
Wherin the Son of Heav'ns eternal King, Nativity 2
Wherwith he wont at Heav'ns high Councel-Table, Nativity 10
Now while the Heav'n by the Suns team untrod, Nativity 19
Could hold all Heav'n and Earth in happier union. Nativity 108
With unexpressive notes to Heav'ns new-born Heir. Nativity 116
And let the Base of Heav'ns deep Organ blow, Nativity 130
And Heav'n as at som festivall, Nativity 147
Heav'ns Queen and Mother both, Nativity 201
Heav'ns youngest teemed Star, Nativity 240
Amazed Heav'n and Earth to shake. Psalm 136, 14
Could Heav'n for pittie thee so strictly doom? Fair Inf 33
Of sheenie Heav'n, and thou some goddess fled Fair Inf 48
As if to shew what creatures Heav'n doth breed, Fair Inf 61
To scorn the sordid world, and unto Heav'n aspire. Fair Inf 63
Above the wheeling poles, and at Heav'ns dore Vacation 34
In Heav'ns defiance mustering all his waves; Vacation 44
That Heav'n and Earth are colour'd with my wo; Passion 32
That was the Casket of Heav'ns richest store, Passion 44
He who with all Heav'ns heraldry whileare Circum 10
Trinity ms 'heav'ns'
Blest pair of *Sirens*, pledges of Heav'ns joy, Musick 1
Trinity ms 'heavens'
And keep in tune with Heav'n, till God ere long Musick 26
Trinity ms 'heav'n' ←'heaven'
Heavn's henshmen Musick Tr. ms 4.16
while all the starrie rounds & arches blue Musick Tr. ms 4.21
'while all the starrie rounds' ←'starrie frame' ←'whilst then' ←'whilst the whole frame of heaven' ←'while all the starrie' ←'that all'
Toward which Time leads me, and the will of Heav'n; Sonnet 7, 12
Trinity ms 'heaven'
Of Death, call'd Life; which us from Life doth sever. Sonnet 14, 4
Trinity ms 'from life' ←'from blis' ←'from life' ←'from heavn'
To Heav'n. Their martyr'd blood and ashes sow Sonnet 18, 10
For other things mild Heav'n a time ordains, Sonnet 21, 11
Trinity ms 'Heaven'
Against heavns hand or will, nor bate a jot Sonnet 22, 7
Trinity ms 'heavns' ←'Gods'
1694 'Heaven's'
Full sight of her in Heaven without restraint, Sonnet 23, 8
Trinity ms 'heaven'
Their twisted cords: he who in Heaven doth dwell Psalm 2, 8
From Heav'n, thy Seat divine, Psalm 80, 58

Heaven-banished
Heav'n-banisht Host, left desert utmost Hell Par Lost 10.437

Heaven-born-child
While the Heav'n-born-childe, Nativity 30

Heaven-fallen
Heav'n-fall'n, in station stood or just array, Par Lost 10.535

Heaven-gifted
With this Heav'n-gifted strength? O glorious strength Samson 36

Heaven-loved
To bless us with thy heav'n-lov'd innocence, Fair Inf 65

Heavenly
Sing Heav'nly Muse, that on the secret top Par Lost 1.6
ms 'heav'nly'
As far as Gods and Heav'nly Essences Par Lost 1.138
ms 'heavenly'
Though of thir Names in heav'nly Records now Par Lost 1.361
ms 'heavenly'
Of heavenly Grace: and God proclaiming peace, Par Lost 2.499
Then shining heav'nly fair, a Goddess arm'd Par Lost 2.757
Though temper'd heav'nly, for that mortal dint, Par Lost 2.813
Both him and thee, and all the heav'nly Host Par Lost 2.824
Taught by the heav'nly Muse to venture down Par Lost 3.19
Say Heav'nly powers, where shall we find such love, Par Lost 3.213
He ask'd, but all the Heav'nly Quire stood mute, Par Lost 3.217
So Heav'nly love shall outdoo Hellish hate Par Lost 3.298
For heav'nly mindes from such distempers foule Par Lost 4.118

Heavenly(*cont*)
Not Spirits, yet to heav'nly Spirits bright Par Lost 4.361
With Heav'nly touch of instrumental sounds Par Lost 4.686
And heav'nly Quires the Hymenaean sung, Par Lost 4.711
And shook his Plumes, that Heav'nly fragrance filld Par Lost 5.286
Our Heav'nly stranger; well we may afford Par Lost 5.316
Our Authour. Heav'nly stranger, please to taste Par Lost 5.397
Here or in Heav'nly Paradises dwell; Par Lost 5.500
To heav'nly Soules had bin all one; but now Par Lost 6.165
O Father, O Supream of heav'nly Thrones, Par Lost 6.723
In heav'nly Spirits could such perverseness dwell? Par Lost 6.788
Of old *Olympus* dwell'st, but Heav'nlie borne, Par Lost 7.7
1669 'Heav'nly born'
For thou art Heav'nlie, shee an empty dreame. Par Lost 7.39
1669 'Heav'nlie'
1667 'Heav'n lie'
Proceeded thus to ask his Heav'nly Guest. Par Lost 7.69
On heav'nly ground they stood, and from the shore Par Lost 7.210
1669 'Heav'nly'
To whom thus *Raphael* answer'd heav'nly meek. Par Lost 8.217
And to the Heav'nly vision thus presum'd. Par Lost 8.356
Let not my words offend thee, Heav'nly Power, Par Lost 8.379
My earthly by his Heav'nly overpowerd, Par Lost 8.453
Led by her Heav'nly Maker, though unseen, Par Lost 8.485
By which to heav'nly Love thou maist ascend, Par Lost 8.592
Love not the heav'nly Spirits, and how thir Love Par Lost 8.615
Go heavenly Guest, Ethereal Messenger, Par Lost 8.646
With Heav'nly spoils, our spoils: What he decreed Par Lost 9.151
Thus earlie, thus alone; her Heav'nly forme Par Lost 9.457
Semblance, and in thy Beauties heav'nly Ray Par Lost 9.607
In heav'nly brests? these, these and many more Par Lost 9.730
And rapture so oft beheld? those heav'nly shapes Par Lost 9.1082
A place so heav'nly, and conniving seem Par Lost 10.624
He ended, and the heav'nly Audience loud Par Lost 10.641
Henceforth; least that too heav'nly form, pretended Par Lost 10.872
Dimentionless through Heav'nly dores; then clad Par Lost 11.17
And slow descends, with somthing heav'nly fraught. Par Lost 11.207
He err'd not, for by this the heav'nly Bands Par Lost 11.208
One of the heav'nly Host, and by his Gate Par Lost 11.230
As present, Heav'nly instructer, I revive Par Lost 11.871
The Heav'nly fires; over the Tent a Cloud Par Lost 12.256
To him his Heavenly Office, nor was long Par Reg 1.28
Yet held it more humane, more heavenly first Par Reg 1.221
Sung Heavenly Anthems of his victory Par Reg 4.594
Sung Victor, and from Heavenly Feast refresht Par Reg 4.637
Sam. Appoint not heavenly disposition, Father, Samson 373
Promisd by Heavenly message twice descending. Samson 635
Seeming at first all heavenly under virgin veil, Samson 1035
Till oft convers with heav'nly habitants Mask 459
Trinity ms 'heavnly'
Bridgewater ms 'hevenly'
What the sage Poets taught by th' heav'nly Muse Mask 515
After the heavenly tune, which none can hear Arcades 72
Say Heav'nly Muse, shall not thy sacred vein Nativity 15
With thousand echo's still prolongs each heav'nly close. Nativity 100
Or any other of that heav'nly brood Fair Inf 55
And joyous news of heav'nly Infants birth, Passion 3
That labour up the Hill of heav'nly Truth, Sonnet 9, 4
Trinity ms 'heavnly'
And Justice from her heavenly bowr Psalm 85, 47

Heavenly-born
Inhabitant of Heav'n, and heav'nlie-born, Par Lost 2.860

Heavenly-guided
When once our heav'nly-guided soul shall clime, On Time 19
Trinity ms 'heavenly-guided'

Heavens
In the Beginning how the Heav'ns and Earth Par Lost 1.9
Before the Heavens thou wert, and at the voice Par Lost 3.9
Hee Heav'n of Heavens and all the Powers therein Par Lost 3.390
That run through all the Heav'ns, or down to th' Earth Par Lost 3.651
Unspeakable, who sitst above these Heavens Par Lost 5.156
Reignd where these Heav'ns now rowl, where Earth now rests Par Lost 5.578
Into the Heav'n of Heav'ns I have presum'd, Par Lost 7.13
1669 'Heavens'
Up to the Heav'n of Heav'ns his high abode, Par Lost 7.553
The Heav'ns and all the Constellations rung, Par Lost 7.562
Open, ye Heav'ns, your living dores; let in Par Lost 7.566
Conjecture, he his Fabric of the Heav'ns Par Lost 8.76
Admitting Motion in the Heav'ns, to shew Par Lost 8.115
Terrestrial Heav'n, danc't round by other Heav'ns Par Lost 9.103
These changes in the Heav'ns, though slow, produc'd Par Lost 10.692
With earths wide bounds, his glory with the Heav'ns. Par Lost 12.371
Then to the Heav'n of Heav'ns he shall ascend Par Lost 12.451
New Heav'ns, new Earth, Ages of endless date Par Lost 12.549
Or range in th' Air, nor from the Heav'n of Heav'ns Par Reg 1.366
Into the Heav'n of Heavens; thou com'st indeed, Par Reg 1.410
Spir. To the Ocean now I fly, Mask 976
B.M. ms 'From the Heav'ns'
Bridgewater ms 'From the heavens'
The painted Heav'ns so full of state. Psalm 136, 18
So as above the Heavens thy praise to set Psalm 8, 3
When I behold thy Heavens, thy Fingers art, Psalm 8, 9
Fowl of the Heavens, and Fish that through the wet Psalm 8, 21

Heaven-warring
Of those Heav'n-warring Champions could be found Par Lost 2.424

Heavier
Or proud return though to his heavier doom, Par Lost 3.159

Heavier*(cont)*
And heavier fall: so should I purchase deare — Par Lost 4.101
Farr heavier load thy self expect to feel — Par Lost 4.972
Of heavier on himself, fearless return'd. — Par Lost 9.57
That burden heavier then the Earth to bear — Par Lost 10.835
Then all the World much heavier, though divided — Par Lost 10.836

Heaviest
Though heaviest by just measure on thy self — Par Lost 6.265
Samson, of all thy sufferings think the heaviest, — Samson 445
Most perfect *Heroe*, try'd in heaviest plight — Passion 13

Heaviness
He di'd for heavines that his Cart went light, — Another 22
line not in 1658 text
1673 'heaviness'
1640, 1657 'heavinesse'

Heavy
Light-arm'd or heavy, sharp, smooth, swift or slow, — Par Lost 2.902
Not distant far with heavie pace the Foe — Par Lost 6.551
Heavie, though in thir place. O fleeting joyes — Par Lost 10.741
Don to his Father, heard this heavie curse, — Par Lost 12.103
Whence heavie persecution shall arise — Par Lost 12.531
But O the heavy change, now thou art gon, — Lycidas 37
Trinity ms 'heavie'
Whose speed is but the heavy Plummets pace; — On Time 3
Trinity ms 'heavie'

Hebe
La. As smooth as *Hebe*'s their unrazor'd lips. — Mask 290
Bridgewater ms 'Hebes'
Such as hang on *Hebe*'s cheek, — Allegro 29
To th' touch of golden wires, while *Hebe* brings — Vacation 38

Hebrew
Our Hebrew Songs and Harps in *Babylon*, — Par Reg 4.336
Sam. Thou knowst I am an *Ebrew*, therefore tell them, — Samson 1319
An *Ebrew*, as I guess, and of our Tribe. — Samson 1540
While the Hebrew Bands did pass. — Psalm 136, 50

Hebrews
Off. *Ebrews*, the Pris'ner *Samson* here I seek. — Samson 1308

Hebrides
Whether beyond the stormy *Hebrides*, — Lycidas 156

Hebron
Up to the Hill by *Hebron*, seat of Giants old, — Samson 148

Hebrus
Down the swift *Hebrus* to the *Lesbian* shore. — Lycidas 63

Hecate
Wherin thou rid'st with *Hecat*', and befriend — Mask 135
Bridgewater ms 'Hecatt''
Trinity ms 'Hecate'
Doing abhorred rites to *Hecate* — Mask 535
Bridgewater ms 'Heccate'

Hecatompylos
And *Hecatompylos* her hunderd gates, — Par Reg 3.287

Hedge
Som roaving Robber calling to his fellows. — Mask 485
Trinity ms 'robber' ←'hedge man' ←'curl'd man of the swoord'
that lurks by hedge or lane of this dead circuit — Mask Tr. ms 16.40
that lurks by hedge or lane, of this dead circuit — Mask Br. ms 393

Hedger
And the swink't hedger at his Supper sate; — Mask 293

Hedgerow
By Hedge-row Elms, on Hillocks green, — Allegro 58

Hedges
Why hast thou laid her Hedges low — Psalm 80, 49

Heed
Gave heed, but waxing more in rage repli'd. — Par Lost 4.969
His great command; take heed least Passion sway — Par Lost 8.635
I have in view, calling to minde with heed — Par Lost 10.1030
But take good heed my hand survey not thee. — Samson 1230
With wanton heed, and giddy cunning, — Allegro 141

Heel
Shaddowd from either heele with featherd maile — Par Lost 5.284
Her Seed shall bruse thy head, thou bruise his heel. — Par Lost 10.181
Mee and Mankinde; I am to bruise his heel; — Par Lost 10.498
Thir fight, what stroke shall bruise the Victors heel. — Par Lost 12.385
Of head or heel: not therefore joynes the Son — Par Lost 12.388
Then temporal death shall bruise the Victors heel, — Par Lost 12.433
And gathers ground fast at the Labourers heel — Par Lost 12.631
Thir plated backs under his heel; — Samson 140
Rough *Satyrs* danc'd, and *Fauns* with clov'n heel, — Lycidas 34
Trinity ms 'heele'

Heels
By force, and at our heels all Hell should rise — Par Lost 2.135
Or at thy heels the dizzy Multitude, — Par Reg 2.420
My heels are fetter'd, but my fist is free. — Samson 1235

Height
That to the highth of this great Argument — Par Lost 1.24
From what highth fall'n, so much the stronger prov'd — Par Lost 1.92
No wonder, fall'n such a pernicious highth. — Par Lost 1.282
ms 'heighth'
To hight of noblest temper Hero's old — Par Lost 1.552
1667 'highth'
ms 'highth'
Stood fixt her stately highth, and strait the dores — Par Lost 1.723
His utmost ire? which to the highth enrag'd, — Par Lost 2.95
Views all things at one view? for from heav'ns highth — Par Lost 2.190
In heighth or depth, still first and last will Reign — Par Lost 2.324
1667 'highth'
Without dimension, where length, breadth, & highth, — Par Lost 2.893

Height*(cont)*
High Thron'd above all highth, bent down his eye, — Par Lost 3.58
Would higth recal high thoughts, how soon unsay — Par Lost 4.95
1667 'highth'
Insuperable highth of loftiest shade, — Par Lost 4.138
This day at highth of Noon came to my Spheare — Par Lost 4.564
The highth of thy aspiring unoppos'd, — Par Lost 6.132
Human imagination to such highth — Par Lost 6.300
Took envie, and aspiring to his highth, — Par Lost 6.793
Heav'ns highth, and with the Center mix the Pole. — Par Lost 7.215
1669 'hight'
The highth and depth of thy Eternal wayes — Par Lost 8.413
Canst raise thy Creature to what highth thou wilt — Par Lost 8.430
Which it had long stood under, streind to the highth — Par Lost 8.454
That to the hight of Deitie aspir'd; — Par Lost 9.167
Scipio the highth of *Rome*. With tract oblique — Par Lost 9.510
Somtimes in highth began, as no delay — Par Lost 9.675
So standing, moving, or to highth upgrown — Par Lost 9.677
Of God, whom to behold was then my highth — Par Lost 10.724
Measur'd by Cubit, length, and breadth, and highth, — Par Lost 11.730
And bear through highth or depth of natures bounds — Par Reg 1.13
To what highth sacred vertue and true worth — Par Reg 1.231
Thy chosen, to what highth thir pow'r unjust — Par Reg 2.45
In highth of all thir flowing wealth dissolv'd: — Par Reg 2.436
Above the highth of Mountains interpos'd. — Par Reg 4.39
The secret wrested from me in her highth — Samson 384
Amidst thir highth of noon, — Samson 683
Up to the highth, whether to hold or break; — Samson 1349
The peerles height of her immortal praise, — Arcades 75

Heightened
Stood scoffing, highthn'd in thir thoughts beyond — Par Lost 6.629
And hight'nd as with Wine, jocond and boon, — Par Lost 9.793

Heinous
Is not so hainous now, foretasted Fruit, — Par Lost 9.929
Meanwhile the hainous and despightfull act — Par Lost 10.1
How hainous had the fact been, how deserving — Samson 493
Nor shall I count it hainous to enjoy — Samson 991

Heir
In full resplendence, Heir of all my might, — Par Lost 5.720
To manifest thee worthiest to be Heir — Par Lost 6.707
Of all things, to be Heir and to be King — Par Lost 6.708
Son, Heir, and Lord, to him Dominion giv'n, — Par Lost 6.887
1667 'Heire'
David's true heir, and his full Scepter sway — Par Reg 3.405
Hail Son of the most High, heir of both worlds, — Par Reg 4.633
Spir. O my lov'd masters heir, and his next joy, — Mask 501
1637 'heire'
Bridgewater ms 'heire'
Trinity ms 'heire'
With unexpressive notes to Heav'ns new-born Heir. — Nativity 116
A Vicounts daughter, an Earls heir,. — Winchester 3
Dear son of memory, great heir of Fame, — Shakespear 5
1632 'Heire'
1663-4 'Heir'
1640 'heire'

Held
By ancient *Tarsus* held, or that Sea-beast — Par Lost 1.200
Th' *Ionian* Gods, of *Javans* Issue held — Par Lost 1.508
With all his Peers: attention held them mute. — Par Lost 1.618
Where Scepter'd Angels held thir residence, — Par Lost 1.734
A solemn Councel forthwith to be held — Par Lost 1.755
This said, he sat; and expectation held — Par Lost 2.417
Portentous held me; but familiar grown, — Par Lost 2.761
His habit fit for speed succinct, and held — Par Lost 3.643
Uriel, though Regent of the Sun, and held — Par Lost 3.690
He held it vain; awe from above had quelld — Par Lost 4.860
And such I held thee; but this question askt — Par Lost 4.887
So saying, he drew nigh, and to me held, — Par Lost 5.82
Even to my mouth of that same fruit held part — Par Lost 5.83
Of counterfeted truth thus held thir ears. — Par Lost 5.771
Through Heav'ns wide Champain held his way, till Morn, — Par Lost 6.2
Held by thy voice, thy potent voice he heares, — Par Lost 7.100
Like a black mist low creeping, he held on — Par Lost 9.180
Held dalliance with his faire *Egyptian* Spouse. — Par Lost 9.443
Thir course through thickest Constellations held — Par Lost 10.411
Impossible is held, as Argument — Par Lost 10.800
Man-slaughter, shall be held the highest pitch — Par Lost 11.693
Yet held it more humane, more heavenly first — Par Reg 1.221
Won *Asia* and the Throne of *Cyrus* held — Par Reg 3.33
But as a man who had been matchless held — Par Reg 4.10
But foul effeminacy held me yok't — Samson 410
Only my love of thee held long debate; — Samson 863
That *Kiriathaim* held, thou knowst me now — Samson 1081
And in your City held my Nuptial Feast: — Samson 1194
Held up their pearled wrists and took her in, — Mask 834
Such mixture was not held a stain) — Penseroso 26
There held in holy passion still, — Penseroso 41
Who had thought this clime had held — Arcades 24
The Sun himself with-held his wonted speed, — Nativity 79
Which 'mongst the wanton gods a foul reproach was held. — Fair Inf 14
Are held with his melodious harmonie — Vacation 51
Which after held the Sun and Moon in fee. — Sonnet 12, 7
Then whome a better Senatour nere held — Sonnet 17, 2
Would have been held in high esteem with *Paul* — Forcers 10
No good from them shall be with-held — Psalm 84, 43

Helena
In *Egypt* gave to *Jove*-born *Helena* — Mask 676
Bridgewater ms 'Hellena'

Helicon
Weept for thee in *Helicon*, Winchester 56
Hell
Nor the deep Tract of Hell, say first what cause Par Lost 1.28
ms 'hell'
Here in the heart of Hell to work in Fire, Par Lost 1.151
Infernal world, and thou profoundest Hell Par Lost 1.251
Can make a Heav'n of Hell, a Hell of Heav'n. Par Lost 1.255
To reign is worth ambition though in Hell: Par Lost 1.262
ms 'hell'
Better to reign in Hell, then serve in Heav'n. Par Lost 1.263
Regaind in Heav'n, or what more lost in Hell? Par Lost 1.270
Of Hell resounded. Princes, Potentates, Par Lost 1.315
Hovering on wing under the Cope of Hell Par Lost 1.345
The chief were those who from the Pit of Hell Par Lost 1.381
And black *Gehenna* call'd, the Type of Hell. Par Lost 1.405
Till good *Josiah* drove them thence to Hell. Par Lost 1.418
ms 'hell'
A shout that tore Hells Concave, and beyond Par Lost 1.542
ms 'hells'
Far round illumin'd hell: highly they rag'd Par Lost 1.666
That riches grow in Hell; that soyle may best Par Lost 1.691
ms 'hell'
With his industrious crew to build in hell. Par Lost 1.751
From Faction; for none sure will claim in Hell Par Lost 2.32
1667 'hell'
Went all his fear: of God, or Hell, or worse Par Lost 2.49
Arm'd with Hell flames and fury all at once Par Lost 2.61
To our destruction: if there be in Hell Par Lost 2.84
By force, and at our heels all Hell should rise Par Lost 2.135
The Deep to shelter us? this Hell then seem'd Par Lost 2.167
Of Hell should spout her Cataracts of Fire, Par Lost 2.176
Must'ring thir rage, and Heav'n resembles Hell? Par Lost 2.268
They dreaded worse then Hell: so much the fear Par Lost 2.293
Princes of Hell? for so the popular vote Par Lost 2.313
By our revolt, but over Hell extend Par Lost 2.326
By sudden onset, either with Hell fire Par Lost 2.364
Of mankind in one root, and Earth with Hell Par Lost 2.383
And hard, that out of Hell leads up to light; Par Lost 2.433
The present misery, and render Hell Par Lost 2.459
Than Hells dread Emperour with pomp Supream, Par Lost 2.510
Heard farr and wide, and all the host of Hell Par Lost 2.519
In whirlwind; Hell scarce holds the wilde uproar. Par Lost 2.541
Suspended Hell, and took with ravishment Par Lost 2.554
Puts on swift wings, and towards the Gates of Hell Par Lost 2.631
Hell bounds high reaching to the horrid Roof, Par Lost 2.644
A cry of Hell Hounds never ceasing bark'd Par Lost 2.654
Fierce as ten Furies, terrible as Hell, Par Lost 2.671
With horrid strides, Hell trembled as he strode. Par Lost 2.676
So frownd the mighty Combatants, that Hell Par Lost 2.719
Had been achiev'd, whereof all Hell had rung, Par Lost 2.723
Fast by Hell Gate, and kept the fatal Key, Par Lost 2.725
T' whom thus the Portress of Hell Gate reply'd; Par Lost 2.746
Hell trembl'd at the hideous Name, and sigh'd Par Lost 2.788
Stood on the brink of Hell and look'd a while, Par Lost 2.918
Weakning the Scepter of old *Night:* first Hell Par Lost 2.1002
From Hell continu'd reaching th' utmost Orbe Par Lost 2.1029
Hell and the Gulf between, and *Satan* there Par Lost 3.70
Prescrib'd, no barrs of Hell, nor all the chains Par Lost 3.82
Yet with revenge accomplish't and to Hell Par Lost 3.160
Must have bin lost, adjudg'd to Death and Hell Par Lost 3.223
Shall lead Hell Captive maugre Hell, and show Par Lost 3.255
In Heaven, or Earth, or under Earth in Hell; Par Lost 3.322
Beneath thy Sentence; Hell her numbers full, Par Lost 3.332
To deepest Hell, and to repair that loss Par Lost 3.678
Of that first Battel, and his flight to Hell: Par Lost 4.12
The Hell within him, for within him Hell Par Lost 4.20
He brings, and round about him, nor from Hell Par Lost 4.21
Which way I flie is Hell; my self am Hell; Par Lost 4.75
To which the Hell I suffer seems a Heav'n. Par Lost 4.78
While they adore me on the Throne of Hell, Par Lost 4.89
O Hell! what doe mine eyes with grief behold, Par Lost 4.358
Which I as freely give; Hell shall unfold, Par Lost 4.381
Of bliss on bliss, while I to Hell am thrust, Par Lost 4.508
The barrs of Hell, on errand bad no doubt: Par Lost 4.795
Which of those rebell Spirits adjudg'd to Hell Par Lost 4.823
And fierce demeanour seems the Prince of Hell, Par Lost 4.871
Who would not, finding way, break loose from Hell, Par Lost 4.889
Unlicenc't from his bounds in Hell prescrib'd; Par Lost 4.909
Seavenfold, and scourge that wisdom back to Hell, Par Lost 4.914
Came not all Hell broke loose? is pain to them Par Lost 4.918
This new created World, whereof in Hell Par Lost 4.937
The facil gates of hell too slightly barrd. Par Lost 4.967
Satan from Hell scap't through the darksom Gulf Par Lost 5.225
Was understood, the injur'd Lovers Hell. Par Lost 5.450
And so from Heav'n to deepest Hell; O fall Par Lost 5.542
Reign thou in Hell thy Kingdom, let mee serve Par Lost 6.183
Yet Chains in Hell, not Realms expect: mean while Par Lost 6.186
Thy ofspring, to the place of evil, Hell, Par Lost 6.276
Or turn this Heav'n it self into the Hell Par Lost 6.291
In Heav'n and Hell thy Power above compare, Par Lost 6.705
Hell heard th' unsufferable noise, Hell saw Par Lost 6.867
Incumberd him with ruin: Hell at last Par Lost 6.874
Hell thir fit habitation fraught with fire Par Lost 6.876
Farr on excursion toward the Gates of Hell; Par Lost 8.231
But the hot Hell that alwayes in him burnes, Par Lost 9.467
Of Paradise for Hell, hope here to taste Par Lost 9.476
I not; so much hath Hell debas'd, and paine Par Lost 9.487

Hell(*cont*)
When first this Tempter cross'd the Gulf from Hell. Par Lost 10.39
All Judgement, whether in Heav'n, or Earth, or Hell. Par Lost 10.57
Within the Gates of Hell sate Sin and Death, Par Lost 10.230
Over this Maine from Hell to that new World Par Lost 10.257
Then Both from out Hell Gates into the waste Par Lost 10.282
From each side shoaling towards the mouth of Hell. Par Lost 10.288
Deep to the Roots of Hell the gather'd beach Par Lost 10.299
Smooth, easie, inoffensive down to Hell. Par Lost 10.305
And of this World, and on the left hand Hell Par Lost 10.322
And tidings fraught, to Hell he now return'd, Par Lost 10.346
Hell could no longer hold us in her bounds, Par Lost 10.365
Within Hell Gates till now, thou us impow'rd Par Lost 10.369
Hell and this World, one Realm, one Continent Par Lost 10.392
If your joynt power prevailes, th' affaires of Hell Par Lost 10.408
The Causey to Hell Gate; on either side Par Lost 10.415
Heav'n-banisht Host, left desert utmost Hell Par Lost 10.437
Then stil at Hels dark threshold to have sate watch, Par Lost 10.594
Alike is Hell, or Paradise, or Heaven, Par Lost 10.598
See with what heat these Dogs of Hell advance Par Lost 10.616
Folly to mee, so doth the Prince of Hell Par Lost 10.621
Through *Chaos* hurld, obstruct the mouth of Hell Par Lost 10.636
Boiles out from under ground, the mouth of Hell; Par Lost 12.42
This our old Conquest, then remember Hell Par Reg 1.46
From Hell's deep-vaulted Den to dwell in light, Par Reg 1.116
All his vast force, and drive him back to Hell, Par Reg 1.153
Be frustrate all ye stratagems of Hell, Par Reg 1.180
Who boast'st release from Hell, and leave to come Par Reg 1.409
So never more in Hell then when in Heaven. Par Reg 1.420
Threat'ns then our expulsion down to Hell; Par Reg 2.128
(Whose ire I dread more then the fire of Hell) Par Reg 3.220
By this repulse receiv'd, and hold'st in Hell Par Reg 4.623
And rifted Rocks whose entrance leads to hell, Mask 518
1673 'Hell'
How are ye joyn'd with hell in triple knot Mask 581
1673 'Hell'
Hence with thy brew'd inchantments, foul deceiver, Mask 696
Trinity ms 'brewd enchauntments' ←'foule brud' ←'hel brewd opiate' ←'hel bru'd liquor' ←'bru'd sorcerie' ←'teacherous (leacherous?) bruage' ←'teacherous kindnesse'
And made Hell grant what Love did seek. Penseroso 108
and heaven and hel deplore Lycidas Tr. ms 29.59
And Hell it self will pass away, Nativity 139
Naught but profoundest Hell can be his shroud, Nativity 218
Eev'n from the lowest Hell set free Psalm 86, 47
Hell-born
Hell-born, not to contend with Spirits of Heav'n. Par Lost 2.687
Hell-doomed
Hell-doom'd, and breath'st defiance here and scorn Par Lost 2.697
1667 'Hell-doomd'
Hellespont
Came to the Sea, and over *Hellespont* Par Lost 10.309
Hell-hounds
My Hell-hounds, to lick up the draff and filth Par Lost 10.630
Hellish
Man had not hellish foes anow besides, Par Lost 2.504
She spake, and at her words the hellish Pest Par Lost 2.735
So Heav'nly love shall outdoo Hellish hate Par Lost 3.298
So dearly to redeem what Hellish hate Par Lost 3.300
Against such hellish mischief fit to oppose. Par Lost 6.636
Waited with hellish rancour imminent Par Lost 9.409
Mean while in Paradise the hellish pair Par Lost 10.585
To hellish falshood, snare them. But for thee Par Lost 10.873
But to vanquish by wisdom hellish wiles. Par Reg 1.175
Infernal Ghosts, and Hellish Furies, round Par Reg 4.422
Be those that quell the might of hellish charms, Mask 613
Helm
Fit well his Helme, gripe fast his orbed Shield, Par Lost 6.543
His starrie Helme unbuckl'd shew'd him prime Par Lost 11.245
Embarqu'd with such a Stears-mate at the Helm? Samson 1045
The helme of Rome, when gownes not armes repelld Sonnet 17, 3
1694 'Helm'
Helmed
O're Shields and Helmes, and helmed heads he rode Par Lost 6.840
The helmed Cherubim Nativity 112
Helmet
Then put on all thy gorgeous arms, thy Helmet Samson 1119
Helmets
Of rigid Spears, and Helmets throng'd, and Shields Par Lost 6.83
Or grovling soild thir crested helmets in the dust. Samson 141
Helms
A Forrest huge of Spears: and thronging Helms Par Lost 1.547
ms 'helms'
Celestial Armourie, Shields, Helmes, and Speares, Par Lost 4.553
O're Shields and Helmes, and helmed heads he rode Par Lost 6.840
Help
Have finisht happie in our mutual help Par Lost 4.727
By conversation with his like to help, Par Lost 8.418
Thy likeness, thy fit help, thy other self, Par Lost 8.450
Alone, without exterior help sustaind? Par Lost 9.336
Help to disburden Nature of her Bearth. Par Lost 9.624
This Woman whom thou mad'st to be my help, Par Lost 10.137
A help, became thy snare; to mee reproach Par Lost 11.165
And with my help thou may'st; to me the power Par Reg 4.103
Is hate, not help to me, it may with mine Samson 1266
Which without help of eye, might be assay'd, Samson 1625
To help you find them. *La*. Gentle villager Mask 304

Help(*cont*)
1637 'helpe'
Bridgewater ms 'helpe'
Trinity ms 'helpe'
To help insnared chastity; Mask 909
1637 'helpe'
Trinity ms 'helpe'
Bridgewater ms 'helpe'
Helpe us to save free Conscience from the paw Sonnet 16, 13
1694 'Help'
Help wast a sullen day; what may be won Sonnet 20, 4
No help for him in God there lies. Psalm 3, 6
Hast broke the teeth. This help was from the Lord Psalm 3, 23
Of him *that help demands*. Psalm 82, 16
Do'st help and comfort me. Psalm 86, 64

Helped
Thir armor help'd thir harm, crush't in and bruis'd Par Lost 6.656

Helpful
And with all helpful service will comply Arcades 38
Trinity ms 'helpfull'

Helping
Helping all urchin blasts, and ill luck signes Mask 845
Bridgewater ms 'helpinge'

Helpless
Left me all helpless with th' irreparable loss Samson 644
Helpless, thence easily contemn'd, and scorn'd, Samson 943
And let a single helpless maiden pass Mask 402
1637 'helplesse'
Trinity ms 'helplesse'
Bridgewater ms 'helpeles'
The aidless innocent Lady his wish't prey, Mask 574
Trinity ms 'aidlesse' ←'helplesse'
Alone, and helpless! Is this the confidence Mask 583
1637 'helplesse'
Trinity ms 'helplesse'
Bridgewater ms 'helpeless'

Hem
Thir Phalanx, and began to hemm him round Par Lost 4.979
Approach, and kiss her sacred vestures hemm. Arcades 83
Trinity ms 'hemme'

Hemisphere
His day, which else as th' other Hemisphere Par Lost 3.725
And light from darkness by the Hemisphere Par Lost 7.250
Spangling the Hemisphere: then first adornd Par Lost 7.384
Nights Hemisphere had veild the Horizon round: Par Lost 9.52
The Hemisphere of Earth in cleerest Ken Par Lost 11.379

Hence
Here for his envy, will not drive us hence: Par Lost 1.260
Satan from hence now on the lower stair Par Lost 3.540
With light from hence, though but reflected, shines; Par Lost 3.723
Hence fills and empties to enlighten th' Earth, Par Lost 3.731
Thir ruine! Hence I will excite thir minds Par Lost 4.522
Not likely to part hence without contest; Par Lost 4.872
From hence, no cloud, or, to obstruct his sight, Par Lost 5.257
Hence then, and evil go with thee along Par Lost 6.275
To chase me hence? erre not that so shall end Par Lost 6.288
And hence the Morning Planet guilds her horns; Par Lost 7.366
Shalt loose, expell'd from hence into a World Par Lost 8.332
But say, where grows the Tree, from hence how far? Par Lost 9.617
Easing thir passage hence, for intercourse, Par Lost 10.260
Forfeit to Death; from hence a passage broad, Par Lost 10.304
This most afflicts me, that departing hence, Par Lost 11.315
Ere thou from hence depart, know I am sent Par Lost 11.356
Greatly instructed I shall hence depart, Par Lost 12.557
Exacts our parting hence; and see the Guards, Par Lost 12.590
Is to go hence unwilling; thou to mee Par Lost 12.617
Who for my wilful crime art banisht hence. Par Lost 12.619
I carry hence; though all by mee is lost, Par Lost 12.621
Will bring me hence, no other Guide I seek. Par Reg 1.336
Mock us with his blest sight, then snatch him hence, Par Reg 2.56
To whom thus Jesus; what conclud'st thou hence? Par Reg 2.317
Thir Superstition yields me; hence with leave Samson 15
The Marriage on; that by occasion hence Samson 224
Come nearer, part not hence so slight inform'd; Samson 1229
My speediest friend, by death to rid me hence, Samson 1263
By order of the Lords new parted hence Samson 1447
No, I am fixt not to part hence without him. Samson 1481
To free him hence! but death who sets all free Samson 1572
To fetch him hence and solemnly attend Samson 1731
Prompt me; and they perhaps are not far off. Mask 229
Trinity ms 'farre hence'
Bridgewater ms 'farr hence'
Hence had the huntress *Dian* her dred bow Mask 441
Hence with thy brew'd inchantments, foul deceiver, Mask 696
There is a gentle Nymph not farr from hence, Mask 824
Hence loathed Melancholy Allegro 1
Hence vain deluding joyes, Penseroso 1
Is that which we from hence descry Arcades 3
Hence with denial vain, and coy excuse, Lycidas 18
To turn Swift-rushing black perdition hence, Fair Inf 67

Henceforth
Consult how we may henceforth most offend Par Lost 1.187
ms 'hence forth'
Henceforth his might we know, and know our own Par Lost 1.643
ms 'Hence forth'
Henceforth, and never shall my Harp thy praise Par Lost 3.414
Henceforth; my dwelling haply may not please Par Lost 4.378
Henceforth an individual solace dear; Par Lost 4.486

Henceforth(*cont*)
And Seale thee so, as henceforth not to scorne Par Lost 4.966
Taste this, and be henceforth among the Gods Par Lost 5.77
Both of thy crime and punishment: henceforth Par Lost 5.881
Open, and henceforth oft; for God will deigne Par Lost 7.569
Created; but henceforth my early care, Par Lost 9.799
Henceforth of God or Angel, earst with joy Par Lost 9.1081
Let none henceforth seek needless cause to approve Par Lost 9.1140
And henceforth Monarchie with thee divide Par Lost 10.379
Henceforth; least that too heav'nly form, pretended Par Lost 10.872
I never from thy side henceforth to stray, Par Lost 11.176
Henceforth I flie not Death, nor would prolong Par Lost 11.547
Henceforth to be foretold what shall befall Par Lost 11.771
Henceforth what is to com I will relate, Par Lost 12.11
Henceforth I learne, that to obey is best, Par Lost 12.561
And high prediction, henceforth I expose Par Reg 1.142
The Gentiles; henceforth Oracles are ceast, Par Reg 1.456
And sends his Spirit of Truth henceforth to dwell Par Reg 1.462
He never more henceforth will dare set foot Par Reg 4.610
Henceforth, nor too much disapprove my own. Samson 970
Hence forth thou art the Genius of the shore, Lycidas 183
Trinity ms 'henceforth'
1638 'Henceforth'

Henchmen
Heavn's henshmen Musick Tr. ms 4.16

Her
Rivers or Mountains in her spotty Globe. Par Lost 1.291
Pour'd never from her frozen loyns, to pass Par Lost 1.352
Rhene or the *Danaw*, when her barbarous Sons Par Lost 1.353
Worshipt in *Rabba* and her watry Plain, Par Lost 1.397
Her Temple on th' offensive Mountain, built Par Lost 1.443
Fanatic *Egypt* and her Priests, to seek Par Lost 1.480
Both her first born and all her bleating Gods. Par Lost 1.489
All her Original brightness, nor appear'd Par Lost 1.592
Stood fixt her stately highth, and strait the dores Par Lost 1.723
Within, her ample spaces, o're the smooth Par Lost 1.725
Wheels her pale course, they on thir mirth and dance Par Lost 1.786
Showrs on her Kings *Barbaric* Pearl and Gold, Par Lost 2.4
For since no deep within her gulf can hold Par Lost 2.12
Her mischief, and purge off the baser fire Par Lost 2.141
Her stores were open'd, and this Firmament Par Lost 2.175
Of Hell should spout her Cataracts of Fire, Par Lost 2.176
Wants not her hidden lustre, Gemms and Gold; Par Lost 2.271
Shall breathe her balme. But first whom shall we send Par Lost 2.402
Loose all her virtue; least bad men should boast Par Lost 2.483
1667 'thir'
Her watrie Labyrinth, whereof who drinks, Par Lost 2.584
With mortal sting: about her middle round Par Lost 2.653
If aught disturb'd thir noyse, into her woomb, Par Lost 2.657
She spake, and at her words the hellish Pest Par Lost 2.735
Forbore, then these to her *Satan* return'd: Par Lost 2.736
From all her Caves, and back resounded *Death*. Par Lost 2.789
His mother bad, and thus bespake her Sire. Par Lost 2.849
Thus saying, from her side the fatal Key, Par Lost 2.871
And towards the Gate rouling her bestial train, Par Lost 2.873
Excel'd her power; the Gates wide op'n stood, Par Lost 2.884
The Womb of nature and perhaps her Grave, Par Lost 2.911
With all her battering Engines bent to rase Par Lost 2.923
In mutinie had from her Axle torn Par Lost 2.926
To her original darkness and your sway Par Lost 2.984
Pourd out by millions her victorious Bands Par Lost 2.997
Her fardest verge, and *Chaos* to retire Par Lost 2.1038
As from her outmost works a brok'd foe Par Lost 2.1039
Tunes her nocturnal Note. Thus with the Year Par Lost 3.40
Shine inward, and the mind through all her powers Par Lost 3.52
And shall grace not find means, that finds her way, Par Lost 3.228
Happie for man, so coming; he her aide Par Lost 3.232
Beneath thy Sentence; Hell her numbers full, Par Lost 3.332
The World shall burn, and from her ashes spring Par Lost 3.334
Rowls o're *Elisian* Flours her Amber stream; Par Lost 3.359
Resigns her charge, while goodness thinks no ill Par Lost 3.688
(So call that opposite fair Starr) her aide Par Lost 3.727
Timely interposes, and her monthly round Par Lost 3.728
With borrowd light her countenance triform Par Lost 3.730
And in her pale dominion checks the night. Par Lost 3.732
Now nearer, Crowns with her enclosure green, Par Lost 4.133
Of *Eden* planted; *Eden* stretchd her Line Par Lost 4.210
Of som irriguous Valley spred her store, Par Lost 4.255
Layes forth her purple Grape, and gently creeps Par Lost 4.259
Her chrystal mirror holds, unite thir streams. Par Lost 4.263
To seek her through the world; nor that sweet Grove Par Lost 4.272
Hid *Amalthea* and her Florid Son Par Lost 4.278
Her unadorned golden tresses wore Par Lost 4.305
As the Vine curles her tendrils, which impli'd Par Lost 4.307
And by her yielded, by him best receivd, Par Lost 4.309
His Sons, the fairest of her Daughters *Eve*. Par Lost 4.324
To entertain you two, her widest Gates, Par Lost 4.382
And send forth all her Kings; there will be room, Par Lost 4.383
On our first Father, half her swelling Breast Par Lost 4.495
Of her loose tresses hid: he in delight Par Lost 4.497
Both of her Beauty and submissive Charms Par Lost 4.498
That shed *May* Flowers; and press'd her Matron lip Par Lost 4.501
Had in her sober Liverie all things clad; Par Lost 4.599
She all night long her amorous descant sung; Par Lost 4.603
Apparent Queen unvaild her peerless light, Par Lost 4.608
And o're the dark her Silver Mantle threw. Par Lost 4.609
Is womans happiest knowledge and her praise. Par Lost 4.638

Her(*cont*)
Sweet is the breath of morn, her rising sweet, Par Lost 4.641
With this her solemn Bird and this fair Moon, Par Lost 4.648
And these the Gemms of Heav'n, her starrie train: Par Lost 4.649
With this her solemn Bird, nor walk by Moon, Par Lost 4.655
Her old possession, and extinguish life Par Lost 4.666
Espoused *Eve* deckt first her nuptial Bed, Par Lost 4.710
Brought her in naked beauty more adorn'd, Par Lost 4.713
Mankind with her faire looks, to be aveng'd Par Lost 4.718
Now had night measur'd with her shaddowie Cone Par Lost 4.776
The Organs of her Fancie, and with them forge Par Lost 4.802
Vertue in her shape how lovly, saw, and pin'd Par Lost 4.848
Her bearded Grove of ears, which way the wind Par Lost 4.982
Now Morn her rosie steps in th' Eastern Clime Par Lost 5.1
Hung over her enamour'd, and beheld Par Lost 5.13
Her hand soft touching, whisperd thus. Awake Par Lost 5.17
How Nature paints her colours, how the Bee Par Lost 5.24
Such whispering wak'd her, but with startl'd eye Par Lost 5.26
To find this but a dream! Thus *Eve* her Night Par Lost 5.93
Her office holds; of all external things, Par Lost 5.103
Into her private Cell when Nature rests. Par Lost 5.109
Oft in her absence mimic Fansie wakes Par Lost 5.110
To imitate her; but misjoyning shapes, Par Lost 5.111
From either eye, and wip'd them with her haire; Par Lost 5.131
To wed her Elm; she spous'd about him twines Par Lost 5.216
Her mariageable arms, and with her brings Par Lost 5.217
Her dowr th' adopted Clusters, to adorn Par Lost 5.218
Wantond as in her prime, and plaid at will Par Lost 5.295
Her Virgin Fancies, pouring forth more sweet, Par Lost 5.296
And *Eve* within, due at her hour prepar'd Par Lost 5.303
Her fertil growth, and by disburd'ning grows Par Lost 5.319
Bestirs her then, and from each tender stalk Par Lost 5.337
Wants her fit vessels pure, then strews the ground Par Lost 5.348
Stood to entertain her guest from Heav'n; no vaile Par Lost 5.383
Alterd her cheek. On whom the Angel *Haile* Par Lost 5.385
And on her ample Square from side to side Par Lost 5.393
Whence in her visage round those spots, unpurg'd Par Lost 5.419
Vapours not yet into her substance turnd. Par Lost 5.420
From her moist Continent to higher Orbes. Par Lost 5.422
Reason receives, and reason is her being, Par Lost 5.487
Upon her Center pois'd, when on a day Par Lost 5.579
Of Planets and of fixt in all her Wheeles Par Lost 5.621
So smooths her charming tones, that Gods own ear Par Lost 5.626
Her shadowie Cloud withdraws, I am to haste, Par Lost 5.686
Obsequious darkness enters, till her houre Par Lost 6.10
Empyreal, from before her vanisht Night, Par Lost 6.14
Had to her Center shook. What wonder? when Par Lost 6.219
From all her Confines. Heav'n the seat of bliss Par Lost 6.273
Now Night her course began, and over Heav'n Par Lost 6.406
Under her Cloudie covert both retir'd, Par Lost 6.409
And all her entrails tore, disgorging foule Par Lost 6.588
Her dark foundations, and too fast had bound. Par Lost 6.870
Her mural breach, returning whence it rowld. Par Lost 6.879
Wisdom thy Sister, and with her didst play Par Lost 7.10
Her Son. So fail not thou, who thee implores: Par Lost 7.38
Haste to thy audience, Night with her will bring Par Lost 7.105
Her Temperance over Appetite, to know Par Lost 7.127
Number sufficient to possess her Realmes Par Lost 7.147
Her ever during Gates, Harmonious sound Par Lost 7.206
And Earth self ballanc't on her Center hung. Par Lost 7.242
Sprung from the Deep, and from her Native East Par Lost 7.245
Prolific humour soft'ning all her Globe, Par Lost 7.280
And Fruit Tree yielding Fruit after her kind; Par Lost 7.311
Her Universal Face with pleasant green, Par Lost 7.316
Her bosom smelling sweet: and these scarce blown, Par Lost 7.319
Embattell'd in her field: and the humble Shrub, Par Lost 7.322
Her sacred shades: though God had yet not rain'd Par Lost 7.331
Transplanted from her cloudie Shrine, and plac'd Par Lost 7.360
Her gather'd beams, great Palace now of Light. Par Lost 7.363
And hence the Morning Planet guilds her horns; Par Lost 7.366
1667 'his'
His mirror, with full face borrowing her Light Par Lost 7.377
Till night, then in the East her turn she shines, Par Lost 7.380
Revolvd on Heav'ns great Axle, and her Reign Par Lost 7.381
Her annual Voiage, born on Windes; the Aire Par Lost 7.431
Ceas'd warbling, but all night tun'd her soft layes: Par Lost 7.436
Between her white wings mantling proudly, Rowes Par Lost 7.439
Her state with Oarie feet: yet oft they quit Par Lost 7.440
Let th' Earth bring forth Foul living in her kinde, Par Lost 7.451
Op'ning her fertil Woomb teem'd at a Birth Par Lost 7.454
Hereafter, join'd in her popular Tribes Par Lost 7.488
The Female Bee that feeds her Husband Drone Par Lost 7.490
Deliciously, and builds her waxen Cells Par Lost 7.491
Now Heav'n in all her Glorie shon, and rowld Par Lost 7.499
Her motions, as the great first-Movers hand Par Lost 7.500
First wheeld thir course; Earth in her rich attire Par Lost 7.501
Surprise thee, and her black attendant Death. Par Lost 7.547
That open'd wide her blazing Portals, led Par Lost 7.575
Earth with her nether Ocean circumfus'd, Par Lost 7.624
And all her numberd Starrs, that seem to rowle Par Lost 8.19
Her end without least motion, and receaves, Par Lost 8.35
Of incorporeal speed, her warmth and light; Par Lost 8.37
With lowliness Majestic from her seat, Par Lost 8.42
And Grace that won who saw to wish her stay, Par Lost 8.43
Rose, and went forth among her Fruits and Flours, Par Lost 8.44
Her Nurserie; they at her coming sprung Par Lost 8.46
And toucht by her fair tendance gladlier grew. Par Lost 8.47
Delighted, or not capable her eare Par Lost 8.49

Her(*cont*)
Her Husband the Relater she preferr'd Par Lost 8.52
Not Words alone pleas'd her. O when meet now Par Lost 8.57
Not unattended, for on her as Queen Par Lost 8.60
And from about her shot Darts of desire Par Lost 8.62
Into all Eyes to wish her still in sight. Par Lost 8.63
Travelling East, and with her part averse Par Lost 8.138
From the Suns beam meet Night, her other part Par Lost 8.139
Sent from her through the wide transpicuous aire, Par Lost 8.141
Enlightning her by Day, as she by Night Par Lost 8.143
Feilds and Inhabitants: Her spots thou seest Par Lost 8.145
Fruits in her soft'nd Soile, for some to eate Par Lost 8.147
Or Shee from West her silent course advance Par Lost 8.163
On her soft Axle, while she paces Eev'n, Par Lost 8.165
Uncheckt, and of her roaving is no end; Par Lost 8.189
Mean, or in her summd up, in her containd Par Lost 8.473
And in her looks, which from that time infus'd Par Lost 8.474
And into all things from her Aire inspir'd Par Lost 8.476
To find her, or for ever to deplore Par Lost 8.479
Her loss, and other pleasures all abjure: Par Lost 8.480
When out of hope, behold her, not farr off, Par Lost 8.481
Such as I saw her in my dream, adornd Par Lost 8.482
To make her amiable: On she came, Par Lost 8.484
Led by her Heav'nly Maker, though unseen, Par Lost 8.485
Grace was in all her steps, Heav'n in her Eye, Par Lost 8.488
Before me; Woman is her Name, of Man Par Lost 8.496
Her vertue and the conscience of her worth, Par Lost 8.502
Wrought in her so, that seeing me, she turn'd; Par Lost 8.507
I follow'd her, she what was Honour knew, Par Lost 8.508
I led her blushing like the Morn: all Heav'n, Par Lost 8.511
More then enough; at least on her bestow'd Par Lost 8.537
Of Nature her th' inferiour, in the mind Par Lost 8.541
In outward also her resembling less Par Lost 8.543
Her loveliness, so absolute she seems Par Lost 8.547
Her own, that what she wills to do or say, Par Lost 8.549
All higher knowledge in her presence falls Par Lost 8.551
Degraded, Wisdom in discourse with her Par Lost 8.552
Authority and Reason on her waite, Par Lost 8.554
Build in her loveliest, and create an awe Par Lost 8.558
About her, as a guard Angelic plac't. Par Lost 8.559
Accuse not Nature, she hath don her part; Par Lost 8.561
Dismiss not her, when most thou needst her nigh, Par Lost 8.564
Not thy subjection: weigh with her thy self; Par Lost 8.570
The more she will acknowledge thee her Head, Par Lost 8.574
And to realities yield all her shows: Par Lost 8.575
What higher in her societie thou findst Par Lost 8.586
Neither her out-side formd so fair, nor aught Par Lost 8.596
From all her words and actions mixt with Love Par Lost 8.602
Sinne and her shadow Death, and Miserie Par Lost 9.12
Her nightly visitation unimplor'd, Par Lost 9.22
And *Eve* first to her Husband thus began. Par Lost 9.204
And good workes in her Husband to promote. Par Lost 9.234
Safest and seemliest by her Husband staies, Par Lost 9.268
Who guards her, or with her the worst endures. Par Lost 9.269
Adam, missthought of her to thee so dear? Par Lost 9.289
Less attributed to her Faith sincere, Par Lost 9.320
Thus her reply with accent sweet renewd. Par Lost 9.321
But bid her well beware, and still erect, Par Lost 9.353
Thus saying, from her Husbands hand her hand Par Lost 9.385
Betook her to the Groves, but *Delia*'s self Par Lost 9.388
Vertumnus, or to *Ceres* in her Prime, Par Lost 9.395
Her long with ardent look his Eye pursu'd Par Lost 9.397
Delighted, but desiring more her stay. Par Lost 9.398
Oft he to her his charge of quick returne Par Lost 9.399
About her glowd, oft stooping to support Par Lost 9.427
From her best prop so farr, and storm so nigh. Par Lost 9.433
What pleasing seemd, for her now pleases more, Par Lost 9.453
She most, and in her look summs all Delight. Par Lost 9.454
Thus earlie, thus alone; her Heav'nly forme Par Lost 9.457
Her graceful Innocence, her every Aire Par Lost 9.459
Her Husband, for I view far round, not nigh, Par Lost 9.482
The way which to her ruin now I tend. Par Lost 9.493
Hee with *Olympias*, this with her who bore Par Lost 9.509
Veres oft, as oft so steers, and shifts her Saile; Par Lost 9.515
To lure her Eye; shee busied heard the sound Par Lost 9.518
To such disport before her through the Field, Par Lost 9.520
From every Beast, more duteous at her call, Par Lost 9.521
Hee boulder now, uncall'd before her stood; Par Lost 9.523
Of her attention gaind, with Serpent Tongue Par Lost 9.529
Help to disburden Nature of her Bearth. Par Lost 9.624
Which when she saw, thus to her guide she spake. Par Lost 9.646
Into her heart too easie entrance won: Par Lost 9.734
Might tempt alone, and in her ears the sound Par Lost 9.736
With Reason, to her seeming, and with Truth; Par Lost 9.738
Sollicited her longing eye; yet first Par Lost 9.743
So saying, her rash hand in evil hour Par Lost 9.780
Earth felt the wound, and Nature from her seat Par Lost 9.782
Sighing through all her Works gave signs of woe, Par Lost 9.783
Intent now wholly on her taste, naught else Par Lost 9.786
Of knowledg, nor was God-head from her thought. Par Lost 9.790
Shall live with her enjoying, I extinct; Par Lost 9.829
So saying, from the Tree her step she turnd, Par Lost 9.834
Waiting desirous her return, had wove Par Lost 9.839
Her Tresses, and her rural labours crown, Par Lost 9.841
Solace in her return, so long delay'd; Par Lost 9.844
And forth to meet her went, the way she took Par Lost 9.847
Of Knowledge he must pass, there he her met, Par Lost 9.849
Scarse from the Tree returning; in her hand Par Lost 9.850

Her(*cont*)
To him she hasted, in her face excuse Par Lost 9.853
Thus *Eve* with Countnance blithe her storie told; Par Lost 9.886
But in her Cheek distemper flushing glowd. Par Lost 9.887
Divine displeasure for her sake, or Death. Par Lost 9.993
Earth trembl'd from her entrails, as again Par Lost 9.1000
Her former trespass fear'd, the more to soothe Par Lost 9.1006
Him with her lov'd societie, that now Par Lost 9.1007
Her hand he seis'd, and to a shadie bank, Par Lost 9.1037
He led her nothing loath; Flours were the Couch, Par Lost 9.1039
In *Malabar* or *Decan* spreds her Armes Par Lost 9.1103
Heard not her lore, both in subjection now Par Lost 9.1128
Lets her will rule; restraint she will not brook, Par Lost 9.1184
Her Husband shee, to taste the fatall fruit, Par Lost 10.4
His free Will, to her own inclining left Par Lost 10.46
Whose failing, while her Faith to me remaines, Par Lost 10.129
That from her hand I could suspect no ill, Par Lost 10.140
Her doing seem'd to justifie the deed; Par Lost 10.142
Was shee thy God, that her thou didst obey Par Lost 10.145
Superior, or but equal, that to her Par Lost 10.147
Wherein God set thee above her made of thee, Par Lost 10.149
Thy Love, not thy Subjection, and her Gifts Par Lost 10.153
Confessing soon, yet not before her Judge Par Lost 10.160
Enmitie, and between thine and her Seed; Par Lost 10.180
Her Seed shall bruse thy head, thou bruise his heel. Par Lost 10.181
Upon her Husband, saw thir shame that sought Par Lost 10.336
Hell could no longer hold us in her bounds, Par Lost 10.365
Habitual habitant; behind her *Death* Par Lost 10.588
Her office they prescrib'd, to th' other five Par Lost 10.657
To end me? Shall Truth fail to keep her word, Par Lost 10.856
Mends not her slowest pace for prayers or cries. Par Lost 10.859
But her with stern regard he thus repell'd. Par Lost 10.866
Through her perversness, but shall see her gaind Par Lost 10.902
He added not, and from her turn'd, but *Eve* Par Lost 10.909
His peace, and thus proceeded in her plaint. Par Lost 10.913
She ended weeping, and her lowlie plight, Par Lost 10.937
Towards her, his life so late and sole delight, Par Lost 10.941
And thus with peaceful words uprais'd her soon. Par Lost 10.946
Broke off the rest; so much of Death her thoughts Par Lost 10.1008
Had entertaind, as di'd her Cheeks with pale. Par Lost 10.1009
Her rosie progress smiling; let us forth, Par Lost 11.175
After short blush of Morn; nigh in her sight Par Lost 11.184
Discover'd soon the place of her retire. Par Lost 11.267
This Hill; let *Eve* (for I have drencht her eyes) Par Lost 11.367
Here Nature seems fulfilld in all her ends. Par Lost 11.602
Twinn'd, and from her hath no dividual being: Par Lost 12.85
Under her own waight groaning till the day Par Lost 12.539
Her also I with gentle Dreams have calm'd Par Lost 12.595
Portending good, and all her spirits compos'd Par Lost 12.596
Let her with thee partake what thou hast heard, Par Lost 12.598
Chiefly what may concern her Faith to know, Par Lost 12.599
The great deliverance by her Seed to come Par Lost 12.600
Lay sleeping ran before, but found her wak't; Par Lost 12.608
Unfold her Crystal Dores, thence on his head Par Reg 1.82
Then toldst her doubting how these things could be Par Reg 1.137
To her a Virgin, that on her should come Par Reg 1.138
O're-shadow her: this man born and now up-grown, Par Reg 1.140
Heaven open'd her eternal doors, from whence Par Reg 1.281
Her dictates from thy mouth? most men admire Par Reg 1.482
Vertue, who follow not her lore: permit me Par Reg 1.483
Night with her sullen wing to double-shade Par Reg 1.500
Others return'd from Baptism, not her Son, Par Reg 2.61
Within her brest, though calm; her brest though pure, Par Reg 2.63
Since first her Salutation heard, with thoughts Par Reg 2.107
The while her Son tracing the Desert wild, Par Reg 2.109
Of beauty and her lures, easily scorn'd Par Reg 2.194
All her assaults, on worthier things intent? Par Reg 2.195
Descend with all her winning charms begirt Par Reg 2.213
Discount'nance her despis'd, and put to rout Par Reg 2.218
All her array; her female pride deject, Par Reg 2.219
Led captive; cease to admire, and all her Plumes Par Reg 2.222
The morns approach, and greet her with his Song: Par Reg 2.281
The Fugitive Bond-woman with her Son Par Reg 2.308
From all the Elements her choicest store Par Reg 2.334
To treat thee as beseems, and as her Lord Par Reg 2.335
To slacken Virtue, and abate her edge, Par Reg 2.455
Then prompt her to do aught may merit praise. Par Reg 2.456
All Earth her wonder at thy acts, thy self Par Reg 3.24
With *Modin* and her Suburbs once content. Par Reg 3.170
Thy Country from her Heathen servitude; Par Reg 3.176
The world thou hast not seen, much less her glory, Par Reg 3.236
Assyria and her Empires antient bounds, Par Reg 3.270
Here *Ninevee*, of length within her wall Par Reg 3.275
Ecbatana her structure vast there shews, Par Reg 3.286
And *Hecatompylos* her hunderd gates, Par Reg 3.287
Have wasted *Sogdiana;* to her aid Par Reg 3.302
The fairest of her Sex *Angelica* Par Reg 3.341
Thy country, and captive lead away her Kings Par Reg 3.366
On the *Tarpeian* rock, her Cittadel Par Reg 4.49
Or hospitable, in her sweet recess, Par Reg 4.242
Trills her thick-warbl'd notes the summer long, Par Reg 4.246
True wisdom, finds her not, or by delusion Par Reg 4.319
Far worse, her false resemblance only meets, Par Reg 4.320
Her shadowy off-spring unsubstantial both, Par Reg 4.399
Who with her radiant finger still'd the roar Par Reg 4.428
The holy City lifted high her Towers, Par Reg 4.545
Her pile, far off appearing like a Mount Par Reg 4.547
Her riddle, and him, who solv'd it not, devour'd; Par Reg 4.573

Her(*cont*)
No triumph; in all her gates *Abaddon* rues Par Reg 4.624
And all her various objects of delight Samson 71
Hid in her vacant interlunar cave. Samson 89
But thee whose strength, while vertue was her mate, Samson 173
Of *Madian* and her vanquisht Kings: Samson 281
That moral verdit quits her of unclean: Samson 324
Unchaste was subsequent, her stain not his. Samson 325
The secret wrested from me in her highth Samson 384
To them who had corrupted her, my Spies, Samson 386
More Faith? who also in her prime of love, Samson 388
Her spurious first-born; Treason against me? Samson 391
Thrice I deluded her, and turn'd to sport Samson 396
Her importunity, each time perceiving Samson 397
Yet the fourth time, when mustring all her wiles, Samson 402
I yielded, and unlock'd her all my heart, Samson 407
Might easily have shook off all her snares: Samson 409
Her Bond-slave; O indignity, O blot Samson 411
In all her functions weary of her self; Samson 596
And on her purest spirits prey, Samson 613
With all her bravery on, and tackle trim, Samson 717
Her harbinger, a damsel train behind; Samson 721
Sam. My Wife, my Traytress, let her not come near me. Samson 725
Wetting the borders of her silk'n veil: Samson 730
Confess, and promise wonders in her change, Samson 753
Her husband, how far urg'd his patience bears, Samson 755
As her at *Timna*, sought by all means therefore Samson 795
Her own transgressions, to upbraid me mine? Samson 820
Goes by the worse, whatever be her cause. Samson 904
Her countrey from a fierce destroyer, chose Samson 985
Chor. She's gone, a manifest Serpent by her sting Samson 997
Sam. So let her go, God sent her to debase me, Samson 999
Adverse and turbulent, or by her charms Samson 1040
Breaking her Marriage Faith to circumvent me. Samson 1115
Mess. *Gaza* yet stands, but all her Sons are fall'n, Samson 1558
From out her ashie womb now teem'd, Samson 1703
And though her body die, her fame survives, Samson 1706
After this mortal change, to her true Servants Mask 10
Excells his Mother at her mighty Art, Mask 63
And Advice with scrupulous head, Mask 108
Trinity ms 'with' ←'with her'
Of Stygian darknes spets her thickest gloom, Mask 132
From her cabin'd loop hole peep, Mask 140
And hugg him into snares. When once her eye Mask 164
And hearken, if I may, her busines here. Mask 169
Turn forth her silver lining on the night? Mask 222
line not in Bridgewater ms
Turn forth her silver lining on the night, Mask 224
line not in Bridgewater ms
Nightly to thee her sad Song mourneth well. Mask 235
And chid her barking waves into attention, Mask 258
I never heard till now. Ile speak to her Mask 264
To give me answer from her mossie Couch. Mask 276
From her thach't pallat rowse, if otherwise Mask 318
Where may she wander now, whether betake her Mask 351
Perhaps som cold bank is her boulster now Mask 353
Leans her unpillow'd head fraught with sad fears. Mask 355
Could stir the constant mood of her calm thoughts, Mask 371
Vertue could see to do what vertue would Mask 373
Trinity ms 'see' ←'ad all her'
By her own radiant light, though Sun and Moon Mask 374
Where with her best nurse Contemplation Mask 377
She plumes her feathers, and lets grow her wings Mask 378
To save her blossoms, and defend her fruit Mask 396
Which if Heav'n gave it, may be term'd her own: Mask 419
Will dare to soyl her Virgin purity, Mask 427
Hence had the huntress *Dian* her dred bow Mask 441
Fear'd her stern frown, and she was queen oth' Woods. Mask 446
Wherwith she freez'd her foes to congeal'd stone? Mask 449
With sudden adoration, and blank aw. Mask 452
Trinity ms 'and blank aw' ←'of bright rays' ←'of her purenesse'
A thousand liveried Angels lacky her, Mask 455
Tell her of things that no gross ear can hear, Mask 458
The divine property of her first being. Mask 469
Or our neglect, we lost her as we came. Mask 510
Till fancy had her fill, but ere a close Mask 548
Deny her nature, and be never more Mask 559
That spreds her verdant leaf to th' morning ray, Mask 622
But you invert the cov'nants of her trust, Mask 682
line not in Bridgewater ms
Wherefore did Nature powre her bounties forth, Mask 710
To deck her Sons, and that no corner might Mask 717
Be vacant of her plenty, in her own loyns Mask 718
To store her children with; if all the world Mask 720
And live like Natures bastards, not her sons, Mask 727
Who would be quite surcharg'd with her own weight, Mask 728
And strangl'd with her waste fertility; Mask 729
The Sea o'refraught would swell, & th' unsought diamonds Mask 732
Trinity ms 'swell' ←'heave her waters up above the shoare'
I hate when vice can bolt her arguments, Mask 760
And vertue has no tongue to check her pride: Mask 761
As if she would her children should be riotous Mask 763
With her abundance, she good cateress Mask 764
Means her provision onely to the good Mask 765
That live according to her sober laws, Mask 766
And she no whit encomber'd with her store, Mask 774
That hath so well been taught her dazling fence, Mask 791

Her(*cont*)
line not in Trinity ms
line not in Bridgewater ms
And the brute Earth would lend her nerves, and shake, Mask 797
line not in Bridgewater ms
line not in Trinity ms
Her words set off by som superior power; Mask 801
line not in Trinity ms
line not in Bridgewater ms
And try her yet more strongly. Com, no more, Mask 806
word not in Trinity ms
word not in Bridgewater ms
Sabrina is her name, a Virgin pure, Mask 826
Of her enraged stepdam *Guendolen*, Mask 830
Commended her fair innocence to the flood Mask 831
That stay'd her flight with his cross-flowing course, Mask 832
Held up their pearled wrists and took her in, Mask 834
Bearing her straight to aged *Nereus* Hall, Mask 835
Who piteous of her woes, rear'd her lank head, Mask 836
And gave her to his daughters to imbathe Mask 837
Her maid'n gentlenes, and oft at Eeve Mask 843
Carrol her goodnes lowd in rustick layes, Mask 849
And throw sweet garland wreaths into her stream Mask 850
And her son that rules the strands, Mask 876
Sleeking her soft alluring locks, Mask 882
To wait in *Amphitrite*'s bowr. Mask 921
Trinity ms 'in Amphitrites' ←'on amphitrite in her'
Then her purfl'd scarf can shew, Mask 995
Celestial *Cupid* her fam'd Son advanc't, Mask 1004
line not in Bridgewater ms
After her wandring labours long, Mask 1006
line not in Bridgewater ms
Make her his eternal Bride, Mask 1008
line not in Bridgewater ms
And from her fair unspotted side Mask 1009
line not in Bridgewater ms
Heav'n it self would stoop to her. Mask 1023
B.M. ms 'Her'
& darknesse wound her in. I Bro. Peace, brother peace Mask Tr. ms 15.53
to have her by my side, though I were sure Mask Tr. ms 16.41
to have her by my side, though I were suer Mask Br. ms 394
As he met her once a Maying, Allegro 20
Fill'd her with thee a daughter fair, Allegro 23
To live with her, and live with thee, Allegro 39
And then in haste her Bowre she leaves, Allegro 87
To win her Grace, whom all commend. Allegro 124
To set her beauties praise above Penseroso 20
He met her, and in secret shades Penseroso 28
In her sweetest, saddest plight, Penseroso 57
While *Cynthia* checks her Dragon yoke, Penseroso 59
Riding neer her highest noon, Penseroso 68
And oft, as if her head she bow'd, Penseroso 71
Her mansion in this fleshly nook: Penseroso 92
That at her flowry work doth sing, Penseroso 143
Fame that her high worth to raise, Arcades 8
Of detraction from her praise, Arcades 11
Envy bid conceal the rest. Arcades 13
Trinity ms 'conceale' ←'her hide'
In circle round her shining throne, Arcades 15
Shooting her beams like silver threds, Arcades 16
In the center of her light. Arcades 19
Juno dare's not give her odds; Arcades 23
And keep unsteddy Nature to her law, Arcades 70
The peerles height of her immortal praise, Arcades 75
Whose lustre leads us, and for her most fit, Arcades 76
I will assay, her worth to celebrate, Arcades 80
And so attend ye toward her glittering state; Arcades 81
Approach, and kiss her sacred vestures hemm. Arcades 83
Her deity. Arcades 93
Yet *Syrinx* well might wait on her. Arcades 107
Trinity ms defective here
What time the Gray-fly winds her sultry horn, Lycidas 28
Nor yet where *Deva* spreads her wisard stream: Lycidas 55
The Muse her self, for her inchanting son Lycidas 59
Sleek *Panope* with all her sisters play'd. Lycidas 99
Had doff't her gawdy trim, Nativity 33
With her great Master so to sympathize: Nativity 34
It was no season then for her Nativity 35
To wanton with the Sun her lusty Paramour. Nativity 36
To hide her guilty front with innocent Snow, Nativity 39
And on her naked shame, Nativity 40
Confounded, that her Makers eyes Nativity 43
Should look so neer upon her foul deformities. Nativity 44
But he her fears to cease, Nativity 45
And waving wide her mirtle wand, Nativity 51
Had given day her room, Nativity 78
To think her part was don, Nativity 105
And that her raign had here its last fulfilling; Nativity 106
And leave her dolorous mansions to the peering day. Nativity 140
Will open wide the Gates of her high Palace Hall. Nativity 148
Hath laid her Babe to rest. Nativity 238
Hath fixt her polisht Car. Nativity 241
Her sleeping Lord with Handmaid Lamp attending. Nativity 242
Amongst her spangled sisters bright. Psalm 136, 34
Unhous'd thy Virgin Soul from her fair biding place. Fair Inf 21
Her false imagin'd loss cease to lament, Fair Inf 72
Immortal Nectar to her Kingly Sire: Vacation 39
When Beldam Nature in her cradle was; Vacation 46

Her(*cont*)
And peace shall lull him in her flowry lap; Vacation 84
Besides what her vertues fair Winchester 4
Added to her noble birth, Winchester 5
Yet had the number of her days Winchester 11
Bin as compleat as was her praise, Winchester 12
In giving limit to her life. Winchester 14
Her high birth, and her graces sweet, Winchester 15
The Virgin quire for her request Winchester 17
To greet her of a lovely son, Winchester 24
And calls *Lucina* to her throws; Winchester 26
The pride of her carnation train, Winchester 37
On her hast'ning funerall. Winchester 46
Next her much like to thee in story, Winchester 62
To him that serv'd for her before, Winchester 66
And at her next birth much like thee, Winchester 67
Like fortunes may her soul acquaint, Winchester 72
Comes dancing from the East, and leads with her May Morn 2
The Flowry *May*, who from her green lap throws May Morn 3
Of *Englands* Counsel, and her Treasury, Sonnet 10, 2
Thou honour'st Verse, and Verse must send her wing Sonnet 13, 9
But as Faith pointed with her golden rod, Sonnet 14, 7
And all her jealous monarchs with amaze, Sonnet 15, 3
her brok'n league, to impe their serpent wings, Sonnet 15, 8
1694 'to Imp her'
To conquer still; peace hath her victories Sonnet 16, 10
Move by her two maine nerves, Iron and Gold Sonnet 17, 8
In all her equipage; besides to know Sonnet 17, 9
In peace, and reck'ns thee her eldest son. Sonnet 17, 14
Whom *Joves* great Son to her glad Husband gave, Sonnet 23, 3
Full sight of her in Heaven without restraint, Sonnet 23, 8
Came vested all in white, pure as her mind: Sonnet 23, 9
Her face was vail'd, yet to my fancied sight, Sonnet 23, 10
Love, sweetness, goodness, in her person shin'd Sonnet 23, 11
With her *green* shade *that* cover'd *all*, Psalm 80, 41
Her Bows as *high as* Cedars tall Psalm 80, 43
Her branches *on the western side* Psalm 80, 45
Her other branches *went*. Psalm 80, 48
Why hast thou laid her Hedges low Psalm 80, 49
And brok'n down her Fence, Psalm 80, 50
That all may pluck her, as they go, Psalm 80, 51
Her Grapes and tender Shoots. Psalm 80, 56
The Swallow there, to lay her young Psalm 84, 11
Hath built her *brooding* nest, Psalm 84, 12
And Justice from her heavenly bowr Psalm 85, 47
Her fruits *to be our food*. Psalm 85, 52
This and this man was born in her, Psalm 87, 19
High God shall fix her fast. Psalm 87, 20

Herald
By Haralds voice explain'd: the hollow Abyss Par Lost 2.518
Thus wore out night, and now the Herald Lark Par Reg 2.279
And listens to the Herald of the Sea Lycidas 89
1638 'herald'

Heraldry
He who with all Heav'ns heraldry whileare Circum 10

Heralds
Mean while the winged Haralds by command Par Lost 1.752
In other part the scepter'd Haralds call Par Lost 11.660

Herb
Grasing the tender herb, were interpos'd, Par Lost 4.253
His orient Beams, on herb, tree, fruit, and flour, Par Lost 4.644
On this delightful land, nor herb, fruit, floure, Par Lost 4.652
Put forth the verdant Grass, Herb yielding Seed, Par Lost 7.310
God made, and every Herb, before it grew Par Lost 7.336
Soft on the flourie herb I found me laid Par Lost 8.254
Productive in Herb, Plant, and nobler birth Par Lost 9.111
Nor nocent yet, but on the grassie Herbe Par Lost 9.186
This Garden, still to tend Plant, Herb and Flour, Par Lost 9.206
The trodden Herb, of abject thoughts and low, Par Lost 9.572
Unbid, and thou shalt eate th' Herb of the Field, Par Lost 10.204
And Fish with Fish; to graze the Herb all leaving, Par Lost 10.711
What it devours not, Herb, or Fruit, or Graine, Par Lost 12.184
Dire inflammation which no cooling herb Samson 626
Had ta'n their supper on the savoury Herb Mask 541
Trinity ms 'herbe'
1637 'herbe'
Bridgewater ms 'herbe'
In every vertuous plant and healing herb Mask 621
Bridgewater ms 'herbe'
1637 'herbe'
Trinity ms 'herbe'
And every Herb that sips the dew; Penseroso 172

Herbs
With Flowers, Garlands, and sweet-smelling Herbs Par Lost 4.709
Then Herbs of every leaf, that sudden flour'd Par Lost 7.317
I mean of Taste, Sight, Smell, Herbs, Fruits, and Flours, Par Lost 8.527
Thou therefore on these Herbs, and Fruits, and Flours Par Lost 10.603
With lavers pure and cleansing herbs wash off Samson 1727
Culling their Potent hearbs, and balefull drugs, Mask 255
Bridgewater ms 'herbs'
Of Hearbs, and other Country Messes, Allegro 85

Herculean
Herculean Samson from the Harlot-lap Par Lost 9.1060

Herd
Down he alights among the sportful Herd Par Lost 4.396
The overthrown he rais'd, and as a Heard Par Lost 6.856
Then at *Circean* call the Herd disguis'd. Par Lost 9.522
A herd of Beeves, faire Oxen and faire Kine Par Lost 11.647

Herd(*cont*)
Corn wine and oyle; and from the herd or flock, Par Lost 12.19
His faithful, left among th' unfaithful herd, Par Lost 12.481
If Cottage were in view, Sheep-cote or Herd; Par Reg 2.287
But Cottage, Herd or Sheep-cote none he saw, Par Reg 2.288
And what the people but a herd confus'd, Par Reg 3.49
And beg to hide them in a herd of Swine, Par Reg 4.630
Be well stock't with as fair a herd as graz'd Mask 152
1637 'Heard'
Trinity ms 'heard'
Bridgewater ms 'heard'

Herdman
That to the faithfull Herdmans art belongs! Lycidas 121
1638 'herdmans'
Trinity ms 'heardsmans'

Herds
The birds thir notes renew, and bleating herds Par Lost 2.494
Or flocks, or heards, or human face divine; Par Lost 3.44
1667 'herds'
Among the bestial herds to raunge, by thee Par Lost 4.754
Pasturing at once, and in broad Herds upsprung. Par Lost 7.462
Shelters in coole, and tends his pasturing Herds Par Lost 9.1109
Were Tents of various hue; by some were herds Par Lost 11.557
Of Herds and Flocks, and numerous servitude; Par Lost 12.132
With herds the pastures throng'd, with flocks the hills, Par Reg 3.260
Far from the cheerfull haunt of men, and herds, Mask 388
1637 'heards'
Trinity ms 'heards'
Bridgewater ms 'heards'
The herds would over-multitude their Lords, Mask 731
1637 'heards'
Bridgewater ms 'heards'
Trinity ms 'heards'
Visits the herds along the twilight meadows, Mask 844
1637 'heards'
Trinity ms 'heards'
Bridgewater ms 'heards'
Or Taint-worm to the weanling Herds that graze, Lycidas 46
1638 'herds'
Trinity ms 'heards'
All Flocks, and Herds, by thy commanding word, Psalm 8, 19

Herdsman
There oft the *Indian* Herdsman shunning heate Par Lost 9.1108

Here
For those rebellious, here thir Prison ordain'd Par Lost 1.71
Here swallow'd up in endless misery. Par Lost 1.142
Here in the heart of Hell to work in Fire, Par Lost 1.151
Whom Thunder hath made greater? Here at least Par Lost 1.258
Here for his envy, will not drive us hence: Par Lost 1.260
Here we may reign secure, and in my choyce Par Lost 1.261
To slumber here, as in the Vales of Heav'n? Par Lost 1.321
Deserve the precious bane. And here let those Par Lost 1.692
Envy from each inferior; but who here Par Lost 2.26
The Signal to ascend, sit lingring here Par Lost 2.56
Then to dwell here, driv'n out from bliss, condemn'd Par Lost 2.86
Thus trampl'd, thus expell'd to suffer here Par Lost 2.195
Inclines, here to continue; and build up here Par Lost 2.314
Us here, as with his Golden those in Heav'n. Par Lost 2.328
To their defence who hold it: here perhaps Par Lost 2.362
Attempting, or to sit in darkness here Par Lost 2.377
Of Angels watching round? Here he had need Par Lost 2.413
While here shall be our home, what best may ease Par Lost 2.458
And they outcast from God, are here condemn'd Par Lost 2.694
Hell-doom'd, and breath'st defiance here and scorn Par Lost 2.697
Without my op'ning. Pensive here I sat Par Lost 2.777
And my fair Son here showst me, the dear pledge Par Lost 2.818
To sit in hateful Office here confin'd, Par Lost 2.859
Here in perpetual agonie and pain, Par Lost 2.861
Strive here for Maistrie, and to Battel bring Par Lost 2.899
Pursuing. I upon my Frontieres here Par Lost 2.998
A glimmering dawn; here Nature first begins Par Lost 2.1037
His words here ended, but his meek aspect Par Lost 3.266
Here shalt thou sit incarnate, here shalt Reign Par Lost 3.315
Here walk'd the Fiend at large in spacious field. Par Lost 3.430
Naught seeking but the praise of men, here find Par Lost 3.453
Till final dissolution, wander here, Par Lost 3.458
Here Pilgrims roam, that stray'd so farr to seek Par Lost 3.476
That stone, or like to that which here below Par Lost 3.600
What wonder then if fields and regions here Par Lost 3.606
Here in the dark so many precious things Par Lost 3.611
Here matter new to gaze the Devil met Par Lost 3.613
For sight no obstacle found here, nor shade, Par Lost 3.615
And here art likeliest by supream decree Par Lost 3.659
And Country whereof here needs no account, Par Lost 4.235
If true, here only, and of delicious taste: Par Lost 4.251
That rais'd us from the dust and plac't us here Par Lost 4.416
The vigilance here plac't, but such as come Par Lost 4.580
Of costliest Emblem: other Creature here Par Lost 4.703
Nor *Faunus* haunted. Here in close recess Par Lost 4.708
Here Love his golden shafts imploies, here lights Par Lost 4.763
Reigns here and revels; not in the bought smile Par Lost 4.765
Here watching at the head of these that sleep? Par Lost 4.826
His loss; but chiefly to find here observd Par Lost 4.849
Whose dwelling God hath planted here in bliss? Par Lost 4.884
Fame is not silent, here in hope to find Par Lost 4.938
To settle here on Earth, or in mid Aire; Par Lost 4.940
Longer thy offerd good, why else set here? Par Lost 5.63
Forbidd'n here, it seems, as onely fit Par Lost 5.69

Here(*cont*)
Here, happie Creature, fair Angelic *Eve*, Par Lost 5.74
A Wilderness of sweets; for Nature here Par Lost 5.294
Beholding shall confess that here on Earth Par Lost 5.329
Created, or such place hast here to dwell, Par Lost 5.373
All *Autumn* pil'd, though *Spring* and *Autumn* here Par Lost 5.394
Cover'd with pearly grain: yet God hath here Par Lost 5.430
Here or in Heav'nly Paradises dwell; Par Lost 5.500
Who formd us from the dust, and plac'd us here Par Lost 5.516
Of midnight march, and hurried meeting here, Par Lost 5.778
Seem twilight here; and now went forth the Morn Par Lost 6.12
Surceas'd, and glad as hoping here to end Par Lost 6.258
And faithful, now prov'd false. But think not here Par Lost 6.271
Thou fablest, here however to dwell free, Par Lost 6.292
Eternize here on Earth; but those elect Par Lost 6.374
Stand still in bright array ye Saints, here stand Par Lost 6.801
Drew many, whom thir place knows here no more; Par Lost 7.144
Not here, till by degrees of merit rais'd Par Lost 7.157
Gave thee, all sorts are here that all th' Earth yields, Par Lost 7.541
Here finish'd hee, and all that he had made Par Lost 7.548
To thee who hast thy dwelling here on Earth. Par Lost 8.118
Tell, if ye saw, how came I thus, how here? Par Lost 8.277
Had lively shadowd: Here had new begun Par Lost 8.311
Eate freely with glad heart; fear here no dearth: Par Lost 8.322
Hast thou not made me here thy substitute, Par Lost 8.381
Walks, and the melodie of Birds; but here Par Lost 8.528
Transported touch; here passion first I felt, Par Lost 8.530
Superiour and unmov'd, here onely weake Par Lost 8.532
But neither here seek I, no nor in Heav'n Par Lost 9.124
How we might best fulfill the work which here Par Lost 9.230
Of Paradise for Hell, hope here to taste Par Lost 9.476
Where universally admir'd; but here Par Lost 9.542
Fruitless to mee, though Fruit be here to excess, Par Lost 9.648
Here grows the Cure of all, this Fruit Divine, Par Lost 9.776
For had the gift bin theirs, it had not here Par Lost 9.806
Insufferably bright. O might I here Par Lost 9.1084
Or here th' attempt, thou couldst not have discernd Par Lost 9.1149
And force upon free will hath here no place. Par Lost 9.1174
My coming seen far off? I miss thee here, Par Lost 10.104
O Son, why sit we here each other viewing Par Lost 10.235
Our foile in Heav'n; here thou shalt Monarch reign, Par Lost 10.375
Which here, though plenteous, all too little seems Par Lost 10.600
Of happiness: yet well, if here would end Par Lost 10.725
From darkness to promote me, or here place Par Lost 10.745
She ended heer, or vehement despaire Par Lost 10.1007
Laborious, till day droop; while here we dwell, Par Lost 11.178
Here let us live, though in fall'n state, content. Par Lost 11.180
His blessed count'nance; here I could frequent, Par Lost 11.317
I heard, here with him at this Fountain talk'd: Par Lost 11.322
God is as here, and will be found alike Par Lost 11.350
Here sleep below while thou to foresight wak'st, Par Lost 11.368
Loose no reward, though here thou see him die, Par Lost 11.459
Better end heer unborn. Why is life giv'n Par Lost 11.502
Here Nature seems fulfilld in all her ends. Par Lost 11.602
And whether here the Race of man will end. Par Lost 11.786
Though bent on speed, so heer th' Arch-angel paus'd Par Lost 12.2
line not in 1667 edition
Mount *Carmel*; here the double-founted stream Par Lost 12.144
Here *Adam* interpos'd. O sent from Heav'n, Par Lost 12.270
Is to stay here; without thee here to stay, Par Lost 12.616
Durst ever, who return'd, and dropt not here Par Reg 1.324
What other way I see not, for we here Par Reg 1.338
Our Fathers here with Manna; in the Mount Par Reg 1.351
Of like succeeding here; I summon all Par Reg 2.143
Of what I suffer here; if Nature need not, Par Reg 2.249
Of *Israel* here had famish'd, had not God Par Reg 2.311
Native of *Thebez* wandring here was fed Par Reg 2.313
Forty and more deserted here indeed. Par Reg 2.316
Lost in a Desert here and hunger-bit: Par Reg 2.416
So spake the Son of God; and here again Par Reg 3.145
The Prospect was, that here and there was room Par Reg 3.263
Cut shorter many a league; here thou behold'st Par Reg 3.269
Here *Ninevee*, of length within her wall Par Reg 3.275
So little here, nay lost; but *Eve* was *Eve*, Par Reg 4.6
These here revolve, or, as thou lik'st, at home, Par Reg 4.281
Of men at thee, for only thou here dwell'st. Par Reg 4.466
And opportunity I here have had Par Reg 4.531
Unwholsom draught: but here I feel amends, Samson 9
With day-spring born; here leave me to respire. Samson 11
Of man or worm; the vilest here excel me, Samson 74
Though Reason here aver Samson 323
But see here comes thy reverend Sire Samson 326
Came lagging after; say if he be here. Samson 337
Here celebrate in *Gaza*; and proclaim Samson 435
Thou must not in the mean while here forgot Samson 479
Of that sollicitation; let me here, Samson 488
Here rather let me drudge and earn my bread, Samson 573
Here I should still enjoy thee day and night Samson 807
Off. Ebrews, the Pris'ner *Samson* here I seek. Samson 1308
Chor. How thou wilt here come off surmounts my reach. Samson 1380
He seems: supposing here to find his Son, Samson 1443
Was not at present here to find my Son, Samson 1446
What shall we do, stay here or run and see? Samson 1520
Chor. Best keep together here, lest running thither Samson 1521
The sufferers then will scarce molest us here, Samson 1525
My Countreymen, whom here I knew remaining, Samson 1549
Man. The accident was loud, & here before thee Samson 1552
1671 printed 'heard', errata 'here'

Here(*cont*)
Nothing is here for tears, nothing to wail — Samson 1721
Confin'd, and pester'd in this pin-fold here, — Mask 7
Trinity ms 'heere'
Bridgewater ms 'heere'
And here their tender age might suffer perill, — Mask 40
Trinity ms 'heere'
Bridgewater ms 'heere'
But here she comes, I fairly step aside — Mask 168
Bridgewater ms 'heere'
Trinity ms 'heere'
And hearken, if I may, her busines here. — Mask 169
Trinity ms 'heere'
Bridgewater ms 'heere'
With this long way, resolving here to lodge — Mask 183
Bridgewater ms 'heere'
Trinity ms 'heere'
Dwell'st here with *Pan*, or *Silvan*, by blest Song — Mask 268
Trinity ms 'heere'
Bridgewater ms 'heere'
And disinherit *Chaos*, that raigns here — Mask 334
Bridgewater ms 'heere'
Trinity ms 'heere'
Either som one like us night-founder'd here, — Mask 483
Trinity ms 'heere'
Bridgewater ms 'heere'
How cam'st thou here good Swain? hath any ram — Mask 497
Bridgewater ms 'heere'
Trinity ms 'heere'
I came not here on such a trivial toy — Mask 502
Bridgewater ms 'heere'
Trinity ms 'heere'
And here to every thirsty wanderer, — Mask 524
Trinity ms 'heere'
Bridgewater ms 'heere'
Into swift flight, till I had found you here, — Mask 579
Trinity ms 'heere'
Bridgewater ms 'heere'
But here thy sword can do thee little stead, — Mask 611
Trinity ms 'heere'
Bridgewater ms 'heere'
Here dwel no frowns, nor anger, from these gates — Mask 667
Bridgewater ms 'heere'
Trinity ms 'heere'
Sorrow flies farr: See here be all the pleasures — Mask 668
Bridgewater ms 'heere'
And first behold this cordial Julep here — Mask 672
Bridgewater ms 'heere'
Trinity ms 'heere'
And timely rest have wanted, but fair Virgin — Mask 689
Bridgewater ms 'heere'
Trinity ms 'but' ←'heere'
And wouldst thou seek again to trap me here — Mask 699
line not in Bridgewater ms
Trinity ms 'heere'
We cannot free the Lady that sits here — Mask 818
Trinity ms 'heere'
Bridgewater ms 'heere'
I am here. — Mask 901
Trinity ms 'heere'
Bridgewater ms 'heere'
Of true Virgin here distrest, — Mask 905
Bridgewater ms 'heere'
Trinity ms 'heere'
And here and there thy banks upon — Mask 936
Bridgewater ms 'heere'
Trinity ms 'heere'
Here be without duck or nod — Mask 960
Bridgewater ms 'heere'
Trinity ms 'heere'
Here behold so goodly grown — Mask 968
Trinity ms 'heere'
Bridgewater ms 'heere'
And sent them here through hard assays — Mask 972
Bridgewater ms 'heere'
Trinity ms 'heere'
he may scratch his forehead. heere be brambles — Mask Tr. ms 17.57
Heer our solemn search hath end. — Arcades 7
Trinity ms 'heere'
Here ye shall have greater grace, — Arcades 104
Trinity ms 'heere'
He laid aside; and here with us to be, — Nativity 12
And that her raign had here its last fulfilling; — Nativity 106
Time is our tedious Song should here have ending, — Nativity 239
Amongst us here below to hide thy nectar'd head. — Fair Inf 49
But oh why didst thou not stay here below — Fair Inf 64
Here I salute thee and thy pardon ask, — Vacation 7
And here though grief my feeble hands up-lock, — Passion 45
Here besides the sorrowing — Winchester 53
Here be tears of perfect moan — Winchester 55
Here lies old *Hobson*, Death hath broke his girt, — Carrier 1
A here alas, hath laid him in the dirt, — Carrier 2
He's here stuck in a slough, and overthrown. — Carrier 4
Here lieth one who did most truly prove, — Another 1
1640, 1657 'Here *Hobson* lyes'
Judgment here thou didst ingage — Psalm 7, 23
And I here pent up thus. — Psalm 88, 36

Hereafter
None yet, but store hereafter from the earth — Par Lost 3.444
Hereafter, join'd in her popular Tribes — Par Lost 7.488
Hereafter, when they come to model Heav'n — Par Lost 8.79
From *Canaan*, to a Land hereafter call'd — Par Lost 12.156
They now, and men hereafter may discern, — Par Reg 1.164
Thy bold attempt; hereafter learn with awe — Par Reg 4.625
Hereby
On Earth, made hereby apter to receive — Par Lost 4.672
But made hereby obnoxious more — Samson 106
Hereditary
The Throne hereditarie, and bound his Reign — Par Lost 12.370
Herein
But herein to our Prophets far beneath, — Par Reg 4.356
Of highest dispensation, which herein — Samson 61
Hereof
For proof hereof, if *Dagon* be thy god, — Samson 1145
Heretics
Must now be nam'd and printed Hereticks — Forcers 11
Hermes
Volatil *Hermes*, and call up unbound — Par Lost 3.603
Of *Japhet* brought by *Hermes*, she ensnar'd — Par Lost 4.717
Of *Hermes*, or his opiate Rod. Mean while — Par Lost 11.133
That *Hermes* once to wise *Ulysses* gave; — Mask 637
Trinity ms 'Hermes once' ←'Mercury'
line not in Bridgewater ms
As *Mercury* did first devise — Mask 963
Trinity ms 'Mercury' ←'Hermes'
With thrice great *Hermes*, or unsphear — Penseroso 88
Hermione
Hermione and *Cadmus*, or the God — Par Lost 9.506
Hermit
For who would rob a Hermit of his Weeds, — Mask 390
Bridgewater ms 'hermitt'
Hermitage
Find out the peacefull hermitage, — Penseroso 168
Hermon
From *Hermon* East to the great Western Sea, — Par Lost 12.141
Mount *Hermon*, yonder Sea, each place behold — Par Lost 12.142
Hero
Most perfect *Heroe*, try'd in heaviest plight — Passion 13
Herod
And his Son *Herod* plac'd on *Juda*'s Throne; — Par Reg 2.424
Heroes
To hight of noblest temper Hero's old — Par Lost 1.552
Of *Sarra*, worn by Kings and Hero's old — Par Lost 11.243
Which greatest Heroes have in battel worn, — Samson 1131
And last of Kings and Queens and *Hero*'s old, — Vacation 47
Heroic
Of *Phlegra* with th' Heroic Race were joyn'd — Par Lost 1.577
Thir own Heroic deeds and hapless fall — Par Lost 2.549
About him exercis'd Heroic Games — Par Lost 4.551
Heroic Ardor to advent'rous deeds — Par Lost 6.66
Not less but more Heroic then the wrauth — Par Lost 9.14
Since first this Subject for Heroic Song — Par Lost 9.25
Heroic deem'd, chief maistrie to dissect — Par Lost 9.29
Of Patience and Heroic Martyrdom — Par Lost 9.32
Not that which justly gives Heroic name — Par Lost 9.40
Heroic built, though of terrestrial mould, — Par Lost 9.485
And Valour and Heroic Vertu call'd; — Par Lost 11.690
Above Heroic, though in secret done, — Par Reg 1.15
Flam'd in my heart, heroic acts, one while — Par Reg 1.216
That Heroic, that Renown'd, — Samson 125
Have prompted this Heroic *Nazarite*, — Samson 318
Of acts indeed heroic, far beyond — Samson 527
With plain Heroic magnitude of mind — Samson 1279
A life Heroic, on his Enemies — Samson 1711
Heroically
Like *Samson*, and heroicly hath finish'd — Samson 1710
Hers
Not Hers who brings it nightly to my Ear. — Par Lost 9.47
Hers in all real dignitie: Adornd — Par Lost 10.151
Herself
Which but her self not all the *Stygian* powers — Par Lost 2.875
Her self a fairer Floure by gloomie *Dis* — Par Lost 4.270
Undeckt, save with her self more lovely fair — Par Lost 5.380
Whose Seed is in her self upon the Earth. — Par Lost 7.312
Serv'd by more noble then her self, attaines — Par Lost 8.34
If Earth industrious of her self fetch Day — Par Lost 8.137
Nature her self, though pure of sinful thought, — Par Lost 8.506
And in her self compleat, so well to know — Par Lost 8.548
Her self, though fairest unsupported Flour, — Par Lost 9.432
Pausing a while, thus to her self she mus'd. — Par Lost 9.744
Thus to her self she pleasingly began. — Par Lost 9.794
And left to her self, if evil thence ensue, — Par Lost 9.1185
Cast her self headlong from th' *Ismenian* steep, — Par Reg 4.575
In all her functions weary of her self; — Samson 596
To aid a Virgin, such as was her self — Mask 856
Trinity ms 'her selfe'
Bridgewater ms 'her selfe'
1637 'her selfe'
What could the Muse her self that *Orpheus* bore, — Lycidas 58
Trinity ms 'muse her selfe' ←'golden hayrd Calliope'
The Muse her self, for her inchanting son — Lycidas 59
Trinity ms 'her selfe'
Then thou our fancy of it self bereaving, — Shakespear 13
1632 'her selfe'
1663-4 'her self'

Hesebon
Of Southmost *Abarim;* in *Hesebon* Par Lost 1.408
ms 'Hesebon'
Heshbon
Of Southmost *Abarim;* in *Hesebon* Par Lost 1.408
ms 'Hesebon'
Hesperian
Fled over *Adria* to th' *Hesperian* Fields, Par Lost 1.520
ms 'Hesperian'
Like those *Hesperian* Gardens fam'd of old, Par Lost 3.568
Hung amiable, *Hesperian* Fables true, Par Lost 4.250
Hesperean sets, my Signal to depart. Par Lost 8.632
But beauty like the fair Hesperian Tree Mask 393
Bridgewater ms 'hesperian'
amidst the Hesperian gardens, on whose bancks Mask Tr. ms 10.05
Hesperides
And Ladies of th' *Hesperides*, that seem'd Par Reg 2.357
Hesperus
With living Saphirs: *Hesperus* that led Par Lost 4.605
Of *Hesperus*, whose Office is to bring Par Lost 9.49
Of *Hesperus*, and his daughters three Mask 982
Trinity ms 'Hesperus' ←'Atlas'
Hether
But on the hether side a different sort Par Lost 11.574
Hewing
Then from the Mountain hewing Timber tall, Par Lost 11.728
Hewn
Hewn on *Norwegian* hills, to be the Mast Par Lost 1.293
From Diamond Quarries hew'n, and Rocks of Gold, Par Lost 5.759
Sore toild, his riv'n Armes to havoc hewn, Par Lost 6.449
Those rugged names to our like mouths grow sleek Sonnet 11, 10
Trinity ms 'rugged' ←'rough hewn' ←'barbarous'
Hid
That in his womb was hid metallic Ore, Par Lost 1.673
For Treasures better hid. Soon had his crew Par Lost 1.688
Sings darkling, and in shadiest Covert hid Par Lost 3.39
His back was turnd, but not his brightness hid; Par Lost 3.624
That brought them forth, but hid thir causes deep. Par Lost 3.707
Hid *Amalthea* and her Florid Son Par Lost 4.278
Of her loose tresses hid: he in delight Par Lost 4.497
What might have else to human Race bin hid; Par Lost 6.896
Fuming from Golden Censers hid the Mount. Par Lost 7.600
Thir wandring course now high, now low, then hid, Par Lost 8.126
Sollicit not thy thoughts with matters hid, Par Lost 8.167
Where to lie hid; Sea he had searcht and Land Par Lost 9.76
Such ambush hid among sweet Flours and Shades Par Lost 9.408
Then voluble and bold, now hid, now seen Par Lost 9.436
And from his presence hid themselves among Par Lost 10.100
Affraid, being naked, hid my self. To whom Par Lost 10.117
Alreadie in part, though hid in gloomiest shade, Par Lost 10.716
As from his face I shall be hid, depriv'd Par Lost 11.316
Not hid, nor those things last which might preserve Par Lost 11.579
And what most merits fame in silence hid. Par Lost 11.699
Hid in her vacant interlunar cave. Samson 89
Hid them in som flowry Cave, Mask 239
Where that damn'd wisard hid in sly disguise Mask 571
Or with the tangles of *Neaera*'s hair? Lycidas 69
1638 'Hid in'
Trinity ms 'or with' ←'hid in'
And hid his head for shame, Nativity 80
Hid from the world in a low delved tombe; Fair Inf 32
Or that his hallow'd reliques should be hid Shakespear 3
Hast hid *where none shall know*. Psalm 85, 8
Hidden
Wants not her hidden lustre, Gemms and Gold; Par Lost 2.271
In Nature none: if other hidden cause Par Lost 6.442
Part hidd'n veins diggd up (nor hath this Earth Par Lost 6.516
To testifie his hidd'n residence; Mask 248
Bridgewater ms 'hidden'
Trinity ms 'hidden'
1637 'hidden'
As you imagine, she has a hidden strength Mask 415
Which you remember not. 2. *Bro*. What hidden strength, Mask 416
Eld. Bro. I mean that too, but yet a hidden strength Mask 418
The hidden soul of harmony. Allegro 144
Hide
Hide thir diminisht heads; to thee I call, Par Lost 4.35
To hide the fraud. At interview both stood Par Lost 6.555
To enter, and his dark suggestions hide Par Lost 9.90
To hide me, and the dark intent I bring. Par Lost 9.162
Hide me, where I may never see them more. Par Lost 9.1090
What best may from the present serve to hide Par Lost 9.1092
To gird thir waste, vain Covering if to hide Par Lost 9.1113
Accurst of blessed, hide me from the face Par Lost 10.723
Living or dying, from thee I will not hide Par Lost 10.974
Through Heav'ns wide bounds; from them I will not hide Par Lost 11.68
Bewailing thir excess, all terror hide. Par Lost 11.111
These God-like Vertues wherefore dost thou hide? Par Reg 3.21
And beg to hide them in a herd of Swine, Par Reg 4.630
Oft he seems to hide his face, Samson 1749
Hide me from Day's garish eie, Penseroso 141
Envy bid conceal the rest. Arcades 13
Trinity ms 'conceale' ←'her hide'
To hide her guilty front with innocent Snow, Nativity 39
And sought to hide his froth-becurled head Psalm 114, 8
Amongst us here below to hide thy nectar'd head. Fair Inf 49
And that one Talent which is death to hide, Sonnet 19, 3
Whom thou dost hide and keep. Psalm 83, 12

Hide(*cont*)
And hide thy face from me, Psalm 88, 58
Hideous
With hideous ruine and combustion down Par Lost 1.46
Under amazement of thir hideous change. Par Lost 1.313
Impendent horrors, threatning hideous fall Par Lost 2.177
A hideous Peal: yet, when they list, would creep, Par Lost 2.656
Ris'n, and with hideous outcry rush'd between. Par Lost 2.726
Hell trembl'd at the hideous Name, and sigh'd Par Lost 2.788
Of hideous length: before the cloudie Van, Par Lost 6.107
The adverse Legions, nor less hideous joyn'd Par Lost 6.206
With hideous orifice gap't on us wide, Par Lost 6.577
Forthwith a hideous gabble rises loud Par Lost 12.56
Yet to that hideous place not so confin'd Par Reg 1.362
Mercy of Heav'n what hideous noise was that! Samson 1509
Uninjur'd in this wilde surrounding wast. Mask 403
Trinity ms 'wide surrounding wast' ←'vast, & hideous wild'
Within the navil of this hideous Wood, Mask 520
Bridgewater ms 'hidious'
When by the rout that made the hideous roar, Lycidas 61
No voice or hideous humm Nativity 174
Deaths hideous house hath barr'd. Psalm 88, 24
Hides
Say first, for Heav'n hides nothing from thy view Par Lost 1.27
But he that hides a dark soul, and foul thoughts Mask 383
Hie
And *up to thee* my praier *doth hie* Psalm 88, 55
Hierarch
To whom the winged Hierarch repli'd. Par Lost 5.468
Warr unproclam'd. The Princely Hierarch Par Lost 11.220
Hierarchal
The great Hierarchal Standard was to move; Par Lost 5.701
Hierarchies
Of Hierarchies, of Orders, and Degrees; Par Lost 5.591
Who speedily through all the Hierarchies Par Lost 5.692
So sang the Hierarchies: Mean while the Son Par Lost 7.192
Hierarchs
Under thir Hierarchs in orders bright Par Lost 5.587
Hierarchy
Each in his Hierarchie, the Orders bright. Par Lost 1.737
1667 'Herarchie'
ms 'hierarchy'
And ride us with a classic Hierarchy Forcers 7
Hies
Accurst, and in a cursed hour he hies. Par Lost 2.1055
High
He trusted to have equal'd the most High, Par Lost 1.40
And high disdain, from sence of injur'd merit, Par Lost 1.98
And put to proof his high Supremacy, Par Lost 1.132
As being the contrary to his high will Par Lost 1.161
And high permission of all-ruling Heaven Par Lost 1.212
High overarch't imbowr; or scatterd sedge Par Lost 1.304
Through Gods high sufferance for the tryal of man, Par Lost 1.366
And downward Fish: yet had his Temple high Par Lost 1.463
Soon recollecting, with high words, that bore Par Lost 1.528
Th' Imperial Ensign, which full high advanc't Par Lost 1.536
In Heav'n by many a Towred structure high, Par Lost 1.733
To have built in Heav'n high Towrs; nor did he scape Par Lost 1.749
At *Pandaemonium*, the high Capital Par Lost 1.756
High on a Throne of Royal State, which far Par Lost 2.1
Thus high uplifted beyond hope, aspires Par Lost 2.7
Beyond thus high, insatiate to pursue Par Lost 2.8
O're Heav'ns high Towrs to force resistless way, Par Lost 2.62
For dignity compos'd and high exploit: Par Lost 2.111
From Heav'ns high jurisdiction, in new League Par Lost 2.319
Heav'n, whose high walls fear no assault or Siege, Par Lost 2.343
And Heav'ns high Arbitrator sit secure Par Lost 2.359
High honourd sits? Go therfore mighty Powers, Par Lost 2.456
His Rivals, winning cheap the high repute Par Lost 2.472
In thoughts more elevate, and reason'd high Par Lost 2.558
Up to the fiery Concave touring high. Par Lost 2.635
Hell bounds high reaching to the horrid Roof, Par Lost 2.644
Fell with us from on high: from them I go Par Lost 2.826
Forthwith the huge Porcullis high up drew, Par Lost 2.874
By which he Reigns: next him high Arbiter Par Lost 2.909
High Thron'd above all highth, bent down his eye, Par Lost 3.58
Him God beholding from his prospect high, Par Lost 3.77
Or high foreknowledge; they themselves decreed Par Lost 3.116
Thir nature, and revoke the high Decree Par Lost 3.126
For which both Heav'n and Earth shall high extoll Par Lost 3.146
Against the high Supremacie of Heav'n, Par Lost 3.205
I through the ample Air in Triumph high Par Lost 3.254
Farr more then Great or High; because in thee Par Lost 3.311
Thir sacred Song, and waken raptures high; Par Lost 3.369
Up to the wall of Heaven a Structure high, Par Lost 3.503
On high behests his Angels to and fro Par Lost 3.533
So high above the circling Canopie Par Lost 3.556
In sight of God's high Throne, gloriously bright, Par Lost 3.655
Which now sat high in his Meridian Towre: Par Lost 4.30
And wrought but malice; lifted up so high Par Lost 4.49
With Diadem and Scepter high advanc'd Par Lost 4.90
Would highth recal high thoughts, how soon unsay Par Lost 4.95
At one slight bound high over leap'd all bound Par Lost 4.181
High eminent, blooming Ambrosial Fruit Par Lost 4.219
That Mountain as his Garden mould high rais'd Par Lost 4.226
A whole days journy high, but wide remote Par Lost 4.284
Into our room of bliss thus high advanc't Par Lost 4.359
Long to continue, and this high seat your Heav'n Par Lost 4.371

High(*cont*)

Then from his loftie stand on that high Tree	Par Lost 4.395
Accessible from Earth, one entrance high;	Par Lost 4.546
Hung high with Diamond flaming, and with Gold.	Par Lost 4.554
Rear'd high thir flourisht heads between, and wrought	Par Lost 4.699
Blown up with high conceits ingendring pride.	Par Lost 4.809
High up in Heav'n, with songs to hymne his Throne,	Par Lost 4.944
To this high exaltation; suddenly	Par Lost 5.90
And when high Noon hast gaind, and when thou fallst.	Par Lost 5.174
With pittie Heav'ns high King, and to him call'd	Par Lost 5.220
And to his message high in honour rise;	Par Lost 5.289
For on som message high they guessd him bound.	Par Lost 5.290
Divine effulgence, whose high Power so far	Par Lost 5.458
At Heav'ns high feasts to have fed: yet what compare?	Par Lost 5.467
From what high state of bliss into what woe!	Par Lost 5.543
High matter thou injoinst me, O prime of men,	Par Lost 5.563
Ten thousand thousand Ensignes high advanc'd,	Par Lost 5.588
From that high mount of God, whence light & shade	Par Lost 5.643
That the most High commanding, now ere Night,	Par Lost 5.699
His name, and high was his degree in Heav'n;	Par Lost 5.707
Were banded to oppose his high Decree;	Par Lost 5.717
This our high place, our Sanctuarie, our Hill.	Par Lost 5.732
High on a Hill, far blazing, as a Mount	Par Lost 5.757
In place thy self so high above thy Peeres.	Par Lost 5.812
They led him high applauded, and present	Par Lost 6.26
Ethereal Trumpet from on high gan blow:	Par Lost 6.60
Thir perfet ranks; for high above the ground	Par Lost 6.71
High in the midst exalted as a God	Par Lost 6.99
So saying, a noble stroke he lifted high,	Par Lost 6.189
From his strong hold of Heav'n high over-rul'd	Par Lost 6.228
Such high advantages thir innocence	Par Lost 6.401
Born eevn or high, for this day will pour down,	Par Lost 6.544
Hymns of high praise, and I among them chief.	Par Lost 6.745
On high: who into Glorie him receav'd,	Par Lost 6.891
Of those too high aspiring, who rebelld	Par Lost 6.899
As a despite don against the most High,	Par Lost 6.906
Of things so high and strange, things to thir thought	Par Lost 7.53
Distant so high, with moving Fires adornd	Par Lost 7.87
This inaccessible high strength, the seat	Par Lost 7.141
Though wide, and this high Temple to frequent	Par Lost 7.148
Glorie they sung to the most High, good will	Par Lost 7.182
So high as heav'd the tumid Hills, so low	Par Lost 7.288
Thir blossoms: with high woods the hills were crownd,	Par Lost 7.326
High in th' expanse of Heaven to divide	Par Lost 7.340
His Longitude through Heav'ns high rode: the gray	Par Lost 7.373
Thir Aierie Caravan high over Sea's	Par Lost 7.428
Up to the Heav'n of Heav'ns his high abode,	Par Lost 7.553
With glorie attributed to the high	Par Lost 8.12
Of what was high: such pleasure she reserv'd,	Par Lost 8.50
Grateful digressions, and solve high dispute	Par Lost 8.55
The Makers high magnificence, who built	Par Lost 8.101
If it presume, might erre in things too high,	Par Lost 8.121
Thir wandring course now high, now low, then hid,	Par Lost 8.126
And thy faire *Eve;* Heav'n is for thee too high	Par Lost 8.172
Therefore from this high pitch let us descend	Par Lost 8.198
But us he sends upon his high behests	Par Lost 8.238
A woodie Mountain; whose high top was plaine,	Par Lost 8.303
As high he soard, obnoxious first or last	Par Lost 9.170
Or Sex, and apprehended nothing high:	Par Lost 9.574
For high from ground the branches would require	Par Lost 9.590
Thenceforth to Speculations high or deep	Par Lost 9.602
Or fansied so, through expectation high	Par Lost 9.789
And I perhaps am secret; Heav'n is high,	Par Lost 9.811
High and remote to see from thence distinct	Par Lost 9.812
Us his prime Creatures, dignifi'd so high,	Par Lost 9.940
Illustrious evidence, example high!	Par Lost 9.962
High overarch't, and echoing Walks between;	Par Lost 9.1107
Raind at thir Eyes, but high Winds worse within	Par Lost 9.1122
Began to rise, high Passions, Anger, Hate,	Par Lost 9.1123
The high Injunction not to taste that Fruit, .	Par Lost 10.13
And easily approv'd; when the most High	Par Lost 10.31
Of high collateral glorie: him Thrones and Powers,	Par Lost 10.86
Of merit high to all th' infernal Host,	Par Lost 10.259
Over the foaming deep high Archt, a Bridge	Par Lost 10.301
From *Susa* his *Memnonian* Palace high	Par Lost 10.308
High proof ye now have giv'n to be the Race	Par Lost 10.385
Ascended his high Throne, which under state	Par Lost 10.445
Thir universal shout and high applause	Par Lost 10.505
Of high *Olympus*, thence by *Saturn* driv'n	Par Lost 10.583
Could alter high Decrees, I to that place	Par Lost 10.953
He ended, and the Son gave signal high	Par Lost 11.72
Hasted, resorting to the Summons high,	Par Lost 11.81
Adam, Heav'ns high behest no Preface needs:	Par Lost 11.251
Instinct through all proportions low and high	Par Lost 11.562
From the high neighbouring Hills, which was thir Seat,	Par Lost 11.575
Such were these Giants, men of high renown;	Par Lost 11.688
To judge them with his Saints: Him the most High	Par Lost 11.705
High in Salvation and the Climes of bliss,	Par Lost 11.708
Fame in the World, high titles, and rich prey,	Par Lost 11.793
Fast on the top of som high mountain fixt.	Par Lost 11.851
For Gods! yet him God the most High voutsafes	Par Lost 12.120
Without Mediator, whose high Office now	Par Lost 12.240
To that proud Citie, whose high Walls thou saw'st	Par Lost 12.342
The Power of the most High; he shall ascend	Par Lost 12.369
High in the love of Heav'n, yet from my Loynes	Par Lost 12.380
Of God most High; So God with Man unites.	Par Lost 12.382
So onely can high Justice rest appaid.	Par Lost 12.401
His Seat at Gods right hand, exalted high	Par Lost 12.457

High(*cont*)

Homeward returning. High in Front advanc't,	Par Lost 12.632
Such high attest was giv'n, a while survey'd	Par Reg 1.37
Of the most High, who in full frequence bright	Par Reg 1.128
And high prediction, henceforth I expose	Par Reg 1.142
And said to me apart, high are thy thoughts	Par Reg 1.229
Can raise them, though above example high;	Par Reg 1.232
To prove him, and illustrate his high worth;	Par Reg 1.370
And on that high Authority had believ'd,	Par Reg 2.5
Alas, from what high hope to what relapse	Par Reg 2.30
O what avails me now that honour high	Par Reg 2.66
My Exaltation to Afflictions high;	Par Reg 2.92
His end of being on Earth, and mission high:	Par Reg 2.114
Of honour, wealth, high fare, aim'd not beyond	Par Reg 2.202
Left his ground-nest, high towring to descry	Par Reg 2.280
From whose high top to ken the prospect round,	Par Reg 2.286
High rooft and walks beneath, and alleys brown	Par Reg 2.293
And all thy heart is set on high designs,	Par Reg 2.410
High actions; but wherewith to be atchiev'd?	Par Reg 2.411
That sole excites to high attempts the flame	Par Reg 3.26
Of the enterprize so hazardous and high;	Par Reg 3.228
The Son of God up to a Mountain high.	Par Reg 3.252
Huge Cities and high towr'd, that well might seem	Par Reg 3.261
To this high mountain top the Tempter brought	Par Reg 3.265
Of that high mountain, whence he might behold	Par Reg 4.26
The Imperial Palace, compass huge, and high	Par Reg 4.51
On what I offer set as high esteem,	Par Reg 4.160
High actions, and high passions best describing:	Par Reg 4.266
Though rooted deep as high, and sturdiest Oaks	Par Reg 4.417
The holy City lifted high her Towers,	Par Reg 4.545
Hail Son of the most High, heir of both worlds,	Par Reg 4.633
Who this high gift of strength committed to me,	Samson 47
For him I reckon not in high estate	Samson 170
To *Dagon*, and advanc'd his praises high	Samson 450
Or th' execution leave to high disposal,	Samson 506
Of birth from Heav'n foretold and high exploits,	Samson 525
But throw'st them lower then thou didst exalt them high,	Samson 689
Though by his blindness maim'd for high attempts,	Samson 1221
Either at home, or through the high street passing,	Samson 1458
With all those high exploits by him atchiev'd,	Samson 1492
Through each high street: little I had dispatch't	Samson 1599
Half round on two main Pillars vaulted high,	Samson 1606
The Feast and noon grew high, and Sacrifice	Samson 1612
Had fill'd thir hearts with mirth, high chear, & wine,	Samson 1613
To matchless valour, and adventures high:	Samson 1740
Took in by lot 'twixt high, and neather *Jove*,	Mask 20
Therfore when any favour'd of high *Jove*,	Mask 78
Storied of old in high immortal vers	Mask 516
Feirce signe of battail make, and menace high,	Mask 654
In courts, at feasts, and high solemnities	Mask 746
line not in Bridgewater ms	
The sublime notion, and high mystery	Mask 785
line not in Bridgewater ms	
line not in Trinity ms	
Till all thy magick structures rear'd so high,	Mask 798
line not in Bridgewater ms	
line not in Trinity ms	
Com let us haste, the Stars grow high,	Mask 956
Through the high wood echoing shrill.	Allegro 56
Boosom'd high in tufted Trees,	Allegro 78
In weeds of Peace high triumphs hold,	Allegro 120
Be seen in som high lonely Towr,	Penseroso 86
And love the high embowed Roof,	Penseroso 157
In Service high, and Anthems cleer,	Penseroso 163
Fame that her high worth to raise,	Arcades 8
Shakes the high thicket, haste I all about,	Arcades 58
Together both, ere the high Lawns appear'd	Lycidas 25
Nor on the shaggy top of *Mona* high,	Lycidas 54
So *Lycidas* sunk low, but mounted high,	Lycidas 172
Wherwith he wont at Heav'ns high Councel-Table,	Nativity 10
The idle spear and shield were high up hung;	Nativity 55
Will open wide the Gates of her high Palace Hall.	Nativity 148
The high, huge-bellied Mountains skip like Rams	Psalm 114, 11
That his mansion hath on high	Psalm 136, 93
Whether above that high first-moving Spheare	Fair Inf 39
High thron'd in secret bliss, for us frail dust	Circum 19
Trinity ms 'high-thron'd'	
Their loud up-lifted Angel trumpets blow,	Musick 11
Trinity ms 'up-lifted' ←'uplifted' ←'high lifted' ←'unsa', ms defective	
in high misterious happie spousall meet	Musick Tr. ms 4.06
Her high birth, and her graces sweet,	Winchester 15
Whilst thou bright Saint high sit'st in glory,	Winchester 61
To that same lot, however mean, or high,	Sonnet 7, 11
Would have been held in high esteem with *Paul*	Forcers 10
Jehovah from on high	Psalm 4, 17
Return on high and in their sight.	Psalm 7, 28
Of Jehovah the most high.	Psalm 7, 64
Her Bows as *high as* Cedars tall	Psalm 80, 43
The Sons of God most high	Psalm 82, 22
Exalt their heads full hie.	Psalm 83, 8
Art the most high, *and thou the same*	Psalm 83, 67
Lord *God* of Hoasts *that raign'st on high*,	Psalm 84, 45
Among the holy Mountains *high*	Psalm 87, 1
High God shall fix her fast.	Psalm 87, 20
Which he who can, and will, deserv's high praise,	Prose 9, 3

High-blessed

Of God high-blest, or to incline his will,	Par Lost 11.145

High-built
Haughty as is his pile high-built and proud. Samson 1069
High-climbing
Obtains the brow of some high-climbing Hill, Par Lost 3.546
Higher
With upright wing against a higher foe. Par Lost 2.72
Satan except, none higher sat, with grave Par Lost 2.300
I sdeind subjection, and thought one step higher Par Lost 4.50
Of stateliest view. Yet higher then thir tops Par Lost 4.142
And higher then that Wall a circling row Par Lost 4.146
Laurel and Mirtle, and what higher grew Par Lost 4.694
From her moist Continent to higher Orbes. Par Lost 5.422
Above mankinde, or aught then mankinde higher, Par Lost 8.358
All higher knowledge in her presence falls Par Lost 8.551
What higher in her societie thou findst Par Lost 8.586
(Though higher of the genial Bed by far, Par Lost 8.598
Nor skilld nor studious, higher Argument Par Lost 9.42
Since higher I fall short, on him who next Par Lost 9.174
Whose higher intellectual more I shun, Par Lost 9.483
Meant mee, by ventring higher then my Lot. Par Lost 9.690
Higher degree of Life, inducement strong Par Lost 9.934
Not higher that Hill nor wider looking round, Par Lost 11.381
Of wisdome; hope no higher, though all the Starrs Par Lost 12.576
Higher design then to enjoy his State; Par Reg 2.203
If I to try whether in higher sort Par Reg 4.198
And his who gave them breath, but higher sung, Par Reg 4.258
In some respect far higher so declar'd. Par Reg 4.521
And higher yet the glorious Temple rear'd Par Reg 4.546
Higher then the Spheary chime; Mask 1021
Yet thou art higher far descended, Penseroso 22
That strain I heard was of a higher mood: Lycidas 87
Dante shall give Fame leave to set thee higher Sonnet 13, 12
The *greedy* flame runs hier and hier Psalm 83, 55
Highest
Thir highest Heav'n; or on the *Delphian* Cliff, Par Lost 1.517
Against the Highest, and fierce with grasped Arms Par Lost 1.667
Will envy whom the highest place exposes Par Lost 2.27
Conscious of highest worth, unmov'd thus spake. Par Lost 2.429
Extoll him equal to the highest in Heav'n: Par Lost 2.479
Satan with thoughts inflam'd of highest design, Par Lost 2.630
Conjur'd against the highest, for which both Thou Par Lost 2.693
Because thou hast, though Thron'd in highest bliss Par Lost 3.305
Interpreter through highest Heav'n to bring, Par Lost 3.657
Would set me highest, and in a moment quit Par Lost 4.51
Of Hill or highest Wall, and sheer within Par Lost 4.182
The middle Tree and highest there that grew, Par Lost 4.195
Shall teach us highest deeds, by proof to try Par Lost 5.865
Such as in highest Heav'n, arrayd in Gold Par Lost 6.13
Among the mightiest, bent on highest deeds, Par Lost 6.112
O Heav'n! that such resemblance of the Highest Par Lost 6.114
Hosanna to the Highest: nor stood at gaze Par Lost 6.205
First, Highest, Holiest, Best, thou alwayes seekst Par Lost 6.724
Our knowing, as to highest wisdom seemd, Par Lost 7.83
Not of Earth onely but of highest Heav'n. Par Lost 8.178
With Gods to sit the highest, am now constraind Par Lost 9.164
Of highest Agents, deemd however wise. Par Lost 9.683
Obscur'd, where highest Woods impenetrable Par Lost 9.1086
Creator wise, that peopl'd highest Heav'n Par Lost 10.889
Of contumacie will provoke the highest Par Lost 10.1027
Of them the Highest, for such of shape may seem Par Lost 11.297
Of Paradise the highest, from whose top Par Lost 11.378
Man-slaughter, shall be held the highest pitch Par Lost 11.693
Above the highest Hills: then shall this Mount Par Lost 11.829
Is fortitude to highest victorie, Par Lost 12.570
Things highest, greatest, multiplies my fear. Par Reg 1.69
The Holy Ghost, and the power of the highest Par Reg 1.139
In lowest poverty to highest deeds; Par Reg 2.438
And dignities and powers all but the highest? Par Reg 3.30
Aim at the highest, without the highest attain'd Par Reg 4.106
There on the highest Pinacle he set Par Reg 4.549
Have brought thee, and highest plac't, highest is best, Par Reg 4.553
Of highest dispensation, which herein Samson 61
Universally crown'd with highest praises. Samson 175
As earst in highest, behold him where he lies. Samson 339
Of highest favours past Samson 685
The highest name for valiant Acts, that honour Samson 1101
Of highest wisdom brings about, Samson 1747
Riding neer her highest noon, Penseroso 68
Highly
Favour'd of Heav'n so highly, to fall off Par Lost 1.30
Far round illumin'd hell: highly they rag'd Par Lost 1.666
Pleas'd highly those infernal States, and joy Par Lost 2.387
He ceas'd, for both seemd highly pleasd, and Death Par Lost 2.845
Who highly thus to entitle me voutsaf'st, Par Lost 11.170
Highly belov'd, being but the Minister Par Lost 12.308
Hale highly favour'd, among women blest; Par Reg 2.68
How highly it concerns his glory now Samson 1148
Off. Regard thy self, this will offend them highly. Samson 1333
The highly favour'd *Joseph* bore Winchester 65
High-raised
And to our high-rais'd phantasie present, Musick 5
Trinity ms 'high-rays'd' ←'high raysd' ←'up rays'd' ←'high rays'd'
High-seated
Of Heav'ns high-seated top, th' Impereal Throne Par Lost 7.585
Hill
Rose out of *Chaos:* Or if *Sion* Hill Par Lost 1.10
ms 'hill'
Hill(*cont*)
Of subterranean wind transports a Hill Par Lost 1.231
ms 'hill'
On that opprobrious Hill, and made his Grove Par Lost 1.403
ms 'hill'
Even to that Hill of scandal, by the Grove Par Lost 1.416
ms 'hill'
There stood a Hill not far whose griesly top Par Lost 1.670
ms 'hill'
Op'nd into the Hill a spacious wound Par Lost 1.689
ms 'hill'
Attest thir joy, that hill and valley rings. Par Lost 2.495
Others apart sat on a Hill retir'd, Par Lost 2.557
With winged course ore Hill or moarie Dale, Par Lost 2.944
Cleer Spring, or shadie Grove, or Sunnie Hill, Par Lost 3.28
Obtains the brow of some high-climbing Hill, Par Lost 3.546
Now to th' ascent of that steep savage Hill Par Lost 4.172
Of Hill or highest Wall, and sheer within Par Lost 4.182
Nor chang'd his course, but through the shaggie hill Par Lost 4.224
Powrd forth profuse on Hill and Dale and Plaine, Par Lost 4.243
Through wood, through waste, o're hill, o're dale his roam. Par Lost 4.538
1667 'hil'
Of echoing Hill or Thicket have we heard Par Lost 4.681
Half way up Hill this vast Sublunar Vault, Par Lost 4.777
From Hill or steaming Lake, duskie or grey, Par Lost 5.186
To Hill, or Valley, Fountain, or fresh shade Par Lost 5.203
My onely Son, and on this holy Hill Par Lost 5.604
In song and dance about the sacred Hill, Par Lost 5.619
This our high place, our Sanctuarie, our Hill. Par Lost 5.732
High on a Hill, far blazing, as a Mount Par Lost 5.757
Returnd not lost: On to the sacred hill Par Lost 6.25
To darken all the Hill, and smoak to rowl Par Lost 6.57
Indissolubly firm; nor obvious Hill, Par Lost 6.69
Of pleasure situate in Hill and Dale) Par Lost 6.641
And with fresh Flourets Hill and Valley smil'd. Par Lost 6.784
Following, above th' *Olympian* Hill I soare, Par Lost 7.3
Soft-ebbing; nor withstood them Rock or Hill, Par Lost 7.300
Hill, Dale, and shadie Woods, and sunnie Plaines, Par Lost 8.262
Gave sign of gratulation, and each Hill; Par Lost 8.514
On his Hill top, to light the bridal Lamp. Par Lost 8.520
Of Hill, and Vallie, Rivers, Woods and Plaines, Par Lost 9.116
Down from a Hill the Beast that reigns in Woods, Par Lost 11.187
In Paradise, and on a Hill made alt, Par Lost 11.210
From yonder blazing Cloud that veils the Hill Par Lost 11.229
This Hill; let *Eve* (for I have drencht her eyes) Par Lost 11.367
In the Visions of God: It was a Hill Par Lost 11.377
Not higher that Hill nor wider looking round, Par Lost 11.381
By mee encampt on yonder Hill, expect Par Lost 12.591
He ended, and they both descend the Hill; Par Lost 12.606
Th' Archangel stood, and from the other Hill Par Lost 12.626
Full forty days he pass'd, whether on hill Par Reg 1.303
Seated as on the top of Vertues hill, Par Reg 2.217
Up to a hill anon his steps he rear'd, Par Reg 2.285
Well have we speeded, and o're hill and dale, Par Reg 3.267
Or where plain was raise hill, or over-lay Par Reg 3.333
There flowrie hill *Hymettus* with the sound Par Reg 4.247
Him walking on a Sunny hill he found, Par Reg 4.447
Up to the Hill by *Hebron*, seat of Giants old, Samson 148
That crawls along the side of yon small hill, Mask 295
From the side of som Hoar Hill, Allegro 55
For we were nurst upon the self-same hill, Lycidas 23
Hill and Dale, doth boast thy blessing. May Morn 8
That labour up the Hill of heav'nly Truth, Sonnet 9, 4
Trinity ms 'hill'
On *Sion* my holi' hill. A firm decree Psalm 2, 13
Hillock
Or palmie hilloc, or the flourie lap Par Lost 4.254
Hillocks
In Hillocks; the swift Stag from under ground Par Lost 7.469
O Woods, O Fountains, Hillocks, Dales and Bowrs, Par Lost 10.860
By Hedge-row Elms, on Hillocks green, Allegro 58
Hills
Hewn on *Norwegian* hills, to be the Mast Par Lost 1.293
Rend up both Rocks and Hills, and ride the Air Par Lost 2.540
On Hills where Flocks are fed, flies toward the Springs Par Lost 3.435
Down the slope hills, disperst, or in a Lake, Par Lost 4.261
Above all Hills. As when by night the Glass Par Lost 5.261
Cherubic Songs by night from neighbouring Hills Par Lost 5.547
Soon banded; others from the dawning Hills Par Lost 6.528
Thir Arms away they threw, and to the Hills Par Lost 6.639
They pluckt the seated Hills with all thir load, Par Lost 6.644
Betook them, and the neighbouring Hills uptore; Par Lost 6.663
So Hills amid the Air encounterd Hills Par Lost 6.664
At his command the uprooted Hills retir'd Par Lost 6.781
Before the Hills appeerd, or Fountain flow'd, Par Lost 7.8
So high as heav'd the tumid Hills, so low Par Lost 7.288
Thir blossoms: with high woods the hills were crownd, Par Lost 7.326
1667 'Hills'
Ye Hills and Dales, ye Rivers, Woods, and Plaines, Par Lost 8.275
From the high neighbouring Hills, which was thir Seat, Par Lost 11.575
From under Heav'n; the Hills to their supplie Par Lost 11.740
Above the highest Hills: then shall this Mount Par Lost 11.829
And now the tops of Hills as Rocks appeer; Par Lost 11.852
Shall dwell to *Senir*, that long ridge of Hills. Par Lost 12.146
With herds the pastures throng'd, with flocks the hills, Par Reg 3.260
To lay hills plain, fell woods, or valleys fill, Par Reg 3.332
To equal length back'd with a ridge of hills Par Reg 4.29
On seven small Hills, with Palaces adorn'd, Par Reg 4.35

Hills(*cont*)

Infamous Hills, and sandy perilous wildes, Mask 424
1637 'hills'
Trinity ms 'hills'
Bridgewater ms 'hills'
That tumble down the snowy hills: Mask 927
And now the Sun had stretch'd out all the hills, Lycidas 190
Amongst their Ews, the little Hills like Lambs. Psalm 114, 12
And hills of Snow and lofts of piled Thunder, Vacation 42
The Vales redoubl'd to the Hills, and they Sonnet 18, 9
The Hills were *over-spread* Psalm 80, 42

Hilly

Tending my flocks hard by i'th hilly crofts, Mask 531
Bridgewater ms 'hillie'
Trinity ms 'hillie' ←'pastur'd'

Him

Had cast him out from Heav'n, with all his Host Par Lost 1.37
With vain attempt. Him the Almighty Power Par Lost 1.44
Reserv'd him to more wrath; for now the thought Par Lost 1.54
Torments him; round he throws his baleful eyes Par Lost 1.56
From him, who in the happy Realms of Light Par Lost 1.85
And him thus answer'd soon his bold Compeer. Par Lost 1.127
Or do him mightier service as his thralls Par Lost 1.149
Shall grieve him, if I fail not, and disturb Par Lost 1.167
Him haply slumbring on the *Norway* foam Par Lost 1.203
Left him at large to his own dark designs, Par Lost 1.213
On Man by him seduc't, but on himself Par Lost 1.219
Of unblest feet. Him followed his next Mate, Par Lost 1.238
ms 'him'
What shall be right: fardest from him is best Par Lost 1.247
So *Satan* spake, and him *Beelzebub* Par Lost 1.271
Behind him cast; the broad circumference Par Lost 1.286
Smote on him sore besides, vaulted with Fire; Par Lost 1.298
Glory of him that made them, to transform Par Lost 1.370
To his grim Idol. Him the *Ammonite* Par Lost 1.396
To do him wanton rites, which cost them woe. Par Lost 1.414
Him follow'd *Rimmon*, whose delightful Seat Par Lost 1.467
Vice for it self: To him no Temple stood Par Lost 1.492
From wing to wing, and half enclose him round Par Lost 1.617
In vision beatific: by him first Par Lost 1.684
Men call'd him *Mulciber;* and how he fell Par Lost 1.740
Fell long before; nor aught avail'd him now Par Lost 1.748
He ceas'd, and next him *Moloc*, Scepter'd King Par Lost 2.43
With him, or who deceive his mind, whose eye Par Lost 2.189
Not peace: and after him thus *Mammon* spake. Par Lost 2.228
Our own right lost: him to unthrone we then Par Lost 2.231
Of him who rules above; so was his will Par Lost 2.351
Suffice, or what evasion bear him safe Par Lost 2.411
Of unessential Night receives him next Par Lost 2.439
Threatens him, plung'd in that abortive gulf. Par Lost 2.441
Or unknown Region, what remains him less Par Lost 2.443
To him who Reigns, and so much to him due Par Lost 2.454
Forbidding; and at once with him they rose; Par Lost 2.475
Of Thunder heard remote. Towards him they bend Par Lost 2.477
Extoll him equal to the highest in Heav'n: Par Lost 2.479
And God-like imitated State; him round Par Lost 2.511
Leads him perplext, where he may likeliest find Par Lost 2.525
Drew after him the third part of Heav'ns Sons Par Lost 2.692
For him who sits above and laughs the while Par Lost 2.731
Sight more detestable then him and thee. Par Lost 2.745
Both him and thee, and all the heav'nly Host Par Lost 2.824
I keep, by him forbidden to unlock Par Lost 2.852
By which he Reigns: next him high Arbiter Par Lost 2.909
Instinct with Fire and Nitre hurried him Par Lost 2.937
Half flying; behoves him now both Oare and Saile. Par Lost 2.942
Wide on the wasteful Deep; with him Enthron'd Par Lost 2.961
Thus *Satan;* and him thus the Anarch old Par Lost 2.988
Pav'd after him a broad and beat'n way Par Lost 2.1026
About him all the Sanctities of Heaven Par Lost 3.60
Him God beholding from his prospect high, Par Lost 3.77
Heapt on him there, nor yet the main Abyss Par Lost 3.83
If him by force he can destroy, or worse, Par Lost 3.91
All he could have; I made him just and right, Par Lost 3.98
Most glorious, in him all his Father shon Par Lost 3.139
Draw after him the whole Race of mankind, Par Lost 3.161
By him corrupted? or wilt thou thy self Par Lost 3.162
For him, what for thy glorie thou hast made? Par Lost 3.164
Yet not of will in him, but grace in me Par Lost 3.174
Dye hee or Justice must; unless for him Par Lost 3.210
Behold mee then, mee for him, life for life Par Lost 3.236
Freely put off, and for him lastly dye Par Lost 3.240
Though last created, that for him I spare Par Lost 3.278
As in him perish all men, so in thee Par Lost 3.287
And dying rise, and rising with him raise Par Lost 3.296
Adore him, who to compass all this dies, Par Lost 3.342
Adore the Son, and honour him as mee. Par Lost 3.343
Not so on Man; him through their malice fall'n, Par Lost 3.400
In *Golgotha* him dead, who lives in Heav'n; Par Lost 3.477
Which else might work him danger or delay: Par Lost 3.635
O're Sea and Land: him *Satan* thus accostes; Par Lost 3.653
His chief delight and favour, him for whom Par Lost 3.664
That I may find him, and with secret gaze, Par Lost 3.671
Or open admiration him behold Par Lost 3.672
That both in him and all things, as is meet, Par Lost 3.675
To serve him better: wise are all his wayes. Par Lost 3.680
The Hell within him, for within him Hell Par Lost 4.20
He brings, and round about him, nor from Hell Par Lost 4.21
What could be less then to afford him praise, Par Lost 4.46

Him(*cont*)

The easiest recompence, and pay him thanks, Par Lost 4.47
Forgetful what from him I still receivd, Par Lost 4.54
Mankind created, and for him this World. Par Lost 4.107
Him counterfet, if any eye beheld. Par Lost 4.117
Uriel once warnd; whose eye pursu'd him down Par Lost 4.125
Saw him disfigur'd, more then could befall Par Lost 4.127
That drove him, though enamourd, from the Spouse Par Lost 4.169
The good before him, but perverts best things Par Lost 4.203
Beneath him with new wonder now he views Par Lost 4.205
Of God the Garden was, by him in the East Par Lost 4.209
Hee for God only, shee for God in him: Par Lost 4.299
And by her yielded, by him best receivd, Par Lost 4.309
Thank him who puts me loath to this revenge Par Lost 4.386
On you who wrong me not for him who wrongd. Par Lost 4.387
Turnd him all eare to hear new utterance flow. Par Lost 4.410
But let us ever praise him, and extoll Par Lost 4.436
For wee to him indeed all praises owe, Par Lost 4.444
Whose image thou art, him thou shalt enjoy Par Lost 4.472
Inseparablie thine, to him shalt beare Par Lost 4.473
Whom fli'st thou? whom thou fli'st, of him thou art, Par Lost 4.482
Or in thick shade retir'd, from him to draw Par Lost 4.532
About him exercis'd Heroic Games Par Lost 4.551
Mine eye pursu'd him still, but under shade Par Lost 4.572
Lost sight of him; one of the banisht crew Par Lost 4.573
New troubles; him thy care must be to find. Par Lost 4.575
Bore him slope downward to the Sun now fall'n Par Lost 4.591
By shorter flight to th' East, had left him there Par Lost 4.595
On him who had stole *Joves* authentic fire. Par Lost 4.719
That neer him stood, and gave them thus in charge. Par Lost 4.787
In search of whom they sought: him there they found Par Lost 4.799
Him thus intent *Ithuriel* with his Spear Par Lost 4.810
Yet thus, unmovd with fear, accost him soon. Par Lost 4.822
To him who sent us, whose charge is to keep Par Lost 4.842
His will who bound us? let him surer barr Par Lost 4.897
And now returns him from his prison scap't, Par Lost 4.906
Or not, who ask what boldness brought him hither Par Lost 4.908
To dispossess him, and thy self to reigne? Par Lost 4.961
Thir Phalanx, and began to hemm him round Par Lost 4.979
Murmuring, and with him fled the shades of night. Par Lost 4.1015
With him I flew, and underneath beheld Par Lost 5.87
Angels, for yee behold him, and with songs Par Lost 5.161
Him first, him last, him midst, and without end. Par Lost 5.165
With thy bright Circlet, praise him in thy Spheare Par Lost 5.169
Acknowledge him thy Greater, sound his praise Par Lost 5.172
To wed her Elm; she spous'd about him twines Par Lost 5.216
With pittie Heav'ns high King, and to him call'd Par Lost 5.220
Thou find'st him from the heat of Noon retir'd, Par Lost 5.231
As may advise him of his happie state, Par Lost 5.234
Yet mutable; whence warne him to beware Par Lost 5.237
He swerve not too secure: tell him withall Par Lost 5.238
But by deceit and lies; this let him know, Par Lost 5.243
The circuit wide. Strait knew him all the Bands Par Lost 5.287
For on som message high they guessd him bound. Par Lost 5.290
Him through the spicie Forrest onward com Par Lost 5.298
Given him by this great Conference to know Par Lost 5.454
All things proceed, and up to him return, Par Lost 5.470
As neerer to him plac't or neerer tending Par Lost 5.476
To him, or possibly his love desert Par Lost 5.515
Not our necessitated, such with him Par Lost 5.530
Our maker, and obey him whose command Par Lost 5.551
Him have anointed, whom ye now behold Par Lost 5.605
At my right hand; your Head I him appoint; Par Lost 5.606
And by my Self have sworn to him shall bow Par Lost 5.607
All knees in Heav'n, and shall confess him Lord: Par Lost 5.608
For ever happie: him who disobeyes Par Lost 5.611
Satan, so call him now, his former name Par Lost 5.658
Awak'ning, thus to him in secret spake. Par Lost 5.672
New Laws from him who reigns, new minds may raise Par Lost 5.680
Under him Regent, tells, as he was taught, Par Lost 5.698
Drew after him the third part of Heav'ns Host: Par Lost 5.710
Nightly before him, saw without thir light Par Lost 5.714
Receive him coming to receive from us Par Lost 5.781
Confess him rightful King? unjust thou saist Par Lost 5.818
With him the points of libertie, who made Par Lost 5.823
Equal to him begotten Son, by whom Par Lost 5.835
By him created in thir bright degrees, Par Lost 5.838
His Laws our Laws, all honour to him done Par Lost 5.844
Nor number, nor example with him wrought Par Lost 5.901
Among those friendly Powers, who him receav'd Par Lost 6.22
They led him high applauded, and present Par Lost 6.26
Incens't, and thus securely him defi'd. Par Lost 6.130
To serve th' unwise, or him who hath rebelld Par Lost 6.179
These Elements, and arm him with the force Par Lost 6.222
And join him nam'd *Almighty* to thy aid, Par Lost 6.294
Was giv'n him temperd so, that neither keen Par Lost 6.322
And writh'd him to and fro convolv'd; so sore Par Lost 6.328
Pass'd through him, but th' Ethereal substance clos'd Par Lost 6.330
Defence, while others bore him on thir Shields Par Lost 6.337
From off the files of warr; there they him laid Par Lost 6.339
Of *Moloc* furious King, who him defi'd, Par Lost 6.357
And at his Chariot wheeles to drag him bound Par Lost 6.358
Of future we may deem him, though till now Par Lost 6.429
In motion or in alt: him soon they met Par Lost 6.532
All power on him transferr'd: whence to his Son Par Lost 6.678
Sate Eagle-wing'd, beside him hung his Bow Par Lost 6.763
And from about him fierce Effusion rowld Par Lost 6.765
Before him Power Divine his way prepar'd; Par Lost 6.780

Him(*cont*)
Before him, such as in thir Soules infix'd Par Lost 6.837
Drove them before him Thunder-struck, pursu'd Par Lost 6.858
Incumberd him with ruin: Hell at last Par Lost 6.874
To meet him all his Saints, who silent stood Par Lost 6.882
Sung Triumph, and him sung Victorious King, Par Lost 6.886
Son, Heir, and Lord, to him Dominion giv'n, Par Lost 6.887
On high: who into Glorie him receav'd, Par Lost 6.891
Thee also from obedience, that with him Par Lost 6.902
What neerer might concern him, how this World Par Lost 7.62
(So call him, brighter once amidst the Host Par Lost 7.132
But least his heart exalt him in the harme Par Lost 7.150
Glorie to him whose just avenging ire Par Lost 7.184
And th' habitations of the just; to him Par Lost 7.186
Immense, and all his Father in him shon. Par Lost 7.196
For *Chaos* heard his voice: him all his Traine Par Lost 7.221
God and his works, Creatour him they sung, Par Lost 7.259
Dawn, and the *Pleiades* before him danc'd Par Lost 7.374
From him, for other light she needed none Par Lost 7.378
Adorns him, colour'd with the Florid hue Par Lost 7.445
And worship God Supream, who made him chief Par Lost 7.515
The Filial Power arriv'd, and sate him down Par Lost 7.587
And worship him, and in reward to rule Par Lost 7.628
Thought him still speaking, still stood fixt to hear; Par Lost 8.3
line not in 1667 edition
Before the Angel, and of him to ask Par Lost 8.53
An Edifice too large for him to fill, Par Lost 8.104
Incited, dance about him various rounds? Par Lost 8.125
Leave them to God above, him serve and feare; Par Lost 8.168
Of other Creatures, as him pleases best, Par Lost 8.169
Wherever plac't, let him dispose: joy thou Par Lost 8.170
Tell me, how may I know him, how adore, Par Lost 8.280
The Soule of Man, or passion in him move. Par Lost 8.585
Him whom to love is to obey, and keep Par Lost 8.634
To sit indulgent, and with him partake Par Lost 9.3
Rural repast, permitting him the while Par Lost 9.4
The Sun was sunk, and after him the Starr Par Lost 9.48
Him after long debate, irresolute Par Lost 9.87
To my relentless thoughts; and him destroyd, Par Lost 9.130
Follow, as to him linkt in weal or woe, Par Lost 9.133
A Creature form'd of Earth, and him endow, Par Lost 9.149
He effected; Man he made, and for him built Par Lost 9.152
Him Lord pronounc'd, and, O indignitie! Par Lost 9.154
Since higher I fall short, on him who next Par Lost 9.174
The Serpent: him fast sleeping soon he found Par Lost 9.182
So bent, the more shall shame him his repulse. Par Lost 9.384
Repeated, shee to him as oft engag'd Par Lost 9.400
But the hot Hell that alwayes in him burnes, Par Lost 9.467
And tortures him now more, the more he sees Par Lost 9.469
Of pleasure not for him ordain'd: then soon Par Lost 9.470
What can your knowledge hurt him, or this Tree Par Lost 9.727
The good befall'n him, Author unsuspect, Par Lost 9.771
About him. But to *Adam* in what sort Par Lost 9.816
Shall I appeer? shall I to him make known Par Lost 9.817
As yet my change, and give him to partake Par Lost 9.818
So dear I love him, that with him all deaths Par Lost 9.832
I could endure, without him live no life. Par Lost 9.833
Misgave him; hee the faultring measure felt; Par Lost 9.846
To him she hasted, in her face excuse Par Lost 9.853
Profan'd first by the Serpent, by him first Par Lost 9.930
Nor yet on him found deadly, he yet lives, Par Lost 9.932
Most Favors, who can please him long; Mee first Par Lost 9.949
So *Adam*, and thus *Eve* to him repli'd. Par Lost 9.960
So saying, she embrac'd him, and for joy Par Lost 9.990
She gave him of that fair enticing Fruit Par Lost 9.996
Him with her lov'd societie, that now Par Lost 9.1007
Began to cast lascivious Eyes, she him Par Lost 9.1014
Him who to worth in Women overtrusting Par Lost 9.1183
Of high collateral glorie: him Thrones and Powers, Par Lost 10.86
He came, and with him *Eve*, more loth, though first Par Lost 10.109
The Guilt on him who made him instrument Par Lost 10.166
Before him naked to the aire, that now Par Lost 10.212
To him with swift ascent he up returnd, Par Lost 10.224
In glory as of old, to him appeas'd Par Lost 10.226
But that success attends him; if mishap, Par Lost 10.239
Met who to meet him came, his Ofspring dear. Par Lost 10.349
There didst not; there let him still Victor sway, Par Lost 10.376
Him first make sure your thrall, and lastly kill. Par Lost 10.402
He sate, and round about him saw unseen: Par Lost 10.448
Was left him, or false glitter: All amaz'd Par Lost 10.452
Congratulant approach'd him, who with hand Par Lost 10.458
Made happie: Him by fraud I have seduc'd Par Lost 10.485
Now rul'd him, punisht in the shape he sin'd, Par Lost 10.516
Him follow'd issuing forth to th' open Field, Par Lost 10.533
And season him thy last and sweetest prey. Par Lost 10.609
Of Man, but fled him, or with count'nance grim Par Lost 10.713
Glar'd on him passing: these were from without Par Lost 10.714
The evil on him brought by me, will curse Par Lost 10.734
That proud excuse? yet him not thy election, Par Lost 10.764
To serve him, thy reward was of his grace, Par Lost 10.767
In sight of God? Him after all Disputes Par Lost 10.828
Befits thee with him leagu'd, thy self as false Par Lost 10.868
Though by the Devil himself, him overweening Par Lost 10.878
Fool'd and beguil'd, by him thou, I by thee, Par Lost 10.880
As some misfortune brings him, or mistake, Par Lost 10.900
How much more, if we pray him, will his ear Par Lost 10.1060
Beseeching him, so as we need not fear Par Lost 10.1082
By him with many comforts, till we end Par Lost 10.1084

Him(*cont*)
Before him reverent, and there confess Par Lost 10.1088
Before him reverent, and both confess'd Par Lost 10.1100
Interpret for him, mee his Advocate Par Lost 11.33
The smell of peace toward Mankinde, let him live Par Lost 11.38
To better life shall yeeld him, where with mee Par Lost 11.42
The Law I gave to Nature him forbids: Par Lost 11.49
Eject him tainted now, and purge him off Par Lost 11.52
And mortal food, as may dispose him best Par Lost 11.54
Created him endowd, with Happiness Par Lost 11.58
Resignes him up with Heav'n and Earth renewd. Par Lost 11.66
Of that defended Fruit; but let him boast Par Lost 11.86
Happier, had it suffic'd him to have known Par Lost 11.88
My motions in him, longer then they move, Par Lost 11.91
For ever, to remove him I decree, Par Lost 11.96
And send him from the Garden forth to Till Par Lost 11.97
For swift descent, with him the Cohort bright Par Lost 11.127
Kneel'd and before him humbl'd all my heart, Par Lost 11.150
Methought I saw him placable and mild, Par Lost 11.151
Two Birds of gayest plume before him drove: Par Lost 11.186
Invests him coming? yet not terrible, Par Lost 11.233
His starrie Helme unbuckl'd shew'd him prime Par Lost 11.245
Thy Husband, him to follow thou art bound; Par Lost 11.291
Of him who all things can, I would not cease Par Lost 11.309
To wearie him with my assiduous cries: Par Lost 11.310
Blown stifling back on him that breaths it forth: Par Lost 11.313
I heard, here with him at this Fountain talk'd: Par Lost 11.322
For though I fled him angrie, yet recall'd Par Lost 11.330
To shew him all Earths Kingdomes and thir Glory. Par Lost 11.384
But him the gentle Angel by the hand Par Lost 11.421
Smote him into the Midriff with a stone Par Lost 11.445
Loose no reward, though here thou see him die, Par Lost 11.459
His best of Man, and gave him up to tears Par Lost 11.497
My dissolution. *Michael* repli'd, Par Lost 11.552
1667 '*Michael* to him repli'd'
Before him, Towns, and rural works between, Par Lost 11.639
And Judgment from above: him old and young Par Lost 11.668
Had not a Cloud descending snatch'd him thence Par Lost 11.670
Ten thousandfould the sin of him who slew Par Lost 11.678
To judge them with his Saints: Him the most High Par Lost 11.705
Him or his Childern, evil he may be sure, Par Lost 11.772
And after him, the surer messenger, Par Lost 11.856
From him, and all his anger to forget. Par Lost 11.878
Though late repenting him of Man deprav'd, Par Lost 11.886
With him or under him to tyrannize, Par Lost 12.39
And famish him of Breath, if not of Bread? Par Lost 12.78
Subjects him from without to violent Lords; Par Lost 12.93
Of him who built the Ark, who for the shame Par Lost 12.102
Him on this side *Euphrates* yet residing, Par Lost 12.114
For Gods! yet him God the most High voutsafes Par Lost 12.120
Which he will shew him, and from him will raise Par Lost 12.123
A mightie Nation, and upon him showre Par Lost 12.124
I see him, but thou canst not, with what Faith Par Lost 12.128
To *Haran*, after him a cumbrous Train Par Lost 12.131
With God, who call'd him, in a land unknown. Par Lost 12.134
Like him in faith, in wisdom, and renown; Par Lost 12.154
Raise him to be the second in that Realme Par Lost 12.162
Swallows him with his Host, but them lets pass Par Lost 12.196
Of two bright Cherubim, before him burn Par Lost 12.254
From *Abraham*, Son of *Isaac*, and from him Par Lost 12.268
Such follow him, as shall be registerd Par Lost 12.335
Unseen before in Heav'n proclaims him com, Par Lost 12.361
Of all mankinde, with him there crucifi'd, Par Lost 12.417
But soon revives, Death over him no power Par Lost 12.420
Returne, the Starres of Morn shall see him rise Par Lost 12.422
Still follow'd him; to them shall leave in charge Par Lost 12.439
To teach all nations what of him they learn'd Par Lost 12.440
Wors with his followers then with him they dealt? Par Lost 12.484
Of him so lately promiss'd to thy aid Par Lost 12.542
His providence, and on him sole depend, Par Lost 12.564
And thus with words not sad she him receav'd. Par Lost 12.609
Against the Spiritual Foe, and broughtst him thence Par Reg 1.10
Unmarkt, unknown; but him the Baptist soon Par Reg 1.25
To him his Heavenly Office, nor was long Par Reg 1.28
His witness unconfirm'd: on him baptiz'd Par Reg 1.29
From Heav'n pronounc'd him his beloved Son. Par Reg 1.32
Delay, for longest time to him is short; Par Reg 1.56
Before him a great Prophet, to proclaim Par Reg 1.70
Purified to receive him pure, or rather Par Reg 1.74
To do him honour as their King; all come, Par Reg 1.75
The Prophet do him reverence, on him rising Par Reg 1.80
This is my Son belov'd, in him am pleas'd. Par Reg 1.85
To him their great Dictator, whose attempt Par Reg 1.113
Temptation and all guile on him to try; Par Reg 1.123
To shew him worthy of his birth divine Par Reg 1.141
To Satan; let him tempt and now assay Par Reg 1.143
All his vast force, and drive him back to Hell, Par Reg 1.153
To exercise him in the Wilderness, Par Reg 1.156
Of his great warfare, e're I send him forth Par Reg 1.158
Where they might see him, and to thee they came; Par Reg 1.246
Me him (for it was shew'n him so from Heaven) Par Reg 1.276
Me him whose Harbinger he was; and first Par Reg 1.277
Or Cedar, to defend him from the dew, Par Reg 1.306
Nor sleeping him nor waking harm'd, his walk Par Reg 1.311
To warm him wet return'd from field at Eve, Par Reg 1.318
Perus'd him, then with words thus utt'red spake. Par Reg 1.320
To prove him, and illustrate his high worth; Par Reg 1.370
Of righteous *Job*, then cruelly to afflict him Par Reg 1.425

Him(*cont*)

To flye or follow what concern'd him most,	Par Reg 1.440
But from him or his Angels President	Par Reg 1.447
If it may stand him more in stead to lye,	Par Reg 1.473
Him whom they heard so late expresly call'd	Par Reg 2.3
And with him talkt, and with him lodg'd, I mean	Par Reg 2.6
Now missing him thir joy so lately found,	Par Reg 2.9
Hath rapt him from us? will he now retire	Par Reg 2.40
Sent his Anointed, and to us reveal'd him,	Par Reg 2.50
In publick, and with him we have convers'd;	Par Reg 2.52
Nor will withdraw him now, nor will recall,	Par Reg 2.55
Mock us with his blest sight, then snatch him hence,	Par Reg 2.56
Nor left at *Jordan*, tydings of him none;	Par Reg 2.62
Could be obtain'd to shelter him or me	Par Reg 2.73
Conceals him: when twelve years he scarce had seen,	Par Reg 2.96
I lost him, but so found, as well I saw	Par Reg 2.97
All his great work to come before him set;	Par Reg 2.112
Had left him vacant, and with speed was gon	Par Reg 2.116
Have found him, view'd him, tasted him, but find	Par Reg 2.131
Of wisest *Solomon*, and made him build,	Par Reg 2.170
And made him bow to the Gods of his Wives.	Par Reg 2.171
Then forthwith to him takes a chosen band	Par Reg 2.236
Commun'd in silent walk, then laid him down	Par Reg 2.261
Him thought, he by the Brook of *Cherith* stood	Par Reg 2.266
The strength whereof suffic'd him forty days;	Par Reg 2.276
When suddenly a man before him stood,	Par Reg 2.298
And with fair speech these words to him address'd.	Par Reg 2.301
Twice by a voice inviting him to eat.	Par Reg 2.314
(Thy throne) but gold that got him puissant friends?	Par Reg 2.425
To him who wears the Regal Diadem,	Par Reg 2.461
Or lawless passions in him which he serves.	Par Reg 2.472
With soothing words renew'd, him thus accosts.	Par Reg 3.6
The just man, and divulges him through Heaven	Par Reg 3.62
Him whom thy wrongs with Saintly patience born,	Par Reg 3.93
From them who could return him nothing else,	Par Reg 3.129
Yet of another Plea bethought him soon.	Par Reg 3.149
With that (such power was giv'n him then) he took	Par Reg 3.251
As antient, but rebuilt by him who twice	Par Reg 3.281
By him thou shalt regain, without him not,	Par Reg 3.371
Still will be tempting him who foyls him still,	Par Reg 4.13
All publick cares, and yet of him suspicious,	Par Reg 4.96
Expel a Devil who first made him such?	Par Reg 4.129
Let his tormenter Conscience find him out,	Par Reg 4.130
For him I was not sent, nor yet to free	Par Reg 4.131
The Lord thy God, and only him shalt serve;	Par Reg 4.177
By him call'd vertue; and his vertuous man,	Par Reg 4.301
Rather accuse him under usual names,	Par Reg 4.316
Brought back the Son of God, and left him there,	Par Reg 4.396
Hungry and cold betook him to his rest,	Par Reg 4.403
Him walking on a Sunny hill he found,	Par Reg 4.447
And in a careless mood thus to him said.	Par Reg 4.450
And staid not, but in brief him answer'd thus.	Par Reg 4.485
To win him, or win from him what I can.	Par Reg 4.530
So saying he caught him up, and without wing	Par Reg 4.541
Her riddle, and him, who solv'd it not, devour'd;	Par Reg 4.573
Who on their plumy Vans receiv'd him soft	Par Reg 4.583
Then in a flowry valley set him down	Par Reg 4.586
On a green bank, and set before him spred	Par Reg 4.587
That soon refresh'd him wearied, and repair'd	Par Reg 4.591
And Thief of Paradise; him long of old	Par Reg 4.604
Ask for this great Deliverer now, and find him	Samson 40
Let us not break in upon him;	Samson 116
For him I reckon not in high estate	Samson 170
Are come upon him his deserts? yet why?	Samson 205
How frequent to desert him, and at last	Samson 275
And tie him to his own prescript,	Samson 308
Whom so it pleases him by choice	Samson 311
Forthwith how thou oughtst to receive him.	Samson 329
As earst in highest, behold him where he lies.	Samson 339
Subject him to so foul indignities,	Samson 371
Such a discomfit, as shall quite despoil him	Samson 469
Him who imploring mercy sues for life,	Samson 512
Wherewith to serve him better then thou hast;	Samson 585
That thou towards him with hand so various,	Samson 668
Behold him in this state calamitous, and turn	Samson 708
I leave him to his lot, and like my own.	Samson 996
Draws him awry enslav'd	Samson 1041
Draws hitherward, I know him by his stride,	Samson 1067
Comes he in peace? what wind hath blown him hither	Samson 1070
With solemnest devotion, spread before him	Samson 1147
Sam. I dread him not, nor all his Giant-brood,	Samson 1247
Though Fame divulge him Father of five Sons	Samson 1248
By his habit I discern him now	Samson 1305
Chor. His manacles remark him, there he sits.	Samson 1309
Or of him bringing to us some glad news?	Samson 1444
Lest I should see him forc't to things unseemly.	Samson 1451
No, I am fixt not to part hence without him.	Samson 1481
And quit: not wanting him, I shall want nothing.	Samson 1484
And view him sitting in the house, enobl'd	Samson 1491
With all those high exploits by him atchiev'd,	Samson 1492
Garrison'd round about him like a Camp	Samson 1497
To use him further yet in some great service,	Samson 1499
Useless, and thence ridiculous about him.	Samson 1501
God will restore him eye-sight to his strength.	Samson 1503
To free him hence! but death who sets all free	Samson 1572
All by him fell thou say'st, by whom fell he,	Samson 1580
Brought him so soon at variance with himself	Samson 1585
The Edifice where all were met to see him	Samson 1588

Him(*cont*)

In thir state Livery clad; before him Pipes	Samson 1616
Both horse and foot before him and behind	Samson 1618
At sight of him the people with a shout	Samson 1620
He patient but undaunted where they led him,	Samson 1623
Came to the place, and what was set before him	Samson 1624
At length for intermission sake they led him	Samson 1629
As over-tir'd to let him lean a while	Samson 1632
He unsuspitious led him; which when *Samson*	Samson 1635
With God not parted from him, as was feard,	Samson 1719
To fetch him hence and solemnly attend	Samson 1731
Home to his Fathers house: there will I build him	Samson 1733
Had by him, ere he parted thence, a Son	Mask 56
Whom therfore she brought up and *Comus* nam'd,	Mask 58
Trinity ms 'nam'd' ←'nam'd him'	
At last betakes him to this ominous Wood,	Mask 61
I shoot from Heav'n to give him safe convoy,	Mask 81
And hugg him into snares. When once her eye	Mask 164
The visage quite transforms of him that drinks,	Mask 527
Who gently ask't if he had seen such two,	Mask 575
Trinity ms 'gently' ←'tooke him'	
Supposing him som neighbour villager;	Mask 576
But for that damn'd magician, let him be girt	Mask 602
'Twixt *Africa* and *Inde*, Ile find him out,	Mask 606
And force him to restore his purchase back,	Mask 607
Or drag him by the curls, to a foul death,	Mask 608
And brandish't blade rush on him, break his glass,	Mask 651
And we should serve him as a grudging master,	Mask 725
Or have I said anough? To him that dares	Mask 780
line not in Bridgewater ms	
line not in Trinity ms	
And bound him fast; without his rod revers't,	Mask 816
Then lies him down the Lubbar Fend,	Allegro 110
Him that yon soars on golden wing,	Penseroso 52
Or call up him that left half told	Penseroso 109
Through the dear might of him that walk'd the waves;	Lycidas 173
There entertain him all the Saints above,	Lycidas 178
To welcom him to this his new abode,	Nativity 18
Nature in aw to him	Nativity 32
Of him that ever was, and ay shall last,	Psalm 114, 16
But then transform'd him to a purple flower	Fair Inf 27
And render him with patience what he lent;	Fair Inf 75
Yet every one shall make him underling,	Vacation 76
And those that cannot live from him asunder	Vacation 77
Ungratefully shall strive to keep him under,	Vacation 78
And peace shall lull him in her flowry lap;	Vacation 84
Then lies him meekly down fast by his Brethrens side.	Passion 21
Of him, t' whose happy-making sight alone,	On Time 18
To him that sits theron	Musick 8
To live with him, and sing in endles morn of light.	Musick 28
To him that serv'd for her before,	Winchester 66
A here alas, hath laid him in the dirt,	Carrier 2
Death was half glad when he had got him down;	Carrier 6
Dodg'd with him, betwixt *Cambridge* and the Bull.	Carrier 8
But lately finding him so long at home,	Carrier 11
Shew'd him his room where he must lodge that night,	Carrier 15
If any ask for him, it shall be sed,	Carrier 17
Rest that gives all men life, gave him his death,	Another 11
And too much breathing put him out of breath;	Another 12
His leasure told him that his time was com,	Another 23
line not in 1658 text	
Guard them, and him within protect from harms,	Sonnet 8, 4
Broke him, as that dishonest victory	Sonnet 10, 6
Madam, me thinks I see him living yet;	Sonnet 10, 11
Bear his milde yoak, they serve him best, his State	Sonnet 19, 11
Happy all those who have in him their stay.	Psalm 2, 28
No help for him in God there lies.	Psalm 3, 6
Will hear my voyce what time to him I crie.	Psalm 4, 18
Him with thy lasting favour and good will.	Psalm 5, 40
Ill to him that meant me peace,	Psalm 7, 10
Or to him have render'd less,	Psalm 7, 11
And overtake it, let him tread	Psalm 7, 14
My defence, and in him lies	Psalm 7, 40
In him who both just and wise	Psalm 7, 41
Already, and for him intended	Psalm 7, 47
The tools of death, that waits him near.	Psalm 7, 48
And think'st upon him; or of man begot	Psalm 8, 13
That him thou visit'st and of him art found;	Psalm 8, 14
With honour and with state thou hast him crown'd.	Psalm 8, 16
O're the works of thy hand thou mad'st him Lord,	Psalm 8, 17
To bow to him and bend,	Psalm 81, 62
Of him *that help demands*.	Psalm 82, 16
Surely to such as do him fear	Psalm 85, 37
Before him Righteousness shall go	Psalm 85, 53
And to be short, at last his guid him brings	Prose 2, 1

Himself

To set himself in Glory above his Peers,	Par Lost 1.39
ms 'himselfe'	
One next himself in power, and next in crime,	Par Lost 1.79
ms 'himselfe'	
Heap on himself damnation, while he sought	Par Lost 1.215
ms 'himselfe'	
On Man by him seduc't, but on himself	Par Lost 1.219
ms 'himselfe'	
Attonement for himself or offering meet,	Par Lost 3.234
Second to thee, offerd himself to die	Par Lost 3.409
Upon himself; horror and doubt distract	Par Lost 4.18
One step no more then from himself can fly	Par Lost 4.22

Himself(*cont*)
Of those fourfooted kindes, himself now one, Par Lost 4.397
Ey'd them askance, and to himself thus plaind. Par Lost 4.504
Through wayes of danger by himself untri'd, Par Lost 4.934
Late falln himself from Heav'n, is plotting now Par Lost 5.240
Perfections, in himself was all his state, Par Lost 5.353
Through pride that sight, & thought himself impaird. Par Lost 5.665
Another now hath to himself ingross't Par Lost 5.775
That argu'd fear; each on himself reli'd, Par Lost 6.238
To find himself not matchless, and his pride Par Lost 6.341
All like himself rebellious, by whose aid Par Lost 7.140
Is hard; for who himself beginning knew? Par Lost 8.251
Of heavier on himself, fearless return'd. Par Lost 9.57
Foul on himself; then wherefore shund or feard Par Lost 9.331
Secure from outward force; within himself Par Lost 9.348
Stood in himself collected, while each part, Par Lost 9.673
First to himself he inward silence broke. Par Lost 9.895
And destin'd Man himself to judge Man fall'n. Par Lost 10.62
Had leasure, wondring at himself now more; Par Lost 10.510
Strange contradiction, which to God himself Par Lost 10.799
Thus *Adam* to himself lamented loud Par Lost 10.845
Though by the Devil himself, him overweening Par Lost 10.878
To save himself and houshold from amidst Par Lost 11.820
Above his Brethren, to himself assuming Par Lost 12.65
He made not Lord; such title to himself Par Lost 12.70
Himself and his rash Armie, where thin Aire Par Lost 12.76
Within himself unworthie Powers to reign Par Lost 12.91
Shall tremble, he descending, will himself Par Lost 12.228
And he himself among them was baptiz'd, Par Reg 1.76
He could not lose himself; but went about Par Reg 2.98
Into himself descended, and at once Par Reg 2.111
Of Spirits likest to himself in guile Par Reg 2.237
Now hungring first, and to himself thus said. Par Reg 2.244
Yet he who reigns within himself, and rules Par Reg 2.466
Subject himself to Anarchy within, Par Reg 2.471
And so of all true good himself despoil'd, Par Reg 3.139
Yet, sacrilegious, to himself would take Par Reg 3.140
Them he himself to glory will advance. Par Reg 3.144
With guilt of his own sin, for he himself Par Reg 3.147
Yet he at length, time to himself best known, Par Reg 3.433
Wise, perfect in himself, and all possessing Par Reg 4.302
Degraded by himself, on grace depending? Par Reg 4.312
Deep verst in books and shallow in himself, Par Reg 4.327
Himself in bonds under *Philistian* yoke; Samson 42
And by himself given over; Samson 121
And weaponless himself, Samson 130
And no man therein Doctor but himself. Samson 299
Who made our Laws to bind us, not himself, Samson 309
Himself an Army, now unequal match Samson 346
To save himself against a coward arm'd Samson 347
Brought him so soon at variance with himself Samson 1585
Pulld down the same destruction on himself; Samson 1658
Nor much more cause, *Samson* hath quit himself Samson 1709
To himself and Fathers house eternal fame; Samson 1717
Himself is his own dungeon. 2. *Bro*. Tis most true Mask 385
Bridgewater ms 'blaze in the summer solstice'
1637 'Himselfe'
Trinity ms 'himselfe is his owne dungeon' ←'blaze in the summer solstice'
Himself to sing, and build the lofty rhyme. Lycidas 11
Trinity ms 'himselfe'
Untill their Lord himself bespake, and bid them go. Nativity 76
The Sun himself with-held his wonted speed, Nativity 79
So both himself and us to glorifie: Nativity 154
And left them both, more in himself content, Sonnet 10, 4
Chose to himself a part Psalm 4, 14

Hind
Goodliest of all the Forrest, Hart and Hinde; Par Lost 11.189

Hinder
His hinder parts, then springs as broke from Bonds, Par Lost 7.465

Hindered
Hinder'd not *Satan* to attempt the minde Par Lost 10.8

Hinders
Of vertue to make wise: what hinders then Par Lost 9.778
For his people of old; what hinders now? Samson 1533
What hinders? as some teachers give to Boyes Prose 6, 2

Hindmost
Rose from the hindmost wheels of *Phoebus* wain. Mask 190
line not in Bridgewater ms

Hinds
Stirs up among the loose unleter'd Hinds, Mask 174
Bridgewater ms 'hindes'
Trinity ms 'hinds'
As when those Hinds that were transform'd to Froggs Sonnet 12, 5
Trinity ms 'hindes'

Hinges
Th' infernal dores, and on thir hinges grate Par Lost 2.881
On golden Hinges turning, as by work Par Lost 5.255
On golden Hinges moving, to let forth Par Lost 7.207
From the four hinges of the world, and fell Par Reg 4.415
And the well-ballanc't world on hinges hung, Nativity 122

Hinnom
The pleasant Vally of *Hinnom*, *Tophet* thence Par Lost 1.404
ms 'Hinnom'

Hippogriff
Of *Hippogrif* bore through the Air sublime Par Reg 4.542

Hippotades
And sage *Hippotades* their answer brings, Lycidas 96

Hips
Curs'd as his life. *Spir*. Alas good ventrous youth, Mask 609
Trinity ms 'downe to the hips' ←'lowest hips' ←'hipps'
1637 'Downe to the hipps'
Bridgewater ms 'downe to the hipps'

Hired
Till they had hir'd a woman with their gold Samson 1114

Hireling
Of hireling wolves whose Gospell is their maw. Sonnet 16, 14
1694 'Hireling'

Hirelings
So since into his Church lewd Hirelings climbe. Par Lost 4.193

His
From thir Creator, and transgress his Will Par Lost 1.31
The Mother of Mankind, what time his Pride Par Lost 1.36
Had cast him out from Heav'n, with all his Host Par Lost 1.37
To set himself in Glory above his Peers, Par Lost 1.39
To mortal men, he with his horrid crew Par Lost 1.51
Confounded though immortal: But his doom Par Lost 1.53
Torments him; round he throws his baleful eyes Par Lost 1.56
There the companions of his fall, o'rewhelm'd Par Lost 1.76
He soon discerns, and weltring by his side Par Lost 1.78
He with his Thunder: and till then who knew Par Lost 1.93
Nor what the Potent Victor in his rage Par Lost 1.95
That durst dislike his reign, and me preferring, Par Lost 1.102
His utmost power with adverse power oppos'd Par Lost 1.103
And shook his throne. What though the field be lost? Par Lost 1.105
That Glory never shall his wrath or might Par Lost 1.110
With suppliant knee, and deifie his power, Par Lost 1.112
Doubted his Empire, that were low indeed, Par Lost 1.114
And him thus answer'd soon his bold Compeer. Par Lost 1.127
And put to proof his high Supremacy, Par Lost 1.132
That we may so suffice his vengeful ire, Par Lost 1.148
Or do him mightier service as his thralls Par Lost 1.149
By right of Warr, what e're his business be Par Lost 1.150
Or do his Errands in the gloomy Deep; Par Lost 1.152
As being the contrary to his high will Par Lost 1.161
Whom we resist. If then his Providence Par Lost 1.162
His inmost counsels from thir destind aim. Par Lost 1.168
His Ministers of vengeance and pursuit Par Lost 1.170
Perhaps hath spent his shafts, and ceases now Par Lost 1.176
Thus Satan talking to his neerest Mate Par Lost 1.192
That sparkling blaz'd, his other Parts besides Par Lost 1.194
Leviathan, which God of all his works Par Lost 1.201
With fixed Anchor in his skaly rind Par Lost 1.206
Moors by his side under the Lee, while Night Par Lost 1.207
Had ris'n or heav'd his head, but that the will Par Lost 1.211
Left him at large to his own dark designs, Par Lost 1.213
How all his malice serv'd but to bring forth Par Lost 1.217
His mighty Stature; on each hand the flames Par Lost 1.222
Then with expanded wings he stears his flight Par Lost 1.225
Of unblest feet. Him followed his next Mate, Par Lost 1.238
Above his equals. Farewel happy Fields Par Lost 1.249
Here for his envy, will not drive us hence: Par Lost 1.260
Was moving toward the shoar; his ponderous shield Par Lost 1.284
Hung on his shoulders like the Moon, whose Orb Par Lost 1.287
His Spear, to equal which the tallest Pine Par Lost 1.292
His Legions, Angel Forms, who lay intrans't Par Lost 1.301
Busiris and his *Memphian* Chivalry, Par Lost 1.307
His swift pursuers from Heav'n Gates discern Par Lost 1.326
Thir Altars by his Altar, Gods ador'd Par Lost 1.384
Within his Sanctuary it self thir Shrines, Par Lost 1.388
His holy Rites, and solemn Feasts profan'd, Par Lost 1.390
And with thir darkness durst affront his light. Par Lost 1.391
To his grim Idol. Him the *Ammonite* Par Lost 1.396
His Temple right against the Temple of God Par Lost 1.402
On that opprobrious Hill, and made his Grove Par Lost 1.403
Peor his other Name, when he entic'd Par Lost 1.412
Yet thence his lustful Orgies he enlarg'd Par Lost 1.415
His righteous Altar, bowing lowly down Par Lost 1.434
The *Syrian* Damsels to lament his fate Par Lost 1.448
While smooth *Adonis* from his native Rock Par Lost 1.450
His eye survay'd the dark Idolatries Par Lost 1.456
Maim'd his brute Image, head and hands lopt off Par Lost 1.459
In his own Temple, on the grunsel edge, Par Lost 1.460
Where he fell flat, and sham'd his Worshipers: Par Lost 1.461
Dagon his Name, Sea Monster, upward Man Par Lost 1.462
And downward Fish: yet had his Temple high Par Lost 1.463
Ahaz his sottish Conquerour, whom he drew Par Lost 1.472
His odious offrings, and adore the Gods Par Lost 1.475
Lik'ning his Maker to the Grazed Ox, Par Lost 1.486
With his enormous brood, and birthright seis'd Par Lost 1.511
His own and *Rhea*'s Son like measure found; Par Lost 1.513
In loss it self; which on his count'nance cast Par Lost 1.526
Like doubtful hue: but he his wonted pride Par Lost 1.527
His mighty Standard; that proud honour claim'd Par Lost 1.533
Azazel as his right, a Cherube tall: Par Lost 1.534
Darts his experienc't eye, and soon traverse Par Lost 1.568
Thir number last he summs. And now his heart Par Lost 1.571
Distends with pride, and hardning in his strength Par Lost 1.572
When *Charlemain* with all his Peerage fell Par Lost 1.586
Stood like a Towr; his form had yet not lost Par Lost 1.591
Shorn of his Beams, or from behind the Moon Par Lost 1.596
Above them all th' Arch Angel: but his face Par Lost 1.600
Sat on his faded cheek, but under Browes Par Lost 1.602
Waiting revenge: cruel his eye, but cast Par Lost 1.604
The fellows of his crime, the followers rather Par Lost 1.606
Millions of Spirits for his fault amerc't Par Lost 1.609

His(*cont*)

For his revolt, yet faithfull how they stood,	Par Lost 1.611
With all his Peers: attention held them mute.	Par Lost 1.618
Sat on his Throne, upheld by old repute,	Par Lost 1.639
Consent or custome, and his Regal State	Par Lost 1.640
Put forth at full, but still his strength conceal'd,	Par Lost 1.641
Henceforth his might we know, and know our own	Par Lost 1.643
By force, hath overcome but half his foe.	Par Lost 1.649
A generation, whom his choice regard	Par Lost 1.653
He spake: and to confirm his words, out-flew	Par Lost 1.663
That in his womb was hid metallic Ore,	Par Lost 1.673
From heav'n, for ev'n in heav'n his looks and thoughts	Par Lost 1.680
Men also, and by his suggestion taught,	Par Lost 1.685
For Treasures better hid. Soon had his crew	Par Lost 1.688
And some the Architect: his hand was known	Par Lost 1.732
Each in his Hierarchie, the Orders bright.	Par Lost 1.737
Nor was his name unheard or unador'd	Par Lost 1.738
By all his Engins, but was headlong sent	Par Lost 1.750
With his industrious crew to build in hell.	Par Lost 1.751
Of Satan and his Peers: thir summons call'd	Par Lost 1.757
Intent, with jocond Music charm his ear;	Par Lost 1.787
At once with joy and fear his heart rebounds.	Par Lost 1.788
His proud imaginations thus displaid.	Par Lost 2.10
His trust was with th' Eternal to be deem'd	Par Lost 2.46
Went all his fear: of God, or Hell, or worse	Par Lost 2.49
The Prison of his Tyranny who Reigns	Par Lost 2.59
Of his Almighty Engin he shall hear	Par Lost 2.65
Among his Angels; and his Throne it self	Par Lost 2.68
His own invented Torments. But perhaps	Par Lost 2.70
Our stronger, some worse way his wrath may find	Par Lost 2.83
The Vassals of his anger, when the Scourge	Par Lost 2.90
His utmost ire? which to the highth enrag'd,	Par Lost 2.95
Our power sufficient to disturb his Heav'n,	Par Lost 2.102
Though inaccessible, his fatal Throne:	Par Lost 2.104
He ended frowning, and his look denounc'd	Par Lost 2.106
But all was false and hollow; though his Tongue	Par Lost 2.112
Maturest Counsels: for his thoughts were low;	Par Lost 2.115
Mistrustful, grounds his courage on despair	Par Lost 2.126
Of all his aim, after some dire revenge.	Par Lost 2.128
All incorruptible would on his Throne	Par Lost 2.138
Th' Almighty Victor to spend all his rage,	Par Lost 2.144
Will he, so wise, let loose at once his ire,	Par Lost 2.155
To give his Enemies thir wish, and end	Par Lost 2.157
Them in his anger, whom his anger saves	Par Lost 2.158
His red right hand to plague us? what if all	Par Lost 2.174
Each on his rock transfixt, the sport and prey	Par Lost 2.181
With him, or who deceive his mind, whose eye	Par Lost 2.189
His anger, and perhaps thus farr remov'd	Par Lost 2.211
Will slack'n, if his breath stir not thir flames.	Par Lost 2.214
Stand in his presence humble, and receive	Par Lost 2.240
Strict Laws impos'd, to celebrate his Throne	Par Lost 2.241
With warbl'd Hymns, and to his Godhead sing	Par Lost 2.242
Our envied Sovran, and his Altar breathes	Par Lost 2.244
Choose to reside, his Glory unobscur'd,	Par Lost 2.265
Covers his Throne; from whence deep thunders roar	Par Lost 2.267
As he our darkness, cannot we his Light	Par Lost 2.269
As *Mammon* ended, and his Sentence pleas'd,	Par Lost 2.291
Aspect he rose, and in his rising seem'd	Par Lost 2.301
A Pillar of State; deep on his Front engraven	Par Lost 2.302
And Princely counsel in his face yet shon,	Par Lost 2.304
The weight of mightiest Monarchies; his look	Par Lost 2.307
Beyond his Potent arm, to live exempt	Par Lost 2.318
Banded against his Throne, but to remaine	Par Lost 2.320
His captive multitude: For he, be sure	Par Lost 2.323
Sole King, and of his Kingdom loose no part	Par Lost 2.325
His Empire, and with Iron Scepter rule	Par Lost 2.327
Us here, as with his Golden those in Heav'n.	Par Lost 2.328
May reap his conquest, and may least rejoyce	Par Lost 2.339
Of him who rules above; so was his will	Par Lost 2.351
In his own strength, this place may lye expos'd	Par Lost 2.360
The utmost border of his Kingdom, left	Par Lost 2.361
To waste his whole Creation, or possess	Par Lost 2.365
Abolish his own works. This would surpass	Par Lost 2.370
Common revenge, and interrupt his joy	Par Lost 2.371
In his disturbance; when his darling Sons	Par Lost 2.373
Pleaded his devilish Counsel, first devis'd	Par Lost 2.379
His glory to augment. The bold design	Par Lost 2.386
They vote: whereat his speech he thus renews.	Par Lost 2.389
His uncouth way, or spread his aerie flight	Par Lost 2.407
His look suspence, awaiting who appeer'd	Par Lost 2.418
In others count'nance read his own dismay	Par Lost 2.422
Above his fellows, with Monarchal pride	Par Lost 2.428
Prudent, least from his resolution rais'd	Par Lost 2.468
His Rivals, winning cheap the high repute	Par Lost 2.472
Dreaded not more th' adventure then his voice	Par Lost 2.474
His own: for neither do the Spirits damn'd	Par Lost 2.482
Extend his ev'ning beam, the fields revive,	Par Lost 2.493
That day and night for his destruction waite.	Par Lost 2.505
Disband, and wandring, each his several way	Par Lost 2.523
Truce to his restless thoughts, and entertain	Par Lost 2.526
The irksom hours, till this great Chief return.	Par Lost 2.527
1667 'his'	
Forthwith his former state and being forgets,	Par Lost 2.585
Explores his solitary flight; som times	Par Lost 2.632
And shook a dreadful Dart; what seem'd his head	Par Lost 2.672
Satan was now at hand, and from his seat	Par Lost 2.674
Admir'd, not fear'd; God and his Son except,	Par Lost 2.678
In th' Artick Sky, and from his horrid hair	Par Lost 2.710

His(*cont*)

Leveld his deadly aime; thir fatall hands	Par Lost 2.712
At thee ordain'd his drudge, to execute	Par Lost 2.732
What e're his wrath, which he calls Justice, bids,	Par Lost 2.733
His wrath which one day will destroy ye both.	Par Lost 2.734
Forth issu'd, brandishing his fatal Dart	Par Lost 2.786
Mee overtook his mother all dismaid,	Par Lost 2.792
And me his Parent would full soon devour	Par Lost 2.805
His end with mine involvd; and knows that I	Par Lost 2.807
Should prove a bitter Morsel, and his bane,	Par Lost 2.808
His deadly arrow; neither vainly hope	Par Lost 2.811
She finish'd, and the suttle Fiend his lore	Par Lost 2.815
His famine should be fill'd, and blest his mawe	Par Lost 2.847
His mother bad, and thus bespake her Sire.	Par Lost 2.849
Death ready stands to interpose his dart,	Par Lost 2.854
But what ow I to his commands above	Par Lost 2.856
Of each his Faction, in thir several Clanns,	Par Lost 2.901
His dark materials to create more Worlds,	Par Lost 2.916
Pondering his Voyage; for no narrow frith	Par Lost 2.919
He had to cross. Nor was his eare less peal'd	Par Lost 2.920
The stedfast Earth. At last his Sail-broad Vannes	Par Lost 2.927
Fluttring his pennons vain plumb down he drops	Par Lost 2.933
Had from his wakeful custody purloind	Par Lost 2.946
With head, hands, wings or feet pursues his way,	Par Lost 2.949
Born through the hollow dark assaults his eare	Par Lost 2.953
Of *Chaos*, and his dark Pavilion spread	Par Lost 2.960
The Consort of his Reign; and by them stood	Par Lost 2.963
But glad that now his Sea should find a shore,	Par Lost 2.1011
Environ'd wins his way; harder beset	Par Lost 2.1016
Following his track, such was the will of Heav'n,	Par Lost 2.1025
Weighs his spread wings, at leasure to behold	Par Lost 2.1046
Of living Saphire, once his native Seat;	Par Lost 2.1050
High Thron'd above all highth, bent down his eye,	Par Lost 3.58
His own works and their works at once to view:	Par Lost 3.59
Stood thick as Starrs, and from his sight receiv'd	Par Lost 3.61
Beatitude past utterance; on his right	Par Lost 3.62
The radiant image of his Glory sat,	Par Lost 3.63
His onely Son; On Earth he first beheld	Par Lost 3.64
Him God beholding from his prospect high,	Par Lost 3.77
Thus to his onely Son foreseeing spake.	Par Lost 3.79
Upon his own rebellious head. And now	Par Lost 3.86
Through all restraint broke loose he wings his way	Par Lost 3.87
For man will hark'n to his glozing lyes,	Par Lost 3.93
Sole pledge of his obedience: So will fall,	Par Lost 3.95
Hee and his faithless Progenie: whose fault?	Par Lost 3.96
Whose but his own? ingrate, he had of mee	Par Lost 3.97
Most glorious, in him all his Father shon	Par Lost 3.139
Substantially express'd, and in his face	Par Lost 3.140
Which uttering thus he to his Father spake.	Par Lost 3.143
With his own folly? that be from thee farr,	Par Lost 3.153
His end, and frustrate thine, shall he fulfill	Par Lost 3.157
His malice, and thy goodness bring to naught,	Par Lost 3.158
Or proud return though to his heavier doom,	Par Lost 3.159
His lapsed powers, though forfeit and enthrall'd	Par Lost 3.176
On even ground against his mortal foe,	Par Lost 3.179
His fall'n condition is, and to me ow	Par Lost 3.181
All his deliv'rance, and to none but me.	Par Lost 3.182
Disloyal breaks his fealtie, and sinns	Par Lost 3.204
To expiate his Treason hath naught left,	Par Lost 3.207
He with his whole posteritie must dye,	Par Lost 3.209
Much less that durst upon his own head draw	Par Lost 3.220
His dearest mediation thus renewd.	Par Lost 3.226
Account mee man; I for his sake will leave	Par Lost 3.238
Well pleas'd, on me let Death wreck all his rage;	Par Lost 3.241
Under his gloomie power I shall not long	Par Lost 3.242
Though now to Death I yield, and am his due	Par Lost 3.245
His prey, nor suffer my unspotted Soule	Par Lost 3.248
My vanquisher, spoild of his vanted spoile;	Par Lost 3.251
Death his deaths wound shall then receive, and stoop	Par Lost 3.252
Inglorious, of his mortall sting disarm'd.	Par Lost 3.253
Death last, and with his Carcass glut the Grave:	Par Lost 3.259
His words here ended, but his meek aspect	Par Lost 3.266
Of his great Father. Admiration seis'd	Par Lost 3.271
His crime makes guiltie all his Sons, thy merit	Par Lost 3.290
His Brethren, ransomd with his own dear life.	Par Lost 3.297
Impresst the effulgence of his Glorie abides,	Par Lost 3.388
Transfus'd on thee his ample Spirit rests.	Par Lost 3.389
To execute fierce vengeance on his foes,	Par Lost 3.399
But in his way lights on the barren Plaines	Par Lost 3.437
Walk'd up and down alone bent on his prey,	Par Lost 3.441
To wait them with his Keys, and now at foot	Par Lost 3.485
His travell'd steps; farr distant he descries	Par Lost 3.501
His sad exclusion from the dores of Bliss.	Par Lost 3.525
On high behests his Angels to and fro	Par Lost 3.533
Pass'd frequent, and his eye with choice regard	Par Lost 3.534
Which to his eye discovers unaware	Par Lost 3.547
Which now the Rising Sun guilds with his beams.	Par Lost 3.551
His flight precipitant, and windes with ease	Par Lost 3.563
Through the pure marble Air his oblique way	Par Lost 3.564
Allur'd his eye: Thither his course he bends	Par Lost 3.573
That from his Lordly eye keep distance due,	Par Lost 3.578
Days, months, & years, towards his all-chearing Lamp	Par Lost 3.581
By his Magnetic beam, that gently warms	Par Lost 3.583
So wondrously was set his Station bright.	Par Lost 3.587
Through his glaz'd Optic Tube yet never saw.	Par Lost 3.590
Draind through a Limbec to his Native forme.	Par Lost 3.605
Undazl'd, farr and wide his eye commands,	Par Lost 3.614
But all Sun-shine, as when his Beams at Noon	Par Lost 3.616

His(*cont*)

No where so cleer, sharp'nd his visual ray	Par Lost 3.620
His back was turnd, but not his brightness hid;	Par Lost 3.624
Circl'd his Head, nor less his Locks behind	Par Lost 3.626
Illustrious on his Shoulders fledge with wings	Par Lost 3.627
To find who might direct his wandring flight	Par Lost 3.631
His journies end and our beginning woe.	Par Lost 3.633
But first he casts to change his proper shape,	Par Lost 3.634
Not of the prime, yet such as in his face	Par Lost 3.637
Under a Coronet his flowing haire	Par Lost 3.640
His habit fit for speed succinct, and held	Par Lost 3.643
Before his decent steps a Silver wand.	Par Lost 3.644
Ere he drew nigh, his radiant visage turnd,	Par Lost 3.646
Admonisht by his ear, and strait was known	Par Lost 3.647
Who in Gods presence, neerest to his Throne	Par Lost 3.649
Stand ready at command, and are his Eyes	Par Lost 3.650
Bear his swift errands over moist and dry,	Par Lost 3.652
The first art wont his great authentic will	Par Lost 3.656
Where all his Sons thy Embassie attend;	Par Lost 3.658
Like honour to obtain, and as his Eye	Par Lost 3.660
All these his wondrous works, but chiefly Man,	Par Lost 3.663
His chief delight and favour, him for whom	Par Lost 3.664
All these his works so wondrous he ordaind,	Par Lost 3.665
His fixed seat, or fixed seat hath none,	Par Lost 3.669
But all these shining Orbes his choice to dwell;	Par Lost 3.670
Who justly hath drivn out his Rebell Foes	Par Lost 3.677
To serve him better: wise are all his wayes.	Par Lost 3.680
By his permissive will, through Heav'n and Earth:	Par Lost 3.685
In his uprightness answer thus returnd.	Par Lost 3.693
For wonderful indeed are all his works,	Par Lost 3.702
I saw when at his Word the formless Mass,	Par Lost 3.708
Confusion heard his voice, and wilde uproar	Par Lost 3.710
Till at his second bidding darkness fled,	Par Lost 3.712
Each had his place appointed, each his course,	Par Lost 3.720
His day, which else as th' other Hemisphere	Par Lost 3.725
Adams abode, those loftie shades his Bowre.	Par Lost 3.734
Throws his steep flight in many an Aerie wheele,	Par Lost 3.741
Haply so scap'd his mortal snare; for now	Par Lost 4.8
To wreck on innocent frail man his loss	Par Lost 4.11
Of that first Battel, and his flight to Hell:	Par Lost 4.12
Yet not rejoycing in his speed, though bold,	Par Lost 4.13
Begins his dire attempt, which nigh the birth	Par Lost 4.15
Now rowling, boiles in his tumultuous brest,	Par Lost 4.16
His troubl'd thoughts, and from the bottom stirr	Par Lost 4.19
Sometimes towards *Eden* which now in his view	Par Lost 4.27
Lay pleasant, his grievd look he fixes sad,	Par Lost 4.28
Which now sat high in his Meridian Towre:	Par Lost 4.30
In that bright eminence, and with his good	Par Lost 4.44
Upbraided none; nor was his service hard.	Par Lost 4.45
How due! yet all his good prov'd ill in me,	Par Lost 4.48
O had his powerful Destiny ordaind	Par Lost 4.58
Drawn to his part; but other Powers as great	Par Lost 4.63
Be then his Love accurst, since love or hate,	Par Lost 4.69
Nay curs'd be thou; since against his thy will	Par Lost 4.71
Of us out-cast, exil'd, his new delight,	Par Lost 4.106
Thus while he spake, each passion dimm'd his face	Par Lost 4.114
Which marrd his borrow'd visage, and betraid	Par Lost 4.116
Spirit of happie sort: his gestures fierce	Par Lost 4.128
Into his neather Empire neighbouring round.	Par Lost 4.145
On which the Sun more glad impress'd his beams	Par Lost 4.150
Meets his approach, and to the heart inspires	Par Lost 4.154
Lights on his feet. As when a prowling Wolfe,	Par Lost 4.183
So since into his Church lewd Hirelings climbe.	Par Lost 4.193
His farr more pleasant Garden God ordaind;	Par Lost 4.215
Nor chang'd his course, but through the shaggie hill	Par Lost 4.224
That Mountain as his Garden mould high rais'd	Par Lost 4.226
Which from his darksom passage now appeers,	Par Lost 4.232
Young *Bacchus* from his Stepdame *Rhea*'s eye;	Par Lost 4.279
His fair large Front and Eye sublime declar'd	Par Lost 4.300
Round from his parted forelock manly hung	Par Lost 4.302
Clustring, but not beneath his shoulders broad:	Par Lost 4.303
And banisht from mans life his happiest life,	Par Lost 4.317
His Sons, the fairest of her Daughters *Eve*.	Par Lost 4.324
Sporting the Lion rampd, and in his paw	Par Lost 4.343
To make them mirth us'd all his might, and wreathd	Par Lost 4.346
His Lithe Proboscis; close the Serpent sly	Par Lost 4.347
His breaded train, and of his fatal guile	Par Lost 4.349
The Tyrants plea, excus'd his devilish deeds.	Par Lost 4.394
Then from his loftie stand on that high Tree	Par Lost 4.395
Now other, as thir shape servd best his end	Par Lost 4.398
Neerer to view his prey, and unespi'd	Par Lost 4.399
His couchant watch, as one who chose his ground	Par Lost 4.406
Be infinitly good, and of his good	Par Lost 4.414
In all this happiness, who at his hand	Par Lost 4.417
His bountie, following our delightful task	Par Lost 4.437
His flesh, his bone; to give thee being I lent	Par Lost 4.483
Naked met his under the flowing Gold	Par Lost 4.496
So saying, his proud step he scornful turn'd,	Par Lost 4.536
Through wood, through waste, o're hill, o're dale his roam.	Par Lost 4.538
Leveld his eevning Rayes: it was a Rock	Par Lost 4.543
From what point of his Compass to beware	Par Lost 4.559
Gods latest Image: I describ'd his way	Par Lost 4.567
Bent all on speed, and markt his Aerie Gate;	Par Lost 4.568
Where he first lighted, soon discernd his looks	Par Lost 4.570
So promis'd hee, and *Uriel* to his charge	Par Lost 4.589
The Clouds that on his Western Throne attend:	Par Lost 4.597
Man hath his daily work of body or mind	Par Lost 4.618
Appointed, which declares his Dignitie,	Par Lost 4.619
And the regard of Heav'n on all his waies;	Par Lost 4.620
His orient Beams, on herb, tree, fruit, and flour,	Par Lost 4.644
All these with ceasless praise his works behold	Par Lost 4.679
Adam from his fair Spouse, nor *Eve* the Rites	Par Lost 4.742
Here Love his golden shafts imploies, here lights	Par Lost 4.763
His constant Lamp, and waves his purple wings,	Par Lost 4.764
To his proud fair, best quitted with disdain.	Par Lost 4.770
When *Gabriel* to his next in power thus spake.	Par Lost 4.781
So saying, on he led his radiant Files,	Par Lost 4.797
Assaying by his Devilish art to reach	Par Lost 4.801
Him thus intent *Ithuriel* with his Spear	Par Lost 4.810
So started up in his own shape the Fiend.	Par Lost 4.819
So spake the Cherube, and his grave rebuke	Par Lost 4.844
His loss; but chiefly to find here observd	Par Lost 4.849
His lustre visibly impar'd; yet seemd	Par Lost 4.850
Chaumping his iron curb: to strive or flie	Par Lost 4.859
His heart, not else dismai'd. Now drew they nigh	Par Lost 4.861
But faded splendor wan; who by his gate	Par Lost 4.870
Stand firm, for in his look defiance lours.	Par Lost 4.873
Puts me in doubt. Lives ther who loves his pain?	Par Lost 4.888
His will who bound us? let him surer barr	Par Lost 4.897
His Iron Gates, if he intends our stay	Par Lost 4.898
And now returns him from his prison scap't,	Par Lost 4.906
Unlicenc't from his bounds in Hell prescrib'd;	Par Lost 4.909
However, and to scape his punishment.	Par Lost 4.911
High up in Heav'n, with songs to hymne his Throne,	Par Lost 4.944
Us'd to the yoak, draw'st his triumphant wheels	Par Lost 4.975
Least on the threshing floore his hopeful sheaves	Par Lost 4.984
Collecting all his might dilated stood,	Par Lost 4.986
His stature reacht the Skie, and on his Crest	Par Lost 4.988
Sat horror Plum'd; nor wanted in his graspe	Par Lost 4.989
Hung forth in Heav'n his golden Scales, yet seen	Par Lost 4.997
His mounted scale aloft: nor more; but fled	Par Lost 4.1014
When *Adam* wak't, so customd, for his sleep	Par Lost 5.3
His wonder was to find unwak'nd *Eve*	Par Lost 5.9
As through unquiet rest: he on his side	Par Lost 5.11
Tunes sweetest his love-labor'd song; now reignes	Par Lost 5.41
If none regard; Heav'n wakes with all his eyes,	Par Lost 5.44
By us oft seen; his dewie locks distill'd	Par Lost 5.56
So cheard he his fair Spouse, and she was cheard,	Par Lost 5.129
Shot paralel to the earth his dewie ray,	Par Lost 5.141
Circle his Throne rejoycing, yee in Heav'n,	Par Lost 5.163
Acknowledge him thy Greater, sound his praise	Par Lost 5.172
His praise, who out of Darkness call'd up Light.	Par Lost 5.179
Rising or falling still advance his praise.	Par Lost 5.191
His praise ye Winds, that from four Quarters blow,	Par Lost 5.192
Melodious murmurs, warbling tune his praise.	Par Lost 5.196
Bear on your wings and in your notes his praise;	Par Lost 5.199
Made vocal by my Song, and taught his praise.	Par Lost 5.204
His barren leaves. Them thus imploid beheld	Par Lost 5.219
His marriage with the seaventimes-wedded Maid.	Par Lost 5.223
To respit his day-labour with repast,	Par Lost 5.232
As may advise him of his happie state,	Par Lost 5.234
Happiness in his power left free to will,	Par Lost 5.235
Left to his own free Will, his Will though free,	Par Lost 5.236
His danger, and from whom, what enemie	Par Lost 5.239
After his charge receivd; but from among	Par Lost 5.248
Vaild with his gorgeous wings, up springing light	Par Lost 5.250
On each hand parting, to his speed gave way	Par Lost 5.252
From hence, no cloud, or, to obstruct his sight,	Par Lost 5.257
When to enshrine his reliques in the Sun's	Par Lost 5.273
He lights, and to his proper shape returns	Par Lost 5.276
His lineaments Divine; the pair that clad	Par Lost 5.278
Each shoulder broad, came mantling o're his brest	Par Lost 5.279
Girt like a Starrie Zone his waste, and round	Par Lost 5.281
Skirted his loines and thighes with downie Gold	Par Lost 5.282
And colours dipt in Heav'n; the third his feet	Par Lost 5.283
And shook his Plumes, that Heav'nly fragrance filld	Par Lost 5.286
Of Angels under watch; and to his state,	Par Lost 5.288
And to his message high in honour rise;	Par Lost 5.289
Of his coole Bowre, while now the mounted Sun	Par Lost 5.300
Shot down direct his fervid Raies to warme	Par Lost 5.301
God hath dispenst his bounties as in Heav'n.	Par Lost 5.330
His god-like Guest, walks forth, without more train	Par Lost 5.351
Accompani'd then with his own compleat	Par Lost 5.352
Perfections, in himself was all his state,	Par Lost 5.353
Neerer his presence *Adam* though not awd,	Par Lost 5.358
From all his alimental recompence	Par Lost 5.424
Varied his bounty so with new delights,	Par Lost 5.431
Of things above his World, and of thir being	Par Lost 5.455
Transcend his own so farr, whose radiant forms	Par Lost 5.457
Exceeded human, and his wary speech	Par Lost 5.459
Unalterably firm his love entire	Par Lost 5.502
To him, or possibly his love desert	Par Lost 5.515
Hath finisht half his journey, and scarce begins	Par Lost 5.559
His other half in the great Zone of Heav'n.	Par Lost 5.560
Under his great Vice-gerent Reign abide	Par Lost 5.609
Into utter darkness, deep ingulft, his place	Par Lost 5.614
So spake th' Omnipotent, and with his words	Par Lost 5.616
Satan, so call him now, his former name	Par Lost 5.658
Honourd by his great Father, and proclaimd	Par Lost 5.663
With all his Legions to dislodge, and leave	Par Lost 5.669
Contemptuous, and his next subordinate	Par Lost 5.671
The great *Messiah*, and his new commands,	Par Lost 5.691
Of his Associate; hee together calls,	Par Lost 5.696
His name, and high was his degree in Heav'n;	Par Lost 5.707
His count'nance, as the Morning Starr that guides	Par Lost 5.708

His(*cont*)
Abstrusest thoughts, from forth his holy Mount Par Lost 5.712
Were banded to oppose his high Decree; Par Lost 5.717
And smiling to his onely Son thus said. Par Lost 5.718
Is rising, who intends to erect his Throne Par Lost 5.725
Nor so content, hath in his thought to try Par Lost 5.727
So spake the Son, but *Satan* with his Powers Par Lost 5.743
They came, and *Satan* to his Royal seat Par Lost 5.756
For thither he assembl'd all his Train, Par Lost 5.767
To one and to his image now proclaim'd? Par Lost 5.784
His equals, if in power and splendor less, Par Lost 5.796
Thus farr his bold discourse without controule Par Lost 5.803
The current of his fury thus oppos'd. Par Lost 5.808
That to his only Son by right endu'd Par Lost 5.815
As by his Word the mighty Father made Par Lost 5.836
Essential Powers, nor by his Reign obscur'd, Par Lost 5.841
His Laws our Laws, all honour to him done Par Lost 5.844
So spake the fervent Angel, but his zeale Par Lost 5.849
From Father to his Son? strange point and new! Par Lost 5.855
Had circl'd his full Orbe, the birth mature Par Lost 5.862
Hoarce murmur echo'd to his words applause Par Lost 5.873
His Thunder on thy head, devouring fire. Par Lost 5.893
His Loyaltie he kept, his Love, his Zeale; Par Lost 5.900
To swerve from truth, or change his constant mind Par Lost 5.902
And with retorted scorn his back he turn'd Par Lost 5.906
Through Heav'ns wide Champain held his way, till Morn, Par Lost 6.2
Within the Mount of God, fast by his Throne, Par Lost 6.5
Reflecting blaze on blaze, first met his view: Par Lost 6.18
His fiery *Chaos* to receave thir fall. Par Lost 6.55
Of God and his *Messiah*. On they move Par Lost 6.68
To win the Mount of God, and on his Throne Par Lost 6.88
To set the envier of his State, the proud Par Lost 6.89
Th' Apostat in his Sun-bright Chariot sate Par Lost 6.100
Then lighted from his gorgeous Throne, for now Par Lost 6.103
And thus his own undaunted heart explores. Par Lost 6.113
His puissance, trusting in th' Almightie's aide, Par Lost 6.119
So pondering, and from his armed Peers Par Lost 6.127
His daring foe, at this prevention more Par Lost 6.129
The Throne of God unguarded, and his side Par Lost 6.133
Against his worthier, as thine now serve thee, Par Lost 6.180
In Heav'n God ever blest, and his Divine Par Lost 6.184
Nor motion of swift thought, less could his Shield Par Lost 6.192
His massie Spear upstaid; as if on Earth Par Lost 6.195
Sidelong, had push't a Mountain from his seat Par Lost 6.197
Half sunk with all his Pines. Amazement seis'd Par Lost 6.198
From his strong hold of Heav'n high over-rul'd Par Lost 6.228
As onely in his arm the moment lay Par Lost 6.239
Of tenfold Adamant, his ample Shield Par Lost 6.255
A vast circumference: At his approach Par Lost 6.256
The great Arch-Angel from his warlike toile Par Lost 6.257
All his right side; then *Satan* first knew pain, Par Lost 6.327
And all his Armour staind ere while so bright. Par Lost 6.334
Forthwith on all sides to his aide was run Par Lost 6.335
Back to his Chariot; where it stood retir'd Par Lost 6.338
To find himself not matchless, and his pride Par Lost 6.341
His confidence to equal God in power. Par Lost 6.343
And at his Chariot wheeles to drag him bound Par Lost 6.358
Refrein'd his tongue blasphemous; but anon Par Lost 6.360
Uriel and *Raphael* his vaunting foe, Par Lost 6.363
Michael and his Angels prevalent Par Lost 6.411
Satan with his rebellious disappeerd, Par Lost 6.414
His Potentates to Councel call'd by night; Par Lost 6.416
Against us from about his Throne, and judg'd Par Lost 6.426
Sufficient to subdue us to his will, Par Lost 6.427
Sore toild, his riv'n Armes to havoc hewn, Par Lost 6.449
The Thunderer of his only dreaded bolt. Par Lost 6.491
He ended, and his words thir drooping chere Par Lost 6.496
This day, fear not his flight; so thick a Cloud Par Lost 6.539
He comes, and settl'd in his face I see Par Lost 6.540
His Adamantine coat gird well, and each Par Lost 6.542
Fit well his Helme, gripe fast his orbed Shield, Par Lost 6.543
Training his devilish Enginrie, impal'd Par Lost 6.553
A Seraph stood, and in his hand a Reed Par Lost 6.579
And to his Mates thus in derision call'd. Par Lost 6.608
So easie, and of his Thunder made a scorn, Par Lost 6.632
And all his Host derided, while they stood Par Lost 6.633
Which God hath in his mighty Angels plac'd) Par Lost 6.638
Shrin'd in his Sanctuarie of Heav'n secure, Par Lost 6.672
That his great purpose he might so fulfill, Par Lost 6.675
To honour his Anointed Son aveng'd Par Lost 6.676
Upon his enemies, and to declare Par Lost 6.677
All power on him transferr'd: whence to his Son Par Lost 6.678
Th' Assessor of his Throne he thus began. Par Lost 6.679
Since *Michael* and his Powers went forth to tame Par Lost 6.686
God and *Messiah* his anointed King. Par Lost 6.718
He said, and on his Son with Rayes direct Par Lost 6.719
Shon full, he all his Father full exprest Par Lost 6.720
Ineffably into his face receiv'd, Par Lost 6.721
So said, he o're his Scepter bowing, rose Par Lost 6.746
Ascended, at his right hand Victorie Par Lost 6.762
Sate Eagle-wing'd, beside him hung his Bow Par Lost 6.763
He onward came, farr off his coming shon, Par Lost 6.768
Illustrious farr and wide, but by his own Par Lost 6.773
Aloft by Angels born, his Sign in Heav'n: Par Lost 6.776
His Armie, circumfus'd on either Wing, Par Lost 6.778
Before him Power Divine his way prepar'd; Par Lost 6.780
At his command the uprooted Hills retir'd Par Lost 6.781
Each to his place, they heard his voice and went Par Lost 6.782

His(*cont*)
Obsequious, Heav'n his wonted face renewd, Par Lost 6.783
This saw his hapless Foes but stood obdur'd, Par Lost 6.785
Grieving to see his Glorie, at the sight Par Lost 6.792
Took envie, and aspiring to his highth, Par Lost 6.793
To all his Host on either hand thus spake. Par Lost 6.800
Accepted, fearless in his righteous Cause, Par Lost 6.804
Vengeance is his, or whose he sole appoints; Par Lost 6.808
Hath honourd me according to his will. Par Lost 6.816
His count'nance too severe to be beheld Par Lost 6.825
And full of wrauth bent on his Enemies. Par Lost 6.826
Of his fierce Chariot rowld, as with the sound Par Lost 6.829
Hee on his impious Foes right onward drove, Par Lost 6.831
Gloomie as Night; under his burning Wheeles Par Lost 6.832
Among them he arriv'd; in his right hand Par Lost 6.835
Thrown on them as a shelter from his ire. Par Lost 6.843
His arrows, from the fourfold-visag'd Foure, Par Lost 6.845
Yet half his strength he put not forth, but check'd Par Lost 6.853
His Thunder in mid Volie, for he meant Par Lost 6.854
Through his wilde Anarchie, so huge a rout Par Lost 6.873
Sole Victor from th' expulsion of his Foes Par Lost 6.880
Messiah his triumphal Chariot turnd: Par Lost 6.881
To meet him all his Saints, who silent stood Par Lost 6.882
Eye witnesses of his Almightie Acts, Par Lost 6.883
And Temple of his mightie Father Thron'd Par Lost 6.890
His punishment, Eternal miserie; Par Lost 6.904
Which would be all his solace and revenge, Par Lost 6.905
Thee once to gaine Companion of his woe. Par Lost 6.907
But list'n not to his Temptations, warne Par Lost 6.908
Of *Bacchus* and his revellers, the Race Par Lost 7.33
In Paradise to *Adam* or his Race, Par Lost 7.45
Though wandring. He with his consorted *Eve* Par Lost 7.50
The doubts that in his heart arose: and now Par Lost 7.60
Before his memorie, as one whose drouth Par Lost 7.66
Proceeded thus to ask his Heav'nly Guest. Par Lost 7.69
Immortal thanks, and his admonishment Par Lost 7.77
Immutably his sovran will, the end Par Lost 7.79
Mov'd the Creator in his holy Rest Par Lost 7.91
Of his Eternal Empire, but the more Par Lost 7.96
To magnifie his works, the more we know. Par Lost 7.97
Much of his Race though steep, suspens in Heav'n Par Lost 7.99
His Generation, and the rising Birth Par Lost 7.102
Or we can bid his absence, till thy Song Par Lost 7.107
Thus *Adam* his illustrious Guest besought: Par Lost 7.109
Fell with his flaming Legions through the Deep Par Lost 7.134
Into his place, and the great Son returnd Par Lost 7.135
Victorious with his Saints, th' Omnipotent Par Lost 7.136
Eternal Father from his Throne beheld Par Lost 7.137
Thir multitude, and to his Son thus spake. Par Lost 7.138
But least his heart exalt him in the harme Par Lost 7.150
His Word, the filial Godhead, gave effect. Par Lost 7.175
Had driven out th' ungodly from his sight Par Lost 7.185
His good to Worlds and Ages infinite. Par Lost 7.191
On his great Expedition now appeer'd, Par Lost 7.193
Immense, and all his Father in him shon. Par Lost 7.196
About his Chariot numberless were pour'd Par Lost 7.197
The King of Glorie in his powerful Word Par Lost 7.208
For *Chaos* heard his voice: him all his Traine Par Lost 7.221
Creation, and the wonders of his might. Par Lost 7.223
Then staid the fervid Wheeles, and in his hand Par Lost 7.224
1669 'the fervid'
His brooding wings the Spirit of God outspred, Par Lost 7.235
God and his works, Creatour him they sung, Par Lost 7.259
Surveying his great Work, that it was good: Par Lost 7.353
And hence the Morning Planet guilds her horns; Par Lost 7.366
1667 'his'
First in his East the glorious Lamp was seen, Par Lost 7.370
His Longitude through Heav'ns high rode: the gray Par Lost 7.373
His mirror, with full face borrowing her Light Par Lost 7.377
And every Bird of wing after his kinde; Par Lost 7.394
And seems a moving Land, and at his Gilles Par Lost 7.415
Draws in, and at his Trunck spouts out a Sea. Par Lost 7.416
As from his Laire the wilde Beast where he wonns Par Lost 7.457
His hinder parts, then springs as broke from Bonds, Par Lost 7.465
And Rampant shakes his Brinded main; the Ounce, Par Lost 7.466
Bore up his branching head: scarse from his mould Par Lost 7.470
His vastness: Fleec't the Flocks and bleating rose, Par Lost 7.472
His Stature, and upright with Front serene Par Lost 7.509
But grateful to acknowledge whence his good Par Lost 7.512
Of all his works: therefore the Omnipotent Par Lost 7.516
Present) thus to his Son audibly spake. Par Lost 7.518
The breath of Life; in his own Image hee Par Lost 7.526
Yet not till the Creator from his work Par Lost 7.551
Up to the Heav'n of Heav'ns his high abode, Par Lost 7.553
Th' addition of his Empire, how it shew'd Par Lost 7.555
In prospect from his Throne, how good, how faire, Par Lost 7.556
Answering his great Idea. Up he rode Par Lost 7.557
The great Creator from his work returnd Par Lost 7.567
Magnificent, his Six days work, a World; Par Lost 7.568
Thither will send his winged Messengers Par Lost 7.572
With his great Father (for he also went Par Lost 7.588
As resting on that day from all his work, Par Lost 7.593
To lessen thee, against his purpose serves Par Lost 7.614
To manifest the more thy might: his evil Par Lost 7.615
Created in his Image, there to dwell Par Lost 7.627
Over his Works, on Earth, in Sea, or Air, Par Lost 7.629
So Charming left his voice, that he a while Par Lost 8.2
line not in 1667 edition

His(*cont*)

So spake our Sire, and by his count'nance seemd	Par Lost 8.39
With conjugal Caresses, from his Lip	Par Lost 8.56
Wherein to read his wondrous Works, and learne	Par Lost 8.68
His Seasons, Hours, or Dayes, or Months, or Yeares:	Par Lost 8.69
His secrets to be scann'd by them who ought	Par Lost 8.74
Conjecture, he his Fabric of the Heav'ns	Par Lost 8.76
His laughter at thir quaint Opinions wide	Par Lost 8.78
His beams, unactive else, thir vigour find.	Par Lost 8.97
So spacious, and his Line stretcht out so farr;	Par Lost 8.102
That Man may know he dwells not in his own;	Par Lost 8.103
Ordain'd for uses to his Lord best known.	Par Lost 8.106
Though numberless, to his Omnipotence,	Par Lost 8.108
God to remove his wayes from human sense,	Par Lost 8.119
By his attractive vertue and thir own	Par Lost 8.124
Or save the Sun his labour, and that swift	Par Lost 8.133
Still luminous by his ray. What if that light	Par Lost 8.140
Hee from the East his flaming rode begin,	Par Lost 8.162
Abundantly his gifts hath also pour'd	Par Lost 8.220
Inward and outward both, his image faire:	Par Lost 8.221
On Man his Equal Love: say therefore on;	Par Lost 8.228
Or enemie, while God was in his work,	Par Lost 8.234
Not that they durst without his leave attempt,	Par Lost 8.237
But us he sends upon his high behests	Par Lost 8.238
In Balmie Sweat, which with his Beames the Sun	Par Lost 8.255
In adoration at his feet I fell	Par Lost 8.315
Not to incur; but soon his cleer aspect	Par Lost 8.336
With blandishment, each Bird stoop'd on his wing.	Par Lost 8.351
But in degree, the cause of his desire	Par Lost 8.417
By conversation with his like to help,	Par Lost 8.418
Or solace his defects. No need that thou	Par Lost 8.419
His single imperfection, and beget	Par Lost 8.423
Like of his like, his Image multipli'd,	Par Lost 8.424
My earthly by his Heav'nly overpowerd,	Par Lost 8.453
The Rib he formd and fashond with his hands;	Par Lost 8.469
Under his forming hands a Creature grew,	Par Lost 8.470
And guided by his voice, nor uninformd	Par Lost 8.486
Father and Mother, and to his Wife adhere;	Par Lost 8.498
On his Hill top, to light the bridal Lamp.	Par Lost 8.520
His Image who made both, and less expressing	Par Lost 8.544
The thoughts, and heart enlarges, hath his seat	Par Lost 8.590
His great command; take heed least Passion sway	Par Lost 8.635
From the thick shade, and *Adam* to his Bowre.	Par Lost 8.653
With Man, as with his Friend, familiar us'd	Par Lost 9.2
Of stern *Achilles* on his Foe pursu'd	Par Lost 9.15
His entrance, and forewarnd the Cherubim	Par Lost 9.61
Most opportune might serve his Wiles, and found	Par Lost 9.85
Of thoughts revolv'd, his final sentence chose	Par Lost 9.88
To enter, and his dark suggestions hide	Par Lost 9.90
As from his wit and native suttletie	Par Lost 9.93
His bursting passion into plaints thus pour'd:	Par Lost 9.98
Or won to what may work his utter loss,	Par Lost 9.131
Of his adorers: hee to be aveng'd,	Par Lost 9.143
And to repaire his numbers thus impair'd,	Par Lost 9.144
Are his Created, or to spite us more,	Par Lost 9.147
Magnificent this World, and Earth his seat,	Par Lost 9.153
Subjected to his service Angel wings,	Par Lost 9.155
Whom us the more to spite his Maker rais'd	Par Lost 9.177
His midnight search, where soonest he might finde	Par Lost 9.181
His head the midst, well stor'd with suttle wiles:	Par Lost 9.184
Fearless unfeard he slept: in at his Mouth	Par Lost 9.187
The Devil enterd, and his brutal sense,	Par Lost 9.188
With act intelligential; but his sleep	Par Lost 9.190
To the Creator, and his Nostrils fill	Par Lost 9.196
Envying our happiness, and of his own	Par Lost 9.254
His wish and best advantage, us asunder,	Par Lost 9.258
Whether his first design be to withdraw	Par Lost 9.261
Enjoy'd by us excites his envie more;	Par Lost 9.264
His violence thou fearst not, being such,	Par Lost 9.282
His fraud is then thy fear, which plain inferrs	Par Lost 9.285
Can by his fraud be shak'n or seduc't;	Par Lost 9.287
Nor thou his malice and false guile contemn;	Par Lost 9.306
So spake domestick *Adam* in his care	Par Lost 9.318
Tempting affronts us with his foul esteem	Par Lost 9.328
Of our integritie: his foul esteeme	Par Lost 9.329
From his surmise prov'd false, find peace within,	Par Lost 9.333
Of God ordain'd them, his creating hand	Par Lost 9.344
Or aught that might his happie State secure,	Par Lost 9.347
The danger lies, yet lies within his power:	Par Lost 9.349
Against his will he can receave no harme.	Par Lost 9.350
For God towards thee hath done his part, do thine.	Par Lost 9.375
So bent, the more shall shame him his repulse.	Par Lost 9.384
Her long with ardent look his Eye pursu'd	Par Lost 9.397
Oft he to her his charge of quick returne	Par Lost 9.399
And on his Quest, where likeliest he might finde	Par Lost 9.414
The whole included Race, his purposd prey.	Par Lost 9.416
He sought them both, but wish'd his hap might find	Par Lost 9.421
Of what so seldom chanc'd, when to his wish,	Par Lost 9.423
Beyond his hope, *Eve* separate he spies,	Par Lost 9.424
Held dalliance with his faire *Egyptian* Spouse.	Par Lost 9.443
His Malice, and with rapine sweet bereav'd	Par Lost 9.461
His fierceness of the fierce intent it brought:	Par Lost 9.462
From his own evil, and for the time remaind	Par Lost 9.464
Though in mid Heav'n, soon ended his delight,	Par Lost 9.468
Fierce hate he recollects, and all his thoughts	Par Lost 9.471
Address'd his way, not with indented wave,	Par Lost 9.496
Prone on the ground, as since, but on his reare,	Par Lost 9.497
Fould above fould a surging Maze, his Head	Par Lost 9.499
Crested aloft, and Carbuncle his Eyes;	Par Lost 9.500
Amidst his circling Spires, that on the grass	Par Lost 9.502
Floted redundant: pleasing was his shape,	Par Lost 9.503
To interrupt, side-long he works his way.	Par Lost 9.512
So varied hee, and of his tortuous Traine	Par Lost 9.516
His turret Crest, and sleek enamel'd Neck,	Par Lost 9.525
His gentle dumb expression turnd at length	Par Lost 9.527
The Eye of *Eve* to mark his play; he glad	Par Lost 9.528
His fraudulent temptation thus began.	Par Lost 9.531
So gloz'd the Tempter, and his Proem tun'd;	Par Lost 9.549
Into the Heart of *Eve* his words made way,	Par Lost 9.550
Bright'ns his Crest, as when a wandring Fire,	Par Lost 9.634
Misleads th' amaz'd Night-wanderer from his way	Par Lost 9.640
Sole Daughter of his voice; the rest, we live	Par Lost 9.653
To Man, and indignation at his wrong,	Par Lost 9.666
Of Preface brooking through his Zeal of Right.	Par Lost 9.676
Is open? or will God incense his ire	Par Lost 9.692
His worshippers; he knows that in the day	Par Lost 9.705
Impart against his will if all be his?	Par Lost 9.728
He ended, and his words replete with guile	Par Lost 9.733
Yet rung of his perswasive words, impregn'd	Par Lost 9.737
Forbids us then to taste, but his forbidding	Par Lost 9.753
Our great Forbidder, safe with all his Spies	Par Lost 9.815
In Femal Sex, the more to draw his Love,	Par Lost 9.822
Great joy he promis'd to his thoughts, and new	Par Lost 9.843
Yet oft his heart, divine of somthing ill,	Par Lost 9.845
Ran through his veins, and all his joynts relax'd;	Par Lost 9.891
From his slack hand the Garland wreath'd for *Eve*	Par Lost 9.892
Thus in calm mood his Words to *Eve* he turnd.	Par Lost 9.920
Us his prime Creatures, dignifi'd so high,	Par Lost 9.940
Set over all his Works, which in our Fall,	Par Lost 9.941
Not well conceav'd of God, who though his Power	Par Lost 9.945
Tenderly wept, much won that he his Love	Par Lost 9.991
Against his better knowledge, not deceav'd,	Par Lost 9.998
Eating his fill, nor *Eve* to iterate	Par Lost 9.1005
To guiltie shame hee cover'd, but his Robe	Par Lost 9.1058
Shorn of his strength, They destitute and bare	Par Lost 9.1062
Shelters in coole, and tends his pasturing Herds	Par Lost 9.1109
Shee first his weak indulgence will accuse.	Par Lost 9.1186
Of God All-seeing, or deceave his Heart	Par Lost 10.6
For Man, for of his state by this they knew,	Par Lost 10.19
Eternal Father from his secret Cloud,	Par Lost 10.32
Amidst in Thunder utter'd thus his voice.	Par Lost 10.33
On his bad Errand, Man should be seduc't	Par Lost 10.41
Against his Maker; no Decree of mine	Par Lost 10.43
Concurring to necessitate his Fall,	Par Lost 10.44
His free Will, to her own inclining left	Par Lost 10.46
On his transgression, Death denounc't that day,	Par Lost 10.49
Mans Friend, his Mediator, his design'd	Par Lost 10.60
Toward the right hand his Glorie, on the Son	Par Lost 10.64
Resplendent all his Father manifest	Par Lost 10.66
Thus saying, from his radiant Seat he rose	Par Lost 10.85
And from his presence hid themselves among	Par Lost 10.100
Before his voice, or was shee made thy guide,	Par Lost 10.146
Of his Creation; justly then accurst,	Par Lost 10.168
Nor alter'd his offence; yet God at last	Par Lost 10.171
To *Satan* first in sin his doom apply'd,	Par Lost 10.172
And on the Serpent thus his curse let fall.	Par Lost 10.174
Her Seed shall bruse thy head, thou bruise his heel.	Par Lost 10.181
Prince of the Aire; then rising from his Grave	Par Lost 10.185
Eevn hee who now foretold his fatal bruise,	Par Lost 10.191
And to the Woman thus his Sentence turn'd.	Par Lost 10.192
As when he wash'd his servants feet so now	Par Lost 10.215
As Father of his Familie he clad	Par Lost 10.216
And thought not much to cloath his Enemies:	Par Lost 10.219
Opprobrious, with his Robe of righteousness,	Par Lost 10.222
Araying cover'd from his Fathers sight.	Par Lost 10.223
Into his blissful bosom reassum'd	Par Lost 10.225
For us his ofspring deare? It cannot be	Par Lost 10.238
By his Avengers, since no place like this	Par Lost 10.241
Can fit his punishment, or their revenge.	Par Lost 10.242
Stay his return perhaps over this Gulfe	Par Lost 10.253
His Nostril wide into the murkie Air,	Par Lost 10.280
Sagacious of his Quarry from so farr.	Par Lost 10.281
Death with his Mace petrific, cold and dry,	Par Lost 10.294
As *Delos* floating once; the rest his look	Par Lost 10.296
From *Susa* his *Memnonian* Palace high	Par Lost 10.308
Bridging his way, *Europe* with *Asia* joyn'd,	Par Lost 10.310
First lighted from his Wing, and landed safe	Par Lost 10.316
His *Zenith*, while the Sun in *Aries* rose:	Par Lost 10.329
Disguis'd he came, but those his Children dear	Par Lost 10.330
To observe the sequel, saw his guileful act	Par Lost 10.334
The present, fearing guiltie what his wrauth	Par Lost 10.340
Thence gatherd his own doom, which understood	Par Lost 10.344
Met who to meet him came, his Ofspring dear.	Par Lost 10.349
Of that stupendious Bridge his joy encreas'd.	Par Lost 10.351
Long hee admiring stood, till Sin, his faire	Par Lost 10.352
Retiring, by his own doom alienated,	Par Lost 10.378
His Quadrature, from thy Orbicular World,	Par Lost 10.381
Or trie thee now more dang'rous to his Throne.	Par Lost 10.382
That scorn'd his indignation: through the Gate,	Par Lost 10.418
As when the *Tartar* from his *Russian* Foe	Par Lost 10.431
The Realm of *Aladule*, in his retreate	Par Lost 10.435
Ascended his high Throne, which under state	Par Lost 10.445
At last as from a Cloud his fulgent head	Par Lost 10.449
With what permissive glory since his fall	Par Lost 10.451
From his Creator, and the more to increase	Par Lost 10.486

His(*cont*)

Both his beloved Man and all his World,	Par Lost 10.489
Mee and Mankinde; I am to bruise his heel;	Par Lost 10.498
His Seed, when is not set, shall bruise my head:	Par Lost 10.499
To fill his eare, when contrary he hears	Par Lost 10.506
His Visage drawn he felt to sharp and spare,	Par Lost 10.511
His Armes clung to his Ribs, his Leggs entwining	Par Lost 10.512
A monstrous Serpent on his Belly prone,	Par Lost 10.514
According to his doom: he would have spoke,	Par Lost 10.517
To his bold Riot: dreadful was the din	Par Lost 10.521
Huge *Python*, and his Power no less he seem'd	Par Lost 10.531
His will who reigns above, to aggravate	Par Lost 10.549
On his pale Horse: to whom *Sin* thus began.	Par Lost 10.590
His thoughts, his looks, words, actions all infect,	Par Lost 10.608
From his transcendent Seat the Saints among,	Par Lost 10.614
To those bright Orders utterd thus his voice.	Par Lost 10.615
And his Adherents, that with so much ease	Par Lost 10.622
For ever, and seal up his ravenous Jawes.	Par Lost 10.637
His mightie Angels gave them several charge,	Par Lost 10.650
Had first his precept so to move, so shine,	Par Lost 10.652
Some say he bid his Angels turne ascanse	Par Lost 10.668
To recompence his distance, in thir sight	Par Lost 10.683
His course intended; else how had the World	Par Lost 10.689
For this we may thank *Adam;* but his thanks	Par Lost 10.736
Wouldst thou admit for his contempt of thee	Par Lost 10.763
God made thee of choice his own, and of his own	Par Lost 10.766
To serve him, thy reward was of his grace,	Par Lost 10.767
Thy punishment then justly is at his Will.	Par Lost 10.768
Be it so, for I submit, his doom is fair,	Par Lost 10.769
His hand to execute what his Decree	Par Lost 10.772
And sleep secure; his dreadful voice no more	Par Lost 10.779
Is his wrauth also? be it, man is not so,	Par Lost 10.795
In punisht man, to satisfie his rigour	Par Lost 10.803
His Sentence beyond dust and Natures Law,	Par Lost 10.805
Which to his evil Conscience represented	Par Lost 10.849
Curs'd his Creation, Death as oft accus'd	Par Lost 10.852
The day of his offence. Why comes not Death,	Par Lost 10.854
Soft words to his fierce passion she assay'd:	Par Lost 10.865
Like his, and colour Serpentine may shew	Par Lost 10.870
By Parents, or his happiest choice too late	Par Lost 10.904
To a fell Adversarie, his hate or shame:	Par Lost 10.906
And tresses all disorderd, at his feet	Par Lost 10.911
His peace, and thus proceeded in her plaint.	Par Lost 10.913
Mee mee onely just object of his ire.	Par Lost 10.936
Commiseration; soon his heart relented	Par Lost 10.940
Towards her, his life so late and sole delight,	Par Lost 10.941
Now at his feet submissive in distress,	Par Lost 10.942
Creature so faire his reconcilement seeking,	Par Lost 10.943
His counsel whom she had displeas'd, his aide;	Par Lost 10.944
As one disarm'd, his anger all he lost,	Par Lost 10.945
His full wrauth whose thou feelst as yet lest part,	Par Lost 10.951
So Death shall be deceav'd his glut, and with us two	Par Lost 10.990
Be forc'd to satisfie his Rav'nous Maw.	Par Lost 10.991
With our own hands his Office on our selves;	Par Lost 10.1002
To better hopes his more attentive minde	Par Lost 10.1011
Hath wiselier arm'd his vengeful ire then so	Par Lost 10.1023
Against us this deceit: to crush his head	Par Lost 10.1035
Shall scape his punishment ordain'd, and wee	Par Lost 10.1039
Reluctance against God and his just yoke	Par Lost 10.1045
Or Heat should injure us, his timely care	Par Lost 10.1057
Hath unbesaught provided, and his hands	Par Lost 10.1058
How much more, if we pray him, will his ear	Par Lost 10.1060
Be open, and his heart to pitie incline,	Par Lost 10.1061
Leave cold the Night, how we his gather'd beams	Par Lost 10.1070
From his displeasure; in whose look serene,	Par Lost 10.1094
Sow'n with contrition in his heart, then those	Par Lost 11.27
Which his own hand manuring all the Trees	Par Lost 11.28
To supplication, heare his sighs though mute;	Par Lost 11.31
Interpret for him, mee his Advocate	Par Lost 11.33
And propitiation, all his works on mee	Par Lost 11.34
Before thee reconcil'd, at least his days	Par Lost 11.39
Numberd, though sad, till Death, his doom (which I	Par Lost 11.40
His final remedie, and after Life	Par Lost 11.62
His Trumpet, heard in *Oreb* since perhaps	Par Lost 11.74
And took thir Seats; till from his Throne supream	Par Lost 11.82
Th' Almighty thus pronouncd his sovran Will.	Par Lost 11.83
To know both Good and Evil, since his taste	Par Lost 11.85
His knowledge of Good lost, and Evil got,	Par Lost 11.87
His heart I know, how variable and vain	Par Lost 11.92
Self-left. Least therefore his now bolder hand	Par Lost 11.93
Of *Hermes*, or his opiate Rod. Mean while	Par Lost 11.133
Which thus to *Eve* his welcome words renewd.	Par Lost 11.140
Of God high-blest, or to incline his will,	Par Lost 11.145
Bending his eare; perswasion in me grew	Par Lost 11.152
His promise, that thy Seed shall bruise our Foe;	Par Lost 11.155
The Bird of *Jove*, stoopt from his aerie tour,	Par Lost 11.185
Adam observ'd, and with his Eye the chase	Par Lost 11.191
Forerunners of his purpose, or to warn	Par Lost 11.195
The field Pavilion'd with his Guardians bright;	Par Lost 11.215
In thir bright stand, there left his Powers to seise	Par Lost 11.221
To find where *Adam* shelterd, took his way,	Par Lost 11.223
One of the heav'nly Host, and by his Gate	Par Lost 11.230
Not in his shape Celestial, but as Man	Par Lost 11.239
Clad to meet Man; over his lucid Armes	Par Lost 11.240
His starrie Helme unbuckl'd shew'd him prime	Par Lost 11.245
In Manhood where Youth ended; by his side	Par Lost 11.246
Satans dire dread, and in his hand the Spear.	Par Lost 11.248
Adam bowd low, hee Kingly from his State	Par Lost 11.249

His(*cont*)

Inclin'd not, but his coming thus declar'd.	Par Lost 11.250
Defeated of his seisure many dayes	Par Lost 11.254
That all his senses bound; *Eve*, who unseen	Par Lost 11.265
Recovering, and his scatterd spirits returnd,	Par Lost 11.294
To *Michael* thus his humble words addressd.	Par Lost 11.295
But prayer against his absolute Decree	Par Lost 11.311
Therefore to his great bidding I submit.	Par Lost 11.314
As from his face I shall be hid, deprivd	Par Lost 11.316
His blessed count'nance; here I could frequent,	Par Lost 11.317
Stood visible, among these Pines his voice	Par Lost 11.321
His bright appearances, or foot step-trace?	Par Lost 11.329
Gladly behold though but his utmost skirts	Par Lost 11.332
Of glory, and farr off his steps adore.	Par Lost 11.333
Adam, thou know'st Heav'n his, and all the Earth.	Par Lost 11.335
Not this Rock onely; his Omnipresence fills	Par Lost 11.336
Fomented by his virtual power and warmd:	Par Lost 11.338
His presence to these narrow bounds confin'd	Par Lost 11.341
Present, and of his presence many a signe	Par Lost 11.351
With goodness and paternal Love, his Face	Par Lost 11.353
Express, and of his steps the track Divine.	Par Lost 11.354
His Eye might there command wherever stood	Par Lost 11.385
Turchestan-born; nor could his eye not ken	Par Lost 11.396
Th' Empire of *Negus* to his utmost Port	Par Lost 11.397
That *Adam* now enforc't to close his eyes,	Par Lost 11.419
Sunk down and all his Spirits became intranst:	Par Lost 11.420
Soon rais'd, and his attention thus recall'd.	Par Lost 11.422
His eyes he op'nd, and beheld a field,	Par Lost 11.429
A sweatie Reaper from his Tillage brought	Par Lost 11.434
More meek came with the Firstlings of his Flock	Par Lost 11.437
His Offring soon propitious Fire from Heav'n	Par Lost 11.441
The others not, for his was not sincere;	Par Lost 11.443
Groand out his Soul with gushing bloud effus'd.	Par Lost 11.447
Much at that sight was *Adam* in his heart	Par Lost 11.448
For envie that his Brothers Offering found	Par Lost 11.456
In his first shape on man; but many shapes	Par Lost 11.467
To his grim Cave, all dismal; yet to sense	Par Lost 11.469
Before his eyes appeard, sad, noysom, dark,	Par Lost 11.478
And over them triumphant Death his Dart	Par Lost 11.491
His best of Man, and gave him up to tears	Par Lost 11.497
And scarce recovering words his plaint renew'd.	Par Lost 11.499
And for his Makers Image sake exempt?	Par Lost 11.514
His Image whom they serv'd, a brutish vice,	Par Lost 11.518
Or if his likeness, by themselves defac't	Par Lost 11.522
Thir stops and chords was seen: his volant touch	Par Lost 11.561
First his own Tooles; then, what might else be wrought	Par Lost 11.572
To worship God aright, and know his works	Par Lost 11.578
Fast caught, they lik'd, and each his liking chose;	Par Lost 11.587
Of wickedness, wherein shall dwell his Race	Par Lost 11.608
Who slew his Brother; studious they appere	Par Lost 11.609
Unmindful of thir Maker, though his Spirit	Par Lost 11.611
Taught them, but they his gifts acknowledg'd none.	Par Lost 11.612
Said th' Angel, who should better hold his place	Par Lost 11.635
Adam was all in tears, and to his guide	Par Lost 11.674
His Brother; for of whom such massacher	Par Lost 11.679
Rescu'd, had in his Righteousness bin lost?	Par Lost 11.682
To judge them with his Saints: Him the most High	Par Lost 11.705
Contending, and remov'd his Tents farr off;	Par Lost 11.727
Thir order: last the Sire, and his three Sons	Par Lost 11.736
His Children, all in view destroyd at once;	Par Lost 11.761
Him or his Childern, evil he may be sure,	Par Lost 11.772
Which neither his foreknowing can prevent,	Par Lost 11.773
The one just Man alive; by his command	Par Lost 11.818
Out of his place, pushd by the horned floud,	Par Lost 11.831
With all his verdure spoil'd, and Trees adrift	Par Lost 11.832
And the cleer Sun on his wide watrie Glass	Par Lost 11.844
His Sluces, as the Heav'n his windows shut.	Par Lost 11.849
Green Tree or ground whereon his foot may light;	Par Lost 11.858
The second time returning, in his Bill	Par Lost 11.859
Anon drie ground appeers, and from his Arke	Par Lost 11.861
The ancient Sire descends with all his Train;	Par Lost 11.862
Grateful to Heav'n, over his head beholds	Par Lost 11.864
Greatly rejoyc'd, and thus his joy broke forth.	Par Lost 11.869
From him, and all his anger to forget.	Par Lost 11.878
So willingly doth God remit his Ire,	Par Lost 11.885
Griev'd at his heart, when looking down he saw	Par Lost 11.887
Such grace shall one just Man find in his sight,	Par Lost 11.890
Surpass his bounds, nor Rain to drown the World	Par Lost 11.894
His triple-colour'd Bow, whereon to look	Par Lost 11.897
And call to mind his Cov'nant: Day and Night,	Par Lost 11.898
As one who in his journey bates at Noone, line not in 1667 edition	Par Lost 12.1
Over his brethren, and quite dispossess	Par Lost 12.28
Hunting (and Men not Beasts shall be his game)	Par Lost 12.30
Subjection to his Empire tyrannous:	Par Lost 12.32
And from Rebellion shall derive his name,	Par Lost 12.36
Above his Brethren, to himself assuming	Par Lost 12.65
By his donation; but Man over men	Par Lost 12.69
But this Usurper his encroachment proud	Par Lost 12.72
Stayes not on Man; to God his Tower intends	Par Lost 12.73
Himself and his rash Armie, where thin Aire	Par Lost 12.76
Above the Clouds will pine his entrails gross,	Par Lost 12.77
His outward freedom: Tyrannie must be,	Par Lost 12.95
Don to his Father, heard this heavie curse,	Par Lost 12.103
Servant of Servants, on his vitious Race.	Par Lost 12.104
His presence from among them, and avert	Par Lost 12.108
His holy Eyes; resolving from thenceforth	Par Lost 12.109
To call by Vision from his Fathers house,	Par Lost 12.121

His(*cont*)
His kindred and false Gods, into a Land Par Lost 12.122
His benediction so, that in his Seed Par Lost 12.125
He leaves his Gods, his Friends, and native Soile Par Lost 12.129
Not wandring poor, but trusting all his wealth Par Lost 12.133
Canaan he now attains, I see his Tents Par Lost 12.135
Gift to his Progenie of all that Land; Par Lost 12.138
Jordan, true limit Eastward; but his Sons Par Lost 12.145
Shall in his Seed be blessed; by that Seed Par Lost 12.148
A Son, and of his Son a Grand-childe leaves, Par Lost 12.153
Of *Pharao:* there he dies, and leaves his Race Par Lost 12.163
His people from enthralment, they return Par Lost 12.171
Frogs, Lice and Flies must all his Palace fill Par Lost 12.177
His Cattel must of Rot and Murren die, Par Lost 12.179
Botches and blaines must all his flesh imboss, Par Lost 12.180
And all his people; Thunder mixt with Haile, Par Lost 12.181
Darkness must overshadow all his bounds, Par Lost 12.187
To let his sojourners depart, and oft Par Lost 12.192
Humbles his stubborn heart, but still as Ice Par Lost 12.193
More hard'nd after thaw, till in his rage Par Lost 12.194
Swallows him with his Host, but them lets pass Par Lost 12.196
Divided, till his rescu'd gain thir shoar: Par Lost 12.199
Such wondrous power God to his Saint will lend, Par Lost 12.200
Though present in his Angel, who shall goe Par Lost 12.201
All night he will pursue, but his approach Par Lost 12.206
God looking forth will trouble all his Host Par Lost 12.209
Moses once more his potent Rod extends Par Lost 12.211
Over the Sea; the Sea his Rod obeys; Par Lost 12.212
That *Moses* might report to them his will, Par Lost 12.237
Obedient to his will, that he voutsafes Par Lost 12.246
Among them to set up his Tabernacle, Par Lost 12.247
By his prescript a Sanctuary is fram'd Par Lost 12.249
An Ark, and in the Ark his Testimony, Par Lost 12.251
The Records of his Cov'nant, over these Par Lost 12.252
Conducted by his Angel to the Land Par Lost 12.259
Promisd to *Abraham* and his Seed: the rest Par Lost 12.260
His whole descent, who thus shall *Canaan* win. Par Lost 12.269
Just *Abraham* and his Seed: now first I finde Par Lost 12.273
His day, in whom all Nations shall be blest, Par Lost 12.277
Of Law, his people into *Canaan* lead; Par Lost 12.309
His Name and Office bearing, who shall quell Par Lost 12.311
Irrevocable, that his Regal Throne Par Lost 12.323
The last, for of his Reign shall be no end. Par Lost 12.330
And his next Son for Wealth and Wisdom fam'd, Par Lost 12.332
Thir Citie, his Temple, and his holy Ark Par Lost 12.340
With all his sacred things, a scorn and prey Par Lost 12.341
Remembring mercie, and his Cov'nant sworn Par Lost 12.346
Barr'd of his right; yet at his Birth a Starr Par Lost 12.360
His place, to offer Incense, Myrrh, and Gold; Par Lost 12.363
His place of birth a solemn Angel tells Par Lost 12.364
Of squadrond Angels hear his Carol sung Par Lost 12.367
A Virgin is his Mother, but his Sire Par Lost 12.368
The Throne hereditarie, and bound his Reign Par Lost 12.370
With earths wide bounds, his glory with the Heav'ns. Par Lost 12.371
Needs must the Serpent now his capital bruise Par Lost 12.383
Not by destroying *Satan*, but his works Par Lost 12.394
In his redemption, and that his obedience Par Lost 12.408
Imputed becomes theirs by Faith, his merits Par Lost 12.409
By his own Nation, slaine for bringing Life; Par Lost 12.414
In this his satisfaction; so he dies, Par Lost 12.419
Out of his grave, fresh as the dawning light, Par Lost 12.423
His death for Man, as many as offerd Life Par Lost 12.425
Shall bruise the head of *Satan*, crush his strength Par Lost 12.430
Defeating Sin and Death, his two maine armes, Par Lost 12.431
And fix farr deeper in his head thir stings Par Lost 12.432
To his Disciples, Men who in his Life Par Lost 12.438
And his Salvation, them who shall beleeve Par Lost 12.441
So in his seed all Nations shall be blest. Par Lost 12.450
Over his foes and thine; there shall surprise Par Lost 12.453
Through all his Realme, and there confounded leave; Par Lost 12.455
His Seat at Gods right hand, exalted high Par Lost 12.457
His faithful, and receave them into bliss, Par Lost 12.462
His faithful, left among th' unfaithful herd, Par Lost 12.481
His people, who defend? will they not deale Par Lost 12.483
Wors with his followers then with him they dealt? Par Lost 12.484
Hee to his own a Comforter will send, Par Lost 12.486
His Spirit within them, and the Law of Faith Par Lost 12.488
Satans assaults, and quench his fierie darts, Par Lost 12.492
Powrd first on his Apostles, whom he sends Par Lost 12.498
His consort Libertie; what, but unbuild Par Lost 12.526
His living Temples, built by Faith to stand, Par Lost 12.527
Satan with his perverted World, then raise Par Lost 12.547
As in his presence, ever to observe Par Lost 12.563
His providence, and on him sole depend, Par Lost 12.564
Mercifull over all his works, with good Par Lost 12.565
Taught this by his example whom I now Par Lost 12.572
In all his wiles, defeated and repuls't, Par Reg 1.6
Into the Desert, his Victorious Field Par Reg 1.9
To all Baptiz'd: to his great Baptism flock'd Par Reg 1.21
As to his worthier, and would have resign'd Par Reg 1.27
To him his Heavenly Office, nor was long Par Reg 1.28
His witness unconfirm'd: on him baptiz'd Par Reg 1.29
From Heav'n pronounc'd him his beloved Son. Par Reg 1.32
Flies to his place, nor rests, but in mid air Par Reg 1.39
To Councel summons all his mighty Peers, Par Reg 1.40
Since *Adam* and his facil consort *Eve* Par Reg 1.51
His birth to our just fear gave no small cause, Par Reg 1.66
But his growth now to youths full flowr, displaying Par Reg 1.67

His(*cont*)
His coming, is sent Harbinger, who all Par Reg 1.71
Unfold her Crystal Dores, thence on his head Par Reg 1.82
His Mother then is mortal, but his Sire, Par Reg 1.86
And what will he not do to advance his Son? Par Reg 1.88
His first-begot we know, and sore have felt, Par Reg 1.89
When his fierce thunder drove us to the deep; Par Reg 1.90
In all his lineaments, though in his face Par Reg 1.92
The glimpses of his Fathers glory shine. Par Reg 1.93
He ended, and his words impression left Par Reg 1.106
His easie steps; girded with snaky wiles, Par Reg 1.120
To end his Raign on Earth so long enjoy'd: Par Reg 1.125
To shew him worthy of his birth divine Par Reg 1.141
His utmost subtilty, because he boasts Par Reg 1.144
And vaunts of his great cunning to the throng Par Reg 1.145
Of his Apostasie; he might have learnt Par Reg 1.146
Whate're his cruel malice could invent. Par Reg 1.149
All his sollicitations, and at length Par Reg 1.152
All his vast force, and drive him back to Hell, Par Reg 1.153
Of his great warfare, e're I send him forth Par Reg 1.158
His weakness shall o'recome Satanic strength Par Reg 1.161
Now entring his great duel, not of arms, Par Reg 1.174
Ventures his filial Vertue, though untri'd, Par Reg 1.177
Musing and much revolving in his brest, Par Reg 1.185
Publish his God-like office now mature, Par Reg 1.188
And his deep thoughts, the better to converse Par Reg 1.190
His holy Meditations thus persu'd. Par Reg 1.195
Before Messiah and his way prepare. Par Reg 1.272
I as all others to his Baptism came, Par Reg 1.273
Refus'd on me his Baptism to confer, Par Reg 1.278
As much his greater, and was hardly won; Par Reg 1.279
Audibly heard from Heav'n, pronounc'd me his, Par Reg 1.284
Me his beloved Son, in whom alone Par Reg 1.285
So spake our Morning Star then in his rise, Par Reg 1.294
Lodg'd in his brest, as well might recommend Par Reg 1.301
Among wild Beasts: they at his sight grew mild, Par Reg 1.310
Nor sleeping him nor waking harm'd, his walk Par Reg 1.311
His Carcass, pin'd with hunger and with droughth? Par Reg 1.325
To prove him, and illustrate his high worth; Par Reg 1.370
And when to all his Angels he propos'd Par Reg 1.371
Of all his flattering Prophets glibb'd with lyes Par Reg 1.375
To his destruction, as I had in charge. Par Reg 1.376
With all inflictions, but his patience won? Par Reg 1.426
And run not sooner to his fatal snare? Par Reg 1.441
Idolatrous, but when his purpose is Par Reg 1.444
Among them to declare his Providence Par Reg 1.445
But from him or his Angels President Par Reg 1.447
God hath now sent his living Oracle Par Reg 1.460
Into the World, to teach his final will, Par Reg 1.461
And sends his Spirit of Truth henceforth to dwell Par Reg 1.462
To tread his Sacred Courts, and minister Par Reg 1.488
About his Altar, handling holy things, Par Reg 1.489
Praying or vowing, and vouchsaf'd his voice Par Reg 1.490
His gray dissimulation, disappear'd Par Reg 1.498
His words, his wisdom full of grace and truth, Par Reg 2.34
Sent his Anointed, and to us reveal'd him, Par Reg 2.50
By his great Prophet, pointed at and shown, Par Reg 2.51
Lay on his Providence; he will not fail Par Reg 2.54
Mock us with his blest sight, then snatch him hence, Par Reg 2.56
But to his Mother *Mary*, when she saw Par Reg 2.60
A Manger his, yet soon enforc't to flye Par Reg 2.75
Were dead, who sought his life, and missing fill'd Par Reg 2.77
Hath been our dwelling many years, his life Par Reg 2.80
Son own'd from Heaven by his Father's voice; Par Reg 2.85
His Father's business; what he meant I mus'd, Par Reg 2.99
Since understand; much more his absence now Par Reg 2.100
All his great work to come before him set; Par Reg 2.112
His end of being on Earth, and mission high: Par Reg 2.114
Where all his Potentates in Council sate; Par Reg 2.118
Each of his reign allotted, rightlier call'd, Par Reg 2.123
Though *Adam* by his Wives allurement fell, Par Reg 2.134
At his command; when from amidst them rose Par Reg 2.149
Set women in his eye and in his walk, Par Reg 2.153
And made him bow to the Gods of his Wives. Par Reg 2.171
In his prime youth the fair *Iberian* maid. Par Reg 2.200
Higher design then to enjoy his State; Par Reg 2.203
On whom his leisure will vouchsafe an eye Par Reg 2.210
How would one look from his Majestick brow Par Reg 2.216
His constancy, with such as have more shew Par Reg 2.226
No advantage, and his strength as oft assay. Par Reg 2.234
To be at hand, and at his beck appear, Par Reg 2.238
Of various persons each to know his part; Par Reg 2.240
Then to the Desert takes with these his flight; Par Reg 2.241
He found his Supper on the coals prepar'd, Par Reg 2.273
Or as a guest with *Daniel* at his pulse. Par Reg 2.278
Left his ground-nest, high towring to descry Par Reg 2.280
The morns approach, and greet her with his Song: Par Reg 2.281
As lightly from his grassy Couch up rose Par Reg 2.282
Up to a hill anon his steps he rear'd, Par Reg 2.285
Thither he bent his way, determin'd there Par Reg 2.291
He spake no dream, for as his words had end, Par Reg 2.337
Our Saviour lifting up his eyes beheld Par Reg 2.338
His invitation earnestly renew'd. Par Reg 2.367
And with these words his temptation pursu'd. Par Reg 2.405
And his Son *Herod* plac'd on *Juda*'s Throne; Par Reg 2.424
When on his shoulders each mans burden lies; Par Reg 2.462
His Honour, Vertue, Merit and chief Praise, Par Reg 2.464
Of his weak arguing, and fallacious drift; Par Reg 3.4

His(*cont*)

At length collecting all his Serpent wiles,	Par Reg 3.5
At his dispose, young *Scipio* had brought down	Par Reg 3.34
His lot who dares be singularly good.	Par Reg 3.57
To all his Angels, who with true applause	Par Reg 3.63
Recount his praises; thus he did to *Job*,	Par Reg 3.64
When to extend his fame through Heaven and Earth,	Par Reg 3.65
His wasted Country freed from *Punic* rage,	Par Reg 3.102
And loses, though but verbal, his reward.	Par Reg 3.104
Oft not deserv'd? I seek not mine, but his	Par Reg 3.106
And for his glory all things made, all things	Par Reg 3.111
By all his Angels glorifi'd, requires	Par Reg 3.113
From us his foes pronounc't glory he exacts.	Par Reg 3.120
And reason; since his word all things produc'd,	Par Reg 3.122
But to shew forth his goodness, and impart	Par Reg 3.124
His good communicable to every soul	Par Reg 3.125
But why should man seek glory? who of his own	Par Reg 3.134
That who advance his glory, not thir own,	Par Reg 3.143
With guilt of his own sin, for he himself	Par Reg 3.147
That by strong hand his Family obtain'd,	Par Reg 3.168
The Father in his purpose hath decreed,	Par Reg 3.186
Lay pleasant; from his side two rivers flow'd,	Par Reg 3.255
His City there thou seest, and *Bactra* there;	Par Reg 3.285
That Empire, under his dominion holds	Par Reg 3.296
Of his great power; for now the *Parthian* King	Par Reg 3.299
In *Ctesiphon* hath gather'd all his Host	Par Reg 3.300
His thousands, in what martial equipage	Par Reg 3.304
When *Agrican* with all his Northern powers	Par Reg 3.338
His daughter, sought by many Prowest Knights,	Par Reg 3.342
And to our Saviour thus his words renew'd.	Par Reg 3.346
In *David*'s royal seat, his true Successour,	Par Reg 3.373
Whose off-spring in his Territory yet serve	Par Reg 3.375
David's true heir, and his full Scepter sway	Par Reg 3.405
For *Israel*, or for *David*, or his Throne,	Par Reg 3.408
When thou stood'st up his Tempter to the pride	Par Reg 3.409
To his due time and providence I leave them.	Par Reg 3.440
Made answer meet, that made void all his wiles.	Par Reg 3.442
Perplex'd and troubl'd at his bad success	Par Reg 4.1
Discover'd in his fraud, thrown from his hope,	Par Reg 4.3
That sleek't his tongue, and won so much on *Eve*,	Par Reg 4.5
This far his over-match, who self deceiv'd	Par Reg 4.7
The strength he was to cope with, or his own:	Par Reg 4.9
To salve his credit, and for very spight	Par Reg 4.12
And never cease, though to his shame the more;	Par Reg 4.14
And his vain importunity pursues.	Par Reg 4.24
Gardens and Groves presented to his eyes,	Par Reg 4.38
And now the Tempter thus his silence broke.	Par Reg 4.43
Above the rest lifting his stately head	Par Reg 4.48
His horrid lusts in private to enjoy,	Par Reg 4.94
Might'st thou expel this monster from his Throne	Par Reg 4.100
Now made a stye, and in his place ascending	Par Reg 4.101
Let his tormenter Conscience find him out,	Par Reg 4.130
Error by his own arms is best evinc't.	Par Reg 4.235
His whispering stream; within the walls then view	Par Reg 4.250
The schools of antient Sages; his who bred	Par Reg 4.251
And his who gave them breath, but higher sung,	Par Reg 4.258
Whose Poem *Phoebus* challeng'd for his own.	Par Reg 4.260
Of *Socrates*, see there his Tenement,	Par Reg 4.274
By him call'd vertue; and his vertuous man,	Par Reg 4.301
For all his tedious talk is but vain boast,	Par Reg 4.307
Incessantly, and to his reading brings not	Par Reg 4.323
The Holiest of Holies, and his Saints;	Par Reg 4.349
Quite at a loss, for all his darts were spent,	Par Reg 4.366
So saying he took (for still he knew his power	Par Reg 4.394
After his aerie jaunt, though hurried sore,	Par Reg 4.402
Hungry and cold betook him to his rest,	Par Reg 4.403
From dews and damps of night his shelter'd head,	Par Reg 4.406
But shelter'd slept in vain, for at his head	Par Reg 4.407
Disturb'd his sleep; and either Tropic now	Par Reg 4.409
Was absent, after all his mischief done,	Par Reg 4.440
Rather by this his last affront resolv'd,	Par Reg 4.444
Desperate of better course, to vent his rage,	Par Reg 4.445
And what he is; his wisdom, power, intent,	Par Reg 4.528
Concerning thee to his Angels, in thir hands	Par Reg 4.557
Receiving from his mother Earth new strength,	Par Reg 4.566
Fresh from his fall, and fiercer grapple joyn'd,	Par Reg 4.567
Renewing fresh assaults, amidst his pride	Par Reg 4.570
Fell whence he stood to see his Victor fall.	Par Reg 4.571
And to his crew, that sat consulting, brought	Par Reg 4.577
Joyless triumphals of his hop't success,	Par Reg 4.578
From his uneasie station, and upbore	Par Reg 4.584
Sung Heavenly Anthems of his victory	Par Reg 4.594
With all his Army, now thou hast aveng'd	Par Reg 4.606
In Paradise to tempt; his snares are broke:	Par Reg 4.611
For *Adam* and his chosen Sons, whom thou	Par Reg 4.614
Under his feet: for proof, e're this thou feel'st	Par Reg 4.621
Shall chase thee with the terror of his voice	Par Reg 4.627
Brought on his way with joy; hee unobserv'd	Par Reg 4.638
Home to his Mothers house private return'd.	Par Reg 4.639
His Godlike presence, and from some great act	Samson 28
When insupportably his foot advanc't,	Samson 136
Fled from his Lion ramp, old Warriors turn'd	Samson 139
Thir plated backs under his heel;	Samson 140
The Jaw of a dead Ass, his sword of bone,	Samson 143
Then by main force pull'd up, and on his shoulders bore	Samson 146
Are come upon him his deserts? yet why?	Samson 205
Yet *Israel* still serves with all his Sons.	Samson 240
Whom God hath of his special favour rais'd	Samson 273

His(*cont*)

Not worse then by his shield and spear	Samson 284
Had not his prowess quell'd thir pride	Samson 286
Yet more there be who doubt his ways not just,	Samson 300
As to his own edicts, found contradicting,	Samson 301
Regardless of his glories diminution;	Samson 303
And tie him to his own prescript,	Samson 308
For with his own Laws he can best dispence.	Samson 314
To set his people free,	Samson 317
Against his vow of strictest purity,	Samson 319
Unchaste was subsequent, her stain not his.	Samson 325
Why are his gifts desirable, to tempt	Samson 358
To *Dagon*, and advanc'd his praises high	Samson 450
His Deity comparing and preferring	Samson 464
But will arise and his great name assert:	Samson 467
And with confusion blank his Worshippers.	Samson 471
To vindicate the glory of his name	Samson 475
The mark of fool set on his front?	Samson 496
But I Gods counsel have not kept, his holy secret	Samson 497
God will relent, and quit thee all his debt;	Samson 509
Home to thy countrey and his sacred house,	Samson 518
His further ire, with praiers and vows renew'd.	Samson 520
Sam. His pardon I implore; but as for life,	Samson 521
His mighty Champion, strong above compare,	Samson 556
His might continues in thee not for naught,	Samson 588
Nor shall his wondrous gifts be frustrate thus.	Samson 589
There exercise all his fierce accidents,	Samson 612
I was his nursling once and choice delight,	Samson 633
His destin'd from the womb,	Samson 634
Under his special eie	Samson 636
Whom I by his appointment had provok't,	Samson 643
But with th' afflicted in his pangs thir sound	Samson 660
Harsh, and of dissonant mood from his complaint,	Samson 662
Secret refreshings, that repair his strength,	Samson 665
Temperst thy providence through his short course,	Samson 670
His labours, for thou canst, to peaceful end.	Samson 709
Her husband, how far urg'd his patience bears,	Samson 755
His vertue or weakness which way to assail:	Samson 756
On both his wings, one black, th' other white,	Samson 973
Bears greatest names in his wild aerie flight.	Samson 974
I leave him to his lot, and like my own.	Samson 996
To such a viper his most sacred trust	Samson 1001
A cleaving mischief, in his way to vertue	Samson 1039
With dotage, and his sense deprav'd	Samson 1042
Happy that house! his way to peace is smooth:	Samson 1049
Over his female in due awe,	Samson 1055
On his whole life, not sway'd	Samson 1059
Draws hitherward, I know him by his stride,	Samson 1067
The Giant *Harapha* of *Gath*, his look	Samson 1068
Haughty as is his pile high-built and proud.	Samson 1069
His habit carries peace, his brow defiance.	Samson 1073
Chor. His fraught we soon shall know, he now arrives.	Samson 1075
Go to his Temple, invocate his aid	Samson 1146
How highly it concerns his glory now	Samson 1148
Offering to combat thee his Champion bold,	Samson 1152
With th' utmost of his Godhead seconded:	Samson 1153
Quite from his people, and delivered up	Samson 1158
Of noble Warriour, so to stain his honour,	Samson 1166
Justly, yet despair not of his final pardon	Samson 1171
Whose ear is ever open; and his eye	Samson 1172
He will accept thee to defend his cause,	Samson 1179
Though by his blindness maim'd for high attempts,	Samson 1221
Chor. His Giantship is gone somewhat crest-fall'n,	Samson 1244
Sam. I dread him not, nor all his Giant-brood,	Samson 1247
His errand on the wicked, who surpris'd	Samson 1285
Making them each his own Deliverer,	Samson 1289
Some other tending, in his hand	Samson 1302
Comes on amain, speed in his look.	Samson 1304
By his habit I discern him now	Samson 1305
His message will be short and voluble.	Samson 1307
Chor. His manacles remark him, there he sits.	Samson 1309
Set God behind: which in his jealousie	Samson 1375
And for a life who will not change his purpose?	Samson 1406
To what may serve his glory best, & spread his name	Samson 1429
Rode up in flames after his message told	Samson 1433
He seems: supposing here to find his Son,	Samson 1443
With good success to work his liberty.	Samson 1454
That part most reverenc'd *Dagon* and his Priests,	Samson 1463
Man. His ransom, if my whole inheritance	Samson 1476
For his redemption all my Patrimony,	Samson 1482
Man. It shall be my delight to tend his eyes,	Samson 1490
And on his shoulders waving down those locks,	Samson 1493
His strength again to grow up with his hair	Samson 1496
Of faithful Souldiery, were not his purpose	Samson 1498
And since his strength with eye-sight was not lost,	Samson 1502
God will restore him eye-sight to his strength.	Samson 1503
Of his delivery, and thy joy thereon	Samson 1505
What if his eye-sight (for to *Israels* God	Samson 1527
He now be dealing dole among his foes,	Samson 1529
And over heaps of slaughter'd walk his way?	Samson 1530
For his people of old; what hinders now?	Samson 1533
Hath paid his ransom now and full discharge.	Samson 1573
Hopeful of his Delivery, which now proves	Samson 1575
What glorious hand gave *Samson* his deaths wound?	Samson 1581
Mess. Unwounded of his enemies he fell.	Samson 1582
Mess. By his own hands. *Man*. Self-violence? what cause	Samson 1584
Among his foes? *Mess*. Inevitable cause	Samson 1586
Upon thir heads and on his own he pull'd.	Samson 1589

His(*cont*)

Proof of his mighty strength in feats and games;	Samson 1602
I sorrow'd at his captive state, but minded	Samson 1603
Between the pillars; he his guide requested	Samson 1630
With both his arms on those two massie Pillars	Samson 1633
Felt in his arms, with head a while enclin'd,	Samson 1636
Or some great matter in his mind revolv'd.	Samson 1638
This utter'd, straining all his nerves he bow'd,	Samson 1646
In *Silo* his bright Sanctuary:	Samson 1674
His fierie vertue rouz'd	Samson 1690
His cloudless thunder bolted on thir heads.	Samson 1696
A life Heroic, on his Enemies	Samson 1711
Sok't in his enemies blood, and from the stream	Samson 1726
Home to his Fathers house: there will I build him	Samson 1733
With all his Trophies hung, and Acts enroll'd	Samson 1736
And from his memory inflame thir breasts	Samson 1739
Visit his Tomb with flowers, only bewailing	Samson 1742
His lot unfortunate in nuptial choice,	Samson 1743
Oft he seems to hide his face,	Samson 1749
And to his faithful Champion hath in place	Samson 1751
His uncontroulable intent,	Samson 1754
His servants he with new acquist	Samson 1755
Which he to grace his tributary gods	Mask 24
The greatest, and the best of all the main	Mask 28
Trinity ms 'maine' ←'his empire'	
He quarters to his blu-hair'd deities,	Mask 29
Has in his charge, with temper'd awe to guide	Mask 32
Where his fair off-spring nurs't in Princely lore,	Mask 34
Whoever tasted, lost his upright shape,	Mask 52
This Nymph that gaz'd upon his clustring locks,	Mask 54
With Ivy berries wreath'd, and his blithe youth,	Mask 55
Much like his Father, but his Mother more,	Mask 57
Who ripe, and frolick of his full grown age,	Mask 59
Excells his Mother at her mighty Art,	Mask 63
His orient liquor in a Crystal Glasse,	Mask 65
Who with his soft Pipe, and smooth-dittied Song,	Mask 86
And in this office of his Mountain watch,	Mask 89
His glowing Axle doth allay	Mask 96
And the slope Sun his upward beam	Mask 98
Of his Chamber in the East.	Mask 101
Whom thrift keeps up about his Country gear,	Mask 167
To testifie his hidd'n residence;	Mask 248
In his loose traces from the furrow came,	Mask 292
And the swink't hedger at his Supper sate;	Mask 293
Count the night watches to his feathery Dames,	Mask 347
What need a man forestall his date of grief,	Mask 362
line not in Trinity ms	
line not in Bridgewater ms	
He that has light within his own cleer brest	Mask 381
Himself is his own dungeon. 2. *Bro*. Tis most true	Mask 385
Bridgewater ms 'blaze in the summer solstice'	
Trinity ms 'himselfe is his owne dungeon' ←'blaze in the summer solstice'	
For who would rob a Hermit of his Weeds,	Mask 390
His few Books, or his Beads, or Maple Dish,	Mask 391
Or do his gray hairs any violence?	Mask 392
That breaks his magick chains at *curfeu* time,	Mask 435
Som roaving Robber calling to his fellows.	Mask 485
The huddling brook to hear his madrigal,	Mask 495
Slip't from the fold, or young Kid lost his dam,	Mask 498
Trinity ms 'his' ←'the' ←'his'	
Spir. O my lov'd masters heir, and his next joy,	Mask 501
Deep skill'd in all his mothers witcheries,	Mask 523
By sly enticement gives his banefull cup,	Mask 525
He and his monstrous rout are heard to howl	Mask 533
The aidless innocent Lady his wish't prey,	Mask 574
And force him to restore his purchase back,	Mask 607
Or drag him by the curls, to a foul death,	Mask 608
Trinity ms 'or drag him by the curls & cleave his scalpe'	
Bridgewater ms 'and cleave his scalpe'	
1637 'and cleave his scalpe'	
Curs'd as his life. *Spir*. Alas good ventrous youth,	Mask 609
1637 'Downe to the hipps'	
Bridgewater ms 'downe to the hipps'	
Trinity ms 'downe to the hips' ←'lowest hips' ←'hipps'	
He with his bare wand can unthred thy joynts,	Mask 614
And in requitall ope his leather'n scrip,	Mask 626
Treads on it daily with his clouted shoon,	Mask 635
line not in Bridgewater ms	
Enter'd the very lime-twigs of his spells,	Mask 646
Boldly assault the necromancers hall;	Mask 649
Trinity ms 'the' ←'his'	
And brandish't blade rush on him, break his glass,	Mask 651
But sease his wand, though he and his curst crew	Mask 653
That flames, and dances in his crystal bounds	Mask 673
Not half his riches known, and yet despis'd,	Mask 724
As a penurious niggard of his wealth,	Mask 726
His praise due paid, for swinish gluttony	Mask 776
Ne're looks to Heav'n amidst his gorgeous feast,	Mask 777
Cramms, and blasphemes his feeder. Shall I go on?	Mask 779
Arm his profane tongue with contemptuous words	Mask 781
line not in Bridgewater ms	
line not in Trinity ms	
O ye mistook, ye should have snatcht his wand	Mask 815
And bound him fast; without his rod revers't,	Mask 816
That had the Scepter from his father *Brute*.	Mask 828
That stay'd her flight with his cross-flowing course,	Mask 832
And gave her to his daughters to imbathe	Mask 837

His(*cont*)

Now the spell hath lost his hold;	Mask 919
His wish't presence, and beside	Mask 950
Where day never shuts his eye,	Mask 978
Of *Hesperus*, and his daughters three	Mask 982
Waxing well of his deep wound	Mask 1000
line not in Bridgewater ms	
Holds his dear *Psyche* sweet intrânc't	Mask 1005
line not in Bridgewater ms	
Make her his eternal Bride,	Mask 1008
line not in Bridgewater ms	
his uninchanted eye, & round the verge	Mask Tr. ms 10.10
his farre-extended armes till with steepe fall	Mask Tr. ms 10.13
halfe his wast flood the wide Atlantique fills	Mask Tr. ms 10.14
he may scratch his forehead. heere be brambles	Mask Tr. ms 17.57
& good heaven cast his best regard upon us	Mask Tr. ms 21.32
where grows the right-borne gold upon his native tree	Mask Tr. ms 27.08
Wher brooding darknes spreads his jealous wings,	Allegro 6
And Laughter holding both his sides.	Allegro 32
To hear the Lark begin his flight,	Allegro 41
From his watch-towre in the skies,	Allegro 43
Stoutly struts his Dames before,	Allegro 52
Wher the great Sun begins his state,	Allegro 60
And the Mower whets his sithe,	Allegro 66
And every Shepherd tells his tale	Allegro 67
To ern his Cream-bowle duly set,	Allegro 106
His shadowy Flale hath thresh'd the Corn	Allegro 108
Basks at the fire his hairy strength;	Allegro 112
Ere the first Cock his Mattin rings.	Allegro 114
Warble his native Wood-notes wilde,	Allegro 134
That *Orpheus* self may heave his head	Allegro 145
His half regain'd *Eurydice*.	Allegro 150
His daughter she (in *Saturns* raign,	Penseroso 25
That in trim Gardens takes his pleasure;	Penseroso 50
Might raise *Musaeus* from his bower,	Penseroso 104
When the gust hath blown his fill,	Penseroso 128
His flaring beams, me Goddes bring	Penseroso 132
Wave at his Wings in Airy stream,	Penseroso 148
Stole under Seas to meet his *Arethuse;*	Arcades 31
For *Lycidas* is dead, dead ere his prime	Lycidas 8
Young *Lycidas*, and hath not left his peer:	Lycidas 9
He must not flote upon his watry bear	Lycidas 12
Toward Heav'ns descent had slop'd his westering wheel.	Lycidas 31
His goary visage down the stream was sent,	Lycidas 62
They knew not of his story,	Lycidas 95
That not a blast was from his dungeon stray'd,	Lycidas 97
His Mantle hairy, and his Bonnet sedge,	Lycidas 104
He shook his Miter'd locks, and stern bespake,	Lycidas 112
Bid *Amaranthus* all his beauty shed,	Lycidas 149
And yet anon repairs his drooping head,	Lycidas 169
And tricks his beams, and with new spangled Ore,	Lycidas 170
With *Nectar* pure his oozy Lock's he laves,	Lycidas 175
And wipe the tears for ever from his eyes.	Lycidas 181
With eager thought warbling his *Dorick* lay:	Lycidas 189
At last he rose, and twitch'd his Mantle blew:	Lycidas 192
to write his owne woes on the vermeil graine	Lycidas Tr. ms 28.18
his goarie scalpe rowle downe the Thracian lee	Lycidas Tr. ms 29.61
And with his Father work us a perpetual peace.	Nativity 7
To welcom him to this his new abode,	Nativity 18
And lay it lowly at his blessed feet;	Nativity 25
From out his secret Altar toucht with hallow'd fire.	Nativity 28
His ready Harbinger,	Nativity 49
His raign of peace upon the earth began:	Nativity 63
The Sun himself with-held his wonted speed,	Nativity 79
And hid his head for shame,	Nativity 80
As his inferiour flame,	Nativity 81
Then his bright Throne, or burning Axletree could bear.	Nativity 84
His constellations set,	Nativity 121
The dreadfull Judge in middle Air shall spread his throne.	Nativity 164
Not half so far casts his usurped sway,	Nativity 170
And wrath to see his Kingdom fail,	Nativity 171
Swindges the scaly Horrour of his foulded tail.	Nativity 172
Apollo from his shrine	Nativity 176
While each peculiar power forgoes his wonted seat.	Nativity 196
The Libyc *Hammon* shrinks his horn,	Nativity 203
His burning Idol all of blackest hue,	Nativity 207
Within his sacred chest,	Nativity 217
Naught but profoundest Hell can be his shroud,	Nativity 218
The sable-stoled Sorcerers bear his worshipt Ark.	Nativity 220
The rayes of *Bethlehem* blind his dusky eyn;	Nativity 223
Our Babe to shew his Godhead true,	Nativity 227
Can in his swadling bands controul the damned crew.	Nativity 228
Pillows his chin upon an Orient wave,	Nativity 231
Each fetter'd Ghost slips to his severall grave,	Nativity 234
His praise and glory was in *Israel* known.	Psalm 114, 6
And sought to hide his froth-becurled head	Psalm 114, 8
Why turned *Jordan* toward his Crystall Fountains?	Psalm 114, 14
For his mercies ay endure,	Psalm 136, 3 etc.
Let us blaze his Name abroad,	Psalm 136, 5
O let us his praises tell,	Psalm 136, 9
That with his miracles doth make	Psalm 136, 13
That by his wisdom did create	Psalm 136, 17
That by his all-commanding might,	Psalm 136, 25
All the day long his cours to run.	Psalm 136, 30
He with his thunder-clasping hand,	Psalm 136, 37
He brought from thence his *Israel*.	Psalm 136, 42
The Tawny King with all his power.	Psalm 136, 54
His chosen people he did bless	Psalm 136, 57

His(*cont*)
He foild bold *Seon* and his host, Psalm 136, 65
With all his over-hardy crew. Psalm 136, 70
And to his servant *Israel*, Psalm 136, 73
His mighty Majesty and worth. Psalm 136, 90
That his mansion hath on high Psalm 136, 93
But kill'd alas, and then bewayl'd his fatal bliss. Fair Inf 7
For since grim Aquilo his charioter Fair Inf 8
He thought it toucht his Deitie full neer, Fair Inf 10
There ended was his quest, there ceast his care. Fair Inf 18
Down he descended from his Snow-soft chaire, Fair Inf 19
But all unwares with his cold-kind embrace Fair Inf 20
Whilome did slay his dearly-loved mate Fair Inf 24
To slake his wrath whom sin hath made our foe Fair Inf 66
In Heav'ns defiance mustering all his waves; Vacation 44
Are held with his melodious harmonie Vacation 51
O're all his Brethren he shall Reign as King, Vacation 75
Yet on his Brothers shall depend for Cloathing. Vacation 82
To find a Foe it shall not be his hap, Vacation 83
Yet shall he live in strife, and at his dore Vacation 85
Yea it shall be his natural property Vacation 87
His thirty Armes along the indented Meads, Vacation 94
He sov'ran Priest stooping his regall head Passion 15
That dropt with odorous oil down his fair eyes, Passion 16
His starry front low-rooft beneath the skies; Passion 18
Then lies him meekly down fast by his Brethrens side. Passion 21
His Godlike acts, and his temptations fierce, Passion 24
His Infancy to sease! Circum 14
Emptied his glory, ev'n to nakednes; Circum 20
Will pierce more neer his heart. Circum 28
To his celestial consort us unite, Musick 27
And in his Garland as he stood, Winchester 21
The haples Babe before his birth Winchester 31
What needs my *Shakespear* for his honour'd Bones, Shakespear 1
Or that his hallow'd reliques should be hid Shakespear 3
Here lies old *Hobson*, Death hath broke his girt, Carrier 1
1658 'hath his desire'
Had not his weekly cours of carriage fail'd; Carrier 10
And thinking now his journeys end was come, Carrier 12
And that he had tane up his latest Inne, Carrier 13
Shew'd him his room where he must lodge that night, Carrier 15
Pull'd off his Boots, and took away the light: Carrier 16
So hung his destiny never to rot Another 3
While he might still jogg on, and keep his trot, Another 4
Untill his revolution was at stay. Another 6
'Gainst old truth) motion number'd out his time; Another 8
His principles being ceast, he ended strait. Another 10
Rest that gives all men life, gave him his death, Another 11
Too long vacation hastned on his term. Another 14
line not in 1658 text
Nay, quoth he, on his swooning bed outstretch'd, Another 17
line not in 1640, 1657, 1658 texts
Ease was his chief disease, and to judge right, Another 21
line not in 1658 text
He di'd for heavines that his Cart went light, Another 22
line not in 1658 text
His leasure told him that his time was com, Another 23
line not in 1658 text
line not in 1658 text
And lack of load, made his life burdensom, Another 24
line not in 1658 text
That even to his last breath (ther be that say't) Another 25
line not in 1640, 1657, 1658 texts
But had his doings lasted as they were, Another 27
Obedient to the Moon he spent his date Another 29
line not in 1658 text
In cours reciprocal, and had his fate Another 30
line not in 1658 text
Yet (strange to think) his wain was his increase: Another 32
line not in 1658 text
His Letters are deliver'd all and gon, Another 33
line not in 1658 text
Whether the Muse, or Love call thee his mate, Sonnet 1, 13
Stoln on his wing my three and twentith yeer! Sonnet 7, 2
Thou, when the Bridegroom with his feastfull friends Sonnet 9, 12
So well your words his noble vertues praise, Sonnet 10, 12
Then his *Casella*, whom he woo'd to sing, Sonnet 13, 13
Trinity ms 'his' ←'old'
Hast reard Gods Trophies and his work pursu'd. Sonnet 16, 6
Either man's work or his own gifts, who best Sonnet 19, 10
Bear his milde yoak, they serve him best, his State Sonnet 19, 11
Is Kingly. Thousands at his bidding speed Sonnet 19, 12
Pronounc't and in his volumes taught our Lawes, Sonnet 21, 3
line not in Trinity ms
And with stiff Vowes renounc'd his Liturgie Forcers 2
Jehovahs Law is ever his delight, Psalm 1, 5
And in his Law he studies day and night. Psalm 1, 6
By watry streams, and in his season knows Psalm 1, 8
To yield his fruit, and his leaf shall not fall, Psalm 1, 9
Against the Lord and his Messiah dear Psalm 2, 5
Speak to them in his wrath, and in his fell Psalm 2, 10
If once his wrath take fire like fuel sere. Psalm 2, 27
And heard me from his holy mount. Psalm 3, 12
For in his faltring mouth unstable Psalm 5, 25
The Lord will own, and have me in his keeping. Psalm 6, 20
His Sword he whets, his Bow hath bended Psalm 7, 46
(His arrows purposely made he Psalm 7, 49
His mischief that due course doth keep, Psalm 7, 57

His(*cont*)
Turns on his head, and his ill trade Psalm 7, 58
Fall on his crown with ruine steep. Psalm 7, 60
According to his justice raise Psalm 7, 62
That bends his rage thy providence to oppose Psalm 8, 8
Scarce to be less then Gods, thou mad'st his lot, Psalm 8, 15
Thou hast put all under his lordly feet, Psalm 8, 18
I set his shoulder free; Psalm 81, 22
His hands from pots, *and mirie soyle* Psalm 81, 23
Mislik'd me for his choice. Psalm 81, 48
But *they, his People, should remain,* Psalm 81, 63
Among the gods on both his hands Psalm 82, 3
For to his people he speaks peace Psalm 85, 31
And to his Saints *full dear*, Psalm 85, 32
To his dear Saints he will speak peace, Psalm 85, 33
His Royal Harbinger, Psalm 85, 54
His footsteps cannot err. Psalm 85, 56
Is his foundation fast, Psalm 87, 2
There Seated in his Sanctuary, Psalm 87, 3
His Temple there is plac't. Psalm 87, 4
And all within his care. Psalm 87, 8
And to be short, at last his guid him brings Prose 2, 1
Who neither can nor will, may hold his peace; Prose 9, 4
But his owne house, and the whole neighbourhood Prose 10, 5
Sees his foule inside through his whited skin. Prose 10, 6

Hispahan
In *Hispahan*, or where the *Russian Ksar* Par Lost 11.394

Hiss
Brusht with the hiss of russling wings. As Bees Par Lost 1.768
ms 'hisse'
Of conflict; over head the dismal hiss Par Lost 6.212
A dismal universal hiss, the sound Par Lost 10.508
But hiss for hiss returnd with forked tongue Par Lost 10.518
And the dire hiss renew'd, and the dire form Par Lost 10.543
Turnd to exploding hiss, triumph to shame Par Lost 10.546
And worn with Famin, long and ceasless hiss, Par Lost 10.573

Hissing
Of hissing through the Hall, thick swarming now Par Lost 10.522

Hist
And the mute Silence hist along, Penseroso 55

Historian
Hystorian, who thus largely hast allayd Par Lost 8.7

Hit
That whom they hit, none on thir feet might stand, Par Lost 6.592
Of harmony in tones and numbers hit Par Reg 4.255
Harder to hit, Samson 1014
La. How easie my misfortune is to hit! Mask 286
To hit the Sense of human sight; Penseroso 14
If my inferior hand or voice could hit Arcades 77

Hither
Who hates me, and hath hither thrust me down Par Lost 2.857
Up hither like Aereal vapours flew Par Lost 3.445
Dissolvd on Earth, fleet hither, and in vain, Par Lost 3.457
Hither of ill-joynd Sons and Daughters born Par Lost 3.463
The more it seems excess, that led thee hither Par Lost 3.698
Look downward on that Globe whose hither side Par Lost 3.722
Such where ye find, seise fast, and hither bring. Par Lost 4.796
Or not, who ask what boldness brought him hither Par Lost 4.908
Haste hither *Eve*, and worth thy sight behold Par Lost 5.308
Up hither, under long obedience tri'd, Par Lost 7.159
Hither as to thir Fountain other Starrs Par Lost 7.364
Up hither, from among the Trees appeer'd Par Lost 8.313
Not hither summond, since they cannot change Par Lost 8.347
What hither brought us, hate, not love, nor hope Par Lost 9.475
Serpent, we might have spar'd our coming hither, Par Lost 9.647
All generations, and had hither come Par Lost 11.344
But on the hether side a different sort Par Lost 11.574
To whom the Son of God. Who brought me hither Par Reg 1.335
Thy coming hither, though I know thy scope, Par Reg 1.494
To what end I have brought thee hither and shewn Par Reg 3.350
My Son now Captive, hither hath inform'd Samson 335
That malice not repentance brought thee hither, Samson 821
Comes he in peace? what wind hath blown him hither Samson 1070
Man. Peace with you brethren; my inducement hither Samson 1445
A little stay will bring some notice hither, Samson 1536
And to our wish I see one hither speeding, Samson 1539
And call the Vales, and bid them hither cast Lycidas 134
Throw hither all your quaint enameld eyes, Lycidas 139
The Timbrel hither bring Psalm 81, 6

Hitherto
Warrs, hitherto the onely Argument Par Lost 9.28
To Sapience, hitherto obscur'd, infam'd, Par Lost 9.797
Hitherto, Lords, what your commands impos'd Samson 1640

Hitherward
Hitherward bent (who could have thought2) escap'd Par Lost 4.794
Draws hitherward, I know him by his stride, Samson 1067

Hitting
Hitting thy aged ear should pierce too deep. Samson 1568

Hive
Pour forth thir populous youth about the Hive Par Lost 1.770
ms 'hive'

Hoar
From the side of som Hoar Hill, Allegro 55
On old *Lycaeus* or *Cyllene* hoar, Arcades 98
Trinity ms 'hoare'

Hoarded
Beauty is natures coyn, must not be hoorded, Mask 739
line not in Bridgewater ms

Hoarse
Had rous'd the Sea, now with hoarse cadence lull — Par Lost 2.287
Calabria from the hoarce *Trinacrian* shore: — Par Lost 2.661
Hoarce murmur echo'd to his words applause — Par Lost 5.873
To hoarce or mute, though fall'n on evil dayes, — Par Lost 7.25
Not understood, till hoarse, and all in rage, — Par Lost 12.58
Hoary
The secrets of the hoarie deep, a dark — Par Lost 2.891
Seed time and Harvest, Heat and hoary Frost — Par Lost 11.899
By hoary *Nereus* wrincled look, — Mask 871
Trinity ms 'hoarie'
1637 'hoarie'
Bridgewater ms 'hoarie'
Hobson
Here lies old *Hobson*, Death hath broke his girt, — Carrier 1
Hobson has supt, and's newly gon to bed. — Carrier 18
Here lieth one who did most truly prove, — Another 1
1640, 1657 'Here *Hobson* lyes'
Hog
Or Ounce, or Tiger, Hog, or bearded Goat, — Mask 71
Bridgewater ms 'Hogg'
Trinity ms 'hog'
Hogs
But this is got by casting Pearl to Hoggs; — Sonnet 12, 8
Trinity ms 'hogs'
Hold
For this Infernal Pit shall never hold — Par Lost 1.657
For since no deep within her gulf can hold — Par Lost 2.12
To their defence who hold it: here perhaps — Par Lost 2.362
And *Chaos*, Ancestors of Nature, hold — Par Lost 2.895
Wide interrupt can hold; so bent he seems — Par Lost 3.84
Translated Saints, or middle Spirits hold — Par Lost 3.461
Divided Empire with Heav'ns King I hold — Par Lost 4.111
Gravely in doubt whether to hold them wise — Par Lost 4.907
She tempers dulcet creams, nor these to hold — Par Lost 5.347
Danc'd hand in hand. A while discourse they hold; — Par Lost 5.395
Hold, as you yours, while our obedience holds; — Par Lost 5.537
We mean to hold what anciently we claim — Par Lost 5.723
From his strong hold of Heav'n high over-rul'd — Par Lost 6.228
Subdue it, and throughout Dominion hold — Par Lost 7.532
How have I then with whom to hold converse — Par Lost 8.408
Devolv'd; though should I hold my peace, yet thou — Par Lost 10.135
Hell could no longer hold us in her bounds, — Par Lost 10.365
My hold of this new Kingdom all depends, — Par Lost 10.406
Thy terms too hard, by which I was to hold — Par Lost 10.751
Said th' Angel, who should better hold his place — Par Lost 11.635
Shall hold thir course, till fire purge all things new, — Par Lost 11.900
Dominion absolute; that right we hold — Par Lost 12.68
So may we hold our place and these mild seats — Par Reg 2.125
Easily done, and hold them all of me; — Par Reg 4.168
Or they with thee hold conversation meet? — Par Reg 4.232
E're thou of *Israel*'s Scepter get fast hold; — Par Reg 4.480
At least might seem to hold all power of thee, — Par Reg 4.494
This day a solemn Feast the people hold — Samson 12
Courted by all the winds that hold them play, — Samson 719
How to endear, and hold thee to me firmest: — Samson 796
Against thee but safe custody, and hold: — Samson 802
Which long shall not with-hold mee from thy head, — Samson 1125
Up to the highth, whether to hold or break; — Samson 1349
Find courage to lay hold on this occasion, — Samson 1716
Now the top of Heav'n doth hold, — Mask 94
And give resounding grace to all Heav'ns Harmonies. — Mask 243
Trinity ms 'give resounding grace' ← 'hold a counterpoint'
Bridgewater ms 'hould a Counterpointe'
B.M. ms 'hold a Counter point'
Which erring men call Chance, this I hold firm, — Mask 588
Bridgewater ms 'hould'
Now the spell hath lost his hold; — Mask 919
In weeds of Peace high triumphs hold, — Allegro 120
What Worlds, or what vast Regions hold — Penseroso 90
And sing to those that hold the vital shears, — Arcades 65
Blind mouthes! that scarce themselves know how to hold — Lycidas 119
Looks toward *Namancos* and *Bayona*'s hold; — Lycidas 162
Could hold all Heav'n and Earth in happier union. — Nativity 108
A Law of Jacobs God, *to hold* — Psalm 81, 15
O God hold not thy peace, — Psalm 83, 2
On whom the grave *hath hold*, — Psalm 88, 46
Who neither can nor will, may hold his peace; — Prose 9, 4
Holdest
By this repulse receiv'd, and hold'st in Hell — Par Reg 4.623
Holding
The clasping charm, and thaw the numming spell, — Mask 853
Trinity ms 'thaw the numming' ← 'melt each' ← 'secret holding'
And Laughter holding both his sides. — Allegro 32
Holds
Sole reigning holds the Tyranny of Heav'n. — Par Lost 1.124
Firm concord holds, men onely disagree — Par Lost 2.497
In whirlwind; Hell scarce holds the wilde uproar. — Par Lost 2.541
And like a weather-beaten Vessel holds — Par Lost 2.1043
Her chrystal mirror holds, unite thir streams. — Par Lost 4.263
Her office holds; of all external things, — Par Lost 5.103
Can turn, or holds it possible to turn — Par Lost 5.441
Hold, as you yours, while our obedience holds; — Par Lost 5.537
With thousand lesser Lights dividual holds, — Par Lost 7.382
Holds on the same, from Woman to begin. — Par Lost 11.633
That Empire, under his dominion holds — Par Reg 3.296
From thy Demoniac holds, possession foul, — Par Reg 4.628

Holds*(cont)*
Sam. No man with-holds thee, nothing from thy hand — Samson 1233
Sam. Where outward force constrains, the sentence holds — Samson 1369
Holds his dear *Psyche* sweet intranc't — Mask 1005
line not in Bridgewater ms
Hole
Could once have mov'd; then in the key-hole turns — Par Lost 2.876
From her cabin'd loop hole peep, — Mask 140
1673 'loop-hole'
Trinity ms 'loopehole'
Bridgewater ms 'loopehole'
Though a rush Candle from the wicker hole — Mask 338
Holiday
Till next Sun-shine holiday, — Mask 959
B.M. ms 'Holiday'
Trinity ms 'Holyday'
On a Sunshine Holyday, — Allegro 98
Holier
Till we com to holier ground, — Mask 943
1637 'holyer'
Trinity ms 'holyer'
Holies
The Holiest of Holies, and his Saints; — Par Reg 4.349
Holiest
Or think thee unbefitting holiest place, — Par Lost 4.759
First, Highest, Holiest, Best, thou alwayes seekst — Par Lost 6.724
Sole but with holiest Meditations fed, — Par Reg 2.110
The Holiest of Holies, and his Saints; — Par Reg 4.349
Hollow
He call'd so loud, that all the hollow Deep — Par Lost 1.314
By strange conveyance fill'd each hollow nook, — Par Lost 1.707
But all was false and hollow; though his Tongue — Par Lost 2.112
Th' Assembly, as when hollow Rocks retain — Par Lost 2.285
By Haralds voice explain'd: the hollow Abyss — Par Lost 2.518
Born through the hollow dark assaults his eare — Par Lost 2.953
Which into hallow Engins long and round — Par Lost 6.484
Approaching gross and huge; in hollow Cube — Par Lost 6.552
Portending hollow truce; at each behind — Par Lost 6.578
The hollow Universal Orb they fill'd, — Par Lost 7.257
Down sunk a hollow bottom broad and deep, — Par Lost 7.289
So many hollow complements and lies, — Par Reg 4.124
this dusky hollow is a paradise & heaven gates ore my head — Mask Tr. ms 13.44
Beneath the hollow round — Nativity 102
With hollow shreik the steep of *Delphos* leaving. — Nativity 178
The drift of hollow states hard to be spelld, — Sonnet 17, 6
With pale and hollow eyes? — Psalm 88, 44
Hollowed
Or hollow'd bodies made of Oak or Firr — Par Lost 6.574
Holocaust
And lay e're while a Holocaust, — Samson 1702
Holy
His holy Rites, and solemn Feasts profan'd, — Par Lost 1.390
Then aught divine or holy else enjoy'd — Par Lost 1.683
Hail holy Light, ofspring of Heav'n first-born, — Par Lost 3.1
To *Beersaba*, where the *Holy Land* — Par Lost 3.536
Nor holy rapture wanted they to praise — Par Lost 5.147
Bestowd, the holy salutation us'd — Par Lost 5.386
Holy Memorials, acts of Zeale and Love — Par Lost 5.593
My onely Son, and on this holy Hill — Par Lost 5.604
Abstrusest thoughts, from forth his holy Mount — Par Lost 5.712
To trouble Holy Rest; Heav'n casts thee out — Par Lost 6.272
Threatn'd, nor from the Holie One of Heav'n — Par Lost 6.359
Farr separate, circling thy holy Mount — Par Lost 6.743
Mov'd the Creator in his holy Rest — Par Lost 7.91
Forerunning Night; when at the holy mount — Par Lost 7.584
But not in silence holy kept; the Harp — Par Lost 7.594
Holy and just: thrice happie if they know — Par Lost 7.631
Holy, divine, good, amiable, or sweet! — Par Lost 9.899
Holie and pure, conformitie divine. — Par Lost 11.606
His holy Eyes; resolving from thenceforth — Par Lost 12.109
The holy One with mortal Men to dwell: — Par Lost 12.248
Thir Citie, his Temple, and his holy Ark — Par Lost 12.340
The Holy Ghost, and the power of the highest — Par Reg 1.139
His holy Meditations thus persu'd. — Par Reg 1.195
Thy Father, who is holy, wise and pure, — Par Reg 1.486
About his Altar, handling holy things, — Par Reg 1.489
With others though in Holy Writ not nam'd, — Par Reg 2.8
The holy City lifted high her Towers, — Par Reg 4.545
Ordain'd thy nurture holy, as of a Plant; — Samson 362
But I Gods counsel have not kept, his holy secret — Samson 497
By prostituting holy things to Idols; — Samson 1358
Chor. Go, and the Holy One — Samson 1427
Sure somthing holy lodges in that brest, — Mask 246
Bridgewater ms 'holye'
And holy dictate of spare Temperance: — Mask 767
Trinity ms 'holie'
Till next Sun-shine holiday, — Mask 959
Bridgewater ms 'holy daye'
Trinity ms 'Holyday'
On a Sunshine Holyday, — Allegro 98
But hail thou Goddes, sage and holy, — Penseroso 11
There held in holy passion still, — Penseroso 41
For so the holy sages once did sing, — Nativity 5
For if such holy Song — Nativity 133
And on the holy Hearth, — Nativity 190
Now sits not girt with Tapers holy shine, — Nativity 202
There doth my soul in holy vision sit — Passion 41
Hymns devout and holy Psalms — Musick 15

Holy(*cont*)
Trinity ms 'holy' ←'holie' ←'sacred'
in high misterious happie spousall meet — Musick Tr. ms 4.06
'happie' ←'holie'
On *Sion* my holi' hill. A firm decree — Psalm 2, 13
And heard me from his holy mount. — Psalm 3, 12
Will towards thy holy temple worship low — Psalm 5, 20
Among the holy Mountains *high* — Psalm 87, 1

Holy-days
No less the people on thir Holy-days — Samson 1421

Homage
Thee homage, and acknowledge thee thir Lord: — Par Reg 2.376

Home
Terror of Heav'n, though fall'n; intend at home, — Par Lost 2.457
While here shall be our home, what best may ease — Par Lost 2.458
Of hard contents, and full of force urg'd home, — Par Lost 6.622
In dust, our final rest and native home. — Par Lost 10.1085
Home to my Brest, and to my memorie — Par Lost 11.154
Nations, and bring home spoils with infinite — Par Lost 11.692
From *Egypt* home return'd, in *Nazareth* — Par Reg 2.79
Bred up in poverty and streights at home; — Par Reg 2.415
At home, scarce view'd the *Gallilean* Towns, — Par Reg 3.233
These here revolve, or, as thou lik'st, at home, — Par Reg 4.281
Home to his Mothers house private return'd. — Par Reg 4.639
Home to thy countrey and his sacred house, — Samson 518
Better at home lie bed-rid, not only idle, — Samson 579
While I at home sate full of cares and fears — Samson 805
Fearless at home of partners in my love. — Samson 810
At home in leisure and domestic ease, — Samson 917
Either at home, or through the high street passing, — Samson 1458
Home to his Fathers house: there will I build him — Samson 1733
And all their friends, and native home forget — Mask 76
It is for homely features to keep home, — Mask 748
line not in Bridgewater ms
us of our selves & native woes beguile — Musick Tr. ms 4.08
'native' ←'home bred' ←'home-bred'
But lately finding him so long at home, — Carrier 11
Victory home, though new rebellions raise — Sonnet 15, 6
And home they fly from round the Coasts — Psalm 84, 15

Home-bred
us of our selves & native woes beguile — Musick Tr. ms 4.08
'native' ←'home bred' ←'home-bred'

Home-felt
But such a sacred, and home-felt delight, — Mask 262
Bridgewater ms 'homefelt'
Trinity ms 'home felt'

Homely
No homely morsels, and whatever thing — Par Lost 10.605
It is for homely features to keep home, — Mask 748
line not in Bridgewater ms
To tend the homely slighted Shepherds trade, — Lycidas 65

Homer
Blind *Melesigenes* thence *Homer* call'd, — Par Reg 4.259

Homeward
Homeward with flying march where we possess — Par Lost 5.688
Homeward returning. High in Front advanc't, — Par Lost 12.632
Look homeward Angel now, and melt with ruth. — Lycidas 163

Homicide
Of *Moloch* homicide, lust hard by hate; — Par Lost 1.417

Honest
Honest and lawful to deserve my food — Samson 1366
And trust thy honest offer'd courtesie, — Mask 322

Honesty
'Twill not restore the truth and honesty — Mask 691
Trinity ms 'honestie'
Bridgewater ms 'honestie'
1637 'honestie'

Honey
With Honey stor'd: the rest are numberless, — Par Lost 7.492
With Honey *for their Meat*. — Psalm 81, 68

Honeyed
The bait of honied words; a rougher tongue — Samson 1066
While the Bee with Honied thie, — Penseroso 142
That on the green terf suck the honied showres, — Lycidas 140

Honeysuckle
With flaunting Hony-suckle, and began — Mask 545
Bridgewater ms 'hony sucle'
Trinity ms 'honiesuckle'
1637 'hony-suckle'

Honour
His mighty Standard; that proud honour claim'd — Par Lost 1.533
Of hazard as of honour, due alike — Par Lost 2.453
Adore the Son, and honour him as mee. — Par Lost 3.343
Like honour to obtain, and as his Eye — Par Lost 3.660
Where honour due and reverence none neglects, — Par Lost 3.738
Godlike erect, with native Honour clad — Par Lost 4.289
Of natures works, honor dishonorable, — Par Lost 4.314
Honour and Empire with revenge enlarg'd, — Par Lost 4.390
In honour to the Worlds great Author rise, — Par Lost 5.188
And to his message high in honour rise; — Par Lost 5.289
Abundance, fit to honour and receive — Par Lost 5.315
To want, and honour these, voutsafe with us — Par Lost 5.365
Thy favour, in this honour done to man, — Par Lost 5.462
Shall bend the knee, and in that honour due — Par Lost 5.817
His Laws our Laws, all honour to him done — Par Lost 5.844
Honour, Dominion, Glorie, and renowne, — Par Lost 6.422
To honour his Anointed Son aveng'd — Par Lost 6.676
Such pairs, in Love and mutual Honour joyn'd? — Par Lost 8.58

Honour(*cont*)
I follow'd her, she what was Honour knew, — Par Lost 8.508
So awful, that with honour thou maist love — Par Lost 8.577
By us? who rather double honour gaine — Par Lost 9.332
And honour from about them, naked left — Par Lost 9.1057
Which leaves us naked thus, of Honour void, — Par Lost 9.1074
Womans domestic honour and chief praise; — Par Lost 11.617
To do him honour as their King; all come, — Par Reg 1.75
To honour thee with Incense, Myrrh, and Gold, — Par Reg 1.251
O what avails me now that honour high — Par Reg 2.66
I look't for some great change; to Honour? no, — Par Reg 2.86
Of honour, wealth, high fare, aim'd not beyond — Par Reg 2.202
Of worth, of honour, glory, and popular praise; — Par Reg 2.227
With honour, only deign to sit and eat. — Par Reg 2.336
Money brings Honour, Friends, Conquest, and Realms; — Par Reg 2.422
His Honour, Vertue, Merit and chief Praise, — Par Reg 2.464
Who names not now with honour patient *Job?* — Par Reg 3.95
From Nations far and nigh; what honour that, — Par Reg 4.122
Rather more honour left and more esteem; — Par Reg 4.207
Since neither wealth, nor honour, arms nor arts, — Par Reg 4.368
Be it but for honours sake of former deeds. — Samson 372
To Honour and Religion! servil mind — Samson 412
That I this honour, I this pomp have brought — Samson 449
The public marks of honour and reward — Samson 992
The highest name for valiant Acts, that honour — Samson 1101
Of noble Warriour, so to stain his honour, — Samson 1166
Har. Fair honour that thou dost thy God, in trusting — Samson 1178
The righteous and all such as honour Truth; — Samson 1276
To honour this great Feast, and great Assembly; — Samson 1315
Vaunting my strength in honour to thir *Dagon?* — Samson 1360
Honour hath left, and freedom, let but them — Samson 1715
To keep my life and honour unassail'd. — Mask 220
line not in Bridgewater ms
Listen for dear honours sake, — Mask 864
Bridgewater ms 'honors'
B.M. ms 'Honours'
And if I give thee honour due, — Allegro 37
I see bright honour sparkle through your eyes, — Arcades 27
Was all in honour and devotion ment — Arcades 35
Have thou the honour first, thy Lord to greet, — Nativity 26
Summers chief honour if thou hadst out-lasted, — Fair Inf 3
If ever deed of honour did thee please, — Sonnet 8, 3
To honour thee, the Priest of *Phoebus* Quire — Sonnet 13, 10
With honour and with state thou hast him crown'd. — Psalm 8, 16
In honour bend thy knee. — Psalm 81, 40
And till they yield thee honour due, — Psalm 83, 59
Thee honour, and adore — Psalm 86, 42

Honourable
How honourable, how glorious to entrap — Samson 855
Sam. Such usage as your honourable Lords — Samson 1108

Honoured
High honourd sits? Go therfore mighty Powers, — Par Lost 2.456
The Author not impair'd, but honourd more? — Par Lost 5.73
Honourd by his great Father, and proclaimd — Par Lost 5.663
Hath honourd me according to his will. — Par Lost 6.816
For God we see hath honour'd thee, and set — Par Lost 8.227
Thy condescension, and shall be honour'd ever — Par Lost 8.649
Of *Jordan* honour'd so, and call'd thee Son — Par Reg 1.329
Lov'd, honour'd, fear'd me, thou alone could hate me — Samson 939
Of my most honour'd Lady, your dear sister. — Mask 564
Bridgewater ms 'honor'd'
In hard besetting need, this will I try — Mask 857
O Fountain *Arethuse*, and thou honour'd floud, — Lycidas 85
Trinity ms 'honour'd' ←'fam'd' ←'smooth'
The honour'd Wife of *Winchester*, — Winchester 2
What needs my *Shakespear* for his honour'd Bones, — Shakespear 1
1632 'honor'd'
1640 'honoured'
And to possess them, Honour'd *Margaret*. — Sonnet 10, 14
Trinity ms 'Honourd'

Honourest
Thou honour'st Verse, and Verse must send her wing — Sonnet 13, 9
Trinity ms 'honourst'

Honouring
Thy cherishing, thy honouring, and thy love, — Par Lost 8.569

Honours
With what may be devis'd of honours new — Par Lost 5.780
Not more; for Honours, Riches, Kingdoms, Glory — Par Reg 4.536

Hooded
They left me then, when the gray-hooded Eev'n — Mask 188
Trinity ms 'gray-hoodded'
line not in Bridgewater ms

Hoods
Cowles, Hoods and Habits with thir wearers tost — Par Lost 3.490

Hook
And the *Carpathian* wisards hook, — Mask 872
Bridgewater ms 'hooke'
Trinity ms 'hooke'
1637 'hooke'
A Sheep-hook, or have learn'd ought els the least — Lycidas 120
Trinity ms 'sheephooke'
1638 'sheephook'

Hooked
The hooked Chariot stood — Nativity 56

Hope
And rest can never dwell, hope never comes — Par Lost 1.66
ms 'Hope'
United thoughts and counsels, equal hope — Par Lost 1.88

Hope(*cont*)
We may with more successful hope resolve   Par Lost 1.120
What reinforcement we may gain from Hope,   Par Lost 1.190
ms 'hope'
Of hope in fears and dangers, heard so oft   Par Lost 1.275
Thus high uplifted beyond hope, aspires   Par Lost 2.7
Must exercise us without hope of end   Par Lost 2.89
Victorious. Thus repuls'd, our final hope   Par Lost 2.142
Besides what hope the never-ending flight   Par Lost 2.221
May hope when everlasting Fate shall yeild   Par Lost 2.232
The former vain to hope argues as vain   Par Lost 2.234
The weight of all and our last hope relies.   Par Lost 2.416
Of Creatures rational, though under hope   Par Lost 2.498
By false presumptuous hope, the ranged powers   Par Lost 2.522
Fallacious hope, or arm th' obdured brest   Par Lost 2.568
His deadly arrow; neither vainly hope   Par Lost 2.811
Glad was the Spirit impure as now in hope   Par Lost 3.630
Then happie; no unbounded hope had rais'd   Par Lost 4.60
All hope excluded thus, behold in stead   Par Lost 4.105
So farwel Hope, and with Hope farwel Fear,   Par Lost 4.108
Beyond the *Cape of Hope*, and now are past   Par Lost 4.160
Farthest from pain, where thou mightst hope to change   Par Lost 4.892
Fame is not silent, here in hope to find   Par Lost 4.938
Heav'ns awful Monarch? wherefore but in hope   Par Lost 4.960
No spot or blame behind: Which gives me hope   Par Lost 5.119
Proud, art thou met? thy hope was to have reacht   Par Lost 6.131
That thou shouldst hope, imperious, and with threats   Par Lost 6.287
Enlightn'd, and thir languisht hope reviv'd.   Par Lost 6.497
Insensate, hope conceiving from despair.   Par Lost 6.787
To ask, nor let thine own inventions hope   Par Lost 7.121
Fond, were it not in hope of thy reply: Par Lost 8.209
When out of hope, behold her, not farr off,   Par Lost 8.481
Nor hope to be my self less miserable   Par Lost 9.126
Watches, no doubt, with greedy hope to find   Par Lost 9.257
Eve separate, he wish'd, but not with hope   Par Lost 9.422
Beyond his hope, *Eve* separate he spies,   Par Lost 9.424
What hither brought us, hate, not love, nor hope   Par Lost 9.475
Of Paradise for Hell, hope here to taste   Par Lost 9.476
To mischief swift. Hope elevates, and joy   Par Lost 9.633
Successful beyond hope, to lead ye forth   Par Lost 10.463
And what thou fearst, alike destroyes all hope   Par Lost 10.838
And with desire to languish without hope,   Par Lost 10.995
That cuts us off from hope, and savours onely   Par Lost 10.1043
Strength added from above, new hope to spring   Par Lost 11.138
Fit haunt of Gods? where I had hope to spend,   Par Lost 11.271
Incessant I could hope to change the will   Par Lost 11.308
With vows, as thir chief good, and final hope.   Par Lost 11.493
Much better seems this Vision, and more hope   Par Lost 11.599
Wandring that watrie Desert: I had hope   Par Lost 11.779
Of utmost hope! now clear I understand   Par Lost 12.376
Of wisedome; hope no higher, though all the Starrs   Par Lost 12.576
Induces best to hope of like success.   Par Reg 1.105
Alas, from what high hope to what relapse   Par Reg 2.30
Soon we shall see our hope, our joy return.   Par Reg 2.57
Thus they out of their plaints new hope resume   Par Reg 2.58
Enerve, and with voluptuous hope dissolve,   Par Reg 2.165
Which way or from what hope dost thou aspire   Par Reg 2.417
Let that come when it comes; all hope is lost   Par Reg 3.204
For where no hope is left, is left no fear;   Par Reg 3.206
Willingly I could flye, and hope thy raign,   Par Reg 3.216
Samaritan or *Jew;* how could'st thou hope   Par Reg 3.359
Discover'd in his fraud, thrown from his hope,   Par Reg 4.3
Without all hope of day!   Samson 82
As one past hope, abandon'd,   Samson 120
This only hope relieves me, that the strife   Samson 460
Man. With cause this hope relieves thee, and these words   Samson 472
Nor am I in the list of them that hope;   Samson 647
My love how couldst thou hope, who tookst the way   Samson 838
To give ye part with me what hope I have   Samson 1453
Cho. That hope would much rejoyce us to partake   Samson 1455
Yet Hope would fain subscribe, and tempts Belief.   Samson 1535
Man. The worst indeed, O all my hope's defeated   Samson 1571
O welcom pure-ey'd Faith, white-handed Hope,   Mask 213
line not in Bridgewater ms
(Not being in danger, as I trust she is not)   Mask 370
Bridgewater ms 'as I hope'
And tell me it is safe, as bid me hope   Mask 400
Trinity ms 'hope' ←'thinke'
Yet where an equall poise of hope and fear   Mask 410
Trinity ms 'hope' ←'hopes'
That I encline to hope, rather then fear,   Mask 412
But the fair Guerdon when we hope to find,   Lycidas 73
And now with second hope she goes,   Winchester 25
Thou with fresh hope the Lovers heart dost fill,   Sonnet 1, 3
And Hope that reaps not shame. Therefore be sure   Sonnet 9, 11
Of heart or hope; but still bear vp and steer   Sonnet 22, 8
1694 'Hope'
But we do hope to find out all your tricks,   Forcers 13
Impudent whoore, where hast thou plac'd thy hope?   Prose 3, 3

Hoped
Down from th' Ecliptic, sped with hop'd success,   Par Lost 3.740
Joyless triumphals of his hop't success,   Par Reg 4.578

Hopeful
Least on the threshing floore his hopeful sheaves   Par Lost 4.984
Of new acceptance, hopeful to regaine   Par Lost 10.972
Hopeful and cheerful, in thy blood will reigne   Par Lost 11.543
Hopeful of his Delivery, which now proves   Samson 1575

Hopeless
Ages of hopeless end; this would be worse.   Par Lost 2.186
Hopeless to circumvent us joynd, where each   Par Lost 9.259
Hopeless are all my evils, all remediless;   Samson 648
Foretell my hopeles doom in som Grove ny: Sonnet 1, 10

Hopes
By mee, have lost our hopes. But he who reigns   Par Lost 1.637
Built thir fond hopes of Glorie or lasting fame,   Par Lost 3.449
Vaine hopes, vaine aimes, inordinate desires   Par Lost 4.808
Augmented, op'nd Eyes, new Hopes, new Joyes,   Par Lost 9.985
To better hopes his more attentive minde   Par Lost 10.1011
All mortals I excell'd, and great in hopes   Samson 523
My hopes all flat, nature within me seems   Samson 595
Chor. Thy hopes are not ill founded nor seem vain   Samson 1504
Hopes thee; of flattering gales   Horace 11

Hoping
Surceas'd, and glad as hoping here to end   Par Lost 6.258
Hee fled, not hoping to escape, but shun   Par Lost 10.339

Horeb
Of *Oreb*, or of *Sinai*, didst inspire   Par Lost 1.7
ms 'Oreb'
The Calf in *Oreb:* and the Rebel King   Par Lost 1.484
ms 'Oreb'
His Trumpet, heard in *Oreb* since perhaps   Par Lost 11.74

Horizon
Beyond th' *Horizon;* then from Pole to Pole   Par Lost 3.560
Farr in th' Horizon to the North appeer'd   Par Lost 6.79
Regent of Day, and all th' Horizon round   Par Lost 7.371
Nights Hemisphere had veild the Horizon round: Par Lost 9.52
Had rounded still th' *Horizon*, and not known   Par Lost 10.684
To this Horizon is my *Phoebus* bound,   Passion 23

Horizontal
Looks through the Horizontal misty Air   Par Lost 1.595
ms 'horizontal'

Horn
With fruits and flowers from *Amalthea*'s horn,   Par Reg 2.356
Nor wanted clouds of foot, nor on each horn,   Par Reg 3.327
Oft list'ning how the Hounds and horn,   Allegro 53
1673 'Horn'
Awakes the slumbring leaves, or tasseld horn   Arcades 57
What time the Gray-fly winds her sultry horn,   Lycidas 28
Trinity ms 'horne'
The Libyc *Hammon* shrinks his horn,   Nativity 203
'Gainst them that rais'd thee dost thou lift thy horn,   Prose 3, 2

Horned
Cerastes hornd, *Hydrus*, and *Ellops* drear,   Par Lost 10.525
Out of his place, pushd by the horned floud,   Par Lost 11.831
The horned Moon to shine by night,   Psalm 136, 33

Hornets
Of Hornets arm'd, no sooner found alone,   Samson 20

Horns
Astarte, Queen of Heav'n, with crescent Horns;   Par Lost 1.439
ms 'horns'
Turnd fierie red, sharpning in mooned hornes   Par Lost 4.978
And hence the Morning Planet guilds her horns;   Par Lost 7.366
Retires, or *Bactrian* Sophi from the hornes   Par Lost 10.433

Horny
And saw the Ravens with their horny beaks   Par Reg 2.267

Horonaim
And *Horonaim*, *Seons* Realm, beyond   Par Lost 1.409
1667 '*Heronaim*', 1668 errata '*Horonaim*'
ms 'Horonaim'
1669 errata '*Honoraim*'

Horrent
With bright imblazonrie, and horrent Arms.   Par Lost 2.513

Horrible
A Dungeon horrible, on all sides round   Par Lost 1.61
In horrible destruction laid thus low,   Par Lost 1.137
Grinnd horrible a gastly smile, to hear   Par Lost 2.846
Horrible discord, and the madding Wheeles   Par Lost 6.210
Of horrible confusion, over which   Par Lost 10.472
Horrid to think, how horrible to feel!   Par Lost 11.465
With horrible convulsion to and fro,   Samson 1649

Horribly
Horribly loud unlike the former shout.   Samson 1510

Horrid
To mortal men, he with his horrid crew   Par Lost 1.51
Breaking the horrid silence thus began.   Par Lost 1.83
In billows, leave i' th' midst a horrid Vale.   Par Lost 1.224
First *Moloch*, horrid King besmear'd with blood   Par Lost 1.392
Advanc't in view, they stand, a horrid Front   Par Lost 1.563
Turning our Tortures into horrid Arms   Par Lost 2.63
Hell bounds high reaching to the horrid Roof,   Par Lost 2.644
With horrid strides, Hell trembled as he strode.   Par Lost 2.676
In th' Artick Sky, and from his horrid hair   Par Lost 2.710
Th' Eternal to prevent such horrid fray   Par Lost 4.996
The horrid shock: now storming furie rose,   Par Lost 6.207
Brandisht aloft the horrid edge came down   Par Lost 6.252
Made horrid Circles; two broad Suns thir Shields   Par Lost 6.305
To this uproar; horrid confusion heapt   Par Lost 6.668
Not yet in horrid Shade or dismal Den,   Par Lost 9.185
And horrid sympathie; for what they saw,   Par Lost 10.540
Horrid, if true! yet why? it was but breath   Par Lost 10.789
Horrid to think, how horrible to feel!   Par Lost 11.465
A pathless Desert, dusk with horrid shades;   Par Reg 1.296
His horrid lusts in private to enjoy,   Par Reg 4.94
From many a horrid rift abortive pour'd   Par Reg 4.411
To thir abyss and horrid pains confin'd.   Samson 501

Horrid(*cont*)
The sight of this so horrid spectacle — Samson 1542
By grots, and caverns shag'd with horrid shades, — Mask 429
'Mongst horrid shapes, and shreiks, and sights unholy, — Allegro 4
With such a horrid clang — Nativity 157
In horrid deeps *to mourn*. — Psalm 88, 28

Horror
Black fire and horror shot with equal rage — Par Lost 2.67
This horror will grow milde, this darkness light, — Par Lost 2.220
With shuddring horror pale, and eyes agast — Par Lost 2.616
Strange horror seise thee, and pangs unfelt before. — Par Lost 2.703
Upon himself; horror and doubt distract — Par Lost 4.18
Sat horror Plum'd; nor wanted in his graspe — Par Lost 4.989
He pluckt, he tasted; mee damp horror chil'd — Par Lost 5.65
In horror; from each hand with speed retir'd — Par Lost 6.307
Strook them with horror backward, but far worse — Par Lost 6.863
Astonied stood and Blank, while horror chill — Par Lost 9.890
Of ugly Serpents; horror on them fell, — Par Lost 10.539
As at some distance from the place of horrour, — Samson 1550
The nodding horror of whose shady brows — Mask 38
Swindges the scaly Horrour of his foulded tail. — Nativity 172

Horrors
Where Joy for ever dwells: Hail horrours, hail — Par Lost 1.250
ms 'Horrours'
Impendent horrors, threatning hideous fall — Par Lost 2.177
And horrors hast thou driv'n me; out of which — Par Lost 10.843

Horse
With Horse and Chariots rankt in loose array; — Par Lost 2.887
The River Horse and scalie Crocodile. — Par Lost 7.474
On his pale Horse: to whom *Sin* thus began. — Par Lost 10.590
Both Horse and Foot, nor idely mustring stood; — Par Lost 11.645
Legions and Cohorts, turmes of horse and wings: — Par Reg 4.66
Both horse and foot before him and behind — Samson 1618
And of the wondrous Hors of Brass, — Penseroso 114

Horsemen
All Horsemen, in which fight they most excel; — Par Reg 3.307

Horses
Of Horses led, and Grooms besmeard with Gold — Par Lost 5.356
In Mail thir horses clad, yet fleet and strong, — Par Reg 3.313

Horus
Osiris, *Isis*, *Orus* and thir Train — Par Lost 1.478
ms 'Orus'
Isis and *Orus*, and the Dog *Anubis* hast. — Nativity 212

Hosanna
Hosanna to the Highest: nor stood at gaze — Par Lost 6.205

Hosannas
With Jubilee, and loud Hosanna's filld — Par Lost 3.348

Hospitable
In *Gibeah*, when the hospitable door — Par Lost 1.504
She turns, on hospitable thoughts intent — Par Lost 5.332
Under the hospitable covert nigh — Par Reg 2.262
Or hospitable, in her sweet recess, — Par Reg 4.242
As the kind hospitable Woods provide. — Mask 187

Host
Had cast him out from Heav'n, with all his Host — Par Lost 1.37
ms 'host'
Hath lost us Heav'n, and all this mighty Host — Par Lost 1.136
ms 'host'
At which the universal Host upsent — Par Lost 1.541
ms 'host'
For mee be witness all the Host of Heav'n, — Par Lost 1.635
ms 'host'
And Trumpets sound throughout the Host proclaim — Par Lost 1.754
ms 'host'
Heard farr and wide, and all the host of Hell — Par Lost 2.519
All th' Host of Heav'n; back they recoild affraid — Par Lost 2.759
Both him and thee, and all the heav'nly Host — Par Lost 2.824
That with extended wings a Bannerd Host — Par Lost 2.885
I saw and heard, for such a numerous Host — Par Lost 2.993
1667 'host'
The starrie Host, rode brightest, till the Moon — Par Lost 4.606
To thy deserted host this cause of flight, — Par Lost 4.922
My self and all th' Angelic Host that stand — Par Lost 5.535
As Heav'ns great Year brings forth, th' Empyreal Host — Par Lost 5.583
Drew after him the third part of Heav'ns Host: — Par Lost 5.710
Far was advanc't on winged speed, an Host — Par Lost 5.744
Through the infinite Host, nor less for that — Par Lost 5.874
Remains thee, aided by this host of friends, — Par Lost 6.38
'Twixt Host and Host but narrow space was left, — Par Lost 6.104
And flying vaulted either Host with fire. — Par Lost 6.214
A numerous Host, in strength each armed hand — Par Lost 6.231
Orewearied, through the faint Satanic Host — Par Lost 6.392
Of Golden Panoplie, refulgent Host, — Par Lost 6.527
Of Iron Globes, which on the Victor Host — Par Lost 6.590
And all his Host derided, while they stood — Par Lost 6.633
Be sure, and terrour seis'd the rebel Host, — Par Lost 6.647
To all his Host on either hand thus spake. — Par Lost 6.800
Of torrent Floods, or of a numerous Host. — Par Lost 6.830
(So call him, brighter once amidst the Host — Par Lost 7.132
Alcinous, host of old *Laertes* Son, — Par Lost 9.441
Of merit high to all th' infernal Host, — Par Lost 10.259
Heav'n-banisht Host, left desert utmost Hell — Par Lost 10.437
One of the heav'nly Host, and by his Gate — Par Lost 11.230
Swallows him with his Host, but them lets pass — Par Lost 12.196
God looking forth will trouble all his Host — Par Lost 12.209
To all the Host of Heaven; the happy place — Par Reg 1.416
In *Ctesiphon* hath gather'd all his Host — Par Reg 3.300
Toucht with the flame: on thir whole Host I flew — Samson 262

Host(*cont*)
And all the spangled host keep watch in squadrons bright? — Nativity 21
As a faint host that hath receiv'd the foil. — Psalm 114, 10
1673 'Host'
He foild bold *Seon* and his host, — Psalm 136, 65
Or wert thou of the golden-winged hoast, — Fair Inf 57
And the Cherubick host in thousand quires — Musick 12
Trinity ms 'hoast'
Thou didst to Jabins *hoast*, — Psalm 83, 36

Hostile
With tumult less and with less hostile din, — Par Lost 2.1040
Long way through hostile scorn, which he susteind — Par Lost 5.904
Rebellious, them with Fire and hostile Arms — Par Lost 6.50
Or Captive drag'd in Chains, with hostile frown — Par Lost 6.260
Raise out of friendship hostil deeds in Peace. — Par Lost 11.796
With Warr and hostile snare such as refuse — Par Lost 12.31
On hostile ground, none daring my affront. — Samson 531
Oft leav'st them to the hostile sword — Samson 692
By worse then hostile deeds, violating the ends — Samson 893
Single Rebellion and did Hostile Acts. — Samson 1210
The desolation of a Hostile City. — Samson 1561
Unstain'd with hostile blood, — Nativity 57

Hostility
But to our power hostility and hate, — Par Lost 2.336
I us'd hostility, and took thir spoil — Samson 1203

Hosting
And in fierce hosting meet, who wont to meet — Par Lost 6.93

Hosts
Lord God of Hosts, how long wilt thou, — Psalm 80, 17
O God of Hosts *vouchsafe* — Psalm 80, 30
Return now, God of Hosts, look down — Psalm 80, 57
Lord God of Hosts *voutsafe*, — Psalm 80, 78
O Lord of Hoasts, how dear — Psalm 84, 2
Ev'n *by* thy Altars Lord of Hoasts — Psalm 84, 13
Lord God of Hoasts hear *now* my praier — Psalm 84, 29
Lord *God* of Hoasts *that raign'st on high*, — Psalm 84, 45

Hot
For hot, cold, moist, and dry, four Champions fierce — Par Lost 2.898
But the hot Hell that alwayes in him burnes, — Par Lost 9.467
Vapour, and Mist, and Exhalation hot, — Par Lost 10.694
Down to the veins of Earth, thence gliding hot — Par Lost 11.568
Gaz'd hot, and of the fresh Wave largely drew, — Par Lost 11.845
Nor in thy hot displeasure me correct; — Psalm 6, 2

Hounds
A cry of Hell Hounds never ceasing bark'd — Par Lost 2.654
My Hell-hounds, to lick up the draff and filth — Par Lost 10.630
Oft list'ning how the Hounds and horn, — Allegro 53

Hour
By Spirits reprobate, and in an hour — Par Lost 1.697
ms 'houre'
Inexorably, and the torturing hour — Par Lost 2.91
1667 'houre'
Destin'd to that good hour: no less rejoyc'd — Par Lost 2.848
Ten thousand fadom deep, and to this hour — Par Lost 2.934
Accurst, and in a cursed hour he hies. — Par Lost 2.1055
Well known from Heav'n; and since Meridian hour — Par Lost 4.581
When *Adam* thus to *Eve*: Fair Consort, th' hour — Par Lost 4.610
Forth issuing at th' accustomd hour stood armd — Par Lost 4.779
Flie thither whence thou fledst: if from this houre — Par Lost 4.963
While day arises, that sweet hour of Prime. — Par Lost 5.170
And *Eve* within, due at her hour prepar'd — Par Lost 5.303
Soon as midnight brought on the duskie houre — Par Lost 5.667
Obsequious darkness enters, till her houre — Par Lost 6.10
Thus answerd. Ill for thee, but in wisht houre — Par Lost 6.150
By sin of disobedience, till that hour — Par Lost 6.396
Who since the Morning hour set out from Heav'n — Par Lost 8.111
And hunger both, from labour, at the houre — Par Lost 8.213
And happie Constellations on that houre — Par Lost 8.512
Early, and th' hour of Supper comes unearn'd. — Par Lost 9.225
Thou never from that houre in Paradise — Par Lost 9.406
I spar'd not, for such pleasure till that hour — Par Lost 9.596
Mean while the hour of Noon drew on, and wak'd — Par Lost 9.739
So saying, her rash hand in evil hour — Par Lost 9.780
O *Eve*, in evil hour thou didst give eare — Par Lost 9.1067
From Noon, and gentle Aires due at thir hour — Par Lost 10.93
Each hour their great adventurer from the search — Par Lost 10.440
O welcom hour whenever! why delayes — Par Lost 10.771
While yet we live, scarse one short hour perhaps, — Par Lost 10.923
One way the self-same hour? why in the East — Par Lost 11.203
Of Speculation; for the hour precise — Par Lost 12.589
It was the hour of night, when thus the Son — Par Reg 2.260
Therefore I watch'd thy footsteps from that hour, — Par Reg 4.522
The miracle of men: then in an hour — Samson 364
Nor from that right to part an hour, — Samson 1056
And I must haste ere morning hour — Mask 920
Trinity ms 'howre'
Bridgewater ms 'howre'
1637 'houre'
Or let my Lamp at midnight hour, — Penseroso 85
Passes to bliss at the mid hour of night, — Sonnet 9, 13
Trinity ms 'the midd night howr' ← 'the midd watch' ← 'that hovre of night'
And when God sends a cheerful hour, refrains. — Sonnet 21, 14
Trinity ms 'houre'

Hourly
Surround me, as thou sawst, hourly conceiv'd — Par Lost 2.796
And hourly born, with sorrow infinite — Par Lost 2.797

Hours
The irksom hours, till this great Chief return. Par Lost 2.527
Thir happie hours in joy and hymning spent. Par Lost 3.417
Knit with the *Graces* and the *Hours* in dance Par Lost 4.267
Oreshades; for these mid-hours, till Eevning rise Par Lost 5.376
Wak't by the circling Hours, with rosie hand Par Lost 6.3
The silent hours, and th' other whose gay Traine Par Lost 7.444
His Seasons, Hours, or Dayes, or Months, or Yeares: Par Lost 8.69
The fruitless hours, but neither self-condemning, Par Lost 9.1188
And now too soon for us the circling hours Par Reg 1.57
Or if I would delight my private hours Par Reg 4.331
The Graces, and the rosie-boosom'd Howres, Mask 986
Trinity ms 'Howrs'
line not in Bridgewater ms
Call on the lazy leaden-stepping hours, On Time 2
Trinity ms 'howres'
While the jolly hours lead on propitious *May*, Sonnet 1, 4
House
He also against the house of God was bold: Par Lost 1.470
With lust and violence the house of God. Par Lost 1.496
From out this dark and dismal house of pain, Par Lost 2.823
Unquenchable, the house of woe and paine. Par Lost 6.877
To Gods Eternal house direct the way, Par Lost 7.576
Abominable, accurst, the house of woe, Par Lost 10.465
A Lazar-house it seemd, wherein were laid Par Lost 11.479
To call by Vision from his Fathers house, Par Lost 12.121
Thir Lords, whom God dispos'd, the house of God Par Lost 12.349
My heart hath been a store-house long of things Par Reg 2.103
Zeal of thy Fathers house, Duty to free Par Reg 3.175
Judah and all thy Father *David*'s house Par Reg 3.282
From Heaven descended to the low-rooft house Par Reg 4.273
Will ask thee skill; I to thy Fathers house Par Reg 4.552
Home to his Mothers house private return'd. Par Reg 4.639
Could have befall'n thee and thy Fathers house. Samson 447
Home to thy countrey and his sacred house, Samson 518
From forth this loathsom prison-house, to abide Samson 922
This Gaol I count the house of Liberty Samson 949
Happy that house! his way to peace is smooth: Samson 1049
Nor in the house with chamber Ambushes Samson 1112
And view him sitting in the house, enobl'd Samson 1491
To himself and Fathers house eternal fame; Samson 1717
Home to his Fathers house: there will I build him Samson 1733
That to the service of this house belongs, Mask 85
And sits as safe as in a Senat house, Mask 389
& yawning dens where glaring monsters house Mask Tr. ms 16.63
and yawninge denns, where glaringe monsters house Mask Br. ms 416
And chose with us a darksom House of mortal Clay. Nativity 14
To house with darknes, and with death. Winchester 10
That thy noble House doth bring, Winchester 54
The house of *Pindarus*, when Temple and Towre Sonnet 8, 11
Into thy house; I in thy fear Psalm 5, 19
Hath found a house of *rest*, Psalm 84, 10
Happy, who in thy house reside Psalm 84, 17
Deaths hideous house hath barr'd. Psalm 88, 24
But his owne house, and the whole neighbourhood Prose 10, 5
Household
In Woman, then to studie houshold good, Par Lost 9.233
To Humane life, and houshold peace confound. Par Lost 10.908
To save himself and houshold from amidst Par Lost 11.820
But to sit idle on the houshold hearth, Samson 566
Houses
Where Houses thick and Sewers annoy the Aire, Par Lost 9.446.
Houses of Gods (so well I have dispos'd Par Reg 4.56
Gods houses, and *will now invade* Psalm 83, 47
Housewife
The sampler, and to teize the huswifes wooll. Mask 751
line not in Bridgewater ms
Hoverest
Tell me bright Spirit where e're thou hoverest Fair Inf 38
Hovering
Hovering on wing under the Cope of Hell Par Lost 1.345
Hov'ring a space, till Winds the signal blow Par Lost 2.717
With wheels yet hov'ring o're the Ocean brim, Par Lost 5.140
Hovering and blazing with delusive Light, Par Lost 9.639
Hovering upon the Waters; what they met Par Lost 10.285
Wide hovering, all the Clouds together drove Par Lost 11.739
Thou hovering Angel girt with golden wings, Mask 214
1637 'flittering Angel'
line not in Bridgewater ms
Trinity ms 'hov'ring' ← 'flittering'
Lingering, and sitting by a new made grave, Mask 472
Trinity ms 'hovering and sitting'
1637 'Hovering and sitting'
Bridgewater ms 'hoveringe and sittinge'
Or likest hovering dreams Penseroso 9
Hovers
Where thickest darkness *hovers round*, Psalm 88, 27
How
In the Beginning how the Heav'ns and Earth Par Lost 1.9
O how unlike the place from whence they fell! Par Lost 1.75
If thou beest he; But O how fall'n! how chang'd Par Lost 1.84
Consult how we may henceforth most offend Par Lost 1.187
Our Enemy, our own loss how repair, Par Lost 1.188
How overcome this dire Calamity, Par Lost 1.189
How all his malice serv'd but to bring forth Par Lost 1.217
For his revolt, yet faithfull how they stood, Par Lost 1.611
How such united force of Gods, how such Par Lost 1.629
Learn how thir greatest Monuments of Fame, Par Lost 1.695

How*(cont)*
Men call'd him *Mulciber;* and how he fell Par Lost 1.740
Can give it, or will ever? how he can Par Lost 2.153
In Heav'n this our delight; how wearisom Par Lost 2.247
Of darkness do we dread? How oft amidst Par Lost 2.263
Of order, how in safety best we may Par Lost 2.280
Yet ever plotting how the Conqueror least Par Lost 2.338
Or substance, how endu'd, and what thir Power, Par Lost 2.356
And where thir weakness, how attempted best, Par Lost 2.357
Nor fail'd they to express how much they prais'd, Par Lost 2.480
By me upheld, that he may know how frail Par Lost 3.180
My sole complacence! well thou know'st how dear, Par Lost 3.276
Numberless, as thou seest, and how they move; Par Lost 3.719
O Sun, to tell thee how I hate thy beams Par Lost 4.37
I fell, how glorious once above thy Spheare; Par Lost 4.39
How due! yet all his good prov'd ill in me, Par Lost 4.48
How dearly I abide that boast so vaine, Par Lost 4.87
By Act of Grace my former state; how soon Par Lost 4.94
Would higth recal high thoughts, how soon unsay Par Lost 4.95
But rather to tell how, if Art could tell, Par Lost 4.236
How from that Saphire Fount the crisped Brooks, Par Lost 4.237
Sin-bred, how have ye troubl'd all mankind Par Lost 4.315
Ah gentle pair, yee little think how nigh Par Lost 4.366
And what I was, whence thither brought, and how. Par Lost 4.452
How beauty is excelld by manly grace Par Lost 4.490
Incredible how swift, had thither rowl'd Par Lost 4.593
Both day and night: how often from the steep Par Lost 4.680
And felt how awful goodness is, and saw Par Lost 4.847
Vertue in her shape how lovly, saw, and pin'd Par Lost 4.848
How busied, in what form and posture coucht. Par Lost 4.876
Where thou art weigh'd, and shown how light, how weak, Par Lost 4.1012
Calls us, we lose the prime, to mark how spring Par Lost 5.21
Our tended Plants, how blows the Citron Grove, Par Lost 5.22
How Nature paints her colours, how the Bee Par Lost 5.24
And fell asleep; but O how glad I wak'd Par Lost 5.92
Thus wondrous fair; thy self how wondrous then! Par Lost 5.155
Hath raisd in Paradise, and how disturbd Par Lost 5.226
This night the human pair, how he designes Par Lost 5.227
Findes no acceptance, nor can find, for how Par Lost 5.531
Sad task and hard, for how shall I relate Par Lost 5.564
Of warring Spirits; how without remorse Par Lost 5.566
And perfet while they stood; how last unfould Par Lost 5.568
Both waking we were one; how then can now Par Lost 5.678
Rebellion rising, saw in whom, how spred Par Lost 5.715
This onely to consult how we may best Par Lost 5.779
Too much to one, but double how endur'd, Par Lost 5.783
Yet by experience taught we know how good, Par Lost 5.826
How provident he is, how farr from thought Par Lost 5.828
No more be troubl'd how to quit the yoke Par Lost 5.882
Or potent tongue; fool, not to think how vain Par Lost 6.135
How few somtimes may know, when thousands err. Par Lost 6.148
Of all thir Regions: how much more of Power Par Lost 6.223
And thy adherents: how hast thou disturb'd Par Lost 6.266
Of thy Rebellion? how hast thou instill'd Par Lost 6.269
Th' invention all admir'd, and each, how hee Par Lost 6.498
That all may see who hate us, how we seek Par Lost 6.559
Who now is plotting how he may seduce Par Lost 6.901
What neerer might concern him, how this World Par Lost 7.62
How first began this Heav'n which we behold Par Lost 7.86
In *Chaos*, and the work begun, how soon Par Lost 7.93
Th' addition of his Empire, how it shew'd Par Lost 7.555
In prospect from his Throne, how good, how faire, Par Lost 7.556
How first this World and face of things began, Par Lost 7.636
How Nature wise and frugal could commit Par Lost 8.26
To visit how they prosper'd, bud and bloom, Par Lost 8.45
And calculate the Starrs, how they will weild Par Lost 8.80
The mightie frame, how build, unbuild, contrive Par Lost 8.81
To save appeerances, how gird the Sphear Par Lost 8.82
How fully hast thou satisfi'd mee, pure Par Lost 8.180
How suttly to detaine thee I devise, Par Lost 8.207
For Man to tell how human Life began Par Lost 8.250
Tell, if ye saw, how came I thus, how here? Par Lost 8.277
Tell me, how may I know him, how adore, Par Lost 8.280
Surpassest farr my naming, how may I Par Lost 8.359
How have I then with whom to hold converse Par Lost 8.408
To see how thou could'st judge of fit and meet: Par Lost 8.448
Love not the heav'nly Spirits, and how thir Love Par Lost 8.615
O Earth, how like to Heav'n, if not preferr'd Par Lost 9.99
Continu'd making, and who knows how long Par Lost 9.138
Then commune how that day they best may ply Par Lost 9.201
How we might best fulfill the work which here Par Lost 9.230
Thoughts, which how found they harbour in thy brest Par Lost 9.288
How are we happie, still in fear of harm? Par Lost 9.326
How cam'st thou speakable of mute, and how Par Lost 9.563
But say, where grows the Tree, from hence how far? Par Lost 9.617
How should ye? by the Fruit? it gives you Life Par Lost 9.686
Of good, how just? of evil, if what is evil Par Lost 9.698
How dies the Serpent? hee hath eat'n and lives, Par Lost 9.764
How art thou lost, how on a sudden lost, Par Lost 9.900
Rather how hast thou yeelded to transgress Par Lost 9.902
The strict forbiddance, how to violate Par Lost 9.903
How can I live without thee, how forgoe Par Lost 9.908
Of thy perfection, how shall I attaine, Par Lost 9.964
Soon found thir Eyes how op'nd, and thir minds Par Lost 9.1053
How dark'nd; innocence, that as a veile Par Lost 9.1054
Be sure then. How shall I behold the face Par Lost 9.1080
Thir guilt and dreaded shame; O how unlike Par Lost 9.1114
Of *Satan* done in Paradise, and how Par Lost 10.2

How(*cont*)
Much wondring how the suttle Fiend had stoln Par Lost 10.20
How all befell: they towards the Throne Supream Par Lost 10.28
But still rejoyc't, how is it now become Par Lost 10.120
Remov'd farr off; then pittying how they stood Par Lost 10.211
Protesting Fate supreame; thence how I found Par Lost 10.480
And Fabl'd how the Serpent, whom they calld Par Lost 10.580
His course intended; else how had the World Par Lost 10.689
To deathless pain? how gladly would I meet Par Lost 10.775
Insensible, how glad would lay me down Par Lost 10.777
But mortal doom'd. How can he exercise Par Lost 10.796
So disinherited how would ye bless Par Lost 10.821
With me? how can they then acquitted stand Par Lost 10.827
In offices of Love, how we may light'n Par Lost 10.960
How little weight my words with thee can finde, Par Lost 10.968
How much more, if we pray him, will his ear Par Lost 10.1060
Leave cold the Night, how we his gather'd beams Par Lost 10.1070
My judgments, how with Mankind I proceed, Par Lost 11.69
As how with peccant Angels late they saw; Par Lost 11.70
His heart I know, how variable and vain Par Lost 11.92
Some days; how long, and what till then our life, Par Lost 11.198
How shall I part, and whither wander down Par Lost 11.282
And wilde, how shall we breath in other Aire Par Lost 11.284
Horrid to think, how horrible to feel! Par Lost 11.465
These painful passages, how we may come Par Lost 11.528
Life much, bent rather how I may be quit Par Lost 11.548
Live well, how long or short permit to Heav'n: Par Lost 11.554
How didst thou grieve then, *Adam*, to behold Par Lost 11.754
How comes it thus? unfould, Celestial Guide, Par Lost 11.785
Thenceforth shall practice how to live secure, Par Lost 11.802
The paths of righteousness, how much more safe, Par Lost 11.814
Were long to tell, how many Battels fought, Par Lost 12.261
How many Kings destroyd, and Kingdoms won, Par Lost 12.262
Or how the Sun shall in mid Heav'n stand still Par Lost 12.263
Among them; how can God with such reside? Par Lost 12.284
How soon hath thy prediction, Seer blest, Par Lost 12.553
How many Ages, as the years of men, Par Reg 1.48
With man or mens affairs, how I begin Par Reg 1.132
Then toldst her doubting how these things could be Par Reg 1.137
How best the mighty work he might begin Par Reg 1.186
Behold the Kings of the Earth how they oppress Par Reg 2.44
How to begin, how to accomplish best Par Reg 2.113
In Courts and Regal Chambers how thou lurk'st, Par Reg 2.183
How many have with a smile made small account Par Reg 2.193
A youth, how all the Beauties of the East Par Reg 2.197
How hee sirnam'd of *Africa* dismiss'd Par Reg 2.199
How would one look from his Majestick brow Par Reg 2.216
He saw the Prophet also how he fled Par Reg 2.270
Into the Desert, and how there he slept Par Reg 2.271
Under a Juniper; then how awakt, Par Reg 2.272
How hast thou hunger then? Satan reply'd, Par Reg 2.319
Alas how simple, to these Cates compar'd, Par Reg 2.348
What I can suffer, how obey? who best Par Reg 3.194
How best their opposition to withstand. Par Reg 3.250
See how in warlike muster they appear, Par Reg 3.308
How quick they wheel'd, and flying behind them shot Par Reg 3.323
Samaritan or *Jew;* how could'st thou hope Par Reg 3.359
Chios and *Creet*, and how they quaff in Gold, Par Reg 4.118
Of the Emperour, how easily subdu'd, Par Reg 4.126
How gloriously; I shall, thou say'st, expel Par Reg 4.127
I see all offers made by me how slight Par Reg 4.155
By thee how fairly is the Giver now Par Reg 4.187
Without thir learning how wilt thou with them, Par Reg 4.231
How wilt thou reason with them, how refute Par Reg 4.233
And how the world began, and how man fell Par Reg 4.311
For both the when and how is no where told, Par Reg 4.472
In what part lodg'd, how easily bereft me, Samson 48
How slight the gift was, hung it in my Hair. Samson 59
See how he lies at random, carelesly diffus'd, Samson 118
By how much from the top of wondrous glory, Samson 167
How counterfeit a coin they are who friends Samson 189
How many evils have enclos'd me round; Samson 194
How could I once look up, or heave the head, Samson 197
In every street, do they not say, how well Samson 204
How frequent to desert him, and at last Samson 275
How *Succoth* and the Fort of *Penuel* Samson 278
And how ingrateful *Ephraim* Samson 282
Forthwith how thou oughtst to receive him. Samson 329
How openly, and with what impudence Samson 398
That saw not how degeneratly I serv'd. Samson 419
Divine impulsion prompting how thou might'st Samson 422
How hainous had the fact been, how deserving Samson 493
By ransom or how else: mean while be calm, Samson 604
What do I beg? how hast thou dealt already? Samson 707
Her husband, how far urg'd his patience bears, Samson 755
How to endear, and hold thee to me firmest: Samson 796
Sam. How cunningly the sorceress displays Samson 819
My love how couldst thou hope, who tookst the way Samson 838
And of Religion, press'd how just it was, Samson 854
How honourable, how glorious to entrap Samson 855
Preaching how meritorious with the gods Samson 859
Bare in thy guilt how foul must thou appear? Samson 902
How wouldst thou use me now, blind, and thereby Samson 941
And last neglected? How wouldst thou insult Samson 944
In perfet thraldom, how again betray me, Samson 946
How highly it concerns his glory now Samson 1148
Sam. Tongue-doubtie Giant, how dost thou prove me these? Samson 1181
Chor. Oh how comely it is and how reviving Samson 1268

How(*cont*)
He's gone, and who knows how he may report Samson 1350
Besides, how vile, contemptible, ridiculous, Samson 1361
Chor. How thou wilt here come off surmounts my reach. Samson 1380
To see me girt with Friends; and how the sight Samson 1415
Thou in old age car'st how to nurse thy Son. Samson 1488
To have guided me aright, I know not how, Samson 1547
How dy'd he? death to life is crown or shame. Samson 1579
Man. Wearied with slaughter then or how? explain. Samson 1583
How sweetly did they float upon the wings Mask 249
How to regain my sever'd company Mask 274
La. How easie my misfortune is to hit! Mask 286
How bitter is such self-delusion? Mask 365
line not in Trinity ms
line not in Bridgewater ms
2. *Bro*. How charming is divine Philosophy! Mask 476
How cam'st thou here good Swain? hath any ram Mask 497
How couldst thou find this dark sequester'd nook? Mask 500
How chance she is not in your company? Mask 508
Bridgewater ms 'howe'
How sweet thou sing'st, how neer the deadly snare! Mask 567
How are ye joyn'd with hell in triple knot Mask 581
How durst thou then thy self approach so neer Mask 616
How to secure the Lady from surprisal, Mask 618
She can teach ye how to clime Mask 1020
how have I bin betrai'd Mask Tr. ms 22.18
Oft list'ning how the Hounds and horn, Allegro 53
How *Faery Mab* the junkets eat, Allegro 102
Tells how the drudging *Goblin* swet, Allegro 105
How little you bested, Penseroso 3
How well could I have spar'd for thee young swain, Lycidas 113
Then how to scramble at the shearers feast, Lycidas 117
Blind mouthes! that scarce themselves know how to hold Lycidas 119
See how from far upon the Eastern rode Nativity 22
How he before the thunderous throne doth lie, Vacation 36
May tell at length how green-ey'd *Neptune* raves, Vacation 43
But fie my wandring Muse how thou dost stray! Vacation 53
Alas, how soon our sin Circum 12
How soon hath Time the suttle theef of youth, Sonnet 7, 1
But from that mark how far they roave we see Sonnet 12, 13
First taught our English Musick how to span Sonnet 13, 2
Then to advise how warr may best, upheld, Sonnet 17, 7
When I consider how my light is spent, Sonnet 19, 1
Plain in thy neatness; O how oft shall he Horace 5
Lord how many are my foes Psalm 3, 1
How many those Psalm 3, 2
Great ones how long will ye Psalm 4, 7
How long be thus forborn Psalm 4, 9
And thou O Lord how long? turn Lord, restore Psalm 6, 7
O Jehovah our Lord how wondrous great Psalm 8, 1
O Jehovah our Lord how wondrous great Psalm 8, 23
Lord God of Hosts, how long wilt thou, Psalm 80, 17
How long wilt thou declare Psalm 80, 18
How long will ye pervert the right Psalm 82, 5
How lovely are thy dwellings fair! Psalm 84, 1
O Lord of Hoasts, how dear Psalm 84, 2
Ah *Constantine*, of how much ill was cause Prose 1, 1

However
However, and to scape his punishment. Par Lost 4.911
Starr interpos'd, however small he sees, Par Lost 5.258
1667 'how ever' in some copies
Thou fablest, here however to dwell free, Par Lost 6.292
But that I doubt, however witness Heaven, Par Lost 6.563
Of highest Agents, deemd however wise. Par Lost 9.683
However I with thee have fixt my Lot, Par Lost 9.952
However insupportable, be all Par Lost 10.134
However some tradition they dispers'd Par Lost 10.578
However chast'ning, to the evil turne Par Lost 11.373
However to this Man inferior far, Par Reg 2.135
An empty cloud. However many books Par Reg 4.321
That mingle with thy fancy. I however Samson 601
To that same lot, however mean, or high, Sonnet 7, 11

Howl
That bred them they return, and howle and gnaw Par Lost 2.799
He and his monstrous rout are heard to howl Mask 533
1637 'howle'
Bridgewater ms 'howle'
Trinity ms 'howle'

Howled
And kennel there, yet there still bark'd and howl'd, Par Lost 2.658
Environ'd thee, some howl'd, some yell'd, some shriek'd, Par Reg 4.423

Hubbub
At length a universal hubbub wilde Par Lost 2.951
And looking down, to see the hubbub strange Par Lost 12.60

Huddling
The huddling brook to hear his madrigal, Mask 495
1673 'hudling'
Bridgewater ms 'hudlinge'

Hue
And such appear'd in hue, as when the force Par Lost 1.230
ms 'hew'
Like doubtful hue: but he his wonted pride Par Lost 1.527
ms 'hew'
Blossoms and Fruits at once of golden hue Par Lost 4.148
Flours of all hue, and without Thorn the Rose: Par Lost 4.256
Adorns him, colour'd with the Florid hue Par Lost 7.445
Celestial rosie red, Loves proper hue, Par Lost 8.619
Were Tents of various hue; by some were herds Par Lost 11.557

Hue(*cont*)
Tall stripling youths rich clad, of fairer hew Par Reg 2.352
Flowers of more mingled hew Mask 994
B.M. ms 'Hew'
Ore laid with black staid Wisdoms hue. Penseroso 16
His burning Idol all of blackest hue, Nativity 207
Hues
Iris all hues, Roses, and Gessamin Par Lost 4.698
And shew me simples of a thousand names Mask 627
Trinity ms 'names' ←'hews'
Their Bels, and Flourets of a thousand hues. Lycidas 135
Hug
And hugg him into snares. When once her eye Mask 164
Trinity ms 'hugge'
Bridgewater ms 'hug'
Huge
That witness'd huge affliction and dismay Par Lost 1.57
Lay floating many a rood, in bulk as huge Par Lost 1.196
So stretcht out huge in length the Arch-fiend lay Par Lost 1.209
A Forrest huge of Spears: and thronging Helms Par Lost 1.547
Anon out of the earth a Fabrick huge Par Lost 1.710
Our prison strong, this huge convex of Fire, Par Lost 2.434
Which he through hazard huge must earn. But they Par Lost 2.473
That fires the length of *Ophiucus* huge Par Lost 2.709
Forthwith the huge Porcullis high up drew, Par Lost 2.874
Such ruin intercept: ten paces huge Par Lost 6.193
Squadrons at once, with huge two-handed sway Par Lost 6.251
Though huge, and in a Rock of Diamond Armd, Par Lost 6.364
Approaching gross and huge; in hollow Cube Par Lost 6.552
Through his wilde Anarchie, so huge a rout Par Lost 6.873
Immediately the Mountains huge appeer Par Lost 7.285
And bended Dolphins play: part huge of bulk Par Lost 7.410
Of huge extent somtimes, with brazen Eyes Par Lost 7.496
Huge *Python*, and his Power no less he seem'd Par Lost 10.531
Began to build a Vessel of huge bulk, Par Lost 11.729
Huge Cities and high towr'd, that well might seem Par Reg 3.261
The Imperial Palace, compass huge, and high Par Reg 4.51
So many, and so huge, that each apart Samson 65
May trace huge Forests, and unharbour'd Heaths, Mask 423
Not *Typhon* huge ending in snaky twine: Nativity 226
Of labours huge and hard, too hard for human wight. Passion 14
Huge pangs and strong Circum 27
Huge-bellied
The high, huge-bellied Mountains skip like Rams Psalm 114, 11
Hugest
Created hugest that swim th' Ocean stream: Par Lost 1.202
Hugest of living Creatures, on the Deep Par Lost 7.413
Hull
He lookd, and saw the Ark hull on the floud, Par Lost 11.840
Hum
And the busie humm of men, Allegro 118
No voice or hideous humm Nativity 174
Human
Excelling human, Princely Dignities, Par Lost 1.359
Of human sacrifice, and parents tears, Par Lost 1.393
Rather then human. Nor did *Israel* scape Par Lost 1.482
Or flocks, or heards, or human face divine; Par Lost 3.44
Betwixt th' Angelical and Human kinde: Par Lost 3.462
To all delight of human sense expos'd Par Lost 4.206
Mother of human Race: what could I doe, Par Lost 4.475
Of human ofsspring, sole proprietie, Par Lost 4.751
This night the human pair, how he designes Par Lost 5.227
Exceeded human, and his wary speech Par Lost 5.459
Human desires can seek or apprehend? Par Lost 5.518
To human sense th' invisible exploits Par Lost 5.565
Of human sense, I shall delineate so, Par Lost 5.572
Human imagination to such highth Par Lost 6.300
What might have else to human Race bin hid; Par Lost 6.896
Unknown, which human knowledg could not reach: Par Lost 7.75
Then time or motion, but to human ears Par Lost 7.177
1669 'humane'
Thir small peculiar, though from human sight Par Lost 7.368
Aught, not surpassing human measure, say. Par Lost 7.640
God to remove his wayes from human sense, Par Lost 8.119
For Man to tell how human Life began Par Lost 8.250
Cannot be human consort; they rejoyce Par Lost 8.392
All human thoughts come short, Supream of things; Par Lost 8.414
Attractive, human, rational, love still; Par Lost 8.587
With grateful Smell, forth came the human pair Par Lost 9.197
Love not the lowest end of human life. Par Lost 9.241
By Tongue of Brute, and human sense exprest? Par Lost 9.554
I knew, but not with human voice endu'd; Par Lost 9.561
I of brute human, yee of human Gods. Par Lost 9.712
Human, to put on Gods, death to be wisht, Par Lost 9.714
Endu'd with human voice and human sense, Par Lost 9.871
The doubt, since humane reach no further knows. Par Lost 10.793
To Humane life, and houshold peace confound. Par Lost 10.908
Or one short sigh of humane breath, up-borne Par Lost 11.147
Of human Glorie, and for Glorie done Par Lost 11.694
Must needs impaire and wearie human sense: Par Lost 12.10
Reserving, human left from human free. Par Lost 12.71
Was difficult, by humane steps untrod; Par Reg 1.298
Nor tasted humane food, nor hunger felt Par Reg 1.308
With more then humane gifts from Heaven adorn'd, Par Reg 2.137
Wandring this woody maze, and humane food Par Reg 2.246
Or human nature can receive, consider Par Reg 3.231
Of human weakness rather then of strength. Par Reg 3.402
Of fate, and chance, and change in human life; Par Reg 4.265

Human(*cont*)
In fleshly Tabernacle, and human form, Par Reg 4.599
Unseemly falls in human eie, Samson 690
In human hearts, nor less in mine towards thee, Samson 792
Thy strength they know surpassing human rate, Samson 1313
Soon as the Potion works, their human count'nance, Mask 68
Bridgewater ms 'humane'
Trinity ms 'humaine'
1637 'humane'
Their port was more then human, as they stood; Mask 297
1637 'humaine'
Trinity ms 'humaine'
Bridgewater ms 'humane'
To hit the Sense of human sight; Penseroso 14
Of human mould with grosse unpurged ear; Arcades 73
Trinity ms 'humaine'
Once bless our human ears, Nativity 126
1673 'humane'
Who having clad thy self in humane weed, Fair Inf 58
Of labours huge and hard, too hard for human wight. Passion 14
Humane
Belial, in act more graceful and humane; Par Lost 2.109
Goddess humane, reach then, and freely taste. Par Lost 9.732
Yet held it more humane, more heavenly first Par Reg 1.221
Humber
Or *Humber* loud that keeps the *Scythians* Name, Vacation 99
Humble
Stand in his presence humble, and receive Par Lost 2.240
Embattell'd in her field: and the humble Shrub, Par Lost 7.322
And humble deprecation thus repli'd. Par Lost 8.378
Fell humble, and imbracing them, besaught Par Lost 10.912
To *Michael* thus his humble words addressd. Par Lost 11.295
Be try'd in humble state, and things adverse, Par Reg 3.189
(Best pleas'd with humble and filial submission) Samson 511
Why do I humble thus my self, and suing Samson 965
O run, prevent them with thy humble ode, Nativity 24
Founded in chast and humble Povertie, Prose 3, 1
Humbled
Humbl'd by such rebuke, so farr beneath Par Lost 6.342
Kneel'd and before him humbl'd all my heart, Par Lost 11.150
So spake, so wish'd much-humbl'd *Eve*, but Fate Par Lost 11.181
Humbled themselves, or penitent besought Par Reg 3.421
Humbles
Humbles his stubborn heart, but still as Ice Par Lost 12.193
Humbling
This annual humbling certain number'd days, Par Lost 10.576
Humbly
Humbly our faults, and pardon beg, with tears Par Lost 10.1089
Humbly thir faults, and pardon beg'd, with tears Par Lost 10.1101
Humid
Then in fair Evening Cloud, or humid Bow, Par Lost 4.151
In humid exhalations, and at Even Par Lost 5.425
Stream, and perpetual draw thir humid traine. Par Lost 7.306
In *Eden* on the humid Flours, that breathd Par Lost 9.193
Iris there with humid bow, Mask 992
Trinity ms 'humid' ←'garish' ←'garnish't'
Humiliation
Therefore thy Humiliation shall exalt Par Lost 3.313
Of sorrow unfeign'd, and humiliation meek. Par Lost 10.1092
Of sorrow unfeign'd, and humiliation meek. Par Lost 10.1104
By Humiliation and strong Sufferance: Par Reg 1.160
Humming
Beat off, returns as oft with humming sound; Par Reg 4.17
Where thou perhaps under the whelming tide Lycidas 157
1638 'humming tide'
Trinity ms 'humming tide'
Humour
Produces with Terrestrial Humor mixt Par Lost 3.610
A stream of Nectarous humor issuing flow'd Par Lost 6.332
Prolific humour soft'ning all her Globe, Par Lost 7.280
That with smooth aire couldst humor best our tongue. Sonnet 13, 8
1648 'humour'
Humours
From anguish of the mind and humours black, Samson 600
Hundred
To be a lyer in four hundred mouths; Par Reg 1.428
And *Hecatompylos* her hunderd gates, Par Reg 3.287
Mother of a hunderd gods; Arcades 22
Trinity ms 'hundred'
1673 'hundred'
Hundredfold
A hunder'd-fold, who having learnt thy way Sonnet 18, 13
Hundreds
With hunderds and with thousands trooping came Par Lost 1.760
1667 'hundreds', 1668 errata 'hunderds'
ms 'hundreds'
Hung
Hung on his shoulders like the Moon, whose Orb Par Lost 1.287
That ore the Realm of impious *Pharaoh* hung Par Lost 1.342
When the fierce Foe hung on our brok'n Rear Par Lost 2.78
Hung ore my Realm, link'd in a golden Chain Par Lost 2.1005
Like Quivers hung, and with Praeamble sweet Par Lost 3.367
Hung amiable, *Hesperian* Fables true, Par Lost 4.250
Round from his parted forelock manly hung Par Lost 4.302
Hung high with Diamond flaming, and with Gold. Par Lost 4.554
Hung forth in Heav'n his golden Scales, yet seen Par Lost 4.997
Hung over her enamour'd, and beheld Par Lost 5.13
Which hung not, but so swift with tempest fell Par Lost 6.190

Hung(*cont*)
The Battel hung; till *Satan*, who that day — Par Lost 6.246
Sate Eagle-wing'd, beside him hung his Bow — Par Lost 6.763
And Earth self ballanc't on her Center hung. — Par Lost 7.242
Thir branches hung with copious Fruit; or gemm'd — Par Lost 7.325
Load'n with fairest Fruit that hung to the Eye — Par Lost 8.307
Hung drooping unsustaind, them she upstaies — Par Lost 9.430
Amid the Tree now got, where plenty hung — Par Lost 9.594
As in a glistering *Zodiac* hung the Sword, — Par Lost 11.247
How slight the gift was, hung it in my Hair. — Samson 59
With all his Trophies hung, and Acts enroll'd — Samson 1736
That nature hung in Heav'n, and fill'd their Lamps — Mask 198
line not in Bridgewater ms
Of Turneys and of Trophies hung; — Penseroso 118
The idle spear and shield were high up hung; — Nativity 55
And the well-ballanc't world on hinges hung, — Nativity 122
So hung his destiny never to rot — Another 3
1640, 1657 'sung'
Picture the sacred wall declares t' have hung — Horace 14

Hunger
Whom hunger drives to seek new haunt for prey, — Par Lost 4.184
Of real hunger, and concoctive heate — Par Lost 5.437
And hunger both, from labour, at the houre — Par Lost 8.213
Not to deferr; hunger and thirst at once, — Par Lost 9.586
Yet parcht with scalding thurst and hunger fierce, — Par Lost 10.556
Hunger and thirst constraining, drugd as oft, — Par Lost 10.568
Nor tasted humane food, nor hunger felt — Par Reg 1.308
His Carcass, pin'd with hunger and with droughth? — Par Reg 1.325
But now I feel I hunger, which declares, — Par Reg 2.252
Though hunger still remain: so it remain — Par Reg 2.255
Not without hunger. Others of some note, — Par Reg 2.306
How hast thou hunger then? Satan reply'd, — Par Reg 2.319
Troubl'd that thou shouldst hunger, hath purvey'd — Par Reg 2.333
Hunger, with sweet restorative delight. — Par Reg 2.373
And with my hunger what hast thou to do? — Par Reg 2.389
By hunger, that each other Creature tames, — Par Reg 2.406
And hunger still: then Embassies thou shew'st — Par Reg 4.121
What hunger, if aught hunger had impair'd, — Par Reg 4.592
Of Savage hunger, or of Savage heat? — Mask 358
line not in Bridgewater ms
line not in Trinity ms

Hunger-bit
Lost in a Desert here and hunger-bit: — Par Reg 2.416

Hungered
Till those days ended, hunger'd then at last — Par Reg 1.309

Hungering
Now hungring first, and to himself thus said. — Par Reg 2.244
Mee hungring more to do my Fathers will. — Par Reg 2.259

Hungers
And now I know he hungers where no food — Par Reg 2.231

Hungry
Hungry and cold betook him to his rest, — Par Reg 4.403
The hungry Sheep look up, and are not fed, — Lycidas 125
Trinity ms 'hungrie'

Hunt
With the Attick Boy to hunt, — Penseroso 124

Hunter
First hunter then, pursu'd a gentle brace, — Par Lost 11.188
1667 'Hunter'
A mightie Hunter thence he shall be styl'd — Par Lost 12.33

Hunting
Hunting (and Men not Beasts shall be his game) — Par Lost 12.30

Huntress
Hence had the huntress *Dian* her dred bow — Mask 441
Trinity ms 'huntresse'
1637 'huntresse'
Goddess of Shades, and Huntress, who at will — Prose 12, 1

Hurdled
In hurdl'd Cotes amid the field secure, — Par Lost 4.186

Hurl
About my Mother *Circe*. Thus I hurl — Mask 153
Bridgewater ms 'hurle'
1637 'hurle'
Trinity ms 'hurle'

Hurled
Hurld headlong flaming from th' Ethereal Skie — Par Lost 1.45
Caught in a fierie Tempest shall be hurl'd — Par Lost 2.180
Hurl'd headlong to partake with us, shall curse — Par Lost 2.374
Hurl'd to and fro with jaculation dire, — Par Lost 6.665
Through *Chaos* hurld, obstruct the mouth of Hell — Par Lost 10.636
Wash far away, where ere thy bones are hurld, — Lycidas 155
1638 'hurl'd'
Trinity ms 'hurl'd'

Hurling
Hurling defiance toward the Vault of Heav'n. — Par Lost 1.669

Hurried
Periods of time, thence hurried back to fire. — Par Lost 2.603
Instinct with Fire and Nitre hurried him — Par Lost 2.937
Of midnight march, and hurried meeting here, — Par Lost 5.778
After his aerie jaunt, though hurried sore, — Par Reg 4.402
Or should I thence hurried on viewles wing, — Passion 50

Hurt
God therefore cannot hurt ye, and be just; — Par Lost 9.700
What can your knowledge hurt him, or this Tree — Par Lost 9.727
Never to hurt them more who rightly trust — Par Lost 12.418
Who hurt thir minds, — Samson 1676
Vertue may be assail'd, but never hurt, — Mask 589
Bridgewater ms 'hurte'

Hurtful
Useful of hurtful, prosperous of adverse — Par Lost 2.259
Hath hurtfull power o're true virginity. — Mask 437
Bridgewater ms 'hurtefull'
Or hurtfull Worm with canker'd venom bites. — Arcades 53

Husband
The Female Bee that feeds her Husband Drone — Par Lost 7.490
Her Husband the Relater she preferr'd — Par Lost 8.52
And *Eve* first to her Husband thus began. — Par Lost 9.204
And good workes in her Husband to promote. — Par Lost 9.234
Safest and seemliest by her Husband staies, — Par Lost 9.268
Thus saying, from her Husbands hand her hand — Par Lost 9.385
Her Husband, for I view far round, not nigh, — Par Lost 9.482
Her Husband shee, to taste the fatall fruit, — Par Lost 10.4
In sorrow forth, and to thy Husbands will — Par Lost 10.195
Upon her Husband, saw thir shame that sought — Par Lost 10.336
Thy Husband, him to follow thou art bound; — Par Lost 11.291
Her husband, how far urg'd his patience bears, — Samson 755
Didst thou at first receive me for thy husband? — Samson 883
Thy Husband, slight me, sell me, and forgo me; — Samson 940
Whom *Joves* great Son to her glad Husband gave, — Sonnet 23, 3
Trinity ms 'husband'

Hush
And hush the waving Woods, nor of lesse faith, — Mask 88

Husk
Rough, or smooth rin'd, or bearded husk, or shell — Par Lost 5.342

Hutched
She hutch't th' all-worshipt ore, and precious gems — Mask 719

Hyacinth
Crocus, and Hyacinth with rich inlay — Par Lost 4.701
And Hyacinth, Earths freshest softest lap. — Par Lost 9.1041
Beds of *Hyacinth*, and roses — Mask 998
Trinity ms 'hyacinth' ←'Hyacinth'
B.M. ms 'Hyacinths'
aeternall roses grow & hyacinth — Mask Tr. ms 10.07
Young *Hyacinth* born on *Eurota*'s strand — Fair Inf 25
Young *Hyacinth* the pride of *Spartan* land; — Fair Inf 26

Hyacinthine
Absolute rule; and Hyacinthin Locks — Par Lost 4.301

Hyaline
On the cleer *Hyaline*, the Glassie Sea; — Par Lost 7.619

Hydaspes
Of *Ganges* or *Hydaspes*, *Indian* streams; — Par Lost 3.436

Hydra
Thir Hydra heads, and the fals North displaies — Sonnet 15, 7
1694 'Hydra-heads'

Hydras
Gorgons and *Hydra's*, and *Chimera*'s dire. — Par Lost 2.628
Harpyies and *Hydra's*, or all the monstrous forms — Mask 605
Bridgewater ms 'Hyidraes'

Hydrus
Cerastes hornd, *Hydrus*, and *Ellops* drear, — Par Lost 10.525

Hyena
Sam. Out, out *Hyaena;* these are thy wonted arts, — Samson 748

Hylas
Then *Ganymed* or *Hylas*, distant more — Par Reg 2.353

Hymen
Hymen, then first to marriage Rites invok't; — Par Lost 11.591
1667 'Hymen'
There let *Hymen* oft appear — Allegro 125

Hymenaean
And heav'nly Quires the Hymenaean sung, — Par Lost 4.711

Hymettus
There flowrie hill *Hymettus* with the sound — Par Reg 4.247

Hymn
High up in Heav'n, with songs to hymne his Throne, — Par Lost 4.944
In Fable, Hymn, or Song, so personating — Par Reg 4.341
Hast thou no vers, no hymn, or solemn strein, — Nativity 17
That tun'st their happiest lines in Hymn, or Story. — Sonnet 13, 11
Trinity ms 'hymn'
1648 'hymne'
Prepare a Hymn, prepare a Song — Psalm 81, 5

Hymning
Thir happie hours in joy and hymning spent. — Par Lost 3.417
Hymning th' Eternal Father: but the shout — Par Lost 6.96
And touch't thir Golden Harps, and hymning prais'd — Par Lost 7.258

Hymns
With warbl'd Hymns, and to his Godhead sing — Par Lost 2.242
Of Hymns and sacred Songs, wherewith thy Throne — Par Lost 3.148
Melodious Hymns about the sovran Throne — Par Lost 5.656
Hymns of high praise, and I among them chief. — Par Lost 6.745
Admiring stood a space, then into Hymns — Par Reg 1.169
With Hymns, our Psalms with artful terms inscrib'd, — Par Reg 4.335
Hymns devout and holy Psalms — Musick 15
Trinity ms 'hymns' ←'hymnes'

Hypocrisy
Hypocrisie, the onely evil that walks — Par Lost 3.683
1667 'Hipocrisie' in some copies
In feign'd Religion, smooth hypocrisie. — Samson 872

Hypocrite
And thou sly hypocrite, who now wouldst seem — Par Lost 4.957
Suffers the Hypocrite or Atheous Priest — Par Reg 1.487

Hypocrites
Whatever Hypocrites austerely talk — Par Lost 4.744

Hyrcanian
And *Margiana* to the *Hyrcanian* cliffs — Par Reg 3.317

Hyrcanus
Antigonus, and old *Hyrcanus* bound, — Par Reg 3.367

I

Fast by the Oracle of God; I thence	Par Lost 1.12
I may assert Eternal Providence,	Par Lost 1.25
Can else inflict, do I repent or change,	Par Lost 1.96
Too well I see and rue the dire event,	Par Lost 1.134
But what if he our Conquerour, (whom I now	Par Lost 1.143
Shall grieve him, if I fail not, and disturb	Par Lost 1.167
What matter where, if I be still the same,	Par Lost 1.256
And what I should be, all but less then he	Par Lost 1.257
I give not Heav'n for lost. From this descent	Par Lost 2.14
More unexpert, I boast not: them let those	Par Lost 2.52
I should be much for open Warr, O Peers,	Par Lost 2.119
I laugh, when those who at the Spear are bold	Par Lost 2.204
All thoughts of warr: ye have what I advise.	Par Lost 2.283
But I should ill become this Throne, O Peers,	Par Lost 2.445
Mee from attempting. Wherefore do I assume	Par Lost 2.450
Against a wakeful Foe, while I abroad	Par Lost 2.463
To yonder Gates? through them I mean to pass,	Par Lost 2.684
Where I reign King, and to enrage thee more,	Par Lost 2.698
Least with a whip of Scorpions I pursue	Par Lost 2.701
What it intends; till first I know of thee,	Par Lost 2.740
I know thee not, nor ever saw till now	Par Lost 2.744
Hast thou forgot me then, and do I seem	Par Lost 2.747
Out of thy head I sprung: amazement seis'd	Par Lost 2.758
I pleas'd, and with attractive graces won	Par Lost 2.762
I also; at which time this powerful Key	Par Lost 2.774
Without my op'ning. Pensive here I sat	Par Lost 2.777
Alone, but long I sat not, till my womb	Par Lost 2.778
Made to destroy: I fled, and cry'd out *Death;*	Par Lost 2.787
I fled, but he pursu'd (though more, it seems,	Par Lost 2.790
That rest or intermission none I find.	Par Lost 2.802
His end with mine involvd; and knows that I	Par Lost 2.807
But thou O Father, I forewarn thee, shun	Par Lost 2.810
I come no enemie, but to set free	Par Lost 2.822
Fell with us from on high: from them I go	Par Lost 2.826
Then this more secret now design'd, I haste	Par Lost 2.838
I keep, by him forbidden to unlock	Par Lost 2.852
But what ow I to his commands above	Par Lost 2.856
My being gav'st me; whom should I obey	Par Lost 2.865
The Gods who live at ease, where I shall Reign	Par Lost 2.868
Chaos and *ancient Night*, I come no Spy,	Par Lost 2.970
Alone, and without guide, half lost, I seek	Par Lost 2.975
I travel this profound, direct my course;	Par Lost 2.980
To your behoof, if I that Region lost,	Par Lost 2.982
Answer'd. I know thee, stranger, who thou art,	Par Lost 2.990
I saw and heard, for such a numerous Host	Par Lost 2.993
Pursuing. I upon my Frontieres here	Par Lost 2.998
Keep residence; if all I can will serve,	Par Lost 2.999
May I express thee unblam'd? since God is light,	Par Lost 3.3
Thee I re-visit now with bolder wing,	Par Lost 3.13
I sung of *Chaos* and *Eternal Night*,	Par Lost 3.18
Though hard and rare: thee I revisit safe,	Par Lost 3.21
Cease I to wander where the Muses haunt	Par Lost 3.27
Nightly I visit: nor somtimes forget	Par Lost 3.32
So were I equal'd with them in renown,	Par Lost 3.34
Purge and disperse, that I may see and tell	Par Lost 3.54
All he could have; I made him just and right,	Par Lost 3.98
Such I created all th' Ethereal Powers	Par Lost 3.100
What pleasure I from such obedience paid,	Par Lost 3.107
Thir own revolt, not I: if I foreknew,	Par Lost 3.117
I formd them free, and free they must remain,	Par Lost 3.124
Till they enthrall themselves: I else must change	Par Lost 3.125
Freely voutsaft; once more I will renew	Par Lost 3.175
Some I have chosen of peculiar grace	Par Lost 3.183
Invites; for I will cleer thir senses dark,	Par Lost 3.188
And I will place within them as a guide	Par Lost 3.194
And none but such from mercy I exclude.	Par Lost 3.202
I offer, on mee let thine anger fall;	Par Lost 3.237
Account mee man; I for his sake will leave	Par Lost 3.238
Under his gloomie power I shall not long	Par Lost 3.242
Life in my self for ever, by thee I live,	Par Lost 3.244
Though now to Death I yield, and am his due	Par Lost 3.245
But I shall rise Victorious, and subdue	Par Lost 3.250
I through the ample Air in Triumph high	Par Lost 3.254
While by thee rais'd I ruin all my Foes,	Par Lost 3.258
Though last created, that for him I spare	Par Lost 3.278
I give thee, reign for ever, and assume	Par Lost 3.318
Thrones, Princedoms, Powers, Dominions I reduce:	Par Lost 3.320
That I may find him, and with secret gaze,	Par Lost 3.671
I saw when at his Word the formless Mass,	Par Lost 3.708
That spot to which I point is *Paradise*,	Par Lost 3.733
Hide thir diminisht heads; to thee I call,	Par Lost 4.35
O Sun, to tell thee how I hate thy beams	Par Lost 4.37
I fell, how glorious once above thy Spheare;	Par Lost 4.39
From me, whom he created what I was	Par Lost 4.43
I sdeind subjection, and thought one step higher	Par Lost 4.50
Forgetful what from him I still receivd,	Par Lost 4.54
Me some inferiour Angel, I had stood	Par Lost 4.59
Me miserable! which way shall I flie	Par Lost 4.73
Which way I flie is Hell; my self am Hell;	Par Lost 4.75
To which the Hell I suffer seems a Heav'n.	Par Lost 4.78
Among the spirits beneath, whom I seduc'd	Par Lost 4.83
Then to submit, boasting I could subdue	Par Lost 4.85
How dearly I abide that boast so vaine,	Par Lost 4.87
Under what torments inwardly I groane;	Par Lost 4.88
The lower still I fall, onely Supream	Par Lost 4.91
But say I could repent and could obtaine	Par Lost 4.93
And heavier fall: so should I purchase deare	Par Lost 4.101

I(*cont*)

From granting hee, as I from begging peace:	Par Lost 4.104
Divided Empire with Heav'ns King I hold	Par Lost 4.111
To you whom I could pittie thus forlorne	Par Lost 4.374
Though I unpittied: League with you I seek,	Par Lost 4.375
That I with you must dwell, or you with me	Par Lost 4.377
Which I as freely give; Hell shall unfold,	Par Lost 4.381
And should I at your harmless innocence	Par Lost 4.388
Melt, as I doe, yet public reason just,	Par Lost 4.389
To do what else though damnd I should abhorre.	Par Lost 4.392
And from whom I was formd flesh of thy flesh,	Par Lost 4.441
And daily thanks, I chiefly who enjoy	Par Lost 4.445
That day I oft remember, when from sleep	Par Lost 4.449
I first awak't, and found my self repos'd	Par Lost 4.450
And what I was, whence thither brought, and how.	Par Lost 4.452
Pure as th' expanse of Heav'n; I thither went	Par Lost 4.456
As I bent down to look, just opposite,	Par Lost 4.460
Bending to look on me, I started back,	Par Lost 4.462
It started back, but pleas'd I soon returnd,	Par Lost 4.463
Of sympathie and love; there I had fixt	Par Lost 4.465
And I will bring thee where no shadow staies	Par Lost 4.470
Mother of human Race: what could I doe,	Par Lost 4.475
Till I espi'd thee, fair indeed and tall,	Par Lost 4.477
Then that smooth watry image; back I turnd,	Par Lost 4.480
His flesh, his bone; to give thee being I lent	Par Lost 4.483
Part of my Soul I seek thee, and thee claim	Par Lost 4.487
Seisd mine, I yielded, and from that time see	Par Lost 4.489
Of bliss on bliss, while I to Hell am thrust,	Par Lost 4.508
Yet let me not forget what I have gain'd	Par Lost 4.512
Thir ruine! Hence I will excite thir minds	Par Lost 4.522
But first with narrow search I must walk round	Par Lost 4.528
A chance but chance may lead where I may meet	Par Lost 4.530
Yet happie pair; enjoy, till I return,	Par Lost 4.534
Gods latest Image: I describ'd his way	Par Lost 4.567
I fear, hath ventur'd from the deep, to raise	Par Lost 4.574
Thou tellst, by morrow dawning I shall know.	Par Lost 4.588
Unargu'd I obey; so God ordains,	Par Lost 4.636
With thee conversing I forget all time,	Par Lost 4.639
Strait side by side were laid, nor turnd I weene	Par Lost 4.741
Farr be it, that I should write thee sin or blame,	Par Lost 4.758
Undaunted. If I must contend, said he,	Par Lost 4.851
O friends, I hear the tread of nimble feet	Par Lost 4.866
And such I held thee; but this question askt	Par Lost 4.887
Dole with delight, which in this place I sought;	Par Lost 4.894
Not that I less endure, or shrink from pain,	Par Lost 4.925
Insulting Angel, well thou knowst I stood	Par Lost 4.926
I therefore, I alone first undertook	Par Lost 4.935
But mark what I arreede thee now, avant;	Par Lost 4.962
Back to th' infernal pit I drag thee chaind,	Par Lost 4.965
Then when I am thy captive talk of chaines,	Par Lost 4.970
Satan, I know thy strength, and thou knowst mine,	Par Lost 4.1006
My Glorie, my Perfection, glad I see	Par Lost 5.29
Thy face, and Morn return'd, for I this Night,	Par Lost 5.30
Such night till this I never pass'd, have dream'd,	Par Lost 5.31
If dream'd, not as I oft am wont, of thee,	Par Lost 5.32
With gentle voice, I thought it thine; it said,	Par Lost 5.37
I rose as at thy call, but found thee not;	Par Lost 5.48
To find thee I directed then my walk;	Par Lost 5.49
And on, methought, alone I pass'd through ways	Par Lost 5.50
And as I wondring lookt, beside it stood	Par Lost 5.54
So quick'nd appetite, that I, methought,	Par Lost 5.85
With him I flew, and underneath beheld	Par Lost 5.87
My Guide was gon, and I, me thought, sunk down,	Par Lost 5.91
And fell asleep; but O how glad I wak'd	Par Lost 5.92
Affects me equally; nor can I like	Par Lost 5.97
This uncouth dream, of evil sprung I fear;	Par Lost 5.98
Som such resemblances methinks I find	Par Lost 5.114
Witness if I be silent, Morn or Eeven,	Par Lost 5.202
But I will haste and from each bough and break,	Par Lost 5.326
Adam, I therefore came, nor art thou such	Par Lost 5.372
I have at will. So to the Silvan Lodge	Par Lost 5.377
To spiritual Natures; only this I know,	Par Lost 5.402
Think not I shall be nice. So down they sat,	Par Lost 5.433
Inhabitant with God, now know I well	Par Lost 5.461
If I refuse not, but convert, as you,	Par Lost 5.492
Divine instructer, I have heard, then when	Par Lost 5.546
Aereal Music send: nor knew I not	Par Lost 5.548
Sad task and hard, for how shall I relate	Par Lost 5.564
Of human sense, I shall delineate so,	Par Lost 5.572
This day I have begot whom I declare	Par Lost 5.603
At my right hand; your Head I him appoint;	Par Lost 5.606
Wast wont, I mine to thee was wont to impart;	Par Lost 5.677
Her shadowie Cloud withdraws, I am to haste,	Par Lost 5.686
Son, thou in whom my glory I behold	Par Lost 5.719
Know whether I be dextrous to subdue	Par Lost 5.741
The supple knee? ye will not, if I trust	Par Lost 5.788
Forsak'n of all good; I see thy fall	Par Lost 5.878
Yet not for thy advise or threats I fly	Par Lost 5.889
I mean to try, whose Reason I have tri'd	Par Lost 6.120
To thee not visible, when I alone	Par Lost 6.145
At first I thought that Libertie and Heav'n	Par Lost 6.164
I see that most through sloth had rather serve,	Par Lost 6.166
I flie not, but have sought thee farr and nigh.	Par Lost 6.295
I might relate of thousands, and thir names	Par Lost 6.373
Believst so main to our success, I bring;	Par Lost 6.471
He comes, and settl'd in his face I see	Par Lost 6.540
If I conjecture aught, no drizling showr,	Par Lost 6.545
But that I doubt, however witness Heaven,	Par Lost 6.563

I(*cont*)
For joy of offerd peace: but I suppose Par Lost 6.617
Visibly, what by Deitie I am, Par Lost 6.682
And in whose hand what by Decree I doe, Par Lost 6.683
For to themselves I left them, and thou knowst, Par Lost 6.689
Insensibly, for I suspend thir doom; Par Lost 6.692
For thee I have ordain'd it, and thus farr Par Lost 6.700
Immense I have transfus'd, that all may know Par Lost 6.704
To glorifie thy Son, I alwayes thee, Par Lost 6.725
As is most just; this I my Glorie account, Par Lost 6.726
Scepter and Power, thy giving, I assume, Par Lost 6.730
Thou shalt be All in All, and I in thee Par Lost 6.732
But whom thou hat'st, I hate, and can put on Par Lost 6.734
Thy terrors, as I put thy mildness on, Par Lost 6.735
Hymns of high praise, and I among them chief. Par Lost 6.745
And twentie thousand (I thir number heard) Par Lost 6.769
Or I alone against them, since by strength Par Lost 6.820
Nor other strife with them do I voutsafe. Par Lost 6.823
By what is past, to thee I have reveal'd Par Lost 6.895
Following, above th' *Olympian* Hill I soare, Par Lost 7.3
The meaning, not the Name I call: for thou Par Lost 7.5
Into the Heav'n of Heav'ns I have presum'd, Par Lost 7.13
Dismounted, on th' *Aleian* Field I fall Par Lost 7.19
More safe I Sing with mortal voice, unchang'd Par Lost 7.24
I have receav'd, to answer thy desire Par Lost 7.119
Yet farr the greater part have kept, I see, Par Lost 7.145
My damage fondly deem'd, I can repaire Par Lost 7.152
This I perform, speak thou, and be it don: Par Lost 7.164
I send along, ride forth, and bid the Deep Par Lost 7.166
Boundless the Deep, because I am who fill Par Lost 7.168
Though I uncircumscrib'd my self retire, Par Lost 7.170
Approach not mee, and what I will is Fate. Par Lost 7.173
And let them be for Lights as I ordaine Par Lost 7.343
Equal have I to render thee, Divine Par Lost 8.6
The thirst I had of knowledge, and voutsaf't Par Lost 8.8
When I behold this goodly Frame, this World Par Lost 8.15
Useless besides, reasoning I oft admire, Par Lost 8.25
To ask or search I blame thee not, for Heav'n Par Lost 8.66
Alreadie by thy reasoning this I guess, Par Lost 8.85
By Numbers that have name. But this I urge, Par Lost 8.114
Not that I so affirm, though so it seem Par Lost 8.117
Thee I have heard relating what was don Par Lost 8.203
How suttly to detaine thee I devise, Par Lost 8.207
Inviting thee to hear while I relate, Par Lost 8.208
For while I sit with thee, I seem in Heav'n, Par Lost 8.210
For I that Day was absent, as befell, Par Lost 8.229
But thy relation now; for I attend, Par Lost 8.247
Soft on the flourie herb I found me laid Par Lost 8.254
Strait toward Heav'n my wondring Eyes I turnd, Par Lost 8.257
By quick instinctive motion up I sprung, Par Lost 8.259
Stood on my feet; about me round I saw Par Lost 8.261
My self I then perus'd, and Limb by Limb Par Lost 8.267
But who I was, or where, or from what cause, Par Lost 8.270
Knew not; to speak I tri'd, and forthwith spake, Par Lost 8.271
What e're I saw. Thou Sun, said I, faire Light, Par Lost 8.273
Tell, if ye saw, how came I thus, how here? Par Lost 8.277
Tell me, how may I know him, how adore, Par Lost 8.280
From whom I have that thus I move and live, Par Lost 8.281
And feel that I am happier then I know, Par Lost 8.282
While thus I call'd, and stray'd I knew not whither, Par Lost 8.283
From where I first drew Aire, and first beheld Par Lost 8.284
Pensive I sate me down; there gentle sleep Par Lost 8.287
My droused sense, untroubl'd, though I thought Par Lost 8.289
I then was passing to my former state Par Lost 8.290
My fancy to believe I yet had being, Par Lost 8.294
First Father, call'd by thee I come thy Guide Par Lost 8.298
Planted, with Walks, and Bowers, that what I saw Par Lost 8.305
To pluck and eate; whereat I wak'd, and found Par Lost 8.309
In adoration at his feet I fell Par Lost 8.315
Submiss: he rear'd me, and Whom thou soughtst I am, Par Lost 8.316
This Paradise I give thee, count it thine Par Lost 8.319
Knowledg of good and ill, which I have set Par Lost 8.324
Remember what I warne thee, shun to taste, Par Lost 8.327
To thee and to thy Race I give; as Lords Par Lost 8.339
After thir kindes; I bring them to receave Par Lost 8.343
I nam'd them, as they pass'd, and understood Par Lost 8.352
I found not what me thought I wanted still; Par Lost 8.355
Surpassest farr my naming, how may I Par Lost 8.359
I see not who partakes. In solitude Par Lost 8.364
Thus I presumptuous; and the vision bright, Par Lost 8.367
So ordering. I with leave of speech implor'd, Par Lost 8.377
My Maker, be propitious while I speak. Par Lost 8.380
Tedious alike: Of fellowship I speak Par Lost 8.389
Such as I seek, fit to participate Par Lost 8.390
A nice and suttle happiness I see Par Lost 8.399
Seem I to thee sufficiently possest Par Lost 8.404
From all Eternitie, for none I know Par Lost 8.406
How have I then with whom to hold converse Par Lost 8.408
Save with the Creatures which I made, and those Par Lost 8.409
He ceas'd, I lowly answer'd. To attaine Par Lost 8.412
I by conversing cannot these erect Par Lost 8.432
Thus I embold'nd spake, and freedom us'd Par Lost 8.434
Thus farr to try thee, *Adam*, I was pleas'd, Par Lost 8.437
And be so minded still; I, ere thou spak'st, Par Lost 8.444
What next I bring shall please thee, be assur'd, Par Lost 8.449
Hee ended, or I heard no more, for now Par Lost 8.452
Abstract as in a transe methought I saw, Par Lost 8.462
Though sleeping, where I lay, and saw the shape Par Lost 8.463

I(*cont*)
Still glorious before whom awake I stood; Par Lost 8.464
Shee disappeerd, and left me dark, I wak'd Par Lost 8.478
Such as I saw her in my dream, adornd Par Lost 8.482
I overjoyd could not forbear aloud. Par Lost 8.490
Of all thy gifts, nor enviest. I now see Par Lost 8.494
I follow'd her, she what was Honour knew, Par Lost 8.508
I led her blushing like the Morn: all Heav'n, Par Lost 8.511
Thus I have told thee all my State, and brought Par Lost 8.521
Which I enjoy, and must confess to find Par Lost 8.523
I mean of Taste, Sight, Smell, Herbs, Fruits, and Flours, Par Lost 8.527
Farr otherwise, transported I behold, Par Lost 8.529
Transported touch; here passion first I felt, Par Lost 8.530
For well I understand in the prime end Par Lost 8.540
O're other Creatures; yet when I approach Par Lost 8.546
And with mysterious reverence I deem) Par Lost 8.599
Yet these subject not; I to thee disclose Par Lost 8.607
What inward thence I feel, not therefore foild, Par Lost 8.608
Approve the best, and follow what I approve. Par Lost 8.611
Bear with me then, if lawful what I ask; Par Lost 8.614
But I can now no more; the parting Sun Par Lost 8.630
I in thy persevering shall rejoyce, Par Lost 8.639
Sent from whose sovran goodness I adore. Par Lost 8.647
Venial discourse unblam'd: I now must change Par Lost 9.5
If answerable style I can obtaine Par Lost 9.20
With what delight could I have walkt thee round, Par Lost 9.114
If I could joy in aught, sweet interchange Par Lost 9.115
Rocks, Dens, and Caves; but I in none of these Par Lost 9.118
Find place or refuge; and the more I see Par Lost 9.119
Pleasures about me, so much more I feel Par Lost 9.120
But neither here seek I, no nor in Heav'n Par Lost 9.124
By what I seek, but others to make such Par Lost 9.127
As I, though thereby worse to me redound: Par Lost 9.128
For onely in destroying I find ease Par Lost 9.129
Not longer then since I in one Night freed Par Lost 9.140
I dread, and to elude, thus wrapt in mist Par Lost 9.158
To hide me, and the dark intent I bring. Par Lost 9.162
O foul descent! that I who erst contended Par Lost 9.163
Let it; I reck not, so it light well aim'd, Par Lost 9.173
Since higher I fall short, on him who next Par Lost 9.174
The clasping Ivie where to climb, while I Par Lost 9.217
Thee satiate, to short absence I could yield. Par Lost 9.248
Our ruin, both by thee informd I learne, Par Lost 9.275
As in a shadie nook I stood behind, Par Lost 9.277
May tempt it, I expected not to hear. Par Lost 9.281
Not diffident of thee do I dissuade Par Lost 9.293
If such affront I labour to avert Par Lost 9.302
I from the influence of thy looks receave Par Lost 9.309
When I am present, and thy trial choose Par Lost 9.316
That I should mind thee oft, and mind thou me. Par Lost 9.358
The willinger I goe, nor much expect Par Lost 9.382
Her Husband, for I view far round, not nigh, Par Lost 9.482
Whose higher intellectual more I shun, Par Lost 9.483
I not; so much hath Hell debas'd, and paine Par Lost 9.487
Infeebl'd me, to what I was in Heav'n. Par Lost 9.488
The way which to her ruin now I tend. Par Lost 9.493
Displeas'd that I approach thee thus, and gaze Par Lost 9.535
Insatiate, I thus single, nor have feard Par Lost 9.536
The first at lest of these I thought denid Par Lost 9.555
The latter I demurre, for in thir looks Par Lost 9.558
I knew, but not with human voice endu'd; Par Lost 9.561
I was at first as other Beasts that graze Par Lost 9.571
Till on a day roaving the field, I chanc'd Par Lost 9.575
Ruddie and Gold: I nearer drew to gaze; Par Lost 9.578
To satisfie the sharp desire I had Par Lost 9.584
Of tasting those fair Apples, I resolv'd Par Lost 9.585
About the mossie Trunk I wound me soon, Par Lost 9.589
I spar'd not, for such pleasure till that hour Par Lost 9.596
At Feed or Fountain never had I found. Par Lost 9.597
Sated at length, ere long I might perceave Par Lost 9.598
I turnd my thoughts, and with capacious mind Par Lost 9.603
United I beheld; no Fair to thine Par Lost 9.608
My conduct, I can bring thee thither soon. Par Lost 9.630
Mother of Science, Now I feel thy Power Par Lost 9.680
That ye should be as Gods, since I as Man, Par Lost 9.710
I of brute human, yee of human Gods. Par Lost 9.712
I question it, for this fair Earth I see, Par Lost 9.720
What fear I then, rather what know to feare Par Lost 9.773
Till dieted by thee I grow mature Par Lost 9.803
Thus grown. Experience, next to thee I owe, Par Lost 9.807
Best guide; not following thee, I had remaind Par Lost 9.808
And I perhaps am secret; Heav'n is high, Par Lost 9.811
Shall I appeer? shall I to him make known Par Lost 9.817
And Death ensue? then I shall be no more, Par Lost 9.827
Shall live with her enjoying, I extinct; Par Lost 9.829
A death to think. Confirm'd then I resolve, Par Lost 9.830
So dear I love him, that with him all deaths Par Lost 9.832
I could endure, without him live no life. Par Lost 9.833
Thee I have misst, and thought it long, depriv'd Par Lost 9.857
Mean I to trie, what rash untri'd I sought, Par Lost 9.860
Perswasively hath so prevaild, that I Par Lost 9.873
Chiefly I sought, without thee can despise. Par Lost 9.878
Disjoyne us, and I then too late renounce Par Lost 9.884
How can I live without thee, how forgoe Par Lost 9.908
Should God create another *Eve*, and I Par Lost 9.911
Would never from my heart; no no, I feel Par Lost 9.913
Nor can I think that God, Creator wise, Par Lost 9.938
However I with thee have fixt my Lot, Par Lost 9.952

I(*cont*)

So forcible within my heart I feel	Par Lost 9.955
Of thy perfection, how shall I attaine,	Par Lost 9.964
Adam, from whose deare side I boast me sprung,	Par Lost 9.965
Were it I thought Death menac't would ensue	Par Lost 9.977
This my attempt, I would sustain alone	Par Lost 9.978
So faithful Love unequald; but I feel	Par Lost 9.983
Eve, now I see thou art exact of taste,	Par Lost 9.1017
And Palate call judicious; I the praise	Par Lost 9.1020
I saw thee first and wedded thee, adorn'd	Par Lost 9.1030
Be sure then. How shall I behold the face	Par Lost 9.1080
Insufferably bright. O might I here	Par Lost 9.1084
Hide me, where I may never see them more.	Par Lost 9.1090
With me, as I besought thee, when that strange	Par Lost 9.1135
I know not whence possessd thee; we had then	Par Lost 9.1137
Was I to have never parted from thy side?	Par Lost 9.1153
Being as I am, why didst not thou the Head	Par Lost 9.1155
Neither had I transgress'd, nor thou with mee.	Par Lost 9.1161
Immutable when thou wert lost, not I,	Par Lost 9.1165
And am I now upbraided, as the cause	Par Lost 9.1168
It seems, in thy restraint: what could I more?	Par Lost 9.1170
I warn'd thee, I admonish'd thee, foretold	Par Lost 9.1171
I also err'd in overmuch admiring	Par Lost 9.1178
What seemd in thee so perfet, that I thought	Par Lost 9.1179
No evil durst attempt thee, but I rue	Par Lost 9.1180
I told ye then he should prevail and speed	Par Lost 10.40
But whom send I to judge them? whom but thee	Par Lost 10.55
Vicegerent Son, to thee I have transferr'd	Par Lost 10.56
Easie it might be seen that I intend	Par Lost 10.58
Mayst ever rest well pleas'd. I go to judge	Par Lost 10.71
When time shall be, for so I undertook	Par Lost 10.74
Of right, that I may mitigate thir doom	Par Lost 10.76
On me deriv'd, yet I shall temper so	Par Lost 10.77
My coming seen far off? I miss thee here,	Par Lost 10.104
Or come I less conspicuous, or what change	Par Lost 10.107
I heard thee in the Garden, and of thy voice	Par Lost 10.116
Whereof I gave thee charge thou shouldst not eat?	Par Lost 10.123
O Heav'n! in evil strait this day I stand	Par Lost 10.125
I should conceal, and not expose to blame	Par Lost 10.130
Devolv'd; though should I hold my peace, yet thou	Par Lost 10.135
Wouldst easily detect what I conceale.	Par Lost 10.136
That from her hand I could suspect no ill,	Par Lost 10.140
Shee gave me of the Tree, and I did eate.	Par Lost 10.143
The Serpent me beguil'd and I did eate.	Par Lost 10.162
Between Thee and the Woman I will put	Par Lost 10.179
Thy sorrow I will greatly multiplie	Par Lost 10.193
I charg'd thee, saying: Thou shalt not eate thereof,	Par Lost 10.200
Methinks I feel new strength within me rise,	Par Lost 10.243
Nor can I miss the way, so strongly drawn	Par Lost 10.262
Leads thee, I shall not lag behinde, nor erre	Par Lost 10.266
The way, thou leading, such a sent I draw	Par Lost 10.267
Nor shall I to the work thou enterprisest	Par Lost 10.270
For I no sooner in my Heart divin'd,	Par Lost 10.357
Now also evidence, but straight I felt	Par Lost 10.361
That I must after thee with this thy Son;	Par Lost 10.363
Of *Satan* (for I glorie in the name,	Par Lost 10.386
Of easie thorough-fare. Therefore while I	Par Lost 10.393
My Substitutes I send ye, and Create	Par Lost 10.403
I call ye and declare ye now, returnd	Par Lost 10.462
What I have don, what sufferd, with what paine	Par Lost 10.470
To expedite your glorious march; but I	Par Lost 10.474
Protesting Fate supreame; thence how I found	Par Lost 10.480
Made happie: Him by fraud I have seduc'd	Par Lost 10.485
Man I deceav'd: that which to mee belongs,	Par Lost 10.496
Mee and Mankinde; I am to bruise his heel;	Par Lost 10.498
There best, where most with ravin I may meet;	Par Lost 10.599
Till I in Man residing through the Race,	Par Lost 10.607
To waste and havoc yonder World, which I	Par Lost 10.617
I suffer them to enter and possess	Par Lost 10.623
Of Passion, I to them had quitted all,	Par Lost 10.627
And know not that I call'd and drew them thither	Par Lost 10.629
The miserie, I deserv'd it, and would beare	Par Lost 10.726
All that I eat or drink, or shall beget,	Par Lost 10.728
Now death to heare! for what can I encrease	Par Lost 10.731
Did I request thee, Maker, from my Clay	Par Lost 10.743
To mould me Man, did I sollicite thee	Par Lost 10.744
All I receav'd, unable to performe	Par Lost 10.750
Thy terms too hard, by which I was to hold	Par Lost 10.751
The good I sought not. To the loss of that,	Par Lost 10.752
I thus contest; then should have been refusd	Par Lost 10.756
Wherefore didst thou beget me? I sought it not	Par Lost 10.762
Be it so, for I submit, his doom is fair,	Par Lost 10.769
That dust I am, and shall to dust returne:	Par Lost 10.770
Fixd on this day? why do I overlive,	Par Lost 10.773
Why am I mockt with death, and length'nd out	Par Lost 10.774
To deathless pain? how gladly would I meet	Par Lost 10.775
As in my Mothers lap? there I should rest	Par Lost 10.778
Pursues me still, least all I cannot die,	Par Lost 10.783
But I shall die a living Death? O thought	Par Lost 10.788
That Death be not one stroak, as I suppos'd,	Par Lost 10.809
From this day onward, which I feel begun	Par Lost 10.811
On my defensless head; both Death and I	Par Lost 10.815
Nor I on my part single, in mee all	Par Lost 10.817
That I must leave ye, Sons; O were I able	Par Lost 10.819
Forc't I absolve: all my evasions vain,	Par Lost 10.829
I find no way, from deep to deeper plung'd!	Par Lost 10.844
With other echo late I taught your Shades	Par Lost 10.861
I had persisted happie, had not thy pride	Par Lost 10.874

I(*cont*)

Fool'd and beguil'd, by him thou, I by thee,	Par Lost 10.880
I beare thee, and unweeting have offended,	Par Lost 10.916
I beg, and clasp thy knees; bereave me not,	Par Lost 10.918
Whereon I live, thy gentle looks, thy aid,	Par Lost 10.919
Whither shall I betake me, where subsist?	Par Lost 10.922
Against God onely, I against God and thee,	Par Lost 10.931
Could alter high Decrees, I to that place	Par Lost 10.953
Since this days Death denounc't, if ought I see,	Par Lost 10.962
Adam, by sad experiment I know	Par Lost 10.967
Restor'd by thee, vile as I am, to place	Par Lost 10.971
Living or dying, from thee I will not hide	Par Lost 10.974
To be forestall'd; much more I fear least Death	Par Lost 10.1024
I have in view, calling to minde with heed	Par Lost 10.1030
Be meant, whom I conjecture, our grand Foe	Par Lost 10.1033
Glanc'd on the ground, with labour I must earne	Par Lost 10.1054
With Incense, I thy Priest before thee bring,	Par Lost 11.25
Numberd, though sad, till Death, his doom (which I	Par Lost 11.40
Made one with me as I with thee am one.	Par Lost 11.44
The Law I gave to Nature him forbids:	Par Lost 11.49
Corrupted. I at first with two fair gifts	Par Lost 11.57
Till I provided Death; so Death becomes	Par Lost 11.61
Through Heav'ns wide bounds; from them I will not hide	Par Lost 11.68
My judgments, how with Mankind I proceed,	Par Lost 11.69
His heart I know, how variable and vain	Par Lost 11.92
For ever, to remove him I decree,	Par Lost 11.96
For I behold them softn'd and with tears	Par Lost 11.110
As I shall thee enlighten, intermix	Par Lost 11.115
Ev'n to the Seat of God. For since I saught	Par Lost 11.148
Methought I saw him placable and mild,	Par Lost 11.151
That I was heard with favour; peace returnd	Par Lost 11.153
Ill worthie I such title should belong	Par Lost 11.163
That I who first brought Death on all, am grac't	Par Lost 11.168
I never from thy side henceforth to stray,	Par Lost 11.176
New Laws to be observ'd; for I descrie	Par Lost 11.228
That I should fear, nor sociably mild,	Par Lost 11.234
As *Raphael*, that I should much confide,	Par Lost 11.235
With reverence I must meet, and thou retire.	Par Lost 11.237
Permits not; to remove thee I am come,	Par Lost 11.260
Must I thus leave thee Paradise? thus leave	Par Lost 11.269
Fit haunt of Gods? where I had hope to spend,	Par Lost 11.271
At Eev'n, which I bred up with tender hand	Par Lost 11.276
How shall I part, and whither wander down	Par Lost 11.282
Incessant I could hope to change the will	Par Lost 11.308
Of him who all things can, I would not cease	Par Lost 11.309
Therefore to his great bidding I submit.	Par Lost 11.314
As from his face I shall be hid, deprivd	Par Lost 11.316
His blessed count'nance; here I could frequent,	Par Lost 11.317
I heard, here with him at this Fountain talk'd:	Par Lost 11.322
So many grateful Altars I would reare	Par Lost 11.323
In yonder nether World where shall I seek	Par Lost 11.328
For though I fled him angrie, yet recall'd	Par Lost 11.330
To life prolongd and promisd Race, I now	Par Lost 11.331
Ere thou from hence depart, know I am sent	Par Lost 11.356
This Hill; let *Eve* (for I have drencht her eyes)	Par Lost 11.367
Ascend, I follow thee, safe Guide, the path	Par Lost 11.371
If so I may attain. So both ascend	Par Lost 11.376
But have I now seen Death? Is this the way	Par Lost 11.462
I must return to native dust? O sight	Par Lost 11.463
I yield it just, said *Adam*, and submit.	Par Lost 11.526
Henceforth I flie not Death, nor would prolong	Par Lost 11.547
Life much, bent rather how I may be quit	Par Lost 11.548
Which I must keep till my appointed day	Par Lost 11.550
But still I see the tenor of Mans woe	Par Lost 11.632
O Visions ill foreseen! better had I	Par Lost 11.763
Wandring that watrie Desert: I had hope	Par Lost 11.779
But I was farr deceav'd; for now I see	Par Lost 11.783
As present, Heav'nly instructer, I revive	Par Lost 11.871
Farr less I now lament for one whole World	Par Lost 11.874
Of wicked Sons destroyd, then I rejoyce	Par Lost 11.875
Much thou hast yet to see, but I perceave	Par Lost 12.8
Henceforth what is to com I will relate,	Par Lost 12.11
I see him, but thou canst not, with what Faith	Par Lost 12.128
Canaan he now attains, I see his Tents	Par Lost 12.135
(Things by thir names I call, though yet unnam'd)	Par Lost 12.140
In prospect, as I point them; on the shoare	Par Lost 12.143
Just *Abraham* and his Seed: now first I finde	Par Lost 12.273
Of mee and all Mankind; but now I see	Par Lost 12.276
This yet I apprehend not, why to those	Par Lost 12.280
Of *David* (so I name this King) shall rise	Par Lost 12.326
Of utmost hope! now clear I understand	Par Lost 12.376
Light out of darkness! full of doubt I stand,	Par Lost 12.473
Whether I should repent me now of sin	Par Lost 12.474
Greatly instructed I shall hence depart,	Par Lost 12.557
Henceforth I learne, that to obey is best,	Par Lost 12.561
Taught this by his example whom I now	Par Lost 12.572
Her also I with gentle Dreams have calm'd	Par Lost 12.595
Whence thou returnst, and whither wentst, I know;	Par Lost 12.610
Wearied I fell asleep: but now lead on;	Par Lost 12.614
I carry hence; though all by mee is lost,	Par Lost 12.621
Such favour I unworthie am voutsaft,	Par Lost 12.622
I Who e're while the happy Garden sung,	Par Reg 1.1
For much more willingly I mention Air,	Par Reg 1.45
For this ill news I bring, the Womans seed	Par Reg 1.64
Thenceforth the Nations may not doubt; I saw	Par Reg 1.79
And out of Heav'n the Sov'raign voice I heard,	Par Reg 1.84
I, when no other durst, sole undertook	Par Reg 1.100
With man or mens affairs, how I begin	Par Reg 1.132

I(*cont*)

On which I sent thee to the Virgin pure Par Reg 1.134
And high prediction, henceforth I expose Par Reg 1.142
He now shall know I can produce a man Par Reg 1.150
By fallacy surpriz'd. But first I mean Par Reg 1.155
Of his great warfare, e're I send him forth Par Reg 1.158
From what consummate vertue I have chose Par Reg 1.165
Awakn'd in me swarm, while I consider Par Reg 1.197
What from within I feel my self, and hear Par Reg 1.198
When I was yet a child, no childish play Par Reg 1.201
What might be publick good; my self I thought Par Reg 1.204
The Law of God I read, and found it sweet, Par Reg 1.207
I went into the Temple, there to hear Par Reg 1.211
This having heard, strait I again revolv'd Par Reg 1.259
I am; this chiefly, that my way must lie Par Reg 1.263
E're I the promis'd Kingdom can attain, Par Reg 1.265
The time prefixt I waited, when behold Par Reg 1.269
The Baptist, (of whose birth I oft had heard, Par Reg 1.270
I as all others to his Baptism came, Par Reg 1.273
Which I believ'd was from above; but he Par Reg 1.274
But as I rose out of the laving stream, Par Reg 1.280
He was well pleas'd; by which I knew the time Par Reg 1.286
Now full, that I no more should live obscure, Par Reg 1.287
The Authority which I deriv'd from Heaven. Par Reg 1.289
And now by some strong motion I am led Par Reg 1.290
I learn not yet, perhaps I need not know; Par Reg 1.292
I ask the rather, and the more admire, Par Reg 1.326
Of God; I saw and heard, for we sometimes Par Reg 1.330
Will bring me hence, no other Guide I seek. Par Reg 1.336
What other way I see not, for we here Par Reg 1.338
(For I discern thee other then thou seem'st) Par Reg 1.348
Wandred this barren waste, the same I now: Par Reg 1.354
Knowing who I am, as I know who thou art? Par Reg 1.356
'Tis true, I am that Spirit unfortunate, Par Reg 1.358
Leaving my dolorous Prison I enjoy Par Reg 1.364
I came among the Sons of God, when he Par Reg 1.368
I undertook that office, and the tongues Par Reg 1.374
To his destruction, as I had in charge. Par Reg 1.376
For what he bids I do; though I have lost Par Reg 1.377
To be belov'd of God, I have not lost Par Reg 1.378
What I see excellent in good, or fair, Par Reg 1.381
Or vertuous, I should so have lost all sense. Par Reg 1.382
To see thee and approach thee, whom I know Par Reg 1.384
To all mankind: why should I? they to me Par Reg 1.388
I lost not what I lost, rather by them Par Reg 1.390
I gain'd what I have gain'd, and with them dwell Par Reg 1.391
Nearer acquainted, now I feel by proof, Par Reg 1.400
Man fall'n shall be restor'd, I never more. Par Reg 1.405
From thee I can and must submiss endure Par Reg 1.476
What wonder then if I delight to hear Par Reg 1.481
To hear thee when I come (since no man comes) Par Reg 1.484
And talk at least, though I despair to attain. Par Reg 1.485
Thy coming hither, though I know thy scope, Par Reg 1.494
I bid not or forbid; do as thou find'st Par Reg 1.495
And with him talkt, and with him lodg'd, I mean Par Reg 2.6
While I to sorrows am no less advanc't, Par Reg 2.69
Of other women, by the birth I bore, Par Reg 2.71
Full grown to Man, acknowledg'd, as I hear, Par Reg 2.83
I look't for some great change; to Honour? no, Par Reg 2.86
Afflicted I may be, it seems, and blest; Par Reg 2.93
I will not argue that, nor will repine. Par Reg 2.94
I lost him, but so found, as well I saw Par Reg 2.97
His Father's business; what he meant I mus'd, Par Reg 2.99
But I to wait with patience am inur'd; Par Reg 2.102
I, as I undertook, and with the vote Par Reg 2.129
Then when I dealt with *Adam* first of Men, Par Reg 2.133
Therefore I am return'd, lest confidence Par Reg 2.140
Of like succeeding here; I summon all Par Reg 2.143
Or counsel to assist; lest I who erst Par Reg 2.145
And now I know he hungers where no food Par Reg 2.231
The rest commit to me, I shall let pass Par Reg 2.233
Where will this end? four times ten days I have pass'd Par Reg 2.245
To Vertue I impute not, or count part Par Reg 2.248
Of what I suffer here; if Nature need not, Par Reg 2.249
But now I feel I hunger, which declares, Par Reg 2.252
Without this bodies wasting, I content me, Par Reg 2.256
With granted leave officious I return, Par Reg 2.302
Of all things destitute, and well I know, Par Reg 2.305
They all had need, I as thou seest have none. Par Reg 2.318
Would'st thou not eat? Thereafter as I like Par Reg 2.321
But tender all their power? nor mention I Par Reg 2.327
Said'st thou not that to all things I had right? Par Reg 2.379
Shall I receive by gift what of my own, Par Reg 2.381
When and where likes me best, I can command? Par Reg 2.382
I can at will, doubt not, as soon as thou, Par Reg 2.383
Thy pompous Delicacies I contemn, Par Reg 2.390
That I have also power to give thou seest, Par Reg 2.393
If of that pow'r I bring thee voluntary Par Reg 2.394
What I might have bestow'd on whom I pleas'd, Par Reg 2.395
Why shouldst thou not accept it? but I see Par Reg 2.398
What I can do or offer is suspect; Par Reg 2.399
They whom I favour thrive in wealth amain, Par Reg 2.430
For I esteem those names of men so poor Par Reg 2.447
And what in me seems wanting, but that I Par Reg 2.450
What if with like aversion I reject Par Reg 2.457
I see thou know'st what is of use to know, Par Reg 3.7
By patience, temperance; I mention still Par Reg 3.92
Shall I seek glory then, as vain men seek Par Reg 3.105

I(*cont*)

Oft not deserv'd? I seek not mine, but his Par Reg 3.106
Who sent me, and thereby witness whence I am. Par Reg 3.107
What if he hath decreed that I shall first Par Reg 3.188
What I can suffer, how obey? who best Par Reg 3.194
Well hath obey'd; just tryal e're I merit Par Reg 3.196
But what concerns it thee when I begin Par Reg 3.198
I would be at the worst; worst is my Port, Par Reg 3.209
The end I would attain, my final good. Par Reg 3.211
Willingly I could flye, and hope thy raign, Par Reg 3.216
(Whose ire I dread more then the fire of Hell) Par Reg 3.220
If I then to the worst that can be hast, Par Reg 3.223
But I will bring thee where thou soon shalt quit Par Reg 3.244
That thou may'st know I seek not to engage Par Reg 3.347
To what end I have brought thee hither and shewn Par Reg 3.350
Means I must use thou say'st, prediction else Par Reg 3.394
My time I told thee, (and that time for thee Par Reg 3.396
I must deliver, if I mean to raign Par Reg 3.404
Should I of these the liberty regard, Par Reg 3.427
To his due time and providence I leave them. Par Reg 3.440
Houses of Gods (so well I have dispos'd Par Reg 4.56
These having shewn thee, I have shewn thee all Par Reg 4.88
Is given, and by that right I give it thee. Par Reg 4.104
(For I have also heard, perhaps have read) Par Reg 4.116
How gloriously; I shall, thou say'st, expel Par Reg 4.127
A brutish monster: what if I withal Par Reg 4.128
For him I was not sent, nor yet to free Par Reg 4.131
I see all offers made by me how slight Par Reg 4.155
On the other side know also thou, that I Par Reg 4.159
On what I offer set as high esteem, Par Reg 4.160
Nor what I part with mean to give for naught; Par Reg 4.161
The Kingdoms of the world to thee I give; Par Reg 4.163
For giv'n to me, I give to whom I please, Par Reg 4.164
I never lik'd thy talk, thy offers less, Par Reg 4.171
But I endure the time, till which expir'd, Par Reg 4.174
That I fall down and worship thee as God? Par Reg 4.192
If I to try whether in higher sort Par Reg 4.198
What both from Men and Angels I receive, Par Reg 4.200
Me naught advantag'd, missing what I aim'd. Par Reg 4.208
The Kingdoms of this world; I shall no more Par Reg 4.210
Think not but that I know these things, or think Par Reg 4.286
I know them not; not therefore am I short Par Reg 4.287
Of knowing what I aught: he who receives Par Reg 4.288
Or if I would delight my private hours Par Reg 4.331
As in our native Language can I find Par Reg 4.333
For thee is fittest place, I found thee there, Par Reg 4.373
What I foretell thee, soon thou shalt have cause Par Reg 4.375
Now contrary, if I read aught in Heaven, Par Reg 4.382
Real or Allegoric I discern not, Par Reg 4.390
After a dismal night; I heard the rack Par Reg 4.452
Did I not tell thee, if thou didst reject Par Reg 4.467
What I foretold thee, many a hard assay Par Reg 4.478
I never fear'd they could, though noising loud Par Reg 4.488
Betok'ning, or ill boding, I contemn Par Reg 4.490
Who knowing I shall raign past thy preventing, Par Reg 4.492
Obtrud'st thy offer'd aid, that I accepting Par Reg 4.493
Of the Messiah I have heard foretold Par Reg 4.502
Announc't by *Gabriel* with the first I knew, Par Reg 4.504
From that time seldom have I ceas'd to eye Par Reg 4.507
Flock'd to the Baptist, I among the rest, Par Reg 4.511
Thenceforth I thought thee worth my nearer view Par Reg 4.514
And narrower Scrutiny, that I might learn Par Reg 4.515
The Son of God I also am, or was, Par Reg 4.518
And if I was, I am; relation stands; Par Reg 4.519
All men are Sons of God; yet thee I thought Par Reg 4.520
Therefore I watch'd thy footsteps from that hour, Par Reg 4.522
Where by all best conjectures I collect Par Reg 4.524
Good reason then, if I before-hand seek Par Reg 4.526
To win him, or win from him what I can. Par Reg 4.530
And opportunity I here have had Par Reg 4.531
Another method I must now begin. Par Reg 4.540
Will ask thee skill; I to thy Fathers house Par Reg 4.552
There I am wont to sit, when any chance Samson 4
Where I a Prisoner chain'd, scarce freely draw Samson 7
Unwholsom draught: but here I feel amends, Samson 9
Retiring from the popular noise, I seek Samson 16
Times past, what once I was, and what am now. Samson 22
Design'd for great exploits; if I must dye Samson 32
Lower then bondslave! Promise was that I Samson 38
Whom have I to complain of but my self? Samson 46
But peace, I must not quarrel with the will Samson 60
O loss of sight, of thee I most complain! Samson 67
They creep, yet see, I dark in light expos'd Samson 75
Scarce half I seem to live, dead more then half. Samson 79
Why am I thus bereav'd thy prime decree? Samson 85
Then had I not been thus exil'd from light; Samson 98
But who are these? for with joint pace I hear Samson 110
Which shall I first bewail, Samson 151
For him I reckon not in high estate Samson 170
Sam. I hear the sound of words, thir sense the air Samson 176
Sam. Your coming, Friends, revives me, for I learn Samson 187
I would be understood) in prosperous days Samson 191
Blindness, for had I sight, confus'd with shame, Samson 196
How could I once look up, or heave the head, Samson 197
Am I not sung and proverbd for a Fool Samson 203
Yet truth to say, I oft have heard men wonder Samson 215
Sam. The first I saw at *Timna*, and she pleas'd Samson 219
Mee, not my Parents, that I sought to wed, Samson 220

I(*cont*)

That what I motion'd was of God; I knew Samson 222
I might begin *Israel*'s Deliverance, Samson 225
The work to which I was divinely call'd; Samson 226
She proving false, the next I took to Wife Samson 227
(O that I never had! fond wish too late.) Samson 228
I thought it lawful from my former act, Samson 231
Israel's oppressours: of what now I suffer Samson 233
She was not the prime cause, but I my self, Samson 234
Thou never wast remiss, I bear thee witness: Samson 239
Sam. That fault I take not on me, but transfer Samson 241
Deliverance offerd: I on th' other side Samson 246
I willingly on some conditions came Samson 258
Toucht with the flame: on thir whole Host I flew Samson 262
As I suppose, towards your once gloried friend, Samson 334
I pray'd for Children, and thought barrenness Samson 352
In wedlock a reproach; I gain'd a Son, Samson 353
But justly; I my self have brought them on, Samson 375
Sole Author I, sole cause: if aught seem vile, Samson 376
This well I knew, nor was at all surpris'd, Samson 381
Thrice I deluded her, and turn'd to sport Samson 396
I yielded, and unlock'd her all my heart, Samson 407
The base degree to which I now am fall'n, Samson 414
That saw not how degenerately I serv'd. Samson 419
Man. I cannot praise thy Marriage choises, Son, Samson 420
I state not that; this I am sure; our Foes Samson 424
Sam. Father, I do acknowledge and confess Samson 448
That I this honour, I this pomp have brought Samson 449
I as a Prophecy receive: for God, Samson 473
Neglected. I already have made way Samson 481
As I deserve, pay on my punishment; Samson 489
But I Gods counsel have not kept, his holy secret Samson 497
Sam. His pardon I implore; but as for life, Samson 521
To what end should I seek it? when in strength Samson 522
All mortals I excell'd, and great in hopes Samson 523
I walk'd about admir'd of all and dreaded Samson 530
Then swoll'n with pride into the snare I fell Samson 532
I drank, from the clear milkie juice allaying Samson 550
To what can I be useful, wherein serve Samson 564
And I perswade me so; why else this strength Samson 586
So much I feel my genial spirits droop, Samson 594
And I shall shortly be with them that rest. Samson 598
That mingle with thy fancy. I however Samson 601
I was his nursling once and choice delight, Samson 633
Abstemious I grew up and thriv'd amain; Samson 637
Whom I by his appointment had provok't, Samson 643
Nor am I in the list of them that hope; Samson 647
This one prayer yet remains, might I be heard, Samson 649
Or might I say contrarious, Samson 669
Nor do I name of men the common rout, Samson 674
What do I beg? how hast thou dealt already? Samson 707
I came, still dreading thy displeasure, *Samson*, Samson 733
I cannot but acknowledge; yet if tears Samson 735
In the perverse event then I foresaw) Samson 737
As I by thee, to Ages an example. Samson 765
Dal. Yet hear me *Samson;* not that I endeavour Samson 766
I may, if possible, thy pardon find Samson 771
First granting, as I do, it was a weakness Samson 773
To what I did thou shewdst me first the way. Samson 781
But I to enemies reveal'd, and should not. Samson 782
E're I to thee, thou to thy self wast cruel. Samson 784
Caus'd what I did? I saw thee mutable Samson 793
No better way I saw then by importuning Samson 797
Why then reveal'd? I was assur'd by those Samson 800
That made for me, I knew that liberty Samson 803
While I at home sate full of cares and fears Samson 805
Here I should still enjoy thee day and night Samson 807
By this appears: I gave, thou say'st, th' example, Samson 822
I led the way; bitter reproach, but true, Samson 823
I to my self was false e're thou to me, Samson 824
Such pardon therefore as I give my folly, Samson 825
And I believe it, weakness to resist Samson 830
Knowing, as needs I must, by thee betray'd? Samson 840
Hear what assaults I had, what snares besides, Samson 845
What sieges girt me round, e're I consented; Samson 846
Dishonourer of *Dagon:* what had I Samson 861
Vertue, as I thought, truth, duty so enjoyning. Samson 870
Sam. I thought where all thy circling wiles would end; Samson 871
I before all the daughters of my Tribe Samson 876
Parents and countrey; nor was I their subject, Samson 886
Witness when I was worried with thy peals. Samson 906
Dal. I was a fool, too rash, and quite mistaken Samson 907
In what I thought would have succeeded best. Samson 908
Towards thee I intend for what I have misdone, Samson 911
I to the Lords will intercede, not doubting Samson 920
Thir favourable ear, that I may fetch thee Samson 921
It fits not; thou and I long since are twain; Samson 929
Where once I have been caught; I know thy trains Samson 932
So much of Adders wisdom I have learn't Samson 936
When I must live uxorious to thy will Samson 945
This Gaol I count the house of Liberty Samson 949
At distance I forgive thee, go with that; Samson 954
Dal. I see thou art implacable, more deaf Samson 960
Why do I humble thus my self, and suing Samson 965
To mix with thy concernments I desist Samson 969
But in my countrey where I most desire, Samson 980
I shall be nam'd among the famousest Samson 982
Nor shall I count it hainous to enjoy Samson 991

I(*cont*)

Which to my countrey I was judg'd to have shewn. Samson 994
I leave him to his lot, and like my own. Samson 996
But had we best retire, I see a storm? Samson 1061
Draws hitherward, I know him by his stride, Samson 1067
I less conjecture then when first I saw Samson 1071
Har. I come not *Samson*, to condole thy chance, Samson 1076
Though for no friendly intent. I am of *Gath*, Samson 1078
If thou at all art known. Much I have heard Samson 1082
That I was never present on the place Samson 1085
Har. Dost thou already single me; I thought Samson 1092
I should have forc'd thee soon wish other arms, Samson 1096
I lose, prevented by thy eyes put out. Samson 1103
Har. To combat with a blind man I disdain, Samson 1106
I only with an Oak'n staff will meet thee, Samson 1123
Sam. I know no Spells, use no forbidden Arts; Samson 1139
Then thine, while I preserv'd these locks unshorn, Samson 1143
Which I to be the power of *Israel*'s God Samson 1150
From thine, these evils I deserve and more, Samson 1169
In confidence whereof I once again Samson 1174
Thine or whom I with *Israel*'s Sons adore. Samson 1177
I chose a Wife, which argu'd me no foe; Samson 1193
That solv'd the riddle which I had propos'd. Samson 1200
When I perceiv'd all set on enmity, Samson 1201
I us'd hostility, and took thir spoil Samson 1203
But I a private person, whom my Countrey Samson 1208
I was no private but a person rais'd Samson 1211
I was to do my part from Heav'n assign'd, Samson 1217
Fear I incurable; bring up thy van, Samson 1234
Sams. Go baffl'd coward, lest I run upon thee, Samson 1237
Sam. I dread him not, nor all his Giant-brood, Samson 1247
Chor. He will directly to the Lords, I fear, Samson 1250
They cannot well impose, nor I sustain; Samson 1258
For I descry this way Samson 1301
By his habit I discern him now Samson 1305
Off. *Ebrews*, the Pris'ner *Samson* here I seek. Samson 1308
Where I will see thee heartn'd and fresh clad Samson 1317
Sam. Thou knowst I am an *Ebrew*, therefore tell them, Samson 1319
My presence; for that cause I cannot come. Samson 1321
Return the way thou cam'st, I will not come. Samson 1332
Joyn'd with extream contempt? I will not come. Samson 1342
Off. I am sorry what this stoutness will produce. Samson 1346
Sam. Shall I abuse this Consecrated gift Samson 1354
Commands are no constraints. If I obey them, Samson 1372
I do it freely; venturing to displease Samson 1373
Sam. Be of good courage, I begin to feel Samson 1381
I with this Messenger will go along, Samson 1384
To thee I am bid say. Art thou our Slave, Samson 1392
Sam. I could be well content to try thir Art, Samson 1399
Like a wild Beast, I am content to go. Samson 1403
Off. I praise thy resolution, doff these links: Samson 1410
I will not wish, lest it perhaps offend them Samson 1414
I know not. Lords are Lordliest in thir wine; Samson 1418
The last of me or no I cannot warrant. Samson 1426
I heard all as I came, the City rings Samson 1449
And numbers thither flock, I had no will, Samson 1450
Lest I should see him forc't to things unseemly. Samson 1451
To give ye part with me what hope I have Samson 1453
Man. I have attempted one by one the Lords Samson 1457
Some much averse I found and wondrous harsh, Samson 1461
And numberd down: much rather I shall chuse Samson 1478
No, I am fixt not to part hence without him. Samson 1481
If need be, I am ready to forgo Samson 1483
And quit: not wanting him, I shall want nothing. Samson 1484
And I perswade me God had not permitted Samson 1495
Man. I know your friendly minds and----O what noise! Samson 1508
Man. Of ruin indeed methought I heard the noise, Samson 1515
Man. He can I know, but doubt to think he will; Samson 1534
And to our wish I see one hither speeding, Samson 1539
An *Ebrew*, as I guess, and of our Tribe. Samson 1540
Mess. O whither shall I run, or which way flie Samson 1541
To have guided me aright, I know not how, Samson 1547
My Countreymen, whom here I knew remaining, Samson 1549
Mess. It would burst forth, but I recover breath Samson 1555
And sense distract, to know well what I utter. Samson 1556
Mess. Ah *Manoa* I refrain, too suddenly Samson 1565
What windy joy this day had I conceiv'd Samson 1574
Yet e're I give the rains to grief, say first, Samson 1578
And as the gates I enter'd with Sun-rise, Samson 1597
Through each high street: little I had dispatch't Samson 1599
I sorrow'd at his captive state, but minded Samson 1603
I among these aloof obscurely stood. Samson 1611
I have perform'd, as reason was, obeying, Samson 1641
I mean to shew you of my strength, yet greater; Samson 1644
The clotted gore. I with what speed the while Samson 1728
Home to his Fathers house: there will I build him Samson 1733
I would not soil these pure Ambrosial weeds, Mask 16
I was dispatcht for their defence, and guard; Mask 42
And listen why, for I will tell ye now Mask 43
I shoot from Heav'n to give him safe convoy, Mask 81
As now I do: But first I must put off Mask 82
Of this occasion. But I hear the tread Mask 91
Of hatefull steps, I must be viewles now. Mask 92
Break off, break off, I feel the different pace, Mask 145
(For so I can distinguish by mine Art) Mask 149
And to my wily trains, I shall e're long Mask 151
About my Mother *Circe*. Thus I hurl Mask 153
I under fair pretence of friendly ends, Mask 160

I(*cont*)
I shall appear som harmles Villager Mask 166
But here she comes, I fairly step aside Mask 168
And hearken, if I may, her busines here. Mask 169
And thank the gods amiss. I should be loath Mask 177
Shall I inform my unacquainted feet Mask 180
This is the place, as well as I may guess, Mask 201
line not in Bridgewater ms
Yet nought but single darknes do I find. Mask 204
line not in Bridgewater ms
I see ye visibly, and now beleeve Mask 216
line not in Bridgewater ms
Trinity ms '& now beleeve' ←'now I beleeve' ←'& while I see yee'
Was I deceiv'd, or did a sable cloud Mask 221
line not in Bridgewater ms
I did not err, there does a sable cloud Mask 223
line not in Bridgewater ms
I cannot hallow to my Brothers, but Mask 226
Such noise as I can make to be heard farthest Mask 227
Of darknes till it smil'd: I have oft heard Mask 252
I never heard till now. Ile speak to her Mask 264
La. No less then if I should my brothers loose. Mask 288
Co. Two such I saw, what time the labour'd Oxe Mask 291
I saw them under a green mantling vine Mask 294
I took it for a faery vision Mask 298
And play i' th plighted clouds. I was aw-strook, Mask 301
And as I past, I worshipt; if those you seek Mask 302
La. To find out that, good Shepherd, I suppose, Mask 307
Co. I know each lane, and every alley green Mask 311
Or shroud within these limits, I shall know Mask 316
I can conduct you Lady to a low Mask 319
Till further quest'. *La*. Shepherd I take thy word, Mask 321
I cannot be, that I should fear to change it. Mask 328
I do not think my sister so to seek, Mask 366
(Not being in danger, as I trust she is not) Mask 370
I fear the dred events that dog them both, Mask 405
Of our unowned sister. *Eld. Bro*. I do not, brother, Mask 407
Inferr, as if I thought my sisters state Mask 408
That I encline to hope, rather then fear, Mask 412
Eld. Bro. I mean that too, but yet a hidden strength Mask 418
Do ye beleeve me yet, or shall I call Mask 438
Where no crude surfet raigns. *Eld. Bro*. List, list, I hear Mask 480
That hallow I should know, what are you? speak; Mask 490
I came not here on such a trivial toy Mask 502
Character'd in the face; this have I learn't Mask 530
I sate me down to watch upon a bank Mask 543
At which I ceas't, and listen'd them a while, Mask 551
Still to be so displac't. I was all eare, Mask 560
Too well I did perceive it was the voice Mask 563
Amaz'd I stood, harrow'd with grief and fear, Mask 565
And O poor hapless Nightingale thought I, Mask 566
Then down the Lawns I ran with headlong hast Mask 568
Till guided by mine ear I found the place Mask 570
(For so by certain signes I knew) had met Mask 572
Longer I durst not stay, but soon I guess't Mask 577
Ye were the two she mean't, with that I sprung Mask 578
Into swift flight, till I had found you here, Mask 579
But furder know I not. 2. *Bro*. O night and shades, Mask 580
Which erring men call Chance, this I hold firm, Mask 588
I love thy courage yet, and bold Emprise, Mask 610
Which when I did, he on the tender grass Mask 624
I purs't it up, but little reck'ning made, Mask 642
But now I find it true; for by this means Mask 644
I knew the foul inchanter though disguis'd, Mask 645
(As I will give you when we go) you may Mask 648
Comus. Nay Lady sit; if I but wave this wand, Mask 659
I would not taste thy treasonous offer; none Mask 702
La. I had not thought to have unlockt my lips Mask 756
I hate when vice can bolt her arguments, Mask 760
Cramms, and blasphemes his feeder. Shall I go on? Mask 779
word not in Bridgewater ms
word not in Trinity ms
Or have I said anough? To him that dares Mask 780
line not in Bridgewater ms
line not in Trinity ms
Fain would I somthing say, yet to what end? Mask 783
line not in Trinity ms
line not in Bridgewater ms
Yet should I try, the uncontrouled worth Mask 793
line not in Trinity ms
line not in Bridgewater ms
Co. She fables not, I feel that I do fear Mask 800
line not in Bridgewater ms
line not in Trinity ms
To som of *Saturns* crew. I must dissemble, Mask 805
line not in Bridgewater ms
line not in Trinity ms
I must not suffer this, yet 'tis but the lees Mask 809
Yet stay, be not disturb'd, now I bethink me, Mask 820
Som other means I have which may be us'd, Mask 821
Trinity ms 'some other meanes I have' ←'there is another way'
Which once of *Meliboeus* old I learnt Mask 822
In hard besetting need, this will I try Mask 857
Thus I set my printless feet Mask 897
That bends not as I tread, Mask 899
I am here. Mask 901

I(*cont*)
Thus I sprinkle on thy brest Mask 911
I have kept of pretious cure, Mask 913
I touch with chaste palms moist and cold, Mask 918
And I must haste ere morning hour Mask 920
I shall be your faithfull guide Mask 944
I have brought ye new delight, Mask 967
Spir. To the Ocean now I fly, Mask 976
There I suck the liquid ayr Mask 980
I can fly, or I can run Mask 1013
but soft I was not sent to court your wonder Mask Tr. ms 10.16
I doubt me gentle mortalls these may seeme Mask Tr. ms 10.16
yet thence I come and oft from thence behold Mask Tr. ms 10.18
I could be willing though now i' th darke to trie Mask Tr. ms 16.38
'I could be willing' ←'beshrew me but I would' ←'beshew me'
to have her by my side, though I were sure Mask Tr. ms 16.41
how have I bin betrai'd Mask Tr. ms 22.18
I throw it on the ground Mask Tr. ms 22.22
'I' ←'lest I'
I could be willinge though now i' th darke to trie Mask Br. ms 391
to have her by my side, though I were suer Mask Br. ms 394
And if I give thee honour due, Allegro 37
Mirth with thee, I mean to live. Allegro 152
I woo to hear thy eeven Song; Penseroso 64
And missing thee, I walk unseen Penseroso 65
I hear the far-off *Curfeu* sound, Penseroso 74
Where I may oft out-watch the *Bear*, Penseroso 87
And as I wake, sweet musick breath Penseroso 151
Where I may sit and rightly spell, Penseroso 170
And I with thee will choose to live. Penseroso 176
I see bright honour sparkle through your eyes, Arcades 27
I know this quest of yours, and free intent Arcades 34
Whom with low reverence I adore as mine, Arcades 37
Which I full oft amidst these shades alone Arcades 42
For know by lot from *Jove* I am the powr Arcades 44
Trinity ms defective here
And all my Plants I save from nightly ill, Arcades 48
When Eev'ning gray doth rise, I fetch my round Arcades 54
Shakes the high thicket, haste I all about, Arcades 58
Hath lockt up mortal sense, then listen I Arcades 62
I will assay, her worth to celebrate, Arcades 80
Follow me as I sing, Arcades 86
I will bring you where she sits, Arcades 91
I com to pluck your Berries harsh and crude, Lycidas 3
Ay me, I fondly dream! Lycidas 56
That strain I heard was of a higher mood: Lycidas 87
How well could I have spar'd for thee young swain, Lycidas 113
Yet can I not perswade me thou art dead Fair Inf 29
Here I salute thee and thy pardon ask, Vacation 7
That now I use thee in my latter task: Vacation 8
I know my tongue but little Grace can do thee Vacation 10
Believe me I have thither packt the worst: Vacation 12
And, if it happen as I did forecast, Vacation 13
I pray thee then deny me not thy aide Vacation 15
For this same small neglect that I have made: Vacation 16
I have some naked thoughts that rove about Vacation 23
Yet I had rather if I were to chuse, Vacation 29
That to the next I may resign my Roome. Vacation 58
For now to sorrow must I tune my song, Passion 8
The leaves should all be black wheron I write, Passion 34
Yet on the softned Quarry would I score Passion 46
Or should I thence hurried on viewles wing, Passion 50
And I (for grief is easily beguild) Passion 54
So have I seen som tender slip Winchester 35
If I may not carry, sure Ile ne're be fetch'd, Another 18
line not in 1640, 1657, 1658 texts
Both them I serve, and of their train am I. Sonnet 1, 14
That I to manhood am arriv'd so near, Sonnet 7, 6
All is, if I have grace to use it so, Sonnet 7, 13
Madam, me thinks I see him living yet; Sonnet 10, 11
A Book was writ of late call'd *Tetrachordon;* Sonnet 11, 1
Trinity ms 'was writ' ←'was writt' ←'I writt'
I did but prompt the age to quit their cloggs Sonnet 12, 1
When I consider how my light is spent, Sonnet 19, 1
I fondly ask; But patience to prevent Sonnet 19, 8
Or man or woman. Yet I argue not Sonnet 22, 6
Content though blind, had I no better guide. Sonnet 22, 14
Methought I saw my late espoused Saint Sonnet 23, 1
And such, as yet once more I trust to have Sonnet 23, 7
I wak'd, she fled, and day brought back my night. Sonnet 23, 14
And fierce ire trouble them; but I saith hee Psalm 2, 11
I will declare; the Lord to me hath say'd Psalm 2, 14
Thou art my Son I have begotten thee Psalm 2, 15
As thy possession I on thee bestow Psalm 2, 17
Th' exalter of my head I count Psalm 3, 9
Aloud I cry'd Psalm 3, 10
I lay and slept, I wak'd again, Psalm 3, 13
I fear not though incamping round about Psalm 3, 17
Answer me when I call Psalm 4, 1
Will hear my voyce what time to him I crie. Psalm 4, 18
In peace at once will I Psalm 4, 37
Me safe where ere I lie Psalm 4, 40
My King and God for unto thee I pray. Psalm 5, 4
Ith' morning I to thee with choyce Psalm 5, 7
But I will in thy mercies dear Psalm 5, 17
Into thy house; I in thy fear Psalm 5, 19
That do observe If I transgress Psalm 5, 23

I(*cont*)
Pity me Lord for I am much deject — Psalm 6, 3
Wearied I am with sighing out my dayes, — Psalm 6, 11
Nightly my Couch I make a kind of Sea; — Psalm 6, 12
My Bed I water with my tears; mine Eie — Psalm 6, 13
Lord my God to thee I flie — Psalm 7, 1
Thy protection while I crie, — Psalm 7, 3
Lord my God if I have thought — Psalm 7, 7
Be in my hands, if I have wrought — Psalm 7, 9
And command which I desire. — Psalm 7, 24
Then will I Jehovah's praise — Psalm 7, 61
When I behold thy Heavens, thy Fingers art, — Psalm 8, 9
The Tongue I heard, was strange. — Psalm 81, 20
I set his shoulder free; — Psalm 81, 22
And I to free thee *did not faile*, — Psalm 81, 27
I answer'd thee in thunder deep — Psalm 81, 29
I tri'd thee at the water *steep* — Psalm 81, 31
I testifie to thee — Psalm 81, 34
I am the Lord thy God which brought — Psalm 81, 41
Ask large enough, and I, *besought*, — Psalm 81, 43
And Israel *whom I lov'd so dear* — Psalm 81, 47
Then did I leave them to their will — Psalm 81, 49
Then would I soon bring down their foes — Psalm 81, 57
I said that ye were Gods, yea all — Psalm 82, 21
I in the temple of my God — Psalm 84, 37
I will *go strait and* hear, — Psalm 85, 30
O hear me *I thee pray*, — Psalm 86, 2
For I am poor, and almost pine — Psalm 86, 3
Preserve my soul, for I have trod — Psalm 86, 5
I call; O make rejoyce — Psalm 86, 10
I lift my soul *and voice*, — Psalm 86, 12
I in the day of my distress — Psalm 86, 21
And answer, *what I pray'd*. — Psalm 86, 24
I in thy truth will bide, — Psalm 86, 38
Thee will I praise O Lord my God — Psalm 86, 41
I mention Egypt, *where proud Kings* — Psalm 87, 11
I mention Babel to my friends, — Psalm 87, 13
All day to thee I cry; — Psalm 88, 2
Reck'n'd I am with them that pass — Psalm 88, 13
I am a man, but weak alas — Psalm 88, 15
And I here pent up thus. — Psalm 88, 36
Lord all the day I thee entreat, — Psalm 88, 39
My hands to thee I spread. — Psalm 88, 40
But I to thee O Lord do cry — Psalm 88, 53
While I thy terrors undergo — Psalm 88, 63
They *fly me now* whom I have lov'd, — Psalm 88, 71
When I dye, let the earth be roul'd in flames. — Prose 5, 1
Tis you that say it, not I, you do the deeds, — Prose 8, 1
What certain Seat, where I may worship thee — Prose 12, 5

I'll
Ile venter, for my new enliv'nd spirits — Mask 228
  Bridgewater ms 'I'le'
I never heard till now. Ile speak to her — Mask 264
Best draw, and stand upon our guard. *Eld. Bro.* Ile hallow, — Mask 487
'Twixt *Africa* and *Inde*, Ile find him out, — Mask 606
  Bridgewater ms 'I'le'
Eld. Bro. Thyrsis lead on apace, Ile follow thee, — Mask 657
  Trinity ms 'I'
  Bridgewater ms 'I'
If I may not carry, sure Ile ne're be fetch'd, — Another 18
  line not in 1640, 1657, 1658 texts
  1673 'I'le'
Spir. Ile tell ye, 'tis not vain, or fabulous, — Mask 513

Iambic
In *Chorus* or *Iambic*, teachers best — Par Reg 4.262

Iberian
In his prime youth the fair *Iberian* maid. — Par Reg 2.200
Of *Caucasus*, and dark *Iberian* dales, — Par Reg 3.318
Roaving the *Celtick*, and *Iberian* fields, — Mask 60

Ice
Of ancient pile; all else deep snow and ice, — Par Lost 2.591
From Beds of raging Fire to starve in Ice — Par Lost 2.600
Mountains of Ice, that stop th' imagin'd way — Par Lost 10.291
Bursting thir brazen Dungeon, armd with ice — Par Lost 10.697
Th' inclement Seasons, Rain, Ice, Hail and Snow, — Par Lost 10.1063
Humbles his stubborn heart, but still as Ice — Par Lost 12.193

Icy-pearled
So mounting up in ycie-pearled carr, — Fair Inf 15

Ida
And *Ida* known, thence on the Snowy top — Par Lost 1.515
  ms 'Ida'
Of three that in Mount *Ida* naked strove, — Par Lost 5.382
Of woody *Ida*'s inmost grove, — Penseroso 29

Idea
Answering his great Idea. Up he rode — Par Lost 7.557

Idiots
Embryo's and Idiots, Eremits and Friers — Par Lost 3.474

Idle
Rove idle unimploid, and less need rest; — Par Lost 4.617
All courage; down thir idle weapons drop'd; — Par Lost 6.839
Main Ocean flow'd, not idle, but with warme — Par Lost 7.279
But to sit idle on the houshold hearth, — Samson 566
Better at home lie bed-rid, not only idle, — Samson 579
Not to sit idle with so great a gift — Samson 1500
Dwell in som idle brain, — Penseroso 5
The idle spear and shield were high up hung; — Nativity 55
Nor to thir idle orbs doth sight appear — Sonnet 22, 4

Idleness
My bread; what harm? Idleness had bin worse; — Par Lost 10.1055

Idly
Idlely, while Satan our great Author thrives — Par Lost 10.236
Both Horse and Foot, nor idely mustring stood; — Par Lost 11.645

Idol
To his grim Idol. Him the *Ammonite* — Par Lost 1.396
Idol of Majestie Divine, enclos'd — Par Lost 6.101
To *Dagon* thir Sea-Idol, and forbid — Samson 13
This Idols day hath bin to thee no day of rest, — Samson 1297
Chaunting thir Idol, and preferring — Samson 1672
His burning Idol all of blackest hue, — Nativity 207

Idolatresses
Beguil'd by fair Idolatresses, fell — Par Lost 1.445

Idolatries
His eye survay'd the dark Idolatries — Par Lost 1.456
Whose foul Idolatries, and other faults — Par Lost 12.337
And all the Idolatries of Heathen round, — Par Reg 3.418

Idolatrous
Idolatrous, but when his purpose is — Par Reg 1.444
By th' Idolatrous rout amidst thir wine; — Samson 443
Idolatrous, uncircumcis'd, unclean. — Samson 1364
Present in Temples at Idolatrous Rites — Samson 1378

Idolatry
Drunk with Idolatry, drunk with Wine, — Samson 1670

Idolisms
Thir Idolisms, Traditions, Paradoxes? — Par Reg 4.234

Idolists
Of Idolists, and Atheists; have brought scandal — Samson 453

Idols
And various Idols through the Heathen World. — Par Lost 1.375
  ms 'Idolls'
To Idols foul. *Thammuz* came next behind, — Par Lost 1.446
  ms 'Idolls'
To Idols, those young *Daniel* could refuse; — Par Reg 2.329
And God with Idols in thir worship joyn'd. — Par Reg 3.426
Thir enemies, who serve Idols with God. — Par Reg 3.432
Besides whom is no God, compar'd with Idols, — Samson 441
To waver, or fall off and joyn with Idols; — Samson 456
By prostituting holy things to Idols; — Samson 1358

Idol-worship
Bred up in Idol-worship; O that men — Par Lost 12.115
Sam. Not in thir Idol-worship, but by labour — Samson 1365

If
Rose out of *Chaos*: Or if *Sion* Hill — Par Lost 1.10
If he oppos'd; and with ambitious aim — Par Lost 1.41
If thou beest he; But O how fall'n! how chang'd — Par Lost 1.84
Myriads though bright: If he whom mutual league, — Par Lost 1.87
  ms 'if'
But what if he our Conquerour, (whom I now — Par Lost 1.143
Whom we resist. If then his Providence — Par Lost 1.162
Shall grieve him, if I fail not, and disturb — Par Lost 1.167
There rest, if any rest can harbour there, — Par Lost 1.185
If not what resolution from despare. — Par Lost 1.191
He lights, if it were Land that ever burn'd — Par Lost 1.228
What matter where, if I be still the same, — Par Lost 1.256
If once they hear that voyce, thir liveliest pledge — Par Lost 1.274
If such astonishment as this can sieze — Par Lost 1.317
If counsels different, or danger shun'd — Par Lost 1.636
Thither, if but to pry, shall be perhaps — Par Lost 1.655
Let such bethink them, if the sleepy drench — Par Lost 2.73
To our destruction: if there be in Hell — Par Lost 2.84
Or if our substance be indeed Divine, — Par Lost 2.99
Which if not Victory is yet Revenge. — Par Lost 2.105
As not behind in hate; if what was urg'd — Par Lost 2.120
What if the breath that kindl'd those grim fires — Par Lost 2.170
His red right hand to plague us? what if all — Par Lost 2.174
If we were wise, against so great a foe — Par Lost 2.202
And vent'rous, if that fail them, shrink and fear — Par Lost 2.205
Our doom; which if we can sustain and bear, — Par Lost 2.209
Will slack'n, if his breath stir not thir flames. — Par Lost 2.214
If we procure not to our selves more woe. — Par Lost 2.225
We warr, if warr be best, or to regain — Par Lost 2.230
Or ambush from the Deep. What if we find — Par Lost 2.344
(if ancient and prophetic fame in Heav'n — Par Lost 2.346
  1667 'If'
The punie habitants, or if not drive, — Par Lost 2.367
Faded so soon. Advise if this be worth — Par Lost 2.376
These past, if any pass, the void profound — Par Lost 2.438
If thence he scape into whatever world, — Par Lost 2.442
With splendor, arm'd with power, if aught propos'd — Par Lost 2.447
More tollerable; if there be cure or charm — Par Lost 2.460
If chance the radiant Sun with farewell sweet — Par Lost 2.492
As if (which might induce us to accord) — Par Lost 2.503
That dismal world, if any Clime perhaps — Par Lost 2.572
If aught disturb'd thir noyse, into her woomb, — Par Lost 2.657
If shape it might be call'd that shape had none — Par Lost 2.667
Som Capital City; or less then if this frame — Par Lost 2.924
Confine with Heav'n; or if som other place — Par Lost 2.977
To your behoof, if I that Region lost, — Par Lost 2.982
Keep residence; if all I can will serve, — Par Lost 2.999
If that way be your walk, you have not farr; — Par Lost 2.1007
If him by force he can destroy, or worse, — Par Lost 3.91
As if predestination over-rul'd — Par Lost 3.114
Thir own revolt, not I: if I foreknew, — Par Lost 3.117
My Umpire *Conscience*, whom if they will hear, — Par Lost 3.195
If mettal, part seemd Gold, part Silver cleer; — Par Lost 3.595
If stone, Carbuncle most or Chrysolite, — Par Lost 3.596

If(*cont*)

What wonder then if fields and regions here	Par Lost 3.606
Him counterfet, if any eye beheld.	Par Lost 4.117
But rather to tell how, if Art could tell,	Par Lost 4.236
If true, here only, and of delicious taste:	Par Lost 4.251
Your numerous ofspring; if no better place,	Par Lost 4.385
Uriel, no wonder if thy perfet sight,	Par Lost 4.577
No Creature thence: if Spirit of other sort,	Par Lost 4.582
But if within the circuit of these walks,	Par Lost 4.586
Ask riddance, if we mean to tread with ease;	Par Lost 4.632
Blest pair; and O yet happiest if ye seek	Par Lost 4.774
Or if, inspiring venom, he might taint	Par Lost 4.804
The lowest of your throng; or if ye know,	Par Lost 4.831
Undaunted. If I must contend, said he,	Par Lost 4.851
His Iron Gates, if he intends our stay	Par Lost 4.898
Flie thither whence thou fledst: if from this houre	Par Lost 4.963
If thou resist. The Fiend lookt up and knew	Par Lost 4.1013
If dream'd, not as I oft am wont, of thee,	Par Lost 5.32
If none regard; Heav'n wakes with all his eyes,	Par Lost 5.44
If better thou belong not to the dawn,	Par Lost 5.167
Witness if I be silent, Morn or Eeven,	Par Lost 5.202
To give us onely good; and if the night	Par Lost 5.206
Through Spirits with ease; nor wonder; if by fire	Par Lost 5.439
Deserving Paradise! if ever, then,	Par Lost 5.446
If not deprav'd from good, created all	Par Lost 5.471
If I refuse not, but convert, as you,	Par Lost 5.492
If ye be found obedient, and retain	Par Lost 5.501
What meant that caution joind, *if ye be found*	Par Lost 5.513
But more desire to hear, if thou consent,	Par Lost 5.555
As may express them best, though what if Earth	Par Lost 5.574
If not the first Arch-Angel, great in Power,	Par Lost 5.660
If these magnific Titles yet remain	Par Lost 5.773
But what if better counsels might erect	Par Lost 5.785
The supple knee? ye will not, if I trust	Par Lost 5.788
To know ye right, or if ye know your selves	Par Lost 5.789
By none, and if not equal all, yet free,	Par Lost 5.791
His equals, if in power and splendor less,	Par Lost 5.796
His massie Spear upstaid; as if on Earth	Par Lost 6.195
To flight, or if to fall, but that they rise	Par Lost 6.285
If not to reign: mean while thy utmost force,	Par Lost 6.293
Great things by small, If Natures concord broke,	Par Lost 6.311
(And if one day, why not Eternal dayes2)	Par Lost 6.424
In Nature none: if other hidden cause	Par Lost 6.442
In future dayes, if Malice should abound,	Par Lost 6.502
Where lodg'd, or whither fled, or if for fight,	Par Lost 6.531
If I conjecture aught, no drizling showr,	Par Lost 6.545
Stand readie to receive them, if they like	Par Lost 6.561
What should they do? if on they rusht, repulse	Par Lost 6.600
If our proposals once again were heard	Par Lost 6.618
If rightly thou art call'd, whose Voice divine	Par Lost 7.2
If they transgress, and slight that sole command,	Par Lost 7.47
Absolv'd, if unforbid thou maist unfould	Par Lost 7.94
Or if the Starr of Eevning and the Moon	Par Lost 7.104
That detriment, if such it be to lose	Par Lost 7.153
If steep, with torrent rapture, if through Plaine,	Par Lost 7.299
Holy and just: thrice happie if they know	Par Lost 7.631
Informd by thee might know; if else thou seekst	Par Lost 7.639
Imports not, if thou reck'n right, the rest	Par Lost 8.71
Rather admire; or if they list to try	Par Lost 8.75
If it presume, might erre in things too high,	Par Lost 8.121
And no advantage gaine. What if the Sun	Par Lost 8.122
In six thou seest, and what if sev'nth to these	Par Lost 8.128
If Earth industrious of her self fetch Day	Par Lost 8.137
Still luminous by his ray. What if that light	Par Lost 8.140
This Earth? reciprocal, if Land be there,	Par Lost 8.144
Tell, if ye saw, how came I thus, how here?	Par Lost 8.277
Of Wisdom, she deserts thee not, if thou	Par Lost 8.563
But if the sense of touch whereby mankind	Par Lost 8.579
To them made common and divulg'd, if aught	Par Lost 8.583
Bear with me then, if lawful what I ask;	Par Lost 8.614
Easier then Air with Air, if Spirits embrace,	Par Lost 8.626
If answerable style I can obtaine	Par Lost 9.20
Depress, and much they may, if all be mine,	Par Lost 9.46
O Earth, how like to Heav'n, if not preferr'd	Par Lost 9.99
If I could joy in aught, sweet interchange	Par Lost 9.115
More Angels to Create, if they at least	Par Lost 9.146
Our taske we choose, what wonder if so near	Par Lost 9.221
Assist us: But if much converse perhaps	Par Lost 9.247
If such affront I labour to avert	Par Lost 9.302
More wise, more watchful, stronger, if need were	Par Lost 9.311
If this be our condition, thus to dwell	Par Lost 9.322
Fraile is our happiness, if this be so,	Par Lost 9.340
Were better, and most likelie if from mee	Par Lost 9.365
But if thou think, trial unsought may finde	Par Lost 9.370
If chance with Nymphlike step fair Virgin pass,	Par Lost 9.452
Wonder not, sovran Mistress, if perhaps	Par Lost 9.532
Of blowing Myrrh and Balme; if thou accept	Par Lost 9.629
Wondrous indeed, if cause of such effects.	Par Lost 9.650
Of good, how just? of evil, if what is evil	Par Lost 9.698
Them nothing: If they all things, who enclos'd	Par Lost 9.722
Impart against his will if all be his?	Par Lost 9.728
Such prohibitions binde not. But if Death	Par Lost 9.760
This may be well: but what if God have seen,	Par Lost 9.826
Certain to undergoe like doom, if Death	Par Lost 9.953
If any be, of tasting this fair Fruit,	Par Lost 9.972
True relish, tasting; if such pleasure be	Par Lost 9.1024
Bad Fruit of Knowledge, if this be to know,	Par Lost 9.1073
To gird thir waste, vain Covering if to hide	Par Lost 9.1113

If(*cont*)

And left to her self, if evil thence ensue,	Par Lost 9.1185
But that success attends him; if mishap,	Par Lost 10.239
So, if great things to small may be compar'd,	Par Lost 10.306
If your joynt power prevailes, th' affaires of Hell	Par Lost 10.408
That laugh, as if transported with some fit	Par Lost 10.626
Of happiness: yet well, if here would end	Par Lost 10.725
Made thee without thy leave, what if thy Son	Par Lost 10.760
Horrid, if true! yet why? it was but breath	Par Lost 10.789
If guiltless? But from me what can proceed,	Par Lost 10.824
Well if thrown out, as supernumerarie	Par Lost 10.887
By a farr worse, or if she love, withheld	Par Lost 10.903
And my displeasure bearst so ill. If Prayers	Par Lost 10.952
Since this days Death denounc't, if ought I see,	Par Lost 10.962
If care of our descent perplex us most,	Par Lost 10.979
But if thou judge it hard and difficult,	Par Lost 10.992
Or if thou covet death, as utmost end	Par Lost 10.1020
How much more, if we pray him, will his ear	Par Lost 10.1060
If patiently thy bidding they obey,	Par Lost 11.112
Nor knowing us nor known: and if by prayer	Par Lost 11.307
If so I may attain. So both ascend	Par Lost 11.376
Obtruded on us thus? who if we knew	Par Lost 11.504
Or if his likeness, by themselves defac't	Par Lost 11.522
There is, said *Michael*, if thou well observe	Par Lost 11.530
No sanctitie, if none be thither brought	Par Lost 11.837
If *Adam* aught perhaps might interpose; line not in 1667 edition	Par Lost 12.4
And famish him of Breath, if not of Bread?	Par Lost 12.78
Pure, and in mind prepar'd, if so befall,	Par Lost 12.444
But say, if our deliverer up to Heav'n	Par Lost 12.479
At least if so we can, and by the head	Par Reg 1.60
But if thou be the Son of God, Command	Par Reg 1.342
If not disposer; lend them oft my aid,	Par Reg 1.393
If it may stand him more in stead to lye,	Par Reg 1.473
What wonder then if I delight to hear	Par Reg 1.481
If he be Man by Mothers side at least,	Par Reg 2.136
If cause were to unfold some active Scene	Par Reg 2.239
Of what I suffer here; if Nature need not,	Par Reg 2.249
If Cottage were in view, Sheep-cote or Herd;	Par Reg 2.287
Tell me if Food were now before thee set,	Par Reg 2.320
If of that pow'r I bring thee voluntary	Par Reg 2.394
Therefore, if at great things thou wouldst arrive,	Par Reg 2.426
Not difficult, if thou hearken to me,	Par Reg 2.428
The wise mans cumbrance if not snare, more apt	Par Reg 2.454
What if with like aversion I reject	Par Reg 2.457
The peoples praise, if always praise unmixt?	Par Reg 3.48
But if there be in glory aught of good,	Par Reg 3.88
Yet if for fame and glory aught be done,	Par Reg 3.100
Aught suffer'd; if young *African* for fame	Par Reg 3.101
If Kingdom move thee not, let move thee Zeal,	Par Reg 3.171
If of my raign Prophetic Writ hath told,	Par Reg 3.184
What if he hath decreed that I shall first	Par Reg 3.188
If there be worse, the expectation more	Par Reg 3.207
If I then to the worst that can be hast,	Par Reg 3.223
These if from servitude thou shalt restore	Par Reg 3.381
I must deliver, if I mean to raign	Par Reg 3.404
A brutish monster: what if I withal	Par Reg 4.128
On this condition, if thou wilt fall down,	Par Reg 4.166
If given, by whom but by the King of Kings,	Par Reg 4.185
God over all supreme? if giv'n to thee,	Par Reg 4.186
If I to try whether in higher sort	Par Reg 4.198
Or if I would delight my private hours	Par Reg 4.331
Now contrary, if I read aught in Heaven,	Par Reg 4.382
And harmless, if not wholsom, as a sneeze	Par Reg 4.458
Did I not tell thee, if thou didst reject	Par Reg 4.467
If thou observe not this, be sure to find,	Par Reg 4.477
And if I was, I am; relation stands;	Par Reg 4.519
Good reason then, if I before-hand seek	Par Reg 4.526
There stand, if thou wilt stand; to stand upright	Par Reg 4.551
Now shew thy Progeny; if not to stand,	Par Reg 4.554
Cast thy self down; safely if Son of God:	Par Reg 4.555
What hunger, if aught hunger had impair'd,	Par Reg 4.592
Design'd for great exploits; if I must dye	Samson 32
Divine Prediction; what if all foretold	Samson 44
And almost life it self, if it be true	Samson 91
To visit or bewail thee, or if better,	Samson 182
As thir Deliverer; if he aught begin,	Samson 274
If any be, they walk obscure;	Samson 296
As if they would confine th' interminable,	Samson 307
Though in this uncouth place; if old respect,	Samson 333
Came lagging after; say if he be here.	Samson 337
To worthiest deeds, if he through frailty err,	Samson 369
Sole Author I, sole cause: if aught seem vile,	Samson 376
And expiate, if possible, my crime,	Samson 490
Repent the sin, but if the punishment	Samson 504
If these they scape, perhaps in poverty	Samson 697
I cannot but acknowledge; yet if tears	Samson 735
If aught in my ability may serve	Samson 743
If not by quick destruction soon cut off	Samson 764
But that on th' other side if it be weigh'd	Samson 768
I may, if possible, thy pardon find	Samson 771
The gentler, if severely thou exact not	Samson 788
And what if Love, which thou interpret'st hate,	Samson 790
If thou in strength all mortals dost exceed,	Samson 817
Philistian gold: if weakness may excuse,	Samson 831
Thou mine, not theirs: if aught against my life	Samson 888
If in my flower of youth and strength, when all men	Samson 938
Fame if not double-fac't is double-mouth'd,	Samson 971

If(*cont*)
If any of these or all, the *Timnian* bride Samson 1018
If thou at all art known. Much I have heard Samson 1082
If thy appearance answer loud report. Samson 1090
For proof hereof, if *Dagon* be thy god, Samson 1145
To free my Countrey; if their servile minds Samson 1213
And had perform'd it if my known offence Samson 1218
If they intend advantage of my labours Samson 1259
Commands are no constraints. If I obey them, Samson 1372
If there be aught of presage in the mind, Samson 1387
With zeal, if aught Religion seem concern'd: Samson 1420
If some convenient ransom were propos'd. Samson 1471
Man. His ransom, if my whole inheritance Samson 1476
If need be, I am ready to forgo Samson 1483
As if the whole inhabitation perish'd, Samson 1512
What if his eye-sight (for to *Israels* God Samson 1527
Are in confusion, give us if thou canst, Samson 1593
And hearken, if I may, her busines here. Mask 169
This way the noise was, if mine ear be true, Mask 170
Would send a glistring Guardian if need were Mask 219
line not in Bridgewater ms
O if thou have Mask 238
La. No less then if I should my brothers loose. Mask 288
And as I past, I worshipt; if those you seek Mask 302
And if your stray attendance be yet lodg'd, Mask 315
From her thach't pallat rowse, if otherwise Mask 318
Or if your influence be quite damm'd up Mask 336
Or *Tyrian* Cynosure. 2. *Bro*. Or if our eyes Mask 342
What if in wild amazement, and affright, Mask 356
Bridgewater ms 'or els in wild'
Trinity ms 'what if' ←'or else'
Or if they be but false alarms of Fear, Mask 364
line not in Bridgewater ms
line not in Trinity ms
Inferr, as if I thought my sisters state Mask 408
Unless the strength of Heav'n, if you mean that? Mask 417
Which if Heav'n gave it, may be term'd her own: Mask 419
If he be friendly he comes well, if not, Mask 488
Who gently ask't if he had seen such two, Mask 575
Self-fed, and self-consum'd, if this fail, Mask 597
And yet came off: if you have this about you Mask 647
Where if he be, with dauntless hardihood, Mask 650
Yet will they soon retire, if he but shrink. Mask 656
Comus. Nay Lady sit; if I but wave this wand, Mask 659
To store her children with; if all the world Mask 720
If you let slip time, like a neglected rose Mask 743
line not in Bridgewater ms
As if she would her children should be riotous Mask 763
If every just man that now pines with want Mask 768
If she be right invok't in warbled Song, Mask 854
(List mortals, if your ears be true) Mask 997
line not in Bridgewater ms
Or if Vertue feeble were, Mask 1022
thou man of lies & falshood, if thou give me it Mask Tr. ms 22.21
And if I give thee honour due, Allegro 37
Or if the earlier season lead Allegro 89
If *Jonsons* learned Sock be on, Allegro 132
These delights, if thou canst give, Allegro 151
And oft, as if her head she bow'd, Penseroso 71
Or if the Ayr will not permit, Penseroso 77
And if ought els, great *Bards* beside, Penseroso 116
If my inferior hand or voice could hit Arcades 77
As if they surely knew their sovran Lord was by. Nativity 60
(If ye have power to touch our senses so) Nativity 127
For if such holy Song Nativity 133
Summers chief honour if thou hadst out-lasted, Fair Inf 3
If likewise he some fair one wedded not, Fair Inf 11
(If so it be that thou these plaints dost hear) Fair Inf 37
Or in the Elisian fields (if such there were.) Fair Inf 40
Oh say me true if thou wert mortal wight Fair Inf 41
As if to shew what creatures Heav'n doth breed, Fair Inf 61
This if thou do he will an off-spring give, Fair Inf 76
And, if it happen as I did forecast, Vacation 13
Yet I had rather if I were to chuse, Vacation 29
What power, what force, what mighty spell, if not Vacation 89
Now mourn, and if sad share with us to bear Circum 6
'Twas such a shifter, that if truth were known, Carrier 5
If any ask for him, it shall be sed, Carrier 17
If I may not carry, sure Ile ne're be fetch'd, Another 18
line not in 1640, 1657, 1658 texts
Portend success in love; O if *Jove*'s will Sonnet 1, 7
All is, if I have grace to use it so, Sonnet 7, 13
If ever deed of honour did thee please, Sonnet 8, 3
If once his wrath take fire like fuel sere. Psalm 2, 27
That do observe If I transgress Psalm 5, 23
Lord my God if I have thought Psalm 7, 7
Or done this, if wickedness Psalm 7, 8
Be in my hands, if I have wrought Psalm 7, 9
If th' unjust will not forbear, Psalm 7, 45
If thou wilt list to mee, Psalm 81, 36
This was that gift (if you the truth will have) Prose 4, 3

Ignoble
Counsel'd ignoble ease, and peaceful sloath, Par Lost 2.227
To noble and ignoble is more sweet Par Lost 12.221
As was my former servitude, ignoble, Samson 416

Ignobly
Ignobly, to the traines and to the smiles Par Lost 11.624

Ignominious
Fled ignominious, to such evil brought Par Lost 6.395
Unmanly, ignominious, infamous, Samson 417

Ignominy
That were an ignominy and shame beneath Par Lost 1.115
Exile, or ignominy, or bonds, or pain, Par Lost 2.207
And ignominie, yet to glorie aspires Par Lost 6.383
But condemnation, ignominy, and shame? Par Reg 3.136

Ignorance
By Ignorance, is that thir happie state, Par Lost 4.519
Under this ignorance of good and Evil, Par Lost 9.774
In ignorance, thou op'nst Wisdoms way, Par Lost 9.809
(Though so esteem'd by shallow ignorance) Mask 514

Ignorant
Why but to keep ye low and ignorant, Par Lost 9.704
Liv'd ignorant of future, so had borne Par Lost 11.764
Ignorant of themselves, of God much more, Par Reg 4.310

Ilissus
To studious musing; there *Ilissus* rouls Par Reg 4.249

Ilium
That fought at *Theb*'s and *Ilium*, on each side Par Lost 1.578
ms 'Ilium'

Ill
But ever to do ill our sole delight, Par Lost 1.160
For happy though but ill, for ill not worst, Par Lost 2.224
But from the Author of all ill could Spring Par Lost 2.381
But I should ill become this Throne, O Peers, Par Lost 2.445
Of this ill Mansion: intermit no watch Par Lost 2.462
Down had been falling, had not by ill chance Par Lost 2.935
Resigns her charge, while goodness thinks no ill Par Lost 3.688
Where no ill seems: Which now for once beguil'd Par Lost 3.689
How due! yet all his good prov'd ill in me, Par Lost 4.48
Knowledge of Good bought dear by knowing ill. Par Lost 4.222
Of God or Angel, for they thought no ill: Par Lost 4.320
Happie, but for so happie ill secur'd Par Lost 4.370
Ill fenc't for Heav'n to keep out such a foe Par Lost 4.372
From hard assaies and ill successes past Par Lost 4.932
Ill matching words and deeds long past or late. Par Lost 5.113
Thus answerd. Ill for thee, but in wisht houre Par Lost 6.150
To thir prepar'd ill Mansion driven down Par Lost 6.738
Knowledg of good and ill, which I have set Par Lost 8.324
Yet oft his heart, divine of somthing ill, Par Lost 9.845
Had shadow'd them from knowing ill, was gon, Par Lost 9.1055
But might as ill have happ'nd thou being by, Par Lost 9.1147
Why hee should mean me ill, or seek to harme. Par Lost 9.1152
That from her hand I could suspect no ill, Par Lost 10.140
My Head, Ill fare our Ancestor impure, Par Lost 10.735
Beare thine own first, ill able to sustaine Par Lost 10.950
And my displeasure bearst so ill. If Prayers Par Lost 10.952
Ill worthie I such title should belong Par Lost 11.163
Of those ill mated Marriages thou saw'st: Par Lost 11.684
1667 'ill-mated'
O Visions ill foreseen! better had I Par Lost 11.763
For this ill news I bring, the Womans seed Par Reg 1.64
Ill sorting with my present state compar'd. Par Reg 1.200
Sir, what ill chance hath brought thee to this place Par Reg 1.321
Extorts, or pleasure to do ill excites? Par Reg 1.423
And who attains not, ill aspires to rule Par Reg 2.469
But govern ill the Nations under yoke, Par Reg 4.135
Ill imitated, while they loudest sing Par Reg 4.339
Or torn up sheer: ill wast thou shrouded then, Par Reg 4.419
They oft fore-signifie and threaten ill: Par Reg 4.464
Betok'ning, or ill boding, I contemn Par Reg 4.490
These two proportiond ill drove me transverse. Samson 209
Chor. Thy hopes are not ill founded nor seem vain Samson 1504
Of Riot, and ill manag'd Merriment, Mask 172
Bridgewater ms 'ill-manag'd'
That he, the Supreme good, t' whom all things ill Mask 217
line not in Bridgewater ms
La. Nay gentle Shepherd ill is lost that praise Mask 271
Lest som ill greeting touch attempt the person Mask 406
And harshly deal like an ill borrower Mask 683
line not in Bridgewater ms
Helping all urchin blasts, and ill luck signes Mask 845
And all my Plants I save from nightly ill, Arcades 48
by leaving out those harsh ill sounding jarres Musick Tr. ms 5.03
'ill sounding' ←'chromatick'
Ill to him that meant me peace, Psalm 7, 10
Turns on his head, and his ill trade Psalm 7, 58
Ah *Constantine*, of how much ill was cause Prose 1, 1
In thy Adulterers, or thy ill got wealth? Prose 3, 4

Illaudable
Illaudable, naught merits but dispraise Par Lost 6.382

Ill-fitted
In slavish habit, ill-fitted weeds Samson 122

Illimitable
Illimitable Ocean without bound, Par Lost 2.892

Ill-joined
Hither of ill-joynd Sons and Daughters born Par Lost 3.463

Ill-mated
Of those ill mated Marriages thou saw'st: Par Lost 11.684
1667 'ill-mated'

Ill-meaning
But your ill-meaning Politician Lords, Samson 1195

Illuminate
To illuminate the Earth, and rule the Day Par Lost 7.350

Illuminated
With inward eyes illuminated Samson 1689

Illumine
Illumin, what is low raise and support; Par Lost 1.23
1667 'Illumine'
ms 'Illumine'
Illumined
Far round illumin'd hell: highly they rag'd Par Lost 1.666
Illusion
Into the same illusion, not as Man Par Lost 10.571
Of power to cheat the eye with blear illusion, Mask 155
Illusions
Illusions as he list, Phantasms and Dreams, Par Lost 4.803
Illustrate
Justice with Mercie, as may illustrate most Par Lost 10.78
To prove him, and illustrate his high worth; Par Reg 1.370
Illustrates
Illustrates, when they see all Regal Power Par Lost 5.739
Illustrious
Illustrious on his Shoulders fledge with wings Par Lost 3.627
But more illustrious made, since he the Head Par Lost 5.842
Illustrious farr and wide, but by his own Par Lost 6.773
Thus *Adam* his illustrious Guest besought: Par Lost 7.109
1667 'illustrous'
1669 'illustrious'
Illustrious evidence, example high! Par Lost 9.962
Detain from following thy illustrious track. Par Lost 10.367
Among illustrious women, faithful wives: Samson 957
To appear as fits before th' illustrious Lords. Samson 1318
Illyria
Lovelier, not those that in *Illyria* chang'd Par Lost 9.505
Image
Oft to the Image of a Brute, adorn'd Par Lost 1.371
ms 'image'
To whose bright Image nightly by the Moon Par Lost 1.440
ms 'image'
Maim'd his brute Image, head and hands lopt off Par Lost 1.459
ms 'image'
Thy self in me thy perfect image viewing Par Lost 2.764
The radiant image of his Glory sat, Par Lost 3.63
The image of thir glorious Maker shon, Par Lost 4.292
Whose image thou art, him thou shalt enjoy Par Lost 4.472
Then that smooth watry image; back I turnd, Par Lost 4.480
Gods latest Image: I describ'd his way Par Lost 4.567
Best Image of my self and dearer half, Par Lost 5.95
To one and to his image now proclaim'd? Par Lost 5.784
Image of thee in all things; and shall soon, Par Lost 6.736
Let us make now Man in our image, Man Par Lost 7.519
The breath of Life; in his own Image hee Par Lost 7.526
Created thee, in the Image of God Par Lost 7.527
Created in his Image, there to dwell Par Lost 7.627
Inward and outward both, his image faire: Par Lost 8.221
Like of his like, his Image multipli'd, Par Lost 8.424
My Image, not imparted to the Brute, Par Lost 8.441
His Image who made both, and less expressing Par Lost 8.544
Th' Image of God in man created once Par Lost 11.508
And for his Makers Image sake exempt? Par Lost 11.514
Thir Makers Image, answerd *Michael*, then Par Lost 11.515
His Image whom they serv'd, a brutish vice, Par Lost 11.518
Gods Image did not reverence in themselves. Par Lost 11.525
True Image of the Father whether thron'd Par Reg 4.596
The Image of thy strength, and mighty minister. Samson 706
Imagination
Human imagination to such highth Par Lost 6.300
For dire imagination still persues me. Samson 1544
Imaginations
His proud imaginations thus displaid. Par Lost 2.10
She forms Imaginations, Aerie shapes, Par Lost 5.105
Imagine
As you imagine, she has a hidden strength Mask 415
Trinity ms 'imagine brother'
Bridgewater ms 'immagine brother'
Imagined
Imagind rather oft then elsewhere seen, Par Lost 3.599
Imagind Lands and Regions in the Moon: Par Lost 5.263
Mountains of Ice, that stop th' imagin'd way Par Lost 10.291
To trust thee from my side, imagin'd wise, Par Lost 10.881
Her false imagin'd loss cease to lament, Fair Inf 72
Imagining
Thir earnest eyes they fix'd, imagining Par Lost 10.553
Imaus
As when a Vultur on *Imaus* bred, Par Lost 3.431
Imbathe
And gave her to his daughters to imbathe Mask 837
Bridgewater ms 'imbath'
Trinity ms 'imbath'
Imbodies
Imbodies, and imbrutes, till she quite loose Mask 468
Imbowered
And in thick shelter of black shades imbowr'd, Mask 62
Trinity ms 'imbour'd'
Imbrued
While Darwen stream with blood of Scotts imbru'd, Sonnet 16, 7
Trinity ms 'imbru'd' ←'embru'd'
Imbrute
This essence to incarnate and imbrute, Par Lost 9.166
Imbrutes
Imbodies, and imbrutes, till she quite loose Mask 468
Bridgewater ms 'imbruts'
Imbued
Imbu'd, bring to thir sweetness no satietie. Par Lost 8.216
Imitate
Imitate when we please? This Desart soile Par Lost 2.270
To imitate her; but misjoyning shapes, Par Lost 5.111
Imitate the Starry Quire, Mask 112
1637 'Immitate'
Imitated
And God-like imitated State; him round Par Lost 2.511
Ill imitated, while they loudest sing Par Reg 4.339
Imitation
In imitation of that Mount whereon Par Lost 5.764
The rest in imitation to like Armes Par Lost 6.662
Immanacled
Thou haste immanacl'd, while Heav'n sees good. Mask 665
Immature
Of Waters, Embryon immature involv'd, Par Lost 7.277
Immeasurable
Of depth immeasurable: Anon they move Par Lost 1.549
They view'd the vast immeasurable Abyss Par Lost 7.211
Immeasurable strength they might behold Samson 206
Immeasurably
Immeasurably, all things shall be your prey. Par Lost 2.844
Immediate
Main reason to perswade immediate Warr, Par Lost 2.121
With nicest touch. Immediate in a flame, Par Lost 6.584
Immediate are the Acts of God, more swift Par Lost 7.176
Irradiance, virtual or immediate touch? Par Lost 8.617
By some immediate stroak; but soon shall find Par Lost 10.52
Immediate dissolution, which we thought Par Lost 10.1049
Immediately
Immediately the Mountains huge appeer Par Lost 7.285
Shall bring on men. Immediately a place Par Lost 11.477
Immediately inordinate desires Par Lost 12.87
When to thir sports they turn'd. Immediately Samson 1614
Immedicable
Nor less then wounds immedicable Samson 620
Immense
Reduc'd thir shapes immense, and were at large, Par Lost 1.790
Th' unfounded deep, and through the void immense Par Lost 2.829
The debt immense of endless gratitude, Par Lost 4.52
1667 'immence' in some copies
The Earth outstretcht immense, a prospect wide Par Lost 5.88
Immense I have transfus'd, that all may know Par Lost 6.704
Immense, and all his Father in him shon. Par Lost 7.196
Of amplitude almost immense, with Starr's Par Lost 7.620
They fasten'd, and the Mole immense wraught on Par Lost 10.300
O goodness infinite, goodness immense! Par Lost 12.469
Imminent
Uplifted imminent one stroke they aim'd Par Lost 6.317
Waited with hellish rancour imminent Par Lost 9.409
In Prison under Judgements imminent: Par Lost 11.725
Immixed
Samson with these immixt, inevitably Samson 1657
Immortal
Confounded though immortal: But his doom Par Lost 1.53
ms 'immortall'
And study of revenge, immortal hate, Par Lost 1.107
ms 'immortall'
From mortal or immortal minds. Thus they Par Lost 1.559
ms 'immortall'
O Myriads of immortal Spirits, O Powers Par Lost 1.622
ms 'immortall'
Immortal vigor, though opprest and fall'n, Par Lost 2.13
(What could it less when Spirits immortal sing2) Par Lost 2.553
Reaping immortal fruits of joy and love, Par Lost 3.67
Silent yet spake, and breath'd immortal love Par Lost 3.267
Immortal Amarant, a Flour which once Par Lost 3.353
Immutable, Immortal, Infinite, Par Lost 3.373
Immortal thanks, and his admonishment Par Lost 7.77
Daughter of God and Man, immortal *Eve*, Par Lost 9.291
Who might have liv'd and joyd immortal bliss, Par Lost 9.1166
Those pure immortal Elements that know Par Lost 11.50
Less pure, accustomd to immortal Fruits? Par Lost 11.285
A gentle wafting to immortal Life. Par Lost 12.435
My mansion is, where those immortal shapes Mask 2
Trinity ms 'immortall'
Bridgewater ms 'immortall'
1637 'immortall'
Till all be made immortal: but when lust Mask 463
Bridgewater ms 'immortall'
Trinity ms 'immortall'
1637 'immortall'
Storied of old in high immortal vers Mask 516
Trinity ms 'immortall'
1637 'immortall'
Bridgewater ms 'immortall'
And underwent a quick immortal change Mask 841
1637 'immortall'
Trinity ms 'immortall'
Bridgewater ms 'immortall'
Married to immortal verse Allegro 137
The immortal mind that hath forsook Penseroso 91
The peerles height of her immortal praise, Arcades 75
Trinity ms 'immortall'
Immortal Nectar to her Kingly Sire: Vacation 39
Touch their immortal Harps of golden wires, Musick 13
Trinity ms 'immortall'

Immortal(*cont*)
He had bin an immortall Carrier. Another 28
1673 'immortal'
And drink thy fill of pure immortal streams. Sonnet 14, 14
Trinity ms 'immortall' ←'immortal'
Warble immortal Notes and *Tuskan* Ayre? Sonnet 20, 12
Immortality
Of immortality. So little knows Par Lost 4.201
1667 'immortalitie'
Quaff immortalitie and joy, secure Par Lost 5.638
line not in 1667 edition
And Immortalitie: that fondly lost, Par Lost 11.59
Immovable
Immovable, infixt, and frozen round, Par Lost 2.602
Immovable of this now fenceless world Par Lost 10.303
1667 'Immoveable'
Immoveable till peace obtain'd from fault Par Lost 10.938
Immured
Immur'd in cypress shades a Sorcerer dwels Mask 521
. Bridgewater ms 'immured'
Immures
Outrageous to devour, immures us round Par Lost 2.435
Immutable
Immutable, Immortal, Infinite, Par Lost 3.373
God made thee perfet, not immutable; Par Lost 5.524
Immutable when thou wert lost, not I, Par Lost 9.1165
Immutably
Or aught by me immutablie foreseen, Par Lost 3.121
Immutably his sovran will, the end Par Lost 7.79
Imp
Fit Vessel, fittest Imp of fraud, in whom Par Lost 9.89
her brok'n league, to impe their serpent wings, Sonnet 15, 8
1694 'Imp'
Impair
Who can impair thee, mighty King, or bound Par Lost 7.608
Must needs impaire and wearie human sense: Par Lost 12.10
Impaired
His lustre visibly impar'd; yet seemd Par Lost 4.850
The Author not impair'd, but honourd more? Par Lost 5.73
Through pride that sight, & thought himself impaird. Par Lost 5.665
Save what sin hath impaird, which yet hath wrought Par Lost 6.691
And to repaire his numbers thus impair'd, Par Lost 9.144
What hunger, if aught hunger had impair'd, Par Reg 4.592
Were all to ruffl'd, and somtimes impair'd. Mask 380
Bridgewater ms 'impayr'd'
Impaled
Impenetrable, impal'd with circling fire, Par Lost 2.647
Training his devilish Enginrie, impal'd Par Lost 6.553
Imparadised
Imparadis't in one anothers arms Par Lost 4.506
Impart
Wast wont, I mine to thee was wont to impart; Par Lost 5.677
Gently for our instruction to impart Par Lost 7.81
Impart against his will if all be his? Par Lost 9.728
Chose to impart to thy apparent need, Par Reg 2.397
But to shew forth his goodness, and impart Par Reg 3.124
Imparted
My Image, not imparted to the Brute, Par Lost 8.441
For never was from Heaven imparted Samson 1438
Impartial
Impartial, self-severe, inexorable, Samson 827
Imparts
The Sun that light imparts to all, receives Par Lost 5.423
Imparts to thee no happiness, no joy, Par Reg 1.417
1671 printed 'imports', errata 'imparts'
Impassable
Impassable, Impervious, let us try Par Lost 10.254
Impassioned
The Tempter all impassiond thus began. Par Lost 9.678
Impassive
Against unpaind, impassive; from which evil Par Lost 6.455
Impatience
Rancor and pride, impatience and despite, Par Lost 10.1044
Impearls
Impearls on every leaf and every flouer. Par Lost 5.747
Impediment
In order, quit of all impediment; Par Lost 6.548
Impendent
Impendent horrors, threatning hideous fall Par Lost 2.177
Impendent, raging into sudden flame Par Lost 5.891
Impenetrable
Impenetrable, impal'd with circling fire, Par Lost 2.647
1667 'Impenitrable'
Obscur'd, where highest Woods impenetrable Par Lost 9.1086
Impenetrably
Invulnerable, impenitrably arm'd: Par Lost 6.400
Impenitence
On thir impenitence; and shall returne Par Lost 11.816
Impenitent
Impenitent, and left a race behind Par Reg 3.423
Imperfect
Left so imperfet by the Maker wise, Par Lost 9.338
Nothing imperfet or deficient left Par Lost 9.345
So law appears imperfet, and but giv'n Par Lost 12.300
And mad'st imperfect words with childish tripps, Vacation 3
Imperfection
His single imperfection, and beget Par Lost 8.423
Imperial
Th' Imperial Ensign, which full high advanc't Par Lost 1.536
ms 'imperial'
Thrones and Imperial Powers, off-spring of heav'n Par Lost 2.310
1667 'imperial'
And this Imperial Sov'ranty, adorn'd Par Lost 2.446
Of Angels by Imperial summons call'd, Par Lost 5.584
Of those Imperial Titles which assert Par Lost 5.801
Of Heav'ns high-seated top, th' Impereal Throne Par Lost 7.585
On each side an Imperial City stood, Par Reg 4.33
The Imperial Palace, compass huge, and high Par Reg 4.51
Imperial rule of all the Sea-girt Iles Mask 21
Bridgewater ms 'imperiall'
Trinity ms 'imperiall rule' ←'the rule & title'
Imperious
That thou shouldst hope, imperious, and with threats Par Lost 6.287
Expect another message more imperious, Samson 1352
Imperishable
Imperishable, and though peirc'd with wound, Par Lost 6.435
Impertinence
Or emptiness, or fond impertinence, Par Lost 8.195
Impervious
Impassable, Impervious, let us try Par Lost 10.254
1667 'impervious'
Impetuous
Wing'd with red Lightning and impetuous rage, Par Lost 1.175
With impetuous recoile and jarring sound Par Lost 2.880
Impetuous winds: he thus began in haste. Par Lost 4.560
Level'd, with such impetuous furie smote, Par Lost 6.591
Impetuous, and continu'd till the Earth Par Lost 11.744
Impetuous, insolent, unquenchable; Samson 1422
Impious
Rais'd impious War in Heav'n and Battel proud Par Lost 1.43
That ore the Realm of impious *Pharaoh* hung Par Lost 1.342
Ransack'd the Center, and with impious hands Par Lost 1.686
Canst thou with impious obloquie condemne Par Lost 5.813
Returns our own. Cease then this impious rage, Par Lost 5.845
This greeting on thy impious Crest receive. Par Lost 6.188
Hee on his impious Foes right onward drove, Par Lost 6.831
The abominable terms, impious condition; Par Reg 4.173
No more thy countrey, but an impious crew Samson 891
Impiously
Thou hast repeld, while impiously they thought Par Lost 7.611
Presumptuously have publish'd, impiously, Samson 498
Implacable
Implacable, and many a dolorous groan, Par Lost 6.658
Dal. I see thou art implacable, more deaf Samson 960
Implanted
From thy implanted Grace in Man, these Sighs Par Lost 11.23
Implements
Such implements of mischief as shall dash Par Lost 6.488
Implicit
And Bush with frizl'd hair implicit: last Par Lost 7.323
Implied
As the Vine curles her tendrils, which impli'd Par Lost 4.307
Implies
But that implies not violence or harme. Par Lost 4.901
That excellence thought in thee, and implies, Par Lost 10.1017
Implore
Sam. His pardon I implore; but as for life, Samson 521
We implore thy powerful hand Mask 903
Bridgewater ms 'ymplore'
Implored
So ordering. I with leave of speech implor'd, Par Lost 8.377
Implores
Her Son. So fail not thou, who thee implores: Par Lost 7.38
Imploring
Him who imploring mercy sues for life, Samson 512
Import
Causes import your need of this fair Fruit. Par Lost 9.731
Important
Not of mean suiters, nor important less Par Lost 11.9
For some important cause, thou needst not doubt. Samson 1379
Imports
Imports not, if thou reck'n right, the rest Par Lost 8.71
Imparts to thee no happiness, no joy, Par Reg 1.417
1671 printed 'imports', errata 'imparts'
Co. Imports their loss, beside the present need? Mask 287
Importune
Mee thus, though importune perhaps, to come Par Lost 9.610
There with my cries importune Heaven, that all Par Lost 10.933
Only the importune Tempter still remain'd, Par Reg 2.404
Curiosity, inquisitive, importune Samson 775
Importuned
Unweetingly importun'd Samson 1680
Importuning
No better way I saw then by importuning Samson 797
Importunity
And his vain importunity pursues. Par Reg 4.24
O'recome with importunity and tears. Samson 51
Her importunity, each time perceiving Samson 397
For importunity, that is for naught, Samson 779
Impose
Had to impose: He through the armed Files Par Lost 1.567
For aught appeers, and on thir Orbs impose Par Lost 8.30
Of us will soon determin, or impose Par Lost 11.227
They cannot well impose, nor I sustain; Samson 1258

Imposed
Strict Laws impos'd, to celebrate his Throne Par Lost 2.241
Thy sleep dissent? new Laws thou seest impos'd; Par Lost 5.679
Inducing darkness, grateful truce impos'd, Par Lost 6.407
Death is the penaltie impos'd, beware, Par Lost 7.545
Yet not so strictly hath our Lord impos'd Par Lost 9.235
To labour calls us now with sweat impos'd, Par Lost 11.172
Obedience to the Law of God, impos'd Par Lost 12.397
My Nation, and the work from Heav'n impos'd, Samson 565
Off. My message was impos'd on me with speed, Samson 1343
Hitherto, Lords, what your commands impos'd Samson 1640
Imposition
From imposition of strict Laws, to free Par Lost 12.304
Impossible
By force impossible, by leave obtain'd Par Lost 2.250
Still as it rose, impossible to climbe. Par Lost 4.548
Impossible: yet haply of thy Race Par Lost 6.501
From whom it sprung, impossible to mix Par Lost 7.58
Impossible is held, as Argument Par Lost 10.800
Impossibly
Since Reason not impossibly may meet Par Lost 9.360
Impostor
Who to the fraudulent Impostor foule Par Lost 3.692
Impostor do not charge most innocent nature, Mask 762
Bridgewater ms 'Imposter'
Trinity ms 'impostor'
Impotence
Belike through impotence, or unaware, Par Lost 2.156
O impotence of mind, in body strong! Samson 52
Impotent
Yet Wealth without these three is impotent, Par Reg 2.433
Impregnable
Impregnable; oft on the bordering Deep Par Lost 2.131
Impregnable, and there Mount *Palatine* Par Reg 4.50
Impregned
Yet rung of his perswasive words, impregn'd Par Lost 9.737
Impregns
On *Juno* smiles, when he impregns the Clouds Par Lost 4.500
Impress
Impress the Air, and shews the Mariner Par Lost 4.558
Impressed
Impresst the effulgence of his Glorie abides, Par Lost 3.388
On which the Sun more glad impress'd his beams Par Lost 4.150
For haste; such flight the great command impress'd Par Lost 7.294
Subscrib'd not; Nature first gave Signs, impress Par Lost 11.182
Impresses
Impreses quaint, Caparisons and Steeds; Par Lost 9.35
Impression
He ended, and his words impression left Par Reg 1.106
Those Delphick lines with deep impression took, Shakespear 12
1663-4 'Impression'
1632 'Impression'
1640 'Impression'
Imprisoned
The air imprison'd also, close and damp, Samson 8
Imprison'd now indeed, Samson 158
Imprisonment
Thou art become (O worst imprisonment!) Samson 155
Improve
What might improve my knowledge or their own; Par Reg 1.213
Improved
Improv'd by tract of time, and wingd ascend Par Lost 5.498
Of *Gabriel* out of *Eden*, now improv'd Par Lost 9.54
Imprudence
Abhor to joyn; and by imprudence mixt, Par Lost 11.686
Impudence
How openly, and with what impudence Samson 398
Impudent
To whom the Tempter impudent repli'd. Par Reg 4.154
Impudent whoore, where hast thou plac'd thy hope? Prose 3, 3
Impulse
So without least impulse or shadow of Fate, Par Lost 3.120
Organic, or impulse of vocal Air, Par Lost 9.530
Or touch with lightest moment of impulse Par Lost 10.45
From intimate impulse, and therefore urg'd Samson 223
Impulsion
Divine impulsion prompting how thou might'st Samson 422
Impure
Glad was the Spirit impure as now in hope Par Lost 3.630
Defaming as impure what God declares Par Lost 4.746
Then shall thy Saints unmixt, and from th' impure Par Lost 6.742
My Head, Ill fare our Ancestor impure, Par Lost 10.735
Nothing dishonourable, impure, unworthy Samson 1424
Impurpled
Impurpl'd with Celestial Roses smil'd. Par Lost 3.364
Impute
Let in these wastful Furies, who impute Par Lost 10.620
Wilt thou impute to obedience what thy fear Par Reg 1.422
To Vertue I impute not, or count part Par Reg 2.248
Imputed
Imputed shall absolve them who renounce Par Lost 3.291
To them by Faith imputed, they may finde Par Lost 12.295
Imputed becomes theirs by Faith, his merits Par Lost 12.409
Imputest
Imput'st thou that to my default, or will Par Lost 9.1145
In
Listings of this word are omitted; see the Introduction.
In the
In billows, leave i' th' midst a horrid Vale. Par Lost 1.224
ms 'ith''
Ith' midst an Altar as the Land-mark stood Par Lost 11.432
La. To seek i' th vally som cool friendly Spring. Mask 282
Bridgewater ms 'in the'
And play i' th plighted clouds. I was aw-strook, Mask 301
Trinity ms 'ith'
May sit i' th center, and enjoy bright day, Mask 382
Trinity ms 'ith'
Tending my flocks hard by i' th hilly crofts, Mask 531
I could be willing though now i' th darke to trie Mask Tr. ms 16.38
I could be willinge though now i' th darke to trie Mask Br. ms 391
In counsel of the wicked, and ith' way Psalm 1, 2
Ith' morning I to thee with choyce Psalm 5, 7
Ith' mid'st of all mine enemies that mark. Psalm 6, 15
Inabstinence
What miserie th' inabstinence of *Eve* Par Lost 11.476
Inaccessible
Though inaccessible, his fatal Throne: Par Lost 2.104
Thron'd inaccessible, but when thou shad'st Par Lost 3.377
This inaccessible high strength, the seat Par Lost 7.141
And inaccessible the *Arabian* drouth: Par Reg 3.274
Inbreathed
Dead things with inbreath'd sense able to pierce, Musick 4
Inbred
Transform'd: but he my inbred enemie Par Lost 2.785
Incapable
Incapable of stain would soon expel Par Lost 2.140
Can comprehend, incapable of more. Par Lost 5.505
Incapable of mortal injurie Par Lost 6.434
Incarnate
Here shalt thou sit incarnate, here shalt Reign Par Lost 3.315
This essence to incarnate and imbrute, Par Lost 9.166
Incense
What fear we then? what doubt we to incense Par Lost 2.94
Choral or Unison: of incense Clouds Par Lost 7.599
Thir morning incense, when all things that breath, Par Lost 9.194
1667 'Incense'
Is open? or will God incense his ire Par Lost 9.692
With incense, where the Golden Altar fum'd, Par Lost 11.18
With Incense, I thy Priest before thee bring, Par Lost 11.25
The Inwards and thir Fat, with Incense strew'd, Par Lost 11.439
Heapt to the popular summe, will so incense Par Lost 12.338
His place, to offer Incense, Myrrh, and Gold; Par Lost 12.363
To honour thee with Incense, Myrrh, and Gold, Par Reg 1.251
Incensed
Incenst with indignation *Satan* stood Par Lost 2.707
1674 'Incenc't' in some copies
1667 'Incenc't'
Th' incensed Deitie, while offerd grace Par Lost 3.187
Th' incensed Father, and th' incensed Son, Par Lost 5.847
Incens't, and thus securely him defi'd. Par Lost 6.130
Least hee incenst at such eruption bold, Par Lost 8.235
To whom then first incenst *Adam* repli'd, Par Lost 9.1162
Incentive
Of missive ruin; part incentive reed Par Lost 6.519
Incessant
What in an age they with incessant toyle Par Lost 1.698
Have rais'd incessant Armies to defeat Par Lost 6.138
Incessant I could hope to change the will Par Lost 11.308
Alas! What boots it with uncessant care Lycidas 64
Trinity ms 'incessant'
Of my *incessant* praiers afford Psalm 86, 19
Incessantly
Incessantly, and to his reading brings not Par Reg 4.323
Incestuous
To whom th' incestuous Mother thus repli'd. Par Lost 10.602
Incestuous, Sacrilegious, but may plead it? Samson 833
Incident
All chances incident to mans frail life Samson 656
In me, but incident to all our sex, Samson 774
Incited
Incited, dance about him various rounds? Par Lost 8.125
Inclement
Of *Chaos* blustring round, inclement skie; Par Lost 3.426
Th' inclement Seasons, Rain, Ice, Hail and Snow, Par Lost 10.1063
Inclinable
Inclinable now grown to touch or taste, Par Lost 9.742
Inclination
Pursues, as inclination or sad choice Par Lost 2.524
Goe whither Fate and inclination strong Par Lost 10.265
Incline
So strictly, but much more to pitie encline: Par Lost 3.402
Be open, and his heart to pitie incline, Par Lost 10.1061
Of God high-blest, or to incline his will, Par Lost 11.145
That I encline to hope, rather then fear, Mask 412
Trinity ms 'incline'
Thy *gracious* ear, O Lord, encline, Psalm 86, 1
Inclined
So strictly, but much more to pitie enclin'd, Par Lost 3.405
Inclin'd not, but his coming thus declar'd. Par Lost 11.250
Of *Adam*, soon enclin'd to admit delight, Par Lost 11.596
And thou thy self seem'st otherwise inclin'd Par Reg 4.212
Felt in his arms, with head a while enclin'd, Samson 1636
But O as to embrace me she enclin'd, Sonnet 23, 13
Inclines
Inclines, here to continue; and build up here Par Lost 2.314

Inclines(*cont*)
Now falling with soft slumbrous weight inclines Par Lost 4.615
Inclining
His free Will, to her own inclining left Par Lost 10.46
Included
The whole included Race, his purposd prey. Par Lost 9.416
Incomposed
With faultring speech and visage incompos'd Par Lost 2.989
Incomprehensible
Spaces incomprehensible (for such Par Lost 8.20
Inconsiderable
Are to the main as inconsiderable, Par Reg 4.457
Incontinence
From the rash hand of bold Incontinence. Mask 397
Trinity ms 'incontinence'
Inconvenient
No inconvenient Diet, nor too light Fare: Par Lost 5.495
Incorporate
Am found Eternal, and incorporate both, Par Lost 10.816
To incorporate with gloomy night; Samson 161
Incorporeal
Thus incorporeal Spirits to smallest forms Par Lost 1.789
And corporeal to incorporeal turn. Par Lost 5.413
Of incorporeal speed, her warmth and light; Par Lost 8.37
Incorrupt
Distemperd all things, and of incorrupt Par Lost 11.56
Incorruptible
All incorruptible would on his Throne Par Lost 2.138
Not incorruptible of Faith, not prooff Par Lost 9.298
Still hanging incorruptible, till men Par Lost 9.622
Increase
Our Maker bids increase, who bids abstain Par Lost 4.748
From his Creator, and the more to increase Par Lost 10.486
Delightfully, *Encrease and multiply*, Par Lost 10.730
Now death to heare! for what can I encrease Par Lost 10.731
That to give the world encrease, Winchester 51
Yet (strange to think) his wain was his increase: Another 32
1640, 1657 'disease'
line not in 1658 text
With vast increase their corn and wine abounds Psalm 4, 36
Increased
Of that stupendious Bridge his joy encreas'd. Par Lost 10.351
The Grandchilde with twelve Sons increast, departs Par Lost 12.155
And as the days increas'd, increas'd thir doubt: Par Reg 2.12
Increate
Bright effluence of bright essence increate. Par Lost 3.6
Incredible
Incredible how swift, had thither rowl'd Par Lost 4.593
Incredible to me, in this displeas'd, Samson 1084
Chor. Yet God hath wrought things as incredible Samson 1532
All with incredible, stupendious force, Samson 1627
Incubus
The fleshliest Incubus, and thus advis'd. Par Reg 2.152
Incumbent
Aloft, incumbent on the dusky Air Par Lost 1.226
Incur
Not to incur; but soon his cleer aspect Par Lost 8.336
Had so enobl'd, as of choice to incurr Par Lost 9.992
Incurable
Fear I incurable; bring up thy van, Samson 1234
Incurred
Incurr'd, what could they less, the penaltie, Par Lost 10.15
Incurrest
Which thou incurr'st by flying, meet thy flight Par Lost 4.913
Incursions
Against the *Scythian*, whose incursions wild Par Reg 3.301
Ind
Outshon the wealth of *Ormus* and of *Ind*, Par Lost 2.2
'Twixt *Africa* and *Inde*, Ile find him out, Mask 606
Indebted
Indebted and undon, hath none to bring: Par Lost 3.235
Indebted and dischargd; what burden then? Par Lost 4.57
Indecent
Repeated, and indecent overthrow Par Lost 6.601
Indeed
Doubted his Empire, that were low indeed, Par Lost 1.114
Or if our substance be indeed Divine, Par Lost 2.99
For wonderful indeed are all his works, Par Lost 3.702
For wee to him indeed all praises owe, Par Lost 4.444
Till I espi'd thee, fair indeed and tall, Par Lost 4.477
Of thir great Potentate; for great indeed Par Lost 5.706
In all things else delight indeed, but such Par Lost 8.524
Wondrous indeed, if cause of such effects. Par Lost 9.650
Indeed? hath God then said that of the Fruit Par Lost 9.656
Op'nd we find indeed, and find we know Par Lost 9.1071
Shee was indeed, and lovely to attract Par Lost 10.152
Would be revenge indeed; which will be lost Par Lost 10.1036
Into the Heav'n of Heavens; thou com'st indeed, Par Reg 1.410
Forty and more deserted here indeed. Par Reg 2.316
So did not *Machabeus:* he indeed Par Reg 3.165
The top of Eloquence, Statists indeed, Par Reg 4.354
Imprison'd now indeed, Samson 158
Mee easily indeed mine may neglect, Samson 291
Of acts indeed heroic, far beyond Samson 527
Sa. Perhaps thou shalt have cause to sorrow indeed. Samson 1347
Man. Of ruin indeed methought I heard the noise, Samson 1515
Man. The worst indeed, O all my hope's defeated Samson 1571
Just law indeed, but more exceeding love! Circum 16

Indefatigable
Upborn with indefatigable wings Par Lost 2.408
Indented
Address'd his way, not with indented wave, Par Lost 9.496
His thirty Armes along the indented Meads, Vacation 94
India
Outshon the wealth of *Ormus* and of *Ind*, Par Lost 2.2
In *India* East or West, or middle shoare Par Lost 5.339
From *India* and the golden *Chersoness*, Par Reg 4.74
'Twixt *Africa* and *Inde*, Ile find him out, Mask 606
Indian
Beyond the *Indian* Mount, or Faerie Elves, Par Lost 1.781
ms 'Indian'
Of *Ganges* or *Hydaspes*, *Indian* streams; Par Lost 3.436
There oft the *Indian* Herdsman shunning heate Par Lost 9.1108
And utmost *Indian* Isle *Taprobane*, Par Reg 4.75
The nice Morn on th' *Indian* steep Mask 139
Indians
But such as at this day to *Indians* known Par Lost 9.1102
Indignant
And scourg'd with many a stroak th' indignant waves. Par Lost 10.311
Indignation
Incenst with indignation *Satan* stood Par Lost 2.707
Gods indignation on these Godless pourd Par Lost 6.811
To Man, and indignation at his wrong, Par Lost 9.666
That scorn'd his indignation: through the Gate, Par Lost 10.418
Thine indignation cause to cease Psalm 85, 15
Indignities
Subject him to so foul indignities, Samson 371
Sam. All these indignities, for such they are Samson 1168
The worst of all indignities, yet on me Samson 1341
Indignity
Him Lord pronounc'd, and, O indignitie! Par Lost 9.154
Her Bond-slave; O indignity, O blot Samson 411
Indirect
Paths indirect, or in the mid way faint! Par Lost 11.631
Indissolubly
Indissolubly firm; nor obvious Hill, Par Lost 6.69
Indite
Not sedulous by Nature to indite Par Lost 9.27
Individual
Henceforth an individual solace dear; Par Lost 4.486
United as one individual Soule Par Lost 5.610
With an individual kiss; On Time 12
Trinity ms 'individuall'
Induce
As if (which might induce us to accord) Par Lost 2.503
Induced
Induc'd me. As new wak't from soundest sleep Par Lost 8.253
Inducement
Higher degree of Life, inducement strong Par Lost 9.934
Man. Peace with you brethren; my inducement hither Samson 1445
Induces
Induces best to hope of like success. Par Reg 1.105
Inducing
Inducing darkness, grateful truce impos'd, Par Lost 6.407
Inductive
Inductive mainly to the sin of *Eve*. Par Lost 11.519
Indulgence
Shee first his weak indulgence will accuse. Par Lost 9.1186
For long indulgence to their fears or grief: Par Reg 1.110
Indulgences
Indulgences, Dispenses, Pardons, Bulls, Par Lost 3.492
Indulgent
Of Gods *Messiah;* those indulgent Laws Par Lost 5.883
To sit indulgent, and with him partake Par Lost 9.3
Indus
Ganges and *Indus:* thus the Orb he roam'd Par Lost 9.82
As far as *Indus* East, *Euphrates* West, Par Reg 3.272
Industrious
With his industrious crew to build in hell. Par Lost 1.751
To vice industrious, but to Nobler deeds Par Lost 2.116
If Earth industrious of her self fetch Day Par Lost 8.137
Of Bees industrious murmur oft invites Par Reg 4.248
Hardy and industrious to support Samson 1274
Ineffable
Sense of new joy ineffable diffus'd: Par Lost 3.137
Light'ning Divine, ineffable, serene, Par Lost 5.734
Ineffably
Ineffably into his face receiv'd, Par Lost 6.721
Ineffectual
Though ineffectual found: misdeem not then, Par Lost 9.301
Inelegant
Tastes, not well joynd, inelegant, but bring Par Lost 5.335
Ineloquent
Nor tongue ineloquent; for God on thee Par Lost 8.219
Inevitable
By my advice; since fate inevitable Par Lost 2.197
Under th' inevitable curb, reserv'd Par Lost 2.322
Among his foes? *Mess*. Inevitable cause Samson 1586
Inevitably
Transgrest, inevitably thou shalt dye; Par Lost 8.330
Samson with these immixt, inevitably Samson 1657
Inexorable
Impartial, self-severe, inexorable, Samson 827
Inexorably
Inexorably, and the torturing hour Par Lost 2.91

Inexperience
Argue thy inexperience what behooves Par Lost 4.931
Inexpert
Warr terrifie them inexpert, and feare Par Lost 12.218
Inexpiable
To raise in me inexpiable hate, Samson 839
Inexplicable
The sense of endless woes? inexplicable Par Lost 10.754
Inexpressible
Of circuit inexpressible they stood, Par Lost 5.595
In *Eden*, distance inexpressible Par Lost 8.113
Inextinguishable
And inextinguishable rage; all Heav'n Par Lost 6.217
Inextricable
Inextricable, or strict necessity; Par Lost 5.528
Infallible
Infallible? yet many will presume: Par Lost 12.530
Infallible; or wert thou sought to deeds Par Reg 3.16
Infamed
To Sapience, hitherto obscur'd, infam'd, Par Lost 9.797
Infamous
Unmanly, ignominious, infamous, Samson 417
Infamous Hills, and sandy perilous wildes, Mask 424
Thereby to wipe away th' infamous blot, Fair Inf 12
Infamy
Vain glorious, and through infamie seeks fame: Par Lost 6.384
Of infamy upon my name denounc't? Samson 968
Infancy
Thy infancy, thy childhood, and thy youth, Par Reg 4.508
The Babe lies yet in smiling Infancy, Nativity 151
His Infancy to sease! Circum 14
Trinity ms 'infancy' ←'infancie'
Infant
Lur'd with the smell of infant blood, to dance Par Lost 2.664
Inhospitably, and kills thir infant Males: Par Lost 12.168
With Infant blood the streets of *Bethlehem;* Par Reg 2.78
Afford a present to the Infant God? Nativity 16
The dredded Infants hand, Nativity 222
And joyous news of heav'nly Infants birth, Passion 3
Mother with Infant down the Rocks. Their moans Sonnet 18, 8
Infant-lips
Half unpronounc't, slide through my infant-lipps, Vacation 4
Infantry
Could merit more then that small infantry Par Lost 1.575
Infect
His thoughts, his looks, words, actions all infect, Par Lost 10.608
Infected
Infected *Sions* daughters with like heat, Par Lost 1.453
Infection
Th' infection when thir borrow'd Gold compos'd Par Lost 1.483
Might think th' infection of my sorrows loud, Passion 55
Infer
To glorifie the Maker, and inferr Par Lost 7.116
Inferr, as if I thought my sisters state Mask 408
Trinity ms 'inferre'
1637 'Inferre'
Inferior
Envy from each inferior; but who here Par Lost 2.26
The luminous inferior Orbs, enclos'd Par Lost 3.420
Me some inferiour Angel, I had stood Par Lost 4.59
Little inferior; whom my thoughts pursue Par Lost 4.362
And these inferiour farr beneath me set? Par Lost 8.382
To me inferiour, infinite descents Par Lost 8.410
Of Nature her th' inferiour, in the mind Par Lost 8.541
Superior; for inferior who is free? Par Lost 9.825
Little inferiour, by my adventure hard Par Lost 10.468
However to this Man inferior far, Par Reg 2.135
Inferiour to the vilest now become Samson 73
The Angelic orders and inferiour creatures mute, Samson 672
If my inferior hand or voice could hit Arcades 77
As his inferiour flame, Nativity 81
Infernal
Th' infernal Serpent; he it was, whose guile Par Lost 1.34
Infernal world, and thou profoundest Hell Par Lost 1.251
For this Infernal Pit shall never hold Par Lost 1.657
ms 'infernal'
Of that infernal Court. But far within Par Lost 1.792
ms 'infernall'
Infernal Thunder, and for Lightning see Par Lost 2.66
Pleas'd highly those infernal States, and joy Par Lost 2.387
In order came the grand infernal Peers, Par Lost 2.507
Of four infernal Rivers that disgorge Par Lost 2.575
In this infernal Vaile first met thou call'st Par Lost 2.742
The key of this infernal Pit by due, Par Lost 2.850
Th' infernal dores, and on thir hinges grate Par Lost 2.881
Who tells of som infernal Spirit seen Par Lost 4.793
Back to th' infernal pit I drag thee chaind, Par Lost 4.965
Shall yield us pregnant with infernal flame, Par Lost 6.483
Infernal noise; Warr seem'd a civil Game Par Lost 6.667
The black tartareous cold Infernal dregs Par Lost 7.238
1667 'infernal'
The infernal Powers, in one day to have marr'd Par Lost 9.136
Of merit high to all th' infernal Host, Par Lost 10.259
Th' infernal Empire, that so neer Heav'ns dore Par Lost 10.389
1667 'Infernal'
Triumphant out of this infernal Pit Par Lost 10.464
Of much amazement to th' infernal Crew, Par Reg 1.107
Infernal Ghosts, and Hellish Furies, round Par Reg 4.422

Infernal(*cont*)
But thou, Infernal Serpent, shalt not long Par Reg 4.618
Troop to th' infernall jail, Nativity 233
1673 'infernal'
Infers
Or Bright inferrs not Excellence: the Earth Par Lost 8.91
His fraud is then thy fear, which plain inferrs Par Lost 9.285
Commends thee more, while it inferrs the good Par Lost 9.754
Infest
Find some occasion to infest our Foes. Samson 423
Infidel
And all who since, Baptiz'd or Infidel Par Lost 1.582
ms 'infidell'
The daughter of an Infidel: they knew not Samson 221
Infinite
Infinite goodness, grace and mercy shewn Par Lost 1.218
The dark unbottom'd infinite Abyss Par Lost 2.405
And hourly born, with sorrow infinite Par Lost 2.797
Won from the void and formless infinite. Par Lost 3.12
Immutable, Immortal, Infinite, Par Lost 3.373
Thir number, or the wisdom infinite Par Lost 3.706
Infinite wrauth, and infinite despaire? Par Lost 4.74
As liberal and free as infinite, Par Lost 4.415
Thy goodness infinite, both when we wake, Par Lost 4.734
Can equal anger infinite provok't. Par Lost 4.916
Orb within Orb, the Father infinite, Par Lost 5.596
Through the infinite Host, nor less for that Par Lost 5.874
Were don, but infinite: for wide was spred Par Lost 6.241
His good to Worlds and Ages infinite. Par Lost 7.191
Great are thy works, *Jehovah*, infinite Par Lost 7.602
To me inferiour, infinite descents Par Lost 8.410
Shouldst propagat, already infinite; Par Lost 8.420
For though the Lord of all be infinite, Par Lost 10.794
For angers sake, finite to infinite Par Lost 10.802
Which infinite calamitie shall cause Par Lost 10.907
But infinite in pardon was my Judge, Par Lost 11.167
Nations, and bring home spoils with infinite Par Lost 11.692
O goodness infinite, goodness immense! Par Lost 12.469
Infinitely
Be infinitly good, and of his good Par Lost 4.414
For which to the infinitly Good we owe Par Lost 7.76
1669 'Infinitely'
Infinitude
Stood rul'd, stood vast infinitude confin'd; Par Lost 3.711
Infinitude, nor vacuous the space. Par Lost 7.169
Infirm
Shee needed, Vertue-proof, no thought infirme Par Lost 5.384
Infirmer
Thy frailtie and infirmer Sex forgiv'n, Par Lost 10.956
Infirmity
Of secrets, then with like infirmity Samson 776
(That last infirmity of Noble mind) Lycidas 71
1638 'infirmitie'
Trinity ms 'infirmitie'
Infixed
Immovable, infixt, and frozen round, Par Lost 2.602
Before him, such as in thir Soules infix'd Par Lost 6.837
Of constancy no root infixt, Samson 1032
Inflame
Whose waves of torrent fire inflame with rage. Par Lost 2.581
With all perfections, so enflame my sense Par Lost 9.1031
And from his memory inflame thir breasts Samson 1739
Inflamed
Of that inflamed Sea, he stood and call'd Par Lost 1.300
Satan with thoughts inflam'd of highest design, Par Lost 2.630
Inflam'd with lust then rage) and swifter far, Par Lost 2.791
Satan, now first inflam'd with rage, came down, Par Lost 4.9
And visage all enflam'd first thus began. Par Lost 6.261
The more he grew in years, the more inflam'd Par Reg 3.40
Inflames
With sudden blaze diffus'd, inflames the Aire: Par Lost 4.818
Rather inflames thy torment, representing Par Reg 1.418
Inflaming
Carnal desire enflaming, hee on *Eve* Par Lost 9.1013
Inflammation
Dire inflammation which no cooling herb Samson 626
Inflexible
As thou art strong, inflexible as steel. Samson 816
Inflict
Can else inflict, do I repent or change, Par Lost 1.96
Might suddenly inflict; that past, return'd Par Lost 10.341
That tyrannie or fortune can inflict, Samson 1291
Inflicted
Inflicted? and what peace can we return, Par Lost 2.335
Because not yet inflicted, as he fear'd, Par Lost 10.51
Shall be inflicted by the Seed of *Eve* Par Reg 1.54
By pains and slaveries, worse then death inflicted Samson 485
Acknowledge them from God inflicted on me Samson 1170
Inflictions
With all inflictions, but his patience won? Par Reg 1.426
Influence
But now at last the sacred influence Par Lost 2.1034
Foreknowledge had no influence on their fault, Par Lost 3.118
Of various influence foment and warme, Par Lost 4.669
Bad influence into th' unwarie brest Par Lost 5.695
Shedding sweet influence: less bright the Moon, Par Lost 7.375
Shed thir selectest influence; the Earth Par Lost 8.513
Of sacred influence: As God in Heav'n Par Lost 9.107

Influence(*cont*)
I from the influence of thy looks receave — Par Lost 9.309
Thir influence malignant when to showre, — Par Lost 10.662
Or if your influence be quite damm'd up — Mask 336
Rain influence, and judge the prise — Allegro 122
Bending one way their pretious influence, — Nativity 71

Inform
Sufficient introduction to inform — Par Reg 3.247
Shall I inform my unacquainted feet — Mask 180
1637 'informe'
Trinity ms 'informe'
Bridgewater ms 'informe'

Informed
Not all parts like, but all alike informd — Par Lost 3.593
Informd by thee might know; if else thou seekst — Par Lost 7.639
Our ruin, both by thee informd I learne, — Par Lost 9.275
My Son now Captive, hither hath inform'd — Samson 335
Come nearer, part not hence so slight inform'd; — Samson 1229

Informidable
Foe not informidable, exempt from wound, — Par Lost 9.486

Informing
Of sacrifice, informing them, by types — Par Lost 12.232

Infringed
To be infring'd, our freedom and our being — Par Reg 1.62

Infuriate
Dilated and infuriate shall send forth — Par Lost 6.486

Infused
So spake the false Arch-Angel, and infus'd — Par Lost 5.694
And vital vertue infus'd, and vital warmth — Par Lost 7.236
And in her looks, which from that time infus'd — Par Lost 8.474
That dwelt within, whose presence had infus'd — Par Lost 9.836

Inglorious
Was not inglorious, though th' event was dire, — Par Lost 1.624
Inglorious, of his mortall sting disarm'd. — Par Lost 3.253
From servitude inglorious welnigh half — Par Lost 9.141
Inglorious life with servitude; for life — Par Lost 12.220
Inglorious: but thou yet art not too late. — Par Reg 3.42
Inglorious, unimploy'd, with age out-worn. — Samson 580
And the inglorious likenes of a beast — Mask 528
Yet art thou not inglorious in thy fate; — Fair Inf 22

Ingraft
Good or not good ingraft, my Merit those — Par Lost 11.35

Ingrate
Whose but his own? ingrate, he had of mee — Par Lost 3.97
Expected, least of all from thee, ingrate — Par Lost 5.811
Turn'd recreant to God, ingrate and false, — Par Reg 3.138

Ingrateful
No ingrateful food: and food alike those pure — Par Lost 5.407
Of mine to thee, ingrateful *Eve*, exprest — Par Lost 9.1164
And how ingrateful *Ephraim* — Samson 282
And condemnation of the ingrateful multitude. — Samson 696

Ingratitude
To heap ingratitude on worthiest deeds? — Samson 276
But with besotted base ingratitude — Mask 778

Ingredients
So deep the power of these Ingredients pierc'd, — Par Lost 11.417

Inhabit
What creatures there inhabit, of what mould, — Par Lost 2.355
Mean while inhabit laxe, ye Powers of Heav'n, — Par Lost 7.162

Inhabitant
Inhabitant of Heav'n, and heav'nlie-born, — Par Lost 2.860
Inhabitant with God, now know I well — Par Lost 5.461

Inhabitants
Wo to the inhabitants on Earth! that now, — Par Lost 4.5
Feilds and Inhabitants: Her spots thou seest — Par Lost 8.145

Inhabitation
As if the whole inhabitation perish'd, — Samson 1512

Inhabited
Inhabited, though sinless, more then now, — Par Lost 10.690

Inherit
That womans love can win or long inherit; — Samson 1012

Inheritance
To claim our just inheritance of old, — Par Lost 2.38
To thir inheritance, then, nor till then, — Par Reg 3.382
Man. His ransom, if my whole inheritance — Samson 1476

Inhospitable
Inhospitable appeer and desolate, — Par Lost 11.306
Jael, who with inhospitable guile — Samson 989

Inhospitably
Inhospitably, and kills thir infant Males: — Par Lost 12.168

Inhuman
Under inhuman pains? Why should not Man, — Par Lost 11.511
Among inhuman foes. — Samson 109

Inhumanly
Inhumanly to men, and multiply — Par Lost 11.677

Inimitable
The Portal shon, inimitable on Earth — Par Lost 3.508
Inimitable sounds, yet as we go, — Arcades 78

Iniquities
Wearied with their iniquities, withdraw — Par Lost 12.107

Iniquity
All workers of iniquity — Psalm 5, 13
Depart all ye that work iniquitie. — Psalm 6, 16
Th' iniquity thou didst forgive — Psalm 85, 5

Injunction
The high Injunction not to taste that Fruit, — Par Lost 10.13

Injure
Or Heat should injure us, his timely care — Par Lost 10.1057

Injured
And high disdain, from sence of injur'd merit, — Par Lost 1.98
Was understood, the injur'd Lovers Hell. — Par Lost 5.450
Till Truth, and Right from Violence be freed, — Sonnet 15, 11
1694 'injur'd Truth'

Injuries
As joyn'd in injuries, one enmitie — Par Lost 10.925
By tribulations, injuries, insults, — Par Reg 3.190
Attends thee, scorns, reproaches, injuries, — Par Reg 4.387

Injurious
Chor. Yet beauty, though injurious, hath strange power, — Samson 1003

Injury
And injury and outrage: And when Night — Par Lost 1.500
Incapable of mortal injurie — Par Lost 6.434

Inlaid
Whereon a Saphir Throne, inlaid with pure — Par Lost 6.758

Inland
Farr to the inland retir'd, about the walls — Par Lost 10.423
1667 'in-land'

Inlay
Crocus, and Hyacinth with rich inlay — Par Lost 4.701
That like to rich, and various gemms inlay — Mask 22
Bridgewater ms 'in laye'

Inlays
That in the channell strayes, — Mask 895
Trinity ms 'in the channell straies' ← 'my rich wheeles inlayes'

Inlet
And through the porch and inlet of each sense — Mask 839

Inly
Whereat hee inlie rag'd, and as they talk'd, — Par Lost 11.444
By words at times cast forth inly rejoyc'd, — Par Reg 1.228
Though inly stung with anger and disdain, — Par Reg 1.466
To whom the Tempter inly rackt reply'd. — Par Reg 3.203

Inmate
In Serpent, Inmate bad, and toward *Eve* — Par Lost 9.495
To stop thir overgrowth, as inmate guests — Par Lost 12.166

Inmost
His inmost counsels from thir destind aim. — Par Lost 1.168
Which God likes best, into thir inmost bowre — Par Lost 4.738
Earths inmost womb, more warmth then *Adam* needs; — Par Lost 5.302
About thir spirits had plaid, and inmost powers — Par Lost 9.1048
Eevn to the inmost seat of mental sight, — Par Lost 11.418
To th' inmost mind, — Samson 611
In their obscured haunts of inmost bowres. — Mask 536
Of woody *Ida*'s inmost grove, — Penseroso 29

Inn
For in the Inn was left no better room: — Par Reg 1.248
And that he had tane up his latest Inne, — Carrier 13

Inner
Governs the inner man, the nobler part, — Par Reg 2.477

Innocence
Simplicitie and spotless innocence. — Par Lost 4.318
And should I at your harmless innocence — Par Lost 4.388
Of puritie and place and innocence, — Par Lost 4.745
With pleasant liquors crown'd: O innocence — Par Lost 5.445
Such high advantages thir innocence — Par Lost 6.401
Yet Innocence and Virgin Modestie, — Par Lost 8.501
Go in thy native innocence, relie — Par Lost 9.373
Despoild of Innocence, of Faith, of Bliss. — Par Lost 9.411
Her graceful Innocence, her every Aire — Par Lost 9.459
How dark'nd; innocence, that as a veile — Par Lost 9.1054
Of Innocence, of Faith, of Puritie, — Par Lost 9.1075
From innocence. Now therefore bend thine eare — Par Lost 11.30
Hast thou betrai'd my credulous innocence — Mask 697
line not in Bridgewater ms
Commended her fair innocence to the flood — Mask 831
Bridgewater ms 'innocense'
To bless us with thy heav'n-lov'd innocence, — Fair Inf 65
And the innocence which is — Psalm 7, 33

Innocent
To wreck on innocent frail man his loss — Par Lost 4.11
So pray'd they innocent, and to thir thoughts — Par Lost 5.209
The aidless innocent Lady his wish't prey, — Mask 574
Impostor do not charge most innocent nature, — Mask 762
To hide her guilty front with innocent Snow, — Nativity 39

Innumerable
Innumerable force of Spirits arm'd — Par Lost 1.101
Innumerable. As when the potent Rod — Par Lost 1.338
And hands innumerable scarce perform. — Par Lost 1.699
Thy praises, with th' innumerable sound — Par Lost 3.147
Amongst innumerable Starrs, that shon — Par Lost 3.565
Innumerable before th' Almighties Throne — Par Lost 5.585
Innumerable as the Starrs of Night, — Par Lost 5.745
Among innumerable false, unmov'd, — Par Lost 5.898
Bristl'd with upright beams innumerable — Par Lost 6.82
None arguing stood, innumerable hands — Par Lost 6.508
Innumerable, and this which yeelds or fills — Par Lost 7.88
Of men innumerable, there to dwell, — Par Lost 7.156
With Frie innumerable swarme, and Shoales — Par Lost 7.400
First Man, of Men innumerable ordain'd — Par Lost 8.297
Ye Cedars, with innumerable boughs — Par Lost 9.1089
Of carnage, prey innumerable, and taste — Par Lost 10.268
On all sides, from innumerable tongues — Par Lost 10.507
And more that shall befall, innumerable — Par Lost 10.896
With maladies innumerable — Samson 608
Thronging the Seas with spawn innumerable, — Mask 713

Innumerous
- Innumerous living Creatures, perfet formes, Par Lost 7.455
- In this close dungeon of innumerous bowes. Mask 349
  - Bridgewater ms 'inumerous'

Inoffensive
- She crushes, inoffensive moust, and meathes Par Lost 5.345
- With inoffensive pace that spinning sleeps Par Lost 8.164
- Smooth, easie, inoffensive down to Hell. Par Lost 10.305

Inordinate
- Vaine hopes, vaine aimes, inordinate desires Par Lost 4.808
- Immediately inordinate desires Par Lost 12.87

Inquire
- He stayd not to enquire: above them all Par Lost 3.571
- Then of our fellow servant, and inquire Par Lost 8.225
- And guides the Eastern Sages, who enquire Par Lost 12.362
- Of Telescope, were curious to enquire: Par Reg 4.42

Inquired
- Shalt be enquir'd at *Delphos* or elsewhere, Par Reg 1.458

Inquisition
- Sollicitous, what moves thy inquisition? Par Reg 3.200

Inquisitive
- Curiosity, inquisitive, importune Samson 775

Inroad
- From *Chaos* and th' inroad of Darkness old, Par Lost 3.421
- With many an inrode gor'd; deformed rout Par Lost 6.387

Inroads
- And with perpetual inrodes to Allarme, Par Lost 2.103

Insatiable
- Insatiable of glory had lost all, Par Reg 3.148

Insatiate
- Beyond thus high, insatiate to pursue Par Lost 2.8
- Insatiate, I thus single, nor have feard Par Lost 9.536

Inscribed
- With Hymns, our Psalms with artful terms inscrib'd, Par Reg 4.335
- Like to that sanguine flower inscrib'd with woe. Lycidas 106

Insect
- Beast, Bird, Insect, or Worm durst enter none; Par Lost 4.704
- Insect or Worme; those wav'd thir limber fans Par Lost 7.476
- Of every Beast, and Bird, and Insect small Par Lost 11.734

Insensate
- Insensate, hope conceiving from despair. Par Lost 6.787
- Insensate left, or to sense reprobate, Samson 1685

Insensible
- Insensible, and forthwith to dissolve: Par Lost 8.291
- Insensible, how glad would lay me down Par Lost 10.777

Insensibly
- Insensibly, for I suspend thir doom; Par Lost 6.692
- Insensibly three different Motions move? Par Lost 8.130

Inseparable
- Inseparable must with mee along: Par Lost 10.250

Inseparably
- Inseparablie thine, to him shalt beare Par Lost 4.473
- Inseparably dark? Samson 154

Inside
- Outside and inside both, pillars and roofs Par Reg 4.58
- Their inside, troubles miserable; Psalm 5, 27
- Sees his foule inside through his whited skin. Prose 10, 6

Insight
- Best school of best experience, quickest in sight Par Reg 3.238

Insinuating
- Insinuating, wove with Gordian twine Par Lost 4.348

Insist
- Bear not too sensibly, nor still insist Samson 913

Insisted
- Sharply thou hast insisted on rebuke, Par Reg 1.468

Insolence
- Of *Belial*, flown with insolence and wine. Par Lost 1.502
- *Har*. This insolence other kind of answer fits. Samson 1236
- To meet the rudenesse, and swill'd insolence Mask 178

Insolent
- Impetuous, insolent, unquenchable; Samson 1422

Inspection
- With narrow search; and with inspection deep Par Lost 9.83

Insphered
- Of bright aereal Spirits live insphear'd Mask 3
  - Bridgewater ms 'inspheard'

Inspire
- Of *Oreb*, or of *Sinai*, didst inspire Par Lost 1.7
- By proof the undoubted Son of God, inspire, Par Reg 1.11
- Hail bounteous *May* that dost inspire May Morn 5
- On smoother, till *Favonius* re-inspire Sonnet 20, 6

Inspired
- Of *Daphne* by *Orontes*, and th' inspir'd Par Lost 4.273
- Of God inspir'd, small store will serve, where store, Par Lost 5.322
- Inspir'd with contradiction durst oppose Par Lost 6.155
- Some one intent on mischief, or inspir'd Par Lost 6.503
- And into all things from her Aire inspir'd Par Lost 8.476
- In heart or head, possessing soon inspir'd Par Lost 9.189
- Which God inspir'd, cannot together perish Par Lost 10.785
- Inspir'd, and wing'd for Heav'n with speedier flight Par Lost 11.7
- Inspir'd; disdain not such access to me. Par Reg 1.492
- Whom well inspir'd the Oracle pronounc'd Par Reg 4.275
- Such are from God inspir'd, not such from thee; Par Reg 4.350

Inspires
- Meets his approach, and to the heart inspires Par Lost 4.154
- And dictates to me slumbring, or inspires Par Lost 9.23
- Inspire's the pale-ey'd Priest from the prophetic cell. Nativity 180
  - 1673 'Inspires'

Inspiring
- Or if, inspiring venom, he might taint Par Lost 4.804

Install
- That which alone can truly reinstall thee Par Reg 3.372
- A Saviour art come down to re-install. Par Reg 4.615

Instant
- Instant without disturb they took Allarm, Par Lost 6.549
- And th' instant stroke of Death denounc't that day Par Lost 10.210
- Not instant, but of future time. With joy Par Lost 10.345

Instantly
- Of sleep, which instantly fell on me, call'd Par Lost 8.458

Instead
- Arming to Battel, and in stead of rage Par Lost 1.553
- But cloud in stead, and ever-during dark Par Lost 3.45
- All hope excluded thus, behold in stead Par Lost 4.105
- With shews instead, meer shews of seeming pure, Par Lost 4.316
- Good out of evil to create, in stead Par Lost 7.188
- They saw, but other sight instead, a crowd Par Lost 10.538
- Thir appetite with gust, instead of Fruit Par Lost 10.565
- Instead shall double ours upon our heads. Par Lost 10.1040
- Regenerate grow instead, that sighs now breath'd Par Lost 11.5
- Quite out thir Native Language, and instead Par Lost 12.54
- Contempt instead, dishonour, obloquy? Par Reg 3.131
- Fixes instead, unmoulding reasons mintage Mask 529
  - Bridgewater ms 'insteed'
  - Trinity ms 'insteed'

Instilled
- Of thy Rebellion? how hast thou instill'd Par Lost 6.269
- And from the Well of Life three drops instill'd. Par Lost 11.416

Instinct
- Instinct with Fire and Nitre hurried him Par Lost 2.937
- It self instinct with Spirit, but convoyd Par Lost 6.752
- By this new felt attraction and instinct. Par Lost 10.263
- Instinct through all proportions low and high Par Lost 11.562
- Full of divine instinct, after some proof Samson 526
- But providence or instinct of nature seems, Samson 1545

Instinctive
- By quick instinctive motion up I sprung, Par Lost 8.259

Instruct
- Instruct me, for Thou know'st; Thou from the first Par Lost 1.19
- Hee will instruct us praying, and of Grace Par Lost 10.1081
- Return'd the wiser, or the more instruct Par Reg 1.439

Instructed
- Instructed that to God is no access Par Lost 12.239
- Greatly instructed I shall hence depart, Par Lost 12.557
- Then with more cautious and instructed skill Samson 757
- For sure so well instructed are my tears, Passion 48

Instruction
- Gently for our instruction to impart Par Lost 7.81

Instructor
- Divine instructer, I have heard, then when Par Lost 5.546
- As present, Heav'nly instructer, I revive Par Lost 11.871

Instructs
- More fruitful, which instructs us not to spare. Par Lost 5.320

Instrument
- Sad instrument of all our woe, she took; Par Lost 2.872
- Like instrument to plague the Sons of men Par Lost 6.505
- The Guilt on him who made him instrument Par Lost 10.166
- And fragile arms, much instrument of war Par Reg 3.388

Instrumental
- With Heav'nly touch of instrumental sounds Par Lost 4.686
- Of instrumental Harmonie that breath'd Par Lost 6.65

Instruments
- Of Instruments that made melodious chime Par Lost 11.559

Insufferably
- Insufferably bright. O might I here Par Lost 9.1084

Insult
- At my affliction, and perhaps to insult, Samson 113
- And last neglected? How wouldst thou insult Samson 944

Insulting
- Insulting, and pursu'd us through the Deep, Par Lost 2.79
- Insulting Angel, well thou knowst I stood Par Lost 4.926
- Of triumph that insulting vanity; Par Reg 4.138

Insults
- By tribulations, injuries, insults, Par Reg 3.190

Insuperable
- Insuperable highth of loftiest shade, Par Lost 4.138

Insupportable
- However insupportable, be all Par Lost 10.134

Insupportably
- When insupportably his foot advanc't, Samson 136

Insurrection
- With blackest Insurrection, to confound Par Lost 2.136
  - 1674 printed 'Iussurrection'

Integrity
- Or taint integritie; but all obey'd Par Lost 5.704
- Of our integritie: his foul esteeme Par Lost 9.329

Intellect
- All Intellect, all Sense, and as they please, Par Lost 6.351

Intellects
- Numbring good intellects; now seldom por'd on. Sonnet 11, 4
  - Trinity ms 'intellects' ← 'wits'

Intellectual
- Though full of pain, this intellectual being, Par Lost 2.147
- To intellectual, give both life and sense, Par Lost 5.485
- Whose higher intellectual more I shun, Par Lost 9.483
- This intellectual food, for beasts reserv'd? Par Lost 9.768

Intelligence
Intelligence of Heav'n, Angel serene, Par Lost 8.181
Intelligent
Intelligent of seasons, and set forth Par Lost 7.427
Th' intelligent among them and the wise Par Reg 3.58
Intelligential
Intelligential substances require Par Lost 5.408
With act intelligential; but his sleep Par Lost 9.190
Intemperance
By Fire, Flood, Famin, by Intemperance more Par Lost 11.472
O're sensual Folly, and Intemperance. Mask 975
Trinity ms 'intemperance'
Intemperate
(For most do taste through fond intemperate thirst) Mask 67
Intend
Terror of Heav'n, though fall'n; intend at home, Par Lost 2.457
No second stroke intend, and such a frown Par Lost 2.713
Whether by supplication we intend Par Lost 5.867
Easie it might be seen that I intend Par Lost 10.58
Towards thee I intend for what I have misdone, Samson 911
If they intend advantage of my labours Samson 1259
And what the *Swede* intend, and what the *French*. Sonnet 21, 8
Trinity ms 'intends'
Intended
Intended to create, and therein plant Par Lost 1.652
Intended thee, for trial onely brought, Par Lost 8.447
As one intended first, not after made Par Lost 8.555
Climat, or Years damp my intended wing Par Lost 9.45
Th' attempt it self, intended by our Foe. Par Lost 9.295
His course intended; else how had the World Par Lost 10.689
Broken be not intended all our power Par Reg 1.61
Already, and for him intended Psalm 7, 47
Intends
That with no middle flight intends to soar Par Lost 1.14
O Father, what intends thy hand, she cry'd, Par Lost 2.727
What it intends; till first I know of thee, Par Lost 2.740
His Iron Gates, if he intends our stay Par Lost 4.898
Intends to pass triumphant, and give Laws. Par Lost 5.693
Is rising, who intends to erect his Throne Par Lost 5.725
Stayes not on Man; to God his Tower intends Par Lost 12.73
Means her provision onely to the good Mask 765
Trinity ms 'means' ← 'intends'
Intense
The one intense, the other still remiss Par Lost 8.387
With answerable pains, but more intense, Samson 615
Intent
Intent, with jocond Music charm his ear; Par Lost 1.787
Though but endevord with sincere intent, Par Lost 3.192
Him thus intent *Ithuriel* with his Spear Par Lost 4.810
She turns, on hospitable thoughts intent Par Lost 5.332
Some one intent on mischief, or inspir'd Par Lost 6.503
To hide me, and the dark intent I bring. Par Lost 9.162
His fierceness of the fierce intent it brought: Par Lost 9.462
Intent now wholly on her taste, naught else Par Lost 9.786
Of amorous intent, well understood Par Lost 9.1035
Into this Wilderness, to what intent Par Reg 1.291
But where delays he now? some great intent Par Reg 2.95
All her assaults, on worthier things intent? Par Reg 2.195
And what he is; his wisdom, power, intent, Par Reg 4.528
Though for no friendly intent. I am of *Gath*, Samson 1078
His uncontroulable intent, Samson 1754
I know this quest of yours, and free intent Arcades 34
Men whose Life, Learning, Faith and pure intent Forcers 9
Inter
This rich Marble doth enterr Winchester 1
Intercede
Presenting, thus to intercede began. Par Lost 11.21
I to the Lords will intercede, not doubting Samson 920
Intercept
And fly, ere evil intercept thy flight. Par Lost 5.871
Such ruin intercept: ten paces huge Par Lost 6.193
To intercept thy way, or send thee back Par Lost 9.410
Might intercept thir Emperour sent, so hee Par Lost 10.429
Intercession
Recounted, mixing intercession sweet. Par Lost 10.228
Intercessor
Patron or Intercessor none appeerd, Par Lost 3.219
Came the mild Judge and Intercessor both Par Lost 10.96
By thir great Intercessor, came in sight Par Lost 11.19
Interchange
If I could joy in aught, sweet interchange Par Lost 9.115
Intercourse
With easie intercourse pass to and fro Par Lost 2.1031
Delighted, and with frequent intercourse Par Lost 7.571
Food of the mind, or this sweet intercourse Par Lost 9.238
Easing thir passage hence, for intercourse, Par Lost 10.260
Interdict
These are not Fruits forbidden, no interdict Par Reg 2.369
Interdicted
Of interdicted Knowledge: fair it seem'd, Par Lost 5.52
Charg'd not to touch the interdicted Tree, Par Lost 7.46
Interdiction
The rigid interdiction, which resounds Par Lost 8.334
Interfused
All space, the ambient Aire wide interfus'd Par Lost 7.89
Interlunar
Hid in her vacant interlunar cave. Samson 89

Interminable
As if they would confine th' interminable, Samson 307
Intermission
That rest or intermission none I find. Par Lost 2.802
Short intermission bought with double smart. Par Lost 4.102
At length for intermission sake they led him Samson 1629
Intermit
Of this ill Mansion: intermit no watch Par Lost 2.462
Intermits
Casual discourse draw on, which intermits Par Lost 9.223
Intermitted
Should intermitted vengeance arm again Par Lost 2.173
Speech intermitted thus to *Eve* renewd. Par Lost 9.1133
Intermix
Chose rather; hee, she knew would intermix Par Lost 8.54
As I shall thee enlighten, intermix Par Lost 11.115
Intermixed
Temper'd soft Tunings, intermixt with Voice Par Lost 7.598
In yonder Spring of Roses intermixt Par Lost 9.218
Internal
Of Fancie my internal sight, by which Par Lost 8.461
Internal Man, is but proportion meet, Par Lost 9.711
Sam. My self? my conscience and internal peace. Samson 1334
And with blindness internal struck. Samson 1686
Interpose
Death ready stands to interpose his dart, Par Lost 2.854
If *Adam* aught perhaps might interpose; Par Lost 12.4
line not in 1667 edition
For so to interpose a little ease, Lycidas 152
To interpose them oft, is not unwise. Sonnet 20, 14
Interposed
Grasing the tender herb, were interpos'd, Par Lost 4.253
Starr interpos'd, however small he sees, Par Lost 5.258
1667 'interposd' in some copies
By Angels many and strong, who interpos'd Par Lost 6.336
With long reach interpos'd; three sev'ral wayes Par Lost 10.323
Here *Adam* interpos'd. O sent from Heav'n, Par Lost 12.270
Above the highth of Mountains interpos'd. Par Reg 4.39
Interposes
Timely interposes, and her monthly round Par Lost 3.728
Interposest
Thou interposest, that my sudden hand Par Lost 2.738
Interposition
Interposition, as a summers cloud. Par Reg 3.222
Interpret
Interpret for him, mee his Advocate Par Lost 11.33
Interpreted
Interpreted) which not long after, he Par Lost 5.762
Interpreter
Interpreter through highest Heav'n to bring, Par Lost 3.657
Divine interpreter, by favour sent Par Lost 7.72
1667 'Interpreter'
Interpretest
And what if Love, which thou interpret'st hate, Samson 790
Interrupt
Common revenge, and interrupt his joy Par Lost 2.371
Wide interrupt can hold; so bent he seems Par Lost 3.84
To interrupt the sweet of Life, from which Par Lost 8.184
To interrupt, side-long he works his way. Par Lost 9.512
National interrupt thir public peace, Par Lost 12.317
Interrupted
Whom thus the Angel interrupted milde. Par Lost 11.286
Intertwined
Whose branching arms thick intertwind might shield Par Reg 4.405
Interval
A dreadful intervall, and Front to Front Par Lost 6.105
1667 'interval'
Interveined
Fair Champain with less rivers interveind, Par Reg 3.257
Intervene
Looks intervene and smiles, or object new Par Lost 9.222
Interview
To hide the fraud. At interview both stood Par Lost 6.555
Such happy interview and fair event Par Lost 11.593
Intervolved
Eccentric, intervolv'd, yet regular Par Lost 5.623
Interwove
Words interwove with sighs found out thir way. Par Lost 1.621
With Ivy canopied, and interwove Mask 544
Interwoven
Of Trees thick interwoven; there he slept, Par Reg 2.263
Intestine
Encroacht on still through our intestine broiles Par Lost 2.1001
Intestine War in Heav'n, the arch foe subdu'd Par Lost 6.259
Intestin Stone and Ulcer, Colic pangs, Par Lost 11.484
Intestin, far within defensive arms Samson 1038
Intimate
From intimate impulse, and therefore urg'd Samson 223
Into
Brought Death into the World, and all our woe, Par Lost 1.3
In equal ruin: into what Pit thou seest Par Lost 1.91
Ten thousand Banners rise into the Air Par Lost 1.545
Op'nd into the Hill a spacious wound Par Lost 1.689
Turning our Tortures into horrid Arms Par Lost 2.63
Scout farr and wide into the Realm of night, Par Lost 2.133
Awak'd should blow them into sevenfold rage Par Lost 2.171
Into their temper; which must needs remove Par Lost 2.277
If thence he scape into whatever world, Par Lost 2.442

Into(*cont*)
Into th' *Euboic* Sea. Others more milde, Par Lost 2.546
Into the burning Lake thir baleful streams; Par Lost 2.576
If aught disturb'd thir noyse, into her woomb, Par Lost 2.657
Into this Deep, and in the general fall Par Lost 2.773
Into my hand was giv'n, with charge to keep Par Lost 2.775
To me, for when they list into the womb Par Lost 2.798
Into this gloom of *Tartarus* profound, Par Lost 2.858
Chance governs all. Into this wilde Abyss, Par Lost 2.910
Into this wild Abyss the warie fiend Par Lost 2.917
Into the wilde expanse, and through the shock Par Lost 2.1014
Shoots farr into the bosom of dim Night Par Lost 2.1036
A God, leap'd fondly into *Aetna* flames, Par Lost 3.470
Plato's *Elysium*, leap'd into the Sea, Par Lost 3.472
Into the devious Air; then might ye see Par Lost 3.489
And flutterd into Raggs, then Reliques, Beads, Par Lost 3.491
Into a *Limbo* large and broad, since calld Par Lost 3.495
Down right into the Worlds first Region throws Par Lost 3.562
Into his neather Empire neighbouring round. Par Lost 4.145
Leaps o're the fence with ease into the Fould: Par Lost 4.187
So clomb this first grand Thief into Gods Fould: Par Lost 4.192
So since into his Church lewd Hirelings climbe. Par Lost 4.193
And now divided into four main Streams, Par Lost 4.233
Into our room of bliss thus high advanc't Par Lost 4.359
Into a liquid Plain, then stood unmov'd Par Lost 4.455
On the green bank, to look into the cleer Par Lost 4.458
Which God likes best, into thir inmost bowre Par Lost 4.738
Into her private Cell when Nature rests. Par Lost 5.109
Evil into the mind of God or Man Par Lost 5.117
Into the blissful field, through Groves of Myrrhe, Par Lost 5.292
Vapours not yet into her substance turnd. Par Lost 5.420
From what high state of bliss into what woe! Par Lost 5.543
Into utter darkness, deep ingulft, his place Par Lost 5.614
Bad influence into th' unwarie brest Par Lost 5.695
Stretcht into Longitude; which having pass'd Par Lost 5.754
At length into the limits of the North Par Lost 5.755
Impendent, raging into sudden flame Par Lost 5.891
Into thir place of punishment, the Gulf Par Lost 6.53
Heav'ns blessed peace, and into Nature brought Par Lost 6.267
Thy malice into thousands, once upright Par Lost 6.270
Or turn this Heav'n it self into the Hell Par Lost 6.291
Which into hallow Engins long and round Par Lost 6.484
To blackest grain, and into store convey'd: Par Lost 6.515
Flew off, and into strange vagaries fell, Par Lost 6.614
Into thir substance pent, which wrought them pain Par Lost 6.657
Can end it. Into thee such Vertue and Grace Par Lost 6.703
From all Heav'ns bounds into the utter Deep: Par Lost 6.716
Ineffably into his face receiv'd, Par Lost 6.721
So spake the Son, and into terrour chang'd Par Lost 6.824
Into the wastful Deep; the monstrous sight Par Lost 6.862
Triumphant through mid Heav'n, into the Courts Par Lost 6.889
On high: who into Glorie him receav'd, Par Lost 6.891
Into the Heav'n of Heav'ns I have presum'd, Par Lost 7.13
Into his place, and the great Son returnd Par Lost 7.135
He trusted to have seis'd, and into fraud Par Lost 7.143
Into thir vacant room, and thence diffuse Par Lost 7.190
Farr into *Chaos*, and the World unborn; Par Lost 7.220
Into one place, and let dry Land appeer. Par Lost 7.284
Into the Clouds, thir tops ascend the Skie: Par Lost 7.287
He brought thee into this delicious Grove, Par Lost 7.537
Into all Eyes to wish her still in sight. Par Lost 8.63
Gladly into the wayes of God with Man: Par Lost 8.226
Shalt loose, expell'd from hence into a World Par Lost 8.332
Sweetness into my heart, unfelt before, Par Lost 8.475
And into all things from her Aire inspir'd Par Lost 8.476
That brought into this World a world of woe, Par Lost 9.11
Into a Gulf shot under ground, till part Par Lost 9.72
His bursting passion into plaints thus pour'd: Par Lost 9.98
Determin'd to advance into our room Par Lost 9.148
Into a Beast, and mixt with bestial slime, Par Lost 9.165
And fall into deception unaware, Par Lost 9.362
Into the Heart of *Eve* his words made way, Par Lost 9.550
So glister'd the dire Snake, and into fraud Par Lost 9.643
Into her heart too easie entrance won: Par Lost 9.734
Into the plant sciential sap, deriv'd Par Lost 9.837
Into the thickest Wood, there soon they chose Par Lost 9.1100
Going into such danger as thou saidst? Par Lost 9.1157
Up into Heav'n from Paradise in haste Par Lost 10.17
Into his blissful bosom reassum'd Par Lost 10.225
Farr into *Chaos*, since the Fiend pass'd through, Par Lost 10.233
His Nostril wide into the murkie Air, Par Lost 10.280
Then Both from out Hell Gates into the waste Par Lost 10.282
Into the Wood fast by, and changing shape Par Lost 10.333
But up and enter now into full bliss. Par Lost 10.503
Into the same illusion, not as Man Par Lost 10.571
O Conscience, into what Abyss of fears Par Lost 10.842
Into this cursed World a woful Race, Par Lost 10.984
Into a lower World, to this obscure Par Lost 11.283
Smote him into the Midriff with a stone Par Lost 11.445
Into thy Mothers lap, or be with ease Par Lost 11.536
Into fit moulds prepar'd; from which he formd Par Lost 11.571
His kindred and false Gods, into a Land Par Lost 12.122
Into the Sea: to sojourn in that Land Par Lost 12.159
Growing into a Nation, and now grown Par Lost 12.164
Of Law, his people into *Canaan* lead; Par Lost 12.309
Then enter into glory, and resume Par Lost 12.456
His faithful, and receave them into bliss, Par Lost 12.462
Into the Desert, his Victorious Field Par Reg 1.9

Into(*cont*)
Admiring stood a space, then into Hymns Par Reg 1.169
I went into the Temple, there to hear Par Reg 1.211
Into this Wilderness, to what intent Par Reg 1.291
Gave up into my hands *Uzzean Job* Par Reg 1.369
To draw the proud King *Ahab* into fraud Par Reg 1.372
Into the Heav'n of Heavens; thou com'st indeed, Par Reg 1.410
Into the World, to teach his final will, Par Reg 1.461
Into thin Air diffus'd: for now began Par Reg 1.499
Into perplexity and new amaze: Par Reg 2.38
Thence into *Egypt*, till the Murd'rous King Par Reg 2.76
Into himself descended, and at once Par Reg 2.111
Fall flat and shrink into a trivial toy, Par Reg 2.223
Into the Desert, and how there he slept Par Reg 2.271
Of my reception into grace; what worse? Par Reg 3.205
Alone into the Temple; there was found Par Reg 4.217
Lest he command them down into the deep Par Reg 4.631
Into thir hands, and they as gladly yield me Samson 259
Into a Dungeon thrust, to work with Slaves? Samson 367
Thee *Samson* bound and blind into thir hands, Samson 438
Then swoll'n with pride into the snare I fell Samson 532
And words addrest seem into tears dissolv'd, Samson 729
To learn thy secrets, get into my power Samson 798
To bring my feet again into the snare Samson 931
Into thy Enemies hand, permitted them Samson 1159
Into the common Prison, there to grind Samson 1161
Into our hands: for hadst thou not committed Samson 1185
When God into the hands of thir deliverer Samson 1270
We unawares run into dangers mouth. Samson 1522
Fall'n into wrath divine, Samson 1683
From under ashes into sudden flame, Samson 1691
And downward fell into a groveling Swine) Mask 53
Into som brutish form of Woolf, or Bear, Mask 70
My dazling Spells into the spungy ayr, Mask 154
Trinity ms 'in to'
Wind me into the easie-hearted man, Mask 163
And hugg him into snares. When once her eye Mask 164
Begin to throng into my memory Mask 206
line not in Bridgewater ms
And chid her barking waves into attention, Mask 258
And put them into mis-becoming plight. Mask 372
Into swift flight, till I had found you here, Mask 579
Were shatter'd into heaps o're thy false head. Mask 799
line not in Bridgewater ms
line not in Trinity ms
And throw sweet garland wreaths into her stream Mask 850
Dissolve me into extasies, Penseroso 165
And think to burst out into sudden blaze, Lycidas 74
Creep and intrude, and climb into the fold? Lycidas 115
And now was dropt into the Western bay; Lycidas 191
Into my heart more joy Psalm 4, 31
Into thy house; I in thy fear Psalm 5, 19
And fell into the pit he made, Psalm 7, 56
Into thy presence let my praier Psalm 88, 5
Into a goodly valley, where he sees Prose 2, 2

Intoxicate
Crude or intoxicate, collecting toys, Par Reg 4.328

Intoxicated
As with new Wine intoxicated both Par Lost 9.1008

Intricacies
And freed from intricacies, taught to live, Par Lost 8.182

Intricate
Th' intricate wards, and every Bolt and Bar Par Lost 2.877
Resembles nearest, mazes intricate, Par Lost 5.622
In tangles, and made intricate seem strait, Par Lost 9.632

Introduce
Of charming symphonie they introduce Par Lost 3.368
In freedome equal? or can introduce Par Lost 5.797
Moses in figure beares, to introduce Par Lost 12.241

Introduced
Death introduc'd through fierce antipathie: Par Lost 10.709

Introduction
Sufficient introduction to inform Par Reg 3.247

Intrude
Creep and intrude, and climb into the fold? Lycidas 115

Intrusion
With loath'd intrusion, and fill all the land; Par Lost 12.178

Intuitive
Discursive, or Intuitive; discourse Par Lost 5.488

Inundation
Beyond all bounds, till inundation rise Par Lost 11.828

Inure
For state, as Sovran King, and to enure Par Lost 8.239

Inured
Thir noxious vapour, or enur'd not feel, Par Lost 2.216
And pious sorrow, equally enur'd Par Lost 11.362
Live on tough roots and stubs, to thirst inur'd Par Reg 1.339
But I to wait with patience am inur'd; Par Reg 2.102
Then cruel, by thir sports to blood enur'd Par Reg 4.139
Deep skill'd in all his mothers witcheries, Mask 523
Trinity ms 'deepe skill'd' ←'deepe learnt' ←'enur'd'
Would grow inur'd to light, and com at last Mask 735
Bridgewater ms 'enur'd'
Trinity ms 'enur'd'

Inutterable
Abominable, inutterable, and worse Par Lost 2.626

Invade
With dangerous expedition to invade Par Lost 2.342

Invade(*cont*)
Night would invade, but there the neighbouring Moon Par Lost 3.726
Or in behalf of Man, or to invade Par Lost 11.102
Is ris'n to invade us, who no less Par Reg 2.127
Gods houses, and *will now invade* Psalm 83, 47
Invaded
Themselves invaded next, and on thir heads Par Lost 6.653
Invaders
Against invaders; therefore coold in zeale Par Lost 11.801
Invading
Of the invading enimy. Psalm 136, 82
Invalid
Invalid that which thee to doubt it mov'd; Par Lost 8.116
Invasion
Found able by invasion to annoy Par Reg 3.365
Inveigle
To inveigle and invite th' unwary sense Mask 538
Invent
All patience. He who therefore can invent Par Lost 6.464
Whate're his cruel malice could invent. Par Reg 1.149
That fancy can beget on youthfull thoughts, Mask 669
Trinity ms 'beget on' ←'invent in' ←'beget on'
Invented
His own invented Torments. But perhaps Par Lost 2.70
Envious commands, invented with designe Par Lost 4.524
Was death invented? or to us deni'd Par Lost 9.767
Invention
Th' invention all admir'd, and each, how hee Par Lost 6.498
Inventions
To match with thir inventions they presum'd Par Lost 6.631
To ask, nor let thine own inventions hope Par Lost 7.121
Inventor
To be th' inventer miss'd, so easie it seemd Par Lost 6.499
Inventors
Of Arts that polish Life, Inventers rare, Par Lost 11.610
Invert
But you invert the cov'nants of her trust, Mask 682
line not in Bridgewater ms
Invest
Of God, as with a Mantle didst invest Par Lost 3.10
Invested
Invested with bright Rayes, jocond to run Par Lost 7.372
Invests
Invests the Sea, and wished Morn delayes: Par Lost 1.208
Invests him coming? yet not terrible, Par Lost 11.233
Invincible
Invincible, and vigour soon returns, Par Lost 1.140
Invincible: abasht the Devil stood, Par Lost 4.846
Invincible, lead forth my armed Saints Par Lost 6.47
Thy temperance invincible besides, Par Reg 2.408
That invincible *Samson*, far renown'd, Samson 341
Puts invincible might Samson 1271
Invincibly
Invincibly; but of this cursed crew Par Lost 6.806
Inviolable
This place inviolable, and these from harm. Par Lost 4.843
Far otherwise th' inviolable Saints Par Lost 6.398
Invisible
God thir Creator, and th' invisible Par Lost 1.369
Of things invisible to mortal sight. Par Lost 3.55
Fountain of Light, thy self invisible Par Lost 3.375
Shoots invisible vertue even to the deep: Par Lost 3.586
Invisible, except to God alone, Par Lost 3.684
To us invisible or dimly seen Par Lost 5.157
To human sense th' invisible exploits Par Lost 5.565
Brightness had made invisible, thus spake. Par Lost 5.599
Son in whose face invisible is beheld Par Lost 6.681
Things not reveal'd, which th' invisible King, Par Lost 7.122
Invisible, yet staid (such priviledge Par Lost 7.589
Invisible else above all Starrs, the Wheele Par Lost 8.135
Of that *Plutonian* Hall, invisible Par Lost 10.444
From eyes of mortals walk invisible, Vacation 66
Invisibly
But follow strait, invisibly thus led? Par Lost 4.476
Invitation
His invitation earnestly renew'd. Par Reg 2.367
Invite
The sensible of pain. All things invite Par Lost 2.278
As may not oft invite, though Spirits of Heav'n Par Lost 5.374
And all things in best order to invite Par Lost 9.402
As thir own ruin on themselves to invite, Samson 1684
To inveigle and invite th' unwary sense Mask 538
The up-land Hamlets will invite, Allegro 92
Invited
He comes invited by a yonger Son Par Lost 12.160
Invites
Invites; for I will cleer thir senses dark, Par Lost 3.188
Invites, and in the Consecrated stream Par Reg 1.72
Of Bees industrious murmur oft invites Par Reg 4.248
Inviting
Inviting thee to hear while I relate, Par Lost 8.208
Fair to the Eye, inviting to the Taste, Par Lost 9.777
Twice by a voice inviting him to eat. Par Reg 2.314
Invocate
Go to his Temple, invocate his aid Samson 1146
Invocated
Consume me, and oft-invocated death Samson 575
Invoke
Invoke thy aid to my adventrous Song, Par Lost 1.13
They light the Nuptial Torch, and bid invoke Par Lost 11.590
Invoked
Shook, but delaid to strike, though oft invok't Par Lost 11.492
Hymen, then first to marriage Rites invok't; Par Lost 11.591
From all the rest, of whom to be invok'd, Par Lost 12.112
God of this world invok't and world beneath; Par Reg 4.203
If she be right invok't in warbled Song, Mask 854
Bridgewater ms 'invok'd'
Invoking
He at their invoking came Winchester 19
Involve
To mingle and involve, done all to spite Par Lost 2.384
Involved
And leave a singed bottom all involv'd Par Lost 1.236
His end with mine involvd; and knows that I Par Lost 2.807
Determind, and thy hapless crew involv'd Par Lost 5.879
Of Waters, Embryon immature involv'd, Par Lost 7.277
Wondrous in length and corpulence involv'd Par Lost 7.483
Satan involv'd in rising Mist, then sought Par Lost 9.75
Within thick Clouds and dark ten-fold involv'd, Par Reg 1.41
Till by thir own perplexities involv'd Samson 304
Invulnerable
To be invulnerable in those bright Arms, Par Lost 2.812
Invulnerable, impenitrably arm'd: Par Lost 6.400
Inward
Shine inward, and the mind through all her powers Par Lost 3.52
The Univers, and to each inward part Par Lost 3.584
Rowld inward, and a spacious Gap disclos'd Par Lost 6.861
Inward and outward both, his image faire: Par Lost 8.221
Whose inward apparition gently mov'd Par Lost 8.293
Elaborate, of inward less exact. Par Lost 8.539
And inward Faculties, which most excell, Par Lost 8.542
What inward thence I feel, not therefore foild, Par Lost 8.608
Thus he resolv'd, but first from inward griefe Par Lost 9.97
Of Reason in my inward Powers, and Speech Par Lost 9.600
Our inward freedom? In the day we eate Par Lost 9.762
First to himself he inward silence broke. Par Lost 9.895
Thir inward State of Mind, calm Region once Par Lost 9.1125
Of Beasts, but inward nakedness, much more Par Lost 10.221
Thy inward fraud, to warn all Creatures from thee Par Lost 10.871
Thir inward lost: Witness th' irreverent Son Par Lost 12.101
With inward consolations recompenc't, Par Lost 12.495
In pious Hearts, an inward Oracle Par Reg 1.463
Or could of inward slaves make outward free? Par Reg 4.145
For inward light alas Samson 162
Sam. Ay me, another inward grief awak't, Samson 330
Repuls't, without much inward passion felt Samson 1006
Was lavish't on thir Sex, that inward gifts Samson 1026
With inward eyes illuminated Samson 1689
Lets in defilement to the inward parts, Mask 466
And inward ripenes doth much less appear, Sonnet 7, 7
Inwardly
Under what torments inwardly I groane; Par Lost 4.88
Rot inwardly, and foul contagion spread: Lycidas 127
Inwards
The Inwards and thir Fat, with Incense strew'd, Par Lost 11.439
Inwove
Thir Crowns inwove with Amarant and Gold, Par Lost 3.352
Inwoven
Of thickest covert was inwoven shade Par Lost 4.693
With flowre-inwov'n tresses torn Nativity 187
Inwreathed
Bind thir resplendent locks inwreath'd with beams, Par Lost 3.361
Inwrought
Inwrought with figures dim, and on the edge Lycidas 105
Trinity ms 'inwraught' ←'scraul'd ore'
Ionian
Th' *Ionian* Gods, of *Javans* Issue held Par Lost 1.508
ms 'Ionian'
Irassa
Small things with greatest) in *Irassa* strove Par Reg 4.564
Ire
That we may so suffice his vengeful ire, Par Lost 1.148
His utmost ire? which to the highth enrag'd, Par Lost 2.95
Will he, so wise, let loose at once his ire, Par Lost 2.155
Thrice chang'd with pale, ire, envie and despair, Par Lost 4.115
Thrown on them as a shelter from his ire. Par Lost 6.843
Glorie to him whose just avenging ire Par Lost 7.184
Or *Neptun*'s ire or *Juno's*, that so long Par Lost 9.18
Is open? or will God incense his ire Par Lost 9.692
Mee mee onely just object of his ire. Par Lost 10.936
Hath wiselier arm'd his vengeful ire then so Par Lost 10.1023
So willingly doth God remit his Ire, Par Lost 11.885
Would stand between me and thy Fathers ire, Par Reg 3.219
(Whose ire I dread more then the fire of Hell) Par Reg 3.220
His further ire, with praiers and vows renew'd. Samson 520
And fierce ire trouble them; but I saith hee Psalm 2, 11
Rise Jehovah in thine ire Psalm 7, 19
They perish at thy dreadfull ire, Psalm 80, 67
Wilt thou thy frowning ire extend Psalm 85, 19
Astonish'd with thine ire. Psalm 88, 64
Iris
Iris all hues, Roses, and Gessamin Par Lost 4.698
In time of Truce; *Iris* had dipt the wooff; Par Lost 11.244
These my skie robes spun out of *Iris* Wooff, Mask 83
Iris there with humid bow, Mask 992

Irksome
The irksom hours, till this great Chief return. Par Lost 2.527
1667 'irksome'
Knew never till this irksom night; methought Par Lost 5.35
For not to irksom toile, but to delight Par Lost 9.242
Iron
His Empire, and with Iron Scepter rule Par Lost 2.327
Three Iron, three of Adamantine Rock, Par Lost 2.646
Of massie Iron or sollid Rock with ease Par Lost 2.878
With radiant light, as glowing Iron with fire; Par Lost 3.594
Chaumping his iron curb: to strive or flie Par Lost 4.859
His Iron Gates, if he intends our stay Par Lost 4.898
Is now an Iron Rod to bruise and breake Par Lost 5.887
Brass, Iron, Stonie mould, had not thir mouthes Par Lost 6.576
Of Iron Globes, which on the Victor Host Par Lost 6.590
Labouring, two massie clods of Iron and Brass Par Lost 11.565
As the Magnetic hardest Iron draws. Par Reg 2.168
The field all iron cast a gleaming brown, Par Reg 3.326
Ran on embattelld Armies clad in Iron, Samson 129
And raise such out-cries on thy clatter'd Iron, Samson 1124
Com not too neer, you fall on iron stakes else. Mask 491
Trinity ms 'iron' ←'pointed'
Bridgewater ms 'Iron'
Drew Iron tears down *Pluto*'s cheek, Penseroso 107
(The Golden opes, the Iron shuts amain) Lycidas 111
1638 'iron'
Trinity ms 'iron'
Move by her two maine nerves, Iron and Gold Sonnet 17, 8
With Iron Scepter bruis'd, and them disperse Psalm 2, 20
Irons
These braveries in Irons loaden on thee. Samson 1243
Irradiance
Irradiance, virtual or immediate touch? Par Lost 8.617
Irradiate
Irradiate, there plant eyes, all mist from thence Par Lost 3.53
Irrational
Irrational till then. For us alone Par Lost 9.766
Daughter of Sin, among th' irrational, Par Lost 10.708
Irrational and brute. Samson 673
Irreconcileable
Irreconcileable, to our grand Foe, Par Lost 1.122
ms 'Irreconcilable'
Irrecoverably
Irrecoverably dark, total Eclipse Samson 81
Irregular
Then most, when most irregular they seem, Par Lost 5.624
Irreligious
It would be to ensnare an irreligious Samson 860
Irreparable
Irreparable; tearms of peace yet none Par Lost 2.331
Left me all helpless with th' irreparable loss Samson 644
Irresistible
Of Union irresistible, mov'd on Par Lost 6.63
Irresistible *Samson?* whom unarm'd Samson 126
1671 printed 'irresistable', errata 'irresistible'
Irresolute
Him after long debate, irresolute Par Lost 9.87
Irresolute, unhardy, unadventrous: Par Reg 3.243
Irreverent
Thir inward lost: Witness th' irreverent Son Par Lost 12.101
Irrevocable
Irrevocable, that his Regal Throne Par Lost 12.323
Irriguous
Of som irriguous Valley spred her store, Par Lost 4.255
Irruption
Lest evil tidings with too rude irruption Samson 1567
Is
And mad'st it pregnant: What in me is dark Par Lost 1.22
Illumin, what is low raise and support; Par Lost 1.23
All is not lost; the unconquerable Will, Par Lost 1.106
And what is else not to be overcome? Par Lost 1.109
Fall'n Cherube, to be weak is miserable Par Lost 1.157
Is this the Region, this the Soil, the Clime, Par Lost 1.242
Who now is Sovran can dispose and bid Par Lost 1.246
What shall be right: fardest from him is best Par Lost 1.247
The mind is its own place, and in it self Par Lost 1.254
To reign is worth ambition though in Hell: Par Lost 1.262
And uncompounded is thir Essence pure, Par Lost 1.425
Full Counsel must mature: Peace is despaird, Par Lost 1.660
Of endless pain? where there is then no good Par Lost 2.30
Precedence, none, whose portion is so small Par Lost 2.33
My sentence is for open Warr: Of Wiles, Par Lost 2.51
To us is adverse. Who but felt of late Par Lost 2.77
We sunk thus low? Th' ascent is easie then; Par Lost 2.81
Th' event is fear'd; should we again provoke Par Lost 2.82
Which if not Victory is yet Revenge. Par Lost 2.105
Is flat despair: we must exasperate Par Lost 2.143
Is doubtful; that he never will is sure. Par Lost 2.154
What can we suffer worse? is this then worst, Par Lost 2.163
Our strength is equal, nor the Law unjust Par Lost 2.200
The sentence of thir Conquerour: This is now Par Lost 2.208
With what is punish't; whence these raging fires Par Lost 2.213
Some easier enterprize? There is a place Par Lost 2.345
Seis'd us, though undismaid: long is the way Par Lost 2.432
(Which is my present journey) and once more Par Lost 2.985
That little which is left so to defend, Par Lost 2.1000
May I express thee unblam'd? since God is light, Par Lost 3.3
When Will and Reason (Reason also is choice) Par Lost 3.108

Is(*cont*)
His fall'n condition is, and to me ow Par Lost 3.181
Elect above the rest; so is my will: Par Lost 3.184
But yet all is not don; Man disobeying, Par Lost 3.203
Father, thy word is past, man shall find grace; Par Lost 3.227
Receive new life. So Man, as is most just, Par Lost 3.294
Melodious part, such concord is in Heav'n. Par Lost 3.371
And waking cri'd, *This is the Gate of Heav'n* Par Lost 3.515
1667 'is'
That both in him and all things, as is meet, Par Lost 3.675
That place is Earth the seat of Man, that light Par Lost 3.724
That spot to which I point is *Paradise*, Par Lost 3.733
As to superior Spirits is wont in Heaven, Par Lost 3.737
Of what he was, what is, and what must be Par Lost 4.25
Which way I flie is Hell; my self am Hell; Par Lost 4.75
O then at last relent: is there no place Par Lost 4.79
Farwel Remorse: all Good to me is lost; Par Lost 4.109
More woe, the more your taste is now of joy; Par Lost 4.369
As now is enterd; yet no purpos'd foe Par Lost 4.373
So neer grows Death to Life, what ere Death is, Par Lost 4.425
And Head, what thou hast said is just and right. Par Lost 4.443
What there thou seest fair Creature is thy self, Par Lost 4.468
How beauty is excelld by manly grace Par Lost 4.490
And wisdom, which alone is truly fair. Par Lost 4.491
From thir own mouths; all is not theirs it seems: Par Lost 4.513
By Ignorance, is that thir happie state, Par Lost 4.519
God is thy Law, thou mine: to know no more Par Lost 4.637
Is womans happiest knowledge and her praise. Par Lost 4.638
Sweet is the breath of morn, her rising sweet, Par Lost 4.641
Or glittering Starr-light without thee is sweet. Par Lost 4.656
Whose bed is undefil'd and chaste pronounc't, Par Lost 4.761
To him who sent us, whose charge is to keep Par Lost 4.842
And felt how awful goodness is, and saw Par Lost 4.847
The rest is true, they found me where they say; Par Lost 4.900
Came not all Hell broke loose? is pain to them Par Lost 4.918
Fame is not silent, here in hope to find Par Lost 4.938
Why sleepst thou *Eve?* now is the pleasant time, Par Lost 5.38
Nor God, nor Man; is Knowledge so despis'd? Par Lost 5.60
Late falln himself from Heav'n, is plotting now Par Lost 5.240
Thir glittering Tents he passd, and now is come Par Lost 5.291
O *Adam*, one Almightie is, from whom Par Lost 5.469
Reason receives, and reason is her being, Par Lost 5.487
Is oftest yours, the latter most is ours, Par Lost 5.489
That is, to thy obedience; therein stand. Par Lost 5.522
Single, is yet so just, my constant thoughts Par Lost 5.552
This is dispenc't, and what surmounts the reach Par Lost 5.571
Each to other like, more then on earth is thought? Par Lost 5.576
Is heard no more in Heav'n; he of the first, Par Lost 5.659
To utter is not safe. Assemble thou Par Lost 5.683
Is rising, who intends to erect his Throne Par Lost 5.725
In battel, what our Power is, or our right. Par Lost 5.728
With speed what force is left, and all imploy Par Lost 5.730
All thy Dominion, *Adam*, is no more Par Lost 5.751
Then what this Garden is to all the Earth, Par Lost 5.752
How provident he is, how farr from thought Par Lost 5.828
Our puissance is our own, our own right hand Par Lost 5.864
Who is our equal: then thou shalt behold Par Lost 5.866
Is now an Iron Rod to bruise and breake Par Lost 5.887
Unbarr'd the gates of Light. There is a Cave Par Lost 6.4
Unsound and false; nor is it aught but just, Par Lost 6.121
Most reason is that Reason overcome. Par Lost 6.126
When he who rules is worthiest, and excells Par Lost 6.177
Them whom he governs. This is servitude, Par Lost 6.178
Omniscient thought. True is, less firmly arm'd, Par Lost 6.430
But live content, which is the calmest life: Par Lost 6.461
But pain is perfet miserie, the worst Par Lost 6.462
Son in whose face invisible is beheld Par Lost 6.681
Two dayes are therefore past, the third is thine; Par Lost 6.699
As is most just; this I my Glorie account, Par Lost 6.726
Fulfill'd, which to fulfil is all my bliss. Par Lost 6.729
Whom to obey is happiness entire. Par Lost 6.741
Vengeance is his, or whose he sole appoints; Par Lost 6.808
Number to this dayes work is not ordain'd Par Lost 6.809
Yet envied; against mee is all thir rage, Par Lost 6.813
By what is past, to thee I have reveal'd Par Lost 6.895
Who now is plotting how he may seduce Par Lost 6.901
Anough is left besides to search and know. Par Lost 7.125
But Knowledge is as food, and needs no less Par Lost 7.126
And put not forth my goodness, which is free Par Lost 7.171
Approach not mee, and what I will is Fate. Par Lost 7.173
Whose Seed is in her self upon the Earth. Par Lost 7.312
Eternal Father (For where is not hee Par Lost 7.517
Is yet distinct by name, thence, as thou know'st Par Lost 7.536
Death is the penaltie impos'd, beware, Par Lost 7.545
A broad and ample rode, whose dust is Gold Par Lost 7.577
Is greater then created to destroy. Par Lost 7.607
With wonder, but delight, and, as is due, Par Lost 8.11
Is as the Book of God before thee set, Par Lost 8.67
Light back to them, is obvious to dispute. Par Lost 8.158
And thy faire *Eve;* Heav'n is for thee too high Par Lost 8.172
But apt the Mind or Fancie is to roave Par Lost 8.188
Uncheckt, and of her roaving is no end; Par Lost 8.189
Is the prime Wisdom, what is more, is fume, Par Lost 8.194
And Day is yet not spent; till then thou seest Par Lost 8.206
And sweeter thy discourse is to my eare Par Lost 8.211
Is hard; for who himself beginning knew? Par Lost 8.251
What call'st thou solitude, is not the Earth Par Lost 8.369
Find pastime, and beare rule; thy Realm is large. Par Lost 8.375

Is(*cont*)

Is no deficience found; not so is Man,	Par Lost 8.416
But Man by number is to manifest	Par Lost 8.422
Before me; Woman is her Name, of Man	Par Lost 8.496
Is propagated seem such dear delight	Par Lost 8.580
In Reason, and is judicious, is the scale	Par Lost 8.591
Leads up to Heav'n, is both the way and guide;	Par Lost 8.613
Him whom to love is to obey, and keep	Par Lost 8.634
The weal or woe in thee is plac't; beware.	Par Lost 8.638
Of *Hesperus*, whose Office is to bring	Par Lost 9.49
Is Center, yet extends to all, so thou	Par Lost 9.108
From dust: spite then with spite is best repaid.	Par Lost 9.178
For solitude somtimes is best societie,	Par Lost 9.249
His fraud is then thy fear, which plain inferrs	Par Lost 9.285
And what is Faith, Love, Vertue unassaid	Par Lost 9.335
Fraile is our happiness, if this be so,	Par Lost 9.340
Reason, is free, and Reason he made right,	Par Lost 9.352
Save what is in destroying, other joy	Par Lost 9.478
To me is lost. Then let me not let pass	Par Lost 9.479
Half what in thee is fair, one man except,	Par Lost 9.545
Who sees thee? (and what is one2) who shouldst be seen	Par Lost 9.546
Easie to mee it is to tell thee all	Par Lost 9.569
Empress, the way is readie, and not long,	Par Lost 9.626
Law to our selves, our Reason is our Law.	Par Lost 9.654
Is open? or will God incense his ire	Par Lost 9.692
Of good, how just? of evil, if what is evil	Par Lost 9.698
Internal Man, is but proportion meet,	Par Lost 9.711
Or is it envie, and can envie dwell	Par Lost 9.729
For good unknown, sure is not had, or had	Par Lost 9.756
And yet unknown, is as not had at all.	Par Lost 9.757
Of this fair Fruit, our doom is, we shall die.	Par Lost 9.763
And I perhaps am secret; Heav'n is high,	Par Lost 9.811
Superior; for inferior who is free?	Par Lost 9.825
This Tree is not as we are told, a Tree	Par Lost 9.863
Hath eat'n of the fruit, and is become,	Par Lost 9.869
For bliss, as thou hast part, to me is bliss,	Par Lost 9.879
Certain my resolution is to Die;	Par Lost 9.907
Is not so hainous now, foretasted Fruit,	Par Lost 9.929
Consort with thee, Death is to mee as Life;	Par Lost 9.954
My own in thee, for what thou art is mine;	Par Lost 9.957
As meet is, after such delicious Fare;	Par Lost 9.1028
Is this the Love, is this the recompence	Par Lost 9.1163
That errour now, which is become my crime,	Par Lost 9.1181
In eevn scale. But fall'n he is, and now	Par Lost 10.47
Father Eternal, thine is to decree,	Par Lost 10.68
Those two; the third best absent is condemn'd,	Par Lost 10.82
But still rejoyc't, how is it now become	Par Lost 10.120
Say Woman, what is this which thou hast done?	Par Lost 10.158
Curs'd is the ground for thy sake, thou in sorrow	Par Lost 10.201
Thine now is all this World, thy vertue hath won	Par Lost 10.372
By Sin and Death a broad way now is pav'd	Par Lost 10.473
True is, mee also he hath judg'd, or rather	Par Lost 10.494
Is enmity, which he will put between	Par Lost 10.497
His Seed, when is not set, shall bruise my head:	Par Lost 10.499
Alike is Hell, or Paradise, or Heaven,	Par Lost 10.598
O miserable of happie! is this the end	Par Lost 10.720
Is propagated curse. O voice once heard	Par Lost 10.729
Thy punishment then justly is at his Will.	Par Lost 10.768
Be it so, for I submit, his doom is fair,	Par Lost 10.769
Is his wrauth also? be it, man is not so,	Par Lost 10.795
Impossible is held, as Argument	Par Lost 10.800
By Death at last, and miserable it is	Par Lost 10.981
O Sons, like one of us Man is become	Par Lost 11.84
Is past, and we shall live. Whence Haile to thee,	Par Lost 11.158
Man is to live, and all things live for Man.	Par Lost 11.161
Thus over-fond, on that which is not thine;	Par Lost 11.289
Thy going is not lonely, with thee goes	Par Lost 11.290
God is as here, and will be found alike	Par Lost 11.350
Is Pietie thus and pure Devotion paid?	Par Lost 11.452
But have I now seen Death? Is this the way	Par Lost 11.462
Better end here unborn. Why is life giv'n	Par Lost 11.502
Therefore so abject is thir punishment,	Par Lost 11.520
But is there yet no other way, besides	Par Lost 11.527
There is, said *Michael*, if thou well observe	Par Lost 11.530
This is old age; but then thou must outlive	Par Lost 11.538
To whom thus *Michael*. Judg not what is best	Par Lost 11.603
Grievous to bear: but that care now is past,	Par Lost 11.776
Man is not whom to warne: those few escap't	Par Lost 11.777
Henceforth what is to com I will relate,	Par Lost 12.11
With some regard to what is just and right	Par Lost 12.16
Is lost, which alwayes with right Reason dwells	Par Lost 12.84
From vertue, which is reason, that no wrong,	Par Lost 12.98
Is meant thy great deliverer, who shall bruise	Par Lost 12.149
To noble and ignoble is more sweet	Par Lost 12.221
To mortal eare is dreadful; they beseech	Par Lost 12.236
Instructed that to God is no access	Par Lost 12.239
By his prescript a Sanctuary is fram'd	Par Lost 12.249
A Virgin is his Mother, but his Sire	Par Lost 12.368
Thy enemie; nor so is overcome	Par Lost 12.390
The Law that is against thee, and the sins	Par Lost 12.416
Till time stand fixt: beyond is all abyss,	Par Lost 12.555
Henceforth I learne, that to obey is best,	Par Lost 12.561
Is fortitude to highest victorie,	Par Lost 12.570
For God is also in sleep, and Dreams advise,	Par Lost 12.611
In mee is no delay; with thee to goe,	Par Lost 12.615
Is to stay here; without thee here to stay,	Par Lost 12.616
Is to go hence unwilling; thou to mee	Par Lost 12.617
I carry hence; though all by mee is lost,	Par Lost 12.621

Is(*cont*)

Delay, for longest time to him is short;	Par Reg 1.56
Destin'd to this, is late of woman born,	Par Reg 1.65
His coming, is sent Harbinger, who all	Par Reg 1.71
The testimony of Heaven, that who he is	Par Reg 1.78
This is my Son belov'd, in him am pleas'd.	Par Reg 1.85
His Mother then is mortal, but his Sire,	Par Reg 1.86
Who this is we must learn, for man he seems	Par Reg 1.91
Thy Father is the Eternal King, who rules	Par Reg 1.236
Or harbour'd in one Cave, is not reveal'd;	Par Reg 1.307
To Town or Village nigh (nighest is far)	Par Reg 1.332
Think'st thou such force in Bread? is it not written	Par Reg 1.347
For lying is thy sustenance, thy food.	Par Reg 1.429
Idolatrous, but when his purpose is	Par Reg 1.444
Thy Father, who is holy, wise and pure,	Par Reg 1.486
Now, now, for sure, deliverance is at hand,	Par Reg 2.35
Thus we rejoyc'd, but soon our joy is turn'd	Par Reg 2.37
For whither is he gone, what accident	Par Reg 2.39
Send thy Messiah forth, the time is come;	Par Reg 2.43
A sword shall pierce, this is my favour'd lot,	Par Reg 2.91
Is ris'n to invade us, who no less	Par Reg 2.127
But he whom we attempt is wiser far	Par Reg 2.205
Is to be found, in the wide Wilderness;	Par Reg 2.232
Though needing, what praise is it to endure?	Par Reg 2.251
And dream'd, as appetite is wont to dream,	Par Reg 2.264
What I can do or offer is suspect;	Par Reg 2.399
And all thy heart is set on high designs,	Par Reg 2.410
Riches are mine, Fortune is in my hand;	Par Reg 2.429
Yet Wealth without these three is impotent,	Par Reg 2.433
To me is not unknown what hath been done	Par Reg 2.444
Golden in shew, is but a wreath of thorns,	Par Reg 2.459
Passions, Desires, and Fears, is more a King;	Par Reg 2.467
Is yet more Kingly, this attracts the Soul,	Par Reg 2.476
I see thou know'st what is of use to know,	Par Reg 3.7
For what is glory but the blaze of fame,	Par Reg 3.47
Are few, and glory scarce of few is rais'd.	Par Reg 3.59
This is true glory and renown, when God	Par Reg 3.60
Where glory is false glory, attributed	Par Reg 3.69
One is the Son of *Jove*, of *Mars* the other,	Par Reg 3.84
Then glory and benediction, that is thanks,	Par Reg 3.127
Yet so much bounty is in God, such grace,	Par Reg 3.142
Obeys *Tiberius;* nor is always rul'd	Par Reg 3.159
And time there is for all things, Truth hath said:	Par Reg 3.183
Know'st thou not that my rising is thy fall,	Par Reg 3.201
Let that come when it comes; all hope is lost	Par Reg 3.204
For where no hope is left, is left no fear;	Par Reg 3.206
I would be at the worst; worst is my Port,	Par Reg 3.209
Why move thy feet so slow to what is best,	Par Reg 3.224
Were better farthest off) is not yet come;	Par Reg 3.397
About the wine-press where sweet moust is powr'd,	Par Reg 4.16
This Emperour hath no Son, and now is old,	Par Reg 4.90
Is given, and by that right I give it thee.	Par Reg 4.104
Is not for thee to know, nor me to tell.	Par Reg 4.153
Thou hast permission on me. It is written	Par Reg 4.175
By thee how fairly is the Giver now	Par Reg 4.187
Repaid? But gratitude in thee is lost	Par Reg 4.188
Who then thou art, whose coming is foretold	Par Reg 4.204
All knowledge is not couch't in *Moses* Law,	Par Reg 4.225
Error by his own arms is best evinc't.	Par Reg 4.235
For all his tedious talk is but vain boast,	Par Reg 4.307
Where God is prais'd aright, and Godlike men,	Par Reg 4.348
Unless where moral vertue is express't	Par Reg 4.351
In them is plainest taught, and easiest learnt,	Par Reg 4.361
For thee is fittest place, I found thee there,	Par Reg 4.373
For both the when and how is no where told,	Par Reg 4.472
The time and means: each act is rightliest done,	Par Reg 4.475
For Son of God to me is yet in doubt,	Par Reg 4.501
And what he is; his wisdom, power, intent,	Par Reg 4.528
Have brought thee, and highest plac't, highest is best,	Par Reg 4.553
For it is written, He will give command	Par Reg 4.556
To whom thus Jesus: also it is written,	Par Reg 4.560
A fairer Paradise is founded now	Par Reg 4.613
But what is strength without a double share	Samson 53
Suffices that to me strength is my bane,	Samson 63
Light the prime work of God to me is extinct,	Samson 70
The Sun to me is dark	Samson 86
Since light so necessary is to life,	Samson 90
That light is in the Soul,	Samson 92
Chor. This, this is he; softly a while,	Samson 115
Man. O miserable change! is this the man,	Samson 340
These rags, this grinding, is not yet so base	Samson 415
Besides whom is no God, compar'd with Idols,	Samson 441
Which is my chief affliction, shame and sorrow,	Samson 457
With me hath end; all the contest is now	Samson 461
God of our Fathers, what is man!	Samson 667
But who is this, what thing of Sea or Land?	Samson 710
Thy mind with what amends is in my power,	Samson 745
For importunity, that is for naught,	Samson 779
Confess it feign'd, weakness is thy excuse,	Samson 829
All wickedness is weakness: that plea therefore	Samson 834
For which our countrey is a name so dear;	Samson 894
No more on me have power, their force is null'd,	Samson 935
Fame if not double-fac't is double-mouth'd,	Samson 971
Chor. She's gone, a manifest Serpent by her sting	Samson 997
Cho. It is not vertue, wisdom, valour, wit,	Samson 1010
But what it is, hard is to say,	Samson 1013
Is it for that such outward ornament	Samson 1025
Or value what is best	Samson 1029

Is(*cont*)
Happy that house! his way to peace is smooth: Samson 1049
Most shines and most is acceptable above. Samson 1052
Haughty as is his pile high-built and proud. Samson 1069
My trust is in the living God who gave me Samson 1140
Soon feel, whose God is strongest, thine or mine. Samson 1155
Whose ear is ever open; and his eye Samson 1172
By combat to decide whose god is God, Samson 1176
Har. Is not thy Nation subject to our Lords? Samson 1182
Is well ejected when the Conquer'd can. Samson 1207
My heels are fetter'd, but my fist is free. Samson 1235
Chor. His Giantship is gone somewhat crest-fall'n, Samson 1244
Is hate, not help to me, it may with mine Samson 1266
Chor. Oh how comely it is and how reviving Samson 1268
But patience is more oft the exercise Samson 1287
Either of these is in thy lot, Samson 1292
And yet perhaps more trouble is behind. Samson 1300
This day to *Dagon* is a solemn Feast, Samson 1311
Brooks no delay: is this thy resolution? Samson 1344
Chor. Thy Son is rather slaying them, that outcry Samson 1517
This evil on the *Philistines* is fall'n, Samson 1523
Nothing is hard) by miracle restor'd, Samson 1528
Man. Suspense in news is torture, speak them out. Samson 1569
Mess. Then take the worst in brief, *Samson* is dead. Samson 1570
Man. The worst indeed, O all my hope's defeated Samson 1571
How dy'd he? death to life is crown or shame. Samson 1579
And which is best and happiest yet, all this Samson 1718
Nothing is here for tears, nothing to wail Samson 1721
(*Gaza* is not in plight to say us nay) Samson 1729
Chor. All is best, though we oft doubt, Samson 1745
My mansion is, where those immortal shapes Mask 2
To such my errand is, and but for such, Mask 15
Th' express resemblance of the gods, is chang'd Mask 69
And they, so perfect is their misery, Mask 73
1637 'in'
Rigor now is gon to bed, Mask 107
Which must not be, for that's against my course; Mask 159
Trinity ms 'thats'
Bridgewater ms 'thats'
Is now the labour of my thoughts, 'tis likeliest Mask 192
This is the place, as well as I may guess, Mask 201
line not in Bridgewater ms
La. Nay gentle Shepherd ill is lost that praise Mask 271
That is addrest to unattending Ears, Mask 272
La. How easie my misfortune is to hit! Mask 286
Which oft is sooner found in lowly sheds Mask 323
And yet is most pretended: In a place Mask 326
Perhaps som cold bank is her boulster now Mask 353
How bitter is such self-delusion? Mask 365
line not in Trinity ms
line not in Bridgewater ms
(Not being in danger, as I trust she is not) Mask 370
Himself is his own dungeon. 2. *Bro*. Tis most true Mask 385
Trinity ms 'himselfe is his owne dungeon' ←'blaze in the summer solstice'
Bridgewater ms 'blaze in the summer solstice'
And tell me it is safe, as bid me hope Mask 400
Does arbitrate th' event, my nature is Mask 411
My sister is not so defenceless left Mask 414
She that has that, is clad in compleat steel, Mask 421
So dear to Heav'n is Saintly chastity, Mask 453
That when a soul is found sincerely so, Mask 454
2. *Bro*. How charming is divine Philosophy! Mask 476
But musical as is *Apollo*'s lute, Mask 478
Defence is a good cause, and Heav'n be for us. Mask 489
Spir. What voice is that, my young Lord? speak agen. Mask 492
That doth enrich these Downs, is worth a thought Mask 505
But O my Virgin Lady, where is she? Mask 507
How chance she is not in your company? Mask 508
For such there be, but unbelief is blind. Mask 519
Alone, and helpless! Is this the confidence Mask 583
Trinity ms 'is'
The pillar'd firmament is rott'nness, Mask 598
And yet more med'cinal is it then that *Moly* Mask 636
line not in Bridgewater ms
Is of such power to stir up joy as this, Mask 677
And that which is not good, is not delicious Mask 704
Beauty is natures coyn, must not be hoorded, Mask 739
line not in Bridgewater ms
Beauty is natures brag, and must be shown Mask 745
line not in Bridgewater ms
It is for homely features to keep home, Mask 748
line not in Bridgewater ms
This is meer moral babble, and direct Mask 807
Som other means I have which may be us'd, Mask 821
Trinity ms 'some other meanes I have' ←'there is another way'
There is a gentle Nymph not farr from hence, Mask 824
Sabrina is her name, a Virgin pure, Mask 826
Is your Fathers residence, Mask 947
But now my task is smoothly don, Mask 1012
Trinity ms 'smoothly' ←'well is don'
Love vertue, she alone is free, Mask 1019
this dusky hollow is a paradise & heaven gates ore my head Mask Tr. ms 13.44
she might be free from perill where she is Mask Tr. ms 16.42
she might be free from perill where she is, Mask Br. ms 395
Whose Saintly visage is too bright Penseroso 13
Where more is meant then meets the ear. Penseroso 120

Is(*cont*)
Is that which we from hence descry Arcades 3
This this is she Arcades 5
This this is she alone, Arcades 17
On which the fate of gods and men is wound. Arcades 67
For *Lycidas* is dead, dead ere his prime Lycidas 8
Fame is the spur that the clear spirit doth raise Lycidas 70
Fame is no plant that grows on mortal soil, Lycidas 78
Return *Alpheus*, the dread voice is past, Lycidas 132
For *Lycidas* your sorrow is not dead, Lycidas 166
This is the Month, and this the happy morn Nativity 1
Full and perfect is, Nativity 166
The parting Genius is with sighing sent, Nativity 186
Nor is *Osiris* seen Nativity 213
Time is our tedious Song should here have ending, Nativity 239
Praise the Lord, for he is kind, Psalm 136, 2
For of gods he is the God; Psalm 136, 6
Small loss it is that thence can come unto thee, Vacation 9
Yet there is something that doth force my fear, Vacation 67
But headlong joy is ever on the wing, Passion 5
To this Horizon is my *Phoebus* bound, Passion 23
And I (for grief is easily beguild) Passion 54
Whose speed is but the heavy Plummets pace; On Time 3
Which is no more then what is false and vain, On Time 5
So little is our loss, On Time 7
So little is thy gain. On Time 8
When every thing that is sincerely good On Time 14
Hobson has supt, and's newly gon to bed. Carrier 18
1658 'and newly'
All is, if I have grace to use it so, Sonnet 7, 13
Thy care is fixt and zealously attends Sonnet 9, 9
Numbring good intellects; now seldom por'd on. Sonnet 11, 4
Trinity ms 'now' ←'but now is'
A title page is this! and some in file Sonnet 11, 6
End Green. Why is it harder Sirs then Gordon, Sonnet 11, 8
But this is got by casting Pearl to Hoggs; Sonnet 12, 8
Of hireling wolves whose Gospell is their maw. Sonnet 16, 14
When I consider how my light is spent, Sonnet 19, 1
And that one Talent which is death to hide, Sonnet 19, 3
Is Kingly. Thousands at his bidding speed Sonnet 19, 12
To interpose them oft, is not unwise. Sonnet 20, 14
New Presbyter is but *Old Priest* writ Large. Forcers 20
Bless'd is the man who hath not walk'd astray Psalm 1, 1
Jehovahs Law is ever his delight, Psalm 1, 5
This day; ask of me, and the grant is made; Psalm 2, 16
No word is firm or sooth Psalm 5, 26
Are troubled, yea my soul is troubled sore Psalm 6, 6
For in death no remembrance is of thee; Psalm 6, 9
Through grief consumes, is waxen old and dark Psalm 6, 14
And the innocence which is Psalm 7, 33
Hearts and reins. On God is cast Psalm 7, 39
God is a just Judge and severe, Psalm 7, 43
And God is every day offended; Psalm 7, 44
And glorious is thy name through all the earth? Psalm 8, 2
O what is man that thou remembrest yet, Psalm 8, 12
And glorious is thy name through all the earth. Psalm 8, 24
But now it is consum'd with fire, Psalm 80, 65
Blow, *as is wont*, in the new Moon Psalm 81, 9
To Sisera, and as *is told* Psalm 83, 35
Jehova is alone, Psalm 83, 66
Is better, *and more blest* Psalm 84, 34
That man is *truly* blest, Psalm 84, 46
Salvation is at hand Psalm 85, 38
Whatever thing is good Psalm 85, 50
Like thee among the gods is none Psalm 86, 25
For great thy mercy is toward me, Psalm 86, 45
Is his foundation fast, Psalm 87, 2
His Temple there is plac't. Psalm 87, 4
This is true Liberty when free born men Prose 9, 1

Isaac
From *Abraham*, Son of *Isaac*, and from him Par Lost 12.268

Ishmael
Of *scornful* Ishmael, Psalm 83, 22

Isis
Osiris, *Isis*, *Orus* and thir Train Par Lost 1.478
ms 'Isis'
Isis and *Orus*, and the Dog *Anubis* hast. Nativity 212

Island
Deeming some Island, oft, as Sea-men tell, Par Lost 1.205
ms 'Iland'
And there take root an Iland salt and bare, Par Lost 11.834
To *Capreae* an Island small but strong Par Reg 4.92
On *Circes* Iland fell (who knows not *Circe* Mask 50
Bridgewater ms 'Island'
Trinity ms 'Island'

Isle
On *Lemnos* th' *Aegaean* Ile: thus they relate, Par Lost 1.746
ms 'ile'
The happy Ile; what strength, what art can then Par Lost 2.410
Of *Eden* strive; nor that *Nyseian* Ile Par Lost 4.275
Bedropt with blood of *Gorgon*, or the Isle Par Lost 10.527
Meroe Nilotic Isle, and more to West, Par Reg 4.71
And utmost *Indian* Isle *Taprobane*, Par Reg 4.75
And weild their little tridents, but this Ile Mask 27
Trinity ms 'Isle'
Bridgewater ms 'Isle'
& sacred limits of this blisfull Isle Mask Tr. ms 10.11

Isles
And ore the *Celtic* roam'd the utmost Isles. Par Lost 1.521
ms 'Iles'
Close sailing from *Bengala*, or the Iles Par Lost 2.638
Or other Worlds they seemd, or happy Iles, Par Lost 3.567
Thrice happy Iles, but who dwelt happy there Par Lost 3.570
To th' Ocean Iles, and in th' ascending Scale Par Lost 4.354
Beyond the Earths green Cape and verdant Isles Par Lost 8.631
Among the Trees on Iles and woodie Shores. Par Lost 9.1118
Of *Tarsus*, bound for th' Isles Samson 715
Imperial rule of all the Sea-girt Iles Mask 21
Trinity ms 'Isles'
Bridgewater ms 'Isles'
Of dire *Chimera*'s and inchanted Iles, Mask 517
Bridgewater ms 'Isles'
Trinity ms 'Isles'

Ismenian
Cast her self headlong from th' *Ismenian* steep, Par Reg 4.575

Ispahan
In *Hispahan*, or where the *Russian Ksar* Par Lost 11.394

Israel
Israel in *Sittim* on thir march from *Nile* Par Lost 1.413
ms 'Israel'
For those the Race of *Israel* oft forsook Par Lost 1.432
ms 'Israel'
Rather then human. Nor did *Israel* scape Par Lost 1.482
ms 'Israel'
Till *Israel* overcome; so call the third Par Lost 12.267
To rescue *Israel* from the *Roman* yoke, Par Reg 1.217
By which they knew thee King of *Israel* born. Par Reg 1.254
The Kingdom shall to *Israel* be restor'd: Par Reg 2.36
Our expectation? God of *Israel*, Par Reg 2.42
Of many in *Israel*, and to a sign Par Reg 2.89
Of *Israel* here had famish'd, had not God Par Reg 2.311
That seat, and reign in *Israel* without end. Par Reg 2.442
Israel in long captivity still mourns; Par Reg 3.279
Thus long from *Israel;* serving as of old Par Reg 3.378
To just extent over all *Israel*'s Sons; Par Reg 3.406
For *Israel*, or for *David*, or his Throne, Par Reg 3.408
Of numbring *Israel*, which cost the lives Par Reg 3.410
To *Israel* then, the same that now to me. Par Reg 3.413
So spake *Israel*'s true King, and to the Fiend Par Reg 3.441
E're thou of *Israel*'s Scepter get fast hold; Par Reg 4.480
Should *Israel* from *Philistian* yoke deliver; Samson 39
The glory late of *Israel*, now the grief; Samson 179
I might begin *Israel*'s Deliverance, Samson 225
Israel's oppressours: of what now I suffer Samson 233
Yet *Israel* still serves with all his Sons. Samson 240
On *Israel*'s Governours, and Heads of Tribes, Samson 242
Defended *Israel* from the *Ammonite*, Samson 285
The dread of *Israel*'s foes, who with a strength Samson 342
To *Israel*, diffidence of God, and doubt Samson 454
Which I to be the power of *Israel*'s God Samson 1150
Thine or whom I with *Israel*'s Sons adore. Samson 1177
Of *Israel* be thy guide Samson 1428
What if his eye-sight (for to *Israels* God Samson 1527
To *Israel*, and now ly'st victorious Samson 1663
Through all *Philistian* bounds. To *Israel* Samson 1714
Jehovah's wonders were in *Israel* shown, Psalm 114, 5
His praise and glory was in *Israel* known. Psalm 114, 6
He brought from thence his *Israel*. Psalm 136, 42
And to his servant *Israel*, Psalm 136, 73
Thou Shepherd that dost Israel *keep* Psalm 80, 1
For Israel *to observe* Psalm 81, 14
Thou antient stock of Israel, Psalm 81, 35
And Israel *whom I lov'd so dear* Psalm 81, 47
And O that Israel would *advise* Psalm 81, 55
That Israels name for ever may Psalm 83, 15

Israelites
Of threescore and ten thousand *Israelites* Par Reg 3.411
Man. Sad, but thou knowst to *Israelites* not saddest Samson 1560

Issue
Th' *Ionian* Gods, of *Javans* Issue held Par Lost 1.508
ms 'issue'
Nor where *Abassin* Kings thir issue Guard, Par Lost 4.280
They issue forth, Steel Bows, and Shafts their arms Par Reg 3.305

Issued
Forth issu'd, brandishing his fatal Dart Par Lost 2.786
Of waters issu'd from a Cave and spread Par Lost 4.454
To see that none thence issu'd forth a spie, Par Lost 8.233
Wisest of men; from whose mouth issu'd forth Par Reg 4.276

Issues
Light issues forth, and at the other dore Par Lost 6.9

Issuing
Forth issuing at th' accustomd hour stood armd Par Lost 4.779
A stream of Nectarous humor issuing flow'd Par Lost 6.332
Forth issuing on a Summers Morn to breathe Par Lost 9.447
Issuing from mee: on your joynt vigor now Par Lost 10.405
Him follow'd issuing forth to th' open Field, Par Lost 10.533
In Triumph issuing forth thir glorious Chief; Par Lost 10.537
What conflux issuing forth, or entring in, Par Reg 4.62

It
Above th' *Aonian* Mount, while it pursues Par Lost 1.15
And mad'st it pregnant: What in me is dark Par Lost 1.22
Th' infernal Serpent; he it was, whose guile Par Lost 1.34
What can it then avail though yet we feel Par Lost 1.153
Or satiate fury yield it from our Foe. Par Lost 1.179
He lights, if it were Land that ever burn'd Par Lost 1.228

It(*cont*)
For that celestial light? Be it so, since he Par Lost 1.245
Of battel when it rag'd, in all assaults Par Lost 1.277
Can give it, or will ever? how he can Par Lost 2.153
To their defence who hold it: here perhaps Par Lost 2.362
(What could it less when Spirits immortal sing2) Par Lost 2.553
All taste of living wight, as once it fled Par Lost 2.613
If shape it might be call'd that shape had none Par Lost 2.667
For each seem'd either; black it stood as Night, Par Lost 2.670
What it intends; till first I know of thee, Par Lost 2.740
I fled, but he pursu'd (though more, it seems, Par Lost 2.790
Directed, no mean recompence it brings Par Lost 2.981
To Heav'n remov'd where first it grew, there grows, Par Lost 3.356
It seem'd, now seems a boundless Continent Par Lost 3.423
The more it seems excess, that led thee hither Par Lost 3.698
To me alike, it deals eternal woe. Par Lost 4.70
Chose freely what it now so justly rues. Par Lost 4.72
Accept your Makers work; he gave it me, Par Lost 4.380
God hath pronounc't it death to taste that Tree, Par Lost 4.427
Which were it toilsom, yet with thee were sweet. Par Lost 4.439
It started back, but pleas'd I soon returnd, Par Lost 4.463
Pleas'd it returnd as soon with answering looks Par Lost 4.464
With thee it came and goes: but follow me, Par Lost 4.469
From thir own mouths; all is not theirs it seems: Par Lost 4.513
Envie them that? can it be sin to know, Par Lost 4.517
Can it be death? and do they onely stand Par Lost 4.518
Leveld his eevning Rayes: it was a Rock Par Lost 4.543
Still as it rose, impossible to climbe. Par Lost 4.548
On purpose, hard thou knowst it to exclude Par Lost 4.584
On to thir blissful Bower; it was a place Par Lost 4.690
Farr be it, that I should write thee sin or blame, Par Lost 4.758
He held it vain; awe from above had quelld Par Lost 4.860
Imploi'd it seems to violate sleep, and those Par Lost 4.883
So wise he judges it to fly from pain Par Lost 4.910
With gentle voice, I thought it thine; it said, Par Lost 5.37
Of interdicted Knowledge: fair it seem'd, Par Lost 5.52
And as I wondring lookt, beside it stood Par Lost 5.54
Forbidd'n here, it seems, as onely fit Par Lost 5.69
Disperse it, as now light dispels the dark. Par Lost 5.208
Can turn, or holds it possible to turn Par Lost 5.441
He left it in thy power, ordaind thy will Par Lost 5.526
Neerly it now concernes us to be sure Par Lost 5.721
United. But to grant it thee unjust, Par Lost 5.831
In the mid way: though strange to us it seemd Par Lost 6.91
On the rough edge of battel ere it joyn'd, Par Lost 6.108
Unsound and false; nor is it aught but just, Par Lost 6.121
Unjustly thou deprav'st it with the name Par Lost 6.174
It sounded, and the faithful Armies rung Par Lost 6.204
Nor solid might resist that edge: it met Par Lost 6.323
Back to his Chariot; where it stood retir'd Par Lost 6.338
But proves not so: then fallible, it seems, Par Lost 6.428
To be th' inventer miss'd, so easie it seemd Par Lost 6.499
Nor serv'd it to relax thir serried files. Par Lost 6.599
For thee I have ordain'd it, and thus farr Par Lost 6.700
Can end it. Into thee such Vertue and Grace Par Lost 6.703
Her mural breach, returning whence it rowld. Par Lost 6.879
Thy weaker; let it profit thee to have heard Par Lost 6.909
From whom it sprung, impossible to mix Par Lost 7.58
That detriment, if such it be to lose Par Lost 7.153
This I perform, speak thou, and be it don: Par Lost 7.164
Amid the Waters, and let it divide Par Lost 7.262
And saw that it was good, and said, Let th' Earth Par Lost 7.309
Plant of the field, which e're it was in the Earth Par Lost 7.335
God made, and every Herb, before it grew Par Lost 7.336
On the green stemm; God saw that it was good. Par Lost 7.337
To give Light on the Earth; and it was so. Par Lost 7.345
Surveying his great Work, that it was good: Par Lost 7.353
And saw that it was good, and bless'd them, saying, Par Lost 7.395
Subdue it, and throughout Dominion hold Par Lost 7.532
Th' addition of his Empire, how it shew'd Par Lost 7.555
And for the Heav'ns wide Circuit, let it speak Par Lost 8.100
Invalid that which thee to doubt it mov'd; Par Lost 8.116
Not that I so affirm, though so it seem Par Lost 8.117
If it presume, might erre in things too high, Par Lost 8.121
Fond, were it not in hope of thy reply: Par Lost 8.209
This Paradise I give thee, count it thine Par Lost 8.319
Possess it, and all things that therein live, Par Lost 8.340
Knew it not good for Man to be alone, Par Lost 8.445
Which it had long stood under, streind to the highth Par Lost 8.454
Whisper'd it to the Woods, and from thir wings Par Lost 8.516
Answer'd. Let it suffice thee that thou know'st Par Lost 8.620
Free in thine own Arbitrement it lies. Par Lost 8.641
Not Hers who brings it nightly to my Ear. Par Lost 9.47
In with the River sunk, and with it rose Par Lost 9.74
Let it; I reck not, so it light well aim'd, Par Lost 9.173
May tempt it, I expected not to hear. Par Lost 9.281
His fierceness of the fierce intent it brought: Par Lost 9.462
Easie to mee it is to tell thee all Par Lost 9.569
Thereof, nor shall ye touch it, least ye die. Par Lost 9.663
How should ye? by the Fruit? it gives you Life Par Lost 9.686
I question it, for this fair Earth I see, Par Lost 9.720
Or is it envie, and can envie dwell Par Lost 9.729
Commends thee more, while it inferrs the good Par Lost 9.754
For Beasts it seems: yet that one Beast which first Par Lost 9.769
For had the gift bin theirs, it had not here Par Lost 9.806
Thee I have misst, and thought it long, depriv'd Par Lost 9.857
Had it been onely coveting to Eye Par Lost 9.923
Much more to taste it under banne to touch. Par Lost 9.925

It(*cont*)

Were it I thought Death menac't would ensue	Par Lost 9.977
In things to us forbidden, it might be wish'd,	Par Lost 9.1025
Of wandring, as thou call'st it, which who knows	Par Lost 9.1146
It seems, in thy restraint: what could I more?	Par Lost 9.1170
And thou th' accuser. Thus it shall befall	Par Lost 9.1182
Easie it might be seen that I intend	Par Lost 10.58
But still rejoyc't, how is it now become	Par Lost 10.120
Thorns also and Thistles it shall bring thee forth	Par Lost 10.203
For us his ofspring deare? It cannot be	Par Lost 10.238
The miserie, I deserv'd it, and would beare	Par Lost 10.726
Concurd not to my being, it were but right	Par Lost 10.747
Wherefore didst thou beget me? I sought it not	Par Lost 10.762
Be it so, for I submit, his doom is fair,	Par Lost 10.769
Horrid, if true! yet why? it was but breath	Par Lost 10.789
Is his wrauth also? be it, man is not so,	Par Lost 10.795
To waste it all my self, and leave ye none!	Par Lost 10.820
By Death at last, and miserable it is	Par Lost 10.981
It lies, yet ere Conception to prevent	Par Lost 10.987
But if thou judge it hard and difficult,	Par Lost 10.992
Happier, had it suffic'd him to have known	Par Lost 11.88
Blown stifling back on him that breaths it forth:	Par Lost 11.313
Thy mortal passage when it comes. Ascend	Par Lost 11.366
In the Visions of God: It was a Hill	Par Lost 11.377
A Lazar-house it seemd, wherein were laid	Par Lost 11.479
Life offer'd, or soon beg to lay it down,	Par Lost 11.506
I yield it just, said *Adam*, and submit.	Par Lost 11.526
From Mans effeminate slackness it begins,	Par Lost 11.634
How comes it thus? unfould, Celestial Guide,	Par Lost 11.785
Least it again dissolve and showr the Earth?	Par Lost 11.883
See where it flows, disgorging at seaven mouthes	Par Lost 12.158
And wheel on th' Earth, devouring where it rouls;	Par Lost 12.183
What it devours not, Herb, or Fruit, or Graine,	Par Lost 12.184
Then loose it to a stranger, that the true	Par Lost 12.358
A perfect Dove descend, what e're it meant,	Par Reg 1.83
The Law of God I read, and found it sweet,	Par Reg 1.207
Made it my whole delight, and in it grew	Par Reg 1.208
Yet held it more humane, more heavenly first	Par Reg 1.221
Affirming it thy Star new grav'n in Heaven,	Par Reg 1.253
Me him (for it was shew'n him so from Heaven)	Par Reg 1.276
Think'st thou such force in Bread? is it not written	Par Reg 1.347
At first it may be; but long since with wo	Par Reg 1.399
This wounds me most (what can it less) that Man,	Par Reg 1.404
If it may stand him more in stead to lye,	Par Reg 1.473
Afflicted I may be, it seems, and blest;	Par Reg 2.93
Though needing, what praise is it to endure?	Par Reg 2.251
Though hunger still remain: so it remain	Par Reg 2.255
Nor mind it, fed with better thoughts that feed	Par Reg 2.258
It was the hour of night, when thus the Son	Par Reg 2.260
Natures own work it seem'd (Nature taught Art)	Par Reg 2.295
Of Wood-Gods and Wood-Nymphs; he view'd it round,	Par Reg 2.297
In vain, where no acceptance it can find,	Par Reg 2.388
Why shouldst thou not accept it? but I see	Par Reg 2.398
To gain dominion or to keep it gain'd.	Par Reg 2.434
They err who count it glorious to subdue	Par Reg 3.71
It may by means far different be attain'd	Par Reg 3.89
Worth or not worth the seeking, let it pass:	Par Reg 3.151
The happier raign the sooner it begins,	Par Reg 3.179
That it shall never end, so when begin	Par Reg 3.185
But what concerns it thee when I begin	Par Reg 3.198
Let that come when it comes; all hope is lost	Par Reg 3.204
It was a Mountain at whose verdant feet	Par Reg 3.253
Without means us'd, what it predicts revokes.	Par Reg 3.356
Long to enjoy it quiet and secure,	Par Reg 3.360
Maugre the *Roman:* it shall be my task	Par Reg 3.368
But whence to thee this zeal, where was it then	Par Reg 3.407
So fares it when with truth falshood contends.	Par Reg 3.443
Is given, and by that right I give it thee.	Par Reg 4.104
On *David*'s Throne, it shall be like a tree	Par Reg 4.147
Thou hast permission on me. It is written	Par Reg 4.175
To me so fatal, me it most concerns.	Par Reg 4.205
In knowledge, all things in it comprehend,	Par Reg 4.224
What makes a Nation happy, and keeps it so,	Par Reg 4.362
For Angels have proclaim'd it, but concealing	Par Reg 4.474
Not when it must, but when it may be best.	Par Reg 4.476
For it is written, He will give command	Par Reg 4.556
To whom thus Jesus: also it is written,	Par Reg 4.560
Her riddle, and him, who solv'd it not, devour'd;	Par Reg 4.573
But weakly to a woman must reveal it,	Samson 50
How slight the gift was, hung it in my Hair.	Samson 59
And almost life it self, if it be true	Samson 91
Dissolves unjointed e're it reach my ear.	Samson 177
I thought it lawful from my former act,	Samson 231
Whom so it pleases him by choice	Samson 311
Be it but for honours sake of former deeds.	Samson 372
Of vow, and have betray'd it to a woman,	Samson 379
Of Nuptial Love profest, carrying it strait	Samson 385
Endure it, doubtful whether God be Lord,	Samson 477
To what end should I seek it? when in strength	Samson 522
What boots it at one gate to make defence,	Samson 560
Femal of sex it seems,	Samson 711
But that on th' other side if it be weigh'd	Samson 768
First granting, as I do, it was a weakness	Samson 773
Was it not weakness also to make known	Samson 778
Confess it feign'd, weakness is thy excuse,	Samson 829
And I believe it, weakness to resist	Samson 830
Incestuous, Sacrilegious, but may plead it?	Samson 833
But Love constrain'd thee; call it furious rage	Samson 836

It(*cont*)

It was not gold, as to my charge thou lay'st,	Samson 849
And of Religion, press'd how just it was,	Samson 854
It would be to ensnare an irreligious	Samson 860
Bin, as it ought, sincere, it would have taught thee	Samson 874
Thy countrey sought of thee, it sought unjustly,	Samson 889
To please thy gods thou didst it; gods unable	Samson 896
It fits not; thou and I long since are twain;	Samson 929
It hath brought forth to make thee memorable	Samson 956
Nor shall I count it hainous to enjoy	Samson 991
Cho. It is not vertue, wisdom, valour, wit,	Samson 1010
But what it is, hard is to say,	Samson 1013
(Which way soever men refer it)	Samson 1015
Is it for that such outward ornament	Samson 1025
What e're it be, to wisest men and best	Samson 1034
As these perhaps, yet wish it had not been,	Samson 1077
What then thou would'st, thou seest it in thy hand.	Samson 1105
How highly it concerns his glory now	Samson 1148
Thir Magistrates confest it, when they took thee	Samson 1183
It was the force of Conquest; force with force	Samson 1206
And had perform'd it if my known offence	Samson 1218
Yet so it may fall out, because thir end	Samson 1265
Is hate, not help to me, it may with mine	Samson 1266
Chor. Oh how comely it is and how reviving	Samson 1268
Sam. So take it with what speed thy message needs.	Samson 1345
I do it freely; venturing to displease	Samson 1373
I will not wish, lest it perhaps offend them	Samson 1414
What noise or shout was that? it tore the Skie.	Samson 1472
May compass it, shall willingly be paid	Samson 1477
Man. It shall be my delight to tend his eyes,	Samson 1490
Chor. Noise call you it or universal groan	Samson 1511
Oh it continues, they have slain my Son.	Samson 1516
Man. Some dismal accident it needs must be;	Samson 1519
With rueful cry, yet what it was we hear not,	Samson 1553
Mess. It would burst forth, but I recover breath	Samson 1555
The sorrow, and converts it nigh to joy.	Samson 1564
Let us go find the body where it lies	Samson 1725
A Monument, and plant it round with shade	Samson 1734
And give it false presentments, lest the place	Mask 156
My best guide now, me thought it was the sound	Mask 171
Of darknes till it smil'd: I have oft heard	Mask 252
1637 'she'	
Bridgewater ms 'she'	
Trinity ms 'she'	
And lap it in *Elysium*, *Scylla* wept,	Mask 257
And in sweet madnes rob'd it of it self,	Mask 261
I took it for a faery vision	Mask 298
It were a journey like the path to Heav'n,	Mask 303
Co. Due west it rises from this shrubby point.	Mask 306
And Courts of Princes, where it first was nam'd,	Mask 325
I cannot be, that I should fear to change it.	Mask 328
T'would be som solace yet, som little chearing	Mask 348
1673 "Twould'	
And tell me it is safe, as bid me hope	Mask 400
Of night, or lonelines it recks me not,	Mask 404
Which if Heav'n gave it, may be term'd her own:	Mask 419
Be it not don in pride, or in presumption.	Mask 431
That when a soul is found sincerely so,	Mask 454
Trinity ms 'when' ←'when it finds'	
And turns it by degrees to the souls essence,	Mask 462
As loath to leave the body that it lov'd,	Mask 473
2. *Bro*. Me thought so too; what should it be? *Eld*. *Bro*. For certain	Mask 482
To this my errand, and the care it brought.	Mask 506
Too well I did perceive it was the voice	Mask 563
You gave me Brother? *Eld*. *Bro*. Yes, and keep it still,	Mask 584
Lean on it safely, not a period	Mask 585
It shall be in eternal restless change	Mask 596
The leaf was darkish, and had prickles on it,	Mask 631
Treads on it daily with his clouted shoon,	Mask 635
line not in Bridgewater ms	
And yet more med'cinal is it then that *Moly*	Mask 636
line not in Bridgewater ms	
He call'd it *Haemony*, and gave it me,	Mask 638
And bad me keep it as of sovran use	Mask 639
I purs't it up, but little reck'ning made,	Mask 642
But now I find it true; for by this means	Mask 644
This will restore all soon. *La*. 'Twill not false traitor,	Mask 690
1637 'T'will'	
Bridgewater ms 't'will'	
Trinity ms 't'will not' ←'stand back'	
'Twill not restore the truth and honesty	Mask 691
Bridgewater ms 'twill'	
Trinity ms 't'will'	
1637 'T'will'	
Were it a draft for *Juno* when she banquets,	Mask 701
I would not taste thy treasonous offer; none	Mask 702
Trinity ms 'would not taste' ←'should reject' ←'hate it from thy hands'	
It withers on the stalk with languish't head.	Mask 744
line not in Bridgewater ms	
It is for homely features to keep home,	Mask 748
line not in Bridgewater ms	
be it not don in pride or in praesumption	Mask Tr. ms 16.56
thou man of lies & falshood, if thou give me it	Mask Tr. ms 22.21
I throw it on the ground	Mask Tr. ms 22.22
Com, and trip it as ye go	Allegro 33
Whilst the Lantskip round it measures,	Allegro 70
Towers, and Battlements it sees	Allegro 77

It(*cont*)
Alas! What boots it with uncessant care — Lycidas 64
Were it not better don as others use, — Lycidas 67
It was that fatall and perfidious Bark — Lycidas 100
What recks it them? What need they? They are sped; — Lycidas 122
And lay it lowly at his blessed feet; — Nativity 25
It was the Winter wilde, — Nativity 29
It was no season then for her — Nativity 35
He thought it toucht his Deitie full neer, — Fair Inf 10
(If so it be that thou these plaints dost hear) — Fair Inf 37
Small loss it is that thence can come unto thee, — Vacation 9
And, if it happen as I did forecast, — Vacation 13
Thou know'st it must be now thy only bent — Vacation 55
For once it was my dismal hap to hear — Vacation 68
Your Son, said she, (nor can you it prevent) — Vacation 73
To find a Foe it shall not be his hap, — Vacation 83
Yea it shall be his natural property — Vacation 87
'Twas such a shifter, that if truth were known, — Carrier 5
If any ask for him, it shall be sed, — Carrier 17
'Gainst old truth) motion number'd out his time; — Another 8
1640, 1657 ''twas motion'
Nor were it contradiction to affirm — Another 13
line not in 1658 text
That even to his last breath (ther be that say't) — Another 25
line not in 1640, 1657, 1658 texts
Yet be it less or more, or soon or slow, — Sonnet 7, 9
It shall be still in strictest measure eev'n, — Sonnet 7, 10
All is, if I have grace to use it so, — Sonnet 7, 13
The Subject new: it walk'd the Town a while, — Sonnet 11, 3
Trinity ms 'walk'd' ←'It went off well about'
End Green. Why is it harder Sirs then Gordon, — Sonnet 11, 8
1673 printed 'is harder', errata 'is it harder'
Both spirituall powre and civill, what each meanes — Sonnet 17, 10
Trinity ms 'each' ←'it'
And overtake it, let him tread — Psalm 7, 14
Lodge it with dishonour foul. — Psalm 7, 18
He dig'd a pit, and delv'd it deep, — Psalm 7, 55
Thy free love made it thine, — Psalm 80, 34
Thou did'st prepare for it a place — Psalm 80, 37
And root it deep and fast — Psalm 80, 38
That it *began to grow apace*, — Psalm 80, 39
Up turns it by the roots, — Psalm 80, 54
But now it is consum'd with fire, — Psalm 80, 65
With shame, *and scape it never*. — Psalm 83, 64
So shall it never slide — Psalm 86, 40
The Lord shall write it in a Scrowle — Psalm 87, 21
Tis you that say it, not I, you do the deeds, — Prose 8, 1
Sea-girt it lies, where Giants dwelt of old, — Prose 12, 9
Now void, it fitts thy people; thether bend — Prose 12, 10

Italian
O're all th' *Italian* fields where still doth sway — Sonnet 18, 11

Iterate
Eating his fill, nor *Eve* to iterate — Par Lost 9.1005

Ithuriel
Ithuriel and *Zephon*, with wingd speed — Par Lost 4.788
Him thus intent *Ithuriel* with his Spear — Par Lost 4.810
Ithuriel and *Zephon* through the shade, — Par Lost 4.868

Its
The mind is its own place, and in it self — Par Lost 1.254
Of force to its own likeness: up he starts — Par Lost 4.813
And that her raign had here its last fulfilling; — Nativity 106

Itself
The mind is its own place, and in it self — Par Lost 1.254
ms 'it selfe'
Within his Sanctuary it self thir Shrines, — Par Lost 1.388
ms 'it selfe'
Vice for it self: To him no Temple stood — Par Lost 1.492
ms 'it selfe'
In loss it self; which on his count'nance cast — Par Lost 1.526
ms 'it selfe'
Among his Angels; and his Throne it self — Par Lost 2.68
The Ford, and of it self the water flies — Par Lost 2.612
Or turn this Heav'n it self into the Hell — Par Lost 6.291
It self instinct with Spirit, but convoyd — Par Lost 6.752
All but the Throne it self of God. Full soon — Par Lost 6.834
Whose vertue on it self workes no effect, — Par Lost 8.95
Remaines, sufficient of it self to raise — Par Lost 9.43
Bitter ere long back on it self recoiles; — Par Lost 9.172
Th' attempt it self, intended by our Foe. — Par Lost 9.295
Your feare it self of Death removes the feare. — Par Lost 9.702
And what she did, whatever in it self, — Par Lost 10.141
The Realm it self of Satan long usurpt, — Par Lost 10.189
Good by it self, and Evil not at all. — Par Lost 11.89
Upon the Temple it self: at last they seise — Par Lost 12.356
But force the Spirit of Grace it self, and binde — Par Lost 12.525
My crime; whatever for it self condemn'd, — Par Reg 3.213
And almost life it self, if it be true — Samson 91
By it self, with aggravations not surcharg'd, — Samson 769
And in sweet madnes rob'd it of it self, — Mask 261
1637 'it selfe'
Trinity ms 'it selfe'
Bridgewater ms 'it selfe'
And link't it self by carnal sensualty — Mask 474
But evil on it self shall back recoyl, — Mask 593
Bridgewater ms 'it selfe'
1637 'it selfe'
Trinity ms 'it selfe'
Gather'd like scum, and setl'd to it self — Mask 595

Itself(*cont*)
1637 'it selfe'
Bridgewater ms 'it selfe'
Trinity ms 'it selfe'
Unsavoury in th' injoyment of it self — Mask 742
1637 'it selfe'
line not in Bridgewater ms
Trinity ms 'it selfe'
Heav'n it self would stoop to her. — Mask 1023
Trinity ms 'it selfe'
Bridgewater ms 'it selfe'
Cardoyn 'it selfe'
1637 'it selfe'
B.M. ms 'its Selfe'
And Hell it self will pass away, — Nativity 139
Then thou our fancy of it self bereaving, — Shakespear 13
1632 'her selfe'
1640 'our selfe'
1663-4 'her self'

Ivory
And from thir Ivorie Port the Cherubim — Par Lost 4.778
In Cedar, Marble, Ivory or Gold. — Par Reg 4.60

Ivy
The clasping Ivie where to climb, while I — Par Lost 9.217
With Ivy berries wreath'd, and his blithe youth, — Mask 55
Trinity ms 'ivie'
Bridgewater ms 'Ivye'
1637 'Ivie'
With Ivy canopied, and interwove — Mask 544
1637 'ivie'
Bridgewater ms 'Ivie'
Trinity ms 'ivie'
Ye Myrtles brown, with Ivy never-sear, — Lycidas 2
1638 'ivy'
Trinity ms 'Ivie'

Ivy-crowned
To Ivy-crowned *Bacchus* bore; — Allegro 16

Jabin
Thou didst to Jabins *hoast*, — Psalm 83, 36

Jacob
The Stairs were such as whereon *Jacob* saw — Par Lost 3.510
Jacob in *Mahanaim*, where he saw — Par Lost 11.214
Ten Sons of *Jacob*, two of *Joseph* lost — Par Reg 3.377
To Jacobs God, *that all may hear* — Psalm 81, 3
A Law of Jacobs God, *to hold* — Psalm 81, 15
O Jacobs God give ear, — Psalm 84, 30
Returned Jacob back. — Psalm 85, 4
Of Jacobs *Land, though there be store*, — Psalm 87, 7

Jaculation
Hurl'd to and fro with jaculation dire, — Par Lost 6.665

Jael
Jael, who with inhospitable guile — Samson 989

Jail
This Gaol I count the house of Liberty — Samson 949
Troop to th' infernall jail, — Nativity 233
1673 'Jail'

Jangling
To sow a jangling noise of words unknown: — Par Lost 12.55

Janus
Had, like a double *Janus*, all thir shape — Par Lost 11.129

Japhet
Of *Japhet* brought by *Hermes*, she ensnar'd — Par Lost 4.717

Jar
Jarr not with liberty, but well consist. — Par Lost 5.793

Jarred
Jarr'd against natures chime, and with harsh din — Musick 20
Trinity ms 'jarr'd against' ←'drown'd'

Jarring
With impetuous recoile and jarring sound — Par Lost 2.880
Should combat, and thir jarring Sphears confound. — Par Lost 6.315

Jars
by leaving out those harsh ill sounding jarres — Musick Tr. ms 5.03

Jasmine
Iris all hues, Roses, and Gessamin — Par Lost 4.698
The tufted Crow-toe, and pale Gessamine, — Lycidas 143
1638 'gessamine'
Trinity ms 'Gessamie'

Jasper
Pavement that like a Sea of Jasper shon — Par Lost 3.363
Of Jasper, or of liquid Pearle, whereon — Par Lost 3.519
Down from a Skie of Jasper lighted now — Par Lost 11.209

Jaunt
After his aerie jaunt, though hurried sore, — Par Reg 4.402

Javan
Th' *Ionian* Gods, of *Javans* Issue held — Par Lost 1.508
ms 'Javans'
Of *Javan* or *Gadier* — Samson 716

Javelin
With Dart and Jav'lin, Stones and sulfurous Fire; — Par Lost 11.658

Jaw
The Jaw of a dead Ass, his sword of bone, — Samson 143
To have wrought such wonders with an Asses Jaw; — Samson 1095

Jaws
With hatefullest disrelish writh'd thir jaws — Par Lost 10.569
For ever, and seal up his ravenous Jawes. — Par Lost 10.637

Jealous
For envie, yet with jealous leer maligne — Par Lost 4.503
That jealous of thir secrets fiercely oppos'd — Par Lost 10.478

Jealous(*cont*)	
the jealous ocean that old river winds	Mask Tr. ms 10.12
Wher brooding darknes spreads his jealous wings,	Allegro 6
And all her jealous monarchs with amaze,	Sonnet 15, 3
1694 'Jealous'	
Jealousies	
Ambiguous words and jealousies, to sound	Par Lost 5.703
Jealousy	
Love unlibidinous reign'd, nor jealousie	Par Lost 5.449
The jealousie of Love, powerful of sway	Samson 791
Set God behind: which in his jealousie	Samson 1375
Jehovah	
Jehovah thundring out of *Sion*, thron'd	Par Lost 1.386
ms 'Jehovah'	
Jehovah, who in one Night when he pass'd	Par Lost 1.487
ms 'Jehovah'	
Great are thy works, *Jehovah*, infinite	Par Lost 7.602
Jehovah's wonders were in *Israel* shown,	Psalm 114, 5
Jehovahs Law is ever his delight,	Psalm 1, 5
Jehovah serve, and let your joy converse	Psalm 2, 24
Unto Jehovah, he full soon reply'd	Psalm 3, 11
Jehovah from on high	Psalm 4, 17
Of righteousness and in Jehovah trust.	Psalm 4, 24
Jehovah to my words give ear	Psalm 5, 1
Jehovah thou my early voyce	Psalm 5, 5
For thou Jehovah wilt be found	Psalm 5, 37
Rise Jehovah in thine ire	Psalm 7, 19
Jehovah judgeth most upright	Psalm 7, 29
Then will I Jehovah's praise	Psalm 7, 61
Of Jehovah the most high.	Psalm 7, 64
O Jehovah our Lord how wondrous great	Psalm 8, 1
O Jehovah our Lord how wondrous great	Psalm 8, 23
Jehova is alone,	Psalm 83, 66
Jephtha	
Gideon and *Jephtha*, and the Shepherd lad,	Par Reg 2.439
Jephthah	
Had dealt with *Jephtha*, who by argument,	Samson 283
Jericho	
Nigh to *Bethabara; in Jerico*	Par Reg 2.20
Jerusalem	
And once a year *Jerusalem*, few days	Par Reg 3.234
Led captive, and *Jerusalem* laid waste,	Par Reg 3.283
Till underneath them fair *Jerusalem*,	Par Reg 4.544
Jessamine	
The tufted Crow-toe, and pale Gessamine,	Lycidas 143
Trinity ms 'Gessamie'	
1638 'gessamine'	
Jest	
Jest and youthful Jollity,	Allegro 26
Jester	
Although thir drudge, to be thir fool or jester,	Samson 1338
Jesting	
Jesting decides great things	Prose 7, 1
Jesus	
When *Jesus* son of *Mary* second *Eve*,	Par Lost 10.183
But *Joshua* whom the Gentiles *Jesus* call,	Par Lost 12.310
Jesus Messiah Son of God declar'd,	Par Reg 2.4
To whom thus Jesus; what conclud'st thou hence?	Par Reg 2.317
The giver, answer'd Jesus. Why should that	Par Reg 2.322
To whom thus Jesus temperately reply'd:	Par Reg 2.378
To whom thus Jesus patiently reply'd;	Par Reg 2.432
To whom thus Jesus: also it is written,	Par Reg 4.560
Jet	
The white Pink, and the Pansie freakt with jeat,	Lycidas 144
Trinity ms 'jet'	
Jew	
Promiscuous from all Nations, Jew, or Greek,	Par Reg 3.118
Samaritan or *Jew;* how could'st thou hope	Par Reg 3.359
Jigs	
With Jiggs, and rural dance resort,	Mask 952
1637 'Iiggs'	
Job	
Less over-weening, since he fail'd in *Job*,	Par Reg 1.147
Gave up into my hands *Uzzean Job*	Par Reg 1.369
Of righteous *Job*, then cruelly to afflict him	Par Reg 1.425
Recount his praises; thus he did to *Job*,	Par Reg 3.64
He ask'd thee, hast thou seen my servant *Job?*	Par Reg 3.67
Who names not now with honour patient *Job?*	Par Reg 3.95
Jocund	
Intent, with jocond Music charm his ear;	Par Lost 1.787
Invested with bright Rayes, jocond to run	Par Lost 7.372
And hight'nd as with Wine, jocond and boon,	Par Lost 9.793
Semichor. While thir hearts were jocund and sublime,	Samson 1669
Such as the jocond Flute, or gamesom Pipe	Mask 173
Bridgewater ms 'iocond'	
Revels the spruce and jocond Spring,	Mask 985
line not in Bridgewater ms	
And the jocond rebecks sound	Allegro 94
Jocundry	
& favour our close jocondrie	Mask Tr. ms 12.29
'jocondrie' ← 'revelrie'	
Jog	
While he might still jogg on, and keep his trot,	Another 4
1640, 1657 'jog'	
John	
The same whom *John* saw also in the Sun:	Par Lost 3.623
Lodg'd in *Bethabara* where *John* baptiz'd,	Par Reg 1.184
By *John* the Baptist, and in publick shown,	Par Reg 2.84

John(*cont*)	
Thy age, like ours, O Soul of Sir *John Cheek*,	Sonnet 11, 12
Join	
To joyn thir dark Encounter in mid air:	Par Lost 2.718
Thir Nature also to thy Nature joyn;	Par Lost 3.282
1667 'joyne'	
No voice exempt, no voice but well could joine	Par Lost 3.370
On Earth joyn all ye Creatures to extoll	Par Lost 5.164
Joyn voices all ye living Souls, ye Birds,	Par Lost 5.197
And join him nam'd *Almighty* to thy aid,	Par Lost 6.294
May joyne us, equal Joy, as equal Love;	Par Lost 9.882
Of noxious efficacie, and when to joyne	Par Lost 10.660
With cruel Tournament the Squadrons joine;	Par Lost 11.652
Abhor to joyn; and by imprudence mixt,	Par Lost 11.686
Places and titles, and with these to joine	Par Lost 12.516
To waver, or fall off and joyn with Idols;	Samson 456
And joyn with thee calm Peace, and Quiet,	Penseroso 45
And joyn thy voice unto the Angel Quire,	Nativity 27
Joined	
Joynd with me once, now misery hath joynd	Par Lost 1.90
Of *Phlegra* with th' Heroic Race were joyn'd	Par Lost 1.577
Fall circumvented thus by fraud, though joynd	Par Lost 3.152
Hither of ill-joynd Sons and Daughters born	Par Lost 3.463
In full harmonic number joind, thir songs	Par Lost 4.687
Just met, and closing stood in squadron joind	Par Lost 4.863
Tastes, not well joynd, inelegant, but bring	Par Lost 5.335
What meant that caution joind, *if ye be found*	Par Lost 5.513
Or all Angelic Nature joind in one,	Par Lost 5.834
That stood for Heav'n, in mighty Quadrate joyn'd	Par Lost 6.62
On the rough edge of battel ere it joyn'd,	Par Lost 6.108
The adverse Legions, nor less hideous joyn'd	Par Lost 6.206
Abandon fear; to strength and counsel joind	Par Lost 6.494
Hereafter, join'd in her popular Tribes	Par Lost 7.488
Such pairs, in Love and mutual Honour joyn'd?	Par Lost 8.58
And joind thir vocal Worship to the Quire	Par Lost 9.198
1667 'joynd'	
He made us, and delight to Reason joyn'd.	Par Lost 9.243
Hopeless to circumvent us joynd, where each	Par Lost 9.259
Thy sweet Converse and Love so dearly joyn'd,	Par Lost 9.909
Bridging his way, *Europe* with *Asia* joyn'd,	Par Lost 10.310
Still moves with thine, join'd in connexion sweet,	Par Lost 10.359
1667 'joyn'd'	
As joyn'd in injuries, one enmitie	Par Lost 10.925
Then meeting joyn'd thir tribute to the Sea:	Par Reg 3.258
And God with Idols in thir worship joyn'd.	Par Reg 3.426
Within thy self, much more with Empire joyn'd.	Par Reg 4.284
But vertue joyn'd with riches and long life, .	Par Reg 4.298
Fresh from his fall, and fiercer grapple joyn'd,	Par Reg 4.567
Had *Judah* that day join'd, or one whole Tribe,	Samson 265
Once join'd, the contrary she proves, a thorn	Samson 1037
Joyn'd with extream contempt? I will not come.	Samson 1342
How are ye joyn'd with hell in triple knot	Mask 581
Bridgewater ms 'ioyn'd'	
Joining	
Which Reason joyning or disjoyning, frames	Par Lost 5.106
Of length prodigious joyning to the Wall	Par Lost 10.302
Between us two let there be peace, both joyning,	Par Lost 10.924
Joins	
Hee with a crew, whom like Ambition joyns	Par Lost 12.38
Of head or heel: not therefore joynes the Son	Par Lost 12.388
Chor. Where the heart joins not, outward acts defile not.	Samson 1368
Joint	
Not ti'd or manacl'd with joynt or limb,	Par Lost 1.426
ms 'joint'	
Distinguishable in member, joynt, or limb,	Par Lost 2.668
Of membrane, joynt, or limb, exclusive barrs:	Par Lost 8.625
These paths & Bowers doubt not but our joynt hands	Par Lost 9.244
Issuing from mee: on your joynt vigor now	Par Lost 10.405
If your joynt power prevailes, th' affaires of Hell	Par Lost 10.408
But who are these? for with joint pace I hear	Samson 110
My sudden rage to tear thee joint by joint.	Samson 953
Wed your divine sounds, and mixt power employ	Musick 3
Trinity ms 'mixt power' ← 'mix't' ← 'happiest sounds' ← 'joynt force'	
Jointed	
In jointed Armour watch: on smooth the Seale,	Par Lost 7.409
Joint-racking	
Dropsies, and Asthma's, and Joint-racking Rheums.	Par Lost 11.488
Joints	
With supple joints, and lively vigour led:	Par Lost 8.269
Ran through his veins, and all his joynts relax'd;	Par Lost 9.891
As on entrails, joints, and limbs,	Samson 614
No less through all my sinews, joints and bones,	Samson 1142
He with his bare wand can unthred thy joynts,	Mask 614
Bridgewater ms 'ioynts'	
Jollity	
All now was turn'd to jollitie and game,	Par Lost 11.714
Tipsie dance, and Jollity.	Mask 104
Trinity ms 'jollity'	
Bridgewater ms 'Jollitie'	
1637 'Jollitie'	
Jest and youthful Jollity,	Allegro 26
Jolly	
While the jolly hours lead on propitious *May*,	Sonnet 1, 4
Jonson	
If *Jonsons* learned Sock be on,	Allegro 132
Jordan	
From *Paneas* the fount of *Jordans* flood	Par Lost 3.535

Jordan(*cont*)
Jordan, true limit Eastward; but his Sons Par Lost 12.145
To the flood *Jordan*, came as then obscure, Par Reg 1.24
So to the Coast of *Jordan* he directs Par Reg 1.119
Of *Jordan* honour'd so, and call'd thee Son Par Reg 1.329
At *Jordan* with the Baptist, and had seen Par Reg 2.2
Then on the bank of *Jordan*, by a Creek: Par Reg 2.25
Nor left at *Jordan*, tydings of him none; Par Reg 2.62
As the Red Sea and *Jordan* once he cleft, Par Reg 3.438
Till at the Ford of *Jordan* whither all Par Reg 4.510
Low in the earth, *Jordans* clear streams recoil, Psalm 114, 9
Why turned *Jordan* toward his Crystall Fountains? Psalm 114, 14
Joseph
From *Nazareth* the Son of *Joseph* deem'd Par Reg 1.23
Ten Sons of *Jacob*, two of *Joseph* lost Par Reg 3.377
The highly favour'd *Joseph* bore Winchester 65
Thy loved Josephs seed, Psalm 80, 4
In Joseph, *not to change*, Psalm 81, 18
Joshua
But *Joshua* whom the Gentiles *Jesus* call, Par Lost 12.310
Josiah
Till good *Josiah* drove them thence to Hell. Par Lost 1.418
ms 'Josiah'
Jostling
Through *Bosporus* betwixt the justling Rocks: Par Lost 2.1018
Justling or pusht with Winds rude in thir shock Par Lost 10.1074
Jot
Against heavns hand or will, nor bate a jot Sonnet 22, 7
Journey
(Which is my present journey) and once more Par Lost 2.985
His journies end and our beginning woe. Par Lost 3.633
A whole days journy high, but wide remote Par Lost 4.284
1667 'journey'
Hath finisht half his journey, and scarce begins Par Lost 5.559
To journie through the airie gloom began, Par Lost 7.246
As Tribute such a sumless journey brought Par Lost 8.36
My journey strange, with clamorous uproare Par Lost 10.479
As one who in his journey bates at Noone, Par Lost 12.1
line not in 1667 edition
To guide them in thir journey, and remove Par Lost 12.204
Save when they journie, and at length they come, Par Lost 12.258
Several days journey, built by *Ninus* old, Par Reg 3.276
No journey of a Sabbath day, and loaded so; Samson 149
It were a journey like the path to Heav'n, Mask 303
1637 'journy'
Trinity ms 'journy'
Bridgewater ms 'Jorney'
And thinking now his journeys end was come, Carrier 12
1658 'journey's'
They journey on from strength to strength Psalm 84, 25
Journeyed
Satan had journied on, pensive and slow; Par Lost 4.173
when as they journey'd from this dark abode Sonnet 14, Tr. ms 41.07
Journeys
The less not bright, nor Heav'n such journies run, Par Lost 8.88
Joust
At Joust and Torneament; then marshal'd Feast Par Lost 9.37
Jousted
Jousted in *Aspramont* or *Montalban*, Par Lost 1.583
Jove
Titanian, or *Earth-born*, that warr'd on *Jove*, Par Lost 1.198
ms 'Jove'
By younger *Saturn*, he from mightier *Jove* Par Lost 1.512
ms 'Jove'
So *Jove* usurping reign'd: these first in *Creet* Par Lost 1.514
ms 'Jove'
From Heav'n, they fabl'd, thrown by angry *Jove* Par Lost 1.741
ms 'Jove'
Whom Gentiles *Ammon* call and *Lybian Jove*, Par Lost 4.277
On him who had stole *Joves* authentic fire. Par Lost 4.719
Yet Virgin of *Proserpina* from *Jove*. Par Lost 9.396
Ammonian Jove, or *Capitoline* was seen, Par Lost 9.508
And *Ops*, ere yet *Dictaean Jove* was born. Par Lost 10.584
The Bird of *Jove*, stoopt from his aerie tour, Par Lost 11.185
Wrought that effect on *Jove*, so Fables tell; Par Reg 2.215
One is the Son of *Jove*, of *Mars* the other, Par Reg 3.84
With *Joves Alcides*, and oft foil'd still rose, Par Reg 4.565
Before the starry threshold of *Joves* Court Mask 1
1637 '*Ioves*'
Took in by lot 'twixt high, and neather *Jove*, Mask 20
1637 '*Iove*'
But that by quick command from Soveran *Jove* Mask 41
1637 '*Iove*'
Therfore when any favour'd of high *Jove*, Mask 78
1637 '*Iove*'
Dips me all o're, as when the wrath of *Jove* Mask 803
line not in Trinity ms
line not in Bridgewater ms
1637 '*Iove*'
Youth and Joy; so *Jove* hath sworn. Mask 1011
line not in Bridgewater ms
1637 '*Iove*'
While yet there was no fear of *Jove*. Penseroso 30
Ay round about *Joves* Altar sing. Penseroso 48
For know by lot from *Jove* I am the powr Arcades 44
Trinity ms 'Jo', ms defective
That from beneath the seat of *Jove* doth spring, Lycidas 16
And perfet witnes of all-judging *Jove*; Lycidas 82

Jove(*cont*)
Which carefull *Jove* in natures true behoofe Fair Inf 45
Portend success in love; O if *Jove*'s will Sonnet 1, 7
Whom *Joves* great Son to her glad Husband gave, Sonnet 23, 3
Jove-born
In *Egypt* gave to *Jove*-born *Helena* Mask 676
1637 '*Iove*-borne'
Trinity ms 'Jove borne'
Bridgewater ms 'Jove-borne'
Joy
Who now triumphs, and in th' excess of joy Par Lost 1.123
Where Joy for ever dwells: Hail horrours, hail Par Lost 1.250
ms 'joy'
Obscure some glimps of joy, to have found thir chief Par Lost 1.524
At once with joy and fear his heart rebounds. Par Lost 1.788
Common revenge, and interrupt his joy Par Lost 2.371
In our Confusion, and our Joy upraise Par Lost 2.372
Pleas'd highly those infernal States, and joy Par Lost 2.387
Attest thir joy, that hill and valley rings. Par Lost 2.495
Forgets both joy and grief, pleasure and pain. Par Lost 2.586
Becam'st enamour'd, and such joy thou took'st Par Lost 2.765
Reaping immortal fruits of joy and love, Par Lost 3.67
Uninterrupted joy, unrivald love Par Lost 3.68
Sense of new joy ineffable diffus'd: Par Lost 3.137
Thenceforth, but in thy presence Joy entire. Par Lost 3.265
With Joy and Love triumphing, and fair Truth. Par Lost 3.338
As from blest voices, uttering joy, Heav'n rung Par Lost 3.347
Thir happie hours in joy and hymning spent. Par Lost 3.417
In miserie; such joy Ambition findes. Par Lost 4.92
Vernal delight and joy, able to drive Par Lost 4.155
More woe, the more your taste is now of joy; Par Lost 4.369
Where neither joy nor love, but fierce desire, Par Lost 4.509
In whose sight all things joy, with ravishment Par Lost 5.46
Quaff immortalitie and joy, secure Par Lost 5.638
line not in 1667 edition
With copious hand, rejoycing in thir joy. Par Lost 5.641
With joy and acclamations loud, that one Par Lost 6.23
So oft in Festivals of joy and love Par Lost 6.94
Thus foil'd thir mightiest, ours joy filld, and shout, Par Lost 6.200
For joy of offerd peace: but I suppose Par Lost 6.617
First seen, them unexpected joy surpriz'd, Par Lost 6.774
One Kingdom, Joy and Union without end. Par Lost 7.161
Birth-day of Heav'n and Earth; with joy and shout Par Lost 7.256
Wherever plac't, let him dispose: joy thou Par Lost 8.170
With fragrance and with joy my heart oreflow'd. Par Lost 8.266
If I could joy in aught, sweet interchange Par Lost 9.115
Save what is in destroying, other joy Par Lost 9.478
To mischief swift. Hope elevates, and joy Par Lost 9.633
Hath tasted, envies not, but brings with joy Par Lost 9.770
Great joy he promis'd to his thoughts, and new Par Lost 9.843
May joyne us, equal Joy, as equal Love; Par Lost 9.882
So saying, she embrac'd him, and for joy Par Lost 9.990
Henceforth of God or Angel, earst with joy Par Lost 9.1081
Where art thou *Adam*, wont with joy to meet Par Lost 10.103
Not instant, but of future time. With joy Par Lost 10.345
Great joy was at thir meeting, and at sight Par Lost 10.350
Of that stupendious Bridge his joy encreas'd. Par Lost 10.351
Rais'd from thir Dark *Divan*, and with like joy Par Lost 10.457
To dash thir pride, and joy for Man seduc't. Par Lost 10.577
And bringing forth, soon recompenc't with joy, Par Lost 10.1052
All my redeemd may dwell in joy and bliss, Par Lost 11.43
In fellowships of joy: the Sons of Light Par Lost 11.80
Out of despaire, joy, but with fear yet linkt; Par Lost 11.139
True patience, and to temper joy with fear Par Lost 11.361
Of these fair Atheists, and now swim in joy, Par Lost 11.625
To whom thus *Adam* of short joy bereft. Par Lost 11.628
Greatly rejoyc'd, and thus his joy broke forth. Par Lost 11.869
Shal spend thir dayes in joy unblam'd, and dwell Par Lost 12.22
He ceas'd, discerning *Adam* with such joy Par Lost 12.372
Replete with joy and wonder thus repli'd. Par Lost 12.468
With joy the tidings brought from Heav'n: at length Par Lost 12.504
To bring forth fruits Joy and eternal Bliss. Par Lost 12.551
Imparts to thee no happiness, no joy, Par Reg 1.417
Now missing him thir joy so lately found, Par Reg 2.9
Thus we rejoyc'd, but soon our joy is turn'd Par Reg 2.37
Soon we shall see our hope, our joy return. Par Reg 2.57
There without sign of boast, or sign of joy, Par Reg 2.119
While to their native land with joy they hast, Par Reg 3.437
Nor yet amidst this joy and brightest morn Par Reg 4.439
Brought on his way with joy; hee unobserv'd Par Reg 4.638
Of his delivery, and thy joy thereon Samson 1505
Man. That were a joy presumptuous to be thought. Samson 1531
The sorrow, and converts it nigh to joy. Samson 1564
What windy joy this day had I conceiv'd Samson 1574
Mean while welcom Joy, and Feast, Mask 102
Bridgewater ms 'Joye'
Spir. O my lov'd masters heir, and his next joy, Mask 501
Bridgewater ms 'Joye'
Is of such power to stir up joy as this, Mask 677
Bridgewater ms 'Joye'
Youth and Joy; so *Jove* hath sworn. Mask 1011
1637 'Ioy'
line not in Bridgewater ms
In the blest Kingdoms meek of joy and love. Lycidas 177
line not in 1638 edition
But headlong joy is ever on the wing, Passion 5
And Joy shall overtake us as a flood, On Time 13
So sweetly sung your Joy the Clouds along Circum 4

Joy(*cont*)
Trinity ms 'joy'
Blest pair of *Sirens*, pledges of Heav'ns joy, Musick 1
Follow'd thee up to joy and bliss for ever. Sonnet 14, 8
Trinity ms 'joy' ←'Joy' ←'joy'
Up to the Realm of peace & Joy for ever, Sonnet 14, Tr. ms 41.08
Jehovah serve, and let your joy converse Psalm 2, 24
Into my heart more joy Psalm 4, 31
Their joy, while thou from blame Psalm 5, 34
With joy and gladsom cheer Psalm 84, 26
Joyed
Who might have liv'd and joyd immortal bliss, Par Lost 9.1166
Joyfully
Now *joyfully* are met Psalm 85, 42
Joyless
Of Harlots, loveless, joyless, unindeard, Par Lost 4.766
Joyless triumphals of his hop't success, Par Reg 4.578
Joyous
Joyous the Birds; fresh Gales and gentle Aires Par Lost 8.515
Fanning their joyous Leaves to thy soft layes. Lycidas 44
And joyous news of heav'nly Infants birth, Passion 3
Joys
Of dalliance had with thee in Heav'n, and joys Par Lost 2.819
Sole partner and sole part of all these joyes, Par Lost 4.411
Augmented, op'nd Eyes, new Hopes, new Joyes, Par Lost 9.985
Heavie, though in thir place. O fleeting joyes Par Lost 10.741
Hence vain deluding joyes, Penseroso 1
Whispering new joyes to the milde Ocean, Nativity 66
Then *in the joyes of Vanity*, Psalm 84, 35
Jubilant
While the bright Pomp ascended jubilant. Par Lost 7.564
Jubilee
With Jubilee, and loud Hosanna's filld Par Lost 3.348
With Jubilie advanc'd; and as they went, Par Lost 6.884
With Saintly shout, and solemn Jubily, Musick 9
Trinity ms 'jubilie' ←'crie'
Judaea
Judaea now and all the promis'd land Par Reg 3.157
Enterd *Judea* seeking mee, who then Samson 252
Judah
Of alienated *Judah*. Next came one Par Lost 1.457
ms 'Judah'
And his Son *Herod* plac'd on *Juda*'s Throne; Par Reg 2.424
Whose off-spring on the Throne of *Juda* sat Par Reg 2.440
Judah and all thy Father *David*'s house Par Reg 3.282
Mean while the men of *Judah* to prevent Samson 256
Had *Judah* that day join'd, or one whole Tribe, Samson 265
In *Dan*, in *Judah*, and the bordering Tribes, Samson 976
He feels from *Juda*'s Land Nativity 221
Judge
To fickle Chance, and *Chaos* judge the strife: Par Lost 2.233
Both what they judge and what they choose; for so Par Lost 3.123
That farr be from thee, Father, who art Judg Par Lost 3.154
1667 'Judge'
Then all thy Saints assembl'd, thou shalt judge Par Lost 3.330
O loss of one in Heav'n to judge of wise, Par Lost 4.904
So judge thou still, presumptuous, till the wrauth, Par Lost 4.912
To see how thou could'st judge of fit and meet: Par Lost 8.448
But whom send I to judge them? whom but thee Par Lost 10.55
And destin'd Man himself to judge Man fall'n. Par Lost 10.62
Mayst ever rest well pleas'd. I go to judge Par Lost 10.71
Came the mild Judge and Intercessor both Par Lost 10.96
The gracious Judge without revile repli'd. Par Lost 10.118
Before my Judge, either to undergoe Par Lost 10.126
Confessing soon, yet not before her Judge Par Lost 10.160
So judg'd he Man, both Judge and Saviour sent, Par Lost 10.209
The Son of God to judge them terrifi'd Par Lost 10.338
But if thou judge it hard and difficult, Par Lost 10.992
But infinite in pardon was my Judge, Par Lost 11.167
To whom thus *Michael*. Judg not what is best Par Lost 11.603
To judge them with his Saints: Him the most High Par Lost 11.705
With glory and power to judge both quick and dead, Par Lost 12.460
To judge th' unfaithful dead, but to reward Par Lost 12.461
Rain influence, and judge the prise Allegro 122
The dreadfull Judge in middle Air shall spread his throne. Nativity 164
Ease was his chief disease, and to judge right, Another 21
line not in 1658 text
That all both judge you to relate them true, Sonnet 10, 13
Before the Judge, who thenceforth bid thee rest Sonnet 14, 13
He who of those delights can judge, And spare Sonnet 20, 13
Judge me Lord, be judge in this Psalm 7, 31
God is a just Judge and severe, Psalm 7, 43
Rise God, judge thou the earth *in might*, Psalm 82, 25
Judged
Well have ye judg'd, well ended long debate, Par Lost 2.390
And judg'd of public moment, in the shape Par Lost 2.448
Shall satisfie for Man, be judg'd and die, Par Lost 3.295
None seconded, as out of season judg'd, Par Lost 5.850
Judg'd thee perverse: the easier conquest now Par Lost 6.37
Against us from about his Throne, and judg'd Par Lost 6.426
Whoever judg'd, the worst on mee must light, Par Lost 10.73
Are to behold the Judgment, but the judg'd, Par Lost 10.81
Though in mysterious terms, judg'd as then best: Par Lost 10.173
So judg'd he Man, both Judge and Saviour sent, Par Lost 10.209
Meanwhile ere thus was sin'd and judg'd on Earth, Par Lost 10.229
True is, mee also he hath judg'd, or rather Par Lost 10.494
And gracious temper he both heard and judg'd Par Lost 10.1047
Cloath'd us unworthie, pitying while he judg'd; Par Lost 10.1059

Judged(*cont*)
Repairing where he judg'd us, prostrate fall Par Lost 10.1087
Repairing where he judg'd them prostrate fell Par Lost 10.1099
Seis'd on by force, judg'd, and to death condemnd Par Lost 12.412
As by that early action may be judg'd, Par Reg 4.215
Yet now am judg'd an enemy. Why then Samson 882
Which to my countrey I was judg'd to have shewn. Samson 994
Judgement
Are to behold the Judgment, but the judg'd, Par Lost 10.81
1667 'Judgement'
And to the place of judgment will return, Par Lost 10.932
1667 'judgement'
And Judgment from above: him old and young Par Lost 11.668
1667 'Judgement'
Would think to charm my judgement, as mine eyes Mask 758
Bridgewater ms 'Judgement'
In judgment, or abide their tryal then, Psalm 1, 13
1673 printed 'jugdment'
Judges
So wise he judges it to fly from pain Par Lost 4.910
By Judges first, then under Kings; of whom Par Lost 12.320
Be taught ye Judges of the earth; with fear Psalm 2, 23
He judges and debates. Psalm 82, 4
Who judges in great suits and controversies, Prose 10, 3
Judgest
Of all things made, and judgest onely right. Par Lost 3.155
Judgeth
Jehovah judgeth most upright Psalm 7, 29
Judging
And perfet witnes of all-judging *Jove;* Lycidas 82
Judgment
Thy Judgement to do aught, which else free Will Par Lost 8.636
Anger and just rebuke, and judgement giv'n, Par Lost 9.10
All Judgement, whether in Heav'n, or Earth, or Hell. Par Lost 10.57
To Judgement he proceeded on th' accus'd Par Lost 10.164
On *Adam* last thus judgement he pronounc'd. Par Lost 10.197
And while the dread of judgement past remains Par Lost 12.14
Over free Reason, God in Judgement just Par Lost 12.92
Yet years, and to ripe years judgment mature, Par Reg 3.37
A spirit and judgment equal or superior, Par Reg 4.324
Were left for hast unfinish't, judgment scant, Samson 1027
Judgment here thou didst ingage Psalm 7, 23
With judgment false and wrong Psalm 82, 6
Judgments
My judgments, how with Mankind I proceed, Par Lost 11.69
In Prison under Judgements imminent: Par Lost 11.725
Must be compelld by Signes and Judgements dire; Par Lost 12.175
Judicious
In Reason, and is judicious, is the scale Par Lost 8.591
And Palate call judicious; I the praise Par Lost 9.1020
Juggler
In this unhallow'd air, but that this Jugler Mask 757
Trinity ms 'juggler'
Jugglers
Juglers and Dancers, Antics, Mummers, Mimics, Samson 1325
Juice
I drank, from the clear milkie juice allaying Samson 550
Juiciest
Each Plant and juciest Gourd will pluck such choice Par Lost 5.327
Julep
And first behold this cordial Julep here Mask 672
1637 'julep'
Trinity ms 'julep'
Julius
Great *Julius*, whom now all the world admires Par Reg 3.39
Juniper
Under a Juniper; then how awakt, Par Reg 2.272
Junkets
How *Faery Mab* the junkets eat, Allegro 102
Iunkets and knacks, that they may learne apace. Prose 6, 3
Juno
On *Juno* smiles, when he impregns the Clouds Par Lost 4.500
Or *Neptun*'s ire or *Juno's*, that so long Par Lost 9.18
Were it a draft for *Juno* when she banquets, Mask 701
1637 '*Iuno*'
Juno dare's not give her odds; Arcades 23
Trinity ms 'Juno' ←'Ceres' ←'Juno'
Jupiter
Smil'd with superior Love, as *Jupiter* Par Lost 4.499
Apollo, *Neptune*, *Jupiter*, or *Pan*, Par Reg 2.190
Jurisdiction
From Heav'ns high jurisdiction, in new League Par Lost 2.319
Just
Mee though just right, and the fixt Laws of Heav'n Par Lost 2.18
To claim our just inheritance of old, Par Lost 2.38
Of Spirits that in our just pretenses arm'd Par Lost 2.825
All he could have; I made him just and right, Par Lost 3.98
Mans mortal crime, and just th' unjust to save, Par Lost 3.215
Receive new life. So Man, as is most just, Par Lost 3.294
New Heav'n and Earth, wherein the just shall dwell, Par Lost 3.335
Melt, as I doe, yet public reason just, Par Lost 4.389
And Head, what thou hast said is just and right. Par Lost 4.443
Founded in Reason, Loyal, Just, and Pure, Par Lost 4.755
Single, is yet so just, my constant thoughts Par Lost 5.552
The just Decree of God, pronounc't and sworn, Par Lost 5.814
Unsound and false; nor is it aught but just, Par Lost 6.121
Though heaviest by just measure on thy self Par Lost 6.265
For strength from Truth divided and from Just, Par Lost 6.381

Just(*cont*)
As is most just; this I my Glorie account, Par Lost 6.726
That from thy just obedience could revolt, Par Lost 6.740
Glorie to him whose just avenging ire Par Lost 7.184
And th' habitations of the just; to him Par Lost 7.186
This be thy just Circumference, O World. Par Lost 7.231
Pattern of just equalitie perhaps Par Lost 7.487
To visit oft the dwellings of just Men Par Lost 7.570
Holy and just: thrice happie if they know Par Lost 7.631
Then self esteem, grounded on just and right Par Lost 8.572
Anger and just rebuke, and judgement giv'n, Par Lost 9.10
Of good, how just? of evil, if what is evil Par Lost 9.698
God therefore cannot hurt ye, and be just; Par Lost 9.700
Not just, not God; not feard then, nor obeyd: Par Lost 9.701
Just confidence, and native righteousness Par Lost 9.1056
Omniscient, who in all things wise and just, Par Lost 10.7
Heav'n-fall'n, in station stood or just array, Par Lost 10.535
Through multitude that sung: Just are thy ways, Par Lost 10.643
Justice Divine not hast'n to be just? Par Lost 10.857
To my just number found. O why did God, Par Lost 10.888
Mee mee onely just object of his ire. Par Lost 10.936
Found so erroneous, thence by just event Par Lost 10.969
Reluctance against God and his just yoke Par Lost 10.1045
Wak't in the renovation of the just, Par Lost 11.65
Out of thy loyns; th' unjust the just hath slain, Par Lost 11.455
I yield it just, said *Adam*, and submit. Par Lost 11.526
Just men they seemd, and all thir study bent Par Lost 11.577
But who was that Just Man, whom had not Heav'n Par Lost 11.681
With Foes for daring single to be just, Par Lost 11.703
The one just Man alive; by his command Par Lost 11.818
For one Man found so perfet and so just, Par Lost 11.876
Such grace shall one just Man find in his sight, Par Lost 11.890
Both Heav'n and Earth, wherein the just shall dwell. Par Lost 11.901
With some regard to what is just and right Par Lost 12.16
Over free Reason, God in Judgement just Par Lost 12.92
Just *Abraham* and his Seed: now first I finde Par Lost 12.273
Just for unjust, that in such righteousness Par Lost 12.294
Appeer of respiration to the just, Par Lost 12.540
His birth to our just fear gave no small cause, Par Reg 1.66
Just *Simeon* and Prophetic *Anna*, warn'd Par Reg 1.255
Owe not all Creatures by just right to thee Par Reg 2.325
Conteins of good, wise, just, the perfect shape. Par Reg 3.11
The just man, and divulges him through Heaven Par Reg 3.62
Well hath obey'd; just tryal e're I merit Par Reg 3.196
And just in time thou com'st to have a view Par Reg 3.298
To just extent over all *Israel*'s Sons; Par Reg 3.406
Deservedly made vassal, who once just, Par Reg 4.133
Chor. In seeking just occasion to provoke Samson 237
Chor. Just are the ways of God, Samson 293
Yet more there be who doubt his ways not just, Samson 300
Nor in respect of the enemy just cause Samson 316
Which argues over-just, and self-displeas'd Samson 514
Just or unjust, alike seem miserable, Samson 703
Or else with just allowance counterpois'd, Samson 770
And of Religion, press'd how just it was, Samson 854
To the Spirits of just men long opprest! Samson 1269
To lay their just hands on that Golden Key Mask 13
Defence is a good cause, and Heav'n be for us. Mask 489
Trinity ms 'defence' ← 'a just Defence'
May never this just sword be lifted up, Mask 601
If every just man that now pines with want Mask 768
Bridgewater ms 'Just'
Or wert thou that just Maid who once before Fair Inf 50
O more exceeding love or law more just? Circum 15
Just law indeed, but more exceeding love! Circum 16
With those just Spirits that wear victorious Palms, Musick 14
Words with just note and accent, not to scan Sonnet 13, 3
Had ripen'd thy just soul to dwell with God, Sonnet 14, 2
And succour our just Fears Forcers 18
Nor sinners in th' assembly of just men. Psalm 1, 14
For the Lord knows th' upright way of the just, Psalm 1, 15
Offer the offerings just Psalm 4, 23
To bless the just man still, Psalm 5, 38
But the just establish fast, Psalm 7, 37
Since thou art the just God that tries Psalm 7, 38
In him who both just and wise Psalm 7, 41
God is a just Judge and severe, Psalm 7, 43
By just and equal Lawes. Psalm 82, 12
Whose waies are just and right. Psalm 84, 44
Thy waies, and love the just, Psalm 86, 6

Just
Just o're the blissful seat of Paradise, Par Lost 3.527
As I bent down to look, just opposite, Par Lost 4.460
Just met, and closing stood in squadron joind Par Lost 4.863
Just then returnd at shut of Evening Flours. Par Lost 9.278

Juster
What can be juster in a State then this? Prose 9, 5

Justice
Such place Eternal Justice had prepar'd Par Lost 1.70
What e're his wrath, which he calls Justice, bids, Par Lost 2.733
The other none: in Mercy and Justice both, Par Lost 3.132
Dye hee or Justice must; unless for him Par Lost 3.210
Of Mercy and Justice in thy face discern'd, Par Lost 3.407
All Justice: nor delaid the winged Saint Par Lost 5.247
Justice shall not return as bountie scorn'd. Par Lost 10.54
Mercie collegue with Justice, sending thee Par Lost 10.59
Justice with Mercie, as may illustrate most Par Lost 10.78
Thy Justice seems; yet to say truth, too late, Par Lost 10.755

Justice(*cont*)
Justice Divine not hast'n to be just? Par Lost 10.857
But Death comes not at call, Justice Divine Par Lost 10.858
Of Justice, of Religion, Truth and Peace, Par Lost 11.667
Justice and Temperance, Truth and Faith forgot; Par Lost 11.807
But Justice, and some fatal curse annext Par Lost 12.99
To civil Justice, part religious Rites Par Lost 12.231
So onely can high Justice rest appaid. Par Lost 12.401
Yea Truth, and justice then Nativity 141
1673 'Justice'
Of vengeful Justice bore for our excess, Circum 24
According to his justice raise Psalm 7, 62
And Justice from her heavenly bowr Psalm 85, 47
Thy justice in the *gloomy* land Psalm 88, 51

Justifiable
And justifiable to Men; Samson 294

Justification
Justification towards God, and peace Par Lost 12.296

Justify
And justifie the wayes of God to men. Par Lost 1.26
Her doing seem'd to justifie the deed; Par Lost 10.142

Justly
So were created, nor can justly accuse Par Lost 3.112
Who justly hath drivn out his Rebell Foes Par Lost 3.677
Chose freely what it now so justly rues. Par Lost 4.72
Justly hast in derision, and secure Par Lost 5.736
Not that which justly gives Heroic name Par Lost 9.40
More justly, Seat worthier of Gods, as built Par Lost 9.100
Of his Creation; justly then accurst, Par Lost 10.168
Thy punishment then justly is at his Will. Par Lost 10.768
What justly thou hast lost; nor set thy heart, Par Lost 11.288
To whom thus *Michael*. Justly thou abhorr'st Par Lost 12.79
For God hath justly giv'n the Nations up Par Reg 1.442
To thy Delusions; justly, since they fell Par Reg 1.443
And long Renown thou justly may'st prefer Par Reg 4.84
But justly; I my self have brought them on, Samson 375
Justly, yet despair not of his final pardon Samson 1171
We may justly now accuse Arcades 10
Trinity ms 'wee may justly now accuse' ← 'now seemes guiltie of abuse'

Keen
Of Theologians, but with keen dispatch Par Lost 5.436
Was giv'n him temperd so, that neither keen Par Lost 6.322
Of that alluring fruit, urg'd me so keene. Par Lost 9.588
Blow moist and keen, shattering the graceful locks Par Lost 10.1066
Drivn by a keen North-winde, that blowing drie Par Lost 11.842
Against a Winters day when winds blow keen, Par Reg 1.317
And like a quiver'd Nymph with Arrows keen Mask 422
1637 'keene'
Bridgewater ms 'keene'
Trinity ms 'keene'

Keep
Into my hand was giv'n, with charge to keep Par Lost 2.775
I keep, by him forbidden to unlock Par Lost 2.852
Keep residence; if all I can will serve, Par Lost 2.999
That from his Lordly eye keep distance due, Par Lost 3.578
Ill fenc't for Heav'n to keep out such a foe Par Lost 4.372
From us no other service then to keep Par Lost 4.420
To keep them low whom knowledge might exalt Par Lost 4.525
While they keep watch, or nightly rounding walk Par Lost 4.685
To him who sent us, whose charge is to keep Par Lost 4.842
To Till and keep, and of the Fruit to eate: Par Lost 8.320
Him whom to love is to obey, and keep Par Lost 8.634
Will keep from Wilderness with ease, as wide Par Lost 9.245
Why but to keep ye low and ignorant, Par Lost 9.704
But keep the odds of Knowledge in my power Par Lost 9.820
To end me? Shall Truth fail to keep her word, Par Lost 10.856
Which I must keep till my appointed day Par Lost 11.550
To gain dominion or to keep it gain'd. Par Reg 2.434
Under the Seal of silence could not keep, Samson 49
Chor. Best keep together here, lest running thither Samson 1521
Strive to keep up a frail, and Feaverish being Mask 8
1637 'keepe'
Trinity ms 'keepe'
Bridgewater ms 'keepe'
Their merry wakes and pastimes keep: Mask 121
Bridgewater ms 'keepe'
1637 'keepe'
Trinity ms 'keepe'
To keep my life and honour unassail'd. Mask 220
line not in Bridgewater ms
1637 'keepe'
Trinity ms 'keepe'
2. *Bro*. Heav'n keep my sister, agen agen and neer, Mask 486
Trinity ms 'keepe'
1637 'keepe'
Bridgewater ms 'keepe'
You gave me Brother? *Eld. Bro*. Yes, and keep it still, Mask 584
Bridgewater ms 'keepe'
Trinity ms 'keepe'
And bad me keep it as of sovran use Mask 639
Bridgewater ms 'keepe'
1637 'keepe'
Trinity ms 'keepe'
It is for homely features to keep home, Mask 748
Trinity ms 'keepe'
line not in Bridgewater ms
1637 'keepe'

Keep(*cont*)
Com, but keep thy wonted state, Penseroso 37
With such consort as they keep, Penseroso 145
And keep unsteddy Nature to her law, Arcades 70
Trinity ms 'keepe'
And all the spangled host keep watch in squadrons bright? Nativity 21
Was all that did their silly thoughts so busie keep. Nativity 92
And bid the weltring waves their oozy channel keep. Nativity 124
To keep in compass of thy Predicament: Vacation 56
Ungratefully shall strive to keep him under, Vacation 78
And keep in tune with Heav'n, till God ere long Musick 26
Trinity ms 'keepe'
While he might still jogg on, and keep his trot, Another 4
1640 'keepe'
For thou alone dost keep Psalm 4, 39
His mischief that due course doth keep, Psalm 7, 57
Thou Shepherd that dost Israel *keep* Psalm 80, 1
Whom thou dost hide and keep. Psalm 83, 12
Had rather keep a dore, Psalm 84, 38
Lord God that dost me save and keep, Psalm 88, 1

Keeping
Not keeping strictest watch, as she was warnd. Par Lost 9.363
To simple Shepherds, keeping watch by night; Par Lost 12.365
The work of many hands, which earns my keeping Samson 1260
The Lord will own, and have me in his keeping. Psalm 6, 20

Keeps
In that aspect, and still that distance keepes Par Lost 7.379
What makes a Nation happy, and keeps it so, Par Reg 4.362
Whom thrift keeps up about his Country gear, Mask 167
1637 'keepes'
the scalie-harnest dragon ever keeps Mask Tr. ms 10.09
'dragon ever keeps' ←'watchfull dragons keep'
Or *Humber* loud that keeps the *Scythians* Name, Vacation 99
Who keepes the lawes and statutes of the Senate, Prose 10, 2

Ken
At once as far as Angels kenn he views Par Lost 1.59
ms 'kenne'
Saw within kenn a glorious Angel stand, Par Lost 3.622
The Hemisphere of Earth in cleerest Ken Par Lost 11.379
Turchestan-born; nor could his eye not ken Par Lost 11.396
From whose high top to ken the prospect round, Par Reg 2.286

Kenelm
Of head bereft li'th poor *Kenelm* King-born. Prose 13, 2

Kennel
And kennel there, yet there still bark'd and howl'd, Par Lost 2.658

Kens
Delos or *Samos* first appeering kenns Par Lost 5.265

Kept
Fast by Hell Gate, and kept the fatal Key, Par Lost 2.725
Reservd from night, and kept for thee in store. Par Lost 5.128
His Loyaltie he kept, his Love, his Zeale; Par Lost 5.900
Yet farr the greater part have kept, I see, Par Lost 7.145
But not in silence holy kept; the Harp Par Lost 7.594
With *Halleluiahs:* Thus was Sabbath kept. Par Lost 7.634
That kept thir watch; thence full of anguish driv'n, Par Lost 9.62
Though kept from Man, and worthy to be admir'd, Par Lost 9.746
There kept thir Watch the Legions, while the Grand Par Lost 10.427
Kept in that State, had not the folly of Man Par Lost 10.619
Kept not my happy Station, but was driv'n Par Reg 1.360
Deposited within thee; which to have kept Samson 429
But I Gods counsel have not kept, his holy secret Samson 497
I have kept of pretious cure, Mask 913
Ev'n them who kept thy truth so pure of old Sonnet 18, 3

Kerchiefed
But Cherchef't in a comly Cloud, Penseroso 125

Kernels
From many a berrie, and from sweet kernels prest Par Lost 5.346

Key
Fast by Hell Gate, and kept the fatal Key, Par Lost 2.725
I also; at which time this powerful Key Par Lost 2.774
The key of this infernal Pit by due, Par Lost 2.850
Thus saying, from her side the fatal Key, Par Lost 2.871
Thy key of strength and safety: thou wilt say, Samson 799
To lay their just hands on that Golden Key Mask 13
Trinity ms 'key'
1637 'key'
Bridgewater ms 'keye'

Keyhole
Could once have mov'd; then in the key-hole turns Par Lost 2.876

Keys
To wait them with his Keys, and now at foot Par Lost 3.485
Two massy Keyes he bore of metals twain, Lycidas 110
Trinity ms 'keys'
1638 'keyes'

Khan
Of *Cambalu*, seat of *Cathaian Can* Par Lost 11.388

Kicked
The latter quick up flew, and kickt the beam; Par Lost 4.1004

Kid
Dandl'd the Kid; Bears, Tygers, Ounces, Pards, Par Lost 4.344
Unsuckt of Lamb or Kid, that tend thir play. Par Lost 9.583
Oft sacrificing Bullock, Lamb, or Kid, Par Lost 12.20
Who tore the Lion, as the Lion tears the Kid, Samson 128
Slip't from the fold, or young Kid lost his dam, Mask 498
Bridgewater ms 'kyd'
1637 'kid'
Trinity ms 'kid'

Kids
To gorge the flesh of Lambs or yeanling Kids Par Lost 3.434

Kill
Him first make sure your thrall, and lastly kill. Par Lost 10.402

Killed
Among thy slain self-kill'd Samson 1664
But kill'd alas, and then bewayl'd his fatal bliss. Fair Inf 7
Kil'd with report that Old man eloquent, Sonnet 10, 8
Trinity ms 'kill'd'
1673 'Kill'd'

Killing
As killing as the Canker to the Rose, Lycidas 45

Kills
Inhospitably, and kills thir infant Males: Par Lost 12.168

Kind
Severing each kind, and scum'd the Bullion dross: Par Lost 1.704
1667 'kinde'
Betwixt th' Angelical and Human kinde: Par Lost 3.462
The Tempter ere th' Accuser of man-kind, Par Lost 4.10
All Trees of noblest kind for sight, smell, taste; Par Lost 4.217
Saw undelighted all delight, all kind Par Lost 4.286
Proportiond to each kind. So from the root Par Lost 5.479
Differing but in degree, of kind the same. Par Lost 5.490
Thir nimble tread, as when the total kind Par Lost 6.73
And Fruit Tree yielding Fruit after her kind; Par Lost 7.311
And every Bird of wing after his kinde; Par Lost 7.394
Let th' Earth bring forth Foul living in her kinde, Par Lost 7.451
Each in their kinde. The Earth obey'd, and strait Par Lost 7.453
Minims of Nature; some of Serpent kinde Par Lost 7.482
Each with thir kinde, Lion with Lioness; Par Lost 8.393
And lovely, never since of Serpent kind Par Lost 9.504
Of brutal kind, that daily are in sight? Par Lost 9.565
Warm'd by the Sun, producing every kind, Par Lost 9.721
The Figtree, not that kind for Fruit renown'd, Par Lost 9.1101
With secret amity things of like kinde Par Lost 10.248
Land, Sea, and Aire, and every kinde that lives, Par Lost 11.337
A shelter and a kind of shading cool Par Reg 3.221
So near related, or the same of kind, Samson 786
Chor. But this another kind of tempest brings. Samson 1063
Har. This insolence other kind of answer fits. Samson 1236
As the kind hospitable Woods provide. Mask 187
Bridgewater ms 'kynde'
Praise the Lord, for he is kind, Psalm 136, 2
But all unwares with his cold-kind embrace Fair Inf 20
In the kind office of a Chamberlin Carrier 14
1658 'Death in the likenesse'
Nightly my Couch I make a kind of Sea; Psalm 6, 12

Kindle
Of this pure cause would kindle my rap't spirits Mask 794
line not in Bridgewater ms
line not in Trinity ms

Kindled
What if the breath that kindl'd those grim fires Par Lost 2.170
Kindl'd through agitation to a Flame, Par Lost 9.637

Kindles
Kindles the gummie bark of Firr or Pine, Par Lost 10.1076

Kindliest
Taste after taste upheld with kindliest change, Par Lost 5.336

Kindly
Of porous Earth with kindly thirst up drawn, Par Lost 4.228
Not only enlighten, but with kindly heate Par Lost 4.668
Bursting with kindly rupture forth disclos'd Par Lost 7.419
Was kindly com to live with them below; Nativity 90

Kindness
Hence with thy brew'd inchantments, foul deceiver, Mask 696
Trinity ms 'brewd enchauntments' ←'foule brud' ←'hel brewd opiate' ←'hel bru'd liquor' ←'bru'd sorcerie' ←'teacherous (leacherous?) bruage' ←'teacherous kindnesse'
Shall they thy loving kindness tell Psalm 88, 45

Kindred
His kindred and false Gods, into a Land Par Lost 12.122
Will send for all my kindred, all my friends Samson 1730

Kinds
Of those fourfooted kindes, himself now one, Par Lost 4.397
Thir stellar vertue on all kinds that grow Par Lost 4.671
Alcinous reign'd, fruit of all kindes, in coate, Par Lost 5.341
The waters generated by thir kindes, Par Lost 7.393
After thir kindes; I bring them to receave Par Lost 8.343
In procreation common to all kindes Par Lost 8.597
All kinds, and for destruction to mature Par Lost 10.612
Of heart-sick Agonie, all feavorous kinds, Par Lost 11.482

Kine
The smell of Grain, or tedded Grass, or Kine, Par Lost 9.450
A herd of Beeves, faire Oxen and faire Kine Par Lost 11.647
Low in a mead of Kine under a Thorn, Prose 13, 1

King
Fearless, endanger'd Heav'ns perpetual King; Par Lost 1.131
First *Moloch*, horrid King besmear'd with blood Par Lost 1.392
ms 'king'
By that uxorious King, whose heart though large, Par Lost 1.444
ms 'king'
A Leper once he lost and gain'd a King, Par Lost 1.471
The Calf in *Oreb:* and the Rebel King Par Lost 1.484
And sat as Princes, whom the supreme King Par Lost 1.735
He ceas'd, and next him *Moloc*, Scepter'd King Par Lost 2.43
Either to disinthrone the King of Heav'n Par Lost 2.229
And know not that the King of Heav'n hath doom'd Par Lost 2.316

King(*cont*)
Sole King, and of his Kingdom loose no part Par Lost 2.325
Where I reign King, and to enrage thee more, Par Lost 2.698
Thy King and Lord? Back to thy punishment, Par Lost 2.699
In bold conspiracy against Heav'ns King, Par Lost 2.751
And by command of Heav'ns all-powerful King Par Lost 2.851
From your Dominion won, th' Ethereal King Par Lost 2.978
Made head against Heav'ns King, though overthrown. Par Lost 2.992
Anointed universal King; all Power Par Lost 3.317
Eternal King; thee Author of all being, Par Lost 3.374
Warring in Heav'n against Heav'ns matchless King: Par Lost 4.41
Divided Empire with Heav'ns King I hold Par Lost 4.111
So sudden to behold the grieslie King; Par Lost 4.821
From my prevailing arme, though Heavens King Par Lost 4.973
With pittie Heav'ns high King, and to him call'd Par Lost 5.220
Excess, before th' all bounteous King, who showrd Par Lost 5.640
Messiah King anointed, could not beare Par Lost 5.664
Fit entertainment to receive our King Par Lost 5.690
About the great reception of thir King, Par Lost 5.769
Of King anointed, for whom all this haste Par Lost 5.777
Confess him rightful King? unjust thou saist Par Lost 5.818
These tidings carrie to th' anointed King; Par Lost 5.870
Right reason for thir Law, and for thir King Par Lost 6.42
Had not th' Eternal King Omnipotent Par Lost 6.227
Of *Moloc* furious King, who him defi'd, Par Lost 6.357
Of all things, to be Heir and to be King Par Lost 6.708
God and *Messiah* his anointed King. Par Lost 6.718
Sung Triumph, and him sung Victorious King, Par Lost 6.886
Things not reveal'd, which th' invisible King, Par Lost 7.122
The King of Glorie in his powerful Word Par Lost 7.208
Who can impair thee, mighty King, or bound Par Lost 7.608
For state, as Sovran King, and to enure Par Lost 8.239
Or that, not Mystic, where the Sapient King Par Lost 9.442
Antagonist of Heav'ns Almightie King) Par Lost 10.387
Against the *Syrian* King, who to surprize Par Lost 11.218
Suspected to a sequent King, who seeks Par Lost 12.165
Behinde them, while th' obdurat King pursues: Par Lost 12.205
Of *David* (so I name this King) shall rise Par Lost 12.326
Anointed King *Messiah* might be born Par Lost 12.359
To do him honour as their King; all come, Par Reg 1.75
Their King, their Leader, and Supream on Earth. Par Reg 1.99
Thy Father is the Eternal King, who rules Par Reg 1.236
By which they knew thee King of *Israel* born. Par Reg 1.254
To draw the proud King *Ahab* into fraud Par Reg 1.372
But thou art serviceable to Heaven's King. Par Reg 1.421
Thence into *Egypt*, till the Murd'rous King Par Reg 2.76
Little suspicious to any King; but now Par Reg 2.82
For therein stands the office of a King, Par Reg 2.463
Passions, Desires, and Fears, is more a King; Par Reg 2.467
The *Pontic* King and in triumph had rode. Par Reg 3.36
And o're a mighty King so oft prevail'd, Par Reg 3.167
That thou who worthiest art should'st be thir King? Par Reg 3.226
Of his great power; for now the *Parthian* King Par Reg 3.299
So spake *Israel*'s true King, and to the Fiend Par Reg 3.441
If given, by whom but by the King of Kings, Par Reg 4.185
These rules will render thee a King compleat Par Reg 4.283
These only with our Law best form a King. Par Reg 4.364
On which the *Tartar* King did ride; Penseroso 115
Wherin the Son of Heav'ns eternal King, Nativity 2
They call the grisly king, Nativity 209
1673 'King'
The Tawny King with all his power. Psalm 136, 54
In solemn Songs at King *Alcinous* feast, Vacation 49
O're all his Brethren he shall Reign as King, Vacation 75
When thou taught'st *Cambridge*, and King *Edward* Greek. Sonnet 11, 14
anointed have my King (though ye rebell) Psalm 2, 12
My King and God for unto thee I pray. Psalm 5, 4
Sing loud to God *our King*, Psalm 81, 2
Toward thee, My King, my God. Psalm 84, 16
Then an unjust and wicked King Prose 11, 3

King-born
Of head bereft li'th poor *Kenelm* King-born. Prose 13, 2

Kingdom
Sole King, and of his Kingdom loose no part Par Lost 2.325
The utmost border of his Kingdom, left Par Lost 2.361
Reign thou in Hell thy Kingdom, let mee serve Par Lost 6.183
Kingdom and Power and Glorie appertains, Par Lost 6.815
One Kingdom, Joy and Union without end. Par Lost 7.161
My hold of this new Kingdom all depends, Par Lost 10.406
Repentance, and Heavens Kingdom nigh at hand Par Reg 1.20
And of thy Kingdom there should be no end. Par Reg 1.241
E're I the promis'd Kingdom can attain, Par Reg 1.265
The Kingdom shall to *Israel* be restor'd: Par Reg 2.36
Besides to give a Kingdom hath been thought Par Reg 2.481
But to a Kingdom thou art born, ordain'd Par Reg 3.152
If Kingdom move thee not, let move thee Zeal, Par Reg 3.171
My everlasting Kingdom, why art thou Par Reg 3.199
(As he who seeking Asses found a Kingdom) Par Reg 3.242
All this fair sight; thy Kingdom though foretold Par Reg 3.351
And of my Kingdom there shall be no end: Par Reg 4.151
Till time mature thee to a Kingdoms waight; Par Reg 4.282
Kingdom nor Empire pleases thee, nor aught Par Reg 4.369
A Kingdom they portend thee, but what Kingdom, Par Reg 4.389
And wrath to see his Kingdom fail, Nativity 171

Kingdoms
To shew him all Earths Kingdomes and thir Glory. Par Lost 11.384
The Kingdoms of *Almansor*, *Fez* and *Sus*, Par Lost 11.403
How many Kings destroyd, and Kingdoms won, Par Lost 12.262

Kingdoms(*cont*)
The Kingdoms of the world, and all thir glory. Par Reg 4.89
The Kingdoms of the world to thee I give; Par Reg 4.163
The Kingdoms of the world to thee were giv'n, Par Reg 4.182
The Kingdoms of this world; I shall no more Par Reg 4.210
What ruins Kingdoms, and lays Cities flat; Par Reg 4.363
Not more; for Honours, Riches, Kingdoms, Glory Par Reg 4.536
In the blest Kingdoms meek of joy and love. Lycidas 177
line not in 1638 edition
Trinity ms 'kingdoms'

Kingly
The likeness of a Kingly Crown had on. Par Lost 2.673
The work as of a Kingly Palace Gate Par Lost 3.505
Adam bowd low, hee Kingly from his State Par Lost 11.249
Is yet more Kingly, this attracts the Soul, Par Reg 2.476
Immortal Nectar to her Kingly Sire: Vacation 39
Is Kingly. Thousands at his bidding speed Sonnet 19, 12

Kings
Of *Babel*, and the works of *Memphian* Kings Par Lost 1.694
ms 'kings'
Thir Kings, when *Aegypt* with *Assyria* strove Par Lost 1.721
ms 'kings'
Showrs on her Kings *Barbaric* Pearl and Gold, Par Lost 2.4
Of great *Seleucia*, built by *Grecian* Kings, Par Lost 4.212
Nor where *Abassin* Kings thir issue Guard, Par Lost 4.280
And send forth all her Kings; there will be room, Par Lost 4.383
Of *Sarra*, worn by Kings and Hero's old Par Lost 11.243
To *Paquin* of *Sinaean* Kings, and thence Par Lost 11.390
Ercoco and the less Maritim Kings Par Lost 11.398
How many Kings destroyd, and Kingdoms won, Par Lost 12.262
By Judges first, then under Kings; of whom Par Lost 12.320
All Nations, and to Kings foretold, of Kings Par Lost 12.329
Returnd from *Babylon* by leave of Kings Par Lost 12.348
Regents and Potentates, and Kings, yea gods Par Reg 1.117
Behold the Kings of the Earth how they oppress Par Reg 2.44
Riches though offer'd from the hand of Kings. Par Reg 2.449
Should Kings and Nations from thy mouth consult, Par Reg 3.12
The drink of none but Kings; of later fame Par Reg 3.289
From the luxurious Kings of *Antioch* won. Par Reg 3.297
Thy country, and captive lead away her Kings Par Reg 3.366
From the *Asian* Kings and *Parthian* among these, Par Reg 4.73
Shar'd among petty Kings too far remov'd; Par Reg 4.87
If given, by whom but by the King of Kings, Par Reg 4.185
Of *Madian* and her vanquisht Kings: Samson 281
And Kings sate still with awfull eye, Nativity 59
Kings of prowess and renown. Psalm 136, 62
And last of Kings and Queens and *Hero*'s old, Vacation 47
That Kings for such a Tomb would wish to die. Shakespear 16
1663-4 '*Kings*'
And rumors loud, that daunt remotest kings, Sonnet 15, 4
1694 'Kings'
muse a vain thing, the Kings of th' earth upstand Psalm 2, 2
And now be wise at length ye Kings averse Psalm 2, 22
Of Kings and lordly States, Psalm 82, 2
I mention Egypt, *where proud Kings* Psalm 87, 11
And *Kings* be born of thee, whose dredded might Prose 12, 13

Kiriathaim
That *Kiriathaim* held, thou knowst me now Samson 1081

Kirtled
Amidst the flowry-kirtl'd *Naiades* Mask 254
Bridgewater ms 'flowrie-kyrtled'
Trinity ms 'flowrie-kirtl'd' ← 'flowrie-kirtled'
1637 'flowrie-kirtl'd'

Kishon
When at the brook of Kishon *old* Psalm 83, 37

Kiss
Approach, and kiss her sacred vestures hemm. Arcades 83
Trinity ms 'kisse'
That did thy cheek envermeil, thought to kiss Fair Inf 6
With an individual kiss; On Time 12
Trinity ms 'kisse'
With trembling; kiss the Son least he appear Psalm 2, 25

Kissed
Kiss'd as the gracious signs of sweet remorse Par Lost 5.134
Smoothly the waters kist, Nativity 65
Sweet Peace and Righteousness have kiss'd Psalm 85, 43

Kisses
With kisses pure: aside the Devil turnd Par Lost 4.502

Knacks
Iunkets and knacks, that they may learne apace. Prose 6, 3

Knee
With suppliant knee, and deifie his power, Par Lost 1.112
The supple knee? ye will not, if I trust Par Lost 5.788
Shall bend the knee, and in that honour due Par Lost 5.817
He back recoild; the tenth on bended knee Par Lost 6.194
In honour bend thy knee. Psalm 81, 40

Kneeled
Kneel'd and before him humbl'd all my heart, Par Lost 11.150

Knees
All knees to thee shall bow, of them that bide Par Lost 3.321
All knees in Heav'n, and shall confess him Lord: Par Lost 5.608
I beg, and clasp thy knees; bereave me not, Par Lost 10.918

Knee-tribute
Knee-tribute yet unpaid, prostration vile, Par Lost 5.782

Knew
He with his Thunder: and till then who knew Par Lost 1.93
Know ye not mee? ye knew me once no mate Par Lost 4.828
If thou resist. The Fiend lookt up and knew Par Lost 4.1013

Knew(*cont*)
Knew never till this irksom night; methought Par Lost 5.35
The circuit wide. Strait knew him all the Bands Par Lost 5.287
Aereal Music send: nor knew I not Par Lost 5.548
All his right side; then *Satan* first knew pain, Par Lost 6.327
Chose rather; hee, she knew would intermix Par Lost 8.54
Is hard; for who himself beginning knew? Par Lost 8.251
Knew not; to speak I tri'd, and forthwith spake, Par Lost 8.271
While thus I call'd, and stray'd I knew not whither, Par Lost 8.283
Knew it not good for Man to be alone, Par Lost 8.445
I follow'd her, she what was Honour knew, Par Lost 8.508
I knew, but not with human voice endu'd; Par Lost 9.561
And knew not eating Death: Satiate at length, Par Lost 9.792
For still they knew, and ought to have still remember'd Par Lost 10.12
For Man, for of his state by this they knew, Par Lost 10.19
Concern'd not Man (since he no further knew) Par Lost 10.170
Obtruded on us thus? who if we knew Par Lost 11.504
By which they knew thee King of *Israel* born. Par Reg 1.254
Not knew by sight) now come, who was to come Par Reg 1.271
Strait knew me, and with loudest voice proclaim'd Par Reg 1.275
He was well pleas'd; by which I knew the time Par Reg 1.286
To know this only, that he nothing knew; Par Reg 4.294
So saying he took (for still he knew his power Par Reg 4.394
Announc't by *Gabriel* with the first I knew, Par Reg 4.504
The daughter of an Infidel: they knew not Samson 221
That what I motion'd was of God; I knew Samson 222
This well I knew, nor was at all surpris'd, Samson 381
That made for me, I knew that liberty Samson 803
My Countreymen, whom here I knew remaining, Samson 1549
(For so by certain signes I knew) had met Mask 572
  Bridgewater ms 'knowe'
I knew the foul inchanter though disguis'd, Mask 645
Who would not sing for *Lycidas?* he knew Lycidas 10
  Trinity ms 'he well knew'
They knew not of his story, Lycidas 95
As if they surely knew their sovran Lord was by. Nativity 60
She knew such harmony alone Nativity 107
Love led them on, and Faith who knew them best Sonnet 14, 9
  Trinity ms 'knew' ←'saw' ←'knew'

Knewest
Thou knewst by name, and all th' ethereal Powers, Par Lost 12.577
My enemies, lov'd thee, as too well thou knew'st, Samson 878

Knight
Captain or Colonel, or Knight in Arms, Sonnet 8, 1

Knights
Begirt with *British* and *Armoric* Knights; Par Lost 1.581
  ms 'knights'
Prick forth the Aerie Knights, and couch thir Spears Par Lost 2.536
With long and tedious havoc fabl'd Knights Par Lost 9.30
Bases and tinsel Trappings, gorgious Knights Par Lost 9.36
By Knights of *Logres*, or of *Lyones*, Par Reg 2.360
His daughter, sought by many Prowest Knights, Par Reg 3.342
Where throngs of Knights and Barons bold, Allegro 119

Knit
Knit with the *Graces* and the *Hours* in dance Par Lost 4.267
Com, knit hands, and beat the ground, Mask 143
  Bridgewater ms 'knitt'

Knitting
In twisted braids of Lillies knitting Mask 862

Knock
Or knock the breast, no weakness, no contempt, Samson 1722
And loudly knock to have their passage out; Vacation 24

Knot
How are ye joyn'd with hell in triple knot Mask 581
  Bridgewater ms 'knott'
Your learned hands, can loose this Gordian knot? Vacation 90
And doth confirm the knot, Psalm 83, 30

Knot-grass
Of Knot-grass dew-besprent, and were in fold, Mask 542
  Bridgewater ms 'knot grasse'
  Trinity ms 'knot grasse'

Knots
In Beds and curious Knots, but Nature boon Par Lost 4.242

Know
As stood like these, could ever know repulse? Par Lost 1.630
Henceforth his might we know, and know our own Par Lost 1.643
What yet they know must follow, to endure Par Lost 2.206
And know not that the King of Heav'n hath doom'd Par Lost 2.316
What it intends; till first I know of thee, Par Lost 2.740
I know thee not, nor ever saw till now Par Lost 2.744
Befalln us unforeseen, unthought of, know Par Lost 2.821
To know, and this once known, shall soon return, Par Lost 2.839
Answer'd. I know thee, stranger, who thou art, Par Lost 2.990
By me upheld, that he may know how frail Par Lost 3.180
Unspeakable desire to see, and know Par Lost 3.662
Fair Angel, thy desire which tends to know Par Lost 3.694
Pleasant to know, and worthiest to be all Par Lost 3.703
Th' Omnipotent. Ay me, they little know Par Lost 4.86
As Man ere long, and this new World shall know. Par Lost 4.113
Envie them that? can it be sin to know, Par Lost 4.517
With more desire to know, and to reject Par Lost 4.523
A Spirit, zealous, as he seem'd, to know Par Lost 4.565
Thou tellst, by morrow dawning I shall know. Par Lost 4.588
God is thy Law, thou mine: to know no more Par Lost 4.637
No happier state, and know to know no more. Par Lost 4.775
Know ye not then said *Satan*, fill'd with scorn, Par Lost 4.827
Know ye not mee? ye knew me once no mate Par Lost 4.828
Not to know mee argues your selves unknown, Par Lost 4.830

Know(*cont*)
The lowest of your throng; or if ye know, Par Lost 4.831
Satan, I know thy strength, and thou knowst mine, Par Lost 4.1006
Created pure. But know that in the Soule Par Lost 5.100
But by deceit and lies; this let him know, Par Lost 5.243
To spiritual Natures; only this I know, Par Lost 5.402
For know, whatever was created, needs Par Lost 5.414
Given him by this great Conference to know Par Lost 5.454
Inhabitant with God, now know I well Par Lost 5.461
Know whether I be dextrous to subdue Par Lost 5.741
To know ye right, or if ye know your selves Par Lost 5.789
Yet by experience taught we know how good, Par Lost 5.826
Doctrin which we would know whence learnt: who saw Par Lost 5.856
We know no time when we were not as now; Par Lost 5.859
Know none before us, self-begot, self-rais'd Par Lost 5.860
When who can uncreate thee thou shalt know. Par Lost 5.895
How few somtimes may know, when thousands err. Par Lost 6.148
(Unanswerd least thou boast) to let thee know; Par Lost 6.163
Immense I have transfus'd, that all may know Par Lost 6.704
Led on, yet sinless, with desire to know Par Lost 7.61
To magnifie his works, the more we know. Par Lost 7.97
Anough is left besides to search and know. Par Lost 7.125
Her Temperance over Appetite, to know Par Lost 7.127
Know then, that after *Lucifer* from Heav'n Par Lost 7.131
Holy and just: thrice happie if they know Par Lost 7.631
Informd by thee might know; if else thou seekst Par Lost 7.639
That Man may know he dwells not in his own; Par Lost 8.103
To know what passes there; be lowlie wise: Par Lost 8.173
That not to know at large of things remote Par Lost 8.191
From use, obscure and suttle, but to know Par Lost 8.192
Tell me, how may I know him, how adore, Par Lost 8.280
And feel that I am happier then I know, Par Lost 8.282
And shun the bitter consequence: for know, Par Lost 8.328
Thir language and thir wayes, they also know, Par Lost 8.373
From all Eternitie, for none I know Par Lost 8.406
And in her self compleat, so well to know Par Lost 8.548
First thy obedience; th' other who can know, Par Lost 9.368
Knowing both Good and Evil as they know. Par Lost 9.709
Th' offence, that Man should thus attain to know? Par Lost 9.726
In plain then, what forbids he but to know, Par Lost 9.758
What fear I then, rather what know to feare Par Lost 9.773
In knowledge, as the Gods who all things know; Par Lost 9.804
Op'nd we find indeed, and find we know Par Lost 9.1071
Bad Fruit of Knowledge, if this be to know, Par Lost 9.1073
I know not whence possessd thee; we had then Par Lost 9.1137
Th' ethereal People ran, to hear and know Par Lost 10.27
As vitiated in Nature: more to know Par Lost 10.169
Out of the ground wast taken, know thy Birth, Par Lost 10.207
And know not that I call'd and drew them thither Par Lost 10.629
Adam, by sad experiment I know Par Lost 10.967
Those pure immortal Elements that know Par Lost 11.50
To know both Good and Evil, since his taste Par Lost 11.85
His heart I know, how variable and vain Par Lost 11.92
Ere thou from hence depart, know I am sent Par Lost 11.356
Before thee shall appear; that thou mayst know Par Lost 11.475
To worship God aright, and know his works Par Lost 11.578
Rational Libertie; yet know withall, Par Lost 12.82
To know thir God, or message to regard, Par Lost 12.174
Chiefly what may concern her Faith to know, Par Lost 12.599
Whence thou returnst, and whither wentst, I know; Par Lost 12.610
Our hated habitation; well ye know Par Reg 1.47
His first-begot we know, and sore have felt, Par Reg 1.89
He now shall know I can produce a man Par Reg 1.150
Serious to learn and know, and thence to do Par Reg 1.203
For know, thou art no Son of mortal man, Par Reg 1.234
I learn not yet, perhaps I need not know; Par Reg 1.292
Knowing who I am, as I know who thou art? Par Reg 1.356
To see thee and approach thee, whom I know Par Reg 1.384
To all truth requisite for men to know. Par Reg 1.464
Thy coming hither, though I know thy scope, Par Reg 1.494
And now I know he hungers where no food Par Reg 2.231
Of various persons each to know his part; Par Reg 2.240
Of all things destitute, and well I know, Par Reg 2.305
To know, and knowing worship God aright, Par Reg 2.475
I see thou know'st what is of use to know, Par Reg 3.7
They praise and they admire they know not what; Par Reg 3.52
And know not whom, but as one leads the other; Par Reg 3.53
Without distrust or doubt, that he may know Par Reg 3.193
And regal Mysteries; that thou may'st know Par Reg 3.249
That thou may'st know I seek not to engage Par Reg 3.347
Know therefore when my season comes to sit Par Reg 4.146
Is not for thee to know, nor me to tell. Par Reg 4.153
On the other side know also thou, that I Par Reg 4.159
The *Gentiles* also know, and write, and teach Par Reg 4.227
Think not but that I know these things, or think Par Reg 4.286
I know them not; not therefore am I short Par Reg 4.287
To know this only, that he nothing knew; Par Reg 4.294
Therefore to know what more thou art then man, Par Reg 4.538
Happ'ly had ends above my reach to know: Samson 62
Lay stor'd, in what part summ'd, that she might know: Samson 395
Once more thy face, and know of thy estate, Samson 742
Where once I have been caught; I know thy trains Samson 932
Draws hitherward, I know him by his stride, Samson 1067
Chor. His fraught we soon shall know, he now arrives. Samson 1075
Sam. The way to know were not to see but taste. Samson 1091
Sam. I know no Spells, use no forbidden Arts; Samson 1139
Thy strength they know surpassing human rate, Samson 1313
I know not. Lords are Lordliest in thir wine; Samson 1418

Know(*cont*)
Man. I know your friendly minds and----O what noise! Samson 1508
Man. He can I know, but doubt to think he will; Samson 1534
To have guided me aright, I know not how, Samson 1547
No Preface needs, thou seest we long to know. Samson 1554
And sense distract, to know well what I utter. Samson 1556
More then anough we know; but while things yet Samson 1592
Co. I know each lane, and every alley green Mask 311
Bridgewater ms 'knowe'
Or shroud within these limits, I shall know Mask 316
That hallow I should know, what are you? speak; Mask 490
Bridgewater ms 'knowe'
But furder know I not. 2. *Bro*. O night and shades, Mask 580
And thou art worthy that thou shouldst not know Mask 788
line not in Trinity ms
line not in Bridgewater ms
I know this quest of yours, and free intent Arcades 34
For know by lot from *Jove* I am the powr Arcades 44
Blind mouthes! that scarce themselves know how to hold Lycidas 119
I know my tongue but little Grace can do thee Vacation 10
My sorrows are too dark for day to know: Passion 33
In all her equipage; besides to know Sonnet 17, 9
To measure life, learn thou betimes, and know Sonnet 21, 9
Yet know the Lord hath chose Psalm 4, 13
Sea-paths in shoals do slide. And know no dearth. Psalm 8, 22
They know not nor will understand, Psalm 82, 17
Then shall they know that thou whose name Psalm 83, 65
Hast hid *where none shall know*. Psalm 85, 8

Knowest
Instruct me, for Thou know'st; Thou from the first Par Lost 1.19
Against thy Fathers head? and know'st for whom; Par Lost 2.730
My sole complacence! well thou know'st how dear, Par Lost 3.276
Som dreadful thing no doubt; for well thou knowst Par Lost 4.426
On purpose, hard thou knowst it to exclude Par Lost 4.584
To thee no reason; who knowst only good, Par Lost 4.895
Insulting Angel, well thou knowst I stood Par Lost 4.926
Satan, I know thy strength, and thou knowst mine, Par Lost 4.1006
For to themselves I left them, and thou knowst, Par Lost 6.689
And thou thir Natures know'st, & gav'st them Names, Par Lost 7.493
Is yet distinct by name, thence, as thou know'st Par Lost 7.536
Of destind habitation; but thou know'st Par Lost 7.622
To come and play before thee, know'st thou not Par Lost 8.372
Well manag'd; of that skill the more thou know'st, Par Lost 8.573
Answer'd. Let it suffice thee that thou know'st Par Lost 8.620
Befall thee sever'd from me; for thou knowst Par Lost 9.252
On Earth these thy transgressors, but thou knowst Par Lost 10.72
So now of what thou knowst not, who desir'st Par Lost 10.948
Adam, thou know'st Heav'n his, and all the Earth. Par Lost 11.335
I see thou know'st what is of use to know, Par Reg 3.7
Know'st thou not that my rising is thy fall, Par Reg 3.201
That wrought with me: thou know'st the Magistrates Samson 850
That *Kiriathaim* held, thou knowst me now Samson 1081
Sam. Thou knowst I am an *Ebrew*, therefore tell them, Samson 1319
Man. Sad, but thou knowst to *Israelites* not saddest Samson 1560
Thou know'st it must be now thy only bent Vacation 55

Knowing
Knowledge of Good bought dear by knowing ill. Par Lost 4.222
Our knowing, as to highest wisdom seemd, Par Lost 7.83
Govern the rest, self-knowing, and from thence Par Lost 7.510
And finde thee knowing not of Beasts alone, Par Lost 8.438
Knowing both Good and Evil as they know. Par Lost 9.709
Had shadow'd them from knowing ill, was gon, Par Lost 9.1055
All, though all-knowing, what had past with Man Par Lost 10.227
Nor knowing us nor known: and if by prayer Par Lost 11.307
Not knowing to what Land, yet firm believes: Par Lost 12.127
Knowing who I am, as I know who thou art? Par Reg 1.356
To know, and knowing worship God aright, Par Reg 2.475
Of knowing what I aught: he who receives Par Reg 4.288
Who knowing I shall raign past thy preventing, Par Reg 4.492
Knowing, as needs I must, by thee betray'd? Samson 840
Yet knowing thir advantages too many, Samson 1401

Knowledge
Of knowledge past or present, could have fear'd, Par Lost 1.628
Cut off, and for the Book of knowledg fair Par Lost 3.47
Our Death the Tree of knowledge grew fast by, Par Lost 4.221
1667 'Knowledge'
Knowledge of Good bought dear by knowing ill. Par Lost 4.222
Of knowledge, planted by the Tree of Life, Par Lost 4.424
One fatal Tree there stands of Knowledge call'd, Par Lost 4.514
Forbidden them to taste: Knowledge forbidd'n? Par Lost 4.515
To keep them low whom knowledge might exalt Par Lost 4.525
Is womans happiest knowledge and her praise. Par Lost 4.638
Of interdicted Knowledge: fair it seem'd, Par Lost 5.52
Nor God, nor Man; is Knowledge so despis'd? Par Lost 5.60
Our knowledge or opinion; then retires Par Lost 5.108
Our knowledge, and the scale of Nature set Par Lost 5.509
Unknown, which human knowledg could not reach: Par Lost 7.75
Of knowledge within bounds; beyond abstain Par Lost 7.120
But Knowledge is as food, and needs no less Par Lost 7.126
1669 'knowledge'
Which tasted works knowledge of Good and Evil, Par Lost 7.543
The thirst I had of knowledge, and voutsaf't Par Lost 8.8
Knowledg of good and ill, which I have set Par Lost 8.324
Thir Nature, with such knowledg God endu'd Par Lost 8.353
All higher knowledge in her presence falls Par Lost 8.551
To Knowledge? By the Threatner, look on mee, Par Lost 9.687
To happier life, knowledge of Good and Evil; Par Lost 9.697
Knowledge of Good and Evil in this Tree, Par Lost 9.723

Knowledge(*cont*)
What can your knowledge hurt him, or this Tree Par Lost 9.727
Of Knowledge, knowledge both of good and evil; Par Lost 9.752
Of knowledg, nor was God-head from her thought. Par Lost 9.790
In knowledge, as the Gods who all things know; Par Lost 9.804
But keep the odds of Knowledge in my power Par Lost 9.820
Of Knowledge he must pass, there he her met, Par Lost 9.849
Against his better knowledge, not deceav'd, Par Lost 9.998
Bad Fruit of Knowledge, if this be to know, Par Lost 9.1073
His knowledge of Good lost, and Evil got, Par Lost 11.87
Forbidd'n knowledge by forbidd'n means. Par Lost 12.279
Of knowledge, what this Vessel can containe; Par Lost 12.559
1669 'Knowledge'
Deeds to thy knowledge answerable, add Faith, Par Lost 12.582
What might improve my knowledge or their own; Par Reg 1.213
For what concerns my knowledge God reveals. Par Reg 1.293
Thir taste no knowledge works, at least of evil, Par Reg 2.371
In knowledge, all things in it comprehend, Par Reg 4.224
All knowledge is not couch't in *Moses* Law, Par Reg 4.225

Known
Long after known in *Palestine*, and nam'd Par Lost 1.80
Then were they known to men by various Names, Par Lost 1.374
Say, Muse, thir Names then known, who first, who last, Par Lost 1.376
And *Ida* known, thence on the Snowy top Par Lost 1.515
And some the Architect: his hand was known Par Lost 1.732
To know, and this once known, shall soon return, Par Lost 2.839
Admonisht by his ear, and strait was known Par Lost 3.647
Well known from Heav'n; and since Meridian hour Par Lost 4.581
Of Father, Son, and Brother first were known. Par Lost 4.757
Or undiminisht brightness, to be known Par Lost 4.836
Already known what he for news had thought Par Lost 6.20
O now in danger tri'd, now known in Armes Par Lost 6.418
Till now not known, but known as soon contemnd, Par Lost 6.432
What may no less perhaps availe us known, Par Lost 7.85
Ordain'd for uses to his Lord best known. Par Lost 8.106
Not in themselves, all thir known vertue appeers Par Lost 9.110
Be real, why not known, since easier shunnd? Par Lost 9.699
Shall I appeer? shall I to him make known Par Lost 9.817
So eminently never had bin known. Par Lost 9.976
From this delightful Fruit, nor known till now Par Lost 9.1023
But such as at this day to *Indians* known Par Lost 9.1102
No ground of enmitie between us known, Par Lost 9.1151
Was known in Heav'n; for what can scape the Eye Par Lost 10.5
And person, had'st thou known thy self aright. Par Lost 10.156
Had rounded still th' *Horizon*, and not known Par Lost 10.684
Happier, had it suffic'd him to have known Par Lost 11.88
Nor knowing us nor known: and if by prayer Par Lost 11.307
Now amplier known thy Saviour and thy Lord, Par Lost 12.544
Known partly, and soon found of whom they spake Par Reg 1.262
And not well understood as good not known? Par Reg 1.437
To thee not known, whence hast thou then thy truth, Par Reg 1.446
Andrew and *Simon*, famous after known Par Reg 2.7
A Carpenter thy Father known, thy self Par Reg 2.414
Famous he was in Heaven, on Earth less known; Par Reg 3.68
Yet he at length, time to himself best known, Par Reg 3.433
But now hath cast me off as never known, Samson 641
Was it not weakness also to make known Samson 778
If thou at all art known. Much I have heard Samson 1082
And had perform'd it if my known offence Samson 1218
Not half his riches known, and yet despis'd, Mask 724
Bridgewater ms 'knowne'
Trinity ms 'knowne'
His praise and glory was in *Israel* known. Psalm 114, 6
'Twas such a shifter, that if truth were known, Carrier 5
Though later born, then to have known the dayes Sonnet 10, 9
By the known rules of antient libertie, Sonnet 12, 2
Trinity ms 'knowne' ←'known'
Or wondrous acts be known, Psalm 88, 50

Knows
Devoid of sense and motion? and who knows, Par Lost 2.151
For want of other prey, but that he knows Par Lost 2.806
His end with mine involvd; and knows that I Par Lost 2.807
This knows my punisher; therefore as farr Par Lost 4.103
Of immortality. So little knows Par Lost 4.201
Drew many, whom thir place knows here no more; Par Lost 7.144
Continu'd making, and who knows how long Par Lost 9.138
His worshippers; he knows that in the day Par Lost 9.705
And knows, and speaks, and reasons, and discerns, Par Lost 9.765
Of wandring, as thou call'st it, which who knows Par Lost 9.1146
Or in some other dismal place who knows Par Lost 10.787
The doubt, since humane reach no further knows. Par Lost 10.793
Who knows, or more then this, that we are dust, Par Lost 11.199
The Father knows the Son; therefore secure Par Reg 1.176
Of gaining *David*'s Throne no man knows when, Par Reg 4.471
Reject not then what offerd means, who knows Samson 516
He's gone, and who knows how he may report Samson 1350
That no second knows nor third, Samson 1701
On *Circes* Iland fell (who knows not *Circe* Mask 50
1637 'knowes'
Well knows to still the wilde winds when they roar, Mask 87
He can requite thee, for he knows the charms Sonnet 8, 5
By watry streams, and in his season knows Psalm 1, 8
For the Lord knows th' upright way of the just, Psalm 1, 15
(For whom to chuse he knows) Psalm 4, 16

Ksar
In *Hispahan*, or where the *Russian Ksar* Par Lost 11.394

Laborious
With what compulsion and laborious flight Par Lost 2.80

Laborious(*cont*)	
Laborious, till day droop; while here we dwell,	Par Lost 11.178
Laborious works, unwillingly this rest	Samson 14
To scorn delights, and live laborious dayes;	Lycidas 72
Labour	
Our labour must be to pervert that end,	Par Lost 1.164
Through labour and indurance. This deep world	Par Lost 2.262
So he with difficulty and labour hard	Par Lost 2.1021
Mov'd on, with difficulty and labour hee;	Par Lost 2.1022
Of thir sweet Gardning labour then suffic'd	Par Lost 4.328
Labour and rest, as day and night to men	Par Lost 4.613
And at our pleasant labour, to reform	Par Lost 4.625
To respit his day-labour with repast,	Par Lost 5.232
Nor long shall be our labour, yet ere dawne,	Par Lost 6.492
Or save the Sun his labour, and that swift	Par Lost 8.133
And hunger both, from labour, at the houre	Par Lost 8.213
Adam, well may we labour still to dress	Par Lost 9.205
Aid us, the work under our labour grows,	Par Lost 9.208
Labour, as to debarr us when we need	Par Lost 9.236
If such affront I labour to avert	Par Lost 9.302
Be frustrate, do, undo, and labour loose,	Par Lost 9.944
Without our hazard, labour, or allarme,	Par Lost 10.491
From the Suns Axle; they with labour push'd	Par Lost 10.670
Glanc'd on the ground, with labour I must earne	Par Lost 10.1054
My labour will sustain me; and least Cold	Par Lost 10.1056
To labour calls us now with sweat impos'd,	Par Lost 11.172
By suffering, and earne rest from labour won,	Par Lost 11.375
Far other labour to be undergon	Par Reg 2.132
Put to the labour of a Beast, debas't	Samson 37
Sam. Not in thir Idol-worship, but by labour	Samson 1365
Is now the labour of my thoughts, 'tis likeliest	Mask 192
The labour of an age in piled Stones,	Shakespear 2
That labour up the Hill of heav'nly Truth,	Sonnet 9, 4
Doth God exact day labour, light deny'd,	Sonnet 19, 7
Laboured	
Tunes sweetest his love-labor'd song; now reignes	Par Lost 5.41
And over-labour'd at thir publick Mill,	Samson 1327
Co. Two such I saw, what time the labour'd Oxe	Mask 291
Labourer	
And gathers ground fast at the Labourers heel	Par Lost 12.631
Labourers	
That ten day-labourers could not end,	Allegro 109
Labouring	
With *Lapland* Witches, while the labouring Moon	Par Lost 2.665
Labouring had rais'd, and thus to *Eve* repli'd.	Par Lost 10.1012
Labouring, two massie clods of Iron and Brass	Par Lost 11.565
Labouring the soile, and reaping plenteous crop,	Par Lost 12.18
Of Archers, nor of labouring Pioners	Par Reg 3.330
Labouring thy mind	Samson 1298
The labouring clouds do often rest:	Allegro 74
Labours	
Let us divide our labours, thou where choice	Par Lost 9.214
Her Tresses, and her rural labours crown,	Par Lost 9.841
Sorrows, and labours, opposition, hate,	Par Reg 4.386
His labours, for thou canst, to peaceful end.	Samson 709
If they intend advantage of my labours	Samson 1259
After her wandring labours long,	Mask 1006
line not in Bridgewater ms	
Of labours huge and hard, too hard for human wight.	Passion 14
Labyrinth	
Her watrie Labyrinth, whereof who drinks,	Par Lost 2.584
In Labyrinth of many a round self-rowld,	Par Lost 9.183
La. Dim darknes, and this leavy Labyrinth.	Mask 278
Trinity ms 'labyrinth'	
Bridgewater ms 'laborinth'	
Lack	
Sam. For want of words no doubt, or lack of breath,	Samson 905
And lack of load, made his life burdensom,	Another 24
line not in 1658 text	
Lackey	
A thousand liveried Angels lacky her,	Mask 455
1637 'lackie'	
Bridgewater ms 'lackey'	
Trinity ms 'lackey' ←'lakey'	
Lad	
Gideon and *Jephtha*, and the Shepherd lad,	Par Reg 2.439
Brought to my mind a certain Shepherd Lad	Mask 619
Trinity ms 'lad'	
Bridgewater ms 'lad'	
1637 'lad'	
Laden	
Thir penance, laden with Fruit, like that	Par Lost 10.550
Laden with blooming gold, had need the guard	Mask 394
Ladies	
And Ladies of th' *Hesperides*, that seem'd	Par Reg 2.357
Lords, Ladies, Captains, Councellors, or Priests,	Samson 1653
With store of Ladies, whose bright eies	Allegro 121
The Faiery Ladies daunc't upon the hearth;	Vacation 60
Ladon	
By sandy *Ladons* Lillied banks.	Arcades 97
Lady	
Co. What chance good Lady hath bereft you thus?	Mask 277
Trinity ms 'La.'	
1637 'Ladie'	
Bridgewater ms 'lady'	
Co. And left your fair side all unguarded Lady?	Mask 283
1637 'Ladie'	
Trinity ms 'Ladie'	
Lady(*cont*)	
Bridgewater ms 'ladye'	
I can conduct you Lady to a low	Mask 319
1637 'Ladie'	
Trinity ms 'Ladie'	
Bridgewater ms 'ladie'	
But O my Virgin Lady, where is she?	Mask 507
Bridgewater ms 'lady'	
1637 'Ladie'	
Trinity ms 'Ladie'	
Of my most honour'd Lady, your dear sister.	Mask 564
Trinity ms 'Ladie'	
Bridgewater ms 'lady'	
The aidless innocent Lady his wish't prey,	Mask 574
Bridgewater ms 'ladie'	
1637 'Ladie'	
Trinity ms 'Ladie'	
How to secure the Lady from surprisal,	Mask 618
Bridgewater ms 'lady'	
1637 'Ladie'	
Trinity ms 'ladie'	
Comus. Nay Lady sit; if I but wave this wand,	Mask 659
Trinity ms 'Ladie'	
Bridgewater ms 'ladye'	
1637 'Ladie'	
Co. Why are you vext Lady? why do you frown?	Mask 666
Bridgewater ms 'ladie'	
Trinity ms 'Ladie'	
1637 'Ladie'	
And timely rest have wanted, but fair Virgin	Mask 689
Trinity ms 'faire virgin' ←'fairest virgin' ←'sweet Ladie'	
List Lady be not coy, and be not cosen'd	Mask 737
1637 'Ladie'	
Trinity ms 'Ladie'	
line not in Bridgewater ms	
We cannot free the Lady that sits here	Mask 818
1637 'Ladie'	
Trinity ms 'La.'	
Bridgewater ms 'lady'	
Brightest Lady look on me,	Mask 910
Trinity ms 'ladie'	
Bridgewater ms 'lady'	
Com Lady while Heaven lends us grace,	Mask 938
1637 'Ladie'	
Bridgewater ms 'sister'	
Trinity ms 'Ladie'	
Noble Lord, and Lady bright,	Mask 966
Trinity ms 'Ladie'	
poore ladie thou hast need of some refreshing	Mask Tr. ms 20.09
'ladie' ←'Ladie'	
poore ladie thou hast neede of some refreshinge	Mask Br. ms 660
To serve the Lady of this place.	Arcades 105
Trinity ms 'Ladie'	
Gentle Lady may thy grave	Winchester 47
Lady that in the prime of earliest youth,	Sonnet 9, 1
Trinity ms 'Ladie'	
Laertes	
Alcinous, host of old *Laertes* Son,	Par Lost 9.441
Lag	
Leads thee, I shall not lag behinde, nor erre	Par Lost 10.266
Lagging	
Came lagging after; say if he be here.	Samson 337
Nipt with the lagging rear of winters frost.	Samson 1577
Lahor	
To *Agra* and *Lahor* of great *Mogul*	Par Lost 11.391
Laid	
In horrible destruction laid thus low,	Par Lost 1.137
ms 'layd'	
Shot after us in storm, oreblown hath laid	Par Lost 1.172
ms 'layd'	
With unexperienc't thought, and laid me downe	Par Lost 4.457
O fair foundation laid whereon to build	Par Lost 4.521
Strait side by side were laid, nor turnd I weene	Par Lost 4.741
Now laid perhaps asleep secure of harme.	Par Lost 4.791
Lights on a heap of nitrous Powder, laid	Par Lost 4.815
From off the files of warr; there they him laid	Par Lost 6.339
A triple mounted row of Pillars laid	Par Lost 6.572
Soft on the flourie herb I found me laid	Par Lost 8.254
Laid on our Necks. Remember with what mild	Par Lost 10.1046
Choicest and best; then sacrificing, laid	Par Lost 11.438
A Lazar-house it seemd, wherein were laid	Par Lost 11.479
Contriv'd, and of provisions laid in large	Par Lost 11.732
And sayings laid up, portending strange events.	Par Reg 2.104
Commun'd in silent walk, then laid him down	Par Reg 2.261
Led captive, and *Jerusalem* laid waste,	Par Reg 3.283
Remove their swelling Epithetes thick laid	Par Reg 4.343
Of thunder, chas'd the clouds, and laid the winds,	Par Reg 4.429
Ore laid with black staid Wisdoms hue.	Penseroso 16
Softly on my eye-lids laid.	Penseroso 150
He laid aside; and here with us to be,	Nativity 12
Hath laid her Babe to rest.	Nativity 238
Had burial, yet not laid in earth,	Winchester 32
A here alas, hath laid him in the dirt,	Carrier 2
1658 'left'	
Why hast thou laid her Hedges low	Psalm 80, 49
Let thy *good* hand be *laid*,	Psalm 80, 70
Lair	
As from his Laire the wilde Beast where he wonns	Par Lost 7.457

Lake
Chain'd on the burning Lake, nor ever thence Par Lost 1.210
ms 'lake'
With solid, as the Lake with liquid fire; Par Lost 1.229
Groveling and prostrate on yon Lake of Fire, Par Lost 1.280
ms 'lake'
Sluc'd from the Lake, a second multitude Par Lost 1.702
ms 'lake'
Of that forgetful Lake benumm not still, Par Lost 2.74
Chain'd on the burning Lake? that sure was worse. Par Lost 2.169
Into the burning Lake thir baleful streams; Par Lost 2.576
Wafted by Angels, or flew o're the Lake Par Lost 3.521
Down the slope hills, disperst, or in a Lake, Par Lost 4.261
Smooth Lake, that to me seemd another Skie. Par Lost 4.459
From Hill or steaming Lake, duskie or grey, Par Lost 5.186
Neer that bituminous Lake where *Sodom* flam'd; Par Lost 10.562
From standing lake to tripping ebbe, that stole Par Lost 11.847
On this side the broad lake *Genezaret*, Par Reg 2.23
Araxes and the *Caspian* lake, thence on Par Reg 3.271
In fog, or fire, by lake, or moorish fen, Mask 433
Goddess of the silver lake, Mask 865
B.M. ms 'Lake'
The Pilot of the *Galilean* lake, Lycidas 109

Lakes
Rocks, Caves, Lakes, Fens, Bogs, Dens, and shades of death, Par Lost 2.621
And Lakes and running Streams the waters fill; Par Lost 7.397
Others on Silver Lakes and Rivers Bath'd Par Lost 7.437

Lamb
Unsuckt of Lamb or Kid, that tend thir play. Par Lost 9.583
Oft sacrificing Bullock, Lamb, or Kid, Par Lost 12.20

Lambs
To gorge the flesh of Lambs or yeanling Kids Par Lost 3.434
Ewes and thir bleating Lambs over the Plaine, Par Lost 11.649
Amongst their Ews, the little Hills like Lambs. Psalm 114, 12

Lament
The *Syrian* Damsels to lament his fate Par Lost 1.448
Torment, and loud lament, and furious rage. Par Lost 8.244
Yet all had heard, with audible lament Par Lost 11.266
Lament not *Eve*, but patiently resigne Par Lost 11.287
Farr less I now lament for one whole World Par Lost 11.874
Har. By *Astaroth* e're long thou shalt lament Samson 1242
Whom Universal nature did lament, Lycidas 60
A voice of weeping heard, and loud lament; Nativity 183
Her false imagin'd loss cease to lament, Fair Inf 72

Lamentable
View'd first thir lamentable lot, and found Par Lost 2.617

Lamentation
Cocytus, nam'd of lamentation loud Par Lost 2.579
Man. Come, come, no time for lamentation now, Samson 1708
And lamentation to the Sons of *Caphtor* Samson 1713

Lamented
Thus *Adam* to himself lamented loud Par Lost 10.845

Lamenting
Then who created thee lamenting learne, Par Lost 5.894
Lamenting turnd full sad; O what are these, Par Lost 11.675

Lamp
And feel thy sovran vital Lamp; but thou Par Lost 3.22
Days, months, & years, towards his all-chearing Lamp Par Lost 3.581
His constant Lamp, and waves his purple wings, Par Lost 4.764
First in his East the glorious Lamp was seen, Par Lost 7.370
On his Hill top, to light the bridal Lamp. Par Lost 8.520
Or let my Lamp at midnight hour, Penseroso 85
Her sleeping Lord with Handmaid Lamp attending. Nativity 242
To fill thy odorous Lamp with deeds of light, Sonnet 9, 10
Trinity ms 'lamp'

Lamps
Of Starry Lamps and blazing Cressets fed Par Lost 1.728
ms 'lamps'
And from within the golden Lamps that burne Par Lost 5.713
That shine, yet bear thir bright officious Lamps, Par Lost 9.104
Seaven Lamps as in a Zodiac representing Par Lost 12.255
That nature hung in Heav'n, and fill'd their Lamps Mask 198
line not in Bridgewater ms
1637 'lamps'
Trinity ms 'lamps'

Lance
To mortal combat or carreer with Lance) Par Lost 1.766
ms 'lance'

Lancelot
Lancelot or *Pelleas*, or *Pellenore*, Par Reg 2.361

Land
That felt unusual weight, till on dry Land Par Lost 1.227
ms 'land'
He lights, if it were Land that ever burn'd Par Lost 1.228
ms 'land'
Like Night, and darken'd all the Land of *Nile:* Par Lost 1.343
Of *Doric* Land; or who with *Saturn* old Par Lost 1.519
ms 'land'
In ancient *Greece;* and in *Ausonian* land Par Lost 1.739
Of Whirlwind and dire Hail, which on firm land Par Lost 2.589
Nor good dry Land: nigh founderd on he fares, Par Lost 2.940
Firm land imbosom'd without Firmament, Par Lost 3.75
So on this windie Sea of Land, the Fiend Par Lost 3.440
Over the *Promis'd Land* to God so dear, Par Lost 3.531
To *Beersaba*, where the *Holy Land* Par Lost 3.536
The goodly prospect of some forein land Par Lost 3.548
O're Sea and Land: him *Satan* thus accostes; Par Lost 3.653
When first on this delightful Land he spreads Par Lost 4.643

Land(*cont*)
On this delightful land, nor herb, fruit, floure, Par Lost 4.652
By morrow Eevning, and from Land to Land Par Lost 4.662
Into one place, and let dry Land appeer. Par Lost 7.284
The dry Land, Earth, and the great receptacle Par Lost 7.307
And seems a moving Land, and at his Gilles Par Lost 7.415
As Plants: ambiguous between Sea and Land Par Lost 7.473
This Earth? reciprocal, if Land be there, Par Lost 8.144
Where to lie hid; Sea he had searcht and Land Par Lost 9.76
At *Darien*, thence to the Land where flowes Par Lost 9.81
Now Land, now Sea, and Shores with Forrest crownd, Par Lost 9.117
Farr to the inland retir'd, about the walls Par Lost 10.423
1667 'in-land'
Like change on Sea and Land, sideral blast, Par Lost 10.693
Land, Sea, and Aire, and every kinde that lives, Par Lost 11.337
His kindred and false Gods, into a Land Par Lost 12.122
Not knowing to what Land, yet firm believes: Par Lost 12.127
With God, who call'd him, in a land unknown. Par Lost 12.134
Gift to his Progenie of all that Land; Par Lost 12.138
From *Canaan*, to a Land hereafter call'd Par Lost 12.156
Into the Sea: to sojourn in that Land Par Lost 12.159
With glory and spoile back to thir promis'd Land. Par Lost 12.172
With loath'd intrusion, and fill all the land; Par Lost 12.178
As on drie land between two christal walls, Par Lost 12.197
Conducted by his Angel to the Land Par Lost 12.259
God, as to leave them, and expose thir Land, Par Lost 12.339
Made famous in a Land and times obscure; Par Reg 3.94
Judaea now and all the promis'd land Par Reg 3.157
Thir Fathers in the land of *Egypt* serv'd, Par Reg 3.379
Nor in the land of their captivity Par Reg 3.420
While to their native land with joy they hast, Par Reg 3.437
When to the promis'd land thir Fathers pass'd; Par Reg 3.439
As in the land of darkness yet in light, Samson 99
The harrass of thir Land, beset me round; Samson 257
But who is this, what thing of Sea or Land? Samson 710
Whistles ore the Furrow'd Land, Allegro 64
The up-land Hamlets will invite, Allegro 92
She strikes a universall Peace through Sea and Land. Nativity 52
He feels from *Juda*'s Land Nativity 221
And past from *Pharian* fields to *Canaan* Land, Psalm 114, 3
Smote the first-born of *Egypt* Land. Psalm 136, 38
He gave their Land therin to dwell. Psalm 136, 74
Young *Hyacinth* the pride of *Spartan* land; Fair Inf 26
While Avarice, and Rapine share the land. Sonnet 15, 14
1694 'Land'
And post o're Land and Ocean without rest: Sonnet 19, 13
Lay deep their plots together through each Land, Psalm 2, 4
And fill'd the land *at last*. Psalm 80, 40
When as he pass'd through Aegypt land; Psalm 81, 19
Through out the land of thy abode Psalm 81, 37
Thee out of Aegypt land Psalm 81, 42
Thy Land to favour graciously Psalm 85, 1
To dwell within our Land. Psalm 85, 40
Our Land shall forth in plenty throw Psalm 85, 51
Of Jacobs *Land, though there be store*, Psalm 87, 7
Thy justice in the *gloomy* land Psalm 88, 51
What Land, what Seat of rest thou bidst me seek, Prose 12, 4
Beyond the Realm of *Gaul*, a Land there lies, Prose 12, 8

Landed
First lighted from his Wing, and landed safe Par Lost 10.316

Landmark
Ith' midst an Altar as the Land-mark stood Par Lost 11.432

Land-pilot
Would overtask the best Land-Pilots art, Mask 309
1637 'land-pilots'
Trinity ms 'land-pilots'
Bridgewater ms 'land pilots'

Lands
Or in *Valdarno*, to descry new Lands, Par Lost 1.290
ms 'lands'
There lands the Fiend, a spot like which perhaps Par Lost 3.588
Imagind Lands and Regions in the Moon: Par Lost 5.263
Flying, and over Lands with mutual wing Par Lost 7.429
In foraign Lands thir memorie be lost Par Lost 12.46
And he can spred thy Name o're Lands and Seas, Sonnet 8, 7
Trinity ms 'lands'

Landscape
Scowls ore the dark'nd lantskip Snow, or showre; Par Lost 2.491
That Lantskip: And of pure now purer aire Par Lost 4.153
Discovering in wide Lantskip all the East Par Lost 5.142
Whilst the Lantskip round it measures, Allegro 70

Lane
Co. I know each lane, and every alley green Mask 311
that lurks by hedge or lane of this dead circuit Mask Tr. ms 16.40
that lurks by hedge or lane, of this dead circuit Mask Br. ms 393

Language
Thir language and thir wayes, they also know, Par Lost 8.373
What may this mean? Language of Man pronounc't Par Lost 9.553
Quite out thir Native Language, and instead Par Lost 12.54
As in our native Language can I find Par Reg 4.333
Hail native Language, that by sinews weak Vacation 1

Languish
And with desire to languish without hope, Par Lost 10.995

Languished
Enlightn'd, and thir languisht hope reviv'd. Par Lost 6.497
With languish't head unpropt, Samson 119
It withers on the stalk with languish't head. Mask 744
line not in Bridgewater ms

Languished(*cont*)
Trinity ms 'with languish't head' ←'and fades away'
And the languisht Mothers Womb Winchester 33
Languishing
Before the present object languishing Par Lost 10.996
Lank
Who piteous of her woes, rear'd her lank head, Mask 836
1637 'lanke'
Bridgewater ms 'lanke'
Trinity ms 'lanck'
Lantern
In thy dark lantern thus close up the Stars, Mask 197
1637 'lanterne'
line not in Bridgewater ms
1673 'Lantern'
Trinity ms 'lanterne'
And he by Friars Lanthorn led Allegro 104
Lap
Or palmie hilloc, or the flourie lap Par Lost 4.254
And Hyacinth, Earths freshest softest lap. Par Lost 9.1041
Herculean Samson from the Harlot-lap Par Lost 9.1060
As in my Mothers lap? there I should rest Par Lost 10.778
Into thy Mothers lap, or be with ease Par Lost 11.536
Of all my strength in the lascivious lap Samson 536
And lap it in *Elysium*, *Scylla* wept, Mask 257
Lap me in soft *Lydian* Aires, Allegro 136
On whose fresh lap the swart Star sparely looks, Lycidas 138
And peace shall lull him in her flowry lap; Vacation 84
The Flowry *May*, who from her green lap throws May Morn 3
Lapland
With *Lapland* Witches, while the labouring Moon Par Lost 2.665
Lapse
And liquid Lapse of murmuring Streams; by these, Par Lost 8.263
Since thy original lapse, true Libertie Par Lost 12.83
Lapsed
His lapsed powers, though forfeit and enthrall'd Par Lost 3.176
Whom they triumph'd once lapst. Thus were they plagu'd Par Lost 10.572
Larboard
Or when *Ulysses* on the Larbord shunnd Par Lost 2.1019
Large
Prone on the Flood, extended long and large Par Lost 1.195
Left him at large to his own dark designs, Par Lost 1.213
Ethereal temper, massy, large and round, Par Lost 1.285
By that uxorious King, whose heart though large, Par Lost 1.444
Reduc'd thir shapes immense, and were at large, Par Lost 1.790
ms defective here
Here walk'd the Fiend at large in spacious field. Par Lost 3.430
Into a *Limbo* large and broad, since calld Par Lost 3.495
Over Mount *Sion*, and, though that were large, Par Lost 3.530
Which to our general Sire gave prospect large Par Lost 4.144
Southward through *Eden* went a River large, Par Lost 4.223
His fair large Front and Eye sublime declar'd Par Lost 4.300
Free leave so large to all things else, and choice Par Lost 4.434
For us too large, where thy abundance wants Par Lost 4.730
Our givers thir own gifts, and large bestow Par Lost 5.317
From large bestowd, where Nature multiplies Par Lost 5.318
She gathers, Tribute large, and on the board Par Lost 5.343
And we have yet large day, for scarce the Sun Par Lost 5.558
And left large field, unsafe within the wind Par Lost 6.309
Of future, in small room large heart enclos'd, Par Lost 7.486
An Edifice too large for him to fill, Par Lost 8.104
That not to know at large of things remote Par Lost 8.191
Find pastime, and beare rule; thy Realm is large. Par Lost 8.375
Wings growing, and Dominion giv'n me large Par Lost 10.244
(Erelong to swim at large) and laugh; for which Par Lost 11.626
1667 'larg'
Contriv'd, and of provisions laid in large Par Lost 11.732
With large Wine-offerings pour'd, and sacred Feast, Par Lost 12.21
Acceptance of large Grace, from servil fear Par Lost 12.305
Large liberty to round this Globe of Earth, Par Reg 1.365
To thy large heart give utterance due, thy heart Par Reg 3.10
Large Countries, and in field great Battels win, Par Reg 3.73
The seats of mightiest Monarchs, and so large Par Reg 3.262
In thy large recompense, and shalt be good Lycidas 184
New Presbyter is but *Old Priest* writ Large. Forcers 20
Trinity ms 'large'
Trinity ms 'large' ←'at large'
And set at large; now spare, Psalm 4, 5
Ask large enough, and I, *besought*, Psalm 81, 43
Large-limbed
And large-lim'd *Og* he did subdue, Psalm 136, 69
1673 'large-limb'd'
Largely
Hystorian, who thus largely hast allayd Par Lost 8.7
Took largely, of thir mutual guilt the Seale, Par Lost 9.1043
Gaz'd hot, and of the fresh Wave largely drew, Par Lost 11.845
And mak'st them largely drink the tears Psalm 80, 23
Larger
Now Dragon grown, larger then whom the Sun Par Lost 10.529
Lark
Thus wore out night, and now the Herald Lark Par Reg 2.279
Ere morrow wake, or the low roosted lark Mask 317
Trinity ms 'low-roosted Larke'
1637 'larke'
Bridgewater ms 'larke'
Trinity ms 'ere morrow wake' ←'ere the larke rowse'
To hear the Lark begin his flight, Allegro 41

Lars
The *Lars*, and *Lemures* moan with midnight plaint, Nativity 191
Lascivious
Began to cast lascivious Eyes, she him Par Lost 9.1014
Old, and lascivious, and from *Rome* retir'd Par Reg 4.91
Of all my strength in the lascivious lap Samson 536
But most by leud and lavish act of sin, Mask 465
Trinity ms 'lewd and lavish' ←'the lascivious'
Last
Say, Muse, thir Names then known, who first, who last, Par Lost 1.376
Belial came last, then whom a Spirit more lewd Par Lost 1.490
Thir number last he summs. And now his heart Par Lost 1.571
Tears such as Angels weep, burst forth: at last Par Lost 1.620
In heighth or depth, still first and last will Reign Par Lost 2.324
The weight of all and our last hope relies. Par Lost 2.416
Alone the dreadful voyage; till at last Par Lost 2.426
Farr off the flying Fiend: at last appeer Par Lost 2.643
At last this odious offspring whom thou seest Par Lost 2.781
The stedfast Earth. At last his Sail-broad Vannes Par Lost 2.927
But now at last the sacred influence Par Lost 2.1034
But Mercy first and last shall brightest shine. Par Lost 3.134
Death last, and with his Carcass glut the Grave: Par Lost 3.259
Though last created, that for him I spare Par Lost 3.278
And long he wanderd, till at last a gleame Par Lost 3.499
All night; at last by break of chearful dawne Par Lost 3.545
O then at last relent: is there no place Par Lost 4.79
Heav'ns last best gift, my ever new delight, Par Lost 5.19
Of our last Eevnings talk, in this thy dream, Par Lost 5.115
Him first, him last, him midst, and without end. Par Lost 5.165
Fairest of Starrs, last in the train of Night, Par Lost 5.166
More aerie, last the bright consummate floure Par Lost 5.481
Your bodies may at last turn all to Spirit, Par Lost 5.497
And perfet while they stood; how last unfould Par Lost 5.568
Tenfold the length of this terrene: at last Par Lost 6.78
Whence in perpetual fight they needs must last Par Lost 6.693
In universal ruin last, and now Par Lost 6.797
Incumberd him with ruin: Hell at last Par Lost 6.874
And Bush with frizl'd hair implicit: last Par Lost 7.323
The Sixt, and of Creation last arose Par Lost 7.449
Smooth sliding without step, last led me up Par Lost 8.302
As high he soard, obnoxious first or last Par Lost 9.170
Persisted, yet submiss, though last, repli'd. Par Lost 9.377
Chiefly by what thy own last reasoning words Par Lost 9.379
O fairest of Creation, last and best Par Lost 9.896
Even shame, the last of evils; of the first Par Lost 9.1079
Nor alter'd his offence; yet God at last Par Lost 10.171
Whom he shall tread at last under our feet; Par Lost 10.190
On *Adam* last thus judgement he pronounc'd. Par Lost 10.197
At last as from a Cloud his fulgent head Par Lost 10.449
And season him thy last and sweetest prey. Par Lost 10.609
Both *Sin*, and *Death*, and yawning *Grave* at last Par Lost 10.635
Both in me, and without me, and so last Par Lost 10.812
But to my own conviction: first and last Par Lost 10.831
With Spirits Masculine, create at last Par Lost 10.890
By Death at last, and miserable it is Par Lost 10.981
That after wretched Life must be at last Par Lost 10.985
My early visitation, and my last Par Lost 11.275
To weigh thy Spirits down, and last consume Par Lost 11.545
Not hid, nor those things last which might preserve Par Lost 11.579
1667 'lost', 1668 errata 'last'
In factious opposition, till at last Par Lost 11.664
Thir order: last the Sire, and his three Sons Par Lost 11.736
By th' Angel, on thy feet thou stoodst at last, Par Lost 11.759
Famin and anguish will at last consume Par Lost 11.778
To whom thus *Michael*. Those whom last thou sawst Par Lost 11.787
At this last sight, assur'd that Man shall live Par Lost 11.872
Still tend from bad to worse, till God at last Par Lost 12.106
Last with one midnight stroke all the first-born Par Lost 12.189
The last, for of his Reign shall be no end. Par Lost 12.330
Upon the Temple it self: at last they seise Par Lost 12.356
Last in the Clouds from Heav'n to be reveald Par Lost 12.545
He ended; and thus *Adam* last reply'd. Par Lost 12.552
To whom thus also th' Angel last repli'd: Par Lost 12.574
Would not be last, and with the voice divine Par Reg 1.35
And last the sum of all, my Father's voice, Par Reg 1.283
Till those days ended, hunger'd then at last Par Reg 1.309
The Stoic last in Philosophic pride, Par Reg 4.300
Rather by this his last affront resolv'd, Par Reg 4.444
Thy manhood last, though yet in private bred; Par Reg 4.509
Thy wound, yet not thy last and deadliest wound Par Reg 4.622
Twice by an Angel, who at last in sight Samson 24
How frequent to desert him, and at last Samson 275
And last neglected? How wouldst thou insult Samson 944
Thir nuptials, nor this last so trecherously Samson 1023
By some great act, or of my days the last. Samson 1389
The last of me or no I cannot warrant. Samson 1426
To utter what will come at last too soon; Samson 1566
Eye-witness of what first or last was done, Samson 1594
At last with head erect thus cryed aloud, Samson 1639
At last betakes him to this ominous Wood, Mask 61
At last a soft and solemn breathing sound Mask 555
And mix no more with goodness, when at last Mask 594
Would grow inur'd to light, and com at last Mask 735
And may at last my weary age Penseroso 167
(That last infirmity of Noble mind) Lycidas 71
Last came, and last did go, Lycidas 108
At last he rose, and twitch'd his Mantle blew: Lycidas 192
And that her raign had here its last fulfilling; Nativity 106

Last(*cont*)
At last surrounds their sight Nativity 109
When at the worlds last session, Nativity 163
And then at last our bliss Nativity 165
Of him that ever was, and ay shall last, Psalm 114, 16
The daintest dishes shall be serv'd up last. Vacation 14
And last of Kings and Queens and *Hero*'s old, Vacation 47
And last of all, thy greedy self consum'd, On Time 10
That even to his last breath (ther be that say't) Another 25
line not in 1640, 1657, 1658 texts
Saves th' upright of Heart at last. Psalm 7, 42
And fill'd the land *at last*. Psalm 80, 40
Be said of Sion *last* Psalm 87, 18
And to be short, at last his guid him brings Prose 2, 1
Lasted
Summers chief honour if thou hadst out-lasted, Fair Inf 3
But had his doings lasted as they were, Another 27
Last-end
That till the worlds last-end shall make thy name to live. Fair Inf 77
Lasting
Both of lost happiness and lasting pain Par Lost 1.55
Built thir fond hopes of Glorie or lasting fame, Par Lost 3.449
Of Paradise, deare bought with lasting woes! Par Lost 10.742
Hast built thy self a live-long Monument. Shakespear 8
1663-4 'lasting *Monument*'
1632 'lasting Monument'
Him with thy lasting favour and good will. Psalm 5, 40
Thy course, there shalt thou find a lasting seat, Prose 12, 11
Lastly
Freely put off, and for him lastly dye Par Lost 3.240
Him first make sure your thrall, and lastly kill. Par Lost 10.402
Thee lastly nuptial Bowre, by mee adornd Par Lost 11.280
Violence and stripes, and lastly cruel death, Par Reg 4.388
Man. O lastly over-strong against thy self! Samson 1590
As he pronounces lastly on each deed, Lycidas 83
Late
Who from the terrour of this Arm so late Par Lost 1.113
To us is adverse. Who but felt of late Par Lost 2.77
That mighty leading Angel, who of late Par Lost 2.991
Thy creature late so lov'd, thy youngest Son Par Lost 3.151
Ill matching words and deeds long past or late. Par Lost 5.113
Late falln himself from Heav'n, is plotting now Par Lost 5.240
Of yesterday, so late hath past the lips Par Lost 5.675
From all: my Sect thou seest, now learn too late Par Lost 6.147
Through all Eternitie so late to build Par Lost 7.92
Pleas'd me long choosing, and beginning late; Par Lost 9.26
That name, unless an age too late, or cold Par Lost 9.44
When *Satan* who late fled before the threats Par Lost 9.53
Disjoyne us, and I then too late renounce Par Lost 9.884
Remarkably so late of thy so true, Par Lost 9.982
To that first naked Glorie. Such of late Par Lost 9.1115
To *Tauris* or *Casbeen*. So these the late Par Lost 10.436
Of this new glorious World, and mee so late Par Lost 10.721
Thy Justice seems; yet to say truth, too late, Par Lost 10.755
With other echo late I taught your Shades Par Lost 10.861
By Parents, or his happiest choice too late Par Lost 10.904
Towards her, his life so late and sole delight, Par Lost 10.941
The Air attrite to Fire, as late the Clouds Par Lost 10.1073
As how with peccant Angels late they saw; Par Lost 11.70
Where Cattle pastur'd late, now scatterd lies Par Lost 11.653
Where luxurie late reign'd, Sea-monsters whelp'd Par Lost 11.751
And stabl'd; of Mankind, so numerous late, Par Lost 11.752
Though late repenting him of Man deprav'd, Par Lost 11.886
Pursuing whom he late dismissd, the Sea Par Lost 12.195
Of Paradise, so late thir happie seat, Par Lost 12.642
Destin'd to this, is late of woman born, Par Reg 1.65
To verifie that solemn message late, Par Reg 1.133
For that to me thou seem'st the man, whom late Par Reg 1.327
Him whom they heard so late expresly call'd Par Reg 2.3
Inglorious: but thou yet art not too late. Par Reg 3.42
By my advice, as nearer and of late Par Reg 3.364
The glory late of *Israel*, now the grief; Samson 179
(O that I never had! fond wish too late.) Samson 228
Though late, yet in some part to recompense Samson 746
Of such late Wassailers; yet O where els Mask 179
This evening late by then the chewing flocks Mask 540
Or did of late earths Sonnes besiege the wall Fair Inf 47
Which takes our late fantasticks with delight, Vacation 20
As thou from yeer to yeer hast sung too late Sonnet 1, 11
But my late spring no bud or blossom shew'th. Sonnet 7, 4
A Book was writ of late call'd *Tetrachordon;* Sonnet 11, 1
Methought I saw my late espoused Saint Sonnet 23, 1
Lately
Possesses lately, thither to arrive Par Lost 2.979
Now lately Heaven and Earth, another World Par Lost 2.1004
Foretold so lately what would come to pass, Par Lost 10.38
Of him so lately promiss'd to thy aid Par Lost 12.542
Now missing him thir joy so lately found, Par Reg 2.9
So lately found, and so abruptly gone, Par Reg 2.10
But lately finding him so long at home, Carrier 11
Later
Gods, yet confest later then Heav'n and Earth Par Lost 1.509
Sooner or later; which th' Almightie seeing, Par Lost 10.613
The drink of none but Kings; of later fame Par Reg 3.289
Or what (though rare) of later age, Penseroso 101
Though later born, then to have known the dayes Sonnet 10, 9
Lateral
Eurus and *Zephir* with thir lateral noise, Par Lost 10.705

Latest
Gods latest Image: I describ'd his way Par Lost 4.567
My fairest, my espous'd, my latest found, Par Lost 5.18
These latter scenes confine my roving vers, Passion 22
1673 'latest scenes'
And that he had tane up his latest Inne, Carrier 13
Out of the tender mouths of latest bearth, Psalm 8, 4
Latona
Might she the wise *Latona* be, Arcades 20
Raild at *Latona*'s twin-born progenie Sonnet 12, 6
Latter
The latter: for what place can be for us Par Lost 2.235
The latter quick up flew, and kickt the beam; Par Lost 4.1004
Is oftest yours, the latter most is ours, Par Lost 5.489
The latter I demurre, for in thir looks Par Lost 9.558
Thus will this latter, as the former World, Par Lost 12.105
That now I use thee in my latter task: Vacation 8
These latter scenes confine my roving vers, Passion 22
1673 'latest scenes'
Laugh
I laugh, when those who at the Spear are bold Par Lost 2.204
That laugh, as if transported with some fit Par Lost 10.626
(Erelong to swim at large) and laugh; for which Par Lost 11.626
Shall laugh, the Lord shall scoff them, then severe Psalm 2, 9
Among themselves they laugh, they play, Psalm 80, 27
Laughest
Laugh'st at thir vain designes and tumults vain, Par Lost 5.737
Laughing
laughing to teach the truth Prose 6, 1
Laughs
For him who sits above and laughs the while Par Lost 2.731
Laughter
And to thir foes a laughter; for in view Par Lost 6.603
His laughter at thir quaint Opinions wide Par Lost 8.78
Offended, worth your laughter, hath giv'n up Par Lost 10.488
As mockt they storm; great laughter was in Heav'n Par Lost 12.59
And Laughter holding both his sides. Allegro 32
Laureate
To strew the Laureat Herse where *Lycid* lies. Lycidas 151
1638 'laureat'
Trinity ms 'laureat'
And Dunbarr feild resounds thy praises loud, Sonnet 16, 8
Trinity ms 'Worsters laureat wreath' ←'Dunbarr feild'
And Worsters laureat wreath; yet much remaines Sonnet 16, 9
Trinity ms 'Worsters laureat wreath' ←'twentie battles more'
1694 'Laureat'
Laurel
Laurel and Mirtle, and what higher grew Par Lost 4.694
Of Laurel ever green, and branching Palm, Samson 1735
Laurels
Yet once more, O ye Laurels, and once more Lycidas 1
1638 'laurels'
Trinity ms 'Laurells' ←'laurells'
Lavers
With lavers pure and cleansing herbs wash off Samson 1727
In nectar'd lavers strew'd with Asphodil, Mask 838
Laves
With *Nectar* pure his oozy Lock's he laves, Lycidas 175
Laving
But as I rose out of the laving stream, Par Reg 1.280
Lavinia
Of *Turnus* for *Lavinia* disespous'd, Par Lost 9.17
Lavish
But most by leud and lavish act of sin, Mask 465
Bridgewater ms 'lascivious'
Trinity ms 'lewd and lavish' ←'the lascivious'
Seem'd erst so lavish and profuse, Arcades 9
Lavished
Was lavish't on thir Sex, that inward gifts Samson 1026
Law
Our strength is equal, nor the Law unjust Par Lost 2.200
God is thy Law, thou mine: to know no more Par Lost 4.637
Haile wedded Love, mysterious Law, true source Par Lost 4.750
Law and Edict on us, who without law Par Lost 5.798
Shalt thou give Law to God, shalt thou dispute Par Lost 5.822
By force, who reason for thir Law refuse, Par Lost 6.41
Right reason for thir Law, and for thir King Par Lost 6.42
Law to our selves, our Reason is our Law. Par Lost 9.654
Of God or Death, of Law or Penaltie? Par Lost 9.775
Convict by flight, and Rebel to all Law Par Lost 10.83
His Sentence beyond dust and Natures Law, Par Lost 10.805
The Law I gave to Nature him forbids: Par Lost 11.49
Proceeded, and Oppression, and Sword-Law Par Lost 11.672
Concord and law of Nature from the Earth, Par Lost 12.29
And therefore was Law given them to evince Par Lost 12.287
Sin against Law to fight; that when they see Par Lost 12.289
Law can discover sin, but not remove, Par Lost 12.290
Of Conscience, which the Law by Ceremonies Par Lost 12.297
So law appears imperfet, and but giv'n Par Lost 12.300
1667 'Law'
To filial, works of Law to works of Faith. Par Lost 12.306
Of Law, his people into *Canaan* lead; Par Lost 12.309
Obedience to the Law of God, impos'd Par Lost 12.397
The Law of God exact he shall fulfill Par Lost 12.402
Alone fulfill the Law; thy punishment Par Lost 12.404
The Law that is against thee, and the sins Par Lost 12.416
His Spirit within them, and the Law of Faith Par Lost 12.488

Law(*cont*)
The Law of God I read, and found it sweet, Par Reg 1.207
The Teachers of our Law, and to propose Par Reg 1.212
The Law and Prophets, searching what was writ Par Reg 1.260
Meats by the Law unclean, or offer'd first Par Reg 2.328
The Temple, oft the Law with foul affronts, Par Reg 3.161
All knowledge is not couch't in *Moses* Law, Par Reg 4.225
That solace? All our Law and Story strew'd Par Reg 4.334
These only with our Law best form a King. Par Reg 4.364
These reasons in Loves law have past for good, Samson 811
Against the law of nature, law of nations, Samson 890
Therefore Gods universal Law Samson 1053
Due by the Law to capital punishment? Samson 1225
Our Law forbids at thir Religious Rites Samson 1320
Our Law, or stain my vow of *Nazarite*. Samson 1386
Scandalous or forbidden in our Law. Samson 1409
Our God, our Law, my Nation, or my self, Samson 1425
Of dire necessity, whose law in death conjoin'd Samson 1666
Of Misers treasure by an out-laws den, Mask 399
Bridgewater ms 'outlawes'
1637 'outlaws'
Trinity ms 'outlaws'
And keep unsteddy Nature to her law, Arcades 70
Trinity ms 'law'
O more exceeding love or law more just? Circum 15
Just law indeed, but more exceeding love! Circum 16
Purification in the old Law did save, Sonnet 23, 6
Trinity ms 'law'
Jehovahs Law is ever his delight, Psalm 1, 5
And in his Law he studies day and night. Psalm 1, 6
A Law of Jacobs God, *to hold* Psalm 81, 15

Lawful
Not lawful to reveal? yet for thy good Par Lost 5.570
Bear with me then, if lawful what I ask; Par Lost 8.614
Lawful desires of Nature, not beyond; Par Reg 2.230
I thought it lawful from my former act, Samson 231
Honest and lawful to deserve my food Samson 1366

Lawless
But first the lawless Tyrant, who denies Par Lost 12.173
Or lawless passions in him which he serves. Par Reg 2.472

Lawn
And sable stole of *Cipres* Lawn, Penseroso 35
The Shepherds on the Lawn, Nativity 85

Lawns
Betwixt them Lawns, or level Downs, and Flocks Par Lost 4.252
Tending my flocks hard by i' th hilly crofts, Mask 531
Trinity ms 'crofts' ←'lawns'
Then down the Lawns I ran with headlong hast Mask 568
Bridgewater ms 'lawnes'
Trinity ms 'lawnes'
1637 'lawns'
On the Lawns, and on the Leas. Mask 965
1637 'lawns'
Bridgewater ms 'lawnes'
Trinity ms 'lawns'
Russet Lawns, and Fallows Gray, Allegro 71
Together both, ere the high Lawns appear'd Lycidas 25
Trinity ms 'Launs'
1638 'lawns'

Lawrence
Lawrence of vertuous Father vertuous Son, Sonnet 20, 1

Laws
Mee though just right, and the fixt Laws of Heav'n Par Lost 2.18
Strict Laws impos'd, to celebrate his Throne Par Lost 2.241
Thy sleep dissent? new Laws thou seest impos'd; Par Lost 5.679
New Laws from him who reigns, new minds may raise Par Lost 5.680
Intends to pass triumphant, and give Laws. Par Lost 5.693
Flatly unjust, to binde with Laws the free, Par Lost 5.819
His Laws our Laws, all honour to him done Par Lost 5.844
Of Gods *Messiah;* those indulgent Laws Par Lost 5.883
New Laws to be observ'd; for I descrie Par Lost 11.228
Through the twelve Tribes, to rule by Laws ordaind: Par Lost 12.226
Ordaine them Lawes; part such as appertaine Par Lost 12.230
Of great *Messiah* shall sing. Thus Laws and Rites Par Lost 12.244
So many and so various Laws are giv'n; Par Lost 12.282
So many Laws argue so many sins Par Lost 12.283
From imposition of strict Laws, to free Par Lost 12.304
Spiritual Lawes by carnal power shall force Par Lost 12.521
On every conscience; Laws which none shall finde Par Lost 12.522
Who made our Laws to bind us, not himself, Samson 309
For with his own Laws he can best dispence. Samson 314
That live according to her sober laws, Mask 766
Bridgewater ms 'lawes'
Against the canon laws of our foundation; Mask 808
Bridgewater ms 'lawes'
Pronounc't and in his volumes taught our Lawes, Sonnet 21, 3
line not in Trinity ms
By just and equal Lawes. Psalm 82, 12
Who keepes the lawes and statutes of the Senate, Prose 10, 2

Lax
Mean while inhabit laxe, ye Powers of Heav'n, Par Lost 7.162

Lay
Lay vanquisht, rowling in the fiery Gulfe Par Lost 1.52
Lay floating many a rood, in bulk as huge Par Lost 1.196
So stretcht out huge in length the Arch-fiend lay Par Lost 1.209
His Legions, Angel Forms, who lay intrans't Par Lost 1.301
Abject and lost lay these, covering the Flood, Par Lost 1.312
A refuge from those wounds: or when we lay Par Lost 2.168

Lay(*cont*)
Then thou thy regal Scepter shalt lay by, Par Lost 3.339
Lay waving round; on som great charge imploy'd Par Lost 3.628
Lay pleasant, his grievd look he fixes sad, Par Lost 4.28
As onely in his arm the moment lay Par Lost 6.239
Chariot and Charioter lay overturnd Par Lost 6.390
Though sleeping, where I lay, and saw the shape Par Lost 8.463
Of Grove or Garden-Plot more pleasant lay, Par Lost 9.418
That lay in wait; beyond this had bin force, Par Lost 9.1173
Eden and all the Coast in prospect lay. Par Lost 10.89
Insensible, how glad would lay me down Par Lost 10.777
Outstretcht he lay, on the cold ground, and oft Par Lost 10.851
Stretcht out to the amplest reach of prospect lay. Par Lost 11.380
Life offer'd, or soon beg to lay it down, Par Lost 11.506
Lay Seige, encampt; by Batterie, Scale, and Mine, Par Lost 11.656
Lay sleeping ran before, but found her wak't; Par Lost 12.608
There he shall first lay down the rudiments Par Reg 1.157
Lay on his Providence; he will not fail Par Reg 2.54
In Valley or Green Meadow to way-lay Par Reg 2.185
Thence to the bait of Women lay expos'd; Par Reg 2.204
Greater and nobler done, and to lay down Par Reg 2.482
Lay pleasant; from his side two rivers flow'd, Par Reg 3.255
To lay hills plain, fell woods, or valleys fill, Par Reg 3.332
Or where plain was raise hill, or over-lay Par Reg 3.333
Lay stor'd, in what part summ'd, that she might know: Samson 395
At length to lay my head and hallow'd pledge Samson 535
Or left thy carkass where the Ass lay thrown: Samson 1097
And with one buffet lay thy structure low, Samson 1239
Chor. Fathers are wont to lay up for thir Sons, Samson 1485
Thou for thy Son art bent to lay out all; Samson 1486
And lay e're while a Holocaust, Samson 1702
Find courage to lay hold on this occasion, Samson 1716
To lay their just hands on that Golden Key Mask 13
Bridgewater ms 'laye'
With eager thought warbling his *Dorick* lay: Lycidas 189
And lay it lowly at his blessed feet; Nativity 25
Have linkt that amorous power to thy soft lay, Sonnet 1, 8
Lay deep their plots together through each Land, Psalm 2, 4
I lay and slept, I wak'd again, Psalm 3, 13
Both lay me down and sleep Psalm 4, 38
The Swallow there, to lay her young Psalm 84, 11

Layest
Directed to the Manger where thou lais't, Par Reg 1.247
Too long, then lay'st thy scapes on names ador'd, Par Reg 2.189
It was not gold, as to my charge thou lay'st, Samson 849

Lays
Layes forth her purple Grape, and gently creeps Par Lost 4.259
Ceas'd warbling, but all night tun'd her soft layes: Par Lost 7.436
What ruins Kingdoms, and lays Cities flat; Par Reg 4.363
Carrol her goodnes lowd in rustick layes, Mask 849
Fanning their joyous Leaves to thy soft layes. Lycidas 44
Trinity ms 'lays'

Lazar-house
A Lazar-house it seemd, wherein were laid Par Lost 11.479

Lazy
Call on the lazy leaden-stepping hours, On Time 2
Trinity ms 'lazie'

Lead
Shall lead Hell Captive maugre Hell, and show Par Lost 3.255
Which would but lead me to a worse relapse Par Lost 4.100
A chance but chance may lead where I may meet Par Lost 4.530
To visit thee; lead on then where thy Bowre Par Lost 5.375
Of all those Myriads which we lead the chief; Par Lost 5.684
Gabriel, lead forth to Battel these my Sons Par Lost 6.46
Invincible, lead forth my armed Saints Par Lost 6.47
Who art to lead thy ofspring, and supposest Par Lost 8.86
Lead then, said *Eve*. Hee leading swiftly rowld Par Lost 9.631
Deterrd not from atchieving what might leade Par Lost 9.696
Or transmigration, as thir lot shall lead. Par Lost 10.261
Successful beyond hope, to lead ye forth Par Lost 10.463
And reasonings, though through Mazes, lead me still Par Lost 10.830
Prosperous or adverse: so shalt thou lead Par Lost 11.364
Of Death, and many are the wayes that lead Par Lost 11.468
Shall lead thir lives, and multiplie apace, Par Lost 12.17
Of Law, his people into *Canaan* lead; Par Lost 12.309
Wearied I fell asleep: but now lead on; Par Lost 12.614
Draw out with credulous desire, and lead Par Reg 2.166
By saving Doctrine, and from errour lead Par Reg 2.474
In all things that to greatest actions lead Par Reg 3.239
Thy country, and captive lead away her Kings Par Reg 3.366
Lead in swift round the Months and Years. Mask 114
Bridgewater ms 'leade'
To my proportion'd strength. Shepherd lead on.---- Mask 330
Bridgewater ms 'leade'
Eld. Bro. Thyrsis lead on apace, Ile follow thee, Mask 657
Bridgewater ms 'leade'
And in thy right hand lead with thee, Allegro 35
Or if the earlier season lead Allegro 89
And lead ye where ye may more neer behold Arcades 40
While the jolly hours lead on propitious *May*, Sonnet 1, 4
This thought might lead me through the worlds vain mask Sonnet 22, 13
Lord lead me in thy righteousness Psalm 5, 21
Lead me because of those Psalm 5, 22

Leaden
With a sad Leaden downward cast, Penseroso 43

Leaden-stepping
Call on the lazy leaden-stepping hours, On Time 2

Leader
Thus answer'd. Leader of those Armies bright, Par Lost 1.272
Did first create your Leader, next free choice, Par Lost 2.19
A faithful Leader, not to hazard all Par Lost 4.933
Argues no Leader but a lyar trac't, Par Lost 4.949
A Legion; led in fight, yet Leader seemd Par Lost 6.232
Deliverer from new Lords, leader to free Par Lost 6.451
Leader, the terms we sent were terms of weight, Par Lost 6.621
Their King, their Leader, and Supream on Earth. Par Reg 1.99

Leaders
The Heads and Leaders thither hast where stood Par Lost 1.357
Under thir God-like Leaders, in the Cause Par Lost 6.67

Leadest
Thou lead'st me, and to the hand of Heav'n submit, Par Lost 11.372
Who leadest like a flock of sheep Psalm 80, 3

Leading
That mighty leading Angel, who of late Par Lost 2.991
Lead then, said *Eve*. Hee leading swiftly rowld Par Lost 9.631
The way, thou leading, such a sent I draw Par Lost 10.267
One day forth walk'd alone, the Spirit leading; Par Reg 1.189

Leads
And hard, that out of Hell leads up to light; Par Lost 2.433
Leads him perplext, where he may likeliest find Par Lost 2.525
What readiest path leads where your gloomie bounds Par Lost 2.976
The great Work-Maister, leads to no excess Par Lost 3.696
Leads up to Heav'n, is both the way and guide; Par Lost 8.613
Leads thee, or where most needs, whether to wind Par Lost 9.215
Leads thee, I shall not lag behinde, nor erre Par Lost 10.266
Untraind in Armes, where rashness leads not on. Par Lost 12.222
And know not whom, but as one leads the other; Par Reg 3.53
And rifted Rocks whose entrance leads to hell, Mask 518
Whose lustre leads us, and for her most fit, Arcades 76
Comes dancing from the East, and leads with her May Morn 2
Toward which Time leads me, and the will of Heav'n; Sonnet 7, 12
Toward solid good what leads the nearest way; Sonnet 21, 10

Leaf
Of firm and fragrant leaf; on either side Par Lost 4.695
Impearls on every leaf and every flouer. Par Lost 5.747
Then Herbs of every leaf, that sudden flour'd Par Lost 7.317
An Olive leafe he brings, pacific signe: Par Lost 11.860
That spreds her verdant leaf to th' morning ray, Mask 622
The leaf was darkish, and had prickles on it, Mask 631
1637 'leafe'
Trinity ms 'leafe'
Bridgewater ms 'leafe'
To yield his fruit, and his leaf shall not fall, Psalm 1, 9

Leafy
La. Dim darknes, and this leavy Labyrinth. Mask 278
Trinity ms 'leavie'
Bridgewater ms 'leavye'

League
Myriads though bright: If he whom mutual league, Par Lost 1.87
From Heav'ns high jurisdiction, in new League Par Lost 2.319
Uplifted spurns the ground, thence many a League Par Lost 2.929
Well pleas'd they slack thir course, and many a League Par Lost 4.164
Fair couple, linkt in happie nuptial League, Par Lost 4.339
Though I unpittied: League with you I seek, Par Lost 4.375
Of ravenous Fowl, though many a League remote, Par Lost 10.274
Many a dark League, reduc't in careful Watch Par Lost 10.438
Cut shorter many a league; here thou behold'st Par Reg 3.269
Chuse which thou wilt by conquest or by league. Par Reg 3.370
By parl, or composition, truce, or league Par Reg 4.529
The *Philistines*, when thou hadst broke the league, Samson 1189
her brok'n league, to impe their serpent wings, Sonnet 15, 8
1694 'League'

League-breaker
As a League-breaker and deliver'd bound Samson 1184
As a league-breaker gave up bound, presum'd Samson 1209

Leagued
Befits thee with him leagu'd, thy self as false Par Lost 10.868
Who leagu'd with millions more in rash revolt Par Reg 1.359

Leagues
Blows them transverse ten thousand Leagues awry Par Lost 3.488
Of enemies, of aids, battels and leagues, Par Reg 3.392

Lean
As over-tir'd to let him lean a while Samson 1632
Lean on it safely, not a period Mask 585
Trinity ms 'leane'
1637 'Leane'
Bridgewater ms 'leane'
Praising the lean and sallow Abstinence. Mask 709
1637 'leane'
Bridgewater ms 'leane'
And when they list, their lean and flashy songs Lycidas 123
Trinity ms 'leane'

Leaned
And meek surrender, half imbracing leand Par Lost 4.494

Leaning
Leaning half-rais'd, with looks of cordial Love Par Lost 5.12

Leans
Leans her unpillow'd head fraught with sad fears. Mask 355
Trinity ms 'leans' ←'she leans'
Bridgewater ms 'leanes'
Therfore on thy firme hand religion leanes Sonnet 17, 13
1694 'leans'

Leaped
A God, leap'd fondly into *Aetna* flames, Par Lost 3.470
Plato's Elysium, leap'd into the Sea, Par Lost 3.472

Leaped*(cont)*
At one slight bound high over leap'd all bound Par Lost 4.181
1667 'overleap'd'
Slip't from the fold, or young Kid lost his dam, Mask 498
Trinity ms 'slip't' ←'leapt'

Leaps
Leaps o're the fence with ease into the Fould: Par Lost 4.187

Learn
Learn how thir greatest Monuments of Fame, Par Lost 1.695
ms 'Learne'
Thither let us bend all our thoughts, to learn Par Lost 2.354
Retire, or taste thy folly, and learn by proof, Par Lost 2.686
To mark what of thir state he more might learn Par Lost 4.400
Then who created thee lamenting learne, Par Lost 5.894
From all: my Sect thou seest, now learn too late Par Lost 6.147
There let them learn, as likes them, to despise Par Lost 6.717
Wherein to read his wondrous Works, and learne Par Lost 8.68
Till warn'd, or by experience taught, she learne, Par Lost 8.190
Our ruin, both by thee informd I learne, Par Lost 9.275
With sinfulness of Men; thereby to learn Par Lost 11.360
Henceforth I learne, that to obey is best, Par Lost 12.561
Who this is we must learn, for man he seems Par Reg 1.91
Serious to learn and know, and thence to do Par Reg 1.203
I learn not yet, perhaps I need not know; Par Reg 1.292
There thou shalt hear and learn the secret power Par Reg 4.254
And narrower Scrutiny, that I might learn Par Reg 4.515
Thy bold attempt; hereafter learn with awe Par Reg 4.625
Sam. Your coming, Friends, revives me, for I learn Samson 187
To learn thy secrets, get into my power Samson 798
And wisely learn to curb thy sorrows wild; Fair Inf 73
That we on Earth with undiscording voice Musick 17
Trinity ms 'on earth' ←'below may learne'
To measure life, learn thou betimes, and know Sonnet 21, 9
Iunkets and knacks, that they may learne apace. Prose 6, 3

Learned
Soon learnd, now milder, and thus answerd smooth. Par Lost 2.816
What further would be learnt. Live while ye may, Par Lost 4.533
Doctrin which we would know whence learnt: who saw Par Lost 5.856
Disdain'd, but meaner thoughts learnd in thir flight, Par Lost 6.367
To teach all nations what of him they learn'd Par Lost 12.440
This having learnt, thou hast attaind the summe Par Lost 12.575
Of his Apostasie; he might have learnt Par Reg 1.146
In them is plainest taught, and easiest learnt, Par Reg 4.361
So much of Adders wisdom I have learn't Samson 936
Deep skill'd in all his mothers witcheries, Mask 523
Trinity ms 'deepe skill'd' ←'deepe learnt' ←'enur'd'
Character'd in the face; this have I learn't Mask 530
Bridgewater ms 'learnt'
Which once of *Meliboeus* old I learnt Mask 822
If *Jonsons* learned Sock be on, Allegro 132
A Sheep-hook, or have learn'd ought els the least Lycidas 120
Trinity ms 'learn't'
Your learned hands, can loose this Gordian knot? Vacation 90
What severs each thou 'hast learnt, which few hav don. Sonnet 17, 11
1662 'learn't'
1694 'learn'd'
A hunder'd-fold, who having learnt thy way Sonnet 18, 13

Learning
Without thir learning how wilt thou with them, Par Reg 4.231
Hated not Learning wors then Toad or Asp; Sonnet 11, 13
Men whose Life, Learning, Faith and pure intent Forcers 9
Trinity ms 'learning'

Leas
On the Lawns, and on the Leas. Mask 965
1637 'leas'
Bridgewater ms 'leas'
Trinity ms 'leas'

Lease
Shortned hast thy own lives lease, Winchester 52

Least
Whom Thunder hath made greater? Here at least Par Lost 1.258
Mammon, the least erected Spirit that fell Par Lost 1.679
Thus farr at least recover'd, hath much more Par Lost 2.22
Yet ever plotting how the Conqueror least Par Lost 2.338
May reap his conquest, and may least rejoyce Par Lost 2.339
So without least impulse or shadow of Fate, Par Lost 3.120
To me are all my works, nor Man the least Par Lost 3.277
Evil be thou my Good; by thee at least Par Lost 4.110
Among our other torments not the least, Par Lost 4.510
At least distemperd, discontented thoughts, Par Lost 4.807
Will save us trial what the least can doe Par Lost 4.855
At least had gon to rack, disturbd and torne Par Lost 4.994
Expected, least of all from thee, ingrate Par Lost 5.811
On either side, the least of whom could weild Par Lost 6.221
Thou canst not. Hast thou turnd the least of these Par Lost 6.284
At least our envious Foe hath fail'd, who thought Par Lost 7.139
Her end without least motion, and receaves, Par Lost 8.35
Wors then can Man with Beast, and least of all. Par Lost 8.397
More then enough; at least on her bestow'd Par Lost 8.537
Thy mate, who sees when thou art seen least wise. Par Lost 8.578
More Angels to Create, if they at least Par Lost 9.146
For hee who tempts, though in vain, at least asperses Par Lost 9.296
Touchd onely, that our trial, when least sought, Par Lost 9.380
Of gesture or lest action overawd Par Lost 9.460
The first at lest of these I thought denid Par Lost 9.555
And wandring vanitie, when lest was safe, Par Lost 10.875
His full wrauth whose thou feelst as yet lest part, Par Lost 10.951
Before thee reconcil'd, at least his days Par Lost 11.39

Least(*cont*)
And live for ever, dream at least to live Par Lost 11.95
At least if so we can, and by the head Par Reg 1.60
At least to try, and teach the erring Soul Par Reg 1.224
To love, at least comtemplate and admire Par Reg 1.380
At least in vain, for they shall find thee mute. Par Reg 1.459
And talk at least, though I despair to attain. Par Reg 1.485
If he be Man by Mothers side at least, Par Reg 2.136
Thir taste no knowledge works, at least of evil, Par Reg 2.371
The deed becomes unprais'd, the man at least, Par Reg 3.103
Think not so slight of glory; therein least Par Reg 3.109
In cunning, over-reach't where least he thought, Par Reg 4.11
At least might seem to hold all power of thee, Par Reg 4.494
Yet that which was the worst now least afflicts me, Samson 195
This with the other should, at least, have paird, Samson 208
At least of thy own Nation, and as noble. Samson 218
Down Reason then, at least vain reasonings down, Samson 322
Weakly at least, and shamefully: A sin Samson 499
That what by me thou hast lost thou least shalt miss. Samson 927
Dal. Let me approach at least, and touch thy hand. Samson 951
So shall he least confusion draw Samson 1058
Where strength can least abide, though all thy hairs Samson 1136
A Sheep-hook, or have learn'd ought els the least Lycidas 120

Leathern
And in requitall ope his leather'n scrip, Mask 626
Trinity ms 'leatherne' ←'letherne'
Bridgewater ms 'letherne'
1673 'leathern'

Leave
In billows, leave i' th' midst a horrid Vale. Par Lost 1.224
And leave a singed bottom all involv'd Par Lost 1.236
By force impossible, by leave obtain'd Par Lost 2.250
That be assur'd, without leave askt of thee: Par Lost 2.685
Account mee man; I for his sake will leave Par Lost 3.238
Thou wilt not leave me in the loathsom grave Par Lost 3.247
Took leave, and toward the coast of Earth beneath, Par Lost 3.739
Free leave so large to all things else, and choice Par Lost 4.434
This Garden, and no corner leave unspi'd; Par Lost 4.529
Search through this Garden, leave unsearcht no nook, Par Lost 4.789
1667 'leav'
May come and go, so unapprov'd, and leave Par Lost 5.118
With all his Legions to dislodge, and leave Par Lost 5.669
Leave them to God above, him serve and feare; Par Lost 8.168
Not that they durst without his leave attempt, Par Lost 8.237
So ordering. I with leave of speech implor'd, Par Lost 8.377
Or this, or worse, leave not the faithful side Par Lost 9.265
Wisdom without their leave? and wherein lies Par Lost 9.725
Made thee without thy leave, what if thy Son Par Lost 10.760
That I must leave ye, Sons; O were I able Par Lost 10.819
To waste it all my self, and leave ye none! Par Lost 10.820
Leave cold the Night, how we his gather'd beams Par Lost 10.1070
Must I thus leave thee Paradise? thus leave Par Lost 11.269
Shall leave them to enjoy; for th' Earth shall bear Par Lost 11.804
To leave them to thir own polluted wayes; Par Lost 12.110
Must eat, and on the ground leave nothing green: Par Lost 12.186
God, as to leave them, and expose thir Land, Par Lost 12.339
Returnd from *Babylon* by leave of Kings Par Lost 12.348
Still follow'd him; to them shall leave in charge Par Lost 12.439
Through all his Realme, and there confounded leave; Par Lost 12.455
To leave this Paradise, but shalt possess Par Lost 12.586
Who boast'st release from Hell, and leave to come Par Reg 1.409
With granted leave officious I return, Par Reg 2.302
Then those thir Conquerours, who leave behind Par Reg 3.78
To his due time and providence I leave them. Par Reg 3.440
Look once more e're we leave this specular Mount Par Reg 4.236
With day-spring born; here leave me to respire. Samson 11
Thir Superstition yields me; hence with leave Samson 15
Or th' execution leave to high disposal, Samson 506
Of fancy, feard lest one day thou wouldst leave me Samson 794
Being once a wife, for me thou wast to leave Samson 885
I leave him to his lot, and like my own. Samson 996
And gives them leave to wear their Saphire crowns, Mask 26
As loath to leave the body that it lov'd, Mask 473
That the shrewd medling Elfe delights to make, Mask 846
Trinity ms 'make' ←'makes' ←'leave'
And leave her dolorous mansions to the peering day. Nativity 140
Dante shall give Fame leave to set thee higher Sonnet 13, 12
Trinity ms 'Dante shall give Fame leave to' ←'Fame by the Tuscan's leav shall'
Then did I leave them to their will Psalm 81, 49

Leaves
Pure, and commands to som, leaves free to all. Par Lost 4.747
Serpent, thy overpraising leaves in doubt Par Lost 9.615
As leaves a greater store of Fruit untoucht, Par Lost 9.621
Which leaves us naked thus, of Honour void, Par Lost 9.1074
Of *Turkish* Crescent, leaves all waste beyond Par Lost 10.434
He leaves his Gods, his Friends, and native Soile Par Lost 12.129
A Son, and of his Son a Grand-childe leaves, Par Lost 12.153
Of *Pharao:* there he dies, and leaves his Race Par Lost 12.163
Which when he lists, he leaves, or boasts he can, Par Reg 4.306
And then in haste her Bowre she leaves, Allegro 87
And from the Boughs brush off the evil dew, Arcades 50
Trinity ms 'bowes' ←'leaves'
Awakes the slumbring leaves, or tasseld horn Arcades 57
Shatter your leaves before the mellowing year. Lycidas 5
Fanning their joyous Leaves to thy soft layes. Lycidas 44
1638 'leaves'
Trinity ms 'leavs'

Leaves(*cont*)
The leaves should all be black wheron I write, Passion 34
Hath from the leaves of thy unvalu'd Book, Shakespear 11

Leaves
Thick as Autumnal Leaves that strow the Brooks Par Lost 1.302
ms 'leaves'
The trembling leaves, while Universal *Pan* Par Lost 4.266
Of leaves and fuming rills, *Aurora*'s fan, Par Lost 5.6
His barren leaves. Them thus imploid beheld Par Lost 5.219
Springs lighter the green stalk, from thence the leaves Par Lost 5.480
Of rusling Leaves, but minded not, as us'd Par Lost 9.519
Some Tree whose broad smooth Leaves together sowd, Par Lost 9.1095
At Loopholes cut through thickest shade: Those Leaves Par Lost 9.1110
Ending on the russling Leaves, Penseroso 129

Leavest
Oft leav'st them to the hostile sword Samson 692

Leaving
And Fish with Fish; to graze the Herb all leaving, Par Lost 10.711
Leaving my dolorous Prison I enjoy Par Reg 1.364
With hollow shreik the steep of *Delphos* leaving. Nativity 178
Fly after the Night-steeds, leaving their Moon-lov'd maze. Nativity 236
by leaving out those harsh ill sounding jarres Musick Tr. ms 5.03

Leavy
La. Dim darknes, and this leavy Labyrinth. Mask 278
Trinity ms 'leavie'
Bridgewater ms 'leavye'

Lebanon
Whose annual wound in *Lebanon* allur'd Par Lost 1.447
ms 'Lebanon'

Lecherous
Hence with thy brew'd inchantments, foul deceiver, Mask 696
Trinity ms 'brewd enchauntments' ←'foule brud' ←'hel brewd opiate' ←'hel bru'd liquor' ←'bru'd sorcerie' ←'teacherous (leacherous?) bruage' ←'teacherous kindnesse'

Lechi
In *Ramath-lechi* famous to this day: Samson 145

Led
That led th' imbattelld Seraphim to Warr Par Lost 1.129
Of *Solomon* he led by fraud to build Par Lost 1.401
Ezekiel saw, when by the Vision led Par Lost 1.455
Or cast a Rampart. *Mammon* led them on, Par Lost 1.678
The more it seems excess, that led thee hither Par Lost 3.698
Led on th' Eternal Spring. Not that faire field Par Lost 4.268
But follow strait, invisibly thus led? Par Lost 4.476
With living Saphirs: *Hesperus* that led Par Lost 4.605
So saying, on he led his radiant Files, Par Lost 4.797
Fruitless imbraces: or they led the Vine Par Lost 5.215
Of Horses led, and Grooms besmeard with Gold Par Lost 5.356
They led him high applauded, and present Par Lost 6.26
A Legion; led in fight, yet Leader seemd Par Lost 6.232
With thy Celestial Song. Up led by thee Par Lost 7.12
Led on, yet sinless, with desire to know Par Lost 7.61
That open'd wide her blazing Portals, led Par Lost 7.575
With supple joints, and lively vigour led: Par Lost 8.269
Smooth sliding without step, last led me up Par Lost 8.302
Led by her Heav'nly Maker, though unseen, Par Lost 8.485
I led her blushing like the Morn: all Heav'n, Par Lost 8.511
Thoughts, whither have ye led me, with what sweet Par Lost 9.473
Led *Eve* our credulous Mother, to the Tree Par Lost 9.644
He led her nothing loath; Flours were the Couch, Par Lost 9.1039
Captivity led captive through the Aire, Par Lost 10.188
In sight, to each of these three places led. Par Lost 10.324
Led them direct, and down the Cliff as fast Par Lost 12.639
In *Adam*'s overthrow, and led thir march Par Reg 1.115
Thought following thought, and step by step led on, Par Reg 1.192
By whose bright course led on they found the place, Par Reg 1.252
And now by some strong motion I am led Par Reg 1.290
And he still on was led, but with such thoughts Par Reg 1.299
Led captive; cease to admire, and all her Plumes Par Reg 2.222
Led captive, and *Jerusalem* laid waste, Par Reg 3.283
By great *Arsaces* led, who founded first Par Reg 3.295
To admiration, led by Natures light; Par Reg 4.228
Ensnar'd, assaulted, overcome, led bound, Samson 365
He led me on to mightiest deeds Samson 638
Hath led me on desirous to behold Samson 741
I led the way; bitter reproach, but true, Samson 823
He patient but undaunted where they led him, Samson 1623
At length for intermission sake they led him Samson 1629
He unsuspitious led him; which when *Samson* Samson 1635
And he by Friars Lanthorn led Allegro 104
Like one that had bin led astray Penseroso 69
The Star-led Wisards haste with odours sweet: Nativity 23
Led by the strength of the Almighties hand, Psalm 114, 4
Love led them on, and Faith who knew them best Sonnet 14, 9
Trinity ms 'Love led them on' ←'Faith shew'd the way' ←'Faith who led on the way'
And led thee out of thrall. Psalm 81, 28

Ledst
Thou Spirit who ledst this glorious Eremite Par Reg 1.8

Lee
Moors by his side under the Lee, while Night Par Lost 1.207
his goarie scalpe rowle downe the Thracian lee Lycidas Tr. ms 29.61
Or Rockie *Avon*, or of Sedgie *Lee*, Vacation 97

Leer
For envie, yet with jealous leer maligne Par Lost 4.503

Lees
I must not suffer this, yet 'tis but the lees Mask 809

Lees*(cont)*
Trinity ms 'but the lees' ←'the tilted lees' ←'the very lees'
Left
Have left us this our spirit and strength intire Par Lost 1.146
Left him at large to his own dark designs, Par Lost 1.213
Thir living strength, and unfrequented left Par Lost 1.433
The utmost border of his Kingdom, left Par Lost 2.361
That little which is left so to defend, Par Lost 2.1000
To expiate his Treason hath naught left, Par Lost 3.207
Left for Repentance, none for Pardon left? Par Lost 4.80
None left but by submission; and that word Par Lost 4.81
The only sign of our obedience left Par Lost 4.428
By shorter flight to th' East, had left him there Par Lost 4.595
Happiness in his power left free to will, Par Lost 5.235
Left to his own free Will, his Will though free, Par Lost 5.236
He left it in thy power, ordaind thy will Par Lost 5.526
With speed what force is left, and all imploy Par Lost 5.730
'Twixt Host and Host but narrow space was left, Par Lost 6.104
And left large field, unsafe within the wind Par Lost 6.309
Left them Superiour, while we can preserve Par Lost 6.443
For to themselves I left them, and thou knowst, Par Lost 6.689
And of thir wonted vigour left them draind, Par Lost 6.851
Anough is left besides to search and know. Par Lost 7.125
So Charming left his voice, that he a while Par Lost 8.2
line not in 1667 edition
Hath left to thir disputes, perhaps to move Par Lost 8.77
Mine eyes he clos'd, but op'n left the Cell Par Lost 8.460
Shee disappeerd, and left me dark, I wak'd Par Lost 8.478
Or Nature faild in mee, and left some part Par Lost 8.534
Th' Angelic Name, and thinner left the throng Par Lost 9.142
Left so imperfet by the Maker wise, Par Lost 9.338
Nothing imperfet or deficient left Par Lost 9.345
But God left free the Will, for what obeyes Par Lost 9.351
God so commanded, and left that Command Par Lost 9.652
Encumberd, now had left them, up they rose Par Lost 9.1051
And honour from about them, naked left Par Lost 9.1057
And left to her self, if evil thence ensue, Par Lost 9.1185
His free Will, to her own inclining left Par Lost 10.46
Appointed to sit there, had left thir charge, Par Lost 10.421
Heav'n-banisht Host, left desert utmost Hell Par Lost 10.437
Was left him, or false glitter: All amaz'd Par Lost 10.452
Where all yet left of that revolted Rout Par Lost 10.534
Self-left. Least therefore his now bolder hand Par Lost 11.93
In thir bright stand, there left his Powers to seise Par Lost 11.221
Recess, and onely consolation left Par Lost 11.304
All left, in one small bottom swum imbark't. Par Lost 11.753
And hear the din; thus was the building left Par Lost 12.61
Reserving, human left from human free. Par Lost 12.71
Left in confusion, *Babylon* thence call'd. Par Lost 12.343
His faithful, left among th' unfaithful herd, Par Lost 12.481
Thir doctrine and thir story written left, Par Lost 12.506
Left onely in those written Records pure, Par Lost 12.513
Left them inrould, or what the Spirit within Par Lost 12.523
And unrecorded left through many an Age, Par Reg 1.16
He ended, and his words impression left Par Reg 1.106
For in the Inn was left no better room: Par Reg 1.248
Nor left at *Jordan*, tydings of him none; Par Reg 2.62
Had left him vacant, and with speed was gon Par Reg 2.116
Left his ground-nest, high towring to descry Par Reg 2.280
For where no hope is left, is left no fear; Par Reg 3.206
Th' one winding, the other strait and left between Par Reg 3.256
Impenitent, and left a race behind Par Reg 3.423
Rather more honour left and more esteem; Par Reg 4.207
Brought back the Son of God, and left him there, Par Reg 4.396
Left me all helpless with th' irreparable loss Samson 644
Were left for hast unfinish't, judgment scant, Samson 1027
Or left thy carkass where the Ass lay thrown: Samson 1097
And he in that calamitous prison left. Samson 1480
Insensate left, or to sense reprobate, Samson 1685
Fully reveng'd, hath left them years of mourning, Samson 1712
Honour hath left, and freedom, let but them Samson 1715
Of all thy dues be done, and none left out, Mask 137
They left me then, when the gray-hooded Eev'n Mask 188
line not in Bridgewater ms
La. They left me weary on a grassie terf. Mask 280
Co. And left your fair side all unguarded Lady? Mask 283
Bridgewater ms 'lefte'
My sister is not so defenceless left Mask 414
Spir. What, have you let the false enchanter scape? Mask 814
Bridgewater ms 'have yee left'
Or call up him that left half told Penseroso 109
What shallow-searching *Fame* hath left untold; Arcades 41
Young *Lycidas*, and hath not left his peer: Lycidas 9
Hath left in shadows dred, Nativity 206
A here alas, hath laid him in the dirt, Carrier 2
1658 'left him'
Who liv'd in both, unstain'd with gold or fee, Sonnet 10, 3
Trinity ms 'liv'd in' ←'left them'
And left them both, more in himself content, Sonnet 10, 4
Left
He scours the right hand coast, som times the left, Par Lost 2.633
Threw forth, till on the left side op'ning wide, Par Lost 2.755
Vanguard, to Right and Left the Front unfould; Par Lost 6.558
Had ended; when to Right and Left the Front Par Lost 6.569
Who stooping op'nd my left side, and took Par Lost 8.465
And of this World, and on the left hand Hell Par Lost 10.322
Legal
To save them, not thir own, though legal works. Par Lost 12.410
Legal*(cont)*
Of sin, or legal debt; Samson 313
Legend
In copious Legend, or sweet Lyric Song. Samson 1737
Legion
As each divided Legion might have seemd Par Lost 6.230
A Legion; led in fight, yet Leader seemd Par Lost 6.232
Squar'd in full Legion (such command we had) Par Lost 8.232
Legions
His Legions, Angel Forms, who lay intrans't Par Lost 1.301
ms 'legions'
That all these puissant Legions, whose exile Par Lost 1.632
ms 'legions'
Encamp thir Legions, or with obscure wing Par Lost 2.132
Till thickest Legions close; with feats of Arms Par Lost 2.537
To that side Heav'n from whence your Legions fell: Par Lost 2.1006
What thou and thy gay Legions dare against; Par Lost 4.942
With all his Legions to dislodge, and leave Par Lost 5.669
In silence thir bright Legions, to the sound Par Lost 6.64
Thy Legions under darkness; but thou seest Par Lost 6.142
The adverse Legions, nor less hideous joyn'd Par Lost 6.206
Came shadowing, and opprest whole Legions arm'd, Par Lost 6.655
Fell with his flaming Legions through the Deep Par Lost 7.134
There kept thir Watch the Legions, while the Grand Par Lost 10.427
Legions and Cohorts, turmes of horse and wings: Par Reg 4.66
Thee and thy Legions, yelling they shall flye, Par Reg 4.629
With all the greisly legions that troop Mask 603
Legs
His Armes clung to his Ribs, his Leggs entwining Par Lost 10.512
Lehi
In *Ramath-lechi* famous to this day: Samson 145
Leisure
Weighs his spread wings, at leasure to behold Par Lost 2.1046
Had leasure, wondring at himself now more; Par Lost 10.510
On whom his leisure will vouchsafe an eye Par Reg 2.210
At home in leisure and domestic ease, Samson 917
And adde to these retired leasure, Penseroso 49
His leasure told him that his time was com, Another 23
line not in 1658 text
Lemnos
On *Lemnos* th' *Aegaean* Ile: thus they relate, Par Lost 1.746
ms 'Lemnos'
Lemures
The *Lars*, and *Lemures* moan with midnight plaint, Nativity 191
Lend
To other speedie aide might lend at need; Par Lost 9.260
Such wondrous power God to his Saint will lend, Par Lost 12.200
If not disposer; lend them oft my aid, Par Reg 1.393
To sage Philosophy next lend thine ear, Par Reg 4.272
Sams. A Little onward lend thy guiding hand Samson 1
Co. O foolishnes of men! that lend their ears Mask 706
And the brute Earth would lend her nerves, and shake, Mask 797
line not in Bridgewater ms
line not in Trinity ms
Thou honour'st Verse, and Verse must send her wing Sonnet 13, 9
1648 'must lend'
Trinity ms 'must lend'
Lends
Com Lady while Heaven lends us grace, Mask 938
Length
So stretcht out huge in length the Arch-fiend lay Par Lost 1.209
Of dreadful length and dazling Arms, in guise Par Lost 1.564
At length from us may find, who overcomes Par Lost 1.648
Or chang'd at length, and to the place conformd Par Lost 2.217
Our torments also may in length of time Par Lost 2.274
That fires the length of *Ophiucus* huge Par Lost 2.709
Without dimension, where length, breadth, & highth, Par Lost 2.893
At length a universal hubbub wilde Par Lost 2.951
Tamely endur'd a Bridge of wondrous length Par Lost 2.1028
Scarce thus at length faild speech recoverd sad. Par Lost 4.357
Rising in clouded Majestie, at length Par Lost 4.607
At length into the limits of the North Par Lost 5.755
Tenfold the length of this terrene: at last Par Lost 6.78
Of hideous length: before the cloudie Van, Par Lost 6.107
Of fighting Seraphim confus'd, at length Par Lost 6.249
Rage prompted them at length, and found them arms Par Lost 6.635
Weening to prosper, and at length prevaile Par Lost 6.795
They open to themselves at length the way Par Lost 7.158
1669 'lenghth'
Wondrous in length and corpulence involv'd Par Lost 7.483
Downward as farr Antartic; and in length Par Lost 9.79
His gentle dumb expression turnd at length Par Lost 9.527
Though at the voice much marveling; at length Par Lost 9.551
Sated at length, ere long I might perceave Par Lost 9.598
And knew not eating Death: Satiate at length, Par Lost 9.792
Speechless he stood and pale, till thus at length Par Lost 9.894
At length gave utterance to these words constraind. Par Lost 9.1066
Of length prodigious joyning to the Wall Par Lost 10.302
At length a Reverend Sire among them came, Par Lost 11.719
Measur'd by Cubit, length, and breadth, and highth, Par Lost 11.730
With length of happy dayes the race of man; Par Lost 11.782
The River-dragon tam'd at length submits Par Lost 12.191
Save when they journie, and at length they come, Par Lost 12.258
With joy the tidings brought from Heav'n: at length Par Lost 12.504
All his sollicitations, and at length Par Reg 1.152
At length collecting all his Serpent wiles, Par Reg 3.5
Here *Ninevee*, of length within her wall Par Reg 3.275
Yet he at length, time to himself best known, Par Reg 3.433

Length(*cont*)
To equal length back'd with a ridge of hills — Par Reg 4.29
By all the Prophets; of thy birth at length — Par Reg 4.503
Throttl'd at length in the Air, expir'd and fell; — Par Reg 4.568
To count them things worth notice, till at length — Samson 250
At one spears length. O ever failing trust — Samson 348
At length to lay my head and hallow'd pledge — Samson 535
Vain monument of strength; till length of years — Samson 570
With hard contest: at length that grounded maxim — Samson 865
Are reconcil'd at length, and Sea to Shore: — Samson 962
At length for intermission sake they led him — Samson 1629
And stretch'd out all the Chimney's length, — Allegro 111
May tell at length how green-ey'd *Neptune* raves, — Vacation 43
And now be wise at length ye Kings averse — Psalm 2, 22
Upon me: cause at length to cease — Psalm 7, 34
Hath at length brought forth a Lie. — Psalm 7, 54
Be not thou silent *now at length* — Psalm 83, 1
Till all before *our* God *at length* — Psalm 84, 27
O turn to me *thy face at length*, — Psalm 86, 57

Lengthened
Why am I mockt with death, and length'nd out — Par Lost 10.774

Lenient
Lenient of grief and anxious thought, — Samson 659

Lent
His flesh, his bone; to give thee being I lent — Par Lost 4.483
And to those dainty limms which nature lent — Mask 680
line not in Bridgewater ms
And render him with patience what he lent; — Fair Inf 75
All these have lent their armed hands — Psalm 83, 31

Leo
By *Leo* and the *Virgin* and the *Scales*, — Par Lost 10.676

Leper
A Leper once he lost and gain'd a King, — Par Lost 1.471
ms 'leper'

Leprous
And leprous sin will melt from earthly mould, — Nativity 138

Lesbian
Down the swift *Hebrus* to the *Lesbian* shore. — Lycidas 63
1645 printed '*Letbian*'

Less
Of force believe Almighty, since no less — Par Lost 1.144
ms 'lesse'
And what I should be, all but less then he — Par Lost 1.257
ms 'lesse'
Less then Arch Angel ruind, and th' excess — Par Lost 1.593
ms 'Lesse'
What force effected not: that he no less — Par Lost 1.647
ms 'lesse'
Now less then smallest Dwarfs, in narrow room — Par Lost 1.779
ms 'lesse'
Equal in strength, and rather then be less — Par Lost 2.47
To less then Gods. On th' other side up rose — Par Lost 2.108
Wrought still within them; and no less desire — Par Lost 2.295
To be created like to us, though less — Par Lost 2.349
All circumspection, and we now no less — Par Lost 2.414
Or unknown Region, what remains him less — Par Lost 2.443
Alone th' Antagonist of Heav'n, nor less — Par Lost 2.509
(What could it less when Spirits immortal sing2) — Par Lost 2.553
Within unseen. Farr less abhorrd than these — Par Lost 2.659
Destin'd to that good hour: no less rejoyc'd — Par Lost 2.848
He had to cross. Nor was his eare less peal'd — Par Lost 2.920
Som Capital City; or less then if this frame — Par Lost 2.924
With tumult less and with less hostile din, — Par Lost 2.1040
That *Satan* with less toil, and now with ease — Par Lost 2.1041
Which had no less prov'd certain unforeknown. — Par Lost 3.119
Much less that durst upon his own head draw — Par Lost 3.220
Love no where to be found less then Divine! — Par Lost 3.411
Of glimmering air less vext with tempest loud: — Par Lost 3.429
Circl'd his Head, nor less his Locks behind — Par Lost 3.626
What could be less then to afford him praise, — Par Lost 4.46
Under a Platan, yet methought less faire, — Par Lost 4.478
Less winning soft, less amiablie milde, — Par Lost 4.479
Diurnal, or this less volubil Earth — Par Lost 4.594
Rove idle unimploid, and less need rest; — Par Lost 4.617
Or less be lost. Thy fear, said *Zephon* bold, — Par Lost 4.854
Less pain, less to be fled, or thou then they — Par Lost 4.919
Less hardie to endure? courageous Chief, — Par Lost 4.920
Not that I less endure, or shrink from pain, — Par Lost 4.925
Of *Galileo*, less assur'd, observes — Par Lost 5.262
His equals, if in power and splendor less, — Par Lost 5.796
Erre not, much less for this to be our Lord, — Par Lost 5.799
To make us less, bent rather to exalt — Par Lost 5.829
Through the infinite Host, nor less for that — Par Lost 5.874
Of wrauth awak't: nor with less dread the loud — Par Lost 6.59
Nor motion of swift thought, less could his Shield — Par Lost 6.192
The adverse Legions, nor less hideous joyn'd — Par Lost 6.206
Two potent Thrones, that to be less then Gods — Par Lost 6.366
Nor of Renown less eager, yet by doome — Par Lost 6.378
Omniscient thought. True is, less firmly arm'd, — Par Lost 6.430
No less then for deliverance what we owe. — Par Lost 6.468
Think nothing hard, much less to be despaird. — Par Lost 6.495
Nor less on either side tempestuous fell — Par Lost 6.844
What may no less perhaps availe us known, — Par Lost 7.85
But Knowledge is as food, and needs no less — Par Lost 7.126
The less by Night alterne: and made the Starrs, — Par Lost 7.348
Shedding sweet influence: less bright the Moon, — Par Lost 7.375
That better might with farr less compass move, — Par Lost 8.33
The less not bright, nor Heav'n such journies run, — Par Lost 8.88

Less(*cont*)
Nor less think wee in Heav'n of thee on Earth — Par Lost 8.224
Pleas'd with thy words no less then thou with mine. — Par Lost 8.248
Much less can Bird with Beast, or Fish with Fowle — Par Lost 8.395
Second to me or like, equal much less. — Par Lost 8.407
Elaborate, of inward less exact. — Par Lost 8.539
In outward also her resembling less — Par Lost 8.543
His Image who made both, and less expressing — Par Lost 8.544
Less excellent, as thou thy self perceav'st. — Par Lost 8.566
Not less but more Heroic then the wrauth — Par Lost 9.14
Nor hope to be my self less miserable — Par Lost 9.126
Less attributed to her Faith sincere, — Par Lost 9.320
Of all that he Created, much less Man, — Par Lost 9.346
May finde us both perhaps farr less prepar'd, — Par Lost 9.381
Thou canst, who art sole Wonder, much less arm — Par Lost 9.533
Till *Adam*, though not less then *Eve* abash't, — Par Lost 9.1065
Incurr'd, what could they less, the penaltie, — Par Lost 10.15
Or come I less conspicuous, or what change — Par Lost 10.107
Huge *Python*, and his Power no less he seem'd — Par Lost 10.531
And torment less then none of what we dread, — Par Lost 10.998
Felt less remorse: they forthwith to the place — Par Lost 10.1098
Not of mean suiters, nor important less — Par Lost 11.9
In Fables old, less ancient yet then these, — Par Lost 11.11
Less pure, accustomd to immortal Fruits? — Par Lost 11.285
Ercoco and the less Maritim Kings — Par Lost 11.398
And hee the future evil shall no less — Par Lost 11.774
Peace to corrupt no less then Warr to waste. — Par Lost 11.784
Farr less I now lament for one whole World — Par Lost 11.874
Less over-weening, since he fail'd in *Job*, — Par Reg 1.147
What can be then less in me then desire — Par Reg 1.383
This wounds me most (what can it less) that Man, — Par Reg 1.404
While I to sorrows am no less advanc't, — Par Reg 2.69
Is ris'n to invade us, who no less — Par Reg 2.127
Famous he was in Heaven, on Earth less known; — Par Reg 3.68
Freely; of whom what could he less expect — Par Reg 3.126
The world thou hast not seen, much less her glory, — Par Reg 3.236
Fair Champain with less rivers interveind, — Par Reg 3.257
Aim therefore at no less then all the world, — Par Reg 4.105
Much less my mind; though thou should'st add to tell — Par Reg 4.113
For what can less so great a gift deserve? — Par Reg 4.169
I never lik'd thy talk, thy offers less, — Par Reg 4.171
To mans less universe, and soon are gone; — Par Reg 4.459
They ravel more, still less resolv'd, — Samson 305
Nor less then wounds immedicable — Samson 620
The easier towards me, or thy hatred less. — Samson 772
In human hearts, nor less in mine towards thee, — Samson 792
Less therefore to be pleas'd, obey'd, or fear'd, — Samson 900
Not less renown'd then in Mount *Ephraim*, — Samson 988
Sam. Be less abstruse, my riddling days are past. — Samson 1064
I less conjecture then when first I saw — Samson 1071
No less through all my sinews, joints and bones, — Samson 1142
Stalking with less unconsci'nable strides, — Samson 1245
No less the people on thir Holy-days — Samson 1421
And hush the waving Woods, nor of lesse faith, — Mask 88
1673 'less'
Bridgewater ms 'less'
La. No less then if I should my brothers loose. — Mask 288
Bridgewater ms 'lesse'
1637 'lesse'
Trinity ms 'lesse'
Less warranted then this, or less secure — Mask 327
Trinity ms both 'lesse'
1637 'Lesse', 'lesse'
Bridgewater ms both 'lesse'
'Less *Philomel* will daign a Song, — Penseroso 56
Less then half we find exprest, — Arcades 12
Trinity ms 'lesse'
And inward ripenes doth much less appear, — Sonnet 7, 7
Trinity ms 'lesse'
Yet be it less or more, or soon or slow, — Sonnet 7, 9
Trinity ms 'lesse'
No less renownd then warr, new foes arise — Sonnet 16, 11
Or to him have render'd less, — Psalm 7, 11
Scarce to be less then Gods, thou mad'st his lot, — Psalm 8, 15

Lessen
Mans Nature, less'n or degrade thine owne. — Par Lost 3.304
To lessen thee, against his purpose serves — Par Lost 7.614
To lessen or extenuate my offence, — Samson 767

Lessens
Man. Relate by whom. *Mess*. By *Samson*. *Man*. That still lessens — Samson 1563

Lesser
Are many lesser Faculties that serve — Par Lost 5.101
With thousand lesser Lights dividual holds, — Par Lost 7.382
What ere the skill of lesser gods can show, — Arcades 79

Lest
Prudent, least from his resolution rais'd — Par Lost 2.468
Loose all her virtue; least bad men should boast — Par Lost 2.483
Least with a whip of Scorpions I pursue — Par Lost 2.701
Least Heav'n surcharg'd with potent multitude — Par Lost 2.836
Least total darkness should by Night regaine — Par Lost 4.665
Least on the threshing floore his hopeful sheaves — Par Lost 4.984
Least wilfully transgressing he pretend — Par Lost 5.244
No fear lest Dinner coole; when thus began — Par Lost 5.396
In our defence, lest unawares we lose — Par Lost 5.731
These wicked Tents devoted, least the wrauth — Par Lost 5.890
(Unanswerd least thou boast) to let thee know; — Par Lost 6.163
Least from this flying Steed unrein'd, (as once — Par Lost 7.17
To those Apostates, least the like befall — Par Lost 7.44

Lest(*cont*)

But least his heart exalt him in the harme	Par Lost 7.150
Of *Chaos* farr remov'd, least fierce extreames	Par Lost 7.272
And govern well thy appetite, least sin	Par Lost 7.546
Least hee incenst at such eruption bold,	Par Lost 8.235
His great command; take heed least Passion sway	Par Lost 8.635
But other doubt possesses me, least harm	Par Lost 9.251
Least by some faire appeering good surpris'd	Par Lost 9.354
Thereof, nor shall ye touch it, least ye die.	Par Lost 9.663
Least thou not tasting, different degree	Par Lost 9.883
Us to abolish, least the Adversary	Par Lost 9.947
Least on my head both sin and punishment,	Par Lost 10.133
But least the difficultie of passing back	Par Lost 10.252
Pursues me still, least all I cannot die,	Par Lost 10.783
Least that pure breath of Life, the Spirit of Man	Par Lost 10.784
Henceforth; least that too heav'nly form, pretended	Par Lost 10.872
To be forestall'd; much more I fear least Death	Par Lost 10.1024
My labour will sustain me; and least Cold	Par Lost 10.1056
Self-left. Least therefore his now bolder hand	Par Lost 11.93
Thy choice of flaming Warriours, least the Fiend	Par Lost 11.101
Perpetual banishment. Yet least they faint	Par Lost 11.108
Least Paradise a receptacle prove	Par Lost 11.123
Least it again dissolve and showr the Earth?	Par Lost 11.883
And get themselves a name, least far disperst	Par Lost 12.45
Least entring on the *Canaanite* allarmd	Par Lost 12.217
Therefore I am return'd, lest confidence	Par Reg 2.140
Or counsel to assist; lest I who erst	Par Reg 2.145
They shall up lift thee, lest at any time	Par Reg 4.558
Lest he command them down into the deep	Par Reg 4.631
Of fancy, feard lest one day thou wouldst leave me	Samson 794
Sam. Not for thy life, lest fierce remembrance wake	Samson 952
Sams. Go baffl'd coward, lest I run upon thee,	Samson 1237
Will not dare mention, lest a question rise	Samson 1254
I will not wish, lest it perhaps offend them	Samson 1414
Lest I should see him forc't to things unseemly.	Samson 1451
Chor. Best keep together here, lest running thither	Samson 1521
Lest evil tidings with too rude irruption	Samson 1567
And give it false presentments, lest the place	Mask 156
Bridgewater ms 'least'	
Trinity ms 'lest' ←'else'	
Lest som ill greeting touch attempt the person	Mask 406
Lest the Sorcerer us intice	Mask 940
Bridgewater ms 'least'	
I throw it on the ground	Mask Tr. ms 22.22
'I' ←'lest I'	
My true account, least he returning chide,	Sonnet 19, 6
With trembling; kiss the Son least he appear	Psalm 2, 25
Least as a Lion (and no wonder)	Psalm 7, 4

Let

Let us not slip th' occasion, whether scorn,	Par Lost 1.178
Casts pale and dreadful? Thither let us tend	Par Lost 1.183
But wherefore let we then our faithful friends,	Par Lost 1.264
And dig'd out ribs of Gold. Let none admire	Par Lost 1.690
Deserve the precious bane. And here let those	Par Lost 1.692
More unexpert, I boast not: them let those	Par Lost 2.52
By our delay? no, let us rather choose	Par Lost 2.60
Let such bethink them, if the sleepy drench	Par Lost 2.73
Let this be good, whether our angry Foe	Par Lost 2.152
Will he, so wise, let loose at once his ire,	Par Lost 2.155
To whom we hate. Let us not then pursue	Par Lost 2.249
Thither let us bend all our thoughts, to learn	Par Lost 2.354
I offer, on mee let thine anger fall;	Par Lost 3.237
Well pleas'd, on me let Death wreck all his rage;	Par Lost 3.241
The Stairs were then let down, whether to dare	Par Lost 3.523
Earth, Aire, and Sea. Then let us not think hard	Par Lost 4.432
But let us ever praise him, and extoll	Par Lost 4.436
Yet let me not forget what I have gain'd	Par Lost 4.512
His will who bound us? let him surer barr	Par Lost 4.897
And let us to our fresh imployments rise	Par Lost 5.125
But silently a gentle tear let fall	Par Lost 5.130
And nourish all things, let your ceasless change	Par Lost 5.183
But by deceit and lies; this let him know,	Par Lost 5.243
In *Adam*, not to let th' occasion pass	Par Lost 5.453
Let us advise, and to this hazard draw	Par Lost 5.729
And equal over equals to let Reigne,	Par Lost 5.820
(Unanswerd least thou boast) to let thee know;	Par Lost 6.163
Reign thou in Hell thy Kingdom, let mee serve	Par Lost 6.183
Nameless in dark oblivion let them dwell.	Par Lost 6.380
Sad resolution and secure: let each	Par Lost 6.541
And to disorder'd rage let loose the reines,	Par Lost 6.696
There let them learn, as likes them, to despise	Par Lost 6.717
Thy weaker; let it profit thee to have heard	Par Lost 6.909
To ask, nor let thine own inventions hope	Par Lost 7.121
On golden Hinges moving, to let forth	Par Lost 7.207
Let ther be Light, said God, and forthwith Light	Par Lost 7.243
Again, God said, let ther be Firmament	Par Lost 7.261
Amid the Waters, and let it divide	Par Lost 7.262
Into one place, and let dry Land appeer.	Par Lost 7.284
And saw that it was good, and said, Let th' Earth	Par Lost 7.309
Again th' Almightie spake: Let there be Lights	Par Lost 7.339
The Day from Night; and let them be for Signes,	Par Lost 7.341
And let them be for Lights as I ordaine	Par Lost 7.343
And God said, let the Waters generate	Par Lost 7.387
And let Fowle flie above the Earth, with wings	Par Lost 7.389
And let the Fowle be multiply'd on the Earth.	Par Lost 7.398
Let th' Earth bring forth Foul living in her kinde,	Par Lost 7.451
Let us make now Man in our image, Man	Par Lost 7.519
In our similitude, and let them rule	Par Lost 7.520

Let(*cont*)

Open, ye Heav'ns, your living dores; let in	Par Lost 7.566
And for the Heav'ns wide Circuit, let it speak	Par Lost 8.100
Wherever plac't, let him dispose: joy thou	Par Lost 8.170
Therefore from this high pitch let us descend	Par Lost 8.198
Let not my words offend thee, Heav'nly Power,	Par Lost 8.379
Answer'd. Let it suffice thee that thou know'st	Par Lost 8.620
Let it; I reck not, so it light well aim'd,	Par Lost 9.173
Let us divide our labours, thou where choice	Par Lost 9.214
Let us not then suspect our happie State	Par Lost 9.337
To me is lost. Then let me not let pass	Par Lost 9.479
And thy fair Fruit let hang, as to no end	Par Lost 9.798
But come, so well refresh't, now let us play,	Par Lost 9.1027
But let us now, as in bad plight, devise	Par Lost 9.1091
Let none henceforth seek needless cause to approve	Par Lost 9.1140
And on the Serpent thus his curse let fall.	Par Lost 10.174
Impassable, Impervious, let us try	Par Lost 10.254
There didst not; there let him still Victor sway,	Par Lost 10.376
Let in these wastful Furies, who impute	Par Lost 10.620
All of me then shall die: let this appease	Par Lost 10.792
Between us two let there be peace, both joyning,	Par Lost 10.924
But rise, let us no more contend, nor blame	Par Lost 10.958
From what we fear for both, let us make short,	Par Lost 10.1000
Let us seek Death, or he not found, supply	Par Lost 10.1001
To make death in us live: Then let us seek	Par Lost 10.1028
Unskilful with what words to pray, let mee	Par Lost 11.32
The smell of peace toward Mankinde, let him live	Par Lost 11.38
But let us call to Synod all the Blest	Par Lost 11.67
Of that defended Fruit; but let him boast	Par Lost 11.86
Her rosie progress smiling; let us forth,	Par Lost 11.175
Here let us live, though in fall'n state, content.	Par Lost 11.180
This Hill; let *Eve* (for I have drencht her eyes)	Par Lost 11.367
The Men though grave, ey'd them, and let thir eyes	Par Lost 11.585
With thought that they must be. Let no man seek	Par Lost 11.770
The Earth again by flood, nor let the Sea	Par Lost 11.893
To let his sojourners depart, and oft	Par Lost 12.192
Let us descend now therefore from this top	Par Lost 12.588
Let her with thee partake what thou hast heard,	Par Lost 12.598
To Satan; let him tempt and now assay	Par Reg 1.143
O Son, but nourish them and let them soar	Par Reg 1.230
But let us wait; thus far he hath perform'd,	Par Reg 2.49
Let us be glad of this, and all our fears	Par Reg 2.53
The rest commit to me, I shall let pass	Par Reg 2.233
Worth or not worth the seeking, let it pass:	Par Reg 3.151
If Kingdom move thee not, let move thee Zeal,	Par Reg 3.171
Let that come when it comes; all hope is lost	Par Reg 3.204
Of *Bethel* and of *Dan*? no, let them serve	Par Reg 3.431
Let his tormenter Conscience find him out,	Par Reg 4.130
Therefore let pass, as they are transitory,	Par Reg 4.209
So let extend thy mind o're all the world,	Par Reg 4.223
Yet stay, let me not rashly call in doubt	Samson 43
Let there be light, and light was over all;	Samson 84
Let us not break in upon him;	Samson 116
Chor. Hee speaks, let us draw nigh. Matchless in might,	Samson 178
Of that sollicitation; let me here,	Samson 488
And let another hand, not thine, exact	Samson 507
And at another to let in the foe	Samson 561
Here rather let me drudge and earn my bread,	Samson 573
Sam. My Wife, my Traytress, let her not come near me.	Samson 725
Let weakness then with weakness come to parl	Samson 785
Let me obtain forgiveness of thee, *Samson*,	Samson 909
Dal. Let me approach at least, and touch thy hand.	Samson 951
Sam. So let her go, God sent her to debase me,	Samson 999
Therefore without feign'd shifts let be assign'd	Samson 1116
As over-tir'd to let him lean a while	Samson 1632
Honour hath left, and freedom, let but them	Samson 1715
Let us go find the body where it lies	Samson 1725
Com let us our rights begin,	Mask 125
And let a single helpless maiden pass	Mask 402
Bridgewater ms 'she'	
And earths base built on stubble. But com let's on.	Mask 599
Trinity ms 'lets'	
Bridgewater ms 'lets'	
But for that damn'd magician, let him be girt	Mask 602
If you let slip time, like a neglected rose	Mask 743
line not in Bridgewater ms	
Spir. What, have you let the false enchanter scape?	Mask 814
Bridgewater ms 'left'	
Let us fly this cursed place,	Mask 939
Com let us haste, the Stars grow high,	Mask 956
There let *Hymen* oft appear	Allegro 125
Or let my Lamp at midnight hour,	Penseroso 85
Som time let Gorgeous Tragedy	Penseroso 97
And let som strange mysterious dream,	Penseroso 147
But let my due feet never fail,	Penseroso 155
There let the pealing Organ blow,	Penseroso 161
And Daffadillies fill their cups with tears,	Lycidas 150
Trinity ms 'and' ←'let'	
Let our frail thoughts dally with false surmise.	Lycidas 153
And let your silver chime	Nativity 128
And let the Base of Heav'ns deep Organ blow,	Nativity 130
Let us with a gladsom mind	Psalm 136, 1
Let us blaze his Name abroad,	Psalm 136, 5
O let us his praises tell,	Psalm 136, 9
Let us therfore warble forth	Psalm 136, 89
Let down in clowdie throne to do the world some good.	Fair Inf 56
Which the sad morn had let fall	Winchester 45
Let *Euclid* rest and *Archimedes* pause,	Sonnet 21, 7

Let(*cont*)
Let us break off, say they, by strength of hand Psalm 2, 6
Jehovah serve, and let your joy converse Psalm 2, 24
But Lord, thus let me pray, Psalm 4, 28
God, find them guilty, let them fall Psalm 5, 29
Let th' enemy pursue my soul Psalm 7, 13
And overtake it, let him tread Psalm 7, 14
Let thy *good* hand be *laid*, Psalm 80, 70
Come let us cut them off say they, Psalm 83, 13
So let their Princes speed Psalm 83, 42
So let their Princes *bleed*. Psalm 83, 44
No quiet let them find, Psalm 83, 50
Giddy and *restless* let *them reel* Psalm 83, 51
Asham'd and troubl'd let them be, Psalm 83, 61
But let them never more Psalm 85, 34
And let my foes *then* see Psalm 86, 62
Into thy presence let my praier Psalm 88, 5
When I dye, let the earth be roul'd in flames. Prose 5, 1
Lethe
Lethe the River of Oblivion roules Par Lost 2.583
Lethean
They ferry over this *Lethean* Sound Par Lost 2.604
Lets
Lets her will rule; restraint she will not brook, Par Lost 9.1184
Swallows him with his Host, but them lets pass Par Lost 12.196
There in captivitie he lets them dwell Par Lost 12.344
She plumes her feathers, and lets grow her wings Mask 378
  Bridgewater ms 'letts'
Lets in defilement to the inward parts, Mask 466
  Bridgewater ms 'letts'
Letters
And letters where my tears have washt a wannish white. Passion 35
His Letters are deliver'd all and gon, Another 33
  line not in 1658 text
  1640, 1657 'letters'
Leucothea
Leucothea wak'd, and with fresh dews imbalmd Par Lost 11.135
By *Leucothea's* lovely hands, Mask 875
  Bridgewater ms 'Lewcotheas'
Levant
Forth rush the *Levant* and the *Ponent* Windes Par Lost 10.704
Level
And level pavement: from the arched roof Par Lost 1.726
Now shaves with level wing the Deep, then soares Par Lost 2.634
Betwixt them Lawns, or level Downs, and Flocks Par Lost 4.252
The Ayr was calm, and on the level brine, Lycidas 98
  Trinity ms 'levell'
Levelled
Leveld his deadly aime; thir fatall hands Par Lost 2.712
  1674 printed 'level d'
Leveld his eevning Rayes: it was a Rock Par Lost 4.543
Level'd, with such impetuous furie smote, Par Lost 6.591
But opposite in leveld West was set Par Lost 7.376
With thy long levell'd rule of streaming light, Mask 340
Leviathan
Leviathan, which God of all his works Par Lost 1.201
  ms 'Leviathan'
Tempest the Ocean: there Leviathan Par Lost 7.412
Levied
Levied to side with warring Winds, and poise Par Lost 2.905
One man, Assassin-like had levied Warr, Par Lost 11.219
Levity
Not out of levity, but over-powr'd Samson 880
Levy
Among themselves, and levie cruel warres, Par Lost 2.501
Lewd
Belial came last, then whom a Spirit more lewd Par Lost 1.490
So since into his Church lewd Hirelings climbe. Par Lost 4.193
But most by leud and lavish act of sin, Mask 465
  Bridgewater ms 'lewde'
  Trinity ms 'lewd and lavish' ←'the lascivious'
Lewdly
Yet leudly dar'st our ministring upbraid. Par Lost 6.182
Lewdly-pampered
Of that which lewdly-pamper'd Luxury Mask 770
  Trinity ms 'lewdly-pamperd'
  1637 'lewdy-pamper'd'
  Bridgewater ms 'leudly-pamper'd'
Liable
Not liable to fear or flight or paine. Par Lost 6.397
Proudly secure, yet liable to fall Samson 55
Liar
Argues no Leader but a lyar trac't, Par Lost 4.949
To be a lyer in four hundred mouths; Par Reg 1.428
Libbard
The Libbard, and the Tyger, as the Moale Par Lost 7.467
Libecchio
Sirocco, and *Libecchio*, Thus began Par Lost 10.706
Liberal
As liberal and free as infinite, Par Lost 4.415
So amply, and with hands so liberal Par Lost 8.362
With liberal hand: he scrupl'd not to eat Par Lost 9.997
Liberty
Hard liberty before the easie yoke Par Lost 2.256
Patron of liberty, who more then thou Par Lost 4.958
Jarr not with liberty, but well consist. Par Lost 5.793
With him the points of libertie, who made Par Lost 5.823
At first I thought that Libertie and Heav'n Par Lost 6.164

Liberty(*cont*)
Found worthy not of Libertie alone, Par Lost 6.420
Xerxes, the Libertie of *Greece* to yoke, Par Lost 10.307
Thou hast atchiev'd our libertie, confin'd Par Lost 10.368
Rational Libertie; yet know withall, Par Lost 12.82
Since thy original lapse, true Libertie Par Lost 12.83
Deprives them of thir outward libertie, Par Lost 12.100
His consort Libertie; what, but unbuild Par Lost 12.526
Large liberty to round this Globe of Earth, Par Reg 1.365
Should I of these the liberty regard, Par Reg 3.427
Then to love Bondage more then Liberty, Samson 270
Bondage with ease then strenuous liberty; Samson 271
That made for me, I knew that liberty Samson 803
This Gaol I count the house of Liberty Samson 949
With good success to work his liberty. Samson 1454
The Mountain Nymph, sweet Liberty; Allegro 36
After long toil their liberty had won, Psalm 114, 2
At *Chaeronea*, fatal to liberty Sonnet 10, 7
By the known rules of antient libertie, Sonnet 12, 2
  Trinity ms 'liberty'
Licence they mean when they cry libertie; Sonnet 12, 11
  Trinity ms 'liberty'
In libertyes defence, my noble task, Sonnet 22, 11
This is true Liberty when free born men Prose 9, 1
Libra
Of *Libra* to the fleecie Starr that bears Par Lost 3.558
Libyan
Beneath *Gibralter* to the *Lybian* sands. Par Lost 1.355
  ms 'Lybian'
Whom Gentiles *Ammon* call and *Lybian Jove*, Par Lost 4.277
  1667 '*Libyan*'
And vapour as the *Libyan* Air adust, Par Lost 12.635
Libyc
The Libyc *Hammon* shrinks his horn, Nativity 203
Lice
Frogs, Lice and Flies must all his Palace fill Par Lost 12.177
Licence
Licence they mean when they cry libertie; Sonnet 12, 11
Lichas
And *Lichas* from the top of *Oeta* threw Par Lost 2.545
Lick
My Hell-hounds, to lick up the draff and filth Par Lost 10.630
Licked
Fawning, and lick'd the ground whereon she trod. Par Lost 9.526
Lickerish
With lickerish baits fit to ensnare a brute? Mask 700
  line not in Bridgewater ms
Lictors
Lictors and rods the ensigns of thir power, Par Reg 4.65
Lids
Our eye-lids; other Creatures all day long Par Lost 4.616
Thy eye-lids? and remembrest what Decree Par Lost 5.674
Softly on my eye-lids laid. Penseroso 150
Under the opening eye-lids of the morn, Lycidas 26
  Trinity ms 'eyelids'
Lie
Lye thus astonisht on th' oblivious Pool, Par Lost 1.266
  ms 'Ly'
New courage and revive, though now they lye Par Lost 1.279
  ms 'ly'
In his own strength, this place may lye expos'd Par Lost 2.360
Lie vanquisht; thou hast givn me to possess Par Lost 3.243
That lie bestrowne unsightly and unsmooth, Par Lost 4.631
Where to lie hid; Sea he had searcht and Land Par Lost 9.76
Where Armies lie encampt, come flying, lur'd Par Lost 10.276
Of *Egypt* must lie dead. Thus with ten wounds Par Lost 12.190
I am; this chiefly, that my way must lie Par Reg 1.263
Lie in this miserable loathsom plight Samson 480
Better at home lie bed-rid, not only idle, Samson 579
With their grave Saws in slumber ly. Mask 110
  Bridgewater ms 'lye'
  Trinity ms 'lie'
And those happy climes that ly Mask 977
  Trinity ms 'lie'
  1637 'lie'
  B.M. ms 'lie'
Such sweet compulsion doth in musick ly, Arcades 68
  Trinity ms 'lie'
Where your old *Bards*, the famous *Druids* ly, Lycidas 53
  1638 'lie'
  Trinity ms 'lie'
Or that thy beauties lie in wormie bed, Fair Inf 31
How he before the thunderous throne doth lie, Vacation 36
Come tripping to the Room where thou didst lie; Vacation 62
And so Sepulcher'd in such pomp dost lie, Shakespear 15
Lie scatter'd on the Alpine mountains cold, Sonnet 18, 2
Me safe where ere I lie Psalm 4, 40
Thou wilt destroy that speak a ly Psalm 5, 15
Hath at length brought forth a Lie. Psalm 7, 54
Before thee *prostrate lie*. Psalm 88, 4
Surcharg'd my Soul doth lie, Psalm 88, 10
That in the grave lie *deep*. Psalm 88, 20
Lie
If it may stand him more in stead to lye, Par Reg 1.473
Lies
Lies dark and wilde, beat with perpetual storms Par Lost 2.588
Which way the neerest coast of darkness lyes Par Lost 2.958
Lies through your spacious Empire up to light, Par Lost 2.974

Lies(*cont*)
But in the Mount that lies from *Eden* North, Par Lost 4.569
That which before us lies in daily life, Par Lost 8.193
Free in thine own Arbitrement it lies. Par Lost 8.641
The danger lies, yet lies within his power: Par Lost 9.349
To us, in such aboundance lies our choice, Par Lost 9.620
Wisdom without their leave? and wherein lies Par Lost 9.725
It lies, yet ere Conception to prevent Par Lost 10.987
Wherere our days work lies, though now enjoind Par Lost 11.177
Where Cattle pastur'd late, now scatterd lies Par Lost 11.653
When on his shoulders each mans burden lies; Par Reg 2.462
See how he lies at random, carelesly diffus'd, Samson 118
As earst in highest, behold him where he lies. Samson 339
Let us go find the body where it lies Samson 1725
Lies through the perplex't paths of this drear Wood, Mask 37
That thou hast banish't from thy tongue with lies, Mask 692
whether deluded and soothing lies & soothing flatteries. Mask Tr. ms 22.20
thou man of lies & falshood, if thou give me it Mask Tr. ms 22.21
Wher perhaps som beauty lies, Allegro 79
Then lies him down the Lubbar Fend, Allegro 110
Set off to th' world, nor in broad rumour lies, Lycidas 80
To strew the Laureat Herse where *Lycid* lies. Lycidas 151
All meanly wrapt in the rude manger lies; Nativity 31
The Babe lies yet in smiling Infancy, Nativity 151
Then lies him meekly down fast by his Brethrens side. Passion 21
Here lies old *Hobson*, Death hath broke his girt, Carrier 1
Here lieth one who did most truly prove, Another 1
1640, 1657 'Here *Hobson* lyes'
No help for him in God there lies. Psalm 3, 6
Things false and vain and nothing else but lies? Psalm 4, 12
My defence, and in him lies Psalm 7, 40
Beyond the Realm of *Gaul*, a Land there lies, Prose 12, 8
Sea-girt it lies, where Giants dwelt of old, Prose 12, 9

Lies
By falsities and lyes the greatest part Par Lost 1.367
For man will hark'n to his glozing lyes, Par Lost 3.93
But by deceit and lies; this let him know, Par Lost 5.243
The starrie flock, allur'd them, and with lyes Par Lost 5.709
And flatter'd out of all, believing lies Par Lost 10.42
Of all his flattering Prophets glibb'd with lyes Par Reg 1.375
Deservedly thou griev'st, compos'd of lyes Par Reg 1.407
From the beginning, and in lies wilt end; Par Reg 1.408
By mixing somewhat true to vent more lyes. Par Reg 1.433
So many hollow complements and lies, Par Reg 4.124

Liest
To *Israel*, and now ly'st victorious Samson 1663

Lieth
Here lieth one who did most truly prove, Another 1
1640, 1657 'Here *Hobson* lyes'
Of head bereft li'th poor *Kenelm* King-born. Prose 13, 2

Life
By thir Rebellion, from the Books of Life. Par Lost 1.363
ms 'life'
Where all life dies, death lives, and Nature breeds, Par Lost 2.624
Behold mee then, mee for him, life for life Par Lost 3.236
Life in my self for ever, by thee I live, Par Lost 3.244
Receive new life. So Man, as is most just, Par Lost 3.294
His Brethren, ransomd with his own dear life. Par Lost 3.297
In Paradise, fast by the Tree of Life Par Lost 3.354
And flours aloft shading the Fount of Life, Par Lost 3.357
Or happiness in this or th' other life; Par Lost 3.450
Thence up he flew, and on the Tree of Life Par Lost 4.194
Sat like a Cormorant; yet not true Life Par Lost 4.196
And all amid them stood the Tree of Life, Par Lost 4.218
Of vegetable Gold; and next to Life Par Lost 4.220
And banisht from mans life his happiest life, Par Lost 4.317
Of knowledge, planted by the Tree of Life, Par Lost 4.424
So neer grows Death to Life, what ere Death is, Par Lost 4.425
Substantial Life, to have thee by my side Par Lost 4.485
Her old possession, and extinguish life Par Lost 4.666
What life the Gods live there, and such live thou. Par Lost 5.81
Of life ambrosial frutage bear, and vines Par Lost 5.427
Of substance, and in things that live, of life; Par Lost 5.474
To intellectual, give both life and sense, Par Lost 5.485
By living Streams among the Trees of Life, Par Lost 5.652
Spare out of life perhaps, and not repine, Par Lost 6.460
But live content, which is the calmest life: Par Lost 6.461
Adverse to life: then founded, then conglob'd Par Lost 7.239
The breath of Life; in his own Image hee Par Lost 7.526
To interrupt the sweet of Life, from which Par Lost 8.184
That which before us lies in daily life, Par Lost 8.193
For Man to tell how human Life began Par Lost 8.250
Amid the Garden by the Tree of Life, Par Lost 8.326
Rose up a Fountain by the Tree of Life; Par Lost 9.73
Of Creatures animate with gradual life Par Lost 9.112
Love not the lowest end of human life. Par Lost 9.241
How should ye? by the Fruit? it gives you Life Par Lost 9.686
And life more perfet have attaind then Fate Par Lost 9.689
To happier life, knowledge of Good and Evil; Par Lost 9.697
I could endure, without him live no life. Par Lost 9.833
Higher degree of Life, inducement strong Par Lost 9.934
Consort with thee, Death is to mee as Life; Par Lost 9.954
Farr otherwise th' event, not Death, but Life Par Lost 9.984
My other self, the partner of my life; Par Lost 10.128
And dust shalt eat all the dayes of thy Life. Par Lost 10.178
Shalt eate thereof all the days of thy Life; Par Lost 10.202
Least that pure breath of Life, the Spirit of Man Par Lost 10.784
Of Life that sinn'd; what dies but what had life Par Lost 10.790

Life(*cont*)
To Humane life, and houshold peace confound. Par Lost 10.908
Towards her, his life so late and sole delight, Par Lost 10.941
That after wretched Life must be at last Par Lost 10.985
Eve, thy contempt of life and pleasure seems Par Lost 10.1013
For loss of life and pleasure overlov'd. Par Lost 10.1019
To pass commodiously this life, sustain'd Par Lost 10.1083
To better life shall yeeld him, where with mee Par Lost 11.42
His final remedie, and after Life Par Lost 11.62
By Faith and faithful works, to second Life, Par Lost 11.64
By the waters of Life, where ere they sate Par Lost 11.79
Reach also of the Tree of Life, and eat, Par Lost 11.94
And guard all passage to the Tree of Life: Par Lost 11.122
The sourse of life; next favourable thou, Par Lost 11.169
Some days; how long, and what till then our life, Par Lost 11.198
To life prolongd and promisd Race, I now Par Lost 11.331
Safest thy life, and best prepar'd endure Par Lost 11.365
As once thou slepst, while Shee to life was formd. Par Lost 11.369
And from the Well of Life three drops instill'd. Par Lost 11.416
That beat out life; he fell, and deadly pale Par Lost 11.446
Better end heer unborn. Why is life giv'n Par Lost 11.502
Life offer'd, or soon beg to lay it down, Par Lost 11.506
The Balme of Life. To whom our Ancestor. Par Lost 11.546
Life much, bent rather how I may be quit Par Lost 11.548
Nor love thy Life, nor hate; but what thou livst Par Lost 11.553
Of Arts that polish Life, Inventers rare, Par Lost 11.610
Thir Bootie; scarce with Life the Shepherds flye, Par Lost 11.650
Select for life shall in the Ark be lodg'd, Par Lost 11.823
Inglorious life with servitude; for life Par Lost 12.220
To a reproachful life and cursed death, Par Lost 12.406
Proclaiming Life to all who shall believe Par Lost 12.407
By his own Nation, slaine for bringing Life; Par Lost 12.414
His death for Man, as many as offerd Life Par Lost 12.425
In sin for ever lost from life; this act Par Lost 12.429
A gentle wafting to immortal Life. Par Lost 12.435
To his Disciples, Men who in his Life Par Lost 12.438
Of washing them from guilt of sin to Life Par Lost 12.443
And to the faithful Death the Gate of Life; Par Lost 12.571
Whereby they may direct their future life. Par Reg 1.396
Were dead, who sought his life, and missing fill'd Par Reg 2.77
Hath been our dwelling many years, his life Par Reg 2.80
But life preserves, destroys life's enemy, Par Reg 2.372
Affecting private life, or more obscure Par Reg 3.22
Thy life hath yet been private, most part spent Par Reg 3.232
Of fate, and chance, and change in human life; Par Reg 4.265
But vertue joyn'd with riches and long life, Par Reg 4.298
Wealth, pleasure, pain or torment, death and life, Par Reg 4.305
By me propos'd in life contemplative, Par Reg 4.370
Ambrosial, Fruits fetcht from the tree of life, Par Reg 4.589
And from the fount of life Ambrosial drink, Par Reg 4.590
Would ask a life to wail, but chief of all, Samson 66
Since light so necessary is to life, Samson 90
And almost life it self, if it be true Samson 91
To live a life half dead, a living death, Samson 100
To all the miseries of life, Samson 107
Life in captivity Samson 108
Him who imploring mercy sues for life, Samson 512
Sam. His pardon I implore; but as for life, Samson 521
Softn'd with pleasure and voluptuous life; Samson 534
Nor th' other light of life continue long, Samson 592
All chances incident to mans frail life Samson 656
To life obscur'd, which were a fair dismission, Samson 688
Thou mine, not theirs: if aught against my life Samson 888
Life yet hath many solaces, enjoy'd Samson 915
Sam. Not for thy life, lest fierce remembrance wake Samson 952
Of secresie, my safety, and my life. Samson 1002
Not wedlock-trechery endangering life. Samson 1009
On his whole life, not sway'd Samson 1059
This day will be remarkable in my life Samson 1388
And for a life who will not change his purpose? Samson 1406
How dy'd he? death to life is crown or shame. Samson 1579
Then all thy life had slain before. Samson 1668
A life Heroic, on his Enemies Samson 1711
To keep my life and honour unassail'd. Mask 220
line not in Bridgewater ms
Curs'd as his life. *Spir*. Alas good ventrous youth, Mask 609
Trinity ms 'downe to the hips' ←'lowest hips' ←'hipps'
1637 'Downe to the hipps'
Bridgewater ms 'downe to the hipps'
To life so friendly, or so cool to thirst. Mask 678
And slits the thin spun life. But not the praise, Lycidas 76
In giving limit to her life. Winchester 14
Shortned hast thy own lives lease, Winchester 52
Rest that gives all men life, gave him his death, Another 11
And lack of load, made his life burdensom, Another 24
line not in 1658 text
Of Death, call'd Life; which us from Life doth sever. Sonnet 14, 4
Trinity ms 'call'd Life' ←'call'd life'
Trinity ms 'from life' ←'from blis' ←'from life' ←'from heavn'
To measure life, learn thou betimes, and know Sonnet 21, 9
Men whose Life, Learning, Faith and pure intent Forcers 9
Trinity ms 'life'
That of my life distrustfully thus say, Psalm 3, 5
My life down to the earth and roul Psalm 7, 15
And life in us renew. Psalm 85, 28
To seek my life, and in their eyes Psalm 86, 51
My life *at deaths uncherful dore* Psalm 88, 11

Life(*cont*)
From life discharg'd and parted quite — Psalm 88, 17
E're yet my life be spent, — Psalm 88, 54
Life-blood
And Life-blood streaming fresh; wide was the wound, — Par Lost 8.467
Life-giving
Of that life-giving Plant, but only us'd — Par Lost 4.199
Lifeless
Living or liveless to be found was none, — Par Lost 3.443
As good have grown there still a liveless Rib. — Par Lost 9.1154
Outrage from liveless things; but Discord first — Par Lost 10.707
Lift
With Head up-lift above the wave, and Eyes — Par Lost 1.193
ms 'uplift'
Will once more lift us up, in spight of Fate, — Par Lost 2.393
Of Heav'ns ascent they lift thir Feet, when loe — Par Lost 3.486
Divide the night, and lift our thoughts to Heaven. — Par Lost 4.688
Liken on Earth conspicuous, that may lift — Par Lost 6.299
They shall up lift thee, lest at any time — Par Reg 4.558
Lift not thy spear against the Muses Bowre, — Sonnet 8, 9
On us lift up the light — Psalm 4, 29
Lift up the favour of thy count'nance bright. — Psalm 4, 30
I lift my soul *and voice*, — Psalm 86, 12
'Gainst them that rais'd thee dost thou lift thy horn, — Prose 3, 2
Lifted
And wrought but malice; lifted up so high — Par Lost 4.49
So saying, a noble stroke he lifted high, — Par Lost 6.189
The holy City lifted high her Towers, — Par Reg 4.545
May never this just sword be lifted up, — Mask 601
Their loud up-lifted Angel trumpets blow, — Musick 11
Trinity ms 'up-lifted' ←'uplifted' ←'high lifted' ←'unsa', ms defective
Lifting
Up lifting bore them in thir hands: Amaze, — Par Lost 6.646
Our Saviour lifting up his eyes beheld — Par Reg 2.338
Above the rest lifting his stately head — Par Reg 4.48
Ligea
And fair *Ligea*'s golden comb, — Mask 880
Trinity ms 'Ligeas', but line deleted
Bridgewater ms 'Ligeas'
Light
No light, but rather darkness visible — Par Lost 1.63
As far remov'd from God and light of Heav'n — Par Lost 1.73
From him, who in the happy Realms of Light — Par Lost 1.85
ms 'light'
The seat of desolation, voyd of light, — Par Lost 1.181
For that celestial light? Be it so, since he — Par Lost 1.245
And with thir darkness durst affront his light. — Par Lost 1.391
With *Naphtha* and *Asphaltus* yeilded light — Par Lost 1.729
Heav'ns purest Light, yet our great Enemy — Par Lost 2.137
This horror will grow milde, this darkness light, — Par Lost 2.220
As he our darkness, cannot we his Light — Par Lost 2.269
Dwell not unvisited of Heav'ns fair Light — Par Lost 2.398
And hard, that out of Hell leads up to light; — Par Lost 2.433
1667 'Light'
To that new world of light and bliss, among — Par Lost 2.867
Bordering on light; when strait behold the Throne — Par Lost 2.959
Lies through your spacious Empire up to light, — Par Lost 2.974
Of light appears, and from the walls of Heav'n — Par Lost 2.1035
Wafts on the calmer wave by dubious light — Par Lost 2.1042
Hail holy Light, ofspring of Heav'n first-born, — Par Lost 3.1
1667 'light'
May I express thee unblam'd? since God is light, — Par Lost 3.3
And never but in unapproached light — Par Lost 3.4
So much the rather thou Celestial light — Par Lost 3.51
Not farr off Heav'n, in the Precincts of light, — Par Lost 3.88
Light after light well us'd they shall attain, — Par Lost 3.196
Fountain of Light, thy self invisible — Par Lost 3.375
Of dawning light turnd thither-ward in haste — Par Lost 3.500
Dispenses Light from farr; they as they move — Par Lost 3.579
With radiant light, as glowing Iron with fire; — Par Lost 3.594
Light shon, and order from disorder sprung: — Par Lost 3.713
With light from hence, though but reflected, shines; — Par Lost 3.723
That place is Earth the seat of Man, that light — Par Lost 3.724
With borrowd light her countenance triform — Par Lost 3.730
Apparent Queen unvaild her peerless light, — Par Lost 4.608
With first approach of light, we must be ris'n, — Par Lost 4.624
Or glittering Starr-light without thee is sweet. — Par Lost 4.656
Ministring light prepar'd, they set and rise; — Par Lost 4.664
Full Orb'd the Moon, and with more pleasing light — Par Lost 5.42
Speak yee who best can tell, ye Sons of light, — Par Lost 5.160
His praise, who out of Darkness call'd up Light. — Par Lost 5.179
Disperse it, as now light dispels the dark. — Par Lost 5.208
The Sun that light imparts to all, receives — Par Lost 5.423
Hear all ye Angels, Progenie of Light, — Par Lost 5.600
From that high mount of God, whence light & shade — Par Lost 5.643
Nightly before him, saw without thir light — Par Lost 5.714
Unbarr'd the gates of Light. There is a Cave — Par Lost 6.4
Where light and darkness in perpetual round — Par Lost 6.6
Light issues forth, and at the other dore — Par Lost 6.9
So beauteous, op'ning to the ambient light. — Par Lost 6.481
Out of such prison, though Spirits of purest light, — Par Lost 6.660
And the great Light of Day yet wants to run — Par Lost 7.98
Let ther be Light, said God, and forthwith Light — Par Lost 7.243
Sojourn'd the while. God saw the Light was good; — Par Lost 7.249
And light from darkness by the Hemisphere — Par Lost 7.250
Divided: Light the Day, and Darkness Night — Par Lost 7.251
By the Celestial Quires, when Orient Light — Par Lost 7.254

Light(*cont*)
To give Light on the Earth; and it was so. — Par Lost 7.345
And Light from Darkness to divide. God saw, — Par Lost 7.352
Of Light by farr the greater part he took, — Par Lost 7.359
And drink the liquid Light, firm to retaine — Par Lost 7.362
Her gather'd beams, great Palace now of Light. — Par Lost 7.363
Repairing, in thir gold'n Urns draw Light, — Par Lost 7.365
His mirror, with full face borrowing her Light — Par Lost 7.377
From him, for other light she needed none — Par Lost 7.378
Diurnal) meerly to officiate light — Par Lost 8.22
Of incorporeal speed, her warmth and light; — Par Lost 8.37
Still luminous by his ray. What if that light — Par Lost 8.140
Communicating Male and Femal Light, — Par Lost 8.150
Each Orb a glimps of Light, conveyd so farr — Par Lost 8.156
Light back to them, is obvious to dispute. — Par Lost 8.158
Glad we return'd up to the coasts of Light — Par Lost 8.245
What e're I saw. Thou Sun, said I, faire Light, — Par Lost 8.273
This happie Light, when answer none return'd, — Par Lost 8.285
On his Hill top, to light the bridal Lamp. — Par Lost 8.520
Light above Light, for thee alone, as seems, — Par Lost 9.105
Now when as sacred Light began to dawne — Par Lost 9.192
Hovering and blazing with delusive Light, — Par Lost 9.639
To Starr or Sun-light, spread thir umbrage broad — Par Lost 9.1087
In fellowships of joy: the Sons of Light — Par Lost 11.80
To resalute the World with sacred Light — Par Lost 11.134
Darkness ere Dayes mid-course, and Morning light — Par Lost 11.204
They light the Nuptial Torch, and bid invoke — Par Lost 11.590
One Man except, the onely Son of light — Par Lost 11.808
Shall long usurp; ere the third dawning light — Par Lost 12.421
Out of his grave, fresh as the dawning light, — Par Lost 12.423
Light out of darkness! full of doubt I stand, — Par Lost 12.473
From Hell's deep-vaulted Den to dwell in light, — Par Reg 1.116
The City gates out powr'd, light armed Troops — Par Reg 3.311
To admiration, led by Natures light; — Par Reg 4.228
Built nobly, pure the air, and light the soil, — Par Reg 4.239
Light from above, from the fountain of light, — Par Reg 4.289
By light of Nature not in all quite lost. — Par Reg 4.352
As day-light sunk, and brought in lowring night — Par Reg 4.398
Privation meer of light and absent day. — Par Reg 4.400
In the bosom of bliss, and light of light — Par Reg 4.597
Light the prime work of God to me is extinct, — Samson 70
They creep, yet see, I dark in light expos'd — Samson 75
Let there be light, and light was over all; — Samson 84
Since light so necessary is to life, — Samson 90
That light is in the Soul, — Samson 92
Then had I not been thus exil'd from light; — Samson 98
As in the land of darkness yet in light, — Samson 99
Shut up from outward light — Samson 160
For inward light alas — Samson 162
Cause light again within thy eies to spring, — Samson 584
That these dark orbs no more shall treat with light, — Samson 591
Nor th' other light of life continue long, — Samson 592
Tis onely day-light that makes Sin — Mask 126
Trinity ms 'daylight'
Bridgewater ms 'day light'
In a light fantastick round. — Mask 144
And envious darknes, e're they could return, — Mask 194
Trinity ms 'and envious darknesse' ←'to the soone parting light'
With everlasting oil, to give due light — Mask 199
line not in Bridgewater ms
In such a scant allowance of Star-light, — Mask 308
1637 'starre light'
Bridgewater ms 'starr light'
Trinity ms 'starre light'
With thy long levell'd rule of streaming light, — Mask 340
As that the single want of light and noise — Mask 369
By her own radiant light, though Sun and Moon — Mask 374
He that has light within his own cleer brest — Mask 381
And so bestudd with Stars, that they below — Mask 734
Trinity ms 'and so bestudde with starres' ←'would so be studde the center with thire starre light'
Would grow inur'd to light, and com at last — Mask 735
Trinity ms 'light' ←'day'
On the light fantastick toe, — Allegro 34
Rob'd in flames, and Amber light, — Allegro 61
Till the live-long day-light fail, — Allegro 99
Teach light to counterfeit a gloom, — Penseroso 80
Casting a dimm religious light. — Penseroso 160
In the center of her light. — Arcades 19
That glorious Form, that Light unsufferable, — Nativity 8
Hath took no print of the approching light, — Nativity 20
Wherin the Prince of light — Nativity 62
For all the morning light, — Nativity 73
A Globe of circular light, — Nativity 110
Did fill the new-made world with light. — Psalm 136, 26
In Wintry solstice like the shortn'd light — Passion 6
To live with him, and sing in endles morn of light. — Musick 28
Of blazing Majesty and Light, — Winchester 70
Pull'd off his Boots, and took away the light: — Carrier 16
He di'd for heavines that his Cart went light, — Another 22
line not in 1658 text
To fill thy odorous Lamp with deeds of light, — Sonnet 9, 10
When I consider how my light is spent, — Sonnet 19, 1
Doth God exact day labour, light deny'd, — Sonnet 19, 7
What neat repast shall feast us, light and choice, — Sonnet 20, 9
Bereft of light thir seeing have forgot, — Sonnet 22, 3
1694 'Sight'

Light(*cont*)	
On us lift up the light	Psalm 4, 29
Shine forth, *and from thy cloud give light*,	Psalm 80, 7
Light	
Thir course, in even ballance down they light	Par Lost 1.349
Light as the Lightning glimps they ran, they flew,	Par Lost 6.642
Let it; I reck not, so it light well aim'd,	Par Lost 9.173
Or daring, first on mee th' assault shall light.	Par Lost 9.305
Whoever judg'd, the worst on mee must light,	Par Lost 10.73
On mee as on thir natural center light	Par Lost 10.740
The sentence from thy head remov'd may light	Par Lost 10.934
The burd'n of many Ages, on me light	Par Lost 11.767
Green Tree or ground whereon his foot may light;	Par Lost 11.858
Yet as being oft times noxious where they light	Par Reg 4.460
Light	
With Sails and Wind thir canie Waggons light:	Par Lost 3.439
Where thou art weigh'd, and shown how light, how weak,	Par Lost 4.1012
Was Aerie light from pure digestion bred,	Par Lost 5.4
Vaild with his gorgeous wings, up springing light	Par Lost 5.250
No inconvenient Diet, nor too light Fare:	Par Lost 5.495
Soft she withdrew, and like a Wood-Nymph light	Par Lost 9.386
Light-armed	
Light-arm'd or heavy, sharp, smooth, swift or slow,	Par Lost 2.902
Lookd round, and Scouts each Coast light-armed scoure,	Par Lost 6.529
Lighted	
Where he first lighted, soon discernd his looks	Par Lost 4.570
Then lighted from his gorgeous Throne, for now	Par Lost 6.103
First lighted from his Wing, and landed safe	Par Lost 10.316
Down from a Skie of Jasper lighted now	Par Lost 11.209
But with a scarce-wel-lighted flame;	Winchester 20
Lighten	
In offices of Love, how we may light'n	Par Lost 10.960
To light'n what thou suffer'st, and appease	Samson 744
Lightens	
Nor lightens aught each mans peculiar load.	Par Reg 1.402
Lighter	
Thir lighter wings. To whom these most adhere,	Par Lost 2.906
Springs lighter the green stalk, from thence the leaves	Par Lost 5.480
Of lighter toes, and such Court guise	Mask 962
Trinity ms 'lighter' ← 'nimbler' ← 'speedier'	
Lightest	
Or touch with lightest moment of impulse	Par Lost 10.45
Lightly	
Touch'd lightly; for no falshood can endure	Par Lost 4.811
Lightly dispers'd, and the shrill Matin Song	Par Lost 5.7
-As lightly from his grassy Couch up rose	Par Reg 2.282
Lightning	
Wing'd with red Lightning and impetuous rage,	Par Lost 1.175
ms 'lightning'	
Infernal Thunder, and for Lightning see	Par Lost 2.66
Light'ning Divine, ineffable, serene,	Par Lost 5.734
Light as the Lightning glimps they ran, they flew,	Par Lost 6.642
Glar'd lightning, and shot forth pernicious fire	Par Lost 6.849
Saw Satan fall like Lightning down from Heav'n,	Par Lost 10.184
Tine the slant Lightning, whose thwart flame driv'n down	Par Lost 10.1075
In Thunder Lightning and loud Trumpets sound	Par Lost 12.229
Fierce rain with lightning mixt, water with fire	Par Reg 4.412
Or Lightning thou shalt fall from Heav'n trod down	Par Reg 4.620
Swift as the lightning glance he executes	Samson 1284
Lights	
Here Love his golden shafts imploies, here lights	Par Lost 4.763
Again th' Almightie spake: Let there be Lights	Par Lost 7.339
And let them be for Lights as I ordaine	Par Lost 7.343
And God made two great Lights, great for thir use	Par Lost 7.346
With thousand lesser Lights dividual holds,	Par Lost 7.382
Lights	
He lights, if it were Land that ever burn'd	Par Lost 1.228
But in his way lights on the barren Plaines	Par Lost 3.437
Nor staid, till on *Niphates* top he lights.	Par Lost 3.742
Lights on his feet. As when a prowling Wolfe,	Par Lost 4.183
Lights on a heap of nitrous Powder, laid	Par Lost 4.815
He lights, and to his proper shape returns	Par Lost 5.276
Of all corruption, all the blame lights due;	Par Lost 10.833
Like	
Dove-like satst brooding on the vast Abyss	Par Lost 1.21
Hung on his shoulders like the Moon, whose Orb	Par Lost 1.287
Over the burning Marle, not like those steps	Par Lost 1.296
Like Night, and darken'd all the Land of *Nile:*	Par Lost 1.343
A multitude, like which the populous North	Par Lost 1.351
Came like a Deluge on the South, and spread	Par Lost 1.354
Like cumbrous flesh; but in what shape they choose	Par Lost 1.428
Shon like a Meteor streaming to the Wind	Par Lost 1.537
Stood like a Towr; his form had yet not lost	Par Lost 1.591
As stood like these, could ever know repulse?	Par Lost 1.630
Rose like an Exhalation, with the sound	Par Lost 1.711
Built like a Temple, where *Pilasters* round	Par Lost 1.713
Dropt from the Zenith like a falling Star,	Par Lost 1.745
(Though like a cover'd field, where Champions bold	Par Lost 1.763
Throng numberless, like that Pigmean Race	Par Lost 1.780
ms defective here	
And in thir own dimensions like themselves	Par Lost 1.793
And God-like imitated State; him round	Par Lost 2.511
Unterrifi'd, and like a Comet burn'd,	Par Lost 2.708
So wide they stood, and like a Furnace mouth	Par Lost 2.888
Springs upward like a Pyramid of fire	Par Lost 2.1013
And like a weather-beaten Vessel holds	Par Lost 2.1043
God-like fruition, quitted all to save	Par Lost 3.307
Pavement that like a Sea of Jasper shon	Par Lost 3.363
Like(*cont*)	
Like Quivers hung, and with Praeamble sweet	Par Lost 3.367
Drawn round about thee like a radiant Shrine,	Par Lost 3.379
Up hither like Aereal vapours flew	Par Lost 3.445
Like those *Hesperian* Gardens fam'd of old,	Par Lost 3.568
There lands the Fiend, a spot like which perhaps	Par Lost 3.588
And like a devillish Engine back recoiles	Par Lost 4.17
Look'st from thy sole Dominion like the God	Par Lost 4.33
Sat like a Cormorant; yet not true Life	Par Lost 4.196
Like this fair Paradise, your sense, yet such	Par Lost 4.379
Not like these narrow limits, to receive	Par Lost 4.384
Multitudes like thy self, and thence be call'd	Par Lost 4.474
Squat like a Toad, close at the eare of *Eve;*	Par Lost 4.800
Like gentle breaths from Rivers pure, thence raise	Par Lost 4.806
Why satst thou like an enemie in waite	Par Lost 4.825
But like a proud Steed reind, went hautie on,	Par Lost 4.858
Like *Teneriff* or *Atlas* unremov'd:	Par Lost 4.987
One shapd and wing'd like one of those from Heav'n	Par Lost 5.55
Girt like a Starrie Zone his waste, and round	Par Lost 5.281
Skie-tinctur'd grain. Like *Maia*'s son he stood,	Par Lost 5.285
His god-like Guest, walks forth, without more train	Par Lost 5.351
They came, that like *Pomona*'s Arbour smil'd	Par Lost 5.378
Grateful vicissitude, like Day and Night;	Par Lost 6.8
Under thir God-like Leaders, in the Cause	Par Lost 6.67
All like himself rebellious, by whose aid	Par Lost 7.140
Stretcht like a Promontorie sleeps or swimmes,	Par Lost 7.414
With Goddess-like demeanour forth she went;	Par Lost 8.59
I led her blushing like the Morn: all Heav'n,	Par Lost 8.511
Looses discount'nanc't, and like folly shewes;	Par Lost 8.553
Like a black mist low creeping, he held on	Par Lost 9.180
Soft she withdrew, and like a Wood-Nymph light	Par Lost 9.386
In gate surpass'd and Goddess-like deport,	Par Lost 9.389
As they, participating God-like food?	Par Lost 9.717
Saw Satan fall like Lightning down from Heav'n,	Par Lost 10.184
By his Avengers, since no place like this	Par Lost 10.241
Thir penance, laden with Fruit, like that	Par Lost 10.550
The Frutage fair to sight, like that which grew	Par Lost 10.561
Like distant breadth to *Taurus* with the Seav'n	Par Lost 10.673
Like his, and colour Serpentine may shew	Par Lost 10.870
O Sons, like one of us Man is become	Par Lost 11.84
Had, like a double *Janus*, all thir shape	Par Lost 11.129
One man, Assassin-like had levied Warr,	Par Lost 11.219
So maist thou live, till like ripe Fruit thou drop	Par Lost 11.535
Like a dark Ceeling stood; down rush'd the Rain	Par Lost 11.743
Like him in faith, in wisdom, and renown;	Par Lost 12.154
Surcharg'd, as had like grief bin dew'd in tears,	Par Lost 12.373
By Faith not void of workes: this God-like act	Par Lost 12.427
Or theirs whom he redeems, a death like sleep,	Par Lost 12.434
For death, like that which the redeemer dy'd.	Par Lost 12.445
Induces best to hope of like success.	Par Reg 1.105
Publish his God-like office now mature,	Par Reg 1.188
Like things of thee to all that present stood.	Par Reg 1.258
The Spirit descended on me like a Dove,	Par Reg 1.282
Thy wisdom, and behold thy God-like deeds?	Par Reg 1.386
Or like a Fawning Parasite obey'st;	Par Reg 1.452
Of like succeeding here; I summon all	Par Reg 2.143
As the noon Skie; more like to Goddesses	Par Reg 2.156
Would'st thou not eat? Thereafter as I like	Par Reg 2.321
What if with like aversion I reject	Par Reg 2.457
These God-like Vertues wherefore dost thou hide?	Par Reg 3.21
Like to themselves, distinguishable scarce	Par Reg 3.424
Many a fair Edifice besides, more like	Par Reg 4.55
On *David*'s Throne, it shall be like a tree	Par Reg 4.147
Like turbulencies in the affairs of men,	Par Reg 4.462
Her pile, far off appearing like a Mount	Par Reg 4.547
Rule in the Clouds; like an Autumnal Star	Par Reg 4.619
From restless thoughts, that like a deadly swarm	Samson 19
Like whom the Gentiles feign to bear up Heav'n.	Samson 150
Who like a foolish Pilot have shipwrack't,	Samson 198
Fearless of danger, like a petty God	Samson 529
Like a tame Weather, all my precious fleece,	Samson 538
Like a stately Ship	Samson 714
Like a fair flower surcharg'd with dew, she weeps	Samson 728
And arts of every woman false like thee,	Samson 749
Of secrets, then with like infirmity	Samson 776
I leave him to his lot, and like my own.	Samson 996
Much like thy riddle, *Samson*, in one day	Samson 1016
Were bristles rang'd like those that ridge the back	Samson 1137
Then like a Robber stripdst them of thir robes?	Samson 1188
Like a wild Beast, I am content to go.	Samson 1403
Garrison'd round about him like a Camp	Samson 1497
Like that self-begott'n bird	Samson 1699
Like *Samson*, and heroicly hath finish'd	Samson 1710
That like to rich, and various gemms inlay	Mask 22
Much like his Father, but his Mother more,	Mask 57
Like a sad Votarist in Palmers weed	Mask 189
line not in Bridgewater ms	
It were a journey like the path to Heav'n,	Mask 303
But beauty like the fair Hesperian Tree	Mask 393
And like a quiver'd Nymph with Arrows keen	Mask 422
Either som one like us night-founder'd here,	Mask 483
Like stabl'd wolves, or tigers at their prey,	Mask 534
Rose like a steam of rich distill'd Perfumes,	Mask 556
Gather'd like scum, and setl'd to it self	Mask 595
Unknown, and like esteem'd, and the dull swayn	Mask 634
line not in Bridgewater ms	
Or like the sons of *Vulcan* vomit smoak,	Mask 655
And harshly deal like an ill borrower	Mask 683

Like(*cont*)
line not in Bridgewater ms
And live like Natures bastards, not her sons, Mask 727
Trinity ms 'like' ←'for' ←'as'
If you let slip time, like a neglected rose Mask 743
line not in Bridgewater ms
Love-darting eyes, or tresses like the Morn? Mask 753
line not in Bridgewater ms
Like one that had bin led astray Penseroso 69
To somthing like Prophetic strain. Penseroso 174
Shooting her beams like silver threds, Arcades 16
Sitting like a Goddes bright, Arcades 18
Like to that sanguine flower inscrib'd with woe. Lycidas 106
Th' enameld *Arras* of the Rainbow wearing, Nativity 143
1673 'Orb'd in a Rain-bow and like glories wearing'
The high, huge-bellied Mountains skip like Rams Psalm 114, 11
Amongst their Ews, the little Hills like Lambs. Psalm 114, 12
The floods stood still like Walls of Glass, Psalm 136, 49
Or *Trent*, who like some earth-born Giant spreads Vacation 93
In Wintry solstice like the shortn'd light Passion 6
His Godlike acts, and his temptations fierce, Passion 24
Next her much like to thee in story, Winchester 62
And at her next birth much like thee, Winchester 67
Like fortunes may her soul acquaint, Winchester 72
And like an Engin mov'd with wheel and waight, Another 9
Those rugged names to our like mouths grow sleek Sonnet 11, 10
Thy age, like ours, O Soul of Sir *John Cheek*, Sonnet 11, 12
Brought to me like *Alcestis* from the grave, Sonnet 23, 2
Like to a potters vessel shiver'd so. Psalm 2, 21
If once his wrath take fire like fuel sere. Psalm 2, 27
Talking like this worlds brood; Psalm 4, 27
Of my foes that urge like fire; Psalm 7, 21
Who leadest like a flock of sheep Psalm 80, 3
But ye shall die like men, and fall Psalm 82, 23
Like stubble from the wind. Psalm 83, 52
Truth from the earth *like to a flowr* Psalm 85, 45
Like thee among the gods is none Psalm 86, 25
Like to thy *glorious* works. Psalm 86, 28
And like the slain *in bloody fight* Psalm 88, 19
Like waves they me persue. Psalm 88, 68

Like
Infected *Sions* daughters with like heat, Par Lost 1.453
His own and *Rhea*'s Son like measure found; Par Lost 1.513
Like doubtful hue: but he his wonted pride Par Lost 1.527
To be created like to us, though less Par Lost 2.349
Synod of Gods, and like to what ye are, Par Lost 2.391
For never but once more was either like Par Lost 2.721
Not all parts like, but all alike informd Par Lost 3.593
That stone, or like to that which here below Par Lost 3.600
Like honour to obtain, and as his Eye Par Lost 3.660
Like consort to thy self canst no where find. Par Lost 4.448
Mind us of like repose, since God hath set Par Lost 4.612
Endowd with all thir gifts, and O too like Par Lost 4.715
Your message, like to end as much in vain? Par Lost 4.833
The fall of others from like state of bliss; Par Lost 5.241
Each to other like, more then on earth is thought? Par Lost 5.576
Mean while in other parts like deeds deservd Par Lost 6.354
Our selves with like defence, to me deserves Par Lost 6.467
Like instrument to plague the Sons of men Par Lost 6.505
On Wheels (for like to Pillars most they seem'd Par Lost 6.573
To whom thus *Belial* in like gamesom mood, Par Lost 6.620
The rest in imitation to like Armes Par Lost 6.662
Thy tempring; with like safetie guided down Par Lost 7.15
To those Apostates, least the like befall Par Lost 7.44
Like things to like, the rest to several place Par Lost 7.240
Seemd like to Heav'n, a seat where Gods might dwell, Par Lost 7.329
Second to me or like, equal much less. Par Lost 8.407
By conversation with his like to help, Par Lost 8.418
Like of his like, his Image multipli'd, Par Lost 8.424
O Earth, how like to Heav'n, if not preferr'd Par Lost 9.99
Why shouldst not thou like sense within thee feel Par Lost 9.315
Single with like defence, wherever met, Par Lost 9.325
All other Beasts that saw, with like desire Par Lost 9.592
Certain to undergoe like doom, if Death Par Lost 9.953
With secret amity things of like kinde Par Lost 10.248
Rais'd from thir Dark *Divan*, and with like joy Par Lost 10.457
Catcht by Contagion, like in punishment, Par Lost 10.544
Like change on Sea and Land, sideral blast, Par Lost 10.693
To *Satan* only like both crime and doom. Par Lost 10.841
With like desire, which would be meserie Par Lost 10.997
Hee with a crew, whom like Ambition joyns Par Lost 12.38
For ever shall endure; the like shall sing Par Lost 12.324

Like
Affects me equally; nor can I like Par Lost 5.97
Stand readie to receive them, if they like Par Lost 6.561

Liked
Fast caught, they lik'd, and each his liking chose; Par Lost 11.587
I never lik'd thy talk, thy offers less, Par Reg 4.171

Likelier
They taste and die: what likelier can ensue? Par Lost 4.527

Likeliest
Leads him perplext, where he may likeliest find Par Lost 2.525
And here art likeliest by supream decree Par Lost 3.659
As likeliest was, when two such Foes met arm'd; Par Lost 6.688
Likeliest she seemd, *Pomona* when she fled Par Lost 9.394
1667 'Likest'
And on his Quest, where likeliest he might finde Par Lost 9.414
Where he might likeliest find this new-declar'd, Par Reg 1.121

Likeliest(*cont*)
And not returning that would likeliest render Par Reg 3.130
Likeliest, and neerest to the present ayd Mask 90
Trinity ms 'likliest'
Is now the labour of my thoughts, 'tis likeliest Mask 192
Trinity ms 'likliest'

Likely
Those argent Fields more likely habitants, Par Lost 3.460
Not likely to part hence without contest; Par Lost 4.872
Were better, and most likelie if from mee Par Lost 9.365
To us, as likely tasting to attaine Par Lost 9.935

Liken
Liken on Earth conspicuous, that may lift Par Lost 6.299

Likeness
The likeness of a Kingly Crown had on. Par Lost 2.673
Of force to its own likeness: up he starts Par Lost 4.813
Thy likeness, thy fit help, thy other self, Par Lost 8.450
Satan in likeness of an Angel bright Par Lost 10.327
Disfiguring not Gods likeness, but thir own, Par Lost 11.521
Or if his likeness, by themselves defac't Par Lost 11.522
Heaven open'd, and in likeness of a Dove Par Reg 1.30
And take the Weeds and likenes of a Swain, Mask 84
1637 'likenesse'
Trinity ms 'liknesse'
Bridgewater ms 'likenesse'
And the inglorious likenes of a beast Mask 528
Trinity ms 'likenesse'
Bridgewater ms 'likeness'
1637 'likenesse'
In the kind office of a Chamberlin Carrier 14
1658 'Death in the likenesse'

Likening
Lik'ning his Maker to the Grazed Ox, Par Lost 1.486
ms 'Likning'
By lik'ning spiritual to corporal forms, Par Lost 5.573

Likes
Which God likes best, into thir inmost bowre Par Lost 4.738
Assume, as likes them best, condense or rare. Par Lost 6.353
There let them learn, as likes them, to despise Par Lost 6.717
When and where likes me best, I can command? Par Reg 2.382

Likest
Likest to thee in shape and count'nance bright, Par Lost 2.756
The golden Sun in splendor likest Heaven Par Lost 3.572
Of Godlike Power: for likest Gods they seemd, Par Lost 6.301
Likeliest she seemd, *Pomona* when she fled Par Lost 9.394
1667 'Likest'
Of Spirits likest to himself in guile Par Reg 2.237
These here revolve, or, as thou lik'st, at home, Par Reg 4.281
That likest thy *Narcissus* are? Mask 237
Or likest hovering dreams Penseroso 9

Likewise
If likewise he some fair one wedded not, Fair Inf 11

Liking
Fast caught, they lik'd, and each his liking chose; Par Lost 11.587

Lilied
By sandy *Ladons* Lillied banks. Arcades 97
Trinity ms 'lillied'

Lilies
In twisted braids of Lillies knitting Mask 862
B.M. ms 'Lillys'
1637 'lillies'
Trinity ms 'lillies'
Bridgewater ms 'lillies'

Lily
The Lillie and Rose, that neither sow'd nor spun. Sonnet 20, 8

Limb
Not ti'd or manacl'd with joynt or limb, Par Lost 1.426
ms 'lim'
Distinguishable in member, joynt, or limb, Par Lost 2.668
Youth smil'd Celestial, and to every Limb Par Lost 3.638
They Limb themselves, and colour, shape or size Par Lost 6.352
My self I then perus'd, and Limb by Limb Par Lost 8.267
Of membrane, joynt, or limb, exclusive barrs: Par Lost 8.625
And strength, of courage hautie, and of limb Par Lost 9.484
Hath walk'd about, and each limb to survey, Samson 1089

Limbec
Draind through a Limbec to his Native forme. Par Lost 3.605

Limbed
Limb'd and full grown: out of the ground up rose Par Lost 7.456
And large-lim'd *Og* he did subdue, Psalm 136, 69
1673 'large-limb'd'

Limber
Insect or Worme; those wav'd thir limber fans Par Lost 7.476

Limbo
Into a *Limbo* large and broad, since calld Par Lost 3.495

Limbs
And on thir naked limbs the flourie roof Par Lost 4.772
Our Limbs benumm'd, ere this diurnal Starr Par Lost 10.1069
And sedentary numness craze my limbs Samson 571
As on entrails, joints, and limbs, Samson 614
And to those dainty limms which nature lent Mask 680
line not in Bridgewater ms
Trinity ms 'lims'

Lime-twigs
Enter'd the very lime-twigs of his spells, Mask 646
Bridgewater ms 'lymetwiggs'
1637 'limetwigs'
Trinity ms 'lime twigs'

Limit
Reaching beyond all limit at one blow Par Lost 6.140
Jordan, true limit Eastward; but his Sons Par Lost 12.145
In giving limit to her life. Winchester 14
Limitary
Proud limitarie Cherube, but ere then Par Lost 4.971
Limited
And limited thir might; though numberd such Par Lost 6.229
Limits
Not like these narrow limits, to receive Par Lost 4.384
Within these hallowd limits thou appeer, Par Lost 4.964
At length into the limits of the North Par Lost 5.755
Or shroud within these limits, I shall know Mask 316
Bridgewater ms 'lymitts'
& sacred limits of this blisfull Isle Mask Tr. ms 10.11
In straiter limits bound, Nativity 169
Line
Of *Eden* planted; *Eden* stretchd her Line Par Lost 4.210
True Paradise under the *Ethiop* Line Par Lost 4.282
These as a line thir long dimension drew, Par Lost 7.480
So spacious, and his Line stretcht out so farr; Par Lost 8.102
With darkness, thrice the Equinoctial Line Par Lost 9.64
Sprung of old *Anchises* line, Mask 923
Bridgewater ms 'lyne'
Presenting *Thebs*, or *Pelops* line, Penseroso 99
Lineaments
His lineaments Divine; the pair that clad Par Lost 5.278
For wings, and smallest Lineaments exact Par Lost 7.477
In all his lineaments, though in his face Par Reg 1.92
Lines
Those Delphick lines with deep impression took, Shakespear 12
1632 'Lines'
1663-4 'Lines'
That tun'st their happiest lines in Hymn, or Story. Sonnet 13, 11
1648 'Lines'
Linger
Will not connive, or linger, thus provok'd, Samson 466
Lingerest
Perhaps thou linger'st in deep thoughts detain'd Par Reg 3.227
Lingering
The Signal to ascend, sit lingring here Par Lost 2.56
Thy lingring, or with one stroke of this Dart Par Lost 2.702
Our lingring Parents, and to th' Eastern Gate Par Lost 12.638
As a lingring disease, Samson 618
Lingering, and sitting by a new made grave, Mask 472
Bridgewater ms 'hoveringe'
Trinity ms 'hovering'
1637 'Hovering'
Lining
Turn forth her silver lining on the night? Mask 222
line not in Bridgewater ms
Turn forth her silver lining on the night, Mask 224
line not in Bridgewater ms
Link
The Link of Nature draw me: Flesh of Flesh, Par Lost 9.914
Linked
Thus drooping, or with linked Thunderbolts Par Lost 1.328
Hung ore my Realm, link'd in a golden Chain Par Lost 2.1005
Fair couple, linkt in happie nuptial League, Par Lost 4.339
Follow, as to him linkt in weal or woe, Par Lost 9.133
Shall separate us, linkt in Love so deare, Par Lost 9.970
Shall meet, alreadie linkt and Wedlock-bound Par Lost 10.905
Out of despaire, joy, but with fear yet linkt; Par Lost 11.139
And link't it self by carnal sensualty Mask 474
Bridgewater ms 'linc'kt'
Of lincked sweetnes long drawn out, Allegro 140
Linkt to the mutual flowing of the Seas, Another 31
1640, 1657 'Linckt'
line not in 1658 text
Have linkt that amorous power to thy soft lay, Sonnet 1, 8
Links
Off. I praise thy resolution, doff these links: Samson 1410
Lion
Sporting the Lion rampd, and in his paw Par Lost 4.343
A Lion now he stalkes with fierie glare, Par Lost 4.402
The Tawnie Lion, pawing to get free Par Lost 7.464
Each with thir kinde, Lion with Lioness; Par Lost 8.393
The Lion and fierce Tiger glar'd aloof. Par Reg 1.313
Who tore the Lion, as the Lion tears the Kid, Samson 128
Fled from his Lion ramp, old Warriors turn'd Samson 139
Least as a Lion (and no wonder) Psalm 7, 4
Lioness
Each with thir kinde, Lion with Lioness; Par Lost 8.393
Wherwith she tam'd the brinded lioness Mask 443
Trinity ms 'lionesse'
Bridgewater ms 'Lyonesse'
1637 'lionesse'
Lip
The lip of *Tantalus*. Thus roving on Par Lost 2.614
That shed *May* Flowers; and press'd her Matron lip Par Lost 4.501
With conjugal Caresses, from his Lip Par Lost 8.56
What need a vermeil-tinctur'd lip for that Mask 752
line not in Bridgewater ms
Thrice upon thy rubied lip, Mask 915
Lips
Flowd from thir lips, in Prose or numerous Verse, Par Lost 5.150
Of yesterday, so late hath past the lips Par Lost 5.675
Nor are thy lips ungraceful, Sire of men, Par Lost 8.218

Lips(*cont*)
What words have past thy Lips, *Adam* severe, Par Lost 9.1144
La. As smooth as *Hebe*'s their unrazor'd lips. Mask 290
Trinity ms 'lipps'
Bridgewater ms 'lipps'
La. I had not thought to have unlockt my lips Mask 756
Bridgewater ms 'lipps'
Half unpronounc't, slide through my infant-lipps, Vacation 4
Liquid
With solid, as the Lake with liquid fire; Par Lost 1.229
That underneath had veins of liquid fire Par Lost 1.701
Of Jasper, or of liquid Pearle, whereon Par Lost 3.519
Into a liquid Plain, then stood unmov'd Par Lost 4.455
Sits on the Bloom extracting liquid sweet. Par Lost 5.25
Nor in thir liquid texture mortal wound Par Lost 6.348
Whose liquid murmur heard new thirst excites, Par Lost 7.68
The Firmament, expanse of liquid, pure, Par Lost 7.264
And drink the liquid Light, firm to retaine Par Lost 7.362
And liquid Lapse of murmuring Streams; by these, Par Lost 8.263
From underground) the liquid Ore he dreind Par Lost 11.570
Whose drink was only from the liquid brook. Samson 557
There I suck the liquid ayr Mask 980
Thy liquid notes that close the eye of Day, Sonnet 1, 5
What slender Youth bedew'd with liquid odours Horace 1
Liquor
Whose heads that turbulent liquor fills with fumes. Samson 552
Or medcinal liquor can asswage, Samson 627
His orient liquor in a Crystal Glasse, Mask 65
Trinity ms 'liquor' ← 'like'
1673 'Liquor'
And shed the lushious liquor on the ground, Mask 652
Trinity ms 'liquor' ← 'potion'
Hence with thy brew'd inchantments, foul deceiver, Mask 696
Trinity ms 'brewd enchauntments' ← 'foule brud' ← 'hel brewd opiate' ← 'hel bru'd liquor' ← 'bru'd sorcerie' ← 'teacherous (leacherous?) bruage' ← 'teacherous kindnesse'
Liquors
With pleasant liquors crown'd: O innocence Par Lost 5.445
Which she with pretious viold liquors heals. Mask 847
line not in Bridgewater ms
List
A hideous Peal: yet, when they list, would creep, Par Lost 2.656
To me, for when they list into the womb Par Lost 2.798
Illusions as he list, Phantasms and Dreams, Par Lost 4.803
Rather admire; or if they list to try Par Lost 8.75
Nor am I in the list of them that hope; Samson 647
Where no crude surfet raigns. *Eld. Bro*. List, list, I hear Mask 480
Bridgewater ms 'list, list'
Trinity ms 'list list' ← 'list bro. list'
List Lady be not coy, and be not cosen'd Mask 737
(List mortals, if your ears be true) Mask 997
line not in Bridgewater ms
And when they list, their lean and flashy songs Lycidas 123
If thou wilt list to mee, Psalm 81, 36
Listed
Conspicuous with three listed colours gay, Par Lost 11.866
Each others force in camp or listed field: Samson 1087
Coasting the *Tyrrhene* shore, as the winds listed, Mask 49
Listen
But list'n not to his Temptations, warne Par Lost 6.908
And listen why, for I will tell ye now Mask 43
Listen where thou art sitting Mask 860
Trinity ms 'Listen' ← 'Listen virgin'
Listen for dear honours sake, Mask 864
Listen and save. Mask 866
B.M. ms 'Listen Listen Listen'
Listen and appear to us Mask 867
Listen and save. Mask 889
Hath lockt up mortal sense, then listen I Arcades 62
Listened
At which I ceas't, and listen'd them a while, Mask 551
Bridgewater ms 'listned'
Trinity ms 'listend' ← 'listen'
Listening
Silence, and Sleep listning to thee will watch, Par Lost 7.106
The Planets in thir station list'ning stood, Par Lost 7.563
By Night, and listening where the hapless Paire Par Lost 10.342
1667 'listning'
Was rife, and perfet in my list'ning ear, Mask 203
Trinity ms 'listening'
1637 'listening'
line not in Bridgewater ms
Oft list'ning how the Hounds and horn, Allegro 53
And hears the unexpressive nuptiall Song, Lycidas 176
Trinity ms '& heares' ← 'listening'
Listening to what unshorn *Apollo* sings Vacation 37
Through the soft silence of the list'ning night; Circum 5
Trinity ms 'listening'
Listens
Listens delighted. Eevning now approach'd Par Lost 5.627
And listens to the Herald of the Sea Lycidas 89
Lists
Which when he lists, he leaves, or boasts he can, Par Reg 4.306
Me overthrown, to enter lists with God, Samson 463
Lithe
His Lithe Proboscis; close the Serpent sly Par Lost 4.347

Litter
That draw the litter of close-curtain'd sleep.   Mask 554
Little
That little which is left so to defend,   Par Lost 2.1000
Th'Omnipotent. Ay me, they little know   Par Lost 4.86
Of immortality. So little knows   Par Lost 4.201
Little inferior; whom my thoughts pursue   Par Lost 4.362
Ah gentle pair, yee little think how nigh   Par Lost 4.366
Our dayes work brought to little, though begun   Par Lost 9.224
And durable; and now in little space   Par Lost 10.320
Little inferiour, by my adventure hard   Par Lost 10.468
Which here, though plenteous, all too little seems   Par Lost 10.600
How little weight my words with thee can finde,   Par Lost 10.968
Little suspicious to any King; but now   Par Reg 2.82
So little here, nay lost; but *Eve* was *Eve*,   Par Reg 4.6
But these are false, or little else but dreams,   Par Reg 4.291
Sams. A Little onward lend thy guiding hand   Samson 1
To these dark steps, a little further on;   Samson 2
Little prevails, or rather seems a tune,   Samson 661
That in a little time while breath remains thee,   Samson 1126
A little stay will bring some notice hither,   Samson 1536
Through each high street: little I had dispatch't   Samson 1599
And weild their little tridents, but this Ile   Mask 27
T'would be som solace yet, som little chearing   Mask 348
But here thy sword can do thee little stead,   Mask 611
Trinity ms 'little stead' ←'small availe' ←'little stead'
I purs't it up, but little reck'ning made,   Mask 642
How little you bested,   Penseroso 3
Of other care they little reck'ning make,   Lycidas 116
Daily devours apace, and nothing sed,   Lycidas 129
Trinity ms 'little' ←'nothing'
1638 'little'
For so to interpose a little ease,   Lycidas 152
Full little thought they than,   Nativity 88
Amongst their Ews, the little Hills like Lambs.   Psalm 114, 12
I know my tongue but little Grace can do thee   Vacation 10
So little is our loss,   On Time 7
So little is thy gain.   On Time 8
Liturgy
And with stiff Vowes renounc'd his Liturgie   Forcers 2
Live
Shall we then live thus vile, the Race of Heav'n   Par Lost 2.194
Live to our selves, though in this vast recess,   Par Lost 2.254
Beyond his Potent arm, to live exempt   Par Lost 2.318
Yet live in hatred, enmity, and strife   Par Lost 2.500
The Gods who live at ease, where I shall Reign   Par Lost 2.868
Life in my self for ever, by thee I live,   Par Lost 3.244
And live in thee transplanted, and from thee   Par Lost 3.293
What further would be learnt. Live while ye may,   Par Lost 4.533
What life the Gods live there, and such live thou.   Par Lost 5.81
Of substance, and in things that live, of life;   Par Lost 5.474
Monarchie over such as live by right   Par Lost 5.795
Yet soon he heal'd; for Spirits that live throughout   Par Lost 6.344
All Heart they live, all Head, all Eye, all Eare,   Par Lost 6.350
But live content, which is the calmest life: Par Lost 6.461
Stor'd in each Orb perhaps with some that live.   Par Lost 8.152
Live, in what state, condition or degree,   Par Lost 8.176
And freed from intricacies, taught to live,   Par Lost 8.182
And ye that live and move, fair Creatures, tell,   Par Lost 8.276
From whom I have that thus I move and live,   Par Lost 8.281
Possess it, and all things that therein live,   Par Lost 8.340
Or live in Sea, or Aire, Beast, Fish, and Fowle.   Par Lost 8.341
Be strong, live happie, and love, but first of all   Par Lost 8.633
Sole Daughter of his voice; the rest, we live   Par Lost 9.653
Mee who have touch'd and tasted, yet both live,   Par Lost 9.688
Shall live with her enjoying, I extinct;   Par Lost 9.829
I could endure, without him live no life.   Par Lost 9.833
How can I live without thee, how forgoe   Par Lost 9.908
To live again in these wilde Woods forlorn?   Par Lost 9.910
Lives, as thou saidst, and gaines to live as Man   Par Lost 9.933
In solitude live savage, in some glade   Par Lost 9.1085
The savour of Death from all things there that live: Par Lost 10.269
Whereon I live, thy gentle looks, thy aid,   Par Lost 10.919
While yet we live, scarse one short hour perhaps,   Par Lost 10.923
To make death in us live: Then let us seek   Par Lost 10.1028
The smell of peace toward Mankinde, let him live   Par Lost 11.38
And live for ever, dream at least to live   Par Lost 11.95
Is past, and we shall live. Whence Haile to thee,   Par Lost 11.158
Man is to live, and all things live for Man.   Par Lost 11.161
Here let us live, though in fall'n state, content.   Par Lost 11.180
So maist thou live, till like ripe Fruit thou drop   Par Lost 11.535
Live well, how long or short permit to Heav'n: Par Lost 11.554
O pittie and shame, that they who to live well   Par Lost 11.629
Thenceforth shall practice how to live secure,   Par Lost 11.802
At this last sight, assur'd that Man shall live   Par Lost 11.872
Perform, and not performing cannot live.   Par Lost 12.299
In mean estate live moderate, till grown   Par Lost 12.351
For this he shall live hated, be blasphem'd,   Par Lost 12.411
That ye may live, which will be many dayes,   Par Lost 12.602
Now full, that I no more should live obscure,   Par Reg 1.287
Live on tough roots and stubs, to thirst inur'd   Par Reg 1.339
To live upon thir tongues and be thir talk,   Par Reg 3.55
Scarce half I seem to live, dead more then half.   Samson 79
To live a life half dead, a living death,   Samson 100
When I must live uxorious to thy will   Samson 945
To live the poorest in my Tribe, then richest,   Samson 1479
Of bright aereal Spirits live insphear'd   Mask 3
That in the colours of the Rainbow live   Mask 300
Live(*cont*)
And live like Natures bastards, not her sons,   Mask 727
Trinity ms '& live' ←'living'
That live according to her sober laws,   Mask 766
And love to live in dimple sleek;   Allegro 30
To live with her, and live with thee,   Allegro 39
Mirth with thee, I mean to live.   Allegro 152
And I with thee will choose to live.   Penseroso 176
Of this fair Wood, and live in Oak'n bowr,   Arcades 45
Trinity ms defective here
To nurse the Saplings tall, and curl the grove   Arcades 46
Trinity ms 'nurse the saplings tall' ←'live a thousand yeares'
Bring your Flocks, and live with us,   Arcades 103
To scorn delights, and live laborious dayes;   Lycidas 72
Was kindly com to live with them below;   Nativity 90
That till the worlds last-end shall make thy name to live.   Fair Inf 77
And those that cannot live from him asunder   Vacation 77
Yet shall he live in strife, and at his dore   Vacation 85
To live with him, and sing in endles morn of light.   Musick 28
Lived
To them who liv'd; nor on the vertue thought   Par Lost 4.198
Spontaneous, for within them Spirit livd,   Par Lost 7.204
Creatures that livd, and movd, and walk'd, or flew,   Par Lost 8.264
And livd: One came, methought, of shape Divine,   Par Lost 8.295
Who might have liv'd and joyd immortal bliss,   Par Lost 9.1166
Liv'd ignorant of future, so had borne   Par Lost 11.764
While yet the Patriark liv'd, who scap'd the Flood,   Par Lost 12.117
For *Solomon* he liv'd at ease, and full   Par Reg 2.201
With glory, wept that he had liv'd so long   Par Reg 3.41
Their choicest youth; they only liv'd who fled.   Samson 264
Who liv'd in both, unstain'd with gold or fee,   Sonnet 10, 3
Trinity ms 'liv'd in' ←'left them'
Livelier
Livelier then *Meliboean*, or the graine   Par Lost 11.242
With youthful steps? much livelier then e're while   Samson 1442
Liveliest
If once they hear that voyce, thir liveliest pledge   Par Lost 1.274
Livelong
Till the live-long day-light fail,   Allegro 99
Hast built thy self a live-long Monument.   Shakespear 8
1663-4 'lasting *Monument*'
1632 'lasting Monument'
Lively
With wonder, and could love, so lively shines   Par Lost 4.363
With supple joints, and lively vigour led: Par Lost 8.269
Had lively shadowd: Here had new begun   Par Lost 8.311
When the fresh blood grows lively, and returns   Mask 670
While the Cock with lively din,   Allegro 49
Of lively portrature display'd,   Penseroso 149
My plaining vers as lively as before;   Passion 47
Liver
In Entrailes, Heart or Head, Liver or Reines;   Par Lost 6.346
Liveried
A thousand liveried Angels lacky her,   Mask 455
Liveries
In all the Liveries dect of Summers pride   Par Lost 7.478
The clouds in thousand Liveries dight,   Allegro 62
Livery
Had in her sober Liverie all things clad;   Par Lost 4.599
In thir state Livery clad; before him Pipes   Samson 1616
Lives
Where all life dies, death lives, and Nature breeds,   Par Lost 2.624
In *Golgotha* him dead, who lives in Heav'n;   Par Lost 3.477
Puts me in doubt. Lives ther who loves his pain?   Par Lost 4.888
How dies the Serpent? hee hath eat'n and lives,   Par Lost 9.764
Nor yet on him found deadly, he yet lives,   Par Lost 9.932
Lives, as thou saidst, and gaines to live as Man   Par Lost 9.933
Land, Sea, and Aire, and every kinde that lives,   Par Lost 11.337
To these that sober Race of Men, whose lives   Par Lost 11.621
Shall lead thir lives, and multiplie apace,   Par Lost 12.17
Man lives not by Bread only, but each Word   Par Reg 1.349
For truths sake suffering death unjust, lives now   Par Reg 3.98
Of numbring *Israel*, which cost the lives   Par Reg 3.410
A secular bird ages of lives.   Samson 1707
But lives and spreds aloft by those pure eyes,   Lycidas 81
& in our lives & in our song   Musick Tr. ms 5.05
Livest
Nor love thy Life, nor hate; but what thou livst   Par Lost 11.553
Sweet Echo, sweetest Nymph that liv'st unseen   Mask 230
Dwell'st here with *Pan*, or *Silvan*, by blest Song   Mask 268
Trinity ms 'dwell'st' ←'liv'st'
Livid
Save what the glimmering of these livid flames   Par Lost 1.182
Living
Thir living strength, and unfrequented left   Par Lost 1.433
All taste of living wight, as once it fled   Par Lost 2.613
Fearless to be o'rmatcht by living might.   Par Lost 2.855
Of living Saphire, once his native Seat;   Par Lost 2.1050
The living, and forthwith the cited dead   Par Lost 3.327
Living or liveless to be found was none,   Par Lost 3.443
Of living Creatures new to sight and strange: Par Lost 4.287
With living Saphirs: *Hesperus* that led   Par Lost 4.605
Joyn voices all ye living Souls, ye Birds,   Par Lost 5.197
By living Streams among the Trees of Life,   Par Lost 5.652
Distinct with eyes, and from the living Wheels   Par Lost 6.846
Reptil with Spawn abundant, living Soule: Par Lost 7.388
Soul living, each that crept, which plenteously   Par Lost 7.392
Hugest of living Creatures, on the Deep   Par Lost 7.413

Living*(cont)*
Let th' Earth bring forth Foul living in her kinde, Par Lost 7.451
Innumerous living Creatures, perfet formes, Par Lost 7.455
Express, and thou becam'st a living Soul. Par Lost 7.528
And every living thing that moves on the Earth. Par Lost 7.534
Open, ye Heav'ns, your living dores; let in Par Lost 7.566
By living Soule, desert and desolate, Par Lost 8.154
With various living creatures, and the Aire Par Lost 8.370
Compare above all living Creatures deare, Par Lost 9.228
Thee all things living gaze on, all things thine Par Lost 9.539
With sent of living Carcasses design'd Par Lost 10.277
But I shall die a living Death? O thought Par Lost 10.788
Living or dying, from thee I will not hide Par Lost 10.974
Mother of all things living, since by thee Par Lost 11.160
As to forsake the living God, and fall Par Lost 12.118
His living Temples, built by Faith to stand, Par Lost 12.527
God hath now sent his living Oracle Par Reg 1.460
To live a life half dead, a living death, Samson 100
Living and dead recorded, who to save Samson 984
My trust is in the living God who gave me Samson 1140
Living or dying thou hast fulfill'd Samson 1661
Before our living Dread who dwells Samson 1673
And live like Natures bastards, not her sons, Mask 727
Trinity ms '& live' ←'living'
All living creatures he doth feed, Psalm 136, 85
Soon swallow'd up in dark and long out-living night. Passion 7
Was not long a living Tomb. Winchester 34
Madam, me thinks I see him living yet; Sonnet 10, 11
O living God, for thee. Psalm 84, 8

Lo
Of Heav'ns ascent they lift thir Feet, when loe Par Lost 3.486
Was meant by Death that day, when lo, to thee Par Lost 10.1050
For Man and Beast: when loe a wonder strange! Par Lost 11.733
For lo thy *furious* foes *now* swell Psalm 83, 5
Lo this man there was born: Psalm 87, 16

Load
Farr heavier load thy self expect to feel Par Lost 4.972
Deigns none to ease thy load and taste thy sweet, Par Lost 5.59
They pluckt the seated Hills with all thir load, Par Lost 6.644
Nor lightens aught each mans peculiar load. Par Reg 1.402
Who hast of sorrow thy full load besides; Samson 214
And lack of load, made his life burdensom, Another 24
line not in 1658 text
Meekly thou didst resign this earthy load Sonnet 14, 3
Trinity ms 'load' ←'clod'

Loaded
No journey of a Sabbath day, and loaded so; Samson 149

Loaden
Of goodliest Trees loaden with fairest Fruit, Par Lost 4.147
Load'n with fairest Fruit that hung to the Eye Par Lost 8.307
Loaden with fruit of fairest colours mixt, Par Lost 9.577
Bow'd their Stiff necks, loaden with stormy blasts, Par Reg 4.418
These braveries in Irons loaden on thee. Samson 1243

Loads
That with superfluous burden loads the day, Sonnet 21, 13

Loath
Thank him who puts me loath to this revenge Par Lost 4.386
Creation could repeate, yet would be loath Par Lost 9.946
He led her nothing loath; Flours were the Couch, Par Lost 9.1039
He came, and with him *Eve*, more loth, though first Par Lost 10.109
Of all the rest: then wilt thou not be loath Par Lost 12.585
Timorous and loth, with novice modesty, Par Reg 3.241
1671 'loah' in some copies
And thank the gods amiss. I should be loath Mask 177
As loath to leave the body that it lov'd, Mask 473
The Air such pleasure loth to lose, Nativity 99

Loathed
With loath'd intrusion, and fill all the land; Par Lost 12.178
Hence loathed Melancholy Allegro 1

Loathsome
Thou wilt not leave me in the loathsom grave Par Lost 3.247
To loathsom sickness, worthily, since they Par Lost 11.524
Lie in this miserable loathsom plight Samson 480
From forth this loathsom prison-house, to abide Samson 922
And praise thee *from their loathsom bed* Psalm 88, 43

Local
As of a Duel, or the local wounds Par Lost 12.387

Lock
And here though grief my feeble hands up-lock, Passion 45
1673 'up lock'

Locked
Hath lockt up mortal sense, then listen I Arcades 62
1673 'lock't'
Trinity ms 'lockt up' ←'chain'd'

Locks
Bind thir resplendent locks inwreath'd with beams, Par Lost 3.361
Circl'd his Head, nor less his Locks behind Par Lost 3.626
Absolute rule; and Hyacinthin Locks Par Lost 4.301
By us oft seen; his dewie locks distill'd Par Lost 5.56
Climbing, sat thicker then the snakie locks Par Lost 10.559
Blow moist and keen, shattering the graceful locks Par Lost 10.1066
With careful step, Locks white as doune, Samson 327
Or pitied object, these redundant locks Samson 568
Miraculous yet remaining in those locks? Samson 587
Then thine, while I preserv'd these locks unshorn, Samson 1143
With those thy boyst'rous locks, no worthy match Samson 1164
And on his shoulders waving down those locks, Samson 1493
This Nymph that gaz'd upon his clustring locks, Mask 54

Locks*(cont)*
Braid your Locks with rosie Twine Mask 105
Bridgewater ms 'locks'
Trinity ms 'locks'
Sleeking her soft alluring locks, Mask 882
As ragged as thy Locks, Allegro 9
He shook his Miter'd locks, and stern bespake, Lycidas 112
With *Nectar* pure his oozy Lock's he laves, Lycidas 175
1638 'locks'
Trinity ms 'locks'

Locrine
Whilom she was the daughter of *Locrine*, Mask 827
Spir. Virgin, daughter of *Locrine* Mask 922

Locusts
Of *Locusts*, warping on the Eastern Wind, Par Lost 1.341
ms 'Locusts'
A darksom Cloud of Locusts swarming down Par Lost 12.185

Lodge
Thus at thir shadie Lodge arriv'd, both stood Par Lost 4.720
But chiefly where those two fair Creatures Lodge, Par Lost 4.790
I have at will. So to the Silvan Lodge Par Lost 5.377
Lodge and dislodge by turns, which makes through Heav'n Par Lost 6.7
With this long way, resolving here to lodge Mask 183
Or whistle from the Lodge, or village cock Mask 346
Trinity ms 'lodge'
Bridgewater ms 'lodge'
Shew'd him his room where he must lodge that night, Carrier 15
Lodge it with dishonour foul. Psalm 7, 18

Lodged
Where lodg'd, or whither fled, or if for fight, Par Lost 6.531
Myriads between two brazen Mountains lodg'd Par Lost 7.201
Lodg'd in a small partition, and the rest Par Lost 8.105
Select for life shall in the Ark be lodg'd, Par Lost 11.823
Lodg'd in *Bethabara* where *John* baptiz'd, Par Reg 1.184
Lodg'd in his brest, as well might recommend Par Reg 1.301
And with him talkt, and with him lodg'd, I mean Par Reg 2.6
In what part lodg'd, how easily bereft me, Samson 48
And if your stray attendance be yet lodg'd, Mask 315
Lodg'd with me useless, though my Soul more bent Sonnet 19, 4

Lodges
Sure somthing holy lodges in that brest, Mask 246

Loftiest
Of riot ascends above thir loftiest Towrs, Par Lost 1.499
Insuperable highth of loftiest shade, Par Lost 4.138

Lofts
And hills of Snow and lofts of piled Thunder, Vacation 42

Lofty
Adams abode, those loftie shades his Bowre. Par Lost 3.734
Then from his loftie stand on that high Tree Par Lost 4.395
Cities of Men with lofty Gates and Towrs, Par Lost 11.640
Thence what the lofty grave Tragoedians taught Par Reg 4.261
May thy lofty head be crown'd Mask 934
Bridgewater ms 'loftie'
1637 'loftie'
Himself to sing, and build the lofty rhyme. Lycidas 11
Trinity ms 'loftie'
Advanc'd their lofty head. Psalm 80, 44
With Trumpets *lofty sound*, Psalm 81, 10

Logres
By Knights of *Logres*, or of *Lyones*, Par Reg 2.360

Loins
Pour'd never from her frozen loyns, to pass Par Lost 1.352
Skirted his loines and thighes with downie Gold Par Lost 5.282
And girded on our loyns, may cover round Par Lost 9.1096
Our own begotten, and of our Loines to bring Par Lost 10.983
Out of thy loyns; th' unjust the just hath slain, Par Lost 11.455
High in the love of Heav'n, yet from my Loynes Par Lost 12.380
Not onely to the Sons of *Abrahams* Loines Par Lost 12.447
Be vacant of her plenty, in her own loyns Mask 718
Bridgewater ms 'loynes'
Trinity ms 'loynes'

London-Bull
Dodg'd with him, betwixt *Cambridge* and the Bull. Carrier 8
1658 *'London-Bull'*

Lone
In this close dungeon of innumerous bowes. Mask 349
Trinity ms 'close' ←'sad' ←'lone'
Bridgewater ms 'lone dungeon'

Loneliness
Of night, or lonelines it recks me not, Mask 404
1673 'loneliness'
Trinity ms 'lonlinesse'
Bridgewater ms 'lonelinesse'
1637 'lonelynesse'

Lonely
My self expose, with lonely steps to tread Par Lost 2.828
Thy going is not lonely, with thee goes Par Lost 11.290
To the misled and lonely Travailer? Mask 200
line not in Bridgewater ms
Be seen in som high lonely Towr, Penseroso 86
The lonely mountains o're, Nativity 181

Long
Long after known in *Palestine*, and nam'd Par Lost 1.80
Prone on the Flood, extended long and large Par Lost 1.195
Thir Seats long after next the Seat of God, Par Lost 1.383
The rest were long to tell, though far renown'd, Par Lost 1.507
There went a fame in Heav'n that he ere long Par Lost 1.651
Long under darkness cover. But these thoughts Par Lost 1.659

Long(*cont*)

Fell long before; nor aught avail'd him now	Par Lost 1.748
The sound of blustring winds, which all night long	Par Lost 2.286
By pollicy, and long process of time,	Par Lost 2.297
Well have ye judg'd, well ended long debate,	Par Lost 2.390
Seis'd us, though undismaid: long is the way	Par Lost 2.432
Alone, but long I sat not, till my womb	Par Lost 2.778
Escap't the *Stygian* Pool, though long detain'd	Par Lost 3.14
This my long sufferance and my day of grace	Par Lost 3.198
Under his gloomie power I shall not long	Par Lost 3.242
Shall enter Heaven long absent, and returne,	Par Lost 3.261
And after all thir tribulations long	Par Lost 3.336
Cleombrotus, and many more too long,	Par Lost 3.473
Long after, now unpeopl'd, and untrod;	Par Lost 3.497
And long he wanderd, till at last a gleame	Par Lost 3.499
Philosophers in vain so long have sought,	Par Lost 3.601
As Man ere long, and this new World shall know.	Par Lost 4.113
Or where the Sons of *Eden* long before	Par Lost 4.213
Yielded them, side-long as they sat recline	Par Lost 4.333
Long to continue, and this high seat your Heav'n	Par Lost 4.371
Short pleasures, for long woes are to succeed.	Par Lost 4.535
She all night long her amorous descant sung;	Par Lost 4.603
Our eye-lids; other Creatures all day long	Par Lost 4.616
But wherfore all night long shine these, for whom	Par Lost 4.657
Ill matching words and deeds long past or late.	Par Lost 5.113
On Princes, when thir rich Retinue long	Par Lost 5.355
Long after to blest *Marie*, second *Eve*.	Par Lost 5.387
Alternate all night long: but not so wak'd	Par Lost 5.657
Interpreted) which not long after, he	Par Lost 5.762
Long way through hostile scorn, which he susteind	Par Lost 5.904
Conflicting Fire: long time in eeven scale	Par Lost 6.245
Not long divisible, and from the gash	Par Lost 6.331
Which into hallow Engins long and round	Par Lost 6.484
Nor long shall be our labour, yet ere dawne,	Par Lost 6.492
Whom fled we thought, will save us long pursuit	Par Lost 6.538
Not long, for sudden all at once thir Reeds	Par Lost 6.582
A while in trouble; but they stood not long,	Par Lost 6.634
Long strugling underneath, ere they could wind	Par Lost 6.659
Up hither, under long obedience tri'd,	Par Lost 7.159
With borders long the Rivers. That Earth now	Par Lost 7.328
These as a line thir long dimension drew,	Par Lost 7.480
But long ere our approaching heard within	Par Lost 8.242
Which it had long stood under, streind to the highth	Par Lost 8.454
Or *Neptun*'s ire or *Juno's*, that so long	Par Lost 9.18
Pleas'd me long choosing, and beginning late;	Par Lost 9.26
With long and tedious havoc fabl'd Knights	Par Lost 9.30
Him after long debate, irresolute	Par Lost 9.87
Continu'd making, and who knows how long	Par Lost 9.138
Bitter ere long back on it self recoiles;	Par Lost 9.172
As we need walk, till younger hands ere long	Par Lost 9.246
Her long with ardent look his Eye pursu'd	Par Lost 9.397
As one who long in populous City pent,	Par Lost 9.445
To interrupt, side-long he works his way.	Par Lost 9.512
Sated at length, ere long I might perceave	Par Lost 9.598
Wanted not long, though to this shape retain'd.	Par Lost 9.601
Empress, the way is readie, and not long,	Par Lost 9.626
Whose taste, too long forborn, at first assay	Par Lost 9.747
Solace in her return, so long delay'd;	Par Lost 9.844
Thee I have misst, and thought it long, depriv'd	Par Lost 9.857
Most Favors, who can please him long; Mee first	Par Lost 9.949
Confounded long they sate, as struck'n mute,	Par Lost 9.1064
Braunching so broad and long, that in the ground	Par Lost 9.1104
Whence *Adam* faultring long, thus answer'd brief.	Par Lost 10.115
The Realm it self of Satan long usurpt,	Par Lost 10.189
With long reach interpos'd; three sev'ral wayes	Par Lost 10.323
Long hee admiring stood, till Sin, his faire	Par Lost 10.352
With peril great atchiev'd. Long were to tell	Par Lost 10.469
Long had foretold, a Fabrick wonderful	Par Lost 10.482
Of public scorn; he wonderd, but not long	Par Lost 10.509
And worn with Famin, long and ceasless hiss,	Par Lost 10.573
A long days dying to augment our paine,	Par Lost 10.964
Some days; how long, and what till then our life,	Par Lost 11.198
Sight so deform what heart of Rock could long	Par Lost 11.494
Live well, how long or short permit to Heav'n:	Par Lost 11.554
Long had not walkt, when from the Tents behold	Par Lost 11.581
(Erelong to swim at large) and laugh; for which	Par Lost 11.626
The world erelong a world of tears must weepe.	Par Lost 11.627
Long time in peace by Families and Tribes	Par Lost 12.23
Shall dwell to *Senir*, that long ridge of Hills.	Par Lost 12.146
Were long to tell, how many Battels fought,	Par Lost 12.261
Through the worlds wilderness long wanderd man	Par Lost 12.313
Long time shall dwell and prosper, but when sins	Par Lost 12.316
But first a long succession must ensue,	Par Lost 12.331
Shall long usurp; ere the third dawning light	Par Lost 12.421
Worthy t' have not remain'd so long unsung.	Par Reg 1.17
To him his Heavenly Office, nor was long	Par Reg 1.28
Upon my head, long the decrees of Heav'n	Par Reg 1.55
Must bide the stroak of that long threatn'd wound,	Par Reg 1.59
Of hazard, which admits no long debate,	Par Reg 1.95
For long indulgence to their fears or grief:	Par Reg 1.110
To end his Raign on Earth so long enjoy'd:	Par Reg 1.125
At first it may be; but long since with wo	Par Reg 1.399
Moses was in the Mount, and missing long;	Par Reg 2.15
Messiah certainly now come, so long	Par Reg 2.32
Thus long to some great purpose he obscures.	Par Reg 2.101
My heart hath been a store-house long of things	Par Reg 2.103
Too long, then lay'st thy scapes on names ador'd,	Par Reg 2.189
In this wild solitude so long should bide	Par Reg 2.304

Long(*cont*)

With glory, wept that he had liv'd so long	Par Reg 3.41
Israel in long captivity still mourns;	Par Reg 3.279
Long to enjoy it quiet and secure,	Par Reg 3.360
Thus long from *Israel;* serving as of old	Par Reg 3.378
Long in preparing, soon to nothing brought,	Par Reg 3.389
Another plain, long but in bredth not wide;	Par Reg 4.27
And long Renown thou justly may'st prefer	Par Reg 4.84
Will be for thee no sitting, or not long	Par Reg 4.107
Long since. Wert thou so void of fear or shame,	Par Reg 4.189
Trills her thick-warbl'd notes the summer long,	Par Reg 4.246
But vertue joyn'd with riches and long life,	Par Reg 4.298
And Thief of Paradise; him long of old	Par Reg 4.604
But thou, Infernal Serpent, shalt not long	Par Reg 4.618
Whom long descent of birth	Samson 171
Dagon must stoop, and shall e're long receive	Samson 468
Nothing more certain, will not long defer	Samson 474
Against all competition, nor will long	Samson 476
Nor th' other light of life continue long,	Samson 592
No long petition, speedy death,	Samson 650
Only my love of thee held long debate;	Samson 863
It fits not; thou and I long since are twain;	Samson 929
That womans love can win or long inherit;	Samson 1012
That either they love nothing, or not long?	Samson 1033
Which long shall not with-hold mee from thy head,	Samson 1125
Har. By *Astaroth* e're long thou shalt lament	Samson 1242
To the Spirits of just men long opprest!	Samson 1269
No Preface needs, thou seest we long to know.	Samson 1554
And to my wily trains, I shall e're long Bridgewater ms 'longe'	Mask 151
With this long way, resolving here to lodge Bridgewater ms 'longe'	Mask 183
With thy long levell'd rule of streaming light,	Mask 340
Under the ribs of Death, but O ere long	Mask 562
After her wandring labours long, line not in Bridgewater ms	Mask 1006
Till the live-long day-light fail,	Allegro 99
Of lincked sweetnes long drawn out,	Allegro 140
Thee bright-hair'd *Vesta* long of yore,	Penseroso 23
From the glad sound would not be absent long,	Lycidas 35
That with long beams the shame-fac't night array'd,	Nativity 111
Enwrap our fancy long,	Nativity 134
After long toil their liberty had won,	Psalm 114, 2
All the day long his cours to run.	Psalm 136, 30
He wanderd long, till thee he spy'd from farr,	Fair Inf 17
And in times long and dark Prospective Glass	Vacation 71
Soon swallow'd up in dark and long out-living night.	Passion 7
Which on our dearest Lord did sease er'e long,	Passion 10
Then long Eternity shall greet our bliss.	On Time 11
This day, but O ere long	Circum 26
And keep in tune with Heav'n, till God ere long	Musick 26
Was not long a living Tomb.	Winchester 34
And welcom thee, and wish thee long.	May Morn 10
Hast built thy self a live-long Monument. 1663-4 'lasting *Monument*' 1632 'lasting Monument'	Shakespear 8
But lately finding him so long at home,	Carrier 11
Too long vacation hastned on his term. line not in 1658 text	Another 14
With *Midas* Ears, committing short and long;	Sonnet 13, 4
Great ones how long will ye	Psalm 4, 7
How long be thus forborn	Psalm 4, 9
And thou O Lord how long? turn Lord, restore	Psalm 6, 7
Lord God of Hosts, how long wilt thou,	Psalm 80, 17
How long wilt thou declare	Psalm 80, 18
Hath set, and planted *long*,	Psalm 80, 62
How long will ye pervert the right	Psalm 82, 5
My Soul doth long and almost die	Psalm 84, 5
And glory shall *ere long appear*	Psalm 85, 39
Mercy and Truth *that long were miss'd*	Psalm 85, 41
And all night long, before thee *weep*	Psalm 88, 3

Longer

He views in bredth, and without longer pause	Par Lost 3.561
Longer thy offerd good, why else set here?	Par Lost 5.63
And longer will delay to heare thee tell	Par Lost 7.101
Desire with thee still longer to converse	Par Lost 8.252
Not longer then since I in one Night freed	Par Lost 9.140
Hell could no longer hold us in her bounds,	Par Lost 10.365
Why stand we longer shivering under feares,	Par Lost 10.1003
But longer in that Paradise to dwell,	Par Lost 11.48
My motions in him, longer then they move,	Par Lost 11.91
But longer in this Paradise to dwell	Par Lost 11.259
Part good, part bad, of bad the longer scrowle,	Par Lost 12.336
Longer on Earth then certaine times to appeer	Par Lost 12.437
We may no longer stay: go, waken *Eve;*	Par Lost 12.594
Longer then thou canst feed them on thy cost?	Par Reg 2.421
Longer I durst not stay, but soon I guess't	Mask 577
Longer dare abide,	Nativity 225

Longest

Delay, for longest time to him is short;	Par Reg 1.56

Longing

Millions that stand in Arms, and longing wait	Par Lost 2.55
Still unfulfill'd with pain of longing pines;	Par Lost 4.511
Longing and envying stood, but could not reach.	Par Lost 9.593
Sollicited her longing eye; yet first	Par Lost 9.743
Not to be trusted, longing to be seen	Par Lost 10.877

Longitude

Or Longitude, where the great Luminarie	Par Lost 3.576

Longitude(*cont*)
Mean while in utmost Longitude, where Heav'n Par Lost 4.539
Stretcht into Longitude; which having pass'd Par Lost 5.754
His Longitude through Heav'ns high rode: the gray Par Lost 7.373
Long-uncoupled
Of long-uncoupled bed, and childless eld, Fair Inf 13
Look
He ended frowning, and his look denounc'd Par Lost 2.106
The weight of mightiest Monarchies; his look Par Lost 2.307
His look suspence, awaiting who appeer'd Par Lost 2.418
And with disdainful look thus first began. Par Lost 2.680
Pleas'd, out of Heaven shalt look down and smile, Par Lost 3.257
Look downward on that Globe whose hither side Par Lost 3.722
Lay pleasant, his grievd look he fixes sad, Par Lost 4.28
On the green bank, to look into the cleer Par Lost 4.458
As I bent down to look, just opposite, Par Lost 4.460
Bending to look on me, I started back, Par Lost 4.462
Stand firm, for in his look defiance lours. Par Lost 4.873
To trample thee as mire: for proof look up, Par Lost 4.1010
And look for adoration to th' abuse Par Lost 5.800
Whereto with look compos'd *Satan* repli'd. Par Lost 6.469
Her long with ardent look his Eye pursu'd Par Lost 9.397
She most, and in her look summs all Delight. Par Lost 9.454
To Knowledge? By the Threatner, look on mee, Par Lost 9.687
Adam, estrang'd in look and alterd stile, Par Lost 9.1132
As *Delos* floating once; the rest his look Par Lost 10.296
From his displeasure; in whose look serene, Par Lost 10.1094
His triple-colour'd Bow, whereon to look Par Lost 11.897
How would one look from his Majestick brow Par Reg 2.216
Look once more e're we leave this specular Mount Par Reg 4.236
That she might look at will through every pore? Samson 97
How could I once look up, or heave the head, Samson 197
Chor. Look now for no inchanting voice, nor fear Samson 1065
The Giant *Harapha* of *Gath*, his look Samson 1068
Comes on amain, speed in his look. Samson 1304
And first behold this cordial Julep here Mask 672
Trinity ms 'first behold' ←'looke upon'
By hoary *Nereus* wrincled look, Mask 871
Bridgewater ms 'looke'
Trinity ms 'looke'
1637 'looke'
Brightest Lady look on me, Mask 910
Bridgewater ms 'looke'
1637 'looke'
Trinity ms 'looke'
he may scratch his forehead. heere be brambles Mask Tr. ms 17.57
'he may scratch' ←'he may chaunce' ←'chance' ←'had best look to'
Where no profaner eye may look, Penseroso 140
Look Nymphs, and Shepherds look, Arcades 1
Trinity ms 'Looke'
The hungry Sheep look up, and are not fed, Lycidas 125
Trinity ms 'looke'
Look homeward Angel now, and melt with ruth. Lycidas 163
Trinity ms 'looke'
Should look so neer upon her foul deformities. Nativity 44
Look in, and see each blissful Deitie Vacation 35
With praise enough for Envy to look wan; Sonnet 13, 6
Trinity ms 'looke' ←'look'
Return now, God of Hosts, look down Psalm 80, 57
Thou God our shield look on the face Psalm 84, 31
Look down *on mortal men*. Psalm 85, 48
On thy third Reigne the Earth look now, and tell Prose 12, 3
Looked
Stood on the brink of Hell and look'd a while, Par Lost 2.918
One Gate there only was, and that look'd East Par Lost 4.178
If thou resist. The Fiend lookt up and knew Par Lost 4.1013
And as I wondring lookt, beside it stood Par Lost 5.54
Lookd round, and Scouts each Coast light-armed scoure, Par Lost 6.529
Spreading thir bane; the blasted Starrs lookt wan, Par Lost 10.412
He lookd and saw a spacious Plaine, whereon Par Lost 11.556
He lookd and saw wide Territorie spred Par Lost 11.638
He look'd, and saw the face of things quite chang'd, Par Lost 11.712
He lookd, and saw the Ark hull on the floud, Par Lost 11.840
I look't for some great change; to Honour? no, Par Reg 2.86
He look't and saw what numbers numberless Par Reg 3.310
Lookest
Look'st from thy sole Dominion like the God Par Lost 4.33
Looking
Of outward strength; while shame, thou looking on, Par Lost 9.312
Conversing, looking, loving, to abstain Par Lost 10.993
Not higher that Hill nor wider looking round, Par Lost 11.381
Griev'd at his heart, when looking down he saw Par Lost 11.887
And looking down, to see the hubbub strange Par Lost 12.60
God looking forth will trouble all his Host Par Lost 12.209
They looking back, all th' Eastern side beheld Par Lost 12.641
And looking round on every side beheld Par Reg 1.295
Looking on the Earth, with approbation marks Par Reg 3.61
Or what the cross dire-looking Planet smites, Arcades 52
Looks
All these and more came flocking; but with looks Par Lost 1.522
Looks through the Horizontal misty Air Par Lost 1.595
From heav'n, for ev'n in heav'n his looks and thoughts Par Lost 1.680
Looks down with wonder at the sudden view Par Lost 3.542
And worthie seemd, for in thir looks Divine Par Lost 4.291
Pleas'd it returnd as soon with answering looks Par Lost 4.464
Where he first lighted, soon discernd his looks Par Lost 4.570
Mankind with her faire looks, to be aveng'd Par Lost 4.718

Looks(*cont*)
Leaning half-rais'd, with looks of cordial Love Par Lost 5.12
Be not disheart'nd then, nor cloud those looks Par Lost 5.122
So saying, with dispatchful looks in haste Par Lost 5.331
And in her looks, which from that time infus'd Par Lost 8.474
Express they, by looks onely, or do they mix Par Lost 8.616
Looks intervene and smiles, or object new Par Lost 9.222
Of looks and smiles, for smiles from Reason flow, Par Lost 9.239
I from the influence of thy looks receave Par Lost 9.309
Thy looks, the Heav'n of mildness, with disdain, Par Lost 9.534
The latter I demurre, for in thir looks Par Lost 9.558
Love was not in thir looks, either to God Par Lost 10.111
That thou on Earth hadst prosper'd, which thy looks Par Lost 10.360
His thoughts, his looks, words, actions all infect, Par Lost 10.608
Whereon I live, thy gentle looks, thy aid, Par Lost 10.919
With looks agast and sad he thus bespake. Par Reg 1.43
Of fair fallacious looks, venereal trains, Samson 533
And lower looks, but in a sultrie chafe. Samson 1246
But rigid looks of Chast austerity, Mask 450
Bridgewater ms 'lookes'
By unchaste looks, loose gestures, and foul talk, Mask 464
Bridgewater ms 'lookes'
Ne're looks to Heav'n amidst his gorgeous feast, Mask 777
And looks commercing with the skies, Penseroso 39
On whose fresh lap the swart Star sparely looks, Lycidas 138
Looks toward *Namancos* and *Bayona*'s hold; Lycidas 162
Loop
From her cabin'd loop hole peep, Mask 140
Bridgewater ms 'loopehole'
1673 'loop-hole'
Trinity ms 'loopehole'
Loopholes
At Loopholes cut through thickest shade: Those Leaves Par Lost 9.1110
Loose
Will he, so wise, let loose at once his ire, Par Lost 2.155
With Horse and Chariots rankt in loose array; Par Lost 2.887
Through all restraint broke loose he wings his way Par Lost 3.87
Now in loose Garlands thick thrown off, the bright Par Lost 3.362
Of her loose tresses hid: he in delight Par Lost 4.497
Who would not, finding way, break loose from Hell, Par Lost 4.889
Came not all Hell broke loose? is pain to them Par Lost 4.918
And to disorder'd rage let loose the reines, Par Lost 6.696
That wandring loose about Samson 675
Stirs up among the loose unleter'd Hinds, Mask 174
In his loose traces from the furrow came, Mask 292
By unchaste looks, loose gestures, and foul talk, Mask 464
The loose train of thy amber-dropping hair, Mask 863
Your learned hands, can loose this Gordian knot? Vacation 90
Loosely
Part loosly wing the Region, part more wise Par Lost 7.425
Nor both so loosly disally'd Samson 1022
Loosening
From thir foundations loosning to and fro Par Lost 6.643
Lop
More hands then ours to lop thir wanton growth: Par Lost 4.629
Lop overgrown, or prune, or prop, or bind, Par Lost 9.210
Lopped
Maim'd his brute Image, head and hands lopt off Par Lost 1.459
With branches lopt, in Wood or Mountain fell'd) Par Lost 6.575
Loquacious
Bold or loquacious, thus abasht repli'd. Par Lost 10.161
Lord
Within Heav'ns bound, unless Heav'ns Lord supream Par Lost 2.236
Thy King and Lord? Back to thy punishment, Par Lost 2.699
Suspicious, reasonless. Why should thir Lord Par Lost 4.516
Whose easier business were to serve thir Lord Par Lost 4.943
Hail universal Lord, be bounteous still Par Lost 5.205
All knees in Heav'n, and shall confess him Lord: Par Lost 5.608
Erre not, much less for this to be our Lord, Par Lost 5.799
What Heavens Lord had powerfullest to send Par Lost 6.425
Son, Heir, and Lord, to him Dominion giv'n, Par Lost 6.887
Attendant on thir Lord: Heav'n op'nd wide Par Lost 7.205
Ordain'd for uses to his Lord best known. Par Lost 8.106
So spake the Universal Lord, and seem'd Par Lost 8.376
Him Lord pronounc'd, and, O indignitie! Par Lost 9.154
Yet not so strictly hath our Lord impos'd Par Lost 9.235
Ofspring of Heav'n and Earth, and all Earths Lord, Par Lost 9.273
Which when the Lord God heard, without delay Par Lost 10.163
Chiefly on Man, sole Lord of all declar'd, Par Lost 10.401
For though the Lord of all be infinite, Par Lost 10.794
Mayst cover: well may then thy Lord appeas'd Par Lost 11.257
Before the Lord, as in despite of Heav'n, Par Lost 12.34
He made not Lord; such title to himself Par Lost 12.70
As did thir Lord before them. Thus they win Par Lost 12.502
Now amplier known thy Saviour and thy Lord, Par Lost 12.544
But thou art plac't above me, thou art Lord; Par Reg 1.475
To treat thee as beseems, and as her Lord Par Reg 2.335
Thee homage, and acknowledge thee thir Lord: Par Reg 2.376
And worship me as thy superior Lord, Par Reg 4.167
The Lord thy God, and only him shalt serve; Par Reg 4.177
Tempt not the Lord thy God, he said and stood. Par Reg 4.561
Endure it, doubtful whether God be Lord, Samson 477
Spir. What voice is that, my young Lord? speak agen. Mask 492
Trinity ms 'lord'
Noble Lord, and Lady bright, Mask 966
Clos'd o're the head of your lov'd *Lycidas*? Lycidas 51
1638 'your lord'
Have thou the honour first, thy Lord to greet, Nativity 26

Lord(*cont*)
As if they surely knew their sovran Lord was by. Nativity 60
Untill their Lord himself bespake, and bid them go. Nativity 76
Her sleeping Lord with Handmaid Lamp attending. Nativity 242
Praise the Lord, for he is kind, Psalm 136, 2
Which on our dearest Lord did sease er'e long, Passion 10
To their great Lord, whose love their motion sway'd Musick 22
Avenge O Lord thy slaughter'd Saints, whose bones Sonnet 18, 1
Because you have thrown of your Prelate Lord, Forcers 1
For the Lord knows th' upright way of the just, Psalm 1, 15
Against the Lord and his Messiah dear Psalm 2, 5
Shall laugh, the Lord shall scoff them, then severe Psalm 2, 9
I will declare; the Lord to me hath say'd Psalm 2, 14
Lord how many are my foes Psalm 3, 1
But thou Lord art my shield my glory, Psalm 3, 7
Was the Lord. Of many millions Psalm 3, 15
Rise Lord, save me my God for thou Psalm 3, 19
Hast broke the teeth. This help was from the Lord Psalm 3, 23
Yet know the Lord hath chose Psalm 4, 13
But Lord, thus let me pray, Psalm 4, 28
Thou Lord alone in safety mak'st me dwell. Psalm 4, 42
Lord lead me in thy righteousness Psalm 5, 21
Lord in thine anger do not reprehend me Psalm 6, 1
Pity me Lord for I am much deject Psalm 6, 3
And thou O Lord how long? turn Lord, restore Psalm 6, 7
The Lord hath heard, the Lord hath heard my prai'r Psalm 6, 18
The Lord will own, and have me in his keeping. Psalm 6, 20
Lord my God to thee I flie Psalm 7, 1
Lord my God if I have thought Psalm 7, 7
Judge me Lord, be judge in this Psalm 7, 31
O Jehovah our Lord how wondrous great Psalm 8, 1
O're the works of thy hand thou mad'st him Lord, Psalm 8, 17
O Jehovah our Lord how wondrous great Psalm 8, 23
Lord God of Hosts, how long wilt thou, Psalm 80, 17
Lord God of Hosts *voutsafe*, Psalm 80, 78
I am the Lord thy God which brought Psalm 81, 41
Who hate the Lord should *then be fain* Psalm 81, 61
Lord fill with shame their face. Psalm 83, 60
O Lord of Hoasts, how dear Psalm 84, 2
Thy Courts O Lord to see, Psalm 84, 6
Ev'n *by* thy Altars Lord of Hoasts Psalm 84, 13
Lord God of Hoasts hear *now* my praier Psalm 84, 29
For God the Lord both Sun and Shield Psalm 84, 41
Lord *God* of Hoasts *that raign'st on high*, Psalm 84, 45
Thou hast not Lord been slack, Psalm 85, 2
Cause us to see thy goodness Lord, Psalm 85, 25
And now what God the Lord will speak Psalm 85, 29
The Lord will also then bestow Psalm 85, 49
Thy *gracious* ear, O Lord, encline, Psalm 86, 1
Pitty me Lord for daily thee Psalm 86, 9
Thy Servants Soul; for Lord to thee Psalm 86, 11
For thou art good, thou Lord art prone Psalm 86, 13
Unto my supplication Lord Psalm 86, 17
O Lord, nor any works Psalm 86, 26
To bow them low before thee Lord, Psalm 86, 31
Teach me O Lord thy way *most right*, Psalm 86, 37
Thee will I praise O Lord my God Psalm 86, 41
But thou Lord art the God most mild Psalm 86, 53
And be asham'd, because thou Lord Psalm 86, 63
Sions *fair* Gates the Lord loves more Psalm 87, 5
The Lord shall write it in a Scrowle Psalm 87, 21
Lord God that dost me save and keep, Psalm 88, 1
Lord all the day I thee entreat, Psalm 88, 39
But I to thee O Lord do cry Psalm 88, 53
Why wilt thou Lord my soul forsake, Psalm 88, 57

Lorded
And lorded over them whom now they serve; Samson 267

Lordliest
I know not. Lords are Lordliest in thir wine; Samson 1418

Lordly
Forc't Halleluiah's; while he Lordly sits Par Lost 2.243
That from his Lordly eye keep distance due, Par Lost 3.578
More Lordly thund'ring then thou well wilt bear. Samson 1353
Thou hast put all under his lordly feet, Psalm 8, 18
Of Kings and lordly States, Psalm 82, 2

Lords
For one restraint, Lords of the World besides? Par Lost 1.32
The great Seraphic Lords and Cherubim Par Lost 1.794
In naked Majestie seemd Lords of all, Par Lost 4.290
Deliverer from new Lords, leader to free Par Lost 6.451
To thee and to thy Race I give; as Lords Par Lost 8.339
Yet Lords declar'd of all in Earth or Aire? Par Lost 9.658
As Lords, a spacious World, to our native Heaven Par Lost 10.467
Worldlie or dissolute, on what thir Lords Par Lost 11.803
Subjects him from without to violent Lords; Par Lost 12.93
Thir Lords, whom God dispos'd, the house of God Par Lost 12.349
Thir Lords the *Philistines* with gather'd powers Samson 251
To some *Philistian* Lords, with whom to treat Samson 482
I to the Lords will intercede, not doubting Samson 920
Bearing my words and doings to the Lords Samson 947
Sam. Such usage as your honourable Lords Samson 1108
Har. Is not thy Nation subject to our Lords? Samson 1182
But your ill-meaning Politician Lords, Samson 1195
My Nation was subjected to your Lords. Samson 1205
Chor. He will directly to the Lords, I fear, Samson 1250
Off. *Samson*, to thee our Lords thus bid me say; Samson 1310
To appear as fits before th' illustrious Lords. Samson 1318
Not dragging? the *Philistian* Lords command. Samson 1371

Lords(*cont*)
Off. *Samson*, this second message from our Lords Samson 1391
By this compliance thou wilt win the Lords Samson 1411
I know not. Lords are Lordliest in thir wine; Samson 1418
By order of the Lords new parted hence Samson 1447
Man. I have attempted one by one the Lords Samson 1457
With seats where all the Lords and each degree Samson 1607
Hitherto, Lords, what your commands impos'd Samson 1640
Lords, Ladies, Captains, Councellors, or Priests, Samson 1653
The herds would over-multitude their Lords, Mask 731

Lore
She finish'd, and the suttle Fiend his lore Par Lost 2.815
Heard not her lore, both in subjection now Par Lost 9.1128
Vertue, who follow not her lore: permit me Par Reg 1.483
Where his fair off-spring nurs't in Princely lore, Mask 34

Lorn
Where the love-lorn Nightingale Mask 234
Bridgewater ms 'love-lorne'
Trinity ms 'love-lorne'
1637 'love-lorne'
B.M. ms 'Love lorn'

Lose
To be no more; sad cure; for who would loose, Par Lost 2.146
Sole King, and of his Kingdom loose no part Par Lost 2.325
Loose all her virtue; least bad men should boast Par Lost 2.483
The tempting stream, with one small drop to loose Par Lost 2.607
Calls us, we lose the prime, to mark how spring Par Lost 5.21
In our defence, lest unawares we lose Par Lost 5.731
That detriment, if such it be to lose Par Lost 7.153
Shalt loose, expell'd from hence into a World Par Lost 8.332
Be frustrate, do, undo, and labour loose, Par Lost 9.944
One Flesh; to loose thee were to loose my self. Par Lost 9.959
Loose no reward, though here thou see him die, Par Lost 11.459
Shall with thir freedom lost all vertu loose Par Lost 11.798
Then loose it to a stranger, that the true Par Lost 12.358
He could not lose himself; but went about Par Reg 2.98
I lose, prevented by thy eyes put out. Samson 1103
Lose thir defence distracted and amaz'd. Samson 1286
La. No less then if I should my brothers loose. Mask 288
1637 'lose'
Imbodies, and imbrutes, till she quite loose Mask 468
The Air such pleasure loth to lose, Nativity 99

Loses
Looses discount'nanc't, and like folly shewes; Par Lost 8.553
And loses, though but verbal, his reward. Par Reg 3.104

Losing
Affecting God-head, and so loosing all, Par Lost 3.206
By loosing thee a while, the whole Race lost. Par Lost 3.280

Loss
With loss of *Eden*, till one greater Man Par Lost 1.4
ms 'losse'
Our Enemy, our own loss how repair, Par Lost 1.188
ms 'losse'
Th' associates and copartners of our loss Par Lost 1.265
ms 'losse'
In loss it self; which on his count'nance cast Par Lost 1.526
For who can yet beleeve, though after loss, Par Lost 1.631
ms 'losse'
Hath bin achievd of merit, yet this loss Par Lost 2.21
Warr hath determin'd us, and foild with loss Par Lost 2.330
Wide gaping, and with utter loss of being Par Lost 2.440
Cleer Victory, to our part loss and rout Par Lost 2.770
A World from utter loss, and hast been found Par Lost 3.308
To deepest Hell, and to repair that loss Par Lost 3.678
To wreck on innocent frail man his loss Par Lost 4.11
His loss; but chiefly to find here observd Par Lost 4.849
O loss of one in Heav'n to judge of wise, Par Lost 4.904
Us timely of what might else have bin our loss, Par Lost 7.74
Her loss, and other pleasures all abjure: Par Lost 8.480
Or won to what may work his utter loss, Par Lost 9.131
Another Rib afford, yet loss of thee Par Lost 9.912
The good I sought not. To the loss of that, Par Lost 10.752
For loss of life and pleasure overlov'd. Par Lost 10.1019
Thir unexpected loss and plaints out breath'd. Par Reg 2.29
Quite at a loss, for all his darts were spent, Par Reg 4.366
O loss of sight, of thee I most complain! Samson 67
Left me all helpless with th' irreparable loss Samson 644
From whence captivity and loss of eyes. Samson 1744
Co. Imports their loss, beside the present need? Mask 287
1637 'losse'
Bridgewater ms 'losse'
Trinity ms 'losse'
Though *Erymanth* your loss deplore, Arcades 100
Trinity ms 'losse'
Such, *Lycidas*, thy loss to Shepherds ear. Lycidas 49
1638 'losse'
Trinity ms 'losse'
Must redeem our loss; Nativity 153
Her false imagin'd loss cease to lament, Fair Inf 72
Small loss it is that thence can come unto thee, Vacation 9
So little is our loss, On Time 7
Trinity ms 'losse'
For all this wast of wealth, and loss of blood. Sonnet 12, 14
Trinity ms 'losse' ←'loss'

Lost
Both of lost happiness and lasting pain Par Lost 1.55
And shook his throne. What though the field be lost? Par Lost 1.105
All is not lost; the unconquerable Will, Par Lost 1.106

Lost(*cont*)
Hath lost us Heav'n, and all this mighty Host Par Lost 1.136
Said then the lost Arch-Angel, this the seat Par Lost 1.243
Regaind in Heav'n, or what more lost in Hell? Par Lost 1.270
Abject and lost lay these, covering the Flood, Par Lost 1.312
Warriers, the Flowr of Heav'n, once yours, now lost, Par Lost 1.316
A Leper once he lost and gain'd a King, Par Lost 1.471
Not in despair, to have found themselves not lost Par Lost 1.525
Stood like a Towr; his form had yet not lost Par Lost 1.591
By mee, have lost our hopes. But he who reigns Par Lost 1.637
I give not Heav'n for lost. From this descent Par Lost 2.14
Car'd not to be at all; with that care lost Par Lost 2.48
A fairer person lost not Heav'n; he seemd Par Lost 2.110
To perish rather, swallowd up and lost Par Lost 2.149
Our own right lost: him to unthrone we then Par Lost 2.231
And found no end, in wandring mazes lost. Par Lost 2.561
And time and place are lost; where eldest Night Par Lost 2.894
Alone, and without guide, half lost, I seek Par Lost 2.975
To your behoof, if I that Region lost, Par Lost 2.982
For should Man finally be lost, should Man Par Lost 3.150
Man shall not quite be lost, but sav'd who will, Par Lost 3.173
Must have bin lost, adjudg'd to Death and Hell Par Lost 3.223
Can never seek, once dead in sins and lost; Par Lost 3.233
By loosing thee a while, the whole Race lost. Par Lost 3.280
Farwel Remorse: all Good to me is lost; Par Lost 4.109
Lost sight of him; one of the banisht crew Par Lost 4.573
Or less be lost. Thy fear, said *Zephon* bold, Par Lost 4.854
Returnd not lost: On to the sacred hill Par Lost 6.25
Plagues; they astonisht all resistance lost, Par Lost 6.838
Self-lost, and in a moment will create Par Lost 7.154
To me is lost. Then let me not let pass Par Lost 9.479
There swallow'd up and lost, from succour farr. Par Lost 9.642
That all was lost. Back to the Thicket slunk Par Lost 9.784
How art thou lost, how on a sudden lost, Par Lost 9.900
Much pleasure we have lost, while we abstain'd Par Lost 9.1022
Both Good and Evil, Good lost, and Evil got, Par Lost 9.1072
Immutable when thou wert lost, not I, Par Lost 9.1165
With odds what Warr hath lost, and fully aveng'd Par Lost 10.374
Till thir lost shape, permitted, they resum'd, Par Lost 10.574
On me alreadie lost, mee then thy self Par Lost 10.929
As one disarm'd, his anger all he lost, Par Lost 10.945
Would be revenge indeed; which will be lost Par Lost 10.1036
And Immortalitie: that fondly lost, Par Lost 11.59
His knowledge of Good lost, and Evil got, Par Lost 11.87
What justly thou hast lost; nor set thy heart, Par Lost 11.288
But this praeeminence thou hast lost, brought down Par Lost 11.347
Not hid, nor those things last which might preserve Par Lost 11.579
1667 'lost', 1668 errata 'last'
Of love and youth not lost, Songs, Garlands, Flours, Par Lost 11.594
Rescu'd, had in his Righteousness bin lost? Par Lost 11.682
Shall with thir freedom lost all vertu loose Par Lost 11.798
In foraign Lands thir memorie be lost Par Lost 12.46
Is lost, which alwayes with right Reason dwells Par Lost 12.84
Thir inward lost: Witness th' irreverent Son Par Lost 12.101
In sin for ever lost from life; this act Par Lost 12.429
I carry hence; though all by mee is lost, Par Lost 12.621
By one mans disobedience lost, now sing Par Reg 1.2
Lost Paradise deceiv'd by me, though since Par Reg 1.52
Winning by Conquest what the first man lost Par Reg 1.154
For what he bids I do; though I have lost Par Reg 1.377
Much lustre of my native brightness, lost Par Reg 1.378
To be belov'd of God, I have not lost Par Reg 1.379
Or vertuous, I should so have lost all sense. Par Reg 1.382
I lost not what I lost, rather by them Par Reg 1.390
Lost bliss, to thee no more communicable, Par Reg 1.419
Sought lost *Eliah*, so in each place these Par Reg 2.19
I lost him, but so found, as well I saw Par Reg 2.97
Lost in a Desert here and hunger-bit: Par Reg 2.416
Insatiable of glory had lost all, Par Reg 3.148
Let that come when it comes; all hope is lost Par Reg 3.204
Ten Sons of *Jacob*, two of *Joseph* lost Par Reg 3.377
So little here, nay lost; but *Eve* was *Eve*, Par Reg 4.6
Repaid? But gratitude in thee is lost Par Reg 4.188
By light of Nature not in all quite lost. Par Reg 4.352
Temptation, hast regain'd lost Paradise, Par Reg 4.608
Thy Bondage or lost Sight, Samson 152
To afflict thy self in vain: though sight be lost, Samson 914
That what by me thou hast lost thou least shalt miss. Samson 927
Made older then thy age through eye-sight lost. Samson 1489
And since his strength with eye-sight was not lost, Samson 1502
So vertue giv'n for lost, Samson 1697
Whoever tasted, lost his upright shape, Mask 52
La. Nay gentle Shepherd ill is lost that praise Mask 271
But O that haples virgin our lost sister Mask 350
Slip't from the fold, or young Kid lost his dam, Mask 498
Or our neglect, we lost her as we came. Mask 510
Now the spell hath lost his hold; Mask 919
Were lost in death, till he that dwelt above Circum 18
The conscience, Friend, to have lost them overply'd Sonnet 22, 10
Be lost in memory. Psalm 83, 16
Things that on earth were lost, or were abus'd. Prose 2, 4

Lot
For ever now to have thir lot in pain, Par Lost 1.608
Worth waiting, since our present lot appeers Par Lost 2.223
View'd first thir lamentable lot, and found Par Lost 2.617
So farr the happier Lot, enjoying thee Par Lost 4.446
Gabriel, to thee thy course by Lot hath giv'n Par Lost 4.561
And read thy Lot in yon celestial Sign Par Lost 4.1011

Lot(*cont*)
Meant mee, by ventring higher then my Lot. Par Lost 9.690
Thou therefore also taste, that equal Lot Par Lost 9.881
However I with thee have fixt my Lot, Par Lost 9.952
Or transmigration, as thir lot shall lead. Par Lost 10.261
My part of evil onely, each dayes lot Par Lost 11.765
And fears as eminent, above the lot Par Reg 2.70
A sword shall pierce, this is my favour'd lot, Par Reg 2.91
His lot who dares be singularly good. Par Reg 3.57
I leave him to his lot, and like my own. Samson 996
Either of these is in thy lot, Samson 1292
His lot unfortunate in nuptial choice, Samson 1743
Took in by lot 'twixt high, and neather *Jove*, Mask 20
Bridgewater ms 'lott'
More happines then this thy present lot. Mask 789
line not in Trinity ms
line not in Bridgewater ms
For know by lot from *Jove* I am the powr Arcades 44
To that same lot, however mean, or high, Sonnet 7, 11
Scarce to be less then Gods, thou mad'st his lot, Psalm 8, 15
To aid the Sons of Lot. Psalm 83, 32

Loud
He call'd so loud, that all the hollow Deep Par Lost 1.314
Though for the noyse of Drums and Timbrels loud Par Lost 1.394
Of Trumpets loud and Clarions be upreard Par Lost 1.532
With deafning shout, return'd them loud acclaim. Par Lost 2.520
Cocytus, nam'd of lamentation loud Par Lost 2.579
With wide *Cerberian* mouths full loud, and rung Par Lost 2.655
With noises loud and ruinous (to compare Par Lost 2.921
Loud as from numbers without number, sweet Par Lost 3.346
With Jubilee, and loud Hosanna's filld Par Lost 3.348
Back from pursuit thy Powers with loud acclaime Par Lost 3.397
Of glimmering air less vext with tempest loud: Par Lost 3.429
Breathe soft or loud; and wave your tops, ye Pines, Par Lost 5.193
With joy and acclamations loud, that one Par Lost 6.23
Of wrauth awak't: nor with less dread the loud Par Lost 6.59
Satan: And thus was heard Commanding loud. Par Lost 6.557
What we propound, and loud that all may hear. Par Lost 6.567
Crystallin Ocean, and the loud misrule Par Lost 7.271
Torment, and loud lament, and furious rage. Par Lost 8.244
1667 'lowd'
Thir mighty Chief returnd: loud was th' acclaime: Par Lost 10.455
He ended, and the heav'nly Audience loud Par Lost 10.641
Boreas and *Caecias* and *Argestes* loud Par Lost 10.699
Thus *Adam* to himself lamented loud Par Lost 10.845
Forthwith a hideous gabble rises loud Par Lost 12.56
In Thunder Lightning and loud Trumpets sound Par Lost 12.229
He ceas'd, and heard thir grant in loud acclaim; Par Reg 2.235
With chaunt of tuneful Birds resounding loud; Par Reg 2.290
I never fear'd they could, though noising loud Par Reg 4.488
The deeds themselves, though mute, spoke loud the dooer; Samson 248
Great Pomp, and Sacrifice, and Praises loud Samson 436
If thy appearance answer loud report. Samson 1090
Horribly loud unlike the former shout. Samson 1510
Man. The accident was loud, & here before thee Samson 1552
Whence eev'n now the tumult of loud Mirth Mask 202
line not in Bridgewater ms
Carrol her goodnes lowd in rustick layes, Mask 849
Bridgewater ms 'loud'
Trinity ms 'loud'
While rocking Winds are Piping loud, Penseroso 126
Harping in loud and solemn quire, Nativity 115
A voice of weeping heard, and loud lament; Nativity 183
Trampling the unshowr'd Grasse with lowings loud: Nativity 215
Or *Humber* loud that keeps the *Scythians* Name, Vacation 99
Loud o're the rest *Cremona*'s Trump doth sound; Passion 26
Might think th' infection of my sorrows loud, Passion 55
Their loud up-lifted Angel trumpets blow, Musick 11
And rumors loud, that daunt remotest kings, Sonnet 15, 4
Trinity ms 'loud' ← 'loudd'
And Dunbarr feild resounds thy praises loud, Sonnet 16, 8
To God our strength sing loud, *and clear* Psalm 81, 1
Sing loud to God *our King*, Psalm 81, 2
Loud acclamations ring. Psalm 81, 4

Louder
Would speed before thee, and be louder heard, Par Lost 10.954

Loudest
With loudest vehemence: thither he plyes, Par Lost 2.954
Then loudest Oratorie: yet thir port Par Lost 11.8
Strait knew me, and with loudest voice proclaim'd Par Reg 1.275
Ill imitated, while they loudest sing Par Reg 4.339

Loudly
Begin, and somwhat loudly sweep the string. Lycidas 17
And loudly knock to have their passage out; Vacation 24

Lour
Smile she or lowre: Samson 1057

Loured
Skie lowr'd and muttering Thunder, som sad drops Par Lost 9.1002

Louring
Heav'ns chearful face, the lowring Element Par Lost 2.490
As day-light sunk, and brought in lowring night Par Reg 4.398

Lours
Stand firm, for in his look defiance lours. Par Lost 4.873

Love
And works of love or enmity fulfill. Par Lost 1.431
Fell not from Heaven, or more gross to love Par Lost 1.491
Smit with the love of sacred Song; but chief Par Lost 3.29
Reaping immortal fruits of joy and love, Par Lost 3.67

Love(*cont*)
Uninterrupted joy, unrivald love Par Lost 3.68
Of true allegiance, constant Faith or Love, Par Lost 3.104
Love without end, and without measure Grace, Par Lost 3.142
Say Heav'nly powers, where shall we find such love, Par Lost 3.213
In whom the fulness dwels of love divine, Par Lost 3.225
Silent yet spake, and breath'd immortal love Par Lost 3.267
So Heav'nly love shall outdoo Hellish hate Par Lost 3.298
Love hath abounded more then Glory abounds, Par Lost 3.312
With Joy and Love triumphing, and fair Truth. Par Lost 3.338
For mans offence. O unexampl'd love, Par Lost 3.410
Love no where to be found less then Divine! Par Lost 3.411
But Heav'ns free Love dealt equally to all? Par Lost 4.68
Be then his Love accurst, since love or hate, Par Lost 4.69
That ever since in loves imbraces met, Par Lost 4.322
With wonder, and could love, so lively shines Par Lost 4.363
Of sympathie and love; there I had fixt Par Lost 4.465
Smil'd with superior Love, as *Jupiter* Par Lost 4.499
Where neither joy nor love, but fierce desire, Par Lost 4.509
And mutual love, the Crown of all our bliss Par Lost 4.728
Mysterious of connubial Love refus'd: Par Lost 4.743
Haile wedded Love, mysterious Law, true source Par Lost 4.750
Here Love his golden shafts imploies, here lights Par Lost 4.763
Leaning half-rais'd, with looks of cordial Love Par Lost 5.12
Love unlibidinous reign'd, nor jealousie Par Lost 5.449
Unalterably firm his love entire Par Lost 5.502
To him, or possibly his love desert Par Lost 5.515
Because wee freely love, as in our will Par Lost 5.539
To love or not; in this we stand or fall: Par Lost 5.540
Yet that we never shall forget to love Par Lost 5.550
Holy Memorials, acts of Zeale and Love Par Lost 5.593
His Loyaltie he kept, his Love, his Zeale; Par Lost 5.900
So oft in Festivals of joy and love Par Lost 6.94
Of Majestie Divine, Sapience and Love Par Lost 7.195
Or wander with delight, and love to haunt Par Lost 7.330
Such pairs, in Love and mutual Honour joyn'd? Par Lost 8.58
On Man his Equal Love: say therefore on; Par Lost 8.228
Collateral love, and deerest amitie. Par Lost 8.426
The spirit of love and amorous delight. Par Lost 8.477
In every gesture dignitie and love. Par Lost 8.489
Thy cherishing, thy honouring, and thy love, Par Lost 8.569
So awful, that with honour thou maist love Par Lost 8.577
Attractive, human, rational, love still; Par Lost 8.587
Wherein true Love consists not; love refines Par Lost 8.589
By which to heav'nly Love thou maist ascend, Par Lost 8.592
From all her words and actions mixt with Love Par Lost 8.602
To love thou blam'st me not, for love thou saist Par Lost 8.612
Love not the heav'nly Spirits, and how thir Love Par Lost 8.615
Celestial rosie red, Loves proper hue, Par Lost 8.619
Us happie, and without Love no happiness. Par Lost 8.621
Be strong, live happie, and love, but first of all Par Lost 8.633
Him whom to love is to obey, and keep Par Lost 8.634
To brute deni'd, and are of Love the food, Par Lost 9.240
Love not the lowest end of human life. Par Lost 9.241
Conjugal Love, then which perhaps no bliss Par Lost 9.263
Thy equal fear that my firm Faith and Love Par Lost 9.286
And Matrimonial Love; but *Eve*, who thought Par Lost 9.319
And what is Faith, Love, Vertue unassaid Par Lost 9.335
Not then mistrust, but tender love enjoynes, Par Lost 9.357
What hither brought us, hate, not love, nor hope Par Lost 9.475
Shee fair, divinely fair, fit Love for Gods, Par Lost 9.489
Not terrible, though terrour be in Love Par Lost 9.490
Hate stronger, under shew of Love well feign'd, Par Lost 9.492
The Tempter, but with shew of Zeale and Love Par Lost 9.665
In Femal Sex, the more to draw his Love, Par Lost 9.822
So dear I love him, that with him all deaths Par Lost 9.832
Thy presence, agonie of love till now Par Lost 9.858
May joyne us, equal Joy, as equal Love; Par Lost 9.882
Thy sweet Converse and Love so dearly joyn'd, Par Lost 9.909
O glorious trial of exceeding Love, Par Lost 9.961
Shall separate us, linkt in Love so deare, Par Lost 9.970
This happie trial of thy Love, which else Par Lost 9.975
So faithful Love unequald; but I feel Par Lost 9.983
Tenderly wept, much won that he his Love Par Lost 9.991
There they thir fill of Love and Loves disport Par Lost 9.1042
Is this the Love, is this the recompence Par Lost 9.1163
Love was not in thir looks, either to God Par Lost 10.111
Thy Love, not thy Subjection, and her Gifts Par Lost 10.153
By a farr worse, or if she love, withheld Par Lost 10.903
What love sincere, and reverence in my heart Par Lost 10.915
In offices of Love, how we may light'n Par Lost 10.960
Thy Love, the sole contentment of my heart Par Lost 10.973
From Loves due Rites, Nuptial imbraces sweet, Par Lost 10.994
With goodness and paternal Love, his Face Par Lost 11.353
Nor love thy Life, nor hate; but what thou livst Par Lost 11.553
And now of love they treat till th' Eevning Star Par Lost 11.588
Loves Harbinger appeerd; then all in heat Par Lost 11.589
Of love and youth not lost, Songs, Garlands, Flours, Par Lost 11.594
High in the love of Heav'n, yet from my Loynes Par Lost 12.380
Both by obedience and by love, though love Par Lost 12.403
Working through love, upon thir hearts shall write, Par Lost 12.489
Founded in righteousness and peace and love Par Lost 12.550
1669 'Love'
And love with fear the onely God, to walk Par Lost 12.562
Add vertue, Patience, Temperance, add Love, Par Lost 12.583
To love, at least comtemplate and admire Par Reg 1.380
Then to love Bondage more then Liberty, Samson 270
Of Nuptial Love profest, carrying it strait Samson 385

Love(*cont*)
More Faith? who also in her prime of love, Samson 388
And what if Love, which thou interpret'st hate, Samson 790
The jealousie of Love, powerful of sway Samson 791
Mine and Loves prisoner, not the *Philistines*, Samson 808
Fearless at home of partners in my love. Samson 810
These reasons in Loves law have past for good, Samson 811
And Love hath oft, well meaning, wrought much wo, Samson 813
But Love constrain'd thee; call it furious rage Samson 836
To satisfie thy lust: Love seeks to have Love; Samson 837
My love how couldst thou hope, who tookst the way Samson 838
Only my love of thee held long debate; Samson 863
But had thy love, still odiously pretended, Samson 873
With me, where my redoubl'd love and care Samson 923
Love once possest, nor can be easily Samson 1005
That womans love can win or long inherit; Samson 1012
Or was too much of self-love mixt, Samson 1031
That either they love nothing, or not long? Samson 1033
Conceiv'd, agreeable to a Fathers love, Samson 1506
Venus now wakes, and wak'ns Love. Mask 124
Bridgewater ms 'love'
That wontst to love the travailers benizon, Mask 332
I love thy courage yet, and bold Emprise, Mask 610
Love vertue, she alone is free, Mask 1019
And love to live in dimple sleek; Allegro 30
And made Hell grant what Love did seek. Penseroso 108
And love the high embowed Roof, Penseroso 157
In the blest Kingdoms meek of joy and love. Lycidas 177
line not in 1638 edition
colouring the pale cheeke of uninjoyd love Lycidas Tr. ms 28.16
With Truth, and Peace, and Love shall ever shine On Time 16
O more exceeding love or law more just? Circum 15
Just law indeed, but more exceeding love! Circum 16
To their great Lord, whose love their motion sway'd Musick 22
Portend success in love; O if *Jove's* will Sonnet 1, 7
Whether the Muse, or Love call thee his mate, Sonnet 1, 13
When Faith and Love which parted from thee never, Sonnet 14, 1
Love led them on, and Faith who knew them best Sonnet 14, 9
Trinity ms 'Love led them on' ←'Faith shew'd the way' ←'Faith who led on the way'
Love, sweetness, goodness, in her person shin'd Sonnet 23, 11
Still to love vanity, Psalm 4, 10
To love, to seek, to prize Psalm 4, 11
And shall triumph in thee, who love thy name. Psalm 5, 36
Thy free love made it thine, Psalm 80, 34
Thy waies, and love the just, Psalm 86, 6

Loved
Thy creature late so lov'd, thy youngest Son Par Lost 3.151
Him with her lov'd societie, that now Par Lost 9.1007
My enemies, lov'd thee, as too well thou knew'st, Samson 878
Lov'd, honour'd, fear'd me, thou alone could hate me Samson 939
As loath to leave the body that it lov'd, Mask 473
Bridgewater ms 'loved'
Spir. O my lov'd masters heir, and his next joy, Mask 501
Bridgewater ms 'Lov'd'
He lov'd me well, and oft would beg me sing, Mask 623
And old *Damoetas* lov'd to hear our song. Lycidas 36
Clos'd o're the head of your lov'd *Lycidas?* Lycidas 51
Trinity ms 'lov'd' ←'youn'
1638 'your lord'
Fly after the Night-steeds, leaving their Moon-lov'd maze. Nativity 236
Whilome did slay his dearly-loved mate Fair Inf 24
To bless us with thy heav'n-lov'd innocence, Fair Inf 65
Thy loved Josephs seed, Psalm 80, 4
And Israel *whom I lov'd so dear* Psalm 81, 47
They *fly me now* whom I have lov'd, Psalm 88, 71

Love-darting
Love-darting eyes, or tresses like the Morn? Mask 753
Trinity ms 'love-darting'
line not in Bridgewater ms

Love-laboured
Tunes sweetest his love-labor'd song; now reignes Par Lost 5.41

Loveless
Of Harlots, loveless, joyless, unindeard, Par Lost 4.766

Lovelier
Unprais'd: for nothing lovelier can be found Par Lost 9.232
Lovelier, not those that in *Illyria* chang'd Par Lost 9.505

Loveliest
So hand in hand they passd, the lovliest pair Par Lost 4.321
Build in her loveliest, and create an awe Par Lost 8.558

Loveliness
Her loveliness, so absolute she seems Par Lost 8.547

Love-lorn
Where the love-lorn Nightingale Mask 234
Trinity ms 'love-lorne'
B.M. ms 'Love lorn'
Bridgewater ms 'love-lorne'
1637 'love-lorne'

Lovely
When God hath showrd the earth; so lovely seemd Par Lost 4.152
More lovely then *Pandora*, whom the Gods Par Lost 4.714
Vertue in her shape how lovly, saw, and pin'd Par Lost 4.848
Undeckt, save with her self more lovely fair Par Lost 5.380
Consummate lovly smil'd; Aire, Water, Earth, Par Lost 7.502
Manlike, but different Sex, so lovly faire, Par Lost 8.471
And lovely, never since of Serpent kind Par Lost 9.504
Shee was indeed, and lovely to attract Par Lost 10.152
Carrol her goodnes lowd in rustick layes, Mask 849

Lovely(*cont*)
Trinity ms 'rustick' ←'lovely'
By *Leucothea*'s lovely hands, Mask 875
Whom lovely *Venus* at a birth Allegro 14
For he being amorous on that lovely die Fair Inf 5
To greet her of a lovely son, Winchester 24
To plant this *lovely* Vine. Psalm 80, 36
How lovely are thy dwellings fair! Psalm 84, 1
Love-quarrels
Sam. Love-quarrels oft in pleasing concord end, Samson 1008
Lover
Or Serenate, which the starv'd Lover sings Par Lost 4.769
Was understood, the injur'd Lovers Hell. Par Lost 5.450
Quickly found a lover meet; Winchester 16
Thou with fresh hope the Lovers heart dost fill, Sonnet 1, 3
Lover and friend thou hast remov'd Psalm 88, 69
Lovers
And lovers of thir Country, as may seem; Par Reg 4.355
Loves
Puts me in doubt. Lives ther who loves his pain? Par Lost 4.888
As one who loves, and some unkindness meets, Par Lost 9.271
For maid'nhood she loves, and will be swift Mask 855
And shadows brown that *Sylvan* loves Penseroso 134
Perhaps their loves, or els their sheep, Nativity 91
For who loves that, must first be wise and good; Sonnet 12, 12
Sions *fair* Gates the Lord loves more Psalm 87, 5
Lovest
For ever, and in mee all whom thou lov'st: Par Lost 6.733
Love-tale
Of *Thammuz* yearly wounded: the Love-tale Par Lost 1.452
ms 'love-tale'
Loving
In loving thou dost well, in passion not, Par Lost 8.588
Conversing, looking, loving, to abstain Par Lost 10.993
Shall they thy loving kindness tell Psalm 88, 45
Low
Illumin, what is low raise and support; Par Lost 1.23
Doubted his Empire, that were low indeed, Par Lost 1.114
In horrible destruction laid thus low, Par Lost 1.137
To bestial Gods; for which thir heads as low Par Lost 1.435
We sunk thus low? Th' ascent is easie then; Par Lost 2.81
Maturest Counsels: for his thoughts were low; Par Lost 2.115
Thus said, he turnd, and *Satan* bowing low, Par Lost 3.736
To keep them low whom knowledge might exalt Par Lost 4.525
As to a superior Nature, bowing low, Par Lost 5.360
So high as heav'd the tumid Hills, so low Par Lost 7.288
Thir wandring course now high, now low, then hid, Par Lost 8.126
With low subjection; understand the same Par Lost 8.345
Approaching two and two, These cowring low Par Lost 8.350
Descend to? who aspires must down as low Par Lost 9.169
Like a black mist low creeping, he held on Par Lost 9.180
The trodden Herb, of abject thoughts and low, Par Lost 9.572
Why but to keep ye low and ignorant, Par Lost 9.704
But first low Reverence don, as to the power Par Lost 9.835
Now was the Sun in Western cadence low Par Lost 10.92
Had unbenighted shon, while the low Sun Par Lost 10.682
Adam bowd low, hee Kingly from his State Par Lost 11.249
Instinct through all proportions low and high Par Lost 11.562
Yet somtimes Nations will decline so low Par Lost 12.97
Though men esteem thee low of Parentage, Par Reg 1.235
He added not; and Satan bowing low Par Reg 1.497
Close in a Cottage low together got Par Reg 2.28
Thou art unknown, unfriended, low of birth, Par Reg 2.413
Chor. As signal now in low dejected state, Samson 338
And with one buffet lay thy structure low, Samson 1239
Ere morrow wake, or the low roosted lark Mask 317
Bridgewater ms 'lowe'
Trinity ms 'low-roosted'
1637 'low-roosted'
I can conduct you Lady to a low Mask 319
Bridgewater ms 'lowe'
Where the bow'd welkin slow doth bend, Mask 1015
Trinity ms 'slow' ←'low' ←'cleere'
Whom with low reverence I adore as mine, Arcades 37
And the low world in measur'd motion draw Arcades 71
That sunk so low that sacred head of thine. Lycidas 102
Ye valleys low where the milde whispers use, Lycidas 136
So *Lycidas* sunk low, but mounted high, Lycidas 172
Low in the earth, *Jordans* clear streams recoil, Psalm 114, 9
Hid from the world in a low delved tombe; Fair Inf 32
Earths utmost bounds: them shalt thou bring full low Psalm 2, 19
Will towards thy holy temple worship low Psalm 5, 20
Why hast thou laid her Hedges low Psalm 80, 49
Of wicked men the low estate Psalm 82, 15
To bow them low before the Lord, Psalm 86, 31
Bruz'd, and afflicted and *so low* Psalm 88, 61
Low in a mead of Kine under a Thorn, Prose 13, 1
Low-browed
There under *Ebon* shades, and low-brow'd Rocks, Allegro 8
Lower
Satan from hence now on the lower stair Par Lost 3.540
And in the lowest deep a lower deep Par Lost 4.76
The lower still I fall, onely Supream Par Lost 4.91
Within them every lower facultie Par Lost 5.410
Bellerophon, though from a lower Clime) Par Lost 7.18
Deign to descend now lower, and relate Par Lost 7.84
A lower flight, and speak of things at hand Par Lost 8.199
Into a lower World, to this obscure Par Lost 11.283

Lower(*cont*)
Lower then bondslave! Promise was that I Samson 38
But throw'st them lower then thou didst exalt them high, Samson 689
And lower looks, but in a sultrie chafe. Samson 1246
Lowest
Great things resolv'd, which from the lowest deep Par Lost 2.392
Harsh Thunder, that the lowest bottom shook Par Lost 2.882
And in the lowest deep a lower deep Par Lost 4.76
The lowest of your throng; or if ye know, Par Lost 4.831
In these thy lowest works, yet these declare Par Lost 5.158
Ethereal, and as lowest first the Moon; Par Lost 5.418
Love not the lowest end of human life. Par Lost 9.241
Of lowest order, past; and from the dore Par Lost 10.443
In lowest poverty to highest deeds; Par Reg 2.438
To lowest pitch of abject fortune thou art fall'n. Samson 169
Curs'd as his life. *Spir*. Alas good ventrous youth, Mask 609
Trinity ms 'downe to the hips' ←'lowest hips' ←'hipps'
Eev'n from the lowest Hell set free Psalm 86, 47
Thou in the lowest pit *profound* Psalm 88, 25
Lowings
Trampling the unshowr'd Grasse with lowings loud: Nativity 215
Lowliest
Thus they in lowliest plight repentant stood Par Lost 11.1
Lowliness
With lowliness Majestic from her seat, Par Lost 8.42
Lowly
His righteous Altar, bowing lowly down Par Lost 1.434
Th' eternal Regions: lowly reverent Par Lost 3.349
Lowly they bow'd adoring, and began Par Lost 5.144
The Earth, and stately tread, or lowly creep; Par Lost 5.201
Under whose lowly roof thou hast voutsaf't Par Lost 5.463
To know what passes there; be lowlie wise: Par Lost 8.173
He ceas'd, I lowly answer'd. To attaine Par Lost 8.412
She ended weeping, and her lowlie plight, Par Lost 10.937
Which oft is sooner found in lowly sheds Mask 323
And lay it lowly at his blessed feet; Nativity 25
Low-roofed
From Heaven descended to the low-rooft house Par Reg 4.273
His starry front low-rooft beneath the skies; Passion 18
Low-thoughted
Which men call Earth, and with low-thoughted care Mask 6
Loyal
Founded in Reason, Loyal, Just, and Pure, Par Lost 4.755
But loyal cottage, where you may be safe Mask 320
Bridgewater ms 'loyall'
Trinity ms 'loyall'
1637 'loyall'
Loyalty
His Loyaltie he kept, his Love, his Zeale; Par Lost 5.900
Lubber
Then lies him down the Lubbar Fend, Allegro 110
Lucent
Astronomer in the Sun's lucent Orbe Par Lost 3.589
Lucid
Of *Abbana* and *Pharphar*, lucid streams. Par Lost 1.469
Clad to meet Man; over his lucid Armes Par Lost 11.240
Lucifer
The Palace of great *Lucifer*, (so call Par Lost 5.760
Know then, that after *Lucifer* from Heav'n Par Lost 7.131
Of *Lucifer*, so by allusion calld, Par Lost 10.425
Or *Lucifer* that often warn'd them thence; Nativity 74
Lucina
And calls *Lucina* to her throws; Winchester 26
Atropos for *Lucina* came; Winchester 28
Luck
Helping all urchin blasts, and ill luck signes Mask 845
1637 'lucke'
Good luck befriend thee Son; for at thy birth Vacation 59
Lucky
With lucky words favour my destin'd Urn, Lycidas 20
Trinity ms 'luckie'
Lucre
Of lucre and ambition, and the truth Par Lost 12.511
Lucrine
Pontus and *Lucrine* Bay, and *Afric* Coast. Par Reg 2.347
Luggage
Luggage of war there shewn me, argument Par Reg 3.401
Lull
Had rous'd the Sea, now with hoarse cadence lull Par Lost 2.287
To lull the daughters of *Necessity*, Arcades 69
And peace shall lull him in her flowry lap; Vacation 84
Lulled
These lulld by Nightingales imbraceing slept, Par Lost 4.771
Yet they in pleasing slumber lull'd the sense, Mask 260
Bridgewater ms 'lulld'
By whispering Windes soon lull'd asleep. Allegro 116
Luminaries
With thir bright Luminaries that Set and Rose, Par Lost 7.385
Yet not to Earth are those bright Luminaries Par Lost 8.98
Luminary
Or Longitude, where the great Luminarie Par Lost 3.576
Luminous
The luminous inferior Orbs, enclos'd Par Lost 3.420
Still luminous by his ray. What if that light Par Lost 8.140
Lure
To lure her Eye; shee busied heard the sound Par Lost 9.518
And airy tongues, that syllable mens names Mask 208
Trinity ms 'syllable mens nams' ←'lure night wanderers'

Lured
Lur'd with the smell of infant blood, to dance — Par Lost 2.664
Where Armies lie encampt, come flying, lur'd — Par Lost 10.276
Lures
Of beauty and her lures, easily scorn'd — Par Reg 2.194
Lurk
In whatsoever shape he lurk, of whom — Par Lost 4.587
Lurkest
In Courts and Regal Chambers how thou lurk'st, — Par Reg 2.183
Lurking
The danger, and the lurking Enemie — Par Lost 9.1172
Lurks
The Wife, where danger or dishonour lurks, — Par Lost 9.267
that lurks by hedge or lane of this dead circuit — Mask Tr. ms 16.40
that lurks by hedge or lane, of this dead circuit — Mask Br. ms 393
Luscious
And shed the lushious liquor on the ground, — Mask 652
Bridgewater ms 'lussious'
Lust
Of *Moloch* homicide, lust hard by hate; — Par Lost 1.417
With lust and violence the house of God. — Par Lost 1.496
Inflam'd with lust then rage) and swifter far, — Par Lost 2.791
By thee adulterous lust was driv'n from men — Par Lost 4.753
As wantonly repaid; in Lust they burne: — Par Lost 9.1015
Surfet, and lust, till wantonness and pride — Par Lost 11.795
By lust and rapine; first ambitious grown — Par Reg 4.137
To satisfie thy lust: Love seeks to have Love; — Samson 837
Till all be made immortal: but when lust — Mask 463
Lustful
Yet thence his lustful Orgies he enlarg'd — Par Lost 1.415
ms 'lustfull'
Of lustful appetence, to sing, to dance, — Par Lost 11.619
Lustre
Though chang'd in outward lustre; that fixt mind — Par Lost 1.97
With Gemms and Golden lustre rich imblaz'd, — Par Lost 1.538
Wants not her hidden lustre, Gemms and Gold; — Par Lost 2.271
His lustre visibly impar'd; yet seemd — Par Lost 4.850
Was plac't in regal lustre. Down a while — Par Lost 10.447
Of lustre from the brook, in memorie, — Par Lost 11.325
Much lustre of my native brightness, lost — Par Reg 1.378
Whose lustre leads us, and for her most fit, — Arcades 76
Lusts
His horrid lusts in private to enjoy, — Par Reg 4.94
Lusty
Before the Flood thou with thy lusty Crew, — Par Reg 2.178
To wanton with the Sun her lusty Paramour. — Nativity 36
Lute
More tuneable then needed Lute or Harp — Par Lost 5.151
But musical as is *Apollo*'s lute, — Mask 478
Of Lute, or Viol still, more apt for mournful things. — Passion 28
To hear the Lute well toucht, or artfull voice — Sonnet 20, 11
Luxuriant
Luxuriant; mean while murmuring waters fall — Par Lost 4.260
Luxurious
And in luxurious Cities, where the noyse — Par Lost 1.498
Luxurious by restraint; what we by day — Par Lost 9.209
In Triumph and luxurious wealth, are they — Par Lost 11.788
From the luxurious Kings of *Antioch* won. — Par Reg 3.297
Luxurious by thir wealth, and greedier still, — Par Reg 4.141
Luxury
In wealth and luxurie. Th' ascending pile — Par Lost 1.722
ms 'luxury'
To luxurie and riot, feast and dance, — Par Lost 11.715
Where luxurie late reign'd, Sea-monsters whelp'd — Par Lost 11.751
Of luxury, though call'd magnificence, — Par Reg 4.111
Of that which lewdly-pamper'd Luxury — Mask 770
Bridgewater ms 'luxurie'
1637 'Luxurie'
Trinity ms 'luxurie'
Luz
To *Padan-Aram* in the field of *Luz*, — Par Lost 3.513
Lybian
Beneath *Gibralter* to the *Lybian* sands. — Par Lost 1.355
ms 'Lybian'
Whom Gentiles *Ammon* call and *Lybian Jove*, — Par Lost 4.277
1667 '*Libyan*'
And vapour as the *Libyan* Air adust, — Par Lost 12.635
Lycaeus
On old *Lycaeus* or *Cyllene* hoar, — Arcades 98
Lyceum
Lyceum there, and painted *Stoa* next: — Par Reg 4.253
Lycid
To strew the Laureat Herse where *Lycid* lies. — Lycidas 151
Trinity ms 'Lycid"
Lycidas
For *Lycidas* is dead, dead ere his prime — Lycidas 8
Young *Lycidas*, and hath not left his peer: — Lycidas 9
Who would not sing for *Lycidas?* he knew — Lycidas 10
Such, *Lycidas*, thy loss to Shepherds ear. — Lycidas 49
Clos'd o're the head of your lov'd *Lycidas?* — Lycidas 51
To strew the Laureat Herse where *Lycid* lies. — Lycidas 151
Trinity ms 'Lycid"
For *Lycidas* your sorrow is not dead, — Lycidas 166
So *Lycidas* sunk low, but mounted high, — Lycidas 172
Now *Lycidas* the Shepherds weep no more; — Lycidas 182
Lydian
Lap me in soft *Lydian* Aires, — Allegro 136
Lying
For lying is thy sustenance, thy food. — Par Reg 1.429
Lyonesse
By Knights of *Logres*, or of *Lyones*, — Par Reg 2.360
Lyre
With other notes then to th' *Orphean* Lyre — Par Lost 3.17
Lyric
Aeolian charms and *Dorian Lyric* Odes, — Par Reg 4.257
In copious Legend, or sweet Lyric Song. — Samson 1737
Mab
How *Faery Mab* the junkets eat, — Allegro 102
Maccabeus
So did not *Machabeus:* he indeed — Par Reg 3.165
Macdonnel
Colkitto, or Macdonnel, or Galasp? — Sonnet 11, 9
Mace
Death with his Mace petrific, cold and dry, — Par Lost 10.294
By the earth-shaking *Neptune*'s mace, — Mask 869
Macedon
To *Macedon*, and *Artaxerxes* Throne; — Par Reg 4.271
Macedonian
Of *Macedonian Philip* had e're these — Par Reg 3.32
Machaerus
Machaerus and each Town or City wall'd — Par Reg 2.22
Machination
With dev'lish machination might devise — Par Lost 6.504
Machinations
And devilish machinations come to nought. — Par Reg 1.181
Mad
He markd and mad demeanour, then alone, — Par Lost 4.129
And mad despight to be so oft repell'd. — Par Reg 4.446
And urg'd them on with mad desire — Samson 1677
She guiltless damsell flying the mad pursuit — Mask 829
Fools or mad men stand not within thy sight. — Psalm 5, 12
Madam
Madam, me thinks I see him living yet; — Sonnet 10, 11
Madding
Horrible discord, and the madding Wheeles — Par Lost 6.210
Made
Whom reason hath equald, force hath made supream — Par Lost 1.248
Whom Thunder hath made greater? Here at least — Par Lost 1.258
Glory of him that made them, to transform — Par Lost 1.370
On that opprobrious Hill, and made his Grove — Par Lost 1.403
And publish Grace to all, on promise made — Par Lost 2.238
Made to destroy: I fled, and cry'd out *Death;* — Par Lost 2.787
Made head against Heav'ns King, though overthrown. — Par Lost 2.992
All he could have; I made him just and right, — Par Lost 3.98
Made passive both, had servd necessitie, — Par Lost 3.110
Of all things made, and judgest onely right. — Par Lost 3.155
For him, what for thy glorie thou hast made? — Par Lost 3.164
Made flesh, when time shall be, of Virgin seed, — Par Lost 3.284
Made visible, th' Almighty Father shines, — Par Lost 3.386
Vows made in pain, as violent and void. — Par Lost 4.97
To recommend coole *Zephyr*, and made ease — Par Lost 4.329
That made us, and for us this ample World — Par Lost 4.413
On Earth, made hereby apter to receive — Par Lost 4.672
The God that made both Skie, Air, Earth and Heav'n — Par Lost 4.722
Thy blasting volied Thunder made all speed — Par Lost 4.928
Made vocal by my Song, and taught his praise. — Par Lost 5.204
God made thee perfet, not immutable; — Par Lost 5.524
And good he made thee, but to persevere — Par Lost 5.525
Thus *Adam* made request, and *Raphael* — Par Lost 5.561
Brightness had made invisible, thus spake. — Par Lost 5.599
Made answer. Mightie Father, thou thy foes — Par Lost 5.735
With him the points of libertie, who made — Par Lost 5.823
As by his Word the mighty Father made — Par Lost 5.836
But more illustrious made, since he the Head — Par Lost 5.842
Made horrid Circles; two broad Suns thir Shields — Par Lost 6.305
Or equal what between us made the odds, — Par Lost 6.441
Or hollow'd bodies made of Oak or Firr — Par Lost 6.574
So easie, and of his Thunder made a scorn, — Par Lost 6.632
The Waters from the Waters: and God made — Par Lost 7.263
Op'ning thir various colours, and made gay — Par Lost 7.318
God made, and every Herb, before it grew — Par Lost 7.336
And God made two great Lights, great for thir use — Par Lost 7.346
The less by Night alterne: and made the Starrs, — Par Lost 7.348
In the Suns Orb, made porous to receive — Par Lost 7.361
And worship God Supream, who made him chief — Par Lost 7.515
Here finish'd hee, and all that he had made — Par Lost 7.548
Witness this new-made World, another Heav'n — Par Lost 7.617
Hast thou not made me here thy substitute, — Par Lost 8.381
Save with the Creatures which I made, and those — Par Lost 8.409
This turn hath made amends; thou hast fulfill'd — Par Lost 8.491
His Image who made both, and less expressing — Par Lost 8.544
As one intended first, not after made — Par Lost 8.555
Made so adorn for thy delight the more, — Par Lost 8.576
To them made common and divulg'd, if aught — Par Lost 8.583
For whom all this was made, all this will soon — Par Lost 9.132
He effected; Man he made, and for him built — Par Lost 9.152
He made us, and delight to Reason joyn'd. — Par Lost 9.243
Reason, is free, and Reason he made right, — Par Lost 9.352
Into the Heart of *Eve* his words made way, — Par Lost 9.550
In tangles, and made intricate seem strait, — Par Lost 9.632
1667 'make'
The Tongue not made for Speech to speak thy praise: — Par Lost 9.749
Made common and unhallowd ere our taste; — Par Lost 9.931
Dependent made; so God shall uncreate, — Par Lost 9.943
Made erre, was now exhal'd, and grosser sleep — Par Lost 9.1049

Made*(cont)*	
Accountable made haste to make appear	Par Lost 10.29
Before his voice, or was shee made thy guide,	Par Lost 10.146
Wherein God set thee above her made of thee,	Par Lost 10.149
The Guilt on him who made him instrument	Par Lost 10.166
And Chains they made all fast, too fast they made	Par Lost 10.319
Mine with this glorious Work, and made one Realm	Par Lost 10.391
Made happie: Him by fraud I have seduc'd	Par Lost 10.485
Then Heav'n and Earth renewd shall be made pure	Par Lost 10.638
Made thee without thy leave, what if thy Son	Par Lost 10.760
God made thee of choice his own, and of his own	Par Lost 10.766
The stonie from thir hearts, & made new flesh	Par Lost 11.4
Made one with me as I with thee am one.	Par Lost 11.44
In Paradise, and on a Hill made alt,	Par Lost 11.210
Of Instruments that made melodious chime	Par Lost 11.559
With thir four Wives; and God made fast the dore.	Par Lost 11.737
As after thirst, which made thir flowing shrink	Par Lost 11.846
He made not Lord; such title to himself	Par Lost 12.70
Made it my whole delight, and in it grew	Par Reg 1.208
That out of these hard stones be made thee bread;	Par Reg 1.343
Of wisest *Solomon*, and made him build,	Par Reg 2.170
And made him bow to the Gods of his Wives.	Par Reg 2.171
How many have with a smile made small account	Par Reg 2.193
Made and set wholly on the accomplishment	Par Reg 2.207
Made Captive, yet deserving freedom more	Par Reg 3.77
Made famous in a Land and times obscure;	Par Reg 3.94
And for his glory all things made, all things	Par Reg 3.111
Made answer meet, that made void all his wiles.	Par Reg 3.442
Now made a stye, and in his place ascending	Par Reg 4.101
Expel a Devil who first made him such?	Par Reg 4.129
Deservedly made vassal, who once just,	Par Reg 4.133
I see all offers made by me how slight	Par Reg 4.155
Made of my Enemies the scorn and gaze;	Samson 34
By weakest suttleties, not made to rule,	Samson 56
But made hereby obnoxious more	Samson 106
Made Arms ridiculous, useless the forgery	Samson 131
Who made our Laws to bind us, not himself,	Samson 309
Neglected. I already have made way	Samson 481
When God with these forbid'n made choice to rear	Samson 555
That made for me, I knew that liberty	Samson 803
Made older then thy age through eye-sight lost.	Samson 1489
Who had made thir dreadful enemy thir thrall.	Samson 1622
Till further quest'. *La*. Shepherd I take thy word,	Mask 321
Trinity ms 'quest' ←'quest be made'	
Till all be made immortal: but when lust	Mask 463
Lingering, and sitting by a new made grave,	Mask 472
I purs't it up, but little reck'ning made,	Mask 642
Made Goddess of the River; still she retains	Mask 842
And made Hell grant what Love did seek.	Penseroso 108
With puissant words, and murmurs made to bless,	Arcades 60
When by the rout that made the hideous roar,	Lycidas 61
Before was never made,	Nativity 118
Did fill the new-made world with light.	Psalm 136, 26
Bleak winters force that made thy blossome drie;	Fair Inf 4
To slake his wrath whom sin hath made our foe	Fair Inf 66
For this same small neglect that I have made:	Vacation 16
Broke the fair musick that all creatures made	Musick 21
Made of sphear-metal, never to decay	Another 5
Untill his revolution was at stay.	Another 6
1658 'made of stay'	
And lack of load, made his life burdensom,	Another 24
line not in 1658 text	
That would have made *Quintilian* stare and gasp.	Sonnet 11, 11
This day; ask of me, and the grant is made;	Psalm 2, 16
(His arrows purposely made he	Psalm 7, 49
And fell into the pit he made,	Psalm 7, 56
Thy free love made it thine,	Psalm 80, 34
Thou hast made firm and strong.	Psalm 80, 64
Strong for thy self hast made.	Psalm 80, 72
The Nations all whom thou hast made	Psalm 86, 29
Madest	
And mad'st it pregnant: What in me is dark	Par Lost 1.22
And starrie Pole: Thou also mad'st the Night,	Par Lost 4.724
This Woman whom thou mad'st to be my help,	Par Lost 10.137
And mad'st imperfect words with childish tripps,	Vacation 3
Scarce to be less then Gods, thou mad'st his lot,	Psalm 8, 15
O're the works of thy hand thou mad'st him Lord,	Psalm 8, 17
Madian	
Of *Madian* and her vanquisht Kings:	Samson 281
Madness	
And Moon-struck madness, pining Atrophie,	Par Lost 11.486
line not in 1667 edition	
Chor. O madness, to think use of strongest wines	Samson 553
And in sweet madnes rob'd it of it self,	Mask 261
1637 'madnesse'	
Trinity ms 'madnesse'	
Madrigal	
The huddling brook to hear his madrigal,	Mask 495
Trinity ms 'madrigall'	
1637 'madrigale'	
Bridgewater ms 'madrigall'	
Maenalus	
From the stony *Maenalus*,	Arcades 102
Maeonides	
Blind *Thamyris* and blind *Maeonides*,	Par Lost 3.35
Maeotis	
Maeotis, up beyond the River *Ob;*	Par Lost 9.78

Magazine	
Fit for the Tun som Magazin to store	Par Lost 4.816
Magazines	
Thir Armories and Magazins contemns,	Samson 1281
Magellan	
Beneath *Magellan*. At that tasted Fruit	Par Lost 10.687
Magic	
Pendant by suttle Magic many a row	Par Lost 1.727
ms 'magic'	
To frustrate and dissolve these Magic spells,	Samson 1149
Hath met the vertue of this Magick dust,	Mask 165
Bridgewater ms 'magick'	
Trinity ms 'magick'	
That breaks his magick chains at *curfeu* time,	Mask 435
1637 'magicke'	
Till all thy magick structures rear'd so high,	Mask 798
line not in Trinity ms	
line not in Bridgewater ms	
To undoe the charmed band	Mask 904
Trinity ms 'charmed' ←'mag'	
Magician	
And black enchantments, some Magicians Art	Samson 1133
But for that damn'd magician, let him be girt	Mask 602
Bridgewater ms 'magitian'	
1673 'Magician'	
Magistrates	
That wrought with me: thou know'st the Magistrates	Samson 850
Thir Magistrates confest it, when they took thee	Samson 1183
Magnanimity	
The rest was magnanimity to remit,	Samson 1470
Magnanimous	
Magnanimous to correspond with Heav'n,	Par Lost 7.511
Far more magnanimous, then to assume.	Par Reg 2.483
With youthful courage and magnanimous thoughts	Samson 524
Magnetic	
By his Magnetic beam, that gently warms	Par Lost 3.583
As the Magnetic hardest Iron draws.	Par Reg 2.168
Magnific	
If these magnific Titles yet remain	Par Lost 5.773
O Parent, these are thy magnific deeds,	Par Lost 10.354
Magnificence	
Nor great *Alcairo* such magnificence	Par Lost 1.718
Magnificence; and what can Heav'n shew more?	Par Lost 2.273
The Makers high magnificence, who built	Par Lost 8.101
Of luxury, though call'd magnificence,	Par Reg 4.111
Magnificent	
Ascending by degrees magnificent	Par Lost 3.502
Magnificent, his Six days work, a World;	Par Lost 7.568
Magnificent this World, and Earth his seat,	Par Lost 9.153
Magnified	
Thy Thunders magnifi'd; but to create	Par Lost 7.606
So *Dagon* shall be magnifi'd, and God,	Samson 440
Magnify	
To magnifie his works, the more we know.	Par Lost 7.97
Magnitude	
Of smallest Magnitude close by the Moon.	Par Lost 2.1053
Globose, and every magnitude of Starrs,	Par Lost 7.357
With plain Heroic magnitude of mind	Samson 1279
Magnitudes	
Thir magnitudes, this Earth a spot, a graine,	Par Lost 8.17
Mahanaim	
Jacob in *Mahanaim*, where he saw	Par Lost 11.214
Maia	
Skie-tinctur'd grain. Like *Maia*'s son he stood,	Par Lost 5.285
Maid	
His marriage with the seaventimes-wedded Maid.	Par Lost 5.223
In his prime youth the fair *Iberian* maid.	Par Reg 2.200
To many a youth, and many a maid,	Allegro 95
Of wedded Maid, and Virgin Mother born,	Nativity 3
Or wert thou that just Maid who once before	Fair Inf 50
And save thy hand-maids Son.	Psalm 86, 60
Maiden	
And let a single helpless maiden pass	Mask 402
1637 'mayden'	
Bridgewater ms 'mayden'	
Trinity ms 'mayden'	
Her maid'n gentlenes, and oft at Eeve	Mask 843
Bridgewater ms 'maiden'	
1637 'maiden'	
Trinity ms 'maiden' ←'maden'	
The Saintly Vail of Maiden white to throw,	Nativity 42
Or *Severn* swift, guilty of Maidens death,	Vacation 96
Maidenhood	
For maid'nhood she loves, and will be swift	Mask 855
Trinity ms 'maidenhood'	
1637 'maidenhood'	
Bridgewater ms 'maydenhood'	
Maids	
In vain the *Tyrian* Maids their wounded *Thamuz* mourn.	Nativity 204
Thy hand-maids, clad them o're with purple beams	Sonnet 14, 10
Trinity ms 'handmaides' ←'handmaids'	
Mail	
Shaddowd from either heele with featherd maile	Par Lost 5.284
Mangl'd with gastly wounds through Plate and Maile,	Par Lost 6.368
In coats of Mail and military pride;	Par Reg 3.312
In Mail thir horses clad, yet fleet and strong,	Par Reg 3.313
Chalybean temper'd steel, and frock of mail	Samson 133

Maimed
Maim'd his brute Image, head and hands lopt off — Par Lost 1.459
Though by his blindness maim'd for high attempts, — Samson 1221
Main
Main reason to perswade immediate Warr, — Par Lost 2.121
Heapt on him there, nor yet the main Abyss — Par Lost 3.83
And now divided into four main Streams, — Par Lost 4.233
Both Battels maine, with ruinous assault — Par Lost 6.216
A standing fight, then soaring on main wing — Par Lost 6.243
Believst so main to our success, I bring; — Par Lost 6.471
Main Promontories flung, which in the Air — Par Lost 6.654
Wild work in Heav'n, and dangerous to the maine. — Par Lost 6.698
Main Ocean flow'd, not idle, but with warme — Par Lost 7.279
Over this Maine from Hell to that new World — Par Lost 10.257
Defeating Sin and Death, his two maine armes, — Par Lost 12.431
And management of this main enterprize — Par Reg 1.112
Are to the main as inconsiderable, — Par Reg 4.457
Then by main force pull'd up, and on his shoulders bore — Samson 146
Half round on two main Pillars vaulted high, — Samson 1606
That to the arched roof gave main support. — Samson 1634
The greatest, and the best of all the main — Mask 28
Bridgewater ms 'Maine'
Trinity ms 'maine' ←'his empire'
1637 'maine'
Of the *Erythraean* main. — Psalm 136, 46
Move by her two maine nerves, Iron and Gold — Sonnet 17, 8
1662, 1694 'main'
Mainly
Inductive mainly to the sin of *Eve*. — Par Lost 11.519
Maintained
The better fight, who single hast maintaind — Par Lost 6.30
Majestic
Majestic though in ruin: sage he stood — Par Lost 2.305
1674 'Majectick' in some copies
1667 'Majestick'
With lowliness Majestic from her seat, — Par Lost 8.42
How would one look from his Majestick brow — Par Reg 2.216
Nor doth this grandeur and majestic show — Par Reg 4.110
In thir majestic unaffected stile — Par Reg 4.359
And *Tethys* grave majestick pace, — Mask 870
Bridgewater ms 'maiestick'
1637 'majesticke'
Flowing with majestick train, — Penseroso 34
Majesty
And with the Majesty of darkness round — Par Lost 2.266
In naked Majestie seemd Lords of all, — Par Lost 4.290
Rising in clouded Majestie, at length — Par Lost 4.607
Idol of Majestie Divine, enclos'd — Par Lost 6.101
Of Majestie Divine, Sapience and Love — Par Lost 7.195
1669 'Majesty'
And with obsequious Majestie approv'd — Par Lost 8.509
To whom the Virgin Majestie of *Eve*, — Par Lost 9.270
Or of the Thrones above, such Majestie — Par Lost 11.232
Perswasive, Virgin majesty with mild — Par Reg 2.159
She may pass on with unblench't majesty, — Mask 430
Bridgewater ms 'maiestie'
1637 'majestie'
Trinity ms 'majestie'
What sudden blaze of majesty — Arcades 2
Trinity ms 'majestie'
1673 'Majesty'
And that far-beaming blaze of Majesty, — Nativity 9
His mighty Majesty and worth. — Psalm 136, 90
Of blazing Majesty and Light, — Winchester 70
Make
Can make a Heav'n of Hell, a Hell of Heav'n. — Par Lost 1.255
Dropt Manna, and could make the worse appear — Par Lost 2.113
To make them mirth us'd all his might, and wreathd — Par Lost 4.346
For God's, yet able to make Gods of Men: — Par Lost 5.70
To make us less, bent rather to exalt — Par Lost 5.829
Let us make now Man in our image, Man — Par Lost 7.519
To make her amiable: On she came, — Par Lost 8.484
By what I seek, but others to make such — Par Lost 9.127
Of vertue to make wise: what hinders then — Par Lost 9.778
Shall I appeer? shall I to him make known — Par Lost 9.817
To open Eyes, and make them Gods who taste; — Par Lost 9.866
Accountable made haste to make appear — Par Lost 10.29
Him first make sure your thrall, and lastly kill. — Par Lost 10.402
Both to destroy, or unimmortal make — Par Lost 10.611
Can he make deathless Death? that were to make — Par Lost 10.798
From what we fear for both, let us make short, — Par Lost 10.1000
To make death in us live: Then let us seek — Par Lost 10.1028
Make they but of thir Brethren, men of men? — Par Lost 11.680
And make perswasion do the work of fear; — Par Reg 1.223
Thou must make sure thy own, the *Parthian* first — Par Reg 3.363
Or could of inward slaves make outward free? — Par Reg 4.145
She sought to make me Traytor to my self; — Samson 401
Found soon occasion thereby to make thee — Samson 425
What boots it at one gate to make defence, — Samson 560
Was it not weakness also to make known — Samson 778
It hath brought forth to make thee memorable — Samson 956
To make them sport with blind activity? — Samson 1328
Or make a game of my calamities? — Samson 1331
Such noise as I can make to be heard farthest — Mask 227
As to make this relation? *Spir*. Care and utmost shifts — Mask 617
Feirce signe of battail make, and menace high, — Mask 654
That the shrewd medling Elfe delights to make, — Mask 846
Trinity ms 'make' ←'makes' ←'leave'

Make(*cont*)
Make her his eternal Bride, — Mask 1008
line not in Bridgewater ms
Of other care they little reck'ning make, — Lycidas 116
Make up full consort to th' Angelike symphony. — Nativity 132
And make soft rills from fiery flint-stones gush. — Psalm 114, 18
That with his miracles doth make — Psalm 136, 13
That till the worlds last-end shall make thy name to live. — Fair Inf 77
Such as may make thee search thy coffers round, — Vacation 31
Yet every one shall make him underling, — Vacation 76
Dost make us Marble with too much conceaving; — Shakespear 14
For one Carrier put down to make six bearers. — Another 20
line not in 1640, 1657, 1658 texts
And still revolt when truth would set them free. — Sonnet 12, 10
Trinity ms 'still revolt when Truth would sett them' ←'make them' ←'set them' ←'hate the truth wherby they should be'
Nightly my Couch I make a kind of Sea; — Psalm 6, 12
Wild Beasts there brouze, and make their food — Psalm 80, 55
My God, oh make them as a wheel — Psalm 83, 49
I call; O make rejoyce — Psalm 86, 10
Maker
Lik'ning his Maker to the Grazed Ox, — Par Lost 1.486
Unless th' Almighty Maker them ordain — Par Lost 2.915
Thir maker, or thir making, or thir Fate, — Par Lost 3.113
The Universal Maker we may praise; — Par Lost 3.676
The image of thir glorious Maker shon, — Par Lost 4.292
Accept your Makers work; he gave it me, — Par Lost 4.380
Maker Omnipotent, and thou the Day, — Par Lost 4.725
Our Maker bids increase, who bids abstain — Par Lost 4.748
Thir Maker, in fit strains pronounc't or sung — Par Lost 5.148
Varie to our great Maker still new praise. — Par Lost 5.184
Our maker, and obey him whose command — Par Lost 5.551
Thy making, while the Maker gave thee being? — Par Lost 5.858
To glorifie the Maker, and inferr — Par Lost 7.116
The Makers high magnificence, who built — Par Lost 8.101
Not of my self; by some great Maker then, — Par Lost 8.278
My Maker, be propitious while I speak. — Par Lost 8.380
Led by her Heav'nly Maker, though unseen, — Par Lost 8.485
Whom us the more to spite his Maker rais'd — Par Lost 9.177
Left so imperfet by the Maker wise, — Par Lost 9.338
Fairest resemblance of thy Maker faire, — Par Lost 9.538
Against his Maker; no Decree of mine — Par Lost 10.43
Did I request thee, Maker, from my Clay — Par Lost 10.743
And for his Makers Image sake exempt? — Par Lost 11.514
Thir Makers Image, answerd *Michael*, then — Par Lost 11.515
Unmindful of thir Maker, though his Spirit — Par Lost 11.611
Confounded, that her Makers eyes — Nativity 43
To serve therewith my Maker, and present — Sonnet 19, 5
Makes
His crime makes guiltie all his Sons, thy merit — Par Lost 3.290
Lodge and dislodge by turns, which makes through Heav'n — Par Lost 6.7
Which all subdues, and makes remiss the hands — Par Lost 6.458
With Mountains as with Weapons arm'd, which makes — Par Lost 6.697
But call in aide, which makes a bloody Fray; — Par Lost 11.651
1667 'tacks'
And makes a Covenant never to destroy — Par Lost 11.892
Too numerous; whence of guests he makes them slaves — Par Lost 12.167
What makes a Nation happy, and keeps it so, — Par Reg 4.362
But now again she makes address to speak. — Samson 731
Tis onely day-light that makes Sin — Mask 126
Bridgewater ms 'maks'
And makes one blot of all the ayr, — Mask 133
Trinity ms 'makes one' ←'throws a' ←'makes a'
And the inglorious likenes of a beast — Mask 528
Trinity ms 'and' ←'and makes' ←'and'
Evil with thee no biding makes — Psalm 5, 11
Makest
Thou Lord alone in safety mak'st me dwell. — Psalm 4, 42
And mak'st them largely drink the tears — Psalm 80, 23
A strife thou mak'st us *and a prey* — Psalm 80, 25
And mak'st me odious, — Psalm 88, 34
Making
Thir maker, or thir making, or thir Fate, — Par Lost 3.113
Thy making, while the Maker gave thee being? — Par Lost 5.858
Continu'd making, and who knows how long — Par Lost 9.138
Making them each his own Deliverer, — Samson 1289
Of him, t' whose happy-making sight alone, — On Time 18
Malabar
In *Malabar* or *Decan* spreds her Armes — Par Lost 9.1103
Maladies
Numbers of all diseas'd, all maladies — Par Lost 11.480
With maladies innumerable — Samson 608
Malcontent
To whom thus answer'd Satan malecontent: — Par Reg 2.392
Male
Of *Baalim* and *Ashtaroth*, those male, — Par Lost 1.422
Male he created thee, but thy consort — Par Lost 7.529
Communicating Male and Femal Light, — Par Lost 8.150
Malediction
With malediction mention'd, and the blot — Samson 978
Males
Inhospitably, and kills thir infant Males: — Par Lost 12.168
Malice
How all his malice serv'd but to bring forth — Par Lost 1.217
So deep a malice, to confound the race — Par Lost 2.382
His malice, and thy goodness bring to naught, — Par Lost 3.158
Not so on Man; him through their malice fall'n, — Par Lost 3.400
And wrought but malice; lifted up so high — Par Lost 4.49

Malice(*cont*)
Deep malice to conceale, couch't with revenge: Par Lost 4.123
Deep malice thence conceiving and disdain, Par Lost 5.666
Thy malice into thousands, once upright Par Lost 6.270
In future dayes, if Malice should abound, Par Lost 6.502
In meditated fraud and malice, bent Par Lost 9.55
Nor thou his malice and false guile contemn; Par Lost 9.306
His Malice, and with rapine sweet bereav'd Par Lost 9.461
Whate're his cruel malice could invent. Par Reg 1.149
What but thy malice mov'd thee to misdeem Par Reg 1.424
That malice not repentance brought thee hither, Samson 821
Of malice or of sorcery, or that power Mask 587

Malicious
What hath bin warn'd us, what malicious Foe Par Lost 9.253
And with malitious counsel stir them up Samson 1251

Malign
The Spirit maligne, but much more envy seis'd Par Lost 3.553
For envie, yet with jealous leer maligne Par Lost 4.503
Two Planets rushing from aspect maligne Par Lost 6.313
Of Spirits maligne a better Race to bring Par Lost 7.189
1669 'malign'

Malignant
Thir influence malignant when to showre, Par Lost 10.662
To good malignant, to bad men benigne, Par Lost 12.538

Mammon
Or cast a Rampart. *Mammon* led them on, Par Lost 1.678
ms 'Mammon'
Mammon, the least erected Spirit that fell Par Lost 1.679
ms 'Mammon'
Not peace: and after him thus *Mammon* spake. Par Lost 2.228
As *Mammon* ended, and his Sentence pleas'd, Par Lost 2.291

Man
Of Mans First Disobedience, and the Fruit Par Lost 1.1
ms 'mans'
With loss of *Eden*, till one greater Man Par Lost 1.4
On Man by him seduc't, but on himself Par Lost 1.219
ms 'man'
Through Gods high sufferance for the tryal of man, Par Lost 1.366
Dagon his Name, Sea Monster, upward Man Par Lost 1.462
ms 'man'
Glories: For never since created man, Par Lost 1.573
Of some new Race call'd *Man*, about this time Par Lost 2.348
Man had not hellish foes anow besides, Par Lost 2.504
Mean while the Adversary of God and Man, Par Lost 2.629
But hee once past, soon after when man fell, Par Lost 2.1023
And Man there plac't, with purpose to assay Par Lost 3.90
For man will hark'n to his glozing lyes, Par Lost 3.93
Self-tempted, self-deprav'd: Man falls deceiv'd Par Lost 3.130
By the other first: Man therefore shall find grace, Par Lost 3.131
Thy sovran sentence, that Man should find grace; Par Lost 3.145
For should Man finally be lost, should Man Par Lost 3.150
Man shall not quite be lost, but sav'd who will, Par Lost 3.173
But yet all is not don; Man disobeying, Par Lost 3.203
Mans mortal crime, and just th' unjust to save, Par Lost 3.215
And silence was in Heav'n: on mans behalf Par Lost 3.218
Father, thy word is past, man shall find grace; Par Lost 3.227
Happie for man, so coming; he her aide Par Lost 3.232
Account mee man; I for his sake will leave Par Lost 3.238
To me are all my works, nor Man the least Par Lost 3.277
And be thy self Man among men on Earth, Par Lost 3.283
Receive new life. So Man, as is most just, Par Lost 3.294
Shall satisfie for Man, be judg'd and die, Par Lost 3.295
Mans Nature, less'n or degrade thine owne. Par Lost 3.304
Both God and Man, Son both of God and Man, Par Lost 3.316
Began to bloom, but soon for mans offence Par Lost 3.355
Not so on Man; him through their malice fall'n, Par Lost 3.400
Perceive thee purpos'd not to doom frail Man Par Lost 3.404
For mans offence. O unexampl'd love, Par Lost 3.410
To Paradise the happie seat of Man, Par Lost 3.632
All these his wondrous works, but chiefly Man, Par Lost 3.663
In which of all these shining Orbes hath Man Par Lost 3.668
For neither Man nor Angel can discern Par Lost 3.682
That place is Earth the seat of Man, that light Par Lost 3.724
To wreck on innocent frail man his loss Par Lost 4.11
As Man ere long, and this new World shall know. Par Lost 4.113
All path of Man or Beast that past that way: Par Lost 4.177
And banisht from mans life his happiest life, Par Lost 4.317
Adam the goodliest man of men since borne Par Lost 4.323
More of th' Almighties works, and chiefly Man Par Lost 4.566
Man hath his daily work of body or mind Par Lost 4.618
Daughter of God and Man, accomplisht *Eve*, Par Lost 4.660
All things to mans delightful use; the roofe Par Lost 4.692
Such was thir awe of Man. In shadie Bower Par Lost 4.705
1667 'man'
But our destroyer, foe to God and Man? Par Lost 4.749
Nor God, nor Man; is Knowledge so despis'd? Par Lost 5.60
Evil into the mind of God or Man Par Lost 5.117
(Whose praise be ever sung) to man in part Par Lost 5.405
Thy favour, in this honour done to man, Par Lost 5.462
Mans nourishment, by gradual scale sublim'd Par Lost 5.483
Vital in every part, not as frail man Par Lost 6.345
Or heart of man suffice to comprehend? Par Lost 7.114
Another World, out of one man a Race Par Lost 7.155
Upon the Earth, and man to till the ground Par Lost 7.332
To Man, the greater to have rule by Day, Par Lost 7.347
Let us make now Man in our image, Man Par Lost 7.519
This said, he formd thee, *Adam*, thee O Man Par Lost 7.524
From Man or Angel the great Architect Par Lost 8.72

Man(*cont*)
That Man may know he dwells not in his own; Par Lost 8.103
Gladly into the wayes of God with Man: Par Lost 8.226
On Man his Equal Love: say therefore on; Par Lost 8.228
For Man to tell how human Life began Par Lost 8.250
First Man, of Men innumerable ordain'd Par Lost 8.297
And all this good to man, for whose well being Par Lost 8.361
Wors then can Man with Beast, and least of all. Par Lost 8.397
Is no deficience found; not so is Man, Par Lost 8.416
But Man by number is to manifest Par Lost 8.422
Knew it not good for Man to be alone, Par Lost 8.445
Before me; Woman is her Name, of Man Par Lost 8.496
The Soule of Man, or passion in him move. Par Lost 8.585
With Man, as with his Friend, familiar us'd Par Lost 9.2
Disloyal on the part of Man, revolt, Par Lost 9.7
On mans destruction, maugre what might hap Par Lost 9.56
Of Growth, Sense, Reason, all summ'd up in Man. Par Lost 9.113
He effected; Man he made, and for him built Par Lost 9.152
Of Heav'n, this Man of Clay, Son of despite, Par Lost 9.176
Daughter of God and Man, immortal *Eve*, Par Lost 9.291
Of all that he Created, much less Man, Par Lost 9.346
Half what in thee is fair, one man except, Par Lost 9.545
What may this mean? Language of Man pronounc't Par Lost 9.553
To Man, and indignation at his wrong, Par Lost 9.666
Shall that be shut to Man, which to the Beast Par Lost 9.691
That ye should be as Gods, since I as Man, Par Lost 9.710
Internal Man, is but proportion meet, Par Lost 9.711
And what are Gods that Man may not become Par Lost 9.716
Th' offence, that Man should thus attain to know? Par Lost 9.726
Though kept from Man, and worthy to be admir'd, Par Lost 9.746
Friendly to man, farr from deceit or guile. Par Lost 9.772
Lives, as thou saidst, and gaines to live as Man Par Lost 9.933
To counterfet Mans voice, true in our Fall, Par Lost 9.1069
Of Man, with strength entire, and free will arm'd, Par Lost 10.9
For Man, for of his state by this they knew, Par Lost 10.19
On his bad Errand, Man should be seduc't Par Lost 10.41
Mans Friend, his Mediator, his design'd Par Lost 10.60
And destin'd Man himself to judge Man fall'n. Par Lost 10.62
To sentence Man: the voice of God they heard Par Lost 10.97
The thickest Trees, both Man and Wife, till God Par Lost 10.101
Concern'd not Man (since he no further knew) Par Lost 10.170
So judg'd he Man, both Judge and Saviour sent, Par Lost 10.209
All, though all-knowing, what had past with Man Par Lost 10.227
Chiefly on Man, sole Lord of all declar'd, Par Lost 10.401
Of absolute perfection, therein Man Par Lost 10.483
Both his beloved Man and all his World, Par Lost 10.489
To range in, and to dwell, and over Man Par Lost 10.492
Man I deceav'd: that which to mee belongs, Par Lost 10.496
Into the same illusion, not as Man Par Lost 10.571
To dash thir pride, and joy for Man seduc't. Par Lost 10.577
Till I in Man residing through the Race, Par Lost 10.607
Kept in that State, had not the folly of Man Par Lost 10.619
Which mans polluting Sin with taint hath shed Par Lost 10.631
Of Man, but fled him, or with count'nance grim Par Lost 10.713
To mould me Man, did I sollicite thee Par Lost 10.744
Least that pure breath of Life, the Spirit of Man Par Lost 10.784
Is his wrauth also? be it, man is not so, Par Lost 10.795
Wrath without end on Man whom Death must end? Par Lost 10.797
In punisht man, to satisfie his rigour Par Lost 10.803
For one mans fault thus guiltless be condemn'd, Par Lost 10.823
Through the still Night, not now, as ere man fell, Par Lost 10.846
From thy implanted Grace in Man, these Sighs Par Lost 11.23
All thy request for Man, accepted Son, Par Lost 11.46
O Sons, like one of us Man is become Par Lost 11.84
Or in behalf of Man, or to invade Par Lost 11.102
With whose stol'n Fruit Man once more to delude. Par Lost 11.125
Man is to live, and all things live for Man. Par Lost 11.161
One man, Assassin-like had levied Warr, Par Lost 11.219
Not in his shape Celestial, but as Man Par Lost 11.239
Clad to meet Man; over his lucid Armes Par Lost 11.240
To that meek man, who well had sacrific'd; Par Lost 11.451
In his first shape on man; but many shapes Par Lost 11.467
His best of Man, and gave him up to tears Par Lost 11.497
Th' Image of God in man created once Par Lost 11.508
Under inhuman pains? Why should not Man, Par Lost 11.511
But still I see the tenor of Mans woe Par Lost 11.632
From Mans effeminate slackness it begins, Par Lost 11.634
But who was that Just Man, whom had not Heav'n Par Lost 11.681
For Man and Beast: when loe a wonder strange! Par Lost 11.733
With thought that they must be. Let no man seek Par Lost 11.770
Man is not whom to warne: those few escap't Par Lost 11.777
With length of happy dayes the race of man; Par Lost 11.782
And whether here the Race of man will end. Par Lost 11.786
One Man except, the onely Son of light Par Lost 11.808
The one just Man alive; by his command Par Lost 11.818
No sooner hee with them of Man and Beast Par Lost 11.822
At this last sight, assur'd that Man shall live Par Lost 11.872
For one Man found so perfet and so just, Par Lost 11.876
Though late repenting him of Man deprav'd, Par Lost 11.886
Such grace shall one just Man find in his sight, Par Lost 11.890
With Man therein or Beast; but when he brings Par Lost 11.895
And Man as from a second stock proceed. Par Lost 12.7
By his donation; but Man over men Par Lost 12.69
Stayes not on Man; to God his Tower intends Par Lost 12.73
Siege and defiance: Wretched man! what food Par Lost 12.74
Reason in man obscur'd, or not obeyd, Par Lost 12.86
Man till then free. Therefore since hee permits Par Lost 12.90
A Nation from one faithful man to spring: Par Lost 12.113

Man(*cont*)
Mans voice commanding, Sun in *Gibeon* stand, Par Lost 12.265
Some bloud more precious must be paid for Man, Par Lost 12.293
Cannot appease, nor Man the moral part Par Lost 12.298
Through the worlds wilderness long wanderd man Par Lost 12.313
Of God most High; So God with Man unites. Par Lost 12.382
Thy ransom paid, which Man from death redeems, Par Lost 12.424
His death for Man, as many as offerd Life Par Lost 12.425
What man can do against them, not affraid, Par Lost 12.493
1667 'Man'
By one mans disobedience lost, now sing Par Reg 1.2
By one mans firm obedience fully tri'd Par Reg 1.4
Nigh Thunder-struck, th' exalted man, to whom Par Reg 1.36
Who this is we must learn, for man he seems Par Reg 1.91
This man of men, attested Son of God, Par Reg 1.122
With man or mens affairs, how I begin Par Reg 1.132
O're-shadow her: this man born and now up-grown, Par Reg 1.140
He now shall know I can produce a man Par Reg 1.150
Winning by Conquest what the first man lost Par Reg 1.154
This perfect Man, by merit call'd my Son, Par Reg 1.166
For know, thou art no Son of mortal man, Par Reg 1.234
But now an aged man in Rural weeds, Par Reg 1.314
For that to me thou seem'st the man, whom late Par Reg 1.327
Man lives not by Bread only, but each Word Par Reg 1.349
Nor lightens aught each mans peculiar load. Par Reg 1.402
Small consolation then, were Man adjoyn'd: Par Reg 1.403
This wounds me most (what can it less) that Man, Par Reg 1.404
Man fall'n shall be restor'd, I never more. Par Reg 1.405
To hear thee when I come (since no man comes) Par Reg 1.484
Full grown to Man, acknowledg'd, as I hear, Par Reg 2.83
However to this Man inferior far, Par Reg 2.135
If he be Man by Mothers side at least, Par Reg 2.136
When suddenly a man before him stood, Par Reg 2.298
The wise mans cumbrance if not snare, more apt Par Reg 2.454
When on his shoulders each mans burden lies; Par Reg 2.462
Which every wise and vertuous man attains: Par Reg 2.468
Governs the inner man, the nobler part, Par Reg 2.477
The just man, and divulges him through Heaven Par Reg 3.62
The deed becomes unprais'd, the man at least, Par Reg 3.103
But why should man seek glory? who of his own Par Reg 3.134
What of perfection can in man be found, Par Reg 3.230
But as a man who had been matchless held Par Reg 4.10
What wise and valiant man would seek to free Par Reg 4.143
Teaching not taught; the childhood shews the man, Par Reg 4.220
By him call'd vertue; and his vertuous man, Par Reg 4.301
As fearing God nor man, contemning all Par Reg 4.304
And how the world began, and how man fell Par Reg 4.311
To mans less universe, and soon are gone; Par Reg 4.459
On man, beast, plant, wastful and turbulent, Par Reg 4.461
Of gaining *David*'s Throne no man knows when, Par Reg 4.471
To the utmost of meer man both wise and good, Par Reg 4.535
Therefore to know what more thou art then man, Par Reg 4.538
Of man or worm; the vilest here excel me, Samson 74
No strength of man, or fiercest wild beast could withstand; Samson 127
Since man on earth unparallel'd! Samson 165
And no man therein Doctor but himself. Samson 299
Man. O miserable change! is this the man, Samson 340
In mortal strength! and oh what not in man Samson 349
All chances incident to mans frail life Samson 656
God of our Fathers, what is man! Samson 667
With God or Man will gain thee no remission. Samson 835
In man or woman, though to thy own condemning, Samson 844
Gave to the man despotic power Samson 1054
Har. To combat with a blind man I disdain, Samson 1106
Har. With thee a Man condemn'd, a Slave enrol'd, Samson 1224
To fight with thee no man of arms will deign. Samson 1226
Sam. No man with-holds thee, nothing from thy hand Samson 1233
God for the fear of Man, and Man prefer, Samson 1374
Chor. In time thou hast resolv'd, the man returns. Samson 1390
Wind me into the easie-hearted man, Mask 163
What need a man forestall his date of grief, Mask 362
line not in Bridgewater ms
line not in Trinity ms
Or els som neighbour Wood-man, or at worst, Mask 484
Trinity ms 'woodman'
1637 'wood man'
Som roaving Robber calling to his fellows. Mask 485
Trinity ms 'robber' ←'hedge man' ←'curl'd man of the swoord'
If every just man that now pines with want Mask 768
thou man of lies & falshood, if thou give me it Mask Tr. ms 22.21
Kil'd with report that Old man eloquent, Sonnet 10, 8
To after age thou shalt be writ the man, Sonnet 13, 7
Of Death, call'd Life; which us from Life doth sever. Sonnet 14, 4
Trinity ms 'us' ←'man'
Either man's work or his own gifts, who best Sonnet 19, 10
Or man or woman. Yet I argue not Sonnet 22, 6
1694 'Man'
Bless'd is the man who hath not walk'd astray Psalm 1, 1
The bloodi' and guileful man God doth detest. Psalm 5, 16
To bless the just man still, Psalm 5, 38
O what is man that thou remembrest yet, Psalm 8, 12
And think'st upon him; or of man begot Psalm 8, 13
Upon the man of thy right hand Psalm 80, 69
Upon the Son of Man, whom thou Psalm 80, 71
Dispatch the poor mans cause, Psalm 82, 10
And raise the man in deep distress Psalm 82, 11
That man is *truly* blest, Psalm 84, 46

Man(*cont*)
Lo this man there was born: Psalm 87, 16
This and this man was born in her, Psalm 87, 19
That this man there was born. Psalm 87, 24
I am a man, but weak alas Psalm 88, 15
Whom doe we count a good man, whom but he Prose 10, 1
Manacled
Not ti'd or manacl'd with joynt or limb, Par Lost 1.426
Manacles
Chor. His manacles remark him, there he sits. Samson 1309
Managed
Well manag'd; of that skill the more thou know'st, Par Lost 8.573
Of Riot, and ill manag'd Merriment, Mask 172
Bridgewater ms 'ill-manag'd'
Management
And management of this main enterprize Par Reg 1.112
Manasseh
And in Manasse's sight Psalm 80, 10
Mane
And Rampant shakes his Brinded main; the Ounce, Par Lost 7.466
And hairie Main terrific, though to thee Par Lost 7.497
Manger
Directed to the Manger where thou lais't, Par Reg 1.247
A Manger his, yet soon enforc't to flye Par Reg 2.75
All meanly wrapt in the rude manger lies; Nativity 31
Mangle
Mangle my apprehensive tenderest parts, Samson 624
Mangled
Mangl'd with gastly wounds through Plate and Maile, Par Lost 6.368
Manhood
With thee thy Manhood also to this Throne; Par Lost 3.314
Thou did'st resigne thy Manhood, and the Place Par Lost 10.148
In Manhood where Youth ended; by his side Par Lost 11.246
Manhood to God-head, with more strength to foil Par Lost 12.389
Thy manhood last, though yet in private bred; Par Reg 4.509
Who with a grain of manhood well resolv'd Samson 408
That I to manhood am arriv'd so near, Sonnet 7, 6
Manifest
To manifest thee worthiest to be Heir Par Lost 6.707
To manifest the more thy might: his evil Par Lost 7.615
But Man by number is to manifest Par Lost 8.422
Resplendent all his Father manifest Par Lost 10.66
Chor. She's gone, a manifest Serpent by her sting Samson 997
Manifold
Unlimited of manifold delights: Par Lost 4.435
Greater so manifold to this one use, Par Lost 8.29
And manifold in sin, deserv'd to fall. Par Lost 10.16
Mankind
The Mother of Mankind, what time his Pride Par Lost 1.36
1667 'Mankinde'
Of Mankind they corrupted to forsake Par Lost 1.368
Of mankind in one root, and Earth with Hell Par Lost 2.383
Of mankind, in the happie Garden plac't, Par Lost 3.66
Draw after him the whole Race of mankind, Par Lost 3.161
And now without redemption all mankind Par Lost 3.222
Found out for mankind under wrauth, O thou Par Lost 3.275
The Head of all mankind, though *Adams* Son. Par Lost 3.286
The Tempter ere th' Accuser of man-kind, Par Lost 4.10
Mankind created, and for him this World. Par Lost 4.107
Sin-bred, how have ye troubl'd all mankind Par Lost 4.315
Mankind with her faire looks, to be aveng'd Par Lost 4.718
In them at once to ruin all mankind. Par Lost 5.228
Haile Mother of Mankind, whose fruitful Womb Par Lost 5.388
To whom the Patriarch of mankind repli'd, Par Lost 5.506
Female for Race; then bless'd Mankinde, and said, Par Lost 7.530
Above mankinde, or aught then mankinde higher, Par Lost 8.358
But if the sense of touch whereby mankind Par Lost 8.579
With grateful Memorie: thou to mankind Par Lost 8.650
So spake the Patriarch of Mankinde, but *Eve* Par Lost 9.376
The onely two of Mankinde, but in them Par Lost 9.415
So spake the Enemie of Mankind, enclos'd Par Lost 9.494
He ruind, now Mankind; whom will he next? Par Lost 9.950
Mee and Mankinde; I am to bruise his heel; Par Lost 10.498
Destin'd restorer of Mankind, by whom Par Lost 10.646
Me now your curse! Ah, why should all mankind Par Lost 10.822
Mankind? this mischief had not then befall'n, Par Lost 10.895
The Race of Mankind drownd, before the Shrine Par Lost 11.13
The smell of peace toward Mankinde, let him live Par Lost 11.38
My judgments, how with Mankind I proceed, Par Lost 11.69
Eve rightly call'd, Mother of all Mankind, Par Lost 11.159
O miserable Mankind, to what fall Par Lost 11.500
Patrons of Mankind, Gods, and Sons of Gods, Par Lost 11.696
And stabl'd; of Mankind, so numerous late, Par Lost 11.752
That he relents, not to blot out mankind, Par Lost 11.891
Mankinds deliverance. But the voice of God Par Lost 12.235
Of mee and all Mankind; but now I see Par Lost 12.276
Of all mankinde, with him there crucifi'd, Par Lost 12.417
(For by the Womans Seed) on all Mankind. Par Lost 12.601
Recover'd Paradise to all mankind, Par Reg 1.3
At first against mankind so well had thriv'd Par Reg 1.114
Of Saviour to mankind, and which way first Par Reg 1.187
Or work Redemption for mankind, whose sins Par Reg 1.266
To all mankind: why should I? they to me Par Reg 1.388
Great Benefactors of mankind, Deliverers, Par Reg 3.82
Now enter, and begin to save mankind. Par Reg 4.635
Manlier
Therefore with manlier objects we must try Par Reg 2.225

Manliest
At will the manliest, resolutest brest, Par Reg 2.167
Manlike
Manlike, but different Sex, so lovly faire, Par Lost 8.471
Manly
Round from his parted forelock manly hung Par Lost 4.302
How beauty is excelld by manly grace Par Lost 4.490
Co. Were they of manly prime, or youthful bloom? Mask 289
Manna
Dropt Manna, and could make the worse appear Par Lost 2.113
Our Fathers here with Manna; in the Mount Par Reg 1.351
Rain'd from Heaven Manna, and that Prophet bold Par Reg 2.312
And drenches with *Elysian* dew Mask 996
Trinity ms 'Elysian' ←'Sabaean' ←'manna'
Bridgewater ms 'with Manna'
Manned
Move by her two maine nerves, Iron and Gold Sonnet 17, 8
1694 'mann'd by'
Manner
In manner at our will th' affairs of Earth, Par Reg 1.50
Manners
Civility of Manners, Arts, and Arms, Par Reg 4.83
After the *Tuscan* Mariners transform'd Mask 48
Bridgewater ms 'manners transformed'
Manoah
Old *Manoah:* advise Samson 328
But wherefore comes old *Manoa* in such hast Samson 1441
To thee first reverend *Manoa*, and to these Samson 1548
Mess. Ah *Manoa* I refrain, too suddenly Samson 1565
Mansion
In this unhappy Mansion, or once more Par Lost 1.268
Of this ill Mansion: intermit no watch Par Lost 2.462
From thy Empyreal Mansion thus alone, Par Lost 3.699
To thir prepar'd ill Mansion driven down Par Lost 6.738
And said, thy Mansion wants thee, *Adam*, rise, Par Lost 8.296
My mansion is, where those immortal shapes Mask 2
Bridgewater ms 'Mansion'
Her mansion in this fleshly nook: Penseroso 92
That his mansion hath on high Psalm 136, 93
Mansions
And leave her dolorous mansions to the peering day. Nativity 140
Manslaughter
Man-slaughter, shall be held the highest pitch Par Lost 11.693
Mansur
The Kingdoms of *Almansor*, *Fez* and *Sus*, Par Lost 11.403
Mantle
Of God, as with a Mantle didst invest Par Lost 3.10
And o're the dark her Silver Mantle threw. Par Lost 4.609
His Mantle hairy, and his Bonnet sedge, Lycidas 104
Trinity ms 'mantle'
1638 'mantle'
At last he rose, and twitch'd his Mantle blew: Lycidas 192
1638 'mantle'
Trinity ms 'mantle'
Over the Pole thy thickest mantle throw, Passion 30
Mantling
Of coole recess, o're which the mantling vine Par Lost 4.258
Each shoulder broad, came mantling o're his brest Par Lost 5.279
Between her white wings mantling proudly, Rowes Par Lost 7.439
I saw them under a green mantling vine Mask 294
Bridgewater ms 'mantlinge'
Manuring
That mock our scant manuring, and require Par Lost 4.628
Which his own hand manuring all the Trees Par Lost 11.28
Many
O Prince, O Chief of many Throned Powers, Par Lost 1.128
Lay floating many a rood, in bulk as huge Par Lost 1.196
Nigh on the Plain in many cells prepar'd, Par Lost 1.700
To many a row of Pipes the sound-board breaths. Par Lost 1.709
Pendant by suttle Magic many a row Par Lost 1.727
In Heav'n by many a Towred structure high, Par Lost 1.733
With notes Angelical to many a Harp Par Lost 2.548
No rest: through many a dark and drearie Vaile Par Lost 2.618
They pass'd, and many a Region dolorous, Par Lost 2.619
O're many a Frozen, many a fierie Alpe, Par Lost 2.620
But ended foul in many a scaly fould Par Lost 2.651
Uplifted spurns the ground, thence many a League Par Lost 2.929
As many miles aloft: that furie stay'd, Par Lost 2.938
As many as are restor'd, without thee none. Par Lost 3.289
With many a vain exploit, though then renownd: Par Lost 3.465
Cleombrotus, and many more too long, Par Lost 3.473
Here in the dark so many precious things Par Lost 3.611
Of many a colourd plume sprinkl'd with Gold, Par Lost 3.642
Throws his steep flight in many an Aerie wheele, Par Lost 3.741
Well pleas'd they slack thir course, and many a League Par Lost 4.164
Rose a fresh Fountain, and with many a rill Par Lost 4.229
Runs divers, wandring many a famous Realme Par Lost 4.234
Among so many signes of power and rule Par Lost 4.429
Are many lesser Faculties that serve Par Lost 5.101
From many a berrie, and from sweet kernels prest Par Lost 5.346
The ruin of so many glorious once Par Lost 5.567
That of so many Myriads fall'n, yet one Par Lost 6.24
Thir names of thee; so over many a tract Par Lost 6.76
Of Heav'n they march'd, and many a Province wide Par Lost 6.77
By Angels many and strong, who interpos'd Par Lost 6.336
With many an inrode gor'd; deformed rout Par Lost 6.387
And stumbl'd many, who receives them right, Par Lost 6.624
Implacable, and many a dolorous groan, Par Lost 6.658

Many*(cont)*
Drew many, whom thir place knows here no more; Par Lost 7.144
So many nobler Bodies to create, Par Lost 8.28
In Labyrinth of many a round self-rowld, Par Lost 9.183
Neerer he drew, and many a walk travers'd Par Lost 9.434
Curld many a wanton wreath in sight of *Eve*, Par Lost 9.517
For many are the Trees of God that grow Par Lost 9.618
In heav'nly brests? these, these and many more Par Lost 9.730
Of ravenous Fowl, though many a League remote, Par Lost 10.274
And scourg'd with many a stroak th' indignant waves. Par Lost 10.311
Many a dark League, reduc't in careful Watch Par Lost 10.438
Of many ways to die the shortest choosing, Par Lost 10.1005
By him with many comforts, till we end Par Lost 10.1084
Defeated of his seisure many dayes Par Lost 11.254
And one bad act with many deeds well done Par Lost 11.256
So many grateful Altars I would reare Par Lost 11.323
Present, and of his presence many a signe Par Lost 11.351
In his first shape on man; but many shapes Par Lost 11.467
Of Death, and many are the wayes that lead Par Lost 11.468
Till many years over thy head return: Par Lost 11.534
The burd'n of many Ages, on me light Par Lost 11.767
Were long to tell, how many Battels fought, Par Lost 12.261
How many Kings destroyd, and Kingdoms won, Par Lost 12.262
So many and so various Laws are giv'n; Par Lost 12.282
So many Laws argue so many sins Par Lost 12.283
His death for Man, as many as offerd Life Par Lost 12.425
Infallible? yet many will presume: Par Lost 12.530
That ye may live, which will be many dayes, Par Lost 12.602
And unrecorded left through many an Age, Par Reg 1.16
How many Ages, as the years of men, Par Reg 1.48
Of many a pleasant Realm and Province wide. Par Reg 1.118
Through many a hard assay even to the death, Par Reg 1.264
Began to doubt, and doubted many days, Par Reg 2.11
Hath been our dwelling many years, his life Par Reg 2.80
Of many in *Israel*, and to a sign Par Reg 2.89
Many are in each Region passing fair Par Reg 2.155
Or *Amymone*, *Syrinx*, many more Par Reg 2.188
How many have with a smile made small account Par Reg 2.193
So many Ages, and shall yet regain Par Reg 2.441
Who for so many benefits receiv'd Par Reg 3.137
Cut shorter many a league; here thou behold'st Par Reg 3.269
Of many Provinces from bound to bound; Par Reg 3.315
His daughter, sought by many Prowest Knights, Par Reg 3.342
Many a fair Edifice besides, more like Par Reg 4.55
So many hollow complements and lies, Par Reg 4.124
An empty cloud. However many books Par Reg 4.321
From many a horrid rift abortive pour'd Par Reg 4.411
What I foretold thee, many a hard assay Par Reg 4.478
So many terrors, voices, prodigies Par Reg 4.482
So after many a foil the Tempter proud, Par Reg 4.569
So many, and so huge, that each apart Samson 65
The tread of many feet stearing this way; Samson 111
How many evils have enclos'd me round; Samson 194
In that sore battel when so many dy'd Samson 287
Them out of thine, who slew'st them many a slain. Samson 439
Which many a famous Warriour overturns, Samson 542
Chor. Many are the sayings of the wise Samson 652
Life yet hath many solaces, enjoy'd Samson 915
Exempt from many a care and chance to which Samson 918
The work of many hands, which earns my keeping Samson 1260
Yet knowing thir advantages too many, Samson 1401
With many murmurs mixt, whose pleasing poison Mask 526
Yet have they many baits, and guilefull spells Mask 537
With many a tower and terrass round, Mask 935
And not many furlongs thence Mask 946
Many a friend to gratulate Mask 949
Where young *Adonis* oft reposes, Mask 999
Trinity ms 'young Adonis oft' ←'many a cherub soft'
B.M. ms 'many'a Cherub soft'
Bridgewater ms 'many a Cherub soft'
To many a youth, and many a maid, Allegro 95
With stories told of many a feat, Allegro 101
In notes, with many a winding bout Allegro 139
Shall subject be to many an Accident. Vacation 74
Lord how many are my foes Psalm 3, 1
How many those Psalm 3, 2
Many are they Psalm 3, 4
Was the Lord. Of many millions Psalm 3, 15
Many there be that say Psalm 4, 25
Maple
His few Books, or his Beads, or Maple Dish, Mask 391
Trinity ms 'maple'
1637 'maple'
Bridgewater ms 'maple'
Marasmus
Marasmus, and wide-wasting Pestilence, Par Lost 11.487
line not in 1667 edition
Marble
Through the pure marble Air his oblique way Par Lost 3.564
In Cedar, Marble, Ivory or Gold. Par Reg 4.60
Next this marble venom'd seat Mask 916
Forget thy self to Marble, till Penseroso 42
And the chill Marble seems to sweat, Nativity 195
This rich Marble doth enterr Winchester 1
Dost make us Marble with too much conceaving; Shakespear 14
1663-4 '*Marble*'
1640 'marble'

March
Israel in *Sittim* on thir march from *Nile* Par Lost 1.413
Four ways thir flying March, along the Banks Par Lost 2.574
In confus'd march forlorn, th' adventrous Bands Par Lost 2.615
Homeward with flying march where we possess Par Lost 5.688
Of midnight march, and hurried meeting here, Par Lost 5.778
Thir march was, and the passive Air upbore Par Lost 6.72
To expedite your glorious march; but I Par Lost 10.474
In *Adam*'s overthrow, and led thir march Par Reg 1.115
Marched
Of Heav'n they march'd, and many a Province wide Par Lost 6.77
Marches
He marches now in hast; see, though from far, Par Reg 3.303
Marching
From *Egypt* marching, equal'd with one stroke Par Lost 1.488
Under spread Ensigns marching might pass through Par Lost 2.886
Marching from *Eden* towards the West, shall finde Par Lost 12.40
Marchioness
No Marchioness, but now a Queen. Winchester 74
Margaret
And to possess them, Honour'd *Margaret*. Sonnet 10, 14
Margent
By slow *Meander*'s margent green, Mask 232
Margiana
And *Margiana* to the *Hyrcanian* cliffs Par Reg 3.317
Marginal
Cropp yee as close as marginall P---s eares Forcers Tr. ms 45.17
Mariner
Impress the Air, and shews the Mariner Par Lost 4.558
Mariners
After the *Tuscan* Mariners transform'd Mask 48
Bridgewater ms 'manners transformed'
Trinity ms 'mariners'
Marish
Ris'n from a River o're the marish glides, Par Lost 12.630
1669 'Marish'
Maritime
Ercoco and the less Maritim Kings Par Lost 11.398
1667 'Maritine'
Mark
To mark what of thir state he more might learn Par Lost 4.400
But mark what I arreede thee now, avant; Par Lost 4.962
Calls us, we lose the prime, to mark how spring Par Lost 5.21
Whatever sleights none would suspicious mark, Par Lost 9.92
The Eye of *Eve* to mark his play; he glad Par Lost 9.528
Ith' midst an Altar as the Land-mark stood Par Lost 11.432
To mark thir doings, them beholding soon, Par Lost 12.50
On no slight grounds thy safety; hear, and mark Par Reg 3.349
The mark of fool set on his front? Samson 496
Mark what radiant state she spreds, Arcades 14
Trinity ms 'Marke'
But from that mark how far they roave we see Sonnet 12, 13
Trinity ms 'marke' ←'mark'
Ith' mid'st of all mine enemies that mark. Psalm 6, 15
Marked
He markd and mad demeanour, then alone, Par Lost 4.129
By word or action markt: about them round Par Lost 4.401
Bent all on speed, and markt his Aerie Gate; Par Lost 4.568
The way he came not having mark'd, return Par Reg 1.297
Marks
Looking on the Earth, with approbation marks Par Reg 3.61
The public marks of honour and reward Samson 992
Marl
Over the burning Marle, not like those steps Par Lost 1.296
Marocco
Damasco, or *Marocco*, or *Trebisond*, Par Lost 1.584
ms 'Marocco'
Marocco and *Algiers*, and *Tremisen;* Par Lost 11.404
Marred
Which marrd his borrow'd visage, and betraid Par Lost 4.116
The infernal Powers, in one day to have marr'd Par Lost 9.136
Marriage
His marriage with the seaventimes-wedded Maid. Par Lost 5.223
Of nuptial Sanctitie and marriage Rites: Par Lost 8.487
Hymen, then first to marriage Rites invok't; Par Lost 11.591
The Marriage on; that by occasion hence Samson 224
To seek in marriage that fallacious Bride, Samson 320
Man. I cannot praise thy Marriage choises, Son, Samson 420
Breaking her Marriage Faith to circumvent me. Samson 1115
The God that sits at marriage feast; Winchester 18
Marriageable
Her mariageable arms, and with her brings Par Lost 5.217
Marriages
Of those ill mated Marriages thou saw'st: Par Lost 11.684
Married
Married to immortal verse Allegro 137
Marrying
Marrying or prostituting, as befell, Par Lost 11.716
Mars
One is the Son of *Jove*, of *Mars* the other, Par Reg 3.84
of clamourous sin that all our musick marres Musick Tr. ms 5.04
Marsh
Ris'n from a River o're the marish glides, Par Lost 12.630
1669 'Marish'
Marshalled
At Joust and Torneament; then marshal'd Feast Par Lost 9.37
Martial
Sonorous mettal blowing Martial sounds: Par Lost 1.540
Martial(*cont*)
ms 'Martiall'
His thousands, in what martial equipage Par Reg 3.304
Martyrdom
Of Patience and Heroic Martyrdom Par Lost 9.32
Martyred
To Heav'n. Their martyr'd blood and ashes sow Sonnet 18, 10
Marveling
Though at the voice much marveling; at length Par Lost 9.551
Mary
Long after to blest *Marie*, second *Eve*. Par Lost 5.387
When *Jesus* son of *Mary* second *Eve*, Par Lost 10.183
But to his Mother *Mary*, when she saw Par Reg 2.60
Thus *Mary* pondering oft, and oft to mind Par Reg 2.105
The better part with *Mary*, and the *Ruth*, Sonnet 9, 5
Masculine
With Spirits Masculine, create at last Par Lost 10.890
Mask
Mixt Dance, or wanton Mask, or Midnight Bal, Par Lost 4.768
With mask, and antique Pageantry, Allegro 128
O what a Mask was there, what a disguise! Passion 19
1673 'mask'
This thought might lead me through the worlds vain mask Sonnet 22, 13
Mass
I saw when at his Word the formless Mass, Par Lost 3.708
Throughout the fluid Mass, but downward purg'd Par Lost 7.237
From the conflagrant mass, purg'd and refin'd, Par Lost 12.548
And all the world, and mass of sinful flesh; Par Reg 1.162
A mighty masse of things strangely confus'd, Prose 2, 3
Massacre
His Brother; for of whom such massacher Par Lost 11.679
Massy
Ethereal temper, massy, large and round, Par Lost 1.285
With wond'rous Art found out the massie Ore, Par Lost 1.703
ms 'massy'
Of massie Iron or sollid Rock with ease Par Lost 2.878
In Pearl, in Diamond, and massie Gold, Par Lost 5.634
His massie Spear upstaid; as if on Earth Par Lost 6.195
Labouring, two massie clods of Iron and Brass Par Lost 11.565
The Gates of *Azza*, Post, and massie Bar Samson 147
With both his arms on those two massie Pillars Samson 1633
When Mountains tremble, those two massie Pillars Samson 1648
With antick Pillars massy proof, Penseroso 158
Two massy Keyes he bore of metals twain, Lycidas 110
Trinity ms 'massie'
1638 'massie'
Mast
Hewn on *Norwegian* hills, to be the Mast Par Lost 1.293
ms 'mast'
Master
The great Work-Maister, leads to no excess Par Lost 3.696
There wanted yet the Master work, the end Par Lost 7.505
Spir. O my lov'd masters heir, and his next joy, Mask 501
Trinity ms 'maisters'
1673 'Masters'
And we should serve him as a grudging master, Mask 725
Trinity ms 'maister'
Bridgewater ms 'Master'
With her great Master so to sympathize: Nativity 34
As ever in my great task Masters eye. Sonnet 7, 14
Trinity ms 'task-maisters'
Mastering
To dwell, unless by maistring Heav'ns Supreame; Par Lost 9.125
Masters
But to thir Masters gave me up for nought, Samson 1215
Masters commands come with a power resistless Samson 1404
Mastery
Strive here for Maistrie, and to Battel bring Par Lost 2.899
Heroic deem'd, chief maistrie to dissect Par Lost 9.29
Match
To match with thir inventions they presum'd Par Lost 6.631
This far his over-match, who self deceiv'd Par Reg 4.7
Himself an Army, now unequal match Samson 346
With those thy boyst'rous locks, no worthy match Samson 1164
Matched
Grew darker at thir frown, so matcht they stood; Par Lost 2.720
Where good with bad were matcht, who of themselves Par Lost 11.685
Thought none my equal, now be over-match'd. Par Reg 2.146
Matching
Ill matching words and deeds long past or late. Par Lost 5.113
Matchless
Matchless, but with th' Almighty, and that strife Par Lost 1.623
Ended rejoycing in thir matchless Chief: Par Lost 2.487
Warring in Heav'n against Heav'ns matchless King: Par Lost 4.41
To find himself not matchless, and his pride Par Lost 6.341
Valour or strength, though matchless, quelld with pain Par Lost 6.457
Plenipotent on Earth, of matchless might Par Lost 10.404
By matchless Deeds express thy matchless Sire. Par Reg 1.233
But as a man who had been matchless held Par Reg 4.10
Chor. Hee speaks, let us draw nigh. Matchless in might, Samson 178
The matchless *Gideon* in pursuit Samson 280
To matchless valour, and adventures high: Samson 1740
Guided by faith and matchless Fortitude Sonnet 16, 3
1694 'Matchless'
Mate
Thus Satan talking to his neerest Mate Par Lost 1.192
Of unblest feet. Him followed his next Mate, Par Lost 1.238
Know ye not mee? ye knew me once no mate Par Lost 4.828

Mate(*cont*)
Bank the mid Sea: part single or with mate — Par Lost 7.403
Thy mate, who sees when thou art seen least wise. — Par Lost 8.578
Among the Beasts no Mate for thee was found. — Par Lost 8.594
He never shall find out fit Mate, but such — Par Lost 10.899
But thee whose strength, while vertue was her mate, — Samson 173
Embarqu'd with such a Stears-mate at the Helm? — Samson 1045
Whilome did slay his dearly-loved mate — Fair Inf 24
Whether the Muse, or Love call thee his mate, — Sonnet 1, 13

Mated
Of those ill mated Marriages thou saw'st: — Par Lost 11.684
1667 'ill-mated'

Material
This worlds material mould, came to a heap: — Par Lost 3.709

Materials
His dark materials to create more Worlds, — Par Lost 2.916
Deep under ground, materials dark and crude, — Par Lost 6.478

Mates
And to his Mates thus in derision call'd. — Par Lost 6.608

Matin
Lightly dispers'd, and the shrill Matin Song — Par Lost 5.7
The matin Trumpet Sung: in Arms they stood — Par Lost 6.526
With Eevning Harps and Mattin, when God said, — Par Lost 7.450
Ere the first Cock his Mattin rings. — Allegro 114

Matrimonial
And Matrimonial Love; but *Eve*, who thought — Par Lost 9.319
Of Matrimonial treason: so farewel. — Samson 959

Matron
Expos'd a Matron to avoid worse rape. — Par Lost 1.505
1667 'Yielded thir Matrons'
That shed *May* Flowers; and press'd her Matron lip — Par Lost 4.501
The Earth, when *Adam* and first Matron *Eve* — Par Lost 11.136
Some rich *Philistian* Matron she may seem, — Samson 722
Or that crown'd Matron sage white-robed truth? — Fair Inf 54

Matrons
Expos'd a Matron to avoid worse rape. — Par Lost 1.505
1667 'Yielded thir Matrons'
Once had the early Matrons run — Winchester 23

Matter
What matter where, if I be still the same, — Par Lost 1.256
Shall be the copious matter of my Song — Par Lost 3.413
Here matter new to gaze the Devil met — Par Lost 3.613
Such to perfection, one first matter all, — Par Lost 5.472
High matter thou injoinst me, O prime of men, — Par Lost 5.563
Matter to mee of Glory, whom thir hate — Par Lost 5.738
Matter unform'd and void: Darkness profound — Par Lost 7.233
Rais'd, as of som great matter to begin. — Par Lost 9.669
Matter of scorne, not to be given the Foe, — Par Lost 9.951
Matter of glorious trial; and perhaps — Par Lost 9.1177
To the reception of thir matter act, — Par Lost 10.807
Reflected, may with matter sere foment, — Par Lost 10.1071
Or some great matter in his mind revolv'd. — Samson 1638
And wov'n close, both matter, form and stile; — Sonnet 11, 2

Matters
Sollicit not thy thoughts with matters hid, — Par Lost 8.167
And trifles for choice matters, worth a spunge; — Par Reg 4.329
Chor. Consider, *Samson;* matters now are strain'd — Samson 1348

Mature
Full Counsel must mature: Peace is despaird, — Par Lost 1.660
Had circl'd his full Orbe, the birth mature — Par Lost 5.862
Till dieted by thee I grow mature — Par Lost 9.803
All kinds, and for destruction to mature — Par Lost 10.612
Constant, mature, proof against all assaults, — Par Lost 10.882
Gatherd, not harshly pluckt, for death mature: — Par Lost 11.537
Publish his God-like office now mature, — Par Reg 1.188
Yet years, and to ripe years judgment mature, — Par Reg 3.37
Till time mature thee to a Kingdoms waight; — Par Reg 4.282

Maturest
Maturest Counsels: for his thoughts were low; — Par Lost 2.115

Maugre
Shall lead Hell Captive maugre Hell, and show — Par Lost 3.255
On mans destruction, maugre what might hap — Par Lost 9.56
Maugre the *Roman:* it shall be my task — Par Reg 3.368

Maw
His famine should be fill'd, and blest his mawe — Par Lost 2.847
To stuff this Maw, this vast unhide-bound Corps. — Par Lost 10.601
Be forc'd to satisfie his Rav'nous Maw. — Par Lost 10.991
Of hireling wolves whose Gospell is their maw. — Sonnet 16, 14
1694 'Maw'

Maxim
With hard contest: at length that grounded maxim — Samson 865

Maxims
Thy politic maxims, or that cumbersome — Par Reg 3.400

May
I may assert Eternal Providence, — Par Lost 1.25
We may with more successful hope resolve — Par Lost 1.120
That we may so suffice his vengeful ire, — Par Lost 1.148
Which oft times may succeed, so as perhaps — Par Lost 1.166
Consult how we may henceforth most offend — Par Lost 1.187
What reinforcement we may gain from Hope, — Par Lost 1.190
Here we may reign secure, and in my choyce — Par Lost 1.261
With rallied Arms to try what may be yet — Par Lost 1.269
At length from us may find, who overcomes — Par Lost 1.648
Space may produce new Worlds; whereof so rife — Par Lost 1.650
That riches grow in Hell; that soyle may best — Par Lost 1.691
We now debate; who can advise, may speak. — Par Lost 2.42
Our stronger, some worse way his wrath may find — Par Lost 2.83
Our Supream Foe in time may much remit — Par Lost 2.210

May(*cont*)
Of future dayes may bring, what chance, what change — Par Lost 2.222
May hope when everlasting Fate shall yeild — Par Lost 2.232
Our torments also may in length of time — Par Lost 2.274
Of order, how in safety best we may — Par Lost 2.280
May reap his conquest, and may least rejoyce — Par Lost 2.339
In his own strength, this place may lye expos'd — Par Lost 2.360
Som advantagious act may be achiev'd — Par Lost 2.363
May prove thir foe, and with repenting hand — Par Lost 2.369
And opportune excursion we may chance — Par Lost 2.396
While here shall be our home, what best may ease — Par Lost 2.458
Leads him perplext, where he may likeliest find — Par Lost 2.525
May I express thee unblam'd? since God is light, — Par Lost 3.3
Purge and disperse, that I may see and tell — Par Lost 3.54
By me upheld, that he may know how frail — Par Lost 3.180
What may suffice, and soft'n stonie hearts — Par Lost 3.189
That they may stumble on, and deeper fall; — Par Lost 3.201
In those who, when they may, accept not grace. — Par Lost 3.302
That I may find him, and with secret gaze, — Par Lost 3.671
The Universal Maker we may praise; — Par Lost 3.676
Henceforth; my dwelling haply may not please — Par Lost 4.378
A chance but chance may lead where I may meet — Par Lost 4.530
What further would be learnt. Live while ye may, — Par Lost 4.533
May come and go, so unapprov'd, and leave — Par Lost 5.118
As may advise him of his happie state, — Par Lost 5.234
Our Heav'nly stranger; well we may afford — Par Lost 5.316
As may not oft invite, though Spirits of Heav'n — Par Lost 5.374
Spiritual, may of purest Spirits be found — Par Lost 5.406
As may compare with Heaven; and to taste — Par Lost 5.432
To proper substance; time may come when men — Par Lost 5.493
With Angels may participate, and find — Par Lost 5.494
Your bodies may at last turn all to Spirit, — Par Lost 5.497
Ethereal, as wee, or may at choice — Par Lost 5.499
By steps we may ascend to God. But say, — Par Lost 5.512
As may express them best, though what if Earth — Par Lost 5.574
New Laws from him who reigns, new minds may raise — Par Lost 5.680
What doubtful may ensue, more in this place — Par Lost 5.682
This onely to consult how we may best — Par Lost 5.779
With what may be devis'd of honours new — Par Lost 5.780
While Pardon may be found in time besought. — Par Lost 5.848
How few somtimes may know, when thousands err. — Par Lost 6.148
From me som Plume, that thy success may show — Par Lost 6.161
Liken on Earth conspicuous, that may lift — Par Lost 6.299
Sanguin, such as Celestial Spirits may bleed, — Par Lost 6.333
Of future we may deem him, though till now — Par Lost 6.429
May serve to better us, and worse our foes, — Par Lost 6.440
Of Mightiest. Sense of pleasure we may well — Par Lost 6.459
With what more forcible we may offend — Par Lost 6.465
That all may see who hate us, how we seek — Par Lost 6.559
What we propound, and loud that all may hear. — Par Lost 6.567
Have sufferd, that the Glorie may be thine — Par Lost 6.701
Immense I have transfus'd, that all may know — Par Lost 6.704
That they may have thir wish, to trie with mee — Par Lost 6.818
Who now is plotting how he may seduce — Par Lost 6.901
What may no less perhaps availe us known, — Par Lost 7.85
Yet what thou canst attain, which best may serve — Par Lost 7.115
In measure what the mind may well contain, — Par Lost 7.128
Nor glistering, may of solid good containe — Par Lost 8.93
That Man may know he dwells not in his own; — Par Lost 8.103
As Clouds, and Clouds may rain, and Rain produce — Par Lost 8.146
Useful, whence haply mention may arise — Par Lost 8.200
Tell me, how may I know him, how adore, — Par Lost 8.280
Surpassest farr my naming, how may I — Par Lost 8.359
Deprest, and much they may, if all be mine, — Par Lost 9.46
Or won to what may work his utter loss, — Par Lost 9.131
In wo then; that destruction wide may range: — Par Lost 9.134
In every Bush and Brake, where hap may finde — Par Lost 9.160
Then commune how that day they best may ply — Par Lost 9.201
Adam, well may we labour still to dress — Par Lost 9.205
May tempt it, I expected not to hear. — Par Lost 9.281
Since Reason not impossibly may meet — Par Lost 9.360
But if thou think, trial unsought may finde — Par Lost 9.370
May finde us both perhaps farr less prepar'd, — Par Lost 9.381
What may this mean? Language of Man pronounc't — Par Lost 9.553
But of this Tree we may not taste nor touch; — Par Lost 9.651
Of each Tree in the Garden we may eate, — Par Lost 9.660
And what are Gods that Man may not become — Par Lost 9.716
May have diverted from continual watch — Par Lost 9.814
This may be well: but what if God have seen, — Par Lost 9.826
May joyne us, equal Joy, as equal Love; — Par Lost 9.882
Hide me, where I may never see them more. — Par Lost 9.1090
What best may from the present serve to hide — Par Lost 9.1092
And girded on our loyns, may cover round — Par Lost 9.1096
Easie it might be seen that I intend — Par Lost 10.58
1667 'may'
Of right, that I may mitigate thir doom — Par Lost 10.76
Justice with Mercie, as may illustrate most — Par Lost 10.78
So, if great things to small may be compar'd, — Par Lost 10.306
There best, where most with ravin I may meet; — Par Lost 10.599
For this we may thank *Adam;* but his thanks — Par Lost 10.736
Like his, and colour Serpentine may shew — Par Lost 10.870
The sentence from thy head remov'd may light — Par Lost 10.934
In offices of Love, how we may light'n — Par Lost 10.960
Reflected, may with matter sere foment, — Par Lost 10.1071
And what may else be remedie or cure — Par Lost 10.1079
All my redeemd may dwell in joy and bliss, — Par Lost 11.43
And mortal food, as may dispose him best — Par Lost 11.54
Eve, easily may Faith admit, that all — Par Lost 11.141

May(*cont*)
Hard to belief may seem; yet this will Prayer, Par Lost 11.146
Mayst cover: well may then thy Lord appeas'd Par Lost 11.257
Of them the Highest, for such of shape may seem Par Lost 11.297
If so I may attain. So both ascend Par Lost 11.376
These painful passages, how we may come Par Lost 11.528
Life much, bent rather how I may be quit Par Lost 11.548
Him or his Childern, evil he may be sure, Par Lost 11.772
More then anough, that temperance may be tri'd: Par Lost 11.805
Green Tree or ground whereon his foot may light; Par Lost 11.858
A Citie and Towre, whose top may reach to Heav'n; Par Lost 12.44
The bloud of Bulls and Goats, they may conclude Par Lost 12.292
To them by Faith imputed, they may finde Par Lost 12.295
We may no longer stay: go, waken *Eve;* Par Lost 12.594
Chiefly what may concern her Faith to know, Par Lost 12.599
That ye may live, which will be many dayes, Par Lost 12.602
Thenceforth the Nations may not doubt; I saw Par Reg 1.79
They now, and men hereafter may discern, Par Reg 1.164
Against whate're may tempt, whate're seduce, Par Reg 1.178
By Miracle he may, reply'd the Swain, Par Reg 1.337
Whereby they may direct their future life. Par Reg 1.396
At first it may be; but long since with wo Par Reg 1.399
If it may stand him more in stead to lye, Par Reg 1.473
Afflicted I may be, it seems, and blest; Par Reg 2.93
So may we hold our place and these mild seats Par Reg 2.125
May also in this poverty as soon Par Reg 2.451
Then prompt her to do aught may merit praise. Par Reg 2.456
It may by means far different be attain'd Par Reg 3.89
Without distrust or doubt, that he may know Par Reg 3.193
May bring them back repentant and sincere, Par Reg 3.435
As by that early action may be judg'd, Par Reg 4.215
And lovers of thir Country, as may seem; Par Reg 4.355
Not when it must, but when it may be best. Par Reg 4.476
May warn thee, as a sure fore-going sign. Par Reg 4.483
Have been before contemn'd, and may agen: Par Reg 4.537
Counsel or Consolation we may bring, Samson 183
Mee easily indeed mine may neglect, Samson 291
About thy ransom: well they may by this Samson 483
Some rich *Philistian* Matron she may seem, Samson 722
May expiate (though the fact more evil drew Samson 736
If aught in my ability may serve Samson 743
I may, if possible, thy pardon find Samson 771
Thine forgive mine; that men may censure thine Samson 787
Philistian gold: if weakness may excuse, Samson 831
Incestuous, Sacrilegious, but may plead it? Samson 833
Thir favourable ear, that I may fetch thee Samson 921
May ever tend about thee to old age Samson 925
To all posterity may stand defam'd, Samson 977
Some narrow place enclos'd, where sight may give thee, Samson 1117
Yet so it may fall out, because thir end Samson 1265
Is hate, not help to me, it may with mine Samson 1266
May chance to number thee with those Samson 1295
He's gone, and who knows how he may report Samson 1350
Yet that he may dispense with me or thee Samson 1377
Nothing to do, be sure, that may dishonour Samson 1385
So dreaded once, may now exasperate them Samson 1417
Happ'n what may, of me expect to hear Samson 1423
To what may serve his glory best, & spread his name Samson 1429
May compass it, shall willingly be paid Samson 1477
Mess. Feed on that first, there may in grief be surfet. Samson 1562
And what may quiet us in a death so noble. Samson 1724
Our number may affright: Som Virgin sure Mask 148
And hearken, if I may, her busines here. Mask 169
This is the place, as well as I may guess, Mask 201
line not in Bridgewater ms
These thoughts may startle well, but not astound Mask 210
line not in Bridgewater ms
But loyal cottage, where you may be safe Mask 320
Where may she wander now, whether betake her Mask 351
May sit i' th center, and enjoy bright day, Mask 382
You may as well spred out the unsun'd heaps Mask 398
Which if Heav'n gave it, may be term'd her own: Mask 419
May trace huge Forests, and unharbour'd Heaths, Mask 423
She may pass on with unblench't majesty, Mask 430
Vertue may be assail'd, but never hurt, Mask 589
May never this just sword be lifted up, Mask 601
(As I will give you when we go) you may Mask 648
Where most may wonder at the workmanship; Mask 747
line not in Bridgewater ms
Som other means I have which may be us'd, Mask 821
May thy brimmed waves for this Mask 924
May thy billows rowl ashoar Mask 932
May thy lofty head be crown'd Mask 934
I doubt me gentle mortalls these may seeme Mask Tr. ms 10.16
& may upon any needfull accident Mask Tr. ms 16.55
be it not don in pride or in praesumption Mask Tr. ms 16.56
'be' ← 'may be' ← 'be'
he may scratch his forehead. heere be brambles Mask Tr. ms 17.57
'he may scratch' ← 'he may chaunce' ← 'chance' ← 'had best look to'
Such as the meeting soul may pierce Allegro 138
That *Orpheus* self may heave his head Allegro 145
Where I may oft out-watch the *Bear*, Penseroso 87
Where no profaner eye may look, Penseroso 140
As may with sweetnes, through mine ear, Penseroso 164
And may at last my weary age Penseroso 167
Where I may sit and rightly spell, Penseroso 170
We may justly now accuse Arcades 10

May(*cont*)
Trinity ms 'wee may justly now accuse' ← 'now seemes guiltie of abuse'
And lead ye where ye may more neer behold Arcades 40
Where ye may all that are of noble stemm Arcades 82
So may som gentle Muse Lycidas 19
That so they may without suspect or fears Vacation 27
Such as may make thee search thy coffers round, Vacation 31
Such where the deep transported mind may soare Vacation 33
May tell at length how green-ey'd *Neptune* raves, Vacation 43
That to the next I may resign my Roome. Vacation 58
That we on Earth with undiscording voice Musick 17
Trinity ms 'on earth' ← 'below may learne'
May rightly answer that melodious noise; Musick 18
O may we soon again renew that Song, Musick 25
And keep in tune with Heav'n, till God ere long Musick 26
Trinity ms 'and' ← 'may'
Gentle Lady may thy grave Winchester 47
Like fortunes may her soul acquaint, Winchester 72
The Flowry *May*, who from her green lap throws May Morn 3
Hail bounteous *May* that dost inspire May Morn 5
If I may not carry, sure Ile ne're be fetch'd, Another 18
line not in 1640, 1657, 1658 texts
While the jolly hours lead on propitious *May*, Sonnet 1, 4
Whose chance on these defenceless dores may sease, Sonnet 8, 2
Then to advise how warr may best, upheld, Sonnet 17, 7
The triple Tyrant: that from these may grow Sonnet 18, 12
Early may fly the *Babylonian* wo. Sonnet 18, 14
Help wast a sullen day; what may be won Sonnet 20, 4
Of Attick tast, with Wine, whence we may rise Sonnet 20, 10
May with their wholsom and preventive Shears Forcers 16
That all may pluck her, as they go, Psalm 80, 51
To Jacobs God, *that all may hear* Psalm 81, 3
That Israels name for ever may Psalm 83, 15
That so thy people may rejoyce Psalm 85, 23
Iunkets and knacks, that they may learne apace. Prose 6, 3
Having to advise the public may speak free, Prose 9, 2
Who neither can nor will, may hold his peace; Prose 9, 4
What certain Seat, where I may worship thee Prose 12, 5

May
That shed *May* Flowers; and press'd her Matron lip Par Lost 4.501

Mayest
Happier thou mayst be, worthier canst not be: Par Lost 5.76
At thy request, and that thou maist beware Par Lost 6.894
Bereavd of happiness thou maist partake Par Lost 6.903
Absolv'd, if unforbid thou maist unfould Par Lost 7.94
Thou mai'st not; in the day thou eat'st, thou di'st; Par Lost 7.544
So awful, that with honour thou maist love Par Lost 8.577
By which to heav'nly Love thou maist ascend, Par Lost 8.592
Mayst ever rest well pleas'd. I go to judge Par Lost 10.71
Giv'n thee of Grace, wherein thou may'st repent, Par Lost 11.255
Mayst cover: well may then thy Lord appeas'd Par Lost 11.257
Which that thou mayst beleeve, and be confirmd Par Lost 11.355
Before thee shall appear; that thou mayst know Par Lost 11.475
So maist thou live, till like ripe Fruit thou drop Par Lost 11.535
As thou to thy reproach mayst well remember, Par Reg 3.66
And regal Mysteries; that thou may'st know Par Reg 3.249
Turning with easie eye thou may'st behold. Par Reg 3.293
That thou may'st know I seek not to engage Par Reg 3.347
My Aerie Microscope) thou may'st behold Par Reg 4.57
And long Renown thou justly may'st prefer Par Reg 4.84
And with my help thou may'st; to me the power Par Reg 4.103
Where thou mayst bring thy off'rings, to avert Samson 519
So maist thou be translated to the skies, Mask 242
Trinity ms 'maist' ← 'mast'
B.M. ms 'may'st'
Bridgewater ms 'mayst'

Maying
As he met her once a Maying, Allegro 20

Maze
Fould above fould a surging Maze, his Head Par Lost 9.499
Wandring this woody maze, and humane food Par Reg 2.246
Fly after the Night-steeds, leaving their Moon-lov'd maze. Nativity 236

Mazes
And found no end, in wandring mazes lost. Par Lost 2.561
Resembles nearest, mazes intricate, Par Lost 5.622
And reasonings, though through Mazes, lead me still Par Lost 10.830
In the blind mazes of this tangl'd Wood? Mask 181
Trinity ms 'mazes' ← 'alleys'
The melting voice through mazes running; Allegro 142

Mazy
With mazie error under pendant shades Par Lost 4.239
The Serpent sleeping, in whose mazie foulds Par Lost 9.161

Me
Instruct me, for Thou know'st; Thou from the first Par Lost 1.19
And mad'st it pregnant: What in me is dark Par Lost 1.22
Joynd with me once, now misery hath joynd Par Lost 1.90
That with the mightiest rais'd me to contend, Par Lost 1.99
That durst dislike his reign, and me preferring, Par Lost 1.102
ms 'mee'
Extort from me. To bow and sue for grace Par Lost 1.111
For mee be witness all the Host of Heav'n, Par Lost 1.635
1667 'me'
ms 'me'
By mee, have lost our hopes. But he who reigns Par Lost 1.637
1674 'me' in some copies
1667 'me'
ms 'me'

Me(*cont*)
Mee though just right, and the fixt Laws of Heav'n Par Lost 2.18
Did not disswade me most, and seem to cast Par Lost 2.122
Mee from attempting. Wherefore do I assume Par Lost 2.450
1667 'Me'
1674 'Me' in some copies
None shall partake with me. Thus saying rose Par Lost 2.466
Me Father, and that Fantasm call'st my Son? Par Lost 2.743
Hast thou forgot me then, and do I seem Par Lost 2.747
At first, and call'd me *Sin*, and for a Sign Par Lost 2.760
Portentous held me; but familiar grown, Par Lost 2.761
Thy self in me thy perfect image viewing Par Lost 2.764
With me in secret, that my womb conceiv'd Par Lost 2.766
Mee overtook his mother all dismaid, Par Lost 2.792
1667 'Me'
Ingendring with me, of that rape begot Par Lost 2.794
Surround me, as thou sawst, hourly conceiv'd Par Lost 2.796
To me, for when they list into the womb Par Lost 2.798
A fresh with conscious terrours vex me round, Par Lost 2.801
And me his Parent would full soon devour Par Lost 2.805
Dear Daughter, since thou claim'st me for thy Sire, Par Lost 2.817
And my fair Son here showst me, the dear pledge Par Lost 2.818
Who hates me, and hath hither thrust me down Par Lost 2.857
My being gav'st me; whom should I obey Par Lost 2.865
But thee, whom follow? thou wilt bring me soon Par Lost 2.866
Those other two equal'd with me in Fate, Par Lost 3.33
Seasons return, but not to me returns Par Lost 3.41
Surrounds me, from the chearful wayes of men Par Lost 3.46
Of Natures works to mee expung'd and ras'd, Par Lost 3.49
Whose but his own? ingrate, he had of mee Par Lost 3.97
1667 'me' in some copies
Not mee. They therefore as to right belongd, Par Lost 3.111
Or aught by me immutablie foreseen, Par Lost 3.121
Yet not of will in him, but grace in me Par Lost 3.174
Upheld by me, yet once more he shall stand Par Lost 3.178
By me upheld, that he may know how frail Par Lost 3.180
His fall'n condition is, and to me ow Par Lost 3.181
All his deliv'rance, and to none but me. Par Lost 3.182
The rest shall hear me call, and oft be warnd Par Lost 3.185
Behold mee then, mee for him, life for life Par Lost 3.236
I offer, on mee let thine anger fall; Par Lost 3.237
Account mee man; I for his sake will leave Par Lost 3.238
Well pleas'd, on me let Death wreck all his rage; Par Lost 3.241
Lie vanquisht; thou hast givn me to possess Par Lost 3.243
All that of me can die, yet that debt paid, Par Lost 3.246
Thou wilt not leave me in the loathsom grave Par Lost 3.247
To me are all my works, nor Man the least Par Lost 3.277
Adore the Son, and honour him as mee. Par Lost 3.343
Hath brought me from the Quires of Cherubim Par Lost 3.666
Thy way thou canst not miss, me mine requires. Par Lost 3.735
Till Pride and worse Ambition threw me down Par Lost 4.40
From me, whom he created what I was Par Lost 4.43
How due! yet all his good prov'd ill in me, Par Lost 4.48
Would set me highest, and in a moment quit Par Lost 4.51
Me some inferiour Angel, I had stood Par Lost 4.59
As great might have aspir'd, and me though mean Par Lost 4.62
To me alike, it deals eternal woe. Par Lost 4.70
Me miserable! which way shall I flie Par Lost 4.73
Still threatning to devour me opens wide, Par Lost 4.77
Disdain forbids me, and my dread of shame Par Lost 4.82
Th' Omnipotent. Ay me, they little know Par Lost 4.86
While they adore me on the Throne of Hell, Par Lost 4.89
Which would but lead me to a worse relapse Par Lost 4.100
Farwel Remorse: all Good to me is lost; Par Lost 4.109
That I with you must dwell, or you with me Par Lost 4.377
Accept your Makers work; he gave it me, Par Lost 4.380
Thank him who puts me loath to this revenge Par Lost 4.386
On you who wrong me not for him who wrongd. Par Lost 4.387
By conquering this new World, compels me now Par Lost 4.391
With unexperienc't thought, and laid me downe Par Lost 4.457
Smooth Lake, that to me seemd another Skie. Par Lost 4.459
Bending to look on me, I started back, Par Lost 4.462
Had not a voice thus warnd me, What thou seest, Par Lost 4.467
With thee it came and goes: but follow me, Par Lost 4.469
Yet let me not forget what I have gain'd Par Lost 4.512
Know ye not mee? ye knew me once no mate Par Lost 4.828
1667 'not me'
Not to know mee argues your selves unknown, Par Lost 4.830
Puts me in doubt. Lives ther who loves his pain? Par Lost 4.888
The rest is true, they found me where they say; Par Lost 4.900
Close at mine ear one call'd me forth to walk Par Lost 5.36
That brought me on a sudden to the Tree Par Lost 5.51
Forbid who will, none shall from me withhold Par Lost 5.62
He pluckt, he tasted; mee damp horror chil'd Par Lost 5.65
So saying, he drew nigh, and to me held, Par Lost 5.82
Affects me equally; nor can I like Par Lost 5.97
No spot or blame behind: Which gives me hope Par Lost 5.119
Assur'd me, and still assure: though what thou tellst Par Lost 5.553
Hath past in Heav'n, som doubt within me move, Par Lost 5.554
High matter thou injoinst me, O prime of men, Par Lost 5.563
Mee disobeyes, breaks union, and that day Par Lost 5.612
Of Heav'ns Almightie. Thou to me thy thoughts Par Lost 5.676
And all who under me thir Banners wave, Par Lost 5.687
Matter to mee of Glory, whom thir hate Par Lost 5.738
Giv'n me to quell thir pride, and in event Par Lost 5.740
From me som Plume, that thy success may show Par Lost 6.161
Reign thou in Hell thy Kingdom, let mee serve Par Lost 6.183
From mee returnd, as erst thou saidst, from flight, Par Lost 6.187

Me(*cont*)
Unvanquisht, easier to transact with mee Par Lost 6.286
To chase me hence? erre not that so shall end Par Lost 6.288
Our selves with like defence, to me deserves Par Lost 6.467
1667 'Mee'
That thou in me well pleas'd, declarst thy will Par Lost 6.728
For ever, and in mee all whom thou lov'st: Par Lost 6.733
By mee, not you but mee they have despis'd, Par Lost 6.812
Yet envied; against mee is all thir rage, Par Lost 6.813
Hath honourd me according to his will. Par Lost 6.816
Therefore to mee thir doom he hath assig'n'd; Par Lost 6.817
That they may have thir wish, to trie with mee Par Lost 6.818
Return me to my Native Element: Par Lost 7.16
Approach not mee, and what I will is Fate. Par Lost 7.173
Things else by me unsearchable, now heard Par Lost 8.10
Speed almost Spiritual; mee thou thinkst not slow, Par Lost 8.110
How fully hast thou satisfi'd mee, pure Par Lost 8.180
Ere my remembrance: now hear mee relate Par Lost 8.204
Induc'd me. As new wak't from soundest sleep Par Lost 8.253
Soft on the flourie herb I found me laid Par Lost 8.254
Stood on my feet; about me round I saw Par Lost 8.261
Tell me, how may I know him, how adore, Par Lost 8.280
Pensive I sate me down; there gentle sleep Par Lost 8.287
First found me, and with soft oppression seis'd Par Lost 8.288
So saying, by the hand he took me rais'd, Par Lost 8.300
Smooth sliding without step, last led me up Par Lost 8.302
Tempting, stirr'd in me sudden appetite Par Lost 8.308
Submiss: he rear'd me, and Whom thou soughtst I am, Par Lost 8.316
Thou hast provided all things: but with mee Par Lost 8.363
Hast thou not made me here thy substitute, Par Lost 8.381
And these inferiour farr beneath me set? Par Lost 8.382
What thinkst thou then of mee, and this my State, Par Lost 8.403
Second to me or like, equal much less. Par Lost 8.407
1667 'mee'
To me inferiour, infinite descents Par Lost 8.410
Of sleep, which instantly fell on me, call'd Par Lost 8.458
Shee disappeerd, and left me dark, I wak'd Par Lost 8.478
Before me; Woman is her Name, of Man Par Lost 8.496
She heard me thus, and though divinely brought, Par Lost 8.500
Wrought in her so, that seeing me, she turn'd; Par Lost 8.507
Or Nature faild in mee, and left some part Par Lost 8.534
So much delights me as those graceful acts, Par Lost 8.600
To love thou blam'st me not, for love thou saist Par Lost 8.612
Bear with me then, if lawful what I ask; Par Lost 8.614
Gentle to me and affable hath been Par Lost 8.648
And dictates to me slumbring, or inspires Par Lost 9.23
Pleas'd me long choosing, and beginning late; Par Lost 9.26
To Person or to Poem. Mee of these Par Lost 9.41
Pleasures about me, so much more I feel Par Lost 9.120
Torment within me, as from the hateful siege Par Lost 9.121
Of contraries; all good to me becomes Par Lost 9.122
As I, though thereby worse to me redound: Par Lost 9.128
To mee shall be the glorie sole among Par Lost 9.135
To hide me, and the dark intent I bring. Par Lost 9.162
Sole *Eve*, Associate sole, to me beyond Par Lost 9.227
God hath assign'd us, nor of me shalt pass Par Lost 9.231
But other doubt possesses me, least harm Par Lost 9.251
Befall thee sever'd from me; for thou knowst Par Lost 9.252
Or daring, first on mee th' assault shall light. Par Lost 9.305
With me, best witness of thy Vertue tri'd. Par Lost 9.317
That I should mind thee oft, and mind thou me. Par Lost 9.358
Were better, and most likelie if from mee Par Lost 9.365
Thoughts, whither have ye led me, with what sweet Par Lost 9.473
To me is lost. Then let me not let pass Par Lost 9.479
Infeebl'd me, to what I was in Heav'n. Par Lost 9.488
To me so friendly grown above the rest Par Lost 9.564
Easie to mee it is to tell thee all Par Lost 9.569
Of that alluring fruit, urg'd me so keene. Par Lost 9.588
About the mossie Trunk I wound me soon, Par Lost 9.589
Strange alteration in me, to degree Par Lost 9.599
Mee thus, though importune perhaps, to come Par Lost 9.610
Fruitless to mee, though Fruit be here to excess, Par Lost 9.648
1667 'me'
Within me cleere, not onely to discerne Par Lost 9.681
To Knowledge? By the Threatner, look on mee, Par Lost 9.687
Mee who have touch'd and tasted, yet both live, Par Lost 9.688
Meant mee, by ventring higher then my Lot. Par Lost 9.690
Full happiness with mee, or rather not, Par Lost 9.819
And render me more equal, and perhaps, Par Lost 9.823
Adam shall share with me in bliss or woe: Par Lost 9.831
Reasoning to admiration, and with mee Par Lost 9.872
For bliss, as thou hast part, to me is bliss, Par Lost 9.879
And mee with thee hath ruind, for with thee Par Lost 9.906
The Link of Nature draw me: Flesh of Flesh, Par Lost 9.914
Most Favors, who can please him long; Mee first Par Lost 9.949
Consort with thee, Death is to mee as Life; Par Lost 9.954
The Bond of Nature draw me to my owne, Par Lost 9.956
Ingaging me to emulate, but short Par Lost 9.963
Adam, from whose deare side I boast me sprung, Par Lost 9.965
To undergoe with mee one Guilt, one Crime, Par Lost 9.971
Since to each meaning savour me apply, Par Lost 9.1019
1667 'we'
And brown as Evening: Cover me ye Pines, Par Lost 9.1088
Hide me, where I may never see them more. Par Lost 9.1090
With me, as I besought thee, when that strange Par Lost 9.1135
Why hee should mean me ill, or seek to harme. Par Lost 9.1152
Command me absolutely not to go, Par Lost 9.1156
Neither had I transgress'd, nor thou with mee. Par Lost 9.1161

Me(*cont*)

Supream, that thou in mee thy Son belov'd	Par Lost 10.70
Whoever judg'd, the worst on mee must light,	Par Lost 10.73
On me deriv'd, yet I shall temper so	Par Lost 10.77
Whose failing, while her Faith to me remaines,	Par Lost 10.129
Subdues me, and calamitous constraint	Par Lost 10.132
And gav'st me as thy perfet gift, so good,	Par Lost 10.138
Shee gave me of the Tree, and I did eate.	Par Lost 10.143
The Serpent me beguil'd and I did eate.	Par Lost 10.162
Methinks I feel new strength within me rise,	Par Lost 10.243
Wings growing, and Dominion giv'n me large	Par Lost 10.244
Beyond this Deep; whatever drawes me on,	Par Lost 10.245
Inseparable must with mee along:	Par Lost 10.250
Amply have merited of me, of all	Par Lost 10.388
Issuing from mee: on your joynt vigor now	Par Lost 10.405
True is, mee also he hath judg'd, or rather	Par Lost 10.494
Mee not, but the brute Serpent in whose shape	Par Lost 10.495
Man I deceav'd: that which to mee belongs,	Par Lost 10.496
Mee and Mankinde; I am to bruise his heel;	Par Lost 10.498
To mee, who with eternal Famin pine,	Par Lost 10.597
Folly to mee, so doth the Prince of Hell	Par Lost 10.621
Of this new glorious World, and mee so late	Par Lost 10.721
Accurst of blessed, hide me from the face	Par Lost 10.723
The evil on him brought by me, will curse	Par Lost 10.734
Mine own that bide upon me, all from mee	Par Lost 10.738
Shall with a fierce reflux on mee redound,	Par Lost 10.739
On mee as on thir natural center light	Par Lost 10.740
To mould me Man, did I sollicite thee	Par Lost 10.744
From darkness to promote me, or here place	Par Lost 10.745
And equal to reduce me to my dust,	Par Lost 10.748
Wherefore didst thou beget me? I sought it not	Par Lost 10.762
Insensible, how glad would lay me down	Par Lost 10.777
To mee and to my ofspring would torment me	Par Lost 10.781
Pursues me still, least all I cannot die,	Par Lost 10.783
All of me then shall die: let this appease	Par Lost 10.792
Both in me, and without me, and so last	Par Lost 10.812
To perpetuitie; Ay me, that fear	Par Lost 10.813
Nor I on my part single, in me all	Par Lost 10.817
Me now your curse! Ah, why should all mankind	Par Lost 10.822
If guiltless? But from me what can proceed,	Par Lost 10.824
1667 'mee'	
With me? how can they then acquitted stand	Par Lost 10.827
And reasonings, though through Mazes, lead me still	Par Lost 10.830
On mee, mee onely, as the sourse and spring	Par Lost 10.832
And horrors hast thou driv'n me; out of which	Par Lost 10.843
To end me? Shall Truth fail to keep her word,	Par Lost 10.856
More to the part sinister from me drawn,	Par Lost 10.886
Forsake me not thus, *Adam*, witness Heav'n	Par Lost 10.914
I beg, and clasp thy knees; bereave me not,	Par Lost 10.918
Whither shall I betake me, where subsist?	Par Lost 10.922
That cruel Serpent: On me exercise not	Par Lost 10.927
On me alreadie lost, mee then thy self	Par Lost 10.929
On me, sole cause to thee of all this woe,	Par Lost 10.935
Mee mee onely just object of his ire.	Par Lost 10.936
To me committed and by me expos'd.	Par Lost 10.957
Fruit of thy Womb: On mee the Curse aslope	Par Lost 10.1053
My labour will sustain me; and least Cold	Par Lost 10.1056
Unskilful with what words to pray, let mee	Par Lost 11.32
1667 'me' in some copies	
Interpret for him, mee his Advocate	Par Lost 11.33
And propitiation, all his works on mee	Par Lost 11.34
Accept me, and in mee from these receave	Par Lost 11.37
To better life shall yeeld him, where with mee	Par Lost 11.42
Made one with me as I with thee am one.	Par Lost 11.44
Bending his eare; perswasion in me grew	Par Lost 11.152
Assures me that the bitterness of death	Par Lost 11.157
To me transgressour, who for thee ordaind	Par Lost 11.164
A help, became thy snare; to mee reproach	Par Lost 11.165
Who highly thus to entitle me voutsaf'st,	Par Lost 11.170
Thee lastly nuptial Bowre, by mee adornd	Par Lost 11.280
This most afflicts me, that departing hence,	Par Lost 11.315
Thou lead'st me, and to the hand of Heav'n submit,	Par Lost 11.372
The burd'n of many Ages, on me light	Par Lost 11.767
Abortive, to torment me ere thir being,	Par Lost 11.769
Of mee and all Mankind; but now I see	Par Lost 12.276
Favour unmerited by me, who sought	Par Lost 12.278
Whether I should repent me now of sin	Par Lost 12.474
By mee done and occasiond, or rejoyce	Par Lost 12.475
By mee encampt on yonder Hill, expect	Par Lost 12.591
1669 'me'	
In mee is no delay; with thee to goe,	Par Lost 12.615
1669 'me'	
Is to go hence unwilling; thou to mee	Par Lost 12.617
I carry hence; though all by mee is lost,	Par Lost 12.621
1669 'me'	
By mee the Promis'd Seed shall all restore.	Par Lost 12.623
1669 'me'	
Lost Paradise deceiv'd by me, though since	Par Reg 1.52
Will waft me; and the way found prosperous once	Par Reg 1.104
Awakn'd in me swarm, while I consider	Par Reg 1.197
To me was pleasing, all my mind was set	Par Reg 1.202
And said to me apart, high are thy thoughts	Par Reg 1.229
Conceiv'd in me a Virgin, he fore-told	Par Reg 1.239
Strait knew me, and with loudest voice proclaim'd	Par Reg 1.275
Me him (for it was shew'n him so from Heaven)	Par Reg 1.276
Me him whose Harbinger he was; and first	Par Reg 1.277
Refus'd on me his Baptism to confer,	Par Reg 1.278
The Spirit descended on me like a Dove,	Par Reg 1.282

Me(*cont*)

Audibly heard from Heav'n, pronounc'd me his,	Par Reg 1.284
Me his beloved Son, in whom alone	Par Reg 1.285
For that to me thou seem'st the man, whom late	Par Reg 1.327
To whom the Son of God. Who brought me hither	Par Reg 1.335
Will bring me hence, no other Guide I seek.	Par Reg 1.336
Why dost thou then suggest to me distrust,	Par Reg 1.355
What can be then less in me then desire	Par Reg 1.383
Men generally think me much a foe	Par Reg 1.387
To all mankind: why should I? they to me	Par Reg 1.388
Envy they say excites me, thus to gain	Par Reg 1.397
This wounds me most (what can it less) that Man,	Par Reg 1.404
And urg'd me hard with doings, which not will	Par Reg 1.469
But misery hath rested from me; where	Par Reg 1.470
But thou art plac't above me, thou art Lord;	Par Reg 1.475
Vertue, who follow not her lore: permit me	Par Reg 1.483
Inspir'd; disdain not such access to me.	Par Reg 1.492
O what avails me now that honour high	Par Reg 2.66
Could be obtain'd to shelter him or me	Par Reg 2.73
The rest commit to me, I shall let pass	Par Reg 2.233
Without this bodies wasting, I content me,	Par Reg 2.256
Mee hungring more to do my Fathers will.	Par Reg 2.259
Tell me if Food were now before thee set,	Par Reg 2.320
When and where likes me best, I can command?	Par Reg 2.382
Not difficult, if thou hearken to me,	Par Reg 2.428
To me is not unknown what hath been done	Par Reg 2.444
And what in me seems wanting, but that I	Par Reg 2.450
Thou neither dost perswade me to seek wealth	Par Reg 3.44
Who sent me, and thereby witness whence I am.	Par Reg 3.107
Of worse torments me then the feeling can.	Par Reg 3.208
Would stand between me and thy Fathers ire,	Par Reg 3.219
Plausible to the world, to me worth naught.	Par Reg 3.393
Will unpredict and fail me of the Throne:	Par Reg 3.395
When that comes think not thou to find me slack	Par Reg 3.398
Luggage of war there shewn me, argument	Par Reg 3.401
To *Israel* then, the same that now to me.	Par Reg 3.413
And with my help thou may'st; to me the power	Par Reg 4.103
And studs of Pearl, to me should'st tell who thirst	Par Reg 4.120
Is not for thee to know, nor me to tell.	Par Reg 4.153
I see all offers made by me how slight	Par Reg 4.155
For giv'n to me, I give to whom I please,	Par Reg 4.164
And worship me as thy superior Lord,	Par Reg 4.167
Easily done, and hold them all of me;	Par Reg 4.168
Thou hast permission on me. It is written	Par Reg 4.175
As offer them to me the Son of God,	Par Reg 4.190
To me my own, on such abhorred pact,	Par Reg 4.191
Get thee behind me; plain thou now appear'st	Par Reg 4.193
To me so fatal, me it most concerns.	Par Reg 4.205
Me naught advantag'd, missing what I aim'd.	Par Reg 4.208
By me propos'd in life contemplative,	Par Reg 4.370
In their conjunction met, give me to spell,	Par Reg 4.385
Directs me in the Starry Rubric set.	Par Reg 4.393
Mee worse then wet thou find'st not; other harm	Par Reg 4.486
Those terrors which thou speak'st of, did me none;	Par Reg 4.487
Mee to thy will; desist, thou art discern'd	Par Reg 4.497
And toil'st in vain, nor me in vain molest.	Par Reg 4.498
For Son of God to me is yet in doubt,	Par Reg 4.501
Relieves me from my task of servile toyl,	Samson 5
Daily in the common Prison else enjoyn'd me,	Samson 6
With day-spring born; here leave me to respire.	Samson 11
Thir Superstition yields me; hence with leave	Samson 15
But rush upon me thronging, and present	Samson 21
Yet stay, let me not rashly call in doubt	Samson 43
Who this high gift of strength committed to me,	Samson 47
In what part lodg'd, how easily bereft me,	Samson 48
God, when he gave me strength, to shew withal	Samson 58
Suffices that to me strength is my bane,	Samson 63
Light the prime work of God to me is extinct,	Samson 70
Of man or worm; the vilest here excel me,	Samson 74
The Sun to me is dark	Samson 86
Thir daily practice to afflict me more.	Samson 114
Sam. Your coming, Friends, revives me, for I learn	Samson 187
How many evils have enclos'd me round;	Samson 194
Yet that which was the worst now least afflicts me,	Samson 195
My Vessel trusted to me from above,	Samson 199
To a deceitful Woman: tell me Friends,	Samson 202
In me, of wisdom nothing more then mean;	Samson 207
These two proportiond ill drove me transverse.	Samson 209
Mee, not my Parents, that I sought to wed,	Samson 220
Sam. That fault I take not on me, but transfer	Samson 241
Singly by me against their Conquerours	Samson 244
Enterd *Judea* seeking mee, who then	Samson 252
The harrass of thir Land, beset me round;	Samson 257
Into thir hands, and they as gladly yield me	Samson 259
Bound with two cords; but cords to me were threds	Samson 261
Sam. Of such examples adde mee to the roul,	Samson 290
Mee easily indeed mine may neglect,	Samson 291
Sam. Ay me, another inward grief awak't,	Samson 330
And such a Son as all Men hail'd me happy;	Samson 354
O wherefore did God grant me my request,	Samson 356
Nothing of all these evils hath befall'n me	Samson 374
The mystery of God giv'n me under pledge	Samson 378
Of *Timna* first betray me, and reveal	Samson 383
The secret wrested from me in her highth	Samson 384
Her spurious first-born; Treason against me?	Samson 391
And amorous reproaches to win from me	Samson 393
She purpos'd to betray me, and (which was worse	Samson 399
She sought to make me Traytor to my self;	Samson 401

Me(*cont*)

To storm me over-watch't, and wearied out,	Samson 405
But foul effeminacy held me yok't	Samson 410
This only hope relieves me, that the strife	Samson 460
With me hath end; all the contest is now	Samson 461
Me overthrown, to enter lists with God,	Samson 463
Of all these boasted Trophies won on me,	Samson 470
Of that sollicitation; let me here,	Samson 488
Of a deceitful Concubine who shore me	Samson 537
Then turn'd me out ridiculous, despoil'd,	Samson 539
Here rather let me drudge and earn my bread,	Samson 573
Consume me, and oft-invocated death	Samson 575
And I perswade me so; why else this strength	Samson 586
Sam. All otherwise to me my thoughts portend,	Samson 590
My hopes all flat, nature within me seems	Samson 595
My griefs not only pain me	Samson 617
Sleep hath forsook and giv'n me o're	Samson 629
He led me on to mightiest deeds	Samson 638
But now hath cast me off as never known,	Samson 641
Left me all helpless with th' irreparable loss	Samson 644
Sam. My Wife, my Traytress, let her not come near me.	Samson 725
Hath led me on desirous to behold	Samson 741
Dal. Yet hear me *Samson;* not that I endeavour	Samson 766
The easier towards me, or thy hatred less.	Samson 772
In me, but incident to all our sex,	Samson 774
To what I did thou shewdst me first the way.	Samson 781
More strength from me, then in thy self was found.	Samson 789
Of fancy, feard lest one day thou wouldst leave me	Samson 794
How to endear, and hold thee to me firmest:	Samson 796
Who tempted me, that nothing was design'd	Samson 801
That made for me, I knew that liberty	Samson 803
Her own transgressions, to upbraid me mine?	Samson 820
I to my self was false e're thou to me,	Samson 824
To raise in me inexpiable hate,	Samson 839
What sieges girt me round, e're I consented;	Samson 846
That wrought with me: thou know'st the Magistrates	Samson 850
Took full possession of me and prevail'd;	Samson 869
Didst thou at first receive me for thy husband?	Samson 883
Being once a wife, for me thou wast to leave	Samson 885
Let me obtain forgiveness of thee, *Samson*,	Samson 909
Afford me place to shew what recompence	Samson 910
With me, where my redoubl'd love and care	Samson 923
With nursing diligence, to me glad office,	Samson 924
That what by me thou hast lost thou least shalt miss.	Samson 927
Nor think me so unwary or accurst	Samson 930
No more on me have power, their force is null'd,	Samson 935
Lov'd, honour'd, fear'd me, thou alone could hate me	Samson 939
Thy Husband, slight me, sell me, and forgo me;	Samson 940
How wouldst thou use me now, blind, and thereby	Samson 941
In perfet thraldom, how again betray me,	Samson 946
Dal. Let me approach at least, and touch thy hand.	Samson 951
Conferr'd upon me, for the piety	Samson 993
Sam. So let her go, God sent her to debase me,	Samson 999
Sam. Or peace or not, alike to me he comes.	Samson 1074
Men call me *Harapha*, oh Soul most surely blest	Samson 1079
That *Kiriathaim* held, thou knowst me now	Samson 1081
Incredible to me, in this displeas'd,	Samson 1084
Har. Dost thou already single me; I thought	Samson 1092
Had brought me to the field where thou art fam'd	Samson 1094
Afford me assassinated and betray'd,	Samson 1109
In fight withstand me single and unarm'd,	Samson 1111
Close-banded durst attaque me, no not sleeping,	Samson 1113
Breaking her Marriage Faith to circumvent me.	Samson 1115
Or rather flight, no great advantage on me;	Samson 1118
Which long shall not with-hold mee from thy head,	Samson 1125
My trust is in the living God who gave me	Samson 1140
Acknowledge them from God inflicted on me	Samson 1170
Sam. Tongue-doubtie Giant, how dost thou prove me these?	Samson 1181
I chose a Wife, which argu'd me no foe;	Samson 1193
Appointed to await me thirty spies,	Samson 1197
To wring from me and tell to them my secret,	Samson 1199
Me their Deliverer sent would not receive,	Samson 1214
But to thir Masters gave me up for nought,	Samson 1215
Had not disabl'd me, not all your force:	Samson 1219
Sam. Cam'st thou for this, vain boaster, to survey me,	Samson 1227
My speediest friend, by death to rid me hence,	Samson 1263
The worst that he can give, to me the best.	Samson 1264
Is hate, not help to me, it may with mine	Samson 1266
Off. *Samson*, to thee our Lords thus bid me say;	Samson 1310
But they must pick me out with shackles tir'd,	Samson 1326
On my refusal to distress me more,	Samson 1330
Can they think me so broken, so debas'd	Samson 1335
The worst of all indignities, yet on me	Samson 1341
Off. My message was impos'd on me with speed,	Samson 1343
Of those who have me in thir civil power.	Samson 1367
But who constrains me to the Temple of *Dagon*,	Samson 1370
Yet that he may dispense with me or thee	Samson 1377
Some rouzing motions in me which dispose	Samson 1382
Because they shall not trail me through thir streets	Samson 1402
To see me girt with Friends; and how the sight	Samson 1415
Of me as of a common Enemy,	Samson 1416
Happ'n what may, of me expect to hear	Samson 1423
The last of me or no I cannot warrant.	Samson 1426
To give ye part with me what hope I have	Samson 1453
And I perswade me God had not permitted	Samson 1495
For dire imagination still persues me.	Samson 1544
To have guided me aright, I know not how,	Samson 1547
Mess. Occasions drew me early to this City,	Samson 1596

Me(*cont*)

Wind me into the easie-hearted man,	Mask 163
My Brothers when they saw me wearied out	Mask 182
To bring me Berries, or such cooling fruit	Mask 186
They left me then, when the gray-hooded Eev'n	Mask 188
line not in Bridgewater ms	
Had stole them from me, els O theevish Night	Mask 195
Prompt me; and they perhaps are not far off.	Mask 229
Canst thou not tell me of a gentle Pair	Mask 236
Tell me but where	Mask 240
Compell'd me to awake the courteous Echo	Mask 275
To give me answer from her mossie Couch.	Mask 276
La. They left me weary on a grassie terf.	Mask 280
What readiest way would bring me to that place?	Mask 305
Eie me blest Providence, and square my triall	Mask 329
Bridgewater ms 'Eye my'	
And tell me it is safe, as bid me hope	Mask 400
Of night, or lonelines it recks me not,	Mask 404
Do ye beleeve me yet, or shall I call	Mask 438
Spir. Ay me unhappy then my fears are true.	Mask 511
I sate me down to watch upon a bank	Mask 543
You gave me Brother? *Eld*. *Bro*. Yes, and keep it still,	Mask 584
Shall be unsaid for me: against the threats	Mask 586
He lov'd me well, and oft would beg me sing,	Mask 623
And shew me simples of a thousand names	Mask 627
But of divine effect, he cull'd me out;	Mask 630
He call'd it *Haemony*, and gave it me,	Mask 638
And bad me keep it as of sovran use	Mask 639
Thou told'st me of? What grim aspects are these,	Mask 694
These oughly-headed Monsters? Mercy guard me!	Mask 695
And wouldst thou seek again to trap me here	Mask 699
line not in Bridgewater ms	
Dips me all o're, as when the wrath of *Jove*	Mask 803
line not in Bridgewater ms	
line not in Trinity ms	
Yet stay, be not disturb'd, now I bethink me,	Mask 820
Brightest Lady look on me,	Mask 910
Mortals that would follow me,	Mask 1018
I doubt me gentle mortalls these may seeme	Mask Tr. ms 10.16
thou man of lies & falshood, if thou give me it	Mask Tr. ms 22.21
Mirth, admit me of thy crue	Allegro 38
Lap me in soft *Lydian* Aires,	Allegro 136
Thus night oft see me in thy pale career,	Penseroso 121
His flaring beams, me Goddes bring	Penseroso 132
Hide me from Day's garish eie,	Penseroso 141
Dissolve me into extasies,	Penseroso 165
Follow me as I sing,	Arcades 86
Follow me,	Arcades 90
Compels me to disturb your season due:	Lycidas 7
Ay me, I fondly dream!	Lycidas 56
Trinity ms 'mee'	
Ay me! Whilst thee the shores, and sounding Seas	Lycidas 154
Trinity ms 'mee'	
Yet can I not perswade me thou art dead	Fair Inf 29
Resolve me then oh Soul most surely blest	Fair Inf 36
Tell me bright Spirit where e're thou hoverest	Fair Inf 38
Oh say me true if thou wert mortal wight	Fair Inf 41
Forsook the hated earth, O tell me sooth	Fair Inf 51
Believe me I have thither packt the worst:	Vacation 12
I pray thee then deny me not thy aide	Vacation 15
But haste thee strait to do me once a Pleasure,	Vacation 17
Me softer airs befit, and softer strings	Passion 27
Befriend me night best Patroness of grief,	Passion 29
To bear me where the Towers of *Salem* stood,	Passion 39
Toward which Time leads me, and the will of Heav'n;	Sonnet 7, 12
When strait a barbarous noise environs me	Sonnet 12, 3
Lodg'd with me useless, though my Soul more bent	Sonnet 19, 4
To day deep thoughts resolve with me to drench	Sonnet 21, 5
Right onward. What supports me dost thou ask?	Sonnet 22, 9
This thought might lead me through the worlds vain mask	Sonnet 22, 13
Brought to me like *Alcestis* from the grave,	Sonnet 23, 2
But O as to embrace me she enclin'd,	Sonnet 23, 13
To whom thou untry'd seem'st fair. Me in my vow'd	Horace 13
I will declare; the Lord to me hath say'd	Psalm 2, 14
This day; ask of me, and the grant is made;	Psalm 2, 16
That in arms against me rise	Psalm 3, 3
And heard me from his holy mount.	Psalm 3, 12
They pitch against me their Pavillions.	Psalm 3, 18
Rise Lord, save me my God for thou	Psalm 3, 19
Answer me when I call	Psalm 4, 1
Thou didst me disinthrall	Psalm 4, 4
Now pity me, and hear my earnest prai'r.	Psalm 4, 6
But Lord, thus let me pray,	Psalm 4, 28
Both lay me down and sleep	Psalm 4, 38
Me safe where ere I lie	Psalm 4, 40
Thou Lord alone in safety mak'st me dwell.	Psalm 4, 42
Lord lead me in thy righteousness	Psalm 5, 21
Lead me because of those	Psalm 5, 22
Lord in thine anger do not reprehend me	Psalm 6, 1
Nor in thy hot displeasure me correct;	Psalm 6, 2
Pity me Lord for I am much deject	Psalm 6, 3
Am very weak and faint; heal and amend me,	Psalm 6, 4
My soul, O save me for thy goodness sake	Psalm 6, 8
Depart from me, for the voice of my weeping	Psalm 6, 17
The Lord will own, and have me in his keeping.	Psalm 6, 20
Save me and secure me under	Psalm 7, 2
Ill to him that meant me peace,	Psalm 7, 10
And wake for me, their furi' asswage;	Psalm 7, 22

Me(*cont*)	
Judge me Lord, be judge in this	Psalm 7, 31
Upon me: cause at length to cease	Psalm 7, 34
Deliver'd were *by me*.	Psalm 81, 24
On me then didst thou call,	Psalm 81, 26
If thou wilt list to mee,	Psalm 81, 36
Mislik'd me for his choice.	Psalm 81, 48
To serve me *all their daies*,	Psalm 81, 54
O hear me *I thee pray*,	Psalm 86, 2
Pitty me Lord for daily thee	Psalm 86, 9
For thou wilt *grant* me *free access*	Psalm 86, 23
Teach me O Lord thy way *most right*,	Psalm 86, 37
For great thy mercy is toward me,	Psalm 86, 45
O God the proud against me rise	Psalm 86, 49
O turn to me *thy face at length*,	Psalm 86, 57
And me have mercy on,	Psalm 86, 58
Some sign of good to me afford,	Psalm 86, 61
Do'st help and comfort me.	Psalm 86, 64
Lord God that dost me save and keep,	Psalm 88, 1
Hast set me *all forlorn*,	Psalm 88, 26
Full sore doth press on me;	Psalm 88, 30
Thou break'st upon me all thy waves,	Psalm 88, 31
And all thy waves break me.	Psalm 88, 32
Thou dost my friends from me estrange,	Psalm 88, 33
And mak'st me odious,	Psalm 88, 34
Me to them odious, *for they change*,	Psalm 88, 35
And hide thy face from me,	Psalm 88, 58
Thy fierce wrath over me doth flow	Psalm 88, 65
Thy threatnings cut me through.	Psalm 88, 66
All day they round about me go,	Psalm 88, 67
Like waves they me persue.	Psalm 88, 68
And sever'd from me far.	Psalm 88, 70
They *fly me now* whom I have lov'd,	Psalm 88, 71
And your ungodly deeds finde me the words.	Prose 8, 2
What Land, what Seat of rest thou bidst me seek,	Prose 12, 4
Mead	
To the tann'd Haycock in the Mead,	Allegro 90
Low in a mead of Kine under a Thorn,	Prose 13, 1
Meadow	
From a fat Meddow ground; or fleecy Flock,	Par Lost 11.648
In Valley or Green Meadow to way-lay	Par Reg 2.185
Low in a mead of Kine under a Thorn,	Prose 13, 1
Meadows	
The Cattel in the Fields and Meddowes green:	Par Lost 7.460
Visits the herds along the twilight meadows,	Mask 844
Trinity ms 'meadows' ←'medows'	
Bridgewater ms 'meadowes'	
Meadows trim with Daisies pide,	Allegro 75
Meads	
His thirty Armes along the indented Meads,	Vacation 94
Meager	
Whom thus the meager Shadow answerd soon.	Par Lost 10.264
Meagre	
Blew meager Hag, or stubborn unlaid ghost,	Mask 434
Bridgewater ms 'meagar'	
Trinity ms 'meager' ←'wrincl'd' ←'wrinckled'	
Mean	
All Heav'n, what this might mean, and whither tend	Par Lost 3.272
I mean of Taste, Sight, Smell, Herbs, Fruits, and Flours,	Par Lost 8.527
What may this mean? Language of Man pronounc't	Par Lost 9.553
But say, what mean those colourd streaks in Heavn,	Par Lost 11.879
By fallacy surpriz'd. But first I mean	Par Reg 1.155
And with him talkt, and with him lodg'd, I mean	Par Reg 2.6
I must deliver, if I mean to raign	Par Reg 3.404
Nor what I part with mean to give for naught;	Par Reg 4.161
I mean to shew you of my strength, yet greater;	Samson 1644
Unless the strength of Heav'n, if you mean that?	Mask 417
Bridgewater ms 'meane'	
1637 'meane'	
Trinity ms 'meane'	
Eld. Bro. I mean that too, but yet a hidden strength	Mask 418
Bridgewater ms 'meane'	
1637 'meane'	
Trinity ms 'meane'	
Mirth with thee, I mean to live.	Allegro 152
Licence they mean when they cry libertie;	Sonnet 12, 11
Trinity ms 'meane' ←'mean'	
Of Brittish *Themis*, with no mean applause	Sonnet 21, 2
line not in Trinity ms	
Mean	
Directed, no mean recompence it brings	Par Lost 2.981
As great might have aspir'd, and me though mean	Par Lost 4.62
Too mean pretense, but what we more affect,	Par Lost 6.421
Mean, or in her summd up, in her containd	Par Lost 8.473
The skill of Artifice or Office mean,	Par Lost 9.39
Not of mean suiters, nor important less	Par Lost 11.9
In mean estate live moderate, till grown	Par Lost 12.351
In me, of wisdom nothing more then mean;	Samson 207
To that same lot, however mean, or high,	Sonnet 7, 11
Trinity ms 'meane'	
Mean	
To yonder Gates? through them I mean to pass,	Par Lost 2.684
Ask riddance, if we mean to tread with ease;	Par Lost 4.632
We mean to hold what anciently we claim	Par Lost 5.723
I mean to try, whose Reason I have tri'd	Par Lost 6.120
The strife of Glorie: which we mean to win,	Par Lost 6.290
Mean I to trie, what rash untri'd I sought,	Par Lost 9.860
Why hee should mean me ill, or seek to harme.	Par Lost 9.1152
Meander	
By slow *Meander's* margent green,	Mask 232
Trinity ms 'Maeanders'	
Bridgewater ms 'Meanders'	
B.M. ms 'Meanders'	
Meaner	
Disdain'd, but meaner thoughts learnd in thir flight,	Par Lost 6.367
Meanest	
To worst abuse, or to thir meanest use.	Par Lost 4.204
None of the meanest, some great Potentate	Par Lost 11.231
Ruling them by perswasion as thou mean'st,	Par Reg 4.230
Meaning	
The meaning, not the Name I call: for thou	Par Lost 7.5
Since to each meaning savour me apply,	Par Lost 9.1019
In what degree or meaning thou art call'd	Par Reg 4.516
And Love hath oft, well meaning, wrought much wo,	Samson 813
But your ill-meaning Politician Lords,	Samson 1195
There was another meaning in these gifts,	Mask 754
line not in Bridgewater ms	
Meanly	
All meanly wrapt in the rude manger lies;	Nativity 31
Means	
Great acts require great means of enterprise,	Par Reg 2.412
It may by means far different be attain'd	Par Reg 3.89
Which to have come to pass by means of thee,	Samson 444
To prosecute the means of thy deliverance	Samson 603
Means her provision onely to the good	Mask 765
Trinity ms 'means' ←'intends'	
Som other means I have which may be us'd,	Mask 821
1637 'meanes'	
Trinity ms 'some other meanes I have' ←'there is another way'	
Bridgewater ms 'meanes'	
Both spirituall powre and civill, what each meanes	Sonnet 17, 10
1694 'means'	
What powre the Church & what the civill meanes	Sonnet 17, Tr. ms 45.11
Means	
And out of good still to find means of evil;	Par Lost 1.165
And shall grace not find means, that finds her way,	Par Lost 3.228
And teach us further by what means to shun	Par Lost 10.1062
The Serpent, by what means he shall achieve	Par Lost 12.234
1667 'meanes'	
Forbidd'n knowledge by forbidd'n means.	Par Lost 12.279
In all things, and all men, supposes means,	Par Reg 3.355
Without means us'd, what it predicts revokes.	Par Reg 3.356
Means I must use thou say'st, prediction else	Par Reg 3.394
Means there shall be to this, but what the means,	Par Reg 4.152
The time and means: each act is rightliest done,	Par Reg 4.475
He would not else who never wanted means,	Samson 315
Reject not then what offerd means, who knows	Samson 516
Effeminatly vanquish't? by which means,	Samson 562
As her at *Timna*, sought by all means therefore	Samson 795
But now I find it true; for by this means	Mask 644
Trinity ms 'meanes'	
Bridgewater ms 'meanes'	
Meant	
Each Stair mysteriously was meant, nor stood	Par Lost 3.516
What meant that caution joind, *if ye be found*	Par Lost 5.513
His Thunder in mid Volie, for he meant	Par Lost 6.854
Meant mee, by ventring higher then my Lot.	Par Lost 9.690
As in thir crime. Thus was th' applause they meant,	Par Lost 10.545
Be meant, whom I conjecture, our grand Foe	Par Lost 10.1033
Was meant by Death that day, when lo, to thee	Par Lost 10.1050
Is meant thy great deliverer, who shall bruise	Par Lost 12.149
A perfect Dove descend, what e're it meant,	Par Reg 1.83
His Father's business; what he meant I mus'd,	Par Reg 2.99
Ye were the two she mean't, with that I sprung	Mask 578
Trinity ms 'meant'	
Bridgewater ms 'meant'	
Yea even that which mischief meant most harm,	Mask 591
Trinity ms 'ment'	
As if she would her children should be riotous	Mask 763
Trinity ms 'would' ←'ment'	
Where more is meant then meets the ear.	Penseroso 120
Was all in honour and devotion ment	Arcades 35
Ill to him that meant me peace,	Psalm 7, 10
Meanwhile	
Mean while the winged Haralds by command	Par Lost 1.752
ms defective here	
Mean while the Adversary of God and Man,	Par Lost 2.629
A growing burden. Mean while Warr arose,	Par Lost 2.767
Thenceforth shall be for ever shut. Mean while	Par Lost 3.333
Mean while upon the firm opacous Globe	Par Lost 3.418
Luxuriant; mean while murmuring waters fall	Par Lost 4.260
Mean while in utmost Longitude, where Heav'n	Par Lost 4.539
Mean while, as Nature wills, Night bids us rest.	Par Lost 4.633
Mean while our Primitive great Sire, to meet	Par Lost 5.350
As from the Mine. Mean while at Table *Eve*	Par Lost 5.443
Whose progenie you are. Mean while enjoy	Par Lost 5.503
Mean while th' Eternal eye, whose sight discernes	Par Lost 5.711
Yet Chains in Hell, not Realms expect: mean while	Par Lost 6.186
If not to reign: mean while thy utmost force,	Par Lost 6.293
Mean while in other parts like deeds deservd	Par Lost 6.354
Effect shall end our wish. Mean while revive;	Par Lost 6.493
Mean while inhabit laxe, ye Powers of Heav'n,	Par Lost 7.162
So sang the Hierarchies: Mean while the Son	Par Lost 7.192
Mean while the tepid Caves, and Fens and shoares	Par Lost 7.417
Mean while the hour of Noon drew on, and wak'd	Par Lost 9.739

Meanwhile(*cont*)
1667 'Meanwhile'
Meanwhile the hainous and despightfull act — Par Lost 10.1
Meanwhile ere thus was sin'd and judg'd on Earth, — Par Lost 10.229
Mean while in Paradise the hellish pair — Par Lost 10.585
Of *Hermes*, or his opiate Rod. Mean while — Par Lost 11.133
Meanwhile the Southwind rose, and with black wings — Par Lost 11.738
Meanwhile they in thir earthly *Canaan* plac't — Par Lost 12.315
Mean while the Son of God, who yet some days — Par Reg 1.183
Mean while the new-baptiz'd, who yet remain'd — Par Reg 2.1
Mean while the men of *Judah* to prevent — Samson 256
Thou must not in the mean while here forgot — Samson 479
By ransom or how else: mean while be calm, — Samson 604
Mean while welcom Joy, and Feast, — Mask 102
1637 'Meane while'
Trinity ms 'meane while'
Bridgewater ms 'meane-while'
Mean while the Rural ditties were not mute, — Lycidas 32
Trinity ms 'meane while'

Measure
His own and *Rhea*'s Son like measure found; — Par Lost 1.513
Love without end, and without measure Grace, — Par Lost 3.142
Full to the utmost measure of what bliss — Par Lost 5.517
Of surfet where full measure onely bounds — Par Lost 5.639
line not in 1667 edition
Though heaviest by just measure on thy self — Par Lost 6.265
They measure all, of other excellence — Par Lost 6.821
In measure what the mind may well contain, — Par Lost 7.128
Thy power; what thought can measure thee or tongue — Par Lost 7.603
Aught, not surpassing human measure, say. — Par Lost 7.640
Misgave him; hee the faultring measure felt; — Par Lost 9.846
Measure of strength so great to mortal seed, — Samson 1439
It shall be still in strictest measure eev'n, — Sonnet 7, 10
To measure life, learn thou betimes, and know — Sonnet 21, 9

Measured
Now had night measur'd with her shaddowie Cone — Par Lost 4.776
Measur'd by Cubit, length, and breadth, and highth, — Par Lost 11.730
Measur'd this transient World, the Race of time, — Par Lost 12.554
Had measur'd twice six years, at our great Feast — Par Reg 1.210
By voice or hand, and various-measur'd verse, — Par Reg 4.256
And the low world in measur'd motion draw — Arcades 71
Harry whose tuneful and well measur'd Song — Sonnet 13, 1
Trinity ms 'well-measur'd'

Measures
Nine times the Space that measures Day and Night — Par Lost 1.50
To motion, measures all things durable — Par Lost 5.581
Burst forth, and in Celestial measures mov'd, — Par Reg 1.170
Whilst the Lantskip round it measures, — Allegro 70

Measuring
Thus measuring things in Heav'n by things on Earth — Par Lost 6.893

Meat
With Honey *for their Meat*. — Psalm 81, 68

Meaths
She crushes, inoffensive moust, and meathes — Par Lost 5.345

Meats
Thus when with meats and drinks they had suffic'd, — Par Lost 5.451
In Meats and Drinks, which on the Earth shall bring — Par Lost 11.473
Of meats and drinks, Natures refreshment sweet; — Par Reg 2.265
Meats by the Law unclean, or offer'd first — Par Reg 2.328
With dishes pil'd, and meats of noblest sort — Par Reg 2.341

Medal
Compar'd with aught on Earth, Medal or Stone; — Par Lost 3.592

Meddling
That the shrewd medling Elfe delights to make, — Mask 846
Bridgewater ms 'medlinge'

Medes
In *Habor*, and among the *Medes* dispers't, — Par Reg 3.376

Media
From *Media* post to *Aegypt*, there fast bound. — Par Lost 4.171
Of *Adiabene*, *Media*, and the South — Par Reg 3.320

Mediation
His dearest mediation thus renewd. — Par Lost 3.226

Mediator
Mans Friend, his Mediator, his design'd — Par Lost 10.60
Without Mediator, whose high Office now — Par Lost 12.240

Medicinal
Or medcinal liquor can asswage, — Samson 627
And yet more med'cinal is it then that *Moly* — Mask 636
Trinity ms 'med'cinall'
line not in Bridgewater ms
1637 'med'cinall'

Meditate
To meditate my rural minstrelsie, — Mask 547
1673 'meditate upon'
And strictly meditate the thankles Muse, — Lycidas 66

Meditated
In meditated fraud and malice, bent — Par Lost 9.55

Meditation
With meditation on the happie end. — Par Lost 12.605
That musing meditation most affects — Mask 386
Bridgewater ms 'meditacion'
My meditation waigh — Psalm 5, 2

Meditations
His holy Meditations thus persu'd. — Par Reg 1.195
Sole but with holiest Meditations fed, — Par Reg 2.110

Medusa
Medusa with *Gorgonian* terror guards — Par Lost 2.611

Medway
Or *Medway* smooth, or Royal Towred *Thame*. — Vacation 100

Meed
Without the meed of som melodious tear. — Lycidas 14
Of so much fame in Heav'n expect thy meed. — Lycidas 84

Meek
His words here ended, but his meek aspect — Par Lost 3.266
And meek surrender, half imbracing lean'd — Par Lost 4.494
Yet with submiss approach and reverence meek, — Par Lost 5.359
To whom thus *Raphael* answer'd heav'nly meek. — Par Lost 8.217
Of sorrow unfeign'd, and humiliation meek. — Par Lost 10.1092
Of sorrow unfeign'd, and humiliation meek. — Par Lost 10.1104
To whom thus *Eve* with sad demeanour meek. — Par Lost 11.162
More meek came with the Firstlings of his Flock — Par Lost 11.437
To that meek man, who well had sacrific'd; — Par Lost 11.451
By simply meek; that suffering for Truths sake — Par Lost 12.569
To meek submission: thou at season fit — Par Lost 12.597
From that placid aspect and meek regard, — Par Reg 3.217
Our Saviour meek and with untroubl'd mind — Par Reg 4.401
Thus they the Son of God our Saviour meek — Par Reg 4.636
Soft, modest, meek, demure, — Samson 1036
In the blest Kingdoms meek of joy and love. — Lycidas 177
line not in 1638 edition
The good and meek of heart — Psalm 4, 15

Meek-eyed
Sent down the meek-eyd Peace, — Nativity 46
1673 'meek-ey'd'

Meekly
Meekly compos'd awaited the fulfilling: — Par Reg 2.108
Then lies him meekly down fast by his Brethrens side. — Passion 21
Meekly thou didst resign this earthy load — Sonnet 14, 3

Meet
Against the Torturer; when to meet the noise — Par Lost 2.64
To meet so great a foe: and now great deeds — Par Lost 2.722
Undaunted to meet there what ever power — Par Lost 2.955
A chance but chance may lead where I may meet — Par Lost 4.530
Which thou incurr'st by flying, meet thy flight — Par Lost 4.913
Mean while our Primitive great Sire, to meet — Par Lost 5.350
And in fierce hosting meet, who wont to meet — Par Lost 6.93
Weapons more violent, when next we meet, — Par Lost 6.439
To meet him all his Saints, who silent stood — Par Lost 6.882
Not Words alone pleas'd her. O when meet now — Par Lost 8.57
From the Suns beam meet Night, her other part — Par Lost 8.139
Who meet with various objects, from the sense — Par Lost 8.609
Since Reason not impossibly may meet — Par Lost 9.360
And forth to meet her went, the way she took — Par Lost 9.847
Either to meet no danger, or to finde — Par Lost 9.1176
Where art thou *Adam*, wont with joy to meet — Par Lost 10.103
Met who to meet him came, his Ofspring dear. — Par Lost 10.349
There best, where most with ravin I may meet; — Par Lost 10.599
To deathless pain? how gladly would I meet — Par Lost 10.775
Shall meet, alreadie linkt and Wedlock-bound — Par Lost 10.905
With reverence I must meet, and thou retire. — Par Lost 11.237
Clad to meet Man; over his lucid Armes — Par Lost 11.240
Made answer meet, that made void all his wiles. — Par Reg 3.442
Or they with thee hold conversation meet? — Par Reg 4.232
I only with an Oak'n staff will meet thee, — Samson 1123
To meet the rudenesse, and swill'd insolence — Mask 178
Bridgewater ms 'meete'
And run to meet what he would most avoid? — Mask 363
line not in Bridgewater ms
line not in Trinity ms
Stole under Seas to meet his *Arethuse;* — Arcades 31
in high misterious happie spousall meet — Musick Tr. ms 4.06
Quickly found a lover meet; — Winchester 16
Where shall we sometimes meet, and by the fire — Sonnet 20, 3
All beasts that in the field or forrest meet, — Psalm 8, 20

Meet
Attonement for himself or offering meet, — Par Lost 3.234
That both in him and all things, as is meet, — Par Lost 3.675
To see how thou could'st judge of fit and meet: — Par Lost 8.448
Internal Man, is but proportion meet, — Par Lost 9.711
As meet is, after such delicious Fare; — Par Lost 9.1028
By pleasure, though to Nature seeming meet, — Par Lost 11.604

Meetest
Moon, that now meetst the orient Sun, now fli'st — Par Lost 5.175

Meeting
Of midnight march, and hurried meeting here, — Par Lost 5.778
Great joy was at thir meeting, and at sight — Par Lost 10.350
To over-reach, but with the Serpent meeting — Par Lost 10.879
Then meeting joyn'd thir tribute to the Sea: — Par Reg 3.258
Such as the meeting soul may pierce — Allegro 138

Meets
Audacious, but that seat soon failing, meets — Par Lost 2.931
Meets his approach, and to the heart inspires — Par Lost 4.154
With Earth and Ocean meets, the setting Sun — Par Lost 4.540
Our circuit meets full West. As flame they part — Par Lost 4.784
As one who loves, and some unkindness meets, — Par Lost 9.271
Far worse, her false resemblance only meets, — Par Reg 4.320
Where more is meant then meets the ear. — Penseroso 120

Megaera
That curld *Megaera:* greedily they pluck'd — Par Lost 10.560

Melancholy
Daemoniac Phrenzie, moaping Melancholie — Par Lost 11.485
line not in 1667 edition
A melancholly damp of cold and dry — Par Lost 11.544
Wrapt in a pleasing fit of melancholy — Mask 546
Bridgewater ms 'melencholy'

Melancholy(*cont*)
And setlings of a melancholy blood; Mask 810
Bridgewater ms 'mellancholy'
Hence loathed Melancholy Allegro 1
Hail divinest Melancholy, Penseroso 12
Most musicall, most melancholy! Penseroso 62
1673 'Melancholy'
These pleasures *Melancholy* give, Penseroso 175
Melesigenes
Blind *Melesigenes* thence *Homer* call'd, Par Reg 4.259
Meliboean
Livelier then *Meliboean*, or the graine Par Lost 11.242
Meliboeus
Which once of *Meliboeus* old I learnt Mask 822
Trinity ms 'Melibaeus'
Bridgewater ms 'Millebeus'
Melind
Mombaza, and *Quiloa*, and *Melind*, Par Lost 11.399
Mellifluous
We brush mellifluous Dewes, and find the ground Par Lost 5.429
Mellifluous streams that water'd all the schools Par Reg 4.277
Mellowing
Shatter your leaves before the mellowing year. Lycidas 5
Melodious
Melodious part, such concord is in Heav'n. Par Lost 3.371
Melodious murmurs, warbling tune his praise. Par Lost 5.196
Melodious Hymns about the sovran Throne Par Lost 5.656
Of Instruments that made melodious chime Par Lost 11.559
Without the meed of som melodious tear. Lycidas 14
Move in melodious time; Nativity 129
Are held with his melodious harmonie Vacation 51
May rightly answer that melodious noise; Musick 18
Melody
Walks, and the melodie of Birds; but here Par Lost 8.528
Melt
Melt, as I doe, yet public reason just, Par Lost 4.389
The clasping charm, and thaw the numming spell, Mask 853
Trinity ms 'thaw the numming' ←'melt each' ←'secret holding'
Look homeward Angel now, and melt with ruth. Lycidas 163
And leprous sin will melt from earthly mould, Nativity 138
Melted
Had melted (whether found where casual fire Par Lost 11.566
Melting
The melting voice through mazes running; Allegro 142
Member
Distinguishable in member, joynt, or limb, Par Lost 2.668
Membrane
Of membrane, joynt, or limb, exclusive barrs: Par Lost 8.625
Memnon
Prince *Memnons* sister might beseem, Penseroso 18
Memnonian
From *Susa* his *Memnonian* Palace high Par Lost 10.308
Memorable
Poor *Socrates* (who next more memorable2) Par Reg 3.96
It hath brought forth to make thee memorable Samson 956
Memorial
Be no memorial blotted out and ras'd Par Lost 1.362
ms 'memoriall'
Memorial, where the might of *Gabriel* fought, Par Lost 6.355
Worthy of Memorial) canst thou not remember Par Reg 2.445
Memorials
Holy Memorials, acts of Zeale and Love Par Lost 5.593
Memory
That slumberd, wakes the bitter memorie Par Lost 4.24
Canceld from Heav'n and sacred memorie, Par Lost 6.379
Before his memorie, as one whose drouth Par Lost 7.66
1669 'memory'
And what before thy memorie was don Par Lost 7.637
With grateful Memorie: thou to mankind Par Lost 8.650
Home to my Brest, and to my memorie Par Lost 11.154
Of lustre from the brook, in memorie, Par Lost 11.325
In foraign Lands thir memorie be lost Par Lost 12.46
And from his memory inflame thir breasts Samson 1739
Begin to throng into my memory Mask 206
Trinity ms 'memorie'
line not in Bridgewater ms
1637 'memorie'
Dear son of memory, great heir of Fame, Shakespear 5
1632 'Memory'
1640 'Memory'
1663-4 '*Memory*'
Be lost in memory. Psalm 83, 16
Memphian
Busiris and his *Memphian* Chivalry, Par Lost 1.307
ms 'Memphian'
Of *Babel*, and the works of *Memphian* Kings Par Lost 1.694
ms 'Memphian'
In *Memphian* Grove, or Green, Nativity 214
Men
And justifie the wayes of God to men. Par Lost 1.26
ms 'Men'
To mortal men, he with his horrid crew Par Lost 1.51
Deeming some Island, oft, as Sea-men tell, Par Lost 1.205
ms 'Seamen'
Upon the wing, as when men wont to watch Par Lost 1.332
Then were they known to men by various Names, Par Lost 1.374
Men also, and by his suggestion taught, Par Lost 1.685

Men(*cont*)
Men call'd him *Mulciber;* and how he fell Par Lost 1.740
Sea-faring men orewatcht, whose Bark by chance Par Lost 2.288
Loose all her virtue; least bad men should boast Par Lost 2.483
O shame to men! Devil with Devil damn'd Par Lost 2.496
Firm concord holds, men onely disagree Par Lost 2.497
Surrounds me, from the chearful wayes of men Par Lost 3.46
To mortal men, above which only shon Par Lost 3.268
And be thy self Man among men on Earth, Par Lost 3.283
As in him perish all men, so in thee Par Lost 3.287
Bad men and Angels, they arraignd shall sink Par Lost 3.331
Hail Son of God, Saviour of Men, thy Name Par Lost 3.412
With vanity had filld the works of men: Par Lost 3.447
Naught seeking but the praise of men, here find Par Lost 3.453
Created this new happie Race of Men Par Lost 3.679
Came furious down to be reveng'd on men, Par Lost 4.4
Whence true autoritie in men; though both Par Lost 4.295
Adam the goodliest man of men since borne Par Lost 4.323
Grip't in each paw: When *Adam* first of men Par Lost 4.408
Labour and rest, as day and night to men Par Lost 4.613
Shine not in vain, nor think, though men were none, Par Lost 4.675
By thee adulterous lust was driv'n from men Par Lost 4.753
For God's, yet able to make Gods of Men: Par Lost 5.70
And why not Gods of Men, since good, the more Par Lost 5.71
To proper substance; time may come when men Par Lost 5.493
High matter thou injoinst me, O prime of men, Par Lost 5.563
That Structure in the Dialect of men Par Lost 5.761
Seek not the praise of men: the other sort Par Lost 6.376
Like instrument to plague the Sons of men Par Lost 6.505
Of men innumerable, there to dwell, Par Lost 7.156
To future men, and in thir dwellings peace: Par Lost 7.183
To visit oft the dwellings of just Men Par Lost 7.570
Thir seasons: among these the seat of men, Par Lost 7.623
Thir pleasant dwelling place. Thrice happie men, Par Lost 7.625
And sons of men, whom God hath thus advanc't, Par Lost 7.626
Nor are thy lips ungraceful, Sire of men, Par Lost 8.218
First Man, of Men innumerable ordain'd Par Lost 8.297
Still hanging incorruptible, till men Par Lost 9.622
With Men as Angels without Feminine, Par Lost 10.893
With sinfulness of Men; thereby to learn Par Lost 11.360
Shall bring on men. Immediately a place Par Lost 11.477
Just men they seemd, and all thir study bent Par Lost 11.577
Freedom and Peace to men: they on the Plain Par Lost 11.580
The Men though grave, ey'd them, and let thir eyes Par Lost 11.585
To these that sober Race of Men, whose lives Par Lost 11.621
Cities of Men with lofty Gates and Towrs, Par Lost 11.640
Grey-headed men and grave, with Warriours mixt, Par Lost 11.662
Deaths Ministers, not Men, who thus deal Death Par Lost 11.676
Inhumanly to men, and multiply Par Lost 11.677
Make they but of thir Brethren, men of men? Par Lost 11.680
Such were these Giants, men of high renown; Par Lost 11.688
Destroyers rightlier call'd and Plagues of men. Par Lost 11.697
By Men who there frequent, or therein dwell. Par Lost 11.838
This second sours of Men, while yet but few; Par Lost 12.13
Hunting (and Men not Beasts shall be his game) Par Lost 12.30
But God who oft descends to visit men Par Lost 12.48
By his donation; but Man over men Par Lost 12.69
That Son, who on the quiet state of men Par Lost 12.80
Bred up in Idol-worship; O that men Par Lost 12.115
Establisht, such delight hath God in Men Par Lost 12.245
The holy One with mortal Men to dwell: Par Lost 12.248
Men who attend the Altar, and should most Par Lost 12.354
To his Disciples, Men who in his Life Par Lost 12.438
To God more glory, more good will to Men Par Lost 12.477
To good malignant, to bad men benigne, Par Lost 12.538
How many Ages, as the years of men, Par Reg 1.48
This man of men, attested Son of God, Par Reg 1.122
With man or mens affairs, how I begin Par Reg 1.132
They now, and men hereafter may discern, Par Reg 1.164
To earn Salvation for the Sons of men. Par Reg 1.167
With solitude, till far from track of men, Par Reg 1.191
Though men esteem thee low of Parentage, Par Reg 1.235
All Heaven and Earth, Angels and Sons of men, Par Reg 1.237
Guided the Wise Men thither from the East, Par Reg 1.250
So far from path or road of men, who pass Par Reg 1.322
Men to much misery and hardship born; Par Reg 1.341
Men generally think me much a foe Par Reg 1.387
To all truth requisite for men to know. Par Reg 1.464
Her dictates from thy mouth? most men admire Par Reg 1.482
Plain Fishermen, no greater men them call, Par Reg 2.27
Then when I dealt with *Adam* first of Men, Par Reg 2.133
Among daughters of men the fairest found; Par Reg 2.154
Cast wanton eyes on the daughters of men, Par Reg 2.180
Delight not all; among the Sons of Men, Par Reg 2.192
Rocks whereon greatest men have oftest wreck'd; Par Reg 2.228
But men endu'd with these have oft attain'd Par Reg 2.437
For I esteem those names of men so poor Par Reg 2.447
Cities of men, or head-strong Multitudes, Par Reg 2.470
To things not glorious, men not worthy of fame. Par Reg 3.70
Till Conquerour Death discover them scarce men, Par Reg 3.85
Shall I seek glory then, as vain men seek Par Reg 3.105
Glory from men, from all men good or bad, Par Reg 3.114
In all things, and all men, supposes means, Par Reg 3.355
That screen'd the fruits of the earth and seats of men Par Reg 4.30
Of fighting beasts, and men to beasts expos'd, Par Reg 4.140
Though Sons of God both Angels are and Men, Par Reg 4.197
What both from Men and Angels I receive, Par Reg 4.200
Wisest of men; from whose mouth issu'd forth Par Reg 4.276

Men(*cont*)
Wise men have said are wearisom; who reads Par Reg 4.322
Where God is prais'd aright, and Godlike men, Par Reg 4.348
As men divinely taught, and better teaching Par Reg 4.357
Like turbulencies in the affairs of men, Par Reg 4.462
Of men at thee, for only thou here dwell'st. Par Reg 4.466
All men are Sons of God; yet thee I thought Par Reg 4.520
(Which Men enjoying sight oft without cause complain) Samson 157
Strongest of mortal men, Samson 168
Chor. Tax not divine disposal, wisest Men Samson 210
Yet truth to say, I oft have heard men wonder Samson 215
Mean while the men of *Judah* to prevent Samson 256
And justifiable to Men; Samson 294
Man. Brethren and men of *Dan*, for such ye seem, Samson 332
And such a Son as all Men hail'd me happy; Samson 354
The miracle of men: then in an hour Samson 364
At times when men seek most repose and rest, Samson 406
Secrets of men, the secrets of a friend, Samson 492
Or taste that cheers the heart of Gods and men, Samson 545
Nor do I name of men the common rout, Samson 674
That wisest and best men full oft beguil'd Samson 759
Thine forgive mine; that men may censure thine Samson 787
Which might have aw'd the best resolv'd of men, Samson 847
Of wisest men; that to the public good Samson 867
Of men conspiring to uphold thir state Samson 892
Dal. In argument with men a woman ever Samson 903
Eye-sight exposes daily men abroad. Samson 919
If in my flower of youth and strength, when all men Samson 938
(Which way soever men refer it) Samson 1015
What e're it be, to wisest men and best Samson 1034
Men call me *Harapha*, of stock renown'd Samson 1079
Notorious murder on those thirty men Samson 1186
To the Spirits of just men long opprest! Samson 1269
The brute and boist'rous force of violent men Samson 1273
Above the Sons of men; but sight bereav'd Samson 1294
(So mutable are all the ways of men) Samson 1407
So fond are mortal men Samson 1682
Which men call Earth, and with low-thoughted care Mask 6
And airy tongues, that syllable mens names Mask 208
line not in Bridgewater ms
Trinity ms 'syllable mens nams' ← 'lure night wanderers'
Far from the cheerfull haunt of men, and herds, Mask 388
The frivolous bolt of *Cupid*, gods and men Mask 445
Which erring men call Chance, this I hold firm, Mask 588
But such as are good men can give good things, Mask 703
Co. O foolishnes of men! that lend their ears Mask 706
And by men, heart-easing Mirth, Allegro 13
And the busie humm of men, Allegro 118
On which the fate of gods and men is wound. Arcades 67
Will down return to men, Nativity 142
Thereby to set the hearts of men on fire Fair Inf 62
Rest that gives all men life, gave him his death, Another 11
1640, 1657 'us'
Cromwell, our cheif of men, who through a cloud Sonnet 16, 1
1694 'Men'
Men whose Life, Learning, Faith and pure intent Forcers 9
Nor sinners in th' assembly of just men. Psalm 1, 14
And the way of bad men to ruine must. Psalm 1, 16
Of men abhor'd Psalm 3, 22
Fools or mad men stand not within thy sight. Psalm 5, 12
Of evil men the wickedness Psalm 7, 35
Of wicked men the low estate Psalm 82, 15
But ye shall die like men, and fall Psalm 82, 23
Look down *on mortal men*. Psalm 85, 48
And violent men are met Psalm 86, 50
This is true Liberty when free born men Prose 9, 1

Menace
Feirce signe of battail make, and menace high, Mask 654

Menaced
Were it I thought Death menac't would ensue Par Lost 9.977

Mends
Mends not her slowest pace for prayers or cries. Par Lost 10.859

Mental
Eevn to the inmost seat of mental sight, Par Lost 11.418

Mention
Then sweet, now sad to mention, through dire change Par Lost 2.820
Useful, whence haply mention may arise Par Lost 8.200
For much more willingly I mention Air, Par Reg 1.45
But tender all their power? nor mention I Par Reg 2.327
By patience, temperance; I mention still Par Reg 3.92
With mention of that name renews th' assault. Samson 331
Will not dare mention, lest a question rise Samson 1254
I mention Egypt, *where proud Kings* Psalm 87, 11
I mention Babel to my friends, Psalm 87, 13

Mentioned
No more mention'd then of violence Par Lost 10.1041
That what I motion'd was of God; I knew Samson 222
1671 printed 'mention'd', errata 'motion'd'
With malediction mention'd, and the blot Samson 978

Merchants
Of *Ternate* and *Tidore*, whence Merchants bring Par Lost 2.639

Mercies
For his mercies ay endure, Psalm 136, 3 etc.
But I will in thy mercies dear Psalm 5, 17
Thy numerous mercies go Psalm 5, 18

Merciful
Mercifull over all his works, with good Par Lost 12.565
1667 'Merciful'

Merciful(*cont*)
Most mercifull, most true. Psalm 86, 56

Mercury
That *Hermes* once to wise *Ulysses* gave; Mask 637
Trinity ms 'Hermes once' ← 'Mercury'
As *Mercury* did first devise Mask 963
Bridgewater ms 'Mercurie'
Trinity ms 'Mercury' ← 'Hermes'

Mercy
Infinite goodness, grace and mercy shewn Par Lost 1.218
The other none: in Mercy and Justice both, Par Lost 3.132
But Mercy first and last shall brightest shine. Par Lost 3.134
And none but such from mercy I exclude. Par Lost 3.202
Father of Mercie and Grace, thou didst not doome Par Lost 3.401
Of Mercy and Justice in thy face discern'd, Par Lost 3.407
Mercie collegue with Justice, sending thee Par Lost 10.59
Justice with Mercie, as may illustrate most Par Lost 10.78
What else but favor, grace, and mercie shon? Par Lost 10.1096
Remembring mercie, and his Cov'nant sworn Par Lost 12.346
Him who imploring mercy sues for life, Samson 512
Mercy of Heav'n what hideous noise was that! Samson 1509
These oughly-headed Monsters? Mercy guard me! Mask 695
Trinity ms 'mercie'
Bridgewater ms 'Mercie'
1637 'Mercie'
And Mercy set between, Nativity 144
1673 'Mercy will sit between'
Or wert thou that sweet smiling Youth! Fair Inf 53
'thou Mercy that' common conjectural emendation
To us thy mercy shew Psalm 85, 26
Mercy and Truth *that long were miss'd* Psalm 85, 41
Art full of mercy, thou *alone* Psalm 86, 15
For great thy mercy is toward me, Psalm 86, 45
And me have mercy on, Psalm 86, 58

Mercy-seat
Praying, for from the Mercie-seat above Par Lost 11.2
A Mercie-seat of Gold between the wings Par Lost 12.253

Mere
With shews instead, meer shews of seeming pure, Par Lost 4.316
Meer Serpent in appearance, forth was come, Par Lost 9.413
Privation meer of light and absent day. Par Reg 4.400
To the utmost of meer man both wise and good, Par Reg 4.535
This is meer moral babble, and direct Mask 807
Bridgewater ms 'meere'
1637 'meere'
Trinity ms 'meere moral bable' ← 'your morall stuffe' ← 'meere morall stuffe'
Taught ye by meer *A. S.* and *Rotherford*? Forcers 8

Merely
Not meerly titular, since by Decree Par Lost 5.774
Diurnal) meerly to officiate light Par Lost 8.22
And meerly mortal dross; On Time 6
Meerly to drive the time away he sickn'd, Another 15
line not in 1640, 1657, 1658 texts

Meriba
Of Meriba *renown'd*. Psalm 81, 32

Meridian
Which now sat high in his Meridian Towre: Par Lost 4.30
Well known from Heav'n; and since Meridian hour Par Lost 4.581
To sit and taste, till this meridian heat Par Lost 5.369

Merit
And high disdain, from sence of injur'd merit, Par Lost 1.98
Could merit more then that small infantry Par Lost 1.575
Satan exalted sat, by merit rais'd Par Lost 2.5
Hath bin achievd of merit, yet this loss Par Lost 2.21
His crime makes guiltie all his Sons, thy merit Par Lost 3.290
By Merit more then Birthright Son of God, Par Lost 3.309
Ascend to Heav'n, by merit thine, and see Par Lost 5.80
Messiah, who by right of merit Reigns. Par Lost 6.43
Not here, till by degrees of merit rais'd Par Lost 7.157
Of merit high to all th' infernal Host, Par Lost 10.259
Good or not good ingraft, my Merit those Par Lost 11.35
This perfect Man, by merit call'd my Son, Par Reg 1.166
Then prompt her to do aught may merit praise. Par Reg 2.456
His Honour, Vertue, Merit and chief Praise, Par Reg 2.464
Well hath obey'd; just tryal e're I merit Par Reg 3.196
Strength, comliness of shape, or amplest merit Samson 1011

Merited
Have nothing merited, nor can performe Par Lost 4.418
Thy merited reward, the first assay Par Lost 6.153
Amply have merited of me, of all Par Lost 10.388
Which to have merited, without excuse, Samson 734

Meritorious
Preaching how meritorious with the gods Samson 859

Merits
Thy Merits; under thee as Head Supream Par Lost 3.319
That reaches blame, but rather merits praise Par Lost 3.697
Illaudable, naught merits but dispraise Par Lost 6.382
Such recompence best merits) from the bough Par Lost 9.995
And what most merits fame in silence hid. Par Lost 11.699
Imputed becomes theirs by Faith, his merits Par Lost 12.409

Meroe
Meroe Nilotic Isle, and more to West, Par Reg 4.71

Merriment
Of Riot, and ill manag'd Merriment, Mask 172
Bridgewater ms 'merriment'
Trinity ms 'merriment'

Merry
Their merry wakes and pastimes keep: Mask 121
Trinity ms 'merrie'
When the merry Bells ring round, Allegro 93
Message
Your message, like to end as much in vain? Par Lost 4.833
And to his message high in honour rise; Par Lost 5.289
For on som message high they guessd him bound. Par Lost 5.290
Thy message, which might else in telling wound, Par Lost 11.299
To know thir God, or message to regard, Par Lost 12.174
To verifie that solemn message late, Par Reg 1.133
Promisd by Heavenly message twice descending. Samson 635
His message will be short and voluble. Samson 1307
Off. My message was impos'd on me with speed, Samson 1343
Sam. So take it with what speed thy message needs. Samson 1345
Expect another message more imperious, Samson 1352
Off. *Samson*, this second message from our Lords Samson 1391
Rode up in flames after his message told Samson 1433
But now my task is smoothly don, Mask 1012
Trinity ms 'taske' ←'buisnesse' ←'message'
Messenger
Go heavenly Guest, Ethereal Messenger, Par Lost 8.646
And after him, the surer messenger, Par Lost 11.856
A messenger from God fore-told thy birth Par Reg 1.238
I with this Messenger will go along, Samson 1384
Messengers
The speediest of thy winged messengers, Par Lost 3.229
Thither will send his winged Messengers Par Lost 7.572
Messes
Of Hearbs, and other Country Messes, Allegro 85
Messiah
Messiah King anointed, could not beare Par Lost 5.664
The great *Messiah*, and his new commands, Par Lost 5.691
Messiah was declar'd in sight of Heav'n, Par Lost 5.765
Of Gods *Messiah;* those indulgent Laws Par Lost 5.883
Messiah, who by right of merit Reigns. Par Lost 6.43
Of God and his *Messiah*. On they move Par Lost 6.68
God and *Messiah* his anointed King. Par Lost 6.718
When the great Ensign of *Messiah* blaz'd Par Lost 6.775
Against God and *Messiah*, or to fall Par Lost 6.796
Messiah his triumphal Chariot turnd: Par Lost 6.881
Of great *Messiah* shall sing. Thus Laws and Rites Par Lost 12.244
Anointed King *Messiah* might be born Par Lost 12.359
And told them the Messiah now was born, Par Reg 1.245
Concerning the Messiah, to our Scribes Par Reg 1.261
Before Messiah and his way prepare. Par Reg 1.272
Jesus Messiah Son of God declar'd, Par Reg 2.4
Messiah certainly now come, so long Par Reg 2.32
Send thy Messiah forth, the time is come; Par Reg 2.43
Of the Messiah I have heard foretold Par Reg 4.502
Against the Lord and his Messiah dear Psalm 2, 5
Met
Met such imbodied force, as nam'd with these Par Lost 1.574
In this infernal Vaile first met thou call'st Par Lost 2.742
Here matter new to gaze the Devil met Par Lost 3.613
Down the steep glade, and met the neather Flood, Par Lost 4.231
That ever since in loves imbraces met, Par Lost 4.322
Naked met his under the flowing Gold Par Lost 4.496
Just met, and closing stood in squadron joind Par Lost 4.863
Reflecting blaze on blaze, first met his view: Par Lost 6.18
Forth stepping opposite, half way he met Par Lost 6.128
Proud, art thou met? thy hope was to have reacht Par Lost 6.131
A third part of the Gods, in Synod met Par Lost 6.156
Prodigious power had shewn, and met in Armes Par Lost 6.247
Nor solid might resist that edge: it met Par Lost 6.323
In motion or in alt: him soon they met Par Lost 6.532
As likeliest was, when two such Foes met arm'd; Par Lost 6.688
Single with like defence, wherever met, Par Lost 9.325
Adjoynd, from each thing met conceaves delight, Par Lost 9.449
Of Knowledge he must pass, there he her met, Par Lost 9.849
Hovering upon the Waters; what they met Par Lost 10.285
The confines met of Empyrean Heav'n Par Lost 10.321
Met who to meet him came, his Ofspring dear. Par Lost 10.349
Triumphal with triumphal act have met, Par Lost 10.390
Not that more glorious, when the Angels met Par Lost 11.213
Frequented thir Assemblies, whereso met, Par Lost 11.722
Of Fairy Damsels met in Forest wide Par Reg 2.359
Such forces met not, nor so wide a camp, Par Reg 3.337
Met ever; and to shameful silence brought, Par Reg 4.22
In their conjunction met, give me to spell, Par Reg 4.385
The Edifice where all were met to see him Samson 1588
Met from all parts to solemnize this Feast. Samson 1656
Hath met the vertue of this Magick dust, Mask 165
(For so by certain signes I knew) had met Mask 572
Where this night are met in state Mask 948
Trinity ms 'met' ←'come'
As he met her once a Maying, Allegro 20
Where *Corydon* and *Thyrsis* met, Allegro 83
He met her, and in secret shades Penseroso 28
Met in the milder shades of Purgatory. Sonnet 13, 14
Now *joyfully* are met Psalm 85, 42
And violent men are met Psalm 86, 50
Metal
Sonorous mettal blowing Martial sounds: Par Lost 1.540
ms 'mettle'
Compar'd with aught on Earth, Medal or Stone; Par Lost 3.592
If mettal, part seemd Gold, part Silver cleer; Par Lost 3.595
Fusil or grav'n in mettle. After these, Par Lost 11.573

Metal(*cont*)
Made of sphear-metal, never to decay Another 5
1640 'spheares mettall'
1657 'spheares metall'
1658 'Sphear mettall'
Metallic
That in his womb was hid metallic Ore, Par Lost 1.673
Metals
Metals of drossiest Ore to perfet Gold Par Lost 5.442
Two massy Keyes he bore of metals twain, Lycidas 110
Trinity ms 'mettalls'
1638 'metalls'
Meteor
Shon like a Meteor streaming to the Wind Par Lost 1.537
Meteorous
Gliding meteorous, as Ev'ning Mist Par Lost 12.629
1669 'Meteorous'
Methinks
Som such resemblances methinks I find Par Lost 5.114
Methinks I feel new strength within me rise, Par Lost 10.243
Some safer resolution, which methinks Par Lost 10.1029
Alas methinks whom God hath chosen once Samson 368
Madam, me thinks I see him living yet; Sonnet 10, 11
Trinity ms 'methinks'
Method
Another method I must now begin. Par Reg 4.540
Methought
Under a Platan, yet methought less faire, Par Lost 4.478
Knew never till this irksom night; methought Par Lost 5.35
And on, methought, alone I pass'd through ways Par Lost 5.50
So quick'nd appetite, that I, methought, Par Lost 5.85
My Guide was gon, and I, me thought, sunk down, Par Lost 5.91
And livd: One came, methought, of shape Divine, Par Lost 8.295
I found not what me thought I wanted still; Par Lost 8.355
Abstract as in a transe methought I saw, Par Lost 8.462
Methought I saw him placable and mild, Par Lost 11.151
Man. Of ruin indeed methought I heard the noise, Samson 1515
My best guide now, me thought it was the sound Mask 171
Bridgewater ms 'methought'
Where no crude surfet raigns. *Eld. Bro*. List, list, I hear Mask 480
Trinity ms 'I heare' ←'I heard' ←'me thought'
2. *Bro*. Me thought so too; what should it be? *Eld. Bro*. For certain Mask 482
Methought I saw my late espoused Saint Sonnet 23, 1
Trinity ms 'Mee thought'
Metropolis
First-seen, or some renown'd Metropolis Par Lost 3.549
Round thir Metropolis, and now expecting Par Lost 10.439
Mews
The haunt of Seales and Orcs, and Sea-mews clang. Par Lost 11.835
Mexico
Rich *Mexico* the seat of *Motezume*, Par Lost 11.407
Michael
Of Thunder and the Sword of *Michael* Par Lost 2.294
Go *Michael* of Celestial Armies Prince, Par Lost 6.44
Of Battel: whereat *Michael* bid sound Par Lost 6.202
Saw where the Sword of *Michael* smote, and fell'd Par Lost 6.250
Of *Michael* from the Armorie of God Par Lost 6.321
Michael and his Angels prevalent Par Lost 6.411
Since *Michael* and his Powers went forth to tame Par Lost 6.686
Under whose conduct *Michael* soon reduc'd Par Lost 6.777
Michael, this my behest have thou in charge, Par Lost 11.99
To *Michael* thus his humble words addressd. Par Lost 11.295
To whom thus *Michael* with regard benigne. Par Lost 11.334
Michael from *Adams* eyes the Filme remov'd Par Lost 11.412
T' whom *Michael* thus, hee also mov'd, repli'd. Par Lost 11.453
To whom thus *Michael*. Death thou hast seen Par Lost 11.466
Thir Makers Image, answerd *Michael*, then Par Lost 11.515
There is, said *Michael*, if thou well observe Par Lost 11.530
My dissolution. *Michael* repli'd, Par Lost 11.552
1667 '*Michael* to him repli'd'
To whom thus *Michael*. Judg not what is best Par Lost 11.603
To whom thus *Michael*. These are the product Par Lost 11.683
To whom thus *Michael*. Those whom last thou sawst Par Lost 11.787
To whom thus *Michael*. Justly thou abhorr'st Par Lost 12.79
To whom thus *Michael*. Doubt not but that sin Par Lost 12.285
To whom thus *Michael*. Dream not of thir fight, Par Lost 12.386
So spake th' Archangel *Michael*, then paus'd, Par Lost 12.466
Mickle
A noble Peer of mickle trust, and power Mask 31
Microscope
My Aerie Microscope) thou may'st behold Par Reg 4.57
Mid
Still ending, still renewing, through mid Heav'n; Par Lost 3.729
In the mid way: though strange to us it seemd Par Lost 6.91
Of fiercest opposition in mid Skie, Par Lost 6.314
His Thunder in mid Volie, for he meant Par Lost 6.854
Triumphant through mid Heav'n, into the Courts Par Lost 6.889
Bank the mid Sea: part single or with mate Par Lost 7.403
The mid Aereal Skie: Others on ground Par Lost 7.442
Though in mid Heav'n, soon ended his delight, Par Lost 9.468
Paths indirect, or in the mid way faint! Par Lost 11.631
Or how the Sun shall in mid Heav'n stand still Par Lost 12.263
Flies to his place, nor rests, but in mid air Par Reg 1.39
But night sits monarch yet in the mid sky. Mask 957
Passes to bliss at the mid hour of night, Sonnet 9, 13
Trinity ms 'the midd night howr' ←'the midd watch' ←'that hovre of night'

Midair
To joyn thir dark Encounter in mid air: Par Lost 2.718
To settle here on Earth, or in mid Aire; Par Lost 4.940
Came flying, and in mid Aire aloud thus cri'd. Par Lost 6.536

Midas
With *Midas* Ears, committing short and long; Sonnet 13, 4

Mid-course
Darkness ere Dayes mid-course, and Morning light Par Lost 11.204

Midday
Where God resides, and ere mid-day arriv'd Par Lost 8.112
Benighted walks under the mid-day Sun; Mask 384
Bridgewater ms 'walks in black vapours though the noone tyde brand'
Trinity ms 'benighted walks under the midday sun' ←'walks in black vapours though the noontyde brand'

Middle
That with no middle flight intends to soar Par Lost 1.14
Of cold *Olympus* rul'd the middle Air Par Lost 1.516
With mortal sting: about her middle round Par Lost 2.653
Through utter and through middle darkness borne Par Lost 3.16
Translated Saints, or middle Spirits hold Par Lost 3.461
The middle Tree and highest there that grew, Par Lost 4.195
With regal Ornament; the middle pair Par Lost 5.280
In *India* East or West, or middle shoare Par Lost 5.339
Or Earth, or Middle, all things fair and good; Par Lost 9.605
Those middle parts, that this new commer, Shame, Par Lost 9.1097
Of middle Age one rising, eminent Par Lost 11.665
Up to the middle Region of thick Air, Par Reg 2.117
The dreadfull Judge in middle Air shall spread his throne. Nativity 164
Through middle empire of the freezing aire Fair Inf 16

Mid-hours
Oreshades; for these mid-hours, till Eevning rise Par Lost 5.376

Midian
Of *Madian* and her vanquisht Kings: Samson 281
Do to them as to Midian *bold* Psalm 83, 33

Midnight
Whose midnight Revels, by a Forrest side Par Lost 1.782
Celestial voices to the midnight air, Par Lost 4.682
Mixt Dance, or wanton Mask, or Midnight Bal, Par Lost 4.768
Soon as midnight brought on the duskie houre Par Lost 5.667
Of midnight march, and hurried meeting here, Par Lost 5.778
By Night he fled, and at Midnight return'd Par Lost 9.58
Of midnight vapor glide obscure, and prie Par Lost 9.159
His midnight search, where soonest he might finde Par Lost 9.181
Last with one midnight stroke all the first-born Par Lost 12.189
Midnight shout, and revelry, Mask 103
Of mid-night Torches burns; mysterious Dame Mask 130
Bridgewater ms 'mid night'
Of *Cerberus*, and blackest midnight born, Allegro 2
Or let my Lamp at midnight hour, Penseroso 85
The *Lars*, and *Lemures* moan with midnight plaint, Nativity 191
Passes to bliss at the mid hour of night, Sonnet 9, 13
Trinity ms 'the midd night howr' ←'the midd watch' ←'that hovre of night'

Midnoon
Ris'n on mid-noon; som great behest from Heav'n Par Lost 5.311

Midriff
Smote him into the Midriff with a stone Par Lost 11.445

Midst
In billows, leave i' th' midst a horrid Vale. Par Lost 1.224
Midst came thir mighty Paramount, and seemd Par Lost 2.508
And where the river of Bliss through midst of Heavn Par Lost 3.358
Him first, him last, him midst, and without end. Par Lost 5.165
Flew through the midst of Heav'n; th' angelic Quires Par Lost 5.251
Amidst as from a flaming Mount, whose top Par Lost 5.598
1667 'A midst'
From midst a Golden Cloud thus milde was heard. Par Lost 6.28
High in the midst exalted as a God Par Lost 6.99
And in the midst thus undismai'd began. Par Lost 6.417
His head the midst, well stor'd with suttle wiles: Par Lost 9.184
Of Forrein Worlds: he through the midst unmarkt, Par Lost 10.441
Ophiusa) but still greatest hee the midst, Par Lost 10.528
Ith' midst an Altar as the Land-mark stood Par Lost 11.432
That open'd in the midst a woody Scene, Par Reg 2.294
From cold *Septentrion* blasts, thence in the midst Par Reg 4.31
And in my midst of sorrow and heart-grief Samson 1339
To sit the midst of Trinal Unity, Nativity 11
Ith' mid'st of all mine enemies that mark. Psalm 6, 15

Might
That with reiterated crimes he might Par Lost 1.214
Evil to others, and enrag'd might see Par Lost 1.216
In Heav'n, which follows dignity, might draw Par Lost 2.25
Contending, and so doubtful what might fall. Par Lost 2.203
To found this nether Empire, which might rise Par Lost 2.296
Others among the chief might offer now Par Lost 2.469
And so refus'd might in opinion stand Par Lost 2.471
As if (which might induce us to accord) Par Lost 2.503
Might yield them easier habitation, bend Par Lost 2.573
If shape it might be call'd that shape had none Par Lost 2.667
Or substance might be call'd that shadow seem'd, Par Lost 2.669
Th' undaunted Fiend what this might be admir'd, Par Lost 2.677
Might hap to move new broiles: Be this or aught Par Lost 2.837
Under spread Ensigns marching might pass through Par Lost 2.886
Might in that noise reside, of whom to ask Par Lost 2.957
All Heav'n, what this might mean, and whither tend Par Lost 3.272
Into the devious Air; then might ye see Par Lost 3.489
Round he surveys, and well might, where he stood Par Lost 3.555
To find who might direct his wandring flight Par Lost 3.631

Might(*cont*)
Which else might work him danger or delay: Par Lost 3.635
As great might have aspir'd, and me though mean Par Lost 4.62
Castalian Spring, might with this Paradise Par Lost 4.274
To mark what of thir state he more might learn Par Lost 4.400
Whence rushing he might surest seize them both Par Lost 4.407
To keep them low whom knowledge might exalt Par Lost 4.525
Or if, inspiring venom, he might taint Par Lost 4.804
Might have ensu'd, nor onely Paradise Par Lost 4.991
Well hast thou taught the way that might direct Par Lost 5.508
But what if better counsels might erect Par Lost 5.785
To veile the Heav'n, though darkness there might well Par Lost 6.11
As each divided Legion might have seemd Par Lost 6.230
That might determine, and not need repeate, Par Lost 6.318
Nor solid might resist that edge: it met Par Lost 6.323
I might relate of thousands, and thir names Par Lost 6.373
With dev'lish machination might devise Par Lost 6.504
That whom they hit, none on thir feet might stand, Par Lost 6.592
The sooner for thir Arms, unarm'd they might Par Lost 6.595
Such as we might perceive amus'd them all, Par Lost 6.623
That his great purpose he might so fulfill, Par Lost 6.675
They hard'nd more by what might most reclame, Par Lost 6.791
That wisht the Mountains now might be again Par Lost 6.842
What might have else to human Race bin hid; Par Lost 6.896
Of disobedience; firm they might have stood, Par Lost 6.911
What neerer might concern him, how this World Par Lost 7.62
Us timely of what might else have bin our loss, Par Lost 7.74
Contiguous might distemper the whole frame: Par Lost 7.273
Seemd like to Heav'n, a seat where Gods might dwell, Par Lost 7.329
With Sanctitie of Reason, might erect Par Lost 7.508
Informd by thee might know; if else thou seekst Par Lost 7.639
That better might with farr less compass move, Par Lost 8.33
If it presume, might erre in things too high, Par Lost 8.121
Destruction with Creation might have mixt. Par Lost 8.236
On mans destruction, maugre what might hap Par Lost 9.56
Most opportune might serve his Wiles, and found Par Lost 9.85
Doubt might beget of Diabolic pow'r Par Lost 9.95
His midnight search, where soonest he might finde Par Lost 9.181
How we might best fulfill the work which here Par Lost 9.230
To other speedie aide might lend at need; Par Lost 9.260
Or aught that might his happie State secure, Par Lost 9.347
And on his Quest, where likeliest he might finde Par Lost 9.414
He sought them both, but wish'd his hap might find Par Lost 9.421
Sated at length, ere long I might perceave Par Lost 9.598
Serpent, we might have spar'd our coming hither, Par Lost 9.647
Deterrd not from atchieving what might leade Par Lost 9.696
Might tempt alone, and in her ears the sound Par Lost 9.736
The guiltie Serpent, and well might, for *Eve* Par Lost 9.785
In things to us forbidden, it might be wish'd, Par Lost 9.1025
Insufferably bright. O might I here Par Lost 9.1084
But might as ill have happ'nd thou being by, Par Lost 9.1147
Who might have liv'd and joyd immortal bliss, Par Lost 9.1166
Easie it might be seen that I intend Par Lost 10.58
1667 'may'
Might suddenly inflict; that past, return'd Par Lost 10.341
Might intercept thir Emperour sent, so hee Par Lost 10.429
As might affect the Earth with cold and heat Par Lost 10.653
So might the wrauth. Fond wish! couldst thou support Par Lost 10.834
That on my head all might be visited, Par Lost 10.955
Which might supplie the Sun: such Fire to use, Par Lost 10.1078
Thy message, which might else in telling wound, Par Lost 11.299
His Eye might there command wherever stood Par Lost 11.385
First his own Tooles; then, what might else be wrought Par Lost 11.572
Not hid, nor those things last which might preserve Par Lost 11.579
If *Adam* aught perhaps might interpose; Par Lost 12.4
line not in 1667 edition
That *Moses* might report to them his will, Par Lost 12.237
Anointed King *Messiah* might be born Par Lost 12.359
Where he might likeliest find this new-declar'd, Par Reg 1.121
Of his Apostasie; he might have learnt Par Reg 1.146
How best the mighty work he might begin Par Reg 1.186
What might be publick good; my self I thought Par Reg 1.204
What might improve my knowledge or their own; Par Reg 1.213
Where they might see him, and to thee they came; Par Reg 1.246
Lodg'd in his brest, as well might recommend Par Reg 1.301
Or wither'd sticks to gather; which might serve Par Reg 1.316
That he might fall in *Ramoth*, they demurring, Par Reg 1.373
Sometimes they thought he might be only shewn, Par Reg 2.13
What I might have bestow'd on whom I pleas'd, Par Reg 2.395
That might require th' array of war, thy skill Par Reg 3.17
Huge Cities and high towr'd, that well might seem Par Reg 3.261
Of that high mountain, whence he might behold Par Reg 4.26
Whose branching arms thick intertwind might shield Par Reg 4.405
At least might seem to hold all power of thee, Par Reg 4.494
And narrower Scrutiny, that I might learn Par Reg 4.515
Annull'd, which might in part my grief have eas'd, Samson 72
That she might look at will through every pore? Samson 97
Might have subdu'd the Earth, Samson 174
Chor. Hee speaks, let us draw nigh. Matchless in might, Samson 178
Immeasurable strength they might behold Samson 206
I might begin *Israel*'s Deliverance, Samson 225
Lay stor'd, in what part summ'd, that she might know: Samson 395
Might easily have shook off all her snares: Samson 409
His might continues in thee not for naught, Samson 588
This one prayer yet remains, might I be heard, Samson 649
Or might I say contrarious, Samson 669
Which might have aw'd the best resolv'd of men, Samson 847
Of thy prodigious might and feats perform'd Samson 1083

Might(*cont*)	
Of those encounters, where we might have tri'd	Samson 1086
Puts invincible might	Samson 1271
Samson, with might endu'd	Samson 1293
Of sort, might sit in order to behold,	Samson 1608
On banks and scaffolds under Skie might stand;	Samson 1610
Which without help of eye, might be assay'd,	Samson 1625
And here their tender age might suffer perill,	Mask 40
What might this be? A thousand fantasies	Mask 205
line not in Bridgewater ms	
Be barr'd that happines, might we but hear	Mask 343
Was took e're she was ware, and wish't she might	Mask 558
And took in strains that might create a soul	Mask 561
Too well I did perceive it was the voice	Mask 563
Trinity ms 'might perceave'	
Bridgewater ms 'might perceive'	
Be those that quell the might of hellish charms,	Mask 613
To deck her Sons, and that no corner might	Mask 717
she might be free from perill where she is	Mask Tr. ms 16.42
she might be free from perill where she is,	Mask Br. ms 395
Prince *Memnons* sister might beseem,	Penseroso 18
Might raise *Musaeus* from his bower,	Penseroso 104
Might she the wise *Latona* be,	Arcades 20
Yet *Syrinx* well might wait on her.	Arcades 107
Trinity ms defective here	
Whom Universal nature did lament,	Lycidas 60
Trinity ms 'did' ←'might'	
Through the dear might of him that walk'd the waves;	Lycidas 173
That by his all-commanding might,	Psalm 136, 25
Might think th' infection of my sorrows loud,	Passion 55
Ye might discern a Cipress bud.	Winchester 22
While he might still jogg on, and keep his trot,	Another 4
1658 'he could but'	
Perhaps my semblance might deceive the truth,	Sonnet 7, 5
Stand spelling fals, while one might walk to Mile-	Sonnet 11, 7
This thought might lead me through the worlds vain mask	Sonnet 22, 13
To save us by thy might.	Psalm 80, 12
From whence they might not swerve.	Psalm 81, 16
Favouring the wicked *by your might.*	Psalm 82, 7
Rise God, judge thou the earth *in might*,	Psalm 82, 25
For they consult with all their might,	Psalm 83, 17
And *Kings* be born of thee, whose dredded might	Prose 12, 13
Might	
That Glory never shall his wrath or might	Par Lost 1.110
These were the prime in order and in might;	Par Lost 1.506
Henceforth his might we know, and know our own	Par Lost 1.643
Not more Almighty to resist our might	Par Lost 2.192
Fearless to be o'rmatcht by living might.	Par Lost 2.855
My word, my wisdom, and effectual might,	Par Lost 3.170
Thee only extoll'd, Son of thy Fathers might,	Par Lost 3.398
To make them mirth us'd all his might, and wreathd	Par Lost 4.346
Collecting all his might dilated stood,	Par Lost 4.986
In full resplendence, Heir of all my might,	Par Lost 5.720
Remain not; wherfore should not strength and might	Par Lost 6.116
And limited thir might; though numberd such	Par Lost 6.229
In might or swift prevention; but the sword	Par Lost 6.320
Memorial, where the might of *Gabriel* fought,	Par Lost 6.355
In might though wondrous and in Acts of Warr,	Par Lost 6.377
All doubt of Victorie, eternal might	Par Lost 6.630
Go then thou Mightiest in thy Fathers might,	Par Lost 6.710
Armd with thy might, rid Heav'n of these rebell'd,	Par Lost 6.737
My overshadowing Spirit and might with thee	Par Lost 7.165
Creation, and the wonders of his might.	Par Lost 7.223
To manifest the more thy might: his evil	Par Lost 7.615
Plenipotent on Earth, of matchless might	Par Lost 10.404
For in those dayes Might onely shall be admir'd,	Par Lost 11.689
Of Paradise by might of Waves be moovd	Par Lost 11.830
Mightest	
Farthest from pain, where thou mightst hope to change	Par Lost 4.892
Might'st thou expel this monster from his Throne	Par Reg 4.100
Divine impulsion prompting how thou might'st	Samson 422
Mightier	
Or do him mightier service as his thralls	Par Lost 1.149
By younger *Saturn*, he from mightier *Jove*	Par Lost 1.512
Of Truth, in word mightier then they in Armes;	Par Lost 6.32
Mightiest	
That with the mightiest rais'd me to contend,	Par Lost 1.99
The weight of mightiest Monarchies; his look	Par Lost 2.307
Among the mightiest, bent on highest deeds,	Par Lost 6.112
Thus foil'd thir mightiest, ours joy filld, and shout,	Par Lost 6.200
And now thir Mightiest quelld, the battel swerv'd,	Par Lost 6.386
1667 'mightiest'	
Of Mightiest. Sense of pleasure we may well	Par Lost 6.459
Go then thou Mightiest in thy Fathers might,	Par Lost 6.710
Of mightiest Empire, from the destind Walls	Par Lost 11.387
The seats of mightiest Monarchs, and so large	Par Reg 3.262
He led me on to mightiest deeds	Samson 638
Mighty	
Wast present, and with mighty wings outspread	Par Lost 1.20
Hath lost us Heav'n, and all this mighty Host	Par Lost 1.136
His mighty Stature; on each hand the flames	Par Lost 1.222
His mighty Standard; that proud honour claim'd	Par Lost 1.533
Awaiting what command thir mighty Chief	Par Lost 1.566
Of mighty Cherubim; the sudden blaze	Par Lost 1.665
High honourd sits? Go therfore mighty Powers,	Par Lost 2.456
Midst came thir mighty Paramount, and seemd	Par Lost 2.508
So frownd the mighty Combatants, that Hell	Par Lost 2.719
That mighty leading Angel, who of late	Par Lost 2.991
Mighty(*cont*)	
Made answer. Mightie Father, thou thy foes	Par Lost 5.735
Regions they pass'd, the mightie Regencies	Par Lost 5.748
As by his Word the mighty Father made	Par Lost 5.836
That stood for Heav'n, in mighty Quadrate joyn'd	Par Lost 6.62
Which God hath in his mighty Angels plac'd)	Par Lost 6.638
Of Thrones and mighty Seraphim prostrate,	Par Lost 6.841
And Temple of his mightie Father Thron'd	Par Lost 6.890
A mightie Spheare he fram'd, unlightsom first,	Par Lost 7.355
Who can impair thee, mighty King, or bound	Par Lost 7.608
The mightie frame, how build, unbuild, contrive	Par Lost 8.81
Thir mighty Chief returnd: loud was th' acclaime:	Par Lost 10.455
His mightie Angels gave them several charge,	Par Lost 10.650
Giants of mightie Bone, and bould emprise;	Par Lost 11.642
A mightie Hunter thence he shall be styl'd	Par Lost 12.33
A mightie Nation, and upon him showre	Par Lost 12.124
To Councel summons all his mighty Peers,	Par Reg 1.40
How best the mighty work he might begin	Par Reg 1.186
Who could do mighty things, and could contemn	Par Reg 2.448
And o're a mighty King so oft prevail'd,	Par Reg 3.167
His mighty Champion, strong above compare,	Samson 556
The Image of thy strength, and mighty minister.	Samson 706
To quell the mighty of the Earth, th' oppressour,	Samson 1272
Proof of his mighty strength in feats and games;	Samson 1602
Excells his Mother at her mighty Art,	Mask 63
1637 'mightie'	
Bridgewater ms 'mightie'	
Trinity ms 'mightie' ←'potent'	
Culling their Potent hearbs, and balefull drugs,	Mask 255
Trinity ms 'potent' ←'myghty' ←'powerfull' ←'potent'	
That the mighty *Pan*	Nativity 89
His mighty Majesty and worth.	Psalm 136, 90
What power, what force, what mighty spell, if not	Vacation 89
In darkness can thy mighty *hand*	Psalm 88, 49
A mighty masse of things strangely confus'd,	Prose 2, 3
Mild	
This horror will grow milde, this darkness light,	Par Lost 2.220
Re-enter Heav'n; or else in some milde Zone	Par Lost 2.397
Into th' *Euboic* Sea. Others more milde,	Par Lost 2.546
Less winning soft, less amiablie milde,	Par Lost 4.479
Of grateful Eevning milde, then silent Night	Par Lost 4.647
Nor grateful Eevning mild, nor silent Night	Par Lost 4.654
Milde, as when *Zephyrus* on *Flora* breathes,	Par Lost 5.16
Whom thus th' Angelic Vertue answered milde.	Par Lost 5.371
From midst a Golden Cloud thus milde was heard.	Par Lost 6.28
And thus the Godlike Angel answerd milde.	Par Lost 7.110
To whom mild answer *Adam* thus return'd.	Par Lost 9.226
Express'd, and thus divinely answer'd milde.	Par Lost 10.67
Came the mild Judge and Intercessor both	Par Lost 10.96
Wholsom and cool, and mild, but with black Air	Par Lost 10.847
Laid on our Necks. Remember with what mild	Par Lost 10.1046
Methought I saw him placable and mild,	Par Lost 11.151
That I should fear, nor sociably mild,	Par Lost 11.234
Whom thus the Angel interrupted milde.	Par Lost 11.286
Among wild Beasts: they at his sight grew mild,	Par Reg 1.310
So may we hold our place and these mild seats	Par Reg 2.125
Perswasive, Virgin majesty with mild	Par Reg 2.159
Frugal, and mild, and temperate, conquer'd well,	Par Reg 4.134
In Regions milde of calm and serene Ayr,	Mask 4
Trinity ms 'mild'	
Bridgewater ms 'mylde'	
1637 'mild'	
Ye valleys low where the milde whispers use,	Lycidas 136
1638 'mild'	
Trinity ms 'mild'	
Whispering new joyes to the milde Ocean,	Nativity 66
Would soon unboosom all thir Echoes milde,	Passion 53
Bear his milde yoak, they serve him best, his State	Sonnet 19, 11
For other things mild Heav'n a time ordains,	Sonnet 21, 11
But thou Lord art the God most mild	Psalm 86, 53
Milder	
Soon learnd, now milder, and thus answerd smooth.	Par Lost 2.816
Of onset ended soon each milder thought.	Par Lost 6.98
Met in the milder shades of Purgatory.	Sonnet 13, 14
Trinity ms 'milder' ←'mildest'	
Mildew	
'Gainst all inchantments, mildew blast, or damp	Mask 640
Mildly	
Said mildely, Author of all this thou seest	Par Lost 8.317
Mildness	
Thy terrors, as I put thy mildness on,	Par Lost 6.735
Thy looks, the Heav'n of mildness, with disdain,	Par Lost 9.534
Mile-end	
Stand spelling fals, while one might walk to Mile-	Sonnet 11, 7
End Green. Why is it harder Sirs then Gordon,	Sonnet 11, 8
Miles	
As many miles aloft: that furie stay'd,	Par Lost 2.938
Militant	
At which command the Powers Militant,	Par Lost 6.61
In shew Plebeian Angel militant	Par Lost 10.442
Military	
Your military obedience, to dissolve	Par Lost 4.955
And thou in Military prowess next	Par Lost 6.45
A militarie Vest of purple flowd	Par Lost 11.241
In coats of Mail and military pride;	Par Reg 3.312
Milk	
Of Ewe or Goat dropping with Milk at Eevn,	Par Lost 9.582

Milkmaid
And the Milkmaid singeth blithe, Allegro 65
Milky
Of nectarous draughts between, from milkie stream, Par Lost 5.306
Seen in the Galaxie, that Milkie way Par Lost 7.579
I drank, from the clear milkie juice allaying Samson 550
Mill
Eyeless in *Gaza* at the Mill with slaves, Samson 41
Gives and the Mill had tam'd thee? O that fortune Samson 1093
And over-labour'd at thir publick Mill, Samson 1327
Our Captive, at the public Mill our drudge, Samson 1393
Millions
Millions of Spirits for his fault amerc't Par Lost 1.609
ms defective here
Millions of flaming swords, drawn from the thighs Par Lost 1.664
Millions that stand in Arms, and longing wait Par Lost 2.55
Pourd out by millions her victorious Bands Par Lost 2.997
Millions of spiritual Creatures walk the Earth Par Lost 4.677
By Thousands and by Millions rang'd for fight; Par Lost 6.48
Millions of fierce encountring Angels fought Par Lost 6.220
Who leagu'd with millions more in rash revolt Par Reg 1.359
And set to work millions of spinning Worms, Mask 715
Was the Lord. Of many millions Psalm 3, 15
Mimic
Oft in her absence mimic Fansie wakes Par Lost 5.110
Mimics
Juglers and Dancers, Antics, Mummers, Mimics, Samson 1325
1671 printed 'Mimirs', errata 'Mimics'
Mincing
With the mincing *Dryades* Mask 964
Bridgewater ms 'mincinge'
Mincius
Smooth-sliding *Mincius*, crown'd with vocall reeds, Lycidas 86
Mind
Though chang'd in outward lustre; that fixt mind Par Lost 1.97
Can perish: for the mind and spirit remains Par Lost 1.139
A mind not to be chang'd by Place or Time. Par Lost 1.253
The mind is its own place, and in it self Par Lost 1.254
Hateful to utter: but what power of mind Par Lost 1.626
Of present pain, that with ambitious mind Par Lost 2.34
With him, or who deceive his mind, whose eye Par Lost 2.189
Not mind us not offending, satisfi'd Par Lost 2.212
Shine inward, and the mind through all her powers Par Lost 3.52
But what created mind can comprehend Par Lost 3.705
And understood not that a grateful mind Par Lost 4.55
Mind us of like repose, since God hath set Par Lost 4.612
Man hath his daily work of body or mind Par Lost 4.618
But of offence and trouble, which my mind Par Lost 5.34
Evil into the mind of God or Man Par Lost 5.117
Not burd'nd Nature, sudden mind arose Par Lost 5.452
To swerve from truth, or change his constant mind Par Lost 5.902
These things, as not to mind from whence they grow Par Lost 6.477
In measure what the mind may well contain, Par Lost 7.128
But apt the Mind or Fancie is to roave Par Lost 8.188
As us'd or not, works in the mind no change, Par Lost 8.525
Of Nature her th' inferiour, in the mind Par Lost 8.541
Greatness of mind and nobleness thir seat Par Lost 8.557
Union of Mind, or in us both one Soule; Par Lost 8.604
Or bear what to my minde first thoughts present, Par Lost 9.213
1667 'mind'
Food of the mind, or this sweet intercourse Par Lost 9.238
That I should mind thee oft, and mind thou me. Par Lost 9.358
I turnd my thoughts, and with capacious mind Par Lost 9.603
To reach, and feed at once both Bodie and Mind? Par Lost 9.779
Coverd, but not at rest or ease of Mind, Par Lost 9.1120
Thir inward State of Mind, calm Region once Par Lost 9.1125
Hinder'd not *Satan* to attempt the minde Par Lost 10.8
But all corrupt, both Mind and Will deprav'd, Par Lost 10.825
To better hopes his more attentive minde Par Lost 10.1011
And excellent then what thy minde contemnes; Par Lost 10.1015
I have in view, calling to minde with heed Par Lost 10.1030
So prevalent as to concerne the mind Par Lost 11.144
Produce prodigious Births of bodie or mind. Par Lost 11.687
And call to mind his Cov'nant: Day and Night, Par Lost 11.898
Pure, and in mind prepar'd, if so befall, Par Lost 12.444
To me was pleasing, all my mind was set Par Reg 1.202
Thus *Mary* pondering oft, and oft to mind Par Reg 2.105
And amplitude of mind to greatest Deeds. Par Reg 2.139
Then *Solomon*, of more exalted mind, Par Reg 2.206
Nor mind it, fed with better thoughts that feed Par Reg 2.258
And oft by force, which to a generous mind Par Reg 2.479
Much less my mind; though thou should'st add to tell Par Reg 4.113
So let extend thy mind o're all the world, Par Reg 4.223
Our Saviour meek and with untroubl'd mind Par Reg 4.401
Ease to the body some, none to the mind Samson 18
O impotence of mind, in body strong! Samson 52
The tumors of a troubl'd mind, Samson 185
To Honour and Religion! servil mind Samson 412
From anguish of the mind and humours black, Samson 600
To th' inmost mind, Samson 611
Thy mind with what amends is in my power, Samson 745
With plain Heroic magnitude of mind Samson 1279
Labouring thy mind Samson 1298
With corporal servitude, that my mind ever Samson 1336
If there be aught of presage in the mind, Samson 1387
Or some great matter in his mind revolv'd. Samson 1638
And calm of mind all passion spent. Samson 1758
The vertuous mind, that ever walks attended Mask 211
Mind(*cont*)
line not in Bridgewater ms
The unpolluted temple of the mind, Mask 461
Bridgewater ms 'mynde'
Brought to my mind a certain Shepherd Lad Mask 619
Trinity ms 'mynd'
Bridgewater ms 'mynd'
Thou canst not touch the freedom of my minde Mask 663
Bridgewater ms 'mynde'
Trinity ms 'mind' ← 'mynd'
1637 'mind'
Or fill the fixed mind with all your toyes; Penseroso 4
The immortal mind that hath forsook Penseroso 91
(That last infirmity of Noble mind) Lycidas 71
Let us with a gladsom mind Psalm 136, 1
Such where the deep transported mind may soare Vacation 33
Came vested all in white, pure as her mind: Sonnet 23, 9
Trinity ms 'minde'
And to their wandring mind; Psalm 81, 50
And all as one in mind Psalm 83, 18
Minded
So minded, have oreleapt these earthie bounds Par Lost 4.583
And be so minded still; I, ere thou spak'st, Par Lost 8.444
Of rusling Leaves, but minded not, as us'd Par Lost 9.519
Which then not minded in dismay, yet now Par Lost 11.156
I sorrow'd at his captive state, but minded Samson 1603
Mindless
Gently with Mirtle band, mindless the while, Par Lost 9.431
Minds
From mortal or immortal minds. Thus they Par Lost 1.559
Thence more at ease thir minds and somwhat rais'd Par Lost 2.521
For heav'nly mindes from such distempers foule Par Lost 4.118
Thir ruine! Hence I will excite thir minds Par Lost 4.522
New Laws from him who reigns, new minds may raise Par Lost 5.680
Our minds and teach us to cast off this Yoke? Par Lost 5.786
Unhurt our mindes, and understanding sound, Par Lost 6.444
Of composition, strait they chang'd thir minds, Par Lost 6.613
Soon found thir Eyes how op'nd, and thir minds Par Lost 9.1053
Fresh in thir mindes, fearing the Deitie, Par Lost 12.15
In the admiration only of weak minds Par Reg 2.221
To free my Countrey; if their servile minds Samson 1213
Man. I know your friendly minds and----O what noise! Samson 1508
Who hurt thir minds, Samson 1676
Mine
Before mine eyes in opposition sits Par Lost 2.803
His end with mine involvd; and knows that I Par Lost 2.807
Of mine own brood, that on my bowels feed: Par Lost 2.863
Yours be th' advantage all, mine the revenge. Par Lost 2.987
Mine ear shall not be slow, mine eye not shut. Par Lost 3.193
Thy way thou canst not miss, me mine requires. Par Lost 3.735
O Hell! what doe mine eyes with grief behold, Par Lost 4.358
Mine eyes till now, and pin'd with vain desire, Par Lost 4.466
Seisd mine, I yielded, and from that time see Par Lost 4.489
Mine eye pursu'd him still, but under shade Par Lost 4.572
God is thy Law, thou mine: to know no more Par Lost 4.637
Satan, I know thy strength, and thou knowst mine, Par Lost 4.1006
Then Heav'n permits, nor mine, though doubld now Par Lost 4.1009
Close at mine ear one call'd me forth to walk Par Lost 5.36
Wast wont, I mine to thee was wont to impart; Par Lost 5.677
Pleas'd with thy words no less then thou with mine. Par Lost 8.248
Before mine Eyes all real, as the dream Par Lost 8.310
Yet dreadful in mine eare, though in my choice Par Lost 8.335
By Nature as in aide, and clos'd mine eyes. Par Lost 8.459
Mine eyes he clos'd, but op'n left the Cell Par Lost 8.460
Deprest, and much they may, if all be mine, Par Lost 9.46
Th' effects to correspond, opener mine Eyes, Par Lost 9.875
Mine never shall be parted, bliss or woe. Par Lost 9.916
My own in thee, for what thou art is mine; Par Lost 9.957
Of mine to thee, ingrateful *Eve*, exprest Par Lost 9.1164
Against his Maker; no Decree of mine Par Lost 10.43
Mine both in Heav'n and Earth to do thy will Par Lost 10.69
Adventrous work, yet to thy power and mine Par Lost 10.255
Mine with this glorious Work, and made one Realm Par Lost 10.391
Mine own that bide upon me, all from mee Par Lost 10.738
True opener of mine eyes, prime Angel blest, Par Lost 11.598
Mine eyes true op'ning, and my heart much eas'd, Par Lost 12.274
Riches are mine, Fortune is in my hand; Par Reg 2.429
Oft not deserv'd? I seek not mine, but his Par Reg 3.106
Before mine eyes thou hast set; and in my ear Par Reg 3.390
More then of arms before, allure mine eye, Par Reg 4.112
Had been fulfilld but through mine own default, Samson 45
Mee easily indeed mine may neglect, Samson 291
Your younger feet, while mine cast back with age Samson 336
Mine eie to harbour sleep, or thoughts to rest. Samson 459
Thine forgive mine; that men may censure thine Samson 787
In human hearts, nor less in mine towards thee, Samson 792
Mine and Loves prisoner, not the *Philistines*, Samson 808
Her own transgressions, to upbraid me mine? Samson 820
Thou mine, not theirs: if aught against my life Samson 888
Soon feel, whose God is strongest, thine or mine. Samson 1155
Is hate, not help to me, it may with mine Samson 1266
(For so I can distinguish by mine Art) Mask 149
Trinity ms 'myne'
Bridgewater ms 'myne'
This way the noise was, if mine ear be true, Mask 170
Trinity ms 'my'
Bridgewater ms 'my'
No goblin, or swart Faery of the mine, Mask 436

Mine(*cont*)
Till guided by mine ear I found the place — Mask 570
Bridgewater ms 'myne'
Trinity ms 'myne'
Would think to charm my judgement, as mine eyes — Mask 758
Trinity ms 'mye'
Bridgewater ms 'my'
Streit mine eye hath caught new pleasures — Allegro 69
As may with sweetnes, through mine ear, — Penseroso 164
And bring all Heav'n before mine eyes. — Penseroso 166
Whom with low reverence I adore as mine, — Arcades 37
Mine eye hath found that sad Sepulchral rock — Passion 43
Mine as whom washt from spot of child-bed taint, — Sonnet 23, 5
My Bed I water with my tears; mine Eie — Psalm 6, 13
Ith' mid'st of all mine enemies that mark. — Psalm 6, 15
Mine enemies shall all be blank and dash't — Psalm 6, 21
Mine eye grows dim and dead, — Psalm 88, 38

Mine
As from the Mine. Mean while at Table *Eve* — Par Lost 5.443
Lay Seige, encampt; by Batterie, Scale, and Mine, — Par Lost 11.656

Mineral
Sublim'd with Mineral fury, aid the Winds, — Par Lost 1.235
ms 'minerall'
Entrails unlike) of Mineral and Stone, — Par Lost 6.517

Minerva
That wise *Minerva* wore, unconquer'd Virgin, — Mask 448

Mingle
To mingle and involve, done all to spite — Par Lost 2.384
Thou and thy wicked crew; there mingle broiles, — Par Lost 6.277
As Earth and Skie would mingle; but my self — Par Reg 4.453
That mingle with thy fancy. I however — Samson 601

Mingled
They found, they mingl'd, and with suttle Art, — Par Lost 6.513
Flowers of more mingled hew — Mask 994

Minims
Minims of Nature; some of Serpent kinde — Par Lost 7.482

Minister
Thus to th' Empyreal Minister he fram'd. — Par Lost 5.460
To the bright Minister that watchd, hee blew — Par Lost 11.73
Highly belov'd, being but the Minister — Par Lost 12.308
To tread his Sacred Courts, and minister — Par Reg 1.488
The Image of thy strength, and mighty minister. — Samson 706

Ministered
Ministerd naked, and thir flowing cups — Par Lost 5.444

Ministeries
With Ministeries due and solemn Rites: — Par Lost 7.149

Ministering
Ministring light prepar'd, they set and rise; — Par Lost 4.664
Ministring Spirits, traind up in Feast and Song; — Par Lost 6.167
Yet leudly dar'st our ministring upbraid. — Par Lost 6.182

Ministers
His Ministers of vengeance and pursuit — Par Lost 1.170
ms 'ministers'
And flaming Ministers to watch and tend — Par Lost 9.156
Deaths Ministers, not Men, who thus deal Death — Par Lost 11.676
Thy gentle Ministers, who come to pay — Par Reg 2.375

Ministrant
Princedoms, and Dominations ministrant — Par Lost 10.87
And call swift flights of Angels ministrant — Par Reg 2.385

Ministry
Thir Ministry perform'd, and race well run, — Par Lost 12.505

Minstrelsy
Such hast thou arm'd, the Minstrelsie of Heav'n, — Par Lost 6.168
To meditate my rural minstrelsie, — Mask 547

Mintage
Fixes instead, unmoulding reasons mintage — Mask 529

Minute
With minute drops from off the Eaves. — Penseroso 130

Minutes
Time counts not, though with swiftest minutes wing'd. — Par Lost 10.91

Miracle
Redouble then this miracle, and say, — Par Lost 9.562
By Miracle he may, reply'd the Swain, — Par Reg 1.337
The miracle of men: then in an hour — Samson 364
Nothing is hard) by miracle restor'd, — Samson 1528

Miracles
To speak all Tongues, and do all Miracles, — Par Lost 12.501
That with his miracles doth make — Psalm 136, 13

Miraculous
Miraculous yet remaining in those locks? — Samson 587

Mire
To trample thee as mire: for proof look up, — Par Lost 4.1010
A here alas, hath laid him in the dirt, — Carrier 2
1658 'in the mire'
Now that the Fields are dank, and ways are mire, — Sonnet 20, 2

Mires
To Boggs and Mires, and oft through Pond or Poole, — Par Lost 9.641

Mirror
Her chrystal mirror holds, unite thir streams. — Par Lost 4.263
His mirror, with full face borrowing her Light — Par Lost 7.377
O mirror of our fickle state, — Samson 164

Mirth
Wheels her pale course, they on thir mirth and dance — Par Lost 1.786
To make them mirth us'd all his might, and wreathd — Par Lost 4.346
They swim in mirth, and fansie that they feel — Par Lost 9.1009
Had fill'd thir hearts with mirth, high chear, & wine, — Samson 1613
Whence eev'n now the tumult of loud Mirth — Mask 202
Trinity ms 'mirth'

Mirth(*cont*)
line not in Bridgewater ms
Will double all their mirth and chere; — Mask 955
And by men, heart-easing Mirth, — Allegro 13
Mirth, admit me of thy crue — Allegro 38
Mirth with thee, I mean to live. — Allegro 152
Far from all resort of mirth, — Penseroso 81
Ere-while of Musick, and Ethereal mirth, — Passion 1
Mirth and youth, and warm desire, — May Morn 6
In mirth, that after no repenting drawes; — Sonnet 21, 6

Miry
His hands from pots, *and mirie soyle* — Psalm 81, 23

Misbecoming
And put them into mis-becoming plight. — Mask 372
1637 'mis-becomming'
Trinity ms 'misbecomming'
Bridgewater ms 'misbecomminge'

Miscellaneous
A miscellaneous rabble, who extol — Par Reg 3.50

Mischance
Of shak't Olympus by mischance didst fall; — Fair Inf 44
But whether by mischance or blame — Winchester 27

Mischief
Her mischief, and purge off the baser fire — Par Lost 2.141
Such implements of mischief as shall dash — Par Lost 6.488
Some one intent on mischief, or inspir'd — Par Lost 6.503
Against such hellish mischief fit to oppose. — Par Lost 6.636
Of mischief, gratulating, thus excites. — Par Lost 9.472
To mischief swift. Hope elevates, and joy — Par Lost 9.633
Of mischief, and polluted from the end — Par Lost 10.167
Mankind? this mischief had not then befall'n, — Par Lost 10.895
O Teacher, some great mischief hath befall'n — Par Lost 11.450
Was absent, after all his mischief done, — Par Reg 4.440
A cleaving mischief, in his way to vertue — Samson 1039
Yea even that which mischief meant most harm, — Mask 591
Trinity ms 'mischeife'
1637 'mischiefe'
Bridgewater ms 'mischiefe'
His mischief that due course doth keep, — Psalm 7, 57

Mischievous
Thither full fraught with mischievous revenge, — Par Lost 2.1054

Miscreated
Thy miscreated Front athwart my way — Par Lost 2.683

Misdeed
My rash but more unfortunate misdeed. — Samson 747

Misdeeds
To evils which our own misdeeds have wrought, — Par Lost 10.1080

Misdeem
Though ineffectual found: misdeem not then, — Par Lost 9.301
What but thy malice mov'd thee to misdeem — Par Reg 1.424

Misdoing
Not wilfully mis-doing, but unware — Par Reg 1.225

Misdone
Towards thee I intend for what I have misdone, — Samson 911

Miser
Of Misers treasure by an out-laws den, — Mask 399
1637 'misers'
Trinity 'misers'
Bridgewater ms 'misers'

Miserable
Fall'n Cherube, to be weak is miserable — Par Lost 1.157
Then miserable to have eternal being: — Par Lost 2.98
All on a sudden miserable pain — Par Lost 2.752
Me miserable! which way shall I flie — Par Lost 4.73
Nor hope to be my self less miserable — Par Lost 9.126
Of all our good, sham'd, naked, miserable. — Par Lost 9.1139
O miserable of happie! is this the end — Par Lost 10.720
Of refuge, and concludes thee miserable — Par Lost 10.839
More miserable; both have sin'd, but thou — Par Lost 10.930
By Death at last, and miserable it is — Par Lost 10.981
O miserable Mankind, to what fall — Par Lost 11.500
As a poor miserable captive thrall, — Par Reg 1.411
Easily canst thou find one miserable, — Par Reg 1.471
And buried; but O yet more miserable! — Samson 101
Man. O miserable change! is this the man, — Samson 340
Lie in this miserable loathsom plight — Samson 480
Just or unjust, alike seem miserable, — Samson 703
Are drawn to wear out miserable days, — Samson 762
Their inside, troubles miserable; — Psalm 5, 27

Miseries
The growing miseries, which *Adam* saw — Par Lost 10.715
And proves the sourse of all my miseries; — Samson 64
To all the miseries of life, — Samson 107
The close of all my miseries, and the balm. — Samson 651

Misery
Joynd with me once, now misery hath joynd — Par Lost 1.90
Here swallow'd up in endless misery. — Par Lost 1.142
The present misery, and render Hell — Par Lost 2.459
Of happiness and final misery, — Par Lost 2.563
In miserie; such joy Ambition findes. — Par Lost 4.92
Miserie, uncreated till the crime — Par Lost 6.268
But pain is perfet miserie, the worst — Par Lost 6.462
His punishment, Eternal miserie; — Par Lost 6.904
Sinne and her shadow Death, and Miserie — Par Lost 9.12
The miserie, I deserv'd it, and would beare — Par Lost 10.726
Bereaving sense, but endless miserie — Par Lost 10.810
Thy hatred for this miserie befall'n, — Par Lost 10.928
To be to others cause of misery, — Par Lost 10.982

Misery(*cont*)
With like desire, which would be meserie — Par Lost 10.997
1667 'miserie'
Of miserie, so thinking to evade — Par Lost 10.1021
What miserie th' inabstinence of *Eve* — Par Lost 11.476
Men to much misery and hardship born; — Par Reg 1.341
Companions of my misery and wo. — Par Reg 1.398
But misery hath rested from me; where — Par Reg 1.470
Thir foe to misery beneath thir fears, — Samson 1469
And they, so perfect is their misery, — Mask 73
Bridgewater ms 'miserie'
1637 'miserie'
Trinity ms 'miserie'
Beheld us in our misery. — Psalm 136, 78
Misfortune
As some misfortune brings him, or mistake, — Par Lost 10.900
La. How easie my misfortune is to hit! — Mask 286
Misgave
Misgave him; hee the faultring measure felt; — Par Lost 9.846
Misguided
Misguided; only what remains past cure — Samson 912
Mishap
But that success attends him; if mishap, — Par Lost 10.239
What hard mishap hath doom'd this gentle swain? — Lycidas 92
Misinform
She dictate false, and missinforme the Will — Par Lost 9.355
Misjoining
To imitate her; but misjoyning shapes, — Par Lost 5.111
Mislead
Alas what can they teach, and not mislead; — Par Reg 4.309
Misleads
Misleads th' amaz'd Night-wanderer from his way — Par Lost 9.640
Misled
Misled; the stubborn only to subdue. — Par Reg 1.226
To the misled and lonely Travailer? — Mask 200
line not in Bridgewater ms
Misliked
Mislik'd me for his choice. — Psalm 81, 48
Misrepresent
Or do my eyes misrepresent? Can this be hee, — Samson 124
Misrule
Crystallin Ocean, and the loud misrule — Par Lost 7.271
At random yielded up to their misrule; — Par Lost 10.628
Miss
Thy way thou canst not miss, me mine requires. — Par Lost 3.735
My coming seen far off? I miss thee here, — Par Lost 10.104
Nor can I miss the way, so strongly drawn — Par Lost 10.262
That what by me thou hast lost thou least shalt miss. — Samson 927
Their full tribute never miss — Mask 925
1637 'misse'
Trinity ms 'misse'
Bridgewater ms 'misse'
Missed
To be th' inventer miss'd, so easie it seemd — Par Lost 6.499
Thee I have misst, and thought it long, depriv'd — Par Lost 9.857
Flew up, nor missd the way, by envious windes — Par Lost 11.15
To gain a Scepter, oftest better miss't. — Par Reg 2.486
Mercy and Truth *that long were miss'd* — Psalm 85, 41
Missing
Now missing him thir joy so lately found, — Par Reg 2.9
Moses was in the Mount, and missing long; — Par Reg 2.15
Were dead, who sought his life, and missing fill'd — Par Reg 2.77
Me naught advantag'd, missing what I aim'd. — Par Reg 4.208
And missing thee, I walk unseen — Penseroso 65
Mission
His end of being on Earth, and mission high: — Par Reg 2.114
Missive
Of missive ruin; part incentive reed — Par Lost 6.519
Mist
Irradiate, there plant eyes, all mist from thence — Par Lost 3.53
The Angel, nor in mist, the common gloss — Par Lost 5.435
None was, but from the Earth a dewie Mist — Par Lost 7.333
Satan involv'd in rising Mist, then sought — Par Lost 9.75
I dread, and to elude, thus wrapt in mist — Par Lost 9.158
Like a black mist low creeping, he held on — Par Lost 9.180
Vapour, and Mist, and Exhalation hot, — Par Lost 10.694
Gliding meteorous, as Ev'ning Mist — Par Lost 12.629
But swoln with wind, and the rank mist they draw, — Lycidas 126
Mistake
As some misfortune brings him, or mistake, — Par Lost 10.900
Mistaken
Dal. I was a fool, too rash, and quite mistaken — Samson 907
Misthought
Adam, missthought of her to thee so dear? — Par Lost 9.289
Mistook
O ye mistook, ye should have snatcht his wand — Mask 815
Trinity ms 'mistooke'
Bridgewater ms 'mistooke'
1637 'mistooke'
Too divine to be mistook: — Arcades 4
Trinity ms 'mistooke'
Mistress
Wonder not, sovran Mistress, if perhaps — Par Lost 9.532
To the great Mistres of yon princely shrine, — Arcades 36
Trinity ms 'mistresse', ms defective
Though *Syrinx* your *Pans* Mistres were, — Arcades 106
1673 'Mistress'
Trinity ms defective here
Mistrust
Not then mistrust, but tender love enjoynes, — Par Lost 9.357
Mistrust, Suspicion, Discord, and shook sore — Par Lost 9.1124
Mistrustful
Mistrustful, grounds his courage on despair — Par Lost 2.126
Mists
Ye Mists and Exhalations that now rise — Par Lost 5.185
With black usurping mists, som gentle taper — Mask 337
Misty
Looks through the Horizontal misty Air — Par Lost 1.595
And mistie Regions of wide air next under, — Vacation 41
Misused
Crush't the sweet poyson of mis-used Wine — Mask 47
Bridgewater ms 'mis-vsed'
Mitigate
Nor wanting power to mitigate and swage — Par Lost 1.556
Of right, that I may mitigate thir doom — Par Lost 10.76
To mitigate thus plead, not to reverse) — Par Lost 11.41
Mitred
He shook his Miter'd locks, and stern bespake, — Lycidas 112
Trinity ms 'mitre'd'
1638 'mitred'
Mix
Perpetual Circle, multiform; and mix — Par Lost 5.182
What order, so contriv'd as not to mix — Par Lost 5.334
From whom it sprung, impossible to mix — Par Lost 7.58
Heav'ns highth, and with the Center mix the Pole. — Par Lost 7.215
Express they, by looks onely, or do they mix — Par Lost 8.616
Total they mix, Union of Pure with Pure — Par Lost 8.627
As Flesh to mix with Flesh, or Soul with Soul. — Par Lost 8.629
To Death, and mix with our connatural dust? — Par Lost 11.529
To mix with thy concernments I desist — Samson 969
And mix no more with goodness, when at last — Mask 594
Trinity ms '& mixe no more' ← 'till all to place'
Bridgewater ms 'mixe'
1637 'mixe'
Wed your divine sounds, and mixt power employ — Musick 3
Trinity ms 'Wed' ← 'wed' ← 'Mixe'
Mixed
Mixt with obdurate pride and stedfast hate: — Par Lost 1.58
ms 'Mix'd'
Mixt with auxiliar Gods; and what resounds — Par Lost 1.579
Mixt with *Tartarean* Sulphur, and strange fire, — Par Lost 2.69
But all these in thir pregnant causes mixt — Par Lost 2.913
Abortive, monstrous, or unkindly mixt, — Par Lost 3.456
Produces with Terrestrial Humor mixt — Par Lost 3.610
Appeerd, with gay enameld colours mixt: — Par Lost 4.149
Mixt Dance, or wanton Mask, or Midnight Bal, — Par Lost 4.768
To have reported: gladly then he mixt — Par Lost 6.21
Destruction with Creation might have mixt. — Par Lost 8.236
From all her words and actions mixt with Love — Par Lost 8.602
Into a Beast, and mixt with bestial slime, — Par Lost 9.165
Loaden with fruit of fairest colours mixt, — Par Lost 9.577
That time Celestial visages, yet mixt — Par Lost 10.24
And Prayers, which in this Golden Censer, mixt — Par Lost 11.24
Grey-headed men and grave, with Warriours mixt, — Par Lost 11.662
Abhor to joyn; and by imprudence mixt, — Par Lost 11.686
And all his people; Thunder mixt with Haile, — Par Lost 12.181
Haile mixt with fire must rend th' *Egyptian* Skie — Par Lost 12.182
Fierce rain with lightning mixt, water with fire — Par Reg 4.412
Or was too much of self-love mixt, — Samson 1031
Samson with these immixt, inevitably — Samson 1657
With many murmurs mixt, whose pleasing poison — Mask 526
With spirits of balm, and fragrant Syrops mixt. — Mask 674
Wed your divine sounds, and mixt power employ — Musick 3
Trinity ms 'mixt power' ← 'mix't' ← 'happiest sounds' ← 'joynt force'
Mixing
Recounted, mixing intercession sweet. — Par Lost 10.228
By mixing somewhat true to vent more lyes. — Par Reg 1.433
Mixture
No gross, no unharmoneous mixture foule, — Par Lost 11.51
Com. Can any mortal mixture of Earths mould — Mask 244
Such mixture was not held a stain) — Penseroso 26
Moab
Next *Chemos*, th' obscene dread of *Moabs* Sons, — Par Lost 1.406
ms 'Moabs'
Moab, with them of Hagars blood — Psalm 83, 23
Moan
The *Lars*, and *Lemures* moan with midnight plaint, — Nativity 191
Here be tears of perfect moan — Winchester 55
Moans
Mother with Infant down the Rocks. Their moans — Sonnet 18, 8
Mock
That mock our scant manuring, and require — Par Lost 4.628
Mock us with his blest sight, then snatch him hence, — Par Reg 2.56
Mocked
Why am I mockt with death, and length'nd out — Par Lost 10.774
As mockt they storm; great laughter was in Heav'n — Par Lost 12.59
Mode
For one of *Syrian* mode, whereon to burn — Par Lost 1.474
In perfect *Phalanx* to the *Dorian* mood — Par Lost 1.550
A Table richly spred, in regal mode, — Par Reg 2.340
Model
By Model, or by shading Pencil drawn. — Par Lost 3.509
Hereafter, when they come to model Heav'n — Par Lost 8.79
Moderate
In mean estate live moderate, till grown — Par Lost 12.351

Moderate(*cont*)
Others more moderate seeming, but thir aim — Samson 1464
Had but a moderate and beseeming share — Mask 769

Moderation
By moderation either state to beare, — Par Lost 11.363

Modern
City of old or modern Fame, the Seat — Par Lost 11.386
In antient and in modern books enroll'd; — Samson 653
From old, or modern Bard in Hall, or Bowr. — Mask 45
1637 'moderne'
Bridgewater ms 'moderne'
Trinity ms 'moderne'

Modest
Yielded with coy submission, modest pride, — Par Lost 4.310
Soft, modest, meek, demure, — Samson 1036

Modesty
Yet Innocence and Virgin Modestie, — Par Lost 8.501
Timorous and loth, with novice modesty, — Par Reg 3.241

Modin
With *Modin* and her Suburbs once content. — Par Reg 3.170

Mogul
To *Agra* and *Lahor* of great *Mogul* — Par Lost 11.391

Moist
For hot, cold, moist, and dry, four Champions fierce — Par Lost 2.898
Bear his swift errands over moist and dry, — Par Lost 3.652
To nourish, and superfluous moist consumes: — Par Lost 5.325
From her moist Continent to higher Orbes. — Par Lost 5.422
Moist nutriment, or under Rocks thir food — Par Lost 7.408
Blow moist and keen, shattering the graceful locks — Par Lost 10.1066
Vapour, and Exhalation dusk and moist, — Par Lost 11.741
That with moist curb sways the smooth Severn stream, — Mask 825
I touch with chaste palms moist and cold, — Mask 918
Or whether thou to our moist vows deny'd, — Lycidas 159

Moisture
Satiate with genial moisture, when God said — Par Lost 7.282
Soon dri'd, and on the reaking moisture fed. — Par Lost 8.256

Mole
The Libbard, and the Tyger, as the Moale — Par Lost 7.467
They fasten'd, and the Mole immense wraught on — Par Lost 10.300
Or sullen *Mole* that runneth underneath, — Vacation 95

Molest
And not molest us, unless we our selves — Par Lost 8.186
And toil'st in vain, nor me in vain molest. — Par Reg 4.498
The sufferers then will scarce molest us here, — Samson 1525

Moloch
First *Moloch*, horrid King besmear'd with blood — Par Lost 1.392
ms 'Moloch'
Of *Moloch* homicide, lust hard by hate; — Par Lost 1.417
ms 'Moloch'
He ceas'd, and next him *Moloc*, Scepter'd King — Par Lost 2.43
Of *Moloc* furious King, who him defi'd, — Par Lost 6.357
And sullen *Moloch* fled, — Nativity 205

Molten
Thy molten crystal fill with mudd, — Mask 931

Moly
And yet more med'cinal is it then that *Moly* — Mask 636
Trinity ms 'Moly' ←'ancient Moly'
line not in Bridgewater ms

Mombaza
Mombaza, and *Quiloa*, and *Melind*, — Par Lost 11.399

Moment
All in a moment through the gloom were seen — Par Lost 1.544
And judg'd of public moment, in the shape — Par Lost 2.448
All in one moment, and so neer the brink; — Par Lost 2.609
Hee rules a moment; *Chaos* Umpire sits, — Par Lost 2.907
Would set me highest, and in a moment quit — Par Lost 4.51
As onely in his arm the moment lay — Par Lost 6.239
Were ready, in a moment up they turnd — Par Lost 6.509
Self-lost, and in a moment will create — Par Lost 7.154
Or touch with lightest moment of impulse — Par Lost 10.45
All these which in a moment thou behold'st, — Par Reg 4.162
All in a moment overwhelm'd and fall'n. — Samson 1559
And in a moment shall be quite abash't. — Psalm 6, 24

Mona
Nor on the shaggy top of *Mona* high, — Lycidas 54

Monarch
Monarch in Heav'n, till then as one secure — Par Lost 1.638
The Monarch, and prevented all reply, — Par Lost 2.467
Heav'ns awful Monarch? wherefore but in hope — Par Lost 4.960
That equal over equals Monarch Reigne: — Par Lost 5.832
Our foile in Heav'n; here thou shalt Monarch reign, — Par Lost 10.375
But night sits monarch yet in the mid sky. — Mask 957
Bridgewater ms 'Monarch'

Monarchal
Above his fellows, with Monarchal pride — Par Lost 2.428

Monarchies
The weight of mightiest Monarchies; his look — Par Lost 2.307
The Monarchies of the Earth, thir pomp and state, — Par Reg 3.246
All Monarchies besides throughout the world, — Par Reg 4.150

Monarchs
Perplexes Monarchs. Dark'n'd so, yet shon — Par Lost 1.599
Empires, and Monarchs, and thir radiant Courts, — Par Reg 3.237
The seats of mightiest Monarchs, and so large — Par Reg 3.262
And all her jealous monarchs with amaze, — Sonnet 15, 3
1694 'Monarchs'

Monarchy
Against the Throne and Monarchy of God — Par Lost 1.42
Monarchie over such as live by right — Par Lost 5.795

Monarchy(*cont*)
And henceforth Monarchie with thee divide — Par Lost 10.379
He who obtains the Monarchy of Heav'n, — Par Reg 1.87
Of that first golden Monarchy the seat, — Par Reg 3.277

Money
Money brings Honour, Friends, Conquest, and Realms; — Par Reg 2.422

Mongst
'Mongst horrid shapes, and shreiks, and sights unholy, — Allegro 4
Which 'mongst the wanton gods a foul reproach was held. — Fair Inf 14

Monster
Dagon his Name, Sea Monster, upward Man — Par Lost 1.462
ms 'monster'
The Monster moving onward came as fast — Par Lost 2.675
Whom thus the Sin-born Monster answerd soon. — Par Lost 10.596
Food for so foule a Monster, in thy power — Par Lost 10.986
Might'st thou expel this monster from his Throne — Par Reg 4.100
A brutish monster: what if I withal — Par Reg 4.128
And as that *Theban* Monster that propos'd — Par Reg 4.572
That specious Monster, my accomplisht snare. — Samson 230

Monsters
These yelling Monsters that with ceasless cry — Par Lost 2.795
With complicated monsters head and taile, — Par Lost 10.523
Where luxurie late reign'd, Sea-monsters whelp'd — Par Lost 11.751
These oughly-headed Monsters? Mercy guard me! — Mask 695
Trinity ms 'monsters'
1637 'monsters'
& yawning dens where glaring monsters house — Mask Tr. ms 16.63
and yawninge denns, where glaringe monsters house — Mask Br. ms 416

Monstrous
As whom the Fables name of monstrous size, — Par Lost 1.197
With monstrous shapes and sorceries abus'd — Par Lost 1.479
Perverse, all monstrous, all prodigious things, — Par Lost 2.625
Abortive, monstrous, or unkindly mixt, — Par Lost 3.456
Into the wastful Deep; the monstrous sight — Par Lost 6.862
A monstrous Serpent on his Belly prone, — Par Lost 10.514
Diseases dire, of which a monstrous crew — Par Lost 11.474
He and his monstrous rout are heard to howl — Mask 533
Harpyies and *Hydra's*, or all the monstrous forms — Mask 605
Visit'st the bottom of the monstrous world; — Lycidas 158

Montalban
Jousted in *Aspramont* or *Montalban*, — Par Lost 1.583
ms 'Montalban'

Montezuma
Rich *Mexico* the seat of *Motezume*, — Par Lost 11.407

Month
This is the Month, and this the happy morn — Nativity 1

Monthly
Timely interposes, and her monthly round — Par Lost 3.728

Months
Days, months, & years, towards his all-chearing Lamp — Par Lost 3.581
His Seasons, Hours, or Dayes, or Months, or Yeares: — Par Lost 8.69
Lead in swift round the Months and Years. — Mask 114
Trinity ms 'months'
Bridgewater ms 'months'

Monument
Where Satan now prevailes, a Monument — Par Lost 10.258
Or monument to Ages, and thereon — Par Lost 11.326
Vain monument of strength; till length of years — Samson 570
A Monument, and plant it round with shade — Samson 1734
Hast built thy self a live-long Monument. — Shakespear 8
1663-4 '*Monument*'

Monumental
Of Pine, or monumental Oake, — Penseroso 135

Monuments
Learn how thir greatest Monuments of Fame, — Par Lost 1.695
ms 'monuments'
Oft seen in Charnell vaults, and Sepulchers — Mask 471
Trinity ms 'sepulchers' ←'monume'

Mood
In perfect *Phalanx* to the *Dorian* mood — Par Lost 1.550
To whom thus *Belial* in like gamesom mood, — Par Lost 6.620
Thus in calm mood his Words to *Eve* he turnd. — Par Lost 9.920
And in a careless mood thus to him said. — Par Reg 4.450
Harsh, and of dissonant mood from his complaint, — Samson 662
Could stir the constant mood of her calm thoughts, — Mask 371
That strain I heard was of a higher mood: — Lycidas 87
That bawle for freedom in their senceless mood, — Sonnet 12, 9

Moon
Hung on his shoulders like the Moon, whose Orb — Par Lost 1.287
ms 'moon'
To whose bright Image nightly by the Moon — Par Lost 1.440
ms 'moon'
Shorn of his Beams, or from behind the Moon — Par Lost 1.596
ms 'moon'
Or dreams he sees, while over-head the Moon — Par Lost 1.784
With *Lapland* Witches, while the labouring Moon — Par Lost 2.665
Of smallest Magnitude close by the Moon. — Par Lost 2.1053
Not in the neighbouring Moon, as some have dreamd; — Par Lost 3.459
Night would invade, but there the neighbouring Moon — Par Lost 3.726
The starrie Host, rode brightest, till the Moon — Par Lost 4.606
With this her solemn Bird and this fair Moon, — Par Lost 4.648
With this her solemn Bird, nor walk by Moon, — Par Lost 4.655
Which they beheld, the Moons resplendent Globe — Par Lost 4.723
Daz'ling the Moon; these to the Bower direct — Par Lost 4.798
Full Orb'd the Moon, and with more pleasing light — Par Lost 5.42
Moon, that now meetst the orient Sun, now fli'st — Par Lost 5.175
Imagind Lands and Regions in the Moon: — Par Lost 5.263
Ethereal, and as lowest first the Moon; — Par Lost 5.418

Moon(*cont*)	
Nor doth the Moon no nourishment exhale	Par Lost 5.421
Or if the Starr of Eevning and the Moon	Par Lost 7.104
Though of Ethereal Mould: then form'd the Moon	Par Lost 7.356
Shedding sweet influence: less bright the Moon,	Par Lost 7.375
To the terrestrial Moon be as a Starr	Par Lost 8.142
Solstitial summers heat. To the blanc Moone	Par Lost 10.656
And thou Moon in the vale of *Aialon*,	Par Lost 12.266
And silent as the Moon,	Samson 87
Now to the Moon in wavering Morrice move,	Mask 116
Bridgewater ms 'moone'	
1637 'Moone'	
Trinity ms 'moone'	
Eld. Bro. Unmuffle ye faint stars, and thou fair Moon	Mask 331
Bridgewater ms 'moone'	
1637 'moon'	
Trinity ms 'moone' ←'M'	
By her own radiant light, though Sun and Moon	Mask 374
Bridgewater ms 'moone'	
Trinity ms 'moone'	
To the corners of the Moon.	Mask 1017
Trinity ms 'Moone' ←'moone'	
1637 'Moone'	
Trinity ms 'Moone'	
To behold the wandring Moon,	Penseroso 67
The horned Moon to shine by night,	Psalm 136, 33
Obedient to the Moon he spent his date	Another 29
line not in 1658 text	
1640 'Moone'	
Which after held the Sun and Moon in fee.	Sonnet 12, 7
Trinity ms 'moone' ←'Moon'	
Of Sun or Moon or Starre throughout the year,	Sonnet 22, 5
The Moon and Starrs which thou so bright hast set,	Psalm 8, 10
Blow, *as is wont*, in the new Moon	Psalm 81, 9
Mooned	
Turnd fierie red, sharpning in mooned hornes	Par Lost 4.978
And mooned *Ashtaroth*,	Nativity 200
Moon-loved	
Fly after the Night-steeds, leaving their Moon-lov'd maze.	Nativity 236
Moons	
With thir attendant Moons thou wilt descrie	Par Lost 8.149
In Rhombs and wedges, and half moons, and wings.	Par Reg 3.309
Moonstruck	
And Moon-struck madness, pining Atrophie,	Par Lost 11.486
line not in 1667 edition	
Moor	
The Realm of *Bocchus* to the Black-moor Sea;	Par Reg 4.72
Moorish	
In fog, or fire, by lake, or moorish fen,	Mask 433
Trinity ms 'moorie'	
Moors	
Moors by his side under the Lee, while Night	Par Lost 1.207
ms 'Moores'	
Moory	
With winged course ore Hill or moarie Dale,	Par Lost 2.944
Moping	
Daemoniac Phrenzie, moaping Melancholie	Par Lost 11.485
line not in 1667 edition	
Moral	
Cannot appease, nor Man the moral part	Par Lost 12.298
Of moral prudence, with delight receiv'd	Par Reg 4.263
Unless where moral vertue is express't	Par Reg 4.351
That moral verdit quits her of unclean:	Samson 324
And try her yet more strongly. Com, no more,	Mask 806
Trinity ms 'no more' ←'y'are too morall'	
This is meer moral babble, and direct	Mask 807
Bridgewater ms 'morrall'	
1637 'morall'	
Trinity ms 'meere moral bable' ←'your morall stuffe' ←'meere morall stuffe'	
More	
Delight thee more, and *Siloa*'s Brook that flow'd	Par Lost 1.11
Reserv'd him to more wrath; for now the thought	Par Lost 1.54
We may with more successful hope resolve	Par Lost 1.120
In this unhappy Mansion, or once more	Par Lost 1.268
Regaind in Heav'n, or what more lost in Hell?	Par Lost 1.270
Belial came last, then whom a Spirit more lewd	Par Lost 1.490
Fell not from Heaven, or more gross to love	Par Lost 1.491
Or Altar smoak'd; yet who more oft then hee	Par Lost 1.493
All these and more came flocking; but with looks	Par Lost 1.522
Could merit more then that small infantry	Par Lost 1.575
Were always downward bent, admiring more	Par Lost 1.681
More glorious and more dread then from no fall,	Par Lost 2.16
Thus farr at least recover'd, hath much more	Par Lost 2.22
Will covet more. With this advantage then	Par Lost 2.35
More then can be in Heav'n, we now return	Par Lost 2.37
More unexpert, I boast not: them let those	Par Lost 2.52
Calls us to Penance? More destroy'd then thus	Par Lost 2.92
Belial, in act more graceful and humane;	Par Lost 2.109
To be no more; sad cure; for who would loose,	Par Lost 2.146
Whatever doing, what can we suffer more,	Par Lost 2.162
Not more Almighty to resist our might	Par Lost 2.192
If we procure not to our selves more woe.	Par Lost 2.225
Magnificence; and what can Heav'n shew more?	Par Lost 2.273
In power and excellence, but favour'd more	Par Lost 2.350
Will once more lift us up, in spight of Fate,	Par Lost 2.393
Of hazard more, as he above the rest	Par Lost 2.455
More tollerable; if there be cure or charm	Par Lost 2.460

More(*cont*)	
Dreaded not more th' adventure then his voice	Par Lost 2.474
Thence more at ease thir minds and somwhat rais'd	Par Lost 2.521
Others with vast *Typhoean* rage more fell	Par Lost 2.539
Into th' *Euboic* Sea. Others more milde,	Par Lost 2.546
The thronging audience. In discourse more sweet	Par Lost 2.555
In thoughts more elevate, and reason'd high	Par Lost 2.558
Of fierce extreams, extreams by change more fierce,	Par Lost 2.599
Where I reign King, and to enrage thee more,	Par Lost 2.698
More dreadful and deform: on th' other side	Par Lost 2.706
For never but once more was either like	Par Lost 2.721
Sight more detestable then him and thee.	Par Lost 2.745
I fled, but he pursu'd (though more, it seems,	Par Lost 2.790
Perhaps our vacant room, though more remov'd,	Par Lost 2.835
Then this more secret now design'd, I haste	Par Lost 2.838
And by decision more imbroiles the fray	Par Lost 2.908
His dark materials to create more Worlds,	Par Lost 2.916
(Which is my present journey) and once more	Par Lost 2.985
And more endanger'd, then when *Argo* pass'd	Par Lost 2.1017
Or dim suffusion veild. Yet not the more	Par Lost 3.26
Freely voutsaft; once more I will renew	Par Lost 3.175
Upheld by me, yet once more he shall stand	Par Lost 3.178
But hard be hard'nd, blind be blinded more,	Par Lost 3.200
And reconcilement; wrauth shall be no more	Par Lost 3.264
By Merit more then Birthright Son of God,	Par Lost 3.309
Farr more then Great or High; because in thee	Par Lost 3.311
Love hath abounded more then Glory abounds,	Par Lost 3.312
For regal Scepter then no more shall need,	Par Lost 3.340
So strictly, but much more to pitie encline:	Par Lost 3.402
So strictly, but much more to pitie enclin'd,	Par Lost 3.405
Those argent Fields more likely habitants,	Par Lost 3.460
Cleombrotus, and many more too long,	Par Lost 3.473
At top whereof, but farr more rich appeerd	Par Lost 3.504
The Spirit maligne, but much more envy seis'd	Par Lost 3.553
The more it seems excess, that led thee hither	Par Lost 3.698
One step no more then from himself can fly	Par Lost 4.22
By thee, and more then half perhaps will reigne;	Par Lost 4.112
Saw him disfigur'd, more then could befall	Par Lost 4.127
On which the Sun more glad impress'd his beams	Par Lost 4.150
In narrow room Natures whole wealth, yea more,	Par Lost 4.207
His farr more pleasant Garden God ordaind;	Par Lost 4.215
They sat them down, and after no more toil	Par Lost 4.327
More easie, wholsom thirst and appetite	Par Lost 4.330
More grateful, to thir Supper Fruits they fell,	Par Lost 4.331
More woe, the more your taste is now of joy;	Par Lost 4.369
To mark what of thir state he more might learn	Par Lost 4.400
With more desire to know, and to reject	Par Lost 4.523
More of th' Almighties works, and chiefly Man	Par Lost 4.566
More hands then ours to lop thir wanton growth:	Par Lost 4.629
God is thy Law, thou mine: to know no more	Par Lost 4.637
Perfection from the Suns more potent Ray.	Par Lost 4.673
Broiderd the ground, more colour'd then with stone	Par Lost 4.702
More sacred and sequesterd, though but feignd,	Par Lost 4.706
Brought her in naked beauty more adorn'd,	Par Lost 4.713
More lovely then *Pandora*, whom the Gods	Par Lost 4.714
No happier state, and know to know no more.	Par Lost 4.775
That Glorie then, when thou no more wast good,	Par Lost 4.838
Or all at once; more glorie will be wonn,	Par Lost 4.853
Though for possession put to try once more	Par Lost 4.941
Patron of liberty, who more then thou	Par Lost 4.958
Gave heed, but waxing more in rage repli'd.	Par Lost 4.969
To boast what Arms can doe, since thine no more	Par Lost 4.1008
His mounted scale aloft: nor more; but fled	Par Lost 4.1014
Of Birds on every bough; so much the more	Par Lost 5.8
Full Orb'd the Moon, and with more pleasing light	Par Lost 5.42
Sweet of thy self, but much more sweet thus cropt,	Par Lost 5.68
And why not Gods of Men, since good, the more	Par Lost 5.71
Communicated, more abundant growes,	Par Lost 5.72
The Author not impair'd, but honourd more?	Par Lost 5.73
That wont to be more chearful and serene	Par Lost 5.123
More tuneable then needed Lute or Harp	Par Lost 5.151
To add more sweetness, and they thus began.	Par Lost 5.152
Her Virgin Fancies, pouring forth more sweet,	Par Lost 5.296
Earths inmost womb, more warmth then *Adam* needs;	Par Lost 5.302
More fruitful, which instructs us not to spare.	Par Lost 5.320
His god-like Guest, walks forth, without more train	Par Lost 5.351
More solemn then the tedious pomp that waits	Par Lost 5.354
Be over, and the Sun more coole decline.	Par Lost 5.370
Undeckt, save with her self more lovely fair	Par Lost 5.380
Shall fill the World more numerous with thy Sons	Par Lost 5.389
As that more willingly thou couldst not seem	Par Lost 5.466
But more refin'd, more spiritous, and pure,	Par Lost 5.475
More aerie, last the bright consummate floure	Par Lost 5.481
Can comprehend, incapable of more.	Par Lost 5.505
Attentive, and with more delighted eare,	Par Lost 5.545
But more desire to hear, if thou consent,	Par Lost 5.555
Each to other like, more then on earth is thought?	Par Lost 5.576
Is heard no more in Heav'n; he of the first,	Par Lost 5.659
What doubtful may ensue, more in this place	Par Lost 5.682
All thy Dominion, *Adam*, is no more	Par Lost 5.751
Abdiel, then whom none with more zeale ador'd	Par Lost 5.805
Our happie state under one Head more neer	Par Lost 5.830
But more illustrious made, since he the Head	Par Lost 5.842
Th' Apostat, and more haughty thus repli'd.	Par Lost 5.852
No more be troubl'd how to quit the yoke	Par Lost 5.882
Back on thy foes more glorious to return	Par Lost 6.39
His daring foe, at this prevention more	Par Lost 6.129
Of all thir Regions: how much more of Power	Par Lost 6.223

More(*cont*)

Or som more sudden vengeance wing'd from God	Par Lost 6.279
Receive, no more then can the fluid Aire:	Par Lost 6.349
Too mean pretense, but what we more affect,	Par Lost 6.421
The remedie; perhaps more valid Armes,	Par Lost 6.438
Weapons more violent, when next we meet,	Par Lost 6.439
With what more forcible we may offend	Par Lost 6.465
Doubl'd, would render them yet more despis'd,	Par Lost 6.602
And Brest, (what could we more2) propounded terms	Par Lost 6.612
They hard'nd more by what might most reclame,	Par Lost 6.791
More safe I Sing with mortal voice, unchang'd	Par Lost 7.24
Of his Eternal Empire, but the more	Par Lost 7.96
To magnifie his works, the more we know.	Par Lost 7.97
Drew many, whom thir place knows here no more;	Par Lost 7.144
Immediate are the Acts of God, more swift	Par Lost 7.176
Part loosly wing the Region, part more wise	Par Lost 7.425
To manifest the more thy might: his evil	Par Lost 7.615
Thou usest, and from thence creat'st more good.	Par Lost 7.616
Serv'd by more noble then her self, attaines	Par Lost 8.34
More plenty then the Sun that barren shines,	Par Lost 8.94
Is the prime Wisdom, what is more, is fume,	Par Lost 8.194
As with a smile more bright'nd, thus repli'd.	Par Lost 8.368
Hee ended, or I heard no more, for now	Par Lost 8.452
The more desirable, or to say all,	Par Lost 8.505
More then enough; at least on her bestow'd	Par Lost 8.537
Then value: Oft times nothing profits more	Par Lost 8.571
Well manag'd; of that skill the more thou know'st,	Par Lost 8.573
The more she will acknowledge thee her Head,	Par Lost 8.574
Made so adorn for thy delight the more,	Par Lost 8.576
More grateful then harmonious sound to the eare.	Par Lost 8.606
But I can now no more; the parting Sun	Par Lost 8.630
No more of talk where God or Angel Guest	Par Lost 9.1
Not less but more Heroic then the wrauth	Par Lost 9.14
More justly, Seat worthier of Gods, as built	Par Lost 9.100
Find place or refuge; and the more I see	Par Lost 9.119
Pleasures about me, so much more I feel	Par Lost 9.120
More Angels to Create, if they at least	Par Lost 9.146
Are his Created, or to spite us more,	Par Lost 9.147
Whom us the more to spite his Maker rais'd	Par Lost 9.177
Our pleasant task enjoyn'd, but till more hands	Par Lost 9.207
Enjoy'd by us excites his envie more;	Par Lost 9.264
More wise, more watchful, stronger, if need were	Par Lost 9.311
Go; for thy stay, not free, absents thee more;	Par Lost 9.372
So bent, the more shall shame him his repulse.	Par Lost 9.384
Delighted, but desiring more her stay.	Par Lost 9.398
Of Grove or Garden-Plot more pleasant lay,	Par Lost 9.418
Spot more delicious then those Gardens feign'd	Par Lost 9.439
Much hee the Place admir'd, the Person more.	Par Lost 9.444
What pleasing seemd, for her now pleases more,	Par Lost 9.453
Angelic, but more soft, and Feminine,	Par Lost 9.458
And tortures him now more, the more he sees	Par Lost 9.469
Whose higher intellectual more I shun,	Par Lost 9.483
From every Beast, more duteous at her call,	Par Lost 9.521
Thy awful brow, more awful thus retir'd.	Par Lost 9.537
Grateful to appetite, more pleas'd my sense	Par Lost 9.580
Yet more amaz'd unwarie thus reply'd.	Par Lost 9.614
Grow up to thir provision, and more hands	Par Lost 9.623
She scarse had said, though brief, when now more bold	Par Lost 9.664
And life more perfet have attaind then Fate	Par Lost 9.689
In heav'nly brests? these, these and many more	Par Lost 9.730
Commends thee more, while it inferrs the good	Par Lost 9.754
In Femal Sex, the more to draw his Love,	Par Lost 9.822
And render me more equal, and perhaps,	Par Lost 9.823
And Death ensue? then I shall be no more,	Par Lost 9.827
Not felt, nor shall be twice, for never more	Par Lost 9.859
Much more to taste it under banne to touch.	Par Lost 9.925
Rather then Death or aught then Death more dread	Par Lost 9.969
Her former trespass fear'd, the more to soothe	Par Lost 9.1006
Uncover'd more, so rose the *Danite* strong	Par Lost 9.1059
Hide me, where I may never see them more.	Par Lost 9.1090
It seems, in thy restraint: what could I more?	Par Lost 9.1170
The Eevning coole when he from wrauth more coole	Par Lost 10.95
He came, and with him *Eve*, more loth, though first	Par Lost 10.109
As vitiated in Nature: more to know	Par Lost 10.169
Of Beasts, but inward nakedness, much more	Par Lost 10.221
Or trie thee now more dang'rous to his Throne.	Par Lost 10.382
From his Creator, and the more to increase	Par Lost 10.486
Or much more grievous pain? Ye have th' account	Par Lost 10.501
Had leasure, wondring at himself now more;	Par Lost 10.510
This more delusive, not the touch, but taste	Par Lost 10.563
The Poles of Earth twice ten degrees and more	Par Lost 10.669
Inhabited, though sinless, more then now,	Par Lost 10.690
And sleep secure; his dreadful voice no more	Par Lost 10.779
More to the part sinister from me drawn,	Par Lost 10.886
And more that shall befall, innumerable	Par Lost 10.896
More miserable; both have sin'd, but thou	Par Lost 10.930
But rise, let us no more contend, nor blame	Par Lost 10.958
To better hopes his more attentive minde	Par Lost 10.1011
To argue in thee somthing more sublime	Par Lost 10.1014
To be forestall'd; much more I fear least Death	Par Lost 10.1024
No more be mention'd then of violence	Par Lost 10.1041
How much more, if we pray him, will his ear	Par Lost 10.1060
Fruits of more pleasing savour from thy seed	Par Lost 11.26
And in thir state, though firm, stood more confirmd.	Par Lost 11.71
When God descended, and perhaps once more	Par Lost 11.75
With whose stol'n Fruit Man once more to delude.	Par Lost 11.125
Spangl'd with eyes more numerous then those	Par Lost 11.130
Of *Argus*, and more wakeful then to drouze,	Par Lost 11.131

More(*cont*)

Who knows, or more then this, that we are dust,	Par Lost 11.199
And thither must return and be no more.	Par Lost 11.200
More orient in yon Western Cloud that draws	Par Lost 11.205
Not that more glorious, when the Angels met	Par Lost 11.213
No more availes then breath against the winde,	Par Lost 11.312
Corruption to bring forth more violent deeds.	Par Lost 11.428
More meek came with the Firstlings of his Flock	Par Lost 11.437
More terrible at th' entrance then within.	Par Lost 11.470
By Fire, Flood, Famin, by Intemperance more	Par Lost 11.472
Much better seems this Vision, and more hope	Par Lost 11.599
No more was seen; the floating Vessel swum	Par Lost 11.745
More then anough, that temperance may be tri'd:	Par Lost 11.805
The paths of righteousness, how much more safe,	Par Lost 11.814
The Ark no more now flotes, but seems on ground	Par Lost 11.850
More hard'nd after thaw, till in his rage	Par Lost 12.194
Moses once more his potent Rod extends	Par Lost 12.211
To noble and ignoble is more sweet	Par Lost 12.221
Some bloud more precious must be paid for Man,	Par Lost 12.293
Manhood to God-head, with more strength to foil	Par Lost 12.389
Never to hurt them more who rightly trust	Par Lost 12.418
And evil turn to good; more wonderful	Par Lost 12.471
Much more, that much more good thereof shall spring,	Par Lost 12.476
To God more glory, more good will to Men	Par Lost 12.477
With cause for evils past, yet much more cheer'd	Par Lost 12.604
More awful then the sound of Trumpet, cri'd	Par Reg 1.19
For much more willingly I mention Air,	Par Reg 1.45
Not thence to be more pure, but to receive	Par Reg 1.77
Yet held it more humane, more heavenly first	Par Reg 1.221
Now full, that I no more should live obscure,	Par Reg 1.287
I ask the rather, and the more admire,	Par Reg 1.326
More then the Camel, and to drink go far,	Par Reg 1.340
Who leagu'd with millions more in rash revolt	Par Reg 1.359
Man fall'n shall be restor'd, I never more.	Par Reg 1.405
Lost bliss, to thee no more communicable,	Par Reg 1.419
So never more in Hell then when in Heaven.	Par Reg 1.420
By thee are giv'n, and what confest more true	Par Reg 1.431
By mixing somewhat true to vent more lyes.	Par Reg 1.433
Return'd the wiser, or the more instruct	Par Reg 1.439
No more shalt thou by oracling abuse	Par Reg 1.455
And thou no more with Pomp and Sacrifice	Par Reg 1.457
If it may stand him more in stead to lye,	Par Reg 1.473
Permission from above; thou canst not more.	Par Reg 1.496
Since understand; much more his absence now	Par Reg 2.100
With more then humane gifts from Heaven adorn'd,	Par Reg 2.137
As the noon Skie; more like to Goddesses	Par Reg 2.156
Or *Amymone*, *Syrinx*, many more	Par Reg 2.188
Then *Solomon*, of more exalted mind,	Par Reg 2.206
His constancy, with such as have more shew	Par Reg 2.226
Mee hungring more to do my Fathers will.	Par Reg 2.259
But much more wonder that the Son of God	Par Reg 2.303
Forty and more deserted here indeed.	Par Reg 2.316
Then *Ganymed* or *Hylas*, distant more	Par Reg 2.353
Accomplish what they did, perhaps and more?	Par Reg 2.452
The wise mans cumbrance if not snare, more apt	Par Reg 2.454
Passions, Desires, and Fears, is more a King;	Par Reg 2.467
Is yet more Kingly, this attracts the Soul,	Par Reg 2.476
Far more magnanimous, then to assume.	Par Reg 2.483
Affecting private life, or more obscure	Par Reg 3.22
The more he grew in years, the more inflam'd	Par Reg 3.40
Made Captive, yet deserving freedom more	Par Reg 3.77
Poor *Socrates* (who next more memorable2)	Par Reg 3.96
If there be worse, the expectation more	Par Reg 3.207
(Whose ire I dread more then the fire of Hell)	Par Reg 3.220
At sight whereof the Fiend yet more presum'd,	Par Reg 3.345
And never cease, though to his shame the more;	Par Reg 4.14
Many a fair Edifice besides, more like	Par Reg 4.55
Meroe Nilotic Isle, and more to West,	Par Reg 4.71
More then of arms before, allure mine eye,	Par Reg 4.112
Or nothing more then still to contradict:	Par Reg 4.158
To worship thee accurst, now more accurst	Par Reg 4.179
And more blasphemous? which expect to rue.	Par Reg 4.181
Rather more honour left and more esteem;	Par Reg 4.207
The Kingdoms of this world; I shall no more	Par Reg 4.210
Then to a worldly Crown, addicted more	Par Reg 4.213
Look once more e're we leave this specular Mount	Par Reg 4.236
Within thy self, much more with Empire joyn'd.	Par Reg 4.284
Ignorant of themselves, of God much more,	Par Reg 4.310
And now the Sun with more effectual beams	Par Reg 4.432
Who all things now behold more fresh and green,	Par Reg 4.435
Not more; for Honours, Riches, Kingdoms, Glory	Par Reg 4.536
Therefore to know what more thou art then man,	Par Reg 4.538
He never more henceforth will dare set foot	Par Reg 4.610
Scarce half I seem to live, dead more then half.	Samson 79
And buried; but O yet more miserable!	Samson 101
But made hereby obnoxious more	Samson 106
Thir daily practice to afflict me more.	Samson 114
In me, of wisdom nothing more then mean;	Samson 207
But what more oft in Nations grown corrupt,	Samson 268
Then to love Bondage more then Liberty,	Samson 270
Yet more there be who doubt his ways not just,	Samson 300
They ravel more, still less resolv'd,	Samson 305
More Faith? who also in her prime of love,	Samson 388
Enough, and more the burden of that fault;	Samson 431
Nothing more certain, will not long defer	Samson 474
On thee, who now no more canst do them harm.	Samson 486
Who evermore approves and more accepts	Samson 510
For self-offence, more then for God offended.	Samson 515

More(*cont*)
Against another object more enticing? Samson 559
That these dark orbs no more shall treat with light, Samson 591
With answerable pains, but more intense, Samson 615
Heads without name no more rememberd, Samson 677
May expiate (though the fact more evil drew Samson 736
Once more thy face, and know of thy estate, Samson 742
My rash but more unfortunate misdeed. Samson 747
Then with more cautious and instructed skill Samson 757
More strength from me, then in thy self was found. Samson 789
Or by evasions thy crime uncoverst more. Samson 842
No more thy countrey, but an impious crew Samson 891
No more on me have power, their force is null'd, Samson 935
Dal. I see thou art implacable, more deaf Samson 960
To *Samson*, but shalt never see *Gath* more. Samson 1129
From thine, these evils I deserve and more, Samson 1169
Much more affliction then already felt Samson 1257
But patience is more oft the exercise Samson 1287
More then the working day thy hands, Samson 1299
And yet perhaps more trouble is behind. Samson 1300
On my refusal to distress me more, Samson 1330
Expect another message more imperious, Samson 1352
More Lordly thund'ring then thou well wilt bear. Samson 1353
What act more execrably unclean, prophane? Samson 1362
Others more moderate seeming, but thir aim Samson 1464
More generous far and civil, who confess'd Samson 1467
More then anough we know; but while things yet Samson 1592
Relation more particular and distinct. Samson 1595
Thee with thy slaughter'd foes in number more Samson 1667
Nor much more cause, *Samson* hath quit himself Samson 1709
Much like his Father, but his Mother more, Mask 57
But boast themselves more comely then before Mask 75
Their port was more then human, as they stood; Mask 297
Som say no evil thing that walks by night Mask 432
  Bridgewater ms 'naye more noe evill'
  Trinity ms 'Some say' ←'Nay more' ←'Some say'
Deny her nature, and be never more Mask 559
And mix no more with goodness, when at last Mask 594
  Trinity ms '& mixe no more' ←'till all to place'
And yet more med'cinal is it then that *Moly* Mask 636
  line not in Bridgewater ms
More happines then this thy present lot. Mask 789
  line not in Trinity ms
  line not in Bridgewater ms
And try her yet more strongly. Com, no more, Mask 806
  Trinity ms 'no more' ←'y'are too morall'
Flowers of more mingled hew Mask 994
With two sister Graces more Allegro 15
Where more is meant then meets the ear. Penseroso 120
And lead ye where ye may more neer behold Arcades 40
Nymphs and Shepherds dance no more Arcades 96
Trip no more in twilight ranks, Arcades 99
Yet once more, O ye Laurels, and once more Lycidas 1
Shall now no more be seen, Lycidas 43
Stands ready to smite once, and smite no more. Lycidas 131
Weep no more, woful Shepherds weep no more, Lycidas 165
Now *Lycidas* the Shepherds weep no more; Lycidas 182
The new-enlightn'd world no more should need; Nativity 82
Can no more divine, Nativity 177
And cam'st again to visit us once more? Fair Inf 52
Yet more; the stroke of death he must abide, Passion 20
Of Lute, or Viol still, more apt for mournful things. Passion 28
Which is no more then what is false and vain, On Time 5
O more exceeding love or law more just? Circum 15
Just law indeed, but more exceeding love! Circum 16
Will pierce more neer his heart. Circum 28
More then she could own from Earth. Winchester 6
As he were prest to death, he cry'd more waight; Another 26
  line not in 1640, 1657, 1658 texts
That som more timely-happy spirits indu'th. Sonnet 7, 8
Yet be it less or more, or soon or slow, Sonnet 7, 9
And left them both, more in himself content, Sonnet 10, 4
And Worsters laureat wreath; yet much remaines Sonnet 16, 9
Lodg'd with me useless, though my Soul more bent Sonnet 19, 4
And such, as yet once more I trust to have Sonnet 23, 7
So clear, as in no face with more delight. Sonnet 23, 12
Their bonds, and cast from us, no more to wear, Psalm 2, 7
Into my heart more joy Psalm 4, 31
Is better, *and more blest* Psalm 84, 34
Toward us, *and chide no more*. Psalm 85, 16
But let them never more Psalm 85, 34
Thy name for ever more. Psalm 86, 44
Sions *fair* Gates the Lord loves more Psalm 87, 5
Whom thou rememberest no more, Psalm 88, 21
Dost never more regard, Psalm 88, 22
No sacrifice to God more acceptable Prose 11, 2

Moreh
Of *Moreh;* there by promise he receaves Par Lost 12.137

Morn
Invests the Sea, and wished Morn delayes: Par Lost 1.208
  ms 'morn'
Sheer o're the Chrystal Battlements; from Morn Par Lost 1.742
Day, or the sweet approach of Ev'n or Morn, Par Lost 3.42
Sweet is the breath of morn, her rising sweet, Par Lost 4.641
But neither breath of Morn when she ascends Par Lost 4.650
Showrd Roses, which the Morn repair'd. Sleep on Par Lost 4.773
Now Morn her rosie steps in th' Eastern Clime Par Lost 5.1
Thy face, and Morn return'd, for I this Night, Par Lost 5.30

Morn(*cont*)
Sure pledge of day, that crownst the smiling Morn Par Lost 5.168
Witness if I be silent, Morn or Eeven, Par Lost 5.202
Comes this way moving; seems another Morn Par Lost 5.310
Yield Nectar, though from off the boughs each Morn Par Lost 5.428
(For wee have also our Eevning and our Morn, Par Lost 5.628
Among the sons of Morn, what multitudes Par Lost 5.716
Through Heav'ns wide Champain held his way, till Morn, Par Lost 6.2
Seem twilight here; and now went forth the Morn Par Lost 6.12
Now when fair Morn Orient in Heav'n appeerd Par Lost 6.524
And the third sacred Morn began to shine Par Lost 6.748
Visit'st my slumbers Nightly, or when Morn Par Lost 7.29
He nam'd. Thus was the first Day Eev'n and Morn: Par Lost 7.252
Both when first Eevning was, and when first Morn. Par Lost 7.260
So Eev'n and Morn recorded the Third Day. Par Lost 7.338
Glad Eevning and glad Morn crownd the fourth day. Par Lost 7.386
Ev'ning and Morn solemniz'd the Fift day. Par Lost 7.448
So Ev'n and Morn accomplish'd the Sixt day: Par Lost 7.550
I led her blushing like the Morn: all Heav'n, Par Lost 8.511
Disturbd not, waiting close th' approach of Morn. Par Lost 9.191
Forth issuing on a Summers Morn to breathe Par Lost 9.447
That Morn when first they parted; by the Tree Par Lost 9.848
Desire of wandring this unhappie Morn, Par Lost 9.1136
Though after sleepless Night; for see the Morn, Par Lost 11.173
After short blush of Morn; nigh in her sight Par Lost 11.184
Returne, the Starres of Morn shall see him rise Par Lost 12.422
Food to *Elijah* bringing Even and Morn, Par Reg 2.268
The morns approach, and greet her with his Song: Par Reg 2.281
To gratulate the sweet return of morn; Par Reg 4.438
Nor yet amidst this joy and brightest morn Par Reg 4.439
The nice Morn on th' *Indian* steep Mask 139
  Trinity ms 'morne'
  1637 'Morne'
  Bridgewater ms 'morne'
Love-darting eyes, or tresses like the Morn? Mask 753
  1637 'Morne'
  line not in Bridgewater ms
  Trinity ms 'morne'
Chearly rouse the slumbring morn, Allegro 54
When in one night, ere glimps of morn, Allegro 107
Till civil-suited Morn appeer, Penseroso 122
And early ere the odorous breath of morn Arcades 56
  Trinity ms 'morne'
Under the opening eye-lids of the morn, Lycidas 26
  Trinity ms 'morne'
While the still morn went out with Sandals gray, Lycidas 187
  Trinity ms 'morne'
This is the Month, and this the happy morn Nativity 1
To live with him, and sing in endles morn of light. Musick 28
  Trinity ms 'morne' ←'birth'
Which the sad morn had let fall Winchester 45
Each morn, and thee prevent. Psalm 88, 56

Morning
Both where the morning Sun first warmly smote Par Lost 4.244
To morrow ere fresh Morning streak the East Par Lost 4.623
Awake, the morning shines, and the fresh field Par Lost 5.20
Then when fair Morning first smiles on the World, Par Lost 5.124
Thir Orisons, each Morning duly paid Par Lost 5.145
On to thir mornings rural work they haste Par Lost 5.211
His count'nance, as the Morning Starr that guides Par Lost 5.708
Or Starrs of Morning, Dew-drops, which the Sun Par Lost 5.746
End, and dismiss thee ere the Morning shine. Par Lost 7.108
And Morning *Chorus* sung the second Day. Par Lost 7.275
And hence the Morning Planet guilds her horns; Par Lost 7.366
Who since the Morning hour set out from Heav'n Par Lost 8.111
Thir morning incense, when all things that breath, Par Lost 9.194
Not without Song, each Morning, and due praise Par Lost 9.800
Darkness ere Dayes mid-course, and Morning light Par Lost 11.204
Darkness defends between till morning Watch; Par Lost 12.207
So spake our Morning Star then in his rise, Par Reg 1.294
As morning shews the day. Be famous then Par Reg 4.221
Thus pass'd the night so foul till morning fair Par Reg 4.426
Fair morning yet betides thee Son of God, Par Reg 4.451
The morning Trumpets Festival proclaim'd Samson 1598
That spreds her verdant leaf to th' morning ray, Mask 622
  Bridgewater ms 'morninge'
And I must haste ere morning hour Mask 920
  Bridgewater ms 'morninge'
Flames in the forehead of the morning sky: Lycidas 171
For all the morning light, Nativity 73
But when of old the sons of morning sung, Nativity 119
Now the bright morning Star, Dayes harbinger, May Morn 1
Shalt in the morning hear Psalm 5, 6
Ith' morning I to thee with choyce Psalm 5, 7

Morocco
Damasco, or *Marocco*, or *Trebisond*, Par Lost 1.584
  ms 'Marocco'
Marocco and *Algiers*, and *Tremisen;* Par Lost 11.404

Morpheus
The fickle Pensioners of *Morpheus* train. Penseroso 10

Morris
Now to the Moon in wavering Morrice move, Mask 116
  Bridgewater ms 'morrice'
  Trinity ms 'morrice'

Morrow
Thou tellst, by morrow dawning I shall know. Par Lost 4.588
To morrow ere fresh Morning streak the East Par Lost 4.623
By morrow Eevning, and from Land to Land Par Lost 4.662

Morrow(*cont*)
Works of day pass't, or morrows next designe, Par Lost 5.33
Ere morrow wake, or the low roosted lark Mask 317
Trinity ms 'ere morrow wake' ←'ere the larke rowse'
Bridgewater ms 'morrowe'
And at my window bid good morrow, Allegro 46
To morrow to fresh Woods, and Pastures new. Lycidas 193

Morsel
Should prove a bitter Morsel, and his bane, Par Lost 2.808

Morsels
No homely morsels, and whatever thing Par Lost 10.605

Mortal
Of that Forbidden Tree, whose mortal tast Par Lost 1.2
ms 'mortall'
To mortal men, he with his horrid crew Par Lost 1.51
ms 'mortall'
From mortal or immortal minds. Thus they Par Lost 1.559
ms 'mortall'
Compare of mortal prowess, yet observ'd Par Lost 1.588
ms 'mortall'
Who boast in mortal things, and wond'ring tell Par Lost 1.693
ms 'mortall'
To mortal combat or carreer with Lance) Par Lost 1.766
ms 'mortall'
With mortal sting: about her middle round Par Lost 2.653
Possesses thee to bend that mortal Dart Par Lost 2.729
Though temper'd heav'nly, for that mortal dint, Par Lost 2.813
Of things invisible to mortal sight. Par Lost 3.55
On even ground against his mortal foe, Par Lost 3.179
Which of ye will be mortal to redeem Par Lost 3.214
Mans mortal crime, and just th' unjust to save, Par Lost 3.215
Inglorious, of his mortall sting disarm'd. Par Lost 3.253
To mortal men, above which only shon Par Lost 3.268
Haply so scap'd his mortal snare; for now Par Lost 4.8
Nor in thir liquid texture mortal wound Par Lost 6.348
Incapable of mortal injurie Par Lost 6.434
More safe I Sing with mortal voice, unchang'd Par Lost 7.24
From that day mortal, and this happie State Par Lost 8.331
Wept at compleating of the mortal Sin Par Lost 9.1003
What rests but that the mortal Sentence pass Par Lost 10.48
Of mortal change on Earth. As when a flock Par Lost 10.273
But mortal doom'd. How can he exercise Par Lost 10.796
And mortal food, as may dispose him best Par Lost 11.54
That must be mortal to us both. O flours, Par Lost 11.273
Thy mortal passage when it comes. Ascend Par Lost 11.366
Thy mortal sight to faile; objects divine Par Lost 12.9
To mortal eare is dreadful; they beseech Par Lost 12.236
The holy One with mortal Men to dwell: Par Lost 12.248
Expect with mortal paine: say where and when Par Lost 12.384
His Mother then is mortal, but his Sire, Par Reg 1.86
For know, thou art no Son of mortal man, Par Reg 1.234
Then Mortal Creatures, graceful and discreet, Par Reg 2.157
Of mortal things. Who therefore seeks in these Par Reg 4.318
Strongest of mortal men, Samson 168
In mortal strength! and oh what not in man Samson 349
Above the nerve of mortal arm Samson 639
Certain to have won by mortal duel from thee, Samson 1102
Defie thee to the trial of mortal fight, Samson 1175
Measure of strength so great to mortal seed, Samson 1439
So fond are mortal men Samson 1682
After this mortal change, to her true Servants Mask 10
Trinity ms 'mortall'
1637 'mortall'
Bridgewater ms 'mortall'
Com. Can any mortal mixture of Earths mould Mask 244
Bridgewater ms 'mortall'
Trinity ms 'mortall'
1637 'mortall'
By which all mortal frailty must subsist, Mask 686
Trinity ms 'mortall'
1637 'mortall'
line not in Bridgewater ms
And though not mortal, yet a cold shuddring dew Mask 802
line not in Bridgewater ms
1637 'mortall'
line not in Trinity ms
beyond the written date of mortall change Mask Tr. ms 10.22
Hath lockt up mortal sense, then listen I Arcades 62
Trinity ms 'mortall sense' ←'mortall eyes' ←'mortalitie'
Fame is no plant that grows on mortal soil, Lycidas 78
Trinity ms 'mortall'
1638 'mortall'
And chose with us a darksom House of mortal Clay. Nativity 14
As never was by mortall finger strook, Nativity 95
1673 'mortal'
Above the reach of mortall ey. Psalm 136, 94
1673 'mortal'
Oh say me true if thou wert mortal wight Fair Inf 41
And meerly mortal dross; On Time 6
Trinity ms 'mortall'
Look down *on mortal men*. Psalm 85, 48

Mortality
Mortalitie my sentence, and be Earth Par Lost 10.776
Hath lockt up mortal sense, then listen I Arcades 62
Trinity ms 'mortall sense' ←'mortall eyes' ←'mortalitie'
Above mortalitie that shew'd thou wast divine. Fair Inf 35

Mortals
To tempt or punish mortals, except whom Par Lost 2.1032

Mortals(*cont*)
Was distant; and these flaws, though mortals fear them Par Reg 4.454
All mortals I excell'd, and great in hopes Samson 523
If thou in strength all mortals dost exceed, Samson 817
(List mortals, if your ears be true) Mask 997
1637 'mortalls'
line not in Bridgewater ms
Mortals that would follow me, Mask 1018
Trinity ms 'mortalls'
1637 'Mortalls'
Bridgewater ms 'Mortalls'
I doubt me gentle mortalls these may seeme Mask Tr. ms 10.16
Sent by som spirit to mortals good, Penseroso 153
From eyes of mortals walk invisible, Vacation 66

Mortification
To black mortification. Samson 622

Mosaic
Mosaic; underfoot the Violet, Par Lost 4.700

Mosco
In *Mosco*, or the Sultan in *Bizance*, Par Lost 11.395

Moscow
In *Mosco*, or the Sultan in *Bizance*, Par Lost 11.395

Moses
Moses and *Aaron*) sent from God to claime Par Lost 12.170
Aw'd by the rod of *Moses* so to stand Par Lost 12.198
Moses once more his potent Rod extends Par Lost 12.211
That *Moses* might report to them his will, Par Lost 12.237
Moses in figure beares, to introduce Par Lost 12.241
And therefore shall not *Moses*, though of God Par Lost 12.307
Moses was forty days, nor eat nor drank, Par Reg 1.352
Moses was in the Mount, and missing long; Par Reg 2.15
On points and questions fitting *Moses* Chair, Par Reg 4.219
All knowledge is not couch't in *Moses* Law, Par Reg 4.225

Mossy
Thir Table was, and mossie seats had round, Par Lost 5.392
About the mossie Trunk I wound me soon, Par Lost 9.589
1667 'Mossie'
In Wood or Grove by mossie Fountain side, Par Reg 2.184
To give me answer from her mossie Couch. Mask 276
Bridgewater ms 'mossy'
The Hairy Gown and Mossy Cell, Penseroso 169

Most
He trusted to have equal'd the most High, Par Lost 1.40
Consult how we may henceforth most offend Par Lost 1.187
Did not disswade me most, and seem to cast Par Lost 2.122
When he who most excels in fact of Arms, Par Lost 2.124
Then most conspicuous, when great things of small, Par Lost 2.258
In doing what we most in suffering feel? Par Lost 2.340
The most averse, thee chiefly, who full oft Par Lost 2.763
Thir lighter wings. To whom these most adhere, Par Lost 2.906
Most glorious, in him all his Father shon Par Lost 3.139
Receive new life. So Man, as is most just, Par Lost 3.294
If stone, Carbuncle most or Chrysolite, Par Lost 3.596
Wilde work produces oft, and most in dreams, Par Lost 5.112
Is oftest yours, the latter most is ours, Par Lost 5.489
Then most, when most irregular they seem, Par Lost 5.624
That the most High commanding, now ere Night, Par Lost 5.699
Most reason is that Reason overcome. Par Lost 6.126
I see that most through sloth had rather serve, Par Lost 6.166
Once found, which yet unfound most would have thought Par Lost 6.500
On Wheels (for like to Pillars most they seem'd Par Lost 6.573
As is most just; this I my Glorie account, Par Lost 6.726
They hard'nd more by what might most reclame, Par Lost 6.791
As a despite don against the most High, Par Lost 6.906
Glorie they sung to the most High, good will Par Lost 7.182
And renders us in things that most concerne Par Lost 8.196
And inward Faculties, which most excell, Par Lost 8.542
Dismiss not her, when most thou needst her nigh, Par Lost 8.564
Most opportune might serve his Wiles, and found Par Lost 9.85
Leads thee, or where most needs, whether to wind Par Lost 9.215
Were better, and most likelie if from mee Par Lost 9.365
She most, and in her look summs all Delight. Par Lost 9.454
Most Favors, who can please him long; Mee first Par Lost 9.949
The Parts of each for other, that seem most Par Lost 9.1093
And easily approv'd; when the most High Par Lost 10.31
Justice with Mercie, as may illustrate most Par Lost 10.78
There best, where most with ravin I may meet; Par Lost 10.599
Or whom he wishes most shall seldom gain Par Lost 10.901
If care of our descent perplex us most, Par Lost 10.979
When angry most he seem'd and most severe, Par Lost 10.1095
This most afflicts me, that departing hence, Par Lost 11.315
And what most merits fame in silence hid. Par Lost 11.699
To judge them with his Saints: Him the most High Par Lost 11.705
For Gods! yet him God the most High voutsafes Par Lost 12.120
Men who attend the Altar, and should most Par Lost 12.354
The Power of the most High; he shall ascend Par Lost 12.369
Of God most High; So God with Man unites. Par Lost 12.382
Of the most High, who in full frequence bright Par Reg 1.128
This wounds me most (what can it less) that Man, Par Reg 1.404
To flye or follow what concern'd him most, Par Reg 1.440
Her dictates from thy mouth? most men admire Par Reg 1.482
Of most erected Spirits, most temper'd pure Par Reg 3.27
Thy life hath yet been private, most part spent Par Reg 3.232
All Horsemen, in which fight they most excel; Par Reg 3.307
To me so fatal, me it most concerns. Par Reg 4.205
This Tempest at this Desert most was bent; Par Reg 4.465
Hail Son of the most High, heir of both worlds, Par Reg 4.633
O loss of sight, of thee I most complain! Samson 67

Most(*cont*)	
Bear in their Superscription (of the most	Samson 190
At times when men seek most repose and rest,	Samson 406
Of all reproach the most with shame that ever	Samson 446
Deceiveable, in most things as a child	Samson 942
And with contrary blast proclaims most deeds,	Samson 972
Of falshood most unconjugal traduc't.	Samson 979
But in my countrey where I most desire,	Samson 980
To such a viper his most sacred trust	Samson 1001
Most shines and most is acceptable above.	Samson 1052
That part most reverenc'd *Dagon* and his Priests,	Samson 1463
Revives, reflourishes, then vigorous most	Samson 1704
When most unactive deem'd,	Samson 1705
(For most do taste through fond intemperate thirst)	Mask 67
And yet is most pretended: In a place	Mask 326
And run to meet what he would most avoid?	Mask 363
line not in Trinity ms	
line not in Bridgewater ms	
Himself is his own dungeon. 2. *Bro*. Tis most true	Mask 385
That musing meditation most affects	Mask 386
But most by leud and lavish act of sin,	Mask 465
Of my most honour'd Lady, your dear sister.	Mask 564
Yea even that which mischief meant most harm,	Mask 591
Shall in the happy trial prove most glory.	Mask 592
Where most may wonder at the workmanship;	Mask 747
line not in Bridgewater ms	
Impostor do not charge most innocent nature,	Mask 762
Most musicall, most melancholy!	Penseroso 62
Whose lustre leads us, and for her most fit,	Arcades 76
Resolve me then oh Soul most surely blest	Fair Inf 36
Most perfect *Heroe*, try'd in heaviest plight	Passion 13
Here lieth one who did most truly prove,	Another 1
when most were wont which till then us'd to scan	Sonnet 13, Tr. ms 40.03
Jehovah judgeth most upright	Psalm 7, 29
Of Jehovah the most high.	Psalm 7, 64
The Sons of God most high	Psalm 82, 22
Art the most high, *and thou the same*	Psalm 83, 67
Teach me O Lord thy way *most right*,	Psalm 86, 37
But thou Lord art the God most mild	Psalm 86, 53
Most mercifull, most true.	Psalm 86, 56
City of God, most glorious things	Psalm 87, 9
Motes	
As the gay motes that people the Sun Beams,	Penseroso 8
Motezume	
Rich *Mexico* the seat of *Motezume*,	Par Lost 11.407
Mother	
The Mother of Mankind, what time his Pride	Par Lost 1.36
Rifl'd the bowels of thir mother Earth	Par Lost 1.687
Mee overtook his mother all dismaid,	Par Lost 2.792
His mother bad, and thus bespake her Sire.	Par Lost 2.849
Mother of human Race: what could I doe,	Par Lost 4.475
So spake our general Mother, and with eyes	Par Lost 4.492
Whatever Earth all-bearing Mother yields	Par Lost 5.338
Haile Mother of Mankind, whose fruitful Womb	Par Lost 5.388
Fermented the great Mother to conceave,	Par Lost 7.281
Father and Mother, and to his Wife adhere;	Par Lost 8.498
Led *Eve* our credulous Mother, to the Tree	Par Lost 9.644
Mother of Science, Now I feel thy Power	Par Lost 9.680
About the Mother Tree, a Pillard shade	Par Lost 9.1106
To whom th' incestuous Mother thus repli'd.	Par Lost 10.602
As in my Mothers lap? there I should rest	Par Lost 10.778
Eve rightly call'd, Mother of all Mankind,	Par Lost 11.159
Mother of all things living, since by thee	Par Lost 11.160
Into thy Mothers lap, or be with ease	Par Lost 11.536
A Virgin is his Mother, but his Sire	Par Lost 12.368
The seed of Woman: Virgin Mother, Haile,	Par Lost 12.379
So spake our Mother *Eve*, and *Adam* heard	Par Lost 12.624
His Mother then is mortal, but his Sire,	Par Reg 1.86
These growing thoughts my Mother soon perceiving	Par Reg 1.227
But to his Mother *Mary*, when she saw	Par Reg 2.60
If he be Man by Mothers side at least,	Par Reg 2.136
By Mothers side thy Father, though thy right	Par Reg 3.154
When slipping from thy Mothers eye thou went'st	Par Reg 4.216
Athens the eye of *Greece*, Mother of Arts	Par Reg 4.240
Receiving from his mother Earth new strength,	Par Reg 4.566
Home to his Mothers house private return'd.	Par Reg 4.639
Much like his Father, but his Mother more,	Mask 57
Trinity ms 'mother'	
Bridgewater ms 'mother'	
Excells his Mother at her mighty Art,	Mask 63
Bridgewater ms 'mother'	
Trinity ms 'mother'	
And to my wily trains, I shall e're long	Mask 151
Trinity ms 'wilie' ← 'mothers'	
About my Mother *Circe*. Thus I hurl	Mask 153
Trinity ms 'mother'	
Bridgewater ms 'mother'	
My Mother *Circe* with the Sirens three,	Mask 253
Bridgewater ms 'mother'	
Trinity ms 'mother'	
1637 'mother'	
Deep skill'd in all his mothers witcheries,	Mask 523
Mother of a hunderd gods;	Arcades 22
Of wedded Maid, and Virgin Mother born,	Nativity 3
Heav'ns Queen and Mother both,	Nativity 201
Then thou the mother of so sweet a child	Fair Inf 71
And the languisht Mothers Womb	Winchester 33
Mother with Infant down the Rocks. Their moans	Sonnet 18, 8

Motherly	
Motherly cares and fears got head, and rais'd	Par Reg 2.64
Motion	
That in our proper motion we ascend	Par Lost 2.75
Devoid of sense and motion? and who knows,	Par Lost 2.151
Prodigious motion felt and rueful throes.	Par Lost 2.780
To motion, measures all things durable	Par Lost 5.581
Nor motion of swift thought, less could his Shield	Par Lost 6.192
Stood they or mov'd, in stature, motion, arms	Par Lost 6.302
In motion or in alt: him soon they met	Par Lost 6.532
Then time or motion, but to human ears	Par Lost 7.177
Her end without least motion, and receaves,	Par Lost 8.35
Admitting Motion in the Heav'ns, to shew	Par Lost 8.115
Attends thee, and each word, each motion formes,	Par Lost 8.223
By quick instinctive motion up I sprung,	Par Lost 8.259
Motion, each act won audience ere the tongue,	Par Lost 9.674
Thir motion, at whose Front a flaming Sword,	Par Lost 12.592
And now by some strong motion I am led	Par Reg 1.290
Habit, or state, or motion, still expressing	Par Reg 4.601
And the low world in measur'd motion draw	Arcades 71
To their great Lord, whose love their motion sway'd	Musick 22
Time numbers motion, yet (without a crime	Another 7
'Gainst old truth) motion number'd out his time;	Another 8
1640, 1657 ''twas motion'	
Motioned	
Well hast thou motion'd, well thy thoughts imployd	Par Lost 9.229
That what I motion'd was of God; I knew	Samson 222
1671 printed 'mention'd', errata 'motion'd'	
Motionless	
In stony fetters fixt, and motionless;	Mask 819
Bridgewater ms 'motionlesse'	
1637 'motionlesse'	
Motions	
All these our motions vain, sees and derides;	Par Lost 2.191
Turn swift thir various motions, or are turnd	Par Lost 3.582
And in thir motions harmonie Divine	Par Lost 5.625
Her motions, as the great first-Movers hand	Par Lost 7.500
Insensibly three different Motions move?	Par Lost 8.130
Thir planetarie motions and aspects	Par Lost 10.658
My motions in him, longer then they move,	Par Lost 11.91
Some rouzing motions in me which dispose	Samson 1382
Mould	
A various mould, and from the boyling cells	Par Lost 1.706
Sit unpolluted, and th' Ethereal mould	Par Lost 2.139
What creatures there inhabit, of what mould,	Par Lost 2.355
This worlds material mould, came to a heap:	Par Lost 3.709
That Mountain as his Garden mould high rais'd	Par Lost 4.226
Creatures of other mould, earth-born perhaps,	Par Lost 4.360
To whom thus *Eve*. *Adam*, earths hallowd mould,	Par Lost 5.321
Of this Ethereous mould whereon we stand,	Par Lost 6.473
Brass, Iron, Stonie mould, had not thir mouthes	Par Lost 6.576
Though of Ethereal Mould: then form'd the Moon	Par Lost 7.356
Bore up his branching head: scarse from his mould	Par Lost 7.470
Heroic built, though of terrestrial mould,	Par Lost 9.485
To mould me Man, did I sollicite thee	Par Lost 10.744
With the rank vapours of this Sin-worn mould.	Mask 17
Bridgewater ms 'moulde'	
Com. Can any mortal mixture of Earths mould	Mask 244
Of human mould with grosse unpurged ear;	Arcades 73
And leprous sin will melt from earthly mould,	Nativity 138
As in a womb, and from that mould	Psalm 7, 53
Moulds	
Into fit moulds prepar'd; from which he formd	Par Lost 11.571
Mound	
As with a rural mound the champain head	Par Lost 4.134
Mount	
Above th' *Aonian* Mount, while it pursues	Par Lost 1.15
Beyond the *Indian* Mount, or Faerie Elves,	Par Lost 1.781
ms defective here	
Betwixt *Damiata* and mount *Casius* old,	Par Lost 2.593
Over Mount *Sion*, and, though that were large,	Par Lost 3.530
The way he went, and on th' *Assyrian* mount	Par Lost 4.126
Mount *Amara*, though this by som suppos'd	Par Lost 4.281
But in the Mount that lies from *Eden* North,	Par Lost 4.569
Of three that in Mount *Ida* naked strove,	Par Lost 5.382
Amidst as from a flaming Mount, whose top	Par Lost 5.598
From that high mount of God, whence light & shade	Par Lost 5.643
Abstrusest thoughts, from forth his holy Mount	Par Lost 5.712
High on a Hill, far blazing, as a Mount	Par Lost 5.757
Rais'd on a Mount, with Pyramids and Towrs	Par Lost 5.758
In imitation of that Mount whereon	Par Lost 5.764
Within the Mount of God, fast by his Throne,	Par Lost 6.5
To win the Mount of God, and on his Throne	Par Lost 6.88
Farr separate, circling thy holy Mount	Par Lost 6.743
Forerunning Night; when at the holy mount	Par Lost 7.584
Fuming from Golden Censers hid the Mount.	Par Lost 7.600
Nor that which on the flaming Mount appeerd	Par Lost 11.216
On this Mount he appeerd, under this Tree	Par Lost 11.320
Or thence from *Niger* Flood to *Atlas* Mount	Par Lost 11.402
Above the highest Hills: then shall this Mount	Par Lost 11.829
Mount *Hermon*, yonder Sea, each place behold	Par Lost 12.142
Mount *Carmel;* here the double-founted stream	Par Lost 12.144
God from the Mount of *Sinai*, whose gray top	Par Lost 12.227
Our Fathers here with Manna; in the Mount	Par Reg 1.351
Moses was in the Mount, and missing long;	Par Reg 2.15
Impregnable, and there Mount *Palatine*	Par Reg 4.50
Look once more e're we leave this specular Mount	Par Reg 4.236
Her pile, far off appearing like a Mount	Par Reg 4.547

Mount(*cont*)
Not less renown'd then in Mount *Ephraim*, Samson 988
Over the mount, and all this hallow'd ground, Arcades 55
Where the great vision of the guarded Mount Lycidas 161
1638 'mount'
Trinity ms 'mount'
As on mount *Sinai* rang Nativity 158
And heard me from his holy mount. Psalm 3, 12
Mountain
Her Temple on th' offensive Mountain, built Par Lost 1.443
ms 'mountain'
Hath scath'd the Forrest Oaks, or Mountain Pines, Par Lost 1.613
ms 'mountain'
As when from mountain tops the dusky clouds Par Lost 2.488
That Mountain as his Garden mould high rais'd Par Lost 4.226
The Mountain of the Congregation call'd; Par Lost 5.766
Sidelong, had push't a Mountain from his seat Par Lost 6.197
With branches lopt, in Wood or Mountain fell'd) Par Lost 6.575
A woodie Mountain; whose high top was plaine, Par Lost 8.303
To shew us in this Mountain, while the Winds Par Lost 10.1065
Had wasted woods on Mountain or in Vale, Par Lost 11.567
Then from the Mountain hewing Timber tall, Par Lost 11.728
Fast on the top of som high mountain fixt. Par Lost 11.851
The Son of God up to a Mountain high. Par Reg 3.252
It was a Mountain at whose verdant feet Par Reg 3.253
To this high mountain top the Tempter brought Par Reg 3.265
Of that high mountain, whence he might behold Par Reg 4.26
And in this office of his Mountain watch, Mask 89
Bridgewater ms 'mountaine'
1637 'Mountaine'
Trinity ms 'mountaine'
And spotted mountain pard, but set at nought Mask 444
1637 'mountaine'
Trinity ms 'mountayne'
Bridgewater ms 'mountaine'
The Mountain Nymph, sweet Liberty; Allegro 36
Then past hee to a flowry Mountaine greene, Prose 4, 1
Mountaineer
No savage fierce, Bandite, or mountaneer Mask 426
Trinity ms 'mountaneere'
1673 'Mountaneer'
Bridgewater ms 'mountaneere'
1637 'mountaneete'
Mountains
Rivers or Mountains in her spotty Globe. Par Lost 1.291
ms 'Mountaines'
The bottom of the Mountains upward turn'd, Par Lost 6.649
Under the weight of Mountains buried deep, Par Lost 6.652
With Mountains as with Weapons arm'd, which makes Par Lost 6.697
That wisht the Mountains now might be again Par Lost 6.842
Myriads between two brazen Mountains lodg'd Par Lost 7.201
And surging waves, as Mountains to assault Par Lost 7.214
Immediately the Mountains huge appeer Par Lost 7.285
Mountains of Ice, that stop th' imagin'd way Par Lost 10.291
Above the highth of Mountains interpos'd. Par Reg 4.39
When Mountains tremble, those two massie Pillars Samson 1648
Mountains on whose barren brest Allegro 73
The lonely mountains o're, Nativity 181
The high, huge-bellied Mountains skip like Rams Psalm 114, 11
Why fled the Ocean? And why skipt the Mountains? Psalm 114, 13
Take up a weeping on the Mountains wilde, Passion 51
Lie scatter'd on the Alpine mountains cold, Sonnet 18, 2
Till all the mountains blaze, Psalm 83, 56
Among the holy Mountains *high* Psalm 87, 1
Mounted
His mounted scale aloft: nor more; but fled Par Lost 4.1014
Of his coole Bowre, while now the mounted Sun Par Lost 5.300
A triple mounted row of Pillars laid Par Lost 6.572
1667 'triple-mounted'
Close following pace for pace, not mounted yet Par Lost 10.589
So *Lycidas* sunk low, but mounted high, Lycidas 172
Mounting
So mounting up in ycie-pearled carr, Fair Inf 15
Mourn
And all their echoes mourn. Lycidas 41
Trinity ms 'mourne'
The Nimphs in twilight shade of tangled thickets mourn. Nativity 188
In vain the *Tyrian* Maids their wounded *Thamuz* mourn. Nativity 204
Now mourn, and if sad share with us to bear Circum 6
Trinity ms 'mourne'
In horrid deeps *to mourn*. Psalm 88, 28
Mourned
Who mourn'd in earnest, when the Captive Ark Par Lost 1.458
Mourners
Had got a race of mourners on som pregnant cloud. Passion 56
Mourneth
Nightly to thee her sad Song mourneth well. Mask 235
Mournful
That we must change for Heav'n, this mournful gloom Par Lost 1.244
ms 'mournfull'
Of Lute, or Viol still, more apt for mournful things. Passion 28
Mourning
Fully reveng'd, hath left them years of mourning, Samson 1712
Mourns
Though comfortless, as when a Father mourns Par Lost 11.760
Israel in long captivity still mourns; Par Reg 3.279
Bore witness gloriously; whence *Gaza* mourns Samson 1752
Mouth
So wide they stood, and like a Furnace mouth Par Lost 2.888
Even to my mouth of that same fruit held part Par Lost 5.83
Fearless unfeard he slept: in at his Mouth Par Lost 9.187
Nigh Rivers mouth or Foreland, where the Wind Par Lost 9.514
From each side shoaling towards the mouth of Hell. Par Lost 10.288
Through *Chaos* hurld, obstruct the mouth of Hell Par Lost 10.636
To som Caves mouth, or whether washt by stream Par Lost 11.569
Boiles out from under ground, the mouth of Hell; Par Lost 12.42
Proceeding from the mouth of God; who fed Par Reg 1.350
Her dictates from thy mouth? most men admire Par Reg 1.482
Should Kings and Nations from thy mouth consult, Par Reg 3.12
Wisest of men; from whose mouth issu'd forth Par Reg 4.276
We unawares run into dangers mouth. Samson 1522
Filling each mouth with envy, or with praise, Sonnet 15, 2
1694 'Mouths'
For in his faltring mouth unstable Psalm 5, 25
Mouthed
Fame if not double-fac't is double-mouth'd, Samson 971
Mouths
Put to thir mouths the sounding Alchymie Par Lost 2.517
With wide *Cerberian* mouths full loud, and rung Par Lost 2.655
And *Discord* with a thousand various mouths. Par Lost 2.967
From thir own mouths; all is not theirs it seems: Par Lost 4.513
Brass, Iron, Stonie mould, had not thir mouthes Par Lost 6.576
Cast on themselves from thir own mouths. There stood Par Lost 10.547
See where it flows, disgorging at seaven mouthes Par Lost 12.158
To be a lyer in four hundred mouths; Par Reg 1.428
Dishonour, obloquie, and op't the mouths Samson 452
So rife and celebrated in the mouths Samson 866
Blind mouthes! that scarce themselves know how to hold Lycidas 119
Trinity ms 'mouths'
Those rugged names to our like mouths grow sleek Sonnet 11, 10
Trinity ms 'mouths' ←'mouthes' ←'mouths'
Out of the tender mouths of latest bearth, Psalm 8, 4
Out of the mouths of babes and sucklings thou Psalm 8, 5
Move
Of depth immeasurable: Anon they move Par Lost 1.549
Might hap to move new broiles: Be this or aught Par Lost 2.837
Then feed on thoughts, that voluntarie move Par Lost 3.37
Dispenses Light from farr; they as they move Par Lost 3.579
Numberless, as thou seest, and how they move; Par Lost 3.719
And yee five other wandring Fires that move Par Lost 5.177
Hath past in Heav'n, som doubt within me move, Par Lost 5.554
The great Hierarchal Standard was to move; Par Lost 5.701
Of God and his *Messiah*. On they move Par Lost 6.68
And onward move Embattelld; when behold Par Lost 6.550
Or Wonders move th' obdurate to relent? Par Lost 6.790
That better might with farr less compass move, Par Lost 8.33
This to attain, whether Heav'n move or Earth, Par Lost 8.70
Hath left to thir disputes, perhaps to move Par Lost 8.77
Insensibly three different Motions move? Par Lost 8.130
And ye that live and move, fair Creatures, tell, Par Lost 8.276
From whom I have that thus I move and live, Par Lost 8.281
The Soule of Man, or passion in him move. Par Lost 8.585
Till *Adam* thus 'gan *Eve* to dalliance move, Par Lost 9.1016
Bound with *Gorgonian* rigor not to move, Par Lost 10.297
Had first his precept so to move, so shine, Par Lost 10.652
My motions in him, longer then they move, Par Lost 11.91
If Kingdom move thee not, let move thee Zeal, Par Reg 3.171
Why move thy feet so slow to what is best, Par Reg 3.224
And reconcilement move with feign'd remorse, Samson 752
Now to the Moon in wavering Morrice move, Mask 116
That sing, and singing in their glory move, Lycidas 180
Move in melodious time; Nativity 129
Didst move my first endeavouring tongue to speak, Vacation 2
That he could never die while he could move, Another 2
Move by her two maine nerves, Iron and Gold Sonnet 17, 8
1694 'mann'd'
Moved
Mov'd our Grand Parents in that happy State, Par Lost 1.29
Mov'd on in silence to soft Pipes that charm'd Par Lost 1.561
Could once have mov'd; then in the key-hole turns Par Lost 2.876
Mov'd on, with difficulty and labour hee; Par Lost 2.1022
The Trepidation talkt, and that first mov'd; Par Lost 3.483
Thus he in scorn. The warlike Angel mov'd, Par Lost 4.902
Of Union irresistible, mov'd on Par Lost 6.63
Stood they or mov'd, in stature, motion, arms Par Lost 6.302
By wound, though from thir place by violence mov'd. Par Lost 6.405
Mov'd the Creator in his holy Rest Par Lost 7.91
Invalid that which thee to doubt it mov'd; Par Lost 8.116
Mov'd contrarie with thwart obliquities, Par Lost 8.132
Creatures that livd, and movd, and walk'd, or flew, Par Lost 8.264
Whose inward apparition gently mov'd Par Lost 8.293
New part puts on, and as to passion mov'd, Par Lost 9.667
To whom soon mov'd with touch of blame thus *Eve*. Par Lost 9.1143
T' whom *Michael* thus, hee also mov'd, repli'd. Par Lost 11.453
Was heard, of Harp and Organ; and who moovd Par Lost 11.560
Of Paradise by might of Waves be moovd Par Lost 11.830
Burst forth, and in Celestial measures mov'd, Par Reg 1.170
What but thy malice mov'd thee to misdeem Par Reg 1.424
Thou art not to be harm'd, therefore not mov'd; Par Reg 2.407
Not therefore to be obey'd. But zeal mov'd thee; Samson 895
But that which mov'd my coming now, was chiefly Samson 1452
That dumb things would be mov'd to sympathize, Mask 796
line not in Trinity ms
line not in Bridgewater ms
And like an Engin mov'd with wheel and waight, Another 9

Moved(*cont*)
1640 'moov'd'
The Earths foundations all are mov'd — Psalm 82, 19

Mover
Her motions, as the great first-Movers hand — Par Lost 7.500

Moves
And every living thing that moves on the Earth. — Par Lost 7.534
Still moves with thine, join'd in connexion sweet, — Par Lost 10.359
Sollicitous, what moves thy inquisition? — Par Reg 3.200
Cho. Yet on she moves, now stands & eies thee fixt, — Samson 726
And with these raptures moves the vocal air — Mask 247

Moving
Was moving toward the shoar; his ponderous shield — Par Lost 1.284
The Monster moving onward came as fast — Par Lost 2.675
To first of women *Eve* thus moving speech, — Par Lost 4.409
Comes this way moving; seems another Morn — Par Lost 5.310
Under spred Ensignes moving nigh, in slow — Par Lost 6.533
Distant so high, with moving Fires adornd — Par Lost 7.87
On golden Hinges moving, to let forth — Par Lost 7.207
And seems a moving Land, and at his Gilles — Par Lost 7.415
So standing, moving, or to highth upgrown — Par Lost 9.677
My self, my Sepulcher, a moving Grave, — Samson 102
Whether above that high first-moving Spheare — Fair Inf 39

Mower
And the Mower whets his sithe, — Allegro 66

Mows
The Sithe of Time mowes down, devour unspar'd, — Par Lost 10.606

Mozambic
Mozambic, off at Sea North-East windes blow — Par Lost 4.161

Much
From what highth fall'n, so much the stronger prov'd — Par Lost 1.92
In Arms not worse, in foresight much advanc't, — Par Lost 1.119
Thus farr at least recover'd, hath much more — Par Lost 2.22
I should be much for open Warr, O Peers, — Par Lost 2.119
Our Supream Foe in time may much remit — Par Lost 2.210
They dreaded worse then Hell: so much the fear — Par Lost 2.293
To him who Reigns, and so much to him due — Par Lost 2.454
Nor fail'd they to express how much they prais'd, — Par Lost 2.480
Of good and evil much they argu'd then, — Par Lost 2.562
So much the neerer danger; go and speed; — Par Lost 2.1008
So much the rather thou Celestial light — Par Lost 3.51
Much less that durst upon his own head draw — Par Lost 3.220
So strictly, but much more to pitie encline: — Par Lost 3.402
So strictly, but much more to pitie enclin'd, — Par Lost 3.405
The Spirit maligne, but much more envy seis'd — Par Lost 3.553
Then much revolving, thus in sighs began. — Par Lost 4.31
Praeeminent by so much odds, while thou — Par Lost 4.447
Under a shade of flours, much wondring where — Par Lost 4.451
Your message, like to end as much in vain? — Par Lost 4.833
In that dark durance: thus much what was askt. — Par Lost 4.899
Of Birds on every bough; so much the more — Par Lost 5.8
Much fairer to my Fancie then by day: — Par Lost 5.53
Sweet of thy self, but much more sweet thus cropt, — Par Lost 5.68
Too much to one, but double how endur'd, — Par Lost 5.783
Erre not, much less for this to be our Lord, — Par Lost 5.799
Of all thir Regions: how much more of Power — Par Lost 6.223
Think nothing hard, much less to be despaird. — Par Lost 6.495
Much of his Race though steep, suspens in Heav'n — Par Lost 7.99
Much less can Bird with Beast, or Fish with Fowle — Par Lost 8.395
Second to me or like, equal much less. — Par Lost 8.407
Too much of Ornament, in outward shew — Par Lost 8.538
So much delights me as those graceful acts, — Par Lost 8.600
Deprest, and much they may, if all be mine, — Par Lost 9.46
Pleasures about me, so much more I feel — Par Lost 9.120
Bane, and in Heav'n much worse would be my state. — Par Lost 9.123
Thir growing work: for much thir work outgrew — Par Lost 9.202
Assist us: But if much converse perhaps — Par Lost 9.247
Of all that he Created, much less Man, — Par Lost 9.346
The willinger I goe, nor much expect — Par Lost 9.382
O much deceav'd, much failing, hapless *Eve*, — Par Lost 9.404
Much hee the Place admir'd, the Person more. — Par Lost 9.444
I not; so much hath Hell debas'd, and paine — Par Lost 9.487
Thou canst, who art sole Wonder, much less arm — Par Lost 9.533
Though at the voice much marveling; at length — Par Lost 9.551
Much reason, and in thir actions oft appeers. — Par Lost 9.559
Much more to taste it under banne to touch. — Par Lost 9.925
Tenderly wept, much won that he his Love — Par Lost 9.991
Much pleasure we have lost, while we abstain'd — Par Lost 9.1022
Too facil then thou didst not much gainsay, — Par Lost 9.1158
Much wondring how the suttle Fiend had stoln — Par Lost 10.20
And thought not much to cloath his Enemies: — Par Lost 10.219
Of Beasts, but inward nakedness, much more — Par Lost 10.221
Or much more grievous pain? Ye have th' account — Par Lost 10.501
And his Adherents, that with so much ease — Par Lost 10.622
Devourd each other; nor stood much in awe — Par Lost 10.712
Then all the World much heavier, though divided — Par Lost 10.836
Broke off the rest; so much of Death her thoughts — Par Lost 10.1008
To be forestall'd; much more I fear least Death — Par Lost 10.1024
How much more, if we pray him, will his ear — Par Lost 10.1060
As *Raphael*, that I should much confide, — Par Lost 11.235
The visual Nerve, for he had much to see; — Par Lost 11.415
Much at that sight was *Adam* in his heart — Par Lost 11.448
The rule of not too much, by temperance taught — Par Lost 11.531
Life much, bent rather how I may be quit — Par Lost 11.548
Much better seems this Vision, and more hope — Par Lost 11.599
Those were of hate and death, or pain much worse, — Par Lost 11.601

Much(*cont*)
In wise deport, spake much of Right and Wrong, — Par Lost 11.666
Who having spilt much blood, and don much waste — Par Lost 11.791
The paths of righteousness, how much more safe, — Par Lost 11.814
Much thou hast yet to see, but I perceave — Par Lost 12.8
Mine eyes true op'ning, and my heart much eas'd, — Par Lost 12.274
Much more, that much more good thereof shall spring, — Par Lost 12.476
With cause for evils past, yet much more cheer'd — Par Lost 12.604
For much more willingly I mention Air, — Par Reg 1.45
Of much amazement to th' infernal Crew, — Par Reg 1.107
Musing and much revolving in his brest, — Par Reg 1.185
As much his greater, and was hardly won; — Par Reg 1.279
Men to much misery and hardship born; — Par Reg 1.341
Much lustre of my native brightness, lost — Par Reg 1.378
Men generally think me much a foe — Par Reg 1.387
Since understand; much more his absence now — Par Reg 2.100
Belial, in much uneven scale thou weigh'st — Par Reg 2.173
But much more wonder that the Son of God — Par Reg 2.303
For so much good, so much beneficence. — Par Reg 3.133
Yet so much bounty is in God, such grace, — Par Reg 3.142
The world thou hast not seen, much less her glory, — Par Reg 3.236
Much ostentation vain of fleshly arm, — Par Reg 3.387
And fragile arms, much instrument of war — Par Reg 3.388
Vented much policy, and projects deep — Par Reg 3.391
That sleek't his tongue, and won so much on *Eve*, — Par Reg 4.5
Much less my mind; though thou should'st add to tell — Par Reg 4.113
And with the *Gentiles* much thou must converse, — Par Reg 4.229
Westward, much nearer by Southwest, behold — Par Reg 4.237
Within thy self, much more with Empire joyn'd. — Par Reg 4.284
Ignorant of themselves, of God much more, — Par Reg 4.310
Much of the Soul they talk, but all awrie, — Par Reg 4.313
By how much from the top of wondrous glory, — Samson 167
So much I feel my genial spirits droop, — Samson 594
With studied argument, and much perswasion sought — Samson 658
And Love hath oft, well meaning, wrought much wo, — Samson 813
Thou wilt renounce thy seeking, and much rather — Samson 828
So much of Adders wisdom I have learn't — Samson 936
Henceforth, nor too much disapprove my own. — Samson 970
Repuls't, without much inward passion felt — Samson 1006
Much like thy riddle, *Samson*, in one day — Samson 1016
Or was too much of self-love mixt, — Samson 1031
If thou at all art known. Much I have heard — Samson 1082
And thou hast need much washing to be toucht. — Samson 1107
Much more affliction then already felt — Samson 1257
With youthful steps? much livelier then e're while — Samson 1442
Cho. That hope would much rejoyce us to partake — Samson 1455
Some much averse I found and wondrous harsh, — Samson 1461
And numberd down: much rather I shall chuse — Samson 1478
From other hands we need not much to fear. — Samson 1526
So in the sad event too much concern'd. — Samson 1551
Nor much more cause, *Samson* hath quit himself — Samson 1709
Much like his Father, but his Mother more, — Mask 57
Of so much fame in Heav'n expect thy meed. — Lycidas 84
Next her much like to thee in story, — Winchester 62
And at her next birth much like thee, — Winchester 67
Dost make us Marble with too much conceaving; — Shakespear 14
And too much breathing put him out of breath; — Another 12
And inward ripenes doth much less appear, — Sonnet 7, 7
And Worsters laureat wreath; yet much remaines — Sonnet 16, 9
Pity me Lord for I am much deject — Psalm 6, 3
With much confusion; then grow red with shame, — Psalm 6, 22
Ah *Constantine*, of how much ill was cause — Prose 1, 1

Much-humbled
So spake, so wish'd much-humbl'd *Eve*, but Fate — Par Lost 11.181

Mud
Thy molten crystal fill with mudd, — Mask 931
Trinity ms 'mud'
1637 'mudde'
Bridgewater ms 'mud'

Mulciber
Men call'd him *Mulciber;* and how he fell — Par Lost 1.740
ms 'Mulciber'

Mules
Mules after these, Camels and Dromedaries, — Par Reg 3.335

Multiform
Perpetual Circle, multiform; and mix — Par Lost 5.182

Multiplied
And let the Fowle be multiply'd on the Earth. — Par Lost 7.398
Like of his like, his Image multipli'd, — Par Lost 8.424
Of vision multiplyed through air, or glass — Par Reg 4.41

Multiplies
From large bestowd, where Nature multiplies — Par Lost 5.318
Things highest, greatest, multiplies my fear. — Par Reg 1.69

Multiply
Be fruitful, multiply, and in the Seas — Par Lost 7.396
Be fruitful, multiplie, and fill the Earth, — Par Lost 7.531
And multiply a Race of Worshippers — Par Lost 7.630
Thy sorrow I will greatly multiplie — Par Lost 10.193
Delightfully, *Encrease and multiply*, — Par Lost 10.730
Or multiplie, but curses on my head? — Par Lost 10.732
Inhumanly to men, and multiply — Par Lost 11.677
Shall lead thir lives, and multiplie apace, — Par Lost 12.17

Multitude
A multitude, like which the populous North — Par Lost 1.351
Sluc'd from the Lake, a second multitude — Par Lost 1.702
As from a sky. The hasty multitude — Par Lost 1.730
His captive multitude: For he, be sure — Par Lost 2.323
Least Heav'n surcharg'd with potent multitude — Par Lost 2.836

Multitude(*cont*)
Then with the multitude of my redeemd — Par Lost 3.260
The multitude of Angels with a shout — Par Lost 3.345
Nor multitude, stand onely and behold — Par Lost 6.810
Distinct alike with multitude of eyes, — Par Lost 6.847
Thir multitude, and to his Son thus spake. — Par Lost 7.138
For one forbidden Tree a multitude — Par Lost 10.554
Through multitude that sung: Just are thy ways, — Par Lost 10.643
In wealth and multitude, factious they grow; — Par Lost 12.352
O what a multitude of thoughts at once — Par Reg 1.196
Or at thy heels the dizzy Multitude, — Par Reg 2.420
A multitude with Spades and Axes arm'd — Par Reg 3.331
And condemnation of the ingrateful multitude. — Samson 696
The herds would over-multitude their Lords, — Mask 731
1637 'over-inultitude'
Bridgewater ms 'overmultitude'
Trinity ms 'over multitude'

Multitudes
Multitudes like thy self, and thence be call'd — Par Lost 4.474
Among the sons of Morn, what multitudes — Par Lost 5.716
Against revolted multitudes the Cause — Par Lost 6.31
About the new-arriv'd, in multitudes — Par Lost 10.26
Cities of men, or head-strong Multitudes, — Par Reg 2.470

Mummers
Juglers and Dancers, Antics, Mummers, Mimics, — Samson 1325

Mural
Her mural breach, returning whence it rowld. — Par Lost 6.879

Murder
Notorious murder on those thirty men — Samson 1186

Murderer
What Murtherer, what Traytor, Parricide, — Samson 832
A Murtherer, a Revolter, and a Robber. — Samson 1180

Murderous
Thence into *Egypt*, till the Murd'rous King — Par Reg 2.76

Murky
His Nostril wide into the murkie Air, — Par Lost 10.280

Murmur
He scarce had finisht, when such murmur filld — Par Lost 2.284
Hoarce murmur echo'd to his words applause — Par Lost 5.873
Whose liquid murmur heard new thirst excites, — Par Lost 7.68
Of Bees industrious murmur oft invites — Par Reg 4.248
That murmur, soon replies, God doth not need — Sonnet 19, 9

Murmured
And fell *Charybdis* murmur'd soft applause: — Mask 259
Bridgewater ms 'murmurd'

Murmuring
Luxuriant; mean while murmuring waters fall — Par Lost 4.260
Not distant far from thence a murmuring sound — Par Lost 4.453
Murmuring, and with him fled the shades of night. — Par Lost 4.1015
And liquid Lapse of murmuring Streams; by these, — Par Lost 8.263
To whom the Tempter murmuring thus reply'd. — Par Reg 3.108
And the Waters murmuring — Penseroso 144

Murmurs
Melodious murmurs, warbling tune his praise. — Par Lost 5.196
With many murmurs mixt, whose pleasing poison — Mask 526
With puissant words, and murmurs made to bless, — Arcades 60

Murrain
His Cattel must of Rot and Murren die, — Par Lost 12.179

Musaeus
Might raise *Musaeus* from his bower, — Penseroso 104

Muse
Sing Heav'nly Muse, that on the secret top — Par Lost 1.6
Say, Muse, thir Names then known, who first, who last, — Par Lost 1.376
Taught by the heav'nly Muse to venture down — Par Lost 3.19
Both Harp and Voice; nor could the Muse defend — Par Lost 7.37
With admiration, and deep Muse to heare — Par Lost 7.52
1669 'muse'
What the sage Poets taught by th' heav'nly Muse, — Mask 515
Bridgewater ms 'muse'
So may som gentle Muse — Lycidas 19
Trinity ms 'muse'
What could the Muse her self that *Orpheus* bore, — Lycidas 58
Trinity ms 'muse her selfe' ←'golden hayrd Calliope'
The Muse her self, for her inchanting son — Lycidas 59
Trinity ms 'muse'
And strictly meditate the thankles Muse, — Lycidas 66
Trinity ms 'muse'
That shrunk thy streams; Return *Sicilian* Muse, — Lycidas 133
Say Heav'nly Muse, shall not thy sacred vein — Nativity 15
But fie my wandring Muse how thou dost stray! — Vacation 53
My muse with Angels did divide to sing; — Passion 4
Whether the Muse, or Love call thee his mate, — Sonnet 1, 13
muse a vain thing, the Kings of th'earth upstand — Psalm 2, 2

Mused
Pausing a while, thus to her self she mus'd. — Par Lost 9.744
His Father's business; what he meant I mus'd, — Par Reg 2.99

Muses
Cease I to wander where the Muses haunt — Par Lost 3.27
Nor of the Muses nine, nor on the top — Par Lost 7.6
And hears the Muses in a ring, — Penseroso 47
Lift not thy spear against the Muses Bowre, — Sonnet 8, 9

Music
Intent, with jocond Music charm his ear; — Par Lost 1.787
ms 'music'
Aereal Music send: nor knew I not — Par Lost 5.548
With Feast and Musick all the Tents resound. — Par Lost 11.592
With Music or with Poem, where so soon — Par Reg 4.332
And as I wake, sweet musick breath — Penseroso 151

Music(*cont*)
Such sweet compulsion doth in musick ly, — Arcades 68
And yet such musick worthiest were to blaze — Arcades 74
When such musick sweet — Nativity 93
Such Musick (as 'tis said) — Nativity 117
Ere-while of Musick, and Ethereal mirth, — Passion 1
That erst with Musick, and triumphant song — Circum 2
Trinity ms 'musick'
Broke the fair musick that all creatures made — Musick 21
of clamourous sin that all our musick marres — Musick Tr. ms 5.04
First taught our English Musick how to span — Sonnet 13, 2
Trinity ms 'Music'
1648 'Music'

Musical
But musical as is *Apollo*'s lute, — Mask 478
1637 'musicall'
Trinity ms 'musicall'
Bridgewater ms 'musicall'
Most musicall, most melancholy! — Penseroso 62
1673 'musical'

Musing
Musing and much revolving in his brest, — Par Reg 1.185
To studious musing; there *Ilissus* rouls — Par Reg 4.249
Or seven, though one should musing sit; — Samson 1017
Leans her unpillow'd head fraught with sad fears. — Mask 355
Trinity ms 'fraught with sad feares' ←'musing at our unkindnesse'
That musing meditation most affects — Mask 386
Bridgewater ms 'musinge'
With eev'n step, and musing gate, — Penseroso 38

Musk-rose
And sweeten'd every muskrose of the dale, — Mask 496
Bridgewater ms 'muskerose'
The Musk-rose, and the well attir'd Woodbine, — Lycidas 146
Trinity ms 'muske rose'
1638 'musk-rose'

Musky
And West winds, with musky wing — Mask 989
1637 'muskie'
Trinity ms 'muskie' ←'musky'
Bridgewater ms 'muskye'

Must
Our labour must be to pervert that end, — Par Lost 1.164
That we must change for Heav'n, this mournful gloom — Par Lost 1.244
Full Counsel must mature: Peace is despaird, — Par Lost 1.660
Open or understood must be resolv'd. — Par Lost 1.662
Must exercise us without hope of end — Par Lost 2.89
Is flat despair: we must exasperate — Par Lost 2.143
And that must end us, that must be our cure, — Par Lost 2.145
What yet they know must follow, to endure — Par Lost 2.206
Our servile offerings. This must be our task — Par Lost 2.246
Into their temper; which must needs remove — Par Lost 2.277
Must we renounce, and changing stile be call'd — Par Lost 2.312
Which he through hazard huge must earn. But they — Par Lost 2.473
Confus'dly, and which thus must ever fight, — Par Lost 2.914
Where onely what they needs must do, appeard, — Par Lost 3.105
I formd them free, and free they must remain, — Par Lost 3.124
Till they enthrall themselves: I else must change — Par Lost 3.125
He with his whole posteritie must dye, — Par Lost 3.209
Dye hee or Justice must; unless for him — Par Lost 3.210
Must have bin lost, adjudg'd to Death and Hell — Par Lost 3.223
Of what he was, what is, and what must be — Par Lost 4.25
Worse; of worse deeds worse sufferings must ensue. — Par Lost 4.26
That I with you must dwell, or you with me — Par Lost 4.377
Dearer thy self then all; needs must the power — Par Lost 4.412
But first with narrow search I must walk round — Par Lost 4.528
New troubles; him thy care must be to find. — Par Lost 4.575
With first approach of light, we must be ris'n, — Par Lost 4.624
Undaunted. If I must contend, said he, — Par Lost 4.851
She crushes, inoffensive moust, and meathes — Par Lost 5.345
Willing or no, who will but what they must — Par Lost 5.533
The full relation, which must needs be strange, — Par Lost 5.556
Ruin must needs ensue; for what availes — Par Lost 6.456
Whence in perpetual fight they needs must last — Par Lost 6.693
Which else to several Sphears thou must ascribe, — Par Lost 8.131
Which must be mutual, in proportion due — Par Lost 8.385
Which I enjoy, and must confess to find — Par Lost 8.523
Venial discourse unblam'd: I now must change — Par Lost 9.5
Descend to? who aspires must down as low — Par Lost 9.169
Suttle he needs must be, who could seduce — Par Lost 9.307
Of Knowledge he must pass, there he her met, — Par Lost 9.849
For us created, needs with us must faile, — Par Lost 9.942
Whoever judg'd, the worst on mee must light, — Par Lost 10.73
Must suffer change, disdain'd not to begin — Par Lost 10.213
Inseparable must with mee along: — Par Lost 10.250
That I must after thee with this thy Son; — Par Lost 10.363
Wrath without end on Man whom Death must end? — Par Lost 10.797
That I must leave ye, Sons; O were I able — Par Lost 10.819
Which must be born to certain woe, devourd — Par Lost 10.980
That after wretched Life must be at last — Par Lost 10.985
Glanc'd on the ground, with labour I must earne — Par Lost 10.1054
And thither must return and be no more. — Par Lost 11.200
With reverence I must meet, and thou retire. — Par Lost 11.237
Must I thus leave thee Paradise? thus leave — Par Lost 11.269
That must be mortal to us both. O flours, — Par Lost 11.273
I must return to native dust? O sight — Par Lost 11.463
This is old age; but then thou must outlive — Par Lost 11.538
Obtuse, all taste of pleasure must forgoe, — Par Lost 11.541

Must(*cont*)
Which I must keep till my appointed day Par Lost 11.550
The world erelong a world of tears must weepe. Par Lost 11.627
With thought that they must be. Let no man seek Par Lost 11.770
Must needs impaire and wearie human sense: Par Lost 12.10
His outward freedom: Tyrannie must be, Par Lost 12.95
Must be compelld by Signes and Judgements dire; Par Lost 12.175
To blood unshed the Rivers must be turnd, Par Lost 12.176
Frogs, Lice and Flies must all his Palace fill Par Lost 12.177
His Cattel must of Rot and Murren die, Par Lost 12.179
Botches and blaines must all his flesh imboss, Par Lost 12.180
Haile mixt with fire must rend th' *Egyptian* Skie Par Lost 12.182
Must eat, and on the ground leave nothing green: Par Lost 12.186
Darkness must overshadow all his bounds, Par Lost 12.187
Of *Egypt* must lie dead. Thus with ten wounds Par Lost 12.190
Some bloud more precious must be paid for Man, Par Lost 12.293
But first a long succession must ensue, Par Lost 12.331
Needs must the Serpent now his capital bruise Par Lost 12.383
Must reascend, what will betide the few Par Lost 12.480
Must bide the stroak of that long threatn'd wound, Par Reg 1.59
Who this is we must learn, for man he seems Par Reg 1.91
But must with something sudden be oppos'd, Par Reg 1.96
I am; this chiefly, that my way must lie Par Reg 1.263
Full weight must be transferr'd upon my head. Par Reg 1.267
From thee I can and must submiss endure Par Reg 1.476
Therefore with manlier objects we must try Par Reg 2.225
Then swell with pride, and must be titl'd Gods, Par Reg 3.81
Thou must make sure thy own, the *Parthian* first Par Reg 3.363
Means I must use thou say'st, prediction else Par Reg 3.394
I must deliver, if I mean to raign Par Reg 3.404
By wisdom; as thy Empire must extend, Par Reg 4.222
And with the *Gentiles* much thou must converse, Par Reg 4.229
Not when it must, but when it may be best. Par Reg 4.476
Another method I must now begin. Par Reg 4.540
Design'd for great exploits; if I must dye Samson 32
But weakly to a woman must reveal it, Samson 50
But peace, I must not quarrel with the will Samson 60
Dagon must stoop, and shall e're long receive Samson 468
Thou must not in the mean while here forgot Samson 479
Must not omit a Fathers timely care Samson 602
But must secret passage find Samson 610
Knowing, as needs I must, by thee betray'd? Samson 840
Private respects must yield; with grave authority Samson 868
Bare in thy guilt how foul must thou appear? Samson 902
When I must live uxorious to thy will Samson 945
What Pilot so expert but needs must wreck Samson 1044
Sam. He must allege some cause, and offer'd fight Samson 1253
Whom Patience finally must crown. Samson 1296
But they must pick me out with shackles tir'd, Samson 1326
Man. Some dismal accident it needs must be; Samson 1519
As now I do: But first I must put off Mask 82
Of hatefull steps, I must be viewles now. Mask 92
Which must not be, for that's against my course; Mask 159
Farr other arms, and other weapons must Mask 612
By which all mortal frailty must subsist, Mask 686
line not in Bridgewater ms
Beauty is natures coyn, must not be hoorded, Mask 739
line not in Bridgewater ms
But must be currant, and the good thereof Mask 740
line not in Bridgewater ms
Beauty is natures brag, and must be shown Mask 745
line not in Bridgewater ms
That must be utter'd to unfold the sage Mask 786
line not in Bridgewater ms
line not in Trinity ms
To som of *Saturns* crew. I must dissemble, Mask 805
line not in Bridgewater ms
line not in Trinity ms
I must not suffer this, yet 'tis but the lees Mask 809
And I must haste ere morning hour Mask 920
He must not flote upon his watry bear Lycidas 12
Now thou art gon, and never must return! Lycidas 38
This must not yet be so, Nativity 150
Must redeem our loss; Nativity 153
The wakefull trump of doom must thunder through the deep, Nativity 156
Thou know'st it must be now thy only bent Vacation 55
For now to sorrow must I tune my song, Passion 8
Yet more; the stroke of death he must abide, Passion 20
Shew'd him his room where he must lodge that night, Carrier 15
For who loves that, must first be wise and good; Sonnet 12, 12
Thou honour'st Verse, and Verse must send her wing Sonnet 13, 9
Must now be nam'd and printed Hereticks Forcers 11
And the way of bad men to ruine must. Psalm 1, 16

Must
About the wine-press where sweet moust is powr'd, Par Reg 4.16

Muster
See how in warlike muster they appear, Par Reg 3.308

Mustering
Must'ring thir rage, and Heav'n resembles Hell? Par Lost 2.268
Both Horse and Foot, nor idely mustring stood; Par Lost 11.645
Yet the fourth time, when mustring all his wiles, Samson 402
In Heav'ns defiance mustering all his waves; Vacation 44

Mutable
Yet mutable; whence warne him to beware Par Lost 5.237
Caus'd what I did? I saw thee mutable Samson 793
(So mutable are all the ways of men) Samson 1407

Mute
With all his Peers: attention held them mute. Par Lost 1.618

Mute(*cont*)
The perilous attempt: but all sat mute, Par Lost 2.420
He ask'd, but all the Heav'nly Quire stood mute, Par Lost 3.217
To hoarce or mute, though fall'n on evil dayes, Par Lost 7.25
Speaking or mute all comliness and grace Par Lost 8.222
Created mute to all articulat sound; Par Lost 9.557
How cam'st thou speakable of mute, and how Par Lost 9.563
Flourishd, since mute, to som great cause addrest, Par Lost 9.672
Gave elocution to the mute, and taught Par Lost 9.748
Confounded long they sate, as struck'n mute, Par Lost 9.1064
Th' Angelic Guards ascended, mute and sad Par Lost 10.18
To supplication, heare his sighs though mute; Par Lost 11.31
Which Heav'n by these mute signs in Nature shews Par Lost 11.194
As thou art wont, my prompted Song else mute, Par Reg 1.12
At least in vain, for they shall find thee mute. Par Reg 1.459
A while as mute confounded what to say, Par Reg 3.2
The deeds themselves, though mute, spoke loud the dooer; Samson 248
The Angelic orders and inferiour creatures mute, Samson 672
And the mute Silence hist along, Penseroso 55
Mean while the Rural ditties were not mute, Lycidas 32

Mutely
Where he had mutely sate two years before: Vacation 6

Mutiny
In mutinie had from her Axle torn Par Lost 2.926

Muttering
Skie lowr'd and muttering Thunder, som sad drops Par Lost 9.1002

Mutters
And backward mutters of dissevering power, Mask 817

Mutual
Myriads though bright: If he whom mutual league, Par Lost 1.87
ms 'mutuall'
And mutual amitie so streight, so close, Par Lost 4.376
Have finisht happie in our mutual help Par Lost 4.727
And mutual love, the Crown of all our bliss Par Lost 4.728
For sin, on warr and mutual slaughter bent. Par Lost 6.506
Flying, and over Lands with mutual wing Par Lost 7.429
Such pairs, in Love and mutual Honour joyn'd? Par Lost 8.58
Which must be mutual, in proportion due Par Lost 8.385
Took largely, of thir mutual guilt the Seale, Par Lost 9.1043
Thus they in mutual accusation spent Par Lost 9.1187
Consists in mutual and partak'n bliss, Mask 741
line not in Bridgewater ms
1637 'mutuall'
Trinity ms 'mutuall'
Linkt to the mutual flowing of the Seas, Another 31
1640, 1657 'mutuall'
line not in 1658 text

Muzzled
These oughly-headed Monsters? Mercy guard me! Mask 695
Trinity ms 'ougly headed' ← 'ougly musl'd' ← 'musl'd'

My
Invoke thy aid to my adventrous Song, Par Lost 1.13
Here we may reign secure, and in my choyce Par Lost 1.261
My sentence is for open Warr: Of Wiles, Par Lost 2.51
My voice disswades; for what can force or guile Par Lost 2.188
By my advice; since fate inevitable Par Lost 2.197
Thy miscreated Front athwart my way Par Lost 2.683
Thou interposest, that my sudden hand Par Lost 2.738
Me Father, and that Fantasm call'st my Son? Par Lost 2.743
With me in secret, that my womb conceiv'd Par Lost 2.766
Into my hand was giv'n, with charge to keep Par Lost 2.775
Without my op'ning. Pensive here I sat Par Lost 2.777
Alone, but long I sat not, till my womb Par Lost 2.778
Tore through my entrails, that with fear and pain Par Lost 2.783
Distorted, all my nether shape thus grew Par Lost 2.784
Transform'd: but he my inbred enemie Par Lost 2.785
My Bowels, thir repast; then bursting forth Par Lost 2.800
Grim *Death* my Son and foe, who sets them on, Par Lost 2.804
And my fair Son here showst me, the dear pledge Par Lost 2.818
Of mine own brood, that on my bowels feed: Par Lost 2.863
Thou art my Father, thou my Author, thou Par Lost 2.864
My being gav'st me; whom should I obey Par Lost 2.865
Wandring this darksome Desart, as my way, Par Lost 2.973
I travel this profound, direct my course; Par Lost 2.980
(Which is my present journey) and once more Par Lost 2.985
Pursuing. I upon my Frontieres here Par Lost 2.998
Hung ore my Realm, link'd in a golden Chain Par Lost 2.1005
Havock and spoil and ruin are my gain. Par Lost 2.1009
In that obscure sojourn, while in my flight Par Lost 3.15
Through Heav'n and Earth, so shall my glorie excel, Par Lost 3.133
O Son, in whom my Soul hath chief delight, Par Lost 3.168
Son of my bosom, Son who art alone Par Lost 3.169
My word, my wisdom, and effectual might, Par Lost 3.170
All hast thou spok'n as my thoughts are, all Par Lost 3.171
As my Eternal purpose hath decreed: Par Lost 3.172
Elect above the rest; so is my will: Par Lost 3.184
My Umpire *Conscience*, whom if they will hear, Par Lost 3.195
This my long sufferance and my day of grace Par Lost 3.198
His prey, nor suffer my unspotted Soule Par Lost 3.248
My vanquisher, spoild of his vanted spoile; Par Lost 3.251
While by thee rais'd I ruin all my Foes, Par Lost 3.258
Then with the multitude of my redeemd Par Lost 3.260
My sole complacence! well thou know'st how dear, Par Lost 3.276
To me are all my works, nor Man the least Par Lost 3.277
Thee from my bosom and right hand, to save, Par Lost 3.279
Shall be the copious matter of my Song Par Lost 3.413
Henceforth, and never shall my Harp thy praise Par Lost 3.414
That bring to my remembrance from what state Par Lost 4.38

My(*cont*)

Disdain forbids me, and my dread of shame	Par Lost 4.82
By Act of Grace my former state; how soon	Par Lost 4.94
This knows my punisher; therefore as farr	Par Lost 4.103
Evil be thou my Good; by thee at least	Par Lost 4.110
Little inferior; whom my thoughts pursue	Par Lost 4.362
Henceforth; my dwelling haply may not please	Par Lost 4.378
And without whom am to no end, my Guide	Par Lost 4.442
Out of my side to thee, neerest my heart	Par Lost 4.484
Substantial Life, to have thee by my side	Par Lost 4.485
Part of my Soul I seek thee, and thee claim	Par Lost 4.487
My other half: with that thy gentle hand	Par Lost 4.488
This day at highth of Noon came to my Spheare	Par Lost 4.564
My Author and Disposer, what thou bidst	Par Lost 4.635
Better abode, and my afflicted Powers	Par Lost 4.939
From my prevailing arme, though Heavens King	Par Lost 4.973
My fairest, my espous'd, my latest found,	Par Lost 5.18
Heav'ns last best gift, my ever new delight,	Par Lost 5.19
O Sole in whom my thoughts find all repose,	Par Lost 5.28
My Glorie, my Perfection, glad I see	Par Lost 5.29
But of offence and trouble, which my mind	Par Lost 5.34
To find thee I directed then my walk;	Par Lost 5.49
Much fairer to my Fancie then by day:	Par Lost 5.53
Even to my mouth of that same fruit held part	Par Lost 5.83
And various: wondring at my flight and change	Par Lost 5.89
My Guide was gon, and I, me thought, sunk down,	Par Lost 5.91
Made vocal by my Song, and taught his praise.	Par Lost 5.204
Single, is yet so just, my constant thoughts	Par Lost 5.552
Hear my Decree, which unrevok't shall stand.	Par Lost 5.602
My onely Son, and on this holy Hill	Par Lost 5.604
At my right hand; your Head I him appoint;	Par Lost 5.606
Son, thou in whom my glory I behold	Par Lost 5.719
In full resplendence, Heir of all my might,	Par Lost 5.720
Gabriel, lead forth to Battel these my Sons	Par Lost 6.46
Invincible, lead forth my armed Saints	Par Lost 6.47
From all: my Sect thou seest, now learn too late	Par Lost 6.147
Of my revenge, first sought for thou returnst	Par Lost 6.151
Effulgence of my Glorie, Son belov'd,	Par Lost 6.680
Ascend my Chariot, guide the rapid Wheeles	Par Lost 6.711
That shake Heav'ns basis, bring forth all my Warr,	Par Lost 6.712
My Bow and Thunder, my Almightie Arms	Par Lost 6.713
As is most just; this I my Glorie account,	Par Lost 6.726
My exaltation, and my whole delight,	Par Lost 6.727
Fulfill'd, which to fulfil is all my bliss.	Par Lost 6.729
Return me to my Native Element:	Par Lost 7.16
Visit'st my slumbers Nightly, or when Morn	Par Lost 7.29
Purples the East: still govern thou my Song,	Par Lost 7.30
My damage fondly deem'd, I can repaire	Par Lost 7.152
And thou my Word, begotten Son, by thee	Par Lost 7.163
My overshadowing Spirit and might with thee	Par Lost 7.165
And put not forth my goodness, which is free	Par Lost 7.171
Ere my remembrance: now hear mee relate	Par Lost 8.204
My Storie, which perhaps thou hast not heard;	Par Lost 8.205
And sweeter thy discourse is to my eare	Par Lost 8.211
Strait toward Heav'n my wondring Eyes I turnd,	Par Lost 8.257
Stood on my feet; about me round I saw	Par Lost 8.261
With fragrance and with joy my heart oreflow'd.	Par Lost 8.266
My Tongue obey'd and readily could name	Par Lost 8.272
My droused sense, untroubl'd, though I thought	Par Lost 8.289
I then was passing to my former state	Par Lost 8.290
When suddenly stood at my Head a dream,	Par Lost 8.292
My fancy to believe I yet had being,	Par Lost 8.294
My wandring, had not hee who was my Guide	Par Lost 8.312
The day thou eat'st thereof, my sole command	Par Lost 8.329
Yet dreadful in mine eare, though in my choice	Par Lost 8.335
My sudden apprehension: but in these	Par Lost 8.354
Surpassest farr my naming, how may I	Par Lost 8.359
Let not my words offend thee, Heav'nly Power,	Par Lost 8.379
My Maker, be propitious while I speak.	Par Lost 8.380
What thinkst thou then of mee, and this my State,	Par Lost 8.403
My Image, not imparted to the Brute,	Par Lost 8.441
My earthly by his Heav'nly overpowerd,	Par Lost 8.453
Of Fancie my internal sight, by which	Par Lost 8.461
Who stooping op'nd my left side, and took	Par Lost 8.465
Sweetness into my heart, unfelt before,	Par Lost 8.475
Such as I saw her in my dream, adornd	Par Lost 8.482
Bone of my Bone, Flesh of my Flesh, my Self	Par Lost 8.495
My pleaded reason. To the Nuptial Bowre	Par Lost 8.510
Thus I have told thee all my State, and brought	Par Lost 8.521
My Storie to the sum of earthly bliss	Par Lost 8.522
Or from my side subducting, took perhaps	Par Lost 8.536
Hesperean sets, my Signal to depart.	Par Lost 8.632
Of my Celestial Patroness, who deignes	Par Lost 9.21
Easie my unpremeditated Verse:	Par Lost 9.24
Climat, or Years damp my intended wing	Par Lost 9.45
Not Hers who brings it nightly to my Ear.	Par Lost 9.47
Bane, and in Heav'n much worse would be my state.	Par Lost 9.123
To my relentless thoughts; and him destroyd,	Par Lost 9.130
Provokes my envie, this new Favorite	Par Lost 9.175
Or bear what to my minde first thoughts present,	Par Lost 9.213
But that thou shouldst my firmness therfore doubt	Par Lost 9.279
Thy equal fear that my firm Faith and Love	Par Lost 9.286
Thy absence from my sight, but to avoid	Par Lost 9.294
As was my food, nor aught but food discern'd	Par Lost 9.573
Grateful to appetite, more pleas'd my sense	Par Lost 9.580
Tempting so nigh, to pluck and eat my fill	Par Lost 9.595
Of Reason in my inward Powers, and Speech	Par Lost 9.600
I turnd my thoughts, and with capacious mind	Par Lost 9.603

My(*cont*)

My conduct, I can bring thee thither soon.	Par Lost 9.630
Meant mee, by ventring higher then my Lot.	Par Lost 9.690
Created; but henceforth my early care,	Par Lost 9.799
As yet my change, and give him to partake	Par Lost 9.818
But keep the odds of Knowledge in my power	Par Lost 9.820
Hast thou not wonderd, *Adam*, at my stay?	Par Lost 9.856
Certain my resolution is to Die;	Par Lost 9.907
Would never from my heart; no no, I feel	Par Lost 9.913
Bone of my Bone thou art, and from thy State	Par Lost 9.915
However I with thee have fixt my Lot,	Par Lost 9.952
So forcible within my heart I feel	Par Lost 9.955
The Bond of Nature draw me to my owne,	Par Lost 9.956
My own in thee, for what thou art is mine;	Par Lost 9.957
This my attempt, I would sustain alone	Par Lost 9.978
Hath toucht my sense, flat seems to this, and harsh.	Par Lost 9.987
On my experience, *Adam*, freely taste,	Par Lost 9.988
With all perfections, so enflame my sense	Par Lost 9.1031
Would thou hadst heark'nd to my words, and stai'd	Par Lost 9.1134
Imput'st thou that to my default, or will	Par Lost 9.1145
That errour now, which is become my crime,	Par Lost 9.1181
My coming seen far off? I miss thee here,	Par Lost 10.104
My voice thou oft hast heard, and hast not fear'd,	Par Lost 10.119
Before my Judge, either to undergoe	Par Lost 10.126
My other self, the partner of my life;	Par Lost 10.128
By my complaint; but strict necessitie	Par Lost 10.131
Least on my head both sin and punishment,	Par Lost 10.133
Devolv'd; though should I hold my peace, yet thou	Par Lost 10.135
This Woman whom thou mad'st to be my help,	Par Lost 10.137
By secretest conveyance. Thou my Shade	Par Lost 10.249
For I no sooner in my Heart divin'd,	Par Lost 10.357
My Heart, which by a secret harmonie	Par Lost 10.358
To my associate Powers, them to acquaint	Par Lost 10.395
My Substitutes I send ye, and Create	Par Lost 10.403
My hold of this new Kingdom all depends,	Par Lost 10.406
Through Sin to Death expos'd by my exploit.	Par Lost 10.407
Little inferiour, by my adventure hard	Par Lost 10.468
Toild out my uncouth passage, forc't to ride	Par Lost 10.475
My journey strange, with clamorous uproare	Par Lost 10.479
His Seed, when is not set, shall bruise my head:	Par Lost 10.499
Of my performance: What remains, ye Gods,	Par Lost 10.502
To gratifie my scornful Enemies,	Par Lost 10.625
My Hell-hounds, to lick up the draff and filth	Par Lost 10.630
Of God, whom to behold was then my highth	Par Lost 10.724
My own deservings; but this will not serve;	Par Lost 10.727
Or multiplie, but curses on my head?	Par Lost 10.732
My Head, Ill fare our Ancestor impure,	Par Lost 10.735
Did I request thee, Maker, from my Clay	Par Lost 10.743
In this delicious Garden? as my Will	Par Lost 10.746
Concurd not to my being, it were but right	Par Lost 10.747
And equal to reduce me to my dust,	Par Lost 10.748
Mortalitie my sentence, and be Earth	Par Lost 10.776
As in my Mothers lap? there I should rest	Par Lost 10.778
Would Thunder in my ears, no fear of worse	Par Lost 10.780
To mee and to my ofspring would torment me	Par Lost 10.781
On my defensless head; both Death and I	Par Lost 10.815
Nor I on my part single, in mee all	Par Lost 10.817
Forc't I absolve: all my evasions vain,	Par Lost 10.829
But to my own conviction: first and last	Par Lost 10.831
Out of my sight, thou Serpent, that name best	Par Lost 10.867
Rejected my forewarning, and disdain'd	Par Lost 10.876
To trust thee from my side, imagin'd wise,	Par Lost 10.881
To my just number found. O why did God,	Par Lost 10.888
What love sincere, and reverence in my heart	Par Lost 10.915
My onely strength and stay: forlorn of thee,	Par Lost 10.921
There with my cries importune Heaven, that all	Par Lost 10.933
And my displeasure bearst so ill. If Prayers	Par Lost 10.952
That on my head all might be visited,	Par Lost 10.955
How little weight my words with thee can finde,	Par Lost 10.968
Thy Love, the sole contentment of my heart	Par Lost 10.973
What thoughts in my unquiet brest are ris'n,	Par Lost 10.975
My bread; what harm? Idleness had bin worse;	Par Lost 10.1055
My labour will sustain me; and least Cold	Par Lost 10.1056
Good or not good ingraft, my Merit those	Par Lost 11.35
Shall perfet, and for these my Death shall pay.	Par Lost 11.36
All my redeemd may dwell in joy and bliss,	Par Lost 11.43
Obtain, all thy request was my Decree:	Par Lost 11.47
My judgments, how with Mankind I proceed,	Par Lost 11.69
My motions in him, longer then they move,	Par Lost 11.91
Michael, this my behest have thou in charge,	Par Lost 11.99
My Cov'nant in the womans seed renewd;	Par Lost 11.116
To Spirits foule, and all my Trees thir prey,	Par Lost 11.124
Kneel'd and before him humbl'd all my heart,	Par Lost 11.150
Home to my Brest, and to my memorie	Par Lost 11.154
But infinite in pardon was my Judge,	Par Lost 11.167
My early visitation, and my last	Par Lost 11.275
To wearie him with my assiduous cries:	Par Lost 11.310
Presence Divine, and to my Sons relate;	Par Lost 11.319
My obvious breast, arming to overcom	Par Lost 11.374
Which I must keep till my appointed day	Par Lost 11.550
My dissolution. *Michael* repli'd, phrase not in 1667 edition	Par Lost 11.552
My part of evil onely, each dayes lot	Par Lost 11.765
At once, by my foreknowledge gaining Birth	Par Lost 11.768
Enlightner of my darkness, gracious things	Par Lost 12.271
Mine eyes true op'ning, and my heart much eas'd,	Par Lost 12.274
What oft my steddiest thoughts have searcht in vain,	Par Lost 12.377
High in the love of Heav'n, yet from my Loynes	Par Lost 12.380

My(*cont*)

Greatly in peace of thought, and have my fill	Par Lost 12.558
Beyond which was my folly to aspire.	Par Lost 12.560
Acknowledge my Redeemer ever blest.	Par Lost 12.573
Who for my wilful crime art banisht hence.	Par Lost 12.619
As thou art wont, my prompted Song else mute,	Par Reg 1.12
Upon my head, long the decrees of Heav'n	Par Reg 1.55
Things highest, greatest, multiplies my fear.	Par Reg 1.69
This is my Son belov'd, in him am pleas'd.	Par Reg 1.85
This perfect Man, by merit call'd my Son,	Par Reg 1.166
What from without comes often to my ears,	Par Reg 1.199
Ill sorting with my present state compar'd.	Par Reg 1.200
To me was pleasing, all my mind was set	Par Reg 1.202
All righteous things: therefore above my years,	Par Reg 1.206
Made it my whole delight, and in it grew	Par Reg 1.208
To such perfection, that e're yet my age	Par Reg 1.209
What might improve my knowledge or their own;	Par Reg 1.213
To which my Spirit aspir'd, victorious deeds	Par Reg 1.215
Flam'd in my heart, heroic acts, one while	Par Reg 1.216
These growing thoughts my Mother soon perceiving	Par Reg 1.227
I am; this chiefly, that my way must lie	Par Reg 1.263
Full weight must be transferr'd upon my head.	Par Reg 1.267
And last the sum of all, my Father's voice,	Par Reg 1.283
For what concerns my knowledge God reveals.	Par Reg 1.293
Kept not my happy Station, but was driv'n	Par Reg 1.360
Leaving my dolorous Prison I enjoy	Par Reg 1.364
Hath he excluded my resort sometimes.	Par Reg 1.367
Gave up into my hands *Uzzean Job*	Par Reg 1.369
Much lustre of my native brightness, lost	Par Reg 1.378
If not disposer; lend them oft my aid,	Par Reg 1.393
Oft my advice by presages and signs,	Par Reg 1.394
Companions of my misery and wo.	Par Reg 1.398
Spoken against, that through my very Soul	Par Reg 2.90
A sword shall pierce, this is my favour'd lot,	Par Reg 2.91
My Exaltation to Afflictions high;	Par Reg 2.92
My heart hath been a store-house long of things	Par Reg 2.103
Of my success with *Eve* in Paradise	Par Reg 2.141
Thought none my equal, now be over-match'd.	Par Reg 2.146
Mee hungring more to do my Fathers will.	Par Reg 2.259
And who withholds my pow'r that right to use?	Par Reg 2.380
Shall I receive by gift what of my own,	Par Reg 2.381
Array'd in Glory on my cup to attend:	Par Reg 2.386
And with my hunger what hast thou to do?	Par Reg 2.389
Riches are mine, Fortune is in my hand;	Par Reg 2.429
He ask'd thee, hast thou seen my servant *Job?*	Par Reg 3.67
If of my raign Prophetic Writ hath told,	Par Reg 3.184
My exaltation without change or end.	Par Reg 3.197
My everlasting Kingdom, why art thou	Par Reg 3.199
Know'st thou not that my rising is thy fall,	Par Reg 3.201
And my promotion will be thy destruction?	Par Reg 3.202
Of my reception into grace; what worse?	Par Reg 3.205
I would be at the worst; worst is my Port,	Par Reg 3.209
My harbour and my ultimate repose,	Par Reg 3.210
The end I would attain, my final good.	Par Reg 3.211
My error was my error, and my crime	Par Reg 3.212
My crime; whatever for it self condemn'd,	Par Reg 3.213
Rather then aggravate my evil state,	Par Reg 3.218
By my advice, as nearer and of late	Par Reg 3.364
Maugre the *Roman:* it shall be my task	Par Reg 3.368
Before mine eyes thou hast set; and in my ear	Par Reg 3.390
My time I told thee, (and that time for thee	Par Reg 3.396
On my part aught endeavouring, or to need	Par Reg 3.399
My brethren, as thou call'st them; those Ten Tribes	Par Reg 3.403
My Aerie Microscope) thou may'st behold	Par Reg 4.57
And with my help thou may'st; to me the power	Par Reg 4.103
Much less my mind; though thou should'st add to tell	Par Reg 4.113
Know therefore when my season comes to sit	Par Reg 4.146
And of my Kingdom there shall be no end:	Par Reg 4.151
To me my own, on such abhorred pact,	Par Reg 4.191
Or if I would delight my private hours	Par Reg 4.331
Nicely or cautiously my offer'd aid,	Par Reg 4.377
The perfet season offer'd with my aid	Par Reg 4.468
Ambitious spirit, and wouldst be thought my God,	Par Reg 4.495
Thenceforth I thought thee worth my nearer view	Par Reg 4.514
Thou art to be my fatal enemy.	Par Reg 4.525
To understand my Adversary, who	Par Reg 4.527
Relieves me from my task of servile toyl,	Samson 5
O wherefore was my birth from Heaven foretold	Samson 23
Of both my Parents all in flames ascended	Samson 25
Why was my breeding order'd and prescrib'd	Samson 30
Betray'd, Captiv'd, and both my Eyes put out,	Samson 33
Made of my Enemies the scorn and gaze;	Samson 34
How slight the gift was, hung it in my Hair.	Samson 59
Happ'ly had ends above my reach to know:	Samson 62
Suffices that to me strength is my bane,	Samson 63
And proves the sourse of all my miseries;	Samson 64
Annull'd, which might in part my grief have eas'd,	Samson 72
In power of others, never in my own;	Samson 78
My self, my Sepulcher, a moving Grave,	Samson 102
Perhaps my enemies who come to stare	Samson 112
At my affliction, and perhaps to insult,	Samson 113
Or do my eyes misrepresent? Can this be hee,	Samson 124
Dissolves unjointed e're it reach my ear.	Samson 177
Now of my own experience, not by talk,	Samson 188
My Vessel trusted to me from above,	Samson 199
Mee, not my Parents, that I sought to wed,	Samson 220
That specious Monster, my accomplish snare.	Samson 230
I thought it lawful from my former act,	Samson 231

My(*cont*)

Gave up my fort of silence to a Woman.	Samson 236
Us'd no ambition to commend my deeds,	Samson 247
Cho. Thy words to my remembrance bring	Samson 277
My Son now Captive, hither hath inform'd	Samson 335
Who would be now a Father in my stead?	Samson 355
O wherefore did God grant me my request,	Samson 356
As vile hath been my folly, who have profan'd	Samson 377
A *Canaanite*, my faithless enemy.	Samson 380
To them who had corrupted her, my Spies,	Samson 386
My capital secret, in what part my strength	Samson 394
I yielded, and unlock'd her all my heart,	Samson 407
As was my former servitude, ignoble,	Samson 416
Which is my chief affliction, shame and sorrow,	Samson 457
The anguish of my Soul, that suffers not	Samson 458
As I deserve, pay on my punishment;	Samson 489
And expiate, if possible, my crime,	Samson 490
On hostile ground, none daring my affront.	Samson 531
At length to lay my head and hallow'd pledge	Samson 535
Of all my strength in the lascivious lap	Samson 536
Like a tame Weather, all my precious fleece,	Samson 538
Shav'n, and disarm'd among my enemies.	Samson 540
My Nation, and the work from Heav'n impos'd,	Samson 565
And sedentary numness craze my limbs	Samson 571
Here rather let me drudge and earn my bread,	Samson 573
Hast'n the welcom end of all my pains.	Samson 576
Sam. All otherwise to me my thoughts portend,	Samson 590
So much I feel my genial spirits droop,	Samson 594
My hopes all flat, nature within me seems	Samson 595
My race of glory run, and race of shame,	Samson 597
My griefs not only pain me	Samson 617
Thoughts my Tormenters arm'd with deadly stings	Samson 623
Mangle my apprehensive tenderest parts,	Samson 624
To deaths benumming Opium as my only cure.	Samson 630
Hopeless are all my evils, all remediless;	Samson 648
The close of all my miseries, and the balm.	Samson 651
Sam. My Wife, my Traytress, let her not come near me.	Samson 725
My penance hath not slack'n'd, though my pardon	Samson 738
If aught in my ability may serve	Samson 743
Thy mind with what amends is in my power,	Samson 745
My rash but more unfortunate misdeed.	Samson 747
To lessen or extenuate my offence,	Samson 767
To learn thy secrets, get into my power	Samson 798
Wailing thy absence in my widow'd bed;	Samson 806
Fearless at home of partners in my love.	Samson 810
Such pardon therefore as I give my folly,	Samson 825
My love how couldst thou hope, who tookst the way	Samson 838
It was not gold, as to my charge thou lay'st,	Samson 849
And Princes of my countrey came in person,	Samson 851
Was not behind, but ever at my ear,	Samson 858
Only my love of thee held long debate;	Samson 863
I before all the daughters of my Tribe	Samson 876
And of my Nation chose thee from among	Samson 877
My enemies, lov'd thee, as too well thou knew'st,	Samson 878
Too well, unbosom'd all my secrets to thee,	Samson 879
Then, as since then, thy countries foe profest:	Samson 884
Nor under their protection but my own,	Samson 887
Thou mine, not theirs: if aught against my life	Samson 888
With me, where my redoubl'd love and care	Samson 923
Sams. No, no, of my condition take no care;	Samson 928
To bring my feet again into the snare	Samson 931
Though dearly to my cost, thy ginns, and toyls;	Samson 933
To fence my ear against thy sorceries.	Samson 937
If in my flower of youth and strength, when all men	Samson 938
Bearing my words and doings to the Lords	Samson 947
To thine whose doors my feet shall never enter.	Samson 950
My sudden rage to tear thee joint by joint.	Samson 953
Of infamy upon my name denounc't?	Samson 968
Henceforth, nor too much disapprove my own.	Samson 970
My name perhaps among the Circumcis'd	Samson 975
But in my countrey where I most desire,	Samson 980
Above the faith of wedlock-bands, my tomb	Samson 986
Which to my countrey I was judg'd to have shewn.	Samson 994
I leave him to his lot, and like my own.	Samson 996
And aggravate my folly who committed	Samson 1000
Of secresie, my safety, and my life.	Samson 1002
Sam. Be less abstruse, my riddling days are past.	Samson 1064
My trust is in the living God who gave me	Samson 1140
At my Nativity this strength, diffus'd	Samson 1141
No less through all my sinews, joints and bones,	Samson 1142
The pledge of my unviolated vow.	Samson 1144
And in your City held my Nuptial Feast:	Samson 1194
To wring from me and tell to them my secret,	Samson 1199
As on my enemies, where ever chanc'd,	Samson 1202
To pay my underminers in thir coin.	Samson 1204
My Nation was subjected to your Lords.	Samson 1205
But I a private person, whom my Countrey	Samson 1208
To free my Countrey; if their servile minds	Samson 1213
I was to do my part from Heav'n assign'd,	Samson 1217
And had perform'd it if my known offence	Samson 1218
To descant on my strength, and give thy verdit?	Samson 1228
But take good heed my hand survey not thee.	Samson 1230
Har. O *Baal-zebub!* can my ears unus'd	Samson 1231
My heels are fetter'd, but my fist is free.	Samson 1235
If they intend advantage of my labours	Samson 1259
The work of many hands, which earns my keeping	Samson 1260
With no small profit daily to my owners.	Samson 1261
But come what will, my deadliest foe will prove	Samson 1262

My(*cont*)
My speediest friend, by death to rid me hence, Samson 1263
My presence; for that cause I cannot come. Samson 1321
On my refusal to distress me more, Samson 1330
Or make a game of my calamities? Samson 1331
Sam. My self? my conscience and internal peace. Samson 1334
With corporal servitude, that my mind ever Samson 1336
And in my midst of sorrow and heart-grief Samson 1339
Off. My message was impos'd on me with speed, Samson 1343
Of strength, again returning with my hair Samson 1355
After my great transgression, so requite Samson 1356
Vaunting my strength in honour to thir *Dagon?* Samson 1360
Honest and lawful to deserve my food Samson 1366
Chor. How thou wilt here come off surmounts my reach. Samson 1380
To something extraordinary my thoughts. Samson 1383
Our Law, or stain my vow of *Nazarite*. Samson 1386
This day will be remarkable in my life Samson 1388
By some great act, or of my days the last. Samson 1389
Our God, our Law, my Nation, or my self, Samson 1425
Man. Peace with you brethren; my inducement hither Samson 1445
Was not at present here to find my Son, Samson 1446
But that which mov'd my coming now, was chiefly Samson 1452
To accept of ransom for my Son thir pris'ner, Samson 1460
Man. His ransom, if my whole inheritance Samson 1476
To live the poorest in my Tribe, then richest, Samson 1479
For his redemption all my Patrimony, Samson 1482
Man. It shall be my delight to tend his eyes, Samson 1490
Oh it continues, they have slain my Son. Samson 1516
Which earst my eyes beheld and yet behold; Samson 1543
My Countreymen, whom here I knew remaining, Samson 1549
Man. The worst indeed, O all my hope's defeated Samson 1571
Now of my own accord such other tryal Samson 1643
I mean to shew you of my strength, yet greater; Samson 1644
Will send for all my kindred, all my friends Samson 1730
My mansion is, where those immortal shapes Mask 2
To such my errand is, and but for such, Mask 15
But to my task. *Neptune* besides the sway Mask 18
Took in by lot 'twixt high, and neather *Jove*, Mask 20
 1637 'my lot'
These my skie robes spun out of *Iris* Wooff, Mask 83
Benighted in these Woods. Now to my charms, Mask 150
And to my wily trains, I shall e're long Mask 151
About my Mother *Circe*. Thus I hurl Mask 153
My dazling Spells into the spungy ayr, Mask 154
And my quaint habits breed astonishment, Mask 157
Which must not be, for that's against my course; Mask 159
This way the noise was, if mine ear be true, Mask 170
 Bridgewater ms 'my eare'
 Trinity ms 'my eare'
My best guide now, me thought it was the sound Mask 171
Shall I inform my unacquainted feet Mask 180
My Brothers when they saw me wearied out Mask 182
Is now the labour of my thoughts, 'tis likeliest Mask 192
Was rife, and perfet in my list'ning ear, Mask 203
 line not in Bridgewater ms
Begin to throng into my memory Mask 206
 line not in Bridgewater ms
To keep my life and honour unassail'd. Mask 220
 line not in Bridgewater ms
I cannot hallow to my Brothers, but Mask 226
Ile venter, for my new enliv'nd spirits Mask 228
My Mother *Circe* with the Sirens three, Mask 253
And she shall be my Queen. Hail forren wonder Mask 265
How to regain my sever'd company Mask 274
La. How easie my misfortune is to hit! Mask 286
La. No less then if I should my brothers loose. Mask 288
My daily walks and ancient neighbourhood, Mask 314
Eie me blest Providence, and square my triall Mask 329
 Trinity ms 'my' ←'this'
 Bridgewater ms 'Eye my'
To my proportion'd strength. Shepherd lead on.···· Mask 330
I do not think my sister so to seek, Mask 366
Inferr, as if I thought my sisters state Mask 408
Does arbitrate th' event, my nature is Mask 411
My sister is not so defenceless left Mask 414
'Tis chastity, my brother, chastity: Mask 420
2. *Bro*. Heav'n keep my sister, agen agen and neer, Mask 486
Spir. What voice is that, my young Lord? speak agen. Mask 492
2. *Bro*. O brother, 'tis my father Shepherd sure. Mask 493
Spir. O my lov'd masters heir, and his next joy, Mask 501
To this my errand, and the care it brought. Mask 506
But O my Virgin Lady, where is she? Mask 507
Spir. Ay me unhappy then my fears are true. Mask 511
Tending my flocks hard by i'th hilly crofts, Mask 531
To meditate my rural minstrelsie, Mask 547
Of my most honour'd Lady, your dear sister. Mask 564
Already, ere my best speed could praevent, Mask 573
Brought to my mind a certain Shepherd Lad Mask 619
Thou canst not touch the freedom of my minde Mask 663
Hast thou betrai'd my credulous innocence Mask 697
 line not in Bridgewater ms
La. I had not thought to have unlockt my lips Mask 756
Would think to charm my judgement, as mine eyes Mask 758
 Trinity ms 'mye eyes'
 Bridgewater ms 'my eyes'
Of this pure cause would kindle my rap't spirits Mask 794
 line not in Bridgewater ms
 line not in Trinity ms

My(*cont*)
My sliding Chariot stayes, Mask 892
That in the channell strayes, Mask 895
 Trinity ms 'in the channell straies' ←'my rich wheeles inlayes'
Thus I set my printless feet Mask 897
Sab. Shepherd 'tis my office best Mask 908
Drops that from my fountain pure, Mask 912
But now my task is smoothly don, Mask 1012
this dusky hollow is a paradise & heaven gates ore my head Mask Tr. ms 13.44
to have her by my side, though I were sure Mask Tr. ms 16.41
O my simplicity what sights are these? with darke disguises Mask Tr. ms 22.19
to have her by my side, though I were suer Mask Br. ms 394
And at my window bid good morrow, Allegro 46
Or let my Lamp at midnight hour, Penseroso 85
Softly on my eye-lids laid. Penseroso 150
But let my due feet never fail, Penseroso 155
And may at last my weary age Penseroso 167
And all my Plants I save from nightly ill, Arcades 48
When Eev'ning gray doth rise, I fetch my round Arcades 54
Number my ranks, and visit every sprout Arcades 59
If my inferior hand or voice could hit Arcades 77
With lucky words favour my destin'd Urn, Lycidas 20
And bid fair peace be to my sable shrowd. Lycidas 22
Phoebus repli'd, and touch'd my trembling ears; Lycidas 77
But now my Oat proceeds, Lycidas 88
Ah! Who hath reft (quoth he) my dearest pledge? Lycidas 107
Didst move my first endeavouring tongue to speak, Vacation 2
Half unpronounc't, slide through my infant-lipps, Vacation 4
That now I use thee in my latter task: Vacation 8
I know my tongue but little Grace can do thee Vacation 10
Before thou cloath my fancy in fit sound: Vacation 32
But fie my wandring Muse how thou dost stray! Vacation 53
That to the next I may resign my Roome. Vacation 58
Yet there is something that doth force my fear, Vacation 67
For once it was my dismal hap to hear Vacation 68
My muse with Angels did divide to sing; Passion 4
For now to sorrow must I tune my song, Passion 8
And set my Harpe to notes of saddest wo, Passion 9
These latter scenes confine my roving vers, Passion 22
To this Horizon is my *Phoebus* bound, Passion 23
And work my flatter'd fancy to belief, Passion 31
That Heav'n and Earth are colour'd with my wo; Passion 32
My sorrows are too dark for day to know: Passion 33
And letters where my tears have washt a wannish white. Passion 35
My spirit som transporting *Cherub* feels, Passion 38
There doth my soul in holy vision sit Passion 41
And here though grief my feeble hands up-lock, Passion 45
My plaining vers as lively as before; Passion 47
For sure so well instructed are my tears, Passion 48
Might think th' infection of my sorrows loud, Passion 55
What needs my *Shakespear* for his honour'd Bones, Shakespear 1
Foretell my hopeles doom in som Grove ny: Sonnet 1, 10
For my relief; yet hadst no reason why, Sonnet 1, 12
Stoln on his wing my three and twentith yeer! Sonnet 7, 2
My hasting dayes flie on with full career, Sonnet 7, 3
But my late spring no bud or blossom shew'th. Sonnet 7, 4
Perhaps my semblance might deceive the truth, Sonnet 7, 5
As ever in my great task Masters eye. Sonnet 7, 14
When I consider how my light is spent, Sonnet 19, 1
E're half my days, in this dark world and wide, Sonnet 19, 2
Lodg'd with me useless, though my Soul more bent Sonnet 19, 4
To serve therewith my Maker, and present Sonnet 19, 5
My true account, least he returning chide, Sonnet 19, 6
In libertyes defence, my noble task, Sonnet 22, 11
Methought I saw my late espoused Saint Sonnet 23, 1
Her face was vail'd, yet to my fancied sight, Sonnet 23, 10
I wak'd, she fled, and day brought back my night. Sonnet 23, 14
To whom thou untry'd seem'st fair. Me in my vow'd Horace 13
My dank and dropping weeds Horace 15
anointed have my King (though ye rebell) Psalm 2, 12
On *Sion* my holi' hill. A firm decree Psalm 2, 13
Thou art my Son I have begotten thee Psalm 2, 15
Lord how many are my foes Psalm 3, 1
That of my life distrustfully thus say, Psalm 3, 5
But thou Lord art my shield my glory, Psalm 3, 7
Thee through my story Psalm 3, 8
Th' exalter of my head I count Psalm 3, 9
For my sustain Psalm 3, 14
Rise Lord, save me my God for thou Psalm 3, 19
On the cheek-bone all my foes, Psalm 3, 21
God of my righteousness Psalm 4, 2
Now pity me, and hear my earnest prai'r. Psalm 4, 6
My glory have in scorn Psalm 4, 8
Will hear my voyce what time to him I crie. Psalm 4, 18
Into my heart more joy Psalm 4, 31
Jehovah to my words give ear Psalm 5, 1
My meditation waigh Psalm 5, 2
The voyce of my complaining hear Psalm 5, 3
My King and God for unto thee I pray. Psalm 5, 4
Jehovah thou my early voyce Psalm 5, 5
Will rank my Prayers, and watch till thou appear. Psalm 5, 8
Set thy wayes right before, where my step goes. Psalm 5, 24
For all my bones, that even with anguish ake, Psalm 6, 5
Are troubled, yea my soul is troubled sore Psalm 6, 6
My soul, O save me for thy goodness sake Psalm 6, 8
Wearied I am with sighing out my dayes, Psalm 6, 11
Nightly my Couch I make a kind of Sea; Psalm 6, 12

My(*cont*)
My Bed I water with my tears; mine Eie Psalm 6, 13
Depart from me, for the voice of my weeping Psalm 6, 17
The Lord hath heard, the Lord hath heard my prai'r Psalm 6, 18
My supplication with acceptance fair Psalm 6, 19
Lord my God to thee I flie Psalm 7, 1
He hast to tear my Soul asunder Psalm 7, 5
Lord my God if I have thought Psalm 7, 7
Be in my hands, if I have wrought Psalm 7, 9
And not fre'd my foe for naught; Psalm 7, 12
Let th' enemy pursue my soul Psalm 7, 13
My life down to the earth and roul Psalm 7, 15
In the dust my glory dead, Psalm 7, 16
Of my foes that urge like fire; Psalm 7, 21
According to my righteousness Psalm 7, 32
My defence, and in him lies Psalm 7, 40
In the pure firmament, then saith my heart, Psalm 8, 11
Hear O my people, *heark'n well*, Psalm 81, 33
And yet my people would not *hear*, Psalm 81, 45
Nor hearken to my voice; Psalm 81, 46
O that my people would *be wise* Psalm 81, 53
To walk my *righteous* waies. Psalm 81, 56
And turn my hand against *all those* Psalm 81, 59
My God, oh make them as a wheel Psalm 83, 49
My Soul doth long and almost die Psalm 84, 5
My heart and flesh aloud do crie, Psalm 84, 7
Toward thee, My King, my God. Psalm 84, 16
Lord God of Hoasts hear *now* my praier Psalm 84, 29
I in the temple of my God Psalm 84, 37
Preserve my soul, for I have trod Psalm 86, 5
Save thou thy servant O my God Psalm 86, 7
I lift my soul *and voice*, Psalm 86, 12
Unto my supplication Lord Psalm 86, 17
Of my *incessant* praiers afford Psalm 86, 19
I in the day of my distress Psalm 86, 21
To fear thy name my heart unite Psalm 86, 39
Thee will I praise O Lord my God Psalm 86, 41
With my whole heart, and blaze abroad Psalm 86, 43
And thou hast free'd my Soul Psalm 86, 46
To seek my life, and in their eyes Psalm 86, 51
And let my foes *then* see Psalm 86, 62
I mention Babel to my friends, Psalm 87, 13
And all my fountains *clear*. Psalm 87, 28
Into thy presence let my praier Psalm 88, 5
And to my cries, that *ceaseless are*, Psalm 88, 7
Surcharg'd my Soul doth lie, Psalm 88, 10
My life *at deaths uncherful dore* Psalm 88, 11
Thou dost my friends from me estrange, Psalm 88, 33
My hands to thee I spread. Psalm 88, 40
E're yet my life be spent, Psalm 88, 54
And *up to thee* my praier *doth hie* Psalm 88, 55
Why wilt thou Lord my soul forsake, Psalm 88, 57

Myriads
Myriads though bright: If he whom mutual league, Par Lost 1.87
O Myriads of immortal Spirits, O Powers Par Lost 1.622
Of all those Myriads which we lead the chief; Par Lost 5.684
That of so many Myriads fall'n, yet one Par Lost 6.24
Myriads between two brazen Mountains lodg'd Par Lost 7.201

Myrrh
What drops the Myrrhe, and what the balmie Reed, Par Lost 5.23
Into the blissful field, through Groves of Myrrhe, Par Lost 5.292
Of blowing Myrrh and Balme; if thou accept Par Lost 9.629
His place, to offer Incense, Myrrh, and Gold; Par Lost 12.363
To honour thee with Incense, Myrrh, and Gold, Par Reg 1.251
With Groves of myrrhe, and cinnamon. Mask 937
Trinity ms 'mirrhe'
Bridgewater ms 'mirhe'

Myrrhine
Crystal and Myrrhine cups imboss'd with Gems Par Reg 4.119

Myrtle
That to the fringed Bank with Myrtle crownd, Par Lost 4.262
Laurel and Mirtle, and what higher grew Par Lost 4.694
With Myrtle, find what to redress till Noon: Par Lost 9.219
Gently with Mirtle band, mindless the while, Par Lost 9.431
About the cedar'n alleys fling Mask 990
Trinity ms 'cedar'ne' ←'myrtle'
And waving wide her mirtle wand, Nativity 51

Myrtles
Beyond a row of Myrtles, on a Flat, Par Lost 9.627
Ye Myrtles brown, with Ivy never-sear, Lycidas 2
Trinity ms 'myrtle's' ←'myrtl's'
Trinity ms 'myrtle's'

Myself
My self expose, with lonely steps to tread Par Lost 2.828
Life in my self for ever, by thee I live, Par Lost 3.244
Which way I flie is Hell; my self am Hell; Par Lost 4.75
I first awak't, and found my self repos'd Par Lost 4.450
Best Image of my self and dearer half, Par Lost 5.95
My self and all th' Angelic Host that stand Par Lost 5.535
And by my Self have sworn to him shall bow Par Lost 5.607
Though I uncircumscrib'd my self retire, Par Lost 7.170
My self I then perus'd, and Limb by Limb Par Lost 8.267
Not of my self; by some great Maker then, Par Lost 8.278
Nor hope to be my self less miserable Par Lost 9.126
One Flesh; to loose thee were to loose my self. Par Lost 9.959
Affraid, being naked, hid my self. To whom Par Lost 10.117
My self the total Crime, or to accuse Par Lost 10.127
To waste it all my self, and leave ye none! Par Lost 10.820

Myself(*cont*)
What from within I feel my self, and hear Par Reg 1.198
What might be publick good; my self I thought Par Reg 1.204
As Earth and Skie would mingle; but my self Par Reg 4.453
Whom have I to complain of but my self? Samson 46
My self, my Sepulcher, a moving Grave, Samson 102
She was not the prime cause, but I my self, Samson 234
But justly; I my self have brought them on, Samson 375
She sought to make me Traytor to my self; Samson 401
Whole to my self, unhazarded abroad, Samson 809
I to my self was false e're thou to me, Samson 824
Why do I humble thus my self, and suing Samson 965
Sam. My self? my conscience and internal peace. Samson 1334
Our God, our Law, my Nation, or my self, Samson 1425

Mysteries
Who all the sacred mysteries of Heav'n Par Lost 12.509
And regal Mysteries; that thou may'st know Par Reg 3.249

Mysterious
Nor those mysterious parts were then conceald, Par Lost 4.312
Mysterious of connubial Love refus'd: Par Lost 4.743
Haile wedded Love, mysterious Law, true source Par Lost 4.750
And with mysterious reverence I deem) Par Lost 8.599
Though in mysterious terms, judg'd as then best: Par Lost 10.173
Of mid-night Torches burns; mysterious Dame Mask 130
Bridgewater ms 'misterious'
And let som strange mysterious dream, Penseroso 147
in high misterious happie spousall meet Musick Tr. ms 4.06

Mysteriously
Each Stair mysteriously was meant, nor stood Par Lost 3.516

Mystery
The mystery of God giv'n me under pledge Samson 378
The sublime notion, and high mystery Mask 785
line not in Bridgewater ms
1637 'mysterie'
line not in Trinity ms

Mystic
In mystic Dance not without Song, resound Par Lost 5.178
Or that, not Mystic, where the Sapient King Par Lost 9.442

Mystical
Mystical dance, which yonder starrie Spheare Par Lost 5.620

Nabaioth
Out cast *Nebaioth*, yet found he relief Par Reg 2.309

Naiades
Nymphs of *Diana*'s train, and *Naiades* Par Reg 2.355
Amidst the flowry-kirtl'd *Naiades* Mask 254
Trinity ms 'Naiades' ←'Naiads' ←'Naiades'
Bridgewater ms 'Niades'

Nailed
A shameful and accurst, naild to the Cross Par Lost 12.413
Smote *Sisera* sleeping through the Temples nail'd. Samson 990

Nails
But to the Cross he nailes thy Enemies, Par Lost 12.415

Naked
In naked Majestie seemd Lords of all, Par Lost 4.290
So passd they naked on, nor shund the sight Par Lost 4.319
Naked met his under the flowing Gold Par Lost 4.496
Brought her in naked beauty more adorn'd, Par Lost 4.713
And on thir naked limbs the flourie roof Par Lost 4.772
Of three that in Mount *Ida* naked strove, Par Lost 5.382
Ministerd naked, and thir flowing cups Par Lost 5.444
And honour from about them, naked left Par Lost 9.1057
Which leaves us naked thus, of Honour void, Par Lost 9.1074
To that first naked Glorie. Such of late Par Lost 9.1115
With featherd Cincture, naked else and wilde Par Lost 9.1117
Of all our good, sham'd, naked, miserable. Par Lost 9.1139
Affraid, being naked, hid my self. To whom Par Lost 10.117
So dreadful to thee? that thou art naked, who Par Lost 10.121
Before him naked to the aire, that now Par Lost 10.212
And on her naked shame, Nativity 40
I have some naked thoughts that rove about Vacation 23

Nakedness
Thir nakedness with Skins of Beasts, or slain, Par Lost 10.217
Of Beasts, but inward nakedness, much more Par Lost 10.221
Emptied his glory, ev'n to nakednes; Circum 20

Namancos
Looks toward *Namancos* and *Bayona*'s hold; Lycidas 162

Name
As whom the Fables name of monstrous size, Par Lost 1.197
Peor his other Name, when he entic'd Par Lost 1.412
ms 'name'
Dagon his Name, Sea Monster, upward Man Par Lost 1.462
ms 'name'
Nor was his name unheard or unador'd Par Lost 1.738
Hell trembl'd at the hideous Name, and sigh'd Par Lost 2.788
Orcus and *Ades*, and the dreaded name Par Lost 2.964
Hail Son of God, Saviour of Men, thy Name Par Lost 3.412
But with no friendly voice, and add thy name Par Lost 4.36
Satan, and couldst thou faithful add? O name, Par Lost 4.950
O sacred name of faithfulness profan'd! Par Lost 4.951
Satan, so call him now, his former name Par Lost 5.658
His name, and high was his degree in Heav'n; Par Lost 5.707
All Power, and us eclipst under the name Par Lost 5.776
Unjustly thou deprav'st it with the name Par Lost 6.174
Descend from Heav'n *Urania*, by that name Par Lost 7.1
The meaning, not the Name I call: for thou Par Lost 7.5
Is yet distinct by name, thence, as thou know'st Par Lost 7.536
By Numbers that have name. But this I urge, Par Lost 8.114
My Tongue obey'd and readily could name Par Lost 8.272

Name(*cont*)
O by what Name, for thou above all these, Par Lost 8.357
Before me; Woman is her Name, of Man Par Lost 8.496
Not that which justly gives Heroic name Par Lost 9.40
That name, unless an age too late, or cold Par Lost 9.44
Th' Angelic Name, and thinner left the throng Par Lost 9.142
Of *Satan* (for I glorie in the name, Par Lost 10.386
While the Creator calling forth by name Par Lost 10.649
Out of my sight, thou Serpent, that name best Par Lost 10.867
Farr other name deserving. But the Field Par Lost 11.171
And from Rebellion shall derive his name, Par Lost 12.36
And get themselves a name, least far disperst Par Lost 12.45
His Name and Office bearing, who shall quell Par Lost 12.311
Of *David* (so I name this King) shall rise Par Lost 12.326
Thou knewst by name, and all th' ethereal Powers, Par Lost 12.577
By name to come call'd Charitie, the soul Par Lost 12.584
And exquisitest name, for which was drain'd Par Reg 2.346
With mention of that name renews th' assault. Samson 331
But will arise and his great name assert: Samson 467
To vindicate the glory of his name Samson 475
Nor do I name of men the common rout, Samson 674
Heads without name no more rememberd, Samson 677
For which our countrey is a name so dear; Samson 894
Of infamy upon my name denounc't? Samson 968
My name perhaps among the Circumcis'd Samson 975
The highest name for valiant Acts, that honour Samson 1101
To what may serve his glory best, & spread his name Samson 1429
With that same vaunted name Virginity, Mask 738
line not in Bridgewater ms
They had their name thence; course complexions Mask 749
line not in Bridgewater ms
Sabrina is her name, a Virgin pure, Mask 826
In name of great *Oceanus*, Mask 868
Let us blaze his Name abroad, Psalm 136, 5
That till the worlds last-end shall make thy name to live. Fair Inf 77
Or *Humber* loud that keeps the *Scythians* Name, Vacation 99
Devoted to thy vertuous name; Winchester 60
What need'st thou such weak witnes of thy name? Shakespear 6
1663-4 '*Name*'
1632 'Name'
And he can spred thy Name o're Lands and Seas, Sonnet 8, 7
Trinity ms 'name'
Fairfax, whose name in armes through Europe rings Sonnet 15, 1
1694 'Name'
And shall triumph in thee, who love thy name. Psalm 5, 36
And sing the Name and Deitie Psalm 7, 63
And glorious is thy name through all the earth? Psalm 8, 2
And glorious is thy name through all the earth. Psalm 8, 24
Shall call upon thy Name. Psalm 80, 76
That Israels name for ever may Psalm 83, 15
Then shall they know that thou whose name Psalm 83, 65
And glorifie thy name. Psalm 86, 32
To fear thy name my heart unite Psalm 86, 39
Thy name for ever more. Psalm 86, 44
And for that name unfit. Psalm 88, 16

Named
Long after known in *Palestine*, and nam'd Par Lost 1.80
Met such imbodied force, as nam'd with these Par Lost 1.574
Cocytus, nam'd of lamentation loud Par Lost 2.579
Crownd them with Glory, and to thir Glory nam'd Par Lost 5.839
And join him nam'd *Almighty* to thy aid, Par Lost 6.294
He nam'd. Thus was the first Day Eev'n and Morn: Par Lost 7.252
And Heav'n he nam'd the Firmament: So Eev'n Par Lost 7.274
I nam'd them, as they pass'd, and understood Par Lost 8.352
Which thou hast rightly nam'd, but of thy self, Par Lost 8.439
Celestial, whether among the Thrones, or nam'd Par Lost 11.296
Ridiculous, and the work Confusion nam'd. Par Lost 12.62
With others though in Holy Writ not nam'd, Par Reg 2.8
I shall be nam'd among the famousest Samson 982
Whom therfore she brought up and *Comus* nam'd, Mask 58
Trinity ms 'nam'd' ←'nam'd him'
And Courts of Princes, where it first was nam'd, Mask 325
Must now be nam'd and printed Hereticks Forcers 11
Trinity ms 'namd'

Nameless
Nameless in dark oblivion let them dwell. Par Lost 6.380

Names
Though of thir Names in heav'nly Records now Par Lost 1.361
ms 'names'
Got them new Names, till wandring ore the Earth, Par Lost 1.365
ms 'names'
Then were they known to men by various Names, Par Lost 1.374
ms 'names'
Say, Muse, thir Names then known, who first, who last, Par Lost 1.376
ms 'names'
Egypt from *Syrian* ground, had general Names Par Lost 1.421
ms 'names'
A crew who under Names of old Renown, Par Lost 1.477
ms 'names'
Thir names of thee; so over many a tract Par Lost 6.76
I might relate of thousands, and thir names Par Lost 6.373
And thou thir Natures know'st, & gav'st them Names, Par Lost 7.493
From thee thir Names, and pay thee fealtie Par Lost 8.344
From the first op'ning bud, and gave ye Names, Par Lost 11.277
(Things by thir names I call, though yet unnam'd) Par Lost 12.140
Above all names in Heav'n; and thence shall come, Par Lost 12.458
Then shall they seek to avail themselves of names, Par Lost 12.515
Too long, then lay'st thy scapes on names ador'd, Par Reg 2.189

Names(*cont*)
For I esteem those names of men so poor Par Reg 2.447
Who names not now with honour patient *Job?* Par Reg 3.95
Rather accuse him under usual names, Par Reg 4.316
Bears greatest names in his wild aerie flight. Samson 974
And airy tongues, that syllable mens names Mask 208
line not in Bridgewater ms
Trinity ms 'syllable mens nams' ←'lure night wanderers'
And shew me simples of a thousand names Mask 627
Trinity ms 'names' ←'hews'
Those rugged names to our like mouths grow sleek Sonnet 11, 10

Naming
Surpassest farr my naming, how may I Par Lost 8.359
Conceales not from us, naming thee the Tree Par Lost 9.751
Worth naming Son of God by voice from Heav'n, Par Reg 4.539

Naphtha
With *Naphtha* and *Asphaltus* yeilded light Par Lost 1.729
ms 'Naptha'

Narcissus
That likest thy *Narcissus* are? Mask 237
next adde Narcissus that still weeps in vaine Lycidas Tr. ms 28.19

Nard
And flouring Odours, Cassia, Nard, and Balme; Par Lost 5.293
Nard, and *Cassia*'s balmy smels. Mask 991
Trinity ms 'Nard' ←'nard' ←'balme'

Narrow
Now less then smallest Dwarfs, in narrow room Par Lost 1.779
Pondering his Voyage; for no narrow frith Par Lost 2.919
In narrow room Natures whole wealth, yea more, Par Lost 4.207
Not like these narrow limits, to receive Par Lost 4.384
But first with narrow search I must walk round Par Lost 4.528
'Twixt Host and Host but narrow space was left, Par Lost 6.104
Put forth, and to a narrow vent appli'd Par Lost 6.583
With narrow search; and with inspection deep Par Lost 9.83
In narrow circuit strait'nd by a Foe, Par Lost 9.323
His presence to these narrow bounds confin'd Par Lost 11.341
Some narrow place enclos'd, where sight may give thee, Samson 1117
Above the smoak and stirr of this dim spot, Mask 5
Trinity ms 'dim' ←'dim, narrow'

Narrower
Half yet remaines unsung, but narrower bound Par Lost 7.21
And narrower Scrutiny, that I might learn Par Reg 4.515

Nathless
Nathless he so endur'd, till on the Beach Par Lost 1.299

Nation
And one peculiar Nation to select Par Lost 12.111
A Nation from one faithful man to spring: Par Lost 12.113
A mightie Nation, and upon him showre Par Lost 12.124
Growing into a Nation, and now grown Par Lost 12.164
By his own Nation, slaine for bringing Life; Par Lost 12.414
Great numbers of each Nation to receave Par Lost 12.503
What makes a Nation happy, and keeps it so, Par Reg 4.362
At least of thy own Nation, and as noble. Samson 218
My Nation, and the work from Heav'n impos'd, Samson 565
Such numbers of our Nation: and the Priest Samson 857
And of my Nation chose thee from among Samson 877
Har. Is not thy Nation subject to our Lords? Samson 1182
My Nation was subjected to your Lords. Samson 1205
Our God, our Law, my Nation, or my self, Samson 1425
That of a Nation arm'd the strength contain'd: Samson 1494
An old, and haughty Nation proud in Arms: Mask 33
Bridgewater ms 'nacion'
Trinity ms 'nation'
So th' assemblies of each Nation Psalm 7, 25
Till they no Nation be Psalm 83, 14

National
National interrupt thir public peace, Par Lost 12.317
From National obstriction, without taint Samson 312

Nations
Among the Nations round, and durst abide Par Lost 1.385
ms 'nations'
On half the Nations, and with fear of change Par Lost 1.598
ms 'nations'
In order, though to Nations yet unborn, Par Lost 4.663
Nations, and bring home spoils with infinite Par Lost 11.692
Subduing Nations, and achievd thereby Par Lost 11.792
Yet somtimes Nations will decline so low Par Lost 12.97
All Nations shall be blest; he straight obeys, Par Lost 12.126
This ponder, that all Nations of the Earth Par Lost 12.147
His day, in whom all Nations shall be blest, Par Lost 12.277
All Nations, and to Kings foretold, of Kings Par Lost 12.329
To teach all nations what of him they learn'd Par Lost 12.440
All Nations they shall teach; for from that day Par Lost 12.446
So in his seed all Nations shall be blest. Par Lost 12.450
To evangelize the Nations, then on all Par Lost 12.499
Thenceforth the Nations may not doubt; I saw Par Reg 1.79
E're in the head of Nations he appear Par Reg 1.98
Among the Nations? that hath been thy craft, Par Reg 1.432
For God hath justly giv'n the Nations up Par Reg 1.442
But to guide Nations in the way of truth Par Reg 2.473
Should Kings and Nations from thy mouth consult, Par Reg 3.12
Peaceable Nations, neighbouring, or remote, Par Reg 3.76
Promiscuous from all Nations, Jew, or Greek, Par Reg 3.118
Of Nations; there the Capitol thou seest Par Reg 4.47
All Nations now to *Rome* obedience pay, Par Reg 4.80
From Nations far and nigh; what honour that, Par Reg 4.122
But govern ill the Nations under yoke, Par Reg 4.135
Nations besides from all the quarter'd winds, Par Reg 4.202

Nations(*cont*)
But what more oft in Nations grown corrupt, Samson 268
Against the law of nature, law of nations, Samson 890
Why do the Gentiles tumult, and the Nations Psalm 2, 1
And drov'st out Nations *proud and haut* Psalm 80, 35
The Nations all possess. Psalm 82, 28
The Nations all whom thou hast made Psalm 86, 29
When he the Nations doth enrowle Psalm 87, 23
Shall aw the World, and Conquer Nations bold. Prose 12, 14

Native
While smooth *Adonis* from his native Rock Par Lost 1.450
Self-rais'd, and repossess thir native seat? Par Lost 1.634
Up to our native seat: descent and fall Par Lost 2.76
Of living Saphire, once his native Seat; Par Lost 2.1050
Draind through a Limbec to his Native forme. Par Lost 3.605
Native perfumes, and whisper whence they stole Par Lost 4.158
Godlike erect, with native Honour clad Par Lost 4.289
Thus said. Native of Heav'n, for other place Par Lost 5.361
Of this our native Heav'n, Ethereal Sons. Par Lost 5.863
Though not destroy, thir happie Native seat; Par Lost 6.226
Soon closing, and by native vigour heal'd. Par Lost 6.436
Return me to my Native Element: Par Lost 7.16
Sprung from the Deep, and from her Native East Par Lost 7.245
As from his wit and native suttletie Par Lost 9.93
Go in thy native innocence, relie Par Lost 9.373
Just confidence, and native righteousness Par Lost 9.1056
As Lords, a spacious World, to our native Heaven Par Lost 10.467
In dust, our final rest and native home. Par Lost 10.1085
Thee Native Soile, these happie Walks and Shades, Par Lost 11.270
Where he abides, think there thy native soile. Par Lost 11.292
I must return to native dust? O sight Par Lost 11.463
Quite out thir Native Language, and instead Par Lost 12.54
He leaves his Gods, his Friends, and native Soile Par Lost 12.129
Much lustre of my native brightness, lost Par Reg 1.378
Native of *Thebez* wandring here was fed Par Reg 2.313
While to their native land with joy they hast, Par Reg 3.437
And Eloquence, native to famous wits Par Reg 4.241
As in our native Language can I find Par Reg 4.333
And all their friends, and native home forget Mask 76
where grows the right-borne gold upon his native tree Mask Tr. ms 27.08
Warble his native Wood-notes wilde, Allegro 134
Hail native Language, that by sinews weak Vacation 1
us of our selves & native woes beguile Musick Tr. ms 4.08
'native' ←'home bred' ←'home-bred'

Natives
Natives and Sons of Heav'n possest before Par Lost 5.790

Nativity
These in thir dark Nativitie the Deep Par Lost 6.482
At thy Nativity a glorious Quire Par Reg 1.242
At my Nativity this strength, diffus'd Samson 1141

Natural
On mee as on thir natural center light Par Lost 10.740
But Natural necessity begot. Par Lost 10.765
Thir natural pravitie, by stirring up Par Lost 12.288
Som natural tears they drop'd, but wip'd them soon; Par Lost 12.645
Yea it shall be his natural property Vacation 87

Nature
In temper and in nature, will receive Par Lost 2.218
Where all life dies, death lives, and Nature breeds, Par Lost 2.624
1667 'nature'
And *Chaos*, Ancestors of Nature, hold Par Lost 2.895
The Womb of nature and perhaps her Grave, Par Lost 2.911
A glimmering dawn; here Nature first begins Par Lost 2.1037
Of Natures works to mee expung'd and ras'd, Par Lost 3.49
Thir nature, and revoke the high Decree Par Lost 3.126
Thir Nature also to thy Nature joyn; Par Lost 3.282
Mans Nature, less'n or degrade thine owne. Par Lost 3.304
All th' unaccomplisht works of Natures hand, Par Lost 3.455
In narrow room Natures whole wealth, yea more, Par Lost 4.207
In Beds and curious Knots, but Nature boon Par Lost 4.242
Of natures works, honor dishonorable, Par Lost 4.314
Mean while, as Nature wills, Night bids us rest. Par Lost 4.633
In Nature and all things, which these soft fires Par Lost 4.667
How Nature paints her colours, how the Bee Par Lost 5.24
Whom to behold but thee, Natures desire, Par Lost 5.45
Into her private Cell when Nature rests. Par Lost 5.109
Of Natures Womb, that in quaternion run Par Lost 5.181
A Wilderness of sweets; for Nature here Par Lost 5.294
From large bestowd, where Nature multiplies Par Lost 5.318
As to a superior Nature, bowing low, Par Lost 5.360
Not burd'nd Nature, sudden mind arose Par Lost 5.452
Our knowledge, and the scale of Nature set Par Lost 5.509
By nature free, not over-rul'd by Fate Par Lost 5.527
Or all Angelic Nature joind in one, Par Lost 5.834
Or Nature; God and Nature bid the same, Par Lost 6.176
Heav'ns blessed peace, and into Nature brought Par Lost 6.267
Great things by small, If Natures concord broke, Par Lost 6.311
In Nature none: if other hidden cause Par Lost 6.442
Th' originals of Nature in thir crude Par Lost 6.511
Of Nature from the unapparent Deep: Par Lost 7.103
Minims of Nature; some of Serpent kinde Par Lost 7.482
How Nature wise and frugal could commit Par Lost 8.26
For such vast room in Nature unpossest Par Lost 8.153
Thir Nature, with such knowledg God endu'd Par Lost 8.353
By Nature as in aide, and clos'd mine eyes. Par Lost 8.459
Nature her self, though pure of sinful thought, Par Lost 8.506
Or Nature faild in mee, and left some part Par Lost 8.534
Of Nature her th' inferiour, in the mind Par Lost 8.541

Nature(*cont*)
Accuse not Nature, she hath don her part; Par Lost 8.561
Not sedulous by Nature to indite Par Lost 9.27
Help to disburden Nature of her Bearth. Par Lost 9.624
Earth felt the wound, and Nature from her seat Par Lost 9.782
The Link of Nature draw me: Flesh of Flesh, Par Lost 9.914
The Bond of Nature draw me to my owne, Par Lost 9.956
In pangs, and Nature gave a second groan, Par Lost 9.1001
As vitiated in Nature: more to know Par Lost 10.169
His Sentence beyond dust and Natures Law, Par Lost 10.805
Crooked by nature, bent, as now appears, Par Lost 10.885
Of Nature, and not fill the World at once Par Lost 10.892
The Law I gave to Nature him forbids: Par Lost 11.49
Subscrib'd not; Nature first gave Signs, imprest Par Lost 11.182
Which Heav'n by these mute signs in Nature shews Par Lost 11.194
While they pervert pure Natures healthful rules Par Lost 11.523
The bent of Nature; which he thus express'd. Par Lost 11.597
Here Nature seems fulfilld in all her ends. Par Lost 11.602
By pleasure, though to Nature seeming meet, Par Lost 11.604
Concord and law of Nature from the Earth, Par Lost 12.29
All secrets of the deep, all Natures works, Par Lost 12.578
And bear through highth or depth of natures bounds Par Reg 1.13
Lawful desires of Nature, not beyond; Par Reg 2.230
Of what I suffer here; if Nature need not, Par Reg 2.249
Or God support Nature without repast Par Reg 2.250
Nature hath need of what she asks; yet God Par Reg 2.253
Of meats and drinks, Natures refreshment sweet; Par Reg 2.265
Natures own work it seem'd (Nature taught Art) Par Reg 2.295
Nature asham'd, or better to express, Par Reg 2.332
Or human nature can receive, consider Par Reg 3.231
To admiration, led by Natures light; Par Reg 4.228
By light of Nature not in all quite lost. Par Reg 4.352
My hopes all flat, nature within me seems Samson 595
Against the law of nature, law of nations, Samson 890
But providence or instinct of nature seems, Samson 1545
And makes one blot of all the ayr, Mask 133
Trinity ms 'all the aire' ←'nature'
That nature hung in Heav'n, and fill'd their Lamps Mask 198
line not in Bridgewater ms
Does arbitrate th' event, my nature is Mask 411
Deny her nature, and be never more Mask 559
And to those dainty limms which nature lent Mask 680
line not in Bridgewater ms
Wherefore did Nature powre her bounties forth, Mask 710
Trinity ms 'nature'
Bridgewater ms 'nature'
And live like Natures bastards, not her sons, Mask 727
Trinity ms 'natures'
Bridgewater ms 'natures'
Beauty is natures coyn, must not be hoorded, Mask 739
line not in Bridgewater ms
Beauty is natures brag, and must be shown Mask 745
line not in Bridgewater ms
Impostor do not charge most innocent nature, Mask 762
Natures full blessings would be well dispenc't Mask 772
Bridgewater ms 'natures'
Trinity ms 'natures'
And keep unsteddy Nature to her law, Arcades 70
Whom Universal nature did lament, Lycidas 60
Nature in aw to him Nativity 32
Nature that heard such sound Nativity 101
Which carefull *Jove* in natures true behoofe Fair Inf 45
When Beldam Nature in her cradle was; Vacation 46
Jarr'd against natures chime, and with harsh din Musick 20
Nature and fate had had no strife Winchester 13

Natures
To spiritual Natures; only this I know, Par Lost 5.402
And thou thir Natures know'st, & gav'st them Names, Par Lost 7.493

Naught
Created thing naught valu'd he nor shun'd; Par Lost 2.679
His malice, and thy goodness bring to naught, Par Lost 3.158
To expiate his Treason hath naught left, Par Lost 3.207
Naught seeking but the praise of men, here find Par Lost 3.453
Illaudable, naught merits but dispraise Par Lost 6.382
Intent now wholly on her taste, naught else Par Lost 9.786
And devilish machinations come to nought. Par Reg 1.181
Plausible to the world, to me worth naught. Par Reg 3.393
Nor what I part with mean to give for naught; Par Reg 4.161
Me naught advantag'd, missing what I aim'd. Par Reg 4.208
His might continues in thee not for naught, Samson 588
For importunity, that is for naught, Samson 779
But to thir Masters gave me up for nought, Samson 1215
Of all thy dues be done, and none left out, Mask 137
Trinity ms 'none' ←'nought'
Yet nought but single darknes do I find. Mask 204
line not in Bridgewater ms
And spotted mountain pard, but set at nought Mask 444
Trinity ms 'naught'
Naught but profoundest Hell can be his shroud, Nativity 218
And not fre'd my foe for naught; Psalm 7, 12

Navel
Within the navil of this hideous Wood, Mask 520
Trinity ms 'navill'
1637 'navill'
Bridgewater ms 'navill'

Nay
Nay curs'd be thou; since against his thy will Par Lost 4.71
Nay didst permit, approve, and fair dismiss. Par Lost 9.1159

Nay(*cont*)
So little here, nay lost; but *Eve* was *Eve*, Par Reg 4.6
Deceivable and vain! Nay what thing good Samson 350
(*Gaza* is not in plight to say us nay) Samson 1729
La. Nay gentle Shepherd ill is lost that praise Mask 271
Som say no evil thing that walks by night Mask 432
Bridgewater ms 'naye more noe evill'
Trinity ms 'Some say' ←'Nay more' ←'Some say'
Comus. Nay Lady sit; if I but wave this wand, Mask 659
Nay, quoth he, on his swooning bed outstretch'd, Another 17
line not in 1640, 1657, 1658 texts
Nazareth
From *Nazareth* the Son of *Joseph* deem'd Par Reg 1.23
From *Egypt* home return'd, in *Nazareth* Par Reg 2.79
Nazarite
Have prompted this Heroic *Nazarite*, Samson 318
A *Nazarite* in place abominable Samson 1359
Our Law, or stain my vow of *Nazarite*. Samson 1386
Neaera
Or with the tangles of *Neaera*'s hair? Lycidas 69
1638 'Neera's'
Near
All in one moment, and so neer the brink; Par Lost 2.609
So neer grows Death to Life, what ere Death is, Par Lost 4.425
That neer him stood, and gave them thus in charge. Par Lost 4.787
Our happie state under one Head more neer Par Lost 5.830
And Warr so neer the Peace of God in bliss Par Lost 7.55
For while so near each other thus all day Par Lost 9.220
Our taske we choose, what wonder if so near Par Lost 9.221
And at the brink of *Chaos*, neer the foot Par Lost 10.347
Th' infernal Empire, that so neer Heav'ns dore Par Lost 10.389
Neer that bituminous Lake where *Sodom* flam'd; Par Lost 10.562
Sam. My Wife, my Traytress, let her not come near me. Samson 725
So near related, or the same of kind, Samson 786
Of som chast footing neer about this ground. Mask 146
1673 'near'
1637 'neere'
Trinity ms 'neere'
Bridgewater ms 'neere'
2. *Bro*. Heav'n keep my sister, agen agen and neer, Mask 486
Trinity ms 'neere'
Bridgewater ms 'neere'
1637 'neere'
Com not too neer, you fall on iron stakes else. Mask 491
Bridgewater ms 'neere'
1637 'neere'
Trinity ms 'neere'
How sweet thou sing'st, how neer the deadly snare! Mask 567
1637 'neere'
1673 'near'
Trinity ms 'neere'
Bridgewater ms 'neere'
How durst thou then thy self approach so neer Mask 616
1637 'neere'
Trinity ms 'neere'
Bridgewater ms 'neere'
All the Swains that there abide, Mask 951
Trinity ms 'neere abide'
Bridgewater ms 'neere abide'
While the Plowman neer at hand, Allegro 63
Riding neer her highest noon, Penseroso 68
And lead ye where ye may more neer behold Arcades 40
1673 'near'
Trinity ms 'neere'
Should look so neer upon her foul deformities. Nativity 44
1673 'near'
He thought it toucht his Deitie full neer, Fair Inf 10
Will pierce more neer his heart. Circum 28
1673 'near'
Trinity ms 'neere'
That I to manhood am arriv'd so near, Sonnet 7, 6
Trinity ms 'neere'
The tools of death, that waits him near. Psalm 7, 48
Where thou do'st dwell so near. Psalm 84, 4
Nearer
Sits Arbitress, and neerer to the Earth Par Lost 1.785
Neerer our ancient Seat; perhaps in view Par Lost 2.394
So much the neerer danger; go and speed; Par Lost 2.1008
Now nearer, Crowns with her enclosure green, Par Lost 4.133
Neerer to view his prey, and unespi'd Par Lost 4.399
Neerer his presence *Adam* though not awd, Par Lost 5.358
As neerer to him plac't or neerer tending Par Lost 5.476
In battailous aspect, and neerer view Par Lost 6.81
What neerer might concern him, how this World Par Lost 7.62
Neerer he drew, and many a walk travers'd Par Lost 9.434
Ruddie and Gold: I nearer drew to gaze; Par Lost 9.578
Nearer acquainted, now I feel by proof, Par Reg 1.400
1671 printed 'never', errata 'nearer'
By my advice, as nearer and of late Par Reg 3.364
Westward, much nearer by Southwest, behold Par Reg 4.237
Thenceforth I thought thee worth my nearer view Par Reg 4.514
And now at nearer view, no other certain Samson 723
Come nearer, part not hence so slight inform'd; Samson 1229
(For so from such as nearer stood we heard) Samson 1631
Nearest
Thus Satan talking to his neerest Mate Par Lost 1.192
Which way the neerest coast of darkness lyes Par Lost 2.958
Who in Gods presence, neerest to his Throne Par Lost 3.649
Nearest(*cont*)
Out of my side to thee, neerest my heart Par Lost 4.484
Resembles nearest, mazes intricate, Par Lost 5.622
Likeliest, and neerest to the present ayd Mask 90
1673 'nearest'
Toward solid good what leads the nearest way; Sonnet 21, 10
Nearly
Neerly it now concernes us to be sure Par Lost 5.721
Near-ushering
Co. Could that divide you from neer-ushering guides? Mask 279
Bridgewater ms 'neere vsheringe'
1637 'neere-ushering'
Trinity ms 'neere ushering' ←'thire ushering'
Neat
Of lighter toes, and such Court guise Mask 962
Trinity ms 'such court guise' ←'such neate guise' ←'courtly guise'
What neat repast shall feast us, light and choice, Sonnet 20, 9
Neat-handed
Which the neat-handed *Phillis* dresses; Allegro 86
Neatness
Plain in thy neatness; O how oft shall he Horace 5
Nebaioth
Out cast *Nebaioth*, yet found he relief Par Reg 2.309
Nebo
From *Aroar* to *Nebo*, and the wild Par Lost 1.407
ms 'Nebo'
Necessary
Since light so necessary is to life, Samson 90
Necessitate
Concurring to necessitate his Fall, Par Lost 10.44
Necessitated
Not our necessitated, such with him Par Lost 5.530
Necessity
Made passive both, had servd necessitie, Par Lost 3.110
So spake the Fiend, and with necessitie, Par Lost 4.393
Inextricable, or strict necessity; Par Lost 5.528
To act or not, Necessitie and Chance Par Lost 7.172
1669 'Necessity'
By my complaint; but strict necessitie Par Lost 10.131
But Natural necessity begot. Par Lost 10.765
Of dire necessity, whose law in death conjoin'd Samson 1666
To lull the daughters of *Necessity*, Arcades 69
Neck
Thir downie Brest; the Swan with Arched neck Par Lost 7.438
With burnisht Neck of verdant Gold, erect Par Lost 9.501
His turret Crest, and sleek enamel'd Neck, Par Lost 9.525
And on the neck of crowned Fortune proud Sonnet 16, 5
line not in 1694 text
Necks
Heav'ns everlasting Frame, while o're the necks Par Lost 3.395
Will ye submit your necks, and chuse to bend Par Lost 5.787
Laid on our Necks. Remember with what mild Par Lost 10.1046
Bow'd their Stiff necks, loaden with stormy blasts, Par Reg 4.418
Necromancer
Boldly assault the necromancers hall; Mask 649
Trinity ms 'necromancers' ←'necromantik'
Bridgewater ms 'Negromancers'
Nectar
Ran Nectar, visiting each plant, and fed Par Lost 4.240
Yield Nectar, though from off the boughs each Morn Par Lost 5.428
With Angels Food, and rubied Nectar flows Par Lost 5.633
From Nectar, drink of Gods. *Adam* the while Par Lost 9.838
bedew'd with nectar, & celestiall songs Mask Tr. ms 10.06
With *Nectar* pure his oozy Lock's he laves, Lycidas 175
Trinity ms 'nectar'
Immortal Nectar to her Kingly Sire: Vacation 39
Nectared
And a perpetual feast of nectar'd sweets, Mask 479
Bridgewater ms 'Nectard'
In nectar'd lavers strew'd with Asphodil, Mask 838
Amongst us here below to hide thy nectar'd head. Fair Inf 49
Nectarine
Nectarine Fruits which the compliant boughes Par Lost 4.332
Nectarous
Of nectarous draughts between, from milkie stream, Par Lost 5.306
A stream of Nectarous humor issuing flow'd Par Lost 6.332
Need
Contrive who need, or when they need, not now Par Lost 2.53
Nor will occasion want, nor shall we need Par Lost 2.341
Of Angels watching round? Here he had need Par Lost 2.413
For regal Scepter then no more shall need, Par Lost 3.340
Aught whereof hee hath need, hee who requires Par Lost 4.419
Rove idle unimploid, and less need rest; Par Lost 4.617
Wee ours for change delectable, not need) Par Lost 5.629
That might determine, and not need repeate, Par Lost 6.318
Had need from head to foot well understand; Par Lost 6.625
Or solace his defects. No need that thou Par Lost 8.419
Desiring; nor restrain'd conveyance need Par Lost 8.628
Labour, as to debarr us when we need Par Lost 9.236
As we need walk, till younger hands ere long Par Lost 9.246
To other speedie aide might lend at need; Par Lost 9.260
More wise, more watchful, stronger, if need were Par Lost 9.311
Causes import your need of this fair Fruit. Par Lost 9.731
Attendance none shall need, nor Train, where none Par Lost 10.80
No detriment need feare, goe and be strong. Par Lost 10.409
Beseeching him, so as we need not fear Par Lost 10.1082
I learn not yet, perhaps I need not know; Par Reg 1.292

Need(*cont*)
Of what I suffer here; if Nature need not, Par Reg 2.249
Nature hath need of what she asks; yet God Par Reg 2.253
Can satisfie that need some other way, Par Reg 2.254
They all had need, I as thou seest have none. Par Reg 2.318
Chose to impart to thy apparent need, Par Reg 2.397
Shalt raign, and *Rome* or *Caesar* not need fear. Par Reg 3.385
On my part aught endeavouring, or to need Par Reg 3.399
And thou hast need much washing to be toucht. Samson 1107
Be efficacious in thee now at need. Samson 1437
If need be, I am ready to forgo Samson 1483
From other hands we need not much to fear. Samson 1526
Would send a glistring Guardian if need were Mask 219
line not in Bridgewater ms
Co. Imports their loss, beside the present need? Mask 287
Bridgewater ms 'neede'
What need a man forestall his date of grief, Mask 362
line not in Trinity ms
line not in Bridgewater ms
Laden with blooming gold, had need the guard Mask 394
Bridgewater ms 'neede'
What need a vermeil-tinctur'd lip for that Mask 752
line not in Bridgewater ms
In hard besetting need, this will I try Mask 857
Bridgewater ms 'neede'
Trinity ms 'need' ←'in honourd vertues cause'
poore ladie thou hast need of some refreshing Mask Tr. ms 20.09
poore ladie thou hast neede of some refreshinge Mask Br. ms 660
What recks it them? What need they? They are sped; Lycidas 122
The new-enlightn'd world no more should need; Nativity 82
And with full hand supplies their need. Psalm 136, 86
From others he shall stand in need of nothing, Vacation 81
That murmur, soon replies, God doth not need Sonnet 19, 9
Give ear *in time of need*, Psalm 80, 2
with need, *and sad decay*. Psalm 86, 4

Needed
More tuneable then needed Lute or Harp Par Lost 5.151
Thir pamperd boughes, and needed hands to check Par Lost 5.214
Shee needed, Vertue-proof, no thought infirme Par Lost 5.384
From him, for other light she needed none Par Lost 7.378

Needest
Dismiss not her, when most thou needst her nigh, Par Lost 8.564
For some important cause, thou needst not doubt. Samson 1379
What need'st thou such weak witnes of thy name? Shakespear 6
1640 'needs'
1632 'needst'

Needful
& may upon any needfull accident Mask Tr. ms 16.55

Needing
Though needing, what praise is it to endure? Par Reg 2.251

Needless
Needless to thee repeated; nor unknown Par Lost 7.494
Let none henceforth seek needless cause to approve Par Lost 9.1140
Riches are needless then, both for themselves, Par Reg 2.484
Not a waste, or needless sound Mask 942
Trinity ms 'needlesse'
1637 'needlesse'
Bridgewater ms 'needles'

Needs
Into their temper; which must needs remove Par Lost 2.277
Where onely what they needs must do, appeard, Par Lost 3.105
And Country whereof here needs no account, Par Lost 4.235
Dearer thy self then all; needs must the power Par Lost 4.412
Earths inmost womb, more warmth then *Adam* needs; Par Lost 5.302
For know, whatever was created, needs Par Lost 5.414
The full relation, which must needs be strange, Par Lost 5.556
Ruin must needs ensue; for what availes Par Lost 6.456
Whence in perpetual fight they needs must last Par Lost 6.693
But Knowledge is as food, and needs no less Par Lost 7.126
Of Day and Night; which needs not thy beleefe, Par Lost 8.136
Leads thee, or where most needs, whether to wind Par Lost 9.215
Suttle he needs must be, who could seduce Par Lost 9.307
For us created, needs with us must faile, Par Lost 9.942
Adam, Heav'ns high behest no Preface needs: Par Lost 11.251
Must needs impaire and wearie human sense: Par Lost 12.10
Needs must the Serpent now his capital bruise Par Lost 12.383
No other doctrine needs, though granted true; Par Reg 4.290
(And what he brings, what needs he elsewhere seek) Par Reg 4.325
Knowing, as needs I must, by thee betray'd? Samson 840
What Pilot so expert but needs must wreck Samson 1044
Sam. So take it with what speed thy message needs. Samson 1345
Man. Some dismal accident it needs must be; Samson 1519
No Preface needs, thou seest we long to know. Samson 1554
What needs my *Shakespear* for his honour'd Bones, Shakespear 1
1663-4 'need'
1632 'neede'
1640 'neede'

Needst
Thou needst not be ambitious to be first, Vacation 11

Neglect
They who neglect and scorn, shall never taste; Par Lost 3.199
Neglect not, and the benefit imbrace Par Lost 12.426
Mee easily indeed mine may neglect, Samson 291
Or our neglect, we lost her as we came. Mask 510
For this same small neglect that I have made: Vacation 16

Neglected
Neglected. I already have made way Samson 481
And last neglected? How wouldst thou insult Samson 944

Neglected(*cont*)
If you let slip time, like a neglected rose Mask 743
line not in Bridgewater ms

Neglects
Where honour due and reverence none neglects, Par Lost 3.738

Negus
Th' Empire of *Negus* to his utmost Port Par Lost 11.397

Neighbour
Or els som neighbour Wood-man, or at worst, Mask 484
Bridgewater ms 'neyghbour'
Supposing him som neighbour villager; Mask 576
Bridgewater ms 'neighbour-villager'
To every neighbour foe, Psalm 80, 26

Neighbourhood
Audacious neighbourhood, the wisest heart Par Lost 1.400
ms 'neighborhood'
My daily walks and ancient neighbourhood, Mask 314
Trinity ms 'neighbourhood' ←'nighbour'
The gentle neighbourhood of grove and spring Passion 52
But his owne house, and the whole neighbourhood Prose 10, 5

Neighbouring
Of those bright confines, whence with neighbouring Arms Par Lost 2.395
Not in the neighbouring Moon, as some have dreamd; Par Lost 3.459
Night would invade, but there the neighbouring Moon Par Lost 3.726
Into his neather Empire neighbouring round. Par Lost 4.145
Cherubic Songs by night from neighbouring Hills Par Lost 5.547
Betook them, and the neighbouring Hills uptore; Par Lost 6.663
From the high neighbouring Hills, which was thir Seat, Par Lost 11.575
Pitcht about *Sechem*, and the neighbouring Plaine Par Lost 12.136
Peaceable Nations, neighbouring, or remote, Par Reg 3.76
From *Atropatia* and the neighbouring plains Par Reg 3.319
The Cynosure of neighbouring eyes. Allegro 80

Neighbours
We come thy friends and neighbours not unknown Samson 180

Neither
His own: for neither do the Spirits damn'd Par Lost 2.482
His deadly arrow; neither vainly hope Par Lost 2.811
Of neither Sea, nor Shore, nor Air, nor Fire, Par Lost 2.912
Quencht in a Boggie *Syrtis*, neither Sea, Par Lost 2.939
For neither Man nor Angel can discern Par Lost 3.682
Where neither joy nor love, but fierce desire, Par Lost 4.509
But neither breath of Morn when she ascends Par Lost 4.650
Neither our own but giv'n; what follie then Par Lost 4.1007
In various style, for neither various style Par Lost 5.146
Was giv'n him temperd so, that neither keen Par Lost 6.322
Neither her out-side formd so fair, nor aught Par Lost 8.596
But neither here seek I, no nor in Heav'n Par Lost 9.124
Neither had I transgress'd, nor thou with mee. Par Lost 9.1161
The fruitless hours, but neither self-condemning, Par Lost 9.1188
And sin? the Bodie properly hath neither. Par Lost 10.791
Which neither his foreknowing can prevent, Par Lost 11.773
Yet neither thus disheartn'd or dismay'd, Par Reg 1.268
Thou neither dost perswade me to seek wealth Par Reg 3.44
Since neither wealth, nor honour, arms nor arts, Par Reg 4.368
For neither were ye playing on the steep, Lycidas 52
The Lillie and Rose, that neither sow'd nor spun. Sonnet 20, 8
Who neither can nor will, may hold his peace; Prose 9, 4

Nepenthes
Not that *Nepenthes* which the wife of *Thone*, Mask 675
Trinity ms 'Nepenthes' ←'nepenthes'

Neptune
Or *Neptun*'s ire or *Juno's*, that so long Par Lost 9.18
Apollo, *Neptune*, *Jupiter*, or *Pan*, Par Reg 2.190
But to my task. *Neptune* besides the sway Mask 18
By the earth-shaking *Neptune*'s mace, Mask 869
Trinity ms 'neptunes'
1637 '*Neptun*'s'
Bridgewater ms 'Neptunes'
That came in *Neptune*'s plea, Lycidas 90
Trinity ms 'Neptunes'
1638 'Neptunes'
May tell at length how green-ey'd *Neptune* raves, Vacation 43

Nereus
Bearing her straight to aged *Nereus* Hall, Mask 835
By hoary *Nereus* wrincled look, Mask 871

Nerve
The visual Nerve, for he had much to see; Par Lost 11.415
Above the nerve of mortal arm Samson 639

Nerves
This utter'd, straining all his nerves he bow'd, Samson 1646
Your nervs are all chain'd up in Alablaster, Mask 660
Bridgewater ms 'nerves'
1673 'nerves'
Trinity ms 'nerves'
And the brute Earth would lend her nerves, and shake, Mask 797
line not in Trinity ms
line not in Bridgewater ms
Move by her two maine nerves, Iron and Gold Sonnet 17, 8
1662, 1694 'Nerves'

Nest
Left his ground-nest, high towring to descry Par Reg 2.280
Hath built her *brooding* nest, Psalm 84, 12

Nests
They to thir grassie Couch, these to thir Nests Par Lost 4.601
The Desert, Fowls in thir clay nests were couch't; Par Reg 1.501
And nests in order rang'd Samson 1694

Net
Rove without rein, till in the amorous Net Par Lost 11.586

Nether
'Twixt upper, nether, and surrounding Fires; Par Lost 1.346
To found this nether Empire, which might rise Par Lost 2.296
Distorted, all my nether shape thus grew Par Lost 2.784
Into his neather Empire neighbouring round. Par Lost 4.145
Down the steep glade, and met the neather Flood, Par Lost 4.231
Earth with her nether Ocean circumfus'd, Par Lost 7.624
In yonder nether World where shall I seek Par Lost 11.328
Took in by lot 'twixt high, and neather *Jove*, Mask 20
Nethermost
Or Spirit of the nethermost Abyss Par Lost 2.956
And Spirits of this nethermost Abyss, Par Lost 2.969
Nets
Hearts after them tangl'd in Amorous Nets. Par Reg 2.162
And hugg him into snares. When once her eye Mask 164
Trinity ms 'snares' ←'nets'
Never
And rest can never dwell, hope never comes Par Lost 1.66
And courage never to submit or yield: Par Lost 1.108
That Glory never shall his wrath or might Par Lost 1.110
To do ought good never will be our task, Par Lost 1.159
Pour'd never from her frozen loyns, to pass Par Lost 1.352
Glories: For never since created man, Par Lost 1.573
For this Infernal Pit shall never hold Par Lost 1.657
Is doubtful; that he never will is sure. Par Lost 2.154
A cry of Hell Hounds never ceasing bark'd Par Lost 2.654
For never but once more was either like Par Lost 2.721
And never but in unapproached light Par Lost 3.4
They who neglect and scorn, shall never taste; Par Lost 3.199
Can never seek, once dead in sins and lost; Par Lost 3.233
With these that never fade the Spirits elect Par Lost 3.360
Henceforth, and never shall my Harp thy praise Par Lost 3.414
Through his glaz'd Optic Tube yet never saw. Par Lost 3.590
For never can true reconcilement grow Par Lost 4.98
Pan or *Silvanus* never slept, nor Nymph, Par Lost 4.707
Such night till this I never pass'd, have dream'd, Par Lost 5.31
Knew never till this irksom night; methought Par Lost 5.35
Waking thou never wilt consent to do. Par Lost 5.121
Yet that we never shall forget to love Par Lost 5.550
Was never, Arms on Armour clashing bray'd Par Lost 6.209
Thou never from that houre in Paradise Par Lost 9.406
And lovely, never since of Serpent kind Par Lost 9.504
At Feed or Fountain never had I found. Par Lost 9.597
In Fruit she never tasted, whether true Par Lost 9.788
Not felt, nor shall be twice, for never more Par Lost 9.859
Would never from my heart; no no, I feel Par Lost 9.913
Mine never shall be parted, bliss or woe. Par Lost 9.916
So eminently never had bin known. Par Lost 9.976
For never did thy Beautie since the day Par Lost 9.1029
Hide me, where I may never see them more. Par Lost 9.1090
Was I to have never parted from thy side? Par Lost 9.1153
Satisfi'd never; that were to extend Par Lost 10.804
He never shall find out fit Mate, but such Par Lost 10.899
I never from thy side henceforth to stray, Par Lost 11.176
That never will in other Climate grow, Par Lost 11.274
In some to spring from thee, who never touch'd Par Lost 11.425
And makes a Covenant never to destroy Par Lost 11.892
Never to hurt them more who rightly trust Par Lost 12.418
Never did wrong or violence, by them Par Reg 1.389
Nearer acquainted, now I feel by proof, Par Reg 1.400
1671 printed 'never', errata 'nearer'
Man fall'n shall be restor'd, I never more. Par Reg 1.405
So never more in Hell then when in Heaven. Par Reg 1.420
That it shall never end, so when begin Par Reg 3.185
Thou never shalt obtain; prediction still Par Reg 3.354
And never cease, though to his shame the more; Par Reg 4.14
I never lik'd thy talk, thy offers less, Par Reg 4.171
To wish thou never hadst rejected thus Par Reg 4.376
I never fear'd they could, though noising loud Par Reg 4.488
He never more henceforth will dare set foot Par Reg 4.610
In power of others, never in my own; Samson 78
And shall again, pretend they ne're so wise. Samson 212
(O that I never had! fond wish too late.) Samson 228
Thou never wast remiss, I bear thee witness: Samson 239
For of such Doctrine never was there School, Samson 297
But never find self-satisfying solution. Samson 306
He would not else who never wanted means, Samson 315
But now hath cast me off as never known, Samson 641
To thine whose doors my feet shall never enter. Samson 950
Eternal tempest never to be calm'd. Samson 964
That I was never present on the place Samson 1085
To *Samson*, but shalt never see *Gath* more. Samson 1129
At *Askalon*, who never did thee harm, Samson 1187
Shall never, unrepented, find forgiveness. Samson 1376
For never was from Heaven imparted Samson 1438
What never yet was heard in Tale or Song Mask 44
Which these dun shades will ne're report. Mask 127
Bridgewater ms 'neere'
That ne're art call'd, but when the Dragon woom Mask 131
Bridgewater ms 'neere'
Trinity ms 'neere'
I never heard till now. Ile speak to her Mask 264
Whom certain these rough shades did never breed Mask 266
Deny her nature, and be never more Mask 559
Vertue may be assail'd, but never hurt, Mask 589
May never this just sword be lifted up, Mask 601
Ne're looks to Heav'n amidst his gorgeous feast, Mask 777
Bridgewater ms 'neere'

Never(*cont*)
Their full tribute never miss Mask 925
Never scorch thy tresses fair, Mask 929
Where day never shuts his eye, Mask 978
his uninchanted eye, & round the verge Mask Tr. ms 10.10
'uninchanted' ←'never charmed'
Was never heard the Nymphs to daunt, Penseroso 137
But let my due feet never fail, Penseroso 155
Now thou art gon, and never must return! Lycidas 38
As never was by mortall finger strook, Nativity 95
Before was never made, Nativity 118
Devouring war shall never cease to roare: Vacation 86
And surely, Death could never have prevail'd, Carrier 9
That he could never die while he could move, Another 2
So hung his destiny never to rot Another 3
Made of sphear-metal, never to decay Another 5
If I may not carry, sure Ile ne're be fetch'd, Another 18
line not in 1640, 1657, 1658 texts
When Faith and Love which parted from thee never, Sonnet 14, 1
Then whome a better Senatour nere held Sonnet 17, 2
1694 'ne're'
1662 'ner'e'
With shame, *and scape it never.* Psalm 83, 64
But let them never more Psalm 85, 34
So shall it never slide Psalm 86, 40
That ne're shall be out-worn Psalm 87, 22
Dost never more regard, Psalm 88, 22
Never-ending
Besides what hope the never-ending flight Par Lost 2.221
Never-parting
To live with him, and sing in endles morn of light. Musick 28
Trinity ms 'endlesse' ←'never-parting' ←'cloudlesse' ←'endlesse' ←'uneclipsed' ←'ever-glorious' ←'ever-endlesse'
Never-sere
Ye Myrtles brown, with Ivy never-sear, Lycidas 2
Trinity ms 'never sere'
1638 'never-sere'
1673 'never sear'
Nevertheless
Found so unfortunate; nevertheless, Par Lost 10.970
New
Receive thy new Possessor: One who brings Par Lost 1.252
New courage and revive, though now they lye Par Lost 1.279
Or in *Valdarno*, to descry new Lands, Par Lost 1.290
Got them new Names, till wandring ore the Earth, Par Lost 1.365
Of Glory obscur'd: As when the Sun new ris'n Par Lost 1.594
New warr, provok't; our better part remains Par Lost 1.645
Space may produce new Worlds; whereof so rife Par Lost 1.650
New rub'd with Baum, expatiate and confer Par Lost 1.774
Of new Subjection; with what eyes could we Par Lost 2.239
From Heav'ns high jurisdiction, in new League Par Lost 2.319
Of some new Race call'd *Man*, about this time Par Lost 2.348
In search of this new world, whom shall we find Par Lost 2.403
Might hap to move new broiles: Be this or aught Par Lost 2.837
To that new world of light and bliss, among Par Lost 2.867
Directly towards the new created World, Par Lost 3.89
Sense of new joy ineffable diffus'd: Par Lost 3.137
Receive new life. So Man, as is most just, Par Lost 3.294
New Heav'n and Earth, wherein the just shall dwell, Par Lost 3.335
New *Babels*, had they wherewithall, would build: Par Lost 3.468
Here matter new to gaze the Devil met Par Lost 3.613
To visit oft this new Creation round; Par Lost 3.661
Created this new happie Race of Men Par Lost 3.679
Of this new World; at whose sight all the Starrs Par Lost 4.34
Of us out-cast, exil'd, his new delight, Par Lost 4.106
As Man ere long, and this new World shall know. Par Lost 4.113
Whom hunger drives to seek new haunt for prey, Par Lost 4.184
Beneath him with new wonder now he views Par Lost 4.205
Of living Creatures new to sight and strange: Par Lost 4.287
By conquering this new World, compels me now Par Lost 4.391
Turnd him all eare to hear new utterance flow. Par Lost 4.410
New troubles; him thy care must be to find. Par Lost 4.575
This new created World, whereof in Hell Par Lost 4.937
Heav'ns last best gift, my ever new delight, Par Lost 5.19
Varie to our great Maker still new praise. Par Lost 5.184
Varied his bounty so with new delights, Par Lost 5.431
Thy sleep dissent? new Laws thou seest impos'd; Par Lost 5.679
New Laws from him who reigns, new minds may raise Par Lost 5.680
In us who serve, new Counsels, to debate Par Lost 5.681
The great *Messiah*, and his new commands, Par Lost 5.691
With what may be devis'd of honours new Par Lost 5.780
From Father to his Son? strange point and new! Par Lost 5.855
Deliverer from new Lords, leader to free Par Lost 6.451
Which to our eyes discoverd new and strange, Par Lost 6.571
Whose liquid murmur heard new thirst excites, Par Lost 7.68
And Spirit coming to create new Worlds. Par Lost 7.209
Thence to behold this new created World Par Lost 7.554
Then as new wak't thus gratefully repli'd. Par Lost 8.4
1667 'To whom thus *Adam*'
Induc'd me. As new wak't from soundest sleep Par Lost 8.253
Had lively shadowd: Here had new begun Par Lost 8.311
Provokes my envie, this new Favorite Par Lost 9.175
Looks intervene and smiles, or object new Par Lost 9.222
New part puts on, and as to passion mov'd, Par Lost 9.667
Great joy he promis'd to his thoughts, and new Par Lost 9.843
New gatherd, and ambrosial smell diffus'd. Par Lost 9.852
Augmented, op'nd Eyes, new Hopes, new Joyes, Par Lost 9.985
As with new Wine intoxicated both Par Lost 9.1008

New(*cont*)
Those middle parts, that this new commer, Shame, Par Lost 9.1097
Methinks I feel new strength within me rise, Par Lost 10.243
Over this Maine from Hell to that new World Par Lost 10.257
By this new felt attraction and instinct. Par Lost 10.263
Of this new wondrous Pontifice, unhop't Par Lost 10.348
As Battel hath adjudg'd, from this new World Par Lost 10.377
My hold of this new Kingdom all depends, Par Lost 10.406
The new created World, which fame in Heav'n Par Lost 10.481
New Heav'n and Earth shall to the Ages rise, Par Lost 10.647
Of this new glorious World, and mee so late Par Lost 10.721
Of new acceptance, hopeful to regaine Par Lost 10.972
The stonie from thir hearts, & made new flesh Par Lost 11.4
Vacant possession som new trouble raise: Par Lost 11.103
Strength added from above, new hope to spring Par Lost 11.138
New Laws to be observ'd; for I descrie Par Lost 11.228
New reapt, the other part sheep-walks and foulds; Par Lost 11.431
Betok'ning peace from God, and Cov'nant new. Par Lost 11.867
Shall hold thir course, till fire purge all things new, Par Lost 11.900
Then with transition sweet new Speech resumes. Par Lost 12.5
line not in 1667 edition
New Heav'ns, new Earth, Ages of endless date Par Lost 12.549
Affirming it thy Star new grav'n in Heaven, Par Reg 1.253
Our new baptizing Prophet at the Ford Par Reg 1.328
What happ'ns new; Fame also finds us out. Par Reg 1.334
Into perplexity and new amaze: Par Reg 2.38
Thus they out of their plaints new hope resume Par Reg 2.58
Without new trouble; such an Enemy Par Reg 2.126
Our Saviour, and new train of words began. Par Reg 3.266
Of Academics old and new, with those Par Reg 4.278
Yet with no new device, they all were spent, Par Reg 4.443
Receiving from his mother Earth new strength, Par Reg 4.566
Do they not seek occasion of new quarrels Samson 1329
By order of the Lords new parted hence Samson 1447
His servants he with new acquist Samson 1755
Ile venter, for my new enliv'nd spirits Mask 228
Trinity ms 'new-enliv'nd'
Lingering, and sitting by a new made grave, Mask 472
And force him to restore his purchase back, Mask 607
Trinity ms 'purchase back' ←'new got prey'
With som other new device. Mask 941
Bridgewater ms 'newe'
I have brought ye new delight, Mask 967
Streit mine eye hath caught new pleasures Allegro 69
And tricks his beams, and with new spangled Ore, Lycidas 170
Trinity ms 'newspangled'
To morrow to fresh Woods, and Pastures new. Lycidas 193
To welcom him to this his new abode, Nativity 18
Whispering new joyes to the milde Ocean, Nativity 66
Not those new fangled toys, and triming slight Vacation 19
New shot up from vernall showr; Winchester 40
There with thee, new welcom Saint, Winchester 71
The Subject new: it walk'd the Town a while, Sonnet 11, 3
Victory home, though new rebellions raise Sonnet 15, 6
No less renownd then warr, new foes arise Sonnet 16, 11
New Presbyter is but *Old Priest* writ Large. Forcers 20
Blow, *as is wont*, in the new Moon Psalm 81, 9

New-arrived
About the new-arriv'd, in multitudes Par Lost 10.26

New-baptized
Mean while the new-baptiz'd, who yet remain'd Par Reg 2.1

New-born
With unexpressive notes to Heav'ns new-born Heir. Nativity 116

New-declared
Where he might likeliest find this new-declar'd, Par Reg 1.121

New-enlightened
The new-enlightn'd world no more should need; Nativity 82
1673 'new enlightn'd'

New-entrusted
And new-entrusted Scepter, but their way Mask 36
Trinity ms 'new entrusted'
Bridgewater ms 'newe entrusted'

Newly
Hobson has supt, and's newly gon to bed. Carrier 18

New-made
Witness this new-made World, another Heav'n Par Lost 7.617
Did fill the new-made world with light. Psalm 136, 26

News
Already known what he for news had thought Par Lost 6.20
Entrance unseen. Soon as th' unwelcome news Par Lost 10.21
He added not, for *Adam* at the newes Par Lost 11.263
For this ill news I bring, the Womans seed Par Reg 1.64
Or of him bringing to us some glad news? Samson 1444
For evil news rides post, while good news baits. Samson 1538
Man. Suspense in news is torture, speak them out. Samson 1569
And joyous news of heav'nly Infants birth, Passion 3

Next
One next himself in power, and next in crime, Par Lost 1.79
Of unblest feet. Him followed his next Mate, Par Lost 1.238
At thir great Emperors call, as next in worth Par Lost 1.378
Thir Seats long after next the Seat of God, Par Lost 1.383
Next *Chemos*, th' obscene dread of *Moabs* Sons, Par Lost 1.406
To Idols foul. *Thammuz* came next behind, Par Lost 1.446
Of alienated *Judah*. Next came one Par Lost 1.457
Did first create your Leader, next free choice, Par Lost 2.19
He ceas'd, and next him *Moloc*, Scepter'd King Par Lost 2.43
Of unessential Night receives him next Par Lost 2.439
By which he Reigns: next him high Arbiter Par Lost 2.909

Next(*cont*)
Of *Demogorgon; Rumor* next and *Chance*, Par Lost 2.965
Thy bosom, and this glorie next to thee Par Lost 3.239
Thee next they sang of all Creation first, Par Lost 3.383
The builders next of *Babel* on the Plain Par Lost 3.466
Of vegetable Gold; and next to Life Par Lost 4.220
When *Gabriel* to his next in power thus spake. Par Lost 4.781
Awaiting next command. To whom thir Chief Par Lost 4.864
Wise to flie pain, professing next the Spie, Par Lost 4.948
Works of day pass't, or morrows next designe, Par Lost 5.33
Reason as chief; among these Fansie next Par Lost 5.102
Contemptuous, and his next subordinate Par Lost 5.671
And thou in Military prowess next Par Lost 6.45
Together both with next to Almightie Arme, Par Lost 6.316
Weapons more violent, when next we meet, Par Lost 6.439
He sat; and in th' assembly next upstood Par Lost 6.446
Themselves invaded next, and on thir heads Par Lost 6.653
Of Commonaltie: swarming next appeer'd Par Lost 7.489
What next I bring shall please thee, be assur'd, Par Lost 8.449
Since higher I fall short, on him who next Par Lost 9.174
Thus grown. Experience, next to thee I owe, Par Lost 9.807
He ruind, now Mankind; whom will he next? Par Lost 9.950
Feed first, on each Beast next, and Fish, and Fowle, Par Lost 10.604
Who can extenuate thee? Next, to the Son, Par Lost 10.645
The sourse of life; next favourable thou, Par Lost 11.169
Uncull'd, as came to hand; a Shepherd next Par Lost 11.436
And his next Son for Wealth and Wisdom fam'd, Par Lost 12.332
Poor *Socrates* (who next more memorable2) Par Reg 3.96
Of *Egypt*, *Baal* next and *Ashtaroth*, Par Reg 3.417
Lyceum there, and painted *Stoa* next: Par Reg 4.253
To sage Philosophy next lend thine ear, Par Reg 4.272
The next to fabling fell and smooth conceits, Par Reg 4.295
She proving false, the next I took to Wife Samson 227
In both which we, as next participate. Samson 1507
Stept as they se'd to the next Thicket side Mask 185
Spir. O my lov'd masters heir, and his next joy, Mask 501
Next this marble venom'd seat Mask 916
Till next Sun-shine holiday, Mask 959
Next *Camus*, reverend Sire, went footing slow, Lycidas 103
next adde Narcissus that still weeps in vaine Lycidas Tr. ms 28.19
And mistie Regions of wide air next under, Vacation 41
That to the next I may resign my Roome. Vacation 58
Next her much like to thee in story, Winchester 62
And at her next birth much like thee, Winchester 67

Nibbling
Where the nibling flocks do stray, Allegro 72

Nice
Flours worthy of Paradise which not nice Art Par Lost 4.241
Think not I shall be nice. So down they sat, Par Lost 5.433
A nice and suttle happiness I see Par Lost 8.399
Nothing will please the difficult and nice, Par Reg 4.157
And Advice with scrupulous head, Mask 108
Trinity ms 'Advice' ←'nice tom', ms defective
The nice Morn on th' *Indian* steep Mask 139

Nicely
Nicely or cautiously my offer'd aid, Par Reg 4.377

Nicest
With nicest touch. Immediate in a flame, Par Lost 6.584

Nieces
Of *Hesperus*, and his daughters three Mask 982
Trinity ms 'daughters' ←'neeces' ←'daughters'

Niger
Or thence from *Niger* Flood to *Atlas* Mount Par Lost 11.402

Niggard
As a penurious niggard of his wealth, Mask 726

Nigh
Nigh on the Plain in many cells prepar'd, Par Lost 1.700
Nor good dry Land: nigh founderd on he fares, Par Lost 2.940
Stars distant, but nigh hand seemd other Worlds, Par Lost 3.566
He drew not nigh unheard, the Angel bright, Par Lost 3.645
Ere he drew nigh, his radiant visage turnd, Par Lost 3.646
Begins his dire attempt, which nigh the birth Par Lost 4.15
Ah gentle pair, yee little think how nigh Par Lost 4.366
Th' unarmed Youth of Heav'n, but nigh at hand Par Lost 4.552
His heart, not else dismai'd. Now drew they nigh Par Lost 4.861
So saying, he drew nigh, and to me held, Par Lost 5.82
I flie not, but have sought thee farr and nigh. Par Lost 6.295
Under spred Ensignes moving nigh, in slow Par Lost 6.533
Dismiss not her, when most thou needst her nigh, Par Lost 8.564
From servitude inglorious welnigh half Par Lost 9.141
By sly assault; and somwhere nigh at hand Par Lost 9.256
From her best prop so farr, and storm so nigh. Par Lost 9.433
Her Husband, for I view far round, not nigh, Par Lost 9.482
Nigh Rivers mouth or Foreland, where the Wind Par Lost 9.514
Tempting so nigh, to pluck and eat my fill Par Lost 9.595
To whom sad *Eve* with shame nigh overwhelm'd, Par Lost 10.159
On what was pure, till cramm'd and gorg'd, nigh burst Par Lost 10.632
Desolate where she sate, approaching nigh, Par Lost 10.864
After short blush of Morn; nigh in her sight Par Lost 11.184
O *Eve*, some furder change awaits us nigh, Par Lost 11.193
He ended; and th' Arch-Angel soon drew nigh, Par Lost 11.238
Well pleas'd, but answer'd not; for now too nigh Par Lost 12.625
Repentance, and Heavens Kingdom nigh at hand Par Reg 1.20
Nigh Thunder-struck, th' exalted man, to whom Par Reg 1.36
To Town or Village nigh (nighest is far) Par Reg 1.332
Nigh to *Bethabara;* in *Jerico* Par Reg 2.20
Under the hospitable covert nigh Par Reg 2.262
From Nations far and nigh; what honour that, Par Reg 4.122

Nigh(*cont*)
And threatning nigh; what they can do as signs Par Reg 4.489
Of Angels on full sail of wing flew nigh, Par Reg 4.582
Chor. Hee speaks, let us draw nigh. Matchless in might, Samson 178
But yield to double darkness nigh at hand: Samson 593
The sorrow, and converts it nigh to joy. Samson 1564
Foretell my hopeles doom in som Grove ny: Sonnet 1, 10
Tearing and no rescue nigh. Psalm 7, 6
Unto the grave draws nigh. Psalm 88, 12
Nighest
To Town or Village nigh (nighest is far) Par Reg 1.332
Night
Nine times the Space that measures Day and Night Par Lost 1.50
ms 'night'
Moors by his side under the Lee, while Night Par Lost 1.207
ms 'night'
Like Night, and darken'd all the Land of *Nile:* Par Lost 1.343
ms 'night'
Jehovah, who in one Night when he pass'd Par Lost 1.487
ms 'night'
And injury and outrage: And when Night Par Lost 1.500
ms 'night'
Witness the Streets of *Sodom*, and that night Par Lost 1.503
Frighted the Reign of *Chaos* and old Night. Par Lost 1.543
Scout farr and wide into the Realm of night, Par Lost 2.133
In the wide womb of uncreated night, Par Lost 2.150
The sound of blustring winds, which all night long Par Lost 2.286
Drew audience and attention still as Night Par Lost 2.308
Of unessential Night receives him next Par Lost 2.439
That day and night for his destruction waite. Par Lost 2.505
For each seem'd either; black it stood as Night, Par Lost 2.670
And time and place are lost; where eldest Night Par Lost 2.894
Sat Sable-vested *Night*, eldest of things, Par Lost 2.962
1667 'Night'
Chaos and *ancient Night*, I come no Spy, Par Lost 2.970
Erect the Standard there of *ancient Night;* Par Lost 2.986
Weakning the Scepter of old *Night:* first Hell Par Lost 2.1002
1667 'Night'
Shoots farr into the bosom of dim Night Par Lost 2.1036
I sung of *Chaos* and *Eternal Night*, Par Lost 3.18
Coasting the wall of Heav'n on this side Night Par Lost 3.71
Dark, waste, and wild, under the frown of Night Par Lost 3.424
Dreaming by night under the open Skie, Par Lost 3.514
All night; at last by break of chearful dawne Par Lost 3.545
Of Nights extended shade; from Eastern Point Par Lost 3.557
Night would invade, but there the neighbouring Moon Par Lost 3.726
And in her pale dominion checks the night. Par Lost 3.732
Chief of th' Angelic Guards, awaiting night; Par Lost 4.550
In *Autumn* thwarts the night, when vapors fir'd Par Lost 4.557
She all night long her amorous descant sung; Par Lost 4.603
Of night, and all things now retir'd to rest Par Lost 4.611
Labour and rest, as day and night to men Par Lost 4.613
Mean while, as Nature wills, Night bids us rest. Par Lost 4.633
Of grateful Eevning milde, then silent Night Par Lost 4.647
Nor grateful Eevning mild, nor silent Night Par Lost 4.654
But wherfore all night long shine these, for whom Par Lost 4.657
Least total darkness should by Night regaine Par Lost 4.665
These then, though unbeheld in deep of night, Par Lost 4.674
Both day and night: how often from the steep Par Lost 4.680
Divide the night, and lift our thoughts to Heaven. Par Lost 4.688
And starrie Pole: Thou also mad'st the Night, Par Lost 4.724
Now had night measur'd with her shaddowie Cone Par Lost 4.776
To thir night watches in warlike Parade, Par Lost 4.780
Murmuring, and with him fled the shades of night. Par Lost 4.1015
Thy face, and Morn return'd, for I this Night, Par Lost 5.30
Such night till this I never pass'd, have dream'd, Par Lost 5.31
Knew never till this irksom night; methought Par Lost 5.35
To find this but a dream! Thus *Eve* her Night Par Lost 5.93
The trouble of thy thoughts this night in sleep Par Lost 5.96
Reservd from night, and kept for thee in store. Par Lost 5.128
And choral symphonies, Day without Night, Par Lost 5.162
Fairest of Starrs, last in the train of Night, Par Lost 5.166
To give us onely good; and if the night Par Lost 5.206
This night the human pair, how he designes Par Lost 5.227
Above all Hills. As when by night the Glass Par Lost 5.261
Cherubic Songs by night from neighbouring Hills Par Lost 5.547
Now when ambrosial Night with Clouds exhal'd Par Lost 5.642
To grateful Twilight (for Night comes not there Par Lost 5.645
Alternate all night long: but not so wak'd Par Lost 5.657
Tell them that by command, ere yet dim Night Par Lost 5.685
That the most High commanding, now ere Night, Par Lost 5.699
Now ere dim Night had disincumberd Heav'n, Par Lost 5.700
Innumerable as the Starrs of Night, Par Lost 5.745
All night the dreadless Angel unpursu'd Par Lost 6.1
Grateful vicissitude, like Day and Night; Par Lost 6.8
Empyreal, from before her vanisht Night, Par Lost 6.14
Now Night her course began, and over Heav'n Par Lost 6.406
His Potentates to Councel call'd by night; Par Lost 6.416
So all ere day-spring, under conscious Night Par Lost 6.521
Gloomie as Night; under his burning Wheeles Par Lost 6.832
Haste to thy audience, Night with her will bring Par Lost 7.105
Onely Omniscient, hath suppress in Night, Par Lost 7.123
Divided: Light the Day, and Darkness Night Par Lost 7.251
The Day from Night; and let them be for Signes, Par Lost 7.341
The less by Night alterne: and made the Starrs, Par Lost 7.348
In thir vicissitude, and rule the Night, Par Lost 7.351
Till night, then in the East her turn she shines, Par Lost 7.380
Ceas'd warbling, but all night tun'd her soft layes: Par Lost 7.436

Night(*cont*)
Forerunning Night; when at the holy mount Par Lost 7.584
One day and night; in all thir vast survey Par Lost 8.24
Of Day and Night; which needs not thy beleefe, Par Lost 8.136
From the Suns beam meet Night, her other part Par Lost 8.139
Enlightning her by Day, as she by Night Par Lost 8.143
Disporting, till the amorous Bird of Night Par Lost 8.518
Twixt Day and Night, and now from end to end Par Lost 9.51
Nights Hemisphere had veild the Horizon round: Par Lost 9.52
By Night he fled, and at Midnight return'd Par Lost 9.58
He circl'd, four times cross'd the Carr of Night Par Lost 9.65
Not longer then since I in one Night freed Par Lost 9.140
One night or two with wanton growth derides Par Lost 9.211
Compact of unctuous vapor, which the Night Par Lost 9.635
By Night, and listening where the hapless Paire Par Lost 10.342
Of unoriginal *Night* and *Chaos* wilde, Par Lost 10.477
Through the still Night, not now, as ere man fell, Par Lost 10.846
Leave cold the Night, how we his gather'd beams Par Lost 10.1070
Though after sleepless Night; for see the Morn, Par Lost 11.173
Raine day and night, all fountains of the Deep Par Lost 11.826
And call to mind his Cov'nant: Day and Night, Par Lost 11.898
By day a Cloud, by night a Pillar of Fire, Par Lost 12.203
All night he will pursue, but his approach Par Lost 12.206
Shall rest by Day, a fiery gleame by Night, Par Lost 12.257
A day entire, and Nights due course adjourne, Par Lost 12.264
To simple Shepherds, keeping watch by night; Par Lost 12.365
To Shepherds watching at their folds by night, Par Reg 1.244
Sometimes, anon in shady vale, each night Par Reg 1.304
Night with her sullen wing to double-shade Par Reg 1.500
It was the hour of night, when thus the Son Par Reg 2.260
Thus wore out night, and now the Herald Lark Par Reg 2.279
As day-light sunk, and brought in lowring night Par Reg 4.398
From dews and damps of night his shelter'd head, Par Reg 4.406
Thus pass'd the night so foul till morning fair Par Reg 4.426
After a night of storm so ruinous, Par Reg 4.436
After a dismal night; I heard the rack Par Reg 4.452
Whereof this ominous night that clos'd thee round, Par Reg 4.481
On thy birth-night, that sung thee Saviour born. Par Reg 4.506
When she deserts the night Samson 88
To incorporate with gloomy night; Samson 161
Tongue-batteries, she surceas'd not day nor night Samson 404
Here I should still enjoy thee day and night Samson 807
What hath night to do with sleep? Mask 122
Night hath better sweets to prove, Mask 123
Of mid-night Torches burns; mysterious Dame Mask 130
Trinity ms 'midnight'
Bridgewater ms 'mid night'
Had stole them from me, els O theevish Night Mask 195
word not in Bridgewater ms
Trinity ms 'night'
And airy tongues, that syllable mens names Mask 208
Trinity ms 'syllable mens nams' ←'lure night wanderers'
Turn forth her silver lining on the night? Mask 222
line not in Bridgewater ms
Turn forth her silver lining on the night, Mask 224
line not in Bridgewater ms
Of silence, through the empty-vaulted night Mask 250
Co. Perhaps fore-stalling night prevented them. Mask 285
In double night of darknes, and of shades; Mask 335
Count the night watches to his feathery Dames, Mask 347
Of night, or lonelines it recks me not, Mask 404
Som say no evil thing that walks by night Mask 432
That brow this bottom glade, whence night by night Mask 532
But furder know I not. 2. *Bro*. O night and shades, Mask 580
Where this night are met in state Mask 948
But night sits monarch yet in the mid sky. Mask 957
And singing startle the dull night, Allegro 42
When in one night, ere glimps of morn, Allegro 107
Smoothing the rugged brow of night, Penseroso 58
Thus night oft see me in thy pale career, Penseroso 121
To further this nights glad solemnity; Arcades 39
But els in deep of night when drowsines Arcades 61
Batt'ning our flocks with the fresh dews of night, Lycidas 29
But peacefull was the night Nativity 61
That with long beams the shame-fac't night array'd, Nativity 111
The horned Moon to shine by night, Psalm 136, 33
Soon swallow'd up in dark and long out-living night. Passion 7
Befriend me night best Patroness of grief, Passion 29
Through the soft silence of the list'ning night; Circum 5
where day dwells without night Musick Tr. ms 4.29
Shew'd him his room where he must lodge that night, Carrier 15
Passes to bliss at the mid hour of night, Sonnet 9, 13
Trinity ms 'the midd night howr' ←'the midd watch' ←'that hovre of night'
I wak'd, she fled, and day brought back my night. Sonnet 23, 14
And in his Law he studies day and night. Psalm 1, 6
And all night long, before thee *weep* Psalm 88, 3
Night-foundered
The Pilot of some small night-founder'd Skiff, Par Lost 1.204
ms 'night-founderd'
Either som one like us night-founder'd here, Mask 483
1637 'night founder'd'
Trinity ms 'night founder'd'
Bridgewater ms 'night founderd'
Night-hag
Nor uglier follow the Night-Hag, when call'd Par Lost 2.662
Nightingale
Were slunk, all but the wakeful Nightingale; Par Lost 4.602

Nightingale(*cont*)
Till Ev'n, nor then the solemn Nightingal — Par Lost 7.435
Where the love-lorn Nightingale — Mask 234
Trinity ms 'nightingale'
Bridgewater ms 'nightingale'
And O poor hapless Nightingale thought I, — Mask 566
Bridgewater ms 'nightingale'
1637 'nightingale'
Trinity ms 'nightingale'
O Nightingale, that on yon bloomy Spray — Sonnet 1, 1

Nightingales
These lulld by Nightingales imbraceing slept, — Par Lost 4.771

Nightly
To whose bright Image nightly by the Moon — Par Lost 1.440
Ply stemming nightly toward the Pole. So seem'd — Par Lost 2.642
Nightly I visit: nor somtimes forget — Par Lost 3.32
While they keep watch, or nightly rounding walk — Par Lost 4.685
Nightly before him, saw without thir light — Par Lost 5.714
Visit'st my slumbers Nightly, or when Morn — Par Lost 7.29
Which nightly as a circling Zone thou seest — Par Lost 7.580
Her nightly visitation unimplor'd, — Par Lost 9.22
Not Hers who brings it nightly to my Ear. — Par Lost 9.47
Who in their nightly watchfull Sphears, — Mask 113
Nightly to thee her sad Song mourneth well. — Mask 235
By all the *Nymphs* that nightly dance — Mask 883
To bless the dores from nightly harm: — Penseroso 84
And all my Plants I save from nightly ill, — Arcades 48
Trinity ms 'nightlie'
No nightly trance, or breathed spell, — Nativity 179
Nightly my Couch I make a kind of Sea; — Psalm 6, 12

Night-raven
And the night-Raven sings; — Allegro 7

Nights
The space of seven continu'd Nights he rode — Par Lost 9.63
What he *Almightie* styl'd, six Nights and Days — Par Lost 9.137
Equal in Days and Nights, except to those — Par Lost 10.680
Brings dangers, troubles, cares, and sleepless nights — Par Reg 2.460

Night-steeds
Fly after the Night-steeds, leaving their Moon-lov'd maze. — Nativity 236

Night-wanderer
Misleads th' amaz'd Night-wanderer from his way — Par Lost 9.640

Night-warbling
To the night-warbling Bird, that now awake — Par Lost 5.40

Nile
Like Night, and darken'd all the Land of *Nile:* — Par Lost 1.343
ms 'Nile'
Israel in *Sittim* on thir march from *Nile* — Par Lost 1.413
ms 'Nile'
By *Nilus* head, enclosd with shining Rock, — Par Lost 4.283
Egypt, divided by the River *Nile;* — Par Lost 12.157
The brutish gods of *Nile* as fast, — Nativity 211

Nilotic
Meroe Nilotic Isle, and more to West, — Par Reg 4.71

Nilus
By *Nilus* head, enclosd with shining Rock, — Par Lost 4.283

Nimble
O friends, I hear the tread of nimble feet — Par Lost 4.866
Thir nimble tread, as when the total kind — Par Lost 6.73
Consum'd with nimble glance, and grateful steame; — Par Lost 11.442

Nimbler
Of lighter toes, and such Court guise — Mask 962
Trinity ms 'lighter' ←'nimbler' ←'speedier'

Nine
Nine times the Space that measures Day and Night — Par Lost 1.50
Nine dayes they fell; confounded *Chaos* roard, — Par Lost 6.871
Nor of the Muses nine, nor on the top — Par Lost 7.6
That sit upon the nine enfolded Sphears, — Arcades 64

Ninefold
Ninefold, and gates of burning Adamant — Par Lost 2.436
And with your ninefold harmony — Nativity 131

Nineveh
Here *Ninevee*, of length within her wall — Par Reg 3.275

Ninus
Several days journey, built by *Ninus* old, — Par Reg 3.276

Nip
Sav'd with care from Winters nip, — Winchester 36

Niphates
Nor staid, till on *Niphates* top he lights. — Par Lost 3.742

Nipped
Nipt with the lagging rear of winters frost. — Samson 1577

Nisibis
The great *Seleucia*, *Nisibis*, and there — Par Reg 3.291

Nisroch
Nisroc, of Principalities the prime; — Par Lost 6.447

Nitre
Instinct with Fire and Nitre hurried him — Par Lost 2.937

Nitrous
Lights on a heap of nitrous Powder, laid — Par Lost 4.815
Conception; Sulphurous and Nitrous Foame — Par Lost 6.512

No
That with no middle flight intends to soar — Par Lost 1.14
No light, but rather darkness visible — Par Lost 1.63
Of force believe Almighty, since no less — Par Lost 1.144
No wonder, fall'n such a pernicious highth. — Par Lost 1.282
Be no memorial blotted out and ras'd — Par Lost 1.362
Vice for it self: To him no Temple stood — Par Lost 1.492
What force effected not: that he no less — Par Lost 1.647
For since no deep within her gulf can hold — Par Lost 2.12

No(*cont*)
More glorious and more dread then from no fall, — Par Lost 2.16
And trust themselves to fear no second fate: — Par Lost 2.17
Of endless pain? where there is then no good — Par Lost 2.30
For which to strive, no strife can grow up there — Par Lost 2.31
By our delay? no, let us rather choose — Par Lost 2.60
To be no more; sad cure; for who would loose, — Par Lost 2.146
Wrought still within them; and no less desire — Par Lost 2.295
Sole King, and of his Kingdom loose no part — Par Lost 2.325
Heav'n, whose high walls fear no assault or Siege, — Par Lost 2.343
All circumspection, and we now no less — Par Lost 2.414
Of this ill Mansion: intermit no watch — Par Lost 2.462
And found no end, in wandring mazes lost. — Par Lost 2.561
No rest: through many a dark and drearie Vaile — Par Lost 2.618
No second stroke intend, and such a frown — Par Lost 2.713
I come no enemie, but to set free — Par Lost 2.822
Destin'd to that good hour: no less rejoyc'd — Par Lost 2.848
Pondering his Voyage; for no narrow frith — Par Lost 2.919
Chaos and *ancient Night*, I come no Spy, — Par Lost 2.970
Directed, no mean recompence it brings — Par Lost 2.981
To find thy piercing ray, and find no dawn; — Par Lost 3.24
Transports our adversarie, whom no bounds — Par Lost 3.81
Prescrib'd, no barrs of Hell, nor all the chains — Par Lost 3.82
Foreknowledge had no influence on their fault, — Par Lost 3.118
Which had no less prov'd certain unforeknown. — Par Lost 3.119
Father, to see thy face, wherein no cloud — Par Lost 3.262
And reconcilement; wrauth shall be no more — Par Lost 3.264
For regal Scepter then no more shall need, — Par Lost 3.340
No sooner had th' Almighty ceas't, but all — Par Lost 3.344
No voice exempt, no voice but well could joine — Par Lost 3.370
Whom else no Creature can behold; on thee — Par Lost 3.387
No sooner did thy dear and onely Son — Par Lost 3.403
For sight no obstacle found here, nor shade, — Par Lost 3.615
Shot upward still direct, whence no way round — Par Lost 3.618
Resigns her charge, while goodness thinks no ill — Par Lost 3.688
Where no ill seems: Which now for once beguil'd — Par Lost 3.689
The great Work-Maister, leads to no excess — Par Lost 3.696
One step no more then from himself can fly — Par Lost 4.22
But with no friendly voice, and add thy name — Par Lost 4.36
Ah wherefore! he deservd no such return — Par Lost 4.42
Then happie; no unbounded hope had rais'd — Par Lost 4.60
O then at last relent: is there no place — Par Lost 4.79
Cross-barrd and bolted fast, fear no assault, — Par Lost 4.190
And Country whereof here needs no account, — Par Lost 4.235
Of God or Angel, for they thought no ill: — Par Lost 4.320
They sat them down, and after no more toil — Par Lost 4.327
As now is enterd; yet no purpos'd foe — Par Lost 4.373
Your numerous ofspring; if no better place, — Par Lost 4.385
From us no other service then to keep — Par Lost 4.420
Som dreadful thing no doubt; for well thou knowst — Par Lost 4.426
And without whom am to no end, my Guide — Par Lost 4.442
And I will bring thee where no shadow staies — Par Lost 4.470
This Garden, and no corner leave unspi'd; — Par Lost 4.529
No evil thing approach or enter in; — Par Lost 4.563
Uriel, no wonder if thy perfet sight, — Par Lost 4.577
No Creature thence: if Spirit of other sort, — Par Lost 4.582
And of thir doings God takes no account. — Par Lost 4.622
God is thy Law, thou mine: to know no more — Par Lost 4.637
No happier state, and know to know no more. — Par Lost 4.775
Search through this Garden, leave unsearcht no nook, — Par Lost 4.789
The barrs of Hell, on errand bad no doubt: — Par Lost 4.795
Touch'd lightly; for no falshood can endure — Par Lost 4.811
Know ye not mee? ye knew me once no mate — Par Lost 4.828
That Glorie then, when thou no more wast good, — Par Lost 4.838
Though thither doom'd? Thou wouldst thy self, no doubt, — Par Lost 4.890
To thee no reason; who knowst only good, — Par Lost 4.895
Which taught thee yet no better, that no pain — Par Lost 4.915
Argues no Leader but a lyar trac't, — Par Lost 4.949
So threatn'd hee, but *Satan* to no threats — Par Lost 4.968
To boast what Arms can doe, since thine no more — Par Lost 4.1008
No spot or blame behind: Which gives me hope — Par Lost 5.119
By violence, no, for that shall be withstood, — Par Lost 5.242
From hence, no cloud, or, to obstruct his sight, — Par Lost 5.257
Stood to entertain her guest from Heav'n; no vaile — Par Lost 5.383
Shee needed, Vertue-proof, no thought infirme — Par Lost 5.384
No fear lest Dinner coole; when thus began — Par Lost 5.396
No ingrateful food: and food alike those pure — Par Lost 5.407
Nor doth the Moon no nourishment exhale — Par Lost 5.421
No inconvenient Diet, nor too light Fare: — Par Lost 5.495
Findes no acceptance, nor can find, for how — Par Lost 5.531
Willing or no, who will but what they must — Par Lost 5.533
By Destinie, and can no other choose? — Par Lost 5.534
Is heard no more in Heav'n; he of the first, — Par Lost 5.659
All thy Dominion, *Adam*, is no more — Par Lost 5.751
Words which no eare ever to hear in Heav'n — Par Lost 5.810
We know no time when we were not as now; — Par Lost 5.859
No more be troubl'd how to quit the yoke — Par Lost 5.882
On the proud Crest of *Satan*, that no sight, — Par Lost 6.191
The ridges of grim Warr; no thought of flight, — Par Lost 6.236
None of retreat, no unbecoming deed — Par Lost 6.237
No equal, raunging through the dire attack — Par Lost 6.248
Receive, no more then can the fluid Aire: — Par Lost 6.349
No less then for deliverance what we owe. — Par Lost 6.468
If I conjecture aught, no drizling showr, — Par Lost 6.545
Endless, and no solution will be found: — Par Lost 6.694
What may no less perhaps availe us known, — Par Lost 7.85
But Knowledge is as food, and needs no less — Par Lost 7.126
Drew many, whom thir place knows here no more; — Par Lost 7.144

No(*cont*)

Wherever thus created, for no place	Par Lost 7.535
Whose vertue on it self workes no effect,	Par Lost 8.95
And no advantage gaine. What if the Sun	Par Lost 8.122
Uncheckt, and of her roaving is no end;	Par Lost 8.189
Imbu'd, bring to thir sweetness no satietie.	Par Lost 8.216
Pleas'd with thy words no less then thou with mine.	Par Lost 8.248
Eate freely with glad heart; fear here no dearth:	Par Lost 8.322
No pleasure, though in pleasure, solitarie.	Par Lost 8.402
Is no deficience found; not so is Man,	Par Lost 8.416
Or solace his defects. No need that thou	Par Lost 8.419
And no such companie as then thou saw'st	Par Lost 8.446
Hee ended, or I heard no more, for now	Par Lost 8.452
As us'd or not, works in the mind no change,	Par Lost 8.525
An outside? fair no doubt, and worthy well	Par Lost 8.568
Among the Beasts no Mate for thee was found.	Par Lost 8.594
Us happie, and without Love no happiness.	Par Lost 8.621
But I can now no more; the parting Sun	Par Lost 8.630
Perfet within, no outward aid require;	Par Lost 8.642
No more of talk where God or Angel Guest	Par Lost 9.1
But neither here seek I, no nor in Heav'n	Par Lost 9.124
Watches, no doubt, with greedy hope to find	Par Lost 9.257
Conjugal Love, then which perhaps no bliss	Par Lost 9.263
Sticks no dishonor on our Front, but turns	Par Lost 9.330
And *Eden* were no *Eden* thus expos'd.	Par Lost 9.341
Against his will he can receave no harme.	Par Lost 9.350
United I beheld; no Fair to thine	Par Lost 9.608
Somtimes in highth began, as no delay	Par Lost 9.675
Though threat'nd, which no worse then this can bring.	Par Lost 9.715
And thy fair Fruit let hang, as to no end	Par Lost 9.798
And Death ensue? then I shall be no more,	Par Lost 9.827
I could endure, without him live no life.	Par Lost 9.833
Would never from my heart; no no, I feel	Par Lost 9.913
Original; while *Adam* took no thought,	Par Lost 9.1004
And elegant, of Sapience no small part,	Par Lost 9.1018
No ground of enmitie between us known,	Par Lost 9.1151
And force upon free will hath here no place.	Par Lost 9.1174
Either to meet no danger, or to finde	Par Lost 9.1176
No evil durst attempt thee, but I rue	Par Lost 9.1180
And of thir vain contest appeer'd no end.	Par Lost 9.1189
Against his Maker; no Decree of mine	Par Lost 10.43
Forbearance no acquittance ere day end.	Par Lost 10.53
That from her hand I could suspect no ill,	Par Lost 10.140
Concern'd not Man (since he no further knew)	Par Lost 10.170
By his Avengers, since no place like this	Par Lost 10.241
For Death from Sin no power can separate.	Par Lost 10.251
For I no sooner in my Heart divin'd,	Par Lost 10.357
Hell could no longer hold us in her bounds,	Par Lost 10.365
No detriment need feare, goe and be strong.	Par Lost 10.409
Huge *Python*, and his Power no less he seem'd	Par Lost 10.531
No homely morsels, and whatever thing	Par Lost 10.605
To sanctitie that shall receive no staine:	Par Lost 10.639
And sleep secure; his dreadful voice no more	Par Lost 10.779
Would Thunder in my ears, no fear of worse	Par Lost 10.780
The doubt, since humane reach no further knows.	Par Lost 10.793
I find no way, from deep to deeper plung'd!	Par Lost 10.844
But rise, let us no more contend, nor blame	Par Lost 10.958
Will prove no sudden, but a slow-pac't evill,	Par Lost 10.963
That shew no end but Death, and have the power,	Par Lost 10.1004
No more be mention'd then of violence	Par Lost 10.1041
No gross, no unharmoneous mixture foule,	Par Lost 11.51
And thither must return and be no more.	Par Lost 11.200
Adam, Heav'ns high behest no Preface needs:	Par Lost 11.251
No more availes then breath against the winde,	Par Lost 11.312
No despicable gift; surmise not then	Par Lost 11.340
Loose no reward, though here thou see him die,	Par Lost 11.459
But is there yet no other way, besides	Par Lost 11.527
No more was seen; the floating Vessel swum	Par Lost 11.745
With thought that they must be. Let no man seek	Par Lost 11.770
And hee the future evil shall no less	Par Lost 11.774
Peace to corrupt no less then Warr to waste.	Par Lost 11.784
In sharp contest of Battel found no aide	Par Lost 11.800
No sooner hee with them of Man and Beast	Par Lost 11.822
No sanctitie, if none be thither brought	Par Lost 11.837
The Ark no more now flotes, but seems on ground	Par Lost 11.850
Twinn'd, and from her hath no dividual being:	Par Lost 12.85
Though to the Tyrant thereby no excuse.	Par Lost 12.96
From vertue, which is reason, that no wrong,	Par Lost 12.98
Instructed that to God is no access	Par Lost 12.239
The last, for of his Reign shall be no end.	Par Lost 12.330
But soon revives, Death over him no power	Par Lost 12.420
Eternitie, whose end no eye can reach.	Par Lost 12.556
Of wisdome; hope no higher, though all the Starrs	Par Lost 12.576
We may no longer stay: go, waken *Eve;*	Par Lost 12.594
In mee is no delay; with thee to goe,	Par Lost 12.615
His birth to our just fear gave no small cause,	Par Reg 1.66
Of hazard, which admits no long debate,	Par Reg 1.95
I, when no other durst, sole undertook	Par Reg 1.100
At these sad tidings; but no time was then	Par Reg 1.109
When I was yet a child, no childish play	Par Reg 1.201
For know, thou art no Son of mortal man,	Par Reg 1.234
And of thy Kingdom there should be no end.	Par Reg 1.241
For in the Inn was left no better room:	Par Reg 1.248
Now full, that I no more should live obscure,	Par Reg 1.287
Will bring me hence, no other Guide I seek.	Par Reg 1.336
Imparts to thee no happiness, no joy,	Par Reg 1.417
Lost bliss, to thee no more communicable,	Par Reg 1.419
No more shalt thou by oracling abuse	Par Reg 1.455

No(*cont*)

And thou no more with Pomp and Sacrifice	Par Reg 1.457
To hear thee when I come (since no man comes)	Par Reg 1.484
Plain Fishermen, no greater men them call,	Par Reg 2.27
While I to sorrows am no less advanc't,	Par Reg 2.69
I look't for some great change; to Honour? no,	Par Reg 2.86
Is ris'n to invade us, who no less	Par Reg 2.127
And now I know he hungers where no food	Par Reg 2.231
No advantage, and his strength as oft assay.	Par Reg 2.234
And from the sting of Famine fear no harm,	Par Reg 2.257
He spake no dream, for as his words had end,	Par Reg 2.337
These are not Fruits forbidden, no interdict	Par Reg 2.369
Thir taste no knowledge works, at least of evil,	Par Reg 2.371
In vain, where no acceptance it can find,	Par Reg 2.388
And count thy specious gifts no gifts but guiles.	Par Reg 2.391
For no allurement yields to appetite,	Par Reg 2.409
So reigning can be no sincere delight.	Par Reg 2.480
Of whom to be disprais'd were no small praise?	Par Reg 3.56
Wise or unwise, no difference, no exemption;	Par Reg 3.115
For where no hope is left, is left no fear;	Par Reg 3.206
No wonder, for though in thee be united	Par Reg 3.229
On no slight grounds thy safety; hear, and mark	Par Reg 3.349
Of *Bethel* and of *Dan?* no, let them serve	Par Reg 3.431
And rash, before-hand had no better weigh'd	Par Reg 4.8
The City which thou seest no other deem	Par Reg 4.44
This Emperour hath no Son, and now is old,	Par Reg 4.90
Aim therefore at no less then all the world,	Par Reg 4.105
Will be for thee no sitting, or not long	Par Reg 4.107
And of my Kingdom there shall be no end:	Par Reg 4.151
No trifle; yet with this reserve, not else,	Par Reg 4.165
The tryal hath indamag'd thee no way,	Par Reg 4.206
The Kingdoms of this world; I shall no more	Par Reg 4.210
No other doctrine needs, though granted true;	Par Reg 4.290
Without beginning; for no date prefixt	Par Reg 4.392
Yet with no new device, they all were spent,	Par Reg 4.443
Of gaining *David*'s Throne no man knows when,	Par Reg 4.471
Thou shalt be what thou art ordain'd, no doubt;	Par Reg 4.473
The Son of God, which bears no single sence;	Par Reg 4.517
No triumph; in all her gates *Abaddon* rues	Par Reg 4.624
Of Hornets arm'd, no sooner found alone,	Samson 20
No strength of man, or fiercest wild beast could withstand;	Samson 127
No journey of a Sabbath day, and loaded so;	Samson 149
Puts forth no visual beam.	Samson 163
Us'd no ambition to commend my deeds,	Samson 247
And no man therein Doctor but himself.	Samson 299
Besides whom is no God, compar'd with Idols,	Samson 441
On thee, who now no more canst do them harm.	Samson 486
Robustious to no purpose clustring down,	Samson 569
That these dark orbs no more shall treat with light,	Samson 591
But finding no redress, ferment and rage,	Samson 619
Dire inflammation which no cooling herb	Samson 626
No long petition, speedy death,	Samson 650
Heads without name no more rememberd,	Samson 677
Changest thy countenance, and thy hand with no regard	Samson 684
And now at nearer view, no other certain	Samson 723
No way assur'd. But conjugal affection	Samson 739
No better way I saw then by importuning	Samson 797
With God or Man will gain thee no remission.	Samson 835
Dal. Since thou determinst weakness for no plea	Samson 843
No more thy countrey, but an impious crew	Samson 891
Sam. For want of words no doubt, or lack of breath,	Samson 905
Sams. No, no, of my condition take no care;	Samson 928
No more on me have power, their force is null'd,	Samson 935
Of constancy no root infixt,	Samson 1032
Chor. Look now for no inchanting voice, nor fear	Samson 1065
Though for no friendly intent. I am of *Gath*,	Samson 1078
Close-banded durst attaque me, no not sleeping,	Samson 1113
Or rather flight, no great advantage on me;	Samson 1118
Sam. I know no Spells, use no forbidden Arts;	Samson 1139
No less through all my sinews, joints and bones,	Samson 1142
As good for nothing else, no better service	Samson 1163
With those thy boyst'rous locks, no worthy match	Samson 1164
To others did no violence nor spoil.	Samson 1191
I chose a Wife, which argu'd me no foe;	Samson 1193
I was no private but a person rais'd	Samson 1211
To fight with thee no man of arms will deign.	Samson 1226
Sam. No man with-holds thee, nothing from thy hand	Samson 1233
With no small profit daily to my owners.	Samson 1261
This Idols day hath bin to thee no day of rest,	Samson 1297
Brooks no delay: is this thy resolution?	Samson 1344
Commands are no constraints. If I obey them,	Samson 1372
Which to no few of them would prove pernicious.	Samson 1400
No less the people on thir Holy-days	Samson 1421
The last of me or no I cannot warrant.	Samson 1426
And numbers thither flock, I had no will,	Samson 1450
No, I am fixt not to part hence without him.	Samson 1481
No Preface needs, thou seest we long to know.	Samson 1554
That no second knows nor third,	Samson 1701
Man. Come, come, no time for lamentation now,	Samson 1708
Or knock the breast, no weakness, no contempt,	Samson 1722
La. No less then if I should my brothers loose.	Mask 288
Bridgewater ms 'noe'	
Secure without all doubt, or controversie:	Mask 409
Bridgewater ms 'doubt or question, no'	
Trinity ms 'doubt or question, no'	
No savage fierce, Bandite, or mountaneer	Mask 426
Bridgewater ms 'noe'	
Som say no evil thing that walks by night	Mask 432

No(*cont*)
Bridgewater ms 'noe'
No goblin, or swart Faery of the mine, Mask 436
Bridgewater ms 'noe'
Tell her of things that no gross ear can hear, Mask 458
Bridgewater ms 'noe'
Where no crude surfet raigns. *Eld. Bro.* List, list, I hear Mask 480
Bridgewater ms 'noe'
And mix no more with goodness, when at last Mask 594
Trinity ms '& mixe no more' ←'till all to place'
Bridgewater ms 'noe'
Here dwel no frowns, nor anger, from these gates Mask 667
Bridgewater ms 'noe'
To deck her Sons, and that no corner might Mask 717
Bridgewater ms 'noe'
And vertue has no tongue to check her pride: Mask 761
Bridgewater ms 'noe'
And she no whit encomber'd with her store, Mask 774
Bridgewater ms 'noe'
And try her yet more strongly. Com, no more, Mask 806
Trinity ms 'no more' ←'y'are too morall'
Bridgewater ms 'noe'
While yet there was no fear of *Jove*. Penseroso 30
Where no profaner eye may look, Penseroso 140
Where no print of step hath been, Arcades 85
Nymphs and Shepherds dance no more Arcades 96
Trip no more in twilight ranks, Arcades 99
Shall now no more be seen, Lycidas 43
Fame is no plant that grows on mortal soil, Lycidas 78
Stands ready to smite once, and smite no more. Lycidas 131
Weep no more, woful Shepherds weep no more, Lycidas 165
Now *Lycidas* the Shepherds weep no more; Lycidas 182
Hast thou no vers, no hymn, or solemn strein, Nativity 17
Hath took no print of the approching light, Nativity 20
It was no season then for her Nativity 35
No War, or Battails sound Nativity 53
The new-enlightn'd world no more should need; Nativity 82
But wisest Fate sayes no, Nativity 149
No voice or hideous humm Nativity 174
Can no more divine, Nativity 177
No nightly trance, or breathed spell, Nativity 179
O Fairest flower no sooner blown but blasted, Fair Inf 1
Alack that so to change thee winter had no power. Fair Inf 28
Oh no? for something in thy face did shine Fair Inf 34
Which is no more then what is false and vain, On Time 5
Your fiery essence can distill no tear, Circum 7
Nature and fate had had no strife Winchester 13
No Marchioness, but now a Queen. Winchester 74
For my relief; yet hadst no reason why, Sonnet 1, 12
But my late spring no bud or blossom shew'th. Sonnet 7, 4
No anger find in thee, but pity and ruth. Sonnet 9, 8
No less renownd then warr, new foes arise Sonnet 16, 11
Of Brittish *Themis*, with no mean applause Sonnet 21, 2
line not in Trinity ms
In mirth, that after no repenting drawes; Sonnet 21, 6
Content though blind, had I no better guide. Sonnet 22, 14
So clear, as in no face with more delight. Sonnet 23, 12
Their bonds, and cast from us, no more to wear, Psalm 2, 7
No help for him in God there lies. Psalm 3, 6
Evil with thee no biding makes Psalm 5, 11
No word is firm or sooth Psalm 5, 26
For in death no remembrance is of thee; Psalm 6, 9
Least as a Lion (and no wonder) Psalm 7, 4
Tearing and no rescue nigh. Psalm 7, 6
Sea-paths in shoals do slide. And know no dearth. Psalm 8, 22
No alien God shall be Psalm 81, 38
Their time should have no end. Psalm 81, 64
Till they no Nation be Psalm 83, 14
No quiet let them find, Psalm 83, 50
No good from them shall be with-held Psalm 84, 43
Toward us, *and chide no more*. Psalm 85, 16
No fear of thee have set. Psalm 86, 52
Whom thou rememberest no more, Psalm 88, 21
Thy wrath *from which no shelter saves* Psalm 88, 29
No sacrifice to God more acceptable Prose 11, 2

Nobility
Thir choice nobility and flower, not only Samson 1654

Noble
So saying, a noble stroke he lifted high, Par Lost 6.189
Serv'd by more noble then her self, attaines Par Lost 8.34
To noble and ignoble is more sweet Par Lost 12.221
Appearing, and beginning noble deeds, Par Reg 4.99
At least of thy own Nation, and as noble. Samson 218
Of noble Warriour, so to stain his honour, Samson 1166
And what may quiet us in a death so noble. Samson 1724
A noble Peer of mickle trust, and power Mask 31
And noble grace that dash't brute violence Mask 451
Noble Lord, and Lady bright, Mask 966
Where ye may all that are of noble stemm Arcades 82
(That last infirmity of Noble mind) Lycidas 71
Trinity ms 'noble'
1638 'noble'
Added to her noble birth, Winchester 5
That thy noble House doth bring, Winchester 54
So well your words his noble vertues praise, Sonnet 10, 12
In libertyes defence, my noble task, Sonnet 22, 11

Nobleness
Greatness of mind and nobleness thir seat Par Lost 8.557

Nobler
To vice industrious, but to Nobler deeds Par Lost 2.116
Two of far nobler shape erect and tall, Par Lost 4.288
So many nobler Bodies to create, Par Lost 8.28
Productive in Herb, Plant, and nobler birth Par Lost 9.111
Call *El Dorado:* but to nobler sights Par Lost 11.411
Created, as thou art, to nobler end Par Lost 11.605
Governs the inner man, the nobler part, Par Reg 2.477
Greater and nobler done, and to lay down Par Reg 2.482
O yet a nobler task awaites thy hand; Sonnet 15, 9
1694 'Nobler'

Noblest
To hight of noblest temper Hero's old Par Lost 1.552
All Trees of noblest kind for sight, smell, taste; Par Lost 4.217
With dishes pil'd, and meats of noblest sort Par Reg 2.341
The Structure, skill of noblest Architects, Par Reg 4.52

Nobly
Built nobly, pure the air, and light the soil, Par Reg 4.239

Nocent
Nor nocent yet, but on the grassie Herbe Par Lost 9.186

Nocturnal
Tunes her nocturnal Note. Thus with the Year Par Lost 3.40
Nocturnal and Diurnal rhomb suppos'd, Par Lost 8.134
Hail Goddesse of Nocturnal sport Mask 128
Trinity ms 'nocturnall'
Bridgewater ms 'nocturnall'
1637 'Nocturnall'

Nod
Here be without duck or nod Mask 960
B.M. ms 'Nod'

Nodding
The nodding horror of whose shady brows Mask 38
Bridgewater ms 'noddinge'

Nods
Nods, and Becks, and Wreathed Smiles, Allegro 28

Noise
Though for the noyse of Drums and Timbrels loud Par Lost 1.394
ms 'noise'
And in luxurious Cities, where the noyse Par Lost 1.498
ms 'noise'
Against the Torturer; when to meet the noise Par Lost 2.64
If aught disturb'd thir noyse, into her woomb, Par Lost 2.657
Eternal *Anarchie*, amidst the noise Par Lost 2.896
Might in that noise reside, of whom to ask Par Lost 2.957
Of brazen Chariots rag'd; dire was the noise Par Lost 6.211
From far with thundring noise among our foes Par Lost 6.487
Emboweld with outragious noise the Air, Par Lost 6.587
Infernal noise; Warr seem'd a civil Game Par Lost 6.667
Hell heard th' unsufferable noise, Hell saw Par Lost 6.867
Noise, other then the sound of Dance or Song, Par Lost 8.243
With spattering noise rejected: oft they assayd, Par Lost 10.567
Eurus and *Zephir* with thir lateral noise, Par Lost 10.705
To sow a jangling noise of words unknown: Par Lost 12.55
Retiring from the popular noise, I seek Samson 16
And now am come to see of whom such noise Samson 1088
What noise or shout was that? it tore the Skie. Samson 1472
Man. I know your friendly minds and----O what noise! Samson 1508
Mercy of Heav'n what hideous noise was that! Samson 1509
Chor. Noise call you it or universal groan Samson 1511
Blood, death, and deathful deeds are in that noise, Samson 1513
Man. Of ruin indeed methought I heard the noise, Samson 1515
This way the noise was, if mine ear be true, Mask 170
Such noise as I can make to be heard farthest Mask 227
As that the single want of light and noise Mask 369
Sweet Bird that shunn'st the noise of folly, Penseroso 61
Answering the stringed noise, Nativity 97
May rightly answer that melodious noise; Musick 18
When strait a barbarous noise environs me Sonnet 12, 3

Noises
With noises loud and ruinous (to compare Par Lost 2.921

Noising
I never fear'd they could, though noising loud Par Reg 4.488

Noisome
Before his eyes appeard, sad, noysom, dark, Par Lost 11.478
Of noisom winds, and blasting vapours chill. Arcades 49
Trinity ms 'noysome'

None
Which but th' Omnipotent none could have foyld, Par Lost 1.273
And dig'd out ribs of Gold. Let none admire Par Lost 1.690
From Faction; for none sure will claim in Hell Par Lost 2.32
Precedence, none, whose portion is so small Par Lost 2.33
Free, and to none accountable, preferring Par Lost 2.255
Satan except, none higher sat, with grave Par Lost 2.300
Irreparable; tearms of peace yet none Par Lost 2.331
Astonisht: none among the choice and prime Par Lost 2.423
None shall partake with me. Thus saying rose Par Lost 2.466
If shape it might be call'd that shape had none Par Lost 2.667
These Gates for ever shut, which none can pass Par Lost 2.776
That rest or intermission none I find. Par Lost 2.802
Save he who reigns above, none can resist. Par Lost 2.814
The other none: in Mercy and Justice both, Par Lost 3.132
All his deliv'rance, and to none but me. Par Lost 3.182
And none but such from mercy I exclude. Par Lost 3.202
Patron or Intercessor none appeerd, Par Lost 3.219
Indebted and undon, hath none to bring: Par Lost 3.235
As many as are restor'd, without thee none. Par Lost 3.289
Living or liveless to be found was none, Par Lost 3.443
None yet, but store hereafter from the earth Par Lost 3.444

None(*cont*)
His fixed seat, or fixed seat hath none, Par Lost 3.669
Where honour due and reverence none neglects, Par Lost 3.738
Upbraided none; nor was his service hard. Par Lost 4.45
Left for Repentance, none for Pardon left? Par Lost 4.80
None left but by submission; and that word Par Lost 4.81
But further way found none, so thick entwin'd, Par Lost 4.174
See farr and wide: in at this Gate none pass Par Lost 4.579
Shine not in vain, nor think, though men were none, Par Lost 4.675
Beast, Bird, Insect, or Worm durst enter none; Par Lost 4.704
Observing none, but adoration pure Par Lost 4.737
If none regard; Heav'n wakes with all his eyes, Par Lost 5.44
Deigns none to ease thy load and taste thy sweet, Par Lost 5.59
Forbid who will, none shall from me withhold Par Lost 5.62
Yet evil whence? in thee can harbour none, Par Lost 5.99
None can then Heav'n such glorious shape contain; Par Lost 5.362
On other surety none; freely we serve, Par Lost 5.538
By none, and if not equal all, yet free, Par Lost 5.791
Abdiel, then whom none with more zeale ador'd Par Lost 5.805
None seconded, as out of season judg'd, Par Lost 5.850
Know none before us, self-begot, self-rais'd Par Lost 5.860
Omnipotence to none. But well thou comst Par Lost 6.159
None of retreat, no unbecoming deed Par Lost 6.237
In Nature none: if other hidden cause Par Lost 6.442
None arguing stood, innumerable hands Par Lost 6.508
That whom they hit, none on thir feet might stand, Par Lost 6.592
Of ending this great Warr, since none but Thou Par Lost 6.702
To none communicable in Earth or Heaven: Par Lost 7.124
None was, but from the Earth a dewie Mist Par Lost 7.333
From him, for other light she needed none Par Lost 7.378
To see that none thence issu'd forth a spie, Par Lost 8.233
This happie Light, when answer none return'd, Par Lost 8.285
From all Eternitie, for none I know Par Lost 8.406
In eminence, and obstacle find none Par Lost 8.624
Whatever sleights none would suspicious mark, Par Lost 9.92
Rocks, Dens, and Caves; but I in none of these Par Lost 9.118
Let none henceforth seek needless cause to approve Par Lost 9.1140
Attendance none shall need, nor Train, where none Par Lost 10.80
Conviction to the Serpent none belongs. Par Lost 10.84
To waste it all my self, and leave ye none! Par Lost 10.820
And torment less then none of what we dread, Par Lost 10.998
None of the meanest, some great Potentate Par Lost 11.231
Taught them, but they his gifts acknowledg'd none. Par Lost 11.612
Through all the Plain, and refuge none was found. Par Lost 11.673
No sanctitie, if none be thither brought Par Lost 11.837
On every conscience; Laws which none shall finde Par Lost 12.522
In Troop or Caravan, for single none Par Reg 1.323
Nor left at *Jordan*, tydings of him none; Par Reg 2.62
Thought none my equal, now be over-match'd. Par Reg 2.146
None are, thou think'st, but taken with such toys. Par Reg 2.177
But Cottage, Herd or Sheep-cote none he saw, Par Reg 2.288
Of thee these forty days none hath regard, Par Reg 2.315
They all had need, I as thou seest have none. Par Reg 2.318
The drink of none but Kings; of later fame Par Reg 3.289
By free consent of all, none opposite, Par Reg 3.358
Other donation none thou canst produce: Par Reg 4.184
All glory arrogate, to God give none, Par Reg 4.315
Those terrors which thou speak'st of, did me none; Par Reg 4.487
Ease to the body some, none to the mind Samson 18
None offering fight; who single combatant Samson 344
On hostile ground, none daring my affront. Samson 531
None daring to appear Antagonist. Samson 1628
Of all thy dues be done, and none left out, Mask 137
Trinity ms 'none' ←'nought'
I would not taste thy treasonous offer; none Mask 702
After the heavenly tune, which none can hear Arcades 72
Hast hid *where none shall know*. Psalm 85, 8
Like thee among the gods is none Psalm 86, 25

Nook
By strange conveyance fill'd each hollow nook, Par Lost 1.707
Search through this Garden, leave unsearcht no nook, Par Lost 4.789
As in a shadie nook I stood behind, Par Lost 9.277
How couldst thou find this dark sequester'd nook? Mask 500
Bridgewater ms 'nooke'
Trinity ms 'nooke'
Her mansion in this fleshly nook: Penseroso 92

Noon
To Noon he fell, from Noon to dewy Eve, Par Lost 1.743
But all Sun-shine, as when his Beams at Noon Par Lost 3.616
This day at highth of Noon came to my Spheare Par Lost 4.564
Our walk at noon, with branches overgrown, Par Lost 4.627
And when high Noon hast gaind, and when thou fallst. Par Lost 5.174
Thou find'st him from the heat of Noon retir'd, Par Lost 5.231
Ris'n on mid-noon; som great behest from Heav'n Par Lost 5.311
With Myrtle, find what to redress till Noon: Par Lost 9.219
To be returnd by Noon amid the Bowre, Par Lost 9.401
Mean while the hour of Noon drew on, and wak'd Par Lost 9.739
From Noon, and gentle Aires due at thir hour Par Lost 10.93
As one who in his journey bates at Noone, Par Lost 12.1
line not in 1667 edition
As the noon Skie; more like to Goddesses Par Reg 2.156
To rest at noon, and entr'd soon the shade Par Reg 2.292
O dark, dark, dark, amid the blaze of noon, Samson 80
Amidst thir highth of noon, Samson 683
The Feast and noon grew high, and Sacrifice Samson 1612
Riding neer her highest noon, Penseroso 68

Noontide
Or Summers Noon-tide air, while thus he spake. Par Lost 2.309

Noontide(*cont*)
Imbround the noontide Bowrs: Thus was this place, Par Lost 4.246
Noontide repast, or Afternoons repose. Par Lost 9.403
Benighted walks under the mid-day Sun; Mask 384
Trinity ms 'benighted walks under the midday sun' ←'walks in black vapours though the noontyde brand'
Bridgewater ms 'walks in black vapours though the noone tyde brand'

Nor
Nor the deep Tract of Hell, say first what cause Par Lost 1.28
Nor what the Potent Victor in his rage Par Lost 1.95
Chain'd on the burning Lake, nor ever thence Par Lost 1.210
Nor did they not perceave the evil plight Par Lost 1.335
Nor had they yet among the Sons of *Eve* Par Lost 1.364
Of utmost *Arnon*. Nor content with such Par Lost 1.399
Nor founded on the brittle strength of bones, Par Lost 1.427
Rather then human. Nor did *Israel* scape Par Lost 1.482
Nor wanting power to mitigate and swage Par Lost 1.556
All her Original brightness, nor appear'd Par Lost 1.592
Caelestial Spirits in Bondage, nor th' Abyss Par Lost 1.658
With Golden Architrave; nor did there want Par Lost 1.715
Nor great *Alcairo* such magnificence Par Lost 1.718
Nor was his name unheard or unador'd Par Lost 1.738
Fell long before; nor aught avail'd him now Par Lost 1.748
To have built in Heav'n high Towrs; nor did he scape Par Lost 1.749
Our strength is equal, nor the Law unjust Par Lost 2.200
Nor want we skill or Art, from whence to raise Par Lost 2.272
Nor will occasion want, nor shall we need Par Lost 2.341
Nor fail'd they to express how much they prais'd, Par Lost 2.480
Alone th' Antagonist of Heav'n, nor less Par Lost 2.509
Nor uglier follow the Night-Hag, when call'd Par Lost 2.662
Created thing naught valu'd he nor shun'd; Par Lost 2.679
I know thee not, nor ever saw till now Par Lost 2.744
Of neither Sea, nor Shore, nor Air, nor Fire, Par Lost 2.912
He had to cross. Nor was his eare less peal'd Par Lost 2.920
Nor good dry Land: nigh founderd on he fares, Par Lost 2.940
Nightly I visit: nor somtimes forget Par Lost 3.32
Prescrib'd, no barrs of Hell, nor all the chains Par Lost 3.82
Heapt on him there, nor yet the main Abyss Par Lost 3.83
So were created, nor can justly accuse Par Lost 3.112
His prey, nor suffer my unspotted Soule Par Lost 3.248
To me are all my works, nor Man the least Par Lost 3.277
Nor shalt thou by descending to assume Par Lost 3.303
Nor stop thy flaming Chariot wheels, that shook Par Lost 3.394
Forget, nor from thy Fathers praise disjoine. Par Lost 3.415
Each Stair mysteriously was meant, nor stood Par Lost 3.516
For sight no obstacle found here, nor shade, Par Lost 3.615
Circl'd his Head, nor less his Locks behind Par Lost 3.626
For neither Man nor Angel can discern Par Lost 3.682
Nor staid, till on *Niphates* top he lights. Par Lost 3.742
Far off and fearless, nor with cause to boast, Par Lost 4.14
He brings, and round about him, nor from Hell Par Lost 4.21
Upbraided none; nor was his service hard. Par Lost 4.45
To them who liv'd; nor on the vertue thought Par Lost 4.198
Nor chang'd his course, but through the shaggie hill Par Lost 4.224
To seek her through the world; nor that sweet Grove Par Lost 4.272
Of *Eden* strive; nor that *Nyseian* Ile Par Lost 4.275
Nor where *Abassin* Kings thir issue Guard, Par Lost 4.280
Nor those mysterious parts were then conceald, Par Lost 4.312
So passd they naked on, nor shund the sight Par Lost 4.319
Nor gentle purpose, nor endearing smiles Par Lost 4.337
Wanted, nor youthful dalliance as beseems Par Lost 4.338
Have nothing merited, nor can performe Par Lost 4.418
Where neither joy nor love, but fierce desire, Par Lost 4.509
With charm of earliest Birds, nor rising Sun Par Lost 4.651
On this delightful land, nor herb, fruit, floure, Par Lost 4.652
Glistring with dew, nor fragrance after showers, Par Lost 4.653
Nor grateful Eevning mild, nor silent Night Par Lost 4.654
With this her solemn Bird, nor walk by Moon, Par Lost 4.655
Shine not in vain, nor think, though men were none, Par Lost 4.675
Pan or *Silvanus* never slept, nor Nymph, Par Lost 4.707
Nor *Faunus* haunted. Here in close recess Par Lost 4.708
Strait side by side were laid, nor turnd I weene Par Lost 4.741
Adam from his fair Spouse, nor *Eve* the Rites Par Lost 4.742
Casual fruition, nor in Court Amours Par Lost 4.767
Sat horror Plum'd; nor wanted in his graspe Par Lost 4.989
Might have ensu'd, nor onely Paradise Par Lost 4.991
Then Heav'n permits, nor mine, though doubld now Par Lost 4.1009
His mounted scale aloft: nor more; but fled Par Lost 4.1014
Nor God, nor Man; is Knowledge so despis'd? Par Lost 5.60
Affects me equally; nor can I like Par Lost 5.97
Be not disheart'nd then, nor cloud those looks Par Lost 5.122
Nor holy rapture wanted they to praise Par Lost 5.147
All Justice: nor delaid the winged Saint Par Lost 5.247
She tempers dulcet creams, nor these to hold Par Lost 5.347
Adam, I therefore came, nor art thou such Par Lost 5.372
Nor doth the Moon no nourishment exhale Par Lost 5.421
And to thir viands fell, nor seemingly Par Lost 5.434
The Angel, nor in mist, the common gloss Par Lost 5.435
Through Spirits with ease; nor wonder; if by fire Par Lost 5.439
Love unlibidinous reign'd, nor jealousie Par Lost 5.449
No inconvenient Diet, nor too light Fare: Par Lost 5.495
Findes no acceptance, nor can find, for how Par Lost 5.531
Aereal Music send: nor knew I not Par Lost 5.548
Nor so content, hath in his thought to try Par Lost 5.727
Essential Powers, nor by his Reign obscur'd, Par Lost 5.841
Through the infinite Host, nor less for that Par Lost 5.874
Nor number, nor example with him wrought Par Lost 5.901

Nor(*cont*)

Superior, nor of violence fear'd aught;	Par Lost 5.905
Of wrauth awak't: nor with less dread the loud	Par Lost 6.59
Indissolubly firm; nor obvious Hill,	Par Lost 6.69
Nor streit'ning Vale, nor Wood, nor Stream divides	Par Lost 6.70
Unsound and false; nor is it aught but just,	Par Lost 6.121
Apostat, still thou errst, nor end wilt find	Par Lost 6.172
Nor motion of swift thought, less could his Shield	Par Lost 6.192
Hosanna to the Highest: nor stood at gaze	Par Lost 6.205
The adverse Legions, nor less hideous joyn'd	Par Lost 6.206
The Adversarie. Nor think thou with wind	Par Lost 6.282
As not of power, at once; nor odds appeerd	Par Lost 6.319
Nor solid might resist that edge: it met	Par Lost 6.323
Descending, and in half cut sheere, nor staid,	Par Lost 6.325
Nor in thir liquid texture mortal wound	Par Lost 6.348
Threatn'd, nor from the Holie One of Heav'n	Par Lost 6.359
Nor stood unmindful *Abdiel* to annoy	Par Lost 6.369
Nor of Renown less eager, yet by doome	Par Lost 6.378
Nor long shall be our labour, yet ere dawne,	Par Lost 6.492
Part hidd'n veins diggd up (nor hath this Earth	Par Lost 6.516
Nor serv'd it to relax thir serried files.	Par Lost 6.599
Nor multitude, stand onely and behold	Par Lost 6.810
Not emulous, nor care who them excells;	Par Lost 6.822
Nor other strife with them do I voutsafe.	Par Lost 6.823
Nor less on either side tempestuous fell	Par Lost 6.844
Nor of the Muses nine, nor on the top	Par Lost 7.6
Both Harp and Voice; nor could the Muse defend	Par Lost 7.37
To ask, nor let thine own inventions hope	Par Lost 7.121
Infinitude, nor vacuous the space.	Par Lost 7.169
Nor staid, but on the Wings of Cherubim	Par Lost 7.218
Nor past uncelebrated, nor unsung	Par Lost 7.253
Soft-ebbing; nor withstood them Rock or Hill,	Par Lost 7.300
Till Ev'n, nor then the solemn Nightingal	Par Lost 7.435
Needless to thee repeated; nor unknown	Par Lost 7.494
The less not bright, nor Heav'n such journies run,	Par Lost 8.88
Nor glistering, may of solid good containe	Par Lost 8.93
The easiest way, nor with perplexing thoughts	Par Lost 8.183
Nor are thy lips ungraceful, Sire of men,	Par Lost 8.218
Nor tongue ineloquent; for God on thee	Par Lost 8.219
Nor less think wee in Heav'n of thee on Earth	Par Lost 8.224
So well converse, nor with the Ox the Ape;	Par Lost 8.396
From prone, nor in thir wayes complacence find.	Par Lost 8.433
And guided by his voice, nor uninformd	Par Lost 8.486
Of all thy gifts, nor enviest. I now see	Par Lost 8.494
Nor vehement desire, these delicacies	Par Lost 8.526
Neither her out-side formd so fair, nor aught	Par Lost 8.596
Desiring; nor restrain'd conveyance need	Par Lost 8.628
Nor skilld nor studious, higher Argument	Par Lost 9.42
But neither here seek I, no nor in Heav'n	Par Lost 9.124
Nor hope to be my self less miserable	Par Lost 9.126
Nor nocent yet, but on the grassie Herbe	Par Lost 9.186
1667 'Not'	
God hath assign'd us, nor of me shalt pass	Par Lost 9.231
Nor thou his malice and false guile contemn;	Par Lost 9.306
Angels, nor think superfluous others aid.	Par Lost 9.308
The willinger I goe, nor much expect	Par Lost 9.382
What hither brought us, hate, not love, nor hope	Par Lost 9.475
In *Epidaurus;* nor to which transformd	Par Lost 9.507
Insatiate, I thus single, nor have feard	Par Lost 9.536
As was my food, nor aught but food discern'd	Par Lost 9.573
But of this Tree we may not taste nor touch;	Par Lost 9.651
Thereof, nor shall ye touch it, least ye die.	Par Lost 9.663
Not just, not God; not feard then, nor obeyd:	Par Lost 9.701
Of knowledg, nor was God-head from her thought.	Par Lost 9.790
Not felt, nor shall be twice, for never more	Par Lost 9.859
Of danger tasted, nor to evil unknown	Par Lost 9.864
Not God Omnipotent, nor Fate, yet so	Par Lost 9.927
Nor yet on him found deadly, he yet lives,	Par Lost 9.932
Nor can I think that God, Creator wise,	Par Lost 9.938
Eating his fill, nor *Eve* to iterate	Par Lost 9.1005
From this delightful Fruit, nor known till now	Par Lost 9.1023
They sate them down to weep, nor onely Teares	Par Lost 9.1121
Neither had I transgress'd, nor thou with mee.	Par Lost 9.1161
Nor troubl'd at these tidings from the Earth,	Par Lost 10.36
Attendance none shall need, nor Train, where none	Par Lost 10.80
Nor alter'd his offence; yet God at last	Par Lost 10.171
Nor hee thir outward onely with the Skins	Par Lost 10.220
Nor can I miss the way, so strongly drawn	Par Lost 10.262
Leads thee, I shall not lag behinde, nor erre	Par Lost 10.266
Nor shall I to the work thou enterprisest	Par Lost 10.270
Nor this unvoyageable Gulf obscure	Par Lost 10.366
Devourd each other; nor stood much in awe	Par Lost 10.712
Nor I on my part single, in mee all	Par Lost 10.817
But rise, let us no more contend, nor blame	Par Lost 10.958
So spake our Father penitent, nor *Eve*	Par Lost 10.1097
Not of mean suiters, nor important less	Par Lost 11.9
Flew up, nor missd the way, by envious windes	Par Lost 11.15
Nor that which on the flaming Mount appeerd	Par Lost 11.216
That I should fear, nor sociably mild,	Par Lost 11.234
What justly thou hast lost; nor set thy heart,	Par Lost 11.288
Nor knowing us nor known: and if by prayer	Par Lost 11.307
Not higher that Hill nor wider looking round,	Par Lost 11.381
Turchestan-born; nor could his eye not ken	Par Lost 11.396
Th' excepted Tree, nor with the Snake conspir'd,	Par Lost 11.426
Nor sinn'd thy sin, yet from that derive	Par Lost 11.427
Henceforth I flie not Death, nor would prolong	Par Lost 11.547
Nor love thy Life, nor hate; but what thou livst	Par Lost 11.553
Not hid, nor those things last which might preserve	Par Lost 11.579

Nor(*cont*)

Both Horse and Foot, nor idely mustring stood;	Par Lost 11.645
The Earth again by flood, nor let the Sea	Par Lost 11.893
Surpass his bounds, nor Rain to drown the World	Par Lost 11.894
Cannot appease, nor Man the moral part	Par Lost 12.298
Thy enemie; nor so is overcome	Par Lost 12.390
In thee and in thy Seed: nor can this be,	Par Lost 12.395
Nor after resurrection shall he stay	Par Lost 12.436
To him his Heavenly Office, nor was long	Par Reg 1.28
Flies to his place, nor rests, but in mid air	Par Reg 1.39
Nor tasted humane food, nor hunger felt	Par Reg 1.308
Nor sleeping him nor waking harm'd, his walk	Par Reg 1.311
Moses was forty days, nor eat nor drank,	Par Reg 1.352
Or range in th' Air, nor from the Heav'n of Heav'ns	Par Reg 1.366
Nor lightens aught each mans peculiar load.	Par Reg 1.402
Nor will withdraw him now, nor will recall,	Par Reg 2.55
Nor left at *Jordan*, tydings of him none;	Par Reg 2.62
I will not argue that, nor will repine.	Par Reg 2.94
Nor tasted, nor had appetite; that Fast	Par Reg 2.247
Nor mind it, fed with better thoughts that feed	Par Reg 2.258
Duty and Service, nor to stay till bid,	Par Reg 2.326
But tender all their power? nor mention I	Par Reg 2.327
Nor proffer'd by an Enemy, though who	Par Reg 2.330
For Empires sake, nor Empire to affect	Par Reg 3.45
Orders and governs, nor content in Heaven	Par Reg 3.112
Or Barbarous, nor exception hath declar'd;	Par Reg 3.119
Obeys *Tiberius;* nor is always rul'd	Par Reg 3.159
Nor wanted clouds of foot, nor on each horn,	Par Reg 3.327
Of Archers, nor of labouring Pioners	Par Reg 3.330
Such forces met not, nor so wide a camp,	Par Reg 3.337
To thir inheritance, then, nor till then,	Par Reg 3.382
Nor in the land of their captivity	Par Reg 3.420
The Tempter stood, nor had what to reply,	Par Reg 4.2
Nor doth this grandeur and majestic show	Par Reg 4.110
For him I was not sent, nor yet to free	Par Reg 4.131
Is not for thee to know, nor me to tell.	Par Reg 4.153
Nor what I part with mean to give for naught;	Par Reg 4.161
As fearing God nor man, contemning all	Par Reg 4.304
Since neither wealth, nor honour, arms nor arts,	Par Reg 4.368
Kingdom nor Empire pleases thee, nor aught	Par Reg 4.369
Nor when, eternal sure, as without end,	Par Reg 4.391
In ruine reconcil'd: nor slept the winds	Par Reg 4.413
Unshaken; nor yet staid the terror there,	Par Reg 4.421
Nor yet amidst this joy and brightest morn	Par Reg 4.439
And toil'st in vain, nor me in vain molest.	Par Reg 4.498
Nor in respect of the enemy just cause	Samson 316
This well I knew, nor was at all surpris'd,	Samson 381
Tongue-batteries, she surceas'd not day nor night	Samson 404
Against all competition, nor will long	Samson 476
Thou couldst repress, nor did the dancing Rubie	Samson 543
Thirst, and refresht; nor envy'd them the grape	Samson 551
Nor shall his wondrous gifts be frustrate thus.	Samson 589
Nor th' other light of life continue long,	Samson 592
Nor less then wounds immedicable	Samson 620
Nor breath of Vernal Air from snowy *Alp*.	Samson 628
Nor am I in the list of them that hope;	Samson 647
Nor do I name of men the common rout,	Samson 674
Nor only dost degrade them, or remit	Samson 687
Nor shouldst thou have trusted that to womans frailty	Samson 783
In human hearts, nor less in mine towards thee,	Samson 792
Parents and countrey; nor was I their subject,	Samson 886
Nor under their protection but my own,	Samson 887
Bear not too sensibly, nor still insist	Samson 913
Nor think me so unwary or accurst	Samson 930
Henceforth, nor too much disapprove my own.	Samson 970
Nor shall I count it hainous to enjoy	Samson 991
Love once possest, nor can be easily	Samson 1005
Nor both so loosly disally'd	Samson 1022
Thir nuptials, nor this last so trecherously	Samson 1023
Nor from that right to part an hour,	Samson 1056
By female usurpation, nor dismay'd.	Samson 1060
Chor. Look now for no inchanting voice, nor fear	Samson 1065
Nor in the house with chamber Ambushes	Samson 1112
For valour to assail, nor by the sword	Samson 1165
To others did no violence nor spoil.	Samson 1191
Sam. I dread him not, nor all his Giant-brood,	Samson 1247
They cannot well impose, nor I sustain;	Samson 1258
Chor. Thy hopes are not ill founded nor seem vain	Samson 1504
That no second knows nor third,	Samson 1701
Nor much more cause, *Samson* hath quit himself	Samson 1709
And hush the waving Woods, nor of lesse faith,	Mask 88
Here dwel no frowns, nor anger, from these gates	Mask 667
Trinity ms 'nor' ← 'or'	
List Lady be not coy, and be not cosen'd	Mask 737
Trinity ms 'nor' ← 'and' ← 'nor'	
Thou hast nor Eare, nor Soul to apprehend	Mask 784
line not in Trinity ms	
line not in Bridgewater ms	
Nor wet *Octobers* torrent flood	Mask 930
Nor on the shaggy top of *Mona* high,	Lycidas 54
Nor yet where *Deva* spreads her wisard stream:	Lycidas 55
Nor in the glistering foil	Lycidas 79
Set off to th' world, nor in broad rumour lies,	Lycidas 80
Nor is *Osiris* seen	Nativity 213
Nor can he be at rest	Nativity 216
Nor all the gods beside,	Nativity 224
Your Son, said she, (nor can you it prevent)	Vacation 73
Nor were it contradiction to affirm	Another 13

Nor(*cont*)
line not in 1658 text
Fainted, and died, nor would with Ale be quickn'd; Another 16
line not in 1640, 1657, 1658 texts
Staid not behind, nor in the grave were trod; Sonnet 14, 6
The Lillie and Rose, that neither sow'd nor spun. Sonnet 20, 8
Nor to thir idle orbs doth sight appear Sonnet 22, 4
Against heavns hand or will, nor bate a jot Sonnet 22, 7
Nor sinners in th' assembly of just men. Psalm 1, 14
Nor in thy hot displeasure me correct; Psalm 6, 2
Nor shalt thou to a forein God Psalm 81, 39
Nor hearken to my voice; Psalm 81, 46
They know not nor will understand, Psalm 82, 17
O Lord, nor any works Psalm 86, 26
Who neither can nor will, may hold his peace; Prose 9, 4

North
A multitude, like which the populous North Par Lost 1.351
Ascending, while the North wind sleeps, o'respread Par Lost 2.489
But in the Mount that lies from *Eden* North, Par Lost 4.569
With strictest watch; these other wheel the North, Par Lost 4.783
The Quarters of the North, there to prepare Par Lost 5.689
Equal to ours, throughout the spacious North; Par Lost 5.726
At length into the limits of the North Par Lost 5.755
Farr in th' Horizon to the North appeer'd Par Lost 6.79
Scarce tollerable, and from the North to call Par Lost 10.654
Corrupt and Pestilent: Now from the North Par Lost 10.695
Wash'd by the Southern Sea, and on the North Par Reg 4.28
Germans and *Scythians*, and *Sarmatians* North Par Reg 4.78
Back'd on the North and West by a thick wood, Par Reg 4.448
Thir Hydra heads, and the fals North displaies Sonnet 15, 7
1694 '*North*'

North-east
Mozambic, off at Sea North-East windes blow Par Lost 4.161

Northern
When *Agrican* with all his Northern powers Par Reg 3.338
Shoots against the dusky Pole, Mask 99
Bridgewater ms 'Northerne'
Trinity ms 'dusky' ← 'northren'

Northward
From *Hamath* Northward to the Desert South Par Lost 12.139

North-wind
Drivn by a keen North-winde, that blowing drie Par Lost 11.842

Norumbega
Of *Norumbega*, and the *Samoed* shoar Par Lost 10.696

Norway
Him haply slumbring on the *Norway* foam Par Lost 1.203
ms 'Norway'

Norwegian
Hewn on *Norwegian* hills, to be the Mast Par Lost 1.293
ms 'Norwegian'

Nostril
His Nostril wide into the murkie Air, Par Lost 10.280

Nostrils
Dust of the ground, and in thy nostrils breath'd Par Lost 7.525
To the Creator, and his Nostrils fill Par Lost 9.196

Not
The force of those dire Arms? yet not for those, Par Lost 1.94
All is not lost; the unconquerable Will, Par Lost 1.106
And what is else not to be overcome? Par Lost 1.109
In Arms not worse, in foresight much advanc't, Par Lost 1.119
Shall grieve him, if I fail not, and disturb Par Lost 1.167
Let us not slip th' occasion, whether scorn, Par Lost 1.178
If not what resolution from despare. Par Lost 1.191
Not by the sufferance of supernal Power. Par Lost 1.241
A mind not to be chang'd by Place or Time. Par Lost 1.253
We shall be free; th' Almighty hath not built Par Lost 1.259
Here for his envy, will not drive us hence: Par Lost 1.260
And call them not to share with us their part Par Lost 1.267
Over the burning Marle, not like those steps Par Lost 1.296
Nor did they not perceave the evil plight Par Lost 1.335
In which they were, or the fierce pains not feel; Par Lost 1.336
Not ti'd or manacl'd with joynt or limb, Par Lost 1.426
In *Sion* also not unsung, where stood Par Lost 1.442
Fell not from Heaven, or more gross to love Par Lost 1.491
Not in despair, to have found themselves not lost Par Lost 1.525
Semblance of worth, not substance, gently rais'd Par Lost 1.529
Stood like a Towr; his form had yet not lost Par Lost 1.591
Was not inglorious, though th' event was dire, Par Lost 1.624
So as not either to provoke, or dread Par Lost 1.644
What force effected not: that he no less Par Lost 1.647
There stood a Hill not far whose griesly top Par Lost 1.670
The Roof was fretted Gold. Not *Babilon*, Par Lost 1.717
I give not Heav'n for lost. From this descent Par Lost 2.14
Car'd not to be at all; with that care lost Par Lost 2.48
He reck'd not, and these words thereafter spake. Par Lost 2.50
More unexpert, I boast not: them let those Par Lost 2.52
Contrive who need, or when they need, not now Par Lost 2.53
Of that forgetful Lake benumm not still, Par Lost 2.74
Which if not Victory is yet Revenge. Par Lost 2.105
A fairer person lost not Heav'n; he seemd Par Lost 2.110
As not behind in hate; if what was urg'd Par Lost 2.120
Did not disswade me most, and seem to cast Par Lost 2.122
Not more Almighty to resist our might Par Lost 2.192
Not mind us not offending, satisfi'd Par Lost 2.212
Will slack'n, if his breath stir not thir flames. Par Lost 2.214
Thir noxious vapour, or enur'd not feel, Par Lost 2.216
For happy though but ill, for ill not worst, Par Lost 2.224
If we procure not to our selves more woe. Par Lost 2.225

Not(*cont*)
Not peace: and after him thus *Mammon* spake. Par Lost 2.228
To whom we hate. Let us not then pursue Par Lost 2.249
Wants not her hidden lustre, Gemms and Gold; Par Lost 2.271
And know not that the King of Heav'n hath doom'd Par Lost 2.316
This place our dungeon, not our safe retreat Par Lost 2.317
Err not) another World, the happy seat Par Lost 2.347
The punie habitants, or if not drive, Par Lost 2.367
Dwell not unvisited of Heav'ns fair Light Par Lost 2.398
These Royalties, and not refuse to Reign, Par Lost 2.451
Dreaded not more th' adventure then his voice Par Lost 2.474
Man had not hellish foes anow besides, Par Lost 2.504
Thaws not, but gathers heap, and ruin seems Par Lost 2.590
Admir'd, not fear'd; God and his Son except, Par Lost 2.678
Created thing naught valu'd he nor shun'd; Par Lost 2.679
Hell-born, not to contend with Spirits of Heav'n. Par Lost 2.687
Had not the Snakie Sorceress that sat Par Lost 2.724
I know thee not, nor ever saw till now Par Lost 2.744
Alone, but long I sat not, till my womb Par Lost 2.778
Which but her self not all the *Stygian* powers Par Lost 2.875
Down had been falling, had not by ill chance Par Lost 2.935
Fled not in silence through the frighted deep Par Lost 2.994
If that way be your walk, you have not farr; Par Lost 2.1007
He ceas'd; and *Satan* staid not to reply, Par Lost 2.1010
Revisit'st not these eyes, that rowle in vain Par Lost 3.23
Or dim suffusiôn veild. Yet not the more Par Lost 3.26
Seasons return, but not to me returns Par Lost 3.41
Not farr off Heav'n, in the Precincts of light, Par Lost 3.88
Not free, what proof could they have givn sincere Par Lost 3.103
Not what they would? what praise could they receive? Par Lost 3.106
Not mee. They therefore as to right belongd, Par Lost 3.111
Thir own revolt, not I: if I foreknew, Par Lost 3.117
Man shall not quite be lost, but sav'd who will, Par Lost 3.173
Yet not of will in him, but grace in me Par Lost 3.174
Mine ear shall not be slow, mine eye not shut. Par Lost 3.193
But yet all is not don; Man disobeying, Par Lost 3.203
By doom severe, had not the Son of God, Par Lost 3.224
And shall grace not find means, that finds her way, Par Lost 3.228
Under his gloomie power I shall not long Par Lost 3.242
Thou wilt not leave me in the loathsom grave Par Lost 3.247
In those who, when they may, accept not grace. Par Lost 3.302
Approach not, but with both wings veil thir eyes. Par Lost 3.382
Thy Fathers dreadful Thunder didst not spare, Par Lost 3.393
Not so on Man; him through their malice fall'n, Par Lost 3.400
Father of Mercie and Grace, thou didst not doome Par Lost 3.401
Perceive thee purpos'd not to doom frail Man Par Lost 3.404
Not in the neighbouring Moon, as some have dreamd; Par Lost 3.459
He stayd not to enquire: above them all Par Lost 3.571
Not all parts like, but all alike informd Par Lost 3.593
His back was turnd, but not his brightness hid; Par Lost 3.624
Not of the prime, yet such as in his face Par Lost 3.637
He drew not nigh unheard, the Angel bright, Par Lost 3.645
Thy way thou canst not miss, me mine requires. Par Lost 3.735
Yet not rejoycing in his speed, though bold, Par Lost 4.13
And understood not that a grateful mind Par Lost 4.55
By owing owes not, but still pays, at once Par Lost 4.56
Ambition. Yet why not? som other Power Par Lost 4.61
Fell not, but stand unshak'n, from within Par Lost 4.64
Yet not anough had practisd to deceive Par Lost 4.124
Sat like a Cormorant; yet not true Life Par Lost 4.196
Flours worthy of Paradise which not nice Art Par Lost 4.241
Led on th' Eternal Spring. Not that faire field Par Lost 4.268
Not equal, as thir sex not equal seemd; Par Lost 4.296
Clustring, but not beneath his shoulders broad: Par Lost 4.303
Then was not guiltie shame, dishonest shame Par Lost 4.313
Not Spirits, yet to heav'nly Spirits bright Par Lost 4.361
Henceforth; my dwelling haply may not please Par Lost 4.378
Not like these narrow limits, to receive Par Lost 4.384
On you who wrong me not for him who wrongd. Par Lost 4.387
So various, not to taste that onely Tree Par Lost 4.423
Earth, Aire, and Sea. Then let us not think hard Par Lost 4.432
Not distant far from thence a murmuring sound Par Lost 4.453
Had not a voice thus warnd me, What thou seest, Par Lost 4.467
Among our other torments not the least, Par Lost 4.510
Yet let me not forget what I have gain'd Par Lost 4.512
From thir own mouths; all is not theirs it seems: Par Lost 4.513
Not only enlighten, but with kindly heate Par Lost 4.668
Shine not in vain, nor think, though men were none, Par Lost 4.675
Reigns here and revels; not in the bought smile Par Lost 4.765
Know ye not then said *Satan*, fill'd with scorn, Par Lost 4.827
Know ye not mee? ye knew me once no mate Par Lost 4.828
For you, there sitting where ye durst not soare; Par Lost 4.829
Not to know mee argues your selves unknown, Par Lost 4.830
Think not, revolted Spirit, thy shape the same, Par Lost 4.835
Best with the best, the Sender not the sent, Par Lost 4.852
The Fiend repli'd not, overcome with rage; Par Lost 4.857
His heart, not else dismai'd. Now drew they nigh Par Lost 4.861
Not likely to part hence without contest; Par Lost 4.872
Of others, who approve not to transgress Par Lost 4.880
Who would not, finding way, break loose from Hell, Par Lost 4.889
But evil hast not tri'd: and wilt object Par Lost 4.896
But that implies not violence or harme. Par Lost 4.901
Or not, who ask what boldness brought him hither Par Lost 4.908
Came not all Hell broke loose? is pain to them Par Lost 4.918
Thou surely hadst not come sole fugitive. Par Lost 4.923
Not that I less endure, or shrink from pain, Par Lost 4.925
And seconded thy else not dreaded Spear. Par Lost 4.929
A faithful Leader, not to hazard all Par Lost 4.933

Not(*cont*)
Fame is not silent, here in hope to find Par Lost 4.938
And practis'd distances to cringe, not fight. Par Lost 4.945
And Seale thee so, as henceforth not to scorne Par Lost 4.966
With violence of this conflict, had not soon Par Lost 4.995
If dream'd, not as I oft am wont, of thee, Par Lost 5.32
I rose as at thy call, but found thee not; Par Lost 5.48
This said he paus'd not, but with ventrous Arme Par Lost 5.64
And why not Gods of Men, since good, the more Par Lost 5.71
The Author not impair'd, but honourd more? Par Lost 5.73
Happier thou mayst be, worthier canst not be: Par Lost 5.76
Thy self a Goddess, not to Earth confind, Par Lost 5.78
Could not but taste. Forthwith up to the Clouds Par Lost 5.86
But with addition strange; yet be not sad. Par Lost 5.116
Be not disheart'nd then, nor cloud those looks Par Lost 5.122
If better thou belong not to the dawn, Par Lost 5.167
In mystic Dance not without Song, resound Par Lost 5.178
He swerve not too secure: tell him withall Par Lost 5.238
Not unconform to other shining Globes, Par Lost 5.259
True appetite, and not disrelish thirst Par Lost 5.305
More fruitful, which instructs us not to spare. Par Lost 5.320
What order, so contriv'd as not to mix Par Lost 5.334
Tastes, not well joynd, inelegant, but bring Par Lost 5.335
Neerer his presence *Adam* though not awd, Par Lost 5.358
As may not oft invite, though Spirits of Heav'n Par Lost 5.374
Vapours not yet into her substance turnd. Par Lost 5.420
Think not I shall be nice. So down they sat, Par Lost 5.433
Not burd'nd Nature, sudden mind arose Par Lost 5.452
In *Adam*, not to let th' occasion pass Par Lost 5.453
Food not of Angels, yet accepted so, Par Lost 5.465
As that more willingly thou couldst not seem Par Lost 5.466
If not deprav'd from good, created all Par Lost 5.471
Wonder not then, what God for you saw good Par Lost 5.491
If I refuse not, but convert, as you, Par Lost 5.492
God made thee perfet, not immutable; Par Lost 5.524
By nature free, not over-rul'd by Fate Par Lost 5.527
Not our necessitated, such with him Par Lost 5.530
Can hearts, not free, be tri'd whether they serve Par Lost 5.532
To love or not; in this we stand or fall: Par Lost 5.540
Aereal Music send: nor knew I not Par Lost 5.548
Not lawful to reveal? yet for thy good Par Lost 5.570
As yet this world was not, and *Chaos* wilde Par Lost 5.577
All seemd well pleas'd, all seem'd, but were not all Par Lost 5.617
Wee ours for change delectable, not need) Par Lost 5.629
To grateful Twilight (for Night comes not there Par Lost 5.645
Alternate all night long: but not so wak'd Par Lost 5.657
If not the first Arch-Angel, great in Power, Par Lost 5.660
Messiah King anointed, could not beare Par Lost 5.664
To utter is not safe. Assemble thou Par Lost 5.683
Interpreted) which not long after, he Par Lost 5.762
Not meerly titular, since by Decree Par Lost 5.774
The supple knee? ye will not, if I trust Par Lost 5.788
By none, and if not equal all, yet free, Par Lost 5.791
Jarr not with liberty, but well consist. Par Lost 5.793
Erre not, much less for this to be our Lord, Par Lost 5.799
Our being ordain'd to govern, not to serve? Par Lost 5.802
And tempt not these; but hast'n to appease Par Lost 5.846
We know no time when we were not as now; Par Lost 5.859
Will not be now voutsaf't, other Decrees Par Lost 5.884
Yet not for thy advise or threats I fly Par Lost 5.889
Distinguish not: for soon expect to feel Par Lost 5.892
Returnd not lost: On to the sacred hill Par Lost 6.25
Abdiel that sight endur'd not, where he stood Par Lost 6.111
Remain not; wherfore should not strength and might Par Lost 6.116
Or potent tongue; fool, not to think how vain Par Lost 6.135
All are not of thy Train; there be who Faith Par Lost 6.143
To thee not visible, when I alone Par Lost 6.145
Thy self not free, but to thy self enthrall'd; Par Lost 6.181
Yet Chains in Hell, not Realms expect: mean while Par Lost 6.186
Which hung not, but so swift with tempest fell Par Lost 6.190
Though not destroy, thir happie Native seat; Par Lost 6.226
Had not th' Eternal King Omnipotent Par Lost 6.227
And faithful, now prov'd false. But think not here Par Lost 6.271
Brooks not the works of violence and Warr. Par Lost 6.274
Thou canst not. Hast thou turnd the least of these Par Lost 6.284
To chase me hence? erre not that so shall end Par Lost 6.288
If not to reign: mean while thy utmost force, Par Lost 6.293
I flie not, but have sought thee farr and nigh. Par Lost 6.295
That might determine, and not need repeate, Par Lost 6.318
As not of power, at once; nor odds appeerd Par Lost 6.319
Not long divisible, and from the gash Par Lost 6.331
To find himself not matchless, and his pride Par Lost 6.341
Vital in every part, not as frail man Par Lost 6.345
Seek not the praise of men: the other sort Par Lost 6.376
Not liable to fear or flight or paine. Par Lost 6.397
Gave them above thir foes, not to have sinnd, Par Lost 6.402
Not to have disobei'd; in fight they stood Par Lost 6.403
Not to be overpowerd, Companions deare, Par Lost 6.419
Found worthy not of Libertie alone, Par Lost 6.420
(And if one day, why not Eternal dayes2) Par Lost 6.424
But proves not so: then fallible, it seems, Par Lost 6.428
Till now not known, but known as soon contemnd, Par Lost 6.432
Spare out of life perhaps, and not repine, Par Lost 6.460
Not uninvented that, which thou aright Par Lost 6.470
These things, as not to mind from whence they grow Par Lost 6.477
This day, fear not his flight; so thick a Cloud Par Lost 6.539
Not distant far with heavie pace the Foe Par Lost 6.551
Our overture, and turn not back perverse; Par Lost 6.562

Not(*cont*)
Brass, Iron, Stonie mould, had not thir mouthes Par Lost 6.576
Not long, for sudden all at once thir Reeds Par Lost 6.582
O Friends, why come not on these Victors proud? Par Lost 6.609
Not understood, this gift they have besides, Par Lost 6.626
They shew us when our foes walk not upright. Par Lost 6.627
A while in trouble; but they stood not long, Par Lost 6.634
Had not th' Almightie Father where he sits Par Lost 6.671
Number to this dayes work is not ordain'd Par Lost 6.809
By mee, not you but mee they have despis'd, Par Lost 6.812
Not emulous, nor care who them excells; Par Lost 6.822
Yet half his strength he put not forth, but check'd Par Lost 6.853
Not to destroy, but root them out of Heav'n: Par Lost 6.855
But list'n not to his Temptations, warne Par Lost 6.908
The meaning, not the Name I call: for thou Par Lost 7.5
Standing on Earth, not rapt above the Pole, Par Lost 7.23
And solitude; yet not alone, while thou Par Lost 7.28
Her Son. So fail not thou, who thee implores: Par Lost 7.38
Charg'd not to touch the interdicted Tree, Par Lost 7.46
Unknown, which human knowledg could not reach: Par Lost 7.75
What wee, not to explore the secrets aske Par Lost 7.95
Thee also happier, shall not be withheld Par Lost 7.117
Things not reveal'd, which th' invisible King, Par Lost 7.122
Not here, till by degrees of merit rais'd Par Lost 7.157
And put not forth my goodness, which is free Par Lost 7.171
To act or not, Necessitie and Chance Par Lost 7.172
Approach not mee, and what I will is Fate. Par Lost 7.173
Was not; shee in a cloudie Tabernacle Par Lost 7.248
Appeer'd not: over all the face of Earth Par Lost 7.278
Main Ocean flow'd, not idle, but with warme Par Lost 7.279
Her sacred shades: though God had yet not rain'd Par Lost 7.331
Streaking the ground with sinuous trace; not all Par Lost 7.481
Not noxious, but obedient at thy call. Par Lost 7.498
Of all yet don; a Creature who not prone Par Lost 7.506
Eternal Father (For where is not hee Par Lost 7.517
Thou mai'st not; in the day thou eat'st, thou di'st; Par Lost 7.544
Yet not till the Creator from his work Par Lost 7.551
But not in silence holy kept; the Harp Par Lost 7.594
Had work and rested not, the solemn Pipe, Par Lost 7.595
From Heaven Gate not farr, founded in view Par Lost 7.618
Aught, not surpassing human measure, say. Par Lost 7.640
Yet went she not, as not with such discourse Par Lost 8.48
Delighted, or not capable her eare Par Lost 8.49
Not Words alone pleas'd her. O when meet now Par Lost 8.57
Not unattended, for on her as Queen Par Lost 8.60
To ask or search I blame thee not, for Heav'n Par Lost 8.66
Imports not, if thou reck'n right, the rest Par Lost 8.71
Did wisely to conceal, and not divulge Par Lost 8.73
That bodies bright and greater should not serve Par Lost 8.87
The less not bright, nor Heav'n such journies run, Par Lost 8.88
Or Bright inferrs not Excellence: the Earth Par Lost 8.91
Yet not to Earth are those bright Luminaries Par Lost 8.98
That Man may know he dwells not in his own; Par Lost 8.103
Speed almost Spiritual; mee thou thinkst not slow, Par Lost 8.110
Not that I so affirm, though so it seem Par Lost 8.117
Of Day and Night; which needs not thy beleefe, Par Lost 8.136
But whether thus these things, or whether not, Par Lost 8.159
Sollicit not thy thoughts with matters hid, Par Lost 8.167
Dream not of other Worlds, what Creatures there Par Lost 8.175
Not of Earth onely but of highest Heav'n. Par Lost 8.178
And not molest us, unless we our selves Par Lost 8.186
That not to know at large of things remote Par Lost 8.191
Of somthing not unseasonable to ask Par Lost 8.201
My Storie, which perhaps thou hast not heard; Par Lost 8.205
And Day is yet not spent; till then thou seest Par Lost 8.206
Fond, were it not in hope of thy reply: Par Lost 8.209
Not that they durst without his leave attempt, Par Lost 8.237
Knew not; to speak I tri'd, and forthwith spake, Par Lost 8.271
Not of my self; by some great Maker then, Par Lost 8.278
While thus I call'd, and stray'd I knew not whither, Par Lost 8.283
My wandring, had not hee who was my Guide Par Lost 8.312
Not to incur; but soon his cleer aspect Par Lost 8.336
Not onely these fair bounds, but all the Earth Par Lost 8.338
Not hither summond, since they cannot change Par Lost 8.347
I found not what me thought I wanted still; Par Lost 8.355
I see not who partakes. In solitude Par Lost 8.364
What call'st thou solitude, is not the Earth Par Lost 8.369
To come and play before thee, know'st thou not Par Lost 8.372
And reason not contemptibly; with these Par Lost 8.374
Let not my words offend thee, Heav'nly Power, Par Lost 8.379
Hast thou not made me here thy substitute, Par Lost 8.381
Wherto th' Almighty answer'd, not displeas'd. Par Lost 8.398
Of happiness, or not? who am alone Par Lost 8.405
Is no deficience found; not so is Man, Par Lost 8.416
Best with thy self accompanied, seek'st not Par Lost 8.428
And finde thee knowing not of Beasts alone, Par Lost 8.438
My Image, not imparted to the Brute, Par Lost 8.441
Knew it not good for Man to be alone, Par Lost 8.445
When out of hope, behold her, not farr off, Par Lost 8.481
I overjoyd could not forbear aloud. Par Lost 8.490
That would be woo'd, and not unsought be won, Par Lost 8.503
Not obvious, not obtrusive, but retir'd, Par Lost 8.504
As us'd or not, works in the mind no change, Par Lost 8.525
Not proof enough such Object to sustain, Par Lost 8.535
As one intended first, not after made Par Lost 8.555
Accuse not Nature, she hath don her part; Par Lost 8.561
Do thou but thine, and be not diffident Par Lost 8.562
Of Wisdom, she deserts thee not, if thou Par Lost 8.563

Not(*cont*)

Dismiss not her, when most thou needst her nigh,	Par Lost 8.564
Not thy subjection: weigh with her thy self;	Par Lost 8.570
To Cattel and each Beast; which would not be	Par Lost 8.582
In loving thou dost well, in passion not,	Par Lost 8.588
Wherein true Love consists not; love refines	Par Lost 8.589
Not sunk in carnal pleasure, for which cause	Par Lost 8.593
Yet these subject not; I to thee disclose	Par Lost 8.607
What inward thence I feel, not therefore foild,	Par Lost 8.608
To love thou blam'st me not, for love thou saist	Par Lost 8.612
Love not the heav'nly Spirits, and how thir Love	Par Lost 8.615
Would not admit; thine and of all thy Sons	Par Lost 8.637
Not less but more Heroic then the wrauth	Par Lost 9.14
Not sedulous by Nature to indite	Par Lost 9.27
Not that which justly gives Heroic name	Par Lost 9.40
Not Hers who brings it nightly to my Ear.	Par Lost 9.47
Now not, though Sin, not Time, first wraught the change,	Par Lost 9.70
O Earth, how like to Heav'n, if not preferr'd	Par Lost 9.99
Not in themselves, all thir known vertue appeers	Par Lost 9.110
Not longer then since I in one Night freed	Par Lost 9.140
But what will not Ambition and Revenge	Par Lost 9.168
Let it; I reck not, so it light well aim'd,	Par Lost 9.173
Not yet in horrid Shade or dismal Den,	Par Lost 9.185
Nor nocent yet, but on the grassie Herbe	Par Lost 9.186
1667 'Not'	
Disturbd not, waiting close th' approach of Morn.	Par Lost 9.191
Yet not so strictly hath our Lord impos'd	Par Lost 9.235
Love not the lowest end of human life.	Par Lost 9.241
For not to irksom toile, but to delight	Par Lost 9.242
These paths & Bowers doubt not but our joynt hands	Par Lost 9.244
Or this, or worse, leave not the faithful side	Par Lost 9.265
May tempt it, I expected not to hear.	Par Lost 9.281
His violence thou fearst not, being such,	Par Lost 9.282
As wee, not capable of death or paine,	Par Lost 9.283
Can either not receave, or can repell.	Par Lost 9.284
Not diffident of thee do I dissuade	Par Lost 9.293
Not incorruptible of Faith, not prooff	Par Lost 9.298
Though ineffectual found: misdeem not then,	Par Lost 9.301
Why shouldst not thou like sense within thee feel	Par Lost 9.315
Suttle or violent, we not endu'd	Par Lost 9.324
But harm precedes not sin: onely our Foe	Par Lost 9.327
Let us not then suspect our happie State	Par Lost 9.337
As not secure to single or combin'd.	Par Lost 9.339
Not then mistrust, but tender love enjoynes,	Par Lost 9.357
Since Reason not impossibly may meet	Par Lost 9.360
Not keeping strictest watch, as she was warnd.	Par Lost 9.363
Seek not temptation then, which to avoide	Par Lost 9.364
Thou sever not: Trial will come unsought.	Par Lost 9.366
Not seeing thee attempted, who attest?	Par Lost 9.369
Go; for thy stay, not free, absents thee more;	Par Lost 9.372
Though not as shee with Bow and Quiver armd,	Par Lost 9.390
Eve separate, he wish'd, but not with hope	Par Lost 9.422
Or that, not Mystic, where the Sapient King	Par Lost 9.442
Of pleasure not for him ordain'd: then soon	Par Lost 9.470
What hither brought us, hate, not love, nor hope	Par Lost 9.475
To me is lost. Then let me not let pass	Par Lost 9.479
Her Husband, for I view far round, not nigh,	Par Lost 9.482
Foe not informidable, exempt from wound,	Par Lost 9.486
I not; so much hath Hell debas'd, and paine	Par Lost 9.487
Not terrible, though terrour be in Love	Par Lost 9.490
And beautie, not approacht by stronger hate,	Par Lost 9.491
Address'd his way, not with indented wave,	Par Lost 9.496
Lovelier, not those that in *Illyria* chang'd	Par Lost 9.505
Of rusling Leaves, but minded not, as us'd	Par Lost 9.519
Wonder not, sovran Mistress, if perhaps	Par Lost 9.532
Not unamaz'd she thus in answer spake.	Par Lost 9.552
I knew, but not with human voice endu'd;	Par Lost 9.561
Not to deferr; hunger and thirst at once,	Par Lost 9.586
Longing and envying stood, but could not reach.	Par Lost 9.593
I spar'd not, for such pleasure till that hour	Par Lost 9.596
Wanted not long, though to this shape retain'd.	Par Lost 9.601
Empress, the way is readie, and not long,	Par Lost 9.626
But of this Tree we may not taste nor touch;	Par Lost 9.651
Of all these Garden Trees ye shall not eate,	Par Lost 9.657
The Garden, God hath said, Ye shall not eate	Par Lost 9.662
Within me cleere, not onely to discerne	Par Lost 9.681
Queen of this Universe, doe not believe	Par Lost 9.684
Those rigid threats of Death; ye shall not Die:	Par Lost 9.685
For such a petty Trespass, and not praise	Par Lost 9.693
Deterrd not from atchieving what might leade	Par Lost 9.696
Be real, why not known, since easier shunnd?	Par Lost 9.699
Not just, not God; not feard then, nor obeyd:	Par Lost 9.701
And what are Gods that Man may not become	Par Lost 9.716
The Tongue not made for Speech to speak thy praise:	Par Lost 9.749
Conceales not from us, naming thee the Tree	Par Lost 9.751
For good unknown, sure is not had, or had	Par Lost 9.756
And yet unknown, is as not had at all.	Par Lost 9.757
Such prohibitions binde not. But if Death	Par Lost 9.760
Hath tasted, envies not, but brings with joy	Par Lost 9.770
And knew not eating Death: Satiate at length,	Par Lost 9.792
Not without Song, each Morning, and due praise	Par Lost 9.800
For had the gift bin theirs, it had not here	Par Lost 9.806
Best guide; not following thee, I had remaind	Par Lost 9.808
Full happiness with mee, or rather not,	Par Lost 9.819
A thing not undesireable, somtime	Par Lost 9.824
Hast thou not wonderd, *Adam*, at my stay?	Par Lost 9.856
Not felt, nor shall be twice, for never more	Par Lost 9.859
This Tree is not as we are told, a Tree	Par Lost 9.863

Not(*cont*)

Or not restraind as wee, or not obeying,	Par Lost 9.868
Not dead, as we are threatn'd, but thenceforth	Par Lost 9.870
Least thou not tasting, different degree	Par Lost 9.883
Deitie for thee, when Fate will not permit.	Par Lost 9.885
Not God Omnipotent, nor Fate, yet so	Par Lost 9.927
Perhaps thou shalt not Die, perhaps the Fact	Par Lost 9.928
Is not so hainous now, foretasted Fruit,	Par Lost 9.929
Not well conceav'd of God, who though his Power	Par Lost 9.945
Matter of scorne, not to be given the Foe,	Par Lost 9.951
The worst, and not perswade thee rather die	Par Lost 9.979
Farr otherwise th' event, not Death, but Life	Par Lost 9.984
With liberal hand: he scrupl'd not to eat	Par Lost 9.997
Against his better knowledge, not deceav'd,	Par Lost 9.998
So said he, and forbore not glance or toy	Par Lost 9.1034
Till *Adam*, though not less then *Eve* abash't,	Par Lost 9.1065
There sit not, and reproach us as unclean,	Par Lost 9.1098
The Figtree, not that kind for Fruit renown'd,	Par Lost 9.1101
Coverd, but not at rest or ease of Mind,	Par Lost 9.1120
For Understanding rul'd not, and the Will	Par Lost 9.1127
Heard not her lore, both in subjection now	Par Lost 9.1128
I know not whence possessd thee; we had then	Par Lost 9.1137
Remaind still happie, not as now, despoild	Par Lost 9.1138
Or here th' attempt, thou couldst not have discernd	Par Lost 9.1149
Being as I am, why didst not thou the Head	Par Lost 9.1155
Command me absolutely not to go,	Par Lost 9.1156
Too facil then thou didst not much gainsay,	Par Lost 9.1158
Immutable when thou wert lost, not I,	Par Lost 9.1165
Of thy transgressing? not enough severe,	Par Lost 9.1169
Lets her will rule; restraint she will not brook,	Par Lost 9.1184
Hinder'd not *Satan* to attempt the minde	Par Lost 10.8
The high Injunction not to taste that Fruit,	Par Lost 10.13
Whoever tempted; which they not obeying,	Par Lost 10.14
All were who heard, dim sadness did not spare	Par Lost 10.23
With pitie, violated not thir bliss.	Par Lost 10.25
From unsuccessful charge, be not dismaid,	Par Lost 10.35
Which your sincerest care could not prevent,	Par Lost 10.37
Because not yet inflicted, as he fear'd,	Par Lost 10.51
Justice shall not return as bountie scorn'd.	Par Lost 10.54
Before thee; and not repenting, this obtaine	Par Lost 10.75
Time counts not, though with swiftest minutes wing'd.	Par Lost 10.91
Not pleas'd, thus entertaind with solitude,	Par Lost 10.105
Love was not in thir looks, either to God	Par Lost 10.111
My voice thou oft hast heard, and hast not fear'd,	Par Lost 10.119
Whereof I gave thee charge thou shouldst not eat?	Par Lost 10.123
I should conceal, and not expose to blame	Par Lost 10.130
Thy Love, not thy Subjection, and her Gifts	Par Lost 10.153
Confessing soon, yet not before her Judge	Par Lost 10.160
Concern'd not Man (since he no further knew)	Par Lost 10.170
I charg'd thee, saying: Thou shalt not eate thereof,	Par Lost 10.200
Must suffer change, disdain'd not to begin	Par Lost 10.213
And thought not much to cloath his Enemies:	Par Lost 10.219
Not unagreeable, to found a path	Par Lost 10.256
Leads thee, I shall not lag behinde, nor erre	Par Lost 10.266
Bound with *Gorgonian* rigor not to move,	Par Lost 10.297
Hee fled, not hoping to escape, but shun	Par Lost 10.339
Not instant, but of future time. With joy	Par Lost 10.345
Thy Trophies, which thou view'st as not thine own,	Par Lost 10.355
What thy hands builded not, thy Wisdom gain'd	Par Lost 10.373
There didst not; there let him still Victor sway,	Par Lost 10.376
For in possession such, not onely of right,	Par Lost 10.461
Mee not, but the brute Serpent in whose shape	Par Lost 10.495
His Seed, when is not set, shall bruise my head:	Par Lost 10.499
A World who would not purchase with a bruise,	Par Lost 10.500
Of public scorn; he wonderd, but not long	Par Lost 10.509
And *Dipsas* (not so thick swarm'd once the Soil	Par Lost 10.526
1667 'Not'	
Though to delude them sent, could not abstain,	Par Lost 10.557
This more delusive, not the touch, but taste	Par Lost 10.563
Into the same illusion, not as Man	Par Lost 10.571
Close following pace for pace, not mounted yet	Par Lost 10.589
With travail difficult, not better farr	Par Lost 10.593
Kept in that State, had not the folly of Man	Par Lost 10.619
And know not that I call'd and drew them thither	Par Lost 10.629
Had rounded still th' *Horizon*, and not known	Par Lost 10.684
My own deservings; but this will not serve;	Par Lost 10.727
Concurd not to my being, it were but right	Par Lost 10.747
The good I sought not. To the loss of that,	Par Lost 10.752
Wherefore didst thou beget me? I sought it not	Par Lost 10.762
That proud excuse? yet him not thy election,	Par Lost 10.764
Is his wrauth also? be it, man is not so,	Par Lost 10.795
Of weakness, not of Power. Will he, draw out,	Par Lost 10.801
Not to th' extent of thir own Spheare. But say	Par Lost 10.808
That Death be not one stroak, as I suppos'd,	Par Lost 10.809
Not to do onely, but to will the same	Par Lost 10.826
Through the still Night, not now, as ere man fell,	Par Lost 10.846
The day of his offence. Why comes not Death,	Par Lost 10.854
Justice Divine not hast'n to be just?	Par Lost 10.857
But Death comes not at call, Justice Divine	Par Lost 10.858
Mends not her slowest pace for prayers or cries.	Par Lost 10.859
I had persisted happie, had not thy pride	Par Lost 10.874
Not to be trusted, longing to be seen	Par Lost 10.877
And understood not all was but a shew	Par Lost 10.883
Of Nature, and not fill the World at once	Par Lost 10.892
Mankind? this mischief had not then befall'n,	Par Lost 10.895
He added not, and from her turn'd, but *Eve*	Par Lost 10.909
Not so repulst, with Tears that ceas'd not flowing,	Par Lost 10.910
Forsake me not thus, *Adam*, witness Heav'n	Par Lost 10.914

Not*(cont)*

I beg, and clasp thy knees; bereave me not,	Par Lost 10.918
That cruel Serpent: On me exercise not	Par Lost 10.927
So now of what thou knowst not, who desir'st	Par Lost 10.948
Living or dying, from thee I will not hide	Par Lost 10.974
Let us seek Death, or he not found, supply	Par Lost 10.1001
Not thy contempt, but anguish and regret	Par Lost 10.1018
The penaltie pronounc't, doubt not but God	Par Lost 10.1022
So snatcht will not exempt us from the paine	Par Lost 10.1025
Beseeching him, so as we need not fear	Par Lost 10.1082
Not of mean suiters, nor important less	Par Lost 11.9
Good or not good ingraft, my Merit those	Par Lost 11.35
To mitigate thus plead, not to reverse)	Par Lost 11.41
Through Heav'ns wide bounds; from them I will not hide	Par Lost 11.68
Good by it self, and Evil not at all.	Par Lost 11.89
Dismiss them not disconsolate; reveale	Par Lost 11.113
Which then not minded in dismay, yet now	Par Lost 11.156
Subscrib'd not; Nature first gave Signs, imprest	Par Lost 11.182
Pursuing, not unmov'd to *Eve* thus spake.	Par Lost 11.192
He err'd not, for by this the heav'nly Bands	Par Lost 11.208
A glorious Apparition, had not doubt	Par Lost 11.211
Not that more glorious, when the Angels met	Par Lost 11.213
Not unperceav'd of *Adam*, who to *Eve*,	Par Lost 11.224
Invests him coming? yet not terrible,	Par Lost 11.233
But solemn and sublime, whom not to offend,	Par Lost 11.236
Not in his shape Celestial, but as Man	Par Lost 11.239
Inclin'd not, but his coming thus declar'd.	Par Lost 11.250
Permits not; to remove thee I am come,	Par Lost 11.260
He added not, for *Adam* at the newes	Par Lost 11.263
Lament not *Eve*, but patiently resigne	Par Lost 11.287
Thus over-fond, on that which is not thine;	Par Lost 11.289
Thy going is not lonely, with thee goes	Par Lost 11.290
Of him who all things can, I would not cease	Par Lost 11.309
Not this Rock onely; his Omnipresence fills	Par Lost 11.336
No despicable gift; surmise not then	Par Lost 11.340
Yet doubt not but in Vallie and in plaine	Par Lost 11.349
Not higher that Hill nor wider looking round,	Par Lost 11.381
Turchestan-born; nor could his eye not ken	Par Lost 11.396
The others not, for his was not sincere;	Par Lost 11.443
Drie-ey'd behold? *Adam* could not, but wept,	Par Lost 11.495
Though not of Woman born; compassion quell'd	Par Lost 11.496
What we receive, would either not accept	Par Lost 11.505
Under inhuman pains? Why should not Man,	Par Lost 11.511
Disfiguring not Gods likeness, but thir own,	Par Lost 11.521
Gods Image did not reverence in themselves.	Par Lost 11.525
The rule of not too much, by temperance taught	Par Lost 11.531
Due nourishment, not gluttonous delight,	Par Lost 11.533
Gatherd, not harshly pluckt, for death mature:	Par Lost 11.537
Henceforth I flie not Death, nor would prolong	Par Lost 11.547
Not hid, nor those things last which might preserve	Par Lost 11.579
Long had not walkt, when from the Tents behold	Par Lost 11.581
Of love and youth not lost, Songs, Garlands, Flours,	Par Lost 11.594
To whom thus *Michael*. Judg not what is best	Par Lost 11.603
Had not a Cloud descending snatch'd him thence	Par Lost 11.670
Deaths Ministers, not Men, who thus deal Death	Par Lost 11.676
But who was that Just Man, whom had not Heav'n	Par Lost 11.681
Man is not whom to warne: those few escap't	Par Lost 11.777
That he relents, not to blot out mankind,	Par Lost 11.891
Of proud ambitious heart, who not content	Par Lost 12.25
Hunting (and Men not Beasts shall be his game)	Par Lost 12.30
Not understood, till hoarse, and all in rage,	Par Lost 12.58
Authoritie usurpt, from God not giv'n:	Par Lost 12.66
He made not Lord; such title to himself	Par Lost 12.70
Stayes not on Man; to God his Tower intends	Par Lost 12.73
And famish him of Breath, if not of Bread?	Par Lost 12.78
Reason in man obscur'd, or not obeyd,	Par Lost 12.86
Not knowing to what Land, yet firm believes:	Par Lost 12.127
I see him, but thou canst not, with what Faith	Par Lost 12.128
Not wandring poor, but trusting all his wealth	Par Lost 12.133
What it devours not, Herb, or Fruit, or Graine,	Par Lost 12.184
Through the wilde Desert, not the readiest way,	Par Lost 12.216
Untraind in Armes, where rashness leads not on.	Par Lost 12.222
This yet I apprehend not, why to those	Par Lost 12.280
To whom thus *Michael*. Doubt not but that sin	Par Lost 12.285
Law can discover sin, but not remove,	Par Lost 12.290
Perform, and not performing cannot live.	Par Lost 12.299
And therefore shall not *Moses*, though of God	Par Lost 12.307
The Scepter, and regard not *Davids* Sons,	Par Lost 12.357
To whom thus *Michael*. Dream not of thir fight,	Par Lost 12.386
Of head or heel: not therefore joynes the Son	Par Lost 12.388
Disabl'd not to give thee thy deaths wound:	Par Lost 12.392
Not by destroying *Satan*, but his works	Par Lost 12.394
To save them, not thir own, though legal works.	Par Lost 12.410
Neglect not, and the benefit imbrace	Par Lost 12.426
By Faith not void of workes: this God-like act	Par Lost 12.427
Not onely to the Sons of *Abrahams* Loines	Par Lost 12.447
His people, who defend? will they not deale	Par Lost 12.483
What man can do against them, not affraid,	Par Lost 12.493
Though not but by the Spirit understood.	Par Lost 12.514
Thir own Faith not anothers: for on Earth	Par Lost 12.528
Of all the rest: then wilt thou not be loath	Par Lost 12.585
And thus with words not sad she him receav'd.	Par Lost 12.609
Well pleas'd, but answer'd not; for now too nigh	Par Lost 12.625
Worthy t' have not remain'd so long unsung.	Par Reg 1.17
Would not be last, and with the voice divine	Par Reg 1.35
Broken be not intended all our power	Par Reg 1.61
Not thence to be more pure, but to receive	Par Reg 1.77
Thenceforth the Nations may not doubt; I saw	Par Reg 1.79

Not*(cont)*

And what will he not do to advance his Son?	Par Reg 1.88
Not force, but well couch't fraud, well woven snares,	Par Reg 1.97
Now entring his great duel, not of arms,	Par Reg 1.174
And was admir'd by all, yet this not all	Par Reg 1.214
Not wilfully mis-doing, but unware	Par Reg 1.225
A Star, not seen before in Heaven appearing	Par Reg 1.249
Not knew by sight) now come, who was to come	Par Reg 1.271
I learn not yet, perhaps I need not know;	Par Reg 1.292
The way he came not having mark'd, return	Par Reg 1.297
Or harbour'd in one Cave, is not reveal'd;	Par Reg 1.307
Durst ever, who return'd, and dropt not here	Par Reg 1.324
What other way I see not, for we here	Par Reg 1.338
Think'st thou such force in Bread? is it not written	Par Reg 1.347
Man lives not by Bread only, but each Word	Par Reg 1.349
Kept not my happy Station, but was driv'n	Par Reg 1.360
Yet to that hideous place not so confin'd	Par Reg 1.362
To be belov'd of God, I have not lost	Par Reg 1.379
I lost not what I lost, rather by them	Par Reg 1.390
If not disposer; lend them oft my aid,	Par Reg 1.393
That fellowship in pain divides not smart,	Par Reg 1.401
And not well understood as good not known?	Par Reg 1.437
And run not sooner to his fatal snare?	Par Reg 1.441
To thee not known, whence hast thou then thy truth,	Par Reg 1.446
And urg'd me hard with doings, which not will	Par Reg 1.469
And not inforc'd oft-times to part from truth;	Par Reg 1.472
Vertue, who follow not her lore: permit me	Par Reg 1.483
Inspir'd; disdain not such access to me.	Par Reg 1.492
I bid not or forbid; do as thou find'st	Par Reg 1.495
Permission from above; thou canst not more.	Par Reg 1.496
He added not; and Satan bowing low	Par Reg 1.497
With others though in Holy Writ not nam'd,	Par Reg 2.8
Lay on his Providence; he will not fail	Par Reg 2.54
Others return'd from Baptism, not her Son,	Par Reg 2.61
I will not argue that, nor will repine.	Par Reg 2.94
He could not lose himself; but went about	Par Reg 2.98
Have we not seen, or by relation heard,	Par Reg 2.182
Delight not all; among the Sons of Men,	Par Reg 2.192
Of honour, wealth, high fare, aim'd not beyond	Par Reg 2.202
Lawful desires of Nature, not beyond;	Par Reg 2.230
To Vertue I impute not, or count part	Par Reg 2.248
Of what I suffer here; if Nature need not,	Par Reg 2.249
Not rustic as before, but seemlier clad,	Par Reg 2.299
Not without hunger. Others of some note,	Par Reg 2.306
Of *Israel* here had famish'd, had not God	Par Reg 2.311
Would'st thou not eat? Thereafter as I like	Par Reg 2.321
Hast thou not right to all Created things,	Par Reg 2.324
Owe not all Creatures by just right to thee	Par Reg 2.325
These are not Fruits forbidden, no interdict	Par Reg 2.369
Said'st thou not that to all things I had right?	Par Reg 2.379
I can at will, doubt not, as soon as thou,	Par Reg 2.383
Why shouldst thou not accept it? but I see	Par Reg 2.398
Thou art not to be harm'd, therefore not mov'd;	Par Reg 2.407
Not difficult, if thou hearken to me,	Par Reg 2.428
To me is not unknown what hath been done	Par Reg 2.444
Worthy of Memorial) canst thou not remember	Par Reg 2.445
Extol not Riches then, the toyl of Fools,	Par Reg 2.453
The wise mans cumbrance if not snare, more apt	Par Reg 2.454
Riches and Realms; yet not for that a Crown,	Par Reg 2.458
And who attains not, ill aspires to rule	Par Reg 2.469
Could not sustain thy Prowess, or subsist	Par Reg 3.19
Quench not the thirst of glory, but augment.	Par Reg 3.38
Inglorious: but thou yet art not too late.	Par Reg 3.42
They praise and they admire they know not what;	Par Reg 3.52
And know not whom, but as one leads the other;	Par Reg 3.53
To things not glorious, men not worthy of fame.	Par Reg 3.70
Who names not now with honour patient *Job?*	Par Reg 3.95
Oft not deserv'd? I seek not mine, but his	Par Reg 3.106
Think not so slight of glory; therein least	Par Reg 3.109
Though chiefly not for glory as prime end,	Par Reg 3.123
And not returning that would likeliest render	Par Reg 3.130
That who advance his glory, not thir own,	Par Reg 3.143
Satan had not to answer, but stood struck	Par Reg 3.146
Worth or not worth the seeking, let it pass:	Par Reg 3.151
Be now in powerful hands, that will not part	Par Reg 3.155
So did not *Machabeus:* he indeed	Par Reg 3.165
If Kingdom move thee not, let move thee Zeal,	Par Reg 3.171
And Duty; Zeal and Duty are not slow;	Par Reg 3.172
Know'st thou not that my rising is thy fall,	Par Reg 3.201
Raign or raign not; though to that gentle brow	Par Reg 3.215
The world thou hast not seen, much less her glory,	Par Reg 3.236
Such forces met not, nor so wide a camp,	Par Reg 3.337
That thou may'st know I seek not to engage	Par Reg 3.347
Thy Vertue, and not every way secure	Par Reg 3.348
By him thou shalt regain, without him not,	Par Reg 3.371
Shalt raign, and *Rome* or *Caesar* not need fear.	Par Reg 3.385
Were better farthest off) is not yet come;	Par Reg 3.397
When that comes think not thou to find me slack	Par Reg 3.398
Yet gives not o're though desperate of success,	Par Reg 4.23
Another plain, long but in bredth not wide;	Par Reg 4.27
Will be for thee no sitting, or not long	Par Reg 4.107
For him I was not sent, nor yet to free	Par Reg 4.131
Is not for thee to know, nor me to tell.	Par Reg 4.153
No trifle; yet with this reserve, not else,	Par Reg 4.165
Be not so sore offended, Son of God;	Par Reg 4.196
Advise thee, gain them as thou canst, or not.	Par Reg 4.211
Teaching not taught; the childhood shews the man,	Par Reg 4.220
All knowledge is not couch't in *Moses* Law,	Par Reg 4.225

Not(*cont*)

Think not but that I know these things, or think	Par Reg 4.286
I know them not; not therefore am I short	Par Reg 4.287
Equal to God, oft shames not to prefer,	Par Reg 4.303
Alas what can they teach, and not mislead;	Par Reg 4.309
True wisdom, finds her not, or by delusion	Par Reg 4.319
Incessantly, and to his reading brings not	Par Reg 4.323
Such are from God inspir'd, not such from thee;	Par Reg 4.350
By light of Nature not in all quite lost.	Par Reg 4.352
Real or Allegoric I discern not,	Par Reg 4.390
Not yet expir'd) and to the Wilderness	Par Reg 4.395
And harmless, if not wholsom, as a sneeze	Par Reg 4.458
Did I not tell thee, if thou didst reject	Par Reg 4.467
Not when it must, but when it may be best.	Par Reg 4.476
If thou observe not this, be sure to find,	Par Reg 4.477
And staid not, but in brief him answer'd thus.	Par Reg 4.485
Mee worse then wet thou find'st not; other harm	Par Reg 4.486
As false portents, not sent from God, but thee;	Par Reg 4.491
Though not to be Baptiz'd, by voice from Heav'n	Par Reg 4.512
Not more; for Honours, Riches, Kingdoms, Glory	Par Reg 4.536
Now shew thy Progeny; if not to stand,	Par Reg 4.554
Tempt not the Lord thy God, he said and stood.	Par Reg 4.561
Her riddle, and him, who solv'd it not, devour'd;	Par Reg 4.573
But thou, Infernal Serpent, shalt not long	Par Reg 4.618
Thy wound, yet not thy last and deadliest wound	Par Reg 4.622
Yet stay, let me not rashly call in doubt	Samson 43
Under the Seal of silence could not keep,	Samson 49
By weakest suttleties, not made to rule,	Samson 56
But peace, I must not quarrel with the will	Samson 60
And not as feeling through all parts diffus'd,	Samson 96
Then had I not been thus exil'd from light;	Samson 98
Buried, yet not exempt	Samson 103
Let us not break in upon him;	Samson 116
For him I reckon not in high estate	Samson 170
We come thy friends and neighbours not unknown	Samson 180
Now of my own experience, not by talk,	Samson 188
Not to be found, though sought. Yee see, O friends,	Samson 193
Am I not sung and proverbd for a Fool	Samson 203
In every street, do they not say, how well	Samson 204
Chor. Tax not divine disposal, wisest Men	Samson 210
Deject not then so overmuch thy self,	Samson 213
Mee, not my Parents, that I sought to wed,	Samson 220
The daughter of an Infidel: they knew not	Samson 221
She was not the prime cause, but I my self,	Samson 234
Sam. That fault I take not on me, but transfer	Samson 241
Acknowledg'd not, or not at all consider'd	Samson 245
But they persisted deaf, and would not seem	Samson 249
Not flying, but fore-casting in what place	Samson 254
Not worse then by his shield and spear	Samson 284
Had not his prowess quell'd thir pride	Samson 286
But Gods propos'd deliverance not so.	Samson 292
Unless there be who think not God at all,	Samson 295
Yet more there be who doubt his ways not just,	Samson 300
Who made our Laws to bind us, not himself,	Samson 309
He would not else who never wanted means,	Samson 315
Unchaste was subsequent, her stain not his.	Samson 325
In mortal strength! and oh what not in man	Samson 349
He should not so o'rewhelm, and as a thrall	Samson 370
Sam. Appoint not heavenly disposition, Father,	Samson 373
But warn'd by oft experience: did not she	Samson 382
Tongue-batteries, she surceas'd not day nor night	Samson 404
These rags, this grinding, is not yet so base	Samson 415
That saw not how degeneratly I serv'd.	Samson 419
Rather approv'd them not; but thou didst plead	Samson 421
I state not that; this I am sure; our Foes	Samson 424
The anguish of my Soul, that suffers not	Samson 458
Will not connive, or linger, thus provok'd,	Samson 466
Nothing more certain, will not long defer	Samson 474
Thou must not in the mean while here forgot	Samson 479
But I Gods counsel have not kept, his holy secret	Samson 497
But act not in thy own affliction, Son,	Samson 503
And let another hand, not thine, exact	Samson 507
Reject not then what offerd means, who knows	Samson 516
Sam. But what avail'd this temperance, not compleat	Samson 558
Better at home lie bed-rid, not only idle,	Samson 579
His might continues in thee not for naught,	Samson 588
Man. Believe not these suggestions which proceed	Samson 599
Must not omit a Fathers timely care	Samson 602
Sam. O that torment should not be confin'd	Samson 606
My griefs not only pain me	Samson 617
Not evenly, as thou rul'st	Samson 671
Though not disordinate, yet causless suffring	Samson 701
So deal not with this once thy glorious Champion,	Samson 705
Sam. My Wife, my Traytress, let her not come near me.	Samson 725
My penance hath not slack'n'd, though my pardon	Samson 738
Not truly penitent, but chief to try	Samson 754
With goodness principl'd not to reject	Samson 760
If not by quick destruction soon cut off	Samson 764
Dal. Yet hear me *Samson;* not that I endeavour	Samson 766
By it self, with aggravations not surcharg'd,	Samson 769
Was it not weakness also to make known	Samson 778
But I to enemies reveal'd, and should not.	Samson 782
The gentler, if severely thou exact not	Samson 788
Mine and Loves prisoner, not the *Philistines*,	Samson 808
Be not unlike all others, not austere	Samson 815
In uncompassionate anger do not so.	Samson 818
That malice not repentance brought thee hither,	Samson 821
It was not gold, as to my charge thou lay'st,	Samson 849

Not(*cont*)

Was not behind, but ever at my ear,	Samson 858
Not out of levity, but over-powr'd	Samson 880
Thou mine, not theirs: if aught against my life	Samson 888
Not therefore to be obey'd. But zeal mov'd thee;	Samson 895
Bear not too sensibly, nor still insist	Samson 913
Where other senses want not their delights	Samson 916
I to the Lords will intercede, not doubting	Samson 920
It fits not; thou and I long since are twain;	Samson 929
Sam. Not for thy life, lest fierce remembrance wake	Samson 952
Fame if not double-fac't is double-mouth'd,	Samson 971
Not less renown'd then in Mount *Ephraim*,	Samson 988
Not wedlock-trechery endangering life.	Samson 1009
Cho. It is not vertue, wisdom, valour, wit,	Samson 1010
Had not so soon preferr'd	Samson 1019
Capacity not rais'd to apprehend	Samson 1028
That either they love nothing, or not long?	Samson 1033
On his whole life, not sway'd	Samson 1059
Sam. Or peace or not, alike to me he comes.	Samson 1074
Har. I come not *Samson*, to condole thy chance,	Samson 1076
As these perhaps, yet wish it had not been,	Samson 1077
Sam. The way to know were not to see but taste.	Samson 1091
Sam. Boast not of what thou wouldst have done, but do	Samson 1104
Who durst not with thir whole united powers	Samson 1110
Close-banded durst attaque me, no not sleeping,	Samson 1113
Which long shall not with-hold mee from thy head,	Samson 1125
Har. Thou durst not thus disparage glorious arms	Samson 1130
Thir ornament and safety, had not spells	Samson 1132
Har. Presume not on thy God, what e're he be,	Samson 1156
Thee he regards not, owns not, hath cut off	Samson 1157
Justly, yet despair not of his final pardon	Samson 1171
Har. Is not thy Nation subject to our Lords?	Samson 1182
Into our hands: for hadst thou not committed	Samson 1185
Me their Deliverer sent would not receive,	Samson 1214
Had not disabl'd me, not all your force:	Samson 1219
Come nearer, part not hence so slight inform'd;	Samson 1229
But take good heed my hand survey not thee.	Samson 1230
Hear these dishonours, and not render death?	Samson 1232
Sam. I dread him not, nor all his Giant-brood,	Samson 1247
Will not dare mention, lest a question rise	Samson 1254
Whether he durst accept the offer or not,	Samson 1255
And that he durst not plain enough appear'd.	Samson 1256
Is hate, not help to me, it may with mine	Samson 1266
Off. This answer, be assur'd, will not content them.	Samson 1322
Sam. Have they not Sword-players, and ev'ry sort	Samson 1323
Do they not seek occasion of new quarrels	Samson 1329
Return the way thou cam'st, I will not come.	Samson 1332
Joyn'd with extream contempt? I will not come.	Samson 1342
Sam. Not in thir Idol-worship, but by labour	Samson 1365
Chor. Where the heart joins not, outward acts defile not.	Samson 1368
Not dragging? the *Philistian* Lords command.	Samson 1371
For some important cause, thou needst not doubt.	Samson 1379
Because they shall not trail me through thir streets	Samson 1402
And for a life who will not change his purpose?	Samson 1406
I will not wish, lest it perhaps offend them	Samson 1414
I know not. Lords are Lordliest in thir wine;	Samson 1418
Was not at present here to find my Son,	Samson 1446
No, I am fixt not to part hence without him.	Samson 1481
And quit: not wanting him, I shall want nothing.	Samson 1484
And I perswade me God had not permitted	Samson 1495
Of faithful Souldiery, were not his purpose	Samson 1498
Not to sit idle with so great a gift	Samson 1500
And since his strength with eye-sight was not lost,	Samson 1502
Chor. Thy hopes are not ill founded nor seem vain	Samson 1504
From slaughter of one foe could not ascend.	Samson 1518
From other hands we need not much to fear.	Samson 1526
To have guided me aright, I know not how,	Samson 1547
With rueful cry, yet what it was we hear not,	Samson 1553
Man. Sad, but thou knowst to *Israelites* not saddest	Samson 1560
Not to be absent at that spectacle.	Samson 1604
Not without wonder or delight beheld.	Samson 1642
Thir choice nobility and flower, not only	Samson 1654
Not willingly, but tangl'd in the fold,	Samson 1665
With God not parted from him, as was feard,	Samson 1719
(*Gaza* is not in plight to say us nay)	Samson 1729
I would not soil these pure Ambrosial weeds,	Mask 16
On *Circes* Iland fell (who knows not *Circe*	Mask 50
Not once perceive their foul disfigurement,	Mask 74
Which must not be, for that's against my course;	Mask 159
Baited with reasons not unplausible	Mask 162
But where they are, and why they came not back,	Mask 191
These thoughts may startle well, but not astound	Mask 210
line not in Bridgewater ms	
I did not err, there does a sable cloud	Mask 223
line not in Bridgewater ms	
Prompt me; and they perhaps are not far off.	Mask 229
Canst thou not tell me of a gentle Pair	Mask 236
Not any boast of skill, but extreme shift	Mask 273
Eld. Bro. Peace brother, be not over-exquisite	Mask 359
line not in Bridgewater ms	
line not in Trinity ms	
I do not think my sister so to seek,	Mask 366
(Not being in danger, as I trust she is not)	Mask 370
Of night, or lonelines it recks me not,	Mask 404
Of our unowned sister. *Eld. Bro*. I do not, brother,	Mask 407
My sister is not so defenceless left	Mask 414
Which you remember not. 2. *Bro*. What hidden strength,	Mask 416
Be it not don in pride, or in presumption.	Mask 431

Not(*cont*)

Not harsh, and crabbed as dull fools suppose,	Mask 477
If he be friendly he comes well, if not,	Mask 488
Com not too neer, you fall on iron stakes else.	Mask 491
I came not here on such a trivial toy	Mask 502
Of pilfering Woolf, not all the fleecy wealth	Mask 504
How chance she is not in your company?	Mask 508
Spir. Ile tell ye, 'tis not vain, or fabulous,	Mask 513
Longer I durst not stay, but soon I guess't	Mask 577
But furder know I not. 2. *Bro*. O night and shades,	Mask 580
Lean on it safely, not a period	Mask 585
Surpriz'd by unjust force, but not enthrall'd,	Mask 590
Bore a bright golden flowre, but not in this soyl:	Mask 633
line not in Bridgewater ms	
Root-bound, that fled *Apollo*, *La*. Fool do not boast,	Mask 662
Trinity ms 'doe not boast' ←'thou art over proud'	
Thou canst not touch the freedom of my minde	Mask 663
Not that *Nepenthes* which the wife of *Thone*,	Mask 675
This will restore all soon. *La*. 'Twill not false traitor,	Mask 690
Trinity ms 't'will not' ←'stand back'	
'Twill not restore the truth and honesty	Mask 691
I would not taste thy treasonous offer; none	Mask 702
Trinity ms 'would not taste' ←'should reject' ←'hate it from thy hands'	
And that which is not good, is not delicious	Mask 704
Not half his riches known, and yet despis'd,	Mask 724
And live like Natures bastards, not her sons,	Mask 727
List Lady be not coy, and be not cosen'd	Mask 737
line not in Bridgewater ms	
Beauty is natures coyn, must not be hoorded,	Mask 739
line not in Bridgewater ms	
La. I had not thought to have unlockt my lips	Mask 756
Impostor do not charge most innocent nature,	Mask 762
And thou art worthy that thou shouldst not know	Mask 788
line not in Trinity ms	
line not in Bridgewater ms	
Thou art not fit to hear thy self convinc't;	Mask 792
line not in Trinity ms	
line not in Bridgewater ms	
Co. She fables not, I feel that I do fear	Mask 800
line not in Bridgewater ms	
line not in Trinity ms	
And though not mortal, yet a cold shuddring dew	Mask 802
line not in Trinity ms	
line not in Bridgewater ms	
I must not suffer this, yet 'tis but the lees	Mask 809
Yet stay, be not disturb'd, now I bethink me,	Mask 820
There is a gentle Nymph not farr from hence,	Mask 824
That bends not as I tread,	Mask 899
Not a waste, or needless sound	Mask 942
And not many furlongs thence	Mask 946
but soft I was not sent to court your wonder	Mask Tr. ms 10.16
be it not don in pride or in praesumption	Mask Tr. ms 16.56
were they not taken thence	Mask Tr. ms 22.07
Som time walking not unseen	Allegro 57
That ten day-labourers could not end,	Allegro 109
Such mixture was not held a stain)	Penseroso 26
Or if the Ayr will not permit,	Penseroso 77
Not trickt and frounc't as she was wont,	Penseroso 123
Juno dare's not give her odds;	Arcades 23
All *Arcadia* hath not seen.	Arcades 95
Trinity ms defective here	
All *Arcadia* hath not seen.	Arcades 109
Young *Lycidas*, and hath not left his peer:	Lycidas 9
Who would not sing for *Lycidas*? he knew	Lycidas 10
He must not flote upon his watry bear	Lycidas 12
Mean while the Rural ditties were not mute,	Lycidas 32
From the glad sound would not be absent long,	Lycidas 35
Were it not better don as others use,	Lycidas 67
And slits the thin spun life. But not the praise,	Lycidas 76
They knew not of his story,	Lycidas 95
That not a blast was from his dungeon stray'd,	Lycidas 97
The hungry Sheep look up, and are not fed,	Lycidas 125
For *Lycidas* your sorrow is not dead,	Lycidas 166
Say Heav'nly Muse, shall not thy sacred vein	Nativity 15
The Trumpet spake not to the armed throng,	Nativity 58
And will not take their flight,	Nativity 72
This must not yet be so,	Nativity 150
Not half so far casts his usurped sway,	Nativity 170
Now sits not girt with Tapers holy shine,	Nativity 202
Not *Typhon* huge ending in snaky twine:	Nativity 226
If likewise he some fair one wedded not,	Fair Inf 11
Yet art thou not inglorious in thy fate;	Fair Inf 22
Yet can I not perswade me thou art dead	Fair Inf 29
But oh why didst thou not stay here below	Fair Inf 64
Thou needst not be ambitious to be first,	Vacation 11
I pray thee then deny me not thy aide	Vacation 15
Not those new fangled toys, and triming slight	Vacation 19
To find a Foe it shall not be his hap,	Vacation 83
What power, what force, what mighty spell, if not	Vacation 89
Had burial, yet not laid in earth,	Winchester 32
Was not long a living Tomb.	Winchester 34
Had not his weekly cours of carriage fail'd;	Carrier 10
If I may not carry, sure Ile ne're be fetch'd,	Another 18
line not in 1640, 1657, 1658 texts	
Lift not thy spear against the Muses Bowre,	Sonnet 8, 9
And Hope that reaps not shame. Therefore be sure	Sonnet 9, 11
Hated not Learning wors then Toad or Asp;	Sonnet 11, 13

Not(*cont*)

Words with just note and accent, not to scan	Sonnet 13, 3
Staid not behind, nor in the grave were trod;	Sonnet 14, 6
Not of warr onely, but detractions rude,	Sonnet 16, 2
The helme of Rome, when gownes not armes repelld	Sonnet 17, 3
Forget not: in thy book record their groanes	Sonnet 18, 5
That murmur, soon replies, God doth not need	Sonnet 19, 9
To interpose them oft, is not unwise.	Sonnet 20, 14
Or man or woman. Yet I argue not	Sonnet 22, 6
From them whose sin ye envi'd, not abhor'd,	Forcers 4
Trinity ms 'nott'	
Bless'd is the man who hath not walk'd astray	Psalm 1, 1
Of sinners hath not stood, and in the seat	Psalm 1, 3
Of scorners hath not sate. But in the great	Psalm 1, 4
To yield his fruit, and his leaf shall not fall,	Psalm 1, 9
Not so the wicked, but as chaff which fann'd	Psalm 1, 11
The wind drives, so the wicked shall not stand	Psalm 1, 12
I fear not though incamping round about	Psalm 3, 17
Be aw'd, and do not sin,	Psalm 4, 19
For thou art not a God that takes	Psalm 5, 9
Fools or mad men stand not within thy sight.	Psalm 5, 12
Lord in thine anger do not reprehend me	Psalm 6, 1
And not fre'd my foe for naught;	Psalm 7, 12
If th' unjust will not forbear,	Psalm 7, 45
So shall we not go back from thee	Psalm 80, 73
From whence they might not swerve.	Psalm 81, 16
In Joseph, *not to change*,	Psalm 81, 18
And I to free thee *did not faile*,	Psalm 81, 27
And yet my people would not *hear*,	Psalm 81, 45
They know not nor will understand,	Psalm 82, 17
Be not thou silent *now at length*	Psalm 83, 1
O God hold not thy peace,	Psalm 83, 2
Sit not thou still O God of *strength*	Psalm 83, 3
We cry and do not cease.	Psalm 83, 4
Thou hast not Lord been slack,	Psalm 85, 2
Wilt thou not turn, and *hear our voice*	Psalm 85, 21
Then will he come, and not be slow	Psalm 85, 55
Not thy Conversion, but those rich demaines	Prose 1, 2
Another *Constantine* comes not in hast.	Prose 3, 5
Tis you that say it, not I, you do the deeds,	Prose 8, 1

Note

Tunes her nocturnal Note. Thus with the Year	Par Lost 3.40
Sole, or responsive each to others note	Par Lost 4.683
Not without hunger. Others of some note,	Par Reg 2.306
Words with just note and accent, not to scan	Sonnet 13, 3
Trinity ms 'note' ←'notes'	

Notes

The birds thir notes renew, and bleating herds	Par Lost 2.494
With notes Angelical to many a Harp	Par Lost 2.548
With other notes then to th' *Orphean* Lyre	Par Lost 3.17
Bear on your wings and in your notes his praise;	Par Lost 5.199
Those Notes to Tragic; foul distrust, and breach	Par Lost 9.6
Trills her thick-warbl'd notes the summer long,	Par Reg 4.246
Clear'd up their choicest notes in bush and spray	Par Reg 4.437
Warble his native Wood-notes wilde,	Allegro 134
In notes, with many a winding bout	Allegro 139
Such notes as warbled to the string,	Penseroso 106
With unexpressive notes to Heav'ns new-born Heir.	Nativity 116
And set my Harpe to notes of saddest wo,	Passion 9
Thy liquid notes that close the eye of Day,	Sonnet 1, 5
Warble immortal Notes and *Tuskan* Ayre?	Sonnet 20, 12

Nothing

Say first, for Heav'n hides nothing from thy view	Par Lost 1.27
To nothing this essential, happier farr	Par Lost 2.97
On this side nothing; and by proof we feel	Par Lost 2.101
Have nothing merited, nor can performe	Par Lost 4.418
Think nothing hard, much less to be despaird.	Par Lost 6.495
Then value: Oft times nothing profits more	Par Lost 8.571
Unprais'd: for nothing lovelier can be found	Par Lost 9.232
Nothing imperfet or deficient left	Par Lost 9.345
Or Sex, and apprehended nothing high:	Par Lost 9.574
Them nothing: If they all things, who enclos'd	Par Lost 9.722
He led her nothing loath; Flours were the Couch,	Par Lost 9.1039
And hateful; nothing wants, but that thy shape,	Par Lost 10.869
But *Adam* with such counsel nothing sway'd,	Par Lost 10.1010
Must eat, and on the ground leave nothing green:	Par Lost 12.186
Women, when nothing else, beguil'd the heart	Par Reg 2.169
Nothing but ruin wheresoe're they rove,	Par Reg 3.79
From them who could return him nothing else,	Par Reg 3.129
Hath nothing, and to whom nothing belongs	Par Reg 3.135
Long in preparing, soon to nothing brought,	Par Reg 3.389
Nothing will please the difficult and nice,	Par Reg 4.157
Or nothing more then still to contradict:	Par Reg 4.158
Conjectures, fancies, built on nothing firm.	Par Reg 4.292
To know this only, that he nothing knew;	Par Reg 4.294
In me, of wisdom nothing more then mean;	Samson 207
Nothing of all these evils hath befall'n me	Samson 374
Nothing more certain, will not long defer	Samson 474
Who tempted me, that nothing was design'd	Samson 801
By thy request, who could deny thee nothing;	Samson 881
For peace, reap nothing but repulse and hate?	Samson 966
That either they love nothing, or not long?	Samson 1033
As good for nothing else, no better service	Samson 1163
Sam. No man with-holds thee, nothing from thy hand	Samson 1233
Nothing to do, be sure, that may dishonour	Samson 1385
Yet this be sure, in nothing to comply	Samson 1408
Nothing dishonourable, impure, unworthy	Samson 1424
And quit: not wanting him, I shall want nothing.	Samson 1484

Nothing(*cont*)
Nothing is hard) by miracle restor'd, Samson 1528
Nothing is here for tears, nothing to wail Samson 1721
Dispraise, or blame, nothing but well and fair, Samson 1723
Drink the clear stream, and nothing wear but Freize, Mask 722
Bridgewater ms 'nothinge'
Daily devours apace, and nothing sed, Lycidas 129
Trinity ms 'little' ←'nothing'
1638 'little'
From others he shall stand in need of nothing, Vacation 81
Things false and vain and nothing else but lies? Psalm 4, 12

Notice
To count them things worth notice, till at length Samson 250
A little stay will bring some notice hither, Samson 1536

Notion
So told as earthly notion can receave. Par Lost 7.179
The sublime notion, and high mystery Mask 785
line not in Trinity ms
line not in Bridgewater ms

Notions
Seek them with wandring thoughts, and notions vain. Par Lost 8.187

Notorious
Notorious murder on those thirty men Samson 1186

Notus
Notus and *Afer* black with thundrous Clouds Par Lost 10.702

Nourish
Temper or nourish, or in part shed down Par Lost 4.670
And nourish all things, let your ceasless change Par Lost 5.183
To nourish, and superfluous moist consumes: Par Lost 5.325
O Son, but nourish them and let them soar Par Reg 1.230

Nourisher
These bounties which our Nourisher, from whom Par Lost 5.398

Nourishment
Nor doth the Moon no nourishment exhale Par Lost 5.421
Mans nourishment, by gradual scale sublim'd Par Lost 5.483
Wisdom to Folly, as Nourishment to Winde. Par Lost 7.130
1669 'nourishment'
Due nourishment, not gluttonous delight, Par Lost 11.533

Novelty
This noveltie on Earth, this fair defect Par Lost 10.891

Novice
Timorous and loth, with novice modesty, Par Reg 3.241

Now
Reserv'd him to more wrath; for now the thought Par Lost 1.54
Joynd with me once, now misery hath joynd Par Lost 1.90
Who now triumphs, and in th' excess of joy Par Lost 1.123
But what if he our Conquerour, (whom I now Par Lost 1.143
Perhaps hath spent his shafts, and ceases now Par Lost 1.176
Who now is Sovran can dispose and bid Par Lost 1.246
New courage and revive, though now they lye Par Lost 1.279
Warriers, the Flowr of Heav'n, once yours, now lost, Par Lost 1.316
To adore the Conquerour? who now beholds Par Lost 1.323
Though of thir Names in heav'nly Records now Par Lost 1.361
Thir painful steps o're the burnt soyle; and now Par Lost 1.562
Thir number last he summs. And now his heart Par Lost 1.571
For ever now to have thir lot in pain, Par Lost 1.608
Stands on the blasted Heath. He now prepar'd Par Lost 1.615
Fell long before; nor aught avail'd him now Par Lost 1.748
Behold a wonder! they but now who seemd Par Lost 1.777
Now less then smallest Dwarfs, in narrow room Par Lost 1.779
More then can be in Heav'n, we now return Par Lost 2.37
We now debate; who can advise, may speak. Par Lost 2.42
That fought in Heav'n; now fiercer by despair: Par Lost 2.45
Contrive who need, or when they need, not now Par Lost 2.53
The sentence of thir Conquerour: This is now Par Lost 2.208
As soft as now severe, our temper chang'd Par Lost 2.276
Had rous'd the Sea, now with hoarse cadence lull Par Lost 2.287
Ethereal Vertues; or these Titles now Par Lost 2.311
All circumspection, and we now no less Par Lost 2.414
Satan, whom now transcendent glory rais'd Par Lost 2.427
Others among the chief might offer now Par Lost 2.469
Now shaves with level wing the Deep, then soares Par Lost 2.634
Satan was now at hand, and from his seat Par Lost 2.674
To meet so great a foe: and now great deeds Par Lost 2.722
I know thee not, nor ever saw till now Par Lost 2.744
Now in thine eye so foul, once deemd so fair Par Lost 2.748
Pregnant by thee, and now excessive grown Par Lost 2.779
Soon learnd, now milder, and thus answerd smooth. Par Lost 2.816
Then sweet, now sad to mention, through dire change Par Lost 2.820
Should be, and, by concurring signs, ere now Par Lost 2.831
Then this more secret now design'd, I haste Par Lost 2.838
Half flying; behoves him now both Oare and Saile. Par Lost 2.942
Now lately Heaven and Earth, another World Par Lost 2.1004
But glad that now his Sea should find a shore, Par Lost 2.1011
But now at last the sacred influence Par Lost 2.1034
That *Satan* with less toil, and now with ease Par Lost 2.1041
Thee I re-visit now with bolder wing, Par Lost 3.13
Now had the Almighty Father from above, Par Lost 3.56
In the dun Air sublime, and ready now Par Lost 3.72
Upon his own rebellious head. And now Par Lost 3.86
And now without redemption all mankind Par Lost 3.222
Though now to Death I yield, and am his due Par Lost 3.245
Now in loose Garlands thick thrown off, the bright Par Lost 3.362
It seem'd, now seems a boundless Continent Par Lost 3.423
And now Saint *Peter* at Heav'ns Wicket seems Par Lost 3.484
To wait them with his Keys, and now at foot Par Lost 3.485
Long after, now unpeopl'd, and untrod; Par Lost 3.497
Satan from hence now on the lower stair Par Lost 3.540

Now(*cont*)
Which now the Rising Sun guilds with his beams. Par Lost 3.551
Culminate from th' *Aequator*, as they now Par Lost 3.617
Glad was the Spirit impure as now in hope Par Lost 3.630
And now a stripling Cherube he appeers, Par Lost 3.636
Where no ill seems: Which now for once beguil'd Par Lost 3.689
Wo to the inhabitants on Earth! that now, Par Lost 4.5
Haply so scap'd his mortal snare; for now Par Lost 4.8
Satan, now first inflam'd with rage, came down, Par Lost 4.9
Now rowling, boiles in his tumultuous brest, Par Lost 4.16
By change of place: Now conscience wakes despair Par Lost 4.23
Sometimes towards *Eden* which now in his view Par Lost 4.27
Which now sat high in his Meridian Towre: Par Lost 4.30
Chose freely what it now so justly rues. Par Lost 4.72
Now nearer, Crowns with her enclosure green, Par Lost 4.133
That Lantskip: And of pure now purer aire Par Lost 4.153
All sadness but despair: now gentle gales Par Lost 4.156
Beyond the *Cape of Hope*, and now are past Par Lost 4.160
Now to th' ascent of that steep savage Hill Par Lost 4.172
Beneath him with new wonder now he views Par Lost 4.205
Which from his darksom passage now appeers, Par Lost 4.232
And now divided into four main Streams, Par Lost 4.233
Coucht, and now fild with pasture gazing sat, Par Lost 4.351
Declin'd was hasting now with prone carreer Par Lost 4.353
More woe, the more your taste is now of joy; Par Lost 4.369
As now is enterd; yet no purpos'd foe Par Lost 4.373
By conquering this new World, compels me now Par Lost 4.391
Of those fourfooted kindes, himself now one, Par Lost 4.397
Now other, as thir shape servd best his end Par Lost 4.398
A Lion now he stalkes with fierie glare, Par Lost 4.402
Mine eyes till now, and pin'd with vain desire, Par Lost 4.466
Returnd on that bright beam, whose point now raisd Par Lost 4.590
Bore him slope downward to the Sun now fall'n Par Lost 4.591
Now came still Eevning on, and Twilight gray Par Lost 4.598
Silence was pleas'd: now glow'd the Firmament Par Lost 4.604
Of night, and all things now retir'd to rest Par Lost 4.611
Now falling with soft slumbrous weight inclines Par Lost 4.615
And when we seek, as now, thy gift of sleep. Par Lost 4.735
Now had night measur'd with her shaddowie Cone Par Lost 4.776
Now laid perhaps asleep secure of harme. Par Lost 4.791
Departed from thee, and thou resembl'st now Par Lost 4.839
His heart, not else dismai'd. Now drew they nigh Par Lost 4.861
Hasting this way, and now by glimps discerne Par Lost 4.867
And now returns him from his prison scap't, Par Lost 4.906
And thou sly hypocrite, who now wouldst seem Par Lost 4.957
But mark what I arreede thee now, avant; Par Lost 4.962
What seemd both Spear and Shield: now dreadful deeds Par Lost 4.990
In counterpoise, now ponders all events, Par Lost 4.1001
Then Heav'n permits, nor mine, though doubld now Par Lost 4.1009
Now Morn her rosie steps in th' Eastern Clime Par Lost 5.1
Why sleepst thou *Eve*? now is the pleasant time, Par Lost 5.38
To the night-warbling Bird, that now awake Par Lost 5.40
Tunes sweetest his love-labor'd song; now reignes Par Lost 5.41
That open now thir choicest bosom'd smells Par Lost 5.127
Moon, that now meetst the orient Sun, now fli'st Par Lost 5.175
Ye Mists and Exhalations that now rise Par Lost 5.185
Disperse it, as now light dispels the dark. Par Lost 5.208
Late falln himself from Heav'n, is plotting now Par Lost 5.240
Now on the polar windes, then with quick Fann Par Lost 5.269
Thir glittering Tents he passd, and now is come Par Lost 5.291
Of his coole Bowre, while now the mounted Sun Par Lost 5.300
Inhabitant with God, now know I well Par Lost 5.461
Reignd where these Heav'ns now rowl, where Earth now rests Par Lost 5.578
Him have anointed, whom ye now behold Par Lost 5.605
Listens delighted. Eevning now approach'd Par Lost 5.627
word not in 1667 edition
Now when ambrosial Night with Clouds exhal'd Par Lost 5.642
Satan, so call him now, his former name Par Lost 5.658
Both waking we were one; how then can now Par Lost 5.678
That the most High commanding, now ere Night, Par Lost 5.699
Now ere dim Night had disincumberd Heav'n, Par Lost 5.700
Neerly it now concernes us to be sure Par Lost 5.721
Another now hath to himself ingross't Par Lost 5.775
To one and to his image now proclaim'd? Par Lost 5.784
We know no time when we were not as now; Par Lost 5.859
Will not be now voutsaf't, other Decrees Par Lost 5.884
Is now an Iron Rod to bruise and breake Par Lost 5.887
Seem twilight here; and now went forth the Morn Par Lost 6.12
Judg'd thee perverse: the easier conquest now Par Lost 6.37
Of Battel now began, and rushing sound Par Lost 6.97
Then lighted from his gorgeous Throne, for now Par Lost 6.103
From all: my Sect thou seest, now learn too late Par Lost 6.147
To heav'nly Soules had bin all one; but now Par Lost 6.165
Against his worthier, as thine now serve thee, Par Lost 6.180
The horrid shock: now storming furie rose, Par Lost 6.207
And clamour such as heard in Heav'n till now Par Lost 6.208
Unnam'd in Heav'n, now plenteous, as thou seest Par Lost 6.263
And faithful, now prov'd false. But think not here Par Lost 6.271
Now wav'd thir fierie Swords, and in the Aire Par Lost 6.304
And now thir Mightiest quelld, the battel swerv'd, Par Lost 6.386
Now Night her course began, and over Heav'n Par Lost 6.406
O now in danger tri'd, now known in Armes Par Lost 6.418
Of future we may deem him, though till now Par Lost 6.429
Till now not known, but known as soon contemnd, Par Lost 6.432
Since now we find this our Empyreal form Par Lost 6.433
Now when fair Morn Orient in Heav'n appeerd Par Lost 6.524
By quick contraction or remove; but now Par Lost 6.597
Purest at first, now gross by sinning grown. Par Lost 6.661

Now(*cont*)

Upon confusion rose: and now all Heav'n	Par Lost 6.669
In universal ruin last, and now	Par Lost 6.797
That wisht the Mountains now might be again	Par Lost 6.842
Where now he sits at the right hand of bliss.	Par Lost 6.892
With *Satan*, hee who envies now thy state,	Par Lost 6.900
Who now is plotting how he may seduce	Par Lost 6.901
The doubts that in his heart arose: and now	Par Lost 7.60
Deign to descend now lower, and relate	Par Lost 7.84
On his great Expedition now appeer'd,	Par Lost 7.193
Celestial Equipage; and now came forth	Par Lost 7.203
Be gather'd now ye Waters under Heav'n	Par Lost 7.283
All but within those banks, where Rivers now	Par Lost 7.305
With borders long the Rivers. That Earth now	Par Lost 7.328
Her gather'd beams, great Palace now of Light.	Par Lost 7.363
The grassie Clods now Calv'd, now half appeer'd	Par Lost 7.463
Now Heav'n in all her Glorie shon, and rowld	Par Lost 7.499
Let us make now Man in our image, Man	Par Lost 7.519
Pouderd with Starrs. And now on Earth the Seventh	Par Lost 7.581
Now resting, bless'd and hallowd the Seav'nth day,	Par Lost 7.592
Relate thee; greater now in thy return	Par Lost 7.604
And thy request think now fulfill'd, that ask'd	Par Lost 7.635
Things else by me unsearchable, now heard	Par Lost 8.10
Not Words alone pleas'd her. O when meet now	Par Lost 8.57
And *Raphael* now to *Adam*'s doubt propos'd	Par Lost 8.64
Thir wandring course now high, now low, then hid,	Par Lost 8.126
Ere my remembrance: now hear mee relate	Par Lost 8.204
But thy relation now; for I attend,	Par Lost 8.247
Hee ended, or I heard no more, for now	Par Lost 8.452
That what seemd fair in all the World, seemd now	Par Lost 8.472
Of all thy gifts, nor enviest. I now see	Par Lost 8.494
But I can now no more; the parting Sun	Par Lost 8.630
Venial discourse unblam'd: I now must change	Par Lost 9.5
Now alienated, distance and distaste,	Par Lost 9.9
Twixt Day and Night, and now from end to end	Par Lost 9.51
Of *Gabriel* out of *Eden*, now improv'd	Par Lost 9.54
Now not, though Sin, not Time, first wraught the change,	Par Lost 9.70
Now Land, now Sea, and Shores with Forrest crownd,	Par Lost 9.117
Whether such vertue spent of old now faild	Par Lost 9.145
With Gods to sit the highest, am now constraind	Par Lost 9.164
Now when as sacred Light began to dawne	Par Lost 9.192
Tending to wilde. Thou therefore now advise	Par Lost 9.212
For now, and since first break of dawne the Fiend,	Par Lost 9.412
Then voluble and bold, now hid, now seen	Par Lost 9.436
What pleasing seemd, for her now pleases more,	Par Lost 9.453
And tortures him now more, the more he sees	Par Lost 9.469
Occasion which now smiles, behold alone	Par Lost 9.480
The way which to her ruin now I tend.	Par Lost 9.493
Hee boulder now, uncall'd before her stood;	Par Lost 9.523
Amid the Tree now got, where plenty hung	Par Lost 9.594
She scarse had said, though brief, when now more bold	Par Lost 9.664
Mother of Science, Now I feel thy Power	Par Lost 9.680
Inclinable now grown to touch or taste,	Par Lost 9.742
Intent now wholly on her taste, naught else	Par Lost 9.786
Thy presence, agonie of love till now	Par Lost 9.858
Defac't, deflourd, and now to Death devote?	Par Lost 9.901
Is not so hainous now, foretasted Fruit,	Par Lost 9.929
He ruind, now Mankind; whom will he next?	Par Lost 9.950
Him with her lov'd societie, that now	Par Lost 9.1007
Eve, now I see thou art exact of taste,	Par Lost 9.1017
From this delightful Fruit, nor known till now	Par Lost 9.1023
But come, so well refresh't, now let us play,	Par Lost 9.1027
With ardor to enjoy thee, fairer now	Par Lost 9.1032
Made erre, was now exhal'd, and grosser sleep	Par Lost 9.1049
Encumberd, now had left them, up they rose	Par Lost 9.1051
Our wonted Ornaments now soild and staind,	Par Lost 9.1076
Will dazle now this earthly, with thir blaze	Par Lost 9.1083
But let us now, as in bad plight, devise	Par Lost 9.1091
And full of Peace, now tost and turbulent:	Par Lost 9.1126
Heard not her lore, both in subjection now	Par Lost 9.1128
Remaind still happie, not as now, despoild	Par Lost 9.1138
And am I now upbraided, as the cause	Par Lost 9.1168
That errour now, which is become my crime,	Par Lost 9.1181
In eevn scale. But fall'n he is, and now	Par Lost 10.47
Now was the Sun in Western cadence low	Par Lost 10.92
To fan the Earth now wak'd, and usher in	Par Lost 10.94
Now walking in the Garden, by soft windes	Par Lost 10.98
But still rejoyc't, how is it now become	Par Lost 10.120
Eevn hee who now foretold his fatal bruise,	Par Lost 10.191
Before him naked to the aire, that now	Par Lost 10.212
As when he wash'd his servants feet so now	Par Lost 10.215
In counterview within the Gates, that now	Par Lost 10.231
Sin opening, who thus now to Death began.	Par Lost 10.234
Where Satan now prevailes, a Monument	Par Lost 10.258
Immovable of this now fenceless world	Par Lost 10.303
Now had they brought the work by wondrous Art	Par Lost 10.312
And durable; and now in little space	Par Lost 10.320
And now thir way to Earth they had descri'd,	Par Lost 10.325
And tidings fraught, to Hell he now return'd,	Par Lost 10.346
Now also evidence, but straight I felt	Par Lost 10.361
Within Hell Gates till now, thou us impow'rd	Par Lost 10.369
Thine now is all this World, thy vertue hath won	Par Lost 10.372
Or trie thee now more dang'rous to his Throne.	Par Lost 10.382
High proof ye now have giv'n to be the Race	Par Lost 10.385
Issuing from mee: on your joynt vigor now	Par Lost 10.405
Round thir Metropolis, and now expecting	Par Lost 10.439
I call ye and declare ye now, returnd	Par Lost 10.462
And Dungeon of our Tyrant: Now possess,	Par Lost 10.466

Now(*cont*)

By Sin and Death a broad way now is pav'd	Par Lost 10.473
But up and enter now into full bliss.	Par Lost 10.503
Had leasure, wondring at himself now more;	Par Lost 10.510
Now rul'd him, punisht in the shape he sin'd,	Par Lost 10.516
To forked tongue, for now were all transform'd	Par Lost 10.519
Of hissing through the Hall, thick swarming now	Par Lost 10.522
Now Dragon grown, larger then whom the Sun	Par Lost 10.529
They felt themselves now changing; down thir arms,	Par Lost 10.541
Now ris'n, to work them furder woe or shame;	Par Lost 10.555
Once actual, now in body, and to dwell	Par Lost 10.587
What thinkst thou of our Empire now, though earnd	Par Lost 10.592
Inhabited, though sinless, more then now,	Par Lost 10.690
Corrupt and Pestilent: Now from the North	Par Lost 10.695
Beast now with Beast gan war, and Fowle with Fowle,	Par Lost 10.710
The Glory of that Glory, who now becom	Par Lost 10.722
Now death to heare! for what can I encrease	Par Lost 10.731
Me now your curse! Ah, why should all mankind	Par Lost 10.822
Through the still Night, not now, as ere man fell,	Par Lost 10.846
Crooked by nature, bent, as now appears,	Par Lost 10.885
Now at his feet submissive in distress,	Par Lost 10.942
So now of what thou knowst not, who desir'st	Par Lost 10.948
Which now the Skie with various Face begins	Par Lost 10.1064
Regenerate grow instead, that sighs now breath'd	Par Lost 11.5
From innocence. Now therefore bend thine eare	Par Lost 11.30
Eject him tainted now, and purge him off	Par Lost 11.52
He sorrows now, repents, and prayes contrite,	Par Lost 11.90
Self-left. Least therefore his now bolder hand	Par Lost 11.93
Had ended now thir Orisons, and found	Par Lost 11.137
Which then not minded in dismay, yet now	Par Lost 11.156
To labour calls us now with sweat impos'd,	Par Lost 11.172
Wherere our days work lies, though now enjoind	Par Lost 11.177
Down from a Skie of Jasper lighted now	Par Lost 11.209
Eve, now expect great tidings, which perhaps	Par Lost 11.226
Who now shall reare ye to the Sun, or ranke	Par Lost 11.278
To life prolongd and promisd Race, I now	Par Lost 11.331
To dwell on eeven ground now with thy Sons:	Par Lost 11.348
That *Adam* now enforc't to close his eyes,	Par Lost 11.419
Adam, now ope thine eyes, and first behold	Par Lost 11.423
But have I now seen Death? Is this the way	Par Lost 11.462
And now prepare thee for another sight.	Par Lost 11.555
And now of love they treat till th' Eevning Star	Par Lost 11.588
Of these fair Atheists, and now swim in joy,	Par Lost 11.625
But now prepare thee for another Scene.	Par Lost 11.637
Where Cattle pastur'd late, now scatterd lies	Par Lost 11.653
Which now direct thine eyes and soon behold.	Par Lost 11.711
All now was turn'd to jollitie and game,	Par Lost 11.714
Sent up amain; and now the thick'nd Skie	Par Lost 11.742
Anough to beare; those now, that were dispenst	Par Lost 11.766
Grievous to bear: but that care now is past,	Par Lost 11.776
But I was farr deceav'd; for now I see	Par Lost 11.783
And now what further shall ensue, behold.	Par Lost 11.839
Which now abated, for the Clouds were fled,	Par Lost 11.841
With soft foot towards the deep, who now had stopt	Par Lost 11.848
The Ark no more now flotes, but seems on ground	Par Lost 11.850
And now the tops of Hills as Rocks appeer;	Par Lost 11.852
Farr less I now lament for one whole World	Par Lost 11.874
Ur of *Chaldaea*, passing now the Ford	Par Lost 12.130
Canaan he now attains, I see his Tents	Par Lost 12.135
Growing into a Nation, and now grown	Par Lost 12.164
Without Mediator, whose high Office now	Par Lost 12.240
Just *Abraham* and his Seed: now first I finde	Par Lost 12.273
Of mee and all Mankind; but now I see	Par Lost 12.276
Of utmost hope! now clear I understand	Par Lost 12.376
Needs must the Serpent now his capital bruise	Par Lost 12.383
Whether I should repent me now of sin	Par Lost 12.474
Now amplier known thy Saviour and thy Lord,	Par Lost 12.544
Taught this by his example whom I now	Par Lost 12.572
Let us descend now therefore from this top	Par Lost 12.588
Wearied I fell asleep: but now lead on;	Par Lost 12.614
Well pleas'd, but answer'd not; for now too nigh	Par Lost 12.625
By one mans disobedience lost, now sing	Par Reg 1.2
Now had the great Proclaimer with a voice	Par Reg 1.18
And now too soon for us the circling hours	Par Reg 1.57
But his growth now to youths full flowr, displaying	Par Reg 1.67
Successfully; a calmer voyage now	Par Reg 1.103
O're-shadow her: this man born and now up-grown,	Par Reg 1.140
To Satan; let him tempt and now assay	Par Reg 1.143
He now shall know I can produce a man	Par Reg 1.150
They now, and men hereafter may discern,	Par Reg 1.164
Now entring his great duel, not of arms,	Par Reg 1.174
Publish his God-like office now mature,	Par Reg 1.188
He entred now the bordering Desert wild,	Par Reg 1.193
And told them the Messiah now was born,	Par Reg 1.245
Not knew by sight) now come, who was to come	Par Reg 1.271
Now full, that I no more should live obscure,	Par Reg 1.287
And now by some strong motion I am led	Par Reg 1.290
But now an aged man in Rural weeds,	Par Reg 1.314
Wandred this barren waste, the same I now:	Par Reg 1.354
Whom thus answer'd th' Arch Fiend now undisguis'd.	Par Reg 1.357
Nearer acquainted, now I feel by proof,	Par Reg 1.400
Among the Prime in Splendour, now depos'd,	Par Reg 1.413
God hath now sent his living Oracle	Par Reg 1.460
Into thin Air diffus'd: for now began	Par Reg 1.499
And now wild Beasts came forth the woods to roam.	Par Reg 1.502
Now missing him thir joy so lately found,	Par Reg 2.9
Messiah certainly now come, so long	Par Reg 2.32
Now, now, for sure, deliverance is at hand,	Par Reg 2.35

Now(*cont*)
Hath rapt him from us? will he now retire Par Reg 2.40
Nor will withdraw him now, nor will recall, Par Reg 2.55
O what avails me now that honour high Par Reg 2.66
Little suspicious to any King; but now Par Reg 2.82
But where delays he now? some great intent Par Reg 2.95
Since understand; much more his absence now Par Reg 2.100
Demonian Spirits now, from the Element Par Reg 2.122
Thought none my equal, now be over-match'd. Par Reg 2.146
And now I know he hungers where no food Par Reg 2.231
Now hungring first, and to himself thus said. Par Reg 2.244
But now I feel I hunger, which declares, Par Reg 2.252
Thus wore out night, and now the Herald Lark Par Reg 2.279
Tell me if Food were now before thee set, Par Reg 2.320
Under the Trees now trip'd, now solemn stood Par Reg 2.354
Such was the Splendour, and the Tempter now Par Reg 2.366
Great *Julius*, whom now all the world admires Par Reg 3.39
Who names not now with honour patient *Job?* Par Reg 3.95
For truths sake suffering death unjust, lives now Par Reg 3.98
Be now in powerful hands, that will not part Par Reg 3.155
Judaea now and all the promis'd land Par Reg 3.157
All these the *Parthian*, now some Ages past, Par Reg 3.294
Of his great power; for now the *Parthian* King Par Reg 3.299
He marches now in hast; see, though from far, Par Reg 3.303
To *Israel* then, the same that now to me. Par Reg 3.413
And now the Tempter thus his silence broke. Par Reg 4.43
All Nations now to *Rome* obedience pay, Par Reg 4.80
This Emperour hath no Son, and now is old, Par Reg 4.90
Now made a stye, and in his place ascending Par Reg 4.101
That people victor once, now vile and base, Par Reg 4.132
Now both abhor, since thou hast dar'd to utter Par Reg 4.172
To worship thee accurst, now more accurst Par Reg 4.179
By thee how fairly is the Giver now Par Reg 4.187
Get thee behind me; plain thou now appear'st Par Reg 4.193
So spake the Son of God; but Satan now Par Reg 4.365
Now at full age, fulness of time, thy season, Par Reg 4.380
Now contrary, if I read aught in Heaven, Par Reg 4.382
Feigning to disappear. Darkness now rose, Par Reg 4.397
Disturb'd his sleep; and either Tropic now Par Reg 4.409
And now the Sun with more effectual beams Par Reg 4.432
Who all things now behold more fresh and green, Par Reg 4.435
To whom the Fiend now swoln with rage reply'd: Par Reg 4.499
Another method I must now begin. Par Reg 4.540
Now shew thy Progeny; if not to stand, Par Reg 4.554
With all his Army, now thou hast aveng'd Par Reg 4.606
A fairer Paradise is founded now Par Reg 4.613
Now enter, and begin to save mankind. Par Reg 4.635
Times past, what once I was, and what am now. Samson 22
Ask for this great Deliverer now, and find him Samson 40
Inferiour to the vilest now become Samson 73
Imprison'd now indeed, Samson 158
The glory late of *Israel*, now the grief; Samson 179
Now of my own experience, not by talk, Samson 188
Yet that which was the worst now least afflicts me, Samson 195
Israel's oppressours: of what now I suffer Samson 233
And lorded over them whom now they serve; Samson 267
My Son now Captive, hither hath inform'd Samson 335
Chor. As signal now in low dejected state, Samson 338
Himself an Army, now unequal match Samson 346
Who would be now a Father in my stead? Samson 355
The base degree to which I now am fall'n, Samson 414
With me hath end; all the contest is now Samson 461
On thee, who now no more canst do them harm. Samson 486
The Sons of *Anac*, famous now and blaz'd, Samson 528
Now blind, disheartn'd, sham'd, dishonour'd, quell'd, Samson 563
But now hath cast me off as never known, Samson 641
And now at nearer view, no other certain Samson 723
Cho. Yet on she moves, now stands & eies thee fixt, Samson 726
About t' have spoke, but now, with head declin'd Samson 727
But now again she makes address to speak. Samson 731
Yet now am judg'd an enemy. Why then Samson 882
How wouldst thou use me now, blind, and thereby Samson 941
Discover'd in the end, till now conceal'd. Samson 998
Chor. Look now for no inchanting voice, nor fear Samson 1065
Chor. His fraught we soon shall know, he now arrives. Samson 1075
That *Kiriathaim* held, thou knowst me now Samson 1081
And now am come to see of whom such noise Samson 1088
How highly it concerns his glory now Samson 1148
Who now defies thee thrice to single fight, Samson 1222
By his habit I discern him now Samson 1305
A Public Officer, and now at hand. Samson 1306
And now some public proof thereof require Samson 1314
Chor. Consider, *Samson;* matters now are strain'd Samson 1348
So dreaded once, may now exasperate them Samson 1417
Of thy conception, and be now a shield Samson 1434
Be efficacious in thee now at need. Samson 1437
But that which mov'd my coming now, was chiefly Samson 1452
He now be dealing dole among his foes, Samson 1529
For his people of old; what hinders now? Samson 1533
Hath paid his ransom now and full discharge. Samson 1573
Hopeful of his Delivery, which now proves Samson 1575
Now of my own accord such other tryal Samson 1643
To *Israel*, and now ly'st victorious Samson 1663
From out her ashie womb now teem'd, Samson 1703
Man. Come, come, no time for lamentation now, Samson 1708
But to my task. *Neptune* besides the sway Mask 18
Trinity ms 'taske' ←'buisnesse now'
And listen why, for I will tell ye now Mask 43

Now(*cont*)
As now I do: But first I must put off Mask 82
Bridgewater ms 'nowe'
Of hatefull steps, I must be viewles now. Mask 92
Bridgewater ms 'nowe'
Now the top of Heav'n doth hold, Mask 94
Rigor now is gon to bed, Mask 107
Now to the Moon in wavering Morrice move, Mask 116
Bridgewater ms 'nowe'
Venus now wakes, and wak'ns Love. Mask 124
Benighted in these Woods. Now to my charms, Mask 150
Trinity ms 'now'
Bridgewater ms 'now'
My best guide now, me thought it was the sound Mask 171
Bridgewater ms 'nowe'
Is now the labour of my thoughts, 'tis likeliest Mask 192
Whence eev'n now the tumult of loud Mirth Mask 202
line not in Bridgewater ms
I see ye visibly, and now beleeve Mask 216
Trinity ms '& now beleeve' ←'now I beleeve' ←'& while I see yee'
line not in Bridgewater ms
I never heard till now. Ile speak to her Mask 264
Where may she wander now, whether betake her Mask 351
Bridgewater ms 'nowe'
Perhaps som cold bank is her boulster now Mask 353
Bridgewater ms 'nowe'
Till now that this extremity compell'd, Mask 643
But now I find it true; for by this means Mask 644
If every just man that now pines with want Mask 768
Now heaps upon som few with vast excess, Mask 771
Yet stay, be not disturb'd, now I bethink me, Mask 820
Bridgewater ms 'nowe'
Now the spell hath lost his hold; Mask 919
Spir. To the Ocean now I fly, Mask 976
Bridgewater ms 'nowe'
But now my task is smoothly don, Mask 1012
I could be willing though now i' th darke to trie Mask Tr. ms 16.38
I could be willinge though now i' th darke to trie Mask Br. ms 391
We may justly now accuse Arcades 10
Trinity ms 'wee may justly now accuse' ←'now seemes guiltie of abuse'
But O the heavy change, now thou art gon, Lycidas 37
Now thou art gon, and never must return! Lycidas 38
Shall now no more be seen, Lycidas 43
But now my Oat proceeds, Lycidas 88
Look homeward Angel now, and melt with ruth. Lycidas 163
Now *Lycidas* the Shepherds weep no more; Lycidas 182
And now the Sun had stretch'd out all the hills, Lycidas 190
And now was dropt into the Western bay; Lycidas 191
Now while the Heav'n by the Suns team untrod, Nativity 19
Who now hath quite forgot to rave, Nativity 67
Now was almost won Nativity 104
But now begins; for from this happy day Nativity 167
Now sits not girt with Tapers holy shine, Nativity 202
That now I use thee in my latter task: Vacation 8
Expectance calls thee now another way, Vacation 54
Thou know'st it must be now thy only bent Vacation 55
For now to sorrow must I tune my song, Passion 8
Once glorious Towers, now sunk in guiltles blood; Passion 40
Now mourn, and if sad share with us to bear Circum 6
Enter'd the world, now bleeds to give us ease; Circum 11
And now with second hope she goes, Winchester 25
No Marchioness, but now a Queen. Winchester 74
Now the bright morning Star, Dayes harbinger, May Morn 1
And thinking now his journeys end was come, Carrier 12
Now timely sing, ere the rude Bird of Hate Sonnet 1, 9
Numbring good intellects; now seldom por'd on. Sonnet 11, 4
Trinity ms 'now' ←'but now is'
Now that the Fields are dank, and ways are mire, Sonnet 20, 2
Must now be nam'd and printed Hereticks Forcers 11
Who now enjoyes thee credulous, all Gold, Horace 9
And now be wise at length ye Kings averse Psalm 2, 22
Hast smote ere now Psalm 3, 20
And set at large; now spare, Psalm 4, 5
Now pity me, and hear my earnest prai'r. Psalm 4, 6
Return now, God of Hosts, look down Psalm 80, 57
But now it is consum'd with fire, Psalm 80, 65
That now so proudly rise, Psalm 81, 58
Be not thou silent *now at length* Psalm 83, 1
For lo thy *furious* foes *now* swell Psalm 83, 5
By right now shall we seize Psalm 83, 46
Gods houses, and *will now invade* Psalm 83, 47
Lord God of Hoasts hear *now* my praier Psalm 84, 29
And now what God the Lord will speak Psalm 85, 29
Now *joyfully* are met Psalm 85, 42
They *fly me now* whom I have lov'd, Psalm 88, 71
Which once smelt sweet, now stinks as odiously; Prose 4, 2
On thy third Reigne the Earth look now, and tell Prose 12, 3
Now void, it fitts thy people; thether bend Prose 12, 10

Nowhere
Love no where to be found less then Divine! Par Lost 3.411
No where so cleer, sharp'nd his visual ray Par Lost 3.620
Like consort to thy self canst no where find. Par Lost 4.448
For both the when and how is no where told, Par Reg 4.472

Noxious
Thir noxious vapour, or enur'd not feel, Par Lost 2.216
Not noxious, but obedient at thy call. Par Lost 7.498

Noxious(*cont*)
Of noxious efficacie, and when to joyne Par Lost 10.660
The fiery Serpent fled, and noxious Worm, Par Reg 1.312
Yet as being oft times noxious where they light Par Reg 4.460
Nulled
No more on me have power, their force is null'd, Samson 935
Number
Thir number last he summs. And now his heart Par Lost 1.571
Though without number still amidst the Hall Par Lost 1.791
Loud as from numbers without number, sweet Par Lost 3.346
Thir number, or the wisdom infinite Par Lost 3.706
In full harmonic number joind, thir songs Par Lost 4.687
One of our number thus reduc't becomes, Par Lost 5.843
Nor number, nor example with him wrought Par Lost 5.901
Equal in number to that Godless crew Par Lost 6.49
And twentie thousand (I thir number heard) Par Lost 6.769
Number to this dayes work is not ordain'd Par Lost 6.809
Number sufficient to possess her Realmes Par Lost 7.147
The number of thy worshippers. Who seekes Par Lost 7.613
Speed, to describe whose swiftness Number failes. Par Lost 8.38
But Man by number is to manifest Par Lost 8.422
To my just number found. O why did God, Par Lost 10.888
May chance to number thee with those Samson 1295
Thee with thy slaughter'd foes in number more Samson 1667
Our number may affright: Som Virgin sure Mask 148
Number my ranks, and visit every sprout Arcades 59
Trinity ms 'number' ←'& number all'
Yet had the number of her days Winchester 11
Numbered
And limited thir might; though numberd such Par Lost 6.229
And all her numberd Starrs, that seem to rowle Par Lost 8.19
This annual humbling certain number'd days, Par Lost 10.576
Numberd, though sad, till Death, his doom (which I Par Lost 11.40
And numberd down: much rather I shall chuse Samson 1478
'Gainst old truth) motion number'd out his time; Another 8
1640, 1657 'numbred'
1658 'numbered'
Numbering
Of numbring *Israel*, which cost the lives Par Reg 3.410
Numbring good intellects; now seldom por'd on. Sonnet 11, 4
Numberless
So numberless were those bad Angels seen Par Lost 1.344
Throng numberless, like that Pigmean Race Par Lost 1.780
Numberless, as thou seest, and how they move; Par Lost 3.719
Pavilions numberless, and sudden reard, Par Lost 5.653
Armie against Armie numberless to raise Par Lost 6.224
About his Chariot numberless were pour'd Par Lost 7.197
With Honey stor'd: the rest are numberless, Par Lost 7.492
Though numberless, to his Omnipotence, Par Lost 8.108
By Angels numberless, thy daily Train. Par Lost 9.548
He look't and saw what numbers numberless Par Reg 3.310
As thick and numberless Penseroso 7
Numbers
Harmonious numbers; as the wakeful Bird Par Lost 3.38
Beneath thy Sentence; Hell her numbers full, Par Lost 3.332
Loud as from numbers without number, sweet Par Lost 3.346
Thir Starry dance in numbers that compute Par Lost 3.580
By Numbers that have name. But this I urge, Par Lost 8.114
And through all numbers absolute, though One; Par Lost 8.421
And to repaire his numbers thus impair'd, Par Lost 9.144
Numbers of all diseas'd, all maladies Par Lost 11.480
Great numbers of each Nation to receave Par Lost 12.503
He look't and saw what numbers numberless Par Reg 3.310
Of harmony in tones and numbers hit Par Reg 4.255
Such numbers of our Nation: and the Priest Samson 857
And numbers thither flock, I had no will, Samson 1450
Thy easie numbers flow, and that each heart Shakespear 10
Time numbers motion, yet (without a crime Another 7
Numbing
The clasping charm, and thaw the numming spell, Mask 853
Bridgewater ms 'numminge'
Trinity ms 'thaw the numming' ←'melt each' ←'secret holding'
Numbness
And sedentary numness craze my limbs Samson 571
Numerous
A numerous Brigad hasten'd. As when Bands Par Lost 1.675
I saw and heard, for such a numerous Host Par Lost 2.993
Your numerous ofspring; if no better place, Par Lost 4.385
Flowd from thir lips, in Prose or numerous Verse, Par Lost 5.150
Shall fill the World more numerous with thy Sons Par Lost 5.389
A numerous Host, in strength each armed hand Par Lost 6.231
Of torrent Floods, or of a numerous Host. Par Lost 6.830
Thir Brood as numerous hatch, from the Egg that soon Par Lost 7.418
Numerous, and every Starr perhaps a World Par Lost 7.621
You two this way, among these numerous Orbs Par Lost 10.397
Spangl'd with eyes more numerous then those Par Lost 11.130
And stabl'd; of Mankind, so numerous late, Par Lost 11.752
Of Herds and Flocks, and numerous servitude; Par Lost 12.132
Too numerous; whence of guests he makes them slaves Par Lost 12.167
Such and so numerous was thir Chivalrie; Par Reg 3.344
Thy numerous mercies go Psalm 5, 18
Nun
Com pensive Nun, devout and pure, Penseroso 31
Nuptial
Fair couple, linkt in happie nuptial League, Par Lost 4.339
Espoused *Eve* deckt first her nuptial Bed, Par Lost 4.710
1667 'Nuptial'

Nuptial(*cont*)
Of nuptial Sanctitie and marriage Rites: Par Lost 8.487
My pleaded reason. To the Nuptial Bowre Par Lost 8.510
From Loves due Rites, Nuptial imbraces sweet, Par Lost 10.994
Thee lastly nuptial Bowre, by mee adornd Par Lost 11.280
They light the Nuptial Torch, and bid invoke Par Lost 11.590
Of Nuptial Love profest, carrying it strait Samson 385
And in your City held my Nuptial Feast: Samson 1194
His lot unfortunate in nuptial choice, Samson 1743
And hears the unexpressive nuptiall Song, Lycidas 176
1673 'nuptial'
Nuptials
Thir nuptials, nor this last so trecherously Samson 1023
Nurse
Sons wont to nurse thir Parents in old age, Samson 1487
Thou in old age car'st how to nurse thy Son. Samson 1488
Where with her best nurse Contemplation Mask 377
To nurse the Saplings tall, and curl the grove Arcades 46
Trinity ms 'nurse the saplings tall' ←'live a thousand yeares'
Thy drowsie Nurse hath sworn she did them spie Vacation 61
Nursed
Where his fair off-spring nurs't in Princely lore, Mask 34
Bridgewater ms 'nurst'
For we were nurst upon the self-same hill, Lycidas 23
Trinity ms 'nurs't'
Nursery
Her Nurserie; they at her coming sprung Par Lost 8.46
Nursing
With nursing diligence, to me glad office, Samson 924
Nursling
I was his nursling once and choice delight, Samson 633
Nurture
Ordain'd thy nurture holy, as of a Plant; Samson 362
Nut-brown
Then to the Spicy Nut-brown Ale, Allegro 100
Nutriment
Moist nutriment, or under Rocks thir food Par Lost 7.408
Nutriments
And from these corporal nutriments perhaps Par Lost 5.496
Nymph
Pan or *Silvanus* never slept, nor Nymph, Par Lost 4.707
Then Wood-Nymph, or the fairest Goddess feign'd Par Lost 5.381
Soft she withdrew, and like a Wood-Nymph light Par Lost 9.386
Thy Paranymph, worthless to thee compar'd, Samson 1020
This Nymph that gaz'd upon his clustring locks, Mask 54
Bridgewater ms 'nimphe'
Trinity ms 'nymph'
Sweet Echo, sweetest Nymph that liv'st unseen Mask 230
Trinity ms 'nymph'
Bridgewater ms 'nymphe'
And like a quiver'd Nymph with Arrows keen Mask 422
1637 'nymph'
Trinity ms 'nymph'
Bridgewater ms 'nimphe'
There is a gentle Nymph not farr from hence, Mask 824
Trinity ms 'nymph'
Bridgewater ms 'Nimphe'
1637 'nymph'
Haste thee nymph, and bring with thee Allegro 25
The Mountain Nymph, sweet Liberty; Allegro 36
Nymphlike
If chance with Nymphlike step fair Virgin pass, Par Lost 9.452
Nymphs
Of Wood-Gods and Wood-Nymphs; he view'd it round, Par Reg 2.297
Nymphs of *Diana*'s train, and *Naiades* Par Reg 2.355
The Wood-Nymphs deckt with Daisies trim, Mask 120
Bridgewater ms 'wood nimphs'
Trinity ms 'wood nimphs'
1637 'Wood-nymphs'
The water Nymphs that in the bottom plaid, Mask 833
Trinity ms 'waternymphs'
Bridgewater ms 'nimphs'
By all the *Nymphs* that nightly dance Mask 883
Trinity ms 'nymphs'
Bridgewater ms 'Nimphes'
The Sea Nymphs, and their powers offended. Penseroso 21
Was never heard the Nymphs to daunt, Penseroso 137
Look Nymphs, and Shepherds look, Arcades 1
Fair silver-buskind Nymphs as great and good, Arcades 33
Nymphs and Shepherds dance no more Arcades 96
Trinity ms 'nymphs'
Where were ye Nymphs when the remorseless deep Lycidas 50
1638 'Nimphs'
Trinity ms 'nymphs'
The Nimphs in twilight shade of tangled thickets mourn. Nativity 188
Nyseian
Of *Eden* strive; nor that *Nyseian* Ile Par Lost 4.275
O
And chiefly Thou O Spirit, that dost prefer Par Lost 1.17
O how unlike the place from whence they fell! Par Lost 1.75
If thou beest he; But O how fall'n! how chang'd Par Lost 1.84
ms 'oh'
O Prince, O Chief of many Throned Powers, Par Lost 1.128
O Myriads of immortal Spirits, O Powers Par Lost 1.622
ms 'o powers'
I should be much for open Warr, O Peers, Par Lost 2.119
O Progeny of Heav'n, Empyreal Thrones, Par Lost 2.430
But I should ill become this Throne, O Peers, Par Lost 2.445

O(*cont*)

O shame to men! Devil with Devil damn'd	Par Lost 2.496
O Father, what intends thy hand, she cry'd,	Par Lost 2.727
Against thy only Son? What fury O Son,	Par Lost 2.728
But thou O Father, I forewarn thee, shun	Par Lost 2.810
O Father, gracious was that word which clos'd	Par Lost 3.144
O Son, in whom my Soul hath chief delight,	Par Lost 3.168
O thou in Heav'n and Earth the only peace	Par Lost 3.274
Found out for mankind under wrauth, O thou	Par Lost 3.275
For mans offence. O unexampl'd love,	Par Lost 3.410
O for that warning voice, which he who saw	Par Lost 4.1
O thou that with surpassing Glory crownd,	Par Lost 4.32
O Sun, to tell thee how I hate thy beams	Par Lost 4.37
O had his powerful Destiny ordaind	Par Lost 4.58
O then at last relent: is there no place	Par Lost 4.79
O Hell! what doe mine eyes with grief behold,	Par Lost 4.358
To whom thus *Eve* repli'd. O thou for whom	Par Lost 4.440
O fair foundation laid whereon to build	Par Lost 4.521
Endowd with all thir gifts, and O too like	Par Lost 4.715
Blest pair; and O yet happiest if ye seek	Par Lost 4.774
O friends, I hear the tread of nimble feet	Par Lost 4.866
O loss of one in Heav'n to judge of wise,	Par Lost 4.904
Satan, and couldst thou faithful add? O name,	Par Lost 4.950
O sacred name of faithfulness profan'd!	Par Lost 4.951
O Sole in whom my thoughts find all repose,	Par Lost 5.28
And O fair Plant, said he, with fruit surcharg'd,	Par Lost 5.58
But he thus overjoy'd, O Fruit Divine,	Par Lost 5.67
And fell asleep; but O how glad I wak'd	Par Lost 5.92
With pleasant liquors crown'd: O innocence	Par Lost 5.445
O *Adam*, one Almightie is, from whom	Par Lost 5.469
O favourable spirit, propitious guest,	Par Lost 5.507
And so from Heav'n to deepest Hell; O fall	Par Lost 5.542
High matter thou injoinst me, O prime of men,	Par Lost 5.563
O argument blasphemous, false and proud!	Par Lost 5.809
O alienate from God, O spirit accurst,	Par Lost 5.877
O Heav'n! that such resemblance of the Highest	Par Lost 6.114
O now in danger tri'd, now known in Armes	Par Lost 6.418
O Friends, why come not on these Victors proud?	Par Lost 6.609
O Father, O Supream of heav'nly Thrones,	Par Lost 6.723
This be thy just Circumference, O World.	Par Lost 7.231
This said, he formd thee, *Adam*, thee O Man	Par Lost 7.524
Not Words alone pleas'd her. O when meet now	Par Lost 8.57
O by what Name, for thou above all these,	Par Lost 8.357
O Earth, how like to Heav'n, if not preferr'd	Par Lost 9.99
Him Lord pronounc'd, and, O indignitie!	Par Lost 9.154
O foul descent! that I who erst contended	Par Lost 9.163
O Woman, best are all things as the will	Par Lost 9.343
O much deceav'd, much failing, hapless *Eve*,	Par Lost 9.404
O Sacred, Wise, and Wisdom-giving Plant,	Par Lost 9.679
O Sovran, vertuous, precious of all Trees	Par Lost 9.795
O fairest of Creation, last and best	Par Lost 9.896
O glorious trial of exceeding Love,	Par Lost 9.961
O *Eve*, in evil hour thou didst give eare	Par Lost 9.1067
Insufferably bright. O might I here	Par Lost 9.1084
Thir guilt and dreaded shame; O how unlike	Par Lost 9.1114
O Heav'n! in evil strait this day I stand	Par Lost 10.125
O Son, why sit we here each other viewing	Par Lost 10.235
O Parent, these are thy magnific deeds,	Par Lost 10.354
O miserable of happie! is this the end	Par Lost 10.720
Is propagated curse. O voice once heard	Par Lost 10.729
Heavie, though in thir place. O fleeting joyes	Par Lost 10.741
O welcom hour whenever! why delayes	Par Lost 10.771
But I shall die a living Death? O thought	Par Lost 10.788
That I must leave ye, Sons; O were I able	Par Lost 10.819
O Conscience, into what Abyss of fears	Par Lost 10.842
O Woods, O Fountains, Hillocks, Dales and Bowrs,	Par Lost 10.860
To my just number found. O why did God,	Par Lost 10.888
And to our Seed (O hapless Seed!) deriv'd.	Par Lost 10.965
O Sons, like one of us Man is become	Par Lost 11.84
O *Eve*, some furder change awaits us nigh,	Par Lost 11.193
O unexpected stroke, worse then of Death!	Par Lost 11.268
That must be mortal to us both. O flours,	Par Lost 11.273
O Teacher, some great mischief hath befall'n	Par Lost 11.450
I must return to native dust? O sight	Par Lost 11.463
O miserable Mankind, to what fall	Par Lost 11.500
O pittie and shame, that they who to live well	Par Lost 11.629
Lamenting turnd full sad; O what are these,	Par Lost 11.675
O Visions ill foreseen! better had I	Par Lost 11.763
O thou who future things canst represent	Par Lost 11.870
O execrable Son so to aspire	Par Lost 12.64
Bred up in Idol-worship; O that men	Par Lost 12.115
Here *Adam* interpos'd. O sent from Heav'n,	Par Lost 12.270
O Prophet of glad tidings, finisher	Par Lost 12.375
O goodness infinite, goodness immense!	Par Lost 12.469
O ancient Powers of Air and this wide world,	Par Reg 1.44
O what a multitude of thoughts at once	Par Reg 1.196
O Son, but nourish them and let them soar	Par Reg 1.230
O what avails me now that honour high	Par Reg 2.66
O patient Son of God, yet only stoodst	Par Reg 4.420
Then hear, O Son of *David*, Virgin-born;	Par Reg 4.500
O wherefore was my birth from Heaven foretold	Samson 23
With this Heav'n-gifted strength? O glorious strength	Samson 36
O impotence of mind, in body strong!	Samson 52
O loss of sight, of thee I most complain!	Samson 67
Blind among enemies, O worse then chains,	Samson 68
O dark, dark, dark, amid the blaze of noon,	Samson 80
O first created Beam, and thou great Word,	Samson 83
And buried; but O yet more miserable!	Samson 101

O(*cont*)

O change beyond report, thought, or belief!	Samson 117
Thou art become (O worst imprisonment!)	Samson 155
O mirror of our fickle state,	Samson 164
Not to be found, though sought. Yee see, O friends,	Samson 193
(O that I never had! fond wish too late.)	Samson 228
Who vanquisht with a peal of words (O weakness!)	Samson 235
Man. O miserable change! is this the man,	Samson 340
At one spears length. O ever failing trust	Samson 348
O wherefore did God grant me my request,	Samson 356
Her Bond-slave; O indignity, O blot	Samson 411
Chor. O madness, to think use of strongest wines	Samson 553
Sam. O that torment should not be confin'd	Samson 606
Gives and the Mill had tam'd thee? O that fortune	Samson 1093
Har. O *Baal-zebub!* can my ears unus'd	Samson 1231
Man. I know your friendly minds and----O what noise!	Samson 1508
Mess. O whither shall I run, or which way flie	Samson 1541
Man. The worst indeed, O all my hope's defeated	Samson 1571
Man. O lastly over-strong against thy self!	Samson 1590
Chor. O dearly-bought revenge, yet glorious!	Samson 1660
Of such late Wassailers; yet O where els	Mask 179
1637 'o'	
Trinity ms 'O' ←'Oh'	
Bridgewater ms 'o'	
Had stole them from me, els O theevish Night	Mask 195
word not in Bridgewater ms	
1637 'o'	
O welcom pure-ey'd Faith, white-handed Hope,	Mask 213
line not in Bridgewater ms	
O if thou have	Mask 238
Trinity ms 'Oh'	
But O that haples virgin our lost sister	Mask 350
Trinity ms 'oh'	
1637 'o'	
2. *Bro*. O brother, 'tis my father Shepherd sure.	Mask 493
Trinity ms 'o' ←'oh'	
Spir. O my lov'd masters heir, and his next joy,	Mask 501
But O my Virgin Lady, where is she?	Mask 507
Trinity ms 'oh'	
1637 'o'	
Under the ribs of Death, but O ere long	Mask 562
1637 'o'	
Trinity ms 'oh'	
And O poor hapless Nightingale thought I,	Mask 566
1637 'o'	
But furder know I not. 2. *Bro*. O night and shades,	Mask 580
Co. O foolishnes of men! that lend their ears	Mask 706
Trinity ms 'O' ←'Oh'	
O ye mistook, ye should have snatcht his wand	Mask 815
Trinity ms 'oh'	
O my simplicity what sights are these? with darke disguises	Mask Tr. ms 22.19
But, O sad Virgin, that thy power	Penseroso 103
Yet once more, O ye Laurels, and once more	Lycidas 1
But O the heavy change, now thou art gon,	Lycidas 37
1638 'oh'	
O Fountain *Arethuse*, and thou honour'd floud,	Lycidas 85
1638 'Oh'	
Trinity ms 'Oh'	
And, O ye *Dolphins*, waft the haples youth.	Lycidas 164
O run, prevent them with thy humble ode,	Nativity 24
O let us his praises tell,	Psalm 136, 9
O Fairest flower no sooner blown but blasted,	Fair Inf 1
Forsook the hated earth, O tell me sooth	Fair Inf 51
O what a Mask was there, what a disguise!	Passion 19
Triumphing over Death, and Chance, and thee O Time.	On Time 22
O more exceeding love or law more just?	Circum 15
Trinity ms 'Oh'	
This day, but O ere long	Circum 26
Trinity ms 'O' ←'Oh'	
O may we soon again renew that Song,	Musick 25
Trinity ms 'oh'	
O Nightingale, that on yon bloomy Spray	Sonnet 1, 1
Portend success in love; O if *Jove's* will	Sonnet 1, 7
Thy age, like ours, O Soul of Sir *John Cheek*,	Sonnet 11, 12
O yet a nobler task awaites thy hand;	Sonnet 15, 9
Avenge O Lord thy slaughter'd Saints, whose bones	Sonnet 18, 1
But O as to embrace me she enclin'd,	Sonnet 23, 13
Trinity ms 'o'	
Plain in thy neatness; O how oft shall he	Horace 5
And thou O Lord how long? turn Lord, restore	Psalm 6, 7
My soul, O save me for thy goodness sake	Psalm 6, 8
O Jehovah our Lord how wondrous great	Psalm 8, 1
O what is man that thou remembrest yet,	Psalm 8, 12
O Jehovah our Lord how wondrous great	Psalm 8, 23
To us O God *vouchsafe;*	Psalm 80, 14
O God of Hosts *vouchsafe*	Psalm 80, 30
Hear O my people, *heark'n well*,	Psalm 81, 33
O that my people would *be wise*	Psalm 81, 53
And O that Israel would *advise*	Psalm 81, 55
O God hold not thy peace,	Psalm 83, 2
Sit not thou still O God of *strength*	Psalm 83, 3
O Lord of Hoasts, how dear	Psalm 84, 2
Thy Courts O Lord to see,	Psalm 84, 6
O living God, for thee.	Psalm 84, 8
O Jacobs God give ear,	Psalm 84, 30
Thy *gracious* ear, O Lord, encline,	Psalm 86, 1
O hear me *I thee pray*,	Psalm 86, 2
Save thou thy servant O my God	Psalm 86, 7

O(*cont*)
I call; O make rejoyce Psalm 86, 10
O Lord, nor any works Psalm 86, 26
Teach me O Lord thy way *most right*, Psalm 86, 37
Thee will I praise O Lord my God Psalm 86, 41
O God the proud against me rise Psalm 86, 49
O turn to me *thy face at length*, Psalm 86, 57
But I to thee O Lord do cry Psalm 88, 53

Oak
Or hollow'd bodies made of Oak or Firr Par Lost 6.574
Under the covert of some ancient Oak, Par Reg 1.305
Gently o're th' accustom'd Oke; Penseroso 60
Of Pine, or monumental Oake, Penseroso 135

Oaken
I only with an Oak'n staff will meet thee, Samson 1123
Of this fair Wood, and live in Oak'n bowr, Arcades 45
Trinity ms defective here

Oaks
Hath scath'd the Forrest Oaks, or Mountain Pines, Par Lost 1.613
ms 'oakes'
Though rooted deep as high, and sturdiest Oaks Par Reg 4.417
From betwixt two aged Okes, Allegro 82
Thus sang the uncouth Swain to th' Okes and rills, Lycidas 186
Trinity ms 'oakes'
1638 'oaks'

Oar
Half flying; behoves him now both Oare and Saile. Par Lost 2.942

Oary
Her state with Oarie feet: yet oft they quit Par Lost 7.440

Oat
But now my Oat proceeds, Lycidas 88
Trinity ms 'oate'
1638 'oat'

Oaten
Or sound of pastoral reed with oaten stops, Mask 345
Temper'd to th' Oaten Flute, Lycidas 33
1638 'oaten'
Trinity ms 'oaten'

Oath
Pronounc'd among the Gods, and by an Oath, Par Lost 2.352

Ob
Maeotis, up beyond the River *Ob;* Par Lost 9.78

Obdurate
Mixt with obdurate pride and stedfast hate: Par Lost 1.58
Or Wonders move th' obdurate to relent? Par Lost 6.790
Behinde them, while th' obdurat King pursues: Par Lost 12.205

Obdured
Fallacious hope, or arm th' obdured brest Par Lost 2.568
This saw his hapless Foes but stood obdur'd, Par Lost 6.785

Obedience
Sole pledge of his obedience: So will fall, Par Lost 3.95
What pleasure I from such obedience paid, Par Lost 3.107
To pray, repent, and bring obedience due. Par Lost 3.190
To Prayer, repentance, and obedience due, Par Lost 3.191
Filial obedience: as a sacrifice Par Lost 3.269
The only sign of our obedience left Par Lost 4.428
The proof of thir obedience and thir faith? Par Lost 4.520
Your military obedience, to dissolve Par Lost 4.955
Obedient? can we want obedience then Par Lost 5.514
That is, to thy obedience; therein stand. Par Lost 5.522
Hold, as you yours, while our obedience holds; Par Lost 5.537
That from thy just obedience could revolt, Par Lost 6.740
Thee also from obedience, that with him Par Lost 6.902
Up hither, under long obedience tri'd, Par Lost 7.159
Our prompt obedience. Fast we found, fast shut Par Lost 8.240
The Pledge of thy Obedience and thy Faith, Par Lost 8.325
First thy obedience; th' other who can know, Par Lost 9.368
Obedience to the Law of God, impos'd Par Lost 12.397
Both by obedience and by love, though love Par Lost 12.403
In his redemption, and that his obedience Par Lost 12.408
By one mans firm obedience fully tri'd Par Reg 1.4
Wilt thou impute to obedience what thy fear Par Reg 1.422
All Nations now to *Rome* obedience pay, Par Reg 4.80
And seals obedience first with wounding smart Circum 25
In first obedience, and their state of good. Musick 24

Obedient
If ye be found obedient, and retain Par Lost 5.501
Obedient? can we want obedience then Par Lost 5.514
Not noxious, but obedient at thy call. Par Lost 7.498
Obedient to his will, that he voutsafes Par Lost 12.246
Obedient to the Moon he spent his date Another 29
line not in 1658 text

Obey
My being gav'st me; whom should I obey Par Lost 2.865
Unargu'd I obey; so God ordains, Par Lost 4.636
Our maker, and obey him whose command Par Lost 5.551
Behests obey, worthiest to be obey'd, Par Lost 6.185
Whom to obey is happiness entire. Par Lost 6.741
Him whom to love is to obey, and keep Par Lost 8.634
Was shee thy God, that her thou didst obey Par Lost 10.145
If patiently thy bidding they obey, Par Lost 11.112
Henceforth I learne, that to obey is best, Par Lost 12.561
What I can suffer, how obey? who best Par Reg 3.194
Commands are no constraints. If I obey them, Samson 1372

Obeyed
Yet to thir Generals Voyce they soon obeyd Par Lost 1.337
ms 'obai'd'
Or taint integritie: but all obey'd Par Lost 5.704

Obeyed(*cont*)
The Deitie, and divine commands obei'd, Par Lost 5.806
Behests obey, worthiest to be obey'd, Par Lost 6.185
So easily obeyd amid the choice Par Lost 7.48
1669 'obey'd'
Each in their kinde. The Earth obey'd, and strait Par Lost 7.453
My Tongue obey'd and readily could name Par Lost 8.272
What thou commandst, and right thou shouldst be obeyd: Par Lost 9.570
Not just, not God; not feard then, nor obeyd: Par Lost 9.701
1667 'obeid'
Reason in man obscur'd, or not obeyd, Par Lost 12.86
Well hath obey'd; just tryal e're I merit Par Reg 3.196
Not therefore to be obey'd. But zeal mov'd thee; Samson 895
Less therefore to be pleas'd, obey'd, or fear'd, Samson 900

Obeyest
Or like a Fawning Parasite obey'st; Par Reg 1.452

Obeying
Or not restraind as wee, or not obeying, Par Lost 9.868
Whoever tempted; which they not obeying, Par Lost 10.14
I have perform'd, as reason was, obeying, Samson 1641

Obeys
But God left free the Will, for what obeyes Par Lost 9.351
All Nations shall be blest; he straight obeys, Par Lost 12.126
Over the Sea; the Sea his Rod obeys; Par Lost 12.212
Obeys *Tiberius;* nor is always rul'd Par Reg 3.159

Object
But evil hast not tri'd: and wilt object Par Lost 4.896
As with an object that excels the sense, Par Lost 8.456
Not proof enough such Object to sustain, Par Lost 8.535
Looks intervene and smiles, or object new Par Lost 9.222
Some specious object by the Foe subornd, Par Lost 9.361
Mee mee onely just object of his ire. Par Lost 10.936
Before the present object languishing Par Lost 10.996
Why else this double object in our sight Par Lost 11.201
Such object hath the power to soft'n and tame Par Reg 2.163
Against another object more enticing? Samson 559
Or pitied object, these redundant locks Samson 568

Objects
To objects distant farr, whereby he soon Par Lost 3.621
Who meet with various objects, from the sense Par Lost 8.609
Thy mortal sight to faile; objects divine Par Lost 12.9
Therefore with manlier objects we must try Par Reg 2.225
And all her various objects of delight Samson 71

Oblige
Deserted, then oblige thee with a fact Par Lost 9.980

Oblique
Through the pure marble Air his oblique way Par Lost 3.564
Scipio the highth of *Rome*. With tract oblique Par Lost 9.510
Oblique the Centric Globe: Som say the Sun Par Lost 10.671

Obliquities
Mov'd contrarie with thwart obliquities, Par Lost 8.132

Oblivion
Lethe the River of Oblivion roules Par Lost 2.583
Nameless in dark oblivion let them dwell. Par Lost 6.380
Of *dark* oblivion? Psalm 88, 52

Oblivious
Lye thus astonisht on th' oblivious Pool, Par Lost 1.266

Obloquy
Canst thou with impious obloquie condemne Par Lost 5.813
Contempt instead, dishonour, obloquy? Par Reg 3.131
Dishonour, obloquie, and op't the mouths Samson 452

Obnoxious
As high he soard, obnoxious first or last Par Lost 9.170
To shame obnoxious, and unseemliest seen, Par Lost 9.1094
But made hereby obnoxious more Samson 106

Obscene
Next *Chemos*, th' obscene dread of *Moabs* Sons, Par Lost 1.406

Obscure
Dilated or condens't, bright or obscure, Par Lost 1.429
Obscure some glimps of joy, to have found thir chief Par Lost 1.524
Encamp thir Legions, or with obscure wing Par Lost 2.132
And through the palpable obscure find out Par Lost 2.406
In that obscure sojourn, while in my flight Par Lost 3.15
Thy sin and place of doom obscure and foule. Par Lost 4.840
Round through the vast profunditie obscure, Par Lost 7.229
From use, obscure and suttle, but to know Par Lost 8.192
Bound on a voyage uncouth and obscure, Par Lost 8.230
Of midnight vapor glide obscure, and prie Par Lost 9.159
Nor this unvoyageable Gulf obscure Par Lost 10.366
Into a lower World, to this obscure Par Lost 11.283
To the flood *Jordan*, came as then obscure, Par Reg 1.24
Now full, that I no more should live obscure, Par Reg 1.287
Affecting private life, or more obscure Par Reg 3.22
Made famous in a Land and times obscure; Par Reg 3.94
If any be, they walk obscure; Samson 296
To a contemptible old age obscure. Samson 572

Obscured
Of Glory obscur'd: As when the Sun new ris'n Par Lost 1.594
Alien from Heav'n, with passions foul obscur'd: Par Lost 4.571
Essential Powers, nor by his Reign obscur'd, Par Lost 5.841
But soon obscur'd with smoak, all Heav'n appeerd, Par Lost 6.585
To Sapience, hitherto obscur'd, infam'd, Par Lost 9.797
Obscur'd, where highest Woods impenetrable Par Lost 9.1086
Reason in man obscur'd, or not obeyd, Par Lost 12.86
To life obscur'd, which were a fair dismission, Samson 688
In their obscured haunts of inmost bowres. Mask 536

Obscurely
The Womans seed, obscurely then foretold, Par Lost 12.543

Obscurely(*cont*)
I among these aloof obscurely stood. Samson 1611
Obscures
Thus long to some great purpose he obscures. Par Reg 2.101
Obsequious
Obsequious darkness enters, till her houre Par Lost 6.10
Obsequious, Heav'n his wonted face renewd, Par Lost 6.783
And with obsequious Majestie approv'd Par Lost 8.509
Obsequy
With silent obsequie and funeral train Samson 1732
Observe
Receave with solemne purpose to observe Par Lost 7.78
To observe the sequel, saw his guileful act Par Lost 10.334
There is, said *Michael*, if thou well observe Par Lost 11.530
As in his presence, ever to observe Par Lost 12.563
Short sojourn; and what thence could'st thou observe? Par Reg 3.235
If thou observe not this, be sure to find, Par Reg 4.477
That do observe If I transgress Psalm 5, 23
For Israel *to observe* Psalm 81, 14
Observed
Compare of mortal prowess, yet observ'd Par Lost 1.588
His loss; but chiefly to find here observd Par Lost 4.849
Proceeding, which in other Beasts observ'd Par Lost 9.94
Departing gave command, and they observ'd. Par Lost 10.430
Adam observ'd, and with his Eye the chase Par Lost 11.191
New Laws to be observ'd; for I descrie Par Lost 11.228
Of them derided, but of God observd Par Lost 11.817
Observes
Of *Galileo*, less assur'd, observes Par Lost 5.262
Observing
Observing none, but adoration pure Par Lost 4.737
Obstacle
For sight no obstacle found here, nor shade, Par Lost 3.615
In eminence, and obstacle find none Par Lost 8.624
Obstinacy
Anger, and obstinacie, and hate, and guile. Par Lost 10.114
Obstriction
From National obstriction, without taint Samson 312
Obstruct
From hence, no cloud, or, to obstruct his sight, Par Lost 5.257
Through *Chaos* hurld, obstruct the mouth of Hell Par Lost 10.636
Obstruct Heav'n Towrs, and in derision sets Par Lost 12.52
Obtain
Or shall the Adversarie thus obtain Par Lost 3.156
Like honour to obtain, and as his Eye Par Lost 3.660
But say I could repent and could obtaine Par Lost 4.93
Obtaine: though to recount Almightie works Par Lost 7.112
1669 'Obtain'
If answerable style I can obtaine Par Lost 9.20
Before thee; and not repenting, this obtaine Par Lost 10.75
Obtain, all thy request was my Decree: Par Lost 11.47
Thou never shalt obtain; prediction still Par Reg 3.354
Let me obtain forgiveness of thee, *Samson*, Samson 909
Obtained
By force impossible, by leave obtain'd Par Lost 2.250
Immoveable till peace obtain'd from fault Par Lost 10.938
Could be obtain'd to shelter him or me Par Reg 2.73
That by strong hand his Family obtain'd, Par Reg 3.168
Yet always pity or pardon hath obtain'd. Samson 814
Obtains
Obtains the brow of some high-climbing Hill, Par Lost 3.546
He who obtains the Monarchy of Heav'n, Par Reg 1.87
Obtrude
Why shouldst thou then obtrude this diligence, Par Reg 2.387
Obtruded
Obtruded on us thus? who if we knew Par Lost 11.504
Obtrudest
Obtrud'st thy offer'd aid, that I accepting Par Reg 4.493
Obtruding
Obtruding false rules pranckt in reasons garb. Mask 759
Bridgewater ms 'obtrudinge'
Obtrusive
Not obvious, not obtrusive, but retir'd, Par Lost 8.504
Obtuse
Obtuse, all taste of pleasure must forgoe, Par Lost 11.541
Obvious
Indissolubly firm; nor obvious Hill, Par Lost 6.69
Light back to them, is obvious to dispute. Par Lost 8.158
Not obvious, not obtrusive, but retir'd, Par Lost 8.504
Where obvious dutie erewhile appear'd unsaught: Par Lost 10.106
My obvious breast, arming to overcom Par Lost 11.374
So obvious and so easie to be quench't, Samson 95
Occasion
Let us not slip th' occasion, whether scorn, Par Lost 1.178
Nor will occasion want, nor shall we need Par Lost 2.341
In *Adam*, not to let th' occasion pass Par Lost 5.453
Occasion which now smiles, behold alone Par Lost 9.480
Direct, or by occasion hath presented Par Lost 9.974
But on Occasions forelock watchful wait. Par Reg 3.173
They themselves rather are occasion best, Par Reg 3.174
The Marriage on; that by occasion hence Samson 224
Chor. In seeking just occasion to provoke Samson 237
Find some occasion to infest our Foes. Samson 423
Found soon occasion thereby to make thee Samson 425
Do they not seek occasion of new quarrels Samson 1329
Find courage to lay hold on this occasion, Samson 1716
Of this occasion. But I hear the tread Mask 91
Bitter constraint, and sad occasion dear, Lycidas 6

Occasionally
Occasionally; and to consummate all, Par Lost 8.556
Occasioned
By mee done and occasiond, or rejoyce Par Lost 12.475
Occasions
Mess. Occasions drew me early to this City, Samson 1596
Ocean
Created hugest that swim th' Ocean stream: Par Lost 1.202
Under yon boyling Ocean, wrapt in Chains; Par Lost 2.183
Illimitable Ocean without bound, Par Lost 2.892
Uncertain which, in Ocean or in Air. Par Lost 3.76
To darkness, such as bound the Ocean wave. Par Lost 3.539
Chear'd with the grateful smell old Ocean smiles. Par Lost 4.165
To th' Ocean Iles, and in th' ascending Scale Par Lost 4.354
With Earth and Ocean meets, the setting Sun Par Lost 4.540
With wheels yet hov'ring o're the Ocean brim, Par Lost 5.140
Sups with the Ocean: though in Heav'n the Trees Par Lost 5.426
Crystallin Ocean, and the loud misrule Par Lost 7.271
Main Ocean flow'd, not idle, but with warme Par Lost 7.279
Tempest the Ocean: there Leviathan Par Lost 7.412
Earth with her nether Ocean circumfus'd, Par Lost 7.624
West from *Orontes* to the Ocean barr'd Par Lost 9.80
Broke up, shall heave the Ocean to usurp Par Lost 11.827
Spir. To the Ocean now I fly, Mask 976
B.M. ms 'From the Heav'ns'
Bridgewater ms 'From the heavens'
the jealous ocean that old river winds Mask Tr. ms 10.12
So sinks the day-star in the Ocean bed, Lycidas 168
Whispering new joyes to the milde Ocean, Nativity 66
Why fled the Ocean? And why skipt the Mountains? Psalm 114, 13
And post o're Land and Ocean without rest: Sonnet 19, 13
Brutus far to the West, in th' Ocean wide Prose 12, 7
Oceanus
In name of great *Oceanus*, Mask 868
October
Nor wet *Octobers* torrent flood Mask 930
1637 'Octobers'
Odds
Praeeminent by so much odds, while thou Par Lost 4.447
As not of power, at once; nor odds appeerd Par Lost 6.319
Or equal what between us made the odds, Par Lost 6.441
But keep the odds of Knowledge in my power Par Lost 9.820
With odds what Warr hath lost, and fully aveng'd Par Lost 10.374
Juno dare's not give her odds; Arcades 23
Ode
O run, prevent them with thy humble ode, Nativity 24
Odes
So they in Heav'n their Odes and Vigils tun'd: Par Reg 1.182
Aeolian charms and *Dorian Lyric* Odes, Par Reg 4.257
Odious
His odious offrings, and adore the Gods Par Lost 1.475
At last this odious offspring whom thou seest Par Lost 2.781
And silence on the odious dinn of Warr: Par Lost 6.408
Tedious, unshar'd with thee, and odious soon. Par Lost 9.880
And utter odious Truth, that God would come Par Lost 11.704
And mak'st me odious, Psalm 88, 34
Me to them odious, *for they change*, Psalm 88, 35
Odiously
But had thy love, still odiously pretended, Samson 873
Which once smelt sweet, now stinks as odiously; Prose 4, 2
Odoriferous
Fanning thir odoriferous wings dispense Par Lost 4.157
Odorous
So entertaind those odorous sweets the Fiend Par Lost 4.166
Groves whose rich Trees wept odorous Gumms and Balme, Par Lost 4.248
Acanthus, and each odorous bushie shrub Par Lost 4.696
Spirits odorous breathes: flours and thir fruit Par Lost 5.482
An Amber sent of odorous perfume Samson 720
Waters the odorous banks that blow Mask 993
B.M. ms 'Od'rous'
And early ere the odorous breath of morn Arcades 56
Trinity ms 'odourous'
That dropt with odorous oil down his fair eyes, Passion 16
To fill thy odorous Lamp with deeds of light, Sonnet 9, 10
Odour
When from the boughes a savorie odour blow'n, Par Lost 9.579
Odours
Ambrosial Odours and Ambrosial Flowers, Par Lost 2.245
With odours; there ye shall be fed and fill'd Par Lost 2.843
Sabean Odours from the spicie shoare Par Lost 4.162
And flouring Odours, Cassia, Nard, and Balme; Par Lost 5.293
With Rose and Odours from the shrub unfum'd. Par Lost 5.349
Flung Rose, flung Odours from the spicie Shrub, Par Lost 8.517
Of gentlest gale *Arabian* odors fann'd Par Reg 2.364
With odours visited and annual flowers. Samson 987
Dropping odours, dropping Wine. Mask 106
Covering the earth with odours, fruits, and flocks, Mask 712
The Star-led Wisards haste with odours sweet: Nativity 23
What slender Youth bedew'd with liquid odours Horace 1
Oealia
As when *Alcides* from *Oechalia* Crown'd Par Lost 2.542
1667 '*Oealia*'
Oechalia
As when *Alcides* from *Oechalia* Crown'd Par Lost 2.542
1667 '*Oealia*'
Oeta
And *Lichas* from the top of *Oeta* threw Par Lost 2.545

Of
Listings of this word are omitted; see the Introduction.
Of the
Fear'd her stern frown, and she was queen oth' Woods. Mask 446
Bridgewater ms 'o'th''
Trinity ms 'o'th'
Off
Favour'd of Heav'n so highly, to fall off Par Lost 1.30
From off the tossing of these fiery waves, Par Lost 1.184
Forthwith upright he rears from off the Pool Par Lost 1.221
Maim'd his brute Image, head and hands lopt off Par Lost 1.459
Her mischief, and purge off the baser fire Par Lost 2.141
Purge off this gloom; the soft delicious Air, Par Lost 2.400
Farr off from these a slow and silent stream, Par Lost 2.582
As when farr off at Sea a Fleet descri'd Par Lost 2.636
Farr off the flying Fiend: at last appeer Par Lost 2.643
Farr off th' Empyreal Heav'n, extended wide Par Lost 2.1047
Cut off, and for the Book of knowledg fair Par Lost 3.47
Not farr off Heav'n, in the Precincts of light, Par Lost 3.88
Freely put off, and for him lastly dye Par Lost 3.240
Now in loose Garlands thick thrown off, the bright Par Lost 3.362
Satan alighted walks: a Globe farr off Par Lost 3.422
Fly o're the backside of the World farr off Par Lost 3.494
Andromeda farr off *Atlantic* Seas Par Lost 3.559
Far off and fearless, nor with cause to boast, Par Lost 4.14
Mozambic, off at Sea North-East windes blow Par Lost 4.161
Handed they went; and eas'd the putting off Par Lost 4.739
Uzziel, half these draw off, and coast the South Par Lost 4.782
Shadowie sets off the face of things; in vain, Par Lost 5.43
Yield Nectar, though from off the boughs each Morn Par Lost 5.428
Our minds and teach us to cast off this Yoke? Par Lost 5.786
From off the files of warr; there they him laid Par Lost 6.339
Flew off, and into strange vagaries fell, Par Lost 6.614
He onward came, farr off his coming shon, Par Lost 6.768
But drive farr off the barbarous dissonance Par Lost 7.32
God hath bid dwell farr off all anxious cares, Par Lost 8.185
When out of hope, behold her, not farr off, Par Lost 8.481
So ye shall die perhaps, by putting off Par Lost 9.713
My coming seen far off? I miss thee here, Par Lost 10.104
Remov'd farr off; then pittying how they stood Par Lost 10.211
Broke off the rest; so much of Death her thoughts Par Lost 10.1008
That cuts us off from hope, and savours onely Par Lost 10.1043
Eject him tainted now, and purge him off Par Lost 11.52
Wide waving, all approach farr off to fright, Par Lost 11.121
Of glory, and farr off his steps adore. Par Lost 11.333
Contending, and remov'd his Tents farr off; Par Lost 11.727
Pretends to wash off sin, and fit them so Par Reg 1.73
Were better farthest off) is not yet come; Par Reg 3.397
Who wrought their own captivity, fell off Par Reg 3.415
Beat off, returns as oft with humming sound; Par Reg 4.17
Her pile, far off appearing like a Mount Par Reg 4.547
From off the Altar, where an Off'ring burn'd, Samson 26
Might easily have shook off all her snares: Samson 409
To waver, or fall off and joyn with Idols; Samson 456
But now hath cast me off as never known, Samson 641
If not by quick destruction soon cut off Samson 764
Thee he regards not, owns not, hath cut off Samson 1157
Chor. How thou wilt here come off surmounts my reach. Samson 1380
With lavers pure and cleansing herbs wash off Samson 1727
As now I do: But first I must put off Mask 82
Break off, break off, I feel the different pace, Mask 145
Bridgewater ms both 'of'
Prompt me; and they perhaps are not far off. Mask 229
Trinity ms 'farre hence'
Bridgewater ms 'farr hence'
Driving far off each thing of sin and guilt, Mask 456
Bridgewater ms 'of'
Som far off hallow break the silent Air. Mask 481
1673 'of'
Trinity ms 'farre-off'
Bridgewater ms 'of'
And yet came off: if you have this about you Mask 647
Her words set off by som superior power; Mask 801
line not in Trinity ms
line not in Bridgewater ms
Whilst from off the waters fleet Mask 896
Bridgewater ms 'of'
I hear the far-off *Curfeu* sound, Penseroso 74
With minute drops from off the Eaves. Penseroso 130
And from the Boughs brush off the evil dew, Arcades 50
Set off to th' world, nor in broad rumour lies, Lycidas 80
That blows from off each beaked Promontory, Lycidas 94
Pull'd off his Boots, and took away the light: Carrier 16
The Subject new: it walk'd the Town a while, Sonnet 11, 3
Trinity ms 'walk'd' ←'It went off well about'
Because you have thrown of your Prelate Lord, Forcers 1
Trinity ms 'off'
Let us break off, say they, by strength of hand Psalm 2, 6
Come let us cut them off say they, Psalm 83, 13
At Endor quite cut off, and rowl'd Psalm 83, 39
Offal
With suckt and glutted offal, at one sling Par Lost 10.633
Offence
Began to bloom, but soon for mans offence Par Lost 3.355
For mans offence. O unexampl'd love, Par Lost 3.410
But of offence and trouble, which my mind Par Lost 5.34
Th' offence, that Man should thus attain to know? Par Lost 9.726
Nor alter'd his offence; yet God at last Par Lost 10.171
Offence(*cont*)
The day of his offence. Why comes not Death, Par Lost 10.854
For self-offence, more then for God offended. Samson 515
To lessen or extenuate my offence, Samson 767
After offence returning, to regain Samson 1004
And had perform'd it if my known offence Samson 1218
Offend
Consult how we may henceforth most offend Par Lost 1.187
With what more forcible we may offend Par Lost 6.465
Let not my words offend thee, Heav'nly Power, Par Lost 8.379
To offend, discount'nanc't both, and discompos'd; Par Lost 10.110
But solemn and sublime, whom not to offend, Par Lost 11.236
Off. Regard thy self, this will offend them highly. Samson 1333
I will not wish, lest it perhaps offend them Samson 1414
Offended
And pious awe, that feard to have offended. Par Lost 5.135
Offended, worth your laughter, hath giv'n up Par Lost 10.488
Chewd bitter Ashes, which th' offended taste Par Lost 10.566
I beare thee, and unweeting have offended, Par Lost 10.916
By Prayer th' offended Deitie to appease, Par Lost 11.149
Offended; fearless of reproach and scorn, Par Lost 11.811
Be not so sore offended, Son of God; Par Reg 4.196
For self-offence, more then for God offended. Samson 515
The Sea Nymphs, and their powers offended. Penseroso 21
And God is every day offended; Psalm 7, 44
Offending
Not mind us not offending, satisfi'd Par Lost 2.212
Offensive
Her Temple on th' offensive Mountain, built Par Lost 1.443
Offer
Others among the chief might offer now Par Lost 2.469
I offer, on mee let thine anger fall; Par Lost 3.237
Offer sweet smelling Gumms and Fruits and Flours: Par Lost 11.327
His place, to offer Incense, Myrrh, and Gold; Par Lost 12.363
What I can do or offer is suspect; Par Reg 2.399
This offer sets before thee to deliver. Par Reg 3.380
On what I offer set as high esteem, Par Reg 4.160
As offer them to me the Son of God, Par Reg 4.190
Whether he durst accept the offer or not, Samson 1255
I would not taste thy treasonous offer; none Mask 702
Offer the offerings just Psalm 4, 23
Offered
Th' incensed Deitie, while offerd grace Par Lost 3.187
Glad to be offer'd, he attends the will Par Lost 3.270
Second to thee, offerd himself to die Par Lost 3.409
Longer thy offerd good, why else set here? Par Lost 5.63
For joy of offerd peace: but I suppose Par Lost 6.617
And anger wouldst resent the offer'd wrong, Par Lost 9.300
Of thy full branches offer'd free to all; Par Lost 9.802
Life offer'd, or soon beg to lay it down, Par Lost 11.506
His death for Man, as many as offerd Life Par Lost 12.425
Meats by the Law unclean, or offer'd first Par Reg 2.328
Riches though offer'd from the hand of Kings. Par Reg 2.449
Thou valu'st, because offer'd, and reject'st: Par Reg 4.156
Nicely or cautiously my offer'd aid, Par Reg 4.377
The perfet season offer'd with my aid Par Reg 4.468
Obtrud'st thy offer'd aid, that I accepting Par Reg 4.493
Deliverance offerd: I on th' other side Samson 246
Though offer'd only, by the sent conceiv'd Samson 390
Reject not then what offerd means, who knows Samson 516
Sam. He must allege some cause, and offer'd fight Samson 1253
And trust thy honest offer'd courtesie, Mask 322
Offering
Attonement for himself or offering meet, Par Lost 3.234
His Offring soon propitious Fire from Heav'n Par Lost 11.441
For envie that his Brothers Offering found Par Lost 11.456
From off the Altar, where an Off'ring burn'd, Samson 26
None offering fight; who single combatant Samson 344
Offering to combat thee his Champion bold, Samson 1152
Offring to every weary Travailer, Mask 64
Bridgewater ms 'offringe'
Offerings
His odious offrings, and adore the Gods Par Lost 1.475
Our servile offerings. This must be our task Par Lost 2.246
With large Wine-offerings pour'd, and sacred Feast, Par Lost 12.21
Where thou mayst bring thy off'rings, to avert Samson 519
Offer the offerings just Psalm 4, 23
Offers
I see all offers made by me how slight Par Reg 4.155
I never lik'd thy talk, thy offers less, Par Reg 4.171
Office
To sit in hateful Office here confin'd, Par Lost 2.859
Her office holds; of all external things, Par Lost 5.103
Thir Office in the Firmament of Heav'n Par Lost 7.344
The skill of Artifice or Office mean, Par Lost 9.39
Of *Hesperus*, whose Office is to bring Par Lost 9.49
Her office they prescrib'd, to th' other five Par Lost 10.657
With our own hands his Office on our selves; Par Lost 10.1002
Without Mediator, whose high Office now Par Lost 12.240
His Name and Office bearing, who shall quell Par Lost 12.311
To him his Heavenly Office, nor was long Par Reg 1.28
Publish his God-like office now mature, Par Reg 1.188
I undertook that office, and the tongues Par Reg 1.374
For therein stands the office of a King, Par Reg 2.463
With nursing diligence, to me glad office, Samson 924
And in this office of his Mountain watch, Mask 89
Sab. Shepherd 'tis my office best Mask 908
But thou canst best perform that office where thou art. Fair Inf 70

Office(*cont*)
In the kind office of a Chamberlin Carrier 14
1658 'Death in the likenesse'
Officer
A Public Officer, and now at hand. Samson 1306
Officers
Are but as slavish officers of vengeance, Mask 218
line not in Bridgewater ms
Offices
In offices of Love, how we may light'n Par Lost 10.960
Officiate
Diurnal) meerly to officiate light Par Lost 8.22
Officious
Officious, but to thee Earths habitant. Par Lost 8.99
That shine, yet bear thir bright officious Lamps, Par Lost 9.104
With granted leave officious I return, Par Reg 2.302
Offspring
Thrones and Imperial Powers, off-spring of heav'n Par Lost 2.310
At last this odious offspring whom thou seest Par Lost 2.781
Hail holy Light, ofspring of Heav'n first-born, Par Lost 3.1
Your numerous ofspring; if no better place, Par Lost 4.385
Of human ofsspring, sole proprietie, Par Lost 4.751
1667 'ofspring'
Thy ofspring, to the place of evil, Hell, Par Lost 6.276
Who art to lead thy ofspring, and supposest Par Lost 8.86
Ofspring of Heav'n and Earth, and all Earths Lord, Par Lost 9.273
For us his ofspring deare? It cannot be Par Lost 10.238
Met who to meet him came, his Ofspring dear. Par Lost 10.349
To mee and to my ofspring would torment me Par Lost 10.781
To thee and to thy Ofspring; good with bad Par Lost 11.358
Yet they a beauteous ofspring shall beget; Par Lost 11.613
The end of all thy Ofspring, end so sad, Par Lost 11.755
Whose off-spring on the Throne of *Juda* sat Par Reg 2.440
Whose off-spring in his Territory yet serve Par Reg 3.375
Her shadowy off-spring unsubstantial both, Par Reg 4.399
Where his fair off-spring nurs't in Princely lore, Mask 34
Bridgewater ms 'ofspringe'
Trinity ms 'ofspring'
This if thou do he will an off-spring give, Fair Inf 76
Oft
Which oft times may succeed, so as perhaps Par Lost 1.166
ms 'oftimes'
Deeming some Island, oft, as Sea-men tell, Par Lost 1.205
Of hope in fears and dangers, heard so oft Par Lost 1.275
Oft to the Image of a Brute, adorn'd Par Lost 1.371
For those the Race of *Israel* oft forsook Par Lost 1.432
Or Altar smoak'd; yet who more oft then hee Par Lost 1.493
Impregnable; oft on the bordering Deep Par Lost 2.131
Of darkness do we dread? How oft amidst Par Lost 2.263
The most averse, thee chiefly, who full oft Par Lost 2.763
The rest shall hear me call, and oft be warnd Par Lost 3.185
By which, to visit oft those happy Tribes, Par Lost 3.532
Imagind rather oft then elsewhere seen, Par Lost 3.599
To visit oft this new Creation round; Par Lost 3.661
And oft though wisdom wake, suspicion sleeps Par Lost 3.686
Strait couches close, then rising changes oft Par Lost 4.405
That day I oft remember, when from sleep Par Lost 4.449
Singing thir great Creator: oft in bands Par Lost 4.684
If dream'd, not as I oft am wont, of thee, Par Lost 5.32
By us oft seen; his dewie locks distill'd Par Lost 5.56
Oft in her absence mimic Fansie wakes Par Lost 5.110
Wilde work produces oft, and most in dreams, Par Lost 5.112
As may not oft invite, though Spirits of Heav'n Par Lost 5.374
So oft in Festivals of joy and love Par Lost 6.94
Glide under the green Wave, in Sculles that oft Par Lost 7.402
Her state with Oarie feet: yet oft they quit Par Lost 7.440
Open, and henceforth oft; for God will deigne Par Lost 7.569
To visit oft the dwellings of just Men Par Lost 7.570
Useless besides, reasoning I oft admire, Par Lost 8.25
Then value: Oft times nothing profits more Par Lost 8.571
Be good and friendly still, and oft return. Par Lost 8.651
That I should mind thee oft, and mind thou me. Par Lost 9.358
Oft he to her his charge of quick returne Par Lost 9.399
Repeated, shee to him as oft engag'd Par Lost 9.400
About her glowd, oft stooping to support Par Lost 9.427
Veres oft, as oft so steers, and shifts her Saile; Par Lost 9.515
But as in gaze admiring: Oft he bowd Par Lost 9.524
Much reason, and in thir actions oft appeers. Par Lost 9.559
Which oft, they say, some evil Spirit attends Par Lost 9.638
To Boggs and Mires, and oft through Pond or Poole, Par Lost 9.641
As Reapers oft are wont thir Harvest Queen. Par Lost 9.842
Yet oft his heart, divine of somthing ill, Par Lost 9.845
And rapture so oft beheld? those heav'nly shapes Par Lost 9.1082
There oft the *Indian* Herdsman shunning heate Par Lost 9.1108
My voice thou oft hast heard, and hast not fear'd, Par Lost 10.119
With spattering noise rejected: oft they assayd, Par Lost 10.567
Hunger and thirst constraining, drugd as oft, Par Lost 10.568
With soot and cinders fill'd; so oft they fell Par Lost 10.570
Outstretcht he lay, on the cold ground, and oft Par Lost 10.851
Curs'd his Creation, Death as oft accus'd Par Lost 10.852
Shook, but delaid to strike, though oft invok't Par Lost 11.492
And testifi'd against thir wayes; hee oft Par Lost 11.721
Oft sacrificing Bullock, Lamb, or Kid, Par Lost 12.20
But God who oft descends to visit men Par Lost 12.48
Who oft as undeservedly enthrall Par Lost 12.94
To let his sojourners depart, and oft Par Lost 12.192
From whom as oft he saves them penitent Par Lost 12.319
What oft my steddiest thoughts have searcht in vain, Par Lost 12.377

Oft(*cont*)
And oft supported so as shall amaze Par Lost 12.496
The Baptist, (of whose birth I oft had heard, Par Reg 1.270
By rigour unconniving, but that oft Par Reg 1.363
If not disposer; lend them oft my aid, Par Reg 1.393
Oft my advice by presages and signs, Par Reg 1.394
Thus *Mary* pondering oft, and oft to mind Par Reg 2.105
No advantage, and his strength as oft assay. Par Reg 2.234
But men endu'd with these have oft attain'd Par Reg 2.437
And oft by force, which to a generous mind Par Reg 2.479
Oft not deserv'd? I seek not mine, but his Par Reg 3.106
With temperate sway; oft have they violated Par Reg 3.160
The Temple, oft the Law with foul affronts, Par Reg 3.161
And o're a mighty King so oft prevail'd, Par Reg 3.167
And oft beyond; to South the *Persian* Bay, Par Reg 3.273
So oft, and the perswasive Rhetoric Par Reg 4.4
Beat off, returns as oft with humming sound; Par Reg 4.17
Of Bees industrious murmur oft invites Par Reg 4.248
Equal to God, oft shames not to prefer, Par Reg 4.303
And mad despight to be so oft repell'd. Par Reg 4.446
They oft fore-signifie and threaten ill: Par Reg 4.464
With *Joves Alcides*, and oft foil'd still rose, Par Reg 4.565
(Which Men enjoying sight oft without cause complain) Samson 157
Yet truth to say, I oft have heard men wonder Samson 215
But what more oft in Nations grown corrupt, Samson 268
But warn'd by oft experience: did not she Samson 382
Yet toward these thus dignifi'd, thou oft Samson 682
Oft leav'st them to the hostile sword Samson 692
For oft alike, both come to evil end. Samson 704
That wisest and best men full oft beguil'd Samson 759
And Love hath oft, well meaning, wrought much wo, Samson 813
Sam. Love-quarrels oft in pleasing concord end, Samson 1008
Sam. Fair days have oft contracted wind and rain. Samson 1062
Thou oft shalt wish thy self at *Gath* to boast Samson 1127
But patience is more oft the exercise Samson 1287
Chor. All is best, though we oft doubt, Samson 1745
Oft he seems to hide his face, Samson 1749
Of darknes till it smil'd: I have oft heard Mask 252
Which oft is sooner found in lowly sheds Mask 323
Bridgewater ms 'ofte'
Oft seeks to sweet retired Solitude, Mask 376
Bridgewater ms 'of'
Till oft convers with heav'nly habitants Mask 459
Oft seen in Charnell vaults, and Sepulchers Mask 471
El. Bro. Thyrsis? Whose artful strains have oft delaid Mask 494
He lov'd me well, and oft would beg me sing, Mask 623
Her maid'n gentlenes, and oft at Eeve Mask 843
Bridgewater ms 'ofte'
And drenches with *Elysian* dew Mask 996
Bridgewater ms 'drenches oft'
Trinity ms 'drenches' ←'drenches oft'
Where young *Adonis* oft reposes, Mask 999
Trinity ms 'young Adonis oft' ←'many a cherub soft'
Bridgewater ms 'many a Cherub soft'
B.M. ms 'many'a Cherub soft'
yet thence I come and oft from thence behold Mask Tr. ms 10.18
Oft list'ning how the Hounds and horn, Allegro 53
There let *Hymen* oft appear Allegro 125
Oft in glimmering Bowres, and glades Penseroso 27
Spare Fast, that oft with gods doth diet, Penseroso 46
Thee Chauntress oft the Woods among, Penseroso 63
And oft, as if her head she bow'd, Penseroso 71
Oft on a Plat of rising ground, Penseroso 73
Where I may oft out-watch the *Bear*, Penseroso 87
Thus night oft see me in thy pale career, Penseroso 121
Which I full oft amidst these shades alone Arcades 42
Oft till the Star that rose, at Ev'ning, bright Lycidas 30
1638 'Oft till the ev'n-starre bright'
To interpose them oft, is not unwise. Sonnet 20, 14
Plain in thy neatness; O how oft shall he Horace 5
Stronglier, and better oft then earnest can. Prose 7, 2
Often
Between the Cherubim; yea, often plac'd Par Lost 1.387
Both day and night: how often from the steep Par Lost 4.680
What from without comes often to my ears, Par Reg 1.199
Pray'd for, but often proves our woe, our bane? Samson 351
Through paths, and turnings oft'n trod by day, Mask 569
Trinity ms 'often'
Bridgewater ms 'often'
1637 'often'
and often takes our cattell with strange pinches Mask Tr. ms 23.51
The labouring clouds do often rest: Allegro 74
Of that renowned flood, so often sung, Arcades 29
Or *Lucifer* that often warn'd them thence; Nativity 74
Which others at their Barr so often wrench; Sonnet 21, 4
line not in Trinity ms
Oftest
Is oftest yours, the latter most is ours, Par Lost 5.489
Rocks whereon greatest men have oftest wreck'd; Par Reg 2.228
To gain a Scepter, oftest better miss't. Par Reg 2.486
In choice, but oftest to affect the wrong? Samson 1030
Oft-invocated
Consume me, and oft-invocated death Samson 575
Oft-times
And not inforc'd oft-times to part from truth; Par Reg 1.472
Yet as being oft times noxious where they light Par Reg 4.460
Og
As *Og* or *Anak* and the *Emims* old Samson 1080

Og(*cont*)
And large-lim'd *Og* he did subdue, Psalm 136, 69
Oh
In mortal strength! and oh what not in man Samson 349
Chor. Oh how comely it is and how reviving Samson 1268
Oh it continues, they have slain my Son. Samson 1516
Oh no? for something in thy face did shine Fair Inf 34
Resolve me then oh Soul most surely blest Fair Inf 36
Oh say me true if thou wert mortal wight Fair Inf 41
But oh why didst thou not stay here below Fair Inf 64
My God, oh make them as a wheel Psalm 83, 49
Oil
Corn wine and oyle; and from the herd or flock, Par Lost 12.19
Fertil of corn the glebe, of oyl and wine, Par Reg 3.259
With everlasting oil, to give due light Mask 199
line not in Bridgewater ms
Trinity ms 'oyle'
1637 'oile'
That dropt with odorous oil down his fair eyes, Passion 16
Oils
Dropt in Ambrosial Oils till she reviv'd, Mask 840
Trinity ms 'oyles'
Bridgewater ms 'oyles'
1637 'oyles'
Old
Of old *Euphrates* to the Brook that parts Par Lost 1.420
A crew who under Names of old Renown, Par Lost 1.477
Of *Doric* Land; or who with *Saturn* old Par Lost 1.519
Frighted the Reign of *Chaos* and old Night. Par Lost 1.543
To hight of noblest temper Hero's old Par Lost 1.552
Of Warriers old with order'd Spear and Shield, Par Lost 1.565
Sat on his Throne, upheld by old repute, Par Lost 1.639
To claim our just inheritance of old, Par Lost 2.38
Betwixt *Damiata* and mount *Casius* old, Par Lost 2.593
Thus *Satan;* and him thus the Anarch old Par Lost 2.988
Weakning the Scepter of old *Night:* first Hell Par Lost 2.1002
And *Tiresias* and *Phineus* Prophets old. Par Lost 3.36
From *Chaos* and th' inroad of Darkness old, Par Lost 3.421
Like those *Hesperian* Gardens fam'd of old, Par Lost 3.568
In various shapes old *Proteus* from the Sea, Par Lost 3.604
Chear'd with the grateful smell old Ocean smiles. Par Lost 4.165
Girt with the River *Triton*, where old *Cham*, Par Lost 4.276
Her old possession, and extinguish life Par Lost 4.666
Of old *Olympus* dwell'st, but Heav'nlie borne, Par Lost 7.7
From the Armoury of God, where stand of old Par Lost 7.200
With second thoughts, reforming what was old! Par Lost 9.101
Whether such vertue spent of old now faild Par Lost 9.145
Alcinous, host of old *Laertes* Son, Par Lost 9.441
As when of old som Orator renound Par Lost 9.670
In glory as of old, to him appeas'd Par Lost 10.226
In Fables old, less ancient yet then these, Par Lost 11.11
Of *Sarra*, worn by Kings and Hero's old Par Lost 11.243
City of old or modern Fame, the Seat Par Lost 11.386
This is old age; but then thou must outlive Par Lost 11.538
And Judgment from above: him old and young Par Lost 11.668
This our old Conquest, then remember Hell Par Reg 1.46
The City of Palms, *Aenon*, and *Salem* Old, Par Reg 2.21
But trouble, as old *Simeon* plain fore-told, Par Reg 2.87
So spake the old Serpent doubting, and from all Par Reg 2.147
All others by thy self; because of old Par Reg 2.174
Fairer then feign'd of old, or fabl'd since Par Reg 2.358
On *Aaron*'s breast: or tongue of Seers old Par Reg 3.15
The Prophets old, who sung thy endless raign, Par Reg 3.178
Several days journey, built by *Ninus* old, Par Reg 3.276
Antigonus, and old *Hyrcanus* bound, Par Reg 3.367
Thus long from *Israel;* serving as of old Par Reg 3.378
This Emperour hath no Son, and now is old, Par Reg 4.90
Old, and lascivious, and from *Rome* retir'd Par Reg 4.91
Of Academics old and new, with those Par Reg 4.278
And Thief of Paradise; him long of old Par Reg 4.604
Fled from his Lion ramp, old Warriors turn'd Samson 139
Up to the Hill by *Hebron*, seat of Giants old, Samson 148
Old *Manoah:* advise Samson 328
Though in this uncouth place; if old respect, Samson 333
To a contemptible old age obscure. Samson 572
In crude old age; Samson 700
May ever tend about thee to old age Samson 925
As *Og* or *Anak* and the *Emims* old Samson 1080
But wherefore comes old *Manoa* in such hast Samson 1441
Sons wont to nurse thir Parents in old age, Samson 1487
Thou in old age car'st how to nurse thy Son. Samson 1488
For his people of old; what hinders now? Samson 1533
An old, and haughty Nation proud in Arms: Mask 33
Bridgewater ms 'ould'
From old, or modern Bard in Hall, or Bowr. Mask 45
Antiquity from the old Schools of Greece Mask 439
Bridgewater ms 'ould'
Storied of old in high immortal vers Mask 516
Which once of *Meliboeus* old I learnt Mask 822
And, as the old Swain said, she can unlock Mask 852
Bridgewater ms 'owld'
And old sooth-saying *Glaucus* spell, Mask 874
Bridgewater ms 'ould'
Sprung of old *Anchises* line, Mask 923
Bridgewater ms 'owld'
the jealous ocean that old river winds Mask Tr. ms 10.12
And young and old com forth to play Allegro 97
Till old experience do attain Penseroso 173

Old(*cont*)
On old *Lycaeus* or *Cyllene* hoar, Arcades 98
And old *Damoetas* lov'd to hear our song. Lycidas 36
Where your old *Bards*, the famous *Druids* ly, Lycidas 53
Sleep'st by the fable of *Bellerus* old, Lycidas 160
But when of old the sons of morning sung, Nativity 119
Th' old Dragon under ground Nativity 168
And last of Kings and Queens and *Hero*'s old, Vacation 47
A *Sybil* old, bow-bent with crooked age, Vacation 69
Here lies old *Hobson*, Death hath broke his girt, Carrier 1
'Gainst old truth) motion number'd out his time; Another 8
word not in 1640 or 1657 texts
Kil'd with report that Old man eloquent, Sonnet 10, 8
Then his *Casella*, whom he woo'd to sing, Sonnet 13, 13
Trinity ms 'his' ←'old'
Vane, young in yeares, but in sage counsell old, Sonnet 17, 1
Ev'n them who kept thy truth so pure of old Sonnet 18, 3
Purification in the old Law did save, Sonnet 23, 6
New Presbyter is but *Old Priest* writ Large. Forcers 20
Trinity ms 'old'
Through grief consumes, is waxen old and dark Psalm 6, 14
Trouble he hath conceav'd of old Psalm 7, 52
This was a Statute *giv'n of old* Psalm 81, 13
When at the brook of Kishon *old* Psalm 83, 37
Sea-girt it lies, where Giants dwelt of old, Prose 12, 9
Older
Made older then thy age through eye-sight lost. Samson 1489
Olive
An Olive leafe he brings, pacific signe: Par Lost 11.860
See there the Olive Grove of *Academe*, Par Reg 4.244
She crown'd with Olive green, came softly sliding Nativity 47
Olympian
As at th' Olympian Games or *Pythian* fields; Par Lost 2.530
Following, above th' *Olympian* Hill I soare, Par Lost 7.3
Olympias
Hee with *Olympias*, this with her who bore Par Lost 9.509
Olympus
Of cold *Olympus* rul'd the middle Air Par Lost 1.516
ms 'Olympus'
Of old *Olympus* dwell'st, but Heav'nlie borne, Par Lost 7.7
Of high *Olympus*, thence by *Saturn* driv'n Par Lost 10.583
Of shak't Olympus by mischance didst fall; Fair Inf 44
Omen
Bid go with evil omen and the brand Samson 967
Ominous
Ominous conjecture on the whole success: Par Lost 2.123
Whereof this ominous night that clos'd thee round, Par Reg 4.481
At last betakes him to this ominous Wood, Mask 61
Omission
Too grievous for the trespass or omission, Samson 691
Omit
Must not omit a Fathers timely care Samson 602
Omnific
Said then th' Omnific Word, your discord end: Par Lost 7.217
Omnipotence
Of our Omnipotence, and with what Arms Par Lost 5.722
Omnipotence to none. But well thou comst Par Lost 6.159
Second Omnipotence, two dayes are past, Par Lost 6.684
Girt with Omnipotence, with Radiance crown'd Par Lost 7.194
Though numberless, to his Omnipotence, Par Lost 8.108
Omnipotent
Who durst defie th' Omnipotent to Arms. Par Lost 1.49
Which but th' Omnipotent none could have foyld, Par Lost 1.273
Subdues us, and Omnipotent Decree, Par Lost 2.198
Thee Father first they sung Omnipotent, Par Lost 3.372
Th' Omnipotent. Ay me, they little know Par Lost 4.86
Maker Omnipotent, and thou the Day, Par Lost 4.725
So spake th' Omnipotent, and with his words Par Lost 5.616
Against th' Omnipotent to rise in Arms; Par Lost 6.136
Had not th' Eternal King Omnipotent Par Lost 6.227
Victorious with his Saints, th' Omnipotent Par Lost 7.136
Of all his works: therefore the Omnipotent Par Lost 7.516
Not God Omnipotent, nor Fate, yet so Par Lost 9.927
Omnipresence
Hath Omnipresence) and the work ordain'd, Par Lost 7.590
Not this Rock onely; his Omnipresence fills Par Lost 11.336
Omniscient
Omniscient thought. True is, less firmly arm'd, Par Lost 6.430
Onely Omniscient, hath suppresst in Night, Par Lost 7.123
Omniscient, who in all things wise and just, Par Lost 10.7
On
Listings of this word are omitted; see the Introduction.
Once
At once as far as Angels kenn he views Par Lost 1.59
Joynd with me once, now misery hath joynd Par Lost 1.90
In this unhappy Mansion, or once more Par Lost 1.268
If once they hear that voyce, thir liveliest pledge Par Lost 1.274
Warriers, the Flowr of Heav'n, once yours, now lost, Par Lost 1.316
A Leper once he lost and gain'd a King, Par Lost 1.471
(Far other once beheld in bliss) condemn'd Par Lost 1.607
At once with joy and fear his heart rebounds. Par Lost 1.788
Arm'd with Hell flames and fury all at once Par Lost 2.61
Will he, so wise, let loose at once his ire, Par Lost 2.155
Will once more lift us up, in spight of Fate, Par Lost 2.393
Forbidding; and at once with him they rose; Par Lost 2.475
Thir rising all at once was as the sound Par Lost 2.476
All taste of living wight, as once it fled Par Lost 2.613
For never but once more was either like Par Lost 2.721

Once(*cont*)

Now in thine eye so foul, once deemd so fair	Par Lost 2.748
To know, and this once known, shall soon return,	Par Lost 2.839
Could once have mov'd; then in the key-hole turns	Par Lost 2.876
(Which is my present journey) and once more	Par Lost 2.985
But hee once past, soon after when man fell,	Par Lost 2.1023
Of living Saphire, once his native Seat;	Par Lost 2.1050
His own works and their works at once to view:	Par Lost 3.59
Freely voutsaft; once more I will renew	Par Lost 3.175
Upheld by me, yet once more he shall stand	Par Lost 3.178
Can never seek, once dead in sins and lost;	Par Lost 3.233
Immortal Amarant, a Flour which once	Par Lost 3.353
Of all this World at once. As when a Scout	Par Lost 3.543
Where no ill seems: Which now for once beguil'd	Par Lost 3.689
I fell, how glorious once above thy Spheare;	Par Lost 4.39
By owing owes not, but still pays, at once	Par Lost 4.56
Uriel once warnd; whose eye pursu'd him down	Par Lost 4.125
Blossoms and Fruits at once of golden hue	Par Lost 4.148
Know ye not mee? ye knew me once no mate	Par Lost 4.828
Or all at once; more glorie will be wonn,	Par Lost 4.853
Though for possession put to try once more	Par Lost 4.941
Once fawn'd, and cring'd, and servilly ador'd	Par Lost 4.959
In them at once to ruin all mankind.	Par Lost 5.228
At once on th' Eastern cliff of Paradise	Par Lost 5.275
The ruin of so many glorious once	Par Lost 5.567
Squadrons at once, with huge two-handed sway	Par Lost 6.251
Thy malice into thousands, once upright	Par Lost 6.270
As not of power, at once; nor odds appeerd	Par Lost 6.319
Once found, which yet unfound most would have thought	Par Lost 6.500
Not long, for sudden all at once thir Reeds	Par Lost 6.582
If our proposals once again were heard	Par Lost 6.618
At once the Four spred out thir Starrie wings	Par Lost 6.827
Thee once to gaine Companion of his woe.	Par Lost 6.907
Least from this flying Steed unrein'd, (as once	Par Lost 7.17
(So call him, brighter once amidst the Host	Par Lost 7.132
Pasturing at once, and in broad Herds upsprung.	Par Lost 7.462
At once came forth whatever creeps the ground,	Par Lost 7.475
From thee alone, which on us both at once	Par Lost 9.303
Not to deferr; hunger and thirst at once,	Par Lost 9.586
To reach, and feed at once both Bodie and Mind?	Par Lost 9.779
Thir inward State of Mind, calm Region once	Par Lost 9.1125
As *Delos* floating once; the rest his look	Par Lost 10.296
And *Dipsas* (not so thick swarm'd once the Soil	Par Lost 10.526
Whom they triumph'd once lapst. Thus were they plagu'd	Par Lost 10.572
Once actual, now in body, and to dwell	Par Lost 10.587
Is propagated curse. O voice once heard	Par Lost 10.729
Of Nature, and not fill the World at once	Par Lost 10.892
Then both our selves and Seed at once to free	Par Lost 10.999
When God descended, and perhaps once more	Par Lost 11.75
With whose stol'n Fruit Man once more to delude.	Par Lost 11.125
As once thou slepst, while Shee to life was formd.	Par Lost 11.369
Th' Image of God in man created once	Par Lost 11.508
His Children, all in view destroyd at once;	Par Lost 11.761
At once, by my foreknowledge gaining Birth	Par Lost 11.768
A Dove sent forth once and agen to spie	Par Lost 11.857
Moses once more his potent Rod extends	Par Lost 12.211
Will waft me; and the way found prosperous once	Par Reg 1.104
O what a multitude of thoughts at once	Par Reg 1.196
And for a time caught up to God, as once	Par Reg 2.14
Rode up to Heaven, yet once again to come.	Par Reg 2.17
Into himself descended, and at once	Par Reg 2.111
To enamour, as the Zone of *Venus* once	Par Reg 2.214
Abominations rather, as did once	Par Reg 3.162
With *Modin* and her Suburbs once content.	Par Reg 3.170
And once a year *Jerusalem*, few days	Par Reg 3.234
As the Red Sea and *Jordan* once he cleft,	Par Reg 3.438
That people victor once, now vile and base,	Par Reg 4.132
Deservedly made vassal, who once just,	Par Reg 4.133
Look once more e're we leave this specular Mount	Par Reg 4.236
That once found out and solv'd, for grief and spight	Par Reg 4.574
Times past, what once I was, and what am now.	Samson 22
How could I once look up, or heave the head,	Samson 197
As I suppose, towards your once gloried friend,	Samson 334
Alas methinks whom God hath chosen once	Samson 368
I was his nursling once and choice delight,	Samson 633
So deal not with this once thy glorious Champion,	Samson 705
Once more thy face, and know of thy estate,	Samson 742
Being once a wife, for me thou wast to leave	Samson 885
Where once I have been caught; I know thy trains	Samson 932
Love once possest, nor can be easily	Samson 1005
Once join'd, the contrary she proves, a thorn	Samson 1037
In confidence whereof I once again	Samson 1174
So dreaded once, may now exasperate them	Samson 1417
Thir once great dread, captive, & blind before them,	Samson 1474
At once both to destroy and be destroy'd;	Samson 1587
Not once perceive their foul disfigurement,	Mask 74
And hugg him into snares. When once her eye	Mask 164
That *Hermes* once to wise *Ulysses* gave;	Mask 637
line not in Bridgewater ms	
Trinity ms 'Hermes once' ←'Mercury'	
Which once of *Meliboeus* old I learnt	Mask 822
As he met her once a Maying,	Allegro 20
Yet once more, O ye Laurels, and once more	Lycidas 1
Stands ready to smite once, and smite no more.	Lycidas 131
For so the holy sages once did sing,	Nativity 5
Once bless our human ears,	Nativity 126
Or wert thou that just Maid who once before	Fair Inf 50
And cam'st again to visit us once more?	Fair Inf 52

Once(*cont*)

But haste thee strait to do me once a Pleasure,	Vacation 17
Such as the wise *Demodocus* once told	Vacation 48
For once it was my dismal hap to hear	Vacation 68
Once glorious Towers, now sunk in guiltles blood;	Passion 40
When once our heav'nly-guided soul shall clime,	On Time 19
As once we did, till disproportion'd sin	Musick 19
Once had the early Matrons run	Winchester 23
Spoil'd at once both fruit and tree:	Winchester 30
His principles being ceast, he ended strait.	Another 10
1658 'once ceas'd'	
Daughter to that good Earl, once President	Sonnet 10, 1
And such, as yet once more I trust to have	Sonnet 23, 7
If once his wrath take fire like fuel sere.	Psalm 2, 27
In peace at once will I	Psalm 4, 37
Which once smelt sweet, now stinks as odiously;	Prose 4, 2

One

With loss of *Eden*, till one greater Man	Par Lost 1.4
For one restraint, Lords of the World besides?	Par Lost 1.32
As one great Furnace flam'd, yet from those flames	Par Lost 1.62
One next himself in power, and next in crime,	Par Lost 1.79
Receive thy new Possessor: One who brings	Par Lost 1.252
Of alienated *Judah*. Next came one	Par Lost 1.457
For one of *Syrian* mode, whereon to burn	Par Lost 1.474
Jehovah, who in one Night when he pass'd	Par Lost 1.487
From *Egypt* marching, equal'd with one stroke	Par Lost 1.488
Monarch in Heav'n, till then as one secure	Par Lost 1.638
As in an Organ from one blast of wind	Par Lost 1.708
One day upon our heads; while we perhaps	Par Lost 2.178
Views all things at one view? he from heav'ns highth	Par Lost 2.190
Of mankind in one root, and Earth with Hell	Par Lost 2.383
The tempting stream, with one small drop to loose	Par Lost 2.607
All in one moment, and so neer the brink;	Par Lost 2.609
The one seem'd Woman to the waste, and fair,	Par Lost 2.650
Thy lingring, or with one stroke of this Dart	Par Lost 2.702
His wrath which one day will destroy ye both.	Par Lost 2.734
This uncouth errand sole, and one for all	Par Lost 2.827
And wisdome at one entrance quite shut out.	Par Lost 3.50
Potable Gold, when with one vertuous touch	Par Lost 3.608
Th' Arch-Angel *Uriel*, one of the seav'n	Par Lost 3.648
One step no more then from himself can fly	Par Lost 4.22
I sdeind subjection, and thought one step higher	Par Lost 4.50
As one continu'd brake, the undergrowth	Par Lost 4.175
One Gate there only was, and that look'd East	Par Lost 4.178
At one slight bound high over leap'd all bound	Par Lost 4.181
Of those fourfooted kindes, himself now one,	Par Lost 4.397
His couchant watch, as one who chose his ground	Par Lost 4.406
This one, this easie charge, of all the Trees	Par Lost 4.421
One easie prohibition, who enjoy	Par Lost 4.433
Imparadis't in one anothers arms	Par Lost 4.506
One fatal Tree there stands of Knowledge call'd,	Par Lost 4.514
Conspicuous farr, winding with one ascent	Par Lost 4.545
Accessible from Earth, one entrance high;	Par Lost 4.546
Lost sight of him; one of the banisht crew	Par Lost 4.573
O loss of one in Heav'n to judge of wise,	Par Lost 4.904
Close at mine ear one call'd me forth to walk	Par Lost 5.36
One shapd and wing'd like one of those from Heav'n	Par Lost 5.55
That one Celestial Father gives to all.	Par Lost 5.403
O *Adam*, one Almightie is, from whom	Par Lost 5.469
Such to perfection, one first matter all,	Par Lost 5.472
United as one individual Soule	Par Lost 5.610
Both waking we were one; how then can now	Par Lost 5.678
Or several one by one, the Regent Powers,	Par Lost 5.697
And all the Sea, from one entire globose	Par Lost 5.753
Too much to one, but double how endur'd,	Par Lost 5.783
To one and to his image now proclaim'd?	Par Lost 5.784
One over all with unsucceeded power.	Par Lost 5.821
Our happie state under one Head more neer	Par Lost 5.830
1667 'our' in some copies	
Or all Angelic Nature joind in one,	Par Lost 5.834
One of our number thus reduc't becomes,	Par Lost 5.843
With joy and acclamations loud, that one	Par Lost 6.23
That of so many Myriads fall'n, yet one	Par Lost 6.24
Unanimous, as sons of one great Sire	Par Lost 6.95
Reaching beyond all limit at one blow	Par Lost 6.140
To heav'nly Soules had bin all one; but now	Par Lost 6.165
Uplifted imminent one stroke they aim'd	Par Lost 6.317
Threatn'd, nor from the Holie One of Heav'n	Par Lost 6.359
Who have sustaind one day in doubtful fight	Par Lost 6.423
(And if one day, why not Eternal dayes2)	Par Lost 6.424
As one he stood escap't from cruel fight,	Par Lost 6.448
Some one intent on mischief, or inspir'd	Par Lost 6.503
Provide, pernicious with one touch to fire.	Par Lost 6.520
Under thir Head imbodied all in one.	Par Lost 6.779
One Spirit in them rul'd, and every eye	Par Lost 6.848
Before his memorie, as one whose drouth	Par Lost 7.66
Another World, out of one man a Race	Par Lost 7.155
One Kingdom, Joy and Union without end.	Par Lost 7.161
One foot he center'd, and the other turn'd	Par Lost 7.228
Into one place, and let dry Land appeer.	Par Lost 7.284
One day and night; in all thir vast survey	Par Lost 8.24
Greater so manifold to this one use,	Par Lost 8.29
And livd: One came, methought, of shape Divine,	Par Lost 8.295
The one intense, the other still remiss	Par Lost 8.387
And through all numbers absolute, though One;	Par Lost 8.421
And they shall be one Flesh, one Heart, one Soule.	Par Lost 8.499
As one intended first, not after made	Par Lost 8.555
Union of Mind, or in us both one Soule;	Par Lost 8.604

One(*cont*)
The infernal Powers, in one day to have marr'd Par Lost 9.136
Not longer then since I in one Night freed Par Lost 9.140
One night or two with wanton growth derides Par Lost 9.211
As one who loves, and some unkindness meets, Par Lost 9.271
As one who long in populous City pent, Par Lost 9.445
That space the Evil one abstracted stood Par Lost 9.463
At first, as one who sought access, but feard Par Lost 9.511
Half what in thee is fair, one man except, Par Lost 9.545
Who sees thee? (and what is one2) who shouldst be seen Par Lost 9.546
Fast by a Fountain, one small Thicket past Par Lost 9.628
For Beasts it seems: yet that one Beast which first Par Lost 9.769
So having said, as one from sad dismay Par Lost 9.917
Our State cannot be severd, we are one, Par Lost 9.958
One Flesh; to loose thee were to loose my self. Par Lost 9.959
One Heart, one Soul in both; whereof good prooff Par Lost 9.967
To undergoe with mee one Guilt, one Crime, Par Lost 9.971
For this one Tree had bin forbidden ten. Par Lost 9.1026
Mine with this glorious Work, and made one Realm Par Lost 10.391
Hell and this World, one Realm, one Continent Par Lost 10.392
For one forbidden Tree a multitude Par Lost 10.554
With suckt and glutted offal, at one sling Par Lost 10.633
With cruel expectation. Yet one doubt Par Lost 10.782
That Death be not one stroak, as I suppos'd, Par Lost 10.809
For one mans fault thus guiltless be condemn'd, Par Lost 10.823
Said hee, with one thrice acceptable stroke Par Lost 10.855
While yet we live, scarse one short hour perhaps, Par Lost 10.923
As joyn'd in injuries, one enmitie Par Lost 10.925
As one disarm'd, his anger all he lost, Par Lost 10.945
Made one with me as I with thee am one. Par Lost 11.44
O Sons, like one of us Man is become Par Lost 11.84
Or one short sigh of humane breath, up-borne Par Lost 11.147
One way the self-same hour? why in the East Par Lost 11.203
One man, Assassin-like had levied Warr, Par Lost 11.219
One of the heav'nly Host, and by his Gate Par Lost 11.230
And one bad act with many deeds well done Par Lost 11.256
In other part stood one who at the Forge Par Lost 11.564
One way a Band select from forage drives Par Lost 11.646
Of middle Age one rising, eminent Par Lost 11.665
All left, in one small bottom swum imbark't. Par Lost 11.753
One Man except, the onely Son of light Par Lost 11.808
The one just Man alive; by his command Par Lost 11.818
Farr less I now lament for one whole World Par Lost 11.874
For one Man found so perfet and so just, Par Lost 11.876
Such grace shall one just Man find in his sight, Par Lost 11.890
As one who in his journey bates at Noone, Par Lost 12.1
line not in 1667 edition
Thus thou hast seen one World begin and end; Par Lost 12.6
Under paternal rule; till one shall rise Par Lost 12.24
And one peculiar Nation to select Par Lost 12.111
A Nation from one faithful man to spring: Par Lost 12.113
Last with one midnight stroke all the first-born Par Lost 12.189
One greater, of whose day he shall foretell, Par Lost 12.242
The holy One with mortal Men to dwell: Par Lost 12.248
And all the rule, one Empire; onely add Par Lost 12.581
Both in one Faith unanimous though sad, Par Lost 12.603
By one mans disobedience lost, now sing Par Reg 1.2
By one mans firm obedience fully tri'd Par Reg 1.4
One day forth walk'd alone, the Spirit leading; Par Reg 1.189
Flam'd in my heart, heroic acts, one while Par Reg 1.216
Or harbour'd in one Cave, is not reveal'd; Par Reg 1.307
Easily canst thou find one miserable, Par Reg 1.471
How would one look from his Majestick brow Par Reg 2.216
As one in City, or Court, or Palace bred, Par Reg 2.300
And know not whom, but as one leads the other; Par Reg 3.53
One is the Son of *Jove*, of *Mars* the other, Par Reg 3.84
Th' one winding, the other strait and left between Par Reg 3.256
Roman and *Parthian?* therefore one of these Par Reg 3.362
That Evil one, Satan for ever damn'd. Par Reg 4.194
Fortune and Fate, as one regardless quite Par Reg 4.317
As one past hope, abandon'd, Samson 120
Had *Judah* that day join'd, or one whole Tribe, Samson 265
At one spears length. O ever failing trust Samson 348
What boots it at one gate to make defence, Samson 560
This one prayer yet remains, might I be heard, Samson 649
Of fancy, feard lest one day thou wouldst leave me Samson 794
On both his wings, one black, th' other white, Samson 973
Much like thy riddle, *Samson*, in one day Samson 1016
Or seven, though one should musing sit; Samson 1017
One vertuous rarely found, Samson 1047
And with one buffet lay thy structure low, Samson 1239
Chor. Go, and the Holy One Samson 1427
Man. I have attempted one by one the Lords Samson 1457
From slaughter of one foe could not ascend. Samson 1518
And to our wish I see one hither speeding, Samson 1539
And eyes fast fixt he stood, as one who pray'd, Samson 1637
And makes one blot of all the ayr, Mask 133
Trinity ms 'makes one' ←'throws a' ←'makes a'
Either som one like us night-founder'd here, Mask 483
Against th' unarmed weakness of one Virgin Mask 582
But this will cure all streight, one sip of this Mask 811
When in one night, ere glimps of morn, Allegro 107
Like one that had bin led astray Penseroso 69
Bending one way their pretious influence, Nativity 71
If likewise he some fair one wedded not, Fair Inf 11
Yet every one shall make him underling, Vacation 76
Summers three times eight save one Winchester 7
Or els the ways being foul, twenty to one, Carrier 3

One(*cont*)
Here lieth one who did most truly prove, Another 1
1640, 1657 'Here *Hobson* lyes'
For one Carrier put down to make six bearers. Another 20
line not in 1640, 1657, 1658 texts
Stand spelling fals, while one might walk to Mile- Sonnet 11, 7
And that one Talent which is death to hide, Sonnet 19, 3
Against heavns hand or will, nor bate a jot Sonnet 22, 7
1694 'one jot'
Upon your beds, each one, Psalm 4, 21
And all as one in mind Psalm 83, 18
O're all the earth *art one*. Psalm 83, 68
For one day in thy Courts *to be* Psalm 84, 33

Ones
Great ones how long will ye Psalm 4, 7

Only
Serv'd onely to discover sights of woe, Par Lost 1.64
ms 'only'
1667 'only'
Firm concord holds, men onely disagree Par Lost 2.497
Created evil, for evil only good, Par Lost 2.623
Against thy only Son? What fury O Son, Par Lost 2.728
His onely Son; On Earth he first beheld Par Lost 3.64
Our two first Parents, yet the onely two Par Lost 3.65
Thus to his onely Son foreseeing spake. Par Lost 3.79
Onely begotten Son, seest thou what rage Par Lost 3.80
Where onely what they needs must do, appeard, Par Lost 3.105
Of all things made, and judgest onely right. Par Lost 3.155
To mortal men, above which only shon Par Lost 3.268
O thou in Heav'n and Earth the only peace Par Lost 3.274
Thou therefore whom thou only canst redeem, Par Lost 3.281
Thee only extoll'd, Son of thy Fathers might, Par Lost 3.398
No sooner did thy dear and onely Son Par Lost 3.403
Hypocrisie, the onely evil that walks Par Lost 3.683
1667 'only'
Contented with report hear onely in heav'n: Par Lost 3.701
The lower still I fall, onely Supream Par Lost 4.91
One Gate there only was, and that look'd East Par Lost 4.178
1667 'onely'
Of that life-giving Plant, but only us'd Par Lost 4.199
If true, here only, and of delicious taste: Par Lost 4.251
1667 'onely'
Hee for God only, shee for God in him: Par Lost 4.299
So various, not to taste that onely Tree Par Lost 4.423
The only sign of our obedience left Par Lost 4.428
Can it be death? and do they onely stand Par Lost 4.518
Not only enlighten, but with kindly heate Par Lost 4.668
To thee no reason; who knowst only good, Par Lost 4.895
Might have ensu'd, nor onely Paradise Par Lost 4.991
And temperat vapors bland, which th' only sound Par Lost 5.5
Forbidd'n here, it seems, as onely fit Par Lost 5.69
To give us onely good; and if the night Par Lost 5.206
Two onely, who yet by sov'ran gift possess Par Lost 5.366
To spiritual Natures; only this I know, Par Lost 5.402
My onely Son, and on this holy Hill Par Lost 5.604
Of surfet where full measure onely bounds Par Lost 5.639
line not in 1667 edition
And smiling to his onely Son thus said. Par Lost 5.718
This onely to consult how we may best Par Lost 5.779
That to his only Son by right endu'd Par Lost 5.815
Among the faithless, faithful only hee; Par Lost 5.897
As onely in his arm the moment lay Par Lost 6.239
The Thunderer of his only dreaded bolt. Par Lost 6.491
Nor multitude, stand onely and behold Par Lost 6.810
Onely Omniscient, hath suppresst in Night, Par Lost 7.123
Which onely thy solution can resolve. Par Lost 8.14
Onely to shine, yet scarce to contribute Par Lost 8.155
Think onely what concernes thee and thy being; Par Lost 8.174
Not of Earth onely but of highest Heav'n. Par Lost 8.178
Not onely these fair bounds, but all the Earth Par Lost 8.338
Intended thee, for trial onely brought, Par Lost 8.447
Superiour and unmov'd, here onely weake Par Lost 8.532
Express they, by looks onely, or do they mix Par Lost 8.616
Warrs, hitherto the onely Argument Par Lost 9.28
For onely in destroying I find ease Par Lost 9.129
But harm precedes not sin: onely our Foe Par Lost 9.327
Touchd onely, that our trial, when least sought, Par Lost 9.380
The onely two of Mankinde, but in them Par Lost 9.415
Within me cleere, not onely to discerne Par Lost 9.681
Had it been onely coveting to Eye Par Lost 9.923
They sate them down to weep, nor onely Teares Par Lost 9.1121
Nor hee thir outward onely with the Skins Par Lost 10.220
For in possession such, not onely of right, Par Lost 10.461
Not to do onely, but to will the same Par Lost 10.826
On mee, mee onely, as the sourse and spring Par Lost 10.832
To *Satan* only like both crime and doom. Par Lost 10.841
1667 'onely'
My onely strength and stay: forlorn of thee, Par Lost 10.921
Against God onely, I against God and thee, Par Lost 10.931
Mee mee onely just object of his ire. Par Lost 10.936
That cuts us off from hope, and savours onely Par Lost 10.1043
Pains onely in Child-bearing were foretold, Par Lost 10.1051
Recess, and onely consolation left Par Lost 11.304
Not this Rock onely; his Omnipresence fills Par Lost 11.336
Bred onely and completed to the taste Par Lost 11.618
For in those dayes Might onely shall be admir'd, Par Lost 11.689
The onely righteous in a World perverse, Par Lost 11.701
My part of evil onely, each dayes lot Par Lost 11.765

Only(*cont*)
One Man except, the onely Son of light Par Lost 11.808
He gave us onely over Beast, Fish, Fowl Par Lost 12.67
So onely can high Justice rest appaid. Par Lost 12.401
Not onely to the Sons of *Abrahams* Loines Par Lost 12.447
Left onely in those written Records pure, Par Lost 12.513
And love with fear the onely God, to walk Par Lost 12.562
And all the rule, one Empire; onely add Par Lost 12.581
Misled; the stubborn only to subdue. Par Reg 1.226
Man lives not by Bread only, but each Word Par Reg 1.349
Sometimes they thought he might be only shewn, Par Reg 2.13
In the admiration only of weak minds Par Reg 2.221
Or that which only seems to satisfie Par Reg 2.229
Only in a bottom saw a pleasant Grove, Par Reg 2.289
With honour, only deign to sit and eat. Par Reg 2.336
Only the importune Tempter still remain'd, Par Reg 2.404
That other o're the body only reigns, Par Reg 2.478
The Lord thy God, and only him shalt serve; Par Reg 4.177
To know this only, that he nothing knew; Par Reg 4.294
Far worse, her false resemblance only meets, Par Reg 4.320
These only with our Law best form a King. Par Reg 4.364
O patient Son of God, yet only stoodst Par Reg 4.420
Of men at thee, for only thou here dwell'st. Par Reg 4.466
Their choicest youth; they only liv'd who fled. Samson 264
Though offer'd only, by the sent conceiv'd Samson 390
This only hope relieves me, that the strife Samson 460
Whose drink was only from the liquid brook. Samson 557
Better at home lie bed-rid, not only idle, Samson 579
My griefs not only pain me Samson 617
To deaths benumming Opium as my only cure. Samson 630
Nor only dost degrade them, or remit Samson 687
Only my love of thee held long debate; Samson 863
Misguided; only what remains past cure Samson 912
I only with an Oak'n staff will meet thee, Samson 1123
Went up with armed powers thee only seeking, Samson 1190
Thir choice nobility and flower, not only Samson 1654
The vulgar only scap'd who stood without. Samson 1659
They only set on sport and play Samson 1679
Visit his Tomb with flowers, only bewailing Samson 1742
Tis onely day-light that makes Sin Mask 126
Trinity ms 'only'
Bridgewater ms 'only'
Means her provision onely to the good Mask 765
Trinity ms 'only'
Onely with speeches fair Nativity 37
1673 'Only'
And wearie of their place do only stay Vacation 25
Thou know'st it must be now thy only bent Vacation 55
Who onely thought to crop the flowr Winchester 39
Onely remains this superscription. Another 34
line not in 1658 text
1673 'Only'
Not of warr onely, but detractions rude, Sonnet 16, 2
1694 'only'
They also serve who only stand and waite. Sonnet 19, 14
Who *only* on thee doth relie, Psalm 84, 47
And in thee only rest. Psalm 84, 48

Onset
By sudden onset, either with Hell fire Par Lost 2.364
Of onset ended soon each milder thought. Par Lost 6.98

Onward
The Monster moving onward came as fast Par Lost 2.675
Him through the spicie Forrest onward com Par Lost 5.298
And onward move Embattelld; when behold Par Lost 6.550
He onward came, farr off his coming shon, Par Lost 6.768
Hee on his impious Foes right onward drove, Par Lost 6.831
From this day onward, which I feel begun Par Lost 10.811
Sams. A Little onward lend thy guiding hand Samson 1
Right onward. What supports me dost thou ask? Sonnet 22, 9
Trinity ms 'Right onward' ←'Vphillward'

Ooze
And on the washie Oose deep Channels wore; Par Lost 7.303

Oozy
With *Nectar* pure his oozy Lock's he laves, Lycidas 175
1638 'oazie'
Trinity ms 'oozie'
And bid the weltring waves their oozy channel keep. Nativity 124

Opacous
Mean while upon the firm opacous Globe Par Lost 3.418
Round this opacous Earth, this punctual spot, Par Lost 8.23

Opal
With Opal Towrs and Battlements adorn'd Par Lost 2.1049

Opaque
Shadow from body opaque can fall, and the Aire, Par Lost 3.619

Ope
Adam, now ope thine eyes, and first behold Par Lost 11.423
And in requitall ope his leather'n scrip, Mask 626

Oped
Dishonour, obloquie, and op't the mouths Samson 452

Open
Open or understood must be resolv'd. Par Lost 1.662
ms 'Op'n'
Whether of open Warr or covert guile, Par Lost 2.41
My sentence is for open Warr: Of Wiles, Par Lost 2.51
I should be much for open Warr, O Peers, Par Lost 2.119
Warr therefore, open or conceal'd, alike Par Lost 2.187
Unfast'ns: on a sudden op'n flie Par Lost 2.879
Excel'd her power; the Gates wide op'n stood, Par Lost 2.884

Open(*cont*)
Dreaming by night under the open Skie, Par Lost 3.514
Or open admiration him behold Par Lost 3.672
The open field, and where the unpierc't shade Par Lost 4.245
Both turnd, and under op'n Skie ador'd Par Lost 4.721
That open now thir choicest bosom'd smells Par Lost 5.127
Soon as they forth were come to open sight Par Lost 5.138
Of Battel, open when, and when to close Par Lost 6.235
Peace and composure, and with open brest Par Lost 6.560
To entertain them fair with open Front Par Lost 6.611
They open to themselves at length the way Par Lost 7.158
Displayd on the op'n Firmament of Heav'n. Par Lost 7.390
Open, ye everlasting Gates, they sung, Par Lost 7.565
Open, ye Heav'ns, your living dores; let in Par Lost 7.566
Open, and henceforth oft; for God will deigne Par Lost 7.569
Mine eyes he clos'd, but op'n left the Cell Par Lost 8.460
Is open? or will God incense his ire Par Lost 9.692
To open Eyes, and make them Gods who taste; Par Lost 9.866
In open shew, and with ascention bright Par Lost 10.187
Stood open wide, belching outrageous flame Par Lost 10.232
Wide open and unguarded, *Satan* pass'd, Par Lost 10.419
Him follow'd issuing forth to th' open Field, Par Lost 10.533
Be open, and his heart to pitie incline, Par Lost 10.1061
Of Heav'n set open on the Earth shall powre Par Lost 11.825
Whose ear is ever open; and his eye Samson 1172
The other side was op'n, where the throng Samson 1609
And in requitall ope his leather'n scrip, Mask 626
Bridgewater ms 'open'
Will open wide the Gates of her high Palace Hall. Nativity 148
An open grave their throat, their tongue they smooth. Psalm 5, 28

Opened
Op'nd into the Hill a spacious wound Par Lost 1.689
ms 'Op'n'd'
Her stores were open'd, and this Firmament Par Lost 2.175
1667 'op'n'd'
Of *Erebus*. She op'nd, but to shut Par Lost 2.883
Direct against which op'nd from beneath, Par Lost 3.526
Of Heav'n arriv'd, the gate self-opend wide Par Lost 5.254
Attendant on thir Lord: Heav'n op'nd wide Par Lost 7.205
1669 'open'd'
That open'd wide her blazing Portals, led Par Lost 7.575
Who stooping op'nd my left side, and took Par Lost 8.465
Op'nd and cleerd, and ye shall be as Gods, Par Lost 9.708
Augmented, op'nd Eyes, new Hopes, new Joyes, Par Lost 9.985
Soon found thir Eyes how op'nd, and thir minds Par Lost 9.1053
Op'nd we find indeed, and find we know Par Lost 9.1071
His eyes he op'nd, and beheld a field, Par Lost 11.429
Heaven open'd, and in likeness of a Dove Par Reg 1.30
Heaven open'd her eternal doors, from whence Par Reg 1.281
That open'd in the midst a woody Scene, Par Reg 2.294

Opener
Th' effects to correspond, opener mine Eyes, Par Lost 9.875
True opener of mine eyes, prime Angel blest, Par Lost 11.598

Openest
In ignorance, thou op'nst Wisdoms way, Par Lost 9.809

Opening
Op'ning thir brazen foulds discover wide Par Lost 1.724
Threw forth, till on the left side op'ning wide, Par Lost 2.755
Without my op'ning. Pensive here I sat Par Lost 2.777
So wide the op'ning seemd, where bounds were set Par Lost 3.538
So beauteous, op'ning to the ambient light. Par Lost 6.481
And Chrystal wall of Heav'n, which op'ning wide, Par Lost 6.860
Op'ning thir various colours, and made gay Par Lost 7.318
Op'ning her fertil Woomb teem'd at a Birth Par Lost 7.454
Op'ning the way, but of Divine effect Par Lost 9.865
Sin opening, who thus now to Death began. Par Lost 10.234
From the first op'ning bud, and gave ye Names, Par Lost 11.277
Down the great River to the op'ning Gulf, Par Lost 11.833
Mine eyes true op'ning, and my heart much eas'd, Par Lost 12.274
Under the opening eye-lids of the morn, Lycidas 26
1638 'glimmering'
Trinity ms 'opening' ←'glimmering'

Openly
But openly begin, as best becomes Par Reg 1.288
How openly, and with what impudence Samson 398

Opens
Still threatning to devour me opens wide, Par Lost 4.77
Of *Tartarus*, which ready opens wide Par Lost 6.54
Passes to bliss at the mid hour of night, Sonnet 9, 13
Trinity ms 'passes to' ←'opens the dore of'

Operation
But of the Tree whose operation brings Par Lost 8.323
In Paradise, of operation blest Par Lost 9.796
Farr other operation first displaid, Par Lost 9.1012

Opes
That ope's the Palace of Eternity: Mask 14
Bridgewater ms 'opes'
Trinity ms 'ope's' ←'shews'
(The Golden opes, the Iron shuts amain) Lycidas 111

Ophion
Ophion with *Eurynome*, the wide- Par Lost 10.581

Ophir
And *Sofala* thought *Ophir*, to the Realme Par Lost 11.400

Ophiucus
That fires the length of *Ophiucus* huge Par Lost 2.709

Ophiusa
Ophiusa) but still greatest hee the midst, Par Lost 10.528

Opiate
Of *Hermes*, or his opiate Rod. Mean while Par Lost 11.133
Hence with thy brew'd inchantments, foul deceiver, Mask 696
Trinity ms 'brewd enchauntments' ←'foule brud' ←'hel brewd opiate' ←'hel bru'd liquor' ←'bru'd sorcerie' ←'teacherous (leacherous?) bruage' ←'teacherous kindnesse'
Opinion
And so refus'd might in opinion stand Par Lost 2.471
Our knowledge or opinion; then retires Par Lost 5.108
Whose witnesse and opinion winnes the cause; Prose 10, 4
Opinions
His laughter at thir quaint Opinions wide Par Lost 8.78
Opium
To deaths benumming Opium as my only cure. Samson 630
Opportune
And opportune excursion we may chance Par Lost 2.396
Most opportune might serve his Wiles, and found Par Lost 9.85
The Woman, opportune to all attempts, Par Lost 9.481
Opportunely
And rather opportunely in this place Par Reg 2.396
Opportunity
And opportunity I here have had Par Reg 4.531
Danger will wink on Opportunity, Mask 401
1637 'opportunitie'
Trinity ms 'opportunity'
Bridgewater ms 'opportunitie'
Oppose
To second, or oppose, or undertake Par Lost 2.419
But Fate withstands, and to oppose th' attempt Par Lost 2.610
Were banded to oppose his high Decree; Par Lost 5.717
Inspir'd with contradiction durst oppose Par Lost 6.155
Against such hellish mischief fit to oppose. Par Lost 6.636
To oppose against such powerful arguments? Samson 862
That bends his rage thy providence to oppose Psalm 8, 8
Opposed
If he oppos'd; and with ambitious aim Par Lost 1.41
His utmost power with adverse power oppos'd Par Lost 1.103
The current of his fury thus oppos'd. Par Lost 5.808
He hasted, and oppos'd the rockie Orb Par Lost 6.254
That jealous of thir secrets fiercely oppos'd Par Lost 10.478
But must with something sudden be oppos'd, Par Reg 1.96
Opposing
Against th' opposing will and arm of Heav'n Mask 600
Bridgewater ms 'opposinge'
Opposite
In emulation opposite to Heav'n. Par Lost 2.298
(So call that opposite fair Starr) her aide Par Lost 3.727
As I bent down to look, just opposite, Par Lost 4.460
Forth stepping opposite, half way he met Par Lost 6.128
Blaz'd opposite, while expectation stood Par Lost 6.306
But opposite in leveld West was set Par Lost 7.376
In *Sextile*, *Square*, and *Trine*, and *Opposite*, Par Lost 10.659
By free consent of all, none opposite, Par Reg 3.358
Opposition
Before mine eyes in opposition sits Par Lost 2.803
Of fiercest opposition in mid Skie, Par Lost 6.314
In factious opposition, till at last Par Lost 11.664
How best their opposition to withstand. Par Reg 3.250
Sorrows, and labours, opposition, hate, Par Reg 4.386
But vertue which breaks through all opposition, Samson 1050
Oppress
Behold the Kings of the Earth how they oppress Par Reg 2.44
And the same end; still watching to oppress Samson 232
Oppressed
Immortal vigor, though opprest and fall'n, Par Lost 2.13
Came shadowing, and opprest whole Legions arm'd, Par Lost 6.655
Oppress'd them, wearied with thir amorous play. Par Lost 9.1045
Would scruple that, with want opprest? behold Par Reg 2.331
To the Spirits of just men long opprest! Samson 1269
Oppresses
Oppresses else with Surfet, and soon turns Par Lost 7.129
Oppression
First found me, and with soft oppression seis'd Par Lost 8.288
Proceeded, and Oppression, and Sword-Law Par Lost 11.672
Oppressor
To quell the mighty of the Earth, th' oppressour, Samson 1272
Oppressors
Israel's oppressours: of what now I suffer Samson 233
Opprobrious
On that opprobrious Hill, and made his Grove Par Lost 1.403
Accept this dark opprobrious Den of shame, Par Lost 2.58
Opprobrious, with his Robe of righteousness, Par Lost 10.222
Ops
And *Ops*, ere yet *Dictaean Jove* was born. Par Lost 10.584
Optic
Through Optic Glass the *Tuscan* Artist views Par Lost 1.288
ms 'optick'
Through his glaz'd Optic Tube yet never saw. Par Lost 3.590
By what strange Parallax or Optic skill Par Reg 4.40
Or
Of *Oreb*, or of *Sinai*, didst inspire Par Lost 1.7
Rose out of *Chaos:* Or if *Sion* Hill Par Lost 1.10
Things unattempted yet in Prose or Rhime. Par Lost 1.16
Can else inflict, do I repent or change, Par Lost 1.96
And courage never to submit or yield: Par Lost 1.108
That Glory never shall his wrath or might Par Lost 1.110
To wage by force or guile eternal Warr Par Lost 1.121

Or(*cont*)
Whether upheld by strength, or Chance, or Fate, Par Lost 1.133
Or do him mightier service as his thralls Par Lost 1.149
Or do his Errands in the gloomy Deep; Par Lost 1.152
Strength undiminisht, or eternal being Par Lost 1.154
Doing or Suffering: but of this be sure, Par Lost 1.158
Or satiate fury yield it from our Foe. Par Lost 1.179
Titanian, or *Earth-born*, that warr'd on *Jove*, Par Lost 1.198
Briareos or *Typhon*, whom the Den Par Lost 1.199
By ancient *Tarsus* held, or that Sea-beast Par Lost 1.200
Had ris'n or heav'd his head, but that the will Par Lost 1.211
Torn from *Pelorus*, or the shatter'd side Par Lost 1.232
A mind not to be chang'd by Place or Time. Par Lost 1.253
In this unhappy Mansion, or once more Par Lost 1.268
Regaind in Heav'n, or what more lost in Hell? Par Lost 1.270
Or in *Valdarno*, to descry new Lands, Par Lost 1.290
Rivers or Mountains in her spotty Globe. Par Lost 1.291
High overarch't imbowr; or scatterd sedge Par Lost 1.304
Eternal spirits; or have ye chos'n this place Par Lost 1.318
Or in this abject posture have ye sworn Par Lost 1.322
Thus drooping, or with linked Thunderbolts Par Lost 1.328
Awake, arise, or be for ever fall'n. Par Lost 1.330
In which they were, or the fierce pains not feel; Par Lost 1.336
Rhene or the *Danaw*, when her barbarous Sons Par Lost 1.353
Can either Sex assume, or both; so soft Par Lost 1.424
Not ti'd or manacl'd with joynt or limb, Par Lost 1.426
Dilated or condens't, bright or obscure, Par Lost 1.429
And works of love or enmity fulfill. Par Lost 1.431
Fell not from Heaven, or more gross to love Par Lost 1.491
Or Altar smoak'd; yet who more oft then hee Par Lost 1.493
Thir highest Heav'n; or on the *Delphian* Cliff, Par Lost 1.517
Or in *Dodona*, and through all the bounds Par Lost 1.518
Of *Doric* Land; or who with *Saturn* old Par Lost 1.519
With dread of death to flight or foul retreat, Par Lost 1.555
From mortal or immortal minds. Thus they Par Lost 1.559
In Fable or *Romance* of *Uthers* Son Par Lost 1.580
And all who since, Baptiz'd or Infidel Par Lost 1.582
Jousted in *Aspramont* or *Montalban*, Par Lost 1.583
Damasco, or *Marocco*, or *Trebisond*, Par Lost 1.584
Or whom *Biserta* sent from *Afric* shore Par Lost 1.585
Shorn of his Beams, or from behind the Moon Par Lost 1.596
Hath scath'd the Forrest Oaks, or Mountain Pines, Par Lost 1.613
Foreseeing or presaging, from the Depth Par Lost 1.627
Of knowledge past or present, could have fear'd, Par Lost 1.628
If counsels different, or danger shun'd Par Lost 1.636
Consent or custome, and his Regal State Par Lost 1.640
So as not either to provoke, or dread Par Lost 1.644
To work in close design, by fraud or guile Par Lost 1.646
Our first eruption, thither or elsewhere: Par Lost 1.656
Open or understood must be resolv'd. Par Lost 1.662
Or cast a Rampart. *Mammon* led them on, Par Lost 1.678
Then aught divine or holy else enjoy'd Par Lost 1.683
Cornice or Freeze, with bossy Sculptures grav'n, Par Lost 1.716
Belus or *Serapis* thir Gods, or seat Par Lost 1.720
Nor was his name unheard or unador'd Par Lost 1.738
By place or choice the worthiest; they anon Par Lost 1.759
To mortal combat or carreer with Lance) Par Lost 1.766
Flie to and fro, or on the smoothed Plank, Par Lost 1.772
Beyond the *Indian* Mount, or Faerie Elves, Par Lost 1.781
Or Fountain some belated Peasant sees, Par Lost 1.783
Or dreams he sees, while over-head the Moon Par Lost 1.784
Or where the gorgeous East with richest hand Par Lost 2.3
With what besides, in Counsel or in Fight, Par Lost 2.20
Whether of open Warr or covert guile, Par Lost 2.41
Went all his fear: of God, or Hell, or worse Par Lost 2.49
Contrive who need, or when they need, not now Par Lost 2.53
Or if our substance be indeed Divine, Par Lost 2.99
Encamp thir Legions, or with obscure wing Par Lost 2.132
Scorning surprize. Or could we break our way Par Lost 2.134
Can give it, or will ever? how he can Par Lost 2.153
Belike through impotence, or unaware, Par Lost 2.156
A refuge from those wounds: or when we lay Par Lost 2.168
And plunge us in the flames? or from above Par Lost 2.172
Designing or exhorting glorious warr, Par Lost 2.179
Of racking whirlwinds, or for ever sunk Par Lost 2.182
Warr therefore, open or conceal'd, alike Par Lost 2.187
My voice disswades; for what can force or guile Par Lost 2.188
With him, or who deceive his mind, whose eye Par Lost 2.189
Exile, or ignominy, or bonds, or pain, Par Lost 2.207
Thir noxious vapour, or enur'd not feel, Par Lost 2.216
Or chang'd at length, and to the place conformd Par Lost 2.217
We warr, if warr be best, or to regain Par Lost 2.230
Nor want we skill or Art, from whence to raise Par Lost 2.272
Or Pinnace anchors in a craggy Bay Par Lost 2.289
Or Summers Noon-tide air, while thus he spake. Par Lost 2.309
Ethereal Vertues; or these Titles now Par Lost 2.311
In heighth or depth, still first and last will Reign Par Lost 2.324
Voutsaf't or sought; for what peace will be giv'n Par Lost 2.332
Heav'n, whose high walls fear no assault or Siege, Par Lost 2.343
Or ambush from the Deep. What if we find Par Lost 2.344
Or substance, how endu'd, and what thir Power, Par Lost 2.356
By force or suttlety: Though Heav'n be shut, Par Lost 2.358
To waste his whole Creation, or possess Par Lost 2.365
The punie habitants, or if not drive, Par Lost 2.367
Attempting, or to sit in darkness here Par Lost 2.377
Re-enter Heav'n; or else in some milde Zone Par Lost 2.397
His uncouth way, or spread his aerie flight Par Lost 2.407
Suffice, or what evasion bear him safe Par Lost 2.411

Or(*cont*)

To second, or oppose, or undertake	Par Lost 2.419
So hardie as to proffer or accept	Par Lost 2.425
Or unknown Region, what remains him less	Par Lost 2.443
Of difficulty or danger could deterr	Par Lost 2.449
More tollerable; if there be cure or charm	Par Lost 2.460
To respite or deceive, or slack the pain	Par Lost 2.461
Or clos ambition varnisht o're with zeal.	Par Lost 2.485
Scowls ore the dark'nd lantskip Snow, or showre;	Par Lost 2.491
Pursues, as inclination or sad choice	Par Lost 2.524
Part on the Plain, or in the Air sublime	Par Lost 2.528
Upon the wing, or in swift Race contend,	Par Lost 2.529
As at th' Olympian Games or *Pythian* fields;	Par Lost 2.530
Part curb thir fierie Steeds, or shun the Goal	Par Lost 2.531
With rapid wheels, or fronted Brigads form.	Par Lost 2.532
Free Vertue should enthrall to Force or Chance.	Par Lost 2.551
Pain for a while or anguish, and excite	Par Lost 2.567
Fallacious hope, or arm th' obdured brest	Par Lost 2.568
Than Fables yet have feign'd, or fear conceiv'd,	Par Lost 2.627
Close sailing from *Bengala*, or the Iles	Par Lost 2.638
Distinguishable in member, joynt, or limb,	Par Lost 2.668
Or substance might be call'd that shadow seem'd,	Par Lost 2.669
Retire, or taste thy folly, and learn by proof,	Par Lost 2.686
Thy lingring, or with one stroke of this Dart	Par Lost 2.702
That rest or intermission none I find.	Par Lost 2.802
Might hap to move new broiles: Be this or aught	Par Lost 2.837
Of massie Iron or sollid Rock with ease	Par Lost 2.878
Light-arm'd or heavy, sharp, smooth, swift or slow,	Par Lost 2.902
Of *Barca* or *Cyrene*'s torrid soil,	Par Lost 2.904
Som Capital City; or less then if this frame	Par Lost 2.924
With winged course ore Hill or moarie Dale,	Par Lost 2.944
Ore bog or steep, through strait, rough, dense, or rare,	Par Lost 2.948
With head, hands, wings or feet pursues his way,	Par Lost 2.949
And swims or sinks, or wades, or creeps, or flyes:	Par Lost 2.950
Or Spirit of the nethermost Abyss	Par Lost 2.956
With purpose to explore or to disturb	Par Lost 2.971
Confine with Heav'n; or if som other place	Par Lost 2.977
Or when *Ulysses* on the Larbord shunnd	Par Lost 2.1019
To tempt or punish mortals, except whom	Par Lost 2.1032
Or in the emptier waste, resembling Air,	Par Lost 2.1045
In circuit, undetermind square or round,	Par Lost 2.1048
Or of th' Eternal Coeternal beam	Par Lost 3.2
Or hear'st thou rather pure Ethereal stream,	Par Lost 3.7
Or dim suffusion veild. Yet not the more	Par Lost 3.26
Cleer Spring, or shadie Grove, or Sunnie Hill,	Par Lost 3.28
Day, or the sweet approach of Ev'n or Morn,	Par Lost 3.42
Or sight of vernal bloom, or Summers Rose,	Par Lost 3.43
Or flocks, or heards, or human face divine;	Par Lost 3.44
Uncertain which, in Ocean or in Air.	Par Lost 3.76
If him by force he can destroy, or worse,	Par Lost 3.91
Of true allegiance, constant Faith or Love,	Par Lost 3.104
Thir maker, or thir making, or thir Fate,	Par Lost 3.113
Or high foreknowledge; they themselves decreed	Par Lost 3.116
So without least impulse or shadow of Fate,	Par Lost 3.120
Or aught by me immutablie foreseen,	Par Lost 3.121
Or shall the Adversarie thus obtain	Par Lost 3.156
Or proud return though to his heavier doom,	Par Lost 3.159
By him corrupted? or wilt thou thy self	Par Lost 3.162
Dye hee or Justice must; unless for him	Par Lost 3.210
Patron or Intercessor none appeerd,	Par Lost 3.219
Attonement for himself or offering meet,	Par Lost 3.234
Mans Nature, less'n or degrade thine owne.	Par Lost 3.304
Farr more then Great or High; because in thee	Par Lost 3.311
In Heaven, or Earth, or under Earth in Hell;	Par Lost 3.322
To gorge the flesh of Lambs or yeanling Kids	Par Lost 3.434
Of *Ganges* or *Hydaspes*, *Indian* streams;	Par Lost 3.436
Living or liveless to be found was none,	Par Lost 3.443
Built thir fond hopes of Glorie or lasting fame,	Par Lost 3.449
Or happiness in this or th' other life;	Par Lost 3.450
Abortive, monstrous, or unkindly mixt,	Par Lost 3.456
Translated Saints, or middle Spirits hold	Par Lost 3.461
Or in *Franciscan* think to pass disguis'd;	Par Lost 3.480
By Model, or by shading Pencil drawn.	Par Lost 3.509
Of Jasper, or of liquid Pearle, whereon	Par Lost 3.519
Wafted by Angels, or flew o're the Lake	Par Lost 3.521
The Fiend by easie ascent, or aggravate	Par Lost 3.524
First-seen, or some renown'd Metropolis	Par Lost 3.549
Or other Worlds they seemd, or happy Iles,	Par Lost 3.567
Through the calm Firmament; but up or downe	Par Lost 3.574
By center, or eccentric, hard to tell,	Par Lost 3.575
Or Longitude, where the great Luminarie	Par Lost 3.576
Turn swift thir various motions, or are turnd	Par Lost 3.582
Compar'd with aught on Earth, Medal or Stone;	Par Lost 3.592
If stone, Carbuncle most or Chrysolite,	Par Lost 3.596
Rubie or Topaz, to the Twelve that shon	Par Lost 3.597
That stone, or like to that which here below	Par Lost 3.600
He seemd, or fixt in cogitation deep.	Par Lost 3.629
Which else might work him danger or delay:	Par Lost 3.635
That run through all the Heav'ns, or down to th' Earth	Par Lost 3.651
His fixed seat, or fixed seat hath none,	Par Lost 3.669
Or open admiration him behold	Par Lost 3.672
Thir number, or the wisdom infinite	Par Lost 3.706
Or from without, to all temptations arm'd.	Par Lost 4.65
Thou hadst: whom hast thou then or what to accuse,	Par Lost 4.67
Be then his Love accurst, since love or hate,	Par Lost 4.69
Then in fair Evening Cloud, or humid Bow,	Par Lost 4.151
All path of Man or Beast that past that way:	Par Lost 4.177
Of Hill or highest Wall, and sheer within	Par Lost 4.182

Or(*cont*)

Or as a Thief bent to unhoord the cash	Par Lost 4.188
In at the window climbs, or o're the tiles;	Par Lost 4.191
To worst abuse, or to thir meanest use.	Par Lost 4.204
Or where the Sons of *Eden* long before	Par Lost 4.213
Betwixt them Lawns, or level Downs, and Flocks	Par Lost 4.252
Or palmie hilloc, or the flourie lap	Par Lost 4.254
Down the slope hills, disperst, or in a Lake,	Par Lost 4.261
Of God or Angel, for they thought no ill:	Par Lost 4.320
In Wood or Wilderness, Forrest or Den;	Par Lost 4.342
Or Bedward ruminating: for the Sun	Par Lost 4.352
That I with you must dwell, or you with me	Par Lost 4.377
By word or action markt: about them round	Par Lost 4.401
Or in thick shade retir'd, from him to draw	Par Lost 4.532
No evil thing approach or enter in;	Par Lost 4.563
Diurnal, or this less volubil Earth	Par Lost 4.594
Man hath his daily work of body or mind	Par Lost 4.618
Or glittering Starr-light without thee is sweet.	Par Lost 4.656
Temper or nourish, or in part shed down	Par Lost 4.670
Of echoing Hill or Thicket have we heard	Par Lost 4.681
Sole, or responsive each to others note	Par Lost 4.683
While they keep watch, or nightly rounding walk	Par Lost 4.685
Beast, Bird, Insect, or Worm durst enter none;	Par Lost 4.704
Pan or *Silvanus* never slept, nor Nymph,	Par Lost 4.707
Farr be it, that I should write thee sin or blame,	Par Lost 4.758
Or think thee unbefitting holiest place,	Par Lost 4.759
Present, or past, as Saints and Patriarchs us'd.	Par Lost 4.762
Mixt Dance, or wanton Mask, or Midnight Bal,	Par Lost 4.768
Or Serenate, which the starv'd Lover sings	Par Lost 4.769
Or if, inspiring venom, he might taint	Par Lost 4.804
The lowest of your throng; or if ye know,	Par Lost 4.831
Or undiminisht brightness, to be known	Par Lost 4.836
Or all at once; more glorie will be wonn,	Par Lost 4.853
Or less be lost. Thy fear, said *Zephon* bold,	Par Lost 4.854
Chaumping his iron curb: to strive or flie	Par Lost 4.859
But that implies not violence or harme.	Par Lost 4.901
Or not, who ask what boldness brought him hither	Par Lost 4.908
Less pain, less to be fled, or thou then they	Par Lost 4.919
Not that I less endure, or shrink from pain,	Par Lost 4.925
To settle here on Earth, or in mid Aire;	Par Lost 4.940
Like *Teneriff* or *Atlas* unremov'd:	Par Lost 4.987
Of Heav'n perhaps, or all the Elements	Par Lost 4.993
Beautie, which whether waking or asleep,	Par Lost 5.14
Works of day pass't, or morrows next designe,	Par Lost 5.33
Or envie, or what reserve forbids to taste?	Par Lost 5.61
Which Reason joyning or disjoyning, frames	Par Lost 5.106
All what we affirm or what deny, and call	Par Lost 5.107
Our knowledge or opinion; then retires	Par Lost 5.108
Ill matching words and deeds long past or late.	Par Lost 5.113
Evil into the mind of God or Man	Par Lost 5.117
No spot or blame behind: Which gives me hope	Par Lost 5.119
Thir Maker, in fit strains pronounc't or sung	Par Lost 5.148
Flowd from thir lips, in Prose or numerous Verse,	Par Lost 5.150
More tuneable then needed Lute or Harp	Par Lost 5.151
To us invisible or dimly seen	Par Lost 5.157
From Hill or steaming Lake, duskie or grey,	Par Lost 5.186
Or wet the thirstie Earth with falling showers,	Par Lost 5.190
Rising or falling still advance his praise.	Par Lost 5.191
Breathe soft or loud; and wave your tops, ye Pines,	Par Lost 5.193
The Earth, and stately tread, or lowly creep;	Par Lost 5.201
Witness if I be silent, Morn or Even,	Par Lost 5.202
To Hill, or Valley, Fountain, or fresh shade	Par Lost 5.203
Have gathered aught of evil or conceald,	Par Lost 5.207
Fruitless imbraces: or they led the Vine	Par Lost 5.215
Converse with *Adam*, in what Bowre or shade	Par Lost 5.230
Or with repose; and such discourse bring on,	Par Lost 5.233
From hence, no cloud, or, to obstruct his sight,	Par Lost 5.257
Or Pilot from amidst the *Cyclades*	Par Lost 5.264
Delos or *Samos* first appeering kenns	Par Lost 5.265
Wilde above Rule or Art; enormous bliss.	Par Lost 5.297
Berrie or Grape: to whom thus *Adam* call'd.	Par Lost 5.307
In *India* East or West, or middle shoare	Par Lost 5.339
In *Pontus* or the *Punic* Coast, or where	Par Lost 5.340
Rough, or smooth rin'd, or bearded husk, or shell	Par Lost 5.342
Created, or such place hast here to dwell,	Par Lost 5.373
Then Wood-Nymph, or the fairest Goddess feign'd	Par Lost 5.381
Can turn, or holds it possible to turn	Par Lost 5.441
As neerer to him plac't or neerer tending	Par Lost 5.476
Discursive, or Intuitive; discourse	Par Lost 5.488
Ethereal, as wee, or may at choice	Par Lost 5.499
Here or in Heav'nly Paradises dwell;	Par Lost 5.500
To him, or possibly his love desert	Par Lost 5.515
Human desires can seek or apprehend?	Par Lost 5.518
Inextricable, or strict necessity;	Par Lost 5.528
Willing or no, who will but what they must	Par Lost 5.533
To love or not; in this we stand or fall:	Par Lost 5.540
Or in thir glittering Tissues bear imblaz'd	Par Lost 5.592
Or several one by one, the Regent Powers,	Par Lost 5.697
Or taint integritie; but all obey'd	Par Lost 5.704
Of Deitie or Empire, such a foe	Par Lost 5.724
In battel, what our Power is, or our right.	Par Lost 5.728
Thy Rebels, or be found the worst in Heav'n.	Par Lost 5.742
Or Starrs of Morning, Dew-drops, which the Sun	Par Lost 5.746
To know ye right, or if ye know your selves	Par Lost 5.789
Who can in reason then or right assume	Par Lost 5.794
In freedome equal? or can introduce	Par Lost 5.797
Or all Angelic Nature joind in one,	Par Lost 5.834
Or singular and rash, whereat rejoic'd	Par Lost 5.851

Or(*cont*)

Beseeching or besieging. This report,	Par Lost 5.869
Yet not for thy advise or threats I fly	Par Lost 5.889
To swerve from truth, or change his constant mind	Par Lost 5.902
That self same day by fight, or by surprize	Par Lost 6.87
There fail where Vertue fails, or weakest prove	Par Lost 6.117
Or potent tongue; fool, not to think how vain	Par Lost 6.135
Thy folly; or with solitarie hand	Par Lost 6.139
Or Nature; God and Nature bid the same,	Par Lost 6.176
To serve th' unwise, or him who hath rebelld	Par Lost 6.179
Winds under ground or waters forcing way	Par Lost 6.196
When to advance, or stand, or turn the sway	Par Lost 6.234
Or Captive drag'd in Chains, with hostile frown	Par Lost 6.260
Or som more sudden vengeance wing'd from God	Par Lost 6.279
To flight, or if to fall, but that they rise	Par Lost 6.285
Or turn this Heav'n it self into the Hell	Par Lost 6.291
Of Angels, can relate, or to what things	Par Lost 6.298
Stood they or mov'd, in stature, motion, arms	Par Lost 6.302
In might or swift prevention; but the sword	Par Lost 6.320
In Entrailes, Heart or Head, Liver or Reines;	Par Lost 6.346
They Limb themselves, and colour, shape or size	Par Lost 6.352
Assume, as likes them best, condense or rare.	Par Lost 6.353
Defensive scarse, or with pale fear surpris'd,	Par Lost 6.393
Not liable to fear or flight or paine.	Par Lost 6.397
Or equal what between us made the odds,	Par Lost 6.441
Valour or strength, though matchless, quelld with pain	Par Lost 6.457
Our yet unwounded Enemies, or arme	Par Lost 6.466
Some one intent on mischief, or inspir'd	Par Lost 6.503
Where lodg'd, or whither fled, or if for fight,	Par Lost 6.531
In motion or in alt: him soon they met	Par Lost 6.532
Born eevn or high, for this day will pour down,	Par Lost 6.544
Or hollow'd bodies made of Oak or Firr	Par Lost 6.574
With branches lopt, in Wood or Mountain fell'd)	Par Lost 6.575
By quick contraction or remove; but now	Par Lost 6.597
Or Wonders move th' obdurate to relent?	Par Lost 6.790
Stood reimbattell'd fierce, by force or fraud	Par Lost 6.794
Against God and *Messiah*, or to fall	Par Lost 6.796
Or faint retreat; when the great Son of God	Par Lost 6.799
Vengeance is his, or whose he sole appoints;	Par Lost 6.808
Or I alone against them, since by strength	Par Lost 6.820
Of torrent Floods, or of a numerous Host.	Par Lost 6.830
Of Goats or timerous flock together throngd	Par Lost 6.857
Before the Hills appeerd, or Fountain flow'd,	Par Lost 7.8
To hoarce or mute, though fall'n on evil dayes,	Par Lost 7.25
Visit'st my slumbers Nightly, or when Morn	Par Lost 7.29
In Paradise to *Adam* or his Race,	Par Lost 7.45
What within *Eden* or without was done	Par Lost 7.65
Innumerable, and this which yeelds or fills	Par Lost 7.88
Or if the Starr of Eevning and the Moon	Par Lost 7.104
Or we can bid his absence, till thy Song	Par Lost 7.107
What words or tongue of Seraph can suffice,	Par Lost 7.113
Or heart of man suffice to comprehend?	Par Lost 7.114
To none communicable in Earth or Heaven:	Par Lost 7.124
To act or not, Necessitie and Chance	Par Lost 7.172
Then time or motion, but to human ears	Par Lost 7.177
Part rise in crystal Wall, or ridge direct,	Par Lost 7.293
Soft-ebbing; nor withstood them Rock or Hill,	Par Lost 7.300
But they, or under ground, or circuit wide	Par Lost 7.301
Thir branches hung with copious Fruit; or gemm'd	Par Lost 7.325
Or wander with delight, and love to haunt	Par Lost 7.330
By tincture or reflection they augment	Par Lost 7.367
Bank the mid Sea: part single or with mate	Par Lost 7.403
Of Coral stray, or sporting with quick glance	Par Lost 7.405
Or in thir Pearlie shells at ease, attend	Par Lost 7.407
Moist nutriment, or under Rocks thir food	Par Lost 7.408
Stretcht like a Promontorie sleeps or swimmes,	Par Lost 7.414
In Forrest wilde, in Thicket, Brake, or Den;	Par Lost 7.458
Insect or Worme; those wav'd thir limber fans	Par Lost 7.476
All sounds on Fret by String or Golden Wire	Par Lost 7.597
Choral or Unison: of incense Clouds	Par Lost 7.599
Thy power; what thought can measure thee or tongue	Par Lost 7.603
Who can impair thee, mighty King, or bound	Par Lost 7.608
Over his Works, on Earth, in Sea, or Air,	Par Lost 7.629
What thanks sufficient, or what recompence	Par Lost 8.5
Delighted, or not capable her eare	Par Lost 8.49
To ask or search I blame thee not, for Heav'n	Par Lost 8.66
His Seasons, Hours, or Dayes, or Months, or Yeares:	Par Lost 8.69
This to attain, whether Heav'n move or Earth,	Par Lost 8.70
From Man or Angel the great Architect	Par Lost 8.72
Rather admire; or if they list to try	Par Lost 8.75
Or Bright inferrs not Excellence: the Earth	Par Lost 8.91
Progressive, retrograde, or standing still,	Par Lost 8.127
Or save the Sun his labour, and that swift	Par Lost 8.133
But whether thus these things, or whether not,	Par Lost 8.159
Rise on the Earth, or Earth rise on the Sun,	Par Lost 8.161
Or Shee from West her silent course advance	Par Lost 8.163
Live, in what state, condition or degree,	Par Lost 8.176
But apt the Mind or Fancie is to roave	Par Lost 8.188
Till warn'd, or by experience taught, she learne,	Par Lost 8.190
Or emptiness, or fond impertinence,	Par Lost 8.195
Speaking or mute all comliness and grace	Par Lost 8.222
Or enemie, while God was in his work,	Par Lost 8.234
Noise, other then the sound of Dance or Song,	Par Lost 8.243
Creatures that livd, and movd, and walk'd, or flew,	Par Lost 8.264
But who I was, or where, or from what cause,	Par Lost 8.270
Above, or round about thee or beneath.	Par Lost 8.318
Or live in Sea, or Aire, Beast, Fish, and Fowle.	Par Lost 8.341
Above mankinde, or aught then mankinde higher,	Par Lost 8.358

Or(*cont*)

Or all enjoying, what contentment find?	Par Lost 8.366
Can sort, what harmonie or true delight?	Par Lost 8.384
Much less can Bird with Beast, or Fish with Fowle	Par Lost 8.395
Of happiness, or not? who am alone	Par Lost 8.405
Second to me or like, equal much less.	Par Lost 8.407
Or solace his defects. No need that thou	Par Lost 8.419
Of Union or Communion, deifi'd;	Par Lost 8.431
Hee ended, or I heard no more, for now	Par Lost 8.452
Mean, or in her summd up, in her containd	Par Lost 8.473
To find her, or for ever to deplore	Par Lost 8.479
With what all Earth or Heaven could bestow	Par Lost 8.483
The more desirable, or to say all,	Par Lost 8.505
As us'd or not, works in the mind no change,	Par Lost 8.525
Or Nature faild in mee, and left some part	Par Lost 8.534
Or from my side subducting, took perhaps	Par Lost 8.536
Her own, that what she wills to do or say,	Par Lost 8.549
The Soule of Man, or passion in him move.	Par Lost 8.585
Union of Mind, or in us both one Soule;	Par Lost 8.604
Express they, by looks onely, or do they mix	Par Lost 8.616
Irradiance, virtual or immediate touch?	Par Lost 8.617
Of membrane, joynt, or limb, exclusive barrs:	Par Lost 8.625
As Flesh to mix with Flesh, or Soul with Soul.	Par Lost 8.629
The weal or woe in thee is plac't; beware.	Par Lost 8.638
And all the Blest: stand fast; to stand or fall	Par Lost 8.640
No more of talk where God or Angel Guest	Par Lost 9.1
Thrice Fugitive about *Troy* Wall; or rage	Par Lost 9.16
Or *Neptun*'s ire or *Juno's*, that so long	Par Lost 9.18
And dictates to me slumbring, or inspires	Par Lost 9.23
Unsung; or to describe Races and Games,	Par Lost 9.33
Or tilting Furniture, emblazon'd Shields,	Par Lost 9.34
The skill of Artifice or Office mean,	Par Lost 9.39
To Person or to Poem. Mee of these	Par Lost 9.41
That name, unless an age too late, or cold	Par Lost 9.44
Climat, or Years damp my intended wing	Par Lost 9.45
From entrance or Cherubic Watch, by stealth	Par Lost 9.68
Find place or refuge; and the more I see	Par Lost 9.119
Or won to what may work his utter loss,	Par Lost 9.131
Follow, as to him linkt in weal or woe,	Par Lost 9.133
Are his Created, or to spite us more,	Par Lost 9.147
As high he soard, obnoxious first or last	Par Lost 9.170
So saying, through each Thicket Danck or Drie,	Par Lost 9.179
Not yet in horrid Shade or dismal Den,	Par Lost 9.185
In heart or head, possessing soon inspir'd	Par Lost 9.189
Lop overgrown, or prune, or prop, or bind,	Par Lost 9.210
One night or two with wanton growth derides	Par Lost 9.211
Or bear what to my minde first thoughts present,	Par Lost 9.213
Leads thee, or where most needs, whether to wind	Par Lost 9.215
The Woodbine round this Arbour, or direct	Par Lost 9.216
Looks intervene and smiles, or object new	Par Lost 9.222
Refreshment, whether food, or talk between,	Par Lost 9.237
Food of the mind, or this sweet intercourse	Par Lost 9.238
Our fealtie from God, or to disturb	Par Lost 9.262
Or this, or worse, leave not the faithful side	Par Lost 9.265
The Wife, where danger or dishonour lurks,	Par Lost 9.267
Who guards her, or with her the worst endures.	Par Lost 9.269
To God or thee, because we have a foe	Par Lost 9.280
As wee, not capable of death or paine,	Par Lost 9.283
Can either not receave, or can repell.	Par Lost 9.284
Can by his fraud be shak'n or seduc't;	Par Lost 9.287
Or daring, first on mee th' assault shall light.	Par Lost 9.305
Shame to be overcome or over-reacht	Par Lost 9.313
Suttle or violent, we not endu'd	Par Lost 9.324
Foul on himself; then wherefore shund or feard	Par Lost 9.331
As not secure to single or combin'd.	Par Lost 9.339
Nothing imperfet or deficient left	Par Lost 9.345
Or aught that might his happie State secure,	Par Lost 9.347
Oread or *Dryad*, or of *Delia*'s Traine,	Par Lost 9.387
Guiltless of fire had formd, or Angels brought.	Par Lost 9.392
To *Pales*, or *Pomona* thus adornd,	Par Lost 9.393
Vertumnus, or to *Ceres* in her Prime,	Par Lost 9.395
Noontide repast, or Afternoons repose.	Par Lost 9.403
Foundst either sweet repast, or sound repose;	Par Lost 9.407
To intercept thy way, or send thee back	Par Lost 9.410
Of Grove or Garden-Plot more pleasant lay,	Par Lost 9.418
Thir tendance or Plantation for delight	Par Lost 9.419
By Fountain or by shadie Rivulet	Par Lost 9.420
Carnation, Purple, Azure, or spect with Gold,	Par Lost 9.429
Of stateliest Covert, Cedar, Pine, or Palme,	Par Lost 9.435
Or of reviv'd *Adonis*, or renownd	Par Lost 9.440
Or that, not Mystic, where the Sapient King	Par Lost 9.442
The smell of Grain, or tedded Grass, or Kine,	Par Lost 9.450
Or Dairie, each rural sight, each rural sound;	Par Lost 9.451
Of gesture or lest action overawd	Par Lost 9.460
Hermione and *Cadmus*, or the God	Par Lost 9.506
Ammonian Jove, or *Capitoline* was seen,	Par Lost 9.508
Nigh Rivers mouth or Foreland, where the Wind	Par Lost 9.514
Organic, or impulse of vocal Air,	Par Lost 9.530
Or Sex, and apprehended nothing high:	Par Lost 9.574
Then smell of sweetest Fenel or the Teats	Par Lost 9.581
Of Ewe or Goat dropping with Milk at Eevn,	Par Lost 9.582
Unsuckt of Lamb or Kid, that tend thir play.	Par Lost 9.583
Thy utmost reach or *Adams:* Round the Tree	Par Lost 9.591
At Feed or Fountain never had I found.	Par Lost 9.597
Thenceforth to Speculations high or deep	Par Lost 9.602
Or Earth, or Middle, all things fair and good;	Par Lost 9.605
Equivalent or second, which compel'd	Par Lost 9.609
To Boggs and Mires, and oft through Pond or Poole,	Par Lost 9.641

Or(*cont*)
Yet Lords declar'd of all in Earth or Aire? Par Lost 9.658
In *Athens* or free *Rome*, where Eloquence Par Lost 9.671
So standing, moving, or to highth upgrown Par Lost 9.677
Is open? or will God incense his ire Par Lost 9.692
What can your knowledge hurt him, or this Tree Par Lost 9.727
Or is it envie, and can envie dwell Par Lost 9.729
Inclinable now grown to touch or taste, Par Lost 9.742
For good unknown, sure is not had, or had Par Lost 9.756
Was death invented? or to us deni'd Par Lost 9.767
Friendly to man, farr from deceit or guile. Par Lost 9.772
Of God or Death, of Law or Penaltie? Par Lost 9.775
Or fansied so, through expectation high Par Lost 9.789
Full happiness with mee, or rather not, Par Lost 9.819
Adam shall share with me in bliss or woe: Par Lost 9.831
Or not restraind as wee, or not obeying, Par Lost 9.868
Whatever can to sight or thought be formd, Par Lost 9.898
Holy, divine, good, amiable, or sweet! Par Lost 9.899
Mine never shall be parted, bliss or woe. Par Lost 9.916
But past who can recall, or don undoe? Par Lost 9.926
But to be Gods, or Angels Demi-gods. Par Lost 9.937
Rather then Death or aught then Death more dread Par Lost 9.969
Direct, or by occasion hath presented Par Lost 9.974
Divine displeasure for her sake, or Death. Par Lost 9.993
So said he, and forbore not glance or toy Par Lost 9.1034
Henceforth of God or Angel, earst with joy Par Lost 9.1081
To Starr or Sun-light, spread thir umbrage broad Par Lost 9.1087
In *Malabar* or *Decan* spreds her Armes Par Lost 9.1103
Coverd, but not at rest or ease of Mind, Par Lost 9.1120
Imput'st thou that to my default, or will Par Lost 9.1145
Or to thy self perhaps: hadst thou been there, Par Lost 9.1148
Or here th' attempt, thou couldst not have discernd Par Lost 9.1149
Why hee should mean me ill, or seek to harme. Par Lost 9.1152
Either to meet no danger, or to finde Par Lost 9.1176
Of God All-seeing, or deceave his Heart Par Lost 10.6
Whatever wiles of Foe or seeming Friend. Par Lost 10.11
Or touch with lightest moment of impulse Par Lost 10.45
All Judgement, whether in Heav'n, or Earth, or Hell. Par Lost 10.57
Or come I less conspicuous, or what change Par Lost 10.107
Absents thee, or what chance detains? Come forth. Par Lost 10.108
Or to each other, but apparent guilt, Par Lost 10.112
My self the total Crime, or to accuse Par Lost 10.127
Before his voice, or was shee made thy guide, Par Lost 10.146
Superior, or but equal, that to her Par Lost 10.147
Bold or loquacious, thus abasht repli'd. Par Lost 10.161
Thir nakedness with Skins of Beasts, or slain, Par Lost 10.217
Or as the Snake with youthful Coate repaid; Par Lost 10.218
Can fit his punishment, or their revenge. Par Lost 10.242
Or sympathie, or som connatural force Par Lost 10.246
Or transmigration, as thir lot shall lead. Par Lost 10.261
Solid or slimie, as in raging Sea Par Lost 10.286
Or trie thee now more dang'rous to his Throne. Par Lost 10.382
Retires, or *Bactrian* Sophi from the hornes Par Lost 10.433
To *Tauris* or *Casbeen*. So these the late Par Lost 10.436
And shape Starr bright appeer'd, or brighter, clad Par Lost 10.450
Was left him, or false glitter: All amaz'd Par Lost 10.452
Without our hazard, labour, or allarme, Par Lost 10.491
True is, mee also he hath judg'd, or rather Par Lost 10.494
Or much more grievous pain? Ye have th' account Par Lost 10.501
Bedropt with blood of *Gorgon*, or the Isle Par Lost 10.527
Heav'n-fall'n, in station stood or just array, Par Lost 10.535
Now ris'n, to work them furder woe or shame; Par Lost 10.555
Alike is Hell, or Paradise, or Heaven, Par Lost 10.598
Both to destroy, or unimmortal make Par Lost 10.611
Sooner or later; which th' Almightie seeing, Par Lost 10.613
Or down from Heav'n descend. Such was thir song, Par Lost 10.648
Which of them rising with the Sun, or falling, Par Lost 10.663
Or East or West, which had forbid the Snow Par Lost 10.685
Of Man, but fled him, or with count'nance grim Par Lost 10.713
All that I eat or drink, or shall beget, Par Lost 10.728
Or multiplie, but curses on my head? Par Lost 10.732
From darkness to promote me, or here place Par Lost 10.745
Or in some other dismal place who knows Par Lost 10.787
Mends not her slowest pace for prayers or cries. Par Lost 10.859
Or find some other way to generate Par Lost 10.894
As some misfortune brings him, or mistake, Par Lost 10.900
Or whom he wishes most shall seldom gain Par Lost 10.901
By a farr worse, or if she love, withheld Par Lost 10.903
By Parents, or his happiest choice too late Par Lost 10.904
To a fell Adversarie, his hate or shame: Par Lost 10.906
Living or dying, from thee I will not hide Par Lost 10.974
Or end, though sharp and sad, yet tolerable, Par Lost 10.977
Let us seek Death, or he not found, supply Par Lost 10.1001
She ended heer, or vehement despaire Par Lost 10.1007
Or if thou covet death, as utmost end Par Lost 10.1020
By death brought on our selves, or childless days Par Lost 10.1037
Without wrauth or reviling; wee expected Par Lost 10.1048
Or Heat should injure us, his timely care Par Lost 10.1057
Or by collision of two bodies grinde Par Lost 10.1072
Justling or pusht with Winds rude in thir shock Par Lost 10.1074
Kindles the gummie bark of Firr or Pine, Par Lost 10.1076
And what may else be remedie or cure Par Lost 10.1079
Blow'n vagabond or frustrate: in they passd Par Lost 11.16
Good or not good ingraft, my Merit those Par Lost 11.35
Of *Amarantin* Shade, Fountain or Spring, Par Lost 11.78
Or in behalf of Man, or to invade Par Lost 11.102
Of *Hermes*, or his opiate Rod. Mean while Par Lost 11.133
Of God high-blest, or to incline his will, Par Lost 11.145

Or(*cont*)
Or one short sigh of humane breath, up-borne Par Lost 11.147
Forerunners of his purpose, or to warn Par Lost 11.195
Who knows, or more then this, that we are dust, Par Lost 11.199
Of us will soon determin, or impose Par Lost 11.227
Or of the Thrones above, such Majestie Par Lost 11.232
Livelier then *Meliboean*, or the graine Par Lost 11.242
Who now shall reare ye to the Sun, or ranke Par Lost 11.278
With what to sight or smell was sweet; from thee Par Lost 11.281
Celestial, whether among the Thrones, or nam'd Par Lost 11.296
Or monument to Ages, and thereon Par Lost 11.326
His bright appearances, or foot step-trace? Par Lost 11.329
Of Paradise or *Eden:* this had been Par Lost 11.342
Prosperous or adverse: so shalt thou lead Par Lost 11.364
City of old or modern Fame, the Seat Par Lost 11.386
Down to the golden *Chersonese*, or where Par Lost 11.392
The *Persian* in *Ecbatan* sate, or since Par Lost 11.393
In *Hispahan*, or where the *Russian Ksar* Par Lost 11.394
In *Mosco*, or the Sultan in *Bizance*, Par Lost 11.395
Or thence from *Niger* Flood to *Atlas* Mount Par Lost 11.402
Of gastly Spasm, or racking torture, qualmes Par Lost 11.481
Life offer'd, or soon beg to lay it down, Par Lost 11.506
Or if his likeness, by themselves defac't Par Lost 11.522
Into thy Mothers lap, or be with ease Par Lost 11.536
Live well, how long or short permit to Heav'n: Par Lost 11.554
Had wasted woods on Mountain or in Vale, Par Lost 11.567
To som Caves mouth, or whether washt by stream Par Lost 11.569
Fusil or grav'n in mettle. After these, Par Lost 11.573
Those were of hate and death, or pain much worse, Par Lost 11.601
Paths indirect, or in the mid way faint! Par Lost 11.631
Single or in Array of Battel rang'd Par Lost 11.644
From a fat Meddow ground; or fleecy Flock, Par Lost 11.648
Produce prodigious Births of bodie or mind. Par Lost 11.687
Marrying or prostituting, as befell, Par Lost 11.716
Rape or Adulterie, where passing faire Par Lost 11.717
Triumphs or Festivals, and to them preachd Par Lost 11.723
Him or his Childern, evil he may be sure, Par Lost 11.772
Worldlie or dissolute, on what thir Lords Par Lost 11.803
Or violence, hee of thir wicked wayes Par Lost 11.812
By Men who there frequent, or therein dwell. Par Lost 11.838
Green Tree or ground whereon his foot may light; Par Lost 11.858
Or serve they as a flourie verge to binde Par Lost 11.881
With Man therein or Beast; but when he brings Par Lost 11.895
Corn wine and oyle; and from the herd or flock, Par Lost 12.19
Oft sacrificing Bullock, Lamb, or Kid, Par Lost 12.20
Or from Heav'n claming second Sovrantie; Par Lost 12.35
With him or under him to tyrannize, Par Lost 12.39
Regardless whether good or evil fame. Par Lost 12.47
Reason in man obscur'd, or not obeyd, Par Lost 12.86
To know thir God, or message to regard, Par Lost 12.174
What it devours not, Herb, or Fruit, or Graine, Par Lost 12.184
Or how the Sun shall in mid Heav'n stand still Par Lost 12.263
As of a Duel, or the local wounds Par Lost 12.387
Of head or heel: not therefore joynes the Son Par Lost 12.388
Or theirs whom he redeems, a death like sleep, Par Lost 12.434
Whether in Heav'n or Earth, for then the Earth Par Lost 12.463
By mee done and occasiond, or rejoyce Par Lost 12.475
Left them inrould, or what the Spirit within Par Lost 12.523
Or works of God in Heav'n, Aire, Earth, or Sea, Par Lost 12.579
And bear through highth or depth of natures bounds Par Reg 1.13
Purified to receive him pure, or rather Par Reg 1.74
For long indulgence to their fears or grief: Par Reg 1.110
With man or mens affairs, how I begin Par Reg 1.132
Allure, or terrifie, or undermine. Par Reg 1.179
What might improve my knowledge or their own; Par Reg 1.213
Or work Redemption for mankind, whose sins Par Reg 1.266
Yet neither thus disheartn'd or dismay'd, Par Reg 1.268
Or Cedar, to defend him from the dew, Par Reg 1.306
Or harbour'd in one Cave, is not reveal'd; Par Reg 1.307
Or wither'd sticks to gather; which might serve Par Reg 1.316
So far from path or road of men, who pass Par Reg 1.322
In Troop or Caravan, for single none Par Reg 1.323
To Town or Village nigh (nighest is far) Par Reg 1.332
Or range in th' Air, nor from the Heav'n of Heav'ns Par Reg 1.366
What I see excellent in good, or fair, Par Reg 1.381
Or vertuous, I should so have lost all sense. Par Reg 1.382
Never did wrong or violence, by them Par Reg 1.389
A spectacle of ruin or of scorn Par Reg 1.415
Extorts, or pleasure to do ill excites? Par Reg 1.423
Return'd the wiser, or the more instruct Par Reg 1.439
To flye or follow what concern'd him most, Par Reg 1.440
But from him or his Angels President Par Reg 1.447
Or like a Fawning Parasite obey'st; Par Reg 1.452
Shalt be enquir'd at *Delphos* or elsewhere, Par Reg 1.458
Say and unsay, feign, flatter, or abjure? Par Reg 1.474
Check or reproof, and glad to scape so quit. Par Reg 1.477
And tuneable as Silvan Pipe or Song; Par Reg 1.480
Suffers the Hypocrite or Atheous Priest Par Reg 1.487
Praying or vowing, and vouchsaf'd his voice Par Reg 1.490
I bid not or forbid; do as thou find'st Par Reg 1.495
Machaerus and each Town or City wall'd Par Reg 2.22
Or in *Perea*, but return'd in vain. Par Reg 2.24
To have conceiv'd of God, or that salute Par Reg 2.67
Could be obtain'd to shelter him or me Par Reg 2.73
There without sign of boast, or sign of joy, Par Reg 2.119
Or counsel to assist; lest I who erst Par Reg 2.145
Have we not seen, or by relation heard, Par Reg 2.182
In Wood or Grove by mossie Fountain side, Par Reg 2.184

Or(*cont*)

In Valley or Green Meadow to way-lay	Par Reg 2.185
Daphne, or *Semele*, *Antiopa*,	Par Reg 2.187
Or *Amymone*, *Syrinx*, many more	Par Reg 2.188
Apollo, *Neptune*, *Jupiter*, or *Pan*,	Par Reg 2.190
Satyr, or Fawn, or Silvan? But these haunts	Par Reg 2.191
Of fond desire? or should she confident,	Par Reg 2.211
Or turn to reverent awe? for Beauty stands	Par Reg 2.220
Or that which only seems to satisfie	Par Reg 2.229
To Vertue I impute not, or count part	Par Reg 2.248
Or God support Nature without repast	Par Reg 2.250
Or as a guest with *Daniel* at his pulse.	Par Reg 2.278
If Cottage were in view, Sheep-cote or Herd;	Par Reg 2.287
But Cottage, Herd or Sheep-cote none he saw,	Par Reg 2.288
As one in City, or Court, or Palace bred,	Par Reg 2.300
Meats by the Law unclean, or offer'd first	Par Reg 2.328
Nature asham'd, or better to express,	Par Reg 2.332
And savour, Beasts of chase, or Fowl of game,	Par Reg 2.342
In pastry built, or from the spit, or boyl'd,	Par Reg 2.343
Gris-amber-steam'd; all Fish from Sea or Shore,	Par Reg 2.344
Freshet, or purling Brook, of shell or fin,	Par Reg 2.345
Then *Ganymed* or *Hylas*, distant more	Par Reg 2.353
Fairer then feign'd of old, or fabl'd since	Par Reg 2.358
By Knights of *Logres*, or of *Lyones*,	Par Reg 2.360
Lancelot or *Pelleas*, or *Pellenore*,	Par Reg 2.361
Of chiming strings, or charming pipes and winds	Par Reg 2.363
What I can do or offer is suspect;	Par Reg 2.399
Which way or from what hope dost thou aspire	Par Reg 2.417
Or at thy heels the dizzy Multitude,	Par Reg 2.420
To gain dominion or to keep it gain'd.	Par Reg 2.434
Cities of men, or head-strong Multitudes,	Par Reg 2.470
Or lawless passions in him which he serves.	Par Reg 2.472
On *Aaron*'s breast: or tongue of Seers old	Par Reg 3.15
Infallible; or wert thou sought to deeds	Par Reg 3.16
Could not sustain thy Prowess, or subsist	Par Reg 3.19
Affecting private life, or more obscure	Par Reg 3.22
Peaceable Nations, neighbouring, or remote,	Par Reg 3.76
Violent or shameful death thir due reward.	Par Reg 3.87
Without ambition, war, or violence;	Par Reg 3.90
Glory from men, from all men good or bad,	Par Reg 3.114
Wise or unwise, no difference, no exemption;	Par Reg 3.115
Above all Sacrifice, or hallow'd gift	Par Reg 3.116
Promiscuous from all Nations, Jew, or Greek,	Par Reg 3.118
Or Barbarous, nor exception hath declar'd;	Par Reg 3.119
Worth or not worth the seeking, let it pass:	Par Reg 3.151
Thy right by sitting still or thus retiring?	Par Reg 3.164
Without distrust or doubt, that he may know	Par Reg 3.193
My exaltation without change or end.	Par Reg 3.197
Raign or raign not; though to that gentle brow	Par Reg 3.215
Or human nature can receive, consider	Par Reg 3.231
Built by *Emathian*, or by *Parthian* hands,	Par Reg 3.290
Of equal dread in flight, or in pursuit;	Par Reg 3.306
Chariots or Elephants endorst with Towers	Par Reg 3.329
To lay hills plain, fell woods, or valleys fill,	Par Reg 3.332
Or where plain was raise hill, or over-lay	Par Reg 3.333
By Prophet or by Angel, unless thou	Par Reg 3.352
Samaritan or *Jew;* how could'st thou hope	Par Reg 3.359
Chuse which thou wilt by conquest or by league.	Par Reg 3.370
Shalt raign, and *Rome* or *Caesar* not need fear.	Par Reg 3.385
On my part aught endeavouring, or to need	Par Reg 3.399
Thy politic maxims, or that cumbersome	Par Reg 3.400
For *Israel*, or for *David*, or his Throne,	Par Reg 3.408
Humbled themselves, or penitent besought	Par Reg 3.421
The strength he was to cope with, or his own:	Par Reg 4.9
Or as a swarm of flies in vintage time,	Par Reg 4.15
Or surging waves against a solid rock,	Par Reg 4.18
Vain battry, and in froth or bubbles end;	Par Reg 4.20
By what strange Parallax or Optic skill	Par Reg 4.40
Of vision multiplyed through air, or glass	Par Reg 4.41
In Cedar, Marble, Ivory or Gold.	Par Reg 4.60
What conflux issuing forth, or entring in,	Par Reg 4.62
Hasting or on return, in robes of State;	Par Reg 4.64
Or Embassies from Regions far remote	Par Reg 4.67
Or on the *Aemilian*, some from farthest South,	Par Reg 4.69
Will be for thee no sitting, or not long	Par Reg 4.107
On *Cittron* tables or *Atlantic* stone;	Par Reg 4.115
Or could of inward slaves make outward free?	Par Reg 4.145
Or as a stone that shall to pieces dash	Par Reg 4.149
Or nothing more then still to contradict:	Par Reg 4.158
Long since. Wert thou so void of fear or shame,	Par Reg 4.189
Advise thee, gain them as thou canst, or not.	Par Reg 4.211
The *Pentateuch* or what the Prophets wrote,	Par Reg 4.226
Or they with thee hold conversation meet?	Par Reg 4.232
Or hospitable, in her sweet recess,	Par Reg 4.242
City or Suburban, studious walks and shades;	Par Reg 4.243
By voice or hand, and various-measur'd verse,	Par Reg 4.256
In *Chorus* or *Iambic*, teachers best	Par Reg 4.262
These here revolve, or, as thou lik'st, at home,	Par Reg 4.281
Think not but that I know these things, or think	Par Reg 4.286
But these are false, or little else but dreams,	Par Reg 4.291
Wealth, pleasure, pain or torment, death and life,	Par Reg 4.305
Which when he lists, he leaves, or boasts he can,	Par Reg 4.306
Or subtle shifts conviction to evade.	Par Reg 4.308
True wisdom, finds her not, or by delusion	Par Reg 4.319
A spirit and judgment equal or superior,	Par Reg 4.324
Crude or intoxicate, collecting toys,	Par Reg 4.328
Or if I would delight my private hours	Par Reg 4.331
With Music or with Poem, where so soon	Par Reg 4.332

Or(*cont*)

In Fable, Hymn, or Song, so personating	Par Reg 4.341
Thin sown with aught of profit or delight,	Par Reg 4.345
Or active, tended on by glory, or fame,	Par Reg 4.371
Nicely or cautiously my offer'd aid,	Par Reg 4.377
On *David*'s Throne; or Throne of all the world,	Par Reg 4.379
Or Heav'n write aught of Fate, by what the Stars	Par Reg 4.383
Voluminous, or single characters,	Par Reg 4.384
Real or Allegoric I discern not,	Par Reg 4.390
Or torn up sheer: ill wast thou shrouded then,	Par Reg 4.419
From drooping plant, or dropping tree; the birds	Par Reg 4.434
Or to the Earths dark basis underneath,	Par Reg 4.456
Betok'ning, or ill boding, I contemn	Par Reg 4.490
In what degree or meaning thou art call'd	Par Reg 4.516
The Son of God I also am, or was,	Par Reg 4.518
By parl, or composition, truce, or league	Par Reg 4.529
To win him, or win from him what I can.	Par Reg 4.530
Or thirst, and as he fed, Angelic Quires	Par Reg 4.593
Conceiving, or remote from Heaven, enshrin'd	Par Reg 4.598
Habit, or state, or motion, still expressing	Par Reg 4.601
Or Lightning thou shalt fall from Heav'n trod down	Par Reg 4.620
For yonder bank hath choice of Sun or shade,	Samson 3
Or benefit reveal'd to *Abraham*'s race?	Samson 29
Dungeon, or beggery, or decrepit age!	Samson 69
Of man or worm; the vilest here excel me,	Samson 74
Within doors, or without, still as a fool,	Samson 77
O change beyond report, thought, or belief!	Samson 117
Or do my eyes misrepresent? Can this be hee,	Samson 124
No strength of man, or fiercest wild beast could withstand;	Samson 127
Or grovling soild thir crested helmets in the dust.	Samson 141
Thy Bondage or lost Sight,	Samson 152
Or the sphear of fortune raises;	Samson 172
To visit or bewail thee, or if better,	Samson 182
Counsel or Consolation we may bring,	Samson 183
How could I once look up, or heave the head,	Samson 197
Then of thine own Tribe fairer, or as fair,	Samson 217
Acknowledg'd not, or not at all consider'd	Samson 245
Had *Judah* that day join'd, or one whole Tribe,	Samson 265
And to despise, or envy, or suspect	Samson 272
Of sin, or legal debt;	Samson 313
Temptation found'st, or over-potent charms	Samson 427
To waver, or fall off and joyn with Idols;	Samson 456
Mine eie to harbour sleep, or thoughts to rest.	Samson 459
Will not connive, or linger, thus provok'd,	Samson 466
Or *Dagon*. But for thee what shall be done?	Samson 478
Or th' execution leave to high disposal,	Samson 506
Sparkling, out-pow'rd, the flavor, or the smell,	Samson 544
Or taste that cheers the heart of Gods and men,	Samson 545
Sam. Where ever fountain or fresh current flow'd	Samson 547
Or pitied object, these redundant locks	Samson 568
Till vermin or the draff of servil food	Samson 574
By ransom or how else: mean while be calm,	Samson 604
Or medcinal liquor can asswage,	Samson 627
The subject of thir cruelty, or scorn.	Samson 646
Little prevails, or rather seems a tune,	Samson 661
Or might I say contrarious,	Samson 669
From thee on them, or them to thee of service.	Samson 686
Nor only dost degrade them, or remit	Samson 687
Too grievous for the trespass or omission,	Samson 691
To dogs and fowls a prey, or else captiv'd:	Samson 694
Or to the unjust tribunals, under change of times,	Samson 695
Just or unjust, alike seem miserable,	Samson 703
But who is this, what thing of Sea or Land?	Samson 710
Of *Javan* or *Gadier*	Samson 716
His vertue or weakness which way to assail:	Samson 756
To lessen or extenuate my offence,	Samson 767
Or else with just allowance counterpois'd,	Samson 770
The easier towards me, or thy hatred less.	Samson 772
So near related, or the same of kind,	Samson 786
Yet always pity or pardon hath obtain'd.	Samson 814
With God or Man will gain thee no remission.	Samson 835
Or by evasions thy crime uncoverst more.	Samson 842
In man or woman, though to thy own condemning,	Samson 844
Less therefore to be pleas'd, obey'd, or fear'd,	Samson 900
Sam. For want of words no doubt, or lack of breath,	Samson 905
Nor think me so unwary or accurst	Samson 930
To gloss upon, and censuring, frown or smile?	Samson 948
At this who ever envies or repines	Samson 995
Strength, comliness of shape, or amplest merit	Samson 1011
That womans love can win or long inherit;	Samson 1012
Or seven, though one should musing sit;	Samson 1017
If any of these or all, the *Timnian* bride	Samson 1018
Or value what is best	Samson 1029
Or was too much of self-love mixt,	Samson 1031
That either they love nothing, or not long?	Samson 1033
Adverse and turbulent, or by her charms	Samson 1040
Smile she or lowre:	Samson 1057
Sam. Or peace or not, alike to me he comes.	Samson 1074
As *Og* or *Anak* and the *Emims* old	Samson 1080
Each others force in camp or listed field:	Samson 1087
Or left thy carkass where the Ass lay thrown:	Samson 1097
Or rather flight, no great advantage on me;	Samson 1118
Arm'd thee or charm'd thee strong, which thou from Heaven	Samson 1134
Of chaf't wild Boars, or ruffl'd Porcupines.	Samson 1138
Then thou shalt see, or rather to thy sorrow	Samson 1154
Soon feel, whose God is strongest, thine or mine.	Samson 1155
Thine or whom I with *Israel*'s Sons adore.	Samson 1177
Or swing thee in the Air, then dash thee down	Samson 1240

Or(*cont*)

Some way or other yet further to afflict thee. Samson 1252
Whether he durst accept the offer or not, Samson 1255
That tyrannie or fortune can inflict, Samson 1291
A Scepter or quaint staff he bears, Samson 1303
Or make a game of my calamities? Samson 1331
Although thir drudge, to be thir fool or jester, Samson 1338
Up to the highth, whether to hold or break; Samson 1349
Yet that he may dispense with me or thee Samson 1377
Our Law, or stain my vow of *Nazarite*. Samson 1386
By some great act, or of my days the last. Samson 1389
Or we shall find such Engines to assail Samson 1396
Scandalous or forbidden in our Law. Samson 1409
Our God, our Law, my Nation, or my self, Samson 1425
The last of me or no I cannot warrant. Samson 1426
Or of him bringing to us some glad news? Samson 1444
Either at home, or through the high street passing, Samson 1458
What noise or shout was that? it tore the Skie. Samson 1472
Or at some proof of strength before them shown. Samson 1475
Chor. Noise call you it or universal groan Samson 1511
What shall we do, stay here or run and see? Samson 1520
Chor. Of good or bad so great, of bad the sooner; Samson 1537
Mess. O whither shall I run, or which way flie Samson 1541
But providence or instinct of nature seems, Samson 1545
Or reason though disturb'd, and scarse consulted Samson 1546
How dy'd he? death to life is crown or shame. Samson 1579
Man. Wearied with slaughter then or how? explain. Samson 1583
Eye-witness of what first or last was done, Samson 1594
To heave, pull, draw, or break, he still perform'd Samson 1626
Or some great matter in his mind revolv'd. Samson 1638
Not without wonder or delight beheld. Samson 1642
Lords, Ladies, Captains, Councellors, or Priests, Samson 1653
Living or dying thou hast fulfill'd Samson 1661
Insensate left, or to sense reprobate, Samson 1685
Or knock the breast, no weakness, no contempt, Samson 1722
Dispraise, or blame, nothing but well and fair, Samson 1723
In copious Legend, or sweet Lyric Song. Samson 1737
What never yet was heard in Tale or Song Mask 44
From old, or modern Bard in Hall, or Bowr. Mask 45
Into som brutish form of Woolf, or Bear, Mask 70
Or Ounce, or Tiger, Hog, or bearded Goat, Mask 71
Such as the jocond Flute, or gamesom Pipe Mask 173
To bring me Berries, or such cooling fruit Mask 186
Was I deceiv'd, or did a sable cloud Mask 221
line not in Bridgewater ms
Dwell'st here with *Pan*, or *Silvan*, by blest Song Mask 268
Co. By falshood, or discourtesie, or why? Mask 281
Co. Were they of manly prime, or youthful bloom? Mask 289
Dingle, or bushy dell of this wilde Wood, Mask 312
Or shroud within these limits, I shall know Mask 316
Ere morrow wake, or the low roosted lark Mask 317
Less warranted then this, or less secure Mask 327
Or if your influence be quite damm'd up Mask 336
Or *Tyrian* Cynosure. 2. *Bro*. Or if our eyes Mask 342
Trinity ms both 'or'
Or sound of pastoral reed with oaten stops, Mask 345
Or whistle from the Lodge, or village cock Mask 346
Or 'gainst the rugged bark of som broad Elm Mask 354
What if in wild amazement, and affright, Mask 356
Bridgewater ms 'or els in wild'
Trinity ms 'what if' ←'or else'
Or while we speak within the direfull grasp Mask 357
line not in Bridgewater ms
line not in Trinity ms
Of Savage hunger, or of Savage heat? Mask 358
line not in Bridgewater ms
line not in Trinity ms
Or if they be but false alarms of Fear, Mask 364
line not in Trinity ms
line not in Bridgewater ms
Or so unprincipl'd in vertues book, Mask 367
Far from the cheerfull haunt of men, and herds, Mask 388
Bridgewater ms 'or herds'
Trinity ms 'and' ←'or'
His few Books, or his Beads, or Maple Dish, Mask 391
Or do his gray hairs any violence? Mask 392
Of night, or lonelines it recks me not, Mask 404
Secure without all doubt, or controversie: Mask 409
No savage fierce, Bandite, or mountaneer Mask 426
Be it not don in pride, or in presumption. Mask 431
In fog, or fire, by lake, or moorish fen, Mask 433
Blew meager Hag, or stubborn unlaid ghost, Mask 434
No goblin, or swart Faery of the mine, Mask 436
Do ye beleeve me yet, or shall I call Mask 438
Or els som neighbour Wood-man, or at worst, Mask 484
Slip't from the fold, or young Kid lost his dam, Mask 498
Or straggling weather the pen't flock forsook? Mask 499
As a stray'd Ewe, or to pursue the stealth Mask 503
Or our neglect, we lost her as we came. Mask 510
Spir. Ile tell ye, 'tis not vain, or fabulous, Mask 513
Like stabl'd wolves, or tigers at their prey, Mask 534
Of malice or of sorcery, or that power Mask 587
Harpyies and *Hydra's*, or all the monstrous forms Mask 605
Or drag him by the curls, to a foul death, Mask 608
'Gainst all inchantments, mildew blast, or damp Mask 640
Or gastly furies apparition; Mask 641
Or like the sons of *Vulcan* vomit smoak, Mask 655
And you a statue; or as *Daphne* was Mask 661

Or(*cont*)

Trinity ms 'or' ←'fixt'
Here dwel no frowns, nor anger, from these gates Mask 667
Trinity ms 'nor' ←'or'
To life so friendly, or so cool to thirst. Mask 678
The sampler, and to teize the huswifes wooll. Mask 751
Trinity ms 'or to'
Love-darting eyes, or tresses like the Morn? Mask 753
line not in Bridgewater ms
Or have I said anough? To him that dares Mask 780
line not in Trinity ms
line not in Bridgewater ms
Summer drouth, or singed air Mask 928
Not a waste, or needless sound Mask 942
Here be without duck or nod Mask 960
I can fly, or I can run Mask 1013
Or if Vertue feeble were, Mask 1022
that lurks by hedge or lane of this dead circuit Mask Tr. ms 16.40
be it not don in pride or in praesumption Mask Tr. ms 16.56
that lurks by hedge or lane, of this dead circuit Mask Br. ms 393
Or whether (as som Sager sing) Allegro 17
Through the Sweet-Briar, or the Vine, Allegro 47
Or the twisted Eglantine. Allegro 48
And to the stack, or the Barn dore, Allegro 51
Or if the earlier season lead Allegro 89
Of Wit, or Arms, while both contend Allegro 123
Or sweetest *Shakespear* fancies childe, Allegro 133
Or fill the fixed mind with all your toyes; Penseroso 4
Or likest hovering dreams Penseroso 9
Or that Starr'd *Ethiope* Queen that strove Penseroso 19
Or if the Ayr will not permit, Penseroso 77
Or the Belmans drousie charm, Penseroso 83
Or let my Lamp at midnight hour, Penseroso 85
With thrice great *Hermes*, or unsphear Penseroso 88
What Worlds, or what vast Regions hold Penseroso 90
In fire, air, flood, or under ground, Penseroso 94
With Planet, or with Element. Penseroso 96
Presenting *Thebs*, or *Pelops* line, Penseroso 99
Or the tale of *Troy* divine. Penseroso 100
Or what (though rare) of later age, Penseroso 101
Or bid the soul of *Orpheus* sing Penseroso 105
Or call up him that left half told Penseroso 109
Or usher'd with a shower still, Penseroso 127
Of Pine, or monumental Oake, Penseroso 135
Or fright them from their hallow'd haunt. Penseroso 138
Above, about, or underneath, Penseroso 152
Or th' unseen Genius of the Wood. Penseroso 154
Or the towred *Cybele*, Arcades 21
Of noisom winds, and blasting vapours chill. Arcades 49
Trinity ms 'winds or'
Or what the cross dire-looking Planet smites, Arcades 52
Trinity ms 'or' ←'&'
Or hurtfull Worm with canker'd venom bites. Arcades 53
Awakes the slumbring leaves, or tasseld horn Arcades 57
If my inferior hand or voice could hit Arcades 77
On old *Lycaeus* or *Cyllene* hoar, Arcades 98
Or Taint-worm to the weanling Herds that graze, Lycidas 46
Or Frost to Flowers, that their gay wardrop wear, Lycidas 47
Or with the tangles of *Neaera's* hair? Lycidas 69
1638 'Hid in'
Trinity ms 'or with' ←'hid in'
A Sheep-hook, or have learn'd ought els the least Lycidas 120
Or whether thou to our moist vows deny'd, Lycidas 159
Hast thou no vers, no hymn, or solemn strein, Nativity 17
No War, or Battails sound Nativity 53
Or *Lucifer* that often warn'd them thence; Nativity 74
Then his bright Throne, or burning Axletree could bear. Nativity 84
Or ere the point of dawn, Nativity 86
Perhaps their loves, or els their sheep, Nativity 91
No voice or hideous humm Nativity 174
No nightly trance, or breathed spell, Nativity 179
In *Memphian* Grove, or Green, Nativity 214
Or that thy coarse corrupts in earths dark wombe, Fair Inf 30
Or that thy beauties lie in wormie bed, Fair Inf 31
Or in the Elisian fields (if such there were.) Fair Inf 40
Or did of late earths Sonnes besiege the wall Fair Inf 47
Or wert thou that just Maid who once before Fair Inf 50
Or wert thou that sweet smiling Youth! Fair Inf 53
Or that crown'd Matron sage white-robed truth? Fair Inf 54
Or any other of that heav'nly brood Fair Inf 55
Or wert thou of the golden-winged hoast, Fair Inf 57
Or drive away the slaughtering pestilence, Fair Inf 68
That so they may without suspect or fears Vacation 27
Of utmost *Tweed*, or *Oose*, or gulphie *Dun*, Vacation 92
Or *Trent*, who like some earth-born Giant spreads Vacation 93
Or sullen *Mole* that runneth underneath, Vacation 95
Or *Severn* swift, guilty of Maidens death, Vacation 96
Or Rockie *Avon*, or of Sedgie *Lee*, Vacation 97
Or Coaly *Tine*, or antient hollowed *Dee*, Vacation 98
Or *Humber* loud that keeps the *Scythians* Name, Vacation 99
Or *Medway* smooth, or Royal Towred *Thame*. Vacation 100
Of Lute, or Viol still, more apt for mournful things. Passion 28
Or should I thence hurried on viewles wing, Passion 50
O more exceeding love or law more just? Circum 15
But whether by mischance or blame Winchester 27
Or that his hallow'd reliques should be hid Shakespear 3
Or els the ways being foul, twenty to one, Carrier 3
Whether the Muse, or Love call thee his mate, Sonnet 1, 13

Or(*cont*)
But my late spring no bud or blossom shew'th. Sonnet 7, 4
Yet be it less or more, or soon or slow, Sonnet 7, 9
To that same lot, however mean, or high, Sonnet 7, 11
Captain or Colonel, or Knight in Arms, Sonnet 8, 1
Who liv'd in both, unstain'd with gold or fee, Sonnet 10, 3
Colkitto, or Macdonnel, or Galasp? Sonnet 11, 9
Hated not Learning wors then Toad or Asp; Sonnet 11, 13
That tun'st their happiest lines in Hymn, or Story. Sonnet 13, 11
Filling each mouth with envy, or with praise, Sonnet 15, 2
Whether to settle peace or to unfold Sonnet 17, 5
Either man's work or his own gifts, who best Sonnet 19, 10
To hear the Lute well toucht, or artfull voice Sonnet 20, 11
To outward view, of blemish or of spot; Sonnet 22, 2
Of Sun or Moon or Starre throughout the year, Sonnet 22, 5
1694 'Or Sun'
Or man or woman. Yet I argue not Sonnet 22, 6
Against heavns hand or will, nor bate a jot Sonnet 22, 7
Of heart or hope; but still bear vp and steer Sonnet 22, 8
In judgment, or abide their tryal then, Psalm 1, 13
Fools or mad men stand not within thy sight. Psalm 5, 12
No word is firm or sooth Psalm 5, 26
Or done this, if wickedness Psalm 7, 8
Or to him have render'd less, Psalm 7, 11
And think'st upon him; or of man begot Psalm 8, 13
All beasts that in the field or forrest meet, Psalm 8, 20
Or they *who* in perdition *dwell* Psalm 88, 47
Or wondrous acts be known, Psalm 88, 50
Things that on earth were lost, or were abus'd. Prose 2, 4
In thy Adulterers, or thy ill got wealth? Prose 3, 4

Oracle
Fast by the Oracle of God; I thence Par Lost 1.12
So spake this Oracle, then verifi'd Par Lost 10.182
God hath now sent his living Oracle Par Reg 1.460
In pious Hearts, an inward Oracle Par Reg 1.463
Thy Counsel would be as the Oracle Par Reg 3.13
Whom well inspir'd the Oracle pronounc'd Par Reg 4.275

Oracles
And answers, oracles, portents and dreams, Par Reg 1.395
Yet thou pretend'st to truth; all Oracles Par Reg 1.430
The Gentiles; henceforth Oracles are ceast, Par Reg 1.456
The Oracles are dumm, Nativity 173

Oracling
No more shalt thou by oracling abuse Par Reg 1.455

Oraculous
Urim and *Thummim*, those oraculous gems Par Reg 3.14

Orator
As when of old som Orator renound Par Lost 9.670

Orators
Thence to the famous Orators repair, Par Reg 4.267
Thir Orators thou then extoll'st, as those Par Reg 4.353

Oratory
Then loudest Oratorie: yet thir port Par Lost 11.8
Then all the Oratory of *Greece* and *Rome*. Par Reg 4.360

Orb
Hung on his shoulders like the Moon, whose Orb Par Lost 1.287
ms 'orb'
From Hell continu'd reaching th' utmost Orbe Par Lost 2.1029
Astronomer in the Sun's lucent Orbe Par Lost 3.589
Beneath th' *Azores;* whither the prime Orb, Par Lost 4.592
With the fixt Starrs, fixt in thir Orb that flies, Par Lost 5.176
Orb within Orb, the Father infinite, Par Lost 5.596
Had circl'd his full Orbe, the birth mature Par Lost 5.862
He hasted, and oppos'd the rockie Orb Par Lost 6.254
The hollow Universal Orb they fill'd, Par Lost 7.257
In the Suns Orb, made porous to receive Par Lost 7.361
Cycle and Epicycle, Orb in Orb: Par Lost 8.84
Stor'd in each Orb perhaps with some that live. Par Lost 8.152
Each Orb a glimps of Light, conveyd so farr Par Lost 8.156
Ganges and *Indus:* thus the Orb he roam'd Par Lost 9.82

Orbed
Full Orb'd the Moon, and with more pleasing light Par Lost 5.42
Fit well his Helme, gripe fast his orbed Shield, Par Lost 6.543
Th' enameld *Arras* of the Rainbow wearing, Nativity 143
1673 'Orb'd in a Rain-bow and like glories wearing'

Orbicular
That rowld orbicular, and turnd to Starrs Par Lost 3.718
His Quadrature, from thy Orbicular World, Par Lost 10.381

Orbs
So thick a drop serene hath quencht thir Orbs, Par Lost 3.25
The luminous inferior Orbs, enclos'd Par Lost 3.420
In which of all these shining Orbes hath Man Par Lost 3.668
But all these shining Orbes his choice to dwell; Par Lost 3.670
From her moist Continent to higher Orbes. Par Lost 5.422
Recorded eminent. Thus when in Orbes Par Lost 5.594
With dreadful shade contiguous, and the Orbes Par Lost 6.828
For aught appeers, and on thir Orbs impose Par Lost 8.30
Centring receav'st from all those Orbs; in thee, Par Lost 9.109
You two this way, among these numerous Orbs Par Lost 10.397
That these dark orbs no more shall treat with light, Samson 591
But in their glimmering Orbs did glow, Nativity 75
Nor to thir idle orbs doth sight appear Sonnet 22, 4
1694 'Orbs'

Orcs
The haunt of Seales and Orcs, and Sea-mews clang. Par Lost 11.835

Orcus
Orcus and *Ades*, and the dreaded name Par Lost 2.964

Ordain
Unless th' Almighty Maker them ordain Par Lost 2.915
And let them be for Lights as I ordaine Par Lost 7.343
Ordaine them Lawes; part such as appertaine Par Lost 12.230
That did the solid Earth ordain Psalm 136, 21

Ordained
For those rebellious, here thir Prison ordain'd Par Lost 1.71
At thee ordain'd his drudge, to execute Par Lost 2.732
Unchangeable, Eternal, which ordain'd Par Lost 3.127
Thir freedom, they themselves ordain'd thir fall. Par Lost 3.128
All these his works so wondrous he ordaind, Par Lost 3.665
O had his powerful Destiny ordaind Par Lost 4.58
His farr more pleasant Garden God ordaind; Par Lost 4.215
Ordaind by thee, and this delicious place Par Lost 4.729
1667 'Ordain'd'
He left it in thy power, ordaind thy will Par Lost 5.526
Ordaind without redemption, without end. Par Lost 5.615
Our being ordain'd to govern, not to serve? Par Lost 5.802
For thee I have ordain'd it, and thus farr Par Lost 6.700
Number to this dayes work is not ordain'd Par Lost 6.809
Glorie and praise, whose wisdom had ordain'd Par Lost 7.187
Hath Omnipresence) and the work ordain'd, Par Lost 7.590
Ordain'd for uses to his Lord best known. Par Lost 8.106
First Man, of Men innumerable ordain'd Par Lost 8.297
Of God ordain'd them, his creating hand Par Lost 9.344
1667 'ordaind'
Of pleasure not for him ordain'd: then soon Par Lost 9.470
Shall scape his punishment ordain'd, and wee Par Lost 10.1039
To me transgressour, who for thee ordaind Par Lost 11.164
Through the twelve Tribes, to rule by Laws ordaind: Par Lost 12.226
The purpos'd Counsel pre-ordain'd and fixt Par Reg 1.127
But to a Kingdom thou art born, ordain'd Par Reg 3.152
Thou shalt be what thou art ordain'd, no doubt; Par Reg 4.473
Ordain'd thy nurture holy, as of a Plant; Samson 362
This he a Testimony ordain'd Psalm 81, 17

Ordains
That so ordains: this was at first resolv'd, Par Lost 2.201
Unargu'd I obey; so God ordains, Par Lost 4.636
Of *Servitude* to serve whom God ordains, Par Lost 6.175
For other things mild Heav'n a time ordains, Sonnet 21, 11

Order
These were the prime in order and in might; Par Lost 1.506
The whole Battalion views, thir order due, Par Lost 1.569
Of order, how in safety best we may Par Lost 2.280
In order came the grand infernal Peers, Par Lost 2.507
Light shon, and order from disorder sprung: Par Lost 3.713
In order, though to Nations yet unborn, Par Lost 4.663
What order, so contriv'd as not to mix Par Lost 5.334
Secret they finish'd, and in order set, Par Lost 6.522
In order, quit of all impediment; Par Lost 6.548
Shaded with branching Palme, each order bright, Par Lost 6.885
And all things in best order to invite Par Lost 9.402
Of lowest order, past; and from the dore Par Lost 10.443
Thir order: last the Sire, and his three Sons Par Lost 11.736
That fragrant smell diffus'd, in order stood Par Reg 2.351
By order of the Lords new parted hence Samson 1447
Of sort, might sit in order to behold, Samson 1608
And nests in order rang'd Samson 1694
Bright-harnest Angels sit in order serviceable. Nativity 244
And out of order gon. Psalm 82, 20

Ordered
Of Warriers old with order'd Spear and Shield, Par Lost 1.565
Why was my breeding order'd and prescrib'd Samson 30
That they would fitly fall in order'd Characters. Passion 49

Ordering
So ordering. I with leave of speech implor'd, Par Lost 8.377

Orderly
Of Birds in orderly array on wing Par Lost 6.74

Orders
Each in his Hierarchie, the Orders bright. Par Lost 1.737
ms 'orders'
Under thir Hierarchs in orders bright Par Lost 5.587
Of Hierarchies, of Orders, and Degrees; Par Lost 5.591
Equally free; for Orders and Degrees Par Lost 5.792
To those bright Orders utterd thus his voice. Par Lost 10.615
Orders and governs, nor content in Heaven Par Reg 3.112
The Angelic orders and inferiour creatures mute, Samson 672

Ore
That in his womb was hid metallic Ore, Par Lost 1.673
With wond'rous Art found out the massie Ore, Par Lost 1.703
Metals of drossiest Ore to perfet Gold Par Lost 5.442
From underground) the liquid Ore he dreind Par Lost 11.570
She hutch't th' all-worshipt ore, and precious gems Mask 719
Bridgewater ms 'oare'
The beryl, and the golden ore, Mask 933
Bridgewater ms 'Oare'
And tricks his beams, and with new spangled Ore, Lycidas 170
1638 'ore'
Trinity ms 'ore'

Oread
Oread or *Dryad*, or of *Delia*'s Traine, Par Lost 9.387

Oreb
Of *Oreb*, or of *Sinai*, didst inspire Par Lost 1.7
ms 'Oreb'
The Calf in *Oreb:* and the Rebel King Par Lost 1.484
ms 'Oreb'
His Trumpet, heard in *Oreb* since perhaps Par Lost 11.74
As Zeb and Oreb evil sped Psalm 83, 41

Organ
As in an Organ from one blast of wind Par Lost 1.708
Was heard, of Harp and Organ; and who moovd Par Lost 11.560
There let the pealing Organ blow, Penseroso 161
And let the Base of Heav'ns deep Organ blow, Nativity 130
Organic
Organic, or impulse of vocal Air, Par Lost 9.530
Organs
The Organs of her Fancie, and with them forge Par Lost 4.802
And Dulcimer, all Organs of sweet stop, Par Lost 7.596
Orgies
Yet thence his lustful Orgies he enlarg'd Par Lost 1.415
Orient
With Orient Colours waving: with them rose Par Lost 1.546
ms 'orient'
Secure, and at the brightning Orient beam Par Lost 2.399
Imbellisht, thick with sparkling orient Gemmes Par Lost 3.507
Rowling on Orient Pearl and sands of Gold, Par Lost 4.238
His orient Beams, on herb, tree, fruit, and flour, Par Lost 4.644
Advancing, sow'd the earth with Orient Pearle, Par Lost 5.2
Moon, that now meetst the orient Sun, now fli'st Par Lost 5.175
Shot through with orient Beams: when all the Plain Par Lost 6.15
Now when fair Morn Orient in Heav'n appeerd Par Lost 6.524
By the Celestial Quires, when Orient Light Par Lost 7.254
More orient in yon Western Cloud that draws Par Lost 11.205
His orient liquor in a Crystal Glasse, Mask 65
Pillows his chin upon an Orient wave, Nativity 231
Orifice
With hideous orifice gap't on us wide, Par Lost 6.577
Original
All her Original brightness, nor appear'd Par Lost 1.592
ms 'original'
Thir frail Original, and faded bliss, Par Lost 2.375
1667 'Originals'
To her original darkness and your sway Par Lost 2.984
Exalted from so base original, Par Lost 9.150
Original; while *Adam* took no thought, Par Lost 9.1004
Th' effects which thy original crime hath wrought Par Lost 11.424
Since thy original lapse, true Libertie Par Lost 12.83
Originals
Thir frail Original, and faded bliss, Par Lost 2.375
1667 'Originals'
Th' originals of Nature in thir crude Par Lost 6.511
Orion
Afloat, when with fierce Winds *Orion* arm'd Par Lost 1.305
ms 'Orion'
Orisons
Thir Orisons, each Morning duly paid Par Lost 5.145
Had ended now thir Orisons, and found Par Lost 11.137
Ormus
Outshon the wealth of *Ormus* and of *Ind*, Par Lost 2.2
Ornament
With regal Ornament; the middle pair Par Lost 5.280
Too much of Ornament, in outward shew Par Lost 8.538
Is it for that such outward ornament Samson 1025
Thir ornament and safety, had not spells Samson 1132
Ornaments
Our wonted Ornaments now soild and staind, Par Lost 9.1076
Ornate
That so bedeckt, ornate, and gay, Samson 712
Orontes
Of *Daphne* by *Orontes*, and th' inspir'd Par Lost 4.273
West from *Orontes* to the Ocean barr'd Par Lost 9.80
Orphean
With other notes then to th' *Orphean* Lyre Par Lost 3.17
Orpheus
That *Orpheus* self may heave his head Allegro 145
Or bid the soul of *Orpheus* sing Penseroso 105
What could the Muse her self that *Orpheus* bore, Lycidas 58
Orus
Osiris, *Isis*, *Orus* and thir Train Par Lost 1.478
ms 'Orus'
Isis and *Orus*, and the Dog *Anubis* hast. Nativity 212
Osier
Where grows the Willow and the Osier dank, Mask 891
Trinity ms 'osier'
1637 'osier'
Osiers
Where winds with Reeds, and Osiers whisp'ring play Par Reg 2.26
Osiris
Osiris, *Isis*, *Orus* and thir Train Par Lost 1.478
ms 'Osiris'
Nor is *Osiris* seen Nativity 213
Ostentation
Much ostentation vain of fleshly arm, Par Reg 3.387
Other
That sparkling blaz'd, his other Parts besides Par Lost 1.194
Peor his other Name, when he entic'd Par Lost 1.412
(Far other once beheld in bliss) condemn'd Par Lost 1.607
To less then Gods. On th' other side up rose Par Lost 2.108
In others count'nance read his own dismay Par Lost 2.422
Wasting the Earth, each other to destroy: Par Lost 2.502
Eclipses at thir charms. The other shape, Par Lost 2.666
More dreadful and deform: on th' other side Par Lost 2.706
Each cast at th' other, as when two black Clouds Par Lost 2.714
For want of other prey, but that he knows Par Lost 2.806
Confine with Heav'n; or if som other place Par Lost 2.977
Charybdis, and by th' other whirlpool steard. Par Lost 2.1020

Other(*cont*)
With other notes then to th' *Orphean* Lyre Par Lost 3.17
Those other two equal'd with me in Fate, Par Lost 3.33
By the other first: Man therefore shall find grace, Par Lost 3.131
The other none: in Mercy and Justice both, Par Lost 3.132
Som other able, and as willing, pay Par Lost 3.211
Alone, for other Creature in this place Par Lost 3.442
Or happiness in this or th' other life; Par Lost 3.450
Stars distant, but nigh hand seemd other Worlds, Par Lost 3.566
Or other Worlds they seemd, or happy Iles, Par Lost 3.567
His day, which else as th' other Hemisphere Par Lost 3.725
Ambition. Yet why not? som other Power Par Lost 4.61
Drawn to his part; but other Powers as great Par Lost 4.63
With other promises and other vaunts Par Lost 4.84
On th' other side: which when th' arch-fellon saw Par Lost 4.179
Creatures of other mould, earth-born perhaps, Par Lost 4.360
Now other, as thir shape servd best his end Par Lost 4.398
From us no other service then to keep Par Lost 4.420
Over all other Creatures that possess Par Lost 4.431
My other half: with that thy gentle hand Par Lost 4.488
Among our other torments not the least, Par Lost 4.510
No Creature thence: if Spirit of other sort, Par Lost 4.582
Our eye-lids; other Creatures all day long Par Lost 4.616
While other Animals unactive range, Par Lost 4.621
Sole, or responsive each to others note Par Lost 4.683
Of costliest Emblem: other Creature here Par Lost 4.703
This said unanimous, and other Rites Par Lost 4.736
With strictest watch; these other wheel the North, Par Lost 4.783
Prove chaff. On th' other side *Satan* allarm'd Par Lost 4.985
Two other precious drops that ready stood, Par Lost 5.132
And yee five other wandring Fires that move Par Lost 5.177
Not unconform to other shining Globes, Par Lost 5.259
Thus said. Native of Heav'n, for other place Par Lost 5.361
By Destinie, and can no other choose? Par Lost 5.534
On other surety none; freely we serve, Par Lost 5.538
His other half in the great Zone of Heav'n. Par Lost 5.560
Each to other like, more then on earth is thought? Par Lost 5.576
That day, as other solemn dayes, they spent Par Lost 5.618
Will not be now voutsaf't, other Decrees Par Lost 5.884
Light issues forth, and at the other dore Par Lost 6.9
Mean while in other parts like deeds deservd Par Lost 6.354
Seek not the praise of men: the other sort Par Lost 6.376
Cherubic waving fires: on th' other part Par Lost 6.413
In Nature none: if other hidden cause Par Lost 6.442
Thick-rammd, at th' other bore with touch of fire Par Lost 6.485
The punishment to other hand belongs, Par Lost 6.807
They measure all, of other excellence Par Lost 6.821
Nor other strife with them do I voutsafe. Par Lost 6.823
One foot he center'd, and the other turn'd Par Lost 7.228
Hither as to thir Fountain other Starrs Par Lost 7.364
From him, for other light she needed none Par Lost 7.378
The silent hours, and th' other whose gay Traine Par Lost 7.444
And Brute as other Creatures, but endu'd Par Lost 7.507
Be Center to the World, and other Starrs Par Lost 8.123
From the Suns beam meet Night, her other part Par Lost 8.139
Allotted there; and other Suns perhaps Par Lost 8.148
Of other Creatures, as him pleases best, Par Lost 8.169
Dream not of other Worlds, what Creatures there Par Lost 8.175
Noise, other then the sound of Dance or Song, Par Lost 8.243
The one intense, the other still remiss Par Lost 8.387
Beneath what other Creatures are to thee? Par Lost 8.411
Thy likeness, thy fit help, thy other self, Par Lost 8.450
Her loss, and other pleasures all abjure: Par Lost 8.480
O're other Creatures; yet when I approach Par Lost 8.546
Beyond all other, think the same voutsaf't Par Lost 8.581
Proceeding, which in other Beasts observ'd Par Lost 9.94
Terrestrial Heav'n, danc't round by other Heav'ns Par Lost 9.103
For while so near each other thus all day Par Lost 9.220
But other doubt possesses me, least harm Par Lost 9.251
To other speedie aide might lend at need; Par Lost 9.260
Angels, nor think superfluous others aid. Par Lost 9.308
First thy obedience; th' other who can know, Par Lost 9.368
Save what is in destroying, other joy Par Lost 9.478
I was at first as other Beasts that graze Par Lost 9.571
All other Beasts that saw, with like desire Par Lost 9.592
Each thing on Earth; and other care perhaps Par Lost 9.813
On th' other side, *Adam*, soon as he heard Par Lost 9.888
Farr other operation first displaid, Par Lost 9.1012
As from unrest, and each the other viewing, Par Lost 9.1052
The Parts of each for other, that seem most Par Lost 9.1093
Or to each other, but apparent guilt, Par Lost 10.112
My other self, the partner of my life; Par Lost 10.128
O Son, why sit we here each other viewing Par Lost 10.235
In other Worlds, and happier Seat provides Par Lost 10.237
Then sufferd. Th' other way *Satan* went down Par Lost 10.414
Each other, till supplanted down he fell Par Lost 10.513
They saw, but other sight instead, a crowd Par Lost 10.538
Her office they prescrib'd, to th' other five Par Lost 10.657
Devourd each other; nor stood much in awe Par Lost 10.712
Or in some other dismal place who knows Par Lost 10.787
With other echo late I taught your Shades Par Lost 10.861
To answer, and resound farr other Song. Par Lost 10.862
Or find some other way to generate Par Lost 10.894
Each other, blam'd enough elsewhere, but strive Par Lost 10.959
Each others burden in our share of woe; Par Lost 10.961
This other serv'd but to eternize woe; Par Lost 11.60
Farr other name deserving. But the Field Par Lost 11.171
That never will in other Climate grow, Par Lost 11.274

Other*(cont)*
And wilde, how shall we breath in other Aire — Par Lost 11.284
New reapt, the other part sheep-walks and foulds; — Par Lost 11.431
The others not, for his was not sincere; — Par Lost 11.443
Will be aveng'd, and th' others Faith approv'd — Par Lost 11.458
But is there yet no other way, besides — Par Lost 11.527
In other part stood one who at the Forge — Par Lost 11.564
In other part the scepter'd Haralds call — Par Lost 11.660
Among the Builders; each to other calls — Par Lost 12.57
Whose foul Idolatries, and other faults — Par Lost 12.337
Th' Archangel stood, and from the other Hill — Par Lost 12.626
I, when no other durst, sole undertook — Par Reg 1.100
Will bring me hence, no other Guide I seek. — Par Reg 1.336
What other way I see not, for we here — Par Reg 1.338
(For I discern thee other then thou seem'st) — Par Reg 1.348
The other service was thy chosen task, — Par Reg 1.427
Of other women, by the birth I bore, — Par Reg 2.71
Far other labour to be undergon — Par Reg 2.132
Can satisfie that need some other way, — Par Reg 2.254
By hunger, that each other Creature tames, — Par Reg 2.406
That other o're the body only reigns, — Par Reg 2.478
And know not whom, but as one leads the other; — Par Reg 3.53
One is the Son of *Jove*, of *Mars* the other, — Par Reg 3.84
Th' one winding, the other strait and left between — Par Reg 3.256
Besides thir other worse then heathenish crimes; — Par Reg 3.419
The City which thou seest no other deem — Par Reg 4.44
On the other side know also thou, that I — Par Reg 4.159
Other donation none thou canst produce: — Par Reg 4.184
No other doctrine needs, though granted true; — Par Reg 4.290
Mee worse then wet thou find'st not; other harm — Par Reg 4.486
From worst of other evils, pains and wrongs, — Samson 105
This with the other should, at least, have paird, — Samson 208
Deliverance offerd: I on th' other side — Samson 246
And Rivals? In this other was there found — Samson 387
Nor th' other light of life continue long, — Samson 592
And now at nearer view, no other certain — Samson 723
But that on th' other side if it be weigh'd — Samson 768
Far other reasonings, brought forth other deeds. — Samson 875
Where other senses want not their delights — Samson 916
On both his wings, one black, th' other white, — Samson 973
Each others force in camp or listed field: — Samson 1087
I should have forc'd thee soon wish other arms, — Samson 1096
Har. This insolence other kind of answer fits. — Samson 1236
Some way or other yet further to afflict thee. — Samson 1252
Some other tending, in his hand — Samson 1302
From other hands we need not much to fear. — Samson 1526
The other side was op'n, where the throng — Samson 1609
Now of my own accord such other tryal — Samson 1643
All other parts remaining as they were, — Mask 72
Pacing toward the other gole — Mask 100
Farr other arms, and other weapons must — Mask 612
But in another Countrey, as he said, — Mask 632
Trinity ms 'an other'
With that which you receiv'd on other terms, — Mask 684
line not in Bridgewater ms
Som other means I have which may be us'd, — Mask 821
Trinity ms 'some other meanes I have' ←'there is another way'
With som other new device. — Mask 941
Other trippings to be trod — Mask 961
Of Hearbs, and other Country Messes, — Allegro 85
Of other care they little reck'ning make, — Lycidas 116
Where other groves, and other streams along, — Lycidas 174
Or any other of that heav'nly brood — Fair Inf 55
And former sufferings other where are found; — Passion 25
For other things mild Heav'n a time ordains, — Sonnet 21, 11
Content though blind, had I no better guide. — Sonnet 22, 14
1694 'other Guide'
Her other branches *went*. — Psalm 80, 48
As other Princes *die*. — Psalm 82, 24
Of all that other gods have done — Psalm 86, 27

Others
Evil to others, and enrag'd might see — Par Lost 1.216
Others among the chief might offer now — Par Lost 2.469
Others with vast *Typhoean* rage more fell — Par Lost 2.539
Into th' *Euboic* Sea. Others more milde, — Par Lost 2.546
Others apart sat on a Hill retir'd, — Par Lost 2.557
Others came single; he who to be deemd — Par Lost 3.469
Others whose fruit burnisht with Golden Rinde — Par Lost 4.249
Gave proof unheeded; others on the grass — Par Lost 4.350
Of others, who approve not to transgress — Par Lost 4.880
The fall of others from like state of bliss; — Par Lost 5.241
Defence, while others bore him on thir Shields — Par Lost 6.337
Soon banded; others from the dawning Hills — Par Lost 6.528
Others on Silver Lakes and Rivers Bath'd — Par Lost 7.437
The mid Aereal Skie: Others on ground — Par Lost 7.442
By what I seek, but others to make such — Par Lost 9.127
Though others envie what they cannot give; — Par Lost 9.805
To be to others cause of misery, — Par Lost 10.982
Of Cattel grazing: others, whence the sound — Par Lost 11.558
Deserted: Others to a Citie strong — Par Lost 11.655
Assaulting; others from the wall defend — Par Lost 11.657
Though of Rebellion others he accuse. — Par Lost 12.37
I as all others to his Baptism came, — Par Reg 1.273
With others though in Holy Writ not nam'd, — Par Reg 2.8
Others return'd from Baptism, not her Son, — Par Reg 2.61
All others by thy self; because of old — Par Reg 2.174
Not without hunger. Others of some note, — Par Reg 2.306

Others*(cont)*
Of these things others quickly will dispose — Par Reg 2.400
Others in vertue plac'd felicity, — Par Reg 4.297
In power of others, never in my own; — Samson 78
Be not unlike all others, not austere — Samson 815
To others did no violence nor spoil. — Samson 1191
Others more moderate seeming, but thir aim — Samson 1464
Were it not better don as others use, — Lycidas 67
From others he shall stand in need of nothing, — Vacation 81
Which others at their Barr so often wrench; — Sonnet 21, 4
line not in Trinity ms

Otherwise
Far otherwise th' inviolable Saints — Par Lost 6.398
Farr otherwise, transported I behold, — Par Lost 8.529
Farr otherwise th' event, not Death, but Life — Par Lost 9.984
And thou thy self seem'st otherwise inclin'd — Par Reg 4.212
Sam. All otherwise to me my thoughts portend, — Samson 590
From her thach't pallat rowse, if otherwise — Mask 318

Ought
His secrets to be scann'd by them who ought — Par Lost 8.74
For still they knew, and ought to have still remember'd — Par Lost 10.12
Of knowing what I aught: he who receives — Par Reg 4.288
Bin, as it ought, sincere, it would have taught thee — Samson 874

Oughtst
Forthwith how thou oughtst to receive him. — Samson 329

Ounce
And Rampant shakes his Brinded main; the Ounce, — Par Lost 7.466
Or Ounce, or Tiger, Hog, or bearded Goat, — Mask 71
Bridgewater ms 'ounce'

Ounces
Dandl'd the Kid; Bears, Tygers, Ounces, Pards, — Par Lost 4.344

Our
Brought Death into the World, and all our woe, — Par Lost 1.3
Mov'd our Grand Parents in that happy State, — Par Lost 1.29
Irreconcileable, to our grand Foe; — Par Lost 1.122
Though all our Glory extinct, and happy state — Par Lost 1.141
But what if he our Conquerour, (whom I now — Par Lost 1.143
Have left us this our spirit and strength intire — Par Lost 1.146
Strongly to suffer and support our pains, — Par Lost 1.147
To do ought good never will be our task, — Par Lost 1.159
But ever to do ill our sole delight, — Par Lost 1.160
Out of our evil seek to bring forth good, — Par Lost 1.163
Our labour must be to pervert that end, — Par Lost 1.164
Or satiate fury yield it from our Foe. — Par Lost 1.179
And reassembling our afflicted Powers, — Par Lost 1.186
Our Enemy, our own loss how repair, — Par Lost 1.188
But wherefore let we then our faithful friends, — Par Lost 1.264
Th' associates and copartners of our loss — Par Lost 1.265
By mee, have lost our hopes. But he who reigns — Par Lost 1.637
Which tempted our attempt, and wrought our fall. — Par Lost 1.642
Henceforth his might we know, and know our own — Par Lost 1.643
New warr, provok't; our better part remains — Par Lost 1.645
Our first eruption, thither or elsewhere: — Par Lost 1.656
ms defective here
To claim our just inheritance of old, — Par Lost 2.38
By our delay? no, let us rather choose — Par Lost 2.60
Turning our Tortures into horrid Arms — Par Lost 2.63
That in our proper motion we ascend — Par Lost 2.75
Up to our native seat: descent and fall — Par Lost 2.76
When the fierce Foe hung on our brok'n Rear — Par Lost 2.78
Our stronger, some worse way his wrath may find — Par Lost 2.83
To our destruction: if there be in Hell — Par Lost 2.84
Or if our substance be indeed Divine, — Par Lost 2.99
Our power sufficient to disturb his Heav'n, — Par Lost 2.102
Scorning surprize. Or could we break our way — Par Lost 2.134
By force, and at our heels all Hell should rise — Par Lost 2.135
Heav'ns purest Light, yet our great Enemy — Par Lost 2.137
Victorious. Thus repuls'd, our final hope — Par Lost 2.142
And that must end us, that must be our cure, — Par Lost 2.145
Let this be good, whether our angry Foe — Par Lost 2.152
One day upon our heads; while we perhaps — Par Lost 2.178
All these our motions vain, sees and derides; — Par Lost 2.191
Not more Almighty to resist our might — Par Lost 2.192
Then wise to frustrate all our plots and wiles. — Par Lost 2.193
Our strength is equal, nor the Law unjust — Par Lost 2.200
Our doom; which if we can sustain and bear, — Par Lost 2.209
Our Supream Foe in time may much remit — Par Lost 2.210
Our purer essence then will overcome — Par Lost 2.215
Worth waiting, since our present lot appeers — Par Lost 2.223
Our own right lost: him to unthrone we then — Par Lost 2.231
Our envied Sovran, and his Altar breathes — Par Lost 2.244
Our servile offerings. This must be our task — Par Lost 2.246
In Heav'n this our delight; how wearisom — Par Lost 2.247
Unacceptable, though in Heav'n, our state — Par Lost 2.251
Our own good from our selves, and from our own — Par Lost 2.253
Of servile Pomp. Our greatness will appeer — Par Lost 2.257
As he our darkness, cannot we his Light — Par Lost 2.269
Our torments also may in length of time — Par Lost 2.274
Become our Elements, these piercing Fires — Par Lost 2.275
As soft as now severe, our temper chang'd — Par Lost 2.276
Compose our present evils, with regard — Par Lost 2.281
This place our dungeon, not our safe retreat — Par Lost 2.317
By our revolt, but over Hell extend — Par Lost 2.326
But to our power hostility and hate, — Par Lost 2.336
Thither let us bend all our thoughts, to learn — Par Lost 2.354
All as our own, and drive as we were driven, — Par Lost 2.366
Seduce them to our Party, that thir God — Par Lost 2.368
In our Confusion, and our Joy upraise — Par Lost 2.372

Our(*cont*)

Neerer our ancient Seat; perhaps in view	Par Lost 2.394
Choice in our suffrage; for on whom we send,	Par Lost 2.415
The weight of all and our last hope relies.	Par Lost 2.416
Our prison strong, this huge convex of Fire,	Par Lost 2.434
While here shall be our home, what best may ease	Par Lost 2.458
(For what could else) to our Almighty Foe	Par Lost 2.769
Cleer Victory, to our part loss and rout	Par Lost 2.770
Of Spirits that in our just pretenses arm'd	Par Lost 2.825
Perhaps our vacant room, though more remov'd,	Par Lost 2.835
Sad instrument of all our woe, she took;	Par Lost 2.872
Encroacht on still through our intestine broiles	Par Lost 2.1001
Our two first Parents, yet the onely two	Par Lost 3.65
Transports our adversarie, whom no bounds	Par Lost 3.81
His journies end and our beginning woe.	Par Lost 3.633
While time was, our first-Parents had bin warnd	Par Lost 4.6
Which to our general Sire gave prospect large	Par Lost 4.144
Our Death the Tree of knowledge grew fast by,	Par Lost 4.221
Into our room of bliss thus high advanc't	Par Lost 4.359
The only sign of our obedience left	Par Lost 4.428
His bountie, following our delightful task	Par Lost 4.437
So spake our general Mother, and with eyes	Par Lost 4.492
On our first Father, half her swelling Breast	Par Lost 4.495
Among our other torments not the least,	Par Lost 4.510
Our eye-lids; other Creatures all day long	Par Lost 4.616
And at our pleasant labour, to reform	Par Lost 4.625
Our walk at noon, with branches overgrown,	Par Lost 4.627
That mock our scant manuring, and require	Par Lost 4.628
To whom our general Ancestor repli'd.	Par Lost 4.659
Divide the night, and lift our thoughts to Heaven.	Par Lost 4.688
What day the genial Angel to our Sire	Par Lost 4.712
Which we in our appointed work imployd	Par Lost 4.726
Have finisht happie in our mutual help	Par Lost 4.727
And mutual love, the Crown of all our bliss	Par Lost 4.728
Our Maker bids increase, who bids abstain	Par Lost 4.748
But our destroyer, foe to God and Man?	Par Lost 4.749
Our circuit meets full West. As flame they part	Par Lost 4.784
His Iron Gates, if he intends our stay	Par Lost 4.898
Neither our own but giv'n; what follie then	Par Lost 4.1007
Our tended Plants, how blows the Citron Grove,	Par Lost 5.22
Our knowledge or opinion; then reties	Par Lost 5.108
Of our last Eevnings talk, in this thy dream,	Par Lost 5.115
And let us to our fresh imployments rise	Par Lost 5.125
Varie to our great Maker still new praise.	Par Lost 5.184
This day to be our Guest. But goe with speed,	Par Lost 5.313
Our Heav'nly stranger; well we may afford	Par Lost 5.316
Our givers thir own gifts, and large bestow	Par Lost 5.317
To entertain our Angel guest, as hee	Par Lost 5.328
Mean while our Primitive great Sire, to meet	Par Lost 5.350
Our Authour. Heav'nly stranger, please to taste	Par Lost 5.397
These bounties which our Nourisher, from whom	Par Lost 5.398
Our knowledge, and the scale of Nature set	Par Lost 5.509
Our voluntarie service he requires,	Par Lost 5.529
Not our necessitated, such with him	Par Lost 5.530
In sight of God enthron'd, our happie state	Par Lost 5.536
Hold, as you yours, while our obedience holds;	Par Lost 5.537
Because wee freely love, as in our will	Par Lost 5.539
To whom our great Progenitor. Thy words	Par Lost 5.544
Our maker, and obey him whose command	Par Lost 5.551
(For wee have also our Eevning and our Morn,	Par Lost 5.628
Fit entertainment to receive our King	Par Lost 5.690
Of our Omnipotence, and with what Arms	Par Lost 5.722
In battel, what our Power is, or our right.	Par Lost 5.728
In our defence, lest unawares we lose	Par Lost 5.731
This our high place, our Sanctuarie, our Hill.	Par Lost 5.732
Our minds and teach us to cast off this Yoke?	Par Lost 5.786
Erre not, much less for this to be our Lord,	Par Lost 5.799
Our being ordain'd to govern, not to serve?	Par Lost 5.802
And of our good, and of our dignitie	Par Lost 5.827
Our happie state under one Head more neer	Par Lost 5.830
1667 'our Head' in some copies	
One of our number thus reduc't becomes,	Par Lost 5.843
His Laws our Laws, all honour to him done	Par Lost 5.844
Returns our own. Cease then this impious rage,	Par Lost 5.845
By our own quick'ning power, when fatal course	Par Lost 5.861
Of this our native Heav'n, Ethereal Sons.	Par Lost 5.863
Our puissance is our own, our own right hand	Par Lost 5.864
Who is our equal: then thou shalt behold	Par Lost 5.866
Yet leudly dar'st our ministring upbraid.	Par Lost 6.182
Since now we find this our Empyreal form	Par Lost 6.433
May serve to better us, and worse our foes,	Par Lost 6.440
Unhurt our mindes, and understanding sound,	Par Lost 6.444
Enjoyment of our right as Gods; yet hard	Par Lost 6.452
Our yet unwounded Enemies, or arme	Par Lost 6.466
Believst so main to our success, I bring;	Par Lost 6.471
From far with thundring noise among our foes	Par Lost 6.487
Nor long shall be our labour, yet ere dawne,	Par Lost 6.492
Effect shall end our wish. Mean while revive;	Par Lost 6.493
Our overture, and turn not back perverse;	Par Lost 6.562
Freely our part; yee who appointed stand	Par Lost 6.565
Which to our eyes discoverd new and strange,	Par Lost 6.571
Collected stood within our thoughts amus'd,	Par Lost 6.581
If our proposals once again were heard	Par Lost 6.618
They shew us when our foes walk not upright.	Par Lost 6.627
Great things, and full of wonder in our eares,	Par Lost 7.70
Us timely of what might else have bin our loss,	Par Lost 7.74
Gently for our instruction to impart	Par Lost 7.81
Our knowing, as to highest wisdom seemd,	Par Lost 7.83

Our(*cont*)

At least our envious Foe hath fail'd, who thought	Par Lost 7.139
Let us make now Man in our image, Man	Par Lost 7.519
In our similitude, and let them rule	Par Lost 7.520
So spake our Sire, and by his count'nance seemd	Par Lost 8.39
Then of our fellow servant, and inquire	Par Lost 8.225
Our prompt obedience. Fast we found, fast shut	Par Lost 8.240
But long ere our approaching heard within	Par Lost 8.242
So spake the Godlike Power, and thus our Sire.	Par Lost 8.249
Determin'd to advance into our room	Par Lost 9.148
With Heav'nly spoils, our spoils: What he decreed	Par Lost 9.151
Our pleasant task enjoyn'd, but till more hands	Par Lost 9.207
Aid us, the work under our labour grows,	Par Lost 9.208
Let us divide our labours, thou where choice	Par Lost 9.214
Our taske we choose, what wonder if so near	Par Lost 9.221
Our dayes work brought to little, though begun	Par Lost 9.224
Yet not so strictly hath our Lord impos'd	Par Lost 9.235
These paths & Bowers doubt not but our joynt hands	Par Lost 9.244
Envying our happiness, and of his own	Par Lost 9.254
Our fealtie from God, or to disturb	Par Lost 9.262
Our ruin, both by thee informd I learne,	Par Lost 9.275
Th' attempt it self, intended by our Foe.	Par Lost 9.295
If this be our condition, thus to dwell	Par Lost 9.322
But harm precedes not sin: onely our Foe	Par Lost 9.327
Of our integritie: his foul esteeme	Par Lost 9.329
Sticks no dishonor on our Front, but turns	Par Lost 9.330
Favour from Heav'n, our witness from th' event.	Par Lost 9.334
Let us not then suspect our happie State	Par Lost 9.337
Fraile is our happiness, if this be so,	Par Lost 9.340
Touchd onely, that our trial, when least sought,	Par Lost 9.380
To us, in such aboundance lies our choice,	Par Lost 9.620
Led *Eve* our credulous Mother, to the Tree	Par Lost 9.644
Of prohibition, root of all our woe;	Par Lost 9.645
Serpent, we might have spar'd our coming hither,	Par Lost 9.647
Law to our selves, our Reason is our Law.	Par Lost 9.654
On our belief, that all from them proceeds;	Par Lost 9.719
By thee communicated, and our want:	Par Lost 9.755
Our inward freedom? In the day we eate	Par Lost 9.762
Of this fair Fruit, our doom is, we shall die.	Par Lost 9.763
Our great Forbidder, safe with all his Spies	Par Lost 9.815
Made common and unhallowd ere our taste;	Par Lost 9.931
Set over all his Works, which in our Fall,	Par Lost 9.941
Our State cannot be severd, we are one,	Par Lost 9.958
And gladly of our Union heare thee speak,	Par Lost 9.966
To counterfet Mans voice, true in our Fall,	Par Lost 9.1069
False in our promis'd Rising; since our Eyes	Par Lost 9.1070
Our wonted Ornaments now soild and staind,	Par Lost 9.1076
And in our Faces evident the signes	Par Lost 9.1077
And girded on our loyns, may cover round	Par Lost 9.1096
Of all our good, sham'd, naked, miserable.	Par Lost 9.1139
Whom he shall tread at last under our feet;	Par Lost 10.190
Idlely, while Satan our great Author thrives	Par Lost 10.236
Thou hast atchiev'd our libertie, confin'd	Par Lost 10.368
Our foile in Heav'n; here thou shalt Monarch reign,	Par Lost 10,375
And Dungeon of our Tyrant: Now possess,	Par Lost 10.466
As Lords, a spacious World, to our native Heaven	Par Lost 10.467
Plac't in a Paradise, by our exile	Par Lost 10.484
Without our hazard, labour, or allarme,	Par Lost 10.491
What thinkst thou of our Empire now, though earnd	Par Lost 10.592
My Head, Ill fare our Ancestor impure,	Par Lost 10.735
Each others burden in our share of woe;	Par Lost 10.961
A long days dying to augment our paine,	Par Lost 10.964
And to our Seed (O hapless Seed!) deriv'd.	Par Lost 10.965
Tending to some relief of our extremes,	Par Lost 10.976
As in our evils, and of easier choice.	Par Lost 10.978
If care of our descent perplex us most,	Par Lost 10.979
Our own begotten, and of our Loines to bring	Par Lost 10.983
With our own hands his Office on our selves;	Par Lost 10.1002
Part of our Sentence, that thy Seed shall bruise	Par Lost 10.1031
Be meant, whom I conjecture, our grand Foe	Par Lost 10.1033
Resolv'd, as thou proposest; so our Foe	Par Lost 10.1038
Instead shall double ours upon our heads.	Par Lost 10.1040
Laid on our Necks. Remember with what mild	Par Lost 10.1046
Our Limbs benumm'd, ere this diurnal Starr	Par Lost 10.1069
To evils which our own misdeeds have wrought,	Par Lost 10.1080
In dust, our final rest and native home.	Par Lost 10.1085
Humbly our faults, and pardon beg, with tears	Par Lost 10.1089
Watering the ground, and with our sighs the Air	Par Lost 10.1090
So spake our Father penitent, nor *Eve*	Par Lost 10.1097
His promise, that thy Seed shall bruise our Foe;	Par Lost 11.155
All unconcern'd with our unrest, begins	Par Lost 11.174
Wherere our days work lies, though now enjoind	Par Lost 11.177
Us haply too secure of our discharge	Par Lost 11.196
Some days; how long, and what till then our life,	Par Lost 11.198
Why else this double object in our sight	Par Lost 11.201
Our frailtie can sustain, thy tidings bring,	Par Lost 11.302
Departure from this happy place, our sweet	Par Lost 11.303
Familiar to our eyes, all places else	Par Lost 11.305
Our second *Adam* in the Wilderness,	Par Lost 11.383
Rowling in dust and gore. To which our Sire.	Par Lost 11.460
To Death, and mix with our connatural dust?	Par Lost 11.529
The Balme of Life. To whom our Ancestor.	Par Lost 11.546
Why our great expectation should be call'd	Par Lost 12.378
As at the Worlds great period; and our Sire	Par Lost 12.467
But say, if our deliverer up to Heav'n	Par Lost 12.479
Exacts our parting hence; and see the Guards,	Par Lost 12.590
So spake our Mother *Eve*, and *Adam* heard	Par Lost 12.624
Our lingring Parents, and to th' Eastern Gate	Par Lost 12.638

Our(*cont*)
This our old Conquest, then remember Hell Par Reg 1.46
Our hated habitation; well ye know Par Reg 1.47
In manner at our will th' affairs of Earth, Par Reg 1.50
Broken be not intended all our power Par Reg 1.61
To be infring'd, our freedom and our being Par Reg 1.62
His birth to our just fear gave no small cause, Par Reg 1.66
Ye see our danger on the utmost edge Par Reg 1.94
Had measur'd twice six years, at our great Feast Par Reg 1.210
The Teachers of our Law, and to propose Par Reg 1.212
Concerning the Messiah, to our Scribes Par Reg 1.261
So spake our Morning Star then in his rise, Par Reg 1.294
Our new baptizing Prophet at the Ford Par Reg 1.328
Our Fathers here with Manna; in the Mount Par Reg 1.351
To whom our Saviour sternly thus reply'd. Par Reg 1.406
So spake our Saviour; but the subtle Fiend, Par Reg 1.465
To whom our Saviour with unalter'd brow. Par Reg 1.493
Unlook'd for are we fall'n, our eyes beheld Par Reg 2.31
Expected of our Fathers; we have heard Par Reg 2.33
Thus we rejoyc'd, but soon our joy is turn'd Par Reg 2.37
Our expectation? God of *Israel*, Par Reg 2.42
Let us be glad of this, and all our fears Par Reg 2.53
Soon we shall see our hope, our joy return. Par Reg 2.57
From the bleak air; a Stable was our warmth, Par Reg 2.74
Hath been our dwelling many years, his life Par Reg 2.80
So may we hold our place and these mild seats Par Reg 2.125
Threat'ns then our expulsion down to Hell; Par Reg 2.128
Our Saviour, and found all was but a dream, Par Reg 2.283
Our Saviour lifting up his eyes beheld Par Reg 2.338
To whom our Saviour calmly thus reply'd. Par Reg 3.43
To whom our Saviour fervently reply'd. Par Reg 3.121
To whom our Saviour answer thus return'd. Par Reg 3.181
Our Saviour, and new train of words began. Par Reg 3.266
And to our Saviour thus his words renew'd. Par Reg 3.346
To whom our Saviour answer'd thus unmov'd. Par Reg 3.386
He brought our Saviour to the western side Par Reg 4.25
Whom thus our Saviour answer'd with disdain. Par Reg 4.170
To whom our Saviour sagely thus repli'd. Par Reg 4.285
As in our native Language can I find Par Reg 4.333
That solace? All our Law and Story strew'd Par Reg 4.334
With Hymns, our Psalms with artful terms inscrib'd, Par Reg 4.335
Our Hebrew Songs and Harps in *Babylon*, Par Reg 4.336
That pleas'd so well our Victors ear, declare Par Reg 4.337
But herein to our Prophets far beneath, Par Reg 4.356
These only with our Law best form a King. Par Reg 4.364
Thus to our Saviour with stern brow reply'd. Par Reg 4.367
Our Saviour meek and with untroubl'd mind Par Reg 4.401
Of this fair change, and to our Saviour came, Par Reg 4.442
Thus they the Son of God our Saviour meek Par Reg 4.636
O mirror of our fickle state, Samson 164
Who made our Laws to bind us, not himself, Samson 309
Pray'd for, but often proves our woe, our bane? Samson 351
Our earnest Prayers, then giv'n with solemn hand Samson 359
Find some occasion to infest our Foes. Samson 423
I state not that; this I am sure; our Foes Samson 424
And strongest drinks our chief support of health, Samson 554
Against the uncircumcis'd, our enemies. Samson 640
God of our Fathers, what is man! Samson 667
In me, but incident to all our sex, Samson 774
Such numbers of our Nation: and the Priest Samson 857
For which our countrey is a name so dear; Samson 894
Har. Is not thy Nation subject to our Lords? Samson 1182
Into our hands: for hadst thou not committed Samson 1185
Off. *Samson*, to thee our Lords thus bid me say; Samson 1310
Our Law forbids at thir Religious Rites Samson 1320
Our Law, or stain my vow of *Nazarite*. Samson 1386
Off. *Samson*, this second message from our Lords Samson 1391
To thee I am bid say. Art thou our Slave, Samson 1392
Our Captive, at the public Mill our drudge, Samson 1393
And dar'st thou at our sending and command Samson 1394
Scandalous or forbidden in our Law. Samson 1409
Our God, our Law, my Nation, or my self, Samson 1425
And to our wish I see one hither speeding, Samson 1539
An *Ebrew*, as I guess, and of our Tribe. Samson 1540
Before our living Dread who dwells Samson 1673
Com let us our rights begin, Mask 125
Our conceal'd Solemnity. Mask 142
Our number may affright: Som Virgin sure Mask 148
And thou shalt be our star of *Arcady*, Mask 341
Or *Tyrian* Cynosure. 2. *Bro*. Or if our eyes Mask 342
But O that haples virgin our lost sister Mask 350
Leans her unpillow'd head fraught with sad fears. Mask 355
Trinity ms 'fraught with sad feares' ←'musing at our unkindnesse'
Of our unowned sister. *Eld*. *Bro*. I do not, brother, Mask 407
Best draw, and stand upon our guard. *Eld*. *Bro*. Ile hallow, Mask 487
Or our neglect, we lost her as we came. Mask 510
Against the canon laws of our foundation; Mask 808
Till thou our summons answer'd have. Mask 888
And our sudden coming there Mask 954
& favour our close jocondrie Mask Tr. ms 12.29
and often takes our cattell with strange pinches Mask Tr. ms 23.51
And therfore to our weaker view, Penseroso 15
To whom our vows and wishes bend, Arcades 6
Heer our solemn search hath end. Arcades 7
Batt'ning our flocks with the fresh dews of night, Lycidas 29
And old *Damoetas* lov'd to hear our song. Lycidas 36
Let our frail thoughts dally with false surmise. Lycidas 153

Our(*cont*)
Or whether thou to our moist vows deny'd, Lycidas 159
Our great redemption from above did bring; Nativity 4
That he our deadly forfeit should release, Nativity 6
Once bless our human ears, Nativity 126
(If ye have power to touch our senses so) Nativity 127
Enwrap our fancy long, Nativity 134
Must redeem our loss; Nativity 153
And then at last our bliss Nativity 165
Our Babe to shew his Godhead true, Nativity 227
Time is our tedious Song should here have ending, Nativity 239
Beheld us in our misery. Psalm 136, 78
To slake his wrath whom sin hath made our foe Fair Inf 66
To stand 'twixt us and our deserved smart Fair Inf 69
Which takes our late fantasticks with delight, Vacation 20
Which on our dearest Lord did sease er'e long, Passion 10
So little is our loss, On Time 7
Then long Eternity shall greet our bliss On Time 11
When once our heav'nly-guided soul shall clime, On Time 19
Seas wept from our deep sorrow, Circum 9
Alas, how soon our sin Circum 12
Of vengeful Justice bore for our excess, Circum 24
And to our high-rais'd phantasie present, Musick 5
of clamourous sin that all our musick marres Musick Tr. ms 5.04
& in our lives & in our song Musick Tr. ms 5.05
Thus we salute thee with our early Song, May Morn 9
Thou in our wonder and astonishment Shakespear 7
Then thou our fancy of it self bereaving, Shakespear 13
1640 'our selfe'
Those rugged names to our like mouths grow sleek Sonnet 11, 10
First taught our English Musick how to span Sonnet 13, 2
That with smooth aire couldst humor best our tongue. Sonnet 13, 8
Cromwell, our cheif of men, who through a cloud Sonnet 16, 1
Threatning to bind our soules with secular chaines: Sonnet 16, 12
When all our Fathers worship't Stocks and Stones, Sonnet 18, 4
Pronounc't and in his volumes taught our Lawes, Sonnet 21, 3
line not in Trinity ms
To force our Consciences that Christ set free, Forcers 6
Trinity ms 'our' ←'the'
And succour our just Fears Forcers 18
O Jehovah our Lord how wondrous great Psalm 8, 1
O Jehovah our Lord how wondrous great Psalm 8, 23
And on our foes thy dread Psalm 80, 8
To God our strength sing loud, *and clear* Psalm 81, 1
Sing loud to God *our King*, Psalm 81, 2
Our solemn Feast *comes round*. Psalm 81, 12
Till all before *our* God *at length* Psalm 84, 27
Thou God our shield look on the face Psalm 84, 31
God of our saving health and peace, Psalm 85, 13
Wilt thou not turn, and *hear our voice* Psalm 85, 21
To dwell within our Land. Psalm 85, 40
Our Land shall forth in plenty throw Psalm 85, 51
Her fruits *to be our food*. Psalm 85, 52
Did our forefathers yoke, Psalm 87, 12
But *twise that praise shall in our ear* Psalm 87, 17

Ours
Then such could hav orepow'rd such force as ours) Par Lost 1.145
More hands then ours to lop thir wanton growth: Par Lost 4.629
Is oftest yours, the latter most is ours, Par Lost 5.489
Wee ours for change delectable, not need) Par Lost 5.629
Equal to ours, throughout the spacious North; Par Lost 5.726
Thus foil'd thir mightiest, ours joy filld, and shout, Par Lost 6.200
Instead shall double ours upon our heads. Par Lost 10.1040
Thy age, like ours, O Soul of Sir *John Cheek*, Sonnet 11, 12

Ourselves
If we procure not to our selves more woe. Par Lost 2.225
Our own good from our selves, and from our own Par Lost 2.253
Live to our selves, though in this vast recess, Par Lost 2.254
Our selves with like defence, to me deserves Par Lost 6.467
And not molest us, unless we our selves Par Lost 8.186
Law to our selves, our Reason is our Law. Par Lost 9.654
Then both our selves and Seed at once to free Par Lost 10.999
With our own hands his Office on our selves; Par Lost 10.1002
By death brought on our selves, or childless days Par Lost 10.1037
Against our selves, and wilful barrenness, Par Lost 10.1042
us of our selves & native woes beguile Musick Tr. ms 4.08

Ouse
Of utmost *Tweed*, or *Oose*, or gulphie *Dun*, Vacation 92

Out
Rose out of *Chaos*: Or if *Sion* Hill Par Lost 1.10
Had cast him out from Heav'n, with all his Host Par Lost 1.37
Out of our evil seek to bring forth good, Par Lost 1.163
And out of good still to find means of evil; Par Lost 1.165
So stretcht out huge in length the Arch-fiend lay Par Lost 1.209
Be no memorial blotted out and ras'd Par Lost 1.362
Jehovah thundring out of *Sion*, thron'd Par Lost 1.386
Words interwove with sighs found out thir way. Par Lost 1.621
And dig'd out ribs of Gold. Let none admire Par Lost 1.690
With wond'rous Art found out the massie Ore, Par Lost 1.703
1667 'founded'
ms 'founded'
Anon out of the earth a Fabrick huge Par Lost 1.710
Then to dwell here, driv'n out from bliss, condemn'd Par Lost 2.86
Thrive under evil, and work ease out of pain Par Lost 2.261
And through the palpable obscure find out Par Lost 2.406
And hard, that out of Hell leads up to light; Par Lost 2.433
Out of thy head I sprung: amazement seis'd Par Lost 2.758
Made to destroy: I fled, and cry'd out *Death*; Par Lost 2.787

Out(*cont*)	
From out this dark and dismal house of pain,	Par Lost 2.823
Pourd out by millions her victorious Bands	Par Lost 2.997
And wisdome at one entrance quite shut out.	Par Lost 3.50
Pleas'd, out of Heaven shalt look down and smile,	Par Lost 3.257
Found out for mankind under wrauth, O thou	Par Lost 3.275
Who justly hath drivn out his Rebell Foes	Par Lost 3.677
Out of the fertil ground he caus'd to grow	Par Lost 4.216
Ill fenc't for Heav'n to keep out such a foe	Par Lost 4.372
Out of my side to thee, neerest my heart	Par Lost 4.484
His praise, who out of Darkness call'd up Light.	Par Lost 5.179
All perfet good unmeasur'd out, descends,	Par Lost 5.399
Cast out from God and blessed vision, falls	Par Lost 5.613
None seconded, as out of season judg'd,	Par Lost 5.850
Pursuing drive them out from God and bliss,	Par Lost 6.52
Who out of smallest things could without end	Par Lost 6.137
To trouble Holy Rest; Heav'n casts thee out	Par Lost 6.272
Spare out of life perhaps, and not repine,	Par Lost 6.460
Out of such prison, though Spirits of purest light,	Par Lost 6.660
Pursue these sons of Darkness, drive them out	Par Lost 6.715
At once the Four spred out thir Starrie wings	Par Lost 6.827
Not to destroy, but root them out of Heav'n:	Par Lost 6.855
Another World, out of one man a Race	Par Lost 7.155
Had driven out th' ungodly from his sight	Par Lost 7.185
Good out of evil to create, in stead	Par Lost 7.188
Disparted, and between spun out the Air,	Par Lost 7.241
Draws in, and at his Trunck spouts out a Sea.	Par Lost 7.416
Limb'd and full grown: out of the ground up rose	Par Lost 7.456
So spacious, and his Line stretcht out so farr;	Par Lost 8.102
Who since the Morning hour set out from Heav'n	Par Lost 8.111
When out of hope, behold her, not farr off,	Par Lost 8.481
Of *Gabriel* out of *Eden*, now improv'd	Par Lost 9.54
And flatter'd out of all, believing lies	Par Lost 10.42
Out of the ground wast taken, know thy Birth,	Par Lost 10.207
Then Both from out Hell Gates into the waste	Par Lost 10.282
From out of *Chaos* to the out side bare	Par Lost 10.317
Triumphant out of this infernal Pit	Par Lost 10.464
Toild out my uncouth passage, forc't to ride	Par Lost 10.475
Why am I mockt with death, and length'nd out	Par Lost 10.774
Of weakness, not of Power. Will he, draw out,	Par Lost 10.801
And horrors hast thou driv'n me; out of which	Par Lost 10.843
Out of my sight, thou Serpent, that name best	Par Lost 10.867
Well if thrown out, as supernumerarie	Par Lost 10.887
He never shall find out fit Mate, but such	Par Lost 10.899
Without remorse drive out the sinful Pair,	Par Lost 11.105
Out of despaire, joy, but with fear yet linkt;	Par Lost 11.139
Stretcht out to the amplest reach of prospect lay.	Par Lost 11.380
That beat out life; he fell, and deadly pale	Par Lost 11.446
Groand out his Soul with gushing bloud effus'd.	Par Lost 11.447
Out of thy loyns; th' unjust the just hath slain,	Par Lost 11.455
Raise out of friendship hostil deeds in Peace.	Par Lost 11.796
Out of his place, pushd by the horned floud,	Par Lost 11.831
Forthwith from out the Arke a Raven flies,	Par Lost 11.855
That he relents, not to blot out mankind,	Par Lost 11.891
Boiles out from under ground, the mouth of Hell;	Par Lost 12.42
Quite out thir Native Language, and instead	Par Lost 12.54
Palpable darkness, and blot out three dayes;	Par Lost 12.188
And due to theirs which out of thine will grow:	Par Lost 12.400
Out of his grave, fresh as the dawning light,	Par Lost 12.423
Light out of darkness! full of doubt I stand,	Par Lost 12.473
Out of the water, Heav'n above the Clouds	Par Reg 1.81
And out of Heav'n the Sov'raign voice I heard,	Par Reg 1.84
The dismal expedition to find out	Par Reg 1.101
But as I rose out of the laving stream,	Par Reg 1.280
What happ'ns new; Fame also finds us out.	Par Reg 1.334
That out of these hard stones be made thee bread;	Par Reg 1.343
Thus they out of their plaints new hope resume	Par Reg 2.58
Draw out with credulous desire, and lead	Par Reg 2.166
Thus wore out night, and now the Herald Lark	Par Reg 2.279
Let his tormenter Conscience find him out,	Par Reg 4.130
Out of the wood he starts in wonted shape;	Par Reg 4.449
That once found out and solv'd, for grief and spight	Par Reg 4.574
Betray'd, Captiv'd, and both my Eyes put out,	Samson 33
To storm me over-watch't, and wearied out,	Samson 405
Them out of thine, who slew'st them many a slain.	Samson 439
Then turn'd me out ridiculous, despoil'd,	Samson 539
Sam. Out, out *Hyaena;* these are thy wonted arts,	Samson 748
Are drawn to wear out miserable days,	Samson 762
Not out of levity, but over-powr'd	Samson 880
I lose, prevented by thy eyes put out.	Samson 1103
To put out both thine eyes, and fetter'd send thee	Samson 1160
Yet so it may fall out, because thir end	Samson 1265
But they must pick me out with shackles tir'd,	Samson 1326
Thou for thy Son art bent to lay out all;	Samson 1486
Man. Suspense in news is torture, speak them out.	Samson 1569
From out her ashie womb now teem'd,	Samson 1703
Bacchus that first from out the purple Grape,	Mask 46
These my skie robes spun out of *Iris* Wooff,	Mask 83
Of all thy dues be done, and none left out,	Mask 137
My Brothers when they saw me wearied out	Mask 182
To help you find them. *La*. Gentle villager	Mask 304
Trinity ms 'them' ← 'them out'	
La. To find out that, good Shepherd, I suppose,	Mask 307
You may as well spred out the unsun'd heaps	Mask 398
'Twixt *Africa* and *Inde*, Ile find him out,	Mask 606
But of divine effect, he cull'd me out;	Mask 630
Find out som uncouth cell,	Allegro 5
And stretch'd out all the Chimney's length,	Allegro 111

Out(*cont*)	
And Crop-full out of dores he flings,	Allegro 113
Of lincked sweetnes long drawn out,	Allegro 140
Find out the peacefull hermitage,	Penseroso 168
And think to burst out into sudden blaze,	Lycidas 74
While the still morn went out with Sandals gray,	Lycidas 187
And now the Sun had stretch'd out all the hills,	Lycidas 190
From out his secret Altar toucht with hallow'd fire.	Nativity 28
Ring out ye Crystall sphears,	Nativity 125
And loudly knock to have their passage out;	Vacation 24
Fly envious *Time*, till thou run out thy race,	On Time 1
by leaving out those harsh ill sounding jarres	Musick Tr. ms 5.03
'Gainst old truth) motion number'd out his time;	Another 8
And too much breathing put him out of breath;	Another 12
But we do hope to find out all your tricks,	Forcers 13
Wearied I am with sighing out my dayes,	Psalm 6, 11
Out of the tender mouths of latest bearth,	Psalm 8, 4
Out of the mouths of babes and sucklings thou	Psalm 8, 5
And drov'st out Nations *proud and haut*	Psalm 80, 35
The *tusked* Boar out of the wood	Psalm 80, 53
And led thee out of thrall.	Psalm 81, 28
Through out the land of thy abode	Psalm 81, 37
Thee out of Aegypt land	Psalm 81, 42
And out of order gon.	Psalm 82, 20
Outbrake	
While the red fire, and smouldring clouds out brake:	Nativity 159
Outbreathed	
Thir unexpected loss and plaints out breath'd.	Par Reg 2.29
Outcast	
And they outcast from God, are here condemn'd	Par Lost 2.694
Of us out-cast, exil'd, his new delight,	Par Lost 4.106
Out cast *Nebaioth*, yet found he relief	Par Reg 2.309
Outcries	
And raise such out-cries on thy clatter'd Iron,	Samson 1124
Outcry	
Ris'n, and with hideous outcry rush'd between.	Par Lost 2.726
So strange thy outcry, and thy words so strange	Par Lost 2.737
Chor. Thy Son is rather slaying them, that outcry	Samson 1517
Outdo	
So Heav'nly love shall outdoo Hellish hate	Par Lost 3.298
Outdone	
And Strength and Art are easily out-done	Par Lost 1.696
ms 'outdon'	
1667 'out done' in some copies, 'outdone' in others	
Outflew	
He spake: and to confirm his words, out-flew	Par Lost 1.663
ms 'out flew'	
Outgo	
In worth and excellence he shall out-go them,	Vacation 79
Outgrew	
Thir growing work: for much thir work outgrew	Par Lost 9.202
Outlandish	
Outlandish flatteries? then proceed'st to talk	Par Reg 4.125
Outlasted	
Summers chief honour if thou hadst out-lasted,	Fair Inf 3
Outlaw	
Of Misers treasure by an out-laws den,	Mask 399
1637 'outlaws'	
Trinity ms 'outlaws'	
Outlive	
This is old age; but then thou must outlive	Par Lost 11.538
Outliving	
Soon swallow'd up in dark and long out-living night.	Passion 7
Outmost	
As from her outmost works a brok'd foe	Par Lost 2.1039
Outpoured	
The City gates out powr'd, light armed Troops	Par Reg 3.311
Sparkling, out-pow'rd, the flavor, or the smell,	Samson 544
Outrage	
And injury and outrage: And when Night	Par Lost 1.500
Outrage from liveless things; but Discord first	Par Lost 10.707
Outrageous	
Outrageous to devour, immures us round	Par Lost 2.435
Emboweld with outragious noise the Air,	Par Lost 6.587
Outrageous as a Sea, dark, wasteful, wilde,	Par Lost 7.212
Stood open wide, belching outrageous flame	Par Lost 10.232
Outrageously	
And storm outrageously,	Psalm 83, 6
Outshine	
Cloth'd with transcendent brightness didst out-shine	Par Lost 1.86
ms 'outshine'	
1667 'outshine'	
Outshone	
Outshon the wealth of *Ormus* and of *Ind*,	Par Lost 2.2
Outside	
On the bare outside of this World, that seem'd	Par Lost 3.74
An outside? fair no doubt, and worthy well	Par Lost 8.568
Neither her out-side formd so fair, nor aught	Par Lost 8.596
From out of *Chaos* to the out side bare	Par Lost 10.317
1667 'outside'	
Outside and inside both, pillars and roofs	Par Reg 4.58
Outspread	
Wast present, and with mighty wings outspread	Par Lost 1.20
Then all this globous Earth in Plain out spred,	Par Lost 5.649
1667 'outspred'	
His brooding wings the Spirit of God outspred,	Par Lost 7.235
In the dust and there out spread	Psalm 7, 17
Between their wings out-spread,	Psalm 80, 6

Outstretched
The Earth outstretcht immense, a prospect wide Par Lost 5.88
Outstretcht he lay, on the cold ground, and oft Par Lost 10.851
A spatious plain out stretch't in circuit wide Par Reg 3.254
Nay, quoth he, on his swooning bed outstretch'd, Another 17
line not in 1640, 1657, 1658 texts
1673 'out-stretch'd'
Outward
Though chang'd in outward lustre; that fixt mind Par Lost 1.97
ms 'out ward'
Each perturbation smooth'd with outward calme, Par Lost 4.120
Inward and outward both, his image faire: Par Lost 8.221
Too much of Ornament, in outward shew Par Lost 8.538
In outward also her resembling less Par Lost 8.543
Perfet within, no outward aid require; Par Lost 8.642
Of outward strength; while shame, thou looking on, Par Lost 9.312
Secure from outward force; within himself Par Lost 9.348
Nor hee thir outward onely with the Skins Par Lost 10.220
His outward freedom: Tyrannie must be, Par Lost 12.95
Deprives them of thir outward libertie, Par Lost 12.100
Well deem in outward Rites and specious formes Par Lost 12.534
Or could of inward slaves make outward free? Par Reg 4.145
Shut up from outward light Samson 160
Is it for that such outward ornament Samson 1025
Chor. Where the heart joins not, outward acts defile not. Samson 1368
Sam. Where outward force constrains, the sentence holds Samson 1369
Begin to cast a beam on th' outward shape, Mask 460
To outward view, of blemish or of spot; Sonnet 22, 2
Outwatch
Where I may oft out-watch the *Bear*, Penseroso 87
Outworn
Inglorious, unimploy'd, with age out-worn. Samson 580
That ne're shall be out-worn Psalm 87, 22
Over
Over the burning Marle, not like those steps Par Lost 1.296
That ore the Realm of impious *Pharaoh* hung Par Lost 1.342
Got them new Names, till wandring ore the Earth, Par Lost 1.365
Fled over *Adria* to th' *Hesperian* Fields, Par Lost 1.520
And ore the *Celtic* roam'd the utmost Isles. Par Lost 1.521
Thir painful steps o're the burnt soyle; and now Par Lost 1.562
Within, her ample spaces, o're the smooth Par Lost 1.725
Sheer o're the Chrystal Battlements; from Morn Par Lost 1.742
O're Heav'ns high Towrs to force resistless way, Par Lost 2.62
By our revolt, but over Hell extend Par Lost 2.326
Over the vast abrupt, ere he arrive Par Lost 2.409
Barr'd over us prohibit all egress. Par Lost 2.437
Or clos ambition varnisht o're with zeal. Par Lost 2.485
Scowls ore the dark'nd lantskip Snow, or showre; Par Lost 2.491
They ferry over this *Lethean* Sound Par Lost 2.604
O're many a Frozen, many a fierie Alpe, Par Lost 2.620
Over the *Caspian*, then stand front to front Par Lost 2.716
With winged course ore Hill or moarie Dale, Par Lost 2.944
Ore bog or steep, through strait, rough, dense, or rare, Par Lost 2.948
Hung ore my Realm, link'd in a golden Chain Par Lost 2.1005
Over the dark Abyss, whose boiling Gulf Par Lost 2.1027
Rowls o're *Elisian* Flours her Amber stream; Par Lost 3.359
Heav'ns everlasting Frame, while o're the necks Par Lost 3.395
Fly o're the backside of the World farr off Par Lost 3.494
Wafted by Angels, or flew o're the Lake Par Lost 3.521
Just o're the blissful seat of Paradise, Par Lost 3.527
Over Mount *Sion*, and, though that were large, Par Lost 3.530
Over the *Promis'd Land* to God so dear, Par Lost 3.531
Bear his swift errands over moist and dry, Par Lost 3.652
O're Sea and Land: him *Satan* thus accostes; Par Lost 3.653
Leaps o're the fence with ease into the Fould: Par Lost 4.187
In at the window climbs, or o're the tiles; Par Lost 4.191
Of coole recess, o're which the mantling vine Par Lost 4.258
Over all other Creatures that possess Par Lost 4.431
Through wood, through waste, o're hill, o're dale his roam. Par Lost 4.538
And o're the dark her Silver Mantle threw. Par Lost 4.609
Hung over her enamour'd, and beheld Par Lost 5.13
With wheels yet hov'ring o're the Ocean brim, Par Lost 5.140
Each shoulder broad, came mantling o're his brest Par Lost 5.279
Be over, and the Sun more coole decline. Par Lost 5.370
Wide over all the Plain, and wider farr Par Lost 5.648
Monarchie over such as live by right Par Lost 5.795
And equal over equals to let Reigne, Par Lost 5.820
One over all with unsucceeded power. Par Lost 5.821
That equal over equals Monarch Reigne: Par Lost 5.832
Came summond over *Eden* to receive Par Lost 6.75
Thir names of thee; so over many a tract Par Lost 6.76
Now Night her course began, and over Heav'n Par Lost 6.406
So said, he o're his Scepter bowing, rose Par Lost 6.746
Over thir heads a chrystal Firmament, Par Lost 6.757
O're Shields and Helmes, and helmed heads he rode Par Lost 6.840
Her Temperance over Appetite, to know Par Lost 7.127
Appeer'd not: over all the face of Earth Par Lost 7.278
Thir Aierie Caravan high over Sea's Par Lost 7.428
Flying, and over Lands with mutual wing Par Lost 7.429
Over the Fish and Fowle of Sea and Aire, Par Lost 7.521
Beast of the Field, and over all the Earth, Par Lost 7.522
Over Fish of the Sea, and Fowle of the Aire, Par Lost 7.533
Over his Works, on Earth, in Sea, or Air, Par Lost 7.629
With Centric and Eccentric scribl'd o're, Par Lost 8.83
And over Fields and Waters, as in Aire Par Lost 8.301
O're other Creatures; yet when I approach Par Lost 8.546
From *Eden* over *Pontus*, and the Poole Par Lost 9.77
Set over all his Works, which in our Fall, Par Lost 9.941

Over(*cont*)
Usurping over sovran Reason claimd Par Lost 9.1130
Thine shall submit, hee over thee shall rule. Par Lost 10.196
Stay his return perhaps over this Gulfe Par Lost 10.253
Over this Maine from Hell to that new World Par Lost 10.257
Over the foaming deep high Archt, a Bridge Par Lost 10.301
Came to the Sea, and over *Hellespont* Par Lost 10.309
Over the vext Abyss, following the track Par Lost 10.314
By *Astracan* over the Snowie Plaines Par Lost 10.432
Of horrible confusion, over which Par Lost 10.472
To range in, and to dwell, and over Man Par Lost 10.492
To rule, as over all he should have rul'd. Par Lost 10.493
Of flight pursu'd in th' Air and ore the ground Par Lost 11.202
O're the blew Firmament a radiant white, Par Lost 11.206
Clad to meet Man; over his lucid Armes Par Lost 11.240
And over them triumphant Death his Dart Par Lost 11.491
Till many years over thy head return: Par Lost 11.534
Ewes and thir bleating Lambs over the Plaine, Par Lost 11.649
Rode tilting o're the Waves, all dwellings else Par Lost 11.747
Grateful to Heav'n, over his head beholds Par Lost 11.864
Over the Earth a Cloud, will therein set Par Lost 11.896
Over his brethren, and quite dispossess Par Lost 12.28
He gave us onely over Beast, Fish, Fowl Par Lost 12.67
By his donation; but Man over men Par Lost 12.69
Over free Reason, God in Judgement just Par Lost 12.92
Over the Sea; the Sea his Rod obeys; Par Lost 12.212
The Records of his Cov'nant, over these Par Lost 12.252
The Heav'nly fires; over the Tent a Cloud Par Lost 12.256
But soon revives, Death over him no power Par Lost 12.420
Over his foes and thine; there shall surprise Par Lost 12.453
From God, and over wrauth grace shall abound. Par Lost 12.478
Mercifull over all his works, with good Par Lost 12.565
Ris'n from a River o're the marish glides, Par Lost 12.630
Wav'd over by that flaming Brand, the Gate Par Lost 12.643
Then to subdue and quell o're all the earth Par Reg 1.218
That other o're the body only reigns, Par Reg 2.478
And o're a mighty King so oft prevail'd, Par Reg 3.167
Well have we speeded, and o're hill and dale, Par Reg 3.267
To just extent over all *Israel*'s Sons; Par Reg 3.406
Yet gives not o're though desperate of success, Par Reg 4.23
God over all supreme? if giv'n to thee, Par Reg 4.186
So let extend thy mind o're all the world, Par Reg 4.223
Shook the Arsenal and fulmin'd over *Greece*, Par Reg 4.270
Over whose heads they rore, and seem to point, Par Reg 4.463
Over the Wilderness and o're the Plain; Par Reg 4.543
Over temptation, and the Tempter proud. Par Reg 4.595
Let there be light, and light was over all; Samson 84
And by himself given over; Samson 121
And lorded over them whom now they serve; Samson 267
Sleep hath forsook and giv'n me o're Samson 629
Prevailing over fear, and timerous doubt Samson 740
Over his female in due awe, Samson 1055
And Victor over all Samson 1290
And over heaps of slaughter'd walk his way? Samson 1530
And casts a gleam over this tufted Grove. Mask 225
line not in Bridgewater ms
Hath hurtfull power o're true virginity. Mask 437
Bridgewater ms 'ore'
Trinity ms 'ore' ←'o'er' ←'over'
1637 'ore'
Slip't from the fold, or young Kid lost his dam, Mask 498
Trinity ms 'from' ←'ore'
Root-bound, that fled *Apollo*, *La*. Fool do not boast, Mask 662
Trinity ms 'doe not boast' ←'thou art over proud'
Were shatter'd into heaps o're thy false head. Mask 799
line not in Bridgewater ms
line not in Trinity ms
1637 'ore'
Dips me all o're, as when the wrath of *Jove* Mask 803
line not in Trinity ms
line not in Bridgewater ms
O're the Cowslips Velvet head, Mask 898
1637 'Ore'
Bridgewater ms 'ore'
Trinity ms 'ore'
On the Lawns, and on the Leas. Mask 965
B.M. ms both 'o're the'
O're sensual Folly, and Intemperance. Mask 975
Trinity ms 'ore'
1637 'Ore'
Bridgewater ms 'ore'
this dusky hollow is a paradise & heaven gates ore my head Mask Tr. ms 13.44
Whistles ore the Furrow'd Land, Allegro 64
Over thy decent shoulders drawn. Penseroso 36
Gently o're th' accustom'd Oke; Penseroso 60
Over som wide-water'd shoar, Penseroso 75
Over the mount, and all this hallow'd ground, Arcades 55
O're the smooth enameld green Arcades 84
Trinity ms 'Ore'
Clos'd o're the head of your lov'd *Lycidas*? Lycidas 51
1638 'ore'
Trinity ms 'ore'
Inwrought with figures dim, and on the edge Lycidas 105
Trinity ms 'inwraught' ←'scraul'd ore'
The lonely mountains o're, Nativity 181
O're all his Brethren he shall Reign as King, Vacation 75
Loud o're the rest *Cremona*'s Trump doth sound; Passion 26
Over the Pole thy thickest mantle throw, Passion 30

Over(*cont*)
Triumphing over Death, and Chance, and thee O Time. On Time 22
And he can spred thy Name o're Lands and Seas, Sonnet 8, 7
Trinity ms 'or'e'
Thy hand-maids, clad them o're with purple beams Sonnet 14, 10
O're all th' *Italian* fields where still doth sway Sonnet 18, 11
And post o're Land and Ocean without rest: Sonnet 19, 13
O're the works of thy hand thou mad'st him Lord, Psalm 8, 17
O're all the earth *art one*. Psalm 83, 68
Them from thy hand deliver'd o're Psalm 88, 23
Thy fierce wrath over me doth flow Psalm 88, 65
Overarched
High overarch't imbowr; or scatterd sedge Par Lost 1.304
ms 'overarcht'
High overarch't, and echoing Walks between; Par Lost 9.1107
Overawed
Of gesture or lest action overawd Par Lost 9.460
Overblown
Shot after us in storm, oreblown hath laid Par Lost 1.172
ms 'oreblow'n'
Overbuilt
Disparted *Chaos* over built exclaimd, Par Lost 10.416
Overcame
Whose constant perseverance overcame Par Reg 1.148
Of thir pursuers, and overcame by flight; Par Reg 3.325
Over-cloy
Their stores doth over-cloy Psalm 4, 34
Overcome
And what is else not to be overcome? Par Lost 1.109
How overcome this dire Calamity, Par Lost 1.189
By force, hath overcome but half his foe. Par Lost 1.649
Our purer essence then will overcome Par Lost 2.215
The Fiend repli'd not, overcome with rage; Par Lost 4.857
Most reason is that Reason overcome. Par Lost 6.126
Shame to be overcome or over-reacht Par Lost 9.313
But fondly overcome with Femal charm. Par Lost 9.999
My obvious breast, arming to overcom Par Lost 11.374
To overcome in Battle, and subdue Par Lost 11.691
Till *Israel* overcome; so call the third Par Lost 12.267
Thy enemie; nor so is overcome Par Lost 12.390
His weakness shall o'recome Satanic strength Par Reg 1.161
O'recome with importunity and tears. Samson 51
Ensnar'd, assaulted, overcome, led bound, Samson 365
Overcomes
At length from us may find, who overcomes Par Lost 1.648
Overcoming
Still overcoming evil, and by small Par Lost 12.566
Over-exquisite
Eld. Bro. Peace brother, be not over-exquisite Mask 359
line not in Trinity ms
line not in Bridgewater ms
1637 'over exquisite'
Overflowed
With fragrance and with joy my heart oreflow'd. Par Lost 8.266
Over-fond
Thus over-fond, on that which is not thine; Par Lost 11.289
1667 'over fond'
Overfraught
The Sea o'refraught would swell, & th' unsought diamonds Mask 732
Bridgewater ms 'orefraught'
Trinity ms 'orefraught'
1637 'ore-fraught'
Overgrown
With thicket overgrown, grottesque and wilde, Par Lost 4.136
Our walk at noon, with branches overgrown, Par Lost 4.627
Lop overgrown, or prune, or prop, or bind, Par Lost 9.210
With wilde Thyme and the gadding Vine o'regrown, Lycidas 40
1638 'oregrown'
Trinity ms 'oregrowne'
Overgrowth
To stop thir overgrowth, as inmate guests Par Lost 12.166
Over-hardy
With all his over-hardy crew. Psalm 136, 70
Overhead
Or dreams he sees, while over-head the Moon Par Lost 1.784
ms 'over head'
1667 'over head'
Access deni'd; and over head up grew Par Lost 4.137
Of conflict; over head the dismal hiss Par Lost 6.212
Thick overhead with verdant roof imbowr'd Par Lost 9.1038
Overheard
And from the parting Angel over-heard Par Lost 9.276
Overhung
The rest was craggie cliff, that overhung Par Lost 4.547
Overjoyed
But he thus overjoy'd, O Fruit Divine, Par Lost 5.67
I overjoyd could not forbear aloud. Par Lost 8.490
Over-just
Which argues over-just, and self-displeas'd Samson 514
Over-laboured
And over-labour'd at thir publick Mill, Samson 1327
Overlaid
Were set, and Doric pillars overlaid Par Lost 1.714
ms 'over-layd'
Of Cedar, overlaid with Gold, therein Par Lost 12.250
Ore laid with black staid Wisdoms hue. Penseroso 16
Overlay
To fortifie thus farr, and overlay Par Lost 10.370

Overlay(*cont*)
Or where plain was raise hill, or over-lay Par Reg 3.333
Overleaped
At one slight bound high over leap'd all bound Par Lost 4.181
1667 'overleap'd'
So minded, have oreleapt these earthie bounds Par Lost 4.583
Overlive
Fixd on this day? why do I overlive, Par Lost 10.773
Overloved
For loss of life and pleasure overlov'd. Par Lost 10.1019
Overmatch
This far his over-match, who self deceiv'd Par Reg 4.7
Overmatched
Fearless to be o'rmatcht by living might. Par Lost 2.855
1667 'o'rematcht'
Thought none my equal, now be over-match'd. Par Reg 2.146
Overmuch
By attributing overmuch to things Par Lost 8.565
I also err'd in overmuch admiring Par Lost 9.1178
Deject not then so overmuch thy self, Samson 213
Over-multitude
The herds would over-multitude their Lords, Mask 731
Bridgewater ms 'overmultitude'
Trinity ms 'over multitude'
1637 'over-inultitude'
Overpassed
He slightly view'd, and slightly over-pass'd; Par Reg 2.198
Overplied
The conscience, Friend, to have lost them overply'd Sonnet 22, 10
1694 'over ply'd'
Over-potent
Temptation found'st, or over-potent charms Samson 427
Overpower
We overpower? Suppose he should relent Par Lost 2.237
Overpowered
Then such could hav orepow'rd such force as ours) Par Lost 1.145
ms 'orepowr'd'
Not to be overpowerd, Companions deare, Par Lost 6.419
My earthly by his Heav'nly overpowerd, Par Lost 8.453
Not out of levity, but over-powr'd Samson 880
Overpraising
Serpent, thy overpraising leaves in doubt Par Lost 9.615
Overreach
To over-reach, but with the Serpent meeting Par Lost 10.879
Over-reached
Shame to be overcome or over-reacht Par Lost 9.313
In cunning, over-reach't where least he thought, Par Reg 4.11
Over-ripe
Thy years are ripe, and over-ripe, the Son Par Reg 3.31
Overruled
As if predestination over-rul'd Par Lost 3.114
By nature free, not over-rul'd by Fate Par Lost 5.527
From his strong hold of Heav'n high over-rul'd Par Lost 6.228
Overrun
By Conquest far and wide, to over-run Par Reg 3.72
Overshades
Oreshades; for these mid-hours, till Eevning rise Par Lost 5.376
Overshadow
Darkness must overshadow all his bounds, Par Lost 12.187
O're-shadow her: this man born and now up-grown, Par Reg 1.140
Overshadowing
My overshadowing Spirit and might with thee Par Lost 7.165
Spreading and over-shadowing all the Earth, Par Reg 4.148
Overspread
Ascending, while the North wind sleeps, o'respread Par Lost 2.489
Had gon to wrack, with ruin overspred, Par Lost 6.670
The Hills were *over-spread* Psalm 80, 42
Over-strong
Man. O lastly over-strong against thy self! Samson 1590
Over-sure
Deceive ye to perswasion over-sure Par Reg 2.142
Overtake
And Joy shall overtake us as a flood, On Time 13
And overtake it, let him tread Psalm 7, 14
Overtask
Would overtask the best Land-Pilots art, Mask 309
Trinity ms 'overtaske'
Bridgewater ms 'overtaske'
Overthrew
Hath vext the Red-Sea Coast, whose waves orethrew Par Lost 1.306
Since *Satan* fell, whom follie overthrew, Par Lost 4.905
Of *Ramiel* scorcht and blasted overthrew. Par Lost 6.372
Overthrow
That with sad overthrow and foul defeat Par Lost 1.135
Repeated, and indecent overthrow Par Lost 6.601
In *Adam*'s overthrow, and led thir march Par Reg 1.115
Overthrown
Made head against Heav'ns King, though overthrown. Par Lost 2.992
The overthrown he rais'd, and as a Heard Par Lost 6.856
Me overthrown, to enter lists with God, Samson 463
Deprest, and overthrown, as seem'd, Samson 1698
He's here stuck in a slough, and overthrown. Carrier 4
Overtired
As over-tir'd to let him lean a while Samson 1632
Overtook
Mee overtook his mother all dismaid, Par Lost 2.792
Overtrusting
Him who to worth in Women overtrusting Par Lost 9.1183

Overture
Our overture, and turn not back perverse; Par Lost 6.562
Overturned
Chariot and Charioter lay overturnd Par Lost 6.390
Overturns
Of evils, and excessive, overturnes Par Lost 6.463
Which many a famous Warriour overturns, Samson 542
Overwatched
Sea-faring men orewatcht, whose Bark by chance Par Lost 2.288
To storm me over-watch't, and wearied out, Samson 405
Overwearied
Orewearied, through the faint Satanic Host Par Lost 6.392
Overween
Chosen thou hast, and they that overween, Sonnet 9, 6
Overweening
Though by the Devil himself, him overweening Par Lost 10.878
Less over-weening, since he fail'd in *Job*, Par Reg 1.147
Overwhelm
To pieces, and orewhelm whatever stands Par Lost 6.489
And overwhelm thir Warr: the Race elect Par Lost 12.214
He should not so o'rewhelm, and as a thrall Samson 370
Overwhelmed
There the companions of his fall, o'rewhelm'd Par Lost 1.76
ms 'orewhelmd'
To whom sad *Eve* with shame nigh overwhelm'd, Par Lost 10.159
Flood overwhelmd, and them with all thir pomp Par Lost 11.748
All in a moment overwhelm'd and fall'n. Samson 1559
Overwoody
Of Fruit-trees overwoodie reachd too farr Par Lost 5.213
Overworn
O're worn and soild; Samson 123
Owe
But what ow I to his commands above Par Lost 2.856
His fall'n condition is, and to me ow Par Lost 3.181
So burthensome still paying, still to ow; Par Lost 4.53
For wee to him indeed all praises owe, Par Lost 4.444
Attend: That thou art happie, owe to God; Par Lost 5.520
That thou continu'st such, owe to thy self, Par Lost 5.521
No less then for deliverance what we owe. Par Lost 6.468
For which to the infinitly Good we owe Par Lost 7.76
Thus grown. Experience, next to thee I owe, Par Lost 9.807
The Faith they owe; when earnestly they seek Par Lost 9.1141
Owe not all Creatures by just right to thee Par Reg 2.325
To such as owe them absolute subjection; Samson 1405
The bounds of either sword to thee wee ow. Sonnet 17, 12
1662, 1694 'owe'
Owes
By owing owes not, but still pays, at once Par Lost 4.56
Owing
By owing owes not, but still pays, at once Par Lost 4.56
Owls
Of Owles and Cuckoes, Asses, Apes and Doggs. Sonnet 12, 4
Trinity ms 'Owles' ←'Owls'
Own
Our Enemy, our own loss how repair, Par Lost 1.188
ms 'owne'
Left him at large to his own dark designs, Par Lost 1.213
As Gods, and by thir own recover'd strength, Par Lost 1.240
The mind is its own place, and in it self Par Lost 1.254
In his own Temple, on the grunsel edge, Par Lost 1.460
His own and *Rhea*'s Son like measure found; Par Lost 1.513
Henceforth his might we know, and know our own Par Lost 1.643
And in thir own dimensions like themselves Par Lost 1.793
His own invented Torments. But perhaps Par Lost 2.70
Our own right lost: him to unthrone we then Par Lost 2.231
Our own good from our selves, and from our own Par Lost 2.253
In his own strength, this place may lye expos'd Par Lost 2.360
All as our own, and drive as we were driven, Par Lost 2.366
Abolish his own works. This would surpass Par Lost 2.370
In others count'nance read his own dismay Par Lost 2.422
His own: for neither do the Spirits damn'd Par Lost 2.482
Thir own Heroic deeds and hapless fall Par Lost 2.549
Thine own begotten, breaking violent way Par Lost 2.782
Of mine own brood, that on my bowels feed: Par Lost 2.863
His own works and their works at once to view: Par Lost 3.59
Upon his own rebellious head. And now Par Lost 3.86
Whose but his own? ingrate, he had of mee Par Lost 3.97
Thir own revolt, not I: if I foreknew, Par Lost 3.117
The first sort by thir own suggestion fell, Par Lost 3.129
With his own folly? that be from thee farr, Par Lost 3.153
Much less that durst upon his own head draw Par Lost 3.220
Thir own both righteous and unrighteous deeds, Par Lost 3.292
His Brethren, ransomd with his own dear life. Par Lost 3.297
Mans Nature, less'n or degrade thine owne. Par Lost 3.304
From thir own mouths; all is not theirs it seems: Par Lost 4.513
Of force to its own likeness: up he starts Par Lost 4.813
So started up in his own shape the Fiend. Par Lost 4.819
Neither our own but giv'n; what follie then Par Lost 4.1007
Left to his own free Will, his Will though free, Par Lost 5.236
Our givers thir own gifts, and large bestow Par Lost 5.317
Accompani'd then with his own compleat Par Lost 5.352
Transcend his own so farr, whose radiant forms Par Lost 5.457
So smooths her charming tones, that Gods own ear Par Lost 5.626
Returns our own. Cease then this impious rage, Par Lost 5.845
By our own quick'ning power, when fatal course Par Lost 5.861
Our puissance is our own, our own right hand Par Lost 5.864
And thus his own undaunted heart explores. Par Lost 6.113
Illustrious farr and wide, but by his own Par Lost 6.773

Own(*cont*)
To ask, nor let thine own inventions hope Par Lost 7.121
The breath of Life; in his own Image hee Par Lost 7.526
That Man may know he dwells not in his own; Par Lost 8.103
By his attractive vertue and thir own Par Lost 8.124
Her own, that what she wills to do or say, Par Lost 8.549
Free in thine own Arbitrement it lies. Par Lost 8.641
Envying our happiness, and of his own Par Lost 9.254
Chiefly by what thy own last reasoning words Par Lost 9.379
From his own evil, and for the time remaind Par Lost 9.464
The Bond of Nature draw me to my owne, Par Lost 9.956
My own in thee, for what thou art is mine; Par Lost 9.957
His free Will, to her own inclining left Par Lost 10.46
Thence gatherd his own doom, which understood Par Lost 10.344
Thy Trophies, which thou view'st as not thine own, Par Lost 10.355
Retiring, by his own doom alienated, Par Lost 10.378
Cast on themselves from thir own mouths. There stood Par Lost 10.547
My own deservings; but this will not serve; Par Lost 10.727
Mine own that bide upon me, all from mee Par Lost 10.738
God made thee of choice his own, and of his own Par Lost 10.766
Not to th' extent of thir own Spheare. But say Par Lost 10.808
But to my own conviction: first and last Par Lost 10.831
Beare thine own first, ill able to sustaine Par Lost 10.950
Our own begotten, and of our Loines to bring Par Lost 10.983
With our own hands his Office on our selves; Par Lost 10.1002
To evils which our own misdeeds have wrought, Par Lost 10.1080
Which his own hand manuring all the Trees Par Lost 11.28
Disfiguring not Gods likeness, but thir own, Par Lost 11.521
First his own Tooles; then, what might else be wrought Par Lost 11.572
To leave them to thir own polluted wayes; Par Lost 12.110
To worship thir own work in Wood and Stone Par Lost 12.119
To save them, not thir own, though legal works. Par Lost 12.410
By his own Nation, slaine for bringing Life; Par Lost 12.414
Hee to his own a Comforter will send, Par Lost 12.486
To thir own vile advantages shall turne Par Lost 12.510
Thir own Faith not anothers: for on Earth Par Lost 12.528
Under her own waight groaning till the day Par Lost 12.539
What might improve my knowledge or their own; Par Reg 1.213
Natures own work it seem'd (Nature taught Art) Par Reg 2.295
Shall I receive by gift what of my own, Par Reg 2.381
But why should man seek glory? who of his own Par Reg 3.134
That who advance his glory, not thir own, Par Reg 3.143
With guilt of his own sin, for he himself Par Reg 3.147
Thou must make sure thy own, the *Parthian* first Par Reg 3.363
Who wrought their own captivity, fell off Par Reg 3.415
The strength he was to cope with, or his own: Par Reg 4.9
To me my own, on such abhorred pact, Par Reg 4.191
Error by his own arms is best evinc't. Par Reg 4.235
Whose Poem *Phoebus* challeng'd for his own. Par Reg 4.260
The vices of thir Deities, and thir own Par Reg 4.340
Had been fulfilld but through mine own default, Samson 45
In power of others, never in my own; Samson 78
Now of my own experience, not by talk, Samson 188
Then of thine own Tribe fairer, or as fair, Samson 217
At least of thy own Nation, and as noble. Samson 218
As to his own edicts, found contradicting, Samson 301
Till by thir own perplexities involv'd Samson 304
And tie him to his own prescript, Samson 308
For with his own Laws he can best dispence. Samson 314
But act not in thy own affliction, Son, Samson 503
Her own transgressions, to upbraid me mine? Samson 820
In man or woman, though to thy own condemning, Samson 844
Nor under their protection but my own, Samson 887
Of their own deity, Gods cannot be: Samson 899
Henceforth, nor too much disapprove my own. Samson 970
I leave him to his lot, and like my own. Samson 996
Draw thir own ruin who attempt the deed. Samson 1267
Making them each his own Deliverer, Samson 1289
Mess. By his own hands. *Man*. Self-violence? what cause Samson 1584
Upon thir heads and on his own he pull'd. Samson 1589
Now of my own accord such other tryal Samson 1643
Thir own destruction to come speedy upon them. Samson 1681
As thir own ruin on themselves to invite, Samson 1684
By her own radiant light, though Sun and Moon Mask 374
1637 'owne'
Bridgewater ms 'owne'
Trinity ms 'owne'
He that has light within his own cleer brest Mask 381
Trinity ms 'owne'
Bridgewater ms 'owne'
1637 'owne'
Himself is his own dungeon. 2. *Bro*. Tis most true Mask 385
1637 'owne'
Trinity ms 'himselfe is his owne dungeon' ←'blaze in the summer solstice'
Bridgewater ms 'blaze in the summer solstice'
Which if Heav'n gave it, may be term'd her own: Mask 419
Trinity ms 'owne'
Bridgewater ms 'owne'
1637 'owne'
Be vacant of her plenty, in her own loyns Mask 718
Trinity ms 'owne'
1637 'owne'
Bridgewater ms 'owne'
Who would be quite surcharg'd with her own weight, Mask 728
Trinity ms 'owne'
Bridgewater ms 'owne'
Three fair branches of your own, Mask 969

Own(*cont*)
1637 'owne'
Trinity ms 'owne'
Bridgewater ms 'owne'
to write his owne woes on the vermeil graine — Lycidas Tr. ms 28.18
More then she could own from Earth. — Winchester 6
Shortned hast thy own lives lease, — Winchester 52
Either man's work or his own gifts, who best — Sonnet 19, 10
By their own counsels quell'd; — Psalm 5, 30
The Lord will own, and have me in his keeping. — Psalm 6, 20
Their own conceits they follow'd still — Psalm 81, 51
Their own devises blind. — Psalm 81, 52
But his owne house, and the whole neighbourhood — Prose 10, 5

Owned
Son own'd from Heaven by his Father's voice; — Par Reg 2.85
That own'd the vertuous Ring and Glass, — Penseroso 113

Owners
With no small profit daily to my owners. — Samson 1261

Owns
Thee he regards not, owns not, hath cut off — Samson 1157

Ox
Lik'ning his Maker to the Grazed Ox, — Par Lost 1.486
ms 'ox'
So well converse, nor with the Ox the Ape; — Par Lost 8.396
Co. Two such I saw, what time the labour'd Oxe — Mask 291
Trinity ms 'oxe'
Bridgewater ms 'oxe'

Oxen
A herd of Beeves, faire Oxen and faire Kine — Par Lost 11.647

Oxus
And *Samarchand* by *Oxus*, *Temirs* Throne, — Par Lost 11.389

P
Cropp yee as close as marginall P---s eares — Forcers Tr. ms 45.17

Pace
Not distant far with heavie pace the Foe — Par Lost 6.551
With inoffensive pace that spinning sleeps — Par Lost 8.164
Close following pace for pace, not mounted yet — Par Lost 10.589
Mends not her slowest pace for prayers or cries. — Par Lost 10.859
But who are these? for with joint pace I hear — Samson 110
Break off, break off, I feel the different pace, — Mask 145
And *Tethys* grave majestick pace, — Mask 870
Whose speed is but the heavy Plummets pace; — On Time 3

Paced
Will prove no sudden, but a slow-pac't evill, — Par Lost 10.963

Paces
Such ruin intercept: ten paces huge — Par Lost 6.193
On her soft Axle, while she paces Eev'n, — Par Lost 8.165

Pacific
An Olive leafe he brings, pacific signe: — Par Lost 11.860

Pacing
Pacing toward the other gole — Mask 100
Bridgewater ms 'pacinge'

Packed
Believe me I have thither packt the worst: — Vacation 12

Packing
Your plots and packing wors then those of *Trent*, — Forcers 14
Trinity ms 'packings'

Pact
To me my own, on such abhorred pact, — Par Reg 4.191

Padan Aram
To *Padan-Aram* in the field of *Luz*, — Par Lost 3.513

Page
A title page is this! and some in file — Sonnet 11, 6

Pageantry
With mask, and antique Pageantry, — Allegro 128

Paid
Sidonian Virgins paid thir Vows and Songs, — Par Lost 1.441
ms 'pay'd'
Eternity so spent in worship paid — Par Lost 2.248
What pleasure I from such obedience paid, — Par Lost 3.107
All that of me can die, yet that debt paid, — Par Lost 3.246
Thir Orisons, each Morning duly paid — Par Lost 5.145
Is Pietie thus and pure Devotion paid? — Par Lost 11.452
Some bloud more precious must be paid for Man, — Par Lost 12.293
Thy ransom paid, which Man from death redeems, — Par Lost 12.424
Bitterly hast thou paid, and still art paying — Samson 432
May compass it, shall willingly be paid — Samson 1477
Hath paid his ransom now and full discharge. — Samson 1573
His praise due paid, for swinish gluttony — Mask 776
Bridgewater ms 'payed'

Pain
Both of lost happiness and lasting pain — Par Lost 1.55
ms 'paine'
So spake th' Apostate Angel, though in pain, — Par Lost 1.125
Anguish and doubt and fear and sorrow and pain — Par Lost 1.558
For ever now to have thir lot in pain, — Par Lost 1.608
Of endless pain? where there is then no good — Par Lost 2.30
Of present pain, that with ambitious mind — Par Lost 2.34
Where pain of unextinguishable fire — Par Lost 2.88
Though full of pain, this intellectual being, — Par Lost 2.147
Exile, or ignominy, or bonds, or pain, — Par Lost 2.207
Familiar the fierce heat, and void of pain; — Par Lost 2.219
Thrive under evil, and work ease out of pain — Par Lost 2.261
The sensible of pain. All things invite — Par Lost 2.278
To respite or deceive, or slack the pain — Par Lost 2.461
Through pain up by the roots *Thessalian* Pines, — Par Lost 2.544
Pain for a while or anguish, and excite — Par Lost 2.567
Forgets both joy and grief, pleasure and pain. — Par Lost 2.586

Pain(*cont*)
In sweet forgetfulness all pain and woe, — Par Lost 2.608
To waste Eternal dayes in woe and pain? — Par Lost 2.695
All on a sudden miserable pain — Par Lost 2.752
Tore through my entrails, that with fear and pain — Par Lost 2.783
From out this dark and dismal house of pain, — Par Lost 2.823
Here in perpetual agonie and pain, — Par Lost 2.861
Vows made in pain, as violent and void. — Par Lost 4.97
Was gatherd, which cost *Ceres* all that pain — Par Lost 4.271
Still unfulfill'd with pain of longing pines; — Par Lost 4.511
Puts me in doubt. Lives ther who loves his pain? — Par Lost 4.888
Farthest from pain, where thou mightst hope to change — Par Lost 4.892
So wise he judges it to fly from pain — Par Lost 4.910
Which taught thee yet no better, that no pain — Par Lost 4.915
Came not all Hell broke loose? is pain to them — Par Lost 4.918
Less pain, less to be fled, or thou then they — Par Lost 4.919
The first in flight from pain, had'st thou alledg'd — Par Lost 4.921
Not that I less endure, or shrink from pain, — Par Lost 4.925
Wise to flie pain, professing next the Spie, — Par Lost 4.948
Precipitate thee with augmented paine. — Par Lost 6.280
All his right side; then *Satan* first knew pain, — Par Lost 6.327
And uncouth paine fled bellowing. On each wing — Par Lost 6.362
Then first with fear surpris'd and sense of paine — Par Lost 6.394
Not liable to fear or flight or paine. — Par Lost 6.397
Some disadvantage we endur'd and paine, — Par Lost 6.431
Against unequal armes to fight in paine, — Par Lost 6.454
Valour or strength, though matchless, quelld with pain — Par Lost 6.457
But pain is perfet miserie, the worst — Par Lost 6.462
Into thir substance pent, which wrought them pain — Par Lost 6.657
Unquenchable, the house of woe and paine. — Par Lost 6.877
As wee, not capable of death or paine, — Par Lost 9.283
I not; so much hath Hell debas'd, and paine — Par Lost 9.487
Rather your dauntless vertue, whom the pain — Par Lost 9.694
The pain of absence from thy sight. But strange — Par Lost 9.861
1667 'paine'
What I have don, what sufferd, with what paine — Par Lost 10.470
Or much more grievous pain? Ye have th' account — Par Lost 10.501
To deathless pain? how gladly would I meet — Par Lost 10.775
A long days dying to augment our paine, — Par Lost 10.964
So snatcht will not exempt us from the paine — Par Lost 10.1025
Those were of hate and death, or pain much worse, — Par Lost 11.601
Expect with mortal paine: say where and when — Par Lost 12.384
That fellowship in pain divides not smart, — Par Reg 1.401
Wealth, pleasure, pain or torment, death and life, — Par Reg 4.305
My griefs not only pain me — Samson 617
Refreshment after toil, ease after pain, — Mask 687
line not in Bridgewater ms
Trinity ms 'paine'
1637 'paine'

Pained
Unwearied, unobnoxious to be pain'd — Par Lost 6.404

Painful
Thir painful steps o're the burnt soyle; and now — Par Lost 1.562
ms 'painfull'
Of painful Superstition and blind Zeal, — Par Lost 3.452
These painful passages, how we may come — Par Lost 11.528
Painful diseases and deform'd, — Samson 699

Pains
Strongly to suffer and support our pains, — Par Lost 1.147
In which they were, or the fierce pains not feel; — Par Lost 1.336
Pains onely in Child-bearing were foretold, — Par Lost 10.1051
Under inhuman pains? Why should not Man, — Par Lost 11.511
Whose pains have earn'd the far fet spoil. With that — Par Reg 2.401
Of dangers, and adversities and pains, — Par Reg 4.479
From worst of other evils, pains and wrongs, — Samson 105
By pains and slaveries, worse then death inflicted — Samson 485
To thir abyss and horrid pains confin'd. — Samson 501
Hast'n the welcom end of all my pains. — Samson 576
With answerable pains, but more intense, — Samson 615

Paint
Till the Sun paint your fleecie skirts with Gold, — Par Lost 5.187

Painted
Solac'd the Woods, and spred thir painted wings — Par Lost 7.434
Lyceum there, and painted *Stoa* next: — Par Reg 4.253
The painted Heav'ns so full of state. — Psalm 136, 18

Paints
How Nature paints her colours, how the Bee — Par Lost 5.24

Pair
So hand in hand they passd, the lovliest pair — Par Lost 4.321
Ah gentle pair, yee little think how nigh — Par Lost 4.366
Yet happie pair; enjoy, till I return, — Par Lost 4.534
Blest pair; and O yet happiest if ye seek — Par Lost 4.774
This night the human pair, how he designes — Par Lost 5.227
His lineaments Divine; the pair that clad — Par Lost 5.278
With regal Ornament; the middle pair — Par Lost 5.280
Harmonie to behold in wedded pair — Par Lost 8.605
With grateful Smell, forth came the human pair — Par Lost 9.197
By Night, and listening where the hapless Paire — Par Lost 10.342
Mean while in Paradise the hellish pair — Par Lost 10.585
Seem'd thir Petition, then when th' ancient Pair — Par Lost 11.10
Without remorse drive out the sinful Pair, — Par Lost 11.105
Canst thou not tell me of a gentle Pair — Mask 236
Trinity ms 'paire'
Bridgewater ms 'payre'
1637 'Paire'
Blest pair of *Sirens*, pledges of Heav'ns joy, — Musick 1
Trinity ms 'paire'

Paired
This with the other should, at least, have paird, Samson 208
Pairs
Among the Trees in Pairs they rose, they walk'd: Par Lost 7.459
Such pairs, in Love and mutual Honour joyn'd? Par Lost 8.58
So fitly them in pairs thou hast combin'd; Par Lost 8.394
Came seavens, and pairs, and enterd in, as taught Par Lost 11.735
Palace
The work as of a Kingly Palace Gate Par Lost 3.505
The Palace of great *Lucifer*, (so call Par Lost 5.760
Her gather'd beams, great Palace now of Light. Par Lost 7.363
From *Susa* his *Memnonian* Palace high Par Lost 10.308
Frogs, Lice and Flies must all his Palace fill Par Lost 12.177
As one in City, or Court, or Palace bred, Par Reg 2.300
The Imperial Palace, compass huge, and high Par Reg 4.51
That ope's the Palace of Eternity: Mask 14
1637 'palace'
Bridgewater ms 'pallace'
Trinity ms 'palace'
Will open wide the Gates of her high Palace Hall. Nativity 148
Palaces
In Courts and Palaces he also Reigns Par Lost 1.497
Sea without shoar; and in thir Palaces Par Lost 11.750
On seven small Hills, with Palaces adorn'd, Par Reg 4.35
Their stately Palaces. Psalm 83, 48
Palate
And Palate call judicious; I the praise Par Lost 9.1020
Palatine
Impregnable, and there Mount *Palatine* Par Reg 4.50
Pale
Casts pale and dreadful? Thither let us tend Par Lost 1.183
Wheels her pale course, they on thir mirth and dance Par Lost 1.786
With shuddring horror pale, and eyes agast Par Lost 2.616
And in her pale dominion checks the night. Par Lost 3.732
Thrice chang'd with pale, ire, envie and despair, Par Lost 4.115
Defensive scarse, or with pale fear surpris'd, Par Lost 6.393
Speechless he stood and pale, till thus at length Par Lost 9.894
On his pale Horse: to whom *Sin* thus began. Par Lost 10.590
Had entertaind, as di'd her Cheeks with pale. Par Lost 10.1009
That beat out life; he fell, and deadly pale Par Lost 11.446
Stoop thy pale visage through an amber cloud, Mask 333
Thus night oft see me in thy pale career, Penseroso 121
To walk the studious Cloysters pale, Penseroso 156
The tufted Crow-toe, and pale Gessamine, Lycidas 143
colouring the pale cheeke of uninjoyd love Lycidas Tr. ms 28.16
Edg'd with poplar pale. Nativity 185
The flocking shadows pale, Nativity 232
The yellow Cowslip, and the pale Primrose. May Morn 4
Rescu'd from death by force though pale and faint. Sonnet 23, 4
With pale and hollow eyes? Psalm 88, 44
Pale-eyed
Inspire's the pale-ey'd Priest from the prophetic cell. Nativity 180
Pales
To *Pales*, or *Pomona* thus adornd, Par Lost 9.393
Palestine
Long after known in *Palestine*, and nam'd Par Lost 1.80
ms 'Palestine'
Of *Palestine*, in *Gath* and *Ascalon* Par Lost 1.465
ms 'Palestine'
A thousand fore-skins fell, the flower of *Palestin* Samson 144
To *Palestine*, won by a *Philistine* Samson 1099
With that twise batter'd god of *Palestine*, Nativity 199
Pall
In Scepter'd Pall com sweeping by, Penseroso 98
Pallet
From her thach't pallat rowse, if otherwise Mask 318
1637 'palate'
Trinity ms 'palate' ←'pallat' ←'palate'
Bridgewater ms 'palat'
Palm
Cedar, and Pine, and Firr, and branching Palm, Par Lost 4.139
Shaded with branching Palme, each order bright, Par Lost 6.885
Of stateliest Covert, Cedar, Pine, or Palme, Par Lost 9.435
Of Laurel ever green, and branching Palm, Samson 1735
Palmer
Like a sad Votarist in Palmers weed Mask 189
Trinity ms 'palmers'
line not in Bridgewater ms
Palms
The City of Palms, *Aenon*, and *Salem* Old, Par Reg 2.21
I touch with chaste palms moist and cold, Mask 918
Trinity ms 'palmes'
Bridgewater ms 'palmes'
1637 'palmes'
With those just Spirits that wear victorious Palms, Musick 14
Trinity ms 'palmes'
Palm-tree
Then Fruits of Palm-tree pleasantest to thirst Par Lost 8.212
Palmy
Or palmie hilloc, or the flourie lap Par Lost 4.254
Palpable
And through the palpable obscure find out Par Lost 2.406
Palpable darkness, and blot out three dayes; Par Lost 12.188
Pampered
Thir pamperd boughes, and needed hands to check Par Lost 5.214
Of that which lewdly-pamper'd Luxury Mask 770
Trinity ms 'lewdly-pamperd'
1637 'lewdy-pamper'd'

Pampered(*cont*)
Bridgewater ms 'leudly-pamper'd'
Pan
The trembling leaves, while Universal *Pan* Par Lost 4.266
Pan or *Silvanus* never slept, nor Nymph, Par Lost 4.707
Apollo, *Neptune*, *Jupiter*, or *Pan*, Par Reg 2.190
In wanton dance they praise the bounteous *Pan*, Mask 176
Dwell'st here with *Pan*, or *Silvan*, by blest Song Mask 268
Though *Syrinx* your *Pans* Mistres were, Arcades 106
Trinity ms defective here
That the mighty *Pan* Nativity 89
and gives thee praise above the pipe of Pan; Sonnet 13, Tr. ms 40.06
Pandemonium
At *Pandaemonium*, the high Capital Par Lost 1.756
ms 'Pandaemonium'
Of *Pandaemonium*, Citie and proud seate Par Lost 10.424
Pandora
More lovely then *Pandora*, whom the Gods Par Lost 4.714
Paneas
From *Paneas* the fount of *Jordans* flood Par Lost 3.535
Pangs
Strange horror seise thee, and pangs unfelt before. Par Lost 2.703
In pangs, and Nature gave a second groan, Par Lost 9.1001
Intestin Stone and Ulcer, Colic pangs, Par Lost 11.484
But with th' afflicted in his pangs thir sound Samson 660
Huge pangs and strong Circum 27
Through pangs fled to felicity, Winchester 68
Panope
Sleek *Panope* with all her sisters play'd. Lycidas 99
Panoply
Of Golden Panoplie, refulgent Host, Par Lost 6.527
Hee in Celestial Panoplie all armd Par Lost 6.760
Pansies
Pansies, and Violets, and Asphodel, Par Lost 9.1040
Of pancies, pinks, and gaudy Daffadils. Mask 851
Pansy
The white Pink, and the Pansie freakt with jeat, Lycidas 144
Trinity ms 'pansie' ←'pancie'
1638 'pansie'
Paquin
To *Paquin* of *Sinaean* Kings, and thence Par Lost 11.390
Parables
That Gentiles in thir Parables condemn Samson 500
Parade
To thir night watches in warlike Parade, Par Lost 4.780
Paradise
In Paradise, fast by the Tree of Life Par Lost 3.354
And they who to be sure of Paradise Par Lost 3.478
The Paradise of Fools, to few unknown Par Lost 3.496
Just o're the blissful seat of Paradise, Par Lost 3.527
To Paradise the happie seat of Man, Par Lost 3.632
That spot to which I point is *Paradise*, Par Lost 3.733
Of *Eden*, where delicious Paradise, Par Lost 4.132
The verdurous wall of paradise up sprung: Par Lost 4.143
1667 'Paradise'
A Heav'n on Earth, for blissful Paradise Par Lost 4.208
Flours worthy of Paradise which not nice Art Par Lost 4.241
Castalian Spring, might with this Paradise Par Lost 4.274
True Paradise under the *Ethiop* Line Par Lost 4.282
Like this fair Paradise, your sense, yet such Par Lost 4.379
In Paradise that bear delicious fruit Par Lost 4.422
Against the eastern Gate of Paradise Par Lost 4.542
In Paradise of all things common else. Par Lost 4.752
Might have ensu'd, nor onely Paradise Par Lost 4.991
Of Paradise and *Edens* happie Plains, Par Lost 5.143
Hath raisd in Paradise, and how disturbd Par Lost 5.226
At once on th' Eastern cliff of Paradise Par Lost 5.275
Deserving Paradise! if ever, then, Par Lost 5.446
In Paradise to *Adam* or his Race, Par Lost 7.45
In what he gives to thee, this Paradise Par Lost 8.171
This Paradise I give thee, count it thine Par Lost 8.319
Where *Tigris* at the foot of Paradise Par Lost 9.71
Thou never from that houre in Paradise Par Lost 9.406
Of Paradise for Hell, hope here to taste Par Lost 9.476
In Paradise, and various, yet unknown Par Lost 9.619
In Paradise, of operation blest Par Lost 9.796
Of *Satan* done in Paradise, and how Par Lost 10.2
Up into Heav'n from Paradise in haste Par Lost 10.17
To Paradise first tending, when behold Par Lost 10.326
All yours, right down to Paradise descend; Par Lost 10.398
Plac't in a Paradise, by our exile Par Lost 10.484
Which grew in Paradise, the bait of *Eve* Par Lost 10.551
Mean while in Paradise the hellish pair Par Lost 10.585
Alike is Hell, or Paradise, or Heaven, Par Lost 10.598
Of Paradise, deare bought with lasting woes! Par Lost 10.742
Of Paradise could have produc't, ere fall'n Par Lost 11.29
But longer in that Paradise to dwell, Par Lost 11.48
Hast thee, and from the Paradise of God Par Lost 11.104
Least Paradise a receptacle prove Par Lost 11.123
In Paradise, and on a Hill made alt, Par Lost 11.210
But longer in this Paradise to dwell Par Lost 11.259
Must I thus leave thee Paradise? thus leave Par Lost 11.269
Of Paradise or *Eden:* this had been Par Lost 11.342
Of Paradise the highest, from whose top Par Lost 11.378
Of Paradise by might of Waves be moovd Par Lost 11.830
Safe to eternal Paradise of rest. Par Lost 12.314
Shall all be Paradise, far happier place Par Lost 12.464
To leave this Paradise, but shalt possess Par Lost 12.586

Paradise(*cont*)
A paradise within thee, happier farr. Par Lost 12.587
1667 'Paradise'
Of Paradise, so late thir happie seat, Par Lost 12.642
Recover'd Paradise to all mankind, Par Reg 1.3
Lost Paradise deceiv'd by me, though since Par Reg 1.52
Of my success with *Eve* in Paradise Par Reg 2.141
And Thief of Paradise; him long of old Par Reg 4.604
Temptation, hast regain'd lost Paradise, Par Reg 4.608
In Paradise to tempt; his snares are broke: Par Reg 4.611
A fairer Paradise is founded now Par Reg 4.613
this dusky hollow is a paradise & heaven gates ore my head Mask Tr. ms 13.44
Paradises
Here or in Heav'nly Paradises dwell; Par Lost 5.500
Paradoxes
Thir Idolisms, Traditions, Paradoxes? Par Reg 4.234
Paragoned
Of that bright Starr to *Satan* paragond. Par Lost 10.426
Parallax
By what strange Parallax or Optic skill Par Reg 4.40
Parallel
Shot paralel to the earth his dewie ray, Par Lost 5.141
Paramount
Midst came thir mighty Paramount, and seemd Par Lost 2.508
Paramour
To wanton with the Sun her lusty Paramour. Nativity 36
Paranymph
Thy Paranymph, worthless to thee compar'd, Samson 1020
Parasite
Or like a Fawning Parasite obey'st; Par Reg 1.452
Parch
Began to parch that temperate Clime; whereat Par Lost 12.636
Parched
Yet parcht with scalding thurst and hunger fierce, Par Lost 10.556
Parching
Where Armies whole have sunk: the parching Air Par Lost 2.594
Unwept, and welter to the parching wind, Lycidas 13
Pard
And spotted mountain pard, but set at nought Mask 444
Bridgewater ms 'Pard'
Pardon
Left for Repentance, none for Pardon left? Par Lost 4.80
While Pardon may be found in time besought. Par Lost 5.848
Humbly our faults, and pardon beg, with tears Par Lost 10.1089
Humbly thir faults, and pardon beg'd, with tears Par Lost 10.1101
But infinite in pardon was my Judge, Par Lost 11.167
Sam. His pardon I implore; but as for life, Samson 521
My penance hath not slack'n'd, though my pardon Samson 738
I may, if possible, thy pardon find Samson 771
Yet always pity or pardon hath obtain'd. Samson 814
Such pardon therefore as I give my folly, Samson 825
Justly, yet despair not of his final pardon Samson 1171
Here I salute thee and thy pardon ask, Vacation 7
To pardon, thou to all Psalm 86, 14
Pardons
Indulgences, Dispenses, Pardons, Bulls, Par Lost 3.492
Pards
Dandl'd the Kid; Bears, Tygers, Ounces, Pards, Par Lost 4.344
Parent
And me his Parent would full soon devour Par Lost 2.805
These are thy glorious works, Parent of good, Par Lost 5.153
Thir Parent soon discern'd, though in disguise. Par Lost 10.331
O Parent, these are thy magnific deeds, Par Lost 10.354
Parentage
Though men esteem thee low of Parentage, Par Reg 1.235
Parents
Mov'd our Grand Parents in that happy State, Par Lost 1.29
ms 'parents'
Of human sacrifice, and parents tears, Par Lost 1.393
Thir boasted Parents; *Titan* Heav'ns first born Par Lost 1.510
ms 'parents'
Our two first Parents, yet the onely two Par Lost 3.65
While time was, our first-Parents had bin warnd Par Lost 4.6
1667 'first Parents'
By Parents, or his happiest choice too late Par Lost 10.904
Our lingring Parents, and to th' Eastern Gate Par Lost 12.638
Of both my Parents all in flames ascended Samson 25
Mee, not my Parents, that I sought to wed, Samson 220
Parents and countrey; nor was I their subject, Samson 886
Sons wont to nurse thir Parents in old age, Samson 1487
Parle
They ended parle, and both addrest for fight Par Lost 6.296
By parl, or composition, truce, or league Par Reg 4.529
Let weakness then with weakness come to parl Samson 785
Parley
Sweet Queen of Parly, Daughter of the Sphear, Mask 241
1637 'Parlie'
B.M. ms 'Queen of Pity'
Trinity ms 'parlie'
Bridgewater ms 'parlie'
Parleys
With blandisht parlies, feminine assaults, Samson 403
Parliament
Till the sad breaking of that Parlament Sonnet 10, 5
That so the Parliament Forcers 15
Trinity ms 'Parlament'
Parricide
What Murtherer, what Traytor, Parricide, Samson 832
Parsimonious
The Parsimonious Emmet, provident Par Lost 7.485
Part
And call them not to share with us their part Par Lost 1.267
By falsities and lyes the greatest part Par Lost 1.367
New warr, provok't; our better part remains Par Lost 1.645
Sole King, and of his Kingdom loose no part Par Lost 2.325
By *Satan*, and in part propos'd: for whence, Par Lost 2.380
Part on the Plain, or in the Air sublime Par Lost 2.528
Part curb thir fierie Steeds, or shun the Goal Par Lost 2.531
Another part in Squadrons and gross Bands, Par Lost 2.570
Drew after him the third part of Heav'ns Sons Par Lost 2.692
Cleer Victory, to our part loss and rout Par Lost 2.770
Melodious part, such concord is in Heav'n. Par Lost 3.371
The Univers, and to each inward part Par Lost 3.584
If mettal, part seemd Gold, part Silver cleer; Par Lost 3.595
Drawn to his part; but other Powers as great Par Lost 4.63
Sole partner and sole part of all these joyes, Par Lost 4.411
Part of my Soul I seek thee, and thee claim Par Lost 4.487
Temper or nourish, or in part shed down Par Lost 4.670
Even to my mouth of that same fruit held part Par Lost 5.83
(Whose praise be ever sung) to man in part Par Lost 5.405
Drew after him the third part of Heav'ns Host: Par Lost 5.710
A third part of the Gods, in Synod met Par Lost 6.156
Vital in every part, not as frail man Par Lost 6.345
Cherubic waving fires: on th' other part Par Lost 6.413
Part hidd'n veins diggd up (nor hath this Earth Par Lost 6.516
Of missive ruin; part incentive reed Par Lost 6.519
Freely our part; yee who appointed stand Par Lost 6.565
Yet farr the greater part have kept, I see, Par Lost 7.145
Part rise in crystal Wall, or ridge direct, Par Lost 7.293
Of Light by farr the greater part he took, Par Lost 7.359
Bank the mid Sea: part single or with mate Par Lost 7.403
And bended Dolphins play: part huge of bulk Par Lost 7.410
Part loosly wing the Region, part more wise Par Lost 7.425
Travelling East, and with her part averse Par Lost 8.138
From the Suns beam meet Night, her other part Par Lost 8.139
Or Nature faild in mee, and left some part Par Lost 8.534
Accuse not Nature, she hath don her part; Par Lost 8.561
Disloyal on the part of Man, revolt, Par Lost 9.7
And disobedience: On the part of Heav'n Par Lost 9.8
Into a Gulf shot under ground, till part Par Lost 9.72
For God towards thee hath done his part, do thine. Par Lost 9.375
New part puts on, and as to passion mov'd, Par Lost 9.667
Stood in himself collected, while each part, Par Lost 9.673
For bliss, as thou hast part, to me is bliss, Par Lost 9.879
And elegant, of Sapience no small part, Par Lost 9.1018
Thus fenc't, and as they thought, thir shame in part Par Lost 9.1119
Unseemly to beare rule, which was thy part Par Lost 10.155
Alreadie in part, though hid in gloomiest shade, Par Lost 10.716
Nor I on my part single, in mee all Par Lost 10.817
More to the part sinister from me drawn, Par Lost 10.886
His full wrauth whose thou feelst as yet lest part, Par Lost 10.951
Part of our Sentence, that thy Seed shall bruise Par Lost 10.1031
Part arable and tilth, whereon were Sheaves Par Lost 11.430
New reapt, the other part sheep-walks and foulds; Par Lost 11.431
In part, from such deformities be free, Par Lost 11.513
In other part stood one who at the Forge Par Lost 11.564
Part wield thir Arms, part courb the foaming Steed, Par Lost 11.643
In other part the scepter'd Haralds call Par Lost 11.660
My part of evil onely, each dayes lot Par Lost 11.765
Ordaine them Lawes; part such as appertaine Par Lost 12.230
To civil Justice, part religious Rites Par Lost 12.231
Cannot appease, nor Man the moral part Par Lost 12.298
Part good, part bad, of bad the longer scrowle, Par Lost 12.336
And not inforc'd oft-times to part from truth; Par Reg 1.472
Of various persons each to know his part; Par Reg 2.240
To Vertue I impute not, or count part Par Reg 2.248
Governs the inner man, the nobler part, Par Reg 2.477
Be now in powerful hands, that will not part Par Reg 3.155
Thy life hath yet been private, most part spent Par Reg 3.232
On my part aught endeavouring, or to need Par Reg 3.399
Nor what I part with mean to give for naught; Par Reg 4.161
In what part lodg'd, how easily bereft me, Samson 48
Annull'd, which might in part my grief have eas'd, Samson 72
She all in every part; why was the sight Samson 93
My capital secret, in what part my strength Samson 394
Lay stor'd, in what part summ'd, that she might know: Samson 395
And peoples safety, which in part they effect: Samson 681
Though late, yet in some part to recompense Samson 746
Nor from that right to part an hour, Samson 1056
I was to do my part from Heav'n assign'd, Samson 1217
Come nearer, part not hence so slight inform'd; Samson 1229
To give ye part with me what hope I have Samson 1453
That part most reverenc'd *Dagon* and his Priests, Samson 1463
No, I am fixt not to part hence without him. Samson 1481
To think her part was don, Nativity 105
Thy easie numbers flow, and that each heart Shakespear 10
1663-4 'each part'
1632 'each part'
The better part with *Mary*, and the *Ruth*, Sonnet 9, 5
Chose to himself a part Psalm 4, 14
Part
Our circuit meets full West. As flame they part Par Lost 4.784
Not likely to part hence without contest; Par Lost 4.872
Follow'd with benediction. Since to part, Par Lost 8.645
How shall I part, and whither wander down Par Lost 11.282
Of Spirit and Truth; the rest, farr greater part, Par Lost 12.533

Partake
Hurl'd headlong to partake with us, shall curse Par Lost 2.374
None shall partake with me. Thus saying rose Par Lost 2.466
Partake thou also; happie though thou art, Par Lost 5.75
Bereavd of happiness thou maist partake Par Lost 6.903
To sit indulgent, and with him partake Par Lost 9.3
Of Creatures wanting voice, that done, partake Par Lost 9.199
As yet my change, and give him to partake Par Lost 9.818
Let her with thee partake what thou hast heard, Par Lost 12.598
Cho. That hope would much rejoyce us to partake Samson 1455
Partaken
Consists in mutual and partak'n bliss, Mask 741
1637 'partaken'
Trinity ms 'partaken'
line not in Bridgewater ms
Partakers
Partakers, and uncropt falls to the ground. Par Lost 4.731
Partakes
I see not who partakes. In solitude Par Lost 8.364
Parted
Round from his parted forelock manly hung Par Lost 4.302
So parted they, the Angel up to Heav'n Par Lost 8.652
That Morn when first they parted; by the Tree Par Lost 9.848
Mine never shall be parted, bliss or woe. Par Lost 9.916
Was I to have never parted from thy side? Par Lost 9.1153
Of all things parted by th' Empyreal bounds, Par Lost 10.380
By order of the Lords new parted hence Samson 1447
With God not parted from him, as was feard, Samson 1719
Had by him, ere he parted thence, a Son Mask 56
When Faith and Love which parted from thee never, Sonnet 14, 1
From life discharg'd and parted quite Psalm 88, 17
Parthenope
By dead *Parthenope*'s dear tomb, Mask 879
Bridgewater ms 'Parthenopes'
Parthian
Built by *Emathian*, or by *Parthian* hands, Par Reg 3.290
All these the *Parthian*, now some Ages past, Par Reg 3.294
Of his great power; for now the *Parthian* King Par Reg 3.299
Roman and *Parthian?* therefore one of these Par Reg 3.362
Thou must make sure thy own, the *Parthian* first Par Reg 3.363
To render thee the *Parthian* at dispose; Par Reg 3.369
From the *Asian* Kings and *Parthian* among these, Par Reg 4.73
Before the *Parthian;* these two Thrones except, Par Reg 4.85
Partial
Thir Song was partial, but the harmony Par Lost 2.552
Participate
With Angels may participate, and find Par Lost 5.494
Such as I seek, fit to participate Par Lost 8.390
In both which we, as next participate. Samson 1507
Participating
As they, participating God-like food? Par Lost 9.717
Particular
Relation more particular and distinct. Samson 1595
Parting
The sequel each of parting and of fight; Par Lost 4.1003
On each hand parting, to his speed gave way Par Lost 5.252
But I can now no more; the parting Sun Par Lost 8.630
And from the parting Angel over-heard Par Lost 9.276
Exacts our parting hence; and see the Guards, Par Lost 12.590
And envious darknes, e're they could return, Mask 194
Trinity ms 'and envious darknesse' ←'to the soone parting light'
The parting Genius is with sighing sent, Nativity 186
To live with him, and sing in endles morn of light. Musick 28
Trinity ms 'endlesse' ←'never-parting' ←'cloudlesse' ←'endlesse' ←'uneclipsed' ←'ever-glorious' ←'ever-endlesse'
Partition
Of this great Round: partition firm and sure, Par Lost 7.267
Lodg'd in a small partition, and the rest Par Lost 8.105
Partly
Known partly, and soon found of whom they spake Par Reg 1.262
Partner
Sole partner and sole part of all these joyes, Par Lost 4.411
My other self, the partner of my life; Par Lost 10.128
Partners
Th' associates and copartners of our loss Par Lost 1.265
Fearless at home of partners in my love. Samson 810
Partook
Sometimes that with *Elijah* he partook, Par Reg 2.277
Parts
That sparkling blaz'd, his other Parts besides Par Lost 1.194
ms 'parts'
Not all parts like, but all alike informd Par Lost 3.593
Nor those mysterious parts were then conceald, Par Lost 4.312
Mean while in other parts like deeds deservd Par Lost 6.354
His hinder parts, then springs as broke from Bonds, Par Lost 7.465
The Parts of each for other, that seem most Par Lost 9.1093
Those middle parts, that this new commer, Shame, Par Lost 9.1097
And not as feeling through all parts diffus'd, Samson 96
Mangle my apprehensive tenderest parts, Samson 624
Met from all parts to solemnize this Feast. Samson 1656
All other parts remaining as they were, Mask 72
Lets in defilement to the inward parts, Mask 466
Bridgewater ms 'partes'
Parts
Of old *Euphrates* to the Brook that parts Par Lost 1.420
Vex'd *Scylla* bathing in the Sea that parts Par Lost 2.660

Party
Seduce them to our Party, that thir God Par Lost 2.368
Pass
Pour'd never from her frozen loyns, to pass Par Lost 1.352
ms 'passe'
These past, if any pass, the void profound Par Lost 2.438
And wish and struggle, as they pass, to reach Par Lost 2.606
To yonder Gates? through them I mean to pass, Par Lost 2.684
These Gates for ever shut, which none can pass Par Lost 2.776
Under spread Ensigns marching might pass through Par Lost 2.886
With easie intercourse pass to and fro Par Lost 2.1031
Or in *Franciscan* think to pass disguis'd; Par Lost 3.480
They pass the Planets seven, and pass the fixt, Par Lost 3.481
See farr and wide: in at this Gate none pass Par Lost 4.579
In *Adam*, not to let th' occasion pass Par Lost 5.453
Intends to pass triumphant, and give Laws. Par Lost 5.693
Floats, as they pass, fann'd with unnumber'd plumes: Par Lost 7.432
God hath assign'd us, nor of me shalt pass Par Lost 9.231
If chance with Nymphlike step fair Virgin pass, Par Lost 9.452
To me is lost. Then let me not let pass Par Lost 9.479
Of Knowledge he must pass, there he her met, Par Lost 9.849
Foretold so lately what would come to pass, Par Lost 10.38
What rests but that the mortal Sentence pass Par Lost 10.48
To pass commodiously this life, sustain'd Par Lost 10.1083
Swallows him with his Host, but them lets pass Par Lost 12.196
So far from path or road of men, who pass Par Reg 1.322
The rest commit to me, I shall let pass Par Reg 2.233
Worth or not worth the seeking, let it pass: Par Reg 3.151
Therefore let pass, as they are transitory, Par Reg 4.209
Which to have come to pass by means of thee, Samson 444
Chances to passe through this adventrous glade, Mask 79
1673 'pass'
Bridgewater ms 'pass'
And let a single helpless maiden pass Mask 402
Trinity ms 'passe'
Bridgewater ms 'passe'
1637 'passe'
She may pass on with unblench't majesty, Mask 430
Trinity ms 'passe'
1637 'passe'
Of them that pass unweeting by the way. Mask 539
1637 'passe'
Trinity ms 'passe'
Bridgewater ms 'passe'
Spir. What, have you let the false enchanter scape? Mask 814
Trinity ms 'scape' ←'passe'
And Hell it self will pass away, Nativity 139
While the Hebrew Bands did pass. Psalm 136, 50
Then sing of secret things that came to pass Vacation 45
Fore-saw what future dayes should bring to pass, Vacation 72
They pass through Baca's *thirstie* Vale, Psalm 84, 21
Reck'n'd I am with them that pass Psalm 88, 13
Passage
A passage down to th' Earth, a passage wide, Par Lost 3.528
Which from his darksom passage now appeers, Par Lost 4.232
Easing thir passage hence, for intercourse, Par Lost 10.260
Forfeit to Death; from hence a passage broad, Par Lost 10.304
Toild out my uncouth passage, forc't to ride Par Lost 10.475
And guard all passage to the Tree of Life: Par Lost 11.122
Thy mortal passage when it comes. Ascend Par Lost 11.366
But must secret passage find Samson 610
And loudly knock to have their passage out; Vacation 24
Passages
These painful passages, how we may come Par Lost 11.528
Passed
Thir childrens cries unheard, that past through fire Par Lost 1.395
Jehovah, who in one Night when he pass'd Par Lost 1.487
ms 'past'
These past, if any pass, the void profound Par Lost 2.438
They pass'd, and many a Region dolorous, Par Lost 2.619
And more endanger'd, then when *Argo* pass'd Par Lost 2.1017
But hee once past, soon after when man fell, Par Lost 2.1023
Father, thy word is past, man shall find grace; Par Lost 3.227
All this dark Globe the Fiend found as he pass'd, Par Lost 3.498
Pass'd frequent, and his eye with choice regard Par Lost 3.534
All path of Man or Beast that past that way: Par Lost 4.177
Pass'd underneath ingulft, for God had thrown Par Lost 4.225
So passd they naked on, nor shund the sight Par Lost 4.319
So hand in hand they passd, the lovliest pair Par Lost 4.321
Thus talking hand in hand alone they pass'd Par Lost 4.689
Such night till this I never pass'd, have dream'd, Par Lost 5.31
And on, methought, alone I pass'd through ways Par Lost 5.50
Thir glittering Tents he passd, and now is come Par Lost 5.291
Hath past in Heav'n, som doubt within me move, Par Lost 5.554
Of yesterday, so late hath past the lips Par Lost 5.675
Regions they pass'd, the mightie Regencies Par Lost 5.748
Stretcht into Longitude; which having pass'd Par Lost 5.754
Though single. From amidst them forth he passd, Par Lost 5.903
Pass'd through him, but th' Ethereal substance clos'd Par Lost 6.330
Nor past uncelebrated, nor unsung Par Lost 7.253
I nam'd them, as they pass'd, and understood Par Lost 8.352
Fast by a Fountain, one small Thicket past Par Lost 9.628
What words have past thy Lips, *Adam* severe, Par Lost 9.1144
All, though all-knowing, what had past with Man Par Lost 10.227
Farr into *Chaos*, since the Fiend pass'd through, Par Lost 10.233
Wide open and unguarded, *Satan* pass'd, Par Lost 10.419
Of lowest order, past; and from the dore Par Lost 10.443
Blow'n vagabond or frustrate: in they passd Par Lost 11.16

Passed(*cont*)
And while the dread of judgement past remains Par Lost 12.14
Full forty days he pass'd, whether on hill Par Reg 1.303
Recalling what remarkably had pass'd Par Reg 2.106
He slightly view'd, and slightly over-pass'd; Par Reg 2.198
Where will this end? four times ten days I have pass'd Par Reg 2.245
When to the promis'd land thir Fathers pass'd; Par Reg 3.439
Thus pass'd the night so foul till morning fair Par Reg 4.426
These reasons in Loves law have past for good, Samson 811
And as I past, I worshipt; if those you seek Mask 302
And past from *Pharian* fields to *Canaan* Land, Psalm 114, 3
When as he pass'd through Aegypt land; Psalm 81, 19
Then past hee to a flowry Mountaine greene, Prose 4, 1
Passenger
Threats the forlorn and wandring Passinger. Mask 39
Trinity ms 'passinger'
Bridgewater ms 'passinger'
Passes
To know what passes there; be lowlie wise: Par Lost 8.173
And as he passes turn, Lycidas 21
Passes to bliss at the mid hour of night, Sonnet 9, 13
Trinity ms 'passes to' ←'opens the dore of'
Passing
I then was passing to my former state Par Lost 8.290
But least the difficultie of passing back Par Lost 10.252
Glar'd on him passing: these were from without Par Lost 10.714
Rape or Adulterie, where passing faire Par Lost 11.717
Ur of *Chaldaea*, passing now the Ford Par Lost 12.130
Many are in each Region passing fair Par Reg 2.155
And at their passing cleave the *Assyrian* flood, Par Reg 3.436
Either at home, or through the high street passing, Samson 1458
Then passing through the Spheres of watchful fire, Vacation 40
Passion
Signs of remorse and passion to behold Par Lost 1.605
Passion and Apathie, and glory and shame, Par Lost 2.564
Thus while he spake, each passion dimm'd his face Par Lost 4.114
Transported touch; here passion first I felt, Par Lost 8.530
The Soule of Man, or passion in him move. Par Lost 8.585
In loving thou dost well, in passion not, Par Lost 8.588
His great command; take heed least Passion sway Par Lost 8.635
His bursting passion into plaints thus pour'd: Par Lost 9.98
New part puts on, and as to passion mov'd, Par Lost 9.667
Of Passion, I to them had quitted all, Par Lost 10.627
And in a troubl'd Sea of passion tost, Par Lost 10.718
Soft words to his fierce passion she assay'd: Par Lost 10.865
Repuls't, without much inward passion felt Samson 1006
And calm of mind all passion spent. Samson 1758
There held in holy passion still, Penseroso 41
Passions
Whose wanton passions in the sacred Porch Par Lost 1.454
Alien from Heav'n, with passions foul obscur'd: Par Lost 4.571
Began to rise, high Passions, Anger, Hate, Par Lost 9.1123
And upstart Passions catch the Government Par Lost 12.88
Passions, Desires, and Fears, is more a King; Par Reg 2.467
Or lawless passions in him which he serves. Par Reg 2.472
High actions, and high passions best describing: Par Reg 4.266
Passive
Made passive both, had servd necessitie, Par Lost 3.110
Thir march was, and the passive Air upbore Par Lost 6.72
Past
Of knowledge past or present, could have fear'd, Par Lost 1.628
Beatitude past utterance; on his right Par Lost 3.62
Wherein past, present, future he beholds, Par Lost 3.78
Father, thy word is past, man shall find grace; Par Lost 3.227
Of all past Ages to the general Doom Par Lost 3.328
Beyond the *Cape of Hope*, and now are past Par Lost 4.160
Present, or past, as Saints and Patriarchs us'd. Par Lost 4.762
From hard assaies and ill successes past Par Lost 4.932
Works of day pass't, or morrows next designe, Par Lost 5.33
Ill matching words and deeds long past or late. Par Lost 5.113
By present, past, and future) on such day Par Lost 5.582
Second Omnipotence, two dayes are past, Par Lost 6.684
Two dayes are therefore past, the third is thine; Par Lost 6.699
By what is past, to thee I have reveal'd Par Lost 6.895
But past who can recall, or don undoe? Par Lost 9.926
Might suddenly inflict; that past, return'd Par Lost 10.341
Beyond all past example and future, Par Lost 10.840
Is past, and we shall live. Whence Haile to thee, Par Lost 11.158
Of peaceful dayes portends, then those two past; Par Lost 11.600
Grievous to bear: but that care now is past, Par Lost 11.776
And while the dread of judgement past remains Par Lost 12.14
With cause for evils past, yet much more cheer'd Par Lost 12.604
Accompanied of things past and to come Par Reg 1.300
All these the *Parthian*, now some Ages past, Par Reg 3.294
Thir Gods ridiculous, and themselves past shame. Par Reg 4.342
Who knowing I shall raign past thy preventing, Par Reg 4.492
Times past, what once I was, and what am now. Samson 22
As one past hope, abandon'd, Samson 120
Of highest favours past Samson 685
Misguided; only what remains past cure Samson 912
Sam. Be less abstruse, my riddling days are past. Samson 1064
Return *Alpheus*, the dread voice is past, Lycidas 132
Pastime
Find pastime, and beare rule; thy Realm is large. Par Lost 8.375
Pastimes
Their merry wakes and pastimes keep: Mask 121
Pastoral
Charm'd with *Arcadian* Pipe, the Pastoral Reed Par Lost 11.132

Pastoral(*cont*)
Or sound of pastoral reed with oaten stops, Mask 345
Trinity ms 'pastorall'
Bridgewater ms 'pastorall'
Pastry
In pastry built, or from the spit, or boyl'd, Par Reg 2.343
Pasture
Coucht, and now fild with pasture gazing sat, Par Lost 4.351
Graze the Sea weed thir pasture, and through Groves Par Lost 7.404
Pastured
Where Cattle pastur'd late, now scatterd lies Par Lost 11.653
Tending my flocks hard by i' th hilly crofts, Mask 531
Trinity ms 'hillie' ←'pastur'd'
Pastures
With herds the pastures throng'd, with flocks the hills, Par Reg 3.260
To morrow to fresh Woods, and Pastures new. Lycidas 193
Trinity ms 'pasturs'
1638 'pastures'
Pasturing
Pasturing at once, and in broad Herds upsprung. Par Lost 7.462
Shelters in coole, and tends his pasturing Herds Par Lost 9.1109
Paternal
The Chariot of Paternal Deitie, Par Lost 6.750
Uplifted, in Paternal Glorie rode Par Lost 7.219
With goodness and paternal Love, his Face Par Lost 11.353
Under paternal rule; till one shall rise Par Lost 12.24
Path
What readiest path leads where your gloomie bounds Par Lost 2.976
All path of Man or Beast that past that way: Par Lost 4.177
Of erring, from the path of truth remote: Par Lost 6.173
Not unagreeable, to found a path Par Lost 10.256
Ascend, I follow thee, safe Guide, the path Par Lost 11.371
So far from path or road of men, who pass Par Reg 1.322
It were a journey like the path to Heav'n, Mask 303
Strait follow'd thee the path that Saints have trod Sonnet 14, Tr. ms 41.06
Pathless
A pathless Desert, dusk with horrid shades; Par Reg 1.296
Through the Heav'ns wide pathles way; Penseroso 70
Paths
These paths & Bowers doubt not but our joynt hands Par Lost 9.244
Paths indirect, or in the mid way faint! Par Lost 11.631
The paths of righteousness, how much more safe, Par Lost 11.814
Lies through the perplex't paths of this drear Wood, Mask 37
Through paths, and turnings oft'n trod by day, Mask 569
Sea-paths in shoals do slide. And know no dearth. Psalm 8, 22
Patience
With stubborn patience as with triple steel. Par Lost 2.569
All patience. He who therefore can invent Par Lost 6.464
Of Patience and Heroic Martyrdom Par Lost 9.32
True patience, and to temper joy with fear Par Lost 11.361
Add vertue, Patience, Temperance, add Love, Par Lost 12.583
With all inflictions, but his patience won? Par Reg 1.426
But I to wait with patience am inur'd; Par Reg 2.102
By patience, temperance; I mention still Par Reg 3.92
Him whom thy wrongs with Saintly patience born, Par Reg 3.93
Extolling Patience as the truest fortitude; Samson 654
Her husband, how far urg'd his patience bears, Samson 755
But patience is more oft the exercise Samson 1287
Whom Patience finally must crown. Samson 1296
Their faith, their patience, and their truth. Mask 971
Trinity ms 'patience' ←'temperance' ←'patience'
B.M. ms 'Patience'
And render him with patience what he lent; Fair Inf 75
I fondly ask; But patience to prevent Sonnet 19, 8
Patient
Who names not now with honour patient *Job*? Par Reg 3.95
O patient Son of God, yet only stoodst Par Reg 4.420
He patient but undaunted where they led him, Samson 1623
Patiently
If patiently thy bidding they obey, Par Lost 11.112
Lament not *Eve*, but patiently resigne Par Lost 11.287
Of rendring up, and patiently attend Par Lost 11.551
phrase not in 1667 edition
To whom thus Jesus patiently reply'd; Par Reg 2.432
Patriarch
To whom the Patriarch of mankind repli'd, Par Lost 5.506
So spake the Patriarch of Mankinde, but *Eve* Par Lost 9.376
While yet the Patriark liv'd, who scap'd the Flood, Par Lost 12.117
Plainlier shall be reveald. This Patriarch blest, Par Lost 12.151
Patriarchs
Present, or past, as Saints and Patriarchs us'd. Par Lost 4.762
Patrimony
Posteritie stands curst: Fair Patrimonie Par Lost 10.818
Who freed, as to thir antient Patrimony, Par Reg 3.428
For his redemption all my Patrimony, Samson 1482
Patron
Patron or Intercessor none appeerd, Par Lost 3.219
Patron of liberty, who more then thou Par Lost 4.958
Patroness
Of my Celestial Patroness, who deignes Par Lost 9.21
Befriend me night best Patroness of grief, Passion 29
Patrons
Patrons of Mankind, Gods, and Sons of Gods, Par Lost 11.696
Pattern
Pattern of just equalitie perhaps Par Lost 7.487
Paul
Would have been held in high esteem with *Paul* Forcers 10

Pause
He views in bredth, and without longer pause Par Lost 3.561
After short pause assenting, thus began. Par Lost 5.562
Destruction to the rest: this pause between Par Lost 6.162
Let *Euclid* rest and *Archimedes* pause, Sonnet 21, 7
Paused
This said he paus'd not, but with ventrous Arme Par Lost 5.64
Though bent on speed, so heer th' Arch-angel paus'd Par Lost 12.2
line not in 1667 edition
So spake th' Archangel *Michael*, then paus'd, Par Lost 12.466
Pausing
Pausing a while, thus to her self she mus'd. Par Lost 9.744
Paved
Pav'd after him a broad and beat'n way Par Lost 2.1026
In progress through the rode of Heav'n Star-pav'd. Par Lost 4.976
By Sin and Death a broad way now is pav'd Par Lost 10.473
From thy coral-pav'n bed, Mask 886
Trinity ms 'corall-paven' ← 'corall-paved'
Pavement
The riches of Heav'ns pavement, trod'n Gold, Par Lost 1.682
And level pavement: from the arched roof Par Lost 1.726
Pavement that like a Sea of Jasper shon Par Lost 3.363
And pavement Starrs, as Starrs to thee appeer, Par Lost 7.578
Paven
From thy coral-pav'n bed, Mask 886
1637 'coral-paven'
Trinity ms 'corall-paven' ← 'corall-paved'
Bridgewater ms 'Corall paven'
Pavilion
Of *Chaos*, and his dark Pavilion spread Par Lost 2.960
Pavilioned
The field Pavilion'd with his Guardians bright; Par Lost 11.215
Pavilions
Pavilions numberless, and sudden reard, Par Lost 5.653
They pitch against me their Pavillions. Psalm 3, 18
Paw
Sporting the Lion rampd, and in his paw Par Lost 4.343
Grip't in each paw: When *Adam* first of men Par Lost 4.408
Besides what the grim Woolf with privy paw Lycidas 128
Helpe us to save free Conscience from the paw Sonnet 16, 13
Pawing
The Tawnie Lion, pawing to get free Par Lost 7.464
Pay
Som other able, and as willing, pay Par Lost 3.211
The easiest recompence, and pay him thanks, Par Lost 4.47
From thee thir Names, and pay thee fealtie Par Lost 8.344
We are by doom to pay; rather such acts Par Lost 10.1026
Shall perfet, and for these my Death shall pay. Par Lost 11.36
Thy gentle Ministers, who come to pay Par Reg 2.375
All Nations now to *Rome* obedience pay, Par Reg 4.80
As I deserve, pay on my punishment; Samson 489
To pay my underminers in thir coin. Samson 1204
Paying
So burthensome still paying, still to ow; Par Lost 4.53
Bitterly hast thou paid, and still art paying Samson 432
Paynim
Defi'd the best of *Panim* chivalry Par Lost 1.765
ms 'Paynim'
Both *Paynim*, and the Peers of *Charlemane*. Par Reg 3.343
Pays
By owing owes not, but still pays, at once Par Lost 4.56
Peace
Regions of sorrow, doleful shades, where peace Par Lost 1.65
Full Counsel must mature: Peace is despaird, Par Lost 1.660
ms 'peace'
Not peace: and after him thus *Mammon* spake. Par Lost 2.228
Advising peace: for such another Field Par Lost 2.292
What sit we then projecting peace and Warr? Par Lost 2.329
1667 'Peace'
Irreparable; tearms of peace yet none Par Lost 2.331
Voutsaf't or sought; for what peace will be giv'n Par Lost 2.332
Inflicted? and what peace can we return, Par Lost 2.335
Of heavenly Grace: and God proclaiming peace, Par Lost 2.499
Who first broke peace in Heav'n and Faith, till then Par Lost 2.690
Of anger shall remain, but peace assur'd, Par Lost 3.263
O thou in Heav'n and Earth the only peace Par Lost 3.274
From granting hee, as I from begging peace: Par Lost 4.104
Firm peace recoverd soon and wonted calm. Par Lost 5.210
Heav'ns blessed peace, and into Nature brought Par Lost 6.267
Peace and composure, and with open brest Par Lost 6.560
For joy of offerd peace: but I suppose Par Lost 6.617
And Warr so neer the Peace of God in bliss Par Lost 7.55
To future men, and in thir dwellings peace: Par Lost 7.183
Silence, ye troubl'd waves, and thou Deep, peace, Par Lost 7.216
From his surmise prov'd false, find peace within, Par Lost 9.333
Pernicious to thy Peace, chiefly assur'd Par Lost 9.981
And full of Peace, now tost and turbulent: Par Lost 9.1126
Devolv'd; though should I hold my peace, yet thou Par Lost 10.135
To Humane life, and houshold peace confound. Par Lost 10.908
His peace, and thus proceeded in her plaint. Par Lost 10.913
Between us two let there be peace, both joyning, Par Lost 10.924
Immoveable till peace obtain'd from fault Par Lost 10.938
The smell of peace toward Mankinde, let him live Par Lost 11.38
So send them forth, though sorrowing, yet in peace: Par Lost 11.117
That I was heard with favour; peace returnd Par Lost 11.153
Glad to be so dismist in peace. Can thus Par Lost 11.507
Freedom and Peace to men: they on the Plain Par Lost 11.580
Of Justice, of Religion, Truth and Peace, Par Lost 11.667
Peace*(cont)*
All would have then gon well, peace would have crownd Par Lost 11.781
Peace to corrupt no less then Warr to waste. Par Lost 11.784
Raise out of friendship hostil deeds in Peace. Par Lost 11.796
And full of peace, denouncing wrauth to come Par Lost 11.815
Betok'ning peace from God, and Cov'nant new. Par Lost 11.867
Long time in peace by Families and Tribes Par Lost 12.23
Justification towards God, and peace Par Lost 12.296
National interrupt thir public peace, Par Lost 12.317
Endeavour Peace: thir strife pollution brings Par Lost 12.355
Founded in righteousness and peace and love Par Lost 12.550
1669 'Peace'
Greatly in peace of thought, and have my fill Par Lost 12.558
And all the flourishing works of peace destroy, Par Reg 3.80
By deeds of peace, by wisdom eminent, Par Reg 3.91
Sat'st unappall'd in calm and sinless peace. Par Reg 4.425
But peace, I must not quarrel with the will Samson 60
For peace, reap nothing but repulse and hate? Samson 966
Happy that house! his way to peace is smooth: Samson 1049
Comes he in peace? what wind hath blown him hither Samson 1070
His habit carries peace, his brow defiance. Samson 1073
Sam. Or peace or not, alike to me he comes. Samson 1074
Sam. My self? my conscience and internal peace. Samson 1334
Man. Peace with you brethren; my inducement hither Samson 1445
With peace and consolation hath dismist, Samson 1757
Eld. Bro. Peace brother, be not over-exquisite Mask 359
line not in Trinity ms
line not in Bridgewater ms
And the sweet peace that goodnes boosoms ever, Mask 368
& darknesse wound her in. I Bro. Peace, brother peace Mask Tr. ms 15.53
In weeds of Peace high triumphs hold, Allegro 120
And joyn with thee calm Peace, and Quiet, Penseroso 45
And bid fair peace be to my sable shrowd. Lycidas 22
And with his Father work us a perpetual peace. Nativity 7
Sent down the meek-eyd Peace, Nativity 46
She strikes a universall Peace through Sea and Land. Nativity 52
His raign of peace upon the earth began: Nativity 63
And peace shall lull him in her flowry lap; Vacation 84
With Truth, and Peace, and Love shall ever shine On Time 16
Peace and quiet ever have; Winchester 48
Up to the Realm of peace & Joy for ever, Sonnet 14, Tr. ms 41.08
To peace and truth thy glorious way hast plough'd, Sonnet 16, 4
1694 'Peace'
To conquer still; peace hath her victories Sonnet 16, 10
1694 'Peace'
Whether to settle peace or to unfold Sonnet 17, 5
1694 'Peace'
In peace, and reck'ns thee her eldest son. Sonnet 17, 14
word not in 1694 text
And be at peace within. Psalm 4, 22
In peace at once will I Psalm 4, 37
Ill to him that meant me peace, Psalm 7, 10
O God hold not thy peace, Psalm 83, 2
God of our saving health and peace, Psalm 85, 13
For to his people he speaks peace Psalm 85, 31
To his dear Saints he will speak peace, Psalm 85, 33
Sweet Peace and Righteousness have kiss'd Psalm 85, 43
Who neither can nor will, may hold his peace; Prose 9, 4
Peaceable
Peaceable Nations, neighbouring, or remote, Par Reg 3.76
Peaceful
Counsel'd ignoble ease, and peaceful sloath, Par Lost 2.227
To peaceful Counsels, and the settl'd State Par Lost 2.279
And thus with peaceful words uprais'd her soon. Par Lost 10.946
Of peaceful dayes portends, then those two past; Par Lost 11.600
His labours, for thou canst, to peaceful end. Samson 709
Find out the peacefull hermitage, Penseroso 168
But peacefull was the night Nativity 61
Peal
A hideous Peal: yet, when they list, would creep, Par Lost 2.656
Shall hast'n, such a peal shall rouse thir sleep. Par Lost 3.329
Who vanquisht with a peal of words (O weakness!) Samson 235
Pealed
He had to cross. Nor was his eare less peal'd Par Lost 2.920
Pealing
There let the pealing Organ blow, Penseroso 161
Peals
Witness when I was worried with thy peals. Samson 906
Pearl
Showrs on her Kings *Barbaric* Pearl and Gold, Par Lost 2.4
Of Jasper, or of liquid Pearle, whereon Par Lost 3.519
Rowling on Orient Pearl and sands of Gold, Par Lost 4.238
Advancing, sow'd the earth with Orient Pearle, Par Lost 5.2
In Pearl, in Diamond, and massie Gold, Par Reg 2.634
And studs of Pearl, to me should'st tell who thirst Par Reg 4.120
But this is got by casting Pearl to Hoggs; Sonnet 12, 8
Trinity ms 'pearle' ← 'peal' ← 'pearl'
Pearled
Held up their pearled wrists and took her in, Mask 834
Bridgewater ms 'peackled'
Trinity ms 'pearled' ← 'white'
So mounting up in ycie-pearled carr, Fair Inf 15
Pearls
And those Pearls of dew she wears, Winchester 43
Pearly
Cover'd with pearly grain: yet God hath here Par Lost 5.430
Or in thir Pearlie shells at ease, attend Par Lost 7.407

Peasant
Or Fountain some belated Peasant sees, Par Lost 1.783
ms 'peasant'
Pebbles
As Children gathering pibles on the shore. Par Reg 4.330
Peccant
As how with peccant Angels late they saw; Par Lost 11.70
Pechora
Beyond *Petsora* Eastward, to the rich Par Lost 10.292
Peculiar
Some I have chosen of peculiar grace Par Lost 3.183
Shot forth peculiar Graces; then with voice Par Lost 5.15
Thir small peculiar, though from human sight Par Lost 7.368
And one peculiar Nation to select Par Lost 12.111
Nor lightens aught each mans peculiar load. Par Reg 1.402
While each peculiar power forgoes his wonted seat. Nativity 196
Peeling
Peeling thir Provinces, exhausted all Par Reg 4.136
Peep
From her cabin'd loop hole peep, Mask 140
Trinity ms 'peepe'
Bridgewater ms 'peepe'
1637 'peepe'
Peer
A noble Peer of mickle trust, and power Mask 31
Trinity ms 'peere'
Bridgewater ms 'Peere'
1637 'Peere'
Young *Lycidas*, and hath not left his peer: Lycidas 9
1638 'peere'
Trinity ms 'peere'
Peerage
When *Charlemain* with all his Peerage fell Par Lost 1.586
ms 'peerage'
Peering
And leave her dolorous mansions to the peering day. Nativity 140
Peerless
Apparent Queen unvaild her peerless light, Par Lost 4.608
The peerles height of her immortal praise, Arcades 75
Trinity ms 'peerelesse'
Peers
To set himself in Glory above his Peers, Par Lost 1.39
ms 'peeres'
With all his Peers: attention held them mute. Par Lost 1.618
ms 'peeres'
Of Satan and his Peers: thir summons call'd Par Lost 1.757
ms 'peers'
I should be much for open Warr, O Peers, Par Lost 2.119
But I should ill become this Throne, O Peers, Par Lost 2.445
In order came the grand infernal Peers, Par Lost 2.507
In place thy self so high above thy Peeres. Par Lost 5.812
So pondering, and from his armed Peers Par Lost 6.127
Forth rush'd in haste the great consulting Peers, Par Lost 10.456
To Councel summons all his mighty Peers, Par Reg 1.40
Both *Paynim*, and the Peers of *Charlemane*. Par Reg 3.343
Pegasean
Above the flight of *Pegasean* wing. Par Lost 7.4
Peking
To *Paquin* of *Sinaean* Kings, and thence Par Lost 11.390
Pellean
Remember that *Pellean* Conquerour, Par Reg 2.196
Pelleas
Lancelot or *Pelleas*, or *Pellenore*, Par Reg 2.361
Pellenore
Lancelot or *Pelleas*, or *Pellenore*, Par Reg 2.361
Pelops
Presenting *Thebs*, or *Pelops* line, Penseroso 99
Pelorus
Torn from *Pelorus*, or the shatter'd side Par Lost 1.232
ms 'Pelorus'
Pen
Watching where Shepherds pen thir Flocks at eeve Par Lost 4.185
Slip't from the fold, or young Kid lost his dam, Mask 498
Trinity ms 'fold' ←'penne'
Penal
In Adamantine Chains and penal Fire, Par Lost 1.48
ms 'penall'
Thy penal forfeit from thy self; perhaps Samson 508
Penalty
Death is the penaltie impos'd, beware, Par Lost 7.545
Of God or Death, of Law or Penaltie? Par Lost 9.775
Incurr'd, what could they less, the penaltie, Par Lost 10.15
Sufficient penaltie, why hast thou added Par Lost 10.753
The penaltie pronounc't, doubt not but God Par Lost 10.1022
From penaltie, because from death releast Par Lost 11.197
On penaltie of death, and suffering death, Par Lost 12.398
The penaltie to thy transgression due, Par Lost 12.399
Penance
Calls us to Penance? More destroy'd then thus Par Lost 2.92
Thir penance, laden with Fruit, like that Par Lost 10.550
My penance hath not slack'n'd, though my pardon Samson 738
Pencil
By Model, or by shading Pencil drawn. Par Lost 3.509
Pendent
Pendant by suttle Magic many a row Par Lost 1.727
This pendant world, in bigness as a Starr Par Lost 2.1052
With mazie error under pendant shades Par Lost 4.239
Pontifical, a ridge of pendent Rock Par Lost 10.313
Pendulous
The pendulous round Earth with ballanc't Aire Par Lost 4.1000
Penetration
With gentle penetration, though unseen, Par Lost 3.585
Penitent
So spake our Father penitent, nor *Eve* Par Lost 10.1097
From whom as oft he saves them penitent Par Lost 12.319
Humbled themselves, or penitent besought Par Reg 3.421
Man. Be penitent and for thy fault contrite, Samson 502
Not truly penitent, but chief to try Samson 754
The penitent, but ever to forgive, Samson 761
Penned
The folded flocks pen'd in their watled cotes, Mask 344
Pennons
Fluttring his pennons vain plumb down he drops Par Lost 2.933
The Dank, and rising on stiff Pennons, towre Par Lost 7.441
Pens
They summ'd thir Penns, and soaring th' air sublime Par Lost 7.421
Pensioners
The fickle Pensioners of *Morpheus* train. Penseroso 10
Pensive
Without my op'ning. Pensive here I sat Par Lost 2.777
Satan had journied on, pensive and slow; Par Lost 4.173
Pensive I sate me down; there gentle sleep Par Lost 8.287
The Pensive secrecy of desert cell, Mask 387
1673 'pensive'
Trinity ms 'pensive'
Bridgewater ms 'pensive'
Com pensive Nun, devout and pure, Penseroso 31
With Cowslips wan that hang the pensive hed, Lycidas 147
In pensive trance, and anguish, and ecstatick fit. Passion 42
Pent
Into thir substance pent, which wrought them pain Par Lost 6.657
As one who long in populous City pent, Par Lost 9.445
As with the force of winds and waters pent, Samson 1647
Or straggling weather the pen't flock forsook? Mask 499
Bridgewater ms 'pent'
And I here pent up thus. Psalm 88, 36
Pentateuch
The *Pentateuch* or what the Prophets wrote, Par Reg 4.226
Penuel
How *Succoth* and the Fort of *Penuel* Samson 278
Penurious
As a penurious niggard of his wealth, Mask 726
People
Th' ethereal People ran, to hear and know Par Lost 10.27
His people from enthralment, they return Par Lost 12.171
And all his people; Thunder mixt with Haile, Par Lost 12.181
Of Law, his people into *Canaan* lead; Par Lost 12.309
His people, who defend? will they not deale Par Lost 12.483
Thy Glory, free thy people from thir yoke, Par Reg 2.48
The peoples praise, if always praise unmixt? Par Reg 3.48
And what the people but a herd confus'd, Par Reg 3.49
A victor people free from servile yoke? Par Reg 4.102
That people victor once, now vile and base, Par Reg 4.132
This day a solemn Feast the people hold Samson 12
To set his people free, Samson 317
And peoples safety, which in part they effect: Samson 681
Quite from his people, and delivered up Samson 1158
No less the people on thir Holy-days Samson 1421
Chor. Doubtless the people shouting to behold Samson 1473
For his people of old; what hinders now? Samson 1533
Samson should be brought forth to shew the people Samson 1601
At sight of him the people with a shout Samson 1620
As the gay motes that people the Sun Beams, Penseroso 8
His chosen people he did bless Psalm 136, 57
Thy blessing on thy people flows. Psalm 3, 24
All people from the worlds foundation. Psalm 7, 30
Against thy peoples praire. Psalm 80, 20
Hear O my people, *heark'n well*, Psalm 81, 33
And yet my people would not *hear*, Psalm 81, 45
O that my people would *be wise* Psalm 81, 53
But *they, his People, should remain*, Psalm 81, 63
Against thy people they contrive Psalm 83, 9
That wrought thy people woe, Psalm 85, 6
That so thy people may rejoyce Psalm 85, 23
For to his people he speaks peace Psalm 85, 31
Now void, it fitts thy people; thether bend Prose 12, 10
Peopled
Creator wise, that peopl'd highest Heav'n Par Lost 10.889
Peor
Peor his other Name, when he entic'd Par Lost 1.412
ms 'Peor'
Peor, and *Baalim*, Nativity 197
Peraea
Or in *Perea*, but return'd in vain. Par Reg 2.24
Perceive
Nor did they not perceave the evil plight Par Lost 1.335
ms 'perceive'
Perceive thee purpos'd not to doom frail Man Par Lost 3.404
Such as we might perceive amus'd them all, Par Lost 6.623
Sated at length, ere long I might perceave Par Lost 9.598
Much thou hast yet to see, but I perceave Par Lost 12.8
Not once perceive their foul disfigurement, Mask 74
Trinity ms 'perceave'
Too well I did perceive it was the voice Mask 563
Trinity ms 'perceave'

Perceived
Which when *Beelzebub* perceiv'd, then whom, Par Lost 2.299
Warr he perceav'd, warr in procinct, and found Par Lost 6.19
When I perceiv'd all set on enmity, Samson 1201
Perceivest
Less excellent, as thou thy self perceav'st. Par Lost 8.566
Perceiving
Perceaving where she sat retir'd in sight, Par Lost 8.41
These growing thoughts my Mother soon perceiving Par Reg 1.227
Her importunity, each time perceiving Samson 397
Perched
Assailant on the perched roosts, Samson 1693
Perdition
To bottomless perdition, there to dwell Par Lost 1.47
To turn Swift-rushing black perdition hence, Fair Inf 67
Or they *who* in perdition *dwell* Psalm 88, 47
Perfect
In perfect *Phalanx* to the *Dorian* mood Par Lost 1.550
ms 'perfet'
Thy self in me thy perfect image viewing Par Lost 2.764
Uriel, no wonder if thy perfet sight, Par Lost 4.577
To whom thus *Eve* with perfet beauty adornd. Par Lost 4.634
All perfet good unmeasur'd out, descends, Par Lost 5.399
Metals of drossiest Ore to perfet Gold Par Lost 5.442
God made thee perfet, not immutable; Par Lost 5.524
And perfet while they stood; how last unfould Par Lost 5.568
Thir perfet ranks; for high above the ground Par Lost 6.71
But pain is perfet miserie, the worst Par Lost 6.462
Innumerous living Creatures, perfet formes, Par Lost 7.455
Thou in thy self art perfet, and in thee Par Lost 8.415
Perfet within, no outward aid require; Par Lost 8.642
And life more perfet have attaind then Fate Par Lost 9.689
What seemd in thee so perfet, that I thought Par Lost 9.1179
And gav'st me as thy perfet gift, so good, Par Lost 10.138
Shall perfet, and for these my Death shall pay. Par Lost 11.36
For one Man found so perfet and so just, Par Lost 11.876
A perfect Dove descend, what e're it meant, Par Reg 1.83
This perfect Man, by merit call'd my Son, Par Reg 1.166
Conteins of good, wise, just, the perfect shape. Par Reg 3.11
Wise, perfect in himself, and all possessing Par Reg 4.302
The perfet season offer'd with my aid Par Reg 4.468
In perfet thraldom, how again betray me, Samson 946
And they, so perfect is their misery, Mask 73
Was rife, and perfet in my list'ning ear, Mask 203
1637 'perfect'
Trinity ms 'perfect'
line not in Bridgewater ms
And perfet witnes of all-judging *Jove;* Lycidas 82
Trinity ms 'perfect'
1638 'perfect'
Full and perfect is, Nativity 166
1673 'perfet'
Most perfect *Heroe*, try'd in heaviest plight Passion 13
In perfect Diapason, whilst they stood Musick 23
1673 'perfet'
Here be tears of perfect moan Winchester 55
Perfection
Perfection from the Suns more potent Ray. Par Lost 4.673
My Glorie, my Perfection, glad I see Par Lost 5.29
Such to perfection, one first matter all, Par Lost 5.472
Of thy perfection, how shall I attaine, Par Lost 9.964
And for thee, whose perfection farr excell'd Par Lost 10.150
Of absolute perfection, therein Man Par Lost 10.483
To such perfection, that e're yet my age Par Reg 1.209
What of perfection can in man be found, Par Reg 3.230
Perfections
Perfections, in himself was all his state, Par Lost 5.353
With all perfections, so enflame my sense Par Lost 9.1031
Perfections absolute, Graces divine, Par Reg 2.138
Perfectly
Yet are but dim, shall perfetly be then Par Lost 9.707
And perfectly divine, On Time 15
Perfidious
While with perfidious hatred they pursu'd Par Lost 1.308
In this perfidious fraud, contagion spred Par Lost 5.880
It was that fatall and perfidious Bark Lycidas 100
Perform
And hands innumerable scarce perform. Par Lost 1.699
Have nothing merited, nor can performe Par Lost 4.418
This I perform, speak thou, and be it don: Par Lost 7.164
All I receav'd, unable to performe Par Lost 10.750
Perform, and not performing cannot live. Par Lost 12.299
But thou canst best perform that office where thou art. Fair Inf 70
Performance
Of my performance: What remains, ye Gods, Par Lost 10.502
Performed
Warr wearied hath perform'd what Warr can do, Par Lost 6.695
On the cleft Wood, and all due Rites perform'd. Par Lost 11.440
Thir Ministry perform'd, and race well run, Par Lost 12.505
And ruine *Adam*, and the exploit perform'd Par Reg 1.102
But let us wait; thus far he hath perform'd, Par Reg 2.49
Of thy prodigious might and feats perform'd Samson 1083
And had perform'd it if my known offence Samson 1218
To heave, pull, draw, or break, he still perform'd Samson 1626
I have perform'd, as reason was, obeying, Samson 1641
Performing
And in performing end us; what besides Par Lost 11.300
Perform, and not performing cannot live. Par Lost 12.299

Performs
Burns frore, and cold performs th' effect of Fire. Par Lost 2.595
Perfume
An Amber sent of odorous perfume Samson 720
Perfumes
Native perfumes, and whisper whence they stole Par Lost 4.158
Rose like a steam of rich distill'd Perfumes, Mask 556
Trinity ms 'perfumes'
Bridgewater ms 'perfumes'
1673 'perfumes'
Perhaps
Which oft times may succeed, so as perhaps Par Lost 1.166
Perhaps hath spent his shafts, and ceases now Par Lost 1.176
Thither, if but to pry, shall be perhaps Par Lost 1.655
His own invented Torments. But perhaps Par Lost 2.70
One day upon our heads; while we perhaps Par Lost 2.178
His anger, and perhaps thus farr remov'd Par Lost 2.211
To their defence who hold it: here perhaps Par Lost 2.362
Neerer our ancient Seat; perhaps in view Par Lost 2.394
That dismal world, if any Clime perhaps Par Lost 2.572
Perhaps our vacant room, though more remov'd, Par Lost 2.835
The Womb of nature and perhaps her Grave, Par Lost 2.911
There lands the Fiend, a spot like which perhaps Par Lost 3.588
To witness with thine eyes what some perhaps Par Lost 3.700
By thee, and more then half perhaps will reigne; Par Lost 4.112
Creatures of other mould, earth-born perhaps, Par Lost 4.360
Now laid perhaps asleep secure of harme. Par Lost 4.791
Of Heav'n perhaps, or all the Elements Par Lost 4.993
To us perhaps he brings, and will voutsafe Par Lost 5.312
The Earth to yield; unsavourie food perhaps Par Lost 5.401
And from these corporal nutriments perhaps Par Lost 5.496
The secrets of another world, perhaps Par Lost 5.569
The remedie; perhaps more valid Armes, Par Lost 6.438
Spare out of life perhaps, and not repine, Par Lost 6.460
Somwhat extravagant and wilde, perhaps Par Lost 6.616
What may no less perhaps availe us known, Par Lost 7.85
Pattern of just equalitie perhaps Par Lost 7.487
Numerous, and every Starr perhaps a World Par Lost 7.621
Hath left to thir disputes, perhaps to move Par Lost 8.77
Allotted there; and other Suns perhaps Par Lost 8.148
Stor'd in each Orb perhaps with some that live. Par Lost 8.152
My Storie, which perhaps thou hast not heard; Par Lost 8.205
Or from my side subducting, took perhaps Par Lost 8.536
Before had bin contriving, though perhaps Par Lost 9.139
Assist us: But if much converse perhaps Par Lost 9.247
Conjugal Love, then which perhaps no bliss Par Lost 9.263
May finde us both perhaps farr less prepar'd, Par Lost 9.381
Wonder not, sovran Mistress, if perhaps Par Lost 9.532
Mee thus, though importune perhaps, to come Par Lost 9.610
So ye shall die perhaps, by putting off Par Lost 9.713
And I perhaps am secret; Heav'n is high, Par Lost 9.811
Each thing on Earth; and other care perhaps Par Lost 9.813
And render me more equal, and perhaps, Par Lost 9.823
Perhaps thou shalt not Die, perhaps the Fact Par Lost 9.928
Or to thy self perhaps: hadst thou been there, Par Lost 9.1148
Matter of glorious trial; and perhaps Par Lost 9.1177
Stay his return perhaps over this Gulfe Par Lost 10.253
Encroaching *Eve* perhaps, had first the rule Par Lost 10.582
While yet we live, scarse one short hour perhaps, Par Lost 10.923
His Trumpet, heard in *Oreb* since perhaps Par Lost 11.74
When God descended, and perhaps once more Par Lost 11.75
Eve, now expect great tidings, which perhaps Par Lost 11.226
Perhaps thy Capital Seate, from whence had spred Par Lost 11.343
The World: in Spirit perhaps he also saw Par Lost 11.406
If *Adam* aught perhaps might interpose; Par Lost 12.4
line not in 1667 edition
I learn not yet, perhaps I need not know; Par Reg 1.292
Accomplish what they did, perhaps and more? Par Reg 2.452
Perhaps thou linger'st in deep thoughts detain'd Par Reg 3.227
Headlong would follow; and to thir Gods perhaps Par Reg 3.430
(For I have also heard, perhaps have read) Par Reg 4.116
Perhaps my enemies who come to stare Samson 112
At my affliction, and perhaps to insult, Samson 113
Thy penal forfeit from thy self; perhaps Samson 508
If these they scape, perhaps in poverty Samson 697
Though fond and reasonless to some perhaps; Samson 812
My name perhaps among the Circumcis'd Samson 975
As these perhaps, yet wish it had not been, Samson 1077
And yet perhaps more trouble is behind. Samson 1300
Sa. Perhaps thou shalt have cause to sorrow indeed. Samson 1347
To favour, and perhaps to set thee free. Samson 1412
I will not wish, lest it perhaps offend them Samson 1414
Prompt me; and they perhaps are not far off. Mask 229
Trinity ms 'perhapps'
Co. Perhaps fore-stalling night prevented them. Mask 285
Trinity ms 'perhapps'
Perhaps som cold bank is her boulster now Mask 353
Trinity ms 'perhaps' ← 'perhapps'
Wher perhaps som beauty lies, Allegro 79
Where thou perhaps under the whelming tide Lycidas 157
Trinity ms 'perhapps'
Perhaps their loves, or els their sheep, Nativity 91
Perhaps my semblance might deceive the truth, Sonnet 7, 5
Trinity ms 'Perhapps'
Peril
Through dark and desart wayes with peril gone Par Lost 3.544
And peril great provok't, who thus hath dar'd Par Lost 9.922
With peril great atchiev'd. Long were to tell Par Lost 10.469

Peril(*cont*)	
And here their tender age might suffer perill,	Mask 40
1673 'peril'	
she might be free from perill where she is	Mask Tr. ms 16.42
she might be free from perill where she is,	Mask Br. ms 395
Perilous	
In worst extreams, and on the perilous edge	Par Lost 1.276
The perilous attempt: but all sat mute,	Par Lost 2.420
Would draw thee forth to perilous enterprises,	Samson 804
Infamous Hills, and sandy perilous wildes,	Mask 424
1637 'perillous'	
Bridgewater ms 'perrilous'	
To all that wander in that perilous flood.	Lycidas 185
1638 'perillous'	
Trinity ms 'perilous' ←'perillous'	
Period	
As at the Worlds great period; and our Sire	Par Lost 12.467
Lean on it safely, not a period	Mask 585
Periods	
Periods of time, thence hurried back to fire.	Par Lost 2.603
Peripatetics	
Sirnam'd *Peripatetics*, and the Sect	Par Reg 4.279
Perish	
Can perish: for the mind and spirit remains	Par Lost 1.139
1667 'Perish'	
To perish rather, swallowd up and lost	Par Lost 2.149
As in him perish all men, so in thee	Par Lost 3.287
Which God inspir'd, cannot together perish	Par Lost 10.785
Grow up and perish, as the summer flie,	Samson 676
In anger and ye perish in the way	Psalm 2, 26
They perish at thy dreadfull ire,	Psalm 80, 67
Perished	
As if the whole inhabitation perish'd,	Samson 1512
Permission	
And high permission of all-ruling Heaven	Par Lost 1.212
With thy permission then, and thus forewarnd	Par Lost 9.378
Permission from above; thou canst not more.	Par Reg 1.496
Thou hast permission on me. It is written	Par Reg 4.175
Permissive	
By his permissive will, through Heav'n and Earth:	Par Lost 3.685
Permissive, and acceptance found, which gain'd	Par Lost 8.435
With what permissive glory since his fall	Par Lost 10.451
Permit	
Deitie for thee, when Fate will not permit.	Par Lost 9.885
Nay didst permit, approve, and fair dismiss.	Par Lost 9.1159
Live well, how long or short permit to Heav'n:	Par Lost 11.554
Vertue, who follow not her lore: permit me	Par Reg 1.483
Or if the Ayr will not permit,	Penseroso 77
Permits	
Then Heav'n permits, nor mine, though doubld now	Par Lost 4.1009
Permits not; to remove thee I am come,	Par Lost 11.260
Man till then free. Therefore since hee permits	Par Lost 12.90
Permitted	
This tumult, and permitted all, advis'd:	Par Lost 6.674
Till thir lost shape, permitted, they resum'd,	Par Lost 10.574
Permitted rather, and by thee usurp't,	Par Reg 4.183
Into thy Enemies hand, permitted them	Samson 1159
And I perswade me God had not permitted	Samson 1495
Permitting	
Rural repast, permitting him the while	Par Lost 9.4
Pernicious	
No wonder, fall'n such a pernicious highth.	Par Lost 1.282
Provide, pernicious with one touch to fire.	Par Lost 6.520
Glar'd lightning, and shot forth pernicious fire	Par Lost 6.849
Pernicious to thy Peace, chiefly assur'd	Par Lost 9.981
Which to no few of them would prove pernicious.	Samson 1400
Perpetual	
Fearless, endanger'd Heav'ns perpetual King;	Par Lost 1.131
ms 'perpetuall'	
And with perpetual inrodes to Allarme,	Par Lost 2.103
Lies dark and wilde, beat with perpetual storms	Par Lost 2.588
Here in perpetual agonie and pain,	Par Lost 2.861
Perpetual Fountain of Domestic sweets,	Par Lost 4.760
Perpetual Circle, multiform; and mix	Par Lost 5.182
Where light and darkness in perpetual round	Par Lost 6.6
Whence in perpetual fight they needs must last	Par Lost 6.693
Stream, and perpetual draw thir humid traine.	Par Lost 7.306
Perpetual smil'd on Earth with vernant Flours,	Par Lost 10.679
Perpetual banishment. Yet least they faint	Par Lost 11.108
And a perpetual feast of nectar'd sweets,	Mask 479
Bridgewater ms 'perpetuall'	
Trinity ms 'perpetuall'	
1637 'perpetuall'	
And with his Father work us a perpetual peace.	Nativity 7
Perpetuity	
To perpetuitie; Ay me, that fear	Par Lost 10.813
Perplex	
The better reason, to perplex and dash	Par Lost 2.114
If care of our descent perplex us most,	Par Lost 10.979
Perplexed	
Leads him perplext, where he may likeliest find	Par Lost 2.525
Of shrubs and tangling bushes had perplext	Par Lost 4.176
Perplex'd the *Greek* and *Cytherea*'s Son;	Par Lost 9.19
Erwhile perplext with thoughts what would becom	Par Lost 12.275
Perplex'd and troubl'd at his bad success	Par Reg 4.1
Lies through the perplex't paths of this drear Wood,	Mask 37
Trinity ms 'perplext'	
Bridgewater ms 'perplext'	
Perplexes	
Perplexes Monarchs. Dark'n'd so, yet shon	Par Lost 1.599
Perplexing	
The easiest way, nor with perplexing thoughts	Par Lost 8.183
Perplexities	
Till by thir own perplexities involv'd	Samson 304
Perplexity	
Into perplexity and new amaze:	Par Reg 2.38
Persecute	
For them that persecute.) Behold	Psalm 7, 50
Persecution	
Whence heavie persecution shall arise	Par Lost 12.531
Persecutors	
Thir proudest persecuters: for the Spirit	Par Lost 12.497
Persepolis	
Till *Cyrus* set them free; *Persepolis*	Par Reg 3.284
Perseverance	
Whose constant perseverance overcame	Par Reg 1.148
Persevere	
And good he made thee, but to persevere	Par Lost 5.525
Thir happiness, and persevere upright.	Par Lost 7.632
On all who in the worship persevere	Par Lost 12.532
Persevering	
I in thy persevering shall rejoyce,	Par Lost 8.639
Persian	
The *Persian* in *Ecbatan* sate, or since	Par Lost 11.393
And oft beyond; to South the *Persian* Bay,	Par Reg 3.273
Persisted	
Persisted, yet submiss, though last, repli'd.	Par Lost 9.377
I had persisted happie, had not thy pride	Par Lost 10.874
But they persisted deaf, and would not seem	Samson 249
Persisting	
And to the end persisting, safe arrive.	Par Lost 3.197
Person	
A fairer person lost not Heav'n; he seemd	Par Lost 2.110
To Person or to Poem. Mee of these	Par Lost 9.41
Much hee the Place admir'd, the Person more.	Par Lost 9.444
And person, had'st thou known thy self aright.	Par Lost 10.156
As of a person separate to God,	Samson 31
And Princes of my countrey came in person,	Samson 851
But I a private person, whom my Countrey	Samson 1208
I was no private but a person rais'd	Samson 1211
Lest som ill greeting touch attempt the person	Mask 406
Love, sweetness, goodness, in her person shin'd	Sonnet 23, 11
Personating	
In Fable, Hymn, or Song, so personating	Par Reg 4.341
Persons	
Of various persons each to know his part;	Par Reg 2.240
Persuade	
Main reason to perswade immediate Warr,	Par Lost 2.121
The worst, and not perswade thee rather die	Par Lost 9.979
Thou neither dost perswade me to seek wealth	Par Reg 3.44
And I perswade me so; why else this strength	Samson 586
And I perswade me God had not permitted	Samson 1495
Yet can I not perswade me thou art dead	Fair Inf 29
Persuaders	
Powerful perswaders, quick'nd at the scent	Par Lost 9.587
Persuasion	
Bending his eare; perswasion in me grew	Par Lost 11.152
And make perswasion do the work of fear;	Par Reg 1.223
Deceive ye to perswasion over-sure	Par Reg 2.142
Ruling them by perswasion as thou mean'st,	Par Reg 4.230
With studied argument, and much perswasion sought	Samson 658
Persuasive	
And with perswasive accent thus began.	Par Lost 2.118
Yet rung of his perswasive words, impregn'd	Par Lost 9.737
Perswasive, Virgin majesty with mild	Par Reg 2.159
So oft, and the perswasive Rhetoric	Par Reg 4.4
Persuasively	
Perswasively hath so prevaild, that I	Par Lost 9.873
Pert	
Trip the pert Fairies and the dapper Elves;	Mask 118
Perturbation	
Each perturbation smooth'd with outward calme,	Par Lost 4.120
And shame, and perturbation, and despaire,	Par Lost 10.113
Peru	
And *Cusco* in *Peru*, the richer seat	Par Lost 11.408
Perused	
My self I then perus'd, and Limb by Limb	Par Lost 8.267
Perus'd him, then with words thus utt'red spake.	Par Reg 1.320
Perverse	
Perverse, all monstrous, all prodigious things,	Par Lost 2.625
Of this frail World; by which the Spirits perverse	Par Lost 2.1030
Judg'd thee perverse: the easier conquest now	Par Lost 6.37
Our overture, and turn not back perverse;	Par Lost 6.562
And this perverse Commotion governd thus,	Par Lost 6.706
Of thy presum'd return! event perverse!	Par Lost 9.405
The onely righteous in a World perverse,	Par Lost 11.701
In the perverse event then I foresaw)	Samson 737
Perverseness	
In heav'nly Spirits could such perverseness dwell?	Par Lost 6.788
Through her perversness, but shall see her gaind	Par Lost 10.902
1667 'perverseness'	
Pervert	
Our labour must be to pervert that end,	Par Lost 1.164
By some false guile pervert; and shall pervert	Par Lost 3.92
While they pervert pure Natures healthful rules	Par Lost 11.523
How long will ye pervert the right	Psalm 82, 5

Perverted
Hee in the Serpent, had perverted *Eve*, Par Lost 10.3
Satan with his perverted World, then raise Par Lost 12.547
Perverts
The good before him, but perverts best things Par Lost 4.203
Pest
She spake, and at her words the hellish Pest Par Lost 2.735
Pestered
Confin'd, and pester'd in this pin-fold here, Mask 7
Bridgewater ms 'pestered'
Pestilence
Shakes Pestilence and Warr. Each at the Head Par Lost 2.711
Marasmus, and wide-wasting Pestilence, Par Lost 11.487
line not in 1667 edition
By three days Pestilence? such was thy zeal Par Reg 3.412
Or drive away the slaughtering pestilence, Fair Inf 68
Pestilent
Corrupt and Pestilent: Now from the North Par Lost 10.695
Pet
Should in a pet of temperance feed on Pulse, Mask 721
Peter
And now Saint *Peter* at Heav'ns Wicket seems Par Lost 3.484
Petition
Seem'd thir Petition, then when th' ancient Pair Par Lost 11.10
No long petition, speedy death, Samson 650
Petrific
Death with his Mace petrific, cold and dry, Par Lost 10.294
Petsora
Beyond *Petsora* Eastward, to the rich Par Lost 10.292
Petty
For such a petty Trespass, and not praise Par Lost 9.693
Shar'd among petty Kings too far remov'd; Par Reg 4.87
Fearless of danger, like a petty God Samson 529
As a petty enterprise of small enforce. Samson 1223
From a thousand petty rills, Mask 926
1637 'pettie'
Bridgewater ms 'pettie'
Phalanx
In perfect *Phalanx* to the *Dorian* mood Par Lost 1.550
ms 'Phalanx'
Thir Phalanx, and began to hemm him round Par Lost 4.979
In Cubic Phalanx firm advanc't entire, Par Lost 6.399
Phantasm
Me Father, and that Fantasm call'st my Son? Par Lost 2.743
Phantasms
Illusions as he list, Phantasms and Dreams, Par Lost 4.803
Pharaoh
That ore the Realm of impious *Pharaoh* hung Par Lost 1.342
ms 'Pharaoh'
Of *Pharao:* there he dies, and leaves his Race Par Lost 12.163
And in despight of *Pharao* fell, Psalm 136, 41
Pharian
And past from *Pharian* fields to *Canaan* Land, Psalm 114, 3
Pharpar
Of *Abbana* and *Pharphar*, lucid streams. Par Lost 1.469
ms 'Pharphar'
Pharphar
Of *Abbana* and *Pharphar*, lucid streams. Par Lost 1.469
ms 'Pharphar'
Philip
Of *Macedonian Philip* had e're these Par Reg 3.32
Philistean
Of *Philistean Dalilah*, and wak'd Par Lost 9.1061
Philistia
Philistia *full of scorn*, Psalm 87, 14
Philistine
Should *Israel* from *Philistian* yoke deliver; Samson 39
Himself in bonds under *Philistian* yoke; Samson 42
Why thou shouldst wed *Philistian* women rather Samson 216
The *Philistine*, thy Countries Enemy, Samson 238
To some *Philistian* Lords, with whom to treat Samson 482
Some rich *Philistian* Matron she may seem, Samson 722
Philistian gold: if weakness may excuse, Samson 831
To *Palestine*, won by a *Philistine* Samson 1099
Not dragging? the *Philistian* Lords command. Samson 1371
Of this but each *Philistian* City round Samson 1655
Through all *Philistian* bounds. To *Israel* Samson 1714
Philistines
Thir Lords the *Philistines* with gather'd powers Samson 251
This day the *Philistines* a popular Feast Samson 434
Man. Wilt thou then serve the *Philistines* with that gift Samson 577
Mine and Loves prisoner, not the *Philistines*, Samson 808
The *Philistines*, when thou hadst broke the league, Samson 1189
Sam. Among the Daughters of the *Philistines* Samson 1192
Chor. Yet with this strength thou serv'st the *Philistines*, Samson 1363
This evil on the *Philistines* is fall'n, Samson 1523
The Philistims, and they of Tyre Psalm 83, 27
Phillis
Which the neat-handed *Phillis* dresses; Allegro 86
Philomel
'Less *Philomel* will daign a Song, Penseroso 56
Philosophers
Philosophers in vain so long have sought, Par Lost 3.601
Philosophic
The Stoic last in Philosophic pride, Par Reg 4.300
Philosophy
Vain wisdom all, and false Philosophie: Par Lost 2.565
To sage Philosophy next lend thine ear, Par Reg 4.272

Philosophy(*cont*)
2. *Bro*. How charming is divine Philosophy! Mask 476
Trinity ms 'philosophy'
1637 'Philosophie'
Bridgewater ms 'philosophie'
Phineus
And *Tiresias* and *Phineus* Prophets old. Par Lost 3.36
Phlegethon
Heard on the ruful stream; fierce *Phlegeton* Par Lost 2.580
Phlegra
Of *Phlegra* with th' Heroic Race were joyn'd Par Lost 1.577
ms 'Phlegra'
Phoebus
Whose Poem *Phoebus* challeng'd for his own. Par Reg 4.260
To quench the drouth of *Phoebus*, which as they taste Mask 66
Bridgewater ms 'Phebus'
Rose from the hindmost wheels of *Phoebus* wain. Mask 190
line not in Bridgewater ms
Phoebus repli'd, and touch'd my trembling ears; Lycidas 77
1638 'Phebus'
To this Horizon is my *Phoebus* bound, Passion 23
To honour thee, the Priest of *Phoebus* Quire Sonnet 13, 10
Phoenicians
Came *Astoreth*, whom the *Phoenicians* call'd Par Lost 1.438
ms 'Phoenicians'
Phoenix
A *Phaenix*, gaz'd by all, as that sole Bird Par Lost 5.272
Phylacteries
Clip your Phylacteries, though bauk your Ears, Forcers 17
Phyllis
Which the neat-handed *Phillis* dresses; Allegro 86
Pick
But they must pick me out with shackles tir'd, Samson 1326
Pickaxe
Of Pioners with Spade and Pickax arm'd Par Lost 1.676
1667 'Pickaxe'
ms 'pick axe'
Picture
Picture the sacred wall declares t' have hung Horace 14
Pieces
To pieces, and orewhelm whatever stands Par Lost 6.489
Or as a stone that shall to pieces dash Par Reg 4.149
Pied
Meadows trim with Daisies pide, Allegro 75
Piemontese
Slayn by the bloody *Piemontese* that roll'd Sonnet 18, 7
Pierce
A sword shall pierce, this is my favour'd lot, Par Reg 2.91
Hitting thy aged ear should pierce too deep. Samson 1568
Such as the meeting soul may pierce Allegro 138
Will pierce more neer his heart. Circum 28
Trinity ms 'peirce'
Dead things with inbreath'd sense able to pierce, Musick 4
Trinity ms 'peirce' ←'pierce' ←'peirce'
Pierced
Where wounds of deadly hate have peirc'd so deep: Par Lost 4.99
And with fierce Ensignes pierc'd the deep array Par Lost 6.356
Imperishable, and though peirc'd with wound, Par Lost 6.435
So deep the power of these Ingredients pierc'd, Par Lost 11.417
Piercing
Become our Elements, these piercing Fires Par Lost 2.275
To find thy piercing ray, and find no dawn; Par Lost 3.24
Piety
Prefer, and Pietie to God, though then Par Lost 6.144
Is Pietie thus and pure Devotion paid? Par Lost 11.452
And fear of God, from whom thir pietie feign'd Par Lost 11.799
The second, both for pietie renownd Par Lost 12.321
Conferr'd upon me, for the piety Samson 993
Pilasters
Built like a Temple, where *Pilasters* round Par Lost 1.713
ms 'pilasters'
Pile
In wealth and luxurie. Th' ascending pile Par Lost 1.722
Of ancient pile; all else deep snow and ice, Par Lost 2.591
Of grassie Terfe, and pile up every Stone Par Lost 11.324
Her pile, far off appearing like a Mount Par Reg 4.547
Haughty as is his pile high-built and proud. Samson 1069
Piled
Of Alablaster, pil'd up to the Clouds, Par Lost 4.544
All *Autumn* pil'd, though *Spring* and *Autumn* here Par Lost 5.394
Tables are set, and on a sudden pil'd Par Lost 5.632
With dishes pil'd, and meats of noblest sort Par Reg 2.341
1671 printed 'pill'd', errata 'pil'd'
And hills of Snow and lofts of piled Thunder, Vacation 42
The labour of an age in piled Stones, Shakespear 2
Pilfering
Of pilfering Woolf, not all the fleecy wealth Mask 504
Bridgewater ms 'pilferinge'
Pilgrim
Came forth with Pilgrim steps in amice gray; Par Reg 4.427
Pilgrims
Here Pilgrims roam, that stray'd so farr to seek Par Lost 3.476
Pillar
A Pillar of State; deep on his Front engraven Par Lost 2.302
Before them in a Cloud, and Pillar of Fire, Par Lost 12.202
By day a Cloud, by night a Pillar of Fire, Par Lost 12.203
1667 'pillar'
Then through the Firey Pillar and the Cloud Par Lost 12.208

Pillared
About the Mother Tree, a Pillard shade — Par Lost 9.1106
As dangerous to the pillard frame of Heaven, — Par Reg 4.455
The pillar'd firmament is rott'nness, — Mask 598
Bridgewater ms 'pillard'
Pillars
Were set, and Doric pillars overlaid — Par Lost 1.714
Betwixt these rockie Pillars *Gabriel* sat — Par Lost 4.549
A triple mounted row of Pillars laid — Par Lost 6.572
On Wheels (for like to Pillars most they seem'd — Par Lost 6.573
Outside and inside both, pillars and roofs — Par Reg 4.58
Half round on two main Pillars vaulted high, — Samson 1606
Between the pillars; he his guide requested — Samson 1630
With both his arms on those two massie Pillars — Samson 1633
When Mountains tremble, those two massie Pillars — Samson 1648
With antick Pillars massy proof, — Penseroso 158
Pillows
Pillows his chin upon an Orient wave, — Nativity 231
Pilot
The Pilot of some small night-founder'd Skiff, — Par Lost 1.204
Or Pilot from amidst the *Cyclades* — Par Lost 5.264
Who like a foolish Pilot have shipwrack't, — Samson 198
What Pilot so expert but needs must wreck — Samson 1044
Would overtask the best Land-Pilots art, — Mask 309
Bridgewater ms 'land pilots'
1637 'land-pilots'
Trinity ms 'land-pilots'
The Pilot of the *Galilean* lake, — Lycidas 109
Trinity ms 'pylot'
Pinched
She was pincht, and pull'd she sed, — Allegro 103
Pinches
and often takes our cattell with strange pinches — Mask Tr. ms 23.51
Pinching
Avoided pinching cold and scorching heate? — Par Lost 10.691
Pindarus
The house of *Pindarus*, when Temple and Towre — Sonnet 8, 11
Pine
His Spear, to equal which the tallest Pine — Par Lost 1.292
ms 'pine'
Thir soft Ethereal warmth, and there to pine — Par Lost 2.601
Cedar, and Pine, and Firr, and branching Palm, — Par Lost 4.139
Of stateliest Covert, Cedar, Pine, or Palme, — Par Lost 9.435
To mee, who with eternal Famin pine, — Par Lost 10.597
Kindles the gummie bark of Firr or Pine, — Par Lost 10.1076
Above the Clouds will pine his entrails gross, — Par Lost 12.77
Of Pine, or monumental Oake, — Penseroso 135
For I am poor, and almost pine — Psalm 86, 3
Pined
Mine eyes till now, and pin'd with vain desire, — Par Lost 4.466
Vertue in her shape how lovly, saw, and pin'd — Par Lost 4.848
His Carcass, pin'd with hunger and with droughth? — Par Reg 1.325
Pines
Hath scath'd the Forrest Oaks, or Mountain Pines, — Par Lost 1.613
ms 'pines'
Through pain up by the roots *Thessalian* Pines, — Par Lost 2.544
Still unfulfill'd with pain of longing pines; — Par Lost 4.511
Breathe soft or loud; and wave your tops, ye Pines, — Par Lost 5.193
Half sunk with all his Pines. Amazement seis'd — Par Lost 6.198
And brown as Evening: Cover me ye Pines, — Par Lost 9.1088
Stood visible, among these Pines his voice — Par Lost 11.321
On the vext Wilderness, whose tallest Pines, — Par Reg 4.416
Under the spreading favour of these Pines, — Mask 184
Trinity ms 'pines'
Bridgewater ms 'pines'
If every just man that now pines with want — Mask 768
Bridgewater ms 'pynes'
Pinfold
Confin'd, and pester'd in this pin-fold here, — Mask 7
Bridgewater ms 'pinfold'
Trinity ms 'pinfold'
Pining
And Moon-struck madness, pining Atrophie, — Par Lost 11.486
line not in 1667 edition
Pink
The white Pink, and the Pansie freakt with jeat, — Lycidas 144
Trinity ms 'pinke'
1638 'pink'
Pinks
Of pancies, pinks, and gaudy Daffadils. — Mask 851
Trinity ms 'pinks' ←'and of'
Bridgewater ms 'pinkes'
Pinnace
Or Pinnace anchors in a craggy Bay — Par Lost 2.289
Pinnacle
There on the highest Pinacle he set — Par Reg 4.549
Pinnacles
With glistering Spires and Pinnacles adornd, — Par Lost 3.550
Pins
Of this round World: with Pinns of Adamant — Par Lost 10.318
Pioners
Of Pioners with Spade and Pickax arm'd — Par Lost 1.676
ms 'pioners'
Of Archers, nor of labouring Pioners — Par Reg 3.330
Pious
And pious awe, that feard to have offended. — Par Lost 5.135
And pious sorrow, equally enur'd — Par Lost 11.362
In pious Hearts, an inward Oracle — Par Reg 1.463

Pious(*cont*)
Bewail thy falshood, and the pious works — Samson 955
Pipe
Had work and rested not, the solemn Pipe, — Par Lost 7.595
Charm'd with *Arcadian* Pipe, the Pastoral Reed — Par Lost 11.132
And tuneable as Silvan Pipe or Song; — Par Reg 1.480
Who with his soft Pipe, and smooth-dittied Song, — Mask 86
Bridgewater ms 'pipe'
Trinity ms 'pipe'
Such as the jocond Flute, or gamesom Pipe — Mask 173
Bridgewater ms 'pipe'
Trinity ms 'pipe'
and gives thee praise above the pipe of Pan; — Sonnet 13, Tr. ms 40.06
Piped
The soothest Shepherd that ere pip't on plains. — Mask 823
Bridgewater ms 'pipt'
1637 'pipe't'
Pipes
Mov'd on in silence to soft Pipes that charm'd — Par Lost 1.561
ms 'pipes'
To many a row of Pipes the sound-board breaths. — Par Lost 1.709
ms 'pipes'
Of chiming strings, or charming pipes and winds — Par Reg 2.363
In thir state Livery clad; before him Pipes — Samson 1616
Grate on their scrannel Pipes of wretched straw, — Lycidas 124
Trinity ms 'pipes'
1638 'pipes'
Piping
While rocking Winds are Piping loud, — Penseroso 126
Pit
In equal ruin: into what Pit thou seest — Par Lost 1.91
ms 'pit'
The chief were those who from the Pit of Hell — Par Lost 1.381
ms 'pit'
For this Infernal Pit shall never hold — Par Lost 1.657
ms 'pit'
The key of this infernal Pit by due, — Par Lost 2.850
Back to th' infernal pit I drag thee chaind, — Par Lost 4.965
Burnt after them to the bottomless pit. — Par Lost 6.866
Triumphant out of this infernal Pit — Par Lost 10.464
He dig'd a pit, and delv'd it deep, — Psalm 7, 55
And fell into the pit he made, — Psalm 7, 56
Down to the *dismal* pit — Psalm 88, 14
Thou in the lowest pit *profound* — Psalm 88, 25
Pitch
Driv'n headlong from the Pitch of Heaven, down — Par Lost 2.772
Therefore from this high pitch let us descend — Par Lost 8.198
Man-slaughter, shall be held the highest pitch — Par Lost 11.693
Smeard round with Pitch, and in the side a dore — Par Lost 11.731
To lowest pitch of abject fortune thou art fall'n. — Samson 169
They pitch against me their Pavillions. — Psalm 3, 18
Pitched
Pitcht about *Sechem*, and the neighbouring Plaine — Par Lost 12.136
Pitchy
Wav'd round the Coast, up call'd a pitchy cloud — Par Lost 1.340
when the big rowling flakes of pitchie clowds — Mask Tr. ms 15.52
when the bigg rowling flakes of pitchie clouds — Mask Br. ms 345
Piteous
The Serpents head; piteous amends, unless — Par Lost 10.1032
Who piteous of her woes, rear'd her lank head, — Mask 836
He hath with a piteous eye — Psalm 136, 77
Pitied
Or pitied object, these redundant locks — Samson 568
Pity
So strictly, but much more to pitie encline: — Par Lost 3.402
So strictly, but much more to pitie enclin'd, — Par Lost 3.405
To you whom I could pittie thus forlorne — Par Lost 4.374
With pittie Heav'ns high King, and to him call'd — Par Lost 5.220
With pitie, violated not thir bliss. — Par Lost 10.25
Be open, and his heart to pitie incline, — Par Lost 10.1061
O pittie and shame, that they who to live well — Par Lost 11.629
Yet always pity or pardon hath obtain'd. — Samson 814
Sweet Queen of Parly, Daughter of the Sphear, — Mask 241
B.M. ms 'Queen of Pity'
Could Heav'n for pittie thee so strictly doom? — Fair Inf 33
No anger find in thee, but pity and ruth. — Sonnet 9, 8
Trinity ms 'pitty'
Now pity me, and hear my earnest prai'r. — Psalm 4, 6
Pity me Lord for I am much deject — Psalm 6, 3
Pitty me Lord for daily thee — Psalm 86, 9
Pitying
Remov'd farr off; then pittying how they stood — Par Lost 10.211
Cloath'd us unworthie, pitying while he judg'd; — Par Lost 10.1059
Placable
Methought I saw him placable and mild, — Par Lost 11.151
Place
Such place Eternal Justice had prepar'd — Par Lost 1.70
O how unlike the place from whence they fell! — Par Lost 1.75
A mind not to be chang'd by Place or Time. — Par Lost 1.253
ms 'place'
The mind is its own place, and in it self — Par Lost 1.254
Eternal spirits; or have ye chos'n this place — Par Lost 1.318
As this place testifies, and this dire change — Par Lost 1.625
By place or choice the worthiest; they anon — Par Lost 1.759
Will envy whom the highest place exposes — Par Lost 2.27
Heav'ns fugitives, and for thir dwelling place — Par Lost 2.57
Or chang'd at length, and to the place conformd — Par Lost 2.217
The latter: for what place can be for us — Par Lost 2.235

Place(*cont*)
We can create, and in what place so e're Par Lost 2.260
This place our dungeon, not our safe retreat Par Lost 2.317
Some easier enterprize? There is a place Par Lost 2.345
In his own strength, this place may lye expos'd Par Lost 2.360
To search with wandring quest a place foretold Par Lost 2.830
Created vast and round, a place of bliss Par Lost 2.832
And bring ye to the place where Thou and Death Par Lost 2.840
And time and place are lost; where eldest Night Par Lost 2.894
Confine with Heav'n; or if som other place Par Lost 2.977
And I will place within them as a guide Par Lost 3.194
Alone, for other Creature in this place Par Lost 3.442
The place he found beyond expression bright, Par Lost 3.591
Each had his place appointed, each his course, Par Lost 3.720
That place is Earth the seat of Man, that light Par Lost 3.724
By change of place: Now conscience wakes despair Par Lost 4.23
O then at last relent: is there no place Par Lost 4.79
Imbround the noontide Bowrs: Thus was this place, Par Lost 4.246
Your numerous ofspring; if no better place, Par Lost 4.385
Charge and strict watch that to this happie Place Par Lost 4.562
1667 'place'
On to thir blissful Bower; it was a place Par Lost 4.690
Ordaind by thee, and this delicious place Par Lost 4.729
Of puritie and place and innocence, Par Lost 4.745
Or think thee unbefitting holiest place, Par Lost 4.759
Thy sin and place of doom obscure and foule. Par Lost 4.840
This place inviolable, and these from harm. Par Lost 4.843
To question thy bold entrance on this place; Par Lost 4.882
And boldly venture to whatever place Par Lost 4.891
Dole with delight, which in this place I sought; Par Lost 4.894
Thus said. Native of Heav'n, for other place Par Lost 5.361
Created, or such place hast here to dwell, Par Lost 5.373
Into utter darkness, deep ingulft, his place Par Lost 5.614
What doubtful may ensue, more in this place Par Lost 5.682
This our high place, our Sanctuarie, our Hill. Par Lost 5.732
In place thy self so high above thy Peeres. Par Lost 5.812
Into thir place of punishment, the Gulf Par Lost 6.53
Thy ofspring, to the place of evil, Hell, Par Lost 6.276
By wound, though from thir place by violence mov'd. Par Lost 6.405
Each to his place, they heard his voice and went Par Lost 6.782
Into his place, and the great Son returnd Par Lost 7.135
Drew many, whom thir place knows here no more; Par Lost 7.144
Like things to like, the rest to several place Par Lost 7.240
Into one place, and let dry Land appeer. Par Lost 7.284
Wherever thus created, for no place Par Lost 7.535
Thir pleasant dwelling place. Thrice happie men, Par Lost 7.625
Found unsuspected way. There was a place, Par Lost 9.69
Find place or refuge; and the more I see Par Lost 9.119
Much hee the Place admir'd, the Person more. Par Lost 9.444
And force upon free will hath here no place. Par Lost 9.1174
Thou did'st resigne thy Manhood, and the Place Par Lost 10.148
By his Avengers, since no place like this Par Lost 10.241
Of *Satan*, to the self same place where hee Par Lost 10.315
A place so heav'nly, and conniving seem Par Lost 10.624
Heavie, though in thir place. O fleeting joyes Par Lost 10.741
From darkness to promote me, or here place Par Lost 10.745
Or in some other dismal place who knows Par Lost 10.787
And to the place of judgment will return, Par Lost 10.932
Could alter high Decrees, I to that place Par Lost 10.953
Restor'd by thee, vile as I am, to place Par Lost 10.971
What better can we do, then to the place Par Lost 10.1086
Felt less remorse: they forthwith to the place Par Lost 10.1098
And on the East side of the Garden place, Par Lost 11.118
Discover'd soon the place of her retire. Par Lost 11.267
Departure from this happy place, our sweet Par Lost 11.303
With worship, place by place where he voutsaf'd Par Lost 11.318
Shall bring on men. Immediately a place Par Lost 11.477
Said th' Angel, who should better hold his place Par Lost 11.635
Out of his place, pushd by the horned floud, Par Lost 11.831
To teach thee that God attributes to place Par Lost 11.836
Mount *Hermon*, yonder Sea, each place behold Par Lost 12.142
His place, to offer Incense, Myrrh, and Gold; Par Lost 12.363
His place of birth a solemn Angel tells Par Lost 12.364
Shall all be Paradise, far happier place Par Lost 12.464
Thir place of rest, and Providence thir guide: Par Lost 12.647
Flies to his place, nor rests, but in mid air Par Reg 1.39
By whose bright course led on they found the place, Par Reg 1.252
Sir, what ill chance hath brought thee to this place Par Reg 1.321
Yet to that hideous place not so confin'd Par Reg 1.362
Comes to the place where he before had sat Par Reg 1.412
To all the Host of Heaven; the happy place Par Reg 1.416
Sought lost *Eliah*, so in each place these Par Reg 2.19
So may we hold our place and these mild seats Par Reg 2.125
And rather opportunely in this place Par Reg 2.396
Now made a stye, and in his place ascending Par Reg 4.101
For thee is fittest place, I found thee there, Par Reg 4.373
Wandring the Wilderness, whatever place, Par Reg 4.600
This unfrequented place to find some ease, Samson 17
Not flying, but fore-casting in what place Samson 254
Though in this uncouth place; if old respect, Samson 333
Afford me place to shew what recompence Samson 910
That I was never present on the place Samson 1085
Some narrow place enclos'd, where sight may give thee, Samson 1117
A *Nazarite* in place abominable Samson 1359
As at some distance from the place of horrour, Samson 1550
Came to the place, and what was set before him Samson 1624
And to his faithful Champion hath in place Samson 1751
And give it false presentments, lest the place Mask 156

Place(*cont*)
This is the place, as well as I may guess, Mask 201
line not in Bridgewater ms
What readiest way would bring me to that place? Mask 305
And yet is most pretended: In a place Mask 326
Till guided by mine ear I found the place Mask 570
Let us fly this cursed place, Mask 939
Som still removed place will fit, Penseroso 78
To serve the Lady of this place. Arcades 105
Unhous'd thy Virgin Soul from her fair biding place. Fair Inf 21
Took up, and in fit place did reinstall? Fair Inf 46
And wearie of their place do only stay Vacation 25
Thou did'st prepare for it a place Psalm 80, 37

Placed
Between the Cherubim; yea, often plac'd Par Lost 1.387
In the Pourlieues of Heav'n, and therein plac't Par Lost 2.833
Of mankind, in the happie Garden plac't, Par Lost 3.66
And Man there plac't, with purpose to assay Par Lost 3.90
Severe but in true filial freedom plac't; Par Lost 4.294
That rais'd us from the dust and plac't us here Par Lost 4.416
The vigilance here plac't, but such as come Par Lost 4.580
As neerer to him plac't or neerer tending Par Lost 5.476
Who formd us from the dust, and plac'd us here Par Lost 5.516
Encamping, plac'd in Guard thir Watches round, Par Lost 6.412
Which God hath in his mighty Angels plac'd) Par Lost 6.638
Transplanted from her cloudie Shrine, and plac'd Par Lost 7.360
Plac'd Heav'n from Earth so farr, that earthly sight, Par Lost 8.120
Wherever plac't, let him dispose: joy thou Par Lost 8.170
About her, as a guard Angelic plac't. Par Lost 8.559
The weal or woe in thee is plac't; beware. Par Lost 8.638
Was plac't in regal lustre. Down a while Par Lost 10.447
Plac't in a Paradise, by our exile Par Lost 10.484
Meanwhile they in thir earthly *Canaan* plac't Par Lost 12.315
But thou art plac't above me, thou art Lord; Par Reg 1.475
And his Son *Herod* plac'd on *Juda*'s Throne; Par Reg 2.424
Others in vertue plac'd felicity, Par Reg 4.297
Have brought thee, and highest plac't, highest is best, Par Reg 4.553
And well plac't words of glozing courtesie Mask 161
Trinity ms 'well-plac't'
His Temple there is plac't. Psalm 87, 4
Impudent whoore, where hast thou plac'd thy hope? Prose 3, 3

Places
Those happie places thou hast deignd a while Par Lost 5.364
In sight, to each of these three places led. Par Lost 10.324
Familiar to our eyes, all places else Par Lost 11.305
Places and titles, and with these to joine Par Lost 12.516
Art all things under Heav'n, all places thou, Par Lost 12.618

Placid
From that placid aspect and meek regard, Par Reg 3.217

Plague
His red right hand to plague us? what if all Par Lost 2.174
Like instrument to plague the Sons of men Par Lost 6.505

Plagued
Whom they triumph'd once lapst. Thus were they plagu'd Par Lost 10.572

Plagues
Plagues; they astonisht all resistance lost, Par Lost 6.838
Destroyers rightlier call'd and Plagues of men. Par Lost 11.697

Plain
Seest thou yon dreary Plain, forlorn and wilde, Par Lost 1.180
ms 'plain'
On the firm brimstone, and fill all the Plain; Par Lost 1.350
ms 'plain'
Worshipt in *Rabba* and her watry Plain, Par Lost 1.397
ms 'plain'
Nigh on the Plain in many cells prepar'd, Par Lost 1.700
ms 'plaine'
Part on the Plain, or in the Air sublime Par Lost 2.528
The builders next of *Babel* on the Plain Par Lost 3.466
Powrd forth profuse on Hill and Dale and Plaine, Par Lost 4.243
Into a liquid Plain, then stood unmov'd Par Lost 4.455
Wide over all the Plain, and wider farr Par Lost 5.648
Then all this globous Earth in Plain out spred, Par Lost 5.649
Shot through with orient Beams: when all the Plain Par Lost 6.15
If steep, with torrent rapture, if through Plaine, Par Lost 7.299
A woodie Mountain; whose high top was plaine, Par Lost 8.303
Yet doubt not but in Vallie and in plaine Par Lost 11.349
1667 'Plaine'
He lookd and saw a spacious Plaine, whereon Par Lost 11.556
Down to the Plain descended: by thir guise Par Lost 11.576
Freedom and Peace to men: they on the Plain Par Lost 11.580
Ewes and thir bleating Lambs over the Plaine, Par Lost 11.649
Through all the Plain, and refuge none was found. Par Lost 11.673
The Plain, wherein a black bituminous gurge Par Lost 12.41
Pitcht about *Sechem*, and the neighbouring Plaine Par Lost 12.136
To the subjected Plaine; then disappeer'd. Par Lost 12.640
Plain Fishermen, no greater men them call, Par Reg 2.27
A spatious plain out stretch't in circuit wide Par Reg 3.254
To lay hills plain, fell woods, or valleys fill, Par Reg 3.332
Or where plain was raise hill, or over-lay Par Reg 3.333
Another plain, long but in bredth not wide; Par Reg 4.27
A third sort doubted all things, though plain sence; Par Reg 4.296
Over the Wilderness and o're the Plain; Par Reg 4.543
And that he durst not plain enough appear'd. Samson 1256
With plain Heroic magnitude of mind Samson 1279
Up in the broad fields of the sky: Mask 979
Trinity ms 'broad' ←'plaine'
To rise above the watry plain. Psalm 136, 22
Plain in thy neatness; O how oft shall he Horace 5

Plain(*cont*)
As dung upon the plain. Psalm 83, 40
Plain
His fraud is then thy fear, which plain inferrs Par Lost 9.285
In plain then, what forbids he but to know, Par Lost 9.758
But trouble, as old *Simeon* plain fore-told, Par Reg 2.87
Get thee behind me; plain thou now appear'st Par Reg 4.193
Plained
Ey'd them askance, and to himself thus plaind. Par Lost 4.504
Plainest
In them is plainest taught, and easiest learnt, Par Reg 4.361
Plaining
My plaining vers as lively as before; Passion 47
Plainlier
Plainlier shall be reveald. This Patriarch blest, Par Lost 12.151
Plains
In dubious Battel on the Plains of Heav'n, Par Lost 1.104
ms 'plain's'
But in his way lights on the barren Plaines Par Lost 3.437
1667 'plaines'
Of Paradise and *Edens* happie Plains, Par Lost 5.143
Hill, Dale, and shadie Woods, and sunnie Plaines, Par Lost 8.262
Ye Hills and Dales, ye Rivers, Woods, and Plaines, Par Lost 8.275
Of Hill, and Vallie, Rivers, Woods and Plaines, Par Lost 9.116
By *Astracan* over the Snowie Plaines Par Lost 10.432
From *Atropatia* and the neighbouring plains Par Reg 3.319
The soothest Shepherd that ere pip't on plains. Mask 823
Bridgewater ms 'playnes'
Trinity ms 'plaines'
Plaint
Sate in thir sad discourse, and various plaint, Par Lost 10.343
His peace, and thus proceeded in her plaint. Par Lost 10.913
And scarce recovering words his plaint renew'd. Par Lost 11.499
And scarce to th' Angel utterdst thus thy plaint. Par Lost 11.762
The *Lars*, and *Lemures* moan with midnight plaint, Nativity 191
Plaints
His bursting passion into plaints thus pour'd: Par Lost 9.98
Thir unexpected loss and plaints out breath'd. Par Reg 2.29
Thus they out of their plaints new hope resume Par Reg 2.58
(If so it be that thou these plaints dost hear) Fair Inf 37
Planet
And hence the Morning Planet guilds her horns; Par Lost 7.366
The Planet Earth, so stedfast though she seem, Par Lost 8.129
With Planet, or with Element. Penseroso 96
Or what the cross dire-looking Planet smites, Arcades 52
Planetary
Thir planetarie motions and aspects Par Lost 10.658
Planets
They pass the Planets seven, and pass the fixt, Par Lost 3.481
Of Planets and of fixt in all her Wheeles Par Lost 5.621
Two Planets rushing from aspect maligne Par Lost 6.313
The Planets in thir station list'ning stood, Par Lost 7.563
And Planets, Planet-strook, real Eclips Par Lost 10.413
Planet-struck
And Planets, Planet-strook, real Eclips Par Lost 10.413
Plank
Flie to and fro, or on the smoothed Plank, Par Lost 1.772
ms 'plank'
Plant
Intended to create, and therein plant Par Lost 1.652
Irradiate, there plant eyes, all mist from thence Par Lost 3.53
Of that life-giving Plant, but only us'd Par Lost 4.199
Ran Nectar, visiting each plant, and fed Par Lost 4.240
And O fair Plant, said he, with fruit surcharg'd, Par Lost 5.58
With every Plant, in sign of Worship wave. Par Lost 5.194
Each Plant and juciest Gourd will pluck such choice Par Lost 5.327
With Plant, Fruit, Flour Ambrosial, Gemms & Gold, Par Lost 6.475
Plant of the field, which e're it was in the Earth Par Lost 7.335
Productive in Herb, Plant, and nobler birth Par Lost 9.111
This Garden, still to tend Plant, Herb and Flour, Par Lost 9.206
O Sacred, Wise, and Wisdom-giving Plant, Par Lost 9.679
Into the plant sciential sap, deriv'd Par Lost 9.837
From drooping plant, or dropping tree; the birds Par Reg 4.434
On man, beast, plant, wastful and turbulent, Par Reg 4.461
Ordain'd thy nurture holy, as of a Plant; Samson 362
A Monument, and plant it round with shade Samson 1734
In every vertuous plant and healing herb Mask 621
Fame is no plant that grows on mortal soil, Lycidas 78
To plant this *lovely* Vine. Psalm 80, 36
Plantation
Thir tendance or Plantation for delight Par Lost 9.419
Planted
Of *Eden* planted; *Eden* stretchd her Line Par Lost 4.210
Of knowledge, planted by the Tree of Life, Par Lost 4.424
Whose dwelling God hath planted here in bliss? Par Lost 4.884
This Garden, planted with the Trees of God, Par Lost 7.538
Planted, with Walks, and Bowers, that what I saw Par Lost 8.305
He shall be as a tree which planted grows Psalm 1, 7
Hath set, and planted *long*, Psalm 80, 62
Planter
Chos'n by the sovran Planter, when he fram'd Par Lost 4.691
Plants
To prune these growing Plants, and tend these Flours, Par Lost 4.438
Our tended Plants, how blows the Citron Grove, Par Lost 5.22
As Plants: ambiguous between Sea and Land Par Lost 7.473
And all my Plants I save from nightly ill, Arcades 48
Trinity ms 'plants'

Plat
This Flourie Plat, the sweet recess of *Eve* Par Lost 9.456
Oft on a Plat of rising ground, Penseroso 73
Platan
Under a Platan, yet methought less faire, Par Lost 4.478
Plate
In *Aarons* Brest-plate, and a stone besides Par Lost 3.598
Mangl'd with gastly wounds through Plate and Maile, Par Lost 6.368
Plated
Thir plated backs under his heel; Samson 140
Plato
Plato's Elysium, leap'd into the Sea, Par Lost 3.472
Plato's retirement, where the *Attic* Bird Par Reg 4.245
The spirit of *Plato* to unfold Penseroso 89
Plausible
Plausible to the world, to me worth naught. Par Reg 3.393
Play
In some Purlieu two gentle Fawnes at play, Par Lost 4.404
Wisdom thy Sister, and with her didst play Par Lost 7.10
And bended Dolphins play: part huge of bulk Par Lost 7.410
To come and play before thee, know'st thou not Par Lost 8.372
The Eye of *Eve* to mark his play; he glad Par Lost 9.528
Unsuckt of Lamb or Kid, that tend thir play. Par Lost 9.583
But come, so well refresh't, now let us play, Par Lost 9.1027
Oppress'd them, wearied with thir amorous play. Par Lost 9.1045
When I was yet a child, no childish play Par Reg 1.201
Where winds with Reeds, and Osiers whisp'ring play Par Reg 2.26
Courted by all the winds that hold them play, Samson 719
To shew them feats, and play before thir god, Samson 1340
To come and play before them at thir Feast. Samson 1448
They only set on sport and play Samson 1679
And play i' th plighted clouds. I was aw-strook, Mask 301
Bridgewater ms 'playe'
Spir. Back Shepherds, back, anough your play, Mask 958
Bridgewater ms 'playe'
And young and old com forth to play Allegro 97
Among themselves they laugh, they play, Psalm 80, 27
Played
In curles on either cheek plaid, wings he wore Par Lost 3.641
Alone as they. About them frisking playd Par Lost 4.340
Wantond as in her prime, and plaid at will Par Lost 5.295
About thir spirits had plaid, and inmost powers Par Lost 9.1048
The water Nymphs that in the bottom plaid, Mask 833
1637 'playd'
Trinity ms 'playd'
Bridgewater ms 'played'
Sleek *Panope* with all her sisters play'd. Lycidas 99
Trinity ms 'plaid'
Players
Sam. Have they not Sword-players, and ev'ry sort Samson 1323
Playing
Zephir with *Aurora* playing, Allegro 19
For neither were ye playing on the steep, Lycidas 52
Plea
The Tyrants plea, excus'd his devilish deeds. Par Lost 4.394
With righteous plea, thir utmost vigilance, Par Lost 10.30
Yet of another Plea bethought him soon. Par Reg 3.149
All wickedness is weakness: that plea therefore Samson 834
Dal. Since thou determinst weakness for no plea Samson 843
That came in *Neptune's* plea, Lycidas 90
Plead
To mitigate thus plead, not to reverse) Par Lost 11.41
Rather approv'd them not; but thou didst plead Samson 421
Incestuous, Sacrilegious, but may plead it? Samson 833
Pleaded
Pleaded his devilish Counsel, first devis'd Par Lost 2.379
My pleaded reason. To the Nuptial Bowre Par Lost 8.510
Pleasant
The pleasant Vally of *Hinnom*, *Tophet* thence Par Lost 1.404
Pleasant to know, and worthiest to be all Par Lost 3.703
Lay pleasant, his grievd look he fixes sad, Par Lost 4.28
Dwelt in *Telassar:* in this pleasant soile Par Lost 4.214
His farr more pleasant Garden God ordaind; Par Lost 4.215
And at our pleasant labour, to reform Par Lost 4.625
With charm of earliest Birds; pleasant the Sun Par Lost 4.642
Why sleepst thou *Eve?* now is the pleasant time, Par Lost 5.38
Which he had pluckt; the pleasant savourie smell Par Lost 5.84
With pleasant liquors crown'd: O innocence Par Lost 5.445
So they among themselves in pleasant veine Par Lost 6.628
Her Universal Face with pleasant green, Par Lost 7.316
And freely all thir pleasant fruit for food Par Lost 7.540
Thir pleasant dwelling place. Thrice happie men, Par Lost 7.625
Though pleasant, but thy words with Grace Divine Par Lost 8.215
Of Earth before scarce pleasant seemd. Each Tree Par Lost 8.306
Our pleasant task enjoyn'd, but till more hands Par Lost 9.207
Of Grove or Garden-Plot more pleasant lay, Par Lost 9.418
Among the pleasant Villages and Farmes Par Lost 9.448
What can be toilsom in these pleasant Walkes? Par Lost 11.179
Those Tents thou sawst so pleasant, were the Tents Par Lost 11.607
Of many a pleasant Realm and Province wide. Par Reg 1.118
Only in a bottom saw a pleasant Grove, Par Reg 2.289
Lay pleasant; from his side two rivers flow'd, Par Reg 3.255
Courts thee on Roses in some pleasant Cave, Horace 2
And Harp *with* pleasant *string*, Psalm 81, 8
The *pleasant* Tabernacles are! Psalm 84, 3
Pleasantest
Then Fruits of Palm-tree pleasantest to thirst Par Lost 8.212

Please	
These Feminine. For Spirits when they please	Par Lost 1.423
Imitate when we please? This Desart soile	Par Lost 2.270
Henceforth; my dwelling haply may not please	Par Lost 4.378
All seasons and thir change, all please alike.	Par Lost 4.640
For dinner savourie fruits, of taste to please	Par Lost 5.304
Our Authour. Heav'nly stranger, please to taste	Par Lost 5.397
All Intellect, all Sense, and as they please,	Par Lost 6.351
Of all tastes else to please thir appetite,	Par Lost 7.49
What next I bring shall please thee, be assur'd,	Par Lost 8.449
Most Favors, who can please him long; Mee first	Par Lost 9.949
Nothing will please the difficult and nice,	Par Reg 4.157
For giv'n to me, I give to whom I please,	Par Reg 4.164
To please thy gods thou didst it; gods unable	Samson 896
But all to please, and sate the curious taste?	Mask 714
Towred Cities please us then,	Allegro 117
If ever deed of honour did thee please,	Sonnet 8, 3
Pleased	
Timorous and slothful: yet he pleas'd the ear,	Par Lost 2.117
As *Mammon* ended, and his Sentence pleas'd,	Par Lost 2.291
Pleas'd highly those infernal States, and joy	Par Lost 2.387
I pleas'd, and with attractive graces won	Par Lost 2.762
He ceas'd, for both seemd highly pleasd, and Death	Par Lost 2.845
Well pleas'd, on me let Death wreck all his rage;	Par Lost 3.241
Pleas'd, out of Heaven shalt look down and smile,	Par Lost 3.257
Well pleas'd they slack thir course, and many a League	Par Lost 4.164
Who came thir bane, though with them better pleas'd	Par Lost 4.167
It started back, but pleas'd I soon returnd,	Par Lost 4.463
1667 'pleasd'	
Pleas'd it returnd as soon with answering looks	Par Lost 4.464
Silence was pleas'd: now glow'd the Firmament	Par Lost 4.604
All seemd well pleas'd, all seem'd, but were not all	Par Lost 5.617
Such as he pleasd, and circumscrib'd thir being?	Par Lost 5.825
That thou in me well pleas'd, declarst thy will	Par Lost 6.728
In presence of th' Almightie Father, pleas'd	Par Lost 7.11
Not Words alone pleas'd her. O when meet now	Par Lost 8.57
Pleas'd with thy words no less then thou with mine.	Par Lost 8.248
Social communication, yet so pleas'd,	Par Lost 8.429
Thus farr to try thee, *Adam*, I was pleas'd,	Par Lost 8.437
Pleas'd me long choosing, and beginning late;	Par Lost 9.26
Grateful to appetite, more pleas'd my sense	Par Lost 9.580
Mayst ever rest well pleas'd. I go to judge	Par Lost 10.71
Not pleas'd, thus entertaind with solitude,	Par Lost 10.105
Well pleas'd, but answer'd not; for now too nigh	Par Lost 12.625
This is my Son belov'd, in him am pleas'd.	Par Reg 1.85
He was well pleas'd; by which I knew the time	Par Reg 1.286
What I might have bestow'd on whom I pleas'd,	Par Reg 2.395
That pleas'd so well our Victors ear, declare	Par Reg 4.337
Sam. The first I saw at *Timna*, and she pleas'd	Samson 219
(Best pleas'd with humble and filial submission)	Samson 511
Less therefore to be pleas'd, obey'd, or fear'd,	Samson 900
Pleases	
Of other Creatures, as him pleases best,	Par Lost 8.169
What pleasing seemd, for her now pleases more,	Par Lost 9.453
Kingdom nor Empire pleases thee, nor aught	Par Reg 4.369
Whom so it pleases him by choice	Samson 311
Pleasing	
Yet with a pleasing sorcerie could charm	Par Lost 2.566
Full Orb'd the Moon, and with more pleasing light	Par Lost 5.42
What pleasing seemd, for her now pleases more,	Par Lost 9.453
Floted redundant: pleasing was his shape,	Par Lost 9.503
Of thy victorious Arm, well-pleasing Son,	Par Lost 10.634
Fruits of more pleasing savour from thy seed	Par Lost 11.26
To me was pleasing, all my mind was set	Par Reg 1.202
Smooth on the tongue discourst, pleasing to th' ear,	Par Reg 1.479
Sam. Love-quarrels oft in pleasing concord end,	Samson 1008
Yet they in pleasing slumber lull'd the sense,	Mask 260
Bridgewater ms 'pleasinge'	
With many murmurs mixt, whose pleasing poison	Mask 526
Bridgewater ms 'pleasinge'	
Wrapt in a pleasing fit of melancholy	Mask 546
Bridgewater ms 'pleasinge'	
Pleasingly	
Thus to her self she pleasingly began.	Par Lost 9.794
Pleasure	
Forgets both joy and grief, pleasure and pain.	Par Lost 2.586
What pleasure I from such obedience paid,	Par Lost 3.107
Of Mightiest. Sense of pleasure we may well	Par Lost 6.459
Of pleasure situate in Hill and Dale)	Par Lost 6.641
Of what was high: such pleasure she reserv'd,	Par Lost 8.50
No pleasure, though in pleasure, solitarie.	Par Lost 8.402
Not sunk in carnal pleasure, for which cause	Par Lost 8.593
Such Pleasure took the Serpent to behold	Par Lost 9.455
Of pleasure not for him ordain'd: then soon	Par Lost 9.470
Of pleasure, but all pleasure to destroy,	Par Lost 9.477
I spar'd not, for such pleasure till that hour	Par Lost 9.596
Much pleasure we have lost, while we abstain'd	Par Lost 9.1022
True relish, tasting; if such pleasure be	Par Lost 9.1024
Eve, thy contempt of life and pleasure seems	Par Lost 10.1013
For loss of life and pleasure overlov'd.	Par Lost 10.1019
Obtuse, all taste of pleasure must forgoe,	Par Lost 11.541
By pleasure, though to Nature seeming meet,	Par Lost 11.604
Shall change thir course to pleasure, ease, and sloth,	Par Lost 11.794
Extorts, or pleasure to do ill excites?	Par Reg 1.423
In corporal pleasure he, and careless ease;	Par Reg 4.299
Wealth, pleasure, pain or torment, death and life,	Par Reg 4.305
Softn'd with pleasure and voluptuous life;	Samson 534
To roule with pleasure in a sensual stie.	Mask 77

Pleasure(*cont*)	
That in trim Gardens takes his pleasure;	Penseroso 50
The Air such pleasure loth to lose,	Nativity 99
But haste thee strait to do me once a Pleasure,	Vacation 17
Pleasures	
Short pleasures, for long woes are to succeed.	Par Lost 4.535
Her loss, and other pleasures all abjure:	Par Lost 8.480
Pleasures about me, so much more I feel	Par Lost 9.120
Aetherial, who all pleasures else despise,	Par Reg 3.28
Sorrow flies farr: See here be all the pleasures	Mask 668
1637 'pleasurs'	
In unreproved pleasures free;	Allegro 40
Streit mine eye hath caught new pleasures	Allegro 69
These pleasures *Melancholy* give,	Penseroso 175
Plebeian	
In shew Plebeian Angel militant	Par Lost 10.442
1667 'plebeian'	
Pledge	
If once they hear that voyce, thir liveliest pledge	Par Lost 1.274
And my fair Son here showst me, the dear pledge	Par Lost 2.818
Sole pledge of his obedience: So will fall,	Par Lost 3.95
For prospect, what well us'd had bin the pledge	Par Lost 4.200
Sure pledge of day, that crownst the smiling Morn	Par Lost 5.168
The Pledge of thy Obedience and thy Faith,	Par Lost 8.325
The mystery of God giv'n me under pledge	Samson 378
At length to lay my head and hallow'd pledge	Samson 535
The pledge of my unviolated vow.	Samson 1144
Ah! Who hath reft (quoth he) my dearest pledge?	Lycidas 107
Pledges	
Blest pair of *Sirens*, pledges of Heav'ns joy,	Musick 1
Pleiades	
Dawn, and the *Pleiades* before him danc'd	Par Lost 7.374
Plenipotent	
Plenipotent on Earth, of matchless might	Par Lost 10.404
Plenteous	
Unnam'd in Heav'n, now plenteous, as thou seest	Par Lost 6.263
Which here, though plenteous, all too little seems	Par Lost 10.600
Labouring the soile, and reaping plenteous crop,	Par Lost 12.18
And from their plenteous grounds	Psalm 4, 35
Plenteously	
Soul living, each that crept, which plenteously	Par Lost 7.392
Plenty	
More plenty then the Sun that barren shines,	Par Lost 8.94
Amid the Tree now got, where plenty hung	Par Lost 9.594
1667 'plentie'	
Be vacant of her plenty, in her own loyns	Mask 718
Trinity ms 'plentie'	
1637 'plentie'	
Bridgewater ms 'plentie'	
Our Land shall forth in plenty throw	Psalm 85, 51
Plied	
The conscience, Friend, to have lost them overply'd	Sonnet 22, 10
1694 'over ply'd'	
Plies	
With loudest vehemence: thither he plyes,	Par Lost 2.954
Plight	
Nor did they not perceave the evil plight	Par Lost 1.335
They worse abhorr'd. *Satan* beheld thir plight,	Par Lost 6.607
But let us now, as in bad plight, devise	Par Lost 9.1091
She ended weeping, and her lowlie plight,	Par Lost 10.937
Thus they in lowliest plight repentant stood	Par Lost 11.1
Lie in this miserable loathsom plight	Samson 480
(*Gaza* is not in plight to say us nay)	Samson 1729
And put them into mis-becoming plight.	Mask 372
In her sweetest, saddest plight,	Penseroso 57
Most perfect *Heroe*, try'd in heaviest plight	Passion 13
Plighted	
And play i' th plighted clouds. I was aw-strook,	Mask 301
Plot	
Of Grove or Garden-Plot more pleasant lay,	Par Lost 9.418
Plots	
Then wise to frustrate all our plots and wiles.	Par Lost 2.193
Your plots and packing wors then those of *Trent*,	Forcers 14
Trinity ms 'plotts'	
Lay deep their plots together through each Land,	Psalm 2, 4
Their Plots and Counsels deep,	Psalm 83, 10
Plotting	
Yet ever plotting how the Conqueror least	Par Lost 2.338
Late falln himself from Heav'n, is plotting now	Par Lost 5.240
Who now is plotting how he may seduce	Par Lost 6.901
Ploughed	
To peace and truth thy glorious way hast plough'd,	Sonnet 16, 4
1694 'Plough'd'	
Ploughman	
While the Plowman neer at hand,	Allegro 63
Plowman	
Swayes them; the careful Plowman doubting stands	Par Lost 4.983
Pluck	
Each Plant and juciest Gourd will pluck such choice	Par Lost 5.327
To pluck and eate; whereat I wak'd, and found	Par Lost 8.309
Tempting so nigh, to pluck and eat my fill	Par Lost 9.595
I com to pluck your Berries harsh and crude,	Lycidas 3
That all may pluck her, as they go,	Psalm 80, 51
Plucked	
He pluckt, he tasted; mee damp horror chil'd	Par Lost 5.65
Which he had pluckt; the pleasant savourie smell	Par Lost 5.84
They pluckt the seated Hills with all thir load,	Par Lost 6.644
Forth reaching to the Fruit, she pluck'd, she eat:	Par Lost 9.781

Plucked(*cont*)
That curld *Megaera:* greedily they pluck'd — Par Lost 10.560
Gatherd, not harshly pluckt, for death mature: — Par Lost 11.537
Pluck't up by som unheedy swain, — Winchester 38
Plucking
Plucking ripe clusters from the tender shoots, — Mask 296
Bridgewater ms 'pluckinge'
Plumb
Fluttring his pennons vain plumb down he drops — Par Lost 2.933
Plume
Of many a colourd plume sprinkl'd with Gold, — Par Lost 3.642
From me som Plume, that thy success may show — Par Lost 6.161
Two Birds of gayest plume before him drove: — Par Lost 11.186
Plumed
Sat horror Plum'd; nor wanted in his graspe — Par Lost 4.989
Plumes
And shook his Plumes, that Heav'nly fragrance filld — Par Lost 5.286
Floats, as they pass, fann'd with unnumber'd plumes: — Par Lost 7.432
Led captive; cease to admire, and all her Plumes — Par Reg 2.222
She plumes her feathers, and lets grow her wings — Mask 378
Trinity ms 'plum'es'
Th' earth cumber'd, and the wing'd air dark't with plumes, — Mask 730
Plummet
Whose speed is but the heavy Plummets pace; — On Time 3
Trinity ms 'plummets'
Plumy
Who on their plumy Vans receiv'd him soft — Par Reg 4.583
Plunge
And plunge us in the flames? or from above — Par Lost 2.172
Plunged
Threatens him, plung'd in that abortive gulf. — Par Lost 2.441
Th' untractable Abysse, plung'd in the womb — Par Lost 10.476
I find no way, from deep to deeper plung'd! — Par Lost 10.844
Plurality
To seise the widdow'd whore Pluralitie — Forcers 3
Trinity ms 'Plurality'
Pluto
Of *Pluto*, to have quite set free — Allegro 149
Drew Iron tears down *Pluto*'s cheek, — Penseroso 107
Plutonian
Of that *Plutonian* Hall, invisible — Par Lost 10.444
Ply
Ply stemming nightly toward the Pole. So seem'd — Par Lost 2.642
Then commune how that day they best may ply — Par Lost 9.201
And cheeks of sorry grain will serve to ply — Mask 750
line not in Bridgewater ms
Poem
To Person or to Poem. Mee of these — Par Lost 9.41
Whose Poem *Phoebus* challeng'd for his own. — Par Reg 4.260
With Music or with Poem, where so soon — Par Reg 4.332
Poet
Of sad *Electra*'s Poet had the power — Sonnet 8, 13
Trinity ms 'poet'
Poets
What the sage Poets taught by th' heav'nly Muse, — Mask 515
Trinity ms 'poets'
Bridgewater ms 'poets'
Such sights as youthfull Poets dream — Allegro 129
Point
Of Nights extended shade; from Eastern Point — Par Lost 3.557
That spot to which I point is *Paradise*, — Par Lost 3.733
From what point of his Compass to beware — Par Lost 4.559
Returnd on that bright beam, whose point now raisd — Par Lost 4.590
The western Point, where those half-rounding guards — Par Lost 4.862
1667 'point'
From Father to his Son? strange point and new! — Par Lost 5.855
In prospect, as I point them; on the shoare — Par Lost 12.143
Over whose heads they rore, and seem to point, — Par Reg 4.463
Ruin, destruction at the utmost point. — Samson 1514
Co. Due west it rises from this shrubby point. — Mask 306
Bridgewater ms 'pointe'
Or ere the point of dawn, — Nativity 86
Pointed
By his great Prophet, pointed at and shown, — Par Reg 2.51
Com not too neer, you fall on iron stakes else. — Mask 491
Trinity ms 'iron' ←'pointed'
But as Faith pointed with her golden rod, — Sonnet 14, 7
Pointing
Drivn backward slope thir pointing spires, and rowld — Par Lost 1.223
ms 'poynting'
Under a Star-ypointing *Pyramid?* — Shakespear 4
1640 'starre-ypointing'
1663-4 'Starre-ypointing'
1632 'starre-ypointed' in some copies, 'starre-ypointing' in others
Points
With him the points of libertie, who made — Par Lost 5.823
On points and questions fitting *Moses* Chair, — Par Reg 4.219
Poise
Levied to side with warring Winds, and poise — Par Lost 2.905
Yet where an equall poise of hope and fear — Mask 410
Poised
Upon her Center pois'd, when on a day — Par Lost 5.579
Poison
Crush't the sweet poyson of mis-used Wine — Mask 47
With many murmurs mixt, whose pleasing poison — Mask 526
Bridgewater ms 'poyson'
Poisonous
Entangl'd with a poysnous bosom snake, — Samson 763
Polar
Now on the polar windes, then with quick Fann — Par Lost 5.269
As when two Polar Winds blowing adverse — Par Lost 10.289
Beyond the Polar Circles; to them Day — Par Lost 10.681
Pole
As from the Center thrice to th' utmost Pole. — Par Lost 1.74
ms 'pole'
Ply stemming nightly toward the Pole. So seem'd — Par Lost 2.642
Beyond th' *Horizon;* then from Pole to Pole — Par Lost 3.560
And starrie Pole: Thou also mad'st the Night, — Par Lost 4.724
Standing on Earth, not rapt above the Pole, — Par Lost 7.23
Heav'ns highth, and with the Center mix the Pole. — Par Lost 7.215
From Pole to Pole, traversing each Colure; — Par Lost 9.66
Shoots against the dusky Pole, — Mask 99
Trinity ms 'pole'
Over the Pole thy thickest mantle throw, — Passion 30
Poles
The Poles of Earth twice ten degrees and more — Par Lost 10.669
Above the wheeling poles, and at Heav'ns dore — Vacation 34
Policy
By pollicy, and long process of time, — Par Lost 2.297
Vented much policy, and projects deep — Par Reg 3.391
Polish
Of Arts that polish Life, Inventers rare, — Par Lost 11.610
Polished
Stay thy cloudy Ebon chair, — Mask 134
Trinity ms 'clowdie' ←'polisht'
Hath fixt her polisht Car. — Nativity 241
Politic
Thy politic maxims, or that cumbersome — Par Reg 3.400
Politician
But your ill-meaning Politician Lords, — Samson 1195
Pollute
Pollute with sinfull blame, — Nativity 41
Polluted
Of mischief, and polluted from the end — Par Lost 10.167
To leave them to thir own polluted wayes; — Par Lost 12.110
Polluting
Which mans polluting Sin with taint hath shed — Par Lost 10.631
Pollution
Endeavour Peace: thir strife pollution brings — Par Lost 12.355
Pomona
They came, that like *Pomona*'s Arbour smil'd — Par Lost 5.378
To *Pales*, or *Pomona* thus adornd, — Par Lost 9.393
Likeliest she seemd, *Pomona* when she fled — Par Lost 9.394
Pomp
With gay Religions full of Pomp and Gold, — Par Lost 1.372
ms 'pomp'
Of servile Pomp. Our greatness will appeer — Par Lost 2.257
Than Hells dread Emperour with pomp Supream, — Par Lost 2.510
More solemn then the tedious pomp that waits — Par Lost 5.354
While the bright Pomp ascended jubilant. — Par Lost 7.564
A pomp of winning Graces waited still, — Par Lost 8.61
Flood overwhelmd, and them with all thir pomp — Par Lost 11.748
And thou no more with Pomp and Sacrifice — Par Reg 1.457
The Monarchies of the Earth, thir pomp and state, — Par Reg 3.246
And as a blessing with such pomp adorn'd? — Samson 357
Great Pomp, and Sacrifice, and Praises loud — Samson 436
That I this honour, I this pomp have brought — Samson 449
With Sacrifices, Triumph, Pomp, and Games; — Samson 1312
And pomp, and feast, and revelry, — Allegro 127
And so Sepulcher'd in such pomp dost lie, — Shakespear 15
1632 'pompe'
1640 'pompe'
Pompey
The *Carthaginian* pride, young *Pompey* quell'd — Par Reg 3.35
Pompous
Thy pompous Delicacies I contemn, — Par Reg 2.390
Pond
To Boggs and Mires, and oft through Pond or Poole, — Par Lost 9.641
Ponder
This ponder, that all Nations of the Earth — Par Lost 12.147
Pondering
Pondering the danger with deep thoughts; and each — Par Lost 2.421
Pondering his Voyage; for no narrow frith — Par Lost 2.919
So pondering, and from his armed Peers — Par Lost 6.127
Thus *Mary* pondering oft, and oft to mind — Par Reg 2.105
Ponderous
Was moving toward the shoar; his ponderous shield — Par Lost 1.284
Ponders
In counterpoise, now ponders all events, — Par Lost 4.1001
Ponent
Forth rush the *Levant* and the *Ponent* Windes — Par Lost 10.704
Pontic
The *Pontic* King and in triumph had rode. — Par Reg 3.36
Pontifical
Pontifical, a ridge of pendent Rock — Par Lost 10.313
Pontifice
Of this new wondrous Pontifice, unhop't — Par Lost 10.348
Pontus
In *Pontus* or the *Punic* Coast, or where — Par Lost 5.340
From *Eden* over *Pontus*, and the Poole — Par Lost 9.77
Pontus and *Lucrine* Bay, and *Afric* Coast. — Par Reg 2.347
Pool
Forthwith upright he rears from off the Pool — Par Lost 1.221
ms 'poole'

Pool*(cont)*
Lye thus astonisht on th' oblivious Pool, Par Lost 1.266
ms 'poole'
And *Eleale* to th' *Asphaltick* Pool. Par Lost 1.411
ms 'poole'
Escap't the *Stygian* Pool, though long detain'd Par Lost 3.14
From *Eden* over *Pontus*, and the Poole Par Lost 9.77
To Boggs and Mires, and oft through Pond or Poole, Par Lost 9.641
Beyond *Danubius* to the *Tauric* Pool. Par Reg 4.79
& halfe the slow unfadom'd Stygian poole Mask Tr. ms 10.15
'Stygian poole' ← 'poole of styx'

Poor
Not wandring poor, but trusting all his wealth Par Lost 12.133
As a poor miserable captive thrall, Par Reg 1.411
For I esteem those names of men so poor Par Reg 2.447
Poor *Socrates* (who next more memorable2) Par Reg 3.96
Thy Foes derision, Captive, Poor, and Blind Samson 366
And O poor hapless Nightingale thought I, Mask 566
Trinity ms 'poore'
Bridgewater ms 'poore'
1637 'poore'
poore ladie thou hast need of some refreshing Mask Tr. ms 20.09
poore ladie thou hast neede of some refreshinge Mask Br. ms 660
Poor fleshly Tabernacle entered, Passion 17
Dispatch the poor mans cause, Psalm 82, 10
Defend the poor and desolate, Psalm 82, 13
For I am poor, and almost pine Psalm 86, 3
Of head bereft li'th poor *Kenelm* King-born. Prose 13, 2

Poorest
To live the poorest in my Tribe, then richest, Samson 1479

Pope
That the first wealthy *Pope* receiv'd of thee. Prose 1, 3

Poplar
Edg'd with poplar pale. Nativity 185

Popular
Princes of Hell? for so the popular vote Par Lost 2.313
Hereafter, join'd in her popular Tribes Par Lost 7.488
Heapt to the popular summe, will so incense Par Lost 12.338
Of worth, of honour, glory, and popular praise; Par Reg 2.227
Retiring from the popular noise, I seek Samson 16
This day the *Philistines* a popular Feast Samson 434

Populous
A multitude, like which the populous North Par Lost 1.351
Pour forth thir populous youth about the Hive Par Lost 1.770
Swarm populous, unnumber'd as the Sands Par Lost 2.903
Thir station, Heav'n yet populous retaines Par Lost 7.146
As one who long in populous City pent, Par Lost 9.445
The populous rout Psalm 3, 16

Porch
Whose wanton passions in the sacred Porch Par Lost 1.454
ms 'porch'
And through the porch and inlet of each sense Mask 839
Bridgewater ms 'portch'

Porches
And Porches wide, but chief the spacious Hall Par Lost 1.762
ms 'porches'
Porches and Theatres, Baths, Aqueducts, Par Reg 4.36

Porcupines
Of chaf't wild Boars, or ruffl'd Porcupines. Samson 1138

Pore
That she might look at will through every pore? Samson 97

Pored
Numbring good intellects; now seldom por'd on. Sonnet 11, 4

Porous
Of porous Earth with kindly thirst up drawn, Par Lost 4.228
In the Suns Orb, made porous to receive Par Lost 7.361

Port
Gladly the Port, though Shrouds and Tackle torn; Par Lost 2.1044
And from thir Ivorie Port the Cherubim Par Lost 4.778
And with them comes a third of Regal port, Par Lost 4.869
Then loudest Oratorie: yet thir port Par Lost 11.8
Th' Empire of *Negus* to his utmost Port Par Lost 11.397
I would be at the worst; worst is my Port, Par Reg 3.209
Their port was more then human, as they stood; Mask 297
Bridgewater ms 'porte'

Portal
The Portal shon, inimitable on Earth Par Lost 3.508
Driving dum silence from the portal dore, Vacation 5

Portals
That open'd wide her blazing Portals, led Par Lost 7.575

Portcullis
Forthwith the huge Porcullis high up drew, Par Lost 2.874

Ported
With ported Spears, as thick as when a field Par Lost 4.980

Portend
A Kingdom they portend thee, but what Kingdom, Par Reg 4.389
Sam. All otherwise to me my thoughts portend, Samson 590
Portend success in love; O if *Jove*'s will Sonnet 1, 7

Portending
Portending hollow truce; at each behind Par Lost 6.578
Portending good, and all her spirits compos'd Par Lost 12.596
And sayings laid up, portending strange events. Par Reg 2.104

Portends
Of peaceful dayes portends, then those two past; Par Lost 11.600

Portentous
Portentous held me; but familiar grown, Par Lost 2.761
With this portentous Bridge the dark Abyss. Par Lost 10.371

Portents
And answers, oracles, portents and dreams, Par Reg 1.395
As false portents, not sent from God, but thee; Par Reg 4.491

Portion
In utter darkness, and thir portion set Par Lost 1.72
Precedence, none, whose portion is so small Par Lost 2.33

Portraiture
Of lively portrature display'd, Penseroso 149

Portrayed
Various, with boastful Argument portraid, Par Lost 6.84

Portress
T' whom thus the Portress of Hell Gate reply'd; Par Lost 2.746

Possess
To waste his whole Creation, or possess Par Lost 2.365
Lie vanquisht; thou hast givn me to possess Par Lost 3.243
Over all other Creatures that possess Par Lost 4.431
1667 'possesse'
Two onely, who yet by sov'ran gift possess Par Lost 5.366
Homeward with flying march where we possess Par Lost 5.688
Number sufficient to possess her Realmes Par Lost 7.147
Possess it, and all things that therein live, Par Lost 8.340
And Dungeon of our Tyrant: Now possess, Par Lost 10.466
I suffer them to enter and possess Par Lost 10.623
All th' Earth he gave thee to possess and rule, Par Lost 11.339
To leave this Paradise, but shalt possess Par Lost 12.586
And fancies fond with gaudy shapes possess, Penseroso 6
And to possess them, Honour'd *Margaret*. Sonnet 10, 14
The Nations all possess. Psalm 82, 28

Possessed
Natives and Sons of Heav'n possest before Par Lost 5.790
Seem I to thee sufficiently possest Par Lost 8.404
I know not whence possessd thee; we had then Par Lost 9.1137
This Universe we have possest, and rul'd Par Reg 1.49
But say thou wer't possess'd of *David*'s Throne Par Reg 3.357
They had by this possess'd the Towers of *Gath*, Samson 266
Love once possest, nor can be easily Samson 1005

Possesses
Possesses thee to bend that mortal Dart Par Lost 2.729
Possesses lately, thither to arrive Par Lost 2.979
But other doubt possesses me, least harm Par Lost 9.251

Possessing
In heart or head, possessing soon inspir'd Par Lost 9.189
Wise, perfect in himself, and all possessing Par Reg 4.302

Possession
Her old possession, and extinguish life Par Lost 4.666
Though for possession put to try once more Par Lost 4.941
For in possession such, not onely of right, Par Lost 10.461
Vacant possession som new trouble raise: Par Lost 11.103
Possession of the Garden; hee alone, Par Lost 11.222
Easily from possession won with arms; Par Reg 3.156
From thy Demoniac holds, possession foul, Par Reg 4.628
Took full possession of me and prevail'd; Samson 869
As thy possession I on thee bestow Psalm 2, 17

Possessor
Receive thy new Possessor: One who brings Par Lost 1.252
ms 'possessour'

Possible
Can turn, or holds it possible to turn Par Lost 5.441
Firm we subsist, yet possible to swerve, Par Lost 9.359
And expiate, if possible, my crime, Samson 490
I may, if possible, thy pardon find Samson 771

Possibly
To him, or possibly his love desert Par Lost 5.515

Post
From *Media* post to *Aegypt*, there fast bound. Par Lost 4.171
The Gates of *Azza*, Post, and massie Bar Samson 147
For evil news rides post, while good news baits. Samson 1538
To earth from thy praefixed seat didst poast, Fair Inf 59
And post o're Land and Ocean without rest: Sonnet 19, 13

Posterity
He with his whole posteritie must dye, Par Lost 3.209
From the beginning, that posteritie Par Lost 7.638
Posteritie stands curst: Fair Patrimonie Par Lost 10.818
To all posterity may stand defam'd, Samson 977

Posture
Or in this abject posture have ye sworn Par Lost 1.322
How busied, in what form and posture coucht. Par Lost 4.876
In posture to displode thir second tire Par Lost 6.605

Potable
Potable Gold, when with one vertuous touch Par Lost 3.608

Potent
Nor what the Potent Victor in his rage Par Lost 1.95
ms 'potent'
Innumerable. As when the potent Rod Par Lost 1.338
Beyond his Potent arm, to live exempt Par Lost 2.318
Least Heav'n surcharg'd with potent multitude Par Lost 2.836
Perfection from the Suns more potent Ray. Par Lost 4.673
Or potent tongue; fool, not to think how vain Par Lost 6.135
Two potent Thrones, that to be less then Gods Par Lost 6.366
Held by thy voice, thy potent voice he heares, Par Lost 7.100
Moses once more his potent Rod extends Par Lost 12.211
Temptation found'st, or over-potent charms Samson 427
Excells his Mother at her mighty Art, Mask 63
Trinity ms 'mightie' ← 'potent'
Culling their Potent hearbs, and balefull drugs, Mask 255
Bridgewater ms 'potent'
1673 'potent'
Trinity ms 'potent' ← 'myghty' ← 'powerfull' ← 'potent'

Potentate
Of thir great Potentate; for great indeed Par Lost 5.706
None of the meanest, some great Potentate Par Lost 11.231
Potentates
Of Hell resounded. Princes, Potentates, Par Lost 1.315
Of Seraphim and Potentates and Thrones Par Lost 5.749
His Potentates to Councel call'd by night; Par Lost 6.416
Cherub and Seraph, Potentates and Thrones, Par Lost 7.198
Regents and Potentates, and Kings, yea gods Par Reg 1.117
Where all his Potentates in Council sate; Par Reg 2.118
Potion
Soon as the Potion works, their human count'nance, Mask 68
Trinity ms 'potion'
Bridgewater ms 'potion'
And shed the lushious liquor on the ground, Mask 652
Trinity ms 'liquor' ←'potion'
Pots
His hands from pots, *and mirie soyle* Psalm 81, 23
Potter
Like to a potters vessel shiver'd so. Psalm 2, 21
Pour
Pour forth thir populous youth about the Hive Par Lost 1.770
1667 'Poure'
ms 'Poure'
And what thy stores contain, bring forth and poure Par Lost 5.314
Born eevn or high, for this day will pour down, Par Lost 6.544
Of Heav'n set open on the Earth shall powre Par Lost 11.825
And shed the lushious liquor on the ground, Mask 652
Trinity ms 'shed' ←'powre'
Wherefore did Nature powre her bounties forth, Mask 710
Bridgewater ms 'power'
Poured
Treble confusion, wrath and vengeance pour'd. Par Lost 1.220
Pour'd never from her frozen loyns, to pass Par Lost 1.352
Pourd out by millions her victorious Bands Par Lost 2.997
Worlds, and on whom hath all these graces powrd; Par Lost 3.674
Powrd forth profuse on Hill and Dale and Plaine, Par Lost 4.243
The hand that formd them on thir shape hath pourd. Par Lost 4.365
Gods indignation on these Godless pourd Par Lost 6.811
About his Chariot numberless were pour'd Par Lost 7.197
Abundantly his gifts hath also pour'd Par Lost 8.220
His bursting passion into plaints thus pour'd: Par Lost 9.98
With large Wine-offerings pour'd, and sacred Feast, Par Lost 12.21
Powrd first on his Apostles, whom he sends Par Lost 12.498
The City gates out powr'd, light armed Troops Par Reg 3.311
About the wine-press where sweet moust is powr'd, Par Reg 4.16
From many a horrid rift abortive pour'd Par Reg 4.411
Sparkling, out-pow'rd, the flavor, or the smell, Samson 544
Pouring
Her Virgin Fancies, pouring forth more sweet, Par Lost 5.296
Poverty
Bred up in poverty and streights at home; Par Reg 2.415
In lowest poverty to highest deeds; Par Reg 2.438
May also in this poverty as soon Par Reg 2.451
If these they scape, perhaps in poverty Samson 697
Founded in chast and humble Povertie, Prose 3, 1
Powder
Lights on a heap of nitrous Powder, laid Par Lost 4.815
Powdered
Pouderd with Starrs. And now on Earth the Seventh Par Lost 7.581
My dazling Spells into the spungy ayr, Mask 154
Trinity ms 'dazling' ←'powder'd'
Power
With vain attempt. Him the Almighty Power Par Lost 1.44
ms 'power'
One next himself in power, and next in crime, Par Lost 1.79
His utmost power with adverse power oppos'd Par Lost 1.103
With suppliant knee, and deifie his power, Par Lost 1.112
Not by the sufferance of supernal Power. Par Lost 1.241
ms 'power'
Nor wanting power to mitigate and swage Par Lost 1.556
Hateful to utter: but what power of mind Par Lost 1.626
ms 'powre'
Exalted to such power, and gave to rule, Par Lost 1.736
Of Sovran power, with awful Ceremony Par Lost 1.753
Our power sufficient to disturb his Heav'n, Par Lost 2.102
But to our power hostility and hate, Par Lost 2.336
In power and excellence, but favour'd more Par Lost 2.350
Or substance, how endu'd, and what thir Power, Par Lost 2.356
With splendor, arm'd with power, if aught propos'd Par Lost 2.447
Excel'd her power; the Gates wide op'n stood, Par Lost 2.884
Undaunted to meet there what ever power Par Lost 2.955
Under his gloomie power I shall not long Par Lost 3.242
Anointed universal King; all Power Par Lost 3.317
Ambition. Yet why not? som other Power Par Lost 4.61
Hadst thou the same free Will and Power to stand? Par Lost 4.66
Dearer thy self then all; needs must the power Par Lost 4.412
1667 'Power'
Among so many signes of power and rule Par Lost 4.429
When *Gabriel* to his next in power thus spake. Par Lost 4.781
By thy example, but have power and right Par Lost 4.881
Allegeance to th' acknowldg'd Power supream? Par Lost 4.956
Thy goodness beyond thought, and Power Divine: Par Lost 5.159
Happiness in his power left free to will, Par Lost 5.235
Divine effulgence, whose high Power so far Par Lost 5.458
He left it in thy power, ordaind thy will Par Lost 5.526
If not the first Arch-Angel, great in Power, Par Lost 5.660
In battel, what our Power is, or our right. Par Lost 5.728

Power(*cont*)
Illustrates, when they see all Regal Power Par Lost 5.739
All Power, and us eclipst under the name Par Lost 5.776
His equals, if in power and splendor less, Par Lost 5.796
One over all with unsucceeded power. Par Lost 5.821
By our own quick'ning power, when fatal course Par Lost 5.861
Abandond at the terror of thy Power Par Lost 6.134
Of all thir Regions: how much more of Power Par Lost 6.223
Prodigious power had shewn, and met in Armes Par Lost 6.247
Of Godlike Power: for likest Gods they seemd, Par Lost 6.301
As not of power, at once; nor odds appeerd Par Lost 6.319
His confidence to equal God in power. Par Lost 6.343
Forthwith (behold the excellence, the power Par Lost 6.637
All power on him transferr'd: whence to his Son Par Lost 6.678
In Heav'n and Hell thy Power above compare, Par Lost 6.705
Scepter and Power, thy giving, I assume, Par Lost 6.730
Before him Power Divine his way prepar'd; Par Lost 6.780
Kingdom and Power and Glorie appertains, Par Lost 6.815
The Filial Power arriv'd, and sate him down Par Lost 7.587
Thy power; what thought can measure thee or tongue Par Lost 7.603
So spake the Godlike Power, and thus our Sire. Par Lost 8.249
In goodness and in power praeeminent; Par Lost 8.279
Let not my words offend thee, Heav'nly Power, Par Lost 8.379
Doubt might beget of Diabolic pow'r Par Lost 9.95
The danger lies, yet lies within his power: Par Lost 9.349
Mother of Science, Now I feel thy Power Par Lost 9.680
But keep the odds of Knowledge in my power Par Lost 9.820
But first low Reverence don, as to the power Par Lost 9.835
Not well conceav'd of God, who though his Power Par Lost 9.945
For Death from Sin no power can separate. Par Lost 10.251
Adventrous work, yet to thy power and mine Par Lost 10.255
Flew divers, and with Power (thir Power was great) Par Lost 10.284
If your joynt power prevailes, th' affaires of Hell Par Lost 10.408
Reluctant, but in vaine, a greater power Par Lost 10.515
Huge *Python*, and his Power no less he seem'd Par Lost 10.531
Too soon arriv'd, *Sin* there in power before, Par Lost 10.586
Of weakness, not of Power. Will he, draw out, Par Lost 10.801
Food for so foule a Monster, in thy power Par Lost 10.986
That shew no end but Death, and have the power, Par Lost 10.1004
He ceas'd; and th' Archangelic Power prepar'd Par Lost 11.126
Fomented by his virtual power and warmd: Par Lost 11.338
So deep the power of these Ingredients pierc'd, Par Lost 11.417
Such wondrous power God to his Saint will lend, Par Lost 12.200
The Power of the most High; he shall ascend Par Lost 12.369
But soon revives, Death over him no power Par Lost 12.420
With glory and power to judge both quick and dead, Par Lost 12.460
Secular power, though feigning still to act Par Lost 12.517
Spiritual Lawes by carnal power shall force Par Lost 12.521
Broken be not intended all our power Par Reg 1.61
The Holy Ghost, and the power of the highest Par Reg 1.139
Brute violence and proud Tyrannick pow'r, Par Reg 1.219
Thy chosen, to what highth thir pow'r unjust Par Reg 2.45
Such object hath the power to soft'n and tame Par Reg 2.163
But tender all their power? nor mention I Par Reg 2.327
And who withholds my pow'r that right to use? Par Reg 2.380
That I have also power to give thou seest, Par Reg 2.393
If of that pow'r I bring thee voluntary Par Reg 2.394
With that (such power was giv'n him then) he took Par Reg 3.251
Of his great power; for now the *Parthian* King Par Reg 3.299
Lictors and rods the ensigns of thir power, Par Reg 4.65
In ample Territory, wealth and power, Par Reg 4.82
And with my help thou may'st; to me the power Par Reg 4.103
There thou shalt hear and learn the secret power Par Reg 4.254
So saying he took (for still he knew his power Par Reg 4.394
At least might seem to hold all power of thee, Par Reg 4.494
And what he is; his wisdom, power, intent, Par Reg 4.528
In power of others, never in my own; Samson 78
Salve to thy Sores, apt words have power to swage Samson 184
Tacit, was in thy power; true; and thou bear'st Samson 430
Thy mind with what amends is in my power, Samson 745
To learn thy secrets, get into my power Samson 798
No more on me have power, their force is null'd, Samson 935
Chor. Yet beauty, though injurious, hath strange power, Samson 1003
Gave to the man despotic power Samson 1054
Which I to be the power of *Israel*'s God Samson 1150
Tyrannic power, but raging to pursue Samson 1275
Of those who have me in thir civil power. Samson 1367
Masters commands come with a power resistless Samson 1404
A noble Peer of mickle trust, and power Mask 31
Of power to cheat the eye with blear illusion, Mask 155
Bridgewater ms 'powre'
Hath hurtfull power o're true virginity. Mask 437
Of malice or of sorcery, or that power Mask 587
Bridgewater ms 'powre'
Is of such power to stir up joy as this, Mask 677
Against the Sun-clad power of Chastity, Mask 782
line not in Bridgewater ms
line not in Trinity ms
Her words set off by som superior power; Mask 801
line not in Trinity ms
line not in Bridgewater ms
And backward mutters of dissevering power, Mask 817
And adde the power of som adjuring verse. Mask 858
Trinity ms 'power' ←'call' ←'power'
Whose power hath a true consent Penseroso 95
But, O sad Virgin, that thy power Penseroso 103
For know by lot from *Jove* I am the powr Arcades 44
Trinity ms 'wer', ms defective

Power(*cont*)
(If ye have power to touch our senses so) Nativity 127
While each peculiar power forgoes his wonted seat. Nativity 196
The Tawny King with all his power. Psalm 136, 54
Alack that so to change thee winter had no power. Fair Inf 28
What power, what force, what mighty spell, if not Vacation 89
Wed your divine sounds, and mixt power employ Musick 3
Trinity ms 'divine sounds' ←'choise chords' ←'divine power'
Have linkt that amorous power to thy soft lay, Sonnet 1, 8
Of sad *Electra*'s Poet had the power Sonnet 8, 13
Trinity ms 'powre'
Both spirituall powre and civill, what each meanes Sonnet 17, 10
1662 'power'
word not in 1694 text
What powre the Church & what the civill meanes Sonnet 17, Tr. ms 45.11
With power, and Princes in their Congregations Psalm 2, 3
And their power that do amiss. Psalm 7, 36

Powered
Not out of levity, but over-powr'd Samson 880

Powerful
I also; at which time this powerful Key Par Lost 2.774
And by command of Heav'ns all-powerful King Par Lost 2.851
In vain, though by thir powerful Art they binde Par Lost 3.602
O had his powerful Destiny ordaind Par Lost 4.58
The King of Glorie in his powerful Word Par Lost 7.208
Against the charm of Beauties powerful glance. Par Lost 8.533
Powerful perswaders, quick'nd at the scent Par Lost 9.587
Powerful at greatest distance to unite Par Lost 10.247
Be now in powerful hands, that will not part Par Reg 3.155
The jealousie of Love, powerful of sway Samson 791
To oppose against such powerful arguments? Samson 862
Culling their Potent hearbs, and balefull drugs, Mask 255
Trinity ms 'potent' ←'myghty' ←'powerfull' ←'potent'
We implore thy powerful hand Mask 903
Trinity ms 'powerfull'
Bridgewater ms 'powerfull'
1637 'powerfull'

Powerfullest
What Heavens Lord had powerfullest to send Par Lost 6.425

Powers
O Prince, O Chief of many Throned Powers, Par Lost 1.128
ms 'powers'
And reassembling our afflicted Powers, Par Lost 1.186
ms 'powers'
And Powers that earst in Heaven sat on Thrones; Par Lost 1.360
ms 'powers'
O Myriads of immortal Spirits, O Powers Par Lost 1.622
ms 'powers'
Powers and Dominions, Deities of Heav'n, Par Lost 2.11
Thrones and Imperial Powers, off-spring of heav'n Par Lost 2.310
High honourd sits? Go therfore mighty Powers, Par Lost 2.456
1667 'powers'
By false presumptuous hope, the ranged powers Par Lost 2.522
Which but her self not all the *Stygian* powers Par Lost 2.875
T' whom *Satan* turning boldly, thus. Ye Powers Par Lost 2.968
Shine inward, and the mind through all her powers Par Lost 3.52
Such I created all th' Ethereal Powers Par Lost 3.100
His lapsed powers, though forfeit and enthrall'd Par Lost 3.176
Say Heav'nly powers, where shall we find such love, Par Lost 3.213
1667 'Powers'
The powers of darkness bound. Thou at the sight Par Lost 3.256
Thrones, Princedoms, Powers, Dominions I reduce: Par Lost 3.320
Hee Heav'n of Heavens and all the Powers therein Par Lost 3.390
Back from pursuit thy Powers with loud acclaime Par Lost 3.397
Drawn to his part; but other Powers as great Par Lost 4.63
Better abode, and my afflicted Powers Par Lost 4.939
Thrones, Dominations, Princedoms, Vertues, Powers, Par Lost 5.601
Or several one by one, the Regent Powers, Par Lost 5.697
So spake the Son, but *Satan* with his Powers Par Lost 5.743
Thrones, Dominations, Princedomes, Vertues, Powers, Par Lost 5.772
Thee what thou art, and formd the Pow'rs of Heav'n Par Lost 5.824
Thrones, Dominations, Princedoms, Vertues, Powers, Par Lost 5.840
Essential Powers, nor by his Reign obscur'd, Par Lost 5.841
Among those friendly Powers, who him receav'd Par Lost 6.22
At which command the Powers Militant, Par Lost 6.61
The banded Powers of *Satan* hasting on Par Lost 6.85
Since *Michael* and his Powers went forth to tame Par Lost 6.686
And to rebellious fight rallied thir Powers Par Lost 6.786
Among th' Angelic Powers, and the deep fall Par Lost 6.898
Mean while inhabit laxe, ye Powers of Heav'n, Par Lost 7.162
The infernal Powers, in one day to have marr'd Par Lost 9.136
Of Reason in my inward Powers, and Speech Par Lost 9.600
About thir spirits had plaid, and inmost powers Par Lost 9.1048
Assembl'd Angels, and ye Powers return'd Par Lost 10.34
Of high collateral glorie: him Thrones and Powers, Par Lost 10.86
Spoild Principalities and Powers, triumpht Par Lost 10.186
To my associate Powers, them to acquaint Par Lost 10.395
Thrones, Dominations, Princedoms, Vertues, Powers, Par Lost 10.460
In thir bright stand, there left his Powers to seise Par Lost 11.221
Within himself unworthie Powers to reign Par Lost 12.91
Thou knewst by name, and all th' ethereal Powers, Par Lost 12.577
O ancient Powers of Air and this wide world, Par Reg 1.44
That all the Angels and Aetherial Powers, Par Reg 1.163
Powers of Fire, Air, Water, and Earth beneath, Par Reg 2.124
And dignities and powers all but the highest? Par Reg 3.30
When *Agrican* with all his Northern powers Par Reg 3.338
Thir Lords the *Philistines* with gather'd powers Samson 251

Powers(*cont*)
Who durst not with thir whole united powers Samson 1110
Went up with armed powers thee only seeking, Samson 1190
The Sea Nymphs, and their powers offended. Penseroso 21
Ye flaming Powers, and winged Warriours bright, Circum 1

Practice
Thir daily practice to afflict me more. Samson 114

Practise
Thenceforth shall practice how to live secure, Par Lost 11.802

Practised
That practisd falshood under saintly shew, Par Lost 4.122
Yet not anough had practisd to deceive Par Lost 4.124
And practis'd distances to cringe, not fight. Par Lost 4.945
Without the sure guess of well-practiz'd feet. Mask 310
Bridgewater ms 'well practiz'd'

Praetors
Pretors, Proconsuls to thir Provinces Par Reg 4.63

Praise
Admiring enter'd, and the work some praise Par Lost 1.731
Not what they would? what praise could they receive? Par Lost 3.106
Henceforth, and never shall my Harp thy praise Par Lost 3.414
Forget, nor from thy Fathers praise disjoine. Par Lost 3.415
Naught seeking but the praise of men, here find Par Lost 3.453
The Universal Maker we may praise; Par Lost 3.676
That reaches blame, but rather merits praise Par Lost 3.697
What could be less then to afford him praise, Par Lost 4.46
But let us ever praise him, and extoll Par Lost 4.436
Is womans happiest knowledge and her praise. Par Lost 4.638
That heav'n would want spectators, God want praise; Par Lost 4.676
All these with ceasless praise his works behold Par Lost 4.679
Nor holy rapture wanted they to praise Par Lost 5.147
With thy bright Circlet, praise him in thy Spheare Par Lost 5.169
Acknowledge him thy Greater, sound his praise Par Lost 5.172
His praise, who out of Darkness call'd up Light. Par Lost 5.179
Varie to our great Maker still new praise. Par Lost 5.184
Rising or falling still advance his praise. Par Lost 5.191
His praise ye Winds, that from four Quarters blow, Par Lost 5.192
Melodious murmurs, warbling tune his praise. Par Lost 5.196
Bear on your wings and in your notes his praise; Par Lost 5.199
Made vocal by my Song, and taught his praise. Par Lost 5.204
(Whose praise be ever sung) to man in part Par Lost 5.405
Seek not the praise of men: the other sort Par Lost 6.376
Hymns of high praise, and I among them chief. Par Lost 6.745
Glorie and praise, whose wisdom had ordain'd Par Lost 7.187
From th' Earths great Altar send up silent praise Par Lost 9.195
For such a petty Trespass, and not praise Par Lost 9.693
The Tongue not made for Speech to speak thy praise: Par Lost 9.749
Thy praise hee also who forbids thy use, Par Lost 9.750
Not without Song, each Morning, and due praise Par Lost 9.800
And Palate call judicious; I the praise Par Lost 9.1020
Womans domestic honour and chief praise; Par Lost 11.617
Of worth, of honour, glory, and popular praise; Par Reg 2.227
Though needing, what praise is it to endure?, Par Reg 2.251
Then prompt her to do aught may merit praise. Par Reg 2.456
His Honour, Vertue, Merit and chief Praise, Par Reg 2.464
The peoples praise, if always praise unmixt? Par Reg 3.48
Things vulgar, & well weigh'd, scarce worth the praise, Par Reg 3.51
They praise and they admire they know not what; Par Reg 3.52
Of whom to be disprais'd were no small praise? Par Reg 3.56
Man. I cannot praise thy Marriage choises, Son, Samson 420
Off. I praise thy resolution, doff these links: Samson 1410
Rifted the Air clamouring thir god with praise, Samson 1621
In wanton dance they praise the bounteous *Pan*, Mask 176
Trinity ms 'they praise' ←'adore' ←'they praise'
La. Nay gentle Shepherd ill is lost that praise Mask 271
His praise due paid, for swinish gluttony Mask 776
With a crown of deathless Praise, Mask 973
Trinity ms 'praise' ←'bays'
Bridgewater ms 'praise'
To set her beauties praise above Penseroso 20
Of detraction from her praise, Arcades 11
The peerles height of her immortal praise, Arcades 75
And slits the thin spun life. But not the praise, Lycidas 76
His praise and glory was in *Israel* known. Psalm 114, 6
Praise the Lord, for he is kind, Psalm 136, 2
Bin as compleat as was her praise, Winchester 12
So well your words his noble vertues praise, Sonnet 10, 12
With praise enough for Envy to look wan; Sonnet 13, 6
and gives thee praise above the pipe of Pan; Sonnet 13, Tr. ms 40.06
Filling each mouth with envy, or with praise, Sonnet 15, 2
1694 'Praise'
What severs each thou 'hast learnt, which few hav don. Sonnet 17, 11
Who in the grave can celebrate thy praise? Psalm 6, 10
Then will I Jehovah's praise Psalm 7, 61
So as above the Heavens thy praise to set Psalm 8, 3
Where thee they ever praise, Psalm 84, 18
Thee will I praise O Lord my God Psalm 86, 41
But *twise that praise shall in our ear* Psalm 87, 17
And praise thee *from their loathsom bed* Psalm 88, 43
Which he who can, and will, deserv's high praise, Prose 9, 3

Praised
Nor fail'd they to express how much they prais'd, Par Lost 2.480
And touch't thir Golden Harps, and hymning prais'd Par Lost 7.258
Where God is prais'd aright, and Godlike men, Par Reg 4.348

Praises
Thy praises, with th' innumerable sound Par Lost 3.147
For wee to him indeed all praises owe, Par Lost 4.444
Recount his praises; thus he did to *Job*, Par Reg 3.64

Praises(*cont*)
Universally crown'd with highest praises. Samson 175
Great Pomp, and Sacrifice, and Praises loud Samson 436
To *Dagon*, and advanc'd his praises high Samson 450
O let us his praises tell, Psalm 136, 9
And Dunbarr feild resounds thy praises loud, Sonnet 16, 8
1694 'Praises'

Praising
Praising the lean and sallow Abstinence. Mask 709
Bridgewater ms 'praisinge'

Prancing
Prauncing their riders bore, the flower and choice Par Reg 3.314

Pranked
Obtruding false rules pranckt in reasons garb. Mask 759
Bridgewater ms 'prank't'
Trinity ms 'pranck't'

Pravity
Thir natural pravitie, by stirring up Par Lost 12.288

Pray
To pray, repent, and bring obedience due. Par Lost 3.190
How much more, if we pray him, will his ear Par Lost 10.1060
Unskilful with what words to pray, let mee Par Lost 11.32
I pray thee then deny me not thy aide Vacation 15
But Lord, thus let me pray, Psalm 4, 28
My King and God for unto thee I pray. Psalm 5, 4
O hear me *I thee pray*, Psalm 86, 2

Prayed
So pray'd they innocent, and to thir thoughts Par Lost 5.209
Pray'd for, but often proves our woe, our bane? Samson 351
I pray'd for Children, and thought barrenness Samson 352
And eyes fast fixt he stood, as one who pray'd, Samson 1637
And answer, *what I pray'd*. Psalm 86, 24

Prayer
To Prayer, repentance, and obedience due, Par Lost 3.191
1667 'prayer'
Unutterable, which the Spirit of prayer Par Lost 11.6
Hard to belief may seem; yet this will Prayer, Par Lost 11.146
By Prayer th' offended Deitie to appease, Par Lost 11.149
Nor knowing us nor known: and if by prayer Par Lost 11.307
But prayer against his absolute Decree Par Lost 11.311
But God who caus'd a fountain at thy prayer Samson 581
This one prayer yet remains, might I be heard, Samson 649
Now pity me, and hear my earnest prai'r. Psalm 4, 6
The Lord hath heard, the Lord hath heard my prai'r Psalm 6, 18
Against thy peoples praire. Psalm 80, 20
Lord God of Hoasts hear *now* my praier Psalm 84, 29
Into thy presence let my praier Psalm 88, 5
And *up to thee* my praier *doth hie* Psalm 88, 55

Prayers
Mends not her slowest pace for prayers or cries. Par Lost 10.859
And my displeasure bearst so ill. If Prayers Par Lost 10.952
Of *Themis* stood devout. To Heav'n thir prayers Par Lost 11.14
And Prayers, which in this Golden Censer, mixt Par Lost 11.24
Sufficient that thy Prayers are heard, and Death, Par Lost 11.252
Our earnest Prayers, then giv'n with solemn hand Samson 359
Thrice she assay'd with flattering prayers and sighs, Samson 392
His further ire, with praiers and vows renew'd. Samson 520
To prayers, then winds and seas, yet winds to seas Samson 961
Will rank my Prayers, and watch till thou appear. Psalm 5, 8
Of my *incessant* praiers afford Psalm 86, 19

Praying
Hee will instruct us praying, and of Grace Par Lost 10.1081
Praying, for from the Mercie-seat above Par Lost 11.2
Praying or vowing, and vouchsaf'd his voice Par Reg 1.490

Prays
He sorrows now, repents, and prayes contrite, Par Lost 11.90

Preached
Triumphs or Festivals, and to them preachd Par Lost 11.723
Salvation shall be Preacht, but to the Sons Par Lost 12.448

Preaching
Preaching how meritorious with the gods Samson 859

Preamble
Like Quivers hung, and with Praeamble sweet Par Lost 3.367

Precedence
Precedence, none, whose portion is so small Par Lost 2.33

Precedes
But harm precedes not sin: onely our Foe Par Lost 9.327
Till then the Curse pronounc't on both precedes. Par Lost 10.640

Precept
Had first his precept so to move, so shine, Par Lost 10.652

Precepts
In brief sententious precepts, while they treat Par Reg 4.264
And fetch their precepts from the *Cynick* Tub, Mask 708
1637 'praecepts'

Precincts
Not farr off Heav'n, in the Precincts of light, Par Lost 3.88

Precious
Deserve the precious bane. And here let those Par Lost 1.692
1667 'pretious'
Here in the dark so many precious things Par Lost 3.611
Two other precious drops that ready stood, Par Lost 5.132
In thee concentring all thir precious beams Par Lost 9.106
O Sovran, vertuous, precious of all Trees Par Lost 9.795
Some bloud more precious must be paid for Man, Par Lost 12.293
Like a tame Weather, all my precious fleece, Samson 538
She hutch't th' all-worshipt ore, and precious gems Mask 719
Bridgewater ms 'pretious'
Which she with pretious viold liquors heals. Mask 847

Precious(*cont*)
Trinity ms 'precious'
line not in Bridgewater ms
1637 'precious'
I have kept of pretious cure, Mask 913
1637 'precious'
Trinity ms 'precious'
Bending one way their pretious influence, Nativity 71

Precipice
The fiery Surge, that from the Precipice Par Lost 1.173
ms 'precipice'

Precipitance
Hasted with glad precipitance, uprowld Par Lost 7.291

Precipitant
His flight precipitant, and windes with ease Par Lost 3.563

Precipitate
Precipitate thee with augmented paine. Par Lost 6.280

Precise
Of Speculation; for the hour precise Par Lost 12.589

Predestination
As if predestination over-rul'd Par Lost 3.114
1667 'Predestination'

Predicament
To keep in compass of thy Predicament: Vacation 56

Prediction
How soon hath thy prediction, Seer blest, Par Lost 12.553
And high prediction, henceforth I expose Par Reg 1.142
Thou never shalt obtain; prediction still Par Reg 3.354
Means I must use thou say'st, prediction else Par Reg 3.394
Divine Prediction; what if all foretold Samson 44

Predicts
Without means us'd, what it predicts revokes. Par Reg 3.356

Predominant
Whether the Sun predominant in Heav'n Par Lost 8.160

Pre-eminence
In favour and praeeminence, yet fraught Par Lost 5.661
But this praeeminence thou hast lost, brought down Par Lost 11.347

Pre-eminent
Praeeminent by so much odds, while thou Par Lost 4.447
1667 'Preeminent'
In goodness and in power praeeminent; Par Lost 8.279

Preface
Of Preface brooking through his Zeal of Right. Par Lost 9.676
Adam, Heav'ns high behest no Preface needs: Par Lost 11.251
For Satan with slye preface to return Par Reg 2.115
No Preface needs, thou seest we long to know. Samson 1554

Prefer
And chiefly Thou O Spirit, that dost prefer Par Lost 1.17
Prefer, and Pietie to God, though then Par Lost 6.144
And long Renown thou justly may'st prefer Par Reg 4.84
Equal to God, oft shames not to prefer, Par Reg 4.303
God for the fear of Man, and Man prefer, Samson 1374

Preferred
Her Husband the Relater she preferr'd Par Lost 8.52
O Earth, how like to Heav'n, if not preferr'd Par Lost 9.99
Had not so soon preferr'd Samson 1019

Preferring
That durst dislike his reign, and me preferring, Par Lost 1.102
Free, and to none accountable, preferring Par Lost 2.255
His Deity comparing and preferring Samson 464
Chaunting thir Idol, and preferring Samson 1672

Prefixed
The time prefixt I waited, when behold Par Reg 1.269
Without beginning; for no date prefixt Par Reg 4.392
To earth from thy praefixed seat didst poast, Fair Inf 59

Pregnant
And mad'st it pregnant: What in me is dark Par Lost 1.22
Pregnant by thee, and now excessive grown Par Lost 2.779
But all these in thir pregnant causes mixt Par Lost 2.913
Shall yield us pregnant with infernal flame, Par Lost 6.483
Had got a race of mourners on som pregnant cloud. Passion 56

Prelate
Because you have thrown of your Prelate Lord, Forcers 1

Pre-ordained
The purpos'd Counsel pre-ordain'd and fixt Par Reg 1.127

Prepare
The Quarters of the North, there to prepare Par Lost 5.689
And now prepare thee for another sight. Par Lost 11.555
But now prepare thee for another Scene. Par Lost 11.637
Before Messiah and his way prepare. Par Reg 1.272
Thou did'st prepare for it a place Psalm 80, 37
Prepare a Hymn, prepare a Song Psalm 81, 5

Prepared
Such place Eternal Justice had prepar'd Par Lost 1.70
Stands on the blasted Heath. He now prepar'd Par Lost 1.615
Nigh on the Plain in many cells prepar'd, Par Lost 1.700
Ministring light prepar'd, they set and rise; Par Lost 4.664
And *Eve* within, due at her hour prepar'd Par Lost 5.303
To thir prepar'd ill Mansion driven down Par Lost 6.738
Before him Power Divine his way prepar'd; Par Lost 6.780
He took the golden Compasses, prepar'd Par Lost 7.225
To the Garden of bliss, thy seat prepar'd. Par Lost 8.299
May finde us both perhaps farr less prepar'd, Par Lost 9.381
He ceas'd; and th' Archangelic Power prepar'd Par Lost 11.126
Safest thy life, and best prepar'd endure Par Lost 11.365
Into fit moulds prepar'd; from which he formd Par Lost 11.571
Pure, and in mind prepar'd, if so befall, Par Lost 12.444
He found his Supper on the coals prepar'd, Par Reg 2.273

Preparing
Long in preparing, soon to nothing brought, Par Reg 3.389
Presage
Presage of Victorie and fierce desire Par Lost 6.201
If there be aught of presage in the mind, Samson 1387
That far events full wisely could presage, Vacation 70
Presages
Oft my advice by presages and signs, Par Reg 1.394
Presaging
Foreseeing or presaging, from the Depth Par Lost 1.627
Presaging, since with sorrow and hearts distress Par Lost 12.613
Prove to be presaging tears Winchester 44
Presbyter
New Presbyter is but *Old Priest* writ Large. Forcers 20
Prescribed
Prescrib'd, no barrs of Hell, nor all the chains Par Lost 3.82
Why hast thou, *Satan*, broke the bounds prescrib'd Par Lost 4.878
Unlicenc't from his bounds in Hell prescrib'd; Par Lost 4.909
Her office they prescrib'd, to th' other five Par Lost 10.657
Why was my breeding order'd and prescrib'd Samson 30
Prescript
By his prescript a Sanctuary is fram'd Par Lost 12.249
And tie him to his own prescript, Samson 308
Presence
Stand in his presence humble, and receive Par Lost 2.240
Thenceforth, but in thy presence Joy entire. Par Lost 3.265
Who in Gods presence, neerest to his Throne Par Lost 3.649
Neerer his presence *Adam* though not awd, Par Lost 5.358
In presence of th' Almightie Father, pleas'd Par Lost 7.11
Presence Divine. Rejoycing, but with aw Par Lost 8.314
All higher knowledge in her presence falls Par Lost 8.551
That dwelt within, whose presence had infus'd Par Lost 9.836
Thy presence, agonie of love till now Par Lost 9.858
And from his presence hid themselves among Par Lost 10.100
To whom the sovran Presence thus repli'd. Par Lost 10.144
Presence Divine, and to my Sons relate; Par Lost 11.319
His presence to these narrow bounds confin'd Par Lost 11.341
Present, and of his presence many a signe Par Lost 11.351
His presence from among them, and avert Par Lost 12.108
As in his presence, ever to observe Par Lost 12.563
His Godlike presence, and from some great act Samson 28
My presence; for that cause I cannot come. Samson 1321
His wish't presence, and beside Mask 950
  Trinity ms 'praesence'
Shake earth, and at the presence be agast Psalm 114, 15
Into thy presence let my praier Psalm 88, 5
Present
Of knowledge past or present, could have fear'd, Par Lost 1.628
Of present pain, that with ambitious mind Par Lost 2.34
Worth waiting, since our present lot appeers Par Lost 2.223
Compose our present evils, with regard Par Lost 2.281
The present misery, and render Hell Par Lost 2.459
(Which is my present journey) and once more Par Lost 2.985
Wherein past, present, future he beholds, Par Lost 3.78
Present, or past, as Saints and Patriarchs us'd. Par Lost 4.762
By present, past, and future) on such day Par Lost 5.582
What best may from the present serve to hide Par Lost 9.1092
The present, fearing guiltie what his wrauth Par Lost 10.340
As sorted best with present things. The Sun Par Lost 10.651
Before the present object languishing Par Lost 10.996
As present, Heav'nly instructer, I revive Par Lost 11.871
Ill sorting with my present state compar'd. Par Reg 1.200
Like things of thee to all that present stood. Par Reg 1.258
But rush upon me thronging, and present Samson 21
That I was never present on the place Samson 1085
Was not at present here to find my Son, Samson 1446
Likeliest, and neerest to the present ayd Mask 90
  Trinity ms 'praesent'
Co. Imports their loss, beside the present need? Mask 287
  1637 'praesent'
  Trinity ms 'praesent'
More happines then this thy present lot. Mask 789
  line not in Bridgewater ms
  1637 'praesent'
  line not in Trinity ms
Afford a present to the Infant God? Nativity 16
  1673 'Present'
Think what a present thou to God hast sent, Fair Inf 74
And to our high-rais'd phantasie present, Musick 5
  Trinity ms 'praesent' ←'present'
To serve therewith my Maker, and present Sonnet 19, 5
Present
Wast present, and with mighty wings outspread Par Lost 1.20
They led him high applauded, and present Par Lost 6.26
Present) thus to his Son audibly spake. Par Lost 7.518
Or bear what to my minde first thoughts present, Par Lost 9.213
When I am present, and thy trial choose Par Lost 9.316
Present, and of his presence many a signe Par Lost 11.351
Though present in his Angel, who shall goe Par Lost 12.201
Present in Temples at Idolatrous Rites Samson 1378
Presented
Presented with a Universal blanc Par Lost 3.48
Presented stood in terrible array Par Lost 6.106
Direct, or by occasion hath presented Par Lost 9.974
Gardens and Groves presented to his eyes, Par Reg 4.38
Presenting
Presenting, thus to intercede began. Par Lost 11.21
Presenting *Thebs*, or *Pelops* line, Penseroso 99
Presentments
And give it false presentments, lest the place Mask 156
  Trinity ms 'praesentments'
Preservation
Thou canst avoid, self-preservation bids; Samson 505
Preserve
Left them Superiour, while we can preserve Par Lost 6.443
Not hid, nor those things last which might preserve Par Lost 11.579
With all the Creatures, and thir seed preserve. Par Lost 11.873
Preserve my soul, for I have trod Psalm 86, 5
Preserved
Then thine, while I preserv'd these locks unshorn, Samson 1143
By thee preserv'd alive. Psalm 85, 24
Preserves
But life preserves, destroys life's enemy, Par Reg 2.372
President
But from him or his Angels President Par Reg 1.447
Daughter to that good Earl, once President Sonnet 10, 1
Press
About the wine-press where sweet moust is powr'd, Par Reg 4.16
Full sore doth press on me; Psalm 88, 30
Pressed
That shed *May* Flowers; and press'd her Matron lip Par Lost 4.501
From many a berrie, and from sweet kernels prest Par Lost 5.346
And of Religion, press'd how just it was, Samson 854
As he were prest to death, he cry'd more waight; Another 26
  line not in 1640, 1657, 1658 texts
Presume
If it presume, might erre in things too high, Par Lost 8.121
Infallible? yet many will presume: Par Lost 12.530
Har. Presume not on thy God, what e're he be, Samson 1156
Presumed
To match with thir inventions they presum'd Par Lost 6.631
Into the Heav'n of Heav'ns I have presum'd, Par Lost 7.13
And to the Heav'nly vision thus presum'd. Par Lost 8.356
Of thy presum'd return! event perverse! Par Lost 9.405
Bold deed thou hast presum'd, adventrous *Eve*, Par Lost 9.921
At sight whereof the Fiend yet more presum'd, Par Reg 3.345
'Twixt God and *Dagon; Dagon* hath presum'd, Samson 462
As a league-breaker gave up bound, presum'd Samson 1209
Presumes
Which he presumes already vain and void, Par Lost 10.50
Presumption
Be it not don in pride, or in presumption. Mask 431
  Trinity ms 'praesumption'
be it not don in pride or in praesumption Mask Tr. ms 16.56
  'or in praesumption' ←'or wilfull tempting'
Presumptuous
By false presumptuous hope, the ranged powers Par Lost 2.522
So judge thou still, presumptuous, till the wrauth, Par Lost 4.912
Thus I presumptuous; and the vision bright, Par Lost 8.367
Man. That were a joy presumptuous to be thought. Samson 1531
Presumptuously
Presumptuously have publish'd, impiously, Samson 498
Pretence
Too mean pretense, but what we more affect, Par Lost 6.421
To all Beleevers; and from that pretense, Par Lost 12.520
Under pretence of Bridal friends and guests, Samson 1196
I under fair pretence of friendly ends, Mask 160
  1637 'praetents'
  Trinity ms 'praetence'
Pretences
Of Spirits that in our just pretenses arm'd Par Lost 2.825
Pretend
Least wilfully transgressing he pretend Par Lost 5.244
And shall again, pretend they ne're so wise. Samson 212
Pretended
Henceforth; least that too heav'nly form, pretended Par Lost 10.872
But had thy love, still odiously pretended, Samson 873
And yet is most pretended: In a place Mask 326
  Trinity ms 'praetended'
  1637 'praetended'
Pretendest
Yet thou pretend'st to truth; all Oracles Par Reg 1.430
Pretending
To say and strait unsay, pretending first Par Lost 4.947
Pretending so commanded to consult Par Lost 5.768
Pretends
Pretends to wash off sin, and fit them so Par Reg 1.73
Pretexts
These false pretexts and varnish'd colours failing, Samson 901
Prevail
Weening to prosper, and at length prevaile Par Lost 6.795
I told ye then he should prevail and speed Par Lost 10.40
If your joynt power prevailes, th' affaires of Hell Par Lost 10.408
  1667 'prevaile'
Prevailed
Perswasively hath so prevaild, that I Par Lost 9.873
And o're a mighty King so oft prevail'd, Par Reg 3.167
Took full possession of me and prevail'd; Samson 869
And surely, Death could never have prevail'd, Carrier 9
Prevailing
From my prevailing arme, though Heavens King Par Lost 4.973
Prevailing over fear, and timerous doubt Samson 740
Prevails
Where Satan now prevailes, a Monument Par Lost 10.258
Little prevails, or rather seems a tune, Samson 661

Prevalent
Michael and his Angels prevalent Par Lost 6.411
So prevalent as to concerne the mind Par Lost 11.144
Prevenient
Prevenient Grace descending had remov'd Par Lost 11.3
Prevent
Th' Eternal to prevent such horrid fray Par Lost 4.996
Which your sincerest care could not prevent, Par Lost 10.37
It lies, yet ere Conception to prevent Par Lost 10.987
Which neither his foreknowing can prevent, Par Lost 11.773
Mean while the men of *Judah* to prevent Samson 256
Already, ere my best speed could praevent, Mask 573
1673 'prevent'
Bridgewater ms 'prevent'
O run, prevent them with thy humble ode, Nativity 24
Your Son, said she, (nor can you it prevent) Vacation 73
I fondly ask; But patience to prevent Sonnet 19, 8
Each morn, and thee prevent. Psalm 88, 56
Prevented
The Monarch, and prevented all reply, Par Lost 2.467
Prevented spares to tell thee yet by deeds Par Lost 2.739
I lose, prevented by thy eyes put out. Samson 1103
Co. Perhaps fore-stalling night prevented them. Mask 285
Trinity ms 'praevented'
1637 'praevented'
Preventing
Who knowing I shall raign past thy preventing, Par Reg 4.492
Prevention
His daring foe, at this prevention more Par Lost 6.129
In might or swift prevention; but the sword Par Lost 6.320
Preventive
May with their wholsom and preventive Shears Forcers 16
Prey
Roaming to seek thir prey on earth, durst fix Par Lost 1.382
Each on his rock transfixt, the sport and prey Par Lost 2.181
For want of other prey, but that he knows Par Lost 2.806
Immeasurably, all things shall be your prey. Par Lost 2.844
His prey, nor suffer my unspotted Soule Par Lost 3.248
Dislodging from a Region scarce of prey Par Lost 3.433
Walk'd up and down alone bent on his prey, Par Lost 3.441
Whom hunger drives to seek new haunt for prey, Par Lost 4.184
Neerer to view his prey, and unespi'd Par Lost 4.399
The whole included Race, his purposd prey. Par Lost 9.416
Of carnage, prey innumerable, and taste Par Lost 10.268
To Sin and Death a prey, and so to us, Par Lost 10.490
And season him thy last and sweetest prey. Par Lost 10.609
To Spirits foule, and all my Trees thir prey, Par Lost 11.124
Fame in the World, high titles, and rich prey, Par Lost 11.793
With all his sacred things, a scorn and prey Par Lost 12.341
To the uncircumcis'd a welcom prey, Samson 260
And on her purest spirits prey, Samson 613
To dogs and fowls a prey, or else captiv'd: Samson 694
Like stabl'd wolves, or tigers at their prey, Mask 534
Bridgewater ms 'preye'
The aidless innocent Lady his wish't prey, Mask 574
And force him to restore his purchase back, Mask 607
Trinity ms 'purchase back' ←'new got prey'
A strife thou mak'st us *and a prey* Psalm 80, 25
Prick
Prick forth the Aerie Knights, and couch thir Spears Par Lost 2.536
1667 'Pric'
Prickles
The leaf was darkish, and had prickles on it, Mask 631
Pride
The Mother of Mankind, what time his Pride Par Lost 1.36
ms 'pride'
Mixt with obdurate pride and stedfast hate: Par Lost 1.58
Like doubtful hue: but he his wonted pride Par Lost 1.527
Distends with pride, and hardning in his strength Par Lost 1.572
Of dauntless courage, and considerate Pride Par Lost 1.603
ms 'pride'
Above his fellows, with Monarchal pride Par Lost 2.428
Till Pride and worse Ambition threw me down Par Lost 4.40
Yielded with coy submission, modest pride, Par Lost 4.310
Blown up with high conceits ingendring pride. Par Lost 4.809
Through pride that sight, & thought himself impaird. Par Lost 5.665
Giv'n me to quell thir pride, and in event Par Lost 5.740
To find himself not matchless, and his pride Par Lost 6.341
In all the Liveries dect of Summers pride Par Lost 7.478
To dash thir pride, and joy for Man seduc't. Par Lost 10.577
I had persisted happie, had not thy pride Par Lost 10.874
Rancor and pride, impatience and despite, Par Lost 10.1044
Surfet, and lust, till wantonness and pride Par Lost 11.795
All her array; her female pride deject, Par Reg 2.219
The *Carthaginian* pride, young *Pompey* quell'd Par Reg 3.35
Then swell with pride, and must be titl'd Gods, Par Reg 3.81
In coats of Mail and military pride; Par Reg 3.312
When thou stood'st up his Tempter to the pride Par Reg 3.409
The Stoic last in Philosophic pride, Par Reg 4.300
Renewing fresh assaults, amidst his pride Par Reg 4.570
Had not his prowess quell'd thir pride Samson 286
Then swoll'n with pride into the snare I fell Samson 532
Be it not don in pride, or in presumption. Mask 431
And vertue has no tongue to check her pride: Mask 761
be it not don in pride or in praesumption Mask Tr. ms 16.56
Young *Hyacinth* the pride of *Spartan* land; Fair Inf 26
The pride of her carnation train, Winchester 37
For they amidst their pride have said Psalm 83, 45

Priest
In Temples and at Altars, when the Priest Par Lost 1.494
ms 'Preist'
With Incense, I thy Priest before thee bring, Par Lost 11.25
Before the Altar and the vested Priest, Par Reg 1.257
Suffers the Hypocrite or Atheous Priest Par Reg 1.487
Worship't with Temple, Priest and Sacrifice; Par Reg 3.83
Such numbers of our Nation: and the Priest Samson 857
1671 'Pirest' in some copies
And the well-feasted Priest then soonest fir'd Samson 1419
Inspire's the pale-ey'd Priest from the prophetic cell. Nativity 180
He sov'ran Priest stooping his regall head Passion 15
To honour thee, the Priest of *Phoebus* Quire Sonnet 13, 10
Trinity ms 'Priest' ←'Preist'
New Presbyter is but *Old Priest* writ Large. Forcers 20
Trinity ms 'Preist'
Priests
Fanatic *Egypt* and her Priests, to seek Par Lost 1.480
ms 'preists'
But first among the Priests dissension springs, Par Lost 12.353
Though Priests, the Crown, and *David*'s Throne usurp'd, Par Reg 3.169
That part most reverenc'd *Dagon* and his Priests, Samson 1463
Lords, Ladies, Captains, Councellors, or Priests, Samson 1653
Us thy vow'd Priests, till utmost end Mask 136
Bridgewater ms 'preists'
Trinity ms 'preists'
Prime
These were the prime in order and in might; Par Lost 1.506
Astonisht: none among the choice and prime Par Lost 2.423
Not of the prime, yet such as in his face Par Lost 3.637
Beneath th' *Azores;* whither the prime Orb, Par Lost 4.592
Calls us, we lose the prime, to mark how spring Par Lost 5.21
While day arises, that sweet hour of Prime. Par Lost 5.170
Wantond as in her prime, and plaid at will Par Lost 5.295
High matter thou injoinst me, O prime of men, Par Lost 5.563
Nisroc, of Principalities the prime; Par Lost 6.447
Is the prime Wisdom, what is more, is fume, Par Lost 8.194
For well I understand in the prime end Par Lost 8.540
The season, prime for sweetest Sents and Aires: Par Lost 9.200
Vertumnus, or to *Ceres* in her Prime, Par Lost 9.395
Us his prime Creatures, dignifi'd so high, Par Lost 9.940
Thou art thir Author and prime Architect: Par Lost 10.356
His starrie Helme unbuckl'd shew'd him prime Par Lost 11.245
True opener of mine eyes, prime Angel blest, Par Lost 11.598
Among the Prime in Splendour, now depos'd, Par Reg 1.413
In his prime youth the fair *Iberian* maid. Par Reg 2.200
Though chiefly not for glory as prime end, Par Reg 3.123
Light the prime work of God to me is extinct, Samson 70
Why am I thus bereav'd thy prime decree? Samson 85
She was not the prime cause, but I my self, Samson 234
More Faith? who also in her prime of love, Samson 388
Co. Were they of manly prime, or youthful bloom? Mask 289
For *Lycidas* is dead, dead ere his prime Lycidas 8
Lady that in the prime of earliest youth, Sonnet 9, 1
Primitive
Mean while our Primitive great Sire, to meet Par Lost 5.350
Primrose
Bring the rathe Primrose that forsaken dies. Lycidas 142
1638 'primerose'
Trinity ms 'primrose'
Soft silken Primrose fading timelesslie, Fair Inf 2
The yellow Cowslip, and the pale Primrose. May Morn 4
Primrose-season
Brisk as the *April* buds in Primrose-season. Mask 671
Bridgewater ms 'primrose season'
1637 'primrose season'
Trinity ms 'primrose season'
Prince
O Prince, O Chief of many Throned Powers, Par Lost 1.128
And fierce demeanour seems the Prince of Hell, Par Lost 4.871
Go *Michael* of Celestial Armies Prince, Par Lost 6.44
So spake the Prince of Angels; to whom thus Par Lost 6.281
Prince of the Aire; then rising from his Grave Par Lost 10.185
Whom thus the Prince of Darkness answerd glad. Par Lost 10.383
Folly to mee, so doth the Prince of Hell Par Lost 10.621
Prince above Princes, gently hast thou tould Par Lost 11.298
The Serpent, Prince of aire, and drag in Chaines Par Lost 12.454
The Prince of darkness, glad would also seem Par Reg 4.441
Prince *Memnons* sister might beseem, Penseroso 18
Wherin the Prince of light Nativity 62
Princedoms
Thrones, Princedoms, Powers, Dominions I reduce: Par Lost 3.320
Thrones, Dominations, Princedoms, Vertues, Powers, Par Lost 5.601
Thrones, Dominations, Princedomes, Vertues, Powers, Par Lost 5.772
Thrones, Dominations, Princedoms, Vertues, Powers, Par Lost 5.840
Princedoms, and Dominations ministrant Par Lost 10.87
Thrones, Dominations, Princedoms, Vertues, Powers, Par Lost 10.460
Princely
Excelling human, Princely Dignities, Par Lost 1.359
And Princely counsel in his face yet shon, Par Lost 2.304
Warr unproclam'd. The Princely Hierarch Par Lost 11.220
Where his fair off-spring nurs't in Princely lore, Mask 34
Trinity ms 'princely'
Bridgewater ms 'princely'
To the great Mistres of yon princely shrine, Arcades 36
Where the bright Seraphim in burning row Musick 10
Trinity ms 'burning' ←'triple' ←'tripled' ←'princely' ←'princly'

Princes
Of Hell resounded. Princes, Potentates, Par Lost 1.315
And sat as Princes, whom the supreme King Par Lost 1.735
ms 'princes'
Princes of Hell? for so the popular vote Par Lost 2.313
On Princes, when thir rich Retinue long Par Lost 5.355
Prince above Princes, gently hast thou tould Par Lost 11.298
Princes, Heavens antient Sons, Aethereal Thrones, Par Reg 2.121
And Princes of my countrey came in person, Samson 851
And Courts of Princes, where it first was nam'd, Mask 325
Trinity ms 'princes'
Bridgewater ms 'princes'
With power, and Princes in their Congregations Psalm 2, 3
As other Princes *die*. Psalm 82, 24
So let their Princes speed Psalm 83, 42
So let their Princes *bleed*. Psalm 83, 44
Principalities
Nisroc, of Principalities the prime; Par Lost 6.447
Spoild Principalities and Powers, triumpht Par Lost 10.186
Principled
With goodness principl'd not to reject Samson 760
Principles
His principles being ceast, he ended strait. Another 10
Print
Where no print of step hath been, Arcades 85
Hath took no print of the approching light, Nativity 20
Printed
Must now be nam'd and printed Hereticks Forcers 11
Printless
Thus I set my printless feet Mask 897
1637 'printlesse'
Trinity ms 'printlesse'
Bridgewater ms 'printles'
Prison
For those rebellious, here thir Prison ordain'd Par Lost 1.71
ms 'pris'on'
The Prison of his Tyranny who Reigns Par Lost 2.59
Our prison strong, this huge convex of Fire, Par Lost 2.434
Com'st thou, escap'd thy prison, and transform'd, Par Lost 4.824
And now returns him from his prison scap't, Par Lost 4.906
Out of such prison, though Spirits of purest light, Par Lost 6.660
In Prison under Judgements imminent: Par Lost 11.725
1667 'prison'
Leaving my dolorous Prison I enjoy Par Reg 1.364
Daily in the common Prison else enjoyn'd me, Samson 6
Prison within Prison Samson 153
Into the common Prison, there to grind Samson 1161
And he in that calamitous prison left. Samson 1480
Prisoned
Who as they sung, would take the prison'd soul, Mask 256
Bridgewater ms 'prisond'
Prisoner
Where I a Prisoner chain'd, scarce freely draw Samson 7
Mine and Loves prisoner, not the *Philistines*, Samson 808
Off. Ebrews, the Pris'ner *Samson* here I seek. Samson 1308
To accept of ransom for my Son thir pris'ner, Samson 1460
Prison-house
From forth this loathsom prison-house, to abide Samson 922
Prithee
El. Bro. What fears good *Thyrsis?* Prethee briefly shew. Mask 512
1637 'prethee'
Bridgewater ms 'prithee'
Trinity ms 'preethee'
And crumble all thy sinews. *Eld. Bro*. Why prethee Shepherd Mask 615
Trinity ms 'preethee'
Bridgewater ms 'prithee'
Private
Into her private Cell when Nature rests. Par Lost 5.109
Private, unactive, calm, contemplative, Par Reg 2.81
Affecting private life, or more obscure Par Reg 3.22
Thy life hath yet been private, most part spent Par Reg 3.232
His horrid lusts in private to enjoy, Par Reg 4.94
Or if I would delight my private hours Par Reg 4.331
Thy manhood last, though yet in private bred; Par Reg 4.509
Home to his Mothers house private return'd. Par Reg 4.639
Private respects must yield; with grave authority Samson 868
But I a private person, whom my Countrey Samson 1208
I was no private but a person rais'd Samson 1211
Private reward, for which both God and State Samson 1465
Privation
Privation meer of light and absent day. Par Reg 4.400
Privilege
Invisible, yet staid (such priviledge Par Lost 7.589
By priviledge of death and burial Samson 104
Privy
Besides what the grim Woolf with privy paw Lycidas 128
Trinity ms 'privie'
Prize
Rain influence, and judge the prise Allegro 122
To love, to seek, to prize Psalm 4, 11
Proboscis
His Lithe Proboscis; close the Serpent sly Par Lost 4.347
Proceed
All things proceed, and up to him return, Par Lost 5.470
If guiltless? But from me what can proceed, Par Lost 10.824
My judgments, how with Mankind I proceed, Par Lost 11.69
And Man as from a second stock proceed. Par Lost 12.7
Thou shalt proceed, and from thy Womb the Son Par Lost 12.381
Proceed*(cont)*
Man. Believe not these suggestions which proceed Samson 599
Proceeded
Proceeded thus to ask his Heav'nly Guest. Par Lost 7.69
To Judgement he proceeded on th' accus'd Par Lost 10.164
His peace, and thus proceeded in her plaint. Par Lost 10.913
Proceeded, and Oppression, and Sword-Law Par Lost 11.672
Proceedest
Outlandish flatteries? then proceed'st to talk Par Reg 4.125
Proceeding
Proceeding, which in other Beasts observ'd Par Lost 9.94
Proceeding from the mouth of God; who fed Par Reg 1.350
Proceeds
On our belief, that all from them proceeds; Par Lost 9.719
Whose vertue, for of good still good proceeds, Par Lost 9.973
But now my Oat proceeds, Lycidas 88
Process
By pollicy, and long process of time, Par Lost 2.297
Cannot without process of speech be told, Par Lost 7.178
Procession
Follow'd in bright procession to behold Par Lost 7.222
Procinct
Warr he perceav'd, warr in procinct, and found Par Lost 6.19
Proclaim
And Trumpets sound throughout the Host proclaim Par Lost 1.754
ms 'proclaime'
The summoning Arch-Angels to proclaime Par Lost 3.325
Before him a great Prophet, to proclaim Par Reg 1.70
Here celebrate in *Gaza;* and proclaim Samson 435
Proclaimed
Honourd by his great Father, and proclaimd Par Lost 5.663
To one and to his image now proclaim'd? Par Lost 5.784
Strait knew me, and with loudest voice proclaim'd Par Reg 1.275
For Angels have proclaim'd it, but concealing Par Reg 4.474
The morning Trumpets Festival proclaim'd Samson 1598
Proclaimer
Now had the great Proclaimer with a voice Par Reg 1.18
Proclaiming
Of heavenly Grace: and God proclaiming peace, Par Lost 2.499
Proclaiming Life to all who shall believe Par Lost 12.407
1667 'Proclaming'
Proclaims
Unseen before in Heav'n proclaims him com, Par Lost 12.361
And with contrary blast proclaims most deeds, Samson 972
Proconsuls
Pretors, Proconsuls to thir Provinces Par Reg 4.63
Procreation
In procreation common to all kindes Par Lost 8.597
Procure
If we procure not to our selves more woe. Par Lost 2.225
Prodigies
So many terrors, voices, prodigies Par Reg 4.482
Prodigious
Perverse, all monstrous, all prodigious things, Par Lost 2.625
Prodigious motion felt and rueful throes. Par Lost 2.780
Prodigious power had shewn, and met in Armes Par Lost 6.247
Of length prodigious joyning to the Wall Par Lost 10.302
Produce prodigious Births of bodie or mind. Par Lost 11.687
Of thy prodigious might and feats perform'd Samson 1083
Produce
Space may produce new Worlds; whereof so rife Par Lost 1.650
As Clouds, and Clouds may rain, and Rain produce Par Lost 8.146
Produce prodigious Births of bodie or mind. Par Lost 11.687
That all this good of evil shall produce, Par Lost 12.470
He now shall know I can produce a man Par Reg 1.150
Other donation none thou canst produce: Par Reg 4.184
Off. I am sorry what this stoutness will produce. Samson 1346
Produced
These changes in the Heav'ns, though slow, produc'd Par Lost 10.692
Of Paradise could have product, ere fall'n Par Lost 11.29
And reason; since his word all things produc'd, Par Reg 3.122
Produces
Produces with Terrestrial Humor mixt Par Lost 3.610
Wilde work produces oft, and most in dreams, Par Lost 5.112
Producing
Warm'd by the Sun, producing every kind, Par Lost 9.721
Product
To whom thus *Michael*. These are the product Par Lost 11.683
Productive
Productive in Herb, Plant, and nobler birth Par Lost 9.111
Proem
So gloz'd the Tempter, and his Proem tun'd; Par Lost 9.549
Profane
Of Heathen and prophane, thir carkasses Samson 693
What act more execrably unclean, prophane? Samson 1362
Arm his profane tongue with contemptuous words Mask 781
line not in Trinity ms
line not in Bridgewater ms
Profaned
His holy Rites, and solemn Feasts profan'd, Par Lost 1.390
O sacred name of faithfulness profan'd! Par Lost 4.951
Profan'd first by the Serpent, by him first Par Lost 9.930
As vile hath been my folly, who have profan'd Samson 377
Profaner
Where no profaner eye may look, Penseroso 140
1673 'prophaner'
Professed
The first and wisest of them all profess'd Par Reg 4.293

Professed(*cont*)
Of Nuptial Love profest, carrying it strait | Samson 385
Then, as since then, thy countries foe profest: | Samson 884
Professing
Wise to flie pain, professing next the Spie, | Par Lost 4.948
Proffer
So hardie as to proffer or accept | Par Lost 2.425
Proffered
Nor proffer'd by an Enemy, though who | Par Reg 2.330
Profit
Thy weaker; let it profit thee to have heard | Par Lost 6.909
Thin sown with aught of profit or delight, | Par Reg 4.345
With no small profit daily to my owners. | Samson 1261
Profits
Then value: Oft times nothing profits more | Par Lost 8.571
Bind us with after-bands, what profits then | Par Lost 9.761
Profluent
Baptizing in the profluent stream, the signe | Par Lost 12.442
Profound
These past, if any pass, the void profound | Par Lost 2.438
A gulf profound as that *Serbonian* Bog | Par Lost 2.592
Into this gloom of *Tartarus* profound, | Par Lost 2.858
I travel this profound, direct my course; | Par Lost 2.980
Matter unform'd and void: Darkness profound | Par Lost 7.233
To contemplation and profound dispute, | Par Reg 4.214
Thou in the lowest pit *profound* | Psalm 88, 25
Profoundest
Infernal world, and thou profoundest Hell | Par Lost 1.251
Naught but profoundest Hell can be his shroud, | Nativity 218
Profundity
Round through the vast profunditie obscure, | Par Lost 7.229
Profuse
Powrd forth profuse on Hill and Dale and Plaine, | Par Lost 4.243
On a green shadie Bank profuse of Flours | Par Lost 8.286
Seem'd erst so lavish and profuse, | Arcades 9
Progenitor
To whom our great Progenitor. Thy words | Par Lost 5.544
And reverence thee thir great Progenitor. | Par Lost 11.346
Progeny
O Progeny of Heav'n, Empyreal Thrones, | Par Lost 2.430
Hee and his faithless Progenie: whose fault? | Par Lost 3.96
Whose progenie you are. Mean while enjoy | Par Lost 5.503
Hear all ye Angels, Progenie of Light, | Par Lost 5.600
To them and to thir Progenie from thence | Par Lost 11.107
Gift to his Progenie of all that Land; | Par Lost 12.138
Now shew thy Progeny; if not to stand, | Par Reg 4.554
Raild at *Latona*'s twin-born progenie | Sonnet 12, 6
Trinity ms 'progeny'
Progress
In progress through the rode of Heav'n Star-pav'd. | Par Lost 4.976
Her rosie progress smiling; let us forth, | Par Lost 11.175
Progressive
Progressive, retrograde, or standing still, | Par Lost 8.127
Prohibit
Barr'd over us prohibit all egress. | Par Lost 2.437
Prohibition
One easie prohibition, who enjoy | Par Lost 4.433
Of prohibition, root of all our woe; | Par Lost 9.645
Prohibitions
Such prohibitions binde not. But if Death | Par Lost 9.760
Projecting
What sit we then projecting peace and Warr? | Par Lost 2.329
Projects
Vented much policy, and projects deep | Par Reg 3.391
Prolific
Prolific humour soft'ning all her Globe, | Par Lost 7.280
Prologue
Came Prologue, and Apologie to prompt, | Par Lost 9.854
Prolong
Henceforth I flie not Death, nor would prolong | Par Lost 11.547
After appearance, and again prolong | Par Reg 2.41
To win thy destin'd seat, but wilt prolong | Par Reg 4.469
Prolonged
To life prolongd and promisd Race, I now | Par Lost 11.331
Prolongs
With thousand echo's still prolongs each heav'nly close. | Nativity 100
Promiscuous
While the promiscuous croud stood yet aloof? | Par Lost 1.380
Promiscuous from all Nations, Jew, or Greek, | Par Reg 3.118
Promise
And publish Grace to all, on promise made | Par Lost 2.238
His promise, that thy Seed shall bruise our Foe; | Par Lost 11.155
Of *Moreh;* there by promise he receaves | Par Lost 12.137
And puissant deeds, a promise shall receive | Par Lost 12.322
The promise of the Father, who shall dwell | Par Lost 12.487
Lower then bondslave! Promise was that I | Samson 38
Confess, and promise wonders in her change, | Samson 753
Promised
Over the *Promis'd Land* to God so dear, | Par Lost 3.531
So promis'd hee, and *Uriel* to his charge | Par Lost 4.589
But thou hast promis'd from us two a Race | Par Lost 4.732
Great joy he promis'd to his thoughts, and new | Par Lost 9.843
False in our promis'd Rising; since our Eyes | Par Lost 9.1070
To life prolongd and promisd Race, I now | Par Lost 11.331
Which that false Fruit that promis'd clearer sight | Par Lost 11.413
With glory and spoile back to thir promis'd Land. | Par Lost 12.172
Promisd to *Abraham* and his Seed: the rest | Par Lost 12.260
The Spirit of God, promisd alike and giv'n | Par Lost 12.519

Promised(*cont*)
Of him so lately promiss'd to thy aid | Par Lost 12.542
1669 'promis'd'
By mee the Promis'd Seed shall all restore. | Par Lost 12.623
E're I the promis'd Kingdom can attain, | Par Reg 1.265
Judaea now and all the promis'd land | Par Reg 3.157
When to the promis'd land thir Fathers pass'd; | Par Reg 3.439
Promisd by Heavenly message twice descending. | Samson 635
Promises
With other promises and other vaunts | Par Lost 4.84
Promontories
Main Promontories flung, which in the Air | Par Lost 6.654
Promontory
Stretcht like a Promontorie sleeps or swimmes, | Par Lost 7.414
That blows from off each beaked Promontory, | Lycidas 94
Trinity ms 'promontorie'
1638 'Promontorie'
Promote
And good workes in her Husband to promote. | Par Lost 9.234
From darkness to promote me, or here place | Par Lost 10.745
Born to that end, born to promote all truth, | Par Reg 1.205
Promotion
And my promotion will be thy destruction? | Par Reg 3.202
Prompt
Unmeditated, such prompt eloquence | Par Lost 5.149
Our prompt obedience. Fast we found, fast shut | Par Lost 8.240
Came Prologue, and Apologie to prompt, | Par Lost 9.854
Then prompt her to do aught may merit praise. | Par Reg 2.456
Prompt me; and they perhaps are not far off. | Mask 229
I did but prompt the age to quit their cloggs | Sonnet 12, 1
Prompted
Rage prompted them at length, and found them arms | Par Lost 6.635
As thou art wont, my prompted Song else mute, | Par Reg 1.12
Have prompted this Heroic *Nazarite*, | Samson 318
Prompting
Divine impulsion prompting how thou might'st | Samson 422
Prone
Prone on the Flood, extended long and large | Par Lost 1.195
With awful reverence prone; and as a God | Par Lost 2.478
Declin'd was hasting now with prone carreer | Par Lost 4.353
A cloudy spot. Down thither prone in flight | Par Lost 5.266
Of all yet don; a Creature who not prone | Par Lost 7.506
From prone, nor in thir wayes complacence find. | Par Lost 8.433
Prone on the ground, as since, but on his reare, | Par Lost 9.497
A monstrous Serpent on his Belly prone, | Par Lost 10.514
With supplication prone and Fathers tears | Samson 1459
For thou art good, thou Lord art prone | Psalm 86, 13
Pronounced
Pronounc'd among the Gods, and by an Oath, | Par Lost 2.352
When ever that shall be; so Fate pronounc'd. | Par Lost 2.809
God hath pronounc't it death to taste that Tree, | Par Lost 4.427
Whose bed is undefil'd and chaste pronounc't, | Par Lost 4.761
Thir Maker, in fit strains pronounc't or sung | Par Lost 5.148
The just Decree of God, pronounc't and sworn, | Par Lost 5.814
Of woe and sorrow. Sternly he pronounc'd | Par Lost 8.333
Him Lord pronounc'd, and, O indignitie! | Par Lost 9.154
What may this mean? Language of Man pronounc't | Par Lost 9.553
On *Adam* last thus judgement he pronounc'd. | Par Lost 10.197
Till then the Curse pronounc't on both precedes. | Par Lost 10.640
The penaltie pronounc't, doubt not but God | Par Lost 10.1022
Th' Almighty thus pronouncd his sovran Will. | Par Lost 11.83
1667 'pronounc'd' in some copies
From Heav'n pronounc'd him his beloved Son. | Par Reg 1.32
Audibly heard from Heav'n, pronounc'd me his, | Par Reg 1.284
From us his foes pronounc't glory he exacts. | Par Reg 3.120
Whom well inspir'd the Oracle pronounc'd | Par Reg 4.275
Heard thee pronounc'd the Son of God belov'd. | Par Reg 4.513
Pronounc't and in his volumes taught our Lawes, | Sonnet 21, 3
line not in Trinity ms
Pronounces
As he pronounces lastly on each deed, | Lycidas 83
Pronouncing
For want of well pronouncing *Shibboleth*. | Samson 289
Proof
And put to proof his high Supremacy, | Par Lost 1.132
On this side nothing; and by proof we feel | Par Lost 2.101
Retire, or taste thy folly, and learn by proof, | Par Lost 2.686
Not free, what proof could they have givn sincere | Par Lost 3.103
Gave proof unheeded; others on the grass | Par Lost 4.350
The proof of thir obedience and thir faith? | Par Lost 4.520
To trample thee as mire: for proof look up, | Par Lost 4.1010
Shee needed, Vertue-proof, no thought infirme | Par Lost 5.384
Shall teach us highest deeds, by proof to try | Par Lost 5.865
Not proof enough such Object to sustain, | Par Lost 8.535
Not incorruptible of Faith, not prooff | Par Lost 9.298
One Heart, one Soul in both; whereof good prooff | Par Lost 9.967
Such proof, conclude, they then begin to faile. | Par Lost 9.1142
High proof ye now have giv'n to be the Race | Par Lost 10.385
Constant, mature, proof against all assaults, | Par Lost 10.882
By proof the undoubted Son of God, inspire, | Par Reg 1.11
Gabriel this day by proof thou shalt behold, | Par Reg 1.130
Nearer acquainted, now I feel by proof, | Par Reg 1.400
Proof against all temptation as a rock | Par Reg 4.533
Under his feet: for proof, e're this thou feel'st | Par Reg 4.621
Adamantean Proof; | Samson 134
Full of divine instinct, after some proof | Samson 526
For proof hereof, if *Dagon* be thy god, | Samson 1145
And now some public proof thereof require | Samson 1314

Proof(*cont*)
Or at some proof of strength before them shown. Samson 1475
Proof of his mighty strength in feats and games; Samson 1602
With antick Pillars massy proof, Penseroso 158
Of branching Elm Star-proof, Arcades 89
1673 'Elm-Star-proof'
Trinity ms 'sta re-proofe', ms defective
Prop
Lop overgrown, or prune, or prop, or bind, Par Lost 9.210
From her best prop so farr, and storm so nigh. Par Lost 9.433
Propagate
Shouldst propagat, already infinite; Par Lost 8.420
Propagated
Is propagated seem such dear delight Par Lost 8.580
Is propagated curse. O voice once heard Par Lost 10.729
Propense
In feeble hearts, propense anough before Samson 455
Proper
That in our proper motion we ascend Par Lost 2.75
But first he casts to change his proper shape, Par Lost 3.634
He lights, and to his proper shape returns Par Lost 5.276
To proper substance; time may come when men Par Lost 5.493
Celestial rosie red, Loves proper hue, Par Lost 8.619
Properly
And sin? the Bodie properly hath neither. Par Lost 10.791
Property
The divine property of her first being. Mask 469
Bridgewater ms 'propertie'
1637 'propertie'
Trinity ms 'propertie'
Yea it shall be his natural property Vacation 87
Prophecies
When Prophesies of thee are best fullfill'd. Par Reg 4.381
Prophecy
All Prophecie, That of the Royal Stock Par Lost 12.325
I as a Prophecy receive: for God, Samson 473
Prophesied
On *David*'s Throne, be propheci'd what will. Par Reg 4.108
Prophet
O Prophet of glad tidings, finisher Par Lost 12.375
Before him a great Prophet, to proclaim Par Reg 1.70
The Prophet do him reverence, on him rising Par Reg 1.80
Our new baptizing Prophet at the Ford Par Reg 1.328
To *Balaam* Reprobate, a Prophet yet Par Reg 1.491
By his great Prophet, pointed at and shown, Par Reg 2.51
He saw the Prophet also how he fled Par Reg 2.270
Rain'd from Heaven Manna, and that Prophet bold Par Reg 2.312
By Prophet or by Angel, unless thou Par Reg 3.352
That whirl'd the Prophet up at *Chebar* flood, Passion 37
Prophetic
(if ancient and prophetic fame in Heav'n Par Lost 2.346
Just *Simeon* and Prophetic *Anna*, warn'd Par Reg 1.255
If of my raign Prophetic Writ hath told, Par Reg 3.184
To somthing like Prophetic strain. Penseroso 174
Inspire's the pale-ey'd Priest from the prophetic cell. Nativity 180
Prophets
And *Tiresias* and *Phineus* Prophets old. Par Lost 3.36
And all the Prophets in thir Age the times Par Lost 12.243
The Law and Prophets, searching what was writ Par Reg 1.260
Of all his flattering Prophets glibb'd with lyes Par Reg 1.375
Therefore as those young Prophets then with care Par Reg 2.18
The Prophets old, who sung thy endless raign, Par Reg 3.178
The *Pentateuch* or what the Prophets wrote, Par Reg 4.226
But herein to our Prophets far beneath, Par Reg 4.356
By all the Prophets; of thy birth at length Par Reg 4.503
Propitiation
And propitiation, all his works on mee Par Lost 11.34
Propitious
O favourable spirit, propitious guest, Par Lost 5.507
My Maker, be propitious while I speak. Par Lost 8.380
His Offring soon propitious Fire from Heav'n Par Lost 11.441
Which he hath sent propitious, some great good Par Lost 12.612
While the jolly hours lead on propitious *May*, Sonnet 1, 4
Proportion
Which must be mutual, in proportion due Par Lost 8.385
Internal Man, is but proportion meet, Par Lost 9.711
In unsuperfluous eeven proportion, Mask 773
Proportional
Proportional ascent, which cannot be Par Lost 9.936
Proportioned
Proportiond to each kind. So from the root Par Lost 5.479
These two proportiond ill drove me transverse. Samson 209
To my proportion'd strength. Shepherd lead on.---- Mask 330
Proportions
Instinct through all proportions low and high Par Lost 11.562
Proposal
Sam. Spare that proposal, Father, spare the trouble Samson 487
Proposals
If our proposals once again were heard Par Lost 6.618
Propose
The Teachers of our Law, and to propose Par Reg 1.212
Proposed
By *Satan*, and in part propos'd: for whence, Par Lost 2.380
With splendor, arm'd with power, if aught propos'd Par Lost 2.447
And *Raphael* now to *Adam*'s doubt propos'd Par Lost 8.64
Those terms whatever, when they were propos'd: Par Lost 10.757
And when to all his Angels he propos'd Par Reg 1.371
Then these thou bear'st that title, have propos'd Par Reg 4.199

Proposed(*cont*)
By me propos'd in life contemplative, Par Reg 4.370
And as that *Theban* Monster that propos'd Par Reg 4.572
But Gods propos'd deliverance not so. Samson 292
That solv'd the riddle which I had propos'd. Samson 1200
If some convenient ransom were propos'd. Samson 1471
Proposest
Thou to thy self proposest, in the choice Par Lost 8.400
Resolv'd, as thou proposest; so our Foe Par Lost 10.1038
Propound
What we propound, and loud that all may hear. Par Lost 6.567
And dar'st thou to the Son of God propound Par Reg 4.178
Propounded
And Brest, (what could we more2) propounded terms Par Lost 6.612
Propriety
Of human ofsspring, sole proprietie, Par Lost 4.751
Prose
Things unattempted yet in Prose or Rhime. Par Lost 1.16
ms 'prose'
Flowd from thir lips, in Prose or numerous Verse, Par Lost 5.150
Prosecute
To prosecute the means of thy deliverance Samson 603
To acquit themselves and prosecute their foes Samson 897
Proserpina
Of *Enna*, where *Proserpin* gathering flours Par Lost 4.269
Yet Virgin of *Proserpina* from *Jove*. Par Lost 9.396
Proserpine
so fares as did forsaken Proserpine Mask Tr. ms 15.52
soe fares as did forsaken Proserpine Mask Br. ms 344
Prospect
Him God beholding from his prospect high, Par Lost 3.77
The goodly prospect of some forein land Par Lost 3.548
Which to our general Sire gave prospect large Par Lost 4.144
For prospect, what well us'd had bin the pledge Par Lost 4.200
The Earth outstretcht immense, a prospect wide Par Lost 5.88
In prospect; there the Eagle and the Stork Par Lost 7.423
In prospect from his Throne, how good, how faire, Par Lost 7.556
Eden and all the Coast in prospect lay. Par Lost 10.89
Us'd by the Tempter: on that prospect strange Par Lost 10.552
Stretcht out to the amplest reach of prospect lay. Par Lost 11.380
In prospect, as I point them; on the shoare Par Lost 12.143
From whose high top to ken the prospect round, Par Reg 2.286
The Prospect was, that here and there was room Par Reg 3.263
Prospective
And in times long and dark Prospective Glass Vacation 71
Prosper
Surer to prosper then prosperity Par Lost 2.39
Weening to prosper, and at length prevaile Par Lost 6.795
Long time shall dwell and prosper, but when sins Par Lost 12.316
And what he takes in hand shall prosper all. Psalm 1, 10
Prospered
To visit how they prosper'd, bud and bloom, Par Lost 8.45
That thou on Earth hadst prosper'd, which thy looks Par Lost 10.360
Prospering
To touch the prosperous growth of this tall Wood. Mask 270
Trinity ms 'prosperous' ← 'prospering'
Bridgewater ms 'prosperinge'
And at thy growing vertues fret their spleen, Sonnet 9, 7
Trinity ms 'growing' ← 'prospering' ← 'blooming'
Prosperity
Surer to prosper then prosperity Par Lost 2.39
Prosperous
Useful of hurtful, prosperous of adverse Par Lost 2.259
Prosperous or adverse: so shalt thou lead Par Lost 11.364
With prosperous wing full summ'd to tell of deeds Par Reg 1.14
Will waft me; and the way found prosperous once Par Reg 1.104
I would be understood) in prosperous days Samson 191
To touch the prosperous growth of this tall Wood. Mask 270
Bridgewater ms 'prosperinge'
Trinity ms 'prosperous' ← 'prospering'
Prostituting
Marrying or prostituting, as befell, Par Lost 11.716
By prostituting holy things to Idols; Samson 1358
Prostrate
Groveling and prostrate on yon Lake of Fire, Par Lost 1.280
Of Thrones and mighty Seraphim prostrate, Par Lost 6.841
Repairing where he judg'd us, prostrate fall Par Lost 10.1087
Repairing where he judg'd them prostrate fell Par Lost 10.1099
Before thee *prostrate lie*. Psalm 88, 4
Prostration
Knee-tribute yet unpaid, prostration vile, Par Lost 5.782
Protect
Guard them, and him within protect from harms, Sonnet 8, 4
Protection
Nor under their protection but my own, Samson 887
Thy protection while I crie, Psalm 7, 3
Protects
That gave thee being, still shades thee and protects. Par Lost 9.266
Protesting
Protesting Fate supreame; thence how I found Par Lost 10.480
Proteus
In various shapes old *Proteus* from the Sea, Par Lost 3.604
Proud
Rais'd impious War in Heav'n and Battel proud Par Lost 1.43
His mighty Standard; that proud honour claim'd Par Lost 1.533
His proud imaginations thus displaid. Par Lost 2.10
As when to warn proud Cities warr appears Par Lost 2.533
Unbrok'n, and in proud rebellious Arms Par Lost 2.691

Proud(*cont*)
Or proud return though to his heavier doom, Par Lost 3.159
So saying, his proud step he scornful turn'd, Par Lost 4.536
To his proud fair, best quitted with disdain. Par Lost 4.770
But like a proud Steed reind, went hautie on, Par Lost 4.858
Proud limitarie Cherube, but ere then Par Lost 4.971
O argument blasphemous, false and proud! Par Lost 5.809
On those proud Towrs to swift destruction doom'd. Par Lost 5.907
To set the envier of his State, the proud Par Lost 6.89
Proud, art thou met? thy hope was to have reacht Par Lost 6.131
On the proud Crest of *Satan*, that no sight, Par Lost 6.191
O Friends, why come not on these Victors proud? Par Lost 6.609
But to convince the proud what Signs availe, Par Lost 6.789
Thy Empire? easily the proud attempt Par Lost 7.609
A Foe so proud will first the weaker seek, Par Lost 9.383
Of *Pandaemonium*, Citie and proud seate Par Lost 10.424
That proud excuse? yet him not thy election, Par Lost 10.764
Of proud ambitious heart, who not content Par Lost 12.25
But this Usurper his encroachment proud Par Lost 12.72
To that proud Citie, whose high Walls thou saw'st Par Lost 12.342
Brute violence and proud Tyrannick pow'r, Par Reg 1.219
To draw the proud King *Ahab* into fraud Par Reg 1.372
With bridges rivers proud, as with a yoke; Par Reg 3.334
So after many a foil the Tempter proud, Par Reg 4.569
Over temptation, and the Tempter proud. Par Reg 4.595
In scorn of thir proud arms and warlike tools, Samson 137
Duell'd thir Armies rank't in proud array, Samson 345
Haughty as is his pile high-built and proud. Samson 1069
Contemptuous, proud, set on revenge and spite; Samson 1462
An old, and haughty Nation proud in Arms: Mask 33
Bridgewater ms 'proude'
Root-bound, that fled *Apollo*, *La*. Fool do not boast, Mask 662
Trinity ms 'doe not boast' ←'thou art over proud'
And on the neck of crowned Fortune proud Sonnet 16, 5
line not in 1694 text
And drov'st out Nations *proud and haut* Psalm 80, 35
And they that hate thee *proud and fell* Psalm 83, 7
O God the proud against me rise Psalm 86, 49
I mention Egypt, *where proud Kings* Psalm 87, 11

Proudest
Thir proudest persecuters: for the Spirit Par Lost 12.497
Equal in fame to proudest Conquerours. Par Reg 3.99

Proudly
In shape and gesture proudly eminent Par Lost 1.590
Between her white wings mantling proudly, Rowes Par Lost 7.439
With Towers and Temples proudly elevate Par Reg 4.34
Who durst so proudly tempt the Son of God. Par Reg 4.580
Proudly secure, yet liable to fall Samson 55
That now so proudly rise, Psalm 81, 58

Prove
May prove thir foe, and with repenting hand Par Lost 2.369
Should prove a bitter Morsel, and his bane, Par Lost 2.808
Prove chaff. On th' other side *Satan* allarm'd Par Lost 4.985
There fail where Vertue fails, or weakest prove Par Lost 6.117
As both thir deeds compar'd this day shall prove. Par Lost 6.170
Cannot well suite with either, but soon prove Par Lost 8.388
Should prove tempestuous: To the Winds they set Par Lost 10.664
Prove disobedient, and reprov'd, retort, Par Lost 10.761
Will prove no sudden, but a slow-pac't evill, Par Lost 10.963
Least Paradise a receptacle prove Par Lost 11.123
To prove him, and illustrate his high worth; Par Reg 1.370
Sam. Tongue-doubtie Giant, how dost thou prove me these? Samson 1181
But come what will, my deadliest foe will prove Samson 1262
Which to no few of them would prove pernicious. Samson 1400
Night hath better sweets to prove, Mask 123
Shall in the happy trial prove most glory. Mask 592
Prove to be presaging tears Winchester 44
Here lieth one who did most truly prove, Another 1

Proved
From what highth fall'n, so much the stronger prov'd Par Lost 1.92
1667 'provd'
Which had no less prov'd certain unforeknown. Par Lost 3.119
How due! yet all his good prov'd ill in me, Par Lost 4.48
Aspirer, but thir thoughts prov'd fond and vain Par Lost 6.90
And faithful, now prov'd false. But think not here Par Lost 6.271
From his surmise prov'd false, find peace within, Par Lost 9.333
The vertue of that Fruit, in thee first prov'd: Par Lost 9.616
From thy fierce wrath which we had prov'd Psalm 85, 11

Proverbed
Am I not sung and proverbd for a Fool Samson 203

Proves
But proves not so: then fallible, it seems, Par Lost 6.428
In Battel which the stronger proves, they all, Par Lost 6.819
And proves the sourse of all my miseries; Samson 64
Pray'd for, but often proves our woe, our bane? Samson 351
Once join'd, the contrary she proves, a thorn Samson 1037
Hopeful of his Delivery, which now proves Samson 1575

Provide
Provide, pernicious with one touch to fire. Par Lost 6.520
As the kind hospitable Woods provide. Mask 187

Provided
Thou hast provided all things: but with mee Par Lost 8.363
Hath unbesaught provided, and his hands Par Lost 10.1058
Till I provided Death; so Death becomes Par Lost 11.61

Providence
I may assert Eternal Providence, Par Lost 1.25
Whom we resist. If then his Providence Par Lost 1.162
ms 'providence'

Providence(*cont*)
Of Providence, Foreknowledge, Will and Fate, Par Lost 2.559
His providence, and on him sole depend, Par Lost 12.564
1669 'Providence'
Thir place of rest, and Providence thir guide: Par Lost 12.647
Among them to declare his Providence Par Reg 1.445
Lay on his Providence; he will not fail Par Reg 2.54
To his due time and providence I leave them. Par Reg 3.440
Temperst thy providence through his short course, Samson 670
But providence or instinct of nature seems, Samson 1545
Eie me blest Providence, and square my triall Mask 329
Bridgewater ms 'providence'
Trinity ms 'providence'
That bends his rage thy providence to oppose Psalm 8, 8

Provident
How provident he is, how farr from thought Par Lost 5.828
The Parsimonious Emmet, provident Par Lost 7.485

Provides
In other Worlds, and happier Seat provides Par Lost 10.237

Providing
By a providing Angel; all the race Par Reg 2.310

Province
Of Heav'n they march'd, and many a Province wide Par Lost 6.77
Of many a pleasant Realm and Province wide. Par Reg 1.118
In every Province, who themselves disdaining Par Reg 1.448
Reduc't a Province under Roman yoke, Par Reg 3.158

Provinces
Of many Provinces from bound to bound; Par Reg 3.315
Pretors, Proconsuls to thir Provinces Par Reg 4.63
Peeling thir Provinces, exhausted all Par Reg 4.136

Proving
She proving false, the next I took to Wife Samson 227

Provision
Grow up to thir provision, and more hands Par Lost 9.623
Both Table and Provision vanish'd quite Par Reg 2.402
Means her provision onely to the good Mask 765

Provisions
Contriv'd, and of provisions laid in large Par Lost 11.732

Provoke
So as not either to provoke, or dread Par Lost 1.644
Th' event is fear'd; should we again provoke Par Lost 2.82
Of contumacie will provoke the highest Par Lost 10.1027
Chor. In seeking just occasion to provoke Samson 237

Provoked
New warr, provok't; our better part remains Par Lost 1.645
ms 'provok'd'
Can equal anger infinite provok't. Par Lost 4.916
Of this right hand provok't, since first that tongue Par Lost 6.154
And peril great provok't, who thus hath dar'd Par Lost 9.922
Will not connive, or linger, thus provok'd, Samson 466
Whom I by his appointment had provok't, Samson 643

Provokes
Provokes my envie, this new Favorite Par Lost 9.175

Provoking
Provoking God to raise them enemies: Par Lost 12.318

Prow
Uplifted; and secure with beaked prow Par Lost 11.746

Prowess
Compare of mortal prowess, yet observ'd Par Lost 1.588
And thou in Military prowess next Par Lost 6.45
First seen in acts of prowess eminent Par Lost 11.789
Could not sustain thy Prowess, or subsist Par Reg 3.19
Had not his prowess quell'd thir pride Samson 286
So had the glory of Prowess been recover'd Samson 1098
Kings of prowess and renown. Psalm 136, 62

Prowest
His daughter, sought by many Prowest Knights, Par Reg 3.342

Prowling
Lights on his feet. As when a prowling Wolfe, Par Lost 4.183

Prudence
Of moral prudence, with delight receiv'd Par Reg 4.263

Prudent
Prudent, least from his resolution rais'd Par Lost 2.468
Easing thir flight; so stears the prudent Crane Par Lost 7.430

Prune
To prune these growing Plants, and tend these Flours, Par Lost 4.438
Lop overgrown, or prune, or prop, or bind, Par Lost 9.210

Pry
Thither, if but to pry, shall be perhaps Par Lost 1.655
1667 'prie'
ms 'prie'
Of midnight vapor glide obscure, and prie Par Lost 9.159

Psalms
With Hymns, our Psalms with artful terms inscrib'd, Par Reg 4.335
Hymns devout and holy Psalms Musick 15
Trinity ms 'psalmes' ←'Psalmes'

Psaltery
The *cheerfull* Psaltry bring along Psalm 81, 7

Psyche
Holds his dear *Psyche* sweet intranc't Mask 1005
line not in Bridgewater ms

Public
Deliberation sat and public care; Par Lost 2.303
1667 'publick'
And judg'd of public moment, in the shape Par Lost 2.448
Melt, as I doe, yet public reason just, Par Lost 4.389
Of public scorn; he wonderd, but not long Par Lost 10.509
National interrupt thir public peace, Par Lost 12.317

Public(*cont*)
What might be publick good; my self I thought — Par Reg 1.204
In publick, and with him we have convers'd; — Par Reg 2.52
By *John* the Baptist, and in publick shown, — Par Reg 2.84
That for the Publick all this weight he bears. — Par Reg 2.465
All publick cares, and yet of him suspicious, — Par Reg 4.96
Of wisest men; that to the public good — Samson 867
The public marks of honour and reward — Samson 992
A Public Officer, and now at hand. — Samson 1306
And now some public proof thereof require — Samson 1314
And over-labour'd at thir publick Mill, — Samson 1327
Our Captive, at the public Mill our drudge, — Samson 1393
Was *Samson* as a public servant brought, — Samson 1615
And Public Faith cleard from the shamefull brand — Sonnet 15, 12
1694 'publick'
Of Public Fraud. In vain doth Valour bleed — Sonnet 15, 13
1694 'publick'
Having to advise the public may speak free, — Prose 9, 2

Publish
And publish Grace to all, on promise made — Par Lost 2.238
Publish his God-like office now mature, — Par Reg 1.188
To publish them, both common female faults: — Samson 777

Published
Presumptuously have publish'd, impiously, — Samson 498

Puissance
Our puissance is our own, our own right hand — Par Lost 5.864
His puissance, trusting in th' Almightie's aide, — Par Lost 6.119

Puissant
That all these puissant Legions, whose exile — Par Lost 1.632
Gird on, and Sword upon thy puissant Thigh; — Par Lost 6.714
And puissant deeds, a promise shall receive — Par Lost 12.322
(Thy throne) but gold that got him puissant friends? — Par Reg 2.425
With puissant words, and murmurs made to bless, — Arcades 60

Pull
To heave, pull, draw, or break, he still perform'd — Samson 1626

Pulled
Then by main force pull'd up, and on his shoulders bore — Samson 146
Upon thir heads and on his own he pull'd. — Samson 1589
Pulld down the same destruction on himself; — Samson 1658
She was pincht, and pull'd she sed, — Allegro 103
Pull'd off his Boots, and took away the light: — Carrier 16

Pulp
The savourie pulp they chew, and in the rinde — Par Lost 4.335

Pulse
Or as a guest with *Daniel* at his pulse. — Par Reg 2.278
Should in a pet of temperance feed on Pulse, — Mask 721
Bridgewater ms 'pulse'
Trinity ms 'pulse' ←'fetches' ←'pulse'

Punctual
Round this opacous Earth, this punctual spot, — Par Lost 8.23

Punic
In *Pontus* or the *Punic* Coast, or where — Par Lost 5.340
His wasted Country freed from *Punic* rage, — Par Reg 3.102

Punish
To punish endless? wherefore cease we then? — Par Lost 2.159
To tempt or punish mortals, except whom — Par Lost 2.1032

Punished
With what is punish't; whence these raging fires — Par Lost 2.213
Now rul'd him, punisht in the shape he sin'd, — Par Lost 10.516
In punisht man, to satisfie his rigour — Par Lost 10.803
And will alike be punish'd; whether thou — Par Reg 3.214

Punisher
This knows my punisher; therefore as farr — Par Lost 4.103

Punishment
To undergo eternal punishment? — Par Lost 1.155
And stripes, and arbitrary punishment — Par Lost 2.334
Thy King and Lord? Back to thy punishment, — Par Lost 2.699
However, and to scape his punishment. — Par Lost 4.911
Both of thy crime and punishment: henceforth — Par Lost 5.881
Into thir place of punishment, the Gulf — Par Lost 6.53
The punishment to other hand belongs, — Par Lost 6.807
His punishment, Eternal miserie; — Par Lost 6.904
Least on my head both sin and punishment, — Par Lost 10.133
Can fit his punishment, or their revenge. — Par Lost 10.242
Catcht by Contagion, like in punishment, — Par Lost 10.544
Thy punishment then justly is at his Will. — Par Lost 10.768
The punishment all on thy self; alas, — Par Lost 10.949
Shall scape his punishment ordain'd, and wee — Par Lost 10.1039
Therefore so abject is thir punishment, — Par Lost 11.520
Awaits the good, the rest what punishment? — Par Lost 11.710
Alone fulfill the Law; thy punishment — Par Lost 12.404
Rewarded well with servil punishment! — Samson 413
As I deserve, pay on my punishment; — Samson 489
Repent the sin, but if the punishment — Samson 504
The punishment of dissolute days, in fine, — Samson 702
Due by the Law to capital punishment? — Samson 1225

Puny
The punie habitants, or if not drive, — Par Lost 2.367

Purchase
And heavier fall: so should I purchase deare — Par Lost 4.101
A World who would not purchase with a bruise, — Par Lost 10.500
Among the Heathen of thir purchase got, — Par Lost 10.579
And force him to restore his purchase back, — Mask 607
Trinity ms 'purchase back' ←'new got prey'

Pure
Before all Temples th' upright heart and pure, — Par Lost 1.18
And uncompounded is thir Essence pure, — Par Lost 1.425
Or hear'st thou rather pure Ethereal stream, — Par Lost 3.7

Pure(*cont*)
From the pure Empyrean where he sits — Par Lost 3.57
Through the pure marble Air his oblique way — Par Lost 3.564
Breathe forth *Elixir* pure, and Rivers run — Par Lost 3.607
That Lantskip: And of pure now purer aire — Par Lost 4.153
Truth, wisdome, Sanctitude severe and pure, — Par Lost 4.293
With shews instead, meer shews of seeming pure, — Par Lost 4.316
Pure as th' expanse of Heav'n; I thither went — Par Lost 4.456
With kisses pure: aside the Devil turnd — Par Lost 4.502
Observing none, but adoration pure — Par Lost 4.737
Pure, and commands to som, leaves free to all. — Par Lost 4.747
Founded in Reason, Loyal, Just, and Pure, — Par Lost 4.755
Th' animal Spirits that from pure blood arise — Par Lost 4.805
Like gentle breaths from Rivers pure, thence raise — Par Lost 4.806
As when thou stoodst in Heav'n upright and pure; — Par Lost 4.837
Was Aerie light from pure digestion bred, — Par Lost 5.4
Created pure. But know that in the Soule — Par Lost 5.100
Wants her fit vessels pure, then strews the ground — Par Lost 5.348
No ingrateful food: and food alike those pure — Par Lost 5.407
But more refin'd, more spiritous, and pure, — Par Lost 5.475
Whereon a Saphir Throne, inlaid with pure — Par Lost 6.758
Ethereal, first of things, quintessence pure — Par Lost 7.244
The Firmament, expanse of liquid, pure, — Par Lost 7.264
How fully hast thou satisfi'd mee, pure — Par Lost 8.180
Nature her self, though pure of sinful thought, — Par Lost 8.506
Whatever pure thou in the body enjoy'st — Par Lost 8.622
(And pure thou wert created) we enjoy — Par Lost 8.623
Total they mix, Union of Pure with Pure — Par Lost 8.627
On what was pure, till cramm'd and gorg'd, nigh burst — Par Lost 10.632
Then Heav'n and Earth renewd shall be made pure — Par Lost 10.638
Least that pure breath of Life, the Spirit of Man — Par Lost 10.784
Those pure immortal Elements that know — Par Lost 11.50
Less pure, accustomd to immortal Fruits? — Par Lost 11.285
Is Pietie thus and pure Devotion paid? — Par Lost 11.452
While they pervert pure Natures healthful rules — Par Lost 11.523
Holie and pure, conformitie divine. — Par Lost 11.606
Pure, and in mind prepar'd, if so befall, — Par Lost 12.444
Left onely in those written Records pure, — Par Lost 12.513
Purified to receive him pure, or rather — Par Reg 1.74
Not thence to be more pure, but to receive — Par Reg 1.77
On which I sent thee to the Virgin pure — Par Reg 1.134
Thy Father, who is holy, wise and pure, — Par Reg 1.486
Within her brest, though calm; her brest though pure, — Par Reg 2.63
Defends the touching of these viands pure, — Par Reg 2.370
Of most erected Spirits, most temper'd pure — Par Reg 3.27
Built nobly, pure the air, and light the soil, — Par Reg 4.239
The breath of Heav'n fresh-blowing, pure and sweet, — Samson 10
Against the Eastern ray, translucent, pure. — Samson 548
With lavers pure and cleansing herbs wash off — Samson 1727
I would not soil these pure Ambrosial weeds, — Mask 16
Of this pure cause would kindle my rap't spirits — Mask 794
line not in Trinity ms
line not in Bridgewater ms
Sabrina is her name, a Virgin pure, — Mask 826
Trinity ms 'pure' ←'chast' ←'goddesse'
Drops that from my fountain pure, — Mask 912
Com pensive Nun, devout and pure, — Penseroso 31
But lives and spreds aloft by those pure eyes, — Lycidas 81
With *Nectar* pure his oozy Lock's he laves, — Lycidas 175
That undisturbed Song of pure content, — Musick 6
Hast gain'd thy entrance, Virgin wise and pure. — Sonnet 9, 14
And drink thy fill of pure immortal streams. — Sonnet 14, 14
Ev'n them who kept thy truth so pure of old — Sonnet 18, 3
Came vested all in white, pure as her mind: — Sonnet 23, 9
Men whose Life, Learning, Faith and pure intent — Forcers 9
In the pure firmament, then saith my heart, — Psalm 8, 11

Pure-eyed
O welcom pure-ey'd Faith, white-handed Hope, — Mask 213
Trinity ms 'pure-eyd'
line not in Bridgewater ms

Pureness
With sudden adoration, and blank aw. — Mask 452
Trinity ms 'and blank aw' ←'of bright rays' ←'of her purenesse'

Purer
Our purer essence then will overcome — Par Lost 2.215
That Lantskip: And of pure now purer aire — Par Lost 4.153
The grosser feeds the purer, Earth the Sea, — Par Lost 5.416
We that are of purer fire — Mask 111

Purest
Heav'ns purest Light, yet our great Enemy — Par Lost 2.137
Spiritual, may of purest Spirits be found — Par Lost 5.406
Out of such prison, though Spirits of purest light, — Par Lost 6.660
Purest at first, now gross by sinning grown. — Par Lost 6.661
And on her purest spirits prey, — Samson 613

Purfled
Then her purfl'd scarf can shew, — Mask 995
Bridgewater ms 'purfld'
Trinity ms 'purfl'd' ←'watchet'
B.M. ms 'purfled'

Purgatory
Met in the milder shades of Purgatory. — Sonnet 13, 14

Purge
Her mischief, and purge off the baser fire — Par Lost 2.141
Purge off this gloom; the soft delicious Air, — Par Lost 2.400
Purge and disperse, that I may see and tell — Par Lost 3.54
Eject him tainted now, and purge him off — Par Lost 11.52
Shall hold thir course, till fire purge all things new, — Par Lost 11.900

Purged
Throughout the fluid Mass, but downward purg'd Par Lost 7.237
Had bred; then purg'd with Euphrasie and Rue Par Lost 11.414
From the conflagrant mass, purg'd and refin'd, Par Lost 12.548
Purification
Purification in the old Law did save, Sonnet 23, 6
Purified
Purified to receive him pure, or rather Par Reg 1.74
Purity
Of puritie and place and innocence, Par Lost 4.745
Of Innocence, of Faith, of Puritie, Par Lost 9.1075
Against his vow of strictest purity, Samson 319
Will dare to soyl her Virgin purity, Mask 427
1637 'puritie'
Bridgewater ms 'puritie'
Trinity ms 'puritie'
Purlieu
In some Purlieu two gentle Fawnes at play, Par Lost 4.404
Purlieus
In the Pourlieues of Heav'n, and therein plac't Par Lost 2.833
Purling
Freshet, or purling Brook, of shell or fin, Par Reg 2.345
Purloined
Had from his wakeful custody purloind Par Lost 2.946
Purple
Ran purple to the Sea, suppos'd with blood Par Lost 1.451
Layes forth her purple Grape, and gently creeps Par Lost 4.259
Arraying with reflected Purple and Gold Par Lost 4.596
His constant Lamp, and waves his purple wings, Par Lost 4.764
With spots of Gold and Purple, azure and green: Par Lost 7.479
Carnation, Purple, Azure, or spect with Gold, Par Lost 9.429
A militarie Vest of purple flowd Par Lost 11.241
Bacchus that first from out the purple Grape, Mask 46
And purple all the ground with vernal flowres. Lycidas 141
But then transform'd him to a purple flower Fair Inf 27
Thy hand-maids, clad them o're with purple beams Sonnet 14, 10
Purples
Purples the East: still govern thou my Song, Par Lost 7.30
Purpose
With purpose to explore or to disturb Par Lost 2.971
And Man there plac't, with purpose to assay Par Lost 3.90
As my Eternal purpose hath decreed: Par Lost 3.172
Nor gentle purpose, nor endearing smiles Par Lost 4.337
On purpose, hard thou knowst it to exclude Par Lost 4.584
That his great purpose he might so fulfill, Par Lost 6.675
Receave with solemne purpose to observe Par Lost 7.78
To lessen thee, against his purpose serves Par Lost 7.614
Return'd and gracious purpose thus renew'd. Par Lost 8.337
Forerunners of his purpose, or to warn Par Lost 11.195
With purpose to resign them in full time Par Lost 12.301
Idolatrous, but when his purpose is Par Reg 1.444
Thus long to some great purpose he obscures. Par Reg 2.101
The Father in his purpose hath decreed, Par Reg 3.186
On the *Campanian* shore, with purpose there Par Reg 4.93
Robustious to no purpose clustring down, Samson 569
And for a life who will not change his purpose? Samson 1406
Of faithful Souldiery, were not his purpose Samson 1498
Purposed
Perceive thee purpos'd not to doom frail Man Par Lost 3.404
As now is enterd; yet no purpos'd foe Par Lost 4.373
The whole included Race, his purposd prey. Par Lost 9.416
The purpos'd Counsel pre-ordain'd and fixt Par Reg 1.127
She purpos'd to betray me, and (which was worse Samson 399
La. They were but twain, and purpos'd quick return. Mask 284
Then quick about thy purpos'd business come, Vacation 57
Purposely
(His arrows purposely made he Psalm 7, 49
Purposes
Can execute thir aerie purposes, Par Lost 1.430
Pursed
I purs't it up, but little reck'ning made, Mask 642
Bridgewater ms 'purst'
Pursue
Beyond thus high, insatiate to pursue Par Lost 2.8
To whom we hate. Let us not then pursue Par Lost 2.249
Least with a whip of Scorpions I pursue Par Lost 2.701
Little inferior; whom my thoughts pursue Par Lost 4.362
Pursue these sons of Darkness, drive them out Par Lost 6.715
All night he will pursue, but his approach Par Lost 12.206
All to the push of Fate, persue thy way Par Reg 4.470
Tyrannic power, but raging to pursue Samson 1275
As a stray'd Ewe, or to pursue the stealth Mask 503
Trinity ms 'persue'
Let th' enemy pursue my soul Psalm 7, 13
So with thy whirlwind them pursue, Psalm 83, 57
Like waves they me persue. Psalm 88, 68
Pursued
While with perfidious hatred they pursu'd Par Lost 1.308
ms 'persu'd'
Insulting, and pursu'd us through the Deep, Par Lost 2.79
What when we fled amain, pursu'd and strook Par Lost 2.165
I fled, but he pursu'd (though more, it seems, Par Lost 2.790
Uriel once warnd; whose eye pursu'd him down Par Lost 4.125
Mine eye pursu'd him still, but under shade Par Lost 4.572
Drove them before him Thunder-struck, pursu'd Par Lost 6.858
Of stern *Achilles* on his Foe pursu'd Par Lost 9.15
Her long with ardent look his Eye pursu'd Par Lost 9.397
First hunter then, pursu'd a gentle brace, Par Lost 11.188

Pursued(*cont*)
Of flight pursu'd in th' Air and ore the ground Par Lost 11.202
Fled and pursu'd transverse the resonant fugue. Par Lost 11.563
His holy Meditations thus persu'd. Par Reg 1.195
And with these words his temptation pursu'd. Par Reg 2.405
Hast reard Gods Trophies and his work pursu'd. Sonnet 16, 6
Pursuers
His swift pursuers from Heav'n Gates discern Par Lost 1.326
ms 'persuers'
Of thir pursuers, and overcame by flight; Par Reg 3.325
Pursues
Above th' *Aonian* Mount, while it pursues Par Lost 1.15
ms 'persues'
Pursues, as inclination or sad choice Par Lost 2.524
Pursues the *Arimaspian*, who by stelth Par Lost 2.945
With head, hands, wings or feet pursues his way, Par Lost 2.949
Pursues me still, least all I cannot die, Par Lost 10.783
Behinde them, while th' obdurat King pursues: Par Lost 12.205
And his vain importunity pursues. Par Reg 4.24
For dire imagination still persues me. Samson 1544
Pursuing
Pursuing. I upon my Frontieres here Par Lost 2.998
Pursuing drive them out from God and bliss, Par Lost 6.52
Pursuing, not unmov'd to *Eve* thus spake. Par Lost 11.192
Pursuing whom he late dismissd, the Sea Par Lost 12.195
Pursuit
His Ministers of vengeance and pursuit Par Lost 1.170
ms 'persuit'
Back from pursuit thy Powers with loud acclaime Par Lost 3.397
Whom fled we thought, will save us long pursuit Par Lost 6.538
Of equal dread in flight, or in pursuit; Par Reg 3.306
The matchless *Gideon* in pursuit Samson 280
She guiltless damsell flying the mad pursuit Mask 829
Bridgewater ms 'pursuite'
Trinity ms 'persuite'
Purveyed
Yeild thee, so well this day thou hast purvey'd. Par Lost 9.1021
Troubl'd that thou shouldst hunger, hath purvey'd Par Reg 2.333
Push
All to the push of Fate, persue thy way Par Reg 4.470
Push them in their rebellions all Psalm 5, 31
Pushed
Sidelong, had push't a Mountain from his seat Par Lost 6.197
From the Suns Axle; they with labour push'd Par Lost 10.670
Justling or pusht with Winds rude in thir shock Par Lost 10.1074
Out of his place, pushd by the horned floud, Par Lost 11.831
Put
And put to proof his high Supremacy, Par Lost 1.132
Put forth at full, but still his strength conceal'd, Par Lost 1.641
Put to thir mouths the sounding Alchymie Par Lost 2.517
Freely put off, and for him lastly dye Par Lost 3.240
Dying put on the weeds of *Dominic*, Par Lost 3.479
Then when the Dragon, put to second rout, Par Lost 4.3
Though for possession put to try once more Par Lost 4.941
Battels and Realms: in these he put two weights Par Lost 4.1002
Put forth, and to a narrow vent appli'd Par Lost 6.583
But whom thou hat'st, I hate, and can put on Par Lost 6.734
Thy terrors, as I put thy mildness on, Par Lost 6.735
Yet half his strength he put not forth, but check'd Par Lost 6.853
And put not forth my goodness, which is free Par Lost 7.171
Put forth the verdant Grass, Herb yielding Seed, Par Lost 7.310
Human, to put on Gods, death to be wisht, Par Lost 9.714
Between Thee and the Woman I will put Par Lost 10.179
Is enmity, which he will put between Par Lost 10.497
Discount'nance her despis'd, and put to rout Par Reg 2.218
Betray'd, Captiv'd, and both my Eyes put out, Samson 33
Put to the labour of a Beast, debas't Samson 37
I lose, prevented by thy eyes put out. Samson 1103
Then put on all thy gorgeous arms, thy Helmet Samson 1119
To put out both thine eyes, and fetter'd send thee Samson 1160
As now I do: But first I must put off Mask 82
And put the Damsel to suspicious flight, Mask 158
And put them into mis-becoming plight. Mask 372
And too much breathing put him out of breath; Another 12
For one Carrier put down to make six bearers. Another 20
line not in 1640, 1657, 1658 texts
And gladness thou hast put Psalm 4, 32
Thou hast put all under his lordly feet, Psalm 8, 18
Puts
Puts on swift wings, and towards the Gates of Hell Par Lost 2.631
Thank him who puts me loath to this revenge Par Lost 4.386
Puts me in doubt. Lives ther who loves his pain? Par Lost 4.888
New part puts on, and as to passion mov'd, Par Lost 9.667
Puts forth no visual beam. Samson 163
Puts invincible might Samson 1271
Putting
Handed they went; and eas'd the putting off Par Lost 4.739
So ye shall die perhaps, by putting off Par Lost 9.713
Pygmean
Throng numberless, like that Pigmean Race Par Lost 1.780
ms 'pigmean'
Pyramid
Springs upward like a Pyramid of fire Par Lost 2.1013
Under a Star-ypointing *Pyramid*? Shakespear 4
Pyramids
Rais'd on a Mount, with Pyramids and Towrs Par Lost 5.758
Pyrrha
Deucalion and chaste *Pyrrha* to restore Par Lost 11.12

Pyrrha(*cont*)
Pyrrha for whom bindst thou — Horace 3
Pythian
As at th' Olympian Games or *Pythian* fields; — Par Lost 2.530
Ingenderd in the *Pythian* Vale on slime, — Par Lost 10.530
Python
Huge *Python*, and his Power no less he seem'd — Par Lost 10.531
Quadrate
That stood for Heav'n, in mighty Quadrate joyn'd — Par Lost 6.62
Quadrature
His Quadrature, from thy Orbicular World, — Par Lost 10.381
Quaff
Quaff immortalitie and joy, secure — Par Lost 5.638
line not in 1667 edition
Chios and *Creet*, and how they quaff in Gold, — Par Reg 4.118
Quaint
His laughter at thir quaint Opinions wide — Par Lost 8.78
Impreses quaint, Caparisons and Steeds; — Par Lost 9.35
A Scepter or quaint staff he bears, — Samson 1303
And my quaint habits breed astonishment, — Mask 157
Bridgewater ms 'quainte'
1637 'queint'
With Ringlets quaint, and wanton windings wove. — Arcades 47
Throw hither all your quaint enameld eyes, — Lycidas 139
Affrights the *Flamins* at their service quaint; — Nativity 194
Qualms
Of gastly Spasm, or racking torture, qualmes — Par Lost 11.481
Quarrel
But peace, I must not quarrel with the will — Samson 60
Quarrels
Sam. Love-quarrels oft in pleasing concord end, — Samson 1008
Do they not seek occasion of new quarrels — Samson 1329
Quarries
From Diamond Quarries hew'n, and Rocks of Gold, — Par Lost 5.759
Quarry
Sagacious of his Quarry from so farr. — Par Lost 10.281
1667 'Quarrey'
Yet on the softned Quarry would I score — Passion 46
Quarter
Each quarter, to descrie the distant foe, — Par Lost 6.530
Quartered
Nations besides from all the quarter'd winds, — Par Reg 4.202
Quarters
Swift to thir several Quarters hasted then — Par Lost 3.714
His praise ye Winds, that from four Quarters blow, — Par Lost 5.192
The Quarters of the North, there to prepare — Par Lost 5.689
He quarters to his blu-hair'd deities, — Mask 29
Quaternion
Of Natures Womb, that in quaternion run — Par Lost 5.181
Queen
Astarte, Queen of Heav'n, with crescent Horns; — Par Lost 1.439
ms 'queen'
Apparent Queen unvaild her peerless light, — Par Lost 4.608
Not unattended, for on her as Queen — Par Lost 8.60
Queen of this Universe, doe not believe — Par Lost 9.684
As Reapers oft are wont thir Harvest Queen. — Par Lost 9.842
As sitting Queen ador'd on Beauties Throne, — Par Reg 2.212
Then great and glorious *Rome*, Queen of the Earth — Par Reg 4.45
Sweet Queen of Parly, Daughter of the Sphear, — Mask 241
Bridgewater ms 'Qweene'
Trinity ms 'Queene'
And she shall be my Queen. Hail forren wonder — Mask 265
1637 'Queene'
Bridgewater ms 'Qweene'
Trinity ms 'queene'
Fair silver-shafted Queen for ever chaste, — Mask 442
Trinity ms 'Q.'
Bridgewater ms 'Qweene'
1637 'Queene'
Fear'd her stern frown, and she was queen oth' Woods. — Mask 446
Trinity ms 'Q.'
Bridgewater ms 'Qweene'
Sadly sits th' *Assyrian* Queen; — Mask 1002
line not in Bridgewater ms
Trinity ms 'Queene'
1637 'Queene'
Or that Starr'd *Ethiope* Queen that strove — Penseroso 19
Such a rural Queen — Arcades 94
Trinity ms 'ueene', ms defective
Such a rural Queen — Arcades 108
Trinity ms 'Queene'
Heav'ns Queen and Mother both, — Nativity 201
No Marchioness, but now a Queen. — Winchester 74
Queens
And last of Kings and Queens and *Hero*'s old, — Vacation 47
Quell
Giv'n me to quell thir pride, and in event — Par Lost 5.740
His Name and Office bearing, who shall quell — Par Lost 12.311
Then to subdue and quell o're all the earth — Par Reg 1.218
To quell the mighty of the Earth, th' oppressour, — Samson 1272
Be those that quell the might of hellish charms, — Mask 613
That doth the wrathfull tyrants quell. — Psalm 136, 10
Quelled
He held it vain; awe from above had quelld — Par Lost 4.860
And now thir Mightiest quelld, the battel swerv'd, — Par Lost 6.386
Valour or strength, though matchless, quelld with pain — Par Lost 6.457
Though not of Woman born; compassion quell'd — Par Lost 11.496
The *Carthaginian* pride, young *Pompey* quell'd — Par Reg 3.35

Quelled(*cont*)
Had not his prowess quell'd thir pride — Samson 286
Now blind, disheartn'd, sham'd, dishonour'd, quell'd, — Samson 563
By their own counsels quell'd; — Psalm 5, 30
Queller
Queller of Satan, on thy glorious work — Par Reg 4.634
Quench
Satans assaults, and quench his fierie darts, — Par Lost 12.492
Quench not the thirst of glory, but augment. — Par Reg 3.38
To quench the drouth of *Phoebus*, which as they taste — Mask 66
Quenched
Quencht in a Boggie *Syrtis*, neither Sea, — Par Lost 2.939
So thick a drop serene hath quencht thir Orbs, — Par Lost 3.25
So obvious and so easie to be quench't, — Samson 95
Quest
To search with wandring quest a place foretold — Par Lost 2.830
And on his Quest, where likeliest he might finde — Par Lost 9.414
Following, as seem'd, the quest of some stray Ewe, — Par Reg 1.315
Till further quest'. *La*. Shepherd I take thy word, — Mask 321
Bridgewater ms 'quest'
Trinity ms 'quest' ←'quest be made'
I know this quest of yours, and free intent — Arcades 34
There ended was his quest, there ceast his care. — Fair Inf 18
Question
To question thy bold entrance on this place; — Par Lost 4.882
And such I held thee; but this question askt — Par Lost 4.887
I question it, for this fair Earth I see, — Par Lost 9.720
Will not dare mention, lest a question rise — Samson 1254
Secure without all doubt, or controversie: — Mask 409
Trinity ms 'doubt or question, no'
Bridgewater ms 'doubt or question, no'
Questioned
Be questiond and blaspheam'd without defence. — Par Lost 3.166
And question'd every gust of rugged wings — Lycidas 93
Questions
On points and questions fitting *Moses* Chair, — Par Reg 4.219
Quick
The latter quick up flew, and kickt the beam; — Par Lost 4.1004
Now on the polar windes, then with quick Fann — Par Lost 5.269
By quick contraction or remove; but now — Par Lost 6.597
We should compel them to a quick result. — Par Lost 6.619
Of Coral stray, or sporting with quick glance — Par Lost 7.405
By quick instinctive motion up I sprung, — Par Lost 8.259
Oft he to her his charge of quick returne — Par Lost 9.399
With glory and power to judge both quick and dead, — Par Lost 12.460
To whom quick answer Satan thus return'd. — Par Reg 2.172
How quick they wheel'd, and flying behing them shot — Par Reg 3.323
If not by quick destruction soon cut off — Samson 764
But that by quick command from Soveran *Jove* — Mask 41
La. They were but twain, and purpos'd quick return. — Mask 284
And underwent a quick immortal change — Mask 841
1637 'quicke'
Then quick about thy purpos'd business come, — Vacation 57
Quicken
Quick'n us thou, then *gladly* wee — Psalm 80, 75
Quickened
So quick'nd appetite, that I, methought, — Par Lost 5.85
Powerful perswaders, quick'nd at the scent — Par Lost 9.587
Fainted, and died, nor would with Ale be quickn'd; — Another 16
line not in 1640, 1657, 1658 texts
Quickening
By our own quick'ning power, when fatal course — Par Lost 5.861
Quickest
Best school of best experience, quickest in sight — Par Reg 3.238
Quickly
Of these things others quickly will dispose — Par Reg 2.400
Quickly to the green earths end, — Mask 1014
Trinity ms 'quickly to' ←'farre beyond'
And why from us so quickly thou didst take thy flight. — Fair Inf 42
Quickly found a lover meet; — Winchester 16
Quiet
Quiet though sad, the respit of that day — Par Lost 11.272
That Son, who on the quiet state of men — Par Lost 12.80
Long to enjoy it quiet and secure, — Par Reg 3.360
And what may quiet us in a death so noble. — Samson 1724
And joyn with thee calm Peace, and Quiet, — Penseroso 45
Peace and quiet ever have; — Winchester 48
No quiet let them find, — Psalm 83, 50
Quietly
Suffering, abstaining, quietly expecting — Par Reg 3.192
Quills
He touch'd the tender stops of various Quills, — Lycidas 188
1638 'quills'
Trinity ms 'quills'
Quiloa
Mombaza, and *Quiloa*, and *Melind*, — Par Lost 11.399
Quintessence
And this Ethereal quintessence of Heav'n — Par Lost 3.716
Ethereal, first of things, quintessence pure — Par Lost 7.244
Quintilian
That would have made *Quintilian* stare and gasp. — Sonnet 11, 11
Quintius
Quintius, Fabricius, Curius, Regulus? — Par Reg 2.446
Quips
Quips and Cranks, and wanton Wiles, — Allegro 27
Quit
Would set me highest, and in a moment quit — Par Lost 4.51
No more be troubl'd how to quit the yoke — Par Lost 5.882

Quit(*cont*)
In order, quit of all impediment; Par Lost 6.548
Her state with Oarie feet: yet oft they quit Par Lost 7.440
Life much, bent rather how I may be quit Par Lost 11.548
Check or reproof, and glad to scape so quit. Par Reg 1.477
But I will bring thee where thou soon shalt quit Par Reg 3.244
God will relent, and quit thee all his debt; Samson 509
And quit: not wanting him, I shall want nothing. Samson 1484
Nor much more cause, *Samson* hath quit himself Samson 1709
Then all this Earthy grosnes quit, On Time 20
I did but prompt the age to quit their cloggs Sonnet 12, 1
Quite
We should be quite abolisht and expire. Par Lost 2.93
Will either quite consume us, and reduce Par Lost 2.96
Of what we are and were, dismissing quite Par Lost 2.282
And wisdome at one entrance quite shut out. Par Lost 3.50
Man shall not quite be lost, but sav'd who will, Par Lost 3.173
Redeem thee quite from Deaths rapacious claime; Par Lost 11.258
He look'd, and saw the face of things quite chang'd, Par Lost 11.712
Over his brethren, and quite dispossess Par Lost 12.28
Quite out thir Native Language, and instead Par Lost 12.54
At every sudden slighting quite abasht: Par Reg 2.224
Both Table and Provision vanish'd quite Par Reg 2.402
Fortune and Fate, as one regardless quite Par Reg 4.317
By light of Nature not in all quite lost. Par Reg 4.352
Quite at a loss, for all his darts were spent, Par Reg 4.366
Such a discomfit, as shall quite despoil him Samson 469
Dal. I was a fool, too rash, and quite mistaken Samson 907
Quite from his people, and delivered up Samson 1158
Despis'd and thought extinguish't quite, Samson 1688
Or if your influence be quite damm'd up Mask 336
Imbodies, and imbrutes, till she quite loose Mask 468
The visage quite transforms of him that drinks, Mask 527
Who would be quite surcharg'd with her own weight, Mask 728
Of *Pluto*, to have quite set free Allegro 149
Who now hath quite forgot to rave, Nativity 67
And in a moment shall be quite abash't. Psalm 6, 24
At Endor quite cut off, and rowl'd Psalm 83, 39
From life discharg'd and parted quite Psalm 88, 17
Quits
That moral verdit quits her of unclean: Samson 324
Quitted
God-like fruition, quitted all to save Par Lost 3.307
To his proud fair, best quitted with disdain. Par Lost 4.770
Of Passion, I to them had quitted all, Par Lost 10.627
Quiver
And Quiver with three-bolted Thunder stor'd, Par Lost 6.764
Though not as shee with Bow and Quiver armd, Par Lost 9.390
Quivered
And like a quiver'd Nymph with Arrows keen Mask 422
Trinity ms 'quiverd'
Quivers
Like Quivers hung, and with Praeamble sweet Par Lost 3.367
Quoth
Ah! Who hath reft (quoth he) my dearest pledge? Lycidas 107
Nay, quoth he, on his swooning bed outstretch'd, Another 17
line not in 1640, 1657, 1658 texts
Rabba
Worshipt in *Rabba* and her watry Plain, Par Lost 1.397
ms 'Rabba'
Rabbis
Among the gravest Rabbies disputant Par Reg 4.218
Rabble
A miscellaneous rabble, who extol Par Reg 3.50
Race
For those the Race of *Israel* oft forsook Par Lost 1.432
ms 'race'
Of *Phlegra* with th' Heroic Race were joyn'd Par Lost 1.577
ms 'race'
Throng numberless, like that Pigmean Race Par Lost 1.780
ms 'race'
Shall we then live thus vile, the Race of Heav'n Par Lost 2.194
1667 'race'
1674 'race' in some copies
Of some new Race call'd *Man*, about this time Par Lost 2.348
So deep a malice, to confound the race Par Lost 2.382
A race of upstart Creatures, to supply Par Lost 2.834
Draw after him the whole Race of mankind, Par Lost 3.161
By loosing thee a while, the whole Race lost. Par Lost 3.280
Created this new happie Race of Men Par Lost 3.679
1667 'race' in some copies
Mother of human Race: what could I doe, Par Lost 4.475
But thou hast promis'd from us two a Race Par Lost 4.732
Impossible: yet haply of thy Race Par Lost 6.501
What might have else to human Race bin hid; Par Lost 6.896
Of *Bacchus* and his revellers, the Race Par Lost 7.33
In Paradise to *Adam* or his Race, Par Lost 7.45
Another World, out of one man a Race Par Lost 7.155
Of Spirits maligne a better Race to bring Par Lost 7.189
Female for Race; then bless'd Mankinde, and said, Par Lost 7.530
And multiply a Race of Worshippers Par Lost 7.630
To thee and to thy Race I give; as Lords Par Lost 8.339
The whole included Race, his purposd prey. Par Lost 9.416
High proof ye now have giv'n to be the Race Par Lost 10.385
Till I in Man residing through the Race, Par Lost 10.607
Into this cursed World a woful Race, Par Lost 10.984
The Race unblest, to being yet unbegot. Par Lost 10.988
The Race of Mankind drownd, before the Shrine Par Lost 11.13
Race(*cont*)
To life prolongd and promisd Race, I now Par Lost 11.331
Of wickedness, wherein shall dwell his Race Par Lost 11.608
To these that sober Race of Men, whose lives Par Lost 11.621
With length of happy dayes the race of man; Par Lost 11.782
And whether here the Race of man will end. Par Lost 11.786
Servant of Servants, on his vitious Race. Par Lost 12.104
Of *Pharao:* there he dies, and leaves his Race Par Lost 12.163
And overwhelm thir Warr: the Race elect Par Lost 12.214
And coupl'd with them, and begot a race. Par Reg 2.181
By a providing Angel; all the race Par Reg 2.310
Impenitent, and left a race behind Par Reg 3.423
Or benefit reveal'd to *Abraham*'s race? Samson 29
My race of glory run, and race of shame, Samson 597
From the unforeskinn'd race, of whom thou bear'st Samson 1100
Thy strength they know surpassing human rate, Samson 1313
1671 printed 'race', errata 'rate'
Had got a race of mourners on som pregnant cloud. Passion 56
Fly envious *Time*, till thou run out thy race, On Time 1
Race
Upon the wing, or in swift Race contend, Par Lost 2.529
1667 'race'
Much of his Race though steep, suspens in Heav'n Par Lost 7.99
Thir Ministry perform'd, and race well run, Par Lost 12.505
Measur'd this transient World, the Race of time, Par Lost 12.554
Races
Unsung; or to describe Races and Games, Par Lost 9.33
Rack
At least had gon to rack, disturbd and torne Par Lost 4.994
A World devote to universal rack. Par Lost 11.821
After a dismal night; I heard the rack Par Reg 4.452
Racked
Vaunting aloud, but rackt with deep despare: Par Lost 1.126
ms 'wrackt'
To whom the Tempter inly rackt reply'd. Par Reg 3.203
Racking
Of racking whirlwinds, or for ever sunk Par Lost 2.182
Of gastly Spasm, or racking torture, qualmes Par Lost 11.481
Dropsies, and Asthma's, and Joint-racking Rheums. Par Lost 11.488
Radiance
Girt with Omnipotence, with Radiance crown'd Par Lost 7.194
Radiant
If chance the radiant Sun with farewell sweet Par Lost 2.492
The radiant image of his Glory sat, Par Lost 3.63
Drawn round about thee like a radiant Shrine, Par Lost 3.379
With radiant light, as glowing Iron with fire; Par Lost 3.594
Ere he drew nigh, his radiant visage turnd, Par Lost 3.646
So saying, on he led his radiant Files, Par Lost 4.797
Transcend his own so farr, whose radiant forms Par Lost 5.457
Of radiant *Urim*, work divinely wrought, Par Lost 6.761
Sphear'd in a radiant Cloud, for yet the Sun Par Lost 7.247
Thus saying, from his radiant Seat he rose Par Lost 10.85
O're the blew Firmament a radiant white, Par Lost 11.206
Empires, and Monarchs, and thir radiant Courts, Par Reg 3.237
Who with her radiant finger still'd the roar Par Reg 4.428
By her own radiant light, though Sun and Moon Mask 374
Mark what radiant state she spreds, Arcades 14
With radiant feet the tissued clouds down stearing, Nativity 146
With thee there clad in radiant sheen, Winchester 73
Rafters
With smoaky rafters, then in tapstry Halls Mask 324
Rage
Nor what the Potent Victor in his rage Par Lost 1.95
Wing'd with red Lightning and impetuous rage, Par Lost 1.175
Arming to Battel, and in stead of rage Par Lost 1.553
Black fire and horror shot with equal rage Par Lost 2.67
Th' Almighty Victor to spend all his rage, Par Lost 2.144
Awak'd should blow them into sevenfold rage Par Lost 2.171
Must'ring thir rage, and Heav'n resembles Hell? Par Lost 2.268
Others with vast *Typhoean* rage more fell Par Lost 2.539
Whose waves of torrent fire inflame with rage. Par Lost 2.581
Inflam'd with lust then rage) and swifter far, Par Lost 2.791
Onely begotten Son, seest thou what rage Par Lost 3.80
Well pleas'd, on me let Death wreck all his rage; Par Lost 3.241
Satan, now first inflam'd with rage, came down, Par Lost 4.9
The Fiend repli'd not, overcome with rage; Par Lost 4.857
Gave heed, but waxing more in rage repli'd. Par Lost 4.969
Returns our own. Cease then this impious rage, Par Lost 5.845
The Rebel Thrones, but greater rage to see Par Lost 6.199
And inextinguishable rage; all Heav'n Par Lost 6.217
Rage prompted them at length, and found them arms Par Lost 6.635
And to disorder'd rage let loose the reines, Par Lost 6.696
Yet envied; against mee is all thir rage, Par Lost 6.813
Torment, and loud lament, and furious rage. Par Lost 8.244
Thrice Fugitive about *Troy* Wall; or rage Par Lost 9.16
Not understood, till hoarse, and all in rage, Par Lost 12.58
More hard'nd after thaw, till in his rage Par Lost 12.194
With wonder, then with envy fraught and rage Par Reg 1.38
His wasted Country freed from *Punic* rage, Par Reg 3.102
Desperate of better course, to vent his rage, Par Reg 4.445
To whom the Fiend now swoln with rage reply'd: Par Reg 4.499
But finding no redress, ferment and rage, Samson 619
But Love constrain'd thee; call it furious rage Samson 836
My sudden rage to tear thee joint by joint. Samson 953
Rouze thy self amidst the rage Psalm 7, 20
That bends his rage thy providence to oppose Psalm 8, 8
Raged
Of battel when it rag'd, in all assaults Par Lost 1.277

Raged(*cont*)
Far round illumin'd hell: highly they rag'd Par Lost 1.666
Of brazen Chariots rag'd; dire was the noise Par Lost 6.211
Whereat hee inlie rag'd, and as they talk'd, Par Lost 11.444
Rages
Thy anger, unappeasable, still rages, Samson 963
Ragged
As ragged as thy Locks, Allegro 9
Raging
With what is punish't; whence these raging fires Par Lost 2.213
From Beds of raging Fire to starve in Ice Par Lost 2.600
Impendent, raging into sudden flame Par Lost 5.891
Solid or slimie, as in raging Sea Par Lost 10.286
Tyrannic power, but raging to pursue Samson 1275
Rags
And flutterd into Raggs, then Reliques, Beads, Par Lost 3.491
These rags, this grinding, is not yet so base Samson 415
Railed
Raild at *Latona*'s twin-born progenie Sonnet 12, 6
Trinity ms 'Rail'd'
Rain
As Clouds, and Clouds may rain, and Rain produce Par Lost 8.146
Th' inclement Seasons, Rain, Ice, Hail and Snow, Par Lost 10.1063
Like a dark Ceeling stood; down rush'd the Rain Par Lost 11.743
Raine day and night, all fountains of the Deep Par Lost 11.826
Surpass his bounds, nor Rain to drown the World Par Lost 11.894
Fierce rain with lightning mixt, water with fire Par Reg 4.412
Sam. Fair days have oft contracted wind and rain. Samson 1062
Rain influence, and judge the prise Allegro 122
Rainbow
That in the colours of the Rainbow live Mask 300
Trinity ms 'rainbow'
Bridgewater ms 'raynebow'
Th' enameld *Arras* of the Rainbow wearing, Nativity 143
1673 'Orb'd in a Rain-bow and like glories wearing'
Rainbows
Of Rainbows and Starrie Eyes. The Waters thus Par Lost 7.446
Rained
Her sacred shades: though God had yet not rain'd Par Lost 7.331
Raind at thir Eyes, but high Winds worse within Par Lost 9.1122
Rain'd from Heaven Manna, and that Prophet bold Par Reg 2.312
Raise
Illumin, what is low raise and support; Par Lost 1.23
Nor want we skill or Art, from whence to raise Par Lost 2.272
And dying rise, and rising with him raise Par Lost 3.296
I fear, hath ventur'd from the deep, to raise Par Lost 4.574
Like gentle breaths from Rivers pure, thence raise Par Lost 4.806
New Laws from him who reigns, new minds may raise Par Lost 5.680
Armie against Armie numberless to raise Par Lost 6.224
Canst raise thy Creature to what highth thou wilt Par Lost 8.430
Remaines, sufficient of it self to raise Par Lost 9.43
Would utmost vigor raise, and rais'd unite. Par Lost 9.314
Vacant possession som new trouble raise: Par Lost 11.103
Raise out of friendship hostil deeds in Peace. Par Lost 11.796
That God voutsafes to raise another World Par Lost 11.877
Which he will shew him, and from him will raise Par Lost 12.123
Raise him to be the second in that Realme Par Lost 12.162
Provoking God to raise them enemies: Par Lost 12.318
Satan with his perverted World, then raise Par Lost 12.547
Can raise them, though above example high; Par Reg 1.232
Or where plain was raise hill, or over-lay Par Reg 3.333
Exasperate, exulcerate, and raise Samson 625
To raise in me inexpiable hate, Samson 839
And raise such out-cries on thy clatter'd Iron, Samson 1124
Might raise *Musaeus* from his bower, Penseroso 104
Fame that her high worth to raise, Arcades 8
Fame is the spur that the clear spirit doth raise Lycidas 70
Victory home, though new rebellions raise Sonnet 15, 6
According to his justice raise Psalm 7, 62
And raise the man in deep distress Psalm 82, 11
Raised
Rais'd impious War in Heav'n and Battel proud Par Lost 1.43
ms 'Raisd'
That with the mightiest rais'd me to contend, Par Lost 1.99
Semblance of worth, not substance, gently rais'd Par Lost 1.529
Of Flutes and soft Recorders; such as rais'd Par Lost 1.551
Self-rais'd, and repossess thir native seat? Par Lost 1.634
ms 'Selfe-rais'd'
Satan exalted sat, by merit rais'd Par Lost 2.5
Satan, whom now transcendent glory rais'd Par Lost 2.427
Prudent, least from his resolution rais'd Par Lost 2.468
Thence more at ease thir minds and somwhat rais'd Par Lost 2.521
While by thee rais'd I ruin all my Foes, Par Lost 3.258
Then happie; no unbounded hope had rais'd Par Lost 4.60
That Mountain as his Garden mould high rais'd Par Lost 4.226
That rais'd us from the dust and plac't us here Par Lost 4.416
Returnd on that bright beam, whose point now raisd Par Lost 4.590
Leaning half-rais'd, with looks of cordial Love Par Lost 5.12
Hath raisd in Paradise, and how disturbd Par Lost 5.226
Have heap'd this Table. Rais'd of grassie terf Par Lost 5.391
Rais'd on a Mount, with Pyramids and Towrs Par Lost 5.758
Know none before us, self-begot, self-rais'd Par Lost 5.860
Have rais'd incessant Armies to defeat Par Lost 6.138
The overthrown he rais'd, and as a Heard Par Lost 6.856
Not here, till by degrees of merit rais'd Par Lost 7.157
And gaz'd a while the ample Skie, till rais'd Par Lost 8.258
So saying, by the hand he took me rais'd, Par Lost 8.300
Whom us the more to spite his Maker rais'd Par Lost 9.177

Raised(*cont*)
Would utmost vigor raise, and rais'd unite. Par Lost 9.314
Rais'd, as of som great matter to begin. Par Lost 9.669
An eager appetite, rais'd by the smell Par Lost 9.740
Rais'd from thir Dark *Divan*, and with like joy Par Lost 10.457
Labouring had rais'd, and thus to *Eve* repli'd. Par Lost 10.1012
Soon rais'd, and his attention thus recall'd. Par Lost 11.422
And *Eden* rais'd in the wast Wilderness. Par Reg 1.7
So to subvert whom he suspected rais'd Par Reg 1.124
Motherly cares and fears got head, and rais'd Par Reg 2.64
What rais'd *Antipater* the *Edomite*, Par Reg 2.423
Are few, and glory scarce of few is rais'd. Par Reg 3.59
And grisly Spectres, which the Fiend had rais'd Par Reg 4.430
Whom God hath of his special favour rais'd Samson 273
Capacity not rais'd to apprehend Samson 1028
I was no private but a person rais'd Samson 1211
And to our high-rais'd phantasie present, Musick 5
Trinity ms 'high-rays'd' ← 'high raysd' ← 'up rays'd' ← 'high rays'd'
'Gainst them that rais'd thee dost thou lift thy horn, Prose 3, 2
Raises
Or the sphear of fortune raises; Samson 172
Rallied
With rallied Arms to try what may be yet Par Lost 1.269
And to rebellious fight rallied thir Powers Par Lost 6.786
Ram
How cam'st thou here good Swain? hath any ram Mask 497
1673 'Ram'
Trinity ms 'ramme'
Ramath
That he might fall in *Ramoth*, they demurring, Par Reg 1.373
Ramath-Lehi
In *Ramath-lechi* famous to this day: Samson 145
Ramiel
Of *Ramiel* scorcht and blasted overthrew. Par Lost 6.372
Rammed
Thick-rammd, at th' other bore with touch of fire Par Lost 6.485
Ramoth
That he might fall in *Ramoth*, they demurring, Par Reg 1.373
Ramp
Fled from his Lion ramp, old Warriors turn'd Samson 139
Rampant
And Rampant shakes his Brinded main; the Ounce, Par Lost 7.466
Rampart
Or cast a Rampart. *Mammon* led them on, Par Lost 1.678
ms 'rampart'
Ramped
Sporting the Lion rampd, and in his paw Par Lost 4.343
Rams
The high, huge-bellied Mountains skip like Rams Psalm 114, 11
Ran
Ran purple to the Sea, suppos'd with blood Par Lost 1.451
Ran Nectar, visiting each plant, and fed Par Lost 4.240
Light as the Lightning glimps they ran, they flew, Par Lost 6.642
Survey'd, and sometimes went, and sometimes ran Par Lost 8.268
Ran through his veins, and all his joynts relax'd; Par Lost 9.891
Th' ethereal People ran, to hear and know Par Lost 10.27
Lay sleeping ran before, but found her wak't; Par Lost 12.608
Ran on embattelld Armies clad in Iron, Samson 129
Then down the Lawns I ran with headlong hast Mask 568
Rancour
Waited with hellish rancour imminent Par Lost 9.409
1667 'rancor'
Rancor and pride, impatience and despite, Par Lost 10.1044
Random
But still thy words at random, as before, Par Lost 4.930
At random yielded up to their misrule; Par Lost 10.628
See how he lies at random, carelesly diffus'd, Samson 118
Rang
As on mount *Sinai* rang Nativity 158
Range
While other Animals unactive range, Par Lost 4.621
Among the bestial herds to raunge, by thee Par Lost 4.754
In wo then; that destruction wide may range: Par Lost 9.134
To range in, and to dwell, and over Man Par Lost 10.492
Or range in th' Air, nor from the Heav'n of Heav'ns Par Reg 1.366
Ranged
By false presumptuous hope, the ranged powers Par Lost 2.522
By Thousands and by Millions rang'd for fight; Par Lost 6.48
In common, rang'd in figure wedge thir way, Par Lost 7.426
Single or in Array of Battel rang'd Par Lost 11.644
He saw them in thir forms of battell rang'd, Par Reg 3.322
Were bristles rang'd like those that ridge the back Samson 1137
And nests in order rang'd Samson 1694
Ranging
No equal, raunging through the dire attack Par Lost 6.248
Rank
Who now shall reare ye to the Sun, or ranke Par Lost 11.278
With the rank vapours of this Sin-worn mould. Mask 17
1637 'ranck'
Bridgewater ms 'ranke'
Trinity ms 'ranck'
But swoln with wind, and the rank mist they draw, Lycidas 126
Will rank my Prayers, and watch till thou appear. Psalm 5, 8
Ranked
With Horse and Chariots rankt in loose array; Par Lost 2.887
Stood rankt of Seraphim another row Par Lost 6.604
Duell'd thir Armies rank't in proud array, Samson 345

Rankle	
Ranckle, and fester, and gangrene,	Samson 621
Ranks	
To speak; whereat thir doubl'd Ranks they bend	Par Lost 1.616
ms 'ranks'	
A Silvan Scene, and as the ranks ascend	Par Lost 4.140
Thir perfet ranks; for high above the ground	Par Lost 6.71
On thir imbattelld ranks the Waves return,	Par Lost 12.213
Number my ranks, and visit every sprout	Arcades 59
Trinity ms 'rancks'	
Trip no more in twilight ranks,	Arcades 99
Trinity ms 'rancks'	
Are seen in glittering ranks with wings displaid,	Nativity 114
Ransacked	
Ransack'd the Center, and with impious hands	Par Lost 1.686
Ransom	
The deadly forfeiture, and ransom set.	Par Lost 3.221
Both Ransom and Redeemer voluntarie,	Par Lost 10.61
Thy ransom paid, which Man from death redeems,	Par Lost 12.424
About thy ransom: well they may by this	Samson 483
By ransom or how else: mean while be calm,	Samson 604
To accept of ransom for my Son thir pris'ner,	Samson 1460
If some convenient ransom were propos'd.	Samson 1471
Man. His ransom, if my whole inheritance	Samson 1476
Hath paid his ransom now and full discharge.	Samson 1573
Ransomed	
His Brethren, ransomd with his own dear life.	Par Lost 3.297
Rapacious	
Redeem thee quite from Deaths rapacious claime;	Par Lost 11.258
Rape	
Expos'd a Matron to avoid worse rape.	Par Lost 1.505
Ingendring with me, of that rape begot	Par Lost 2.794
Rape or Adulterie, where passing faire	Par Lost 11.717
By boistrous rape th' Athenian damsel got,	Fair Inf 9
Raphael	
Raphael, the sociable Spirit, that deign'd	Par Lost 5.221
Raphael, said hee, thou hear'st what stir on Earth	Par Lost 5.224
Thus *Adam* made request, and *Raphael*	Par Lost 5.561
Uriel and *Raphael* his vaunting foe,	Par Lost 6.363
Say Goddess, what ensu'd when *Raphael*,	Par Lost 7.40
And *Raphael* now to *Adam*'s doubt propos'd	Par Lost 8.64
To whom thus *Raphael* answer'd heav'nly meek.	Par Lost 8.217
As *Raphael*, that I should much confide,	Par Lost 11.235
Rapid	
With rapid wheels, or fronted Brigads form.	Par Lost 2.532
Upon the rapid current, which through veins	Par Lost 4.227
Ascend my Chariot, guide the rapid Wheeles	Par Lost 6.711
With clamor thence the rapid Currents drive	Par Lost 11.853
Rapine	
His Malice, and with rapine sweet bereav'd	Par Lost 9.461
By lust and rapine; first ambitious grown	Par Reg 4.137
While Avarice, and Rapine share the land.	Sonnet 15, 14
Rapt	
Rapt in a Chariot drawn by fiery Steeds.	Par Lost 3.522
Standing on Earth, not rapt above the Pole,	Par Lost 7.23
Rapt in a balmie Cloud with winged Steeds	Par Lost 11.706
Hath rapt him from us? will he now retire	Par Reg 2.40
Of this pure cause would kindle my rap't spirits	Mask 794
line not in Trinity ms	
line not in Bridgewater ms	
Thy rapt soul sitting in thine eyes:	Penseroso 40
Rapture	
Nor holy rapture wanted they to praise	Par Lost 5.147
To rapture, till the savage clamor dround	Par Lost 7.36
If steep, with torrent rapture, if through Plaine,	Par Lost 7.299
And rapture so oft beheld? those heav'nly shapes	Par Lost 9.1082
As all their souls in blisfull rapture took:	Nativity 98
Raptures	
Thir sacred Song, and waken raptures high;	Par Lost 3.369
And with these raptures moves the vocal air	Mask 247
and as your equall raptures temper'd sweet	Musick Tr. ms 4.05
'your equall raptures' ←'your raptures'	
Rare	
Ore bog or steep, through strait, rough, dense, or rare,	Par Lost 2.948
Though hard and rare: thee I revisit safe,	Par Lost 3.21
Of colour glorious and effect so rare?	Par Lost 3.612
Assume, as likes them best, condense or rare.	Par Lost 6.353
Those rare and solitarie, these in flocks	Par Lost 7.461
Of Arts that polish Life, Inventers rare,	Par Lost 11.610
Some beauty rare, *Calisto*, *Clymene*,	Par Reg 2.186
Or what (though rare) of later age,	Penseroso 101
Rarely	
Rarely be found: so shall the World goe on,	Par Lost 12.537
One vertuous rarely found,	Samson 1047
Rarer	
The rarer thy example stands,	Samson 166
Rash	
Or singular and rash, whereat rejoic'd	Par Lost 5.851
So saying, her rash hand in evil hour	Par Lost 9.780
Mean I to trie, what rash untri'd I sought,	Par Lost 9.860
Himself and his rash Armie, where thin Aire	Par Lost 12.76
Who leagu'd with millions more in rash revolt	Par Reg 1.359
And rash, before-hand had no better weigh'd	Par Reg 4.8
My rash but more unfortunate misdeed.	Samson 747
Dal. I was a fool, too rash, and quite mistaken	Samson 907
From the rash hand of bold Incontinence.	Mask 397
Bridgewater ms 'rashe'	
Rashly	
Yet stay, let me not rashly call in doubt	Samson 43
Rashness	
Untraind in Armes, where rashness leads not on.	Par Lost 12.222
Rate	
Thy strength they know surpassing human rate,	Samson 1313
1671 printed 'race', errata 'rate'	
Rathe	
Bring the rathe Primrose that forsaken dies.	Lycidas 142
Rather	
No light, but rather darkness visible	Par Lost 1.63
Rather then human. Nor did *Israel* scape	Par Lost 1.482
The fellows of his crime, the followers rather	Par Lost 1.606
Equal in strength, and rather then be less	Par Lost 2.47
By our delay? no, let us rather choose	Par Lost 2.60
To perish rather, swallowd up and lost	Par Lost 2.149
Of splendid vassalage, but rather seek	Par Lost 2.252
Or hear'st thou rather pure Ethereal stream,	Par Lost 3.7
So much the rather thou Celestial light	Par Lost 3.51
Imagind rather oft then elsewhere seen,	Par Lost 3.599
That reaches blame, but rather merits praise	Par Lost 3.697
But rather to tell how, if Art could tell,	Par Lost 4.236
To make us less, bent rather to exalt	Par Lost 5.829
I see that most through sloth had rather serve,	Par Lost 6.166
Chose rather; hee, she knew would intermix	Par Lost 8.54
Rather admire; or if they list to try	Par Lost 8.75
By us? who rather double honour gaine	Par Lost 9.332
Rather your dauntless vertue, whom the pain	Par Lost 9.694
What fear I then, rather what know to feare	Par Lost 9.773
Full happiness with mee, or rather not,	Par Lost 9.819
Rather how hast thou yeelded to transgress	Par Lost 9.902
Rather then Death or aught then Death more dread	Par Lost 9.969
The worst, and not perswade thee rather die	Par Lost 9.979
Yet willingly chose rather Death with thee:	Par Lost 9.1167
True is, mee also he hath judg'd, or rather	Par Lost 10.494
Rather then solid vertu, all but a Rib	Par Lost 10.884
We are by doom to pay; rather such acts	Par Lost 10.1026
Rather belongs, distrust and all dispraise:	Par Lost 11.166
To be thus wrested from us? rather why	Par Lost 11.503
Life much, bent rather how I may be quit	Par Lost 11.548
Return them back to *Egypt*, choosing rather	Par Lost 12.219
Purified to receive him pure, or rather	Par Reg 1.74
I ask the rather, and the more admire,	Par Reg 1.326
I lost not what I lost, rather by them	Par Reg 1.390
Rather inflames thy torment, representing	Par Reg 1.418
Rather to be in readiness, with hand	Par Reg 2.144
And rather opportunely in this place	Par Reg 2.396
Abominations rather, as did once	Par Reg 3.162
They themselves rather are occasion best,	Par Reg 3.174
Rather then aggravate my evil state,	Par Reg 3.218
Of human weakness rather then of strength.	Par Reg 3.402
Permitted rather, and by thee usurp't,	Par Reg 4.183
Rather more honour left and more esteem;	Par Reg 4.207
Rather accuse him under usual names,	Par Reg 4.316
That rather *Greece* from us these Arts deriv'd;	Par Reg 4.338
Rather by this his last affront resolv'd,	Par Reg 4.444
Why thou shouldst wed *Philistian* women rather	Samson 216
Rather approv'd them not; but thou didst plead	Samson 421
Here rather let me drudge and earn my bread,	Samson 573
Little prevails, or rather seems a tune,	Samson 661
Thou wilt renounce thy seeking, and much rather	Samson 828
Or rather flight, no great advantage on me;	Samson 1118
Then thou shalt see, or rather to thy sorrow	Samson 1154
And numberd down: much rather I shall chuse	Samson 1478
Chor. Thy Son is rather slaying them, that outcry	Samson 1517
That I encline to hope, rather then fear,	Mask 412
Yet I had rather if I were to chuse,	Vacation 29
Had rather keep a dore,	Psalm 84, 38
Rational	
Of Creatures rational, though under hope	Par Lost 2.498
As doth your Rational; and both contain	Par Lost 5.409
All rational delight, wherein the brute	Par Lost 8.391
Attractive, human, rational, love still;	Par Lost 8.587
Rational Libertie; yet know withall,	Par Lost 12.82
Rattling	
With Heav'ns Artillery fraught, come rattling on	Par Lost 2.715
But ratling storm of Arrows barbd with fire.	Par Lost 6.546
Rave	
Who now hath quite forgot to rave,	Nativity 67
Ravel	
They ravel more, still less resolv'd,	Samson 305
Raven	
Forthwith from out the Arke a Raven flies,	Par Lost 11.855
At every fall smoothing the Raven doune	Mask 251
Bridgewater ms 'raven'	
Trinity ms 'raven'	
And the night-Raven sings;	Allegro 7
Ravenous	
Of ravenous Fowl, though many a League remote,	Par Lost 10.274
For ever, and seal up his ravenous Jawes.	Par Lost 10.637
Be forc'd to satisfie his Rav'nous Maw.	Par Lost 10.991
Though ravenous, taught to abstain from what they brought:	Par Reg 2.269
Ravens	
And saw the Ravens with their horny beaks	Par Reg 2.267
Raves	
May tell at length how green-ey'd *Neptune* raves,	Vacation 43
Ravin	
There best, where most with ravin I may meet;	Par Lost 10.599

Ravishment
Suspended Hell, and took with ravishment — Par Lost 2.554
In whose sight all things joy, with ravishment — Par Lost 5.46
With ravishment beheld, there best beheld — Par Lost 9.541
Breath such Divine inchanting ravishment? — Mask 245

Ray
To find thy piercing ray, and find no dawn; — Par Lost 3.24
No where so cleer, sharp'nd his visual ray — Par Lost 3.620
Perfection from the Suns more potent Ray. — Par Lost 4.673
Shot paralel to the earth his dewie ray, — Par Lost 5.141
With Heav'ns ray, and temperd they shoot forth — Par Lost 6.480
Still luminous by his ray. What if that light — Par Lost 8.140
Semblance, and in thy Beauties heav'nly Ray — Par Lost 9.607
Against the Eastern ray, translucent, pure. — Samson 548
That spreds her verdant leaf to th' morning ray, — Mask 622

Rays
Of beaming sunnie Raies, a golden tiar — Par Lost 3.625
Leveld his eevning Rayes: it was a Rock — Par Lost 4.543
Shot down direct his fervid Raies to warme — Par Lost 5.301
1667 'raies' in some copies
He said, and on his Son with Rayes direct — Par Lost 6.719
Invested with bright Rayes, jocond to run — Par Lost 7.372
Where through the sacred rayes of Chastity, — Mask 425
Trinity ms 'rays' ←'aw'
1637 'rays'
With sudden adoration, and blank aw. — Mask 452
Trinity ms 'and blank aw' ←'of bright rays' ←'of her purenesse'
The rayes of *Bethlehem* blind his dusky eyn; — Nativity 223

Raze
With all her battering Engines bent to rase — Par Lost 2.923
Upon thir Tongues a various Spirit to rase — Par Lost 12.53

Razed
Be no memorial blotted out and ras'd — Par Lost 1.362
ms 'raz'd'
Of Natures works to mee expung'd and ras'd, — Par Lost 3.49

Razor
But by the Barbers razor best subdu'd. — Samson 1167

Reach
And wish and struggle, as they pass, to reach — Par Lost 2.606
Assaying by his Devilish art to reach — Par Lost 4.801
This is dispenc't, and what surmounts the reach — Par Lost 5.571
Unknown, which human knowledg could not reach: — Par Lost 7.75
Thy utmost reach or *Adams:* Round the Tree — Par Lost 9.591
Longing and envying stood, but could not reach. — Par Lost 9.593
Goddess humane, reach then, and freely taste. — Par Lost 9.732
To reach, and feed at once both Bodie and Mind? — Par Lost 9.779
With long reach interpos'd; three sev'ral wayes — Par Lost 10.323
The doubt, since humane reach no further knows. — Par Lost 10.793
To over-reach, but with the Serpent meeting — Par Lost 10.879
Reach also of the Tree of Life, and eat, — Par Lost 11.94
Stretcht out to the amplest reach of prospect lay. — Par Lost 11.380
A Citie and Towre, whose top may reach to Heav'n; — Par Lost 12.44
Eternitie, whose end no eye can reach. — Par Lost 12.556
Happ'ly had ends above my reach to know: — Samson 62
Dissolves unjointed e're it reach my ear. — Samson 177
Chor. How thou wilt here come off surmounts my reach. — Samson 1380
Above the reach of mortall ey. — Psalm 136, 94

Reached
His stature reacht the Skie, and on his Crest — Par Lost 4.988
Of Fruit-trees overwoodie reachd too farr — Par Lost 5.213
Proud, art thou met? thy hope was to have reacht — Par Lost 6.131
Shame to be overcome or over-reacht — Par Lost 9.313
In cunning, over-reach't where least he thought, — Par Reg 4.11

Reaches
That reaches blame, but rather merits praise — Par Lost 3.697

Reaching
Hell bounds high reaching to the horrid Roof, — Par Lost 2.644
From Hell continu'd reaching th' utmost Orbe — Par Lost 2.1029
Reaching beyond all limit at one blow — Par Lost 6.140
Forth reaching to the Fruit, she pluck'd, she eat: — Par Lost 9.781

Read
And summons read, the great consult began. — Par Lost 1.798
In others count'nance read his own dismay — Par Lost 2.422
1667 'red'
And read thy Lot in yon celestial Sign — Par Lost 4.1011
Wherein to read his wondrous Works, and learne — Par Lost 8.68
The Law of God I read, and found it sweet, — Par Reg 1.207
(For I have also heard, perhaps have read) — Par Reg 4.116
Now contrary, if I read aught in Heaven, — Par Reg 4.382
When they shall read this clearly in your charge — Forcers 19

Reader
Cries the stall-reader, bless us! what a word on — Sonnet 11, 5

Readiest
What readiest path leads where your gloomie bounds — Par Lost 2.976
Through the wilde Desert, not the readiest way, — Par Lost 12.216
The slightest, easiest, readiest recompence — Par Reg 3.128
What readiest way would bring me to that place? — Mask 305
Readiest thy grace to shew, — Psalm 86, 54

Readily
My Tongue obey'd and readily could name — Par Lost 8.272

Readiness
Rather to be in readiness, with hand — Par Reg 2.144

Reading
Incessantly, and to his reading brings not — Par Reg 4.323

Readmit
Gracious to re-admit the suppliant; — Samson 1173

Reads
Wise men have said are wearisom; who reads — Par Reg 4.322

Ready
Death ready stands to interpose his dart, — Par Lost 2.854
In the dun Air sublime, and ready now — Par Lost 3.72
Stand ready at command, and are his Eyes — Par Lost 3.650
Two other precious drops that ready stood, — Par Lost 5.132
Of *Tartarus*, which ready opens wide — Par Lost 6.54
Were ready, in a moment up they turnd — Par Lost 6.509
Stand readie to receive them, if they like — Par Lost 6.561
Empress, the way is readie, and not long, — Par Lost 9.626
If need be, I am ready to forgo — Samson 1483
Stands ready to smite once, and smite no more. — Lycidas 131
Trinity ms 'readie'
His ready Harbinger, — Nativity 49
As ready to expire, — Psalm 88, 62

Real
Of real hunger, and concoctive heate — Par Lost 5.437
Before mine Eyes all real, as the dream — Par Lost 8.310
Be real, why not known, since easier shunnd? — Par Lost 9.699
Hers in all real dignitie: Adornd — Par Lost 10.151
And Planets, Planet-strook, real Eclips — Par Lost 10.413
Real or Allegoric I discern not, — Par Reg 4.390
In real darkness of the body dwells, — Samson 159

Realities
And to realities yield all her shows: — Par Lost 8.575

Realm
That ore the Realm of impious *Pharaoh* hung — Par Lost 1.342
ms 'realm'
And *Horonaim*, *Seons* Realm, beyond — Par Lost 1.409
ms 'realm'
Scout farr and wide into the Realm of night, — Par Lost 2.133
The secrets of your Realm, but by constraint — Par Lost 2.972
Hung ore my Realm, link'd in a golden Chain — Par Lost 2.1005
Runs divers, wandring many a famous Realme — Par Lost 4.234
Find pastime, and beare rule; thy Realm is large. — Par Lost 8.375
The Realm it self of Satan long usurpt, — Par Lost 10.189
1667 'Realme'
Mine with this glorious Work, and made one Realm — Par Lost 10.391
Hell and this World, one Realm, one Continent — Par Lost 10.392
The Realm of *Aladule*, in his retreate — Par Lost 10.435
1667 'Realme'
And *Sofala* thought *Ophir*, to the Realme — Par Lost 11.400
Raise him to be the second in that Realme — Par Lost 12.162
Through all his Realme, and there confounded leave; — Par Lost 12.455
1667 'realme'
Of many a pleasant Realm and Province wide. — Par Reg 1.118
The Realm of *Bocchus* to the Black-moor Sea; — Par Reg 4.72
Up to the Realm of peace & Joy for ever, — Sonnet 14, Tr. ms 41.08
Beyond the Realm of *Gaul*, a Land there lies, — Prose 12, 8

Realms
From him, who in the happy Realms of Light — Par Lost 1.85
ms 'realmes'
Battels and Realms: in these he put two weights — Par Lost 4.1002
Yet Chains in Hell, not Realms expect: mean while — Par Lost 6.186
Number sufficient to possess her Realmes — Par Lost 7.147
Money brings Honour, Friends, Conquest, and Realms; — Par Reg 2.422
Riches and Realms; yet not for that a Crown, — Par Reg 2.458

Realty
Should yet remain, where faith and realtie — Par Lost 6.115

Reap
May reap his conquest, and may least rejoyce — Par Lost 2.339
For peace, reap nothing but repulse and hate? — Samson 966

Reaped
New reapt, the other part sheep-walks and foulds; — Par Lost 11.431

Reaper
A sweatie Reaper from his Tillage brought — Par Lost 11.434

Reapers
As Reapers oft are wont thir Harvest Queen. — Par Lost 9.842

Reaping
Reaping immortal fruits of joy and love, — Par Lost 3.67
Labouring the soile, and reaping plenteous crop, — Par Lost 12.18

Reaps
And Hope that reaps not shame. Therefore be sure — Sonnet 9, 11

Rear
When the fierce Foe hung on our brok'n Rear — Par Lost 2.78
Standards, and Gonfalons twixt Van and Reare — Par Lost 5.589
Prone on the ground, as since, but on his reare, — Par Lost 9.497
Who now shall reare ye to the Sun, or ranke — Par Lost 11.278
So many grateful Altars I would reare — Par Lost 11.323
When God with these forbid'n made choice to rear — Samson 555
Nipt with the lagging rear of winters frost. — Samson 1577
Scatters the rear of darknes thin, — Allegro 50

Reared
Rear'd in *Azotus*, dreaded through the Coast — Par Lost 1.464
Rear'd high thir flourisht heads between, and wrought — Par Lost 4.699
Pavilions numberless, and sudden reard, — Par Lost 5.653
Submiss: he rear'd me, and Whom thou soughtst I am, — Par Lost 8.316
And sunk thee as thy Sons; till gently reard — Par Lost 11.758
Up to a hill anon his steps he rear'd, — Par Reg 2.285
And higher yet the glorious Temple rear'd — Par Reg 4.546
Till all thy magick structures rear'd so high, — Mask 798
line not in Bridgewater ms
line not in Trinity ms
Who piteous of her woes, rear'd her lank head, — Mask 836
1637 'reatd'
Bridgewater ms 'reard'
Hast reard Gods Trophies and his work pursu'd. — Sonnet 16, 6

Reared(*cont*)
1694 'And Fought God's Battels'
Rears
Forthwith upright he rears from off the Pool Par Lost 1.221
Reascend
Hath emptied Heav'n, shall fail to re-ascend Par Lost 1.633
ms 'reascend'
The dark descent, and up to reascend, Par Lost 3.20
Must reascend, what will betide the few Par Lost 12.480
Reason
Whom reason hath equald, force hath made supream Par Lost 1.248
The better reason, to perplex and dash Par Lost 2.114
Main reason to perswade immediate Warr, Par Lost 2.121
Thus *Belial* with words cloath'd in reasons garb Par Lost 2.226
With reason hath deep silence and demurr Par Lost 2.431
When Will and Reason (Reason also is choice) Par Lost 3.108
Melt, as I doe, yet public reason just, Par Lost 4.389
Founded in Reason, Loyal, Just, and Pure, Par Lost 4.755
To thee no reason; who knowst only good, Par Lost 4.895
Reason as chief; among these Fansie next Par Lost 5.102
Which Reason joyning or disjoyning, frames Par Lost 5.106
Reason receives, and reason is her being, Par Lost 5.487
Who can in reason then or right assume Par Lost 5.794
By force, who reason for thir Law refuse, Par Lost 6.41
Right reason for thir Law, and for thir King Par Lost 6.42
I mean to try, whose Reason I have tri'd Par Lost 6.120
When Reason hath to deal with force, yet so Par Lost 6.125
Most reason is that Reason overcome. Par Lost 6.126
With Sanctitie of Reason, might erect Par Lost 7.508
And reason not contemptibly; with these Par Lost 8.374
Good reason was thou freely shouldst dislike, Par Lost 8.443
My pleaded reason. To the Nuptial Bowre Par Lost 8.510
Authority and Reason on her waite, Par Lost 8.554
In Reason, and is judicious, is the scale Par Lost 8.591
Of Growth, Sense, Reason, all summ'd up in Man. Par Lost 9.113
Of looks and smiles, for smiles from Reason flow, Par Lost 9.239
He made us, and delight to Reason joyn'd. Par Lost 9.243
Reason, is free, and Reason he made right, Par Lost 9.352
Since Reason not impossibly may meet Par Lost 9.360
Much reason, and in thir actions oft appeers. Par Lost 9.559
Of Reason in my inward Powers, and Speech Par Lost 9.600
Law to our selves, our Reason is our Law. Par Lost 9.654
With Reason, to her seeming, and with Truth; Par Lost 9.738
Usurping over sovran Reason claimd Par Lost 9.1130
Is lost, which alwayes with right Reason dwells Par Lost 12.84
Reason in man obscur'd, or not obeyd, Par Lost 12.86
From Reason, and to servitude reduce Par Lost 12.89
Over free Reason, God in Judgement just Par Lost 12.92
From vertue, which is reason, that no wrong, Par Lost 12.98
And for thy reason why they should be sought, Par Reg 2.485
And reason; since his word all things produc'd, Par Reg 3.122
How wilt thou reason with them, how refute Par Reg 4.233
Good reason then, if I before-hand seek Par Reg 4.526
Down Reason then, at least vain reasonings down, Samson 322
Though Reason here aver Samson 323
Or reason though disturb'd, and scarse consulted Samson 1546
I have perform'd, as reason was, obeying, Samson 1641
Fixes instead, unmoulding reasons mintage Mask 529
Obtruding false rules pranckt in reasons garb. Mask 759
For my relief; yet hadst no reason why, Sonnet 1, 12
Reasoned
In thoughts more elevate, and reason'd high Par Lost 2.558
Reasoning
Useless besides, reasoning I oft admire, Par Lost 8.25
Alreadie by thy reasoning this I guess, Par Lost 8.85
Chiefly by what thy own last reasoning words Par Lost 9.379
Reasoning to admiration, and with mee Par Lost 9.872
Reasonings
And reasonings, though through Mazes, lead me still Par Lost 10.830
Down Reason then, at least vain reasonings down, Samson 322
Far other reasonings, brought forth other deeds. Samson 875
Reasonless
Suspicious, reasonless. Why should thir Lord Par Lost 4.516
Though fond and reasonless to some perhaps; Samson 812
Reasons
And knows, and speaks, and reasons, and discerns, Par Lost 9.765
These reasons in Loves law have past for good, Samson 811
And combated in silence all these reasons Samson 864
Baited with reasons not unplausible Mask 162
Reassembling
And reassembling our afflicted Powers, Par Lost 1.186
Reassumed
Into his blissful bosom reassum'd Par Lost 10.225
Rebecks
And the jocond rebecks sound Allegro 94
Rebel
Of Rebel Angels, by whose aid aspiring Par Lost 1.38
ms 'rebell'
The Calf in *Oreb:* and the Rebel King Par Lost 1.484
ms 'rebell'
Who justly hath drivn out his Rebell Foes Par Lost 3.677
Which of those rebell Spirits adjudg'd to Hell Par Lost 4.823
The Rebel Thrones, but greater rage to see Par Lost 6.199
Be sure, and terrour seis'd the rebel Host, Par Lost 6.647
Convict by flight, and Rebel to all Law Par Lost 10.83
anointed have my King (though ye rebell) Psalm 2, 12
Rebelled
To serve th' unwise, or him who hath rebelld Par Lost 6.179
Rebelled(*cont*)
Armd with thy might, rid Heav'n of these rebell'd, Par Lost 6.737
Of those too high aspiring, who rebelld Par Lost 6.899
Still on; for against thee they have rebell'd; Psalm 5, 32
Rebellion
By thir Rebellion, from the Books of Life. Par Lost 1.363
ms 'rebellion'
Rebellion rising, saw in whom, how spred Par Lost 5.715
Of thy Rebellion? how hast thou instill'd Par Lost 6.269
And from Rebellion shall derive his name, Par Lost 12.36
Though of Rebellion others he accuse. Par Lost 12.37
Single Rebellion and did Hostile Acts. Samson 1210
Rebellions
Victory home, though new rebellions raise Sonnet 15, 6
1694 'Rebellions'
Push them in their rebellions all Psalm 5, 31
Rebellious
For those rebellious, here thir Prison ordain'd Par Lost 1.71
Erring; for he with this rebellious rout Par Lost 1.747
Unbrok'n, and in proud rebellious Arms Par Lost 2.691
Upon his own rebellious head. And now Par Lost 3.86
Faithful to whom? to thy rebellious crew? Par Lost 4.952
Rebellious, them with Fire and hostile Arms Par Lost 6.50
Satan with his rebellious disappeerd, Par Lost 6.414
And to rebellious fight rallied thir Powers Par Lost 6.786
All like himself rebellious, by whose aid Par Lost 7.140
Rebels
Thy Rebels, or be found the worst in Heav'n. Par Lost 5.742
Rebounding
And with rebounding surge the barrs assaild, Par Lost 10.417
Rebounds
At once with joy and fear his heart rebounds. Par Lost 1.788
Rebuff
The strong rebuff of som tumultuous cloud Par Lost 2.936
Rebuilt
As antient, but rebuilt by him who twice Par Reg 3.281
Rebuke
So spake the Cherube, and his grave rebuke Par Lost 4.844
Humbl'd by such rebuke, so farr beneath Par Lost 6.342
Anger and just rebuke, and judgement giv'n, Par Lost 9.10
Sharply thou hast insisted on rebuke, Par Reg 1.468
At thy rebuke and frown. Psalm 80, 68
Recall
Would higth recal high thoughts, how soon unsay Par Lost 4.95
Against thee are gon forth without recall; Par Lost 5.885
But past who can recall, or don undoe? Par Lost 9.926
Nor will withdraw him now, nor will recall, Par Reg 2.55
Recalled
But see the angry Victor hath recall'd Par Lost 1.169
For though I fled him angrie, yet recall'd Par Lost 11.330
Soon rais'd, and his attention thus recall'd. Par Lost 11.422
Recalling
Recalling what remarkably had pass'd Par Reg 2.106
Recant
What feign'd submission swore: ease would recant Par Lost 4.96
Receive
Receive thy new Possessor: One who brings Par Lost 1.252
In temper and in nature, will receive Par Lost 2.218
Stand in his presence humble, and receive Par Lost 2.240
Not what they would? what praise could they receive? Par Lost 3.106
Death his deaths wound shall then receive, and stoop Par Lost 3.252
Receive new life. So Man, as is most just, Par Lost 3.294
Not like these narrow limits, to receive Par Lost 4.384
On Earth, made hereby apter to receive Par Lost 4.672
Abundance, fit to honour and receive Par Lost 5.315
Fit entertainment to receive our King Par Lost 5.690
Receive him coming to receive from us Par Lost 5.781
His fiery *Chaos* to receave thir fall. Par Lost 6.55
Came summond over *Eden* to receive Par Lost 6.75
From flight, seditious Angel, to receave Par Lost 6.152
This greeting on thy impious Crest receive. Par Lost 6.188
Receive, no more then can the fluid Aire: Par Lost 6.349
Stand readie to receive them, if they like Par Lost 6.561
Receave with solemne purpose to observe Par Lost 7.78
So told as earthly notion can receave. Par Lost 7.179
In the Suns Orb, made porous to receive Par Lost 7.361
After thir kindes; I bring them to receave Par Lost 8.343
Can either not receave, or can repell. Par Lost 9.284
I from the influence of thy looks receave Par Lost 9.309
Against his will he can receave no harme. Par Lost 9.350
To sanctitie that shall receive no staine: Par Lost 10.639
Accept me, and in mee from these receave Par Lost 11.37
What we receive, would either not accept Par Lost 11.505
Did, as thou sawst, receave, to walk with God Par Lost 11.707
And puissant deeds, a promise shall receive Par Lost 12.322
His faithful, and receave them into bliss, Par Lost 12.462
Great numbers of each Nation to receave Par Lost 12.503
Purified to receive him pure, or rather Par Reg 1.74
Not thence to be more pure, but to receive Par Reg 1.77
Shall I receive by gift what of my own, Par Reg 2.381
Or human nature can receive, consider Par Reg 3.231
What both from Men and Angels I receive, Par Reg 4.200
Forthwith how thou oughtst to receive him. Samson 329
Dagon must stoop, and shall e're long receive Samson 468
I as a Prophecy receive: for God, Samson 473
Didst thou at first receive me for thy husband? Samson 883
Me their Deliverer sent would not receive, Samson 1214
Held up their pearled wrists and took her in, Mask 834

Receive(*cont*)
Trinity ms '& took' ←'to take' ←'carie' ←'receave'
Received
Of Heav'n receiv'd us falling, and the Thunder, Par Lost 1.174
Stood thick as Starrs, and from his sight receiv'd Par Lost 3.61
Forgetful what from him I still receivd, Par Lost 4.54
And by her yielded, by him best receivd, Par Lost 4.309
After his charge receivd; but from among Par Lost 5.248
Among those friendly Powers, who him receav'd Par Lost 6.22
Ineffably into his face receiv'd, Par Lost 6.721
And as ye have receivd, so have ye don Par Lost 6.805
Yawning receavd them whole, and on them clos'd, Par Lost 6.875
On high: who into Glorie him receav'd, Par Lost 6.891
I have receav'd, to answer thy desire Par Lost 7.119
But in the fruitful Earth; there first receavd Par Lost 8.96
Giv'n and receiv'd; but in disparitie Par Lost 8.386
All I receav'd, unable to performe Par Lost 10.750
By wisdome, and superiour gifts receav'd. Par Lost 11.636
1667 'receavd'
And thus with words not sad she him receav'd. Par Lost 12.609
Who for so many benefits receiv'd Par Reg 3.137
Of moral prudence, with delight receiv'd Par Reg 4.263
Who on their plumy Vans receiv'd him soft Par Reg 4.583
By this repulse receiv'd, and hold'st in Hell Par Reg 4.623
With that which you receiv'd on other terms, Mask 684
Trinity ms 'receav'd'
line not in Bridgewater ms
As a faint host that hath receiv'd the foil. Psalm 114, 10
That the first wealthy *Pope* receiv'd of thee. Prose 1, 3
Receives
Of unessential Night receives him next Par Lost 2.439
The Sun that light imparts to all, receives Par Lost 5.423
Reason receives, and reason is her being, Par Lost 5.487
And stumbl'd many, who receives them right, Par Lost 6.624
Her end without least motion, and receaves, Par Lost 8.35
Earth sitting still, when she alone receaves Par Lost 8.89
Of *Moreh;* there by promise he receaves Par Lost 12.137
Glory he requires, and glory he receives Par Reg 3.117
Of knowing what I aught: he who receives Par Reg 4.288
Receivest
Centring receav'st from all those Orbs; in thee, Par Lost 9.109
Receiving
Receiving from his mother Earth new strength, Par Reg 4.566
Receptacle
The dry Land, Earth, and the great receptacle Par Lost 7.307
Least Paradise a receptacle prove Par Lost 11.123
Reception
About the great reception of thir King, Par Lost 5.769
To the reception of thir matter act, Par Lost 10.807
Of my reception into grace; what worse? Par Reg 3.205
Recess
In close recess and secret conclave sat Par Lost 1.795
ms 'recesse'
Live to our selves, though in this vast recess, Par Lost 2.254
Of coole recess, o're which the mantling vine Par Lost 4.258
Nor *Faunus* haunted. Here in close recess Par Lost 4.708
This Flourie Plat, the sweet recess of *Eve* Par Lost 9.456
Recess, and onely consolation left Par Lost 11.304
Or hospitable, in her sweet recess, Par Reg 4.242
Reciprocal
This Earth? reciprocal, if Land be there, Par Lost 8.144
In cours reciprocal, and had his fate Another 30
line not in 1658 text
1640 'reciprocall'
Reck
Let it; I reck not, so it light well aim'd, Par Lost 9.173
Recked
He reck'd not, and these words thereafter spake. Par Lost 2.50
1667 'reckd'
Reckon
Imports not, if thou reck'n right, the rest Par Lost 8.71
For him I reckon not in high estate Samson 170
Reckoned
Reck'n'd I am with them that pass Psalm 88, 13
Reckonest
And reck'n'st thou thy self with Spirits of Heav'n, Par Lost 2.696
Reckoning
I purs't it up, but little reck'ning made, Mask 642
Bridgewater ms 'reckoninge'
Trinity ms 'reckoning'
Of other care they little reck'ning make, Lycidas 116
1638 'reckoning'
Trinity ms 'reckning'
Reckons
In peace, and reck'ns thee her eldest son. Sonnet 17, 14
1662, 1694 'reckons'
Recks
Of night, or lonelines it recks me not, Mask 404
What recks it them? What need they? They are sped; Lycidas 122
Reclaim
They hard'nd more by what might most reclame, Par Lost 6.791
Recline
Yielded them, side-long as they sat recline Par Lost 4.333
Recoil
With impetuous recoile and jarring sound Par Lost 2.880
But evil on it self shall back recoyl, Mask 593
Bridgewater ms 'recoyle'
1637 'recoyle'
Recoil(*cont*)
Trinity ms 'recoyle'
Low in the earth, *Jordans* clear streams recoil, Psalm 114, 9
Recoiled
All th' Host of Heav'n; back they recoild affraid Par Lost 2.759
He back recoild; the tenth on bended knee Par Lost 6.194
And fierie foaming Steeds; what stood, recoyld Par Lost 6.391
Recoils
And like a devillish Engine back recoiles Par Lost 4.17
Bitter ere long back on it self recoiles; Par Lost 9.172
Recollecting
Soon recollecting, with high words, that bore Par Lost 1.528
Recollects
Fierce hate he recollects, and all his thoughts Par Lost 9.471
Recomforted
Recomforted, and after thoughts disturbd Par Lost 9.918
Recommend
To recommend coole *Zephyr*, and made ease Par Lost 4.329
Lodg'd in his brest, as well might recommend Par Reg 1.301
Recompence
Directed, no mean recompence it brings Par Lost 2.981
The easiest recompence, and pay him thanks, Par Lost 4.47
Torment with ease, and soonest recompence Par Lost 4.893
From all his alimental recompence Par Lost 5.424
What thanks sufficient, or what recompence Par Lost 8.5
In recompence (for such compliance bad Par Lost 9.994
Such recompence best merits) from the bough Par Lost 9.995
Is this the Love, is this the recompence Par Lost 9.1163
To recompence his distance, in thir sight Par Lost 10.683
The slightest, easiest, readiest recompence Par Reg 3.128
Hard recompence, unsutable return Par Reg 3.132
Though late, yet in some part to recompense Samson 746
Afford me place to shew what recompence Samson 910
In thy large recompense, and shalt be good Lycidas 184
Trinity ms 'recompence'
Recompenced
And bringing forth, soon recompenc't with joy, Par Lost 10.1052
With inward consolations recompenc't, Par Lost 12.495
Reconciled
Before thee reconcil'd, at least his days Par Lost 11.39
In ruine reconcil'd: nor slept the winds Par Reg 4.413
Are reconcil'd at length, and Sea to Shore: Samson 962
Reconcilement
And reconcilement; wrauth shall be no more Par Lost 3.264
For never can true reconcilement grow Par Lost 4.98
Creature so faire his reconcilement seeking, Par Lost 10.943
And reconcilement move with feign'd remorse, Samson 752
Record
Forget not: in thy book record their groanes Sonnet 18, 5
Recorded
Recorded eminent. Thus when in Orbes Par Lost 5.594
So Eev'n and Morn recorded the Third Day. Par Lost 7.338
Living and dead recorded, who to save Samson 984
Recorders
Of Flutes and soft Recorders; such as rais'd Par Lost 1.551
ms 'recorders'
Records
Though of thir Names in heav'nly Records now Par Lost 1.361
ms 'records'
The Records of his Cov'nant, over these Par Lost 12.252
Left onely in those written Records pure, Par Lost 12.513
Recount
Obtaine: though to recount Almightie works Par Lost 7.112
Recount his praises; thus he did to *Job*, Par Reg 3.64
Recounted
Recounted, mixing intercession sweet. Par Lost 10.228
Recover
Mess. It would burst forth, but I recover breath Samson 1555
Recovered
As Gods, and by thir own recover'd strength, Par Lost 1.240
Thus farr at least recover'd, hath much more Par Lost 2.22
Scarce thus at length faild speech recoverd sad. Par Lost 4.357
Firm peace recoverd soon and wonted calm. Par Lost 5.210
Recover'd Paradise to all mankind, Par Reg 1.3
So had the glory of Prowess been recover'd Samson 1098
Recovering
To whom thus *Eve*, recovering heart, repli'd. Par Lost 10.966
Recovering, and his scatterd spirits returnd, Par Lost 11.294
And scarce recovering words his plaint renew'd. Par Lost 11.499
Recreant
Turn'd recreant to God, ingrate and false, Par Reg 3.138
Recure
Which hee, who comes thy Saviour, shall recure, Par Lost 12.393
Red
Wing'd with red Lightning and impetuous rage, Par Lost 1.175
Hath vext the Red-Sea Coast, whose waves orethrew Par Lost 1.306
ms 'red-sea'
His red right hand to plague us? what if all Par Lost 2.174
Turnd fierie red, sharpning in mooned hornes Par Lost 4.978
Celestial rosie red, Loves proper hue, Par Lost 8.619
As the Red Sea and *Jordan* once he cleft, Par Reg 3.438
While the red fire, and smouldring clouds out brake: Nativity 159
Curtain'd with cloudy red, Nativity 230
With much confusion; then grow red with shame, Psalm 6, 22
Redeem
Which of ye will be mortal to rédeem Par Lost 3.214
Thou therefore whom thou only canst redeem, Par Lost 3.281
1667 'redeeme'

Redeem(*cont*)
Giving to death, and dying to redeeme, Par Lost 3.299
So dearly to redeem what Hellish hate Par Lost 3.300
Redeem thee quite from Deaths rapacious claime; Par Lost 11.258
Must redeem our loss; Nativity 153
Redeemed
Then with the multitude of my redeemd Par Lost 3.260
All my redeemd may dwell in joy and bliss, Par Lost 11.43
Redeemer
Both Ransom and Redeemer voluntarie, Par Lost 10.61
For death, like that which the redeemer dy'd. Par Lost 12.445
Acknowledge my Redeemer ever blest. Par Lost 12.573
Redeems
Thy ransom paid, which Man from death redeems, Par Lost 12.424
Or theirs whom he redeems, a death like sleep, Par Lost 12.434
Redemption
And now without redemption all mankind Par Lost 3.222
Ordaind without redemption, without end. Par Lost 5.615
In his redemption, and that his obedience Par Lost 12.408
Or work Redemption for mankind, whose sins Par Reg 1.266
For his redemption all my Patrimony, Samson 1482
Our great redemption from above did bring; Nativity 4
1673 'Redemption'
Redouble
Redouble then this miracle, and say, Par Lost 9.562
Redoubled
The Atheist crew, but with redoubl'd blow Par Lost 6.370
With me, where my redoubl'd love and care Samson 923
The Vales redoubl'd to the Hills, and they Sonnet 18, 9
Redound
On desparate reveng, that shall redound Par Lost 3.85
As I, though thereby worse to me redound: Par Lost 9.128
Shall with a fierce reflux on mee redound, Par Lost 10.739
Redounded
Driv'n back redounded as a flood on those Par Lost 7.57
Redounding
Cast forth redounding smoak and ruddy flame. Par Lost 2.889
Redounds
To transubstantiate; what redounds, transpires Par Lost 5.438
Redress
With Myrtle, find what to redress till Noon: Par Lost 9.219
But finding no redress, ferment and rage, Samson 619
This *wicked* earth redress, Psalm 82, 26
Red-Sea
Hath vext the Red-Sea Coast, whose waves orethrew Par Lost 1.306
ms 'red-sea'
Reduce
Will either quite consume us, and reduce Par Lost 2.96
All usurpation thence expell'd, reduce Par Lost 2.983
Thrones, Princedoms, Powers, Dominions I reduce: Par Lost 3.320
And equal to reduce me to my dust, Par Lost 10.748
From Reason, and to servitude reduce Par Lost 12.89
Reduced
Reduc'd thir shapes immense, and were at large, Par Lost 1.790
One of our number thus reduc't becomes, Par Lost 5.843
Concocted and adusted they reduc'd Par Lost 6.514
Under whose conduct *Michael* soon reduc'd Par Lost 6.777
Many a dark League, reduc't in careful Watch Par Lost 10.438
Reduc't a Province under Roman yoke, Par Reg 3.158
They had anough reveng'd, having reduc't Samson 1468
Redundant
Floted redundant: pleasing was his shape, Par Lost 9.503
Or pitied object, these redundant locks Samson 568
Reed
What drops the Myrrhe, and what the balmie Reed, Par Lost 5.23
Of missive ruin; part incentive reed Par Lost 6.519
A Seraph stood, and in his hand a Reed Par Lost 6.579
The swelling Gourd, up stood the cornie Reed Par Lost 7.321
Charm'd with *Arcadian* Pipe, the Pastoral Reed Par Lost 11.132
Or sound of pastoral reed with oaten stops, Mask 345
Bridgewater ms 'reede'
Re-edify
They first re-edifie, and for a while Par Lost 12.350
Reeds
Not long, for sudden all at once thir Reeds Par Lost 6.582
Where winds with Reeds, and Osiers whisp'ring play Par Reg 2.26
Smooth-sliding *Mincius*, crown'd with vocall reeds, Lycidas 86
Reeking
Soon dri'd, and on the reaking moisture fed. Par Lost 8.256
Reel
Giddy and *restless* let *them reel* Psalm 83, 51
Re-embattled
Stood reimbattell'd fierce, by force or fraud Par Lost 6.794
Re-enter
Re-enter Heav'n; or else in some milde Zone Par Lost 2.397
Refection
They eate, they drink, and in communion sweet Par Lost 5.637
1667 'with refection'
Refer
(Which way soever men refer it) Samson 1015
Refined
But more refin'd, more spiritous, and pure, Par Lost 5.475
Tri'd in sharp tribulation, and refin'd Par Lost 11.63
From the conflagrant mass, purg'd and refin'd, Par Lost 12.548
Refines
Wherein true Love consists not; love refines Par Lost 8.589
Reflected
With light from hence, though but reflected, shines; Par Lost 3.723

Reflected(*cont*)
Arraying with reflected Purple and Gold Par Lost 4.596
Reflected, may with matter sere foment, Par Lost 10.1071
Reflecting
Reflecting blaze on blaze, first met his view: Par Lost 6.18
Reflection
Though distant farr som small reflection gaines Par Lost 3.428
By tincture or reflection they augment Par Lost 7.367
Reflourishes
Revives, reflourishes, then vigorous most Samson 1704
Reflux
Shall with a fierce reflux on mee redound, Par Lost 10.739
Reform
And at our pleasant labour, to reform Par Lost 4.625
that didst reform thy art, the cheif among Sonnet 13, Tr. ms 40.08
Reforming
With second thoughts, reforming what was old! Par Lost 9.101
Refrain
Mess. Ah *Manoa* I refrain, too suddenly Samson 1565
Refrained
Refrein'd his tongue blasphemous; but anon Par Lost 6.360
Refrains
And when God sends a cheerful hour, refrains. Sonnet 21, 14
Refreshed
But come, so well refresh't, now let us play, Par Lost 9.1027
That soon refresh'd him wearied, and repair'd Par Reg 4.591
Sung Victor, and from Heavenly Feast refresht Par Reg 4.637
Thirst, and refresht; nor envy'd them the grape Samson 551
Refreshing
poore ladie thou hast need of some refreshing Mask Tr. ms 20.09
poore ladie thou hast neede of some refreshinge Mask Br. ms 660
Refreshings
Secret refreshings, that repair his strength, Samson 665
Refreshment
Refreshment, whether food, or talk between, Par Lost 9.237
Of meats and drinks, Natures refreshment sweet; Par Reg 2.265
Refreshment after toil, ease after pain, Mask 687
line not in Bridgewater ms
Reft
Ah! Who hath reft (quoth he) my dearest pledge? Lycidas 107
Refuge
A refuge from those wounds: or when we lay Par Lost 2.168
Find place or refuge; and the more I see Par Lost 9.119
Of refuge, and concludes thee miserable Par Lost 10.839
Through all the Plain, and refuge none was found. Par Lost 11.673
Refulgent
Of Golden Panoplie, refulgent Host, Par Lost 6.527
Refusal
Cause thy refusal, said the subtle Fiend, Par Reg 2.323
On my refusal to distress me more, Samson 1330
Refuse
These Royalties, and not refuse to Reign, Par Lost 2.451
If I refuse not, but convert, as you, Par Lost 5.492
By force, who reason for thir Law refuse, Par Lost 6.41
With Warr and hostile snare such as refuse Par Lost 12.31
To Idols, those young *Daniel* could refuse; Par Reg 2.329
Refused
(Certain to be refus'd) what erst they feard; Par Lost 2.470
And so refus'd might in opinion stand Par Lost 2.471
Mysterious of connubial Love refus'd: Par Lost 4.743
I thus contest; then should have been refusd Par Lost 10.756
Refus'd on me his Baptism to confer, Par Reg 1.278
And storm'st refus'd, thinking to terrifie Par Reg 4.496
Refusing
Refusing to accept as great a share Par Lost 2.452
Refute
How wilt thou reason with them, how refute Par Reg 4.233
Refuted
These shifts refuted, answer thy appellant Samson 1220
Refutes
But self-destruction therefore saught, refutes Par Lost 10.1016
Regain
Restore us, and regain the blissful Seat, Par Lost 1.5
ms 'regaine'
We warr, if warr be best, or to regain Par Lost 2.230
Least total darkness should by Night regaine Par Lost 4.665
Of new acceptance, hopeful to regaine Par Lost 10.972
So many Ages, and shall yet regain Par Reg 2.441
Antiochus: and think'st thou to regain Par Reg 3.163
By him thou shalt regain, without him not, Par Reg 3.371
After offence returning, to regain Samson 1004
How to regain my sever'd company Mask 274
Bridgewater ms 'regayne'
Trinity ms 'regaine'
1637 'regaine'
Regained
Regaind in Heav'n, or what more lost in Hell? Par Lost 1.270
Thereby regaind, but sat devising Death Par Lost 4.197
Temptation, hast regain'd lost Paradise, Par Reg 4.608
His half regain'd *Eurydice*. Allegro 150
Regal
Consent or custome, and his Regal State Par Lost 1.640
ms 'regal'
With Trumpets regal sound the great result: Par Lost 2.515
Then thou thy regal Scepter shalt lay by, Par Lost 3.339
For regal Scepter then no more shall need, Par Lost 3.340
And with them comes a third of Regal port, Par Lost 4.869
With regal Ornament; the middle pair Par Lost 5.280

Regal(*cont*)
Illustrates, when they see all Regal Power — Par Lost 5.739
With Regal Scepter, every Soule in Heav'n — Par Lost 5.816
Was plac't in regal lustre. Down a while — Par Lost 10.447
Irrevocable, that his Regal Throne — Par Lost 12.323
In Courts and Regal Chambers how thou lurk'st, — Par Reg 2.183
A Table richly spred, in regal mode, — Par Reg 2.340
To him who wears the Regal Diadem, — Par Reg 2.461
Thee, of thy self so apt, in regal Arts, — Par Reg 3.248
And regal Mysteries; that thou may'st know — Par Reg 3.249
Indu'd with Regal Vertues as thou art, — Par Reg 4.98
He sov'ran Priest stooping his regall head — Passion 15
1673 'regal'
Regard
A generation, whom his choice regard — Par Lost 1.653
Compose our present evils, with regard — Par Lost 2.281
Pass'd frequent, and his eye with choice regard — Par Lost 3.534
And the regard of Heav'n on all his waies; — Par Lost 4.620
To whom with stern regard thus *Gabriel* spake. — Par Lost 4.877
If none regard; Heav'n wakes with all his eyes, — Par Lost 5.44
But her with stern regard he thus repell'd. — Par Lost 10.866
To whom thus *Michael* with regard benigne. — Par Lost 11.334
With some regard to what is just and right — Par Lost 12.16
To know thir God, or message to regard, — Par Lost 12.174
The Scepter, and regard not *Davids* Sons, — Par Lost 12.357
Of thee these forty days none hath regard, — Par Reg 2.315
From that placid aspect and meek regard, — Par Reg 3.217
Should I of these the liberty regard, — Par Reg 3.427
Changest thy countenance, and thy hand with no regard — Samson 684
Off. Regard thy self, this will offend them highly. — Samson 1333
Of small regard to see to, yet well skill'd — Mask 620
& good heaven cast his best regard upon us — Mask Tr. ms 21.32
Regard the weak and fatherless — Psalm 82, 9
Dost never more regard, — Psalm 88, 22
Regarded
Regarded, such delight till then, as seemd, — Par Lost 9.787
Regardless
Regardless of the Bliss wherein hee sat — Par Lost 3.408
Regardless whether good or evil fame. — Par Lost 12.47
Fortune and Fate, as one regardless quite — Par Reg 4.317
Regardless of his glories diminution; — Samson 303
Regards
Thee he regards not, owns not, hath cut off — Samson 1157
Regencies
Regions they pass'd, the mightie Regencies — Par Lost 5.748
Regenerate
Regenerate grow instead, that sighs now breath'd — Par Lost 11.5
1667 'Regenerat'
Regent
Uriel, though Regent of the Sun, and held — Par Lost 3.690
1667 'regent' in some copies
Or several one by one, the Regent Powers, — Par Lost 5.697
Under him Regent, tells, as he was taught, — Par Lost 5.698
Regent of Day, and all th' Horizon round — Par Lost 7.371
Since *Uriel* Regent of the Sun descri'd — Par Lost 9.60
Regents
Regents and Potentates, and Kings, yea gods — Par Reg 1.117
Regiment
From every Band and squared Regiment — Par Lost 1.758
ms 'regiment'
Region
Is this the Region, this the Soil, the Clime, — Par Lost 1.242
ms 'region'
Or unknown Region, what remains him less — Par Lost 2.443
They pass'd, and many a Region dolorous, — Par Lost 2.619
To your behoof, if I that Region lost, — Par Lost 2.982
Dislodging from a Region scarce of prey — Par Lost 3.433
Down right into the Worlds first Region throws — Par Lost 3.562
From skirt to skirt a fierie Region, stretcht — Par Lost 6.80
Part loosly wing the Region, part more wise — Par Lost 7.425
Thir inward State of Mind, calm Region once — Par Lost 9.1125
Up to the middle Region of thick Air, — Par Reg 2.117
Many are in each Region passing fair — Par Reg 2.155
Of *Cynthia*'s seat, the Airy region thrilling, — Nativity 103
Regions
Regions of sorrow, doleful shades, where peace — Par Lost 1.65
Th' eternal Regions: lowly reverent — Par Lost 3.349
What wonder then if fields and regions here — Par Lost 3.606
Imagind Lands and Regions in the Moon: — Par Lost 5.263
Regions they pass'd, the mightie Regencies — Par Lost 5.748
In thir triple Degrees, Regions to which — Par Lost 5.750
Of all thir Regions: how much more of Power — Par Lost 6.223
Filld all the Regions: from thir blissful Bowrs — Par Lost 11.77
With aw the Regions round, and with them came — Par Reg 1.22
Copartner in these Regions of the World, — Par Reg 1.392
Or Embassies from Regions far remote — Par Reg 4.67
In Regions milde of calm and serene Ayr, — Mask 4
Bridgewater ms 'regions'
Trinity ms 'regions'
What Worlds, or what vast Regions hold — Penseroso 90
And mistie Regions of wide air next under, — Vacation 41
Registered
Such follow him, as shall be registerd — Par Lost 12.335
Regorged
And fat regorg'd of Bulls and Goats, — Samson 1671
Regret
Not thy contempt, but anguish and regret — Par Lost 10.1018
Regular
Eccentric, intervolv'd, yet regular — Par Lost 5.623
Regulus
Quintius, Fabricius, Curius, Regulus? — Par Reg 2.446
Reign
That durst dislike his reign, and me preferring, — Par Lost 1.102
ms 'raign'
Here we may reign secure, and in my choyce — Par Lost 1.261
To reign is worth ambition though in Hell: — Par Lost 1.262
Better to reign in Hell, then serve in Heav'n. — Par Lost 1.263
Frighted the Reign of *Chaos* and old Night. — Par Lost 1.543
ms 'reign'
In heighth or depth, still first and last will Reign — Par Lost 2.324
These Royalties, and not refuse to Reign, — Par Lost 2.451
Where I reign King, and to enrage thee more, — Par Lost 2.698
The Gods who live at ease, where I shall Reign — Par Lost 2.868
The Consort of his Reign; and by them stood — Par Lost 2.963
Here shalt thou sit incarnate, here shalt Reign — Par Lost 3.315
1667 'Reigne'
I give thee, reign for ever, and assume — Par Lost 3.318
By thee, and more then half perhaps will reigne; — Par Lost 4.112
To dispossess him, and thy self to reign? — Par Lost 4.961
Under his great Vice-gerent Reign abide — Par Lost 5.609
And equal over equals to let Reigne, — Par Lost 5.820
That equal over equals Monarch Reigne: — Par Lost 5.832
Essential Powers, nor by his Reign obscur'd, — Par Lost 5.841
Reign thou in Hell thy Kingdom, let mee serve — Par Lost 6.183
If not to reign: mean while thy utmost force, — Par Lost 6.293
Worthiest to Reign: he celebrated rode — Par Lost 6.888
Revolvd on Heav'ns great Axle, and her Reign — Par Lost 7.381
Our foile in Heav'n; here thou shalt Monarch reign, — Par Lost 10.375
There dwell and Reign in bliss, thence on the Earth — Par Lost 10.399
Hopeful and cheerful, in thy blood will reigne — Par Lost 11.543
Within himself unworthie Powers to reign — Par Lost 12.91
Will reign among them, as of thee begot; — Par Lost 12.286
The last, for of his Reign shall be no end. — Par Lost 12.330
The Throne hereditarie, and bound his Reign — Par Lost 12.370
To end his Raign on Earth so long enjoy'd: — Par Reg 1.125
Each of his reign allotted, rightlier call'd, — Par Reg 2.123
That seat, and reign in *Israel* without end. — Par Reg 2.442
The Prophets old, who sung thy endless raign, — Par Reg 3.178
The happier raign the sooner it begins, — Par Reg 3.179
Raign then; what canst thou better do the while? — Par Reg 3.180
If of my raign Prophetic Writ hath told, — Par Reg 3.184
Can suffer, best can do; best reign, who first — Par Reg 3.195
Raign or raign not; though to that gentle brow — Par Reg 3.215
Willingly I could flye, and hope thy raign, — Par Reg 3.216
Shalt raign, and *Rome* or *Caesar* not need fear. — Par Reg 3.385
I must deliver, if I mean to raign — Par Reg 3.404
Who knowing I shall raign past thy preventing, — Par Reg 4.492
His daughter she (in *Saturns* raign, — Penseroso 25
His raign of peace upon the earth began: — Nativity 63
And that her raign had here its last fulfilling; — Nativity 106
1673 'reign'
O're all his Brethren he shall Reign as King, — Vacation 75
On thy third Reigne the Earth look now, and tell — Prose 12, 3
Reigned
So *Jove* usurping reign'd: these first in *Creet* — Par Lost 1.514
Alcinous reign'd, fruit of all kindes, in coate, — Par Lost 5.341
Love unlibidinous reign'd, nor jealousie — Par Lost 5.449
Reignd where these Heav'ns now rowl, where Earth now rests — Par Lost 5.578
Where luxurie late reign'd, Sea-monsters whelp'd — Par Lost 11.751
Reignest
Lord *God* of Hoasts *that raign'st on high*, — Psalm 84, 45
Reigning
Sole reigning holds the Tyranny of Heav'n. — Par Lost 1.124
ms 'raigning'
So reigning can be no sincere delight. — Par Reg 2.480
Reigns
In Courts and Palaces he also Reigns — Par Lost 1.497
ms 'reigns'
By mee, have lost our hopes. But he who reigns — Par Lost 1.637
ms 'reignes'
The Prison of his Tyranny who Reigns — Par Lost 2.59
To him who Reigns, and so much to him due — Par Lost 2.454
Save he who reigns above, none can resist. — Par Lost 2.814
By which he Reigns: next him high Arbiter — Par Lost 2.909
Reigns here and revels; not in the bought smile — Par Lost 4.765
Tunes sweetest his love-labor'd song; now reignes — Par Lost 5.41
New Laws from him who reigns, new minds may raise — Par Lost 5.680
Messiah, who by right of merit Reigns. — Par Lost 6.43
His will who reigns above, to aggravate — Par Lost 10.549
Down from a Hill the Beast that reigns in Woods, — Par Lost 11.187
Yet he who reigns within himself, and rules — Par Reg 2.466
That other o're the body only reigns, — Par Reg 2.478
And disinherit *Chaos*, that raigns here — Mask 334
Bridgewater ms 'raignes'
Trinity ms 'raignes'
Where no crude surfet raigns. *Eld*. *Bro*. List, list, I hear — Mask 480
Trinity ms 'reigns'
Bridgewater ms 'raignes'
But night sits monarch yet in the mid sky. — Mask 957
Trinity ms 'sitts' ←'raignes'
Rein
Rove without rein, till in the amorous Net — Par Lost 11.586
Reined
But like a proud Steed reind, went hautie on, — Par Lost 4.858

Reinforcement
What reinforcement we may gain from Hope, Par Lost 1.190
Reins
In Entrailes, Heart or Head, Liver or Reines; Par Lost 6.346
And to disorder'd rage let loose the reines, Par Lost 6.696
Was bid turn Reines from th' Equinoctial Rode Par Lost 10.672
Then give the rains to wandring thought, Samson 302
In heart, head, brest, and reins; Samson 609
Yet e're I give the rains to grief, say first, Samson 1578
Hearts and reins. On God is cast Psalm 7, 39
Reinspire
On smoother, till *Favonius* re-inspire Sonnet 20, 6
Reinstall
That which alone can truly reinstall thee Par Reg 3.372
A Saviour art come down to re-install. Par Reg 4.615
Took up, and in fit place did reinstall? Fair Inf 46
Reiterated
That with reiterated crimes he might Par Lost 1.214
Reject
With more desire to know, and to reject Par Lost 4.523
That Golden Scepter which thou didst reject Par Lost 5.886
What if with like aversion I reject Par Reg 2.457
Did I not tell thee, if thou didst reject Par Reg 4.467
Reject not then what offerd means, who knows Samson 516
With goodness principl'd not to reject Samson 760
I would not taste thy treasonous offer; none Mask 702
Trinity ms 'would not taste' ←'should reject' ←'hate it from thy hands'
Rejected
With spattering noise rejected: oft they assayd, Par Lost 10.567
Rejected my forewarning, and disdain'd Par Lost 10.876
To wish thou never hadst rejected thus Par Reg 4.376
Rejectest
Thou valu'st, because offer'd, and reject'st: Par Reg 4.156
Rejoice
May reap his conquest, and may least rejoyce Par Lost 2.339
Cannot be human consort; they rejoyce Par Lost 8.392
I in thy persevering shall rejoyce, Par Lost 8.639
With these successes, and with them rejoyce, Par Lost 10.396
Of wicked Sons destroyd, then I rejoyce Par Lost 11.875
By mee done and occasiond, or rejoyce Par Lost 12.475
Cho. That hope would much rejoyce us to partake Samson 1455
That so thy people may rejoyce Psalm 85, 23
I call; O make rejoyce Psalm 86, 10
Rejoiced
Destin'd to that good hour: no less rejoyc'd Par Lost 2.848
Or singular and rash, whereat rejoic'd Par Lost 5.851
Disburd'nd Heav'n rejoic'd, and soon repaird Par Lost 6.878
But still rejoyc't, how is it now become Par Lost 10.120
Greatly rejoyc'd, and thus his joy broke forth. Par Lost 11.869
By words at times cast forth inly rejoyc'd, Par Reg 1.228
Thus we rejoyc'd, but soon our joy is turn'd Par Reg 2.37
Rejoicing
Ended rejoycing in thir matchless Chief: Par Lost 2.487
Yet not rejoycing in his speed, though bold, Par Lost 4.13
Circle his Throne rejoycing, yee in Heav'n, Par Lost 5.163
With copious hand, rejoycing in thir joy. Par Lost 5.641
Great triumph and rejoycing was in Heav'n Par Lost 7.180
Presence Divine. Rejoycing, but with aw Par Lost 8.314
Relapse
Which would but lead me to a worse relapse Par Lost 4.100
Alas, from what high hope to what relapse Par Reg 2.30
Relate
On *Lemnos* th' *Aegaean* Ile: thus they relate, Par Lost 1.746
Sad task and hard, for how shall I relate Par Lost 5.564
Of Angels, can relate, or to what things Par Lost 6.298
I might relate of thousands, and thir names Par Lost 6.373
Deign to descend now lower, and relate Par Lost 7.84
Relate thee; greater now in thy return Par Lost 7.604
This friendly condescention to relate Par Lost 8.9
Ere my remembrance: now hear mee relate Par Lost 8.204
Inviting thee to hear while I relate, Par Lost 8.208
Presence Divine, and to my Sons relate; Par Lost 11.319
Henceforth what is to com I will relate, Par Lost 12.11
Man. Relate by whom. *Mess*. By *Samson*. *Man*. That still lessens Samson 1563
That all both judge you to relate them true, Sonnet 10, 13
Related
And brief related whom they brought, where found, Par Lost 4.875
Related, and thus *Adam* answerd sad. Par Lost 5.94
So near related, or the same of kind, Samson 786
Relater
Her Husband the Relater she preferr'd Par Lost 8.52
Relating
Adam relating, she sole Auditress; Par Lost 8.51
Thee I have heard relating what was don Par Lost 8.203
Relation
The full relation, which must needs be strange, Par Lost 5.556
But thy relation now; for I attend, Par Lost 8.247
Have we not seen, or by relation heard, Par Reg 2.182
And if I was, I am; relation stands; Par Reg 4.519
Relation more particular and distinct. Samson 1595
As to make this relation? *Spir*. Care and utmost shifts Mask 617
1673 'Relation'
Bridgewater ms 'relacion'
Relations
Relations dear, and all the Charities Par Lost 4.756
Relax
Nor serv'd it to relax thir serried files. Par Lost 6.599
Relaxed
Ran through his veins, and all his joynts relax'd; Par Lost 9.891
Release
Who boast'st release from Hell, and leave to come Par Reg 1.409
And force him to restore his purchase back, Mask 607
Trinity ms 'restore' ←'release'
That he our deadly forfeit should release, Nativity 6
Released
From penaltie, because from death releast Par Lost 11.197
Relent
We overpower? Suppose he should relent Par Lost 2.237
O then at last relent: is there no place Par Lost 4.79
Or Wonders move th' obdurate to relent? Par Lost 6.790
Undoubtedly he will relent and turn Par Lost 10.1093
God will relent, and quit thee all his debt; Samson 509
Relented
Commiseration; soon his heart relented Par Lost 10.940
Relentless
To my relentless thoughts; and him destroyd, Par Lost 9.130
Relents
That he relents, not to blot out mankind, Par Lost 11.891
Relics
And flutterd into Raggs, then Reliques, Beads, Par Lost 3.491
When to enshrine his reliques in the Sun's Par Lost 5.273
Or that his hallow'd reliques should be hid Shakespear 3
1640 'Relikes'
1632 'Reliques'
1663-4 'Reliques'
Relied
That argu'd fear; each on himself reli'd, Par Lost 6.238
Relief
Tending to some relief of our extremes, Par Lost 10.976
Out cast *Nebaioth*, yet found he relief Par Reg 2.309
For my relief; yet hadst no reason why, Sonnet 1, 12
Relies
The weight of all and our last hope relies. Par Lost 2.416
Relieve
So shalt thou save thy self and us relieve Par Reg 1.344
Relieves
Relieves me from my task of servile toyl, Samson 5
This only hope relieves me, that the strife Samson 460
Man. With cause this hope relieves thee, and these words Samson 472
Religion
Of Justice, of Religion, Truth and Peace, Par Lost 11.667
Religion satisfi'd; Truth shall retire Par Lost 12.535
To Honour and Religion! servil mind Samson 412
And of Religion, press'd how just it was, Samson 854
In feign'd Religion, smooth hypocrisie. Samson 872
With zeal, if aught Religion seem concern'd: Samson 1420
Therfore on thy firme hand religion leanes Sonnet 17, 13
1662, 1694 'Religion'
Religions
With gay Religions full of Pomp and Gold, Par Lost 1.372
ms 'religions'
Religious
Religious titl'd them the Sons of God, Par Lost 11.622
To civil Justice, part religious Rites Par Lost 12.231
Our Law forbids at thir Religious Rites Samson 1320
Casting a dimm religious light. Penseroso 160
Relish
True relish, tasting; if such pleasure be Par Lost 9.1024
Reluctance
Untam'd reluctance, and revenge though slow, Par Lost 2.337
Reluctance against God and his just yoke Par Lost 10.1045
Reluctant
And sweet reluctant amorous delay. Par Lost 4.311
In duskie wreathes, reluctant flames, the signe Par Lost 6.58
Reluctant, but in vaine, a greater power Par Lost 10.515
Rely
Go in thy native innocence, relie Par Lost 9.373
Who *only* on thee doth relie, Psalm 84, 47
Remain
Banded against his Throne, but to remaine Par Lost 2.320
I formd them free, and free they must remain, Par Lost 3.124
Of anger shall remain, but peace assur'd, Par Lost 3.263
If these magnific Titles yet remain Par Lost 5.773
Should yet remain, where faith and realtie Par Lost 6.115
Remain not; wherfore should not strength and might Par Lost 6.116
Childless thou art, Childless remaine: Par Lost 10.989
Though hunger still remain: so it remain Par Reg 2.255
But *they, his People, should remain*, Psalm 81, 63
Remained
And fields were fought in Heav'n; wherein remaind Par Lost 2.768
Frequent; and of the Sixt day yet remain'd; Par Lost 7.504
From his own evil, and for the time remaind Par Lost 9.464
Best guide; not following thee, I had remaind Par Lost 9.808
Remaind still happie, not as now, despoild Par Lost 9.1138
Worthy t' have not remain'd so long unsung. Par Reg 1.17
Mean while the new-baptiz'd, who yet remain'd Par Reg 2.1
After forty days fasting had remain'd, Par Reg 2.243
Only the importune Tempter still remain'd, Par Reg 2.404
Remainest
Remainest God alone. Psalm 86, 36
Remaining
Miraculous yet remaining in those locks? Samson 587
My Countreymen, whom here I knew remaining, Samson 1549
All other parts remaining as they were, Mask 72
Bridgewater ms 'remayninge'

Remains
Can perish: for the mind and spirit remains — Par Lost 1.139
ms 'remaines'
New warr, provok't; our better part remains — Par Lost 1.645
ms 'remaines'
Or unknown Region, what remains him less — Par Lost 2.443
Remains thee, aided by this host of friends, — Par Lost 6.38
Half yet remaines unsung, but narrower bound — Par Lost 7.21
1669 'remains'
Creator; something yet of doubt remaines, — Par Lost 8.13
Remaines, sufficient of it self to raise — Par Lost 9.43
Whose failing, while her Faith to me remaines, — Par Lost 10.129
Of my performance: What remains, ye Gods, — Par Lost 10.502
1667 'remaines'
And while the dread of judgement past remains — Par Lost 12.14
Uncertain and unsettl'd still remains, — Par Reg 4.326
That rigid score. A worse thing yet remains, — Samson 433
This one prayer yet remains, might I be heard, — Samson 649
Misguided; only what remains past cure — Samson 912
That in a little time while breath remains thee, — Samson 1126
We cannot free the Lady that sits here — Mask 818
Trinity ms 'sits' ←'remaines'
Onely remains this superscription. — Another 34
1640, 1657 'remaines'
line not in 1658 text
And Worsters laureat wreath; yet much remaines — Sonnet 16, 9
1694 'remains'

Remark
Chor. His manacles remark him, there he sits. — Samson 1309

Remarkable
This day will be remarkable in my life — Samson 1388

Remarkably
Remarkably so late of thy so true, — Par Lost 9.982
Recalling what remarkably had pass'd — Par Reg 2.106

Remediless
Submitting to what seemd remediless, — Par Lost 9.919
Hopeless are all my evils, all remediless; — Samson 648
For we by rightfull doom remedíles — Circum 17
Trinity ms 'remedilesse'

Remedy
The remedie; perhaps more valid Armes, — Par Lost 6.438
And what may else be remedie or cure — Par Lost 10.1079
His final remedie, and after Life — Par Lost 11.62

Remember
That day I oft remember, when from sleep — Par Lost 4.449
Yet fell; remember, and fear to transgress. — Par Lost 6.912
Remember what I warne thee, shun to taste, — Par Lost 8.327
Laid on our Necks. Remember with what mild — Par Lost 10.1046
This our old Conquest, then remember Hell — Par Reg 1.46
Remember that *Pellean* Conquerour, — Par Reg 2.196
Worthy of Memorial) canst thou not remember — Par Reg 2.445
As thou to thy reproach mayst well remember, — Par Reg 3.66
And thither will return thee, yet remember — Par Reg 4.374
Which you remember not. 2. *Bro*. What hidden strength, — Mask 416

Remembered
For still they knew, and ought to have still remember'd — Par Lost 10.12
Heads without name no more rememberd, — Samson 677

Rememberest
Thy eye-lids? and remembrest what Decree — Par Lost 5.674
When this creation was? rememberst thou — Par Lost 5.857
Resounded, (thou remember'st, for thou heardst) — Par Lost 7.561
O what is man that thou remembrest yet, — Psalm 8, 12
Whom thou rememberest no more, — Psalm 88, 21

Remembering
Remembring mercie, and his Cov'nant sworn — Par Lost 12.346
Remembring *Abraham* by some wond'rous call — Par Reg 3.434

Remembrance
Had in remembrance alwayes with delight; — Par Lost 3.704
That bring to my remembrance from what state — Par Lost 4.38
Ere my remembrance: now hear mee relate — Par Lost 8.204
Cho. Thy words to my remembrance bring — Samson 277
Sam. Not for thy life, lest fierce remembrance wake — Samson 952
For in death no remembrance is of thee; — Psalm 6, 9

Remiss
Which all subdues, and makes remiss the hands — Par Lost 6.458
The one intense, the other still remiss — Par Lost 8.387
Thou never wast remiss, I bear thee witness: — Samson 239

Remission
With God or Man will gain thee no remission. — Samson 835

Remit
Our Supream Foe in time may much remit — Par Lost 2.210
So willingly doth God remit his Ire, — Par Lost 11.885
Nor only dost degrade them, or remit — Samson 687
The rest was magnanimity to remit, — Samson 1470

Remorse
Signs of remorse and passion to behold — Par Lost 1.605
Farwel Remorse: all Good to me is lost; — Par Lost 4.109
Kiss'd as the gracious signs of sweet remorse — Par Lost 5.134
Of warring Spirits; how without remorse — Par Lost 5.566
Felt less remorse: they forthwith to the place — Par Lost 10.1098
Without remorse drive out the sinful Pair, — Par Lost 11.105
And reconcilement move with feign'd remorse, — Samson 752
And secret sting of amorous remorse. — Samson 1007

Remorseless
Where were ye Nymphs when the remorseless deep — Lycidas 50
1638 'remorselesse'
Trinity ms 'remorselesse'
And with remorsles cruelty, — Winchester 29

Remote
Of Thunder heard remote. Towards him they bend — Par Lost 2.477
Th' Arch-chimic Sun so farr from us remote — Par Lost 3.609
A whole days journy high, but wide remote — Par Lost 4.284
Of erring, from the path of truth remote: — Par Lost 6.173
So farr remote, with diminution seen. — Par Lost 7.369
That not to know at large of things remote — Par Lost 8.191
High and remote to see from thence distinct — Par Lost 9.812
Of ravenous Fowl, though many a League remote, — Par Lost 10.274
Peaceable Nations, neighbouring, or remote, — Par Reg 3.76
Or Embassies from Regions far remote — Par Reg 4.67
Conceiving, or remote from Heaven, enshrin'd — Par Reg 4.598

Remotest
And rumors loud, that daunt remotest kings, — Sonnet 15, 4

Remove
Into their temper; which must needs remove — Par Lost 2.277
By quick contraction or remove; but now — Par Lost 6.597
God to remove his wayes from human sense, — Par Lost 8.119
For ever, to remove him I decree, — Par Lost 11.96
Permits not; to remove thee I am come, — Par Lost 11.260
To guide them in thir journey, and remove — Par Lost 12.204
Law can discover sin, but not remove, — Par Lost 12.290
In signal of remove, waves fiercely round; — Par Lost 12.593
Remove their swelling Epithetes thick laid — Par Reg 4.343
And all temptation can remove, — Samson 1051

Removed
As far remov'd from God and light of Heav'n — Par Lost 1.73
His anger, and perhaps thus farr remov'd — Par Lost 2.211
In strictest bondage, though thus far remov'd, — Par Lost 2.321
Perhaps our vacant room, though more remov'd, — Par Lost 2.835
To Heav'n remov'd where first it grew, there grows, — Par Lost 3.356
Of *Chaos* farr remov'd, least fierce extreames — Par Lost 7.272
Remov'd farr off; then pittying how they stood — Par Lost 10.211
The sentence from thy head remov'd may light — Par Lost 10.934
Prevenient Grace descending had remov'd — Par Lost 11.3
Michael from *Adams* eyes the Filme remov'd — Par Lost 11.412
Contending, and remov'd his Tents farr off; — Par Lost 11.727
Corrupting each thir way; yet those remoov'd, — Par Lost 11.889
Shar'd among petty Kings too far remov'd; — Par Reg 4.87
with distant worlds, & strange removed clim — Mask Tr. ms 10.17
Som still removed place will fit, — Penseroso 78
Thine anger all thou hadst remov'd, — Psalm 85, 9
Lover and friend thou hast remov'd — Psalm 88, 69

Removes
Your feare it self of Death removes the feare. — Par Lost 9.702

Rend
Rend up both Rocks and Hills, and ride the Air — Par Lost 2.540
And *Thrascias* rend the Woods and Seas upturn; — Par Lost 10.700
Haile mixt with fire must rend th' *Egyptian* Skie — Par Lost 12.182

Render
With Armed watch, that render all access — Par Lost 2.130
The present misery, and render Hell — Par Lost 2.459
Doubl'd, would render them yet more despis'd, — Par Lost 6.602
Equal have I to render thee, Divine — Par Lost 8.6
And render me more equal, and perhaps, — Par Lost 9.823
Desirous to resigne, and render back — Par Lost 10.749
And not returning that would likeliest render — Par Reg 3.130
To render thee the *Parthian* at dispose; — Par Reg 3.369
These rules will render thee a King compleat — Par Reg 4.283
Hear these dishonours, and not render death? — Samson 1232
And render him with patience what he lent; — Fair Inf 75

Rendered
Or to him have render'd less, — Psalm 7, 11

Rendering
Of rendring up, and patiently attend — Par Lost 11.551

Renders
And renders us in things that most concerne — Par Lost 8.196
Renders them useless, while — Samson 1282

Renew
The birds thir notes renew, and bleating herds — Par Lost 2.494
Freely voutsaft; once more I will renew — Par Lost 3.175
Though all to shivers dash't, the assault renew, — Par Reg 4.19
O may we soon again renew that Song, — Musick 25
And life in us renew. — Psalm 85, 28

Renewed
With fresh alacritie and force renew'd — Par Lost 2.1012
His dearest mediation thus renewd. — Par Lost 3.226
Obsequious, Heav'n his wonted face renewd, — Par Lost 6.783
Return'd and gracious purpose thus renew'd. — Par Lost 8.337
Thus her reply with accent sweet renewd. — Par Lost 9.321
Speech intermitted thus to *Eve* renewd. — Par Lost 9.1133
And the dire hiss renew'd, and the dire form — Par Lost 10.543
Then Heav'n and Earth renewd shall be made pure — Par Lost 10.638
Resignes him up with Heav'n and Earth renewd. — Par Lost 11.66
My Cov'nant in the womans seed renewd; — Par Lost 11.116
Which thus to *Eve* his welcome words renewd. — Par Lost 11.140
And scarce recovering words his plaint renew'd. — Par Lost 11.499
His invitation earnestly renew'd. — Par Reg 2.367
With soothing words renew'd, him thus accosts. — Par Reg 3.6
And to our Saviour thus his words renew'd. — Par Reg 3.346
His further ire, with praiers and vows renew'd. — Samson 520
Favour renew'd, and add a greater sin — Samson 1357

Renewing
Still ending, still renewing, through mid Heav'n; — Par Lost 3.729
Renewing fresh assaults, amidst his pride — Par Reg 4.570

Renews
They vote: whereat his speech he thus renews. — Par Lost 2.389
With mention of that name renews th' assault. — Samson 331

Renounce
Must we renounce, and changing stile be call'd Par Lost 2.312
Imputed shall absolve them who renounce Par Lost 3.291
Disjoyne us, and I then too late renounce Par Lost 9.884
Thou wilt renounce thy seeking, and much rather Samson 828
Renounced
And with stiff Vowes renounc'd his Liturgie Forcers 2
Trinity ms 'renouncd'
Renovation
Wak't in the renovation of the just, Par Lost 11.65
Renown
A crew who under Names of old Renown, Par Lost 1.477
ms 'renown'
So were I equal'd with them in renown, Par Lost 3.34
Nor of Renown less eager, yet by doome Par Lost 6.378
Honour, Dominion, Glorie, and renowne, Par Lost 6.422
Such were these Giants, men of high renown; Par Lost 11.688
Thus Fame shall be atchiev'd, renown on Earth, Par Lost 11.698
Like him in faith, in wisdom, and renown; Par Lost 12.154
Great in Renown, and call'd the Son of God; Par Reg 1.136
This is true glory and renown, when God Par Reg 3.60
And long Renown thou justly may'st prefer Par Reg 4.84
Kings of prowess and renown. Psalm 136, 62
Renowned
The rest were long to tell, though far renown'd, Par Lost 1.507
With many a vain exploit, though then renownd: Par Lost 3.465
First-seen, or some renown'd Metropolis Par Lost 3.549
1667 'renownd'
Or of reviv'd *Adonis*, or renownd Par Lost 9.440
As when of old som Orator renound Par Lost 9.670
The Figtree, not that kind for Fruit renown'd, Par Lost 9.1101
The second, both for pietie renownd Par Lost 12.321
So far renown'd, and with the spoils enricht Par Reg 4.46
That Heroic, that Renown'd, Samson 125
That invincible *Samson*, far renown'd, Samson 341
Not less renown'd then in Mount *Ephraim*, Samson 988
Men call me *Harapha*, of stock renown'd Samson 1079
Of that renowned flood, so often sung, Arcades 29
Trinity ms 'renouned'
No less renownd then warr, new foes arise Sonnet 16, 11
1694 'than those of War'
Of Meriba *renown'd*. Psalm 81, 32
Repaid
From dust: spite then with spite is best repaid. Par Lost 9.178
As wantonly repaid; in Lust they burne: Par Lost 9.1015
Or as the Snake with youthful Coate repaid; Par Lost 10.218
Repaid? But gratitude in thee is lost Par Reg 4.188
Repair
Our Enemy, our own loss how repair, Par Lost 1.188
To deepest Hell, and to repair that loss Par Lost 3.678
My damage fondly deem'd, I can repaire Par Lost 7.152
Dazl'd and spent, sunk down, and sought repair Par Lost 8.457
And to repaire his numbers thus impair'd, Par Lost 9.144
Thence to the famous Orators repair, Par Reg 4.267
Secret refreshings, that repair his strength, Samson 665
Repaired
Showrd Roses, which the Morn repair'd. Sleep on Par Lost 4.773
Disburd'nd Heav'n rejoic'd, and soon repaird Par Lost 6.878
That soon refresh'd him wearied, and repair'd Par Reg 4.591
Repairing
Repairing, in thir gold'n Urns draw Light, Par Lost 7.365
Repairing where he judg'd us, prostrate fall Par Lost 10.1087
Repairing where he judg'd them prostrate fell Par Lost 10.1099
Repairs
And yet anon repairs his drooping head, Lycidas 169
Repast
My Bowels, thir repast; then bursting forth Par Lost 2.800
To respit his day-labour with repast, Par Lost 5.232
Forthwith from dance to sweet repast they turn Par Lost 5.630
Of sweet repast; they satiate, and soon fill, Par Lost 8.214
Rural repast, permitting him the while Par Lost 9.4
Noontide repast, or Afternoons repose. Par Lost 9.403
Foundst either sweet repast, or sound repose; Par Lost 9.407
Or God support Nature without repast Par Reg 2.250
That have been tir'd all day without repast, Mask 688
What neat repast shall feast us, light and choice, Sonnet 20, 9
Repealed
With Blessedness. Whence *Adam* soon repeal'd Par Lost 7.59
Repeat
That might determine, and not need repeate, Par Lost 6.318
Creation could repeate, yet would be loath Par Lost 9.946
Repeated
Repeated, and indecent overthrow Par Lost 6.601
Needless to thee repeated; nor unknown Par Lost 7.494
1667 'repeaed'
Repeated, while the sedentarie Earth, Par Lost 8.32
Repeated, shee to him as oft engag'd Par Lost 9.400
Of sight, reserv'd alive to be repeated Samson 645
Went to the ground: And the repeated air Sonnet 8, 12
Repel
And all temptation to transgress repel. Par Lost 8.643
Can either not receave, or can repell. Par Lost 9.284
Repelled
Thou hast repeld, while impiously they thought Par Lost 7.611
But her with stern regard he thus repell'd. Par Lost 10.866
And mad despight to be so oft repell'd. Par Reg 4.446
The helme of Rome, when gownes not armes repelld Sonnet 17, 3
1662, 1694 'repell'd'

Repent
Can else inflict, do I repent or change, Par Lost 1.96
To pray, repent, and bring obedience due. Par Lost 3.190
But say I could repent and could obtaine Par Lost 4.93
Giv'n thee of Grace, wherein thou may'st repent, Par Lost 11.255
Whether I should repent me now of sin Par Lost 12.474
Repent the sin, but if the punishment Samson 504
Repentance
To Prayer, repentance, and obedience due, Par Lost 3.191
Left for Repentance, none for Pardon left? Par Lost 4.80
Conversion and Repentance, as to Souls Par Lost 11.724
Repentance, and Heavens Kingdom nigh at hand Par Reg 1.20
That malice not repentance brought thee hither, Samson 821
Repentant
Thus they in lowliest plight repentant stood Par Lost 11.1
May bring them back repentant and sincere, Par Reg 3.435
Then as repentant to submit, beseech, Samson 751
Repenting
May prove thir foe, and with repenting hand Par Lost 2.369
Before thee; and not repenting, this obtaine Par Lost 10.75
Though late repenting him of Man deprav'd, Par Lost 11.886
In mirth, that after no repenting drawes; Sonnet 21, 6
Repents
He sorrows now, repents, and prayes contrite, Par Lost 11.90
Repine
Spare out of life perhaps, and not repine, Par Lost 6.460
I will not argue that, nor will repine. Par Reg 2.94
Repines
At this who ever envies or repines Samson 995
Replenished
With Fish replenisht, and the Aire with Fowle, Par Lost 7.447
Replenisht, and all these at thy command Par Lost 8.371
Replete
He ended, and his words replete with guile Par Lost 9.733
Replete with joy and wonder thus repli'd. Par Lost 12.468
Replied
Whereto with speedy words th' Arch-fiend reply'd. Par Lost 1.156
To whom the Goblin full of wrauth reply'd, Par Lost 2.688
T'whom thus the Portress of Hell Gate reply'd; Par Lost 2.746
To whom the great Creatour thus reply'd. Par Lost 3.167
Wondring; but soon th' Almighty thus reply'd: Par Lost 3.273
To whom thus *Eve* repli'd. O thou for whom Par Lost 4.440
To whom our general Ancestor repli'd. Par Lost 4.659
The Fiend repli'd not, overcome with rage; Par Lost 4.857
Disdainfully half smiling thus repli'd. Par Lost 4.903
To whom the warriour Angel, soon repli'd. Par Lost 4.946
Gave heed, but waxing more in rage repli'd. Par Lost 4.969
To whom the winged Hierarch repli'd. Par Lost 5.468
To whom the Patriarch of mankind repli'd, Par Lost 5.506
Th' Apostat, and more haughty thus repli'd. Par Lost 5.852
To whom in brief thus *Abdiel* stern repli'd. Par Lost 6.171
Whereto with look compos'd *Satan* repli'd. Par Lost 6.469
Then as new wak't thus gratefully repli'd. Par Lost 8.4
Benevolent and facil thus repli'd. Par Lost 8.65
To whom thus *Adam* cleerd of doubt, repli'd. Par Lost 8.179
As with a smile more bright'nd, thus repli'd. Par Lost 8.368
And humble deprecation thus repli'd. Par Lost 8.378
To whom thus half abash't *Adam* repli'd. Par Lost 8.595
With sweet austeer composure thus reply'd, Par Lost 9.272
To whom with healing words *Adam* replyd. Par Lost 9.290
1667 'reply'd'
To whom thus *Adam* fervently repli'd. Par Lost 9.342
Persisted, yet submiss, though last, repli'd. Par Lost 9.377
To whom the guileful Tempter thus reply'd. Par Lost 9.567
Yet more amaz'd unwarie thus reply'd. Par Lost 9.614
To whom the Tempter guilefully repli'd. Par Lost 9.655
So *Adam*, and thus *Eve* to him repli'd. Par Lost 9.960
To whom then first incenst *Adam* repli'd, Par Lost 9.1162
The gracious Judge without revile repli'd. Par Lost 10.118
To whom thus *Adam* sore beset repli'd. Par Lost 10.124
To whom the sovran Presence thus repli'd. Par Lost 10.144
Bold or loquacious, thus abasht repli'd. Par Lost 10.161
To whom th' incestuous Mother thus repli'd. Par Lost 10.602
To whom thus *Eve*, recovering heart, repli'd. Par Lost 10.966
Labouring had rais'd, and thus to *Eve* repli'd. Par Lost 10.1012
To whom thus *Adam* gratefully repli'd. Par Lost 11.370
T'whom *Michael* thus, hee also mov'd, repli'd. Par Lost 11.453
My dissolution. *Michael* repli'd, Par Lost 11.552
1667 '*Michael* to him repli'd'
Replete with joy and wonder thus repli'd. Par Lost 12.468
He ended; and thus *Adam* last reply'd. Par Lost 12.552
To whom thus also th' Angel last repli'd: Par Lost 12.574
By Miracle he may, reply'd the Swain, Par Reg 1.337
He ended, and the Son of God reply'd. Par Reg 1.346
To whom our Saviour sternly thus reply'd. Par Reg 1.406
How hast thou hunger then? Satan reply'd, Par Reg 2.319
To whom thus Jesus temperately reply'd: Par Reg 2.378
To whom thus Jesus patiently reply'd; Par Reg 2.432
To whom our Saviour calmly thus reply'd. Par Reg 3.43
To whom the Tempter murmuring thus reply'd. Par Reg 3.108
To whom our Saviour fervently reply'd. Par Reg 3.121
To whom the Tempter inly rackt reply'd. Par Reg 3.203
To whom the Son of God unmov'd reply'd. Par Reg 4.109
To whom the Tempter impudent repli'd. Par Reg 4.154
To whom the Fiend with fear abasht reply'd. Par Reg 4.195
To whom our Saviour sagely thus repli'd. Par Reg 4.285
Thus to our Saviour with stern brow reply'd. Par Reg 4.367
To whom the Fiend now swoln with rage reply'd: Par Reg 4.499

Replied(*cont*)
Phoebus repli'd, and touch'd my trembling ears; Lycidas 77
Unto Jehovah, he full soon reply'd Psalm 3, 11
Replies
That murmur, soon replies, God doth not need Sonnet 19, 9
Reply
The Monarch, and prevented all reply, Par Lost 2.467
He ceas'd; and *Satan* staid not to reply, Par Lost 2.1010
Fond, were it not in hope of thy reply: Par Lost 8.209
Thus her reply with accent sweet renewd. Par Lost 9.321
What to reply, confuted and convinc't Par Reg 3.3
The Tempter stood, nor had what to reply, Par Reg 4.2
Report
Contented with report hear onely in heav'n: Par Lost 3.701
Beseeching or besieging. This report, Par Lost 5.869
That *Moses* might report to them his will, Par Lost 12.237
O change beyond report, thought, or belief! Samson 117
If thy appearance answer loud report. Samson 1090
He's gone, and who knows how he may report Samson 1350
Which these dun shades will ne're report. Mask 127
Kil'd with report that Old man eloquent, Sonnet 10, 8
Reported
To have reported: gladly then he mixt Par Lost 6.21
Repose
After the toyl of Battel to repose Par Lost 1.319
Mind us of like repose, since God hath set Par Lost 4.612
O Sole in whom my thoughts find all repose, Par Lost 5.28
Or with repose; and such discourse bring on, Par Lost 5.233
Noontide repast, or Afternoons repose. Par Lost 9.403
Foundst either sweet repast, or sound repose; Par Lost 9.407
And eat the second time after repose, Par Reg 2.275
My harbour and my ultimate repose, Par Reg 3.210
At times when men seek most repose and rest, Samson 406
Reposed
I first awak't, and found my self repos'd Par Lost 4.450
On flours repos'd, and with fresh flourets crownd, Par Lost 5.636
line not in 1667 edition
Reposes
Where young *Adonis* oft reposes, Mask 999
Repossess
Self-rais'd, and repossess thir native seat? Par Lost 1.634
ms 'repossesse'
Reprehend
Lord in thine anger do not reprehend me Psalm 6, 1
Represent
Which the five watchfull Senses represent, Par Lost 5.104
O thou who future things canst represent Par Lost 11.870
Represented
Which to his evil Conscience represented Par Lost 10.849
Representing
Variously representing; yet still free Par Lost 8.610
Seaven Lamps as in a Zodiac representing Par Lost 12.255
Rather inflames thy torment, representing Par Reg 1.418
Repress
Thou couldst repress, nor did the dancing Rubie Samson 543
Reprieve
Without Reprieve adjudg'd to death, Samson 288
Reproach
Universal reproach, far worse to beare Par Lost 6.34
There sit not, and reproach us as unclean, Par Lost 9.1098
A help, became thy snare; to mee reproach Par Lost 11.165
Offended; fearless of reproach and scorn, Par Lost 11.811
As thou to thy reproach mayst well remember, Par Reg 3.66
In wedlock a reproach; I gain'd a Son, Samson 353
Of all reproach the most with shame that ever Samson 446
I led the way; bitter reproach, but true, Samson 823
Which 'mongst the wanton gods a foul reproach was held. Fair Inf 14
Reproaches
Attends thee, scorns, reproaches, injuries, Par Reg 4.387
And amorous reproaches to win from me Samson 393
Reproachful
To a reproachful life and cursed death, Par Lost 12.406
Arm his profane tongue with contemptuous words Mask 781
1637 'reproachfull words'
Reprobate
By Spirits reprobate, and in an hour Par Lost 1.697
To *Balaam* Reprobate, a Prophet yet Par Reg 1.491
Insensate left, or to sense reprobate, Samson 1685
Reproof
Check or reproof, and glad to scape so quit. Par Reg 1.477
Reproved
Prove disobedient, and reprov'd, retort, Par Lost 10.761
Reptile
Reptil with Spawn abundant, living Soule: Par Lost 7.388
Repulse
As stood like these, could ever know repulse? Par Lost 1.630
What should they do? if on they rusht, repulse Par Lost 6.600
So bent, the more shall shame him his repulse. Par Lost 9.384
So Satan, whom repulse upon repulse Par Reg 4.21
By this repulse receiv'd, and hold'st in Hell Par Reg 4.623
For peace, reap nothing but repulse and hate? Samson 966
Repulsed
Victorious. Thus repuls'd, our final hope Par Lost 2.142
Complete to have discover'd and repulst Par Lost 10.10
Not so repulst, with Tears that ceas'd not flowing, Par Lost 10.910
In all his wiles, defeated and repuls't, Par Reg 1.6
Repuls't, without much inward passion felt Samson 1006
They were repulst and slain, Psalm 83, 38

Repute
Sat on his Throne, upheld by old repute, Par Lost 1.639
His Rivals, winning cheap the high repute Par Lost 2.472
Request
Thus *Adam* made request, and *Raphael* Par Lost 5.561
At thy request, and that thou maist beware Par Lost 6.894
This also thy request with caution askt Par Lost 7.111
And thy request think now fulfill'd, that ask'd Par Lost 7.635
Did I request thee, Maker, from my Clay Par Lost 10.743
All thy request for Man, accepted Son, Par Lost 11.46
Obtain, all thy request was my Decree: Par Lost 11.47
O wherefore did God grant me my request, Samson 356
By thy request, who could deny thee nothing; Samson 881
Gentle swain at thy request Mask 900
Trinity ms 'request' ← 'behe'
The Virgin quire for her request Winchester 17
Requested
Between the pillars; he his guide requested Samson 1630
Require
That mock our scant manuring, and require Par Lost 4.628
Intelligential substances require Par Lost 5.408
Perfet within, no outward aid require; Par Lost 8.642
For high from ground the branches would require Par Lost 9.590
Great acts require great means of enterprise, Par Reg 2.412
That might require th' array of war, thy skill Par Reg 3.17
And now some public proof thereof require Samson 1314
Required
Subjection, but requir'd with gentle sway, Par Lost 4.308
Requires
Thy way thou canst not miss, me mine requires. Par Lost 3.735
Aught whereof hee hath need, hee who requires Par Lost 4.419
Our voluntarie service he requires, Par Lost 5.529
In unitie defective, which requires Par Lost 8.425
By all his Angels glorifi'd, requires Par Reg 3.113
Glory he requires, and glory he receives Par Reg 3.117
Requisite
To all truth requisite for men to know. Par Reg 1.464
Requital
And in requitall ope his leather'n scrip, Mask 626
1673 'requital'
Requite
After my great transgression, so requite Samson 1356
He can requite thee, for he knows the charms Sonnet 8, 5
Resalute
To resalute the World with sacred Light Par Lost 11.134
Rescue
To rescue *Israel* from the *Roman* yoke, Par Reg 1.217
Tearing and no rescue nigh. Psalm 7, 6
And rescue from the hands Psalm 82, 14
Rescued
Rescu'd, had in his Righteousness bin lost? Par Lost 11.682
Divided, till his rescu'd gain thir shoar: Par Lost 12.199
And Public Faith cleard from the shamefull brand Sonnet 15, 12
1694 'be rescu'd'
Rescu'd from death by force though pale and faint. Sonnet 23, 4
Resemblance
In them Divine resemblance, and such grace Par Lost 4.364
O Heav'n! that such resemblance of the Highest Par Lost 6.114
Fairest resemblance of thy Maker faire, Par Lost 9.538
Far worse, her false resemblance only meets, Par Reg 4.320
Th' express resemblance of the gods, is chang'd Mask 69
Resemblances
Som such resemblances methinks I find Par Lost 5.114
Resembles
Must'ring thir rage, and Heav'n resembles Hell? Par Lost 2.268
Resembles nearest, mazes intricate, Par Lost 5.622
Resemblest
Departed from thee, and thou resembl'st now Par Lost 4.839
Resembling
Or in the emptier waste, resembling Air, Par Lost 2.1045
In outward also her resembling less Par Lost 8.543
Resembling thy great Father: he seeks glory, Par Reg 3.110
Resent
And anger wouldst resent the offer'd wrong, Par Lost 9.300
Reserve
Or envie, or what reserve forbids to taste? Par Lost 5.61
No trifle; yet with this reserve, not else, Par Reg 4.165
Reserved
Reserv'd him to more wrath; for now the thought Par Lost 1.54
ms 'Reservd'
Reserv'd and destin'd to Eternal woe; Par Lost 2.161
Under th' inevitable curb, reserv'd Par Lost 2.322
Reservd from night, and kept for thee in store. Par Lost 5.128
Of what was high: such pleasure she reserv'd, Par Lost 8.50
This intellectual food, for beasts reserv'd? Par Lost 9.768
Degraded, to what wretched state reserv'd! Par Lost 11.501
Of sight, reserv'd alive to be repeated Samson 645
Reserving
Reserving, human left from human free. Par Lost 12.71
Reside
Choose to reside, his Glory unobscur'd, Par Lost 2.265
Might in that noise reside, of whom to ask Par Lost 2.957
Among them; how can God with such reside? Par Lost 12.284
Happy, who in thy house reside Psalm 84, 17
Residence
Where Scepter'd Angels held thir residence, Par Lost 1.734
Keep residence; if all I can will serve, Par Lost 2.999
Of Fish within thir watry residence, Par Lost 8.346

Residence(*cont*)
To testifie his hidd'n residence; Mask 248
Is your Fathers residence, Mask 947
Resides
Where God resides, and ere mid-day arriv'd Par Lost 8.112
Residing
Till I in Man residing through the Race, Par Lost 10.607
Him on this side *Euphrates* yet residing, Par Lost 12.114
Resign
And gladlier shall resign, when in the end Par Lost 6.731
Thou did'st resigne thy Manhood, and the Place Par Lost 10.148
Desirous to resigne, and render back Par Lost 10.749
Lament not *Eve*, but patiently resigne Par Lost 11.287
With purpose to resign them in full time Par Lost 12.301
That to the next I may resign my Roome. Vacation 58
Meekly thou didst resign this earthy load Sonnet 14, 3
Trinity ms 'resigne'
Resigned
As to his worthier, and would have resign'd Par Reg 1.27
Resigns
Resigns her charge, while goodness thinks no ill Par Lost 3.688
Resignes him up with Heav'n and Earth renewd. Par Lost 11.66
Resist
Whom we resist. If then his Providence Par Lost 1.162
Not more Almighty to resist our might Par Lost 2.192
Save he who reigns above, none can resist. Par Lost 2.814
If thou resist. The Fiend lookt up and knew Par Lost 4.1013
Nor solid might resist that edge: it met Par Lost 6.323
With spiritual Armour, able to resist Par Lost 12.491
Of female Seed, far abler to resist Par Reg 1.151
And I believe it, weakness to resist Samson 830
And all that band them to resist Samson 1753
Resistance
Plagues; they astonisht all resistance lost, Par Lost 6.838
Resistless
O're Heav'ns high Towrs to force resistless way, Par Lost 2.62
Those antient, whose resistless eloquence Par Reg 4.268
Masters commands come with a power resistless Samson 1404
Resolutest
At will the manliest, resolutest brest, Par Reg 2.167
Resolution
If not what resolution from despare. Par Lost 1.191
Prudent, least from his resolution rais'd Par Lost 2.468
Sad resolution and secure: let each Par Lost 6.541
Certain my resolution is to Die; Par Lost 9.907
Some safer resolution, which methinks Par Lost 10.1029
Dal. With doubtful feet and wavering resolution Samson 732
Brooks no delay: is this thy resolution? Samson 1344
Off. I praise thy resolution, doff these links: Samson 1410
Untill his revolution was at stay. Another 6
1640, 1658 'resolution'
Resolve
We may with more successful hope resolve Par Lost 1.120
Which onely thy solution can resolve. Par Lost 8.14
A death to think. Confirm'd then I resolve, Par Lost 9.830
Resolve me then oh Soul most surely blest Fair Inf 36
To day deep thoughts resolve with me to drench Sonnet 21, 5
Resolved
Open or understood must be resolv'd. Par Lost 1.662
That so ordains: this was at first resolv'd, Par Lost 2.201
Great things resolv'd, which from the lowest deep Par Lost 2.392
Friendliest to sleep and silence, he resolv'd Par Lost 5.668
Thus he resolv'd, but first from inward griefe Par Lost 9.97
Of tasting those fair Apples, I resolv'd Par Lost 9.585
This day affords, declaring thee resolvd, Par Lost 9.968
Resolv'd, as thou proposest; so our Foe Par Lost 10.1038
Rather by this his last affront resolv'd, Par Reg 4.444
They ravel more, still less resolv'd, Samson 305
Who with a grain of manhood well resolv'd Samson 408
Which might have aw'd the best resolv'd of men, Samson 847
Chor. In time thou hast resolv'd, the man returns. Samson 1390
Resolving
His holy Eyes; resolving from thenceforth Par Lost 12.109
With this long way, resolving here to lodge Mask 183
Bridgewater ms 'resolvinge'
Resonant
Fled and pursu'd transverse the resonant fugue. Par Lost 11.563
Resort
Hath he excluded my resort sometimes. Par Reg 1.367
Thither shall all the valiant youth resort, Samson 1738
That in the various bussle of resort Mask 379
Bridgewater ms 'resorte'
With Jiggs, and rural dance resort, Mask 952
Bridgewater ms 'resorte'
Far from all resort of mirth, Penseroso 81
Resorting
Hasted, resorting to the Summons high, Par Lost 11.81
Resound
Encompass'd shall resound thee ever blest. Par Lost 3.149
In mystic Dance not without Song, resound Par Lost 5.178
To answer, and resound farr other Song. Par Lost 10.862
With Feast and Musick all the Tents resound. Par Lost 11.592
resound and eccho Hallelu Musick Tr. ms 4.22
Resounded
Of Hell resounded. Princes, Potentates, Par Lost 1.315
From all her Caves, and back resounded *Death*. Par Lost 2.789
Resounded, and had Earth bin then, all Earth Par Lost 6.218
Resounded, (thou remember'st, for thou heardst) Par Lost 7.561
Resounding
With chaunt of tuneful Birds resounding loud; Par Reg 2.290
And give resounding grace to all Heav'ns Harmonies. Mask 243
Trinity ms 'give resounding grace' ←'hold a counterpoint'
Bridgewater ms 'hould a Counterpointe'
B.M. ms 'hold a Counter point'
And the resounding shore, Nativity 182
Resounds
Mixt with auxiliar Gods; and what resounds Par Lost 1.579
The rigid interdiction, which resounds Par Lost 8.334
And Dunbarr feild resounds thy praises loud, Sonnet 16, 8
1694 'resound'
Respect
In some respect far higher so declar'd. Par Reg 4.521
Nor in respect of the enemy just cause Samson 316
Though in this uncouth place; if old respect, Samson 333
Respects
Private respects must yield; with grave authority Samson 868
Respiration
Appeer of respiration to the just, Par Lost 12.540
Respire
With day-spring born; here leave me to respire. Samson 11
Respite
To respite or deceive, or slack the pain Par Lost 2.461
To respit his day-labour with repast, Par Lost 5.232
Quiet though sad, the respit of that day Par Lost 11.272
Gave respit to the drowsie frighted steeds Mask 553
Bridgewater ms 'respite'
Resplendence
In full resplendence, Heir of all my might, Par Lost 5.720
Resplendent
Bind thir resplendent locks inwreath'd with beams, Par Lost 3.361
Which they beheld, the Moons resplendent Globe Par Lost 4.723
Empress of this fair World, resplendent *Eve*, Par Lost 9.568
Resplendent all his Father manifest Par Lost 10.66
Responsive
Sole, or responsive each to others note Par Lost 4.683
Rest
And rest can never dwell, hope never comes Par Lost 1.66
There rest, if any rest can harbour there, Par Lost 1.185
No rest: through many a dark and drearie Vaile Par Lost 2.618
That rest or intermission none I find. Par Lost 2.802
Of night, and all things now retir'd to rest Par Lost 4.611
Labour and rest, as day and night to men Par Lost 4.613
Rove idle unimploid, and less need rest; Par Lost 4.617
Mean while, as Nature wills, Night bids us rest. Par Lost 4.633
As through unquiet rest: he on his side Par Lost 5.11
To rest, and what the Garden choicest bears Par Lost 5.368
All but the unsleeping eyes of God to rest, Par Lost 5.647
To trouble Holy Rest; Heav'n casts thee out Par Lost 6.272
Far in the dark dislodg'd, and void of rest, Par Lost 6.415
Ye Angels arm'd, this day from Battel rest; Par Lost 6.802
Mov'd the Creator in his holy Rest Par Lost 7.91
The credit of whose vertue rest with thee, Par Lost 9.649
Coverd, but not at rest or ease of Mind, Par Lost 9.1120
Mayst ever rest well pleas'd. I go to judge Par Lost 10.71
As in my Mothers lap? there I should rest Par Lost 10.778
In dust, our final rest and native home. Par Lost 10.1085
By suffering, and earne rest from labour won, Par Lost 11.375
Shall rest by Day, a fiery gleame by Night, Par Lost 12.257
Safe to eternal Paradise of rest. Par Lost 12.314
So onely can high Justice rest appaid. Par Lost 12.401
Thir place of rest, and Providence thir guide: Par Lost 12.647
The rest commit to me, I shall let pass Par Reg 2.233
To rest at noon, and entr'd soon the shade Par Reg 2.292
Above the rest lifting his stately head Par Reg 4.48
The rest are barbarous, and scarce worth the sight, Par Reg 4.86
As varnish on a Harlots cheek, the rest, Par Reg 4.344
Hungry and cold betook him to his rest, Par Reg 4.403
Flock'd to the Baptist, I among the rest, Par Reg 4.511
Laborious works, unwillingly this rest Samson 14
At times when men seek most repose and rest, Samson 406
Mine eie to harbour sleep, or thoughts to rest. Samson 459
And I shall shortly be with them that rest. Samson 598
This Idols day hath bin to thee no day of rest, Samson 1297
The rest was magnanimity to remit, Samson 1470
For grant they be so, while they rest unknown, Mask 361
line not in Bridgewater ms
line not in Trinity ms
Amongst the rest a small unsightly root, Mask 629
And timely rest have wanted, but fair Virgin Mask 689
Thus I set my printless feet Mask 897
Bridgewater ms 'I rest'
The labouring clouds do often rest: Allegro 74
Envy bid conceal the rest. Arcades 13
Nor can he be at rest Nativity 216
Hath laid her Babe to rest. Nativity 238
While sad *Ulisses* soul and all the rest Vacation 50
Loud o're the rest *Cremona*'s Trump doth sound; Passion 26
Sweet rest sease thee evermore, Winchester 50
Rest that gives all men life, gave him his death, Another 11
Before the Judge, who thenceforth bid thee rest Sonnet 14, 13
And post o're Land and Ocean without rest: Sonnet 19, 13
Let *Euclid* rest and *Archimedes* pause, Sonnet 21, 7
Hath found a house of *rest*, Psalm 84, 10
And in thee only rest. Psalm 84, 48
What Land, what Seat of rest thou bidst me seek, Prose 12, 4

Rest
The rest were long to tell, though far renown'd, Par Lost 1.507
Thir dread commander: he above the rest Par Lost 1.589
Belch'd fire and rowling smoak; the rest entire Par Lost 1.671
For while they sit contriving, shall the rest, Par Lost 2.54
Of hazard more, as he above the rest Par Lost 2.455
Elect above the rest; so is my will: Par Lost 3.184
The rest shall hear me call, and oft be warnd Par Lost 3.185
The rest in circuit walles this Universe. Par Lost 3.721
The rest was craggie cliff, that overhung Par Lost 4.547
The rest is true, they found me where they say; Par Lost 4.900
Destruction to the rest: this pause between Par Lost 6.162
The rest in imitation to like Armes Par Lost 6.662
Like things to like, the rest to several place Par Lost 7.240
With Honey stor'd: the rest are numberless, Par Lost 7.492
Govern the rest, self-knowing, and from thence Par Lost 7.510
Imports not, if thou reck'n right, the rest Par Lost 8.71
Lodg'd in a small partition, and the rest Par Lost 8.105
To me so friendly grown above the rest Par Lost 9.564
The credit of whose vertue rest with thee, Par Lost 9.649
Sole Daughter of his voice; the rest, we live Par Lost 9.653
As *Delos* floating once; the rest his look Par Lost 10.296
Flown to the upper World; the rest were all Par Lost 10.422
Above the rest still to retain; they all Par Lost 10.532
Broke off the rest; so much of Death her thoughts Par Lost 10.1008
Awaits the good, the rest what punishment? Par Lost 11.710
From all the rest, of whom to be invok'd, Par Lost 12.112
Promisd to *Abraham* and his Seed: the rest Par Lost 12.260
Of Spirit and Truth; the rest, farr greater part, Par Lost 12.533
Of all the rest: then wilt thou not be loath Par Lost 12.585

Rested
Had work and rested not, the solemn Pipe, Par Lost 7.595

Resting
With stench and smoak: Such resting found the sole Par Lost 1.237
Now resting, bless'd and hallowd the Seav'nth day, Par Lost 7.592
As resting on that day from all his work, Par Lost 7.593

Restless
Truce to his restless thoughts, and entertain Par Lost 2.526
Such restless revolution day by day Par Lost 8.31
From restless thoughts, that like a deadly swarm Samson 19
It shall be in eternal restless change Mask 596
Trinity ms 'restlesse'
1637 'restlesse'
Giddy and *restless* let *them reel* Psalm 83, 51

Restorative
Hunger, with sweet restorative delight. Par Reg 2.373

Restore
Restore us, and regain the blissful Seat, Par Lost 1.5
Deucalion and chaste *Pyrrha* to restore Par Lost 11.12
By mee the Promis'd Seed shall all restore. Par Lost 12.623
These if from servitude thou shalt restore Par Reg 3.381
God will restore him eye-sight to his strength. Samson 1503
And force him to restore his purchase back, Mask 607
Trinity ms 'restore' ← 'release'
This will restore all soon. *La*. 'Twill not false traitor, Mask 690
'Twill not restore the truth and honesty Mask 691
And thou O Lord how long? turn Lord, restore Psalm 6, 7
Turn us, and us restore, Psalm 85, 14

Restored
As from a second root shall be restor'd, Par Lost 3.288
As many as are restor'd, without thee none. Par Lost 3.289
Restor'd by thee, vile as I am, to place Par Lost 10.971
Betwixt the world destroy'd and world restor'd, Par Lost 12.3
line not in 1667 edition
Till truth were freed, and equity restor'd: Par Reg 1.220
Man fall'n shall be restor'd, I never more. Par Reg 1.405
The Kingdom shall to *Israel* be restor'd: Par Reg 2.36
Nothing is hard) by miracle restor'd, Samson 1528

Restorer
Destin'd restorer of Mankind, by whom Par Lost 10.646

Restrained
Desiring; nor restrain'd conveyance need Par Lost 8.628
Or not restraind as wee, or not obeying, Par Lost 9.868
A space, till firmer thoughts restraind excess, Par Lost 11.498

Restraint
For one restraint, Lords of the World besides? Par Lost 1.32
Through all restraint broke loose he wings his way Par Lost 3.87
Luxurious by restraint; what we by day Par Lost 9.209
Greedily she ingorg'd without restraint, Par Lost 9.791
It seems, in thy restraint: what could I more? Par Lost 9.1170
Lets her will rule; restraint she will not brook, Par Lost 9.1184
Full sight of her in Heaven without restraint, Sonnet 23, 8

Rests
Transfus'd on thee his ample Spirit rests. Par Lost 3.389
Into her private Cell when Nature rests. Par Lost 5.109
Reignd where these Heav'ns now rowl, where Earth now rests Par Lost 5.578
What rests but that the mortal Sentence pass Par Lost 10.48
Flies to his place, nor rests, but in mid air Par Reg 1.39

Result
With Trumpets regal sound the great result: Par Lost 2.515
We should compel them to a quick result. Par Lost 6.619

Resume
Thir surest signal, they will soon resume Par Lost 1.278
Then enter into glory, and resume Par Lost 12.456
Thus they out of their plaints new hope resume Par Reg 2.58

Resumed
Till thir lost shape, permitted, they resum'd, Par Lost 10.574

Resumes
Then with transition sweet new Speech resumes. Par Lost 12.5
line not in 1667 edition

Resurrection
Nor after resurrection shall he stay Par Lost 12.436

Retain
Th' Assembly, as when hollow Rocks retain Par Lost 2.285
If ye be found obedient, and retain Par Lost 5.501
And drink the liquid Light, firm to retaine Par Lost 7.362
Above the rest still to retain; they all Par Lost 10.532

Retained
Wanted not long, though to this shape retain'd. Par Lost 9.601
1667 'retaind'

Retaining
Retaining still Divine similitude Par Lost 11.512

Retains
Thir station, Heav'n yet populous retaines Par Lost 7.146
Made Goddess of the River; still she retains Mask 842
1637 'retaines'
Trinity ms 'retaines'
Bridgewater ms 'retaines'

Retinue
On Princes, when thir rich Retinue long Par Lost 5.355
What Followers, what Retinue canst thou gain, Par Reg 2.419

Retire
Retire, or taste thy folly, and learn by proof, Par Lost 2.686
Her fardest verge, and *Chaos* to retire Par Lost 2.1038
Though I uncircumscrib'd my self retire, Par Lost 7.170
And giv'st access, though secret she retire. Par Lost 9.810
With reverence I must meet, and thou retire. Par Lost 11.237
Discover'd soon the place of her retire. Par Lost 11.267
Religion satisfi'd; Truth shall retire Par Lost 12.535
Hath rapt him from us? will he now retire Par Reg 2.40
Skill'd to retire, and in retiring draw Par Reg 2.161
But had we best retire, I see a storm? Samson 1061
Yet will they soon retire, if he but shrink. Mask 656

Retired
Others apart sat on a Hill retir'd, Par Lost 2.557
Or in thick shade retir'd, from him to draw Par Lost 4.532
Of night, and all things now retir'd to rest Par Lost 4.611
Thou find'st him from the heat of Noon retir'd, Par Lost 5.231
In horror; from each hand with speed retir'd Par Lost 6.307
Back to his Chariot; where it stood retir'd Par Lost 6.338
Under her Cloudie covert both retir'd, Par Lost 6.409
Divided, and to either Flank retir'd. Par Lost 6.570
At his command the uprooted Hills retir'd Par Lost 6.781
Perceaving where she sat retir'd in sight, Par Lost 8.41
Not obvious, not obtrusive, but retir'd, Par Lost 8.504
Thy awful brow, more awful thus retir'd. Par Lost 9.537
Farr to the inland retir'd, about the walls Par Lost 10.423
Retir'd unto the Desert, but with arms; Par Reg 3.166
Old, and lascivious, and from *Rome* retir'd Par Reg 4.91
Safe to the rock of *Etham* was retir'd, Samson 253
Oft seeks to sweet retired Solitude, Mask 376
Trinity ms 'sweet retired solitude' ← 'solitarie sweet retire'
And adde to these retired leasure, Penseroso 49

Retirement
And short retirement urges sweet returne. Par Lost 9.250
Plato's retirement, where the *Attic* Bird Par Reg 4.245

Retires
Our knowledge or opinion; then retires Par Lost 5.108
Retires, or *Bactrian* Sophi from the hornes Par Lost 10.433

Retiring
Retiring, by his own doom alienated, Par Lost 10.378
Skill'd to retire, and in retiring draw Par Reg 2.161
Thy right by sitting still or thus retiring? Par Reg 3.164
Retiring from the popular noise, I seek Samson 16

Retort
Prove disobedient, and reprov'd, retort, Par Lost 10.761

Retorted
And with retorted scorn his back he turn'd Par Lost 5.906

Retreat
With dread of death to flight or foul retreat, Par Lost 1.555
This place our dungeon, not our safe retreat Par Lost 2.317
None of retreat, no unbecoming deed Par Lost 6.237
Or faint retreat; when the great Son of God Par Lost 6.799
The Realm of *Aladule*, in his retreate Par Lost 10.435

Retreated
Retreated in a silent valley, sing Par Lost 2.547

Retreating
Towards the retreating Sea thir furious tyde. Par Lost 11.854

Retrenched
But this thy glory shall be soon retrench'd; Par Reg 1.454

Retribution
Fit retribution, emptie as thir deeds; Par Lost 3.454

Retrograde
Progressive, retrograde, or standing still, Par Lost 8.127

Return
More then can be in Heav'n, we now return Par Lost 2.37
Inflicted? and what peace can we return, Par Lost 2.335
The irksom hours, till this great Chief return. Par Lost 2.527
That bred them they return, and howle and gnaw Par Lost 2.799
To know, and this once known, shall soon return, Par Lost 2.839
Seasons return, but not to me returns Par Lost 3.41
Or proud return though to his heavier doom, Par Lost 3.159
Shall enter Heaven long absent, and returne, Par Lost 3.261
Ah wherefore! he deservd no such return Par Lost 4.42
Thou following cryd'st aloud, Return faire *Eve;* Par Lost 4.481

Return(*cont*)
Yet happie pair; enjoy, till I return, Par Lost 4.534
All things proceed, and up to him return, Par Lost 5.470
Back on thy foes more glorious to return Par Lost 6.39
Of Thunder: back defeated to return Par Lost 6.606
Return me to my Native Element: Par Lost 7.16
Relate thee; greater now in thy return Par Lost 7.604
Thir distance argues and thir swift return Par Lost 8.21
Be good and friendly still, and oft return. Par Lost 8.651
And short retirement urges sweet returne. Par Lost 9.250
Oft he to her his charge of quick returne Par Lost 9.399
Of thy presum'd return! event perverse! Par Lost 9.405
Waiting desirous her return, had wove Par Lost 9.839
Solace in her return, so long delay'd; Par Lost 9.844
Justice shall not return as bountie scorn'd. Par Lost 10.54
Till thou return unto the ground, for thou Par Lost 10.206
For dust thou art, and shalt to dust returne. Par Lost 10.208
Stay his return perhaps over this Gulfe Par Lost 10.253
1667 'returne'
That dust I am, and shall to dust returne: Par Lost 10.770
And to the place of judgment will return, Par Lost 10.932
And thither must return and be no more. Par Lost 11.200
I must return to native dust? O sight Par Lost 11.463
Till many years over thy head return: Par Lost 11.534
On thir impenitence; and shall returne Par Lost 11.816
His people from enthralment, they return Par Lost 12.171
On thir imbattelld ranks the Waves return, Par Lost 12.213
Return them back to *Egypt*, choosing rather Par Lost 12.219
Returne, the Starres of Morn shall see him rise Par Lost 12.422
And vengeance to the wicked, at return Par Lost 12.541
The way he came not having mark'd, return Par Reg 1.297
Soon we shall see our hope, our joy return. Par Reg 2.57
For Satan with slye preface to return Par Reg 2.115
With granted leave officious I return, Par Reg 2.302
From them who could return him nothing else, Par Reg 3.129
Hard recompence, unsutable return Par Reg 3.132
Hasting or on return, in robes of State; Par Reg 4.64
And thither will return thee, yet remember Par Reg 4.374
To gratulate the sweet return of morn; Par Reg 4.438
But God hath set before us, to return thee Samson 517
Return the way thou cam'st, I will not come. Samson 1332
And envious darknes, e're they could return, Mask 194
Bridgewater ms 'retorne'
1637 'returne'
Trinity ms 'returne'
La. They were but twain, and purpos'd quick return. Mask 284
Bridgewater ms 'returne'
Trinity ms 'returne'
Now thou art gon, and never must return! Lycidas 38
Trinity ms 'returne'
Return *Alpheus*, the dread voice is past, Lycidas 132
Trinity ms 'Returne'
That shrunk thy streams; Return *Sicilian* Muse, Lycidas 133
1638 'return'
Trinity ms 'returne'
Will down return to men, Nativity 142
They shall return in hast the way they came Psalm 6, 23
Return on high and in their sight. Psalm 7, 28
Return us, *and thy grace divine*, Psalm 80, 29
Return now, God of Hosts, look down Psalm 80, 57
Return us, *and thy grace divine* Psalm 80, 77
And *calmly* didst return Psalm 85, 10
Return to folly, *but surcease* Psalm 85, 35

Returned
With deafning shout, return'd them loud acclaim. Par Lost 2.520
Forbore, then these to her *Satan* return'd: Par Lost 2.736
In his uprightness answer thus returnd. Par Lost 3.693
It started back, but pleas'd I soon returnd, Par Lost 4.463
Pleas'd it returnd as soon with answering looks Par Lost 4.464
To whom the winged Warriour thus returnd: Par Lost 4.576
Returnd on that bright beam, whose point now raisd Par Lost 4.590
Thy face, and Morn return'd, for I this Night, Par Lost 5.30
Returnd not lost: On to the sacred hill Par Lost 6.25
From mee returnd, as erst thou saidst, from flight, Par Lost 6.187
Into his place, and the great Son returnd Par Lost 7.135
Desisting, though unwearied, up returnd Par Lost 7.552
The great Creator from his work returnd Par Lost 7.567
Glad we return'd up to the coasts of Light Par Lost 8.245
This happie Light, when answer none return'd, Par Lost 8.285
Return'd and gracious purpose thus renew'd. Par Lost 8.337
Of heavier on himself, fearless return'd. Par Lost 9.57
By Night he fled, and at Midnight return'd Par Lost 9.58
On the eighth return'd, and on the Coast averse Par Lost 9.67
To whom mild answer *Adam* thus return'd. Par Lost 9.226
Just then returnd at shut of Evening Flours. Par Lost 9.278
To be returnd by Noon amid the Bowre, Par Lost 9.401
Assembl'd Angels, and ye Powers return'd Par Lost 10.34
To him with swift ascent he up returnd, Par Lost 10.224
Ere this he had return'd, with fury driv'n Par Lost 10.240
Might suddenly inflict; that past, return'd Par Lost 10.341
And tidings fraught, to Hell he now return'd, Par Lost 10.346
Thir mighty Chief returnd: loud was th' acclaime: Par Lost 10.455
I call ye and declare ye now, returnd Par Lost 10.462
But hiss for hiss returnd with forked tongue Par Lost 10.518
That I was heard with favour; peace returnd Par Lost 11.153
Recovering, and his scatterd spirits returnd, Par Lost 11.294
Returnd from *Babylon* by leave of Kings Par Lost 12.348
To warm him wet return'd from field at Eve, Par Reg 1.318

Returned(*cont*)
Durst ever, who return'd, and dropt not here Par Reg 1.324
Return'd the wiser, or the more instruct Par Reg 1.439
Dissembl'd, and this Answer smooth return'd. Par Reg 1.467
Or in *Perea*, but return'd in vain. Par Reg 2.24
Others return'd from Baptism, not her Son, Par Reg 2.61
From *Egypt* home return'd, in *Nazareth* Par Reg 2.79
Therefore I am return'd, lest confidence Par Reg 2.140
To whom quick answer Satan thus return'd. Par Reg 2.172
To whom our Saviour answer thus return'd. Par Reg 3.181
Home to his Mothers house private return'd. Par Reg 4.639
Returned Jacob back. Psalm 85, 4

Returnest
Of my revenge, first sought for thou returnst Par Lost 6.151
Whence thou returnst, and whither wentst, I know; Par Lost 12.610

Returning
Her mural breach, returning whence it rowld. Par Lost 6.879
Scarse from the Tree returning; in her hand Par Lost 9.850
The second time returning, in his Bill Par Lost 11.859
Homeward returning. High in Front advanc't, Par Lost 12.632
And not returning that would likeliest render Par Reg 3.130
After offence returning, to regain Samson 1004
Of strength, again returning with my hair Samson 1355
My true account, least he returning chide, Sonnet 19, 6

Returns
Invincible, and vigour soon returns, Par Lost 1.140
ms 'returnes'
Seasons return, but not to me returns Par Lost 3.41
Touch of Celestial temper, but returns Par Lost 4.812
And now returns him from his prison scap't, Par Lost 4.906
He lights, and to his proper shape returns Par Lost 5.276
Returns our own. Cease then this impious rage, Par Lost 5.845
Down to this habitable, which returnes Par Lost 8.157
Beat off, returns as oft with humming sound; Par Reg 4.17
Chor. In time thou hast resolv'd, the man returns. Samson 1390
But unexpectedly returns Samson 1750
When the fresh blood grows lively, and returns Mask 670
Bridgewater ms 'returnes'
Trinity ms 'returnes'

Reveal
Not lawful to reveal? yet for thy good Par Lost 5.570
Dismiss them not disconsolate; reveale Par Lost 11.113
But weakly to a woman must reveal it, Samson 50
Of *Timna* first betray me, and reveal Samson 383

Revealed
By what is past, to thee I have reveal'd Par Lost 6.895
Farr differing from this World, thou hast reveal'd Par Lost 7.71
Things not reveal'd, which th' invisible King, Par Lost 7.122
Contented that thus farr hath been reveal'd Par Lost 8.177
Plainlier shall be reveald. This Patriarch blest, Par Lost 12.151
Thou hast reveald, those chiefly which concerne Par Lost 12.272
Last in the Clouds from Heav'n to be reveald Par Lost 12.545
1669 'reveal'd'
Or harbour'd in one Cave, is not reveal'd; Par Reg 1.307
Sent his Anointed, and to us reveal'd him, Par Reg 2.50
Or benefit reveal'd to *Abraham*'s race? Samson 29
Shameful garrulity. To have reveal'd Samson 491
But I to enemies reveal'd, and should not. Samson 782
Why then reveal'd? I was assur'd by those Samson 800

Reveals
For what concerns my knowledge God reveals. Par Reg 1.293

Revellers
Of *Bacchus* and his revellers, the Race Par Lost 7.33
1667 'Revellers'

Revelry
Midnight shout, and revelry, Mask 103
1637 'revelrie'
& favour our close jocondrie Mask Tr. ms 12.29
'jocondrie' ←'revelrie'
And pomp, and feast, and revelry, Allegro 127

Revels
Whose midnight Revels, by a Forrest side Par Lost 1.782
ms 'revells'
Reigns here and revels; not in the bought smile Par Lost 4.765
Revels the spruce and jocond Spring, Mask 985
1637 'Revells'
line not in Bridgewater ms
Trinity ms 'revells'

Revenge
Stird up with Envy and Revenge, deceiv'd Par Lost 1.35
ms 'revenge'
And study of revenge, immortal hate, Par Lost 1.107
Waiting revenge: cruel his eye, but cast Par Lost 1.604
Which if not Victory is yet Revenge. Par Lost 2.105
Desperate revenge, and Battel dangerous Par Lost 2.107
Of all his aim, after some dire revenge. Par Lost 2.128
First, what Revenge? the Towrs of Heav'n are fill'd Par Lost 2.129
Untam'd reluctance, and revenge though slow, Par Lost 2.337
Common revenge, and interrupt his joy Par Lost 2.371
Yours be th' advantage all, mine the revenge. Par Lost 2.987
Thither full fraught with mischievous revenge, Par Lost 2.1054
On desparate reveng, that shall redound Par Lost 3.85
1667 'revenge'
Yet with revenge accomplish't and to Hell Par Lost 3.160
Deep malice to conceale, couch't with revenge: Par Lost 4.123
Thank him who puts me loath to this revenge Par Lost 4.386
Honour and Empire with revenge enlarg'd, Par Lost 4.390
Of my revenge, first sought for thou returnst Par Lost 6.151

Revenge(*cont*)
Which would be all his solace and revenge, Par Lost 6.905
But what will not Ambition and Revenge Par Lost 9.168
To basest things. Revenge, at first though sweet, Par Lost 9.171
Of guile, of hate, of envie, of revenge; Par Lost 9.466
Can fit his punishment, or their revenge. Par Lost 10.242
Would be revenge indeed; which will be lost Par Lost 10.1036
Have satisfi'd thir utmost of revenge Samson 484
Contemptuous, proud, set on revenge and spite; Samson 1462
A dreadful way thou took'st to thy revenge. Samson 1591
Chor. O dearly-bought revenge, yet glorious! Samson 1660

Revenged
Came furious down to be reveng'd on men, Par Lost 4.4
They had anough reveng'd, having reduc't Samson 1468
Fully reveng'd, hath left them years of mourning, Samson 1712

Reverence
With awful reverence prone; and as a God Par Lost 2.478
Where honour due and reverence none neglects, Par Lost 3.738
Yet with submiss approach and reverence meek, Par Lost 5.359
And with mysterious reverence I deem) Par Lost 8.599
But first low Reverence don, as to the power Par Lost 9.835
What love sincere, and reverence in my heart Par Lost 10.915
With reverence I must meet, and thou retire. Par Lost 11.237
And reverence thee thir great Progenitor. Par Lost 11.346
Gods Image did not reverence in themselves. Par Lost 11.525
The Prophet do him reverence, on him rising Par Reg 1.80
Whom with low reverence I adore as mine, Arcades 37

Reverenced
That part most reverenc'd *Dagon* and his Priests, Samson 1463

Reverend
At length a Reverend Sire among them came, Par Lost 11.719
But see here comes thy reverend Sire Samson 326
With thee; say reverend Sire, we thirst to hear. Samson 1456
To thee first reverend *Manoa*, and to these Samson 1548
Next *Camus*, reverend Sire, went footing slow, Lycidas 103

Reverent
Th' eternal Regions: lowly reverent Par Lost 3.349
Before him reverent, and there confess Par Lost 10.1088
Before him reverent, and both confess'd Par Lost 10.1100
Or turn to reverent awe? for Beauty stands Par Reg 2.220

Reverse
But with swift wheele reverse, deep entring shar'd Par Lost 6.326
To mitigate thus plead, not to reverse) Par Lost 11.41

Reversed
And bound him fast; without his rod revers't, Mask 816
Bridgewater ms 'reverst'

Revile
The gracious Judge without revile repli'd. Par Lost 10.118

Reviling
Without wrauth or reviling; wee expected Par Lost 10.1048

Revisit
Thee I re-visit now with bolder wing, Par Lost 3.13
Though hard and rare: thee I revisit safe, Par Lost 3.21

Revisitest
Revisit'st not these eyes, that rowle in vain Par Lost 3.23

Revive
New courage and revive, though now they lye Par Lost 1.279
Extend his ev'ning beam, the fields revive, Par Lost 2.493
Effect shall end our wish. Mean while revive; Par Lost 6.493
As present, Heav'nly instructer, I revive Par Lost 11.871
And us again revive, Psalm 85, 22

Revived
Enlightn'd, and thir languisht hope reviv'd. Par Lost 6.497
Or of reviv'd *Adonis*, or renownd Par Lost 9.440
Dropt in Ambrosial Oils till she reviv'd, Mask 840
Bridgewater ms 'revived'

Revives
But soon revives, Death over him no power Par Lost 12.420
Sam. Your coming, Friends, revives me, for I learn Samson 187
Revives, reflourishes, then vigorous most Samson 1704

Reviving
Chor. Oh how comely it is and how reviving Samson 1268

Revoke
Thir nature, and revoke the high Decree Par Lost 3.126

Revokes
Without means us'd, what it predicts revokes. Par Reg 3.356

Revolt
Who first seduc'd them to that foul revolt? Par Lost 1.33
For his revolt, yet faithfull how they stood, Par Lost 1.611
By our revolt, but over Hell extend Par Lost 2.326
Thir own revolt, not I: if I foreknew, Par Lost 3.117
Author of evil, unknown till thy revolt, Par Lost 6.262
That from thy just obedience could revolt, Par Lost 6.740
Disloyal on the part of Man, revolt, Par Lost 9.7
Who leagu'd with millions more in rash revolt Par Reg 1.359
And still revolt when truth would set them free. Sonnet 12, 10
Trinity ms 'still revolt when Truth would sett them' ←'make them' ←'set them' ←'hate the truth wherby they should be'

Revolted
Think not, revolted Spirit, thy shape the same, Par Lost 4.835
Against revolted multitudes the Cause Par Lost 6.31
Where all yet left of that revolted Rout Par Lost 10.534

Revolter
A Murtherer, a Revolter, and a Robber. Samson 1180

Revolution
Such restless revolution day by day Par Lost 8.31
Comes thundring back with dreadful revolution Par Lost 10.814
Untill his revolution was at stay. Another 6

Revolution(*cont*)
1640, 1658 'resolution'

Revolutions
At certain revolutions all the damn'd Par Lost 2.597

Revolve
These here revolve, or, as thou lik'st, at home, Par Reg 4.281

Revolved
Revolvd on Heav'ns great Axle, and her Reign Par Lost 7.381
Of thoughts revolv'd, his final sentence chose Par Lost 9.88
This having heard, strait I again revolv'd Par Reg 1.259
Or some great matter in his mind revolv'd. Samson 1638

Revolving
Then much revolving, thus in sighs began. Par Lost 4.31
Musing and much revolving in his brest, Par Reg 1.185

Reward
All who have thir reward on Earth, the fruits Par Lost 3.451
Thy merited reward, the first assay Par Lost 6.153
By terrible Example the reward Par Lost 6.910
And worship him, and in reward to rule Par Lost 7.628
To serve him, thy reward was of his grace, Par Lost 10.767
Loose no reward, though here thou see him die, Par Lost 11.459
Exempt from Death; to shew thee what reward Par Lost 11.709
To judge th' unfaithful dead, but to reward Par Lost 12.461
The fame and glory, glory the reward Par Reg 3.25
Violent or shameful death thir due reward. Par Reg 3.87
And loses, though but verbal, his reward. Par Reg 3.104
The public marks of honour and reward Samson 992
Private reward, for which both God and State Samson 1465

Rewarded
Rewarded well with servil punishment! Samson 413

Rhea
His own and *Rhea*'s Son like measure found; Par Lost 1.513
ms 'Rhea's'
Young *Bacchus* from his Stepdame *Rhea*'s eye; Par Lost 4.279

Rhene
Rhene or the *Danaw*, when her barbarous Sons Par Lost 1.353
ms 'Rhene'

Rhetoric
So oft, and the perswasive Rhetoric Par Reg 4.4
Enjoy your deer Wit, and gay Rhetorick Mask 790
line not in Trinity ms
line not in Bridgewater ms

Rheums
Dropsies, and Asthma's, and Joint-racking Rheums. Par Lost 11.488

Rhine
Rhene or the *Danaw*, when her barbarous Sons Par Lost 1.353
ms 'Rhene'

Rhodope
In *Rhodope*, where Woods and Rocks had Eares Par Lost 7.35

Rhomb
Nocturnal and Diurnal rhomb suppos'd, Par Lost 8.134

Rhombs
In Rhombs and wedges, and half moons, and wings. Par Reg 3.309

Rhyme
Things unattempted yet in Prose or Rhime. Par Lost 1.16
ms 'rime'
Himself to sing, and build the lofty rhyme. Lycidas 11
Trinity ms 'rime'

Rib
From thence a Rib, with cordial spirits warme; Par Lost 8.466
The Rib he formd and fashond with his hands; Par Lost 8.469
Another Rib afford, yet loss of thee Par Lost 9.912
As good have grown there still a liveless Rib. Par Lost 9.1154
Rather then solid vertu, all but a Rib Par Lost 10.884

Ribs
And dig'd out ribs of Gold. Let none admire Par Lost 1.690
His Armes clung to his Ribs, his Leggs entwining Par Lost 10.512
Under the ribs of Death, but O ere long Mask 562
Trinity ms 'ribbs'
Bridgewater ms 'ribbs'

Rich
With Gemms and Golden lustre rich imblaz'd, Par Lost 1.538
At top whereof, but farr more rich appeerd Par Lost 3.504
Of some rich Burgher, whose substantial dores, Par Lost 4.189
Groves whose rich Trees wept odorous Gumms and Balme, Par Lost 4.248
Crocus, and Hyacinth with rich inlay Par Lost 4.701
On Princes, when thir rich Retinue long Par Lost 5.355
First wheeld thir course; Earth in her rich attire Par Lost 7.501
Beyond *Petsora* Eastward, to the rich Par Lost 10.292
Rich *Mexico* the seat of *Motezume*, Par Lost 11.407
Fame in the World, high titles, and rich prey, Par Lost 11.793
Tall stripling youths rich clad, of fairer hew Par Reg 2.352
Some rich *Philistian* Matron she may seem, Samson 722
That like to rich, and various gemms inlay Mask 22
Rose like a steam of rich distill'd Perfumes, Mask 556
Bridgewater ms 'the softe steame of'
Trinity ms 'rich' ←'slow' ←'the softe steame of'
That in the channell strayes, Mask 895
Trinity ms 'in the channell straies' ←'my rich wheeles inlayes'
This rich Marble doth enterr Winchester 1
Then dwell in Tents, *and rich abode* Psalm 84, 39
Not thy Conversion, but those rich demaines Prose 1, 2

Richer
And *Cusco* in *Peru*, the richer seat Par Lost 11.408

Riches
The riches of Heav'ns pavement, trod'n Gold, Par Lost 1.682
That riches grow in Hell; that soyle may best Par Lost 1.691

Riches(*cont*)
And all the riches of this World enjoydst, Par Lost 12.580
Get Riches first, get Wealth, and Treasure heap, Par Reg 2.427
Riches are mine, Fortune is in my hand; Par Reg 2.429
Riches though offer'd from the hand of Kings. Par Reg 2.449
Extol not Riches then, the toyl of Fools, Par Reg 2.453
Riches and Realms; yet not for that a Crown, Par Reg 2.458
Riches are needless then, both for themselves, Par Reg 2.484
But vertue joyn'd with riches and long life, Par Reg 4.298
Not more; for Honours, Riches, Kingdoms, Glory Par Reg 4.536
Not half his riches known, and yet despis'd, Mask 724
Richest
Or where the gorgeous East with richest hand Par Lost 2.3
Of richest texture spred, at th' upper end Par Lost 10.446
To live the poorest in my Tribe, then richest, Samson 1479
But cull those richest Robes, and gay'st attire Vacation 21
That was the Casket of Heav'ns richest store, Passion 44
Richly
A Beavie of fair Women, richly gay Par Lost 11.582
A Table richly spred, in regal mode, Par Reg 2.340
And storied Windows richly dight, Penseroso 159
Rid
Armd with thy might, rid Heav'n of these rebell'd, Par Lost 6.737
Better at home lie bed-rid, not only idle, Samson 579
My speediest friend, by death to rid me hence, Samson 1263
Riddance
Ask riddance, if we mean to tread with ease; Par Lost 4.632
Riddle
Her riddle, and him, who solv'd it not, devour'd; Par Reg 4.573
Much like thy riddle, *Samson*, in one day Samson 1016
That solv'd the riddle which I had propos'd. Samson 1200
Riddling
Sam. Be less abstruse, my riddling days are past. Samson 1064
Ride
Wont ride in arm'd, and at the Soldans chair Par Lost 1.764
Rend up both Rocks and Hills, and ride the Air Par Lost 2.540
Ride on thy wings, and thou with thy Compeers, Par Lost 4.974
I send along, ride forth, and bid the Deep Par Lost 7.166
Toild out my uncouth passage, forc't to ride Par Lost 10.475
On which the *Tartar* King did ride; Penseroso 115
And ride us with a classic Hierarchy Forcers 7
Riders
Prauncing their riders bore, the flower and choice Par Reg 3.314
Of Gymnic Artists, Wrestlers, Riders, Runners, Samson 1324
Rides
In spring time, when the Sun with *Taurus* rides, Par Lost 1.769
As in a cloudy Chair ascending rides Par Lost 2.930
For evil news rides post, while good news baits. Samson 1538
Ridest
Wherin thou rid'st with *Hecat'*, and befriend Mask 135
Trinity ms 'ridst'
Ridge
Whose snowie ridge the roving *Tartar* bounds, Par Lost 3.432
Part rise in crystal Wall, or ridge direct, Par Lost 7.293
Pontifical, a ridge of pendent Rock Par Lost 10.313
Shall dwell to *Senir*, that long ridge of Hills. Par Lost 12.146
To equal length back'd with a ridge of hills Par Reg 4.29
Were bristles rang'd like those that ridge the back Samson 1137
Ridges
The ridges of grim Warr; no thought of flight, Par Lost 6.236
Ridiculous
Ridiculous, and the work Confusion nam'd. Par Lost 12.62
Thir Gods ridiculous, and themselves past shame. Par Reg 4.342
Made Arms ridiculous, useless the forgery Samson 131
Then turn'd me out ridiculous, despoil'd, Samson 539
Besides, how vile, contemptible, ridiculous, Samson 1361
Useless, and thence ridiculous about him. Samson 1501
Riding
In secret, riding through the Air she comes Par Lost 2.663
Riding neer her highest noon, Penseroso 68
Rife
Space may produce new Worlds; whereof so rife Par Lost 1.650
So rife and celebrated in the mouths Samson 866
Was rife, and perfet in my list'ning ear, Mask 203
line not in Bridgewater ms
Rifled
Rifl'd the bowels of thir mother Earth Par Lost 1.687
Rift
From many a horrid rift abortive pour'd Par Reg 4.411
Rifted
Rifted the Air clamouring thir god with praise, Samson 1621
And rifted Rocks whose entrance leads to hell, Mask 518
Rigged
Gloriously rigg'd; and for a word, a tear, Samson 200
Built in th' eclipse, and rigg'd with curses dark, Lycidas 101
Right
By right of Warr, what e're his business be Par Lost 1.150
What shall be right: fardest from him is best Par Lost 1.247
His Temple right against the Temple of God Par Lost 1.402
Azazel as his right, a Cherube tall: Par Lost 1.534
Mee though just right, and the fixt Laws of Heav'n Par Lost 2.18
Our own right lost: him to unthrone we then Par Lost 2.231
All he could have; I made him just and right, Par Lost 3.98
Not mee. They therefore as to right belongd, Par Lost 3.111
Of all things made, and judgest onely right. Par Lost 3.155
Down right into the Worlds first Region throws Par Lost 3.562
Any, but God alone, to value right Par Lost 4.202
And Head, what thou hast said is just and right. Par Lost 4.443

Right(*cont*)
Slowly descended, and with right aspect Par Lost 4.541
By thy example, but have power and right Par Lost 4.881
In battel, what our Power is, or our right. Par Lost 5.728
To know ye right, or if ye know your selves Par Lost 5.789
Who can in reason then or right assume Par Lost 5.794
Monarchie over such as live by right Par Lost 5.795
That to his only Son by right endu'd Par Lost 5.815
Right reason for thir Law, and for thir King Par Lost 6.42
Messiah, who by right of merit Reigns. Par Lost 6.43
Enjoyment of our right as Gods; yet hard Par Lost 6.452
And stumbl'd many, who receives them right, Par Lost 6.624
By Sacred Unction, thy deserved right. Par Lost 6.709
Hee on his impious Foes right onward drove, Par Lost 6.831
Imports not, if thou reck'n right, the rest Par Lost 8.71
Then self esteem, grounded on just and right Par Lost 8.572
Reason, is free, and Reason he made right, Par Lost 9.352
What thou commandst, and right thou shouldst be obeyd: Par Lost 9.570
And gaze, and worship thee of right declar'd Par Lost 9.611
Of Preface brooking through his Zeal of Right. Par Lost 9.676
Of right, that I may mitigate thir doom Par Lost 10.76
All yours, right down to Paradise descend; Par Lost 10.398
For in possession such, not onely of right, Par Lost 10.461
Concurd not to my being, it were but right Par Lost 10.747
In wise deport, spake much of Right and Wrong, Par Lost 11.666
With some regard to what is just and right Par Lost 12.16
Dominion absolute; that right we hold Par Lost 12.68
Is lost, which alwayes with right Reason dwells Par Lost 12.84
Barr'd of his right; yet at his Birth a Starr Par Lost 12.360
Hast thou not right to all Created things, Par Reg 2.324
Owe not all Creatures by just right to thee Par Reg 2.325
Said'st thou not that to all things I had right? Par Reg 2.379
And who withholds my pow'r that right to use? Par Reg 2.380
That which to God alone of right belongs; Par Reg 3.141
By Mothers side thy Father, though thy right Par Reg 3.154
Thy right by sitting still or thus retiring? Par Reg 3.164
Is given, and by that right I give it thee. Par Reg 4.104
And hath full right to exempt Samson 310
Nor from that right to part an hour, Samson 1056
If she be right invok't in warbled Song, Mask 854
And in thy right hand lead with thee, Allegro 35
Right against the Eastern gate, Allegro 59
Ease was his chief disease, and to judge right, Another 21
line not in 1658 text
Till Truth, and Right from Violence be freed, Sonnet 15, 11
1694 'injur'd Truth'
Therfore on thy firme hand religion leanes Sonnet 17, 13
Trinity ms 'firme' ←'right'
1694 'Right'
Right onward. What supports me dost thou ask? Sonnet 22, 9
Trinity ms 'Right onward' ←'Vphillward'
Set thy wayes right before, where my step goes. Psalm 5, 24
Will surround thee, seeking right, Psalm 7, 26
Visit this Vine, which thy right hand Psalm 80, 61
Upon the man of thy right hand Psalm 80, 69
How long will ye pervert the right Psalm 82, 5
For thou art he who shalt by right Psalm 82, 27
By right now shall we seize Psalm 83, 46
Whose waies are just and right. Psalm 84, 44
Teach me O Lord thy way *most right*, Psalm 86, 37
Right
His red right hand to plague us? what if all Par Lost 2.174
He scours the right hand coast, som times the left, Par Lost 2.633
At thy right hand voluptuous, as beseems Par Lost 2.869
Beatitude past utterance; on his right Par Lost 3.62
Thee from my bosom and right hand, to save, Par Lost 3.279
At my right hand; your Head I him appoint; Par Lost 5.606
Our puissance is our own, our own right hand Par Lost 5.864
Of this right hand provok't, since first that tongue Par Lost 6.154
All his right side; then *Satan* first knew pain, Par Lost 6.327
Vanguard, to Right and Left the Front unfould; Par Lost 6.558
Had ended; when to Right and Left the Front Par Lost 6.569
From the right hand of Glorie where he sate, Par Lost 6.747
Ascended, at his right hand Victorie Par Lost 6.762
Among them he arriv'd; in his right hand Par Lost 6.835
Where now he sits at the right hand of bliss. Par Lost 6.892
Toward the right hand his Glorie, on the Son Par Lost 10.64
His Seat at Gods right hand, exalted high Par Lost 12.457
Right-borne
where grows the right-borne gold upon his native tree Mask Tr. ms 27.08
Righteous
His righteous Altar, bowing lowly down Par Lost 1.434
Thir own both righteous and unrighteous deeds, Par Lost 3.292
Accepted, fearless in his righteous Cause, Par Lost 6.804
With righteous plea, thir utmost vigilance, Par Lost 10.30
Righteous are thy Decrees on all thy Works; Par Lost 10.644
The onely righteous in a World perverse, Par Lost 11.701
All righteous things: therefore above my years, Par Reg 1.206
Of righteous *Job*, then cruelly to afflict him Par Reg 1.425
1671 'irghteous' in some copies
The righteous and all such as honour Truth; Samson 1276
To walk my *righteous* waies. Psalm 81, 56
Righteousness
Just confidence, and native righteousness Par Lost 9.1056
Opprobrious, with his Robe of righteousness, Par Lost 10.222
Rescu'd, had in his Righteousness bin lost? Par Lost 11.682
The paths of righteousness, how much more safe, Par Lost 11.814
Just for unjust, that in such righteousness Par Lost 12.294

Righteousness*(cont)*
Founded in righteousness and peace and love Par Lost 12.550
1669 'Righteousness'
God of my righteousness Psalm 4, 2
Of righteousness and in Jehovah trust. Psalm 4, 24
Lord lead me in thy righteousness Psalm 5, 21
According to my righteousness Psalm 7, 32
Sweet Peace and Righteousness have kiss'd Psalm 85, 43
Before him Righteousness shall go Psalm 85, 53
Rightful
Confess him rightful King? unjust thou saist Par Lost 5.818
For we by rightfull doom remediles Circum 17
1673 'rightful'
Rightlier
Destroyers rightlier call'd and Plagues of men. Par Lost 11.697
Each of his reign allotted, rightlier call'd, Par Reg 2.123
Rightliest
The time and means: each act is rightliest done, Par Reg 4.475
Rightly
If rightly thou art call'd, whose Voice divine Par Lost 7.2
Which thou hast rightly nam'd, but of thy self, Par Lost 8.439
Eve rightly call'd, Mother of all Mankind, Par Lost 11.159
Never to hurt them more who rightly trust Par Lost 12.418
Where I may sit and rightly spell, Penseroso 170
May rightly answer that melodious noise; Musick 18
Trinity ms 'may rightly' ←'rightly to'
Rigid
The rigid satisfaction, death for death. Par Lost 3.212
Of rigid Spears, and Helmets throng'd, and Shields Par Lost 6.83
The rigid interdiction, which resounds Par Lost 8.334
Those rigid threats of Death; ye shall not Die: Par Lost 9.685
That rigid score. A worse thing yet remains, Samson 433
But rigid looks of Chast austerity, Mask 450
Rigor
Bound with *Gorgonian* rigor not to move, Par Lost 10.297
Rigorous
Then who self-rigorous chooses death as due; Samson 513
Rigorously
At the sad Sentence rigorously urg'd, Par Lost 11.109
Rigour
In punisht man, to satisfie his rigour Par Lost 10.803
By rigour unconniving, but that oft Par Reg 1.363
Rigor now is gon to bed, Mask 107
Rill
Rose a fresh Fountain, and with many a rill Par Lost 4.229
Fed the same flock, by fountain, shade, and rill. Lycidas 24
Rills
Of leaves and fuming rills, *Aurora*'s fan, Par Lost 5.6
From a thousand petty rills, Mask 926
Thus sang the uncouth Swain to th' Okes and rills, Lycidas 186
And make soft rills from fiery flint-stones gush. Psalm 114, 18
Rimmon
Him follow'd *Rimmon*, whose delightful Seat Par Lost 1.467
ms 'Rimmon'
Rind
With fixed Anchor in his skaly rind Par Lost 1.206
ms 'rinde'
Others whose fruit burnisht with Golden Rinde Par Lost 4.249
The savourie pulp they chew, and in the rinde Par Lost 4.335
Rough, or smooth rin'd, or bearded husk, or shell Par Lost 5.342
Withall thy charms, although this corporal rinde Mask 664
Bridgewater ms 'rind'
1637 'rind'
Trinity ms 'rind'
& fruits of golden rind, on whose faire tree Mask Tr. ms 10.08
Rined
Rough, or smooth rin'd, or bearded husk, or shell Par Lost 5.342
Ring
When the merry Bells ring round, Allegro 93
And hears the Muses in a ring, Penseroso 47
That own'd the vertuous Ring and Glass, Penseroso 113
Ring out ye Crystall sphears, Nativity 125
In vain with Cymbals ring, Nativity 208
Wherwith the stage of Ayr and Earth did ring, Passion 2
Loud acclamations ring. Psalm 81, 4
Ringlets
Dissheveld, but in wanton ringlets wav'd Par Lost 4.306
With Ringlets quaint, and wanton windings wove. Arcades 47
Trinity ms 'ringlets'
Rings
Attest thir joy, that hill and valley rings. Par Lost 2.495
I heard all as I came, the City rings Samson 1449
Ere the first Cock his Mattin rings. Allegro 114
Fairfax, whose name in armes through Europe rings Sonnet 15, 1
Of which all Europe talks from side to side. Sonnet 22, 12
1694 '*Europe* rings'
Riot
Of riot ascends above thir loftiest Towrs, Par Lost 1.499
To his bold Riot: dreadful was the din Par Lost 10.521
To luxurie and riot, feast and dance, Par Lost 11.715
Of Riot, and ill manag'd Merriment, Mask 172
Bridgewater ms 'riott'
Trinity ms 'riot'
Riotous
As if she would her children should be riotous Mask 763
Ripe
Of *Ceres* ripe for harvest waving bends Par Lost 4.981
All seasons, ripe for use hangs on the stalk; Par Lost 5.323

Ripe*(cont)*
So maist thou live, till like ripe Fruit thou drop Par Lost 11.535
When this worlds disolution shall be ripe, Par Lost 12.459
Thy years are ripe, and over-ripe, the Son Par Reg 3.31
Yet years, and to ripe years judgment mature, Par Reg 3.37
Who ripe, and frolick of his full grown age, Mask 59
Plucking ripe clusters from the tender shoots, Mask 296
Ripened
Had ripen'd thy just soul to dwell with God, Sonnet 14, 2
Trinity ms 'rip'nd' ←'rip'n'd'
Ripeness
And inward ripenes doth much less appear, Sonnet 7, 7
Trinity ms 'ripenesse'
Rise
Ten thousand Banners rise into the Air Par Lost 1.545
By force, and at our heels all Hell should rise Par Lost 2.135
To found this nether Empire, which might rise Par Lost 2.296
But I shall rise Victorious, and subdue Par Lost 3.250
And dying rise, and rising with him raise Par Lost 3.296
Ministring light prepar'd, they set and rise; Par Lost 4.664
And let us to our fresh imployments rise Par Lost 5.125
Ye Mists and Exhalations that now rise Par Lost 5.185
In honour to the Worlds great Author rise, Par Lost 5.188
And to his message high in honour rise; Par Lost 5.289
Oreshades; for these mid-hours, till Eevning rise Par Lost 5.376
Against th' Omnipotent to rise in Arms; Par Lost 6.136
To flight, or if to fall, but that they rise Par Lost 6.285
Part rise in crystal Wall, or ridge direct, Par Lost 7.293
Rise on the Earth, or Earth rise on the Sun, Par Lost 8.161
And said, thy Mansion wants thee, *Adam*, rise, Par Lost 8.296
Began to rise, high Passions, Anger, Hate, Par Lost 9.1123
Methinks I feel new strength within me rise, Par Lost 10.243
New Heav'n and Earth shall to the Ages rise, Par Lost 10.647
But rise, let us no more contend, nor blame Par Lost 10.958
Beyond all bounds, till inundation rise Par Lost 11.828
Under paternal rule; till one shall rise Par Lost 12.24
Of *David* (so I name this King) shall rise Par Lost 12.326
Returne, the Starres of Morn shall see him rise Par Lost 12.422
So spake our Morning Star then in his rise, Par Reg 1.294
And by the Angel was bid rise and eat, Par Reg 2.274
Will not dare mention, lest a question rise Samson 1254
Rise therefore with all speed and come along, Samson 1316
And as the gates I enter'd with Sun-rise, Samson 1597
Rise, rise, and heave thy rosie head Mask 885
Till the dappled dawn doth rise; Allegro 44
When Eev'ning gray doth rise, I fetch my round Arcades 54
To rise above the watry plain. Psalm 136, 22
Of Attick tast, with Wine, whence we may rise Sonnet 20, 10
That in arms against me rise Psalm 3, 3
Rise Lord, save me my God for thou Psalm 3, 19
Rise Jehovah in thine ire Psalm 7, 19
That now so proudly rise, Psalm 81, 58
Rise God, judge thou the earth *in might*, Psalm 82, 25
O God the proud against me rise Psalm 86, 49
There to thy Sons another *Troy* shall rise, Prose 12, 12
Risen
Had ris'n or heav'd his head, but that the will Par Lost 1.211
ms 'risen'
Of Glory obscur'd: As when the Sun new ris'n Par Lost 1.594
Ris'n, and with hideous outcry rush'd between. Par Lost 2.726
With first approach of light, we must be ris'n, Par Lost 4.624
Of day-spring, and the Sun, who scarce up risen Par Lost 5.139
Ris'n on mid-noon; som great behest from Heav'n Par Lost 5.311
Now ris'n, to work them furder woe or shame; Par Lost 10.555
What thoughts in my unquiet brest are ris'n, Par Lost 10.975
Ris'n from a River o're the marish glides, Par Lost 12.630
Is ris'n to invade us, who no less Par Reg 2.127
Rises
Forthwith a hideous gabble rises loud Par Lost 12.56
Co. Due west it rises from this shrubby point. Mask 306
Rising
Celestial vertues rising, will appear Par Lost 2.15
Aspect he rose, and in his rising seem'd Par Lost 2.301
Thir rising all at once was as the sound Par Lost 2.476
The rising world of waters dark and deep, Par Lost 3.11
And dying rise, and rising with him raise Par Lost 3.296
Which now the Rising Sun guilds with his beams. Par Lost 3.551
Strait couches close, then rising changes oft Par Lost 4.405
Rising in clouded Majestie, at length Par Lost 4.607
Sweet is the breath of morn, her rising sweet, Par Lost 4.641
With charm of earliest Birds, nor rising Sun Par Lost 4.651
Rising or falling still advance his praise. Par Lost 5.191
Rebellion rising, saw in whom, how spred Par Lost 5.715
Is rising, who intends to erect his Throne Par Lost 5.725
His Generation, and the rising Birth Par Lost 7.102
The Dank, and rising on stiff Pennons, towre Par Lost 7.441
Rising, the crumbl'd Earth above them threw Par Lost 7.468
Satan involv'd in rising Mist, then sought Par Lost 9.75
Circular base of rising foulds, that tour'd Par Lost 9.498
False in our promis'd Rising; since our Eyes Par Lost 9.1070
Prince of the Aire; then rising from his Grave Par Lost 10.185
Which of them rising with the Sun, or falling, Par Lost 10.663
Of middle Age one rising, eminent Par Lost 11.665
The Prophet do him reverence, on him rising Par Reg 1.80
That to the fall and rising he should be Par Reg 2.88
Know'st thou not that my rising is thy fall, Par Reg 3.201
Oft on a Plat of rising ground, Penseroso 73

Rites
His holy Rites, and solemn Feasts profan'd, Par Lost 1.390
ms 'rites'
To do him wanton rites, which cost them woe. Par Lost 1.414
This said unanimous, and other Rites Par Lost 4.736
Adam from his fair Spouse, nor *Eve* the Rites Par Lost 4.742
With Ministeries due and solemn Rites: Par Lost 7.149
Of nuptial Sanctitie and marriage Rites: Par Lost 8.487
From Loves due Rites, Nuptial imbraces sweet, Par Lost 10.994
On the cleft Wood, and all due Rites perform'd. Par Lost 11.440
Hymen, then first to marriage Rites invok't; Par Lost 11.591
To civil Justice, part religious Rites Par Lost 12.231
Of great *Messiah* shall sing. Thus Laws and Rites Par Lost 12.244
Well deem in outward Rites and specious formes Par Lost 12.534
1669 'Rights' in some copies
Our Law forbids at thir Religious Rites Samson 1320
Present in Temples at Idolatrous Rites Samson 1378
Com let us our rights begin, Mask 125
Doing abhorred rites to *Hecate* Mask 535

Rivals
His Rivals, winning cheap the high repute Par Lost 2.472
1667 'rivals'
And Rivals? In this other was there found Samson 387

Riven
Sore toild, his riv'n Armes to havoc hewn, Par Lost 6.449

River
Lethe the River of Oblivion roules Par Lost 2.583
And where the river of Bliss through midst of Heavn Par Lost 3.358
Southward through *Eden* went a River large, Par Lost 4.223
Girt with the River *Triton*, where old *Cham*, Par Lost 4.276
The River Horse and scalie Crocodile. Par Lost 7.474
In with the River sunk, and with it rose Par Lost 9.74
Maeotis, up beyond the River *Ob;* Par Lost 9.78
Nigh Rivers mouth or Foreland, where the Wind Par Lost 9.514
Down the great River to the op'ning Gulf, Par Lost 11.833
Egypt, divided by the River *Nile;* Par Lost 12.157
Ris'n from a River o're the marish glides, Par Lost 12.630
Divided by a river, of whose banks Par Reg 4.32
Made Goddess of the River; still she retains Mask 842
1637 'river'
Trinity ms 'river'
the jealous ocean that old river winds Mask Tr. ms 10.12
And *upward* to that river *wide* Psalm 80, 47

River-dragon
The River-dragon tam'd at length submits Par Lost 12.191

Rivers
Rivers or Mountains in her spotty Globe. Par Lost 1.291
Of four infernal Rivers that disgorge Par Lost 2.575
Breathe forth *Elixir* pure, and Rivers run Par Lost 3.607
Like gentle breaths from Rivers pure, thence raise Par Lost 4.806
All but within those banks, where Rivers now Par Lost 7.305
With borders long the Rivers. That Earth now Par Lost 7.328
Others on Silver Lakes and Rivers Bath'd Par Lost 7.437
Ye Hills and Dales, ye Rivers, Woods, and Plaines, Par Lost 8.275
Of Hill, and Vallie, Rivers, Woods and Plaines, Par Lost 9.116
To blood unshed the Rivers must be turnd, Par Lost 12.176
Lay pleasant; from his side two rivers flow'd, Par Reg 3.255
Fair Champain with less rivers interveind, Par Reg 3.257
With bridges rivers proud, as with a yoke; Par Reg 3.334
Shallow Brooks, and Rivers wide. Allegro 76
Rivers arise; whether thou be the Son, Vacation 91

Rivulet
By Fountain or by shadie Rivulet Par Lost 9.420

Road
In progress through the rode of Heav'n Star-pav'd. Par Lost 4.976
Through all th' Empyreal road; till at the Gate Par Lost 5.253
His Longitude through Heav'ns high rode: the gray Par Lost 7.373
A broad and ample rode, whose dust is Gold Par Lost 7.577
Hee from the East his flaming rode begin, Par Lost 8.162
Descend through Darkness, on your Rode with ease Par Lost 10.394
Was bid turn Reines from th' Equinoctial Rode Par Lost 10.672
So far from path or road of men, who pass Par Reg 1.322
In various habits on the *Appian* road, Par Reg 4.68
See how from far upon the Eastern rode Nativity 22

Roam
Here Pilgrims roam, that stray'd so farr to seek Par Lost 3.476
Through wood, through waste, o're hill, o're dale his roam. Par Lost 4.538
And now wild Beasts came forth the woods to roam. Par Reg 1.502

Roamed
And ore the *Celtic* roam'd the utmost Isles. Par Lost 1.521
Ganges and *Indus:* thus the Orb he roam'd Par Lost 9.82

Roaming
Roaming to seek thir prey on earth, durst fix Par Lost 1.382
False titl'd Sons of God, roaming the Earth Par Reg 2.179

Roar
Covers his Throne; from whence deep thunders roar Par Lost 2.267
From those deep throated Engins belcht, whose roar Par Lost 6.586
The brazen Throat of Warr had ceast to roar, Par Lost 11.713
Who with her radiant finger still'd the roar Par Reg 4.428
Over whose heads they rore, and seem to point, Par Reg 4.463
Well knows to still the wilde winds when they roar, Mask 87
1637 'roare'
Bridgewater ms 'roare'
Trinity ms 'roare'
The wonted roar was up amidst the Woods, Mask 549
1637 'roare'
Bridgewater ms 'roare'
Trinity ms 'roare'

Roar(*cont*)
Swinging slow with sullen roar; Penseroso 76
When by the rout that made the hideous roar, Lycidas 61
Trinity ms 'roare'
1638 'rore'
Devouring war shall never cease to roare: Vacation 86

Roared
Nine dayes they fell; confounded *Chaos* roard, Par Lost 6.871

Rob
But rob and spoil, burn, slaughter, and enslave Par Reg 3.75
For who would rob a Hermit of his Weeds, Mask 390
Bridgewater ms 'robb'

Robbed
And in sweet madnes rob'd it of it self, Mask 261

Robber
A Murtherer, a Revolter, and a Robber. Samson 1180
Then like a Robber stripdst them of thir robes? Samson 1188
Som roaving Robber calling to his fellows. Mask 485
Trinity ms 'robber' ←'hedge man' ←'curl'd man of the swoord'
Bridgewater ms 'robber'
1637 'robber'

Robe
With conquest, felt th' envenom'd robe, and tore Par Lost 2.543
To guiltie shame hee cover'd, but his Robe Par Lost 9.1058
Opprobrious, with his Robe of righteousness, Par Lost 10.222
In Saffron robe, with Taper clear, Allegro 126
All in a robe of darkest grain, Penseroso 33

Robed
Rob'd in flames, and Amber light, Allegro 61
1673 'Roab'd'
Or that crown'd Matron sage white-robed truth? Fair Inf 54

Robes
Hasting or on return, in robes of State; Par Reg 4.64
Then like a Robber stripdst them of thir robes? Samson 1188
These my skie robes spun out of *Iris* Wooff, Mask 83
Bridgewater ms 'skye webs'
But cull those richest Robes, and gay'st attire Vacation 21

Robustious
Robustious to no purpose clustring down, Samson 569

Rock
While smooth *Adonis* from his native Rock Par Lost 1.450
ms 'rock'
Each on his rock transfixt, the sport and prey Par Lost 2.181
Three Iron, three of Adamantine Rock, Par Lost 2.646
Of massie Iron or sollid Rock with ease Par Lost 2.878
By *Nilus* head, enclosd with shining Rock, Par Lost 4.283
Leveld his eevning Rayes: it was a Rock Par Lost 4.543
Though huge, and in a Rock of Diamond Armd, Par Lost 6.364
Soft-ebbing; nor withstood them Rock or Hill, Par Lost 7.300
Pontifical, a ridge of pendent Rock Par Lost 10.313
Not this Rock onely; his Omnipresence fills Par Lost 11.336
Sight so deform what heart of Rock could long Par Lost 11.494
Or surging waves against a solid rock, Par Reg 4.18
On the *Tarpeian* rock, her Cittadel Par Reg 4.49
Proof against all temptation as a rock Par Reg 4.533
Safe to the rock of *Etham* was retir'd, Samson 253
Though thou wert firmlier fastn'd then a rock. Samson 1398
Mine eye hath found that sad Sepulchral rock Passion 43
And satisfie them from the rock Psalm 81, 67

Rocking
While rocking Winds are Piping loud, Penseroso 126

Rocks
Th' Assembly, as when hollow Rocks retain Par Lost 2.285
Rend up both Rocks and Hills, and ride the Air Par Lost 2.540
Rocks, Caves, Lakes, Fens, Bogs, Dens, and shades of death, Par Lost 2.621
Through *Bosporus* betwixt the justling Rocks: Par Lost 2.1018
From Diamond Quarries hew'n, and Rocks of Gold, Par Lost 5.759
Though standing else as Rocks, but down they fell Par Lost 6.593
Rocks, Waters, Woods, and by the shaggie tops Par Lost 6.645
In *Rhodope*, where Woods and Rocks had Eares Par Lost 7.35
Moist nutriment, or under Rocks thir food Par Lost 7.408
Rocks, Dens, and Caves; but I in none of these Par Lost 9.118
And now the tops of Hills as Rocks appeer; Par Lost 11.852
And with dark shades and rocks environ'd round, Par Reg 1.194
Rocks whereon greatest men have oftest wreck'd; Par Reg 2.228
And rifted Rocks whose entrance leads to hell, Mask 518
1637 'rocks'
Bridgewater ms 'rocks'
Trinity ms 'rocks'
Wherwith she sits on diamond rocks Mask 881
There under *Ebon* shades, and low-brow'd Rocks, Allegro 8
That glassy flouds from rugged rocks can crush, Psalm 114, 17
Mother with Infant down the Rocks. Their moans Sonnet 18, 8

Rocky
Betwixt these rockie Pillars *Gabriel* sat Par Lost 4.549
He hasted, and oppos'd the rockie Orb Par Lost 6.254
Or Rockie *Avon*, or of Sedgie *Lee*, Vacation 97
As in a rocky Cell Psalm 4, 41

Rod
Innumerable. As when the potent Rod Par Lost 1.338
ms 'rod'
Is now an Iron Rod to bruise and breake Par Lost 5.887
Of *Hermes*, or his opiate Rod. Mean while Par Lost 11.133
Aw'd by the rod of *Moses* so to stand Par Lost 12.198
Moses once more his potent Rod extends Par Lost 12.211
Over the Sea; the Sea his Rod obeys; Par Lost 12.212
With touch aetherial of Heav'ns fiery rod Samson 549

Rod(*cont*)
And bound him fast; without his rod revers't, — Mask 816
Trinity ms 'rod' ←'art'
But as Faith pointed with her golden rod, — Sonnet 14, 7

Rode
The starrie Host, rode brightest, till the Moon — Par Lost 4.606
Hee on the wings of Cherub rode sublime — Par Lost 6.771
O're Shields and Helmes, and helmed heads he rode — Par Lost 6.840
Worthiest to Reign: he celebrated rode — Par Lost 6.888
Uplifted, in Paternal Glorie rode — Par Lost 7.219
Answering his great Idea. Up he rode — Par Lost 7.557
The space of seven continu'd Nights he rode — Par Lost 9.63
Rode tilting o're the Waves, all dwellings else — Par Lost 11.747
Rode up to Heaven, yet once again to come. — Par Reg 2.17
The *Pontic* King and in triumph had rode. — Par Reg 3.36
Rode up in flames after his message told — Samson 1433

Rods
Lictors and rods the ensigns of thir power, — Par Reg 4.65

Roll
Revisit'st not these eyes, that rowle in vain — Par Lost 3.23
Reignd where these Heav'ns now rowl, where Earth now rests — Par Lost 5.578
To darken all the Hill, and smoak to rowl — Par Lost 6.57
And all her numberd Starrs, that seem to rowle — Par Lost 8.19
Sea, Aire, and Shoar, the Thunder when to rowle — Par Lost 10.666
To dress, and troule the Tongue, and roule the Eye. — Par Lost 11.620
He in whose hand all times and seasons roul. — Par Reg 3.187
Sam. Of such examples adde mee to the roul, — Samson 290
To roule with pleasure in a sensual stie. — Mask 77
Bridgewater ms 'rowle'
May thy billows rowl ashoar — Mask 932
Trinity ms 'roule'
1637 'rowle'
Bridgewater ms 'rowle'
his goarie scalpe rowle downe the Thracian lee — Lycidas Tr. ms 29.61
My life down to the earth and roul — Psalm 7, 15

Rolled
Drivn backward slope thir pointing spires, and rowld — Par Lost 1.223
That rowld orbicular, and turnd to Starrs — Par Lost 3.718
Incredible how swift, had thither rowl'd — Par Lost 4.593
By thousands, Angel on Arch-Angel rowl'd; — Par Lost 6.594
And from about him fierce Effusion rowld — Par Lost 6.765
Of his fierce Chariot rowld, as with the sound — Par Lost 6.829
Rowld inward, and a spacious Gap disclos'd — Par Lost 6.861
Her mural breach, returning whence it rowld. — Par Lost 6.879
Now Heav'n in all her Glorie shon, and rowld — Par Lost 7.499
In Labyrinth of many a round self-rowld, — Par Lost 9.183
Lead then, said *Eve*. Hee leading swiftly rowld — Par Lost 9.631
But on thy rould in heaps, and up the Trees — Par Lost 10.558
Deep under water rould; Sea cover'd Sea, — Par Lost 11.749
Slayn by the bloody *Piemontese* that roll'd — Sonnet 18, 7
At Endor quite cut off, and rowl'd — Psalm 83, 39
When I dye, let the earth be roul'd in flames. — Prose 5, 1

Rolling
Lay vanquisht, rowling in the fiery Gulfe — Par Lost 1.52
Cherube and Seraph rowling in the Flood — Par Lost 1.324
Belch'd fire and rowling smoak; the rest entire — Par Lost 1.671
And towards the Gate rouling her bestial train, — Par Lost 2.873
Now rowling, boiles in his tumultuous brest, — Par Lost 4.16
Rowling on Orient Pearl and sands of Gold, — Par Lost 4.238
Wave rowling after Wave, where way they found, — Par Lost 7.298
Rowling in dust and gore. To which our Sire. — Par Lost 11.460
Rowling in brutish vices, and deform'd, — Par Reg 3.86
when the big rowling flakes of pitchie clowds — Mask Tr. ms 15.52
'rowling' ←'wallowing'
when the bigg rowling flakes of pitchie clouds — Mask Br. ms 345
Walk'st on the rowling Sphear, and through the deep, — Prose 12, 2

Rolls
Lethe the River of Oblivion roules — Par Lost 2.583
Rowls o're *Elisian* Flours her Amber stream; — Par Lost 3.359
And wheel on th' Earth, devouring where it rouls; — Par Lost 12.183
To studious musing; there *Ilissus* rouls — Par Reg 4.249

Roman
To rescue *Israel* from the *Roman* yoke, — Par Reg 1.217
Reduc't a Province under Roman yoke, — Par Reg 3.158
Roman and *Parthian?* therefore one of these — Par Reg 3.362
Maugre the *Roman:* it shall be my task — Par Reg 3.368

Romance
In Fable or *Romance* of *Uthers* Son — Par Lost 1.580
ms 'Romance'

Romances
Besieg'd *Albracca*, as Romances tell; — Par Reg 3.339

Rome
Scipio the highth of *Rome*. With tract oblique — Par Lost 9.510
In *Athens* or free *Rome*, where Eloquence — Par Lost 9.671
On *Europe* thence, and where *Rome* was to sway — Par Lost 11.405
Shalt raign, and *Rome* or *Caesar* not need fear. — Par Reg 3.385
Then great and glorious *Rome*, Queen of the Earth — Par Reg 4.45
All Nations now to *Rome* obedience pay, — Par Reg 4.80
To *Rome*'s great Emperour, whose wide domain — Par Reg 4.81
Old, and lascivious, and from *Rome* retir'd — Par Reg 4.91
Then all the Oratory of *Greece* and *Rome*. — Par Reg 4.360
The helme of Rome, when gownes not armes repelld — Sonnet 17, 3
1662, 1694 '*Rome*'

Rood
Lay floating many a rood, in bulk as huge — Par Lost 1.196

Roof
The Roof was fretted Gold. Not *Babilon*, — Par Lost 1.717
ms 'roof'

Roof(*cont*)
And level pavement: from the arched roof — Par Lost 1.726
Hell bounds high reaching to the horrid Roof, — Par Lost 2.644
All things to mans delightful use; the roofe — Par Lost 4.692
And on thir naked limbs the flourie roof — Par Lost 4.772
But first from under shadie arborous roof, — Par Lost 5.137
Under whose lowly roof thou hast voutsaf't — Par Lost 5.463
Thick overhead with verdant roof imbowr'd — Par Lost 9.1038
That to the arched roof gave main support. — Samson 1634
The whole roof after them, with burst of thunder — Samson 1651
And love the high embowed Roof, — Penseroso 157
Under the shady roof — Arcades 88
Trinity ms 'fe', ms defective
Runs through the arched roof in words deceiving. — Nativity 175
Wert thou some Starr which from the ruin'd roofe — Fair Inf 43

Roofed
High rooft and walks beneath, and alleys brown — Par Reg 2.293
From Heaven descended to the low-rooft house — Par Reg 4.273
His starry front low-rooft beneath the skies; — Passion 18

Roofs
Outside and inside both, pillars and roofs — Par Reg 4.58

Room
Now less then smallest Dwarfs, in narrow room — Par Lost 1.779
Perhaps our vacant room, though more remov'd, — Par Lost 2.835
By wondrous birth: Be thou in *Adams* room — Par Lost 3.285
In narrow room Natures whole wealth, yea more, — Par Lost 4.207
Into our room of bliss thus high advanc't — Par Lost 4.359
And send forth all her Kings; there will be room, — Par Lost 4.383
Into thir vacant room, and thence diffuse — Par Lost 7.190
Of future, in small room large heart enclos'd, — Par Lost 7.486
For such vast room in Nature unpossest — Par Lost 8.153
Determin'd to advance into our room — Par Lost 9.148
They die; but in thir room, as they forewarne, — Par Lost 12.507
For in the Inn was left no better room: — Par Reg 1.248
The Prospect was, that here and there was room — Par Reg 3.263
Where glowing Embers through the room — Penseroso 79
Had given day her room, — Nativity 78
That to the next I may resign my Roome. — Vacation 58
Come tripping to the Room where thou didst lie; — Vacation 62
Shew'd him his room where he must lodge that night, — Carrier 15

Roosted
Ere morrow wake, or the low roosted lark — Mask 317
1637 'low-roosted'
Trinity ms 'low-roosted'
Bridgewater ms 'rooster'

Roosts
Assailant on the perched roosts, — Samson 1693

Root
Of mankind in one root, and Earth with Hell — Par Lost 2.383
As from a second root shall be restor'd, — Par Lost 3.288
Proportiond to each kind. So from the root — Par Lost 5.479
Not to destroy, but root them out of Heav'n: — Par Lost 6.855
Of prohibition, root of all our woe; — Par Lost 9.645
The bended Twigs take root, and Daughters grow — Par Lost 9.1105
And there take root an Iland salt and bare, — Par Lost 11.834
Of constancy no root infixt, — Samson 1032
Amongst the rest a small unsightly root, — Mask 629
Bridgewater ms 'roote'
And root it deep and fast — Psalm 80, 38

Root-bound
Root-bound, that fled *Apollo*, *La*. Fool do not boast, — Mask 662
1637 'Root bound'
Trinity ms 'root-bound'
Bridgewater ms 'roote bound'

Rooted
Though rooted deep as high, and sturdiest Oaks — Par Reg 4.417

Roots
Through pain up by the roots *Thessalian* Pines, — Par Lost 2.544
Deep to the Roots of Hell the gather'd beach — Par Lost 10.299
Live on tough roots and stubs, to thirst inur'd — Par Reg 1.339
Up turns it by the roots, — Psalm 80, 54

Rose
Rose out of *Chaos:* Or if *Sion* Hill — Par Lost 1.10
With Orient Colours waving: with them rose — Par Lost 1.546
Rose like an Exhalation, with the sound — Par Lost 1.711
To less then Gods. On th' other side up rose — Par Lost 2.108
Aspect he rose, and in his rising seem'd — Par Lost 2.301
None shall partake with me. Thus saying rose — Par Lost 2.466
Forbidding; and at once with him they rose; — Par Lost 2.475
Rose a fresh Fountain, and with many a rill — Par Lost 4.229
Of Heav'n the Starrs that usher Evening rose: — Par Lost 4.355
Still as it rose, impossible to climbe. — Par Lost 4.548
I rose as at thy call, but found thee not; — Par Lost 5.48
The horrid shock: now storming furie rose, — Par Lost 6.207
Up rose the Victor Angels, and to Arms — Par Lost 6.525
Upon confusion rose: and now all Heav'n — Par Lost 6.669
So said, he o're his Scepter bowing, rose — Par Lost 6.746
Rose as in Dance the stately Trees, and spred — Par Lost 7.324
With thir bright Luminaries that Set and Rose, — Par Lost 7.385
Limb'd and full grown: out of the ground up rose — Par Lost 7.456
Among the Trees in Pairs they rose, they walk'd: — Par Lost 7.459
His vastness: Fleec't the Flocks and bleating rose, — Par Lost 7.472
Rose, and went forth among her Fruits and Flours, — Par Lost 8.44
Rose up a Fountain by the Tree of Life; — Par Lost 9.73
In with the River sunk, and with it rose — Par Lost 9.74
Encumberd, now had left them, up they rose — Par Lost 9.1051
Uncover'd more, so rose the *Danite* strong — Par Lost 9.1059
Thus saying, from his radiant Seat he rose — Par Lost 10.85

Rose(*cont*)
His *Zenith*, while the Sun in *Aries* rose: Par Lost 10.329
Meanwhile the Southwind rose, and with black wings Par Lost 11.738
But as I rose out of the laving stream, Par Reg 1.280
At his command; when from amidst them rose Par Reg 2.149
As lightly from his grassy Couch up rose Par Reg 2.282
Feigning to disappear. Darkness now rose, Par Reg 4.397
With *Joves Alcides*, and oft foil'd still rose, Par Reg 4.565
Rose from the hindmost wheels of *Phoebus* wain. Mask 190
line not in Bridgewater ms
And sweeten'd every muskrose of the dale, Mask 496
Bridgewater ms 'muskerose'
Rose like a steam of rich distill'd Perfumes, Mask 556
If you let slip time, like a neglected rose Mask 743
line not in Bridgewater ms
Oft till the Star that rose, at Ev'ning, bright Lycidas 30
1638 'Oft till the ev'n-starre bright'
Trinity ms 'starre that rose' ←'ev'n starre bright'
As killing as the Canker to the Rose, Lycidas 45
Trinity ms 'rose'
1638 'rose'
The Musk-rose, and the well attir'd Woodbine, Lycidas 146
Trinity ms 'muske rose'
1638 'musk-rose'
At last he rose, and twitch'd his Mantle blew: Lycidas 192
The Lillie and Rose, that neither sow'd nor spun. Sonnet 20, 8

Rose
Or sight of vernal bloom, or Summers Rose, Par Lost 3.43
Flours of all hue, and without Thorn the Rose: Par Lost 4.256
With Rose and Odours from the shrub unfum'd. Par Lost 5.349
Flung Rose, flung Odours from the spicie Shrub, Par Lost 8.517

Roseate
In darker veile) and roseat Dews dispos'd Par Lost 5.646

Roses
Impurpl'd with Celestial Roses smil'd. Par Lost 3.364
Iris all hues, Roses, and Gessamin Par Lost 4.698
Showrd Roses, which the Morn repair'd. Sleep on Par Lost 4.773
In yonder Spring of Roses intermixt Par Lost 9.218
Half spi'd, so thick the Roses bushing round Par Lost 9.426
Down drop'd, and all the faded Roses shed: Par Lost 9.893
Beds of *Hyacinth*, and roses Mask 998
B.M. ms 'Roses'
Bridgewater ms 'Roses'
1673 'Roses'
aeternall roses grow & hyacinth Mask Tr. ms 10.07
And fresh-blown Roses washt in dew, Allegro 22
And ye the breathing Roses of the Wood, Arcades 32
Trinity ms 'roses'
Courts thee on Roses in some pleasant Cave, Horace 2

Rosy
Now Morn her rosie steps in th' Eastern Clime Par Lost 5.1
Wak't by the circling Hours, with rosie hand Par Lost 6.3
Celestial rosie red, Loves proper hue, Par Lost 8.619
Her rosie progress smiling; let us forth, Par Lost 11.175
Braid your Locks with rosie Twine Mask 105
Rise, rise, and heave thy rosie head Mask 885

Rosy-bosomed
The Graces, and the rosie-boosom'd Howres, Mask 986
1637 'rosie-bosom'd'
Trinity ms 'rosie-bosom'd'
line not in Bridgewater ms

Rot
His Cattel must of Rot and Murren die, Par Lost 12.179
Rot inwardly, and foul contagion spread: Lycidas 127
So hung his destiny never to rot Another 3

Rottenness
The pillar'd firmament is rott'nness, Mask 598
Trinity ms 'rottennesse'
Bridgewater ms 'rottennesse'
1637 'rottennesse'

Rough
Ore bog or steep, through strait, rough, dense, or rare, Par Lost 2.948
Rough, or smooth rin'd, or bearded husk, or shell Par Lost 5.342
On the rough edge of battel ere it joyn'd, Par Lost 6.108
Hard are the ways of truth, and rough to walk, Par Reg 1.478
Whom certain these rough shades did never breed Mask 266
Rough *Satyrs* danc'd, and *Fauns* with clov'n heel, Lycidas 34
Those rugged names to our like mouths grow sleek Sonnet 11, 10
Trinity ms 'rugged' ←'rough hewn' ←'barbarous'
Rough with black winds and storms Horace 7

Rougher
The bait of honied words; a rougher tongue Samson 1066

Round
Torments him; round he throws his baleful eyes Par Lost 1.56
A Dungeon horrible, on all sides round Par Lost 1.61
Ethereal temper, massy, large and round, Par Lost 1.285
Wav'd round the Coast, up call'd a pitchy cloud Par Lost 1.340
Among the Nations round, and durst abide Par Lost 1.385
From wing to wing, and half enclose him round Par Lost 1.617
Far round illumin'd hell: highly they rag'd Par Lost 1.666
Built like a Temple, where *Pilasters* round Par Lost 1.713
And with the Majesty of darkness round Par Lost 2.266
Of Angels watching round? Here he had need Par Lost 2.413
Outrageous to devour, immures us round Par Lost 2.435
And God-like imitated State; him round Par Lost 2.511
Immovable, infixt, and frozen round, Par Lost 2.602
With mortal sting: about her middle round Par Lost 2.653
A fresh with conscious terrours vex me round, Par Lost 2.801

Round(*cont*)
Created vast and round, a place of bliss Par Lost 2.832
With terrors and with clamors compasst round Par Lost 2.862
Of fighting Elements, on all sides round Par Lost 2.1015
In circuit, undetermind square or round, Par Lost 2.1048
Drawn round about thee like a radiant Shrine, Par Lost 3.379
Of this round World, whose first convex divides Par Lost 3.419
Of *Chaos* blustring round, inclement skie; Par Lost 3.426
Round he surveys, and well might, where he stood Par Lost 3.555
Shot upward still direct, whence no way round Par Lost 3.618
Lay waving round; on som great charge imploy'd Par Lost 3.628
To visit oft this new Creation round; Par Lost 3.661
Timely interposes, and her monthly round Par Lost 3.728
He brings, and round about him, nor from Hell Par Lost 4.21
Into his neather Empire neighbouring round. Par Lost 4.145
Round from his parted forelock manly hung Par Lost 4.302
By word or action markt: about them round Par Lost 4.401
But first with narrow search I must walk round Par Lost 4.528
Those have thir course to finish, round the Earth, Par Lost 4.661
Thir Phalanx, and began to hemm him round Par Lost 4.979
The pendulous round Earth with ballanc't Aire Par Lost 4.1000
Girt like a Starrie Zone his waste, and round Par Lost 5.281
Thir Table was, and mossie seats had round, Par Lost 5.392
Whence in her visage round those spots, unpurg'd Par Lost 5.419
Encompass'd round with foes, thus answerd bold. Par Lost 5.876
Where light and darkness in perpetual round Par Lost 6.6
Encamping, plac'd in Guard thir Watches round, Par Lost 6.412
Which into hallow Engins long and round Par Lost 6.484
Lookd round, and Scouts each Coast light-armed scoure, Par Lost 6.529
In darkness, and with dangers compast round, Par Lost 7.27
1667 printed 'rouud'
Imbracing round this florid Earth, what cause Par Lost 7.90
Round through the vast profunditie obscure, Par Lost 7.229
Of this great Round: partition firm and sure, Par Lost 7.267
Regent of Day, and all th' Horizon round Par Lost 7.371
Round this opacous Earth, this punctual spot, Par Lost 8.23
Stood on my feet; about me round I saw Par Lost 8.261
Above, or round about thee or beneath. Par Lost 8.318
Nights Hemisphere had veild the Horizon round: Par Lost 9.52
Terrestrial Heav'n, danc't round by other Heav'ns Par Lost 9.103
With what delight could I have walkt thee round, Par Lost 9.114
In Labyrinth of many a round self-rowld, Par Lost 9.183
The Woodbine round this Arbour, or direct Par Lost 9.216
Half spi'd, so thick the Roses bushing round Par Lost 9.426
Her Husband, for I view far round, not nigh, Par Lost 9.482
Thy utmost reach or *Adams:* Round the Tree Par Lost 9.591
Condenses, and the cold invirons round, Par Lost 9.636
And girded on our loyns, may cover round Par Lost 9.1096
Of this round World: with Pinns of Adamant Par Lost 10.318
Round thir Metropolis, and now expecting Par Lost 10.439
He sate, and round about him saw unseen: Par Lost 10.448
Still following thee, still compassing thee round Par Lost 11.352
Not higher that Hill nor wider looking round, Par Lost 11.381
Smeard round with Pitch, and in the side a dore Par Lost 11.731
And shelterd round, but all the Cataracts Par Lost 11.824
In signal of remove, waves fiercely round; Par Lost 12.593
With aw the Regions round, and with them came Par Reg 1.22
And with dark shades and rocks environ'd round, Par Reg 1.194
And looking round on every side beheld Par Reg 1.295
Large liberty to round this Globe of Earth, Par Reg 1.365
From whose high top to ken the prospect round, Par Reg 2.286
Of Wood-Gods and Wood-Nymphs; he view'd it round, Par Reg 2.297
And all the Idolatries of Heathen round, Par Reg 3.418
Thence to the gates cast round thine eye, and see Par Reg 4.61
Infernal Ghosts, and Hellish Furies, round Par Reg 4.422
Whereof this ominous night that clos'd thee round, Par Reg 4.481
How many evils have enclos'd me round; Samson 194
The harrass of thir Land, beset me round; Samson 257
Among the Heathen round; to God have brought Samson 451
What sieges girt me round, e're I consented; Samson 846
Great among the Heathen round: Samson 1430
Garrison'd round about him like a Camp Samson 1497
Half round on two main Pillars vaulted high, Samson 1606
Of this but each *Philistian* City round Samson 1655
A Monument, and plant it round with shade Samson 1734
Lead in swift round the Months and Years. Mask 114
In a light fantastick round. Mask 144
With many a tower and terrass round, Mask 935
his uninchanted eye, & round the verge Mask Tr. ms 10.10
Whilst the Lantskip round it measures, Allegro 70
When the merry Bells ring round, Allegro 93
Ay round about *Joves* Altar sing. Penseroso 48
In circle round her shining throne, Arcades 15
When Eev'ning gray doth rise, I fetch my round Arcades 54
And turn the Adamantine spindle round, Arcades 66
Beneath the hollow round Nativity 102
In Urns, and Altars round, Nativity 192
Such as may make thee search thy coffers round, Vacation 31
And sweetly singing round about thy Bed Vacation 63
I fear not though incamping round about Psalm 3, 17
Our solemn Feast *comes round*. Psalm 81, 12
With clouds encompass'd round; Psalm 81, 30
And home they fly from round the Coasts Psalm 84, 15
Where thickest darkness *hovers round*, Psalm 88, 27
All day they round about me go, Psalm 88, 67

Rounded
Had rounded still th' *Horizon*, and not known Par Lost 10.684

Rounding
While they keep watch, or nightly rounding walk — Par Lost 4.685
The western Point, where those half-rounding guards — Par Lost 4.862
Rounds
Incited, dance about him various rounds? — Par Lost 8.125
while all the starrie rounds & arches blue — Musick Tr. ms 4.21
Rouse
Rouse and bestir themselves ere well awake. — Par Lost 1.334
Shall hast'n, such a peal shall rouse thir sleep. — Par Lost 3.329
Ere morrow wake, or the low roosted lark — Mask 317
Trinity ms 'ere morrow wake' ←'ere the larke rowse'
From her thach't pallat rowse, if otherwise — Mask 318
Chearly rouse the slumbring morn, — Allegro 54
Rouze thy self amidst the rage — Psalm 7, 20
Roused
Rous'd from the slumber, on that fiery Couch, — Par Lost 1.377
Had rous'd the Sea, now with hoarse cadence lull — Par Lost 2.287
His fierie vertue rouz'd — Samson 1690
Rousing
Some rouzing motions in me which dispose — Samson 1382
Rout
Erring; for he with this rebellious rout — Par Lost 1.747
Cleer Victory, to our part loss and rout — Par Lost 2.770
With ruin upon ruin, rout on rout, — Par Lost 2.995
Then when the Dragon, put to second rout, — Par Lost 4.3
With many an inrode gor'd; deformed rout — Par Lost 6.387
Foule dissipation follow'd and forc't rout; — Par Lost 6.598
Through his wilde Anarchie, so huge a rout — Par Lost 6.873
Of that wilde Rout that tore the *Thracian* Bard — Par Lost 7.34
Where all yet left of that revolted Rout — Par Lost 10.534
Discount'nance her despis'd, and put to rout — Par Reg 2.218
By th' Idolatrous rout amidst thir wine; — Samson 443
Nor do I name of men the common rout, — Samson 674
He and his monstrous rout are heard to howl — Mask 533
Bridgewater ms 'route'
When by the rout that made the hideous roar, — Lycidas 61
The populous rout — Psalm 3, 16
Rove
Rove idle unimploid, and less need rest; — Par Lost 4.617
But apt the Mind or Fancie is to roave — Par Lost 8.188
Rove without rein, till in the amorous Net — Par Lost 11.586
Nothing but ruin wheresoe're they rove, — Par Reg 3.79
I have some naked thoughts that rove about — Vacation 23
But from that mark how far they roave we see — Sonnet 12, 13
Trinity ms 'roave' ←'roav'
Roving
The lip of *Tantalus*. Thus roving on — Par Lost 2.614
Whose snowie ridge the roving *Tartar* bounds, — Par Lost 3.432
Uncheckt, and of her roaving is no end; — Par Lost 8.189
Till on a day roaving the field, I chanc'd — Par Lost 9.575
That heard the Adversary, who roving still — Par Reg 1.33
Roaving the *Celtick*, and *Iberian* fields, — Mask 60
Bridgewater ms 'roavinge'
Som roaving Robber calling to his fellows. — Mask 485
Bridgewater ms 'roavinge'
These latter scenes confine my roving vers, — Passion 22
Row
To many a row of Pipes the sound-board breaths. — Par Lost 1.709
Pendant by suttle Magic many a row — Par Lost 1.727
And higher then that Wall a circling row — Par Lost 4.146
Among sweet dewes and flours; where any row — Par Lost 5.212
A triple mounted row of Pillars laid — Par Lost 6.572
Stood rankt of Seraphim another row — Par Lost 6.604
Till on those cursed Engins triple-row — Par Lost 6.650
Beyond a row of Myrtles, on a Flat, — Par Lost 9.627
By Hedge-row Elms, on Hillocks green, — Allegro 58
Sate simply chatting in a rustick row; — Nativity 87
Where the bright Seraphim in burning row — Musick 10
Rows
Between her white wings mantling proudly, Rowes — Par Lost 7.439
Royal
Forerun the Royal Camp, to trench a Field, — Par Lost 1.677
ms 'royall'
High on a Throne of Royal State, which far — Par Lost 2.1
From *Auran* Eastward to the Royal Towrs — Par Lost 4.211
They came, and *Satan* to his Royal seat — Par Lost 5.756
All Prophecie, That of the Royal Stock — Par Lost 12.325
In *David*'s royal seat, his true Successour, — Par Reg 3.373
Or *Medway* smooth, or Royal Towred *Thame*. — Vacation 100
Cyriack, whose Grandsire on the Royal Bench — Sonnet 21, 1
line not in Trinity ms
His Royal Harbinger, — Psalm 85, 54
Royalties
These Royalties, and not refuse to Reign, — Par Lost 2.451
Rubbed
New rub'd with Baum, expatiate and confer — Par Lost 1.774
Rubied
With Angels Food, and rubied Nectar flows — Par Lost 5.633
Thrice upon thy rubied lip, — Mask 915
Rubric
Directs me in the Starry Rubric set. — Par Reg 4.393
Ruby
Rubie or Topaz, to the Twelve that shon — Par Lost 3.597
Thou couldst repress, nor did the dancing Rubie — Samson 543
Ruddy
Cast forth redounding smoak and ruddy flame. — Par Lost 2.889
Ruddie and Gold: I nearer drew to gaze; — Par Lost 9.578
The ruddy waves he cleft in twain, — Psalm 136, 45

Rude
But with such Gardning Tools as Art yet rude, — Par Lost 9.391
Beholders rude, and shallow to discerne — Par Lost 9.544
Justling or pusht with Winds rude in thir shock — Par Lost 10.1074
Lest evil tidings with too rude irruption — Samson 1567
From the chill dew, amongst rude burrs and thistles? — Mask 352
Trinity ms 'amoungst rude burrs & thistles' ←'in this surrounding wilde' ←'in this dead solitude'
Where the rude Ax with heaved stroke, — Penseroso 136
And with forc'd fingers rude, — Lycidas 4
All meanly wrapt in the rude manger lies; — Nativity 31
Now timely sing, ere the rude Bird of Hate — Sonnet 1, 9
Not of warr onely, but detractions rude, — Sonnet 16, 2
Rudeness
To meet the rudenesse, and swill'd insolence — Mask 178
1673 'rudeness'
Bridgewater ms 'rudenes'
Rudest
With rudest violence? — Psalm 80, 52
Rudiments
There he shall first lay down the rudiments — Par Reg 1.157
Those rudiments, and see before thine eyes — Par Reg 3.245
Rue
Too well I see and rue the dire event, — Par Lost 1.134
No evil durst attempt thee, but I rue — Par Lost 9.1180
Had bred; then purg'd with Euphrasie and Rue — Par Lost 11.414
And more blasphemous? which expect to rue. — Par Reg 4.181
Rueful
Heard on the ruful stream; fierce *Phlegeton* — Par Lost 2.580
Prodigious motion felt and rueful throes. — Par Lost 2.780
With rueful cry, yet what it was we hear not, — Samson 1553
Rues
Chose freely what it now so justly rues. — Par Lost 4.72
No triumph; in all her gates *Abaddon* rues — Par Reg 4.624
Ruffian
a tough encounter with the shaggiest ruffian — Mask Tr. ms 16.39
a tough encounter, with the shaggiest ruffian — Mask Br. ms 392
Ruffled
Of chaf't wild Boars, or ruffl'd Porcupines. — Samson 1138
Were all to ruffl'd, and somtimes impair'd. — Mask 380
Rugged
Or 'gainst the rugged bark of som broad Elm — Mask 354
Smoothing the rugged brow of night, — Penseroso 58
And question'd every gust of rugged wings — Lycidas 93
That glassy flouds from rugged rocks can crush, — Psalm 114, 17
Those rugged names to our like mouths grow sleek — Sonnet 11, 10
Trinity ms 'rugged' ←'rough hewn' ←'barbarous'
Ruggedest
Severest temper, smooth the rugged'st brow, — Par Reg 2.164
Ruin
With hideous ruine and combustion down — Par Lost 1.46
In equal ruin: into what Pit thou seest — Par Lost 1.91
Majestic though in ruin: sage he stood — Par Lost 2.305
Thaws not, but gathers heap, and ruin seems — Par Lost 2.590
With ruin upon ruin, rout on rout, — Par Lost 2.995
Havock and spoil and ruin are my gain. — Par Lost 2.1009
While by thee rais'd I ruin all my Foes, — Par Lost 3.258
Thir ruine! Hence I will excite thir minds — Par Lost 4.522
In them at once to ruin all mankind. — Par Lost 5.228
The ruin of so many glorious once — Par Lost 5.567
Such ruin intercept: ten paces huge — Par Lost 6.193
Ruin must needs ensue; for what availes — Par Lost 6.456
Of missive ruin; part incentive reed — Par Lost 6.519
Had gon to wrack, with ruin overspred, — Par Lost 6.670
In universal ruin last, and now — Par Lost 6.797
Incumberd him with ruin: Hell at last — Par Lost 6.874
Our ruin, both by thee informd I learne, — Par Lost 9.275
The way which to her ruin now I tend. — Par Lost 9.493
And ruine *Adam*, and the exploit perform'd — Par Reg 1.102
A spectacle of ruin or of scorn — Par Reg 1.415
Nothing but ruin wheresoe're they rove, — Par Reg 3.79
In ruine reconcil'd: nor slept the winds — Par Reg 4.413
Ruin, and desperation, and dismay, — Par Reg 4.579
To folly and shameful deeds which ruin ends. — Samson 1043
Draw thir own ruin who attempt the deed. — Samson 1267
Ruin, destruction at the utmost point. — Samson 1514
Man. Of ruin indeed methought I heard the noise, — Samson 1515
As thir own ruin on themselves to invite, — Samson 1684
To save th' *Athenian* Walls from ruine bare. — Sonnet 8, 14
And the way of bad men to ruine must. — Psalm 1, 16
Fall on his crown with ruine steep. — Psalm 7, 60
Ruined
Less then Arch Angel ruind, and th' excess — Par Lost 1.593
ms 'ruin'd'
And mee with thee hath ruind, for with thee — Par Lost 9.906
He ruind, now Mankind; whom will he next? — Par Lost 9.950
Wert thou some Starr which from the ruin'd roofe — Fair Inf 43
Ruining
Heav'n ruining from Heav'n and would have fled — Par Lost 6.868
Ruinous
With noises loud and ruinous (to compare — Par Lost 2.921
Both Battels maine, with ruinous assault — Par Lost 6.216
After a night of storm so ruinous, — Par Reg 4.436
Ruins
What ruins Kingdoms, and lays Cities flat; — Par Reg 4.363
Rule
Exalted to such power, and gave to rule, — Par Lost 1.736
His Empire, and with Iron Scepter rule — Par Lost 2.327

Rule(*cont*)
Absolute rule; and Hyacinthin Locks Par Lost 4.301
Among so many signes of power and rule Par Lost 4.429
Wilde above Rule or Art; enormous bliss. Par Lost 5.297
1667 'rule'
To Man, the greater to have rule by Day, Par Lost 7.347
To illuminate the Earth, and rule the Day Par Lost 7.350
In thir vicissitude, and rule the Night, Par Lost 7.351
In our similitude, and let them rule Par Lost 7.520
And worship him, and in reward to rule Par Lost 7.628
Find pastime, and beare rule; thy Realm is large. Par Lost 8.375
Lets her will rule; restraint she will not brook, Par Lost 9.1184
Unseemly to beare rule, which was thy part Par Lost 10.155
Thine shall submit, hee over thee shall rule. Par Lost 10.196
To rule, as over all he should have rul'd. Par Lost 10.493
Encroaching *Eve* perhaps, had first the rule Par Lost 10.582
All th' Earth he gave thee to possess and rule, Par Lost 11.339
The rule of not too much, by temperance taught Par Lost 11.531
Under paternal rule; till one shall rise Par Lost 12.24
Through the twelve Tribes, to rule by Laws ordaind: Par Lost 12.226
And all the rule, one Empire; onely add Par Lost 12.581
And who attains not, ill aspires to rule Par Reg 2.469
Rule in the Clouds; like an Autumnal Star Par Reg 4.619
By weakest suttleties, not made to rule, Samson 56
Imperial rule of all the Sea-girt Iles Mask 21
Trinity ms 'imperiall rule' ←'the rule & title'
With thy long levell'd rule of streaming light, Mask 340

Ruled
Of cold *Olympus* rul'd the middle Air Par Lost 1.516
As if predestination over-rul'd Par Lost 3.114
Stood rul'd, stood vast infinitude confin'd; Par Lost 3.711
By nature free, not over-rul'd by Fate Par Lost 5.527
From his strong hold of Heav'n high over-rul'd Par Lost 6.228
One Spirit in them rul'd, and every eye Par Lost 6.848
For Understanding rul'd not, and the Will Par Lost 9.1127
To rule, as over all he should have rul'd. Par Lost 10.493
Now rul'd him, punisht in the shape he sin'd, Par Lost 10.516
This Universe we have possest, and rul'd Par Reg 1.49
Obeys *Tiberius;* nor is always rul'd Par Reg 3.159
That rul'd the *Amorrean* coast. Psalm 136, 66

Rules
Of him who rules above; so was his will Par Lost 2.351
Hee rules a moment; *Chaos* Umpire sits, Par Lost 2.907
When he who rules is worthiest, and excells Par Lost 6.177
While they pervert pure Natures healthful rules Par Lost 11.523
Thy Father is the Eternal King, who rules Par Reg 1.236
Yet he who reigns within himself, and rules Par Reg 2.466
These rules will render thee a King compleat Par Reg 4.283
The solid rules of Civil Government Par Reg 4.358
Obtruding false rules pranckt in reasons garb. Mask 759
And her son that rules the strands, Mask 876
By the known rules of antient libertie, Sonnet 12, 2

Rulest
Not evenly, as thou rul'st Samson 671

Ruling
And high permission of all-ruling Heaven Par Lost 1.212
ms 'all-ruleing'
Thick clouds and dark doth Heav'ns all-ruling Sire Par Lost 2.264
Ruling them by perswasion as thou mean'st, Par Reg 4.230

Ruminating
Or Bedward ruminating: for the Sun Par Lost 4.352

Rumour
Of *Demogorgon; Rumor* next and *Chance*, Par Lost 2.965
1667 'Rumor'
Set off to th' world, nor in broad rumour lies, Lycidas 80
Trinity ms 'rumor'

Rumoured
Against a rumord Warr, the Smuttie graine Par Lost 4.817
When all abroad was rumour'd that this day Samson 1600

Rumours
And rumors loud, that daunt remotest kings, Sonnet 15, 4
1694 'Rumours'

Run
Breathe forth *Elixir* pure, and Rivers run Par Lost 3.607
That run through all the Heav'ns, or down to th' Earth Par Lost 3.651
Of Natures Womb, that in quaternion run Par Lost 5.181
Forthwith on all sides to his aide was run Par Lost 6.335
And the great Light of Day yet wants to run Par Lost 7.98
Invested with bright Rayes, jocond to run Par Lost 7.372
The less not bright, nor Heav'n such journies run, Par Lost 8.88
Thir Ministry perform'd, and race well run, Par Lost 12.505
And run not sooner to his fatal snare? Par Reg 1.441
By Conquest far and wide, to over-run Par Reg 3.72
My race of glory run, and race of shame, Samson 597
Sams. Go baffl'd coward, lest I run upon thee, Samson 1237
What shall we do, stay here or run and see? Samson 1520
We unawares run into dangers mouth. Samson 1522
Mess. O whither shall I run, or which way flie Samson 1541
Run to your shrouds, within these Brakes and Trees, Mask 147
And run to meet what he would most avoid? Mask 363
line not in Bridgewater ms
line not in Trinity ms
I can fly, or I can run Mask 1013
O run, prevent them with thy humble ode, Nativity 24
Time will run back, and fetch the age of gold, Nativity 135
All the day long his cours to run. Psalm 136, 30
Fly envious *Time*, till thou run out thy race, On Time 1
Once had the early Matrons run Winchester 23

Run(*cont*)
From the hard Season gaining: time will run Sonnet 20, 5

Rung
With wide *Cerberian* mouths full loud, and rung Par Lost 2.655
Had been achiev'd, whereof all Hell had rung, Par Lost 2.723
As from blest voices, uttering joy, Heav'n rung Par Lost 3.347
It sounded, and the faithful Armies rung Par Lost 6.204
The Heav'ns and all the Constellations rung, Par Lost 7.562
So sung they, and the Empyrean rung, Par Lost 7.633
Yet rung of his perswasive words, impregn'd Par Lost 9.737

Runners
Of Gymnic Artists, Wrestlers, Riders, Runners, Samson 1324

Runneth
Or sullen *Mole* that runneth underneath, Vacation 95

Running
And Lakes and running Streams the waters fill; Par Lost 7.397
Chor. Best keep together here, lest running thither Samson 1521
The melting voice through mazes running; Allegro 142

Runs
Runs divers, wandring many a famous Realme Par Lost 4.234
Runs through the arched roof in words deceiving. Nativity 175
The *greedy* flame runs hier and hier Psalm 83, 55

Rupture
Bursting with kindly rupture forth disclos'd Par Lost 7.419

Rural
As with a rural mound the champain head Par Lost 4.134
A happy rural seat of various view; Par Lost 4.247
On to thir mornings rural work they haste Par Lost 5.211
Rural repast, permitting him the while Par Lost 9.4
Or Dairie, each rural sight, each rural sound; Par Lost 9.451
Her Tresses, and her rural labours crown, Par Lost 9.841
Before him, Towns, and rural works between, Par Lost 11.639
But now an aged man in Rural weeds, Par Reg 1.314
Unlesse the Goddes that in rurall shrine Mask 267
1673 'rural'
To meditate my rural minstrelsie, Mask 547
Trinity ms 'rurall'
Bridgewater ms 'rurall'
With Jiggs, and rural dance resort, Mask 952
1637 'rurall'
Bridgewater ms 'rurall'
Trinity ms 'rurall'
Such a rural Queen Arcades 94
Trinity ms defective here
Such a rural Queen Arcades 108
Trinity ms 'rurall'
Mean while the Rural ditties were not mute, Lycidas 32
1638 'rurall'
Trinity ms 'rurall'

Rush
Wag'd in the troubl'd Skie, and Armies rush Par Lost 2.534
Forth rush the *Levant* and the *Ponent* Windes Par Lost 10.704
But rush upon me thronging, and present Samson 21
Though a rush Candle from the wicker hole Mask 338
Bridgewater ms 'rushe'
And brandish't blade rush on him, break his glass, Mask 651
Bridgewater ms 'rushe'

Rushed
Ris'n, and with hideous outcry rush'd between. Par Lost 2.726
So under fierie Cope together rush'd Par Lost 6.215
What should they do? if on they rusht, repulse Par Lost 6.600
Dawning through Heav'n: forth rush'd with whirlwind sound Par Lost 6.749
Forth rush'd in haste the great consulting Peers, Par Lost 10.456
Like a dark Ceeling stood; down rush'd the Rain Par Lost 11.743
Within thir stony caves, but rush'd abroad Par Reg 4.414
Of fire; that Spirit that first rusht on thee Samson 1435

Rushing
Whence rushing he might surest seize them both Par Lost 4.407
Of Battel now began, and rushing sound Par Lost 6.97
Two Planets rushing from aspect maligne Par Lost 6.313
To turn Swift-rushing black perdition hence, Fair Inf 67
See see the Chariot, and those rushing wheels, Passion 36

Rushy-fringed
By the rushy-fringed bank, Mask 890
1637 'rushie fringed'
Bridgewater ms 'rushie fringed'
Trinity ms 'rushie-fringed'

Russet
Russet Lawns, and Fallows Gray, Allegro 71

Russian
As when the *Tartar* from his *Russian* Foe Par Lost 10.431
In *Hispahan*, or where the *Russian Ksar* Par Lost 11.394

Rustic
Rustic, of grassie sord; thither anon Par Lost 11.433
Not rustic as before, but seemlier clad, Par Reg 2.299
Carrol her goodnes lowd in rustick layes, Mask 849
Trinity ms 'rustick' ←'lovely'
1637 'rusticke'
Sate simply chatting in a rustick row; Nativity 87

Rustling
Brusht with the hiss of russling wings. As Bees Par Lost 1.768
Of rusling Leaves, but minded not, as us'd Par Lost 9.519
Ending on the russling Leaves, Penseroso 129

Ruth
Look homeward Angel now, and melt with ruth. Lycidas 163
The better part with *Mary*, and the *Ruth*, Sonnet 9, 5
No anger find in thee, but pity and ruth. Sonnet 9, 8

Rutherford
Taught ye by meer *A . S*. and *Rotherford?* Forcers 8
S
Taught ye by meer *A . S*. and *Rotherford?* Forcers 8
Sabaean
And drenches with *Elysian* dew Mask 996
Trinity ms 'Elysian' ←'Sabaean' ←'manna'
Sabbath
With *Halleluiahs:* Thus was Sabbath kept. Par Lost 7.634
Ere Sabbath Eev'ning: so we had in charge. Par Lost 8.246
No journey of a Sabbath day, and loaded so; Samson 149
Sabean
Sabean Odours from the spicie shoare Par Lost 4.162
Sable
Was I deceiv'd, or did a sable cloud Mask 221
line not in Bridgewater ms
I did not err, there does a sable cloud Mask 223
line not in Bridgewater ms
1637 'sables'
And sable stole of *Cipres* Lawn, Penseroso 35
And bid fair peace be to my sable shrowd. Lycidas 22
Sable-stoled
The sable-stoled Sorcerers bear his worshipt Ark. Nativity 220
Sable-vested
Sat Sable-vested *Night*, eldest of things, Par Lost 2.962
Sabrina
Sabrina is her name, a Virgin pure, Mask 826
Sabrina fair Mask 859
B.M. ms 'Sabrina Sabrina'
Sacred
Whose wanton passions in the sacred Porch Par Lost 1.454
But now at last the sacred influence Par Lost 2.1034
Smit with the love of sacred Song; but chief Par Lost 3.29
Of Hymns and sacred Songs, wherewith thy Throne Par Lost 3.148
But to destruction sacred and devote, Par Lost 3.208
Thir sacred Song, and waken raptures high; Par Lost 3.369
More sacred and sequesterd, though but feignd, Par Lost 4.706
O sacred name of faithfulness profan'd! Par Lost 4.951
Worthy of Sacred silence to be heard; Par Lost 5.557
In song and dance about the sacred Hill, Par Lost 5.619
Returnd not lost: On to the sacred hill Par Lost 6.25
Canceld from Heav'n and sacred memorie, Par Lost 6.379
By Sacred Unction, thy deserved right. Par Lost 6.709
And the third sacred Morn began to shine Par Lost 6.748
Her sacred shades: though God had yet not rain'd Par Lost 7.331
Of sacred influence: As God in Heav'n Par Lost 9.107
Now when as sacred Light began to dawne Par Lost 9.192
O Sacred, Wise, and Wisdom-giving Plant, Par Lost 9.679
The sacred Fruit forbidd'n? som cursed fraud Par Lost 9.904
That sacred Fruit, sacred to abstinence, Par Lost 9.924
To resalute the World with sacred Light Par Lost 11.134
With large Wine-offerings pour'd, and sacred Feast, Par Lost 12.21
With all his sacred things, a scorn and prey Par Lost 12.341
Who all the sacred mysteries of Heav'n Par Lost 12.509
To what highth sacred vertue and true worth Par Reg 1.231
To tread his Sacred Courts, and minister Par Reg 1.488
Select, and Sacred, Glorious for a while, Samson 363
To violate the sacred trust of silence Samson 428
Home to thy countrey and his sacred house, Samson 518
To such a viper his most sacred trust Samson 1001
But such a sacred, and home-felt delight, Mask 262
Where through the sacred rayes of Chastity, Mask 425
To such a flame of sacred vehemence, Mask 795
line not in Bridgewater ms
line not in Trinity ms
& sacred limits of this blisfull Isle Mask Tr. ms 10.11
Approach, and kiss her sacred vestures hemm. Arcades 83
Begin then, Sisters of the sacred well, Lycidas 15
That sunk so low that sacred head of thine. Lycidas 102
Say Heav'nly Muse, shall not thy sacred vein Nativity 15
Within his sacred chest, Nativity 217
Hymns devout and holy Psalms Musick 15
Trinity ms 'holy' ←'holie' ←'sacred'
Picture the sacred wall declares t' have hung Horace 14
With sacred Songs are there, Psalm 87, 26
Sacrifice
Of human sacrifice, and parents tears, Par Lost 1.393
Filial obedience: as a sacrifice Par Lost 3.269
Of sacrifice, informing them, by types Par Lost 12.232
And thou no more with Pomp and Sacrifice Par Reg 1.457
Worship't with Temple, Priest and Sacrifice; Par Reg 3.83
Above all Sacrifice, or hallow'd gift Par Reg 3.116
Great Pomp, and Sacrifice, and Praises loud Samson 436
The Feast and noon grew high, and Sacrifice Samson 1612
No sacrifice to God more acceptable Prose 11, 2
Sacrificed
To that meek man, who well had sacrific'd; Par Lost 11.451
Sacrifices
With Sacrifices, Triumph, Pomp, and Games; Samson 1312
Sacrificing
Choicest and best; then sacrificing, laid Par Lost 11.438
Oft sacrificing Bullock, Lamb, or Kid, Par Lost 12.20
Sacrilegious
Yet, sacrilegious, to himself would take Par Reg 3.140
Incestuous, Sacrilegious, but may plead it? Samson 833
Sad
That with sad overthrow and foul defeat Par Lost 1.135
To be no more; sad cure; for who would loose, Par Lost 2.146

Sad*(cont)*
Pursues, as inclination or sad choice Par Lost 2.524
Sad *Acheron* of sorrow, black and deep; Par Lost 2.578
Then sweet, now sad to mention, through dire change Par Lost 2.820
Sad instrument of all our woe, she took; Par Lost 2.872
His sad exclusion from the dores of Bliss. Par Lost 3.525
Lay pleasant, his grievd look he fixes sad, Par Lost 4.28
Scarce thus at length faild speech recoverd sad. Par Lost 4.357
In sad event, when to the unwiser Son Par Lost 4.716
Related, and thus *Adam* answerd sad. Par Lost 5.94
But with addition strange; yet be not sad. Par Lost 5.116
Sad task and hard, for how shall I relate Par Lost 5.564
Sad resolution and secure: let each Par Lost 6.541
Deaths Harbinger: Sad task, yet argument Par Lost 9.13
So having said, as one from sad dismay Par Lost 9.917
Skie lowr'd and muttering Thunder, som sad drops Par Lost 9.1002
Th' Angelic Guards ascended, mute and sad Par Lost 10.18
To whom sad *Eve* with shame nigh overwhelm'd, Par Lost 10.159
Sate in thir sad discourse, and various plaint, Par Lost 10.343
Thus to disburd'n sought with sad complaint. Par Lost 10.719
Whom thus afflicted when sad *Eve* beheld, Par Lost 10.863
Adam, by sad experiment I know Par Lost 10.967
Or end, though sharp and sad, yet tolerable, Par Lost 10.977
Numberd, though sad, till Death, his doom (which I Par Lost 11.40
At the sad Sentence rigorously urg'd, Par Lost 11.109
To whom thus *Eve* with sad demeanour meek. Par Lost 11.162
Quiet though sad, the respit of that day Par Lost 11.272
Before his eyes appeard, sad, noysom, dark, Par Lost 11.478
Lamenting turnd full sad; O what are these, Par Lost 11.675
The end of all thy Ofspring, end so sad, Par Lost 11.755
Whereat the heart of *Adam* erst so sad Par Lost 11.868
Both in one Faith unanimous though sad, Par Lost 12.603
And thus with words not sad she him receav'd. Par Lost 12.609
With looks agast and sad he thus bespake. Par Reg 1.43
At these sad tidings; but no time was then Par Reg 1.109
So in the sad event too much concern'd. Samson 1551
Man. Sad, but thou knowst to *Israelites* not saddest Samson 1560
Like a sad Votarist in Palmers weed Mask 189
line not in Bridgewater ms
Nightly to thee her sad Song mourneth well. Mask 235
In this close dungeon of innumerous bowes. Mask 349
Trinity ms 'close' ←'sad' ←'lone'
Leans her unpillow'd head fraught with sad fears. Mask 355
Trinity ms 'fraught with sad feares' ←'musing at our unkindnesse'
With a sad Leaden downward cast, Penseroso 43
But, O sad Virgin, that thy power Penseroso 103
Bitter constraint, and sad occasion dear, Lycidas 6
And every flower that sad embroidery wears: Lycidas 148
Trinity ms 'sad' ←'sorrows'
Let our frail thoughts dally with false surmise. Lycidas 153
Trinity ms 'fraile' ←'sad'
and that sad floure that strove Lycidas Tr. ms 28.17
While sad *Ulisses* soul and all the rest Vacation 50
Mine eye hath found that sad Sepulchral rock Passion 43
Now mourn, and if sad share with us to bear Circum 6
Which the sad morn had let fall Winchester 45
Of sad *Electra*'s Poet had the power Sonnet 8, 13
Till the sad breaking of that Parlament Sonnet 10, 5
with need, *and sad decay*. Psalm 86, 4
Saddest
Man. Sad, but thou knowst to *Israelites* not saddest Samson 1560
In her sweetest, saddest plight, Penseroso 57
And set my Harpe to notes of saddest wo, Passion 9
Sadly
Eld. Bro. To tell thee sadly Shepherd, without blame, Mask 509
Sadly sits th' *Assyrian* Queen; Mask 1002
line not in Bridgewater ms
Sadness
All sadness but despair: now gentle gales Par Lost 4.156
All were who heard, dim sadness did not spare Par Lost 10.23
Safe
From the safe shore thir floating Carkases Par Lost 1.310
Establisht in a safe unenvied Throne Par Lost 2.23
This place our dungeon, not our safe retreat Par Lost 2.317
Suffice, or what evasion bear him safe Par Lost 2.411
Though hard and rare: thee I revisit safe, Par Lost 3.21
And to the end persisting, safe arrive. Par Lost 3.197
To utter is not safe. Assemble thou Par Lost 5.683
More safe I Sing with mortal voice, unchang'd Par Lost 7.24
Our great Forbidder, safe with all his Spies Par Lost 9.815
First lighted from his Wing, and landed safe Par Lost 10.316
And wandring vanitie, when lest was safe, Par Lost 10.875
Ascend, I follow thee, safe Guide, the path Par Lost 11.371
The paths of righteousness, how much more safe, Par Lost 11.814
Safe towards *Canaan* from the shoar advance Par Lost 12.215
Safe to eternal Paradise of rest. Par Lost 12.314
Safe to the rock of *Etham* was retir'd, Samson 253
Against thee but safe custody, and hold: Samson 802
I shoot from Heav'n to give him safe convoy, Mask 81
Bridgewater ms 'salfe'
But loyal cottage, where you may be safe Mask 320
And sits as safe as in a Senat house, Mask 389
And tell me it is safe, as bid me hope Mask 400
Was this the cottage, and the safe abode Mask 693
Me safe where ere I lie Psalm 4, 40
And then we shall be safe. Psalm 80, 16
And then we shall be safe. Psalm 80, 32

Safe(*cont*)
And then we shall be safe. Psalm 80, 80
They find their safe abode, Psalm 84, 14
Safely
Cast thy self down; safely if Son of God: Par Reg 4.555
Lean on it safely, not a period Mask 585
Bridgewater ms 'salfly'
Safer
Some safer resolution, which methinks Par Lost 10.1029
Safest
Safest and seemliest by her Husband staies, Par Lost 9.268
Safest thy life, and best prepar'd endure Par Lost 11.365
But safest he who stood aloof, Samson 135
Safety
Of order, how in safety best we may Par Lost 2.280
That for the general safety he despis'd Par Lost 2.481
Thy tempring; with like safetie guided down Par Lost 7.15
1669 'safety'
On no slight grounds thy safety; hear, and mark Par Reg 3.349
And peoples safety, which in part they effect: Samson 681
Wherein consisted all thy strength and safety? Samson 780
Thy key of strength and safety: thou wilt say, Samson 799
Of secresie, my safety, and my life. Samson 1002
Again in safety what thou wouldst have done Samson 1128
Thir ornament and safety, had not spells Samson 1132
Thou Lord alone in safety mak'st me dwell. Psalm 4, 42
Saffron
In Saffron robe, with Taper clear, Allegro 126
Sagacious
Sagacious of his Quarry from so farr. Par Lost 10.281
Sage
Majestic though in ruin: sage he stood Par Lost 2.305
To sage Philosophy next lend thine ear, Par Reg 4.272
What the sage Poets taught by th' heav'nly Muse, Mask 515
That must be utter'd to unfold the sage Mask 786
line not in Trinity ms
line not in Bridgewater ms
But hail thou Goddes, sage and holy, Penseroso 11
In sage and solemn tunes have sung, Penseroso 117
And sage *Hippotades* their answer brings, Lycidas 96
Or that crown'd Matron sage white-robed truth? Fair Inf 54
Vane, young in yeares, but in sage counsell old, Sonnet 17, 1
1694 'Sage'
Sagely
To whom our Saviour sagely thus repli'd. Par Reg 4.285
Sager
Or whether (as som Sager sing) Allegro 17
Sages
And guides the Eastern Sages, who enquire Par Lost 12.362
The schools of antient Sages; his who bred Par Reg 4.251
For so the holy sages once did sing, Nativity 5
1673 'Sages'
Said
Said then the lost Arch-Angel, this the seat Par Lost 1.243
This said, he sat; and expectation held Par Lost 2.417
Thus said, he turnd, and *Satan* bowing low, Par Lost 3.736
And Head, what thou hast said is just and right. Par Lost 4.443
This said unanimous, and other Rites Par Lost 4.736
Know ye not then said *Satan*, fill'd with scorn, Par Lost 4.827
Undaunted. If I must contend, said he, Par Lost 4.851
Or less be lost. Thy fear, said *Zephon* bold, Par Lost 4.854
With gentle voice, I thought it thine; it said, Par Lost 5.37
And O fair Plant, said he, with fruit surcharg'd, Par Lost 5.58
This said he paus'd not, but with ventrous Arme Par Lost 5.64
Raphael, said hee, thou hear'st what stir on Earth Par Lost 5.224
Thus said. Native of Heav'n, for other place Par Lost 5.361
And smiling to his onely Son thus said. Par Lost 5.718
He said, and as the sound of waters deep Par Lost 5.872
He said, and on his Son with Rayes direct Par Lost 6.719
So said, he o're his Scepter bowing, rose Par Lost 6.746
Said then th' Omnific Word, your discord end: Par Lost 7.217
And said, thus farr extend, thus farr thy bounds, Par Lost 7.230
Let ther be Light, said God, and forthwith Light Par Lost 7.243
Again, God said, let ther be Firmament Par Lost 7.261
Satiate with genial moisture, when God said Par Lost 7.282
And saw that it was good, and said, Let th' Earth Par Lost 7.309
He scarce had said, when the bare Earth, till then Par Lost 7.313
And God said, let the Waters generate Par Lost 7.387
With Eevning Harps and Mattin, when God said, Par Lost 7.450
This said, he formd thee, *Adam*, thee O Man Par Lost 7.524
Female for Race; then bless'd Mankinde, and said, Par Lost 7.530
What e're I saw. Thou Sun, said I, faire Light, Par Lost 8.273
And said, thy Mansion wants thee, *Adam*, rise, Par Lost 8.296
Said mildely, Author of all this thou seest Par Lost 8.317
Lead then, said *Eve*. Hee leading swiftly rowld Par Lost 9.631
Indeed? hath God then said that of the Fruit Par Lost 9.656
The Garden, God hath said, Ye shall not eate Par Lost 9.662
She scarse had said, though brief, when now more bold Par Lost 9.664
So having said, as one from sad dismay Par Lost 9.917
So said he, and forbore not glance or toy Par Lost 9.1034
So having said, he thus to *Eve* in few: Par Lost 10.157
So having said, a while he stood, expecting Par Lost 10.504
This said, they both betook them several wayes, Par Lost 10.610
Said hee, with one thrice acceptable stroke Par Lost 10.855
I yield it just, said *Adam*, and submit. Par Lost 11.526
There is, said *Michael*, if thou well observe Par Lost 11.530
Said th' Angel, who should better hold his place Par Lost 11.635
Be sure they will, said th' Angel; but from Heav'n Par Lost 12.485

Said(*cont*)
And said to me apart, high are thy thoughts Par Reg 1.229
Now hungring first, and to himself thus said. Par Reg 2.244
Cause thy refusal, said the subtle Fiend, Par Reg 2.323
Of glory as thou wilt, said he, so deem, Par Reg 3.150
And time there is for all things, Truth hath said: Par Reg 3.183
Wise men have said are wearisom; who reads Par Reg 4.322
And in a careless mood thus to him said. Par Reg 4.450
Tempt not the Lord thy God, he said and stood. Par Reg 4.561
Stept as they se'd to the next Thicket side Mask 185
Trinity ms 'sed'
Bridgewater ms 's'ed'
But in another Countrey, as he said, Mask 632
line not in Bridgewater ms
Or have I said anough? To him that dares Mask 780
line not in Bridgewater ms
line not in Trinity ms
And, as the old Swain said, she can unlock Mask 852
Trinity ms 'sed'
She was pincht, and pull'd she sed, Allegro 103
Daily devours apace, and nothing sed, Lycidas 129
1638 'said'
Such Musick (as 'tis said) Nativity 117
Your Son, said she, (nor can you it prevent) Vacation 73
If any ask for him, it shall be sed, Carrier 17
I will declare; the Lord to me hath say'd Psalm 2, 14
I said that ye were Gods, yea all Psalm 82, 21
For they amidst their pride have said Psalm 83, 45
Be said of Sion *last* Psalm 87, 18
Saidest
From mee returnd, as erst thou saidst, from flight, Par Lost 6.187
Lives, as thou saidst, and gaines to live as Man Par Lost 9.933
Going into such danger as thou saidst? Par Lost 9.1157
Said'st thou not that to all things I had right? Par Reg 2.379
Sail
Half flying; behoves him now both Oare and Saile. Par Lost 2.942
Those balmie spoiles. As when to them who saile Par Lost 4.159
But firm Battalion; back with speediest Sail Par Lost 6.534
Veres oft, as oft so steers, and shifts her Saile; Par Lost 9.515
Of Angels on full sail of wing flew nigh, Par Reg 4.582
Sail-broad
The stedfast Earth. At last his Sail-broad Vannes Par Lost 2.927
Sailing
Close sailing from *Bengala*, or the Iles Par Lost 2.638
Who after came from Earth, sayling arriv'd, Par Lost 3.520
Comes this way sailing Samson 713
Sails
With Sails and Wind thir canie Waggons light: Par Lost 3.439
Sailes between worlds and worlds, with steddie wing Par Lost 5.268
Sails fill'd, and streamers waving, Samson 718
Saint
And now Saint *Peter* at Heav'ns Wicket seems Par Lost 3.484
All Justice: nor delaid the winged Saint Par Lost 5.247
Such wondrous power God to his Saint will lend, Par Lost 12.200
Whilst thou bright Saint high sit'st in glory, Winchester 61
There with thee, new welcom Saint, Winchester 71
Methought I saw my late espoused Saint Sonnet 23, 1
Trinity ms 'saint'
Sainted
Amongst the enthron'd gods on Sainted seats. Mask 11
Bridgewater ms 'sainted'
Trinity ms 'sainted'
Saintly
That practisd falshood under saintly shew, Par Lost 4.122
Him whom thy wrongs with Saintly patience born, Par Reg 3.93
So dear to Heav'n is Saintly chastity, Mask 453
1637 'saintly'
Trinity ms 'sainctly'
Bridgewater ms 'sainctly'
Whose Saintly visage is too bright Penseroso 13
The Saintly Vail of Maiden white to throw, Nativity 42
With Saintly shout, and solemn Jubily, Musick 9
Trinity ms 'saintly' ←'saintlie'
Saints
Then all thy Saints assembl'd, thou shalt judge Par Lost 3.330
Translated Saints, or middle Spirits hold Par Lost 3.461
Present, or past, as Saints and Patriarchs us'd. Par Lost 4.762
Invincible, lead forth my armed Saints Par Lost 6.47
Far otherwise th' inviolable Saints Par Lost 6.398
Then shall thy Saints unmixt, and from th' impure Par Lost 6.742
Attended with ten thousand thousand Saints, Par Lost 6.767
Stand still in bright array ye Saints, here stand Par Lost 6.801
To meet him all his Saints, who silent stood Par Lost 6.882
Victorious with his Saints, th' Omnipotent Par Lost 7.136
From his transcendent Seat the Saints among, Par Lost 10.614
To judge them with his Saints: Him the most High Par Lost 11.705
The Holiest of Holies, and his Saints; Par Reg 4.349
Of Saints, the trial of thir fortitude, Samson 1288
There entertain him all the Saints above, Lycidas 178
Trinity ms 'Sts'
Strait follow'd thee the path that Saints have trod Sonnet 14, Tr. ms 41.06
Avenge O Lord thy slaughter'd Saints, whose bones Sonnet 18, 1
And to his Saints *full dear*, Psalm 85, 32
To his dear Saints he will speak peace, Psalm 85, 33
Saith
And fierce ire trouble them; but I saith hee Psalm 2, 11
In the pure firmament, then saith my heart, Psalm 8, 11

Sake
Account mee man; I for his sake will leave — Par Lost 3.238
Divine displeasure for her sake, or Death. — Par Lost 9.993
Curs'd is the ground for thy sake, thou in sorrow — Par Lost 10.201
For angers sake, finite to infinite — Par Lost 10.802
And for his Makers Image sake exempt? — Par Lost 11.514
By simply meek; that suffering for Truths sake — Par Lost 12.569
For Empires sake, nor Empire to affect — Par Reg 3.45
For glories sake by all thy argument. — Par Reg 3.46
For truths sake suffering death unjust, lives now — Par Reg 3.98
Be it but for honours sake of former deeds. — Samson 372
At length for intermission sake they led him — Samson 1629
Listen for dear honours sake, — Mask 864
Anow of such as for their bellies sake, — Lycidas 114
My soul, O save me for thy goodness sake — Psalm 6, 8

Sale
They easily would set to sale, a third — Samson 1466

Salem
The City of Palms, *Aenon*, and *Salem* Old, — Par Reg 2.21
To bear me where the Towers of *Salem* stood, — Passion 39

Sallow
Praising the lean and sallow Abstinence. — Mask 709
  Bridgewater ms 'shallow'

Salmanassar
And seat of *Salmanassar*, whose success — Par Reg 3.278

Salt
And there take root an Iland salt and bare, — Par Lost 11.834
Of every salt Flood, and each ebbing Stream, — Mask 19
  Bridgewater ms 'salte'

Salutation
Bestowd, the holy salutation us'd — Par Lost 5.386
Since first her Salutation heard, with thoughts — Par Reg 2.107

Salute
To have conceiv'd of God, or that salute — Par Reg 2.67
Here I salute thee and thy pardon ask, — Vacation 7
Thus we salute thee with our early Song, — May Morn 9

Salvation
High in Salvation and the Climes of bliss, — Par Lost 11.708
And his Salvation, them who shall beleeve — Par Lost 12.441
Salvation shall be Preacht, but to the Sons — Par Lost 12.448
To earn Salvation for the Sons of men. — Par Reg 1.167
Salvation is at hand — Psalm 85, 38

Salve
To salve his credit, and for very spight — Par Reg 4.12
Salve to thy Sores, apt words have power to swage — Samson 184

Samarchand
And *Samarchand* by *Oxus*, *Temirs* Throne, — Par Lost 11.389

Samaritan
Samaritan or *Jew;* how could'st thou hope — Par Reg 3.359

Same
What matter where, if I be still the same, — Par Lost 1.256
The same whom *John* saw also in the Sun: — Par Lost 3.623
Hadst thou the same free Will and Power to stand? — Par Lost 4.66
Think not, revolted Spirit, thy shape the same, — Par Lost 4.835
Even to my mouth of that same fruit held part — Par Lost 5.83
Differing but in degree, of kind the same. — Par Lost 5.490
That self same day by fight, or by surprize — Par Lost 6.87
Or Nature; God and Nature bid the same, — Par Lost 6.176
With low subjection; understand the same — Par Lost 8.345
Beyond all other, think the same voutsaf't — Par Lost 8.581
Of *Satan*, to the self same place where hee — Par Lost 10.315
Into the same illusion, not as Man — Par Lost 10.571
Not to do onely, but to will the same — Par Lost 10.826
One way the self-same hour? why in the East — Par Lost 11.203
Holds on the same, from Woman to begin. — Par Lost 11.633
The fluid skirts of that same watrie Cloud, — Par Lost 11.882
Wandred this barren waste, the same I now: — Par Reg 1.354
To *Israel* then, the same that now to me. — Par Reg 3.413
And the same end; still watching to oppress — Samson 232
So near related, or the same of kind, — Samson 786
Pulld down the same destruction on himself; — Samson 1658
With that same vaunted name Virginity, — Mask 738
  line not in Bridgewater ms
For we were nurst upon the self-same hill, — Lycidas 23
  Trinity ms 'selfe same'
Fed the same flock, by fountain, shade, and rill. — Lycidas 24
For this same small neglect that I have made: — Vacation 16
To that same lot, however mean, or high, — Sonnet 7, 11
Art the most high, *and thou the same* — Psalm 83, 67

Samoed
Of *Norumbega*, and the *Samoed* shoar — Par Lost 10.696

Samos
Delos or *Samos* first appeering kenns — Par Lost 5.265

Sampler
The sampler, and to teize the huswifes wooll. — Mask 751
  line not in Bridgewater ms
  Trinity ms 'sample'

Samson
Herculean Samson from the Harlot-lap — Par Lost 9.1060
Irresistible *Samson?* whom unarm'd — Samson 126
That invincible *Samson*, far renown'd, — Samson 341
Thee *Samson* bound and blind into thir hands, — Samson 438
Samson, of all thy sufferings think the heaviest, — Samson 445
I came, still dreading thy displeasure, *Samson*, — Samson 733
Dal. Yet hear me *Samson;* not that I endeavour — Samson 766
Let me obtain forgiveness of thee, *Samson*, — Samson 909
Much like thy riddle, *Samson*, in one day — Samson 1016
Har. I come not *Samson*, to condole thy chance, — Samson 1076

Samson(*cont*)
To *Samson*, but shalt never see *Gath* more. — Samson 1129
Samson, with might endu'd — Samson 1293
Off. *Ebrews*, the Pris'ner *Samson* here I seek. — Samson 1308
Off. *Samson*, to thee our Lords thus bid me say; — Samson 1310
Chor. Consider, *Samson;* matters now are strain'd — Samson 1348
Off. *Samson*, this second message from our Lords — Samson 1391
Man. Relate by whom. *Mess*. By *Samson*. *Man*. That still lessens — Samson 1563
Mess. Then take the worst in brief, *Samson* is dead. — Samson 1570
What glorious hand gave *Samson* his deaths wound? — Samson 1581
Samson should be brought forth to shew the people — Samson 1601
Was *Samson* as a public servant brought, — Samson 1615
He unsuspitious led him; which when *Samson* — Samson 1635
Samson with these immixt, inevitably — Samson 1657
Nor much more cause, *Samson* hath quit himself — Samson 1709
Like *Samson*, and heroicly hath finish'd — Samson 1710

Sanctities
About him all the Sanctities of Heaven — Par Lost 3.60

Sanctitude
Truth, wisdome, Sanctitude severe and pure, — Par Lost 4.293

Sanctity
With Sanctitie of Reason, might erect — Par Lost 7.508
Of nuptial Sanctitie and marriage Rites: — Par Lost 8.487
To sanctitie that shall receive no staine: — Par Lost 10.639
No sanctitie, if none be thither brought — Par Lost 11.837

Sanctuary
Within his Sanctuary it self thir Shrines, — Par Lost 1.388
  ms 'sanctuary'
This our high place, our Sanctuarie, our Hill. — Par Lost 5.732
Shrin'd in his Sanctuarie of Heav'n secure, — Par Lost 6.672
By his prescript a Sanctuary is fram'd — Par Lost 12.249
In *Silo* his bright Sanctuary: — Samson 1674
There Seated in his Sanctuary, — Psalm 87, 3

Sandals
While the still morn went out with Sandals gray, — Lycidas 187
  Trinity ms 'sandals'
  1638 'sandals'

Sands
Beneath *Gibralter* to the *Lybian* sands. — Par Lost 1.355
Swarm populous, unnumber'd as the Sands — Par Lost 2.903
Rowling on Orient Pearl and sands of Gold, — Par Lost 4.238
And on the Tawny Sands and Shelves, — Mask 117
  1637 'sands'
  Trinity ms 'sands'
  Bridgewater ms 'sands'
On Sands, and Shoars, and desert Wildernesses. — Mask 209
  Trinity ms 'sands'
  line not in Bridgewater ms

Sandy
Infamous Hills, and sandy perilous wildes, — Mask 424
  Bridgewater ms 'sandie'
  1637 'sandie'
  Trinity ms 'sandie'
By sandy *Ladons* Lillied banks. — Arcades 97
  Trinity ms 'sandie'

Sang
Thee next they sang of all Creation first, — Par Lost 3.383
So sang the Hierarchies: Mean while the Son — Par Lost 7.192
Thus sang the uncouth Swain to th' Okes and rills, — Lycidas 186
  Trinity ms 'sung'

Sanguine
Sanguin, such as Celestial Spirits may bleed, — Par Lost 6.333
Like to that sanguine flower inscrib'd with woe. — Lycidas 106

Sap
Into the plant sciential sap, deriv'd — Par Lost 9.837

Sapience
Of Majestie Divine, Sapience and Love — Par Lost 7.195
To Sapience, hitherto obscur'd, infam'd, — Par Lost 9.797
And elegant, of Sapience no small part, — Par Lost 9.1018

Sapient
Or that, not Mystic, where the Sapient King — Par Lost 9.442

Saplings
To nurse the Saplings tall, and curl the grove — Arcades 46
  Trinity ms 'nurse the saplings tall' ← 'live a thousand yeares'

Sapphire
Of living Saphire, once his native Seat; — Par Lost 2.1050
How from that Saphire Fount the crisped Brooks, — Par Lost 4.237
Whereon a Saphir Throne, inlaid with pure — Par Lost 6.758
On the Chrystallin Skie, in Saphir Thron'd. — Par Lost 6.772
And gives them leave to wear their Saphire crowns, — Mask 26
  Bridgewater ms 'saphire'
  Trinity ms 'saphire'

Sapphire-coloured
Ay sung before the saphire-colour'd throne — Musick 7
  Trinity ms 'sapphire-couour'd' ← 'saphire-colour'd'
  ← 'saphire-colourd' ← 'soveraigne'

Sapphires
With living Saphirs: *Hesperus* that led — Par Lost 4.605

Sarmatians
Germans and *Scythians*, and *Sarmatians* North — Par Reg 4.78

Sarra
Of *Sarra*, worn by Kings and Hero's old — Par Lost 11.243

Sat
And Powers that earst in Heaven sat on Thrones; — Par Lost 1.360
Sat on his faded cheek, but under Browes — Par Lost 1.602
Sat on his Throne, upheld by old repute, — Par Lost 1.639
And sat as Princes, whom the supreme King — Par Lost 1.735
In close recess and secret conclave sat — Par Lost 1.795

Sat(*cont*)
Satan exalted sat, by merit rais'd — Par Lost 2.5
Satan except, none higher sat, with grave — Par Lost 2.300
Deliberation sat and public care; — Par Lost 2.303
This said, he sat; and expectation held — Par Lost 2.417
The perilous attempt: but all sat mute, — Par Lost 2.420
Others apart sat on a Hill retir'd, — Par Lost 2.557
Yet unconsum'd. Before the Gates there sat — Par Lost 2.648
Had not the Snakie Sorceress that sat — Par Lost 2.724
Without my op'ning. Pensive here I sat — Par Lost 2.777
Alone, but long I sat not, till my womb — Par Lost 2.778
Sat Sable-vested *Night*, eldest of things, — Par Lost 2.962
The radiant image of his Glory sat, — Par Lost 3.63
Regardless of the Bliss wherein hee sat — Par Lost 3.408
Which now sat high in his Meridian Towre: — Par Lost 4.30
Sat like a Cormorant; yet not true Life — Par Lost 4.196
Thereby regaind, but sat devising Death — Par Lost 4.197
They sat them down, and after no more toil — Par Lost 4.327
Yielded them, side-long as they sat recline — Par Lost 4.333
Coucht, and now fild with pasture gazing sat, — Par Lost 4.351
Betwixt these rockie Pillars *Gabriel* sat — Par Lost 4.549
Sat horror Plum'd; nor wanted in his graspe — Par Lost 4.989
Adam discernd, as in the dore he sat — Par Lost 5.299
Think not I shall be nice. So down they sat, — Par Lost 5.433
By whom in bliss imbosom'd sat the Son, — Par Lost 5.597
Th' Apostat in his Sun-bright Chariot sate — Par Lost 6.100
He sat; and in th' assembly next upstood — Par Lost 6.446
From the right hand of Glorie where he sate, — Par Lost 6.747
Sate Eagle-wing'd, beside him hung his Bow — Par Lost 6.763
The Filial Power arriv'd, and sate him down — Par Lost 7.587
Perceaving where she sat retir'd in sight, — Par Lost 8.41
Pensive I sate me down; there gentle sleep — Par Lost 8.287
Confounded long they sate, as struck'n mute, — Par Lost 9.1064
They sate them down to weep, nor onely Teares — Par Lost 9.1121
Within the Gates of Hell sate Sin and Death, — Par Lost 10.230
Sate in thir sad discourse, and various plaint, — Par Lost 10.343
In Council sate, sollicitous what chance — Par Lost 10.428
He sate, and round about him saw unseen: — Par Lost 10.448
Climbing, sat thicker then the snakie locks — Par Lost 10.559
Then stil at Hels dark threshold to have sate watch, — Par Lost 10.594
Desolate where she sate, approaching nigh, — Par Lost 10.864
By the waters of Life, where ere they sate — Par Lost 11.79
The *Persian* in *Ecbatan* sate, or since — Par Lost 11.393
Comes to the place where he before had sat — Par Reg 1.412
Where all his Potentates in Council sate; — Par Reg 2.118
Whose off-spring on the Throne of *Juda* sat — Par Reg 2.440
And to his crew, that sat consulting, brought — Par Reg 4.577
While I at home sate full of cares and fears — Samson 805
Upon the heads of all who sate beneath, — Samson 1652
And the swink't hedger at his Supper sate; — Mask 293
I sate me down to watch upon a bank — Mask 543
Have sate to wonder at, and gaze upon: — Arcades 43
Trinity ms 'sat'
And Kings sate still with awfull eye, — Nativity 59
Sate simply chatting in a rustick row; — Nativity 87
Where he had mutely sate two years before: — Vacation 6
Of scorners hath not sate. But in the great — Psalm 1, 4

Satan
And thence in Heav'n call'd Satan, with bold words — Par Lost 1.82
Thus Satan talking to his neerest Mate — Par Lost 1.192
So *Satan* spake, and him *Beelzebub* — Par Lost 1.271
ms 'Satan'
Of Satan and his Peers: thir summons call'd — Par Lost 1.757
ms defective here
Satan exalted sat, by merit rais'd — Par Lost 2.5
Satan except, none higher sat, with grave — Par Lost 2.300
By *Satan*, and in part propos'd: for whence, — Par Lost 2.380
Satan, whom now transcendent glory rais'd — Par Lost 2.427
Satan with thoughts inflam'd of highest design, — Par Lost 2.630
Satan was now at hand, and from his seat — Par Lost 2.674
Incenst with indignation *Satan* stood — Par Lost 2.707
Forbore, then these to her *Satan* return'd: — Par Lost 2.736
T' whom *Satan* turning boldly, thus. Ye Powers — Par Lost 2.968
Thus *Satan;* and him thus the Anarch old — Par Lost 2.988
He ceas'd; and *Satan* staid not to reply, — Par Lost 2.1010
That *Satan* with less toil, and now with ease — Par Lost 2.1041
Hell and the Gulf between, and *Satan* there — Par Lost 3.70
Satan alighted walks: a Globe farr off — Par Lost 3.422
Satan from hence now on the lower stair — Par Lost 3.540
O're Sea and Land: him *Satan* thus accostes; — Par Lost 3.653
Thus said, he turnd, and *Satan* bowing low, — Par Lost 3.736
Satan, now first inflam'd with rage, came down, — Par Lost 4.9
Satan had journied on, pensive and slow; — Par Lost 4.173
When *Satan* still in gaze, as first he stood, — Par Lost 4.356
Know ye not then said *Satan*, fill'd with scorn, — Par Lost 4.827
Why hast thou, *Satan*, broke the bounds prescrib'd — Par Lost 4.878
To whom thus *Satan*, with contemptuous brow. — Par Lost 4.885
Since *Satan* fell, whom follie overthrew, — Par Lost 4.905
Satan, and couldst thou faithful add? O name, — Par Lost 4.950
So threatn'd hee, but *Satan* to no threats — Par Lost 4.968
Prove chaff. On th' other side *Satan* allarm'd — Par Lost 4.985
Satan, I know thy strength, and thou knowst mine, — Par Lost 4.1006
Satan from Hell scap't through the darksom Gulf — Par Lost 5.225
Satan, so call him now, his former name — Par Lost 5.658
So spake the Son, but *Satan* with his Powers — Par Lost 5.743
They came, and *Satan* to his Royal seat — Par Lost 5.756
The banded Powers of *Satan* hasting on — Par Lost 6.85
Satan with vast and haughtie strides advanc't, — Par Lost 6.109

Satan(*cont*)
On the proud Crest of *Satan*, that no sight, — Par Lost 6.191
The Battel hung; till *Satan*, who that day — Par Lost 6.246
The sword of *Satan* with steep force to smite — Par Lost 6.324
All his right side; then *Satan* first knew pain, — Par Lost 6.327
Satan with his rebellious disappeerd, — Par Lost 6.414
Whereto with look compos'd *Satan* repli'd. — Par Lost 6.469
Satan: And thus was heard Commanding loud. — Par Lost 6.557
They worse abhorr'd. *Satan* beheld thir plight, — Par Lost 6.607
With *Satan*, hee who envies now thy state, — Par Lost 6.900
When *Satan* who late fled before the threats — Par Lost 9.53
Satan involv'd in rising Mist, then sought — Par Lost 9.75
Of *Satan* done in Paradise, and how — Par Lost 10.2
Hinder'd not *Satan* to attempt the minde — Par Lost 10.8
To *Satan* first in sin his doom apply'd, — Par Lost 10.172
Saw Satan fall like Lightning down from Heav'n, — Par Lost 10.184
The Realm it self of Satan long usurpt, — Par Lost 10.189
Idlely, while Satan our great Author thrives — Par Lost 10.236
Where Satan now prevailes, a Monument — Par Lost 10.258
Of *Satan*, to the self same place where hee — Par Lost 10.315
Satan in likeness of an Angel bright — Par Lost 10.327
Of *Satan* (for I glorie in the name, — Par Lost 10.386
Then sufferd. Th' other way *Satan* went down — Par Lost 10.414
Wide open and unguarded, *Satan* pass'd, — Par Lost 10.419
Of that bright Starr to *Satan* paragond. — Par Lost 10.426
Second of *Satan* sprung, all conquering *Death*, — Par Lost 10.591
To *Satan* only like both crime and doom. — Par Lost 10.841
Satan, who in the Serpent hath contriv'd — Par Lost 10.1034
Satans dire dread, and in his hand the Spear. — Par Lost 11.248
Satan, whose fall from Heav'n, a deadlier bruise, — Par Lost 12.391
Not by destroying *Satan*, but his works — Par Lost 12.394
Shall bruise the head of *Satan*, crush his strength — Par Lost 12.430
Satans assaults, and quench his fierie darts, — Par Lost 12.492
Satan with his perverted World, then raise — Par Lost 12.547
To Satan; let him tempt and now assay — Par Reg 1.143
He added not; and Satan bowing low — Par Reg 1.497
For Satan with slye preface to return — Par Reg 2.115
To whom quick answer Satan thus return'd. — Par Reg 2.172
How hast thou hunger then? Satan reply'd, — Par Reg 2.319
To whom thus answer'd Satan malecontent: — Par Reg 2.392
So spake the Son of God, and Satan stood — Par Reg 3.1
Satan had not to answer, but stood struck — Par Reg 3.146
So Satan, whom repulse upon repulse — Par Reg 4.21
That Evil one, Satan for ever damn'd. — Par Reg 4.194
So spake the Son of God; but Satan now — Par Reg 4.365
But Satan smitten with amazement fell — Par Reg 4.562
So Satan fell and strait a fiery Globe — Par Reg 4.581
Queller of Satan, on thy glorious work — Par Reg 4.634

Satanic
Orewearied, through the faint Satanic Host — Par Lost 6.392
His weakness shall o'recome Satanic strength — Par Reg 1.161

Sate
But all to please, and sate the curious taste? — Mask 714

Sated
Sated at length, ere long I might perceave — Par Lost 9.598

Satiate
Or satiate fury yield it from our Foe. — Par Lost 1.179
Satiate with genial moisture, when God said — Par Lost 7.282
Of sweet repast; they satiate, and soon fill, — Par Lost 8.214
Thee satiate, to short absence I could yield. — Par Lost 9.248
And knew not eating Death: Satiate at length, — Par Lost 9.792

Satiety
Imbu'd, bring to thir sweetness no satietie. — Par Lost 8.216

Satisfaction
The rigid satisfaction, death for death. — Par Lost 3.212
In this his satisfaction; so he dies, — Par Lost 12.419

Satisfied
Not mind us not offending, satisfi'd — Par Lost 2.212
How fully hast thou satisfi'd mee, pure — Par Lost 8.180
Them fully satisfied, and thee appease. — Par Lost 10.79
Satisfi'd never; that were to extend — Par Lost 10.804
Religion satisfi'd; Truth shall retire — Par Lost 12.535
Have satisfi'd thir utmost of revenge — Samson 484
Intirely satisfi'd, — Circum 22

Satisfy
Shall satisfie for Man, be judg'd and die, — Par Lost 3.295
To satisfie the sharp desire I had — Par Lost 9.584
In punisht man, to satisfie his rigour — Par Lost 10.803
Be forc'd to satisfie his Rav'nous Maw. — Par Lost 10.991
Or that which only seems to satisfie — Par Reg 2.229
Can satisfie that need some other way, — Par Reg 2.254
To satisfie thy lust: Love seeks to have Love; — Samson 837
And satisfie them from the rock — Psalm 81, 67

Satisfying
But never find self-satisfying solution. — Samson 306

Satst
Dove-like satst brooding on the vast Abyss — Par Lost 1.21
Why satst thou like an enemie in waite — Par Lost 4.825
Sat'st unappall'd in calm and sinless peace. — Par Reg 4.425

Saturn
By younger *Saturn*, he from mightier *Jove* — Par Lost 1.512
ms 'Saturn'
Of *Doric* Land; or who with *Saturn* old — Par Lost 1.519
ms 'Saturn'
Of high *Olympus*, thence by *Saturn* driv'n — Par Lost 10.583
To som of *Saturns* crew. I must dissemble, — Mask 805
line not in Bridgewater ms
line not in Trinity ms

Saturn(*cont*)
To solitary *Saturn* bore; Penseroso 24
His daughter she (in *Saturns* raign, Penseroso 25

Satyr
Satyr, or Fawn, or Silvan? But these haunts Par Reg 2.191

Satyrs
Rough *Satyrs* danc'd, and *Fauns* with clov'n heel, Lycidas 34
1638 'Satyres'

Savage
Now to th' ascent of that steep savage Hill Par Lost 4.172
To rapture, till the savage clamor dround Par Lost 7.36
In solitude live savage, in some glade Par Lost 9.1085
In savage Wilderness, wherefore deprive Par Reg 3.23
Of Savage hunger, or of Savage heat? Mask 358
line not in Bridgewater ms
line not in Trinity ms
No savage fierce, Bandite, or mountaneer Mask 426
Trinity ms 'salvage'
Bridgewater ms 'salvage'

Save
Save what the glimmering of these livid flames Par Lost 1.182
Save he who reigns above, none can resist. Par Lost 2.814
Mans mortal crime, and just th' unjust to save, Par Lost 3.215
Thee from my bosom and right hand, to save, Par Lost 3.279
God-like fruition, quitted all to save Par Lost 3.307
Save on that side which from the wall of Heav'n Par Lost 3.427
Will save us trial what the least can doe Par Lost 4.855
The cool, the silent, save where silence yields Par Lost 5.39
Save what by frugal storing firmness gains Par Lost 5.324
Undeckt, save with her self more lovely fair Par Lost 5.380
Fannd with coole Winds, save those who in thir course Par Lost 5.655
Whom fled we thought, will save us long pursuit Par Lost 6.538
Save what sin hath impaird, which yet hath wrought Par Lost 6.691
To save appeerances, how gird the Sphear Par Lost 8.82
Or save the Sun his labour, and that swift Par Lost 8.133
Save with the Creatures which I made, and those Par Lost 8.409
Save what is in destroying, other joy Par Lost 9.478
To save himself and houshold from amidst Par Lost 11.820
Save when they journie, and at length they come, Par Lost 12.258
Save by those shadowie expiations weak, Par Lost 12.291
To save them, not thir own, though legal works. Par Lost 12.410
So shalt thou save thy self and us relieve Par Reg 1.344
Now enter, and begin to save mankind. Par Reg 4.635
To save himself against a coward arm'd Samson 347
Living and dead recorded, who to save Samson 984
To save her blossoms, and defend her fruit Mask 396
Listen and save. Mask 866
Listen and save. Mask 889
Save the Cricket on the hearth, Penseroso 82
And all my Plants I save from nightly ill, Arcades 48
Summers three times eight save one Winchester 7
To save th' *Athenian* Walls from ruine bare. Sonnet 8, 14
Trinity ms 'saue'
Helpe us to save free Conscience from the paw Sonnet 16, 13
Purification in the old Law did save, Sonnet 23, 6
Rise Lord, save me my God for thou Psalm 3, 19
My soul, O save me for thy goodness sake Psalm 6, 8
Save me and secure me under Psalm 7, 2
To save us by thy might. Psalm 80, 12
Save thou thy servant O my God Psalm 86, 7
And save thy hand-maids Son. Psalm 86, 60
Lord God that dost me save and keep, Psalm 88, 1

Saved
Man shall not quite be lost, but sav'd who will, Par Lost 3.173
Sav'd with care from Winters nip, Winchester 36

Saves
Them in his anger, whom his anger saves Par Lost 2.158
From whom as oft he saves them penitent Par Lost 12.319
Saves th' upright of Heart at last. Psalm 7, 42
Thy wrath *from which no shelter saves* Psalm 88, 29

Saving
By saving Doctrine, and from errour lead Par Reg 2.474
God of our saving health and peace, Psalm 85, 13
Thy saving health to us afford Psalm 85, 27

Saviour
Hail Son of God, Saviour of Men, thy Name Par Lost 3.412
So judg'd he Man, both Judge and Saviour sent, Par Lost 10.209
Which hee, who comes thy Saviour, shall recure, Par Lost 12.393
Now amplier known thy Saviour and thy Lord, Par Lost 12.544
Of Saviour to mankind, and which way first Par Reg 1.187
To whom our Saviour sternly thus reply'd. Par Reg 1.406
So spake our Saviour; but the subtle Fiend, Par Reg 1.465
To whom our Saviour with unalter'd brow. Par Reg 1.493
Our Saviour, and found all was but a dream, Par Reg 2.283
Our Saviour lifting up his eyes beheld Par Reg 2.338
To whom our Saviour calmly thus reply'd. Par Reg 3.43
To whom our Saviour fervently reply'd. Par Reg 3.121
To whom our Saviour answer thus return'd. Par Reg 3.181
Our Saviour, and new train of words began. Par Reg 3.266
And to our Saviour thus his words renew'd. Par Reg 3.346
To whom our Saviour answer'd thus unmov'd. Par Reg 3.386
He brought our Saviour to the western side Par Reg 4.25
Whom thus our Saviour answer'd with disdain. Par Reg 4.170
To whom our Saviour sagely thus repli'd. Par Reg 4.285
Thus to our Saviour with stern brow reply'd. Par Reg 4.367
Our Saviour meek and with untroubl'd mind Par Reg 4.401
Of this fair change, and to our Saviour came, Par Reg 4.442
On thy birth-night, that sung thee Saviour born. Par Reg 4.506

Saviour(*cont*)
A Saviour art come down to re-install. Par Reg 4.615
Thus they the Son of God our Saviour meek Par Reg 4.636

Savour
Since to each meaning savour me apply, Par Lost 9.1019
The savour of Death from all things there that live: Par Lost 10.269
Fruits of more pleasing savour from thy seed Par Lost 11.26
And savour, Beasts of chase, or Fowl of game, Par Reg 2.342

Savours
That cuts us off from hope, and savours onely Par Lost 10.1043

Savoury
The savourie pulp they chew, and in the rinde Par Lost 4.335
Which he had pluckt; the pleasant savourie smell Par Lost 5.84
For dinner savourie fruits, of taste to please Par Lost 5.304
When from the boughes a savorie odour blow'n, Par Lost 9.579
So savorie of that Fruit, which with desire, Par Lost 9.741
Had ta'n their supper on the savoury Herb Mask 541
Bridgewater ms 'savorie'
Trinity ms 'savourie'
1637 'savourie'
Are at their savory dinner set Allegro 84

Saw
Ezekiel saw, when by the Vision led Par Lost 1.455
I know thee not, nor ever saw till now Par Lost 2.744
I saw and heard, for such a numerous Host Par Lost 2.993
The Stairs were such as whereon *Jacob* saw Par Lost 3.510
Through his glaz'd Optic Tube yet never saw. Par Lost 3.590
Saw within kenn a glorious Angel stand, Par Lost 3.622
The same whom *John* saw also in the Sun: Par Lost 3.623
I saw when at his Word the formless Mass, Par Lost 3.708
O for that warning voice, which he who saw Par Lost 4.1
Saw him disfigur'd, more then could befall Par Lost 4.127
On th' other side: which when th' arch-fellon saw Par Lost 4.179
Saw undelighted all delight, all kind Par Lost 4.286
And felt how awful goodness is, and saw Par Lost 4.847
Vertue in her shape how lovly, saw, and pin'd Par Lost 4.848
Who dwell in Heav'n, whose excellence he saw Par Lost 5.456
Wonder not then, what God for you saw good Par Lost 5.491
Nightly before him, saw without thir light Par Lost 5.714
Rebellion rising, saw in whom, how spred Par Lost 5.715
Doctrin which we would know whence learnt: who saw Par Lost 5.856
Saw where the Sword of *Michael* smote, and fell'd Par Lost 6.250
Wide the Celestial soile, and saw beneath Par Lost 6.510
When coming towards them so dread they saw Par Lost 6.648
They saw them whelm'd, and all thir confidence Par Lost 6.651
This saw his hapless Foes but stood obdur'd, Par Lost 6.785
Hell heard th' unsufferable noise, Hell saw Par Lost 6.867
Sojourn'd the while. God saw the Light was good; Par Lost 7.249
And saw that it was good, and said, Let th' Earth Par Lost 7.309
On the green stemm; God saw that it was good. Par Lost 7.337
And Light from Darkness to divide. God saw, Par Lost 7.352
And saw that it was good, and bless'd them, saying, Par Lost 7.395
And Grace that won who saw to wish her stay, Par Lost 8.43
Stood on my feet; about me round I saw Par Lost 8.261
What e're I saw. Thou Sun, said I, faire Light, Par Lost 8.273
Tell, if ye saw, how came I thus, how here? Par Lost 8.277
Planted, with Walks, and Bowers, that what I saw Par Lost 8.305
Abstract as in a transe methought I saw, Par Lost 8.462
Though sleeping, where I lay, and saw the shape Par Lost 8.463
Such as I saw her in my dream, adornd Par Lost 8.482
All other Beasts that saw, with like desire Par Lost 9.592
Which when she saw, thus to her guide she spake. Par Lost 9.646
I saw thee first and wedded thee, adorn'd Par Lost 9.1030
Saw Satan fall like Lightning down from Heav'n, Par Lost 10.184
To observe the sequel, saw his guileful act Par Lost 10.334
Upon her Husband, saw thir shame that sought Par Lost 10.336
Vain covertures; but when he saw descend Par Lost 10.337
He sate, and round about him saw unseen: Par Lost 10.448
They saw, but other sight instead, a crowd Par Lost 10.538
And horrid sympathie; for what they saw, Par Lost 10.540
The growing miseries, which *Adam* saw Par Lost 10.715
As how with peccant Angels late they saw; Par Lost 11.70
Methought I saw him placable and mild, Par Lost 11.151
Jacob in *Mahanaim*, where he saw Par Lost 11.214
The World: in Spirit perhaps he also saw Par Lost 11.406
He lookd and saw a spacious Plaine, whereon Par Lost 11.556
He lookd and saw wide Territorie spred Par Lost 11.638
He look'd, and saw the face of things quite chang'd, Par Lost 11.712
But all in vain: which when he saw, he ceas'd Par Lost 11.726
He lookd, and saw the Ark hull on the floud, Par Lost 11.840
Griev'd at his heart, when looking down he saw Par Lost 11.887
Thenceforth the Nations may not doubt; I saw Par Reg 1.79
He saw approach, who first with curious eye Par Reg 1.319
Of God; I saw and heard, for we sometimes Par Reg 1.330
But to his Mother *Mary*, when she saw Par Reg 2.60
I lost him, but so found, as well I saw Par Reg 2.97
And saw the Ravens with their horny beaks Par Reg 2.267
He saw the Prophet also how he fled Par Reg 2.270
But Cottage, Herd or Sheep-cote none he saw, Par Reg 2.288
Only in a bottom saw a pleasant Grove, Par Reg 2.289
He look't and saw what numbers numberless Par Reg 3.310
He saw them in thir forms of battell rang'd, Par Reg 3.322
Sam. The first I saw at *Timna*, and she pleas'd Samson 219
That saw not how degenerately I serv'd. Samson 419
Caus'd what I did? I saw thee mutable Samson 793
No better way I saw then by importuning Samson 797
I less conjecture then when first I saw Samson 1071
My Brothers when they saw me wearied out Mask 182

Saw(*cont*)
Bridgewater ms 'sawe'
Co. Two such I saw, what time the labour'd Oxe — Mask 291
Bridgewater ms 'sawe'
I saw them under a green mantling vine — Mask 294
Bridgewater ms 'sawe'
Trinity ms 'saw''
He saw a greater Sun appear — Nativity 83
That saw the troubl'd Sea, and shivering fled, — Psalm 114, 7
Fore-saw what future dayes should bring to pass, — Vacation 72
Love led them on, and Faith who knew them best — Sonnet 14, 9
Trinity ms 'knew' ←'saw' ←'knew'
Methought I saw my late espoused Saint — Sonnet 23, 1

Sawest
Surround me, as thou sawst, hourly conceiv'd — Par Lost 2.796
And no such companie as then thou saw'st — Par Lost 8.446
Some, as thou saw'st, by violent stroke shall die, — Par Lost 11.471
Those Tents thou sawst so pleasant, were the Tents — Par Lost 11.607
For that fair femal Troop thou sawst, that seemd — Par Lost 11.614
Of those ill mated Marriages thou saw'st: — Par Lost 11.684
Did, as thou sawst, receave, to walk with God — Par Lost 11.707
To whom thus *Michael*. Those whom last thou sawst — Par Lost 11.787
To that proud Citie, whose high Walls thou saw'st — Par Lost 12.342

Saws
With their grave Saws in slumber ly. — Mask 110
Trinity ms 'saws'
1637 'Sawes'
Bridgewater ms 'sawes'

Say
Say first, for Heav'n hides nothing from thy view — Par Lost 1.27
Nor the deep Tract of Hell, say first what cause — Par Lost 1.28
Say, Muse, thir Names then known, who first, who last, — Par Lost 1.376
Say they who counsel Warr, we are decreed, — Par Lost 2.160
Say Heav'nly powers, where shall we find such love, — Par Lost 3.213
But say I could repent and could obtaine — Par Lost 4.93
The rest is true, they found me where they say; — Par Lost 4.900
To say and strait unsay, pretending first — Par Lost 4.947
By steps we may ascend to God. But say, — Par Lost 5.512
Say Goddess, what ensu'd when *Raphael*, — Par Lost 7.40
Aught, not surpassing human measure, say. — Par Lost 7.640
On Man his Equal Love: say therefore on; — Par Lost 8.228
The more desirable, or to say all, — Par Lost 8.505
Her own, that what she wills to do or say, — Par Lost 8.549
Redouble then this miracle, and say, — Par Lost 9.562
Say, for such wonder claims attention due. — Par Lost 9.566
But say, where grows the Tree, from hence how far? — Par Lost 9.617
Which oft, they say, some evil Spirit attends — Par Lost 9.638
Triumph and say; Fickle their State whom God — Par Lost 9.948
Say Woman, what is this which thou hast done? — Par Lost 10.158
Yearly enjoynd, some say, to undergo — Par Lost 10.575
Some say he bid his Angels turne ascanse — Par Lost 10.668
Oblique the Centric Globe: Som say the Sun — Par Lost 10.671
Thy Justice seems; yet to say truth, too late, — Par Lost 10.755
Not to th' extent of thir own Spheare. But say — Par Lost 10.808
But say, what mean those colourd streaks in Heavn, — Par Lost 11.879
Expect with mortal paine: say where and when — Par Lost 12.384
But say, if our deliverer up to Heav'n — Par Lost 12.479
Envy they say excites me, thus to gain — Par Reg 1.397
What to the smallest tittle thou shalt say — Par Reg 1.450
Say and unsay, feign, flatter, or abjure? — Par Reg 1.474
A while as mute confounded what to say, — Par Reg 3.2
What best to say canst say, to do canst do; — Par Reg 3.8
But say thou wer't possess'd of *David's* Throne — Par Reg 3.357
In every street, do they not say, how well — Samson 204
Yet truth to say, I oft have heard men wonder — Samson 215
Came lagging after; say if he be here. — Samson 337
Or might I say contrarious, — Samson 669
Thy key of strength and safety: thou wilt say, — Samson 799
But what it is, hard is to say, — Samson 1013
Off. Samson, to thee our Lords thus bid me say; — Samson 1310
To thee I am bid say. Art thou our Slave, — Samson 1392
With thee; say reverend Sire, we thirst to hear. — Samson 1456
Yet e're I give the rains to grief, say first, — Samson 1578
(*Gaza* is not in plight to say us nay) — Samson 1729
Som say no evil thing that walks by night — Mask 432
Bridgewater ms 'naye more'
Trinity ms 'Some say' ←'Nay more' ←'Some say'
Fain would I somthing say, yet to what end? — Mask 783
line not in Bridgewater ms
line not in Trinity ms
Say Heav'nly Muse, shall not thy sacred vein — Nativity 15
Oh say me true if thou wert mortal wight — Fair Inf 41
That even to his last breath (ther be that say't) — Another 25
line not in 1640, 1657, 1658 texts
Let us break off, say they, by strength of hand — Psalm 2, 6
That of my life distrustfully thus say, — Psalm 3, 5
Many there be that say — Psalm 4, 25
Come let us cut them off say they, — Psalm 83, 13
Tis you that say it, not I, you do the deeds, — Prose 8, 1

Sayest
Confess him rightful King? unjust thou saist — Par Lost 5.818
That we were formd then saist thou? and the work — Par Lost 5.853
To love thou blam'st me not, for love thou saist — Par Lost 8.612
Means I must use thou say'st, prediction else — Par Reg 3.394
How gloriously; I shall, thou say'st, expel — Par Reg 4.127
By this appears: I gave, thou say'st, th' example, — Samson 822
All by him fell thou say'st, by whom fell he, — Samson 1580

Saying
None shall partake with me. Thus saying rose — Par Lost 2.466
Thus saying, from her side the fatal Key, — Par Lost 2.871
So saying, his proud step he scornful turn'd, — Par Lost 4.536
So saying, on he led his radiant Files, — Par Lost 4.797
So saying, he drew nigh, and to me held, — Par Lost 5.82
So saying, with dispatchful looks in haste — Par Lost 5.331
So saying, a noble stroke he lifted high, — Par Lost 6.189
And saw that it was good, and bless'd them, saying, — Par Lost 7.395
So saying, by the hand he took me rais'd, — Par Lost 8.300
So saying, he arose; whom *Adam* thus — Par Lost 8.644
So saying, through each Thicket Danck or Drie, — Par Lost 9.179
Thus saying, from her Husbands hand her hand — Par Lost 9.385
So saying, her rash hand in evil hour — Par Lost 9.780
So saying, from the Tree her step she turnd, — Par Lost 9.834
So saying, she embrac'd him, and for joy — Par Lost 9.990
Thus saying, from his radiant Seat he rose — Par Lost 10.85
I charg'd thee, saying: Thou shalt not eate thereof, — Par Lost 10.200
So saying, with delight he snuff'd the smell — Par Lost 10.272
So saying he dismiss'd them, they with speed — Par Lost 10.410
So saying he took (for still he knew his power — Par Reg 4.394
So saying he caught him up, and without wing — Par Reg 4.541
And old sooth-saying *Glaucus* spell, — Mask 874
Bridgewater ms 'sooth-sayinge'
1637 'sooth saying'

Sayings
And sayings laid up, portending strange events. — Par Reg 2.104
Chor. Many are the sayings of the wise — Samson 652

Says
But wisest Fate sayes no, — Nativity 149

Scaffolds
On banks and scaffolds under Skie might stand; — Samson 1610

Scalding
Yet parcht with scalding thurst and hunger fierce, — Par Lost 10.556

Scale
The way seems difficult and steep to scale — Par Lost 2.71
To th' Ocean Iles, and in th' ascending Scale — Par Lost 4.354
His mounted scale aloft: nor more; but fled — Par Lost 4.1014
Mans nourishment, by gradual scale sublim'd — Par Lost 5.483
Our knowledge, and the scale of Nature set — Par Lost 5.509
Conflicting Fire: long time in eeven scale — Par Lost 6.245
In Reason, and is judicious, is the scale — Par Lost 8.591
In eevn scale. But fall'n he is, and now — Par Lost 10.47
Lay Seige, encampt; by Batterie, Scale, and Mine, — Par Lost 11.656
Belial, in much uneven scale thou weigh'st — Par Reg 2.173

Scaled
That scal'd by steps of Gold to Heav'n Gate — Par Lost 3.541

Scales
Hung forth in Heav'n his golden Scales, yet seen — Par Lost 4.997
Of Fish that with thir Finns and shining Scales — Par Lost 7.401
By *Leo* and the *Virgin* and the *Scales*, — Par Lost 10.676

Scalp
Or drag him by the curls, to a foul death, — Mask 608
Bridgewater ms 'and cleave his scalpe'
1637 'and cleave his scalpe'
Trinity ms 'or drag him by the curls & cleave his scalpe'
His goary visage down the stream was sent, — Lycidas 62
Trinity ms 'visage' ←'head' ←'scalpe'
his goarie scalpe rowle downe the Thracian lee — Lycidas Tr. ms 29.61

Scaly
With fixed Anchor in his skaly rind — Par Lost 1.206
ms 'Scaly'
But ended foul in many a scaly fould — Par Lost 2.651
The River Horse and scalie Crocodile. — Par Lost 7.474
By scaly *Tritons* winding shell, — Mask 873
1637 'scalie'
Bridgewater ms 'scalie'
Swindges the scaly Horrour of his foulded tail. — Nativity 172

Scaly-harnessed
the scalie-harnest dragon ever keeps — Mask Tr. ms 10.09

Scan
Words with just note and accent, not to scan — Sonnet 13, 3
when most were wont which till then us'd to scan — Sonnet 13, Tr. ms 40.03

Scandal
Even to that Hill of scandal, by the Grove — Par Lost 1.416
ms 'scandall'
Of Idolists, and Atheists; have brought scandal — Samson 453

Scandalous
Scandalous or forbidden in our Law. — Samson 1409

Scanned
His secrets to be scann'd by them who ought — Par Lost 8.74

Scant
That mock our scant manuring, and require — Par Lost 4.628
Were left for hast unfinish't, judgment scant, — Samson 1027
In such a scant allowance of Star-light, — Mask 308

Scape
Rather then human. Nor did *Israel* scape — Par Lost 1.482
To have built in Heav'n high Towrs; nor did he scape — Par Lost 1.749
If thence he scape into whatever world, — Par Lost 2.442
However, and to scape his punishment. — Par Lost 4.911
Was known in Heav'n; for what can scape the Eye — Par Lost 10.5
Shall scape his punishment ordain'd, and wee — Par Lost 10.1039
Check or reproof, and glad to scape so quit. — Par Reg 1.477
If these they scape, perhaps in poverty — Samson 697
Spir. What, have you let the false enchanter scape? — Mask 814
Trinity ms 'scape' ←'passe'
With shame, *and scape it never*. — Psalm 83, 64

Scaped
Both glorying to have scap't the *Stygian* flood Par Lost 1.239
The coming of thir secret foe, and scap'd Par Lost 4.7
Haply so scap'd his mortal snare; for now Par Lost 4.8
And now returns him from his prison scap't, Par Lost 4.906
Satan from Hell scap't through the darksom Gulf Par Lost 5.225
While yet the Patriark liv'd, who scap'd the Flood, Par Lost 12.117
The vulgar only scap'd who stood without. Samson 1659
Scapes
Too long, then lay'st thy scapes on names ador'd, Par Reg 2.189
Scar
To heal the scarr of these corrosive Fires Par Lost 2.401
Scarce
He scarce had ceas't when the superiour Fiend Par Lost 1.283
And hands innumerable scarce perform. Par Lost 1.699
He scarce had finisht, when such murmur filld Par Lost 2.284
In whirlwind; Hell scarce holds the wilde uproar. Par Lost 2.541
Dislodging from a Region scarce of prey Par Lost 3.433
Scarce thus at length faild speech recoverd sad. Par Lost 4.357
He scarce had ended, when those two approachd Par Lost 4.874
Of day-spring, and the Sun, who scarce up risen Par Lost 5.139
And we have yet large day, for scarce the Sun Par Lost 5.558
Hath finisht half his journey, and scarce begins Par Lost 5.559
Defensive scarse, or with pale fear surpris'd, Par Lost 6.393
So scoffing in ambiguous words he scarce, Par Lost 6.568
Yet scarce allay'd still eyes the current streame, Par Lost 7.67
He scarce had said, when the bare Earth, till then Par Lost 7.313
Her bosom smelling sweet: and these scarce blown, Par Lost 7.319
Bore up his branching head: scarse from his mould Par Lost 7.470
Onely to shine, yet scarce to contribute Par Lost 8.155
Of Earth before scarce pleasant seemd. Each Tree Par Lost 8.306
1667 'scarse'
She scarse had said, though brief, when now more bold Par Lost 9.664
Scarse from the Tree returning; in her hand Par Lost 9.850
Scarce tollerable, and from the North to call Par Lost 10.654
While yet we live, scarse one short hour perhaps, Par Lost 10.923
And scarce recovering words his plaint renew'd. Par Lost 11.499
Thir Bootie; scarse with Life the Shepherds flye, Par Lost 11.650
And scarce to th' Angel utterdst thus thy plaint. Par Lost 11.762
In such a season born when scarce a Shed Par Reg 2.72
Conceals him: when twelve years he scarce had seen, Par Reg 2.96
Things vulgar, & well weigh'd, scarce worth the praise, Par Reg 3.51
Are few, and glory scarce of few is rais'd. Par Reg 3.59
Till Conquerour Death discover them scarce men, Par Reg 3.85
At home, scarce view'd the *Gallilean* Towns, Par Reg 3.233
Like to themselves, distinguishable scarce Par Reg 3.424
The rest are barbarous, and scarce worth the sight, Par Reg 4.86
Where I a Prisoner chain'd, scarce freely draw Samson 7
Scarce half I seem to live, dead more then half. Samson 79
The sufferers then will scarce molest us here, Samson 1525
Or reason though disturb'd, and scarse consulted Samson 1546
Blind mouthes! that scarce themselves know how to hold Lycidas 119
Trinity ms 'scarse'
Scarce to be less then Gods, thou mad'st his lot, Psalm 8, 15
Scarce-well-lighted
But with a scarce-wel-lighted flame; Winchester 20
Scarf
Then her purfl'd scarf can shew, Mask 995
Trinity ms 'scarfe'
1637 'scarfe'
B.M. ms 'Scarfe'
Bridgewater ms 'scarfe'
Scars
Deep scars of Thunder had intrencht, and care Par Lost 1.601
ms 'scarrs'
Scathed
Hath scath'd the Forrest Oaks, or Mountain Pines, Par Lost 1.613
Scattered
High overarch't imbowr; or scatterd sedge Par Lost 1.304
With scatter'd Arms and Ensigns, till anon Par Lost 1.325
Recovering, and his scatterd spirits returnd, Par Lost 11.294
Where Cattle pastur'd late, now scatterd lies Par Lost 11.653
Lie scatter'd on the Alpine mountains cold, Sonnet 18, 2
Scatters
Scatters the rear of darknes thin, Allegro 50
Scene
A Silvan Scene, and as the ranks ascend Par Lost 4.140
But now prepare thee for another Scene. Par Lost 11.637
If cause were to unfold some active Scene Par Reg 2.239
That open'd in the midst a woody Scene, Par Reg 2.294
And from the daily Scene effeminate. Par Reg 4.142
Scenes
These latter scenes confine my roving vers, Passion 22
Scent
Powerful perswaders, quick'nd at the scent Par Lost 9.587
The way, thou leading, such a sent I draw Par Lost 10.267
With sent of living Carcasses design'd Par Lost 10.277
Though offer'd only, by the sent conceiv'd Samson 390
An Amber sent of odorous perfume Samson 720
Scented
So sented the grim Feature, and upturn'd Par Lost 10.279
Scents
The season, prime for sweetest Sents and Aires: Par Lost 9.200
Sceptre
To gain a Scepter, oftest better miss't. Par Reg 2.486
With Iron Scepter bruis'd, and them disperse Psalm 2, 20
His Empire, and with Iron Scepter rule Par Lost 2.327
Weakning the Scepter of old *Night:* first Hell Par Lost 2.1002

Sceptre(*cont*)
Then thou thy regal Scepter shalt lay by, Par Lost 3.339
For regal Scepter then no more shall need, Par Lost 3.340
With Diadem and Scepter high advanc'd Par Lost 4.90
With Regal Scepter, every Soule in Heav'n Par Lost 5.816
That Golden Scepter which thou didst reject Par Lost 5.886
Scepter and Power, thy giving, I assume, Par Lost 6.730
So said, he o're his Scepter bowing, rose Par Lost 6.746
The Scepter, and regard not *Davids* Sons, Par Lost 12.357
David's true heir, and his full Scepter sway Par Reg 3.405
E're thou of *Israel*'s Scepter get fast hold; Par Reg 4.480
A Scepter or quaint staff he bears, Samson 1303
And new-entrusted Scepter, but their way Mask 36
Trinity ms 'scepter'
Bridgewater ms 'scepter'
That had the Scepter from his father *Brute*. Mask 828
1637 'scepter'
Trinity ms 'scepter'
Bridgewater ms 'scepter'
Sceptred
Where Scepter'd Angels held thir residence, Par Lost 1.734
ms 'scepter'd'
He ceas'd, and next him *Moloc*, Scepter'd King Par Lost 2.43
In other part the scepter'd Haralds call Par Lost 11.660
In Scepter'd Pall com sweeping by, Penseroso 98
School
Best school of best experience, quickest in sight Par Reg 3.238
For of such Doctrine never was there School, Samson 297
Schools
The schools of antient Sages; his who bred Par Reg 4.251
Mellifluous streams that water'd all the schools Par Reg 4.277
Antiquity from the old Schools of Greece Mask 439
Trinity ms 'schooles'
Bridgewater ms 'schooles'
1637 'schools'
Science
Mother of Science, Now I feel thy Power Par Lost 9.680
Sciential
Into the plant sciential sap, deriv'd Par Lost 9.837
Scipio
Scipio the highth of *Rome*. With tract oblique Par Lost 9.510
At his dispose, young *Scipio* had brought down Par Reg 3.34
Scoff
Shall laugh, the Lord shall scoff them, then severe Psalm 2, 9
Scoffing
So scoffing in ambiguous words he scarce, Par Lost 6.568
Stood scoffing, highthn'd in thir thoughts beyond Par Lost 6.629
Scoop
Still as they thirsted scoop the brimming stream; Par Lost 4.336
Scope
And utter dissolution, as the scope Par Lost 2.127
Thy coming hither, though I know thy scope, Par Reg 1.494
Scorch
Never scorch thy tresses fair, Mask 929
Bridgewater ms 'scortch'
Scorched
Of *Ramiel* scorcht and blasted overthrew. Par Lost 6.372
Scorching
Avoided pinching cold and scorching heate? Par Lost 10.691
Score
That rigid score. A worse thing yet remains, Samson 433
Yet on the softned Quarry would I score Passion 46
Scorn
Let us not slip th' occasion, whether scorn, Par Lost 1.178
Thrice he assayd, and thrice in spight of scorn, Par Lost 1.619
Hell-doom'd, and breath'st defiance here and scorn Par Lost 2.697
They who neglect and scorn, shall never taste; Par Lost 3.199
Know ye not then said *Satan*, fill'd with scorn, Par Lost 4.827
To whom thus *Zephon*, answering scorn with scorn. Par Lost 4.834
Thus he in scorn. The warlike Angel mov'd, Par Lost 4.902
And Seale thee so, as henceforth not to scorne Par Lost 4.966
Long way through hostile scorn, which he susteind Par Lost 5.904
And with retorted scorn his back he turn'd Par Lost 5.906
So easie, and of his Thunder made a scorn, Par Lost 6.632
Against temptation: thou thy self with scorne Par Lost 9.299
Matter of scorne, not to be given the Foe, Par Lost 9.951
Wherewith to scorne the Earth: but that false Fruit Par Lost 9.1011
1667 'scorn'
Of public scorn; he wonderd, but not long Par Lost 10.509
Offended; fearless of reproach and scorn, Par Lost 11.811
With all his sacred things, a scorn and prey Par Lost 12.341
A spectacle of ruin or of scorn Par Reg 1.415
The Son of God; and added thus in scorn: Par Reg 4.550
Made of my Enemies the scorn and gaze; Samson 34
In scorn of thir proud arms and warlike tools, Samson 137
Disglorifi'd, blasphem'd, and had in scorn Samson 442
Contempt, and scorn of all, to be excluded Samson 494
The subject of thir cruelty, or scorn. Samson 646
To scorn delights, and live laborious dayes; Lycidas 72
Trinity ms 'scorne'
To scorn the sordid world, and unto Heav'n aspire. Fair Inf 63
My glory have in scorn Psalm 4, 8
Philistia *full of scorn*, Psalm 87, 14
Scorned
Then scornd thou didst depart, and to subdue Par Lost 6.40
Justice shall not return as bountie scorn'd. Par Lost 10.54
That scorn'd his indignation: through the Gate, Par Lost 10.418
Of beauty and her lures, easily scorn'd Par Reg 2.194

Scorned(*cont*)
Helpless, thence easily contemn'd, and scorn'd, Samson 943
Scorners
Of scorners hath not sate. But in the great Psalm 1, 4
Scornful
So saying, his proud step he scornful turn'd, Par Lost 4.536
Whom the grand foe with scornful eye askance Par Lost 6.149
To gratifie my scornful Enemies, Par Lost 10.625
Of *scornful* Ishmael, Psalm 83, 22
Scorning
Scorning surprize. Or could we break our way Par Lost 2.134
Scorning the unexempt condition Mask 685
line not in Bridgewater ms
Scorns
Contempts, and scorns, and snares, and violence, Par Reg 3.191
Attends thee, scorns, reproaches, injuries, Par Reg 4.387
Scorpion
Betwixt *Astrea* and the *Scorpion* signe, Par Lost 4.998
Betwixt the *Centaure* and the *Scorpion* stearing Par Lost 10.328
Scorpion and Asp, and *Amphisbaena* dire, Par Lost 10.524
As Graces, draw a Scorpions tail behind? Samson 360
Scorpions
Least with a whip of Scorpions I pursue Par Lost 2.701
Scotch
By shallow *Edwards* and Scotch what d' ye call: Forcers 12
Scots
While Darwen stream with blood of Scotts imbru'd, Sonnet 16, 7
1694 *'Scots'*
Scour
Lookd round, and Scouts each Coast light-armed scoure, Par Lost 6.529
Scourge
The Vassals of his anger, when the Scourge Par Lost 2.90
Seavenfold, and scourge that wisdom back to Hell, Par Lost 4.914
Scourged
And scourg'd with many a stroak th' indignant waves. Par Lost 10.311
Scours
He scours the right hand coast, som times the left, Par Lost 2.633
Scout
Scout farr and wide into the Realm of night, Par Lost 2.133
Of all this World at once. As when a Scout Par Lost 3.543
Ere the blabbing Eastern scout, Mask 138
Bridgewater ms 'scoute'
Scouts
Lookd round, and Scouts each Coast light-armed scoure, Par Lost 6.529
Scowls
Scowls ore the dark'nd lantskip Snow, or showre; Par Lost 2.491
Scramble
Then how to scramble at the shearers feast, Lycidas 117
Scrannel
Grate on their scrannel Pipes of wretched straw, Lycidas 124
Scratch
he may scratch his forehead. heere be brambles Mask Tr. ms 17.57
'he may scratch' ←'he may chaunce' ←'chance' ←'had best look to'
Scrawled
Inwrought with figures dim, and on the edge Lycidas 105
Trinity ms 'inwraught' ←'scraul'd ore'
Screened
That screen'd the fruits of the earth and seats of men Par Reg 4.30
Scribbled
With Centric and Eccentric scribl'd o're, Par Lost 8.83
Scribes
Concerning the Messiah, to our Scribes Par Reg 1.261
Scrip
And in requitall ope his leather'n scrip, Mask 626
Scroll
Part good, part bad, of bad the longer scrowle, Par Lost 12.336
The Lord shall write it in a Scrowle Psalm 87, 21
Scruple
Would scruple that, with want opprest? behold Par Reg 2.331
Scrupled
With liberal hand: he scrupl'd not to eat Par Lost 9.997
Scrupulous
And Advice with scrupulous head, Mask 108
Scrutiny
And narrower Scrutiny, that I might learn Par Reg 4.515
Sculls
Glide under the green Wave, in Sculles that oft Par Lost 7.402
Sculptures
Cornice or Freeze, with bossy Sculptures grav'n, Par Lost 1.716
ms 'sculptures'
Scum
Gather'd like scum, and setl'd to it self Mask 595
Scummed
Severing each kind, and scum'd the Bullion dross: Par Lost 1.704
Scurf
Shon with a glossie scurff, undoubted sign Par Lost 1.672
ms 'scurf'
Scylla
Vex'd *Scylla* bathing in the Sea that parts Par Lost 2.660
And lap it in *Elysium*, *Scylla* wept, Mask 257
Bridgewater ms 'Scilla'
Scythe
The Sithe of Time mowes down, devour unspar'd, Par Lost 10.606
And the Mower whets his sithe, Allegro 66
Scythian
Against the *Scythian*, whose incursions wild Par Reg 3.301
Or *Humber* loud that keeps the *Scythians* Name, Vacation 99
Scythians
Germans and *Scythians*, and *Sarmatians* North Par Reg 4.78
Sdained
I sdeind subjection, and thought one step higher Par Lost 4.50
Sea
Invests the Sea, and wished Morn delayes: Par Lost 1.208
ms 'sea'
Of that inflamed Sea, he stood and call'd Par Lost 1.300
ms 'sea'
Hath vext the Red-Sea Coast, whose waves orethrew Par Lost 1.306
ms 'red-sea'
Ran purple to the Sea, suppos'd with blood Par Lost 1.451
ms 'sea'
Dagon his Name, Sea Monster, upward Man Par Lost 1.462
ms 'sea'
Had rous'd the Sea, now with hoarse cadence lull Par Lost 2.287
Into th' *Euboic* Sea. Others more milde, Par Lost 2.546
As when farr off at Sea a Fleet descri'd Par Lost 2.636
Vex'd *Scylla* bathing in the Sea that parts Par Lost 2.660
Of neither Sea, nor Shore, nor Air, nor Fire, Par Lost 2.912
Quencht in a Boggie *Syrtis*, neither Sea, Par Lost 2.939
But glad that now his Sea should find a shore, Par Lost 2.1011
Pavement that like a Sea of Jasper shon Par Lost 3.363
So on this windie Sea of Land, the Fiend Par Lost 3.440
Plato's *Elysium*, leap'd into the Sea, Par Lost 3.472
Viewless, and underneath a bright Sea flow'd Par Lost 3.518
In various shapes old *Proteus* from the Sea, Par Lost 3.604
O're Sea and Land: him *Satan* thus accostes; Par Lost 3.653
Mozambic, off at Sea North-East windes blow Par Lost 4.161
Earth, Aire, and Sea. Then let us not think hard Par Lost 4.432
The grosser feeds the purer, Earth the Sea, Par Lost 5.416
1667 'sea'
Earth and the Sea feed Air, the Air those Fires Par Lost 5.417
And all the Sea, from one entire globose Par Lost 5.753
Outrageous as a Sea, dark, wasteful, wilde, Par Lost 7.212
Bank the mid Sea: part single or with mate Par Lost 7.403
Graze the Sea weed thir pasture, and through Groves Par Lost 7.404
Draws in, and at his Trunck spouts out a Sea. Par Lost 7.416
As Plants: ambiguous between Sea and Land Par Lost 7.473
Over the Fish and Fowle of Sea and Aire, Par Lost 7.521
Over Fish of the Sea, and Fowle of the Aire, Par Lost 7.533
On the cleer *Hyaline*, the Glassie Sea; Par Lost 7.619
Over his Works, on Earth, in Sea, or Air, Par Lost 7.629
Or live in Sea, or Aire, Beast, Fish, and Fowle. Par Lost 8.341
Where to lie hid; Sea he had searcht and Land Par Lost 9.76
Now Land, now Sea, and Shores with Forrest crownd, Par Lost 9.117
Solid or slimie, as in raging Sea Par Lost 10.286
Upon the *Cronian* Sea, together drive Par Lost 10.290
Came to the Sea, and over *Hellespont* Par Lost 10.309
Sea, Aire, and Shoar, the Thunder when to rowle Par Lost 10.666
Like change on Sea and Land, sideral blast, Par Lost 10.693
And in a troubl'd Sea of passion tost, Par Lost 10.718
Land, Sea, and Aire, and every kinde that lives, Par Lost 11.337
Deep under water rould; Sea cover'd Sea, Par Lost 11.749
Sea without shoar; and in thir Palaces Par Lost 11.750
Towards the retreating Sea thir furious tyde. Par Lost 11.854
The Earth again by flood, nor let the Sea Par Lost 11.893
From *Hermon* East to the great Western Sea, Par Lost 12.141
Mount *Hermon*, yonder Sea, each place behold Par Lost 12.142
Into the Sea: to sojourn in that Land Par Lost 12.159
Pursuing whom he late dismissd, the Sea Par Lost 12.195
Over the Sea; the Sea his Rod obeys; Par Lost 12.212
Or works of God in Heav'n, Aire, Earth, or Sea, Par Lost 12.579
Gris-amber-steam'd; all Fish from Sea or Shore, Par Reg 2.344
Then meeting joyn'd thir tribute to the Sea: Par Reg 3.258
As the Red Sea and *Jordan* once he cleft, Par Reg 3.438
Wash'd by the Southern Sea, and on the North Par Reg 4.28
The Realm of *Bocchus* to the Black-moor Sea; Par Reg 4.72
But who is this, what thing of Sea or Land? Samson 710
Are reconcil'd at length, and Sea to Shore: Samson 962
Were in the flat Sea sunk. And Wisdoms self Mask 375
Trinity ms 'sea'
Bridgewater ms 'sea'
The Sea o'refraught would swell, & th' unsought diamonds Mask 732
Trinity ms 'sea'
1637 'sea'
Bridgewater ms 'sea'
And listens to the Herald of the Sea Lycidas 89
1638 'sea'
She strikes a universall Peace through Sea and Land. Nativity 52
That saw the troubl'd Sea, and shivering fled, Psalm 114, 7
To the stern God of Sea. Horace 16
Nightly my Couch I make a kind of Sea; Psalm 6, 12
Down to the Sea she sent, Psalm 80, 46
Whose bounds the Sea doth check. Psalm 83, 28
Sea-beast
By ancient *Tarsus* held, or that Sea-beast Par Lost 1.200
Sea-faring
Sea-faring men orewatcht, whose Bark by chance Par Lost 2.288
Sea-girt
Imperial rule of all the Sea-girt Iles Mask 21
Trinity ms 'sea-girt'
Sea-girt it lies, where Giants dwelt of old, Prose 12, 9
Sea-idol
To *Dagon* thir Sea-Idol, and forbid Samson 13
Seal
And Seale thee so, as henceforth not to scorne Par Lost 4.966
In jointed Armour watch: on smooth the Seale, Par Lost 7.409

Seal(*cont*)
Took largely, of thir mutual guilt the Seale, Par Lost 9.1043
For ever, and seal up his ravenous Jawes. Par Lost 10.637
Under the Seal of silence could not keep, Samson 49

Seals
The haunt of Seales and Orcs, and Sea-mews clang. Par Lost 11.835
And seals obedience first with wounding smart Circum 25

Seamen
Deeming some Island, oft, as Sea-men tell, Par Lost 1.205
ms 'Seamen'

Seamews
The haunt of Seales and Orcs, and Sea-mews clang. Par Lost 11.835

Sea-monsters
Where luxurie late reign'd, Sea-monsters whelp'd Par Lost 11.751

Sea-nymphs
The Sea Nymphs, and their powers offended. Penseroso 21

Sea-paths
Sea-paths in shoals do slide. And know no dearth. Psalm 8, 22

Search
In search of this new world, whom shall we find Par Lost 2.403
To search with wandring quest a place foretold Par Lost 2.830
But first with narrow search I must walk round Par Lost 4.528
Search through this Garden, leave unsearcht no nook, Par Lost 4.789
In search of whom they sought: him there they found Par Lost 4.799
Due search and consultation will disclose. Par Lost 6.445
Anough is left besides to search and know. Par Lost 7.125
To ask or search I blame thee not, for Heav'n Par Lost 8.66
With narrow search; and with inspection deep Par Lost 9.83
His midnight search, where soonest he might finde Par Lost 9.181
Each hour their great adventurer from the search Par Lost 10.440
Heer our solemn search hath end. Arcades 7
Trinity ms 'search' ←'seach'
Such as may make thee search thy coffers round, Vacation 31

Searched
Where to lie hid; Sea he had searcht and Land Par Lost 9.76
What oft my steddiest thoughts have searcht in vain, Par Lost 12.377

Searching
The Law and Prophets, searching what was writ Par Reg 1.260
What shallow-searching *Fame* hath left untold; Arcades 41
Trinity ms 'shallow searching' ←'vertues which dull'

Seas
Andromeda farr off *Atlantic* Seas Par Lost 3.559
Of congregated Waters he call'd Seas: Par Lost 7.308
Be fruitful, multiply, and in the Seas Par Lost 7.396
Forthwith the Sounds and Seas, each Creek and Bay Par Lost 7.399
Thir Aierie Caravan high over Sea's Par Lost 7.428
Sung *Halleluia*, as the sound of Seas, Par Lost 10.642
And *Thrascias* rend the Woods and Seas upturn; Par Lost 10.700
To prayers, then winds and seas, yet winds to seas Samson 961
The Sounds, and Seas with all their finny drove Mask 115
Bridgewater ms 'seas'
Trinity ms 'seas'
Thronging the Seas with spawn innumerable, Mask 713
Bridgewater ms 'seas'
Trinity ms 'seas'
1637 'seas'
Stole under Seas to meet his *Arethuse;* Arcades 31
Trinity ms 'seas'
Ay me! Whilst thee the shores, and sounding Seas Lycidas 154
Trinity ms 'seas'
1638 'seas'
Seas wept from our deep sorrow, Circum 9
Trinity ms 'seas'
Linkt to the mutual flowing of the Seas, Another 31
line not in 1658 text
1640, 1657 'seas'
And he can spred thy Name o're Lands and Seas, Sonnet 8, 7
Trinity ms 'seas'
On Faith and changed Gods complain: and Seas Horace 6

Season
None seconded, as out of season judg'd, Par Lost 5.850
The season, prime for sweetest Sents and Aires: Par Lost 9.200
And season him thy last and sweetest prey. Par Lost 10.609
To meek submission: thou at season fit Par Lost 12.597
In such a season born when scarce a Shed Par Reg 2.72
Know therefore when my season comes to sit Par Reg 4.146
Now at full age, fulness of time, thy season, Par Reg 4.380
The perfet season offer'd with my aid Par Reg 4.468
Brisk as the *April* buds in Primrose-season. Mask 671
1637 'primrose season'
Bridgewater ms 'primrose season'
Trinity ms 'primrose season'
Or if the earlier season lead Allegro 89
Compels me to disturb your season due: Lycidas 7
It was no season then for her Nativity 35
From the hard Season gaining: time will run Sonnet 20, 5
By watry streams, and in his season knows Psalm 1, 8

Seasons
Seasons return, but not to me returns Par Lost 3.41
All seasons and thir change, all please alike. Par Lost 4.640
All seasons, ripe for use hangs on the stalk; Par Lost 5.323
For Seasons, and for Dayes, and circling Years, Par Lost 7.342
Intelligent of seasons, and set forth Par Lost 7.427
Thir seasons: among these the seat of men, Par Lost 7.623
His Seasons, Hours, or Dayes, or Months, or Yeares: Par Lost 8.69
Of Seasons to each Clime; else had the Spring Par Lost 10.678
Th' inclement Seasons, Rain, Ice, Hail and Snow, Par Lost 10.1063
He in whose hand all times and seasons roul. Par Reg 3.187

Seat
Restore us, and regain the blissful Seat, Par Lost 1.5
ms 'seate'
The seat of desolation, voyd of light, Par Lost 1.181
Said then the lost Arch-Angel, this the seat Par Lost 1.243
Thir Seats long after next the Seat of God, Par Lost 1.383
ms 'seat'
Him follow'd *Rimmon*, whose delightful Seat Par Lost 1.467
ms 'seat'
Self-rais'd, and repossess thir native seat? Par Lost 1.634
ms 'seate'
Belus or *Serapis* thir Gods, or seat Par Lost 1.720
ms 'seate'
Up to our native seat: descent and fall Par Lost 2.76
Err not) another World, the happy seat Par Lost 2.347
Neerer our ancient Seat; perhaps in view Par Lost 2.394
Satan was now at hand, and from his seat Par Lost 2.674
Audacious, but that seat soon failing, meets Par Lost 2.931
Of living Saphire, once his native Seat; Par Lost 2.1050
Just o're the blissful seat of Paradise, Par Lost 3.527
To Paradise the happie seat of Man, Par Lost 3.632
His fixed seat, or fixed seat hath none, Par Lost 3.669
That place is Earth the seat of Man, that light Par Lost 3.724
A happy rural seat of various view; Par Lost 4.247
Long to continue, and this high seat your Heav'n Par Lost 4.371
They came, and *Satan* to his Royal seat Par Lost 5.756
Before the seat supream; from whence a voice Par Lost 6.27
Sidelong, had push't a Mountain from his seat Par Lost 6.197
Though not destroy, thir happie Native seat; Par Lost 6.226
From all her Confines. Heav'n the seat of bliss Par Lost 6.273
This inaccessible high strength, the seat Par Lost 7.141
Seemd like to Heav'n, a seat where Gods might dwell, Par Lost 7.329
Thir seasons: among these the seat of men, Par Lost 7.623
With lowliness Majestic from her seat, Par Lost 8.42
To the Garden of bliss, thy seat prepar'd. Par Lost 8.299
Greatness of mind and nobleness thir seat Par Lost 8.557
The thoughts, and heart enlarges, hath his seat Par Lost 8.590
More justly, Seat worthier of Gods, as built Par Lost 9.100
Magnificent this World, and Earth his seat, Par Lost 9.153
Earth felt the wound, and Nature from her seat Par Lost 9.782
Thus saying, from his radiant Seat he rose Par Lost 10.85
In other Worlds, and happier Seat provides Par Lost 10.237
Of *Pandaemonium*, Citie and proud seate Par Lost 10.424
From his transcendent Seat the Saints among, Par Lost 10.614
Praying, for from the Mercie-seat above Par Lost 11.2
Ev'n to the Seat of God. For since I saught Par Lost 11.148
Perhaps thy Capital Seate, from whence had spred Par Lost 11.343
City of old or modern Fame, the Seat Par Lost 11.386
Of *Cambalu*, seat of *Cathaian Can* Par Lost 11.388
Rich *Mexico* the seat of *Motezume*, Par Lost 11.407
And *Cusco* in *Peru*, the richer seat Par Lost 11.408
Eevn to the inmost seat of mental sight, Par Lost 11.418
From the high neighbouring Hills, which was thir Seat, Par Lost 11.575
A Mercie-seat of Gold between the wings Par Lost 12.253
His Seat at Gods right hand, exalted high Par Lost 12.457
Of Paradise, so late thir happie seat, Par Lost 12.642
That seat, and reign in *Israel* without end. Par Reg 2.442
Of that first golden Monarchy the seat, Par Reg 3.277
And seat of *Salmanassar*, whose success Par Reg 3.278
In *David*'s royal seat, his true Successour, Par Reg 3.373
To win thy destin'd seat, but wilt prolong Par Reg 4.469
For though that seat of earthly bliss be fail'd, Par Reg 4.612
Up to the Hill by *Hebron*, seat of Giants old, Samson 148
Next this marble venom'd seat Mask 916
1637 'seate'
Bridgewater ms 'seate'
Trinity ms 'seate'
That from beneath the seat of *Jove* doth spring, Lycidas 16
Trinity ms 'seate'
Of *Cynthia*'s seat, the Airy region thrilling, Nativity 103
While each peculiar power forgoes his wonted seat. Nativity 196
To earth from thy praefixed seat didst poast, Fair Inf 59
Of sinners hath not stood, and in the seat Psalm 1, 3
From Heav'n, thy Seat divine, Psalm 80, 58
Thou *in thy everlasting Seat* Psalm 86, 35
What Land, what Seat of rest thou bidst me seek, Prose 12, 4
What certain Seat, where I may worship thee Prose 12, 5
Thy course, there shalt thou find a lasting seat, Prose 12, 11

Seated
They pluckt the seated Hills with all thir load, Par Lost 6.644
Of Heav'ns high-seated top, th' Impereal Throne Par Lost 7.585
Seated as on the top of Vertues hill, Par Reg 2.217
Sitting like a Goddes bright, Arcades 18
Trinity ms 'sitting' ←'seated'
There Seated in his Sanctuary, Psalm 87, 3

Seats
Thir Seats long after next the Seat of God, Par Lost 1.383
ms 'seats'
A thousand Demy-Gods on golden seat's, Par Lost 1.796
Thir Table was, and mossie seats had round, Par Lost 5.392
And took thir Seats; till from his Throne supream Par Lost 11.82
So may we hold our place and these mild seats Par Reg 2.125
The seats of mightiest Monarchs, and so large Par Reg 3.262
That screen'd the fruits of the earth and seats of men Par Reg 4.30
With seats where all the Lords and each degree Samson 1607
Amongst the enthron'd gods on Sainted seats. Mask 11
Trinity ms 'seates'

Sechem
Pitcht about *Sechem*, and the neighbouring Plaine Par Lost 12.136
Second
Sluc'd from the Lake, a second multitude Par Lost 1.702
And trust themselves to fear no second fate: Par Lost 2.17
To second, or oppose, or undertake Par Lost 2.419
No second stroke intend, and such a frown Par Lost 2.713
As from a second root shall be restor'd, Par Lost 3.288
Second to thee, offerd himself to die Par Lost 3.409
Till at his second bidding darkness fled, Par Lost 3.712
Then when the Dragon, put to second rout, Par Lost 4.3
Long after to blest *Marie*, second *Eve*. Par Lost 5.387
In posture to displode thir second tire Par Lost 6.605
Second Omnipotence, two dayes are past, Par Lost 6.684
And Morning *Chorus* sung the second Day. Par Lost 7.275
Second to me or like, equal much less. Par Lost 8.407
With second thoughts, reforming what was old! Par Lost 9.101
Equivalent or second, which compel'd Par Lost 9.609
In pangs, and Nature gave a second groan, Par Lost 9.1001
When *Jesus* son of *Mary* second *Eve*, Par Lost 10.183
Second of *Satan* sprung, all conquering *Death*, Par Lost 10.591
By Faith and faithful works, to second Life, Par Lost 11.64
Our second *Adam* in the Wilderness, Par Lost 11.383
The second time returning, in his Bill Par Lost 11.859
And Man as from a second stock proceed. Par Lost 12.7
This second sours of Men, while yet but few; Par Lost 12.13
Or from Heav'n claming second Sovrantie; Par Lost 12.35
Raise him to be the second in that Realme Par Lost 12.162
The second, both for pietie renownd Par Lost 12.321
And eat the second time after repose, Par Reg 2.275
Off. Samson, this second message from our Lords Samson 1391
That no second knows nor third, Samson 1701
And now with second hope she goes, Winchester 25
Secondary
Of secondarie hands, by task transferd Par Lost 5.854
Seconded
And seconded thy else not dreaded Spear. Par Lost 4.929
None seconded, as out of season judg'd, Par Lost 5.850
By *Eve*, though all unweeting, seconded Par Lost 10.335
With th' utmost of his Godhead seconded: Samson 1153
Secrecy
Thou in thy secresie although alone, Par Lost 8.427
Of secresie, my safety, and my life. Samson 1002
The Pensive secrecy of desert cell, Mask 387
1637 'secrecie'
Trinity ms 'secrecie'
Bridgewater ms 'secrecie'
Secret
Sing Heav'nly Muse, that on the secret top Par Lost 1.6
In close recess and secret conclave sat Par Lost 1.795
In secret, riding through the Air she comes Par Lost 2.663
With me in secret, that my womb conceiv'd Par Lost 2.766
Then this more secret now design'd, I haste Par Lost 2.838
That I may find him, and with secret gaze, Par Lost 3.671
The coming of thir secret foe, and scap'd Par Lost 4.7
Awak'ning, thus to him in secret spake. Par Lost 5.672
Secret they finish'd, and in order set, Par Lost 6.522
And giv'st access, though secret she retire. Par Lost 9.810
And I perhaps am secret; Heav'n is high, Par Lost 9.811
Eternal Father from his secret Cloud, Par Lost 10.32
With secret amity things of like kinde Par Lost 10.248
My Heart, which by a secret harmonie Par Lost 10.358
Above Heroic, though in secret done, Par Reg 1.15
There thou shalt hear and learn the secret power Par Reg 4.254
Fool, have divulg'd the secret gift of God Samson 201
The secret wrested from me in her highth Samson 384
My capital secret, in what part my strength Samson 394
But I Gods counsel have not kept, his holy secret Samson 497
But must secret passage find Samson 610
Secret refreshings, that repair his strength, Samson 665
And secret sting of amorous remorse. Samson 1007
To wring from me and tell to them my secret, Samson 1199
Dark vaild *Cotytto*, t' whom the secret flame Mask 129
The clasping charm, and thaw the numming spell, Mask 853
Trinity ms 'thaw the numming' ←'melt each' ←'secret holding'
He met her, and in secret shades Penseroso 28
Divine *Alpheus*, who by secret sluse, Arcades 30
From out his secret Altar toucht with hallow'd fire. Nativity 28
Then sing of secret things that came to pass Vacation 45
High thron'd in secret bliss, for us frail dust Circum 19
Secretest
By secretest conveyance. Thou my Shade Par Lost 10.249
Secrets
The secrets of the hoarie deep, a dark Par Lost 2.891
The secrets of your Realm, but by constraint Par Lost 2.972
The secrets of another world, perhaps Par Lost 5.569
What wee, not to explore the secrets aske Par Lost 7.95
His secrets to be scann'd by them who ought Par Lost 8.74
That jealous of thir secrets fiercely oppos'd Par Lost 10.478
All secrets of the deep, all Natures works, Par Lost 12.578
Secrets of men, the secrets of a friend, Samson 492
Of secrets, then with like infirmity Samson 776
To learn thy secrets, get into my power Samson 798
Too well, unbosom'd all my secrets to thee, Samson 879
Sect
From all: my Sect thou seest, now learn too late Par Lost 6.147
Sirnam'd *Peripatetics*, and the Sect Par Reg 4.279

Secular
Secular power, though feigning still to act Par Lost 12.517
A secular bird ages of lives. Samson 1707
Threatning to bind our soules with secular chaines: Sonnet 16, 12
Secure
Here we may reign secure, and in my choyce Par Lost 1.261
Monarch in Heav'n, till then as one secure Par Lost 1.638
And Heav'ns high Arbitrator sit secure Par Lost 2.359
Secure, and at the brightning Orient beam Par Lost 2.399
In hurdl'd Cotes amid the field secure, Par Lost 4.186
Now laid perhaps asleep secure of harme. Par Lost 4.791
He swerve not too secure: tell him withall Par Lost 5.238
Quaff immortalitie and joy, secure Par Lost 5.638
line not in 1667 edition
Justly hast in derision, and secure Par Lost 5.736
Sad resolution and secure: let each Par Lost 6.541
Shrin'd in his Sanctuarie of Heav'n secure, Par Lost 6.672
As not secure to single or combin'd. Par Lost 9.339
Or aught that might his happie State secure, Par Lost 9.347
Secure from outward force; within himself Par Lost 9.348
But confidence then bore thee on, secure Par Lost 9.1175
And sleep secure; his dreadful voice no more Par Lost 10.779
Us haply too secure of our discharge Par Lost 11.196
Uplifted; and secure with beaked prow Par Lost 11.746
Thenceforth shall practice how to live secure, Par Lost 11.802
This further consolation yet secure Par Lost 12.620
The Father knows the Son; therefore secure Par Reg 1.176
Thy Vertue, and not every way secure Par Reg 3.348
Long to enjoy it quiet and secure, Par Reg 3.360
Where they shall dwell secure, when time shall be Par Reg 4.616
Proudly secure, yet liable to fall Samson 55
Less warranted then this, or less secure Mask 327
Secure without all doubt, or controversie: Mask 409
How to secure the Lady from surprisal, Mask 618
Som times with secure delight Allegro 91
Save me and secure me under Psalm 7, 2
Secured
Happie, but for so happie ill secur'd Par Lost 4.370
To travel with *Tobias*, and secur'd Par Lost 5.222
Securely
Incens't, and thus securely him defi'd. Par Lost 6.130
Securer
Us both securer then thus warnd thou seemst, Par Lost 9.371
Sedentary
Repeated, while the sedentarie Earth, Par Lost 8.32
And sedentary numness craze my limbs Samson 571
Sedge
High overarch't imbowr; or scatterd sedge Par Lost 1.304
His Mantle hairy, and his Bonnet sedge, Lycidas 104
Sedgy
Or Rockie *Avon*, or of Sedgie *Lee*, Vacation 97
Seditious
From flight, seditious Angel, to receave Par Lost 6.152
Seduce
Seduce them to our Party, that thir God Par Lost 2.368
Who now is plotting how he may seduce Par Lost 6.901
Suttle he needs must be, who could seduce Par Lost 9.307
Against whate're may tempt, whate're seduce, Par Reg 1.178
Seduced
Who first seduc'd them to that foul revolt? Par Lost 1.33
On Man by him seduc't, but on himself Par Lost 1.219
Among the spirits beneath, whom I seduc'd Par Lost 4.83
Can by his fraud be shak'n or seduc't; Par Lost 9.287
On his bad Errand, Man should be seduc't Par Lost 10.41
Hee after *Eve* seduc't, unminded slunk Par Lost 10.332
Made happie: Him by fraud I have seduc'd Par Lost 10.485
To dash thir pride, and joy for Man seduc't. Par Lost 10.577
Sedulous
Not sedulous by Nature to indite Par Lost 9.27
See
Too well I see and rue the dire event, Par Lost 1.134
But see the angry Victor hath recall'd Par Lost 1.169
Evil to others, and enrag'd might see Par Lost 1.216
Infernal Thunder, and for Lightning see Par Lost 2.66
Purge and disperse, that I may see and tell Par Lost 3.54
Father, to see thy face, wherein no cloud Par Lost 3.262
See golden days, fruitful of golden deeds, Par Lost 3.337
Into the devious Air; then might ye see Par Lost 3.489
Unspeakable desire to see, and know Par Lost 3.662
Seisd mine, I yielded, and from that time see Par Lost 4.489
See farr and wide: in at this Gate none pass Par Lost 4.579
My Glorie, my Perfection, glad I see Par Lost 5.29
Ascend to Heav'n, by merit thine, and see Par Lost 5.80
Of sense, whereby they hear, see, smell, touch, taste, Par Lost 5.411
Illustrates, when they see all Regal Power Par Lost 5.739
Forsak'n of all good; I see thy fall Par Lost 5.878
I see that most through sloth had rather serve, Par Lost 6.166
The Rebel Thrones, but greater rage to see Par Lost 6.199
He comes, and settl'd in his face I see Par Lost 6.540
That all may see who hate us, how we seek Par Lost 6.559
Grieving to see his Glorie, at the sight Par Lost 6.792
Yet farr the greater part have kept, I see, Par Lost 7.145
For God we see hath honour'd thee, and set Par Lost 8.227
To see that none thence issu'd forth a spie, Par Lost 8.233
I see not who partakes. In solitude Par Lost 8.364
A nice and suttle happiness I see Par Lost 8.399
To see how thou could'st judge of fit and meet: Par Lost 8.448
Of all thy gifts, nor enviest. I now see Par Lost 8.494

See(*cont*)
Find place or refuge; and the more I see — Par Lost 9.119
I question it, for this fair Earth I see, — Par Lost 9.720
High and remote to see from thence distinct — Par Lost 9.812
Eve, now I see thou art exact of taste, — Par Lost 9.1017
Hide me, where I may never see them more. — Par Lost 9.1090
Sublime with expectation when to see — Par Lost 10.536
See with what heat these Dogs of Hell advance — Par Lost 10.616
Through her perversness, but shall see her gaind — Par Lost 10.902
Since this days Death denounc't, if ought I see, — Par Lost 10.962
See Father, what first fruits on Earth are sprung — Par Lost 11.22
Though after sleepless Night; for see the Morn, — Par Lost 11.173
The visual Nerve, for he had much to see; — Par Lost 11.415
Loose no reward, though here thou see him die, — Par Lost 11.459
But still I see the tenor of Mans woe — Par Lost 11.632
But I was farr deceav'd; for now I see — Par Lost 11.783
Much thou hast yet to see, but I perceave — Par Lost 12.8
Comes down to see thir Citie, ere the Tower — Par Lost 12.51
And looking down, to see the hubbub strange — Par Lost 12.60
I see him, but thou canst not, with what Faith — Par Lost 12.128
Canaan he now attains, I see his Tents — Par Lost 12.135
See where it flows, disgorging at seaven mouthes — Par Lost 12.158
Of mee and all Mankind; but now I see — Par Lost 12.276
Sin against Law to fight; that when they see — Par Lost 12.289
Returne, the Starres of Morn shall see him rise — Par Lost 12.422
Exacts our parting hence; and see the Guards, — Par Lost 12.590
Ye see our danger on the utmost edge — Par Reg 1.94
Where they might see him, and to thee they came; — Par Reg 1.246
What other way I see not, for we here — Par Reg 1.338
What I see excellent in good, or fair, — Par Reg 1.381
To see thee and approach thee, whom I know — Par Reg 1.384
Soon we shall see our hope, our joy return. — Par Reg 2.57
Why shouldst thou not accept it? but I see — Par Reg 2.398
I see thou know'st what is of use to know, — Par Reg 3.7
Those rudiments, and see before thine eyes — Par Reg 3.245
He marches now in hast; see, though from far, — Par Reg 3.303
See how in warlike muster they appear, — Par Reg 3.308
Thence to the gates cast round thine eye, and see — Par Reg 4.61
I see all offers made by me how slight — Par Reg 4.155
See there the Olive Grove of *Academe*, — Par Reg 4.244
Of *Socrates*, see there his Tenement, — Par Reg 4.274
Fell whence he stood to see his Victor fall. — Par Reg 4.571
They creep, yet see, I dark in light expos'd — Samson 75
See how he lies at random, carelesly diffus'd, — Samson 118
Not to be found, though sought. Yee see, O friends, — Samson 193
But see here comes thy reverend Sire — Samson 326
Dal. I see thou art implacable, more deaf — Samson 960
But had we best retire, I see a storm? — Samson 1061
And now am come to see of whom such noise — Samson 1088
Sam. The way to know were not to see but taste. — Samson 1091
To *Samson*, but shalt never see *Gath* more. — Samson 1129
Then thou shalt see, or rather to thy sorrow — Samson 1154
Where I will see thee heartn'd and fresh clad — Samson 1317
To see me girt with Friends; and how the sight — Samson 1415
Lest I should see him forc't to things unseemly. — Samson 1451
What shall we do, stay here or run and see? — Samson 1520
And to our wish I see one hither speeding, — Samson 1539
The Edifice where all were met to see him — Samson 1588
I see ye visibly, and now beleeve — Mask 216
 line not in Bridgewater ms
Vertue could see to do what vertue would — Mask 373
 Trinity ms 'see' ← 'ad all her'
Of small regard to see to, yet well skill'd — Mask 620
Sorrow flies farr: See here be all the pleasures — Mask 668
 Trinity ms 'see'
 1637 'see'
 Bridgewater ms 'see'
Thus night oft see me in thy pale career, — Penseroso 121
I see bright honour sparkle through your eyes, — Arcades 27
See how from far upon the Eastern rode — Nativity 22
And wrath to see his Kingdom fail, — Nativity 171
But see the Virgin blest, — Nativity 237
Look in, and see each blissful Deitie — Vacation 35
See see the Chariot, and those rushing wheels, — Passion 36
Madam, me thinks I see him living yet; — Sonnet 10, 11
But from that mark how far they roave we see — Sonnet 12, 13
Thy Courts O Lord to see, — Psalm 84, 6
Cause us to see thy goodness Lord, — Psalm 85, 25
And let my foes *then* see — Psalm 86, 62

Seed
That Shepherd, who first taught the chosen Seed, — Par Lost 1.8
 ms 'seed'
Made flesh, when time shall be, of Virgin seed, — Par Lost 3.284
Put forth the verdant Grass, Herb yielding Seed, — Par Lost 7.310
Whose Seed is in her self upon the Earth. — Par Lost 7.312
Enmitie, and between thine and her Seed; — Par Lost 10.180
Her Seed shall bruse thy head, thou bruise his heel. — Par Lost 10.181
His Seed, when is not set, shall bruise my head: — Par Lost 10.499
And to our Seed (O hapless Seed!) deriv'd. — Par Lost 10.965
Then both our selves and Seed at once to free — Par Lost 10.999
Part of our Sentence, that thy Seed shall bruise — Par Lost 10.1031
Fruits of more pleasing savour from thy seed — Par Lost 11.26
My Cov'nant in the womans seed renewd; — Par Lost 11.116
His promise, that thy Seed shall bruise our Foe; — Par Lost 11.155
With all the Creatures, and thir seed preserve. — Par Lost 11.873
Seed time and Harvest, Heat and hoary Frost — Par Lost 11.899
His benediction so, that in his Seed — Par Lost 12.125
Shall in his Seed be blessed; by that Seed — Par Lost 12.148

Seed(*cont*)
And shadows, of that destind Seed to bruise — Par Lost 12.233
Promisd to *Abraham* and his Seed: the rest — Par Lost 12.260
Just *Abraham* and his Seed: now first I finde — Par Lost 12.273
A Son, the Womans Seed to thee foretold, — Par Lost 12.327
The seed of Woman: Virgin Mother, Haile, — Par Lost 12.379
In thee and in thy Seed: nor can this be, — Par Lost 12.395
So in his seed all Nations shall be blest. — Par Lost 12.450
The Womans seed, obscurely then foretold, — Par Lost 12.543
The great deliverance by her Seed to come — Par Lost 12.600
(For by the Womans Seed) on all Mankind. — Par Lost 12.601
 1669 'seed'
By mee the Promis'd Seed shall all restore. — Par Lost 12.623
Shall be inflicted by the Seed of *Eve* — Par Reg 1.54
For this ill news I bring, the Womans seed — Par Reg 1.64
Of female Seed, far abler to resist — Par Reg 1.151
Measure of strength so great to mortal seed, — Samson 1439
When the blest seed of *Terah*'s faithfull Son, — Psalm 114, 1
Thy loved Josephs seed, — Psalm 80, 4

Seeing
Wrought in her so, that seeing me, she turn'd; — Par Lost 8.507
Not seeing thee attempted, who attest? — Par Lost 9.369
Of God All-seeing, or deceave his Heart — Par Lost 10.6
Sooner or later; which th' Almightie seeing, — Par Lost 10.613
Who seeing those great acts which God had done — Samson 243
Bereft of light thir seeing have forgot, — Sonnet 22, 3
 1694 'Seeing'

Seek
Out of our evil seek to bring forth good, — Par Lost 1.163
Roaming to seek thir prey on earth, durst fix — Par Lost 1.382
Fanatic *Egypt* and her Priests, to seek — Par Lost 1.480
Of splendid vassalage, but rather seek — Par Lost 2.252
Through all the Coasts of dark destruction seek — Par Lost 2.464
Alone, and without guide, half lost, I seek — Par Lost 2.975
Can never seek, once dead in sins and lost; — Par Lost 3.233
Here Pilgrims roam, that stray'd so farr to seek — Par Lost 3.476
Whom hunger drives to seek new haunt for prey, — Par Lost 4.184
To seek her through the world; nor that sweet Grove — Par Lost 4.272
Though I unpittied: League with you I seek, — Par Lost 4.375
Part of my Soul I seek thee, and thee claim — Par Lost 4.487
And when we seek, as now, thy gift of sleep. — Par Lost 4.735
Blest pair; and O yet happiest if ye seek — Par Lost 4.774
Human desires can seek or apprehend? — Par Lost 5.518
Seek not the praise of men: the other sort — Par Lost 6.376
That all may see who hate us, how we seek — Par Lost 6.559
Seek them with wandring thoughts, and notions vain. — Par Lost 8.187
Unpractis'd, unprepar'd, and still to seek. — Par Lost 8.197
Such as I seek, fit to participate — Par Lost 8.390
But neither here seek I, no nor in Heav'n — Par Lost 9.124
By what I seek, but others to make such — Par Lost 9.127
Seek not temptation then, which to avoide — Par Lost 9.364
A Foe so proud will first the weaker seek, — Par Lost 9.383
Let none henceforth seek needless cause to approve — Par Lost 9.1140
The Faith they owe; when earnestly they seek — Par Lost 9.1141
Why hee should mean me ill, or seek to harme. — Par Lost 9.1152
Let us seek Death, or he not found, supply — Par Lost 10.1001
To make death in us live: Then let us seek — Par Lost 10.1028
Of these fair spreading Trees; which bids us seek — Par Lost 10.1067
In yonder nether World where shall I seek — Par Lost 11.328
With thought that they must be. Let no man seek — Par Lost 11.770
Then shall they seek to avail themselves of names, — Par Lost 12.515
Will bring me hence, no other Guide I seek. — Par Reg 1.336
Thou neither dost perswade me to seek wealth — Par Reg 3.44
Shall I seek glory then, as vain men seek — Par Reg 3.105
Oft not deserv'd? I seek not mine, but his — Par Reg 3.106
But why should man seek glory? who of his own — Par Reg 3.134
That thou may'st know I seek not to engage — Par Reg 3.347
What wise and valiant man would seek to free — Par Reg 4.143
And in themselves seek vertue, and to themselves — Par Reg 4.314
(And what he brings, what needs he elsewhere seek) — Par Reg 4.325
Good reason then, if I before-hand seek — Par Reg 4.526
Retiring from the popular noise, I seek — Samson 16
To seek in marriage that fallacious Bride, — Samson 320
At times when men seek most repose and rest, — Samson 406
To what end should I seek it? when in strength — Samson 522
Off. *Ebrews*, the Pris'ner *Samson* here I seek. — Samson 1308
Do they not seek occasion of new quarrels — Samson 1329
La. To seek i' th vally som cool friendly Spring. — Mask 282
 Bridgewater ms 'seeke'
 Trinity ms 'seeke'
 1637 'seeke'
And as I past, I worshipt; if those you seek — Mask 302
 Bridgewater ms 'seeke'
 Trinity ms 'seeke'
 1637 'seeke'
I do not think my sister so to seek, — Mask 366
 Trinity ms 'seeke'
 Bridgewater ms 'seeke'
 1637 'seeke'
And wouldst thou seek again to trap me here — Mask 699
 Trinity ms 'seeke'
 line not in Bridgewater ms
And made Hell grant what Love did seek. — Penseroso 108
To love, to seek, to prize — Psalm 4, 11
To seek my life, and in their eyes — Psalm 86, 51
What Land, what Seat of rest thou bidst me seek, — Prose 12, 4

Seekest
First, Highest, Holiest, Best, thou alwayes seekst — Par Lost 6.724

Seekest(*cont*)
Informd by thee might know; if else thou seekst Par Lost 7.639
Best with thy self accompanied, seek'st not Par Lost 8.428
Seeking
Naught seeking but the praise of men, here find Par Lost 3.453
Creature so faire his reconcilement seeking, Par Lost 10.943
In what thou eatst and drinkst, seeking from thence Par Lost 11.532
Worth or not worth the seeking, let it pass: Par Reg 3.151
(As he who seeking Asses found a Kingdom) Par Reg 3.242
Chor. In seeking just occasion to provoke Samson 237
Enterd *Judea* seeking mee, who then Samson 252
Thou wilt renounce thy seeking, and much rather Samson 828
Went up with armed powers thee only seeking, Samson 1190
Will surround thee, seeking right, Psalm 7, 26
Seeks
Vain glorious, and through infamie seeks fame: Par Lost 6.384
The number of thy worshippers. Who seekes Par Lost 7.613
Despairing, seeks to work us woe and shame Par Lost 9.255
That such an Enemie we have, who seeks Par Lost 9.274
Suspected to a sequent King, who seeks Par Lost 12.165
Resembling thy great Father: he seeks glory, Par Reg 3.110
Of mortal things. Who therefore seeks in these Par Reg 4.318
To satisfie thy lust: Love seeks to have Love; Samson 837
Oft seeks to sweet retired Solitude, Mask 376
Seem
Did not disswade me most, and seem to cast Par Lost 2.122
Hast thou forgot me then, and do I seem Par Lost 2.747
And thou sly hypocrite, who now wouldst seem Par Lost 4.957
As that more willingly thou couldst not seem Par Lost 5.466
Then most, when most irregular they seem, Par Lost 5.624
Seem twilight here; and now went forth the Morn Par Lost 6.12
And all her numberd Starrs, that seem to rowle Par Lost 8.19
Not that I so affirm, though so it seem Par Lost 8.117
The Planet Earth, so stedfast though she seem, Par Lost 8.129
For while I sit with thee, I seem in Heav'n, Par Lost 8.210
Seem I to thee sufficiently possest Par Lost 8.404
Is propagated seem such dear delight Par Lost 8.580
In tangles, and made intricate seem strait, Par Lost 9.632
Ye Eate thereof, your Eyes that seem so cleere, Par Lost 9.706
The Parts of each for other, that seem most Par Lost 9.1093
A place so heav'nly, and conniving seem Par Lost 10.624
Hard to belief may seem; yet this will Prayer, Par Lost 11.146
Of them the Highest, for such of shape may seem Par Lost 11.297
Huge Cities and high towr'd, that well might seem Par Reg 3.261
And lovers of thir Country, as may seem; Par Reg 4.355
The Prince of darkness, glad would also seem Par Reg 4.441
Over whose heads they rore, and seem to point, Par Reg 4.463
At least might seem to hold all power of thee, Par Reg 4.494
Scarce half I seem to live, dead more then half. Samson 79
But they persisted deaf, and would not seem Samson 249
Man. Brethren and men of *Dan*, for such ye seem, Samson 332
Sole Author I, sole cause: if aught seem vile, Samson 376
Just or unjust, alike seem miserable, Samson 703
Some rich *Philistian* Matron she may seem, Samson 722
And words addrest seem into tears dissolv'd, Samson 729
With zeal, if aught Religion seem concern'd: Samson 1420
Chor. Thy hopes are not ill founded nor seem vain Samson 1504
I doubt me gentle mortalls these may seeme Mask Tr. ms 10.16
Seemed
Behold a wonder! they but now who seemd Par Lost 1.777
A fairer person lost not Heav'n; he seemd Par Lost 2.110
The Deep to shelter us? this Hell then seem'd Par Lost 2.167
Aspect he rose, and in his rising seem'd Par Lost 2.301
Midst came thir mighty Paramount, and seemd Par Lost 2.508
Ply stemming nightly toward the Pole. So seem'd Par Lost 2.642
The one seem'd Woman to the waste, and fair, Par Lost 2.650
Or substance might be call'd that shadow seem'd, Par Lost 2.669
For each seem'd either; black it stood as Night, Par Lost 2.670
And shook a dreadful Dart; what seem'd his head Par Lost 2.672
He ceas'd, for both seemd highly pleasd, and Death Par Lost 2.845
On the bare outside of this World, that seem'd Par Lost 3.74
It seem'd, now seems a boundless Continent Par Lost 3.423
So wide the op'ning seemd, where bounds were set Par Lost 3.538
Stars distant, but nigh hand seemd other Worlds, Par Lost 3.566
Or other Worlds they seemd, or happy Iles, Par Lost 3.567
If mettal, part seemd Gold, part Silver cleer; Par Lost 3.595
He seemd, or fixt in cogitation deep. Par Lost 3.629
When God hath showrd the earth; so lovely seemd Par Lost 4.152
In naked Majestie seemd Lords of all, Par Lost 4.290
And worthie seemd, for in thir looks Divine Par Lost 4.291
Not equal, as thir sex not equal seemd; Par Lost 4.296
Smooth Lake, that to me seemd another Skie. Par Lost 4.459
A Spirit, zealous, as he seem'd, to know Par Lost 4.565
His lustre visibly impar'd; yet seemd Par Lost 4.850
What seemd both Spear and Shield: now dreadful deeds Par Lost 4.990
Of interdicted Knowledge: fair it seem'd, Par Lost 5.52
All seemd well pleas'd, all seem'd, but were not all Par Lost 5.617
In the mid way: though strange to us it seemd Par Lost 6.91
Seemd in thy World erroneous to dissent Par Lost 6.146
As each divided Legion might have seemd Par Lost 6.230
A Legion; led in fight, yet Leader seemd Par Lost 6.232
Tormented all the Air; all Air seemd then Par Lost 6.244
Of Godlike Power: for likest Gods they seemd, Par Lost 6.301
To be th' inventer miss'd, so easie it seemd Par Lost 6.499
On Wheels (for like to Pillars most they seem'd Par Lost 6.573
As they would dance, yet for a dance they seemd Par Lost 6.615
Infernal noise; Warr seem'd a civil Game Par Lost 6.667
Our knowing, as to highest wisdom seemd, Par Lost 7.83
Seemed(*cont*)
Seemd like to Heav'n, a seat where Gods might dwell, Par Lost 7.329
So spake our Sire, and by his count'nance seemd Par Lost 8.39
Of Earth before scarce pleasant seemd. Each Tree Par Lost 8.306
So spake the Universal Lord, and seem'd Par Lost 8.376
That what seemd fair in all the World, seemd now Par Lost 8.472
Likeliest she seemd, *Pomona* when she fled Par Lost 9.394
What pleasing seemd, for her now pleases more, Par Lost 9.453
Regarded, such delight till then, as seemd, Par Lost 9.787
Submitting to what seemd remediless, Par Lost 9.919
What seemd in thee so perfet, that I thought Par Lost 9.1179
Her doing seem'd to justifie the deed; Par Lost 10.142
Were such as under Government well seem'd, Par Lost 10.154
Huge *Python*, and his Power no less he seem'd Par Lost 10.531
When angry most he seem'd and most severe, Par Lost 10.1095
Seem'd thir Petition, then when th' ancient Pair Par Lost 11.10
A Lazar-house it seemd, wherein were laid Par Lost 11.479
Just men they seemd, and all thir study bent Par Lost 11.577
For that fair femal Troop thou sawst, that seemd Par Lost 11.614
Following, as seem'd, the quest of some stray Ewe, Par Reg 1.315
Natures own work it seem'd (Nature taught Art) Par Reg 2.295
And Ladies of th' *Hesperides*, that seem'd Par Reg 2.357
Deprest, and overthrown, as seem'd, Samson 1698
Seem'd erst so lavish and profuse, Arcades 9
Seemest
Us both securer then thus warnd thou seemst, Par Lost 9.371
For that to me thou seem'st the man, whom late Par Reg 1.327
(For I discern thee other then thou seem'st) Par Reg 1.348
And thou thy self seem'st otherwise inclin'd Par Reg 4.212
To whom thou untry'd seem'st fair. Me in my vow'd Horace 13
Seeming
With shews instead, meer shews of seeming pure, Par Lost 4.316
With Reason, to her seeming, and with Truth; Par Lost 9.738
Whatever wiles of Foe or seeming Friend. Par Lost 10.11
By pleasure, though to Nature seeming meet, Par Lost 11.604
Seeming at first all heavenly under virgin veil, Samson 1035
Others more moderate seeming, but thir aim Samson 1464
Seemingly
And to thir viands fell, nor seemingly Par Lost 5.434
Seemlier
Not rustic as before, but seemlier clad, Par Reg 2.299
Seemliest
Safest and seemliest by her Husband staies, Par Lost 9.268
Seems
The way seems difficult and steep to scale Par Lost 2.71
Thaws not, but gathers heap, and ruin seems Par Lost 2.590
I fled, but he pursu'd (though more, it seems, Par Lost 2.790
Wide interrupt can hold; so bent he seems Par Lost 3.84
It seem'd, now seems a boundless Continent Par Lost 3.423
And now Saint *Peter* at Heav'ns Wicket seems Par Lost 3.484
Where no ill seems: Which now for once beguil'd Par Lost 3.689
The more it seems excess, that led thee hither Par Lost 3.698
To which the Hell I suffer seems a Heav'n. Par Lost 4.78
From thir own mouths; all is not theirs it seems: Par Lost 4.513
And fierce demeanour seems the Prince of Hell, Par Lost 4.871
Imploi'd it seems to violate sleep, and those Par Lost 4.883
Forbidd'n here, it seems, as onely fit Par Lost 5.69
Of Towring Eagles, to all the Fowles he seems Par Lost 5.271
Comes this way moving; seems another Morn Par Lost 5.310
But proves not so: then fallible, it seems, Par Lost 6.428
And seems a moving Land, and at his Gilles Par Lost 7.415
Her loveliness, so absolute she seems Par Lost 8.547
Seems wisest, vertuousest, discreetest, best; Par Lost 8.550
Light above Light, for thee alone, as seems, Par Lost 9.105
For Beasts it seems: yet that one Beast which first Par Lost 9.769
Hath toucht my sense, flat seems to this, and harsh. Par Lost 9.987
It seems, in thy restraint: what could I more? Par Lost 9.1170
Which here, though plenteous, all too little seems Par Lost 10.600
Thy Justice seems; yet to say truth, too late, Par Lost 10.755
Eve, thy contempt of life and pleasure seems Par Lost 10.1013
Much better seems this Vision, and more hope Par Lost 11.599
Here Nature seems fulfilld in all her ends. Par Lost 11.602
The Ark no more now flotes, but seems on ground Par Lost 11.850
Who this is we must learn, for man he seems Par Reg 1.91
Afflicted I may be, it seems, and blest; Par Reg 2.93
Or that which only seems to satisfie Par Reg 2.229
And what in me seems wanting, but that I Par Reg 2.450
My hopes all flat, nature within me seems Samson 595
Little prevails, or rather seems a tune, Samson 661
Femal of sex it seems, Samson 711
He seems: supposing here to find his Son, Samson 1443
But providence or instinct of nature seems, Samson 1545
Oft he seems to hide his face, Samson 1749
We may justly now accuse Arcades 10
Trinity ms 'wee may justly now accuse' ←'now seemes guiltie of abuse'
And the chill Marble seems to sweat, Nativity 195
Seen
So numberless were those bad Angels seen Par Lost 1.344
All in a moment through the gloom were seen Par Lost 1.544
Beyond compare the Son of God was seen Par Lost 3.138
First-seen, or some renown'd Metropolis Par Lost 3.549
Such wonder seis'd, though after Heaven seen, Par Lost 3.552
Imagind rather oft then elsewhere seen, Par Lost 3.599
Who tells of som infernal Spirit seen Par Lost 4.793
Hung forth in Heav'n his golden Scales, yet seen Par Lost 4.997
By us oft seen; his dewie locks distill'd Par Lost 5.56
To us invisible or dimly seen Par Lost 5.157

Seen(*cont*)
Chariots of God, half on each hand were seen: Par Lost 6.770
First seen, them unexpected joy surpriz'd, Par Lost 6.774
So farr remote, with diminution seen. Par Lost 7.369
First in his East the glorious Lamp was seen, Par Lost 7.370
Seen in the Galaxie, that Milkie way Par Lost 7.579
Thy mate, who sees when thou art seen least wise. Par Lost 8.578
Then voluble and bold, now hid, now seen Par Lost 9.436
Ammonian Jove, or *Capitoline* was seen, Par Lost 9.508
Who sees thee? (and what is one2) who shouldst be seen Par Lost 9.546
This may be well: but what if God have seen, Par Lost 9.826
To shame obnoxious, and unseemliest seen, Par Lost 9.1094
Easie it might be seen that I intend Par Lost 10.58
My coming seen far off? I miss thee here, Par Lost 10.104
Not to be trusted, longing to be seen Par Lost 10.877
But have I now seen Death? Is this the way Par Lost 11.462
To whom thus *Michael*. Death thou hast seen Par Lost 11.466
Thir stops and chords was seen: his volant touch Par Lost 11.561
No more was seen; the floating Vessel swum Par Lost 11.745
First seen in acts of prowess eminent Par Lost 11.789
Thus thou hast seen one World begin and end; Par Lost 12.6
A Star, not seen before in Heaven appearing Par Reg 1.249
At *Jordan* with the Baptist, and had seen Par Reg 2.2
Conceals him: when twelve years he scarce had seen, Par Reg 2.96
Have we not seen, or by relation heard, Par Reg 2.182
He ask'd thee, hast thou seen my servant *Job?* Par Reg 3.67
The world thou hast not seen, much less her glory, Par Reg 3.236
As in thy wond'rous actions hath been seen. Samson 1440
Oft seen in Charnell vaults, and Sepulchers Mask 471
Trinity ms 'seene'
1637 'seene'
Bridgewater ms 'seene'
Who gently ask't if he had seen such two, Mask 575
1637 'seene'
Trinity ms 'seene'
Be seen in som high lonely Towr, Penseroso 86
All *Arcadia* hath not seen. Arcades 95
Trinity ms 'seene'
All *Arcadia* hath not seen. Arcades 109
Trinity ms 'seene'
Shall now no more be seen, Lycidas 43
Trinity ms 'seene'
Are seen in glittering ranks with wings displaid, Nativity 114
Nor is *Osiris* seen Nativity 213
So have I seen som tender slip Winchester 35
And with those few art eminently seen, Sonnet 9, 3
Awake thy strength, come, and *be seen* Psalm 80, 11

Seer
How soon hath thy prediction, Seer blest, Par Lost 12.553

Seers
On *Aaron*'s breast: or tongue of Seers old Par Reg 3.15

Sees
Or Fountain some belated Peasant sees, Par Lost 1.783
Or dreams he sees, while over-head the Moon Par Lost 1.784
All these our motions vain, sees and derides; Par Lost 2.191
Starr interpos'd, however small he sees, Par Lost 5.258
Thy mate, who sees when thou art seen least wise. Par Lost 8.578
And tortures him now more, the more he sees Par Lost 9.469
Who sees thee? (and what is one2) who shouldst be seen Par Lost 9.546
Thou haste immanacl'd, while Heav'n sees good. Mask 665
Towers, and Battlements it sees Allegro 77
Into a goodly valley, where he sees Prose 2, 2
Sees his foule inside through his whited skin. Prose 10, 6

Seest
In equal ruin: into what Pit thou seest Par Lost 1.91
Seest thou yon dreary Plain, forlorn and wilde, Par Lost 1.180
At last this odious offspring whom thou seest Par Lost 2.781
Onely begotten Son, seest thou what rage Par Lost 3.80
Numberless, as thou seest, and how they move; Par Lost 3.719
Had not a voice thus warnd me, What thou seest, Par Lost 4.467
What there thou seest fair Creature is thy self, Par Lost 4.468
Thy sleep dissent? new Laws thou seest impos'd; Par Lost 5.679
Thy Legions under darkness; but thou seest Par Lost 6.142
From all: my Sect thou seest, now learn too late Par Lost 6.147
Unnam'd in Heav'n, now plenteous, as thou seest Par Lost 6.263
Which nightly as a circling Zone thou seest Par Lost 7.580
In six thou seest, and what if sev'nth to these Par Lost 8.128
Feilds and Inhabitants: Her spots thou seest Par Lost 8.145
And Day is yet not spent; till then thou seest Par Lost 8.206
Said mildely, Author of all this thou seest Par Lost 8.317
They all had need, I as thou seest have none. Par Reg 2.318
That I have also power to give thou seest, Par Reg 2.393
His City there thou seest, and *Bactra* there; Par Reg 3.285
The City which thou seest no other deem Par Reg 4.44
Of Nations; there the Capitol thou seest Par Reg 4.47
Take to thy wicked deed: which when thou seest Samson 826
What then thou would'st, thou seest it in thy hand. Samson 1105
No Preface needs, thou seest we long to know. Samson 1554

Seize
If such astonishment as this can sieze Par Lost 1.317
ms 'seise'
Strange horror seise thee, and pangs unfelt before. Par Lost 2.703
Whence rushing he might surest seize them both Par Lost 4.407
1667 'seise'
Such where ye find, seise fast, and hither bring. Par Lost 4.796
In thir bright stand, there left his Powers to seise Par Lost 11.221
Upon the Temple it self: at last they seise Par Lost 12.356
But sease his wand, though he and his curst crew Mask 653

Seize(*cont*)
Bridgewater ms 'cease'
Which on our dearest Lord did sease er'e long, Passion 10
His Infancy to sease! Circum 14
Sweet rest sease thee evermore, Winchester 50
Whose chance on these defenceless dores may sease, Sonnet 8, 2
To seise the widdow'd whore Pluralitie Forcers 3
By right now shall we seize Psalm 83, 46

Seized
With his enormous brood, and birthright seis'd Par Lost 1.511
Seis'd us, though undismaid: long is the way Par Lost 2.432
Out of thy head I sprung: amazement seis'd Par Lost 2.758
Of his great Father. Admiration seis'd Par Lost 3.271
Such wonder seis'd, though after Heaven seen, Par Lost 3.552
The Spirit maligne, but much more envy seis'd Par Lost 3.553
Seisd mine, I yielded, and from that time see Par Lost 4.489
Half sunk with all his Pines. Amazement seis'd Par Lost 6.198
Be sure, and terrour seis'd the rebel Host, Par Lost 6.647
He trusted to have seis'd, and into fraud Par Lost 7.143
First found me, and with soft oppression seis'd Par Lost 8.288
Her hand he seis'd, and to a shadie bank, Par Lost 9.1037
Exploded and had seiz'd with violent hands, Par Lost 11.669
Seis'd on by force, judg'd, and to death condemnd Par Lost 12.412

Seizure
Defeated of his seisure many dayes Par Lost 11.254

Seldom
Of what so seldom chanc'd, when to his wish, Par Lost 9.423
Or whom he wishes most shall seldom gain Par Lost 10.901
With Food, whereof we wretched seldom taste. Par Reg 1.345
Which they who ask'd have seldom understood, Par Reg 1.436
From that time seldom have I ceas'd to eye Par Reg 4.507
Numbring good intellects; now seldom por'd on. Sonnet 11, 4

Select
One way a Band select from forage drives Par Lost 11.646
Select for life shall in the Ark be lodg'd, Par Lost 11.823
And one peculiar Nation to select Par Lost 12.111
Select, and Sacred, Glorious for a while, Samson 363

Selectest
Shed thir selectest influence; the Earth Par Lost 8.513

Seleucia
Of great *Seleucia*, built by *Grecian* Kings, Par Lost 4.212
The great *Seleucia*, *Nisibis*, and there Par Reg 3.291

Self
The mind is its own place, and in it self Par Lost 1.254
ms 'selfe'
Within his Sanctuary it self thir Shrines, Par Lost 1.388
ms 'selfe'
Vice for it self: To him no Temple stood Par Lost 1.492
ms 'selfe'
In loss it self; which on his count'nance cast Par Lost 1.526
ms 'selfe'
Among his Angels; and his Throne it self Par Lost 2.68
The Ford, and of it self the water flies Par Lost 2.612
And reck'n'st thou thy self with Spirits of Heav'n, Par Lost 2.696
Thy self in me thy perfect image viewing Par Lost 2.764
My self expose, with lonely steps to tread Par Lost 2.828
Which but her self not all the *Stygian* powers Par Lost 2.875
By him corrupted? or wilt thou thy self Par Lost 3.162
Life in my self for ever, by thee I live, Par Lost 3.244
And be thy self Man among men on Earth, Par Lost 3.283
Fountain of Light, thy self invisible Par Lost 3.375
Which way I flie is Hell; my self am Hell; Par Lost 4.75
Her self a fairer Floure by gloomie *Dis* Par Lost 4.270
Dearer thy self then all; needs must the power Par Lost 4.412
Like consort to thy self canst no where find. Par Lost 4.448
I first awak't, and found my self repos'd Par Lost 4.450
What there thou seest fair Creature is thy self, Par Lost 4.468
Multitudes like thy self, and thence be call'd Par Lost 4.474
Though thither doomd? Thou wouldst thy self, no doubt, Par Lost 4.890
To dispossess him, and thy self to reigne? Par Lost 4.961
Farr heavier load thy self expect to feel Par Lost 4.972
Sweet of thy self, but much more sweet thus cropt, Par Lost 5.68
Thy self a Goddess, not to Earth confind, Par Lost 5.78
Best Image of my self and dearer half, Par Lost 5.95
Thus wondrous fair; thy self how wondrous then! Par Lost 5.155
Undeckt, save with her self more lovely fair Par Lost 5.380
That thou continu'st such, owe to thy self, Par Lost 5.521
My self and all th' Angelic Host that stand Par Lost 5.535
And by my Self have sworn to him shall bow Par Lost 5.607
In place thy self so high above thy Peeres. Par Lost 5.812
Thy self though great and glorious dost thou count, Par Lost 5.833
Thy self not free, but to thy self enthrall'd; Par Lost 6.181
Though heaviest by just measure on thy self Par Lost 6.265
Or turn this Heav'n it self into the Hell Par Lost 6.291
It self instinct with Spirit, but convoyd Par Lost 6.752
All but the Throne it self of God. Full soon Par Lost 6.834
Though I uncircumscrib'd my self retire, Par Lost 7.170
And Earth self ballanc't on her Center hung. Par Lost 7.242
1667 'self-ballanc't'
Whose Seed is in her self upon the Earth. Par Lost 7.312
Serv'd by more noble then her self, attaines Par Lost 8.34
Whose vertue on it self workes no effect, Par Lost 8.95
If Earth industrious of her self fetch Day Par Lost 8.137
My self I then perus'd, and Limb by Limb Par Lost 8.267
Not of my self; by some great Maker then, Par Lost 8.278
Thou to thy self proposest, in the choice Par Lost 8.400
Thou in thy self art perfet, and in thee Par Lost 8.415
Best with thy self accompanied, seek'st not Par Lost 8.428

Self(*cont*)
Which thou hast rightly nam'd, but of thy self, Par Lost 8.439
Thy likeness, thy fit help, thy other self, Par Lost 8.450
Bone of my Bone, Flesh of my Flesh, my Self Par Lost 8.495
Nature her self, though pure of sinful thought, Par Lost 8.506
And in her self compleat, so well to know Par Lost 8.548
Less excellent, as thou thy self perceav'st. Par Lost 8.566
Not thy subjection: weigh with her thy self; Par Lost 8.570
Then self esteem, grounded on just and right Par Lost 8.572
1667 'self-esteem'
Remaines, sufficient of it self to raise Par Lost 9.43
Nor hope to be my self less miserable Par Lost 9.126
Bitter ere long back on it self recoiles; Par Lost 9.172
Th' attempt it self, intended by our Foe. Par Lost 9.295
Against temptation: thou thy self with scorne Par Lost 9.299
Betook her to the Groves, but *Delia*'s self Par Lost 9.388
Her self, though fairest unsupported Flour, Par Lost 9.432
Your feare it self of Death removes the feare. Par Lost 9.702
Pausing a while, thus to her self she mus'd. Par Lost 9.744
Thus to her self she pleasingly began. Par Lost 9.794
One Flesh; to loose thee were to loose my self. Par Lost 9.959
Or to thy self perhaps: hadst thou been there, Par Lost 9.1148
And left to her self, if evil thence ensue, Par Lost 9.1185
Affraid, being naked, hid my self. To whom Par Lost 10.117
My self the total Crime, or to accuse Par Lost 10.127
My other self, the partner of my life; Par Lost 10.128
And what she did, whatever in it self, Par Lost 10.141
And person, had'st thou known thy self aright. Par Lost 10.156
The Realm it self of Satan long usurpt, Par Lost 10.189
Unnam'd, undreaded, and thy self half starv'd? Par Lost 10.595
To waste it all my self, and leave ye none! Par Lost 10.820
Befits thee with him leagu'd, thy self as false Par Lost 10.868
On me alreadie lost, mee then thy self Par Lost 10.929
The punishment all on thy self; alas, Par Lost 10.949
Good by it self, and Evil not at all. Par Lost 11.89
Upon the Temple it self: at last they seise Par Lost 12.356
But force the Spirit of Grace it self, and binde Par Lost 12.525
What from within I feel my self, and hear Par Reg 1.198
What might be publick good; my self I thought Par Reg 1.204
So shalt thou save thy self and us relieve Par Reg 1.344
Then to thy self ascrib'st the truth fore-told. Par Reg 1.453
All others by thy self; because of old Par Reg 2.174
Thou thy self doat'st on womankind, admiring Par Reg 2.175
A Carpenter thy Father known, thy self Par Reg 2.414
All Earth her wonder at thy acts, thy self Par Reg 3.24
My crime; whatever for it self condemn'd, Par Reg 3.213
Happiest both to thy self and all the world, Par Reg 3.225
Thee, of thy self so apt, in regal Arts, Par Reg 3.248
This far his over-match, who self deceiv'd Par Reg 4.7
And thou thy self seem'st otherwise inclin'd Par Reg 4.212
Within thy self, much more with Empire joyn'd. Par Reg 4.284
As Earth and Skie would mingle; but my self Par Reg 4.453
Cast thy self down; safely if Son of God: Par Reg 4.555
Cast her self headlong from th' *Ismenian* steep, Par Reg 4.575
Whom have I to complain of but my self? Samson 46
And almost life it self, if it be true Samson 91
My self, my Sepulcher, a moving Grave, Samson 102
The Dungeon of thy self; thy Soul Samson 156
Deject not then so overmuch thy self, Samson 213
She was not the prime cause, but I my self, Samson 234
But justly; I my self have brought them on, Samson 375
She sought to make me Traytor to my self; Samson 401
Thy penal forfeit from thy self; perhaps Samson 508
In all her functions weary of her self; Samson 596
By it self, with aggravations not surcharg'd, Samson 769
E're I to thee, thou to thy self wast cruel. Samson 784
More strength from me, then in thy self was found. Samson 789
Whole to my self, unhazarded abroad, Samson 809
I to my self was false e're thou to me, Samson 824
To afflict thy self in vain: though sight be lost, Samson 914
Why do I humble thus my self, and suing Samson 965
Thou oft shalt wish thy self at *Gath* to boast Samson 1127
Off. Regard thy self, this will offend them highly. Samson 1333
Sam. My self? my conscience and internal peace. Samson 1334
Our God, our Law, my Nation, or my self, Samson 1425
Man. O lastly over-strong against thy self! Samson 1590
And in sweet madnes rob'd it of it self, Mask 261
Trinity ms 'selfe'
Bridgewater ms 'selfe'
1637 'selfe'
Were in the flat Sea sunk. And Wisdoms self Mask 375
1637 'selfe'
Trinity ms 'selfe'
Bridgewater ms 'selfe'
And link't it self by carnal sensualty Mask 474
Trinity ms 'selfe'
Bridgewater ms 'selfe'
1637 'selfe'
But evil on it self shall back recoyl, Mask 593
1637 'it selfe'
Trinity ms 'it selfe'
Bridgewater ms 'it selfe'
Gather'd like scum, and setl'd to it self Mask 595
1637 'it selfe'
Trinity ms 'it selfe'
Bridgewater ms 'it selfe'
How durst thou then thy self approach so neer Mask 616
word not in Bridgewater ms

Self(*cont*)
1637 'selfe'
Trinity ms 'selfe'
Why should you be so cruel to your self, Mask 679
1637 'selfe'
line not in Bridgewater ms
Trinity ms 'selfe'
Unsavoury in th' injoyment of it self Mask 742
1637 'selfe'
Trinity ms 'selfe'
line not in Bridgewater ms
Thou art not fit to hear thy self convinc't; Mask 792
line not in Bridgewater ms
1637 'selfe'
line not in Trinity ms
To aid a Virgin, such as was her self Mask 856
Trinity ms 'selfe'
1637 'selfe'
Bridgewater ms 'selfe'
Heav'n it self would stoop to her. Mask 1023
Bridgewater ms 'selfe'
B.M. ms 'Self'
1637 'selfe'
cardoyn 'selfe'
Trinity ms 'selfe'
That *Orpheus* self may heave his head Allegro 145
Forget thy self to Marble, till Penseroso 42
What could the Muse her self that *Orpheus* bore, Lycidas 58
Trinity ms 'muse her selfe' ←'golden hayrd Calliope'
The Muse her self, for her inchanting son Lycidas 59
Trinity ms 'her selfe'
And Hell it self will pass away, Nativity 139
Who having clad thy self in humane weed, Fair Inf 58
And glut thy self with what thy womb devours, On Time 4
Trinity ms 'selfe'
And last of all, thy greedy self consum'd, On Time 10
Trinity ms 'selfe'
Hast built thy self a live-long Monument. Shakespear 8
1632 'selfe'
1640 'selfe'
Then thou our fancy of it self bereaving, Shakespear 13
1632 'selfe'
1640 'selfe'
Rouze thy self amidst the rage Psalm 7, 20
And the young branch, that for thy self Psalm 80, 63
Strong for thy self hast made. Psalm 80, 72

Self-balanced
And Earth self ballanc't on her Center hung. Par Lost 7.242
1667 'self-ballanc't'

Self-begot
Know none before us, self-begot, self-rais'd Par Lost 5.860

Self-begotten
Like that self-begott'n bird Samson 1699

Self-condemning
The fruitless hours, but neither self-condemning, Par Lost 9.1188

Self-consumed
Self-fed, and self-consum'd, if this fail, Mask 597
1637 'selfe consum'd'
Trinity ms 'selfe consum'd'
Bridgewater ms 'selfe consum'd'

Self-delusion
How bitter is such self-delusion? Mask 365
line not in Bridgewater ms
1637 'selfe-delusion'
line not in Trinity ms

Self-depraved
Self-tempted, self-deprav'd: Man falls deceiv'd Par Lost 3.130

Self-destruction
But self-destruction therefore saught, refutes Par Lost 10.1016

Self-displeased
Which argues over-just, and self-displeas'd Samson 514

Self-esteem
Then self esteem, grounded on just and right Par Lost 8.572
1667 'self-esteem'

Self-fed
Self-fed, and self-consum'd, if this fail, Mask 597
1637 'Selfe fed'
Trinity ms 'selfe fed'
Bridgewater ms 'selfe fed'

Self-killed
Among thy slain self-kill'd Samson 1664

Self-knowing
Govern the rest, self-knowing, and from thence Par Lost 7.510

Self-left
Self-left. Least therefore his now bolder hand Par Lost 11.93

Self-lost
Self-lost, and in a moment will create Par Lost 7.154

Self-love
Or was too much of self-love mixt, Samson 1031

Self-offence
For self-offence, more then for God offended. Samson 515

Self-opened
Of Heav'n arriv'd, the gate self-opend wide Par Lost 5.254

Self-preservation
Thou canst avoid, self-preservation bids; Samson 505

Self-raised
Self-rais'd, and repossess thir native seat? Par Lost 1.634
ms 'Selfe-rais'd'

Self-raised(*cont*)
Know none before us, self-begot, self-rais'd Par Lost 5.860
Self-rigorous
Then who self-rigorous chooses death as due; Samson 513
Self-rolled
In Labyrinth of many a round self-rowld, Par Lost 9.183
Selfsame
That self same day by fight, or by surprize Par Lost 6.87
Of *Satan*, to the self same place where hee Par Lost 10.315
One way the self-same hour? why in the East Par Lost 11.203
For we were nurst upon the self-same hill, Lycidas 23
Trinity ms 'selfe same'
Self-satisfying
But never find self-satisfying solution. Samson 306
Self-severe
Impartial, self-severe, inexorable, Samson 827
Self-tempted
Self-tempted, self-deprav'd: Man falls deceiv'd Par Lost 3.130
Self-violence
Mess. By his own hands. *Man*. Self-violence? what cause Samson 1584
Sell
Thy Husband, slight me, sell me, and forgo me; Samson 940
Selves
If we procure not to our selves more woe. Par Lost 2.225
Our own good from our selves, and from our own Par Lost 2.253
Live to our selves, though in this vast recess, Par Lost 2.254
Not to know mee argues your selves unknown, Par Lost 4.830
To know ye right, or if ye know your selves Par Lost 5.789
Our selves with like defence, to me deserves Par Lost 6.467
And not molest us, unless we our selves Par Lost 8.186
Law to our selves, our Reason is our Law. Par Lost 9.654
Then both our selves and Seed at once to free Par Lost 10.999
With our own hands his Office on our selves; Par Lost 10.1002
By death brought on our selves, or childless days Par Lost 10.1037
Against our selves, and wilful barrenness, Par Lost 10.1042
us of our selves & native woes beguile Musick Tr. ms 4.08
Semblance
Semblance of worth, not substance, gently rais'd Par Lost 1.529
Semblance, and in thy Beauties heav'nly Ray Par Lost 9.607
Perhaps my semblance might deceive the truth, Sonnet 7, 5
Semele
Daphne, or *Semele*, *Antiopa*, Par Reg 2.187
Senate
Thir government, and thir great Senate choose Par Lost 12.225
And sits as safe as in a Senat house, Mask 389
Bridgewater ms 'senate'
Trinity ms 'senate'
Who keepes the lawes and statutes of the Senate, Prose 10, 2
Senator
Then whome a better Senatour nere held Sonnet 17, 2
1694 'Senator'
Send
Shall breathe her balme. But first whom shall we send Par Lost 2.402
Choice in our suffrage; for on whom we send, Par Lost 2.415
Shalt in the Sky appeer, and from thee send Par Lost 3.324
And send forth all her Kings; there will be room, Par Lost 4.383
Aereal Music send: nor knew I not Par Lost 5.548
What Heavens Lord had powerfullest to send Par Lost 6.425
Dilated and infuriate shall send forth Par Lost 6.486
I send along, ride forth, and bid the Deep Par Lost 7.166
Thither will send his winged Messengers Par Lost 7.572
From th' Earths great Altar send up silent praise Par Lost 9.195
To intercept thy way, or send thee back Par Lost 9.410
But whom send I to judge them? whom but thee Par Lost 10.55
My Substitutes I send ye, and Create Par Lost 10.403
And send him from the Garden forth to Till Par Lost 11.97
So send them forth, though sorrowing, yet in peace: Par Lost 11.117
And send thee from the Garden forth to till Par Lost 11.261
Hee to his own a Comforter will send, Par Lost 12.486
Of his great warfare, e're I send him forth Par Reg 1.158
Send thy Messiah forth, the time is come; Par Reg 2.43
To put out both thine eyes, and fetter'd send thee Samson 1160
Send thee the Angel of thy Birth, to stand Samson 1431
Will send for all my kindred, all my friends Samson 1730
Would send a glistring Guardian if need were Mask 219
line not in Bridgewater ms
Thou honour'st Verse, and Verse must send her wing Sonnet 13, 9
1648 'lend'
Trinity ms 'lend'
Sender
Best with the best, the Sender not the sent, Par Lost 4.852
Sending
Mercie collegue with Justice, sending thee Par Lost 10.59
And dar'st thou at our sending and command Samson 1394
Sends
But us he sends upon his high behests Par Lost 8.238
And sends a comfortable heat from farr, Par Lost 10.1077
Powrd first on his Apostles, whom he sends Par Lost 12.498
And sends his Spirit of Truth henceforth to dwell Par Reg 1.462
And when God sends a cheerful hour, refrains. Sonnet 21, 14
Seneschals
Serv'd up in Hall with Sewers, and Seneshals; Par Lost 9.38
Senir
Shall dwell to *Senir*, that long ridge of Hills. Par Lost 12.146
Sennaar
Of *Sennaar*, and still with vain designe Par Lost 3.467
Sense
And high disdain, from sence of injur'd merit, Par Lost 1.98

Sense(*cont*)
ms 'sense'
Devoid of sense and motion? and who knows, Par Lost 2.151
(For Eloquence the Soul, Song charms the Sense,) Par Lost 2.556
Sense of new joy ineffable diffus'd: Par Lost 3.137
To all delight of human sense expos'd Par Lost 4.206
Like this fair Paradise, your sense, yet such Par Lost 4.379
Of sense, whereby they hear, see, smell, touch, taste, Par Lost 5.411
To intellectual, give both life and sense, Par Lost 5.485
To human sense th' invisible exploits Par Lost 5.565
Of human sense, I shall delineate so, Par Lost 5.572
All Intellect, all Sense, and as they please, Par Lost 6.351
Then first with fear surpris'd and sense of paine Par Lost 6.394
Of Mightiest. Sense of pleasure we may well Par Lost 6.459
God to remove his wayes from human sense, Par Lost 8.119
My droused sense, untroubl'd, though I thought Par Lost 8.289
As with an object that excels the sense, Par Lost 8.456
But if the sense of touch whereby mankind Par Lost 8.579
Who meet with various objects, from the sense Par Lost 8.609
Active within beyond the sense of brute. Par Lost 9.96
Of Growth, Sense, Reason, all summ'd up in Man. Par Lost 9.113
The Devil enterd, and his brutal sense, Par Lost 9.188
Why shouldst not thou like sense within thee feel Par Lost 9.315
By Tongue of Brute, and human sense exprest? Par Lost 9.554
Grateful to appetite, more pleas'd my sense Par Lost 9.580
Endu'd with human voice and human sense, Par Lost 9.871
Hath toucht my sense, flat seems to this, and harsh. Par Lost 9.987
With all perfections, so enflame my sense Par Lost 9.1031
The sense of endless woes? inexplicable Par Lost 10.754
Bereaving sense, but endless miserie Par Lost 10.810
To his grim Cave, all dismal; yet to sense Par Lost 11.469
Must needs impaire and wearie human sense: Par Lost 12.10
Or vertuous, I should so have lost all sense. Par Reg 1.382
Ambiguous and with double sense deluding, Par Reg 1.435
A third sort doubted all things, though plain sence; Par Reg 4.296
The Son of God, which bears no single sence; Par Reg 4.517
Sam. I hear the sound of words, thir sense the air Samson 176
Though void of corporal sense. Samson 616
And sense of Heav'ns desertion. Samson 632
With dotage, and his sense deprav'd Samson 1042
And sense distract, to know well what I utter. Samson 1556
Insensate left, or to sense reprobate, Samson 1685
Yet they in pleasing slumber lull'd the sense, Mask 260
Bridgewater ms 'sence'
To inveigle and invite th' unwary sense Mask 538
Trinity ms 'sense' ← 'spell'
Bridgewater ms 'sence'
And through the porch and inlet of each sense Mask 839
Bridgewater ms 'sence'
Trinity ms 'sence'
To hit the Sense of human sight; Penseroso 14
Hath lockt up mortal sense, then listen I Arcades 62
Trinity ms 'mortall sense' ← 'mortall eyes' ← 'mortalitie'
Dead things with inbreath'd sense able to pierce, Musick 4
Senseless
That bawle for freedom in their senceless mood, Sonnet 12, 9
Trinity ms 'sensles' ← 'senseles'
Senses
Invites; for I will cleer thir senses dark, Par Lost 3.188
Which the five watchful Senses represent, Par Lost 5.104
That all his senses bound; *Eve*, who unseen Par Lost 11.265
To witherd weak and gray; thy Senses then Par Lost 11.540
Where other senses want not their delights Samson 916
(If ye have power to touch our senses so) Nativity 127
Sensible
The sensible of pain. All things invite Par Lost 2.278
Sensibly
Bear not too sensibly, nor still insist Samson 913
Sensual
To sensual Appetite, who from beneathe Par Lost 9.1129
To roule with pleasure in a sensual stie. Mask 77
1637 'sensuall'
Trinity ms 'sensuall'
Bridgewater ms 'sensuall'
O're sensual Folly, and Intemperance. Mask 975
Trinity ms 'sensuall'
Bridgewater ms 'sensuall'
1637 'sensuall'
Sensualest
The sensuallest, and after *Asmodai* Par Reg 2.151
Sensuality
And link't it self by carnal sensualty Mask 474
Trinity ms 'sensualtie'
1673 'sensuality'
Bridgewater ms 'sensualitie'
1637 'sensualitie'
Sent
Or whom *Biserta* sent from *Afric* shore Par Lost 1.585
By all his Engins, but was headlong sent Par Lost 1.750
Of *Tobits* Son, and with a vengeance sent Par Lost 4.170
To him who sent us, whose charge is to keep Par Lost 4.842
Best with the best, the Sender not the sent, Par Lost 4.852
Leader, the terms we sent were terms of weight, Par Lost 6.621
Grasping ten thousand Thunders, which he sent Par Lost 6.836
Divine interpreter, by favour sent Par Lost 7.72
Sent from her through the wide transpicuous aire, Par Lost 8.141
Sent from whose sovran goodness I adore. Par Lost 8.647
So judg'd he Man, both Judge and Saviour sent, Par Lost 10.209

Sent(*cont*)
Might intercept thir Emperour sent, so hee — Par Lost 10.429
Though to delude them sent, could not abstain, — Par Lost 10.557
Frequenting, sent from hearts contrite, in sign — Par Lost 10.1091
Frequenting, sent from hearts contrite, in sign — Par Lost 10.1103
Ere thou from hence depart, know I am sent — Par Lost 11.356
Sent up amain; and now the thick'nd Skie — Par Lost 11.742
A Dove sent forth once and agen to spie — Par Lost 11.857
Moses and *Aaron*) sent from God to claime — Par Lost 12.170
Here *Adam* interpos'd. O sent from Heav'n, — Par Lost 12.270
Which he hath sent propitious, some great good — Par Lost 12.612
His coming, is sent Harbinger, who all — Par Reg 1.71
On which I sent thee to the Virgin pure — Par Reg 1.134
God hath now sent his living Oracle — Par Reg 1.460
Sent his Anointed, and to us reveal'd him, — Par Reg 2.50
Who sent me, and thereby witness whence I am. — Par Reg 3.107
For him I was not sent, nor yet to free — Par Reg 4.131
As false portents, not sent from God, but thee; — Par Reg 4.491
Bound, and to torment sent before thir time. — Par Reg 4.632
Sam. So let her go, God sent her to debase me, — Samson 999
Me their Deliverer sent would not receive, — Samson 1214
Among them he a spirit of phrenzie sent, — Samson 1675
And sent them here through hard assays — Mask 972
but soft I was not sent to court your wonder — Mask Tr. ms 10.16
Sent by som spirit to mortals good, — Penseroso 153
His goary visage down the stream was sent, — Lycidas 62
Sent down the meek-eyd Peace, — Nativity 46
The parting Genius is with sighing sent, — Nativity 186
Think what a present thou to God hast sent, — Fair Inf 74
Sent thee from the banks of *Came*, — Winchester 59
Down to the Sea she sent, — Psalm 80, 46
With terror sent from thee; — Psalm 88, 60

Sentence
My sentence is for open Warr: Of Wiles, — Par Lost 2.51
The sentence of thir Conquerour: This is now — Par Lost 2.208
As *Mammon* ended, and his Sentence pleas'd, — Par Lost 2.291
Thy sovran sentence, that Man should find grace; — Par Lost 3.145
Beneath thy Sentence; Hell her numbers full, — Par Lost 3.332
Of thoughts revolv'd, his final sentence chose — Par Lost 9.88
What rests but that the mortal Sentence pass — Par Lost 10.48
To sentence Man: the voice of God they heard — Par Lost 10.97
And to the Woman thus his Sentence turn'd. — Par Lost 10.192
Mortalitie my sentence, and be Earth — Par Lost 10.776
His Sentence beyond dust and Natures Law, — Par Lost 10.805
The sentence from thy head remov'd may light — Par Lost 10.934
Part of our Sentence, that thy Seed shall bruise — Par Lost 10.1031
At the sad Sentence rigorously urg'd, — Par Lost 11.109
Then due by sentence when thou didst transgress, — Par Lost 11.253
Sam. Where outward force constrains, the sentence holds — Samson 1369

Sententious
In brief sententious precepts, while they treat — Par Reg 4.264

Sentries
Through the strict Senteries and Stations thick — Par Lost 2.412

Seon
And *Horonaim*, *Seons* Realm, beyond — Par Lost 1.409
ms 'Seons'
He foild bold *Seon* and his host, — Psalm 136, 65

Separate
Farr separate, circling thy holy Mount — Par Lost 6.743
Eve separate, he wish'd, but not with hope — Par Lost 9.422
Beyond his hope, *Eve* separate he spies, — Par Lost 9.424
Shall separate us, linkt in Love so deare, — Par Lost 9.970
For Death from Sin no power can separate. — Par Lost 10.251
As of a person separate to God, — Samson 31

Septentrion
From cold *Septentrion* blasts, thence in the midst — Par Reg 4.31

Sepulchral
Mine eye hath found that sad Sepulchral rock — Passion 43

Sepulchre
My self, my Sepulcher, a moving Grave, — Samson 102

Sepulchred
And so Sepulcher'd in such pomp dost lie, — Shakespear 15
1663-4 '*Sepulcher'd*'

Sepulchres
Oft seen in Charnell vaults, and Sepulchers — Mask 471
Trinity ms 'sepulchers' ←'monume'
Bridgewater ms 'sepulchers'

Sequel
The sequel each of parting and of fight; — Par Lost 4.1003
To observe the sequel, saw his guileful act — Par Lost 10.334

Sequent
Suspected to a sequent King, who seeks — Par Lost 12.165

Sequestered
More sacred and sequesterd, though but feignd, — Par Lost 4.706
How couldst thou find this dark sequester'd nook? — Mask 500
Trinity ms 'sequeste'rd'
Bridgewater ms 'sequesterd'

Seraph
Cherube and Seraph rowling in the Flood — Par Lost 1.324
Alone thus wandring. Brightest Seraph tell — Par Lost 3.667
A Seraph wingd; six wings he wore, to shade — Par Lost 5.277
1667 '*Seraph*' in some copies
The flaming Seraph fearless, though alone — Par Lost 5.875
So spake the Seraph *Abdiel* faithful found, — Par Lost 5.896
A Seraph stood, and in his hand a Reed — Par Lost 6.579
What words or tongue of Seraph can suffice, — Par Lost 7.113
Cherub and Seraph, Potentates and Thrones, — Par Lost 7.198

Seraphic
Seraphic arms and Trophies: all the while — Par Lost 1.539
The great Seraphic Lords and Cherubim — Par Lost 1.794

Seraphim
That led th' imbattelld Seraphim to Warr — Par Lost 1.129
A Globe of fierie Seraphim inclos'd — Par Lost 2.512
Of all the Seraphim with thee combin'd — Par Lost 2.750
Yet dazle Heav'n, that brightest Seraphim — Par Lost 3.381
Of Seraphim and Potentates and Thrones — Par Lost 5.749
Had audience, when among the Seraphim — Par Lost 5.804
Of fighting Seraphim confus'd, at length — Par Lost 6.249
Stood rankt of Seraphim another row — Par Lost 6.604
Of Thrones and mighty Seraphim prostrate, — Par Lost 6.841
And sworded Seraphim, — Nativity 113
Where the bright Seraphim in burning row — Musick 10

Serapis
Belus or *Serapis* thir Gods, or seat — Par Lost 1.720
ms 'Serapis'

Serbonian
A gulf profound as that *Serbonian* Bog — Par Lost 2.592

Sere
Reflected, may with matter sere foment, — Par Lost 10.1071
Ye Myrtles brown, with Ivy never-sear, — Lycidas 2
1673 'never sear'
Trinity ms 'never sere'
1638 'never-sere'
If once his wrath take fire like fuel sere. — Psalm 2, 27

Serenate
Or Serenate, which the starv'd Lover sings — Par Lost 4.769

Serene
So thick a drop serene hath quencht thir Orbs, — Par Lost 3.25
That wont to be more chearful and serene — Par Lost 5.123
Light'ning Divine, ineffable, serene, — Par Lost 5.734
His Stature, and upright with Front serene — Par Lost 7.509
Intelligence of Heav'n, Angel serene, — Par Lost 8.181
From his displeasure; in whose look serene, — Par Lost 10.1094
To whom the Father, without Cloud, serene. — Par Lost 11.45
In Regions milde of calm and serene Ayr, — Mask 4
Bridgewater ms 'Cerene'

Sericana
Of *Sericana*, where *Chineses* drive — Par Lost 3.438

Serious
Serious to learn and know, and thence to do — Par Reg 1.203
And serious doctrine of Virginity, — Mask 787
line not in Trinity ms
line not in Bridgewater ms

Serpent
Th' infernal Serpent; he it was, whose guile — Par Lost 1.34
Voluminous and vast, a Serpent arm'd — Par Lost 2.652
His Lithe Proboscis; close the Serpent sly — Par Lost 4.347
With Serpent errour wandring, found thir way, — Par Lost 7.302
Minims of Nature; some of Serpent kinde — Par Lost 7.482
The Serpent suttl'st Beast of all the field, — Par Lost 7.495
The Serpent suttlest Beast of all the Field. — Par Lost 9.86
The Serpent sleeping, in whose mazie foulds — Par Lost 9.161
The Serpent: him fast sleeping soon he found — Par Lost 9.182
Meer Serpent in appearance, forth was come, — Par Lost 9.413
Such Pleasure took the Serpent to behold — Par Lost 9.455
In Serpent, Inmate bad, and toward *Eve* — Par Lost 9.495
And lovely, never since of Serpent kind — Par Lost 9.504
Of her attention gaind, with Serpent Tongue — Par Lost 9.529
Thee, Serpent, suttlest beast of all the field — Par Lost 9.560
Serpent, thy overpraising leaves in doubt — Par Lost 9.615
Serpent, we might have spar'd our coming hither, — Par Lost 9.647
How dies the Serpent? hee hath eat'n and lives, — Par Lost 9.764
The guiltie Serpent, and well might, for *Eve* — Par Lost 9.785
And hath bin tasted such: the Serpent wise, — Par Lost 9.867
Profan'd first by the Serpent, by him first — Par Lost 9.930
Fraud in the Serpent, speaking as he spake; — Par Lost 9.1150
Hee in the Serpent, had perverted *Eve*, — Par Lost 10.3
Conviction to the Serpent none belongs. — Par Lost 10.84
The Serpent me beguil'd and I did eate. — Par Lost 10.162
Serpent though brute, unable to transferre — Par Lost 10.165
And on the Serpent thus his curse let fall. — Par Lost 10.174
Mee not, but the brute Serpent in whose shape — Par Lost 10.495
A monstrous Serpent on his Belly prone, — Par Lost 10.514
And Fabl'd how the Serpent, whom they calld — Par Lost 10.580
Out of my sight, thou Serpent, that name best — Par Lost 10.867
To over-reach, but with the Serpent meeting — Par Lost 10.879
That cruel Serpent: On me exercise not — Par Lost 10.927
The Serpents head; piteous amends, unless — Par Lost 10.1032
Satan, who in the Serpent hath contriv'd — Par Lost 10.1034
The Serpents head; whereof to thee anon — Par Lost 12.150
The Serpent, by what means he shall achieve — Par Lost 12.234
The adversarie Serpent, and bring back — Par Lost 12.312
Needs must the Serpent now his capital bruise — Par Lost 12.383
The Serpent, Prince of aire, and drag in Chaines — Par Lost 12.454
The fiery Serpent fled, and noxious Worm, — Par Reg 1.312
So spake the old Serpent doubting, and from all — Par Reg 2.147
At length collecting all his Serpent wiles, — Par Reg 3.5
But thou, Infernal Serpent, shalt not long — Par Reg 4.618
Chor. She's gone, a manifest Serpent by her sting — Samson 997
her brok'n league, to impe their serpent wings, — Sonnet 15, 8
1694 'Serpent'

Serpentine
Like his, and colour Serpentine may shew — Par Lost 10.870

Serpents
Alike, to Serpents all as accessories — Par Lost 10.520

Serpents(*cont*)
Of ugly Serpents; horror on them fell, Par Lost 10.539
Serraliona
From *Serraliona;* thwart of these as fierce Par Lost 10.703
Serried
Appear'd, and serried Shields in thick array Par Lost 1.548
Nor serv'd it to relax thir serried files. Par Lost 6.599
Servant
Servant of God, well done, well hast thou fought Par Lost 6.29
Then of our fellow servant, and inquire Par Lost 8.225
Thenceforth the form of servant to assume, Par Lost 10.214
Servant of Servants, on his vitious Race. Par Lost 12.104
He ask'd thee, hast thou seen my servant *Job?* Par Reg 3.67
Was *Samson* as a public servant brought, Samson 1615
And to his servant *Israel*, Psalm 136, 73
1673 'Servant'
Save thou thy servant O my God Psalm 86, 7
Thy Servants Soul; for Lord to thee Psalm 86, 11
Unto thy servant give thy strength, Psalm 86, 59
Servants
As when he wash'd his servants feet so now Par Lost 10.215
Servant of Servants, on his vitious Race. Par Lost 12.104
His servants he with new acquist Samson 1755
After this mortal change, to her true Servants Mask 10
Trinity ms 'servants'
Bridgewater ms 'servants'
Serve
Better to reign in Hell, then serve in Heav'n. Par Lost 1.263
Keep residence; if all I can will serve, Par Lost 2.999
To serve him better: wise are all his wayes. Par Lost 3.680
Whose easier business were to serve thir Lord Par Lost 4.943
Are many lesser Faculties that serve Par Lost 5.101
Of God inspir'd, small store will serve, where store, Par Lost 5.322
Can hearts, not free, be tri'd whether they serve Par Lost 5.532
On other surety none; freely we serve, Par Lost 5.538
Streame in the Aire, and for distinction serve Par Lost 5.590
In us who serve, new Counsels, to debate Par Lost 5.681
Our being ordain'd to govern, not to serve? Par Lost 5.802
I see that most through sloth had rather serve, Par Lost 6.166
Of *Servitude* to serve whom God ordains, Par Lost 6.175
To serve th' unwise, or him who hath rebelld Par Lost 6.179
Against his worthier, as thine now serve thee, Par Lost 6.180
Reign thou in Hell thy Kingdom, let mee serve Par Lost 6.183
May serve to better us, and worse our foes, Par Lost 6.440
Yet what thou canst attain, which best may serve Par Lost 7.115
That bodies bright and greater should not serve Par Lost 8.87
Leave them to God above, him serve and feare; Par Lost 8.168
Most opportune might serve his Wiles, and found Par Lost 9.85
What best may from the present serve to hide Par Lost 9.1092
My own deservings; but this will not serve; Par Lost 10.727
To serve him, thy reward was of his grace, Par Lost 10.767
To serve ungovern'd appetite, and took Par Lost 11.517
Or serve they as a flourie verge to binde Par Lost 11.881
Or wither'd sticks to gather; which might serve Par Reg 1.316
Whose off-spring in his Territory yet serve Par Reg 3.375
Of *Bethel* and of *Dan?* no, let them serve Par Reg 3.431
Thir enemies, who serve Idols with God. Par Reg 3.432
The Lord thy God, and only him shalt serve; Par Reg 4.177
And lorded over them whom now they serve; Samson 267
To what can I be useful, wherein serve Samson 564
Man. Wilt thou then serve the *Philistines* with that gift Samson 577
Wherewith to serve him better then thou hast; Samson 585
If aught in my ability may serve Samson 743
Th' unworthier they; whence to this day they serve. Samson 1216
To what may serve his glory best, & spread his name Samson 1429
And we should serve him as a grudging master, Mask 725
And cheeks of sorry grain will serve to ply Mask 750
line not in Bridgewater ms
To serve the Lady of this place. Arcades 105
Both them I serve, and of their train am I. Sonnet 1, 14
To serve therewith my Maker, and present Sonnet 19, 5
Bear his milde yoak, they serve him best, his State Sonnet 19, 11
They also serve who only stand and waite. Sonnet 19, 14
Jehovah serve, and let your joy converse Psalm 2, 24
To serve me *all their daies*, Psalm 81, 54
Served
Serv'd onely to discover sights of woe, Par Lost 1.64
How all his malice serv'd but to bring forth Par Lost 1.217
Made passive both, had servd necessitie, Par Lost 3.110
Now other, as thir shape servd best his end Par Lost 4.398
Nor serv'd it to relax thir serried files. Par Lost 6.599
Serv'd by more noble then her self, attaines Par Lost 8.34
Serv'd up in Hall with Sewers, and Seneshals; Par Lost 9.38
A Goddess among Gods, ador'd and serv'd Par Lost 9.547
This other serv'd but to eternize woe; Par Lost 11.60
His Image whom they serv'd, a brutish vice, Par Lost 11.518
Thir Fathers in the land of *Egypt* serv'd, Par Reg 3.379
That saw not how degeneratly I serv'd. Samson 419
The daintest dishes shall be serv'd up last. Vacation 14
To him that serv'd for her before, Winchester 66
Serves
The great Creatour? But thir spite still serves Par Lost 2.385
To lessen thee, against his purpose serves Par Lost 7.614
Or lawless passions in him which he serves. Par Reg 2.472
Yet *Israel* still serves with all his Sons. Samson 240
What severs each thou 'hast learnt, which few hav don. Sonnet 17, 11
1694 'serves each'
Servest
Chor. Yet with this strength thou serv'st the *Philistines*, Samson 1363
Service
Or do him mightier service as his thralls Par Lost 1.149
Upbraided none; nor was his service hard. Par Lost 4.45
From us no other service then to keep Par Lost 4.420
Our voluntarie service he requires, Par Lost 5.529
Subjected to his service Angel wings, Par Lost 9.155
The other service was thy chosen task, Par Reg 1.427
Duty and Service, nor to stay till bid, Par Reg 2.326
From thee on them, or them to thee of service. Samson 686
As good for nothing else, no better service Samson 1163
To use him further yet in some great service, Samson 1499
That to the service of this house belongs, Mask 85
In Service high, and Anthems cleer, Penseroso 163
And with all helpful service will comply Arcades 38
Affrights the *Flamins* at their service quaint; Nativity 194
Thy service in some graver subject use, Vacation 30
Serviceable
But thou art serviceable to Heaven's King. Par Reg 1.421
Bright-harnest Angels sit in order serviceable. Nativity 244
Servile
Our servile offerings. This must be our task Par Lost 2.246
Of servile Pomp. Our greatness will appeer Par Lost 2.257
Acceptance of large Grace, from servil fear Par Lost 12.305
A victor people free from servile yoke? Par Reg 4.102
Relieves me from my task of servile toyl, Samson 5
To Honour and Religion! servil mind Samson 412
Rewarded well with servil punishment! Samson 413
Till vermin or the draff of servil food Samson 574
To free my Countrey; if their servile minds Samson 1213
Servilely
Once fawn'd, and cring'd, and servilly ador'd Par Lost 4.959
Servility
Servilitie with freedom to contend, Par Lost 6.169
Serving
Thus long from *Israel;* serving as of old Par Reg 3.378
Servitude
Of *Servitude* to serve whom God ordains, Par Lost 6.175
Them whom he governs. This is servitude, Par Lost 6.178
From servitude inglorious welnigh half Par Lost 9.141
From Reason, and to servitude reduce Par Lost 12.89
Of Herds and Flocks, and numerous servitude; Par Lost 12.132
Inglorious life with servitude; for life Par Lost 12.220
Thy Country from her Heathen servitude; Par Reg 3.176
These if from servitude thou shalt restore Par Reg 3.381
And by thir vices brought to servitude, Samson 269
As was my former servitude, ignoble, Samson 416
With corporal servitude, that my mind ever Samson 1336
Session
Then of thir Session ended they bid cry Par Lost 2.514
When at the worlds last session, Nativity 163
Set
To set himself in Glory above his Peers, Par Lost 1.39
In utter darkness, and thir portion set Par Lost 1.72
Were set, and Doric pillars overlaid Par Lost 1.714
I come no enemie, but to set free Par Lost 2.822
The deadly forfeiture, and ransom set. Par Lost 3.221
So wide the op'ning seemd, where bounds were set Par Lost 3.538
So wondrously was set his Station bright. Par Lost 3.587
Would set me highest, and in a moment quit Par Lost 4.51
Mind us of like repose, since God hath set Par Lost 4.612
Ministring light prepar'd, they set and rise; Par Lost 4.664
Longer thy offerd good, why else set here? Par Lost 5.63
Our knowledge, and the scale of Nature set Par Lost 5.509
Tables are set, and on a sudden pil'd Par Lost 5.632
To set the envier of his State, the proud Par Lost 6.89
Of such commotion, such as to set forth Par Lost 6.310
Secret they finish'd, and in order set, Par Lost 6.522
And Wings were set with Eyes, with Eyes the wheels Par Lost 6.755
And set them in the Firmament of Heav'n Par Lost 7.349
But opposite in leveld West was set Par Lost 7.376
With thir bright Luminaries that Set and Rose, Par Lost 7.385
Intelligent of seasons, and set forth Par Lost 7.427
Was set, and twilight from the East came on, Par Lost 7.583
Is as the Book of God before thee set, Par Lost 8.67
Who since the Morning hour set out from Heav'n Par Lost 8.111
For God we see hath honour'd thee, and set Par Lost 8.227
Knowledg of good and ill, which I have set Par Lost 8.324
And these inferiour farr beneath me set? Par Lost 8.382
Set over all his Works, which in our Fall, Par Lost 9.941
Wherein God set thee above her made of thee, Par Lost 10.149
His Seed, when is not set, shall bruise my head: Par Lost 10.499
Should prove tempestuous: To the Winds they set Par Lost 10.664
What justly thou hast lost; nor set thy heart, Par Lost 11.288
Whereon for different cause the Tempter set Par Lost 11.382
Shall them admonish, and before them set Par Lost 11.813
Of Heav'n set open on the Earth shall powre Par Lost 11.825
Over the Earth a Cloud, will therein set Par Lost 11.896
Among them to set up his Tabernacle, Par Lost 12.247
To me was pleasing, all my mind was set Par Reg 1.202
All his great work to come before him set; Par Reg 2.112
Set women in his eye and in his walk, Par Reg 2.153
Made and set wholly on the accomplishment Par Reg 2.207
Tell me if Food were now before thee set, Par Reg 2.320
And all thy heart is set on high designs, Par Reg 2.410
Till *Cyrus* set them free; *Persepolis* Par Reg 3.284
Before mine eyes thou hast set; and in my ear Par Reg 3.390

Set(*cont*)
On what I offer set as high esteem, Par Reg 4.160
Which would have set thee in short time with ease Par Reg 4.378
Directs me in the Starry Rubric set. Par Reg 4.393
There on the highest Pinacle he set Par Reg 4.549
Then in a flowry valley set him down Par Reg 4.586
On a green bank, and set before him spred Par Reg 4.587
He never more henceforth will dare set foot Par Reg 4.610
To set upon them, what advantag'd best; Samson 255
To set his people free, Samson 317
The mark of fool set on his front? Samson 496
But God hath set before us, to return thee Samson 517
When I perceiv'd all set on enmity, Samson 1201
Set God behind: which in his jealousie Samson 1375
To favour, and perhaps to set thee free. Samson 1412
Contemptuous, proud, set on revenge and spite; Samson 1462
They easily would set to sale, a third Samson 1466
Came to the place, and what was set before him Samson 1624
They only set on sport and play Samson 1679
And spotted mountain pard, but set at nought Mask 444
Bridgewater ms 'sett'
And set to work millions of spinning Worms, Mask 715
Her words set off by som superior power; Mask 801
line not in Trinity ms
line not in Bridgewater ms
Thick set with Agat, and the azurn sheen Mask 893
Bridgewater ms 'sett'
Thus I set my printless feet Mask 897
Bridgewater ms 'rest'
Are at their savory dinner set Allegro 84
To ern his Cream-bowle duly set, Allegro 106
Of *Pluto*, to have quite set free Allegro 149
To set her beauties praise above Penseroso 20
Set off to th' world, nor in broad rumour lies, Lycidas 80
His constellations set, Nativity 121
And Mercy set between, Nativity 144
1673 'Mercy will sit between'
Thereby to set the hearts of men on fire Fair Inf 62
And set my Harpe to notes of saddest wo, Passion 9
And still revolt when truth would set them free. Sonnet 12, 10
Trinity ms 'still revolt when Truth would sett them' ←'make them' ←'set them' ←'hate the truth wherby they should be'
Dante shall give Fame leave to set thee higher Sonnet 13, 12
To force our Consciences that Christ set free, Forcers 6
Trinity ms 'sett'
And set at large; now spare, Psalm 4, 5
Set thy wayes right before, where my step goes. Psalm 5, 24
So as above the Heavens thy praise to set Psalm 8, 3
The Moon and Starrs which thou so bright hast set, Psalm 8, 10
Hath set, and planted *long*, Psalm 80, 62
I set his shoulder free; Psalm 81, 22
And hand in hand are set. Psalm 85, 44
Eev'n from the lowest Hell set free Psalm 86, 47
No fear of thee have set. Psalm 86, 52
Hast set me *all forlorn*, Psalm 88, 26

Setia
Their wines of *Setia*, *Cales*, and *Falerne*, Par Reg 4.117

Sets
Grim *Death* my Son and foe, who sets them on, Par Lost 2.804
Shadowie sets off the face of things; in vain, Par Lost 5.43
Dazles the croud, and sets them all agape. Par Lost 5.357
Hesperean sets, my Signal to depart. Par Lost 8.632
Obstruct Heav'n Towrs, and in derision sets Par Lost 12.52
This offer sets before thee to deliver. Par Reg 3.380
To free him hence! but death who sets all free Samson 1572

Setting
A Summers day; and with the setting Sun Par Lost 1.744
With Earth and Ocean meets, the setting Sun Par Lost 4.540

Settle
To settle here on Earth, or in mid Aire; Par Lost 4.940
Whether to settle peace or to unfold Sonnet 17, 5

Settled
To peaceful Counsels, and the settl'd State Par Lost 2.279
He comes, and settl'd in his face I see Par Lost 6.540
Gather'd like scum, and setl'd to it self Mask 595
Trinity ms 'setled'

Settlings
And setlings of a melancholy blood; Mask 810
Bridgewater ms 'setlinge'

Seven
They pass the Planets seven, and pass the fixt, Par Lost 3.481
Th' Arch-Angel *Uriel*, one of the seav'n Par Lost 3.648
Uriel, for thou of those seav'n Spirits that stand Par Lost 3.654
The space of seven continu'd Nights he rode Par Lost 9.63
Like distant breadth to *Taurus* with the Seav'n Par Lost 10.673
See where it flows, disgorging at seaven mouthes Par Lost 12.158
Seaven Lamps as in a Zodiac representing Par Lost 12.255
On seven small Hills, with Palaces adorn'd, Par Reg 4.35
Or seven, though one should musing sit; Samson 1017

Sevenfold
Awak'd should blow them into sevenfold rage Par Lost 2.171
Seavenfold, and scourge that wisdom back to Hell, Par Lost 4.914

Sevens
Came seavens, and pairs, and enterd in, as taught Par Lost 11.735

Seventh
Pouderd with Starrs. And now on Earth the Seventh Par Lost 7.581
1667 'Seaventh'
Now resting, bless'd and hallowd the Seav'nth day, Par Lost 7.592

Seventh(*cont*)
In six thou seest, and what if sev'nth to these Par Lost 8.128
But hee the seventh from thee, whom thou beheldst Par Lost 11.700

Seven-times-folded
A Weavers beam, and seven-times-folded shield, Samson 1122

Seven-times-wedded
His marriage with the seaventimes-wedded Maid. Par Lost 5.223

Seventy
The space of seventie years, then brings them back, Par Lost 12.345

Sever
Thou sever not: Trial will come unsought. Par Lost 9.366
Of Death, call'd Life; which us from Life doth sever. Sonnet 14, 4

Several
Disband, and wandring, each his several way Par Lost 2.523
Of each his Faction, in thir several Clanns, Par Lost 2.901
Swift to thir several Quarters hasted then Par Lost 3.714
Each in thir several active Sphears assignd, Par Lost 5.477
Or several one by one, the Regent Powers, Par Lost 5.697
Like things to like, the rest to several place Par Lost 7.240
Which else to several Sphears thou must ascribe, Par Lost 8.131
With long reach interpos'd; three sev'ral wayes Par Lost 10.323
This said, they both betook them several wayes, Par Lost 10.610
His mightie Angels gave them several charge, Par Lost 10.650
Several days journey, built by *Ninus* old, Par Reg 3.276
By course commits to severall goverment, Mask 25
Bridgewater ms 'seuerall'
1673 'several'
Each fetter'd Ghost slips to his severall grave, Nativity 234
1673 'several'

Severe
As soft as now severe, our temper chang'd Par Lost 2.276
To us enslav'd, but custody severe, Par Lost 2.333
By doom severe, had not the Son of God, Par Lost 3.224
Truth, wisdome, Sanctitude severe and pure, Par Lost 4.293
Severe but in true filial freedom plac't; Par Lost 4.294
Severe in youthful beautie, added grace Par Lost 4.845
Stood up, and in a flame of zeale severe Par Lost 5.807
His count'nance too severe to be beheld Par Lost 6.825
What words have past thy Lips, *Adam* severe, Par Lost 9.1144
Of thy transgressing? not enough severe, Par Lost 9.1169
When angry most he seem'd and most severe, Par Lost 10.1095
Epicurean, and the *Stoic* severe; Par Reg 4.280
Impartial, self-severe, inexorable, Samson 827
Shall laugh, the Lord shall scoff them, then severe Psalm 2, 9
God is a just Judge and severe, Psalm 7, 43

Severed
Befall thee sever'd from me; for thou knowst Par Lost 9.252
Our State cannot be severd, we are one, Par Lost 9.958
How to regain my sever'd company Mask 274
Bridgewater ms 'severd'
And sever'd from me far. Psalm 88, 70

Severely
The gentler, if severely thou exact not Samson 788

Severest
Severest temper, smooth the rugged'st brow, Par Reg 2.164

Severing
Severing each kind, and scum'd the Bullion dross: Par Lost 1.704
ms defective here

Severity
Strict Age, and sowre Severity, Mask 109
Bridgewater ms 'severitie'
Trinity ms 'severity'
1637 'Severitie'

Severn
That with moist curb sways the smooth Severn stream, Mask 825
Bridgewater ms 'seaverne'
Trinity ms 'Severne'
Or *Severn* swift, guilty of Maidens death, Vacation 96

Severs
What severs each thou 'hast learnt, which few hav don. Sonnet 17, 11
1694 'serves'

Sewed
Some Tree whose broad smooth Leaves together sowd, Par Lost 9.1095
And with what skill they had, together sowd, Par Lost 9.1112

Sewers
Serv'd up in Hall with Sewers, and Seneshals; Par Lost 9.38
Where Houses thick and Sewers annoy the Aire, Par Lost 9.446

Sex
Can either Sex assume, or both; so soft Par Lost 1.424
ms 'sex'
Not equal, as thir sex not equal seemd; Par Lost 4.296
Manlike, but different Sex, so lovly faire, Par Lost 8.471
1667 'sex'
Or Sex, and apprehended nothing high: Par Lost 9.574
In Femal Sex, the more to draw his Love, Par Lost 9.822
And straight conjunction with this Sex: for either Par Lost 10.898
Thy frailtie and infirmer Sex forgiv'n, Par Lost 10.956
The fairest of her Sex *Angelica* Par Reg 3.341
Femal of sex it seems, Samson 711
In me, but incident to all our sex, Samson 774
Was lavish't on thir Sex, that inward gifts Samson 1026

Sexes
Which two great Sexes animate the World, Par Lost 8.151

Sextile
In *Sextile*, *Square*, and *Trine*, and *Opposite*, Par Lost 10.659

Shackles
But they must pick me out with shackles tir'd, Samson 1326

Shade
Of Nights extended shade; from Eastern Point Par Lost 3.557
For sight no obstacle found here, nor shade, Par Lost 3.615
Insuperable highth of loftiest shade, Par Lost 4.138
Shade above shade, a woodie Theatre Par Lost 4.141
The open field, and where the unpierc't shade Par Lost 4.245
Under a tuft of shade that on a green Par Lost 4.325
Under a shade of flours, much wondring where Par Lost 4.451
Or in thick shade retir'd, from him to draw Par Lost 4.532
Mine eye pursu'd him still, but under shade Par Lost 4.572
Of thickest covert was inwoven shade Par Lost 4.693
Ithuriel and *Zephon* through the shade, Par Lost 4.868
To Hill, or Valley, Fountain, or fresh shade Par Lost 5.203
Converse with *Adam*, in what Bowre or shade Par Lost 5.230
A Seraph wingd; six wings he wore, to shade Par Lost 5.277
From that high mount of God, whence light & shade Par Lost 5.643
That under ground, they fought in dismal shade; Par Lost 6.666
With dreadful shade contiguous, and the Orbes Par Lost 6.828
From the thick shade, and *Adam* to his Bowre. Par Lost 8.653
Not yet in horrid Shade or dismal Den, Par Lost 9.185
About the Mother Tree, a Pillard shade Par Lost 9.1106
At Loopholes cut through thickest shade: Those Leaves Par Lost 9.1110
By secretest conveyance. Thou my Shade Par Lost 10.249
Alreadie in part, though hid in gloomiest shade, Par Lost 10.716
Of *Amarantin* Shade, Fountain or Spring, Par Lost 11.78
Night with her sullen wing to double-shade Par Reg 1.500
Where still from shade to shade the Son of God Par Reg 2.242
To rest at noon, and entr'd soon the shade Par Reg 2.292
In ample space under the broadest shade Par Reg 2.339
For yonder bank hath choice of Sun or shade, Samson 3
A Monument, and plant it round with shade Samson 1734
Dancing in the Chequer'd shade; Allegro 96
Fed the same flock, by fountain, shade, and rill. Lycidas 24
To sport with *Amaryllis* in the shade, Lycidas 68
The Nimphs in twilight shade of tangled thickets mourn. Nativity 188
With her *green* shade *that* cover'd *all*, Psalm 80, 41

Shaded
Shaded with branching Palme, each order bright, Par Lost 6.885

Shades
Regions of sorrow, doleful shades, where peace Par Lost 1.65
In *Vallombrosa*, where th' *Etrurian* shades Par Lost 1.303
Rocks, Caves, Lakes, Fens, Bogs, Dens, and shades of death, Par Lost 2.621
Adams abode, those loftie shades his Bowre. Par Lost 3.734
With mazie error under pendant shades Par Lost 4.239
Murmuring, and with him fled the shades of night. Par Lost 4.1015
Her sacred shades: though God had yet not rain'd Par Lost 7.331
That gave thee being, still shades thee and protects. Par Lost 9.266
Such ambush hid among sweet Flours and Shades Par Lost 9.408
With other echo late I taught your Shades Par Lost 10.861
Thee Native Soile, these happie Walks and Shades, Par Lost 11.270
And with dark shades and rocks environ'd round, Par Reg 1.194
A pathless Desert, dusk with horrid shades; Par Reg 1.296
City or Suburban, studious walks and shades; Par Reg 4.243
Wherever, under some concourse of shades Par Reg 4.404
And in thick shelter of black shades imbowr'd, Mask 62
Trinity ms 'shade'
Which these dun shades will ne're report. Mask 127
Whom certain these rough shades did never breed Mask 266
In double night of darknes, and of shades; Mask 335
By grots, and caverns shag'd with horrid shades, Mask 429
Trinity ms 'shads'
Immur'd in cypress shades a Sorcerer dwels Mask 521
But furder know I not. 2. *Bro*. O night and shades, Mask 580
Along the crisped shades and bowres Mask 984
line not in Bridgewater ms
There under *Ebon* shades, and low-brow'd Rocks, Allegro 8
He met her, and in secret shades Penseroso 28
Which I full oft amidst these shades alone Arcades 42
Trinity ms defective here
Of shades and wanton winds, and gushing brooks, Lycidas 137
Met in the milder shades of Purgatory. Sonnet 13, 14
Goddess of Shades, and Huntress, who at will Prose 12, 1

Shadest
Thron'd inaccessible, but when thou shad'st Par Lost 3.377

Shadier
Such was thir awe of Man. In shadie Bower Par Lost 4.705
1667 'shadier'

Shadiest
Sings darkling, and in shadiest Covert hid Par Lost 3.39

Shading
And flours aloft shading the Fount of Life, Par Lost 3.357
By Model, or by shading Pencil drawn. Par Lost 3.509
A shelter and a kind of shading cool Par Reg 3.221

Shadow
Or substance might be call'd that shadow seem'd, Par Lost 2.669
So without least impulse or shadow of Fate, Par Lost 3.120
Shadow from body opaque can fall, and the Aire, Par Lost 3.619
And I will bring thee where no shadow staies Par Lost 4.470
Be but the shaddow of Heav'n, and things therein Par Lost 5.575
Sinne and her shadow Death, and Miserie Par Lost 9.12
Whom thus the meager Shadow answerd soon. Par Lost 10.264
O're-shadow her: this man born and now up-grown, Par Reg 1.140
Syene, and where the shadow both way falls, Par Reg 4.70

Shadowed
Shaddowd from either heele with featherd maile Par Lost 5.284
Had lively shadowd: Here had new begun Par Lost 8.311
Had shadow'd them from knowing ill, was gon, Par Lost 9.1055

Shadowing
On every side with shaddowing Squadrons Deep, Par Lost 6.554
Came shadowing, and opprest whole Legions arm'd, Par Lost 6.655
Spreading and over-shadowing all the Earth, Par Reg 4.148

Shadows
And shadows, of that destind Seed to bruise Par Lost 12.233
1667 'shadowes'
Of calling shapes, and beckning shadows dire, Mask 207
line not in Bridgewater ms
Such are those thick and gloomy shadows damp Mask 470
Bridgewater ms 'shadowes'
And shadows brown that *Sylvan* loves Penseroso 134
Hath left in shadows dred, Nativity 206
The flocking shadows pale, Nativity 232

Shadowy
Now had night measur'd with her shaddowie Cone Par Lost 4.776
Shadowie sets off the face of things; in vain, Par Lost 5.43
Her shadowie Cloud withdraws, I am to haste, Par Lost 5.686
Save by those shadowie expiations weak, Par Lost 12.291
From shadowie Types to Truth, from Flesh to Spirit, Par Lost 12.303
Her shadowy off-spring unsubstantial both, Par Reg 4.399
His shadowy Flale hath thresh'd the Corn Allegro 108

Shady
Cleer Spring, or shadie Grove, or Sunnie Hill, Par Lost 3.28
Such was thir awe of Man. In shadie Bower Par Lost 4.705
1667 'shadier'
Thus at thir shadie Lodge arriv'd, both stood Par Lost 4.720
But first from under shadie arborous roof, Par Lost 5.137
This spacious ground, in yonder shadie Bowre Par Lost 5.367
Hill, Dale, and shadie Woods, and sunnie Plaines, Par Lost 8.262
On a green shadie Bank profuse of Flours Par Lost 8.286
As in a shadie nook I stood behind, Par Lost 9.277
By Fountain or by shadie Rivulet Par Lost 9.420
Her hand he seis'd, and to a shadie bank, Par Lost 9.1037
Sometimes, anon in shady vale, each night Par Reg 1.304
The nodding horror of whose shady brows Mask 38
1637 'shadie'
Trinity ms 'shadie'
Bridgewater ms 'shadie'
Under the shady roof Arcades 88
Trinity ms 'shadie'
And though the shady gloom Nativity 77

Shafted
Fair silver-shafted Queen for ever chaste, Mask 442
Bridgewater ms 'silver shafter'

Shafts
Perhaps hath spent his shafts, and ceases now Par Lost 1.176
Here Love his golden shafts imploies, here lights Par Lost 4.763
They issue forth, Steel Bows, and Shafts their arms Par Reg 3.305

Shagged
By grots, and caverns shag'd with horrid shades, Mask 429

Shaggiest
a tough encounter with the shaggiest ruffian Mask Tr. ms 16.39
a tough encounter, with the shaggiest ruffian Mask Br. ms 392

Shaggy
Nor chang'd his course, but through the shaggie hill Par Lost 4.224
Rocks, Waters, Woods, and by the shaggie tops Par Lost 6.645
Nor on the shaggy top of *Mona* high, Lycidas 54
Trinity ms 'shaggie'
1638 'shaggie'

Shake
That shake Heav'ns basis, bring forth all my Warr, Par Lost 6.712
And the brute Earth would lend her nerves, and shake, Mask 797
line not in Trinity ms
line not in Bridgewater ms
Shall from the surface to the center shake; Nativity 162
Shake earth, and at the presence be agast Psalm 114, 15
Amazed Heav'n and Earth to shake. Psalm 136, 14
That am already bruis'd, and shake Psalm 88, 59

Shaked
Of shak't Olympus by mischance didst fall; Fair Inf 44

Shaken
Can by his fraud be shak'n or seduc't; Par Lost 9.287

Shakes
Shakes Pestilence and Warr. Each at the Head Par Lost 2.711
And Rampant shakes his Brinded main; the Ounce, Par Lost 7.466
Shakes the high thicket, haste I all about, Arcades 58

Shakespeare
Or sweetest *Shakespear* fancies childe, Allegro 133
What needs my *Shakespear* for his honour'd Bones, Shakespear 1
1640 '*Shakespeare*'
1663-4 '*Shakespeare*'
1632 '*Shakespeare*'

Shaking
By the earth-shaking *Neptune*'s mace, Mask 869
Trinity ms 'earth shaking'
Bridgewater ms 'earth-shakinge'
1637 'earth shaking'

Shall
That Glory never shall his wrath or might Par Lost 1.110
Shall grieve him, if I fail not, and disturb Par Lost 1.167
What shall be right: fardest from him is best Par Lost 1.247
We shall be free; th' Almighty hath not built Par Lost 1.259
Hath emptied Heav'n, shall fail to re-ascend Par Lost 1.633
Thither, if but to pry, shall be perhaps Par Lost 1.655
For this Infernal Pit shall never hold Par Lost 1.657
For while they sit contriving, shall the rest, Par Lost 2.54
Of his Almighty Engin he shall hear Par Lost 2.65

Shall(*cont*)

Caught in a fierie Tempest shall be hurl'd	Par Lost 2.180
Shall we then live thus vile, the Race of Heav'n	Par Lost 2.194
May hope when everlasting Fate shall yeild	Par Lost 2.232
Nor will occasion want, nor shall we need	Par Lost 2.341
Hurl'd headlong to partake with us, shall curse	Par Lost 2.374
Shall breathe her balme. But first whom shall we send	Par Lost 2.402
In search of this new world, whom shall we find	Par Lost 2.403
Sufficient? who shall tempt with wandring feet	Par Lost 2.404
While here shall be our home, what best may ease	Par Lost 2.458
None shall partake with me. Thus saying rose	Par Lost 2.466
When ever that shall be; so Fate pronounc'd.	Par Lost 2.809
To know, and this once known, shall soon return,	Par Lost 2.839
Shall dwell at ease, and up and down unseen	Par Lost 2.841
With odours; there ye shall be fed and fill'd	Par Lost 2.843
Immeasurably, all things shall be your prey.	Par Lost 2.844
The Gods who live at ease, where I shall Reign	Par Lost 2.868
Whose Fountain who shall tell? before the Sun,	Par Lost 3.8
On desparate reveng, that shall redound	Par Lost 3.85
By some false guile pervert; and shall pervert	Par Lost 3.92
By the other first: Man therefore shall find grace,	Par Lost 3.131
Through Heav'n and Earth, so shall my glorie excel,	Par Lost 3.133
But Mercy first and last shall brightest shine.	Par Lost 3.134
For which both Heav'n and Earth shall high extoll	Par Lost 3.146
Encompass'd shall resound thee ever blest.	Par Lost 3.149
Or shall the Adversarie thus obtain	Par Lost 3.156
His end, and frustrate thine, shall he fulfill	Par Lost 3.157
Man shall not quite be lost, but sav'd who will,	Par Lost 3.173
Upheld by me, yet once more he shall stand	Par Lost 3.178
The rest shall hear me call, and oft be warnd	Par Lost 3.185
Mine ear shall not be slow, mine eye not shut.	Par Lost 3.193
Light after light well us'd they shall attain,	Par Lost 3.196
They who neglect and scorn, shall never taste;	Par Lost 3.199
Say Heav'nly powers, where shall we find such love,	Par Lost 3.213
Father, thy word is past, man shall find grace;	Par Lost 3.227
And shall grace not find means, that finds her way,	Par Lost 3.228
Under his gloomie power I shall not long	Par Lost 3.242
But I shall rise Victorious, and subdue	Par Lost 3.250
Death his deaths wound shall then receive, and stoop	Par Lost 3.252
Shall lead Hell Captive maugre Hell, and show	Par Lost 3.255
Shall enter Heaven long absent, and returne,	Par Lost 3.261
Of anger shall remain, but peace assur'd,	Par Lost 3.263
And reconcilement; wrauth shall be no more	Par Lost 3.264
Made flesh, when time shall be, of Virgin seed,	Par Lost 3.284
As from a second root shall be restor'd,	Par Lost 3.288
Imputed shall absolve them who renounce	Par Lost 3.291
Shall satisfie for Man, be judg'd and die,	Par Lost 3.295
So Heav'nly love shall outdoo Hellish hate 1667 'shal'	Par Lost 3.298
Therefore thy Humiliation shall exalt	Par Lost 3.313
All knees to thee shall bow, of them that bide	Par Lost 3.321
Shall hast'n, such a peal shall rouse thir sleep.	Par Lost 3.329
Bad men and Angels, they arraignd shall sink	Par Lost 3.331
Thenceforth shall be for ever shut. Mean while	Par Lost 3.333
The World shall burn, and from her ashes spring	Par Lost 3.334
New Heav'n and Earth, wherein the just shall dwell,	Par Lost 3.335
For regal Scepter then no more shall need,	Par Lost 3.340
God shall be All in All. But all ye Gods,	Par Lost 3.341
Shall be the copious matter of my Song	Par Lost 3.413
Henceforth, and never shall my Harp thy praise	Par Lost 3.414
Me miserable! which way shall I flie	Par Lost 4.73
As Man ere long, and this new World shall know.	Par Lost 4.113
Which I as freely give; Hell shall unfold,	Par Lost 4.381
The happier *Eden*, shall enjoy thir fill	Par Lost 4.507
Thou tellst, by morrow dawning I shall know.	Par Lost 4.588
To fill the Earth, who shall with us extoll	Par Lost 4.733
Forbid who will, none shall from me withhold	Par Lost 5.62
By violence, no, for that shall be withstood,	Par Lost 5.242
Beholding shall confess that here on Earth	Par Lost 5.329
Shall fill the World more numerous with thy Sons	Par Lost 5.389
Think not I shall be nice. So down they sat,	Par Lost 5.433
Yet that we never shall forget to love	Par Lost 5.550
Sad task and hard, for how shall I relate	Par Lost 5.564
Of human sense, I shall delineate so,	Par Lost 5.572
Hear my Decree, which unrevok't shall stand.	Par Lost 5.602
And by my Self have sworn to him shall bow	Par Lost 5.607
All knees in Heav'n, and shall confess him Lord:	Par Lost 5.608
Shall bend the knee, and in that honour due	Par Lost 5.817
Shall teach us highest deeds, by proof to try	Par Lost 5.865
As both thir deeds compar'd this day shall prove.	Par Lost 6.170
To chase me hence? erre not that so shall end	Par Lost 6.288
Shall yield us pregnant with infernal flame,	Par Lost 6.483
Dilated and infuriate shall send forth	Par Lost 6.486
Such implements of mischief as shall dash	Par Lost 6.488
Adverse, that they shall fear we have disarmd	Par Lost 6.490
Nor long shall be our labour, yet ere dawne,	Par Lost 6.492
Effect shall end our wish. Mean while revive;	Par Lost 6.493
And gladlier shall resign, when in the end	Par Lost 6.731
Image of thee in all things; and shall soon,	Par Lost 6.736
Then shall thy Saints unmixt, and from th' impure	Par Lost 6.742
Thee also happier, shall not be withheld	Par Lost 7.117
What next I bring shall please thee, be assur'd,	Par Lost 8.449
Extracted; for this cause he shall forgoe	Par Lost 8.497
And they shall be one Flesh, one Heart, one Soule.	Par Lost 8.499
I in thy persevering shall rejoyce,	Par Lost 8.639
Thy condescension, and shall be honour'd ever	Par Lost 8.649
To mee shall be the glorie sole among	Par Lost 9.135
Or daring, first on mee th' assault shall light.	Par Lost 9.305

Shall(*cont*)

So bent, the more shall shame him his repulse.	Par Lost 9.384
Of all these Garden Trees ye shall not eate,	Par Lost 9.657
The Garden, God hath said, Ye shall not eate	Par Lost 9.662
Thereof, nor shall ye touch it, least ye die.	Par Lost 9.663
Those rigid threats of Death; ye shall not Die:	Par Lost 9.685
Shall that be shut to Man, which to the Beast	Par Lost 9.691
Yet are but dim, shall perfetly be then	Par Lost 9.707
Op'nd and cleerd, and ye shall be as Gods,	Par Lost 9.708
So ye shall die perhaps, by putting off	Par Lost 9.713
Of this fair Fruit, our doom is, we shall die.	Par Lost 9.763
Shall tend thee, and the fertil burden ease	Par Lost 9.801
Shall I appeer? shall I to him make known	Par Lost 9.817
And Death ensue? then I shall be no more,	Par Lost 9.827
Shall live with her enjoying, I extinct;	Par Lost 9.829
Adam shall share with me in bliss or woe:	Par Lost 9.831
Not felt, nor shall be twice, for never more	Par Lost 9.859
Mine never shall be parted, bliss or woe.	Par Lost 9.916
Dependent made; so God shall uncreate,	Par Lost 9.943
Of thy perfection, how shall I attaine,	Par Lost 9.964
Shall separate us, linkt in Love so deare,	Par Lost 9.970
Be sure then. How shall I behold the face	Par Lost 9.1080
And thou th' accuser. Thus it shall befall	Par Lost 9.1182
By some immediate stroak; but soon shall find	Par Lost 10.52
Justice shall not return as bountie scorn'd.	Par Lost 10.54
When time shall be, for so I undertook	Par Lost 10.74
On me deriv'd, yet I shall temper so	Par Lost 10.77
Attendance none shall need, nor Train, where none	Par Lost 10.80
Her Seed shall bruse thy head, thou bruise his heel.	Par Lost 10.181
Whom he shall tread at last under our feet;	Par Lost 10.190
Thine shall submit, hee over thee shall rule.	Par Lost 10.196
Thorns also and Thistles it shall bring thee forth	Par Lost 10.203
Or transmigration, as thir lot shall lead.	Par Lost 10.261
Leads thee, I shall not lag behinde, nor erre	Par Lost 10.266
Nor shall I to the work thou enterprisest	Par Lost 10.270
His Seed, when is not set, shall bruise my head:	Par Lost 10.499
Then Heav'n and Earth renewd shall be made pure	Par Lost 10.638
To sanctitie that shall receive no staine:	Par Lost 10.639
New Heav'n and Earth shall to the Ages rise,	Par Lost 10.647
All that I eat or drink, or shall beget,	Par Lost 10.728
Shall be the execration; so besides	Par Lost 10.737
Shall with a fierce reflux on mee redound,	Par Lost 10.739
That dust I am, and shall to dust returne:	Par Lost 10.770
But I shall die a living Death? O thought	Par Lost 10.788
All of me then shall die: let this appease	Par Lost 10.792
To end me? Shall Truth fail to keep her word,	Par Lost 10.856
And more that shall befall, innumerable	Par Lost 10.896
He never shall find out fit Mate, but such	Par Lost 10.899
Or whom he wishes most shall seldom gain	Par Lost 10.901
Through her perversness, but shall see her gaind	Par Lost 10.902
Shall meet, alreadie linkt and Wedlock-bound	Par Lost 10.905
Which infinite calamitie shall cause	Par Lost 10.907
Whither shall I betake me, where subsist?	Par Lost 10.922
So Death shall be deceav'd his glut, and with us two	Par Lost 10.990
Part of our Sentence, that thy Seed shall bruise	Par Lost 10.1031
Shall scape his punishment ordain'd, and wee	Par Lost 10.1039
Instead shall double ours upon our heads.	Par Lost 10.1040
Shall perfet, and for these my Death shall pay.	Par Lost 11.36
To better life shall yeeld him, where with mee	Par Lost 11.42
To *Adam* what shall come in future dayes,	Par Lost 11.114
As I shall thee enlighten, intermix	Par Lost 11.115
His promise, that thy Seed shall bruise our Foe;	Par Lost 11.155
Is past, and we shall live. Whence Haile to thee,	Par Lost 11.158
Who now shall reare ye to the Sun, or ranke	Par Lost 11.278
How shall I part, and whither wander down	Par Lost 11.282
And wilde, how shall we breath in other Aire	Par Lost 11.284
As from his face I shall be hid, deprivd	Par Lost 11.316
In yonder nether World where shall I seek	Par Lost 11.328
To shew thee what shall come in future dayes	Par Lost 11.357
Some, as thou saw'st, by violent stroke shall die,	Par Lost 11.471
In Meats and Drinks, which on the Earth shall bring 1667 'shal'	Par Lost 11.473
Before thee shall appear; that thou mayst know	Par Lost 11.475
Shall bring on men. Immediately a place	Par Lost 11.477
Of wickedness, wherein shall dwell his Race	Par Lost 11.608
Yet they a beauteous ofspring shall beget;	Par Lost 11.613
Shall yield up all thir vertue, all thir fame	Par Lost 11.623
For in those dayes Might onely shall be admir'd,	Par Lost 11.689
Man-slaughter, shall be held the highest pitch	Par Lost 11.693
Thus Fame shall be atchiev'd, renown on Earth,	Par Lost 11.698
Henceforth to be foretold what shall befall	Par Lost 11.771
And hee the future evil shall no less	Par Lost 11.774
Shall change thir course to pleasure, ease, and sloth,	Par Lost 11.794
Shall with thir freedom lost all vertu loose	Par Lost 11.798
Thenceforth shall practice how to live secure,	Par Lost 11.802
Shall leave them to enjoy; for th' Earth shall bear	Par Lost 11.804
So all shall turn degenerate, all deprav'd,	Par Lost 11.806
Shall them admonish, and before them set	Par Lost 11.813
On thir impenitence; and shall returne	Par Lost 11.816
Shall build a wondrous Ark, as thou beheldst,	Par Lost 11.819
Select for life shall in the Ark be lodg'd,	Par Lost 11.823
Of Heav'n set open on the Earth shall powre	Par Lost 11.825
Broke up, shall heave the Ocean to usurp	Par Lost 11.827
Above the highest Hills: then shall this Mount	Par Lost 11.829
And now what further shall ensue, behold.	Par Lost 11.839
At this last sight, assur'd that Man shall live	Par Lost 11.872
Such grace shall one just Man find in his sight,	Par Lost 11.890
Shall hold thir course, till fire purge all things new,	Par Lost 11.900

Shall(*cont*)

Both Heav'n and Earth, wherein the just shall dwell.	Par Lost 11.901
Shall lead thir lives, and multiplie apace,	Par Lost 12.17
Shal spend thir dayes in joy unblam'd, and dwell	Par Lost 12.22
Under paternal rule; till one shall rise	Par Lost 12.24
Hunting (and Men not Beasts shall be his game)	Par Lost 12.30
A mightie Hunter thence he shall be styl'd	Par Lost 12.33
And from Rebellion shall derive his name,	Par Lost 12.36
Marching from *Eden* towards the West, shall finde	Par Lost 12.40
All Nations shall be blest; he straight obeys,	Par Lost 12.126
Shall dwell to *Senir*, that long ridge of Hills.	Par Lost 12.146
Shall in his Seed be blessed; by that Seed	Par Lost 12.148
Is meant thy great deliverer, who shall bruise	Par Lost 12.149
Plainlier shall be reveald. This Patriarch blest,	Par Lost 12.151
Whom *faithful Abraham* due time shall call,	Par Lost 12.152
Though present in his Angel, who shall goe	Par Lost 12.201
This also shall they gain by thir delay	Par Lost 12.223
In the wide Wilderness, there they shall found	Par Lost 12.224
Shall tremble, he descending, will himself	Par Lost 12.228
The Serpent, by what means he shall achieve	Par Lost 12.234
One greater, of whose day he shall foretell,	Par Lost 12.242
Of great *Messiah* shall sing. Thus Laws and Rites	Par Lost 12.244
Shall rest by Day, a fiery gleame by Night,	Par Lost 12.257
Or how the Sun shall in mid Heav'n stand still	Par Lost 12.263
His whole descent, who thus shall *Canaan* win.	Par Lost 12.269
His day, in whom all Nations shall be blest,	Par Lost 12.277
And therefore shall not *Moses*, though of God	Par Lost 12.307
His Name and Office bearing, who shall quell	Par Lost 12.311
Long time shall dwell and prosper, but when sins	Par Lost 12.316
And puissant deeds, a promise shall receive	Par Lost 12.322
For ever shall endure; the like shall sing	Par Lost 12.324
Of *David* (so I name this King) shall rise	Par Lost 12.326
Foretold to *Abraham*, as in whom shall trust	Par Lost 12.328
The last, for of his Reign shall be no end.	Par Lost 12.330
Wandring, shall in a glorious Temple enshrine.	Par Lost 12.334
Such follow him, as shall be registerd	Par Lost 12.335
The Power of the most High; he shall ascend	Par Lost 12.369
Thir fight, what stroke shall bruise the Victors heel.	Par Lost 12.385
Which hee, who comes thy Saviour, shall recure,	Par Lost 12.393
The Law of God exact he shall fulfill	Par Lost 12.402
He shall endure by coming in the Flesh	Par Lost 12.405
Proclaiming Life to all who shall believe	Par Lost 12.407
For this he shall live hated, be blasphem'd,	Par Lost 12.411
Shall long usurp; ere the third dawning light	Par Lost 12.421
Returne, the Starres of Morn shall see him rise	Par Lost 12.422
Shall bruise the head of *Satan*, crush his strength	Par Lost 12.430
Then temporal death shall bruise the Victors heel,	Par Lost 12.433
Nor after resurrection shall he stay	Par Lost 12.436
Still follow'd him; to them shall leave in charge	Par Lost 12.439
And his Salvation, them who shall beleeve	Par Lost 12.441
All Nations they shall teach; for from that day	Par Lost 12.446
Salvation shall be Preacht, but to the Sons	Par Lost 12.448
So in his seed all Nations shall be blest.	Par Lost 12.450
Then to the Heav'n of Heav'ns he shall ascend	Par Lost 12.451
Over his foes and thine; there shall surprise	Par Lost 12.453
Above all names in Heav'n; and thence shall come,	Par Lost 12.458
When this worlds dissolution shall be ripe,	Par Lost 12.459
Shall all be Paradise, far happier place	Par Lost 12.464
That all this good of evil shall produce,	Par Lost 12.470
Much more, that much more good thereof shall spring,	Par Lost 12.476
From God, and over wrauth grace shall abound.	Par Lost 12.478
The enemies of truth; who then shall guide	Par Lost 12.482
The promise of the Father, who shall dwell	Par Lost 12.487
Working through love, upon thir hearts shall write,	Par Lost 12.489
And oft supported so as shall amaze	Par Lost 12.496
Baptiz'd, shall them with wondrous gifts endue	Par Lost 12.500
Wolves shall succeed for teachers, grievous Wolves,	Par Lost 12.508
To thir own vile advantages shall turne	Par Lost 12.510
Then shall they seek to avail themselves of names,	Par Lost 12.515
Spiritual Lawes by carnal power shall force	Par Lost 12.521
On every conscience; Laws which none shall finde	Par Lost 12.522
Shall on the heart engrave. What will they then	Par Lost 12.524
Whence heavie persecution shall arise	Par Lost 12.531
Religion satisfi'd; Truth shall retire	Par Lost 12.535
Rarely be found: so shall the World goe on,	Par Lost 12.537
Greatly instructed I shall hence depart,	Par Lost 12.557
By mee the Promis'd Seed shall all restore.	Par Lost 12.623
Shall be inflicted by the Seed of *Eve*	Par Reg 1.54
He now shall know I can produce a man	Par Reg 1.150
There he shall first lay down the rudiments	Par Reg 1.157
His weakness shall o'recome Satanic strength	Par Reg 1.161
Man fall'n shall be restor'd, I never more.	Par Reg 1.405
But this thy glory shall be soon retrench'd;	Par Reg 1.454
At least in vain, for they shall find thee mute.	Par Reg 1.459
The Kingdom shall to *Israel* be restor'd:	Par Reg 2.36
Soon we shall see our hope, our joy return.	Par Reg 2.57
A sword shall pierce, this is my favour'd lot,	Par Reg 2.91
The rest commit to me, I shall let pass	Par Reg 2.233
Shall I receive by gift what of my own,	Par Reg 2.381
So many Ages, and shall yet regain	Par Reg 2.441
Shall I seek glory then, as vain men seek	Par Reg 3.105
That it shall never end, so when begin	Par Reg 3.185
What if he hath decreed that I shall first	Par Reg 3.188
Maugre the *Roman:* it shall be my task	Par Reg 3.368
How gloriously; I shall, thou say'st, expel	Par Reg 4.127
On *David*'s Throne, it shall be like a tree	Par Reg 4.147
Or as a stone that shall to pieces dash	Par Reg 4.149
And of my Kingdom there shall be no end:	Par Reg 4.151

Shall(*cont*)

Means there shall be to this, but what the means,	Par Reg 4.152
The Kingdoms of this world; I shall no more	Par Reg 4.210
Who knowing I shall raign past thy preventing,	Par Reg 4.492
They shall up lift thee, lest at any time	Par Reg 4.558
Where they shall dwell secure, when time shall be	Par Reg 4.616
Shall chase thee with the terror of his voice	Par Reg 4.627
Thee and thy Legions, yelling they shall flye,	Par Reg 4.629
Which shall I first bewail,	Samson 151
And shall again, pretend they ne're so wise.	Samson 212
So *Dagon* shall be magnifi'd, and God,	Samson 440
Dagon must stoop, and shall e're long receive	Samson 468
Such a discomfit, as shall quite despoil him	Samson 469
Or *Dagon*. But for thee what shall be done?	Samson 478
Nor shall his wondrous gifts be frustrate thus.	Samson 589
That these dark orbs no more shall treat with light,	Samson 591
And I shall shortly be with them that rest.	Samson 598
That what by me thou hast lost thou least shalt miss.	Samson 927
To thine whose doors my feet shall never enter.	Samson 950
I shall be nam'd among the famousest	Samson 982
Nor shall I count it hainous to enjoy	Samson 991
So shall he least confusion draw	Samson 1058
Chor. His fraught we soon shall know, he now arrives.	Samson 1075
Which long shall not with-hold mee from thy head,	Samson 1125
Sam. Shall I abuse this Consecrated gift	Samson 1354
Shall never, unrepented, find forgiveness.	Samson 1376
Or we shall find such Engines to assail	Samson 1396
Because they shall not trail me through thir streets	Samson 1402
May compass it, shall willingly be paid	Samson 1477
And numberd down: much rather I shall chuse	Samson 1478
And quit: not wanting him, I shall want nothing.	Samson 1484
Man. It shall be my delight to tend his eyes,	Samson 1490
What shall we do, stay here or run and see?	Samson 1520
Mess. O whither shall I run, or which way flie	Samson 1541
As with amaze shall strike all who behold.	Samson 1645
Thither shall all the valiant youth resort,	Samson 1738
The Virgins also shall on feastful days	Samson 1741
And to my wily trains, I shall e're long	Mask 151
I shall appear som harmles Villager	Mask 166
Shall I inform my unacquainted feet	Mask 180
And she shall be my Queen. Hail forren wonder	Mask 265
Bridgewater ms 'shalbe'	
Or shroud within these limits, I shall know	Mask 316
Will dare to soyl her Virgin purity,	Mask 427
Trinity ms 'will' ←'shall'	
Do ye beleeve me yet, or shall I call	Mask 438
Shall be unsaid for me: against the threats	Mask 586
Bridgewater ms 'shalbe'	
Shall in the happy trial prove most glory.	Mask 592
But evil on it self shall back recoyl,	Mask 593
It shall be in eternal restless change	Mask 596
Bridgewater ms 'shalbe'	
Cramms, and blasphemes his feeder. Shall I go on?	Mask 779
word not in Trinity ms	
word not in Bridgewater ms	
I shall be your faithfull guide	Mask 944
Bridgewater ms 'shalbe'	
We shall catch them at their sport,	Mask 953
A better soyl shall give ye thanks.	Arcades 101
Here ye shall have greater grace,	Arcades 104
Shall now no more be seen,	Lycidas 43
Say Heav'nly Muse, shall not thy sacred vein	Nativity 15
Shall from the surface to the center shake;	Nativity 162
The dreadfull Judge in middle Air shall spread his throne.	Nativity 164
Of him that ever was, and ay shall last,	Psalm 114, 16
That till the worlds last-end shall make thy name to live.	Fair Inf 77
The daintest dishes shall be serv'd up last.	Vacation 14
Shall subject be to many an Accident.	Vacation 74
O're all his Brethren he shall Reign as King,	Vacation 75
Yet every one shall make him underling,	Vacation 76
Ungratefully shall strive to keep him under,	Vacation 78
In worth and excellence he shall out-go them,	Vacation 79
Yet being above them, he shall be below them;	Vacation 80
From others he shall stand in need of nothing,	Vacation 81
Yet on his Brothers shall depend for Cloathing.	Vacation 82
To find a Foe it shall not be his hap,	Vacation 83
And peace shall lull him in her flowry lap;	Vacation 84
Yet shall he live in strife, and at his dore	Vacation 85
Devouring war shall never cease to roare:	Vacation 86
Yea it shall be his natural property	Vacation 87
Then long Eternity shall greet our bliss	On Time 11
And Joy shall overtake us as a flood,	On Time 13
With Truth, and Peace, and Love shall ever shine	On Time 16
When once our heav'nly-guided soul shall clime,	On Time 19
Attir'd with Stars, we shall for ever sit,	On Time 21
Will pierce more neer his heart.	Circum 28
Trinity ms 'will' ←'Shall' ←'will'	
If any ask for him, it shall be sed,	Carrier 17
It shall be still in strictest measure eev'n,	Sonnet 7, 10
Dante shall give Fame leave to set thee higher	Sonnet 13, 12
Trinity ms 'Dante shall give Fame leave to' ←'Fame by the Tuscan's leav shall'	
Where shall we sometimes meet, and by the fire	Sonnet 20, 3
What neat repast shall feast us, light and choice,	Sonnet 20, 9
When they shall read this clearly in your charge	Forcers 19
Plain in thy neatness; O how oft shall he	Horace 5
Unwonted shall admire:	Horace 8
He shall be as a tree which planted grows	Psalm 1, 7

Shall(*cont*)
To yield his fruit, and his leaf shall not fall, Psalm 1, 9
And what he takes in hand shall prosper all. Psalm 1, 10
The wind drives, so the wicked shall not stand Psalm 1, 12
Shall laugh, the Lord shall scoff them, then severe Psalm 2, 9
Then all who trust in thee shall bring Psalm 5, 33
Defend'st them, they shall ever sing Psalm 5, 35
And shall triumph in thee, who love thy name. Psalm 5, 36
Mine enemies shall all be blank and dash't Psalm 6, 21
They shall return in hast the way they came Psalm 6, 23
And in a moment shall be quite abash't. Psalm 6, 24
And then we shall be safe. Psalm 80, 16
And then we shall be safe. Psalm 80, 32
So shall we not go back from thee Psalm 80, 73
Shall call upon thy Name. Psalm 80, 76
And then we shall be safe. Psalm 80, 80
No alien God shall be Psalm 81, 38
But ye shall die like men, and fall Psalm 82, 23
By right now shall we seize Psalm 83, 46
Then shall they know that thou whose name Psalm 83, 65
No good from them shall be with-held Psalm 84, 43
Hast hid *where none shall know*. Psalm 85, 8
And glory shall *ere long appear* Psalm 85, 39
Shall bud and blossom *then*, Psalm 85, 46
Our Land shall forth in plenty throw Psalm 85, 51
Before him Righteousness shall go Psalm 85, 53
Shall come, *and all shall frame* Psalm 86, 30
So shall it never slide Psalm 86, 40
But *twise that praise shall in our ear* Psalm 87, 17
High God shall fix her fast. Psalm 87, 20
The Lord shall write it in a Scrowle Psalm 87, 21
That ne're shall be out-worn Psalm 87, 22
Shall the deceas'd arise Psalm 88, 42
Shall they thy loving kindness tell Psalm 88, 45
There to thy Sons another *Troy* shall rise, Prose 12, 12
Shall aw the World, and Conquer Nations bold. Prose 12, 14

Shallow
Beholders rude, and shallow to discerne Par Lost 9.544
Deep verst in books and shallow in himself, Par Reg 4.327
(Though so esteem'd by shallow ignorance) Mask 514
Bridgewater ms 'shallowe'
Shallow Brooks, and Rivers wide. Allegro 76
First heard before the shallow Cuccoo's bill Sonnet 1, 6
By shallow *Edwards* and Scotch what d' ye call: Forcers 12
Trinity ms 'shallow' ←'hare braind' ←'haire braind'

Shallow-searching
What shallow-searching *Fame* hath left untold; Arcades 41
Trinity ms 'shallow searching' ←'vertues which dull'

Shalmaneser
And seat of *Salmanassar*, whose success Par Reg 3.278

Shalt
Pleas'd, out of Heaven shalt look down and smile, Par Lost 3.257
Nor shalt thou by descending to assume Par Lost 3.303
Here shalt thou sit incarnate, here shalt Reign Par Lost 3.315
Shalt in the Sky appeer, and from thee send Par Lost 3.324
Then all thy Saints assembl'd, thou shalt judge Par Lost 3.330
Then thou thy regal Scepter shalt lay by, Par Lost 3.339
Whose image thou art, him thou shalt enjoy Par Lost 4.472
Inseparablie thine, to him shalt beare Par Lost 4.473
But come, for thou, besure, shalt give account Par Lost 4.841
Shalt thou give Law to God, shalt thou dispute Par Lost 5.822
Who is our equal: then thou shalt behold Par Lost 5.866
When who can uncreate thee thou shalt know. Par Lost 5.895
Thou shalt be All in All, and I in thee Par Lost 6.732
Transgrest, inevitably thou shalt dye; Par Lost 8.330
Shalt loose, expell'd from hence into a World Par Lost 8.332
God hath assign'd us, nor of me shalt pass Par Lost 9.231
Perhaps thou shalt not Die, perhaps the Fact Par Lost 9.928
Upon thy Belly groveling thou shalt goe, Par Lost 10.177
And dust shalt eat all the dayes of thy Life. Par Lost 10.178
By thy Conception; Children thou shalt bring Par Lost 10.194
I charg'd thee, saying: Thou shalt not eate thereof, Par Lost 10.200
Shalt eate thereof all the days of thy Life; Par Lost 10.202
Unbid, and thou shalt eate th' Herb of the Field, Par Lost 10.204
In the sweat of thy Face shalt thou eat Bread, Par Lost 10.205
For dust thou art, and shalt to dust returne. Par Lost 10.208
Our foile in Heav'n; here thou shalt Monarch reign, Par Lost 10.375
Prosperous or adverse: so shalt thou lead Par Lost 11.364
Thou shalt proceed, and from thy Womb the Son Par Lost 12.381
To leave this Paradise, but shalt possess Par Lost 12.586
Gabriel this day by proof thou shalt behold, Par Reg 1.130
So shalt thou save thy self and us relieve Par Reg 1.344
What to the smallest tittle thou shalt say Par Reg 1.450
No more shalt thou by oracling abuse Par Reg 1.455
Shalt be enquir'd at *Delphos* or elsewhere, Par Reg 1.458
So shalt thou best fullfil, best verifie Par Reg 3.177
But I will bring thee where thou soon shalt quit Par Reg 3.244
Thou never shalt obtain; prediction still Par Reg 3.354
By him thou shalt regain, without him not, Par Reg 3.371
These if from servitude thou shalt restore Par Reg 3.381
Shalt raign, and *Rome* or *Caesar* not need fear. Par Reg 3.385
The first of all Commandments, Thou shalt worship Par Reg 4.176
The Lord thy God, and only him shalt serve; Par Reg 4.177
There thou shalt hear and learn the secret power Par Reg 4.254
What I foretell thee, soon thou shalt have cause Par Reg 4.375
Thou shalt be what thou art ordain'd, no doubt; Par Reg 4.473
But thou, Infernal Serpent, shalt not long Par Reg 4.618
Or Lightning thou shalt fall from Heav'n trod down Par Reg 4.620

Shalt(*cont*)
Thou oft shalt wish thy self at *Gath* to boast Samson 1127
To *Samson*, but shalt never see *Gath* more. Samson 1129
Then thou shalt see, or rather to thy sorrow Samson 1154
Har. By *Astaroth* e're long thou shalt lament Samson 1242
Sa. Perhaps thou shalt have cause to sorrow indeed. Samson 1347
And hamper thee, as thou shalt come of force, Samson 1397
And thou shalt be our star of *Arcady*, Mask 341
In thy large recompense, and shalt be good Lycidas 184
To after age thou shalt be writ the man, Sonnet 13, 7
Earths utmost bounds: them shalt thou bring full low Psalm 2, 19
Shalt in the morning hear Psalm 5, 6
Nor shalt thou to a forein God Psalm 81, 39
For thou art he who shalt by right Psalm 82, 27
Thy course, there shalt thou find a lasting seat, Prose 12, 11

Shame
That were an ignominy and shame beneath Par Lost 1.115
Accept this dark opprobrious Den of shame, Par Lost 2.58
O shame to men! Devil with Devil damn'd Par Lost 2.496
Passion and Apathie, and glory and shame, Par Lost 2.564
Disdain forbids me, and my dread of shame Par Lost 4.82
Then was not guiltie shame, dishonest shame Par Lost 4.313
Gnashing for anguish and despite and shame Par Lost 6.340
Despairing, seeks to work us woe and shame Par Lost 9.255
Of outward strength; while shame, thou looking on, Par Lost 9.312
Shame to be overcome or over-reacht Par Lost 9.313
So bent, the more shall shame him his repulse. Par Lost 9.384
To guiltie shame hee cover'd, but his Robe Par Lost 9.1058
Even shame, the last of evils; of the first Par Lost 9.1079
To shame obnoxious, and unseemliest seen, Par Lost 9.1094
Those middle parts, that this new commer, Shame, Par Lost 9.1097
Thir guilt and dreaded shame; O how unlike Par Lost 9.1114
Thus fenc't, and as they thought, thir shame in part Par Lost 9.1119
And shame, and perturbation, and despaire, Par Lost 10.113
To whom sad *Eve* with shame nigh overwhelm'd, Par Lost 10.159
Upon her Husband, saw thir shame that sought Par Lost 10.336
Turnd to exploding hiss, triumph to shame Par Lost 10.546
Now ris'n, to work them furder woe or shame; Par Lost 10.555
To a fell Adversarie, his hate or shame: Par Lost 10.906
O pittie and shame, that they who to live well Par Lost 11.629
Of him who built the Ark, who for the shame Par Lost 12.102
But condemnation, ignominy, and shame? Par Reg 3.136
And never cease, though to his shame the more; Par Reg 4.14
Long since. Wert thou so void of fear or shame, Par Reg 4.189
Thir Gods ridiculous, and themselves past shame. Par Reg 4.342
Blindness, for had I sight, confus'd with shame, Samson 196
Of all reproach the most with shame that ever Samson 446
Which is my chief affliction, shame and sorrow, Samson 457
My race of glory run, and race of shame, Samson 597
In vain thou striv'st to cover shame with shame, Samson 841
How dy'd he? death to life is crown or shame. Samson 1579
And on her naked shame, Nativity 40
And hid his head for shame, Nativity 80
For whilst to th' shame of slow-endeavouring art, Shakespear 9
And Hope that reaps not shame. Therefore be sure Sonnet 9, 11
With much confusion; then grow red with shame, Psalm 6, 22
To wayes of sin and shame, Psalm 80, 74
Lord fill with shame their face. Psalm 83, 60
With shame, *and scape it never*. Psalm 83, 64

Shamed
Where he fell flat, and sham'd his Worshipers: Par Lost 1.461
Of all our good, sham'd, naked, miserable. Par Lost 9.1139
Now blind, disheartn'd, sham'd, dishonour'd, quell'd, Samson 563
Troubl'd and sham'd for ever, Psalm 83, 62

Shamefaced
That with long beams the shame-fac't night array'd, Nativity 111

Shameful
A shameful and accurst, naild to the Cross Par Lost 12.413
Violent or shameful death thir due reward. Par Reg 3.87
Met ever; and to shameful silence brought, Par Reg 4.22
Shameful garrulity. To have reveal'd Samson 491
To folly and shameful deeds which ruin ends. Samson 1043
And Public Faith cleard from the shamefull brand Sonnet 15, 12
word not in 1694 text

Shamefully
Weakly at least, and shamefully: A sin Samson 499

Shameless
To gaze upon the Sun with shameless brows. Mask 736
Trinity ms 'shamelesse'
Bridgewater ms 'shameles'

Shames
Equal to God, oft shames not to prefer, Par Reg 4.303

Shape
Like cumbrous flesh; but in what shape they choose Par Lost 1.428
In shape and gesture proudly eminent Par Lost 1.590
And judg'd of public moment, in the shape Par Lost 2.448
On either side a formidable shape; Par Lost 2.649
Eclipses at thir charms. The other shape, Par Lost 2.666
If shape it might be call'd that shape had none Par Lost 2.667
Whence and what art thou, execrable shape, Par Lost 2.681
So spake the grieslie terrour, and in shape, Par Lost 2.704
Likest to thee in shape and count'nance bright, Par Lost 2.756
Distorted, all my nether shape thus grew Par Lost 2.784
But first he casts to change his proper shape, Par Lost 3.634
Two of far nobler shape erect and tall, Par Lost 4.288
The hand that formd them on thir shape hath pourd. Par Lost 4.365
Now other, as thir shape servd best his end Par Lost 4.398
A Shape within the watry gleam appeerd Par Lost 4.461

Shape(*cont*)
In whatsoever shape he lurk, of whom Par Lost 4.587
So started up in his own shape the Fiend. Par Lost 4.819
Think not, revolted Spirit, thy shape the same, Par Lost 4.835
Vertue in her shape how lovly, saw, and pin'd Par Lost 4.848
He lights, and to his proper shape returns Par Lost 5.276
Eastward among those Trees, what glorious shape Par Lost 5.309
None can then Heav'n such glorious shape contain; Par Lost 5.362
They Limb themselves, and colour, shape or size Par Lost 6.352
And livd: One came, methought, of shape Divine, Par Lost 8.295
Though sleeping, where I lay, and saw the shape Par Lost 8.463
Floted redundant: pleasing was his shape, Par Lost 9.503
Wanted not long, though to this shape retain'd. Par Lost 9.601
Into the Wood fast by, and changing shape Par Lost 10.333
And shape Starr bright appeer'd, or brighter, clad Par Lost 10.450
Mee not, but the brute Serpent in whose shape Par Lost 10.495
Now rul'd him, punisht in the shape he sin'd, Par Lost 10.516
Till thir lost shape, permitted, they resum'd, Par Lost 10.574
And hateful; nothing wants, but that thy shape, Par Lost 10.869
Had, like a double *Janus*, all thir shape Par Lost 11.129
Not in his shape Celestial, but as Man Par Lost 11.239
Of them the Highest, for such of shape may seem Par Lost 11.297
In his first shape on man; but many shapes Par Lost 11.467
Thir shape, thir colour, and attractive grace, Par Reg 2.176
Conteins of good, wise, just, the perfect shape. Par Reg 3.11
Out of the wood he starts in wonted shape; Par Reg 4.449
Strength, comliness of shape, or amplest merit Samson 1011
Whoever tasted, lost his upright shape, Mask 52
Begin to cast a beam on th' outward shape, Mask 460

Shaped
One shapd and wing'd like one of those from Heav'n Par Lost 5.55
1674 printed 'shap d'

Shapes
Thir great Commander; Godlike shapes and forms Par Lost 1.358
ms 'shap's'
With monstrous shapes and sorceries abus'd Par Lost 1.479
Reduc'd thir shapes immense, and were at large, Par Lost 1.790
In various shapes old *Proteus* from the Sea, Par Lost 3.604
She forms Imaginations, Aerie shapes, Par Lost 5.105
To imitate her; but misjoyning shapes, Par Lost 5.111
By four Cherubic shapes, four Faces each Par Lost 6.753
And rapture so oft beheld? those heav'nly shapes Par Lost 9.1082
In his first shape on man; but many shapes Par Lost 11.467
My mansion is, where those immortal shapes Mask 2
1673 'shape'
Of calling shapes, and beckning shadows dire, Mask 207
Trinity ms 'shaps'
line not in Bridgewater ms
'Mongst horrid shapes, and shreiks, and sights unholy, Allegro 4
And fancies fond with gaudy shapes possess, Penseroso 6

Share
And call them not to share with us their part Par Lost 1.267
Your bulwark, and condemns to greatest share Par Lost 2.29
Refusing to accept as great a share Par Lost 2.452
Adam shall share with me in bliss or woe: Par Lost 9.831
Each others burden in our share of woe; Par Lost 10.961
But what is strength without a double share Samson 53
Had but a moderate and beseeming share Mask 769
Now mourn, and if sad share with us to bear Circum 6
While Avarice, and Rapine share the land. Sonnet 15, 14
1694 'shares'

Shared
But with swift wheele reverse, deep entring shar'd Par Lost 6.326
Shar'd among petty Kings too far remov'd; Par Reg 4.87

Sharp
Light-arm'd or heavy, sharp, smooth, swift or slow, Par Lost 2.902
To satisfie the sharp desire I had Par Lost 9.584
His Visage drawn he felt to sharp and spare, Par Lost 10.511
Or end, though sharp and sad, yet tolerable, Par Lost 10.977
Tri'd in sharp tribulation, and refin'd Par Lost 11.63
In sharp contest of Battel found no aide Par Lost 11.800
Sharp sleet of arrowie showers against the face Par Reg 3.324

Sharpened
No where so cleer, sharp'nd his visual ray Par Lost 3.620

Sharpening
Turnd fierie red, sharpning in mooned hornes Par Lost 4.978

Sharpest
The sharpest sighted Spirit of all in Heav'n; Par Lost 3.691
From sharpest sight: for in the wilie Snake, Par Lost 9.91

Sharply
Sharply thou hast insisted on rebuke, Par Reg 1.468

Shatter
Shatter your leaves before the mellowing year. Lycidas 5
Trinity ms 'shatter' ←'and crop your young'

Shattered
Torn from *Pelorus*, or the shatter'd side Par Lost 1.232
Down clov'n to the waste, with shatterd Armes Par Lost 6.361
To the hazard of thy brains and shatter'd sides. Samson 1241
Were shatter'd into heaps o're thy false head. Mask 799
line not in Bridgewater ms
line not in Trinity ms

Shattering
Blow moist and keen, shattering the graceful locks Par Lost 10.1066

Shaven
Shav'n, and disarm'd among my enemies. Samson 540
On the dry smooth-shaven Green, Penseroso 66

Shaves
Now shaves with level wing the Deep, then soares Par Lost 2.634

She
In secret, riding through the Air she comes Par Lost 2.663
O Father, what intends thy hand, she cry'd, Par Lost 2.727
She spake, and at her words the hellish Pest Par Lost 2.735
She finish'd, and the suttle Fiend his lore Par Lost 2.815
Sad instrument of all our woe, she took; Par Lost 2.872
Of *Erebus*. She op'nd, but to shut Par Lost 2.883
For softness shee and sweet attractive Grace, Par Lost 4.298
Hee for God only, shee for God in him: Par Lost 4.299
Shee as a vail down to the slender waste Par Lost 4.304
She all night long her amorous descant sung; Par Lost 4.603
But neither breath of Morn when she ascends Par Lost 4.650
Of *Japhet* brought by *Hermes*, she ensnar'd Par Lost 4.717
On *Adam*, whom imbracing, thus she spake. Par Lost 5.27
She forms Imaginations, Aerie shapes, Par Lost 5.105
So cheard he his fair Spouse, and she was cheard, Par Lost 5.129
To wed her Elm; she spous'd about him twines Par Lost 5.216
She turns, on hospitable thoughts intent Par Lost 5.332
She gathers, Tribute large, and on the board Par Lost 5.343
She crushes, inoffensive moust, and meathes Par Lost 5.345
She tempers dulcet creams, nor these to hold Par Lost 5.347
Shee needed, Vertue-proof, no thought infirme Par Lost 5.384
For thou art Heav'nlie, shee an empty dreame. Par Lost 7.39
Was not; shee in a cloudie Tabernacle Par Lost 7.248
From him, for other light she needed none Par Lost 7.378
Till night, then in the East her turn she shines, Par Lost 7.380
Perceaving where she sat retir'd in sight, Par Lost 8.41
Yet went she not, as not with such discourse Par Lost 8.48
Of what was high: such pleasure she reserv'd, Par Lost 8.50
Adam relating, she sole Auditress; Par Lost 8.51
Her Husband the Relater she preferr'd Par Lost 8.52
Chose rather; hee, she knew would intermix Par Lost 8.54
With Goddess-like demeanour forth she went; Par Lost 8.59
Earth sitting still, when she alone receaves Par Lost 8.89
The Planet Earth, so stedfast though she seem, Par Lost 8.129
Enlightning her by Day, as she by Night Par Lost 8.143
Or Shee from West her silent course advance Par Lost 8.163
On her soft Axle, while she paces Eev'n, Par Lost 8.165
Till warn'd, or by experience taught, she learne, Par Lost 8.190
Shee disappeerd, and left me dark, I wak'd Par Lost 8.478
1667 'She'
To make her amiable: On she came, Par Lost 8.484
She heard me thus, and though divinely brought, Par Lost 8.500
Wrought in her so, that seeing me, she turn'd; Par Lost 8.507
I follow'd her, she what was Honour knew, Par Lost 8.508
Her loveliness, so absolute she seems Par Lost 8.547
Her own, that what she wills to do or say, Par Lost 8.549
Accuse not Nature, she hath don her part; Par Lost 8.561
Of Wisdom, she deserts thee not, if thou Par Lost 8.563
The more she will acknowledge thee her Head, Par Lost 8.574
She dictate false, and missinforme the Will Par Lost 9.355
Not keeping strictest watch, as she was warnd. Par Lost 9.363
Soft she withdrew, and like a Wood-Nymph light Par Lost 9.386
Though not as shee with Bow and Quiver armd, Par Lost 9.390
Likeliest she seemd, *Pomona* when she fled Par Lost 9.394
Repeated, shee to him as oft engag'd Par Lost 9.400
Veild in a Cloud of Fragrance, where she stood, Par Lost 9.425
Hung drooping unsustaind, them she upstaies Par Lost 9.430
She most, and in her look summs all Delight. Par Lost 9.454
Shee fair, divinely fair, fit Love for Gods, Par Lost 9.489
To lure her Eye; shee busied heard the sound Par Lost 9.518
Fawning, and lick'd the ground whereon she trod. Par Lost 9.526
Not unamaz'd she thus in answer spake. Par Lost 9.552
Which when she saw, thus to her guide she spake. Par Lost 9.646
She scarse had said, though brief, when now more bold Par Lost 9.664
Fixt on the Fruit she gaz'd, which to behold Par Lost 9.735
Pausing a while, thus to her self she mus'd. Par Lost 9.744
Forth reaching to the Fruit, she pluck'd, she eat: Par Lost 9.781
In Fruit she never tasted, whether true Par Lost 9.788
Greedily she ingorg'd without restraint, Par Lost 9.791
Thus to her self she pleasingly began. Par Lost 9.794
And giv'st access, though secret she retire. Par Lost 9.810
So saying, from the Tree her step she turnd, Par Lost 9.834
And forth to meet her went, the way she took Par Lost 9.847
To him she hasted, in her face excuse Par Lost 9.853
Which with bland words at will she thus addrest. Par Lost 9.855
So saying, she embrac'd him, and for joy Par Lost 9.990
She gave him of that fair enticing Fruit Par Lost 9.996
Began to cast lascivious Eyes, she him Par Lost 9.1014
Lets her will rule; restraint she will not brook, Par Lost 9.1184
Shee first his weak indulgence will accuse. Par Lost 9.1186
Her Husband shee, to taste the fatall fruit, Par Lost 10.4
And what she did, whatever in it self, Par Lost 10.141
Shee gave me of the Tree, and I did eate. Par Lost 10.143
Was shee thy God, that her thou didst obey Par Lost 10.145
Before his voice, or was shee made thy guide, Par Lost 10.146
Shee was indeed, and lovely to attract Par Lost 10.152
1667 'She'
Desolate where she sate, approaching nigh, Par Lost 10.864
Soft words to his fierce passion she assay'd: Par Lost 10.865
By a farr worse, or if she love, withheld Par Lost 10.903
She ended weeping, and her lowlie plight, Par Lost 10.937
His counsel whom she had displeas'd, his aide; Par Lost 10.944
She ended heer, or vehement despaire Par Lost 10.1007
As once thou slepst, while Shee to life was formd. Par Lost 11.369
And thus with words not sad she him receav'd. Par Lost 12.609
In *Galilee*, that she should bear a Son Par Reg 1.135
But to his Mother *Mary*, when she saw Par Reg 2.60

She(*cont*)	
Some troubl'd thoughts, which she in sighs thus clad.	Par Reg 2.65
Of fond desire? or should she confident,	Par Reg 2.211
Nature hath need of what she asks; yet God	Par Reg 2.253
When she deserts the night	Samson 88
She all in every part; why was the sight	Samson 93
That she might look at will through every pore?	Samson 97
Sam. The first I saw at *Timna*, and she pleas'd	Samson 219
She proving false, the next I took to Wife	Samson 227
She was not the prime cause, but I my self,	Samson 234
But warn'd by oft experience: did not she	Samson 382
Thrice she assay'd with flattering prayers and sighs,	Samson 392
Lay stor'd, in what part summ'd, that she might know:	Samson 395
She purpos'd to betray me, and (which was worse	Samson 399
She sought to make me Traytor to my self;	Samson 401
Tongue-batteries, she surceas'd not day nor night	Samson 404
Some rich *Philistian* Matron she may seem,	Samson 722
Cho. Yet on she moves, now stands & eies thee fixt,	Samson 726
Like a fair flower surcharg'd with dew, she weeps	Samson 728
But now again she makes address to speak.	Samson 731
Chor. She's gone, a manifest Serpent by her sting	Samson 997
Once join'd, the contrary she proves, a thorn	Samson 1037
Smile she or lowre:	Samson 1057
Whom therfore she brought up and *Comus* nam'd,	Mask 58
But here she comes, I fairly step aside	Mask 168
Of darkness till it smil'd: I have oft heard	Mask 252
1637 'she smiled'	
Trinity ms 'she smiled'	
Bridgewater ms 'she smiled'	
And she shall be my Queen. Hail forren wonder	Mask 265
Where may she wander now, whether betake her	Mask 351
Leans her unpillow'd head fraught with sad fears.	Mask 355
Trinity ms 'leans' ←'she leans'	
(Not being in danger, as I trust she is not)	Mask 370
She plumes her feathers, and lets grow her wings	Mask 378
And let a single helpless maiden pass	Mask 402
Bridgewater ms 'and she'	
As you imagine, she has a hidden strength	Mask 415
She that has that, is clad in compleat steel,	Mask 421
She may pass on with unblench't majesty,	Mask 430
Wherwith she tam'd the brinded lioness	Mask 443
1637 'we'	
Fear'd her stern frown, and she was queen oth' Woods.	Mask 446
Wherwith she freez'd her foes to congeal'd stone?	Mask 449
Imbodies, and imbrutes, till she quite loose	Mask 468
But O my Virgin Lady, where is she?	Mask 507
How chance she is not in your company?	Mask 508
Was took e're she was ware, and wish't she might	Mask 558
Ye were the two she mean't, with that I sprung	Mask 578
Were it a draft for *Juno* when she banquets,	Mask 701
She hutch't th' all-worshipt ore, and precious gems	Mask 719
As if she would her children should be riotous	Mask 763
With her abundance, she good cateress	Mask 764
Trinity ms 'The'	
And she no whit encomber'd with her store,	Mask 774
Co. She fables not, I feel that I do fear	Mask 800
line not in Bridgewater ms	
line not in Trinity ms	
Whilom she was the daughter of *Locrine*,	Mask 827
1637 'shee'	
She guiltless damsell flying the mad pursuit	Mask 829
1673 'The'	
Dropt in Ambrosial Oils till she reviv'd,	Mask 840
Made Goddess of the River; still she retains	Mask 842
Which she with pretious viold liquors heals.	Mask 847
line not in Bridgewater ms	
And, as the old Swain said, she can unlock	Mask 852
If she be right invok't in warbled Song,	Mask 854
For maid'nhood she loves, and will be swift	Mask 855
Wherwith she sits on diamond rocks	Mask 881
Love vertue, she alone is free,	Mask 1019
She can teach ye how to clime	Mask 1020
she might be free from perill where she is	Mask Tr. ms 16.42
she might be free from perill where she is,	Mask Br. ms 395
And then in haste her Bowre she leaves,	Allegro 87
She was pincht, and pull'd she sed,	Allegro 103
His daughter she (in *Saturns* raign,	Penseroso 25
And oft, as if her head she bow'd,	Penseroso 71
Not trickt and frounc't as she was wont,	Penseroso 123
This this is she	Arcades 5
Trinity ms 'shee'	
Less then half we find exprest,	Arcades 12
Trinity ms 'wee find' ←'she hath'	
Mark what radiant state she spreds,	Arcades 14
This this is she alone,	Arcades 17
Might she the wise *Latona* be,	Arcades 20
I will bring you where she sits,	Arcades 91
when she beheld (the gods farre sighted bee)	Lycidas Tr. ms 29.60
She woo's the gentle Air	Nativity 38
She crown'd with Olive green, came softly sliding	Nativity 47
She strikes a universall Peace through Sea and Land.	Nativity 52
She knew such harmony alone	Nativity 107
Thy drowsie Nurse hath sworn she did them spie	Vacation 61
She heard them give thee this, that thou should'st still	Vacation 65
Your Son, said she, (nor can you it prevent)	Vacation 73
More then she could own from Earth.	Winchester 6
She had told, alas too soon,	Winchester 8
And now with second hope she goes,	Winchester 25
She(*cont*)	
And those Pearls of dew she wears,	Winchester 43
Love led them on, and Faith who knew them best	Sonnet 14, 9
Trinity ms 'Faith' ←'she' ←'shee'	
But O as to embrace me she enclin'd,	Sonnet 23, 13
I wak'd, she fled, and day brought back my night.	Sonnet 23, 14
Down to the Sea she sent,	Psalm 80, 46
Sheaf	
First Fruits, the green Eare, and the yellow Sheaf,	Par Lost 11.435
Sheared	
But with swift wheele reverse, deep entring shar'd	Par Lost 6.326
Shearers	
Then how to scramble at the shearers feast,	Lycidas 117
Shears	
And sing to those that hold the vital shears,	Arcades 65
Trinity ms 'sheares'	
Comes the blind *Fury* with th' abhorred shears,	Lycidas 75
Trinity ms 'sheares'	
May with their wholsom and preventive Shears	Forcers 16
Trinity ms 'sheares'	
Sheaves	
Least on the threshing floore his hopeful sheaves	Par Lost 4.984
Part arable and tilth, whereon were Sheaves	Par Lost 11.430
With *Thestylis* to bind the Sheaves;	Allegro 88
Shebean	
Sabean Odours from the spicie shoare	Par Lost 4.162
Shechem	
Pitcht about *Sechem*, and the neighbouring Plaine	Par Lost 12.136
Shed	
That shed *May* Flowers; and press'd her Matron lip	Par Lost 4.501
Temper or nourish, or in part shed down	Par Lost 4.670
Shed thir selectest influence; the Earth	Par Lost 8.513
Down drop'd, and all the faded Roses shed:	Par Lost 9.893
Which mans polluting Sin with taint hath shed	Par Lost 10.631
In such a season born when scarce a Shed	Par Reg 2.72
And shed the lushious liquor on the ground,	Mask 652
Trinity ms 'shed' ←'powre'	
Bid *Amaranthus* all his beauty shed,	Lycidas 149
Shedding	
Shedding sweet influence: less bright the Moon,	Par Lost 7.375
Sheds	
In dim Eclips disastrous twilight sheds	Par Lost 1.597
Which oft is sooner found in lowly sheds	Mask 323
Sheen	
Thick set with Agat, and the azurn sheen	Mask 893
1637 'sheene'	
Bridgewater ms 'sheene'	
Trinity ms 'sheene'	
But farr above in spangled sheen	Mask 1003
Trinity ms 'sheene'	
line not in Bridgewater ms	
1637 'sheene'	
Thron'd in Celestiall sheen,	Nativity 145
With thee there clad in radiant sheen,	Winchester 73
Sheeny	
Of sheenie Heav'n, and thou some goddess fled	Fair Inf 48
Sheep	
The hungry Sheep look up, and are not fed,	Lycidas 125
Trinity ms 'sheepe'	
1638 'sheep'	
Perhaps their loves, or els their sheep,	Nativity 91
Who were thy Sheep and in their antient Fold	Sonnet 18, 6
Who leadest like a flock of sheep	Psalm 80, 3
Sheepcote	
If Cottage were in view, Sheep-cote or Herd;	Par Reg 2.287
But Cottage, Herd or Sheep-cote none he saw,	Par Reg 2.288
Sheep-hook	
A Sheep-hook, or have learn'd ought els the least	Lycidas 120
1638 'sheephook'	
Trinity ms 'sheephooke'	
Sheep-walks	
New reapt, the other part sheep-walks and foulds;	Par Lost 11.431
Sheer	
Sheer o're the Chrystal Battlements; from Morn	Par Lost 1.742
ms 'Sheere'	
Of Hill or highest Wall, and sheer within	Par Lost 4.182
Descending, and in half cut sheere, nor staid,	Par Lost 6.325
Or torn up sheer: ill wast thou shrouded then,	Par Reg 4.419
Shell	
Rough, or smooth rin'd, or bearded husk, or shell	Par Lost 5.342
Freshet, or purling Brook, of shell or fin,	Par Reg 2.345
Within thy airy shell	Mask 231
Trinity ms 'shell', 'cell' written in margin	
By scaly *Tritons* winding shell,	Mask 873
Shells	
Or in thir Pearlie shells at ease, attend	Par Lost 7.407
Shelter	
The Deep to shelter us? this Hell then seem'd	Par Lost 2.167
Thrown on them as a shelter from his ire.	Par Lost 6.843
Could be obtain'd to shelter him or me	Par Reg 2.73
A shelter and a kind of shading cool	Par Reg 3.221
And in thick shelter of black shades imbowr'd,	Mask 62
Trinity ms 'shelter' ←'covert'	
Thy wrath *from which no shelter saves*	Psalm 88, 29
Sheltered	
To find where *Adam* shelterd, took his way,	Par Lost 11.223
And shelterd round, but all the Cataracts	Par Lost 11.824
From dews and damps of night his shelter'd head,	Par Reg 4.406

Sheltered(*cont*)
But shelter'd slept in vain, for at his head Par Reg 4.407
Shelters
Shelters in coole, and tends his pasturing Herds Par Lost 9.1109
Shelves
And on the Tawny Sands and Shelves, Mask 117
1637 'shelves'
Bridgewater ms 'shelves'
Trinity ms 'shelves'
Shepherd
That Shepherd, who first taught the chosen Seed, Par Lost 1.8
ms 'shepherd'
Uncull'd, as came to hand; a Shepherd next Par Lost 11.436
Gideon and *Jephtha*, and the Shepherd lad, Par Reg 2.439
Comus. The Star that bids the Shepherd fold, Mask 93
Bridgewater ms 'shepheard'
Trinity ms 'shepheard'
1637 'Shepheard'
La. Nay gentle Shepherd ill is lost that praise Mask 271
Bridgewater ms 'Shepheard'
Trinity ms 'shepheard'
La. To find out that, good Shepherd, I suppose, Mask 307
Bridgewater ms 'shepheard'
1637 'shepheard'
Trinity ms 'Shepheard'
Till further quest'. *La*. Shepherd I take thy word, Mask 321
Bridgewater ms 'Shepheard'
Trinity ms 'Shepheard'
1637 'Shepheard'
To my proportion'd strength. Shepherd lead on.---- Mask 330
Trinity ms 'shepheard'
1637 'Shepheard'
Bridgewater ms 'shepheard'
2. *Bro*. O brother, 'tis my father Shepherd sure. Mask 493
1637 'Shepheard'
Trinity ms 'shepheard'
Bridgewater ms 'shepheard'
How cam'st thou here good Swain? hath any ram Mask 497
Trinity ms 'good shepheard'
Bridgewater ms 'good shepheard'
Eld. *Bro*. To tell thee sadly Shepherd, without blame, Mask 509
1637 'shepheard'
Trinity ms 'shepheard'
Bridgewater ms 'shepheard'
El. *Bro*. What fears good *Thyrsis?* Prethee briefly shew. Mask 512
And crumble all thy sinews. *Eld*. *Bro*. Why prethee Shepherd Mask 615
Bridgewater ms 'shepheard'
Trinity ms 'shep.'
1637 'shepheard'
Brought to my mind a certain Shepherd Lad Mask 619
Bridgewater ms 'shepheard'
1637 'shepheard'
Trinity ms 'shepheard'
The soothest Shepherd that ere pip't on plains. Mask 823
1637 'shepheard'
Trinity ms 'shepheard'
Bridgewater ms 'shepheard'
Sab. Shepherd 'tis my office best Mask 908
Bridgewater ms 'Shepheard'
Trinity ms 'Shepheard'
1637 'Shepheard'
And every Shepherd tells his tale Allegro 67
Thee Shepherd, thee the Woods, and desert Caves, Lycidas 39
Trinity ms 'shepheard'
1638 'shepherds'
Such, *Lycidas*, thy loss to Shepherds ear. Lycidas 49
1638 'shepherds'
Trinity ms 'shepheards'
To tend the homely slighted Shepherds trade, Lycidas 65
Trinity ms 'shepheards'
1638 'shepherds'
Thou Shepherd that dost Israel *keep* Psalm 80, 1
Shepherdess
That fair *Syrian* Shepherdess, Winchester 63
Shepherds
Watching where Shepherds pen thir Flocks at eeve Par Lost 4.185
Thir Bootie; scarce with Life the Shepherds flye, Par Lost 11.650
To simple Shepherds, keeping watch by night; Par Lost 12.365
To Shepherds watching at their folds by night, Par Reg 1.244
For which the Shepherds at their festivals Mask 848
Trinity ms 'shepheads'
1637 'shepheards'
Bridgewater ms 'shepheards'
Spir. Back Shepherds, back, anough your play, Mask 958
B.M. ms 'shepherds'
Trinity ms 'shepheards'
1637 'shepheards'
Bridgewater ms 'shepheards'
Look Nymphs, and Shepherds look, Arcades 1
Trinity ms 'shepherds'
Nymphs and Shepherds dance no more Arcades 96
Trinity ms 'shepherds'
Weep no more, woful Shepherds weep no more, Lycidas 165
Trinity ms 'shepherds' ←'shepheards'
Now *Lycidas* the Shepherds weep no more; Lycidas 182
1638 'shepherds'
Trinity ms 'shepherds'
The Shepherds on the Lawn, Nativity 85

Shepherds(*cont*)
First heard by happy watchful Shepherds ear, Circum 3
Trinity ms 'shepheards'
Shibboleth
For want of well pronouncing *Shibboleth*. Samson 289
Shield
Was moving toward the shoar; his ponderous shield Par Lost 1.284
Of Warriers old with order'd Spear and Shield, Par Lost 1.565
ms 'shield'
Half wheeling to the Shield, half to the Spear. Par Lost 4.785
What seemd both Spear and Shield: now dreadful deeds Par Lost 4.990
Nor motion of swift thought, less could his Shield Par Lost 6.192
Of tenfold Adamant, his ample Shield Par Lost 6.255
Fit well his Helme, gripe fast his orbed Shield, Par Lost 6.543
Down fell both Spear and Shield, down they as fast, Par Lost 10.542
Whose branching arms thick intertwind might shield Par Reg 4.405
Of brazen shield and spear, the hammer'd Cuirass, Samson 132
Not worse then by his shield and spear Samson 284
A Weavers beam, and seven-times-folded shield, Samson 1122
Of thy conception, and be now a shield Samson 1434
What was that snaky-headed *Gorgon* sheild Mask 447
And som good angel bear a sheild before us. Mask 658
1673 'shield'
Bridgewater ms 'shield'
The idle spear and shield were high up hung; Nativity 55
1673 'Shield'
But thou Lord art my shield my glory, Psalm 3, 7
As with a shield thou wilt surround Psalm 5, 39
Thou God our shield look on the face Psalm 84, 31
For God the Lord both Sun and Shield Psalm 84, 41
Shields
Appear'd, and serried Shields in thick array Par Lost 1.548
ms 'sheilds'
Clash'd on thir sounding Shields the din of war, Par Lost 1.668
1667 'shields'
ms 'shields'
Celestial Armourie, Shields, Helmes, and Speares, Par Lost 4.553
Of rigid Spears, and Helmets throng'd, and Shields Par Lost 6.83
With Flaming Cherubim, and golden Shields; Par Lost 6.102
Made horrid Circles; two broad Suns thir Shields Par Lost 6.305
Defence, while others bore him on thir Shields Par Lost 6.337
O're Shields and Helmes, and helmed heads he rode Par Lost 6.840
Or tilting Furniture, emblazon'd Shields, Par Lost 9.34
Shift
Not any boast of skill, but extreme shift Mask 273
Bridgewater ms 'shifte'
Shifter
'Twas such a shifter, that if truth were known, Carrier 5
Shifts
Veres oft, as oft so steers, and shifts her Saile; Par Lost 9.515
Or subtle shifts conviction to evade. Par Reg 4.308
Therefore without feign'd shifts let be assign'd Samson 1116
These shifts refuted, answer thy appellant Samson 1220
As to make this relation? *Spir*. Care and utmost shifts Mask 617
Shiloh
In *Silo* his bright Sanctuary: Samson 1674
Shinar
Of *Sennaar*, and still with vain designe Par Lost 3.467
Shine
Cloth'd with transcendent brightness didst out-shine Par Lost 1.86
1667 'outshine'
ms 'outshine'
Shine inward, and the mind through all her powers Par Lost 3.52
But Mercy first and last shall brightest shine. Par Lost 3.134
But all Sun-shine, as when his Beams at Noon Par Lost 3.616
But wherfore all night long shine these, for whom Par Lost 4.657
Shine not in vain, nor think, though men were none, Par Lost 4.675
And the third sacred Morn began to shine Par Lost 6.748
End, and dismiss thee ere the Morning shine. Par Lost 7.108
Onely to shine, yet scarce to contribute Par Lost 8.155
That shine, yet bear thir bright officious Lamps, Par Lost 9.104
Had first his precept so to move, so shine, Par Lost 10.652
The glimpses of his Fathers glory shine. Par Reg 1.93
Till next Sun-shine holiday, Mask 959
B.M. ms 'sunshine'
Trinity ms 'sunshine'
Bridgewater ms 'sunshine'
Now sits not girt with Tapers holy shine, Nativity 202
The horned Moon to shine by night, Psalm 136, 33
Oh no? for something in thy face did shine Fair Inf 34
With Truth, and Peace, and Love shall ever shine On Time 16
Shine forth, *and from thy cloud give light*, Psalm 80, 7
Cause thou thy face on us to shine Psalm 80, 15
Cause thou thy face on us to shine, Psalm 80, 31
Cause thou thy face on us to shine, Psalm 80, 79
Shined
Love, sweetness, goodness, in her person shin'd Sonnet 23, 11
Shines
Made visible, th' Almighty Father shines, Par Lost 3.386
With light from hence, though but reflected, shines; Par Lost 3.723
With wonder, and could love, so lively shines Par Lost 4.363
Awake, the morning shines, and the fresh field Par Lost 5.20
Till night, then in the East her turn she shines, Par Lost 7.380
More plenty then the Sun that barren shines, Par Lost 8.94
Most shines and most is acceptable above. Samson 1052
Shining
Then shining heav'nly fair, a Goddess arm'd Par Lost 2.757
In which of all these shining Orbes hath Man Par Lost 3.668

Shining(*cont*)
But all these shining Orbes his choice to dwell; Par Lost 3.670
By *Nilus* head, enclosd with shining Rock, Par Lost 4.283
Not unconform to other shining Globes, Par Lost 5.259
Of Fish that with thir Finns and shining Scales Par Lost 7.401
In circle round her shining throne, Arcades 15

Ship
As when a Ship by skilful Stearsman wrought Par Lost 9.513
Like a stately Ship Samson 714

Shipwrecked
Who like a foolish Pilot have shipwrack't, Samson 198

Shittim
Israel in *Sittim* on thir march from *Nile* Par Lost 1.413
ms 'Sittim'

Shivered
With shiverd armour strow'n, and on a heap Par Lost 6.389
Like to a potters vessel shiver'd so. Psalm 2, 21

Shivering
Why stand we longer shivering under feares, Par Lost 10.1003
That saw the troubl'd Sea, and shivering fled, Psalm 114, 7

Shivers
Though all to shivers dash't, the assault renew, Par Reg 4.19

Shoaling
From each side shoaling towards the mouth of Hell. Par Lost 10.288

Shoals
With Frie innumerable swarme, and Shoales Par Lost 7.400
Sea-paths in shoals do slide. And know no dearth. Psalm 8, 22

Shock
Into the wilde expanse, and through the shock Par Lost 2.1014
The horrid shock: now storming furie rose, Par Lost 6.207
Justling or pusht with Winds rude in thir shock Par Lost 10.1074
And we would feed them *from the shock* Psalm 81, 65

Shoes
Treads on it daily with his clouted shoon, Mask 635
line not in Bridgewater ms
1637 'shoone'
Trinity ms 'shoone'

Shone
Shon like a Meteor streaming to the Wind Par Lost 1.537
Perplexes Monarchs. Dark'n'd so, yet shon Par Lost 1.599
Shon with a glossie scurff, undoubted sign Par Lost 1.672
And Princely counsel in his face yet shon, Par Lost 2.304
Most glorious, in him all his Father shon Par Lost 3.139
To mortal men, above which only shon Par Lost 3.268
Pavement that like a Sea of Jasper shon Par Lost 3.363
The Portal shon, inimitable on Earth Par Lost 3.508
Amongst innumerable Starrs, that shon Par Lost 3.565
Rubie or Topaz, to the Twelve that shon Par Lost 3.597
Light shon, and order from disorder sprung: Par Lost 3.713
The image of thir glorious Maker shon, Par Lost 4.292
Shon full, he all his Father full exprest Par Lost 6.720
He onward came, farr off his coming shon, Par Lost 6.768
Immense, and all his Father in him shon: Par Lost 7.196
Now Heav'n in all her Glorie shon, and rowld Par Lost 7.499
Had unbenighted shon, while the low Sun Par Lost 10.682
What else but favor, grace, and mercie shon? Par Lost 10.1096

Shook
And shook his throne. What though the field be lost? Par Lost 1.105
That shook Heav'ns whol circumference, confirm'd. Par Lost 2.353
And shook a dreadful Dart; what seem'd his head Par Lost 2.672
Harsh Thunder, that the lowest bottom shook Par Lost 2.882
Nor stop thy flaming Chariot wheels, that shook Par Lost 3.394
And shook his Plumes, that Heav'nly fragrance filld Par Lost 5.286
Had to her Center shook. What wonder? when Par Lost 6.219
The stedfast Empyrean shook throughout, Par Lost 6.833
Mistrust, Suspicion, Discord, and shook sore Par Lost 9.1124
Shook, but delaid to strike, though oft invok't Par Lost 11.492
Shook the Arsenal and fulmin'd over *Greece*, Par Reg 4.270
Might easily have shook off all her snares: Samson 409
He tugg'd, he shook, till down they came and drew Samson 1650
He shook his Miter'd locks, and stern bespake, Lycidas 112
Trinity ms 'shooke'

Shoon
Treads on it daily with his clouted shoon, Mask 635

Shoot
With Heav'ns ray, and temperd they shoot forth Par Lost 6.480
I shoot from Heav'n to give him safe convoy, Mask 81
Trinity ms 'shoote'
Bridgewater ms 'shoote'
1637 'shoote'

Shooting
On a Sun beam, swift as a shooting Starr Par Lost 4.556
Shooting her beams like silver threds, Arcades 16

Shoots
Shoots farr into the bosom of dim Night Par Lost 2.1036
Shoots invisible vertue even to the deep: Par Lost 3.586
Shoots against the dusky Pole, Mask 99
Plucking ripe clusters from the tender shoots, Mask 296
Her Grapes and tender Shoots. Psalm 80, 56

Shops
That in their green shops weave the smooth-hair'd silk Mask 716
Bridgewater ms 'shopps'

Shore
Was moving toward the shoar; his ponderous shield Par Lost 1.284
1667 'shore'
ms 'shore'
From the safe shore thir floating Carkases Par Lost 1.310
Or whom *Biserta* sent from *Afric* shore Par Lost 1.585

Shore(*cont*)
Calabria from the hoarce *Trinacrian* shore: Par Lost 2.661
Of neither Sea, nor Shore, nor Air, nor Fire, Par Lost 2.912
But glad that now his Sea should find a shore, Par Lost 2.1011
Borders on *Aegypt* and the *Arabian* shoare; Par Lost 3.537
Sabean Odours from the spicie shoare Par Lost 4.162
In *India* East or West, or middle shoare Par Lost 5.339
On heav'nly ground they stood, and from the shore Par Lost 7.210
Sea, Aire, and Shoar, the Thunder when to rowle Par Lost 10.666
Of *Norumbega*, and the *Samoed* shoar Par Lost 10.696
Sea without shoar; and in thir Palaces Par Lost 11.750
In prospect, as I point them; on the shoare Par Lost 12.143
Divided, till his rescu'd gain thir shoar: Par Lost 12.199
Safe towards *Canaan* from the shoar advance Par Lost 12.215
Gris-amber-steam'd; all Fish from Sea or Shore, Par Reg 2.344
On the *Campanian* shore, with purpose there Par Reg 4.93
Where on the *Aegean* shore a City stands Par Reg 4.238
As Children gathering pibles on the shore. Par Reg 4.330
Of a deceitful Concubine who shore me Samson 537
Are reconcil'd at length, and Sea to Shore: Samson 962
Coasting the *Tyrrhene* shore, as the winds listed, Mask 49
The Sea o'refraught would swell, & th' unsought diamonds Mask 732
Trinity ms 'swell' ←'heave her waters up above the shoare'
May thy billows rowl ashoar Mask 932
1637 'a shoare'
Bridgewater ms 'a shoare'
Trinity ms 'a shore'
Over som wide-water'd shoar, Penseroso 75
Down the swift *Hebrus* to the *Lesbian* shore. Lycidas 63
Trinity ms 'shoare' ←'shore'
Hence forth thou art the Genius of the shore, Lycidas 183
Trinity ms 'shoare'
And the resounding shore, Nativity 182

Shores
Mean while the tepid Caves, and Fens and shoares Par Lost 7.417
Now Land, now Sea, and Shores with Forrest crownd, Par Lost 9.117
Among the Trees on Iles and woodie Shores. Par Lost 9.1118
On Sands, and Shoars, and desert Wildernesses. Mask 209
line not in Bridgewater ms
Trinity ms 'shoars'
Ay me! Whilst thee the shores, and sounding Seas Lycidas 154
Trinity ms 'shoars' ←'floods'

Shorn
Shorn of his Beams, or from behind the Moon Par Lost 1.596
Shorn of his strength, They destitute and bare Par Lost 9.1062
Had shorn the fatal harvest of thy head. Samson 1024

Short
Frequent and full. After short silence then Par Lost 1.797
Short intermission bought with double smart. Par Lost 4.102
Short pleasures, for long woes are to succeed. Par Lost 4.535
After short pause assenting, thus began. Par Lost 5.562
All human thoughts come short, Supream of things; Par Lost 8.414
Twilight upon the Earth, short Arbiter Par Lost 9.50
Since higher I fall short, on him who next Par Lost 9.174
Thee satiate, to short absence I could yield. Par Lost 9.248
And short retirement urges sweet returne. Par Lost 9.250
Ingaging me to emulate, but short Par Lost 9.963
While yet we live, scarse one short hour perhaps, Par Lost 10.923
From what we fear for both, let us make short, Par Lost 10.1000
Or one short sigh of humane breath, up-borne Par Lost 11.147
After short blush of Morn; nigh in her sight Par Lost 11.184
Live well, how long or short permit to Heav'n: Par Lost 11.554
To whom thus *Adam* of short joy bereft. Par Lost 11.628
Delay, for longest time to him is short; Par Reg 1.56
Short sojourn; and what thence could'st thou observe? Par Reg 3.235
I know them not; not therefore am I short Par Reg 4.287
Which would have set thee in short time with ease Par Reg 4.378
Temperst thy providence through his short course, Samson 670
His message will be short and voluble. Samson 1307
And after short abode flie back with speed, Fair Inf 60
After so short time of breath, Winchester 9
With *Midas* Ears, committing short and long; Sonnet 13, 4
And to be short, at last his guid him brings Prose 2, 1

Shortened
In Wintry solstice like the shortn'd light Passion 6
Shortned hast thy own lives lease, Winchester 52

Shorter
By shorter flight to th' East, had left him there Par Lost 4.595
Cut shorter many a league; here thou behold'st Par Reg 3.269

Shortest
Of many ways to die the shortest choosing, Par Lost 10.1005

Shortly
And I shall shortly be with them that rest. Samson 598

Shot
Shot after us in storm, oreblown hath laid Par Lost 1.172
Black fire and horror shot with equal rage Par Lost 2.67
Shot upward still direct, whence no way round Par Lost 3.618
Shot forth peculiar Graces; then with voice Par Lost 5.15
Shot paralel to the earth his dewie ray, Par Lost 5.141
Shot down direct his fervid Raies to warme Par Lost 5.301
Shot through with orient Beams: when all the Plain Par Lost 6.15
Glar'd lightning, and shot forth pernicious fire Par Lost 6.849
And from about her shot Darts of desire Par Lost 8.62
Into a Gulf shot under ground, till part Par Lost 9.72
How quick they wheel'd, and flying behind them shot Par Reg 3.323
New shot up from vernall showr; Winchester 40

Should
And what I should be, all but less then he Par Lost 1.257

Should(*cont*)
Should favour equal to the Sons of Heaven: Par Lost 1.654
Th' event is fear'd; should we again provoke Par Lost 2.82
We should be quite abolisht and expire. Par Lost 2.93
I should be much for open Warr, O Peers, Par Lost 2.119
By force, and at our heels all Hell should rise Par Lost 2.135
Awak'd should blow them into sevenfold rage Par Lost 2.171
Should intermitted vengeance arm again Par Lost 2.173
Of Hell should spout her Cataracts of Fire, Par Lost 2.176
We overpower? Suppose he should relent Par Lost 2.237
But I should ill become this Throne, O Peers, Par Lost 2.445
Loose all her virtue; least bad men should boast Par Lost 2.483
Free Vertue should enthrall to Force or Chance. Par Lost 2.551
Should prove a bitter Morsel, and his bane, Par Lost 2.808
Should be, and, by concurring signs, ere now Par Lost 2.831
His famine should be fill'd, and blest his mawe Par Lost 2.847
My being gav'st me; whom should I obey Par Lost 2.865
But glad that now his Sea should find a shore, Par Lost 2.1011
Thy sovran sentence, that Man should find grace; Par Lost 3.145
For should Man finally be lost, should Man Par Lost 3.150
So should thy goodness and thy greatness both Par Lost 3.165
And heavier fall: so should I purchase deare Par Lost 4.101
And should I at your harmless innocence Par Lost 4.388
To do what else though damnd I should abhorre. Par Lost 4.392
Suspicious, reasonless. Why should thir Lord Par Lost 4.516
Least total darkness should by Night regaine Par Lost 4.665
Farr be it, that I should write thee sin or blame, Par Lost 4.758
At first, that Angel should with Angel warr, Par Lost 6.92
Should yet remain, where faith and realtie Par Lost 6.115
Remain not; wherfore should not strength and might Par Lost 6.116
Should win in Arms, in both disputes alike Par Lost 6.123
Should combat, and thir jarring Sphears confound. Par Lost 6.315
In future dayes, if Malice should abound, Par Lost 6.502
What should they do? if on they rusht, repulse Par Lost 6.600
We should compel them to a quick result. Par Lost 6.619
That bodies bright and greater should not serve Par Lost 8.87
That I should mind thee oft, and mind thou me. Par Lost 9.358
How should ye? by the Fruit? it gives you Life Par Lost 9.686
That ye should be as Gods, since I as Man, Par Lost 9.710
Th' offence, that Man should thus attain to know? Par Lost 9.726
Should God create another *Eve*, and I Par Lost 9.911
Why hee should mean me ill, or seek to harme. Par Lost 9.1152
I told ye then he should prevail and speed Par Lost 10.40
On his bad Errand, Man should be seduc't Par Lost 10.41
I should conceal, and not expose to blame Par Lost 10.130
Devolv'd; though should I hold my peace, yet thou Par Lost 10.135
To rule, as over all he should have rul'd. Par Lost 10.493
Should prove tempestuous: To the Winds they set Par Lost 10.664
I thus contest; then should have been refusd Par Lost 10.756
As in my Mothers lap? there I should rest Par Lost 10.778
Me now your curse! Ah, why should all mankind Par Lost 10.822
Or Heat should injure us, his timely care Par Lost 10.1057
But that from us ought should ascend to Heav'n Par Lost 11.143
Ill worthie I such title should belong Par Lost 11.163
That I should fear, nor sociably mild, Par Lost 11.234
As *Raphael*, that I should much confide, Par Lost 11.235
Under inhuman pains? Why should not Man, Par Lost 11.511
Enterd so faire, should turn aside to tread Par Lost 11.630
Said th' Angel, who should better hold his place Par Lost 11.635
(Canst thou believe2) should be so stupid grown, Par Lost 12.116
Men who attend the Altar, and should most Par Lost 12.354
Why our great expectation should be call'd Par Lost 12.378
Whether I should repent me now of sin Par Lost 12.474
In *Galilee*, that she should bear a Son Par Reg 1.135
To her a Virgin, that on her should come Par Reg 1.138
And of thy Kingdom there should be no end. Par Reg 1.241
Now full, that I no more should live obscure, Par Reg 1.287
Or vertuous, I should so have lost all sense. Par Reg 1.382
To all mankind: why should I? they to me Par Reg 1.388
That to the fall and rising he should be Par Reg 2.88
Of fond desire? or should she confident, Par Reg 2.211
In this wild solitude so long should bide Par Reg 2.304
The giver, answer'd Jesus. Why should that Par Reg 2.322
And for thy reason why they should be sought, Par Reg 2.485
Should Kings and Nations from thy mouth consult, Par Reg 3.12
But why should man seek glory? who of his own Par Reg 3.134
Should I of these the liberty regard, Par Reg 3.427
Should *Israel* from *Philistian* yoke deliver; Samson 39
This with the other should, at least, have paird, Samson 208
He should not so o'rewhelm, and as a thrall Samson 370
To what end should I seek it? when in strength Samson 522
Sam. O that torment should not be confin'd Samson 606
But I to enemies reveal'd, and should not. Samson 782
Here I should still enjoy thee day and night Samson 807
Or seven, though one should musing sit; Samson 1017
I should have forc'd thee soon wish other arms, Samson 1096
Lest I should see him forc't to things unseemly. Samson 1451
Hitting thy aged ear should pierce too deep. Samson 1568
Samson should be brought forth to shew the people Samson 1601
And thank the gods amiss. I should be loath Mask 177
La. No less then if I should my brothers loose. Mask 288
I cannot be, that I should fear to change it. Mask 328
2. *Bro*. Me thought so too; what should it be? *Eld*. *Bro*. For certain Mask 482
That hallow I should know, what are you? speak; Mask 490
Why should you be so cruel to your self, Mask 679
line not in Bridgewater ms
I would not taste thy treasonous offer; none Mask 702
Trinity ms 'would not taste' ←'should reject' ←'hate it from thy hands'
Should in a pet of temperance feed on Pulse, Mask 721
And we should serve him as a grudging master, Mask 725
As if she would her children should be riotous Mask 763
Yet should I try, the uncontrouled worth Mask 793
line not in Trinity ms
line not in Bridgewater ms
O ye mistook, ye should have snatcht his wand Mask 815
That he our deadly forfeit should release, Nativity 6
Should look so neer upon her foul deformities. Nativity 44
The new-enlightn'd world no more should need; Nativity 82
Time is our tedious Song should here have ending, Nativity 239
Fore-saw what future dayes should bring to pass, Vacation 72
The leaves should all be black wheron I write, Passion 34
Or should I thence hurried on viewles wing, Passion 50
Or that his hallow'd reliques should be hid Shakespear 3
And still revolt when truth would set them free. Sonnet 12, 10
Trinity ms 'still revolt when Truth would sett them' ←'make them' ←'set them' ←'hate the truth wherby they should be'
Who hate the Lord should *then be fain* Psalm 81, 61
But *they*, *his People*, *should remain*, Psalm 81, 63
Their time should have no end. Psalm 81, 64

Shoulder
Each shoulder broad, came mantling o're his brest Par Lost 5.279
I set his shoulder free; Psalm 81, 22

Shoulders
Hung on his shoulders like the Moon, whose Orb Par Lost 1.287
With *Atlantean* shoulders fit to bear Par Lost 2.306
Illustrious on his Shoulders fledge with wings Par Lost 3.627
Clustring, but not beneath his shoulders broad: Par Lost 4.303
When on his shoulders each mans burden lies; Par Reg 2.462
Then by main force pull'd up, and on his shoulders bore Samson 146
And on his shoulders waving down those locks, Samson 1493
Over thy decent shoulders drawn. Penseroso 36

Shouldst
That thou shouldst hope, imperious, and with threats Par Lost 6.287
Shouldst propagat, already infinite; Par Lost 8.420
Good reason was thou freely shouldst dislike, Par Lost 8.443
But that thou shouldst my firmness therfore doubt Par Lost 9.279
Why shouldst not thou like sense within thee feel Par Lost 9.315
Who sees thee? (and what is one2) who shouldst be seen Par Lost 9.546
What thou commandst, and right thou shouldst be obeyd: Par Lost 9.570
Whereof I gave thee charge thou shouldst not eat? Par Lost 10.123
Annuls thy doom, the death thou shouldst have dy'd, Par Lost 12.428
Thou shouldst be great and sit on *David*'s Throne, Par Reg 1.240
Troubl'd that thou shouldst hunger, hath purvey'd Par Reg 2.333
Why shouldst thou then obtrude this diligence, Par Reg 2.387
Why shouldst thou not accept it? but I see Par Reg 2.398
That thou who worthiest art should'st be thir King? Par Reg 3.226
Much less my mind; though thou should'st add to tell Par Reg 4.113
And studs of Pearl, to me should'st tell who thirst Par Reg 4.120
Why thou shouldst wed *Philistian* women rather Samson 216
Nor shouldst thou have trusted that to womans frailty Samson 783
Why shouldst thou, but for som fellonious end, Mask 196
line not in Bridgewater ms
And thou art worthy that thou shouldst not know Mask 788
line not in Bridgewater ms
line not in Trinity ms
She heard them give thee this, that thou should'st still Vacation 65

Shout
A shout that tore Hells Concave, and beyond Par Lost 1.542
With deafning shout, return'd them loud acclaim. Par Lost 2.520
The multitude of Angels with a shout Par Lost 3.345
Hymning th' Eternal Father: but the shout Par Lost 6.96
Thus foil'd thir mightiest, ours joy filld, and shout, Par Lost 6.200
Birth-day of Heav'n and Earth; with joy and shout Par Lost 7.256
Thir universal shout and high applause Par Lost 10.505
What noise or shout was that? it tore the Skie. Samson 1472
Horribly loud unlike the former shout. Samson 1510
At sight of him the people with a shout Samson 1620
Midnight shout, and revelry, Mask 103
Bridgewater ms 'shoute'
With Saintly shout, and solemn Jubily, Musick 9

Shouting
Chor. Doubtless the people shouting to behold Samson 1473

Shove
And shove away the worthy bidden guest. Lycidas 118

Show
Magnificence; and what can Heav'n shew more? Par Lost 2.273
Shall lead Hell Captive maugre Hell, and show Par Lost 3.255
That practisd falshood under saintly shew, Par Lost 4.122
From me som Plume, that thy success may show Par Lost 6.161
They shew us when our foes walk not upright. Par Lost 6.627
Show to the Sun thir wav'd coats dropt with Gold, Par Lost 7.406
Admitting Motion in the Heav'ns, to shew Par Lost 8.115
Too much of Ornament, in outward shew Par Lost 8.538
Hate stronger, under shew of Love well feign'd, Par Lost 9.492
The Tempter, but with shew of Zeale and Love Par Lost 9.665
In open shew, and with ascention bright Par Lost 10.187
In shew Plebeian Angel militant Par Lost 10.442
Like his, and colour Serpentine may shew Par Lost 10.870
And understood not all was but a shew Par Lost 10.883
That shew no end but Death, and have the power, Par Lost 10.1004
To shew us in this Mountain, while the Winds Par Lost 10.1065
To shew thee what shall come in future dayes Par Lost 11.357
To shew him all Earths Kingdomes and thir Glory. Par Lost 11.384
Exempt from Death; to shew thee what reward Par Lost 11.709

Show(*cont*)
Which he will shew him, and from him will raise — Par Lost 12.123
To shew him worthy of his birth divine — Par Reg 1.141
His constancy, with such as have more shew — Par Reg 2.226
Golden in shew, is but a wreath of thorns, — Par Reg 2.459
But to shew forth his goodness, and impart — Par Reg 3.124
Nor doth this grandeur and majestic show — Par Reg 4.110
Now shew thy Progeny; if not to stand, — Par Reg 4.554
God, when he gave me strength, to shew withal — Samson 58
Afford me place to shew what recompence — Samson 910
To shew them feats, and play before thir god, — Samson 1340
Samson should be brought forth to shew the people — Samson 1601
I mean to shew you of my strength, yet greater; — Samson 1644
El. Bro. What fears good *Thyrsis?* Prethee briefly shew. — Mask 512
Bridgewater ms 'showe'
And shew me simples of a thousand names — Mask 627
Then her purfl'd scarf can shew, — Mask 995
Of every Star that Heav'n doth shew, — Penseroso 171
What ere the skill of lesser gods can show, — Arcades 79
Our Babe to shew his Godhead true, — Nativity 227
As if to shew what creatures Heav'n doth breed, — Fair Inf 61
And disapproves that care, though wise in show, — Sonnet 21, 12
Who yet will shew us good? — Psalm 4, 26
To us thy mercy shew — Psalm 85, 26
Readiest thy grace to shew, — Psalm 86, 54

Showed
Th' addition of his Empire, how it shew'd — Par Lost 7.555
His starrie Helme unbuckl'd shew'd him prime — Par Lost 11.245
Above mortalitie that shew'd thou wast divine. — Fair Inf 35
Shew'd him his room where he must lodge that night, — Carrier 15
Love led them on, and Faith who knew them best — Sonnet 14, 9
Trinity ms 'Love led them on' ←'Faith shew'd the way' ←'Faith who led on the way'

Showedst
To what I did thou shewdst me first the way. — Samson 781

Shower
Scowls ore the dark'nd lantskip Snow, or showre; — Par Lost 2.491
If I conjecture aught, no drizling showr, — Par Lost 6.545
Thir influence malignant when to showre, — Par Lost 10.662
Least it again dissolve and showr the Earth? — Par Lost 11.883
A mightie Nation, and upon him showre — Par Lost 12.124
Or usher'd with a shower still, — Penseroso 127
New shot up from vernall showr; — Winchester 40

Showered
When God hath showrd the earth; so lovely seemd — Par Lost 4.152
Showrd Roses, which the Morn repair'd. Sleep on — Par Lost 4.773
Excess, before th' all bounteous King, who showrd — Par Lost 5.640

Showers
Showrs on her Kings *Barbaric* Pearl and Gold, — Par Lost 2.4
After soft showers; and sweet the coming on — Par Lost 4.646
Glistring with dew, nor fragrance after showers, — Par Lost 4.653
Or wet the thirstie Earth with falling showers, — Par Lost 5.190
Sharp sleet of arrowie showers against the face — Par Reg 3.324
1671 printed 'shower', errata 'showers'
That on the green terf suck the honied showres, — Lycidas 140
Trinity ms 'showrs'
Where Springs and Showrs abound. — Psalm 84, 24

Showery
Amber, and colours of the showrie Arch. — Par Lost 6.759

Showest
And my fair Son here showst me, the dear pledge — Par Lost 2.818
And hunger still: then Embassies thou shew'st — Par Reg 4.121

Showeth
But my late spring no bud or blossom shew'th. — Sonnet 7, 4

Shown
Infinite goodness, grace and mercy shewn — Par Lost 1.218
Where thou art weigh'd, and shown how light, how weak, — Par Lost 4.1012
Prodigious power had shewn, and met in Armes — Par Lost 6.247
Me him (for it was shew'n him so from Heaven) — Par Reg 1.276
Sometimes they thought he might be only shewn, — Par Reg 2.13
By his great Prophet, pointed at and shown, — Par Reg 2.51
By *John* the Baptist, and in publick shown, — Par Reg 2.84
To what end I have brought thee hither and shewn — Par Reg 3.350
Luggage of war there shewn me, argument — Par Reg 3.401
These having shewn thee, I have shewn thee all — Par Reg 4.88
Which to my countrey I was judg'd to have shewn. — Samson 994
Or at some proof of strength before them shown. — Samson 1475
Beauty is natures brag, and must be shown — Mask 745
Trinity ms 'shewne'
1637 'showne'
line not in Bridgewater ms
Jehovah's wonders were in *Israel* shown, — Psalm 114, 5

Shows
With shews instead, meer shews of seeming pure, — Par Lost 4.316
Impress the Air, and shews the Mariner — Par Lost 4.558
Looses discount'nanc't, and like folly shewes; — Par Lost 8.553
And to realities yield all her shows: — Par Lost 8.575
Which Heav'n by these mute signs in Nature shews — Par Lost 11.194
Ecbatana her structure vast there shews, — Par Reg 3.286
Teaching not taught; the childhood shews the man, — Par Reg 4.220
As morning shews the day. Be famous then — Par Reg 4.221
That ope's the Palace of Eternity: — Mask 14
Trinity ms 'ope's' ←'shews'

Shrewd
That the shrewd medling Elfe delights to make, — Mask 846

Shriek
With hollow shreik the steep of *Delphos* leaving. — Nativity 178

Shrieked
Environ'd thee, some howl'd, some yell'd, some shriek'd, — Par Reg 4.423

Shrieks
'Mongst horrid shapes, and shreiks, and sights unholy, — Allegro 4

Shrill
Lightly dispers'd, and the shrill Matin Song — Par Lost 5.7
Through the high wood echoing shrill. — Allegro 56

Shrine
Drawn round about thee like a radiant Shrine, — Par Lost 3.379
Transplanted from her cloudie Shrine, and plac'd — Par Lost 7.360
The Race of Mankind drownd, before the Shrine — Par Lost 11.13
Who ever by consulting at thy shrine — Par Reg 1.438
Unlesse the Goddes that in rurall shrine — Mask 267
To the great Mistres of yon princely shrine, — Arcades 36
Apollo from his shrine — Nativity 176

Shrined
Shrin'd in his Sanctuarie of Heav'n secure, — Par Lost 6.672

Shrines
Within his Sanctuary it self thir Shrines, — Par Lost 1.388
ms 'shrines'

Shrink
And vent'rous, if that fail them, shrink and fear — Par Lost 2.205
Not that I less endure, or shrink from pain, — Par Lost 4.925
As after thirst, which made thir flowing shrink — Par Lost 11.846
Fall flat and shrink into a trivial toy, — Par Reg 2.223
Yet will they soon retire, if he but shrink. — Mask 656
1637 'shrinke'
Bridgewater ms 'shrinke'
Trinity ms 'shrinke'

Shrinks
The Libyc *Hammon* shrinks his horn, — Nativity 203

Shroud
Som better shroud, som better warmth to cherish — Par Lost 10.1068
Or shroud within these limits, I shall know — Mask 316
Trinity ms 'shroud' ←'shrouded'
Trinity ms 'these' ←'these shroudie'
And bid fair peace be to my sable shrowd. — Lycidas 22
1638 'shroud'
Trinity ms 'shroud'
Naught but profoundest Hell can be his shroud, — Nativity 218

Shrouded
Or torn up sheer: ill wast thou shrouded then, — Par Reg 4.419

Shrouds
Gladly the Port, though Shrouds and Tackle torn; — Par Lost 2.1044
Run to your shrouds, within these Brakes and Trees, — Mask 147

Shrub
Acanthus, and each odorous bushie shrub — Par Lost 4.696
With Rose and Odours from the shrub unfum'd. — Par Lost 5.349
Embattell'd in her field: and the humble Shrub, — Par Lost 7.322
Flung Rose, flung Odours from the spicie Shrub, — Par Lost 8.517

Shrubby
Co. Due west it rises from this shrubby point. — Mask 306
Bridgewater ms 'shrubbie'
1637 'shrubbie'
Trinity ms 'shrubbie'

Shrubs
Of shrubs and tangling bushes had perplext — Par Lost 4.176

Shrunk
That shrunk thy streams; Return *Sicilian* Muse, — Lycidas 133

Shuddering
With shuddring horror pale, and eyes agast — Par Lost 2.616
And though not mortal, yet a cold shuddring dew — Mask 802
line not in Trinity ms
line not in Bridgewater ms

Shun
Part curb thir fierie Steeds, or shun the Goal — Par Lost 2.531
But thou O Father, I forewarn thee, shun — Par Lost 2.810
Remember what I warne thee, shun to taste, — Par Lost 8.327
And shun the bitter consequence: for know, — Par Lost 8.328
Whose higher intellectual more I shun, — Par Lost 9.483
Hee fled, not hoping to escape, but shun — Par Lost 10.339
And teach us further by what means to shun — Par Lost 10.1062

Shunned
If counsels different, or danger shun'd — Par Lost 1.636
ms 'shunn'd'
Created thing naught valu'd he nor shun'd; — Par Lost 2.679
Or when *Ulysses* on the Larbord shunnd — Par Lost 2.1019
So passd they naked on, nor shund the sight — Par Lost 4.319
Foul on himself; then wherefore shund or feard — Par Lost 9.331
Be real, why not known, since easier shunnd? — Par Lost 9.699
Ejected, emptyed, gaz'd, unpityed, shun'd, — Par Reg 1.414
Wisely hast shun'd the broad way and the green, — Sonnet 9, 2

Shunnest
Sweet Bird that shunn'st the noise of folly, — Penseroso 61

Shunning
There oft the *Indian* Herdsman shunning heate — Par Lost 9.1108

Shut
By force or suttlety: Though Heav'n be shut, — Par Lost 2.358
These Gates for ever shut, which none can pass — Par Lost 2.776
Of *Erebus*. She op'nd, but to shut — Par Lost 2.883
And wisdome at one entrance quite shut out. — Par Lost 3.50
Mine ear shall not be slow, mine eye not shut. — Par Lost 3.193
Thenceforth shall be for ever shut. Mean while — Par Lost 3.333
This glorious sight, when sleep hath shut all eyes? — Par Lost 4.658
Our prompt obedience. Fast we found, fast shut — Par Lost 8.240
Just then returnd at shut of Evening Flours. — Par Lost 9.278
Shall that be shut to Man, which to the Beast — Par Lost 9.691
His Sluces, as the Heav'n his windows shut. — Par Lost 11.849

Shut(*cont*)
Shut up from outward light Samson 160
Shuts
Where day never shuts his eye, Mask 978
Bridgewater ms 'shutts'
(The Golden opes, the Iron shuts amain) Lycidas 111
Sibma
The flowry Dale of *Sibma* clad with Vines, Par Lost 1.410
ms 'Sibma'
Sibyl
A *Sybil* old, bow-bent with crooked age, Vacation 69
Sicilian
That shrunk thy streams; Return *Sicilian* Muse, Lycidas 133
Sick
Of heart-sick Agonie, all feavorous kinds, Par Lost 11.482
Tended the sick busiest from Couch to Couch; Par Lost 11.490
Sicken
Will sicken soon and die, Nativity 137
Sickened
Meerly to drive the time away he sickn'd, Another 15
line not in 1640, 1657, 1658 texts
Sickness
To loathsom sickness, worthily, since they Par Lost 11.524
With sickness and disease thou bow'st them down, Samson 698
Side
He soon discerns, and weltring by his side Par Lost 1.78
Moors by his side under the Lee, while Night Par Lost 1.207
Torn from *Pelorus*, or the shatter'd side Par Lost 1.232
That fought at *Theb*'s and *Ilium*, on each side Par Lost 1.578
Whose midnight Revels, by a Forrest side Par Lost 1.782
On this side nothing; and by proof we feel Par Lost 2.101
To less then Gods. On th' other side up rose Par Lost 2.108
On either side a formidable shape; Par Lost 2.649
More dreadful and deform: on th' other side Par Lost 2.706
Threw forth, till on the left side op'ning wide, Par Lost 2.755
Thus saying, from her side the fatal Key, Par Lost 2.871
Levied to side with warring Winds, and poise Par Lost 2.905
To that side Heav'n from whence your Legions fell: Par Lost 2.1006
Coasting the wall of Heav'n on this side Night Par Lost 3.71
Harps ever tun'd, that glittering by thir side Par Lost 3.366
Save on that side which from the wall of Heav'n Par Lost 3.427
Look downward on that Globe whose hither side Par Lost 3.722
On th' other side: which when th' arch-fellon saw Par Lost 4.179
Another side, umbrageous Grots and Caves Par Lost 4.257
Stood whispering soft, by a fresh Fountain side Par Lost 4.326
Out of my side to thee, neerest my heart Par Lost 4.484
Substantial Life, to have thee by my side Par Lost 4.485
Some wandring Spirit of Heav'n, by Fountain side, Par Lost 4.531
Of firm and fragrant leaf; on either side Par Lost 4.695
Strait side by side were laid, nor turnd I weene Par Lost 4.741
Prove chaff. On th' other side *Satan* allarm'd Par Lost 4.985
As through unquiet rest: he on his side Par Lost 5.11
And on her ample Square from side to side Par Lost 5.393
The Throne of God unguarded, and his side Par Lost 6.133
On either side, the least of whom could weild Par Lost 6.221
All his right side; then *Satan* first knew pain, Par Lost 6.327
On every side with shaddowing Squadrons Deep, Par Lost 6.554
Nor less on either side tempestuous fell Par Lost 6.844
With tufts the vallies and each fountain side, Par Lost 7.327
Who stooping op'nd my left side, and took Par Lost 8.465
Or from my side subducting, took perhaps Par Lost 8.536
Neither her out-side formd so fair, nor aught Par Lost 8.596
Or this, or worse, leave not the faithful side Par Lost 9.265
On th' other side, *Adam*, soon as he heard Par Lost 9.888
Adam, from whose deare side I boast me sprung, Par Lost 9.965
Was I to have never parted from thy side? Par Lost 9.1153
From each side shoaling towards the mouth of Hell. Par Lost 10.288
From out of *Chaos* to the out side bare Par Lost 10.317
1667 'outside'
The Causey to Hell Gate; on either side Par Lost 10.415
To trust thee from my side, imagin'd wise, Par Lost 10.881
And on the East side of the Garden place, Par Lost 11.118
I never from thy side henceforth to stray, Par Lost 11.176
In Manhood where Youth ended; by his side Par Lost 11.246
But on the hether side a different sort Par Lost 11.574
Smeard round with Pitch, and in the side a dore Par Lost 11.731
Him on this side *Euphrates* yet residing, Par Lost 12.114
They looking back, all th' Eastern side beheld Par Lost 12.641
And looking round on every side beheld Par Reg 1.295
On this side the broad lake *Genezaret*, Par Reg 2.23
If he be Man by Mothers side at least, Par Reg 2.136
In Wood or Grove by mossie Fountain side, Par Reg 2.184
By Mothers side thy Father, though thy right Par Reg 3.154
Lay pleasant; from his side two rivers flow'd, Par Reg 3.255
He brought our Saviour to the western side Par Reg 4.25
On each side an Imperial City stood, Par Reg 4.33
On the other side know also thou, that I Par Reg 4.159
Deliverance offerd: I on th' other side Samson 246
But that on th' other side if it be weigh'd Samson 768
Fast by thy side, who from thy Fathers field Samson 1432
The other side was op'n, where the throng Samson 1609
And Timbrels, on each side went armed guards, Samson 1617
Stept as they se'd to the next Thicket side Mask 185
Co. And left your fair side all unguarded Lady? Mask 283
That crawls along the side of yon small hill, Mask 295
And every bosky bourn from side to side Mask 313
And from her fair unspotted side Mask 1009
line not in Bridgewater ms

Side(*cont*)
to have her by my side, though I were sure Mask Tr. ms 16.41
to have her by my side, though I were suer Mask Br. ms 394
From the side of som Hoar Hill, Allegro 55
Then lies him meekly down fast by his Brethrens side. Passion 21
Of which all Europe talks from side to side. Sonnet 22, 12
Her branches *on the western side* Psalm 80, 45
Sideboard
And at a stately side-board by the wine Par Reg 2.350
Sidelong
Yielded them, side-long as they sat recline Par Lost 4.333
Sidelong, had push't a Mountain from his seat Par Lost 6.197
To interrupt, side-long he works his way. Par Lost 9.512
Sideral
Like change on Sea and Land, sideral blast, Par Lost 10.693
Sides
A Dungeon horrible, on all sides round Par Lost 1.61
Of fighting Elements, on all sides round Par Lost 2.1015
Of a steep wilderness, whose hairie sides Par Lost 4.135
Forthwith on all sides to his aide was run Par Lost 6.335
On all sides, from innumerable tongues Par Lost 10.507
To the hazard of thy brains and shatter'd sides. Samson 1241
And Laughter holding both his sides. Allegro 32
Sideways
Side-ways as on a dying bed, Winchester 42
Siding
By a strong siding champion Conscience.------ Mask 212
line not in Bridgewater ms
Sidonian
Sidonian Virgins paid thir Vows and Songs, Par Lost 1.441
ms 'Sidonian'
Siege
Heav'n, whose high walls fear no assault or Siege, Par Lost 2.343
Torment within me, as from the hateful siege Par Lost 9.121
Lay Seige, encampt; by Batterie, Scale, and Mine, Par Lost 11.656
Siege and defiance: Wretched man! what food Par Lost 12.74
Sieges
What sieges girt me round, e're I consented; Samson 846
Sierra Leone
From *Serraliona;* thwart of these as fierce Par Lost 10.703
Sift
To try thee, sift thee, and confess have found thee Par Reg 4.532
Sigh
Or one short sigh of humane breath, up-borne Par Lost 11.147
Sighed
Hell trembl'd at the hideous Name, and sigh'd Par Lost 2.788
Sighing
Sighing through all her Works gave signs of woe, Par Lost 9.783
The parting Genius is with sighing sent, Nativity 186
Wearied I am with sighing out my dayes, Psalm 6, 11
Sighs
Words interwove with sighs found out thir way. Par Lost 1.621
Then much revolving, thus in sighs began. Par Lost 4.31
Watering the ground, and with our sighs the Air Par Lost 10.1090
Watering the ground, and with thir sighs the Air Par Lost 10.1102
Regenerate grow instead, that sighs now breath'd Par Lost 11.5
From thy implanted Grace in Man, these Sighs Par Lost 11.23
To supplication, heare his sighs though mute; Par Lost 11.31
Some troubl'd thoughts, which she in sighs thus clad. Par Reg 2.65
Thrice she assay'd with flattering prayers and sighs, Samson 392
Burn in your sighs, and borrow Circum 8
With sighs devout ascend Psalm 88, 6
Sight
Sight more detestable then him and thee. Par Lost 2.745
In Heav'n, when at th' Assembly, and in sight Par Lost 2.749
Or sight of vernal bloom, or Summers Rose, Par Lost 3.43
Of things invisible to mortal sight. Par Lost 3.55
Stood thick as Starrs, and from his sight receiv'd Par Lost 3.61
1667 'siight' in some copies
The powers of darkness bound. Thou at the sight Par Lost 3.256
At sight of all this World beheld so faire. Par Lost 3.554
For sight no obstacle found here, nor shade, Par Lost 3.615
In sight of God's high Throne, gloriously bright, Par Lost 3.655
Of this new World; at whose sight all the Starrs Par Lost 4.34
All Trees of noblest kind for sight, smell, taste; Par Lost 4.217
Of living Creatures new to sight and strange: Par Lost 4.287
So passd they naked on, nor shund the sight Par Lost 4.319
Sight hateful, sight tormenting! thus these two Par Lost 4.505
Lost sight of him; one of the banisht crew Par Lost 4.573
Uriel, no wonder if thy perfet sight, Par Lost 4.577
This glorious sight, when sleep hath shut all eyes? Par Lost 4.658
In whose sight all things joy, with ravishment Par Lost 5.46
Soon as they forth were come to open sight Par Lost 5.138
From hence, no cloud, or, to obstruct his sight, Par Lost 5.257
Haste hither *Eve*, and worth thy sight behold Par Lost 5.308
Enamour'd at that sight; but in those hearts Par Lost 5.448
In sight of God enthron'd, our happie state Par Lost 5.536
Through pride that sight, & thought himself impaird. Par Lost 5.665
Mean while th' Eternal eye, whose sight discernes Par Lost 5.711
Messiah was declar'd in sight of Heav'n, Par Lost 5.765
To stand approv'd in sight of God, though Worlds Par Lost 6.36
Abdiel that sight endur'd not, where he stood Par Lost 6.111
Where boldest; though to sight unconquerable? Par Lost 6.118
On the proud Crest of *Satan*, that no sight, Par Lost 6.191
Grieving to see his Glorie, at the sight Par Lost 6.792
Into the wastful Deep; the monstrous sight Par Lost 6.862
Had driven out th' ungodly from his sight Par Lost 7.185
Thir small peculiar, though from human sight Par Lost 7.368

Sight(*cont*)
Perceaving where she sat retir'd in sight, Par Lost 8.41
Into all Eyes to wish her still in sight. Par Lost 8.63
Plac'd Heav'n from Earth so farr, that earthly sight, Par Lost 8.120
Of Fancie my internal sight, by which Par Lost 8.461
I mean of Taste, Sight, Smell, Herbs, Fruits, and Flours, Par Lost 8.527
From sharpest sight: for in the wilie Snake, Par Lost 9.91
Thy absence from my sight, but to avoid Par Lost 9.294
Access in every Vertue, in thy sight Par Lost 9.310
Or Dairie, each rural sight, each rural sound; Par Lost 9.451
Curld many a wanton wreath in sight of *Eve*, Par Lost 9.517
Of brutal kind, that daily are in sight? Par Lost 9.565
The pain of absence from thy sight. But strange Par Lost 9.861
Whatever can to sight or thought be formd, Par Lost 9.898
Arraying cover'd from his Fathers sight. Par Lost 10.223
In sight, to each of these three places led. Par Lost 10.324
Great joy was at thir meeting, and at sight Par Lost 10.350
They saw, but other sight instead, a crowd Par Lost 10.538
The Frutage fair to sight, like that which grew Par Lost 10.561
To recompence his distance, in thir sight Par Lost 10.683
In sight of God? Him after all Disputes Par Lost 10.828
Out of my sight, thou Serpent, that name best Par Lost 10.867
By thir great Intercessor, came in sight Par Lost 11.19
After short blush of Morn; nigh in her sight Par Lost 11.184
Why else this double object in our sight Par Lost 11.201
1674 printed 'fight'
With what to sight or smell was sweet; from thee Par Lost 11.281
Which that false Fruit that promis'd clearer sight Par Lost 11.413
Eevn to the inmost seat of mental sight, Par Lost 11.418
Much at that sight was *Adam* in his heart Par Lost 11.448
I must return to native dust? O sight Par Lost 11.463
Sight so deform what heart of Rock could long Par Lost 11.494
And now prepare thee for another sight. Par Lost 11.555
At this last sight, assur'd that Man shall live Par Lost 11.872
Such grace shall one just Man find in his sight, Par Lost 11.890
Thy mortal sight to faile; objects divine Par Lost 12.9
Not knew by sight) now come, who was to come Par Reg 1.271
Among wild Beasts: they at his sight grew mild, Par Reg 1.310
Mock us with his blest sight, then snatch him hence, Par Reg 2.56
Best school of best experience, quickest in sight Par Reg 3.238
At sight whereof the Fiend yet more presum'd, Par Reg 3.345
All this fair sight; thy Kingdom though foretold Par Reg 3.351
The rest are barbarous, and scarce worth the sight, Par Reg 4.86
Twice by an Angel, who at last in sight Samson 24
O loss of sight, of thee I most complain! Samson 67
She all in every part; why was the sight Samson 93
Thy Bondage or lost Sight, Samson 152
(Which Men enjoying sight oft without cause complain) Samson 157
Blindness, for had I sight, confus'd with shame, Samson 196
Of sight, reserv'd alive to be repeated Samson 645
To afflict thy self in vain: though sight be lost, Samson 914
Eye-sight exposes daily men abroad. Samson 919
Some narrow place enclos'd, where sight may give thee, Samson 1117
Above the Sons of men; but sight bereav'd Samson 1294
To see me girt with Friends; and how the sight Samson 1415
Made older then thy age through eye-sight lost. Samson 1489
And since his strength with eye-sight was not lost, Samson 1502
God will restore him eye-sight to his strength. Samson 1503
What if his eye-sight (for to *Israels* God Samson 1527
The sight of this so horrid spectacle Samson 1542
At sight of him the people with a shout Samson 1620
Semichor. But he though blind of sight, Samson 1687
To hit the Sense of human sight; Penseroso 14
At last surrounds their sight Nativity 109
Of him, t' whose happy-making sight alone, On Time 18
Bereft of light thir seeing have forgot, Sonnet 22, 3
1694 'of Sight'
Nor to thir idle orbs doth sight appear Sonnet 22, 4
1694 'day'
Full sight of her in Heaven without restraint, Sonnet 23, 8
Her face was vail'd, yet to my fancied sight, Sonnet 23, 10
Fools or mad men stand not within thy sight. Psalm 5, 12
Return on high and in their sight. Psalm 7, 28
And in Manasse's sight Psalm 80, 10

Sighted
The sharpest sighted Spirit of all in Heav'n; Par Lost 3.691
when she beheld (the gods farre sighted bee) Lycidas Tr. ms 29.60

Sights
Serv'd onely to discover sights of woe, Par Lost 1.64
Call *El Dorado:* but to nobler sights Par Lost 11.411
O my simplicity what sights are these? with darke disguises Mask Tr. ms 22.19
'Mongst horrid shapes, and shreiks, and sights unholy, Allegro 4
Such sights as youthfull Poets dream Allegro 129

Sign
Shon with a glossie scurff, undoubted sign Par Lost 1.672
ms 'signe'
At first, and call'd me *Sin*, and for a Sign Par Lost 2.760
The only sign of our obedience left Par Lost 4.428
Betwixt *Astrea* and the *Scorpion* signe, Par Lost 4.998
And read thy Lot in yon celestial Sign Par Lost 4.1011
With every Plant, in sign of Worship wave. Par Lost 5.194
In duskie wreathes, reluctant flames, the signe Par Lost 6.58
Aloft by Angels born, his Sign in Heav'n: Par Lost 6.776
In signe whereof each Bird and Beast behold Par Lost 8.342
Gave sign of gratulation, and each Hill; Par Lost 8.514
Frequenting, sent from hearts contrite, in sign Par Lost 10.1091
Frequenting, sent from hearts contrite, in sign Par Lost 10.1103
Present, and of his presence many a signe Par Lost 11.351

Sign(*cont*)
An Olive leafe he brings, pacific signe: Par Lost 11.860
Baptizing in the profluent stream, the signe Par Lost 12.442
Of many in *Israel*, and to a sign Par Reg 2.89
There without sign of boast, or sign of joy, Par Reg 2.119
May warn thee, as a sure fore-going sign. Par Reg 4.483
Feirce signe of battail make, and menace high, Mask 654
Some sign of good to me afford, Psalm 86, 61

Signal
Thir surest signal, they will soon resume Par Lost 1.278
ms 'signall'
Till, as a signal giv'n, th' uplifted Spear Par Lost 1.347
Swarm'd and were straitn'd; till the Signal giv'n, Par Lost 1.776
ms 'signall'
The Signal to ascend, sit lingring here Par Lost 2.56
Hov'ring a space, till Winds the signal blow Par Lost 2.717
The wonted signal, and superior voice Par Lost 5.705
Hesperean sets, my Signal to depart. Par Lost 8.632
He ended, and the Son gave signal high Par Lost 11.72
In signal of remove, waves fiercely round; Par Lost 12.593
Chor. As signal now in low dejected state, Samson 338

Signify
They oft fore-signifie and threaten ill: Par Reg 4.464

Signs
Signs of remorse and passion to behold Par Lost 1.605
ms 'Signes'
Should be, and, by concurring signs, ere now Par Lost 2.831
Among so many signes of power and rule Par Lost 4.429
Kiss'd as the gracious signs of sweet remorse Par Lost 5.134
But to convince the proud what Signs availe, Par Lost 6.789
The Day from Night; and let them be for Signes, Par Lost 7.341
Sighing through all her Works gave signs of woe, Par Lost 9.783
And in our Faces evident the signes Par Lost 9.1077
Subscrib'd not; Nature first gave Signs, impress Par Lost 11.182
Which Heav'n by these mute signs in Nature shews Par Lost 11.194
Must be compelld by Signes and Judgements dire; Par Lost 12.175
Oft my advice by presages and signs, Par Reg 1.394
And threatning nigh; what they can do as signs Par Reg 4.489
(For so by certain signes I knew) had met Mask 572
1637 'signs'
Helping all urchin blasts, and ill luck signes Mask 845

Sihon
And *Horonaim*, *Seons* Realm, beyond Par Lost 1.409
ms 'Seons'

Silence
Breaking the horrid silence thus began. Par Lost 1.83
Mov'd on in silence to soft Pipes that charm'd Par Lost 1.561
Frequent and full. After short silence then Par Lost 1.797
With reason hath deep silence and demurr Par Lost 2.431
Fled not in silence through the frighted deep Par Lost 2.994
And silence was in Heav'n: on mans behalf Par Lost 3.218
Silence accompanied, for Beast and Bird, Par Lost 4.600
Silence was pleas'd: now glow'd the Firmament Par Lost 4.604
The cool, the silent, save where silence yields Par Lost 5.39
Worthy of Sacred silence to be heard; Par Lost 5.557
Friendliest to sleep and silence, he resolv'd Par Lost 5.668
In silence thir bright Legions, to the sound Par Lost 6.64
Therfore Eternal silence be thir doome. Par Lost 6.385
And silence on the odious dinn of Warr: Par Lost 6.408
Silence, and Sleep listning to thee will watch, Par Lost 7.106
Silence, ye troubl'd waves, and thou Deep, peace, Par Lost 7.216
But not in silence holy kept; the Harp Par Lost 7.594
First to himself he inward silence broke. Par Lost 9.895
Inchanting Daughter, thus the silence broke. Par Lost 10.353
Silence, and with these words attention won. Par Lost 10.459
And what most merits fame in silence hid. Par Lost 11.699
Met ever; and to shameful silence brought, Par Reg 4.22
And now the Tempter thus his silence broke. Par Reg 4.43
Under the Seal of silence could not keep, Samson 49
Gave up my fort of silence to a Woman. Samson 236
To violate the sacred trust of silence Samson 428
And combated in silence all these reasons Samson 864
Of silence, through the empty-vaulted night Mask 250
1637 'Silence'
Till an unusuall stop of sudden silence Mask 552
And stole upon the Air, that even Silence Mask 557
Bridgewater ms 'silence'
Trinity ms 'silence'
And the mute Silence hist along, Penseroso 55
Driving dum silence from the portal dore, Vacation 5
Through the soft silence of the list'ning night; Circum 5

Silent
Retreated in a silent valley, sing Par Lost 2.547
Farr off from these a slow and silent stream, Par Lost 2.582
Silent yet spake, and breath'd immortal love Par Lost 3.267
Of grateful Eevning milde, then silent Night Par Lost 4.647
Nor grateful Eevning mild, nor silent Night Par Lost 4.654
Fame is not silent, here in hope to find Par Lost 4.938
The cool, the silent, save where silence yields Par Lost 5.39
Witness if I be silent, Morn or Eeven, Par Lost 5.202
With silent circumspection unespi'd. Par Lost 6.523
To meet him all his Saints, who silent stood Par Lost 6.882
The silent hours, and th' other whose gay Traine Par Lost 7.444
Or Shee from West her silent course advance Par Lost 8.163
From th' Earths great Altar send up silent praise Par Lost 9.195
Of all thir vertue: silent, and in face Par Lost 9.1063
Commun'd in silent walk, then laid him down Par Reg 2.261
And silent as the Moon, Samson 87

Silent(*cont*)	
With silent obsequie and funeral train	Samson 1732
Som far off hallow break the silent Air.	Mask 481
Be not thou silent *now at length*	Psalm 83, 1
Silently	
Wing silently the buxom Air, imbalm'd	Par Lost 2.842
But silently a gentle tear let fall	Par Lost 5.130
Silk	
That in their green shops weave the smooth-hair'd silk	Mask 716
Trinity ms 'silke'	
Bridgewater ms 'silke'	
Silken	
Dusk faces with white silken Turbants wreath'd:	Par Reg 4.76
Wetting the borders of her silk'n veil:	Samson 730
Soft silken Primrose fading timelesslie,	Fair Inf 2
Silly	
Was all that did their silly thoughts so busie keep.	Nativity 92
Silo	
In *Silo* his bright Sanctuary:	Samson 1674
Siloa	
Delight thee more, and *Siloa*'s Brook that flow'd	Par Lost 1.11
ms 'Siloa's'	
Silvan	
Dwell'st here with *Pan*, or *Silvan*, by blest Song	Mask 268
Silver	
If mettal, part seemd Gold, part Silver cleer;	Par Lost 3.595
Before his decent steps a Silver wand.	Par Lost 3.644
And o're the dark her Silver Mantle threw.	Par Lost 4.609
Others on Silver Lakes and Rivers Bath'd	Par Lost 7.437
Turn forth her silver lining on the night?	Mask 222
line not in Bridgewater ms	
Turn forth her silver lining on the night,	Mask 224
line not in Bridgewater ms	
Goddess of the silver lake,	Mask 865
Shooting her beams like silver threds,	Arcades 16
And let your silver chime	Nativity 128
Their loud up-lifted Angel trumpets blow,	Musick 11
Trinity ms 'angell' ←'arch-angell' ←'symphonie of silver'	
Silver-buskined	
Fair silver-buskind Nymphs as great and good,	Arcades 33
1673 'silver-buskin'd'	
Trinity ms 'silver-buskin'd'	
Silver-shafted	
Fair silver-shafted Queen for ever chaste,	Mask 442
Bridgewater ms 'silver shafter'	
Simeon	
Just *Simeon* and Prophetic *Anna*, warn'd	Par Reg 1.255
But trouble, as old *Simeon* plain fore-told,	Par Reg 2.87
Similitude	
Begotten Son, Divine Similitude,	Par Lost 3.384
In our similitude, and let them rule	Par Lost 7.520
Retaining still Divine similitude	Par Lost 11.512
Simon	
Andrew and *Simon*, famous after known	Par Reg 2.7
Simple	
To simple Shepherds, keeping watch by night;	Par Lost 12.365
Alas how simple, to these Cates compar'd,	Par Reg 2.348
Simples	
And shew me simples of a thousand names	Mask 627
Simplicity	
At wisdoms Gate, and to simplicitie	Par Lost 3.687
Simplicitie and spotless innocence.	Par Lost 4.318
O my simplicity what sights are these? with darke disguises	Mask Tr. ms 22.19
Simply	
By simply meek; that suffering for Truths sake	Par Lost 12.569
Sate simply chatting in a rustick row;	Nativity 87
Sin	
Doubl'd that sin in *Bethel* and in *Dan*,	Par Lost 1.485
At first, and call'd me *Sin*, and for a Sign	Par Lost 2.760
Strange alteration! Sin and Death amain	Par Lost 2.1024
By sin to foul exorbitant desires;	Par Lost 3.177
Of all things transitorie and vain, when Sin	Par Lost 3.446
Envie them that? can it be sin to know,	Par Lost 4.517
Farr be it, that I should write thee sin or blame,	Par Lost 4.758
Thy sin and place of doom obscure and foule.	Par Lost 4.840
By sin of disobedience, till that hour	Par Lost 6.396
1667 'sinne'	
For sin, on warr and mutual slaughter bent.	Par Lost 6.506
Save what sin hath impaird, which yet hath wrought	Par Lost 6.691
And govern well thy appetite, least sin	Par Lost 7.546
Sinne and her shadow Death, and Miserie	Par Lost 9.12
Now not, though Sin, not Time, first wraught the change,	Par Lost 9.70
For such thou art, from sin and blame entire:	Par Lost 9.292
But harm precedes not sin: onely our Foe	Par Lost 9.327
Wept at compleating of the mortal Sin	Par Lost 9.1003
The solace of thir sin, till dewie sleep	Par Lost 9.1044
And manifold in sin, deserv'd to fall.	Par Lost 10.16
Least on my head both sin and punishment,	Par Lost 10.133
To *Satan* first in sin his doom apply'd,	Par Lost 10.172
Within the Gates of Hell sate Sin and Death,	Par Lost 10.230
Sin opening, who thus now to Death began.	Par Lost 10.234
For Death from Sin no power can separate.	Par Lost 10.251
Long hee admiring stood, till Sin, his faire	Par Lost 10.352
Through Sin to Death expos'd by my exploit.	Par Lost 10.407
By Sin and Death a broad way now is pav'd	Par Lost 10.473
To Sin and Death a prey, and so to us,	Par Lost 10.490
Too soon arriv'd, *Sin* there in power before,	Par Lost 10.586
On his pale Horse: to whom *Sin* thus began.	Par Lost 10.590

Sin(*cont*)	
Which mans polluting Sin with taint hath shed	Par Lost 10.631
Both *Sin*, and *Death*, and yawning *Grave* at last	Par Lost 10.635
Daughter of Sin, among th' irrational,	Par Lost 10.708
And sin? the Bodie properly hath neither.	Par Lost 10.791
For dissolution wrought by Sin, that first	Par Lost 11.55
Nor sinn'd thy sin, yet from that derive	Par Lost 11.427
1667 'that sin derive'	
Inductive mainly to the sin of *Eve*.	Par Lost 11.519
Ten thousandfould the sin of him who slew	Par Lost 11.678
To whom thus *Michael*. Doubt not but that sin	Par Lost 12.285
Sin against Law to fight; that when they see	Par Lost 12.289
Law can discover sin, but not remove,	Par Lost 12.290
In sin for ever lost from life; this act	Par Lost 12.429
Defeating Sin and Death, his two maine armes,	Par Lost 12.431
Of washing them from guilt of sin to Life	Par Lost 12.443
Whether I should repent me now of sin	Par Lost 12.474
Pretends to wash off sin, and fit them so	Par Reg 1.73
To conquer Sin and Death the two grand foes,	Par Reg 1.159
With guilt of his own sin, for he himself	Par Reg 3.147
Of sin, or legal debt;	Samson 313
Weakly at least, and shamefully: A sin	Samson 499
Repent the sin, but if the punishment	Samson 504
Favour renew'd, and add a greater sin	Samson 1357
Tis onely day-light that makes Sin	Mask 126
Trinity ms 'sin'	
Bridgewater ms 'sin'	
Driving far off each thing of sin and guilt,	Mask 456
1637 'sinne'	
But most by leud and lavish act of sin,	Mask 465
And leprous sin will melt from earthly mould,	Nativity 138
To slake his wrath whom sin hath made our foe	Fair Inf 66
Alas, how soon our sin	Circum 12
As once we did, till disproportion'd sin	Musick 19
Trinity ms 'sin' ←'Sin'	
of clamourous sin that all our musick marres	Musick Tr. ms 5.04
'of clamourous sin' ←'of sin'	
Of Death, call'd Life; which us from Life doth sever.	Sonnet 14, 4
Trinity ms 'death' ←'Flesh & sin'	
From them whose sin ye envi'd, not abhor'd,	Forcers 4
Be aw'd, and do not sin,	Psalm 4, 19
To wayes of sin and shame,	Psalm 80, 74
With Sin *for evermore.*	Psalm 84, 40
And all their Sin, *that did thee grieve*	Psalm 85, 7
Sinaean	
To *Paquin* of *Sinaean* Kings, and thence	Par Lost 11.390
Sinai	
Of *Oreb*, or of *Sinai*, didst inspire	Par Lost 1.7
ms 'Sinai'	
God from the Mount of *Sinai*, whose gray top	Par Lost 12.227
As on mount *Sinai* rang	Nativity 158
Sin-born	
Whom thus the Sin-born Monster answerd soon.	Par Lost 10.596
Sin-bred	
Sin-bred, how have ye troubl'd all mankind	Par Lost 4.315
Since	
This downfall; since by Fate the strength of Gods	Par Lost 1.116
ms 'Since'	
Since through experience of this great event	Par Lost 1.118
Of force believe Almighty, since no less	Par Lost 1.144
For that celestial light? Be it so, since he	Par Lost 1.245
Glories: For never since created man,	Par Lost 1.573
And all who since, Baptiz'd or Infidel	Par Lost 1.582
For since no deep within her gulf can hold	Par Lost 2.12
By my advice; since fate inevitable	Par Lost 2.197
Worth waiting, since our present lot appeers	Par Lost 2.223
Dear Daughter, since thou claim'st me for thy Sire,	Par Lost 2.817
May I express thee unblam'd? since God is light,	Par Lost 3.3
Into a *Limbo* large and broad, since calld	Par Lost 3.495
Be then his Love accurst, since love or hate,	Par Lost 4.69
Nay curs'd be thou; since against his thy will	Par Lost 4.71
So since into his Church lewd Hirelings climbe.	Par Lost 4.193
That ever since in loves imbraces met,	Par Lost 4.322
Adam the goodliest man of men since borne	Par Lost 4.323
All Beasts of th' Earth, since wilde, and of all chase	Par Lost 4.341
Well known from Heav'n; and since Meridian hour	Par Lost 4.581
Mind us of like repose, since God hath set	Par Lost 4.612
Since *Satan* fell, whom follie overthrew,	Par Lost 4.905
To boast what Arms can doe, since thine no more	Par Lost 4.1008
And why not Gods of Men, since good, the more	Par Lost 5.71
Since by descending from the Thrones above,	Par Lost 5.363
Not meerly titular, since by Decree	Par Lost 5.774
But more illustrious made, since he the Head	Par Lost 5.842
Of this right hand provok't, since first that tongue	Par Lost 6.154
Since now we find this our Empyreal form	Par Lost 6.433
Since *Michael* and his Powers went forth to tame	Par Lost 6.686
Of ending this great Warr, since none but Thou	Par Lost 6.702
Or I alone against them, since by strength	Par Lost 6.820
Of what we are. But since thou hast voutsaf't	Par Lost 7.80
Who since the Morning hour set out from Heav'n	Par Lost 8.111
Not hither summond, since they cannot change	Par Lost 8.347
Follow'd with benediction. Since to part,	Par Lost 8.645
Since first this Subject for Heroic Song	Par Lost 9.25
Since *Uriel* Regent of the Sun descri'd	Par Lost 9.60
Not longer then since I in one Night freed	Par Lost 9.140
Since higher I fall short, on him who next	Par Lost 9.174
Since Reason not impossibly may meet	Par Lost 9.360
For now, and since first break of dawne the Fiend,	Par Lost 9.412

Since(*cont*)	
Prone on the ground, as since, but on his reare,	Par Lost 9.497
And lovely, never since of Serpent kind	Par Lost 9.504
Flourishd, since mute, to som great cause addrest,	Par Lost 9.672
Be real, why not known, since easier shunnd?	Par Lost 9.699
That ye should be as Gods, since I as Man,	Par Lost 9.710
Since to each meaning savour me apply,	Par Lost 9.1019
For never did thy Beautie since the day	Par Lost 9.1029
False in our promis'd Rising; since our Eyes	Par Lost 9.1070
Concern'd not Man (since he no further knew)	Par Lost 10.170
Farr into *Chaos*, since the Fiend pass'd through,	Par Lost 10.233
By his Avengers, since no place like this	Par Lost 10.241
With what permissive glory since his fall	Par Lost 10.451
The doubt, since humane reach no further knows.	Par Lost 10.793
Of tardie execution, since denounc't	Par Lost 10.853
Since this days Death denounc't, if ought I see,	Par Lost 10.962
His Trumpet, heard in *Oreb* since perhaps	Par Lost 11.74
To know both Good and Evil, since his taste	Par Lost 11.85
Ev'n to the Seat of God. For since I saught	Par Lost 11.148
Mother of all things living, since by thee	Par Lost 11.160
The *Persian* in *Ecbatan* sate, or since	Par Lost 11.393
So goodly and erect, though faultie since,	Par Lost 11.509
To loathsom sickness, worthily, since they	Par Lost 11.524
Since thy original lapse, true Libertie	Par Lost 12.83
Man till then free. Therefore since hee permits	Par Lost 12.90
Presaging, since with sorrow and hearts distress	Par Lost 12.613
Since *Adam* and his facil consort *Eve*	Par Reg 1.51
Lost Paradise deceiv'd by me, though since	Par Reg 1.52
Less over-weening, since he fail'd in *Job*,	Par Reg 1.147
At first it may be; but long since with wo	Par Reg 1.399
To thy Delusions; justly, since they fell	Par Reg 1.443
To hear thee when I come (since no man comes)	Par Reg 1.484
Since understand; much more his absence now	Par Reg 2.100
Since first her Salutation heard, with thoughts	Par Reg 2.107
Fairer then feign'd of old, or fabl'd since	Par Reg 2.358
And reason; since his word all things produc'd,	Par Reg 3.122
Now both abhor, since thou hast dar'd to utter	Par Reg 4.172
Long since. Wert thou so void of fear or shame,	Par Reg 4.189
Since neither wealth, nor honour, arms nor arts,	Par Reg 4.368
Since light so necessary is to life,	Samson 90
Since man on earth unparallel'd!	Samson 165
Dal. Since thou determinst weakness for no plea	Samson 843
Then, as since then, thy countries foe profest:	Samson 884
It fits not; thou and I long since are twain;	Samson 929
And since his strength with eye-sight was not lost,	Samson 1502
For since grim Aquilo his charioter	Fair Inf 8
Since thou art the just God that tries	Psalm 7, 38
Sincere	
Not free, what proof could they have givn sincere	Par Lost 3.103
Though but endevord with sincere intent,	Par Lost 3.192
Less attributed to her Faith sincere,	Par Lost 9.320
What love sincere, and reverence in my heart	Par Lost 10.915
The others not, for his was not sincere;	Par Lost 11.443
So reigning can be no sincere delight.	Par Reg 2.480
May bring them back repentant and sincere,	Par Reg 3.435
Bin, as it ought, sincere, it would have taught thee	Samson 874
Sincerely	
That when a soul is found sincerely so,	Mask 454
Bridgewater ms 'cinceerely'	
When every thing that is sincerely good	On Time 14
Sincerest	
Which your sincerest care could not prevent,	Par Lost 10.37
Sinews	
No less through all my sinews, joints and bones,	Samson 1142
And crumble all thy sinews. *Eld. Bro*. Why prethee Shepherd	Mask 615
Bridgewater ms 'sinewes'	
1637 'sinewes'	
Hail native Language, that by sinews weak	Vacation 1
Sinful	
Thir sinful state, and to appease betimes	Par Lost 3.186
Nature her self, though pure of sinful thought,	Par Lost 8.506
Without remorse drive out the sinful Pair,	Par Lost 11.105
And all the world, and mass of sinful flesh;	Par Reg 1.162
Pollute with sinfull blame,	Nativity 41
Sinfulness	
With sinfulness of Men; thereby to learn	Par Lost 11.360
Sing	
Sing Heav'nly Muse, that on the secret top	Par Lost 1.6
With warbl'd Hymns, and to his Godhead sing	Par Lost 2.242
Retreated in a silent valley, sing	Par Lost 2.547
(What could it less when Spirits immortal sing2)	Par Lost 2.553
Unfained *Halleluiahs* to thee sing,	Par Lost 6.744
More safe I Sing with mortal voice, unchang'd	Par Lost 7.24
1669 'sing'	
Of lustful appetence, to sing, to dance,	Par Lost 11.619
Of great *Messiah* shall sing. Thus Laws and Rites	Par Lost 12.244
For ever shall endure; the like shall sing	Par Lost 12.324
By one mans disobedience lost, now sing	Par Reg 1.2
Ill imitated, while they loudest sing	Par Reg 4.339
He lov'd me well, and oft would beg me sing,	Mask 623
Bridgewater ms 'singe'	
That sing about the golden tree:	Mask 983
Bridgewater ms 'singe'	
Or whether (as som Sager sing)	Allegro 17
Ay round about *Joves* Altar sing.	Penseroso 48
Or bid the soul of *Orpheus* sing	Penseroso 105
That at her flowry work doth sing,	Penseroso 143
And sing to those that hold the vital shears,	Arcades 65
Sing(*cont*)	
Follow me as I sing,	Arcades 86
Who would not sing for *Lycidas?* he knew	Lycidas 10
Himself to sing, and build the lofty rhyme.	Lycidas 11
That sing, and singing in their glory move,	Lycidas 180
For so the holy sages once did sing,	Nativity 5
Then sing of secret things that came to pass	Vacation 45
My muse with Angels did divide to sing;	Passion 4
To live with him, and sing in endles morn of light.	Musick 28
Now timely sing, ere the rude Bird of Hate	Sonnet 1, 9
Then his *Casella*, whom he woo'd to sing,	Sonnet 13, 13
Defend'st them, they shall ever sing	Psalm 5, 35
And sing the Name and Deitie	Psalm 7, 63
To God our strength sing loud, *and clear*	Psalm 81, 1
Sing loud to God *our King*,	Psalm 81, 2
Both they who sing, and they who dance	Psalm 87, 25
Singed	
And leave a singed bottom all involv'd	Par Lost 1.236
With singed top thir stately growth though bare	Par Lost 1.614
Summer drouth, or singed air	Mask 928
Singest	
How sweet thou sing'st, how neer the deadly snare!	Mask 567
Bridgewater ms 'singst'	
Singeth	
And the Milkmaid singeth blithe,	Allegro 65
Singing	
Singing thir great Creator: oft in bands	Par Lost 4.684
That singing up to Heaven Gate ascend,	Par Lost 5.198
Circling the Throne and Singing, while the hand	Par Reg 1.171
And singing startle the dull night,	Allegro 42
That sing, and singing in their glory move,	Lycidas 180
And sweetly singing round about thy Bed	Vacation 63
Singing everlastingly;	Musick 16
Single	
Others came single; he who to be deemd	Par Lost 3.469
Single against thee wicked, and thence weak.	Par Lost 4.856
Single, is yet so just, my constant thoughts	Par Lost 5.552
Though single. From amidst them forth he passd,	Par Lost 5.903
The better fight, who single hast maintaind	Par Lost 6.30
Each Warriour single as in Chief, expert	Par Lost 6.233
Bank the mid Sea: part single or with mate	Par Lost 7.403
His single imperfection, and beget	Par Lost 8.423
Single with like defence, wherever met,	Par Lost 9.325
As not secure to single or combin'd.	Par Lost 9.339
Insatiate, I thus single, nor have feard	Par Lost 9.536
Nor I on my part single, in mee all	Par Lost 10.817
Single or in Array of Battel rang'd	Par Lost 11.644
With Foes for daring single to be just,	Par Lost 11.703
In Troop or Caravan, for single none	Par Reg 1.323
Voluminous, or single characters,	Par Reg 4.384
The Son of God, which bears no single sence;	Par Reg 4.517
None offering fight; who single combatant	Samson 344
Har. Dost thou already single me; I thought	Samson 1092
In fight withstand me single and unarm'd,	Samson 1111
Single Rebellion and did Hostile Acts.	Samson 1210
Who now defies thee thrice to single fight,	Samson 1222
Yet nought but single darknes do I find.	Mask 204
line not in Bridgewater ms	
As that the single want of light and noise	Mask 369
And let a single helpless maiden pass	Mask 402
Singly	
Came singly where he stood on the bare strand,	Par Lost 1.379
Singly by me against their Conquerours	Samson 244
Sings	
Sings darkling, and in shadiest Covert hid	Par Lost 3.39
Or Serenate, which the starv'd Lover sings	Par Lost 4.769
And the night-Raven sings;	Allegro 7
Listening to what unshorn *Apollo* sings	Vacation 37
Singular	
Or singular and rash, whereat rejoic'd	Par Lost 5.851
Singularly	
His lot who dares be singularly good.	Par Reg 3.57
Sinister	
More to the part sinister from me drawn,	Par Lost 10.886
Sink	
Bad men and Angels, they arraignd shall sink	Par Lost 3.331
Sinks	
And swims or sinks, or wades, or creeps, or flyes:	Par Lost 2.950
So sinks the day-star in the Ocean bed,	Lycidas 168
Sinless	
Led on, yet sinless, with desire to know	Par Lost 7.61
To whom thus *Eve* yet sinless. Of the Fruit	Par Lost 9.659
Inhabited, though sinless, more then now,	Par Lost 10.690
Sat'st unappall'd in calm and sinless peace.	Par Reg 4.425
Sinned	
Gave them above thir foes, not to have sinnd,	Par Lost 6.402
Meanwhile ere thus was sin'd and judg'd on Earth,	Par Lost 10.229
Now rul'd him, punisht in the shape he sin'd,	Par Lost 10.516
Of Life that sinn'd; what dies but what had life	Par Lost 10.790
More miserable; both have sin'd, but thou	Par Lost 10.930
Nor sinn'd thy sin, yet from that derive	Par Lost 11.427
Sinners	
Of sinners hath not stood, and in the seat	Psalm 1, 3
Nor sinners in th' assembly of just men.	Psalm 1, 14
Sinning	
Purest at first, now gross by sinning grown.	Par Lost 6.661
Sins	
Disloyal breaks his fealtie, and sinns	Par Lost 3.204

Sins*(cont)*
Can never seek, once dead in sins and lost; Par Lost 3.233
So many Laws argue so many sins Par Lost 12.283
Long time shall dwell and prosper, but when sins Par Lost 12.316
The Law that is against thee, and the sins Par Lost 12.416
Or work Redemption for mankind, whose sins Par Reg 1.266

Sinuous
Streaking the ground with sinuous trace; not all Par Lost 7.481

Sin-worn
With the rank vapours of this Sin-worn mould. Mask 17
Bridgewater ms 'sin-worne'
Trinity ms 'sin-worne'
1637 'Sin-worne'

Sion
Rose out of *Chaos:* Or if *Sion* Hill Par Lost 1.10
ms 'Sion'
Jehovah thundring out of *Sion*, thron'd Par Lost 1.386
ms 'Sion'
In *Sion* also not unsung, where stood Par Lost 1.442
ms 'Sion'
Infected *Sions* daughters with like heat, Par Lost 1.453
ms 'Sions'
Thee *Sion* and the flowrie Brooks beneath Par Lost 3.30
Over Mount *Sion*, and, though that were large, Par Lost 3.530
With *Sion*'s songs, to all true tasts excelling, Par Reg 4.347
On *Sion* my holi' hill. A firm decree Psalm 2, 13
In Sion do appear. Psalm 84, 28
Sions *fair* Gates the Lord loves more Psalm 87, 5
Be said of Sion *last* Psalm 87, 18

Sip
But this will cure all streight, one sip of this Mask 811

Sips
And every Herb that sips the dew; Penseroso 172

Sir
Sir, what ill chance hath brought thee to this place Par Reg 1.321
Thy age, like ours, O Soul of Sir *John Cheek*, Sonnet 11, 12

Sire
Thick clouds and dark doth Heav'ns all-ruling Sire Par Lost 2.264
Dear Daughter, since thou claim'st me for thy Sire, Par Lost 2.817
His mother bad, and thus bespake her Sire. Par Lost 2.849
Which to our general Sire gave prospect large Par Lost 4.144
What day the genial Angel to our Sire Par Lost 4.712
Mean while our Primitive great Sire, to meet Par Lost 5.350
Unanimous, as sons of one great Sire Par Lost 6.95
So spake our Sire, and by his count'nance seemd Par Lost 8.39
Nor are thy lips ungraceful, Sire of men, Par Lost 8.218
So spake the Godlike Power, and thus our Sire. Par Lost 8.249
Rowling in dust and gore. To which our Sire. Par Lost 11.460
At length a Reverend Sire among them came, Par Lost 11.719
Thir order: last the Sire, and his three Sons Par Lost 11.736
The ancient Sire descends with all his Train; Par Lost 11.862
A Virgin is his Mother, but his Sire Par Lost 12.368
As at the Worlds great period; and our Sire Par Lost 12.467
His Mother then is mortal, but his Sire, Par Reg 1.86
By matchless Deeds express thy matchless Sire. Par Reg 1.233
But see here comes thy reverend Sire Samson 326
With thee; say reverend Sire, we thirst to hear. Samson 1456
Next *Camus*, reverend Sire, went footing slow, Lycidas 103
1638 'sire'
Trinity ms 'sire'
Immortal Nectar to her Kingly Sire: Vacation 39

Sirens
My Mother *Circe* with the Sirens three, Mask 253
And the Songs of *Sirens* sweet, Mask 878
Bridgewater ms 'sirens'
To the celestial *Sirens* harmony, Arcades 63
Trinity ms 'sirens'
Blest pair of *Sirens*, pledges of Heav'ns joy, Musick 1

Sirocco
Sirocco, and *Libecchio*, Thus began Par Lost 10.706

Sirs
End Green. Why is it harder Sirs then Gordon, Sonnet 11, 8
Trinity ms 'sirs' ←'Sirs'

Sisera
Smote *Sisera* sleeping through the Temples nail'd. Samson 990
To Sisera, and as *is told* Psalm 83, 35

Sister
Wisdom thy Sister, and with her didst play Par Lost 7.10
But O that hapless virgin our lost sister Mask 350
I do not think my sister so to seek, Mask 366
Of our unowned sister. *Eld. Bro*. I do not, brother, Mask 407
Inferr, as if I thought my sisters state Mask 408
My sister is not so defenceless left Mask 414
2. *Bro*. Heav'n keep my sister, agen agen and neer, Mask 486
Of my most honour'd Lady, your dear sister. Mask 564
Com Lady while Heaven lends us grace, Mask 938
Bridgewater ms 'come sister'
With two sister Graces more Allegro 15
Prince *Memnons* sister might beseem, Penseroso 18

Sisters
Atlantick Sisters, and the *Spartan* Twins Par Lost 10.674
Begin then, Sisters of the sacred well, Lycidas 15
Sleek *Panope* with all her sisters play'd. Lycidas 99
Amongst her spangled sisters bright. Psalm 136, 34
Sphear-born harmonious Sisters, Voice, and Vers, Musick 2
Trinity ms 'sisters'

Sit
For while they sit contriving, shall the rest, Par Lost 2.54

Sit*(cont)*
The Signal to ascend, sit lingring here Par Lost 2.56
Sit unpolluted, and th' Ethereal mould Par Lost 2.139
What sit we then projecting peace and Warr? Par Lost 2.329
And Heav'ns high Arbitrator sit secure Par Lost 2.359
Attempting, or to sit in darkness here Par Lost 2.377
To sit in hateful Office here confin'd, Par Lost 2.859
Here shalt thou sit incarnate, here shalt Reign Par Lost 3.315
To sit and taste, till this meridian heat Par Lost 5.369
For while I sit with thee, I seem in Heav'n, Par Lost 8.210
To sit indulgent, and with him partake Par Lost 9.3
With Gods to sit the highest, am now constraind Par Lost 9.164
There sit not, and reproach us as unclean, Par Lost 9.1098
O Son, why sit we here each other viewing Par Lost 10.235
Appointed to sit there, had left thir charge, Par Lost 10.421
Thou shouldst be great and sit on *David*'s Throne, Par Reg 1.240
With honour, only deign to sit and eat. Par Reg 2.336
What doubts the Son of God to sit and eat? Par Reg 2.368
What doubt'st thou Son of God? sit down and eat. Par Reg 2.377
While Virtue, Valour, Wisdom sit in want. Par Reg 2.431
To sit upon thy Father *David*'s Throne; Par Reg 3.153
But tedious wast of time to sit and hear Par Reg 4.123
Know therefore when my season comes to sit Par Reg 4.146
There I am wont to sit, when any chance Samson 4
But to sit idle on the houshold hearth, Samson 566
Or seven, though one should musing sit; Samson 1017
Not to sit idle with so great a gift Samson 1500
Of sort, might sit in order to behold, Samson 1608
May sit i' th center, and enjoy bright day, Mask 382
Would sit, and hearken even to extasie, Mask 625
Comus. Nay Lady sit; if I but wave this wand, Mask 659
Where I may sit and rightly spell, Penseroso 170
That sit upon the nine enfolded Sphears, Arcades 64
To sit the midst of Trinal Unity, Nativity 11
While Birds of Calm sit brooding on the charmed wave. Nativity 68
And Mercy set between, Nativity 144
1673 'Mercy will sit between'
Bright-harnest Angels sit in order serviceable. Nativity 244
There doth my soul in holy vision sit Passion 41
Attir'd with Stars, we shall for ever sit, On Time 21
Sit not thou still O God of *strength* Psalm 83, 3

Sits
Sits Arbitress, and neerer to the Earth Par Lost 1.785
Forc't Halleluiah's; while he Lordly sits Par Lost 2.243
High honourd sits? Go therfore mighty Powers, Par Lost 2.456
For him who sits above and laughs the while Par Lost 2.731
Before mine eyes in opposition sits Par Lost 2.803
Hee rules a moment; *Chaos* Umpire sits, Par Lost 2.907
From the pure Empyrean where he sits Par Lost 3.57
Sits on the Bloom extracting liquid sweet. Par Lost 5.25
Had not th' Almightie Father where he sits Par Lost 6.671
Where now he sits at the right hand of bliss. Par Lost 6.892
Chor. His manacles remark him, there he sits. Samson 1309
And sits as safe as in a Senat house, Mask 389
Bridgewater ms 'sitts'
We cannot free the Lady that sits here Mask 818
Trinity ms 'sits' ←'remaines'
Bridgewater ms 'sitts'
Wherwith she sits on diamond rocks Mask 881
Bridgewater ms 'sitts'
But night sits monarch yet in the mid sky. Mask 957
Bridgewater ms 'sitts'
Trinity ms 'sitts' ←'raignes'
Sadly sits th' *Assyrian* Queen; Mask 1002
line not in Bridgewater ms
I will bring you where she sits, Arcades 91
Now sits not girt with Tapers holy shine, Nativity 202
To him that sits theron Musick 8
Trinity ms 'sitts' ←'sits'
The God that sits at marriage feast; Winchester 18

Sitst
Amidst the glorious brightness where thou sit'st Par Lost 3.376
Amid the Suns bright circle where thou sitst, Par Lost 4.578
Unspeakable, who sitst above these Heavens Par Lost 5.156

Sittest
Listen where thou art sitting Mask 860
Trinity ms 'art sitting' ←'sit'st'
Whilst thou bright Saint high sit'st in glory, Winchester 61
That sitt'st between the Cherubs *bright* Psalm 80, 5

Sittim
Israel in *Sittim* on thir march from *Nile* Par Lost 1.413
ms 'Sittim'

Sitting
Thus sitting, thus consulting, thus in Arms? Par Lost 2.164
For you, there sitting where ye durst not soare; Par Lost 4.829
Earth sitting still, when she alone receaves Par Lost 8.89
As sitting Queen ador'd on Beauties Throne, Par Reg 2.212
Thy right by sitting still or thus retiring? Par Reg 3.164
Will be for thee no sitting, or not long Par Reg 4.107
And view him sitting in the house, enobl'd Samson 1491
Amidst the flowry-kirtl'd *Naiades* Mask 254
Trinity ms 'amidst' ←'sitting amidst'
Lingering, and sitting by a new made grave, Mask 472
Bridgewater ms 'sittinge'
Listen where thou art sitting Mask 860
Thy rapt soul sitting in thine eyes: Penseroso 40
Sitting like a Goddes bright, Arcades 18
Trinity ms 'sitting' ←'seated'

Situate
Of pleasure situate in Hill and Dale) Par Lost 6.641
Situation
The dismal Situation waste and wilde, Par Lost 1.60
ms 'scituation'
Six
A Seraph wingd; six wings he wore, to shade Par Lost 5.277
Magnificent, his Six days work, a World; Par Lost 7.568
Creation and the Six dayes acts they sung, Par Lost 7.601
In six thou seest, and what if sev'nth to these Par Lost 8.128
What he *Almightie* styl'd, six Nights and Days Par Lost 9.137
Had measur'd twice six years, at our great Feast Par Reg 1.210
For one Carrier put down to make six bearers. Another 20
line not in 1640, 1657, 1658 texts
Sixth
The Sixt, and of Creation last arose Par Lost 7.449
Frequent; and of the Sixt day yet remain'd; Par Lost 7.504
So Ev'n and Morn accomplish'd the Sixt day: Par Lost 7.550
Size
As whom the Fables name of monstrous size, Par Lost 1.197
They Limb themselves, and colour, shape or size Par Lost 6.352
All of Gigantic size, *Goliah* chief. Samson 1249
Skies
So maist thou be translated to the skies, Mask 242
Bridgewater ms 'skyes'
B.M. ms 'Skyes'
From his watch-towre in the skies, Allegro 43
And looks commercing with the skies, Penseroso 39
His starry front low-rooft beneath the skies; Passion 18
Skiff
The Pilot of some small night-founder'd Skiff, Par Lost 1.204
ms 'skiff'
Skilful
As when a Ship by skilful Stearsman wrought Par Lost 9.513
Skill
Nor want we skill or Art, from whence to raise Par Lost 2.272
Well manag'd; of that skill the more thou know'st, Par Lost 8.573
The skill of Artifice or Office mean, Par Lost 9.39
And with what skill they had, together sowd, Par Lost 9.1112
That might require th' array of war, thy skill Par Reg 3.17
By what strange Parallax or Optic skill Par Reg 4.40
The Structure, skill of noblest Architects, Par Reg 4.52
Will ask thee skill; I to thy Fathers house Par Reg 4.552
Then with more cautious and instructed skill Samson 757
Not any boast of skill, but extreme shift Mask 273
What ere the skill of lesser gods can show, Arcades 79
Thy worth and skill exempts thee from the throng, Sonnet 13, 5
Skilled
Nor skilld nor studious, higher Argument Par Lost 9.42
Skill'd to retire, and in retiring draw Par Reg 2.161
Deep skill'd in all his mothers witcheries, Mask 523
Bridgewater ms 'skild'
Trinity ms 'deepe skill'd' ←'deepe learnt' ←'enur'd'
Of small regard to see to, yet well skill'd Mask 620
Skin
Sees his foule inside through his whited skin. Prose 10, 6
Skins
Thir nakedness with Skins of Beasts, or slain, Par Lost 10.217
Nor hee thir outward onely with the Skins Par Lost 10.220
A thousand fore-skins fell, the flower of *Palestin* Samson 144
Skip
The high, huge-bellied Mountains skip like Rams Psalm 114, 11
Skipped
Why fled the Ocean? And why skipt the Mountains? Psalm 114, 13
Skirt
From skirt to skirt a fierie Region, stretcht Par Lost 6.80
Skirted
Skirted his loines and thighes with downie Gold Par Lost 5.282
And the yellow-skirted *Fayes*, Nativity 235
Skirts
Dark with excessive bright thy skirts appeer, Par Lost 3.380
Till the Sun paint your fleecie skirts with Gold, Par Lost 5.187
Gladly behold though but his utmost skirts Par Lost 11.332
The fluid skirts of that same watrie Cloud, Par Lost 11.882
Sky
Hurld headlong flaming from th' Ethereal Skie Par Lost 1.45
ms 'skie'
As from a sky. The hasty multitude Par Lost 1.730
Wag'd in the troubl'd Skie, and Armies rush Par Lost 2.534
In th' Artick Sky, and from his horrid hair Par Lost 2.710
Shalt in the Sky appeer, and from thee send Par Lost 3.324
1667 'Skie'
Of *Chaos* blustring round, inclement skie; Par Lost 3.426
Dreaming by night under the open Skie, Par Lost 3.514
Smooth Lake, that to me seemd another Skie. Par Lost 4.459
Both turnd, and under op'n Skie ador'd Par Lost 4.721
The God that made both Skie, Air, Earth and Heav'n Par Lost 4.722
His stature reacht the Skie, and on his Crest Par Lost 4.988
Whether to deck with Clouds the uncolourd skie, Par Lost 5.189
He speeds, and through the vast Ethereal Skie Par Lost 5.267
Of fiercest opposition in mid Skie, Par Lost 6.314
On the Chrystallin Skie, in Saphir Thron'd. Par Lost 6.772
Into the Clouds, thir tops ascend the Skie: Par Lost 7.287
The mid Aereal Skie: Others on ground Par Lost 7.442
And gaz'd a while the ample Skie, till rais'd Par Lost 8.258
Skie lowr'd and muttering Thunder, som sad drops Par Lost 9.1002
Which now the Skie with various Face begins Par Lost 10.1064
Down from a Skie of Jasper lighted now Par Lost 11.209

Sky(*cont*)
Sent up amain; and now the thick'nd Skie Par Lost 11.742
Haile mixt with fire must rend th' *Egyptian* Skie Par Lost 12.182
As the noon Skie; more like to Goddesses Par Reg 2.156
As Earth and Skie would mingle; but my self Par Reg 4.453
What noise or shout was that? it tore the Skie. Samson 1472
On banks and scaffolds under Skie might stand; Samson 1610
These my skie robes spun out of *Iris* Wooff, Mask 83
Trinity ms 'sky'
Bridgewater ms 'skye'
But night sits monarch yet in the mid sky. Mask 957
Trinity ms 'skie'
Bridgewater ms 'skye'
1637 'skie'
Up in the broad fields of the sky: Mask 979
1637 'skie'
B.M. ms 'Sky'
Trinity ms 'skie'
Bridgewater ms 'skye'
Flames in the forehead of the morning sky: Lycidas 171
Trinity ms 'skie'
1638 'skie'
Sky-tinctured
Skie-tinctur'd grain. Like *Maia*'s son he stood, Par Lost 5.285
Slack
To respite or deceive, or slack the pain Par Lost 2.461
Well pleas'd they slack thir course, and many a League Par Lost 4.164
From his slack hand the Garland wreath'd for *Eve* Par Lost 9.892
When that comes think not thou to find me slack Par Reg 3.398
To stint th' enemy, and slack th' avengers brow Psalm 8, 7
Thou hast not Lord been slack, Psalm 85, 2
Slacken
Will slack'n, if his breath stir not thir flames. Par Lost 2.214
To slacken Virtue, and abate her edge, Par Reg 2.455
Slackened
My penance hath not slack'n'd, though my pardon Samson 738
Slackness
From Mans effeminate slackness it begins, Par Lost 11.634
Slain
Thir nakedness with Skins of Beasts, or slain, Par Lost 10.217
Out of thy loyns; th' unjust the just hath slain, Par Lost 11.455
By his own Nation, slaine for bringing Life; Par Lost 12.414
Them out of thine, who slew'st them many a slain. Samson 439
Oh it continues, they have slain my Son. Samson 1516
Among thy slain self-kill'd Samson 1664
Then all thy life had slain before. Samson 1668
Slayn by the bloody *Piemontese* that roll'd Sonnet 18, 7
They were repulst and slain, Psalm 83, 38
And like the slain *in bloody fight* Psalm 88, 19
There can be slaine Prose 11, 1
Slake
To slake his wrath whom sin hath made our foe Fair Inf 66
Slanderous
Bestuck with slandrous darts, and works of Faith Par Lost 12.536
Slant
Tine the slant Lightning, whose thwart flame driv'n down Par Lost 10.1075
Slaughter
For sin, on warr and mutual slaughter bent. Par Lost 6.506
On each hand slaughter and gigantic deeds. Par Lost 11.659
Man-slaughter, shall be held the highest pitch Par Lost 11.693
But rob and spoil, burn, slaughter, and enslave Par Reg 3.75
From slaughter of one foe could not ascend. Samson 1518
Man. Wearied with slaughter then or how? explain. Samson 1583
Slaughtered
And over heaps of slaughter'd walk his way? Samson 1530
Thee with thy slaughter'd foes in number more Samson 1667
Avenge O Lord thy slaughter'd Saints, whose bones Sonnet 18, 1
Slaughtering
Or drive away the slaughtering pestilence, Fair Inf 68
Slave
Lower then bondslave! Promise was that I Samson 38
Her Bond-slave; O indignity, O blot Samson 411
Har. With thee a Man condemn'd, a Slave enrol'd, Samson 1224
To thee I am bid say. Art thou our Slave, Samson 1392
Slaveries
By pains and slaveries, worse then death inflicted Samson 485
Slavery
True slavery, and that blindness worse then this, Samson 418
And freed us from the slavery Psalm 136, 81
Slaves
Too numerous; whence of guests he makes them slaves Par Lost 12.167
Or could of inward slaves make outward free? Par Reg 4.145
Eyeless in *Gaza* at the Mill with slaves, Samson 41
Into a Dungeon thrust, to work with Slaves? Samson 367
Among the Slaves and Asses thy comrades, Samson 1162
Slavish
In slavish habit, ill-fitted weeds Samson 122
Are but as slavish officers of vengeance, Mask 218
line not in Bridgewater ms
From burden, *and from slavish toyle* Psalm 81, 21
Slay
Whilome did slay his dearly-loved mate Fair Inf 24
Slaying
Chor. Thy Son is rather slaying them, that outcry Samson 1517
Sleek
His turret Crest, and sleek enamel'd Neck, Par Lost 9.525
And love to live in dimple sleek; Allegro 30
Sleek *Panope* with all her sisters play'd. Lycidas 99

Sleek(*cont*)
Trinity ms 'sleeke'
Those rugged names to our like mouths grow sleek — Sonnet 11, 10
Sleeked
That sleek't his tongue, and won so much on *Eve*, — Par Reg 4.5
Sleeking
Sleeking her soft alluring locks, — Mask 882
Bridgewater ms 'sleekinge'
Sleep
Shall hast'n, such a peal shall rouse thir sleep. — Par Lost 3.329
That day I oft remember, when from sleep — Par Lost 4.449
Successive, and the timely dew of sleep — Par Lost 4.614
This glorious sight, when sleep hath shut all eyes? — Par Lost 4.658
Unseen, both when we wake, and when we sleep: — Par Lost 4.678
And when we seek, as now, thy gift of sleep. — Par Lost 4.735
Showrd Roses, which the Morn repair'd. Sleep on — Par Lost 4.773
Here watching at the head of these that sleep? — Par Lost 4.826
Imploi'd it seems to violate sleep, and those — Par Lost 4.883
When *Adam* wak't, so customd, for his sleep — Par Lost 5.3
The trouble of thy thoughts this night in sleep — Par Lost 5.96
That what in sleep thou didst abhorr to dream, — Par Lost 5.120
Friendliest to sleep and silence, he resolv'd — Par Lost 5.668
Sleepst thou Companion dear, what sleep can close — Par Lost 5.673
Thy sleep dissent? new Laws thou seest impos'd; — Par Lost 5.679
Silence, and Sleep listning to thee will watch, — Par Lost 7.106
1669 'sleep'
Induc'd me. As new wak't from soundest sleep — Par Lost 8.253
Pensive I sate me down; there gentle sleep — Par Lost 8.287
Of sleep, which instantly fell on me, call'd — Par Lost 8.458
With act intelligential; but his sleep — Par Lost 9.190
The solace of thir sin, till dewie sleep — Par Lost 9.1044
Made erre, was now exhal'd, and grosser sleep — Par Lost 9.1049
And sleep secure; his dreadful voice no more — Par Lost 10.779
Here sleep below while thou to foresight wak'st, — Par Lost 11.368
Or theirs whom he redeems, a death like sleep, — Par Lost 12.434
For God is also in sleep, and Dreams advise, — Par Lost 12.611
Fasting he went to sleep, and fasting wak'd. — Par Reg 2.284
Disturb'd his sleep; and either Tropic now — Par Reg 4.409
Mine eie to harbour sleep, or thoughts to rest. — Samson 459
Sleep hath forsook and giv'n me o're — Samson 629
What hath night to do with sleep? — Mask 122
Bridgewater ms 'sleepe'
1637 'sleepe'
Trinity ms 'sleepe'
That draw the litter of close-curtain'd sleep. — Mask 554
Trinity ms 'sleepe'
1637 'sleepe'
Bridgewater ms 'sleepe'
Entice the dewy-feather'd Sleep; — Penseroso 146
Yet first to those ychain'd in sleep, — Nativity 155
Both lay me down and sleep — Psalm 4, 38
Among the dead *to sleep*, — Psalm 88, 18
Sleepest
Why sleepst thou *Eve?* now is the pleasant time, — Par Lost 5.38
Sleepst thou Companion dear, what sleep can close — Par Lost 5.673
Sleep'st by the fable of *Bellerus* old, — Lycidas 160
Sleeping
On duty, sleeping found by whom they dread, — Par Lost 1.333
Though sleeping, where I lay, and saw the shape — Par Lost 8.463
The Serpent sleeping, in whose mazie foulds — Par Lost 9.161
The Serpent: him fast sleeping soon he found — Par Lost 9.182
Lay sleeping ran before, but found her wak't; — Par Lost 12.608
Nor sleeping him nor waking harm'd, his walk — Par Reg 1.311
Smote *Sisera* sleeping through the Temples nail'd. — Samson 990
Close-banded durst attaque me, no not sleeping, — Samson 1113
Her sleeping Lord with Handmaid Lamp attending. — Nativity 242
Strew all their blessings on thy sleeping Head. — Vacation 64
Sleepless
Though after sleepless Night; for see the Morn, — Par Lost 11.173
Brings dangers, troubles, cares, and sleepless nights — Par Reg 2.460
Sleeps
Ascending, while the North wind sleeps, o'respread — Par Lost 2.489
And oft though wisdom wake, suspicion sleeps — Par Lost 3.686
Stretcht like a Promontorie sleeps or swimmes, — Par Lost 7.414
With inoffensive pace that spinning sleeps — Par Lost 8.164
Sleepy
Let such bethink them, if the sleepy drench — Par Lost 2.73
Sleet
Sharp sleet of arrowie showers against the face — Par Reg 3.324
Sleight
Of power to cheat the eye with blear illusion, — Mask 155
Trinity ms 'bleare' ←'blind' ←'sleight'
Sleights
Whatever sleights none would suspicious mark, — Par Lost 9.92
1667 'fleights'
Slender
Shee as a vail down to the slender waste — Par Lost 4.304
Each Flour of slender stalk, whose head though gay — Par Lost 9.428
What slender Youth bedew'd with liquid odours — Horace 1
Slept
Pan or *Silvanus* never slept, nor Nymph, — Par Lost 4.707
These lulld by Nightingales imbraceing slept, — Par Lost 4.771
Celestial Tabernacles, where they slept — Par Lost 5.654
Fearless unfeard he slept: in at his Mouth — Par Lost 9.187
Of Trees thick interwoven; there he slept, — Par Reg 2.263
Into the Desert, and how there he slept — Par Reg 2.271
But shelter'd slept in vain, for at his head — Par Reg 4.407
In ruine reconcil'd: nor slept the winds — Par Reg 4.413

Slept(*cont*)
I lay and slept, I wak'd again, — Psalm 3, 13
Sleptest
As once thou slepst, while Shee to life was formd. — Par Lost 11.369
Slew
Who slew his Brother; studious they appere — Par Lost 11.609
Ten thousandfould the sin of him who slew — Par Lost 11.678
Slewest
Them out of thine, who slew'st them many a slain. — Samson 439
Slide
Half unpronounc't, slide through my infant-lipps, — Vacation 4
Sea-paths in shoals do slide. And know no dearth. — Psalm 8, 22
So shall it never slide — Psalm 86, 40
Sliding
Smooth sliding without step, last led me up — Par Lost 8.302
My sliding Chariot stayes, — Mask 892
Bridgewater ms 'slydinge'
Smooth-sliding *Mincius*, crown'd with vocall reeds, — Lycidas 86
Trinity ms 'smooth sliding' ←'soft sliding'
She crown'd with Olive green, came softly sliding — Nativity 47
Slight
At one slight bound high over leap'd all bound — Par Lost 4.181
If they transgress, and slight that sole command, — Par Lost 7.47
Think not so slight of glory; therein least — Par Reg 3.109
On no slight grounds thy safety; hear, and mark — Par Reg 3.349
I see all offers made by me how slight — Par Reg 4.155
How slight the gift was, hung it in my Hair. — Samson 59
Thy Husband, slight me, sell me, and forgo me; — Samson 940
Come nearer, part not hence so slight inform'd; — Samson 1229
Not those new fangled toys, and triming slight — Vacation 19
Slighted
To tend the homely slighted Shepherds trade, — Lycidas 65
Trinity ms 'slighted' ←'slighteds'
Slightest
The slightest, easiest, readiest recompence — Par Reg 3.128
Slighting
At every sudden slighting quite abasht: — Par Reg 2.224
Slightly
The facil gates of hell too slightly barrd. — Par Lost 4.967
He slightly view'd, and slightly over-pass'd; — Par Reg 2.198
Slime
Into a Beast, and mixt with bestial slime, — Par Lost 9.165
And with *Asphaltic* slime; broad as the Gate, — Par Lost 10.298
Ingenderd in the *Pythian* Vale on slime, — Par Lost 10.530
Slimy
Solid or slimie, as in raging Sea — Par Lost 10.286
Sling
With suckt and glutted offal, at one sling — Par Lost 10.633
Slingers
Archers, and Slingers, Cataphracts and Spears. — Samson 1619
Slip
Let us not slip th' occasion, whether scorn, — Par Lost 1.178
If you let slip time, like a neglected rose — Mask 743
line not in Bridgewater ms
So have I seen som tender slip — Winchester 35
Slipped
Slip't from the fold, or young Kid lost his dam, — Mask 498
Trinity ms 'slip't' ←'leapt'
1673 'slipt'
Bridgewater ms 'slipt'
Slippered
By *Thetis* tinsel-slipper'd feet, — Mask 877
Bridgewater ms 'tinsel-slipperd'
Slipping
When slipping from thy Mothers eye thou went'st — Par Reg 4.216
Slips
Each fetter'd Ghost slips to his severall grave, — Nativity 234
Slits
And slits the thin spun life. But not the praise, — Lycidas 76
Slope
Drivn backward slope thir pointing spires, and rowld — Par Lost 1.223
Down the slope hills, disperst, or in a Lake, — Par Lost 4.261
Bore him slope downward to the Sun now fall'n — Par Lost 4.591
And the slope Sun his upward beam — Mask 98
Sloped
Toward Heav'ns descent had slop'd his westering wheel. — Lycidas 31
Trinity ms 'sloapt'
Sloth
Counsel'd ignoble ease, and peaceful sloath, — Par Lost 2.227
I see that most through sloth had rather serve, — Par Lost 6.166
Shall change thir course to pleasure, ease, and sloth, — Par Lost 11.794
Slothful
Timorous and slothful: yet he pleas'd the ear, — Par Lost 2.117
Slough
He's here stuck in a slough, and overthrown. — Carrier 4
Slow
Untam'd reluctance, and revenge though slow, — Par Lost 2.337
Farr off from these a slow and silent stream, — Par Lost 2.582
Light-arm'd or heavy, sharp, smooth, swift or slow, — Par Lost 2.902
Mine ear shall not be slow, mine eye not shut. — Par Lost 3.193
Satan had journied on, pensive and slow; — Par Lost 4.173
Under spred Ensignes moving nigh, in slow — Par Lost 6.533
Speed almost Spiritual; mee thou thinkst not slow, — Par Lost 8.110
These changes in the Heav'ns, though slow, produc'd — Par Lost 10.692
And slow descends, with somthing heav'nly fraught. — Par Lost 11.207
They hand in hand with wandring steps and slow, — Par Lost 12.648
And Duty; Zeal and Duty are not slow; — Par Reg 3.172
Why move thy feet so slow to what is best, — Par Reg 3.224

Slow(*cont*)
By slow *Meander*'s margent green, Mask 232
Bridgewater ms 'slowe'
Rose like a steam of rich distill'd Perfumes, Mask 556
Trinity ms 'rich' ← 'slow' ← 'the softe steame of'
Where the bow'd welkin slow doth bend, Mask 1015
Trinity ms 'slow' ← 'low' ← 'cleere'
& halfe the slow unfadom'd Stygian poole Mask Tr. ms 10.15
Swinging slow with sullen roar; Penseroso 76
Next *Camus*, reverend Sire, went footing slow, Lycidas 103
Yet be it less or more, or soon or slow, Sonnet 7, 9
Then will he come, and not be slow Psalm 85, 55
Slow to be angry, and *art stil'd* Psalm 86, 55
Slow-endeavouring
For whilst to th' shame of slow-endeavouring art, Shakespear 9
1632 'slow-endevouring'
1640 'slow-endevouring'
Slowest
Mends not her slowest pace for prayers or cries. Par Lost 10.859
Slowly
Slowly descended, and with right aspect Par Lost 4.541
Slow-paced
Will prove no sudden, but a slow-pac't evill, Par Lost 10.963
Sluice
Each in thir Chrystal sluce, hee ere they fell Par Lost 5.133
Divine *Alpheus*, who by secret sluse, Arcades 30
Sluiced
Sluc'd from the Lake, a second multitude Par Lost 1.702
Sluices
His Sluces, as the Heav'n his windows shut. Par Lost 11.849
Slumber
To slumber here, as in the Vales of Heav'n? Par Lost 1.321
Rous'd from the slumber, on that fiery Couch, Par Lost 1.377
With their grave Saws in slumber ly. Mask 110
Yet they in pleasing slumber lull'd the sense, Mask 260
In slumber soft, and on the ground Mask 1001
line not in Bridgewater ms
From golden slumber on a bed Allegro 146
Slumbered
That slumberd, wakes the bitter memorie Par Lost 4.24
Slumbering
Him haply slumbring on the *Norway* foam Par Lost 1.203
And dictates to me slumbring, or inspires Par Lost 9.23
Chearly rouse the slumbring morn, Allegro 54
Awakes the slumbring leaves, or tasseld horn Arcades 57
Slumbers
Visit'st my slumbers Nightly, or when Morn Par Lost 7.29
Slumbrous
Now falling with soft slumbrous weight inclines Par Lost 4.615
Slunk
Were slunk, all but the wakeful Nightingale; Par Lost 4.602
That all was lost. Back to the Thicket slunk Par Lost 9.784
Hee after *Eve* seduc't, unminded slunk Par Lost 10.332
Sly
His Lithe Proboscis; close the Serpent sly Par Lost 4.347
But with sly circumspection, and began Par Lost 4.537
And thou sly hypocrite, who now wouldst seem Par Lost 4.957
By sly assault; and somwhere nigh at hand Par Lost 9.256
So talk'd the spirited sly Snake; and *Eve* Par Lost 9.613
For Satan with slye preface to return Par Reg 2.115
By sly enticement gives his banefull cup, Mask 525
1637 'slie'
Bridgewater ms 'slye'
Where that damn'd wisard hid in sly disguise Mask 571
Bridgewater ms 'slye'
1637 'slie'
Small
The Pilot of some small night-founder'd Skiff, Par Lost 1.204
Could merit more then that small infantry Par Lost 1.575
Precedence, none, whose portion is so small Par Lost 2.33
Then most conspicuous, when great things of small, Par Lost 2.258
The tempting stream, with one small drop to loose Par Lost 2.607
Great things with small) then when *Bellona* storms, Par Lost 2.922
Though distant farr som small reflection gaines Par Lost 3.428
Starr interpos'd, however small he sees, Par Lost 5.258
Of God inspir'd, small store will serve, where store, Par Lost 5.322
Great things by small, If Natures concord broke, Par Lost 6.311
Of evil then so small as easie think Par Lost 6.437
Thir small peculiar, though from human sight Par Lost 7.368
Of future, in small room large heart enclos'd, Par Lost 7.486
Though, in comparison of Heav'n, so small, Par Lost 8.92
Lodg'd in a small partition, and the rest Par Lost 8.105
Fast by a Fountain, one small Thicket past Par Lost 9.628
And elegant, of Sapience no small part, Par Lost 9.1018
So, if great things to small may be compar'd, Par Lost 10.306
Of every Beast, and Bird, and Insect small Par Lost 11.734
All left, in one small bottom swum imbark't. Par Lost 11.753
Still overcoming evil, and by small Par Lost 12.566
His birth to our just fear gave no small cause, Par Reg 1.66
Small consolation then, were Man adjoyn'd: Par Reg 1.403
How many have with a smile made small account Par Reg 2.193
Of whom to be disprais'd were no small praise? Par Reg 3.56
On seven small Hills, with Palaces adorn'd, Par Reg 4.35
To *Capreae* an Island small but strong Par Reg 4.92
Small things with greatest) in *Irassa* strove Par Reg 4.564
As a petty enterprise of small enforce. Samson 1223
With no small profit daily to my owners. Samson 1261
That crawls along the side of yon small hill, Mask 295
Small(*cont*)
Trinity ms 'smal'
Bridgewater ms 'smale'
But here thy sword can do thee little stead, Mask 611
Trinity ms 'little stead' ← 'small availe' ← 'little stead'
Of small regard to see to, yet well skill'd Mask 620
Bridgewater ms 'smale'
Amongst the rest a small unsightly root, Mask 629
Bridgewater ms 'smale'
Small loss it is that thence can come unto thee, Vacation 9
For this same small neglect that I have made: Vacation 16
Smaller
From Branch to Branch the smaller Birds with song Par Lost 7.433
Smallest
Now less then smallest Dwarfs, in narrow room Par Lost 1.779
Thus incorporeal Spirits to smallest forms Par Lost 1.789
Of smallest Magnitude close by the Moon. Par Lost 2.1053
Who out of smallest things could without end Par Lost 6.137
For wings, and smallest Lineaments exact Par Lost 7.477
What to the smallest tittle thou shalt say Par Reg 1.450
Smart
Short intermission bought with double smart. Par Lost 4.102
That fellowship in pain divides not smart, Par Reg 1.401
To stand 'twixt us and our deserved smart Fair Inf 69
And seals obedience first with wounding smart Circum 25
Smeared
Smeard round with Pitch, and in the side a dore Par Lost 11.731
Smear'd with gumms of glutenous heat Mask 917
Bridgewater ms 'smeard'
Smell
Lur'd with the smell of infant blood, to dance Par Lost 2.664
Chear'd with the grateful smell old Ocean smiles. Par Lost 4.165
All Trees of noblest kind for sight, smell, taste; Par Lost 4.217
Breathing the smell of field and grove, attune Par Lost 4.265
Which he had pluckt; the pleasant savourie smell Par Lost 5.84
Of sense, whereby they hear, see, smell, touch, taste, Par Lost 5.411
I mean of Taste, Sight, Smell, Herbs, Fruits, and Flours, Par Lost 8.527
With grateful Smell, forth came the human pair Par Lost 9.197
The smell of Grain, or tedded Grass, or Kine, Par Lost 9.450
Then smell of sweetest Fenel or the Teats Par Lost 9.581
An eager appetite, rais'd by the smell Par Lost 9.740
New gatherd, and ambrosial smell diffus'd. Par Lost 9.852
So saying, with delight he snuff'd the smell Par Lost 10.272
The smell of peace toward Mankinde, let him live Par Lost 11.38
With what to sight or smell was sweet; from thee Par Lost 11.281
That fragrant smell diffus'd, in order stood Par Reg 2.351
Sparkling, out-pow'rd, the flavor, or the smell, Samson 544
Smelling
With Flowers, Garlands, and sweet-smelling Herbs Par Lost 4.709
Her bosom smelling sweet: and these scarce blown, Par Lost 7.319
Offer sweet smelling Gumms and Fruits and Flours: Par Lost 11.327
Smells
That open now thir choicest bosom'd smells Par Lost 5.127
With flourets deck't and fragrant smells; but *Eve* Par Lost 5.379
From their soft wings, and *Flora*'s earliest smells. Par Reg 2.365
Nard, and *Cassia*'s balmy smels. Mask 991
1637 'smells'
Bridgewater ms 'smells'
Trinity ms 'smells'
Smelt
Which once smelt sweet, now stinks as odiously; Prose 4, 2
Smile
Grinnd horrible a gastly smile, to hear Par Lost 2.846
Pleas'd, out of Heaven shalt look down and smile, Par Lost 3.257
Reigns here and revels; not in the bought smile Par Lost 4.765
As with a smile more bright'nd, thus repli'd. Par Lost 8.368
To whom the Angel with a smile that glow'd Par Lost 8.618
How many have with a smile made small account Par Reg 2.193
To gloss upon, and censuring, frown or smile? Samson 948
Smile she or lowre: Samson 1057
Smiled
Impurpl'd with Celestial Roses smil'd. Par Lost 3.364
Youth smil'd Celestial, and to every Limb Par Lost 3.638
Smil'd with superior Love, as *Jupiter* Par Lost 4.499
They came, that like *Pomona*'s Arbour smil'd Par Lost 5.378
And with fresh Flourets Hill and Valley smil'd. Par Lost 6.784
Consummate lovly smil'd; Aire, Water, Earth, Par Lost 7.502
Birds on the branches warbling; all things smil'd, Par Lost 8.265
A bough of fairest fruit that downie smil'd, Par Lost 9.851
Perpetual smil'd on Earth with vernant Flours, Par Lost 10.679
Of darknes till it smil'd: I have oft heard Mask 252
Smiles
Chear'd with the grateful smell old Ocean smiles. Par Lost 4.165
Nor gentle purpose, nor endearing smiles Par Lost 4.337
On *Juno* smiles, when he impregns the Clouds Par Lost 4.500
Then when fair Morning first smiles on the World, Par Lost 5.124
Looks intervene and smiles, or object new Par Lost 9.222
Of looks and smiles, for smiles from Reason flow, Par Lost 9.239
Occasion which now smiles, behold alone Par Lost 9.480
Ignobly, to the traines and to the smiles Par Lost 11.624
Nods, and Becks, and Wreathed Smiles, Allegro 28
Smiling
Disdainfully half smiling thus repli'd. Par Lost 4.903
Sure pledge of day, that crownst the smiling Morn Par Lost 5.168
And smiling to his onely Son thus said. Par Lost 5.718
Her rosie progress smiling; let us forth, Par Lost 11.175
Of Angels, thus to *Gabriel* smiling spake. Par Reg 1.129
The Babe lies yet in smiling Infancy, Nativity 151

Smiling(*cont*)
Or wert thou that sweet smiling Youth! Fair Inf 53
Smit
Smit with the love of sacred Song; but chief Par Lost 3.29
Smite
The sword of *Satan* with steep force to smite Par Lost 6.324
Stands ready to smite once, and smite no more. Lycidas 131
1638 'smites no'
Smites
Or what the cross dire-looking Planet smites, Arcades 52
Smitten
But Satan smitten with amazement fell Par Reg 4.562
Smoke
With stench and smoak: Such resting found the sole Par Lost 1.237
ms 'smoake'
Belch'd fire and rowling smoak; the rest entire Par Lost 1.671
Cast forth redounding smoak and ruddy flame. Par Lost 2.889
He spreads for flight, and in the surging smoak Par Lost 2.928
To darken all the Hill, and smoak to rowl Par Lost 6.57
But soon obscur'd with smoak, all Heav'n appeerd, Par Lost 6.585
Of smoak and bickering flame, and sparkles dire; Par Lost 6.766
Above the smoak and stirr of this dim spot, Mask 5
Bridgewater ms 'smoake'
1637 'smoake'
Trinity ms 'smoake' ←'smoke'
Or like the sons of *Vulcan* vomit smoak, Mask 655
Trinity ms 'smoake'
Bridgewater ms 'smoake'
1637 'smoake'
Smoked
Or Altar smoak'd; yet who more oft then hee Par Lost 1.493
Smokes
Hard by, a Cottage chimney smokes, Allegro 81
Smoking
Thy smoaking wrath, *and angry brow* Psalm 80, 19
Smoky
With smoaky rafters, then in tapstry Halls Mask 324
1637 'smoakie'
Bridgewater ms 'smoakie'
Trinity ms 'smoakie'
Smooth
While smooth *Adonis* from his native Rock Par Lost 1.450
Within, her ample spaces, o're the smooth Par Lost 1.725
Soon learnd, now milder, and thus answerd smooth. Par Lost 2.816
Light-arm'd or heavy, sharp, smooth, swift or slow, Par Lost 2.902
Smooth Lake, that to me seemd another Skie. Par Lost 4.459
Then that smooth watry image; back I turnd, Par Lost 4.480
Rough, or smooth rin'd, or bearded husk, or shell Par Lost 5.342
In jointed Armour watch: on smooth the Seale, Par Lost 7.409
And beares thee soft with the smooth Air along, Par Lost 8.166
Smooth sliding without step, last led me up Par Lost 8.302
Some Tree whose broad smooth Leaves together sowd, Par Lost 9.1095
Smooth, easie, inoffensive down to Hell. Par Lost 10.305
Of Goddesses, so blithe, so smooth, so gay, Par Lost 11.615
Dissembl'd, and this Answer smooth return'd. Par Reg 1.467
Smooth on the tongue discourst, pleasing to th' ear, Par Reg 1.479
Severest temper, smooth the rugged'st brow, Par Reg 2.164
The next to fabling fell and smooth conceits, Par Reg 4.295
In feign'd Religion, smooth hypocrisie. Samson 872
Happy that house! his way to peace is smooth: Samson 1049
La. As smooth as *Hebe*'s their unrazor'd lips. Mask 290
That with moist curb sways the smooth Severn stream, Mask 825
Bridgewater ms 'smoote'
O're the smooth enameld green Arcades 84
O Fountain *Arethuse*, and thou honour'd floud, Lycidas 85
Trinity ms 'honour'd' ←'fam'd' ←'smooth'
Or *Medway* smooth, or Royal Towred *Thame*. Vacation 100
That with smooth aire couldst humor best our tongue. Sonnet 13, 8
An open grave their throat, their tongue they smooth. Psalm 5, 28
Smooth-dittied
Who with his soft Pipe, and smooth-dittied Song, Mask 86
Bridgewater ms 'smooth dittied'
1673 'smooth dittied'
Trinity ms 'smoth dittied'
Smoothed
Flie to and fro, or on the smoothed Plank, Par Lost 1.772
Each perturbation smooth'd with outward calme, Par Lost 4.120
Smoother
On smoother, till *Favonius* re-inspire Sonnet 20, 6
Smooth-haired
That in their green shops weave the smooth-hair'd silk Mask 716
Trinity ms 'smooth haird'
Bridgewater ms 'smoote-haired'
Smoothing
At every fall smoothing the Raven doune Mask 251
Bridgewater ms 'smoothinge'
Smoothing the rugged brow of night, Penseroso 58
Smoothly
But now my task is smoothly don, Mask 1012
Trinity ms 'smoothly' ←'well is don'
Smoothly the waters kist, Nativity 65
Smooths
So smooths her charming tones, that Gods own ear Par Lost 5.626
Smooth-shaven
On the dry smooth-shaven Green, Penseroso 66
Smooth-sliding
Smooth-sliding *Mincius*, crown'd with vocall reeds, Lycidas 86
Trinity ms 'smooth sliding' ←'soft sliding'

Smote
Smote on him sore besides, vaulted with Fire; Par Lost 1.298
Both where the morning Sun first warmly smote Par Lost 4.244
Saw where the Sword of *Michael* smote, and fell'd Par Lost 6.250
Level'd, with such impetuous furie smote, Par Lost 6.591
As with a Trident smote, and fix't as firm Par Lost 10.295
Smote him into the Midriff with a stone Par Lost 11.445
Smote *Sisera* sleeping through the Temples nail'd. Samson 990
Smote the first-born of *Egypt* Land. Psalm 136, 38
1645 printed 'mote'
Hast smote ere now Psalm 3, 20
Smouldering
While the red fire, and smouldring clouds out brake: Nativity 159
Smutty
Against a rumord Warr, the Smuttie graine Par Lost 4.817
Snake
From sharpest sight: for in the wilie Snake, Par Lost 9.91
So talk'd the spirited sly Snake; and *Eve* Par Lost 9.613
So glister'd the dire Snake, and into fraud Par Lost 9.643
Or as the Snake with youthful Coate repaid; Par Lost 10.218
Th' excepted Tree, nor with the Snake conspir'd, Par Lost 11.426
Entangl'd with a poysnous bosom snake, Samson 763
Snaky
Had not the Snakie Sorceress that sat Par Lost 2.724
Thir Snakie foulds, and added wings. First crept Par Lost 7.484
Climbing, sat thicker then the snakie locks Par Lost 10.559
His easie steps; girded with snaky wiles, Par Reg 1.120
Not *Typhon* huge ending in snaky twine: Nativity 226
Snaky-headed
What was that snaky-headed *Gorgon* sheild Mask 447
1637 'snakie headed'
Trinity ms 'snakie-headed'
Bridgewater ms 'snakie headed'
Snare
Haply so scap'd his mortal snare; for now Par Lost 4.8
To hellish falshood, snare them. But for thee Par Lost 10.873
A help, became thy snare; to mee reproach Par Lost 11.165
With Warr and hostile snare such as refuse Par Lost 12.31
And run not sooner to his fatal snare? Par Reg 1.441
The wise mans cumbrance if not snare, more apt Par Reg 2.454
That specious Monster, my accomplisht snare. Samson 230
Then swoll'n with pride into the snare I fell Samson 532
To bring my feet again into the snare Samson 931
How sweet thou sing'st, how neer the deadly snare! Mask 567
Snares
Disturbances on Earth through Femal snares, Par Lost 10.897
Not force, but well couch't fraud, well woven snares, Par Reg 1.97
Contempts, and scorns, and snares, and violence, Par Reg 3.191
In Paradise to tempt; his snares are broke: Par Reg 4.611
Might easily have shook off all her snares: Samson 409
Hear what assaults I had, what snares besides, Samson 845
And hugg him into snares. When once her eye Mask 164
Trinity ms 'snares' ←'nets'
Dangers, and snares, and wrongs, and worse then so, Passion 11
Snatch
Mock us with his blest sight, then snatch him hence, Par Reg 2.56
snatch us from earth a while Musick Tr. ms 4.07
Snatched
So snatcht will not exempt us from the paine Par Lost 10.1025
Had not a Cloud descending snatch'd him thence Par Lost 11.670
O ye mistook, ye should have snatcht his wand Mask 815
Trinity ms 'snatch't'
Sneeze
And harmless, if not wholsom, as a sneeze Par Reg 4.458
Snow
Scowls ore the dark'nd lantskip Snow, or showre; Par Lost 2.491
Of ancient pile; all else deep snow and ice, Par Lost 2.591
Or East or West, which had forbid the Snow Par Lost 10.685
And snow and haile and stormie gust and flaw, Par Lost 10.698
Th' inclement Seasons, Rain, Ice, Hail and Snow, Par Lost 10.1063
To hide her guilty front with innocent Snow, Nativity 39
And hills of Snow and lofts of piled Thunder, Vacation 42
Snow-soft
Down he descended from his Snow-soft chaire, Fair Inf 19
Snowy
And *Ida* known, thence on the Snowy top Par Lost 1.515
ms 'snowy'
Whose snowie ridge the roving *Tartar* bounds, Par Lost 3.432
By *Astracan* over the Snowie Plaines Par Lost 10.432
Nor breath of Vernal Air from snowy *Alp*. Samson 628
That tumble down the snowy hills: Mask 927
Trinity ms 'snowie'
Bridgewater ms 'snowie'
1637 'snowie'
Snuffed
So saying, with delight he snuff'd the smell Par Lost 10.272
So
Favour'd of Heav'n so highly, to fall off Par Lost 1.30
From what highth fall'n, so much the stronger prov'd Par Lost 1.92
Who from the terrour of this Arm so late Par Lost 1.113
So spake th' Apostate Angel, though in pain, Par Lost 1.125
That we may so suffice his vengeful ire, Par Lost 1.148
Which oft times may succeed, so as perhaps Par Lost 1.166
So stretcht out huge in length the Arch-fiend lay Par Lost 1.209
For that celestial light? Be it so, since he Par Lost 1.245
So *Satan* spake, and him *Beelzebub* Par Lost 1.271
Of hope in fears and dangers, heard so oft Par Lost 1.275
Nathless he so endur'd, till on the Beach Par Lost 1.299

So(*cont*)

And broken Chariot Wheels, so thick bestrown	Par Lost 1.311
He call'd so loud, that all the hollow Deep	Par Lost 1.314
So numberless were those bad Angels seen	Par Lost 1.344
Can either Sex assume, or both; so soft	Par Lost 1.424
So *Jove* usurping reign'd: these first in *Creet*	Par Lost 1.514
Perplexes Monarchs. Dark'n'd so, yet shon	Par Lost 1.599
So as not either to provoke, or dread	Par Lost 1.644
Space may produce new Worlds; whereof so rife	Par Lost 1.650
Thir State affairs. So thick the aerie crowd	Par Lost 1.775
Precedence, none, whose portion is so small	Par Lost 2.33
Will he, so wise, let loose at once his ire,	Par Lost 2.155
That so ordains: this was at first resolv'd,	Par Lost 2.201
If we were wise, against so great a foe	Par Lost 2.202
Contending, and so doubtful what might fall.	Par Lost 2.203
Eternity so spent in worship paid	Par Lost 2.248
They dreaded worse then Hell: so much the fear	Par Lost 2.293
Princes of Hell? for so the popular vote	Par Lost 2.313
Of him who rules above; so was his will	Par Lost 2.351
Faded so soon. Advise if this be worth	Par Lost 2.376
So deep a malice, to confound the race	Par Lost 2.382
So hardie as to proffer or accept	Par Lost 2.425
To him who Reigns, and so much to him due	Par Lost 2.454
And so refus'd might in opinion stand	Par Lost 2.471
All in one moment, and so neer the brink;	Par Lost 2.609
Ply stemming nightly toward the Pole. So seem'd	Par Lost 2.642
So spake the grieslie terrour, and in shape,	Par Lost 2.704
So speaking and so threatning, grew tenfold	Par Lost 2.705
So frownd the mighty Combatants, that Hell	Par Lost 2.719
Grew darker at thir frown, so matcht they stood;	Par Lost 2.720
To meet so great a foe: and now great deeds	Par Lost 2.722
So strange thy outcry, and thy words so strange	Par Lost 2.737
Now in thine eye so foul, once deemd so fair	Par Lost 2.748
When ever that shall be; so Fate pronounc'd.	Par Lost 2.809
So wide they stood, and like a Furnace mouth	Par Lost 2.888
The guarded Gold: So eagerly the fiend	Par Lost 2.947
That little which is left so to defend,	Par Lost 2.1000
So much the neerer danger; go and speed;	Par Lost 2.1008
So he with difficulty and labour hard	Par Lost 2.1021
So thick a drop serene hath quencht thir Orbs,	Par Lost 3.25
So were I equal'd with them in renown,	Par Lost 3.34
So much the rather thou Celestial light	Par Lost 3.51
Wide interrupt can hold; so bent he seems	Par Lost 3.84
Sole pledge of his obedience: So will fall,	Par Lost 3.95
So were created, nor can justly accuse	Par Lost 3.112
So without least impulse or shadow of Fate,	Par Lost 3.120
Both what they judge and what they choose; for so	Par Lost 3.123
Through Heav'n and Earth, so shall my glorie excel,	Par Lost 3.133
Thy creature late so lov'd, thy youngest Son	Par Lost 3.151
So should thy goodness and thy greatness both	Par Lost 3.165
Elect above the rest; so is my will:	Par Lost 3.184
Affecting God-head, and so loosing all,	Par Lost 3.206
Dwels in all Heaven charitie so deare?	Par Lost 3.216
Happie for man, so coming; he her aide	Par Lost 3.232
As in him perish all men, so in thee	Par Lost 3.287
Receive new life. So Man, as is most just,	Par Lost 3.294
So Heav'nly love shall outdoo Hellish hate	Par Lost 3.298
So dearly to redeem what Hellish hate	Par Lost 3.300
So easily destroy'd, and still destroyes	Par Lost 3.301
Found worthiest to be so by being Good,	Par Lost 3.310
Not so on Man; him through their malice fall'n,	Par Lost 3.400
So strictly, but much more to pitie encline:	Par Lost 3.402
So strictly, but much more to pitie enclin'd,	Par Lost 3.405
So on this windie Sea of Land, the Fiend	Par Lost 3.440
Here Pilgrims roam, that stray'd so farr to seek	Par Lost 3.476
Over the *Promis'd Land* to God so dear,	Par Lost 3.531
So wide the op'ning seemd, where bounds were set	Par Lost 3.538
At sight of all this World beheld so faire.	Par Lost 3.554
So high above the circling Canopie	Par Lost 3.556
So wondrously was set his Station bright.	Par Lost 3.587
Philosophers in vain so long have sought,	Par Lost 3.601
Th' Arch-chimic Sun so farr from us remote	Par Lost 3.609
Here in the dark so many precious things	Par Lost 3.611
Of colour glorious and effect so rare?	Par Lost 3.612
No where so cleer, sharp'nd his visual ray	Par Lost 3.620
Sutable grace diffus'd, so well he feignd;	Par Lost 3.639
All these his works so wondrous he ordaind,	Par Lost 3.665
So spake the false dissembler unperceivd;	Par Lost 3.681
(So call that opposite fair Starr) her aide	Par Lost 3.727
Haply so scap'd his mortal snare; for now	Par Lost 4.8
And wrought but malice; lifted up so high	Par Lost 4.49
So burthensome still paying, still to ow;	Par Lost 4.53
Chose freely what it now so justly rues.	Par Lost 4.72
How dearly I abide that boast so vaine,	Par Lost 4.87
Where wounds of deadly hate have peirc'd so deep:	Par Lost 4.99
And heavier fall: so should I purchase deare	Par Lost 4.101
So farwel Hope, and with Hope farwel Fear,	Par Lost 4.108
So on he fares, and to the border comes,	Par Lost 4.131
When God hath showrd the earth; so lovely seemd	Par Lost 4.152
So entertaind those odorous sweets the Fiend	Par Lost 4.166
But further way found none, so thick entwin'd,	Par Lost 4.174
So clomb this first grand Thief into Gods Fould:	Par Lost 4.192
So since into his Church lewd Hirelings climbe.	Par Lost 4.193
Of immortality. So little knows	Par Lost 4.201
So passd they naked on, nor shund the sight	Par Lost 4.319
So hand in hand they passd, the lovliest pair	Par Lost 4.321
With wonder, and could love, so lively shines	Par Lost 4.363
Happie, but for so happie ill secur'd	Par Lost 4.370

So(*cont*)

And mutual amitie so streight, so close,	Par Lost 4.376
So spake the Fiend, and with necessitie,	Par Lost 4.393
So various, not to taste that onely Tree	Par Lost 4.423
So neer grows Death to Life, what ere Death is,	Par Lost 4.425
Among so many signes of power and rule	Par Lost 4.429
Free leave so large to all things else, and choice	Par Lost 4.434
So farr the happier Lot, enjoying thee	Par Lost 4.446
Praeeminent by so much odds, while thou	Par Lost 4.447
So spake our general Mother, and with eyes	Par Lost 4.492
So saying, his proud step he scornful turn'd,	Par Lost 4.536
So minded, have oreleapt these earthie bounds	Par Lost 4.583
So promis'd hee, and *Uriel* to his charge	Par Lost 4.589
Unargu'd I obey; so God ordains,	Par Lost 4.636
So saying, on he led his radiant Files,	Par Lost 4.797
So started up in his own shape the Fiend.	Par Lost 4.819
So sudden to behold the grieslie King;	Par Lost 4.821
So spake the Cherube, and his grave rebuke	Par Lost 4.844
So wise he judges it to fly from pain	Par Lost 4.910
So judge thou still, presumptuous, till the wrauth,	Par Lost 4.912
And Seale thee so, as henceforth not to scorne	Par Lost 4.966
So threatn'd hee, but *Satan* to no threats	Par Lost 4.968
When *Adam* wak't, so customd, for his sleep	Par Lost 5.3
Of Birds on every bough; so much the more	Par Lost 5.8
Nor God, nor Man; is Knowledge so despis'd?	Par Lost 5.60
At such bold words voucht with a deed so bold:	Par Lost 5.66
So saying, he drew nigh, and to me held,	Par Lost 5.82
So quick'nd appetite, that I, methought,	Par Lost 5.85
May come and go, so unapprov'd, and leave	Par Lost 5.118
So cheard he his fair Spouse, and she was cheard,	Par Lost 5.129
So all was cleard, and to the Field they haste.	Par Lost 5.136
So pray'd they innocent, and to thir thoughts	Par Lost 5.209
So spake th' Eternal Father, and fulfilld	Par Lost 5.246
So saying, with dispatchful looks in haste	Par Lost 5.331
What order, so contriv'd as not to mix	Par Lost 5.334
I have at will. So to the Silvan Lodge	Par Lost 5.377
Varied his bounty so with new delights,	Par Lost 5.431
Think not I shall be nice. So down they sat,	Par Lost 5.433
Transcend his own so farr, whose radiant forms	Par Lost 5.457
Divine effulgence, whose high Power so far	Par Lost 5.458
Food not of Angels, yet accepted so,	Par Lost 5.465
Proportiond to each kind. So from the root	Par Lost 5.479
And so from Heav'n to deepest Hell; O fall	Par Lost 5.542
Single, is yet so just, my constant thoughts	Par Lost 5.552
The ruin of so many glorious once	Par Lost 5.567
Of human sense, I shall delineate so,	Par Lost 5.572
So spake th' Omnipotent, and with his words	Par Lost 5.616
So smooths her charming tones, that Gods own ear	Par Lost 5.626
Alternate all night long: but not so wak'd	Par Lost 5.657
Satan, so call him now, his former name	Par Lost 5.658
Of yesterday, so late hath past the lips	Par Lost 5.675
So spake the false Arch-Angel, and infus'd	Par Lost 5.694
Nor so content, hath in his thought to try	Par Lost 5.727
So spake the Son, but *Satan* with his Powers	Par Lost 5.743
The Palace of great *Lucifer*, (so call	Par Lost 5.760
Pretending so commanded to consult	Par Lost 5.768
In place thy self so high above thy Peeres.	Par Lost 5.812
So spake the fervent Angel, but his zeale	Par Lost 5.849
So spake the Seraph *Abdiel* faithful found,	Par Lost 5.896
That of so many Myriads fall'n, yet one	Par Lost 6.24
So spake the Sovran voice, and Clouds began	Par Lost 6.56
Thir names of thee; so over many a tract	Par Lost 6.76
So oft in Festivals of joy and love	Par Lost 6.94
When Reason hath to deal with force, yet so	Par Lost 6.125
So pondering, and from his armed Peers	Par Lost 6.127
So saying, a noble stroke he lifted high,	Par Lost 6.189
Which hung not, but so swift with tempest fell	Par Lost 6.190
So under fierie Cope together rush'd	Par Lost 6.215
1667 'Sounder', 1668 errata 'So under'	
So spake the Prince of Angels; to whom thus	Par Lost 6.281
To chase me hence? erre not that so shall end	Par Lost 6.288
Was giv'n him temperd so, that neither keen	Par Lost 6.322
And writh'd him to and fro convolv'd; so sore	Par Lost 6.328
And all his Armour staind ere while so bright.	Par Lost 6.334
Humbl'd by such rebuke, so farr beneath	Par Lost 6.342
But proves not so: then fallible, it seems,	Par Lost 6.428
Of evil then so small as easie think	Par Lost 6.437
Believst so main to our success, I bring;	Par Lost 6.471
Whose Eye so superficially surveyes	Par Lost 6.476
So beauteous, op'ning to the ambient light.	Par Lost 6.481
To be th' inventer miss'd, so easie it seemd	Par Lost 6.499
So all ere day-spring, under conscious Night	Par Lost 6.521
This day, fear not his flight; so thick a Cloud	Par Lost 6.539
So warnd he them aware themselves, and soon	Par Lost 6.547
So scoffing in ambiguous words he scarce,	Par Lost 6.568
So they among themselves in pleasant veine	Par Lost 6.628
So easie, and of his Thunder made a scorn,	Par Lost 6.632
When coming towards them so dread they saw	Par Lost 6.648
So Hills amid the Air encounterd Hills	Par Lost 6.664
That his great purpose he might so fulfill,	Par Lost 6.675
So said, he o're his Scepter bowing, rose	Par Lost 6.746
And as ye have receivd, so have ye don	Par Lost 6.805
So spake the Son, and into terrour chang'd	Par Lost 6.824
Through his wilde Anarchie, so huge a rout	Par Lost 6.873
Her Son. So fail not thou, who thee implores:	Par Lost 7.38
So easily obeyd amid the choice	Par Lost 7.48
Of things so high and strange, things to thir thought	Par Lost 7.53
So unimaginable as hate in Heav'n,	Par Lost 7.54

So(*cont*)
And Warr so neer the Peace of God in bliss Par Lost 7.55
Distant so high, with moving Fires adornd Par Lost 7.87
Through all Eternitie so late to build Par Lost 7.92
(So call him, brighter once amidst the Host Par Lost 7.132
So spake th' Almightie, and to what he spake Par Lost 7.174
So told as earthly notion can receave. Par Lost 7.179
So sang the Hierarchies: Mean while the Son Par Lost 7.192
Dividing: for as Earth, so he the World Par Lost 7.269
And Heav'n he nam'd the Firmament: So Eev'n Par Lost 7.274
So high as heav'd the tumid Hills, so low Par Lost 7.288
Troop to thir Standard, so the watrie throng, Par Lost 7.297
So Eev'n and Morn recorded the Third Day. Par Lost 7.338
To give Light on the Earth; and it was so. Par Lost 7.345
So farr remote, with diminution seen. Par Lost 7.369
Easing thir flight; so stears the prudent Crane Par Lost 7.430
So Ev'n and Morn accomplish'd the Sixt day: Par Lost 7.550
On errands of supernal Grace. So sung Par Lost 7.573
So sung they, and the Empyrean rung, Par Lost 7.633
So Charming left his voice, that he a while Par Lost 8.2
line not in 1667 edition
So many nobler Bodies to create, Par Lost 8.28
Greater so manifold to this one use, Par Lost 8.29
So spake our Sire, and by his count'nance seemd Par Lost 8.39
Though, in comparison of Heav'n, so small, Par Lost 8.92
So spacious, and his Line stretcht out so farr; Par Lost 8.102
Not that I so affirm, though so it seem Par Lost 8.117
Plac'd Heav'n from Earth so farr, that earthly sight, Par Lost 8.120
The Planet Earth, so stedfast though she seem, Par Lost 8.129
Each Orb a glimps of Light, conveyd so farr Par Lost 8.156
Ere Sabbath Eev'ning: so we had in charge. Par Lost 8.246
So spake the Godlike Power, and thus our Sire. Par Lost 8.249
And thou enlight'nd Earth, so fresh and gay, Par Lost 8.274
So saying, by the hand he took me rais'd, Par Lost 8.300
So amply, and with hands so liberal Par Lost 8.362
So spake the Universal Lord, and seem'd Par Lost 8.376
So ordering. I with leave of speech implor'd, Par Lost 8.377
So fitly them in pairs thou hast combin'd; Par Lost 8.394
So well converse, nor with the Ox the Ape; Par Lost 8.396
Is no deficience found; not so is Man, Par Lost 8.416
Social communication, yet so pleas'd, Par Lost 8.429
And be so minded still; I, ere thou spak'st, Par Lost 8.444
Manlike, but different Sex, so lovly faire, Par Lost 8.471
Wrought in her so, that seeing me, she turn'd; Par Lost 8.507
Her loveliness, so absolute she seems Par Lost 8.547
And in her self compleat, so well to know Par Lost 8.548
For what admir'st thou, what transports thee so, Par Lost 8.567
Made so adorn for thy delight the more, Par Lost 8.576
So awful, that with honour thou maist love Par Lost 8.577
Neither her out-side formd so fair, nor aught Par Lost 8.596
So much delights me as those graceful acts, Par Lost 8.600
So saying, he arose; whom *Adam* thus Par Lost 8.644
So parted they, the Angel up to Heav'n Par Lost 8.652
Or *Neptun*'s ire or *Juno's*, that so long Par Lost 9.18
Is Center, yet extends to all, so thou Par Lost 9.108
Pleasures about me, so much more I feel Par Lost 9.120
Exalted from so base original, Par Lost 9.150
Let it; I reck not, so it light well aim'd, Par Lost 9.173
So saying, through each Thicket Danck or Drie, Par Lost 9.179
The hands dispatch of two Gardning so wide. Par Lost 9.203
For while so near each other thus all day Par Lost 9.220
Our taske we choose, what wonder if so near Par Lost 9.221
Yet not so strictly hath our Lord impos'd Par Lost 9.235
Adam, missthought of her to thee so dear? Par Lost 9.289
So spake domestick *Adam* in his care Par Lost 9.318
Left so imperfet by the Maker wise, Par Lost 9.338
Fraile is our happiness, if this be so, Par Lost 9.340
So spake the Patriarch of Mankinde, but *Eve* Par Lost 9.376
A Foe so proud will first the weaker seek, Par Lost 9.383
So bent, the more shall shame him his repulse. Par Lost 9.384
Of what so seldom chanc'd, when to his wish, Par Lost 9.423
Half spi'd, so thick the Roses bushing round Par Lost 9.426
From her best prop so farr, and storm so nigh. Par Lost 9.433
I not; so much hath Hell debas'd, and paine Par Lost 9.487
So spake the Enemie of Mankind, enclos'd Par Lost 9.494
Veres oft, as oft so steers, and shifts her Saile; Par Lost 9.515
So varied hee, and of his tortuous Traine Par Lost 9.516
So gloz'd the Tempter, and his Proem tun'd; Par Lost 9.549
To me so friendly grown above the rest Par Lost 9.564
Of that alluring fruit, urg'd me so keene. Par Lost 9.588
Tempting so nigh, to pluck and eat my fill Par Lost 9.595
So talk'd the spirited sly Snake; and *Eve* Par Lost 9.613
So glister'd the dire Snake, and into fraud Par Lost 9.643
God so commanded, and left that Command Par Lost 9.652
So standing, moving, or to highth upgrown Par Lost 9.677
Ye Eate thereof, your Eyes that seem so cleere, Par Lost 9.706
So ye shall die perhaps, by putting off Par Lost 9.713
So savorie of that Fruit, which with desire, Par Lost 9.741
So saying, her rash hand in evil hour Par Lost 9.780
Or fansied so, through expectation high Par Lost 9.789
Without Copartner? so to add what wants Par Lost 9.821
So dear I love him, that with him all deaths Par Lost 9.832
So saying, from the Tree her step she turnd, Par Lost 9.834
Solace in her return, so long delay'd; Par Lost 9.844
Perswasively hath so prevaild, that I Par Lost 9.873
Thy sweet Converse and Love so dearly joyn'd, Par Lost 9.909
So having said, as one from sad dismay Par Lost 9.917
Not God Omnipotent, nor Fate, yet so Par Lost 9.927

So(*cont*)
Is not so hainous now, foretasted Fruit, Par Lost 9.929
Though threatning, will in earnest so destroy Par Lost 9.939
Us his prime Creatures, dignifi'd so high, Par Lost 9.940
Dependent made; so God shall uncreate, Par Lost 9.943
So forcible within my heart I feel Par Lost 9.955
So *Adam*, and thus *Eve* to him repli'd. Par Lost 9.960
Shall separate us, linkt in Love so deare, Par Lost 9.970
So eminently never had bin known. Par Lost 9.976
Remarkably so late of thy so true, Par Lost 9.982
So faithful Love unequald; but I feel Par Lost 9.983
Taste so Divine, that what of sweet before Par Lost 9.986
So saying, she embrac'd him, and for joy Par Lost 9.990
Had so enobl'd, as of choice to incurr Par Lost 9.992
Yeild thee, so well this day thou hast purvey'd. Par Lost 9.1021
But come, so well refresh't, now let us play, Par Lost 9.1027
With all perfections, so enflame my sense Par Lost 9.1031
So said he, and forbore not glance or toy Par Lost 9.1034
Uncover'd more, so rose the *Danite* strong Par Lost 9.1059
1667 'more. So'
And rapture so oft beheld? those heav'nly shapes Par Lost 9.1082
So counsel'd hee, and both together went Par Lost 9.1099
Braunching so broad and long, that in the ground Par Lost 9.1104
Columbus found th' *American* so girt Par Lost 9.1116
What seemd in thee so perfet, that I thought Par Lost 9.1179
Foretold so lately what would come to pass, Par Lost 10.38
So spake the Father, and unfoulding bright Par Lost 10.63
When time shall be, for so I undertook Par Lost 10.74
On me deriv'd, yet I shall temper so Par Lost 10.77
So dreadful to thee? that thou art naked, who Par Lost 10.121
And gav'st me as thy perfet gift, so good, Par Lost 10.138
So fit, so acceptable, so Divine, Par Lost 10.139
So having said, he thus to *Eve* in few: Par Lost 10.157
So spake this Oracle, then verifi'd Par Lost 10.182
So judg'd he Man, both Judge and Saviour sent, Par Lost 10.209
As when he wash'd his servants feet so now Par Lost 10.215
Nor can I miss the way, so strongly drawn Par Lost 10.262
So saying, with delight he snuff'd the smell Par Lost 10.272
So sented the grim Feature, and upturn'd Par Lost 10.279
Sagacious of his Quarry from so farr. Par Lost 10.281
So, if great things to small may be compar'd, Par Lost 10.306
Th' infernal Empire, that so neer Heav'ns dore Par Lost 10.389
So saying he dismiss'd them, they with speed Par Lost 10.410
Of *Lucifer*, so by allusion calld, Par Lost 10.425
Might intercept thir Emperour sent, so hee Par Lost 10.429
To *Tauris* or *Casbeen*. So these the late Par Lost 10.436
At that so sudden blaze the *Stygian* throng Par Lost 10.453
To Sin and Death a prey, and so to us, Par Lost 10.490
So having said, a while he stood, expecting Par Lost 10.504
And *Dipsas* (not so thick swarm'd once the Soil Par Lost 10.526
With soot and cinders fill'd; so oft they fell Par Lost 10.570
So fair and good created, and had still Par Lost 10.618
Folly to mee, so doth the Prince of Hell Par Lost 10.621
And his Adherents, that with so much ease Par Lost 10.622
A place so heav'nly, and conniving seem Par Lost 10.624
Had first his precept so to move, so shine, Par Lost 10.652
Of this new glorious World, and mee so late Par Lost 10.721
Shall be the execration; so besides Par Lost 10.737
Be it so, for I submit, his doom is fair, Par Lost 10.769
Is his wrauth also? be it, man is not so, Par Lost 10.795
Both in me, and without me, and so last Par Lost 10.812
So disinherited how would ye bless Par Lost 10.821
So might the wrauth. Fond wish! couldst thou support Par Lost 10.834
Not so repulst, with Tears that ceas'd not flowing, Par Lost 10.910
Towards her, his life so late and sole delight, Par Lost 10.941
Creature so faire his reconcilement seeking, Par Lost 10.943
So now of what thou knowst not, who desir'st Par Lost 10.948
And my displeasure bearst so ill. If Prayers Par Lost 10.952
Found so erroneous, thence by just event Par Lost 10.969
Found so unfortunate; nevertheless, Par Lost 10.970
Food for so foule a Monster, in thy power Par Lost 10.986
So Death shall be deceav'd his glut, and with us two Par Lost 10.990
Broke off the rest; so much of Death her thoughts Par Lost 10.1008
Of miserie, so thinking to evade Par Lost 10.1021
Hath wiselier arm'd his vengeful ire then so Par Lost 10.1023
So snatcht will not exempt us from the paine Par Lost 10.1025
Resolv'd, as thou proposest; so our Foe Par Lost 10.1038
Beseeching him, so as we need not fear Par Lost 10.1082
So spake our Father penitent, nor *Eve* Par Lost 10.1097
Till I provided Death; so Death becomes Par Lost 11.61
So send them forth, though sorrowing, yet in peace: Par Lost 11.117
So prevalent as to concerne the mind Par Lost 11.144
So spake, so wish'd much-humbl'd *Eve*, but Fate Par Lost 11.181
So many grateful Altars I would reare Par Lost 11.323
Prosperous or adverse: so shalt thou lead Par Lost 11.364
If so I may attain. So both ascend Par Lost 11.376
So deep the power of these Ingredients pierc'd, Par Lost 11.417
Sight so deform what heart of Rock could long Par Lost 11.494
Glad to be so dismist in peace. Can thus Par Lost 11.507
So goodly and erect, though faultie since, Par Lost 11.509
Therefore so abject is thir punishment, Par Lost 11.520
So maist thou live, till like ripe Fruit thou drop Par Lost 11.535
Those Tents thou sawst so pleasant, were the Tents Par Lost 11.607
Of Goddesses, so blithe, so smooth, so gay, Par Lost 11.615
Enterd so faire, should turn aside to tread Par Lost 11.630
Unseen amid the throng: so violence Par Lost 11.671
And therefore hated, therefore so beset Par Lost 11.702
And stabl'd; of Mankind, so numerous late, Par Lost 11.752

So(*cont*)

The end of all thy Ofspring, end so sad,	Par Lost 11.755
Liv'd ignorant of future, so had borne	Par Lost 11.764
So all shall turn degenerate, all deprav'd,	Par Lost 11.806
Whereat the heart of *Adam* erst so sad	Par Lost 11.868
For one Man found so perfet and so just,	Par Lost 11.876
So willingly doth God remit his Ire,	Par Lost 11.885
Though bent on speed, so heer th' Arch-angel paus'd	Par Lost 12.2
line not in 1667 edition	
O execrable Son so to aspire	Par Lost 12.64
Yet somtimes Nations will decline so low	Par Lost 12.97
(Canst thou believe2) should be so stupid grown,	Par Lost 12.116
His benediction so, that in his Seed	Par Lost 12.125
Aw'd by the rod of *Moses* so to stand	Par Lost 12.198
Till *Israel* overcome; so call the third	Par Lost 12.267
So many and so various Laws are giv'n;	Par Lost 12.282
So many Laws argue so many sins	Par Lost 12.283
So law appears imperfet, and but giv'n	Par Lost 12.300
Of *David* (so I name this King) shall rise	Par Lost 12.326
Heapt to the popular summe, will so incense	Par Lost 12.338
Of God most High; So God with Man unites.	Par Lost 12.382
Thy enemie; nor so is overcome	Par Lost 12.390
So onely can high Justice rest appaid.	Par Lost 12.401
In this his satisfaction; so he dies,	Par Lost 12.419
Pure, and in mind prepar'd, if so befall,	Par Lost 12.444
So in his seed all Nations shall be blest.	Par Lost 12.450
So spake th' Archangel *Michael*, then paus'd,	Par Lost 12.466
And oft supported so as shall amaze	Par Lost 12.496
Rarely be found: so shall the World goe on,	Par Lost 12.537
Of him so lately promiss'd to thy aid	Par Lost 12.542
So spake our Mother *Eve*, and *Adam* heard	Par Lost 12.624
Of Paradise, so late thir happie seat,	Par Lost 12.642
Worthy t' have not remain'd so long unsung.	Par Reg 1.17
At least if so we can, and by the head	Par Reg 1.60
Pretends to wash off sin, and fit them so	Par Reg 1.73
At first against mankind so well had thriv'd	Par Reg 1.114
So to the Coast of *Jordan* he directs	Par Reg 1.119
So to subvert whom he suspected rais'd	Par Reg 1.124
To end his Raign on Earth so long enjoy'd:	Par Reg 1.125
So spake the Eternal Father, and all Heaven	Par Reg 1.168
So they in Heav'n their Odes and Vigils tun'd:	Par Reg 1.182
Me him (for it was shew'n him so from Heaven)	Par Reg 1.276
So spake our Morning Star then in his rise,	Par Reg 1.294
So far from path or road of men, who pass	Par Reg 1.322
Of *Jordan* honour'd so, and call'd thee Son	Par Reg 1.329
So shalt thou save thy self and us relieve	Par Reg 1.344
Yet to that hideous place not so confin'd	Par Reg 1.362
Or vertuous, I should so have lost all sense.	Par Reg 1.382
So never more in Hell then when in Heaven.	Par Reg 1.420
So spake our Saviour; but the subtle Fiend,	Par Reg 1.465
Check or reproof, and glad to scape so quit.	Par Reg 1.477
Him whom they heard so late expresly call'd	Par Reg 2.3
Now missing him thir joy so lately found,	Par Reg 2.9
So lately found, and so abruptly gone,	Par Reg 2.10
Sought lost *Eliah*, so in each place these	Par Reg 2.19
Messiah certainly now come, so long	Par Reg 2.32
I lost him, but so found, as well I saw	Par Reg 2.97
So may we hold our place and these mild seats	Par Reg 2.125
So spake the old Serpent doubting, and from all	Par Reg 2.147
Wrought that effect on *Jove*, so Fables tell;	Par Reg 2.215
Though hunger still remain: so it remain	Par Reg 2.255
In this wild solitude so long should bide	Par Reg 2.304
So many Ages, and shall yet regain	Par Reg 2.441
For I esteem those names of men so poor	Par Reg 2.447
So reigning can be no sincere delight.	Par Reg 2.480
So spake the Son of God, and Satan stood	Par Reg 3.1
With glory, wept that he had liv'd so long	Par Reg 3.41
By what he taught and suffer'd for so doing,	Par Reg 3.97
Think not so slight of glory; therein least	Par Reg 3.109
For so much good, so much beneficence.	Par Reg 3.133
Who for so many benefits receiv'd	Par Reg 3.137
And so of all true good himself despoil'd,	Par Reg 3.139
Yet so much bounty is in God, such grace,	Par Reg 3.142
So spake the Son of God; and here again	Par Reg 3.145
Of glory as thou wilt, said he, so deem,	Par Reg 3.150
So did not *Machabeus:* he indeed	Par Reg 3.165
And o're a mighty King so oft prevail'd,	Par Reg 3.167
So shalt thou best fullfil, best verifie	Par Reg 3.177
That it shall never end, so when begin	Par Reg 3.185
Why move thy feet so slow to what is best,	Par Reg 3.224
Of the enterprize so hazardous and high;	Par Reg 3.228
Thee, of thy self so apt, in regal Arts,	Par Reg 3.248
The seats of mightiest Monarchs, and so large	Par Reg 3.262
Such forces met not, nor so wide a camp,	Par Reg 3.337
Such and so numerous was thir Chivalrie;	Par Reg 3.344
The God of their fore-fathers; but so dy'd	Par Reg 3.422
So spake *Israel*'s true King, and to the Fiend	Par Reg 3.441
So fares it when with truth falshood contends.	Par Reg 3.443
So oft, and the perswasive Rhetoric	Par Reg 4.4
That sleek't his tongue, and won so much on *Eve*,	Par Reg 4.5
So little here, nay lost; but *Eve* was *Eve*,	Par Reg 4.6
So Satan, whom repulse upon repulse	Par Reg 4.21
So far renown'd, and with the spoils enricht	Par Reg 4.46
Houses of Gods (so well I have dispos'd	Par Reg 4.56
So many hollow complements and lies,	Par Reg 4.124
For what can less so great a gift deserve?	Par Reg 4.169
Long since. Wert thou so void of fear or shame,	Par Reg 4.189
Be not so sore offended, Son of God;	Par Reg 4.196

So(*cont*)

To me so fatal, me it most concerns.	Par Reg 4.205
So let extend thy mind o're all the world,	Par Reg 4.223
With Music or with Poem, where so soon	Par Reg 4.332
That pleas'd so well our Victors ear, declare	Par Reg 4.337
In Fable, Hymn, or Song, so personating	Par Reg 4.341
What makes a Nation happy, and keeps it so,	Par Reg 4.362
So spake the Son of God; but Satan now	Par Reg 4.365
So saying he took (for still he knew his power	Par Reg 4.394
Thus pass'd the night so foul till morning fair	Par Reg 4.426
After a night of storm so ruinous,	Par Reg 4.436
And mad despight to be so oft repell'd.	Par Reg 4.446
So many terrors, voices, prodigies	Par Reg 4.482
So talk'd he, while the Son of God went on	Par Reg 4.484
In some respect far higher so declar'd.	Par Reg 4.521
So saying he caught him up, and without wing	Par Reg 4.541
So after many a foil the Tempter proud,	Par Reg 4.569
So strook with dread and anguish fell the Fiend,	Par Reg 4.576
Who durst so proudly tempt the Son of God.	Par Reg 4.580
So Satan fell and strait a fiery Globe	Par Reg 4.581
So many, and so huge, that each apart	Samson 65
Since light so necessary is to life,	Samson 90
So obvious and so easie to be quench't,	Samson 95
No journey of a Sabbath day, and loaded so;	Samson 149
And shall again, pretend they ne're so wise.	Samson 212
Deject not then so overmuch thy self,	Samson 213
In that sore battel when so many dy'd	Samson 287
But Gods propos'd deliverance not so.	Samson 292
Whom so it pleases him by choice	Samson 311
He should not so o'rewhelm, and as a thrall	Samson 370
Subject him to so foul indignities,	Samson 371
These rags, this grinding, is not yet so base	Samson 415
So *Dagon* shall be magnifi'd, and God,	Samson 440
And I perswade me so; why else this strength	Samson 586
So much I feel my genial spirits droop,	Samson 594
That thou towards him with hand so various,	Samson 668
So deal not with this once thy glorious Champion,	Samson 705
That so bedeckt, ornate, and gay,	Samson 712
So near related, or the same of kind,	Samson 786
In uncompassionate anger do not so.	Samson 818
So rife and celebrated in the mouths	Samson 866
Vertue, as I thought, truth, duty so enjoyning.	Samson 870
For which our countrey is a name so dear;	Samson 894
With all things grateful chear'd, and so suppli'd,	Samson 926
Nor think me so unwary or accurst	Samson 930
So much of Adders wisdom I have learn't	Samson 936
Of Matrimonial treason: so farewel.	Samson 959
Sam. So let her go, God sent her to debase me,	Samson 999
Had not so soon preferr'd	Samson 1019
Nor both so loosly disally'd	Samson 1022
Thir nuptials, nor this last so trecherously	Samson 1023
What Pilot so expert but needs must wreck	Samson 1044
So shall he least confusion draw	Samson 1058
So had the glory of Prowess been recover'd	Samson 1098
Of noble Warriour, so to stain his honour,	Samson 1166
Come nearer, part not hence so slight inform'd;	Samson 1229
Yet so it may fall out, because thir end	Samson 1265
Can they think me so broken, so debas'd	Samson 1335
Sam. So take it with what speed thy message needs.	Samson 1345
After my great transgression, so requite	Samson 1356
(So mutable are all the ways of men)	Samson 1407
So dreaded once, may now exasperate them	Samson 1417
Measure of strength so great to mortal seed,	Samson 1439
Not to sit idle with so great a gift	Samson 1500
Chor. Of good or bad so great, of bad the sooner;	Samson 1537
The sight of this so horrid spectacle	Samson 1542
So in the sad event too much concern'd.	Samson 1551
Brought him so soon at variance with himself	Samson 1585
(For so from such as nearer stood we heard)	Samson 1631
So fond are mortal men	Samson 1682
So vertue giv'n for lost,	Samson 1697
And what may quiet us in a death so noble.	Samson 1724
And they, so perfect is their misery,	Mask 73
Bridgewater ms 'soe'	
(For so I can distinguish by mine Art)	Mask 149
Bridgewater ms 'soe'	
So maist thou be translated to the skies,	Mask 242
Bridgewater ms 'soe'	
For grant they be so, while they rest unknown,	Mask 361
line not in Trinity ms	
line not in Bridgewater ms	
I do not think my sister so to seek,	Mask 366
Bridgewater ms 'soe'	
Or so unprincipl'd in vertues book,	Mask 367
Bridgewater ms 'soe'	
My sister is not so defenceless left	Mask 414
Bridgewater ms 'soe'	
So dear to Heav'n is Saintly chastity,	Mask 453
Bridgewater ms 'soe'	
That when a soul is found sincerely so,	Mask 454
Bridgewater ms 'soe'	
2. *Bro*. Me thought so too; what should it be? *Eld*. *Bro*. For certain	Mask 482
Bridgewater ms 'soe'	
(Though so esteem'd by shallow ignorance)	Mask 514
Bridgewater ms 'soe'	
Still to be so displac't. I was all eare,	Mask 560
Bridgewater ms 'soe'	
(For so by certain signes I knew) had met	Mask 572

So(*cont*)
Bridgewater ms 'soe'
How durst thou then thy self approach so neer — Mask 616
Bridgewater ms 'soe'
To life so friendly, or so cool to thirst. — Mask 678
Bridgewater ms both 'soe'
Why should you be so cruel to your self, — Mask 679
line not in Bridgewater ms
Would so emblaze the forhead of the Deep, — Mask 733
Bridgewater ms 'soe'
And so bestudd with Stars, that they below — Mask 734
Bridgewater ms 'would soe emblaze with starrs that they belowe'
That hath so well been taught her dazling fence, — Mask 791
line not in Bridgewater ms
line not in Trinity ms
Till all thy magick structures rear'd so high, — Mask 798
line not in Bridgewater ms
line not in Trinity ms
Here behold so goodly grown — Mask 968
Bridgewater ms 'soe'
Youth and Joy; so *Jove* hath sworn. — Mask 1011
line not in Bridgewater ms
so fares as did forsaken Proserpine — Mask Tr. ms 15.52
soe fares as did forsaken Proserpine — Mask Br. ms 344
So bucksom, blith, and debonair. — Allegro 24
Seem'd erst so lavish and profuse, — Arcades 9
A deity so unparalel'd? — Arcades 25
Of that renowned flood, so often sung, — Arcades 29
And so attend ye toward her glittering state; — Arcades 81
So may som gentle Muse — Lycidas 19
Of so much fame in Heav'n expect thy meed. — Lycidas 84
That sunk so low that sacred head of thine. — Lycidas 102
For so to interpose a little ease, — Lycidas 152
So sinks the day-star in the Ocean bed, — Lycidas 168
So *Lycidas* sunk low, but mounted high, — Lycidas 172
For so the holy sages once did sing, — Nativity 5
With her great Master so to sympathize: — Nativity 34
Should look so neer upon her foul deformities. — Nativity 44
Was all that did their silly thoughts so busie keep. — Nativity 92
(If ye have power to touch our senses so) — Nativity 127
This must not yet be so, — Nativity 150
So both himself and us to glorifie: — Nativity 154
Not half so far casts his usurped sway, — Nativity 170
So when the Sun in bed, — Nativity 229
The painted Heav'ns so full of state. — Psalm 136, 18
So mounting up in ycie-pearled carr, — Fair Inf 15
For so *Apollo*, with unweeting hand — Fair Inf 23
Alack that so to change thee winter had no power. — Fair Inf 28
Could Heav'n for pittie thee so strictly doom? — Fair Inf 33
(If so it be that thou these plaints dost hear) — Fair Inf 37
And why from us so quickly thou didst take thy flight. — Fair Inf 42
Then thou the mother of so sweet a child — Fair Inf 71
That so they may without suspect or fears — Vacation 27
Dangers, and snares, and wrongs, and worse then so, — Passion 11
For sure so well instructed are my tears, — Passion 48
So little is our loss, — On Time 7
So little is thy gain. — On Time 8
So sweetly sung your Joy the Clouds along — Circum 4
After so short time of breath, — Winchester 9
So have I seen som tender slip — Winchester 35
And so Sepulcher'd in such pomp dost lie, — Shakespear 15
But lately finding him so long at home, — Carrier 11
So hung his destiny never to rot — Another 3
That I to manhood am arriv'd so near, — Sonnet 7, 6
All is, if I have grace to use it so, — Sonnet 7, 13
So well your words his noble vertues praise, — Sonnet 10, 12
And azure wings, that up they flew so drest, — Sonnet 14, 11
Trinity ms 'soe' ← 'so'
Ev'n them who kept thy truth so pure of old — Sonnet 18, 3
Which others at their Barr so often wrench; — Sonnet 21, 4
line not in Trinity ms
So clear, as in no face with more delight. — Sonnet 23, 12
Trinity ms 'soe'
That so the Parliament — Forcers 15
Not so the wicked, but as chaff which fann'd — Psalm 1, 11
The wind drives, so the wicked shall not stand — Psalm 1, 12
Like to a potters vessel shiver'd so. — Psalm 2, 21
So th' assemblies of each Nation — Psalm 7, 25
So as above the Heavens thy praise to set — Psalm 8, 3
The Moon and Starrs which thou so bright hast set, — Psalm 8, 10
So shall we not go back from thee — Psalm 80, 73
And Israel *whom I lov'd so dear* — Psalm 81, 47
That now so proudly rise, — Psalm 81, 58
So let their Princes speed — Psalm 83, 42
So let their Princes *bleed*. — Psalm 83, 44
So with thy whirlwind them pursue, — Psalm 83, 57
Ever confounded, and so die — Psalm 83, 63
Where thou do'st dwell so near. — Psalm 84, 4
That so thy people may rejoyce — Psalm 85, 23
So shall it never slide — Psalm 86, 40
Bruz'd, and afflicted and *so low* — Psalm 88, 61

Soaked
Sok't in his enemies blood, and from the stream — Samson 1726

Soar
That with no middle flight intends to soar — Par Lost 1.14
ms 'soare'
For you, there sitting where ye durst not soare; — Par Lost 4.829

Soar(*cont*)
Winnows the buxom Air; till within soare — Par Lost 5.270
Following, above th' *Olympian* Hill I soare, — Par Lost 7.3
O Son, but nourish them and let them soar — Par Reg 1.230
And from thence can soar as soon — Mask 1016
1637 'soare'
Bridgewater ms 'soare'
Trinity ms 'soare'
Such where the deep transported mind may soare — Vacation 33

Soared
As high he soard, obnoxious first or last — Par Lost 9.170

Soaring
A standing fight, then soaring on main wing — Par Lost 6.243
They summ'd thir Penns, and soaring th' air sublime — Par Lost 7.421

Soars
Now shaves with level wing the Deep, then soares — Par Lost 2.634
Him that yon soars on golden wing, — Penseroso 52

Sober
Had in her sober Liverie all things clad; — Par Lost 4.599
To these that sober Race of Men, whose lives — Par Lost 11.621
Such sober certainty of waking bliss — Mask 263
That live according to her sober laws, — Mask 766
Sober, stedfast, and demure, — Penseroso 32

Sociable
Raphael, the sociable Spirit, that deign'd — Par Lost 5.221

Sociably
That I should fear, nor sociably mild, — Par Lost 11.234

Social
Social communication, yet so pleas'd, — Par Lost 8.429

Societies
In solemn troops, and sweet Societies — Lycidas 179
1638 'societies'
Trinity ms 'societies'

Society
Among unequals what societie — Par Lost 8.383
What higher in her societie thou findst — Par Lost 8.586
For solitude somtimes is best societie, — Par Lost 9.249
Him with her lov'd societie, that now — Par Lost 9.1007
Such Solitude before choicest Society. — Par Reg 1.302

Sock
If *Jonsons* learned Sock be on, — Allegro 132

Socrates
Poor *Socrates* (who next more memorable2) — Par Reg 3.96
Of *Socrates*, see there his Tenement, — Par Reg 4.274

Sodom
Witness the Streets of *Sodom*, and that night — Par Lost 1.503
ms 'Sodom'
Neer that bituminous Lake where *Sodom* flam'd; — Par Lost 10.562

Soever
We can create, and in what place so e're — Par Lost 2.260
(Which way soever men refer it) — Samson 1015

Sofala
And *Sofala* thought *Ophir*, to the Realme — Par Lost 11.400

Soft
Can either Sex assume, or both; so soft — Par Lost 1.424
Of Flutes and soft Recorders; such as rais'd — Par Lost 1.551
Mov'd on in silence to soft Pipes that charm'd — Par Lost 1.561
As soft as now severe, our temper chang'd — Par Lost 2.276
Purge off this gloom; the soft delicious Air, — Par Lost 2.400
Thir soft Ethereal warmth, and there to pine — Par Lost 2.601
Stood whispering soft, by a fresh Fountain side — Par Lost 4.326
On the soft downie Bank damaskt with flours: — Par Lost 4.334
Thy coming, and thy soft imbraces, hee — Par Lost 4.471
Less winning soft, less amiablie milde, — Par Lost 4.479
Now falling with soft slumbrous weight inclines — Par Lost 4.615
After soft showers; and sweet the coming on — Par Lost 4.646
In Nature and all things, which these soft fires — Par Lost 4.667
Her hand soft touching, whisperd thus. Awake — Par Lost 5.17
Breathe soft or loud; and wave your tops, ye Pines, — Par Lost 5.193
Ceas'd warbling, but all night tun'd her soft layes: — Par Lost 7.436
Temper'd soft Tunings, intermixt with Voice — Par Lost 7.598
On her soft Axle, while she paces Eev'n, — Par Lost 8.165
And beares thee soft with the smooth Air along, — Par Lost 8.166
Soft on the flourie herb I found me laid — Par Lost 8.254
First found me, and with soft oppression seis'd — Par Lost 8.288
Soft she withdrew, and like a Wood-Nymph light — Par Lost 9.386
Angelic, but more soft, and Feminine, — Par Lost 9.458
Now walking in the Garden, by soft windes — Par Lost 10.98
Soft words to his fierce passion she assay'd: — Par Lost 10.865
Soft amorous Ditties, and in dance came on: — Par Lost 11.584
With soft foot towards the deep, who now had stopt — Par Lost 11.848
From their soft wings, and *Flora*'s earliest smells. — Par Reg 2.365
Who on their plumy Vans receiv'd him soft — Par Reg 4.583
Soft, modest, meek, demure, — Samson 1036
Who with his soft Pipe, and smooth-dittied Song, — Mask 86
Bridgewater ms 'softe'
And fell *Charybdis* murmur'd soft applause: — Mask 259
At last a soft and solemn breathing sound — Mask 555
Trinity ms 'soft' ← 'sweet' ← 'still' ← 'soft'
Bridgewater ms 'sweete'
Rose like a steam of rich distill'd Perfumes, — Mask 556
Bridgewater ms 'the softe steame of'
Trinity ms 'a steame' ← 'the softe steame'
For gentle usage, and soft delicacy? — Mask 681
line not in Bridgewater ms
Sleeking her soft alluring locks, — Mask 882
Where young *Adonis* oft reposes, — Mask 999
Bridgewater ms 'many a Cherub soft'

Soft(*cont*)
B.M. ms 'many'a Cherub soft'
Trinity ms 'young Adonis oft' ←'many a cherub soft'
In slumber soft, and on the ground — Mask 1001
line not in Bridgewater ms
but soft I was not sent to court your wonder — Mask Tr. ms 10.16
Lap me in soft *Lydian* Aires, — Allegro 136
Fanning their joyous Leaves to thy soft layes. — Lycidas 44
Smooth-sliding *Mincius*, crown'd with vocall reeds, — Lycidas 86
Trinity ms 'smooth sliding' ←'soft sliding'
And make soft rills from fiery flint-stones gush. — Psalm 114, 18
Soft silken Primrose fading timelesslie, — Fair Inf 2
Down he descended from his Snow-soft chaire, — Fair Inf 19
Through the soft silence of the list'ning night; — Circum 5
Have linkt that amorous power to thy soft lay, — Sonnet 1, 8
In thee *fresh brooks, and soft streams glance* — Psalm 87, 27

Soft-ebbing
Soft-ebbing; nor withstood them Rock or Hill, — Par Lost 7.300

Soften
What may suffice, and soft'n stonie hearts — Par Lost 3.189
Such object hath the power to soft'n and tame — Par Reg 2.163

Softened
Fruits in her soft'nd Soile, for some to eate — Par Lost 8.147
For I behold them softn'd and with tears — Par Lost 11.110
1667 'soft'nd'
Softn'd with pleasure and voluptuous life; — Samson 534
Yet on the softned Quarry would I score — Passion 46

Softening
Prolific humour soft'ning all her Globe, — Par Lost 7.280

Softer
Me softer airs befit, and softer strings — Passion 27

Softest
And Hyacinth, Earths freshest softest lap. — Par Lost 9.1041

Softly
Chor. This, this is he; softly a while, — Samson 115
Softly on my eye-lids laid. — Penseroso 150
She crown'd with Olive green, came softly sliding — Nativity 47

Softness
For softness shee and sweet attractive Grace, — Par Lost 4.298

Sogdiana
Have wasted *Sogdiana;* to her aid — Par Reg 3.302

Soil
Is this the Region, this the Soil, the Clime, — Par Lost 1.242
ms 'soile'
Thir painful steps o're the burnt soyle; and now — Par Lost 1.562
That riches grow in Hell; that soyle may best — Par Lost 1.691
Imitate when we please? This Desart soile — Par Lost 2.270
Of *Barca* or *Cyrene*'s torrid soil, — Par Lost 2.904
Dwelt in *Telassar:* in this pleasant soile — Par Lost 4.214
Wide the Celestial soile, and saw beneath — Par Lost 6.510
Fruits in her soft'nd Soile, for some to eate — Par Lost 8.147
Cathaian Coast. The aggregated Soyle — Par Lost 10.293
And *Dipsas* (not so thick swarm'd once the Soil — Par Lost 10.526
The Ground whence he was taken, fitter soile. — Par Lost 11.98
The ground whence thou wast tak'n, fitter Soile. — Par Lost 11.262
Thee Native Soile, these happie Walks and Shades, — Par Lost 11.270
Where he abides, think there thy native soile. — Par Lost 11.292
Labouring the soile, and reaping plenteous crop, — Par Lost 12.18
He leaves his Gods, his Friends, and native Soile — Par Lost 12.129
Built nobly, pure the air, and light the soil, — Par Reg 4.239
I would not soil these pure Ambrosial weeds, — Mask 16
Trinity ms 'soyle'
Bridgewater ms 'soile'
1637 'soile'
Will dare to soyl her Virgin purity, — Mask 427
Bridgewater ms 'soile'
Trinity ms 'soile'
1637 'soyle'
Bore a bright golden flowre, but not in this soyl: — Mask 633
Trinity ms 'soile'
line not in Bridgewater ms
1637 'soyle'
A better soyl shall give ye thanks. — Arcades 101
Trinity ms 'soyle'
Fame is no plant that grows on mortal soil, — Lycidas 78
Trinity ms 'soile'
His hands from pots, *and mirie soyle* — Psalm 81, 23

Soiled
Our wonted Ornaments now soild and staind, — Par Lost 9.1076
O're worn and soild; — Samson 123
Or grovling soild thir crested helmets in the dust. — Samson 141

Sojourn
In that obscure sojourn, while in my flight — Par Lost 3.15
Into the Sea: to sojourn in that Land — Par Lost 12.159
Short sojourn; and what thence could'st thou observe? — Par Reg 3.235

Sojourned
Sojourn'd the while. God saw the Light was good; — Par Lost 7.249

Sojourners
The Sojourners of *Goshen*, who beheld — Par Lost 1.309
ms 'sojourners'
To let his sojourners depart, and oft — Par Lost 12.192

Solace
Henceforth an individual solace dear; — Par Lost 4.486
Which would be all his solace and revenge, — Par Lost 6.905
Or solace his defects. No need that thou — Par Lost 8.419
Solace in her return, so long delay'd; — Par Lost 9.844
The solace of thir sin, till dewie sleep — Par Lost 9.1044
That solace? All our Law and Story strew'd — Par Reg 4.334

Solace(*cont*)
T'would be som solace yet, som little chearing — Mask 348

Solaced
Solac'd the Woods, and spred thir painted wings — Par Lost 7.434

Solaces
Life yet hath many solaces, enjoy'd — Samson 915

Soldan
Wont ride in arm'd, and at the Soldans chair — Par Lost 1.764

Soldiery
Of faithful Souldiery, were not his purpose — Samson 1498

Sole
Sole reigning holds the Tyranny of Heav'n. — Par Lost 1.124
But ever to do ill our sole delight, — Par Lost 1.160
With stench and smoak: Such resting found the sole — Par Lost 1.237
Sole King, and of his Kingdom loose no part — Par Lost 2.325
This uncouth errand sole, and one for all — Par Lost 2.827
And easily transgress the sole Command, — Par Lost 3.94
Sole pledge of his obedience: So will fall, — Par Lost 3.95
My sole complacence! well thou know'st how dear, — Par Lost 3.276
Look'st from thy sole Dominion like the God — Par Lost 4.33
Sole partner and sole part of all these joyes, — Par Lost 4.411
Sole, or responsive each to others note — Par Lost 4.683
Of human ofsspring, sole proprietie, — Par Lost 4.751
Thou surely hadst not come sole fugitive. — Par Lost 4.923
O Sole in whom my thoughts find all repose, — Par Lost 5.28
A *Phaenix*, gaz'd by all, as that sole Bird — Par Lost 5.272
Vengeance is his, or whose he sole appoints; — Par Lost 6.808
Sole Victor from th' expulsion of his Foes — Par Lost 6.880
If they transgress, and slight that sole command, — Par Lost 7.47
Adam relating, she sole Auditress; — Par Lost 8.51
The day thou eat'st thereof, my sole command — Par Lost 8.329
To mee shall be the glorie sole among — Par Lost 9.135
Sole *Eve*, Associate sole, to me beyond — Par Lost 9.227
Thou canst, who art sole Wonder, much less arm — Par Lost 9.533
Sole Daughter of his voice; the rest, we live — Par Lost 9.653
Chiefly on Man, sole Lord of all declar'd, — Par Lost 10.401
On me, sole cause to thee of all this woe, — Par Lost 10.935
Towards her, his life so late and sole delight, — Par Lost 10.941
Thy Love, the sole contentment of my heart — Par Lost 10.973
His providence, and on him sole depend, — Par Lost 12.564
I, when no other durst, sole undertook — Par Reg 1.100
Sole but with holiest Meditations fed, — Par Reg 2.110
That sole excites to high attempts the flame — Par Reg 3.26
Sole Author I, sole cause: if aught seem vile, — Samson 376

Solemn
His holy Rites, and solemn Feasts profan'd, — Par Lost 1.390
With solemn touches, troubl'd thoughts, and chase — Par Lost 1.557
A solemn Councel forthwith to be held — Par Lost 1.755
ms defective here
With solemn adoration down they cast — Par Lost 3.351
With this her solemn Bird and this fair Moon, — Par Lost 4.648
With this her solemn Bird, nor walk by Moon, — Par Lost 4.655
More solemn then the tedious pomp that waits — Par Lost 5.354
That day, as other solemn dayes, they spent — Par Lost 5.618
1667 'solem'
Receave with solemne purpose to observe — Par Lost 7.78
1669 'solemn'
With Ministeries due and solemn Rites: — Par Lost 7.149
Against a solemn day, harnest at hand, — Par Lost 7.202
Till Ev'n, nor then the solemn Nightingal — Par Lost 7.435
Had work and rested not, the solemn Pipe, — Par Lost 7.595
But solemn and sublime, whom not to offend, — Par Lost 11.236
His place of birth a solemn Angel tells — Par Lost 12.364
To verifie that solemn message late, — Par Reg 1.133
Under the Trees now trip'd, now solemn stood — Par Reg 2.354
This day a solemn Feast the people hold — Samson 12
Our earnest Prayers, then giv'n with solemn hand — Samson 359
Of Women, sung at solemn festivals, — Samson 983
This day to *Dagon* is a solemn Feast, — Samson 1311
And in cleer dream, and solemn vision — Mask 457
1637 'solemne'
Bridgewater ms 'solemne'
Trinity ms 'sollemne'
At last a soft and solemn breathing sound — Mask 555
1637 'solemne'
Bridgewater ms 'solemne'
Trinity ms 'sollemne'
In sage and solemn tunes have sung, — Penseroso 117
Heer our solemn search hath end. — Arcades 7
Trinity ms 'sollemne'
In solemn troops, and sweet Societies — Lycidas 179
Trinity ms 'sollemne'
Hast thou no vers, no hymn, or solemn strein, — Nativity 17
Harping in loud and solemn quire, — Nativity 115
In solemn Songs at King *Alcinous* feast, — Vacation 49
With Saintly shout, and solemn Jubily, — Musick 9
Trinity ms 'sollemne'
Our solemn Feast *comes round*. — Psalm 81, 12

Solemnest
With solemnest devotion, spread before him — Samson 1147

Solemnities
In courts, at feasts, and high solemnities — Mask 746
Trinity ms 'sollemnities'
line not in Bridgewater ms

Solemnity
Our conceal'd Solemnity. — Mask 142
Trinity ms 'sollemnity'
Bridgewater ms 'solempnitie'

Solemnity(*cont*)
To further this nights glad solemnity; Arcades 39
Trinity ms 'sole tie', ms defective
Solemnize
Met from all parts to solemnize this Feast. Samson 1656
Solemnized
Ev'ning and Morn solemniz'd the Fift day. Par Lost 7.448
Solemnly
But such as thou hast solemnly elected, Samson 678
To fetch him hence and solemnly attend Samson 1731
Solicit
Sollicit not thy thoughts with matters hid, Par Lost 8.167
To mould me Man, did I sollicite thee Par Lost 10.744
Solicitation
Of that sollicitation; let me here, Samson 488
Solicitations
All his sollicitations, and at length Par Reg 1.152
Solicited
Sollicited her longing eye; yet first Par Lost 9.743
Sollicited, commanded, threatn'd, urg'd, Samson 852
Solicitous
In Council sate, sollicitous what chance Par Lost 10.428
Sollicitous and blank he thus began. Par Reg 2.120
Sollicitous, what moves thy inquisition? Par Reg 3.200
Solid
With solid, as the Lake with liquid fire; Par Lost 1.229
Of massie Iron or sollid Rock with ease Par Lost 2.878
Nor solid might resist that edge: it met Par Lost 6.323
Nor glistering, may of solid good containe Par Lost 8.93
Solid or slimie, as in raging Sea Par Lost 10.286
Rather then solid vertu, all but a Rib Par Lost 10.884
Or surging waves against a solid rock, Par Reg 4.18
The solid rules of Civil Government Par Reg 4.358
That did the solid Earth ordain Psalm 136, 21
Toward solid good what leads the nearest way; Sonnet 21, 10
Solitary
Explores his solitary flight; som times Par Lost 2.632
Thy folly; or with solitarie hand Par Lost 6.139
Those rare and solitarie, these in flocks Par Lost 7.461
No pleasure, though in pleasure, solitarie. Par Lost 8.402
Through *Eden* took thir solitarie way. Par Lost 12.649
Oft seeks to sweet retired Solitude, Mask 376
Trinity ms 'sweet retired solitude' ←'solitarie sweet retire'
To solitary *Saturn* bore; Penseroso 24
Solitude
In blissful solitude; he then survey'd Par Lost 3.69
And solitude; yet not alone, while thou Par Lost 7.28
1669 'sollitude'
I see not who partakes. In solitude Par Lost 8.364
What call'st thou solitude, is not the Earth Par Lost 8.369
For solitude somtimes is best societie, Par Lost 9.249
In solitude live savage, in some glade Par Lost 9.1085
Not pleas'd, thus entertaind with solitude, Par Lost 10.105
With solitude, till far from track of men, Par Reg 1.191
Such Solitude before choicest Society. Par Reg 1.302
In this wild solitude so long should bide Par Reg 2.304
From the chill dew, amongst rude burrs and thistles? Mask 352
Trinity ms 'amoungst rude burrs & thistles' ←'in this surrounding wilde' ←'in this dead solitude'
Oft seeks to sweet retired Solitude, Mask 376
Bridgewater ms 'solitude'
Trinity ms 'sweet retired solitude' ←'solitarie sweet retire'
Solomon
Of *Solomon* he led by fraud to build Par Lost 1.401
ms 'Solomon'
Of wisest *Solomon*, and made him build, Par Reg 2.170
For *Solomon* he liv'd at ease, and full Par Reg 2.201
Then *Solomon*, of more exalted mind, Par Reg 2.206
Solstice
Himself is his own dungeon. 2. *Bro*. Tis most true Mask 385
Trinity ms 'himselfe is his owne dungeon' ←'blaze in the summer solstice'
Bridgewater ms 'blaze in the summer solstice'
In Wintry solstice like the shortn'd light Passion 6
Solstitial
Solstitial summers heat. To the blanc Moone Par Lost 10.656
Solution
Endless, and no solution will be found: Par Lost 6.694
Which onely thy solution can resolve. Par Lost 8.14
But never find self-satisfying solution. Samson 306
Solve
Grateful digressions, and solve high dispute Par Lost 8.55
Solved
Her riddle, and him, who solv'd it not, devour'd; Par Reg 4.573
That once found out and solv'd, for grief and spight Par Reg 4.574
That solv'd the riddle which I had propos'd. Samson 1200
Some
The Pilot of some small night-founder'd Skiff, Par Lost 1.204
Deeming some Island, oft, as Sea-men tell, Par Lost 1.205
Of some great Ammiral, were but a wand, Par Lost 1.294
Obscure some glimps of joy, to have found thir chief Par Lost 1.524
1667 'som'
Admiring enter'd, and the work some praise Par Lost 1.731
And some the Architect: his hand was known Par Lost 1.732
Or Fountain some belated Peasant sees, Par Lost 1.783
Our stronger, some worse way his wrath may find Par Lost 2.83
Of all his aim, after some dire revenge. Par Lost 2.128
Some easier enterprize? There is a place Par Lost 2.345

Some(*cont*)
Of some new Race call'd *Man*, about this time Par Lost 2.348
1667 'som'
Som advantagious act may be achiev'd Par Lost 2.363
Re-enter Heav'n; or else in some milde Zone Par Lost 2.397
Som Capital City; or less then if this frame Par Lost 2.924
The strong rebuff of som tumultuous cloud Par Lost 2.936
Confine with Heav'n; or if som other place Par Lost 2.977
By some false guile pervert; and shall pervert Par Lost 3.92
1667 'som'
Some I have chosen of peculiar grace Par Lost 3.183
Som other able, and as willing, pay Par Lost 3.211
Though distant farr som small reflection gaines Par Lost 3.428
Not in the neighbouring Moon, as some have dreamd; Par Lost 3.459
Obtains the brow of some high-climbing Hill, Par Lost 3.546
The goodly prospect of some forein land Par Lost 3.548
First-seen, or some renown'd Metropolis Par Lost 3.549
Lay waving round; on som great charge imploy'd Par Lost 3.628
To witness with thine eyes what some perhaps Par Lost 3.700
Me some inferiour Angel, I had stood Par Lost 4.59
Ambition. Yet why not? som other Power Par Lost 4.61
Of some rich Burgher, whose substantial dores, Par Lost 4.189
Of som irriguous Valley spred her store, Par Lost 4.255
Mount *Amara*, though this by som suppos'd Par Lost 4.281
In some Purlieu two gentle Fawnes at play, Par Lost 4.404
Som dreadful thing no doubt; for well thou knowst Par Lost 4.426
Some wandring Spirit of Heav'n, by Fountain side, Par Lost 4.531
Pure, and commands to som, leaves free to all. Par Lost 4.747
Who tells of som infernal Spirit seen Par Lost 4.793
Fit for the Tun som Magazin to store Par Lost 4.816
Som such resemblances methinks I find Par Lost 5.114
For on som message high they guessd him bound. Par Lost 5.290
Ris'n on mid-noon; som great behest from Heav'n Par Lost 5.311
And som are fall'n, to disobedience fall'n, Par Lost 5.541
Hath past in Heav'n, som doubt within me move, Par Lost 5.554
From me som Plume, that thy success may show Par Lost 6.161
Or som more sudden vengeance wing'd from God Par Lost 6.279
Some disadvantage we endur'd and paine, Par Lost 6.431
Some one intent on mischief, or inspir'd Par Lost 6.503
Minims of Nature; some of Serpent kinde Par Lost 7.482
Fruits in her soft'nd Soile, for some to eate Par Lost 8.147
Stor'd in each Orb perhaps with some that live. Par Lost 8.152
Not of my self; by some great Maker then, Par Lost 8.278
Or Nature faild in mee, and left some part Par Lost 8.534
As one who loves, and some unkindness meets, Par Lost 9.271
Least by some faire appeering good surpris'd Par Lost 9.354
Some specious object by the Foe subornd, Par Lost 9.361
Which oft, they say, some evil Spirit attends Par Lost 9.638
Rais'd, as of som great matter to begin. Par Lost 9.669
As when of old som Orator renound Par Lost 9.670
Flourishd, since mute, to som great cause addrest, Par Lost 9.672
The sacred Fruit forbidd'n? som cursed fraud Par Lost 9.904
Skie lowr'd and muttering Thunder, som sad drops Par Lost 9.1002
In solitude live savage, in some glade Par Lost 9.1085
Some Tree whose broad smooth Leaves together sowd, Par Lost 9.1095
By some immediate stroak; but soon shall find Par Lost 10.52
Or sympathie, or som connatural force Par Lost 10.246
Yearly enjoynd, some say, to undergo Par Lost 10.575
However some tradition they dispers'd Par Lost 10.578
That laugh, as if transported with some fit Par Lost 10.626
Some say he bid his Angels turne ascanse Par Lost 10.668
Oblique the Centric Globe: Som say the Sun Par Lost 10.671
Or in some other dismal place who knows Par Lost 10.787
Or find some other way to generate Par Lost 10.894
As some misfortune brings him, or mistake, Par Lost 10.900
Tending to some relief of our extremes, Par Lost 10.976
1667 'som'
Some safer resolution, which methinks Par Lost 10.1029
1667 'Som'
Som better shroud, som better warmth to cherish Par Lost 10.1068
Vacant possession som new trouble raise: Par Lost 11.103
O *Eve*, some furder change awaits us nigh, Par Lost 11.193
Some days; how long, and what till then our life, Par Lost 11.198
None of the meanest, some great Potentate Par Lost 11.231
In some to spring from thee, who never touch'd Par Lost 11.425
O Teacher, some great mischief hath befall'n Par Lost 11.450
Some, as thou saw'st, by violent stroke shall die, Par Lost 11.471
Were Tents of various hue; by some were herds Par Lost 11.557
To som Caves mouth, or whether washt by stream Par Lost 11.569
Fast on the top of som high mountain fixt. Par Lost 11.851
With some regard to what is just and right Par Lost 12.16
But Justice, and some fatal curse annext Par Lost 12.99
Some bloud more precious must be paid for Man, Par Lost 12.293
Which he hath sent propitious, some great good Par Lost 12.612
Som natural tears they drop'd, but wip'd them soon; Par Lost 12.645
1669 'Some'
Mean while the Son of God, who yet some days Par Reg 1.183
And now by some strong motion I am led Par Reg 1.290
Under the covert of some ancient Oak, Par Reg 1.305
Following, as seem'd, the quest of some stray Ewe, Par Reg 1.315
Some troubl'd thoughts, which she in sighs thus clad. Par Reg 2.65
I look't for some great change; to Honour? no, Par Reg 2.86
But where delays he now? some great intent Par Reg 2.95
Thus long to some great purpose he obscures. Par Reg 2.101
Some beauty rare, *Calisto*, *Clymene*, Par Reg 2.186
If cause were to unfold some active Scene Par Reg 2.239
Can satisfie that need some other way, Par Reg 2.254
Not without hunger. Others of some note, Par Reg 2.306

Some(*cont*)
All these the *Parthian*, now some Ages past, — Par Reg 3.294
Remembring *Abraham* by some wond'rous call — Par Reg 3.434
Or on the *Aemilian*, some from farthest South, — Par Reg 4.69
Wherever, under some concourse of shades — Par Reg 4.404
Environ'd thee, some howl'd, some yell'd, some shriek'd, — Par Reg 4.423
Some bent at thee thir fiery darts, while thou — Par Reg 4.424
In some respect far higher so declar'd. — Par Reg 4.521
This unfrequented place to find some ease, — Samson 17
Ease to the body some, none to the mind — Samson 18
His Godlike presence, and from some great act — Samson 28
I willingly on some conditions came — Samson 258
Find some occasion to infest our Foes. — Samson 423
To some *Philistian* Lords, with whom to treat — Samson 482
Full of divine instinct, after some proof — Samson 526
Some sourse of consolation from above; — Samson 664
To some great work, thy glory, — Samson 680
Some rich *Philistian* Matron she may seem, — Samson 722
Though late, yet in some part to recompense — Samson 746
Though fond and reasonless to some perhaps; — Samson 812
Some narrow place enclos'd, where sight may give thee, — Samson 1117
And black enchantments, some Magicians Art — Samson 1133
Some way or other yet further to afflict thee. — Samson 1252
Sam. He must allege some cause, and offer'd fight — Samson 1253
Some other tending, in his hand — Samson 1302
And now some public proof thereof require — Samson 1314
For some important cause, thou needst not doubt. — Samson 1379
Some rouzing motions in me which dispose — Samson 1382
By some great act, or of my days the last. — Samson 1389
Or of him bringing to us some glad news? — Samson 1444
Some much averse I found and wondrous harsh, — Samson 1461
If some convenient ransom were propos'd. — Samson 1471
Or at some proof of strength before them shown. — Samson 1475
To use him further yet in some great service, — Samson 1499
Man. Some dismal accident it needs must be; — Samson 1519
A little stay will bring some notice hither, — Samson 1536
As at some distance from the place of horrour, — Samson 1550
Or some great matter in his mind revolv'd. — Samson 1638
Yet som there be that by due steps aspire — Mask 12
  Bridgewater ms 'some'
  Trinity ms 'some'
  1637 'some'
Into som brutish form of Woolf, or Bear, — Mask 70
  1637 'some'
  Trinity ms 'some'
  Bridgewater ms 'some'
Of som chast footing neer about this ground. — Mask 146
  Bridgewater ms 'some'
  1637 'some'
  Trinity ms 'some'
Our number may affright: Som Virgin sure — Mask 148
  Bridgewater ms 'some'
  Trinity ms 'Some'
I shall appear som harmles Villager — Mask 166
  Trinity ms 'some'
  Bridgewater ms 'some'
Why shouldst thou, but for som fellonious end, — Mask 196
  1637 'some'
  Trinity ms 'some'
  line not in Bridgewater ms
Hid them in som flowry Cave, — Mask 239
  1637 'some'
  Trinity ms 'some'
  Bridgewater ms 'some'
  B.M. ms 'some'
La. To seek i'th vally som cool friendly Spring. — Mask 282
  Trinity ms 'some'
  Bridgewater ms 'some'
  1637 'some'
Of som gay creatures of the element — Mask 299
  Bridgewater ms 'some'
  1637 'some'
  Trinity ms 'some'
With black usurping mists, som gentle taper — Mask 337
  1637 'some'
  Bridgewater ms 'some'
  Trinity ms 'some'
Of som clay habitation visit us — Mask 339
  Bridgewater ms 'some'
  1637 'some'
  Trinity ms 'some'
T'would be som solace yet, som little chearing — Mask 348
  Trinity ms both 'some'
  Bridgewater ms both 'some'
Perhaps som cold bank is her boulster now — Mask 353
  1637 'some'
  Trinity ms 'some'
  Bridgewater ms 'some'
Or 'gainst the rugged bark of som broad Elm — Mask 354
  Bridgewater ms 'some'
  1637 'some'
  Trinity ms 'some'
Lest som ill greeting touch attempt the person — Mask 406
  Bridgewater ms 'some'
  Trinity ms 'some'
  1637 'some'
Som say no evil thing that walks by night — Mask 432
  Bridgewater ms 'naye more'

Some(*cont*)
  1637 'Some'
  Trinity ms 'Some say' ←'Nay more' ←'Some say'
Som far off hallow break the silent Air. — Mask 481
  Trinity ms 'some'
  Bridgewater ms 'some'
  1637 'Some'
Either som one like us night-founder'd here, — Mask 483
  Trinity ms 'some'
  1637 'some'
  Bridgewater ms 'some'
Or els som neighbour Wood-man, or at worst, — Mask 484
  Trinity ms 'some'
  Bridgewater ms 'some'
Som roaving Robber calling to his fellows. — Mask 485
  1637 'Some'
  Bridgewater ms 'some'
  Trinity ms 'some'
Supposing him som neighbour villager; — Mask 576
  Bridgewater ms 'some'
  Trinity ms 'some'
  1637 'some'
And som good angel bear a sheild before us. — Mask 658
  Trinity ms 'some'
  Bridgewater ms 'some'
  1637 'some'
Now heaps upon som few with vast excess, — Mask 771
  1637 'some'
  Bridgewater ms 'some'
  Trinity ms 'some'
Her words set off by som superior power; — Mask 801
  1637 'some'
  line not in Trinity ms
  line not in Bridgewater ms
To som of *Saturns* crew. I must dissemble, — Mask 805
  line not in Bridgewater ms
  line not in Trinity ms
  1637 'some'
Som other means I have which may be us'd, — Mask 821
  Trinity ms 'some other meanes I have' ←'there is another way'
  Bridgewater ms 'some'
  1637 'Some'
And adde the power of som adjuring verse. — Mask 858
  1637 'some'
  Bridgewater ms 'some'
With som other new device. — Mask 941
  1637 'some'
  Bridgewater ms 'some'
  Trinity ms 'some'
poore ladie thou hast need of some refreshing — Mask Tr. ms 20.09
poore ladie thou hast neede of some refreshinge — Mask Br. ms 660
Find out som uncouth cell, — Allegro 5
  1673 'some'
Or whether (as som Sager sing) — Allegro 17
From the side of som Hoar Hill, — Allegro 55
Som time walking not unseen — Allegro 57
Wher perhaps som beauty lies, — Allegro 79
Som times with secure delight — Allegro 91
  1673 'Some'
Dwell in som idle brain, — Penseroso 5
  1673 'some'
Over som wide-water'd shoar, — Penseroso 75
  1673 'some'
Som still removed place will fit, — Penseroso 78
Be seen in som high lonely Towr, — Penseroso 86
  1673 'some'
There in close covert by som Brook, — Penseroso 139
  1673 'some'
And let som strange mysterious dream, — Penseroso 147
Sent by som spirit to mortals good, — Penseroso 153
Without the meed of som melodious tear. — Lycidas 14
  1638 'some'
  Trinity ms 'some'
So may som gentle Muse — Lycidas 19
  1638 'some'
  Trinity ms 'some'
And Heav'n as at som festivall, — Nativity 147
  1673 'some'
If likewise he some fair one wedded not, — Fair Inf 11
Wert thou some Starr which from the ruin'd roofe — Fair Inf 43
Of sheenie Heav'n, and thou some goddess fled — Fair Inf 48
Let down in clowdie throne to do the world some good. — Fair Inf 56
I have some naked thoughts that rove about — Vacation 23
Thy service in some graver subject use, — Vacation 30
Or *Trent*, who like some earth-born Giant spreads — Vacation 93
My spirit som transporting *Cherub* feels, — Passion 38
Had got a race of mourners on som pregnant cloud. — Passion 56
So have I seen som tender slip — Winchester 35
  1673 'some'
Pluck't up by som unheedy swain, — Winchester 38
And som Flowers, and som Bays, — Winchester 57
  1673 'some Bays'
And like an Engin mov'd with wheel and waight, — Another 9
  1640, 1657 'some engine'
  1658 'some Engine'
Foretell my hopeles doom in som Grove ny: — Sonnet 1, 10
That som more timely-happy spirits indu'th. — Sonnet 7, 8

Some(*cont*)

Trinity ms 'some'	
A title page is this! and some in file	Sonnet 11, 6
Trinity ms 'some' ←'som'	
Courts thee on Roses in some pleasant Cave,	Horace 2
Some sign of good to me afford,	Psalm 86, 61
What hinders? as some teachers give to Boyes	Prose 6, 2

Someone

Some one intent on mischief, or inspir'd	Par Lost 6.503

Something

Creator; something yet of doubt remaines,	Par Lost 8.13
1667 'some thing'	
Of somthing not unseasonable to ask	Par Lost 8.201
Yet oft his heart, divine of somthing ill,	Par Lost 9.845
To argue in thee somthing more sublime	Par Lost 10.1014
And slow descends, with somthing heav'nly fraught.	Par Lost 11.207
But must with something sudden be oppos'd,	Par Reg 1.96
To something extraordinary my thoughts.	Samson 1383
Sure somthing holy lodges in that brest,	Mask 246
1637 'something'	
Bridgewater ms 'somethinge'	
Fain would I somthing say, yet to what end?	Mask 783
line not in Bridgewater ms	
line not in Trinity ms	
1637 'something'	
To somthing like Prophetic strain.	Penseroso 174
1673 'something'	
Oh no? for something in thy face did shine	Fair Inf 34
Yet there is something that doth force my fear,	Vacation 67

Sometime

A thing not undesireable, somtime	Par Lost 9.824
Som time walking not unseen	Allegro 57
Som time let Gorgeous Tragedy	Penseroso 97

Sometimes

Explores his solitary flight; som times	Par Lost 2.632
He scours the right hand coast, som times the left,	Par Lost 2.633
Nightly I visit: nor somtimes forget	Par Lost 3.32
There alwayes, but drawn up to Heav'n somtimes	Par Lost 3.517
Sometimes towards *Eden* which now in his view	Par Lost 4.27
Sometimes towards Heav'n and the full-blazing Sun,	Par Lost 4.29
But somtimes in the Air, as wee, somtimes	Par Lost 5.79
How few somtimes may know, when thousands err.	Par Lost 6.148
That Warr and various; somtimes on firm ground	Par Lost 6.242
Of huge extent somtimes, with brazen Eyes	Par Lost 7.496
Survey'd, and sometimes went, and sometimes ran	Par Lost 8.268
For solitude somtimes is best societie,	Par Lost 9.249
Somtimes in highth began, as no delay	Par Lost 9.675
Yet somtimes Nations will decline so low	Par Lost 12.97
Sometimes, anon in shady vale, each night	Par Reg 1.304
Of God; I saw and heard, for we sometimes	Par Reg 1.330
Hath he excluded my resort sometimes.	Par Reg 1.367
Sometimes they thought he might be only shewn,	Par Reg 2.13
Sometimes that with *Elijah* he partook,	Par Reg 2.277
Were all to ruffl'd, and somtimes impair'd.	Mask 380
Bridgewater ms 'sometyms'	
1637 'sometimes'	
Trinity ms 'sometymes'	
Som times with secure delight	Allegro 91
Where shall we sometimes meet, and by the fire	Sonnet 20, 3

Somewhat

Thence more at ease thir minds and somwhat rais'd	Par Lost 2.521
Somwhat extravagant and wilde, perhaps	Par Lost 6.616
By mixing somewhat true to vent more lyes.	Par Reg 1.433
Chor. His Giantship is gone somewhat crest-fall'n,	Samson 1244
Begin, and somwhat loudly sweep the string.	Lycidas 17
1638, 1673 'somewhat'	

Somewhere

By sly assault; and somwhere nigh at hand	Par Lost 9.256

Son

Of *Amrams* Son in *Egypts* evill day	Par Lost 1.339
ms 'son'	
His own and *Rhea*'s Son like measure found;	Par Lost 1.513
ms 'sonne'	
In Fable or *Romance* of *Uthers* Son	Par Lost 1.580
ms 'sonne'	
Admir'd, not fear'd; God and his Son except,	Par Lost 2.678
Against thy only Son? What fury O Son,	Par Lost 2.728
Me Father, and that Fantasm call'st my Son?	Par Lost 2.743
Grim *Death* my Son and foe, who sets them on,	Par Lost 2.804
And my fair Son here showst me, the dear pledge	Par Lost 2.818
His onely Son; On Earth he first beheld	Par Lost 3.64
Thus to his onely Son foreseeing spake.	Par Lost 3.79
Onely begotten Son, seest thou what rage	Par Lost 3.80
Beyond compare the Son of God was seen	Par Lost 3.138
Thy creature late so lov'd, thy youngest Son	Par Lost 3.151
O Son, in whom my Soul hath chief delight,	Par Lost 3.168
Son of my bosom, Son who art alone	Par Lost 3.169
By doom severe, had not the Son of God,	Par Lost 3.224
The Head of all mankind, though *Adams* Son.	Par Lost 3.286
By Merit more then Birthright Son of God,	Par Lost 3.309
Both God and Man, Son both of God and Man,	Par Lost 3.316
Adore the Son, and honour him as mee.	Par Lost 3.343
Begotten Son, Divine Similitude,	Par Lost 3.384
Thee only extoll'd, Son of thy Fathers might,	Par Lost 3.398
No sooner did thy dear and onely Son	Par Lost 3.403
Hail Son of God, Saviour of Men, thy Name	Par Lost 3.412
Of *Tobits* Son, and with a vengeance sent	Par Lost 4.170
Hid *Amalthea* and her Florid Son	Par Lost 4.278

Son(*cont*)

In sad event, when to the unwiser Son	Par Lost 4.716
Of Father, Son, and Brother first were known.	Par Lost 4.757
Skie-tinctur'd grain. Like *Maia*'s son he stood,	Par Lost 5.285
To whom the Angel. Son of Heav'n and Earth,	Par Lost 5.519
By whom in bliss imbosom'd sat the Son,	Par Lost 5.597
My onely Son, and on this holy Hill	Par Lost 5.604
With envie against the Son of God, that day	Par Lost 5.662
And smiling to his onely Son thus said.	Par Lost 5.718
Son, thou in whom my glory I behold	Par Lost 5.719
To whom the Son with calm aspect and cleer	Par Lost 5.733
So spake the Son, but *Satan* with his Powers	Par Lost 5.743
That to his only Son by right endu'd	Par Lost 5.815
Equal to him begotten Son, by whom	Par Lost 5.835
Th' incensed Father, and th' incensed Son,	Par Lost 5.847
From Father to his Son? strange point and new!	Par Lost 5.855
To honour his Anointed Son aveng'd	Par Lost 6.676
All power on him transferr'd: whence to his Son	Par Lost 6.678
Effulgence of my Glorie, Son bêlov'd,	Par Lost 6.680
Son in whose face invisible is beheld	Par Lost 6.681
He said, and on his Son with Rayes direct	Par Lost 6.719
To glorifie thy Son, I alwayes thee,	Par Lost 6.725
Or faint retreat; when the great Son of God	Par Lost 6.799
So spake the Son, and into terrour chang'd	Par Lost 6.824
Son, Heir, and Lord, to him Dominion giv'n,	Par Lost 6.887
Her Son. So fail not thou, who thee implores:	Par Lost 7.38
Into his place, and the great Son returnd	Par Lost 7.135
Thir multitude, and to his Son thus spake.	Par Lost 7.138
And thou my Word, begotten Son, by thee	Par Lost 7.163
So sang the Hierarchies: Mean while the Son	Par Lost 7.192
Present) thus to his Son audibly spake.	Par Lost 7.518
Perplex'd the *Greek* and *Cytherea*'s Son;	Par Lost 9.19
Of Heav'n, this Man of Clay, Son of despite,	Par Lost 9.176
Alcinous, host of old *Laertes* Son,	Par Lost 9.441
Vicegerent Son, to thee I have transferr'd	Par Lost 10.56
Toward the right hand his Glorie, on the Son	Par Lost 10.64
Supream, that thou in mee thy Son belov'd	Par Lost 10.70
When *Jesus* son of *Mary* second *Eve*,	Par Lost 10.183
O Son, why sit we here each other viewing	Par Lost 10.235
The Son of God to judge them terrifi'd	Par Lost 10.338
That I must after thee with this thy Son;	Par Lost 10.363
Fair Daughter, and thou Son and Grandchild both,	Par Lost 10.384
Of thy victorious Arm, well-pleasing Son,	Par Lost 10.634
Who can extenuate thee? Next, to the Son,	Par Lost 10.645
Made thee without thy leave, what if thy Son	Par Lost 10.760
Before the Fathers Throne: Them the glad Son	Par Lost 11.20
All thy request for Man, accepted Son,	Par Lost 11.46
He ended, and the Son gave signal high	Par Lost 11.72
One Man except, the onely Son of light	Par Lost 11.808
O execrable Son so to aspire	Par Lost 12.64
That Son, who on the quiet state of men	Par Lost 12.80
Thir inward lost: Witness th' irreverent Son	Par Lost 12.101
A Son, and of his Son a Grand-childe leaves,	Par Lost 12.153
He comes invited by a yonger Son	Par Lost 12.160
In time of dearth, a Son whose worthy deeds	Par Lost 12.161
From *Abraham*, Son of *Isaac*, and from him	Par Lost 12.268
A Son, the Womans Seed to thee foretold,	Par Lost 12.327
And his next Son for Wealth and Wisdom fam'd,	Par Lost 12.332
Thou shalt proceed, and from thy Womb the Son	Par Lost 12.381
Of head or heel: not therefore joynes the Son	Par Lost 12.388
By proof the undoubted Son of God, inspire,	Par Reg 1.11
From *Nazareth* the Son of *Joseph* deem'd	Par Reg 1.23
From Heav'n pronounc'd him his beloved Son.	Par Reg 1.32
This is my Son belov'd, in him am pleas'd.	Par Reg 1.85
And what will he not do to advance his Son?	Par Reg 1.88
This man of men, attested Son of God,	Par Reg 1.122
In *Galilee*, that she should bear a Son	Par Reg 1.135
Great in Renown, and call'd the Son of God;	Par Reg 1.136
This perfect Man, by merit call'd my Son,	Par Reg 1.166
Victory and Triumph to the Son of God	Par Reg 1.173
The Father knows the Son; therefore secure	Par Reg 1.176
Mean while the Son of God, who yet some days	Par Reg 1.183
O Son, but nourish them and let them soar	Par Reg 1.230
For know, thou art no Son of mortal man,	Par Reg 1.234
Me his beloved Son, in whom alone	Par Reg 1.285
Of *Jordan* honour'd so, and call'd thee Son	Par Reg 1.329
To whom the Son of God. Who brought me hither	Par Reg 1.335
But if thou be the Son of God, Command	Par Reg 1.342
He ended, and the Son of God reply'd.	Par Reg 1.346
Declar'd the Son of God, to hear attent	Par Reg 1.385
Jesus Messiah Son of God declar'd,	Par Reg 2.4
Others return'd from Baptism, not her Son,	Par Reg 2.61
Son own'd from Heaven by his Father's voice;	Par Reg 2.85
The while her Son tracing the Desert wild,	Par Reg 2.109
Where still from shade to shade the Son of God	Par Reg 2.242
It was the hour of night, when thus the Son	Par Reg 2.260
But much more wonder that the Son of God	Par Reg 2.303
The Fugitive Bond-woman with her Son	Par Reg 2.308
What doubts the Son of God to sit and eat?	Par Reg 2.368
What doubt'st thou Son of God? sit down and eat.	Par Reg 2.377
And his Son *Herod* plac'd on *Juda*'s Throne;	Par Reg 2.424
So spake the Son of God, and Satan stood	Par Reg 3.1
Thy years are ripe, and over-ripe, the Son	Par Reg 3.31
One is the Son of *Jove*, of *Mars* the other,	Par Reg 3.84
So spake the Son of God; and here again	Par Reg 3.145
The Son of God up to a Mountain high.	Par Reg 3.252
This Emperour hath no Son, and now is old,	Par Reg 4.90
To whom the Son of God unmov'd reply'd.	Par Reg 4.109

Son(*cont*)
And dar'st thou to the Son of God propound Par Reg 4.178
As offer them to me the Son of God, Par Reg 4.190
Be not so sore offended, Son of God; Par Reg 4.196
So spake the Son of God; but Satan now Par Reg 4.365
Brought back the Son of God, and left him there, Par Reg 4.396
O patient Son of God, yet only stoodst Par Reg 4.420
To tempt the Son of God with terrors dire. Par Reg 4.431
Fair morning yet betides thee Son of God, Par Reg 4.451
So talk'd he, while the Son of God went on Par Reg 4.484
Then hear, O Son of *David*, Virgin-born; Par Reg 4.500
For Son of God to me is yet in doubt, Par Reg 4.501
Heard thee pronounc'd the Son of God belov'd. Par Reg 4.513
The Son of God, which bears no single sence; Par Reg 4.517
The Son of God I also am, or was, Par Reg 4.518
Worth naming Son of God by voice from Heav'n, Par Reg 4.539
The Son of God; and added thus in scorn: Par Reg 4.550
Cast thy self down; safely if Son of God: Par Reg 4.555
As when Earths Son *Antaeus* (to compare Par Reg 4.563
Who durst so proudly tempt the Son of God. Par Reg 4.580
The Son of God, with Godlike force indu'd Par Reg 4.602
To dread the Son of God: he all unarm'd Par Reg 4.626
Hail Son of the most High, heir of both worlds, Par Reg 4.633
Thus they the Son of God our Saviour meek Par Reg 4.636
My Son now Captive, hither hath inform'd Samson 335
In wedlock a reproach; I gain'd a Son, Samson 353
And such a Son as all Men hail'd me happy; Samson 354
Man. I cannot praise thy Marriage choises, Son, Samson 420
But act not in thy own affliction, Son, Samson 503
He seems: supposing here to find his Son, Samson 1443
Was not at present here to find my Son, Samson 1446
To accept of ransom for my Son thir pris'ner, Samson 1460
Thou for thy Son art bent to lay out all; Samson 1486
Thou in old age car'st how to nurse thy Son. Samson 1488
Oh it continues, they have slain my Son. Samson 1516
Chor. Thy Son is rather slaying them, that outcry Samson 1517
Had by him, ere he parted thence, a Son Mask 56
Bridgewater ms 'sonne'
Trinity ms 'son'
And her son that rules the strands, Mask 876
Bridgewater ms 'sonne'
Celestial *Cupid* her fam'd Son advanc't, Mask 1004
Trinity ms 'son'
line not in Bridgewater ms
The Muse her self, for her inchanting son Lycidas 59
1638 'sonne'
Wherin the Son of Heav'ns eternal King, Nativity 2
When the blest seed of *Terah*'s faithfull Son, Psalm 114, 1
Good luck befriend thee Son; for at thy birth Vacation 59
Your Son, said she, (nor can you it prevent) Vacation 73
Rivers arise; whether thou be the Son, Vacation 91
To greet her of a lovely son, Winchester 24
Dear son of memory, great heir of Fame, Shakespear 5
1640 'Sonne'
1663-4 'Son'
1632 'Sonne'
In peace, and reck'ns thee her eldest son. Sonnet 17, 14
1662 'Son'
Lawrence of vertuous Father vertuous Son, Sonnet 20, 1
Whom *Joves* great Son to her glad Husband gave, Sonnet 23, 3
Trinity ms 'son'
Thou art my Son I have begotten thee Psalm 2, 15
With trembling; kiss the Son least he appear Psalm 2, 25
Upon the Son of Man, whom thou Psalm 80, 71
And save thy hand-maids Son. Psalm 86, 60

Song
Invoke thy aid to my adventrous Song, Par Lost 1.13
ms 'song'
Thir Song was partial, but the harmony Par Lost 2.552
1667 'song'
(For Eloquence the Soul, Song charms the Sense,) Par Lost 2.556
Smit with the love of sacred Song; but chief Par Lost 3.29
1667 'song'
Thir sacred Song, and waken raptures high; Par Lost 3.369
Shall be the copious matter of my Song Par Lost 3.413
Lightly dispers'd, and the shrill Matin Song Par Lost 5.7
Tunes sweetest his love-labor'd song; now reignes Par Lost 5.41
In mystic Dance not without Song, resound Par Lost 5.178
Made vocal by my Song, and taught his praise. Par Lost 5.204
In song and dance about the sacred Hill, Par Lost 5.619
Ministring Spirits, traind up in Feast and Song; Par Lost 6.167
With thy Celestial Song. Up led by thee Par Lost 7.12
Purples the East: still govern thou my Song, Par Lost 7.30
Or we can bid his absence, till thy Song Par Lost 7.107
From Branch to Branch the smaller Birds with song Par Lost 7.433
Noise, other then the sound of Dance or Song, Par Lost 8.243
Since first this Subject for Heroic Song Par Lost 9.25
Not without Song, each Morning, and due praise Par Lost 9.800
Or down from Heav'n descend. Such was thir song, Par Lost 10.648
To answer, and resound farr other Song. Par Lost 10.862
As thou art wont, my prompted Song else mute, Par Reg 1.12
And tuneable as Silvan Pipe or Song; Par Reg 1.480
The morns approach, and greet her with his Song: Par Reg 2.281
In Fable, Hymn, or Song, so personating Par Reg 4.341
And of the Angelic Song in *Bethlehem* field, Par Reg 4.505
In copious Legend, or sweet Lyric Song. Samson 1737
What never yet was heard in Tale or Song Mask 44
Bridgewater ms 'songe'

Song(*cont*)
Trinity ms 'song'
Who with his soft Pipe, and smooth-dittied Song, Mask 86
Trinity ms 'song'
Bridgewater ms 'songe'
Nightly to thee her sad Song mourneth well. Mask 235
Trinity ms 'song'
B.M. ms 'song'
Bridgewater ms 'song'
Dwell'st here with *Pan*, or *Silvan*, by blest Song Mask 268
Bridgewater ms 'song'
Trinity ms 'song'
If she be right invok't in warbled Song, Mask 854
Bridgewater ms 'songe'
Trinity ms 'song'
'Less *Philomel* will daign a Song, Penseroso 56
I woo to hear thy eeven Song; Penseroso 64
1673 'Even-Song'
And old *Damoetas* lov'd to hear our song. Lycidas 36
And hears the unexpressive nuptiall Song, Lycidas 176
Trinity ms 'song'
1638 'song'
For if such holy Song Nativity 133
Time is our tedious Song should here have ending, Nativity 239
For now to sorrow must I tune my song, Passion 8
That erst with Musick, and triumphant song Circum 2
That undisturbed Song of pure content, Musick 6
Trinity ms 'song'
O may we soon again renew that Song, Musick 25
Trinity ms 'song'
& in our lives & in our song Musick Tr. ms 5.05
Thus we salute thee with our early Song, May Morn 9
Harry whose tuneful and well measur'd Song Sonnet 13, 1
1648 'song'
Trinity ms 'Song' ←'song'
Prepare a Hymn, prepare a Song Psalm 81, 5

Songs
Sidonian Virgins paid thir Vows and Songs, Par Lost 1.441
ms 'songs'
Of Hymns and sacred Songs, wherewith thy Throne Par Lost 3.148
In full harmonic number joind, thir songs Par Lost 4.687
High up in Heav'n, with songs to hymne his Throne, Par Lost 4.944
Angels, for yee behold him, and with songs Par Lost 5.161
Cherubic Songs by night from neighbouring Hills Par Lost 5.547
Of love and youth not lost, Songs, Garlands, Flours, Par Lost 11.594
Our Hebrew Songs and Harps in *Babylon*, Par Reg 4.336
With *Sion*'s songs, to all true tasts excelling, Par Reg 4.347
And the Songs of *Sirens* sweet, Mask 878
1637 'songs'
Trinity ms 'songs'
Bridgewater ms 'songs'
bedew'd with nectar, & celestiall songs Mask Tr. ms 10.06
And when they list, their lean and flashy songs Lycidas 123
In solemn Songs at King *Alcinous* feast, Vacation 49
With sacred Songs are there, Psalm 87, 26

Sonorous
Sonorous mettal blowing Martial sounds: Par Lost 1.540

Sons
Rhene or the *Danaw*, when her barbarous Sons Par Lost 1.353
ms 'sons'
Nor had they yet among the Sons of *Eve* Par Lost 1.364
ms 'sons'
Next *Chemos*, th' obscene dread of *Moabs* Sons, Par Lost 1.406
ms 'sons'
Turns Atheist, as did *Ely*'s Sons, who fill'd Par Lost 1.495
ms 'sonns'
Darkens the Streets, then wander forth the Sons Par Lost 1.501
ms 'sonns'
Should favour equal to the Sons of Heaven: Par Lost 1.654
ms 'sonns'
In bigness to surpass Earths Giant Sons Par Lost 1.778
ms 'giant-sons'
In his disturbance; when his darling Sons Par Lost 2.373
Drew after him the third part of Heav'ns Sons Par Lost 2.692
His crime makes guiltie all his Sons, thy merit Par Lost 3.290
Hither of ill-joynd Sons and Daughters born Par Lost 3.463
Where all his Sons thy Embassie attend; Par Lost 3.658
Or where the Sons of *Eden* long before Par Lost 4.213
His Sons, the fairest of her Daughters *Eve*. Par Lost 4.324
Speak yee who best can tell, ye Sons of light, Par Lost 5.160
1667 'sons' in some copies
Shall fill the World more numerous with thy Sons Par Lost 5.389
Then had the Sons of God excuse to have bin Par Lost 5.447
Among the sons of Morn, what multitudes Par Lost 5.716
Natives and Sons of Heav'n possest before Par Lost 5.790
Of this our native Heav'n, Ethereal Sons. Par Lost 5.863
Gabriel, lead forth to Battel these my Sons Par Lost 6.46
Unanimous, as sons of one great Sire Par Lost 6.95
Like instrument to plague the Sons of men Par Lost 6.505
Pursue these sons of Darkness, drive them out Par Lost 6.715
And sons of men, whom God hath thus advanc't, Par Lost 7.626
Would not admit; thine and of all thy Sons Par Lost 8.637
That I must leave ye, Sons; O were I able Par Lost 10.819
In fellowships of joy: the Sons of Light Par Lost 11.80
O Sons, like one of us Man is become Par Lost 11.84
Presence Divine, and to my Sons relate; Par Lost 11.319
To dwell on eeven ground now with thy Sons: Par Lost 11.348
Guiana, whose great Citie *Geryons* Sons Par Lost 11.410

Sons(*cont*)
Religious titl'd them the Sons of God, Par Lost 11.622
Patrons of Mankind, Gods, and Sons of Gods, Par Lost 11.696
Thir order: last the Sire, and his three Sons Par Lost 11.736
And sunk thee as thy Sons; till gently reard Par Lost 11.758
Of wicked Sons destroyd, then I rejoyce Par Lost 11.875
Jordan, true limit Eastward; but his Sons Par Lost 12.145
The Grandchilde with twelve Sons increast, departs Par Lost 12.155
The Scepter, and regard not *Davids* Sons, Par Lost 12.357
Not onely to the Sons of *Abrahams* Loines Par Lost 12.447
Salvation shall be Preacht, but to the Sons Par Lost 12.448
To earn Salvation for the Sons of men. Par Reg 1.167
All Heaven and Earth, Angels and Sons of men, Par Reg 1.237
I came among the Sons of God, when he Par Reg 1.368
Princes, Heavens antient Sons, Aethereal Thrones, Par Reg 2.121
False titl'd Sons of God, roaming the Earth Par Reg 2.179
Delight not all; among the Sons of Men, Par Reg 2.192
Ten Sons of *Jacob*, two of *Joseph* lost Par Reg 3.377
To just extent over all *Israel*'s Sons; Par Reg 3.406
Though Sons of God both Angels are and Men, Par Reg 4.197
All men are Sons of God; yet thee I thought Par Reg 4.520
For *Adam* and his chosen Sons, whom thou Par Reg 4.614
Yet *Israel* still serves with all his Sons. Samson 240
The Sons of *Anac*, famous now and blaz'd, Samson 528
Thine or whom I with *Israel*'s Sons adore. Samson 1177
Though Fame divulge him Father of five Sons Samson 1248
Above the Sons of men; but sight bereav'd Samson 1294
Chor. Fathers are wont to lay up for thir Sons, Samson 1485
Sons wont to nurse thir Parents in old age, Samson 1487
Mess. *Gaza* yet stands, but all her Sons are fall'n, Samson 1558
And lamentation to the Sons of *Caphtor* Samson 1713
Or like the sons of *Vulcan* vomit smoak, Mask 655
  1673 'Sons'
  Bridgewater ms 'sonns'
To deck her Sons, and that no corner might Mask 717
  Trinity ms 'sons'
  Bridgewater ms 'sonns'
And live like Natures bastards, not her sons, Mask 727
  Bridgewater ms 'sonns'
But when of old the sons of morning sung, Nativity 119
Or did of late earths Sonnes besiege the wall Fair Inf 47
The Sons of God most high Psalm 82, 22
To aid the Sons of Lot. Psalm 83, 32
There to thy Sons another *Troy* shall rise, Prose 12, 12

Soon
He soon discerns, and weltring by his side Par Lost 1.78
  ms 'soone'
And him thus answer'd soon his bold Compeer. Par Lost 1.127
Invincible, and vigour soon returns, Par Lost 1.140
Thir surest signal, they will soon resume Par Lost 1.278
Yet to thir Generals Voyce they soon obeyd Par Lost 1.337
Soon recollecting, with high words, that bore Par Lost 1.528
Darts his experienc't eye, and soon traverse Par Lost 1.568
For Treasures better hid. Soon had his crew Par Lost 1.688
A third as soon had form'd within the ground Par Lost 1.705
Incapable of stain would soon expel Par Lost 2.140
Faded so soon. Advise if this be worth Par Lost 2.376
And me his Parent would full soon devour Par Lost 2.805
Soon learnd, now milder, and thus answerd smooth. Par Lost 2.816
To know, and this once known, shall soon return, Par Lost 2.839
But thee, whom follow? thou wilt bring me soon Par Lost 2.866
Audacious, but that seat soon failing, meets Par Lost 2.931
But hee once past, soon after when man fell, Par Lost 2.1023
Wondring; but soon th' Almighty thus reply'd: Par Lost 3.273
Began to bloom, but soon for mans offence Par Lost 3.355
To objects distant farr, whereby he soon Par Lost 3.621
By Act of Grace my former state; how soon Par Lost 4.94
Would higth recal high thoughts, how soon unsay Par Lost 4.95
Are ever cleer. Whereof hee soon aware, Par Lost 4.119
It started back, but pleas'd I soon returnd, Par Lost 4.463
Pleas'd it returnd as soon with answering looks Par Lost 4.464
Where he first lighted, soon discernd his looks Par Lost 4.570
Yet thus, unmovd with fear, accost him soon. Par Lost 4.822
To whom the warriour Angel, soon repli'd. Par Lost 4.946
With violence of this conflict, had not soon Par Lost 4.995
Soon as they forth were come to open sight Par Lost 5.138
Firm peace recoverd soon and wonted calm. Par Lost 5.210
Soon as midnight brought on the duskie houre Par Lost 5.667
Distinguish not: for soon expect to feel Par Lost 5.892
Of onset ended soon each milder thought. Par Lost 6.98
Yet soon he heal'd; for Spirits that live throughout Par Lost 6.344
Till now not known, but known as soon contemnd, Par Lost 6.432
Soon closing, and by native vigour heal'd. Par Lost 6.436
Soon banded; others from the dawning Hills Par Lost 6.528
In motion or in alt: him soon they met Par Lost 6.532
So warnd he them aware themselves, and soon Par Lost 6.547
But soon obscur'd with smoak, all Heav'n appeerd, Par Lost 6.585
Image of thee in all things; and shall soon, Par Lost 6.736
Under whose conduct *Michael* soon reduc'd Par Lost 6.777
All but the Throne it self of God. Full soon Par Lost 6.834
Disburd'nd Heav'n rejoic'd, and soon repaird Par Lost 6.878
With such confusion: but the evil soon Par Lost 7.56
With Blessedness. Whence *Adam* soon repeal'd Par Lost 7.59
In *Chaos*, and the work begun, how soon Par Lost 7.93
Oppresses else with Surfet, and soon turns Par Lost 7.129
Thir Brood as numerous hatch, from the Egg that soon Par Lost 7.418
Thir callow young, but featherd soon and fledge Par Lost 7.420
Of sweet repast; they satiate, and soon fill, Par Lost 8.214

Soon(*cont*)
Soon dri'd, and on the reaking moisture fed. Par Lost 8.256
Not to incur; but soon his cleer aspect Par Lost 8.336
Cannot well suite with either, but soon prove Par Lost 8.388
For whom all this was made, all this will soon Par Lost 9.132
The Serpent: him fast sleeping soon he found Par Lost 9.182
In heart or head, possessing soon inspir'd Par Lost 9.189
Though in mid Heav'n, soon ended his delight, Par Lost 9.468
Of pleasure not for him ordain'd: then soon Par Lost 9.470
About the mossie Trunk I wound me soon, Par Lost 9.589
My conduct, I can bring thee thither soon. Par Lost 9.630
Tedious, unshar'd with thee, and odious soon. Par Lost 9.880
On th' other side, *Adam*, soon as he heard Par Lost 9.888
Soon as the force of that fallacious Fruit, Par Lost 9.1046
Soon found thir Eyes how op'nd, and thir minds Par Lost 9.1053
Into the thickest Wood, there soon they chose Par Lost 9.1100
To whom soon mov'd with touch of blame thus *Eve*. Par Lost 9.1143
Entrance unseen. Soon as th' unwelcome news Par Lost 10.21
By some immediate stroak; but soon shall find Par Lost 10.52
Confessing soon, yet not before her Judge Par Lost 10.160
Whom thus the meager Shadow answerd soon. Par Lost 10.264
Thir Parent soon discern'd, though in disguise. Par Lost 10.331
Too soon arriv'd, *Sin* there in power before, Par Lost 10.586
Whom thus the Sin-born Monster answerd soon. Par Lost 10.596
Commiseration; soon his heart relented Par Lost 10.940
And thus with peaceful words uprais'd her soon. Par Lost 10.946
And bringing forth, soon recompenc't with joy, Par Lost 10.1052
Of us will soon determin, or impose Par Lost 11.227
He ended; and th' Arch-Angel soon drew nigh, Par Lost 11.238
Discover'd soon the place of her retire. Par Lost 11.267
Soon rais'd, and his attention thus recall'd. Par Lost 11.422
His Offring soon propitious Fire from Heav'n Par Lost 11.441
Life offer'd, or soon beg to lay it down, Par Lost 11.506
Of *Adam*, soon enclin'd to admit delight, Par Lost 11.596
Assemble, and Harangues are heard, but soon Par Lost 11.663
Which now direct thine eyes and soon behold. Par Lost 11.711
To mark thir doings, them beholding soon, Par Lost 12.50
But soon revives, Death over him no power Par Lost 12.420
How soon hath thy prediction, Seer blest, Par Lost 12.553
Som natural tears they drop'd, but wip'd them soon; Par Lost 12.645
Unmarkt, unknown; but him the Baptist soon Par Reg 1.25
And now too soon for us the circling hours Par Reg 1.57
These growing thoughts my Mother soon perceiving Par Reg 1.227
Known partly, and soon found of whom they spake Par Reg 1.262
But this thy glory shall be soon retrench'd; Par Reg 1.454
Thus we rejoyc'd, but soon our joy is turn'd Par Reg 2.37
Soon we shall see our hope, our joy return. Par Reg 2.57
A Manger his, yet soon enforc't to flye Par Reg 2.75
To rest at noon, and entr'd soon the shade Par Reg 2.292
I can at will, doubt not, as soon as thou, Par Reg 2.383
May also in this poverty as soon Par Reg 2.451
Yet of another Plea bethought him soon. Par Reg 3.149
But I will bring thee where thou soon shalt quit Par Reg 3.244
Long in preparing, soon to nothing brought, Par Reg 3.389
With Music or with Poem, where so soon Par Reg 4.332
What I foretell thee, soon thou shalt have cause Par Reg 4.375
The Tempter watch'd, and soon with ugly dreams Par Reg 4.408
To mans less universe, and soon are gone; Par Reg 4.459
That soon refresh'd him wearied, and repair'd Par Reg 4.591
Found soon occasion thereby to make thee Samson 425
If not by quick destruction soon cut off Samson 764
Had not so soon preferr'd Samson 1019
Chor. His fraught we soon shall know, he now arrives. Samson 1075
I should have forc'd thee soon wish other arms, Samson 1096
Soon feel, whose God is strongest, thine or mine. Samson 1155
To utter what will come at last too soon; Samson 1566
Brought him so soon at variance with himself Samson 1585
Soon as the Potion works, their human count'nance, Mask 68
  Bridgewater ms 'soone'
  1637 'Soone'
  Trinity ms 'soone'
And envious darknes, e're they could return, Mask 194
  Trinity ms 'and envious darknesse' ←'to the soone parting light'
Longer I durst not stay, but soon I guess't Mask 577
  1637 'soone'
  Bridgewater ms 'soone'
  Trinity ms 'soone'
Yet will they soon retire, if he but shrink. Mask 656
  1637 'soone'
  Trinity ms 'soone'
  Bridgewater ms 'soone'
This will restore all soon. *La*. 'Twill not false traitor, Mask 690
  Bridgewater ms 'soone'
  Trinity ms 'soone'
  1637 'soone'
And from thence can soar as soon Mask 1016
  Bridgewater ms 'soone'
  1637 'soone'
  Trinity ms 'soone'
By whispering Windes soon lull'd asleep. Allegro 116
Will sicken soon and die, Nativity 137
But full soon they did devour Psalm 136, 53
Soon swallow'd up in dark and long out-living night. Passion 7
Would soon unboosom all thir Echoes milde, Passion 53
Alas, how soon our sin Circum 12
  Trinity ms 'soon' ←'soone'
O may we soon again renew that Song, Musick 25

Soon(*cont*)
Trinity ms 'soone'
She had told, alas too soon, Winchester 8
How soon hath Time the suttle theef of youth, Sonnet 7, 1
Trinity ms 'soone'
Yet be it less or more, or soon or slow, Sonnet 7, 9
Trinity ms 'soone'
That murmur, soon replies, God doth not need Sonnet 19, 9
Unto Jehovah, he full soon reply'd Psalm 3, 11
Then would I soon bring down their foes Psalm 81, 57
Sooner
No sooner had th' Almighty ceas't, but all Par Lost 3.344
No sooner did thy dear and onely Son Par Lost 3.403
The sooner for thir Arms, unarm'd they might Par Lost 6.595
For I no sooner in my Heart divin'd, Par Lost 10.357
Sooner or later; which th' Almightie seeing, Par Lost 10.613
No sooner hee with them of Man and Beast Par Lost 11.822
And run not sooner to his fatal snare? Par Reg 1.441
The happier raign the sooner it begins, Par Reg 3.179
Of Hornets arm'd, no sooner found alone, Samson 20
Thir Captive, and thir triumph; thou the sooner Samson 426
Chor. Of good or bad so great, of bad the sooner; Samson 1537
Which oft is sooner found in lowly sheds Mask 323
O Fairest flower no sooner blown but blasted, Fair Inf 1
Soonest
Torment with ease, and soonest recompence Par Lost 4.893
His midnight search, where soonest he might finde Par Lost 9.181
And the well-feasted Priest then soonest fir'd Samson 1419
Soot
With soot and cinders fill'd; so oft they fell Par Lost 10.570
Sooth
Forsook the hated earth, O tell me sooth Fair Inf 51
No word is firm or sooth Psalm 5, 26
Soothe
Her former trespass fear'd, the more to soothe Par Lost 9.1006
Soothest
The soothest Shepherd that ere pip't on plains. Mask 823
Soothing
With soothing words renew'd, him thus accosts. Par Reg 3.6
whether deluded and soothing lies & soothing flatteries. Mask Tr. ms 22.20
Soothsaying
And old sooth-saying *Glaucus* spell, Mask 874
1637 'sooth saying'
Bridgewater ms 'sooth-sayinge'
Sooty
Of sooty coal the Empiric Alchimist Par Lost 5.440
Under the sooty flag of *Acheron*, Mask 604
1637 'sootie'
Trinity ms 'sootie'
Bridgewater ms 'sootie'
Sophi
Retires, or *Bactrian* Sophi from the hornes Par Lost 10.433
Sorcerer
Immur'd in cypress shades a Sorcerer dwels Mask 521
Bridgewater ms 'sorserer'
Trinity ms 'sorcerer'
Lest the Sorcerer us intice Mask 940
Trinity ms 'sorcerer'
1637 'sorcerer'
Sorcerers
The sable-stoled Sorcerers bear his worshipt Ark. Nativity 220
Sorceress
Had not the Snakie Sorceress that sat Par Lost 2.724
Sam. How cunningly the sorceress displays Samson 819
Sorceries
With monstrous shapes and sorceries abus'd Par Lost 1.479
To fence my ear against thy sorceries. Samson 937
Sorcery
Yet with a pleasing sorcerie could charm Par Lost 2.566
Of malice or of sorcery, or that power Mask 587
Trinity ms 'sorcerie'
Bridgewater ms 'Sorcerie'
1637 'sorcerie'
Hence with thy brew'd inchantments, foul deceiver, Mask 696
Trinity ms 'brewd enchauntments' ←'foule brud' ←'hel brewd opiate' ←'hel bru'd liquor' ←'bru'd sorcerie' ←'teacherous (leacherous?) bruage' ←'teacherous kindnesse'
Sord
Rustic, of grassie sord; thither anon Par Lost 11.433
Sordid
To scorn the sordid world, and unto Heav'n aspire. Fair Inf 63
Sore
Smote on him sore besides, vaulted with Fire; Par Lost 1.298
And writh'd him to and fro convolv'd; so sore Par Lost 6.328
Sore toild, his riv'n Armes to havoc hewn, Par Lost 6.449
These disobedient; sore hath been thir fight, Par Lost 6.687
Mistrust, Suspicion, Discord, and shook sore Par Lost 9.1124
To whom thus *Adam* sore beset repli'd. Par Lost 10.124
His first-begot we know, and sore have felt, Par Reg 1.89
Be not so sore offended, Son of God; Par Reg 4.196
After his aerie jaunt, though hurried sore, Par Reg 4.402
In that sore battel when so many dy'd Samson 287
Sore doth begin Circum 13
After this thy travail sore Winchester 49
Are troubled, yea my soul is troubled sore Psalm 6, 6
When trouble did thee sore assaile, Psalm 81, 25
Full sore doth press on me; Psalm 88, 30
Sorek
Was in the Vale of *Sorec*, *Dalila*, Samson 229
Sores
Salve to thy Sores, apt words have power to swage Samson 184
To the bodies wounds and sores Samson 607
Sorrow
Regions of sorrow, doleful shades, where peace Par Lost 1.65
Anguish and doubt and fear and sorrow and pain Par Lost 1.558
Sad *Acheron* of sorrow, black and deep; Par Lost 2.578
Both to and fro, thir sorrow to augment, Par Lost 2.605
And hourly born, with sorrow infinite Par Lost 2.797
Of woe and sorrow. Sternly he pronounc'd Par Lost 8.333
Thy sorrow I will greatly multiplie Par Lost 10.193
In sorrow forth, and to thy Husbands will Par Lost 10.195
Curs'd is the ground for thy sake, thou in sorrow Par Lost 10.201
To sorrow abandond, but worse felt within, Par Lost 10.717
Of sorrow unfeign'd, and humiliation meek. Par Lost 10.1092
Of sorrow unfeign'd, and humiliation meek. Par Lost 10.1104
Heart-strook with chilling gripe of sorrow stood, Par Lost 11.264
Of sorrow and dejection and despair Par Lost 11.301
And pious sorrow, equally enur'd Par Lost 11.362
Of tears and sorrow a Floud thee also drown'd, Par Lost 11.757
Presaging, since with sorrow and hearts distress Par Lost 12.613
Who hast of sorrow thy full load besides; Samson 214
Which is my chief affliction, shame and sorrow, Samson 457
Then thou shalt see, or rather to thy sorrow Samson 1154
And in my midst of sorrow and heart-grief Samson 1339
Sa. Perhaps thou shalt have cause to sorrow indeed. Samson 1347
The sorrow, and converts it nigh to joy. Samson 1564
Sorrow flies farr: See here be all the pleasures Mask 668
Bridgewater ms 'sorrowe'
Then to com in spight of sorrow, Allegro 45
For *Lycidas* your sorrow is not dead, Lycidas 166
For now to sorrow must I tune my song, Passion 8
Seas wept from our deep sorrow, Circum 9
Through sorrow, and affliction great Psalm 88, 37
Sorrowed
I sorrow'd at his captive state, but minded Samson 1603
Sorrowing
So send them forth, though sorrowing, yet in peace: Par Lost 11.117
Here besides the sorrowing Winchester 53
Sorrows
He sorrows now, repents, and prayes contrite, Par Lost 11.90
While I to sorrows am no less advanc't, Par Reg 2.69
Sorrows, and labours, opposition, hate, Par Reg 4.386
And every flower that sad embroidery wears: Lycidas 148
Trinity ms 'sad' ←'sorrows'
And wisely learn to curb thy sorrows wild; Fair Inf 73
My sorrows are too dark for day to know: Passion 33
Might think th' infection of my sorrows loud, Passion 55
Sorry
Off. I am sorry what this stoutness will produce. Samson 1346
And cheeks of sorry grain will serve to ply Mask 750
line not in Bridgewater ms
1637 'sorrie'
Trinity ms 'sorrie'
Sort
The first sort by thir own suggestion fell, Par Lost 3.129
Spirit of happie sort: his gestures fierce Par Lost 4.128
No Creature thence: if Spirit of other sort, Par Lost 4.582
Seek not the praise of men: the other sort Par Lost 6.376
Can sort, what harmonie or true delight? Par Lost 8.384
About him. But to *Adam* in what sort Par Lost 9.816
But on the hether side a different sort Par Lost 11.574
With dishes pil'd, and meats of noblest sort Par Reg 2.341
If I to try whether in higher sort Par Reg 4.198
A third sort doubted all things, though plain sence; Par Reg 4.296
Sam. Have they not Sword-players, and ev'ry sort Samson 1323
Of sort, might sit in order to behold, Samson 1608
Sorted
As sorted best with present things. The Sun Par Lost 10.651
Sorting
Ill sorting with my present state compar'd. Par Reg 1.200
Sorts
Gave thee, all sorts are here that all th' Earth yields, Par Lost 7.541
Sottish
Ahaz his sottish Conquerour, whom he drew Par Lost 1.472
But with besotted base ingratitude Mask 778
Trinity ms 'besotted' ←'a sottish'
Sought
Heap on himself damnation, while he sought Par Lost 1.215
Voutsaf't or sought; for what peace will be giv'n Par Lost 2.332
Philosophers in vain so long have sought, Par Lost 3.601
In search of whom they sought: him there they found Par Lost 4.799
Dole with delight, which in this place I sought; Par Lost 4.894
Of my revenge, first sought for thou returnst Par Lost 6.151
I flie not, but have sought thee farr and nigh. Par Lost 6.295
Dazl'd and spent, sunk down, and sought repair Par Lost 8.457
Satan involv'd in rising Mist, then sought Par Lost 9.75
Touchd onely, that our trial, when least sought, Par Lost 9.380
In Bowre and Field he sought, where any tuft Par Lost 9.417
He sought them both, but wish'd his hap might find Par Lost 9.421
At first, as one who sought access, but feard Par Lost 9.511
Mean I to trie, what rash untri'd I sought, Par Lost 9.860
Chiefly I sought, without thee can despise. Par Lost 9.878
Upon her Husband, saw thir shame that sought Par Lost 10.336
Thus to disburd'n sought with sad complaint. Par Lost 10.719
The good I sought not. To the loss of that, Par Lost 10.752

Sought(*cont*)
Wherefore didst thou beget me? I sought it not Par Lost 10.762
But self-destruction therefore saught, refutes Par Lost 10.1016
Ev'n to the Seat of God. For since I saught Par Lost 11.148
Favour unmerited by me, who sought Par Lost 12.278
Sought lost *Eliah*, so in each place these Par Reg 2.19
Were dead, who sought his life, and missing fill'd Par Reg 2.77
And for thy reason why they should be sought, Par Reg 2.485
Infallible; or wert thou sought to deeds Par Reg 3.16
His daughter, sought by many Prowest Knights, Par Reg 3.342
Not to be found, though sought. Yee see, O friends, Samson 193
Mee, not my Parents, that I sought to wed, Samson 220
She sought to make me Traytor to my self; Samson 401
With studied argument, and much perswasion sought Samson 658
As her at *Timna*, sought by all means therefore Samson 795
Thy countrey sought of thee, it sought unjustly, Samson 889
And sought to hide his froth-becurled head Psalm 114, 8

Soughtest
Submiss: he rear'd me, and Whom thou soughtst I am, Par Lost 8.316

Soul
(For Eloquence the Soul, Song charms the Sense,) Par Lost 2.556
O Son, in whom my Soul hath chief delight, Par Lost 3.168
His prey, nor suffer my unspotted Soule Par Lost 3.248
Part of my Soul I seek thee, and thee claim Par Lost 4.487
Created pure. But know that in the Soule Par Lost 5.100
Thou Sun, of this great World both Eye and Soule, Par Lost 5.171
Fansie and understanding, whence the Soule Par Lost 5.486
1667 'soule'
United as one individual Soule Par Lost 5.610
With Regal Scepter, every Soule in Heav'n Par Lost 5.816
Reptil with Spawn abundant, living Soule: Par Lost 7.388
Soul living, each that crept, which plenteously Par Lost 7.392
Express, and thou becam'st a living Soul. Par Lost 7.528
By living Soule, desert and desolate, Par Lost 8.154
And they shall be one Flesh, one Heart, one Soule. Par Lost 8.499
The Soule of Man, or passion in him move. Par Lost 8.585
Union of Mind, or in us both one Soule; Par Lost 8.604
As Flesh to mix with Flesh, or Soul with Soul. Par Lost 8.629
One Heart, one Soul in both; whereof good prooff Par Lost 9.967
Groand out his Soul with gushing bloud effus'd. Par Lost 11.447
By name to come call'd Charitie, the soul Par Lost 12.584
At least to try, and teach the erring Soul Par Reg 1.224
Spoken against, that through my very Soul Par Reg 2.90
Is yet more Kingly, this attracts the Soul, Par Reg 2.476
His good communicable to every soul Par Reg 3.125
Much of the Soul they talk, but all awrie, Par Reg 4.313
That light is in the Soul, Samson 92
The Dungeon of thy self; thy Soul Samson 156
The anguish of my Soul, that suffers not Samson 458
Who as they sung, would take the prison'd soul, Mask 256
Trinity ms 'soule'
Bridgewater ms 'soule'
1637 'soule'
But he that hides a dark soul, and foul thoughts Mask 383
Trinity ms 'soule'
Bridgewater ms 'sowle'
1637 'soule'
That when a soul is found sincerely so, Mask 454
1637 'soule'
Trinity ms 'soule'
Bridgewater ms 'sowle'
And turns it by degrees to the souls essence, Mask 462
The soul grows clotted by contagion, Mask 467
1637 'soule'
Bridgewater ms 'soule'
Trinity ms 'soule'
And took in strains that might create a soul Mask 561
1637 'soule'
Bridgewater ms 'sowle'
Trinity ms 'soule'
Thou hast nor Eare, nor Soul to apprehend Mask 784
line not in Bridgewater ms
line not in Trinity ms
1637 'Soule'
Such as the meeting soul may pierce Allegro 138
The hidden soul of harmony. Allegro 144
Thy rapt soul sitting in thine eyes: Penseroso 40
Or bid the soul of *Orpheus* sing Penseroso 105
Unhous'd thy Virgin Soul from her fair biding place. Fair Inf 21
Resolve me then oh Soul most surely blest Fair Inf 36
While sad *Ulisses* soul and all the rest Vacation 50
There doth my soul in holy vision sit Passion 41
When once our heav'nly-guided soul shall clime, On Time 19
Trinity ms 'soule'
Like fortunes may her soul acquaint, Winchester 72
Thy age, like ours, O Soul of Sir *John Cheek*, Sonnet 11, 12
Trinity ms 'soule' ←'soul'
Had ripen'd thy just soul to dwell with God, Sonnet 14, 2
Trinity ms 'soule' ←'soul'
Lodg'd with me useless, though my Soul more bent Sonnet 19, 4
Are troubled, yea my soul is troubled sore Psalm 6, 6
My soul, O save me for thy goodness sake Psalm 6, 8
He hast to tear my Soul asunder Psalm 7, 5
Let th' enemy pursue my soul Psalm 7, 13
My Soul doth long and almost die Psalm 84, 5
Preserve my soul, for I have trod Psalm 86, 5
Thy Servants Soul; for Lord to thee Psalm 86, 11
I lift my soul *and voice*, Psalm 86, 12

Soul(*cont*)
And thou hast free'd my Soul Psalm 86, 46
Surcharg'd my Soul doth lie, Psalm 88, 10
Why wilt thou Lord my soul forsake, Psalm 88, 57

Souls
Joyn voices all ye living Souls, ye Birds, Par Lost 5.197
To heav'nly Soules had bin all one; but now Par Lost 6.165
Before him, such as in thir Soules infix'd Par Lost 6.837
Conversion and Repentance, as to Souls Par Lost 11.724
As all their souls in blisfull rapture took: Nativity 98
Threatning to bind our soules with secular chaines: Sonnet 16, 12
1694 'Souls'

Sound
Then strait commands that at the warlike sound Par Lost 1.531
Rose like an Exhalation, with the sound Par Lost 1.711
And Trumpets sound throughout the Host proclaim Par Lost 1.754
The sound of blustring winds, which all night long Par Lost 2.286
Thir rising all at once was as the sound Par Lost 2.476
With Trumpets regal sound the great result: Par Lost 2.515
With impetuous recoile and jarring sound Par Lost 2.880
Thy praises, with th' innumerable sound Par Lost 3.147
Not distant far from thence a murmuring sound Par Lost 4.453
And temperat vapors bland, which th' only sound Par Lost 5.5
Acknowledge him thy Greater, sound his praise Par Lost 5.172
Ambiguous words and jealousies, to sound Par Lost 5.703
He said, and as the sound of waters deep Par Lost 5.872
In silence thir bright Legions, to the sound Par Lost 6.64
Of Battel now began, and rushing sound Par Lost 6.97
Of Battel: whereat *Michael* bid sound Par Lost 6.202
Dawning through Heav'n: forth rush'd with whirlwind sound Par Lost 6.749
Of his fierce Chariot rowld, as with the sound Par Lost 6.829
Her ever during Gates, Harmonious sound Par Lost 7.206
Followd with acclamation and the sound Par Lost 7.558
Noise, other then the sound of Dance or Song, Par Lost 8.243
More grateful then harmonious sound to the eare. Par Lost 8.606
Or Dairie, each rural sight, each rural sound; Par Lost 9.451
To lure her Eye; shee busied heard the sound Par Lost 9.518
Created mute to all articulat sound; Par Lost 9.557
Might tempt alone, and in her ears the sound Par Lost 9.736
A dismal universal hiss, the sound Par Lost 10.508
Sung *Halleluia*, as the sound of Seas, Par Lost 10.642
To sound at general Doom. Th' Angelic blast Par Lost 11.76
Of Cattel grazing: others, whence the sound Par Lost 11.558
In Thunder Lightning and loud Trumpets sound Par Lost 12.229
More awful then the sound of Trumpet, cri'd Par Reg 1.19
With sound of Harpies wings, and Talons heard; Par Reg 2.403
Beat off, returns as oft with humming sound; Par Reg 4.17
There flowrie hill *Hymettus* with the sound Par Reg 4.247
Sam. I hear the sound of words, thir sense the air Samson 176
But with th' afflicted in his pangs thir sound Samson 660
My best guide now, me thought it was the sound Mask 171
Or sound of pastoral reed with oaten stops, Mask 345
At last a soft and solemn breathing sound Mask 555
Not a waste, or needless sound Mask 942
And the jocond rebecks sound Allegro 94
I hear the far-off *Curfeu* sound, Penseroso 74
From the glad sound would not be absent long, Lycidas 35
No War, or Battails sound Nativity 53
Nature that heard such sound Nativity 101
A drear, and dying sound Nativity 193
Before thou cloath my fancy in fit sound: Vacation 32
Loud o're the rest *Cremona*'s Trump doth sound; Passion 26
With Trumpets *lofty sound*, Psalm 81, 10

Sound
Unhurt our mindes, and understanding sound, Par Lost 6.444
Foundst either sweet repast, or sound repose; Par Lost 9.407

Sound
They ferry over this *Lethean* Sound Par Lost 2.604

Sound-board
To many a row of Pipes the sound-board breaths. Par Lost 1.709
ms 'sound-bord'

Sounded
It sounded, and the faithful Armies rung Par Lost 6.204

Soundest
Induc'd me. As new wak't from soundest sleep Par Lost 8.253

Sounding
Clash'd on thir sounding Shields the din of war, Par Lost 1.668
Put to thir mouths the sounding Alchymie Par Lost 2.517
Ay me! Whilst thee the shores, and sounding Seas Lycidas 154
by leaving out those harsh ill sounding jarres Musick Tr. ms 5.03
'ill sounding' ←'chromatick'

Sounds
Sonorous mettal blowing Martial sounds: Par Lost 1.540
Of stunning sounds and voices all confus'd Par Lost 2.952
With Heav'nly touch of instrumental sounds Par Lost 4.686
Forthwith the Sounds and Seas, each Creek and Bay Par Lost 7.399
Walk'd firm; the crested Cock whose clarion sounds Par Lost 7.443
All sounds on Fret by String or Golden Wire Par Lost 7.597
The Sounds, and Seas with all their finny drove Mask 115
Bridgewater ms 'sounds'
Trinity ms 'sounds'
Inimitable sounds, yet as we go, Arcades 78
Wed your divine sounds, and mixt power employ Musick 3
Trinity ms 'divine sounds' ←'choise chords' ←'divine power'
Trinity ms 'mixt power' ←'mix't' ←'happiest sounds' ←'joynt force'

Sour
Strict Age, and sowre Severity, Mask 109
Source
Haile wedded Love, mysterious Law, true source Par Lost 4.750
1667 'sourse'
On mee, mee onely, as the sourse and spring Par Lost 10.832
The sourse of life; next favourable thou, Par Lost 11.169
This second sours of Men, while yet but few; Par Lost 12.13
And proves the sourse of all my miseries; Samson 64
Some sourse of consolation from above; Samson 664
South
Came like a Deluge on the South, and spread Par Lost 1.354
Uzziel, half these draw off, and coast the South Par Lost 4.782
Decrepit Winter, from the South to bring Par Lost 10.655
From cold *Estotiland*, and South as farr Par Lost 10.686
With adverse blast up-turns them from the South Par Lost 10.701
Of *Congo*, and *Angola* fardest South; Par Lost 11.401
From *Hamath* Northward to the Desert South Par Lost 12.139
And oft beyond; to South the *Persian* Bay, Par Reg 3.273
Of *Adiabene*, *Media*, and the South Par Reg 3.320
Or on the *Aemilian*, some from farthest South, Par Reg 4.69
Southern
Wash'd by the Southern Sea, and on the North Par Reg 4.28
Southmost
Of Southmost *Abarim;* in *Hesebon* Par Lost 1.408
Southward
Southward through *Eden* went a River large, Par Lost 4.223
Southwest
Westward, much nearer by Southwest, behold Par Reg 4.237
Southwind
Meanwhile the Southwind rose, and with black wings Par Lost 11.738
Sovereign
Who now is Sovran can dispose and bid Par Lost 1.246
Of Sovran power, with awful Ceremony Par Lost 1.753
ms 'sovran'
Our envied Sovran, and his Altar breathes Par Lost 2.244
And feel thy sovran vital Lamp; but thou Par Lost 3.22
Thy sovran sentence, that Man should find grace; Par Lost 3.145
Chos'n by the sovran Planter, when he fram'd Par Lost 4.691
Divine the sov'ran Architect had fram'd. Par Lost 5.256
Two onely, who yet by sov'ran gift possess Par Lost 5.366
Melodious Hymns about the sovran Throne Par Lost 5.656
So spake the Sovran voice, and Clouds began Par Lost 6.56
Immutably his sovran will, the end Par Lost 7.79
For state, as Sovran King, and to enure Par Lost 8.239
Sent from whose sovran goodness I adore. Par Lost 8.647
Wonder not, sovran Mistress, if perhaps Par Lost 9.532
Sovran of Creatures, universal Dame. Par Lost 9.612
O Sovran, vertuous, precious of all Trees Par Lost 9.795
Usurping over sovran Reason claimd Par Lost 9.1130
To whom the sovran Presence thus repli'd. Par Lost 10.144
Th' Almighty thus pronouncd his sovran Will. Par Lost 11.83
And out of Heav'n the Sov'raign voice I heard, Par Reg 1.84
But that by quick command from Soveran *Jove* Mask 41
1637 'Soveraigne'
Trinity ms 'soveraigne'
Bridgewater ms 'soveraigne'
And bad me keep it as of sovran use Mask 639
Trinity ms 'soveraine'
Bridgewater ms 'soveraigne'
1673 'sov'ran'
1637 'soveraine'
As if they surely knew their sovran Lord was by. Nativity 60
He sov'ran Priest stooping his regall head Passion 15
Ay sung before the saphire-colour'd throne Musick 7
Trinity ms 'sapphire-coulour'd ←'saphire-colour'd'
←'saphire-colourd' ←'soveraigne'
Sovereignty
And this Imperial Sov'ranty, adorn'd Par Lost 2.446
Or from Heav'n claming second Sovrantie; Par Lost 12.35
Sow
To sow a jangling noise of words unknown: Par Lost 12.55
To Heav'n. Their martyr'd blood and ashes sow Sonnet 18, 10
1673 printed 'so', errata 'sow'
Sowed
Advancing, sow'd the earth with Orient Pearle, Par Lost 5.2
And sowd with Starrs the Heav'n thick as a field: Par Lost 7.358
The Lillie and Rose, that neither sow'd nor spun. Sonnet 20, 8
Sown
Sow'n with contrition in his heart, then those Par Lost 11.27
Thin sown with aught of profit or delight, Par Reg 4.345
Space
Nine times the Space that measures Day and Night Par Lost 1.50
ms 'space'
Space may produce new Worlds; whereof so rife Par Lost 1.650
Hov'ring a space, till Winds the signal blow Par Lost 2.717
'Twixt Host and Host but narrow space was left, Par Lost 6.104
All space, the ambient Aire wide interfus'd Par Lost 7.89
Infinitude, nor vacuous the space. Par Lost 7.169
The space of seven continu'd Nights he rode Par Lost 9.63
That space the Evil one abstracted stood Par Lost 9.463
And durable; and now in little space Par Lost 10.320
A space, till firmer thoughts restraind excess, Par Lost 11.498
The space of seventie years, then brings them back, Par Lost 12.345
Admiring stood a space, then into Hymns Par Reg 1.169
In ample space under the broadest shade Par Reg 2.339
Spaces
Within, her ample spaces, o're the smooth Par Lost 1.725
Spaces(*cont*)
Spaces incomprehensible (for such Par Lost 8.20
Spacious
Op'nd into the Hill a spacious wound Par Lost 1.689
And Porches wide, but chief the spacious Hall Par Lost 1.762
Lies through your spacious Empire up to light, Par Lost 2.974
Here walk'd the Fiend at large in spacious field. Par Lost 3.430
This spacious ground, in yonder shadie Bowre Par Lost 5.367
Equal to ours, throughout the spacious North; Par Lost 5.726
This continent of spacious Heav'n, adornd Par Lost 6.474
Rowld inward, and a spacious Gap disclos'd Par Lost 6.861
So spacious, and his Line stretcht out so farr; Par Lost 8.102
As Lords, a spacious World, to our native Heaven Par Lost 10.467
He lookd and saw a spacious Plaine, whereon Par Lost 11.556
A spatious plain out stretch't in circuit wide Par Reg 3.254
The building was a spacious Theatre Samson 1605
Spade
Of Pioners with Spade and Pickax arm'd Par Lost 1.676
ms 'spade'
Spades
A multitude with Spades and Axes arm'd Par Reg 3.331
Spake
So spake th' Apostate Angel, though in pain, Par Lost 1.125
So *Satan* spake, and him *Beelzebub* Par Lost 1.271
He spake: and to confirm his words, out-flew Par Lost 1.663
He reck'd not, and these words thereafter spake. Par Lost 2.50
Not peace: and after him thus *Mammon* spake. Par Lost 2.228
Or Summers Noon-tide air, while thus he spake. Par Lost 2.309
Conscious of highest worth, unmov'd thus spake. Par Lost 2.429
So spake the grieslie terrour, and in shape, Par Lost 2.704
She spake, and at her words the hellish Pest Par Lost 2.735
Thus to his onely Son foreseeing spake. Par Lost 3.79
Thus while God spake, ambrosial fragrance fill'd Par Lost 3.135
Which uttering thus he to his Father spake. Par Lost 3.143
Silent yet spake, and breath'd immortal love Par Lost 3.267
So spake the false dissembler unperceivd; Par Lost 3.681
Thus while he spake, each passion dimm'd his face Par Lost 4.114
So spake the Fiend, and with necessitie, Par Lost 4.393
So spake our general Mother, and with eyes Par Lost 4.492
When *Gabriel* to his next in power thus spake. Par Lost 4.781
So spake the Cherube, and his grave rebuke Par Lost 4.844
To whom with stern regard thus *Gabriel* spake. Par Lost 4.877
While thus he spake, th' Angelic Squadron bright Par Lost 4.977
On *Adam*, whom imbracing, thus she spake. Par Lost 5.27
So spake th' Eternal Father, and fulfilld Par Lost 5.246
Brightness had made invisible, thus spake. Par Lost 5.599
So spake th' Omnipotent, and with his words Par Lost 5.616
Awak'ning, thus to him in secret spake. Par Lost 5.672
So spake the false Arch-Angel, and infus'd Par Lost 5.694
So spake the Son, but *Satan* with his Powers Par Lost 5.743
So spake the fervent Angel, but his zeale Par Lost 5.849
So spake the Seraph *Abdiel* faithful found, Par Lost 5.896
So spake the Sovran voice, and Clouds began Par Lost 6.56
So spake the Prince of Angels; to whom thus Par Lost 6.281
And cloudie in aspect thus answering spake. Par Lost 6.450
And thus the filial Godhead answering spake. Par Lost 6.722
To all his Host on either hand thus spake. Par Lost 6.800
So spake the Son, and into terrour chang'd Par Lost 6.824
Thir multitude, and to his Son thus spake. Par Lost 7.138
So spake th' Almightie, and to what he spake Par Lost 7.174
Again th' Almightie spake: Let there be Lights Par Lost 7.339
Present) thus to his Son audibly spake. Par Lost 7.518
So spake our Sire, and by his count'nance seemd Par Lost 8.39
So spake the Godlike Power, and thus our Sire. Par Lost 8.249
Knew not; to speak I tri'd, and forthwith spake, Par Lost 8.271
As thus he spake, each Bird and Beast behold Par Lost 8.349
So spake the Universal Lord, and seem'd Par Lost 8.376
Thus I embold'nd spake, and freedom us'd Par Lost 8.434
So spake domestick *Adam* in his care Par Lost 9.318
So spake the Patriarch of Mankinde, but *Eve* Par Lost 9.376
So spake the Enemie of Mankind, enclos'd Par Lost 9.494
Not unamaz'd she thus in answer spake. Par Lost 9.552
Which when she saw, thus to her guide she spake. Par Lost 9.646
Fraud in the Serpent, speaking as he spake; Par Lost 9.1150
So spake the Father, and unfoulding bright Par Lost 10.63
So spake this Oracle, then verifi'd Par Lost 10.182
So spake our Father penitent, nor *Eve* Par Lost 10.1097
So spake, so wish'd much-humbl'd *Eve*, but Fate Par Lost 11.181
Pursuing, not unmov'd to *Eve* thus spake. Par Lost 11.192
While the great Visitant approachd, thus spake. Par Lost 11.225
In wise deport, spake much of Right and Wrong, Par Lost 11.666
So spake th' Archangel *Michael*, then paus'd, Par Lost 12.466
So spake our Mother *Eve*, and *Adam* heard Par Lost 12.624
Of Angels, thus to *Gabriel* smiling spake. Par Reg 1.129
So spake the Eternal Father, and all Heaven Par Reg 1.168
By Vision, found thee in the Temple, and spake Par Reg 1.256
Known partly, and soon found of whom they spake Par Reg 1.262
So spake our Morning Star then in his rise, Par Reg 1.294
Perus'd him, then with words thus utt'red spake. Par Reg 1.320
So spake our Saviour; but the subtle Fiend, Par Reg 1.465
So spake the old Serpent doubting, and from all Par Reg 2.147
He spake no dream, for as his words had end, Par Reg 2.337
So spake the Son of God, and Satan stood Par Reg 3.1
So spake the Son of God; and here again Par Reg 3.145
So spake *Israel*'s true King, and to the Fiend Par Reg 3.441
So spake the Son of God; but Satan now Par Reg 4.365
The Trumpet spake not to the armed throng, Nativity 58
And speak the truth of thee on glorious Theams Sonnet 14, 12

Spake*(cont)*
Trinity ms 'spake'
Spakest
And be so minded still; I, ere thou spak'st, Par Lost 8.444
Span
First taught our English Musick how to span Sonnet 13, 2
Spangled
Spangl'd with eyes more numerous then those Par Lost 11.130
But farr above in spangled sheen Mask 1003
line not in Bridgewater ms
And tricks his beams, and with new spangled Ore, Lycidas 170
Trinity ms 'newspangled'
And all the spangled host keep watch in squadrons bright? Nativity 21
Amongst her spangled sisters bright. Psalm 136, 34
Spangling
Spangling the Hemisphere: then first adornd Par Lost 7.384
Spare
Though last created, that for him I spare Par Lost 3.278
Thy Fathers dreadful Thunder didst not spare, Par Lost 3.393
More fruitful, which instructs us not to spare. Par Lost 5.320
Spare out of life perhaps, and not repine, Par Lost 6.460
All were who heard, dim sadness did not spare Par Lost 10.23
His Visage drawn he felt to sharp and spare, Par Lost 10.511
Sam. Spare that proposal, Father, spare the trouble Samson 487
And holy dictate of spare Temperance: Mask 767
Spare Fast, that oft with gods doth diet, Penseroso 46
The great *Emathian* Conqueror bid spare Sonnet 8, 10
He who of those delights can judge, And spare Sonnet 20, 13
And set at large; now spare, Psalm 4, 5
Spared
I spar'd not, for such pleasure till that hour Par Lost 9.596
Serpent, we might have spar'd our coming hither, Par Lost 9.647
How well could I have spar'd for thee young swain, Lycidas 113
Sparely
On whose fresh lap the swart Star sparely looks, Lycidas 138
Trinity ms 'sparely' ←'faintly' ←'sparely'
Spares
Prevented spares to tell thee yet by deeds Par Lost 2.739
Spark
Discoverd and surpriz'd. As when a spark Par Lost 4.814
Sparkle
Swift as the Sparkle of a glancing Star, Mask 80
Trinity ms 'sparkle'
Bridgewater ms 'sparcle'
I see bright honour sparkle through your eyes, Arcades 27
Sparkled
Sparkl'd in all thir eyes; with full assent Par Lost 2.388
Sparkles
Of smoak and bickering flame, and sparkles dire; Par Lost 6.766
Sparkling
That sparkling blaz'd, his other Parts besides Par Lost 1.194
Imbellisht, thick with sparkling orient Gemmes Par Lost 3.507
Sparkling, out-pow'rd, the flavor, or the smell, Samson 544
Sparrow
There ev'n the Sparrow *freed from wrong* Psalm 84, 9
Spartan
Atlantick Sisters, and the *Spartan* Twins Par Lost 10.674
Young *Hyacinth* the pride of *Spartan* land; Fair Inf 26
Spasm
Of gastly Spasm, or racking torture, qualmes Par Lost 11.481
Spattering
With spattering noise rejected: oft they assayd, Par Lost 10.567
Spawn
Reptil with Spawn abundant, living Soule: Par Lost 7.388
Thronging the Seas with spawn innumerable, Mask 713
Bridgewater ms 'spawne'
1637 'spawne'
Trinity ms 'spawne'
Speak
To speak; whereat thir doubl'd Ranks they bend Par Lost 1.616
We now debate; who can advise, may speak. Par Lost 2.42
Speak yee who best can tell, ye Sons of light, Par Lost 5.160
This I perform, speak thou, and be it don: Par Lost 7.164
And for the Heav'ns wide Circuit, let it speak Par Lost 8.100
A lower flight, and speak of things at hand Par Lost 8.199
Knew not; to speak I tri'd, and forthwith spake, Par Lost 8.271
My Maker, be propitious while I speak. Par Lost 8.380
Tedious alike: Of fellowship I speak Par Lost 8.389
The Tongue not made for Speech to speak thy praise: Par Lost 9.749
And gladly of our Union heare thee speak, Par Lost 9.966
To speak all Tongues, and do all Miracles, Par Lost 12.501
But now again she makes address to speak. Samson 731
Man. Suspense in news is torture, speak them out. Samson 1569
I never heard till now. Ile speak to her Mask 264
Bridgewater ms 'speake'
Trinity ms 'speake'
1637 'speake'
Or while we speak within the direfull grasp Mask 357
line not in Bridgewater ms
line not in Trinity ms
1637 'speake'
That hallow I should know, what are you? speak; Mask 490
Bridgewater ms 'speake'
1637 'speake'
Trinity ms 'speake'
Spir. What voice is that, my young Lord? speak agen. Mask 492
Bridgewater ms 'speake'
Trinity ms 'speake'

Speak*(cont)*
Didst move my first endeavouring tongue to speak, Vacation 2
And speak the truth of thee on glorious Theams Sonnet 14, 12
Trinity ms 'spake'
Speak to them in his wrath, and in his fell Psalm 2, 10
Speak to your hearts alone, Psalm 4, 20
Thou wilt destroy that speak a ly Psalm 5, 15
And now what God the Lord will speak Psalm 85, 29
To his dear Saints he will speak peace, Psalm 85, 33
Having to advise the public may speak free, Prose 9, 2
Speakable
How cam'st thou speakable of mute, and how Par Lost 9.563
Speakest
Those terrors which thou speak'st of, did me none; Par Reg 4.487
Speaking
So speaking and so threatning, grew tenfold Par Lost 2.705
Thought him still speaking, still stood fixt to hear; Par Lost 8.3
line not in 1667 edition
Speaking or mute all comliness and grace Par Lost 8.222
Fraud in the Serpent, speaking as he spake; Par Lost 9.1150
Speaks
And knows, and speaks, and reasons, and discerns, Par Lost 9.765
Chor. Hee speaks, let us draw nigh. Matchless in might, Samson 178
Speaks thunder, and the chains of *Erebus* Mask 804
line not in Bridgewater ms
line not in Trinity ms
For to his people he speaks peace Psalm 85, 31
Spear
His Spear, to equal which the tallest Pine Par Lost 1.292
ms 'speare'
Till, as a signal giv'n, th' uplifted Spear Par Lost 1.347
ms 'speare'
Bow'd down in Battel, sunk before the Spear Par Lost 1.436
ms 'spear'
Of Warriers old with order'd Spear and Shield, Par Lost 1.565
ms 'spear'
I laugh, when those who at the Spear are bold Par Lost 2.204
Half wheeling to the Shield, half to the Spear. Par Lost 4.785
Him thus intent *Ithuriel* with his Spear Par Lost 4.810
And seconded thy else not dreaded Spear. Par Lost 4.929
What seemd both Spear and Shield: now dreadful deeds Par Lost 4.990
His massie Spear upstaid; as if on Earth Par Lost 6.195
Down fell both Spear and Shield, down they as fast, Par Lost 10.542
Satans dire dread, and in his hand the Spear. Par Lost 11.248
Of brazen shield and spear, the hammer'd Cuirass, Samson 132
Not worse then by his shield and spear Samson 284
At one spears length. O ever failing trust Samson 348
Vant-brass and Greves, and Gauntlet, add thy Spear Samson 1121
The idle spear and shield were high up hung; Nativity 55
1673 'Spear'
Lift not thy spear against the Muses Bowre, Sonnet 8, 9
Trinity ms 'speare'
Spears
A Forrest huge of Spears: and thronging Helms Par Lost 1.547
ms 'speares'
Prick forth the Aerie Knights, and couch thir Spears Par Lost 2.536
1667 'spears'
Celestial Armourie, Shields, Helmes, and Speares, Par Lost 4.553
With ported Spears, as thick as when a field Par Lost 4.980
Of rigid Spears, and Helmets throng'd, and Shields Par Lost 6.83
Archers, and Slingers, Cataphracts and Spears. Samson 1619
Special
God and good Angels guard by special grace. Par Lost 2.1033
Whom God hath of his special favour rais'd Samson 273
Under his special eie Samson 636
Specious
Thir specious deeds on earth, which glory excites, Par Lost 2.484
Some specious object by the Foe suborn'd, Par Lost 9.361
Well deem in outward Rites and specious formes Par Lost 12.534
And count thy specious gifts no gifts but guiles. Par Reg 2.391
That specious Monster, my accomplisht snare. Samson 230
Specked
Carnation, Purple, Azure, or spect with Gold, Par Lost 9.429
Speckled
And speckl'd vanity Nativity 136
Spectacle
A spectacle of ruin or of scorn Par Reg 1.415
The sight of this so horrid spectacle Samson 1542
Not to be absent at that spectacle. Samson 1604
Spectators
That heav'n would want spectators, God want praise; Par Lost 4.676
Spectres
And grisly Spectres, which the Fiend had rais'd Par Reg 4.430
Specular
Look once more e're we leave this specular Mount Par Reg 4.236
Speculation
Of Speculation; for the hour precise Par Lost 12.589
Speculations
Thenceforth to Speculations high or deep Par Lost 9.602
Sped
Down from th' Ecliptic, sped with hop'd success, Par Lost 3.740
What recks it them? What need they? They are sped; Lycidas 122
As Zeb and Oreb evil sped Psalm 83, 41
Speech
They vote: whereat his speech he thus renews. Par Lost 2.389
With faultring speech and visage incompos'd Par Lost 2.989
Scarce thus at length faild speech recoverd sad. Par Lost 4.357
To first of women *Eve* thus moving speech, Par Lost 4.409

Speech(*cont*)
Exceeded human, and his wary speech — Par Lost 5.459
Cannot without process of speech be told, — Par Lost 7.178
So ordering. I with leave of speech implor'd, — Par Lost 8.377
Of Reason in my inward Powers, and Speech — Par Lost 9.600
The Tongue not made for Speech to speak thy praise: — Par Lost 9.749
Speech intermitted thus to *Eve* renewd. — Par Lost 9.1133
Then with transition sweet new Speech resumes. — Par Lost 12.5
line not in 1667 edition
And with fair speech these words to him address'd. — Par Reg 2.301
Speeches
Onely with speeches fair — Nativity 37
Speechless
Speechless he stood and pale, till thus at length — Par Lost 9.894
Speed
The work of Sulphur. Thither wing'd with speed — Par Lost 1.674
False fugitive, and to thy speed add wings, — Par Lost 2.700
So much the neerer danger; go and speed; — Par Lost 2.1008
His habit fit for speed succinct, and held — Par Lost 3.643
Yet not rejoycing in his speed, though bold, — Par Lost 4.13
Bent all on speed, and markt his Aerie Gate; — Par Lost 4.568
Ithuriel and *Zephon*, with wingd speed — Par Lost 4.788
Thy blasting volied Thunder made all speed — Par Lost 4.928
On each hand parting, to his speed gave way — Par Lost 5.252
This day to be our Guest. But goe with speed, — Par Lost 5.313
With speed what force is left, and all imploy — Par Lost 5.730
Far was advanc't on winged speed, an Host — Par Lost 5.744
In horror; from each hand with speed retir'd — Par Lost 6.307
Of incorporeal speed, her warmth and light; — Par Lost 8.37
Speed, to describe whose swiftness Number failes. — Par Lost 8.38
Speed almost Spiritual; mee thou thinkst not slow, — Par Lost 8.110
I told ye then he should prevail and speed — Par Lost 10.40
Down he descended strait; the speed of Gods — Par Lost 10.90
So saying he dismiss'd them, they with speed — Par Lost 10.410
Would speed before thee, and be louder heard, — Par Lost 10.954
Though bent on speed, so heer th' Arch-angel paus'd — Par Lost 12.2
line not in 1667 edition
Had left him vacant, and with speed was gon — Par Reg 2.116
Comes on amain, speed in his look. — Samson 1304
Rise therefore with all speed and come along, — Samson 1316
Off. My message was impos'd on me with speed, — Samson 1343
Sam. So take it with what speed thy message needs. — Samson 1345
The clotted gore. I with what speed the while — Samson 1728
Already, ere my best speed could praevent, — Mask 573
Bridgewater ms 'speede'
The Sun himself with-held his wonted speed, — Nativity 79
And after short abode flie back with speed, — Fair Inf 60
Whose speed is but the heavy Plummets pace; — On Time 3
Is Kingly. Thousands at his bidding speed — Sonnet 19, 12
So let their Princes speed — Psalm 83, 42
Speeded
Well have we speeded, and o're hill and dale, — Par Reg 3.267
Speedier
Inspir'd, and wing'd for Heav'n with speedier flight — Par Lost 11.7
Of lighter toes, and such Court guise — Mask 962
Trinity ms 'lighter' ←'nimbler' ←'speedier'
Speediest
The speediest of thy winged messengers, — Par Lost 3.229
But firm Battalion; back with speediest Sail — Par Lost 6.534
My speediest friend, by death to rid me hence, — Samson 1263
Speedily
Who speedily through all the Hierarchies — Par Lost 5.692
Speeding
And to our wish I see one hither speeding, — Samson 1539
Speeds
He speeds, and through the vast Ethereal Skie — Par Lost 5.267
Speedy
Whereto with speedy words th' Arch-fiend reply'd. — Par Lost 1.156
Toward the four winds four speedy Cherubim — Par Lost 2.516
To other speedie aide might lend at need; — Par Lost 9.260
No long petition, speedy death, — Samson 650
Thir own destruction to come speedy upon them. — Samson 1681
Spell
In their conjunction met, give me to spell, — Par Reg 4.385
To inveigle and invite th' unwary sense — Mask 538
Trinity ms 'sense' ←'spell'
The clasping charm, and thaw the numming spell, — Mask 853
And old sooth-saying *Glaucus* spell, — Mask 874
Now the spell hath lost his hold; — Mask 919
Where I may sit and rightly spell, — Penseroso 170
No nightly trance, or breathed spell, — Nativity 179
What power, what force, what mighty spell, if not — Vacation 89
Spelled
The drift of hollow states hard to be spelld, — Sonnet 17, 6
1694 'Spell'd'
1662 'spell'd'
Spelling
Stand spelling fals, while one might walk to Mile- — Sonnet 11, 7
Spells
Thir ornament and safety, had not spells — Samson 1132
Sam. I know no Spells, use no forbidden Arts; — Samson 1139
To frustrate and dissolve these Magic spells, — Samson 1149
My dazling Spells into the spungy ayr, — Mask 154
Trinity ms 'spells'
Bridgewater ms 'spells'
Yet have they many baits, and guilefull spells — Mask 537
Enter'd the very lime-twigs of his spells, — Mask 646
Spend
Th' Almighty Victor to spend all his rage, — Par Lost 2.144
Fit haunt of Gods? where I had hope to spend, — Par Lost 11.271
Shal spend thir dayes in joy unblam'd, and dwell — Par Lost 12.22
Spent
Perhaps hath spent his shafts, and ceases now — Par Lost 1.176
Eternity so spent in worship paid — Par Lost 2.248
Thir happie hours in joy and hymning spent. — Par Lost 3.417
That day, as other solemn dayes, they spent — Par Lost 5.618
And Day is yet not spent; till then thou seest — Par Lost 8.206
Dazl'd and spent, sunk down, and sought repair — Par Lost 8.457
Whether such vertue spent of old now faild — Par Lost 9.145
Thus they in mutual accusation spent — Par Lost 9.1187
Thy life hath yet been private, most part spent — Par Reg 3.232
Quite at a loss, for all his darts were spent, — Par Reg 4.366
Yet with no new device, they all were spent, — Par Reg 4.443
And calm of mind all passion spent. — Samson 1758
Obedient to the Moon he spent his date — Another 29
line not in 1658 text
When I consider how my light is spent, — Sonnet 19, 1
E're yet my life be spent, — Psalm 88, 54
Spets
Of Stygian darknes spets her thickest gloom, — Mask 132
Bridgewater ms 'spetts'
Trinity ms 'spitts'
Sphere
Thus they in Heav'n, above the starry Sphear, — Par Lost 3.416
And that Crystalline Sphear whose ballance weighs — Par Lost 3.482
I fell, how glorious once above thy Spheare; — Par Lost 4.39
This day at highth of Noon came to my Spheare — Par Lost 4.564
With thy bright Circlet, praise him in thy Spheare — Par Lost 5.169
Mystical dance, which yonder starrie Spheare — Par Lost 5.620
Within the visible Diurnal Spheare; — Par Lost 7.22
A mightie Spheare he fram'd, unlightsom first, — Par Lost 7.355
To save appeerances, how gird the Sphear — Par Lost 8.82
Not to th' extent of thir own Spheare. But say — Par Lost 10.808
Or the sphear of fortune raises; — Samson 172
Sweet Queen of Parly, Daughter of the Sphear, — Mask 241
1637 'Sphaere'
Trinity ms 'spheare'
Bridgewater ms 'spheare'
B.M. ms 'Sphere'
Down through the turning sphear — Nativity 48
Whether above that high first-moving Spheare — Fair Inf 39
Walk'st on the rowling Sphear, and through the deep, — Prose 12, 2
Sphere-born
Sphear-born harmonious Sisters, Voice, and Vers, — Musick 2
Trinity ms 'Spheare borne' ←'Spheare-borne'
Sphered
Sphear'd in a radiant Cloud, for yet the Sun — Par Lost 7.247
Sphere-metal
Made of sphear-metal, never to decay — Another 5
1657 'spheares metall'
1640 'spheares mettall'
1658 'Sphear mettall'
Spheres
Each in thir several active Sphears assignd, — Par Lost 5.477
Should combat, and thir jarring Sphears confound. — Par Lost 6.315
Which else to several Sphears thou must ascribe, — Par Lost 8.131
Who in their nightly watchfull Sphears, — Mask 113
1637 'Spheares'
Trinity ms 'spheares'
Bridgewater ms 'sphears'
That sit upon the nine enfolded Sphears, — Arcades 64
Ring out ye Crystall sphears, — Nativity 125
Then passing through the Spheres of watchful fire, — Vacation 40
1673 printed 'Spherse'
Sphery
Higher then the Spheary chime; — Mask 1021
Bridgewater ms 'sphearie'
B.M. ms 'sphaery'
1637 'Sphaerie'
Trinity ms 'speharie' ←'sphaerie'
Spicy
Thir spicie Drugs: they on the Trading Flood — Par Lost 2.640
Sabean Odours from the spicie shoare — Par Lost 4.162
Him through the spicie Forrest onward com — Par Lost 5.298
Flung Rose, flung Odours from the spicie Shrub, — Par Lost 8.517
Then to the Spicy Nut-brown Ale, — Allegro 100
Spied
Then as a Tyger, who by chance hath spi'd — Par Lost 4.403
Half spi'd, so thick the Roses bushing round — Par Lost 9.426
He wanderd long, till thee he spy'd from farr, — Fair Inf 17
Spies
Beyond his hope, *Eve* separate he spies, — Par Lost 9.424
Our great Forbidder, safe with all his Spies — Par Lost 9.815
To them who had corrupted her, my Spies, — Samson 386
Appointed to await me thirty spies, — Samson 1197
Spilt
Who having spilt much blood, and don much waste — Par Lost 11.791
Spindle
And turn the Adamantine spindle round, — Arcades 66
Spinning
With inoffensive pace that spinning sleeps — Par Lost 8.164
And set to work millions of spinning Worms, — Mask 715
Bridgewater ms 'spinninge'
Spires
Drivn backward slope thir pointing spires, and rowld — Par Lost 1.223

Spires(*cont*)
With glistering Spires and Pinnacles adornd, Par Lost 3.550
Amidst his circling Spires, that on the grass Par Lost 9.502
Turrets and Terrases, and glittering Spires. Par Reg 4.54
Of Alabaster, top't with Golden Spires: Par Reg 4.548

Spirit
And chiefly Thou O Spirit, that dost prefer Par Lost 1.17
Can perish: for the mind and spirit remains Par Lost 1.139
Have left us this our spirit and strength intire Par Lost 1.146
Belial came last, then whom a Spirit more lewd Par Lost 1.490
ms 'spirit'
Mammon, the least erected Spirit that fell Par Lost 1.679
ms 'spirit'
Stood up, the strongest and the fiercest Spirit Par Lost 2.44
Or Spirit of the nethermost Abyss Par Lost 2.956
Transfus'd on thee his ample Spirit rests. Par Lost 3.389
The Spirit maligne, but much more envy seis'd Par Lost 3.553
Glad was the Spirit impure as now in hope Par Lost 3.630
The sharpest sighted Spirit of all in Heav'n; Par Lost 3.691
Spirit of happie sort: his gestures fierce Par Lost 4.128
Some wandring Spirit of Heav'n, by Fountain side, Par Lost 4.531
A Spirit, zealous, as he seem'd, to know Par Lost 4.565
No Creature thence: if Spirit of other sort, Par Lost 4.582
Who tells of som infernal Spirit seen Par Lost 4.793
Think not, revolted Spirit, thy shape the same, Par Lost 4.835
Raphael, the sociable Spirit, that deign'd Par Lost 5.221
Till body up to spirit work, in bounds Par Lost 5.478
Your bodies may at last turn all to Spirit, Par Lost 5.497
O favourable spirit, propitious guest, Par Lost 5.507
O alienate from God, O spirit accurst, Par Lost 5.877
It self instinct with Spirit, but convoyd Par Lost 6.752
One Spirit in them rul'd, and every eye Par Lost 6.848
My overshadowing Spirit and might with thee Par Lost 7.165
Spontaneous, for within them Spirit livd, Par Lost 7.204
And Spirit coming to create new Worlds. Par Lost 7.209
His brooding wings the Spirit of God outspred, Par Lost 7.235
Expressing well the spirit within thee free, Par Lost 8.440
The spirit of love and amorous delight. Par Lost 8.477
Which oft, they say, some evil Spirit attends Par Lost 9.638
Least that pure breath of Life, the Spirit of Man Par Lost 10.784
Unutterable, which the Spirit of prayer Par Lost 11.6
The World: in Spirit perhaps he also saw Par Lost 11.406
Unmindful of thir Maker, though his Spirit Par Lost 11.611
Upon thir Tongues a various Spirit to rase Par Lost 12.53
From shadowie Types to Truth, from Flesh to Spirit, Par Lost 12.303
His Spirit within them, and the Law of Faith Par Lost 12.488
Thir proudest persecuters: for the Spirit Par Lost 12.497
Though not but by the Spirit understood. Par Lost 12.514
The Spirit of God, promisd alike and giv'n Par Lost 12.519
Left them inrould, or what the Spirit within Par Lost 12.523
But force the Spirit of Grace it self, and binde Par Lost 12.525
Of Spirit and Truth; the rest, farr greater part, Par Lost 12.533
Thou Spirit who ledst this glorious Eremite Par Reg 1.8
The Spirit descended, while the Fathers voice Par Reg 1.31
One day forth walk'd alone, the Spirit leading; Par Reg 1.189
To which my Spirit aspir'd, victorious deeds Par Reg 1.215
The Spirit descended on me like a Dove, Par Reg 1.282
'Tis true, I am that Spirit unfortunate, Par Reg 1.358
And sends his Spirit of Truth henceforth to dwell Par Reg 1.462
Belial the dislolutest Spirit that fell, Par Reg 2.150
A spirit and judgment equal or superior, Par Reg 4.324
Ambitious spirit, and wouldst be thought my God, Par Reg 4.495
Though in these chains, bulk without spirit vast, Samson 1238
Of fire; that Spirit that first rusht on thee Samson 1435
Among them he a spirit of phrenzie sent, Samson 1675
The spirit of *Plato* to unfold Penseroso 89
Sent by som spirit to mortals good, Penseroso 153
Fame is the spur that the clear spirit doth raise Lycidas 70
Tell me bright Spirit where e're thou hoverest Fair Inf 38
My spirit som transporting *Cherub* feels, Passion 38

Spirited
Flew upward, spirited with various forms, Par Lost 3.717
So talk'd the spirited sly Snake; and *Eve* Par Lost 9.613

Spiritless
Exhausted, spiritless, afflicted, fall'n. Par Lost 6.852

Spiritous
But more refin'd, more spiritous, and pure, Par Lost 5.475
Of spiritous and fierie spume, till toucht Par Lost 6.479

Spirits
Innumerable force of Spirits arm'd Par Lost 1.101
Eternal spirits; or have ye chos'n this place Par Lost 1.318
These Feminine. For Spirits when they please Par Lost 1.423
ms 'spirits'
Millions of Spirits for his fault amerc't Par Lost 1.609
ms 'spirits'
O Myriads of immortal Spirits, O Powers Par Lost 1.622
ms 'spirits'
Caelestial Spirits in Bondage, nor th' Abyss Par Lost 1.658
By Spirits reprobate, and in an hour Par Lost 1.697
ms 'spirits'
Thus incorporeal Spirits to smallest forms Par Lost 1.789
ms 'spirits'
His own: for neither do the Spirits damn'd Par Lost 2.482
(What could it less when Spirits immortal sing2) Par Lost 2.553
Hell-born, not to contend with Spirits of Heav'n. Par Lost 2.687
And reck'n'st thou thy self with Spirits of Heav'n, Par Lost 2.696
Of Spirits that in our just pretenses arm'd Par Lost 2.825
And Spirits of this nethermost Abyss, Par Lost 2.969

Spirits(*cont*)
Of this frail World; by which the Spirits perverse Par Lost 2.1030
And Spirits, both them who stood and them who faild; Par Lost 3.101
All Heav'n, and in the blessed Spirits elect Par Lost 3.136
With these that never fade the Spirits elect Par Lost 3.360
Translated Saints, or middle Spirits hold Par Lost 3.461
Uriel, for thou of those seav'n Spirits that stand Par Lost 3.654
As to superior Spirits is wont in Heaven, Par Lost 3.737
Among the spirits beneath, whom I seduc'd Par Lost 4.83
1667 'Spirits' in some copies
Not Spirits, yet to heav'nly Spirits bright Par Lost 4.361
From these, two strong and suttle Spirits he calld Par Lost 4.786
Th' animal Spirits that from pure blood arise Par Lost 4.805
Which of those rebell Spirits adjudg'd to Hell Par Lost 4.823
As may not oft invite, though Spirits of Heav'n Par Lost 5.374
Spiritual, may of purest Spirits be found Par Lost 5.406
Through Spirits with ease; nor wonder; if by fire Par Lost 5.439
Spirits odorous breathes: flours and thir fruit Par Lost 5.482
To vital Spirits aspire, to animal, Par Lost 5.484
Of warring Spirits; how without remorse Par Lost 5.566
All things, ev'n thee, and all the Spirits of Heav'n Par Lost 5.837
Ministring Spirits, traind up in Feast and Song; Par Lost 6.167
Sanguin, such as Celestial Spirits may bleed, Par Lost 6.333
Yet soon he heal'd; for Spirits that live throughout Par Lost 6.344
Have easily as Spirits evaded swift Par Lost 6.596
Out of such prison, though Spirits of purest light, Par Lost 6.660
In heav'nly Spirits could such perverseness dwell? Par Lost 6.788
Of Spirits maligne a better Race to bring Par Lost 7.189
And Vertues, winged Spirits, and Chariots wing'd, Par Lost 7.199
Of Spirits apostat and thir Counsels vaine Par Lost 7.610
From thence a Rib, with cordial spirits warme; Par Lost 8.466
Love not the heav'nly Spirits, and how thir Love Par Lost 8.615
Easier then Air with Air, if Spirits embrace, Par Lost 8.626
Dimm erst, dilated Spirits, ampler Heart, Par Lost 9.876
About thir spirits had plaid, and inmost powers Par Lost 9.1048
With Spirits Masculine, create at last Par Lost 10.890
To Spirits foule, and all my Trees thir prey, Par Lost 11.124
Recovering, and his scatterd spirits returnd, Par Lost 11.294
Sunk down and all his Spirits became intranst: Par Lost 11.420
To weigh thy Spirits down, and last consume Par Lost 11.545
1667 'spirits'
Portending good, and all her spirits compos'd Par Lost 12.596
Demonian Spirits now, from the Element Par Reg 2.122
Of Spirits likest to himself in guile Par Reg 2.237
All these are Spirits of Air, and Woods, and Springs, Par Reg 2.374
Of most erected Spirits, most temper'd pure Par Reg 3.27
So much I feel my genial spirits droop, Samson 594
And on her purest spirits prey, Samson 613
And fainting spirits uphold. Samson 666
To the Spirits of just men long oppress! Samson 1269
Of bright aereal Spirits live insphear'd Mask 3
Trinity ms 'spirits'
Bridgewater ms 'spiritts'
Ile venter, for my new enliv'nd spirits Mask 228
Bridgewater ms 'speritts'
With spirits of balm, and fragrant Syrops mixt. Mask 674
Bridgewater ms 'spiritts'
Of this pure cause would kindle my rap't spirits Mask 794
line not in Bridgewater ms
line not in Trinity ms
Will bathe the drooping spirits in delight Mask 812
Bridgewater ms 'spiritts'
Which deepest Spirits, and choicest Wits desire: Vacation 22
With those just Spirits that wear victorious Palms, Musick 14
Trinity ms 'spirits'
That som more timely-happy spirits indu'th. Sonnet 7, 8

Spiritual
Spiritual substance with corporeal barr. Par Lost 4.585
Millions of spiritual Creatures walk the Earth Par Lost 4.677
To spiritual Natures; only this I know, Par Lost 5.402
Spiritual, may of purest Spirits be found Par Lost 5.406
By lik'ning spiritual to corporal forms, Par Lost 5.573
Speed almost Spiritual; mee thou thinkst not slow, Par Lost 8.110
With spiritual Armour, able to resist Par Lost 12.491
By spiritual, to themselves appropriating Par Lost 12.518
Spiritual Lawes by carnal power shall force Par Lost 12.521
Against the Spiritual Foe, and broughtst him thence Par Reg 1.10
Both spirituall powre and civill, what each meanes Sonnet 17, 10
1662 'spiritual'
1694 'Spiritual'

Spit
In pastry built, or from the spit, or boyl'd, Par Reg 2.343

Spite
Thrice he assayd, and thrice in spight of scorn, Par Lost 1.619
1667 'spite'
To mingle and involve, done all to spite Par Lost 2.384
The great Creatour? But thir spite still serves Par Lost 2.385
Will once more lift us up, in spight of Fate, Par Lost 2.393
Are his Created, or to spite us more, Par Lost 9.147
Whom us the more to spite his Maker rais'd Par Lost 9.177
From dust: spite then with spite is best repaid. Par Lost 9.178
To salve his credit, and for very spight Par Reg 4.12
That once found out and solv'd, for grief and spight Par Reg 4.574
Contemptuous, proud, set on revenge and spite; Samson 1462
Then to com in spight of sorrow, Allegro 45

Spits
Of Stygian darknes spets her thickest gloom, Mask 132
Bridgewater ms 'spetts'

Spits(*cont*)
Trinity ms 'spitts'
Spleen
And at thy growing vertues fret their spleen, — Sonnet 9, 7
Splendid
Of splendid vassalage, but rather seek — Par Lost 2.252
Splendour
With splendor, arm'd with power, if aught propos'd — Par Lost 2.447
The golden Sun in splendor likest Heaven — Par Lost 3.572
But faded splendor wan; who by his gate — Par Lost 4.870
His equals, if in power and splendor less, — Par Lost 5.796
Among the Prime in Splendour, now depos'd, — Par Reg 1.413
Such was the Splendour, and the Tempter now — Par Reg 2.366
Clad in splendor as befits — Arcades 92
Splendours
Of Heav'n, and from Eternal Splendors flung — Par Lost 1.610
ms 'splendors'
Spoil
Havock and spoil and ruin are my gain. — Par Lost 2.1009
My vanquisher, spoild of his vanted spoile; — Par Lost 3.251
With glory and spoile back to thir promis'd Land. — Par Lost 12.172
Whose pains have earn'd the far fet spoil. With that — Par Reg 2.401
But rob and spoil, burn, slaughter, and enslave — Par Reg 3.75
To others did no violence nor spoil. — Samson 1191
I us'd hostility, and took thir spoil — Samson 1203
Spoiled
My vanquisher, spoild of his vanted spoile; — Par Lost 3.251
Spoild Principalities and Powers, triumpht — Par Lost 10.186
With all his verdure spoil'd, and Trees adrift — Par Lost 11.832
Spoil'd at once both fruit and tree: — Winchester 30
Spoils
Those balmie spoiles. As when to them who saile — Par Lost 4.159
With Heav'nly spoils, our spoils: What he decreed — Par Lost 9.151
Nations, and bring home spoils with infinite — Par Lost 11.692
So far renown'd, and with the spoils enricht — Par Reg 4.46
Spoke
According to his doom: he would have spoke, — Par Lost 10.517
The deeds themselves, though mute, spoke loud the dooer; — Samson 248
About t' have spoke, but now, with head declin'd — Samson 727
Of thee *abroad* are spoke; — Psalm 87, 10
Spoken
All hast thou spok'n as my thoughts are, all — Par Lost 3.171
Spoken against, that through my very Soul — Par Reg 2.90
Sponge
And trifles for choice matters, worth a spunge; — Par Reg 4.329
Spongy
My dazling Spells into the spungy ayr, — Mask 154
Trinity ms 'spungie'
Bridgewater ms 'spungie'
1637 'spungie'
Spontaneous
Spontaneous, for within them Spirit livd, — Par Lost 7.204
Sport
Each on his rock transfixt, the sport and prey — Par Lost 2.181
The sport of Winds: all these upwhirld aloft — Par Lost 3.493
Thrice I deluded her, and turn'd to sport — Samson 396
To make them sport with blind activity? — Samson 1328
They only set on sport and play — Samson 1679
Hail Goddesse of Nocturnal sport — Mask 128
We shall catch them at their sport, — Mask 953
Bridgewater ms 'sporte'
Sport that wrincled Care derides, — Allegro 31
To sport with *Amaryllis* in the shade, — Lycidas 68
Sportful
Down he alights among the sportful Herd — Par Lost 4.396
Sporting
Sporting the Lion rampd, and in his paw — Par Lost 4.343
Of Coral stray, or sporting with quick glance — Par Lost 7.405
Sports
Then cruel, by thir sports to blood enur'd — Par Reg 4.139
When to thir sports they turn'd. Immediately — Samson 1614
Spot
There lands the Fiend, a spot like which perhaps — Par Lost 3.588
That spot to which I point is *Paradise*, — Par Lost 3.733
No spot or blame behind: Which gives me hope — Par Lost 5.119
A cloudy spot. Down thither prone in flight — Par Lost 5.266
Thir magnitudes, this Earth a spot, a graine, — Par Lost 8.17
Round this opacous Earth, this punctual spot, — Par Lost 8.23
Spot more delicious then those Gardens feign'd — Par Lost 9.439
Above the smoak and stirr of this dim spot, — Mask 5
Bridgewater ms 'spott'
To outward view, of blemish or of spot; — Sonnet 22, 2
1694 'Spot'
Mine as whom washt from spot of child-bed taint, — Sonnet 23, 5
Spotless
Simplicitie and spotless innocence. — Par Lost 4.318
Spots
Whence in her visage round those spots, unpurg'd — Par Lost 5.419
With spots of Gold and Purple, azure and green: — Par Lost 7.479
Feilds and Inhabitants: Her spots thou seest — Par Lost 8.145
Spotted
And spotted mountain pard, but set at nought — Mask 444
Spotty
Rivers or Mountains in her spotty Globe. — Par Lost 1.291
Spousal
Sung Spousal, and bid haste the Eevning Starr — Par Lost 8.519
Spousal embraces, vitiated with Gold, — Samson 389
in high misterious happie spousall meet — Musick Tr. ms 4.06
Spousal(*cont*)
'spousall' ←'spousal'
Spouse
That drove him, though enamourd, from the Spouse — Par Lost 4.169
Adam from his fair Spouse, nor *Eve* the Rites — Par Lost 4.742
So cheard he his fair Spouse, and she was cheard, — Par Lost 5.129
Held dalliance with his faire *Egyptian* Spouse. — Par Lost 9.443
Spoused
To wed her Elm; she spous'd about him twines — Par Lost 5.216
Spout
Of Hell should spout her Cataracts of Fire, — Par Lost 2.176
Spouts
Draws in, and at his Trunck spouts out a Sea. — Par Lost 7.416
Spray
Clear'd up their choicest notes in bush and spray — Par Reg 4.437
O Nightingale, that on yon bloomy Spray — Sonnet 1, 1
Spread
Came like a Deluge on the South, and spread — Par Lost 1.354
His uncouth way, or spread his aerie flight — Par Lost 2.407
Under spread Ensigns marching might pass through — Par Lost 2.886
Of *Chaos*, and his dark Pavilion spread — Par Lost 2.960
Weighs his spread wings, at leasure to behold — Par Lost 2.1046
Of som irriguous Valley spred her store, — Par Lost 4.255
1667 'spread'
Of waters issu'd from a Cave and spread — Par Lost 4.454
Then all this globous Earth in Plain out spred, — Par Lost 5.649
1667 'outspred'
Rebellion rising, saw in whom, how spred — Par Lost 5.715
In this perfidious fraud, contagion spred — Par Lost 5.880
Were don, but infinite: for wide was spred — Par Lost 6.241
Under spred Ensignes moving nigh, in slow — Par Lost 6.533
At once the Four spred out thir Starrie wings — Par Lost 6.827
Rose as in Dance the stately Trees, and spred — Par Lost 7.324
Solac'd the Woods, and spred thir painted wings — Par Lost 7.434
To Starr or Sun-light, spread thir umbrage broad — Par Lost 9.1087
Of richest texture spred, at th' upper end — Par Lost 10.446
Perhaps thy Capital Seate, from whence had spred — Par Lost 11.343
He lookd and saw wide Territorie spred — Par Lost 11.638
A Table richly spred, in regal mode, — Par Reg 2.340
On a green bank, and set before him spred — Par Reg 4.587
With solemnest devotion, spread before him — Samson 1147
To what may serve his glory best, & spread his name — Samson 1429
You may as well spred out the unsun'd heaps — Mask 398
1637 'spread'
Bridgewater ms 'spreade'
Trinity ms 'spread'
Rot inwardly, and foul contagion spread: — Lycidas 127
Trinity ms 'spred'
The dreadfull Judge in middle Air shall spread his throne. — Nativity 164
And he can spred thy Name o're Lands and Seas, — Sonnet 8, 7
Trinity ms 'spread'
In the dust and there out spread — Psalm 7, 17
Between their wings out-spread, — Psalm 80, 6
The Hills were *over-spread* — Psalm 80, 42
My hands to thee I spread. — Psalm 88, 40
Spreading
Spreading thir bane; the blasted Starrs lookt wan, — Par Lost 10.412
Of these fair spreading Trees; which bids us seek — Par Lost 10.1067
Spreading and over-shadowing all the Earth, — Par Reg 4.148
Under the spreading favour of these Pines, — Mask 184
Trinity ms 'spredding'
Bridgewater ms 'spreadinge'
Spreads
He spreads for flight, and in the surging smoak — Par Lost 2.928
When first on this delightful Land he spreads — Par Lost 4.643
In *Malabar* or *Decan* spreds her Armes — Par Lost 9.1103
That spreds her verdant leaf to th' morning ray, — Mask 622
Bridgewater ms 'spreades'
Wher brooding darknes spreads his jealous wings, — Allegro 6
Mark what radiant state she spreds, — Arcades 14
Nor yet where *Deva* spreads her wisard stream: — Lycidas 55
Trinity ms 'spreds'
But lives and spreds aloft by those pure eyes, — Lycidas 81
1638 'spreads'
Or *Trent*, who like some earth-born Giant spreads — Vacation 93
Spring
Thrones and Imperial Powers, off-spring of heav'n — Par Lost 2.310
But from the Author of all ill could Spring — Par Lost 2.381
The World shall burn, and from her ashes spring — Par Lost 3.334
Calls us, we lose the prime, to mark how spring — Par Lost 5.21
Of day-spring, and the Sun, who scarce up risen — Par Lost 5.139
Spring both, the face of brightest Heav'n had changd — Par Lost 5.644
So all ere day-spring, under conscious Night — Par Lost 6.521
1667 'day spring' in some copies
In yonder Spring of Roses intermixt — Par Lost 9.218
On mee, mee onely, as the sourse and spring — Par Lost 10.832
Strength added from above, new hope to spring — Par Lost 11.138
In some to spring from thee, who never touch'd — Par Lost 11.425
A Nation from one faithful man to spring: — Par Lost 12.113
Much more, that much more good thereof shall spring, — Par Lost 12.476
Whose off-spring on the Throne of *Juda* sat — Par Reg 2.440
Whose off-spring in his Territory yet serve — Par Reg 3.375
Her shadowy off-spring unsubstantial both, — Par Reg 4.399
With day-spring born; here leave me to respire. — Samson 11
From the dry ground to spring, thy thirst to allay — Samson 582
Cause light again within thy eies to spring, — Samson 584
Abortive as the first-born bloom of spring — Samson 1576
Where his fair off-spring nurs't in Princely lore, — Mask 34

Spring(*cont*)
Bridgewater ms 'ofspringe'
Trinity ms 'ofspring'
La. To seek i' th vally som cool friendly Spring. Mask 282
Trinity ms 'spring'
Bridgewater ms 'springe'
Revels the spruce and jocond Spring, Mask 985
line not in Bridgewater ms
The frolick Wind that breathes the Spring, Allegro 18
That from beneath the seat of *Jove* doth spring, Lycidas 16
From haunted spring, and dale Nativity 184
This if thou do he will an off-spring give, Fair Inf 76
The gentle neighbourhood of grove and spring Passion 52
But my late spring no bud or blossom shew'th. Sonnet 7, 4
Spring
In spring time, when the Sun with *Taurus* rides, Par Lost 1.769
Led on th' Eternal Spring. Not that faire field Par Lost 4.268
All *Autumn* pil'd, though *Spring* and *Autumn* here Par Lost 5.394
Of Seasons to each Clime; else had the Spring Par Lost 10.678
Spring
Cleer Spring, or shadie Grove, or Sunnie Hill, Par Lost 3.28
Castalian Spring, might with this Paradise Par Lost 4.274
Of *Amarantin* Shade, Fountain or Spring, Par Lost 11.78
Springing
Vaild with his gorgeous wings, up springing light Par Lost 5.250
Springs
Springs upward like a Pyramid of fire Par Lost 2.1013
On Hills where Flocks are fed, flies toward the Springs Par Lost 3.435
Springs lighter the green stalk, from thence the leaves Par Lost 5.480
His hinder parts, then springs as broke from Bonds, Par Lost 7.465
But first among the Priests dissension springs, Par Lost 12.353
All these are Spirits of Air, and Woods, and Springs, Par Reg 2.374
Where Springs and Showrs abound. Psalm 84, 24
Springtime
In spring time, when the Sun with *Taurus* rides, Par Lost 1.769
Sprinkle
Thus I sprinkle on thy brest Mask 911
Bridgewater ms 'spincle'
1637 'sprinckle'
Trinity ms 'sprinckle'
Sprinkled
Of many a colourd plume sprinkl'd with Gold, Par Lost 3.642
Sprout
Number my ranks, and visit every sprout Arcades 59
Spruce
Revels the spruce and jocond Spring, Mask 985
line not in Bridgewater ms
Sprung
They heard, and were abasht, and up they sprung Par Lost 1.331
Out of thy head I sprung: amazement seis'd Par Lost 2.758
Light shon, and order from disorder sprung: Par Lost 3.713
The verdurous wall of paradise up sprung: Par Lost 4.143
This uncouth dream, of evil sprung I fear; Par Lost 5.98
Among the Constellations warr were sprung, Par Lost 6.312
From whom it sprung, impossible to mix Par Lost 7.58
Sprung from the Deep, and from her Native East Par Lost 7.245
Her Nurserie; they at her coming sprung Par Lost 8.46
By quick instinctive motion up I sprung, Par Lost 8.259
Adam, from whose deare side I boast me sprung, Par Lost 9.965
A Grove hard by, sprung up with this thir change, Par Lost 10.548
Second of *Satan* sprung, all conquering *Death*, Par Lost 10.591
See Father, what first fruits on Earth are sprung Par Lost 11.22
Ye were the two she mean't, with that I sprung Mask 578
Sprung of old *Anchises* line, Mask 923
Of famous *Arcady* ye are, and sprung Arcades 28
Spume
Of spiritous and fierie spume, till toucht Par Lost 6.479
Spun
Disparted, and between spun out the Air, Par Lost 7.241
These my skie robes spun out of *Iris* Wooff, Mask 83
And slits the thin spun life. But not the praise, Lycidas 76
1638 'thin-spun'
Trinity ms 'thin-spun'
The Lillie and Rose, that neither sow'd nor spun. Sonnet 20, 8
Spur
Fame is the spur that the clear spirit doth raise Lycidas 70
Trinity ms 'spurre'
1638 'spurre'
Spurious
Her spurious first-born; Treason against me? Samson 391
Spurned
Spurn'd them to death by Troops. The bold *Ascalonite* Samson 138
Spurns
Uplifted spurns the ground, thence many a League Par Lost 2.929
Spy
Chaos and *ancient Night*, I come no Spy, Par Lost 2.970
1667 'Spie'
To wing the desolate Abyss, and spie Par Lost 4.936
Wise to flie pain, professing next the Spie, Par Lost 4.948
To see that none thence issu'd forth a spie, Par Lost 8.233
A Dove sent forth once and agen to spie Par Lost 11.857
Thy drowsie Nurse hath sworn she did them spie Vacation 61
Spying
Which *Gabriel* spying, thus bespake the Fiend. Par Lost 4.1005
Squadron
Forthwith from every Squadron and each Band Par Lost 1.356
ms 'squadron'
Just met, and closing stood in squadron joind Par Lost 4.863
Squadron(*cont*)
While thus he spake, th' Angelic Squadron bright Par Lost 4.977
Squadroned
Of squadrond Angels hear his Carol sung. Par Lost 12.367
Squadrons
Another part in Squadrons and gross Bands, Par Lost 2.570
Coverd with thick embatteld Squadrons bright, Par Lost 6.16
Squadrons at once, with huge two-handed sway Par Lost 6.251
On every side with shaddowing Squadrons Deep, Par Lost 6.554
With cruel Tournament the Squadrons joine; Par Lost 11.652
And all the spangled host keep watch in squadrons bright? Nativity 21
Square
In circuit, undetermind square or round, Par Lost 2.1048
And on her ample Square from side to side Par Lost 5.393
In *Sextile*, *Square*, and *Trine*, and *Opposite*, Par Lost 10.659
Eie me blest Providence, and square my triall Mask 329
Squared
From every Band and squared Regiment Par Lost 1.758
Squar'd in full Legion (such command we had) Par Lost 8.232
Squat
Squat like a Toad, close at the eare of *Eve;* Par Lost 4.800
Squint
And gladly banish squint suspicion. Mask 413
Squires
And the Cherubick host in thousand quires Musick 12
Trinity ms 'in thousand quires' ← 'sweet-winged squires'
Stable
From the bleak air; a Stable was our warmth, Par Reg 2.74
And all about the Courtly Stable, Nativity 243
Stabled
And stabl'd; of Mankind, so numerous late, Par Lost 11.752
Like stabl'd wolves, or tigers at their prey, Mask 534
Bridgewater ms 'stabled'
Stablished
To *David*, stablisht as the dayes of Heav'n. Par Lost 12.347
Stack
And to the stack, or the Barn dore, Allegro 51
Staff
Who forthwith from the glittering Staff unfurld Par Lost 1.535
ms 'staff'
I only with an Oak'n staff will meet thee, Samson 1123
A Scepter or quaint staff he bears, Samson 1303
Stag
In Hillocks; the swift Stag from under ground Par Lost 7.469
Stage
Then to the well-trod stage anon, Allegro 131
Ennobled hath the Buskind stage. Penseroso 102
Wherwith the stage of Ayr and Earth did ring, Passion 2
Staid
Ore laid with black staid Wisdoms hue. Penseroso 16
Stain
Incapable of stain would soon expel Par Lost 2.140
To sanctitie that shall receive no staine: Par Lost 10.639
Unchaste was subsequent, her stain not his. Samson 325
Of noble Warriour, so to stain his honour, Samson 1166
Our Law, or stain my vow of *Nazarite*. Samson 1386
Such mixture was not held a stain) Penseroso 26
Stained
And all his Armour staind ere while so bright. Par Lost 6.334
Our wonted Ornaments now soild and staind, Par Lost 9.1076
Stair
Each Stair mysteriously was meant, nor stood Par Lost 3.516
Satan from hence now on the lower stair Par Lost 3.540
Stairs
The Stairs were such as whereon *Jacob* saw Par Lost 3.510
The Stairs were then let down, whether to dare Par Lost 3.523
Stakes
Com not too neer, you fall on iron stakes else. Mask 491
Stalk
All seasons, ripe for use hangs on the stalk; Par Lost 5.323
Bestirs her then, and from each tender stalk Par Lost 5.337
Springs lighter the green stalk, from thence the leaves Par Lost 5.480
Each Flour of slender stalk, whose head though gay Par Lost 9.428
It withers on the stalk with languish't head. Mask 744
Trinity ms 'stalke'
1637 'stalke'
line not in Bridgewater ms
Stalking
Stalking with less unconsci'nable strides, Samson 1245
Stalks
A Lion now he stalkes with fierie glare, Par Lost 4.402
Stalling
Co. Perhaps fore-stalling night prevented them. Mask 285
Bridgewater ms 'forestallinge'
Trinity ms 'fore stalling'
Stall-reader
Cries the stall-reader, bless us! what a word on Sonnet 11, 5
Stand
Advanc't in view, they stand, a horrid Front Par Lost 1.563
Formost to stand against the Thunderers aim Par Lost 2.28
Millions that stand in Arms, and longing wait Par Lost 2.55
Stand in his presence humble, and receive Par Lost 2.240
And so refus'd might in opinion stand Par Lost 2.471
Over the *Caspian*, then stand front to front Par Lost 2.716
Of endless Warrs, and by confusion stand. Par Lost 2.897
Upheld by me, yet once more he shall stand Par Lost 3.178
Saw within kenn a glorious Angel stand, Par Lost 3.622
Stand ready at command, and are his Eyes Par Lost 3.650

Stand(*cont*)
Uriel, for thou of those seav'n Spirits that stand Par Lost 3.654
Fell not, but stand unshak'n, from within Par Lost 4.64
Hadst thou the same free Will and Power to stand? Par Lost 4.66
Then from his loftie stand on that high Tree Par Lost 4.395
Can it be death? and do they onely stand Par Lost 4.518
Stand firm, for in his look defiance lours. Par Lost 4.873
That is, to thy obedience; therein stand. Par Lost 5.522
My self and all th' Angelic Host that stand Par Lost 5.535
To love or not; in this we stand or fall: Par Lost 5.540
Hear my Decree, which unrevok't shall stand. Par Lost 5.602
To stand approv'd in sight of God, though Worlds Par Lost 6.36
When to advance, or stand, or turn the sway Par Lost 6.234
Of this Ethereous mould whereon we stand, Par Lost 6.473
Stand readie to receive them, if they like Par Lost 6.561
Freely our part; yee who appointed stand Par Lost 6.565
That whom they hit, none on thir feet might stand, Par Lost 6.592
Stand still in bright array ye Saints, here stand Par Lost 6.801
Nor multitude, stand onely and behold Par Lost 6.810
From the Armoury of God, where stand of old Par Lost 7.200
And all the Blest: stand fast; to stand or fall Par Lost 8.640
O Heav'n! in evil strait this day I stand Par Lost 10.125
With me? how can they then acquitted stand Par Lost 10.827
Why stand we longer shivering under feares, Par Lost 10.1003
In thir bright stand, there left his Powers to seise Par Lost 11.221
Aw'd by the rod of *Moses* so to stand Par Lost 12.198
Or how the Sun shall in mid Heav'n stand still Par Lost 12.263
Mans voice commanding, Sun in *Gibeon* stand, Par Lost 12.265
Light out of darkness! full of doubt I stand, Par Lost 12.473
His living Temples, built by Faith to stand, Par Lost 12.527
Till time stand fixt: beyond is all abyss, Par Lost 12.555
If it may stand him more in stead to lye, Par Reg 1.473
Would stand between me and thy Fathers ire, Par Reg 3.219
There stand, if thou wilt stand; to stand upright Par Reg 4.551
Now shew thy Progeny; if not to stand, Par Reg 4.554
To all posterity may stand defam'd, Samson 977
Send thee the Angel of thy Birth, to stand Samson 1431
On banks and scaffolds under Skie might stand; Samson 1610
Best draw, and stand upon our guard. *Eld. Bro*. Ile hallow, Mask 487
This will restore all soon. *La*. 'Twill not false traitor, Mask 690
Trinity ms 't'will not' ←'stand back'
Stand fixt in stedfast gaze, Nativity 70
To stand 'twixt us and our deserved smart Fair Inf 69
From others he shall stand in need of nothing, Vacation 81
Stand spelling fals, while one might walk to Mile- Sonnet 11, 7
They also serve who only stand and waite. Sonnet 19, 14
The wind drives, so the wicked shall not stand Psalm 1, 12
Fools or mad men stand not within thy sight. Psalm 5, 12

Standard
His mighty Standard; that proud honour claim'd Par Lost 1.533
ms 'standard'
Erect the Standard there of *ancient Night;* Par Lost 2.986
1667 'standerd' in some copies
1667 'Standerd' in some copies
The great Hierarchal Standard was to move; Par Lost 5.701
Troop to thir Standard, so the watrie throng, Par Lost 7.297

Standards
Standards, and Gonfalons twixt Van and Reare Par Lost 5.589

Standing
A standing fight, then soaring on main wing Par Lost 6.243
Though standing else as Rocks, but down they fell Par Lost 6.593
Standing on Earth, not rapt above the Pole, Par Lost 7.23
Progressive, retrograde, or standing still, Par Lost 8.127
So standing, moving, or to highth upgrown Par Lost 9.677
From standing lake to tripping ebbe, that stole Par Lost 11.847
Cuirassiers all in steel for standing fight; Par Reg 3.328

Stands
Stands on the blasted Heath. He now prepar'd Par Lost 1.615
Death ready stands to interpose his dart, Par Lost 2.854
One fatal Tree there stands of Knowledge call'd, Par Lost 4.514
Swayes them; the careful Plowman doubting stands Par Lost 4.983
To pieces, and orewhelm whatever stands Par Lost 6.489
Posteritie stands curst: Fair Patrimonie Par Lost 10.818
Or turn to reverent awe? for Beauty stands Par Reg 2.220
For therein stands the office of a King, Par Reg 2.463
Where on the *Aegean* shore a City stands Par Reg 4.238
And if I was, I am; relation stands; Par Reg 4.519
The rarer thy example stands, Samson 166
Cho. Yet on she moves, now stands & eies thee fixt, Samson 726
Mess. *Gaza* yet stands, but all her Sons are fall'n, Samson 1558
Stands ready to smite once, and smite no more. Lycidas 131
God in the great assembly stands Psalm 82, 1

Star
Dropt from the Zenith like a falling Star, Par Lost 1.745
ms 'starr'
This pendant world, in bigness as a Starr Par Lost 2.1052
Of *Libra* to the fleecie Starr that bears Par Lost 3.558
(So call that opposite fair Starr) her aide Par Lost 3.727
On a Sun beam, swift as a shooting Starr Par Lost 4.556
Starr interpos'd, however small he sees, Par Lost 5.258
His count'nance, as the Morning Starr that guides Par Lost 5.708
Or if the Starr of Eevning and the Moon Par Lost 7.104
1669 'Star'
Of Angels, then that Starr the Starrs among) Par Lost 7.133
Numerous, and every Starr perhaps a World Par Lost 7.621
To the terrestrial Moon be as a Starr Par Lost 8.142
Sung Spousal, and bid haste the Eevning Starr Par Lost 8.519
The Sun was sunk, and after him the Starr Par Lost 9.48

Star(*cont*)
To Starr or Sun-light, spread thir umbrage broad Par Lost 9.1087
Of that bright Starr to *Satan* paragond. Par Lost 10.426
And shape Starr bright appeer'd, or brighter, clad Par Lost 10.450
1667 'Starr-bright'
Our Limbs benumm'd, ere this diurnal Starr Par Lost 10.1069
And now of love they treat till th' Eevning Star Par Lost 11.588
Barr'd of his right; yet at his Birth a Starr Par Lost 12.360
A Star, not seen before in Heaven appearing Par Reg 1.249
Affirming it thy Star new grav'n in Heaven, Par Reg 1.253
So spake our Morning Star then in his rise, Par Reg 1.294
Rule in the Clouds; like an Autumnal Star Par Reg 4.619
Swift as the Sparkle of a glancing Star, Mask 80
1637 'Starre'
Trinity ms 'starre'
Bridgewater ms 'starre'
Comus. The Star that bids the Shepherd fold, Mask 93
Trinity ms 'starre'
1637 'starre'
Bridgewater ms 'starr'
And thou shalt be our star of *Arcady*, Mask 341
1637 'starre'
Trinity ms 'starre'
Bridgewater ms 'starr'
Of every Star that Heav'n doth shew, Penseroso 171
Oft till the Star that rose, at Ev'ning, bright Lycidas 30
Trinity ms 'starre that rose' ←'ev'n starre bright'
1638 'Oft till the ev'n-starre bright'
On whose fresh lap the swart Star sparely looks, Lycidas 138
Trinity ms 'starre'
1638 'starre'
So sinks the day-star in the Ocean bed, Lycidas 168
1638 'day-starre'
Trinity ms 'day starre'
Heav'ns youngest teemed Star, Nativity 240
Wert thou some Starr which from the ruin'd roofe Fair Inf 43
Now the bright morning Star, Dayes harbinger, May Morn 1
Of Sun or Moon or Starre throughout the year, Sonnet 22, 5
1694 'Star'

Star-bright
And shape Starr bright appeer'd, or brighter, clad Par Lost 10.450
1667 'Starr-bright'

Stare
Perhaps my enemies who come to stare Samson 112
That would have made *Quintilian* stare and gasp. Sonnet 11, 11

Star-led
The Star-led Wisards haste with odours sweet: Nativity 23

Starless
Starless expos'd, and ever-threatning storms Par Lost 3.425

Starlight
Or glittering Starr-light without thee is sweet. Par Lost 4.656
In such a scant allowance of Star-light, Mask 308
1637 'starre light'
Trinity ms 'starre light'
Bridgewater ms 'starr light'
And so bestudd with Stars, that they below Mask 734

Star-paved
In progress through the rode of Heav'n Star-pav'd. Par Lost 4.976

Star-proof
Of branching Elm Star-proof, Arcades 89
1673 'Elm-Star-proof'
Trinity ms 'sta re-proofe', ms defective

Starred
Or that Starr'd *Ethiope* Queen that strove Penseroso 19
1673 'starr'd'

Starry
Of Starry Lamps and blazing Cressets fed Par Lost 1.728
Thus they in Heav'n, above the starry Sphear, Par Lost 3.416
Thir Starry dance in numbers that compute Par Lost 3.580
1667 'Sarry'
The starrie Host, rode brightest, till the Moon Par Lost 4.606
And these the Gemms of Heav'n, her starrie train: Par Lost 4.649
And starrie Pole: Thou also mad'st the Night, Par Lost 4.724
In this commotion, but the Starrie Cope Par Lost 4.992
Girt like a Starrie Zone his waste, and round Par Lost 5.281
Mystical dance, which yonder starrie Spheare Par Lost 5.620
The starrie flock, allur'd them, and with lyes Par Lost 5.709
At once the Four spred out thir Starrie wings Par Lost 6.827
Of Rainbows and Starrie Eyes. The Waters thus Par Lost 7.446
His starrie Helme unbuckl'd shew'd him prime Par Lost 11.245
Directs me in the Starry Rubric set. Par Reg 4.393
Before the starry threshold of *Joves* Court Mask 1
1637 'starrie'
Trinity ms 'starrie'
Bridgewater ms 'starrie'
Imitate the Starry Quire, Mask 112
Trinity ms 'starrie'
1637 'starrie'
Bridgewater ms 'starrie'
His starry front low-rooft beneath the skies; Passion 18
while all the starrie rounds & arches blue Musick Tr. ms 4.21
'while all the starrie rounds' ←'starrie frame' ←'whilst then' ←'whilst the whole frame of' ←'while all the' ←'that all'

Stars
Stood thick as Starrs, and from his sight receiv'd Par Lost 3.61
Amongst innumerable Starrs, that shon Par Lost 3.565
Stars distant, but nigh hand seemd other Worlds, Par Lost 3.566

Stars(*cont*)
That rowld orbicular, and turnd to Starrs Par Lost 3.718
Of this new World; at whose sight all the Starrs Par Lost 4.34
Of Heav'n the Starrs that usher Evening rose: Par Lost 4.355
Fairest of Starrs, last in the train of Night, Par Lost 5.166
With the fixt Starrs, fixt in thir Orb that flies, Par Lost 5.176
Innumerable as the Starrs of Night, Par Lost 5.745
Or Starrs of Morning, Dew-drops, which the Sun Par Lost 5.746
Had wondrous, as with Starrs thir bodies all Par Lost 6.754
Of Angels, then that Starr the Starrs among) Par Lost 7.133
The less by Night alterne: and made the Starrs, Par Lost 7.348
Globose, and every magnitude of Starrs, Par Lost 7.357
And sowd with Starrs the Heav'n thick as a field: Par Lost 7.358
Hither as to thir Fountain other Starrs Par Lost 7.364
With thousand thousand Starres, that then appeer'd Par Lost 7.383
And pavement Starrs, as Starrs to thee appeer, Par Lost 7.578
Pouderd with Starrs. And now on Earth the Seventh Par Lost 7.581
Of amplitude almost immense, with Starr's Par Lost 7.620
And all her numberd Starrs, that seem to rowle Par Lost 8.19
And calculate the Starrs, how they will weild Par Lost 8.80
Be Center to the World, and other Starrs Par Lost 8.123
Invisible else above all Starrs, the Wheele Par Lost 8.135
Spreading thir bane; the blasted Starrs lookt wan, Par Lost 10.412
Returne, the Starres of Morn shall see him rise Par Lost 12.422
Of wisdome; hope no higher, though all the Starrs Par Lost 12.576
Or Heav'n write aught of Fate, by what the Stars Par Reg 4.383
In thy dark lantern thus close up the Stars, Mask 197
line not in Bridgewater ms
Trinity ms 'starres'
Eld. Bro. Unmuffle ye faint stars, and thou fair Moon Mask 331
1673 'Stars'
Trinity ms 'starres'
Bridgewater ms 'starrs'
And so bestudd with Stars, that they below Mask 734
Bridgewater ms 'starrs'
Trinity ms 'starres'
1637 'stars'
Com let us haste, the Stars grow high, Mask 956
1637 'starrs'
Trinity ms 'starres'
Bridgewater ms 'starrs'
The Stars with deep amaze Nativity 69
Attir'd with Stars, we shall for ever sit, On Time 21
Trinity ms 'starres'
The Moon and Starrs which thou so bright hast set, Psalm 8, 10

Started
Bending to look on me, I started back, Par Lost 4.462
It started back, but pleas'd I soon returnd, Par Lost 4.463
So started up in his own shape the Fiend. Par Lost 4.819

Startle
These thoughts may startle well, but not astound Mask 210
line not in Bridgewater ms
And singing startle the dull night, Allegro 42

Startled
Such whispering wak'd her, but with startl'd eye Par Lost 5.26

Starts
Of force to its own likeness: up he starts Par Lost 4.813
Out of the wood he starts in wonted shape; Par Reg 4.449

Starve
From Beds of raging Fire to starve in Ice Par Lost 2.600

Starved
Or Serenate, which the starv'd Lover sings Par Lost 4.769
Unnam'd, undreaded, and thy self half starv'd? Par Lost 10.595

Star-ypointing
Under a Star-ypointing *Pyramid?* Shakespear 4
1663-4 'Starre-ypointing'
1640 'starre-ypointing'
1632 'starre-ypointed' in some copies, 'starre-ypointing' in others

State
Mov'd our Grand Parents in that happy State, Par Lost 1.29
ms 'state'
Though all our Glory extinct, and happy state Par Lost 1.141
Consent or custome, and his Regal State Par Lost 1.640
ms 'state'
Thir State affairs. So thick the aerie crowd Par Lost 1.775
ms 'state'
High on a Throne of Royal State, which far Par Lost 2.1
Yielded with full consent. The happier state Par Lost 2.24
Unacceptable, though in Heav'n, our state Par Lost 2.251
To peaceful Counsels, and the settl'd State Par Lost 2.279
A Pillar of State; deep on his Front engraven Par Lost 2.302
And God-like imitated State; him round Par Lost 2.511
Forthwith his former state and being forgets, Par Lost 2.585
Thir sinful state, and to appease betimes Par Lost 3.186
That bring to my remembrance from what state Par Lost 4.38
By Act of Grace my former state; how soon Par Lost 4.94
To mark what of thir state he more might learn Par Lost 4.400
By Ignorance, is that thir happie state, Par Lost 4.519
No happier state, and know to know no more. Par Lost 4.775
As may advise him of his happie state, Par Lost 5.234
The fall of others from like state of bliss; Par Lost 5.241
Of Angels under watch; and to his state, Par Lost 5.288
Perfections, in himself was all his state, Par Lost 5.353
Your fill what happiness this happie state Par Lost 5.504
In sight of God enthron'd, our happie state Par Lost 5.536
From what high state of bliss into what woe! Par Lost 5.543
Our happie state under one Head more neer Par Lost 5.830

State(*cont*)
To set the envier of his State, the proud Par Lost 6.89
With *Satan*, hee who envies now thy state, Par Lost 6.900
Her state with Oarie feet: yet oft they quit Par Lost 7.440
Live, in what state, condition or degree, Par Lost 8.176
For state, as Sovran King, and to enure Par Lost 8.239
I then was passing to my former state Par Lost 8.290
From that day mortal, and this happie State Par Lost 8.331
What thinkst thou then of mee, and this my State, Par Lost 8.403
Thus I have told thee all my State, and brought Par Lost 8.521
Bane, and in Heav'n much worse would be my state. Par Lost 9.123
Let us not then suspect our happie State Par Lost 9.337
Or aught that might his happie State secure, Par Lost 9.347
Bone of my Bone thou art, and from thy State Par Lost 9.915
Triumph and say; Fickle their State whom God Par Lost 9.948
Our State cannot be severd, we are one, Par Lost 9.958
Thir inward State of Mind, calm Region once Par Lost 9.1125
For Man, for of his state by this they knew, Par Lost 10.19
Ascended his high Throne, which under state Par Lost 10.445
Kept in that State, had not the folly of Man Par Lost 10.619
1667 'state'
And in thir state, though firm, stood more confirmd. Par Lost 11.71
Here let us live, though in fall'n state, content. Par Lost 11.180
Adam bowd low, hee Kingly from his State Par Lost 11.249
By moderation either state to beare, Par Lost 11.363
Degraded, to what wretched state reserv'd! Par Lost 11.501
With fair equalitie, fraternal state, Par Lost 12.26
That Son, who on the quiet state of men Par Lost 12.80
Ill sorting with my present state compar'd. Par Reg 1.200
Higher design then to enjoy his State; Par Reg 2.203
Be try'd in humble state, and things adverse, Par Reg 3.189
Rather then aggravate my evil state, Par Reg 3.218
The Monarchies of the Earth, thir pomp and state, Par Reg 3.246
Hasting or on return, in robes of State; Par Reg 4.64
Habit, or state, or motion, still expressing Par Reg 4.601
O mirror of our fickle state, Samson 164
Chor. As signal now in low dejected state, Samson 338
I state not that; this I am sure; our Foes Samson 424
Behold him in this state calamitous, and turn Samson 708
Of men conspiring to uphold thir state Samson 892
Private reward, for which both God and State Samson 1465
I sorrow'd at his captive state, but minded Samson 1603
In thir state Livery clad; before him Pipes Samson 1616
Are coming to attend their Fathers state, Mask 35
Inferr, as if I thought my sisters state Mask 408
To a degenerate and degraded state. Mask 475
Where this night are met in state Mask 948
Wher the great Sun begins his state, Allegro 60
Com, but keep thy wonted state, Penseroso 37
Mark what radiant state she spreds, Arcades 14
And so attend ye toward her glittering state; Arcades 81
The painted Heav'ns so full of state. Psalm 136, 18
In first obedience, and their state of good. Musick 24
Bear his milde yoak, they serve him best, his State Sonnet 19, 11
With honour and with state thou hast him crown'd. Psalm 8, 16
What can be juster in a State then this? Prose 9, 5

Stateliest
Of stateliest view. Yet higher then thir tops Par Lost 4.142
Of stateliest Covert, Cedar, Pine, or Palme, Par Lost 9.435

Stately
With singed top thir stately growth though bare Par Lost 1.614
Stood fixt her stately highth, and strait the dores Par Lost 1.723
The Earth, and stately tread, or lowly creep; Par Lost 5.201
Rose as in Dance the stately Trees, and spred Par Lost 7.324
And at a stately side-board by the wine Par Reg 2.350
Above the rest lifting his stately head Par Reg 4.48
Like a stately Ship Samson 714
Their stately Palaces. Psalm 83, 48

States
Pleas'd highly those infernal States, and joy Par Lost 2.387
The drift of hollow states hard to be spelld, Sonnet 17, 6
1694 'States'
Of Kings and lordly States, Psalm 82, 2

Station
So wondrously was set his Station bright. Par Lost 3.587
Thir station, Heav'n yet populous retaines Par Lost 7.146
The Planets in thir station list'ning stood, Par Lost 7.563
1667 'stations'
Heav'n-fall'n, in station stood or just array, Par Lost 10.535
To thir fixt Station, all in bright array Par Lost 12.627
Kept not my happy Station, but was driv'n Par Reg 1.360
From his uneasie station, and upbore Par Reg 4.584

Stations
Through the strict Senteries and Stations thick Par Lost 2.412
The Planets in thir station list'ning stood, Par Lost 7.563
1667 'stations'

Statists
The top of Eloquence, Statists indeed, Par Reg 4.354

Statue
And you a statue; or as *Daphne* was Mask 661

Statues
Statues and Trophees, and Triumphal Arcs, Par Reg 4.37

Stature
His mighty Stature; on each hand the flames Par Lost 1.222
ms 'stature'
Thir visages and stature as of Gods, Par Lost 1.570
His stature reacht the Skie, and on his Crest Par Lost 4.988
Stood they or mov'd, in stature, motion, arms Par Lost 6.302

Stature(*cont*)
His Stature, and upright with Front serene Par Lost 7.509
Statute
This was a Statute *giv'n of old* Psalm 81, 13
Statutes
Who keepes the lawes and statutes of the Senate, Prose 10, 2
Stay
His Iron Gates, if he intends our stay Par Lost 4.898
And Grace that won who saw to wish her stay, Par Lost 8.43
Go; for thy stay, not free, absents thee more; Par Lost 9.372
Delighted, but desiring more her stay. Par Lost 9.398
Hast thou not wonderd, *Adam*, at my stay? Par Lost 9.856
Stay his return perhaps over this Gulfe Par Lost 10.253
My onely strength and stay: forlorn of thee, Par Lost 10.921
Nor after resurrection shall he stay Par Lost 12.436
We may no longer stay: go, waken *Eve;* Par Lost 12.594
Is to stay here; without thee here to stay, Par Lost 12.616
Duty and Service, nor to stay till bid, Par Reg 2.326
Yet stay, let me not rashly call in doubt Samson 43
What shall we do, stay here or run and see? Samson 1520
A little stay will bring some notice hither, Samson 1536
Stay thy cloudy Ebon chair, Mask 134
Bridgewater ms 'staye'
Longer I durst not stay, but soon I guess't Mask 577
Yet stay, be not disturb'd, now I bethink me, Mask 820
Bridgewater ms 'staye'
Gen. Stay gentle Swains, for though in this disguise, Arcades 26
But oh why didst thou not stay here below Fair Inf 64
And wearie of their place do only stay Vacation 25
Untill his revolution was at stay. Another 6
1658 'made of stay'
Happy all those who have in him their stay. Psalm 2, 28
Stayed
As many miles aloft: that furie stay'd, Par Lost 2.938
He ceas'd; and *Satan* staid not to reply, Par Lost 2.1010
He stayd not to enquire: above them all Par Lost 3.571
Nor staid, till on *Niphates* top he lights. Par Lost 3.742
Descending, and in half cut sheere, nor staid, Par Lost 6.325
Nor staid, but on the Wings of Cherubim Par Lost 7.218
Then staid the fervid Wheeles, and in his hand Par Lost 7.224
Invisible, yet staid (such priviledge Par Lost 7.589
Would thou hadst heark'nd to my words, and stai'd Par Lost 9.1134
Unshaken; nor yet staid the terror there, Par Reg 4.421
And staid not, but in brief him answer'd thus. Par Reg 4.485
That stay'd her flight with his cross-flowing course, Mask 832
Bridgewater ms 'stayed'
Trinity ms 'stayd'
Staid not behind, nor in the grave were trod; Sonnet 14, 6
Stays
And I will bring thee where no shadow staies Par Lost 4.470
Safest and seemliest by her Husband staies, Par Lost 9.268
Stayes not on Man; to God his Tower intends Par Lost 12.73
My sliding Chariot stayes, Mask 892
Stead
Arming to Battel, and in stead of rage Par Lost 1.553
But cloud in stead, and ever-during dark Par Lost 3.45
All hope excluded thus, behold in stead Par Lost 4.105
Good out of evil to create, in stead Par Lost 7.188
If it may stand him more in stead to lye, Par Reg 1.473
Who would be now a Father in my stead? Samson 355
But here thy sword can do thee little stead, Mask 611
Trinity ms 'little stead' ←'small availe' ←'little stead'
Steadfast
Mixt with obdurate pride and stedfast hate: Par Lost 1.58
The stedfast Earth. At last his Sail-broad Vannes Par Lost 2.927
The stedfast Empyrean shook throughout, Par Lost 6.833
The Planet Earth, so stedfast though she seem, Par Lost 8.129
Sober, stedfast, and demure, Penseroso 32
Stand fixt in stedfast gaze, Nativity 70
Steadiest
What oft my steddiest thoughts have searcht in vain, Par Lost 12.377
Steady
Sailes between worlds and worlds, with steddie wing Par Lost 5.268
Could stir the constant mood of her calm thoughts, Mask 371
Trinity ms 'constant' ←'steadie'
Stealth
Pursues the *Arimaspian*, who by stelth Par Lost 2.945
From entrance or Cherubic Watch, by stealth Par Lost 9.68
As a stray'd Ewe, or to pursue the stealth Mask 503
Steam
Consum'd with nimble glance, and grateful steame; Par Lost 11.442
Rose like a steam of rich distill'd Perfumes, Mask 556
Trinity ms 'a steame' ←'the softe steame'
Bridgewater ms 'the softe steame of'
1637 'steame'
1673 'stream'
Steamed
Gris-amber-steam'd; all Fish from Sea or Shore, Par Reg 2.344
Steaming
From Hill or steaming Lake, duskie or grey, Par Lost 5.186
Steed
But like a proud Steed reind, went hautie on, Par Lost 4.858
Least from this flying Steed unrein'd, (as once Par Lost 7.17
Part wield thir Arms, part courb the foaming Steed, Par Lost 11.643
Steeds
Part curb thir fierie Steeds, or shun the Goal Par Lost 2.531
Rapt in a Chariot drawn by fiery Steeds. Par Lost 3.522
Chariots and flaming Armes, and fierie Steeds Par Lost 6.17

Steeds(*cont*)
And fierie foaming Steeds; what stood, recoyld Par Lost 6.391
Impreses quaint, Caparisons and Steeds; Par Lost 9.35
Rapt in a balmie Cloud with winged Steeds Par Lost 11.706
Gave respit to the drowsie frighted steeds Mask 553
Fly after the Night-steeds, leaving their Moon-lov'd maze. Nativity 236
Steel
With stubborn patience as with triple steel. Par Lost 2.569
They issue forth, Steel Bows, and Shafts their arms Par Reg 3.305
Cuirassiers all in steel for standing fight; Par Reg 3.328
Chalybean temper'd steel, and frock of mail Samson 133
As thou art strong, inflexible as steel. Samson 816
She that has that, is clad in compleat steel, Mask 421
1637 'steele'
Trinity ms 'steele'
Bridgewater ms 'steele'
But here thy sword can do thee little stead, Mask 611
Trinity ms 'swoord' ←'steele' ←'swo'
Steep
The way seems difficult and steep to scale Par Lost 2.71
Ore bog or steep, through strait, rough, dense, or rare, Par Lost 2.948
Throws his steep flight in many an Aerie wheele, Par Lost 3.741
Of a steep wilderness, whose hairie sides Par Lost 4.135
Now to th' ascent of that steep savage Hill Par Lost 4.172
Down the steep glade, and met the neather Flood, Par Lost 4.231
Both day and night: how often from the steep Par Lost 4.680
The sword of *Satan* with steep force to smite Par Lost 6.324
Much of his Race though steep, suspens in Heav'n Par Lost 7.99
If steep, with torrent rapture, if through Plaine, Par Lost 7.299
Cast her self headlong from th' *Ismenian* steep, Par Reg 4.575
In the steep *Atlantick* stream, Mask 97
1637 'steepe'
Bridgewater ms 'steepe'
Trinity ms 'steepe'
The nice Morn on th' *Indian* steep Mask 139
Trinity ms 'steepe'
1637 'steepe'
Bridgewater ms 'steepe'
his farre-extended armes till with steepe fall Mask Tr. ms 10.13
For neither were ye playing on the steep, Lycidas 52
Trinity ms 'steepe'
With hollow shreik the steep of *Delphos* leaving. Nativity 178
Fall on his crown with ruine steep. Psalm 7, 60
I tri'd thee at the water *steep* Psalm 81, 31
Steer
Of heart or hope; but still bear vp and steer Sonnet 22, 8
Steerage
Without the sure guess of well-practiz'd feet. Mask 310
Steered
Charybdis, and by th' other whirlpool steard. Par Lost 2.1020
Steering
Betwixt the *Centaure* and the *Scorpion* stearing Par Lost 10.328
The tread of many feet stearing this way; Samson 111
With radiant feet the tissued clouds down stearing, Nativity 146
Steers
Then with expanded wings he stears his flight Par Lost 1.225
ms 'steares'
Easing thir flight; so stears the prudent Crane Par Lost 7.430
Veres oft, as oft so steers, and shifts her Saile; Par Lost 9.515
Steersman
As when a Ship by skilful Stearsman wrought Par Lost 9.513
Steers-mate
Embarqu'd with such a Stears-mate at the Helm? Samson 1045
Stellar
Thir stellar vertue on all kinds that grow Par Lost 4.671
Stem
On the green stemm; God saw that it was good. Par Lost 7.337
Where ye may all that are of noble stemm Arcades 82
Trinity ms 'stemme'
Stemming
Ply stemming nightly toward the Pole. So seem'd Par Lost 2.642
Stench
With stench and smoak: Such resting found the sole Par Lost 1.237
Step
One step no more then from himself can fly Par Lost 4.22
I sdeind subjection, and thought one step higher Par Lost 4.50
So saying, his proud step he scornful turn'd, Par Lost 4.536
Smooth sliding without step, last led me up Par Lost 8.302
If chance with Nymphlike step fair Virgin pass, Par Lost 9.452
So saying, from the Tree her step she turnd, Par Lost 9.834
His bright appearances, or foot step-trace? Par Lost 11.329
1667 'footstep trace'
Thought following thought, and step by step led on, Par Reg 1.192
With careful step, Locks white as doune, Samson 327
But here she comes, I fairly step aside Mask 168
With eev'n step, and musing gate, Penseroso 38
Where no print of step hath been, Arcades 85
Set thy wayes right before, where my step goes. Psalm 5, 24
Stepdame
Young *Bacchus* from his Stepdame *Rhea*'s eye; Par Lost 4.279
Of her enraged stepdam *Guendolen*, Mask 830
Bridgewater ms 'stepdame'
Trinity ms 'stepdame'
Stepped
Back stept those two faire Angels half amaz'd Par Lost 4.820
Stept as they se'd to the next Thicket side Mask 185
Stepping
Forth stepping opposite, half way he met Par Lost 6.128

Stepping(*cont*)
Call on the lazy leaden-stepping hours, On Time 2
Steps
He walkt with to support uneasie steps Par Lost 1.295
Over the burning Marle, not like those steps Par Lost 1.296
Thir painful steps o're the burnt soyle; and now Par Lost 1.562
My self expose, with lonely steps to tread Par Lost 2.828
His travell'd steps; farr distant he descries Par Lost 3.501
That scal'd by steps of Gold to Heav'n Gate Par Lost 3.541
Before his decent steps a Silver wand. Par Lost 3.644
Now Morn her rosie steps in th' Eastern Clime Par Lost 5.1
By steps we may ascend to God. But say, Par Lost 5.512
Grace was in all her steps, Heav'n in her Eye, Par Lost 8.488
Of glory, and farr off his steps adore. Par Lost 11.333
Express, and of his steps the track Divine. Par Lost 11.354
They hand in hand with wandring steps and slow, Par Lost 12.648
His easie steps; girded with snaky wiles, Par Reg 1.120
Was difficult, by humane steps untrod; Par Reg 1.298
Up to a hill anon his steps he rear'd, Par Reg 2.285
Came forth with Pilgrim steps in amice gray; Par Reg 4.427
To these dark steps, a little further on; Samson 2
With youthful steps? much livelier then e're while Samson 1442
Yet som there be that by due steps aspire Mask 12
Bridgewater ms 'stepps'
Of hatefull steps, I must be viewles now. Mask 92
Bridgewater ms 'stepps'
They had ingag'd their wandring steps too far, Mask 193
Bridgewater ms 'stepps'
Stern
To whom with stern regard thus *Gabriel* spake. Par Lost 4.877
To which the Fiend thus answerd frowning stern. Par Lost 4.924
To whom in brief thus *Abdiel* stern repli'd. Par Lost 6.171
Of stern *Achilles* on his Foe pursu'd Par Lost 9.15
But her with stern regard he thus repell'd. Par Lost 10.866
Thus to our Saviour with stern brow reply'd. Par Reg 4.367
Fear'd her stern frown, and she was queen oth' Woods. Mask 446
1637 'sterne'
Trinity ms 'sterne'
Bridgewater ms 'sterne'
He shook his Miter'd locks, and stern bespake, Lycidas 112
Trinity ms 'sterne'
To the stern God of Sea. Horace 16
Sternly
Of woe and sorrow. Sternly he pronounc'd Par Lost 8.333
To whom our Saviour sternly thus reply'd. Par Reg 1.406
Sticks
Sticks no dishonor on our Front, but turns Par Lost 9.330
Or wither'd sticks to gather; which might serve Par Reg 1.316
Stiff
The Dank, and rising on stiff Pennons, towre Par Lost 7.441
Bow'd their Stiff necks, loaden with stormy blasts, Par Reg 4.418
And with stiff Vowes renounc'd his Liturgie Forcers 2
Stifling
Blown stifling back on him that breaths it forth: Par Lost 11.313
Still
Still urges, and a fiery Deluge, fed Par Lost 1.68
And out of good still to find means of evil; Par Lost 1.165
What matter where, if I be still the same, Par Lost 1.256
Put forth at full, but still his strength conceal'd, Par Lost 1.641
Though without number still amidst the Hall Par Lost 1.791
Of that forgetful Lake benumm not still, Par Lost 2.74
Wrought still within them; and no less desire Par Lost 2.295
In heighth or depth, still first and last will Reign Par Lost 2.324
The great Creatour? But thir spite still serves Par Lost 2.385
And kennel there, yet there still bark'd and howl'd, Par Lost 2.658
Encroacht on still through our intestine broiles Par Lost 2.1001
So easily destroy'd, and still destroyes Par Lost 3.301
Of *Sennaar*, and still with vain designe Par Lost 3.467
Shot upward still direct, whence no way round Par Lost 3.618
Still ending, still renewing, through mid Heav'n; Par Lost 3.729
So burthensome still paying, still to ow; Par Lost 4.53
Forgetful what from him I still receivd, Par Lost 4.54
By owing owes not, but still pays, at once Par Lost 4.56
Still threatning to devour me opens wide, Par Lost 4.77
The lower still I fall, onely Supream Par Lost 4.91
Still as they thirsted scoop the brimming stream; Par Lost 4.336
When *Satan* still in gaze, as first he stood, Par Lost 4.356
Still unfulfill'd with pain of longing pines; Par Lost 4.511
Still as it rose, impossible to climbe. Par Lost 4.548
Mine eye pursu'd him still, but under shade Par Lost 4.572
So judge thou still, presumptuous, till the wrauth, Par Lost 4.912
But still thy words at random, as before, Par Lost 4.930
Attracted by thy beauty still to gaze. Par Lost 5.47
Varie to our great Maker still new praise. Par Lost 5.184
Rising or falling still advance his praise. Par Lost 5.191
Hail universal Lord, be bounteous still Par Lost 5.205
Assur'd me, and still assure: though what thou tellst Par Lost 5.553
Apostat, still thou errst, nor end wilt find Par Lost 6.172
Stand still in bright array ye Saints, here stand Par Lost 6.801
Purples the East: still govern thou my Song, Par Lost 7.30
1669 'Still'
Yet scarce allay'd still eyes the current streame, Par Lost 7.67
In that aspect, and still that distance keepes Par Lost 7.379
Thought him still speaking, still stood fixt to hear; Par Lost 8.3
line not in 1667 edition
A pomp of winning Graces waited still, Par Lost 8.61
Into all Eyes to wish her still in sight. Par Lost 8.63
Still luminous by his ray. What if that light Par Lost 8.140

Still(*cont*)
Unpractis'd, unprepar'd, and still to seek. Par Lost 8.197
Desire with thee still longer to converse Par Lost 8.252
I found not what me thought I wanted still; Par Lost 8.355
The one intense, the other still remiss Par Lost 8.387
And be so minded still; I, ere thou spak'st, Par Lost 8.444
Still glorious before whom awake I stood; Par Lost 8.464
Attractive, human, rational, love still; Par Lost 8.587
Variously representing; yet still free Par Lost 8.610
Be good and friendly still, and oft return. Par Lost 8.651
Adam, well may we labour still to dress Par Lost 9.205
This Garden, still to tend Plant, Herb and Flour, Par Lost 9.206
That gave thee being, still shades thee and protects. Par Lost 9.266
1667 'stil'
How are we happie, still in fear of harm? Par Lost 9.326
But bid her well beware, and still erect, Par Lost 9.353
Still hanging incorruptible, till men Par Lost 9.622
Whose vertue, for of good still good proceeds, Par Lost 9.973
Remaind still happie, not as now, despoild Par Lost 9.1138
As good have grown there still a liveless Rib. Par Lost 9.1154
For still they knew, and ought to have still remember'd Par Lost 10.12
But still rejoyc't, how is it now become Par Lost 10.120
Still moves with thine, join'd in connexion sweet, Par Lost 10.359
There didst not; there let him still Victor sway, Par Lost 10.376
Ophiusa) but still greatest hee the midst, Par Lost 10.528
Above the rest still to retain; they all Par Lost 10.532
Then stil at Hels dark threshold to have sate watch, Par Lost 10.594
So fair and good created, and had still Par Lost 10.618
Had rounded still th' *Horizon*, and not known Par Lost 10.684
Pursues me still, least all I cannot die, Par Lost 10.783
By which all Causes else according still Par Lost 10.806
And reasonings, though through Mazes, lead me still Par Lost 10.830
Still following thee, still compassing thee round Par Lost 11.352
Retaining still Divine similitude Par Lost 11.512
But still I see the tenor of Mans woe Par Lost 11.632
Still tend from bad to worse, till God at last Par Lost 12.106
Humbles his stubborn heart, but still as Ice Par Lost 12.193
Still follow'd him; to them shall leave in charge Par Lost 12.439
Secular power, though feigning still to act Par Lost 12.517
Still overcoming evil, and by small Par Lost 12.566
That heard the Adversary, who roving still Par Reg 1.33
And he still on was led, but with such thoughts Par Reg 1.299
Where still from shade to shade the Son of God Par Reg 2.242
Though hunger still remain: so it remain Par Reg 2.255
Only the importune Tempter still remain'd, Par Reg 2.404
By patience, temperance; I mention still Par Reg 3.92
Thy right by sitting still or thus retiring? Par Reg 3.164
Israel in long captivity still mourns; Par Reg 3.279
Thou never shalt obtain; prediction still Par Reg 3.354
Still will be tempting him who foyls him still, Par Reg 4.13
And hunger still: then Embassies thou shew'st Par Reg 4.121
Luxurious by thir wealth, and greedier still, Par Reg 4.141
Or nothing more then still to contradict: Par Reg 4.158
Uncertain and unsettl'd still remains, Par Reg 4.326
So saying he took (for still he knew his power Par Reg 4.394
And follow'd thee still on to this wast wild; Par Reg 4.523
With *Joves Alcides*, and oft foil'd still rose, Par Reg 4.565
Habit, or state, or motion, still expressing Par Reg 4.601
Within doors, or without, still as a fool, Samson 77
And the same end; still watching to oppress Samson 232
Yet *Israel* still serves with all his Sons. Samson 240
They ravel more, still less resolv'd, Samson 305
Bitterly hast thou paid, and still art paying Samson 432
I came, still dreading thy displeasure, *Samson*, Samson 733
Here I should still enjoy thee day and night Samson 807
But had thy love, still odiously pretended, Samson 873
Bear not too sensibly, nor still insist Samson 913
Thy anger, unappeasable, still rages, Samson 963
For dire imagination still persues me. Samson 1544
Man. Relate by whom. *Mess*. By *Samson*. *Man*. That still lessens Samson 1563
To heave, pull, draw, or break, he still perform'd Samson 1626
Well knows to still the wilde winds when they roar, Mask 87
At last a soft and solemn breathing sound Mask 555
Trinity ms 'soft' ← 'sweet' ← 'still' ← 'soft'
Still to be so displac't. I was all eare, Mask 560
You gave me Brother? *Eld. Bro*. Yes, and keep it still, Mask 584
Made Goddess of the River; still she retains Mask 842
There held in holy passion still, Penseroso 41
Som still removed place will fit, Penseroso 78
Or usher'd with a shower still, Penseroso 127
While the still morn went out with Sandals gray, Lycidas 187
next adde Narcissus that still weeps in vaine Lycidas Tr. ms 28.19
And Kings sate still with awfull eye, Nativity 59
With thousand echo's still prolongs each heav'nly close. Nativity 100
The floods stood still like Walls of Glass, Psalm 136, 49
She heard them give thee this, that thou should'st still Vacation 65
Of Lute, or Viol still, more apt for mournful things. Passion 28
And that great Cov'nant which we still transgress Circum 21
While he might still jogg on, and keep his trot, Another 4
1658 'he could but'
Warbl'st at eeve, when all the Woods are still, Sonnet 1, 2
It shall be still in strictest measure eev'n, Sonnet 7, 10
And still revolt when truth would set them free. Sonnet 12, 10
Trinity ms 'still revolt when Truth would sett them' ← 'make them' ← 'set them' ← 'hate the truth wherby they should be'
when as they journey'd from this dark abode Sonnet 14, Tr. ms 41.07
'when as' ← 'Still as'
For what can Warr, but endless warr still breed, Sonnet 15, 10

Still(*cont*)
To conquer still; peace hath her victories — Sonnet 16, 10
O're all th' *Italian* fields where still doth sway — Sonnet 18, 11
Of heart or hope; but still bear vp and steer — Sonnet 22, 8
Still to love vanity, — Psalm 4, 10
Still on; for against thee they have rebell'd; — Psalm 5, 32
To bless the just man still, — Psalm 5, 38
Their own conceits they follow'd still — Psalm 81, 51
Sit not thou still O God of *strength* — Psalm 83, 3
Who *still* in thee doth trust. — Psalm 86, 8
Still
Drew audience and attention still as Night — Par Lost 2.308
Now came still Eevning on, and Twilight gray — Par Lost 4.598
Stand still in bright array ye Saints, here stand — Par Lost 6.801
Earth sitting still, when she alone receaves — Par Lost 8.89
Progressive, retrograde, or standing still, — Par Lost 8.127
Through the still Night, not now, as ere man fell, — Par Lost 10.846
Or how the Sun shall in mid Heav'n stand still — Par Lost 12.263
Stilled
Who with her radiant finger still'd the roar — Par Reg 4.428
Sting
With mortal sting: about her middle round — Par Lost 2.653
Inglorious, of his mortall sting disarm'd. — Par Lost 3.253
And from the sting of Famine fear no harm, — Par Reg 2.257
Chor. She's gone, a manifest Serpent by her sting — Samson 997
And secret sting of amorous remorse. — Samson 1007
Stings
And fix farr deeper in his head thir stings — Par Lost 12.432
Thoughts my Tormenters arm'd with deadly stings — Samson 623
Stinks
Which once smelt sweet, now stinks as odiously; — Prose 4, 2
Stint
To stint th' enemy, and slack th' avengers brow — Psalm 8, 7
Stir
Will slack'n, if his breath stir not thir flames. — Par Lost 2.214
His troubl'd thoughts, and from the bottom stirr — Par Lost 4.19
Raphael, said hee, thou hear'st what stir on Earth — Par Lost 5.224
And with malitious counsel stir them up — Samson 1251
Above the smoak and stirr of this dim spot, — Mask 5
1637 'stirre'
Trinity ms 'stirre'
Could stir the constant mood of her calm thoughts, — Mask 371
Trinity ms 'stirre'
Bridgewater ms 'stirr'
Is of such power to stir up joy as this, — Mask 677
Trinity ms 'stirre'
Bridgewater ms 'stirre'
1637 'stirre'
Stirred
Stird up with Envy and Revenge, deceiv'd — Par Lost 1.35
ms 'Stirrd'
Tempting, stirr'd in me sudden appetite — Par Lost 8.308
Stirring
Thir natural pravitie, by stirring up — Par Lost 12.288
Stirs
Stirs up among the loose unleter'd Hinds, — Mask 174
Bridgewater ms 'stirrs'
Trinity ms 'stirrs'
Stoa
Lyceum there, and painted *Stoa* next: — Par Reg 4.253
Stock
And Man as from a second stock proceed. — Par Lost 12.7
All Prophecie, That of the Royal Stock — Par Lost 12.325
Men call me *Harapha*, of stock renown'd — Samson 1079
Stocked
Be well stock't with as fair a herd as graz'd — Mask 152
Bridgewater ms 'stockt'
Stocks
When all our Fathers worship't Stocks and Stones, — Sonnet 18, 4
Stoic
Epicurean, and the *Stoic* severe; — Par Reg 4.280
The Stoic last in Philosophic pride, — Par Reg 4.300
To those budge doctors of the *Stoick* Furr, — Mask 707
Trinity ms 'stoick'
Stole
Native perfumes, and whisper whence they stole — Par Lost 4.158
On him who had stole *Joves* authentic fire. — Par Lost 4.719
From standing lake to tripping ebbe, that stole — Par Lost 11.847
Had stole them from me, els O theevish Night — Mask 195
Trinity ms 'stolne'
1637 'stolne'
Bridgewater ms 'stolne'
And stole upon the Air, that even Silence — Mask 557
And sable stole of *Cipres* Lawn, — Penseroso 35
Stole under Seas to meet his *Arethuse;* — Arcades 31
Stoled
The sable-stoled Sorcerers bear his worshipt Ark. — Nativity 220
Stolen
Much wondring how the suttle Fiend had stoln — Par Lost 10.20
With whose stol'n Fruit Man once more to delude. — Par Lost 11.125
Stoln on his wing my three and twentith yeer! — Sonnet 7, 2
Trinity ms 'stolne'
1673 'Soln'
Stone
Compar'd with aught on Earth, Medal or Stone; — Par Lost 3.592
If stone, Carbuncle most or Chrysolite, — Par Lost 3.596
In *Aarons* Brest-plate, and a stone besides — Par Lost 3.598
That stone, or like to that which here below — Par Lost 3.600

Stone(*cont*)
Broiderd the ground, more colour'd then with stone — Par Lost 4.702
Entrails unlike) of Mineral and Stone, — Par Lost 6.517
Of grassie Terfe, and pile up every Stone — Par Lost 11.324
Smote him into the Midriff with a stone — Par Lost 11.445
Intestin Stone and Ulcer, Colic pangs, — Par Lost 11.484
To worship thir own work in Wood and Stone — Par Lost 12.119
On *Cittron* tables or *Atlantic* stone; — Par Reg 4.115
Or as a stone that shall to pieces dash — Par Reg 4.149
Thou chance to dash thy foot against a stone. — Par Reg 4.559
Wherwith she freez'd her foes to congeal'd stone? — Mask 449
Stones
With Dart and Jav'lin, Stones and sulfurous Fire; — Par Lost 11.658
That out of these hard stones be made thee bread; — Par Reg 1.343
And make soft rills from fiery flint-stones gush. — Psalm 114, 18
The labour of an age in piled Stones, — Shakespear 2
1632 'stones'
1640 'stones'
1663-4 'stones'
When all our Fathers worship't Stocks and Stones, — Sonnet 18, 4
Stony
What may suffice, and soft'n stonie hearts — Par Lost 3.189
Brass, Iron, Stonie mould, had not thir mouthes — Par Lost 6.576
The stonie from thir hearts, & made new flesh — Par Lost 11.4
Within thir stony caves, but rush'd abroad — Par Reg 4.414
In stony fetters fixt, and motionless; — Mask 819
1637 'stonie'
Bridgewater ms 'stonie'
Trinity ms 'stonie'
From the stony *Maenalus*, — Arcades 102
Stood
Of that inflamed Sea, he stood and call'd — Par Lost 1.300
The Heads and Leaders thither hast where stood — Par Lost 1.357
Came singly where he stood on the bare strand, — Par Lost 1.379
While the promiscuous croud stood yet aloof? — Par Lost 1.380
In *Sion* also not unsung, where stood — Par Lost 1.442
Vice for it self: To him no Temple stood — Par Lost 1.492
Stood like a Towr; his form had yet not lost — Par Lost 1.591
For his revolt, yet faithfull how they stood, — Par Lost 1.611
As stood like these, could ever know repulse? — Par Lost 1.630
There stood a Hill not far whose griesly top — Par Lost 1.670
Stood fixt her stately highth, and strait the dores — Par Lost 1.723
Stood up, the strongest and the fiercest Spirit — Par Lost 2.44
Majestic though in ruin: sage he stood — Par Lost 2.305
For each seem'd either; black it stood as Night, — Par Lost 2.670
Incenst with indignation *Satan* stood — Par Lost 2.707
Grew darker at thir frown, so matcht they stood; — Par Lost 2.720
Excel'd her power; the Gates wide op'n stood, — Par Lost 2.884
So wide they stood, and like a Furnace mouth — Par Lost 2.888
Stood on the brink of Hell and look'd a while, — Par Lost 2.918
The Consort of his Reign; and by them stood — Par Lost 2.963
Stood thick as Starrs, and from his sight receiv'd — Par Lost 3.61
Sufficient to have stood, though free to fall. — Par Lost 3.99
And Spirits, both them who stood and them who faild; — Par Lost 3.101
Freely they stood who stood, and fell who fell. — Par Lost 3.102
He ask'd, but all the Heav'nly Quire stood mute, — Par Lost 3.217
Each Stair mysteriously was meant, nor stood — Par Lost 3.516
Round he surveys, and well might, where he stood — Par Lost 3.555
Stood rul'd, stood vast infinitude confin'd; — Par Lost 3.711
Me some inferiour Angel, I had stood — Par Lost 4.59
And all amid them stood the Tree of Life, — Par Lost 4.218
Stood whispering soft, by a fresh Fountain side — Par Lost 4.326
When *Satan* still in gaze, as first he stood, — Par Lost 4.356
Into a liquid Plain, then stood unmov'd — Par Lost 4.455
Thus at thir shadie Lodge arriv'd, both stood — Par Lost 4.720
Forth issuing at th' accustomd hour stood armd — Par Lost 4.779
That neer him stood, and gave them thus in charge. — Par Lost 4.787
Invincible: abasht the Devil stood, — Par Lost 4.846
Just met, and closing stood in squadron joind — Par Lost 4.863
Insulting Angel, well thou knowst I stood — Par Lost 4.926
Collecting all his might dilated stood, — Par Lost 4.986
And as I wondring lookt, beside it stood — Par Lost 5.54
Two other precious drops that ready stood, — Par Lost 5.132
Thousand Celestial Ardors, where he stood — Par Lost 5.249
Skie-tinctur'd grain. Like *Maia*'s son he stood, — Par Lost 5.285
Stood to entertain her guest from Heav'n; no vaile — Par Lost 5.383
And perfet while they stood; how last unfould — Par Lost 5.568
Of circuit inexpressible they stood, — Par Lost 5.595
Desirous; all in Circles as they stood, — Par Lost 5.631
Stood up, and in a flame of zeale severe — Par Lost 5.807
That stood for Heav'n, in mighty Quadrate joyn'd — Par Lost 6.62
Presented stood in terrible array — Par Lost 6.106
Abdiel that sight endur'd not, where he stood — Par Lost 6.111
Hosanna to the Highest: nor stood at gaze — Par Lost 6.205
Stood they or mov'd, in stature, motion, arms — Par Lost 6.302
Blaz'd opposite, while expectation stood — Par Lost 6.306
Back to his Chariot; where it stood retir'd — Par Lost 6.338
Nor stood unmindful *Abdiel* to annoy — Par Lost 6.369
And fierie foaming Steeds; what stood, recoyld — Par Lost 6.391
Not to have disobei'd; in fight they stood — Par Lost 6.403
As one he stood escap't from cruel fight, — Par Lost 6.448
None arguing stood, innumerable hands — Par Lost 6.508
The matin Trumpet Sung: in Arms they stood — Par Lost 6.526
To hide the fraud. At interview both stood — Par Lost 6.555
A Seraph stood, and in his hand a Reed — Par Lost 6.579
Stood waving tipt with fire; while we suspense, — Par Lost 6.580
Collected stood within our thoughts amus'd, — Par Lost 6.581
Stood rankt of Seraphim another row — Par Lost 6.604

Stood(*cont*)
Stood scoffing, highthn'd in thir thoughts beyond Par Lost 6.629
And all his Host derided, while they stood Par Lost 6.633
A while in trouble; but they stood not long, Par Lost 6.634
This saw his hapless Foes but stood obdur'd, Par Lost 6.785
Stood reimbattell'd fierce, by force or fraud Par Lost 6.794
To meet him all his Saints, who silent stood Par Lost 6.882
Of disobedience; firm they might have stood, Par Lost 6.911
On heav'nly ground they stood, and from the shore Par Lost 7.210
The swelling Gourd, up stood the cornie Reed Par Lost 7.321
The Planets in thir station list'ning stood, Par Lost 7.563
Thought him still speaking, still stood fixt to hear; Par Lost 8.3
line not in 1667 edition
Stood on my feet; about me round I saw Par Lost 8.261
When suddenly stood at my Head a dream, Par Lost 8.292
Which it had long stood under, streind to the highth Par Lost 8.454
Still glorious before whom awake I stood; Par Lost 8.464
As in a shadie nook I stood behind, Par Lost 9.277
Veild in a Cloud of Fragrance, where she stood, Par Lost 9.425
That space the Evil one abstracted stood Par Lost 9.463
Hee boulder now, uncall'd before her stood; Par Lost 9.523
Longing and envying stood, but could not reach. Par Lost 9.593
Stood in himself collected, while each part, Par Lost 9.673
Astonied stood and Blank, while horror chill Par Lost 9.890
Speechless he stood and pale, till thus at length Par Lost 9.894
Remov'd farr off; then pittying how they stood Par Lost 10.211
Stood open wide, belching outrageous flame Par Lost 10.232
Long hee admiring stood, till Sin, his faire Par Lost 10.352
So having said, a while he stood, expecting Par Lost 10.504
Heav'n-fall'n, in station stood or just array, Par Lost 10.535
Cast on themselves from thir own mouths. There stood Par Lost 10.547
Devourd each other; nor stood much in awe Par Lost 10.712
Thus they in lowliest plight repentant stood Par Lost 11.1
Of *Themis* stood devout. To Heav'n thir prayers Par Lost 11.14
And in thir state, though firm, stood more confirmd. Par Lost 11.71
Heart-strook with chilling gripe of sorrow stood, Par Lost 11.264
Stood visible, among these Pines his voice Par Lost 11.321
His Eye might there command wherever stood Par Lost 11.385
Ith' midst an Altar as the Land-mark stood Par Lost 11.432
In other part stood one who at the Forge Par Lost 11.564
Both Horse and Foot, nor idely mustring stood; Par Lost 11.645
Like a dark Ceeling stood; down rush'd the Rain Par Lost 11.743
Th' Archangel stood, and from the other Hill Par Lost 12.626
Admiring stood a space, then into Hymns Par Reg 1.169
Like things of thee to all that present stood. Par Reg 1.258
Him thought, he by the Brook of *Cherith* stood Par Reg 2.266
When suddenly a man before him stood, Par Reg 2.298
That fragrant smell diffus'd, in order stood Par Reg 2.351
Under the Trees now trip'd, now solemn stood Par Reg 2.354
So spake the Son of God, and Satan stood Par Reg 3.1
Satan had not to answer, but stood struck Par Reg 3.146
The Tempter stood, nor had what to reply, Par Reg 4.2
On each side an Imperial City stood, Par Reg 4.33
Tempt not the Lord thy God, he said and stood. Par Reg 4.561
Fell whence he stood to see his Victor fall. Par Reg 4.571
But safest he who stood aloof, Samson 135
I among these aloof obscurely stood. Samson 1611
(For so from such as nearer stood we heard) Samson 1631
And eyes fast fixt he stood, as one who pray'd, Samson 1637
The vulgar only scap'd who stood without. Samson 1659
Their port was more then human, as they stood; Mask 297
Amaz'd I stood, harrow'd with grief and fear, Mask 565
The hooked Chariot stood Nativity 56
The floods stood still like Walls of Glass, Psalm 136, 49
To bear me where the Towers of *Salem* stood, Passion 39
In perfect Diapason, whilst they stood Musick 23
And in his Garland as he stood, Winchester 21
But vow though the cross Doctors all stood hearers, Another 19
line not in 1640, 1657, 1658 texts
Of sinners hath not stood, and in the seat Psalm 1, 3

Stoodest
By th' Angel, on thy feet thou stoodst at last, Par Lost 11.759

Stoodst
As when thou stoodst in Heav'n upright and pure; Par Lost 4.837
When thou stood'st up his Tempter to the pride Par Reg 3.409
O patient Son of God, yet only stoodst Par Reg 4.420

Stoop
To stoop with wearied wings, and willing feet Par Lost 3.73
Death his deaths wound shall then receive, and stoop Par Lost 3.252
Dagon must stoop, and shall e're long receive Samson 468
Stoop thy pale visage through an amber cloud, Mask 333
Bridgewater ms 'stoope'
1637 'Stoope'
Trinity ms 'stoope'
Heav'n it self would stoop to her. Mask 1023
Cardoyn 'stoope'
1637 'stoope'
Bridgewater ms 'stoope'
Trinity ms 'stoope' ←'bow'

Stooped
With blandishment, each Bird stoop'd on his wing. Par Lost 8.351
The Bird of *Jove*, stoopt from his aerie tour, Par Lost 11.185

Stooping
Who stooping op'nd my left side, and took Par Lost 8.465
About her glowd, oft stooping to support Par Lost 9.427
Stooping through a fleecy cloud. Penseroso 72
He sov'ran Priest stooping his regall head Passion 15

Stop
Nor stop thy flaming Chariot wheels, that shook Par Lost 3.394
And Dulcimer, all Organs of sweet stop, Par Lost 7.596
Mountains of Ice, that stop th' imagin'd way Par Lost 10.291
To stop thir overgrowth, as inmate guests Par Lost 12.166
Till an unusuall stop of sudden silence Mask 552

Stopped
With soft foot towards the deep, who now had stopt Par Lost 11.848

Stops
Thir stops and chords was seen: his volant touch Par Lost 11.561
Or sound of pastoral reed with oaten stops, Mask 345
Bridgewater ms 'stopps'
Trinity ms 'stopps'
He touch'd the tender stops of various Quills, Lycidas 188

Store
None yet, but store hereafter from the earth Par Lost 3.444
Of som irriguous Valley spred her store, Par Lost 4.255
Fit for the Tun som Magazin to store Par Lost 4.816
Reservd from night, and kept for thee in store. Par Lost 5.128
Of God inspir'd, small store will serve, where store, Par Lost 5.322
To blackest grain, and into store convey'd: Par Lost 6.515
In Gods Eternal store, to circumscribe Par Lost 7.226
As leaves a greater store of Fruit untoucht, Par Lost 9.621
Of foul concupiscence; whence evil store; Par Lost 9.1078
From all the Elements her choicest store Par Reg 2.334
To store her children with; if all the world Mask 720
And she no whit encomber'd with her store, Mask 774
With store of Ladies, whose bright eies Allegro 121
That was the Casket of Heav'ns richest store, Passion 44
Of Jacobs *Land, though there be store*, Psalm 87, 7
For cloy'd with woes and trouble store Psalm 88, 9

Stored
And Quiver with three-bolted Thunder stor'd, Par Lost 6.764
With Honey stor'd: the rest are numberless, Par Lost 7.492
Stor'd in each Orb perhaps with some that live. Par Lost 8.152
His head the midst, well stor'd with suttle wiles: Par Lost 9.184
Lay stor'd, in what part summ'd, that she might know: Samson 395

Storehouse
My heart hath been a store-house long of things Par Reg 2.103

Stores
Her stores were open'd, and this Firmament Par Lost 2.175
And what thy stores contain, bring forth and poure Par Lost 5.314
Their stores doth over-cloy Psalm 4, 34

Storied
Storied of old in high immortal vers Mask 516
And storied Windows richly dight, Penseroso 159

Stories
With stories told of many a feat, Allegro 101

Storing
Save what by frugal storing firmness gains Par Lost 5.324

Stork
In prospect; there the Eagle and the Stork Par Lost 7.423

Storm
Shot after us in storm, oreblown hath laid Par Lost 1.172
But ratling storm of Arrows barbd with fire. Par Lost 6.546
From her best prop so farr, and storm so nigh. Par Lost 9.433
As mockt they storm; great laughter was in Heav'n Par Lost 12.59
After a night of storm so ruinous, Par Reg 4.436
To storm me over-watch't, and wearied out, Samson 405
But had we best retire, I see a storm? Samson 1061
And storm outrageously, Psalm 83, 6

Stormest
And storm'st refus'd, thinking to terrifie Par Reg 4.496

Storming
The horrid shock: now storming furie rose, Par Lost 6.207

Storms
Lies dark and wilde, beat with perpetual storms Par Lost 2.588
Great things with small) then when *Bellona* storms, Par Lost 2.922
Starless expos'd, and ever-threatning storms Par Lost 3.425
Rough with black winds and storms Horace 7

Stormy
And snow and haile and stormie gust and flaw, Par Lost 10.698
Bow'd their Stiff necks, loaden with stormy blasts, Par Reg 4.418
Whether beyond the stormy *Hebrides*, Lycidas 156
Trinity ms 'stormie'

Story
The storie heard attentive, and was fill'd Par Lost 7.51
My Storie, which perhaps thou hast not heard; Par Lost 8.205
My Storie to the sum of earthly bliss Par Lost 8.522
Thus *Eve* with Countnance blithe her storie told; Par Lost 9.886
Thir doctrine and thir story written left, Par Lost 12.506
As story tells, have trod this Wilderness; Par Reg 2.307
That solace? All our Law and Story strew'd Par Reg 4.334
The story of *Cambuscan* bold, Penseroso 110
They knew not of his story, Lycidas 95
1638 'storie'
Trinity ms 'storie'
Next her much like to thee in story, Winchester 62
That tun'st their happiest lines in Hymn, or Story. Sonnet 13, 11
Trinity ms 'story'
1648 'story'
Thee through my story Psalm 3, 8

Stoutly
Stoutly struts his Dames before, Allegro 52

Stoutness
Off. I am sorry what this stoutness will produce. Samson 1346

Straggling
Or straggling weather the pen't flock forsook? Mask 499

Straggling(*cont*)
Bridgewater ms 'straglinge'

Straight
Then strait commands that at the warlike sound — Par Lost 1.531
Stood fixt her stately highth, and strait the dores — Par Lost 1.723
Bordering on light; when strait behold the Throne — Par Lost 2.959
Admonisht by his ear, and strait was known — Par Lost 3.647
Strait couches close, then rising changes oft — Par Lost 4.405
But follow strait, invisibly thus led? — Par Lost 4.476
Strait side by side were laid, nor turnd I weene — Par Lost 4.741
To say and strait unsay, pretending first — Par Lost 4.947
The circuit wide. Strait knew him all the Bands — Par Lost 5.287
Of composition, strait they chang'd thir minds, — Par Lost 6.613
Each in their kinde. The Earth obey'd, and strait — Par Lost 7.453
Strait toward Heav'n my wondring Eyes I turnd, — Par Lost 8.257
In tangles, and made intricate seem strait, — Par Lost 9.632
Down he descended strait; the speed of Gods — Par Lost 10.90
Now also evidence, but straight I felt — Par Lost 10.361
And straight conjunction with this Sex: for either — Par Lost 10.898
All Nations shall be blest; he straight obeys, — Par Lost 12.126
This having heard, strait I again revolv'd — Par Reg 1.259
Strait knew me, and with loudest voice proclaim'd — Par Reg 1.275
Th' one winding, the other strait and left between — Par Reg 3.256
So Satan fell and strait a fiery Globe — Par Reg 4.581
Of Nuptial Love profest, carrying it strait — Samson 385
But this will cure all streight, one sip of this — Mask 811
Bridgewater ms 'streite'
Trinity ms 'streite'
Bearing her straight to aged *Nereus* Hall, — Mask 835
Trinity ms 'straite'
Bridgewater ms 'straite'
1637 'straite'
Streit mine eye hath caught new pleasures — Allegro 69
But haste thee strait to do me once a Pleasure, — Vacation 17
His principles being ceast, he ended strait. — Another 10
1640, 1657 'straight'
1658 'streight'
When strait a barbarous noise environs me — Sonnet 12, 3
Strait follow'd thee the path that Saints have trod — Sonnet 14, Tr. ms 41.06
I will *go strait and* hear, — Psalm 85, 30

Strain
To somthing like Prophetic strain. — Penseroso 174
That strain I heard was of a higher mood: — Lycidas 87
Trinity ms 'straine'
Hast thou no vers, no hymn, or solemn strein, — Nativity 17

Strained
Which it had long stood under, streind to the highth — Par Lost 8.454
Chor. Consider, *Samson;* matters now are strain'd — Samson 1348

Straining
This utter'd, straining all his nerves he bow'd, — Samson 1646

Strains
Thir Maker, in fit strains pronounc't or sung — Par Lost 5.148
El. Bro. Thyrsis? Whose artful strains have oft delaid — Mask 494
Trinity ms 'streines'
Bridgewater ms 'streynes'
And took in strains that might create a soul — Mask 561
Bridgewater ms 'streines'
Trinity ms 'streins'
Such streins as would have won the ear — Allegro 148

Strait
Ore bog or steep, through strait, rough, dense, or rare, — Par Lost 2.948
And mutual amitie so streight, so close, — Par Lost 4.376
O Heav'n! in evil strait this day I stand — Par Lost 10.125
And straight conjunction with this Sex: for either — Par Lost 10.898

Straitened
Swarm'd and were straitn'd; till the Signal giv'n, — Par Lost 1.776
In narrow circuit strait'nd by a Foe, — Par Lost 9.323

Straitening
Nor streit'ning Vale, nor Wood, nor Stream divides — Par Lost 6.70

Straiter
In straiter limits bound, — Nativity 169

Straits
Bred up in poverty and streights at home; — Par Reg 2.415
In straights and in distress — Psalm 4, 3

Strand
Came singly where he stood on the bare strand, — Par Lost 1.379
Young *Hyacinth* born on *Eurota*'s strand — Fair Inf 25

Strands
And her son that rules the strands, — Mask 876

Strange
By strange conveyance fill'd each hollow nook, — Par Lost 1.707
ms defective here
Mixt with *Tartarean* Sulphur, and strange fire, — Par Lost 2.69
Strange horror seise thee, and pangs unfelt before. — Par Lost 2.703
So strange thy outcry, and thy words so strange — Par Lost 2.737
Strange alteration! Sin and Death amain — Par Lost 2.1024
Of living Creatures new to sight and strange: — Par Lost 4.287
But with addition strange; yet be not sad. — Par Lost 5.116
The full relation, which must needs be strange, — Par Lost 5.556
From Father to his Son? strange point and new! — Par Lost 5.855
In the mid way: though strange to us it seemd — Par Lost 6.91
Which to our eyes discoverd new and strange, — Par Lost 6.571
Flew off, and into strange vagaries fell, — Par Lost 6.614
Of things so high and strange, things to thir thought — Par Lost 7.53
Commotion strange, in all enjoyments else — Par Lost 8.531
Strange alteration in me, to degree — Par Lost 9.599
The pain of absence from thy sight. But strange — Par Lost 9.861
With me, as I besought thee, when that strange — Par Lost 9.1135

Strange(*cont*)
My journey strange, with clamorous uproare — Par Lost 10.479
Us'd by the Tempter: on that prospect strange — Par Lost 10.552
Strange contradiction, which to God himself — Par Lost 10.799
For Man and Beast: when loe a wonder strange! — Par Lost 11.733
And looking down, to see the hubbub strange — Par Lost 12.60
And sayings laid up, portending strange events. — Par Reg 2.104
By what strange Parallax or Optic skill — Par Reg 4.40
Chor. Yet beauty, though injurious, hath strange power, — Samson 1003
Telling their strange and vigorous faculties; — Mask 628
with distant worlds, & strange removed clim — Mask Tr. ms 10.17
strange distances to heare & unknowne climes — Mask Tr. ms 10.17
and often takes our cattell with strange pinches — Mask Tr. ms 23.51
And let som strange mysterious dream, — Penseroso 147
Yet (strange to think) his wain was his increase: — Another 32
line not in 1658 text
The Tongue I heard, was strange. — Psalm 81, 20

Strangely
A mighty masse of things strangely confus'd, — Prose 2, 3

Stranger
Answer'd. I know thee, stranger, who thou art, — Par Lost 2.990
Our Heav'nly stranger; well we may afford — Par Lost 5.316
Our Authour. Heav'nly stranger, please to taste — Par Lost 5.397
Then loose it to a stranger, that the true — Par Lost 12.358

Strangled
And strangl'd with her waste fertility; — Mask 729

Stratagems
Be frustrate all ye stratagems of Hell, — Par Reg 1.180

Straw
Grate on their scrannel Pipes of wretched straw, — Lycidas 124

Straw-built
The suburb of thir Straw-built Cittadel, — Par Lost 1.773
ms 'straw-built'

Stray
Of Coral stray, or sporting with quick glance — Par Lost 7.405
I never from thy side henceforth to stray, — Par Lost 11.176
Following, as seem'd, the quest of some stray Ewe, — Par Reg 1.315
And if your stray attendance be yet lodg'd, — Mask 315
Bridgewater ms 'straye'
Where the nibling flocks do stray, — Allegro 72
But fie my wandring Muse how thou dost stray! — Vacation 53

Strayed
Here Pilgrims roam, that stray'd so farr to seek — Par Lost 3.476
While thus I call'd, and stray'd I knew not whither, — Par Lost 8.283
As a stray'd Ewe, or to pursue the stealth — Mask 503
Bridgewater ms 'strayed'
1637 'strayd'
That not a blast was from his dungeon stray'd, — Lycidas 97
Trinity ms 'straid'

Strays
That in the channell strayes, — Mask 895
Trinity ms 'in the channell straies' ←'my rich wheeles inlayes'
Which on a sudden straies, — Psalm 83, 54

Streak
To morrow ere fresh Morning streak the East — Par Lost 4.623

Streaking
Streaking the ground with sinuous trace; not all — Par Lost 7.481

Streaks
But say, what mean those colourd streaks in Heavn, — Par Lost 11.879

Stream
Created hugest that swim th' Ocean stream: — Par Lost 1.202
In *Argob* and in *Basan*, to the stream — Par Lost 1.398
Heard on the ruful stream; fierce *Phlegeton* — Par Lost 2.580
Farr off from these a slow and silent stream, — Par Lost 2.582
The tempting stream, with one small drop to loose — Par Lost 2.607
Or hear'st thou rather pure Ethereal stream, — Par Lost 3.7
Rowls o're *Elisian* Flours her Amber stream; — Par Lost 3.359
Still as they thirsted scoop the brimming stream; — Par Lost 4.336
Of nectarous draughts between, from milkie stream, — Par Lost 5.306
Streame in the Aire, and for distinction serve — Par Lost 5.590
Nor streit'ning Vale, nor Wood, nor Stream divides — Par Lost 6.70
A stream of Nectarous humor issuing flow'd — Par Lost 6.332
Yet scarce allay'd still eyes the current streame, — Par Lost 7.67
Stream, and perpetual draw thir humid traine. — Par Lost 7.306
To som Caves mouth, or whether washt by stream — Par Lost 11.569
Mount *Carmel;* here the double-founted stream — Par Lost 12.144
Baptizing in the profluent stream, the signe — Par Lost 12.442
1667 'streame'
Invites, and in the Consecrated stream — Par Reg 1.72
But as I rose out of the laving stream, — Par Reg 1.280
There *Susa* by *Choaspes*, amber stream, — Par Reg 3.288
His whispering stream; within the walls then view — Par Reg 4.250
Allure thee from the cool Crystalline stream. — Samson 546
Sok't in his enemies blood, and from the stream — Samson 1726
Of every salt Flood, and each ebbing Stream, — Mask 19
1637 'Streame'
1673 'stream'
Trinity ms 'streame'
Bridgewater ms 'streame'
In the steep *Atlantick* stream, — Mask 97
1637 'streame'
Bridgewater ms 'streame'
Trinity ms 'streame'
Drink the clear stream, and nothing wear but Freize, — Mask 722
Trinity ms 'streame'
1637 'streame'
Bridgewater ms 'streame'

Stream(*cont*)
That with moist curb sways the smooth Severn stream, Mask 825
Bridgewater ms 'streame'
Trinity ms 'streame'
Commended her fair innocence to the flood Mask 831
Trinity ms 'floud' ←'streame' ←'floud'
And throw sweet garland wreaths into her stream Mask 850
Trinity ms 'streame'
1637 'streame'
Bridgewater ms 'streame'
On Summer eeves by haunted stream. Allegro 130
Wave at his Wings in Airy stream, Penseroso 148
Nor yet where *Deva* spreads her wisard stream: Lycidas 55
Trinity ms 'streame'
His goary visage down the stream was sent, Lycidas 62
Trinity ms 'streame'
While Darwen stream with blood of Scotts imbru'd, Sonnet 16, 7
1694 'Streams'

Streamers
Sails fill'd, and streamers waving, Samson 718

Streaming
Shon like a Meteor streaming to the Wind Par Lost 1.537
And Life-blood streaming fresh; wide was the wound, Par Lost 8.467
With thy long levell'd rule of streaming light, Mask 340

Streams
Of *Abbana* and *Pharphar*, lucid streams. Par Lost 1.469
ms 'streames'
Into the burning Lake thir baleful streams; Par Lost 2.576
Of *Ganges* or *Hydaspes*, *Indian* streams; Par Lost 3.436
And now divided into four main Streams, Par Lost 4.233
Her chrystal mirror holds, unite thir streams. Par Lost 4.263
By living Streams among the Trees of Life, Par Lost 5.652
And Lakes and running Streams the waters fill; Par Lost 7.397
And liquid Lapse of murmuring Streams; by these, Par Lost 8.263
Mellifluous streams that water'd all the schools Par Reg 4.277
Upon thy streams with wily glance, Mask 884
Bridgewater ms 'streames'
That shrunk thy streams; Return *Sicilian* Muse, Lycidas 133
Where other groves, and other streams along, Lycidas 174
Low in the earth, *Jordans* clear streams recoil, Psalm 114, 9
And drink thy fill of pure immortal streams. Sonnet 14, 14
Trinity ms 'streames'
By watry streams, and in his season knows Psalm 1, 8
In thee *fresh brooks, and soft streams glance* Psalm 87, 27

Street
In every street, do they not say, how well Samson 204
Either at home, or through the high street passing, Samson 1458
Through each high street: little I had dispatch't Samson 1599

Streets
Darkens the Streets, then wander forth the Sons Par Lost 1.501
ms 'streets'
Witness the Streets of *Sodom*, and that night Par Lost 1.503
ms 'streets'
With Infant blood the streets of *Bethlehem;* Par Reg 2.78
Equivalent to Angels walk'd thir streets, Samson 343
Because they shall not trail me through thir streets Samson 1402

Strength
This downfall; since by Fate the strength of Gods Par Lost 1.116
Whether upheld by strength, or Chance, or Fate, Par Lost 1.133
Have left us this our spirit and strength intire Par Lost 1.146
Strength undiminisht, or eternal being Par Lost 1.154
As Gods, and by thir own recover'd strength, Par Lost 1.240
Nor founded on the brittle strength of bones, Par Lost 1.427
Thir living strength, and unfrequented left Par Lost 1.433
Distends with pride, and hardning in his strength Par Lost 1.572
Put forth at full, but still his strength conceal'd, Par Lost 1.641
And Strength and Art are easily out-done Par Lost 1.696
ms 'strength'
Equal in strength, and rather then be less Par Lost 2.47
Our strength is equal, nor the Law unjust Par Lost 2.200
In his own strength, this place may lye expos'd Par Lost 2.360
The happy Ile; what strength, what art can then Par Lost 2.410
Satan, I know thy strength, and thou knowst mine, Par Lost 4.1006
Remain not; wherfore should not strength and might Par Lost 6.116
A numerous Host, in strength each armed hand Par Lost 6.231
For strength from Truth divided and from Just, Par Lost 6.381
Valour or strength, though matchless, quelld with pain Par Lost 6.457
Abandon fear; to strength and counsel joind Par Lost 6.494
Or I alone against them, since by strength Par Lost 6.820
Among th' accurst, that witherd all thir strength, Par Lost 6.850
Yet half his strength he put not forth, but check'd Par Lost 6.853
This inaccessible high strength, the seat Par Lost 7.141
Of outward strength; while shame, thou looking on, Par Lost 9.312
And strength, of courage hautie, and of limb Par Lost 9.484
Shorn of his strength, They destitute and bare Par Lost 9.1062
Of Man, with strength entire, and free will arm'd, Par Lost 10.9
Methinks I feel new strength within me rise, Par Lost 10.243
My onely strength and stay: forlorn of thee, Par Lost 10.921
Strength added from above, new hope to spring Par Lost 11.138
Thy youth, thy strength, thy beauty, which will change Par Lost 11.539
Manhood to God-head, with more strength to foil Par Lost 12.389
Shall bruise the head of *Satan*, crush his strength Par Lost 12.430
His weakness shall o'recome Satanic strength Par Reg 1.161
No advantage, and his strength as oft assay. Par Reg 2.234
The strength whereof suffic'd him forty days; Par Reg 2.276
Of human weakness rather then of strength. Par Reg 3.402
The strength he was to cope with, or his own: Par Reg 4.9
Receiving from his mother Earth new strength, Par Reg 4.566

Strength(*cont*)
With this Heav'n-gifted strength? O glorious strength Samson 36
Who this high gift of strength committed to me, Samson 47
But what is strength without a double share Samson 53
God, when he gave me strength, to shew withal Samson 58
Suffices that to me strength is my bane, Samson 63
No strength of man, or fiercest wild beast could withstand; Samson 127
But thee whose strength, while vertue was her mate, Samson 173
Immeasurable strength they might behold Samson 206
The dread of *Israel*'s foes, who with a strength Samson 342
In mortal strength! and oh what not in man Samson 349
My capital secret, in what part my strength Samson 394
To what end should I seek it? when in strength Samson 522
Of all my strength in the lascivious lap Samson 536
Vain monument of strength; till length of years Samson 570
And I perswade me so; why else this strength Samson 586
Secret refreshings, that repair his strength, Samson 665
The Image of thy strength, and mighty minister. Samson 706
Wherein consisted all thy strength and safety? Samson 780
More strength from me, then in thy self was found. Samson 789
Thy key of strength and safety: thou wilt say, Samson 799
If thou in strength all mortals dost exceed, Samson 817
If in my flower of youth and strength, when all men Samson 938
Strength, comliness of shape, or amplest merit Samson 1011
Where strength can least abide, though all thy hairs Samson 1136
At my Nativity this strength, diffus'd Samson 1141
With strength sufficient and command from Heav'n Samson 1212
To descant on my strength, and give thy verdit? Samson 1228
Thy strength they know surpassing human rate, Samson 1313
Of strength, again returning with my hair Samson 1355
Vaunting my strength in honour to thir *Dagon?* Samson 1360
Chor. Yet with this strength thou serv'st the *Philistines*, Samson 1363
Measure of strength so great to mortal seed, Samson 1439
Or at some proof of strength before them shown. Samson 1475
That of a Nation arm'd the strength contain'd: Samson 1494
His strength again to grow up with his hair Samson 1496
And since his strength with eye-sight was not lost, Samson 1502
God will restore him eye-sight to his strength. Samson 1503
Proof of his mighty strength in feats and games; Samson 1602
I mean to shew you of my strength, yet greater; Samson 1644
To my proportion'd strength. Shepherd lead on.---- Mask 330
Bridgewater ms 'streingth'
As you imagine, she has a hidden strength Mask 415
Which you remember not. 2. *Bro*. What hidden strength, Mask 416
Trinity ms 'strenth'
Unless the strength of Heav'n, if you mean that? Mask 417
Eld. *Bro*. I mean that too, but yet a hidden strength Mask 418
Trinity ms 'strength' ←'strenth'
Basks at the fire his hairy strength; Allegro 112
Led by the strength of the Almighties hand, Psalm 114, 4
Let us break off, say they, by strength of hand Psalm 2, 6
Hast founded strength because of all thy foes Psalm 8, 6
Awake thy strength, come, and *be seen* Psalm 80, 11
To God our strength sing loud, *and clear* Psalm 81, 1
Sit not thou still O God of *strength* Psalm 83, 3
Happy, whose strength in thee doth bide, Psalm 84, 19
They journey on from strength to strength Psalm 84, 25
Unto thy servant give thy strength, Psalm 86, 59

Strenuous
Bondage with ease then strenuous liberty; Samson 271

Stretched
So stretcht out huge in length the Arch-fiend lay Par Lost 1.209
Of *Eden* planted; *Eden* stretchd her Line Par Lost 4.210
Stretcht into Longitude; which having pass'd Par Lost 5.754
From skirt to skirt a fierie Region, stretcht Par Lost 6.80
Stretcht like a Promontorie sleeps or swimmes, Par Lost 7.414
So spacious, and his Line stretcht out so farr; Par Lost 8.102
Stretcht out to the amplest reach of prospect lay. Par Lost 11.380
A spatious plain out stretch't in circuit wide Par Reg 3.254
And stretch'd out all the Chimney's length, Allegro 111
And now the Sun had stretch'd out all the hills, Lycidas 190
Trinity ms 'stretcht'

Stretching
Your dungeon stretching far and wide beneath; Par Lost 2.1003

Strew
Thick as Autumnal Leaves that strow the Brooks Par Lost 1.302
To strew the Laureat Herse where *Lycid* lies. Lycidas 151
Strew all their blessings on thy sleeping Head. Vacation 64
For thy Hears to strew the ways, Winchester 58

Strewed
The Inwards and thir Fat, with Incense strew'd, Par Lost 11.439
That solace? All our Law and Story strew'd Par Reg 4.334
In nectar'd lavers strew'd with Asphodil, Mask 838
Bridgewater ms 'strewd'
1637 'strewd'

Strewn
With shiverd armour strow'n, and on a heap Par Lost 6.389

Strews
Wants her fit vessels pure, then strews the ground Par Lost 5.348

Strict
Strict Laws impos'd, to celebrate his Throne Par Lost 2.241
Through the strict Senteries and Stations thick Par Lost 2.412
Charge and strict watch that to this happie Place Par Lost 4.562
Inextricable, or strict necessity; Par Lost 5.528
Affrighted; but strict Fate had cast too deep Par Lost 6.869
The strict forbiddance, how to violate Par Lost 9.903
By my complaint; but strict necessitie Par Lost 10.131
From imposition of strict Laws, to free Par Lost 12.304

Strict(*cont*)
Strict Age, and sowre Severity, Mask 109
Strictest
In strictest bondage, though thus far remov'd, Par Lost 2.321
With strictest watch; these other wheel the North, Par Lost 4.783
Not keeping strictest watch, as she was warnd. Par Lost 9.363
Against his vow of strictest purity, Samson 319
It shall be still in strictest measure eev'n, Sonnet 7, 10
Strictly
So strictly, but much more to pitie encline: Par Lost 3.402
So strictly, but much more to pitie enclin'd, Par Lost 3.405
Yet not so strictly hath our Lord impos'd Par Lost 9.235
And strictly meditate the thankles Muse, Lycidas 66
1638 'stridly'
Could Heav'n for pittie thee so strictly doom? Fair Inf 33
Stride
Draws hitherward, I know him by his stride, Samson 1067
Strides
With horrid strides, Hell trembled as he strode. Par Lost 2.676
Satan with vast and haughtie strides advanc't, Par Lost 6.109
Stalking with less unconsci'nable strides, Samson 1245
Strife
Matchless, but with th' Almighty, and that strife Par Lost 1.623
For which to strive, no strife can grow up there Par Lost 2.31
To fickle Chance, and *Chaos* judge the strife: Par Lost 2.233
Yet live in hatred, enmity, and strife Par Lost 2.500
He to appease thy wrauth, and end the strife Par Lost 3.406
These Acts of hateful strife, hateful to all, Par Lost 6.264
The strife which thou call'st evil, but wee style Par Lost 6.289
The strife of Glorie: which we mean to win, Par Lost 6.290
Nor other strife with them do I voutsafe. Par Lost 6.823
Endeavour Peace: thir strife pollution brings Par Lost 12.355
This only hope relieves me, that the strife Samson 460
Yet shall he live in strife, and at his dore Vacation 85
Nature and fate had had no strife Winchester 13
A strife thou mak'st us *and a prey* Psalm 80, 25
Strike
Shook, but delaid to strike, though oft invok't Par Lost 11.492
As with amaze shall strike all who behold. Samson 1645
Strikes
She strikes a universall Peace through Sea and Land. Nativity 52
String
All sounds on Fret by String or Golden Wire Par Lost 7.597
Such notes as warbled to the string, Penseroso 106
And touch the warbled string. Arcades 87
Trinity ms defective here
Begin, and somwhat loudly sweep the string. Lycidas 17
And Harp *with* pleasant *string*, Psalm 81, 8
Stringed
Answering the stringed noise, Nativity 97
Strings
Of chiming strings, or charming pipes and winds Par Reg 2.363
Me softer airs befit, and softer strings Passion 27
Stripes
And stripes, and arbitrary punishment Par Lost 2.334
Violence and stripes, and lastly cruel death, Par Reg 4.388
Stripling
And now a stripling Cherube he appeers, Par Lost 3.636
Tall stripling youths rich clad, of fairer hew Par Reg 2.352
Strippedst
Then like a Robber stripdst them of thir robes? Samson 1188
Strive
For which to strive, no strife can grow up there Par Lost 2.31
Strive here for Maistrie, and to Battel bring Par Lost 2.899
Of *Eden* strive; nor that *Nyseian* Ile Par Lost 4.275
Chaumping his iron curb: to strive or flie Par Lost 4.859
Each other, blam'd enough elsewhere, but strive Par Lost 10.959
Strive to keep up a frail, and Feaverish being Mask 8
Ungratefully shall strive to keep him under, Vacation 78
Them to ensnare they chiefly strive Psalm 83, 11
Strivest
In vain thou striv'st to cover shame with shame, Samson 841
Strode
With horrid strides, Hell trembled as he strode. Par Lost 2.676
Stroke
From *Egypt* marching, equal'd with one stroke Par Lost 1.488
Thy lingring, or with one stroke of this Dart Par Lost 2.702
1674 printed 'strokc'
No second stroke intend, and such a frown Par Lost 2.713
So saying, a noble stroke he lifted high, Par Lost 6.189
Uplifted imminent one stroke they aim'd Par Lost 6.317
By some immediate stroak; but soon shall find Par Lost 10.52
And th' instant stroke of Death denounc't that day Par Lost 10.210
And scourg'd with many a stroak th' indignant waves. Par Lost 10.311
That Death be not one stroak, as I suppos'd, Par Lost 10.809
Said hee, with one thrice acceptable stroke Par Lost 10.855
O unexpected stroke, worse then of Death! Par Lost 11.268
Some, as thou saw'st, by violent stroke shall die, Par Lost 11.471
Last with one midnight stroke all the first-born Par Lost 12.189
Thir fight, what stroke shall bruise the Victors heel. Par Lost 12.385
Must bide the stroak of that long threatn'd wound, Par Reg 1.59
Where the rude Ax with heaved stroke, Penseroso 136
Yet more; the stroke of death he must abide, Passion 20
Strong
Our prison strong, this huge convex of Fire, Par Lost 2.434
The strong rebuff of som tumultuous cloud Par Lost 2.936
From these, two strong and suttle Spirits he calld Par Lost 4.786
From his strong hold of Heav'n high over-rul'd Par Lost 6.228

Strong(*cont*)
By Angels many and strong, who interpos'd Par Lost 6.336
The dismal Gates, and barricado'd strong; Par Lost 8.241
Be strong, live happie, and love, but first of all Par Lost 8.633
Higher degree of Life, inducement strong Par Lost 9.934
Uncover'd more, so rose the *Danite* strong Par Lost 9.1059
Goe whither Fate and inclination strong Par Lost 10.265
No detriment need feare, goe and be strong. Par Lost 10.409
Deserted: Others to a Citie strong Par Lost 11.655
Subverting worldly strong, and worldly wise Par Lost 12.568
By Humiliation and strong Sufferance: Par Reg 1.160
And now by some strong motion I am led Par Reg 1.290
Cities of men, or head-strong Multitudes, Par Reg 2.470
That by strong hand his Family obtain'd, Par Reg 3.168
In Mail thir horses clad, yet fleet and strong, Par Reg 3.313
To *Capreae* an Island small but strong Par Reg 4.92
O impotence of mind, in body strong! Samson 52
His mighty Champion, strong above compare, Samson 556
As thou art strong, inflexible as steel. Samson 816
Arm'd thee or charm'd thee strong, which thou from Heaven Samson 1134
Man. O lastly over-strong against thy self! Samson 1590
By a strong siding champion Conscience.------ Mask 212
line not in Bridgewater ms
And adde the power of som adjuring verse. Mask 858
Trinity ms 'adjuring' ←'strong'
Huge pangs and strong Circum 27
Thou hast made firm and strong. Psalm 80, 64
Strong for thy self hast made. Psalm 80, 72
Who thence grow bold and strong Psalm 82, 8
By thy strong hand are done, Psalm 86, 34
Stronger
From what highth fall'n, so much the stronger prov'd Par Lost 1.92
Our stronger, some worse way his wrath may find Par Lost 2.83
In Battel which the stronger proves, they all, Par Lost 6.819
More wise, more watchful, stronger, if need were Par Lost 9.311
And beautie, not approacht by stronger hate, Par Lost 9.491
Hate stronger, under shew of Love well feign'd, Par Lost 9.492
Strongest
Stood up, the strongest and the fiercest Spirit Par Lost 2.44
Strongest of mortal men, Samson 168
Chor. O madness, to think use of strongest wines Samson 553
And strongest drinks our chief support of health, Samson 554
Soon feel, whose God is strongest, thine or mine. Samson 1155
Stronghold
From his strong hold of Heav'n high over-rul'd Par Lost 6.228
Stronglier
Stronglier, and better oft then earnest can. Prose 7, 2
Strongly
Strongly to suffer and support our pains, Par Lost 1.147
Nor can I miss the way, so strongly drawn Par Lost 10.262
And try her yet more strongly. Com, no more, Mask 806
word not in Trinity ms
word not in Bridgewater ms
Strove
Thir Kings, when *Aegypt* with *Assyria* strove Par Lost 1.721
Of three that in Mount *Ida* naked strove, Par Lost 5.382
Small things with greatest) in *Irassa* strove Par Reg 4.564
Or that Starr'd *Ethiope* Queen that strove Penseroso 19
and that sad floure that strove Lycidas Tr. ms 28.17
Struck
What when we fled amain, pursu'd and strook Par Lost 2.165
Drove them before him Thunder-struck, pursu'd Par Lost 6.858
Strook them with horror backward, but far worse Par Lost 6.863
And Planets, Planet-strook, real Eclips Par Lost 10.413
Heart-strook with chilling gripe of sorrow stood, Par Lost 11.264
And Moon-struck madness, pining Atrophie, Par Lost 11.486
line not in 1667 edition
Nigh Thunder-struck, th' exalted man, to whom Par Reg 1.36
Satan had not to answer, but stood struck Par Reg 3.146
So strook with dread and anguish fell the Fiend, Par Reg 4.576
And with blindness internal struck. Samson 1686
And play i' th plighted clouds. I was aw-strook, Mask 301
1637 'aw-strooke'
Bridgewater ms 'awe-strooke'
Trinity ms 'aw strooke'
As never was by mortall finger strook, Nativity 95
Strucken
Confounded long they sate, as struck'n mute, Par Lost 9.1064
Structure
In Heav'n by many a Towred structure high, Par Lost 1.733
Up to the wall of Heaven a Structure high, Par Lost 3.503
That Structure in the Dialect of men Par Lost 5.761
Ecbatana her structure vast there shews, Par Reg 3.286
The Structure, skill of noblest Architects, Par Reg 4.52
And with one buffet lay thy structure low, Samson 1239
Structures
Till all thy magick structures rear'd so high, Mask 798
line not in Trinity ms
line not in Bridgewater ms
Struggle
And wish and struggle, as they pass, to reach Par Lost 2.606
Struggling
Long strugling underneath, ere they could wind Par Lost 6.659
Struts
Stoutly struts his Dames before, Allegro 52
Stubble
And earths base built on stubble. But com let's on. Mask 599
Like stubble from the wind. Psalm 83, 52

Stubborn
With stubborn patience as with triple steel. Par Lost 2.569
Humbles his stubborn heart, but still as Ice Par Lost 12.193
Misled; the stubborn only to subdue. Par Reg 1.226
Blew meager Hag, or stubborn unlaid ghost, Mask 434
1637 'stubborne'
Bridgewater ms 'stubborne'
Trinity ms 'stubborne'
Stubs
Live on tough roots and stubs, to thirst inur'd Par Reg 1.339
Stuck
He's here stuck in a slough, and overthrown. Carrier 4
Studied
With studied argument, and much perswasion sought Samson 658
Studies
And in his Law he studies day and night. Psalm 1, 6
Studious
Entring on studious thoughts abstruse, which *Eve* Par Lost 8.40
Nor skilld nor studious, higher Argument Par Lost 9.42
Who slew his Brother; studious they appere Par Lost 11.609
City or Suburban, studious walks and shades; Par Reg 4.243
To studious musing; there *Ilissus* rouls Par Reg 4.249
To walk the studious Cloysters pale, Penseroso 156
Studs
And studs of Pearl, to me should'st tell who thirst Par Reg 4.120
Study
And study of revenge, immortal hate, Par Lost 1.107
In Woman, then to studie houshold good, Par Lost 9.233
Just men they seemd, and all thir study bent Par Lost 11.577
Stuff
To stuff this Maw, this vast unhide-bound Corps. Par Lost 10.601
Of Brick, and of that stuff they cast to build Par Lost 12.43
This is meer moral babble, and direct Mask 807
Trinity ms 'meere moral bable' ←'your morall stuffe' ←'meere morall stuffe'
Stumble
That they may stumble on, and deeper fall; Par Lost 3.201
Stumbled
And stumbl'd many, who receives them right, Par Lost 6.624
Stung
Though inly stung with anger and disdain, Par Reg 1.466
Stunning
Of stunning sounds and voices all confus'd Par Lost 2.952
Stupendous
Of that stupendious Bridge his joy encreas'd. Par Lost 10.351
All with incredible, stupendious force, Samson 1627
Stupid
(Canst thou believe2) should be so stupid grown, Par Lost 12.116
Stupidly
Stupidly good, of enmitie disarm'd, Par Lost 9.465
Sturdiest
Though rooted deep as high, and sturdiest Oaks Par Reg 4.417
Sty
Now made a stye, and in his place ascending Par Reg 4.101
To roule with pleasure in a sensual stie. Mask 77
Stygian
Both glorying to have scap't the *Stygian* flood Par Lost 1.239
ms 'Stygian'
The *Stygian* Counsel thus dissolv'd; and forth Par Lost 2.506
Which but her self not all the *Stygian* powers Par Lost 2.875
Escap't the *Stygian* Pool, though long detain'd Par Lost 3.14
At that so sudden blaze the *Stygian* throng Par Lost 10.453
Of Stygian darknes spets her thickest gloom, Mask 132
Bridgewater ms 'stigian'
& halfe the slow unfadom'd Stygian poole Mask Tr. ms 10.15
'Stygian poole' ←'poole of styx'
In *Stygian* Cave forlorn Allegro 3
Style
Must we renounce, and changing stile be call'd Par Lost 2.312
In various style, for neither various style Par Lost 5.146
The strife which thou call'st evil, but wee style Par Lost 6.289
If answerable style I can obtaine Par Lost 9.20
Adam, estrang'd in look and alterd stile, Par Lost 9.1132
In thir majestic unaffected stile Par Reg 4.359
And wov'n close, both matter, form and stile; Sonnet 11, 2
Styled
What he *Almightie* styl'd, six Nights and Days Par Lost 9.137
Of triumph, to be styl'd great Conquerours, Par Lost 11.695
A mightie Hunter thence he shall be styl'd Par Lost 12.33
Slow to be angry, and *art stil'd* Psalm 86, 55
Styx
Abhorred *Styx* the flood of deadly hate, Par Lost 2.577
& halfe the slow unfadom'd Stygian poole Mask Tr. ms 10.15
'Stygian poole' ←'poole of styx'
Subducting
Or from my side subducting, took perhaps Par Lost 8.536
Subdue
But I shall rise Victorious, and subdue Par Lost 3.250
Then to submit, boasting I could subdue Par Lost 4.85
Know whether I be dextrous to subdue Par Lost 5.741
Then scornd thou didst depart, and to subdue Par Lost 6.40
Sufficient to subdue us to his will, Par Lost 6.427
Subdue it, and throughout Dominion hold Par Lost 7.532
Therein enjoy'd were worthy to subdue Par Lost 8.584
To overcome in Battle, and subdue Par Lost 11.691
Such trouble brought, affecting to subdue Par Lost 12.81
Then to subdue and quell o're all the earth Par Reg 1.218
Misled; the stubborn only to subdue. Par Reg 1.226
Subdue(*cont*)
1671 printed 'destroy', errata 'subdue'
They err who count it glorious to subdue Par Reg 3.71
Great *Alexander* to subdue the world, Par Reg 4.252
And large-lim'd *Og* he did subdue, Psalm 136, 69
Subdued
Intestine War in Heav'n, the arch foe subdu'd Par Lost 6.259
Of the Emperour, how easily subdu'd, Par Reg 4.126
Might have subdu'd the Earth, Samson 174
But by the Barbers razor best subdu'd. Samson 1167
Subdues
Subdues us, and Omnipotent Decree, Par Lost 2.198
Which all subdues, and makes remiss the hands Par Lost 6.458
Subdues me, and calamitous constraint Par Lost 10.132
Subduing
Subduing Nations, and achievd thereby Par Lost 11.792
Subject
Yet these subject not; I to thee disclose Par Lost 8.607
Since first this Subject for Heroic Song Par Lost 9.25
Subject himself to Anarchy within, Par Reg 2.471
Subject him to so foul indignities, Samson 371
The subject of thir cruelty, or scorn. Samson 646
Parents and countrey; nor was I their subject, Samson 886
Har. Is not thy Nation subject to our Lords? Samson 1182
Thy service in some graver subject use, Vacation 30
Shall subject be to many an Accident. Vacation 74
The Subject new: it walk'd the Town a while, Sonnet 11, 3
Trinity ms 'subject'
Subjected
Subjected to his service Angel wings, Par Lost 9.155
To the subjected Plaine; then disappear'd. Par Lost 12.640
My Nation was subjected to your Lords. Samson 1205
Subjection
Of new Subjection; with what eyes could we Par Lost 2.239
I sdeind subjection, and thought one step higher Par Lost 4.50
Subjection, but requir'd with gentle sway, Par Lost 4.308
With low subjection; understand the same Par Lost 8.345
Not thy subjection: weigh with her thy self; Par Lost 8.570
Heard not her lore, both in subjection now Par Lost 9.1128
Thy Love, not thy Subjection, and her Gifts Par Lost 10.153
Subjection to his Empire tyrannous: Par Lost 12.32
To such as owe them absolute subjection; Samson 1405
Subjects
Subjects him from without to violent Lords; Par Lost 12.93
Sublime
Part on the Plain, or in the Air sublime Par Lost 2.528
In the dun Air sublime, and ready now Par Lost 3.72
His fair large Front and Eye sublime declar'd Par Lost 4.300
Hee on the wings of Cherub rode sublime Par Lost 6.771
They summ'd thir Penns, and soaring th' air sublime Par Lost 7.421
In that celestial Colloquie sublime, Par Lost 8.455
Sublime with expectation when to see Par Lost 10.536
To argue in thee somthing more sublime Par Lost 10.1014
But solemn and sublime, whom not to offend, Par Lost 11.236
Of *Hippogrif* bore through the Air sublime Par Reg 4.542
Semichor. While thir hearts were jocund and sublime, Samson 1669
The sublime notion, and high mystery Mask 785
line not in Trinity ms
line not in Bridgewater ms
Sublimed
Sublim'd with Mineral fury, aid the Winds, Par Lost 1.235
Mans nourishment, by gradual scale sublim'd Par Lost 5.483
Sublunar
Half way up Hill this vast Sublunar Vault, Par Lost 4.777
Submiss
Yet with submiss approach and reverence meek, Par Lost 5.359
Submiss: he rear'd me, and Whom thou soughtst I am, Par Lost 8.316
Persisted, yet submiss, though last, repli'd. Par Lost 9.377
From thee I can and must submiss endure Par Reg 1.476
Submission
For who can think Submission? Warr then, Warr Par Lost 1.661
ms 'submission'
None left but by submission; and that word Par Lost 4.81
What feign'd submission swore: ease would recant Par Lost 4.96
Yielded with coy submission, modest pride, Par Lost 4.310
To meek submission: thou at season fit Par Lost 12.597
(Best pleas'd with humble and filial submission) Samson 511
Submissive
Both of her Beauty and submissive Charms Par Lost 4.498
Now at his feet submissive in distress, Par Lost 10.942
Submit
And courage never to submit or yield: Par Lost 1.108
ms 'submitt'
Then to submit, boasting I could subdue Par Lost 4.85
Will ye submit your necks, and chuse to bend Par Lost 5.787
Thine shall submit, hee over thee shall rule. Par Lost 10.196
Be it so, for I submit, his doom is fair, Par Lost 10.769
Therefore to his great bidding I submit. Par Lost 11.314
Thou lead'st me, and to the hand of Heav'n submit, Par Lost 11.372
I yield it just, said *Adam*, and submit. Par Lost 11.526
Then as repentant to submit, beseech, Samson 751
Submits
The River-dragon tam'd at length submits Par Lost 12.191
Again transgresses, and again submits; Samson 758
Submitting
Submitting to what seemd remediless, Par Lost 9.919
Subordinate
Contemptuous, and his next subordinate Par Lost 5.671

Suborned
Some specious object by the Foe subornd, Par Lost 9.361
Subscribe
Yet Hope would fain subscribe, and tempts Belief. Samson 1535
Subscribed
Subscrib'd not; Nature first gave Signs, imprest Par Lost 11.182
Subsequent
Unchaste was subsequent, her stain not his. Samson 325
Subserve
But to subserve where wisdom bears command. Samson 57
Subsist
Firm we subsist, yet possible to swerve, Par Lost 9.359
Whither shall I betake me, where subsist? Par Lost 10.922
Could not sustain thy Prowess, or subsist Par Reg 3.19
By which all mortal frailty must subsist, Mask 686
line not in Bridgewater ms
Substance
And this Empyreal substance cannot fail, Par Lost 1.117
Semblance of worth, not substance, gently rais'd Par Lost 1.529
Or if our substance be indeed Divine, Par Lost 2.99
Or substance, how endu'd, and what thir Power, Par Lost 2.356
Or substance might be call'd that shadow seem'd, Par Lost 2.669
Spiritual substance with corporeal barr. Par Lost 4.585
Vapours not yet into her substance turnd. Par Lost 5.420
Of substance, and in things that live, of life; Par Lost 5.474
To proper substance; time may come when men Par Lost 5.493
Pass'd through him, but th' Ethereal substance clos'd Par Lost 6.330
Into thir substance pent, which wrought them pain Par Lost 6.657
In apprehension then in substance feel Par Lost 11.775
Substances
Intelligential substances require Par Lost 5.408
That to corporeal substances could adde Par Lost 8.109
Substantial
Of some rich Burgher, whose substantial dores, Par Lost 4.189
Substantial Life, to have thee by my side Par Lost 4.485
Substantially
Substantially express'd, and in his face Par Lost 3.140
Substitute
Hast thou not made me here thy substitute, Par Lost 8.381
Substitutes
My Substitutes I send ye, and Create Par Lost 10.403
Subterranean
Of subterranean wind transports a Hill Par Lost 1.231
Subtle
Pendant by suttle Magic many a row Par Lost 1.727
ms defective here
She finish'd, and the suttle Fiend his lore Par Lost 2.815
From these, two strong and suttle Spirits he calld Par Lost 4.786
They found, they mingl'd, and with suttle Art, Par Lost 6.513
From use, obscure and suttle, but to know Par Lost 8.192
A nice and suttle happiness I see Par Lost 8.399
His head the midst, well stor'd with suttle wiles: Par Lost 9.184
Suttle he needs must be, who could seduce Par Lost 9.307
Suttle or violent, we not endu'd Par Lost 9.324
Much wondring how the suttle Fiend had stoln Par Lost 10.20
So spake our Saviour; but the subtle Fiend, Par Reg 1.465
Cause thy refusal, said the subtle Fiend, Par Reg 2.323
Or subtle shifts conviction to evade. Par Reg 4.308
How soon hath Time the suttle theef of youth, Sonnet 7, 1
Subtlest
The Serpent suttl'st Beast of all the field, Par Lost 7.495
The Serpent suttlest Beast of all the Field. Par Lost 9.86
Thee, Serpent, suttlest beast of all the field Par Lost 9.560
Subtleties
By weakest suttleties, not made to rule, Samson 56
Subtlety
By force or suttlety: Though Heav'n be shut, Par Lost 2.358
As from his wit and native suttletie Par Lost 9.93
His utmost subtilty, because he boasts Par Reg 1.144
Subtly
How suttly to detaine thee I devise, Par Lost 8.207
Suburb
The suburb of thir Straw-built Cittadel, Par Lost 1.773
Suburban
City or Suburban, studious walks and shades; Par Reg 4.243
Suburbs
With *Modin* and her Suburbs once content. Par Reg 3.170
Subvert
So to subvert whom he suspected rais'd Par Reg 1.124
Subverting
Subverting worldly strong, and worldly wise Par Lost 12.568
Succeed
Which oft times may succeed, so as perhaps Par Lost 1.166
Short pleasures, for long woes are to succeed. Par Lost 4.535
Who of all Ages to succeed, but feeling Par Lost 10.733
Wolves shall succeed for teachers, grievous Wolves, Par Lost 12.508
Succeeded
In what I thought would have succeeded best. Samson 908
Succeeding
Of like succeeding here; I summon all Par Reg 2.143
Success
Vain Warr with Heav'n, and by success untaught Par Lost 2.9
Ominous conjecture on the whole success: Par Lost 2.123
Down from th' Ecliptic, sped with hop'd success, Par Lost 3.740
From me som Plume, that thy success may show Par Lost 6.161
Believst so main to our success, I bring; Par Lost 6.471
But that success attends him; if mishap, Par Lost 10.239
Induces best to hope of like success. Par Reg 1.105

Success*(cont)*
Of my success with *Eve* in Paradise Par Reg 2.141
And seat of *Salmanassar*, whose success Par Reg 3.278
Perplex'd and troubl'd at his bad success Par Reg 4.1
Yet gives not o're though desperate of success, Par Reg 4.23
Joyless triumphals of his hop't success, Par Reg 4.578
With good success to work his liberty. Samson 1454
Portend success in love; O if *Jove*'s will Sonnet 1, 7
Successes
From hard assaies and ill successes past Par Lost 4.932
With these successes, and with them rejoyce, Par Lost 10.396
Successful
We may with more successful hope resolve Par Lost 1.120
ms 'successfull'
Successful beyond hope, to lead ye forth Par Lost 10.463
Successfully
Successfully; a calmer voyage now Par Reg 1.103
Succession
But first a long succession must ensue, Par Lost 12.331
Successive
Successive, and the timely dew of sleep Par Lost 4.614
Successor
In *David*'s royal seat, his true Successour, Par Reg 3.373
Successour in thy bed, Samson 1021
Succinct
His habit fit for speed succinct, and held Par Lost 3.643
Succoth
How *Succoth* and the Fort of *Penuel* Samson 278
Succour
There swallow'd up and lost, from succour farr. Par Lost 9.642
And succour our just Fears Forcers 18
Such
Such place Eternal Justice had prepar'd Par Lost 1.70
Then such could hav orepow'rd such force as ours) Par Lost 1.145
And such appear'd in hue, as when the force Par Lost 1.230
With stench and smoak: Such resting found the sole Par Lost 1.237
No wonder, fall'n such a pernicious highth. Par Lost 1.282
If such astonishment as this can sieze Par Lost 1.317
Of utmost *Arnon*. Nor content with such Par Lost 1.399
Down cast and damp, yet such wherein appear'd Par Lost 1.523
Of Flutes and soft Recorders; such as rais'd Par Lost 1.551
Met such imbodied force, as nam'd with these Par Lost 1.574
Tears such as Angels weep, burst forth: at last Par Lost 1.620
How such united force of Gods, how such Par Lost 1.629
Nor great *Alcairo* such magnificence Par Lost 1.718
Exalted to such power, and gave to rule, Par Lost 1.736
Let such bethink them, if the sleepy drench Par Lost 2.73
He scarce had finisht, when such murmur filld Par Lost 2.284
After the Tempest: Such applause was heard Par Lost 2.290
Advising peace: for such another Field Par Lost 2.292
No second stroke intend, and such a frown Par Lost 2.713
Becam'st enamour'd, and such joy thou took'st Par Lost 2.765
I saw and heard, for such a numerous Host Par Lost 2.993
Following his track, such was the will of Heav'n, Par Lost 2.1025
Such I created all th' Ethereal Powers Par Lost 3.100
What pleasure I from such obedience paid, Par Lost 3.107
And none but such from mercy I exclude. Par Lost 3.202
Say Heav'nly powers, where shall we find such love, Par Lost 3.213
Shall hast'n, such a peal shall rouse thir sleep. Par Lost 3.329
Melodious part, such concord is in Heav'n. Par Lost 3.371
The Stairs were such as whereon *Jacob* saw Par Lost 3.510
To darkness, such as bound the Ocean wave. Par Lost 3.539
Such wonder seis'd, though after Heaven seen, Par Lost 3.552
Not of the prime, yet such as in his face Par Lost 3.637
Ah wherefore! he deservd no such return Par Lost 4.42
In miserie; such joy Ambition findes. Par Lost 4.92
For heav'nly mindes from such distempers foule Par Lost 4.118
Of *Arabie* the blest, with such delay Par Lost 4.163
In them Divine resemblance, and such grace Par Lost 4.364
Ill fenc't for Heav'n to keep out such a foe Par Lost 4.372
Like this fair Paradise, your sense, yet such Par Lost 4.379
Equal with Gods; aspiring to be such, Par Lost 4.526
The vigilance here plac't, but such as come Par Lost 4.580
Such was thir awe of Man. In shadie Bower Par Lost 4.705
Such where ye find, seise fast, and hither bring. Par Lost 4.796
And such I held thee; but this question askt Par Lost 4.887
Th' Eternal to prevent such horrid fray Par Lost 4.996
Such whispering wak'd her, but with startl'd eye Par Lost 5.26
Such night till this I never pass'd, have dream'd, Par Lost 5.31
At such bold words voucht with a deed so bold: Par Lost 5.66
What life the Gods live there, and such live thou. Par Lost 5.81
Som such resemblances methinks I find Par Lost 5.114
Unmeditated, such prompt eloquence Par Lost 5.149
Or with repose; and such discourse bring on, Par Lost 5.233
Each Plant and juciest Gourd will pluck such choice Par Lost 5.327
None can then Heav'n such glorious shape contain; Par Lost 5.362
Adam, I therefore came, nor art thou such Par Lost 5.372
Created, or such place hast here to dwell, Par Lost 5.373
Such to perfection, one first matter all, Par Lost 5.472
That thou continu'st such, owe to thy self, Par Lost 5.521
Not our necessitated, such with him Par Lost 5.530
By present, past, and future) on such day Par Lost 5.582
(Such are the Courts of God) Th' Angelic throng Par Lost 5.650
Of Deitie or Empire, such a foe Par Lost 5.724
Monarchie over such as live by right Par Lost 5.795
Such as he pleasd, and circumscrib'd thir being? Par Lost 5.825
Such as in highest Heav'n, arrayd in Gold Par Lost 6.13
O Heav'n! that such resemblance of the Highest Par Lost 6.114

Such(*cont*)
Such hast thou arm'd, the Minstrelsie of Heav'n, Par Lost 6.168
Such ruin intercept: ten paces huge Par Lost 6.193
And clamour such as heard in Heav'n till now Par Lost 6.208
And limited thir might; though numberd such Par Lost 6.229
Wide wasting; such destruction to withstand Par Lost 6.253
Human imagination to such highth Par Lost 6.300
Of such commotion, such as to set forth Par Lost 6.310
Sanguin, such as Celestial Spirits may bleed, Par Lost 6.333
Humbl'd by such rebuke, so farr beneath Par Lost 6.342
Fled ignominious, to such evil brought Par Lost 6.395
Such high advantages thir innocence Par Lost 6.401
Such implements of mischief as shall dash Par Lost 6.488
Level'd, with such impetuous furie smote, Par Lost 6.591
Such as we might perceive amus'd them all, Par Lost 6.623
Against such hellish mischief fit to oppose. Par Lost 6.636
Out of such prison, though Spirits of purest light, Par Lost 6.660
As likeliest was, when two such Foes met arm'd; Par Lost 6.688
Can end it. Into thee such Vertue and Grace Par Lost 6.703
In heav'nly Spirits could such perverseness dwell? Par Lost 6.788
Before him, such as in thir Soules infix'd Par Lost 6.837
With such confusion: but the evil soon Par Lost 7.56
Thy hearing, such Commission from above Par Lost 7.118
That detriment, if such it be to lose Par Lost 7.153
When such was heard declar'd th' Almightie's will; Par Lost 7.181
For haste; such flight the great command impress'd Par Lost 7.294
Invisible, yet staid (such priviledge Par Lost 7.589
Spaces incomprehensible (for such Par Lost 8.20
Such disproportions, with superfluous hand Par Lost 8.27
Such restless revolution day by day Par Lost 8.31
As Tribute such a sumless journey brought Par Lost 8.36
Yet went she not, as not with such discourse Par Lost 8.48
Of what was high: such pleasure she reserv'd, Par Lost 8.50
Such pairs, in Love and mutual Honour joyn'd? Par Lost 8.58
The less not bright, nor Heav'n such journies run, Par Lost 8.88
For such vast room in Nature unpossest Par Lost 8.153
Squar'd in full Legion (such command we had) Par Lost 8.232
Least hee incenst at such eruption bold, Par Lost 8.235
Thir Nature, with such knowledg God endu'd Par Lost 8.353
Such as I seek, fit to participate Par Lost 8.390
And no such companie as then thou saw'st Par Lost 8.446
Such as I saw her in my dream, adornd Par Lost 8.482
In all things else delight indeed, but such Par Lost 8.524
Not proof enough such Object to sustain, Par Lost 8.535
Is propagated seem such dear delight Par Lost 8.580
By what I seek, but others to make such Par Lost 9.127
Whether such vertue spent of old now faild Par Lost 9.145
That such an Enemie we have, who seeks Par Lost 9.274
His violence thou fearst not, being such, Par Lost 9.282
For such thou art, from sin and blame entire: Par Lost 9.292
If such affront I labour to avert Par Lost 9.302
But with such Gardning Tools as Art yet rude, Par Lost 9.391
Such ambush hid among sweet Flours and Shades Par Lost 9.408
Such Pleasure took the Serpent to behold Par Lost 9.455
To such disport before her through the Field, Par Lost 9.520
Say, for such wonder claims attention due. Par Lost 9.566
I spar'd not, for such pleasure till that hour Par Lost 9.596
To us, in such aboundance lies our choice, Par Lost 9.620
Wondrous indeed, if cause of such effects. Par Lost 9.650
For such a petty Trespass, and not praise Par Lost 9.693
Such prohibitions binde not. But if Death Par Lost 9.760
Regarded, such delight till then, as seemd, Par Lost 9.787
And hath bin tasted such: the Serpent wise, Par Lost 9.867
In recompence (for such compliance bad Par Lost 9.994
Such recompence best merits) from the bough Par Lost 9.995
True relish, tasting; if such pleasure be Par Lost 9.1024
As meet is, after such delicious Fare; Par Lost 9.1028
But such as at this day to *Indians* known Par Lost 9.1102
To that first naked Glorie. Such of late Par Lost 9.1115
Such proof, conclude, they then begin to faile. Par Lost 9.1142
Going into such danger as thou saidst? Par Lost 9.1157
Were such as under Government well seem'd, Par Lost 10.154
The way, thou leading, such a sent I draw Par Lost 10.267
Such fatal consequence unites us three: Par Lost 10.364
For in possession such, not onely of right, Par Lost 10.461
Or down from Heav'n descend. Such was thir song, Par Lost 10.648
He never shall find out fit Mate, but such Par Lost 10.899
But *Adam* with such counsel nothing sway'd, Par Lost 10.1010
We are by doom to pay; rather such acts Par Lost 10.1026
Which might supplie the Sun: such Fire to use, Par Lost 10.1078
Ill worthie I such title should belong Par Lost 11.163
Or of the Thrones above, such Majestie Par Lost 11.232
Of them the Highest, for such of shape may seem Par Lost 11.297
To such unsightly sufferings be debas't Par Lost 11.510
In part, from such deformities be free, Par Lost 11.513
Such happy interview and fair event Par Lost 11.593
His Brother; for of whom such massacher Par Lost 11.679
Such were these Giants, men of high renown; Par Lost 11.688
Such grace shall one just Man find in his sight, Par Lost 11.890
With Warr and hostile snare such as refuse Par Lost 12.31
He made not Lord; such title to himself Par Lost 12.70
Such trouble brought, affecting to subdue Par Lost 12.81
Such wondrous power God to his Saint will lend, Par Lost 12.200
Ordaine them Lawes; part such as appertaine Par Lost 12.230
Establisht, such delight hath God in Men Par Lost 12.245
Among them; how can God with such reside? Par Lost 12.284
Just for unjust, that in such righteousness Par Lost 12.294
Such follow him, as shall be registerd Par Lost 12.335

Such(*cont*)
He ceas'd, discerning *Adam* with such joy Par Lost 12.372
Though to the death, against such cruelties Par Lost 12.494
Such favour I unworthie am voutsaft, Par Lost 12.622
Such high attest was giv'n, a while survey'd Par Reg 1.37
To such perfection, that e're yet my age Par Reg 1.209
And he still on was led, but with such thoughts Par Reg 1.299
Such Solitude before choicest Society. Par Reg 1.302
Think'st thou such force in Bread? is it not written Par Reg 1.347
Inspir'd; disdain not such access to me. Par Reg 1.492
In such a season born when scarce a Shed Par Reg 2.72
Without new trouble; such an Enemy Par Reg 2.126
Such object hath the power to soft'n and tame Par Reg 2.163
None are, thou think'st, but taken with such toys. Par Reg 2.177
His constancy, with such as have more shew Par Reg 2.226
Such was the Splendour, and the Tempter now Par Reg 2.366
Of conduct would be such, that all the world Par Reg 3.18
And what delight to be by such extoll'd, Par Reg 3.54
Yet so much bounty is in God, such grace, Par Reg 3.142
With that (such power was giv'n him then) he took Par Reg 3.251
Such forces met not, nor so wide a camp, Par Reg 3.337
Such and so numerous was thir Chivalrie; Par Reg 3.344
Between two such enclosing enemies Par Reg 3.361
By three days Pestilence? such was thy zeal Par Reg 3.412
Expel a Devil who first made him such? Par Reg 4.129
To me my own, on such abhorred pact, Par Reg 4.191
Such are from God inspir'd, not such from thee; Par Reg 4.350
To such a tender ball as th' eye confin'd? Samson 94
Sam. Of such examples adde mee to the roul, Samson 290
For of such Doctrine never was there School, Samson 297
Man. Brethren and men of *Dan*, for such ye seem, Samson 332
And such a Son as all Men hail'd me happy; Samson 354
And as a blessing with such pomp adorn'd? Samson 357
Such a discomfit, as shall quite despoil him Samson 469
But such as thou hast solemnly elected, Samson 678
Such pardon therefore as I give my folly, Samson 825
Such numbers of our Nation: and the Priest Samson 857
To oppose against such powerful arguments? Samson 862
To such a viper his most sacred trust Samson 1001
Is it for that such outward ornament Samson 1025
Embarqu'd with such a Stears-mate at the Helm? Samson 1045
And now am come to see of whom such noise Samson 1088
To have wrought such wonders with an Asses Jaw; Samson 1095
Sam. Such usage as your honourable Lords Samson 1108
And raise such out-cries on thy clatter'd Iron, Samson 1124
Sam. All these indignities, for such they are Samson 1168
The righteous and all such as honour Truth; Samson 1276
Will condescend to such absurd commands? Samson 1337
Or we shall find such Engines to assail Samson 1396
To such as owe them absolute subjection; Samson 1405
But wherefore comes old *Manoa* in such hast Samson 1441
(For so from such as nearer stood we heard) Samson 1631
Now of my own accord such other tryal Samson 1643
To such my errand is, and but for such, Mask 15
1645 printed 'To snch'
Such as the jocond Flute, or gamesom Pipe Mask 173
Of such late Wassailers; yet O where els Mask 179
To bring me Berries, or such cooling fruit Mask 186
Such noise as I can make to be heard farthest Mask 227
Breath such Divine inchanting ravishment? Mask 245
But such a sacred, and home-felt delight, Mask 262
Such sober certainty of waking bliss Mask 263
Co. Two such I saw, what time the labour'd Oxe Mask 291
In such a scant allowance of Star-light, Mask 308
How bitter is such self-delusion? Mask 365
line not in Bridgewater ms
line not in Trinity ms
Such are those thick and gloomy shadows damp Mask 470
I came not here on such a trivial toy Mask 502
For such there be, but unbelief is blind. Mask 519
Who gently ask't if he had seen such two, Mask 575
Is of such power to stir up joy as this, Mask 677
But such as are good men can give good things, Mask 703
With such a full and unwithdrawing hand, Mask 711
To such a flame of sacred vehemence, Mask 795
line not in Trinity ms
line not in Bridgewater ms
To aid a Virgin, such as was her self Mask 856
Of lighter toes, and such Court guise Mask 962
Trinity ms 'such court' ←'such neate' ←'courtly'
As *Mercury* did first devise Mask 963
Trinity ms 'as' ←'such as'
Such as hang on *Hebe*'s cheek, Allegro 29
Such sights as youthfull Poets dream Allegro 129
Such as the meeting soul may pierce Allegro 138
Such streins as would have won the ear Allegro 148
Black, but such as in esteem, Penseroso 17
Such mixture was not held a stain) Penseroso 26
Such notes as warbled to the string, Penseroso 106
With such consort as they keep, Penseroso 145
Such sweet compulsion doth in musick ly, Arcades 68
And yet such musick worthiest were to blaze Arcades 74
Such a rural Queen Arcades 94
Such a rural Queen Arcades 108
Such, *Lycidas*, thy loss to Shepherds ear. Lycidas 49
Anow of such as for their bellies sake, Lycidas 114
When such musick sweet Nativity 93
The Air such pleasure loth to lose, Nativity 99

Such(*cont*)
Nature that heard such sound   Nativity 101
She knew such harmony alone   Nativity 107
Such Musick (as 'tis said)   Nativity 117
For if such holy Song   Nativity 133
With such a horrid clang   Nativity 157
Or in the Elisian fields (if such there were.)   Fair Inf 40
Such as may make thee search thy coffers round,   Vacation 31
Such where the deep transported mind may soare   Vacation 33
Such as the wise *Demodocus* once told   Vacation 48
What need'st thou such weak witnes of thy name?   Shakespear 6
And so Sepulcher'd in such pomp dost lie,   Shakespear 15
That Kings for such a Tomb would wish to die.   Shakespear 16
'Twas such a shifter, that if truth were known,   Carrier 5
That call Fame on such gentle acts as these,   Sonnet 8, 6
And such, as yet once more I trust to have   Sonnet 23, 7
Surely to such as do him fear   Psalm 85, 37

Suck
There I suck the liquid ayr   Mask 980
That on the green terf suck the honied showres,   Lycidas 140

Sucked
With suckt and glutted offal, at one sling   Par Lost 10.633

Suckle
With flaunting Hony-suckle, and began   Mask 545
Bridgewater ms 'hony sucle'
1637 'hony-suckle'
Trinity ms 'honiesuckle'

Suckling
With flaunting Hony-suckle, and began   Mask 545
Trinity ms 'flaunting' ←'blowing' ←'suckling'

Sucklings
Out of the mouths of babes and sucklings thou   Psalm 8, 5

Sudden
Of mighty Cherubim; the sudden blaze   Par Lost 1.665
By sudden onset, either with Hell fire   Par Lost 2.364
Thou interposest, that my sudden hand   Par Lost 2.738
All on a sudden miserable pain   Par Lost 2.752
Unfast'ns: on a sudden op'n flie   Par Lost 2.879
Before thir eyes in sudden view appear   Par Lost 2.890
Looks down with wonder at the sudden view   Par Lost 3.542
With sudden blaze diffus'd, inflames the Aire: Par Lost 4.818
So sudden to behold the grieslie King;   Par Lost 4.821
That brought me on a sudden to the Tree   Par Lost 5.51
Not burd'nd Nature, sudden mind arose   Par Lost 5.452
Tables are set, and on a sudden pil'd   Par Lost 5.632
Pavilions numberless, and sudden reard,   Par Lost 5.653
Impendent, raging into sudden flame   Par Lost 5.891
Or som more sudden vengeance wing'd from God   Par Lost 6.279
Not long, for sudden all at once thir Reeds   Par Lost 6.582
Then Herbs of every leaf, that sudden flour'd   Par Lost 7.317
Tempting, stirr'd in me sudden appetite   Par Lost 8.308
My sudden apprehension: but in these   Par Lost 8.354
How art thou lost, how on a sudden lost,   Par Lost 9.900
At that so sudden blaze the *Stygian* throng   Par Lost 10.453
Will prove no sudden, but a slow-pac't evill,   Par Lost 10.963
Adam by this from the cold sudden damp   Par Lost 11.293
But must with something sudden be oppos'd,   Par Reg 1.96
At every sudden slighting quite abasht: Par Reg 2.224
My sudden rage to tear thee joint by joint.   Samson 953
From under ashes into sudden flame,   Samson 1691
With sudden adoration, and blank aw.   Mask 452
Trinity ms 'suddaine'
Till an unusuall stop of sudden silence   Mask 552
Bridgewater ms 'suddaine'
Trinity ms 'suddaine'
Where if he be, with dauntless hardihood,   Mask 650
Trinity ms 'dauntless hardyhood' ←'suddaine violence'
And our sudden coming there   Mask 954
Bridgewater ms 'suddaine'
1637 'suddaine'
Trinity ms 'suddaine'
What sudden blaze of majesty   Arcades 2
And think to burst out into sudden blaze,   Lycidas 74
Which on a sudden straies,   Psalm 83, 54

Suddenly
To this high exaltation; suddenly   Par Lost 5.90
A while, but suddenly at head appeerd   Par Lost 6.556
When suddenly stood at my Head a dream,   Par Lost 8.292
But suddenly with flesh fill'd up and heal'd: Par Lost 8.468
Might suddenly inflict; that past, return'd   Par Lost 10.341
On Bird, Beast, Aire, Aire suddenly eclips'd   Par Lost 11.183
When suddenly a man before him stood,   Par Reg 2.298
Mess. Ah *Manoa* I refrain, too suddenly   Samson 1565

Sue
Extort from me. To bow and sue for grace   Par Lost 1.111

Sues
Him who imploring mercy sues for life,   Samson 512

Suffer
Strongly to suffer and support our pains,   Par Lost 1.147
Whatever doing, what can we suffer more,   Par Lost 2.162
What can we suffer worse? is this then worst,   Par Lost 2.163
Thus trampl'd, thus expell'd to suffer here   Par Lost 2.195
The Victors will. To suffer, as to doe,   Par Lost 2.199
His prey, nor suffer my unspotted Soule   Par Lost 3.248
To which the Hell I suffer seems a Heav'n.   Par Lost 4.78
Must suffer change, disdain'd not to begin   Par Lost 10.213
I suffer them to enter and possess   Par Lost 10.623
Of what I suffer here; if Nature need not,   Par Reg 2.249

Suffer(*cont*)
What I can suffer, how obey? who best   Par Reg 3.194
Can suffer, best can do; best reign, who first   Par Reg 3.195
Israel's oppressours: of what now I suffer   Samson 233
And here their tender age might suffer perill,   Mask 40
I must not suffer this, yet 'tis but the lees   Mask 809

Sufferance
Not by the sufferance of supernal Power.   Par Lost 1.241
Through Gods high sufferance for the tryal of man,   Par Lost 1.366
This my long sufferance and my day of grace   Par Lost 3.198
By sufferance, and thy wonted favour deign'd.   Par Lost 8.202
By Humiliation and strong Sufferance: Par Reg 1.160

Suffered
Have sufferd, that the Glorie may be thine   Par Lost 6.701
Then sufferd. Th' other way *Satan* went down   Par Lost 10.414
What I have don, what sufferd, with what paine   Par Lost 10.470
By what he taught and suffer'd for so doing,   Par Reg 3.97
Aught suffer'd; if young *African* for fame   Par Reg 3.101

Sufferers
The sufferers then will scarce molest us here,   Samson 1525

Sufferest
To light'n what thou suffer'st, and appease   Samson 744

Suffering
Doing or Suffering: but of this be sure,   Par Lost 1.158
ms 'suffering'
In doing what we most in suffering feel?   Par Lost 2.340
By suffering, and earne rest from labour won,   Par Lost 11.375
On penaltie of death, and suffering death,   Par Lost 12.398
By simply meek; that suffering for Truths sake   Par Lost 12.569
For truths sake suffering death unjust, lives now   Par Reg 3.98
Suffering, abstaining, quietly expecting   Par Reg 3.192
Though not disordinate, yet causless suffring   Samson 701

Sufferings
Worse; of worse deeds worse sufferings must ensue.   Par Lost 4.26
To such unsightly sufferings be debas't   Par Lost 11.510
Samson, of all thy sufferings think the heaviest,   Samson 445
And former sufferings other where are found;   Passion 25

Suffers
Suffers the Hypocrite or Atheous Priest   Par Reg 1.487
The anguish of my Soul, that suffers not   Samson 458

Suffice
That we may so suffice his vengeful ire,   Par Lost 1.148
Suffice, or what evasion bear him safe   Par Lost 2.411
What may suffice, and soft'n stonie hearts   Par Lost 3.189
What words or tongue of Seraph can suffice,   Par Lost 7.113
Or heart of man suffice to comprehend?   Par Lost 7.114
Answer'd. Let it suffice thee that thou know'st   Par Lost 8.620

Sufficed
Of thir sweet Gardning labour then suffic'd   Par Lost 4.328
Thus when with meats and drinks they had suffic'd,   Par Lost 5.451
Happier, had it suffic'd him to have known   Par Lost 11.88
The strength whereof suffic'd him forty days;   Par Reg 2.276

Suffices
Suffices that to me strength is my bane,   Samson 63

Sufficient
Our power sufficient to disturb his Heav'n,   Par Lost 2.102
Sufficient? who shall tempt with wandring feet   Par Lost 2.404
Sufficient to have stood, though free to fall.   Par Lost 3.99
Sufficient to subdue us to his will,   Par Lost 6.427
Number sufficient to possess her Realmes   Par Lost 7.147
What thanks sufficient, or what recompence   Par Lost 8.5
Remaines, sufficient of it self to raise   Par Lost 9.43
Sufficient penaltie, why hast thou added   Par Lost 10.753
Sufficient that thy Prayers are heard, and Death,   Par Lost 11.252
Sufficient introduction to inform   Par Reg 3.247
With strength sufficient and command from Heav'n   Samson 1212

Sufficiently
Seem I to thee sufficiently possest   Par Lost 8.404

Suffrage
Choice in our suffrage; for on whom we send,   Par Lost 2.415

Suffusion
Or dim suffusion veild. Yet not the more   Par Lost 3.26

Suggest
Why dost thou then suggest to me distrust,   Par Reg 1.355

Suggested
Tells the suggested cause, and casts between   Par Lost 5.702

Suggestion
Men also, and by his suggestion taught,   Par Lost 1.685
The first sort by thir own suggestion fell,   Par Lost 3.129

Suggestions
To enter, and his dark suggestions hide   Par Lost 9.90
Man. Believe not these suggestions which proceed   Samson 599

Suing
Why do I humble thus my self, and suing   Samson 965

Suit
Cannot well suite with either, but soon prove   Par Lost 8.388

Suitable
Sutable grace diffus'd, so well he feignd;   Par Lost 3.639

Suited
Till civil-suited Morn appeer,   Penseroso 122

Suitors
Not of mean suiters, nor important less   Par Lost 11.9

Suits
Who judges in great suits and controversies,   Prose 10, 3

Sullen
Night with her sullen wing to double-shade   Par Reg 1.500
Swinging slow with sullen roar;   Penseroso 76
And sullen *Moloch* fled,   Nativity 205

Sullen(*cont*)
Or sullen *Mole* that runneth underneath, Vacation 95
Help wast a sullen day; what may be won Sonnet 20, 4
Sulphur
With ever-burning Sulphur unconsum'd: Par Lost 1.69
ms 'sulphur'
The work of Sulphur. Thither wing'd with speed Par Lost 1.674
Mixt with *Tartarean* Sulphur, and strange fire, Par Lost 2.69
Sulphurous
Back to the Gates of Heav'n: the Sulphurous Hail Par Lost 1.171
ms 'sulphurous'
Conception; Sulphurous and Nitrous Foame Par Lost 6.512
With Dart and Jav'lin, Stones and sulfurous Fire; Par Lost 11.658
Sultan
Of thir great Sultan waving to direct Par Lost 1.348
Wont ride in arm'd, and at the Soldans chair Par Lost 1.764
In *Mosco*, or the Sultan in *Bizance*, Par Lost 11.395
Sultry
And lower looks, but in a sultrie chafe. Samson 1246
What time the Gray-fly winds her sultry horn, Lycidas 28
Trinity ms 'sultrie'
Sum
Consulting on the sum of things, foreseen Par Lost 6.673
My Storie to the sum of earthly bliss Par Lost 8.522
Heapt to the popular summe, will so incense Par Lost 12.338
This having learnt, thou hast attaind the summe Par Lost 12.575
And last the sum of all, my Father's voice, Par Reg 1.283
Man. Tell us the sum, the circumstance defer. Samson 1557
Sumless
As Tribute such a sumless journey brought Par Lost 8.36
Summed
They summ'd thir Penns, and soaring th' air sublime Par Lost 7.421
Mean, or in her summd up, in her containd Par Lost 8.473
Of Growth, Sense, Reason, all summ'd up in Man. Par Lost 9.113
With prosperous wing full summ'd to tell of deeds Par Reg 1.14
Lay stor'd, in what part summ'd, that she might know: Samson 395
Summer
In amorous dittyes all a Summers day, Par Lost 1.449
ms 'summers'
A Summers day; and with the setting Sun Par Lost 1.744
ms 'summers'
Or Summers Noon-tide air, while thus he spake. Par Lost 2.309
Or sight of vernal bloom, or Summers Rose, Par Lost 3.43
In all the Liveries dect of Summers pride Par Lost 7.478
Forth issuing on a Summers Morn to breathe Par Lost 9.447
Solstitial summers heat. To the blanc Moone Par Lost 10.656
Interposition, as a summers cloud. Par Reg 3.222
Trills her thick-warbl'd notes the summer long, Par Reg 4.246
Grow up and perish, as the summer flie, Samson 676
Himself is his own dungeon. 2. *Bro*. Tis most true Mask 385
Trinity ms 'himselfe is his owne dungeon' ←'blaze in the summer solstice'
Bridgewater ms 'blaze in the summer solstice'
Summer drouth, or singed air Mask 928
That there eternal Summer dwels, Mask 988
Bridgewater ms 'summer'
Trinity ms 'Summer' ←'summer'
On Summer eeves by haunted stream. Allegro 130
Summers chief honour if thou hadst out-lasted, Fair Inf 3
Summers
Summers three times eight save one Winchester 7
Summon
On what thou hast of vertue, summon all, Par Lost 9.374
Of like succeeding here; I summon all Par Reg 2.143
Summoned
Came summond over *Eden* to receive Par Lost 6.75
Not hither summond, since they cannot change Par Lost 8.347
Summoning
The summoning Arch-Angels to proclaime Par Lost 3.325
Summons
Of Satan and his Peers: thir summons call'd Par Lost 1.757
And summons read, the great consult began. Par Lost 1.798
Of Angels by Imperial summons call'd, Par Lost 5.584
Hasted, resorting to the Summons high, Par Lost 11.81
To Councel summons all his mighty Peers, Par Reg 1.40
Till thou our summons answer'd have. Mask 888
Sumptuous
Thir sumptuous gluttonies, and gorgeous feasts Par Reg 4.114
The sumptuous *Dalila* floating this way: Samson 1072
Sums
Thir number last he summs. And now his heart Par Lost 1.571
She most, and in her look summs all Delight. Par Lost 9.454
Sun
Of Glory obscur'd: As when the Sun new ris'n Par Lost 1.594
ms 'sun'
A Summers day; and with the setting Sun Par Lost 1.744
ms 'sun'
In spring time, when the Sun with *Taurus* rides, Par Lost 1.769
ms 'sun'
If chance the radiant Sun with farewell sweet Par Lost 2.492
Whose Fountain who shall tell? before the Sun, Par Lost 3.8
Which now the Rising Sun guilds with his beams. Par Lost 3.551
The golden Sun in splendor likest Heaven Par Lost 3.572
Astronomer in the Sun's lucent Orbe Par Lost 3.589
Th' Arch-chimic Sun so farr from us remote Par Lost 3.609
The same whom *John* saw also in the Sun: Par Lost 3.623
Uriel, though Regent of the Sun, and held Par Lost 3.690
Sometimes towards Heav'n and the full-blazing Sun, Par Lost 4.29

Sun(*cont*)
O Sun, to tell thee how I hate thy beams Par Lost 4.37
On which the Sun more glad impress'd his beams Par Lost 4.150
Both where the morning Sun first warmly smote Par Lost 4.244
Or Bedward ruminating: for the Sun Par Lost 4.352
With Earth and Ocean meets, the setting Sun Par Lost 4.540
On a Sun beam, swift as a shooting Starr Par Lost 4.556
Amid the Suns bright circle where thou sitst, Par Lost 4.578
Bore him slope downward to the Sun now fall'n Par Lost 4.591
With charm of earliest Birds; pleasant the Sun Par Lost 4.642
With charm of earliest Birds, nor rising Sun Par Lost 4.651
Perfection from the Suns more potent Ray. Par Lost 4.673
This Eevning from the Sun's decline arriv'd Par Lost 4.792
Of day-spring, and the Sun, who scarce up risen Par Lost 5.139
Thou Sun, of this great World both Eye and Soule, Par Lost 5.171
Moon, that now meetst the orient Sun, now fli'st Par Lost 5.175
Till the Sun paint your fleecie skirts with Gold, Par Lost 5.187
When to enshrine his reliques in the Sun's Par Lost 5.273
1667 'Sunn's' in some copies
Of his coole Bowre, while now the mounted Sun Par Lost 5.300
Be over, and the Sun more coole decline. Par Lost 5.370
The Sun that light imparts to all, receives Par Lost 5.423
And we have yet large day, for scarce the Sun Par Lost 5.558
Or Starrs of Morning, Dew-drops, which the Sun Par Lost 5.746
Sphear'd in a radiant Cloud, for yet the Sun Par Lost 7.247
For of Celestial Bodies first the Sun Par Lost 7.354
In the Suns Orb, made porous to receive Par Lost 7.361
Show to the Sun thir wav'd coats dropt with Gold, Par Lost 7.406
Eev'ning arose in *Eden*, for the Sun Par Lost 7.582
More plenty then the Sun that barren shines, Par Lost 8.94
And no advantage gaine. What if the Sun Par Lost 8.122
Or save the Sun his labour, and that swift Par Lost 8.133
From the Suns beam meet Night, her other part Par Lost 8.139
Whether the Sun predominant in Heav'n Par Lost 8.160
Rise on the Earth, or Earth rise on the Sun, Par Lost 8.161
In Balmie Sweat, which with his Beames the Sun Par Lost 8.255
What e're I saw. Thou Sun, said I, faire Light, Par Lost 8.273
But I can now no more; the parting Sun Par Lost 8.630
The Sun was sunk, and after him the Starr Par Lost 9.48
Since *Uriel* Regent of the Sun descri'd Par Lost 9.60
Warm'd by the Sun, producing every kind, Par Lost 9.721
Now was the Sun in Western cadence low Par Lost 10.92
His *Zenith*, while the Sun in *Aries* rose: Par Lost 10.329
Now Dragon grown, larger then whom the Sun Par Lost 10.529
As sorted best with present things. The Sun Par Lost 10.651
Which of them rising with the Sun, or falling, Par Lost 10.663
From the Suns Axle; they with labour push'd Par Lost 10.670
Oblique the Centric Globe: Som say the Sun Par Lost 10.671
Had unbenighted shon, while the low Sun Par Lost 10.682
The Sun, as from *Thyestean* Banquet, turn'd Par Lost 10.688
Which might supplie the Sun: such Fire to use, Par Lost 10.1078
Who now shall reare ye to the Sun, or ranke Par Lost 11.278
And the cleer Sun on his wide watrie Glass Par Lost 11.844
Or how the Sun shall in mid Heav'n stand still Par Lost 12.263
Mans voice commanding, Sun in *Gibeon* stand, Par Lost 12.265
And now the Sun with more effectual beams Par Reg 4.432
For yonder bank hath choice of Sun or shade, Samson 3
The Sun to me is dark Samson 86
And all this tract that fronts the falling Sun Mask 30
Bridgewater ms 'sunn'
Trinity ms 'sun'
The daughter of the Sun? Whose charmed Cup Mask 51
Trinity ms 'sun'
Bridgewater ms 'Sunn'
And the slope Sun his upward beam Mask 98
Trinity ms 'sun'
Bridgewater ms 'sun'
And to the tel-tale Sun discry Mask 141
Bridgewater ms 'sun'
Trinity ms 'sun'
By her own radiant light, though Sun and Moon Mask 374
Trinity ms 'sun'
Bridgewater ms 'sun'
Benighted walks under the mid-day Sun; Mask 384
Bridgewater ms 'walks in black vapours though the noone tyde brand'
Trinity ms 'benighted walks under the midday sun' ←'walks in black vapours though the noontyde brand'
To gaze upon the Sun with shameless brows. Mask 736
Trinity ms 'sun'
Bridgewater ms 'sunn'
Wher the great Sun begins his state, Allegro 60
And when the Sun begins to fling Penseroso 131
And now the Sun had stretch'd out all the hills, Lycidas 190
1638 'sunne'
Now while the Heav'n by the Suns team untrod, Nativity 19
To wanton with the Sun her lusty Paramour. Nativity 36
The Sun himself with-held his wonted speed, Nativity 79
He saw a greater Sun appear Nativity 83
So when the Sun in bed, Nativity 229
And caus'd the Golden-tressed Sun, Psalm 136, 29
What ever clime the Suns bright circle warms. Sonnet 8, 8
Trinity ms 'sun's'
Which after held the Sun and Moon in fee. Sonnet 12, 7
Trinity ms 'sun' ←'Sun'
Of Sun or Moon or Starre throughout the year, Sonnet 22, 5
For God the Lord both Sun and Shield Psalm 84, 41

Sunbeams
As the gay motes that people the Sun Beams, Penseroso 8
Sun-bright
Th' Apostat in his Sun-bright Chariot sate Par Lost 6.100
Sun-clad
Against the Sun-clad power of Chastity, Mask 782
line not in Bridgewater ms
line not in Trinity ms
Sung
I sung of *Chaos* and *Eternal Night*, Par Lost 3.18
Thee Father first they sung Omnipotent, Par Lost 3.372
She all night long her amorous descant sung; Par Lost 4.603
And heav'nly Quires the Hymenaean sung, Par Lost 4.711
Thir Maker, in fit strains pronounc't or sung Par Lost 5.148
(Whose praise be ever sung) to man in part Par Lost 5.405
The matin Trumpet Sung: in Arms they stood Par Lost 6.526
Sung Triumph, and him sung Victorious King, Par Lost 6.886
Glorie they sung to the most High, good will Par Lost 7.182
God and his works, Creatour him they sung, Par Lost 7.259
And Morning *Chorus* sung the second Day. Par Lost 7.275
Open, ye everlasting Gates, they sung, Par Lost 7.565
On errands of supernal Grace. So sung Par Lost 7.573
Creation and the Six dayes acts they sung, Par Lost 7.601
So sung they, and the Empyrean rung, Par Lost 7.633
Sung Spousal, and bid haste the Eevning Starr Par Lost 8.519
Sung *Halleluia*, as the sound of Seas, Par Lost 10.642
Through multitude that sung: Just are thy ways, Par Lost 10.643
In Gems and wanton dress; to the Harp they sung Par Lost 11.583
Of squadrond Angels hear his Carol sung. Par Lost 12.367
I Who e're while the happy Garden sung, Par Reg 1.1
Sung with the voice, and this the argument. Par Reg 1.172
Of Angels in the fields of *Bethlehem* sung Par Reg 1.243
The Prophets old, who sung thy endless raign, Par Reg 3.178
And his who gave them breath, but higher sung, Par Reg 4.258
On thy birth-night, that sung thee Saviour born. Par Reg 4.506
Sung Heavenly Anthems of his victory Par Reg 4.594
Sung Victor, and from Heavenly Feast refresht Par Reg 4.637
Am I not sung and proverbd for a Fool Samson 203
Of Women, sung at solemn festivals, Samson 983
Who as they sung, would take the prison'd soul, Mask 256
In sage and solemn tunes have sung, Penseroso 117
Of that renowned flood, so often sung, Arcades 29
But when of old the sons of morning sung, Nativity 119
So sweetly sung your Joy the Clouds along Circum 4
Ay sung before the saphire-colour'd throne Musick 7
So hung his destiny never to rot Another 3
1640, 1657 'So sung'
As thou from yeer to yeer hast sung too late Sonnet 1, 11
Sunk
Bow'd down in Battel, sunk before the Spear Par Lost 1.436
We sunk thus low? Th' ascent is easie then; Par Lost 2.81
Of racking whirlwinds, or for ever sunk Par Lost 2.182
Where Armies whole have sunk: the parching Air Par Lost 2.594
My Guide was gon, and I, me thought, sunk down, Par Lost 5.91
Half sunk with all his Pines. Amazement seis'd Par Lost 6.198
Down sunk a hollow bottom broad and deep, Par Lost 7.289
Dazl'd and spent, sunk down, and sought repair Par Lost 8.457
Not sunk in carnal pleasure, for which cause Par Lost 8.593
The Sun was sunk, and after him the Starr Par Lost 9.48
In with the River sunk, and with it rose Par Lost 9.74
Sunk down and all his Spirits became intranst: Par Lost 11.420
And sunk thee as thy Sons; till gently reard Par Lost 11.758
As day-light sunk, and brought in lowring night Par Reg 4.398
Were in the flat Sea sunk. And Wisdoms self Mask 375
Bridgewater ms 'sunke'
Trinity ms 'sunke'
1637 'sunck'
That sunk so low that sacred head of thine. Lycidas 102
Sunk though he be beneath the watry floar, Lycidas 167
Trinity ms 'sunck'
So *Lycidas* sunk low, but mounted high, Lycidas 172
Once glorious Towers, now sunk in guiltles blood; Passion 40
Sunlight
To Starr or Sun-light, spread thir umbrage broad Par Lost 9.1087
Sunny
Cleer Spring, or shadie Grove, or Sunnie Hill, Par Lost 3.28
Of beaming sunnie Raies, a golden tiar Par Lost 3.625
Hill, Dale, and shadie Woods, and sunnie Plaines, Par Lost 8.262
Him walking on a Sunny hill he found, Par Reg 4.447
Sunrise
And as the gates I enter'd with Sun-rise, Samson 1597
Suns
Made horrid Circles; two broad Suns thir Shields Par Lost 6.305
Allotted there; and other Suns perhaps Par Lost 8.148
Sunshine
But all Sun-shine, as when his Beams at Noon Par Lost 3.616
Till next Sun-shine holiday, Mask 959
B.M. ms 'sunshine'
Bridgewater ms 'sunshine'
Trinity ms 'sunshine'
On a Sunshine Holyday, Allegro 98
Superficially
Whose Eye so superficially surveyes Par Lost 6.476
Superfluous
Why ask ye, and superfluous begin Par Lost 4.832
To nourish, and superfluous moist consumes: Par Lost 5.325
Such disproportions, with superfluous hand Par Lost 8.27
Angels, nor think superfluous others aid. Par Lost 9.308

Superfluous*(cont)*
That with superfluous burden loads the day, Sonnet 21, 13
Superior
He scarce had ceas't when the superiour Fiend Par Lost 1.283
As to superior Spirits is wont in Heaven, Par Lost 3.737
Smil'd with superior Love, as *Jupiter* Par Lost 4.499
As to a superior Nature, bowing low, Par Lost 5.360
The wonted signal, and superior voice Par Lost 5.705
Superior, nor of violence fear'd aught; Par Lost 5.905
Left them Superiour, while we can preserve Par Lost 6.443
Superiour and unmov'd, here onely weake Par Lost 8.532
Superior; for inferior who is free? Par Lost 9.825
Superior sway: from thus distemperd brest, Par Lost 9.1131
Superior, or but equal, that to her Par Lost 10.147
By wisdome, and superiour gifts receav'd. Par Lost 11.636
And worship me as thy superior Lord, Par Reg 4.167
A spirit and judgment equal or superior, Par Reg 4.324
Her words set off by som superior power; Mask 801
line not in Bridgewater ms
line not in Trinity ms
Supernal
Not by the sufferance of supernal Power. Par Lost 1.241
ms 'supernall'
On errands of supernal Grace. So sung Par Lost 7.573
Expect to hear, supernal Grace contending Par Lost 11.359
Supernumerary
Well if thrown out, as supernumerarie Par Lost 10.887
Superscription
Bear in their Superscription (of the most Samson 190
Onely remains this superscription. Another 34
line not in 1658 text
Superstition
Of painful Superstition and blind Zeal, Par Lost 3.452
Thir Superstition yields me; hence with leave Samson 15
Superstitions
With superstitions and traditions taint, Par Lost 12.512
Superstitious
And to a Superstitious eye the haunt Par Reg 2.296
Supped
Hobson has supt, and's newly gon to bed. Carrier 18
Supper
More grateful, to thir Supper Fruits they fell, Par Lost 4.331
Early, and th' hour of Supper comes unearn'd. Par Lost 9.225
He found his Supper on the coals prepar'd, Par Reg 2.273
And the swink't hedger at his Supper sate; Mask 293
Trinity ms 'supper'
Bridgewater ms 'supper'
Had ta'n their supper on the savoury Herb Mask 541
Supplanted
Each other, till supplanted down he fell Par Lost 10.513
Supplanted *Adam*, and by vanquishing Par Reg 4.607
Supple
The supple knee? ye will not, if I trust Par Lost 5.788
With supple joints, and lively vigour led: Par Lost 8.269
Suppliant
With suppliant knee, and deifie his power, Par Lost 1.112
Unhappilie deceav'd; thy suppliant Par Lost 10.917
Gracious to re-admit the suppliant; Samson 1173
Supplication
Whether by supplication we intend Par Lost 5.867
To supplication, heare his sighs though mute; Par Lost 11.31
With supplication prone and Fathers tears Samson 1459
My supplication with acceptance fair Psalm 6, 19
Unto my supplication Lord Psalm 86, 17
Supplied
With all things grateful chear'd, and so suppli'd, Samson 926
Supplies
And with full hand supplies their need. Psalm 136, 86
Supply
A race of upstart Creatures, to supply Par Lost 2.834
Let us seek Death, or he not found, supply Par Lost 10.1001
Which might supplie the Sun: such Fire to use, Par Lost 10.1078
1667 'supply' in some copies
From under Heav'n; the Hills to their supplie Par Lost 11.740
Support
Illumin, what is low raise and support; Par Lost 1.23
Strongly to suffer and support our pains, Par Lost 1.147
He walkt with to support uneasie steps Par Lost 1.295
About her glowd, oft stooping to support Par Lost 9.427
So might the wrauth. Fond wish! couldst thou support Par Lost 10.834
Or God support Nature without repast Par Reg 2.250
And strongest drinks our chief support of health, Samson 554
Hardy and industrious to support Samson 1274
That to the arched roof gave main support. Samson 1634
Supported
And oft supported so as shall amaze Par Lost 12.496
Supports
Right onward. What supports me dost thou ask? Sonnet 22, 9
Suppose
We overpower? Suppose he should relent Par Lost 2.237
For joy of offerd peace: but I suppose Par Lost 6.617
As I suppose, towards your once gloried friend, Samson 334
La. To find out that, good Shepherd, I suppose, Mask 307
Not harsh, and crabbed as dull fools suppose, Mask 477
Supposed
Ran purple to the Sea, suppos'd with blood Par Lost 1.451
As he suppos'd, all unobserv'd, unseen. Par Lost 4.130
Mount *Amara*, though this by som suppos'd Par Lost 4.281

Supposed(*cont*)
Nocturnal and Diurnal rhomb suppos'd, Par Lost 8.134
The tempted with dishonour foul, suppos'd Par Lost 9.297
That Death be not one stroak, as I suppos'd, Par Lost 10.809
Supposes
In all things, and all men, supposes means, Par Reg 3.355
Supposest
Who art to lead thy ofspring, and supposest Par Lost 8.86
Supposing
He seems: supposing here to find his Son, Samson 1443
Supposing him som neighbour villager; Mask 576
Bridgewater ms 'supposinge'
Suppressed
Onely Omniscient, hath suppresst in Night, Par Lost 7.123
Supremacy
And put to proof his high Supremacy, Par Lost 1.132
Against the high Supremacie of Heav'n, Par Lost 3.205
Supreme
Whom reason hath equald, force hath made supream Par Lost 1.248
And sat as Princes, whom the supreme King Par Lost 1.735
Our Supream Foe in time may much remit Par Lost 2.210
Within Heav'ns bound, unless Heav'ns Lord supream Par Lost 2.236
Than Hells dread Emperour with pomp Supream, Par Lost 2.510
Thy Merits; under thee as Head Supream Par Lost 3.319
And here art likeliest by supream decree Par Lost 3.659
The lower still I fall, onely Supream Par Lost 4.91
1667 'supream' in some copies
Allegeance to th' acknowldg'd Power supream? Par Lost 4.956
Unworshipt, unobey'd the Throne supream Par Lost 5.670
Before the seat supream; from whence a voice Par Lost 6.27
O Father, O Supream of heav'nly Thrones, Par Lost 6.723
Because the Father, t' whom in Heav'n supream Par Lost 6.814
Of Deitie supream, us dispossest, Par Lost 7.142
And worship God Supream, who made him chief Par Lost 7.515
All human thoughts come short, Supream of things; Par Lost 8.414
To dwell, unless by maistring Heav'ns Supreame; Par Lost 9.125
How all befell: they towards the Throne Supream Par Lost 10.28
Supream, that thou in mee thy Son belov'd Par Lost 10.70
Protesting Fate supreame; thence how I found Par Lost 10.480
And took thir Seats; till from his Throne supream Par Lost 11.82
Their King, their Leader, and Supream on Earth. Par Reg 1.99
God over all supreme? if giv'n to thee, Par Reg 4.186
That he, the Supreme good, t' whom all things ill Mask 217
line not in Bridgewater ms
Trinity ms 'supreme'
About the supreme Throne On Time 17
Sups
Sups with the Ocean: though in Heav'n the Trees Par Lost 5.426
Surcease
Return to folly, *but surcease* Psalm 85, 35
Surceased
Surceas'd, and glad as hoping here to end Par Lost 6.258
Tongue-batteries, she surceas'd not day nor night Samson 404
Surcharged
Least Heav'n surcharg'd with potent multitude Par Lost 2.836
And O fair Plant, said he, with fruit surcharg'd, Par Lost 5.58
Surcharg'd, as had like grief bin dew'd in tears, Par Lost 12.373
Like a fair flower surcharg'd with dew, she weeps Samson 728
By it self, with aggravations not surcharg'd, Samson 769
Who would be quite surcharg'd with her own weight, Mask 728
Surcharg'd my Soul doth lie, Psalm 88, 10
Sure
Doing or Suffering: but of this be sure, Par Lost 1.158
From Faction; for none sure will claim in Hell Par Lost 2.32
Is doubtful; that he never will is sure. Par Lost 2.154
Chain'd on the burning Lake? that sure was worse. Par Lost 2.169
His captive multitude: For he, be sure Par Lost 2.323
And they who to be sure of Paradise Par Lost 3.478
But come, for thou, besure, shalt give account Par Lost 4.841
Sure pledge of day, that crownst the smiling Morn Par Lost 5.168
Neerly it now concernes us to be sure Par Lost 5.721
Be sure, and terrour seis'd the rebel Host, Par Lost 6.647
Of this great Round: partition firm and sure, Par Lost 7.267
Of Godhead, fixt for ever firm and sure, Par Lost 7.586
For good unknown, sure is not had, or had Par Lost 9.756
Be sure then. How shall I behold the face Par Lost 9.1080
Him first make sure your thrall, and lastly kill. Par Lost 10.402
Him or his Childern, evil he may be sure, Par Lost 11.772
Be sure they will, said th' Angel; but from Heav'n Par Lost 12.485
Now, now, for sure, deliverance is at hand, Par Reg 2.35
Deceive ye to perswasion over-sure Par Reg 2.142
Thou must make sure thy own, the *Parthian* first Par Reg 3.363
Nor when, eternal sure, as without end, Par Reg 4.391
If thou observe not this, be sure to find, Par Reg 4.477
May warn thee, as a sure fore-going sign. Par Reg 4.483
I state not that; this I am sure; our Foes Samson 424
Before the God of *Abraham*. He, be sure, Samson 465
Nothing to do, be sure, that may dishonour Samson 1385
Yet this be sure, in nothing to comply Samson 1408
Our number may affright: Som Virgin sure Mask 148
Sure somthing holy lodges in that brest, Mask 246
Without the sure guess of well-practiz'd feet. Mask 310
2. *Bro*. O brother, 'tis my father Shepherd sure. Mask 493
to have her by my side, though I were sure Mask Tr. ms 16.41
to have her by my side, though I were suer Mask Br. ms 394
Ever faithfull, ever sure. Psalm 136, 4 etc.
For sure so well instructed are my tears, Passion 48
If I may not carry, sure Ile ne're be fetch'd, Another 18
Sure(*cont*)
line not in 1640, 1657, 1658 texts
And Hope that reaps not shame. Therefore be sure Sonnet 9, 11
Surely
Thou surely hadst not come sole fugitive. Par Lost 4.923
As if they surely knew their sovran Lord was by. Nativity 60
Resolve me then oh Soul most surely blest Fair Inf 36
And surely, Death could never have prevail'd, Carrier 9
Surely to such as do him fear Psalm 85, 37
Surer
Surer to prosper then prosperity Par Lost 2.39
His will who bound us? let him surer barr Par Lost 4.897
And after him, the surer messenger, Par Lost 11.856
Surest
Thir surest signal, they will soon resume Par Lost 1.278
Whence rushing he might surest seize them both Par Lost 4.407
Surety
On other surety none; freely we serve, Par Lost 5.538
Surface
Which of us who beholds the bright surface Par Lost 6.472
Shall from the surface to the center shake; Nativity 162
Surfeit
Of surfet where full measure onely bounds Par Lost 5.639
line not in 1667 edition
Oppresses else with Surfet, and soon turns Par Lost 7.129
Surfet, and lust, till wantonness and pride Par Lost 11.795
Mess. Feed on that first, there may in grief be surfet. Samson 1562
Where no crude surfet raigns. *Eld. Bro*. List, list, I hear Mask 480
Bridgewater ms 'surfeit'
Trinity ms 'surfeit'
Surge
The fiery Surge, that from the Precipice Par Lost 1.173
And with rebounding surge the barrs assaild, Par Lost 10.417
Surging
He spreads for flight, and in the surging smoak Par Lost 2.928
And surging waves, as Mountains to assault Par Lost 7.214
Fould above fould a surging Maze, his Head Par Lost 9.499
Or surging waves against a solid rock, Par Reg 4.18
Surmise
From his surmise prov'd false, find peace within, Par Lost 9.333
No despicable gift; surmise not then Par Lost 11.340
Let our frail thoughts dally with false surmise. Lycidas 153
Surmounts
This is dispenc't, and what surmounts the reach Par Lost 5.571
Chor. How thou wilt here come off surmounts my reach. Samson 1380
Surnamed
How hee sirnam'd of *Africa* dismiss'd Par Reg 2.199
Sirnam'd *Peripatetics*, and the Sect Par Reg 4.279
Surpass
In bigness to surpass Earths Giant Sons Par Lost 1.778
ms defective here
Abolish his own works. This would surpass Par Lost 2.370
Surpass his bounds, nor Rain to drown the World Par Lost 11.894
Surpassed
In gate surpass'd and Goddess-like deport, Par Lost 9.389
Surpassest
Surpassest farr my naming, how may I Par Lost 8.359
Surpassing
O thou that with surpassing Glory crownd, Par Lost 4.32
Aught, not surpassing human measure, say. Par Lost 7.640
Thy strength they know surpassing human rate, Samson 1313
Surprisal
Surprisal, unadmonisht, unforewarnd. Par Lost 5.245
How to secure the Lady from surprisal, Mask 618
1637 'surprisall'
Bridgewater ms 'surprisall'
Surprise
Scorning surprize. Or could we break our way Par Lost 2.134
That self same day by fight, or by surprize Par Lost 6.87
Surprise thee, and her black attendant Death. Par Lost 7.547
Against the *Syrian* King, who to surprize Par Lost 11.218
Over his foes and thine; there shall surprise Par Lost 12.453
Surprised
Surpris'd thee, dim thine eyes, and dizzie swumm Par Lost 2.753
Discoverd and surpriz'd. As when a spark Par Lost 4.814
Defensive scarse, or with pale fear surpris'd, Par Lost 6.393
Then first with fear surpris'd and sense of paine Par Lost 6.394
First seen, them unexpected joy surpriz'd, Par Lost 6.774
Least by some faire appeering good surpris'd Par Lost 9.354
Distracted and surpriz'd with deep dismay Par Reg 1.108
By fallacy surpriz'd. But first I mean Par Reg 1.155
This well I knew, nor was at all surpris'd, Samson 381
His errand on the wicked, who surpris'd Samson 1285
Surpriz'd by unjust force, but not enthrall'd, Mask 590
Trinity ms 'surpris'd'
Bridgewater ms 'surpris'd'
Surrender
And meek surrender, half imbracing leand Par Lost 4.494
Surround
Surround me, as thou sawst, hourly conceiv'd Par Lost 2.796
As with a shield thou wilt surround Psalm 5, 39
Will surround thee, seeking right, Psalm 7, 26
Surrounding
'Twixt upper, nether, and surrounding Fires; Par Lost 1.346
From the chill dew, amongst rude burrs and thistles? Mask 352
Trinity ms 'amoungst rude burrs & thistles' ←'in this surrounding wilde' ←'in this dead solitude'
Uninjur'd in this wilde surrounding wast. Mask 403

Surrounding(*cont*)
Trinity ms 'wide surrounding wast' ←'vast, & hideous wild'
Bridgewater ms 'surroundinge'
Surrounds
Surrounds me, from the chearful wayes of men Par Lost 3.46
At last surrounds their sight Nativity 109
Survey
One day and night; in all thir vast survey Par Lost 8.24
Hath walk'd about, and each limb to survey, Samson 1089
Sam. Cam'st thou for this, vain boaster, to survey me, Samson 1227
But take good heed my hand survey not thee. Samson 1230
Surveyed
His eye survay'd the dark Idolatries Par Lost 1.456
In blissful solitude; he then survey'd Par Lost 3.69
Survey'd, and sometimes went, and sometimes ran Par Lost 8.268
Such high attest was giv'n, a while survey'd Par Reg 1.37
Surveying
Surveying his great Work, that it was good: Par Lost 7.353
Surveys
Round he surveys, and well might, where he stood Par Lost 3.555
Whose Eye so superficially surveyes Par Lost 6.476
Survives
And though her body die, her fame survives, Samson 1706
Sus
The Kingdoms of *Almansor*, *Fez* and *Sus*, Par Lost 11.403
Susa
From *Susa* his *Memnonian* Palace high Par Lost 10.308
There *Susa* by *Choaspes*, amber stream, Par Reg 3.288
Susiana
Of *Susiana* to *Balsara*'s hav'n. Par Reg 3.321
Suspect
Let us not then suspect our happie State Par Lost 9.337
That from her hand I could suspect no ill, Par Lost 10.140
What I can do or offer is suspect; Par Reg 2.399
And to despise, or envy, or suspect Samson 272
That so they may without suspect or fears Vacation 27
Suspected
Suspected to a sequent King, who seeks Par Lost 12.165
So to subvert whom he suspected rais'd Par Reg 1.124
Suspend
Insensibly, for I suspend thir doom; Par Lost 6.692
Suspended
Suspended Hell, and took with ravishment Par Lost 2.554
Suspense
His look suspence, awaiting who appeer'd Par Lost 2.418
Stood waving tipt with fire; while we suspense, Par Lost 6.580
Much of his Race though steep, suspens in Heav'n Par Lost 7.99
Man. Suspense in news is torture, speak them out. Samson 1569
Suspicion
And oft though wisdom wake, suspicion sleeps Par Lost 3.686
Mistrust, Suspicion, Discord, and shook sore Par Lost 9.1124
And gladly banish squint suspicion. Mask 413
Bridgewater ms 'suspition'
Trinity ms 'suspicion' ←'suspition'
Suspicious
Suspicious, reasonless. Why should thir Lord Par Lost 4.516
Whatever sleights none would suspicious mark, Par Lost 9.92
Little suspicious to any King; but now Par Reg 2.82
All publick cares, and yet of him suspicious, Par Reg 4.96
And put the Damsel to suspicious flight, Mask 158
Bridgewater ms 'suspitious'
Sustain
Our doom; which if we can sustain and bear, Par Lost 2.209
Not proof enough such Object to sustain, Par Lost 8.535
This my attempt, I would sustain alone Par Lost 9.978
Beare thine own first, ill able to sustaine Par Lost 10.950
My labour will sustain me; and least Cold Par Lost 10.1056
Our frailtie can sustain, thy tidings bring, Par Lost 11.302
Will he convey up thither to sustain Par Lost 12.75
Could not sustain thy Prowess, or subsist Par Reg 3.19
They cannot well impose, nor I sustain; Samson 1258
For my sustain Psalm 3, 14
Sustained
To be sustaind and fed; of Elements Par Lost 5.415
Long way through hostile scorn, which he susteind Par Lost 5.904
Who have sustaind one day in doubtful fight Par Lost 6.423
Alone, without exterior help sustaind? Par Lost 9.336
To pass commodiously this life, sustain'd Par Lost 10.1083
Sustenance
For lying is thy sustenance, thy food. Par Reg 1.429
Swaddling
Can in his swadling bands controul the damned crew. Nativity 228
Swage
Nor wanting power to mitigate and swage Par Lost 1.556
Salve to thy Sores, apt words have power to swage Samson 184
Swain
By Miracle he may, reply'd the Swain, Par Reg 1.337
And take the Weeds and likenes of a Swain, Mask 84
Bridgewater ms 'Swayne'
Trinity ms 'swayne'
1637 'Swaine'
How cam'st thou here good Swain? hath any ram Mask 497
1637 'Swaine'
Bridgewater ms 'shepheard'
Trinity ms 'shepheard'
Unknown, and like esteem'd, and the dull swayn Mask 634
1673 'swain'
1637 'swayne'

Swain(*cont*)
Trinity ms 'swayne'
line not in Bridgewater ms
And, as the old Swain said, she can unlock Mask 852
Bridgewater ms 'swayne'
Trinity ms 'swaine'
1637 'Swaine'
Gentle swain at thy request Mask 900
1637 'swaine'
Trinity ms 'swaine'
What hard mishap hath doom'd this gentle swain? Lycidas 92
Trinity ms 'swaine'
How well could I have spar'd for thee young swain, Lycidas 113
Trinity ms 'swaine'
Thus sang the uncouth Swain to th' Okes and rills, Lycidas 186
1638 'swain'
Trinity ms 'swaine'
Pluck't up by som unheedy swain, Winchester 38
Swains
All the Swains that there abide, Mask 951
Bridgewater ms 'swaynes'
Trinity ms 'swayns'
Gen. Stay gentle Swains, for though in this disguise, Arcades 26
Trinity ms 'Swayns'
Swallow
The Swallow there, to lay her young Psalm 84, 11
Swallowed
Here swallow'd up in endless misery. Par Lost 1.142
To perish rather, swallowd up and lost Par Lost 2.149
There swallow'd up and lost, from succour farr. Par Lost 9.642
Soon swallow'd up in dark and long out-living night. Passion 7
Swallows
Swallows him with his Host, but them lets pass Par Lost 12.196
Swan
Thir downie Brest; the Swan with Arched neck Par Lost 7.438
Sward
Rustic, of grassie sord; thither anon Par Lost 11.433
Swarm
Swarm populous, unnumber'd as the Sands Par Lost 2.903
With Frie innumerable swarme, and Shoales Par Lost 7.400
Awakn'd in me swarm, while I consider Par Reg 1.197
Or as a swarm of flies in vintage time, Par Reg 4.15
From restless thoughts, that like a deadly swarm Samson 19
They swarm, but in adverse withdraw their head Samson 192
Swarmed
Thick swarm'd, both on the ground and in the air, Par Lost 1.767
Swarm'd and were straitn'd; till the Signal giv'n, Par Lost 1.776
And *Dipsas* (not so thick swarm'd once the Soil Par Lost 10.526
Swarming
Of Commonaltie: swarming next appeer'd Par Lost 7.489
Of hissing through the Hall, thick swarming now Par Lost 10.522
A darksom Cloud of Locusts swarming down Par Lost 12.185
Swart
No goblin, or swart Faery of the mine, Mask 436
Bridgewater ms 'swarte'
On whose fresh lap the swart Star sparely looks, Lycidas 138
Sway
To her original darkness and your sway Par Lost 2.984
Subjection, but requir'd with gentle sway, Par Lost 4.308
When to advance, or stand, or turn the sway Par Lost 6.234
Squadrons at once, with huge two-handed sway Par Lost 6.251
His great command; take heed least Passion sway Par Lost 8.635
Superior sway: from thus distemperd brest, Par Lost 9.1131
There didst not; there let him still Victor sway, Par Lost 10.376
On *Europe* thence, and where *Rome* was to sway Par Lost 11.405
With temperate sway; oft have they violated Par Reg 3.160
David's true heir, and his full Scepter sway Par Reg 3.405
The jealousie of Love, powerful of sway Samson 791
But to my task. *Neptune* besides the sway Mask 18
Bridgewater ms 'swaye'
Not half so far casts his usurped sway, Nativity 170
O're all th' *Italian* fields where still doth sway Sonnet 18, 11
Swayed
But *Adam* with such counsel nothing sway'd, Par Lost 10.1010
On his whole life, not sway'd Samson 1059
To their great Lord, whose love their motion sway'd Musick 22
Trinity ms 'sway'd' ←'swaid'
Th' Heathen, and as thy conquest to be sway'd Psalm 2, 18
Sways
Swayes them; the careful Plowman doubting stands Par Lost 4.983
That with moist curb sways the smooth Severn stream, Mask 825
Bridgewater ms 'swayes'
Trinity ms 'swaies'
Sweat
In Balmie Sweat, which with his Beames the Sun Par Lost 8.255
In the sweat of thy Face shalt thou eat Bread, Par Lost 10.205
To labour calls us now with sweat impos'd, Par Lost 11.172
Tells how the drudging *Goblin* swet, Allegro 105
And the chill Marble seems to sweat, Nativity 195
Sweaty
A sweatie Reaper from his Tillage brought Par Lost 11.434
Swede
And what the *Swede* intend, and what the *French*. Sonnet 21, 8
Sweep
Begin, and somwhat loudly sweep the string. Lycidas 17
Trinity ms 'sweepe'
Sweeping
In Scepter'd Pall com sweeping by, Penseroso 98

Sweet
Of Dulcet Symphonies and voices sweet, Par Lost 1.712
If chance the radiant Sun with farewell sweet Par Lost 2.492
The thronging audience. In discourse more sweet Par Lost 2.555
In sweet forgetfulness all pain and woe, Par Lost 2.608
Then sweet, now sad to mention, through dire change Par Lost 2.820
Day, or the sweet approach of Ev'n or Morn, Par Lost 3.42
Loud as from numbers without number, sweet Par Lost 3.346
Like Quivers hung, and with Praeamble sweet Par Lost 3.367
To seek her through the world; nor that sweet Grove Par Lost 4.272
For softness shee and sweet attractive Grace, Par Lost 4.298
And sweet reluctant amorous delay. Par Lost 4.311
Of thir sweet Gardning labour then suffic'd Par Lost 4.328
Which were it toilsom, yet with thee were sweet. Par Lost 4.439
Sweet is the breath of morn, her rising sweet, Par Lost 4.641
After soft showers; and sweet the coming on Par Lost 4.646
Or glittering Starr-light without thee is sweet. Par Lost 4.656
Sits on the Bloom extracting liquid sweet. Par Lost 5.25
Deigns none to ease thy load and taste thy sweet, Par Lost 5.59
Sweet of thy self, but much more sweet thus cropt, Par Lost 5.68
Kiss'd as the gracious signs of sweet remorse Par Lost 5.134
While day arises, that sweet hour of Prime. Par Lost 5.170
Among sweet dewes and flours; where any row Par Lost 5.212
Her Virgin Fancies, pouring forth more sweet, Par Lost 5.296
From many a berrie, and from sweet kernels prest Par Lost 5.346
Forthwith from dance to sweet repast they turn Par Lost 5.630
They eate, they drink, and in communion sweet Par Lost 5.637
Her bosom smelling sweet: and these scarce blown, Par Lost 7.319
Shedding sweet influence: less bright the Moon, Par Lost 7.375
And Dulcimer, all Organs of sweet stop, Par Lost 7.596
To interrupt the sweet of Life, from which Par Lost 8.184
Of sweet repast; they satiate, and soon fill, Par Lost 8.214
And sweet compliance, which declare unfeign'd Par Lost 8.603
If I could joy in aught, sweet interchange Par Lost 9.115
To basest things. Revenge, at first though sweet, Par Lost 9.171
Food of the mind, or this sweet intercourse Par Lost 9.238
And short retirement urges sweet returne. Par Lost 9.250
With sweet austeer composure thus reply'd, Par Lost 9.272
Thus her reply with accent sweet renewd. Par Lost 9.321
Foundst either sweet repast, or sound repose; Par Lost 9.407
Such ambush hid among sweet Flours and Shades Par Lost 9.408
This Flourie Plat, the sweet recess of *Eve* Par Lost 9.456
His Malice, and with rapine sweet bereav'd Par Lost 9.461
Thoughts, whither have ye led me, with what sweet Par Lost 9.473
Holy, divine, good, amiable, or sweet! Par Lost 9.899
Thy sweet Converse and Love so dearly joyn'd, Par Lost 9.909
Taste so Divine, that what of sweet before Par Lost 9.986
Recounted, mixing intercession sweet. Par Lost 10.228
Still moves with thine, join'd in connexion sweet, Par Lost 10.359
From Loves due Rites, Nuptial imbraces sweet, Par Lost 10.994
With what to sight or smell was sweet; from thee Par Lost 11.281
Departure from this happy place, our sweet Par Lost 11.303
Offer sweet smelling Gumms and Fruits and Flours: Par Lost 11.327
Then with transition sweet new Speech resumes. Par Lost 12.5
line not in 1667 edition
To noble and ignoble is more sweet Par Lost 12.221
The Law of God I read, and found it sweet, Par Reg 1.207
And sweet allay'd, yet terrible to approach, Par Reg 2.160
Of meats and drinks, Natures refreshment sweet; Par Reg 2.265
Hunger, with sweet restorative delight. Par Reg 2.373
About the wine-press where sweet moust is powr'd, Par Reg 4.16
Or hospitable, in her sweet recess, Par Reg 4.242
To gratulate the sweet return of morn; Par Reg 4.438
The breath of Heav'n fresh-blowing, pure and sweet, Samson 10
In copious Legend, or sweet Lyric Song. Samson 1737
Crush't the sweet poyson of mis-used Wine Mask 47
Bridgewater ms 'sweete'
Sweet Echo, sweetest Nymph that liv'st unseen Mask 230
Bridgewater ms 'Sweete'
Sweet Queen of Parly, Daughter of the Sphear, Mask 241
Bridgewater ms 'sweete'
And in sweet madnes rob'd it of it self, Mask 261
Bridgewater ms 'sweete'
And the sweet peace that goodnes boosoms ever, Mask 368
Bridgewater ms 'sweete'
Oft seeks to sweet retired Solitude, Mask 376
Bridgewater ms 'sweete'
Trinity ms 'sweet retired solitude' ←'solitarie sweet retire'
At last a soft and solemn breathing sound Mask 555
Trinity ms 'soft' ←'sweet' ←'still' ←'soft'
Bridgewater ms 'sweete and'
How sweet thou sing'st, how neer the deadly snare! Mask 567
Bridgewater ms 'sweete'
And timely rest have wanted, but fair Virgin Mask 689
Trinity ms 'faire virgin' ←'fairest virgin' ←'sweet Ladie'
And throw sweet garland wreaths into her stream Mask 850
Bridgewater ms 'sweete'
And the Songs of *Sirens* sweet, Mask 878
Bridgewater ms 'sweete'
Holds his dear *Psyche* sweet intranc't Mask 1005
line not in Bridgewater ms
The Mountain Nymph, sweet Liberty; Allegro 36
Sweet Bird that shunn'st the noise of folly, Penseroso 61
And as I wake, sweet musick breath Penseroso 151
Such sweet compulsion doth in musick ly, Arcades 68
In solemn troops, and sweet Societies Lycidas 179
The Star-led Wisards haste with odours sweet: Nativity 23
When such musick sweet Nativity 93

Sweet(*cont*)
Or wert thou that sweet smiling Youth! Fair Inf 53
Then thou the mother of so sweet a child Fair Inf 71
In willing chains and sweet captivitie. Vacation 52
and as your equall raptures temper'd sweet Musick Tr. ms 4.05
Her high birth, and her graces sweet, Winchester 15
Sweet rest sease thee evermore, Winchester 50
Sweet Peace and Righteousness have kiss'd Psalm 85, 43
Which once smelt sweet, now stinks as odiously; Prose 4, 2

Sweet-briar
Through the Sweet-Briar, or the Vine, Allegro 47

Sweetened
And sweeten'd every muskrose of the dale, Mask 496
Trinity ms 'sweetned'
1673 'sweetn'd'
Bridgewater ms 'sweetned'

Sweeter
And sweeter thy discourse is to my eare Par Lost 8.211

Sweetest
Tunes sweetest his love-labor'd song; now reignes Par Lost 5.41
The season, prime for sweetest Sents and Aires: Par Lost 9.200
Then smell of sweetest Fenel or the Teats Par Lost 9.581
And season him thy last and sweetest prey. Par Lost 10.609
Sweet Echo, sweetest Nymph that liv'st unseen Mask 230
Or sweetest *Shakespear* fancies childe, Allegro 133
In her sweetest, saddest plight, Penseroso 57

Sweetly
How sweetly did they float upon the wings Mask 249
Bridgewater ms 'sweetely'
And sweetly singing round about thy Bed Vacation 63
So sweetly sung your Joy the Clouds along Circum 4

Sweetness
To add more sweetness, and they thus began. Par Lost 5.152
Imbu'd, bring to thir sweetness no satietie. Par Lost 8.216
Sweetness into my heart, unfelt before, Par Lost 8.475
Of lincked sweetnes long drawn out, Allegro 140
1673 'sweetness'
As may with sweetnes, through mine ear, Penseroso 164
1673 'sweetness'
Love, sweetness, goodness, in her person shin'd Sonnet 23, 11

Sweets
So entertaind those odorous sweets the Fiend Par Lost 4.166
Perpetual Fountain of Domestic sweets, Par Lost 4.760
A Wilderness of sweets; for Nature here Par Lost 5.294
Night hath better sweets to prove, Mask 123
And a perpetual feast of nectar'd sweets, Mask 479

Sweet-smelling
With Flowers, Garlands, and sweet-smelling Herbs Par Lost 4.709

Sweet-winged
And the Cherubick host in thousand quires Musick 12
Trinity ms 'in thousand quires' ←'sweet-winged squires'

Swell
Then swell with pride, and must be titl'd Gods, Par Reg 3.81
The Sea o'refraught would swell, & th' unsought diamonds Mask 732
Trinity ms 'swell' ←'heave her waters up above the shoare'
1673 'swel'
For lo thy *furious* foes *now* swell Psalm 83, 5

Swelling
On our first Father, half her swelling Breast Par Lost 4.495
The swelling Gourd, up stood the cornie Reed Par Lost 7.321
Remove their swelling Epithetes thick laid Par Reg 4.343

Swerve
He swerve not too secure: tell him withall Par Lost 5.238
To swerve from truth, or change his constant mind Par Lost 5.902
Firm we subsist, yet possible to swerve, Par Lost 9.359
From whence they might not swerve. Psalm 81, 16

Swerved
And now thir Mightiest quelld, the battel swerv'd, Par Lost 6.386

Swift
His swift pursuers from Heav'n Gates discern Par Lost 1.326
Upon the wing, or in swift Race contend, Par Lost 2.529
Puts on swift wings, and towards the Gates of Hell Par Lost 2.631
Light-arm'd or heavy, sharp, smooth, swift or slow, Par Lost 2.902
Turn swift thir various motions, or are turnd Par Lost 3.582
Bear his swift errands over moist and dry, Par Lost 3.652
Swift to thir several Quarters hasted then Par Lost 3.714
On a Sun beam, swift as a shooting Starr Par Lost 4.556
Incredible how swift, had thither rowl'd Par Lost 4.593
On those proud Towrs to swift destruction doom'd. Par Lost 5.907
Which hung not, but so swift with tempest fell Par Lost 6.190
Nor motion of swift thought, less could his Shield Par Lost 6.192
In might or swift prevention; but the sword Par Lost 6.320
But with swift wheele reverse, deep entring shar'd Par Lost 6.326
Have easily as Spirits evaded swift Par Lost 6.596
Immediate are the Acts of God, more swift Par Lost 7.176
On the swift flouds: as Armies at the call Par Lost 7.295
In Hillocks; the swift Stag from under ground Par Lost 7.469
Thir distance argues and thir swift return Par Lost 8.21
Or save the Sun his labour, and that swift Par Lost 8.133
To mischief swift. Hope elevates, and joy Par Lost 9.633
To him with swift ascent he up returnd, Par Lost 10.224
For swift descent, with him the Cohort bright Par Lost 11.127
And call swift flights of Angels ministrant Par Reg 2.385
Swift as the lightning glance he executes Samson 1284
Swift as the Sparkle of a glancing Star, Mask 80
Lead in swift round the Months and Years. Mask 114
Into swift flight, till I had found you here, Mask 579
For maid'nhood she loves, and will be swift Mask 855

Swift(*cont*)
Bridgewater ms 'swifte'
Down the swift *Hebrus* to the *Lesbian* shore. Lycidas 63
Or *Severn* swift, guilty of Maidens death, Vacation 96
Swifter
Inflam'd with lust then rage) and swifter far, Par Lost 2.791
Swiftest
Zophiel, of Cherubim the swiftest wing, Par Lost 6.535
Time counts not, though with swiftest minutes wing'd. Par Lost 10.91
Swiftly
Lead then, said *Eve*. Hee leading swiftly rowld Par Lost 9.631
Fly swiftly to this fair Assembly's ears; Vacation 28
Swiftness
Speed, to describe whose swiftness Number failes. Par Lost 8.38
The swiftness of those Circles attribute, Par Lost 8.107
Swift-rushing
To turn Swift-rushing black perdition hence, Fair Inf 67
Swilled
To meet the rudenesse, and swill'd insolence Mask 178
Swim
Created hugest that swim th' Ocean stream: Par Lost 1.202
They swim in mirth, and fansie that they feel Par Lost 9.1009
Of these fair Atheists, and now swim in joy, Par Lost 11.625
(Erelong to swim at large) and laugh; for which Par Lost 11.626
Swims
And swims or sinks, or wades, or creeps, or flyes: Par Lost 2.950
Stretcht like a Promontorie sleeps or swimmes, Par Lost 7.414
Swine
And beg to hide them in a herd of Swine, Par Reg 4.630
And downward fell into a groveling Swine) Mask 53
Trinity ms 'swine'
Bridgewater ms 'Swyne'
Swing
Or swing thee in the Air, then dash thee down Samson 1240
Swinges
Swindges the scaly Horrour of his foulded tail. Nativity 172
Swinging
Swinging slow with sullen roar; Penseroso 76
Swinish
His praise due paid, for swinish gluttony Mask 776
Swinked
And the swink't hedger at his Supper sate; Mask 293
Trinity ms 'swinck't'
Swollen
To whom the Fiend now swoln with rage reply'd: Par Reg 4.499
Then swoll'n with pride into the snare I fell Samson 532
But swoln with wind, and the rank mist they draw, Lycidas 126
Trinity ms 'swolne'
Swooning
Nay, quoth he, on his swooning bed outstretch'd, Another 17
line not in 1640, 1657, 1658 texts
Swoonings
Thence faintings, swounings of despair, Samson 631
Sword
Of Thunder and the Sword of *Michael* Par Lost 2.294
Saw where the Sword of *Michael* smote, and fell'd Par Lost 6.250
Ere this avenging Sword begin thy doome, Par Lost 6.278
In might or swift prevention; but the sword Par Lost 6.320
The sword of *Satan* with steep force to smite Par Lost 6.324
The griding sword with discontinuous wound Par Lost 6.329
Gird on, and Sword upon thy puissant Thigh; Par Lost 6.714
Cherubic watch, and of a Sword the flame Par Lost 11.120
As in a glistering *Zodiac* hung the Sword, Par Lost 11.247
Thir motion, at whose Front a flaming Sword, Par Lost 12.592
The brandisht Sword of God before them blaz'd Par Lost 12.633
1669 'sword'
A sword shall pierce, this is my favour'd lot, Par Reg 2.91
The Jaw of a dead Ass, his sword of bone, Samson 143
Oft leav'st them to the hostile sword Samson 692
For valour to assail, nor by the sword Samson 1165
Som roaving Robber calling to his fellows. Mask 485
Trinity ms 'robber' ←'hedge man' ←'curl'd man of the swoord'
May never this just sword be lifted up, Mask 601
Trinity ms 'swoord'
But here thy sword can do thee little stead, Mask 611
Trinity ms 'swoord' ←'steele' ←'swo'
The bounds of either sword to thee wee ow. Sonnet 17, 12
1662, 1694 'Sword'
Dare ye for this adjure the Civill Sword Forcers 5
Trinity ms 'sword'
His Sword he whets, his Bow hath bended Psalm 7, 46
Sworded
And sworded Seraphim, Nativity 113
Sword-law
Proceeded, and Oppression, and Sword-Law Par Lost 11.672
Sword-players
Sam. Have they not Sword-players, and ev'ry sort Samson 1323
Swords
Millions of flaming swords, drawn from the thighs Par Lost 1.664
Now wav'd thir fierie Swords, and in the Aire Par Lost 6.304
Swore
What feign'd submission swore: ease would recant Par Lost 4.96
Sworn
Or in this abject posture have ye sworn Par Lost 1.322
ms 'sworne'
And by my Self have sworn to him shall bow Par Lost 5.607
The just Decree of God, pronounc't and sworn, Par Lost 5.814

Sworn(*cont*)
Remembring mercie, and his Cov'nant sworn Par Lost 12.346
Youth and Joy; so *Jove* hath sworn. Mask 1011
line not in Bridgewater ms
Trinity ms 'sworne'
1637 'sworne'
Thy drowsie Nurse hath sworn she did them spie Vacation 61
Swum
Surpris'd thee, dim thine eyes, and dizzie swumm Par Lost 2.753
By Fowl, Fish, Beast, was flown, was swum, was walkt Par Lost 7.503
No more was seen; the floating Vessel swum Par Lost 11.745
All left, in one small bottom swum imbark't. Par Lost 11.753
Syene
Syene, and where the shadow both way falls, Par Reg 4.70
Syllable
And airy tongues, that syllable mens names Mask 208
Trinity ms 'syllable mens nams' ←'lure night wanderers'
line not in Bridgewater ms
Sylvan
A Silvan Scene, and as the ranks ascend Par Lost 4.140
I have at will. So to the Silvan Lodge Par Lost 5.377
And tuneable as Silvan Pipe or Song; Par Reg 1.480
Satyr, or Fawn, or Silvan? But these haunts Par Reg 2.191
Dwell'st here with *Pan*, or *Silvan*, by blest Song Mask 268
And shadows brown that *Sylvan* loves Penseroso 134
Sylvanus
Pan or *Silvanus* never slept, nor Nymph, Par Lost 4.707
Sylvestro
That *Constantine* to good *Sylvestro* gave. Prose 4, 4
Sympathize
That dumb things would be mov'd to sympathize, Mask 796
line not in Trinity ms
line not in Bridgewater ms
With her great Master so to sympathize: Nativity 34
Sympathy
Of sympathie and love; there I had fixt Par Lost 4.465
Or sympathie, or som connatural force Par Lost 10.246
And horrid sympathie; for what they saw, Par Lost 10.540
Symphonies
Of Dulcet Symphonies and voices sweet, Par Lost 1.712
ms 'symphonies'
And choral symphonies, Day without Night, Par Lost 5.162
And charming Symphonies attach'd the heart Par Lost 11.595
Symphonious
Symphonious of ten thousand Harpes that tun'd Par Lost 7.559
Symphony
Of charming symphonie they introduce Par Lost 3.368
Make up full consort to th' Angelike symphony. Nativity 132
Their loud up-lifted Angel trumpets blow, Musick 11
Trinity ms 'angell' ←'arch-angell' ←'symphonie of silver'
Synod
Synod of Gods, and like to what ye are, Par Lost 2.391
A third part of the Gods, in Synod met Par Lost 6.156
In Synod unbenigne, and taught the fixt Par Lost 10.661
But let us call to Synod all the Blest Par Lost 11.67
Syrian
Egypt from *Syrian* ground, had general Names Par Lost 1.421
ms 'Syrian'
The *Syrian* Damsels to lament his fate Par Lost 1.448
ms 'Syrian'
For one of *Syrian* mode, whereon to burn Par Lost 1.474
ms 'Syrian'
Against the *Syrian* King, who to surprize Par Lost 11.218
That fair *Syrian* Shepherdess, Winchester 63
Syrinx
Or *Amymone*, *Syrinx*, many more Par Reg 2.188
Though *Syrinx* your *Pans* Mistres were, Arcades 106
Trinity ms defective here
Yet *Syrinx* well might wait on her. Arcades 107
Syrtis
Quencht in a Boggie *Syrtis*, neither Sea, Par Lost 2.939
Syrups
With spirits of balm, and fragrant Syrops mixt. Mask 674
1637 'syrops'
Bridgewater ms 'sirrops'
Trinity ms 'syrops'
Tabernacle
Was not; shee in a cloudie Tabernacle Par Lost 7.248
Among them to set up his Tabernacle, Par Lost 12.247
In fleshly Tabernacle, and human form, Par Reg 4.599
Poor fleshly Tabernacle entered, Passion 17
Tabernacles
Celestial Tabernacles, where they slept Par Lost 5.654
The *pleasant* Tabernacles are! Psalm 84, 3
Table
Have heap'd this Table. Rais'd of grassie terf Par Lost 5.391
Thir Table was, and mossie seats had round, Par Lost 5.392
As from the Mine. Mean while at Table *Eve* Par Lost 5.443
A Table richly spred, in regal mode, Par Reg 2.340
Command a Table in this Wilderness, Par Reg 2.384
Both Table and Provision vanish'd quite Par Reg 2.402
A table of Celestial Food, Divine, Par Reg 4.588
Wherwith he wont at Heav'ns high Councel-Table, Nativity 10
Tables
Tables are set, and on a sudden pil'd Par Lost 5.632
On *Cittron* tables or *Atlantic* stone; Par Reg 4.115
Tabriz
To *Tauris* or *Casbeen*. So these the late Par Lost 10.436

Tacit
Tacit, was in thy power; true; and thou bear'st — Samson 430
Tackle
Gladly the Port, though Shrouds and Tackle torn; — Par Lost 2.1044
With all her bravery on, and tackle trim, — Samson 717
Tacks
But call in aide, which makes a bloody Fray; — Par Lost 11.651
1667 'tacks'
Tail
With complicated monsters head and taile, — Par Lost 10.523
As Graces, draw a Scorpions tail behind? — Samson 360
Swindges the scaly Horrour of his foulded tail. — Nativity 172
Taint
Or if, inspiring venom, he might taint — Par Lost 4.804
Or taint integritie; but all obey'd — Par Lost 5.704
Which mans polluting Sin with taint hath shed — Par Lost 10.631
With superstitions and traditions taint, — Par Lost 12.512
From National obstriction, without taint — Samson 312
Mine as whom washt from spot of child-bed taint, — Sonnet 23, 5
Tainted
Eject him tainted now, and purge him off — Par Lost 11.52
Taint-worm
Or Taint-worm to the weanling Herds that graze, — Lycidas 46
Trinity ms 'taint-worme'
1638 'taint-worm'
Take
His great command; take heed least Passion sway — Par Lost 8.635
The bended Twigs take root, and Daughters grow — Par Lost 9.1105
Take to thee from among the Cherubim — Par Lost 11.100
And there take root an Iland salt and bare, — Par Lost 11.834
Yet, sacrilegious, to himself would take — Par Reg 3.140
Sam. That fault I take not on me, but transfer — Samson 241
Take to thy wicked deed: which when thou seest — Samson 826
Sams. No, no, of my condition take no care; — Samson 928
But take good heed my hand survey not thee. — Samson 1230
Sam. So take it with what speed thy message needs. — Samson 1345
Mess. Then take the worst in brief, *Samson* is dead. — Samson 1570
And take the Weeds and likenes of a Swain, — Mask 84
Who as they sung, would take the prison'd soul, — Mask 256
Till further quest'. *La*. Shepherd I take thy word, — Mask 321
Held up their pearled wrists and took her in, — Mask 834
Trinity ms '& took' ←'to take' ←'carie' ←'receave'
And will not take their flight, — Nativity 72
And why from us so quickly thou didst take thy flight. — Fair Inf 42
Take up a weeping on the Mountains wilde, — Passion 51
If once his wrath take fire like fuel sere. — Psalm 2, 27
Taken
Out of the ground wast taken, know thy Birth, — Par Lost 10.207
The Ground whence he was taken, fitter soile. — Par Lost 11.98
The ground whence thou wast tak'n, fitter Soile. — Par Lost 11.262
None are, thou think'st, but taken with such toys. — Par Reg 2.177
Had ta'n their supper on the savoury Herb — Mask 541
Bridgewater ms 'tane'
1637 'ta'ne'
Trinity ms 'tane'
were they not taken thence — Mask Tr. ms 22.07
And that he had tane up his latest Inne, — Carrier 13
Takes
And of thir doings God takes no account. — Par Lost 4.622
Then forthwith to him takes a chosen band — Par Reg 2.236
Then to the Desert takes with these his flight; — Par Reg 2.241
and often takes our cattell with strange pinches — Mask Tr. ms 23.51
That in trim Gardens takes his pleasure; — Penseroso 50
Which takes our late fantasticks with delight, — Vacation 20
And what he takes in hand shall prosper all. — Psalm 1, 10
For thou art not a God that takes — Psalm 5, 9
As *when* an *aged* wood takes fire — Psalm 83, 53
Tale
Of *Thammuz* yearly wounded: the Love-tale — Par Lost 1.452
ms 'love-tale'
What never yet was heard in Tale or Song — Mask 44
Trinity ms 'tale'
Bridgewater ms 'tale'
And to the tel-tale Sun discry — Mask 141
1673 'tell-tale'
Trinity ms 'telltale'
Bridgewater ms 'tell tale'
And every Shepherd tells his tale — Allegro 67
Or the tale of *Troy* divine. — Penseroso 100
Talent
And that one Talent which is death to hide, — Sonnet 19, 3
Tales
Thus don the Tales, to bed they creep, — Allegro 115
Talk
Whatever Hypocrites austerely talk — Par Lost 4.744
Then when I am thy captive talk of chaines, — Par Lost 4.970
Of our last Eevnings talk, in this thy dream, — Par Lost 5.115
No more of talk where God or Angel Guest — Par Lost 9.1
Refreshment, whether food, or talk between, — Par Lost 9.237
And talk at least, though I despair to attain. — Par Reg 1.485
To live upon thir tongues and be thir talk, — Par Reg 3.55
Outlandish flatteries? then proceed'st to talk — Par Reg 4.125
I never lik'd thy talk, thy offers less, — Par Reg 4.171
For all his tedious talk is but vain boast, — Par Reg 4.307
Much of the Soul they talk, but all awrie, — Par Reg 4.313
Now of my own experience, not by talk, — Samson 188
By unchaste looks, loose gestures, and foul talk, — Mask 464
1637 'talke'

Talk(*cont*)
Bridgewater ms 'talke'
Trinity ms 'talke'
Talked
The Trepidation talkt, and that first mov'd; — Par Lost 3.483
So talk'd the spirited sly Snake; and *Eve* — Par Lost 9.613
I heard, here with him at this Fountain talk'd: — Par Lost 11.322
Whereat hee inlie rag'd, and as they talk'd, — Par Lost 11.444
And with him talkt, and with him lodg'd, I mean — Par Reg 2.6
So talk'd he, while the Son of God went on — Par Reg 4.484
Talking
Thus Satan talking to his neerest Mate — Par Lost 1.192
Thus talking hand in hand alone they pass'd — Par Lost 4.689
Talking like this worlds brood; — Psalm 4, 27
Talks
Of which all Europe talks from side to side. — Sonnet 22, 12
1694 '*Europe* rings'
Tall
Azazel as his right, a Cherube tall: — Par Lost 1.534
Two of far nobler shape erect and tall, — Par Lost 4.288
Till I espi'd thee, fair indeed and tall, — Par Lost 4.477
Then from the Mountain hewing Timber tall, — Par Lost 11.728
Tall stripling youths rich clad, of fairer hew — Par Reg 2.352
To touch the prosperous growth of this tall Wood. — Mask 270
To nurse the Saplings tall, and curl the grove — Arcades 46
Trinity ms 'nurse the saplings tall' ←'live a thousand yeares'
Her Bows as *high as* Cedars tall — Psalm 80, 43
Tallest
His Spear, to equal which the tallest Pine — Par Lost 1.292
On the vext Wilderness, whose tallest Pines, — Par Reg 4.416
Talons
With sound of Harpies wings, and Talons heard; — Par Reg 2.403
Tamberlane
And *Samarchand* by *Oxus*, *Temirs* Throne, — Par Lost 11.389
Tame
Since *Michael* and his Powers went forth to tame — Par Lost 6.686
Such object hath the power to soft'n and tame — Par Reg 2.163
Like a tame Weather, all my precious fleece, — Samson 538
Of tame villatic Fowl; but as an Eagle — Samson 1695
Tamed
The River-dragon tam'd at length submits — Par Lost 12.191
Gives and the Mill had tam'd thee? O that fortune — Samson 1093
Wherwith she tam'd the brinded lioness — Mask 443
Tamely
Tamely endur'd a Bridge of wondrous length — Par Lost 2.1028
Tames
By hunger, that each other Creature tames, — Par Reg 2.406
Tangled
Hearts after them tangl'd in Amorous Nets. — Par Reg 2.162
Not willingly, but tangl'd in the fold, — Samson 1665
In the blind mazes of this tangl'd Wood? — Mask 181
Trinity ms 'tangled' ←'arched'
1637 'tangled'
Bridgewater ms 'tangled'
The Nimphs in twilight shade of tangled thickets mourn. — Nativity 188
Tangles
In tangles, and made intricate seem strait, — Par Lost 9.632
Or with the tangles of *Neaera*'s hair? — Lycidas 69
Tangling
Of shrubs and tangling bushes had perplext — Par Lost 4.176
Tanned
To the tann'd Haycock in the Mead, — Allegro 90
Tantalus
The lip of *Tantalus*. Thus roving on — Par Lost 2.614
Taper
With black usurping mists, som gentle taper — Mask 337
In Saffron robe, with Taper clear, — Allegro 126
Tapers
Now sits not girt with Tapers holy shine, — Nativity 202
Tapestry
With smoaky rafters, then in tapstry Halls — Mask 324
Bridgewater ms 'tap'strie'
Trinity ms 'tapstrie'
1637 'tapstrie'
Taprobane
And utmost *Indian* Isle *Taprobane*, — Par Reg 4.75
Tardy
Of tardie execution, since denounc't — Par Lost 10.853
Targe
They gatherd, broad as *Amazonian* Targe, — Par Lost 9.1111
Tarpeian
On the *Tarpeian* rock, her Cittadel — Par Reg 4.49
Tarshish
By ancient *Tarsus* held, or that Sea-beast — Par Lost 1.200
ms 'Tarsus'
Tarsus
By ancient *Tarsus* held, or that Sea-beast — Par Lost 1.200
ms 'Tarsus'
Of *Tarsus*, bound for th' Isles — Samson 715
Tartar
Whose snowie ridge the roving *Tartar* bounds, — Par Lost 3.432
As when the *Tartar* from his *Russian* Foe — Par Lost 10.431
On which the *Tartar* King did ride; — Penseroso 115
Tartarean
Mixt with *Tartarean* Sulphur, and strange fire, — Par Lost 2.69
Tartareous
The black tartareous cold Infernal dregs — Par Lost 7.238

Tartarus
Into this gloom of *Tartarus* profound, Par Lost 2.858
Of *Tartarus*, which ready opens wide Par Lost 6.54
Tartessian
In the steep *Atlantick* stream, Mask 97
Trinity ms 'Atlantick' ←'Tartessian'
Task
To do ought good never will be our task, Par Lost 1.159
Our servile offerings. This must be our task Par Lost 2.246
His bountie, following our delightful task Par Lost 4.437
Sad task and hard, for how shall I relate Par Lost 5.564
Of secondarie hands, by task transferd Par Lost 5.854
Deaths Harbinger: Sad task, yet argument Par Lost 9.13
Our pleasant task enjoyn'd, but till more hands Par Lost 9.207
Our taske we choose, what wonder if so near Par Lost 9.221
1667 'task'
The other service was thy chosen task, Par Reg 1.427
Maugre the *Roman:* it shall be my task Par Reg 3.368
Relieves me from my task of servile toyl, Samson 5
To grind in Brazen Fetters under task Samson 35
But to my task. *Neptune* besides the sway Mask 18
Bridgewater ms 'taske'
Trinity ms 'taske' ←'buisnesse now'
But now my task is smoothly don, Mask 1012
B.M. ms 'Task'
1637 'taske'
Trinity ms 'taske' ←'buisnesse' ←'message'
That now I use thee in my latter task: Vacation 8
O yet a nobler task awaites thy hand; Sonnet 15, 9
In libertyes defence, my noble task, Sonnet 22, 11
Taskmaster
As ever in my great task Masters eye. Sonnet 7, 14
Trinity ms 'task-maisters'
Tasseled
Awakes the slumbring leaves, or tasseld horn Arcades 57
Trinity ms 'tassel'd'
Taste
Of that Forbidden Tree, whose mortal tast Par Lost 1.2
All taste of living wight, as once it fled Par Lost 2.613
Retire, or taste thy folly, and learn by proof, Par Lost 2.686
They who neglect and scorn, shall never taste; Par Lost 3.199
All Trees of noblest kind for sight, smell, taste; Par Lost 4.217
If true, here only, and of delicious taste: Par Lost 4.251
More woe, the more your taste is now of joy; Par Lost 4.369
So various, not to taste that onely Tree Par Lost 4.423
God hath pronounc't it death to taste that Tree, Par Lost 4.427
Forbidden them to taste: Knowledge forbidd'n? Par Lost 4.515
They taste and die: what likelier can ensue? Par Lost 4.527
Deigns none to ease thy load and taste thy sweet, Par Lost 5.59
Or envie, or what reserve forbids to taste? Par Lost 5.61
Taste this, and be henceforth among the Gods Par Lost 5.77
Could not but taste. Forthwith up to the Clouds Par Lost 5.86
For dinner savourie fruits, of taste to please Par Lost 5.304
Taste after taste upheld with kindliest change, Par Lost 5.336
To sit and taste, till this meridian heat Par Lost 5.369
Our Authour. Heav'nly stranger, please to taste Par Lost 5.397
Of sense, whereby they hear, see, smell, touch, taste, Par Lost 5.411
As may compare with Heaven; and to taste Par Lost 5.432
To enter, and these earthly fruits to taste, Par Lost 5.464
Delectable both to behold and taste; Par Lost 7.539
Remember what I warne thee, shun to taste, Par Lost 8.327
Of thy Associates, *Adam*, and wilt taste Par Lost 8.401
I mean of Taste, Sight, Smell, Herbs, Fruits, and Flours, Par Lost 8.527
Of Paradise for Hell, hope here to taste Par Lost 9.476
But of this Tree we may not taste nor touch; Par Lost 9.651
Goddess humane, reach then, and freely taste. Par Lost 9.732
Inclinable now grown to touch or taste, Par Lost 9.742
Whose taste, too long forborn, at first assay Par Lost 9.747
Forbids us then to taste, but his forbidding Par Lost 9.753
Fair to the Eye, inviting to the Taste, Par Lost 9.777
Intent now wholly on her taste, naught else Par Lost 9.786
To open Eyes, and make them Gods who taste; Par Lost 9.866
Thou therefore also taste, that equal Lot Par Lost 9.881
Much more to taste it under banne to touch. Par Lost 9.925
Made common and unhallowd ere our taste; Par Lost 9.931
Taste so Divine, that what of sweet before Par Lost 9.986
On my experience, *Adam*, freely taste, Par Lost 9.988
Eve, now I see thou art exact of taste, Par Lost 9.1017
Her Husband shee, to taste the fatall fruit, Par Lost 10.4
The high Injunction not to taste that Fruit, Par Lost 10.13
Of carnage, prey innumerable, and taste Par Lost 10.268
This more delusive, not the touch, but taste Par Lost 10.563
Chewd bitter Ashes, which th' offended taste Par Lost 10.566
To know both Good and Evil, since his taste Par Lost 11.85
Obtuse, all taste of pleasure must forgoe, Par Lost 11.541
Bred onely and completed to the taste Par Lost 11.618
With Food, whereof we wretched seldom taste. Par Reg 1.345
Thir taste no knowledge works, at least of evil, Par Reg 2.371
Or taste that cheers the heart of Gods and men, Samson 545
Sam. The way to know were not to see but taste. Samson 1091
To quench the drouth of *Phoebus*, which as they taste Mask 66
1637 'tast'
Trinity ms 'tast'
(For most do taste through fond intemperate thirst) Mask 67
Trinity ms 'tast'
1637 'tast'
Bridgewater ms 'tast'
I would not taste thy treasonous offer; none Mask 702
Taste(*cont*)
Trinity ms 'would not taste' ←'should reject' ←'hate it from thy hands'
1637 'tast'
But all to please, and sate the curious taste? Mask 714
1637 'tast'
Bridgewater ms 'tast'
Beyond the bliss of dreams. Be wise, and taste.---- Mask 813
1637 'tast'
Bridgewater ms 'tast'
Trinity ms 'tast'
Of Attick tast, with Wine, whence we may rise Sonnet 20, 10
Tasted
He pluckt, he tasted; mee damp horror chil'd Par Lost 5.65
Which tasted works knowledge of Good and Evil, Par Lost 7.543
Mee who have touch'd and tasted, yet both live, Par Lost 9.688
Hath tasted, envies not, but brings with joy Par Lost 9.770
In Fruit she never tasted, whether true Par Lost 9.788
Of danger tasted, nor to evil unknown Par Lost 9.864
And hath bin tasted such: the Serpent wise, Par Lost 9.867
Have also tasted, and have also found Par Lost 9.874
Beneath *Magellan*. At that tasted Fruit Par Lost 10.687
Nor tasted humane food, nor hunger felt Par Reg 1.308
Have found him, view'd him, tasted him, but find Par Reg 2.131
Nor tasted, nor had appetite; that Fast Par Reg 2.247
Whoever tasted, lost his upright shape, Mask 52
Tastes
Tastes, not well joynd, inelegant, but bring Par Lost 5.335
Of all tastes else to please thir appetite, Par Lost 7.49
1669 'tastes'
1667 'tasts'
With *Sion*'s songs, to all true tasts excelling, Par Reg 4.347
Tasting
Tasting concoct, digest, assimilate, Par Lost 5.412
Of tasting those fair Apples, I resolv'd Par Lost 9.585
Least thou not tasting, different degree Par Lost 9.883
To us, as likely tasting to attaine Par Lost 9.935
If any be, of tasting this fair Fruit, Par Lost 9.972
True relish, tasting; if such pleasure be Par Lost 9.1024
Taught
That Shepherd, who first taught the chosen Seed, Par Lost 1.8
Men also, and by his suggestion taught, Par Lost 1.685
Taught by the heav'nly Muse to venture down Par Lost 3.19
Which taught thee yet no better, that no pain Par Lost 4.915
Made vocal by my Song, and taught his praise. Par Lost 5.204
Well hast thou taught the way that might direct Par Lost 5.508
Under him Regent, tells, as he was taught, Par Lost 5.698
Yet by experience taught we know how good, Par Lost 5.826
And freed from intricacies, taught to live, Par Lost 8.182
Till warn'd, or by experience taught, she learne, Par Lost 8.190
Gave elocution to the mute, and taught Par Lost 9.748
To that false Worm, of whomsoever taught Par Lost 9.1068
In Synod unbenigne, and taught the fixt Par Lost 10.661
With other echo late I taught your Shades Par Lost 10.861
The rule of not too much, by temperance taught Par Lost 11.531
Taught them, but they his gifts acknowledg'd none. Par Lost 11.612
Came seavens, and pairs, and enterd in, as taught Par Lost 11.735
Taught this by his example whom I now Par Lost 12.572
Though ravenous, taught to abstain from what they brought: Par Reg 2.269
Natures own work it seem'd (Nature taught Art) Par Reg 2.295
By what he taught and suffer'd for so doing, Par Reg 3.97
Teaching not taught; the childhood shews the man, Par Reg 4.220
Thence what the lofty grave Tragoedians taught Par Reg 4.261
As men divinely taught, and better teaching Par Reg 4.357
In them is plainest taught, and easiest learnt, Par Reg 4.361
Bin, as it ought, sincere, it would have taught thee Samson 874
What the sage Poets taught by th' heav'nly Muse, Mask 515
That hath so well been taught her dazling fence, Mask 791
line not in Bridgewater ms
line not in Trinity ms
First taught our English Musick how to span Sonnet 13, 2
Pronounc't and in his volumes taught our Lawes, Sonnet 21, 3
line not in Trinity ms
Taught ye by meer *A. S.* and *Rotherford*? Forcers 8
Be taught ye Judges of the earth; with fear Psalm 2, 23
Taughtst
When thou taught'st *Cambridge*, and King *Edward* Greek. Sonnet 11, 14
Tauric
Beyond *Danubius* to the *Tauric* Pool. Par Reg 4.79
Tauris
To *Tauris* or *Casbeen*. So these the late Par Lost 10.436
Taurus
In spring time, when the Sun with *Taurus* rides, Par Lost 1.769
1667 'Taurus'
ms 'Taurus'
Like distant breadth to *Taurus* with the Seav'n Par Lost 10.673
Tawny
The Tawnie Lion, pawing to get free Par Lost 7.464
And on the Tawny Sands and Shelves, Mask 117
Bridgewater ms 'tawny'
Trinity ms 'tawnie' ←'yellow'
1637 'tawny'
The Tawny King with all his power. Psalm 136, 54
Tax
Chor. Tax not divine disposal, wisest Men Samson 210
Teach
Our minds and teach us to cast off this Yoke? Par Lost 5.786
Shall teach us highest deeds, by proof to try Par Lost 5.865

Teach(*cont*)
And teach us further by what means to shun Par Lost 10.1062
To teach thee that God attributes to place Par Lost 11.836
To teach all nations what of him they learn'd Par Lost 12.440
All Nations they shall teach; for from that day Par Lost 12.446
At least to try, and teach the erring Soul Par Reg 1.224
Into the World, to teach his final will, Par Reg 1.461
The *Gentiles* also know, and write, and teach Par Reg 4.227
Alas what can they teach, and not mislead; Par Reg 4.309
She can teach ye how to clime Mask 1020
Teach light to counterfeit a gloom, Penseroso 80
Teach me O Lord thy way *most right*, Psalm 86, 37
laughing to teach the truth Prose 6, 1

Teacher
O Teacher, some great mischief hath befall'n Par Lost 11.450

Teachers
Wolves shall succeed for teachers, grievous Wolves, Par Lost 12.508
The Teachers of our Law, and to propose Par Reg 1.212
In *Chorus* or *Iambic*, teachers best Par Reg 4.262
What hinders? as some teachers give to Boyes Prose 6, 2

Teaches
What severs each thou 'hast learnt, which few hav don. Sonnet 17, 11

Teaching
Teaching not taught; the childhood shews the man, Par Reg 4.220
As men divinely taught, and better teaching Par Reg 4.357

Team
Now while the Heav'n by the Suns team untrod, Nativity 19

Tear
But silently a gentle tear let fall Par Lost 5.130
Gloriously rigg'd; and for a word, a tear, Samson 200
My sudden rage to tear thee joint by joint. Samson 953
Without the meed of som melodious tear. Lycidas 14
Trinity ms 'teare'
Your fiery essence can distill no tear, Circum 7
Trinity ms 'teare'
He hast to tear my Soul asunder Psalm 7, 5

Tearing
Tearing and no rescue nigh. Psalm 7, 6

Tears
Of human sacrifice, and parents tears, Par Lost 1.393
ms 'teares'
Tears such as Angels weep, burst forth: at last Par Lost 1.620
They sate them down to weep, nor onely Teares Par Lost 9.1121
Not so repulst, with Tears that ceas'd not flowing, Par Lost 10.910
Humbly our faults, and pardon beg, with tears Par Lost 10.1089
Humbly thir faults, and pardon beg'd, with tears Par Lost 10.1101
For I behold them softn'd and with tears Par Lost 11.110
His best of Man, and gave him up to tears Par Lost 11.497
The world erelong a world of tears must weepe. Par Lost 11.627
Adam was all in tears, and to his guide Par Lost 11.674
Of tears and sorrow a Floud thee also drown'd, Par Lost 11.757
Surcharg'd, as had like grief bin dew'd in tears, Par Lost 12.373
Som natural tears they drop'd, but wip'd them soon; Par Lost 12.645
O'recome with importunity and tears. Samson 51
Who tore the Lion, as the Lion tears the Kid, Samson 128
And words addrest seem into tears dissolv'd, Samson 729
I cannot but acknowledge; yet if tears Samson 735
With supplication prone and Fathers tears Samson 1459
Nothing is here for tears, nothing to wail Samson 1721
Drew Iron tears down *Pluto*'s cheek, Penseroso 107
And Daffadillies fill their cups with tears, Lycidas 150
Trinity ms 'teares'
And wipe the tears for ever from his eyes. Lycidas 181
Trinity ms 'teares'
And letters where my tears have washt a wannish white. Passion 35
For sure so well instructed are my tears, Passion 48
Prove to be presaging tears Winchester 44
Here be tears of perfect moan Winchester 55
My Bed I water with my tears; mine Eie Psalm 6, 13
Thou feed'st them with the bread of tears, Psalm 80, 21
Their bread with tears they eat, Psalm 80, 22
And mak'st them largely drink the tears Psalm 80, 23

Tease
The sampler, and to teize the huswifes wooll. Mask 751
line not in Bridgewater ms

Teats
Then smell of sweetest Fenel or the Teats Par Lost 9.581

Tedded
The smell of Grain, or tedded Grass, or Kine, Par Lost 9.450

Tedious
More solemn then the tedious pomp that waits Par Lost 5.354
Tedious alike: Of fellowship I speak Par Lost 8.389
With long and tedious havoc fabl'd Knights Par Lost 9.30
Tedious, unshar'd with thee, and odious soon. Par Lost 9.880
But tedious wast of time to sit and hear Par Reg 4.123
For all his tedious talk is but vain boast, Par Reg 4.307
Time is our tedious Song should here have ending, Nativity 239

Teemed
Op'ning her fertil Woomb teem'd at a Birth Par Lost 7.454
From out her ashie womb now teem'd, Samson 1703
Heav'ns youngest teemed Star, Nativity 240

Teeming
When for their teeming Flocks, and granges full Mask 175
Bridgewater ms 'teeminge'

Teeth
Hast broke the teeth. This help was from the Lord Psalm 3, 23

Telassar
Dwelt in *Telassar:* in this pleasant soile Par Lost 4.214

Telescope
Of Telescope, were curious to enquire: Par Reg 4.42

Tell
Deeming some Island, oft, as Sea-men tell, Par Lost 1.205
The rest were long to tell, though far renown'd, Par Lost 1.507
Who boast in mortal things, and wond'ring tell Par Lost 1.693
Prevented spares to tell thee yet by deeds Par Lost 2.739
Whose Fountain who shall tell? before the Sun, Par Lost 3.8
Purge and disperse, that I may see and tell Par Lost 3.54
By center, or eccentric, hard to tell, Par Lost 3.575
Alone thus wandring. Brightest Seraph tell Par Lost 3.667
O Sun, to tell thee how I hate thy beams Par Lost 4.37
But rather to tell how, if Art could tell, Par Lost 4.236
Speak yee who best can tell, ye Sons of light, Par Lost 5.160
He swerve not too secure: tell him withall Par Lost 5.238
Tell them that by command, ere yet dim Night Par Lost 5.685
And longer will delay to heare thee tell Par Lost 7.101
For Man to tell how human Life began Par Lost 8.250
And ye that live and move, fair Creatures, tell, Par Lost 8.276
Tell, if ye saw, how came I thus, how here? Par Lost 8.277
Tell me, how may I know him, how adore, Par Lost 8.280
Easie to mee it is to tell thee all Par Lost 9.569
With peril great atchiev'd. Long were to tell Par Lost 10.469
Were long to tell, how many Battels fought, Par Lost 12.261
With prosperous wing full summ'd to tell of deeds Par Reg 1.14
Wrought that effect on *Jove*, so Fables tell; Par Reg 2.215
Tell me if Food were now before thee set, Par Reg 2.320
Besieg'd *Albracca*, as Romances tell; Par Reg 3.339
Much less my mind; though thou should'st add to tell Par Reg 4.113
And studs of Pearl, to me should'st tell who thirst Par Reg 4.120
Is not for thee to know, nor me to tell. Par Reg 4.153
Did I not tell thee, if thou didst reject Par Reg 4.467
To a deceitful Woman: tell me Friends, Samson 202
To wring from me and tell to them my secret, Samson 1199
Sam. Thou knowst I am an *Ebrew*, therefore tell them, Samson 1319
Man. Tell us the sum, the circumstance defer. Samson 1557
And listen why, for I will tell ye now Mask 43
Canst thou not tell me of a gentle Pair Mask 236
Tell me but where Mask 240
And tell me it is safe, as bid me hope Mask 400
Tell her of things that no gross ear can hear, Mask 458
Eld. Bro. To tell thee sadly Shepherd, without blame, Mask 509
O let us his praises tell, Psalm 136, 9
Tell me bright Spirit where e're thou hoverest Fair Inf 38
Forsook the hated earth, O tell me sooth Fair Inf 51
May tell at length how green-ey'd *Neptune* raves, Vacation 43
Shall they thy loving kindness tell Psalm 88, 45
On thy third Reigne the Earth look now, and tell Prose 12, 3

Tellest
Thou tellst, by morrow dawning I shall know. Par Lost 4.588
1667 'telst'
Assur'd me, and still assure: though what thou tellst Par Lost 5.553

Telling
Thy message, which might else in telling wound, Par Lost 11.299
Telling their strange and vigorous faculties; Mask 628
Bridgewater ms 'tellinge'

Tells
Who tells of som infernal Spirit seen Par Lost 4.793
Under him Regent, tells, as he was taught, Par Lost 5.698
Tells the suggested cause, and casts between Par Lost 5.702
His place of birth a solemn Angel tells Par Lost 12.364
As story tells, have trod this Wilderness; Par Reg 2.307
And every Shepherd tells his tale Allegro 67
Tells how the drudging *Goblin* swet, Allegro 105

Tell-tale
And to the tel-tale Sun discry Mask 141
Bridgewater ms 'tell tale'
1673 'tell-tale'
Trinity ms 'telltale'

Temir
And *Samarchand* by *Oxus*, *Temirs* Throne, Par Lost 11.389

Temper
Ethereal temper, massy, large and round, Par Lost 1.285
To hight of noblest temper Hero's old Par Lost 1.552
In temper and in nature, will receive Par Lost 2.218
As soft as now severe, our temper chang'd Par Lost 2.276
Into their temper; which must needs remove Par Lost 2.277
Temper or nourish, or in part shed down Par Lost 4.670
Touch of Celestial temper, but returns Par Lost 4.812
On me deriv'd, yet I shall temper so Par Lost 10.77
And gracious temper he both heard and judg'd Par Lost 10.1047
True patience, and to temper joy with fear Par Lost 11.361
Severest temper, smooth the rugged'st brow, Par Reg 2.164

Temperance
Her Temperance over Appetite, to know Par Lost 7.127
The rule of not too much, by temperance taught Par Lost 11.531
More then anough, that temperance may be tri'd: Par Lost 11.805
Justice and Temperance, Truth and Faith forgot; Par Lost 11.807
Add vertue, Patience, Temperance, add Love, Par Lost 12.583
Thy temperance invincible besides, Par Reg 2.408
By patience, temperance; I mention still Par Reg 3.92
Sam. But what avail'd this temperance, not compleat Samson 558
Should in a pet of temperance feed on Pulse, Mask 721
And holy dictate of spare Temperance: Mask 767
Bridgewater ms 'temperance'
Trinity ms 'temperance'
Their faith, their patience, and their truth. Mask 971
Trinity ms 'patience' ← 'temperance' ← 'patience'

Temperate
And temperat vapors bland, which th' only sound Par Lost 5.5
Began to parch that temperate Clime; whereat Par Lost 12.636
With temperate sway; oft have they violated Par Reg 3.160
Frugal, and mild, and temperate, conquer'd well, Par Reg 4.134
Temperately
To whom thus Jesus temperately reply'd: Par Reg 2.378
Tempered
Though temper'd heav'nly, for that mortal dint, Par Lost 2.813
Was giv'n him temperd so, that neither keen Par Lost 6.322
With Heav'ns ray, and temperd they shoot forth Par Lost 6.480
Temper'd soft Tunings, intermixt with Voice Par Lost 7.598
Of most erected Spirits, most temper'd pure Par Reg 3.27
Chalybean temper'd steel, and frock of mail Samson 133
Has in his charge, with temper'd awe to guide Mask 32
Bridgewater ms 'tempred'
Temper'd to th' Oaten Flute, Lycidas 33
Trinity ms 'temperd'
and as your equall raptures temper'd sweet Musick Tr. ms 4.05
Temperest
Temperst thy providence through his short course, Samson 670
Tempering
Thy tempring; with like safetie guided down Par Lost 7.15
Tempers
She tempers dulcet creams, nor these to hold Par Lost 5.347
Tempest
Caught in a fierie Tempest shall be hurl'd Par Lost 2.180
After the Tempest: Such applause was heard Par Lost 2.290
Of glimmering air less vext with tempest loud: Par Lost 3.429
Which hung not, but so swift with tempest fell Par Lost 6.190
Tempest the Ocean: there Leviathan Par Lost 7.412
This Tempest at this Desert most was bent; Par Reg 4.465
Eternal tempest never to be calm'd. Samson 964
Chor. But this another kind of tempest brings. Samson 1063
And with thy tempest chase; Psalm 83, 58
Tempestuous
With Floods and Whirlwinds of tempestuous fire, Par Lost 1.77
Nor less on either side tempestuous fell Par Lost 6.844
Should prove tempestuous: To the Winds they set Par Lost 10.664
Temple
His Temple right against the Temple of God Par Lost 1.402
ms both 'temple'
Her Temple on th' offensive Mountain, built Par Lost 1.443
ms 'temple'
In his own Temple, on the grunsel edge, Par Lost 1.460
ms 'temple'
And downward Fish: yet had his Temple high Par Lost 1.463
ms 'temple'
Vice for it self: To him no Temple stood Par Lost 1.492
ms 'temple'
Built like a Temple, where *Pilasters* round Par Lost 1.713
ms 'temple'
Bright Temple, to *Aegyptian Theb*'s he flies. Par Lost 5.274
And Temple of his mightie Father Thron'd Par Lost 6.890
Though wide, and this high Temple to frequent Par Lost 7.148
Wandring, shall in a glorious Temple enshrine. Par Lost 12.334
Thir Citie, his Temple, and his holy Ark Par Lost 12.340
Upon the Temple it self: at last they seise Par Lost 12.356
I went into the Temple, there to hear Par Reg 1.211
By Vision, found thee in the Temple, and spake Par Reg 1.256
Worship't with Temple, Priest and Sacrifice; Par Reg 3.83
The Temple, oft the Law with foul affronts, Par Reg 3.161
Alone into the Temple; there was found Par Reg 4.217
And higher yet the glorious Temple rear'd Par Reg 4.546
Go to his Temple, invocate his aid Samson 1146
But who constrains me to the Temple of *Dagon*, Samson 1370
The unpolluted temple of the mind, Mask 461
The house of *Pindarus*, when Temple and Towre Sonnet 8, 11
Trinity ms 'temple''
Will towards thy holy temple worship low Psalm 5, 20
I in the temple of my God Psalm 84, 37
His Temple there is plac't. Psalm 87, 4
Temples
Before all Temples th' upright heart and pure, Par Lost 1.18
ms 'temples'
In Temples and at Altars, when the Priest Par Lost 1.494
ms 'temples'
His living Temples, built by Faith to stand, Par Lost 12.527
To approach thy Temples, give thee in command Par Reg 1.449
Forest and field, and flood, Temples and Towers Par Reg 3.268
With Towers and Temples proudly elevate Par Reg 4.34
Smote *Sisera* sleeping through the Temples nail'd. Samson 990
Present in Temples at Idolatrous Rites Samson 1378
Forsake their Temples dim, Nativity 198
For aye, with Temples vow'd, and Virgin quires. Prose 12, 6
Temporal
Then temporal death shall bruise the Victors heel, Par Lost 12.433
Tempt
Sufficient? who shall tempt with wandring feet Par Lost 2.404
To tempt or punish mortals, except whom Par Lost 2.1032
And tempt not these; but hast'n to appease Par Lost 5.846
May tempt it, I expected not to hear. Par Lost 9.281
Might tempt alone, and in her ears the sound Par Lost 9.736
To Satan; let him tempt and now assay Par Reg 1.143
Against whate're may tempt, whate're seduce, Par Reg 1.178
To tempt the Son of God with terrors dire. Par Reg 4.431
Tempt not the Lord thy God, he said and stood. Par Reg 4.561
Who durst so proudly tempt the Son of God. Par Reg 4.580

Tempt(*cont*)
In Paradise to tempt; his snares are broke: Par Reg 4.611
Why are his gifts desirable, to tempt Samson 358
Temptation
And all temptation to transgress repel. Par Lost 8.643
Against temptation: thou thy self with scorne Par Lost 9.299
Seek not temptation then, which to avoide Par Lost 9.364
His fraudulent temptation thus began. Par Lost 9.531
Through all temptation, and the Tempter foil'd Par Reg 1.5
Temptation and all guile on him to try; Par Reg 1.123
And with these words his temptation pursu'd. Par Reg 2.405
Proof against all temptation as a rock Par Reg 4.533
Over temptation, and the Tempter proud. Par Reg 4.595
Temptation, hast regain'd lost Paradise, Par Reg 4.608
Of Tempter and Temptation without fear. Par Reg 4.617
Temptation found'st, or over-potent charms Samson 427
And all temptation can remove, Samson 1051
Temptations
Or from without, to all temptations arm'd. Par Lost 4.65
But list'n not to his Temptations, warne Par Lost 6.908
His Godlike acts, and his temptations fierce, Passion 24
Tempted
Which tempted our attempt, and wrought our fall. Par Lost 1.642
Self-tempted, self-deprav'd: Man falls deceiv'd Par Lost 3.130
The tempted with dishonour foul, suppos'd Par Lost 9.297
Whoever tempted; which they not obeying, Par Lost 10.14
Who tempted me, that nothing was design'd Samson 801
Tempter
The Tempter ere th' Accuser of man-kind, Par Lost 4.10
So gloz'd the Tempter, and his Proem tun'd; Par Lost 9.549
To whom the guileful Tempter thus reply'd. Par Lost 9.567
To whom the Tempter guilefully repli'd. Par Lost 9.655
The Tempter, but with shew of Zeale and Love Par Lost 9.665
The Tempter all impassiond thus began. Par Lost 9.678
When first this Tempter cross'd the Gulf from Hell. Par Lost 10.39
Us'd by the Tempter: on that prospect strange Par Lost 10.552
Whereon for different cause the Tempter set Par Lost 11.382
Through all temptation, and the Tempter foil'd Par Reg 1.5
Such was the Splendour, and the Tempter now Par Reg 2.366
Only the importune Tempter still remain'd, Par Reg 2.404
To whom the Tempter murmuring thus reply'd. Par Reg 3.108
To whom the Tempter inly rackt reply'd. Par Reg 3.203
To this high mountain top the Tempter brought Par Reg 3.265
When thou stood'st up his Tempter to the pride Par Reg 3.409
The Tempter stood, nor had what to reply, Par Reg 4.2
And now the Tempter thus his silence broke. Par Reg 4.43
To whom the Tempter impudent repli'd. Par Reg 4.154
The Tempter watch'd, and soon with ugly dreams Par Reg 4.408
So after many a foil the Tempter proud, Par Reg 4.569
Over temptation, and the Tempter proud. Par Reg 4.595
Of Tempter and Temptation without fear. Par Reg 4.617
Tempting
The tempting stream, with one small drop to loose Par Lost 2.607
Tempting, stirr'd in me sudden appetite Par Lost 8.308
Tempting affronts us with his foul esteem Par Lost 9.328
Tempting so nigh, to pluck and eat my fill Par Lost 9.595
Still will be tempting him who foyls him still, Par Reg 4.13
be it not don in pride or in praesumption Mask Tr. ms 16.56
'or in praesumption' ←'or wilfull tempting'
Tempts
For hee who tempts, though in vain, at least asperses Par Lost 9.296
Yet Hope would fain subscribe, and tempts Belief. Samson 1535
Ten
Ten thousand Banners rise into the Air Par Lost 1.545
Fierce as ten Furies, terrible as Hell, Par Lost 2.671
Ten thousand fadom deep, and to this hour Par Lost 2.934
Blows them transverse ten thousand Leagues awry Par Lost 3.488
Ten thousand thousand Ensignes high advanc'd, Par Lost 5.588
Such ruin intercept: ten paces huge Par Lost 6.193
Attended with ten thousand thousand Saints, Par Lost 6.767
Grasping ten thousand Thunders, which he sent Par Lost 6.836
Symphonious of ten thousand Harpes that tun'd Par Lost 7.559
For this one Tree had bin forbidden ten. Par Lost 9.1026
The Poles of Earth twice ten degrees and more Par Lost 10.669
Ten thousandfould the sin of him who slew Par Lost 11.678
Of *Egypt* must lie dead. Thus with ten wounds Par Lost 12.190
Where will this end? four times ten days I have pass'd Par Reg 2.245
Deliverance of thy brethren, those ten Tribes Par Reg 3.374
Ten Sons of *Jacob*, two of *Joseph* lost Par Reg 3.377
My brethren, as thou call'st them; those Ten Tribes Par Reg 3.403
Of threescore and ten thousand *Israelites* Par Reg 3.411
That ten day-labourers could not end, Allegro 109
in ten thous Musick Tr. ms 4.16
ms defective
For he had any time this ten yeers full, Carrier 7
Tend
Casts pale and dreadful? Thither let us tend Par Lost 1.183
All Heav'n, what this might mean, and whither tend Par Lost 3.272
To prune these growing Plants, and tend these Flours, Par Lost 4.438
And flaming Ministers to watch and tend Par Lost 9.156
This Garden, still to tend Plant, Herb and Flour, Par Lost 9.206
The way which to her ruin now I tend. Par Lost 9.493
Unsuckt of Lamb or Kid, that tend thir play. Par Lost 9.583
Shall tend thee, and the fertil burden ease Par Lost 9.801
Still tend from bad to worse, till God at last Par Lost 12.106
May ever tend about thee to old age Samson 925
Man. It shall be my delight to tend his eyes, Samson 1490

Tend(*cont*)
To tend the homely slighted Shepherds trade, Lycidas 65
1673 'end'
Tendance
And toucht by her fair tendance gladlier grew. Par Lost 8.47
Thir tendance or Plantation for delight Par Lost 9.419
Tended
Our tended Plants, how blows the Citron Grove, Par Lost 5.22
Tended the sick busiest from Couch to Couch; Par Lost 11.490
Or active, tended on by glory, or fame, Par Reg 4.371
Tender
Grasing the tender herb, were interpos'd, Par Lost 4.253
Bestirs her then, and from each tender stalk Par Lost 5.337
Brought forth the tender Grass, whose verdure clad Par Lost 7.315
Not then mistrust, but tender love enjoynes, Par Lost 9.357
At Eev'n, which I bred up with tender hand Par Lost 11.276
But tender all their power? nor mention I Par Reg 2.327
To such a tender ball as th' eye confin'd? Samson 94
And here their tender age might suffer perill, Mask 40
Plucking ripe clusters from the tender shoots, Mask 296
Which when I did, he on the tender grass Mask 624
He touch'd the tender stops of various Quills, Lycidas 188
So have I seen som tender slip Winchester 35
Out of the tender mouths of latest bearth, Psalm 8, 4
Her Grapes and tender Shoots. Psalm 80, 56
Tenderest
Mangle my apprehensive tenderest parts, Samson 624
Tenderly
Tenderly wept, much won that he his Love Par Lost 9.991
Tending
As neerer to him plac't or neerer tending Par Lost 5.476
Tending to wilde. Thou therefore now advise Par Lost 9.212
To Paradise first tending, when behold Par Lost 10.326
Tending to some relief of our extremes, Par Lost 10.976
Some other tending, in his hand Samson 1302
Tending my flocks hard by i' th hilly crofts, Mask 531
Bridgewater ms 'tendinge'
Tendrils
As the Vine curles her tendrils, which impli'd Par Lost 4.307
Tends
Fair Angel, thy desire which tends to know Par Lost 3.694
Shelters in coole, and tends his pasturing Herds Par Lost 9.1109
Tenement
Of *Socrates*, see there his Tenement, Par Reg 4.274
Teneriff
Like *Teneriff* or *Atlas* unremov'd: Par Lost 4.987
Tenfold
So speaking and so threatning, grew tenfold Par Lost 2.705
1667 'ten fold'
Tenfold the length of this terrene: at last Par Lost 6.78
Of tenfold Adamant, his ample Shield Par Lost 6.255
And felt tenfold confusion in thir fall Par Lost 6.872
Within thick Clouds and dark ten-fold involv'd, Par Reg 1.41
Tenor
But still I see the tenor of Mans woe Par Lost 11.632
Tent
The Heav'nly fires; over the Tent a Cloud Par Lost 12.256
Tenth
He back recoild; the tenth on bended knee Par Lost 6.194
Tents
Thir glittering Tents he passd, and now is come Par Lost 5.291
These wicked Tents devoted, least the wrauth Par Lost 5.890
Were Tents of various hue; by some were herds Par Lost 11.557
Long had not walkt, when from the Tents behold Par Lost 11.581
With Feast and Musick all the Tents resound. Par Lost 11.592
Those Tents thou sawst so pleasant, were the Tents Par Lost 11.607
Contending, and remov'd his Tents farr off; Par Lost 11.727
Canaan he now attains, I see his Tents Par Lost 12.135
The clouded Ark of God till then in Tents Par Lost 12.333
The tents of Edom, and the brood Psalm 83, 21
Then dwell in Tents, *and rich abode* Psalm 84, 39
Tepid
Mean while the tepid Caves, and Fens and shoares Par Lost 7.417
Terah
When the blest seed of *Terah*'s faithfull Son, Psalm 114, 1
Teredon
Artaxata, *Teredon*, *Tesiphon*, Par Reg 3.292
Term
Too long vacation hastned on his term. Another 14
1640 '*Terme*'
1657 '*Term*'
line not in 1658 text
Termed
Which if Heav'n gave it, may be term'd her own: Mask 419
Bridgewater ms 'tearm'd'
Terms
Irreparable; tearms of peace yet none Par Lost 2.331
And Brest, (what could we more2) propounded terms Par Lost 6.612
Leader, the terms we sent were terms of weight, Par Lost 6.621
Though in mysterious terms, judg'd as then best: Par Lost 10.173
Thy terms too hard, by which I was to hold Par Lost 10.751
Those terms whatever, when they were propos'd: Par Lost 10.757
The abominable terms, impious condition; Par Reg 4.173
With Hymns, our Psalms with artful terms inscrib'd, Par Reg 4.335
With that which you receiv'd on other terms, Mask 684
line not in Bridgewater ms
1637 'termes'

Ternate
Of *Ternate* and *Tidore*, whence Merchants bring Par Lost 2.639
Terrace
With many a tower and terrass round, Mask 935
1673 'terras'
Trinity ms 'terrace'
1637 'terrasse'
Bridgewater ms 'terrace'
Terraces
Turrets and Terrases, and glittering Spires. Par Reg 4.54
Terrene
Tenfold the length of this terrene: at last Par Lost 6.78
Terrestrial
Produces with Terrestrial Humor mixt Par Lost 3.610
To the terrestrial Moon be as a Starr Par Lost 8.142
Terrestrial Heav'n, danc't round by other Heav'ns Par Lost 9.103
Heroic built, though of terrestrial mould, Par Lost 9.485
Terrible
Fierce as ten Furies, terrible as Hell, Par Lost 2.671
That dar'st, though grim and terrible, advance Par Lost 2.682
Presented stood in terrible array Par Lost 6.106
By terrible Example the reward Par Lost 6.910
Not terrible, though terrour be in Love Par Lost 9.490
Invests him coming? yet not terrible, Par Lost 11.233
More terrible at th' entrance then within. Par Lost 11.470
And sweet allay'd, yet terrible to approach, Par Reg 2.160
Terrific
And hairie Main terrific, though to thee Par Lost 7.497
Terrified
The Son of God to judge them terrifi'd Par Lost 10.338
Terrify
Warr terrifie them inexpert, and feare Par Lost 12.218
Allure, or terrifie, or undermine. Par Reg 1.179
And storm'st refus'd, thinking to terrifie Par Reg 4.496
Territory
He lookd and saw wide Territorie spred Par Lost 11.638
Whose off-spring in his Territory yet serve Par Reg 3.375
In ample Territory, wealth and power, Par Reg 4.82
Terror
Who from the terrour of this Arm so late Par Lost 1.113
ms 'terror'
Terror of Heav'n, though fall'n; intend at home, Par Lost 2.457
Medusa with *Gorgonian* terror guards Par Lost 2.611
So spake the grieslie terrour, and in shape, Par Lost 2.704
Abandond at the terror of thy Power Par Lost 6.134
Be sure, and terrour seis'd the rebel Host, Par Lost 6.647
So spake the Son, and into terrour chang'd Par Lost 6.824
Not terrible, though terrour be in Love Par Lost 9.490
With terror through the dark Aereal Hall. Par Lost 10.667
All things with double terror: On the Ground Par Lost 10.850
Bewailing thir excess, all terror hide. Par Lost 11.111
Of terrour, foul and ugly to behold, Par Lost 11.464
And terror cease; he grants what they besaught Par Lost 12.238
Unshaken; nor yet staid the terror there, Par Reg 4.421
Shall chase thee with the terror of his voice Par Reg 4.627
With terrour of that blast, Nativity 161
With terror sent from thee; Psalm 88, 60
Terrors
A fresh with conscious terrours vex me round, Par Lost 2.801
With terrors and with clamors compasst round Par Lost 2.862
Thy terrors, as I put thy mildness on, Par Lost 6.735
With terrors and with furies to the bounds Par Lost 6.859
To tempt the Son of God with terrors dire. Par Reg 4.431
So many terrors, voices, prodigies Par Reg 4.482
Those terrors which thou speak'st of, did me none; Par Reg 4.487
While I thy terrors undergo Psalm 88, 63
Tesiphon
Artaxata, *Teredon*, *Tesiphon*, Par Reg 3.292
Test
Avow, and challenge *Dagon* to the test, Samson 1151
Testified
And testifi'd against thir wayes; hee oft Par Lost 11.721
Testifies
As this place testifies, and this dire change Par Lost 1.625
Testify
To testifie his hidd'n residence; Mask 248
To testifie the arms of Chastity? Mask 440
I testifie to thee Psalm 81, 34
Testimony
And for the testimonie of Truth hast born Par Lost 6.33
An Ark, and in the Ark his Testimony, Par Lost 12.251
The testimony of Heaven, that who he is Par Reg 1.78
This he a Testimony ordain'd Psalm 81, 17
Tethys
And *Tethys* grave majestick pace, Mask 870
Bridgewater ms 'Tethis'
Tetrachordon
A Book was writ of late call'd *Tetrachordon;* Sonnet 11, 1
Tetrarchs
Tetrarchs of fire, air, flood, and on the earth Par Reg 4.201
Texture
Nor in thir liquid texture mortal wound Par Lost 6.348
Of richest texture spred, at th' upper end Par Lost 10.446
Th
Each cast at th' other, as when two black Clouds Par Lost 2.714
Th' unarmed Youth of Heav'n, but nigh at hand Par Lost 4.552
Through all th' Empyreal road; till at the Gate Par Lost 5.253
Th' Assessor of his Throne he thus began. Par Lost 6.679

Th(*cont*)
Will be aveng'd, and th' others Faith approv'd Par Lost 11.458
Thame
Or *Medway* smooth, or Royal Towred *Thame*. Vacation 100
Thammuz
To Idols foul. *Thammuz* came next behind, Par Lost 1.446
ms 'Thammuz'
Of *Thammuz* yearly wounded: the Love-tale Par Lost 1.452
ms 'Thammuz'
In vain the *Tyrian* Maids their wounded *Thamuz* mourn. Nativity 204
Thamyris
Blind *Thamyris* and blind *Maeonides*, Par Lost 3.35
Than
Then such could hav orepow'rd such force as ours) Par Lost 1.145
And what I should be, all but less then he Par Lost 1.257
Better to reign in Hell, then serve in Heav'n. Par Lost 1.263
Rather then human. Nor did *Israel* scape Par Lost 1.482
Belial came last, then whom a Spirit more lewd Par Lost 1.490
Or Altar smoak'd; yet who more oft then hee Par Lost 1.493
Gods, yet confest later then Heav'n and Earth Par Lost 1.509
Could merit more then that small infantry Par Lost 1.575
Less then Arch Angel ruind, and th' excess Par Lost 1.593
Then aught divine or holy else enjoy'd Par Lost 1.683
Now less then smallest Dwarfs, in narrow room Par Lost 1.779
More glorious and more dread then from no fall, Par Lost 2.16
More then can be in Heav'n, we now return Par Lost 2.37
Surer to prosper then prosperity Par Lost 2.39
Equal in strength, and rather then be less Par Lost 2.47
Then to dwell here, driv'n out from bliss, condemn'd Par Lost 2.86
Calls us to Penance? More destroy'd then thus Par Lost 2.92
Then miserable to have eternal being: Par Lost 2.98
To less then Gods. On th' other side up rose Par Lost 2.108
Then wise to frustrate all our plots and wiles. Par Lost 2.193
Chains and these Torments? better these then worse Par Lost 2.196
They dreaded worse then Hell: so much the fear Par Lost 2.293
Which when *Beelzebub* perceiv'd, then whom, Par Lost 2.299
Then unknown dangers and as hard escape. Par Lost 2.444
Dreaded not more th' adventure then his voice Par Lost 2.474
Than Hells dread Emperour with pomp Supream, Par Lost 2.510
1667 'Then'
Than Fables yet have feign'd, or fear conceiv'd, Par Lost 2.627
1667 'Then'
Within unseen. Farr less abhorrd than these Par Lost 2.659
1667 'then'
Sight more detestable then him and thee. Par Lost 2.745
Inflam'd with lust then rage) and swifter far, Par Lost 2.791
Then this more secret now design'd, I haste Par Lost 2.838
Great things with small) then when *Bellona* storms, Par Lost 2.922
Som Capital City; or less then if this frame Par Lost 2.924
And more endanger'd, then when *Argo* pass'd Par Lost 2.1017
With other notes then to th' *Orphean* Lyre Par Lost 3.17
By Merit more then Birthright Son of God, Par Lost 3.309
Farr more then Great or High; because in thee Par Lost 3.311
Love hath abounded more then Glory abounds, Par Lost 3.312
Love no where to be found less then Divine! Par Lost 3.411
Wider by farr then that of after-times Par Lost 3.529
Imagind rather oft then elsewhere seen, Par Lost 3.599
One step no more then from himself can fly Par Lost 4.22
What could be less then to afford him praise, Par Lost 4.46
Then to submit, boasting I could subdue Par Lost 4.85
By thee, and more then half perhaps will reigne; Par Lost 4.112
Saw him disfigur'd, more then could befall Par Lost 4.127
Of stateliest view. Yet higher then thir tops Par Lost 4.142
And higher then that Wall a circling row Par Lost 4.146
Then in fair Evening Cloud, or humid Bow, Par Lost 4.151
Then *Asmodeus* with the fishie fume, Par Lost 4.168
Of thir sweet Gardning labour then suffic'd Par Lost 4.328
Dearer thy self then all; needs must the power Par Lost 4.412
From us no other service then to keep Par Lost 4.420
Then that smooth watry image; back I turnd, Par Lost 4.480
More hands then ours to lop thir wanton growth: Par Lost 4.629
Broiderd the ground, more colour'd then with stone Par Lost 4.702
More lovely then *Pandora*, whom the Gods Par Lost 4.714
Less pain, less to be fled, or thou then they Par Lost 4.919
Patron of liberty, who more then thou Par Lost 4.958
Then Heav'n permits, nor mine, though doubld now Par Lost 4.1009
Much fairer to my Fancie then by day: Par Lost 5.53
Then when fair Morning first smiles on the World, Par Lost 5.124
More tuneable then needed Lute or Harp Par Lost 5.151
Earths inmost womb, more warmth then *Adam* needs; Par Lost 5.302
Accompani'd then with his own compleat Par Lost 5.352
More solemn then the tedious pomp that waits Par Lost 5.354
None can then Heav'n such glorious shape contain; Par Lost 5.362
Then Wood-Nymph, or the fairest Goddess feign'd Par Lost 5.381
Then with these various fruits the Trees of God Par Lost 5.390
Divine instructer, I have heard, then when Par Lost 5.546
Each to other like, more then on earth is thought? Par Lost 5.576
Then all this globous Earth in Plain out spred, Par Lost 5.649
Then what this Garden is to all the Earth, Par Lost 5.752
Abdiel, then whom none with more zeale ador'd Par Lost 5.805
Of Truth, in word mightier then they in Armes; Par Lost 6.32
Then violence: for this was all thy care Par Lost 6.35
Then scornd thou didst depart, and to subdue Par Lost 6.40
Receive, no more then can the fluid Aire: Par Lost 6.349
Two potent Thrones, that to be less then Gods Par Lost 6.366
No less then for deliverance what we owe. Par Lost 6.468
Of Angels, then that Starr the Starrs among) Par Lost 7.133
Then time or motion, but to human ears Par Lost 7.177

Than(*cont*)
Then from the Giant Angels; thee that day Par Lost 7.605
Is greater then created to destroy. Par Lost 7.607
Serv'd by more noble then her self, attaines Par Lost 8.34
More plenty then the Sun that barren shines, Par Lost 8.94
Then Fruits of Palm-tree pleasantest to thirst Par Lost 8.212
Then of our fellow servant, and inquire Par Lost 8.225
Noise, other then the sound of Dance or Song, Par Lost 8.243
Pleas'd with thy words no less then thou with mine. Par Lost 8.248
And feel that I am happier then I know, Par Lost 8.282
Above mankinde, or aught then mankinde higher, Par Lost 8.358
More then enough; at least on her bestow'd Par Lost 8.537
Then self esteem, grounded on just and right Par Lost 8.572
More grateful then harmonious sound to the eare. Par Lost 8.606
Easier then Air with Air, if Spirits embrace, Par Lost 8.626
Not less but more Heroic then the wrauth Par Lost 9.14
Not longer then since I in one Night freed Par Lost 9.140
In Woman, then to studie houshold good, Par Lost 9.233
Conjugal Love, then which perhaps no bliss Par Lost 9.263
Us both securer then thus warnd thou seemst, Par Lost 9.371
Spot more delicious then those Gardens feign'd Par Lost 9.439
Then at *Circean* call the Herd disguis'd. Par Lost 9.522
Then smell of sweetest Fenel or the Teats Par Lost 9.581
And life more perfet have attaind then Fate Par Lost 9.689
Meant mee, by ventring higher then my Lot. Par Lost 9.690
Though threat'nd, which no worse then this can bring. Par Lost 9.715
Rather then Death or aught then Death more dread Par Lost 9.969
Deserted, then oblige thee with a fact Par Lost 9.980
Then ever, bountie of this vertuous Tree. Par Lost 9.1033
Till *Adam*, though not less then *Eve* abash't, Par Lost 9.1065
Now Dragon grown, larger then whom the Sun Par Lost 10.529
Climbing, sat thicker then the snakie locks Par Lost 10.559
Then stil at Hels dark threshold to have sate watch, Par Lost 10.594
Inhabited, though sinless, more then now, Par Lost 10.690
That burden heavier then the Earth to bear Par Lost 10.835
Then all the World much heavier, though divided Par Lost 10.836
Rather then solid vertu, all but a Rib Par Lost 10.884
On me alreadie lost, mee then thy self Par Lost 10.929
And torment less then none of what we dread, Par Lost 10.998
And excellent then what thy minde contemnes; Par Lost 10.1015
Hath wiselier arm'd his vengeful ire then so Par Lost 10.1023
What better can we do, then to the place Par Lost 10.1086
Then loudest Oratorie: yet thir port Par Lost 11.8
Seem'd thir Petition, then when th' ancient Pair Par Lost 11.10
In Fables old, less ancient yet then these, Par Lost 11.11
Sow'n with contrition in his heart, then those Par Lost 11.27
My motions in him, longer then they move, Par Lost 11.91
Spangl'd with eyes more numerous then those Par Lost 11.130
Of *Argus*, and more wakeful then to drouze, Par Lost 11.131
Who knows, or more then this, that we are dust, Par Lost 11.199
Livelier then *Meliboean*, or the graine Par Lost 11.242
O unexpected stroke, worse then of Death! Par Lost 11.268
No more availes then breath against the winde, Par Lost 11.312
More terrible at th' entrance then within. Par Lost 11.470
Of peaceful dayes portends, then those two past; Par Lost 11.600
In apprehension then in substance feel Par Lost 11.775
Peace to corrupt no less then Warr to waste. Par Lost 11.784
More then enough, that temperance may be tri'd: Par Lost 11.805
Of wicked Sons destroyd, then I rejoyce Par Lost 11.875
Then temporal death shall bruise the Victors heel, Par Lost 12.433
Longer on Earth then certaine times to appeer Par Lost 12.437
Then this of *Eden*, and far happier daies. Par Lost 12.465
Then that which by creation first brought forth Par Lost 12.472
Wors with his followers then with him they dealt? Par Lost 12.484
More awful then the sound of Trumpet, cri'd Par Reg 1.19
This our old Conquest, then remember Hell Par Reg 1.46
More then the Camel, and to drink go far, Par Reg 1.340
(For I discern thee other then thou seem'st) Par Reg 1.348
What can be then less in me then desire Par Reg 1.383
So never more in Hell then when in Heaven. Par Reg 1.420
Threat'ns then our expulsion down to Hell; Par Reg 2.128
1671 printed 'Threat'ns our', errata 'Threat'ns then our'
Then when I dealt with *Adam* first of Men, Par Reg 2.133
With more then humane gifts from Heaven adorn'd, Par Reg 2.137
Then Mortal Creatures, graceful and discreet, Par Reg 2.157
Higher design then to enjoy his State; Par Reg 2.203
Then *Solomon*, of more exalted mind, Par Reg 2.206
Then *Ganymed* or *Hylas*, distant more Par Reg 2.353
Fairer then feign'd of old, or fabl'd since Par Reg 2.358
Longer then thou canst feed them on thy cost? Par Reg 2.421
Then prompt her to do aught may merit praise. Par Reg 2.456
Far more magnanimous, then to assume. Par Reg 2.483
Then those thir Conquerours, who leave behind Par Reg 3.78
Then glory and benediction, that is thanks, Par Reg 3.127
Of worse torments me then the feeling can. Par Reg 3.208
Rather then aggravate my evil state, Par Reg 3.218
(Whose ire I dread more then the fire of Hell) Par Reg 3.220
Of human weakness rather then of strength. Par Reg 3.402
Besides thir other worse then heathenish crimes; Par Reg 3.419
Then great and glorious *Rome*, Queen of the Earth Par Reg 4.45
Aim therefore at no less then all the world, Par Reg 4.105
More then of arms before, allure mine eye, Par Reg 4.112
Or nothing more then still to contradict: Par Reg 4.158
For this attempt bolder then that on *Eve*, Par Reg 4.180
Then these thou bear'st that title, have propos'd Par Reg 4.199
Then to a worldly Crown, addicted more Par Reg 4.213
Then all the Oratory of *Greece* and *Rome*. Par Reg 4.360
Mee worse then wet thou find'st not; other harm Par Reg 4.486

Than(*cont*)

Therefore to know what more thou art then man, Par Reg 4.538
Lower then bondslave! Promise was that I Samson 38
Blind among enemies, O worse then chains, Samson 68
Scarce half I seem to live, dead more then half. Samson 79
In me, of wisdom nothing more then mean; Samson 207
Then of thine own Tribe fairer, or as fair, Samson 217
Then to love Bondage more then Liberty, Samson 270
Bondage with ease then strenuous liberty; Samson 271
Not worse then by his shield and spear Samson 284
Then undissembl'd hate) with what contempt Samson 400
True slavery, and that blindness worse then this, Samson 418
By pains and slaveries, worse then death inflicted Samson 485
Then who self-rigorous chooses death as due; Samson 513
For self-offence, more then for God offended. Samson 515
Wherewith to serve him better then thou hast; Samson 585
Nor less then wounds immedicable Samson 620
But throw'st them lower then thou didst exalt them high, Samson 689
Then *Dalila* thy wife. Samson 724
In the perverse event then I foresaw) Samson 737
More strength from me, then in thy self was found. Samson 789
No better way I saw then by importuning Samson 797
By worse then hostile deeds, violating the ends Samson 893
To prayers, then winds and seas, yet winds to seas Samson 961
Not less renown'd then in Mount *Ephraim*, Samson 988
I less conjecture then when first I saw Samson 1071
Then thine, while I preserv'd these locks unshorn, Samson 1143
Much more affliction then already felt Samson 1257
More then the working day thy hands, Samson 1299
More Lordly thund'ring then thou well wilt bear. Samson 1353
Though thou wert firmlier fastn'd then a rock. Samson 1398
With youthful steps? much livelier then e're while Samson 1442
To live the poorest in my Tribe, then richest, Samson 1479
Made older then thy age through eye-sight lost. Samson 1489
More then anough we know; but while things yet Samson 1592
Then all thy life had slain before. Samson 1668
But boast themselves more comely then before Mask 75
La. No less then if I should my brothers loose. Mask 288
Their port was more then human, as they stood; Mask 297
With smoaky rafters, then in tapstry Halls Mask 324
Less warranted then this, or less secure Mask 327
That I encline to hope, rather then fear, Mask 412
And yet more med'cinal is it then that *Moly* Mask 636
line not in Bridgewater ms
More happines then this thy present lot. Mask 789
line not in Bridgewater ms
line not in Trinity ms
Then her purfl'd scarf can shew, Mask 995
B.M. ms 'than'
Higher then the Spheary chime; Mask 1021
B.M. ms 'than'
Where more is meant then meets the ear. Penseroso 120
Less then half we find exprest, Arcades 12
Then how to scramble at the shearers feast, Lycidas 117
Then his bright Throne, or burning Axletree could bear. Nativity 84
Dangers, and snares, and wrongs, and worse then so, Passion 11
Which is no more then what is false and vain, On Time 5
More then she could own from Earth. Winchester 6
Though later born, then to have known the dayes Sonnet 10, 9
End Green. Why is it harder Sirs then Gordon, Sonnet 11, 8
Hated not Learning wors then Toad or Asp; Sonnet 11, 13
Then his *Casella*, whom he woo'd to sing, Sonnet 13, 13
No less renownd then warr, new foes arise Sonnet 16, 11
1694 'than those of War'
Then whome a better Senatour nere held Sonnet 17, 2
Your plots and packing wors then those of *Trent*, Forcers 14
Then when a year of glut Psalm 4, 33
Scarce to be less then Gods, thou mad'st his lot, Psalm 8, 15
Then *in the joyes of Vanity*, Psalm 84, 35
Then dwell in Tents, *and rich abode* Psalm 84, 39
Far worse then fire to burn. Psalm 85, 12
Then all the dwellings *faire* Psalm 87, 6
Stronglier, and better oft then earnest can. Prose 7, 2
What can be juster in a State then this? Prose 9, 5
Then an unjust and wicked King Prose 11, 3

Thank

Thank him who puts me loath to this revenge Par Lost 4.386
For this we may thank *Adam;* but his thanks Par Lost 10.736
And thank the gods amiss. I should be loath Mask 177
Bridgewater ms 'thanke'
1637 'thanke'
Trinity ms 'thanke'

Thanked

And then the giver would be better thank't, Mask 775
Trinity ms 'thankt'

Thankless

And strictly meditate the thankles Muse, Lycidas 66
1673 'thankless'
1638 'thanklesse'
Trinity ms 'thanklesse'

Thanks

The easiest recompence, and pay him thanks, Par Lost 4.47
And daily thanks, I chiefly who enjoy Par Lost 4.445
Immortal thanks, and his admonishment Par Lost 7.77
What thanks sufficient, or what recompence Par Lost 8.5
For this we may thank *Adam;* but his thanks Par Lost 10.736
Then glory and benediction, that is thanks, Par Reg 3.127
A better soyl shall give ye thanks. Arcades 101

That

Of that Forbidden Tree, whose mortal tast Par Lost 1.2
Sing Heav'nly Muse, that on the secret top Par Lost 1.6
That Shepherd, who first taught the chosen Seed, Par Lost 1.8
Delight thee more, and *Siloa's* Brook that flow'd Par Lost 1.11
That with no middle flight intends to soar Par Lost 1.14
And chiefly Thou O Spirit, that dost prefer Par Lost 1.17
That to the highth of this great Argument Par Lost 1.24
Mov'd our Grand Parents in that happy State, Par Lost 1.29
Who first seduc'd them to that foul revolt? Par Lost 1.33
Nine times the Space that measures Day and Night Par Lost 1.50
That witness'd huge affliction and dismay Par Lost 1.57
That comes to all; but torture without end Par Lost 1.67
Though chang'd in outward lustre; that fixt mind Par Lost 1.97
That with the mightiest rais'd me to contend, Par Lost 1.99
That durst dislike his reign, and me preferring, Par Lost 1.102
That Glory never shall his wrath or might Par Lost 1.110
Doubted his Empire, that were low indeed, Par Lost 1.114
That were an ignominy and shame beneath Par Lost 1.115
That led th' imbattelld Seraphim to Warr Par Lost 1.129
That with sad overthrow and foul defeat Par Lost 1.135
That we may so suffice his vengeful ire, Par Lost 1.148
Our labour must be to pervert that end, Par Lost 1.164
The fiery Surge, that from the Precipice Par Lost 1.173
That sparkling blaz'd, his other Parts besides Par Lost 1.194
Titanian, or *Earth-born*, that warr'd on *Jove*, Par Lost 1.198
By ancient *Tarsus* held, or that Sea-beast Par Lost 1.200
Created hugest that swim th' Ocean stream: Par Lost 1.202
Had ris'n or heav'd his head, but that the will Par Lost 1.211
That with reiterated crimes he might Par Lost 1.214
That felt unusual weight, till on dry Land Par Lost 1.227
He lights, if it were Land that ever burn'd Par Lost 1.228
That we must change for Heav'n, this mournful gloom Par Lost 1.244
For that celestial light? Be it so, since he Par Lost 1.245
If once they hear that voyce, thir liveliest pledge Par Lost 1.274
Of that inflamed Sea, he stood and call'd Par Lost 1.300
Thick as Autumnal Leaves that strow the Brooks Par Lost 1.302
He call'd so loud, that all the hollow Deep Par Lost 1.314
That ore the Realm of impious *Pharaoh* hung Par Lost 1.342
And Powers that earst in Heaven sat on Thrones; Par Lost 1.360
Glory of him that made them, to transform Par Lost 1.370
Rous'd from the slumber, on that fiery Couch, Par Lost 1.377
Thir childrens cries unheard, that past through fire Par Lost 1.395
On that opprobrious Hill, and made his Grove Par Lost 1.403
Even to that Hill of scandal, by the Grove Par Lost 1.416
Of old *Euphrates* to the Brook that parts Par Lost 1.420
By that uxorious King, whose heart though large, Par Lost 1.444
Doubl'd that sin in *Bethel* and in *Dan*, Par Lost 1.485
Witness the Streets of *Sodom*, and that night Par Lost 1.503
Soon recollecting, with high words, that bore Par Lost 1.528
Then strait commands that at the warlike sound Par Lost 1.531
His mighty Standard; that proud honour claim'd Par Lost 1.533
A shout that tore Hells Concave, and beyond Par Lost 1.542
Mov'd on in silence to soft Pipes that charm'd Par Lost 1.561
Could merit more then that small infantry Par Lost 1.575
That fought at *Theb's* and *Ilium*, on each side Par Lost 1.578
Matchless, but with th' Almighty, and that strife Par Lost 1.623
That all these puissant Legions, whose exile Par Lost 1.632
What force effected not: that he no less Par Lost 1.647
There went a fame in Heav'n that he ere long Par Lost 1.651
That in his womb was hid metallic Ore, Par Lost 1.673
Mammon, the least erected Spirit that fell Par Lost 1.679
That riches grow in Hell; that soyle may best Par Lost 1.691
That underneath had veins of liquid fire Par Lost 1.701
Throng numberless, like that Pigmean Race Par Lost 1.780
Of that infernal Court. But far within Par Lost 1.792
To that bad eminence; and from despair Par Lost 2.6
Of present pain, that with ambitious mind Par Lost 2.34
That fought in Heav'n; now fiercer by despair: Par Lost 2.45
Car'd not to be at all; with that care lost Par Lost 2.48
Millions that stand in Arms, and longing wait Par Lost 2.55
Of that forgetful Lake benumm not still, Par Lost 2.74
That in our proper motion we ascend Par Lost 2.75
With Armed watch, that render all access Par Lost 2.130
And that must end us, that must be our cure, Par Lost 2.145
Those thoughts that wander through Eternity, Par Lost 2.148
Is doubtful; that he never will is sure. Par Lost 2.154
Chain'd on the burning Lake? that sure was worse. Par Lost 2.169
What if the breath that kindl'd those grim fires Par Lost 2.170
That so ordains: this was at first resolv'd, Par Lost 2.201
And vent'rous, if that fail them, shrink and fear Par Lost 2.205
And know not that the King of Heav'n hath doom'd Par Lost 2.316
That shook Heav'ns whol circumference, confirm'd. Par Lost 2.353
Seduce them to our Party, that thir God Par Lost 2.368
And hard, that out of Hell leads up to light; Par Lost 2.433
Threatens him, plung'd in that abortive gulf. Par Lost 2.441
That for the general safety he despis'd Par Lost 2.481
Attest thir joy, that hill and valley rings. Par Lost 2.495
That day and night for his destruction waite. Par Lost 2.505
By doom of Battel; and complain that Fate Par Lost 2.550
That dismal world, if any Clime perhaps Par Lost 2.572
Of four infernal Rivers that disgorge Par Lost 2.575
A gulf profound as that *Serbonian* Bog Par Lost 2.592
Vex'd *Scylla* bathing in the Sea that parts Par Lost 2.660
If shape it might be call'd that shape had none Par Lost 2.667
Or substance might be call'd that shadow seem'd, Par Lost 2.669
That dar'st, though grim and terrible, advance Par Lost 2.682
That be assur'd, without leave askt of thee: Par Lost 2.685

That(*cont*)
Art thou that Traitor Angel, art thou hee, Par Lost 2.689
That fires the length of *Ophiucus* huge Par Lost 2.709
So frownd the mighty Combatants, that Hell Par Lost 2.719
Had not the Snakie Sorceress that sat Par Lost 2.724
Possesses thee to bend that mortal Dart Par Lost 2.729
Thou interposest, that my sudden hand Par Lost 2.738
Me Father, and that Fantasm call'st my Son? Par Lost 2.743
With me in secret, that my womb conceiv'd Par Lost 2.766
Tore through my entrails, that with fear and pain Par Lost 2.783
Ingendring with me, of that rape begot Par Lost 2.794
These yelling Monsters that with ceasless cry Par Lost 2.795
That bred them they return, and howle and gnaw Par Lost 2.799
That rest or intermission none I find. Par Lost 2.802
For want of other prey, but that he knows Par Lost 2.806
His end with mine involvd; and knows that I Par Lost 2.807
When ever that shall be; so Fate pronounc'd. Par Lost 2.809
Though temper'd heav'nly, for that mortal dint, Par Lost 2.813
Of Spirits that in our just pretenses arm'd Par Lost 2.825
Destin'd to that good hour: no less rejoyc'd Par Lost 2.848
Of mine own brood, that on my bowels feed: Par Lost 2.863
To that new world of light and bliss, among Par Lost 2.867
Harsh Thunder, that the lowest bottom shook Par Lost 2.882
That with extended wings a Bannerd Host Par Lost 2.885
Audacious, but that seat soon failing, meets Par Lost 2.931
As many miles aloft: that furie stay'd, Par Lost 2.938
Might in that noise reside, of whom to ask Par Lost 2.957
To your behoof, if I that Region lost, Par Lost 2.982
That mighty leading Angel, who of late Par Lost 2.991
That little which is left so to defend, Par Lost 2.1000
To that side Heav'n from whence your Legions fell: Par Lost 2.1006
If that way be your walk, you have not farr; Par Lost 2.1007
But glad that now his Sea should find a shore, Par Lost 2.1011
That *Satan* with less toil, and now with ease Par Lost 2.1041
In that obscure sojourn, while in my flight Par Lost 3.15
Revisit'st not these eyes, that rowle in vain Par Lost 3.23
That wash thy hallowd feet, and warbling flow, Par Lost 3.31
Then feed on thoughts, that voluntarie move Par Lost 3.37
Purge and disperse, that I may see and tell Par Lost 3.54
On the bare outside of this World, that seem'd Par Lost 3.74
On desparate reveng, that shall redound Par Lost 3.85
O Father, gracious was that word which clos'd Par Lost 3.144
Thy sovran sentence, that Man should find grace; Par Lost 3.145
With his own folly? that be from thee farr, Par Lost 3.153
That farr be from thee, Father, who art Judg Par Lost 3.154
By me upheld, that he may know how frail Par Lost 3.180
That they may stumble on, and deeper fall; Par Lost 3.201
Much less that durst upon his own head draw Par Lost 3.220
And shall grace not find means, that finds her way, Par Lost 3.228
All that of me can die, yet that debt paid, Par Lost 3.246
Though last created, that for him I spare Par Lost 3.278
All knees to thee shall bow, of them that bide Par Lost 3.321
With these that never fade the Spirits elect Par Lost 3.360
Pavement that like a Sea of Jasper shon Par Lost 3.363
Harps ever tun'd, that glittering by thir side Par Lost 3.366
Yet dazle Heav'n, that brightest Seraphim Par Lost 3.381
Th' aspiring Dominations: thou that day Par Lost 3.392
Nor stop thy flaming Chariot wheels, that shook Par Lost 3.394
Save on that side which from the wall of Heav'n Par Lost 3.427
Here Pilgrims roam, that stray'd so farr to seek Par Lost 3.476
And that Crystalline Sphear whose ballance weighs Par Lost 3.482
The Trepidation talkt, and that first mov'd; Par Lost 3.483
Wider by farr then that of after-times Par Lost 3.529
Over Mount *Sion*, and, though that were large, Par Lost 3.530
That scal'd by steps of Gold to Heav'n Gate Par Lost 3.541
Of *Libra* to the fleecie Starr that bears Par Lost 3.558
Amongst innumerable Starrs, that shon Par Lost 3.565
That from his Lordly eye keep distance due, Par Lost 3.578
Thir Starry dance in numbers that compute Par Lost 3.580
By his Magnetic beam, that gently warms Par Lost 3.583
Rubie or Topaz, to the Twelve that shon Par Lost 3.597
That stone, or like to that which here below Par Lost 3.600
That run through all the Heav'ns, or down to th' Earth Par Lost 3.651
Uriel, for thou of those seav'n Spirits that stand Par Lost 3.654
That I may find him, and with secret gaze, Par Lost 3.671
That both in him and all things, as is meet, Par Lost 3.675
To deepest Hell, and to repair that loss Par Lost 3.678
Hypocrisie, the onely evil that walks Par Lost 3.683
That reaches blame, but rather merits praise Par Lost 3.697
The more it seems excess, that led thee hither Par Lost 3.698
That brought them forth, but hid thir causes deep. Par Lost 3.707
That rowld orbicular, and turnd to Starrs Par Lost 3.718
Look downward on that Globe whose hither side Par Lost 3.722
That place is Earth the seat of Man, that light Par Lost 3.724
(So call that opposite fair Starr) her aide Par Lost 3.727
That spot to which I point is *Paradise*, Par Lost 3.733
O for that warning voice, which he who saw Par Lost 4.1
Wo to the inhabitants on Earth! that now, Par Lost 4.5
Of that first Battel, and his flight to Hell: Par Lost 4.12
That slumberd, wakes the bitter memorie Par Lost 4.24
O thou that with surpassing Glory crownd, Par Lost 4.32
That bring to my remembrance from what state Par Lost 4.38
In that bright eminence, and with his good Par Lost 4.44
And understood not that a grateful mind Par Lost 4.55
None left but by submission; and that word Par Lost 4.81
How dearly I abide that boast so vaine, Par Lost 4.87
That practisd falshood under saintly shew, Par Lost 4.122
And higher then that Wall a circling row Par Lost 4.146

That(*cont*)
That Lantskip: And of pure now purer aire Par Lost 4.153
That drove him, though enamourd, from the Spouse Par Lost 4.169
Now to th' ascent of that steep savage Hill Par Lost 4.172
All path of Man or Beast that past that way: Par Lost 4.177
One Gate there only was, and that look'd East Par Lost 4.178
The middle Tree and highest there that grew, Par Lost 4.195
Of that life-giving Plant, but only us'd Par Lost 4.199
That Mountain as his Garden mould high rais'd Par Lost 4.226
How from that Saphire Fount the crisped Brooks, Par Lost 4.237
That to the fringed Bank with Myrtle crownd, Par Lost 4.262
Led on th' Eternal Spring. Not that faire field Par Lost 4.268
Was gatherd, which cost *Ceres* all that pain Par Lost 4.271
To seek her through the world; nor that sweet Grove Par Lost 4.272
Of *Eden* strive; nor that *Nyseian* Ile Par Lost 4.275
That ever since in loves imbraces met, Par Lost 4.322
Under a tuft of shade that on a green Par Lost 4.325
Of Heav'n the Starrs that usher Evening rose: Par Lost 4.355
The hand that formd them on thir shape hath pourd. Par Lost 4.365
That I with you must dwell, or you with me Par Lost 4.377
Then from his loftie stand on that high Tree Par Lost 4.395
That made us, and for us this ample World Par Lost 4.413
That rais'd us from the dust and plac't us here Par Lost 4.416
In Paradise that bear delicious fruit Par Lost 4.422
So various, not to taste that onely Tree Par Lost 4.423
God hath pronounc't it death to taste that Tree, Par Lost 4.427
Over all other Creatures that possess Par Lost 4.431
That day I oft remember, when from sleep Par Lost 4.449
Smooth Lake, that to me seemd another Skie. Par Lost 4.459
Then that smooth watry image; back I turnd, Par Lost 4.480
My other half: with that thy gentle hand Par Lost 4.488
Seisd mine, I yielded, and from that time see Par Lost 4.489
That shed *May* Flowers; and press'd her Matron lip Par Lost 4.501
Envie them that? can it be sin to know, Par Lost 4.517
By Ignorance, is that thir happie state, Par Lost 4.519
The rest was craggie cliff, that overhung Par Lost 4.547
Charge and strict watch that to this happie Place Par Lost 4.562
But in the Mount that lies from *Eden* North, Par Lost 4.569
Returnd on that bright beam, whose point now raisd Par Lost 4.590
The Clouds that on his Western Throne attend: Par Lost 4.597
With living Saphirs: *Hesperus* that led Par Lost 4.605
That mock our scant manuring, and require Par Lost 4.628
That lie bestrowne unsightly and unsmooth, Par Lost 4.631
Thir stellar vertue on all kinds that grow Par Lost 4.671
That heav'n would want spectators, God want praise; Par Lost 4.676
The God that made both Skie, Air, Earth and Heav'n Par Lost 4.722
Farr be it, that I should write thee sin or blame, Par Lost 4.758
That neer him stood, and gave them thus in charge. Par Lost 4.787
Th' animal Spirits that from pure blood arise Par Lost 4.805
Here watching at the head of these that sleep? Par Lost 4.826
That Glorie then, when thou no more wast good, Par Lost 4.838
In that dark durance: thus much what was askt. Par Lost 4.899
But that implies not violence or harme. Par Lost 4.901
Seavenfold, and scourge that wisdom back to Hell, Par Lost 4.914
Which taught thee yet no better, that no pain Par Lost 4.915
Not that I less endure, or shrink from pain, Par Lost 4.925
To the night-warbling Bird, that now awake Par Lost 5.40
That brought me on a sudden to the Tree Par Lost 5.51
Ambrosia; on that Tree he also gaz'd; Par Lost 5.57
Even to my mouth of that same fruit held part Par Lost 5.83
So quick'nd appetite, that I, methought, Par Lost 5.85
Created pure. But know that in the Soule Par Lost 5.100
Are many lesser Faculties that serve Par Lost 5.101
That what in sleep thou didst abhorr to dream, Par Lost 5.120
That wont to be more chearful and serene Par Lost 5.123
That open now thir choicest bosom'd smells Par Lost 5.127
Two other precious drops that ready stood, Par Lost 5.132
And pious awe, that feard to have offended. Par Lost 5.135
Sure pledge of day, that crownst the smiling Morn Par Lost 5.168
While day arises, that sweet hour of Prime. Par Lost 5.170
Moon, that now meetst the orient Sun, now fli'st Par Lost 5.175
With the fixt Starrs, fixt in thir Orb that flies, Par Lost 5.176
And yee five other wandring Fires that move Par Lost 5.177
Of Natures Womb, that in quaternion run Par Lost 5.181
Ye Mists and Exhalations that now rise Par Lost 5.185
His praise ye Winds, that from four Quarters blow, Par Lost 5.192
Fountains and yee, that warble, as ye flow, Par Lost 5.195
That singing up to Heaven Gate ascend, Par Lost 5.198
Yee that in Waters glide, and yee that walk Par Lost 5.200
Raphael, the sociable Spirit, that deign'd Par Lost 5.221
By violence, no, for that shall be withstood, Par Lost 5.242
A *Phaenix*, gaz'd by all, as that sole Bird Par Lost 5.272
His lineaments Divine; the pair that clad Par Lost 5.278
And shook his Plumes, that Heav'nly fragrance filld Par Lost 5.286
Beholding shall confess that here on Earth Par Lost 5.329
More solemn then the tedious pomp that waits Par Lost 5.354
They came, that like *Pomona*'s Arbour smil'd Par Lost 5.378
Of three that in Mount *Ida* naked strove, Par Lost 5.382
That one Celestial Father gives to all. Par Lost 5.403
The Sun that light imparts to all, receives Par Lost 5.423
Enamour'd at that sight; but in those hearts Par Lost 5.448
As that more willingly thou couldst not seem Par Lost 5.466
Of substance, and in things that live, of life; Par Lost 5.474
Well hast thou taught the way that might direct Par Lost 5.508
What meant that caution joind, *if ye be found* Par Lost 5.513
Attend: That thou art happie, owe to God; Par Lost 5.520
That thou continu'st such, owe to thy self, Par Lost 5.521
That is, to thy obedience; therein stand. Par Lost 5.522

That(*cont*)

This was that caution giv'n thee; be advis'd.	Par Lost 5.523
My self and all th' Angelic Host that stand	Par Lost 5.535
Yet that we never shall forget to love	Par Lost 5.550
Mee disobeyes, breaks union, and that day	Par Lost 5.612
That day, as other solemn dayes, they spent	Par Lost 5.618
So smooths her charming tones, that Gods own ear	Par Lost 5.626
From that high mount of God, whence light & shade	Par Lost 5.643
With envie against the Son of God, that day	Par Lost 5.662
Through pride that sight, & thought himself impaird.	Par Lost 5.665
Tell them that by command, ere yet dim Night	Par Lost 5.685
That the most High commanding, now ere Night,	Par Lost 5.699
His count'nance, as the Morning Starr that guides	Par Lost 5.708
And from within the golden Lamps that burne	Par Lost 5.713
That Structure in the Dialect of men	Par Lost 5.761
In imitation of that Mount whereon	Par Lost 5.764
That to his only Son by right endu'd	Par Lost 5.815
Shall bend the knee, and in that honour due	Par Lost 5.817
That equal over equals Monarch Reigne:	Par Lost 5.832
That we were formd then saist thou? and the work	Par Lost 5.853
Through the infinite Host, nor less for that	Par Lost 5.874
That Golden Scepter which thou didst reject	Par Lost 5.886
With joy and acclamations loud, that one	Par Lost 6.23
That of so many Myriads fall'n, yet one	Par Lost 6.24
Equal in number to that Godless crew	Par Lost 6.49
That stood for Heav'n, in mighty Quadrate joyn'd	Par Lost 6.62
Of instrumental Harmonie that breath'd	Par Lost 6.65
That self same day by fight, or by surprize	Par Lost 6.87
At first, that Angel should with Angel warr,	Par Lost 6.92
Abdiel that sight endur'd not, where he stood	Par Lost 6.111
O Heav'n! that such resemblance of the Highest	Par Lost 6.114
That he who in debate of Truth hath won,	Par Lost 6.122
Victor; though brutish that contest and foule,	Par Lost 6.124
Most reason is that Reason overcome.	Par Lost 6.126
Of this right hand provok't, since first that tongue	Par Lost 6.154
From me som Plume, that thy success may show	Par Lost 6.161
At first I thought that Libertie and Heav'n	Par Lost 6.164
I see that most through sloth had rather serve,	Par Lost 6.166
On the proud Crest of *Satan*, that no sight,	Par Lost 6.191
That argu'd fear; each on himself reli'd,	Par Lost 6.238
That Warr and various; somtimes on firm ground	Par Lost 6.242
The Battel hung; till *Satan*, who that day	Par Lost 6.246
To flight, or if to fall, but that they rise	Par Lost 6.285
That thou shouldst hope, imperious, and with threats	Par Lost 6.287
To chase me hence? erre not that so shall end	Par Lost 6.288
Liken on Earth conspicuous, that may lift	Par Lost 6.299
That might determine, and not need repeate,	Par Lost 6.318
Was giv'n him temperd so, that neither keen	Par Lost 6.322
Nor solid might resist that edge: it met	Par Lost 6.323
Yet soon he heal'd; for Spirits that live throughout	Par Lost 6.344
Two potent Thrones, that to be less then Gods	Par Lost 6.366
By sin of disobedience, till that hour	Par Lost 6.396
Not uninvented that, which thou aright	Par Lost 6.470
Adverse, that they shall fear we have disarmd	Par Lost 6.490
That all may see who hate us, how we seek	Par Lost 6.559
But that I doubt, however witness Heaven,	Par Lost 6.563
What we propound, and loud that all may hear.	Par Lost 6.567
That whom they hit, none on thir feet might stand,	Par Lost 6.592
That under ground, they fought in dismal shade;	Par Lost 6.666
That his great purpose he might so fulfill,	Par Lost 6.675
Have sufferd, that the Glorie may be thine	Par Lost 6.701
Immense I have transfus'd, that all may know	Par Lost 6.704
That shake Heav'ns basis, bring forth all my Warr,	Par Lost 6.712
That thou in me well pleas'd, declarst thy will	Par Lost 6.728
That from thy just obedience could revolt,	Par Lost 6.740
That they may have thir wish, to trie with mee	Par Lost 6.818
That wisht the Mountains now might be again	Par Lost 6.842
Among th' accurst, that witherd all thir strength,	Par Lost 6.850
At thy request, and that thou maist beware	Par Lost 6.894
Thee also from obedience, that with him	Par Lost 6.902
Descend from Heav'n *Urania*, by that name	Par Lost 7.1
Of that wilde Rout that tore the *Thracian* Bard	Par Lost 7.34
If they transgress, and slight that sole command,	Par Lost 7.47
The doubts that in his heart arose: and now	Par Lost 7.60
Know then, that after *Lucifer* from Heav'n	Par Lost 7.131
Of Angels, then that Starr the Starrs among)	Par Lost 7.133
That detriment, if such it be to lose	Par Lost 7.153
And saw that it was good, and said, Let th' Earth	Par Lost 7.309
Then Herbs of every leaf, that sudden flour'd	Par Lost 7.317
With borders long the Rivers. That Earth now	Par Lost 7.328
On the green stemm; God saw that it was good.	Par Lost 7.337
Surveying his great Work, that it was good:	Par Lost 7.353
In that aspect, and still that distance keepes	Par Lost 7.379
With thousand thousand Starres, that then appeer'd	Par Lost 7.383
With thir bright Luminaries that Set and Rose,	Par Lost 7.385
Soul living, each that crept, which plenteously	Par Lost 7.392
And saw that it was good, and bless'd them, saying,	Par Lost 7.395
Of Fish that with thir Finns and shining Scales	Par Lost 7.401
Glide under the green Wave, in Sculles that oft	Par Lost 7.402
Thir Brood as numerous hatch, from the Egg that soon	Par Lost 7.418
The Female Bee that feeds her Husband Drone	Par Lost 7.490
And every creeping thing that creeps the ground.	Par Lost 7.523
And every living thing that moves on the Earth.	Par Lost 7.534
Gave thee, all sorts are here that all th' Earth yields,	Par Lost 7.541
Here finish'd hee, and all that he had made	Par Lost 7.548
Symphonious of ten thousand Harpes that tun'd	Par Lost 7.559
That open'd wide her blazing Portals, led	Par Lost 7.575
Seen in the Galaxie, that Milkie way	Par Lost 7.579

That(*cont*)

As resting on that day from all his work,	Par Lost 7.593
Then from the Giant Angels; thee that day	Par Lost 7.605
And thy request think now fulfill'd, that ask'd	Par Lost 7.635
From the beginning, that posteritie	Par Lost 7.638
So Charming left his voice, that he a while	Par Lost 8.2
line not in 1667 edition	
And all her numberd Starrs, that seem to rowle	Par Lost 8.19
That better might with farr less compass move,	Par Lost 8.33
And Grace that won who saw to wish her stay,	Par Lost 8.43
That bodies bright and greater should not serve	Par Lost 8.87
The benefit: consider first, that Great	Par Lost 8.90
More plenty then the Sun that barren shines,	Par Lost 8.94
That Man may know he dwells not in his own;	Par Lost 8.103
That to corporeal substances could adde	Par Lost 8.109
By Numbers that have name. But this I urge,	Par Lost 8.114
Invalid that which thee to doubt it mov'd;	Par Lost 8.116
Not that I so affirm, though so it seem	Par Lost 8.117
Plac'd Heav'n from Earth so farr, that earthly sight,	Par Lost 8.120
Or save the Sun his labour, and that swift	Par Lost 8.133
Still luminous by his ray. What if that light	Par Lost 8.140
Stor'd in each Orb perhaps with some that live.	Par Lost 8.152
With inoffensive pace that spinning sleeps	Par Lost 8.164
Contented that thus farr hath been reveal'd	Par Lost 8.177
That not to know at large of things remote	Par Lost 8.191
That which before us lies in daily life,	Par Lost 8.193
And renders us in things that most concerne	Par Lost 8.196
For I that Day was absent, as befell,	Par Lost 8.229
To see that none thence issu'd forth a spie,	Par Lost 8.233
Not that they durst without his leave attempt,	Par Lost 8.237
Creatures that livd, and movd, and walk'd, or flew,	Par Lost 8.264
And ye that live and move, fair Creatures, tell,	Par Lost 8.276
From whom I have that thus I move and live,	Par Lost 8.281
And feel that I am happier then I know,	Par Lost 8.282
Planted, with Walks, and Bowers, that what I saw	Par Lost 8.305
Load'n with fairest Fruit that hung to the Eye	Par Lost 8.307
Of every Tree that in the Garden growes	Par Lost 8.321
From that day mortal, and this happie State	Par Lost 8.331
Possess it, and all things that therein live,	Par Lost 8.340
Or solace his defects. No need that thou	Par Lost 8.419
In that celestial Colloquie sublime,	Par Lost 8.455
As with an object that excels the sense,	Par Lost 8.456
That what seemd fair in all the World, seemd now	Par Lost 8.472
And in her looks, which from that time infus'd	Par Lost 8.474
That would be woo'd, and not unsought be won,	Par Lost 8.503
Wrought in her so, that seeing me, she turn'd;	Par Lost 8.507
And happie Constellations on that houre	Par Lost 8.512
The character of that Dominion giv'n	Par Lost 8.545
Her own, that what she wills to do or say,	Par Lost 8.549
Well manag'd; of that skill the more thou know'st,	Par Lost 8.573
So awful, that with honour thou maist love	Par Lost 8.577
Those thousand decencies that daily flow	Par Lost 8.601
To whom the Angel with a smile that glow'd	Par Lost 8.618
Answer'd. Let it suffice thee that thou know'st	Par Lost 8.620
That brought into this World a world of woe,	Par Lost 9.11
Or *Neptun*'s ire or *Juno's*, that so long	Par Lost 9.18
Not that which justly gives Heroic name	Par Lost 9.40
That name, unless an age too late, or cold	Par Lost 9.44
That kept thir watch; thence full of anguish driv'n,	Par Lost 9.62
That shine, yet bear thir bright officious Lamps,	Par Lost 9.104
In wo then; that destruction wide may range:	Par Lost 9.134
O foul descent! that I who erst contended	Par Lost 9.163
That to the hight of Deitie aspir'd;	Par Lost 9.167
In *Eden* on the humid Flours, that breathd	Par Lost 9.193
Thir morning incense, when all things that breath,	Par Lost 9.194
Of Creatures wanting voice, that done, partake	Par Lost 9.199
Then commune how that day they best may ply	Par Lost 9.201
That gave thee being, still shades thee and protects.	Par Lost 9.266
That such an Enemie we have, who seeks	Par Lost 9.274
But that thou shouldst my firmness therfore doubt	Par Lost 9.279
Thy equal fear that my firm Faith and Love	Par Lost 9.286
Of all that he Created, much less Man,	Par Lost 9.346
Or aught that might his happie State secure,	Par Lost 9.347
That I should mind thee oft, and mind thou me.	Par Lost 9.358
Touchd onely, that our trial, when least sought,	Par Lost 9.380
Thou never from that houre in Paradise	Par Lost 9.406
Or that, not Mystic, where the Sapient King	Par Lost 9.442
That space the Evil one abstracted stood	Par Lost 9.463
But the hot Hell that alwayes in him burnes,	Par Lost 9.467
Circular base of rising foulds, that tour'd	Par Lost 9.498
Amidst his circling Spires, that on the grass	Par Lost 9.502
Lovelier, not those that in *Illyria* chang'd	Par Lost 9.505
Displeas'd that I approach thee thus, and gaze	Par Lost 9.535
Of brutal kind, that daily are in sight?	Par Lost 9.565
I was at first as other Beasts that graze	Par Lost 9.571
Unsuckt of Lamb or Kid, that tend thir play.	Par Lost 9.583
Of that alluring fruit, urg'd me so keene.	Par Lost 9.588
All other Beasts that saw, with like desire	Par Lost 9.592
I spar'd not, for such pleasure till that hour	Par Lost 9.596
But all that fair and good in thy Divine	Par Lost 9.606
The vertue of that Fruit, in thee first prov'd:	Par Lost 9.616
For many are the Trees of God that grow	Par Lost 9.618
God so commanded, and left that Command	Par Lost 9.652
Indeed? hath God then said that of the Fruit	Par Lost 9.656
Shall that be shut to Man, which to the Beast	Par Lost 9.691
His worshippers; he knows that in the day	Par Lost 9.705
Ye Eate thereof, your Eyes that seem so cleere,	Par Lost 9.706
That ye should be as Gods, since I as Man,	Par Lost 9.710

That(*cont*)

And what are Gods that Man may not become	Par Lost 9.716
The Gods are first, and that advantage use	Par Lost 9.718
On our belief, that all from them proceeds;	Par Lost 9.719
That whoso eats thereof, forthwith attains	Par Lost 9.724
Th' offence, that Man should thus attain to know?	Par Lost 9.726
So savorie of that Fruit, which with desire,	Par Lost 9.741
For Beasts it seems: yet that one Beast which first	Par Lost 9.769
That all was lost. Back to the Thicket slunk	Par Lost 9.784
So dear I love him, that with him all deaths	Par Lost 9.832
That dwelt within, whose presence had infus'd	Par Lost 9.836
That Morn when first they parted; by the Tree	Par Lost 9.848
A bough of fairest fruit that downie smil'd,	Par Lost 9.851
Perswasively hath so prevaild, that I	Par Lost 9.873
Thou therefore also taste, that equal Lot	Par Lost 9.881
That sacred Fruit, sacred to abstinence,	Par Lost 9.924
Nor can I think that God, Creator wise,	Par Lost 9.938
Taste so Divine, that what of sweet before	Par Lost 9.986
Tenderly wept, much won that he his Love	Par Lost 9.991
She gave him of that fair enticing Fruit	Par Lost 9.996
Him with her lov'd societie, that now	Par Lost 9.1007
They swim in mirth, and fansie that they feel	Par Lost 9.1009
Wherewith to scorne the Earth: but that false Fruit	Par Lost 9.1011
Soon as the force of that fallacious Fruit,	Par Lost 9.1046
That with exhilerating vapour bland	Par Lost 9.1047
How dark'nd; innocence, that as a veile	Par Lost 9.1054
To that false Worm, of whomsoever taught	Par Lost 9.1068
The Parts of each for other, that seem most	Par Lost 9.1093
Those middle parts, that this new commer, Shame,	Par Lost 9.1097
The Figtree, not that kind for Fruit renown'd,	Par Lost 9.1101
Braunching so broad and long, that in the ground	Par Lost 9.1104
To that first naked Glorie. Such of late	Par Lost 9.1115
With me, as I besought thee, when that strange	Par Lost 9.1135
Imput'st thou that to my default, or will	Par Lost 9.1145
That lay in wait; beyond this had bin force,	Par Lost 9.1173
What seemd in thee so perfet, that I thought	Par Lost 9.1179
That errour now, which is become my crime,	Par Lost 9.1181
The high Injunction not to taste that Fruit,	Par Lost 10.13
That time Celestial visages, yet mixt	Par Lost 10.24
What rests but that the mortal Sentence pass	Par Lost 10.48
On his transgression, Death denounc't that day,	Par Lost 10.49
Easie it might be seen that I intend	Par Lost 10.58
Supream, that thou in mee thy Son belov'd	Par Lost 10.70
Of right, that I may mitigate thir doom	Par Lost 10.76
So dreadful to thee? that thou art naked, who	Par Lost 10.121
That from her hand I could suspect no ill,	Par Lost 10.140
Was shee thy God, that her thou didst obey	Par Lost 10.145
Superior, or but equal, that to her	Par Lost 10.147
And th' instant stroke of Death denounc't that day	Par Lost 10.210
Before him naked to the aire, that now	Par Lost 10.212
In counterview within the Gates, that now	Par Lost 10.231
But that success attends him; if mishap,	Par Lost 10.239
Over this Maine from Hell to that new World	Par Lost 10.257
The savour of Death from all things there that live:	Par Lost 10.269
Mountains of Ice, that stop th' imagin'd way	Par Lost 10.291
Upon her Husband, saw thir shame that sought	Par Lost 10.336
Might suddenly inflict; that past, return'd	Par Lost 10.341
Of that stupendious Bridge his joy encreas'd.	Par Lost 10.351
That thou on Earth hadst prosper'd, which thy looks	Par Lost 10.360
That I must after thee with this thy Son;	Par Lost 10.363
Th' infernal Empire, that so neer Heav'ns dore	Par Lost 10.389
That scorn'd his indignation: through the Gate,	Par Lost 10.418
Of that bright Starr to *Satan* paragond.	Par Lost 10.426
Of that *Plutonian* Hall, invisible	Par Lost 10.444
At that so sudden blaze the *Stygian* throng	Par Lost 10.453
That jealous of thir secrets fiercely oppos'd	Par Lost 10.478
Man I deceav'd: that which to mee belongs,	Par Lost 10.496
Where all yet left of that revolted Rout	Par Lost 10.534
Thir penance, laden with Fruit, like that	Par Lost 10.550
Us'd by the Tempter: on that prospect strange	Par Lost 10.552
That curld *Megaera:* greedily they pluck'd	Par Lost 10.560
The Frutage fair to sight, like that which grew	Par Lost 10.561
Neer that bituminous Lake where *Sodom* flam'd;	Par Lost 10.562
Kept in that State, had not the folly of Man	Par Lost 10.619
And his Adherents, that with so much ease	Par Lost 10.622
That laugh, as if transported with some fit.	Par Lost 10.626
And know not that I call'd and drew them thither	Par Lost 10.629
To sanctitie that shall receive no staine:	Par Lost 10.639
Through multitude that sung: Just are thy ways,	Par Lost 10.643
Beneath *Magellan*. At that tasted Fruit	Par Lost 10.687
The Glory of that Glory, who now becom	Par Lost 10.722
All that I eat or drink, or shall beget,	Par Lost 10.728
Mine own that bide upon me, all from mee	Par Lost 10.738
The good I sought not. To the loss of that,	Par Lost 10.752
That proud excuse? yet him not thy election,	Par Lost 10.764
That dust I am, and shall to dust returne:	Par Lost 10.770
Least that pure breath of Life, the Spirit of Man	Par Lost 10.784
Of Life that sinn'd; what dies but what had life	Par Lost 10.790
Can he make deathless Death? that were to make	Par Lost 10.798
Satisfi'd never; that were to extend	Par Lost 10.804
That Death be not one stroak, as I suppos'd,	Par Lost 10.809
To perpetuitie; Ay me, that fear	Par Lost 10.813
That I must leave ye, Sons; O were I able	Par Lost 10.819
That burden heavier then the Earth to bear	Par Lost 10.835
With that bad Woman? Thus what thou desir'st	Par Lost 10.837
Out of my sight, thou Serpent, that name best	Par Lost 10.867
And hateful; nothing wants, but that thy shape,	Par Lost 10.869
Henceforth; least that too heav'nly form, pretended	Par Lost 10.872

That(*cont*)

Creator wise, that peopl'd highest Heav'n	Par Lost 10.889
And more that shall befall, innumerable	Par Lost 10.896
Not so repulst, with Tears that ceas'd not flowing,	Par Lost 10.910
That cruel Serpent: On me exercise not	Par Lost 10.927
There with my cries importune Heaven, that all	Par Lost 10.933
Could alter high Decrees, I to that place	Par Lost 10.953
That on my head all might be visited,	Par Lost 10.955
That after wretched Life must be at last	Par Lost 10.985
That shew no end but Death, and have the power,	Par Lost 10.1004
That excellence thought in thee, and implies,	Par Lost 10.1017
Part of our Sentence, that thy Seed shall bruise	Par Lost 10.1031
That cuts us off from hope, and savours onely	Par Lost 10.1043
Was meant by Death that day, when lo, to thee	Par Lost 10.1050
Regenerate grow instead, that sighs now breath'd	Par Lost 11.5
But longer in that Paradise to dwell,	Par Lost 11.48
Those pure immortal Elements that know	Par Lost 11.50
For dissolution wrought by Sin, that first	Par Lost 11.55
And Immortalitie: that fondly lost,	Par Lost 11.59
To the bright Minister that watchd, hee blew	Par Lost 11.73
Of that defended Fruit; but let him boast	Par Lost 11.86
Eve, easily may Faith admit, that all	Par Lost 11.141
But that from us ought should ascend to Heav'n	Par Lost 11.143
That I was heard with favour; peace returnd	Par Lost 11.153
His promise, that thy Seed shall bruise our Foe;	Par Lost 11.155
Assures me that the bitterness of death	Par Lost 11.157
That I who first brought Death on all, am grac't	Par Lost 11.168
Down from a Hill the Beast that reigns in Woods,	Par Lost 11.187
Who knows, or more then this, that we are dust,	Par Lost 11.199
More orient in yon Western Cloud that draws	Par Lost 11.205
And carnal fear that day dimm'd *Adams* eye.	Par Lost 11.212
Not that more glorious, when the Angels met	Par Lost 11.213
Nor that which on the flaming Mount appeerd	Par Lost 11.216
From yonder blazing Cloud that veils the Hill	Par Lost 11.229
That I should fear, nor sociably mild,	Par Lost 11.234
As *Raphael*, that I should much confide,	Par Lost 11.235
Sufficient that thy Prayers are heard, and Death,	Par Lost 11.252
That all his senses bound; *Eve*, who unseen	Par Lost 11.265
Quiet though sad, the respit of that day	Par Lost 11.272
That must be mortal to us both. O flours,	Par Lost 11.273
That never will in other Climate grow,	Par Lost 11.274
Thus over-fond, on that which is not thine;	Par Lost 11.289
Blown stifling back on him that breaths it forth:	Par Lost 11.313
This most afflicts me, that departing hence,	Par Lost 11.315
Land, Sea, and Aire, and every kinde that lives,	Par Lost 11.337
Which that thou mayst beleeve, and be confirmd	Par Lost 11.355
Not higher that Hill nor wider looking round,	Par Lost 11.381
Which that false Fruit that promis'd clearer sight	Par Lost 11.413
That *Adam* now enforc't to close his eyes,	Par Lost 11.419
Nor sinn'd thy sin, yet from that derive	Par Lost 11.427
1667 'that sin derive'	
That beat out life; he fell, and deadly pale	Par Lost 11.446
Much at that sight was *Adam* in his heart	Par Lost 11.448
To that meek man, who well had sacrific'd;	Par Lost 11.451
For envie that his Brothers Offering found	Par Lost 11.456
Of Death, and many are the wayes that lead	Par Lost 11.468
Before thee shall appear; that thou mayst know	Par Lost 11.475
Of Instruments that made melodious chime	Par Lost 11.559
Of Arts that polish Life, Inventers rare,	Par Lost 11.610
For that fair femal Troop thou sawst, that seemd	Par Lost 11.614
To these that sober Race of Men, whose lives	Par Lost 11.621
O pittie and shame, that they who to live well	Par Lost 11.629
But who was that Just Man, whom had not Heav'n	Par Lost 11.681
And utter odious Truth, that God would come	Par Lost 11.704
Anough to beare; those now, that were dispenst	Par Lost 11.766
With thought that they must be. Let no man seek	Par Lost 11.770
Grievous to bear: but that care now is past,	Par Lost 11.776
Wandring that watrie Desert: I had hope	Par Lost 11.779
More then anough, that temperance may be tri'd:	Par Lost 11.805
To teach thee that God attributes to place	Par Lost 11.836
Drivn by a keen North-winde, that blowing drie	Par Lost 11.842
From standing lake to tripping ebbe, that stole	Par Lost 11.847
O thou who future things canst represent	Par Lost 11.870
1667 'that'	
At this last sight, assur'd that Man shall live	Par Lost 11.872
That God voutsafes to raise another World	Par Lost 11.877
The fluid skirts of that same watrie Cloud,	Par Lost 11.882
That he relents, not to blot out mankind,	Par Lost 11.891
Of Brick, and of that stuff they cast to build	Par Lost 12.43
Dominion absolute; that right we hold	Par Lost 12.68
That Son, who on the quiet state of men	Par Lost 12.80
From vertue, which is reason, that no wrong,	Par Lost 12.98
Bred up in Idol-worship; O that men	Par Lost 12.115
His benediction so, that in his Seed	Par Lost 12.125
Gift to his Progenie of all that Land;	Par Lost 12.138
Shall dwell to *Senir*, that long ridge of Hills.	Par Lost 12.146
This ponder, that all Nations of the Earth	Par Lost 12.147
Shall in his Seed be blessed; by that Seed	Par Lost 12.148
Into the Sea: to sojourn in that Land	Par Lost 12.159
Raise him to be the second in that Realme	Par Lost 12.162
And shadows, of that destind Seed to bruise	Par Lost 12.233
That *Moses* might report to them his will,	Par Lost 12.237
Instructed that to God is no access	Par Lost 12.239
Obedient to his will, that he voutsafes	Par Lost 12.246
To whom thus *Michael*. Doubt not but that sin	Par Lost 12.285
Sin against Law to fight; that when they see	Par Lost 12.289
Just for unjust, that in such righteousness	Par Lost 12.294
Irrevocable, that his Regal Throne	Par Lost 12.323

That(*cont*)
All Prophecie, That of the Royal Stock Par Lost 12.325
To that proud Citie, whose high Walls thou saw'st Par Lost 12.342
Then loose it to a stranger, that the true Par Lost 12.358
But by fulfilling that which thou didst want, Par Lost 12.396
In his redemption, and that his obedience Par Lost 12.408
The Law that is against thee, and the sins Par Lost 12.416
For death, like that which the redeemer dy'd. Par Lost 12.445
All Nations they shall teach; for from that day Par Lost 12.446
That all this good of evil shall produce, Par Lost 12.470
Then that which by creation first brought forth Par Lost 12.472
Much more, that much more good thereof shall spring, Par Lost 12.476
To all Beleevers; and from that pretense, Par Lost 12.520
Henceforth I learne, that to obey is best, Par Lost 12.561
By simply meek; that suffering for Truths sake Par Lost 12.569
That ye may live, which will be many dayes, Par Lost 12.602
Began to parch that temperate Clime; whereat Par Lost 12.636
Wav'd over by that flaming Brand, the Gate Par Lost 12.643
That heard the Adversary, who roving still Par Reg 1.33
About the world, at that assembly fam'd Par Reg 1.34
With dread attending when that fatal wound Par Reg 1.53
Must bide the stroak of that long threatn'd wound, Par Reg 1.59
The testimony of Heaven, that who he is Par Reg 1.78
To verifie that solemn message late, Par Reg 1.133
In *Galilee*, that she should bear a Son Par Reg 1.135
To her a Virgin, that on her should come Par Reg 1.138
That all the Angels and Aetherial Powers, Par Reg 1.163
Born to that end, born to promote all truth, Par Reg 1.205
To such perfection, that e're yet my age Par Reg 1.209
Like things of thee to all that present stood. Par Reg 1.258
I am; this chiefly, that my way must lie Par Reg 1.263
Now full, that I no more should live obscure, Par Reg 1.287
For that to me thou seem'st the man, whom late Par Reg 1.327
That out of these hard stones be made thee bread; Par Reg 1.343
'Tis true, I am that Spirit unfortunate, Par Reg 1.358
Yet to that hideous place not so confin'd Par Reg 1.362
By rigour unconniving, but that oft Par Reg 1.363
That he might fall in *Ramoth*, they demurring, Par Reg 1.373
I undertook that office, and the tongues Par Reg 1.374
That fellowship in pain divides not smart, Par Reg 1.401
This wounds me most (what can it less) that Man, Par Reg 1.404
Among the Nations? that hath been thy craft, Par Reg 1.432
And on that high Authority had believ'd, Par Reg 2.5
O what avails me now that honour high Par Reg 2.66
To have conceiv'd of God, or that salute Par Reg 2.67
That to the fall and rising he should be Par Reg 2.88
Spoken against, that through my very Soul Par Reg 2.90
I will not argue that, nor will repine. Par Reg 2.94
Belial the dislolutest Spirit that fell, Par Reg 2.150
Remember that *Pellean* Conquerour, Par Reg 2.196
Wrought that effect on *Jove*, so Fables tell; Par Reg 2.215
Or that which only seems to satisfie Par Reg 2.229
Nor tasted, nor had appetite; that Fast Par Reg 2.247
Can satisfie that need some other way, Par Reg 2.254
Nor mind it, fed with better thoughts that feed Par Reg 2.258
Sometimes that with *Elijah* he partook, Par Reg 2.277
That open'd in the midst a woody Scene, Par Reg 2.294
But much more wonder that the Son of God Par Reg 2.303
Rain'd from Heaven Manna, and that Prophet bold Par Reg 2.312
The giver, answer'd Jesus. Why should that Par Reg 2.322
Would scruple that, with want oppress'? behold Par Reg 2.331
Troubl'd that thou shouldst hunger, hath purvey'd Par Reg 2.333
Was that crude Apple that diverted *Eve!* Par Reg 2.349
That fragrant smell diffus'd, in order stood Par Reg 2.351
And Ladies of th' *Hesperides*, that seem'd Par Reg 2.357
Said'st thou not that to all things I had right? Par Reg 2.379
And who withholds my pow'r that right to use? Par Reg 2.380
That I have also power to give thou seest, Par Reg 2.393
If of that pow'r I bring thee voluntary Par Reg 2.394
Whose pains have earn'd the far fet spoil. With that Par Reg 2.401
By hunger, that each other Creature tames, Par Reg 2.406
(Thy throne) but gold that got him puissant friends? Par Reg 2.425
That seat, and reign in *Israel* without end. Par Reg 2.442
And what in me seems wanting, but that I Par Reg 2.450
Riches and Realms; yet not for that a Crown, Par Reg 2.458
That for the Publick all this weight he bears. Par Reg 2.465
That other o're the body only reigns, Par Reg 2.478
That might require th' array of war, thy skill Par Reg 3.17
Of conduct would be such, that all the world Par Reg 3.18
That sole excites to high attempts the flame Par Reg 3.26
With glory, wept that he had liv'd so long Par Reg 3.41
Then glory and benediction, that is thanks, Par Reg 3.127
And not returning that would likeliest render Par Reg 3.130
That which to God alone of right belongs; Par Reg 3.141
That who advance his glory, not thir own, Par Reg 3.143
Be now in powerful hands, that will not part Par Reg 3.155
That by strong hand his Family obtain'd, Par Reg 3.168
That it shall never end, so when begin Par Reg 3.185
What if he hath decreed that I shall first Par Reg 3.188
Without distrust or doubt, that he may know Par Reg 3.193
Know'st thou not that my rising is thy fall, Par Reg 3.201
Let that come when it comes; all hope is lost Par Reg 3.204
Raign or raign not; though to that gentle brow Par Reg 3.215
From that placid aspect and meek regard, Par Reg 3.217
If I then to the worst that can be hast, Par Reg 3.223
That thou who worthiest art should'st be thir King? Par Reg 3.226
In all things that to greatest actions lead. Par Reg 3.239
And regal Mysteries; that thou may'st know Par Reg 3.249

That(*cont*)
With that (such power was giv'n him then) he took Par Reg 3.251
Huge Cities and high towr'd, that well might seem Par Reg 3.261
The Prospect was, that here and there was room Par Reg 3.263
Of that first golden Monarchy the seat, Par Reg 3.277
That Empire, under his dominion holds Par Reg 3.296
That thou may'st know I seek not to engage Par Reg 3.347
That which alone can truly reinstall thee Par Reg 3.372
My time I told thee, (and that time for thee Par Reg 3.396
When that comes think not thou to find me slack Par Reg 3.398
Thy politic maxims, or that cumbersome Par Reg 3.400
To *Israel* then, the same that now to me. Par Reg 3.413
Made answer meet, that made void all his wiles. Par Reg 3.442
That sleek't his tongue, and won so much on *Eve*, Par Reg 4.5
Of that high mountain, whence he might behold Par Reg 4.26
That screen'd the fruits of the earth and seats of men Par Reg 4.30
Is given, and by that right I give it thee. Par Reg 4.104
From Nations far and nigh; what honour that, Par Reg 4.122
That people victor once, now vile and base, Par Reg 4.132
Of triumph that insulting vanity; Par Reg 4.138
Or as a stone that shall to pieces dash Par Reg 4.149
On the other side know also thou, that I Par Reg 4.159
For this attempt bolder then that on *Eve*, Par Reg 4.180
That I fall down and worship thee as God? Par Reg 4.192
That Evil one, Satan for ever damn'd. Par Reg 4.194
Then these thou bear'st that title, have propos'd Par Reg 4.199
As by that early action may be judg'd, Par Reg 4.215
Wielded at will that fierce Democratie, Par Reg 4.269
Mellifluous streams that water'd all the schools Par Reg 4.277
Think not but that I know these things, or think Par Reg 4.286
To know this only, that he nothing knew; Par Reg 4.294
That solace? All our Law and Story strew'd Par Reg 4.334
That pleas'd so well our Victors ear, declare Par Reg 4.337
That rather *Greece* from us these Arts deriv'd; Par Reg 4.338
Whereof this ominous night that clos'd thee round, Par Reg 4.481
Obtrud'st thy offer'd aid, that I accepting Par Reg 4.493
On thy birth-night, that sung thee Saviour born. Par Reg 4.506
From that time seldom have I ceas'd to eye Par Reg 4.507
And narrower Scrutiny, that I might learn Par Reg 4.515
Therefore I watch'd thy footsteps from that hour, Par Reg 4.522
And as that *Theban* Monster that propos'd Par Reg 4.572
That once found out and solv'd, for grief and spight Par Reg 4.574
And to his crew, that sat consulting, brought Par Reg 4.577
That soon refresh'd him wearied, and repair'd Par Reg 4.591
For though that seat of earthly bliss be fail'd, Par Reg 4.612
From restless thoughts, that like a deadly swarm Samson 19
Lower then bondslave! Promise was that I Samson 38
Suffices that to me strength is my bane, Samson 63
So many, and so huge, that each apart Samson 65
That light is in the Soul, Samson 92
That she might look at will through every pore? Samson 97
That Heroic, that Renown'd, Samson 125
Yet that which was the worst now least afflicts me, Samson 195
Mee, not my Parents, that I sought to wed, Samson 220
That what I motion'd was of God; I knew Samson 222
The Marriage on; that by occasion hence Samson 224
(O that I never had! fond wish too late.) Samson 228
That specious Monster, my accomplisht snare. Samson 230
Sam. That fault I take not on me, but transfer Samson 241
Had *Judah* that day join'd, or one whole Tribe, Samson 265
In that sore battel when so many dy'd Samson 287
To seek in marriage that fallacious Bride, Samson 320
That moral verdit quits her of unclean: Samson 324
With mention of that name renews th' assault. Samson 331
That invincible *Samson*, far renown'd, Samson 341
Lay stor'd, in what part summ'd, that she might know: Samson 395
True slavery, and that blindness worse then this, Samson 418
That saw not how degenerately I serv'd. Samson 419
I state not that; this I am sure; our Foes Samson 424
Enough, and more the burden of that fault; Samson 431
That rigid score. A worse thing yet remains, Samson 433
Of all reproach the most with shame that ever Samson 446
That I this honour, I this pomp have brought Samson 449
The anguish of my Soul, that suffers not Samson 458
This only hope relieves me, that the strife Samson 460
Sam. Spare that proposal, Father, spare the trouble Samson 487
Of that sollicitation; let me here, Samson 488
That Gentiles in thir Parables condemn Samson 500
Or taste that cheers the heart of Gods and men, Samson 545
Whose heads that turbulent liquor fills with fumes. Samson 552
Man. Wilt thou then serve the *Philistines* with that gift Samson 577
That these dark orbs no more shall treat with light, Samson 591
And I shall shortly be with them that rest. Samson 598
That mingle with thy fancy. I however Samson 601
Sam. O that torment should not be confin'd Samson 606
Nor am I in the list of them that hope; Samson 647
Secret refreshings, that repair his strength, Samson 665
That thou towards him with hand so various, Samson 668
That wandring loose about Samson 675
That so bedeckt, ornate, and gay, Samson 712
Courted by all the winds that hold them play, Samson 719
That wisest and best men full oft beguil'd Samson 759
Dal. Yet hear me *Samson;* not that I endeavour Samson 766
But that on th' other side if it be weigh'd Samson 768
For importunity, that is for naught, Samson 779
Nor shouldst thou have trusted that to womans frailty Samson 783
Thine forgive mine; that men may censure thine Samson 787
Who tempted me, that nothing was design'd Samson 801

That(*cont*)
That made for me, I knew that liberty Samson 803
That malice not repentance brought thee hither, Samson 821
All wickedness is weakness: that plea therefore Samson 834
That wrought with me: thou know'st the Magistrates Samson 850
With hard contest: at length that grounded maxim Samson 865
Of wisest men; that to the public good Samson 867
Thir favourable ear, that I may fetch thee Samson 921
That what by me thou hast lost thou least shalt miss. Samson 927
At distance I forgive thee, go with that; Samson 954
That womans love can win or long inherit; Samson 1012
Is it for that such outward ornament Samson 1025
Was lavish't on thir Sex, that inward gifts Samson 1026
That either they love nothing, or not long? Samson 1033
That in domestic good combines: Samson 1048
Happy that house! his way to peace is smooth: Samson 1049
Nor from that right to part an hour, Samson 1056
That *Kiriathaim* held, thou knowst me now Samson 1081
That I was never present on the place Samson 1085
Gives and the Mill had tam'd thee? O that fortune Samson 1093
The highest name for valiant Acts, that honour Samson 1101
That in a little time while breath remains thee, Samson 1126
Were bristles rang'd like those that ridge the back Samson 1137
Har. Fair honour that thou dost thy God, in trusting Samson 1178
That solv'd the riddle which I had propos'd. Samson 1200
And that he durst not plain enough appear'd. Samson 1256
The worst that he can give, to me the best. Samson 1264
That tyrannie or fortune can inflict, Samson 1291
My presence; for that cause I cannot come. Samson 1321
With corporal servitude, that my mind ever Samson 1336
Yet that he may dispense with me or thee Samson 1377
Nothing to do, be sure, that may dishonour Samson 1385
Of fire; that Spirit that first rusht on thee Samson 1435
But that which mov'd my coming now, was chiefly Samson 1452
Cho. That hope would much rejoyce us to partake Samson 1455
That part most reverenc'd *Dagon* and his Priests, Samson 1463
What noise or shout was that? it tore the Skie. Samson 1472
And he in that calamitous prison left. Samson 1480
That of a Nation arm'd the strength contain'd: Samson 1494
Mercy of Heav'n what hideous noise was that! Samson 1509
Blood, death, and deathful deeds are in that noise, Samson 1513
Chor. Thy Son is rather slaying them, that outcry Samson 1517
Man. That were a joy presumptuous to be thought. Samson 1531
Mess. Feed on that first, there may in grief be surfet. Samson 1562
Man. Relate by whom. *Mess*. By *Samson*. *Man*. That still lessens Samson 1563
When all abroad was rumour'd that this day Samson 1600
Not to be absent at that spectacle. Samson 1604
That to the arched roof gave main support. Samson 1634
Like that self-begott'n bird Samson 1699
That no second knows nor third, Samson 1701
And all that band them to resist Samson 1753
Unmindfull of the crown that Vertue gives Mask 9
Yet som there be that by due steps aspire Mask 12
To lay their just hands on that Golden Key Mask 13
That ope's the Palace of Eternity: Mask 14
That like to rich, and various gemms inlay Mask 22
And all this tract that fronts the falling Sun Mask 30
But that by quick command from Soveran *Jove* Mask 41
Bacchus that first from out the purple Grape, Mask 46
This Nymph that gaz'd upon his clustring locks, Mask 54
That to the service of this house belongs, Mask 85
Comus. The Star that bids the Shepherd fold, Mask 93
We that are of purer fire Mask 111
Tis onely day-light that makes Sin Mask 126
That ne're art call'd, but when the Dragon woom Mask 131
Which must not be, for that's against my course; Mask 159
Trinity ms 'thats'
Bridgewater ms 'thats'
When for their teeming Flocks, and granges full Mask 175
Trinity ms 'when' ←'that' ←'when'
That nature hung in Heav'n, and fill'd their Lamps Mask 198
line not in Bridgewater ms
And airy tongues, that syllable mens names Mask 208
line not in Bridgewater ms
The vertuous mind, that ever walks attended Mask 211
line not in Bridgewater ms
That he, the Supreme good, t' whom all things ill Mask 217
line not in Bridgewater ms
Sweet Echo, sweetest Nymph that liv'st unseen Mask 230
That likest thy *Narcissus* are? Mask 237
Sure somthing holy lodges in that brest, Mask 246
Unlesse the Goddes that in rurall shrine Mask 267
La. Nay gentle Shepherd ill is lost that praise Mask 271
That is addrest to unattending Ears, Mask 272
Co. Could that divide you from neer-ushering guides? Mask 279
That crawls along the side of yon small hill, Mask 295
That in the colours of the Rainbow live Mask 300
What readiest way would bring me to that place? Mask 305
La. To find out that, good Shepherd, I suppose, Mask 307
I cannot be, that I should fear to change it. Mask 328
That wontst to love the travailers benizon, Mask 332
And disinherit *Chaos*, that raigns here Mask 334
Be barr'd that happines, might we but hear Mask 343
But O that haples virgin our lost sister Mask 350
And the sweet peace that goodnes boosoms ever, Mask 368
As that the single want of light and noise Mask 369
That in the various bussle of resort Mask 379
He that has light within his own cleer brest Mask 381

That(*cont*)
But he that hides a dark soul, and foul thoughts Mask 383
That musing meditation most affects Mask 386
I fear the dred events that dog them both, Mask 405
That I encline to hope, rather then fear, Mask 412
Unless the strength of Heav'n, if you mean that? Mask 417
Eld. Bro. I mean that too, but yet a hidden strength Mask 418
She that has that, is clad in compleat steel, Mask 421
Som say no evil thing that walks by night Mask 432
That breaks his magick chains at *curfeu* time, Mask 435
What was that snaky-headed *Gorgon* sheild Mask 447
That wise *Minerva* wore, unconquer'd Virgin, Mask 448
Bridgewater ms 'the'
And noble grace that dash't brute violence Mask 451
That when a soul is found sincerely so, Mask 454
Tell her of things that no gross ear can hear, Mask 458
As loath to leave the body that it lov'd, Mask 473
That hallow I should know, what are you? speak; Mask 490
Spir. What voice is that, my young Lord? speak agen. Mask 492
That doth enrich these Downs, is worth a thought Mask 505
The visage quite transforms of him that drinks, Mask 527
That brow this bottom glade, whence night by night Mask 532
Of them that pass unweeting by the way. Mask 539
That draw the litter of close-curtain'd sleep. Mask 554
And stole upon the Air, that even Silence Mask 557
And took in strains that might create a soul Mask 561
Where that damn'd wisard hid in sly disguise Mask 571
Ye were the two she mean't, with that I sprung Mask 578
Of malice or of sorcery, or that power Mask 587
Yea even that which mischief meant most harm, Mask 591
But for that damn'd magician, let him be girt Mask 602
With all the greisly legions that troop Mask 603
Be those that quell the might of hellish charms, Mask 613
That spreds her verdant leaf to th' morning ray, Mask 622
And yet more med'cinal is it then that *Moly* Mask 636
That *Hermes* once to wise *Ulysses* gave; Mask 637
Trinity ms 'that' ←'which' ←'that'
line not in Bridgewater ms
Till now that this extremity compell'd, Mask 643
Root-bound, that fled *Apollo*, *La*. Fool do not boast, Mask 662
That fancy can beget on youthfull thoughts, Mask 669
That flames, and dances in his crystal bounds Mask 673
Not that *Nepenthes* which the wife of *Thone*, Mask 675
With that which you receiv'd on other terms, Mask 684
line not in Bridgewater ms
That have been tir'd all day without repast, Mask 688
That thou hast banish't from thy tongue with lies, Mask 692
And that which is not good, is not delicious Mask 704
Co. O foolishnes of men! that lend their ears Mask 706
That in their green shops weave the smooth-hair'd silk Mask 716
To deck her Sons, and that no corner might Mask 717
And so bestudd with Stars, that they below Mask 734
With that same vaunted name Virginity, Mask 738
line not in Bridgewater ms
What need a vermeil-tinctur'd lip for that Mask 752
line not in Bridgewater ms
In this unhallow'd air, but that this Jugler Mask 757
That live according to her sober laws, Mask 766
If every just man that now pines with want Mask 768
Of that which lewdly-pamper'd Luxury Mask 770
Or have I said anough? To him that dares Mask 780
line not in Trinity ms
line not in Bridgewater ms
That must be utter'd to unfold the sage Mask 786
line not in Bridgewater ms
line not in Trinity ms
And thou art worthy that thou shouldst not know Mask 788
line not in Bridgewater ms
line not in Trinity ms
That hath so well been taught her dazling fence, Mask 791
line not in Bridgewater ms
line not in Trinity ms
That dumb things would be mov'd to sympathize, Mask 796
line not in Bridgewater ms
line not in Trinity ms
Co. She fables not, I feel that I do fear Mask 800
line not in Trinity ms
line not in Bridgewater ms
We cannot free the Lady that sits here Mask 818
Som other means I have which may be us'd, Mask 821
Trinity ms 'that may'
Bridgewater ms 'that may'
The soothest Shepherd that ere pip't on plains. Mask 823
That with moist curb sways the smooth Severn stream, Mask 825
That had the Scepter from his father *Brute*. Mask 828
Bridgewater ms 'whoe'
That stay'd her flight with his cross-flowing course, Mask 832
The water Nymphs that in the bottom plaid, Mask 833
That the shrewd medling Elfe delights to make, Mask 846
And her son that rules the strands, Mask 876
By all the *Nymphs* that nightly dance Mask 883
Bridgewater ms 'of'
That in the channell strayes, Mask 895
That bends not as I tread, Mask 899
Drops that from my fountain pure, Mask 912
That tumble down the snowy hills: Mask 927
All the Swains that there abide, Mask 951
And those happy climes that ly Mask 977

That(*cont*)
That sing about the golden tree: Mask 983
That there eternal Summer dwels, Mask 988
word not in Bridgewater ms
Waters the odorous banks that blow Mask 993
Mortals that would follow me, Mask 1018
the jealous ocean that old river winds Mask Tr. ms 10.12
that lurks by hedge or lane of this dead circuit Mask Tr. ms 16.40
that lurks by hedge or lane, of this dead circuit Mask Br. ms 393
The frolick Wind that breathes the Spring, Allegro 18
Sport that wrincled Care derides, Allegro 31
That ten day-labourers could not end, Allegro 109
Untwisting all the chains that ty Allegro 143
That *Orpheus* self may heave his head Allegro 145
As the gay motes that people the Sun Beams, Penseroso 8
Or that Starr'd *Ethiope* Queen that strove Penseroso 19
Spare Fast, that oft with gods doth diet, Penseroso 46
That in trim Gardens takes his pleasure; Penseroso 50
Him that yon soars on golden wing, Penseroso 52
Sweet Bird that shunn'st the noise of folly, Penseroso 61
Like one that had bin led astray Penseroso 69
The immortal mind that hath forsook Penseroso 91
And of those *Daemons* that are found Penseroso 93
But, O sad Virgin, that thy power Penseroso 103
Or call up him that left half told Penseroso 109
That own'd the vertuous Ring and Glass, Penseroso 113
And shadows brown that *Sylvan* loves Penseroso 134
That at her flowry work doth sing, Penseroso 143
Of every Star that Heav'n doth shew, Penseroso 171
And every Herb that sips the dew; Penseroso 172
Is that which we from hence descry Arcades 3
Fame that her high worth to raise, Arcades 8
Of that renowned flood, so often sung, Arcades 29
That sit upon the nine enfolded Sphears, Arcades 64
And sing to those that hold the vital shears, Arcades 65
Where ye may all that are of noble stemm Arcades 82
That from beneath the seat of *Jove* doth spring, Lycidas 16
Oft till the Star that rose, at Ev'ning, bright Lycidas 30
Trinity ms 'starre that rose' ←'ev'n starre bright'
1638 'Oft till the ev'n-starre bright'
Or Taint-worm to the weanling Herds that graze, Lycidas 46
Or Frost to Flowers, that their gay wardrop wear, Lycidas 47
Had ye bin there---for what could that have don? Lycidas 57
What could the Muse her self that *Orpheus* bore, Lycidas 58
When by the rout that made the hideous roar, Lycidas 61
Fame is the spur that the clear spirit doth raise Lycidas 70
(That last infirmity of Noble mind) Lycidas 71
Fame is no plant that grows on mortal soil, Lycidas 78
That strain I heard was of a higher mood: Lycidas 87
That came in *Neptune*'s plea, Lycidas 90
That blows from off each beaked Promontory, Lycidas 94
That not a blast was from his dungeon stray'd, Lycidas 97
It was that fatall and perfidious Bark Lycidas 100
That sunk so low that sacred head of thine. Lycidas 102
Like to that sanguine flower inscrib'd with woe. Lycidas 106
Blind mouthes! that scarce themselves know how to hold Lycidas 119
That to the faithfull Herdmans art belongs! Lycidas 121
But that two-handed engine at the door, Lycidas 130
That shrunk thy streams; Return *Sicilian* Muse, Lycidas 133
That on the green terf suck the honied showres, Lycidas 140
Bring the rathe Primrose that forsaken dies. Lycidas 142
With Cowslips wan that hang the pensive hed, Lycidas 147
And every flower that sad embroidery wears: Lycidas 148
Through the dear might of him that walk'd the waves; Lycidas 173
That sing, and singing in their glory move, Lycidas 180
To all that wander in that perilous flood. Lycidas 185
and that sad floure that strove Lycidas Tr. ms 28.17
next adde Narcissus that still weeps in vaine Lycidas Tr. ms 28.19
That he our deadly forfeit should release, Nativity 6
That glorious Form, that Light unsufferable, Nativity 8
And that far-beaming blaze of Majesty, Nativity 9
Confounded, that her Makers eyes Nativity 43
Or *Lucifer* that often warn'd them thence; Nativity 74
That the mighty *Pan* Nativity 89
Was all that did their silly thoughts so busie keep. Nativity 92
Nature that heard such sound Nativity 101
And that her raign had here its last fulfilling; Nativity 106
That with long beams the shame-fac't night array'd, Nativity 111
That on the bitter cross Nativity 152
With terrour of that blast, Nativity 161
With that twise batter'd god of *Palestine*, Nativity 199
That saw the troubl'd Sea, and shivering fled, Psalm 114, 7
As a faint host that hath receiv'd the foil. Psalm 114, 10
Of him that ever was, and ay shall last, Psalm 114, 16
That glassy flouds from rugged rocks can crush, Psalm 114, 17
That doth the wrathfull tyrants quell. Psalm 136, 10
1673 'Who'
That with his miracles doth make Psalm 136, 13
1673 'Who'
That by his wisdom did create Psalm 136, 17
1673 'Who'
That did the solid Earth ordain Psalm 136, 21
1673 'Who'
That by his all-commanding might, Psalm 136, 25
1673 'Who'
That rul'd the *Amorrean* coast. Psalm 136, 66
That his mansion hath on high Psalm 136, 93
Bleak winters force that made thy blossome drie; Fair Inf 4

That(*cont*)
For he being amorous on that lovely die Fair Inf 5
That did thy cheek envermeil, thought to kiss Fair Inf 6
Alack that so to change thee winter had no power. Fair Inf 28
Or that thy coarse corrupts in earths dark wombe, Fair Inf 30
Or that thy beauties lie in wormie bed, Fair Inf 31
Above mortalitie that shew'd thou wast divine. Fair Inf 35
(If so it be that thou these plaints dost hear) Fair Inf 37
Whether above that high first-moving Spheare Fair Inf 39
Or wert thou that just Maid who once before Fair Inf 50
Or wert thou that sweet smiling Youth! Fair Inf 53
Or that crown'd Matron sage white-robed truth? Fair Inf 54
Or any other of that heav'nly brood Fair Inf 55
But thou canst best perform that office where thou art. Fair Inf 70
That till the worlds last-end shall make thy name to live. Fair Inf 77
Hail native Language, that by sinews weak Vacation 1
That now I use thee in my latter task: Vacation 8
Small loss it is that thence can come unto thee, Vacation 9
For this same small neglect that I have made: Vacation 16
I have some naked thoughts that rove about Vacation 23
That so they may without suspect or fears Vacation 27
Then sing of secret things that came to pass Vacation 45
That to the next I may resign my Roome. Vacation 58
She heard them give thee this, that thou should'st still Vacation 65
Yet there is something that doth force my fear, Vacation 67
That far events full wisely could presage, Vacation 70
And those that cannot live from him asunder Vacation 77
To harbour those that are at enmity. Vacation 88
Or sullen *Mole* that runneth underneath, Vacation 95
Or *Humber* loud that keeps the *Scythians* Name, Vacation 99
That dropt with odorous oil down his fair eyes, Passion 16
That Heav'n and Earth are colour'd with my wo; Passion 32
That whirl'd the Prophet up at *Chebar* flood, Passion 37
Mine eye hath found that sad Sepulchral rock Passion 43
That was the Casket of Heav'ns richest store, Passion 44
That they would fitly fall in order'd Characters. Passion 49
When every thing that is sincerely good On Time 14
That erst with Musick, and triumphant song Circum 2
Were lost in death, till he that dwelt above Circum 18
And that great Cov'nant which we still transgress Circum 21
That undisturbed Song of pure content, Musick 6
To him that sits theron Musick 8
With those just Spirits that wear victorious Palms, Musick 14
That we on Earth with undiscording voice Musick 17
May rightly answer that melodious noise; Musick 18
Broke the fair musick that all creatures made Musick 21
O may we soon again renew that Song, Musick 25
while all the starrie rounds & arches blue Musick Tr. ms 4.21
'while all the starrie rounds' ←'starrie frame' ←'whilst then' ←'whilst the whole frame of' ←'while all the' ←'that all'
of clamourous sin that all our musick marres Musick Tr. ms 5.04
The God that sits at marriage feast; Winchester 18
That to give the world encrease, Winchester 51
That thy noble House doth bring, Winchester 54
That fair *Syrian* Shepherdess, Winchester 63
To him that serv'd for her before, Winchester 66
Hail bounteous *May* that dost inspire May Morn 5
Or that his hallow'd reliques should be hid Shakespear 3
Thy easie numbers flow, and that each heart Shakespear 10
That Kings for such a Tomb would wish to die. Shakespear 16
'Twas such a shifter, that if truth were known, Carrier 5
Death was half glad when he had got him down; Carrier 6
1658 'glad that'
And that he had tane up his latest Inne, Carrier 13
Shew'd him his room where he must lodge that night, Carrier 15
That he could never die while he could move, Another 2
Rest that gives all men life, gave him his death, Another 11
He di'd for heavines that his Cart went light, Another 22
line not in 1658 text
His leasure told him that his time was com, Another 23
line not in 1658 text
That even to his last breath (ther be that say't) Another 25
line not in 1640, 1657, 1658 texts
line not in 1640, 1657, 1658 texts
O Nightingale, that on yon bloomy Spray Sonnet 1, 1
Thy liquid notes that close the eye of Day, Sonnet 1, 5
Have linkt that amorous power to thy soft lay, Sonnet 1, 8
That I to manhood am arriv'd so near, Sonnet 7, 6
That som more timely-happy spirits indu'th. Sonnet 7, 8
To that same lot, however mean, or high, Sonnet 7, 11
That call Fame on such gentle acts as these, Sonnet 8, 6
Lady that in the prime of earliest youth, Sonnet 9, 1
That labour up the Hill of heav'nly Truth, Sonnet 9, 4
Chosen thou hast, and they that overween, Sonnet 9, 6
And Hope that reaps not shame. Therefore be sure Sonnet 9, 11
Passes to bliss at the mid hour of night, Sonnet 9, 13
Trinity ms 'the midd night howr' ←'the midd watch' ←'that hovre of night'
Daughter to that good Earl, once President Sonnet 10, 1
Till the sad breaking of that Parlament Sonnet 10, 5
Broke him, as that dishonest victory Sonnet 10, 6
Kil'd with report that Old man eloquent, Sonnet 10, 8
That all both judge you to relate them true, Sonnet 10, 13
That would have made *Quintilian* stare and gasp. Sonnet 11, 11
As when those Hinds that were transform'd to Froggs Sonnet 12, 5
That bawle for freedom in their senceless mood, Sonnet 12, 9
For who loves that, must first be wise and good; Sonnet 12, 12

That(*cont*)
But from that mark how far they roave we see — Sonnet 12, 13
That with smooth aire couldst humor best our tongue. — Sonnet 13, 8
That tun'st their happiest lines in Hymn, or Story. — Sonnet 13, 11
that didst reform thy art, the cheif among — Sonnet 13, Tr. ms 40.08
When Faith and Love which parted from thee never, — Sonnet 14, 1
Trinity ms 'which' ←'that'
And azure wings, that up they flew so drest, — Sonnet 14, 11
Trinity ms 'that' ←'thence'
Strait follow'd thee the path that Saints have trod — Sonnet 14, Tr. ms 41.06
And rumors loud, that daunt remotest kings, — Sonnet 15, 4
1694 'which'
Cromwell, our cheif of men, who through a cloud — Sonnet 16, 1
1694 'that through'
Slayn by the bloody *Piemontese* that roll'd — Sonnet 18, 7
The triple Tyrant: that from these may grow — Sonnet 18, 12
And that one Talent which is death to hide, — Sonnet 19, 3
That murmur, soon replies, God doth not need — Sonnet 19, 9
Now that the Fields are dank, and ways are mire, — Sonnet 20, 2
The Lillie and Rose, that neither sow'd nor spun. — Sonnet 20, 8
In mirth, that after no repenting drawes; — Sonnet 21, 6
And disapproves that care, though wise in show, — Sonnet 21, 12
That with superfluous burden loads the day, — Sonnet 21, 13
To force our Consciences that Christ set free, — Forcers 6
That so the Parliament — Forcers 15
That in arms against me rise — Psalm 3, 3
That of my life distrustfully thus say, — Psalm 3, 5
Many there be that say — Psalm 4, 25
For thou art not a God that takes — Psalm 5, 9
Thou wilt destroy that speak a ly — Psalm 5, 15
That do observe If I transgress — Psalm 5, 23
For all my bones, that even with anguish ake, — Psalm 6, 5
Ith' mid'st of all mine enemies that mark. — Psalm 6, 15
Depart all ye that work iniquitie. — Psalm 6, 16
Ill to him that meant me peace, — Psalm 7, 10
Of my foes that urge like fire; — Psalm 7, 21
And their power that do amiss. — Psalm 7, 36
Since thou art the just God that tries — Psalm 7, 38
The tools of death, that waits him near. — Psalm 7, 48
For them that persecute.) Behold — Psalm 7, 50
As in a womb, and from that mould — Psalm 7, 53
His mischief that due course doth keep, — Psalm 7, 57
That bends his rage thy providence to oppose — Psalm 8, 8
O what is man that thou remembrest yet, — Psalm 8, 12
That him thou visit'st and of him art found; — Psalm 8, 14
All beasts that in the field or forrest meet, — Psalm 8, 20
Fowl of the Heavens, and Fish that through the wet — Psalm 8, 21
Thou Shepherd that dost Israel *keep* — Psalm 80, 1
That sitt'st between the Cherubs *bright* — Psalm 80, 5
That it *began to grow apace*, — Psalm 80, 39
With her *green* shade *that* cover'd *all*, — Psalm 80, 41
And *upward* to that river *wide* — Psalm 80, 47
That all may pluck her, as they go, — Psalm 80, 51
And the young branch, that for thy self — Psalm 80, 63
To Jacobs God, *that all may hear* — Psalm 81, 3
O that my people would *be wise* — Psalm 81, 53
And O that Israel would *advise* — Psalm 81, 55
That now so proudly rise, — Psalm 81, 58
That are their enemies. — Psalm 81, 60
Of him *that help demands*. — Psalm 82, 16
I said that ye were Gods, yea all — Psalm 82, 21
And they that hate thee *proud and fell* — Psalm 83, 7
That Israels name for ever may — Psalm 83, 15
That in the Desart dwell, — Psalm 83, 24
That wasted all the Coast — Psalm 83, 34
Then shall they know that thou whose name — Psalm 83, 65
That dry and barren ground — Psalm 84, 22
Lord *God* of Hoasts *that raign'st on high*, — Psalm 84, 45
That man is *truly* blest, — Psalm 84, 46
That wrought thy people woe, — Psalm 85, 6
And all their Sin, *that did thee grieve* — Psalm 85, 7
That so thy people may rejoyce — Psalm 85, 23
Mercy and Truth *that long were miss'd* — Psalm 85, 41
To them that on thee call. — Psalm 86, 16
Of all that other gods have done — Psalm 86, 27
But *twise that praise shall in our ear* — Psalm 87, 17
That ne're shall be out-worn — Psalm 87, 22
That this man there was born. — Psalm 87, 24
Lord God that dost me save and keep, — Psalm 88, 1
And to my cries, that *ceaseless are*, — Psalm 88, 7
Reck'n'd I am with them that pass — Psalm 88, 13
And for that name unfit. — Psalm 88, 16
That in the grave lie *deep*. — Psalm 88, 20
That am already bruis'd, and shake — Psalm 88, 59
That the first wealthy *Pope* receiv'd of thee. — Prose 1, 3
Things that on earth were lost, or were abus'd. — Prose 2, 4
'Gainst them that rais'd thee dost thou lift thy horn, — Prose 3, 2
This was that gift (if you the truth will have) — Prose 4, 3
That *Constantine* to good *Sylvestro* gave. — Prose 4, 4
Iunkets and knacks, that they may learne apace. — Prose 6, 3
Tis you that say it, not I, you do the deeds, — Prose 8, 1

Thatched
From her thach't pallat rowse, if otherwise — Mask 318
Trinity ms 'thetch't'
1673 'thatch't'
Bridgewater ms 'thatcht'

Thaw
More hard'nd after thaw, till in his rage — Par Lost 12.194

Thaw(*cont*)
The clasping charm, and thaw the numming spell, — Mask 853
Bridgewater ms 'thawe'
Trinity ms 'thaw the numming' ←'melt each' ←'secret holding'

Thaws
Thaws not, but gathers heap, and ruin seems — Par Lost 2.590

Thay
Whereby they may direct their future life. — Par Reg 1.396

The
Listings of this word are omitted; see the Introduction.

Theatre
Shade above shade, a woodie Theatre — Par Lost 4.141
The building was a spacious Theatre — Samson 1605

Theatres
Porches and Theatres, Baths, Aqueducts, — Par Reg 4.36

Theban
And as that *Theban* Monster that propos'd — Par Reg 4.572

Thebes
That fought at *Theb*'s and *Ilium*, on each side — Par Lost 1.578
ms 'Theb's'
Bright Temple, to *Aegyptian Theb*'s he flies. — Par Lost 5.274
Presenting *Thebs*, or *Pelops* line, — Penseroso 99

Thebez
Native of *Thebez* wandring here was fed — Par Reg 2.313
1671 printed '*Thebes*', errata '*Thebez*'

Thee
Delight thee more, and *Siloa*'s Brook that flow'd — Par Lost 1.11
That be assur'd, without leave askt of thee: — Par Lost 2.685
Where I reign King, and to enrage thee more, — Par Lost 2.698
Strange horror seise thee, and pangs unfelt before. — Par Lost 2.703
Possesses thee to bend that mortal Dart — Par Lost 2.729
At thee ordain'd his drudge, to execute — Par Lost 2.732
Prevented spares to tell thee yet by deeds — Par Lost 2.739
What it intends; till first I know of thee, — Par Lost 2.740
I know thee not, nor ever saw till now — Par Lost 2.744
Sight more detestable then him and thee. — Par Lost 2.745
Of all the Seraphim with thee combin'd — Par Lost 2.750
Surpris'd thee, dim thine eyes, and dizzie swumm — Par Lost 2.753
Likest to thee in shape and count'nance bright, — Par Lost 2.756
The most averse, thee chiefly, who full oft — Par Lost 2.763
Pregnant by thee, and now excessive grown — Par Lost 2.779
But thou O Father, I forewarn thee, shun — Par Lost 2.810
Of dalliance had with thee in Heav'n, and joys — Par Lost 2.819
Both him and thee, and all the heav'nly Host — Par Lost 2.824
But thee, whom follow? thou wilt bring me soon — Par Lost 2.866
Answer'd. I know thee, stranger, who thou art, — Par Lost 2.990
May I express thee unblam'd? since God is light, — Par Lost 3.3
Dwelt from Eternitie, dwelt then in thee, — Par Lost 3.5
Thee I re-visit now with bolder wing, — Par Lost 3.13
Though hard and rare: thee I revisit safe, — Par Lost 3.21
Thee *Sion* and the flowrie Brooks beneath — Par Lost 3.30
Encompass'd shall resound thee ever blest. — Par Lost 3.149
With his own folly? that be from thee farr, — Par Lost 3.153
That farr be from thee, Father, who art Judg — Par Lost 3.154
Thy bosom, and this glorie next to thee — Par Lost 3.239
Life in my self for ever, by thee I live, — Par Lost 3.244
While by thee rais'd I ruin all my Foes, — Par Lost 3.258
Thee from my bosom and right hand, to save, — Par Lost 3.279
By loosing thee a while, the whole Race lost. — Par Lost 3.280
As in him perish all men, so in thee — Par Lost 3.287
As many as are restor'd, without thee none. — Par Lost 3.289
And live in thee transplanted, and from thee — Par Lost 3.293
Farr more then Great or High; because in thee — Par Lost 3.311
With thee thy Manhood also to this Throne; — Par Lost 3.314
I give thee, reign for ever, and assume — Par Lost 3.318
Thy Merits; under thee as Head Supream — Par Lost 3.319
All knees to thee shall bow, of them that bide — Par Lost 3.321
Shalt in the Sky appeer, and from thee send — Par Lost 3.324
Thee Father first they sung Omnipotent, — Par Lost 3.372
Eternal King; thee Author of all being, — Par Lost 3.374
Drawn round about thee like a radiant Shrine, — Par Lost 3.379
Thee next they sang of all Creation first, — Par Lost 3.383
Whom else no Creature can behold; on thee — Par Lost 3.387
Transfus'd on thee his ample Spirit rests. — Par Lost 3.389
By thee created, and by thee threw down — Par Lost 3.391
Thee only extoll'd, Son of thy Fathers might, — Par Lost 3.398
Perceive thee purpos'd not to doom frail Man — Par Lost 3.404
Second to thee, offerd himself to die — Par Lost 3.409
The more it seems excess, that led thee hither — Par Lost 3.698
Hide thir diminisht heads; to thee I call, — Par Lost 4.35
O Sun, to tell thee how I hate thy beams — Par Lost 4.37
Evil be thou my Good; by thee at least — Par Lost 4.110
By thee, and more then half perhaps will reigne; — Par Lost 4.112
Which were it toilsom, yet with thee were sweet. — Par Lost 4.439
So farr the happier Lot, enjoying thee — Par Lost 4.446
With thee it came and goes: but follow me, — Par Lost 4.469
And I will bring thee where no shadow staies — Par Lost 4.470
Till I espi'd thee, fair indeed and tall, — Par Lost 4.477
His flesh, his bone; to give thee being I lent — Par Lost 4.483
Out of my side to thee, neerest my heart — Par Lost 4.484
Substantial Life, to have thee by my side — Par Lost 4.485
Part of my Soul I seek thee, and thee claim — Par Lost 4.487
Gabriel, to thee thy course by Lot hath giv'n — Par Lost 4.561
With thee conversing I forget all time, — Par Lost 4.639
Or glittering Starr-light without thee is sweet. — Par Lost 4.656
Ordaind by thee, and this delicious place — Par Lost 4.729
By thee adulterous lust was driv'n from men — Par Lost 4.753

Thee(*cont*)
Among the bestial herds to raunge, by thee Par Lost 4.754
Farr be it, that I should write thee sin or blame, Par Lost 4.758
Or think thee unbefitting holiest place, Par Lost 4.759
Departed from thee, and thou resembl'st now Par Lost 4.839
Single against thee wicked, and thence weak. Par Lost 4.856
And such I held thee; but this question askt Par Lost 4.887
To thee no reason; who knowst only good, Par Lost 4.895
Which taught thee yet no better, that no pain Par Lost 4.915
But wherefore thou alone? wherefore with thee Par Lost 4.917
But mark what I arreede thee now, avant; Par Lost 4.962
Back to th' infernal pit I drag thee chaind, Par Lost 4.965
And Seale thee so, as henceforth not to scorne Par Lost 4.966
To trample thee as mire: for proof look up, Par Lost 4.1010
If dream'd, not as I oft am wont, of thee, Par Lost 5.32
Whom to behold but thee, Natures desire, Par Lost 5.45
I rose as at thy call, but found thee not; Par Lost 5.48
To find thee I directed then my walk; Par Lost 5.49
Yet evil whence? in thee can harbour none, Par Lost 5.99
Reservd from night, and kept for thee in store. Par Lost 5.128
To visit thee; lead on then where thy Bowre Par Lost 5.375
This was that caution giv'n thee; be advis'd. Par Lost 5.523
God made thee perfet, not immutable; Par Lost 5.524
And good he made thee, but to persevere Par Lost 5.525
Wast wont, I mine to thee was wont to impart; Par Lost 5.677
Expected, least of all from thee, ingrate Par Lost 5.811
Thee what thou art, and formd the Pow'rs of Heav'n Par Lost 5.824
United. But to grant it thee unjust, Par Lost 5.831
All things, ev'n thee, and all the Spirits of Heav'n Par Lost 5.837
Thy making, while the Maker gave thee being? Par Lost 5.858
Against thee are gon forth without recall; Par Lost 5.885
Then who created thee lamenting learne, Par Lost 5.894
When who can uncreate thee thou shalt know. Par Lost 5.895
Judg'd thee perverse: the easier conquest now Par Lost 6.37
Remains thee, aided by this host of friends, Par Lost 6.38
Thir names of thee; so over many a tract Par Lost 6.76
Unaided could have finisht thee, and whelmd Par Lost 6.141
To thee not visible, when I alone Par Lost 6.145
Thus answerd. Ill for thee, but in wisht houre Par Lost 6.150
(Unanswerd least thou boast) to let thee know; Par Lost 6.163
Against his worthier, as thine now serve thee, Par Lost 6.180
To trouble Holy Rest; Heav'n casts thee out Par Lost 6.272
Hence then, and evil go with thee along Par Lost 6.275
Precipitate thee with augmented paine. Par Lost 6.280
I flie not, but have sought thee farr and nigh. Par Lost 6.295
For thee I have ordain'd it, and thus farr Par Lost 6.700
Can end it. Into thee such Vertue and Grace Par Lost 6.703
To manifest thee worthiest to be Heir Par Lost 6.707
To glorifie thy Son, I alwayes thee, Par Lost 6.725
Thou shalt be All in All, and I in thee Par Lost 6.732
Image of thee in all things; and shall soon, Par Lost 6.736
Unfained *Halleluiahs* to thee sing, Par Lost 6.744
By what is past, to thee I have reveal'd Par Lost 6.895
Thee also from obedience, that with him Par Lost 6.902
Thee once to gaine Companion of his woe. Par Lost 6.907
Thy weaker; let it profit thee to have heard Par Lost 6.909
With thy Celestial Song. Up led by thee Par Lost 7.12
Her Son. So fail not thou, who thee implores: Par Lost 7.38
And longer will delay to heare thee tell Par Lost 7.101
Silence, and Sleep listning to thee will watch, Par Lost 7.106
End, and dismiss thee ere the Morning shine. Par Lost 7.108
Thee also happier, shall not be withheld Par Lost 7.117
And thou my Word, begotten Son, by thee Par Lost 7.163
My overshadowing Spirit and might with thee Par Lost 7.165
Needless to thee repeated; nor unknown Par Lost 7.494
And hairie Main terrific, though to thee Par Lost 7.497
This said, he formd thee, *Adam*, thee O Man Par Lost 7.524
Created thee, in the Image of God Par Lost 7.527
Male he created thee, but thy consort Par Lost 7.529
He brought thee into this delicious Grove, Par Lost 7.537
Gave thee, all sorts are here that all th' Earth yields, Par Lost 7.541
Surprise thee, and her black attendant Death. Par Lost 7.547
And pavement Starrs, as Starrs to thee appeer, Par Lost 7.578
Thy power; what thought can measure thee or tongue Par Lost 7.603
Relate thee; greater now in thy return Par Lost 7.604
Then from the Giant Angels; thee that day Par Lost 7.605
Who can impair thee, mighty King, or bound Par Lost 7.608
Thee to diminish, and from thee withdraw Par Lost 7.612
To lessen thee, against his purpose serves Par Lost 7.614
Informd by thee might know; if else thou seekst Par Lost 7.639
Equal have I to render thee, Divine Par Lost 8.6
To ask or search I blame thee not, for Heav'n Par Lost 8.66
Is as the Book of God before thee set, Par Lost 8.67
Officious, but to thee Earths habitant. Par Lost 8.99
Invalid that which thee to doubt it mov'd; Par Lost 8.116
To thee who hast thy dwelling here on Earth. Par Lost 8.118
And beares thee soft with the smooth Air along, Par Lost 8.166
In what he gives to thee, this Paradise Par Lost 8.171
And thy faire *Eve;* Heav'n is for thee too high Par Lost 8.172
Think onely what concernes thee and thy being; Par Lost 8.174
Thee I have heard relating what was don Par Lost 8.203
How suttly to detaine thee I devise, Par Lost 8.207
Inviting thee to hear while I relate, Par Lost 8.208
For while I sit with thee, I seem in Heav'n, Par Lost 8.210
Nor tongue ineloquent; for God on thee Par Lost 8.219
Attends thee, and each word, each motion formes, Par Lost 8.223
Nor less think wee in Heav'n of thee on Earth Par Lost 8.224
For God we see hath honour'd thee, and set Par Lost 8.227

Thee(*cont*)
Desire with thee still longer to converse Par Lost 8.252
And said, thy Mansion wants thee, *Adam*, rise, Par Lost 8.296
First Father, call'd by thee I come thy Guide Par Lost 8.298
Above, or round about thee or beneath. Par Lost 8.318
This Paradise I give thee, count it thine Par Lost 8.319
Remember what I warne thee, shun to taste, Par Lost 8.327
To thee and to thy Race I give; as Lords Par Lost 8.339
From thee thir Names, and pay thee fealtie Par Lost 8.344
Adore thee, Author of this Universe, Par Lost 8.360
To come and play before thee, know'st thou not Par Lost 8.372
Let not my words offend thee, Heav'nly Power, Par Lost 8.379
Seem I to thee sufficiently possest Par Lost 8.404
Beneath what other Creatures are to thee? Par Lost 8.411
Thou in thy self art perfet, and in thee Par Lost 8.415
Thus farr to try thee, *Adam*, I was pleas'd, Par Lost 8.437
And finde thee knowing not of Beasts alone, Par Lost 8.438
Expressing well the spirit within thee free, Par Lost 8.440
Whose fellowship therefore unmeet for thee Par Lost 8.442
Intended thee, for trial onely brought, Par Lost 8.447
What next I bring shall please thee, be assur'd, Par Lost 8.449
Thus I have told thee all my State, and brought Par Lost 8.521
Of Wisdom, she deserts thee not, if thou Par Lost 8.563
For what admir'st thou, what transports thee so, Par Lost 8.567
The more she will acknowledge thee her Head, Par Lost 8.574
Among the Beasts no Mate for thee was found. Par Lost 8.594
Yet these subject not; I to thee disclose Par Lost 8.607
Answer'd. Let it suffice thee that thou know'st Par Lost 8.620
The weal or woe in thee is plac't; beware. Par Lost 8.638
Light above Light, for thee alone, as seems, Par Lost 9.105
In thee concentring all thir precious beams Par Lost 9.106
Centring receav'st from all those Orbs; in thee, Par Lost 9.109
With what delight could I have walkt thee round, Par Lost 9.114
Leads thee, or where most needs, whether to wind Par Lost 9.215
Thee satiate, to short absence I could yield. Par Lost 9.248
Befall thee sever'd from me; for thou knowst Par Lost 9.252
That gave thee being, still shades thee and protects. Par Lost 9.266
Our ruin, both by thee informd I learne, Par Lost 9.275
To God or thee, because we have a foe Par Lost 9.280
Adam, missthought of her to thee so dear? Par Lost 9.289
Not diffident of thee do I dissuade Par Lost 9.293
From thee alone, which on us both at once Par Lost 9.303
Why shouldst not thou like sense within thee feel Par Lost 9.315
That I should mind thee oft, and mind thou me. Par Lost 9.358
Not seeing thee attempted, who attest? Par Lost 9.369
Go; for thy stay, not free, absents thee more; Par Lost 9.372
For God towards thee hath done his part, do thine. Par Lost 9.375
To intercept thy way, or send thee back Par Lost 9.410
Displeas'd that I approach thee thus, and gaze Par Lost 9.535
Thee all things living gaze on, all things thine Par Lost 9.539
Half what in thee is fair, one man except, Par Lost 9.545
Who sees thee? (and what is one2) who shouldst be seen Par Lost 9.546
Thee, Serpent, suttlest beast of all the field Par Lost 9.560
Easie to mee it is to tell thee all Par Lost 9.569
And gaze, and worship thee of right declar'd Par Lost 9.611
The vertue of that Fruit, in thee first prov'd: Par Lost 9.616
My conduct, I can bring thee thither soon. Par Lost 9.630
The credit of whose vertue rest with thee, Par Lost 9.649
Conceales not from us, naming thee the Tree Par Lost 9.751
Commends thee more, while it inferrs the good Par Lost 9.754
By thee communicated, and our want: Par Lost 9.755
Shall tend thee, and the fertil burden ease Par Lost 9.801
Till dieted by thee I grow mature Par Lost 9.803
Thus grown. Experience, next to thee I owe, Par Lost 9.807
Best guide; not following thee, I had remaind Par Lost 9.808
Thee I have misst, and thought it long, depriv'd Par Lost 9.857
And growing up to Godhead; which for thee Par Lost 9.877
Chiefly I sought, without thee can despise. Par Lost 9.878
Tedious, unshar'd with thee, and odious soon. Par Lost 9.880
Deitie for thee, when Fate will not permit. Par Lost 9.885
Of Enemie hath beguil'd thee, yet unknown, Par Lost 9.905
And mee with thee hath ruind, for with thee Par Lost 9.906
How can I live without thee, how forgoe Par Lost 9.908
Another Rib afford, yet loss of thee Par Lost 9.912
However I with thee have fixt my Lot, Par Lost 9.952
Consort with thee, Death is to mee as Life; Par Lost 9.954
My own in thee, for what thou art is mine; Par Lost 9.957
One Flesh; to loose thee were to loose my self. Par Lost 9.959
And gladly of our Union heare thee speak, Par Lost 9.966
This day affords, declaring thee resolvd, Par Lost 9.968
The worst, and not perswade thee rather die Par Lost 9.979
Deserted, then oblige thee with a fact Par Lost 9.980
Yeild thee, so well this day thou hast purvey'd. Par Lost 9.1021
I saw thee first and wedded thee, adorn'd Par Lost 9.1030
With ardor to enjoy thee, fairer now Par Lost 9.1032
With me, as I besought thee, when that strange Par Lost 9.1135
I know not whence possessd thee; we had then Par Lost 9.1137
Of mine to thee, ingrateful *Eve*, exprest Par Lost 9.1164
Yet willingly chose rather Death with thee: Par Lost 9.1167
I warn'd thee, I admonish'd thee, foretold Par Lost 9.1171
But confidence then bore thee on, secure Par Lost 9.1175
What seemd in thee so perfet, that I thought Par Lost 9.1179
No evil durst attempt thee, but I rue Par Lost 9.1180
But whom send I to judge them? whom but thee Par Lost 10.55
Vicegerent Son, to thee I have transferr'd Par Lost 10.56
Mercie collegue with Justice, sending thee Par Lost 10.59
Before thee; and not repenting, this obtaine Par Lost 10.75
Them fully satisfied, and thee appease. Par Lost 10.79

Thee(*cont*)

My coming seen far off? I miss thee here,	Par Lost 10.104
Absents thee, or what chance detains? Come forth.	Par Lost 10.108
I heard thee in the Garden, and of thy voice	Par Lost 10.116
So dreadful to thee? that thou art naked, who	Par Lost 10.121
Hath told thee? hast thou eaten of the Tree	Par Lost 10.122
Whereof I gave thee charge thou shouldst not eat?	Par Lost 10.123
Wherein God set thee above her made of thee,	Par Lost 10.149
And for thee, whose perfection farr excell'd	Par Lost 10.150
Between Thee and the Woman I will put	Par Lost 10.179
Thine shall submit, hee over thee shall rule.	Par Lost 10.196
I charg'd thee, saying: Thou shalt not eate thereof,	Par Lost 10.200
Thorns also and Thistles it shall bring thee forth	Par Lost 10.203
Leads thee, I shall not lag behinde, nor erre	Par Lost 10.266
Be wanting, but afford thee equal aid,	Par Lost 10.271
Though distant from thee Worlds between, yet felt	Par Lost 10.362
That I must after thee with this thy Son;	Par Lost 10.363
And henceforth Monarchie with thee divide	Par Lost 10.379
Or trie thee now more dang'rous to his Throne.	Par Lost 10.382
Who can extenuate thee? Next, to the Son,	Par Lost 10.645
Did I request thee, Maker, from my Clay	Par Lost 10.743
To mould me Man, did I sollicite thee	Par Lost 10.744
Made thee without thy leave, what if thy Son	Par Lost 10.760
Wouldst thou admit for his contempt of thee	Par Lost 10.763
God made thee of choice his own, and of his own	Par Lost 10.766
Of refuge, and concludes thee miserable	Par Lost 10.839
Befits thee with him leagu'd, thy self as false	Par Lost 10.868
Thy inward fraud, to warn all Creatures from thee	Par Lost 10.871
To hellish falshood, snare them. But for thee	Par Lost 10.873
Fool'd and beguil'd, by him thou, I by thee,	Par Lost 10.880
To trust thee from my side, imagin'd wise,	Par Lost 10.881
I beare thee, and unweeting have offended,	Par Lost 10.916
My onely strength and stay: forlorn of thee,	Par Lost 10.921
Against God onely, I against God and thee,	Par Lost 10.931
On me, sole cause to thee of all this woe,	Par Lost 10.935
Would speed before thee, and be louder heard,	Par Lost 10.954
How little weight my words with thee can finde,	Par Lost 10.968
Restor'd by thee, vile as I am, to place	Par Lost 10.971
Living or dying, from thee I will not hide	Par Lost 10.974
To argue in thee somthing more sublime	Par Lost 10.1014
That excellence thought in thee, and implies,	Par Lost 10.1017
Was meant by Death that day, when lo, to thee	Par Lost 10.1050
With Incense, I thy Priest before thee bring,	Par Lost 11.25
Before thee reconcil'd, at least his days	Par Lost 11.39
Made one with me as I with thee am one.	Par Lost 11.44
Take to thee from among the Cherubim	Par Lost 11.100
Hast thee, and from the Paradise of God	Par Lost 11.104
As I shall thee enlighten, intermix	Par Lost 11.115
Is past, and we shall live. Whence Haile to thee,	Par Lost 11.158
Mother of all things living, since by thee	Par Lost 11.160
To me transgressour, who for thee ordaind	Par Lost 11.164
Giv'n thee of Grace, wherein thou may'st repent,	Par Lost 11.255
Redeem thee quite from Deaths rapacious claime;	Par Lost 11.258
Permits not; to remove thee I am come,	Par Lost 11.260
And send thee from the Garden forth to till	Par Lost 11.261
Must I thus leave thee Paradise? thus leave	Par Lost 11.269
Thee Native Soile, these happie Walks and Shades,	Par Lost 11.270
Thee lastly nuptial Bowre, by mee adornd	Par Lost 11.280
With what to sight or smell was sweet; from thee	Par Lost 11.281
Thy going is not lonely, with thee goes	Par Lost 11.290
All th' Earth he gave thee to possess and rule,	Par Lost 11.339
And reverence thee thir great Progenitor.	Par Lost 11.346
Still following thee, still compassing thee round	Par Lost 11.352
To shew thee what shall come in future dayes	Par Lost 11.357
To thee and to thy Ofspring; good with bad	Par Lost 11.358
Ascend, I follow thee, safe Guide, the path	Par Lost 11.371
In some to spring from thee, who never touch'd	Par Lost 11.425
Before thee shall appear; that thou mayst know	Par Lost 11.475
And now prepare thee for another sight.	Par Lost 11.555
But now prepare thee for another Scene.	Par Lost 11.637
But hee the seventh from thee, whom thou beheldst	Par Lost 11.700
Exempt from Death; to shew thee what reward	Par Lost 11.709
Depopulation; thee another Floud,	Par Lost 11.756
Of tears and sorrow a Floud thee also drown'd,	Par Lost 11.757
And sunk thee as thy Sons; till gently reard	Par Lost 11.758
To teach thee that God attributes to place	Par Lost 11.836
The Serpents head; whereof to thee anon	Par Lost 12.150
Will reign among them, as of thee begot;	Par Lost 12.286
A Son, the Womans Seed to thee foretold,	Par Lost 12.327
Disabl'd not to give thee thy deaths wound:	Par Lost 12.392
In thee and in thy Seed: nor can this be,	Par Lost 12.395
The Law that is against thee, and the sins	Par Lost 12.416
A paradise within thee, happier farr.	Par Lost 12.587
Let her with thee partake what thou hast heard,	Par Lost 12.598
In mee is no delay; with thee to goe,	Par Lost 12.615
Is to stay here; without thee here to stay,	Par Lost 12.616
On which I sent thee to the Virgin pure	Par Reg 1.134
Though men esteem thee low of Parentage,	Par Reg 1.235
Where they might see him, and to thee they came;	Par Reg 1.246
To honour thee with Incense, Myrrh, and Gold,	Par Reg 1.251
By which they knew thee King of *Israel* born.	Par Reg 1.254
By Vision, found thee in the Temple, and spake	Par Reg 1.256
Like things of thee to all that present stood.	Par Reg 1.258
Sir, what ill chance hath brought thee to this place	Par Reg 1.321
Of *Jordan* honour'd so, and call'd thee Son	Par Reg 1.329
That out of these hard stones be made thee bread;	Par Reg 1.343
(For I discern thee other then thou seem'st)	Par Reg 1.348
To see thee and approach thee, whom I know	Par Reg 1.384

Thee(*cont*)

Imparts to thee no happiness, no joy,	Par Reg 1.417
Lost bliss, to thee no more communicable,	Par Reg 1.419
What but thy malice mov'd thee to misdeem	Par Reg 1.424
By thee are giv'n, and what confest more true	Par Reg 1.431
To thee not known, whence hast thou then thy truth,	Par Reg 1.446
To approach thy Temples, give thee in command	Par Reg 1.449
At least in vain, for they shall find thee mute.	Par Reg 1.459
From thee I can and must submiss endure	Par Reg 1.476
To hear thee when I come (since no man comes)	Par Reg 1.484
All fear of thee, arise and vindicate	Par Reg 2.47
Of thee these forty days none hath regard,	Par Reg 2.315
Tell me if Food were now before thee set,	Par Reg 2.320
Owe not all Creatures by just right to thee	Par Reg 2.325
To treat thee as beseems, and as her Lord	Par Reg 2.335
Thee homage, and acknowledge thee thir Lord:	Par Reg 2.376
If of that pow'r I bring thee voluntary	Par Reg 2.394
He ask'd thee, hast thou seen my servant *Job?*	Par Reg 3.67
If Kingdom move thee not, let move thee Zeal,	Par Reg 3.171
But what concerns it thee when I begin	Par Reg 3.198
No wonder, for though in thee be united	Par Reg 3.229
But I will bring thee where thou soon shalt quit	Par Reg 3.244
Thee, of thy self so apt, in regal Arts,	Par Reg 3.248
To what end I have brought thee hither and shewn	Par Reg 3.350
To render thee the *Parthian* at dispose;	Par Reg 3.369
That which alone can truly reinstall thee	Par Reg 3.372
This offer sets before thee to deliver.	Par Reg 3.380
My time I told thee, (and that time for thee	Par Reg 3.396
But whence to thee this zeal, where was it then	Par Reg 3.407
These having shewn thee, I have shewn thee all	Par Reg 4.88
Is given, and by that right I give it thee.	Par Reg 4.104
Will be for thee no sitting, or not long	Par Reg 4.107
Is not for thee to know, nor me to tell.	Par Reg 4.153
The Kingdoms of the world to thee I give;	Par Reg 4.163
To worship thee accurst, now more accurst	Par Reg 4.179
The Kingdoms of the world to thee were giv'n,	Par Reg 4.182
Permitted rather, and by thee usurp't,	Par Reg 4.183
God over all supreme? if giv'n to thee,	Par Reg 4.186
By thee how fairly is the Giver now	Par Reg 4.187
Repaid? But gratitude in thee is lost	Par Reg 4.188
That I fall down and worship thee as God?	Par Reg 4.192
Get thee behind me; plain thou now appear'st	Par Reg 4.193
The tryal hath indamag'd thee no way,	Par Reg 4.206
Advise thee, gain them as thou canst, or not.	Par Reg 4.211
Or they with thee hold conversation meet?	Par Reg 4.232
Till time mature thee to a Kingdoms waight;	Par Reg 4.282
These rules will render thee a King compleat	Par Reg 4.283
Such are from God inspir'd, not such from thee;	Par Reg 4.350
Kingdom nor Empire pleases thee, nor aught	Par Reg 4.369
For thee is fittest place, I found thee there,	Par Reg 4.373
And thither will return thee, yet remember	Par Reg 4.374
What I foretell thee, soon thou shalt have cause	Par Reg 4.375
Which would have set thee in short time with ease	Par Reg 4.378
When Prophesies of thee are best fullfill'd.	Par Reg 4.381
Attends thee, scorns, reproaches, injuries,	Par Reg 4.387
A Kingdom they portend thee, but what Kingdom,	Par Reg 4.389
Environ'd thee, some howl'd, some yell'd, some shriek'd,	Par Reg 4.423
Some bent at thee thir fiery darts, while thou	Par Reg 4.424
Fair morning yet betides thee Son of God,	Par Reg 4.451
Of men at thee, for only thou here dwell'st.	Par Reg 4.466
Did I not tell thee, if thou didst reject	Par Reg 4.467
What I foretold thee, many a hard assay	Par Reg 4.478
Whereof this ominous night that clos'd thee round,	Par Reg 4.481
May warn thee, as a sure fore-going sign.	Par Reg 4.483
As false portents, not sent from God, but thee;	Par Reg 4.491
At least might seem to hold all power of thee,	Par Reg 4.494
On thy birth-night, that sung thee Saviour born.	Par Reg 4.506
Heard thee pronounc'd the Son of God belov'd.	Par Reg 4.513
Thenceforth I thought thee worth my nearer view	Par Reg 4.514
All men are Sons of God; yet thee I thought	Par Reg 4.520
And follow'd thee still on to this wast wild;	Par Reg 4.523
To try thee, sift thee, and confess have found thee	Par Reg 4.532
Will ask thee skill; I to thy Fathers house	Par Reg 4.552
Have brought thee, and highest plac't, highest is best,	Par Reg 4.553
Concerning thee to his Angels, in thir hands	Par Reg 4.557
They shall up lift thee, lest at any time	Par Reg 4.558
Shall chase thee with the terror of his voice	Par Reg 4.627
Thee and thy Legions, yelling they shall flye,	Par Reg 4.629
O loss of sight, of thee I most complain!	Samson 67
But thee whose strength, while vertue was her mate,	Samson 173
To visit or bewail thee, or if better,	Samson 182
Thou never wast remiss, I bear thee witness:	Samson 239
Found soon occasion thereby to make thee	Samson 425
Deposited within thee; which to have kept	Samson 429
Thee *Samson* bound and blind into thir hands,	Samson 438
Which to have come to pass by means of thee,	Samson 444
Could have befall'n thee and thy Fathers house.	Samson 447
Man. With cause this hope relieves thee, and these words	Samson 472
Or *Dagon*. But for thee what shall be done?	Samson 478
On thee, who now no more canst do them harm.	Samson 486
God will relent, and quit thee all his debt;	Samson 509
But God hath set before us, to return thee	Samson 517
Allure thee from the cool Crystalline stream.	Samson 546
Which was expresly giv'n thee to annoy them?	Samson 578
His might continues in thee not for naught,	Samson 588
From thee on them, or them to thee of service.	Samson 686
Cho. Yet on she moves, now stands & eies thee fixt,	Samson 726
And arts of every woman false like thee,	Samson 749

Thee(*cont*)
As I by thee, to Ages an example. Samson 765
E're I to thee, thou to thy self wast cruel. Samson 784
In human hearts, nor less in mine towards thee, Samson 792
Caus'd what I did? I saw thee mutable Samson 793
How to endear, and hold thee to me firmest: Samson 796
Against thee but safe custody, and hold: Samson 802
Would draw thee forth to perilous enterprises, Samson 804
Here I should still enjoy thee day and night Samson 807
That malice not repentance brought thee hither, Samson 821
With God or Man will gain thee no remission. Samson 835
But Love constrain'd thee; call it furious rage Samson 836
Knowing, as needs I must, by thee betray'd? Samson 840
Only my love of thee held long debate; Samson 863
Bin, as it ought, sincere, it would have taught thee Samson 874
And of my Nation chose thee from among Samson 877
My enemies, lov'd thee, as too well thou knew'st, Samson 878
Too well, unbosom'd all my secrets to thee, Samson 879
By thy request, who could deny thee nothing; Samson 881
Thy countrey sought of thee, it sought unjustly, Samson 889
Not therefore to be obey'd. But zeal mov'd thee; Samson 895
Let me obtain forgiveness of thee, *Samson*, Samson 909
Towards thee I intend for what I have misdone, Samson 911
Thir favourable ear, that I may fetch thee Samson 921
May ever tend about thee to old age Samson 925
My sudden rage to tear thee joint by joint. Samson 953
At distance I forgive thee, go with that; Samson 954
It hath brought forth to make thee memorable Samson 956
Thy Paranymph, worthless to thee compar'd, Samson 1020
Gives and the Mill had tam'd thee? O that fortune Samson 1093
1671 'thee;' in some copies
I should have forc'd thee soon wish other arms, Samson 1096
Certain to have won by mortal duel from thee, Samson 1102
Some narrow place enclos'd, where sight may give thee, Samson 1117
I only with an Oak'n staff will meet thee, Samson 1123
That in a little time while breath remains thee, Samson 1126
Arm'd thee or charm'd thee strong, which thou from Heaven Samson 1134
Feigndst at thy birth was giv'n thee in thy hair, Samson 1135
Offering to combat thee his Champion bold, Samson 1152
Thee he regards not, owns not, hath cut off Samson 1157
To put out both thine eyes, and fetter'd send thee Samson 1160
Defie thee to the trial of mortal fight, Samson 1175
He will accept thee to defend his cause, Samson 1179
Thir Magistrates confest it, when they took thee Samson 1183
At *Askalon*, who never did thee harm, Samson 1187
Went up with armed powers thee only seeking, Samson 1190
Who now defies thee thrice to single fight, Samson 1222
Har. With thee a Man condemn'd, a Slave enrol'd, Samson 1224
To fight with thee no man of arms will deign. Samson 1226
But take good heed my hand survey not thee. Samson 1230
Sam. No man with-holds thee, nothing from thy hand Samson 1233
Sams. Go baffl'd coward, lest I run upon thee, Samson 1237
Or swing thee in the Air, then dash thee down Samson 1240
These braveries in Irons loaden on thee. Samson 1243
Some way or other yet further to afflict thee. Samson 1252
May chance to number thee with those Samson 1295
This Idols day hath bin to thee no day of rest, Samson 1297
Off. *Samson*, to thee our Lords thus bid me say; Samson 1310
Where I will see thee heartn'd and fresh clad Samson 1317
Yet that he may dispense with me or thee Samson 1377
To thee I am bid say. Art thou our Slave, Samson 1392
And hamper thee, as thou shalt come of force, Samson 1397
To favour, and perhaps to set thee free. Samson 1412
Send thee the Angel of thy Birth, to stand Samson 1431
Of fire; that Spirit that first rusht on thee Samson 1435
Be efficacious in thee now at need. Samson 1437
With thee; say reverend Sire, we thirst to hear. Samson 1456
To thee first reverend *Manoa*, and to these Samson 1548
Man. The accident was loud, & here before thee Samson 1552
Thee with thy slaughter'd foes in number more Samson 1667
Nightly to thee her sad Song mourneth well. Mask 235
Eld. *Bro*. To tell thee sadly Shepherd, without blame, Mask 509
But here thy sword can do thee little stead, Mask 611
Eld. *Bro*. *Thyrsis* lead on apace, Ile follow thee, Mask 657
Fill'd her with thee a daughter fair, Allegro 23
Haste thee nymph, and bring with thee Allegro 25
And in thy right hand lead with thee, Allegro 35
And if I give thee honour due, Allegro 37
To live with her, and live with thee, Allegro 39
Mirth with thee, I mean to live. Allegro 152
Thee bright-hair'd *Vesta* long of yore, Penseroso 23
And joyn with thee calm Peace, and Quiet, Penseroso 45
But first, and chiefest, with thee bring, Penseroso 51
Thee Chauntress oft the Woods among, Penseroso 63
And missing thee, I walk unseen Penseroso 65
And I with thee will choose to live. Penseroso 176
Thee Shepherd, thee the Woods, and desert Caves, Lycidas 39
How well could I have spar'd for thee young swain, Lycidas 113
Ay me! Whilst thee the shores, and sounding Seas Lycidas 154
He wanderd long, till thee he spy'd from farr, Fair Inf 17
Alack that so to change thee winter had no power. Fair Inf 28
Could Heav'n for pittie thee so strictly doom? Fair Inf 33
Here I salute thee and thy pardon ask, Vacation 7
That now I use thee in my latter task: Vacation 8
Small loss it is that thence can come unto thee, Vacation 9
I know my tongue but little Grace can do thee Vacation 10
I pray thee then deny me not thy aide Vacation 15
But haste thee strait to do me once a Pleasure, Vacation 17

Thee(*cont*)
Such as may make thee search thy coffers round, Vacation 31
Expectance calls thee now another way, Vacation 54
Good luck befriend thee Son; for at thy birth Vacation 59
She heard them give thee this, that thou should'st still Vacation 65
Triumphing over Death, and Chance, and thee O Time. On Time 22
Sweet rest sease thee evermore, Winchester 50
Weept for thee in *Helicon*, Winchester 56
Sent thee from the banks of *Came*, Winchester 59
Next her much like to thee in story, Winchester 62
And at her next birth much like thee, Winchester 67
There with thee, new welcom Saint, Winchester 71
With thee there clad in radiant sheen, Winchester 73
Thus we salute thee with our early Song, May Morn 9
And welcom thee, and wish thee long. May Morn 10
Whether the Muse, or Love call thee his mate, Sonnet 1, 13
If ever deed of honour did thee please, Sonnet 8, 3
He can requite thee, for he knows the charms Sonnet 8, 5
No anger find in thee, but pity and ruth. Sonnet 9, 8
Thy worth and skill exempts thee from the throng, Sonnet 13, 5
To honour thee, the Priest of *Phoebus* Quire Sonnet 13, 10
Dante shall give Fame leave to set thee higher Sonnet 13, 12
and gives thee praise above the pipe of Pan; Sonnet 13, Tr. ms 40.06
When Faith and Love which parted from thee never, Sonnet 14, 1
Trinity ms 'the' ← 'thee'
Follow'd thee up to joy and bliss for ever. Sonnet 14, 8
And speak the truth of thee on glorious Theams Sonnet 14, 12
Before the Judge, who thenceforth bid thee rest Sonnet 14, 13
Strait follow'd thee the path that Saints have trod Sonnet 14, Tr. ms 41.06
The bounds of either sword to thee wee ow. Sonnet 17, 12
In peace, and reck'ns thee her eldest son. Sonnet 17, 14
1694 'thee in chief'
Courts thee on Roses in some pleasant Cave, Horace 2
Who now enjoyes thee credulous, all Gold, Horace 9
Hopes thee; of flattering gales Horace 11
Thou art my Son I have begotten thee Psalm 2, 15
As thy possession I on thee bestow Psalm 2, 17
Thee through my story Psalm 3, 8
My King and God for unto thee I pray. Psalm 5, 4
Ith' morning I to thee with choyce Psalm 5, 7
Evil with thee no biding makes Psalm 5, 11
Still on; for against thee they have rebell'd; Psalm 5, 32
Then all who trust in thee shall bring Psalm 5, 33
And shall triumph in thee, who love thy name. Psalm 5, 36
For in death no remembrance is of thee; Psalm 6, 9
Lord my God to thee I flie Psalm 7, 1
Will surround thee, seeking right, Psalm 7, 26
So shall we not go back from thee Psalm 80, 73
When trouble did thee sore assaile, Psalm 81, 25
And I to free thee *did not faile*, Psalm 81, 27
And led thee out of thrall. Psalm 81, 28
I answer'd thee in thunder deep Psalm 81, 29
I tri'd thee at the water *steep* Psalm 81, 31
I testifie to thee Psalm 81, 34
Thee out of Aegypt land Psalm 81, 42
And they that hate thee *proud and fell* Psalm 83, 7
Themselves against thee they unite Psalm 83, 19
And till they yield thee honour due, Psalm 83, 59
O living God, for thee. Psalm 84, 8
Toward thee, My King, my God. Psalm 84, 16
Where thee they ever praise, Psalm 84, 18
Happy, whose strength in thee doth bide, Psalm 84, 19
Who *only* on thee doth relie, Psalm 84, 47
And in thee only rest. Psalm 84, 48
And all their Sin, *that did thee grieve* Psalm 85, 7
By thee preserv'd alive. Psalm 85, 24
O hear me *I thee pray*, Psalm 86, 2
Who *still* in thee doth trust. Psalm 86, 8
Pitty me Lord for daily thee Psalm 86, 9
Thy Servants Soul; for Lord to thee Psalm 86, 11
To them that on thee call. Psalm 86, 16
Will call on thee *for aid;* Psalm 86, 22
Like thee among the gods is none Psalm 86, 25
To bow them low before thee Lord, Psalm 86, 31
Thee will I praise O Lord my God Psalm 86, 41
Thee honour, and adore Psalm 86, 42
No fear of thee have set. Psalm 86, 52
Of thee *abroad* are spoke; Psalm 87, 10
In thee *fresh brooks, and soft streams glance* Psalm 87, 27
All day to thee I cry; Psalm 88, 2
And all night long, before thee *weep* Psalm 88, 3
Before thee *prostrate lie*. Psalm 88, 4
Lord all the day I thee entreat, Psalm 88, 39
My hands to thee I spread. Psalm 88, 40
And praise thee *from their loathsom bed* Psalm 88, 43
But I to thee O Lord do cry Psalm 88, 53
And *up to thee* my praier *doth hie* Psalm 88, 55
Each morn, and thee prevent. Psalm 88, 56
With terror sent from thee; Psalm 88, 60
That the first wealthy *Pope* receiv'd of thee. Prose 1, 3
'Gainst them that rais'd thee dost thou lift thy horn, Prose 3, 2
What certain Seat, where I may worship thee Prose 12, 5
And *Kings* be born of thee, whose dredded might Prose 12, 13

Their
From thir Creator, and transgress his Will Par Lost 1.31
1667 'their'
For those rebellious, here thir Prison ordain'd Par Lost 1.71
1674 'their' in some copies

Their(*cont*)
1667 'their'
In utter darkness, and thir portion set Par Lost 1.72
1667 'their'
His inmost counsels from thir destind aim. Par Lost 1.168
1667 'their'
Drivn backward slope thir pointing spires, and rowld Par Lost 1.223
1667 'their'
As Gods, and by thir own recover'd strength, Par Lost 1.240
1667 'their'
And call them not to share with us their part Par Lost 1.267
ms 'thir'
If once they hear that voyce, thir liveliest pledge Par Lost 1.274
1667 'their'
Thir surest signal, they will soon resume Par Lost 1.278
1667 'Their'
From the safe shore thir floating Carkases Par Lost 1.310
1667 'their'
Under amazement of thir hideous change. Par Lost 1.313
1667 'their'
Yet to thir Generals Voyce they soon obeyd Par Lost 1.337
1667 'their'
ms 'their'
Of thir great Sultan waving to direct Par Lost 1.348
1667 'their'
Thir course, in even ballance down they light Par Lost 1.349
ms 'Their'
1667 'Their'
Thir great Commander; Godlike shapes and forms Par Lost 1.358
1667 'Their'
Though of thir Names in heav'nly Records now Par Lost 1.361
1667 'their'
By thir Rebellion, from the Books of Life. Par Lost 1.363
God thir Creator, and th' invisible Par Lost 1.369
1667 'their'
Say, Muse, thir Names then known, who first, who last, Par Lost 1.376
1667 'their'
At thir great Emperors call, as next in worth Par Lost 1.378
Roaming to seek thir prey on earth, durst fix Par Lost 1.382
1667 'their'
Thir Seats long after next the Seat of God, Par Lost 1.383
ms 'Their'
1667 'Their'
Thir Altars by his Altar, Gods ador'd Par Lost 1.384
1667 'Their'
Within his Sanctuary it self thir Shrines, Par Lost 1.388
1667 'their'
And with thir darkness durst affront his light. Par Lost 1.391
1667 'their'
Thir childrens cries unheard, that past through fire Par Lost 1.395
1667 'Their'
Israel in *Sittim* on thir march from *Nile* Par Lost 1.413
1667 'their'
And uncompounded is thir Essence pure, Par Lost 1.425
1667 'their'
Can execute thir aerie purposes, Par Lost 1.430
1667 'their'
Thir living strength, and unfrequented left Par Lost 1.433
1667 'Their'
To bestial Gods; for which thir heads as low Par Lost 1.435
1667 'their'
Sidonian Virgins paid thir Vows and Songs, Par Lost 1.441
1667 'their'
Osiris, *Isis*, *Orus* and thir Train Par Lost 1.478
1667 'their'
ms 'their'
1674 'their' in some copies
Thir wandring Gods disguis'd in brutish forms Par Lost 1.481
Th' infection when thir borrow'd Gold compos'd Par Lost 1.483
1667 'their'
Of riot ascends above thir loftiest Towrs, Par Lost 1.499
1674 'their' in some copies
Expos'd a Matron to avoid worse rape. Par Lost 1.505
1667 'Yielded thir Matrons'
Thir boasted Parents; *Titan* Heav'ns first born Par Lost 1.510
Thir highest Heav'n; or on the *Delphian* Cliff, Par Lost 1.517
Obscure some glimps of joy, to have found thir chief Par Lost 1.524
Thir fanting courage, and dispel'd thir fears. Par Lost 1.530
1667 'Their fainting'
ms 'Their fainting'
1667 'their fears'
Thir painful steps o're the burnt soyle; and now Par Lost 1.562
Awaiting what command thir mighty Chief Par Lost 1.566
The whole Battalion views, thir order due, Par Lost 1.569
Thir visages and stature as of Gods, Par Lost 1.570
Thir number last he summs. And now his heart Par Lost 1.571
Thir dread commander: he above the rest Par Lost 1.589
For ever now to have thir lot in pain, Par Lost 1.608
1667 'their'
Thir Glory witherd. As when Heavens Fire Par Lost 1.612
With singed top thir stately growth though bare Par Lost 1.614
1667 'their'
To speak; whereat thir doubl'd Ranks they bend Par Lost 1.616
1667 'their'
Words interwove with sighs found out thir way. Par Lost 1.621
1667 'their'
Self-rais'd, and repossess thir native seat? Par Lost 1.634
1667 'their'

Their(*cont*)
Clash'd on thir sounding Shields the din of war, Par Lost 1.668
1667 'their'
Rifl'd the bowels of thir mother Earth Par Lost 1.687
Learn how thir greatest Monuments of Fame, Par Lost 1.695
Equal'd in all thir glories, to inshrine Par Lost 1.719
Belus or *Serapis* thir Gods, or seat Par Lost 1.720
Thir Kings, when *Aegypt* with *Assyria* strove Par Lost 1.721
Op'ning thir brazen foulds discover wide Par Lost 1.724
Where Scepter'd Angels held thir residence, Par Lost 1.734
Of Satan and his Peers: thir summons call'd Par Lost 1.757
Pour forth thir populous youth about the Hive Par Lost 1.770
The suburb of thir Straw-built Cittadel, Par Lost 1.773
Thir State affairs. So thick the aerie crowd Par Lost 1.775
Wheels her pale course, they on thir mirth and dance Par Lost 1.786
Reduc'd thir shapes immense, and were at large, Par Lost 1.790
And in thir own dimensions like themselves Par Lost 1.793
Heav'ns fugitives, and for thir dwelling place Par Lost 2.57
Encamp thir Legions, or with obscure wing Par Lost 2.132
To give his Enemies thir wish, and end Par Lost 2.157
The sentence of thir Conquerour: This is now Par Lost 2.208
Will slack'n, if his breath stir not thir flames. Par Lost 2.214
Thir noxious vapour, or enur'd not feel, Par Lost 2.216
Must'ring thir rage, and Heav'n resembles Hell? Par Lost 2.268
Into their temper; which must needs remove Par Lost 2.277
Or substance, how endu'd, and what thir Power, Par Lost 2.356
And where thir weakness, how attempted best, Par Lost 2.357
To their defence who hold it: here perhaps Par Lost 2.362
Seduce them to our Party, that thir God Par Lost 2.368
May prove thir foe, and with repenting hand Par Lost 2.369
Thir frail Original, and faded bliss, Par Lost 2.375
The great Creatour? But thir spite still serves Par Lost 2.385
Sparkl'd in all thir eyes; with full assent Par Lost 2.388
Thir rising all at once was as the sound Par Lost 2.476
Loose all her virtue; least bad men should boast Par Lost 2.483
1667 'thir'
Thir specious deeds on earth, which glory excites, Par Lost 2.484
Thus they thir doubtful consultations dark Par Lost 2.486
Ended rejoycing in thir matchless Chief: Par Lost 2.487
The birds thir notes renew, and bleating herds Par Lost 2.494
Attest thir joy, that hill and valley rings. Par Lost 2.495
Midst came thir mighty Paramount, and seemd Par Lost 2.508
Then of thir Session ended they bid cry Par Lost 2.514
Put to thir mouths the sounding Alchymie Par Lost 2.517
Thence more at ease thir minds and somwhat rais'd Par Lost 2.521
Part curb thir fierie Steeds, or shun the Goal Par Lost 2.531
Prick forth the Aerie Knights, and couch thir Spears Par Lost 2.536
Thir own Heroic deeds and hapless fall Par Lost 2.549
Thir Song was partial, but the harmony Par Lost 2.552
Four ways thir flying March, along the Banks Par Lost 2.574
Into the burning Lake thir baleful streams; Par Lost 2.576
Thir soft Ethereal warmth, and there to pine Par Lost 2.601
Both to and fro, thir sorrow to augment, Par Lost 2.605
View'd first thir lamentable lot, and found Par Lost 2.617
Thir spicie Drugs: they on the Trading Flood Par Lost 2.640
If aught disturb'd thir noyse, into her woomb, Par Lost 2.657
Eclipses at thir charms. The other shape, Par Lost 2.666
Leveld his deadly aime; thir fatall hands Par Lost 2.712
To joyn thir dark Encounter in mid air: Par Lost 2.718
Grew darker at thir frown, so matcht they stood; Par Lost 2.720
My Bowels, thir repast; then bursting forth Par Lost 2.800
1667 'their'
Th' infernal dores, and on thir hinges grate Par Lost 2.881
Before thir eyes in sudden view appear Par Lost 2.890
Thir embryon Atoms; they around the flag Par Lost 2.900
Of each his Faction, in thir several Clanns, Par Lost 2.901
Thir lighter wings. To whom these most adhere, Par Lost 2.906
But all these in thir pregnant causes mixt Par Lost 2.913
So thick a drop serene hath quencht thir Orbs, Par Lost 3.25
His own works and their works at once to view: Par Lost 3.59
Thir maker, or thir making, or thir Fate, Par Lost 3.113
Thir will, dispos'd by absolute Decree Par Lost 3.115
Thir own revolt, not I: if I foreknew, Par Lost 3.117
Foreknowledge had no influence on their fault, Par Lost 3.118
Thir nature, and revoke the high Decree Par Lost 3.126
Thir freedom, they themselves ordain'd thir fall. Par Lost 3.128
The first sort by thir own suggestion fell, Par Lost 3.129
Thir sinful state, and to appease betimes Par Lost 3.186
Invites; for I will cleer thir senses dark, Par Lost 3.188
Thir Nature also to thy Nature joyn; Par Lost 3.282
Thir own both righteous and unrighteous deeds, Par Lost 3.292
Shall hast'n, such a peal shall rouse thir sleep. Par Lost 3.329
And after all thir tribulations long Par Lost 3.336
Thir Crowns inwove with Amarant and Gold, Par Lost 3.352
Bind thir resplendent locks inwreath'd with beams, Par Lost 3.361
Then Crown'd again thir gold'n Harps they took, Par Lost 3.365
Harps ever tun'd, that glittering by thir side Par Lost 3.366
1667 'their'
Thir sacred Song, and waken raptures high; Par Lost 3.369
Approach not, but with both wings veil thir eyes. Par Lost 3.382
Not so on Man; him through their malice fall'n, Par Lost 3.400
Thir happie hours in joy and hymning spent. Par Lost 3.417
With Sails and Wind thir canie Waggons light: Par Lost 3.439
Built thir fond hopes of Glorie or lasting fame, Par Lost 3.449
All who have thir reward on Earth, the fruits Par Lost 3.451
Fit retribution, emptie as thir deeds; Par Lost 3.454
White, Black and Grey, with all thir trumperie. Par Lost 3.475
Of Heav'ns ascent they lift thir Feet, when loe Par Lost 3.486

Their(*cont*)
Cowles, Hoods and Habits with thir wearers tost Par Lost 3.490
Thir Starry dance in numbers that compute Par Lost 3.580
Turn swift thir various motions, or are turnd Par Lost 3.582
1667 'their'
In vain, though by thir powerful Art they binde Par Lost 3.602
Thir number, or the wisdom infinite Par Lost 3.706
That brought them forth, but hid thir causes deep. Par Lost 3.707
Swift to thir several Quarters hasted then Par Lost 3.714
The coming of thir secret foe, and scap'd Par Lost 4.7
Hide thir diminisht heads; to thee I call, Par Lost 4.35
Of stateliest view. Yet higher then thir tops Par Lost 4.142
Fanning thir odoriferous wings dispense Par Lost 4.157
Well pleas'd they slack thir course, and many a League Par Lost 4.164
Who came thir bane, though with them better pleas'd Par Lost 4.167
Watching where Shepherds pen thir Flocks at eeve Par Lost 4.185
To worst abuse, or to thir meanest use. Par Lost 4.204
Her chrystal mirror holds, unite thir streams. Par Lost 4.263
The Birds thir quire apply; aires, vernal aires, Par Lost 4.264
Nor where *Abassin* Kings thir issue Guard, Par Lost 4.280
And worthie seemd, for in thir looks Divine Par Lost 4.291
The image of thir glorious Maker shon, Par Lost 4.292
Not equal, as thir sex not equal seemd; Par Lost 4.296
Of thir sweet Gardning labour then suffic'd Par Lost 4.328
More grateful, to thir Supper Fruits they fell, Par Lost 4.331
The hand that formd them on thir shape hath pourd. Par Lost 4.365
Now other, as thir shape servd best his end Par Lost 4.398
To mark what of thir state he more might learn Par Lost 4.400
The happier *Eden*, shall enjoy thir fill Par Lost 4.507
From thir own mouths; all is not theirs it seems: Par Lost 4.513
Suspicious, reasonless. Why should thir Lord Par Lost 4.516
By Ignorance, is that thir happie state, Par Lost 4.519
The proof of thir obedience and thir faith? Par Lost 4.520
Thir ruine! Hence I will excite thir minds Par Lost 4.522
They to thir grassie Couch, these to thir Nests Par Lost 4.601
And of thir doings God takes no account. Par Lost 4.622
More hands then ours to lop thir wanton growth: Par Lost 4.629
All seasons and thir change, all please alike. Par Lost 4.640
Those have thir course to finish, round the Earth, Par Lost 4.661
Thir stellar vertue on all kinds that grow Par Lost 4.671
Singing thir great Creator: oft in bands Par Lost 4.684
In full harmonic number joind, thir songs Par Lost 4.687
On to thir blissful Bower; it was a place Par Lost 4.690
Rear'd high thir flourisht heads between, and wrought Par Lost 4.699
Such was thir awe of Man. In shadie Bower Par Lost 4.705
Endowd with all thir gifts, and O too like Par Lost 4.715
Thus at thir shadie Lodge arriv'd, both stood Par Lost 4.720
Which God likes best, into thir inmost bowre Par Lost 4.738
And on thir naked limbs the flourie roof Par Lost 4.772
And from thir Ivorie Port the Cherubim Par Lost 4.778
To thir night watches in warlike Parade, Par Lost 4.780
Awaiting next command. To whom thir Chief Par Lost 4.864
Whose easier business were to serve thir Lord Par Lost 4.943
Thir Phalanx, and began to hemm him round Par Lost 4.979
That open now thir choicest bosom'd smells Par Lost 5.127
Each in thir Chrystal sluce, hee ere they fell Par Lost 5.133
Thir Orisons, each Morning duly paid Par Lost 5.145
Thir Maker, in fit strains pronounc't or sung Par Lost 5.148
Flowd from thir lips, in Prose or numerous Verse, Par Lost 5.150
1667 'their' in some copies
With the fixt Starrs, fixt in thir Orb that flies, Par Lost 5.176
So pray'd they innocent, and to thir thoughts Par Lost 5.209
On to thir mornings rural work they haste Par Lost 5.211
Thir pamperd boughes, and needed hands to check Par Lost 5.214
Thir glittering Tents he passd, and now is come Par Lost 5.291
Our givers thir own gifts, and large bestow Par Lost 5.317
On Princes, when thir rich Retinue long Par Lost 5.355
Thir Table was, and mossie seats had round, Par Lost 5.392
And to thir viands fell, nor seemingly Par Lost 5.434
Ministerd naked, and thir flowing cups Par Lost 5.444
Of things above his World, and of thir being Par Lost 5.455
Each in thir several active Sphears assignd, Par Lost 5.477
Spirits odorous breathes: flours and thir fruit Par Lost 5.482
Under thir Hierarchs in orders bright Par Lost 5.587
Or in thir glittering Tissues bear imblaz'd Par Lost 5.592
And in thir motions harmonie Divine Par Lost 5.625
With copious hand, rejoycing in thir joy. Par Lost 5.641
Disperst in Bands and Files thir Camp extend Par Lost 5.651
Fannd with coole Winds, save those who in thir course Par Lost 5.655
And all who under me thir Banners wave, Par Lost 5.687
Of thir great Potentate; for great indeed Par Lost 5.706
Nightly before him, saw without thir light Par Lost 5.714
Laugh'st at thir vain designes and tumults vain, Par Lost 5.737
Matter to mee of Glory, whom thir hate Par Lost 5.738
Giv'n me to quell thir pride, and in event Par Lost 5.740
In thir triple Degrees, Regions to which Par Lost 5.750
About the great reception of thir King, Par Lost 5.769
Of counterfeted truth thus held thir ears. Par Lost 5.771
Such as he pleasd, and circumscrib'd thir being? Par Lost 5.825
By him created in thir bright degrees, Par Lost 5.838
Crownd them with Glory, and to thir Glory nam'd Par Lost 5.839
By force, who reason for thir Law refuse, Par Lost 6.41
Right reason for thir Law, and for thir King Par Lost 6.42
Into thir place of punishment, the Gulf Par Lost 6.53
His fiery *Chaos* to receave thir fall. Par Lost 6.55
In silence thir bright Legions, to the sound Par Lost 6.64
Under thir God-like Leaders, in the Cause Par Lost 6.67
Thir perfet ranks; for high above the ground Par Lost 6.71

Their(*cont*)
Thir march was, and the passive Air upbore Par Lost 6.72
Thir nimble tread, as when the total kind Par Lost 6.73
Thir names of thee; so over many a tract Par Lost 6.76
Aspirer, but thir thoughts prov'd fond and vain Par Lost 6.90
Thir Deities to assert, who while they feel Par Lost 6.157
As both thir deeds compar'd this day shall prove. Par Lost 6.170
Thus foil'd thir mightiest, ours joy filld, and shout, Par Lost 6.200
Of all thir Regions: how much more of Power Par Lost 6.223
Though not destroy, thir happie Native seat; Par Lost 6.226
And limited thir might; though numberd such Par Lost 6.229
Now wav'd thir fierie Swords, and in the Aire Par Lost 6.304
Made horrid Circles; two broad Suns thir Shields Par Lost 6.305
Should combat, and thir jarring Sphears confound. Par Lost 6.315
Defence, while others bore him on thir Shields Par Lost 6.337
Nor in thir liquid texture mortal wound Par Lost 6.348
Disdain'd, but meaner thoughts learnd in thir flight, Par Lost 6.367
I might relate of thousands, and thir names Par Lost 6.373
Angels contented with thir fame in Heav'n Par Lost 6.375
Therfore Eternal silence be thir doome. Par Lost 6.385
And now thir Mightiest quelld, the battel swerv'd, Par Lost 6.386
Such high advantages thir innocence Par Lost 6.401
Gave them above thir foes, not to have sinnd, Par Lost 6.402
By wound, though from thir place by violence mov'd. Par Lost 6.405
Encamping, plac'd in Guard thir Watches round, Par Lost 6.412
These in thir dark Nativitie the Deep Par Lost 6.482
He ended, and his words thir drooping chere Par Lost 6.496
Enlightn'd, and thir languisht hope reviv'd. Par Lost 6.497
Th' originals of Nature in thir crude Par Lost 6.511
Whereof to found thir Engins and thir Balls Par Lost 6.518
Brass, Iron, Stonie mould, had not thir mouthes Par Lost 6.576
Not long, for sudden all at once thir Reeds Par Lost 6.582
Thir devilish glut, chaind Thunderbolts and Hail Par Lost 6.589
That whom they hit, none on thir feet might stand, Par Lost 6.592
The sooner for thir Arms, unarm'd they might Par Lost 6.595
Nor serv'd it to relax thir serried files. Par Lost 6.599
And to thir foes a laughter; for in view Par Lost 6.603
In posture to displode thir second tire Par Lost 6.605
They worse abhorr'd. *Satan* beheld thir plight, Par Lost 6.607
Of composition, strait they chang'd thir minds, Par Lost 6.613
Stood scoffing, highthn'd in thir thoughts beyond Par Lost 6.629
To match with thir inventions they presum'd Par Lost 6.631
Thir Arms away they threw, and to the Hills Par Lost 6.639
From thir foundations loosning to and fro Par Lost 6.643
They pluckt the seated Hills with all thir load, Par Lost 6.644
Up lifting bore them in thir hands: Amaze, Par Lost 6.646
They saw them whelm'd, and all thir confidence Par Lost 6.651
Themselves invaded next, and on thir heads Par Lost 6.653
Thir armor help'd thir harm, crush't in and bruis'd Par Lost 6.656
Into thir substance pent, which wrought them pain Par Lost 6.657
These disobedient; sore hath been thir fight, Par Lost 6.687
Equal in their Creation they were form'd, Par Lost 6.690
Insensibly, for I suspend thir doom; Par Lost 6.692
To thir prepar'd ill Mansion driven down Par Lost 6.738
Had wondrous, as with Starrs thir bodies all Par Lost 6.754
Over thir heads a chrystal Firmament, Par Lost 6.757
And twentie thousand (I thir number heard) Par Lost 6.769
Under thir Head imbodied all in one. Par Lost 6.779
And to rebellious fight rallied thir Powers Par Lost 6.786
Yet envied; against mee is all thir rage, Par Lost 6.813
Therefore to mee thir doom he hath assig'n'd; Par Lost 6.817
That they may have thir wish, to trie with mee Par Lost 6.818
At once the Four spred out thir Starrie wings Par Lost 6.827
Before him, such as in thir Soules infix'd Par Lost 6.837
All courage; down thir idle weapons drop'd; Par Lost 6.839
Among th' accurst, that witherd all thir strength, Par Lost 6.850
And of thir wonted vigour left them draind, Par Lost 6.851
And felt tenfold confusion in thir fall Par Lost 6.872
Hell thir fit habitation fraught with fire Par Lost 6.876
Of all tastes else to please thir appetite, Par Lost 7.49
Of things so high and strange, things to thir thought Par Lost 7.53
Thir multitude, and to his Son thus spake. Par Lost 7.138
Drew many, whom thir place knows here no more; Par Lost 7.144
Thir station, Heav'n yet populous retaines Par Lost 7.146
To future men, and in thir dwellings peace: Par Lost 7.183
Into thir vacant room, and thence diffuse Par Lost 7.190
Attendant on thir Lord: Heav'n op'nd wide Par Lost 7.205
And touch't thir Golden Harps, and hymning prais'd Par Lost 7.258
Emergent, and thir broad bare backs upheave Par Lost 7.286
Into the Clouds, thir tops ascend the Skie: Par Lost 7.287
Troop to thir Standard, so the watrie throng, Par Lost 7.297
With Serpent errour wandring, found thir way, Par Lost 7.302
Stream, and perpetual draw thir humid traine. Par Lost 7.306
Op'ning thir various colours, and made gay Par Lost 7.318
Thir branches hung with copious Fruit; or gemm'd Par Lost 7.325
Thir blossoms: with high woods the hills were crownd, Par Lost 7.326
Thir Office in the Firmament of Heav'n Par Lost 7.344
And God made two great Lights, great for thir use Par Lost 7.346
In thir vicissitude, and rule the Night, Par Lost 7.351
Hither as to thir Fountain other Starrs Par Lost 7.364
Repairing, in thir gold'n Urns draw Light, Par Lost 7.365
Thir small peculiar, though from human sight Par Lost 7.368
With thir bright Luminaries that Set and Rose, Par Lost 7.385
The waters generated by thir kindes, Par Lost 7.393
Of Fish that with thir Finns and shining Scales Par Lost 7.401
Graze the Sea weed thir pasture, and through Groves Par Lost 7.404
Show to the Sun thir wav'd coats dropt with Gold, Par Lost 7.406
Or in thir Pearlie shells at ease, attend Par Lost 7.407

Their(*cont*)

Moist nutriment, or under Rocks thir food Par Lost 7.408
Wallowing unweildie, enormous in thir Gate Par Lost 7.411
Thir Brood as numerous hatch, from the Egg that soon Par Lost 7.418
Thir callow young, but featherd soon and fledge Par Lost 7.420
They summ'd thir Penns, and soaring th' air sublime Par Lost 7.421
On Cliffs and Cedar tops thir Eyries build: Par Lost 7.424
In common, rang'd in figure wedge thir way, Par Lost 7.426
Thir Aierie Caravan high over Sea's Par Lost 7.428
Easing thir flight; so stears the prudent Crane Par Lost 7.430
Solac'd the Woods, and spred thir painted wings Par Lost 7.434
Thir downie Brest; the Swan with Arched neck Par Lost 7.438
Each in their kinde. The Earth obey'd, and strait Par Lost 7.453
Insect or Worme; those wav'd thir limber fans Par Lost 7.476
These as a line thir long dimension drew, Par Lost 7.480
Thir Snakie foulds, and added wings. First crept Par Lost 7.484
And thou thir Natures know'st, & gav'st them Names, Par Lost 7.493
First wheeld thir course; Earth in her rich attire Par Lost 7.501
And freely all thir pleasant fruit for food Par Lost 7.540
The Planets in thir station list'ning stood, Par Lost 7.563
Of Spirits apostat and thir Counsels vaine Par Lost 7.610
Thir seasons: among these the seat of men, Par Lost 7.623
Thir pleasant dwelling place. Thrice happie men, Par Lost 7.625
Thir happiness, and persevere upright. Par Lost 7.632
Thir magnitudes, this Earth a spot, a graine, Par Lost 8.17
Thir distance argues and thir swift return Par Lost 8.21
One day and night; in all thir vast survey Par Lost 8.24
For aught appeers, and on thir Orbs impose Par Lost 8.30
Hath left to thir disputes, perhaps to move Par Lost 8.77
His laughter at thir quaint Opinions wide Par Lost 8.78
His beams, unactive else, thir vigour find. Par Lost 8.97
By his attractive vertue and thir own Par Lost 8.124
Thir wandring course now high, now low, then hid, Par Lost 8.126
With thir attendant Moons thou wilt descrie Par Lost 8.149
Imbu'd, bring to thir sweetness no satietie. Par Lost 8.216
After thir kindes; I bring them to receave Par Lost 8.343
From thee thir Names, and pay thee fealtie Par Lost 8.344
Of Fish within thir watry residence, Par Lost 8.346
Thir Element to draw the thinner Aire. Par Lost 8.348
Thir Nature, with such knowledg God endu'd Par Lost 8.353
Thir language and thir wayes, they also know, Par Lost 8.373
Each with thir kinde, Lion with Lioness; Par Lost 8.393
From prone, nor in thir wayes complacence find. Par Lost 8.433
Shed thir selectest influence; the Earth Par Lost 8.513
Whisper'd it to the Woods, and from thir wings Par Lost 8.516
Greatness of mind and nobleness thir seat Par Lost 8.557
Love not the heav'nly Spirits, and how thir Love Par Lost 8.615
That kept thir watch; thence full of anguish driv'n, Par Lost 9.62
That shine, yet bear thir bright officious Lamps, Par Lost 9.104
In thee concentring all thir precious beams Par Lost 9.106
Not in themselves, all thir known vertue appeers Par Lost 9.110
Thir earthy Charge: Of these the vigilance Par Lost 9.157
Thir morning incense, when all things that breath, Par Lost 9.194
And joind thir vocal Worship to the Quire Par Lost 9.198
Thir growing work: for much thir work outgrew Par Lost 9.202
Thir tendance or Plantation for delight Par Lost 9.419
To Beasts, whom God on thir Creation-Day Par Lost 9.556
The latter I demurre, for in thir looks Par Lost 9.558
Much reason, and in thir actions oft appeers. Par Lost 9.559
Unsuckt of Lamb or Kid, that tend thir play. Par Lost 9.583
Grow up to thir provision, and more hands Par Lost 9.623
Things in thir Causes, but to trace the wayes Par Lost 9.682
Wisdom without their leave? and wherein lies Par Lost 9.725
As Reapers oft are wont thir Harvest Queen. Par Lost 9.842
Triumph and say; Fickle their State whom God Par Lost 9.948
There they thir fill of Love and Loves disport Par Lost 9.1042
Took largely, of thir mutual guilt the Seale, Par Lost 9.1043
The solace of thir sin, till dewie sleep Par Lost 9.1044
Oppress'd them, wearied with thir amorous play. Par Lost 9.1045
About thir spirits had plaid, and inmost powers Par Lost 9.1048
Soon found thir Eyes how op'nd, and thir minds Par Lost 9.1053
Of all thir vertue: silent, and in face Par Lost 9.1063
Will dazle now this earthly, with thir blaze Par Lost 9.1083
To Starr or Sun-light, spread thir umbrage broad Par Lost 9.1087
To gird thir waste, vain Covering if to hide Par Lost 9.1113
Thir guilt and dreaded shame; O how unlike Par Lost 9.1114
Thus fenc't, and as they thought, thir shame in part Par Lost 9.1119
Raind at thir Eyes, but high Winds worse within Par Lost 9.1122
Thir inward State of Mind, calm Region once Par Lost 9.1125
And of thir vain contest appeer'd no end. Par Lost 9.1189
With pitie, violated not thir bliss. Par Lost 10.25
With righteous plea, thir utmost vigilance, Par Lost 10.30
Of right, that I may mitigate thir doom Par Lost 10.76
From Noon, and gentle Aires due at thir hour Par Lost 10.93
Brought to thir Ears, while day declin'd, they heard, Par Lost 10.99
Love was not in thir looks, either to God Par Lost 10.111
Thir nakedness with Skins of Beasts, or slain, Par Lost 10.217
Nor hee thir outward onely with the Skins Par Lost 10.220
Can fit his punishment, or their revenge. Par Lost 10.242
Easing thir passage hence, for intercourse, Par Lost 10.260
Or transmigration, as thir lot shall lead. Par Lost 10.261
Flew divers, and with Power (thir Power was great) Par Lost 10.284
And now thir way to Earth they had descri'd, Par Lost 10.325
Thir Parent soon discern'd, though in disguise. Par Lost 10.331
Upon her Husband, saw thir shame that sought Par Lost 10.336
Sate in thir sad discourse, and various plaint, Par Lost 10.343
Great joy was at thir meeting, and at sight Par Lost 10.350
Thou art thir Author and prime Architect: Par Lost 10.356

Their(*cont*)

Thir course through thickest Constellations held Par Lost 10.411
Spreading thir bane; the blasted Starrs lookt wan, Par Lost 10.412
Appointed to sit there, had left thir charge, Par Lost 10.421
There kept thir Watch the Legions, while the Grand Par Lost 10.427
Might intercept thir Emperour sent, so hee Par Lost 10.429
Round thir Metropolis, and now expecting Par Lost 10.439
Each hour their great adventurer from the search Par Lost 10.440
Bent thir aspect, and whom they wish'd beheld, Par Lost 10.454
Thir mighty Chief returnd: loud was th' acclaime: Par Lost 10.455
Rais'd from thir Dark *Divan*, and with like joy Par Lost 10.457
That jealous of thir secrets fiercely oppos'd Par Lost 10.478
Thir universal shout and high applause Par Lost 10.505
In Triumph issuing forth thir glorious Chief; Par Lost 10.537
They felt themselves now changing; down thir arms, Par Lost 10.541
As in thir crime. Thus was th' applause they meant, Par Lost 10.545
Cast on themselves from thir own mouths. There stood Par Lost 10.547
A Grove hard by, sprung up with this thir change, Par Lost 10.548
Thir penance, laden with Fruit, like that Par Lost 10.550
Thir earnest eyes they fix'd, imagining Par Lost 10.553
Thir appetite with gust, instead of Fruit Par Lost 10.565
With hatefullest disrelish writh'd thir jaws Par Lost 10.569
Till thir lost shape, permitted, they resum'd, Par Lost 10.574
To dash thir pride, and joy for Man seduc't. Par Lost 10.577
Among the Heathen of thir purchase got, Par Lost 10.579
At random yielded up to their misrule; Par Lost 10.628
Or down from Heav'n descend. Such was thir song, Par Lost 10.648
Thir planetarie motions and aspects Par Lost 10.658
Thir influence malignant when to showre, Par Lost 10.662
Thir corners, when with bluster to confound Par Lost 10.665
To recompence his distance, in thir sight Par Lost 10.683
Bursting thir brazen Dungeon, armd with ice Par Lost 10.697
Eurus and *Zephir* with thir lateral noise, Par Lost 10.705
On mee as on thir natural center light Par Lost 10.740
Heavie, though in thir place. O fleeting joyes Par Lost 10.741
To the reception of thir matter act, Par Lost 10.807
Not to th' extent of thir own Spheare. But say Par Lost 10.808
Justling or pusht with Winds rude in thir shock Par Lost 10.1074
Humbly thir faults, and pardon beg'd, with tears Par Lost 10.1101
Watering the ground, and with thir sighs the Air Par Lost 10.1102
The stonie from thir hearts, & made new flesh Par Lost 11.4
Then loudest Oratorie: yet thir port Par Lost 11.8
Seem'd thir Petition, then when th' ancient Pair Par Lost 11.10
Of *Themis* stood devout. To Heav'n thir prayers Par Lost 11.14
By thir great Intercessor, came in sight Par Lost 11.19
And in thir state, though firm, stood more confirmd. Par Lost 11.71
Filld all the Regions: from thir blissful Bowrs Par Lost 11.77
And took thir Seats; till from his Throne supream Par Lost 11.82
To them and to thir Progenie from thence Par Lost 11.107
Bewailing thir excess, all terror hide. Par Lost 11.111
To Spirits foule, and all my Trees thir prey, Par Lost 11.124
Had, like a double *Janus*, all thir shape Par Lost 11.129
Had ended now thir Orisons, and found Par Lost 11.137
Direct to th' Eastern Gate was bent thir flight. Par Lost 11.190
In thir bright stand, there left his Powers to seise Par Lost 11.221
And reverence thee thir great Progenitor. Par Lost 11.346
To shew him all Earths Kingdomes and thir Glory. Par Lost 11.384
The Inwards and thir Fat, with Incense strew'd, Par Lost 11.439
With vows, as thir chief good, and final hope. Par Lost 11.493
Thir Makers Image, answerd *Michael*, then Par Lost 11.515
Therefore so abject is thir punishment, Par Lost 11.520
Disfiguring not Gods likeness, but thir own, Par Lost 11.521
Thir stops and chords was seen: his volant touch Par Lost 11.561
From the high neighbouring Hills, which was thir Seat, Par Lost 11.575
Down to the Plain descended: by thir guise Par Lost 11.576
Just men they seemd, and all thir study bent Par Lost 11.577
The Men though grave, ey'd them, and let thir eyes Par Lost 11.585
Unmindful of thir Maker, though his Spirit Par Lost 11.611
Shall yield up all thir vertue, all thir fame Par Lost 11.623
Part wield thir Arms, part courb the foaming Steed, Par Lost 11.643
Ewes and thir bleating Lambs over the Plaine, Par Lost 11.649
Thir Bootie; scarce with Life the Shepherds flye, Par Lost 11.650
Make they but of thir Brethren, men of men? Par Lost 11.680
And of thir doings great dislike declar'd, Par Lost 11.720
And testifi'd against thir wayes; hee oft Par Lost 11.721
Frequented thir Assemblies, whereso met, Par Lost 11.722
Thir order: last the Sire, and his three Sons Par Lost 11.736
With thir four Wives; and God made fast the dore. Par Lost 11.737
From under Heav'n; the Hills to their supplie Par Lost 11.740
Flood overwhelmd, and them with all thir pomp Par Lost 11.748
Sea without shoar; and in thir Palaces Par Lost 11.750
Abortive, to torment me ere thir being, Par Lost 11.769
Shall change thir course to pleasure, ease, and sloth, Par Lost 11.794
Shall with thir freedom lost all vertu loose Par Lost 11.798
And fear of God, from whom thir pietie feign'd Par Lost 11.799
Worldlie or dissolute, on what thir Lords Par Lost 11.803
Or violence, hee of thir wicked wayes Par Lost 11.812
On thir impenitence; and shall returne Par Lost 11.816
As after thirst, which made thir flowing shrink Par Lost 11.846
Towards the retreating Sea thir furious tyde. Par Lost 11.854
With all the Creatures, and thir seed preserve. Par Lost 11.873
Corrupting each thir way; yet those remoov'd, Par Lost 11.889
1667 'thir'
Shall hold thir course, till fire purge all things new, Par Lost 11.900
Fresh in thir mindes, fearing the Deitie, Par Lost 12.15
Shall lead thir lives, and multiplie apace, Par Lost 12.17
Shal spend thir dayes in joy unblam'd, and dwell Par Lost 12.22
In foraign Lands thir memorie be lost Par Lost 12.46

Their(*cont*)
Unseen, and through thir habitations walks Par Lost 12.49
To mark thir doings, them beholding soon, Par Lost 12.50
Comes down to see thir Citie, ere the Tower Par Lost 12.51
Upon thir Tongues a various Spirit to rase Par Lost 12.53
Quite out thir Native Language, and instead Par Lost 12.54
Deprives them of thir outward libertie, Par Lost 12.100
Thir inward lost: Witness th' irreverent Son Par Lost 12.101
Wearied with their iniquities, withdraw Par Lost 12.107
To leave them to thir own polluted wayes; Par Lost 12.110
To worship thir own work in Wood and Stone Par Lost 12.119
(Things by thir names I call, though yet unnam'd) Par Lost 12.140
To stop thir overgrowth, as inmate guests Par Lost 12.166
Inhospitably, and kills thir infant Males: Par Lost 12.168
With glory and spoile back to thir promis'd Land. Par Lost 12.172
To know thir God, or message to regard, Par Lost 12.174
Divided, till his rescu'd gain thir shoar: Par Lost 12.199
To guide them in thir journey, and remove Par Lost 12.204
And craze thir Chariot wheels: when by command Par Lost 12.210
On thir imbattelld ranks the Waves return, Par Lost 12.213
And overwhelm thir Warr: the Race elect Par Lost 12.214
This also shall they gain by thir delay Par Lost 12.223
Thir government, and thir great Senate choose Par Lost 12.225
And terror cease; he grants what they besaught Par Lost 12.238
1667 'them thir desire'
And all the Prophets in thir Age the times Par Lost 12.243
Thir natural pravitie, by stirring up Par Lost 12.288
Meanwhile they in thir earthly *Canaan* plac't Par Lost 12.315
National interrupt thir public peace, Par Lost 12.317
God, as to leave them, and expose thir Land, Par Lost 12.339
Thir Citie, his Temple, and his holy Ark Par Lost 12.340
Thir Lords, whom God dispos'd, the house of God Par Lost 12.349
Endeavour Peace: thir strife pollution brings Par Lost 12.355
Thir fight, what stroke shall bruise the Victors heel. Par Lost 12.385
To whom thus *Michael*. Dream not of thir fight, Par Lost 12.386
To save them, not thir own, though legal works. Par Lost 12.410
And fix farr deeper in his head thir stings Par Lost 12.432
Working through love, upon thir hearts shall write, Par Lost 12.489
Thir proudest persecuters: for the Spirit Par Lost 12.497
As did thir Lord before them. Thus they win Par Lost 12.502
Thir Ministry perform'd, and race well run, Par Lost 12.505
Thir doctrine and thir story written left, Par Lost 12.506
They die; but in thir room, as they forewarne, Par Lost 12.507
To thir own vile advantages shall turne Par Lost 12.510
Thir own Faith not anothers: for on Earth Par Lost 12.528
Thir motion, at whose Front a flaming Sword, Par Lost 12.592
To thir fixt Station, all in bright array Par Lost 12.627
Of Paradise, so late thir happie seat, Par Lost 12.642
Thir place of rest, and Providence thir guide: Par Lost 12.647
Through *Eden* took thir solitarie way. Par Lost 12.649
1669 'their' in some copies
To do him honour as their King; all come, Par Reg 1.75
Their King, their Leader, and Supream on Earth. Par Reg 1.99
For long indulgence to their fears or grief: Par Reg 1.110
To him their great Dictator, whose attempt Par Reg 1.113
In *Adam*'s overthrow, and led thir march Par Reg 1.115
So they in Heav'n their Odes and Vigils tun'd: Par Reg 1.182
What might improve my knowledge or their own; Par Reg 1.213
To Shepherds watching at their folds by night, Par Reg 1.244
Whereby they may direct their future life. Par Reg 1.396
The Desert, Fowls in thir clay nests were couch't; Par Reg 1.501
Now missing him thir joy so lately found, Par Reg 2.9
And as the days increas'd, increas'd thir doubt: Par Reg 2.12
Thir unexpected loss and plaints out breath'd. Par Reg 2.29
Thy chosen, to what highth thir pow'r unjust Par Reg 2.45
Thy Glory, free thy people from thir yoke, Par Reg 2.48
Thus they out of their plaints new hope resume Par Reg 2.58
With clamour was assur'd thir utmost aid Par Reg 2.148
Thir shape, thir colour, and attractive grace, Par Reg 2.176
He ceas'd, and heard thir grant in loud acclaim; Par Reg 2.235
And saw the Ravens with their horny beaks Par Reg 2.267
But tender all their power? nor mention I Par Reg 2.327
From their soft wings, and *Flora*'s earliest smells. Par Reg 2.365
Thir taste no knowledge works, at least of evil, Par Reg 2.371
Thee homage, and acknowledge thee thir Lord: Par Reg 2.376
In highth of all thir flowing wealth dissolv'd: Par Reg 2.436
To live upon thir tongues and be thir talk, Par Reg 3.55
Then those thir Conquerours, who leave behind Par Reg 3.78
Violent or shameful death thir due reward. Par Reg 3.87
That who advance his glory, not thir own, Par Reg 3.143
All things are best fullfil'd in their due time, Par Reg 3.182
That thou who worthiest art should'st be thir King? Par Reg 3.226
Empires, and Monarchs, and thir radiant Courts, Par Reg 3.237
The Monarchies of the Earth, thir pomp and state, Par Reg 3.246
How best their opposition to withstand. Par Reg 3.250
Then meeting joyn'd thir tribute to the Sea: Par Reg 3.258
They issue forth, Steel Bows, and Shafts their arms Par Reg 3.305
In Mail thir horses clad, yet fleet and strong, Par Reg 3.313
Prauncing their riders bore, the flower and choice Par Reg 3.314
He saw them in thir forms of battell rang'd, Par Reg 3.322
Of thir pursuers, and overcame by flight; Par Reg 3.325
Such and so numerous was thir Chivalrie; Par Reg 3.344
Thir Fathers in the land of *Egypt* serv'd, Par Reg 3.379
To thir inheritance, then, nor till then, Par Reg 3.382
Who wrought their own captivity, fell off Par Reg 3.415
Besides thir other worse then heathenish crimes; Par Reg 3.419
Nor in the land of their captivity Par Reg 3.420
The God of their fore-fathers; but so dy'd Par Reg 3.422
And God with Idols in thir worship joyn'd. Par Reg 3.426
Who freed, as to thir antient Patrimony, Par Reg 3.428
Headlong would follow; and to thir Gods perhaps Par Reg 3.430
Thir enemies, who serve Idols with God. Par Reg 3.432
And at their passing cleave the *Assyrian* flood, Par Reg 3.436
While to their native land with joy they hast, Par Reg 3.437
When to the promis'd land thir Fathers pass'd; Par Reg 3.439
Pretors, Proconsuls to thir Provinces Par Reg 4.63
Lictors and rods the ensigns of thir power, Par Reg 4.65
The Kingdoms of the world, and all thir glory. Par Reg 4.89
Thir sumptuous gluttonies, and gorgeous feasts Par Reg 4.114
Their wines of *Setia*, *Cales*, and *Falerne*, Par Reg 4.117
Peeling thir Provinces, exhausted all Par Reg 4.136
Then cruel, by thir sports to blood enur'd Par Reg 4.139
Luxurious by thir wealth, and greedier still, Par Reg 4.141
Without thir learning how wilt thou with them, Par Reg 4.231
Thir Idolisms, Traditions, Paradoxes? Par Reg 4.234
The vices of thir Deities, and thir own Par Reg 4.340
Thir Gods ridiculous, and themselves past shame. Par Reg 4.342
Remove their swelling Epithetes thick laid Par Reg 4.343
Thir Orators thou then extoll'st, as those Par Reg 4.353
And lovers of thir Country, as may seem; Par Reg 4.355
In thir majestic unaffected stile Par Reg 4.359
In their conjunction met, give me to spell, Par Reg 4.385
Within thir stony caves, but rush'd abroad Par Reg 4.414
Bow'd their Stiff necks, loaden with stormy blasts, Par Reg 4.418
Some bent at thee thir fiery darts, while thou Par Reg 4.424
1671 'thir' in some copies
Clear'd up their choicest notes in bush and spray Par Reg 4.437
Concerning thee to his Angels, in thir hands Par Reg 4.557
Who on their plumy Vans receiv'd him soft Par Reg 4.583
Bound, and to torment sent before thir time. Par Reg 4.632
To *Dagon* thir Sea-Idol, and forbid Samson 13
Thir Superstition yields me; hence with leave Samson 15
Thir daily practice to afflict me more. Samson 114
In scorn of thir proud arms and warlike tools, Samson 137
Thir plated backs under his heel; Samson 140
Or grovling soild thir crested helmets in the dust. Samson 141
Sam. I hear the sound of words, thir sense the air Samson 176
Bear in their Superscription (of the most Samson 190
They swarm, but in adverse withdraw their head Samson 192
Singly by me against their Conquerours Samson 244
Thir Lords the *Philistines* with gather'd powers Samson 251
The harrass of thir Land, beset me round; Samson 257
Into thir hands, and they as gladly yield me Samson 259
Toucht with the flame: on thir whole Host I flew Samson 262
Their choicest youth; they only liv'd who fled. Samson 264
And by thir vices brought to servitude, Samson 269
As thir Deliverer; if he aught begin, Samson 274
Thir great Deliverer contemn'd, Samson 279
Had not his prowess quell'd thir pride Samson 286
Till by thir own perplexities involv'd Samson 304
Equivalent to Angels walk'd thir streets, Samson 343
Duell'd thir Armies rank't in proud array, Samson 345
Thir Captive, and thir triumph; thou the sooner Samson 426
To *Dagon*, as their God who hath deliver'd Samson 437
Thee *Samson* bound and blind into thir hands, Samson 438
By th' Idolatrous rout amidst thir wine; Samson 443
Have satisfi'd thir utmost of revenge Samson 484
That Gentiles in thir Parables condemn Samson 500
To thir abyss and horrid pains confin'd. Samson 501
The subject of thir cruelty, or scorn. Samson 646
But with th' afflicted in his pangs thir sound Samson 660
Amidst thir highth of noon, Samson 683
Of Heathen and prophane, thir carkasses Samson 693
Parents and countrey; nor was I their subject, Samson 886
Nor under their protection but my own, Samson 887
Of men conspiring to uphold thir state Samson 892
To acquit themselves and prosecute their foes Samson 897
Of their own deity, Gods cannot be: Samson 899
Where other senses want not their delights Samson 916
Thir favourable ear, that I may fetch thee Samson 921
No more on me have power, their force is null'd, Samson 935
Thir nuptials, nor this last so trecherously Samson 1023
Was lavish't on thir Sex, that inward gifts Samson 1026
Who durst not with thir whole united powers Samson 1110
Till they had hir'd a woman with their gold Samson 1114
Thir ornament and safety, had not spells Samson 1132
Thir Magistrates confest it, when they took thee Samson 1183
1671 'Their' in some copies
Then like a Robber stripdst them of thir robes? Samson 1188
I us'd hostility, and took thir spoil Samson 1203
To pay my underminers in thir coin. Samson 1204
To free my Countrey; if their servile minds Samson 1213
Me their Deliverer sent would not receive, Samson 1214
But to thir Masters gave me up for nought, Samson 1215
Yet so it may fall out, because thir end Samson 1265
Draw thir own ruin who attempt the deed. Samson 1267
When God into the hands of thir deliverer Samson 1270
He all thir Ammunition Samson 1277
Thir Armories and Magazins contemns, Samson 1281
Lose thir defence distracted and amaz'd. Samson 1286
Of Saints, the trial of thir fortitude, Samson 1288
Our Law forbids at thir Religious Rites Samson 1320
And over-labour'd at thir publick Mill, Samson 1327
Although thir drudge, to be thir fool or jester, Samson 1338
To shew them feats, and play before thir god, Samson 1340

Their(*cont*)
Vaunting my strength in honour to thir *Dagon?* Samson 1360
Sam. Not in thir Idol-worship, but by labour Samson 1365
Of those who have me in thir civil power. Samson 1367
Sam. I could be well content to try thir Art, Samson 1399
Yet knowing thir advantages too many, Samson 1401
Because they shall not trail me through thir streets Samson 1402
I know not. Lords are Lordliest in thir wine; Samson 1418
No less the people on thir Holy-days Samson 1421
To come and play before them at thir Feast. Samson 1448
To accept of ransom for my Son thir pris'ner, Samson 1460
Others more moderate seeming, but thir aim Samson 1464
Thir foe to misery beneath thir fears, Samson 1469
Thir once great dread, captive, & blind before them, Samson 1474
Chor. Fathers are wont to lay up for thir Sons, Samson 1485
Sons wont to nurse thir Parents in old age, Samson 1487
Upon thir heads and on his own he pull'd. Samson 1589
Had fill'd thir hearts with mirth, high chear, & wine, Samson 1613
When to thir sports they turn'd. Immediately Samson 1614
In thir state Livery clad; before him Pipes Samson 1616
Rifted the Air clamouring thir god with praise, Samson 1621
Who had made thir dreadful enemy thir thrall. Samson 1622
Thir choice nobility and flower, not only Samson 1654
Semichor. While thir hearts were jocund and sublime, Samson 1669
Chaunting thir Idol, and preferring Samson 1672
Who hurt thir minds, Samson 1676
To call in hast for thir destroyer; Samson 1678
Thir own destruction to come speedy upon them. Samson 1681
As thir own ruin on themselves to invite, Samson 1684
His cloudless thunder bolted on thir heads. Samson 1696
And from his memory inflame thir breasts Samson 1739
To lay their just hands on that Golden Key Mask 13
Trinity ms 'thire'
And gives them leave to wear their Saphire crowns, Mask 26
Trinity ms 'thire'
And weild their little tridents, but this Ile Mask 27
Trinity ms 'thire'
Are coming to attend their Fathers state, Mask 35
Trinity ms 'thire'
And new-entrusted Scepter, but their way Mask 36
Trinity ms 'thire'
And here their tender age might suffer perill, Mask 40
Trinity ms 'thire'
I was dispatcht for their defence, and guard; Mask 42
Trinity ms 'thire'
Soon as the Potion works, their human count'nance, Mask 68
Trinity ms 'thire'
And they, so perfect is their misery, Mask 73
Trinity ms 'thire'
Not once perceive their foul disfigurement, Mask 74
Trinity ms 'thire'
And all their friends, and native home forget Mask 76
Trinity ms 'thire'
With their grave Saws in slumber ly. Mask 110
Trinity ms 'thire'
Who in their nightly watchfull Sphears, Mask 113
Trinity ms 'thire'
The Sounds, and Seas with all their finny drove Mask 115
Trinity ms 'thire'
Their merry wakes and pastimes keep: Mask 121
Trinity ms 'thire'
When for their teeming Flocks, and granges full Mask 175
Trinity ms 'thire'
They had ingag'd their wandring steps too far, Mask 193
Trinity ms 'thire'
That nature hung in Heav'n, and fill'd their Lamps Mask 198
line not in Bridgewater ms
Trinity ms 'thire'
With everlasting oil, to give due light Mask 199
Trinity ms 'due' ←'thire'
Culling their Potent hearbs, and balefull drugs, Mask 255
Trinity ms 'thire'
Co. Could that divide you from neer-ushering guides? Mask 279
Trinity ms 'neere ushering' ←'thire ushering'
Co. Imports their loss, beside the present need? Mask 287
Trinity ms 'thire'
La. As smooth as *Hebe*'s their unrazor'd lips. Mask 290
Trinity ms 'thire'
Their port was more then human, as they stood; Mask 297
Trinity ms 'thire'
The folded flocks pen'd in their watled cotes, Mask 344
Trinity ms 'thire'
Like stabl'd wolves, or tigers at their prey, Mask 534
Trinity ms 'thire'
In their obscured haunts of inmost bowres. Mask 536
Trinity ms 'thire'
Had ta'n their supper on the savoury Herb Mask 541
Trinity ms 'thire'
Telling their strange and vigorous faculties; Mask 628
Trinity ms 'thire'
Co. O foolishnes of men! that lend their ears Mask 706
Trinity ms 'thire'
And fetch their precepts from the *Cynick* Tub, Mask 708
Trinity ms 'thire'
That in their green shops weave the smooth-hair'd silk Mask 716
Trinity ms 'thire'
The herds would over-multitude their Lords, Mask 731
Trinity ms 'thire'

Their(*cont*)
And so bestudd with Stars, that they below Mask 734
Trinity ms 'and so bestudde with starres' ←'would so be studde the center with thire starre light'
They had their name thence; course complexions Mask 749
Trinity ms 'thire'
line not in Bridgewater ms
Held up their pearled wrists and took her in, Mask 834
Trinity ms 'thire'
For which the Shepherds at their festivals Mask 848
Trinity ms 'thire'
Their full tribute never miss Mask 925
Trinity ms 'thire'
We shall catch them at their sport, Mask 953
Trinity ms 'thire'
Bridgewater ms 'this'
Will double all their mirth and chere; Mask 955
Trinity ms 'thire'
Heav'n hath timely tri'd their youth, Mask 970
Trinity ms 'thire'
Their faith, their patience, and their truth. Mask 971
Trinity ms all three 'thire'
Thither all their bounties bring, Mask 987
line not in Bridgewater ms
Trinity ms 'thire'
Are at their savory dinner set Allegro 84
The Sea Nymphs, and their powers offended. Penseroso 21
Or fright them from their hallow'd haunt. Penseroso 138
And all their echoes mourn. Lycidas 41
Trinity ms 'thire'
Fanning their joyous Leaves to thy soft layes. Lycidas 44
Trinity ms 'thire'
Or Frost to Flowers, that their gay wardrop wear, Lycidas 47
Trinity ms 'thire'
And sage *Hippotades* their answer brings, Lycidas 96
Trinity ms 'thire'
Anow of such as for their bellies sake, Lycidas 114
Trinity ms 'thire'
And when they list, their lean and flashy songs Lycidas 123
Trinity ms 'thire'
Grate on their scrannel Pipes of wretched straw, Lycidas 124
Trinity ms 'thire'
Their Bels, and Flourets of a thousand hues. Lycidas 135
Trinity ms 'thire'
And Daffadillies fill their cups with tears, Lycidas 150
Trinity ms 'thire'
That sing, and singing in their glory move, Lycidas 180
Trinity ms 'thire'
As if they surely knew their sovran Lord was by. Nativity 60
Bending one way their pretious influence, Nativity 71
And will not take their flight, Nativity 72
But in their glimmering Orbs did glow, Nativity 75
Untill their Lord himself bespake, and bid them go. Nativity 76
Perhaps their loves, or els their sheep, Nativity 91
Was all that did their silly thoughts so busie keep. Nativity 92
Their hearts and ears did greet, Nativity 94
As all their souls in blisfull rapture took: Nativity 98
At last surrounds their sight Nativity 109
And bid the weltring waves their oozy channel keep. Nativity 124
Affrights the *Flamins* at their service quaint; Nativity 194
Forsake their Temples dim, Nativity 198
In vain the *Tyrian* Maids their wounded *Thamuz* mourn. Nativity 204
Fly after the Night-steeds, leaving their Moon-lov'd maze. Nativity 236
After long toil their liberty had won, Psalm 114, 2
Amongst their Ews, the little Hills like Lambs. Psalm 114, 12
He gave their Land therin to dwell. Psalm 136, 74
And with full hand supplies their need. Psalm 136, 86
And loudly knock to have their passage out; Vacation 24
And wearie of their place do only stay Vacation 25
Strew all their blessings on thy sleeping Head. Vacation 64
Would soon unboosom all thir Echoes milde, Passion 53
1673 'their'
Their loud up-lifted Angel trumpets blow, Musick 11
Trinity ms 'thire'
Touch their immortal Harps of golden wires, Musick 13
Trinity ms 'thire'
To their great Lord, whose love their motion sway'd Musick 22
Trinity ms both 'thire'
In first obedience, and their state of good. Musick 24
Trinity ms 'thire'
He at their invoking came Winchester 19
Both them I serve, and of their train am I. Sonnet 1, 14
And at thy growing vertues fret their spleen, Sonnet 9, 7
I did but prompt the age to quit their cloggs Sonnet 12, 1
Trinity ms 'theire' ←'thir'
That bawle for freedom in their senceless mood, Sonnet 12, 9
Trinity ms 'their' ←'thir'
That tun'st their happiest lines in Hymn, or Story. Sonnet 13, 11
Trinity ms 'theire' ←'thir'
Thir Hydra heads, and the fals North displaies Sonnet 15, 7
1694 'Their'
her brok'n league, to impe their serpent wings, Sonnet 15, 8
1694 'her'
Of hireling wolves whose Gospell is their maw. Sonnet 16, 14
Forget not: in thy book record their groanes Sonnet 18, 5
Who were thy Sheep and in their antient Fold Sonnet 18, 6
Mother with Infant down the Rocks. Their moans Sonnet 18, 8
To Heav'n. Their martyr'd blood and ashes sow Sonnet 18, 10

Their(*cont*)	
Which others at their Barr so often wrench;	Sonnet 21, 4
line not in Trinity ms	
Bereft of light thir seeing have forgot,	Sonnet 22, 3
1694 'their'	
Trinity ms 'thir' ←'their'	
Nor to thir idle orbs doth sight appear	Sonnet 22, 4
1694 'their'	
May with their wholsom and preventive Shears	Forcers 16
In judgment, or abide their tryal then,	Psalm 1, 13
With power, and Princes in their Congregations	Psalm 2, 3
Lay deep their plots together through each Land,	Psalm 2, 4
Their bonds, and cast from us, no more to wear,	Psalm 2, 7
Their twisted cords: he who in Heaven doth dwell	Psalm 2, 8
Happy all those who have in him their stay.	Psalm 2, 28
They pitch against me their Pavillions.	Psalm 3, 18
Their stores doth over-cloy	Psalm 4, 34
And from their plenteous grounds	Psalm 4, 35
With vast increase their corn and wine abounds	Psalm 4, 36
Their inside, troubles miserable;	Psalm 5, 27
An open grave their throat, their tongue they smooth.	Psalm 5, 28
By their own counsels quell'd;	Psalm 5, 30
Push them in their rebellions all	Psalm 5, 31
Their joy, while thou from blame	Psalm 5, 34
And wake for me, their furi' asswage;	Psalm 7, 22
Return on high and in their sight.	Psalm 7, 28
And their power that do amiss.	Psalm 7, 36
Between their wings out-spread,	Psalm 80, 6
Their bread with tears they eat,	Psalm 80, 22
Wherwith their cheeks are wet.	Psalm 80, 24
Advanc'd their lofty head.	Psalm 80, 44
Wild Beasts there brouze, and make their food	Psalm 80, 55
Then did I leave them to their will	Psalm 81, 49
And to their wandring mind;	Psalm 81, 50
Their own conceits they follow'd still	Psalm 81, 51
Their own devises blind.	Psalm 81, 52
To serve me *all their daies*,	Psalm 81, 54
Then would I soon bring down their foes	Psalm 81, 57
That are their enemies.	Psalm 81, 60
Their time should have no end.	Psalm 81, 64
With Honey *for their Meat*.	Psalm 81, 68
Exalt their heads full hie.	Psalm 83, 8
Their Plots and Counsels deep,	Psalm 83, 10
For they consult with all their might,	Psalm 83, 17
All these have lent their armed hands	Psalm 83, 31
So let their Princes speed	Psalm 83, 42
So let their Princes *bleed*.	Psalm 83, 44
For they amidst their pride have said	Psalm 83, 45
Their stately Palaces.	Psalm 83, 48
Lord fill with shame their face.	Psalm 83, 60
They find their safe abode,	Psalm 84, 14
And in their hearts thy waies.	Psalm 84, 20
And all their Sin, *that did thee grieve*	Psalm 85, 7
To seek my life, and in their eyes	Psalm 86, 51
And praise thee *from their loathsom bed*	Psalm 88, 43
Theirs	
From thir own mouths; all is not theirs it seems:	Par Lost 4.513
For had the gift bin theirs, it had not here	Par Lost 9.806
And due to theirs which out of thine will grow:	Par Lost 12.400
Imputed becomes theirs by Faith, his merits	Par Lost 12.409
Or theirs whom he redeems, a death like sleep,	Par Lost 12.434
Thou mine, not theirs: if aught against my life	Samson 888
Them	
Who first seduc'd them to that foul revolt?	Par Lost 1.33
And call them not to share with us their part	Par Lost 1.267
Got them new Names, till wandring ore the Earth,	Par Lost 1.365
Glory of him that made them, to transform	Par Lost 1.370
To do him wanton rites, which cost them woe.	Par Lost 1.414
Till good *Josiah* drove them thence to Hell.	Par Lost 1.418
With Orient Colours waving: with them rose	Par Lost 1.546
Above them all th' Arch Angel: but his face	Par Lost 1.600
With all his Peers: attention held them mute.	Par Lost 1.618
Or cast a Rampart. *Mammon* led them on,	Par Lost 1.678
More unexpert, I boast not: them let those	Par Lost 2.52
Let such bethink them, if the sleepy drench	Par Lost 2.73
Them in his anger, whom his anger saves	Par Lost 2.158
Awak'd should blow them into sevenfold rage	Par Lost 2.171
And vent'rous, if that fail them, shrink and fear	Par Lost 2.205
Wrought still within them; and no less desire	Par Lost 2.295
Seduce them to our Party, that thir God	Par Lost 2.368
With deafning shout, return'd them loud acclaim.	Par Lost 2.520
Might yield them easier habitation, bend	Par Lost 2.573
To yonder Gates? through them I mean to pass,	Par Lost 2.684
That bred them they return, and howle and gnaw	Par Lost 2.799
Grim *Death* my Son and foe, who sets them on,	Par Lost 2.804
Fell with us from on high: from them I go	Par Lost 2.826
Unless th' Almighty Maker them ordain	Par Lost 2.915
The Consort of his Reign; and by them stood	Par Lost 2.963
So were I equal'd with them in renown,	Par Lost 3.34
And Spirits, both them who stood and them who faild;	Par Lost 3.101
I formd them free, and free they must remain,	Par Lost 3.124
And I will place within them as a guide	Par Lost 3.194
Imputed shall absolve them who renounce	Par Lost 3.291
All knees to thee shall bow, of them that bide	Par Lost 3.321
To wait them with his Keys, and now at foot	Par Lost 3.485
Blows them transverse ten thousand Leagues awry	Par Lost 3.488
He stayd not to enquire: above them all	Par Lost 3.571
That brought them forth, but hid thir causes deep.	Par Lost 3.707

Them(*cont*)	
Those balmie spoiles. As when to them who saile	Par Lost 4.159
Who came thir bane, though with them better pleas'd	Par Lost 4.167
To them who liv'd; nor on the vertue thought	Par Lost 4.198
And all amid them stood the Tree of Life,	Par Lost 4.218
Betwixt them Lawns, or level Downs, and Flocks	Par Lost 4.252
They sat them down, and after no more toil	Par Lost 4.327
Yielded them, side-long as they sat recline	Par Lost 4.333
Alone as they. About them frisking playd	Par Lost 4.340
Gambold before them, th' unwieldy Elephant	Par Lost 4.345
To make them mirth us'd all his might, and wreathd	Par Lost 4.346
In them Divine resemblance, and such grace	Par Lost 4.364
The hand that formd them on thir shape hath pourd.	Par Lost 4.365
By word or action markt: about them round	Par Lost 4.401
Whence rushing he might surest seize them both	Par Lost 4.407
Ey'd them askance, and to himself thus plaind.	Par Lost 4.504
Forbidden them to taste: Knowledge forbidd'n?	Par Lost 4.515
Envie them that? can it be sin to know,	Par Lost 4.517
To keep them low whom knowledge might exalt	Par Lost 4.525
That neer him stood, and gave them thus in charge.	Par Lost 4.787
The Organs of her Fancie, and with them forge	Par Lost 4.802
And with them comes a third of Regal port,	Par Lost 4.869
Gravely in doubt whether to hold them wise	Par Lost 4.907
Came not all Hell broke loose? is pain to them	Par Lost 4.918
Swayes them; the careful Plowman doubting stands	Par Lost 4.983
From either eye, and wip'd them with her haire;	Par Lost 5.131
His barren leaves. Them thus imploid beheld	Par Lost 5.219
In them at once to ruin all mankind.	Par Lost 5.228
Dazles the croud, and sets them all agape.	Par Lost 5.357
Within them every lower facultie	Par Lost 5.410
As may express them best, though what if Earth	Par Lost 5.574
Tell them that by command, ere yet dim Night	Par Lost 5.685
The starrie flock, allur'd them, and with lyes	Par Lost 5.709
Crownd them with Glory, and to thir Glory nam'd	Par Lost 5.839
Though single. From amidst them forth he passd,	Par Lost 5.903
Rebellious, them with Fire and hostile Arms	Par Lost 6.50
Pursuing drive them out from God and bliss,	Par Lost 6.52
Vigour Divine within them, can allow	Par Lost 6.158
Them whom he governs. This is servitude,	Par Lost 6.178
Assume, as likes them best, condense or rare.	Par Lost 6.353
Nameless in dark oblivion let them dwell.	Par Lost 6.380
Gave them above thir foes, not to have sinnd,	Par Lost 6.402
Left them Superiour, while we can preserve	Par Lost 6.443
So warnd he them aware themselves, and soon	Par Lost 6.547
Stand readie to receive them, if they like	Par Lost 6.561
Doubl'd, would render them yet more despis'd,	Par Lost 6.602
To entertain them fair with open Front	Par Lost 6.611
We should compel them to a quick result.	Par Lost 6.619
Such as we might perceive amus'd them all,	Par Lost 6.623
And stumbl'd many, who receives them right,	Par Lost 6.624
Rage prompted them at length, and found them arms	Par Lost 6.635
Up lifting bore them in thir hands: Amaze,	Par Lost 6.646
When coming towards them so dread they saw	Par Lost 6.648
They saw them whelm'd, and all thir confidence	Par Lost 6.651
Into thir substance pent, which wrought them pain	Par Lost 6.657
Betook them, and the neighbouring Hills uptore;	Par Lost 6.663
For to themselves I left them, and thou knowst,	Par Lost 6.689
Pursue these sons of Darkness, drive them out	Par Lost 6.715
There let them learn, as likes them, to despise	Par Lost 6.717
Hymns of high praise, and I among them chief.	Par Lost 6.745
First seen, them unexpected joy surpriz'd,	Par Lost 6.774
Or I alone against them, since by strength	Par Lost 6.820
Not emulous, nor care who them excells;	Par Lost 6.822
Nor other strife with them do I voutsafe.	Par Lost 6.823
Among them he arriv'd; in his right hand	Par Lost 6.835
Thrown on them as a shelter from his ire.	Par Lost 6.843
One Spirit in them rul'd, and every eye	Par Lost 6.848
And of thir wonted vigour left them draind,	Par Lost 6.851
Not to destroy, but root them out of Heav'n:	Par Lost 6.855
Drove them before him Thunder-struck, pursu'd	Par Lost 6.858
Strook them with horror backward, but far worse	Par Lost 6.863
Urg'd them behind; headlong themselves they threw	Par Lost 6.864
Burnt after them to the bottomless pit.	Par Lost 6.866
Yawning receavd them whole, and on them clos'd,	Par Lost 6.875
Spontaneous, for within them Spirit livd,	Par Lost 7.204
Soft-ebbing; nor withstood them Rock or Hill,	Par Lost 7.300
The Day from Night; and let them be for Signes,	Par Lost 7.341
And let them be for Lights as I ordaine	Par Lost 7.343
And set them in the Firmament of Heav'n	Par Lost 7.349
And saw that it was good, and bless'd them, saying,	Par Lost 7.395
Rising, the crumbl'd Earth above them threw	Par Lost 7.468
And thou thir Natures know'st, & gav'st them Names,	Par Lost 7.493
In our similitude, and let them rule	Par Lost 7.520
His secrets to be scann'd by them who ought	Par Lost 8.74
Light back to them, is obvious to dispute.	Par Lost 8.158
Leave them to God above, him serve and feare;	Par Lost 8.168
Seek them with wandring thoughts, and notions vain.	Par Lost 8.187
After thir kindes; I bring them to receave	Par Lost 8.343
I nam'd them, as they pass'd, and understood	Par Lost 8.352
So fitly them in pairs thou hast combin'd;	Par Lost 8.394
To them made common and divulg'd, if aught	Par Lost 8.583
Of God ordain'd them, his creating hand	Par Lost 9.344
The onely two of Mankinde, but in them	Par Lost 9.415
He sought them both, but wish'd his hap might find	Par Lost 9.421
Hung drooping unsustaind, them she upstaies	Par Lost 9.430
On our belief, that all from them proceeds;	Par Lost 9.719
Them nothing: If they all things, who enclos'd	Par Lost 9.722
To open Eyes, and make them Gods who taste;	Par Lost 9.866

Them(*cont*)
Divinitie within them breeding wings Par Lost 9.1010
Oppress'd them, wearied with thir amorous play. Par Lost 9.1045
Encumberd, now had left them, up they rose Par Lost 9.1051
Had shadow'd them from knowing ill, was gon, Par Lost 9.1055
And honour from about them, naked left Par Lost 9.1057
Hide me, where I may never see them more. Par Lost 9.1090
They sate them down to weep, nor onely Teares Par Lost 9.1121
But whom send I to judge them? whom but thee Par Lost 10.55
Them fully satisfied, and thee appease. Par Lost 10.79
The Son of God to judge them terrifi'd Par Lost 10.338
To my associate Powers, them to acquaint Par Lost 10.395
With these successes, and with them rejoyce, Par Lost 10.396
So saying he dismiss'd them, they with speed Par Lost 10.410
Of ugly Serpents; horror on them fell, Par Lost 10.539
Now ris'n, to work them furder woe or shame; Par Lost 10.555
Though to delude them sent, could not abstain, Par Lost 10.557
This said, they both betook them several wayes, Par Lost 10.610
I suffer them to enter and possess Par Lost 10.623
Of Passion, I to them had quitted all, Par Lost 10.627
And know not that I call'd and drew them thither Par Lost 10.629
His mightie Angels gave them several charge, Par Lost 10.650
Which of them rising with the Sun, or falling, Par Lost 10.663
Beyond the Polar Circles; to them Day Par Lost 10.681
With adverse blast up-turns them from the South Par Lost 10.701
Thou didst accept them; wilt thou enjoy the good, Par Lost 10.758
To hellish falshood, snare them. But for thee Par Lost 10.873
Fell humble, and imbracing them, besaught Par Lost 10.912
Repairing where he judg'd them prostrate fell Par Lost 10.1099
Before the Fathers Throne: Them the glad Son Par Lost 11.20
Through Heav'ns wide bounds; from them I will not hide Par Lost 11.68
To them and to thir Progenie from thence Par Lost 11.107
For I behold them softn'd and with tears Par Lost 11.110
Dismiss them not disconsolate; reveale Par Lost 11.113
So send them forth, though sorrowing, yet in peace: Par Lost 11.117
Of them the Highest, for such of shape may seem Par Lost 11.297
And over them triumphant Death his Dart Par Lost 11.491
Forsook them, when themselves they villifi'd Par Lost 11.516
The Men though grave, ey'd them, and let thir eyes Par Lost 11.585
Taught them, but they his gifts acknowledg'd none. Par Lost 11.612
Religious titl'd them the Sons of God, Par Lost 11.622
To judge them with his Saints: Him the most High Par Lost 11.705
Allurd them; thence from Cups to civil Broiles. Par Lost 11.718
At length a Reverend Sire among them came, Par Lost 11.719
Triumphs or Festivals, and to them preachd Par Lost 11.723
Flood overwhelmd, and them with all thir pomp Par Lost 11.748
Shall leave them to enjoy; for th' Earth shall bear Par Lost 11.804
Shall them admonish, and before them set Par Lost 11.813
Of them derided, but of God observd Par Lost 11.817
No sooner hee with them of Man and Beast Par Lost 11.822
To mark thir doings, them beholding soon, Par Lost 12.50
Deprives them of thir outward libertie, Par Lost 12.100
His presence from among them, and avert Par Lost 12.108
To leave them to thir own polluted wayes; Par Lost 12.110
In prospect, as I point them; on the shoare Par Lost 12.143
Too numerous; whence of guests he makes them slaves Par Lost 12.167
Swallows him with his Host, but them lets pass Par Lost 12.196
Before them in a Cloud, and Pillar of Fire, Par Lost 12.202
To guide them in thir journey, and remove Par Lost 12.204
Behinde them, while th' obdurat King pursues: Par Lost 12.205
Warr terrifie them inexpert, and feare Par Lost 12.218
Return them back to *Egypt*, choosing rather Par Lost 12.219
Ordaine them Lawes; part such as appertaine Par Lost 12.230
Of sacrifice, informing them, by types Par Lost 12.232
That *Moses* might report to them his will, Par Lost 12.237
And terror cease; he grants what they besaught Par Lost 12.238
1667 'them thir desire'
Among them to set up his Tabernacle, Par Lost 12.247
Among them; how can God with such reside? Par Lost 12.284
Will reign among them, as of thee begot; Par Lost 12.286
And therefore was Law given them to evince Par Lost 12.287
To them by Faith imputed, they may finde Par Lost 12.295
With purpose to resign them in full time Par Lost 12.301
Provoking God to raise them enemies: Par Lost 12.318
From whom as oft he saves them penitent Par Lost 12.319
God, as to leave them, and expose thir Land, Par Lost 12.339
There in captivitie he lets them dwell Par Lost 12.344
The space of seventie years, then brings them back, Par Lost 12.345
To save them, not thir own, though legal works. Par Lost 12.410
Never to hurt them more who rightly trust Par Lost 12.418
Still follow'd him; to them shall leave in charge Par Lost 12.439
And his Salvation, them who shall beleeve Par Lost 12.441
Of washing them from guilt of sin to Life Par Lost 12.443
His faithful, and receave them into bliss, Par Lost 12.462
His Spirit within them, and the Law of Faith Par Lost 12.488
To guide them in all truth, and also arme Par Lost 12.490
What man can do against them, not affraid, Par Lost 12.493
Baptiz'd, shall them with wondrous gifts endue Par Lost 12.500
As did thir Lord before them. Thus they win Par Lost 12.502
Left them inrould, or what the Spirit within Par Lost 12.523
The brandisht Sword of God before them blaz'd Par Lost 12.633
Led them direct, and down the Cliff as fast Par Lost 12.639
Som natural tears they drop'd, but wip'd them soon; Par Lost 12.645
The World was all before them, where to choose Par Lost 12.646
With aw the Regions round, and with them came Par Reg 1.22
A gloomy Consistory; and them amidst Par Reg 1.42
Pretends to wash off sin, and fit them so Par Reg 1.73
And he himself among them was baptiz'd, Par Reg 1.76

Them(*cont*)
O Son, but nourish them and let them soar Par Reg 1.230
Can raise them, though above example high; Par Reg 1.232
And told them the Messiah now was born, Par Reg 1.245
With them from bliss to the bottomless deep, Par Reg 1.361
Never did wrong or violence, by them Par Reg 1.389
I lost not what I lost, rather by them Par Reg 1.390
I gain'd what I have gain'd, and with them dwell Par Reg 1.391
If not disposer; lend them oft my aid, Par Reg 1.393
Among them to declare his Providence Par Reg 1.445
Plain Fishermen, no greater men them call, Par Reg 2.27
They have exalted, and behind them cast Par Reg 2.46
At his command; when from amidst them rose Par Reg 2.149
Hearts after them tangl'd in Amorous Nets. Par Reg 2.162
And coupl'd with them, and begot a race. Par Reg 2.181
Longer then thou canst feed them on thy cost? Par Reg 2.421
Th' intelligent among them and the wise Par Reg 3.58
Till Conquerour Death discover them scarce men, Par Reg 3.85
From them who could return him nothing else, Par Reg 3.129
Them he himself to glory will advance. Par Reg 3.144
Till *Cyrus* set them free; *Persepolis* Par Reg 3.284
He saw them in thir forms of battell rang'd, Par Reg 3.322
How quick they wheel'd, and flying behind them shot Par Reg 3.323
My brethren, as thou call'st them; those Ten Tribes Par Reg 3.403
Of *Bethel* and of *Dan*? no, let them serve Par Reg 3.431
May bring them back repentant and sincere, Par Reg 3.435
To his due time and providence I leave them. Par Reg 3.440
Easily done, and hold them all of me; Par Reg 4.168
As offer them to me the Son of God, Par Reg 4.190
Advise thee, gain them as thou canst, or not. Par Reg 4.211
Ruling them by perswasion as thou mean'st, Par Reg 4.230
Without thir learning how wilt thou with them, Par Reg 4.231
How wilt thou reason with them, how refute Par Reg 4.233
And his who gave them breath, but higher sung, Par Reg 4.258
I know them not; not therefore am I short Par Reg 4.287
The first and wisest of them all profess'd Par Reg 4.293
In them is plainest taught, and easiest learnt, Par Reg 4.361
Was distant; and these flaws, though mortals fear them Par Reg 4.454
Till underneath them fair *Jerusalem*, Par Reg 4.544
And beg to hide them in a herd of Swine, Par Reg 4.630
Lest he command them down into the deep Par Reg 4.631
Spurn'd them to death by Troops. The bold *Ascalonite* Samson 138
To count them things worth notice, till at length Samson 250
To set upon them, what advantag'd best; Samson 255
And lorded over them whom now they serve; Samson 267
But justly; I my self have brought them on, Samson 375
To them who had corrupted her, my Spies, Samson 386
Rather approv'd them not; but thou didst plead Samson 421
Them out of thine, who slew'st them many a slain. Samson 439
On thee, who now no more canst do them harm. Samson 486
Thirst, and refresht; nor envy'd them the grape Samson 551
Which was expresly giv'n thee to annoy them? Samson 578
And I shall shortly be with them that rest. Samson 598
Nor am I in the list of them that hope; Samson 647
From thee on them, or them to thee of service. Samson 686
Nor only dost degrade them, or remit Samson 687
But throw'st them lower then thou didst exalt them high, Samson 689
Oft leav'st them to the hostile sword Samson 692
With sickness and disease thou bow'st them down, Samson 698
Courted by all the winds that hold them play, Samson 719
To publish them, both common female faults: Samson 777
Into thy Enemies hand, permitted them Samson 1159
Acknowledge them from God inflicted on me Samson 1170
Then like a Robber stripdst them of thir robes? Samson 1188
To wring from me and tell to them my secret, Samson 1199
And with malitious counsel stir them up Samson 1251
Renders them useless, while Samson 1282
Making them each his own Deliverer, Samson 1289
Sam. Thou knowst I am an *Ebrew*, therefore tell them, Samson 1319
Off. This answer, be assur'd, will not content them. Samson 1322
To make them sport with blind activity? Samson 1328
Off. Regard thy self, this will offend them highly. Samson 1333
To shew them feats, and play before thir god, Samson 1340
Commands are no constraints. If I obey them, Samson 1372
Which to no few of them would prove pernicious. Samson 1400
To such as owe them absolute subjection; Samson 1405
I will not wish, lest it perhaps offend them Samson 1414
So dreaded once, may now exasperate them Samson 1417
To come and play before them at thir Feast. Samson 1448
Thir once great dread, captive, & blind before them, Samson 1474
Or at some proof of strength before them shown. Samson 1475
Chor. Thy Son is rather slaying them, that outcry Samson 1517
Man. Suspense in news is torture, speak them out. Samson 1569
The whole roof after them, with burst of thunder Samson 1651
Among them he a spirit of phrenzie sent, Samson 1675
And urg'd them on with mad desire Samson 1677
Thir own destruction to come speedy upon them. Samson 1681
Fully reveng'd, hath left them years of mourning, Samson 1712
Honour hath left, and freedom, let but them Samson 1715
And all that band them to resist Samson 1753
And gives them leave to wear their Saphire crowns, Mask 26
Had stole them from me, els O theevish Night Mask 195
Hid them in som flowry Cave, Mask 239
Co. Perhaps fore-stalling night prevented them. Mask 285
I saw them under a green mantling vine Mask 294
Bridgewater ms 'em'
Trinity ms 'em'
To help you find them. *La*. Gentle villager Mask 304

Them(*cont*)
Trinity ms 'them' ←'them out'
And put them into mis-becoming plight. Mask 372
I fear the dred events that dog them both, Mask 405
Of them that pass unweeting by the way. Mask 539
At which I ceas't, and listen'd them a while, Mask 551
We shall catch them at their sport, Mask 953
And sent them here through hard assays Mask 972
Thou fix them on the earth as fast. Penseroso 44
Or fright them from their hallow'd haunt. Penseroso 138
What recks it them? What need they? They are sped; Lycidas 122
And call the Vales, and bid them hither cast Lycidas 134
O run, prevent them with thy humble ode, Nativity 24
Or *Lucifer* that often warn'd them thence; Nativity 74
Untill their Lord himself bespake, and bid them go. Nativity 76
Was kindly com to live with them below; Nativity 90
Till thou hast deck't them in thy best aray; Vacation 26
Thy drowsie Nurse hath sworn she did them spie Vacation 61
She heard them give thee this, that thou should'st still Vacation 65
In worth and excellence he shall out-go them, Vacation 79
Yet being above them, he shall be below them; Vacation 80
Both them I serve, and of their train am I. Sonnet 1, 14
Guard them, and him within protect from harms, Sonnet 8, 4
Who liv'd in both, unstain'd with gold or fee, Sonnet 10, 3
Trinity ms 'liv'd in' ←'left them'
And left them both, more in himself content, Sonnet 10, 4
That all both judge you to relate them true, Sonnet 10, 13
And to possess them, Honour'd *Margaret*. Sonnet 10, 14
And still revolt when truth would set them free. Sonnet 12, 10
Trinity ms 'still revolt when Truth would sett them' ←'make them' ←'set them' ←'hate the truth wherby they should be'
Love led them on, and Faith who knew them best Sonnet 14, 9
Trinity ms 'Love led them on' ←'Faith shew'd the way' ←'Faith who led on the way'
Thy hand-maids, clad them o're with purple beams Sonnet 14, 10
Ev'n them who kept thy truth so pure of old Sonnet 18, 3
To interpose them oft, is not unwise. Sonnet 20, 14
The conscience, Friend, to have lost them overply'd Sonnet 22, 10
From them whose sin ye envi'd, not abhor'd, Forcers 4
Shall laugh, the Lord shall scoff them, then severe Psalm 2, 9
Speak to them in his wrath, and in his fell Psalm 2, 10
And fierce ire trouble them; but I saith hee Psalm 2, 11
Earths utmost bounds: them shalt thou bring full low Psalm 2, 19
With Iron Scepter bruis'd, and them disperse Psalm 2, 20
Thou hat'st; and them unblest Psalm 5, 14
God, find them guilty, let them fall Psalm 5, 29
Push them in their rebellions all Psalm 5, 31
Defend'st them, they shall ever sing Psalm 5, 35
For them that persecute.) Behold Psalm 7, 50
Thou feed'st them with the bread of tears, Psalm 80, 21
And mak'st them largely drink the tears Psalm 80, 23
Then did I leave them to their will Psalm 81, 49
And we would feed them *from the shock* Psalm 81, 65
And satisfie them from the rock Psalm 81, 67
Them to ensnare they chiefly strive Psalm 83, 11
Come let us cut them off say they, Psalm 83, 13
Moab, with them of Hagars blood Psalm 83, 23
With them *great* Asshur also bands Psalm 83, 29
Do to them as to Midian *bold* Psalm 83, 33
My God, oh make them as a wheel Psalm 83, 49
No quiet let them find, Psalm 83, 50
Giddy and *restless* let *them reel* Psalm 83, 51
So with thy whirlwind them pursue, Psalm 83, 57
Asham'd and troubl'd let them be, Psalm 83, 61
No good from them shall be with-held Psalm 84, 43
But let them never more Psalm 85, 34
To them that on thee call. Psalm 86, 16
To bow them low before thee Lord, Psalm 86, 31
Reck'n'd I am with them that pass Psalm 88, 13
Them from thy hand deliver'd o're Psalm 88, 23
Me to them odious, *for they change*, Psalm 88, 35
'Gainst them that rais'd thee dost thou lift thy horn, Prose 3, 2

Themes
And speak the truth of thee on glorious Theams Sonnet 14, 12
Trinity ms 'theames' ←'themes' ←'theames'

Themis
Of *Themis* stood devout. To Heav'n thir prayers Par Lost 11.14
Of Brittish *Themis*, with no mean applause Sonnet 21, 2
line not in Trinity ms

Themselves
Rouse and bestir themselves ere well awake. Par Lost 1.334
Not in despair, to have found themselves not lost Par Lost 1.525
ms 'themselues'
And in thir own dimensions like themselves Par Lost 1.793
And trust themselves to fear no second fate: Par Lost 2.17
Among themselves, and levie cruel warres, Par Lost 2.501
Or high foreknowledge; they themselves decreed Par Lost 3.116
They trespass, Authors to themselves in all Par Lost 3.122
Till they enthrall themselves: I else must change Par Lost 3.125
Thir freedom, they themselves ordain'd thir fall. Par Lost 3.128
They Limb themselves, and colour, shape or size Par Lost 6.352
So warnd he them aware themselves, and soon Par Lost 6.547
So they among themselves in pleasant veine Par Lost 6.628
Themselves invaded next, and on thir heads Par Lost 6.653
For to themselves I left them, and thou knowst, Par Lost 6.689
Urg'd them behind; headlong themselves they threw Par Lost 6.864
1667 'themselvs'
They open to themselves at length the way Par Lost 7.158

Themselves(*cont*)
Not in themselves, all thir known vertue appeers Par Lost 9.110
And from his presence hid themselves among Par Lost 10.100
They felt themselves now changing; down thir arms, Par Lost 10.541
Cast on themselves from thir own mouths. There stood Par Lost 10.547
Forsook them, when themselves they villifi'd Par Lost 11.516
Or if his likeness, by themselves defac't Par Lost 11.522
Gods Image did not reverence in themselves. Par Lost 11.525
Where good with bad were matcht, who of themselves Par Lost 11.685
And get themselves a name, least far disperst Par Lost 12.45
Then shall they seek to avail themselves of names, Par Lost 12.515
By spiritual, to themselves appropriating Par Lost 12.518
In every Province, who themselves disdaining Par Reg 1.448
Riches are needless then, both for themselves, Par Reg 2.484
They themselves rather are occasion best, Par Reg 3.174
As for those captive Tribes, themselves were they Par Reg 3.414
Humbled themselves, or penitent besought Par Reg 3.421
Like to themselves, distinguishable scarce Par Reg 3.424
These thus degenerate, by themselves enslav'd, Par Reg 4.144
Ignorant of themselves, of God much more, Par Reg 4.310
And in themselves seek vertue, and to themselves Par Reg 4.314
Thir Gods ridiculous, and themselves past shame. Par Reg 4.342
The deeds themselves, though mute, spoke loud the dooer; Samson 248
To acquit themselves and prosecute their foes Samson 897
As thir own ruin on themselves to invite, Samson 1684
But boast themselves more comely then before Mask 75
Blind mouthes! that scarce themselves know how to hold Lycidas 119
Among themselves they laugh, they play, Psalm 80, 27
Themselves against thee they unite Psalm 83, 19

Then
He with his Thunder: and till then who knew Par Lost 1.93
What can it then avail though yet we feel Par Lost 1.153
Whom we resist. If then his Providence Par Lost 1.162
Then with expanded wings he stears his flight Par Lost 1.225
Said then the lost Arch-Angel, this the seat Par Lost 1.243
But wherefore let we then our faithful friends, Par Lost 1.264
Then were they known to men by various Names, Par Lost 1.374
Say, Muse, thir Names then known, who first, who last, Par Lost 1.376
Darkens the Streets, then wander forth the Sons Par Lost 1.501
Then strait commands that at the warlike sound Par Lost 1.531
Monarch in Heav'n, till then as one secure Par Lost 1.638
For who can think Submission? Warr then, Warr Par Lost 1.661
Frequent and full. After short silence then Par Lost 1.797
Of endless pain? where there is then no good Par Lost 2.30
Will covet more. With this advantage then Par Lost 2.35
We sunk thus low? Th' ascent is easie then; Par Lost 2.81
What fear we then? what doubt we to incense Par Lost 2.94
To punish endless? wherefore cease we then? Par Lost 2.159
What can we suffer worse? is this then worst, Par Lost 2.163
The Deep to shelter us? this Hell then seem'd Par Lost 2.167
Shall we then live thus vile, the Race of Heav'n Par Lost 2.194
Our purer essence then will overcome Par Lost 2.215
Our own right lost: him to unthrone we then Par Lost 2.231
To whom we hate. Let us not then pursue Par Lost 2.249
Then most conspicuous, when great things of small, Par Lost 2.258
What sit we then projecting peace and Warr? Par Lost 2.329
The happy Ile; what strength, what art can then Par Lost 2.410
Then of thir Session ended they bid cry Par Lost 2.514
Of good and evil much they argu'd then, Par Lost 2.562
Now shaves with level wing the Deep, then soares Par Lost 2.634
Who first broke peace in Heav'n and Faith, till then Par Lost 2.690
Over the *Caspian*, then stand front to front Par Lost 2.716
Forbore, then these to her *Satan* return'd: Par Lost 2.736
Hast thou forgot me then, and do I seem Par Lost 2.747
Then shining heav'nly fair, a Goddess arm'd Par Lost 2.757
My Bowels, thir repast; then bursting forth Par Lost 2.800
Then sweet, now sad to mention, through dire change Par Lost 2.820
Could once have mov'd; then in the key-hole turns Par Lost 2.876
Dwelt from Eternitie, dwelt then in thee, Par Lost 3.5
Then feed on thoughts, that voluntarie move Par Lost 3.37
In blissful solitude; he then survey'd Par Lost 3.69
Behold mee then, mee for him, life for life Par Lost 3.236
Death his deaths wound shall then receive, and stoop Par Lost 3.252
Then with the multitude of my redeemd Par Lost 3.260
Then all thy Saints assembl'd, thou shalt judge Par Lost 3.330
Then thou thy regal Scepter shalt lay by, Par Lost 3.339
For regal Scepter then no more shall need, Par Lost 3.340
Then Crown'd again thir gold'n Harps they took, Par Lost 3.365
With many a vain exploit, though then renownd: Par Lost 3.465
Into the devious Air; then might ye see Par Lost 3.489
And flutterd into Raggs, then Reliques, Beads, Par Lost 3.491
The Stairs were then let down, whether to dare Par Lost 3.523
Beyond th' *Horizon;* then from Pole to Pole Par Lost 3.560
What wonder then if fields and regions here Par Lost 3.606
Swift to thir several Quarters hasted then Par Lost 3.714
Then when the Dragon, put to second rout, Par Lost 4.3
Then much revolving, thus in sighs began. Par Lost 4.31
Indebted and dischargd; what burden then? Par Lost 4.57
Then happie; no unbounded hope had rais'd Par Lost 4.60
Thou hadst: whom hast thou then or what to accuse, Par Lost 4.67
Be then his Love accurst, since love or hate, Par Lost 4.69
O then at last relent: is there no place Par Lost 4.79
He markd and mad demeanour, then alone, Par Lost 4.129
Nor those mysterious parts were then conceald, Par Lost 4.312
Then was not guiltie shame, dishonest shame Par Lost 4.313
Then from his loftie stand on that high Tree Par Lost 4.395
Then as a Tyger, who by chance hath spi'd Par Lost 4.403
Strait couches close, then rising changes oft Par Lost 4.405

Then(*cont*)

Earth, Aire, and Sea. Then let us not think hard	Par Lost 4.432
Into a liquid Plain, then stood unmov'd	Par Lost 4.455
Of grateful Eevning milde, then silent Night	Par Lost 4.647
These then, though unbeheld in deep of night,	Par Lost 4.674
Know ye not then said *Satan*, fill'd with scorn,	Par Lost 4.827
That Glorie then, when thou no more wast good,	Par Lost 4.838
Then when I am thy captive talk of chaines,	Par Lost 4.970
Proud limitarie Cherube, but ere then	Par Lost 4.971
Neither our own but giv'n; what follie then	Par Lost 4.1007
Shot forth peculiar Graces; then with voice	Par Lost 5.15
To find thee I directed then my walk;	Par Lost 5.49
Our knowledge or opinion; then retires	Par Lost 5.108
Be not disheart'nd then, nor cloud those looks	Par Lost 5.122
Thus wondrous fair; thy self how wondrous then!	Par Lost 5.155
Now on the polar windes, then with quick Fann	Par Lost 5.269
Bestirs her then, and from each tender stalk	Par Lost 5.337
Wants her fit vessels pure, then strews the ground	Par Lost 5.348
To visit thee; lead on then where thy Bowre	Par Lost 5.375
Deserving Paradise! if ever, then,	Par Lost 5.446
Then had the Sons of God excuse to have bin	Par Lost 5.447
Wonder not then, what God for you saw good	Par Lost 5.491
Obedient? can we want obedience then	Par Lost 5.514
Then most, when most irregular they seem,	Par Lost 5.624
Both waking we were one; how then can now	Par Lost 5.678
Who can in reason then or right assume	Par Lost 5.794
Returns our own. Cease then this impious rage,	Par Lost 5.845
That we were formd then saist thou? and the work	Par Lost 5.853
Who is our equal: then thou shalt behold	Par Lost 5.866
Then who created thee lamenting learne,	Par Lost 5.894
To have reported: gladly then he mixt	Par Lost 6.21
Then lighted from his gorgeous Throne, for now	Par Lost 6.103
Prefer, and Pietie to God, though then	Par Lost 6.144
Resounded, and had Earth bin then, all Earth	Par Lost 6.218
A standing fight, then soaring on main wing	Par Lost 6.243
Tormented all the Air; all Air seemd then	Par Lost 6.244
Hence then, and evil go with thee along	Par Lost 6.275
All his right side; then *Satan* first knew pain,	Par Lost 6.327
Then first with fear surpris'd and sense of paine	Par Lost 6.394
But proves not so: then fallible, it seems,	Par Lost 6.428
Of evil then so small as easie think	Par Lost 6.437
Go then thou Mightiest in thy Fathers might,	Par Lost 6.710
Then shall thy Saints unmixt, and from th' impure	Par Lost 6.742
Know then, that after *Lucifer* from Heav'n	Par Lost 7.131
Said then th' Omnific Word, your discord end:	Par Lost 7.217
Then staid the fervid Wheeles, and in his hand	Par Lost 7.224
Adverse to life: then founded, then conglob'd	Par Lost 7.239
He scarce had said, when the bare Earth, till then	Par Lost 7.313
Then Herbs of every leaf, that sudden flour'd	Par Lost 7.317
Though of Ethereal Mould: then form'd the Moon	Par Lost 7.356
Till night, then in the East her turn she shines,	Par Lost 7.380
With thousand thousand Starres, that then appeer'd	Par Lost 7.383
Spangling the Hemisphere: then first adornd	Par Lost 7.384
Till Ev'n, nor then the solemn Nightingal	Par Lost 7.435
His hinder parts, then springs as broke from Bonds,	Par Lost 7.465
Female for Race; then bless'd Mankinde, and said,	Par Lost 7.530
Then as new wak't thus gratefully repli'd.	Par Lost 8.4
1667 'To whom thus *Adam*'	
Thir wandring course now high, now low, then hid,	Par Lost 8.126
And Day is yet not spent; till then thou seest	Par Lost 8.206
My self I then perus'd, and Limb by Limb	Par Lost 8.267
Not of my self; by some great Maker then,	Par Lost 8.278
I then was passing to my former state	Par Lost 8.290
Wors then can Man with Beast, and least of all.	Par Lost 8.397
What thinkst thou then of mee, and this my State,	Par Lost 8.403
How have I then with whom to hold converse	Par Lost 8.408
And no such companie as then thou saw'st	Par Lost 8.446
Then value: Oft times nothing profits more	Par Lost 8.571
Bear with me then, if lawful what I ask;	Par Lost 8.614
At Joust and Torneament; then marshal'd Feast	Par Lost 9.37
Satan involv'd in rising Mist, then sought	Par Lost 9.75
In wo then; that destruction wide may range:	Par Lost 9.134
From dust: spite then with spite is best repaid.	Par Lost 9.178
Then commune how that day they best may ply	Par Lost 9.201
Just then returnd at shut of Evening Flours.	Par Lost 9.278
His fraud is then thy fear, which plain inferrs	Par Lost 9.285
Though ineffectual found: misdeem not then,	Par Lost 9.301
Foul on himself; then wherefore shund or feard	Par Lost 9.331
Let us not then suspect our happie State	Par Lost 9.337
Not then mistrust, but tender love enjoynes,	Par Lost 9.357
Seek not temptation then, which to avoide	Par Lost 9.364
With thy permission then, and thus forewarnd	Par Lost 9.378
Then voluble and bold, now hid, now seen	Par Lost 9.436
Of pleasure not for him ordain'd: then soon	Par Lost 9.470
To me is lost. Then let me not let pass	Par Lost 9.479
Redouble then this miracle, and say,	Par Lost 9.562
Lead then, said *Eve*. Hee leading swiftly rowld	Par Lost 9.631
Indeed? hath God then said that of the Fruit	Par Lost 9.656
Not just, not God; not feard then, nor obeyd:	Par Lost 9.701
Why then was this forbid? Why but to awe,	Par Lost 9.703
Yet are but dim, shall perfetly be then	Par Lost 9.707
Goddess humane, reach then, and freely taste.	Par Lost 9.732
Forbids us then to taste, but his forbidding	Par Lost 9.753
In plain then, what forbids he but to know,	Par Lost 9.758
Bind us with after-bands, what profits then	Par Lost 9.761
Irrational till then. For us alone	Par Lost 9.766
What fear I then, rather what know to feare	Par Lost 9.773
Of vertue to make wise: what hinders then	Par Lost 9.778
Regarded, such delight till then, as seemd,	Par Lost 9.787
And Death ensue? then I shall be no more,	Par Lost 9.827
A death to think. Confirm'd then I resolve,	Par Lost 9.830
Disjoyne us, and I then too late renounce	Par Lost 9.884
Be sure then. How shall I behold the face	Par Lost 9.1080
I know not whence possessd thee; we had then	Par Lost 9.1137
Such proof, conclude, they then begin to faile.	Par Lost 9.1142
Too facil then thou didst not much gainsay,	Par Lost 9.1158
To whom then first incenst *Adam* repli'd,	Par Lost 9.1162
But confidence then bore thee on, secure	Par Lost 9.1175
I told ye then he should prevail and speed	Par Lost 10.40
Of his Creation; justly then accurst,	Par Lost 10.168
Though in mysterious terms, judg'd as then best:	Par Lost 10.173
So spake this Oracle, then verifi'd	Par Lost 10.182
Prince of the Aire; then rising from his Grave	Par Lost 10.185
Remov'd farr off; then pittying how they stood	Par Lost 10.211
Then Both from out Hell Gates into the waste	Par Lost 10.282
Then sufferd. Th' other way *Satan* went down	Par Lost 10.414
Then Heav'n and Earth renewd shall be made pure	Par Lost 10.638
Till then the Curse pronounc't on both precedes.	Par Lost 10.640
Of God, whom to behold was then my highth	Par Lost 10.724
I thus contest; then should have been refusd	Par Lost 10.756
Then cavil the conditions? and though God	Par Lost 10.759
Thy punishment then justly is at his Will.	Par Lost 10.768
With this corporeal Clod; then in the Grave,	Par Lost 10.786
All of me then shall die: let this appease	Par Lost 10.792
With me? how can they then acquitted stand	Par Lost 10.827
word not in 1667 edition	
Mankind? this mischief had not then befall'n,	Par Lost 10.895
Then both our selves and Seed at once to free	Par Lost 10.999
To make death in us live: Then let us seek	Par Lost 10.1028
No more be mention'd then of violence	Par Lost 10.1041
What better can we do, then to the place	Par Lost 10.1086
Dimentionless through Heav'nly dores; then clad	Par Lost 11.17
Which then not minded in dismay, yet now	Par Lost 11.156
First hunter then, pursu'd a gentle brace,	Par Lost 11.188
Some days; how long, and what till then our life,	Par Lost 11.198
Then due by sentence when thou didst transgress,	Par Lost 11.253
Mayst cover: well may then thy Lord appeas'd	Par Lost 11.257
No despicable gift; surmise not then	Par Lost 11.340
Had bred; then purg'd with Euphrasie and Rue	Par Lost 11.414
Choicest and best; then sacrificing, laid	Par Lost 11.438
Thir Makers Image, answerd *Michael*, then	Par Lost 11.515
This is old age; but then thou must outlive	Par Lost 11.538
To witherd weak and gray; thy Senses then	Par Lost 11.540
First his own Tooles; then, what might else be wrought	Par Lost 11.572
Loves Harbinger appeerd; then all in heat	Par Lost 11.589
Hymen, then first to marriage Rites invok't;	Par Lost 11.591
Then from the Mountain hewing Timber tall,	Par Lost 11.728
How didst thou grieve then, *Adam*, to behold	Par Lost 11.754
All would have then gon well, peace would have crownd	Par Lost 11.781
Above the highest Hills: then shall this Mount	Par Lost 11.829
Then with uplifted hands, and eyes devout,	Par Lost 11.863
Then with transition sweet new Speech resumes.	Par Lost 12.5
line not in 1667 edition	
Man till then free. Therefore since hee permits	Par Lost 12.90
Then through the Firey Pillar and the Cloud	Par Lost 12.208
By Judges first, then under Kings; of whom	Par Lost 12.320
The clouded Ark of God till then in Tents	Par Lost 12.333
The space of seventie years, then brings them back,	Par Lost 12.345
Then loose it to a stranger, that the true	Par Lost 12.358
Then to the Heav'n of Heav'ns he shall ascend	Par Lost 12.451
Then enter into glory, and resume	Par Lost 12.456
Whether in Heav'n or Earth, for then the Earth	Par Lost 12.463
So spake th' Archangel *Michael*, then paus'd,	Par Lost 12.466
The enemies of truth; who then shall guide	Par Lost 12.482
To evangelize the Nations, then on all	Par Lost 12.499
Then shall they seek to avail themselves of names,	Par Lost 12.515
Shall on the heart engrave. What will they then	Par Lost 12.524
The Womans seed, obscurely then foretold,	Par Lost 12.543
Satan with his perverted World, then raise	Par Lost 12.547
Of all the rest: then wilt thou not be loath	Par Lost 12.585
To the subjected Plaine; then disappeer'd.	Par Lost 12.640
To the flood *Jordan*, came as then obscure,	Par Reg 1.24
With wonder, then with envy fraught and rage	Par Reg 1.38
His Mother then is mortal, but his Sire,	Par Reg 1.86
At these sad tidings; but no time was then	Par Reg 1.109
Then toldst her doubting how these things could be	Par Reg 1.137
Admiring stood a space, then into Hymns	Par Reg 1.169
Then to subdue and quell o're all the earth	Par Reg 1.218
So spake our Morning Star then in his rise,	Par Reg 1.294
Till those days ended, hunger'd then at last	Par Reg 1.309
Perus'd him, then with words thus utt'red spake.	Par Reg 1.320
Why dost thou then suggest to me distrust,	Par Reg 1.355
What can be then less in me then desire	Par Reg 1.383
Small consolation then, were Man adjoyn'd:	Par Reg 1.403
Of righteous *Job*, then cruelly to afflict him	Par Reg 1.425
To thee not known, whence hast thou then thy truth,	Par Reg 1.446
Then to thy self ascrib'st the truth fore-told.	Par Reg 1.453
What wonder then if I delight to hear	Par Reg 1.481
Therefore as those young Prophets then with care	Par Reg 2.18
Then on the bank of *Jordan*, by a Creek:	Par Reg 2.25
Mock us with his blest sight, then snatch him hence,	Par Reg 2.56
Too long, then lay'st thy scapes on names ador'd,	Par Reg 2.189
Then forthwith to him takes a chosen band	Par Reg 2.236
Then to the Desert takes with these his flight;	Par Reg 2.241
Commun'd in silent walk, then laid him down	Par Reg 2.261

Then(*cont*)
Under a Juniper; then how awakt, Par Reg 2.272
How hast thou hunger then? Satan reply'd, Par Reg 2.319
Why shouldst thou then obtrude this diligence, Par Reg 2.387
Extol not Riches then, the toyl of Fools, Par Reg 2.453
Riches are needless then, both for themselves, Par Reg 2.484
Then swell with pride, and must be titl'd Gods, Par Reg 3.81
Shall I seek glory then, as vain men seek Par Reg 3.105
Raign then; what canst thou better do the while? Par Reg 3.180
If I then to the worst that can be hast, Par Reg 3.223
With that (such power was giv'n him then) he took Par Reg 3.251
Then meeting joyn'd thir tribute to the Sea: Par Reg 3.258
To thir inheritance, then, nor till then, Par Reg 3.382
But whence to thee this zeal, where was it then Par Reg 3.407
To *Israel* then, the same that now to me. Par Reg 3.413
And hunger still: then Embassies thou shew'st Par Reg 4.121
Outlandish flatteries? then proceed'st to talk Par Reg 4.125
Then cruel, by thir sports to blood enur'd Par Reg 4.139
Who then thou art, whose coming is foretold Par Reg 4.204
As morning shews the day. Be famous then Par Reg 4.221
His whispering stream; within the walls then view Par Reg 4.250
Thir Orators thou then extoll'st, as those Par Reg 4.353
Or torn up sheer: ill wast thou shrouded then, Par Reg 4.419
Then hear, O Son of *David*, Virgin-born; Par Reg 4.500
Good reason then, if I before-hand seek Par Reg 4.526
Then in a flowry valley set him down Par Reg 4.586
Then had I not been thus exil'd from light; Samson 98
Then with what trivial weapon came to hand, Samson 142
Then by main force pull'd up, and on his shoulders bore Samson 146
Deject not then so overmuch thy self, Samson 213
Enterd *Judea* seeking mee, who then Samson 252
Then give the rains to wandring thought, Samson 302
Down Reason then, at least vain reasonings down, Samson 322
Our earnest Prayers, then giv'n with solemn hand Samson 359
The miracle of men: then in an hour Samson 364
Reject not then what offerd means, who knows Samson 516
Then swoll'n with pride into the snare I fell Samson 532
Then turn'd me out ridiculous, despoil'd, Samson 539
Man. Wilt thou then serve the *Philistines* with that gift Samson 577
Then as repentant to submit, beseech, Samson 751
Then with more cautious and instructed skill Samson 757
Of secrets, then with like infirmity Samson 776
Let weakness then with weakness come to parl Samson 785
Why then reveal'd? I was assur'd by those Samson 800
Yet now am judg'd an enemy. Why then Samson 882
Then, as since then, thy countries foe profest: Samson 884
What then thou would'st, thou seest it in thy hand. Samson 1105
Then put on all thy gorgeous arms, thy Helmet Samson 1119
Then thou shalt see, or rather to thy sorrow Samson 1154
Then like a Robber stripdst them of thir robes? Samson 1188
Or swing thee in the Air, then dash thee down Samson 1240
And the well-feasted Priest then soonest fir'd Samson 1419
The sufferers then will scarce molest us here, Samson 1525
Mess. Then take the worst in brief, *Samson* is dead. Samson 1570
Man. Wearied with slaughter then or how? explain. Samson 1583
Revives, reflourishes, then vigorous most Samson 1704
They left me then, when the gray-hooded Eev'n Mask 188
line not in Bridgewater ms
Spir. Ay me unhappy then my fears are true. Mask 511
This evening late by then the chewing flocks Mask 540
Then down the Lawns I ran with headlong hast Mask 568
How durst thou then thy self approach so neer Mask 616
And then the giver would be better thank't, Mask 775
Then to com in spight of sorrow, Allegro 45
And then in haste her Bowre she leaves, Allegro 87
Then to the Spicy Nut-brown Ale, Allegro 100
Then lies him down the Lubbar Fend, Allegro 110
Towred Cities please us then, Allegro 117
Then to the well-trod stage anon, Allegro 131
Hath lockt up mortal sense, then listen I Arcades 62
Begin then, Sisters of the sacred well, Lycidas 15
It was no season then for her Nativity 35
Full little thought they than, Nativity 88
Yea Truth, and Justice then Nativity 141
And then at last our bliss Nativity 165
But kill'd alas, and then bewayl'd his fatal bliss. Fair Inf 7
But then transform'd him to a purple flower Fair Inf 27
Resolve me then oh Soul most surely blest Fair Inf 36
Then thou the mother of so sweet a child Fair Inf 71
I pray thee then deny me not thy aide Vacation 15
Then passing through the Spheres of watchful fire, Vacation 40
Then sing of secret things that came to pass Vacation 45
Then quick about thy purpos'd business come, Vacation 57
Then lies him meekly down fast by his Brethrens side. Passion 21
Then long Eternity shall greet our bliss On Time 11
Then all this Earthy grosnes quit, On Time 20
And to our high-rais'd phantasie present, Musick 5
Trinity ms 'phantasie' ← 'Phantasie' ← 'fantasie' ← 'fancies then'
while all the starrie rounds & arches blue Musick Tr. ms 4.21
'while all the starrie rounds' ← 'starrie frame' ← 'whilst then' ← 'whilst the whole frame of' ← 'while all the' ← 'that all'
Then thou our fancy of it self bereaving, Shakespear 13
when most were wont which till then us'd to scan Sonnet 13, Tr. ms 40.03
Then to advise how warr may best, upheld, Sonnet 17, 7
Trinity ms 'Then' ← 'and'
In judgment, or abide their tryal then, Psalm 1, 13

Then(*cont*)
Shall laugh, the Lord shall scoff them, then severe Psalm 2, 9
Then all who trust in thee shall bring Psalm 5, 33
With much confusion; then grow red with shame, Psalm 6, 22
Then will I Jehovah's praise Psalm 7, 61
In the pure firmament, then saith my heart, Psalm 8, 11
And then we shall be safe. Psalm 80, 16
And then we shall be safe. Psalm 80, 32
Quick'n us thou, then *gladly* wee Psalm 80, 75
And then we shall be safe. Psalm 80, 80
On me then didst thou call, Psalm 81, 26
Then did I leave them to their will Psalm 81, 49
Then would I soon bring down their foes Psalm 81, 57
Who hate the Lord should *then be fain* Psalm 81, 61
Then shall they know that thou whose name Psalm 83, 65
Shall bud and blossom *then*, Psalm 85, 46
The Lord will also then bestow Psalm 85, 49
Then will he come, and not be slow Psalm 85, 55
And let my foes *then* see Psalm 86, 62
Then past hee to a flowry Mountaine greene, Prose 4, 1

Thence
Fast by the Oracle of God; I thence Par Lost 1.12
And thence in Heav'n call'd Satan, with bold words Par Lost 1.82
Chain'd on the burning Lake, nor ever thence Par Lost 1.210
And fewel'd entrals thence conceiving Fire, Par Lost 1.234
The pleasant Vally of *Hinnom*, *Tophet* thence Par Lost 1.404
Yet thence his lustful Orgies he enlarg'd Par Lost 1.415
Till good *Josiah* drove them thence to Hell. Par Lost 1.418
And *Ida* known, thence on the Snowy top Par Lost 1.515
If thence he scape into whatever world, Par Lost 2.442
Thence more at ease thir minds and somwhat rais'd Par Lost 2.521
Periods of time, thence hurried back to fire. Par Lost 2.603
Uplifted spurns the ground, thence many a League Par Lost 2.929
All usurpation thence expell'd, reduce Par Lost 2.983
Irradiate, there plant eyes, all mist from thence Par Lost 3.53
Thence up he flew, and on the Tree of Life Par Lost 4.194
Waterd the Garden; thence united fell Par Lost 4.230
Not distant far from thence a murmuring sound Par Lost 4.453
Multitudes like thy self, and thence be call'd Par Lost 4.474
No Creature thence: if Spirit of other sort, Par Lost 4.582
Like gentle breaths from Rivers pure, thence raise Par Lost 4.806
Single against thee wicked, and thence weak. Par Lost 4.856
Springs lighter the green stalk, from thence the leaves Par Lost 5.480
Deep malice thence conceiving and disdain, Par Lost 5.666
Into thir vacant room, and thence diffuse Par Lost 7.190
Govern the rest, self-knowing, and from thence Par Lost 7.510
Is yet distinct by name, thence, as thou know'st Par Lost 7.536
Thence to behold this new created World Par Lost 7.554
Thou usest, and from thence creat'st more good. Par Lost 7.616
To see that none thence issu'd forth a spie, Par Lost 8.233
From thence a Rib, with cordial spirits warme; Par Lost 8.466
What inward thence I feel, not therefore foild, Par Lost 8.608
That kept thir watch; thence full of anguish driv'n, Par Lost 9.62
At *Darien*, thence to the Land where flowes Par Lost 9.81
High and remote to see from thence distinct Par Lost 9.812
And left to her self, if evil thence ensue, Par Lost 9.1185
Thence gatherd his own doom, which understood Par Lost 10.344
There dwell and Reign in bliss, thence on the Earth Par Lost 10.399
Protesting Fate supreame; thence how I found Par Lost 10.480
Of high *Olympus*, thence by *Saturn* driv'n Par Lost 10.583
Up to the *Tropic* Crab; thence down amaine Par Lost 10.675
Found so erroneous, thence by just event Par Lost 10.969
To them and to thir Progenie from thence Par Lost 11.107
To *Paquin* of *Sinaean* Kings, and thence Par Lost 11.390
Or thence from *Niger* Flood to *Atlas* Mount Par Lost 11.402
On *Europe* thence, and where *Rome* was to sway Par Lost 11.405
In what thou eatst and drinkst, seeking from thence Par Lost 11.532
Down to the veins of Earth, thence gliding hot Par Lost 11.568
Had not a Cloud descending snatch'd him thence Par Lost 11.670
Allurd them; thence from Cups to civil Broiles. Par Lost 11.718
With clamor thence the rapid Currents drive Par Lost 11.853
A mightie Hunter thence he shall be styl'd Par Lost 12.33
Left in confusion, *Babylon* thence call'd. Par Lost 12.343
Above all names in Heav'n; and thence shall come, Par Lost 12.458
Against the Spiritual Foe, and broughtst him thence Par Reg 1.10
Not thence to be more pure, but to receive Par Reg 1.77
Unfold her Crystal Dores, thence on his head Par Reg 1.82
Serious to learn and know, and thence to do Par Reg 1.203
Thence into *Egypt*, till the Murd'rous King Par Reg 2.76
Thence to the bait of Women lay expos'd; Par Reg 2.204
Short sojourn; and what thence could'st thou observe? Par Reg 3.235
Araxes and the *Caspian* lake, thence on Par Reg 3.271
The City of *Gallaphrone*, from thence to win Par Reg 3.340
From cold *Septentrion* blasts, thence in the midst Par Reg 4.31
Thence to the gates cast round thine eye, and see Par Reg 4.61
Blind *Melesigenes* thence *Homer* call'd, Par Reg 4.259
Thence what the lofty grave Tragoedians taught Par Reg 4.261
Thence to the famous Orators repair, Par Reg 4.267
Thence faintings, swounings of despair, Samson 631
Helpless, thence easily contemn'd, and scorn'd, Samson 943
Useless, and thence ridiculous about him. Samson 1501
Had by him, ere he parted thence, a Son Mask 56
They had their name thence; course complexions Mask 749
line not in Bridgewater ms
Trinity ms 'thence' ← 'from thence' ← 'thence'
And not many furlongs thence Mask 946
And from thence can soar as soon Mask 1016
yet thence I come and oft from thence behold Mask Tr. ms 10.18

Thence(*cont*)	
were they not taken thence	Mask Tr. ms 22.07
Or *Lucifer* that often warn'd them thence;	Nativity 74
He brought from thence his *Israel*.	Psalm 136, 42
Small loss it is that thence can come unto thee,	Vacation 9
Or should I thence hurried on viewles wing,	Passion 50
And azure wings, that up they flew so drest,	Sonnet 14, 11
Trinity ms 'that' ←'thence'	
Thence to thy glorious habitation	Psalm 7, 27
Who thence grow bold and strong	Psalm 82, 8
Thenceforth	
Thenceforth, but in thy presence Joy entire.	Par Lost 3.265
Thenceforth shall be for ever shut. Mean while	Par Lost 3.333
Thenceforth to Speculations high or deep	Par Lost 9.602
Not dead, as we are threatn'd, but thenceforth	Par Lost 9.870
Thenceforth the form of servant to assume,	Par Lost 10.214
Thenceforth shall practice how to live secure,	Par Lost 11.802
His holy Eyes; resolving from thenceforth	Par Lost 12.109
Thenceforth the Nations may not doubt; I saw	Par Reg 1.79
Thenceforth I thought thee worth my nearer view	Par Reg 4.514
Before the Judge, who thenceforth bid thee rest	Sonnet 14, 13
Theologians	
Of Theologians, but with keen dispatch	Par Lost 5.436
There	
To bottomless perdition, there to dwell	Par Lost 1.47
There the companions of his fall, o'rewhelm'd	Par Lost 1.76
There rest, if any rest can harbour there,	Par Lost 1.185
There went a fame in Heav'n that he ere long	Par Lost 1.651
There stood a Hill not far whose griesly top	Par Lost 1.670
With Golden Architrave; nor did there want	Par Lost 1.715
Of endless pain? where there is then no good	Par Lost 2.30
For which to strive, no strife can grow up there	Par Lost 2.31
To our destruction: if there be in Hell	Par Lost 2.84
There to converse with everlasting groans,	Par Lost 2.184
Some easier enterprize? There is a place	Par Lost 2.345
What creatures there inhabit, of what mould,	Par Lost 2.355
More tollerable; if there be cure or charm	Par Lost 2.460
Thir soft Ethereal warmth, and there to pine	Par Lost 2.601
Yet unconsum'd. Before the Gates there sat	Par Lost 2.648
And kennel there, yet there still bark'd and howl'd,	Par Lost 2.658
With odours; there ye shall be fed and fill'd	Par Lost 2.843
Undaunted to meet there what ever power	Par Lost 2.955
Erect the Standard there of *ancient Night;*	Par Lost 2.986
Irradiate, there plant eyes, all mist from thence	Par Lost 3.53
Hell and the Gulf between, and *Satan* there	Par Lost 3.70
Heapt on him there, nor yet the main Abyss	Par Lost 3.83
And Man there plac't, with purpose to assay	Par Lost 3.90
For ever with corruption there to dwell;	Par Lost 3.249
To Heav'n remov'd where first it grew, there grows,	Par Lost 3.356
There alwayes, but drawn up to Heav'n somtimes	Par Lost 3.517
Thrice happy Iles, but who dwelt happy there	Par Lost 3.570
There lands the Fiend, a spot like which perhaps	Par Lost 3.588
Night would invade, but there the neighbouring Moon	Par Lost 3.726
O then at last relent: is there no place	Par Lost 4.79
From *Media* post to *Aegypt*, there fast bound.	Par Lost 4.171
One Gate there only was, and that look'd East	Par Lost 4.178
The middle Tree and highest there that grew,	Par Lost 4.195
And send forth all her Kings; there will be room,	Par Lost 4.383
Of sympathie and love; there I had fixt	Par Lost 4.465
What there thou seest fair Creature is thy self,	Par Lost 4.468
One fatal Tree there stands of Knowledge call'd,	Par Lost 4.514
By shorter flight to th' East, had left him there	Par Lost 4.595
In search of whom they sought: him there they found	Par Lost 4.799
For you, there sitting where ye durst not soare;	Par Lost 4.829
Puts me in doubt. Lives ther who loves his pain?	Par Lost 4.888
What life the Gods live there, and such live thou.	Par Lost 5.81
To grateful Twilight (for Night comes not there	Par Lost 5.645
The Quarters of the North, there to prepare	Par Lost 5.689
Unbarr'd the gates of Light. There is a Cave	Par Lost 6.4
To veile the Heav'n, though darkness there might well	Par Lost 6.11
There fail where Vertue fails, or weakest prove	Par Lost 6.117
All are not of thy Train; there be who Faith	Par Lost 6.143
Thou and thy wicked crew; there mingle broiles,	Par Lost 6.277
From off the files of warr; there they him laid	Par Lost 6.339
There let them learn, as likes them, to despise	Par Lost 6.717
Erroneous there to wander and forlorne.	Par Lost 7.20
Of men innumerable, there to dwell,	Par Lost 7.156
Let ther be Light, said God, and forthwith Light	Par Lost 7.243
Again, God said, let ther be Firmament	Par Lost 7.261
Again th' Almightie spake: Let there be Lights	Par Lost 7.339
Tempest the Ocean: there Leviathan	Par Lost 7.412
In prospect; there the Eagle and the Stork	Par Lost 7.423
There wanted yet the Master work, the end	Par Lost 7.505
Created in his Image, there to dwell	Par Lost 7.627
But in the fruitful Earth; there first receavd	Par Lost 8.96
This Earth? reciprocal, if Land be there,	Par Lost 8.144
Allotted there; and other Suns perhaps	Par Lost 8.148
To know what passes there; be lowlie wise:	Par Lost 8.173
Dream not of other Worlds, what Creatures there	Par Lost 8.175
Pensive I sate me down; there gentle sleep	Par Lost 8.287
Found unsuspected way. There was a place,	Par Lost 9.69
With ravishment beheld, there best beheld	Par Lost 9.541
There swallow'd up and lost, from succour farr.	Par Lost 9.642
Of Knowledge he must pass, there he her met,	Par Lost 9.849
There they thir fill of Love and Loves disport	Par Lost 9.1042
There sit not, and reproach us as unclean,	Par Lost 9.1098
Into the thickest Wood, there soon they chose	Par Lost 9.1100
There oft the *Indian* Herdsman shunning heate	Par Lost 9.1108
There(*cont*)	
Or to thy self perhaps: hadst thou been there,	Par Lost 9.1148
As good have grown there still a liveless Rib.	Par Lost 9.1154
The savour of Death from all things there that live:	Par Lost 10.269
There didst not; there let him still Victor sway,	Par Lost 10.376
There dwell and Reign in bliss, thence on the Earth	Par Lost 10.399
Appointed to sit there, had left thir charge,	Par Lost 10.421
There kept thir Watch the Legions, while the Grand	Par Lost 10.427
Cast on themselves from thir own mouths. There stood	Par Lost 10.547
Too soon arriv'd, *Sin* there in power before,	Par Lost 10.586
There best, where most with ravin I may meet;	Par Lost 10.599
As in my Mothers lap? there I should rest	Par Lost 10.778
Between us two let there be peace, both joyning,	Par Lost 10.924
There with my cries importune Heaven, that all	Par Lost 10.933
Before him reverent, and there confess	Par Lost 10.1088
In thir bright stand, there left his Powers to seise	Par Lost 11.221
Where he abides, think there thy native soile.	Par Lost 11.292
His Eye might there command wherever stood	Par Lost 11.385
But is there yet no other way, besides	Par Lost 11.527
There is, said *Michael*, if thou well observe	Par Lost 11.530
And there take root an Iland salt and bare,	Par Lost 11.834
By Men who there frequent, or therein dwell.	Par Lost 11.838
Of *Moreh;* there by promise he receaves	Par Lost 12.137
Of *Pharao:* there he dies, and leaves his Race	Par Lost 12.163
In the wide Wilderness, there they shall found	Par Lost 12.224
There in captivitie he lets them dwell	Par Lost 12.344
Of all mankinde, with him there crucifi'd,	Par Lost 12.417
Over his foes and thine; there shall surprise	Par Lost 12.453
Through all his Realme, and there confounded leave;	Par Lost 12.455
There he shall first lay down the rudiments	Par Reg 1.157
I went into the Temple, there to hear	Par Reg 1.211
And of thy Kingdom there should be no end.	Par Reg 1.241
There without sign of boast, or sign of joy,	Par Reg 2.119
Of Trees thick interwoven; there he slept,	Par Reg 2.263
Into the Desert, and how there he slept	Par Reg 2.271
Thither he bent his way, determin'd there	Par Reg 2.291
But if there be in glory aught of good,	Par Reg 3.88
And time there is for all things, Truth hath said:	Par Reg 3.183
If there be worse, the expectation more	Par Reg 3.207
The Prospect was, that here and there was room	Par Reg 3.263
There *Babylon* the wonder of all tongues,	Par Reg 3.280
His City there thou seest, and *Bactra* there;	Par Reg 3.285
Ecbatana her structure vast there shews,	Par Reg 3.286
There *Susa* by *Choaspes*, amber stream,	Par Reg 3.288
The great *Seleucia*, *Nisibis*, and there	Par Reg 3.291
Luggage of war there shewn me, argument	Par Reg 3.401
Of Nations; there the Capitol thou seest	Par Reg 4.47
Impregnable, and there Mount *Palatine*	Par Reg 4.50
On the *Campanian* shore, with purpose there	Par Reg 4.93
And of my Kingdom there shall be no end:	Par Reg 4.151
Means there shall be to this, but what the means,	Par Reg 4.152
Alone into the Temple; there was found	Par Reg 4.217
See there the Olive Grove of *Academe*,	Par Reg 4.244
There flowrie hill *Hymettus* with the sound	Par Reg 4.247
To studious musing; there *Ilissus* rouls	Par Reg 4.249
Lyceum there, and painted *Stoa* next:	Par Reg 4.253
There thou shalt hear and learn the secret power	Par Reg 4.254
Of *Socrates*, see there his Tenement,	Par Reg 4.274
For thee is fittest place, I found thee there,	Par Reg 4.373
Brought back the Son of God, and left him there,	Par Reg 4.396
Unshaken; nor yet staid the terror there,	Par Reg 4.421
There on the highest Pinacle he set	Par Reg 4.549
There stand, if thou wilt stand; to stand upright	Par Reg 4.551
There I am wont to sit, when any chance	Samson 4
Let there be light, and light was over all;	Samson 84
Unless there be who think not God at all,	Samson 295
For of such Doctrine never was there School,	Samson 297
Yet more there be who doubt his ways not just,	Samson 300
And Rivals? In this other was there found	Samson 387
There exercise all his fierce accidents,	Samson 612
Into the common Prison, there to grind	Samson 1161
Chor. His manacles remark him, there he sits.	Samson 1309
If there be aught of presage in the mind,	Samson 1387
Mess. Feed on that first, there may in grief be surfet.	Samson 1562
Home to his Fathers house: there will I build him	Samson 1733
Yet som there be that by due steps aspire	Mask 12
I did not err, there does a sable cloud	Mask 223
line not in Bridgewater ms	
Yea there, where very desolation dwels	Mask 428
Bridgewater ms 'even'	
Trinity ms 'even'	
For such there be, but unbelief is blind.	Mask 519
There was another meaning in these gifts,	Mask 754
line not in Bridgewater ms	
Som other means I have which may be us'd,	Mask 821
Trinity ms 'some other meanes I have' ←'there is another way'	
There is a gentle Nymph not farr from hence,	Mask 824
And here and there thy banks upon	Mask 936
All the Swains that there abide,	Mask 951
Bridgewater ms 'neere'	
Trinity ms 'neere'	
And our sudden coming there	Mask 954
There I suck the liquid ayr	Mask 980
Trinity ms 'there' ←'ther'	
That there eternal Summer dwels,	Mask 988
Iris there with humid bow,	Mask 992
There under *Ebon* shades, and low-brow'd Rocks,	Allegro 8

There(*cont*)	
There on Beds of Violets blew,	Allegro 21
There let *Hymen* oft appear	Allegro 125
While yet there was no fear of *Jove*.	Penseroso 30
There held in holy passion still,	Penseroso 41
There in close covert by som Brook,	Penseroso 139
There let the pealing Organ blow,	Penseroso 161
Had ye bin there---for what could that have don?	Lycidas 57
There entertain him all the Saints above,	Lycidas 178
There ended was his quest, there ceast his care.	Fair Inf 18
Or in the Elisian fields (if such there were.)	Fair Inf 40
Yet there is something that doth force my fear,	Vacation 67
O what a Mask was there, what a disguise!	Passion 19
There doth my soul in holy vision sit	Passion 41
There with thee, new welcom Saint,	Winchester 71
With thee there clad in radiant sheen,	Winchester 73
That even to his last breath (ther be that say't)	Another 25
line not in 1640, 1657, 1658 texts	
No help for him in God there lies.	Psalm 3, 6
Many there be that say	Psalm 4, 25
In the dust and there out spread	Psalm 7, 17
Wild Beasts there brouze, and make their food	Psalm 80, 55
Gebal and Ammon *there conspire*,	Psalm 83, 25
There ev'n the Sparrow *freed from wrong*	Psalm 84, 9
The Swallow there, to lay her young	Psalm 84, 11
There Seated in his Sanctuary,	Psalm 87, 3
His Temple there is plac't.	Psalm 87, 4
Of Jacobs *Land, though there be store*,	Psalm 87, 7
Lo this man there was born:	Psalm 87, 16
That this man there was born.	Psalm 87, 24
With sacred Songs are there,	Psalm 87, 26
There can be slaine	Prose 11, 1
Beyond the Realm of *Gaul*, a Land there lies,	Prose 12, 8
Thy course, there shalt thou find a lasting seat,	Prose 12, 11
There to thy Sons another *Troy* shall rise,	Prose 12, 12
Thereafter	
He reck'd not, and these words thereafter spake.	Par Lost 2.50
Would'st thou not eat? Thereafter as I like	Par Reg 2.321
Thereat	
Your wonder, with an Apple; he thereat	Par Lost 10.487
Thereby	
The works of God, thereby to glorifie	Par Lost 3.695
Thereby regaind, but sat devising Death	Par Lost 4.197
As I, though thereby worse to me redound:	Par Lost 9.128
With sinfulness of Men; thereby to learn	Par Lost 11.360
Subduing Nations, and achievd thereby	Par Lost 11.792
Though to the Tyrant thereby no excuse.	Par Lost 12.96
Who sent me, and thereby witness whence I am.	Par Reg 3.107
Found soon occasion thereby to make thee	Samson 425
How wouldst thou use me now, blind, and thereby	Samson 941
Thereby to wipe away th' infamous blot,	Fair Inf 12
Thereby to set the hearts of men on fire	Fair Inf 62
Therefore	
Warr therefore, open or conceal'd, alike	Par Lost 2.187
High honourd sits? Go therfore mighty Powers,	Par Lost 2.456
Not mee. They therefore as to right belongd,	Par Lost 3.111
By the other first: Man therefore shall find grace,	Par Lost 3.131
Thou therefore whom thou only canst redeem,	Par Lost 3.281
Therefore thy Humiliation shall exalt	Par Lost 3.313
This knows my punisher; therefore as farr	Par Lost 4.103
I therefore, I alone first undertook	Par Lost 4.935
Go therefore, half this day as friend with friend	Par Lost 5.229
Adam, I therefore came, nor art thou such	Par Lost 5.372
To whom the Angel. Therefore what he gives	Par Lost 5.404
Therfore Eternal silence be thir doome.	Par Lost 6.385
All patience. He who therefore can invent	Par Lost 6.464
Two dayes are therefore past, the third is thine;	Par Lost 6.699
Therefore to mee thir doom he hath assig'n'd;	Par Lost 6.817
Of all his works: therefore the Omnipotent	Par Lost 7.516
Therefore from this high pitch let us descend	Par Lost 8.198
On Man his Equal Love: say therefore on;	Par Lost 8.228
Whose fellowship therefore unmeet for thee	Par Lost 8.442
What inward thence I feel, not therefore foild,	Par Lost 8.608
Tending to wilde. Thou therefore now advise	Par Lost 9.212
But that thou shouldst my firmness therfore doubt	Par Lost 9.279
God therefore cannot hurt ye, and be just;	Par Lost 9.700
Thou therefore also taste, that equal Lot	Par Lost 9.881
1667 'therfore'	
Of easie thorough-fare. Therefore while I	Par Lost 10.393
Thou therefore on these Herbs, and Fruits, and Flours	Par Lost 10.603
But self-destruction therefore saught, refutes	Par Lost 10.1016
From innocence. Now therefore bend thine eare	Par Lost 11.30
Self-left. Least therefore his now bolder hand	Par Lost 11.93
Therefore to his great bidding I submit.	Par Lost 11.314
Therefore so abject is thir punishment,	Par Lost 11.520
And therefore hated, therefore so beset	Par Lost 11.702
Against invaders; therefore coold in zeale	Par Lost 11.801
Thou therefore give due audience, and attend.	Par Lost 12.12
Man till then free. Therefore since hee permits	Par Lost 12.90
And therefore was Law given them to evince	Par Lost 12.287
And therefore shall not *Moses*, though of God	Par Lost 12.307
Of head or heel: not therefore joynes the Son	Par Lost 12.388
Let us descend now therefore from this top	Par Lost 12.588
The Father knows the Son; therefore secure	Par Reg 1.176
All righteous things: therefore above my years,	Par Reg 1.206
Therefore as those young Prophets then with care	Par Reg 2.18
Therefore I am return'd, lest confidence	Par Reg 2.140
Therefore with manlier objects we must try	Par Reg 2.225
Therefore(*cont*)	
Thou art not to be harm'd, therefore not mov'd;	Par Reg 2.407
Therefore, if at great things thou wouldst arrive,	Par Reg 2.426
Roman and *Parthian*? therefore one of these	Par Reg 3.362
Aim therefore at no less then all the world,	Par Reg 4.105
Know therefore when my season comes to sit	Par Reg 4.146
Therefore let pass, as they are transitory,	Par Reg 4.209
I know them not; not therefore am I short	Par Reg 4.287
Of mortal things. Who therefore seeks in these	Par Reg 4.318
Therefore I watch'd thy footsteps from that hour,	Par Reg 4.522
Therefore to know what more thou art then man,	Par Reg 4.538
From intimate impulse, and therefore urg'd	Samson 223
As her at *Timna*, sought by all means therefore	Samson 795
Such pardon therefore as I give my folly,	Samson 825
All wickedness is weakness: that plea therefore	Samson 834
Not therefore to be obey'd. But zeal mov'd thee;	Samson 895
Less therefore to be pleas'd, obey'd, or fear'd,	Samson 900
Therefore Gods universal Law	Samson 1053
Therefore without feign'd shifts let be assign'd	Samson 1116
Rise therefore with all speed and come along,	Samson 1316
Sam. Thou knowst I am an *Ebrew*, therefore tell them,	Samson 1319
Whom therfore she brought up and *Comus* nam'd,	Mask 58
Bridgewater ms 'which therefore'	
Therfore when any favour'd of high *Jove*,	Mask 78
Bridgewater ms 'Therefore'	
And therfore to our weaker view,	Penseroso 15
1673 'therefore'	
Let us therfore warble forth	Psalm 136, 89
1673 'therefore'	
And Hope that reaps not shame. Therefore be sure	Sonnet 9, 11
Trinity ms 'Therfore'	
Therfore on thy firme hand religion leanes	Sonnet 17, 13
1662, 1694 'Therefore'	
Therein	
Intended to create, and therein plant	Par Lost 1.652
ms 'there-in'	
In the Pourlieues of Heav'n, and therein plac't	Par Lost 2.833
Hee Heav'n of Heavens and all the Powers therein	Par Lost 3.390
That is, to thy obedience; therein stand.	Par Lost 5.522
Be but the shaddow of Heav'n, and things therein	Par Lost 5.575
Possess it, and all things that therein live,	Par Lost 8.340
Therein enjoy'd were worthy to subdue	Par Lost 8.584
Of absolute perfection, therein Man	Par Lost 10.483
By Men who there frequent, or therein dwell.	Par Lost 11.838
With Man therein or Beast; but when he brings	Par Lost 11.895
Over the Earth a Cloud, will therein set	Par Lost 11.896
Of Cedar, overlaid with Gold, therein	Par Lost 12.250
For therein stands the office of a King,	Par Reg 2.463
Think not so slight of glory; therein least	Par Reg 3.109
And no man therein Doctor but himself.	Samson 299
He gave their Land therin to dwell.	Psalm 136, 74
1673 'therein'	
Thereof	
The day thou eat'st thereof, my sole command	Par Lost 8.329
Thereof, nor shall ye touch it, least ye die.	Par Lost 9.663
Ye Eate thereof, your Eyes that seem so cleere,	Par Lost 9.706
That whoso eats thereof, forthwith attains	Par Lost 9.724
I charg'd thee, saying: Thou shalt not eate thereof,	Par Lost 10.200
Shalt eate thereof all the days of thy Life;	Par Lost 10.202
Much more, that much more good thereof shall spring,	Par Lost 12.476
And now some public proof thereof require	Samson 1314
But must be currant, and the good thereof	Mask 740
Trinity ms 'therof'	
line not in Bridgewater ms	
Thereon	
Or monument to Ages, and thereon	Par Lost 11.326
Of his delivery, and thy joy thereon	Samson 1505
To him that sits theron	Musick 8
1673 'thereon'	
Trinity ms 'theron' ←'thereon'	
Therewith	
To serve therewith my Maker, and present	Sonnet 19, 5
These	
For those rebellious, here thir Prison ordain'd	Par Lost 1.71
ms 'these'	
Save what the glimmering of these livid flames	Par Lost 1.182
From off the tossing of these fiery waves,	Par Lost 1.184
Abject and lost lay these, covering the Flood,	Par Lost 1.312
With these came they, who from the bordring flood	Par Lost 1.419
These Feminine. For Spirits when they please	Par Lost 1.423
For those the Race of *Israel* oft forsook	Par Lost 1.432
ms 'these'	
Of despicable foes. With these in troop	Par Lost 1.437
Whom he had vanquisht. After these appear'd	Par Lost 1.476
These were the prime in order and in might;	Par Lost 1.506
So *Jove* usurping reign'd: these first in *Creet*	Par Lost 1.514
All these and more came flocking; but with looks	Par Lost 1.522
Met such imbodied force, as nam'd with these	Par Lost 1.574
By *Fontarabbia*. Thus far these beyond	Par Lost 1.587
As stood like these, could ever know repulse?	Par Lost 1.630
That all these puissant Legions, whose exile	Par Lost 1.632
Long under darkness cover. But these thoughts	Par Lost 1.659
He reck'd not, and these words thereafter spake.	Par Lost 2.50
All these our motions vain, sees and derides;	Par Lost 2.191
Chains and these Torments? better these then worse	Par Lost 2.196
With what is punish't; whence these raging fires	Par Lost 2.213
Become our Elements, these piercing Fires	Par Lost 2.275
Ethereal Vertues; or these Titles now	Par Lost 2.311

These(*cont*)

To heal the scarr of these corrosive Fires	Par Lost 2.401
These past, if any pass, the void profound	Par Lost 2.438
These Royalties, and not refuse to Reign,	Par Lost 2.451
Farr off from these a slow and silent stream,	Par Lost 2.582
Within unseen. Farr less abhorrd than these	Par Lost 2.659
Forbore, then these to her *Satan* return'd:	Par Lost 2.736
These Gates for ever shut, which none can pass	Par Lost 2.776
These yelling Monsters that with ceasless cry	Par Lost 2.795
These Adamantine Gates; against all force	Par Lost 2.853
Thir lighter wings. To whom these most adhere,	Par Lost 2.906
But all these in thir pregnant causes mixt	Par Lost 2.913
Of Heav'n were falling, and these Elements	Par Lost 2.925
Revisit'st not these eyes, that rowle in vain	Par Lost 3.23
With these that never fade the Spirits elect	Par Lost 3.360
The sport of Winds: all these upwhirld aloft	Par Lost 3.493
All these his wondrous works, but chiefly Man,	Par Lost 3.663
All these his works so wondrous he ordaind,	Par Lost 3.665
In which of all these shining Orbes hath Man	Par Lost 3.668
But all these shining Orbes his choice to dwell;	Par Lost 3.670
Worlds, and on whom hath all these graces powrd;	Par Lost 3.674
Your change approaches, when all these delights	Par Lost 4.367
Not like these narrow limits, to receive	Par Lost 4.384
Sole partner and sole part of all these joyes,	Par Lost 4.411
To prune these growing Plants, and tend these Flours,	Par Lost 4.438
Sight hateful, sight tormenting! thus these two	Par Lost 4.505
Betwixt these rockie Pillars *Gabriel* sat	Par Lost 4.549
So minded, have oreleapt these earthie bounds	Par Lost 4.583
But if within the circuit of these walks,	Par Lost 4.586
They to thir grassie Couch, these to thir Nests	Par Lost 4.601
And these the Gemms of Heav'n, her starrie train:	Par Lost 4.649
But wherfore all night long shine these, for whom	Par Lost 4.657
In Nature and all things, which these soft fires	Par Lost 4.667
These then, though unbeheld in deep of night,	Par Lost 4.674
All these with ceasless praise his works behold	Par Lost 4.679
These troublesom disguises which wee wear,	Par Lost 4.740
These lulld by Nightingales imbraceing slept,	Par Lost 4.771
Uzziel, half these draw off, and coast the South	Par Lost 4.782
With strictest watch; these other wheel the North,	Par Lost 4.783
From these, two strong and suttle Spirits he calld	Par Lost 4.786
Daz'ling the Moon; these to the Bower direct	Par Lost 4.798
Here watching at the head of these that sleep?	Par Lost 4.826
This place inviolable, and these from harm.	Par Lost 4.843
Within these hallowd limits thou appeer,	Par Lost 4.964
Battels and Realms: in these he put two weights	Par Lost 4.1002
Reason as chief; among these Fansie next	Par Lost 5.102
These are thy glorious works, Parent of good,	Par Lost 5.153
Unspeakable, who sitst above these Heavens	Par Lost 5.156
In these thy lowest works, yet these declare	Par Lost 5.158
She tempers dulcet creams, nor these to hold	Par Lost 5.347
To want, and honour these, voutsafe with us	Par Lost 5.365
Oreshades; for these mid-hours, till Eevning rise	Par Lost 5.376
Then with these various fruits the Trees of God	Par Lost 5.390
These bounties which our Nourisher, from whom	Par Lost 5.398
To enter, and these earthly fruits to taste,	Par Lost 5.464
And from these corporal nutriments perhaps	Par Lost 5.496
Reignd where these Heav'ns now rowl, where Earth now rests	Par Lost 5.578
If these magnific Titles yet remain	Par Lost 5.773
And tempt not these; but hast'n to appease	Par Lost 5.846
These tidings carrie to th' anointed King;	Par Lost 5.870
These wicked Tents devoted, least the wrauth	Par Lost 5.890
Gabriel, lead forth to Battel these my Sons	Par Lost 6.46
These Elements, and arm him with the force	Par Lost 6.222
These Acts of hateful strife, hateful to all,	Par Lost 6.264
Thou canst not. Hast thou turnd the least of these	Par Lost 6.284
These things, as not to mind from whence they grow	Par Lost 6.477
These in thir dark Nativitie the Deep	Par Lost 6.482
O Friends, why come not on these Victors proud?	Par Lost 6.609
These disobedient; sore hath been thir fight,	Par Lost 6.687
Pursue these sons of Darkness, drive them out	Par Lost 6.715
Armd with thy might, rid Heav'n of these rebell'd,	Par Lost 6.737
Gods indignation on these Godless pourd	Par Lost 6.811
Her bosom smelling sweet: and these scarce blown,	Par Lost 7.319
Those rare and solitarie, these in flocks	Par Lost 7.461
These as a line thir long dimension drew,	Par Lost 7.480
Thir seasons: among these the seat of men,	Par Lost 7.623
In six thou seest, and what if sev'nth to these	Par Lost 8.128
But whether thus these things, or whether not,	Par Lost 8.159
And liquid Lapse of murmuring Streams; by these,	Par Lost 8.263
Not onely these fair bounds, but all the Earth	Par Lost 8.338
Approaching two and two, These cowring low	Par Lost 8.350
My sudden apprehension: but in these	Par Lost 8.354
O by what Name, for thou above all these,	Par Lost 8.357
Replenisht, and all these at thy command	Par Lost 8.371
And reason not contemptibly; with these	Par Lost 8.374
And these inferiour farr beneath me set?	Par Lost 8.382
I by conversing cannot these erect	Par Lost 8.432
Nor vehement desire, these delicacies	Par Lost 8.526
Yet these subject not; I to thee disclose	Par Lost 8.607
To Person or to Poem. Mee of these	Par Lost 9.41
Rocks, Dens, and Caves; but I in none of these	Par Lost 9.118
Thir earthy Charge: Of these the vigilance	Par Lost 9.157
These paths & Bowers doubt not but our joynt hands	Par Lost 9.244
In this enclosure wild, these Beasts among,	Par Lost 9.543
The first at lest of these I thought denid	Par Lost 9.555
Of all these Garden Trees ye shall not eate,	Par Lost 9.657
In heav'nly brests? these, these and many more	Par Lost 9.730
To live again in these wilde Woods forlorn?	Par Lost 9.910

These(*cont*)

At length gave utterance to these words constraind.	Par Lost 9.1066
Nor troubl'd at these tidings from the Earth,	Par Lost 10.36
On Earth these thy transgressors, but thou knowst	Par Lost 10.72
In sight, to each of these three places led.	Par Lost 10.324
O Parent, these are thy magnific deeds,	Par Lost 10.354
With these successes, and with them rejoyce,	Par Lost 10.396
You two this way, among these numerous Orbs	Par Lost 10.397
1667 'those'	
To *Tauris* or *Casbeen*. So these the late	Par Lost 10.436
Silence, and with these words attention won.	Par Lost 10.459
Thou therefore on these Herbs, and Fruits, and Flours	Par Lost 10.603
See with what heat these Dogs of Hell advance	Par Lost 10.616
Let in these wastful Furies, who impute	Par Lost 10.620
These changes in the Heav'ns, though slow, produc'd	Par Lost 10.692
From *Serraliona;* thwart of these as fierce	Par Lost 10.703
Glar'd on him passing: these were from without	Par Lost 10.714
Of these fair spreading Trees; which bids us seek	Par Lost 10.1067
In Fables old, less ancient yet then these,	Par Lost 11.11
From thy implanted Grace in Man, these Sighs	Par Lost 11.23
Shall perfet, and for these my Death shall pay.	Par Lost 11.36
Accept me, and in mee from these receave	Par Lost 11.37
What can be toilsom in these pleasant Walkes?	Par Lost 11.179
Which Heav'n by these mute signs in Nature shews	Par Lost 11.194
Thee Native Soile, these happie Walks and Shades,	Par Lost 11.270
Stood visible, among these Pines his voice	Par Lost 11.321
His presence to these narrow bounds confin'd	Par Lost 11.341
So deep the power of these Ingredients pierc'd,	Par Lost 11.417
These two are Brethren, *Adam*, and to come	Par Lost 11.454
These painful passages, how we may come	Par Lost 11.528
Fusil or grav'n in mettle. After these,	Par Lost 11.573
To these that sober Race of Men, whose lives	Par Lost 11.621
Of these fair Atheists, and now swim in joy,	Par Lost 11.625
Lamenting turnd full sad; O what are these,	Par Lost 11.675
To whom thus *Michael*. These are the product	Par Lost 11.683
Such were these Giants, men of high renown;	Par Lost 11.688
The Records of his Cov'nant, over these	Par Lost 12.252
Without the vent of words, which these he breathd.	Par Lost 12.374
Places and titles, and with these to joine	Par Lost 12.516
At these sad tidings; but no time was then	Par Reg 1.109
Then toldst her doubting how these things could be	Par Reg 1.137
These growing thoughts my Mother soon perceiving	Par Reg 1.227
That out of these hard stones be made thee bread;	Par Reg 1.343
Copartner in these Regions of the World,	Par Reg 1.392
Sought lost *Eliah*, so in each place these	Par Reg 2.19
So may we hold our place and these mild seats	Par Reg 2.125
Satyr, or Fawn, or Silvan? But these haunts	Par Reg 2.191
Then to the Desert takes with these his flight;	Par Reg 2.241
And with fair speech these words to him address'd.	Par Reg 2.301
Of thee these forty days none hath regard,	Par Reg 2.315
Alas how simple, to these Cates compar'd,	Par Reg 2.348
These are not Fruits forbidden, no interdict	Par Reg 2.369
Defends the touching of these viands pure,	Par Reg 2.370
All these are Spirits of Air, and Woods, and Springs,	Par Reg 2.374
Of these things others quickly will dispose	Par Reg 2.400
And with these words his temptation pursu'd.	Par Reg 2.405
Yet Wealth without these three is impotent,	Par Reg 2.433
But men endu'd with these have oft attain'd	Par Reg 2.437
These God-like Vertues wherefore dost thou hide?	Par Reg 3.21
Of *Macedonian Philip* had e're these	Par Reg 3.32
Great Cities by assault: what do these Worthies,	Par Reg 3.74
All these the *Parthian*, now some Ages past,	Par Reg 3.294
Mules after these, Camels and Dromedaries,	Par Reg 3.335
Roman and *Parthian?* therefore one of these	Par Reg 3.362
These if from servitude thou shalt restore	Par Reg 3.381
Should I of these the liberty regard,	Par Reg 3.427
From the *Asian* Kings and *Parthian* among these,	Par Reg 4.73
Before the *Parthian;* these two Thrones except,	Par Reg 4.85
These having shewn thee, I have shewn thee all	Par Reg 4.88
These thus degenerate, by themselves enslav'd,	Par Reg 4.144
All these which in a moment thou behold'st,	Par Reg 4.162
Then these thou bear'st that title, have propos'd	Par Reg 4.199
These here revolve, or, as thou lik'st, at home,	Par Reg 4.281
These rules will render thee a King compleat	Par Reg 4.283
Think not but that I know these things, or think	Par Reg 4.286
But these are false, or little else but dreams,	Par Reg 4.291
Of mortal things. Who therefore seeks in these	Par Reg 4.318
That rather *Greece* from us these Arts deriv'd;	Par Reg 4.338
These only with our Law best form a King.	Par Reg 4.364
Was distant; and these flaws, though mortals fear them	Par Reg 4.454
To these dark steps, a little further on;	Samson 2
But who are these? for with joint pace I hear	Samson 110
These two proportiond ill drove me transverse.	Samson 209
Nothing of all these evils hath befall'n me	Samson 374
These rags, this grinding, is not yet so base	Samson 415
Of all these boasted Trophies won on me,	Samson 470
Man. With cause this hope relieves thee, and these words	Samson 472
When God with these forbid'n made choice to rear	Samson 555
Or pitied object, these redundant locks	Samson 568
That these dark orbs no more shall treat with light,	Samson 591
Man. Believe not these suggestions which proceed	Samson 599
And healing words from these thy friends admit.	Samson 605
Yet toward these thus dignifi'd, thou oft	Samson 682
If these they scape, perhaps in poverty	Samson 697
Sam. Out, out *Hyaena;* these are thy wonted arts,	Samson 748
These reasons in Loves law have past for good,	Samson 811
And combated in silence all these reasons	Samson 864
These false pretexts and varnish'd colours failing,	Samson 901

These(*cont*)	
If any of these or all, the *Timnian* bride	Samson 1018
As these perhaps, yet wish it had not been,	Samson 1077
Then thine, while I preserv'd these locks unshorn,	Samson 1143
To frustrate and dissolve these Magic spells,	Samson 1149
Sam. All these indignities, for such they are	Samson 1168
From thine, these evils I deserve and more,	Samson 1169
Sam. Tongue-doubtie Giant, how dost thou prove me these?	Samson 1181
These shifts refuted, answer thy appellant	Samson 1220
Hear these dishonours, and not render death?	Samson 1232
Though in these chains, bulk without spirit vast,	Samson 1238
These braveries in Irons loaden on thee.	Samson 1243
Either of these is in thy lot,	Samson 1292
Off. I praise thy resolution, doff these links:	Samson 1410
To thee first reverend *Manoa*, and to these	Samson 1548
I among these aloof obscurely stood.	Samson 1611
Samson with these immixt, inevitably	Samson 1657
I would not soil these pure Ambrosial weeds,	Mask 16
Bridgewater ms 'theese'	
These my skie robes spun out of *Iris* Wooff,	Mask 83
Which these dun shades will ne're report.	Mask 127
Run to your shrouds, within these Brakes and Trees,	Mask 147
Benighted in these Woods. Now to my charms,	Mask 150
In the blind mazes of this tangl'd Wood?	Mask 181
Trinity ms 'this' ←'these'	
Under the spreading favour of these Pines,	Mask 184
These thoughts may startle well, but not astound	Mask 210
line not in Bridgewater ms	
And with these raptures moves the vocal air	Mask 247
Whom certain these rough shades did never breed	Mask 266
Or shroud within these limits, I shall know	Mask 316
Trinity ms 'these' ←'these shroudie'	
That doth enrich these Downs, is worth a thought	Mask 505
Here dwel no frowns, nor anger, from these gates	Mask 667
Thou told'st me of? What grim aspects are these,	Mask 694
These oughly-headed Monsters? Mercy guard me!	Mask 695
There was another meaning in these gifts,	Mask 754
line not in Bridgewater ms	
Three fair branches of your own,	Mask 969
B.M. ms 'these fair'	
I doubt me gentle mortalls these may seeme	Mask Tr. ms 10.16
O my simplicity what sights are these? with darke disguises	Mask Tr. ms 22.19
These delights, if thou canst give,	Allegro 151
And adde to these retired leasure,	Penseroso 49
These pleasures *Melancholy* give,	Penseroso 175
Which I full oft amidst these shades alone	Arcades 42
Trinity ms 'the', ms defective	
(If so it be that thou these plaints dost hear)	Fair Inf 37
These latter scenes confine my roving vers,	Passion 22
Whose chance on these defenceless dores may sease,	Sonnet 8, 2
That call Fame on such gentle acts as these,	Sonnet 8, 6
The triple Tyrant: that from these may grow	Sonnet 18, 12
Cyriack, this three years day these eys, though clear	Sonnet 22, 1
All these have lent their armed hands	Psalm 83, 31
Thessalian	
Through pain up by the roots *Thessalian* Pines,	Par Lost 2.544
Thestylis	
With *Thestylis* to bind the Sheaves;	Allegro 88
Thetis	
By *Thetis* tinsel-slipper'd feet,	Mask 877
They	
O how unlike the place from whence they fell!	Par Lost 1.75
If once they hear that voyce, thir liveliest pledge	Par Lost 1.274
Thir surest signal, they will soon resume	Par Lost 1.278
New courage and revive, though now they lye	Par Lost 1.279
While with perfidious hatred they pursu'd	Par Lost 1.308
They heard, and were abasht, and up they sprung	Par Lost 1.331
On duty, sleeping found by whom they dread,	Par Lost 1.333
Nor did they not perceave the evil plight	Par Lost 1.335
In which they were, or the fierce pains not feel;	Par Lost 1.336
Yet to thir Generals Voyce they soon obeyd	Par Lost 1.337
Thir course, in even ballance down they light	Par Lost 1.349
Nor had they yet among the Sons of *Eve*	Par Lost 1.364
Of Mankind they corrupted to forsake	Par Lost 1.368
Then were they known to men by various Names,	Par Lost 1.374
With these came they, who from the bordring flood	Par Lost 1.419
These Feminine. For Spirits when they please	Par Lost 1.423
Like cumbrous flesh; but in what shape they choose	Par Lost 1.428
Of depth immeasurable: Anon they move	Par Lost 1.549
From mortal or immortal minds. Thus they	Par Lost 1.559
Advanc't in view, they stand, a horrid Front	Par Lost 1.563
For his revolt, yet faithfull how they stood,	Par Lost 1.611
To speak; whereat thir doubl'd Ranks they bend	Par Lost 1.616
Far round illumin'd hell: highly they rag'd	Par Lost 1.666
What in an age they with incessant toyle	Par Lost 1.698
From Heav'n, they fabl'd, thrown by angry *Jove*	Par Lost 1.741
On *Lemnos* th' *Aegaean* Ile: thus they relate,	Par Lost 1.746
By place or choice the worthiest; they anon	Par Lost 1.759
In clusters; they among fresh dews and flowers	Par Lost 1.771
Behold a wonder! they but now who seemd	Par Lost 1.777
Wheels her pale course, they on thir mirth and dance	Par Lost 1.786
Contrive who need, or when they need, not now	Par Lost 2.53
For while they sit contriving, shall the rest,	Par Lost 2.54
Say they who counsel Warr, we are decreed,	Par Lost 2.160
What yet they know must follow, to endure	Par Lost 2.206
They dreaded worse then Hell: so much the fear	Par Lost 2.293
They vote: whereat his speech he thus renews.	Par Lost 2.389
(Certain to be refus'd) what erst they feard;	Par Lost 2.470
They(*cont*)	
Which he through hazard huge must earn. But they	Par Lost 2.473
Forbidding; and at once with him they rose;	Par Lost 2.475
Of Thunder heard remote. Towards him they bend	Par Lost 2.477
Nor fail'd they to express how much they prais'd,	Par Lost 2.480
Thus they thir doubtful consultations dark	Par Lost 2.486
Then of thir Session ended they bid cry	Par Lost 2.514
Of good and evil much they argu'd then,	Par Lost 2.562
They ferry over this *Lethean* Sound	Par Lost 2.604
And wish and struggle, as they pass, to reach	Par Lost 2.606
They pass'd, and many a Region dolorous,	Par Lost 2.619
Thir spicie Drugs: they on the Trading Flood	Par Lost 2.640
A hideous Peal: yet, when they list, would creep,	Par Lost 2.656
And they outcast from God, are here condemn'd	Par Lost 2.694
Grew darker at thir frown, so matcht they stood;	Par Lost 2.720
All th' Host of Heav'n; back they recoild affraid	Par Lost 2.759
Through all the Empyrean: down they fell	Par Lost 2.771
To me, for when they list into the womb	Par Lost 2.798
That bred them they return, and howle and gnaw	Par Lost 2.799
So wide they stood, and like a Furnace mouth	Par Lost 2.888
Thir embryon Atoms; they around the flag	Par Lost 2.900
Freely they stood who stood, and fell who fell.	Par Lost 3.102
Not free, what proof could they have givn sincere	Par Lost 3.103
Where onely what they needs must do, appeard,	Par Lost 3.105
Not what they would? what praise could they receive?	Par Lost 3.106
Not mee. They therefore as to right belongd,	Par Lost 3.111
Or high foreknowledge; they themselves decreed	Par Lost 3.116
They trespass, Authors to themselves in all	Par Lost 3.122
Both what they judge and what they choose; for so	Par Lost 3.123
I formd them free, and free they must remain,	Par Lost 3.124
Till they enthrall themselves: I else must change	Par Lost 3.125
Thir freedom, they themselves ordain'd thir fall.	Par Lost 3.128
My Umpire *Conscience*, whom if they will hear,	Par Lost 3.195
Light after light well us'd they shall attain,	Par Lost 3.196
They who neglect and scorn, shall never taste;	Par Lost 3.199
That they may stumble on, and deeper fall;	Par Lost 3.201
In those who, when they may, accept not grace.	Par Lost 3.302
Bad men and Angels, they arraignd shall sink	Par Lost 3.331
Towards either Throne they bow, and to the ground	Par Lost 3.350
With solemn adoration down they cast	Par Lost 3.351
Then Crown'd again thir gold'n Harps they took,	Par Lost 3.365
Of charming symphonie they introduce	Par Lost 3.368
Thee Father first they sung Omnipotent,	Par Lost 3.372
Thee next they sang of all Creation first,	Par Lost 3.383
Thus they in Heav'n, above the starry Sphear,	Par Lost 3.416
New *Babels*, had they wherewithall, would build:	Par Lost 3.468
And they who to be sure of Paradise	Par Lost 3.478
They pass the Planets seven, and pass the fixt,	Par Lost 3.481
Of Heav'ns ascent they lift thir Feet, when loe	Par Lost 3.486
Or other Worlds they seemd, or happy Iles,	Par Lost 3.567
Dispenses Light from farr; they as they move	Par Lost 3.579
In vain, though by thir powerful Art they binde	Par Lost 3.602
Culminate from th' *Aequator*, as they now	Par Lost 3.617
Numberless, as thou seest, and how they move;	Par Lost 3.719
Th' Omnipotent. Ay me, they little know	Par Lost 4.86
While they adore me on the Throne of Hell,	Par Lost 4.89
Native perfumes, and whisper whence they stole	Par Lost 4.158
Well pleas'd they slack thir course, and many a League	Par Lost 4.164
So passd they naked on, nor shund the sight	Par Lost 4.319
Of God or Angel, for they thought no ill:	Par Lost 4.320
So hand in hand they passd, the lovliest pair	Par Lost 4.321
They sat them down, and after no more toil	Par Lost 4.327
More grateful, to thir Supper Fruits they fell,	Par Lost 4.331
Yielded them, side-long as they sat recline	Par Lost 4.333
The savourie pulp they chew, and in the rinde	Par Lost 4.335
Still as they thirsted scoop the brimming stream;	Par Lost 4.336
Alone as they. About them frisking playd	Par Lost 4.340
Can it be death? and do they onely stand	Par Lost 4.518
They taste and die: what likelier can ensue?	Par Lost 4.527
They to thir grassie Couch, these to thir Nests	Par Lost 4.601
Ministring light prepar'd, they set and rise;	Par Lost 4.664
While they keep watch, or nightly rounding walk	Par Lost 4.685
Thus talking hand in hand alone they pass'd	Par Lost 4.689
Which they beheld, the Moons resplendent Globe	Par Lost 4.723
Handed they went; and eas'd the putting off	Par Lost 4.739
Our circuit meets full West. As flame they part	Par Lost 4.784
In search of whom they sought: him there they found	Par Lost 4.799
His heart, not else dismai'd. Now drew they nigh	Par Lost 4.861
And brief related whom they brought, where found,	Par Lost 4.875
The rest is true, they found me where they say;	Par Lost 4.900
Less pain, less to be fled, or thou then they	Par Lost 4.919
Each in thir Chrystal sluce, hee ere they fell	Par Lost 5.133
So all was cleard, and to the Field they haste.	Par Lost 5.136
Soon as they forth were come to open sight	Par Lost 5.138
Lowly they bow'd adoring, and began	Par Lost 5.144
Nor holy rapture wanted they to praise	Par Lost 5.147
To add more sweetness, and they thus began.	Par Lost 5.152
So pray'd they innocent, and to thir thoughts	Par Lost 5.209
On to thir mornings rural work they haste	Par Lost 5.211
Fruitless imbraces: or they led the Vine	Par Lost 5.215
For on som message high they guessd him bound.	Par Lost 5.290
They came, that like *Pomona*'s Arbour smil'd	Par Lost 5.378
Danc'd hand in hand. A while discourse they hold;	Par Lost 5.395
Of sense, whereby they hear, see, smell, touch, taste,	Par Lost 5.411
Think not I shall be nice. So down they sat,	Par Lost 5.433
Thus when with meats and drinks they had suffic'd,	Par Lost 5.451
Can hearts, not free, be tri'd whether they serve	Par Lost 5.532
Willing or no, who will but what they must	Par Lost 5.533

They(*cont*)

And perfet while they stood; how last unfould	Par Lost 5.568
Of circuit inexpressible they stood,	Par Lost 5.595
That day, as other solemn dayes, they spent	Par Lost 5.618
Then most, when most irregular they seem,	Par Lost 5.624
Forthwith from dance to sweet repast they turn	Par Lost 5.630
Desirous; all in Circles as they stood,	Par Lost 5.631
They eate, they drink, and in communion sweet	Par Lost 5.637
Celestial Tabernacles, where they slept	Par Lost 5.654
Illustrates, when they see all Regal Power	Par Lost 5.739
Regions they pass'd, the mightie Regencies	Par Lost 5.748
They came, and *Satan* to his Royal seat	Par Lost 5.756
They led him high applauded, and present	Par Lost 6.26
Of Truth, in word mightier then they in Armes;	Par Lost 6.32
Of God and his *Messiah*. On they move	Par Lost 6.68
Of Heav'n they march'd, and many a Province wide	Par Lost 6.77
With furious expedition; for they weend	Par Lost 6.86
Thir Deities to assert, who while they feel	Par Lost 6.157
To flight, or if to fall, but that they rise	Par Lost 6.285
They ended parle, and both addrest for fight	Par Lost 6.296
Of Godlike Power: for likest Gods they seemd,	Par Lost 6.301
Stood they or mov'd, in stature, motion, arms	Par Lost 6.302
Uplifted imminent one stroke they aim'd	Par Lost 6.317
From off the files of warr; there they him laid	Par Lost 6.339
All Heart they live, all Head, all Eye, all Eare,	Par Lost 6.350
All Intellect, all Sense, and as they please,	Par Lost 6.351
They Limb themselves, and colour, shape or size	Par Lost 6.352
Not to have disobei'd; in fight they stood	Par Lost 6.403
These things, as not to mind from whence they grow	Par Lost 6.477
With Heav'ns ray, and temperd they shoot forth	Par Lost 6.480
Adverse, that they shall fear we have disarmd	Par Lost 6.490
Forthwith from Councel to the work they flew,	Par Lost 6.507
Were ready, in a moment up they turnd	Par Lost 6.509
They found, they mingl'd, and with suttle Art,	Par Lost 6.513
Concocted and adusted they reduc'd	Par Lost 6.514
Secret they finish'd, and in order set,	Par Lost 6.522
The matin Trumpet Sung: in Arms they stood	Par Lost 6.526
In motion or in alt: him soon they met	Par Lost 6.532
Instant without disturb they took Allarm,	Par Lost 6.549
Stand readie to receive them, if they like	Par Lost 6.561
On Wheels (for like to Pillars most they seem'd	Par Lost 6.573
That whom they hit, none on thir feet might stand,	Par Lost 6.592
Though standing else as Rocks, but down they fell	Par Lost 6.593
The sooner for thir Arms, unarm'd they might	Par Lost 6.595
What should they do? if on they rusht, repulse	Par Lost 6.600
They worse abhorr'd. *Satan* beheld thir plight,	Par Lost 6.607
Ere while they fierce were coming, and when wee,	Par Lost 6.610
Of composition, strait they chang'd thir minds,	Par Lost 6.613
As they would dance, yet for a dance they seemd	Par Lost 6.615
Not understood, this gift they have besides,	Par Lost 6.626
They shew us when our foes walk not upright.	Par Lost 6.627
So they among themselves in pleasant veine	Par Lost 6.628
To match with thir inventions they presum'd	Par Lost 6.631
And all his Host derided, while they stood	Par Lost 6.633
A while in trouble; but they stood not long,	Par Lost 6.634
Thir Arms away they threw, and to the Hills	Par Lost 6.639
Light as the Lightning glimps they ran, they flew,	Par Lost 6.642
They pluckt the seated Hills with all thir load,	Par Lost 6.644
When coming towards them so dread they saw	Par Lost 6.648
They saw them whelm'd, and all thir confidence	Par Lost 6.651
Long strugling underneath, ere they could wind	Par Lost 6.659
That under ground, they fought in dismal shade;	Par Lost 6.666
Equal in their Creation they were form'd,	Par Lost 6.690
Whence in perpetual fight they needs must last	Par Lost 6.693
Each to his place, they heard his voice and went	Par Lost 6.782
They hard'nd more by what might most reclame,	Par Lost 6.791
By mee, not you but mee they have despis'd,	Par Lost 6.812
That they may have thir wish, to trie with mee	Par Lost 6.818
In Battel which the stronger proves, they all,	Par Lost 6.819
They measure all, of other excellence	Par Lost 6.821
Plagues; they astonisht all resistance lost,	Par Lost 6.838
Urg'd them behind; headlong themselves they threw	Par Lost 6.864
Nine dayes they fell; confounded *Chaos* roard,	Par Lost 6.871
With Jubilie advanc'd; and as they went,	Par Lost 6.884
Of disobedience; firm they might have stood,	Par Lost 6.911
If they transgress, and slight that sole command,	Par Lost 7.47
They open to themselves at length the way	Par Lost 7.158
Glorie they sung to the most High, good will	Par Lost 7.182
On heav'nly ground they stood, and from the shore	Par Lost 7.210
They view'd the vast immeasurable Abyss	Par Lost 7.211
Exhaling first from Darkness they beheld;	Par Lost 7.255
The hollow Universal Orb they fill'd,	Par Lost 7.257
God and his works, Creatour him they sung,	Par Lost 7.259
Capacious bed of Waters: thither they	Par Lost 7.290
Wave rowling after Wave, where way they found,	Par Lost 7.298
But they, or under ground, or circuit wide	Par Lost 7.301
By tincture or reflection they augment	Par Lost 7.367
They summ'd thir Penns, and soaring th' air sublime	Par Lost 7.421
Floats, as they pass, fann'd with unnumber'd plumes:	Par Lost 7.432
Her state with Oarie feet: yet oft they quit	Par Lost 7.440
Among the Trees in Pairs they rose, they walk'd:	Par Lost 7.459
Open, ye everlasting Gates, they sung,	Par Lost 7.565
Creation and the Six dayes acts they sung,	Par Lost 7.601
Thou hast repeld, while impiously they thought	Par Lost 7.611
Holy and just: thrice happie if they know	Par Lost 7.631
So sung they, and the Empyrean rung,	Par Lost 7.633
To visit how they prosper'd, bud and bloom,	Par Lost 8.45
Her Nurserie; they at her coming sprung	Par Lost 8.46

They(*cont*)

Rather admire; or if they list to try	Par Lost 8.75
Hereafter, when they come to model Heav'n	Par Lost 8.79
And calculate the Starrs, how they will weild	Par Lost 8.80
Of sweet repast; they satiate, and soon fill,	Par Lost 8.214
Not that they durst without his leave attempt,	Par Lost 8.237
Not hither summond, since they cannot change	Par Lost 8.347
I nam'd them, as they pass'd, and understood	Par Lost 8.352
Thir language and thir wayes, they also know,	Par Lost 8.373
Cannot be human consort; they rejoyce	Par Lost 8.392
And they shall be one Flesh, one Heart, one Soule.	Par Lost 8.499
Express they, by looks onely, or do they mix	Par Lost 8.616
Total they mix, Union of Pure with Pure	Par Lost 8.627
So parted they, the Angel up to Heav'n	Par Lost 8.652
Deprest, and much they may, if all be mine,	Par Lost 9.46
More Angels to Create, if they at least	Par Lost 9.146
Then commune how that day they best may ply	Par Lost 9.201
Thoughts, which how found they harbour in thy brest	Par Lost 9.288
Which oft, they say, some evil Spirit attends	Par Lost 9.638
Knowing both Good and Evil as they know.	Par Lost 9.709
As they, participating God-like food?	Par Lost 9.717
Them nothing: If they all things, who enclos'd	Par Lost 9.722
Though others envie what they cannot give;	Par Lost 9.805
That Morn when first they parted; by the Tree	Par Lost 9.848
They swim in mirth, and fansie that they feel	Par Lost 9.1009
As wantonly repaid; in Lust they burne:	Par Lost 9.1015
There they thir fill of Love and Loves disport	Par Lost 9.1042
Encumberd, now had left them, up they rose	Par Lost 9.1051
Shorn of his strength, They destitute and bare	Par Lost 9.1062
Confounded long they sate, as struck'n mute,	Par Lost 9.1064
Into the thickest Wood, there soon they chose	Par Lost 9.1100
They gatherd, broad as *Amazonian* Targe,	Par Lost 9.1111
And with what skill they had, together sowd,	Par Lost 9.1112
Thus fenc't, and as they thought, thir shame in part	Par Lost 9.1119
They sate them down to weep, nor onely Teares	Par Lost 9.1121
The Faith they owe; when earnestly they seek	Par Lost 9.1141
Such proof, conclude, they then begin to faile.	Par Lost 9.1142
Thus they in mutual accusation spent	Par Lost 9.1187
For still they knew, and ought to have still remember'd	Par Lost 10.12
Whoever tempted; which they not obeying,	Par Lost 10.14
Incurr'd, what could they less, the penaltie,	Par Lost 10.15
For Man, for of his state by this they knew,	Par Lost 10.19
How all befell: they towards the Throne Supream	Par Lost 10.28
To sentence Man: the voice of God they heard	Par Lost 10.97
Brought to thir Ears, while day declin'd, they heard,	Par Lost 10.99
Remov'd farr off; then pittying how they stood	Par Lost 10.211
Hovering upon the Waters; what they met	Par Lost 10.285
They fasten'd, and the Mole immense wraught on	Par Lost 10.300
Now had they brought the work by wondrous Art	Par Lost 10.312
And Chains they made all fast, too fast they made	Par Lost 10.319
And now thir way to Earth they had descri'd,	Par Lost 10.325
So saying he dismiss'd them, they with speed	Par Lost 10.410
Departing gave command, and they observ'd.	Par Lost 10.430
Bent thir aspect, and whom they wish'd beheld,	Par Lost 10.454
Above the rest still to retain; they all	Par Lost 10.532
They saw, but other sight instead, a crowd	Par Lost 10.538
And horrid sympathie; for what they saw,	Par Lost 10.540
They felt themselves now changing; down thir arms,	Par Lost 10.541
Down fell both Spear and Shield, down they as fast,	Par Lost 10.542
As in thir crime. Thus was th' applause they meant,	Par Lost 10.545
Thir earnest eyes they fix'd, imagining	Par Lost 10.553
But on thy rould in heaps, and up the Trees 1667 'thy'	Par Lost 10.558
That curld *Megaera:* greedily they pluck'd	Par Lost 10.560
Deceav'd; they fondly thinking to allay	Par Lost 10.564
With spattering noise rejected: oft they assayd,	Par Lost 10.567
With soot and cinders fill'd; so oft they fell	Par Lost 10.570
Whom they triumph'd once lapst. Thus were they plagu'd	Par Lost 10.572
Till thir lost shape, permitted, they resum'd,	Par Lost 10.574
However some tradition they dispers'd	Par Lost 10.578
And Fabl'd how the Serpent, whom they calld	Par Lost 10.580
This said, they both betook them several wayes,	Par Lost 10.610
Her office they prescrib'd, to th' other five	Par Lost 10.657
Should prove tempestuous: To the Winds they set	Par Lost 10.664
From the Suns Axle; they with labour push'd	Par Lost 10.670
Those terms whatever, when they were propos'd:	Par Lost 10.757
With me? how can they then acquitted stand	Par Lost 10.827
Felt less remorse: they forthwith to the place	Par Lost 10.1098
Thus they in lowliest plight repentant stood	Par Lost 11.1
Blow'n vagabond or frustrate: in they passd	Par Lost 11.16
As how with peccant Angels late they saw;	Par Lost 11.70
By the waters of Life, where ere they sate	Par Lost 11.79
My motions in him, longer then they move,	Par Lost 11.91
Perpetual banishment. Yet least they faint	Par Lost 11.108
If patiently thy bidding they obey,	Par Lost 11.112
Whereat hee inlie rag'd, and as they talk'd,	Par Lost 11.444
Forsook them, when themselves they villifi'd	Par Lost 11.516
His Image whom they serv'd, a brutish vice,	Par Lost 11.518
While they pervert pure Natures healthful rules	Par Lost 11.523
To loathsom sickness, worthily, since they	Par Lost 11.524
Just men they seemd, and all thir study bent	Par Lost 11.577
Freedom and Peace to men: they on the Plain	Par Lost 11.580
In Gems and wanton dress; to the Harp they sung	Par Lost 11.583
Fast caught, they lik'd, and each his liking chose;	Par Lost 11.587
And now of love they treat till th' Eevning Star	Par Lost 11.588
They light the Nuptial Torch, and bid invoke	Par Lost 11.590
Who slew his Brother; studious they appere	Par Lost 11.609
Taught them, but they his gifts acknowledg'd none.	Par Lost 11.612

They(*cont*)
Yet they a beauteous ofspring shall beget; Par Lost 11.613
O pittie and shame, that they who to live well Par Lost 11.629
Make they but of thir Brethren, men of men? Par Lost 11.680
With thought that they must be. Let no man seek Par Lost 11.770
In Triumph and luxurious wealth, are they Par Lost 11.788
Or serve they as a flourie verge to binde Par Lost 11.881
Of Brick, and of that stuff they cast to build Par Lost 12.43
As mockt they storm; great laughter was in Heav'n Par Lost 12.59
His people from enthralment, they return Par Lost 12.171
This also shall they gain by thir delay Par Lost 12.223
In the wide Wilderness, there they shall found Par Lost 12.224
To mortal eare is dreadful; they beseech Par Lost 12.236
And terror cease; he grants what they besaught Par Lost 12.238
1667 'them thir desire'
Save when they journie, and at length they come, Par Lost 12.258
Sin against Law to fight; that when they see Par Lost 12.289
The bloud of Bulls and Goats, they may conclude Par Lost 12.292
To them by Faith imputed, they may finde Par Lost 12.295
Meanwhile they in thir earthly *Canaan* plac't Par Lost 12.315
They first re-edifie, and for a while Par Lost 12.350
In wealth and multitude, factious they grow; Par Lost 12.352
Upon the Temple it self: at last they seise Par Lost 12.356
They gladly thither haste, and by a Quire Par Lost 12.366
To teach all nations what of him they learn'd Par Lost 12.440
All Nations they shall teach; for from that day Par Lost 12.446
His people, who defend? will they not deale Par Lost 12.483
Wors with his followers then with him they dealt? Par Lost 12.484
Be sure they will, said th' Angel; but from Heav'n Par Lost 12.485
As did thir Lord before them. Thus they win Par Lost 12.502
They die; but in thir room, as they forewarne, Par Lost 12.507
Then shall they seek to avail themselves of names, Par Lost 12.515
Shall on the heart engrave. What will they then Par Lost 12.524
He ended, and they both descend the Hill; Par Lost 12.606
They looking back, all th' Eastern side beheld Par Lost 12.641
Som natural tears they drop'd, but wip'd them soon; Par Lost 12.645
They hand in hand with wandring steps and slow, Par Lost 12.648
Unanimous they all commit the care Par Reg 1.111
They now, and men hereafter may discern, Par Reg 1.164
So they in Heav'n their Odes and Vigils tun'd: Par Reg 1.182
Where they might see him, and to thee they came; Par Reg 1.246
By whose bright course led on they found the place, Par Reg 1.252
By which they knew thee King of *Israel* born. Par Reg 1.254
Known partly, and soon found of whom they spake Par Reg 1.262
Among wild Beasts: they at his sight grew mild, Par Reg 1.310
That he might fall in *Ramoth*, they demurring, Par Reg 1.373
To all mankind: why should I? they to me Par Reg 1.388
Envy they say excites me, thus to gain Par Reg 1.397
Which they who ask'd have seldom understood, Par Reg 1.436
To thy Delusions; justly, since they fell Par Reg 1.443
At least in vain, for they shall find thee mute. Par Reg 1.459
Him whom they heard so late expresly call'd Par Reg 2.3
Sometimes they thought he might be only shewn, Par Reg 2.13
Behold the Kings of the Earth how they oppress Par Reg 2.44
They have exalted, and behind them cast Par Reg 2.46
Thus they out of their plaints new hope resume Par Reg 2.58
To find whom at the first they found unsought: Par Reg 2.59
Though ravenous, taught to abstain from what they brought: Par Reg 2.269
They all had need, I as thou seest have none. Par Reg 2.318
They whom I favour thrive in wealth amain, Par Reg 2.430
Accomplish what they did, perhaps and more? Par Reg 2.452
And for thy reason why they should be sought, Par Reg 2.485
They praise and they admire they know not what; Par Reg 3.52
They err who count it glorious to subdue Par Reg 3.71
Nothing but ruin wheresoe're they rove, Par Reg 3.79
With temperate sway; oft have they violated Par Reg 3.160
They themselves rather are occasion best, Par Reg 3.174
They issue forth, Steel Bows, and Shafts their arms Par Reg 3.305
All Horsemen, in which fight they most excel; Par Reg 3.307
See how in warlike muster they appear, Par Reg 3.308
How quick they wheel'd, and flying behind them shot Par Reg 3.323
As for those captive Tribes, themselves were they Par Reg 3.414
While to their native land with joy they hast, Par Reg 3.437
Chios and *Creet*, and how they quaff in Gold, Par Reg 4.118
Therefore let pass, as they are transitory, Par Reg 4.209
Or they with thee hold conversation meet? Par Reg 4.232
In brief sententious precepts, while they treat Par Reg 4.264
Alas what can they teach, and not mislead; Par Reg 4.309
Much of the Soul they talk, but all awrie, Par Reg 4.313
Ill imitated, while they loudest sing Par Reg 4.339
A Kingdom they portend thee, but what Kingdom, Par Reg 4.389
Yet with no new device, they all were spent, Par Reg 4.443
Yet as being oft times noxious where they light Par Reg 4.460
Over whose heads they rore, and seem to point, Par Reg 4.463
They oft fore-signifie and threaten ill: Par Reg 4.464
I never fear'd they could, though noising loud Par Reg 4.488
And threatning nigh; what they can do as signs Par Reg 4.489
They shall up lift thee, lest at any time Par Reg 4.558
Where they shall dwell secure, when time shall be Par Reg 4.616
Thee and thy Legions, yelling they shall flye, Par Reg 4.629
Thus they the Son of God our Saviour meek Par Reg 4.636
They creep, yet see, I dark in light expos'd Samson 75
How counterfeit a coin they are who friends Samson 189
They swarm, but in adverse withdraw their head Samson 192
In every street, do they not say, how well Samson 204
Immeasurable strength they might behold Samson 206
And shall again, pretend they ne're so wise. Samson 212
The daughter of an Infidel: they knew not Samson 221

They(*cont*)
But they persisted deaf, and would not seem Samson 249
Into thir hands, and they as gladly yield me Samson 259
Their choicest youth; they only liv'd who fled. Samson 264
They had by this possess'd the Towers of *Gath*, Samson 266
And lorded over them whom now they serve; Samson 267
If any be, they walk obscure; Samson 296
They ravel more, still less resolv'd, Samson 305
As if they would confine th' interminable, Samson 307
About thy ransom: well they may by this Samson 483
And peoples safety, which in part they effect: Samson 681
If these they scape, perhaps in poverty Samson 697
That either they love nothing, or not long? Samson 1033
Till they had hir'd a woman with their gold Samson 1114
Sam. All these indignities, for such they are Samson 1168
Thir Magistrates confest it, when they took thee Samson 1183
Th' unworthier they; whence to this day they serve. Samson 1216
They cannot well impose, nor I sustain; Samson 1258
If they intend advantage of my labours Samson 1259
Thy strength they know surpassing human rate, Samson 1313
Sam. Have they not Sword-players, and ev'ry sort Samson 1323
But they must pick me out with shackles tir'd, Samson 1326
Do they not seek occasion of new quarrels Samson 1329
Can they think me so broken, so debas'd Samson 1335
Because they shall not trail me through thir streets Samson 1402
They easily would set to sale, a third Samson 1466
They had anough reveng'd, having reduc't Samson 1468
Oh it continues, they have slain my Son. Samson 1516
When to thir sports they turn'd. Immediately Samson 1614
He patient but undaunted where they led him, Samson 1623
At length for intermission sake they led him Samson 1629
He tugg'd, he shook, till down they came and drew Samson 1650
They only set on sport and play Samson 1679
To quench the drouth of *Phoebus*, which as they taste Mask 66
All other parts remaining as they were, Mask 72
Trinity ms 'they were' ← 'before'
And they, so perfect is their misery, Mask 73
Well knows to still the wilde winds when they roar, Mask 87
In wanton dance they praise the bounteous *Pan*, Mask 176
Trinity ms 'they praise' ← 'adore' ← 'they praise'
My Brothers when they saw me wearied out Mask 182
Stept as they se'd to the next Thicket side Mask 185
They left me then, when the gray-hooded Eev'n Mask 188
line not in Bridgewater ms
But where they are, and why they came not back, Mask 191
They had ingag'd their wandring steps too far, Mask 193
And envious darknes, e're they could return, Mask 194
Prompt me; and they perhaps are not far off. Mask 229
How sweetly did they float upon the wings Mask 249
Who as they sung, would take the prison'd soul, Mask 256
Yet they in pleasing slumber lull'd the sense, Mask 260
La. They left me weary on a grassie terf. Mask 280
La. They were but twain, and purpos'd quick return. Mask 284
Co. Were they of manly prime, or youthful bloom? Mask 289
Their port was more then human, as they stood; Mask 297
For grant they be so, while they rest unknown, Mask 361
line not in Bridgewater ms
line not in Trinity ms
Or if they be but false alarms of Fear, Mask 364
line not in Trinity ms
line not in Bridgewater ms
Yet have they many baits, and guilefull spells Mask 537
word deleted in trinity ms
Yet will they soon retire, if he but shrink. Mask 656
And so bestudd with Stars, that they below Mask 734
They had their name thence; course complexions Mask 749
line not in Bridgewater ms
were they not taken thence Mask Tr. ms 22.07
Thus don the Tales, to bed they creep, Allegro 115
With such consort as they keep, Penseroso 145
They knew not of his story, Lycidas 95
Of other care they little reck'ning make, Lycidas 116
What recks it them? What need they? They are sped; Lycidas 122
Trinity ms 'they are'
1638 'they are'
And when they list, their lean and flashy songs Lycidas 123
But swoln with wind, and the rank mist they draw, Lycidas 126
As if they surely knew their sovran Lord was by. Nativity 60
Full little thought they than, Nativity 88
They call the grisly king, Nativity 209
But full soon they did devour Psalm 136, 53
That so they may without suspect or fears Vacation 27
That they would fitly fall in order'd Characters. Passion 49
In perfect Diapason, whilst they stood Musick 23
But had his doings lasted as they were, Another 27
Chosen thou hast, and they that overween, Sonnet 9, 6
And still revolt when truth would set them free. Sonnet 12, 10
Trinity ms 'still revolt when Truth would sett them' ← 'make them' ← 'set them' ← 'hate the truth wherby they should be'
Licence they mean when they cry libertie; Sonnet 12, 11
But from that mark how far they roave we see Sonnet 12, 13
And azure wings, that up they flew so drest, Sonnet 14, 11
when as they journey'd from this dark abode Sonnet 14, Tr. ms 41.07
The Vales redoubl'd to the Hills, and they Sonnet 18, 9
Bear his milde yoak, they serve him best, his State Sonnet 19, 11
They also serve who only stand and waite. Sonnet 19, 14
When they shall read this clearly in your charge Forcers 19
Trinity ms 'they' ← 'you'

They(*cont*)
Unmindfull. Hapless they Horace 12
Let us break off, say they, by strength of hand Psalm 2, 6
Many are they Psalm 3, 4
They pitch against me their Pavillions. Psalm 3, 18
An open grave their throat, their tongue they smooth. Psalm 5, 28
Still on; for against thee they have rebell'd; Psalm 5, 32
Defend'st them, they shall ever sing Psalm 5, 35
They shall return in hast the way they came Psalm 6, 23
Their bread with tears they eat, Psalm 80, 22
Among themselves they laugh, they play, Psalm 80, 27
And flouts at us they throw Psalm 80, 28
That all may pluck her, as they go, Psalm 80, 51
They perish at thy dreadfull ire, Psalm 80, 67
From whence they might not swerve. Psalm 81, 16
Their own conceits they follow'd still Psalm 81, 51
But *they, his People, should remain,* Psalm 81, 63
They know not nor will understand, Psalm 82, 17
In darkness they walk on Psalm 82, 18
And they that hate thee *proud and fell* Psalm 83, 7
Against thy people they contrive Psalm 83, 9
Them to ensnare they chiefly strive Psalm 83, 11
Come let us cut them off say they, Psalm 83, 13
Till they no Nation be Psalm 83, 14
For they consult with all their might, Psalm 83, 17
Themselves against thee they unite Psalm 83, 19
The Philistims, and they of Tyre Psalm 83, 27
They were repulst and slain, Psalm 83, 38
For they amidst their pride have said Psalm 83, 45
And till they yield thee honour due, Psalm 83, 59
Then shall they know that thou whose name Psalm 83, 65
They find their safe abode, Psalm 84, 14
And home they fly from round the Coasts Psalm 84, 15
Where thee they ever praise, Psalm 84, 18
They pass through Baca's *thirstie* Vale, Psalm 84, 21
They journey on from strength to strength Psalm 84, 25
Both they who sing, and they who dance Psalm 87, 25
Me to them odious, *for they change,* Psalm 88, 35
Shall they thy loving kindness tell Psalm 88, 45
Or they *who* in perdition *dwell* Psalm 88, 47
All day they round about me go, Psalm 88, 67
Like waves they me persue. Psalm 88, 68
They *fly me now* whom I have lov'd, Psalm 88, 71
Iunkets and knacks, that they may learne apace. Prose 6, 3

Thick
Thick as Autumnal Leaves that strow the Brooks Par Lost 1.302
And broken Chariot Wheels, so thick bestrown Par Lost 1.311
Appear'd, and serried Shields in thick array Par Lost 1.548
Thick swarm'd, both on the ground and in the air, Par Lost 1.767
Thir State affairs. So thick the aerie crowd Par Lost 1.775
Thick clouds and dark doth Heav'ns all-ruling Sire Par Lost 2.264
Through the strict Senteries and Stations thick Par Lost 2.412
In darkness, while thy head flames thick and fast Par Lost 2.754
So thick a drop serene hath quencht thir Orbs, Par Lost 3.25
Stood thick as Starrs, and from his sight receiv'd Par Lost 3.61
Now in loose Garlands thick thrown off, the bright Par Lost 3.362
Imbellisht, thick with sparkling orient Gemmes Par Lost 3.507
Alooff the vulgar Constellations thick, Par Lost 3.577
But further way found none, so thick entwin'd, Par Lost 4.174
Or in thick shade retir'd, from him to draw Par Lost 4.532
With ported Spears, as thick as when a field Par Lost 4.980
Coverd with thick embatteld Squadrons bright, Par Lost 6.16
This day, fear not his flight; so thick a Cloud Par Lost 6.539
Flashing thick flames, Wheele within Wheele undrawn, Par Lost 6.751
Forth flourish't thick the clustring Vine, forth crept Par Lost 7.320
And sowd with Starrs the Heav'n thick as a field: Par Lost 7.358
From the thick shade, and *Adam* to his Bowre. Par Lost 8.653
Half spi'd, so thick the Roses bushing round Par Lost 9.426
Where Houses thick and Sewers annoy the Aire, Par Lost 9.446
Thick overhead with verdant roof imbowr'd Par Lost 9.1038
Of hissing through the Hall, thick swarming now Par Lost 10.522
And *Dipsas* (not so thick swarm'd once the Soil Par Lost 10.526
Within thick Clouds and dark ten-fold involv'd, Par Reg 1.41
Up to the middle Region of thick Air, Par Reg 2.117
Of Trees thick interwoven; there he slept, Par Reg 2.263
Remove their swelling Epithetes thick laid Par Reg 4.343
Whose branching arms thick intertwind might shield Par Reg 4.405
Back'd on the North and West by a thick wood, Par Reg 4.448
And in thick shelter of black shades imbowr'd, Mask 62
Such are those thick and gloomy shadows damp Mask 470
Thick set with Agat, and the azurn sheen Mask 893
1637 'Thicke'
As thick and numberless Penseroso 7

Thickened
Sent up amain; and now the thick'nd Skie Par Lost 11.742

Thicker
Climbing, sat thicker then the snakie locks Par Lost 10.559

Thickest
Till thickest Legions close; with feats of Arms Par Lost 2.537
Of thickest covert was inwoven shade Par Lost 4.693
Where erst was thickest fight, th' Angelic throng, Par Lost 6.308
Into the thickest Wood, there soon they chose Par Lost 9.1100
At Loopholes cut through thickest shade: Those Leaves Par Lost 9.1110
The thickest Trees, both Man and Wife, till God Par Lost 10.101
Thir course through thickest Constellations held Par Lost 10.411
Of Stygian darknes spets her thickest gloom, Mask 132
Over the Pole thy thickest mantle throw, Passion 30
Where thickest darkness *hovers round,* Psalm 88, 27

Thicket
With thicket overgrown, grottesque and wilde, Par Lost 4.136
Of echoing Hill or Thicket have we heard Par Lost 4.681
In Forrest wilde, in Thicket, Brake, or Den; Par Lost 7.458
So saying, through each Thicket Danck or Drie, Par Lost 9.179
Fast by a Fountain, one small Thicket past Par Lost 9.628
That all was lost. Back to the Thicket slunk Par Lost 9.784
Stept as they se'd to the next Thicket side Mask 185
Bridgewater ms 'thickett'
Trinity ms 'thicket'
Shakes the high thicket, haste I all about, Arcades 58

Thickets
The Nimphs in twilight shade of tangled thickets mourn. Nativity 188

Thick-rammed
Thick-rammd, at th' other bore with touch of fire Par Lost 6.485

Thick-warbled
Trills her thick-warbl'd notes the summer long, Par Reg 4.246

Thick-woven
Among thick-wov'n Arborets and Flours Par Lost 9.437

Thief
Or as a Thief bent to unhoord the cash Par Lost 4.188
So clomb this first grand Thief into Gods Fould: Par Lost 4.192
And Thief of Paradise; him long of old Par Reg 4.604
How soon hath Time the suttle theef of youth, Sonnet 7, 1
Trinity ms 'theefe'

Thievish
Had stole them from me, els O theevish Night Mask 195
word not in Bridgewater ms

Thigh
Gird on, and Sword upon thy puissant Thigh; Par Lost 6.714
While the Bee with Honied thie, Penseroso 142

Thighs
Millions of flaming swords, drawn from the thighs Par Lost 1.664
Skirted his loines and thighes with downie Gold Par Lost 5.282

Thin
Himself and his rash Armie, where thin Aire Par Lost 12.76
Into thin Air diffus'd: for now began Par Reg 1.499
Thin sown with aught of profit or delight, Par Reg 4.345
Scatters the rear of darknes thin, Allegro 50
And slits the thin spun life. But not the praise, Lycidas 76
Trinity ms 'thin-spun'
1638 'thin-spun'

Thine
Now in thine eye so foul, once deemd so fair Par Lost 2.748
Surpris'd thee, dim thine eyes, and dizzie swumm Par Lost 2.753
Thine own begotten, breaking violent way Par Lost 2.782
His end, and frustrate thine, shall he fulfill Par Lost 3.157
I offer, on mee let thine anger fall; Par Lost 3.237
Mans Nature, less'n or degrade thine owne. Par Lost 3.304
To witness with thine eyes what some perhaps Par Lost 3.700
Inseparablie thine, to him shalt beare Par Lost 4.473
To boast what Arms can doe, since thine no more Par Lost 4.1008
With gentle voice, I thought it thine; it said, Par Lost 5.37
Ascend to Heav'n, by merit thine, and see Par Lost 5.80
Almightie, thine this universal Frame, Par Lost 5.154
Against his worthier, as thine now serve thee, Par Lost 6.180
Two dayes are therefore past, the third is thine; Par Lost 6.699
Have sufferd, that the Glorie may be thine Par Lost 6.701
To ask, nor let thine own inventions hope Par Lost 7.121
This Paradise I give thee, count it thine Par Lost 8.319
Do thou but thine, and be not diffident Par Lost 8.562
Would not admit; thine and of all thy Sons Par Lost 8.637
Free in thine own Arbitrement it lies. Par Lost 8.641
For God towards thee hath done his part, do thine. Par Lost 9.375
Thee all things living gaze on, all things thine Par Lost 9.539
United I beheld; no Fair to thine Par Lost 9.608
Father Eternal, thine is to decree, Par Lost 10.68
Enmitie, and between thine and her Seed; Par Lost 10.180
Thine shall submit, hee over thee shall rule. Par Lost 10.196
Thy Trophies, which thou view'st as not thine own, Par Lost 10.355
Still moves with thine, join'd in connexion sweet, Par Lost 10.359
Thine now is all this World, thy vertue hath won Par Lost 10.372
Beare thine own first, ill able to sustaine Par Lost 10.950
From innocence. Now therefore bend thine eare Par Lost 11.30
Thus over-fond, on that which is not thine; Par Lost 11.289
Adam, now ope thine eyes, and first behold Par Lost 11.423
Which now direct thine eyes and soon behold. Par Lost 11.711
And due to theirs which out of thine will grow: Par Lost 12.400
Over his foes and thine; there shall surprise Par Lost 12.453
Those rudiments, and see before thine eyes Par Reg 3.245
Thence to the gates cast round thine eye, and see Par Reg 4.61
To sage Philosophy next lend thine ear, Par Reg 4.272
Then of thine own Tribe fairer, or as fair, Samson 217
Them out of thine, who slew'st them many a slain. Samson 439
And let another hand, not thine, exact Samson 507
Thine forgive mine; that men may censure thine Samson 787
To thine whose doors my feet shall never enter. Samson 950
Then thine, while I preserv'd these locks unshorn, Samson 1143
Soon feel, whose God is strongest, thine or mine. Samson 1155
To put out both thine eyes, and fetter'd send thee Samson 1160
From thine, these evils I deserve and more, Samson 1169
Thine or whom I with *Israel*'s Sons adore. Samson 1177
Thy rapt soul sitting in thine eyes: Penseroso 40
That sunk so low that sacred head of thine. Lycidas 102
Lord in thine anger do not reprehend me Psalm 6, 1
Rise Jehovah in thine ire Psalm 7, 19
Thy free love made it thine, Psalm 80, 34
Thine anger all thou hadst remov'd, Psalm 85, 9

Thine(*cont*)	
Thine indignation cause to cease	Psalm 85, 15
Thine ear with favour bend.	Psalm 88, 8
Astonish'd with thine ire.	Psalm 88, 64
Thing	
Created thing naught valu'd he nor shun'd;	Par Lost 2.679
What thing thou art, thus double-form'd, and why	Par Lost 2.741
Som dreadful thing no doubt; for well thou knowst	Par Lost 4.426
No evil thing approach or enter in;	Par Lost 4.563
And every creeping thing that creeps the ground.	Par Lost 7.523
And every living thing that moves on the Earth.	Par Lost 7.534
Creator; something yet of doubt remaines,	Par Lost 8.13
1667 'some thing'	
Adjoynd, from each thing met conceaves delight,	Par Lost 9.449
Of Death denounc't, whatever thing Death be,	Par Lost 9.695
Each thing on Earth; and other care perhaps	Par Lost 9.813
A thing not undesireable, somtime	Par Lost 9.824
No homely morsels, and whatever thing	Par Lost 10.605
Deceivable and vain! Nay what thing good	Samson 350
That rigid score. A worse thing yet remains,	Samson 433
But who is this, what thing of Sea or Land?	Samson 710
Som say no evil thing that walks by night	Mask 432
Bridgewater ms 'thinge'	
Driving far off each thing of sin and guilt,	Mask 456
For when as each thing bad thou hast entomb'd,	On Time 9
When every thing that is sincerely good	On Time 14
muse a vain thing, the Kings of th' earth upstand	Psalm 2, 2
Whatever thing is good	Psalm 85, 50
Things	
Things unattempted yet in Prose or Rhime.	Par Lost 1.16
Abominations; and with cursed things	Par Lost 1.389
Who boast in mortal things, and wond'ring tell	Par Lost 1.693
Views all things at one view? he from heav'ns highth	Par Lost 2.190
Then most conspicuous, when great things of small,	Par Lost 2.258
The sensible of pain. All things invite	Par Lost 2.278
Great things resolv'd, which from the lowest deep	Par Lost 2.392
Perverse, all monstrous, all prodigious things,	Par Lost 2.625
Immeasurably, all things shall be your prey.	Par Lost 2.844
Great things with small) then when *Bellona* storms,	Par Lost 2.922
Sat Sable-vested *Night*, eldest of things,	Par Lost 2.962
Of things invisible to mortal sight.	Par Lost 3.55
Of all things made, and judgest onely right.	Par Lost 3.155
Of all things transitorie and vain, when Sin	Par Lost 3.446
Both all things vain, and all who in vain things	Par Lost 3.448
Here in the dark so many precious things	Par Lost 3.611
That both in him and all things, as is meet,	Par Lost 3.675
The good before him, but perverts best things	Par Lost 4.203
Free leave so large to all things else, and choice	Par Lost 4.434
Had in her sober Liverie all things clad;	Par Lost 4.599
Of night, and all things now retir'd to rest	Par Lost 4.611
In Nature and all things, which these soft fires	Par Lost 4.667
All things to mans delightful use; the roofe	Par Lost 4.692
In Paradise of all things common else.	Par Lost 4.752
Wherein all things created first he weighd,	Par Lost 4.999
Shadowie sets off the face of things; in vain,	Par Lost 5.43
In whose sight all things joy, with ravishment	Par Lost 5.46
Her office holds; of all external things,	Par Lost 5.103
And nourish all things, let your ceasless change	Par Lost 5.183
Of things above his World, and of thir being	Par Lost 5.455
All things proceed, and up to him return,	Par Lost 5.470
Of substance, and in things that live, of life;	Par Lost 5.474
In contemplation of created things	Par Lost 5.511
Be but the shaddow of Heav'n, and things therein	Par Lost 5.575
To motion, measures all things durable	Par Lost 5.581
All things, ev'n thee, and all the Spirits of Heav'n	Par Lost 5.837
Who out of smallest things could without end	Par Lost 6.137
Of Angels, can relate, or to what things	Par Lost 6.298
Great things by small, If Natures concord broke,	Par Lost 6.311
These things, as not to mind from whence they grow	Par Lost 6.477
Consulting on the sum of things, foreseen	Par Lost 6.673
Of all things, to be Heir and to be King	Par Lost 6.708
Image of thee in all things; and shall soon,	Par Lost 6.736
Thus measuring things in Heav'n by things on Earth	Par Lost 6.893
Of things so high and strange, things to thir thought	Par Lost 7.53
Great things, and full of wonder in our eares,	Par Lost 7.70
Things above Earthly thought, which yet concernd	Par Lost 7.82
Things not reveal'd, which th' invisible King,	Par Lost 7.122
This Universe, and all created things:	Par Lost 7.227
Like things to like, the rest to several place	Par Lost 7.240
Ethereal, first of things, quintessence pure	Par Lost 7.244
Cattel and Creeping things, and Beast of the Earth,	Par Lost 7.452
Author and end of all things, and from work	Par Lost 7.591
How first this World and face of things began,	Par Lost 7.636
Things else by me unsearchable, now heard	Par Lost 8.10
If it presume, might erre in things too high,	Par Lost 8.121
But whether thus these things, or whether not,	Par Lost 8.159
That not to know at large of things remote	Par Lost 8.191
And renders us in things that most concerne	Par Lost 8.196
A lower flight, and speak of things at hand	Par Lost 8.199
Birds on the branches warbling; all things smil'd,	Par Lost 8.265
Possess it, and all things that therein live,	Par Lost 8.340
Thou hast provided all things: but with mee	Par Lost 8.363
All human thoughts come short, Supream of things;	Par Lost 8.414
And into all things from her Aire inspir'd	Par Lost 8.476
Giver of all things faire, but fairest this	Par Lost 8.493
In all things else delight indeed, but such	Par Lost 8.524
By attributing overmuch to things	Par Lost 8.565
To basest things. Revenge, at first though sweet,	Par Lost 9.171
Things(*cont*)	
Thir morning incense, when all things that breath,	Par Lost 9.194
O Woman, best are all things as the will	Par Lost 9.343
And all things in best order to invite	Par Lost 9.402
Thee all things living gaze on, all things thine	Par Lost 9.539
Considerd all things visible in Heav'n,	Par Lost 9.604
Or Earth, or Middle, all things fair and good;	Par Lost 9.605
Things in thir Causes, but to trace the wayes	Par Lost 9.682
Them nothing: If they all things, who enclos'd	Par Lost 9.722
In knowledge, as the Gods who all things know;	Par Lost 9.804
In things to us forbidden, it might be wish'd,	Par Lost 9.1025
Omniscient, who in all things wise and just,	Par Lost 10.7
With secret amity things of like kinde	Par Lost 10.248
The savour of Death from all things there that live:	Par Lost 10.269
So, if great things to small may be compar'd,	Par Lost 10.306
Of all things parted by th' Empyreal bounds,	Par Lost 10.380
As sorted best with present things. The Sun	Par Lost 10.651
Outrage from liveless things; but Discord first	Par Lost 10.707
All things with double terror: On the Ground	Par Lost 10.850
Distemperd all things, and of incorrupt	Par Lost 11.56
Mother of all things living, since by thee	Par Lost 11.160
Man is to live, and all things live for Man.	Par Lost 11.161
Of him who all things can, I would not cease	Par Lost 11.309
Not hid, nor those things last which might preserve	Par Lost 11.579
He look'd, and saw the face of things quite chang'd,	Par Lost 11.712
O thou who future things canst represent	Par Lost 11.870
Shall hold thir course, till fire purge all things new,	Par Lost 11.900
(Things by thir names I call, though yet unnam'd)	Par Lost 12.140
Enlightner of my darkness, gracious things	Par Lost 12.271
With all his sacred things, a scorn and prey	Par Lost 12.341
Accomplishing great things, by things deemd weak	Par Lost 12.567
Art all things under Heav'n, all places thou,	Par Lost 12.618
Things highest, greatest, multiplies my fear.	Par Reg 1.69
Then toldst her doubting how these things could be	Par Reg 1.137
All righteous things: therefore above my years,	Par Reg 1.206
Like things of thee to all that present stood.	Par Reg 1.258
Accompanied of things past and to come	Par Reg 1.300
About his Altar, handling holy things,	Par Reg 1.489
My heart hath been a store-house long of things	Par Reg 2.103
All her assaults, on worthier things intent?	Par Reg 2.195
Of greatest things; what woman will you find,	Par Reg 2.208
Of all things destitute, and well I know,	Par Reg 2.305
Hast thou not right to all Created things,	Par Reg 2.324
Said'st thou not that to all things I had right?	Par Reg 2.379
Of these things others quickly will dispose	Par Reg 2.400
Therefore, if at great things thou wouldst arrive,	Par Reg 2.426
Who could do mighty things, and could contemn	Par Reg 2.448
Things vulgar, & well weigh'd, scarce worth the praise,	Par Reg 3.51
To things not glorious, men not worthy of fame.	Par Reg 3.70
And for his glory all things made, all things	Par Reg 3.111
And reason; since his word all things produc'd,	Par Reg 3.122
All things are best fullfil'd in their due time,	Par Reg 3.182
And time there is for all things, Truth hath said:	Par Reg 3.183
Be try'd in humble state, and things adverse,	Par Reg 3.189
In all things that to greatest actions lead.	Par Reg 3.239
In all things, and all men, supposes means,	Par Reg 3.355
In knowledge, all things in it comprehend,	Par Reg 4.224
Think not but that I know these things, or think	Par Reg 4.286
A third sort doubted all things, though plain sence;	Par Reg 4.296
Of mortal things. Who therefore seeks in these	Par Reg 4.318
Who all things now behold more fresh and green,	Par Reg 4.435
Small things with greatest) in *Irassa* strove	Par Reg 4.564
To count them things worth notice, till at length	Samson 250
With all things grateful chear'd, and so suppli'd,	Samson 926
Deceiveable, in most things as a child	Samson 942
By prostituting holy things to Idols;	Samson 1358
Lest I should see him forc't to things unseemly.	Samson 1451
Chor. Yet God hath wrought things as incredible	Samson 1532
More then anough we know; but while things yet	Samson 1592
That he, the Supreme good, t' whom all things ill	Mask 217
line not in Bridgewater ms	
Tell her of things that no gross ear can hear,	Mask 458
But such as are good men can give good things,	Mask 703
That dumb things would be mov'd to sympathize,	Mask 796
line not in Trinity ms	
line not in Bridgewater ms	
Then sing of secret things that came to pass	Vacation 45
Of Lute, or Viol still, more apt for mournful things.	Passion 28
Dead things with inbreath'd sense able to pierce,	Musick 4
For other things mild Heav'n a time ordains,	Sonnet 21, 11
Things false and vain and nothing else but lies?	Psalm 4, 12
City of God, most glorious things	Psalm 87, 9
A mighty masse of things strangely confus'd,	Prose 2, 3
Things that on earth were lost, or were abus'd.	Prose 2, 4
Jesting decides great things	Prose 7, 1
Think	
For who can think Submission? Warr then, Warr	Par Lost 1.661
Or in *Franciscan* think to pass disguis'd;	Par Lost 3.480
Ah gentle pair, yee little think how nigh	Par Lost 4.366
Earth, Aire, and Sea. Then let us not think hard	Par Lost 4.432
Shine not in vain, nor think, though men were none,	Par Lost 4.675
Or think thee unbefitting holiest place,	Par Lost 4.759
Think not, revolted Spirit, thy shape the same,	Par Lost 4.835
Think not I shall be nice. So down they sat,	Par Lost 5.433
Or potent tongue; fool, not to think how vain	Par Lost 6.135
And faithful, now prov'd false. But think not here	Par Lost 6.271
The Adversarie. Nor think thou with wind	Par Lost 6.282
Of evil then so small as easie think	Par Lost 6.437

Think(*cont*)
Think nothing hard, much less to be despaird. — Par Lost 6.495
And thy request think now fulfill'd, that ask'd — Par Lost 7.635
Think onely what concernes thee and thy being; — Par Lost 8.174
Nor less think wee in Heav'n of thee on Earth — Par Lost 8.224
Beyond all other, think the same voutsaf't — Par Lost 8.581
Angels, nor think superfluous others aid. — Par Lost 9.308
But if thou think, trial unsought may finde — Par Lost 9.370
A death to think. Confirm'd then I resolve, — Par Lost 9.830
Nor can I think that God, Creator wise, — Par Lost 9.938
Where he abides, think there thy native soile. — Par Lost 11.292
Horrid to think, how horrible to feel! — Par Lost 11.465
Men generally think me much a foe — Par Reg 1.387
Think not so slight of glory; therein least — Par Reg 3.109
When that comes think not thou to find me slack — Par Reg 3.398
Think not but that I know these things, or think — Par Reg 4.286
Unless there be who think not God at all, — Samson 295
Samson, of all thy sufferings think the heaviest, — Samson 445
Chor. O madness, to think use of strongest wines — Samson 553
Nor think me so unwary or accurst — Samson 930
Can they think me so broken, so debas'd — Samson 1335
Man. He can I know, but doubt to think he will; — Samson 1534
I do not think my sister so to seek, — Mask 366
Trinity ms 'thinke'
1637 'thinke'
Bridgewater ms 'thinke'
And tell me it is safe, as bid me hope — Mask 400
Trinity ms 'hope' ← 'thinke'
Think what, and be adviz'd, you are but young yet. — Mask 755
1637 'Thinke'
line not in Bridgewater ms
Trinity ms 'thinke'
Would think to charm my judgement, as mine eyes — Mask 758
Trinity ms 'thinke'
Bridgewater ms 'thinke'
1637 'thinke'
And think to burst out into sudden blaze, — Lycidas 74
Trinity ms 'thinke'
To think her part was don, — Nativity 105
Think what a present thou to God hast sent, — Fair Inf 74
Might think th' infection of my sorrows loud, — Passion 55
Yet (strange to think) his wain was his increase: — Another 32
line not in 1658 text
1640 'thinke'

Thinkest
Speed almost Spiritual; mee thou thinkst not slow, — Par Lost 8.110
What thinkst thou then of mee, and this my State, — Par Lost 8.403
What thinkst thou of our Empire now, though earnd — Par Lost 10.592
Think'st thou such force in Bread? is it not written — Par Reg 1.347
None are, thou think'st, but taken with such toys. — Par Reg 2.177
Antiochus: and think'st thou to regain — Par Reg 3.163
And think'st upon him; or of man begot — Psalm 8, 13

Thinking
Deceav'd; they fondly thinking to allay — Par Lost 10.564
Of miserie, so thinking to evade — Par Lost 10.1021
And storm'st refus'd, thinking to terrifie — Par Reg 4.496
And thinking now his journeys end was come, — Carrier 12

Thinks
Resigns her charge, while goodness thinks no ill — Par Lost 3.688
Madam, me thinks I see him living yet; — Sonnet 10, 11
Trinity ms 'methinks'

Thinner
Thir Element to draw the thinner Aire. — Par Lost 8.348
Th' Angelic Name, and thinner left the throng — Par Lost 9.142

Third
A third as soon had form'd within the ground — Par Lost 1.705
ms defective here
Drew after him the third part of Heav'ns Sons — Par Lost 2.692
And with them comes a third of Regal port, — Par Lost 4.869
And colours dipt in Heav'n; the third his feet — Par Lost 5.283
Drew after him the third part of Heav'ns Host: — Par Lost 5.710
A third part of the Gods, in Synod met — Par Lost 6.156
Two dayes are therefore past, the third is thine; — Par Lost 6.699
And the third sacred Morn began to shine — Par Lost 6.748
So Eev'n and Morn recorded the Third Day. — Par Lost 7.338
Those two; the third best absent is condemn'd, — Par Lost 10.82
Till *Israel* overcome; so call the third — Par Lost 12.267
Shall long usurp; ere the third dawning light — Par Lost 12.421
A third sort doubted all things, though plain sence; — Par Reg 4.296
They easily would set to sale, a third — Samson 1466
That no second knows nor third, — Samson 1701
On thy third Reigne the Earth look now, and tell — Prose 12, 3

Thirst
Of porous Earth with kindly thirst up drawn, — Par Lost 4.228
More easie, wholsom thirst and appetite — Par Lost 4.330
True appetite, and not disrelish thirst — Par Lost 5.305
Whose liquid murmur heard new thirst excites, — Par Lost 7.68
The thirst I had of knowledge, and voutsaf't — Par Lost 8.8
Then Fruits of Palm-tree pleasantest to thirst — Par Lost 8.212
Not to deferr; hunger and thirst at once, — Par Lost 9.586
Yet parcht with scalding thurst and hunger fierce, — Par Lost 10.556
Hunger and thirst constraining, drug'd as oft, — Par Lost 10.568
As after thirst, which made thir flowing shrink — Par Lost 11.846
Live on tough roots and stubs, to thirst inur'd — Par Reg 1.339
Quench not the thirst of glory, but augment. — Par Reg 3.38
And studs of Pearl, to me should'st tell who thirst — Par Reg 4.120
Or thirst, and as he fed, Angelic Quires — Par Reg 4.593
Thirst, and refresht; nor envy'd them the grape — Samson 551

Thirst(*cont*)
From the dry ground to spring, thy thirst to allay — Samson 582
With thee; say reverend Sire, we thirst to hear. — Samson 1456
(For most do taste through fond intemperate thirst) — Mask 67
Whom thrift keeps up about his Country gear, — Mask 167
Trinity ms 'thrift', 'thirst' written in margin
To life so friendly, or so cool to thirst. — Mask 678

Thirsted
Still as they thirsted scoop the brimming stream; — Par Lost 4.336

Thirsty
Or wet the thirstie Earth with falling showers, — Par Lost 5.190
And here to every thirsty wanderer, — Mask 524
Trinity ms 'thirstie'
Bridgewater ms 'thirstie'
1637 'thirstie'
They pass through Baca's *thirstie* Vale, — Psalm 84, 21

Thirty
Notorious murder on those thirty men — Samson 1186
Appointed to await me thirty spies, — Samson 1197
His thirty Armes along the indented Meads, — Vacation 94

This
That to the highth of this great Argument — Par Lost 1.24
Who from the terrour of this Arm so late — Par Lost 1.113
This downfall; since by Fate the strength of Gods — Par Lost 1.116
And this Empyreal substance cannot fail, — Par Lost 1.117
Since through experience of this great event — Par Lost 1.118
Hath lost us Heav'n, and all this mighty Host — Par Lost 1.136
Have left us this our spirit and strength intire — Par Lost 1.146
Doing or Suffering: but of this be sure, — Par Lost 1.158
The fiery Surge, that from the Precipice — Par Lost 1.173
ms 'This fiery'
How overcome this dire Calamity, — Par Lost 1.189
Is this the Region, this the Soil, the Clime, — Par Lost 1.242
Said then the lost Arch-Angel, this the seat — Par Lost 1.243
That we must change for Heav'n, this mournful gloom — Par Lost 1.244
In this unhappy Mansion, or once more — Par Lost 1.268
If such astonishment as this can sieze — Par Lost 1.317
Eternal spirits; or have ye chos'n this place — Par Lost 1.318
Or in this abject posture have ye sworn — Par Lost 1.322
Transfix us to the bottom of this Gulfe. — Par Lost 1.329
As this place testifies, and this dire change — Par Lost 1.625
For this Infernal Pit shall never hold — Par Lost 1.657
Erring; for he with this rebellious rout — Par Lost 1.747
I give not Heav'n for lost. From this descent — Par Lost 2.14
Hath bin achievd of merit, yet this loss — Par Lost 2.21
Will covet more. With this advantage then — Par Lost 2.35
Accept this dark opprobrious Den of shame, — Par Lost 2.58
In this abhorred deep to utter woe; — Par Lost 2.87
To nothing this essential, happier farr — Par Lost 2.97
On this side nothing; and by proof we feel — Par Lost 2.101
Though full of pain, this intellectual being, — Par Lost 2.147
Let this be good, whether our angry Foe — Par Lost 2.152
What can we suffer worse? is this then worst, — Par Lost 2.163
The Deep to shelter us? this Hell then seem'd — Par Lost 2.167
Her stores were open'd, and this Firmament — Par Lost 2.175
Ages of hopeless end; this would be worse. — Par Lost 2.186
That so ordains: this was at first resolv'd, — Par Lost 2.201
The sentence of thir Conquerour: This is now — Par Lost 2.208
This horror will grow milde, this darkness light, — Par Lost 2.220
Our servile offerings. This must be our task — Par Lost 2.246
In Heav'n this our delight; how wearisom — Par Lost 2.247
Live to our selves, though in this vast recess, — Par Lost 2.254
Through labour and indurance. This deep world — Par Lost 2.262
Imitate when we please? This Desart soile — Par Lost 2.270
To found this nether Empire, which might rise — Par Lost 2.296
This place our dungeon, not our safe retreat — Par Lost 2.317
Of some new Race call'd *Man*, about this time — Par Lost 2.348
In his own strength, this place may lye expos'd — Par Lost 2.360
Abolish his own works. This would surpass — Par Lost 2.370
Faded so soon. Advise if this be worth — Par Lost 2.376
Purge off this gloom; the soft delicious Air, — Par Lost 2.400
In search of this new world, whom shall we find — Par Lost 2.403
This said, he sat; and expectation held — Par Lost 2.417
Our prison strong, this huge convex of Fire, — Par Lost 2.434
But I should ill become this Throne, O Peers, — Par Lost 2.445
And this Imperial Sov'ranty, adorn'd — Par Lost 2.446
Of this ill Mansion: intermit no watch — Par Lost 2.462
Deliverance for us all: this enterprize — Par Lost 2.465
The irksom hours, till this great Chief return. — Par Lost 2.527
1667 'his'
Beyond this flood a frozen Continent — Par Lost 2.587
They ferry over this *Lethean* Sound — Par Lost 2.604
Th' undaunted Fiend what this might be admir'd, — Par Lost 2.677
Thy lingring, or with one stroke of this Dart — Par Lost 2.702
In this infernal Vaile first met thou call'st — Par Lost 2.742
Into this Deep, and in the general fall — Par Lost 2.773
I also; at which time this powerful Key — Par Lost 2.774
At last this odious offspring whom thou seest — Par Lost 2.781
From out this dark and dismal house of pain, — Par Lost 2.823
This uncouth errand sole, and one for all — Par Lost 2.827
Might hap to move new broiles: Be this or aught — Par Lost 2.837
Then this more secret now design'd, I haste — Par Lost 2.838
To know, and this once known, shall soon return, — Par Lost 2.839
The key of this infernal Pit by due, — Par Lost 2.850
Into this gloom of *Tartarus* profound, — Par Lost 2.858
Chance governs all. Into this wilde Abyss, — Par Lost 2.910
Into this wild Abyss the warie fiend — Par Lost 2.917
Som Capital City; or less then if this frame — Par Lost 2.924

This(*cont*)

Ten thousand fadom deep, and to this hour	Par Lost 2.934
And Spirits of this nethermost Abyss,	Par Lost 2.969
Wandring this darksome Desart, as my way,	Par Lost 2.973
I travel this profound, direct my course;	Par Lost 2.980
Of this frail World; by which the Spirits perverse	Par Lost 2.1030
This pendant world, in bigness as a Starr	Par Lost 2.1052
Coasting the wall of Heav'n on this side Night	Par Lost 3.71
On the bare outside of this World, that seem'd	Par Lost 3.74
This my long sufferance and my day of grace	Par Lost 3.198
Thy bosom, and this glorie next to thee	Par Lost 3.239
All Heav'n, what this might mean, and whither tend	Par Lost 3.272
With thee thy Manhood also to this Throne;	Par Lost 3.314
Adore him, who to compass all this dies,	Par Lost 3.342
Of this round World, whose first convex divides	Par Lost 3.419
So on this windie Sea of Land, the Fiend	Par Lost 3.440
Alone, for other Creature in this place	Par Lost 3.442
Or happiness in this or th' other life;	Par Lost 3.450
All this dark Globe the Fiend found as he pass'd,	Par Lost 3.498
And waking cri'd, *This is the Gate of Heav'n*	Par Lost 3.515
1667 'This'	
Of all this World at once. As when a Scout	Par Lost 3.543
At sight of all this World beheld so faire.	Par Lost 3.554
To visit oft this new Creation round;	Par Lost 3.661
Created this new happie Race of Men	Par Lost 3.679
This worlds material mould, came to a heap:	Par Lost 3.709
And this Ethereal quintessence of Heav'n	Par Lost 3.716
The rest in circuit walles this Universe.	Par Lost 3.721
Of this new World; at whose sight all the Starrs	Par Lost 4.34
This knows my punisher; therefore as farr	Par Lost 4.103
Mankind created, and for him this World.	Par Lost 4.107
As Man ere long, and this new World shall know.	Par Lost 4.113
So clomb this first grand Thief into Gods Fould:	Par Lost 4.192
Dwelt in *Telassar:* in this pleasant soile	Par Lost 4.214
Imbround the noontide Bowrs: Thus was this place,	Par Lost 4.246
Castalian Spring, might with this Paradise	Par Lost 4.274
Mount *Amara*, though this by som suppos'd	Par Lost 4.281
From this *Assyrian* Garden, where the Fiend	Par Lost 4.285
Long to continue, and this high seat your Heav'n	Par Lost 4.371
Like this fair Paradise, your sense, yet such	Par Lost 4.379
Thank him who puts me loath to this revenge	Par Lost 4.386
By conquering this new World, compels me now	Par Lost 4.391
That made us, and for us this ample World	Par Lost 4.413
In all this happiness, who at his hand	Par Lost 4.417
This one, this easie charge, of all the Trees	Par Lost 4.421
This Garden, and no corner leave unspi'd;	Par Lost 4.529
Charge and strict watch that to this happie Place	Par Lost 4.562
This day at highth of Noon came to my Spheare	Par Lost 4.564
See farr and wide: in at this Gate none pass	Par Lost 4.579
Diurnal, or this less volubil Earth	Par Lost 4.594
When first on this delightful Land he spreads	Par Lost 4.643
With this her solemn Bird and this fair Moon,	Par Lost 4.648
On this delightful land, nor herb, fruit, floure,	Par Lost 4.652
With this her solemn Bird, nor walk by Moon,	Par Lost 4.655
This glorious sight, when sleep hath shut all eyes?	Par Lost 4.658
Ordaind by thee, and this delicious place	Par Lost 4.729
This said unanimous, and other Rites	Par Lost 4.736
Half way up Hill this vast Sublunar Vault,	Par Lost 4.777
Search through this Garden, leave unsearcht no nook,	Par Lost 4.789
This Eevning from the Sun's decline arriv'd	Par Lost 4.792
This place inviolable, and these from harm.	Par Lost 4.843
Hasting this way, and now by glimps discerne	Par Lost 4.867
To question thy bold entrance on this place;	Par Lost 4.882
And such I held thee; but this question askt	Par Lost 4.887
Dole with delight, which in this place I sought;	Par Lost 4.894
To thy deserted host this cause of flight,	Par Lost 4.922
This new created World, whereof in Hell	Par Lost 4.937
Was this your discipline and faith ingag'd,	Par Lost 4.954
Flie thither whence thou fledst: if from this houre	Par Lost 4.963
In this commotion, but the Starrie Cope	Par Lost 4.992
With violence of this conflict, had not soon	Par Lost 4.995
Thy face, and Morn return'd, for I this Night,	Par Lost 5.30
Such night till this I never pass'd, have dream'd,	Par Lost 5.31
Knew never till this irksom night; methought	Par Lost 5.35
This said he paus'd not, but with ventrous Arme	Par Lost 5.64
Taste this, and be henceforth among the Gods	Par Lost 5.77
To this high exaltation; suddenly	Par Lost 5.90
To find this but a dream! Thus *Eve* her Night	Par Lost 5.93
The trouble of thy thoughts this night in sleep	Par Lost 5.96
This uncouth dream, of evil sprung I fear;	Par Lost 5.98
Of our last Eevnings talk, in this thy dream,	Par Lost 5.115
Almightie, thine this universal Frame,	Par Lost 5.154
Thou Sun, of this great World both Eye and Soule,	Par Lost 5.171
This night the human pair, how he designes	Par Lost 5.227
Go therefore, half this day as friend with friend	Par Lost 5.229
But by deceit and lies; this let him know,	Par Lost 5.243
Comes this way moving; seems another Morn	Par Lost 5.310
This day to be our Guest. But goe with speed,	Par Lost 5.313
This spacious ground, in yonder shadie Bowre	Par Lost 5.367
To sit and taste, till this meridian heat	Par Lost 5.369
Have heap'd this Table. Rais'd of grassie terf	Par Lost 5.391
To spiritual Natures; only this I know,	Par Lost 5.402
Given him by this great Conference to know	Par Lost 5.454
Thy favour, in this honour done to man,	Par Lost 5.462
Your fill what happiness this happie state	Par Lost 5.504
This was that caution giv'n thee; be advis'd.	Par Lost 5.523
To love or not; in this we stand or fall:	Par Lost 5.540
This is dispenc't, and what surmounts the reach	Par Lost 5.571

This(*cont*)

As yet this world was not, and *Chaos* wilde	Par Lost 5.577
This day I have begot whom I declare	Par Lost 5.603
My onely Son, and on this holy Hill	Par Lost 5.604
Then all this globous Earth in Plain out spred,	Par Lost 5.649
What doubtful may ensue, more in this place	Par Lost 5.682
Let us advise, and to this hazard draw	Par Lost 5.729
This our high place, our Sanctuarie, our Hill.	Par Lost 5.732
Then what this Garden is to all the Earth,	Par Lost 5.752
Of King anointed, for whom all this haste	Par Lost 5.777
This onely to consult how we may best	Par Lost 5.779
Our minds and teach us to cast off this Yoke?	Par Lost 5.786
Erre not, much less for this to be our Lord,	Par Lost 5.799
Returns our own. Cease then this impious rage,	Par Lost 5.845
When this creation was? rememberst thou	Par Lost 5.857
Of this our native Heav'n, Ethereal Sons.	Par Lost 5.863
Beseeching or besieging. This report,	Par Lost 5.869
In this perfidious fraud, contagion spred	Par Lost 5.880
Then violence: for this was all thy care	Par Lost 6.35
Remains thee, aided by this host of friends,	Par Lost 6.38
Tenfold the length of this terrene: at last	Par Lost 6.78
His daring foe, at this prevention more	Par Lost 6.129
Of this right hand provok't, since first that tongue	Par Lost 6.154
Destruction to the rest: this pause between	Par Lost 6.162
As both thir deeds compar'd this day shall prove.	Par Lost 6.170
Them whom he governs. This is servitude,	Par Lost 6.178
This greeting on thy impious Crest receive.	Par Lost 6.188
Ere this avenging Sword begin thy doome,	Par Lost 6.278
Or turn this Heav'n it self into the Hell	Par Lost 6.291
Since now we find this our Empyreal form	Par Lost 6.433
Of this Ethereous mould whereon we stand,	Par Lost 6.473
This continent of spacious Heav'n, adornd	Par Lost 6.474
Part hidd'n veins diggd up (nor hath this Earth	Par Lost 6.516
This day, fear not his flight; so thick a Cloud	Par Lost 6.539
Born eevn or high, for this day will pour down,	Par Lost 6.544
Not understood, this gift they have besides,	Par Lost 6.626
(For Earth hath this variety from Heav'n	Par Lost 6.640
To this uproar; horrid confusion heapt	Par Lost 6.668
This tumult, and permitted all, advis'd:	Par Lost 6.674
Of ending this great Warr, since none but Thou	Par Lost 6.702
And this perverse Commotion governd thus,	Par Lost 6.706
As is most just; this I my Glorie account,	Par Lost 6.726
This saw his hapless Foes but stood obdur'd,	Par Lost 6.785
Ye Angels arm'd, this day from Battel rest;	Par Lost 6.802
Invincibly; but of this cursed crew	Par Lost 6.806
Number to this dayes work is not ordain'd	Par Lost 6.809
Least from this flying Steed unrein'd, (as once	Par Lost 7.17
What neerer might concern him, how this World	Par Lost 7.62
Farr differing from this World, thou hast reveal'd	Par Lost 7.71
How first began this Heav'n which we behold	Par Lost 7.86
Innumerable, and this which yeelds or fills	Par Lost 7.88
Imbracing round this florid Earth, what cause	Par Lost 7.90
This also thy request with caution askt	Par Lost 7.111
This inaccessible high strength, the seat	Par Lost 7.141
Though wide, and this high Temple to frequent	Par Lost 7.148
This I perform, speak thou, and be it don:	Par Lost 7.164
This Universe, and all created things:	Par Lost 7.227
This be thy just Circumference, O World.	Par Lost 7.231
Of this great Round: partition firm and sure,	Par Lost 7.267
This said, he formd thee, *Adam*, thee O Man	Par Lost 7.524
He brought thee into this delicious Grove,	Par Lost 7.537
This Garden, planted with the Trees of God,	Par Lost 7.538
Thence to behold this new created World	Par Lost 7.554
Witness this new-made World, another Heav'n	Par Lost 7.617
How first this World and face of things began,	Par Lost 7.636
This friendly condescention to relate	Par Lost 8.9
When I behold this goodly Frame, this World	Par Lost 8.15
Thir magnitudes, this Earth a spot, a graine,	Par Lost 8.17
Round this opacous Earth, this punctual spot,	Par Lost 8.23
Greater so manifold to this one use,	Par Lost 8.29
This to attain, whether Heav'n move or Earth,	Par Lost 8.70
Alreadie by thy reasoning this I guess,	Par Lost 8.85
By Numbers that have name. But this I urge,	Par Lost 8.114
This Earth? reciprocal, if Land be there,	Par Lost 8.144
Down to this habitable, which returnes	Par Lost 8.157
In what he gives to thee, this Paradise	Par Lost 8.171
Therefore from this high pitch let us descend	Par Lost 8.198
This happie Light, when answer none return'd,	Par Lost 8.285
Said mildely, Author of all this thou seest	Par Lost 8.317
This Paradise I give thee, count it thine	Par Lost 8.319
From that day mortal, and this happie State	Par Lost 8.331
Adore thee, Author of this Universe,	Par Lost 8.360
And all this good to man, for whose well being	Par Lost 8.361
What thinkst thou then of mee, and this my State,	Par Lost 8.403
This answer from the gratious voice Divine.	Par Lost 8.436
This turn hath made amends; thou hast fulfill'd	Par Lost 8.491
Giver of all things faire, but fairest this	Par Lost 8.493
Extracted; for this cause he shall forgoe	Par Lost 8.497
That brought into this World a world of woe,	Par Lost 9.11
Since first this Subject for Heroic Song	Par Lost 9.25
For whom all this was made, all this will soon	Par Lost 9.132
Magnificent this World, and Earth his seat,	Par Lost 9.153
This essence to incarnate and imbrute,	Par Lost 9.166
Provokes my envie, this new Favorite	Par Lost 9.175
Of Heav'n, this Man of Clay, Son of despite,	Par Lost 9.176
This Garden, still to tend Plant, Herb and Flour,	Par Lost 9.206
The Woodbine round this Arbour, or direct	Par Lost 9.216
Food of the mind, or this sweet intercourse	Par Lost 9.238

This(*cont*)

Or this, or worse, leave not the faithful side	Par Lost 9.265
If this be our condition, thus to dwell	Par Lost 9.322
Fraile is our happiness, if this be so,	Par Lost 9.340
This Flourie Plat, the sweet recess of *Eve*	Par Lost 9.456
Hee with *Olympias*, this with her who bore	Par Lost 9.509
In this enclosure wild, these Beasts among,	Par Lost 9.543
What may this mean? Language of Man pronounc't	Par Lost 9.553
Redouble then this miracle, and say,	Par Lost 9.562
Empress of this fair World, resplendent *Eve*,	Par Lost 9.568
Wanted not long, though to this shape retain'd.	Par Lost 9.601
But of this Tree we may not taste nor touch;	Par Lost 9.651
But of the Fruit of this fair Tree amidst	Par Lost 9.661
Queen of this Universe, doe not believe	Par Lost 9.684
Why then was this forbid? Why but to awe,	Par Lost 9.703
Though threat'nd, which no worse then this can bring.	Par Lost 9.715
I question it, for this fair Earth I see,	Par Lost 9.720
Knowledge of Good and Evil in this Tree,	Par Lost 9.723
What can your knowledge hurt him, or this Tree	Par Lost 9.727
Causes import your need of this fair Fruit.	Par Lost 9.731
Of this fair Fruit, our doom is, we shall die.	Par Lost 9.763
This intellectual food, for beasts reserv'd?	Par Lost 9.768
Under this ignorance of good and Evil,	Par Lost 9.774
Here grows the Cure of all, this Fruit Divine,	Par Lost 9.776
This may be well: but what if God have seen,	Par Lost 9.826
This Tree is not as we are told, a Tree	Par Lost 9.863
This day affords, declaring thee resolvd,	Par Lost 9.968
If any be, of tasting this fair Fruit,	Par Lost 9.972
This happie trial of thy Love, which else	Par Lost 9.975
This my attempt, I would sustain alone	Par Lost 9.978
Hath toucht my sense, flat seems to this, and harsh.	Par Lost 9.987
Yeild thee, so well this day thou hast purvey'd.	Par Lost 9.1021
From this delightful Fruit, nor known till now	Par Lost 9.1023
For this one Tree had bin forbidden ten.	Par Lost 9.1026
Then ever, bountie of this vertuous Tree.	Par Lost 9.1033
Bad Fruit of Knowledge, if this be to know,	Par Lost 9.1073
Will dazle now this earthly, with thir blaze	Par Lost 9.1083
Those middle parts, that this new commer, Shame,	Par Lost 9.1097
But such as at this day to *Indians* known	Par Lost 9.1102
Desire of wandring this unhappie Morn,	Par Lost 9.1136
Is this the Love, is this the recompence	Par Lost 9.1163
That lay in wait; beyond this had bin force,	Par Lost 9.1173
For Man, for of his state by this they knew,	Par Lost 10.19
When first this Tempter cross'd the Gulf from Hell.	Par Lost 10.39
Before thee; and not repenting, this obtaine	Par Lost 10.75
O Heav'n! in evil strait this day I stand	Par Lost 10.125
This Woman whom thou mad'st to be my help,	Par Lost 10.137
Say Woman, what is this which thou hast done?	Par Lost 10.158
Because thou hast done this, thou art accurst	Par Lost 10.175
So spake this Oracle, then verifi'd	Par Lost 10.182
Ere this he had return'd, with fury driv'n	Par Lost 10.240
By his Avengers, since no place like this	Par Lost 10.241
Beyond this Deep; whatever drawes me on,	Par Lost 10.245
Stay his return perhaps over this Gulfe	Par Lost 10.253
Over this Maine from Hell to that new World	Par Lost 10.257
By this new felt attraction and instinct.	Par Lost 10.263
Immovable of this now fenceless world	Par Lost 10.303
Of this round World: with Pinns of Adamant	Par Lost 10.318
And of this World, and on the left hand Hell	Par Lost 10.322
Of this new wondrous Pontifice, unhop't	Par Lost 10.348
That I must after thee with this thy Son;	Par Lost 10.363
Nor this unvoyageable Gulf obscure	Par Lost 10.366
With this portentous Bridge the dark Abyss.	Par Lost 10.371
Thine now is all this World, thy vertue hath won	Par Lost 10.372
As Battel hath adjudg'd, from this new World	Par Lost 10.377
Mine with this glorious Work, and made one Realm	Par Lost 10.391
Hell and this World, one Realm, one Continent	Par Lost 10.392
You two this way, among these numerous Orbs	Par Lost 10.397
My hold of this new Kingdom all depends,	Par Lost 10.406
Triumphant out of this infernal Pit	Par Lost 10.464
A Grove hard by, sprung up with this thir change,	Par Lost 10.548
This more delusive, not the touch, but taste	Par Lost 10.563
This annual humbling certain number'd days,	Par Lost 10.576
To stuff this Maw, this vast unhide-bound Corps.	Par Lost 10.601
This said, they both betook them several wayes,	Par Lost 10.610
O miserable of happie! is this the end	Par Lost 10.720
Of this new glorious World, and mee so late	Par Lost 10.721
My own deservings; but this will not serve;	Par Lost 10.727
For this we may thank *Adam;* but his thanks	Par Lost 10.736
In this delicious Garden? as my Will	Par Lost 10.746
Fixd on this day? why do I overlive,	Par Lost 10.773
With this corporeal Clod; then in the Grave,	Par Lost 10.786
All of me then shall die: let this appease	Par Lost 10.792
From this day onward, which I feel begun	Par Lost 10.811
This noveltie on Earth, this fair defect	Par Lost 10.891
Mankind? this mischief had not then befall'n,	Par Lost 10.895
And straight conjunction with this Sex: for either	Par Lost 10.898
Thy counsel in this uttermost distress,	Par Lost 10.920
Thy hatred for this miserie befall'n,	Par Lost 10.928
On me, sole cause to thee of all this woe,	Par Lost 10.935
Since this days Death denounc't, if ought I see,	Par Lost 10.962
Into this cursed World a woful Race,	Par Lost 10.984
Against us this deceit: to crush his head	Par Lost 10.1035
To shew us in this Mountain, while the Winds	Par Lost 10.1065
Our Limbs benumm'd, ere this diurnal Starr	Par Lost 10.1069
To pass commodiously this life, sustain'd	Par Lost 10.1083
And Prayers, which in this Golden Censer, mixt	Par Lost 11.24
This other serv'd but to eternize woe;	Par Lost 11.60

This(*cont*)

Michael, this my behest have thou in charge,	Par Lost 11.99
Hard to belief may seem; yet this will Prayer,	Par Lost 11.146
Who knows, or more then this, that we are dust,	Par Lost 11.199
Why else this double object in our sight	Par Lost 11.201
He err'd not, for by this the heav'nly Bands	Par Lost 11.208
But longer in this Paradise to dwell	Par Lost 11.259
Into a lower World, to this obscure	Par Lost 11.283
Adam by this from the cold sudden damp	Par Lost 11.293
Departure from this happy place, our sweet	Par Lost 11.303
This most afflicts me, that departing hence,	Par Lost 11.315
On this Mount he appeerd, under this Tree	Par Lost 11.320
I heard, here with him at this Fountain talk'd:	Par Lost 11.322
Not this Rock onely; his Omnipresence fills	Par Lost 11.336
Of Paradise or *Eden:* this had been	Par Lost 11.342
But this praeeminence thou hast lost, brought down	Par Lost 11.347
This Hill; let *Eve* (for I have drencht her eyes)	Par Lost 11.367
But have I now seen Death? Is this the way	Par Lost 11.462
This is old age; but then thou must outlive	Par Lost 11.538
Fairest and easiest of this combrous charge,	Par Lost 11.549
Much better seems this Vision, and more hope	Par Lost 11.599
Above the highest Hills: then shall this Mount	Par Lost 11.829
At this last sight, assur'd that Man shall live	Par Lost 11.872
This second sours of Men, while yet but few;	Par Lost 12.13
But this Usurper his encroachment proud	Par Lost 12.72
Don to his Father, heard this heavie curse,	Par Lost 12.103
Thus will this latter, as the former World,	Par Lost 12.105
Him on this side *Euphrates* yet residing,	Par Lost 12.114
This ponder, that all Nations of the Earth	Par Lost 12.147
Plainlier shall be reveald. This Patriarch blest,	Par Lost 12.151
The River-dragon tam'd at length submits 1667 'This'	Par Lost 12.191
This also shall they gain by thir delay	Par Lost 12.223
This yet I apprehend not, why to those	Par Lost 12.280
Of *David* (so I name this King) shall rise	Par Lost 12.326
In thee and in thy Seed: nor can this be,	Par Lost 12.395
For this he shall live hated, be blasphem'd,	Par Lost 12.411
In this his satisfaction; so he dies,	Par Lost 12.419
By Faith not void of workes: this God-like act	Par Lost 12.427
In sin for ever lost from life; this act	Par Lost 12.429
When this worlds disolution shall be ripe,	Par Lost 12.459
Then this of *Eden*, and far happier daies.	Par Lost 12.465
That all this good of evil shall produce,	Par Lost 12.470
Measur'd this transient World, the Race of time,	Par Lost 12.554
Of knowledge, what this Vessel can containe;	Par Lost 12.559
Taught this by his example whom I now	Par Lost 12.572
This having learnt, thou hast attaind the summe	Par Lost 12.575
And all the riches of this World enjoydst,	Par Lost 12.580
To leave this Paradise, but shalt possess	Par Lost 12.586
Let us descend now therefore from this top	Par Lost 12.588
This further consolation yet secure	Par Lost 12.620
Thou Spirit who ledst this glorious Eremite	Par Reg 1.8
O ancient Powers of Air and this wide world,	Par Reg 1.44
This our old Conquest, then remember Hell	Par Reg 1.46
This Universe we have possest, and rul'd	Par Reg 1.49
This dreaded time have compast, wherein we	Par Reg 1.58
In this fair Empire won of Earth and Air;	Par Reg 1.63
For this ill news I bring, the Womans seed	Par Reg 1.64
Destin'd to this, is late of woman born,	Par Reg 1.65
This is my Son belov'd, in him am pleas'd.	Par Reg 1.85
Who this is we must learn, for man he seems	Par Reg 1.91
And management of this main enterprize	Par Reg 1.112
Where he might likeliest find this new-declar'd,	Par Reg 1.121
This man of men, attested Son of God,	Par Reg 1.122
Gabriel this day by proof thou shalt behold,	Par Reg 1.130
O're-shadow her: this man born and now up-grown,	Par Reg 1.140
This perfect Man, by merit call'd my Son,	Par Reg 1.166
Sung with the voice, and this the argument.	Par Reg 1.172
And was admir'd by all, yet this not all	Par Reg 1.214
This having heard, strait I again revolv'd	Par Reg 1.259
I am; this chiefly, that my way must lie	Par Reg 1.263
Into this Wilderness, to what intent	Par Reg 1.291
Sir, what ill chance hath brought thee to this place	Par Reg 1.321
Who dwell this wild, constrain'd by want, come forth	Par Reg 1.331
Wandred this barren waste, the same I now:	Par Reg 1.354
Large liberty to round this Globe of Earth,	Par Reg 1.365
This wounds me most (what can it less) that Man,	Par Reg 1.404
But this thy glory shall be soon retrench'd;	Par Reg 1.454
Dissembl'd, and this Answer smooth return'd.	Par Reg 1.467
On this side the broad lake *Genezaret*,	Par Reg 2.23
Let us be glad of this, and all our fears	Par Reg 2.53
A sword shall pierce, this is my favour'd lot,	Par Reg 2.91
However to this Man inferior far,	Par Reg 2.135
Though of this Age the wonder and the fame,	Par Reg 2.209
Where will this end? four times ten days I have pass'd	Par Reg 2.245
Wandring this woody maze, and humane food	Par Reg 2.246
Without this bodies wasting, I content me,	Par Reg 2.256
In this wild solitude so long should bide	Par Reg 2.304
As story tells, have trod this Wilderness;	Par Reg 2.307
Command a Table in this Wilderness,	Par Reg 2.384
Why shouldst thou then obtrude this diligence,	Par Reg 2.387
And rather opportunely in this place	Par Reg 2.396
May also in this poverty as soon	Par Reg 2.451
That for the Publick all this weight he bears.	Par Reg 2.465
Is yet more Kingly, this attracts the Soul,	Par Reg 2.476
This is true glory and renown, when God	Par Reg 3.60
To this high mountain top the Tempter brought	Par Reg 3.265
All this fair sight; thy Kingdom though foretold	Par Reg 3.351

This(*cont*)

This offer sets before thee to deliver.	Par Reg 3.380
But whence to thee this zeal, where was it then	Par Reg 3.407
This far his over-match, who self deceiv'd	Par Reg 4.7
This Emperour hath no Son, and now is old,	Par Reg 4.90
Might'st thou expel this monster from his Throne	Par Reg 4.100
Nor doth this grandeur and majestic show	Par Reg 4.110
Means there shall be to this, but what the means,	Par Reg 4.152
No trifle; yet with this reserve, not else,	Par Reg 4.165
On this condition, if thou wilt fall down,	Par Reg 4.166
For this attempt bolder then that on *Eve*,	Par Reg 4.180
God of this world invok't and world beneath;	Par Reg 4.203
The Kingdoms of this world; I shall no more	Par Reg 4.210
Look once more e're we leave this specular Mount	Par Reg 4.236
To know this only, that he nothing knew;	Par Reg 4.294
What dost thou in this World? the Wilderness	Par Reg 4.372
Nor yet amidst this joy and brightest morn	Par Reg 4.439
Of this fair change, and to our Saviour came,	Par Reg 4.442
Rather by this his last affront resolv'd,	Par Reg 4.444
This Tempest at this Desert most was bent;	Par Reg 4.465
If thou observe not this, be sure to find,	Par Reg 4.477
Whereof this ominous night that clos'd thee round,	Par Reg 4.481
And follow'd thee still on to this wast wild;	Par Reg 4.523
Under his feet: for proof, e're this thou feel'st	Par Reg 4.621
By this repulse receiv'd, and hold'st in Hell	Par Reg 4.623
This day a solemn Feast the people hold	Samson 12
Laborious works, unwillingly this rest	Samson 14
This unfrequented place to find some ease,	Samson 17
With this Heav'n-gifted strength? O glorious strength	Samson 36
Ask for this great Deliverer now, and find him	Samson 40
Who this high gift of strength committed to me,	Samson 47
The tread of many feet stearing this way;	Samson 111
Chor. This, this is he; softly a while,	Samson 115
Or do my eyes misrepresent? Can this be hee,	Samson 124
In *Ramath-lechi* famous to this day:	Samson 145
This with the other should, at least, have paird,	Samson 208
They had by this possess'd the Towers of *Gath*,	Samson 266
Have prompted this Heroic *Nazarite*,	Samson 318
Though in this uncouth place; if old respect,	Samson 333
Man. O miserable change! is this the man,	Samson 340
For this did the Angel twice descend? for this	Samson 361
This well I knew, nor was at all surpris'd,	Samson 381
And Rivals? In this other was there found	Samson 387
These rags, this grinding, is not yet so base	Samson 415
True slavery, and that blindness worse then this,	Samson 418
I state not that; this I am sure; our Foes	Samson 424
This day the *Philistines* a popular Feast	Samson 434
That I this honour, I this pomp have brought	Samson 449
This only hope relieves me, that the strife	Samson 460
Man. With cause this hope relieves thee, and these words	Samson 472
Lie in this miserable loathsom plight	Samson 480
About thy ransom: well they may by this	Samson 483
Sam. But what avail'd this temperance, not compleat	Samson 558
And I perswade me so; why else this strength	Samson 586
This one prayer yet remains, might I be heard,	Samson 649
So deal not with this once thy glorious Champion,	Samson 705
Behold him in this state calamitous, and turn	Samson 708
But who is this, what thing of Sea or Land?	Samson 710
Comes this way sailing	Samson 713
By this appears: I gave, thou say'st, th' example,	Samson 822
From forth this loathsom prison-house, to abide	Samson 922
This Gaol I count the house of Liberty	Samson 949
At this who ever envies or repines	Samson 995
Thir nuptials, nor this last so trecherously	Samson 1023
Chor. But this another kind of tempest brings.	Samson 1063
The sumptuous *Dalila* floating this way:	Samson 1072
Incredible to me, in this displeas'd,	Samson 1084
At my Nativity this strength, diffus'd	Samson 1141
Th' unworthier they; whence to this day they serve.	Samson 1216
Sam. Cam'st thou for this, vain boaster, to survey me,	Samson 1227
Har. This insolence other kind of answer fits.	Samson 1236
This Idols day hath bin to thee no day of rest,	Samson 1297
For I descry this way	Samson 1301
This day to *Dagon* is a solemn Feast,	Samson 1311
To honour this great Feast, and great Assembly;	Samson 1315
Off. This answer, be assur'd, will not content them.	Samson 1322
Off. Regard thy self, this will offend them highly.	Samson 1333
Brooks no delay: is this thy resolution?	Samson 1344
Off. I am sorry what this stoutness will produce.	Samson 1346
Sam. Shall I abuse this Consecrated gift	Samson 1354
Chor. Yet with this strength thou serv'st the *Philistines*,	Samson 1363
I with this Messenger will go along,	Samson 1384
This day will be remarkable in my life	Samson 1388
Off. *Samson*, this second message from our Lords	Samson 1391
Yet this be sure, in nothing to comply	Samson 1408
By this compliance thou wilt win the Lords	Samson 1411
This evil on the *Philistines* is fall'n,	Samson 1523
The sight of this so horrid spectacle	Samson 1542
What windy joy this day had I conceiv'd	Samson 1574
Mess. Occasions drew me early to this City,	Samson 1596
When all abroad was rumour'd that this day	Samson 1600
This utter'd, straining all his nerves he bow'd,	Samson 1646
Of this but each *Philistian* City round	Samson 1655
Met from all parts to solemnize this Feast.	Samson 1656
Find courage to lay hold on this occasion,	Samson 1716
And which is best and happiest yet, all this	Samson 1718
Of true experience from this great event	Samson 1756
Above the smoak and stirr of this dim spot,	Mask 5

This(*cont*)

Confin'd, and pester'd in this pin-fold here,	Mask 7
After this mortal change, to her true Servants	Mask 10
With the rank vapours of this Sin-worn mould.	Mask 17
And weild their little tridents, but this Ile	Mask 27
And all this tract that fronts the falling Sun	Mask 30
Lies through the perplex't paths of this drear Wood,	Mask 37
This Nymph that gaz'd upon his clustring locks,	Mask 54
At last betakes him to this ominous Wood,	Mask 61
Chances to passe through this adventrous glade,	Mask 79
That to the service of this house belongs,	Mask 85
And in this office of his Mountain watch,	Mask 89
Of this occasion. But I hear the tread	Mask 91
Of som chast footing neer about this ground.	Mask 146
Hath met the vertue of this Magick dust,	Mask 165
This way the noise was, if mine ear be true,	Mask 170
In the blind mazes of this tangl'd Wood?	Mask 181
Trinity ms 'this' ←'these'	
With this long way, resolving here to lodge	Mask 183
This is the place, as well as I may guess,	Mask 201
line not in Bridgewater ms	
What might this be? A thousand fantasies	Mask 205
line not in Bridgewater ms	
And casts a gleam over this tufted Grove.	Mask 225
line not in Bridgewater ms	
To touch the prosperous growth of this tall Wood.	Mask 270
La. Dim darknes, and this leavy Labyrinth.	Mask 278
Co. Due west it rises from this shrubby point.	Mask 306
Dingle, or bushy dell of this wilde Wood,	Mask 312
Less warranted then this, or less secure	Mask 327
Eie me blest Providence, and square my triall	Mask 329
Trinity ms 'my' ←'this'	
In this close dungeon of innumerous bowes.	Mask 349
From the chill dew, amongst rude burrs and thistles?	Mask 352
Trinity ms 'amoungst rude burrs & thistles' ←'in this surrounding wilde' ←'in this dead solitude'	
Uninjur'd in this wilde surrounding wast.	Mask 403
How couldst thou find this dark sequester'd nook?	Mask 500
To this my errand, and the care it brought.	Mask 506
Within the navil of this hideous Wood,	Mask 520
Character'd in the face; this have I learn't	Mask 530
Bridgewater ms 'This'	
That brow this bottom glade, whence night by night	Mask 532
This evening late by then the chewing flocks	Mask 540
But furder know I not. 2. *Bro*. O night and shades,	Mask 580
Trinity ms 'but' ←'and this'	
Alone, and helpless! Is this the confidence	Mask 583
Which erring men call Chance, this I hold firm,	Mask 588
Self-fed, and self-consum'd, if this fail,	Mask 597
May never this just sword be lifted up,	Mask 601
As to make this relation? *Spir*. Care and utmost shifts	Mask 617
Bore a bright golden flowre, but not in this soyl:	Mask 633
line not in Bridgewater ms	
Till now that this extremity compell'd,	Mask 643
But now I find it true; for by this means	Mask 644
And yet came off: if you have this about you	Mask 647
Comus. Nay Lady sit; if I but wave this wand,	Mask 659
Withall thy charms, although this corporal rinde	Mask 664
And first behold this cordial Julep here	Mask 672
Is of such power to stir up joy as this,	Mask 677
This will restore all soon. *La*. 'Twill not false traitor,	Mask 690
Was this the cottage, and the safe abode	Mask 693
In this unhallow'd air, but that this Jugler	Mask 757
More happines then this thy present lot.	Mask 789
line not in Bridgewater ms	
line not in Trinity ms	
Of this pure cause would kindle my rap't spirits	Mask 794
line not in Bridgewater ms	
line not in Trinity ms	
This is meer moral babble, and direct	Mask 807
I must not suffer this, yet 'tis but the lees	Mask 809
But this will cure all streight, one sip of this	Mask 811
In hard besetting need, this will I try	Mask 857
Thus I sprinkle on thy brest	Mask 911
Bridgewater ms 'on this'	
Next this marble venom'd seat	Mask 916
May thy brimmed waves for this	Mask 924
Let us fly this cursed place,	Mask 939
Through this gloomy covert wide,	Mask 945
Where this night are met in state	Mask 948
We shall catch them at their sport,	Mask 953
Bridgewater ms 'this sporte'	
& sacred limits of this blisfull Isle	Mask Tr. ms 10.11
this dusky hollow is a paradise & heaven gates ore my head	Mask Tr. ms 13.44
that lurks by hedge or lane of this dead circuit	Mask Tr. ms 16.40
that lurks by hedge or lane, of this dead circuit	Mask Br. ms 393
Her mansion in this fleshly nook:	Penseroso 92
This this is she	Arcades 5
This this is she alone,	Arcades 17
Who had thought this clime had held	Arcades 24
Gen. Stay gentle Swains, for though in this disguise,	Arcades 26
I know this quest of yours, and free intent	Arcades 34
To further this nights glad solemnity;	Arcades 39
Trinity ms defective here	
Of this fair Wood, and live in Oak'n bowr,	Arcades 45
Over the mount, and all this hallow'd ground,	Arcades 55
To serve the Lady of this place.	Arcades 105
What hard mishap hath doom'd this gentle swain?	Lycidas 92

This(*cont*)
This is the Month, and this the happy morn Nativity 1
To welcom him to this his new abode, Nativity 18
This must not yet be so, Nativity 150
But now begins; for from this happy day Nativity 167
This if thou do he will an off-spring give, Fair Inf 76
For this same small neglect that I have made: Vacation 16
Fly swiftly to this fair Assembly's ears; Vacation 28
She heard them give thee this, that thou should'st still Vacation 65
Your learned hands, can loose this Gordian knot? Vacation 90
To this Horizon is my *Phoebus* bound, Passion 23
Then all this Earthy grosnes quit, On Time 20
This day, but O ere long Circum 26
This rich Marble doth enterr Winchester 1
After this thy travail sore Winchester 49
For he had any time this ten yeers full, Carrier 7
Onely remains this superscription. Another 34
line not in 1658 text
A title page is this! and some in file Sonnet 11, 6
But this is got by casting Pearl to Hoggs; Sonnet 12, 8
For all this wast of wealth, and loss of blood. Sonnet 12, 14
Meekly thou didst resign this earthy load Sonnet 14, 3
when as they journey'd from this dark abode Sonnet 14, Tr. ms 41.07
E're half my days, in this dark world and wide, Sonnet 19, 2
Cyriack, this three years day these eys, though clear Sonnet 22, 1
This thought might lead me through the worlds vain mask Sonnet 22, 13
1694 'this World's'
Dare ye for this adjure the Civill Sword Forcers 5
When they shall read this clearly in your charge Forcers 19
This day; ask of me, and the grant is made; Psalm 2, 16
Hast broke the teeth. This help was from the Lord Psalm 3, 23
Talking like this worlds brood; Psalm 4, 27
Or done this, if wickedness Psalm 7, 8
Judge me Lord, be judge in this Psalm 7, 31
To plant this *lovely* Vine. Psalm 80, 36
And visit this *thy* Vine. Psalm 80, 60
Visit this Vine, which thy right hand Psalm 80, 61
This was a Statute *giv'n of old* Psalm 81, 13
This he a Testimony ordain'd Psalm 81, 17
This *wicked* earth redress, Psalm 82, 26
Lo this man there was born: Psalm 87, 16
This and this man was born in her, Psalm 87, 19
That this man there was born. Psalm 87, 24
This was that gift (if you the truth will have) Prose 4, 3
This is true Liberty when free born men Prose 9, 1
What can be juster in a State then this? Prose 9, 5

Thisbite
And the great *Thisbite* who on fiery wheels Par Reg 2.16

Thistles
Thorns also and Thistles it shall bring thee forth Par Lost 10.203
From the chill dew, amongst rude burrs and thistles? Mask 352
Trinity ms 'amoungst rude burrs & thistles' ←'in this surrounding wilde' ←'in this dead solitude'

Thither
Casts pale and dreadful? Thither let us tend Par Lost 1.183
The Heads and Leaders thither hast where stood Par Lost 1.357
Thither, if but to pry, shall be perhaps Par Lost 1.655
Our first eruption, thither or elsewhere: Par Lost 1.656
The work of Sulphur. Thither wing'd with speed Par Lost 1.674
Thither let us bend all our thoughts, to learn Par Lost 2.354
Thither by harpy-footed Furies hail'd, Par Lost 2.596
With loudest vehemence: thither he plyes, Par Lost 2.954
Possesses lately, thither to arrive Par Lost 2.979
Thither full fraught with mischievous revenge, Par Lost 2.1054
Allur'd his eye: Thither his course he bends Par Lost 3.573
And what I was, whence thither brought, and how. Par Lost 4.452
Pure as th' expanse of Heav'n; I thither went Par Lost 4.456
Thither came *Uriel*, gliding through the Eeven Par Lost 4.555
Incredible how swift, had thither rowl'd Par Lost 4.593
Though thither doomd? Thou wouldst thy self, no doubt, Par Lost 4.890
Flie thither whence thou fledst: if from this houre Par Lost 4.963
A cloudy spot. Down thither prone in flight Par Lost 5.266
For thither he assembl'd all his Train, Par Lost 5.767
Thither to come, and with calumnious Art Par Lost 5.770
Capacious bed of Waters: thither they Par Lost 7.290
Descends, thither with heart and voice and eyes Par Lost 7.513
Thither will send his winged Messengers Par Lost 7.572
My conduct, I can bring thee thither soon. Par Lost 9.630
And know not that I call'd and drew them thither Par Lost 10.629
And thither must return and be no more. Par Lost 11.200
Rustic, of grassie sord; thither anon Par Lost 11.433
No sanctitie, if none be thither brought Par Lost 11.837
Will he convey up thither to sustain Par Lost 12.75
They gladly thither haste, and by a Quire Par Lost 12.366
Guided the Wise Men thither from the East, Par Reg 1.250
Thither he bent his way, determin'd there Par Reg 2.291
And thither will return thee, yet remember Par Reg 4.374
And numbers thither flock, I had no will, Samson 1450
Chor. Best keep together here, lest running thither Samson 1521
Thither shall all the valiant youth resort, Samson 1738
Thither all their bounties bring, Mask 987
line not in Bridgewater ms
Believe me I have thither packt the worst: Vacation 12
Now void, it fitts thy people; thether bend Prose 12, 10

Thitherward
Of dawning light turnd thither-ward in haste Par Lost 3.500
As thitherward endevoring, and upright Par Lost 8.260

Thone
Not that *Nepenthes* which the wife of *Thone*, Mask 675
Trinity ms 'Thone' ←'Thon'

Thorn
Flours of all hue, and without Thorn the Rose: Par Lost 4.256
Once join'd, the contrary she proves, a thorn Samson 1037
When first the White thorn blows; Lycidas 48
Trinity ms 'white thorne'
1673 'White Thorn'
1638 'white-thorn'
Low in a mead of Kine under a Thorn, Prose 13, 1

Thorns
Thorns also and Thistles it shall bring thee forth Par Lost 10.203
1667 'Thornes'
Golden in shew, is but a wreath of thorns, Par Reg 2.459

Thoroughfare
Of easie thorough-fare. Therefore while I Par Lost 10.393

Those
As one great Furnace flam'd, yet from those flames Par Lost 1.62
For those rebellious, here thir Prison ordain'd Par Lost 1.71
ms 'these'
The force of those dire Arms? yet not for those, Par Lost 1.94
Thus answer'd. Leader of those Armies bright, Par Lost 1.272
Over the burning Marle, not like those steps Par Lost 1.296
So numberless were those bad Angels seen Par Lost 1.344
The chief were those who from the Pit of Hell Par Lost 1.381
Of *Baalim* and *Ashtaroth*, those male, Par Lost 1.422
For those the Race of *Israel* oft forsook Par Lost 1.432
ms 'these'
Deserve the precious bane. And here let those Par Lost 1.692
More unexpert, I boast not: them let those Par Lost 2.52
Those thoughts that wander through Eternity, Par Lost 2.148
A refuge from those wounds: or when we lay Par Lost 2.168
What if the breath that kindl'd those grim fires Par Lost 2.170
I laugh, when those who at the Spear are bold Par Lost 2.204
Us here, as with his Golden those in Heav'n. Par Lost 2.328
Pleas'd highly those infernal States, and joy Par Lost 2.387
Of those bright confines, whence with neighbouring Arms Par Lost 2.395
Of those Heav'n-warring Champions could be found Par Lost 2.424
To be invulnerable in those bright Arms, Par Lost 2.812
Those other two equal'd with me in Fate, Par Lost 3.33
In those who, when they may, accept not grace. Par Lost 3.302
Those argent Fields more likely habitants, Par Lost 3.460
First from the ancient World those Giants came Par Lost 3.464
By which, to visit oft those happy Tribes, Par Lost 3.532
Like those *Hesperian* Gardens fam'd of old, Par Lost 3.568
Uriel, for thou of those seav'n Spirits that stand Par Lost 3.654
Adams abode, those loftie shades his Bowre. Par Lost 3.734
Those balmie spoiles. As when to them who saile Par Lost 4.159
So entertaind those odorous sweets the Fiend Par Lost 4.166
Nor those mysterious parts were then conceald, Par Lost 4.312
Of those fourfooted kindes, himself now one, Par Lost 4.397
Those Blossoms also, and those dropping Gumms, Par Lost 4.630
Those have thir course to finish, round the Earth, Par Lost 4.661
But chiefly where those two fair Creatures Lodge, Par Lost 4.790
Back stept those two faire Angels half amaz'd Par Lost 4.820
Which of those rebell Spirits adjudg'd to Hell Par Lost 4.823
The western Point, where those half-rounding guards Par Lost 4.862
He scarce had ended, when those two approachd Par Lost 4.874
Imploi'd it seems to violate sleep, and those Par Lost 4.883
One shapd and wing'd like one of those from Heav'n Par Lost 5.55
Be not disheart'nd then, nor cloud those looks Par Lost 5.122
Eastward among those Trees, what glorious shape Par Lost 5.309
Those happie places thou hast deignd a while Par Lost 5.364
No ingrateful food: and food alike those pure Par Lost 5.407
Earth and the Sea feed Air, the Air those Fires Par Lost 5.417
Whence in her visage round those spots, unpurg'd Par Lost 5.419
Enamour'd at that sight; but in those hearts Par Lost 5.448
Fannd with coole Winds, save those who in thir course Par Lost 5.655
Of all those Myriads which we lead the chief; Par Lost 5.684
Of those Imperial Titles which assert Par Lost 5.801
Of Gods *Messiah;* those indulgent Laws Par Lost 5.883
On those proud Towrs to swift destruction doom'd. Par Lost 5.907
Among those friendly Powers, who him receav'd Par Lost 6.22
Eternize here on Earth; but those elect Par Lost 6.374
From those deep throated Engins belcht, whose roar Par Lost 6.586
Till on those cursed Engins triple-row Par Lost 6.650
Of those too high aspiring, who rebelld Par Lost 6.899
To those Apostates, least the like befall Par Lost 7.44
Driv'n back redounded as a flood on those Par Lost 7.57
The Waters underneath from those above Par Lost 7.268
All but within those banks, where Rivers now Par Lost 7.305
Those rare and solitarie, these in flocks Par Lost 7.461
Insect or Worme; those wav'd thir limber fans Par Lost 7.476
Yet not to Earth are those bright Luminaries Par Lost 8.98
The swiftness of those Circles attribute, Par Lost 8.107
Save with the Creatures which I made, and those Par Lost 8.409
So much delights me as those graceful acts, Par Lost 8.600
Those thousand decencies that daily flow Par Lost 8.601
Those Notes to Tragic; foul distrust, and breach Par Lost 9.6
Centring receav'st from all those Orbs; in thee, Par Lost 9.109
Spot more delicious then those Gardens feign'd Par Lost 9.439
Lovelier, not those that in *Illyria* chang'd Par Lost 9.505
Of tasting those fair Apples, I resolv'd Par Lost 9.585
Those rigid threats of Death; ye shall not Die: Par Lost 9.685
And rapture so oft beheld? those heav'nly shapes Par Lost 9.1082
Those middle parts, that this new commer, Shame, Par Lost 9.1097
At Loopholes cut through thickest shade: Those Leaves Par Lost 9.1110

Those(*cont*)
Those two; the third best absent is condemn'd, Par Lost 10.82
Disguis'd he came, but those his Children dear Par Lost 10.330
You two this way, among these numerous Orbs Par Lost 10.397
1667 'those'
And all about found desolate; for those Par Lost 10.420
To those bright Orders utterd thus his voice. Par Lost 10.615
Equal in Days and Nights, except to those Par Lost 10.680
Those terms whatever, when they were propos'd: Par Lost 10.757
Sow'n with contrition in his heart, then those Par Lost 11.27
Good or not good ingraft, my Merit those Par Lost 11.35
Those pure immortal Elements that know Par Lost 11.50
Spangl'd with eyes more numerous then those Par Lost 11.130
Not hid, nor those things last which might preserve Par Lost 11.579
Of peaceful dayes portends, then those two past; Par Lost 11.600
Those were of hate and death, or pain much worse, Par Lost 11.601
Those Tents thou sawst so pleasant, were the Tents Par Lost 11.607
Of those ill mated Marriages thou saw'st: Par Lost 11.684
For in those dayes Might onely shall be admir'd, Par Lost 11.689
Anough to beare; those now, that were dispenst Par Lost 11.766
Man is not whom to warne: those few escap't Par Lost 11.777
To whom thus *Michael*. Those whom last thou sawst Par Lost 11.787
But say, what mean those colourd streaks in Heavn, Par Lost 11.879
Corrupting each thir way; yet those remoov'd, Par Lost 11.889
Till by two brethren (those two brethren call Par Lost 12.169
Thou hast reveald, those chiefly which concerne Par Lost 12.272
This yet I apprehend not, why to those Par Lost 12.280
Save by those shadowie expiations weak, Par Lost 12.291
Left onely in those written Records pure, Par Lost 12.513
Till those days ended, hunger'd then at last Par Reg 1.309
Therefore as those young Prophets then with care Par Reg 2.18
To Idols, those young *Daniel* could refuse; Par Reg 2.329
Witness those antient Empires of the Earth, Par Reg 2.435
For I esteem those names of men so poor Par Reg 2.447
Urim and *Thummim*, those oraculous gems Par Reg 3.14
Then those thir Conquerours, who leave behind Par Reg 3.78
Those rudiments, and see before thine eyes Par Reg 3.245
Deliverance of thy brethren, those ten Tribes Par Reg 3.374
My brethren, as thou call'st them; those Ten Tribes Par Reg 3.403
As for those captive Tribes, themselves were they Par Reg 3.414
Those antient, whose resistless eloquence Par Reg 4.268
Of Academics old and new, with those Par Reg 4.278
Thir Orators thou then extoll'st, as those Par Reg 4.353
Those terrors which thou speak'st of, did me none; Par Reg 4.487
Who seeing those great acts which God had done Samson 243
Miraculous yet remaining in those locks? Samson 587
And to those cruel enemies, Samson 642
Why then reveal'd? I was assur'd by those Samson 800
Of those encounters, where we might have tri'd Samson 1086
Were bristles rang'd like those that ridge the back Samson 1137
With those thy boyst'rous locks, no worthy match Samson 1164
Notorious murder on those thirty men Samson 1186
May chance to number thee with those Samson 1295
Of those who have me in thir civil power. Samson 1367
With all those high exploits by him atchiev'd, Samson 1492
And on his shoulders waving down those locks, Samson 1493
With both his arms on those two massie Pillars. Samson 1633
When Mountains tremble, those two massie Pillars Samson 1648
My mansion is, where those immortal shapes Mask 2
And as I past, I worshipt; if those you seek Mask 302
Such are those thick and gloomy shadows damp Mask 470
Be those that quell the might of hellish charms, Mask 613
And to those dainty limms which nature lent Mask 680
line not in Bridgewater ms
To those budge doctors of the *Stoick* Furr, Mask 707
And those happy climes that ly Mask 977
And of those *Daemons* that are found Penseroso 93
And sing to those that hold the vital shears, Arcades 65
But lives and spreds aloft by those pure eyes, Lycidas 81
Yet first to those ychain'd in sleep, Nativity 155
Not those new fangled toys, and triming slight Vacation 19
But cull those richest Robes, and gay'st attire Vacation 21
And those that cannot live from him asunder Vacation 77
To harbour those that are at enmity. Vacation 88
See see the Chariot, and those rushing wheels, Passion 36
With those just Spirits that wear victorious Palms, Musick 14
by leaving out those harsh ill sounding jarres Musick Tr. ms 5.03
And those Pearls of dew she wears, Winchester 43
Those Delphick lines with deep impression took, Shakespear 12
And with those few art eminently seen, Sonnet 9, 3
Those rugged names to our like mouths grow sleek Sonnet 11, 10
As when those Hinds that were transform'd to Froggs Sonnet 12, 5
No less renownd then warr, new foes arise Sonnet 16, 11
1694 'than those of War'
He who of those delights can judge, And spare Sonnet 20, 13
Your plots and packing wors then those of *Trent*, Forcers 14
Happy all those who have in him their stay. Psalm 2, 28
How many those Psalm 3, 2
Lead me because of those Psalm 5, 22
And turn my hand against *all those* Psalm 81, 59
Not thy Conversion, but those rich demaines Prose 1, 2

Thou
And chiefly Thou O Spirit, that dost prefer Par Lost 1.17
ms 'thou'
Instruct me, for Thou know'st; Thou from the first Par Lost 1.19
ms 'thou know'st; thou'
If thou beest he; But O how fall'n! how chang'd Par Lost 1.84
In equal ruin: into what Pit thou seest Par Lost 1.91

Thou(*cont*)
Seest thou yon dreary Plain, forlorn and wilde, Par Lost 1.180
Infernal world, and thou profoundest Hell Par Lost 1.251
Whence and what art thou, execrable shape, Par Lost 2.681
Art thou that Traitor Angel, art thou hee, Par Lost 2.689
Conjur'd against the highest, for which both Thou Par Lost 2.693
And reck'n'st thou thy self with Spirits of Heav'n, Par Lost 2.696
Thou interposest, that my sudden hand Par Lost 2.738
What thing thou art, thus double-form'd, and why Par Lost 2.741
In this infernal Vaile first met thou call'st Par Lost 2.742
Hast thou forgot me then, and do I seem Par Lost 2.747
Becam'st enamour'd, and such joy thou took'st Par Lost 2.765
At last this odious offspring whom thou seest Par Lost 2.781
Surround me, as thou sawst, hourly conceiv'd Par Lost 2.796
But thou O Father, I forewarn thee, shun Par Lost 2.810
Dear Daughter, since thou claim'st me for thy Sire, Par Lost 2.817
And bring ye to the place where Thou and Death Par Lost 2.840
Thou art my Father, thou my Author, thou Par Lost 2.864
But thee, whom follow? thou wilt bring me soon Par Lost 2.866
Answer'd. I know thee, stranger, who thou art, Par Lost 2.990
Or hear'st thou rather pure Ethereal stream, Par Lost 3.7
Before the Heavens thou wert, and at the voice Par Lost 3.9
And feel thy sovran vital Lamp; but thou Par Lost 3.22
So much the rather thou Celestial light Par Lost 3.51
Onely begotten Son, seest thou what rage Par Lost 3.80
By him corrupted? or wilt thou thy self Par Lost 3.162
For him, what for thy glorie thou hast made? Par Lost 3.164
All hast thou spok'n as my thoughts are, all Par Lost 3.171
Lie vanquisht; thou hast givn me to possess Par Lost 3.243
Thou wilt not leave me in the loathsom grave Par Lost 3.247
The powers of darkness bound. Thou at the sight Par Lost 3.256
O thou in Heav'n and Earth the only peace Par Lost 3.274
Found out for mankind under wrauth, O thou Par Lost 3.275
My sole complacence! well thou know'st how dear, Par Lost 3.276
Thou therefore whom thou only canst redeem, Par Lost 3.281
By wondrous birth: Be thou in *Adams* room Par Lost 3.285
Nor shalt thou by descending to assume Par Lost 3.303
Because thou hast, though Thron'd in highest bliss Par Lost 3.305
Here shalt thou sit incarnate, here shalt Reign Par Lost 3.315
When thou attended gloriously from Heav'n Par Lost 3.323
Then all thy Saints assembl'd, thou shalt judge Par Lost 3.330
Then thou thy regal Scepter shalt lay by, Par Lost 3.339
Amidst the glorious brightness where thou sit'st Par Lost 3.376
Thron'd inaccessible, but when thou shad'st Par Lost 3.377
Th' aspiring Dominations: thou that day Par Lost 3.392
Thou drov'st of warring Angels disarraid. Par Lost 3.396
Father of Mercie and Grace, thou didst not doome Par Lost 3.401
Uriel, for thou of those seav'n Spirits that stand Par Lost 3.654
Numberless, as thou seest, and how they move; Par Lost 3.719
Thy way thou canst not miss, me mine requires. Par Lost 3.735
O thou that with surpassing Glory crownd, Par Lost 4.32
Hadst thou the same free Will and Power to stand? Par Lost 4.66
Thou hadst: whom hast thou then or what to accuse, Par Lost 4.67
Nay curs'd be thou; since against his thy will Par Lost 4.71
Evil be thou my Good; by thee at least Par Lost 4.110
Som dreadful thing no doubt; for well thou knowst Par Lost 4.426
To whom thus *Eve* repli'd. O thou for whom Par Lost 4.440
And Head, what thou hast said is just and right. Par Lost 4.443
Praeeminent by so much odds, while thou Par Lost 4.447
Had not a voice thus warnd me, What thou seest, Par Lost 4.467
What there thou seest fair Creature is thy self, Par Lost 4.468
Whose image thou art, him thou shalt enjoy Par Lost 4.472
Thou following cryd'st aloud, Return faire *Eve;* Par Lost 4.481
Whom fli'st thou? whom thou fli'st, of him thou art, Par Lost 4.482
Amid the Suns bright circle where thou sitst, Par Lost 4.578
On purpose, hard thou knowst it to exclude Par Lost 4.584
Thou tellst, by morrow dawning I shall know. Par Lost 4.588
My Author and Disposer, what thou bidst Par Lost 4.635
God is thy Law, thou mine: to know no more Par Lost 4.637
And starrie Pole: Thou also mad'st the Night, Par Lost 4.724
Maker Omnipotent, and thou the Day, Par Lost 4.725
But thou hast promis'd from us two a Race Par Lost 4.732
Com'st thou, escap'd thy prison, and transform'd, Par Lost 4.824
Why satst thou like an enemie in waite Par Lost 4.825
As when thou stoodst in Heav'n upright and pure; Par Lost 4.837
That Glorie then, when thou no more wast good, Par Lost 4.838
Departed from thee, and thou resembl'st now Par Lost 4.839
But come, for thou, besure, shalt give account Par Lost 4.841
Why hast thou, *Satan*, broke the bounds prescrib'd Par Lost 4.878
Gabriel, thou hadst in Heav'n th' esteem of wise, Par Lost 4.886
Though thither doomd? Thou wouldst thy self, no doubt, Par Lost 4.890
Farthest from pain, where thou mightst hope to change Par Lost 4.892
So judge thou still, presumptuous, till the wrauth, Par Lost 4.912
Which thou incurr'st by flying, meet thy flight Par Lost 4.913
But wherefore thou alone? wherefore with thee Par Lost 4.917
Less pain, less to be fled, or thou then they Par Lost 4.919
The first in flight from pain, had'st thou alledg'd Par Lost 4.921
Thou surely hadst not come sole fugitive. Par Lost 4.923
Insulting Angel, well thou knowst I stood Par Lost 4.926
What thou and thy gay Legions dare against; Par Lost 4.942
Satan, and couldst thou faithful add? O name, Par Lost 4.950
And thou sly hypocrite, who now wouldst seem Par Lost 4.957
Patron of liberty, who more then thou Par Lost 4.958
Flie thither whence thou fledst: if from this houre Par Lost 4.963
Within these hallowd limits thou appeer, Par Lost 4.964
Ride on thy wings, and thou with thy Compeers, Par Lost 4.974
Satan, I know thy strength, and thou knowst mine, Par Lost 4.1006
Where thou art weigh'd, and shown how light, how weak, Par Lost 4.1012

Thou(*cont*)

If thou resist. The Fiend lookt up and knew	Par Lost 4.1013
Why sleepst thou *Eve?* now is the pleasant time,	Par Lost 5.38
Partake thou also; happie though thou art,	Par Lost 5.75
Happier thou mayst be, worthier canst not be:	Par Lost 5.76
What life the Gods live there, and such live thou.	Par Lost 5.81
That what in sleep thou didst abhorr to dream,	Par Lost 5.120
Waking thou never wilt consent to do.	Par Lost 5.121
If better thou belong not to the dawn,	Par Lost 5.167
Thou Sun, of this great World both Eye and Soule,	Par Lost 5.171
In thy eternal course, both when thou climbst,	Par Lost 5.173
And when high Noon hast gaind, and when thou fallst.	Par Lost 5.174
Raphael, said hee, thou hear'st what stir on Earth	Par Lost 5.224
Thou find'st him from the heat of Noon retir'd,	Par Lost 5.231
Those happie places thou hast deignd a while	Par Lost 5.364
Adam, I therefore came, nor art thou such	Par Lost 5.372
Under whose lowly roof thou hast voutsaf't	Par Lost 5.463
As that more willingly thou couldst not seem	Par Lost 5.466
Well hast thou taught the way that might direct	Par Lost 5.508
Attend: That thou art happie, owe to God;	Par Lost 5.520
That thou continu'st such, owe to thy self,	Par Lost 5.521
Assur'd me, and still assure: though what thou tellst	Par Lost 5.553
But more desire to hear, if thou consent,	Par Lost 5.555
High matter thou injoinst me, O prime of men,	Par Lost 5.563
Sleepst thou Companion dear, what sleep can close	Par Lost 5.673
Of Heav'ns Almightie. Thou to me thy thoughts	Par Lost 5.676
Thy sleep dissent? new Laws thou seest impos'd;	Par Lost 5.679
To utter is not safe. Assemble thou	Par Lost 5.683
Son, thou in whom my glory I behold	Par Lost 5.719
Made answer. Mightie Father, thou thy foes	Par Lost 5.735
Canst thou with impious obloquie condemne	Par Lost 5.813
Confess him rightful King? unjust thou saist	Par Lost 5.818
Shalt thou give Law to God, shalt thou dispute	Par Lost 5.822
Thee what thou art, and formd the Pow'rs of Heav'n	Par Lost 5.824
Thy self though great and glorious dost thou count,	Par Lost 5.833
That we were formd then saist thou? and the work	Par Lost 5.853
When this creation was? rememberst thou	Par Lost 5.857
Who is our equal: then thou shalt behold	Par Lost 5.866
That Golden Scepter which thou didst reject	Par Lost 5.886
Thy disobedience. Well thou didst advise,	Par Lost 5.888
When who can uncreate thee thou shalt know.	Par Lost 5.895
Servant of God, well done, well hast thou fought	Par Lost 6.29
Then scornd thou didst depart, and to subdue	Par Lost 6.40
And thou in Military prowess next	Par Lost 6.45
Proud, art thou met? thy hope was to have reacht	Par Lost 6.131
Thy Legions under darkness; but thou seest	Par Lost 6.142
From all: my Sect thou seest, now learn too late	Par Lost 6.147
Of my revenge, first sought for thou returnst	Par Lost 6.151
Omnipotence to none. But well thou comst	Par Lost 6.159
(Unanswerd least thou boast) to let thee know;	Par Lost 6.163
Such hast thou arm'd, the Minstrelsie of Heav'n,	Par Lost 6.168
Apostat, still thou errst, nor end wilt find	Par Lost 6.172
Unjustly thou deprav'st it with the name	Par Lost 6.174
Reign thou in Hell thy Kingdom, let mee serve	Par Lost 6.183
From mee returnd, as erst thou saidst, from flight,	Par Lost 6.187
Unnam'd in Heav'n, now plenteous, as thou seest	Par Lost 6.263
And thy adherents: how hast thou disturb'd	Par Lost 6.266
Of thy Rebellion? how hast thou instill'd	Par Lost 6.269
Thou and thy wicked crew; there mingle broiles,	Par Lost 6.277
The Adversarie. Nor think thou with wind	Par Lost 6.282
Thou canst not. Hast thou turnd the least of these	Par Lost 6.284
That thou shouldst hope, imperious, and with threats	Par Lost 6.287
The strife which thou call'st evil, but wee style	Par Lost 6.289
Thou fablest, here however to dwell free,	Par Lost 6.292
Not uninvented that, which thou aright	Par Lost 6.470
Heav'n witness thou anon, while we discharge	Par Lost 6.564
For to themselves I left them, and thou knowst,	Par Lost 6.689
Of ending this great Warr, since none but Thou	Par Lost 6.702
Go then thou Mightiest in thy Fathers might,	Par Lost 6.710
First, Highest, Holiest, Best, thou alwayes seekst	Par Lost 6.724
That thou in me well pleas'd, declarst thy will	Par Lost 6.728
Thou shalt be All in All, and I in thee	Par Lost 6.732
For ever, and in mee all whom thou lov'st:	Par Lost 6.733
But whom thou hat'st, I hate, and can put on	Par Lost 6.734
At thy request, and that thou maist beware	Par Lost 6.894
Bereavd of happiness thou maist partake	Par Lost 6.903
If rightly thou art call'd, whose Voice divine	Par Lost 7.2
The meaning, not the Name I call: for thou	Par Lost 7.5
Thou with Eternal wisdom didst converse,	Par Lost 7.9
And solitude; yet not alone, while thou	Par Lost 7.28
Purples the East: still govern thou my Song,	Par Lost 7.30
Her Son. So fail not thou, who thee implores:	Par Lost 7.38
For thou art Heav'nlie, shee an empty dreame.	Par Lost 7.39
Farr differing from this World, thou hast reveal'd	Par Lost 7.71
Of what we are. But since thou hast voutsaf't	Par Lost 7.80
Absolv'd, if unforbid thou maist unfould	Par Lost 7.94
Yet what thou canst attain, which best may serve	Par Lost 7.115
And thou my Word, begotten Son, by thee	Par Lost 7.163
This I perform, speak thou, and be it don:	Par Lost 7.164
Silence, ye troubl'd waves, and thou Deep, peace,	Par Lost 7.216
Of Trumpet (for of Armies thou hast heard)	Par Lost 7.296
And thou thir Natures know'st, & gav'st them Names,	Par Lost 7.493
Express, and thou becam'st a living Soul.	Par Lost 7.528
Is yet distinct by name, thence, as thou know'st	Par Lost 7.536
Thou mai'st not; in the day thou eat'st, thou di'st;	Par Lost 7.544
Resounded, (thou remember'st, for thou heardst)	Par Lost 7.561
Which nightly as a circling Zone thou seest	Par Lost 7.580
Thou hast repeld, while impiously they thought	Par Lost 7.611

Thou(*cont*)

Thou usest, and from thence creat'st more good.	Par Lost 7.616
Of destind habitation; but thou know'st	Par Lost 7.622
Informd by thee might know; if else thou seekst	Par Lost 7.639
Imports not, if thou reck'n right, the rest	Par Lost 8.71
Speed almost Spiritual; mee thou thinkst not slow,	Par Lost 8.110
In six thou seest, and what if sev'nth to these	Par Lost 8.128
Which else to several Sphears thou must ascribe,	Par Lost 8.131
Feilds and Inhabitants: Her spots thou seest	Par Lost 8.145
With thir attendant Moons thou wilt descrie	Par Lost 8.149
Wherever plac't, let him dispose: joy thou	Par Lost 8.170
How fully hast thou satisfi'd mee, pure	Par Lost 8.180
My Storie, which perhaps thou hast not heard;	Par Lost 8.205
And Day is yet not spent; till then thou seest	Par Lost 8.206
Pleas'd with thy words no less then thou with mine.	Par Lost 8.248
What e're I saw. Thou Sun, said I, faire Light,	Par Lost 8.273
And thou enlight'nd Earth, so fresh and gay,	Par Lost 8.274
Submiss: he rear'd me, and Whom thou soughtst I am,	Par Lost 8.316
Said mildely, Author of all this thou seest	Par Lost 8.317
The day thou eat'st thereof, my sole command	Par Lost 8.329
Transgrest, inevitably thou shalt dye;	Par Lost 8.330
O by what Name, for thou above all these,	Par Lost 8.357
Thou hast provided all things: but with mee	Par Lost 8.363
What call'st thou solitude, is not the Earth	Par Lost 8.369
To come and play before thee, know'st thou not	Par Lost 8.372
Hast thou not made me here thy substitute,	Par Lost 8.381
So fitly them in pairs thou hast combin'd;	Par Lost 8.394
Thou to thy self proposest, in the choice	Par Lost 8.400
What thinkst thou then of mee, and this my State,	Par Lost 8.403
Thou in thy self art perfet, and in thee	Par Lost 8.415
Or solace his defects. No need that thou	Par Lost 8.419
Thou in thy secresie although alone,	Par Lost 8.427
Canst raise thy Creature to what highth thou wilt	Par Lost 8.430
Which thou hast rightly nam'd, but of thy self,	Par Lost 8.439
Good reason was thou freely shouldst dislike,	Par Lost 8.443
And be so minded still; I, ere thou spak'st,	Par Lost 8.444
And no such companie as then thou saw'st	Par Lost 8.446
To see how thou could'st judge of fit and meet:	Par Lost 8.448
This turn hath made amends; thou hast fulfill'd	Par Lost 8.491
Do thou but thine, and be not diffident	Par Lost 8.562
Of Wisdom, she deserts thee not, if thou	Par Lost 8.563
Dismiss not her, when most thou needst her nigh,	Par Lost 8.564
Less excellent, as thou thy self perceav'st.	Par Lost 8.566
For what admir'st thou, what transports thee so,	Par Lost 8.567
Well manag'd; of that skill the more thou know'st,	Par Lost 8.573
So awful, that with honour thou maist love	Par Lost 8.577
Thy mate, who sees when thou art seen least wise.	Par Lost 8.578
What higher in her societie thou findst	Par Lost 8.586
In loving thou dost well, in passion not,	Par Lost 8.588
By which to heav'nly Love thou maist ascend,	Par Lost 8.592
To love thou blam'st me not, for love thou saist	Par Lost 8.612
Answer'd. Let it suffice thee that thou know'st	Par Lost 8.620
Whatever pure thou in the body enjoy'st	Par Lost 8.622
(And pure thou wert created) we enjoy	Par Lost 8.623
With grateful Memorie: thou to mankind	Par Lost 8.650
Is Center, yet extends to all, so thou	Par Lost 9.108
Tending to wilde. Thou therefore now advise	Par Lost 9.212
Let us divide our labours, thou where choice	Par Lost 9.214
Well hast thou motion'd, well thy thoughts imployd	Par Lost 9.229
Befall thee sever'd from me; for thou knowst	Par Lost 9.252
But that thou shouldst my firmness therfore doubt	Par Lost 9.279
His violence thou fearst not, being such,	Par Lost 9.282
For such thou art, from sin and blame entire:	Par Lost 9.292
Against temptation: thou thy self with scorne	Par Lost 9.299
Nor thou his malice and false guile contemn;	Par Lost 9.306
Of outward strength; while shame, thou looking on,	Par Lost 9.312
Why shouldst not thou like sense within thee feel	Par Lost 9.315
That I should mind thee oft, and mind thou me.	Par Lost 9.358
Thou sever not: Trial will come unsought.	Par Lost 9.366
Wouldst thou approve thy constancie, approve	Par Lost 9.367
But if thou think, trial unsought may finde	Par Lost 9.370
Us both securer then thus warnd thou seemst,	Par Lost 9.371
On what thou hast of vertue, summon all,	Par Lost 9.374
Thou never from that houre in Paradise	Par Lost 9.406
Thou canst, who art sole Wonder, much less arm	Par Lost 9.533
How cam'st thou speakable of mute, and how	Par Lost 9.563
What thou commandst, and right thou shouldst be obeyd:	Par Lost 9.570
Of blowing Myrrh and Balme; if thou accept	Par Lost 9.629
In ignorance, thou op'nst Wisdoms way,	Par Lost 9.809
Hast thou not wonderd, *Adam*, at my stay?	Par Lost 9.856
For bliss, as thou hast part, to me is bliss,	Par Lost 9.879
Thou therefore also taste, that equal Lot	Par Lost 9.881
Least thou not tasting, different degree	Par Lost 9.883
How art thou lost, how on a sudden lost,	Par Lost 9.900
Rather how hast thou yeelded to transgress	Par Lost 9.902
Bone of my Bone thou art, and from thy State	Par Lost 9.915
Bold deed thou hast presum'd, adventrous *Eve*,	Par Lost 9.921
Perhaps thou shalt not Die, perhaps the Fact	Par Lost 9.928
Lives, as thou saidst, and gaines to live as Man	Par Lost 9.933
My own in thee, for what thou art is mine;	Par Lost 9.957
Eve, now I see thou art exact of taste,	Par Lost 9.1017
Yeild thee, so well this day thou hast purvey'd.	Par Lost 9.1021
O *Eve*, in evil hour thou didst give eare	Par Lost 9.1067
Would thou hadst heark'nd to my words, and stai'd	Par Lost 9.1134
Imput'st thou that to my default, or will	Par Lost 9.1145
Of wandring, as thou call'st it, which who knows	Par Lost 9.1146
But might as ill have happ'nd thou being by,	Par Lost 9.1147
Or to thy self perhaps: hadst thou been there,	Par Lost 9.1148

Thou(*cont*)
Or here th' attempt, thou couldst not have discernd Par Lost 9.1149
Being as I am, why didst not thou the Head Par Lost 9.1155
Going into such danger as thou saidst? Par Lost 9.1157
Too facil then thou didst not much gainsay, Par Lost 9.1158
Hadst thou bin firm and fixt in thy dissent, Par Lost 9.1160
Neither had I transgress'd, nor thou with mee. Par Lost 9.1161
Immutable when thou wert lost, not I, Par Lost 9.1165
And thou th' accuser. Thus it shall befall Par Lost 9.1182
Supream, that thou in mee thy Son belov'd Par Lost 10.70
On Earth these thy transgressors, but thou knowst Par Lost 10.72
Where art thou *Adam*, wont with joy to meet Par Lost 10.103
My voice thou oft hast heard, and hast not fear'd, Par Lost 10.119
So dreadful to thee? that thou art naked, who Par Lost 10.121
Hath told thee? hast thou eaten of the Tree Par Lost 10.122
Whereof I gave thee charge thou shouldst not eat? Par Lost 10.123
Devolv'd; though should I hold my peace, yet thou Par Lost 10.135
This Woman whom thou mad'st to be my help, Par Lost 10.137
Was shee thy God, that her thou didst obey Par Lost 10.145
Thou did'st resigne thy Manhood, and the Place Par Lost 10.148
And person, had'st thou known thy self aright. Par Lost 10.156
Say Woman, what is this which thou hast done? Par Lost 10.158
Because thou hast done this, thou art accurst Par Lost 10.175
Upon thy Belly groveling thou shalt goe, Par Lost 10.177
Her Seed shall bruse thy head, thou bruise his heel. Par Lost 10.181
By thy Conception; Children thou shalt bring Par Lost 10.194
Because thou hast heark'nd to the voice of thy Wife, Par Lost 10.198
I charg'd thee, saying: Thou shalt not eate thereof, Par Lost 10.200
Curs'd is the ground for thy sake, thou in sorrow Par Lost 10.201
Unbid, and thou shalt eate th' Herb of the Field, Par Lost 10.204
In the sweat of thy Face shalt thou eat Bread, Par Lost 10.205
Till thou return unto the ground, for thou Par Lost 10.206
For dust thou art, and shalt to dust returne. Par Lost 10.208
By secretest conveyance. Thou my Shade Par Lost 10.249
The way, thou leading, such a sent I draw Par Lost 10.267
Nor shall I to the work thou enterprisest Par Lost 10.270
Thy Trophies, which thou view'st as not thine own, Par Lost 10.355
Thou art thir Author and prime Architect: Par Lost 10.356
That thou on Earth hadst prosper'd, which thy looks Par Lost 10.360
Thou hast atchiev'd our libertie, confin'd Par Lost 10.368
Within Hell Gates till now, thou us impow'rd Par Lost 10.369
Our foile in Heav'n; here thou shalt Monarch reign, Par Lost 10.375
Fair Daughter, and thou Son and Grandchild both, Par Lost 10.384
What thinkst thou of our Empire now, though earnd Par Lost 10.592
Thou therefore on these Herbs, and Fruits, and Flours Par Lost 10.603
Sufficient penaltie, why hast thou added Par Lost 10.753
Thou didst accept them; wilt thou enjoy the good, Par Lost 10.758
Wherefore didst thou beget me? I sought it not Par Lost 10.762
Wouldst thou admit for his contempt of thee Par Lost 10.763
So might the wrauth. Fond wish! couldst thou support Par Lost 10.834
With that bad Woman? Thus what thou desir'st Par Lost 10.837
And what thou fearst, alike destroyes all hope Par Lost 10.838
And horrors hast thou driv'n me; out of which Par Lost 10.843
Out of my sight, thou Serpent, that name best Par Lost 10.867
Fool'd and beguil'd, by him thou, I by thee, Par Lost 10.880
More miserable; both have sin'd, but thou Par Lost 10.930
So now of what thou knowst not, who desir'st Par Lost 10.948
His full wrauth whose thou feelst as yet lest part, Par Lost 10.951
Childless thou art, Childless remaine: Par Lost 10.989
But if thou judge it hard and difficult, Par Lost 10.992
Or if thou covet death, as utmost end Par Lost 10.1020
Resolv'd, as thou proposest; so our Foe Par Lost 10.1038
Michael, this my behest have thou in charge, Par Lost 11.99
The sourse of life; next favourable thou, Par Lost 11.169
With reverence I must meet, and thou retire. Par Lost 11.237
Then due by sentence when thou didst transgress, Par Lost 11.253
Giv'n thee of Grace, wherein thou may'st repent, Par Lost 11.255
The ground whence thou wast tak'n, fitter Soile. Par Lost 11.262
What justly thou hast lost; nor set thy heart, Par Lost 11.288
Thy Husband, him to follow thou art bound; Par Lost 11.291
Prince above Princes, gently hast thou tould Par Lost 11.298
Adam, thou know'st Heav'n his, and all the Earth. Par Lost 11.335
But this praeeminence thou hast lost, brought down Par Lost 11.347
Which that thou mayst beleeve, and be confirmd Par Lost 11.355
Ere thou from hence depart, know I am sent Par Lost 11.356
Prosperous or adverse: so shalt thou lead Par Lost 11.364
Here sleep below while thou to foresight wak'st, Par Lost 11.368
As once thou slepst, while Shee to life was formd. Par Lost 11.369
Thou lead'st me, and to the hand of Heav'n submit, Par Lost 11.372
Loose no reward, though here thou see him die, Par Lost 11.459
To whom thus *Michael*. Death thou hast seen Par Lost 11.466
Some, as thou saw'st, by violent stroke shall die, Par Lost 11.471
Before thee shall appear; that thou mayst know Par Lost 11.475
There is, said *Michael*, if thou well observe Par Lost 11.530
In what thou eatst and drinkst, seeking from thence Par Lost 11.532
So maist thou live, till like ripe Fruit thou drop Par Lost 11.535
This is old age; but then thou must outlive Par Lost 11.538
To what thou hast, and for the Aire of youth Par Lost 11.542
Nor love thy Life, nor hate; but what thou livst Par Lost 11.553
Created, as thou art, to nobler end Par Lost 11.605
Those Tents thou sawst so pleasant, were the Tents Par Lost 11.607
For that fair femal Troop thou sawst, that seemd Par Lost 11.614
Of those ill mated Marriages thou saw'st: Par Lost 11.684
But hee the seventh from thee, whom thou beheldst Par Lost 11.700
Did, as thou sawst, receave, to walk with God Par Lost 11.707
How didst thou grieve then, *Adam*, to behold Par Lost 11.754
By th' Angel, on thy feet thou stoodst at last, Par Lost 11.759
To whom thus *Michael*. Those whom last thou sawst Par Lost 11.787

Thou(*cont*)
Shall build a wondrous Ark, as thou beheldst, Par Lost 11.819
O thou who future things canst represent Par Lost 11.870
To whom th' Archangel. Dextrously thou aim'st; Par Lost 11.884
Thus thou hast seen one World begin and end; Par Lost 12.6
Much thou hast yet to see, but I perceave Par Lost 12.8
Thou therefore give due audience, and attend. Par Lost 12.12
To whom thus *Michael*. Justly thou abhorr'st Par Lost 12.79
(Canst thou believe2) should be so stupid grown, Par Lost 12.116
I see him, but thou canst not, with what Faith Par Lost 12.128
And thou Moon in the vale of *Aialon*, Par Lost 12.266
Thou hast reveald, those chiefly which concerne Par Lost 12.272
To that proud Citie, whose high Walls thou saw'st Par Lost 12.342
Thou shalt proceed, and from thy Womb the Son Par Lost 12.381
But by fulfilling that which thou didst want, Par Lost 12.396
Annuls thy doom, the death thou shouldst have dy'd, Par Lost 12.428
This having learnt, thou hast attaind the summe Par Lost 12.575
Thou knewst by name, and all th' ethereal Powers, Par Lost 12.577
Of all the rest: then wilt thou not be loath Par Lost 12.585
To meek submission: thou at season fit Par Lost 12.597
Let her with thee partake what thou hast heard, Par Lost 12.598
Whence thou returnst, and whither wentst, I know; Par Lost 12.610
Is to go hence unwilling; thou to mee Par Lost 12.617
Art all things under Heav'n, all places thou, Par Lost 12.618
Thou Spirit who ledst this glorious Eremite Par Reg 1.8
As thou art wont, my prompted Song else mute, Par Reg 1.12
Gabriel this day by proof thou shalt behold, Par Reg 1.130
Thou and all Angels conversant on Earth Par Reg 1.131
For know, thou art no Son of mortal man, Par Reg 1.234
Thou shouldst be great and sit on *David*'s Throne, Par Reg 1.240
Directed to the Manger where thou lais't, Par Reg 1.247
For that to me thou seem'st the man, whom late Par Reg 1.327
But if thou be the Son of God, Command Par Reg 1.342
So shalt thou save thy self and us relieve Par Reg 1.344
Think'st thou such force in Bread? is it not written Par Reg 1.347
(For I discern thee other then thou seem'st) Par Reg 1.348
Why dost thou then suggest to me distrust, Par Reg 1.355
Knowing who I am, as I know who thou art? Par Reg 1.356
Deservedly thou griev'st, compos'd of lyes Par Reg 1.407
Into the Heav'n of Heavens; thou com'st indeed, Par Reg 1.410
But thou art serviceable to Heaven's King. Par Reg 1.421
Wilt thou impute to obedience what thy fear Par Reg 1.422
Yet thou pretend'st to truth; all Oracles Par Reg 1.430
To thee not known, whence hast thou then thy truth, Par Reg 1.446
What to the smallest tittle thou shalt say Par Reg 1.450
To thy Adorers; thou with trembling fear, Par Reg 1.451
No more shalt thou by oracling abuse Par Reg 1.455
And thou no more with Pomp and Sacrifice Par Reg 1.457
Sharply thou hast insisted on rebuke, Par Reg 1.468
Easily canst thou find one miserable, Par Reg 1.471
But thou art plac't above me, thou art Lord; Par Reg 1.475
I bid not or forbid; do as thou find'st Par Reg 1.495
Permission from above; thou canst not more. Par Reg 1.496
Belial, in much uneven scale thou weigh'st Par Reg 2.173
Thou thy self doat'st on womankind, admiring Par Reg 2.175
None are, thou think'st, but taken with such toys. Par Reg 2.177
Before the Flood thou with thy lusty Crew, Par Reg 2.178
In Courts and Regal Chambers how thou lurk'st, Par Reg 2.183
To whom thus Jesus; what conclud'st thou hence? Par Reg 2.317
They all had need, I as thou seest have none. Par Reg 2.318
How hast thou hunger then? Satan reply'd, Par Reg 2.319
Would'st thou not eat? Thereafter as I like Par Reg 2.321
Hast thou not right to all Created things, Par Reg 2.324
Troubl'd that thou shouldst hunger, hath purvey'd Par Reg 2.333
What doubt'st thou Son of God? sit down and eat. Par Reg 2.377
Said'st thou not that to all things I had right? Par Reg 2.379
I can at will, doubt not, as soon as thou, Par Reg 2.383
Why shouldst thou then obtrude this diligence, Par Reg 2.387
And with my hunger what hast thou to do? Par Reg 2.389
That I have also power to give thou seest, Par Reg 2.393
Why shouldst thou not accept it? but I see Par Reg 2.398
Thou art not to be harm'd, therefore not mov'd; Par Reg 2.407
Thou art unknown, unfriended, low of birth, Par Reg 2.413
Which way or from what hope dost thou aspire Par Reg 2.417
What Followers, what Retinue canst thou gain, Par Reg 2.419
Longer then thou canst feed them on thy cost? Par Reg 2.421
Therefore, if at great things thou wouldst arrive, Par Reg 2.426
Not difficult, if thou hearken to me, Par Reg 2.428
Worthy of Memorial) canst thou not remember Par Reg 2.445
I see thou know'st what is of use to know, Par Reg 3.7
Infallible; or wert thou sought to deeds Par Reg 3.16
These God-like Vertues wherefore dost thou hide? Par Reg 3.21
Inglorious: but thou yet art not too late. Par Reg 3.42
Thou neither dost perswade me to seek wealth Par Reg 3.44
As thou to thy reproach mayst well remember, Par Reg 3.66
He ask'd thee, hast thou seen my servant *Job?* Par Reg 3.67
Of glory as thou wilt, said he, so deem, Par Reg 3.150
But to a Kingdom thou art born, ordain'd Par Reg 3.152
Antiochus: and think'st thou to regain Par Reg 3.163
So shalt thou best fullfil, best verifie Par Reg 3.177
Raign then; what canst thou better do the while? Par Reg 3.180
My everlasting Kingdom, why art thou Par Reg 3.199
Know'st thou not that my rising is thy fall, Par Reg 3.201
And will alike be punish'd; whether thou Par Reg 3.214
That thou who worthiest art should'st be thir King? Par Reg 3.226
Perhaps thou linger'st in deep thoughts detain'd Par Reg 3.227
Short sojourn; and what thence could'st thou observe? Par Reg 3.235
The world thou hast not seen, much less her glory, Par Reg 3.236

Thou(*cont*)

But I will bring thee where thou soon shalt quit	Par Reg 3.244
And regal Mysteries; that thou may'st know	Par Reg 3.249
Cut shorter many a league; here thou behold'st	Par Reg 3.269
His City there thou seest, and *Bactra* there;	Par Reg 3.285
Turning with easie eye thou may'st behold.	Par Reg 3.293
And just in time thou com'st to have a view	Par Reg 3.298
That thou may'st know I seek not to engage	Par Reg 3.347
By Prophet or by Angel, unless thou	Par Reg 3.352
Thou never shalt obtain; prediction still	Par Reg 3.354
But say thou wer't possess'd of *David*'s Throne	Par Reg 3.357
Samaritan or *Jew;* how could'st thou hope	Par Reg 3.359
Thou must make sure thy own, the *Parthian* first	Par Reg 3.363
Chuse which thou wilt by conquest or by league.	Par Reg 3.370
By him thou shalt regain, without him not,	Par Reg 3.371
These if from servitude thou shalt restore	Par Reg 3.381
Thou on the Throne of *David* in full glory,	Par Reg 3.383
Before mine eyes thou hast set; and in my ear	Par Reg 3.390
Means I must use thou say'st, prediction else	Par Reg 3.394
When that comes think not thou to find me slack	Par Reg 3.398
My brethren, as thou call'st them; those Ten Tribes	Par Reg 3.403
When thou stood'st up his Tempter to the pride	Par Reg 3.409
The City which thou seest no other deem	Par Reg 4.44
Of Nations; there the Capitol thou seest	Par Reg 4.47
My Aerie Microscope) thou may'st behold	Par Reg 4.57
And long Renown thou justly may'st prefer	Par Reg 4.84
Indu'd with Regal Vertues as thou art,	Par Reg 4.98
Might'st thou expel this monster from his Throne	Par Reg 4.100
And with my help thou may'st; to me the power	Par Reg 4.103
Much less my mind; though thou should'st add to tell	Par Reg 4.113
And hunger still: then Embassies thou shew'st	Par Reg 4.121
How gloriously; I shall, thou say'st, expel	Par Reg 4.127
Thou valu'st, because offer'd, and reject'st:	Par Reg 4.156
On the other side know also thou, that I	Par Reg 4.159
All these which in a moment thou behold'st,	Par Reg 4.162
On this condition, if thou wilt fall down,	Par Reg 4.166
Now both abhor, since thou hast dar'd to utter	Par Reg 4.172
Thou hast permission on me. It is written	Par Reg 4.175
The first of all Commandments, Thou shalt worship	Par Reg 4.176
And dar'st thou to the Son of God propound	Par Reg 4.178
Other donation none thou canst produce:	Par Reg 4.184
Long since. Wert thou so void of fear or shame,	Par Reg 4.189
Get thee behind me; plain thou now appear'st	Par Reg 4.193
Then these thou bear'st that title, have propos'd	Par Reg 4.199
Who then thou art, whose coming is foretold	Par Reg 4.204
Advise thee, gain them as thou canst, or not.	Par Reg 4.211
And thou thy self seem'st otherwise inclin'd	Par Reg 4.212
When slipping from thy Mothers eye thou went'st	Par Reg 4.216
And with the *Gentiles* much thou must converse,	Par Reg 4.229
Ruling them by perswasion as thou mean'st,	Par Reg 4.230
Without thir learning how wilt thou with them,	Par Reg 4.231
How wilt thou reason with them, how refute	Par Reg 4.233
There thou shalt hear and learn the secret power	Par Reg 4.254
These here revolve, or, as thou lik'st, at home,	Par Reg 4.281
Thir Orators thou then extoll'st, as those	Par Reg 4.353
What dost thou in this World? the Wilderness	Par Reg 4.372
What I foretell thee, soon thou shalt have cause	Par Reg 4.375
To wish thou never hadst rejected thus	Par Reg 4.376
Or torn up sheer: ill wast thou shrouded then,	Par Reg 4.419
Some bent at thee thir fiery darts, while thou	Par Reg 4.424
Of men at thee, for only thou here dwell'st.	Par Reg 4.466
Did I not tell thee, if thou didst reject	Par Reg 4.467
Thou shalt be what thou art ordain'd, no doubt;	Par Reg 4.473
If thou observe not this, be sure to find,	Par Reg 4.477
E're thou of *Israel*'s Scepter get fast hold;	Par Reg 4.480
Mee worse then wet thou find'st not; other harm	Par Reg 4.486
Those terrors which thou speak'st of, did me none;	Par Reg 4.487
Mee to thy will; desist, thou art discern'd	Par Reg 4.497
In what degree or meaning thou art call'd	Par Reg 4.516
Thou art to be my fatal enemy.	Par Reg 4.525
Therefore to know what more thou art then man,	Par Reg 4.538
There stand, if thou wilt stand; to stand upright	Par Reg 4.551
Thou chance to dash thy foot against a stone.	Par Reg 4.559
Thou didst debel, and down from Heav'n cast	Par Reg 4.605
With all his Army, now thou hast aveng'd	Par Reg 4.606
For *Adam* and his chosen Sons, whom thou	Par Reg 4.614
But thou, Infernal Serpent, shalt not long	Par Reg 4.618
Or Lightning thou shalt fall from Heav'n trod down	Par Reg 4.620
Under his feet: for proof, e're this thou feel'st	Par Reg 4.621
O first created Beam, and thou great Word,	Samson 83
Thou art become (O worst imprisonment!)	Samson 155
To lowest pitch of abject fortune thou art fall'n.	Samson 169
Why thou shouldst wed *Philistian* women rather	Samson 216
Thou never wast remiss, I bear thee witness:	Samson 239
Forthwith how thou oughtst to receive him.	Samson 329
Rather approv'd them not; but thou didst plead	Samson 421
Divine impulsion prompting how thou might'st	Samson 422
Thir Captive, and thir triumph; thou the sooner	Samson 426
Tacit, was in thy power; true; and thou bear'st	Samson 430
Bitterly hast thou paid, and still art paying	Samson 432
Thou must not in the mean while here forgot	Samson 479
Thou canst avoid, self-preservation bids;	Samson 505
Where thou mayst bring thy off'rings, to avert	Samson 519
Thou couldst repress, nor did the dancing Rubie	Samson 543
Man. Wilt thou then serve the *Philistines* with that gift	Samson 577
Wherewith to serve him better then thou hast;	Samson 585
That thou towards him with hand so various,	Samson 668
Not evenly, as thou rul'st	Samson 671

Thou(*cont*)

But such as thou hast solemnly elected,	Samson 678
Yet toward these thus dignifi'd, thou oft	Samson 682
But throw'st them lower then thou didst exalt them high,	Samson 689
With sickness and disease thou bow'st them down,	Samson 698
What do I beg? how hast thou dealt already?	Samson 707
His labours, for thou canst, to peaceful end.	Samson 709
To light'n what thou suffer'st, and appease	Samson 744
To what I did thou shewdst me first the way.	Samson 781
Nor shouldst thou have trusted that to womans frailty	Samson 783
E're I to thee, thou to thy self wast cruel.	Samson 784
The gentler, if severely thou exact not	Samson 788
And what if Love, which thou interpret'st hate,	Samson 790
Of fancy, feard lest one day thou wouldst leave me	Samson 794
Thy key of strength and safety: thou wilt say,	Samson 799
As thou art strong, inflexible as steel.	Samson 816
If thou in strength all mortals dost exceed,	Samson 817
By this appears: I gave, thou say'st, th' example,	Samson 822
I to my self was false e're thou to me,	Samson 824
Take to thy wicked deed: which when thou seest	Samson 826
Thou wilt renounce thy seeking, and much rather	Samson 828
My love how couldst thou hope, who tookst the way	Samson 838
In vain thou striv'st to cover shame with shame,	Samson 841
Dal. Since thou determinst weakness for no plea	Samson 843
It was not gold, as to my charge thou lay'st,	Samson 849
That wrought with me: thou know'st the Magistrates	Samson 850
My enemies, lov'd thee, as too well thou knew'st,	Samson 878
Didst thou at first receive me for thy husband?	Samson 883
Being once a wife, for me thou wast to leave	Samson 885
Thou mine, not theirs: if aught against my life	Samson 888
To please thy gods thou didst it; gods unable	Samson 896
Bare in thy guilt how foul must thou appear?	Samson 902
That what by me thou hast lost thou least shalt miss.	Samson 927
It fits not; thou and I long since are twain;	Samson 929
Lov'd, honour'd, fear'd me, thou alone could hate me	Samson 939
How wouldst thou use me now, blind, and thereby	Samson 941
And last neglected? How wouldst thou insult	Samson 944
Dal. I see thou art implacable, more deaf	Samson 960
That *Kiriathaim* held, thou knowst me now	Samson 1081
If thou at all art known. Much I have heard	Samson 1082
Har. Dost thou already single me; I thought	Samson 1092
Had brought me to the field where thou art fam'd	Samson 1094
From the unforeskinn'd race, of whom thou bear'st	Samson 1100
Sam. Boast not of what thou wouldst have done, but do	Samson 1104
What then thou would'st, thou seest it in thy hand.	Samson 1105
And thou hast need much washing to be toucht.	Samson 1107
Thou oft shalt wish thy self at *Gath* to boast	Samson 1127
Again in safety what thou wouldst have done	Samson 1128
Har. Thou durst not thus disparage glorious arms	Samson 1130
Arm'd thee or charm'd thee strong, which thou from Heaven	Samson 1134
Then thou shalt see, or rather to thy sorrow	Samson 1154
Har. Fair honour that thou dost thy God, in trusting	Samson 1178
Sam. Tongue-doubtie Giant, how dost thou prove me these?	Samson 1181
Into our hands: for hadst thou not committed	Samson 1185
The *Philistines*, when thou hadst broke the league,	Samson 1189
Sam. Cam'st thou for this, vain boaster, to survey me,	Samson 1227
Har. By *Astaroth* e're long thou shalt lament	Samson 1242
Sam. Thou knowst I am an *Ebrew*, therefore tell them,	Samson 1319
Return the way thou cam'st, I will not come.	Samson 1332
Sa. Perhaps thou shalt have cause to sorrow indeed.	Samson 1347
More Lordly thund'ring then thou well wilt bear.	Samson 1353
Chor. Yet with this strength thou serv'st the *Philistines*,	Samson 1363
For some important cause, thou needst not doubt.	Samson 1379
Chor. How thou wilt here come off surmounts my reach.	Samson 1380
Chor. In time thou hast resolv'd, the man returns.	Samson 1390
To thee I am bid say. Art thou our Slave,	Samson 1392
And dar'st thou at our sending and command	Samson 1394
And hamper thee, as thou shalt come of force,	Samson 1397
Though thou wert firmlier fastn'd then a rock.	Samson 1398
By this compliance thou wilt win the Lords	Samson 1411
Thou for thy Son art bent to lay out all;	Samson 1486
Thou in old age car'st how to nurse thy Son.	Samson 1488
No Preface needs, thou seest we long to know.	Samson 1554
Man. Sad, but thou knowst to *Israelites* not saddest	Samson 1560
All by him fell thou say'st, by whom fell he,	Samson 1580
A dreadful way thou took'st to thy revenge.	Samson 1591
Are in confusion, give us if thou canst,	Samson 1593
Living or dying thou hast fulfill'd	Samson 1661
The work for which thou wast foretold	Samson 1662
Wherin thou rid'st with *Hecat*', and befriend	Mask 135
Why shouldst thou, but for som fellonious end, line not in Bridgewater ms	Mask 196
Thou hovering Angel girt with golden wings, line not in Bridgewater ms	Mask 214
And thou unblemish't form of Chastity, line not in Bridgewater ms	Mask 215
Canst thou not tell me of a gentle Pair	Mask 236
O if thou have	Mask 238
So maist thou be translated to the skies,	Mask 242
Eld. Bro. Unmuffle ye faint stars, and thou fair Moon	Mask 331
And thou shalt be our star of *Arcady*,	Mask 341
How cam'st thou here good Swain? hath any ram word not in Bridgewater ms	Mask 497
How couldst thou find this dark sequester'd nook?	Mask 500
How sweet thou sing'st, how neer the deadly snare!	Mask 567
How durst thou then thy self approach so neer	Mask 616
Root-bound, that fled *Apollo*, *La*. Fool do not boast, Trinity ms 'doe not boast' ← 'thou art over proud'	Mask 662

Thou(*cont*)

Thou canst not touch the freedom of my minde	Mask 663
Thou haste immanacl'd, while Heav'n sees good.	Mask 665
That thou hast banish't from thy tongue with lies,	Mask 692
Thou told'st me of? What grim aspects are these,	Mask 694
Hast thou betrai'd my credulous innocence	Mask 697
line not in Bridgewater ms	
And wouldst thou seek again to trap me here	Mask 699
line not in Bridgewater ms	
Thou hast nor Eare, nor Soul to apprehend	Mask 784
line not in Bridgewater ms	
line not in Trinity ms	
And thou art worthy that thou shouldst not know	Mask 788
line not in Bridgewater ms	
line not in Trinity ms	
Thou art not fit to hear thy self convinc't;	Mask 792
line not in Trinity ms	
line not in Bridgewater ms	
Listen where thou art sitting	Mask 860
Till thou our summons answer'd have.	Mask 888
poore ladie thou hast need of some refreshing	Mask Tr. ms 20.09
thou man of lies & falshood, if thou give me it	Mask Tr. ms 22.21
poore ladie thou hast neede of some refreshinge	Mask Br. ms 660
But com thou Goddes fair and free,	Allegro 11
These delights, if thou canst give,	Allegro 151
But hail thou Goddes, sage and holy,	Penseroso 11
Yet thou art higher far descended,	Penseroso 22
Thou fix them on the earth as fast.	Penseroso 44
But O the heavy change, now thou art gon,	Lycidas 37
Now thou art gon, and never must return!	Lycidas 38
O Fountain *Arethuse*, and thou honour'd floud,	Lycidas 85
Where thou perhaps under the whelming tide	Lycidas 157
Or whether thou to our moist vows deny'd,	Lycidas 159
Hence forth thou art the Genius of the shore,	Lycidas 183
Hast thou no vers, no hymn, or solemn strein,	Nativity 17
Have thou the honour first, thy Lord to greet,	Nativity 26
Summers chief honour if thou hadst out-lasted,	Fair Inf 3
Yet art thou not inglorious in thy fate;	Fair Inf 22
Yet can I not perswade me thou art dead	Fair Inf 29
Above mortalitie that shew'd thou wast divine.	Fair Inf 35
(If so it be that thou these plaints dost hear)	Fair Inf 37
Tell me bright Spirit where e're thou hoverest	Fair Inf 38
Oh say me true if thou wert mortal wight	Fair Inf 41
And why from us so quickly thou didst take thy flight.	Fair Inf 42
Wert thou some Starr which from the ruin'd roofe	Fair Inf 43
Of sheenie Heav'n, and thou some goddess fled	Fair Inf 48
Or wert thou that just Maid who once before	Fair Inf 50
Or wert thou that sweet smiling Youth!	Fair Inf 53
Or wert thou of the golden-winged hoast,	Fair Inf 57
But oh why didst thou not stay here below	Fair Inf 64
But thou canst best perform that office where thou art.	Fair Inf 70
Then thou the mother of so sweet a child	Fair Inf 71
Think what a present thou to God hast sent,	Fair Inf 74
This if thou do he will an off-spring give,	Fair Inf 76
Thou needst not be ambitious to be first,	Vacation 11
Till thou hast deck't them in thy best aray;	Vacation 26
Before thou cloath my fancy in fit sound:	Vacation 32
But fie my wandring Muse how thou dost stray!	Vacation 53
Thou know'st it must be now thy only bent	Vacation 55
Come tripping to the Room where thou didst lie;	Vacation 62
She heard them give thee this, that thou should'st still	Vacation 65
Rivers arise; whether thou be the Son,	Vacation 91
Fly envious *Time*, till thou run out thy race,	On Time 1
For when as each thing bad thou hast entomb'd,	On Time 9
Whilst thou bright Saint high sit'st in glory,	Winchester 61
What need'st thou such weak witnes of thy name?	Shakespear 6
Thou in our wonder and astonishment	Shakespear 7
Then thou our fancy of it self bereaving,	Shakespear 13
Thou with fresh hope the Lovers heart dost fill,	Sonnet 1, 3
As thou from yeer to yeer hast sung too late	Sonnet 1, 11
Chosen thou hast, and they that overween,	Sonnet 9, 6
Thou, when the Bridegroom with his feastfull friends	Sonnet 9, 12
When thou taught'st *Cambridge*, and King *Edward* Greek.	Sonnet 11, 14
To after age thou shalt be writ the man,	Sonnet 13, 7
Thou honour'st Verse, and Verse must send her wing	Sonnet 13, 9
Meekly thou didst resign this earthy load	Sonnet 14, 3
What severs each thou 'hast learnt, which few hav don.	Sonnet 17, 11
To measure life, learn thou betimes, and know	Sonnet 21, 9
Right onward. What supports me dost thou ask?	Sonnet 22, 9
Pyrrha for whom bindst thou	Horace 3
To whom thou untry'd seem'st fair. Me in my vow'd	Horace 13
Thou art my Son I have begotten thee	Psalm 2, 15
Earths utmost bounds: them shalt thou bring full low	Psalm 2, 19
But thou Lord art my shield my glory,	Psalm 3, 7
Rise Lord, save me my God for thou	Psalm 3, 19
Thou didst me disinthrall	Psalm 4, 4
And gladness thou hast put	Psalm 4, 32
For thou alone dost keep	Psalm 4, 39
Thou Lord alone in safety mak'st me dwell.	Psalm 4, 42
Jehovah thou my early voyce	Psalm 5, 5
Will rank my Prayers, and watch till thou appear.	Psalm 5, 8
For thou art not a God that takes	Psalm 5, 9
Thou hat'st; and them unblest	Psalm 5, 14
Thou wilt destroy that speak a ly	Psalm 5, 15
Their joy, while thou from blame	Psalm 5, 34
For thou Jehovah wilt be found	Psalm 5, 37
As with a shield thou wilt surround	Psalm 5, 39
And thou O Lord how long? turn Lord, restore	Psalm 6, 7

Thou(*cont*)

Judgment here thou didst ingage	Psalm 7, 23
Since thou art the just God that tries	Psalm 7, 38
Out of the mouths of babes and sucklings thou	Psalm 8, 5
The Moon and Starrs which thou so bright hast set,	Psalm 8, 10
O what is man that thou remembrest yet,	Psalm 8, 12
That him thou visit'st and of him art found;	Psalm 8, 14
Scarce to be less then Gods, thou mad'st his lot,	Psalm 8, 15
With honour and with state thou hast him crown'd.	Psalm 8, 16
O're the works of thy hand thou mad'st him Lord,	Psalm 8, 17
Thou hast put all under his lordly feet,	Psalm 8, 18
Thou Shepherd that dost Israel *keep*	Psalm 80, 1
Cause thou thy face on us to shine	Psalm 80, 15
Lord God of Hosts, how long wilt thou,	Psalm 80, 17
How long wilt thou declare	Psalm 80, 18
Thou feed'st them with the bread of tears,	Psalm 80, 21
A strife thou mak'st us *and a prey*	Psalm 80, 25
Cause thou thy face on us to shine,	Psalm 80, 31
A Vine from Aegypt thou hast brought,	Psalm 80, 33
Thou did'st prepare for it a place	Psalm 80, 37
Why hast thou laid her Hedges low	Psalm 80, 49
Thou hast made firm and strong.	Psalm 80, 64
Upon the Son of Man, whom thou	Psalm 80, 71
Quick'n us thou, then *gladly* wee	Psalm 80, 75
Cause thou thy face on us to shine,	Psalm 80, 79
On me then didst thou call,	Psalm 81, 26
Thou antient stock of Israel,	Psalm 81, 35
If thou wilt list to mee,	Psalm 81, 36
Nor shalt thou to a forein God	Psalm 81, 39
Rise God, judge thou the earth *in might*,	Psalm 82, 25
For thou art he who shalt by right	Psalm 82, 27
Be not thou silent *now at length*	Psalm 83, 1
Sit not thou still O God of *strength*	Psalm 83, 3
Whom thou dost hide and keep.	Psalm 83, 12
Thou didst to Jabins *hoast*,	Psalm 83, 36
Then shall they know that thou whose name	Psalm 83, 65
Art the most high, *and thou the same*	Psalm 83, 67
Where thou do'st dwell so near.	Psalm 84, 4
Thou God our shield look on the face	Psalm 84, 31
Thou hast not Lord been slack,	Psalm 85, 2
Thou hast from *hard* Captivity	Psalm 85, 3
Th' iniquity thou didst forgive	Psalm 85, 5
Thine anger all thou hadst remov'd,	Psalm 85, 9
Wilt thou be angry without end,	Psalm 85, 17
Wilt thou thy frowning ire extend	Psalm 85, 19
Wilt thou not turn, and *hear our voice*	Psalm 85, 21
Save thou thy servant O my God	Psalm 86, 7
For thou art good, thou Lord art prone	Psalm 86, 13
To pardon, thou to all	Psalm 86, 14
Art full of mercy, thou *alone*	Psalm 86, 15
For thou wilt *grant* me *free access*	Psalm 86, 23
The Nations all whom thou hast made	Psalm 86, 29
For great thou art, and wonders great	Psalm 86, 33
Thou *in thy everlasting Seat*	Psalm 86, 35
And thou hast free'd my Soul	Psalm 86, 46
But thou Lord art the God most mild	Psalm 86, 53
And be asham'd, because thou Lord	Psalm 86, 63
Whom thou rememberest no more,	Psalm 88, 21
Thou in the lowest pit *profound*	Psalm 88, 25
Thou break'st upon me all thy waves,	Psalm 88, 31
Thou dost my friends from me estrange,	Psalm 88, 33
Wilt thou do wonders on the dead,	Psalm 88, 41
Why wilt thou Lord my soul forsake,	Psalm 88, 57
Lover and friend thou hast remov'd	Psalm 88, 69
'Gainst them that rais'd thee dost thou lift thy horn,	Prose 3, 2
Impudent whoore, where hast thou plac'd thy hope?	Prose 3, 3
What Land, what Seat of rest thou bidst me seek,	Prose 12, 4
Thy course, there shalt thou find a lasting seat,	Prose 12, 11

Though

Confounded though immortal: But his doom	Par Lost 1.53
Myriads though bright: If he whom mutual league,	Par Lost 1.87
Though chang'd in outward lustre; that fixt mind	Par Lost 1.97
And shook his throne. What though the field be lost?	Par Lost 1.105
So spake th' Apostate Angel, though in pain,	Par Lost 1.125
Though all our Glory extinct, and happy state	Par Lost 1.141
What can it then avail though yet we feel	Par Lost 1.153
To reign is worth ambition though in Hell:	Par Lost 1.262
New courage and revive, though now they lye	Par Lost 1.279
Though of thir Names in heav'nly Records now	Par Lost 1.361
Though for the noyse of Drums and Timbrels loud	Par Lost 1.394
By that uxorious King, whose heart though large,	Par Lost 1.444
The rest were long to tell, though far renown'd,	Par Lost 1.507
Warr'd on by Cranes: though all the Giant brood	Par Lost 1.576
With singed top thir stately growth though bare	Par Lost 1.614
Was not inglorious, though th' event was dire,	Par Lost 1.624
For who can yet beleeve, though after loss,	Par Lost 1.631
(Though like a cover'd field, where Champions bold	Par Lost 1.763
Though without number still amidst the Hall	Par Lost 1.791
Immortal vigor, though opprest and fall'n,	Par Lost 2.13
Mee though just right, and the fixt Laws of Heav'n	Par Lost 2.18
Though inaccessible, his fatal Throne:	Par Lost 2.104
But all was false and hollow; though his Tongue	Par Lost 2.112
Though full of pain, this intellectual being,	Par Lost 2.147
For happy though but ill, for ill not worst,	Par Lost 2.224
Unacceptable, though in Heav'n, our state	Par Lost 2.251
Live to our selves, though in this vast recess,	Par Lost 2.254
Majestic though in ruin: sage he stood	Par Lost 2.305
In strictest bondage, though thus far remov'd,	Par Lost 2.321

Though(*cont*)
Untam'd reluctance, and revenge though slow, Par Lost 2.337
To be created like to us, though less Par Lost 2.349
By force or suttlety: Though Heav'n be shut, Par Lost 2.358
Seis'd us, though undismaid: long is the way Par Lost 2.432
Terror of Heav'n, though fall'n; intend at home, Par Lost 2.457
Of Creatures rational, though under hope Par Lost 2.498
That dar'st, though grim and terrible, advance Par Lost 2.682
I fled, but he pursu'd (though more, it seems, Par Lost 2.790
Though temper'd heav'nly, for that mortal dint, Par Lost 2.813
Perhaps our vacant room, though more remov'd, Par Lost 2.835
Made head against Heav'ns King, though overthrown. Par Lost 2.992
Gladly the Port, though Shrouds and Tackle torn; Par Lost 2.1044
Escap't the *Stygian* Pool, though long detain'd Par Lost 3.14
Though hard and rare: thee I revisit safe, Par Lost 3.21
Sufficient to have stood, though free to fall. Par Lost 3.99
Fall circumvented thus by fraud, though joynd Par Lost 3.152
Or proud return though to his heavier doom, Par Lost 3.159
His lapsed powers, though forfeit and enthrall'd Par Lost 3.176
Though but endevord with sincere intent, Par Lost 3.192
Though now to Death I yield, and am his due Par Lost 3.245
Though last created, that for him I spare Par Lost 3.278
The Head of all mankind, though *Adams* Son. Par Lost 3.286
Because thou hast, though Thron'd in highest bliss Par Lost 3.305
Though distant farr som small reflection gaines Par Lost 3.428
With many a vain exploit, though then renownd: Par Lost 3.465
Over Mount *Sion*, and, though that were large, Par Lost 3.530
Such wonder seis'd, though after Heaven seen, Par Lost 3.552
With gentle penetration, though unseen, Par Lost 3.585
In vain, though by thir powerful Art they binde Par Lost 3.602
And oft though wisdom wake, suspicion sleeps Par Lost 3.686
Uriel, though Regent of the Sun, and held Par Lost 3.690
With light from hence, though but reflected, shines; Par Lost 3.723
Yet not rejoycing in his speed, though bold, Par Lost 4.13
As great might have aspir'd, and me though mean Par Lost 4.62
Who came thir bane, though with them better pleas'd Par Lost 4.167
That drove him, though enamourd, from the Spouse Par Lost 4.169
Mount *Amara*, though this by som suppos'd Par Lost 4.281
Whence true autoritie in men; though both Par Lost 4.295
Though I unpittied: League with you I seek, Par Lost 4.375
To do what else though damnd I should abhorre. Par Lost 4.392
In order, though to Nations yet unborn, Par Lost 4.663
These then, though unbeheld in deep of night, Par Lost 4.674
Shine not in vain, nor think, though men were none, Par Lost 4.675
More sacred and sequesterd, though but feignd, Par Lost 4.706
Though thither doomd? Thou wouldst thy self, no doubt, Par Lost 4.890
Though for possession put to try once more Par Lost 4.941
From my prevailing arme, though Heavens King Par Lost 4.973
Then Heav'n permits, nor mine, though doubld now Par Lost 4.1009
Partake thou also; happie though thou art, Par Lost 5.75
Left to his own free Will, his Will though free, Par Lost 5.236
Neerer his presence *Adam* though not awd, Par Lost 5.358
As may not oft invite, though Spirits of Heav'n Par Lost 5.374
All *Autumn* pil'd, though *Spring* and *Autumn* here Par Lost 5.394
Sups with the Ocean: though in Heav'n the Trees Par Lost 5.426
Yield Nectar, though from off the boughs each Morn Par Lost 5.428
Assur'd me, and still assure: though what thou tellst Par Lost 5.553
As may express them best, though what if Earth Par Lost 5.574
(For time, though in Eternitie, appli'd Par Lost 5.580
Thy self though great and glorious dost thou count, Par Lost 5.833
The flaming Seraph fearless, though alone Par Lost 5.875
Though single. From amidst them forth he passd, Par Lost 5.903
To veile the Heav'n, though darkness there might well Par Lost 6.11
To stand approv'd in sight of God, though Worlds Par Lost 6.36
In the mid way: though strange to us it seemd Par Lost 6.91
Where boldest; though to sight unconquerable? Par Lost 6.118
Victor; though brutish that contest and foule, Par Lost 6.124
Prefer, and Pietie to God, though then Par Lost 6.144
Though not destroy, thir happie Native seat; Par Lost 6.226
And limited thir might; though numberd such Par Lost 6.229
Though heaviest by just measure on thy self Par Lost 6.265
Unspeakable; for who, though with the tongue Par Lost 6.297
Though huge, and in a Rock of Diamond Armd, Par Lost 6.364
In might though wondrous and in Acts of Warr, Par Lost 6.377
By wound, though from thir place by violence mov'd. Par Lost 6.405
Of future we may deem him, though till now Par Lost 6.429
Imperishable, and though peirc'd with wound, Par Lost 6.435
Valour or strength, though matchless, quelld with pain Par Lost 6.457
Though standing else as Rocks, but down they fell Par Lost 6.593
Out of such prison, though Spirits of purest light, Par Lost 6.660
Bellerophon, though from a lower Clime) Par Lost 7.18
To hoarce or mute, though fall'n on evil dayes, Par Lost 7.25
On evil dayes though fall'n, and evil tongues; Par Lost 7.26
Urania, and fit audience find, though few. Par Lost 7.31
Though wandring. He with his consorted *Eve* Par Lost 7.50
Much of his Race though steep, suspens in Heav'n Par Lost 7.99
Obtaine: though to recount Almightie works Par Lost 7.112
Though wide, and this high Temple to frequent Par Lost 7.148
Though I uncircumscrib'd my self retire, Par Lost 7.170
Her sacred shades: though God had yet not rain'd Par Lost 7.331
Though of Ethereal Mould: then form'd the Moon Par Lost 7.356
Thir small peculiar, though from human sight Par Lost 7.368
And hairie Main terrific, though to thee Par Lost 7.497
Desisting, though unwearied, up returnd Par Lost 7.552
Though, in comparison of Heav'n, so small, Par Lost 8.92
Though numberless, to his Omnipotence, Par Lost 8.108
Not that I so affirm, though so it seem Par Lost 8.117
The Planet Earth, so stedfast though she seem, Par Lost 8.129

Though(*cont*)
Though pleasant, but thy words with Grace Divine Par Lost 8.215
My droused sense, untroubl'd, though I thought Par Lost 8.289
Yet dreadful in mine eare, though in my choice Par Lost 8.335
No pleasure, though in pleasure, solitarie. Par Lost 8.402
And through all numbers absolute, though One; Par Lost 8.421
Though sleeping, where I lay, and saw the shape Par Lost 8.463
Led by her Heav'nly Maker, though unseen, Par Lost 8.485
She heard me thus, and though divinely brought, Par Lost 8.500
Nature her self, though pure of sinful thought, Par Lost 8.506
(Though higher of the genial Bed by far, Par Lost 8.598
Now not, though Sin, not Time, first wraught the change, Par Lost 9.70
As I, though thereby worse to me redound: Par Lost 9.128
Before had bin contriving, though perhaps Par Lost 9.139
To basest things. Revenge, at first though sweet, Par Lost 9.171
Our dayes work brought to little, though begun Par Lost 9.224
For hee who tempts, though in vain, at least asperses Par Lost 9.296
Though ineffectual found: misdeem not then, Par Lost 9.301
The Enemie, though bold, will hardly dare, Par Lost 9.304
Persisted, yet submiss, though last, repli'd. Par Lost 9.377
Though not as shee with Bow and Quiver armd, Par Lost 9.390
Each Flour of slender stalk, whose head though gay Par Lost 9.428
Her self, though fairest unsupported Flour, Par Lost 9.432
Though in mid Heav'n, soon ended his delight, Par Lost 9.468
Heroic built, though of terrestrial mould, Par Lost 9.485
Not terrible, though terrour be in Love Par Lost 9.490
Though at the voice much marveling; at length Par Lost 9.551
Wanted not long, though to this shape retain'd. Par Lost 9.601
Mee thus, though importune perhaps, to come Par Lost 9.610
Fruitless to mee, though Fruit be here to excess, Par Lost 9.648
She scarse had said, though brief, when now more bold Par Lost 9.664
Though threat'nd, which no worse then this can bring. Par Lost 9.715
Though kept from Man, and worthy to be admir'd, Par Lost 9.746
Though others envie what they cannot give; Par Lost 9.805
And giv'st access, though secret she retire. Par Lost 9.810
Though threatning, will in earnest so destroy Par Lost 9.939
Not well conceav'd of God, who though his Power Par Lost 9.945
Till *Adam*, though not less then *Eve* abash't, Par Lost 9.1065
Time counts not, though with swiftest minutes wing'd. Par Lost 10.91
He came, and with him *Eve*, more loth, though first Par Lost 10.109
Devolv'd; though should I hold my peace, yet thou Par Lost 10.135
Serpent though brute, unable to transferre Par Lost 10.165
Though in mysterious terms, judg'd as then best: Par Lost 10.173
All, though all-knowing, what had past with Man Par Lost 10.227
Of ravenous Fowl, though many a League remote, Par Lost 10.274
Thir Parent soon discern'd, though in disguise. Par Lost 10.331
By *Eve*, though all unweeting, seconded Par Lost 10.335
Though distant from thee Worlds between, yet felt Par Lost 10.362
Though to delude them sent, could not abstain, Par Lost 10.557
What thinkst thou of our Empire now, though earnd Par Lost 10.592
Which here, though plenteous, all too little seems Par Lost 10.600
Inhabited, though sinless, more then now, Par Lost 10.690
These changes in the Heav'ns, though slow, produc'd Par Lost 10.692
Alreadie in part, though hid in gloomiest shade, Par Lost 10.716
Heavie, though in thir place. O fleeting joyes Par Lost 10.741
Then cavil the conditions? and though God Par Lost 10.759
For though the Lord of all be infinite, Par Lost 10.794
And reasonings, though through Mazes, lead me still Par Lost 10.830
Then all the World much heavier, though divided Par Lost 10.836
Though by the Devil himself, him overweening Par Lost 10.878
Or end, though sharp and sad, yet tolerable, Par Lost 10.977
To supplication, heare his sighs though mute; Par Lost 11.31
Numberd, though sad, till Death, his doom (which I Par Lost 11.40
And in thir state, though firm, stood more confirmd. Par Lost 11.71
So send them forth, though sorrowing, yet in peace: Par Lost 11.117
Though after sleepless Night; for see the Morn, Par Lost 11.173
Wherere our days work lies, though now enjoind Par Lost 11.177
Here let us live, though in fall'n state, content. Par Lost 11.180
Quiet though sad, the respit of that day Par Lost 11.272
For though I fled him angrie, yet recall'd Par Lost 11.330
Gladly behold though but his utmost skirts Par Lost 11.332
Loose no reward, though here thou see him die, Par Lost 11.459
Shook, but delaid to strike, though oft invok't Par Lost 11.492
Though not of Woman born; compassion quell'd Par Lost 11.496
So goodly and erect, though faultie since, Par Lost 11.509
The Men though grave, ey'd them, and let thir eyes Par Lost 11.585
By pleasure, though to Nature seeming meet, Par Lost 11.604
Unmindful of thir Maker, though his Spirit Par Lost 11.611
Though comfortless, as when a Father mourns Par Lost 11.760
Though late repenting him of Man deprav'd, Par Lost 11.886
Though bent on speed, so heer th' Arch-angel paus'd Par Lost 12.2
line not in 1667 edition
Though of Rebellion others he accuse. Par Lost 12.37
Though to the Tyrant thereby no excuse. Par Lost 12.96
(Things by thir names I call, though yet unnam'd) Par Lost 12.140
Though present in his Angel, who shall goe Par Lost 12.201
And therefore shall not *Moses*, though of God Par Lost 12.307
Both by obedience and by love, though love Par Lost 12.403
To save them, not thir own, though legal works. Par Lost 12.410
Though to the death, against such cruelties Par Lost 12.494
Though not but by the Spirit understood. Par Lost 12.514
Secular power, though feigning still to act Par Lost 12.517
Of wisdome; hope no higher, though all the Starrs Par Lost 12.576
Both in one Faith unanimous though sad, Par Lost 12.603
I carry hence; though all by mee is lost, Par Lost 12.621
Above Heroic, though in secret done, Par Reg 1.15
Lost Paradise deceiv'd by me, though since Par Reg 1.52
In all his lineaments, though in his face Par Reg 1.92

Though(*cont*)
Ventures his filial Vertue, though untri'd, Par Reg 1.177
Can raise them, though above example high; Par Reg 1.232
Though men esteem thee low of Parentage, Par Reg 1.235
For what he bids I do; though I have lost Par Reg 1.377
Though inly stung with anger and disdain, Par Reg 1.466
And talk at least, though I despair to attain. Par Reg 1.485
Thy coming hither, though I know thy scope, Par Reg 1.494
With others though in Holy Writ not nam'd, Par Reg 2.8
Within her brest, though calm; her brest though pure, Par Reg 2.63
Though *Adam* by his Wives allurement fell, Par Reg 2.134
Though of this Age the wonder and the fame, Par Reg 2.209
Though needing, what praise is it to endure? Par Reg 2.251
Though hunger still remain: so it remain Par Reg 2.255
Though ravenous, taught to abstain from what they brought: Par Reg 2.269
Nor proffer'd by an Enemy, though who Par Reg 2.330
Riches though offer'd from the hand of Kings. Par Reg 2.449
In battel, though against thy few in arms. Par Reg 3.20
And loses, though but verbal, his reward. Par Reg 3.104
Though chiefly not for glory as prime end, Par Reg 3.123
By Mothers side thy Father, though thy right Par Reg 3.154
Though Priests, the Crown, and *David*'s Throne usurp'd, Par Reg 3.169
Raign or raign not; though to that gentle brow Par Reg 3.215
No wonder, for though in thee be united Par Reg 3.229
He marches now in hast; see, though from far, Par Reg 3.303
All this fair sight; thy Kingdom though foretold Par Reg 3.351
And never cease, though to his shame the more; Par Reg 4.14
Though all to shivers dash't, the assault renew, Par Reg 4.19
Yet gives not o're though desperate of success, Par Reg 4.23
Of luxury, though call'd magnificence, Par Reg 4.111
Much less my mind; though thou should'st add to tell Par Reg 4.113
Though Sons of God both Angels are and Men, Par Reg 4.197
No other doctrine needs, though granted true; Par Reg 4.290
A third sort doubted all things, though plain sence; Par Reg 4.296
After his aerie jaunt, though hurried sore, Par Reg 4.402
Though rooted deep as high, and sturdiest Oaks Par Reg 4.417
Was distant; and these flaws, though mortals fear them Par Reg 4.454
I never fear'd they could, though noising loud Par Reg 4.488
Thy manhood last, though yet in private bred; Par Reg 4.509
Though not to be Baptiz'd, by voice from Heav'n Par Reg 4.512
For though that seat of earthly bliss be fail'd, Par Reg 4.612
Not to be found, though sought. Yee see, O friends, Samson 193
The deeds themselves, though mute, spoke loud the dooer; Samson 248
Though Reason here aver Samson 323
Though in this uncouth place; if old respect, Samson 333
Though offer'd only, by the sent conceiv'd Samson 390
Though void of corporal sense. Samson 616
Though not disordinate, yet causless suffring Samson 701
May expiate (though the fact more evil drew Samson 736
My penance hath not slack'n'd, though my pardon Samson 738
Though late, yet in some part to recompense Samson 746
Though fond and reasonless to some perhaps; Samson 812
In man or woman, though to thy own condemning, Samson 844
To afflict thy self in vain: though sight be lost, Samson 914
Though dearly to my cost, thy ginns, and toyls; Samson 933
Chor. Yet beauty, though injurious, hath strange power, Samson 1003
Or seven, though one should musing sit; Samson 1017
Though for no friendly intent. I am of *Gath*, Samson 1078
Where strength can least abide, though all thy hairs Samson 1136
Though by his blindness maim'd for high attempts, Samson 1221
Though in these chains, bulk without spirit vast, Samson 1238
Though Fame divulge him Father of five Sons Samson 1248
Though thou wert firmlier fastn'd then a rock. Samson 1398
Or reason though disturb'd, and scarse consulted Samson 1546
Semichor. But he though blind of sight, Samson 1687
And though her body die, her fame survives, Samson 1706
Chor. All is best, though we oft doubt, Samson 1745
Though a rush Candle from the wicker hole Mask 338
By her own radiant light, though Sun and Moon Mask 374
Benighted walks under the mid-day Sun; Mask 384
  Trinity ms 'benighted walks under the midday sun' ←'walks in black vapours though the noontyde brand'
  Bridgewater ms 'walks in black vapours though the noone tyde brand'
(Though so esteem'd by shallow ignorance) Mask 514
I knew the foul inchanter though disguis'd, Mask 645
But sease his wand, though he and his curst crew Mask 653
And though not mortal, yet a cold shuddring dew Mask 802
  line not in Bridgewater ms
  line not in Trinity ms
I could be willing though now i' th darke to trie Mask Tr. ms 16.38
to have her by my side, though I were sure Mask Tr. ms 16.41
I could be willinge though now i' th darke to trie Mask Br. ms 391
to have her by my side, though I were suer Mask Br. ms 394
Or what (though rare) of later age, Penseroso 101
Gen. Stay gentle Swains, for though in this disguise, Arcades 26
Though *Erymanth* your loss deplore, Arcades 100
Though *Syrinx* your *Pans* Mistres were, Arcades 106
Sunk though he be beneath the watry floar, Lycidas 167
And though the shady gloom Nativity 77
And here though grief my feeble hands up-lock, Passion 45
But vow though the cross Doctors all stood hearers, Another 19
  line not in 1640, 1657, 1658 texts
Though later born, then to have known the dayes Sonnet 10, 9
Victory home, though new rebellions raise Sonnet 15, 6
  1694 'while'
Lodg'd with me useless, though my Soul more bent Sonnet 19, 4
And disapproves that care, though wise in show, Sonnet 21, 12

Though(*cont*)
Cyriack, this three years day these eys, though clear Sonnet 22, 1
Content though blind, had I no better guide. Sonnet 22, 14
Rescu'd from death by force though pale and faint. Sonnet 23, 4
Clip your Phylacteries, though bauk your Ears, Forcers 17
anointed have my King (though ye rebell) Psalm 2, 12
I fear not though incamping round about Psalm 3, 17
Of Jacobs *Land, though there be store*, Psalm 87, 7

Thought
Reserv'd him to more wrath; for now the thought Par Lost 1.54
Breathing united force with fixed thought Par Lost 1.560
I sdeind subjection, and thought one step higher Par Lost 4.50
To them who liv'd; nor on the vertue thought Par Lost 4.198
Of God or Angel, for they thought no ill: Par Lost 4.320
With unexperienc't thought, and laid me downe Par Lost 4.457
Hitherward bent (who could have thought2) escap'd Par Lost 4.794
With gentle voice, I thought it thine; it said, Par Lost 5.37
My Guide was gon, and I, me thought, sunk down, Par Lost 5.91
Thy goodness beyond thought, and Power Divine: Par Lost 5.159
Shee needed, Vertue-proof, no thought infirme Par Lost 5.384
Each to other like, more then on earth is thought? Par Lost 5.576
Through pride that sight, & thought himself impaird. Par Lost 5.665
Nor so content, hath in his thought to try Par Lost 5.727
How provident he is, how farr from thought Par Lost 5.828
Already known what he for news had thought Par Lost 6.20
Of onset ended soon each milder thought. Par Lost 6.98
At first I thought that Libertie and Heav'n Par Lost 6.164
Nor motion of swift thought, less could his Shield Par Lost 6.192
The ridges of grim Warr; no thought of flight, Par Lost 6.236
Omniscient thought. True is, less firmly arm'd, Par Lost 6.430
Once found, which yet unfound most would have thought Par Lost 6.500
Whom fled we thought, will save us long pursuit Par Lost 6.538
Of things so high and strange, things to thir thought Par Lost 7.53
Things above Earthly thought, which yet concernd Par Lost 7.82
At least our envious Foe hath fail'd, who thought Par Lost 7.139
Thy power; what thought can measure thee or tongue Par Lost 7.603
Thou hast repeld, while impiously they thought Par Lost 7.611
Thought him still speaking, still stood fixt to hear; Par Lost 8.3
  line not in 1667 edition
My drousèd sense, untroubl'd, though I thought Par Lost 8.289
I found not what me thought I wanted still; Par Lost 8.355
Nature her self, though pure of sinful thought, Par Lost 8.506
And Matrimonial Love; but *Eve*, who thought Par Lost 9.319
The first at lest of these I thought denid Par Lost 9.555
Of knowledg, nor was God-head from her thought. Par Lost 9.790
Thee I have misst, and thought it long, depriv'd Par Lost 9.857
Whatever can to sight or thought be formd, Par Lost 9.898
Were it I thought Death menac't would ensue Par Lost 9.977
Original; while *Adam* took no thought, Par Lost 9.1004
Thus fenc't, and as they thought, thir shame in part Par Lost 9.1119
What seemd in thee so perfet, that I thought Par Lost 9.1179
And thought not much to cloath his Enemies: Par Lost 10.219
But I shall die a living Death? O thought Par Lost 10.788
That excellence thought in thee, and implies, Par Lost 10.1017
Immediate dissolution, which we thought Par Lost 10.1049
And *Sofala* thought *Ophir*, to the Realme Par Lost 11.400
With thought that they must be. Let no man seek Par Lost 11.770
Greatly in peace of thought, and have my fill Par Lost 12.558
Thought following thought, and step by step led on, Par Reg 1.192
What might be publick good; my self I thought Par Reg 1.204
Sometimes they thought he might be only shewn, Par Reg 2.13
Thought none my equal, now be over-match'd. Par Reg 2.146
Him thought, he by the Brook of *Cherith* stood Par Reg 2.266
Besides to give a Kingdom hath been thought Par Reg 2.481
In cunning, over-reach't where least he thought, Par Reg 4.11
Ambitious spirit, and wouldst be thought my God, Par Reg 4.495
Thenceforth I thought thee worth my nearer view Par Reg 4.514
All men are Sons of God; yet thee I thought Par Reg 4.520
O change beyond report, thought, or belief! Samson 117
I thought it lawful from my former act, Samson 231
Then give the rains to wandring thought, Samson 302
I pray'd for Children, and thought barrenness Samson 352
Lenient of grief and anxious thought, Samson 659
Vertue, as I thought, truth, duty so enjoyning. Samson 870
Sam. I thought where all thy circling wiles would end; Samson 871
In what I thought would have succeeded best. Samson 908
Har. Dost thou already single me; I thought Samson 1092
Man. That were a joy presumptuous to be thought. Samson 1531
Despis'd and thought extinguish't quite, Samson 1688
My best guide now, me thought it was the sound Mask 171
  Bridgewater ms 'methought'
Inferr, as if I thought my sisters state Mask 408
Where no crude surfet raigns. *Eld. Bro*. List, list, I hear Mask 480
  Trinity ms 'I heare' ←'I heard' ←'me thought'
2. *Bro*. Me thought so too; what should it be? *Eld. Bro*. For certain Mask 482
That doth enrich these Downs, is worth a thought Mask 505
And O poor hapless Nightingale thought I, Mask 566
La. I had not thought to have unlockt my lips Mask 756
Who had thought this clime had held Arcades 24
With eager thought warbling his *Dorick* lay: Lycidas 189
Full little thought they than, Nativity 88
That did thy cheek envermeil, thought to kiss Fair Inf 6
He thought it toucht his Deitie full neer, Fair Inf 10
Who onely thought to crop the flowr Winchester 39
This thought might lead me through the worlds vain mask Sonnet 22, 13
Lord my God if I have thought Psalm 7, 7

Thoughted
Which men call Earth, and with low-thoughted care Mask 6

Thoughtful
Leans her unpillow'd head fraught with sad fears. Mask 355
Trinity ms 'unpillow'd' ←'thoughtfull'
Thoughts
United thoughts and counsels, equal hope Par Lost 1.88
With solemn touches, troubl'd thoughts, and chase Par Lost 1.557
Long under darkness cover. But these thoughts Par Lost 1.659
From heav'n, for ev'n in heav'n his looks and thoughts Par Lost 1.680
ms defective here
Maturest Counsels: for his thoughts were low; Par Lost 2.115
Those thoughts that wander through Eternity, Par Lost 2.148
All thoughts of warr: ye have what I advise. Par Lost 2.283
Thither let us bend all our thoughts, to learn Par Lost 2.354
Pondering the danger with deep thoughts; and each Par Lost 2.421
Truce to his restless thoughts, and entertain Par Lost 2.526
In thoughts more elevate, and reason'd high Par Lost 2.558
Satan with thoughts inflam'd of highest design, Par Lost 2.630
Then feed on thoughts, that voluntarie move Par Lost 3.37
All hast thou spok'n as my thoughts are, all Par Lost 3.171
His troubl'd thoughts, and from the bottom stirr Par Lost 4.19
Would higth recal high thoughts, how soon unsay Par Lost 4.95
Little inferior; whom my thoughts pursue Par Lost 4.362
Divide the night, and lift our thoughts to Heaven. Par Lost 4.688
At least distemperd, discontented thoughts, Par Lost 4.807
O Sole in whom my thoughts find all repose, Par Lost 5.28
The trouble of thy thoughts this night in sleep Par Lost 5.96
So pray'd they innocent, and to thir thoughts Par Lost 5.209
She turns, on hospitable thoughts intent Par Lost 5.332
Single, is yet so just, my constant thoughts Par Lost 5.552
Of Heav'ns Almightie. Thou to me thy thoughts Par Lost 5.676
Abstrusest thoughts, from forth his holy Mount Par Lost 5.712
Aspirer, but thir thoughts prov'd fond and vain Par Lost 6.90
Disdain'd, but meaner thoughts learnd in thir flight, Par Lost 6.367
Collected stood within our thoughts amus'd, Par Lost 6.581
Stood scoffing, highthn'd in thir thoughts beyond Par Lost 6.629
Entring on studious thoughts abstruse, which *Eve* Par Lost 8.40
Sollicit not thy thoughts with matters hid, Par Lost 8.167
The easiest way, nor with perplexing thoughts Par Lost 8.183
Seek them with wandring thoughts, and notions vain. Par Lost 8.187
All human thoughts come short, Supream of things; Par Lost 8.414
The thoughts, and heart enlarges, hath his seat Par Lost 8.590
Of thoughts revolv'd, his final sentence chose Par Lost 9.88
With second thoughts, reforming what was old! Par Lost 9.101
To my relentless thoughts; and him destroyd, Par Lost 9.130
Or bear what to my minde first thoughts present, Par Lost 9.213
Well hast thou motion'd, well thy thoughts imployd Par Lost 9.229
Thoughts, which how found they harbour in thy brest Par Lost 9.288
Fierce hate he recollects, and all his thoughts Par Lost 9.471
Thoughts, whither have ye led me, with what sweet Par Lost 9.473
The trodden Herb, of abject thoughts and low, Par Lost 9.572
I turnd my thoughts, and with capacious mind Par Lost 9.603
Great joy he promis'd to his thoughts, and new Par Lost 9.843
Recomforted, and after thoughts disturbd Par Lost 9.918
His thoughts, his looks, words, actions all infect, Par Lost 10.608
What thoughts in my unquiet brest are ris'n, Par Lost 10.975
Broke off the rest; so much of Death her thoughts Par Lost 10.1008
A space, till firmer thoughts restraind excess, Par Lost 11.498
Erwhile perplext with thoughts what would becom Par Lost 12.275
What oft my steddiest thoughts have searcht in vain, Par Lost 12.377
And his deep thoughts, the better to converse Par Reg 1.190
O what a multitude of thoughts at once Par Reg 1.196
These growing thoughts my Mother soon perceiving Par Reg 1.227
And said to me apart, high are thy thoughts Par Reg 1.229
And he still on was led, but with such thoughts Par Reg 1.299
Some troubl'd thoughts, which she in sighs thus clad. Par Reg 2.65
Since first her Salutation heard, with thoughts Par Reg 2.107
Nor mind it, fed with better thoughts that feed Par Reg 2.258
Perhaps thou linger'st in deep thoughts detain'd Par Reg 3.227
From restless thoughts, that like a deadly swarm Samson 19
Mine eie to harbour sleep, or thoughts to rest. Samson 459
With youthful courage and magnanimous thoughts Samson 524
Sam. All otherwise to me my thoughts portend, Samson 590
Thoughts my Tormenters arm'd with deadly stings Samson 623
To something extraordinary my thoughts. Samson 1383
Is now the labour of my thoughts, 'tis likeliest Mask 192
These thoughts may startle well, but not astound Mask 210
line not in Bridgewater ms
Could stir the constant mood of her calm thoughts, Mask 371
But he that hides a dark soul, and foul thoughts Mask 383
That fancy can beget on youthfull thoughts, Mask 669
Let our frail thoughts dally with false surmise. Lycidas 153
Was all that did their silly thoughts so busie keep. Nativity 92
I have some naked thoughts that rove about Vacation 23
To day deep thoughts resolve with me to drench Sonnet 21, 5
Thousand
Ten thousand Banners rise into the Air Par Lost 1.545
A thousand Demy-Gods on golden seat's, Par Lost 1.796
Ten thousand fadom deep, and to this hour Par Lost 2.934
And *Discord* with a thousand various mouths. Par Lost 2.967
Blows them transverse ten thousand Leagues awry Par Lost 3.488
Thousand Celestial Ardors, where he stood Par Lost 5.249
Ten thousand thousand Ensignes high advanc'd, Par Lost 5.588
Attended with ten thousand thousand Saints, Par Lost 6.767
And twentie thousand (I thir number heard) Par Lost 6.769
Grasping ten thousand Thunders, which he sent Par Lost 6.836
With thousand lesser Lights dividual holds, Par Lost 7.382
With thousand thousand Starres, that then appeer'd Par Lost 7.383
Symphonious of ten thousand Harpes that tun'd Par Lost 7.559

Thousand(*cont*)
Those thousand decencies that daily flow Par Lost 8.601
Of threescore and ten thousand *Israelites* Par Reg 3.411
A thousand fore-skins fell, the flower of *Palestin* Samson 144
What might this be? A thousand fantasies Mask 205
line not in Bridgewater ms
A thousand liveried Angels lacky her, Mask 455
And shew me simples of a thousand names Mask 627
From a thousand petty rills, Mask 926
The clouds in thousand Liveries dight, Allegro 62
To nurse the Saplings tall, and curl the grove Arcades 46
Trinity ms 'nurse the saplings tall' ←'live a thousand yeares'
Their Bels, and Flourets of a thousand hues. Lycidas 135
With thousand echo's still prolongs each heav'nly close. Nativity 100
And the Cherubick host in thousand quires Musick 12
Trinity ms 'in thousand quires' ←'sweet-winged squires'
in ten thous Musick Tr. ms 4.16
ms defective
A thousand daies *at best*. Psalm 84, 36
Thousandfold
Ten thousandfould the sin of him who slew Par Lost 11.678
1667 'thousand fould'
Thousands
With hunderds and with thousands trooping came Par Lost 1.760
By Thousands and by Millions rang'd for fight; Par Lost 6.48
How few somtimes may know, when thousands err. Par Lost 6.148
Thy malice into thousands, once upright Par Lost 6.270
I might relate of thousands, and thir names Par Lost 6.373
By thousands, Angel on Arch-Angel rowl'd; Par Lost 6.594
His thousands, in what martial equipage Par Reg 3.304
Is Kingly. Thousands at his bidding speed Sonnet 19, 12
Thracian
Of that wilde Rout that tore the *Thracian* Bard Par Lost 7.34
his goarie scalpe rowle downe the Thracian lee Lycidas Tr. ms 29.61
Thraldom
In perfet thraldom, how again betray me, Samson 946
Thrall
Him first make sure your thrall, and lastly kill. Par Lost 10.402
As a poor miserable captive thrall, Par Reg 1.411
He should not so o'rewhelm, and as a thrall Samson 370
Who had made thir dreadful enemy thir thrall. Samson 1622
And led thee out of thrall. Psalm 81, 28
Thralls
Or do him mightier service as his thralls Par Lost 1.149
Thrascias
And *Thrascias* rend the Woods and Seas upturn; Par Lost 10.700
Threads
Bound with two cords; but cords to me were threds Samson 261
Shooting her beams like silver threds, Arcades 16
Threaten
They oft fore-signifie and threaten ill: Par Reg 4.464
Threatened
So threatn'd hee, but *Satan* to no threats Par Lost 4.968
Threatn'd, nor from the Holie One of Heav'n Par Lost 6.359
Though threat'nd, which no worse then this can bring. Par Lost 9.715
Not dead, as we are threatn'd, but thenceforth Par Lost 9.870
Must bide the stroak of that long threatn'd wound, Par Reg 1.59
Sollicited, commanded, threatn'd, urg'd, Samson 852
Threatener
To Knowledge? By the Threatner, look on mee, Par Lost 9.687
Threatening
Impendent horrors, threatning hideous fall Par Lost 2.177
So speaking and so threatning, grew tenfold Par Lost 2.705
Starless expos'd, and ever-threatning storms Par Lost 3.425
Still threatning to devour me opens wide, Par Lost 4.77
Though threatning, will in earnest so destroy Par Lost 9.939
Concours in Arms, fierce Faces threatning Warr, Par Lost 11.641
And threatning nigh; what they can do as signs Par Reg 4.489
Who threatning cruel death constrain'd the bride Samson 1198
Threatning to bind our soules with secular chaines: Sonnet 16, 12
Threatenings
Thy threatnings cut me through. Psalm 88, 66
Threatens
Threatens him, plung'd in that abortive gulf. Par Lost 2.441
Threat'ns then our expulsion down to Hell; Par Reg 2.128
Threats
So threatn'd hee, but *Satan* to no threats Par Lost 4.968
Yet not for thy advise or threats I fly Par Lost 5.889
Of airie threats to aw whom yet with deeds Par Lost 6.283
That thou shouldst hope, imperious, and with threats Par Lost 6.287
When *Satan* who late fled before the threats Par Lost 9.53
Those rigid threats of Death; ye shall not Die: Par Lost 9.685
Threats the forlorn and wandring Passinger. Mask 39
Shall be unsaid for me: against the threats Mask 586
Three
And thrice threefold the Gates; three folds were Brass, Par Lost 2.645
Three Iron, three of Adamantine Rock, Par Lost 2.646
Of three that in Mount *Ida* naked strove, Par Lost 5.382
Insensibly three different Motions move? Par Lost 8.130
With long reach interpos'd; three sev'ral wayes Par Lost 10.323
In sight, to each of these three places led. Par Lost 10.324
Such fatal consequence unites us three: Par Lost 10.364
And from the Well of Life three drops instill'd. Par Lost 11.416
Thir order: last the Sire, and his three Sons Par Lost 11.736
Conspicuous with three listed colours gay, Par Lost 11.866
Palpable darkness, and blot out three dayes; Par Lost 12.188
Yet Wealth without these three is impotent, Par Reg 2.433

Three(*cont*)
By three days Pestilence? such was thy zeal — Par Reg 3.412
My Mother *Circe* with the Sirens three, — Mask 253
Three fair branches of your own, — Mask 969
B.M. ms 'these'
Of *Hesperus*, and his daughters three — Mask 982
Summers three times eight save one — Winchester 7
Stoln on his wing my three and twentith yeer! — Sonnet 7, 2
Cyriack, this three years day these eys, though clear — Sonnet 22, 1
1694 'Three'

Three-bolted
And Quiver with three-bolted Thunder stor'd, — Par Lost 6.764

Threefold
And thrice threefold the Gates; three folds were Brass, — Par Lost 2.645

Threescore
Of threescore and ten thousand *Israelites* — Par Reg 3.411

Threshed
His shadowy Flale hath thresh'd the Corn — Allegro 108

Threshing
Least on the threshing floore his hopeful sheaves — Par Lost 4.984

Threshold
Then stil at Hels dark threshold to have sate watch, — Par Lost 10.594
Before the starry threshold of *Joves* Court — Mask 1

Threw
And *Lichas* from the top of *Oeta* threw — Par Lost 2.545
Threw forth, till on the left side op'ning wide, — Par Lost 2.755
By thee created, and by thee threw down — Par Lost 3.391
Till Pride and worse Ambition threw me down — Par Lost 4.40
And o're the dark her Silver Mantle threw. — Par Lost 4.609
Thir Arms away they threw, and to the Hills — Par Lost 6.639
Urg'd them behind; headlong themselves they threw — Par Lost 6.864
Rising, the crumbl'd Earth above them threw — Par Lost 7.468

Thrice
As from the Center thrice to th' utmost Pole. — Par Lost 1.74
Thrice he assayd, and thrice in spight of scorn, — Par Lost 1.619
And thrice threefold the Gates; three folds were Brass, — Par Lost 2.645
Thrice happy Iles, but who dwelt happy there — Par Lost 3.570
Thrice chang'd with pale, ire, envie and despair, — Par Lost 4.115
Thir pleasant dwelling place. Thrice happie men, — Par Lost 7.625
Holy and just: thrice happie if they know — Par Lost 7.631
Thrice Fugitive about *Troy* Wall; or rage — Par Lost 9.16
With darkness, thrice the Equinoctial Line — Par Lost 9.64
Said hee, with one thrice acceptable stroke — Par Lost 10.855
Thrice she assay'd with flattering prayers and sighs, — Samson 392
Thrice I deluded her, and turn'd to sport — Samson 396
Who now defies thee thrice to single fight, — Samson 1222
Thrice upon thy fingers tip, — Mask 914
Thrice upon thy rubied lip, — Mask 915
With thrice great *Hermes*, or unsphear — Penseroso 88

Thrift
Whom thrift keeps up about his Country gear, — Mask 167
Trinity ms 'thrift', 'thirst' written in margin
Bridgewater ms 'thrifte'

Thrilling
Of *Cynthia*'s seat, the Airy region thrilling, — Nativity 103

Thrive
Thrive under evil, and work ease out of pain — Par Lost 2.261
They whom I favour thrive in wealth amain, — Par Reg 2.430

Thrived
At first against mankind so well had thriv'd — Par Reg 1.114
Abstemious I grew up and thriv'd amain; — Samson 637

Thrives
Idlely, while Satan our great Author thrives — Par Lost 10.236

Throat
The brazen Throat of Warr had ceast to roar, — Par Lost 11.713
An open grave their throat, their tongue they smooth. — Psalm 5, 28

Throated
From those deep throated Engins belcht, whose roar — Par Lost 6.586
1667 'deep-throated'

Throes
Prodigious motion felt and rueful throes. — Par Lost 2.780
And calls *Lucina* to her throws; — Winchester 26

Throne
Against the Throne and Monarchy of God — Par Lost 1.42
ms 'throne'
And shook his throne. What though the field be lost? — Par Lost 1.105
Sat on his Throne, upheld by old repute, — Par Lost 1.639
ms 'throne'
High on a Throne of Royal State, which far — Par Lost 2.1
Establisht in a safe unenvied Throne — Par Lost 2.23
Among his Angels; and his Throne it self — Par Lost 2.68
Though inaccessible, his fatal Throne: — Par Lost 2.104
All incorruptible would on his Throne — Par Lost 2.138
Strict Laws impos'd, to celebrate his Throne — Par Lost 2.241
Covers his Throne; from whence deep thunders roar — Par Lost 2.267
Banded against his Throne, but to remaine — Par Lost 2.320
But I should ill become this Throne, O Peers, — Par Lost 2.445
Bordering on light; when strait behold the Throne — Par Lost 2.959
Of Hymns and sacred Songs, wherewith thy Throne — Par Lost 3.148
With thee thy Manhood also to this Throne; — Par Lost 3.314
Towards either Throne they bow, and to the ground — Par Lost 3.350
Who in Gods presence, neerest to his Throne — Par Lost 3.649
In sight of God's high Throne, gloriously bright, — Par Lost 3.655
While they adore me on the Throne of Hell, — Par Lost 4.89
The Clouds that on his Western Throne attend: — Par Lost 4.597
High up in Heav'n, with songs to hymne his Throne, — Par Lost 4.944
Circle his Throne rejoycing, yee in Heav'n, — Par Lost 5.163
Innumerable before th' Almighties Throne — Par Lost 5.585

Throne(*cont*)
Melodious Hymns about the sovran Throne — Par Lost 5.656
Unworshipt, unobey'd the Throne supream — Par Lost 5.670
Is rising, who intends to erect his Throne — Par Lost 5.725
Address, and to begirt th' Almighty Throne — Par Lost 5.868
Within the Mount of God, fast by his Throne, — Par Lost 6.5
To win the Mount of God, and on his Throne — Par Lost 6.88
Then lighted from his gorgeous Throne, for now — Par Lost 6.103
The Throne of God unguarded, and his side — Par Lost 6.133
Against us from about his Throne, and judg'd — Par Lost 6.426
Th' Assessor of his Throne he thus began. — Par Lost 6.679
Whereon a Saphir Throne, inlaid with pure — Par Lost 6.758
All but the Throne it self of God. Full soon — Par Lost 6.834
Eternal Father from his Throne beheld — Par Lost 7.137
In prospect from his Throne, how good, how faire, — Par Lost 7.556
Of Heav'ns high-seated top, th' Impereal Throne — Par Lost 7.585
How all befell: they towards the Throne Supream — Par Lost 10.28
Or trie thee now more dang'rous to his Throne. — Par Lost 10.382
Ascended his high Throne, which under state — Par Lost 10.445
Before the Fathers Throne: Them the glad Son — Par Lost 11.20
And took thir Seats; till from his Throne supream — Par Lost 11.82
And *Samarchand* by *Oxus*, *Temirs* Throne, — Par Lost 11.389
Irrevocable, that his Regal Throne — Par Lost 12.323
The Throne hereditarie, and bound his Reign — Par Lost 12.370
Circling the Throne and Singing, while the hand — Par Reg 1.171
Thou shouldst be great and sit on *David*'s Throne, — Par Reg 1.240
As sitting Queen ador'd on Beauties Throne, — Par Reg 2.212
And his Son *Herod* plac'd on *Juda*'s Throne; — Par Reg 2.424
(Thy throne) but gold that got him puissant friends? — Par Reg 2.425
Whose off-spring on the Throne of *Juda* sat — Par Reg 2.440
Won *Asia* and the Throne of *Cyrus* held — Par Reg 3.33
To sit upon thy Father *David*'s Throne; — Par Reg 3.153
Though Priests, the Crown, and *David*'s Throne usurp'd, — Par Reg 3.169
But say thou wer't possess'd of *David*'s Throne — Par Reg 3.357
Thou on the Throne of *David* in full glory, — Par Reg 3.383
Will unpredict and fail me of the Throne: — Par Reg 3.395
For *Israel*, or for *David*, or his Throne, — Par Reg 3.408
Might'st thou expel this monster from his Throne — Par Reg 4.100
On *David*'s Throne, be propheci'd what will. — Par Reg 4.108
On *David*'s Throne, it shall be like a tree — Par Reg 4.147
To *Macedon*, and *Artaxerxes* Throne; — Par Reg 4.271
On *David*'s Throne; or Throne of all the world, — Par Reg 4.379
Of gaining *David*'s Throne no man knows when, — Par Reg 4.471
Against th' Attempter of thy Fathers Throne, — Par Reg 4.603
Guiding the fiery-wheeled throne, — Penseroso 53
In circle round her shining throne, — Arcades 15
Then his bright Throne, or burning Axletree could bear. — Nativity 84
The dreadfull Judge in middle Air shall spread his throne. — Nativity 164
Let down in clowdie throne to do the world some good. — Fair Inf 56
How he before the thunderous throne doth lie, — Vacation 36
About the supreme Throne — On Time 17
Trinity ms 'throne'
Ay sung before the saphire-colour'd throne — Musick 7
Trinity ms 'throne' ← 'Throne' ← 'throne'

Throned
O Prince, O Chief of many Throned Powers, — Par Lost 1.128
ms 'throned'
Jehovah thundring out of *Sion*, thron'd — Par Lost 1.386
High Thron'd above all highth, bent down his eye, — Par Lost 3.58
Because thou hast, though Thron'd in highest bliss — Par Lost 3.305
Thron'd inaccessible, but when thou shad'st — Par Lost 3.377
On the Chrystallin Skie, in Saphir Thron'd. — Par Lost 6.772
And Temple of his mightie Father Thron'd — Par Lost 6.890
True Image of the Father whether thron'd — Par Reg 4.596
Thron'd in Celestiall sheen, — Nativity 145
High thron'd in secret bliss, for us frail dust — Circum 19
Trinity ms 'high-thron'd'

Thrones
And Powers that earst in Heaven sat on Thrones; — Par Lost 1.360
ms 'thrones'
Thrones and Imperial Powers, off-spring of heav'n — Par Lost 2.310
O Progeny of Heav'n, Empyreal Thrones, — Par Lost 2.430
Thrones, Princedoms, Powers, Dominions I reduce: — Par Lost 3.320
Since by descending from the Thrones above, — Par Lost 5.363
Thrones, Dominations, Princedoms, Vertues, Powers, — Par Lost 5.601
Of Seraphim and Potentates and Thrones — Par Lost 5.749
Thrones, Dominations, Princedomes, Vertues, Powers, — Par Lost 5.772
Thrones, Dominations, Princedoms, Vertues, Powers, — Par Lost 5.840
The Rebel Thrones, but greater rage to see — Par Lost 6.199
Two potent Thrones, that to be less then Gods — Par Lost 6.366
O Father, O Supream of heav'nly Thrones, — Par Lost 6.723
Of Thrones and mighty Seraphim prostrate, — Par Lost 6.841
Cherub and Seraph, Potentates and Thrones, — Par Lost 7.198
Of high collateral glorie: him Thrones and Powers, — Par Lost 10.86
Thrones, Dominations, Princedoms, Vertues, Powers, — Par Lost 10.460
Or of the Thrones above, such Majestie — Par Lost 11.232
Celestial, whether among the Thrones, or nam'd — Par Lost 11.296
Princes, Heavens antient Sons, Aethereal Thrones, — Par Reg 2.121
Before the *Parthian*; these two Thrones except, — Par Reg 4.85

Throng
Throng numberless, like that Pigmean Race — Par Lost 1.780
The lowest of your throng; or if ye know, — Par Lost 4.831
(Such are the Courts of God) Th' Angelic throng — Par Lost 5.650
Where erst was thickest fight, th' Angelic throng, — Par Lost 6.308
Troop to thir Standard, so the watrie throng, — Par Lost 7.297
Th' Angelic Name, and thinner left the throng — Par Lost 9.142
At that so sudden blaze the *Stygian* throng — Par Lost 10.453
Unseen amid the throng: so violence — Par Lost 11.671

Throng(*cont*)
And vaunts of his great cunning to the throng — Par Reg 1.145
The other side was op'n, where the throng — Samson 1609
Begin to throng into my memory — Mask 206
line not in Bridgewater ms
The Trumpet spake not to the armed throng, — Nativity 58
Thy worth and skill exempts thee from the throng, — Sonnet 13, 5

Thronged
Attended: all access was throng'd, the Gates — Par Lost 1.761
Of rigid Spears, and Helmets throng'd, and Shields — Par Lost 6.83
Of Goats or timerous flock together throngd — Par Lost 6.857
With dreadful Faces throng'd and fierie Armes: — Par Lost 12.644
With herds the pastures throng'd, with flocks the hills, — Par Reg 3.260

Thronging
A Forrest huge of Spears: and thronging Helms — Par Lost 1.547
The thronging audience. In discourse more sweet — Par Lost 2.555
But rush upon me thronging, and present — Samson 21
Thronging the Seas with spawn innumerable, — Mask 713
Trinity ms 'thronging' ←'cramming'
Bridgewater ms 'throngeinge'

Throngs
Where throngs of Knights and Barons bold, — Allegro 119

Throttled
Throttl'd at length in the Air, expir'd and fell; — Par Reg 4.568

Through
Since through experience of this great event — Par Lost 1.118
To bellow through the vast and boundless Deep. — Par Lost 1.177
Through Optic Glass the *Tuscan* Artist views — Par Lost 1.288
Through Gods high sufferance for the tryal of man, — Par Lost 1.366
And various Idols through the Heathen World. — Par Lost 1.375
Thir childrens cries unheard, that past through fire — Par Lost 1.395
Rear'd in *Azotus*, dreaded through the Coast — Par Lost 1.464
Or in *Dodona*, and through all the bounds — Par Lost 1.518
All in a moment through the gloom were seen — Par Lost 1.544
Had to impose: He through the armed Files — Par Lost 1.567
Looks through the Horizontal misty Air — Par Lost 1.595
Insulting, and pursu'd us through the Deep, — Par Lost 2.79
Those thoughts that wander through Eternity, — Par Lost 2.148
Belike through impotence, or unaware, — Par Lost 2.156
Through labour and indurance. This deep world — Par Lost 2.262
And through the palpable obscure find out — Par Lost 2.406
Through the strict Senteries and Stations thick — Par Lost 2.412
Through all the Coasts of dark destruction seek — Par Lost 2.464
Which he through hazard huge must earn. But they — Par Lost 2.473
Through pain up by the roots *Thessalian* Pines, — Par Lost 2.544
No rest: through many a dark and drearie Vaile — Par Lost 2.618
Through the wide *Ethiopian* to the Cape — Par Lost 2.641
In secret, riding through the Air she comes — Par Lost 2.663
To yonder Gates? through them I mean to pass, — Par Lost 2.684
Through all the Empyrean: down they fell — Par Lost 2.771
Tore through my entrails, that with fear and pain — Par Lost 2.783
Then sweet, now sad to mention, through dire change — Par Lost 2.820
Th' unfounded deep, and through the void immense — Par Lost 2.829
Under spread Ensigns marching might pass through — Par Lost 2.886
As when a Gryfon through the Wilderness — Par Lost 2.943
Ore bog or steep, through strait, rough, dense, or rare, — Par Lost 2.948
Born through the hollow dark assaults his eare — Par Lost 2.953
Lies through your spacious Empire up to light, — Par Lost 2.974
Fled not in silence through the frighted deep — Par Lost 2.994
Encroacht on still through our intestine broiles — Par Lost 2.1001
Into the wilde expanse, and through the shock — Par Lost 2.1014
Through *Bosporus* betwixt the justling Rocks: — Par Lost 2.1018
Through utter and through middle darkness borne — Par Lost 3.16
Shine inward, and the mind through all her powers — Par Lost 3.52
Through all restraint broke loose he wings his way — Par Lost 3.87
Through Heav'n and Earth, so shall my glorie excel, — Par Lost 3.133
I through the ample Air in Triumph high — Par Lost 3.254
And where the river of Bliss through midst of Heavn — Par Lost 3.358
The full blaze of thy beams, and through a cloud — Par Lost 3.378
Not so on Man; him through their malice fall'n, — Par Lost 3.400
Through dark and desart wayes with peril gone — Par Lost 3.544
Through the pure marble Air his oblique way — Par Lost 3.564
Through the calm Firmament; but up or downe — Par Lost 3.574
Through his glaz'd Optic Tube yet never saw. — Par Lost 3.590
Draind through a Limbec to his Native forme. — Par Lost 3.605
That run through all the Heav'ns, or down to th' Earth — Par Lost 3.651
Interpreter through highest Heav'n to bring, — Par Lost 3.657
By his permissive will, through Heav'n and Earth: — Par Lost 3.685
Still ending, still renewing, through mid Heav'n; — Par Lost 3.729
Southward through *Eden* went a River large, — Par Lost 4.223
Nor chang'd his course, but through the shaggie hill — Par Lost 4.224
Upon the rapid current, which through veins — Par Lost 4.227
To seek her through the world; nor that sweet Grove — Par Lost 4.272
Through wood, through waste, o're hill, o're dale his roam. — Par Lost 4.538
Thither came *Uriel*, gliding through the Eeven — Par Lost 4.555
Search through this Garden, leave unsearcht no nook, — Par Lost 4.789
Ithuriel and *Zephon* through the shade, — Par Lost 4.868
Through wayes of danger by himself untri'd, — Par Lost 4.934
In progress through the rode of Heav'n Star-pav'd. — Par Lost 4.976
As through unquiet rest: he on his side — Par Lost 5.11
And on, methought, alone I pass'd through ways — Par Lost 5.50
Satan from Hell scap't through the darksom Gulf — Par Lost 5.225
Flew through the midst of Heav'n; th' angelic Quires — Par Lost 5.251
Through all th' Empyreal road; till at the Gate — Par Lost 5.253
He speeds, and through the vast Ethereal Skie — Par Lost 5.267
Into the blissful field, through Groves of Myrrhe, — Par Lost 5.292
Him through the spicie Forrest onward com — Par Lost 5.298
Through Spirits with ease; nor wonder; if by fire — Par Lost 5.439

Through(*cont*)
Through pride that sight, & thought himself impaird. — Par Lost 5.665
Who speedily through all the Hierarchies — Par Lost 5.692
Through the infinite Host, nor less for that — Par Lost 5.874
Long way through hostile scorn, which he susteind — Par Lost 5.904
Through Heav'ns wide Champain held his way, till Morn, — Par Lost 6.2
Lodge and dislodge by turns, which makes through Heav'n — Par Lost 6.7
Shot through with orient Beams: when all the Plain — Par Lost 6.15
I see that most through sloth had rather serve, — Par Lost 6.166
Th' Arch-Angel trumpet; through the vast of Heaven — Par Lost 6.203
No equal, raunging through the dire attack — Par Lost 6.248
Pass'd through him, but th' Ethereal substance clos'd — Par Lost 6.330
Mangl'd with gastly wounds through Plate and Maile, — Par Lost 6.368
Vain glorious, and through infamie seeks fame: — Par Lost 6.384
Orewearied, through the faint Satanic Host — Par Lost 6.392
Dawning through Heav'n: forth rush'd with whirlwind sound — Par Lost 6.749
Through his wilde Anarchie, so huge a rout — Par Lost 6.873
Triumphant through mid Heav'n, into the Courts — Par Lost 6.889
Through all Eternitie so late to build — Par Lost 7.92
Fell with his flaming Legions through the Deep — Par Lost 7.134
Round through the vast profunditie obscure, — Par Lost 7.229
To journie through the airie gloom began, — Par Lost 7.246
If steep, with torrent rapture, if through Plaine, — Par Lost 7.299
His Longitude through Heav'n high rode: the gray — Par Lost 7.373
Graze the Sea weed thir pasture, and through Groves — Par Lost 7.404
The glorious Train ascending: He through Heav'n, — Par Lost 7.574
Sent from her through the wide transpicuous aire, — Par Lost 8.141
And through all numbers absolute, though One; — Par Lost 8.421
So saying, through each Thicket Danck or Drie, — Par Lost 9.179
To such disport before her through the Field, — Par Lost 9.520
Kindl'd through agitation to a Flame, — Par Lost 9.637
To Boggs and Mires, and oft through Pond or Poole, — Par Lost 9.641
Of Preface brooking through his Zeal of Right. — Par Lost 9.676
Sighing through all her Works gave signs of woe, — Par Lost 9.783
Or fansied so, through expectation high — Par Lost 9.789
Ran through his veins, and all his joynts relax'd; — Par Lost 9.891
At Loopholes cut through thickest shade: Those Leaves — Par Lost 9.1110
Captivity led captive through the Aire, — Par Lost 10.188
Farr into *Chaos*, since the Fiend pass'd through, — Par Lost 10.233
Descend through Darkness, on your Rode with ease — Par Lost 10.394
Through Sin to Death expos'd by my exploit. — Par Lost 10.407
Thir course through thickest Constellations held — Par Lost 10.411
That scorn'd his indignation: through the Gate, — Par Lost 10.418
Of Forrein Worlds: he through the midst unmarkt, — Par Lost 10.441
Of hissing through the Hall, thick swarming now — Par Lost 10.522
Till I in Man residing through the Race, — Par Lost 10.607
Through *Chaos* hurld, obstruct the mouth of Hell — Par Lost 10.636
Through multitude that sung: Just are thy ways, — Par Lost 10.643
With terror through the dark Aereal Hall. — Par Lost 10.667
Death introduc'd through fierce antipathie: — Par Lost 10.709
And reasonings, though through Mazes, lead me still — Par Lost 10.830
Through the still Night, not now, as ere man fell, — Par Lost 10.846
Disturbances on Earth through Femal snares, — Par Lost 10.897
Through her perversness, but shall see her gaind — Par Lost 10.902
Dimentionless through Heav'nly dores; then clad — Par Lost 11.17
Through Heav'ns wide bounds; from them I will not hide — Par Lost 11.68
Instinct through all proportions low and high — Par Lost 11.562
Through all the Plain, and refuge none was found. — Par Lost 11.673
Unseen, and through thir habitations walks — Par Lost 12.49
Then through the Firey Pillar and the Cloud — Par Lost 12.208
Through the wilde Desert, not the readiest way, — Par Lost 12.216
Through the twelve Tribes, to rule by Laws ordaind: — Par Lost 12.226
Through the worlds wilderness long wanderd man — Par Lost 12.313
Of *Abrahams* Faith wherever through the world; — Par Lost 12.449
With victory, triumphing through the aire — Par Lost 12.452
Through all his Realme, and there confounded leave; — Par Lost 12.455
Working through love, upon thir hearts shall write, — Par Lost 12.489
Through *Eden* took thir solitarie way. — Par Lost 12.649
Through all temptation, and the Tempter foil'd — Par Reg 1.5
And bear through highth or depth of natures bounds — Par Reg 1.13
And unrecorded left through many an Age, — Par Reg 1.16
Through many a hard assay even to the death, — Par Reg 1.264
Spoken against, that through my very Soul — Par Reg 2.90
The just man, and divulges him through Heaven — Par Reg 3.62
When to extend his fame through Heaven and Earth, — Par Reg 3.65
Of vision multiplyed through air, or glass — Par Reg 4.41
Of *Hippogrif* bore through the Air sublime — Par Reg 4.542
As on a floating couch through the blithe Air, — Par Reg 4.585
Had been fulfilld but through mine own default, — Samson 45
And not as feeling through all parts diffus'd, — Samson 96
That she might look at will through every pore? — Samson 97
To worthiest deeds, if he through frailty err, — Samson 369
Temperst thy providence through his short course, — Samson 670
Smote *Sisera* sleeping through the Temples nail'd. — Samson 990
But vertue which breaks through all opposition, — Samson 1050
No less through all my sinews, joints and bones, — Samson 1142
Because they shall not trail me through thir streets — Samson 1402
Either at home, or through the high street passing, — Samson 1458
Made older then thy age through eye-sight lost. — Samson 1489
Through each high street: little I had dispatch't — Samson 1599
Through all *Philistian* bounds. To *Israel* — Samson 1714
Lies through the perplex't paths of this drear Wood, — Mask 37
(For most do taste through fond intemperate thirst) — Mask 67
Chances to passe through this adventrous glade, — Mask 79
Of silence, through the empty-vaulted night — Mask 250
Stoop thy pale visage through an amber cloud, — Mask 333
May trace huge Forests, and unharbour'd Heaths, — Mask 423
Trinity ms 'trace' ←'walke through'

Through(*cont*)
Where through the sacred rayes of Chastity, Mask 425
Through paths, and turnings oft'n trod by day, Mask 569
And through the porch and inlet of each sense Mask 839
Through the force, and through the wile Mask 906
Through this gloomy covert wide, Mask 945
And sent them here through hard assays Mask 972
B.M. ms 'thro''
Through the Sweet-Briar, or the Vine, Allegro 47
Through the high wood echoing shrill. Allegro 56
The melting voice through mazes running; Allegro 142
Through the Heav'ns wide pathles way; Penseroso 70
Stooping through a fleecy cloud. Penseroso 72
Where glowing Embers through the room Penseroso 79
As may with sweetnes, through mine ear, Penseroso 164
I see bright honour sparkle through your eyes, Arcades 27
Through the dear might of him that walk'd the waves; Lycidas 173
Down through the turning sphear Nativity 48
She strikes a universall Peace through Sea and Land. Nativity 52
The wakefull trump of doom must thunder through the deep, Nativity 156
Runs through the arched roof in words deceiving. Nativity 175
Through middle empire of the freezing aire Fair Inf 16
Half unpronounc't, slide through my infant-lipps, Vacation 4
Then passing through the Spheres of watchful fire, Vacation 40
Through the soft silence of the list'ning night; Circum 5
Through pangs fled to felicity, Winchester 68
Fairfax, whose name in armes through Europe rings Sonnet 15, 1
Cromwell, our cheif of men, who through a cloud Sonnet 16, 1
This thought might lead me through the worlds vain mask Sonnet 22, 13
Lay deep their plots together through each Land, Psalm 2, 4
Thee through my story Psalm 3, 8
Through grief consumes, is waxen old and dark Psalm 6, 14
And glorious is thy name through all the earth? Psalm 8, 2
Fowl of the Heavens, and Fish that through the wet Psalm 8, 21
And glorious is thy name through all the earth. Psalm 8, 24
When as he pass'd through Aegypt land; Psalm 81, 19
They pass through Baca's *thirstie* Vale, Psalm 84, 21
As through a fruitfull watry Dale Psalm 84, 23
Through sorrow, and affliction great Psalm 88, 37
Thy threatnings cut me through. Psalm 88, 66
Sees his foule inside through his whited skin. Prose 10, 6
Walk'st on the rowling Sphear, and through the deep, Prose 12, 2

Throughout
And Trumpets sound throughout the Host proclaim Par Lost 1.754
ms 'through out'
Equal to ours, throughout the spacious North; Par Lost 5.726
Yet soon he heal'd; for Spirits that live throughout Par Lost 6.344
The stedfast Empyrean shook throughout, Par Lost 6.833
Throughout the fluid Mass, but downward purg'd Par Lost 7.237
Subdue it, and throughout Dominion hold Par Lost 7.532
Among the Heathen, (for throughout the World Par Reg 2.443
All Monarchies besides throughout the world, Par Reg 4.150
Of Sun or Moon or Starre throughout the year, Sonnet 22, 5
Through out the land of thy abode Psalm 81, 37

Throw
And throw sweet garland wreaths into her stream Mask 850
Bridgewater ms 'throwe'
I throw it on the ground Mask Tr. ms 22.22
Throw hither all your quaint enameld eyes, Lycidas 139
Trinity ms 'throw' ← 'bring'
The Saintly Vail of Maiden white to throw, Nativity 42
Over the Pole thy thickest mantle throw, Passion 30
And flouts at us they throw Psalm 80, 28
Our Land shall forth in plenty throw Psalm 85, 51

Throwest
But throw'st them lower then thou didst exalt them high, Samson 689

Thrown
From Heav'n, they fabl'd, thrown by angry *Jove* Par Lost 1.741
Now in loose Garlands thick thrown off, the bright Par Lost 3.362
Pass'd underneath ingulft, for God had thrown Par Lost 4.225
Thrown on them as a shelter from his ire. Par Lost 6.843
Well if thrown out, as supernumerarie Par Lost 10.887
Discover'd in his fraud, thrown from his hope, Par Reg 4.3
Or left thy carkass where the Ass lay thrown: Samson 1097
Because you have thrown of your Prelate Lord, Forcers 1

Throws
Torments him; round he throws his baleful eyes Par Lost 1.56
Down right into the Worlds first Region throws Par Lost 3.562
Throws his steep flight in many an Aerie wheele, Par Lost 3.741
And makes one blot of all the ayr, Mask 133
Trinity ms 'makes one' ← 'throws a' ← 'makes a'
The Flowry *May*, who from her green lap throws May Morn 3

Thrust
Who hates me, and hath hither thrust me down Par Lost 2.857
Of bliss on bliss, while I to Hell am thrust, Par Lost 4.508
Into a Dungeon thrust, to work with Slaves? Samson 367

Thummim
Urim and *Thummim*, those oraculous gems Par Reg 3.14

Thunder
He with his Thunder: and till then who knew Par Lost 1.93
ms 'thunder'
Of Heav'n receiv'd us falling, and the Thunder, Par Lost 1.174
ms 'thunder'
Whom Thunder hath made greater? Here at least Par Lost 1.258
ms 'thunder'
Deep scars of Thunder had intrencht, and care Par Lost 1.601
ms 'thunder'
Infernal Thunder, and for Lightning see Par Lost 2.66

Thunder(*cont*)
With Heav'ns afflicting Thunder, and besought Par Lost 2.166
Of Thunder and the Sword of *Michael* Par Lost 2.294
Of Thunder heard remote. Towards him they bend Par Lost 2.477
Harsh Thunder, that the lowest bottom shook Par Lost 2.882
Thy Fathers dreadful Thunder didst not spare, Par Lost 3.393
Thy blasting volied Thunder made all speed Par Lost 4.928
His Thunder on thy head, devouring fire. Par Lost 5.893
Of Thunder: back defeated to return Par Lost 6.606
So easie, and of his Thunder made a scorn, Par Lost 6.632
My Bow and Thunder, my Almightie Arms Par Lost 6.713
And Quiver with three-bolted Thunder stor'd, Par Lost 6.764
His Thunder in mid Volie, for he meant Par Lost 6.854
Skie lowr'd and muttering Thunder, som sad drops Par Lost 9.1002
Amidst in Thunder utter'd thus his voice. Par Lost 10.33
Sea, Aire, and Shoar, the Thunder when to rowle Par Lost 10.666
Would Thunder in my ears, no fear of worse Par Lost 10.780
And all his people; Thunder mixt with Haile, Par Lost 12.181
In Thunder Lightning and loud Trumpets sound Par Lost 12.229
When his fierce thunder drove us to the deep; Par Reg 1.90
Gan thunder, and both ends of Heav'n, the Clouds Par Reg 4.410
Of thunder, chas'd the clouds, and laid the winds, Par Reg 4.429
The whole roof after them, with burst of thunder Samson 1651
His cloudless thunder bolted on thir heads. Samson 1696
Speaks thunder, and the chains of *Erebus* Mask 804
line not in Trinity ms
line not in Bridgewater ms
And heal the harms of thwarting thunder blew, Arcades 51
The wakefull trump of doom must thunder through the deep, Nativity 156
And hills of Snow and lofts of piled Thunder, Vacation 42
I answer'd thee in thunder deep Psalm 81, 29

Thunderbolts
Thus drooping, or with linked Thunderbolts Par Lost 1.328
ms 'thunderbolts'
Thir devilish glut, chaind Thunderbolts and Hail Par Lost 6.589

Thunder-clasping
He with his thunder-clasping hand, Psalm 136, 37

Thunderer
Formost to stand against the Thunderers aim Par Lost 2.28
The Thunderer of his only dreaded bolt. Par Lost 6.491

Thundering
Of thundring *Aetna*, whose combustible Par Lost 1.233
Jehovah thundring out of *Sion*, thron'd Par Lost 1.386
From far with thundring noise among our foes Par Lost 6.487
Comes thundring back with dreadful revolution Par Lost 10.814
More Lordly thund'ring then thou well wilt bear. Samson 1353

Thunderous
Notus and *Afer* black with thundrous Clouds Par Lost 10.702
How he before the thunderous throne doth lie, Vacation 36

Thunders
Covers his Throne; from whence deep thunders roar Par Lost 2.267
Grasping ten thousand Thunders, which he sent Par Lost 6.836
Thy Thunders magnifi'd; but to create Par Lost 7.606

Thunderstruck
Drove them before him Thunder-struck, pursu'd Par Lost 6.858
Nigh Thunder-struck, th' exalted man, to whom Par Reg 1.36

Thus
Breaking the horrid silence thus began. Par Lost 1.83
And him thus answer'd soon his bold Compeer. Par Lost 1.127
In horrible destruction laid thus low, Par Lost 1.137
Thus Satan talking to his neerest Mate Par Lost 1.192
Lye thus astonisht on th' oblivious Pool, Par Lost 1.266
Thus answer'd. Leader of those Armies bright, Par Lost 1.272
Thus drooping, or with linked Thunderbolts Par Lost 1.328
From mortal or immortal minds. Thus they Par Lost 1.559
By *Fontarabbia*. Thus far these beyond Par Lost 1.587
On *Lemnos* th' *Aegaean* Ile: thus they relate, Par Lost 1.746
Thus incorporeal Spirits to smallest forms Par Lost 1.789
Thus high uplifted beyond hope, aspires Par Lost 2.7
Beyond thus high, insatiate to pursue Par Lost 2.8
His proud imaginations thus displaid. Par Lost 2.10
Thus farr at least recover'd, hath much more Par Lost 2.22
We sunk thus low? Th' ascent is easie then; Par Lost 2.81
Calls us to Penance? More destroy'd then thus Par Lost 2.92
And with perswasive accent thus began. Par Lost 2.118
Victorious. Thus repuls'd, our final hope Par Lost 2.142
Thus sitting, thus consulting, thus in Arms? Par Lost 2.164
Shall we then live thus vile, the Race of Heav'n Par Lost 2.194
Thus trampl'd, thus expell'd to suffer here Par Lost 2.195
His anger, and perhaps thus farr remov'd Par Lost 2.211
Thus *Belial* with words cloath'd in reasons garb Par Lost 2.226
Not peace: and after him thus *Mammon* spake. Par Lost 2.228
Or Summers Noon-tide air, while thus he spake. Par Lost 2.309
In strictest bondage, though thus far remov'd, Par Lost 2.321
Hatching vain Empires. Thus *Beelzebub* Par Lost 2.378
They vote: whereat his speech he thus renews. Par Lost 2.389
Conscious of highest worth, unmov'd thus spake. Par Lost 2.429
None shall partake with me. Thus saying rose Par Lost 2.466
Thus they thir doubtful consultations dark Par Lost 2.486
The *Stygian* Counsel thus dissolv'd; and forth Par Lost 2.506
The lip of *Tantalus*. Thus roving on Par Lost 2.614
And with disdainful look thus first began. Par Lost 2.680
What thing thou art, thus double-form'd, and why Par Lost 2.741
T' whom thus the Portress of Hell Gate reply'd; Par Lost 2.746
Distorted, all my nether shape thus grew Par Lost 2.784
Soon learnd, now milder, and thus answerd smooth. Par Lost 2.816
His mother bad, and thus bespake her Sire. Par Lost 2.849
Thus saying, from her side the fatal Key, Par Lost 2.871

Thus(*cont*)

Confus'dly, and which thus must ever fight,	Par Lost 2.914
T' whom *Satan* turning boldly, thus. Ye Powers	Par Lost 2.968
Thus *Satan;* and him thus the Anarch old	Par Lost 2.988
Tunes her nocturnal Note. Thus with the Year	Par Lost 3.40
Thus to his onely Son foreseeing spake.	Par Lost 3.79
Thus while God spake, ambrosial fragrance fill'd	Par Lost 3.135
Which uttering thus he to his Father spake.	Par Lost 3.143
Fall circumvented thus by fraud, though joynd	Par Lost 3.152
Or shall the Adversarie thus obtain	Par Lost 3.156
To whom the great Creatour thus reply'd.	Par Lost 3.167
His dearest mediation thus renewd.	Par Lost 3.226
Wondring; but soon th' Almighty thus reply'd:	Par Lost 3.273
Thus they in Heav'n, above the starry Sphear,	Par Lost 3.416
O're Sea and Land: him *Satan* thus accostes;	Par Lost 3.653
Alone thus wandring. Brightest Seraph tell	Par Lost 3.667
In his uprightness answer thus returnd.	Par Lost 3.693
From thy Empyreal Mansion thus alone,	Par Lost 3.699
Thus said, he turnd, and *Satan* bowing low,	Par Lost 3.736
Then much revolving, thus in sighs began.	Par Lost 4.31
All hope excluded thus, behold in stead	Par Lost 4.105
Thus while he spake, each passion dimm'd his face	Par Lost 4.114
Imbround the noontide Bowrs: Thus was this place,	Par Lost 4.246
Scarce thus at length faild speech recoverd sad.	Par Lost 4.357
Into our room of bliss thus high advanc't	Par Lost 4.359
To you whom I could pittie thus forlorne	Par Lost 4.374
To first of women *Eve* thus moving speech,	Par Lost 4.409
To whom thus *Eve* repli'd. O thou for whom	Par Lost 4.440
Had not a voice thus warnd me, What thou seest,	Par Lost 4.467
But follow strait, invisibly thus led?	Par Lost 4.476
Ey'd them askance, and to himself thus plaind.	Par Lost 4.504
Sight hateful, sight tormenting! thus these two	Par Lost 4.505
Impetuous winds: he thus began in haste.	Par Lost 4.560
To whom the winged Warriour thus returnd:	Par Lost 4.576
When *Adam* thus to *Eve:* Fair Consort, th' hour	Par Lost 4.610
To whom thus *Eve* with perfet beauty adornd.	Par Lost 4.634
Thus talking hand in hand alone they pass'd	Par Lost 4.689
Thus at thir shadie Lodge arriv'd, both stood	Par Lost 4.720
When *Gabriel* to his next in power thus spake.	Par Lost 4.781
That neer him stood, and gave them thus in charge.	Par Lost 4.787
Him thus intent *Ithuriel* with his Spear	Par Lost 4.810
Yet thus, unmovd with fear, accost him soon.	Par Lost 4.822
To whom thus *Zephon*, answering scorn with scorn.	Par Lost 4.834
Gabriel from the Front thus calld aloud.	Par Lost 4.865
To whom with stern regard thus *Gabriel* spake.	Par Lost 4.877
To whom thus *Satan*, with contemptuous brow.	Par Lost 4.885
In that dark durance: thus much what was askt.	Par Lost 4.899
Thus he in scorn. The warlike Angel mov'd,	Par Lost 4.902
Disdainfully half smiling thus repli'd.	Par Lost 4.903
To which the Fiend thus answerd frowning stern.	Par Lost 4.924
While thus he spake, th' Angelic Squadron bright	Par Lost 4.977
Which *Gabriel* spying, thus bespake the Fiend.	Par Lost 4.1005
Her hand soft touching, whisperd thus. Awake	Par Lost 5.17
On *Adam*, whom imbracing, thus she spake.	Par Lost 5.27
But he thus overjoy'd, O Fruit Divine,	Par Lost 5.67
Sweet of thy self, but much more sweet thus cropt,	Par Lost 5.68
To find this but a dream! Thus *Eve* her Night	Par Lost 5.93
Related, and thus *Adam* answerd sad.	Par Lost 5.94
To add more sweetness, and they thus began.	Par Lost 5.152
Thus wondrous fair; thy self how wondrous then!	Par Lost 5.155
His barren leaves. Them thus imploid beheld	Par Lost 5.219
Berrie or Grape: to whom thus *Adam* call'd.	Par Lost 5.307
To whom thus *Eve*. *Adam*, earths hallowd mould,	Par Lost 5.321
Thus said. Native of Heav'n, for other place	Par Lost 5.361
Whom thus th' Angelic Vertue answerd milde.	Par Lost 5.371
No fear lest Dinner coole; when thus began	Par Lost 5.396
Thus when with meats and drinks they had suffic'd,	Par Lost 5.451
Thus to th' Empyreal Minister he fram'd.	Par Lost 5.460
Thus *Adam* made request, and *Raphael*	Par Lost 5.561
After short pause assenting, thus began.	Par Lost 5.562
Recorded eminent. Thus when in Orbes	Par Lost 5.594
Brightness had made invisible, thus spake.	Par Lost 5.599
Awak'ning, thus to him in secret spake.	Par Lost 5.672
And smiling to his onely Son thus said.	Par Lost 5.718
Of counterfeted truth thus held thir ears.	Par Lost 5.771
Thus farr his bold discourse without controule	Par Lost 5.803
The current of his fury thus oppos'd.	Par Lost 5.808
One of our number thus reduc't becomes,	Par Lost 5.843
Th' Apostat, and more haughty thus repli'd.	Par Lost 5.852
Encompass'd round with foes, thus answerd bold.	Par Lost 5.876
From midst a Golden Cloud thus milde was heard.	Par Lost 6.28
And thus his own undaunted heart explores.	Par Lost 6.113
Incens't, and thus securely him defi'd.	Par Lost 6.130
Thus answerd. Ill for thee, but in wisht houre	Par Lost 6.150
To whom in brief thus *Abdiel* stern repli'd.	Par Lost 6.171
Thus foil'd thir mightiest, ours joy filld, and shout,	Par Lost 6.200
And visage all enflam'd first thus began.	Par Lost 6.261
So spake the Prince of Angels; to whom thus	Par Lost 6.281
And in the midst thus undismai'd began.	Par Lost 6.417
And cloudie in aspect thus answering spake.	Par Lost 6.450
Came flying, and in mid Aire aloud thus cri'd.	Par Lost 6.536
Satan: And thus was heard Commanding loud.	Par Lost 6.557
And to his Mates thus in derision call'd.	Par Lost 6.608
To whom thus *Belial* in like gamesom mood,	Par Lost 6.620
Th' Assessor of his Throne he thus began.	Par Lost 6.679
For thee I have ordain'd it, and thus farr	Par Lost 6.700
And this perverse Commotion governd thus,	Par Lost 6.706
And thus the filial Godhead answering spake.	Par Lost 6.722

Thus(*cont*)

To all his Host on either hand thus spake.	Par Lost 6.800
Thus measuring things in Heav'n by things on Earth	Par Lost 6.893
Proceeded thus to ask his Heav'nly Guest.	Par Lost 7.69
Thus *Adam* his illustrious Guest besought:	Par Lost 7.109
And thus the Godlike Angel answerd milde.	Par Lost 7.110
Thir multitude, and to his Son thus spake.	Par Lost 7.138
And said, thus farr extend, thus farr thy bounds,	Par Lost 7.230
Thus God the Heav'n created, thus the Earth,	Par Lost 7.232
He nam'd. Thus was the first Day Eev'n and Morn:	Par Lost 7.252
Of Rainbows and Starrie Eyes. The Waters thus	Par Lost 7.446
Present) thus to his Son audibly spake.	Par Lost 7.518
Wherever thus created, for no place	Par Lost 7.535
And sons of men, whom God hath thus advanc't,	Par Lost 7.626
With *Halleluiahs:* Thus was Sabbath kept.	Par Lost 7.634
Then as new wak't thus gratefully repli'd.	Par Lost 8.4
1667 'To whom thus *Adam*'	
Hystorian, who thus largely hast allayd	Par Lost 8.7
Benevolent and facil thus repli'd.	Par Lost 8.65
But whether thus these things, or whether not,	Par Lost 8.159
Contented that thus farr hath been reveal'd	Par Lost 8.177
To whom thus *Adam* cleerd of doubt, repli'd.	Par Lost 8.179
To whom thus *Raphael* answer'd heav'nly meek.	Par Lost 8.217
So spake the Godlike Power, and thus our Sire.	Par Lost 8.249
Tell, if ye saw, how came I thus, how here?	Par Lost 8.277
From whom I have that thus I move and live,	Par Lost 8.281
While thus I call'd, and stray'd I knew not whither,	Par Lost 8.283
Return'd and gracious purpose thus renew'd.	Par Lost 8.337
As thus he spake, each Bird and Beast behold	Par Lost 8.349
And to the Heav'nly vision thus presum'd.	Par Lost 8.356
Thus I presumptuous; and the vision bright,	Par Lost 8.367
As with a smile more bright'nd, thus repli'd.	Par Lost 8.368
And humble deprecation thus repli'd.	Par Lost 8.378
Thus I embold'nd spake, and freedom us'd	Par Lost 8.434
Thus farr to try thee, *Adam*, I was pleas'd,	Par Lost 8.437
She heard me thus, and though divinely brought,	Par Lost 8.500
Thus I have told thee all my State, and brought	Par Lost 8.521
To whom thus half abash't *Adam* repli'd.	Par Lost 8.595
So saying, he arose; whom *Adam* thus	Par Lost 8.644
Ganges and *Indus:* thus the Orb he roam'd	Par Lost 9.82
Thus he resolv'd, but first from inward griefe	Par Lost 9.97
His bursting passion into plaints thus pour'd:	Par Lost 9.98
And to repaire his numbers thus impair'd,	Par Lost 9.144
I dread, and to elude, thus wrapt in mist	Par Lost 9.158
And *Eve* first to her Husband thus began.	Par Lost 9.204
For while so near each other thus all day	Par Lost 9.220
To whom mild answer *Adam* thus return'd.	Par Lost 9.226
With sweet austeer composure thus reply'd,	Par Lost 9.272
Thus her reply with accent sweet renewd.	Par Lost 9.321
If this be our condition, thus to dwell	Par Lost 9.322
And *Eden* were no *Eden* thus expos'd.	Par Lost 9.341
To whom thus *Adam* fervently repli'd.	Par Lost 9.342
Us both securer then thus warnd thou seemst,	Par Lost 9.371
With thy permission then, and thus forewarnd	Par Lost 9.378
Thus saying, from her Husbands hand her hand	Par Lost 9.385
To *Pales*, or *Pomona* thus adornd,	Par Lost 9.393
Thus earlie, thus alone; her Heav'nly forme	Par Lost 9.457
Of mischief, gratulating, thus excites.	Par Lost 9.472
Compulsion thus transported to forget	Par Lost 9.474
His fraudulent temptation thus began.	Par Lost 9.531
Displeas'd that I approach thee thus, and gaze	Par Lost 9.535
Insatiate, I thus single; nor have feard	Par Lost 9.536
Thy awful brow, more awful thus retir'd.	Par Lost 9.537
Not unamaz'd she thus in answer spake.	Par Lost 9.552
To whom the guileful Tempter thus reply'd.	Par Lost 9.567
Mee thus, though importune perhaps, to come	Par Lost 9.610
Yet more amaz'd unwarie thus reply'd.	Par Lost 9.614
Which when she saw, thus to her guide she spake.	Par Lost 9.646
To whom thus *Eve* yet sinless. Of the Fruit	Par Lost 9.659
The Tempter all impassiond thus began.	Par Lost 9.678
Th' offence, that Man should thus attain to know?	Par Lost 9.726
Pausing a while, thus to her self she mus'd.	Par Lost 9.744
Thus to her self she pleasingly began.	Par Lost 9.794
Thus grown. Experience, next to thee I owe,	Par Lost 9.807
Which with bland words at will she thus addrest.	Par Lost 9.855
Thus *Eve* with Countnance blithe her storie told;	Par Lost 9.886
Speechless he stood and pale, till thus at length	Par Lost 9.894
Thus in calm mood his Words to *Eve* he turnd.	Par Lost 9.920
And peril great provok't, who thus hath dar'd	Par Lost 9.922
So *Adam*, and thus *Eve* to him repli'd.	Par Lost 9.960
Till *Adam* thus 'gan *Eve* to dalliance move,	Par Lost 9.1016
Which leaves us naked thus, of Honour void,	Par Lost 9.1074
Thus fenc't, and as they thought, thir shame in part	Par Lost 9.1119
Superior sway: from thus distemperd brest,	Par Lost 9.1131
Speech intermitted thus to *Eve* renewd.	Par Lost 9.1133
To whom soon mov'd with touch of blame thus *Eve*.	Par Lost 9.1143
And thou th' accuser. Thus it shall befall	Par Lost 9.1182
Thus they in mutual accusation spent	Par Lost 9.1187
Amidst in Thunder utter'd thus his voice.	Par Lost 10.33
Express'd, and thus divinely answer'd milde.	Par Lost 10.67
Thus saying, from his radiant Seat he rose	Par Lost 10.85
Approaching, thus to *Adam* call'd aloud.	Par Lost 10.102
Not pleas'd, thus entertaind with solitude,	Par Lost 10.105
Whence *Adam* faultring long, thus answer'd brief.	Par Lost 10.115
To whom thus *Adam* sore beset repli'd.	Par Lost 10.124
To whom the sovran Presence thus repli'd.	Par Lost 10.144
So having said, he thus to *Eve* in few:	Par Lost 10.157
Bold or loquacious, thus abasht repli'd.	Par Lost 10.161

Thus(*cont*)
And on the Serpent thus his curse let fall. Par Lost 10.174
And to the Woman thus his Sentence turn'd. Par Lost 10.192
On *Adam* last thus judgement he pronounc'd. Par Lost 10.197
Meanwhile ere thus was sin'd and judg'd on Earth, Par Lost 10.229
Sin opening, who thus now to Death began. Par Lost 10.234
Whom thus the meager Shadow answerd soon. Par Lost 10.264
Inchanting Daughter, thus the silence broke. Par Lost 10.353
To fortifie thus farr, and overlay Par Lost 10.370
Whom thus the Prince of Darkness answerd glad. Par Lost 10.383
As in thir crime. Thus was th' applause they meant, Par Lost 10.545
Whom they triumph'd once lapst. Thus were they plagu'd Par Lost 10.572
On his pale Horse: to whom *Sin* thus began. Par Lost 10.590
Whom thus the Sin-born Monster answerd soon. Par Lost 10.596
To whom th' incestuous Mother thus repli'd. Par Lost 10.602
To those bright Orders utterd thus his voice. Par Lost 10.615
Sirocco, and *Libecchio*, Thus began Par Lost 10.706
Thus to disburd'n sought with sad complaint. Par Lost 10.719
I thus contest; then should have been refusd Par Lost 10.756
For one mans fault thus guiltless be condemn'd, Par Lost 10.823
With that bad Woman? Thus what thou desir'st Par Lost 10.837
Thus *Adam* to himself lamented loud Par Lost 10.845
Whom thus afflicted when sad *Eve* beheld, Par Lost 10.863
But her with stern regard he thus repell'd. Par Lost 10.866
His peace, and thus proceeded in her plaint. Par Lost 10.913
Forsake me not thus, *Adam*, witness Heav'n Par Lost 10.914
And thus with peaceful words uprais'd her soon. Par Lost 10.946
To whom thus *Eve*, recovering heart, repli'd. Par Lost 10.966
Labouring had rais'd, and thus to *Eve* repli'd. Par Lost 10.1012
Thus they in lowliest plight repentant stood Par Lost 11.1
Presenting, thus to intercede began. Par Lost 11.21
To mitigate thus plead, not to reverse) Par Lost 11.41
Th' Almighty thus pronounced his sovran Will. Par Lost 11.83
Which thus to *Eve* his welcome words renewd. Par Lost 11.140
To whom thus *Eve* with sad demeanour meek. Par Lost 11.162
Who highly thus to entitle me voutsaf'st, Par Lost 11.170
Pursuing, not unmov'd to *Eve* thus spake. Par Lost 11.192
While the great Visitant approachd, thus spake. Par Lost 11.225
Inclin'd not, but his coming thus declar'd. Par Lost 11.250
Must I thus leave thee Paradise? thus leave Par Lost 11.269
Whom thus the Angel interrupted milde. Par Lost 11.286
Thus over-fond, on that which is not thine; Par Lost 11.289
To *Michael* thus his humble words addressd. Par Lost 11.295
To whom thus *Michael* with regard benigne. Par Lost 11.334
To whom thus *Adam* gratefully repli'd. Par Lost 11.370
Soon rais'd, and his attention thus recall'd. Par Lost 11.422
Dismai'd, and thus in haste to th' Angel cri'd. Par Lost 11.449
Is Pietie thus and pure Devotion paid? Par Lost 11.452
T' whom *Michael* thus, hee also mov'd, repli'd. Par Lost 11.453
To whom thus *Michael*. Death thou hast seen Par Lost 11.466
To be thus wrested from us? rather why Par Lost 11.503
Obtruded on us thus? who if we knew Par Lost 11.504
Glad to be so dismist in peace. Can thus Par Lost 11.507
The bent of Nature; which he thus express'd. Par Lost 11.597
To whom thus *Michael*. Judg not what is best Par Lost 11.603
To whom thus *Adam* of short joy bereft. Par Lost 11.628
Deaths Ministers, not Men, who thus deal Death Par Lost 11.676
To whom thus *Michael*. These are the product Par Lost 11.683
Thus Fame shall be atchiev'd, renown on Earth, Par Lost 11.698
And scarce to th' Angel utterdst thus thy plaint. Par Lost 11.762
How comes it thus? unfould, Celestial Guide, Par Lost 11.785
To whom thus *Michael*. Those whom last thou sawst Par Lost 11.787
Greatly rejoyc'd, and thus his joy broke forth. Par Lost 11.869
Thus thou hast seen one World begin and end; Par Lost 12.6
And hear the din; thus was the building left Par Lost 12.61
Whereto thus *Adam* fatherly displeas'd. Par Lost 12.63
To whom thus *Michael*. Justly thou abhorr'st Par Lost 12.79
Thus will this latter, as the former World, Par Lost 12.105
Of *Egypt* must lie dead. Thus with ten wounds Par Lost 12.190
Of great *Messiah* shall sing. Thus Laws and Rites Par Lost 12.244
His whole descent, who thus shall *Canaan* win. Par Lost 12.269
To whom thus *Michael*. Doubt not but that sin Par Lost 12.285
To whom thus *Michael*. Dream not of thir fight, Par Lost 12.386
Replete with joy and wonder thus repli'd. Par Lost 12.468
As did thir Lord before them. Thus they win Par Lost 12.502
He ended; and thus *Adam* last reply'd. Par Lost 12.552
To whom thus also th' Angel last repli'd: Par Lost 12.574
And thus with words not sad she him receav'd. Par Lost 12.609
With looks agast and sad he thus bespake. Par Reg 1.43
Of Angels, thus to *Gabriel* smiling spake. Par Reg 1.129
His holy Meditations thus persu'd. Par Reg 1.195
Yet neither thus disheartn'd or dismay'd, Par Reg 1.268
Perus'd him, then with words thus utt'red spake. Par Reg 1.320
Whom thus answer'd th' Arch Fiend now undisguis'd. Par Reg 1.357
Envy they say excites me, thus to gain Par Reg 1.397
To whom our Saviour sternly thus reply'd. Par Reg 1.406
Thus we rejoyc'd, but soon our joy is turn'd Par Reg 2.37
But let us wait; thus far he hath perform'd, Par Reg 2.49
Thus they out of their plaints new hope resume Par Reg 2.58
Some troubl'd thoughts, which she in sighs thus clad. Par Reg 2.65
Thus long to some great purpose he obscures. Par Reg 2.101
Thus *Mary* pondering oft, and oft to mind Par Reg 2.105
Sollicitous and blank he thus began. Par Reg 2.120
The fleshliest Incubus, and thus advis'd. Par Reg 2.152
To whom quick answer Satan thus return'd. Par Reg 2.172
Now hungring first, and to himself thus said. Par Reg 2.244
It was the hour of night, when thus the Son Par Reg 2.260
Thus wore out night, and now the Herald Lark Par Reg 2.279

Thus(*cont*)
To whom thus Jesus; what conclud'st thou hence? Par Reg 2.317
To whom thus Jesus temperately reply'd: Par Reg 2.378
To whom thus answer'd Satan malecontent: Par Reg 2.392
To whom thus Jesus patiently reply'd; Par Reg 2.432
With soothing words renew'd, him thus accosts. Par Reg 3.6
To whom our Saviour calmly thus reply'd. Par Reg 3.43
Recount his praises; thus he did to *Job*, Par Reg 3.64
To whom the Tempter murmuring thus reply'd. Par Reg 3.108
Thy right by sitting still or thus retiring? Par Reg 3.164
To whom our Saviour answer thus return'd. Par Reg 3.181
And to our Saviour thus his words renew'd. Par Reg 3.346
Thus long from *Israel;* serving as of old Par Reg 3.378
To whom our Saviour answer'd thus unmov'd. Par Reg 3.386
And now the Tempter thus his silence broke. Par Reg 4.43
These thus degenerate, by themselves enslav'd, Par Reg 4.144
Whom thus our Saviour answer'd with disdain. Par Reg 4.170
To whom our Saviour sagely thus repli'd. Par Reg 4.285
Thus to our Saviour with stern brow reply'd. Par Reg 4.367
To wish thou never hadst rejected thus Par Reg 4.376
Thus pass'd the night so foul till morning fair Par Reg 4.426
And in a careless mood thus to him said. Par Reg 4.450
And staid not, but in brief him answer'd thus. Par Reg 4.485
The Son of God; and added thus in scorn: Par Reg 4.550
To whom thus Jesus: also it is written, Par Reg 4.560
Thus they the Son of God our Saviour meek Par Reg 4.636
Why am I thus bereav'd thy prime decree? Samson 85
Then had I not been thus exil'd from light; Samson 98
Will not connive, or linger, thus provok'd, Samson 466
Nor shall his wondrous gifts be frustrate thus. Samson 589
Yet toward these thus dignifi'd, thou oft Samson 682
Why do I humble thus my self, and suing Samson 965
Har. Thou durst not thus disparage glorious arms Samson 1130
Off. *Samson*, to thee our Lords thus bid me say; Samson 1310
At last with head erect thus cryed aloud, Samson 1639
About my Mother *Circe*. Thus I hurl Mask 153
Bridgewater ms 'thus'
Trinity ms 'thus'
In thy dark lantern thus close up the Stars, Mask 197
line not in Bridgewater ms
Co. What chance good Lady hath bereft you thus? Mask 277
Thus I set my printless feet Mask 897
Thus I sprinkle on thy brest Mask 911
Thus don the Tales, to bed they creep, Allegro 115
Thus night oft see me in thy pale career, Penseroso 121
Thus sang the uncouth Swain to th' Okes and rills, Lycidas 186
Thus we salute thee with our early Song, May Morn 9
That of my life distrustfully thus say, Psalm 3, 5
How long be thus forborn Psalm 4, 9
But Lord, thus let me pray, Psalm 4, 28
For ever angry thus Psalm 85, 18
And I here pent up thus. Psalm 88, 36

Thwart
Mov'd contrarie with thwart obliquities, Par Lost 8.132
From *Serraliona;* thwart of these as fierce Par Lost 10.703
Tine the slant Lightning, whose thwart flame driv'n down Par Lost 10.1075

Thwarting
And heal the harms of thwarting thunder blew, Arcades 51

Thwarts
In *Autumn* thwarts the night, when vapors fir'd Par Lost 4.557

Thy
Invoke thy aid to my adventrous Song, Par Lost 1.13
Say first, for Heav'n hides nothing from thy view Par Lost 1.27
Under thy conduct, and in dreadful deeds Par Lost 1.130
Receive thy new Possessor: One who brings Par Lost 1.252
Thy miscreated Front athwart my way Par Lost 2.683
Retire, or taste thy folly, and learn by proof, Par Lost 2.686
Thy King and Lord? Back to thy punishment, Par Lost 2.699
False fugitive, and to thy speed add wings, Par Lost 2.700
Thy lingring, or with one stroke of this Dart Par Lost 2.702
O Father, what intends thy hand, she cry'd, Par Lost 2.727
Against thy only Son? What fury O Son, Par Lost 2.728
Against thy Fathers head? and know'st for whom; Par Lost 2.730
So strange thy outcry, and thy words so strange Par Lost 2.737
In darkness, while thy head flames thick and fast Par Lost 2.754
Out of thy head I sprung: amazement seis'd Par Lost 2.758
Thy self in me thy perfect image viewing Par Lost 2.764
Dear Daughter, since thou claim'st me for thy Sire, Par Lost 2.817
At thy right hand voluptuous, as beseems Par Lost 2.869
Thy daughter and thy darling, without end. Par Lost 2.870
And feel thy sovran vital Lamp; but thou Par Lost 3.22
To find thy piercing ray, and find no dawn; Par Lost 3.24
That wash thy hallowd feet, and warbling flow, Par Lost 3.31
Thy sovran sentence, that Man should find grace; Par Lost 3.145
Thy praises, with th' innumerable sound Par Lost 3.147
Of Hymns and sacred Songs, wherewith thy Throne Par Lost 3.148
Thy creature late so lov'd, thy youngest Son Par Lost 3.151
His malice, and thy goodness bring to naught, Par Lost 3.158
Abolish thy Creation, and unmake, Par Lost 3.163
For him, what for thy glorie thou hast made? Par Lost 3.164
So should thy goodness and thy greatness both Par Lost 3.165
Father, thy word is past, man shall find grace; Par Lost 3.227
The speediest of thy winged messengers, Par Lost 3.229
To visit all thy creatures, and to all Par Lost 3.230
Thy bosom, and this glorie next to thee Par Lost 3.239
Father, to see thy face, wherein no cloud Par Lost 3.262
Thenceforth, but in thy presence Joy entire. Par Lost 3.265
Thir Nature also to thy Nature joyn; Par Lost 3.282

Thy(*cont*)
His crime makes guiltie all his Sons, thy merit Par Lost 3.290
Therefore thy Humiliation shall exalt Par Lost 3.313
With thee thy Manhood also to this Throne; Par Lost 3.314
Thy Merits; under thee as Head Supream Par Lost 3.319
Thy dread Tribunal: forthwith from all Windes Par Lost 3.326
Then all thy Saints assembl'd, thou shalt judge Par Lost 3.330
Beneath thy Sentence; Hell her numbers full, Par Lost 3.332
Then thou thy regal Scepter shalt lay by, Par Lost 3.339
The full blaze of thy beams, and through a cloud Par Lost 3.378
Dark with excessive bright thy skirts appeer, Par Lost 3.380
Thy Fathers dreadful Thunder didst not spare, Par Lost 3.393
Nor stop thy flaming Chariot wheels, that shook Par Lost 3.394
Back from pursuit thy Powers with loud acclaime Par Lost 3.397
Thee only extoll'd, Son of thy Fathers might, Par Lost 3.398
No sooner did thy dear and onely Son Par Lost 3.403
He to appease thy wrauth, and end the strife Par Lost 3.406
Of Mercy and Justice in thy face discern'd, Par Lost 3.407
Hail Son of God, Saviour of Men, thy Name Par Lost 3.412
Henceforth, and never shall my Harp thy praise Par Lost 3.414
Forget, nor from thy Fathers praise disjoine. Par Lost 3.415
Where all his Sons thy Embassie attend; Par Lost 3.658
Fair Angel, thy desire which tends to know Par Lost 3.694
From thy Empyreal Mansion thus alone, Par Lost 3.699
Thy way thou canst not miss, me mine requires. Par Lost 3.735
Look'st from thy sole Dominion like the God Par Lost 4.33
But with no friendly voice, and add thy name Par Lost 4.36
O Sun, to tell thee how I hate thy beams Par Lost 4.37
I fell, how glorious once above thy Spheare; Par Lost 4.39
Nay curs'd be thou; since against his thy will Par Lost 4.71
And from whom I was formd flesh of thy flesh, Par Lost 4.441
Thy coming, and thy soft imbraces, hee Par Lost 4.471
My other half: with that thy gentle hand Par Lost 4.488
Gabriel, to thee thy course by Lot hath giv'n Par Lost 4.561
New troubles; him thy care must be to find. Par Lost 4.575
Uriel, no wonder if thy perfet sight, Par Lost 4.577
God is thy Law, thou mine: to know no more Par Lost 4.637
For us too large, where thy abundance wants Par Lost 4.730
Thy goodness infinite, both when we wake, Par Lost 4.734
And when we seek, as now, thy gift of sleep. Par Lost 4.735
Com'st thou, escap'd thy prison, and transform'd, Par Lost 4.824
Think not, revolted Spirit, thy shape the same, Par Lost 4.835
Thy sin and place of doom obscure and foule. Par Lost 4.840
Or less be lost. Thy fear, said *Zephon* bold, Par Lost 4.854
To thy transgressions, and disturbd the charge Par Lost 4.879
By thy example, but have power and right Par Lost 4.881
To question thy bold entrance on this place; Par Lost 4.882
Which thou incurr'st by flying, meet thy flight Par Lost 4.913
To thy deserted host this cause of flight, Par Lost 4.922
Thy fiercest, when in Battel to thy aide Par Lost 4.927
Thy blasting volied Thunder made all speed Par Lost 4.928
1667 'The'
And seconded thy else not dreaded Spear. Par Lost 4.929
But still thy words at random, as before, Par Lost 4.930
Argue thy inexperience what behooves Par Lost 4.931
What thou and thy gay Legions dare against; Par Lost 4.942
Faithful to whom? to thy rebellious crew? Par Lost 4.952
Then when I am thy captive talk of chaines, Par Lost 4.970
Ride on thy wings, and thou with thy Compeers, Par Lost 4.974
Satan, I know thy strength, and thou knowst mine, Par Lost 4.1006
And read thy Lot in yon celestial Sign Par Lost 4.1011
Thy face, and Morn return'd, for I this Night, Par Lost 5.30
Attracted by thy beauty still to gaze. Par Lost 5.47
I rose as at thy call, but found thee not; Par Lost 5.48
Deigns none to ease thy load and taste thy sweet, Par Lost 5.59
Longer thy offerd good, why else set here? Par Lost 5.63
The trouble of thy thoughts this night in sleep Par Lost 5.96
Of our last Eevnings talk, in this thy dream, Par Lost 5.115
These are thy glorious works, Parent of good, Par Lost 5.153
In these thy lowest works, yet these declare Par Lost 5.158
Thy goodness beyond thought, and Power Divine: Par Lost 5.159
With thy bright Circlet, praise him in thy Spheare Par Lost 5.169
Acknowledge him thy Greater, sound his praise Par Lost 5.172
In thy eternal course, both when thou climbst, Par Lost 5.173
Haste hither *Eve*, and worth thy sight behold Par Lost 5.308
And what thy stores contain, bring forth and poure Par Lost 5.314
To visit thee; lead on then where thy Bowre Par Lost 5.375
Shall fill the World more numerous with thy Sons Par Lost 5.389
Thy favour, in this honour done to man, Par Lost 5.462
That is, to thy obedience; therein stand. Par Lost 5.522
He left it in thy power, ordaind thy will Par Lost 5.526
To whom our great Progenitor. Thy words Par Lost 5.544
Not lawful to reveal? yet for thy good Par Lost 5.570
Thy eye-lids? and remembrest what Decree Par Lost 5.674
Of Heav'ns Almightie. Thou to me thy thoughts Par Lost 5.676
Thy sleep dissent? new Laws thou seest impos'd; Par Lost 5.679
Made answer. Mightie Father, thou thy foes Par Lost 5.735
Thy Rebels, or be found the worst in Heav'n. Par Lost 5.742
All thy Dominion, *Adam*, is no more Par Lost 5.751
In place thy self so high above thy Peeres. Par Lost 5.812
Thy making, while the Maker gave thee being? Par Lost 5.858
And fly, ere evil intercept thy flight. Par Lost 5.871
Forsak'n of all good; I see thy fall Par Lost 5.878
Determind, and thy hapless crew involv'd Par Lost 5.879
Both of thy crime and punishment: henceforth Par Lost 5.881
Thy disobedience. Well thou didst advise, Par Lost 5.888
Yet not for thy advise or threats I fly Par Lost 5.889
His Thunder on thy head, devouring fire. Par Lost 5.893

Thy(*cont*)
Then violence: for this was all thy care Par Lost 6.35
Back on thy foes more glorious to return Par Lost 6.39
Proud, art thou met? thy hope was to have reacht Par Lost 6.131
The highth of thy aspiring unoppos'd, Par Lost 6.132
Abandond at the terror of thy Power Par Lost 6.134
Thy folly; or with solitarie hand Par Lost 6.139
Thy Legions under darkness; but thou seest Par Lost 6.142
All are not of thy Train; there be who Faith Par Lost 6.143
Seemd in thy World erroneous to dissent Par Lost 6.146
Thy merited reward, the first assay Par Lost 6.153
Before thy fellows, ambitious to win Par Lost 6.160
From me som Plume, that thy success may show Par Lost 6.161
Reign thou in Hell thy Kingdom, let mee serve Par Lost 6.183
This greeting on thy impious Crest receive. Par Lost 6.188
Author of evil, unknown till thy revolt, Par Lost 6.262
And thy adherents: how hast thou disturb'd Par Lost 6.266
Of thy Rebellion? how hast thou instill'd Par Lost 6.269
Thy malice into thousands, once upright Par Lost 6.270
Thy ofspring, to the place of evil, Hell, Par Lost 6.276
Thou and thy wicked crew; there mingle broiles, Par Lost 6.277
Ere this avenging Sword begin thy doome, Par Lost 6.278
If not to reign: mean while thy utmost force, Par Lost 6.293
And join him nam'd *Almighty* to thy aid, Par Lost 6.294
Impossible: yet haply of thy Racc Par Lost 6.501
In Heav'n and Hell thy Power above compare, Par Lost 6.705
By Sacred Unction, thy deserved right. Par Lost 6.709
Go then thou Mightiest in thy Fathers might, Par Lost 6.710
Gird on, and Sword upon thy puissant Thigh; Par Lost 6.714
To glorifie thy Son, I alwayes thee, Par Lost 6.725
That thou in me well pleas'd, declarst thy will Par Lost 6.728
Scepter and Power, thy giving, I assume, Par Lost 6.730
Thy terrors, as I put thy mildness on, Par Lost 6.735
Armd with thy might, rid Heav'n of these rebell'd, Par Lost 6.737
That from thy just obedience could revolt, Par Lost 6.740
Then shall thy Saints unmixt, and from th' impure Par Lost 6.742
Farr separate, circling thy holy Mount Par Lost 6.743
At thy request, and that thou maist beware Par Lost 6.894
With *Satan*, hee who envies now thy state, Par Lost 6.900
Thy weaker; let it profit thee to have heard Par Lost 6.909
Wisdom thy Sister, and with her didst play Par Lost 7.10
With thy Celestial Song. Up led by thee Par Lost 7.12
Thy tempring; with like safetie guided down Par Lost 7.15
Held by thy voice, thy potent voice he heares, Par Lost 7.100
Haste to thy audience, Night with her will bring Par Lost 7.105
Or we can bid his absence, till thy Song Par Lost 7.107
This also thy request with caution askt Par Lost 7.111
Thy hearing, such Commission from above Par Lost 7.118
I have receav'd, to answer thy desire Par Lost 7.119
And said, thus farr extend, thus farr thy bounds, Par Lost 7.230
This be thy just Circumference, O World. Par Lost 7.231
Not noxious, but obedient at thy call. Par Lost 7.498
Dust of the ground, and in thy nostrils breath'd Par Lost 7.525
Male he created thee, but thy consort Par Lost 7.529
And govern well thy appetite, least sin Par Lost 7.546
Great are thy works, *Jehovah*, infinite Par Lost 7.602
Thy power; what thought can measure thee or tongue Par Lost 7.603
Relate thee; greater now in thy return Par Lost 7.604
Thy Thunders magnifi'd; but to create Par Lost 7.606
Thy Empire? easily the proud attempt Par Lost 7.609
The number of thy worshippers. Who seekes Par Lost 7.613
To manifest the more thy might: his evil Par Lost 7.615
And thy request think now fulfill'd, that ask'd Par Lost 7.635
And what before thy memorie was don Par Lost 7.637
Which onely thy solution can resolve. Par Lost 8.14
Alreadie by thy reasoning this I guess, Par Lost 8.85
Who art to lead thy ofspring, and supposest Par Lost 8.86
To thee who hast thy dwelling here on Earth. Par Lost 8.118
Of Day and Night; which needs not thy beleefe, Par Lost 8.136
Sollicit not thy thoughts with matters hid, Par Lost 8.167
And thy faire *Eve;* Heav'n is for thee too high Par Lost 8.172
Think onely what concernes thee and thy being; Par Lost 8.174
By sufferance, and thy wonted favour deign'd. Par Lost 8.202
Fond, were it not in hope of thy reply: Par Lost 8.209
And sweeter thy discourse is to my eare Par Lost 8.211
Though pleasant, but thy words with Grace Divine Par Lost 8.215
Nor are thy lips ungraceful, Sire of men, Par Lost 8.218
But thy relation now; for I attend, Par Lost 8.247
Pleas'd with thy words no less then thou with mine. Par Lost 8.248
And said, thy Mansion wants thee, *Adam*, rise, Par Lost 8.296
First Father, call'd by thee I come thy Guide Par Lost 8.298
To the Garden of bliss, thy seat prepar'd. Par Lost 8.299
The Pledge of thy Obedience and thy Faith, Par Lost 8.325
To thee and to thy Race I give; as Lords Par Lost 8.339
Replenisht, and all these at thy command Par Lost 8.371
Find pastime, and beare rule; thy Realm is large. Par Lost 8.375
Hast thou not made me here thy substitute, Par Lost 8.381
Of thy Associates, *Adam*, and wilt taste Par Lost 8.401
The highth and depth of thy Eternal wayes Par Lost 8.413
Thou in thy secresie although alone, Par Lost 8.427
Canst raise thy Creature to what highth thou wilt Par Lost 8.430
Thy likeness, thy fit help, thy other self, Par Lost 8.450
Thy wish exactly to thy hearts desire. Par Lost 8.451
Thy words, Creator bounteous and benigne, Par Lost 8.492
Of all thy gifts, nor enviest. I now see Par Lost 8.494
Thy cherishing, thy honouring, and thy love, Par Lost 8.569
Not thy subjection: weigh with her thy self; Par Lost 8.570
Made so adorn for thy delight the more, Par Lost 8.576

Thy(*cont*)

Thy mate, who sees when thou art seen least wise.	Par Lost 8.578
Thy Judgement to do aught, which else free Will	Par Lost 8.636
Would not admit; thine and of all thy Sons	Par Lost 8.637
I in thy persevering shall rejoyce,	Par Lost 8.639
Thy condescension, and shall be honour'd ever	Par Lost 8.649
Well hast thou motion'd, well thy thoughts imployd	Par Lost 9.229
His fraud is then thy fear, which plain inferrs	Par Lost 9.285
Thy equal fear that my firm Faith and Love	Par Lost 9.286
Thoughts, which how found they harbour in thy brest	Par Lost 9.288
Thy absence from my sight, but to avoid	Par Lost 9.294
I from the influence of thy looks receave	Par Lost 9.309
Access in every Vertue, in thy sight	Par Lost 9.310
When I am present, and thy trial choose	Par Lost 9.316
With me, best witness of thy Vertue tri'd.	Par Lost 9.317
Wouldst thou approve thy constancie, approve	Par Lost 9.367
First thy obedience; th' other who can know,	Par Lost 9.368
Go; for thy stay, not free, absents thee more;	Par Lost 9.372
Go in thy native innocence, relie	Par Lost 9.373
With thy permission then, and thus forewarnd	Par Lost 9.378
Chiefly by what thy own last reasoning words	Par Lost 9.379
Of thy presum'd return! event perverse!	Par Lost 9.405
To intercept thy way, or send thee back	Par Lost 9.410
Thy looks, the Heav'n of mildness, with disdain,	Par Lost 9.534
Thy awful brow, more awful thus retir'd.	Par Lost 9.537
Fairest resemblance of thy Maker faire,	Par Lost 9.538
By gift, and thy Celestial Beautie adore	Par Lost 9.540
By Angels numberless, thy daily Train.	Par Lost 9.548
Thy utmost reach or *Adams:* Round the Tree	Par Lost 9.591
But all that fair and good in thy Divine	Par Lost 9.606
Semblance, and in thy Beauties heav'nly Ray	Par Lost 9.607
Serpent, thy overpraising leaves in doubt	Par Lost 9.615
Mother of Science, Now I feel thy Power	Par Lost 9.680
Great are thy Vertues, doubtless, best of Fruits.	Par Lost 9.745
The Tongue not made for Speech to speak thy praise:	Par Lost 9.749
Thy praise hee also who forbids thy use,	Par Lost 9.750
And thy fair Fruit let hang, as to no end	Par Lost 9.798
Of thy full branches offer'd free to all;	Par Lost 9.802
Thy presence, agonie of love till now	Par Lost 9.858
The pain of absence from thy sight. But strange	Par Lost 9.861
Thy sweet Converse and Love so dearly joyn'd,	Par Lost 9.909
Bone of my Bone thou art, and from thy State	Par Lost 9.915
Of thy perfection, how shall I attaine,	Par Lost 9.964
This happie trial of thy Love, which else	Par Lost 9.975
Pernicious to thy Peace, chiefly assur'd	Par Lost 9.981
Remarkably so late of thy so true,	Par Lost 9.982
For never did thy Beautie since the day	Par Lost 9.1029
What words have past thy Lips, *Adam* severe,	Par Lost 9.1144
Was I to have never parted from thy side?	Par Lost 9.1153
Hadst thou bin firm and fixt in thy dissent,	Par Lost 9.1160
Of thy transgressing? not enough severe,	Par Lost 9.1169
It seems, in thy restraint: what could I more?	Par Lost 9.1170
Mine both in Heav'n and Earth to do thy will	Par Lost 10.69
Supream, that thou in mee thy Son belov'd	Par Lost 10.70
On Earth these thy transgressors, but thou knowst	Par Lost 10.72
I heard thee in the Garden, and of thy voice	Par Lost 10.116
And gav'st me as thy perfet gift, so good,	Par Lost 10.138
Was shee thy God, that her thou didst obey	Par Lost 10.145
Before his voice, or was shee made thy guide,	Par Lost 10.146
Thou did'st resigne thy Manhood, and the Place	Par Lost 10.148
Thy Love, not thy Subjection, and her Gifts	Par Lost 10.153
Unseemly to beare rule, which was thy part	Par Lost 10.155
Upon thy Belly groveling thou shalt goe,	Par Lost 10.177
And dust shalt eat all the dayes of thy Life.	Par Lost 10.178
Her Seed shall bruse thy head, thou bruise his heel.	Par Lost 10.181
Thy sorrow I will greatly multiplie	Par Lost 10.193
By thy Conception; Children thou shalt bring	Par Lost 10.194
In sorrow forth, and to thy Husbands will	Par Lost 10.195
Because thou hast heark'nd to the voice of thy Wife,	Par Lost 10.198
Curs'd is the ground for thy sake, thou in sorrow	Par Lost 10.201
Shalt eate thereof all the days of thy Life;	Par Lost 10.202
In the sweat of thy Face shalt thou eat Bread,	Par Lost 10.205
Out of the ground wast taken, know thy Birth,	Par Lost 10.207
Adventrous work, yet to thy power and mine	Par Lost 10.255
O Parent, these are thy magnific deeds,	Par Lost 10.354
Thy Trophies, which thou view'st as not thine own,	Par Lost 10.355
That thou on Earth hadst prosper'd, which thy looks	Par Lost 10.360
That I must after thee with this thy Son;	Par Lost 10.363
Detain from following thy illustrious track.	Par Lost 10.367
Thine now is all this World, thy vertue hath won	Par Lost 10.372
What thy hands builded not, thy Wisdom gain'd	Par Lost 10.373
His Quadrature, from thy Orbicular World,	Par Lost 10.381
But on thy rould in heaps, and up the Trees	Par Lost 10.558
1667 'they'	
And season him thy last and sweetest prey.	Par Lost 10.609
Of thy victorious Arm, well-pleasing Son,	Par Lost 10.634
Through multitude that sung: Just are thy ways,	Par Lost 10.643
Righteous are thy Decrees on all thy Works;	Par Lost 10.644
Thy terms too hard, by which I was to hold	Par Lost 10.751
Thy Justice seems; yet to say truth, too late,	Par Lost 10.755
Made thee without thy leave, what if thy Son	Par Lost 10.760
That proud excuse? yet him not thy election,	Par Lost 10.764
To serve him, thy reward was of his grace,	Par Lost 10.767
Thy punishment then justly is at his Will.	Par Lost 10.768
And hateful; nothing wants, but that thy shape,	Par Lost 10.869
Thy inward fraud, to warn all Creatures from thee	Par Lost 10.871
I had persisted happie, had not thy pride	Par Lost 10.874
Unhappilie deceav'd; thy suppliant	Par Lost 10.917

Thy(*cont*)

I beg, and clasp thy knees; bereave me not,	Par Lost 10.918
Whereon I live, thy gentle looks, thy aid,	Par Lost 10.919
Thy counsel in this uttermost distress,	Par Lost 10.920
Thy hatred for this miserie befall'n,	Par Lost 10.928
The sentence from thy head remov'd may light	Par Lost 10.934
Thy frailtie and infirmer Sex forgiv'n,	Par Lost 10.956
Thy Love, the sole contentment of my heart	Par Lost 10.973
Food for so foule a Monster, in thy power	Par Lost 10.986
Eve, thy contempt of life and pleasure seems	Par Lost 10.1013
And excellent then what thy minde contemnes;	Par Lost 10.1015
Not thy contempt, but anguish and regret	Par Lost 10.1018
Part of our Sentence, that thy Seed shall bruise	Par Lost 10.1031
Fruit of thy Womb: On mee the Curse aslope	Par Lost 10.1053
From thy implanted Grace in Man, these Sighs	Par Lost 11.23
With Incense, I thy Priest before thee bring,	Par Lost 11.25
Fruits of more pleasing savour from thy seed	Par Lost 11.26
All thy request for Man, accepted Son,	Par Lost 11.46
Obtain, all thy request was my Decree:	Par Lost 11.47
Thy choice of flaming Warriours, least the Fiend	Par Lost 11.101
If patiently thy bidding they obey,	Par Lost 11.112
His promise, that thy Seed shall bruise our Foe;	Par Lost 11.155
A help, became thy snare; to mee reproach	Par Lost 11.165
I never from thy side henceforth to stray,	Par Lost 11.176
Sufficient that thy Prayers are heard, and Death,	Par Lost 11.252
Mayst cover: well may then thy Lord appeas'd	Par Lost 11.257
What justly thou hast lost; nor set thy heart,	Par Lost 11.288
Thy going is not lonely, with thee goes	Par Lost 11.290
Thy Husband, him to follow thou art bound;	Par Lost 11.291
Where he abides, think there thy native soile.	Par Lost 11.292
Thy message, which might else in telling wound,	Par Lost 11.299
Our frailtie can sustain, thy tidings bring,	Par Lost 11.302
Perhaps thy Capital Seate, from whence had spred	Par Lost 11.343
To dwell on eeven ground now with thy Sons:	Par Lost 11.348
To thee and to thy Ofspring; good with bad	Par Lost 11.358
Safest thy life, and best prepar'd endure	Par Lost 11.365
Thy mortal passage when it comes. Ascend	Par Lost 11.366
Th' effects which thy original crime hath wrought	Par Lost 11.424
Nor sinn'd thy sin, yet from that derive	Par Lost 11.427
Out of thy loyns; th' unjust the just hath slain,	Par Lost 11.455
Till many years over thy head return:	Par Lost 11.534
Into thy Mothers lap, or be with ease	Par Lost 11.536
Thy youth, thy strength, thy beauty, which will change	Par Lost 11.539
To witherd weak and gray; thy Senses then	Par Lost 11.540
Hopeful and cheerful, in thy blood will reigne	Par Lost 11.543
To weigh thy Spirits down, and last consume	Par Lost 11.545
Nor love thy Life, nor hate; but what thou livst	Par Lost 11.553
The end of all thy Ofspring, end so sad,	Par Lost 11.755
And sunk thee as thy Sons; till gently reard	Par Lost 11.758
By th' Angel, on thy feet thou stoodst at last,	Par Lost 11.759
And scarce to th' Angel utterdst thus thy plaint.	Par Lost 11.762
Thy mortal sight to faile; objects divine	Par Lost 12.9
Since thy original lapse, true Libertie	Par Lost 12.83
Is meant thy great deliverer, who shall bruise	Par Lost 12.149
Thou shalt proceed, and from thy Womb the Son	Par Lost 12.381
Thy enemie; nor so is overcome	Par Lost 12.390
Disabl'd not to give thee thy deaths wound:	Par Lost 12.392
Which hee, who comes thy Saviour, shall recure,	Par Lost 12.393
In thee and in thy Seed: nor can this be,	Par Lost 12.395
The penaltie to thy transgression due,	Par Lost 12.399
Alone fulfill the Law; thy punishment	Par Lost 12.404
But to the Cross he nailes thy Enemies,	Par Lost 12.415
Thy ransom paid, which Man from death redeems,	Par Lost 12.424
Annuls thy doom, the death thou shouldst have dy'd,	Par Lost 12.428
Of him so lately promiss'd to thy aid	Par Lost 12.542
Now amplier known thy Saviour and thy Lord,	Par Lost 12.544
How soon hath thy prediction, Seer blest,	Par Lost 12.553
Deeds to thy knowledge answerable, add Faith,	Par Lost 12.582
And said to me apart, high are thy thoughts	Par Reg 1.229
By matchless Deeds express thy matchless Sire.	Par Reg 1.233
Thy Father is the Eternal King, who rules	Par Reg 1.236
A messenger from God fore-told thy birth	Par Reg 1.238
And of thy Kingdom there should be no end.	Par Reg 1.241
At thy Nativity a glorious Quire	Par Reg 1.242
Affirming it thy Star new grav'n in Heaven,	Par Reg 1.253
Thy wisdom, and behold thy God-like deeds?	Par Reg 1.386
Rather inflames thy torment, representing	Par Reg 1.418
Wilt thou impute to obedience what thy fear	Par Reg 1.422
What but thy malice mov'd thee to misdeem	Par Reg 1.424
The other service was thy chosen task,	Par Reg 1.427
For lying is thy sustenance, thy food.	Par Reg 1.429
Among the Nations? that hath been thy craft,	Par Reg 1.432
But what have been thy answers, what but dark	Par Reg 1.434
Who ever by consulting at thy shrine	Par Reg 1.438
To thy Delusions; justly, since they fell	Par Reg 1.443
To thee not known, whence hast thou then thy truth,	Par Reg 1.446
To approach thy Temples, give thee in command	Par Reg 1.449
To thy Adorers; thou with trembling fear,	Par Reg 1.451
But this thy glory shall be soon retrench'd;	Par Reg 1.454
Her dictates from thy mouth? most men admire	Par Reg 1.482
Thy Father, who is holy, wise and pure,	Par Reg 1.486
Thy coming hither, though I know thy scope,	Par Reg 1.494
Send thy Messiah forth, the time is come;	Par Reg 2.43
Thy chosen, to what highth thir pow'r unjust	Par Reg 2.45
Thy Glory, free thy people from thir yoke,	Par Reg 2.48
Before the Flood thou with thy lusty Crew,	Par Reg 2.178
Too long, then lay'st thy scapes on names ador'd,	Par Reg 2.189
Cause thy refusal, said the subtle Fiend,	Par Reg 2.323

Thy(*cont*)

Thy gentle Ministers, who come to pay	Par Reg 2.375
Thy pompous Delicacies I contemn,	Par Reg 2.390
And count thy specious gifts no gifts but guiles.	Par Reg 2.391
Chose to impart to thy apparent need,	Par Reg 2.397
Thy temperance invincible besides,	Par Reg 2.408
And all thy heart is set on high designs,	Par Reg 2.410
A Carpenter thy Father known, thy self	Par Reg 2.414
Or at thy heels the dizzy Multitude,	Par Reg 2.420
Longer then thou canst feed them on thy cost?	Par Reg 2.421
(Thy throne) but gold that got him puissant friends?	Par Reg 2.425
And for thy reason why they should be sought,	Par Reg 2.485
Thy actions to thy words accord, thy words	Par Reg 3.9
To thy large heart give utterance due, thy heart	Par Reg 3.10
Should Kings and Nations from thy mouth consult,	Par Reg 3.12
Thy Counsel would be as the Oracle	Par Reg 3.13
That might require th' array of war, thy skill	Par Reg 3.17
Could not sustain thy Prowess, or subsist	Par Reg 3.19
In battel, though against thy few in arms.	Par Reg 3.20
All Earth her wonder at thy acts, thy self	Par Reg 3.24
Thy years are ripe, and over-ripe, the Son	Par Reg 3.31
For glories sake by all thy argument.	Par Reg 3.46
As thou to thy reproach mayst well remember,	Par Reg 3.66
Him whom thy wrongs with Saintly patience born,	Par Reg 3.93
Resembling thy great Father: he seeks glory,	Par Reg 3.110
To sit upon thy Father *David*'s Throne;	Par Reg 3.153
By Mothers side thy Father, though thy right	Par Reg 3.154
Thy right by sitting still or thus retiring?	Par Reg 3.164
Zeal of thy Fathers house, Duty to free	Par Reg 3.175
Thy Country from her Heathen servitude;	Par Reg 3.176
The Prophets old, who sung thy endless raign,	Par Reg 3.178
Sollicitous, what moves thy inquisition?	Par Reg 3.200
Know'st thou not that my rising is thy fall,	Par Reg 3.201
And my promotion will be thy destruction?	Par Reg 3.202
Willingly I could flye, and hope thy raign,	Par Reg 3.216
Would stand between me and thy Fathers ire,	Par Reg 3.219
Why move thy feet so slow to what is best,	Par Reg 3.224
Thy life hath yet been private, most part spent	Par Reg 3.232
Judah and all thy Father *David*'s house	Par Reg 3.282
Thy Vertue, and not every way secure	Par Reg 3.348
On no slight grounds thy safety; hear, and mark	Par Reg 3.349
All this fair sight; thy Kingdom though foretold	Par Reg 3.351
Endeavour, as thy Father *David* did,	Par Reg 3.353
Thou must make sure thy own, the *Parthian* first	Par Reg 3.363
Thy country, and captive lead away her Kings	Par Reg 3.366
Deliverance of thy brethren, those ten Tribes	Par Reg 3.374
Thy politic maxims, or that cumbersome	Par Reg 3.400
By three days Pestilence? such was thy zeal	Par Reg 3.412
And worship me as thy superior Lord,	Par Reg 4.167
I never lik'd thy talk, thy offers less,	Par Reg 4.171
The Lord thy God, and only him shalt serve;	Par Reg 4.177
When slipping from thy Mothers eye thou went'st	Par Reg 4.216
By wisdom; as thy Empire must extend,	Par Reg 4.222
So let extend thy mind o're all the world,	Par Reg 4.223
Now at full age, fulness of time, thy season,	Par Reg 4.380
To win thy destin'd seat, but wilt prolong	Par Reg 4.469
All to the push of Fate, persue thy way	Par Reg 4.470
Who knowing I shall raign past thy preventing,	Par Reg 4.492
Obtrud'st thy offer'd aid, that I accepting	Par Reg 4.493
Mee to thy will; desist, thou art discern'd	Par Reg 4.497
By all the Prophets; of thy birth at length	Par Reg 4.503
On thy birth-night, that sung thee Saviour born.	Par Reg 4.506
Thy infancy, thy childhood, and thy youth,	Par Reg 4.508
Thy manhood last, though yet in private bred;	Par Reg 4.509
Therefore I watch'd thy footsteps from that hour,	Par Reg 4.522
Will ask thee skill; I to thy Fathers house	Par Reg 4.552
Now shew thy Progeny; if not to stand,	Par Reg 4.554
Thou chance to dash thy foot against a stone.	Par Reg 4.559
Tempt not the Lord thy God, he said and stood.	Par Reg 4.561
Against th' Attempter of thy Fathers Throne,	Par Reg 4.603
Thy wound, yet not thy last and deadliest wound	Par Reg 4.622
Thy bold attempt; hereafter learn with awe	Par Reg 4.625
From thy Demoniac holds, possession foul,	Par Reg 4.628
Thee and thy Legions, yelling they shall flye,	Par Reg 4.629
Queller of Satan, on thy glorious work	Par Reg 4.634
Sams. A Little onward lend thy guiding hand	Samson 1
Why am I thus bereav'd thy prime decree?	Samson 85
Thy Bondage or lost Sight,	Samson 152
The Dungeon of thy self; thy Soul	Samson 156
The rarer thy example stands,	Samson 166
We come thy friends and neighbours not unknown	Samson 180
Salve to thy Sores, apt words have power to swage	Samson 184
Who hast of sorrow thy full load besides;	Samson 214
At least of thy own Nation, and as noble.	Samson 218
The *Philistine*, thy Countries Enemy,	Samson 238
Cho. Thy words to my remembrance bring	Samson 277
But see here comes thy reverend Sire	Samson 326
Ordain'd thy nurture holy, as of a Plant;	Samson 362
Thy Foes derision, Captive, Poor, and Blind	Samson 366
Man. I cannot praise thy Marriage choises, Son,	Samson 420
Tacit, was in thy power; true; and thou bear'st	Samson 430
Samson, of all thy sufferings think the heaviest,	Samson 445
Could have befall'n thee and thy Fathers house.	Samson 447
About thy ransom: well they may by this	Samson 483
Man. Be penitent and for thy fault contrite,	Samson 502
But act not in thy own affliction, Son,	Samson 503
Thy penal forfeit from thy self; perhaps	Samson 508
Home to thy countrey and his sacred house,	Samson 518

Thy(*cont*)

Where thou mayst bring thy off'rings, to avert	Samson 519
But God who caus'd a fountain at thy prayer	Samson 581
From the dry ground to spring, thy thirst to allay	Samson 582
Cause light again within thy eies to spring,	Samson 584
That mingle with thy fancy. I however	Samson 601
To prosecute the means of thy deliverance	Samson 603
And healing words from these thy friends admit.	Samson 605
Temperst thy providence through his short course,	Samson 670
To some great work, thy glory,	Samson 680
Changest thy countenance, and thy hand with no regard	Samson 684
So deal not with this once thy glorious Champion,	Samson 705
The Image of thy strength, and mighty minister.	Samson 706
Then *Dalila* thy wife.	Samson 724
I came, still dreading thy displeasure, *Samson*,	Samson 733
Once more thy face, and know of thy estate,	Samson 742
Thy mind with what amends is in my power,	Samson 745
Sam. Out, out *Hyaena;* these are thy wonted arts,	Samson 748
I may, if possible, thy pardon find	Samson 771
The easier towards me, or thy hatred less.	Samson 772
Wherein consisted all thy strength and safety?	Samson 780
To learn thy secrets, get into my power	Samson 798
Thy key of strength and safety: thou wilt say,	Samson 799
Wailing thy absence in my widow'd bed;	Samson 806
Take to thy wicked deed: which when thou seest	Samson 826
Thou wilt renounce thy seeking, and much rather	Samson 828
Confess it feign'd, weakness is thy excuse,	Samson 829
To satisfie thy lust: Love seeks to have Love;	Samson 837
Or by evasions thy crime uncoverst more.	Samson 842
In man or woman, though to thy own condemning,	Samson 844
Sam. I thought where all thy circling wiles would end;	Samson 871
But had thy love, still odiously pretended,	Samson 873
By thy request, who could deny thee nothing;	Samson 881
Didst thou at first receive me for thy husband?	Samson 883
Thy countrey sought of thee, it sought unjustly,	Samson 889
No more thy countrey, but an impious crew	Samson 891
To please thy gods thou didst it; gods unable	Samson 896
Bare in thy guilt how foul must thou appear?	Samson 902
Witness when I was worried with thy peals.	Samson 906
Where once I have been caught; I know thy trains	Samson 932
Though dearly to my cost, thy ginns, and toyls;	Samson 933
Thy fair enchanted cup, and warbling charms	Samson 934
To fence my ear against thy sorceries.	Samson 937
Thy Husband, slight me, sell me, and forgo me;	Samson 940
When I must live uxorious to thy will	Samson 945
Dal. Let me approach at least, and touch thy hand.	Samson 951
Sam. Not for thy life, lest fierce remembrance wake	Samson 952
Bewail thy falshood, and the pious works	Samson 955
Cherish thy hast'n'd widowhood with the gold	Samson 958
Thy anger, unappeasable, still rages,	Samson 963
To mix with thy concernments I desist	Samson 969
Much like thy riddle, *Samson*, in one day	Samson 1016
Thy Paranymph, worthless to thee compar'd,	Samson 1020
Successour in thy bed,	Samson 1021
Had shorn the fatal harvest of thy head.	Samson 1024
Har. I come not *Samson*, to condole thy chance,	Samson 1076
Of thy prodigious might and feats perform'd	Samson 1083
If thy appearance answer loud report.	Samson 1090
Or left thy carkass where the Ass lay thrown:	Samson 1097
I lose, prevented by thy eyes put out.	Samson 1103
What then thou would'st, thou seest it in thy hand.	Samson 1105
Then put on all thy gorgeous arms, thy Helmet	Samson 1119
And Brigandine of brass, thy broad Habergeon,	Samson 1120
Vant-brass and Greves, and Gauntlet, add thy Spear	Samson 1121
And raise such out-cries on thy clatter'd Iron,	Samson 1124
Which long shall not with-hold mee from thy head,	Samson 1125
Feigndst at thy birth was giv'n thee in thy hair,	Samson 1135
Where strength can least abide, though all thy hairs	Samson 1136
For proof hereof, if *Dagon* be thy god,	Samson 1145
Then thou shalt see, or rather to thy sorrow	Samson 1154
Har. Presume not on thy God, what e're he be,	Samson 1156
Into thy Enemies hand, permitted them	Samson 1159
Among the Slaves and Asses thy comrades,	Samson 1162
With those thy boyst'rous locks, no worthy match	Samson 1164
Har. Fair honour that thou dost thy God, in trusting	Samson 1178
Har. Is not thy Nation subject to our Lords?	Samson 1182
These shifts refuted, answer thy appellant	Samson 1220
To descant on my strength, and give thy verdit?	Samson 1228
Sam. No man with-holds thee, nothing from thy hand	Samson 1233
Fear I incurable; bring up thy van,	Samson 1234
And with one buffet lay thy structure low,	Samson 1239
To the hazard of thy brains and shatter'd sides.	Samson 1241
Either of these is in thy lot,	Samson 1292
Labouring thy mind	Samson 1298
More then the working day thy hands,	Samson 1299
Thy strength they know surpassing human rate,	Samson 1313
Brooks no delay: is this thy resolution?	Samson 1344
Sam. So take it with what speed thy message needs.	Samson 1345
Thy words by adding fuel to the flame?	Samson 1351
Dispute thy coming? come without delay;	Samson 1395
Off. I praise thy resolution, doff these links:	Samson 1410
Of *Israel* be thy guide	Samson 1428
Send thee the Angel of thy Birth, to stand	Samson 1431
Fast by thy side, who from thy Fathers field	Samson 1432
Of thy conception, and be now a shield	Samson 1434
As in thy wond'rous actions hath been seen.	Samson 1440
Thou for thy Son art bent to lay out all;	Samson 1486
Thou in old age car'st how to nurse thy Son.	Samson 1488

Thy(*cont*)

Made older then thy age through eye-sight lost.	Samson 1489
Chor. Thy hopes are not ill founded nor seem vain	Samson 1504
Of his delivery, and thy joy thereon	Samson 1505
Chor. Thy Son is rather slaying them, that outcry	Samson 1517
Hitting thy aged ear should pierce too deep.	Samson 1568
A dreadful way thou took'st to thy revenge.	Samson 1591
Among thy slain self-kill'd	Samson 1664
Thee with thy slaughter'd foes in number more	Samson 1667
Then all thy life had slain before.	Samson 1668
Stay thy cloudy Ebon chair,	Mask 134
Us thy vow'd Priests, till utmost end	Mask 136
Of all thy dues be done, and none left out,	Mask 137
In thy dark lantern thus close up the Stars,	Mask 197
line not in Bridgewater ms	
Within thy airy shell	Mask 231
And in the violet-imbroider'd vale	Mask 233
B.M. ms 'thy violet embroiderd Vale'	
That likest thy *Narcissus* are?	Mask 237
Till further quest'. *La*. Shepherd I take thy word,	Mask 321
And trust thy honest offer'd courtesie,	Mask 322
Stoop thy pale visage through an amber cloud,	Mask 333
With thy long levell'd rule of streaming light,	Mask 340
Trinity ms 'thy' ←'a'	
I love thy courage yet, and bold Emprise,	Mask 610
Bridgewater ms 'the'	
But here thy sword can do thee little stead,	Mask 611
He with his bare wand can unthred thy joynts,	Mask 614
And crumble all thy sinews. *Eld. Bro*. Why prethee Shepherd	Mask 615
Trinity ms 'all thy' ←'every'	
Withall thy charms, although this corporal rinde	Mask 664
That thou hast banish't from thy tongue with lies,	Mask 692
Hence with thy brew'd inchantments, foul deceiver,	Mask 696
I would not taste thy treasonous offer; none	Mask 702
Trinity ms 'would not taste' ←'should reject' ←'hate it from thy hands'	
More happines then this thy present lot.	Mask 789
line not in Bridgewater ms	
line not in Trinity ms	
Till all thy magick structures rear'd so high,	Mask 798
line not in Bridgewater ms	
line not in Trinity ms	
Were shatter'd into heaps o're thy false head.	Mask 799
line not in Trinity ms	
line not in Bridgewater ms	
The loose train of thy amber-dropping hair,	Mask 863
Upon thy streams with wily glance,	Mask 884
Rise, rise, and heave thy rosie head	Mask 885
From thy coral-pav'n bed,	Mask 886
And bridle in thy headlong wave,	Mask 887
Gentle swain at thy request	Mask 900
We implore thy powerful hand	Mask 903
Thus I sprinkle on thy brest	Mask 911
Bridgewater ms 'this'	
Thrice upon thy fingers tip,	Mask 914
Thrice upon thy rubied lip,	Mask 915
May thy brimmed waves for this	Mask 924
Never scorch thy tresses fair,	Mask 929
Thy molten crystal fill with mudd,	Mask 931
May thy billows rowl ashoar	Mask 932
May thy lofty head be crown'd	Mask 934
And here and there thy banks upon	Mask 936
As ragged as thy Locks,	Allegro 9
And in thy right hand lead with thee,	Allegro 35
Mirth, admit me of thy crue	Allegro 38
Over thy decent shoulders drawn.	Penseroso 36
Com, but keep thy wonted state,	Penseroso 37
Thy rapt soul sitting in thine eyes:	Penseroso 40
I woo to hear thy eeven Song;	Penseroso 64
But, O sad Virgin, that thy power	Penseroso 103
Thus night oft see me in thy pale career,	Penseroso 121
Fanning their joyous Leaves to thy soft layes.	Lycidas 44
Such, *Lycidas*, thy loss to Shepherds ear.	Lycidas 49
Of so much fame in Heav'n expect thy meed.	Lycidas 84
That shrunk thy streams; Return *Sicilian* Muse,	Lycidas 133
Wash far away, where ere thy bones are hurld,	Lycidas 155
In thy large recompense, and shalt be good	Lycidas 184
Say Heav'nly Muse, shall not thy sacred vein	Nativity 15
O run, prevent them with thy humble ode,	Nativity 24
Have thou the honour first, thy Lord to greet,	Nativity 26
And joyn thy voice unto the Angel Quire,	Nativity 27
Bleak winters force that made thy blossome drie;	Fair Inf 4
That did thy cheek envermeil, thought to kiss	Fair Inf 6
Unhous'd thy Virgin Soul from her fair biding place.	Fair Inf 21
Yet art thou not inglorious in thy fate;	Fair Inf 22
Or that thy coarse corrupts in earths dark wombe,	Fair Inf 30
Or that thy beauties lie in wormie bed,	Fair Inf 31
Oh no? for something in thy face did shine	Fair Inf 34
And why from us so quickly thou didst take thy flight.	Fair Inf 42
Amongst us here below to hide thy nectar'd head.	Fair Inf 49
To earth from thy praefixed seat didst poast,	Fair Inf 59
To bless us with thy heav'n-lov'd innocence,	Fair Inf 65
And wisely learn to curb thy sorrows wild;	Fair Inf 73
That till the worlds last-end shall make thy name to live.	Fair Inf 77
Here I salute thee and thy pardon ask,	Vacation 7
I pray thee then deny me not thy aide	Vacation 15
And from thy wardrope bring thy chiefest treasure;	Vacation 18
Till thou hast deck't them in thy best aray;	Vacation 26

Thy(*cont*)

Thy service in some graver subject use,	Vacation 30
Such as may make thee search thy coffers round,	Vacation 31
Thou know'st it must be now thy only bent	Vacation 55
To keep in compass of thy Predicament:	Vacation 56
Then quick about thy purpos'd business come,	Vacation 57
Good luck befriend thee Son; for at thy birth	Vacation 59
Thy drowsie Nurse hath sworn she did them spie	Vacation 61
And sweetly singing round about thy Bed	Vacation 63
Strew all their blessings on thy sleeping Head.	Vacation 64
Over the Pole thy thickest mantle throw,	Passion 30
Fly envious *Time*, till thou run out thy race,	On Time 1
And glut thy self with what thy womb devours,	On Time 4
So little is thy gain.	On Time 8
And last of all, thy greedy self consum'd,	On Time 10
Gentle Lady may thy grave	Winchester 47
After this thy travail sore	Winchester 49
Shortned hast thy own lives lease,	Winchester 52
That thy noble House doth bring,	Winchester 54
For thy Hears to strew the ways,	Winchester 58
Devoted to thy vertuous name;	Winchester 60
Woods and Groves, are of thy dressing,	May Morn 7
Hill and Dale, doth boast thy blessing.	May Morn 8
What need'st thou such weak witnes of thy name?	Shakespear 6
Thy easie numbers flow, and that each heart	Shakespear 10
Hath from the leaves of thy unvalu'd Book,	Shakespear 11
Thy liquid notes that close the eye of Day,	Sonnet 1, 5
Have linkt that amorous power to thy soft lay,	Sonnet 1, 8
And he can spred thy Name o're Lands and Seas,	Sonnet 8, 7
Lift not thy spear against the Muses Bowre,	Sonnet 8, 9
And at thy growing vertues fret their spleen,	Sonnet 9, 7
Thy care is fixt and zealously attends	Sonnet 9, 9
To fill thy odorous Lamp with deeds of light,	Sonnet 9, 10
Hast gain'd thy entrance, Virgin wise and pure.	Sonnet 9, 14
Thy age, like ours, O Soul of Sir *John Cheek*,	Sonnet 11, 12
Thy worth and skill exempts thee from the throng,	Sonnet 13, 5
that didst reform thy art, the cheif among	Sonnet 13, Tr. ms 40.08
Had ripen'd thy just soul to dwell with God,	Sonnet 14, 2
Trinity ms 'thy' ←'thye'	
Thy Works and Alms and all thy good Endeavour	Sonnet 14, 5
Thy hand-maids, clad them o're with purple beams	Sonnet 14, 10
And drink thy fill of pure immortal streams.	Sonnet 14, 14
Thy firm unshak'n vertue ever brings	Sonnet 15, 5
O yet a nobler task awaites thy hand;	Sonnet 15, 9
To peace and truth thy glorious way hast plough'd,	Sonnet 16, 4
And Dunbarr feild resounds thy praises loud,	Sonnet 16, 8
Therfore on thy firme hand religion leanes	Sonnet 17, 13
Avenge O Lord thy slaughter'd Saints, whose bones	Sonnet 18, 1
Ev'n them who kept thy truth so pure of old	Sonnet 18, 3
Forget not: in thy book record their groanes	Sonnet 18, 5
Who were thy Sheep and in their antient Fold	Sonnet 18, 6
A hunder'd-fold, who having learnt thy way	Sonnet 18, 13
In wreaths thy golden Hair,	Horace 4
Plain in thy neatness; O how oft shall he	Horace 5
As thy possession I on thee bestow	Psalm 2, 17
Th' Heathen, and as thy conquest to be sway'd	Psalm 2, 18
Thy blessing on thy people flows.	Psalm 3, 24
Lift up the favour of thy count'nance bright.	Psalm 4, 30
Fools or mad men stand not within thy sight.	Psalm 5, 12
But I will in thy mercies dear	Psalm 5, 17
Thy numerous mercies go	Psalm 5, 18
Into thy house; I in thy fear	Psalm 5, 19
Will towards thy holy temple worship low	Psalm 5, 20
Lord lead me in thy righteousness	Psalm 5, 21
Set thy wayes right before, where my step goes.	Psalm 5, 24
And shall triumph in thee, who love thy name.	Psalm 5, 36
Him with thy lasting favour and good will.	Psalm 5, 40
Nor in thy hot displeasure me correct;	Psalm 6, 2
My soul, O save me for thy goodness sake	Psalm 6, 8
Who in the grave can celebrate thy praise?	Psalm 6, 10
Thy protection while I crie,	Psalm 7, 3
Thence to thy glorious habitation	Psalm 7, 27
And glorious is thy name through all the earth?	Psalm 8, 2
So as above the Heavens thy praise to set	Psalm 8, 3
Hast founded strength because of all thy foes	Psalm 8, 6
That bends his rage thy providence to oppose	Psalm 8, 8
When I behold thy Heavens, thy Fingers art,	Psalm 8, 9
O're the works of thy hand thou mad'st him Lord,	Psalm 8, 17
All Flocks, and Herds, by thy commanding word,	Psalm 8, 19
And glorious is thy name through all the earth.	Psalm 8, 24
Thy loved Josephs seed,	Psalm 80, 4
Shine forth, *and from thy cloud give light*,	Psalm 80, 7
And on our foes thy dread	Psalm 80, 8
Awake thy strength, come, and *be seen*	Psalm 80, 11
To save us *by thy might*.	Psalm 80, 12
Turn us again, *thy grace divine*	Psalm 80, 13
Cause thou thy face on us to shine	Psalm 80, 15
Thy smoking wrath, *and angry brow*	Psalm 80, 19
Against thy peoples praire.	Psalm 80, 20
Return us, *and thy grace divine*,	Psalm 80, 29
Cause thou thy face on us to shine,	Psalm 80, 31
Thy free love made it thine,	Psalm 80, 34
From Heav'n, thy Seat divine,	Psalm 80, 58
And visit this *thy* Vine.	Psalm 80, 60
Visit this Vine, which thy right hand	Psalm 80, 61
They perish at thy dreadfull ire,	Psalm 80, 67
At thy rebuke and frown.	Psalm 80, 68
Upon the man of thy right hand	Psalm 80, 69

Thy(*cont*)
Let thy *good* hand be *laid*, Psalm 80, 70
Shall call upon thy Name. Psalm 80, 76
Return us, *and thy grace divine* Psalm 80, 77
Cause thou thy face on us to shine, Psalm 80, 79
Through out the land of thy abode Psalm 81, 37
In honour bend thy knee. Psalm 81, 40
I am the Lord thy God which brought Psalm 81, 41
Will grant thy full demand. Psalm 81, 44
O God hold not thy peace, Psalm 83, 2
For lo thy *furious* foes *now* swell Psalm 83, 5
Against thy people they contrive Psalm 83, 9
So with thy whirlwind them pursue, Psalm 83, 57
And with thy tempest chase; Psalm 83, 58
How lovely are thy dwellings fair! Psalm 84, 1
Thy Courts O Lord to see, Psalm 84, 6
Ev'n *by* thy Altars Lord of Hoasts Psalm 84, 13
Happy, who in thy house reside Psalm 84, 17
And in their hearts thy waies. Psalm 84, 20
Of thy anointed *dear*. Psalm 84, 32
For one day in thy Courts *to be* Psalm 84, 33
Thy Land to favour graciously Psalm 85, 1
That wrought thy people woe, Psalm 85, 6
From thy fierce wrath which we had prov'd Psalm 85, 11
Wilt thou thy frowning ire extend Psalm 85, 19
That so thy people may rejoyce Psalm 85, 23
Cause us to see thy goodness Lord, Psalm 85, 25
To us thy mercy shew Psalm 85, 26
Thy saving health to us afford Psalm 85, 27
Thy *gracious* ear, O Lord, encline, Psalm 86, 1
Thy waies, and love the just, Psalm 86, 6
Save thou thy servant O my God Psalm 86, 7
Thy Servants Soul; for Lord to thee Psalm 86, 11
Thy hearing graciously. Psalm 86, 20
Like to thy *glorious* works. Psalm 86, 28
And glorifie thy name. Psalm 86, 32
By thy strong hand are done, Psalm 86, 34
Thou *in thy everlasting Seat* Psalm 86, 35
Teach me O Lord thy way *most right*, Psalm 86, 37
I in thy truth will bide, Psalm 86, 38
To fear thy name my heart unite Psalm 86, 39
Thy name for ever more. Psalm 86, 44
For great thy mercy is toward me, Psalm 86, 45
Readiest thy grace to shew, Psalm 86, 54
O turn to me *thy face at length*, Psalm 86, 57
Unto thy servant give thy strength, Psalm 86, 59
And save thy hand-maids Son. Psalm 86, 60
Into thy presence let my praier Psalm 88, 5
Them from thy hand deliver'd o're Psalm 88, 23
Thy wrath *from which no shelter saves* Psalm 88, 29
Thou break'st upon me all thy waves, Psalm 88, 31
And all thy waves break me. Psalm 88, 32
Shall they thy loving kindness tell Psalm 88, 45
Thy faithfulness *unfold?* Psalm 88, 48
In darkness can thy mighty *hand* Psalm 88, 49
Thy justice in the *gloomy* land Psalm 88, 51
And hide thy face from me, Psalm 88, 58
While I thy terrors undergo Psalm 88, 63
Thy fierce wrath over me doth flow Psalm 88, 65
Thy threatnings cut me through. Psalm 88, 66
Not thy Conversion, but those rich demaines Prose 1, 2
'Gainst them that rais'd thee dost thou lift thy horn, Prose 3, 2
Impudent whoore, where hast thou plac'd thy hope? Prose 3, 3
In thy Adulterers, or thy ill got wealth? Prose 3, 4
Walk'st on the rowling Sphear, and through the deep, Prose 12, 2
On thy third Reigne the Earth look now, and tell Prose 12, 3
Now void, it fitts thy people; thether bend Prose 12, 10
Thy course, there shalt thou find a lasting seat, Prose 12, 11
There to thy Sons another *Troy* shall rise, Prose 12, 12

Thyestean
The Sun, as from *Thyestean* Banquet, turn'd Par Lost 10.688

Thyme
With wilde Thyme and the gadding Vine o'regrown, Lycidas 40
1638 'thyme'

Thyrsis
El. Bro. Thyrsis? Whose artful strains have oft delaid Mask 494
Bridgewater ms 'Thirsis'
El. Bro. What fears good *Thyrsis?* Prethee briefly shew. Mask 512
Bridgewater ms 'Thirsis'
Trinity ms 'Thyrsis' ←'shep.'
Eld. Bro. Thyrsis lead on apace, Ile follow thee, Mask 657
Bridgewater ms 'Thirsis'
Where *Corydon* and *Thyrsis* met, Allegro 83

Thyself
And reck'n'st thou thy self with Spirits of Heav'n, Par Lost 2.696
Thy self in me thy perfect image viewing Par Lost 2.764
By him corrupted? or wilt thou thy self Par Lost 3.162
And be thy self Man among men on Earth, Par Lost 3.283
Fountain of Light, thy self invisible Par Lost 3.375
Dearer thy self then all; needs must the power Par Lost 4.412
Like consort to thy self canst no where find. Par Lost 4.448
What there thou seest fair Creature is thy self, Par Lost 4.468
Multitudes like thy self, and thence be call'd Par Lost 4.474
Though thither doomd? Thou wouldst thy self, no doubt, Par Lost 4.890
To dispossess him, and thy self to reigne? Par Lost 4.961
Farr heavier load thy self expect to feel Par Lost 4.972
Sweet of thy self, but much more sweet thus cropt, Par Lost 5.68
Thy self a Goddess, not to Earth confind, Par Lost 5.78

Thyself(*cont*)
Thus wondrous fair; thy self how wondrous then! Par Lost 5.155
That thou continu'st such, owe to thy self, Par Lost 5.521
In place thy self so high above thy Peeres. Par Lost 5.812
Thy self though great and glorious dost thou count, Par Lost 5.833
Thy self not free, but to thy self enthrall'd; Par Lost 6.181
Though heaviest by just measure on thy self Par Lost 6.265
Thou to thy self proposest, in the choice Par Lost 8.400
Thou in thy self art perfet, and in thee Par Lost 8.415
Best with thy self accompanied, seek'st not Par Lost 8.428
Which thou hast rightly nam'd, but of thy self, Par Lost 8.439
Less excellent, as thou thy self perceav'st. Par Lost 8.566
Not thy subjection: weigh with her thy self; Par Lost 8.570
Against temptation: thou thy self with scorne Par Lost 9.299
Or to thy self perhaps: hadst thou been there, Par Lost 9.1148
And person, had'st thou known thy self aright. Par Lost 10.156
Unnam'd, undreaded, and thy self half starv'd? Par Lost 10.595
Befits thee with him leagu'd, thy self as false Par Lost 10.868
On me alreadie lost, mee then thy self Par Lost 10.929
The punishment all on thy self; alas, Par Lost 10.949
So shalt thou save thy self and us relieve Par Reg 1.344
Then to thy self ascrib'st the truth fore-told. Par Reg 1.453
All others by thy self; because of old Par Reg 2.174
Thou thy self doat'st on womankind, admiring Par Reg 2.175
A Carpenter thy Father known, thy self Par Reg 2.414
All Earth her wonder at thy acts, thy self Par Reg 3.24
Happiest both to thy self and all the world, Par Reg 3.225
Thee, of thy self so apt, in regal Arts, Par Reg 3.248
And thou thy self seem'st otherwise inclin'd Par Reg 4.212
Within thy self, much more with Empire joyn'd. Par Reg 4.284
Cast thy self down; safely if Son of God: Par Reg 4.555
The Dungeon of thy self; thy Soul Samson 156
Deject not then so overmuch thy self, Samson 213
Thy penal forfeit from thy self; perhaps Samson 508
E're I to thee, thou to thy self wast cruel. Samson 784
More strength from me, then in thy self was found. Samson 789
To afflict thy self in vain: though sight be lost, Samson 914
Thou oft shalt wish thy self at *Gath* to boast Samson 1127
Off. Regard thy self, this will offend them highly. Samson 1333
Man. O lastly over-strong against thy self! Samson 1590
How durst thou then thy self approach so neer Mask 616
Trinity ms 'thy selfe'
word not in Bridgewater ms
1637 'thy selfe'
Thou art not fit to hear thy self convinc't; Mask 792
line not in Bridgewater ms
1637 'thy selfe'
Forget thy self to Marble, till Penseroso 42
Who having clad thy self in humane weed, Fair Inf 58
And glut thy self with what thy womb devours, On Time 4
Trinity ms 'thy selfe'
Hast built thy self a live-long Monument. Shakespear 8
1640 'thy selfe'
1632 'thy selfe'
Rouze thy self amidst the rage Psalm 7, 20
And the young branch, that for thy self Psalm 80, 63
Strong for thy self hast made. Psalm 80, 72

Tiar
Of beaming sunnie Raies, a golden tiar Par Lost 3.625

Tiberius
Obeys *Tiberius;* nor is always rul'd Par Reg 3.159

Tide
Or Summers Noon-tide air, while thus he spake. Par Lost 2.309
Towards the retreating Sea thir furious tyde. Par Lost 11.854
Benighted walks under the mid-day Sun; Mask 384
Bridgewater ms 'walks in black vapours though the noone tyde brand'
Trinity ms 'benighted walks under the midday sun' ←'walks in black vapours though the noontyde brand'
Where thou perhaps under the whelming tide Lycidas 157

Tidings
These tidings carrie to th' anointed King; Par Lost 5.870
Nor troubl'd at these tidings from the Earth, Par Lost 10.36
And tidings fraught, to Hell he now return'd, Par Lost 10.346
Eve, now expect great tidings, which perhaps Par Lost 11.226
Our frailtie can sustain, thy tidings bring, Par Lost 11.302
O Prophet of glad tidings, finisher Par Lost 12.375
With joy the tidings brought from Heav'n: at length Par Lost 12.504
At these sad tidings; but no time was then Par Reg 1.109
Nor left at *Jordan*, tydings of him none; Par Reg 2.62
Lest evil tidings with too rude irruption Samson 1567

Tidore
Of *Ternate* and *Tidore*, whence Merchants bring Par Lost 2.639

Tie
And tie him to his own prescript, Samson 308
Untwisting all the chains that ty Allegro 143

Tied
Not ti'd or manacl'd with joynt or limb, Par Lost 1.426

Tiger
Then as a Tyger, who by chance hath spi'd Par Lost 4.403
1667 'Tiger'
The Libbard, and the Tyger, as the Moale Par Lost 7.467
The Lion and fierce Tiger glar'd aloof. Par Reg 1.313
Or Ounce, or Tiger, Hog, or bearded Goat, Mask 71
Trinity ms 'tiger'

Tigers
Dandl'd the Kid; Bears, Tygers, Ounces, Pards, Par Lost 4.344
Like stabl'd wolves, or tigers at their prey, Mask 534

Tigris

Where *Tigris* at the foot of Paradise	Par Lost 9.71

Tiles

In at the window climbs, or o're the tiles;	Par Lost 4.191

Till

With loss of *Eden*, till one greater Man	Par Lost 1.4
He with his Thunder: and till then who knew	Par Lost 1.93
That felt unusual weight, till on dry Land	Par Lost 1.227
Nathless he so endur'd, till on the Beach	Par Lost 1.299
With scatter'd Arms and Ensigns, till anon	Par Lost 1.325
Till, as a signal giv'n, th' uplifted Spear	Par Lost 1.347
Got them new Names, till wandring ore the Earth,	Par Lost 1.365
Till good *Josiah* drove them thence to Hell.	Par Lost 1.418
Monarch in Heav'n, till then as one secure	Par Lost 1.638
Swarm'd and were straitn'd; till the Signal giv'n,	Par Lost 1.776
Alone the dreadful voyage; till at last	Par Lost 2.426
The irksom hours, till this great Chief return.	Par Lost 2.527
Till thickest Legions close; with feats of Arms	Par Lost 2.537
Who first broke peace in Heav'n and Faith, till then	Par Lost 2.690
Hov'ring a space, till Winds the signal blow	Par Lost 2.717
What it intends; till first I know of thee,	Par Lost 2.740
I know thee not, nor ever saw till now	Par Lost 2.744
Threw forth, till on the left side op'ning wide,	Par Lost 2.755
Alone, but long I sat not, till my womb	Par Lost 2.778
Till they enthrall themselves: I else must change	Par Lost 3.125
Till final dissolution, wander here,	Par Lost 3.458
And long he wanderd, till at last a gleame	Par Lost 3.499
Till at his second bidding darkness fled,	Par Lost 3.712
Nor staid, till on *Niphates* top he lights.	Par Lost 3.742
Till Pride and worse Ambition threw me down	Par Lost 4.40
Mine eyes till now, and pin'd with vain desire,	Par Lost 4.466
Till I espi'd thee, fair indeed and tall,	Par Lost 4.477
Yet happie pair; enjoy, till I return,	Par Lost 4.534
The starrie Host, rode brightest, till the Moon	Par Lost 4.606
So judge thou still, presumptuous, till the wrauth,	Par Lost 4.912
Such night till this I never pass'd, have dream'd,	Par Lost 5.31
Knew never till this irksom night; methought	Par Lost 5.35
Till the Sun paint your fleecie skirts with Gold,	Par Lost 5.187
Through all th' Empyreal road; till at the Gate	Par Lost 5.253
Winnows the buxom Air; till within soare	Par Lost 5.270
To sit and taste, till this meridian heat	Par Lost 5.369
Oreshades; for these mid-hours, till Eevning rise	Par Lost 5.376
Till body up to spirit work, in bounds	Par Lost 5.478
Through Heav'ns wide Champain held his way, till Morn,	Par Lost 6.2
Obsequious darkness enters, till her houre	Par Lost 6.10
And clamour such as heard in Heav'n till now	Par Lost 6.208
The Battel hung; till *Satan*, who that day	Par Lost 6.246
Author of evil, unknown till thy revolt,	Par Lost 6.262
Miserie, uncreated till the crime	Par Lost 6.268
By sin of disobedience, till that hour	Par Lost 6.396
Of future we may deem him, though till now	Par Lost 6.429
Till now not known, but known as soon contemnd,	Par Lost 6.432
Of spiritous and fierie spume, till toucht	Par Lost 6.479
Till on those cursed Engins triple-row	Par Lost 6.650
To rapture, till the savage clamor dround	Par Lost 7.36
Or we can bid his absence, till thy Song	Par Lost 7.107
Not here, till by degrees of merit rais'd	Par Lost 7.157
He scarce had said, when the bare Earth, till then	Par Lost 7.313
Till night, then in the East her turn she shines,	Par Lost 7.380
Till Ev'n, nor then the solemn Nightingal	Par Lost 7.435
Yet not till the Creator from his work	Par Lost 7.551
Till warn'd, or by experience taught, she learne,	Par Lost 8.190
And Day is yet not spent; till then thou seest	Par Lost 8.206
And gaz'd a while the ample Skie, till rais'd	Par Lost 8.258
Disporting, till the amorous Bird of Night	Par Lost 8.518
Into a Gulf shot under ground, till part	Par Lost 9.72
Our pleasant task enjoyn'd, but till more hands	Par Lost 9.207
With Myrtle, find what to redress till Noon:	Par Lost 9.219
As we need walk, till younger hands ere long	Par Lost 9.246
Till on a day roaving the field, I chanc'd	Par Lost 9.575
I spar'd not, for such pleasure till that hour	Par Lost 9.596
Still hanging incorruptible, till men	Par Lost 9.622
Irrational till then. For us alone	Par Lost 9.766
Regarded, such delight till then, as seemd,	Par Lost 9.787
Till dieted by thee I grow mature	Par Lost 9.803
Thy presence, agonie of love till now	Par Lost 9.858
Speechless he stood and pale, till thus at length	Par Lost 9.894
Till *Adam* thus 'gan *Eve* to dalliance move,	Par Lost 9.1016
From this delightful Fruit, nor known till now	Par Lost 9.1023
The solace of thir sin, till dewie sleep	Par Lost 9.1044
Till *Adam*, though not less then *Eve* abash't,	Par Lost 9.1065
The thickest Trees, both Man and Wife, till God	Par Lost 10.101
Till thou return unto the ground, for thou	Par Lost 10.206
Long hee admiring stood, till Sin, his faire	Par Lost 10.352
Within Hell Gates till now, thou us impow'rd	Par Lost 10.369
Each other, till supplanted down he fell	Par Lost 10.513
Till thir lost shape, permitted, they resum'd,	Par Lost 10.574
Till I in Man residing through the Race,	Par Lost 10.607
On what was pure, till cramm'd and gorg'd, nigh burst	Par Lost 10.632
Till then the Curse pronounc't on both precedes.	Par Lost 10.640
Immoveable till peace obtain'd from fault	Par Lost 10.938
By him with many comforts, till we end	Par Lost 10.1084
Numberd, though sad, till Death, his doom (which I	Par Lost 11.40
Till I provided Death; so Death becomes	Par Lost 11.61
And took thir Seats; till from his Throne supream	Par Lost 11.82
Laborious, till day droop; while here we dwell,	Par Lost 11.178
Some days; how long, and what till then our life,	Par Lost 11.198
A space, till firmer thoughts restraind excess,	Par Lost 11.498

Till(*cont*)

Till many years over thy head return:	Par Lost 11.534
So maist thou live, till like ripe Fruit thou drop	Par Lost 11.535
Which I must keep till my appointed day	Par Lost 11.550
Rove without rein, till in the amorous Net	Par Lost 11.586
And now of love they treat till th' Eevning Star	Par Lost 11.588
In factious opposition, till at last	Par Lost 11.664
Impetuous, and continu'd till the Earth	Par Lost 11.744
And sunk thee as thy Sons; till gently reard	Par Lost 11.758
Surfet, and lust, till wantonness and pride	Par Lost 11.795
Beyond all bounds, till inundation rise	Par Lost 11.828
Shall hold thir course, till fire purge all things new,	Par Lost 11.900
Under paternal rule; till one shall rise	Par Lost 12.24
Not understood, till hoarse, and all in rage,	Par Lost 12.58
Man till then free. Therefore since hee permits	Par Lost 12.90
Still tend from bad to worse, till God at last	Par Lost 12.106
Till by two brethren (those two brethren call	Par Lost 12.169
More hard'nd after thaw, till in his rage	Par Lost 12.194
Divided, till his rescu'd gain thir shoar:	Par Lost 12.199
Darkness defends between till morning Watch;	Par Lost 12.207
Till *Israel* overcome; so call the third	Par Lost 12.267
The clouded Ark of God till then in Tents	Par Lost 12.333
In mean estate live moderate, till grown	Par Lost 12.351
Under her own waight groaning till the day	Par Lost 12.539
Till time stand fixt: beyond is all abyss,	Par Lost 12.555
With solitude, till far from track of men,	Par Reg 1.191
Till truth were freed, and equity restor'd:	Par Reg 1.220
Till those days ended, hunger'd then at last	Par Reg 1.309
Thence into *Egypt*, till the Murd'rous King	Par Reg 2.76
Duty and Service, nor to stay till bid,	Par Reg 2.326
Till Conquerour Death discover them scarce men,	Par Reg 3.85
Till *Cyrus* set them free; *Persepolis*	Par Reg 3.284
To thir inheritance, then, nor till then,	Par Reg 3.382
But I endure the time, till which expir'd,	Par Reg 4.174
Till time mature thee to a Kingdoms waight;	Par Reg 4.282
Thus pass'd the night so foul till morning fair	Par Reg 4.426
Till at the Ford of *Jordan* whither all	Par Reg 4.510
Till underneath them fair *Jerusalem*,	Par Reg 4.544
To count them things worth notice, till at length	Samson 250
Till by thir own perplexities involv'd	Samson 304
Vain monument of strength; till length of years	Samson 570
Till vermin or the draff of servil food	Samson 574
Discover'd in the end, till now conceal'd.	Samson 998
Till they had hir'd a woman with their gold	Samson 1114
He tugg'd, he shook, till down they came and drew	Samson 1650
Us thy vow'd Priests, till utmost end	Mask 136
Of all thy dues be done, and none left out,	Mask 137
Trinity ms 'of' ← 'till'	
Of darknes till it smil'd: I have oft heard	Mask 252
I never heard till now. Ile speak to her	Mask 264
Till further quest'. *La*. Shepherd I take thy word,	Mask 321
Till oft convers with heav'nly habitants	Mask 459
Till all be made immortal: but when lust	Mask 463
Imbodies, and imbrutes, till she quite loose	Mask 468
Till fancy had her fill, but ere a close	Mask 548
Till an unusuall stop of sudden silence	Mask 552
Till guided by mine ear I found the place	Mask 570
Into swift flight, till I had found you here,	Mask 579
Till now that this extremity compell'd,	Mask 643
Till all thy magick structures rear'd so high,	Mask 798
line not in Bridgewater ms	
line not in Trinity ms	
Dropt in Ambrosial Oils till she reviv'd,	Mask 840
Till thou our summons answer'd have.	Mask 888
Till we com to holier ground,	Mask 943
Till next Sun-shine holiday,	Mask 959
B.M. ms 'till the'	
Till free consent the gods among	Mask 1007
line not in Bridgewater ms	
his farre-extended armes till with steepe fall	Mask Tr. ms 10.13
Till the dappled dawn doth rise;	Allegro 44
Till the live-long day-light fail,	Allegro 99
Forget thy self to Marble, till	Penseroso 42
Till civil-suited Morn appeer,	Penseroso 122
Till old experience do attain	Penseroso 173
Oft till the Star that rose, at Ev'ning, bright	Lycidas 30
1638 'Oft till the ev'n-starre bright'	
He wanderd long, till thee he spy'd from farr,	Fair Inf 17
That till the worlds last-end shall make thy name to live.	Fair Inf 77
Till thou hast deck't them in thy best aray;	Vacation 26
Fly envious *Time*, till thou run out thy race,	On Time 1
Were lost in death, till he that dwelt above	Circum 18
As once we did, till disproportion'd sin	Musick 19
And keep in tune with Heav'n, till God ere long	Musick 26
Till the sad breaking of that Parlament	Sonnet 10, 5
when most were wont which till then us'd to scan	Sonnet 13, Tr. ms 40.03
Till Truth, and Right from Violence be freed,	Sonnet 15, 11
On smoother, till *Favonius* re-inspire	Sonnet 20, 6
Will rank my Prayers, and watch till thou appear.	Psalm 5, 8
Till they no Nation be	Psalm 83, 14
Till all the mountains blaze,	Psalm 83, 56
And till they yield thee honour due,	Psalm 83, 59
Till all before *our* God *at length*	Psalm 84, 27

Till

Upon the Earth, and man to till the ground	Par Lost 7.332
To Till and keep, and of the Fruit to eate:	Par Lost 8.320
And send him from the Garden forth to Till	Par Lost 11.97
And send thee from the Garden forth to till	Par Lost 11.261

Tillage
A sweatie Reaper from his Tillage brought Par Lost 11.434
Tilted
I must not suffer this, yet 'tis but the lees Mask 809
Trinity ms 'but the lees' ← 'the tilted lees' ← 'the very lees'
Tilth
Part arable and tilth, whereon were Sheaves Par Lost 11.430
Tilting
Or tilting Furniture, emblazon'd Shields, Par Lost 9.34
Rode tilting o're the Waves, all dwellings else Par Lost 11.747
Timber
Then from the Mountain hewing Timber tall, Par Lost 11.728
Timbrel
The Timbrel hither bring Psalm 81, 6
Timbreled
In vain with Timbrel'd Anthems dark Nativity 219
Timbrels
Though for the noyse of Drums and Timbrels loud Par Lost 1.394
ms 'timbrells'
And Timbrels, on each side went armed guards, Samson 1617
Time
The Mother of Mankind, what time his Pride Par Lost 1.36
A mind not to be chang'd by Place or Time. Par Lost 1.253
ms 'time'
In spring time, when the Sun with *Taurus* rides, Par Lost 1.769
Our Supream Foe in time may much remit Par Lost 2.210
Our torments also may in length of time Par Lost 2.274
By pollicy, and long process of time, Par Lost 2.297
Of some new Race call'd *Man*, about this time Par Lost 2.348
Periods of time, thence hurried back to fire. Par Lost 2.603
I also; at which time this powerful Key Par Lost 2.774
And time and place are lost; where eldest Night Par Lost 2.894
Made flesh, when time shall be, of Virgin seed, Par Lost 3.284
While time was, our first-Parents had bin warnd Par Lost 4.6
Seisd mine, I yielded, and from that time see Par Lost 4.489
With thee conversing I forget all time, Par Lost 4.639
Why sleepst thou *Eve?* now is the pleasant time, Par Lost 5.38
To proper substance; time may come when men Par Lost 5.493
Improv'd by tract of time, and wingd ascend Par Lost 5.498
(For time, though in Eternitie, appli'd Par Lost 5.580
1667 'Time'
While Pardon may be found in time besought. Par Lost 5.848
We know no time when we were not as now; Par Lost 5.859
Conflicting Fire: long time in eeven scale Par Lost 6.245
Then time or motion, but to human ears Par Lost 7.177
And in her looks, which from that time infus'd Par Lost 8.474
Now not, though Sin, not Time, first wraught the change, Par Lost 9.70
From his own evil, and for the time remaind Par Lost 9.464
That time Celestial visages, yet mixt Par Lost 10.24
When time shall be, for so I undertook Par Lost 10.74
Time counts not, though with swiftest minutes wing'd. Par Lost 10.91
Not instant, but of future time. With joy Par Lost 10.345
The Sithe of Time mowes down, devour unspar'd, Par Lost 10.606
In time of Truce; *Iris* had dipt the wooff; Par Lost 11.244
The second time returning, in his Bill Par Lost 11.859
Seed time and Harvest, Heat and hoary Frost Par Lost 11.899
Long time in peace by Families and Tribes Par Lost 12.23
Whom *faithful Abraham* due time shall call, Par Lost 12.152
In time of dearth, a Son whose worthy deeds Par Lost 12.161
With purpose to resign them in full time Par Lost 12.301
Long time shall dwell and prosper, but when sins Par Lost 12.316
Measur'd this transient World, the Race of time, Par Lost 12.554
Till time stand fixt: beyond is all abyss, Par Lost 12.555
Delay, for longest time to him is short; Par Reg 1.56
This dreaded time have compast, wherein we Par Reg 1.58
At these sad tidings; but no time was then Par Reg 1.109
The time prefixt I waited, when behold Par Reg 1.269
He was well pleas'd; by which I knew the time Par Reg 1.286
And for a time caught up to God, as once Par Reg 2.14
Send thy Messiah forth, the time is come; Par Reg 2.43
And eat the second time after repose, Par Reg 2.275
All things are best fullfil'd in their due time, Par Reg 3.182
And time there is for all things, Truth hath said: Par Reg 3.183
And just in time thou com'st to have a view Par Reg 3.298
My time I told thee, (and that time for thee Par Reg 3.396
Yet he at length, time to himself best known, Par Reg 3.433
To his due time and providence I leave them. Par Reg 3.440
Or as a swarm of flies in vintage time, Par Reg 4.15
But tedious wast of time to sit and hear Par Reg 4.123
But I endure the time, till which expir'd, Par Reg 4.174
Till time mature thee to a Kingdoms waight; Par Reg 4.282
Which would have set thee in short time with ease Par Reg 4.378
Now at full age, fulness of time, thy season, Par Reg 4.380
The time and means: each act is rightliest done, Par Reg 4.475
From that time seldom have I ceas'd to eye Par Reg 4.507
They shall up lift thee, lest at any time Par Reg 4.558
Where they shall dwell secure, when time shall be Par Reg 4.616
Bound, and to torment sent before thir time. Par Reg 4.632
Her importunity, each time perceiving Samson 397
Yet the fourth time, when mustring all her wiles, Samson 402
That in a little time while breath remains thee, Samson 1126
Chor. In time thou hast resolv'd, the man returns. Samson 1390
Man. Come, come, no time for lamentation now, Samson 1708
Co. Two such I saw, what time the labour'd Oxe Mask 291
Bridgewater ms 'tyme'
Trinity ms 'tyme'
That breaks his magick chains at *curfeu* time, Mask 435
Bridgewater ms 'tyme'
Time(*cont*)
Trinity ms 'tyme'
If you let slip time, like a neglected rose Mask 743
line not in Bridgewater ms
Trinity ms 'tyme'
Som time walking not unseen Allegro 57
Som time let Gorgeous Tragedy Penseroso 97
What time the Gray-fly winds her sultry horn, Lycidas 28
Trinity ms 'tyme'
Move in melodious time; Nativity 129
Time will run back, and fetch the age of gold, Nativity 135
Time is our tedious Song should here have ending, Nativity 239
And in times long and dark Prospective Glass Vacation 71
Fly envious *Time*, till thou run out thy race, On Time 1
Triumphing over Death, and Chance, and thee O Time. On Time 22
After so short time of breath, Winchester 9
For he had any time this ten yeers full, Carrier 7
Time numbers motion, yet (without a crime Another 7
'Gainst old truth) motion number'd out his time; Another 8
Meerly to drive the time away he sickn'd, Another 15
line not in 1640, 1657, 1658 texts
His leasure told him that his time was com, Another 23
line not in 1658 text
How soon hath Time the suttle theef of youth, Sonnet 7, 1
1673 'time'
Toward which Time leads me, and the will of Heav'n; Sonnet 7, 12
Trinity ms 'Tyme'
From the hard Season gaining: time will run Sonnet 20, 5
For other things mild Heav'n a time ordains, Sonnet 21, 11
Will hear my voyce what time to him I crie. Psalm 4, 18
Give ear *in time of need*, Psalm 80, 2
Th' appointed time, the day wheron Psalm 81, 11
Their time should have no end. Psalm 81, 64
Timelessly
Soft silken Primrose fading timelesslie, Fair Inf 2
Timely
Timely interposes, and her monthly round Par Lost 3.728
Successive, and the timely dew of sleep Par Lost 4.614
Us timely of what might else have bin our loss, Par Lost 7.74
Or Heat should injure us, his timely care Par Lost 10.1057
Must not omit a Fathers timely care Samson 602
And timely rest have wanted, but fair Virgin Mask 689
Heav'n hath timely tri'd their youth, Mask 970
Now timely sing, ere the rude Bird of Hate Sonnet 1, 9
Timely-happy
That som more timely-happy spirits indu'th. Sonnet 7, 8
Trinity ms 'tymely-happie'
Times
Nine times the Space that measures Day and Night Par Lost 1.50
Which oft times may succeed, so as perhaps Par Lost 1.166
ms 'oftimes'
Explores his solitary flight; som times Par Lost 2.632
He scours the right hand coast, som times the left, Par Lost 2.633
Wider by farr then that of after-times Par Lost 3.529
His marriage with the seaventimes-wedded Maid. Par Lost 5.223
Then value: Oft times nothing profits more Par Lost 8.571
He circl'd, four times cross'd the Carr of Night Par Lost 9.65
And all the Prophets in thir Age the times Par Lost 12.243
Longer on Earth then certaine times to appeer Par Lost 12.437
By words at times cast forth inly rejoyc'd, Par Reg 1.228
And not inforc'd oft-times to part from truth; Par Reg 1.472
Where will this end? four times ten days I have pass'd Par Reg 2.245
Made famous in a Land and times obscure; Par Reg 3.94
He in whose hand all times and seasons roul. Par Reg 3.187
Yet as being oft times noxious where they light Par Reg 4.460
Times past, what once I was, and what am now. Samson 22
At times when men seek most repose and rest, Samson 406
Or to the unjust tribunals, under change of times, Samson 695
A Weavers beam, and seven-times-folded shield, Samson 1122
Som times with secure delight Allegro 91
Summers three times eight save one Winchester 7
Timnah
Sam. The first I saw at *Timna*, and she pleas'd Samson 219
Of *Timna* first betray me, and reveal Samson 383
As her at *Timna*, sought by all means therefore Samson 795
Timnian
If any of these or all, the *Timnian* bride Samson 1018
Timorous
Timorous and slothful: yet he pleas'd the ear, Par Lost 2.117
Of Goats or timerous flock together throngd Par Lost 6.857
Timorous and loth, with novice modesty, Par Reg 3.241
Prevailing over fear, and timerous doubt Samson 740
Tincture
By tincture or reflection they augment Par Lost 7.367
Tinctured
Skie-tinctur'd grain. Like *Maia*'s son he stood, Par Lost 5.285
What need a vermeil-tinctur'd lip for that Mask 752
Trinity ms 'veirmeil tinctur'd'
line not in Bridgewater ms
Tine
Tine the slant Lightning, whose thwart flame driv'n down Par Lost 10.1075
Tinsel
Bases and tinsel Trappings, gorgious Knights Par Lost 9.36
Tinsel-slippered
By *Thetis* tinsel-slipper'd feet, Mask 877
Bridgewater ms 'tinsel-slipperd'
Tip
Thrice upon thy fingers tip, Mask 914

Tipped
Stood waving tipt with fire; while we suspense, Par Lost 6.580
Tipsy
Tipsie dance, and Jollity. Mask 104
Tire
In posture to displode thir second tire Par Lost 6.605
Tired
But they must pick me out with shackles tir'd, Samson 1326
As over-tir'd to let him lean a while Samson 1632
That have been tir'd all day without repast, Mask 688
Bridgewater ms 'tired'
Tiresias
And *Tiresias* and *Phineus* Prophets old. Par Lost 3.36
Tis
'Tis true, I am that Spirit unfortunate, Par Reg 1.358
Tis onely day-light that makes Sin Mask 126
Is now the labour of my thoughts, 'tis likeliest Mask 192
Bridgewater ms 'tis'
Trinity ms 'tiz'
Himself is his own dungeon. 2. *Bro*. Tis most true Mask 385
Bridgewater ms 'tis'
1637 ''Tis'
Trinity ms 'tis'
'Tis chastity, my brother, chastity: Mask 420
Bridgewater ms 'tis'
Trinity ms 'tis'
2. *Bro*. O brother, 'tis my father Shepherd sure. Mask 493
Trinity ms 'tis'
Bridgewater ms 'tis'
Spir. Ile tell ye, 'tis not vain, or fabulous, Mask 513
Bridgewater ms 'tis'
Trinity ms 'Tis'
I must not suffer this, yet 'tis but the lees Mask 809
Trinity ms 'tis'
Bridgewater ms 'tis'
Sab. Shepherd 'tis my office best Mask 908
1637 'tis'
Trinity ms 'tis'
Bridgewater ms 'tis'
Such Musick (as 'tis said) Nativity 117
Tis you that say it, not I, you do the deeds, Prose 8, 1
Tissued
With radiant feet the tissued clouds down stearing, Nativity 146
Tissues
Or in thir glittering Tissues bear imblaz'd Par Lost 5.592
Titan
Thir boasted Parents; *Titan* Heav'ns first born Par Lost 1.510
ms 'Titan'
Titanian
Titanian, or *Earth-born*, that warr'd on *Jove*, Par Lost 1.198
ms 'Titanian'
Title
Ill worthie I such title should belong Par Lost 11.163
He made not Lord; such title to himself Par Lost 12.70
Then these thou bear'st that title, have propos'd Par Reg 4.199
Imperial rule of all the Sea-girt Iles Mask 21
Trinity ms 'imperiall rule' ← 'the rule & title'
A title page is this! and some in file Sonnet 11, 6
Titled
Religious titl'd them the Sons of God, Par Lost 11.622
False titl'd Sons of God, roaming the Earth Par Reg 2.179
Then swell with pride, and must be titl'd Gods, Par Reg 3.81
Titles
Ethereal Vertues; or these Titles now Par Lost 2.311
If these magnific Titles yet remain Par Lost 5.773
Of those Imperial Titles which assert Par Lost 5.801
Fame in the World, high titles, and rich prey, Par Lost 11.793
Places and titles, and with these to joine Par Lost 12.516
Tittle
What to the smallest tittle thou shalt say Par Reg 1.450
Titular
Not meerly titular, since by Decree Par Lost 5.774
Tlemcen
Marocco and *Algiers*, and *Tremisen;* Par Lost 11.404
To
Listings of this word are omitted; see the Introduction.
Toad
Squat like a Toad, close at the eare of *Eve;* Par Lost 4.800
Hated not Learning wors then Toad or Asp; Sonnet 11, 13
Tobias
To travel with *Tobias*, and secur'd Par Lost 5.222
Tobit
Of *Tobits* Son, and with a vengeance sent Par Lost 4.170
Today
To day deep thoughts resolve with me to drench Sonnet 21, 5
Toe
On the light fantastick toe, Allegro 34
The tufted Crow-toe, and pale Gessamine, Lycidas 143
1638 'crow-toe'
Trinity ms 'crowtoe'
Toeing
Of lighter toes, and such Court guise Mask 962
Trinity ms 'toes' ← 'toeing'
Toes
Of lighter toes, and such Court guise Mask 962
B.M. ms 'Toes'
Trinity ms 'toes' ← 'toeing'

Together
Of his Associate; hee together calls, Par Lost 5.696
So under fierie Cope together rush'd Par Lost 6.215
Together both with next to Almightie Arme, Par Lost 6.316
Of Goats or timerous flock together throngd Par Lost 6.857
Some Tree whose broad smooth Leaves together sowd, Par Lost 9.1095
So counsel'd hee, and both together went Par Lost 9.1099
And with what skill they had, together sowd, Par Lost 9.1112
Tost up and down, together crowded drove Par Lost 10.287
Upon the *Cronian* Sea, together drive Par Lost 10.290
Which God inspir'd, cannot together perish Par Lost 10.785
Wide hovering, all the Clouds together drove Par Lost 11.739
Close in a Cottage low together got Par Reg 2.28
Chor. Best keep together here, lest running thither Samson 1521
Together both, ere the high Lawns appear'd Lycidas 25
We drove a field, and both together heard Lycidas 27
Lay deep their plots together through each Land, Psalm 2, 4
Toil
After the toyl of Battel to repose Par Lost 1.319
ms 'toyle'
What in an age they with incessant toyle Par Lost 1.698
That *Satan* with less toil, and now with ease Par Lost 2.1041
They sat them down, and after no more toil Par Lost 4.327
The great Arch-Angel from his warlike toile Par Lost 6.257
For not to irksom toile, but to delight Par Lost 9.242
Extol not Riches then, the toyl of Fools, Par Reg 2.453
Relieves me from my task of servile toyl, Samson 5
Refreshment after toil, ease after pain, Mask 687
line not in Bridgewater ms
Trinity ms 'toile'
1637 'toile'
After long toil their liberty had won, Psalm 114, 2
From burden, *and from slavish toyle* Psalm 81, 21
Toiled
Sore toild, his riv'n Armes to havoc hewn, Par Lost 6.449
Toild out my uncouth passage, forc't to ride Par Lost 10.475
Toilest
And toil'st in vain, nor me in vain molest. Par Reg 4.498
Toils
Though dearly to my cost, thy ginns, and toyls; Samson 933
Toilsome
Which were it toilsom, yet with thee were sweet. Par Lost 4.439
What can be toilsom in these pleasant Walkes? Par Lost 11.179
Told
Cannot without process of speech be told, Par Lost 7.178
So told as earthly notion can receave. Par Lost 7.179
Thus I have told thee all my State, and brought Par Lost 8.521
This Tree is not as we are told, a Tree Par Lost 9.863
Thus *Eve* with Countnance blithe her storie told; Par Lost 9.886
I told ye then he should prevail and speed Par Lost 10.40
Hath told thee? hast thou eaten of the Tree Par Lost 10.122
Prince above Princes, gently hast thou tould Par Lost 11.298
A messenger from God fore-told thy birth Par Reg 1.238
Conceiv'd in me a Virgin, he fore-told Par Reg 1.239
And told them the Messiah now was born, Par Reg 1.245
Then to thy self ascrib'st the truth fore-told. Par Reg 1.453
But trouble, as old *Simeon* plain fore-told, Par Reg 2.87
If of my raign Prophetic Writ hath told, Par Reg 3.184
My time I told thee, (and that time for thee Par Reg 3.396
For both the when and how is no where told, Par Reg 4.472
Rode up in flames after his message told Samson 1433
With stories told of many a feat, Allegro 101
Or call up him that left half told Penseroso 109
Such as the wise *Demodocus* once told Vacation 48
She had told, alas too soon, Winchester 8
His leasure told him that his time was com, Another 23
line not in 1658 text
To Sisera, and as *is told* Psalm 83, 35
Toldest
Then toldst her doubting how these things could be Par Reg 1.137
Thou told'st me of? What grim aspects are these, Mask 694
Trinity ms 'toldst'
Bridgewater ms 'touldst'
Tolerable
More tollerable; if there be cure or charm Par Lost 2.460
Scarce tollerable, and from the North to call Par Lost 10.654
Or end, though sharp and sad, yet tolerable, Par Lost 10.977
Tomb
Above the faith of wedlock-bands, my tomb Samson 986
Visit his Tomb with flowers, only bewailing Samson 1742
By dead *Parthenope*'s dear tomb, Mask 879
Bridgewater ms 'tombe'
Hid from the world in a low delved tombe; Fair Inf 32
Was not long a living Tomb. Winchester 34
That Kings for such a Tomb would wish to die. Shakespear 16
1663-4 '*Tomb*'
1640 'Tombe'
1632 'Tombe'
Tomorrow
To morrow ere fresh Morning streak the East Par Lost 4.623
To morrow to fresh Woods, and Pastures new. Lycidas 193
Tones
So smooths her charming tones, that Gods own ear Par Lost 5.626
Of harmony in tones and numbers hit Par Reg 4.255
Tongue
But all was false and hollow; though his Tongue Par Lost 2.112
Or potent tongue; fool, not to think how vain Par Lost 6.135
Of this right hand provok't, since first that tongue Par Lost 6.154

Tongue(*cont*)
Unspeakable; for who, though with the tongue Par Lost 6.297
Refrein'd his tongue blasphemous; but anon Par Lost 6.360
What words or tongue of Seraph can suffice, Par Lost 7.113
Thy power; what thought can measure thee or tongue Par Lost 7.603
Nor tongue ineloquent; for God on thee Par Lost 8.219
My Tongue obey'd and readily could name Par Lost 8.272
Of her attention gaind, with Serpent Tongue Par Lost 9.529
By Tongue of Brute, and human sense exprest? Par Lost 9.554
Motion, each act won audience ere the tongue, Par Lost 9.674
The Tongue not made for Speech to speak thy praise: Par Lost 9.749
But hiss for hiss returnd with forked tongue Par Lost 10.518
To forked tongue, for now were all transform'd Par Lost 10.519
To dress, and troule the Tongue, and roule the Eye. Par Lost 11.620
Smooth on the tongue discourst, pleasing to th' ear, Par Reg 1.479
On *Aaron*'s breast: or tongue of Seers old Par Reg 3.15
That sleek't his tongue, and won so much on *Eve*, Par Reg 4.5
The bait of honied words; a rougher tongue Samson 1066
That thou hast banish't from thy tongue with lies, Mask 692
Trinity ms 'toungue'
And vertue has no tongue to check her pride: Mask 761
Arm his profane tongue with contemptuous words Mask 781
line not in Trinity ms
line not in Bridgewater ms
Didst move my first endeavouring tongue to speak, Vacation 2
I know my tongue but little Grace can do thee Vacation 10
That with smooth aire couldst humor best our tongue. Sonnet 13, 8
1673 printed 'tongu'
An open grave their throat, their tongue they smooth. Psalm 5, 28
The Tongue I heard, was strange. Psalm 81, 20

Tongue-batteries
Tongue-batteries, she surceas'd not day nor night Samson 404

Tongue-doughty
Sam. Tongue-doubtie Giant, how dost thou prove me these? Samson 1181

Tongues
To hoarce or mute, though fall'n on evil dayes, Par Lost 7.25
1669 'tongues'
On evil dayes though fall'n, and evil tongues; Par Lost 7.26
On all sides, from innumerable tongues Par Lost 10.507
Upon thir Tongues a various Spirit to rase Par Lost 12.53
To speak all Tongues, and do all Miracles, Par Lost 12.501
I undertook that office, and the tongues Par Reg 1.374
Expert in amorous Arts, enchanting tongues Par Reg 2.158
To live upon thir tongues and be thir talk, Par Reg 3.55
There *Babylon* the wonder of all tongues, Par Reg 3.280
And airy tongues, that syllable mens names Mask 208
Trinity ms 'toungs'
line not in Bridgewater ms

Too
Too well I see and rue the dire event, Par Lost 1.134
Cleombrotus, and many more too long, Par Lost 3.473
Endowd with all thir gifts, and O too like Par Lost 4.715
For us too large, where thy abundance wants Par Lost 4.730
The facil gates of hell too slightly barrd. Par Lost 4.967
Of Fruit-trees overwoodie reachd too farr Par Lost 5.213
He swerve not too secure: tell him withall Par Lost 5.238
No inconvenient Diet, nor too light Fare: Par Lost 5.495
Too much to one, but double how endur'd, Par Lost 5.783
From all: my Sect thou seest, now learn too late Par Lost 6.147
Too mean pretense, but what we more affect, Par Lost 6.421
For Gods, and too unequal work we find Par Lost 6.453
His count'nance too severe to be beheld Par Lost 6.825
Affrighted; but strict Fate had cast too deep Par Lost 6.869
Her dark foundations, and too fast had bound. Par Lost 6.870
Of those too high aspiring, who rebelld Par Lost 6.899
An Edifice too large for him to fill, Par Lost 8.104
If it presume, might erre in things too high, Par Lost 8.121
And thy faire *Eve*; Heav'n is for thee too high Par Lost 8.172
Too much of Ornament, in outward shew Par Lost 8.538
That name, unless an age too late, or cold Par Lost 9.44
Into her heart too easie entrance won: Par Lost 9.734
Whose taste, too long forborn, at first assay Par Lost 9.747
Disjoyne us, and I then too late renounce Par Lost 9.884
Too facil then thou didst not much gainsay, Par Lost 9.1158
And Chains they made all fast, too fast they made Par Lost 10.319
Too soon arriv'd, *Sin* there in power before, Par Lost 10.586
Which here, though plenteous, all too little seems Par Lost 10.600
Thy terms too hard, by which I was to hold Par Lost 10.751
Thy Justice seems; yet to say truth, too late, Par Lost 10.755
Henceforth; least that too heav'nly form, pretended Par Lost 10.872
By Parents, or his happiest choice too late Par Lost 10.904
Unwarie, and too desirous, as before, Par Lost 10.947
Us haply too secure of our discharge Par Lost 11.196
The rule of not too much, by temperance taught Par Lost 11.531
Too numerous; whence of guests he makes them slaves Par Lost 12.167
Well pleas'd, but answer'd not; for now too nigh Par Lost 12.625
And now too soon for us the circling hours Par Reg 1.57
Too long, then lay'st thy scapes on names ador'd, Par Reg 2.189
Inglorious: but thou yet art not too late. Par Reg 3.42
Shar'd among petty Kings too far remov'd; Par Reg 4.87
(O that I never had! fond wish too late.) Samson 228
Too grievous for the trespass or omission, Samson 691
My enemies, lov'd thee, as too well thou knew'st, Samson 878
Too well, unbosom'd all my secrets to thee, Samson 879
Dal. I was a fool, too rash, and quite mistaken Samson 907
Bear not too sensibly, nor still insist Samson 913
Henceforth, nor too much disapprove my own. Samson 970
Or was too much of self-love mixt, Samson 1031

Too(*cont*)
Yet knowing thir advantages too many, Samson 1401
So in the sad event too much concern'd. Samson 1551
Mess. Ah *Manoa* I refrain, too suddenly Samson 1565
To utter what will come at last too soon; Samson 1566
Lest evil tidings with too rude irruption Samson 1567
Hitting thy aged ear should pierce too deep. Samson 1568
They had ingag'd their wandring steps too far, Mask 193
Eld. Bro. I mean that too, but yet a hidden strength Mask 418
2. *Bro*. Me thought so too; what should it be? *Eld. Bro*. For certain Mask 482
Com not too neer, you fall on iron stakes else. Mask 491
Too well I did perceive it was the voice Mask 563
Bridgewater ms 'two'
And try her yet more strongly. Com, no more, Mask 806
Trinity ms 'no more' ←'y'are too morall'
Whose Saintly visage is too bright Penseroso 13
Too divine to be mistook: Arcades 4
Of labours huge and hard, too hard for human wight. Passion 14
My sorrows are too dark for day to know: Passion 33
She had told, alas too soon, Winchester 8
Dost make us Marble with too much conceaving; Shakespear 14
And too much breathing put him out of breath; Another 12
Too long vacation hastned on his term. Another 14
line not in 1658 text
As thou from yeer to yeer hast sung too late Sonnet 1, 11

Took
Suspended Hell, and took with ravishment Par Lost 2.554
Sad instrument of all our woe, she took; Par Lost 2.872
Then Crown'd again thir gold'n Harps they took, Par Lost 3.365
Took leave, and toward the coast of Earth beneath, Par Lost 3.739
Instant without disturb they took Allarm, Par Lost 6.549
Took envie, and aspiring to his highth, Par Lost 6.793
He took the golden Compasses, prepar'd Par Lost 7.225
Of Light by farr the greater part he took, Par Lost 7.359
So saying, by the hand he took me rais'd, Par Lost 8.300
Who stooping op'nd my left side, and took Par Lost 8.465
Or from my side subducting, took perhaps Par Lost 8.536
Such Pleasure took the Serpent to behold Par Lost 9.455
And forth to meet her went, the way she took Par Lost 9.847
Original; while *Adam* took no thought, Par Lost 9.1004
Took largely, of thir mutual guilt the Seale, Par Lost 9.1043
And took thir Seats; till from his Throne supream Par Lost 11.82
To find where *Adam* shelterd, took his way, Par Lost 11.223
To serve ungovern'd appetite, and took Par Lost 11.517
Through *Eden* took thir solitarie way. Par Lost 12.649
With that (such power was giv'n him then) he took Par Reg 3.251
So saying he took (for still he knew his power Par Reg 4.394
She proving false, the next I took to Wife Samson 227
Took full possession of me and prevail'd; Samson 869
Thir Magistrates confest it, when they took thee Samson 1183
I us'd hostility, and took thir spoil Samson 1203
Took in by lot 'twixt high, and neather *Jove*, Mask 20
1637 'Tooke'
Trinity ms 'tooke'
Bridgewater ms 'tooke'
I took it for a faery vision Mask 298
1637 'tooke'
Bridgewater ms 'tooke'
Trinity ms 'tooke'
Was took e're she was ware, and wish't she might Mask 558
Trinity ms 'tooke'
Bridgewater ms 'tooke'
1637 'tooke'
And took in strains that might create a soul Mask 561
Bridgewater ms 'tooke'
Trinity ms 'tooke'
Who gently ask't if he had seen such two, Mask 575
Trinity ms 'gently' ←'tooke him'
Held up their pearled wrists and took her in, Mask 834
Trinity ms '& took' ←'to take' ←'carie' ←'receave'
Bridgewater ms 'tooke'
1637 'tooke'
Hath took no print of the approching light, Nativity 20
As all their souls in blisfull rapture took: Nativity 98
Took up, and in fit place did reinstall? Fair Inf 46
Those Delphick lines with deep impression took, Shakespear 12
1632 'tooke'
1640 'tooke'
Pull'd off his Boots, and took away the light: Carrier 16

Tookest
Becam'st enamour'd, and such joy thou took'st Par Lost 2.765
My love how couldst thou hope, who tookst the way Samson 838
A dreadful way thou took'st to thy revenge. Samson 1591

Tools
But with such Gardning Tools as Art yet rude, Par Lost 9.391
First his own Tooles; then, what might else be wrought Par Lost 11.572
In scorn of thir proud arms and warlike tools, Samson 137
The tools of death, that waits him near. Psalm 7, 48

Top
Sing Heav'nly Muse, that on the secret top Par Lost 1.6
At Ev'ning from the top of *Fesole*, Par Lost 1.289
And *Ida* known, thence on the Snowy top Par Lost 1.515
With singed top thir stately growth though bare Par Lost 1.614
There stood a Hill not far whose griesly top Par Lost 1.670
And *Lichas* from the top of *Oeta* threw Par Lost 2.545
At top whereof, but farr more rich appeerd Par Lost 3.504
Nor staid, till on *Niphates* top he lights. Par Lost 3.742
Amidst as from a flaming Mount, whose top Par Lost 5.598

Top(*cont*)
Nor of the Muses nine, nor on the top — Par Lost 7.6
Of Heav'ns high-seated top, th' Impereal Throne — Par Lost 7.585
A woodie Mountain; whose high top was plaine, — Par Lost 8.303
On his Hill top, to light the bridal Lamp. — Par Lost 8.520
Of Paradise the highest, from whose top — Par Lost 11.378
Fast on the top of som high mountain fixt. — Par Lost 11.851
A Citie and Towre, whose top may reach to Heav'n; — Par Lost 12.44
God from the Mount of *Sinai*, whose gray top — Par Lost 12.227
Let us descend now therefore from this top — Par Lost 12.588
Seated as on the top of Vertues hill, — Par Reg 2.217
From whose high top to ken the prospect round, — Par Reg 2.286
To this high mountain top the Tempter brought — Par Reg 3.265
The top of Eloquence, Statists indeed, — Par Reg 4.354
By how much from the top of wondrous glory, — Samson 167
Now the top of Heav'n doth hold, — Mask 94
Nor on the shaggy top of *Mona* high, — Lycidas 54

Topaz
Rubie or Topaz, to the Twelve that shon — Par Lost 3.597

Tophet
The pleasant Vally of *Hinnom*, *Tophet* thence — Par Lost 1.404
ms 'Tophet'

Topped
Of Alabaster, top't with Golden Spires: — Par Reg 4.548

Tops
As when from mountain tops the dusky clouds — Par Lost 2.488
Of stateliest view. Yet higher then thir tops — Par Lost 4.142
Breathe soft or loud; and wave your tops, ye Pines, — Par Lost 5.193
Rocks, Waters, Woods, and by the shaggie tops — Par Lost 6.645
Into the Clouds, thir tops ascend the Skie: — Par Lost 7.287
On Cliffs and Cedar tops thir Eyries build: — Par Lost 7.424
And now the tops of Hills as Rocks appeer; — Par Lost 11.852

Torch
They light the Nuptial Torch, and bid invoke — Par Lost 11.590

Torches
Of mid-night Torches burns; mysterious Dame — Mask 130
Trinity ms 'torches'
Bridgewater ms 'torches'

Tore
A shout that tore Hells Concave, and beyond — Par Lost 1.542
With conquest, felt th' envenom'd robe, and tore — Par Lost 2.543
Tore through my entrails, that with fear and pain — Par Lost 2.783
And all her entrails tore, disgorging foule — Par Lost 6.588
Of that wilde Rout that tore the *Thracian* Bard — Par Lost 7.34
Who tore the Lion, as the Lion tears the Kid, — Samson 128
What noise or shout was that? it tore the Skie. — Samson 1472

Torment
Torment with ease, and soonest recompence — Par Lost 4.893
Torment, and loud lament, and furious rage. — Par Lost 8.244
Torment within me, as from the hateful siege — Par Lost 9.121
To mee and to my ofspring would torment me — Par Lost 10.781
And torment less then none of what we dread, — Par Lost 10.998
Abortive, to torment me ere thir being, — Par Lost 11.769
Rather inflames thy torment, representing — Par Reg 1.418
Wealth, pleasure, pain or torment, death and life, — Par Reg 4.305
Bound, and to torment sent before thir time. — Par Reg 4.632
Sam. O that torment should not be confin'd — Samson 606

Tormented
Tormented all the Air; all Air seemd then — Par Lost 6.244

Tormenting
Sight hateful, sight tormenting! thus these two — Par Lost 4.505

Tormentor
Let his tormenter Conscience find him out, — Par Reg 4.130

Tormentors
Thoughts my Tormenters arm'd with deadly stings — Samson 623

Torments
Torments him; round he throws his baleful eyes — Par Lost 1.56
His own invented Torments. But perhaps — Par Lost 2.70
Chains and these Torments? better these then worse — Par Lost 2.196
Our torments also may in length of time — Par Lost 2.274
Under what torments inwardly I groane; — Par Lost 4.88
Among our other torments not the least, — Par Lost 4.510
Of worse torments me then the feeling can. — Par Reg 3.208

Torn
Torn from *Pelorus*, or the shatter'd side — Par Lost 1.232
In mutinie had from her Axle torn — Par Lost 2.926
Gladly the Port, though Shrouds and Tackle torn; — Par Lost 2.1044
At least had gon to rack, disturbd and torne — Par Lost 4.994
Or torn up sheer: ill wast thou shrouded then, — Par Reg 4.419
With flowre-inwov'n tresses torn — Nativity 187

Torrent
Whose waves of torrent fire inflame with rage. — Par Lost 2.581
Of torrent Floods, or of a numerous Host. — Par Lost 6.830
If steep, with torrent rapture, if through Plaine, — Par Lost 7.299
Nor wet *Octobers* torrent flood — Mask 930

Torrid
On Heavens Azure, and the torrid Clime — Par Lost 1.297
Of *Barca* or *Cyrene*'s torrid soil, — Par Lost 2.904
Fierce as a Comet; which with torrid heat, — Par Lost 12.634

Tortuous
So varied hee, and of his tortuous Traine — Par Lost 9.516

Torture
That comes to all; but torture without end — Par Lost 1.67
Of gastly Spasm, or racking torture, qualmes — Par Lost 11.481
Man. Suspense in news is torture, speak them out. — Samson 1569

Torturer
Against the Torturer; when to meet the noise — Par Lost 2.64

Tortures
Turning our Tortures into horrid Arms — Par Lost 2.63
And tortures him now more, the more he sees — Par Lost 9.469

Torturing
Inexorably, and the torturing hour — Par Lost 2.91

To-ruffled
Were all to ruffl'd, and somtimes impair'd. — Mask 380

Tossed
Cowles, Hoods and Habits with thir wearers tost — Par Lost 3.490
And full of Peace, now tost and turbulent: — Par Lost 9.1126
Tost up and down, together crowded drove — Par Lost 10.287
And in a troubl'd Sea of passion tost, — Par Lost 10.718

Tossing
From off the tossing of these fiery waves, — Par Lost 1.184
Dire was the tossing, deep the groans, despair — Par Lost 11.489

Total
Least total darkness should by Night regaine — Par Lost 4.665
Thir nimble tread, as when the total kind — Par Lost 6.73
Total they mix, Union of Pure with Pure — Par Lost 8.627
My self the total Crime, or to accuse — Par Lost 10.127
Irrecoverably dark, total Eclipse — Samson 81

Touch
Potable Gold, when with one vertuous touch — Par Lost 3.608
With Heav'nly touch of instrumental sounds — Par Lost 4.686
Touch of Celestial temper, but returns — Par Lost 4.812
Of sense, whereby they hear, see, smell, touch, taste, — Par Lost 5.411
Thick-rammd, at th' other bore with touch of fire — Par Lost 6.485
Provide, pernicious with one touch to fire. — Par Lost 6.520
Do as you have in charge, and briefly touch — Par Lost 6.566
With nicest touch. Immediate in a flame, — Par Lost 6.584
Charg'd not to touch the interdicted Tree, — Par Lost 7.46
Transported touch; here passion first I felt, — Par Lost 8.530
But if the sense of touch whereby mankind — Par Lost 8.579
Irradiance, virtual or immediate touch? — Par Lost 8.617
But of this Tree we may not taste nor touch; — Par Lost 9.651
Thereof, nor shall ye touch it, least ye die. — Par Lost 9.663
Inclinable now grown to touch or taste, — Par Lost 9.742
Much more to taste it under banne to touch. — Par Lost 9.925
To whom soon mov'd with touch of blame thus *Eve*. — Par Lost 9.1143
Or touch with lightest moment of impulse — Par Lost 10.45
This more delusive, not the touch, but taste — Par Lost 10.563
Thir stops and chords was seen: his volant touch — Par Lost 11.561
With touch aetherial of Heav'ns fiery rod — Samson 549
Dal. Let me approach at least, and touch thy hand. — Samson 951
To touch the prosperous growth of this tall Wood. — Mask 270
Lest som ill greeting touch attempt the person — Mask 406
Thou canst not touch the freedom of my minde — Mask 663
I touch with chaste palms moist and cold, — Mask 918
And touch the warbled string. — Arcades 87
(If ye have power to touch our senses so) — Nativity 127
To th' touch of golden wires, while *Hebe* brings — Vacation 38
Touch their immortal Harps of golden wires, — Musick 13

Touched
Touch'd lightly; for no falshood can endure — Par Lost 4.811
Of spiritous and fierie spume, till toucht — Par Lost 6.479
And touch't thir Golden Harps, and hymning prais'd — Par Lost 7.258
And toucht by her fair tendance gladlier grew. — Par Lost 8.47
Touchd onely, that our trial, when least sought, — Par Lost 9.380
Mee who have touch'd and tasted, yet both live, — Par Lost 9.688
Hath toucht my sense, flat seems to this, and harsh. — Par Lost 9.987
In some to spring from thee, who never touch'd — Par Lost 11.425
Toucht with the flame: on thir whole Host I flew — Samson 262
And thou hast need much washing to be toucht. — Samson 1107
Phoebus repli'd, and touch'd my trembling ears; — Lycidas 77
Trinity ms 'touch't'
He touch'd the tender stops of various Quills, — Lycidas 188
Trinity ms 'toucht'
From out his secret Altar toucht with hallow'd fire. — Nativity 28
He thought it toucht his Deitie full neer, — Fair Inf 10
To hear the Lute well toucht, or artfull voice — Sonnet 20, 11

Touches
With solemn touches, troubl'd thoughts, and chase — Par Lost 1.557

Touching
Her hand soft touching, whisperd thus. Awake — Par Lost 5.17
Defends the touching of these viands pure, — Par Reg 2.370

Tough
Live on tough roots and stubs, to thirst inur'd — Par Reg 1.339
a tough encounter with the shaggiest ruffian — Mask Tr. ms 16.39
a tough encounter, with the shaggiest ruffian — Mask Br. ms 392

Tournament
At Joust and Torneament; then marshal'd Feast — Par Lost 9.37
With cruel Tournament the Squadrons joine; — Par Lost 11.652

Tourneys
Of Turneys and of Trophies hung; — Penseroso 118

Toward
Was moving toward the shoar; his ponderous shield — Par Lost 1.284
Hurling defiance toward the Vault of Heav'n. — Par Lost 1.669
Toward the four winds four speedy Cherubim — Par Lost 2.516
Ply stemming nightly toward the Pole. So seem'd — Par Lost 2.642
On Hills where Flocks are fed, flies toward the Springs — Par Lost 3.435
Took leave, and toward the coast of Earth beneath, — Par Lost 3.739
Farr on excursion toward the Gates of Hell; — Par Lost 8.231
Strait toward Heav'n my wondring Eyes I turnd, — Par Lost 8.257
In Serpent, Inmate bad, and toward *Eve* — Par Lost 9.495
Toward the right hand his Glorie, on the Son — Par Lost 10.64
The smell of peace toward Mankinde, let him live — Par Lost 11.38
Yet toward these thus dignifi'd, thou oft — Samson 682
Pacing toward the other gole — Mask 100

Toward(*cont*)
And so attend ye toward her glittering state; Arcades 81
Trinity ms 'towards'
Toward Heav'ns descent had slop'd his westering wheel. Lycidas 31
Looks toward *Namancos* and *Bayona*'s hold; Lycidas 162
Why turned *Jordan* toward his Crystall Fountains? Psalm 114, 14
Toward which Time leads me, and the will of Heav'n; Sonnet 7, 12
Toward solid good what leads the nearest way; Sonnet 21, 10
Toward thee, My King, my God. Psalm 84, 16
Toward us, *and chide no more*. Psalm 85, 16
For great thy mercy is toward me, Psalm 86, 45

Towards
Of Thunder heard remote. Towards him they bend Par Lost 2.477
Puts on swift wings, and towards the Gates of Hell Par Lost 2.631
1667 'toward'
And towards the Gate rouling her bestial train, Par Lost 2.873
Directly towards the new created World, Par Lost 3.89
Towards either Throne they bow, and to the ground Par Lost 3.350
Days, months, & years, towards his all-chearing Lamp Par Lost 3.581
Sometimes towards *Eden* which now in his view Par Lost 4.27
Sometimes towards Heav'n and the full-blazing Sun, Par Lost 4.29
When coming towards them so dread they saw Par Lost 6.648
For God towards thee hath done his part, do thine. Par Lost 9.375
How all befell: they towards the Throne Supream Par Lost 10.28
From each side shoaling towards the mouth of Hell. Par Lost 10.288
Towards her, his life so late and sole delight, Par Lost 10.941
With soft foot towards the deep, who now had stopt Par Lost 11.848
Towards the retreating Sea thir furious tyde. Par Lost 11.854
Marching from *Eden* towards the West, shall finde Par Lost 12.40
Safe towards *Canaan* from the shoar advance Par Lost 12.215
Justification towards God, and peace Par Lost 12.296
As I suppose, towards your once gloried friend, Samson 334
That thou towards him with hand so various, Samson 668
The easier towards me, or thy hatred less. Samson 772
In human hearts, nor less in mine towards thee, Samson 792
Towards thee I intend for what I have misdone, Samson 911
Will towards thy holy temple worship low Psalm 5, 20

Tower
Stood like a Towr; his form had yet not lost Par Lost 1.591
ms 'towre'
Which now sat high in his Meridian Towre: Par Lost 4.30
The Dank, and rising on stiff Pennons, towre Par Lost 7.441
The Bird of *Jove*, stoopt from his aerie tour, Par Lost 11.185
A Citie and Towre, whose top may reach to Heav'n; Par Lost 12.44
Comes down to see thir Citie, ere the Tower Par Lost 12.51
Stayes not on Man; to God his Tower intends Par Lost 12.73
With many a tower and terrass round, Mask 935
Bridgewater ms 'towre'
Trinity ms 'towre'
From his watch-towre in the skies, Allegro 43
Be seen in som high lonely Towr, Penseroso 86
The house of *Pindarus*, when Temple and Towre Sonnet 8, 11
Trinity ms 'towre'

Towered
In Heav'n by many a Towred structure high, Par Lost 1.733
ms 'towred'
Circular base of rising foulds, that tour'd Par Lost 9.498
Huge Cities and high towr'd, that well might seem Par Reg 3.261
Towred Cities please us then, Allegro 117
Or the towred *Cybele*, Arcades 21
Or *Medway* smooth, or Royal Towred *Thame*. Vacation 100

Towering
Up to the fiery Concave touring high. Par Lost 2.635
Of Towring Eagles, to all the Fowles he seems Par Lost 5.271
Came towring, armd in Adamant and Gold; Par Lost 6.110
Left his ground-nest, high towring to descry Par Reg 2.280

Towers
Of riot ascends above thir loftiest Towrs, Par Lost 1.499
ms 'towers'
To have built in Heav'n high Towrs; nor did he scape Par Lost 1.749
ms 'Towers'
O're Heav'ns high Towrs to force resistless way, Par Lost 2.62
First, what Revenge? the Towrs of Heav'n are fill'd Par Lost 2.129
With Opal Towrs and Battlements adorn'd Par Lost 2.1049
From *Auran* Eastward to the Royal Towrs Par Lost 4.211
Rais'd on a Mount, with Pyramids and Towrs Par Lost 5.758
On those proud Towrs to swift destruction doom'd. Par Lost 5.907
Cities of Men with lofty Gates and Towrs, Par Lost 11.640
Obstruct Heav'n Towrs, and in derision sets Par Lost 12.52
Forest and field, and flood, Temples and Towers Par Reg 3.268
Chariots or Elephants endorst with Towers Par Reg 3.329
With Towers and Temples proudly elevate Par Reg 4.34
The holy City lifted high her Towers, Par Reg 4.545
They had by this possess'd the Towers of *Gath*, Samson 266
Towers, and Battlements it sees Allegro 77
To bear me where the Towers of *Salem* stood, Passion 39
Once glorious Towers, now sunk in guiltles blood; Passion 40

Town
To Town or Village nigh (nighest is far) Par Reg 1.332
Machaerus and each Town or City wall'd Par Reg 2.22
The Subject new: it walk'd the Town a while, Sonnet 11, 3
Trinity ms 'towne' ←'town'

Towns
Before him, Towns, and rural works between, Par Lost 11.639
At home, scarce view'd the *Gallilean* Towns, Par Reg 3.233

Toy
So said he, and forbore not glance or toy Par Lost 9.1034
Fall flat and shrink into a trivial toy, Par Reg 2.223

Toy(*cont*)
I came not here on such a trivial toy Mask 502
Bridgewater ms 'toye'

Toys
None are, thou think'st, but taken with such toys. Par Reg 2.177
Crude or intoxicate, collecting toys, Par Reg 4.328
Or fill the fixed mind with all your toyes; Penseroso 4
Not those new fangled toys, and triming slight Vacation 19

Trace
Streaking the ground with sinuous trace; not all Par Lost 7.481
Things in thir Causes, but to trace the wayes Par Lost 9.682
His bright appearances, or foot step-trace? Par Lost 11.329
1667 'footstep trace'
May trace huge Forests, and unharbour'd Heaths, Mask 423
Trinity ms 'trace' ←'walke through'

Traced
Argues no Leader but a lyar trac't, Par Lost 4.949

Traces
In his loose traces from the furrow came, Mask 292

Tracing
The while her Son tracing the Desert wild, Par Reg 2.109

Track
Following his track, such was the will of Heav'n, Par Lost 2.1025
Over the vext Abyss, following the track Par Lost 10.314
Detain from following thy illustrious track. Par Lost 10.367
Express, and of his steps the track Divine. Par Lost 11.354
With solitude, till far from track of men, Par Reg 1.191

Tract
Nor the deep Tract of Hell, say first what cause Par Lost 1.28
ms 'tract'
Improv'd by tract of time, and wingd ascend Par Lost 5.498
Thir names of thee; so over many a tract Par Lost 6.76
Scipio the highth of *Rome*. With tract oblique Par Lost 9.510
And all this tract that fronts the falling Sun Mask 30

Trade
To tend the homely slighted Shepherds trade, Lycidas 65
Turns on his head, and his ill trade Psalm 7, 58

Trading
Thir spicie Drugs: they on the Trading Flood Par Lost 2.640
1667 'trading'

Tradition
However some tradition they dispers'd Par Lost 10.578

Traditions
With superstitions and traditions taint, Par Lost 12.512
Thir Idolisms, Traditions, Paradoxes? Par Reg 4.234

Traduced
Of falshood most unconjugal traduc't. Samson 979

Tragedians
Thence what the lofty grave Tragoedians taught Par Reg 4.261

Tragedy
Som time let Gorgeous Tragedy Penseroso 97

Tragic
Those Notes to Tragic; foul distrust, and breach Par Lost 9.6

Trail
Because they shall not trail me through thir streets Samson 1402

Train
Osiris, *Isis*, *Orus* and thir Train Par Lost 1.478
ms 'train'
And towards the Gate rouling her bestial train, Par Lost 2.873
His breaded train, and of his fatal guile Par Lost 4.349
And these the Gemms of Heav'n, her starrie train: Par Lost 4.649
Fairest of Starrs, last in the train of Night, Par Lost 5.166
His god-like Guest, walks forth, without more train Par Lost 5.351
For thither he assembl'd all his Train, Par Lost 5.767
All are not of thy Train; there be who Faith Par Lost 6.143
For *Chaos* heard his voice: him all his Traine Par Lost 7.221
Stream, and perpetual draw thir humid traine. Par Lost 7.306
The silent hours, and th' other whose gay Traine Par Lost 7.444
The glorious Train ascending: He through Heav'n, Par Lost 7.574
Oread or *Dryad*, or of *Delia*'s Traine, Par Lost 9.387
So varied hee, and of his tortuous Traine Par Lost 9.516
By Angels numberless, thy daily Train. Par Lost 9.548
Attendance none shall need, nor Train, where none Par Lost 10.80
The ancient Sire descends with all his Train; Par Lost 11.862
To *Haran*, after him a cumbrous Train Par Lost 12.131
Nymphs of *Diana*'s train, and *Naiades* Par Reg 2.355
Our Saviour, and new train of words began. Par Reg 3.266
Her harbinger, a damsel train behind; Samson 721
With silent obsequie and funeral train Samson 1732
The loose train of thy amber-dropping hair, Mask 863
1637 'traine'
Trinity ms 'traine'
Bridgewater ms 'traine'
B.M. ms 'Train'
The fickle Pensioners of *Morpheus* train. Penseroso 10
Flowing with majestick train, Penseroso 34
The pride of her carnation train, Winchester 37
Both them I serve, and of their train am I. Sonnet 1, 14

Trained
Ministring Spirits, traind up in Feast and Song; Par Lost 6.167

Training
Training his devilish Enginrie, impal'd Par Lost 6.553

Trains
Ignobly, to the traines and to the smiles Par Lost 11.624
Of fair fallacious looks, venereal trains, Samson 533
Where once I have been caught; I know thy trains Samson 932
Benighted in these Woods. Now to my charms, Mask 150
Trinity ms 'charmes' ←'traines'

Trains(*cont*)
And to my wily trains, I shall e're long — Mask 151
Trinity ms 'trains' ←'charmes'
Bridgewater ms 'traynes'
Traitor
Art thou that Traitor Angel, art thou hee, — Par Lost 2.689
She sought to make me Traytor to my self; — Samson 401
What Murtherer, what Traytor, Parricide, — Samson 832
This will restore all soon. *La*. 'Twill not false traitor, — Mask 690
Bridgewater ms 'traytor'
Traitress
Sam. My Wife, my Traytress, let her not come near me. — Samson 725
Trample
To trample thee as mire: for proof look up, — Par Lost 4.1010
Trampled
Thus trampl'd, thus expell'd to suffer here — Par Lost 2.195
Trampling
Trampling the unshowr'd Grasse with lowings loud: — Nativity 215
Trance
Abstract as in a transe methought I saw, — Par Lost 8.462
No nightly trance, or breathed spell, — Nativity 179
In pensive trance, and anguish, and ecstatick fit. — Passion 42
Transact
Unvanquisht, easier to transact with mee — Par Lost 6.286
Transcend
Transcend his own so farr, whose radiant forms — Par Lost 5.457
Transcendent
Cloth'd with transcendent brightness didst out-shine — Par Lost 1.86
Satan, whom now transcendent glory rais'd — Par Lost 2.427
From his transcendent Seat the Saints among, — Par Lost 10.614
Transfer
Serpent though brute, unable to transferre — Par Lost 10.165
Sam. That fault I take not on me, but transfer — Samson 241
Transferred
Of secondarie hands, by task transferd — Par Lost 5.854
All power on him transferr'd: whence to his Son — Par Lost 6.678
Vicegerent Son, to thee I have transferr'd — Par Lost 10.56
Full weight must be transferr'd upon my head. — Par Reg 1.267
Transfix
Transfix us to the bottom of this Gulfe. — Par Lost 1.329
Transfixed
Each on his rock transfixt, the sport and prey — Par Lost 2.181
Transform
Glory of him that made them, to transform — Par Lost 1.370
Transformed
Transform'd: but he my inbred enemie — Par Lost 2.785
Com'st thou, escap'd thy prison, and transform'd, — Par Lost 4.824
In *Epidaurus;* nor to which transformd — Par Lost 9.507
To forked tongue, for now were all transform'd — Par Lost 10.519
After the *Tuscan* Mariners transform'd — Mask 48
Bridgewater ms 'manners transformed'
But then transform'd him to a purple flower — Fair Inf 27
As when those Hinds that were transform'd to Froggs — Sonnet 12, 5
Transforms
The visage quite transforms of him that drinks, — Mask 527
Bridgewater ms 'transformes'
Transfused
Transfus'd on thee his ample Spirit rests. — Par Lost 3.389
Immense I have transfus'd, that all may know — Par Lost 6.704
Transgress
From thir Creator, and transgress his Will — Par Lost 1.31
ms 'transgresse'
And easily transgress the sole Command, — Par Lost 3.94
Of others, who approve not to transgress — Par Lost 4.880
Yet fell; remember, and fear to transgress. — Par Lost 6.912
If they transgress, and slight that sole command, — Par Lost 7.47
And all temptation to transgress repel. — Par Lost 8.643
Rather how hast thou yeelded to transgress — Par Lost 9.902
Then due by sentence when thou didst transgress, — Par Lost 11.253
And that great Cov'nant which we still transgress — Circum 21
Trinity ms 'transgresse'
That do observe If I transgress — Psalm 5, 23
Transgressed
Transgrest, inevitably thou shalt dye; — Par Lost 8.330
Neither had I transgress'd, nor thou with mee. — Par Lost 9.1161
Transgresses
Again transgresses, and again submits; — Samson 758
Transgressing
Least wilfully transgressing he pretend — Par Lost 5.244
Of thy transgressing? not enough severe, — Par Lost 9.1169
Transgression
On his transgression, Death denounc't that day, — Par Lost 10.49
The penaltie to thy transgression due, — Par Lost 12.399
After my great transgression, so requite — Samson 1356
Transgressions
To thy transgressions, and disturbd the charge — Par Lost 4.879
Her own transgressions, to upbraid me mine? — Samson 820
Transgressor
To me transgressour, who for thee ordaind — Par Lost 11.164
Transgressors
On Earth these thy transgressors, but thou knowst — Par Lost 10.72
Transient
Measur'd this transient World, the Race of time, — Par Lost 12.554
Transition
Then with transition sweet new Speech resumes. — Par Lost 12.5
line not in 1667 edition
Transitory
Of all things transitorie and vain, when Sin — Par Lost 3.446

Transitory(*cont*)
Therefore let pass, as they are transitory, — Par Reg 4.209
Translated
Translated Saints, or middle Spirits hold — Par Lost 3.461
So maist thou be translated to the skies, — Mask 242
B.M. ms 'Transplanted'
Translucent
Against the Eastern ray, translucent, pure. — Samson 548
Under the glassie, cool, translucent wave, — Mask 861
Bridgewater ms 'transelucent'
Transmigration
Or transmigration, as thir lot shall lead. — Par Lost 10.261
Transparent
Transparent, Elemental Air, diffus'd — Par Lost 7.265
Transpicuous
Sent from her through the wide transpicuous aire, — Par Lost 8.141
Transpires
To transubstantiate; what redounds, transpires — Par Lost 5.438
Transplanted
And live in thee transplanted, and from thee — Par Lost 3.293
Transplanted from her cloudie Shrine, and plac'd — Par Lost 7.360
So maist thou be translated to the skies, — Mask 242
B.M. ms 'Transplanted'
Transported
Farr otherwise, transported I behold, — Par Lost 8.529
Transported touch; here passion first I felt, — Par Lost 8.530
Compulsion thus transported to forget — Par Lost 9.474
That laugh, as if transported with some fit — Par Lost 10.626
Such where the deep transported mind may soare — Vacation 33
Transporting
My spirit som transporting *Cherub* feels, — Passion 38
Transports
Of subterranean wind transports a Hill — Par Lost 1.231
Transports our adversarie, whom no bounds — Par Lost 3.81
For what admir'st thou, what transports thee so, — Par Lost 8.567
Transubstantiate
To transubstantiate; what redounds, transpires — Par Lost 5.438
Transverse
Blows them transverse ten thousand Leagues awry — Par Lost 3.488
Fled and pursu'd transverse the resonant fugue. — Par Lost 11.563
These two proportiond ill drove me transverse. — Samson 209
Trap
And wouldst thou seek again to trap me here — Mask 699
line not in Bridgewater ms
Trappings
Bases and tinsel Trappings, gorgious Knights — Par Lost 9.36
Travail
With travail difficult, not better farr — Par Lost 10.593
After this thy travail sore — Winchester 49
1673 'travel'
Travel
I travel this profound, direct my course; — Par Lost 2.980
To travel with *Tobias*, and secur'd — Par Lost 5.222
Travelled
His travell'd steps; farr distant he descries — Par Lost 3.501
Traveller
Offring to every weary Travailer, — Mask 64
1673 'Traveller'
Bridgewater ms 'traveller'
Trinity ms 'travailer'
To the misled and lonely Travailer? — Mask 200
Trinity ms 'travailer'
1673 'Traveller'
line not in Bridgewater ms
That wontst to love the travailers benizon, — Mask 332
1673 'travellers'
Travelling
Travelling East, and with her part averse — Par Lost 8.138
Travels
He travels big with vanitie, — Psalm 7, 51
Traverse
Darts his experienc't eye, and soon traverse — Par Lost 1.568
ms 'travers'
Traversed
Neerer he drew, and many a walk travers'd — Par Lost 9.434
Traversing
From Pole to Pole, traversing each Colure; — Par Lost 9.66
Treacherous
Hence with thy brew'd inchantments, foul deceiver, — Mask 696
Trinity ms 'brewd enchauntments' ←'foule brud' ←'hel brewd opiate' ←'hel bru'd liquor' ←'bru'd sorcerie' ←'teacherous (leacherous?) bruage' ←'teacherous kindnesse'
Treacherously
Thir nuptials, nor this last so trecherously — Samson 1023
Treachery
Not wedlock-trechery endangering life. — Samson 1009
Tread
Th' advantage, and descending tread us down — Par Lost 1.327
My self expose, with lonely steps to tread — Par Lost 2.828
Ask riddance, if we mean to tread with ease; — Par Lost 4.632
O friends, I hear the tread of nimble feet — Par Lost 4.866
The Earth, and stately tread, or lowly creep; — Par Lost 5.201
Thir nimble tread, as when the total kind — Par Lost 6.73
Whom he shall tread at last under our feet; — Par Lost 10.190
Enterd so faire, should turn aside to tread — Par Lost 11.630
To tread his Sacred Courts, and minister — Par Reg 1.488
The tread of many feet stearing this way; — Samson 111

Tread(*cont*)
Of this occasion. But I hear the tread Mask 91
That bends not as I tread, Mask 899
And overtake it, let him tread Psalm 7, 14
Treading
Treading the crude consistence, half on foot, Par Lost 2.941
Treads
Treads on it daily with his clouted shoon, Mask 635
line not in Bridgewater ms
Treason
To expiate his Treason hath naught left, Par Lost 3.207
Her spurious first-born; Treason against me? Samson 391
Of Matrimonial treason: so farewel. Samson 959
Treasonous
I would not taste thy treasonous offer; none Mask 702
Treasure
Get Riches first, get Wealth, and Treasure heap, Par Reg 2.427
Of Misers treasure by an out-laws den, Mask 399
Bridgewater ms 'treasures'
And from thy wardrope bring thy chiefest treasure; Vacation 18
Treasures
For Treasures better hid. Soon had his crew Par Lost 1.688
· ms 'treasures'
All treasures and all gain esteem as dross, Par Reg 3.29
Treasury
Of *Englands* Counsel, and her Treasury, Sonnet 10, 2
Treat
And now of love they treat till th' Eevning Star Par Lost 11.588
To treat thee as beseems, and as her Lord Par Reg 2.335
In brief sententious precepts, while they treat Par Reg 4.264
To some *Philistian* Lords, with whom to treat Samson 482
That these dark orbs no more shall treat with light, Samson 591
Trebisond
Damasco, or *Marocco*, or *Trebisond*, Par Lost 1.584
ms 'Trebisond'
Trebizond
Damasco, or *Marocco*, or *Trebisond*, Par Lost 1.584
ms 'Trebisond'
Treble
Treble confusion, wrath and vengeance pour'd. Par Lost 1.220
Tree
Of that Forbidden Tree, whose mortal tast Par Lost 1.2
ms 'tree'
In Paradise, fast by the Tree of Life Par Lost 3.354
Thence up he flew, and on the Tree of Life Par Lost 4.194
The middle Tree and highest there that grew, Par Lost 4.195
And all amid them stood the Tree of Life, Par Lost 4.218
Our Death the Tree of knowledge grew fast by, Par Lost 4.221
Then from his loftie stand on that high Tree Par Lost 4.395
So various, not to taste that onely Tree Par Lost 4.423
Of knowledge, planted by the Tree of Life, Par Lost 4.424
God hath pronounc't it death to taste that Tree, Par Lost 4.427
One fatal Tree there stands of Knowledge call'd, Par Lost 4.514
His orient Beams, on herb, tree, fruit, and flour, Par Lost 4.644
That brought me on a sudden to the Tree Par Lost 5.51
Ambrosia; on that Tree he also gaz'd; Par Lost 5.57
Charg'd not to touch the interdicted Tree, Par Lost 7.46
And Fruit Tree yielding Fruit after her kind; Par Lost 7.311
Varietie without end; but of the Tree Par Lost 7.542
Then Fruits of Palm-tree pleasantest to thirst Par Lost 8.212
Of Earth before scarce pleasant seemd. Each Tree Par Lost 8.306
Of every Tree that in the Garden growes Par Lost 8.321
But of the Tree whose operation brings Par Lost 8.323
Amid the Garden by the Tree of Life, Par Lost 8.326
Rose up a Fountain by the Tree of Life; Par Lost 9.73
A goodly Tree farr distant to behold Par Lost 9.576
Thy utmost reach or *Adams:* Round the Tree Par Lost 9.591
Amid the Tree now got, where plenty hung Par Lost 9.594
But say, where grows the Tree, from hence how far? Par Lost 9.617
Led *Eve* our credulous Mother, to the Tree Par Lost 9.644
But of this Tree we may not taste nor touch; Par Lost 9.651
Of each Tree in the Garden we may eate, Par Lost 9.660
But of the Fruit of this fair Tree amidst Par Lost 9.661
Knowledge of Good and Evil in this Tree, Par Lost 9.723
What can your knowledge hurt him, or this Tree Par Lost 9.727
Conceales not from us, naming thee the Tree Par Lost 9.751
So saying, from the Tree her step she turnd, Par Lost 9.834
That Morn when first they parted; by the Tree Par Lost 9.848
Scarse from the Tree returning; in her hand Par Lost 9.850
This Tree is not as we are told, a Tree Par Lost 9.863
For this one Tree had bin forbidden ten. Par Lost 9.1026
Then ever, bountie of this vertuous Tree. Par Lost 9.1033
Some Tree whose broad smooth Leaves together sowd, Par Lost 9.1095
The Figtree, not that kind for Fruit renown'd, Par Lost 9.1101
About the Mother Tree, a Pillard shade Par Lost 9.1106
Hath told thee? hast thou eaten of the Tree Par Lost 10.122
Shee gave me of the Tree, and I did eate. Par Lost 10.143
And eaten of the Tree concerning which Par Lost 10.199
For one forbidden Tree a multitude Par Lost 10.554
Reach also of the Tree of Life, and eat, Par Lost 11.94
And guard all passage to the Tree of Life: Par Lost 11.122
On this Mount he appeerd, under this Tree Par Lost 11.320
Th' excepted Tree, nor with the Snake conspir'd, Par Lost 11.426
Green Tree or ground whereon his foot may light; Par Lost 11.858
On *David*'s Throne, it shall be like a tree Par Reg 4.147
From drooping plant, or dropping tree; the birds Par Reg 4.434
Ambrosial, Fruits fetcht from the tree of life, Par Reg 4.589
But beauty like the fair Hesperian Tree Mask 393

Tree(*cont*)
Bridgewater ms 'tree'
Trinity ms 'tree'
1637 'tree'
That sing about the golden tree: Mask 983
B.M. ms 'Tree'
& fruits of golden rind, on whose faire tree Mask Tr. ms 10.08
where grows the right-borne gold upon his native tree Mask Tr. ms 27.08
Spoil'd at once both fruit and tree: Winchester 30
He shall be as a tree which planted grows Psalm 1, 7
Trees
Of goodliest Trees loaden with fairest Fruit, Par Lost 4.147
All Trees of noblest kind for sight, smell, taste; Par Lost 4.217
Groves whose rich Trees wept odorous Gumms and Balme, Par Lost 4.248
This one, this easie charge, of all the Trees Par Lost 4.421
Of Fruit-trees overwoodie reachd too farr Par Lost 5.213
Eastward among those Trees, what glorious shape Par Lost 5.309
Then with these various fruits the Trees of God Par Lost 5.390
Sups with the Ocean: though in Heav'n the Trees Par Lost 5.426
By living Streams among the Trees of Life, Par Lost 5.652
Rose as in Dance the stately Trees, and spred Par Lost 7.324
Among the Trees in Pairs they rose, they walk'd: Par Lost 7.459
This Garden, planted with the Trees of God, Par Lost 7.538
A Circuit wide, enclos'd, with goodliest Trees Par Lost 8.304
Up hither, from among the Trees appeer'd Par Lost 8.313
For many are the Trees of God that grow Par Lost 9.618
Of all these Garden Trees ye shall not eate, Par Lost 9.657
O Sovran, vertuous, precious of all Trees Par Lost 9.795
Among the Trees on Iles and woodie Shores. Par Lost 9.1118
The thickest Trees, both Man and Wife, till God Par Lost 10.101
But on thy rould in heaps, and up the Trees Par Lost 10.558
Of these fair spreading Trees; which bids us seek Par Lost 10.1067
Which his own hand manuring all the Trees Par Lost 11.28
To Spirits foule, and all my Trees thir prey, Par Lost 11.124
With all his verdure spoil'd, and Trees adrift Par Lost 11.832
Of Trees thick interwoven; there he slept, Par Reg 2.263
Under the Trees now trip'd, now solemn stood Par Reg 2.354
Run to your shrouds, within these Brakes and Trees, Mask 147
Trinity ms 'trees'
Bridgewater ms 'trees'
Boosom'd high in tufted Trees, Allegro 78
Tremble
Shall tremble, he descending, will himself Par Lost 12.228
When Mountains tremble, those two massie Pillars Samson 1648
Trembled
With horrid strides, Hell trembled as he strode. Par Lost 2.676
Hell trembl'd at the hideous Name, and sigh'd Par Lost 2.788
Earth trembl'd from her entrails, as again Par Lost 9.1000
Trembling
The trembling leaves, while Universal *Pan* Par Lost 4.266
To thy Adorers; thou with trembling fear, Par Reg 1.451
Phoebus repli'd, and touch'd my trembling ears; Lycidas 77
With trembling; kiss the Son least he appear Psalm 2, 25
Tremisen
Marocco and *Algiers*, and *Tremisen;* Par Lost 11.404
Trench
Forerun the Royal Camp, to trench a Field, Par Lost 1.677
Trent
Or *Trent*, who like some earth-born Giant spreads Vacation 93
Your plots and packing wors then those of *Trent*, Forcers 14
Trepidation
The Trepidation talkt, and that first mov'd; Par Lost 3.483
Trespass
They trespass, Authors to themselves in all Par Lost 3.122
For such a petty Trespass, and not praise Par Lost 9.693
The fatal Trespass don by *Eve*, amaz'd, Par Lost 9.889
Her former trespass fear'd, the more to soothe Par Lost 9.1006
Too grievous for the trespass or omission, Samson 691
To trespass as before. Psalm 85, 36
Tressed
And caus'd the Golden-tressed Sun, Psalm 136, 29
Tresses
Her unadorned golden tresses wore Par Lost 4.305
Of her loose tresses hid: he in delight Par Lost 4.497
With Tresses discompos'd, and glowing Cheek, Par Lost 5.10
Her Tresses, and her rural labours crown, Par Lost 9.841
And tresses all disorderd, at his feet Par Lost 10.911
Love-darting eyes, or tresses like the Morn? Mask 753
line not in Bridgewater ms
Never scorch thy tresses fair, Mask 929
With flowre-inwov'n tresses torn Nativity 187
Trial
Through Gods high sufferance for the tryal of man, Par Lost 1.366
ms 'trial'
Will save us trial what the least can doe Par Lost 4.855
Intended thee, for trial onely brought, Par Lost 8.447
When I am present, and thy trial choose Par Lost 9.316
Thou sever not: Trial will come unsought. Par Lost 9.366
But if thou think, trial unsought may finde Par Lost 9.370
Touchd onely, that our trial, when least sought, Par Lost 9.380
O glorious trial of exceeding Love, Par Lost 9.961
This happie trial of thy Love, which else Par Lost 9.975
Matter of glorious trial; and perhaps Par Lost 9.1177
Well hath obey'd; just tryal e're I merit Par Reg 3.196
The tryal hath indamag'd thee no way, Par Reg 4.206
Defie thee to the trial of mortal fight, Samson 1175
Of Saints, the trial of thir fortitude, Samson 1288
Now of my own accord such other tryal Samson 1643

Trial(*cont*)
Eie me blest Providence, and square my triall — Mask 329
Trinity ms 'tryall'
Bridgewater ms 'tryall'
Shall in the happy trial prove most glory. — Mask 592
Trinity ms 'triall'
Bridgewater ms 'triall'
1637 'triall'
In judgment, or abide their tryal then, — Psalm 1, 13

Tribe
Then of thine own Tribe fairer, or as fair, — Samson 217
Had *Judah* that day join'd, or one whole Tribe, — Samson 265
I before all the daughters of my Tribe — Samson 876
To live the poorest in my Tribe, then richest, — Samson 1479
An *Ebrew*, as I guess, and of our Tribe. — Samson 1540

Tribes
By which, to visit oft those happy Tribes, — Par Lost 3.532
Hereafter, join'd in her popular Tribes — Par Lost 7.488
Your Tribes, and water from th' ambrosial Fount? — Par Lost 11.279
Long time in peace by Families and Tribes — Par Lost 12.23
Through the twelve Tribes, to rule by Laws ordaind: — Par Lost 12.226
Deliverance of thy brethren, those ten Tribes — Par Reg 3.374
My brethren, as thou call'st them; those Ten Tribes — Par Reg 3.403
As for those captive Tribes, themselves were they — Par Reg 3.414
On *Israel*'s Governours, and Heads of Tribes, — Samson 242
In *Dan*, in *Judah*, and the bordering Tribes, — Samson 976

Tribulation
Tri'd in sharp tribulation, and refin'd — Par Lost 11.63

Tribulations
And after all thir tribulations long — Par Lost 3.336
By tribulations, injuries, insults, — Par Reg 3.190

Tribunal
Thy dread Tribunal: forthwith from all Windes — Par Lost 3.326

Tribunals
Or to the unjust tribunals, under change of times, — Samson 695

Tributary
Which he to grace his tributary gods — Mask 24
Bridgewater ms 'tributarie'
Trinity ms 'tributarie'
1637 'tributarie'

Tribute
She gathers, Tribute large, and on the board — Par Lost 5.343
Knee-tribute yet unpaid, prostration vile, — Par Lost 5.782
As Tribute such a sumless journey brought — Par Lost 8.36
Then meeting joyn'd thir tribute to the Sea: — Par Reg 3.258
Their full tribute never miss — Mask 925

Tricked
Not trickt and frounc't as she was wont, — Penseroso 123

Tricks
And tricks his beams, and with new spangled Ore, — Lycidas 170
But we do hope to find out all your tricks, — Forcers 13

Trident
As with a Trident smote, and fix't as firm — Par Lost 10.295

Tridents
And weild their little tridents, but this Ile — Mask 27

Tried
But evil hast not tri'd: and wilt object — Par Lost 4.896
Can hearts, not free, be tri'd whether they serve — Par Lost 5.532
I mean to try, whose Reason I have tri'd — Par Lost 6.120
O now in danger tri'd, now known in Armes — Par Lost 6.418
Up hither, under long obedience tri'd, — Par Lost 7.159
Knew not; to speak I tri'd, and forthwith spake, — Par Lost 8.271
With me, best witness of thy Vertue tri'd. — Par Lost 9.317
Tri'd in sharp tribulation, and refin'd — Par Lost 11.63
More then anough, that temperance may be tri'd: — Par Lost 11.805
By one mans firm obedience fully tri'd — Par Reg 1.4
Be try'd in humble state, and things adverse, — Par Reg 3.189
Of those encounters, where we might have tri'd — Samson 1086
Heav'n hath timely tri'd their youth, — Mask 970
Trinity ms 'try'd'
B.M. ms 'try'd'
Most perfect *Heroe*, try'd in heaviest plight — Passion 13
I tri'd thee at the water *steep* — Psalm 81, 31

Tries
Since thou art the just God that tries — Psalm 7, 38

Trifle
No trifle; yet with this reserve, not else, — Par Reg 4.165

Trifles
And trifles for choice matters, worth a spunge; — Par Reg 4.329

Triform
With borrowd light her countenance triform — Par Lost 3.730

Trills
Trills her thick-warbl'd notes the summer long, — Par Reg 4.246

Trim
With all her bravery on, and tackle trim, — Samson 717
The Wood-Nymphs deckt with Daisies trim, — Mask 120
Meadows trim with Daisies pide, — Allegro 75
That in trim Gardens takes his pleasure; — Penseroso 50
Had doff't her gawdy trim, — Nativity 33

Trimming
Not those new fangled toys, and triming slight — Vacation 19

Trinacrian
Calabria from the hoarce *Trinacrian* shore: — Par Lost 2.661

Trinal
To sit the midst of Trinal Unity, — Nativity 11

Trine
In *Sextile*, *Square*, and *Trine*, and *Opposite*, — Par Lost 10.659

Trip
Trip the pert Fairies and the dapper Elves; — Mask 118
Com, and trip it as ye go — Allegro 33
Trip no more in twilight ranks, — Arcades 99

Triple
With stubborn patience as with triple steel. — Par Lost 2.569
In thir triple Degrees, Regions to which — Par Lost 5.750
A triple mounted row of Pillars laid — Par Lost 6.572
1667 'triple-mounted'
How are ye joyn'd with hell in triple knot — Mask 581
1673 'tripple'
Where the bright Seraphim in burning row — Musick 10
Trinity ms 'burning' ←'triple' ←'tripled' ←'princely' ←'princly'
The triple Tyrant: that from these may grow — Sonnet 18, 12

Triple-coloured
His triple-colour'd Bow, whereon to look — Par Lost 11.897

Triple-mounted
A triple mounted row of Pillars laid — Par Lost 6.572
1667 'triple-mounted'

Triple-row
Till on those cursed Engins triple-row — Par Lost 6.650

Tripped
Under the Trees now trip'd, now solemn stood — Par Reg 2.354

Tripping
From standing lake to tripping ebbe, that stole — Par Lost 11.847
Come tripping to the Room where thou didst lie; — Vacation 62

Trippings
Other trippings to be trod — Mask 961

Trips
And mad'st imperfect words with childish tripps, — Vacation 3
1673 printed 'tripp s'

Triton
Girt with the River *Triton*, where old *Cham*, — Par Lost 4.276
By scaly *Tritons* winding shell, — Mask 873

Triumph
I through the ample Air in Triumph high — Par Lost 3.254
Sung Triumph, and him sung Victorious King, — Par Lost 6.886
Great triumph and rejoycing was in Heav'n — Par Lost 7.180
Triumph and say; Fickle their State whom God — Par Lost 9.948
In Triumph issuing forth thir glorious Chief; — Par Lost 10.537
Turnd to exploding hiss, triumph to shame — Par Lost 10.546
Of triumph, to be styl'd great Conquerours, — Par Lost 11.695
In Triumph and luxurious wealth, are they — Par Lost 11.788
1667 'triumph'
Victory and Triumph to the Son of God — Par Reg 1.173
The *Pontic* King and in triumph had rode. — Par Reg 3.36
Of triumph that insulting vanity; — Par Reg 4.138
No triumph; in all her gates *Abaddon* rues — Par Reg 4.624
Thir Captive, and thir triumph; thou the sooner — Samson 426
With Sacrifices, Triumph, Pomp, and Games; — Samson 1312
To triumph in victorious dance — Mask 974
Bridgewater ms 'triumphe'
And shall triumph in thee, who love thy name. — Psalm 5, 36

Triumphal
Messiah his triumphal Chariot turnd: — Par Lost 6.881
Triumphal with triumphal act have met, — Par Lost 10.390
Statues and Trophees, and Triumphal Arcs, — Par Reg 4.37

Triumphals
Joyless triumphals of his hop't success, — Par Reg 4.578
1671 'tryumphals' in some copies

Triumphant
Us'd to the yoak, draw'st his triumphant wheels — Par Lost 4.975
Intends to pass triumphant, and give Laws. — Par Lost 5.693
Triumphant through mid Heav'n, into the Courts — Par Lost 6.889
Triumphant out of this infernal Pit — Par Lost 10.464
And over them triumphant Death his Dart — Par Lost 11.491
That erst with Musick, and triumphant song — Circum 2

Triumphed
Spoild Principalities and Powers, triumpht — Par Lost 10.186
Whom they triumph'd once lapst. Thus were they plagu'd — Par Lost 10.572

Triumphing
With Joy and Love triumphing, and fair Truth. — Par Lost 3.338
With victory, triumphing through the aire — Par Lost 12.452
Triumphing over Death, and Chance, and thee O Time. — On Time 22

Triumphs
Who now triumphs, and in th' excess of joy — Par Lost 1.123
Triumphs or Festivals, and to them preachd — Par Lost 11.723
In weeds of Peace high triumphs hold, — Allegro 120

Trivial
Fall flat and shrink into a trivial toy, — Par Reg 2.223
Then with what trivial weapon came to hand, — Samson 142
Unarm'd, and with a trivial weapon fell'd — Samson 263
I came not here on such a trivial toy — Mask 502
Bridgewater ms 'triviall'
1637 'triviall'
Trinity ms 'triviall'

Trod
Fawning, and lick'd the ground whereon she trod. — Par Lost 9.526
As story tells, have trod this Wilderness; — Par Reg 2.307
Or Lightning thou shalt fall from Heav'n trod down — Par Reg 4.620
Through paths, and turnings oft'n trod by day, — Mask 569
Other trippings to be trod — Mask 961
Then to the well-trod stage anon, — Allegro 131
Staid not behind, nor in the grave were trod; — Sonnet 14, 6
Strait follow'd thee the path that Saints have trod — Sonnet 14, Tr. ms 41.06
Preserve my soul, for I have trod — Psalm 86, 5

Trodden
The riches of Heav'ns pavement, trod'n Gold, Par Lost 1.682
The trodden Herb, of abject thoughts and low, Par Lost 9.572

Troll
To dress, and troule the Tongue, and roule the Eye. Par Lost 11.620

Troop
Of despicable foes. With these in troop Par Lost 1.437
Troop to thir Standard, so the watrie throng, Par Lost 7.297
For that fair femal Troop thou sawst, that seemd Par Lost 11.614
In Troop or Caravan, for single none Par Reg 1.323
With all the greisly legions that troop Mask 603
1637 'troope'
Trinity ms 'troope'
Bridgewater ms 'troope'
Troop to th' infernall jail, Nativity 233

Trooping
With hunderds and with thousands trooping came Par Lost 1.760

Troops
The City gates out powr'd, light armed Troops Par Reg 3.311
Spurn'd them to death by Troops. The bold *Ascalonite* Samson 138
In solemn troops, and sweet Societies Lycidas 179
1638 'troups'

Trophies
Seraphic arms and Trophies: all the while Par Lost 1.539
ms 'trophies'
Thy Trophies, which thou view'st as not thine own, Par Lost 10.355
Statues and Trophees, and Triumphal Arcs, Par Reg 4.37
Of all these boasted Trophies won on me, Samson 470
With all his Trophies hung, and Acts enroll'd Samson 1736
Of Turneys and of Trophies hung; Penseroso 118
Hast reard Gods Trophies and his work pursu'd. Sonnet 16, 6
1694 'And Fought God's Battels'

Tropic
Up to the *Tropic* Crab; thence down amaine Par Lost 10.675
Disturb'd his sleep; and either Tropic now Par Reg 4.409

Trot
While he might still jogg on, and keep his trot, Another 4

Trouble
But of offence and trouble, which my mind Par Lost 5.34
The trouble of thy thoughts this night in sleep Par Lost 5.96
To trouble Holy Rest; Heav'n casts thee out Par Lost 6.272
A while in trouble; but they stood not long, Par Lost 6.634
Vacant possession som new trouble raise: Par Lost 11.103
Such trouble brought, affecting to subdue Par Lost 12.81
God looking forth will trouble all his Host Par Lost 12.209
But trouble, as old *Simeon* plain fore-told, Par Reg 2.87
Without new trouble; such an Enemy Par Reg 2.126
Sam. Spare that proposal, Father, spare the trouble Samson 487
And yet perhaps more trouble is behind. Samson 1300
And fierce ire trouble them; but I saith hee Psalm 2, 11
Trouble he hath conceav'd of old Psalm 7, 52
When trouble did thee sore assaile, Psalm 81, 25
For cloy'd with woes and trouble store Psalm 88, 9

Troubled
With solemn touches, troubl'd thoughts, and chase Par Lost 1.557
Wag'd in the troubl'd Skie, and Armies rush Par Lost 2.534
His troubl'd thoughts, and from the bottom stirr Par Lost 4.19
Sin-bred, how have ye troubl'd all mankind Par Lost 4.315
No more be troubl'd how to quit the yoke Par Lost 5.882
Silence, ye troubl'd waves, and thou Deep, peace, Par Lost 7.216
1669 'troubled'
Nor troubl'd at these tidings from the Earth, Par Lost 10.36
And in a troubl'd Sea of passion tost, Par Lost 10.718
Some troubl'd thoughts, which she in sighs thus clad. Par Reg 2.65
Troubl'd that thou shouldst hunger, hath purvey'd Par Reg 2.333
Perplex'd and troubl'd at his bad success Par Reg 4.1
The tumors of a troubl'd mind, Samson 185
That saw the troubl'd Sea, and shivering fled, Psalm 114, 7
1673 'troubled'
Are troubled, yea my soul is troubled sore Psalm 6, 6
Asham'd and troubl'd let them be, Psalm 83, 61
Troubl'd and sham'd for ever, Psalm 83, 62

Troubles
New troubles; him thy care must be to find. Par Lost 4.575
Brings dangers, troubles, cares, and sleepless nights Par Reg 2.460
Their inside, troubles miserable; Psalm 5, 27

Troublesome
These troublesom disguises which wee wear, Par Lost 4.740

Troy
Thrice Fugitive about *Troy* Wall; or rage Par Lost 9.16
Or the tale of *Troy* divine. Penseroso 100
There to thy Sons another *Troy* shall rise, Prose 12, 12

Truce
Truce to his restless thoughts, and entertain Par Lost 2.526
Inducing darkness, grateful truce impos'd, Par Lost 6.407
Portending hollow truce; at each behind Par Lost 6.578
In time of Truce; *Iris* had dipt the wooff; Par Lost 11.244
By parl, or composition, truce, or league Par Reg 4.529

True
Of true allegiance, constant Faith or Love, Par Lost 3.104
For never can true reconcilement grow Par Lost 4.98
Sat like a Cormorant; yet not true Life Par Lost 4.196
Hung amiable, *Hesperian* Fables true, Par Lost 4.250
If true, here only, and of delicious taste: Par Lost 4.251
True Paradise under the *Ethiop* Line Par Lost 4.282
Severe but in true filial freedom plac't; Par Lost 4.294
Whence true autoritie in men; though both Par Lost 4.295
Haile wedded Love, mysterious Law, true source Par Lost 4.750

True(*cont*)
The rest is true, they found me where they say; Par Lost 4.900
True appetite, and not disrelish thirst Par Lost 5.305
Omniscient thought. True is, less firmly arm'd, Par Lost 6.430
Can sort, what harmonie or true delight? Par Lost 8.384
Wherein true Love consists not; love refines Par Lost 8.589
In Fruit she never tasted, whether true Par Lost 9.788
Remarkably so late of thy so true, Par Lost 9.982
True relish, tasting; if such pleasure be Par Lost 9.1024
To counterfet Mans voice, true in our Fall, Par Lost 9.1069
True is, mee also he hath judg'd, or rather Par Lost 10.494
Horrid, if true! yet why? it was but breath Par Lost 10.789
True patience, and to temper joy with fear Par Lost 11.361
True opener of mine eyes, prime Angel blest, Par Lost 11.598
And great exploits, but of true vertu void; Par Lost 11.790
Since thy original lapse, true Libertie Par Lost 12.83
Jordan, true limit Eastward; but his Sons Par Lost 12.145
Mine eyes true op'ning, and my heart much eas'd, Par Lost 12.274
Then loose it to a stranger, that the true Par Lost 12.358
To what highth sacred vertue and true worth Par Reg 1.231
'Tis true, I am that Spirit unfortunate, Par Reg 1.358
By thee are giv'n, and what confest more true Par Reg 1.431
By mixing somewhat true to vent more lyes. Par Reg 1.433
This is true glory and renown, when God Par Reg 3.60
To all his Angels, who with true applause Par Reg 3.63
And so of all true good himself despoil'd, Par Reg 3.139
In *David*'s royal seat, his true Successour, Par Reg 3.373
David's true heir, and his full Scepter sway Par Reg 3.405
So spake *Israel*'s true King, and to the Fiend Par Reg 3.441
No other doctrine needs, though granted true; Par Reg 4.290
True wisdom, finds her not, or by delusion Par Reg 4.319
With *Sion*'s songs, to all true tasts excelling, Par Reg 4.347
True Image of the Father whether thron'd Par Reg 4.596
And almost life it self, if it be true Samson 91
True slavery, and that blindness worse then this, Samson 418
Tacit, was in thy power; true; and thou bear'st Samson 430
I led the way; bitter reproach, but true, Samson 823
Of true experience from this great event Samson 1756
After this mortal change, to her true Servants Mask 10
This way the noise was, if mine ear be true, Mask 170
Himself is his own dungeon. 2. *Bro*. Tis most true Mask 385
Hath hurtfull power o're true virginity. Mask 437
Spir. Ay me unhappy then my fears are true. Mask 511
But now I find it true; for by this means Mask 644
Of true Virgin here distrest, Mask 905
(List mortals, if your ears be true) Mask 997
line not in Bridgewater ms
Whose power hath a true consent Penseroso 95
Our Babe to shew his Godhead true, Nativity 227
Oh say me true if thou wert mortal wight Fair Inf 41
Which carefull *Jove* in natures true behoofe Fair Inf 45
That all both judge you to relate them true, Sonnet 10, 13
My true account, least he returning chide, Sonnet 19, 6
Most mercifull, most true. Psalm 86, 56
This is true Liberty when free born men Prose 9, 1

Truest
Extolling Patience as the truest fortitude; Samson 654

Truly
And wisdom, which alone is truly fair. Par Lost 4.491
That which alone can truly reinstall thee Par Reg 3.372
Not truly penitent, but chief to try Samson 754
Here lieth one who did most truly prove, Another 1
1640, 1657, 1658 'truely'
That man is *truly* blest, Psalm 84, 46

Trump
The wakefull trump of doom must thunder through the deep, Nativity 156
Loud o're the rest *Cremona*'s Trump doth sound; Passion 26

Trumpery
White, Black and Grey, with all thir trumperie. Par Lost 3.475

Trumpet
Ethereal Trumpet from on high gan blow: Par Lost 6.60
Th' Arch-Angel trumpet; through the vast of Heaven Par Lost 6.203
The matin Trumpet Sung: in Arms they stood Par Lost 6.526
Of Trumpet (for of Armies thou hast heard) Par Lost 7.296
His Trumpet, heard in *Oreb* since perhaps Par Lost 11.74
More awful then the sound of Trumpet, cri'd Par Reg 1.19
The Trumpet spake not to the armed throng, Nativity 58
With Trumpets *lofty sound*, Psalm 81, 10

Trumpets
Of Trumpets loud and Clarions be upreard Par Lost 1.532
ms 'trumpets'
And Trumpets sound throughout the Host proclaim Par Lost 1.754
ms 'trumpets'
With Trumpets regal sound the great result: Par Lost 2.515
In Thunder Lightning and loud Trumpets sound Par Lost 12.229
The morning Trumpets Festival proclaim'd Samson 1598
Their loud up-lifted Angel trumpets blow, Musick 11
Trinity ms 'trumpetts'

Trunk
Draws in, and at his Trunck spouts out a Sea. Par Lost 7.416
About the mossie Trunk I wound me soon, Par Lost 9.589

Trust
And trust themselves to fear no second fate: Par Lost 2.17
His trust was with th' Eternal to be deem'd Par Lost 2.46
The supple knee? ye will not, if I trust Par Lost 5.788
To trust thee from my side, imagin'd wise, Par Lost 10.881
Foretold to *Abraham*, as in whom shall trust Par Lost 12.328
Never to hurt them more who rightly trust Par Lost 12.418

Trust(*cont*)
At one spears length. O ever failing trust Samson 348
To violate the sacred trust of silence Samson 428
To such a viper his most sacred trust Samson 1001
My trust is in the living God who gave me Samson 1140
A noble Peer of mickle trust, and power Mask 31
And trust thy honest offer'd courtesie, Mask 322
(Not being in danger, as I trust she is not) Mask 370
  Bridgewater ms 'hope'
But you invert the cov'nants of her trust, Mask 682
  line not in Bridgewater ms
And such, as yet once more I trust to have Sonnet 23, 7
Of righteousness and in Jehovah trust. Psalm 4, 24
Then all who trust in thee shall bring Psalm 5, 33
Who *still* in thee doth trust. Psalm 86, 8
Trusted
He trusted to have equal'd the most High, Par Lost 1.40
He trusted to have seis'd, and into fraud Par Lost 7.143
Not to be trusted, longing to be seen Par Lost 10.877
My Vessel trusted to me from above, Samson 199
Nor shouldst thou have trusted that to womans frailty Samson 783
Trusting
His puissance, trusting in th' Almightie's aide, Par Lost 6.119
Not wandring poor, but trusting all his wealth Par Lost 12.133
Har. Fair honour that thou dost thy God, in trusting Samson 1178
Truth
With Joy and Love triumphing, and fair Truth. Par Lost 3.338
Truth, wisdome, Sanctitude severe and pure, Par Lost 4.293
Of counterfeted truth thus held thir ears. Par Lost 5.771
To swerve from truth, or change his constant mind Par Lost 5.902
Of Truth, in word mightier then they in Armes; Par Lost 6.32
And for the testimonie of Truth hast born Par Lost 6.33
That he who in debate of Truth hath won, Par Lost 6.122
Of erring, from the path of truth remote: Par Lost 6.173
For strength from Truth divided and from Just, Par Lost 6.381
With Reason, to her seeming, and with Truth; Par Lost 9.738
Thy Justice seems; yet to say truth, too late, Par Lost 10.755
To end me? Shall Truth fail to keep her word, Par Lost 10.856
Of Justice, of Religion, Truth and Peace, Par Lost 11.667
And utter odious Truth, that God would come Par Lost 11.704
Justice and Temperance, Truth and Faith forgot; Par Lost 11.807
From shadowie Types to Truth, from Flesh to Spirit, Par Lost 12.303
The enemies of truth; who then shall guide Par Lost 12.482
To guide them in all truth, and also arme Par Lost 12.490
Of lucre and ambition, and the truth Par Lost 12.511
Of Spirit and Truth; the rest, farr greater part, Par Lost 12.533
Religion satisfi'd; Truth shall retire Par Lost 12.535
By simply meek; that suffering for Truths sake Par Lost 12.569
Born to that end, born to promote all truth, Par Reg 1.205
Till truth were freed, and equity restor'd: Par Reg 1.220
Yet thou pretend'st to truth; all Oracles Par Reg 1.430
To thee not known, whence hast thou then thy truth, Par Reg 1.446
Then to thy self ascrib'st the truth fore-told. Par Reg 1.453
And sends his Spirit of Truth henceforth to dwell Par Reg 1.462
To all truth requisite for men to know. Par Reg 1.464
And not inforc'd oft-times to part from truth; Par Reg 1.472
Hard are the ways of truth, and rough to walk, Par Reg 1.478
His words, his wisdom full of grace and truth, Par Reg 2.34
But to guide Nations in the way of truth Par Reg 2.473
For truths sake suffering death unjust, lives now Par Reg 3.98
And time there is for all things, Truth hath said: Par Reg 3.183
So fares it when with truth falshood contends. Par Reg 3.443
Yet truth to say, I oft have heard men wonder Samson 215
Vertue, as I thought, truth, duty so enjoyning. Samson 870
The righteous and all such as honour Truth; Samson 1276
'Twill not restore the truth and honesty Mask 691
  Bridgewater ms 'trueth'
Their faith, their patience, and their truth. Mask 971
  B.M. ms 'Truth'
Yea Truth, and justice then Nativity 141
Or that crown'd Matron sage white-robed truth? Fair Inf 54
With Truth, and Peace, and Love shall ever shine On Time 16
'Twas such a shifter, that if truth were known, Carrier 5
'Gainst old truth) motion number'd out his time; Another 8
Perhaps my semblance might deceive the truth, Sonnet 7, 5
That labour up the Hill of heav'nly Truth, Sonnet 9, 4
And still revolt when truth would set them free. Sonnet 12, 10
  Trinity ms 'still revolt when Truth would sett them' ← 'make them' ← 'set them' ← 'hate the truth wherby they should be'
But as Faith pointed with her golden rod, Sonnet 14, 7
  Trinity ms 'Faith' ← 'Truth'
And speak the truth of thee on glorious Theams Sonnet 14, 12
Till Truth, and Right from Violence be freed, Sonnet 15, 11
  1694 'injur'd Truth'
To peace and truth thy glorious way hast plough'd, Sonnet 16, 4
  1694 'Truth'
Ev'n them who kept thy truth so pure of old Sonnet 18, 3
Mercy and Truth *that long were miss'd* Psalm 85, 41
Truth from the earth *like to a flowr* Psalm 85, 45
I in thy truth will bide, Psalm 86, 38
This was that gift (if you the truth will have) Prose 4, 3
laughing to teach the truth Prose 6, 1
Try
With rallied Arms to try what may be yet Par Lost 1.269
Though for possession put to try once more Par Lost 4.941
Nor so content, hath in his thought to try Par Lost 5.727
  1667 'trie'
Shall teach us highest deeds, by proof to try Par Lost 5.865

Try(*cont*)
I mean to try, whose Reason I have tri'd Par Lost 6.120
That they may have thir wish, to trie with mee Par Lost 6.818
Rather admire; or if they list to try Par Lost 8.75
Thus farr to try thee, *Adam*, I was pleas'd, Par Lost 8.437
Mean I to trie, what rash untri'd I sought, Par Lost 9.860
Impassable, Impervious, let us try Par Lost 10.254
Or trie thee now more dang'rous to his Throne. Par Lost 10.382
Temptation and all guile on him to try; Par Reg 1.123
At least to try, and teach the erring Soul Par Reg 1.224
Therefore with manlier objects we must try Par Reg 2.225
If I to try whether in higher sort Par Reg 4.198
To try thee, sift thee, and confess have found thee Par Reg 4.532
Not truly penitent, but chief to try Samson 754
Sam. I could be well content to try thir Art, Samson 1399
Yet should I try, the uncontrouled worth Mask 793
  line not in Bridgewater ms
  line not in Trinity ms
  1637 'trie'
And try her yet more strongly. Com, no more, Mask 806
  word not in Trinity ms
  word not in Bridgewater ms
In hard besetting need, this will I try Mask 857
  1637 'trie'
  Trinity ms 'trie'
  Bridgewater ms 'trie'
I could be willing though now i' th darke to trie Mask Tr. ms 16.38
I could be willinge though now i' th darke to trie Mask Br. ms 391
Tub
And fetch their precepts from the *Cynick* Tub, Mask 708
  Bridgewater ms 'tub'
  1637 'tub'
  Trinity ms 'tub'
Tube
Through his glaz'd Optic Tube yet never saw. Par Lost 3.590
Tuft
Under a tuft of shade that on a green Par Lost 4.325
In Bowre and Field he sought, where any tuft Par Lost 9.417
Tufted
And casts a gleam over this tufted Grove. Mask 225
  line not in Bridgewater ms
Boosom'd high in tufted Trees, Allegro 78
The tufted Crow-toe, and pale Gessamine, Lycidas 143
Tufts
With tufts the vallies and each fountain side, Par Lost 7.327
Tugged
He tugg'd, he shook, till down they came and drew Samson 1650
Tumble
That tumble down the snowy hills: Mask 927
  1673 'tumbled'
Tumid
So high as heav'd the tumid Hills, so low Par Lost 7.288
Tumours
The tumors of a troubl'd mind, Samson 185
Tumult
And *Tumult* and *Confusion* all imbroild, Par Lost 2.966
  1667 'Tumult'
With tumult less and with less hostile din, Par Lost 2.1040
This tumult, and permitted all, advis'd: Par Lost 6.674
Whence eev'n now the tumult of loud Mirth Mask 202
  line not in Bridgewater ms
Why do the Gentiles tumult, and the Nations Psalm 2, 1
Tumults
Laugh'st at thir vain designes and tumults vain, Par Lost 5.737
Tumultuous
The strong rebuff of som tumultuous cloud Par Lost 2.936
Now rowling, boiles in his tumultuous brest, Par Lost 4.16
Jarr'd against natures chime, and with harsh din Musick 20
  Trinity ms 'harsh' ← 'tumultuous'
Tun
Fit for the Tun som Magazin to store Par Lost 4.816
Tunable
And tuneable as Silvan Pipe or Song; Par Reg 1.480
Tune
Melodious murmurs, warbling tune his praise. Par Lost 5.196
Little prevails, or rather seems a tune, Samson 661
After the heavenly tune, which none can hear Arcades 72
For now to sorrow must I tune my song, Passion 8
And keep in tune with Heav'n, till God ere long Musick 26
Tuneable
More tuneable then needed Lute or Harp Par Lost 5.151
Tuned
Harps ever tun'd, that glittering by thir side Par Lost 3.366
Ceas'd warbling, but all night tun'd her soft layes: Par Lost 7.436
Symphonious of ten thousand Harpes that tun'd Par Lost 7.559
So gloz'd the Tempter, and his Proem tun'd; Par Lost 9.549
So they in Heav'n their Odes and Vigils tun'd: Par Reg 1.182
Tuneful
With chaunt of tuneful Birds resounding loud; Par Reg 2.290
Harry whose tuneful and well measur'd Song Sonnet 13, 1
  Trinity ms 'tunefull'
  1648 'tunefull'
Tunes
Tunes her nocturnal Note. Thus with the Year Par Lost 3.40
Tunes sweetest his love-labor'd song; now reignes Par Lost 5.41
In sage and solemn tunes have sung, Penseroso 117
Tunest
That tun'st their happiest lines in Hymn, or Story. Sonnet 13, 11

Tunings
Temper'd soft Tunings, intermixt with Voice — Par Lost 7.598
Turbans
Dusk faces with white silken Turbants wreath'd: — Par Reg 4.76
Turbulencies
Like turbulencies in the affairs of men, — Par Reg 4.462
Turbulent
And full of Peace, now tost and turbulent: — Par Lost 9.1126
On man, beast, plant, wastful and turbulent, — Par Reg 4.461
Whose heads that turbulent liquor fills with fumes. — Samson 552
Adverse and turbulent, or by her charms — Samson 1040
Turchestan-born
Turchestan-born; nor could his eye not ken — Par Lost 11.396
Turf
Have heap'd this Table. Rais'd of grassie terf — Par Lost 5.391
Of grassie Terfe, and pile up every Stone — Par Lost 11.324
La. They left me weary on a grassie terf. — Mask 280
Trinity ms 'terfe'
Bridgewater ms 'terfe'
1637 'terfe'
That on the green terf suck the honied showres, — Lycidas 140
1638 'turf'
Trinity ms 'terfe'
Turkestan-born
Turchestan-born; nor could his eye not ken — Par Lost 11.396
Turkis
Of Turkis blew, and Emrauld green — Mask 894
Trinity ms 'turkis' ←'turquis'
Bridgewater ms 'Turkie' ←'Turkies'
Turkish
Of *Turkish* Crescent, leaves all waste beyond — Par Lost 10.434
Turms
Legions and Cohorts, turmes of horse and wings: — Par Reg 4.66
Turn
Turn swift thir various motions, or are turnd — Par Lost 3.582
And corporeal to incorporeal turn. — Par Lost 5.413
Can turn, or holds it possible to turn — Par Lost 5.441
Your bodies may at last turn all to Spirit, — Par Lost 5.497
Forthwith from dance to sweet repast they turn — Par Lost 5.630
When to advance, or stand, or turn the sway — Par Lost 6.234
Or turn this Heav'n it self into the Hell — Par Lost 6.291
Our overture, and turn not back perverse; — Par Lost 6.562
Till night, then in the East her turn she shines, — Par Lost 7.380
This turn hath made amends; thou hast fulfill'd — Par Lost 8.491
Some say he bid his Angels turne ascanse — Par Lost 10.668
Was bid turn Reines from th' Equinoctial Rode — Par Lost 10.672
Undoubtedly he will relent and turn — Par Lost 10.1093
However chast'ning, to the evil turne — Par Lost 11.373
Enterd so faire, should turn aside to tread — Par Lost 11.630
So all shall turn degenerate, all deprav'd, — Par Lost 11.806
And evil turn to good; more wonderful — Par Lost 12.471
To thir own vile advantages shall turne — Par Lost 12.510
Or turn to reverent awe? for Beauty stands — Par Reg 2.220
Behold him in this state calamitous, and turn — Samson 708
Turn forth her silver lining on the night? — Mask 222
1637 'Turne'
Trinity ms 'turne'
line not in Bridgewater ms
Turn forth her silver lining on the night, — Mask 224
line not in Bridgewater ms
Trinity ms 'turne'
1637 'Turne'
And turn the Adamantine spindle round, — Arcades 66
Trinity ms 'turn' ←'turning'
And as he passes turn, — Lycidas 21
Trinity ms 'turne'
To turn Swift-rushing black perdition hence, — Fair Inf 67
And thou O Lord how long? turn Lord, restore — Psalm 6, 7
Turn us again, *thy grace divine* — Psalm 80, 13
And turn my hand against *all those* — Psalm 81, 59
Turn us, and us restore, — Psalm 85, 14
Wilt thou not turn, and *hear our voice* — Psalm 85, 21
O turn to me *thy face at length*, — Psalm 86, 57
Turned
Of dawning light turnd thither-ward in haste — Par Lost 3.500
Turn swift thir various motions, or are turnd — Par Lost 3.582
His back was turnd, but not his brightness hid; — Par Lost 3.624
Ere he drew nigh, his radiant visage turnd, — Par Lost 3.646
That rowld orbicular, and turnd to Starrs — Par Lost 3.718
Thus said, he turnd, and *Satan* bowing low, — Par Lost 3.736
Turnd him all eare to hear new utterance flow. — Par Lost 4.410
Then that smooth watry image; back I turnd, — Par Lost 4.480
With kisses pure: aside the Devil turnd — Par Lost 4.502
So saying, his proud step he scornful turn'd, — Par Lost 4.536
Both turnd, and under op'n Skie ador'd — Par Lost 4.721
Strait side by side were laid, nor turnd I weene — Par Lost 4.741
Turnd fierie red, sharpning in mooned hornes — Par Lost 4.978
Vapours not yet into her substance turnd. — Par Lost 5.420
And with retorted scorn his back he turn'd — Par Lost 5.906
Thou canst not. Hast thou turnd the least of these — Par Lost 6.284
Were ready, in a moment up they turnd — Par Lost 6.509
The bottom of the Mountains upward turn'd, — Par Lost 6.649
Messiah his triumphal Chariot turnd: — Par Lost 6.881
Up from the bottom turn'd by furious windes — Par Lost 7.213
One foot he center'd, and the other turn'd — Par Lost 7.228
Strait toward Heav'n my wondring Eyes I turnd, — Par Lost 8.257
Wrought in her so, that seeing me, she turn'd; — Par Lost 8.507
His gentle dumb expression turnd at length — Par Lost 9.527
Turned(*cont*)
I turnd my thoughts, and with capacious mind — Par Lost 9.603
So saying, from the Tree her step she turnd, — Par Lost 9.834
Thus in calm mood his Words to *Eve* he turnd. — Par Lost 9.920
And to the Woman thus his Sentence turn'd. — Par Lost 10.192
Turnd to exploding hiss, triumph to shame — Par Lost 10.546
The Sun, as from *Thyestean* Banquet, turn'd — Par Lost 10.688
He added not, and from her turn'd, but *Eve* — Par Lost 10.909
Lamenting turnd full sad; O what are these, — Par Lost 11.675
All now was turn'd to jollitie and game, — Par Lost 11.714
To blood unshed the Rivers must be turnd, — Par Lost 12.176
Thus we rejoyc'd, but soon our joy is turn'd — Par Reg 2.37
Turn'd recreant to God, ingrate and false, — Par Reg 3.138
Fled from his Lion ramp, old Warriors turn'd — Samson 139
Thrice I deluded her, and turn'd to sport — Samson 396
Then turn'd me out ridiculous, despoil'd, — Samson 539
When to thir sports they turn'd. Immediately — Samson 1614
Why turned *Jordan* toward his Crystall Fountains? — Psalm 114, 14
Turning
Turning our Tortures into horrid Arms — Par Lost 2.63
T' whom *Satan* turning boldly, thus. Ye Powers — Par Lost 2.968
On golden Hinges turning, as by work — Par Lost 5.255
Turning with easie eye thou may'st behold. — Par Reg 3.293
And turn the Adamantine spindle round, — Arcades 66
Trinity ms 'turn' ←'turning'
Down through the turning sphear — Nativity 48
Turnings
Through paths, and turnings oft'n trod by day, — Mask 569
Turns
Turns Atheist, as did *Ely*'s Sons, who fill'd — Par Lost 1.495
Are brought: and feel by turns the bitter change — Par Lost 2.598
Could once have mov'd; then in the key-hole turns — Par Lost 2.876
She turns, on hospitable thoughts intent — Par Lost 5.332
Lodge and dislodge by turns, which makes through Heav'n — Par Lost 6.7
Oppresses else with Surfet, and soon turns — Par Lost 7.129
Sticks no dishonor on our Front, but turns — Par Lost 9.330
With adverse blast up-turns them from the South — Par Lost 10.701
And turns it by degrees to the souls essence, — Mask 462
Trinity ms 'turnes'
Bridgewater ms 'turnes'
1637 'turnes'
Turns on his head, and his ill trade — Psalm 7, 58
Up turns it by the roots, — Psalm 80, 54
Turnus
Of *Turnus* for *Lavinia* disespous'd, — Par Lost 9.17
Turquoise
Of Turkis blew, and Emrauld green — Mask 894
Bridgewater ms 'Turkie' ←'Turkies'
Trinity ms 'turkis' ←'turquis'
Turret
His turret Crest, and sleek enamel'd Neck, — Par Lost 9.525
Turrets
Turrets and Terrases, and glittering Spires. — Par Reg 4.54
Turtle
With Turtle wing the amorous clouds dividing, — Nativity 50
Tuscan
Through Optic Glass the *Tuscan* Artist views — Par Lost 1.288
ms 'Tuscan'
After the *Tuscan* Mariners transform'd — Mask 48
Bridgewater ms 'Tuscane'
Trinity ms 'Tuscaine'
Dante shall give Fame leave to set thee higher — Sonnet 13, 12
Trinity ms 'Dante shall give Fame leave to' ←'Fame by the Tuscan's leav shall'
Warble immortal Notes and *Tuskan* Ayre? — Sonnet 20, 12
Tusked
The *tusked* Boar out of the wood — Psalm 80, 53
Twain
It fits not; thou and I long since are twain; — Samson 929
La. They were but twain, and purpos'd quick return. — Mask 284
Trinity ms 'twaine'
Bridgewater ms 'twaine'
Two massy Keyes he bore of metals twain, — Lycidas 110
Trinity ms 'twaine'
The ruddy waves he cleft in twain, — Psalm 136, 45
Twas
'Twas such a shifter, that if truth were known, — Carrier 5
'Gainst old truth) motion number'd out his time; — Another 8
1640, 1657 ''twas motion'
Tweed
Of utmost *Tweed*, or *Oose*, or gulphie *Dun*, — Vacation 92
Twelve
Rubie or Topaz, to the Twelve that shon — Par Lost 3.597
The Grandchilde with twelve Sons increast, departs — Par Lost 12.155
Through the twelve Tribes, to rule by Laws ordaind: — Par Lost 12.226
Conceals him: when twelve years he scarce had seen, — Par Reg 2.96
Twentieth
Stoln on his wing my three and twentith yeer! — Sonnet 7, 2
1673 'twentieth'
Twenty
And twentie thousand (I thir number heard) — Par Lost 6.769
Or els the ways being foul, twenty to one, — Carrier 3
And Worsters laureat wreath; yet much remaines — Sonnet 16, 9
Twice
Not felt, nor shall be twice, for never more — Par Lost 9.859
The Poles of Earth twice ten degrees and more — Par Lost 10.669
Had measur'd twice six years, at our great Feast — Par Reg 1.210
Twice by a voice inviting him to eat. — Par Reg 2.314

Twice*(cont)*
As antient, but rebuilt by him who twice — Par Reg 3.281
Twice by an Angel, who at last in sight — Samson 24
For this did the Angel twice descend? for this — Samson 361
Promisd by Heavenly message twice descending. — Samson 635
With that twise batter'd god of *Palestine*, — Nativity 199
1673 'twice'
But *twise that praise shall in our ear* — Psalm 87, 17

Twigs
The bended Twigs take root, and Daughters grow — Par Lost 9.1105
Enter'd the very lime-twigs of his spells, — Mask 646
Trinity ms 'lime twigs'
1637 'limetwigs'
Bridgewater ms 'lymetwiggs'

Twilight
In dim Eclips disastrous twilight sheds — Par Lost 1.597
Now came still Eevning on, and Twilight gray — Par Lost 4.598
To grateful Twilight (for Night comes not there — Par Lost 5.645
Seem twilight here; and now went forth the Morn — Par Lost 6.12
Was set, and twilight from the East came on, — Par Lost 7.583
Twilight upon the Earth, short Arbiter — Par Lost 9.50
Visits the herds along the twilight meadows, — Mask 844
To arched walks of twilight groves, — Penseroso 133
Trip no more in twilight ranks, — Arcades 99
The Nimphs in twilight shade of tangled thickets mourn. — Nativity 188

Twill
This will restore all soon. *La*. 'Twill not false traitor, — Mask 690
Trinity ms 't'will not' ← 'stand back'
Bridgewater ms 't'will'
1637 'T'will'
'Twill not restore the truth and honesty — Mask 691
1637 'T'will'
Bridgewater ms 'twill'
Trinity ms 't'will'

Twin-born
Raild at *Latona*'s twin-born progenie — Sonnet 12, 6

Twine
Insinuating, wove with Gordian twine — Par Lost 4.348
Braid your Locks with rosie Twine — Mask 105
Bridgewater ms 'twine'
Trinity ms 'twine'
Not *Typhon* huge ending in snaky twine: — Nativity 226

Twines
To wed her Elm; she spous'd about him twines — Par Lost 5.216

Twinned
Twinn'd, and from her hath no dividual being: — Par Lost 12.85

Twins
Atlantick Sisters, and the *Spartan* Twins — Par Lost 10.674
Two blissful twins are to be born, — Mask 1010
line not in Bridgewater ms

Twisted
In twisted braids of Lillies knitting — Mask 862
Or the twisted Eglantine. — Allegro 48
Their twisted cords: he who in Heaven doth dwell — Psalm 2, 8

Twitched
At last he rose, and twitch'd his Mantle blew: — Lycidas 192
Trinity ms 'twitcht'

Twixt
'Twixt upper, nether, and surrounding Fires; — Par Lost 1.346
ms 'T'wixt'
Standards, and Gonfalons twixt Van and Reare — Par Lost 5.589
'Twixt Host and Host but narrow space was left, — Par Lost 6.104
Twixt Day and Night, and now from end to end — Par Lost 9.51
'Twixt God and *Dagon; Dagon* hath presum'd, — Samson 462
Took in by lot 'twixt high, and neather *Jove*, — Mask 20
Trinity ms 'twixt'
Bridgewater ms 'twixt'
'Twixt *Africa* and *Inde*, Ile find him out, — Mask 606
Bridgewater ms 'twixt'
Trinity ms 'twixt'
To stand 'twixt us and our deserved smart — Fair Inf 69
Dodg'd with him, betwixt *Cambridge* and the Bull. — Carrier 8
1658 ''twixt'

Two
Each cast at th' other, as when two black Clouds — Par Lost 2.714
Those other two equal'd with me in Fate, — Par Lost 3.33
Our two first Parents, yet the onely two — Par Lost 3.65
Two of far nobler shape erect and tall, — Par Lost 4.288
To entertain you two, her widest Gates, — Par Lost 4.382
In some Purlieu two gentle Fawnes at play, — Par Lost 4.404
Sight hateful, sight tormenting! thus these two — Par Lost 4.505
But thou hast promis'd from us two a Race — Par Lost 4.732
From these, two strong and suttle Spirits he calld — Par Lost 4.786
But chiefly where those two fair Creatures Lodge, — Par Lost 4.790
Back stept those two faire Angels half amaz'd — Par Lost 4.820
He scarce had ended, when those two approachd — Par Lost 4.874
Battels and Realms: in these he put two weights — Par Lost 4.1002
Two other precious drops that ready stood, — Par Lost 5.132
Two onely, who yet by sov'ran gift possess — Par Lost 5.366
Made horrid Circles; two broad Suns thir Shields — Par Lost 6.305
Two Planets rushing from aspect maligne — Par Lost 6.313
Two potent Thrones, that to be less then Gods — Par Lost 6.366
Second Omnipotence, two dayes are past, — Par Lost 6.684
Two dayes, as we compute the dayes of Heav'n, — Par Lost 6.685
As likeliest was, when two such Foes met arm'd; — Par Lost 6.688
Two dayes are therefore past, the third is thine; — Par Lost 6.699
Myriads between two brazen Mountains lodg'd — Par Lost 7.201
And God made two great Lights, great for thir use — Par Lost 7.346

Two*(cont)*
Which two great Sexes animate the World, — Par Lost 8.151
Approaching two and two, These cowring low — Par Lost 8.350
The hands dispatch of two Gardning so wide. — Par Lost 9.203
One night or two with wanton growth derides — Par Lost 9.211
The onely two of Mankinde, but in them — Par Lost 9.415
Those two; the third best absent is condemn'd, — Par Lost 10.82
As when two Polar Winds blowing adverse — Par Lost 10.289
You two this way, among these numerous Orbs — Par Lost 10.397
Between us two let there be peace, both joyning, — Par Lost 10.924
So Death shall be deceav'd his glut, and with us two — Par Lost 10.990
Or by collision of two bodies grinde — Par Lost 10.1072
Corrupted. I at first with two fair gifts — Par Lost 11.57
Two Birds of gayest plume before him drove: — Par Lost 11.186
These two are Brethren, *Adam*, and to come — Par Lost 11.454
Labouring, two massie clods of Iron and Brass — Par Lost 11.565
Of peaceful dayes portends, then those two past; — Par Lost 11.600
Till by two brethren (those two brethren call — Par Lost 12.169
As on drie land between two christal walls, — Par Lost 12.197
Of two bright Cherubim, before him burn — Par Lost 12.254
Defeating Sin and Death, his two maine armes, — Par Lost 12.431
To conquer Sin and Death the two grand foes, — Par Reg 1.159
Lay pleasant; from his side two rivers flow'd, — Par Reg 3.255
Between two such enclosing enemies — Par Reg 3.361
Ten Sons of *Jacob*, two of *Joseph* lost — Par Reg 3.377
Before the *Parthian;* these two Thrones except, — Par Reg 4.85
These two proportiond ill drove me transverse. — Samson 209
Bound with two cords; but cords to me were threds — Samson 261
Half round on two main Pillars vaulted high, — Samson 1606
With both his arms on those two massie Pillars — Samson 1633
When Mountains tremble, those two massie Pillars — Samson 1648
Co. Two such I saw, what time the labour'd Oxe — Mask 291
Trinity ms 'tow'
Who gently ask't if he had seen such two, — Mask 575
Trinity ms 'tow'
Ye were the two she mean't, with that I sprung — Mask 578
Trinity ms 'tow'
Two blissful twins are to be born, — Mask 1010
line not in Bridgewater ms
Trinity ms 'tow'
With two sister Graces more — Allegro 15
From betwixt two aged Okes, — Allegro 82
Two massy Keyes he bore of metals twain, — Lycidas 110
Trinity ms 'tow'
Where he had mutely sate two years before: — Vacation 6
Move by her two maine nerves, Iron and Gold — Sonnet 17, 8
1694 'Two'

Two-handed
Squadrons at once, with huge two-handed sway — Par Lost 6.251
But that two-handed engine at the door, — Lycidas 130
Trinity ms 'tow-handed'

Twould
T'would be som solace yet, som little chearing — Mask 348
1673 ''Twould'

Tyne
Or Coaly *Tine*, or antient hallowed *Dee*, — Vacation 98

Type
And black *Gehenna* call'd, the Type of Hell. — Par Lost 1.405
ms 'type'

Types
Of sacrifice, informing them, by types — Par Lost 12.232
From shadowie Types to Truth, from Flesh to Spirit, — Par Lost 12.303

Typhoean
Others with vast *Typhoean* rage more fell — Par Lost 2.539

Typhon
Briareos or *Typhon*, whom the Den — Par Lost 1.199
ms 'Typhon'
Not *Typhon* huge ending in snaky twine: — Nativity 226

Tyrannic
Brute violence and proud Tyrannick pow'r, — Par Reg 1.219
Tyrannic power, but raging to pursue — Samson 1275

Tyrannize
With him or under him to tyrannize, — Par Lost 12.39

Tyrannous
Subjection to his Empire tyrannous: — Par Lost 12.32

Tyranny
Sole reigning holds the Tyranny of Heav'n. — Par Lost 1.124
The Prison of his Tyranny who Reigns — Par Lost 2.59
His outward freedom: Tyrannie must be, — Par Lost 12.95
That tyrannie or fortune can inflict, — Samson 1291

Tyrant
The Tyrants plea, excus'd his devilish deeds. — Par Lost 4.394
And Dungeon of our Tyrant: Now possess, — Par Lost 10.466
Though to the Tyrant thereby no excuse. — Par Lost 12.96
But first the lawless Tyrant, who denies — Par Lost 12.173
The triple Tyrant: that from these may grow — Sonnet 18, 12

Tyrants
That doth the wrathfull tyrants quell. — Psalm 136, 10

Tyre
The Philistims, and they of Tyre — Psalm 83, 27
And Tyre with Ethiops *utmost ends*, — Psalm 87, 15

Tyrian
Or *Tyrian* Cynosure. 2. *Bro*. Or if our eyes — Mask 342
Bridgewater ms 'Tirian'
In vain the *Tyrian* Maids their wounded *Thamuz* mourn. — Nativity 204

Tyrrhene
Coasting the *Tyrrhene* shore, as the winds listed, — Mask 49

Uglier
Nor uglier follow the Night-Hag, when call'd — Par Lost 2.662
Ugly
Of ugly Serpents; horror on them fell, — Par Lost 10.539
Of terrour, foul and ugly to behold, — Par Lost 11.464
The Tempter watch'd, and soon with ugly dreams — Par Reg 4.408
Ugly-headed
These oughly-headed Monsters? Mercy guard me! — Mask 695
Trinity ms 'ougly headed' ←'ougly musl'd' ←'musl'd'
Bridgewater ms 'ougley headed'
1637 'ougly-headed'
Ulcer
Intestin Stone and Ulcer, Colic pangs, — Par Lost 11.484
Ultimate
My harbour and my ultimate repose, — Par Reg 3.210
Ulysses
Or when *Ulysses* on the Larbord shunnd — Par Lost 2.1019
That *Hermes* once to wise *Ulysses* gave; — Mask 637
line not in Bridgewater ms
1637 '*Vlysses*'
While sad *Ulisses* soul and all the rest — Vacation 50
Umbrage
To Starr or Sun-light, spread thir umbrage broad — Par Lost 9.1087
Umbrageous
Another side, umbrageous Grots and Caves — Par Lost 4.257
Umpire
Hee rules a moment; *Chaos* Umpire sits, — Par Lost 2.907
My Umpire *Conscience*, whom if they will hear, — Par Lost 3.195
Unable
Serpent though brute, unable to transferre — Par Lost 10.165
All I receav'd, unable to performe — Par Lost 10.750
To please thy gods thou didst it; gods unable — Samson 896
Unacceptable
Unacceptable, though in Heav'n, our state — Par Lost 2.251
Unaccomplished
All th' unaccomplisht works of Natures hand, — Par Lost 3.455
Unacquainted
Shall I inform my unacquainted feet — Mask 180
Bridgewater ms 'vnacquainted'
Unactive
While other Animals unactive range, — Par Lost 4.621
His beams, unactive else, thir vigour find. — Par Lost 8.97
Private, unactive, calm, contemplative, — Par Reg 2.81
When most unactive deem'd, — Samson 1705
Unadmonished
Surprisal, unadmonisht, unforewarnd. — Par Lost 5.245
Unadored
Nor was his name unheard or unador'd — Par Lost 1.738
ms 'vnador'd'
Unadorned
Her unadorned golden tresses wore — Par Lost 4.305
Desert and bare, unsightly, unadornd, — Par Lost 7.314
1674 printed 'unadorn d'
The unadorned boosom of the Deep, — Mask 23
Bridgewater ms 'vnadorned'
Unadventurous
Irresolute, unhardy, unadventrous: — Par Reg 3.243
Unaffected
In thir majestic unaffected stile — Par Reg 4.359
Unagreeable
Not unagreeable, to found a path — Par Lost 10.256
Unaided
Unaided could have finisht thee, and whelmd — Par Lost 6.141
Unalterably
Unalterably firm his love entire — Par Lost 5.502
Unaltered
To whom our Saviour with unalter'd brow. — Par Reg 1.493
Unamazed
Not unamaz'd she thus in answer spake. — Par Lost 9.552
Unanimous
This said unanimous, and other Rites — Par Lost 4.736
Unanimous, as sons of one great Sire — Par Lost 6.95
Both in one Faith unanimous though sad, — Par Lost 12.603
Unanimous they all commit the care — Par Reg 1.111
Unanswered
(Unanswerd least thou boast) to let thee know; — Par Lost 6.163
Unappalled
Sat'st unappall'd in calm and sinless peace. — Par Reg 4.425
Unapparent
Of Nature from the unapparent Deep: — Par Lost 7.103
Unappeasable
Thy anger, unappeasable, still rages, — Samson 963
Unapproached
And never but in unapproached light — Par Lost 3.4
Unapproved
May come and go, so unapprov'd, and leave — Par Lost 5.118
Unargued
Unargu'd I obey; so God ordains, — Par Lost 4.636
Unarmed
Th' unarmed Youth of Heav'n, but nigh at hand — Par Lost 4.552
The sooner for thir Arms, unarm'd they might — Par Lost 6.595
To dread the Son of God: he all unarm'd — Par Reg 4.626
Irresistible *Samson*? whom unarm'd — Samson 126
Unarm'd, and with a trivial weapon fell'd — Samson 263
In fight withstand me single and unarm'd, — Samson 1111
Against th' unarmed weakness of one Virgin — Mask 582
Bridgewater ms 'vnarmed'
Unassailed
To keep my life and honour unassail'd. — Mask 220
line not in Bridgewater ms
Trinity ms 'unassaild'
Unassayed
And what is Faith, Love, Vertue unassaid — Par Lost 9.335
Unattempted
Things unattempted yet in Prose or Rhime. — Par Lost 1.16
ms 'vnattempted'
Unattended
Not unattended, for on her as Queen — Par Lost 8.60
Unattending
That is addrest to unattending Ears, — Mask 272
Bridgewater ms 'vnattendinge'
Unaware
Belike through impotence, or unaware, — Par Lost 2.156
Which to his eye discovers unaware — Par Lost 3.547
And fall into deception unaware, — Par Lost 9.362
Unawares
A vast vacuitie: all unawares — Par Lost 2.932
In our defence, lest unawares we lose — Par Lost 5.731
We unawares run into dangers mouth. — Samson 1522
Unbarred
Unbarr'd the gates of Light. There is a Cave — Par Lost 6.4
Unbecoming
None of retreat, no unbecoming deed — Par Lost 6.237
Unbefitting
Or think thee unbefitting holiest place, — Par Lost 4.759
Unbegot
The Race unblest, to being yet unbegot. — Par Lost 10.988
Unbeheld
These then, though unbeheld in deep of night, — Par Lost 4.674
Unbelief
For such there be, but unbelief is blind. — Mask 519
Bridgewater ms 'vnbeliefe'
Trinity ms 'unbeleife'
1637 'unbeliefe'
Unbenighted
Had unbenighted shon, while the low Sun — Par Lost 10.682
Unbenign
In Synod unbenigne, and taught the fixt — Par Lost 10.661
Unbesought
Hath unbesaught provided, and his hands — Par Lost 10.1058
Unbid
Unbid, and thou shalt eate th' Herb of the Field, — Par Lost 10.204
Unblamed
May I express thee unblam'd? since God is light, — Par Lost 3.3
Venial discourse unblam'd: I now must change — Par Lost 9.5
Shal spend thir dayes in joy unblam'd, and dwell — Par Lost 12.22
Unblemished
And thou unblemish't form of Chastity, — Mask 215
Trinity ms 'unblemish't' ←'unspotted'
line not in Bridgewater ms
Unblenched
She may pass on with unblench't majesty, — Mask 430
Trinity ms 'unblensh't'
Bridgewater ms 'vnblensh't'
Unblessed
Of unblest feet. Him followed his next Mate, — Par Lost 1.238
ms 'vnblest'
The Race unblest, to being yet unbegot. — Par Lost 10.988
Of unblest inchanter vile. — Mask 907
Bridgewater ms 'vnblest'
Thou hat'st; and them unblest — Psalm 5, 14
Unborn
In order, though to Nations yet unborn, — Par Lost 4.663
Farr into *Chaos*, and the World unborn; — Par Lost 7.220
Better end heer unborn. Why is life giv'n — Par Lost 11.502
Unbosom
Would soon unboosom all thir Echoes milde, — Passion 53
1673 'unbosom'
Unbosomed
Too well, unbosom'd all my secrets to thee, — Samson 879
Unbottomed
The dark unbottom'd infinite Abyss — Par Lost 2.405
Unbound
Volatil *Hermes*, and call up unbound — Par Lost 3.603
Unbounded
Then happie; no unbounded hope had rais'd — Par Lost 4.60
Voyag'd th' unreal, vast, unbounded deep — Par Lost 10.471
Unbroken
Unbrok'n, and in proud rebellious Arms — Par Lost 2.691
Unbuckled
His starrie Helme unbuckl'd shew'd him prime — Par Lost 11.245
Unbuild
The mightie frame, how build, unbuild, contrive — Par Lost 8.81
His consort Libertie; what, but unbuild — Par Lost 12.526
Uncalled
Hee boulder now, uncall'd before her stood; — Par Lost 9.523
Uncelebrated
Nor past uncelebrated, nor unsung — Par Lost 7.253
Uncertain
Uncertain which, in Ocean or in Air. — Par Lost 3.76
Uncertain and unsettl'd still remains, — Par Reg 4.326
To cast the fashion of uncertain evils; — Mask 360
line not in Trinity ms
1637 'uncertaine'
line not in Bridgewater ms

Uncessant
Alas! What boots it with uncessant care Lycidas 64
Trinity ms 'incessant'
Unchangeable
Unchangeable, Eternal, which ordain'd Par Lost 3.127
Unchanged
More safe I Sing with mortal voice, unchang'd Par Lost 7.24
Unchaste
Unclean, unchaste. Samson 321
Unchaste was subsequent, her stain not his. Samson 325
By unchaste looks, loose gestures, and foul talk, Mask 464
Trinity ms 'unchast'
Bridgewater ms 'vnchast'
1637 'unchast'
Unchecked
Uncheckt, and of her roaving is no end; Par Lost 8.189
Uncheerful
My life *at deaths uncherful dore* Psalm 88, 11
Uncircumcised
To the uncircumcis'd a welcom prey, Samson 260
Against the uncircumcis'd, our enemies. Samson 640
Idolatrous, uncircumcis'd, unclean. Samson 1364
Uncircumscribed
Though I uncircumscrib'd my self retire, Par Lost 7.170
Unclean
There sit not, and reproach us as unclean, Par Lost 9.1098
Meats by the Law unclean, or offer'd first Par Reg 2.328
Unclean, unchaste. Samson 321
That moral verdit quits her of unclean: Samson 324
What act more execrably unclean, prophane? Samson 1362
Idolatrous, uncircumcis'd, unclean. Samson 1364
Unclouded
Blaz'd forth unclouded Deitie; he full Par Lost 10.65
Uncoloured
Whether to deck with Clouds the uncolourd skie, Par Lost 5.189
Uncompassionate
In uncompassionate anger do not so. Samson 818
Uncompounded
And uncompounded is thir Essence pure, Par Lost 1.425
ms 'vncompounded'
Unconcerned
All unconcern'd with our unrest, begins Par Lost 11.174
Unconfirmed
His witness unconfirm'd: on him baptiz'd Par Reg 1.29
Unconform
Not unconform to other shining Globes, Par Lost 5.259
1667 'unconforme' in some copies
Unconjugal
Of falshood most unconjugal traduc't. Samson 979
Unconniving
By rigour unconniving, but that oft Par Reg 1.363
Unconquerable
All is not lost; the unconquerable Will, Par Lost 1.106
ms 'vnconquerable'
Where boldest; though to sight unconquerable? Par Lost 6.118
Unconquered
That wise *Minerva* wore, unconquer'd Virgin, Mask 448
Trinity ms 'unconquer'd' ←'unvanquish't' ←'aeternall'
Bridgewater ms 'vnconquer'd'
Unconscionable
Stalking with less unconsci'nable strides, Samson 1245
Unconsumed
With ever-burning Sulphur unconsum'd: Par Lost 1.69
ms 'vnconsum'd'
Yet unconsum'd. Before the Gates there sat Par Lost 2.648
Uncontrollable
His uncontroulable intent, Samson 1754
Uncontrolled
Yet should I try, the uncontrouled worth Mask 793
line not in Trinity ms
line not in Bridgewater ms
Uncoupled
Of long-uncoupled bed, and childless eld, Fair Inf 13
Uncouth
His uncouth way, or spread his aerie flight Par Lost 2.407
This uncouth errand sole, and one for all Par Lost 2.827
This uncouth dream, of evil sprung I fear; Par Lost 5.98
And uncouth paine fled bellowing. On each wing Par Lost 6.362
Bound on a voyage uncouth and obscure, Par Lost 8.230
Toild out my uncouth passage, forc't to ride Par Lost 10.475
Though in this uncouth place; if old respect, Samson 333
Find out som uncouth cell, Allegro 5
Thus sang the uncouth Swain to th' Okes and rills, Lycidas 186
Uncovered
Uncover'd more, so rose the *Danite* strong Par Lost 9.1059
Uncoverest
Or by evasions thy crime uncoverst more. Samson 842
Uncreate
When who can uncreate thee thou shalt know. Par Lost 5.895
Dependent made; so God shall uncreate, Par Lost 9.943
Uncreated
In the wide womb of uncreated night, Par Lost 2.150
Miserie, uncreated till the crime Par Lost 6.268
Uncropped
Partakers, and uncropt falls to the ground. Par Lost 4.731
Unction
By Sacred Unction, thy deserved right. Par Lost 6.709
Unctuous
Compact of unctuous vapor, which the Night Par Lost 9.635
Unculled
Uncull'd, as came to hand; a Shepherd next Par Lost 11.436
Undaunted
Th' undaunted Fiend what this might be admir'd, Par Lost 2.677
Undaunted to meet there what ever power Par Lost 2.955
Undaunted. If I must contend, said he, Par Lost 4.851
And thus his own undaunted heart explores. Par Lost 6.113
He patient but undaunted where they led him, Samson 1623
Undazzled
Undazl'd, farr and wide his eye commands, Par Lost 3.614
Undecked
Undeckt, save with her self more lovely fair Par Lost 5.380
Undefiled
Whose bed is undefil'd and chaste pronounc't, Par Lost 4.761
Undelayed
Of violence will undelay'd Psalm 7, 59
Undelighted
Saw undelighted all delight, all kind Par Lost 4.286
Under
Under thy conduct, and in dreadful deeds Par Lost 1.130
ms 'Vnder'
Moors by his side under the Lee, while Night Par Lost 1.207
Under amazement of thir hideous change. Par Lost 1.313
ms 'Vnder'
Hovering on wing under the Cope of Hell Par Lost 1.345
ms 'vnder'
A crew who under Names of old Renown, Par Lost 1.477
ms 'vnder'
Sat on his faded cheek, but under Browes Par Lost 1.602
ms 'vnder'
Long under darkness cover. But these thoughts Par Lost 1.659
ms 'vnder'
Under yon boyling Ocean, wrapt in Chains; Par Lost 2.183
Thrive under evil, and work ease out of pain Par Lost 2.261
Under th' inevitable curb, reserv'd Par Lost 2.322
Of Creatures rational, though under hope Par Lost 2.498
Under spread Ensigns marching might pass through Par Lost 2.886
Under his gloomie power I shall not long Par Lost 3.242
Found out for mankind under wrauth, O thou Par Lost 3.275
Thy Merits; under thee as Head Supream Par Lost 3.319
In Heaven, or Earth, or under Earth in Hell; Par Lost 3.322
Dark, waste, and wild, under the frown of Night Par Lost 3.424
Dreaming by night under the open Skie, Par Lost 3.514
Under a Coronet his flowing haire Par Lost 3.640
Under what torments inwardly I groane; Par Lost 4.88
That practisd falshood under saintly shew, Par Lost 4.122
With mazie error under pendant shades Par Lost 4.239
True Paradise under the *Ethiop* Line Par Lost 4.282
Under a tuft of shade that on a green Par Lost 4.325
Under a shade of flours, much wondring where Par Lost 4.451
Under a Platan, yet methought less faire, Par Lost 4.478
Naked met his under the flowing Gold Par Lost 4.496
Mine eye pursu'd him still, but under shade Par Lost 4.572
Both turnd, and under op'n Skie ador'd Par Lost 4.721
But first from under shadie arborous roof, Par Lost 5.137
Of Angels under watch; and to his state, Par Lost 5.288
Under whose lowly roof thou hast voutsaf't Par Lost 5.463
Under thir Hierarchs in orders bright Par Lost 5.587
Under his great Vice-gerent Reign abide Par Lost 5.609
And all who under me thir Banners wave, Par Lost 5.687
Under him Regent, tells, as he was taught, Par Lost 5.698
All Power, and us eclipst under the name Par Lost 5.776
Our happie state under one Head more neer Par Lost 5.830
Under thir God-like Leaders, in the Cause Par Lost 6.67
Thy Legions under darkness; but thou seest Par Lost 6.142
So under fierie Cope together rush'd Par Lost 6.215
1667 'Sounder', 1668 errata 'So under'
Under her Cloudie covert both retir'd, Par Lost 6.409
So all ere day-spring, under conscious Night Par Lost 6.521
Under spred Ensignes moving nigh, in slow Par Lost 6.533
Under the weight of Mountains buried deep, Par Lost 6.652
Under whose conduct *Michael* soon reduc'd Par Lost 6.777
Under thir Head imbodied all in one. Par Lost 6.779
Gloomie as Night; under his burning Wheeles Par Lost 6.832
Up hither, under long obedience tri'd, Par Lost 7.159
Be gather'd now ye Waters under Heav'n Par Lost 7.283
Glide under the green Wave, in Sculles that oft Par Lost 7.402
Moist nutriment, or under Rocks thir food Par Lost 7.408
With clang despis'd the ground, under a cloud Par Lost 7.422
Which it had long stood under, streind to the highth Par Lost 8.454
Under his forming hands a Creature grew, Par Lost 8.470
Aid us, the work under our labour grows, Par Lost 9.208
Hate stronger, under shew of Love well feign'd, Par Lost 9.492
Under this ignorance of good and Evil, Par Lost 9.774
Much more to taste it under banne to touch. Par Lost 9.925
Were such as under Government well seem'd, Par Lost 10.154
Whom he shall tread at last under our feet; Par Lost 10.190
Ascended his high Throne, which under state Par Lost 10.445
Why stand we longer shivering under feares, Par Lost 10.1003
On this Mount he appeerd, under this Tree Par Lost 11.320
Under inhuman pains? Why should not Man, Par Lost 11.511
In Prison under Judgements imminent: Par Lost 11.725
From under Heav'n; the Hills to their supplie Par Lost 11.740
Deep under water rould; Sea cover'd Sea, Par Lost 11.749
Under paternal rule; till one shall rise Par Lost 12.24
With him or under him to tyrannize, Par Lost 12.39

Under(*cont*)
By Judges first, then under Kings; of whom Par Lost 12.320
Under her own waight groaning till the day Par Lost 12.539
Art all things under Heav'n, all places thou, Par Lost 12.618
Under the covert of some ancient Oak, Par Reg 1.305
Under the hospitable covert nigh Par Reg 2.262
Under a Juniper; then how awakt, Par Reg 2.272
In ample space under the broadest shade Par Reg 2.339
Under the Trees now trip'd, now solemn stood Par Reg 2.354
Reduc't a Province under Roman yoke, Par Reg 3.158
That Empire, under his dominion holds Par Reg 3.296
But govern ill the Nations under yoke, Par Reg 4.135
Rather accuse him under usual names, Par Reg 4.316
Wherever, under some concourse of shades Par Reg 4.404
Under his feet: for proof, e're this thou feel'st Par Reg 4.621
To grind in Brazen Fetters under task Samson 35
Himself in bonds under *Philistian* yoke; Samson 42
Under the Seal of silence could not keep, Samson 49
Thir plated backs under his heel; Samson 140
The mystery of God giv'n me under pledge Samson 378
Under his special eie Samson 636
Or to the unjust tribunals, under change of times, Samson 695
Nor under their protection but my own, Samson 887
Seeming at first all heavenly under virgin veil, Samson 1035
Under pretence of Bridal friends and guests, Samson 1196
On banks and scaffolds under Skie might stand; Samson 1610
From under ashes into sudden flame, Samson 1691
I under fair pretence of friendly ends, Mask 160
Bridgewater ms 'vnder'
Under the spreading favour of these Pines, Mask 184
1637 'Vnder'
Bridgewater ms 'vnder'
I saw them under a green mantling vine Mask 294
Bridgewater ms 'vnder'
Benighted walks under the mid-day Sun; Mask 384
Bridgewater ms 'walks in black vapours though the noone tyde brand'
Trinity ms 'benighted walks under the midday sun' ←'walks in black vapours though the noontyde brand'
Under the ribs of Death, but O ere long Mask 562
Bridgewater ms 'vnder'
1637 'Vnder'
Under the sooty flag of *Acheron*, Mask 604
1637 'Vnder'
Bridgewater ms 'vnder'
Under the glassie, cool, translucent wave, Mask 861
Bridgewater ms 'vnder'
1637 'Vnder'
There under *Ebon* shades, and low-brow'd Rocks, Allegro 8
Under the Hawthorn in the dale. Allegro 68
In fire, air, flood, or under ground, Penseroso 94
Stole under Seas to meet his *Arethuse*; Arcades 31
Under the shady roof Arcades 88
Under the opening eye-lids of the morn, Lycidas 26
Where thou perhaps under the whelming tide Lycidas 157
Th' old Dragon under ground Nativity 168
And mistie Regions of wide air next under, Vacation 41
Ungratefully shall strive to keep him under, Vacation 78
Under a Star-ypointing *Pyramid*? Shakespear 4
1640 'Vnder'
1632 'Vnder'
Save me and secure me under Psalm 7, 2
Thou hast put all under his lordly feet, Psalm 8, 18
Low in a mead of Kine under a Thorn, Prose 13, 1

Underfoot
Mosaic; underfoot the Violet, Par Lost 4.700

Undergo
To undergo eternal punishment? Par Lost 1.155
ms 'vndergoe'
Certain to undergoe like doom, if Death Par Lost 9.953
To undergoe with mee one Guilt, one Crime, Par Lost 9.971
Before my Judge, either to undergoe Par Lost 10.126
Yearly enjoynd, some say, to undergo Par Lost 10.575
Which he for us did freely undergo. Passion 12
While I thy terrors undergo Psalm 88, 63

Undergone
Far other labour to be undergon Par Reg 2.132

Underground
Winds under ground or waters forcing way Par Lost 6.196
Deep under ground, materials dark and crude, Par Lost 6.478
That under ground, they fought in dismal shade; Par Lost 6.666
But they, or under ground, or circuit wide Par Lost 7.301
In Hillocks; the swift Stag from under ground Par Lost 7.469
Into a Gulf shot under ground, till part Par Lost 9.72
From underground) the liquid Ore he dreind Par Lost 11.570
Boiles out from under ground, the mouth of Hell; Par Lost 12.42
In fire, air, flood, or under ground, Penseroso 94
Th' old Dragon under ground Nativity 168

Undergrowth
As one continu'd brake, the undergrowth Par Lost 4.175

Underling
Yet every one shall make him underling, Vacation 76

Undermine
Allure, or terrifie, or undermine. Par Reg 1.179

Underminers
To pay my underminers in thir coin. Samson 1204

Underneath
That underneath had veins of liquid fire Par Lost 1.701

Underneath(*cont*)
Viewless, and underneath a bright Sea flow'd Par Lost 3.518
Pass'd underneath ingulft, for God had thrown Par Lost 4.225
With him I flew, and underneath beheld Par Lost 5.87
Long strugling underneath, ere they could wind Par Lost 6.659
The Waters underneath from those above Par Lost 7.268
Or to the Earths dark basis underneath, Par Reg 4.456
Till underneath them fair *Jerusalem*, Par Reg 4.544
Above, about, or underneath, Penseroso 152
Or sullen *Mole* that runneth underneath, Vacation 95

Understand
Had need from head to foot well understand; Par Lost 6.625
With low subjection; understand the same Par Lost 8.345
For well I understand in the prime end Par Lost 8.540
Of utmost hope! now clear I understand Par Lost 12.376
Since understand; much more his absence now Par Reg 2.100
To understand my Adversary, who Par Reg 4.527
They know not nor will understand, Psalm 82, 17

Understanding
Fansie and understanding, whence the Soule Par Lost 5.486
Unhurt our mindes, and understanding sound, Par Lost 6.444
For Understanding rul'd not, and the Will Par Lost 9.1127

Understood
Open or understood must be resolv'd. Par Lost 1.662
ms 'vnderstood'
And understood not that a grateful mind Par Lost 4.55
Was understood, the injur'd Lovers Hell. Par Lost 5.450
Not understood, this gift they have besides, Par Lost 6.626
I nam'd them, as they pass'd, and understood Par Lost 8.352
Of amorous intent, well understood Par Lost 9.1035
Thence gatherd his own doom, which understood Par Lost 10.344
And understood not all was but a shew Par Lost 10.883
Not understood, till hoarse, and all in rage, Par Lost 12.58
Though not but by the Spirit understood. Par Lost 12.514
Which they who ask'd have seldom understood, Par Reg 1.436
And not well understood as good not known? Par Reg 1.437
I would be understood) in prosperous days Samson 191

Undertake
To second, or oppose, or undertake Par Lost 2.419

Undertook
I therefore, I alone first undertook Par Lost 4.935
When time shall be, for so I undertook Par Lost 10.74
I, when no other durst, sole undertook Par Reg 1.100
I undertook that office, and the tongues Par Reg 1.374
I, as I undertook, and with the vote Par Reg 2.129

Underwent
And underwent a quick immortal change Mask 841
Bridgewater ms 'vnderwent'

Undeserved
Will arrogate Dominion undeserv'd Par Lost 12.27

Undeservedly
Who oft as undeservedly enthrall Par Lost 12.94

Undesirable
A thing not undesireable, somtime Par Lost 9.824

Undetermined
In circuit, undetermind square or round, Par Lost 2.1048

Undiminished
Strength undiminisht, or eternal being Par Lost 1.154
ms 'vndiminish'd'
Or undiminisht brightness, to be known Par Lost 4.836

Undiscording
That we on Earth with undiscording voice Musick 17

Undisguised
Whom thus answer'd th' Arch Fiend now undisguis'd. Par Reg 1.357

Undismayed
Seis'd us, though undismaid: long is the way Par Lost 2.432
And in the midst thus undismai'd began. Par Lost 6.417

Undissembled
Then undissembl'd hate) with what contempt Samson 400

Undisturbed
That undisturbed Song of pure content, Musick 6

Undo
But past who can recall, or don undoe? Par Lost 9.926
Be frustrate, do, undo, and labour loose, Par Lost 9.944
To undoe the charmed band Mask 904
1673 'undo'
Bridgewater ms 'vndoe'

Undone
Indebted and undon, hath none to bring: Par Lost 3.235

Undoubted
Shon with a glossie scurff, undoubted sign Par Lost 1.672
ms 'vndoubted'
By proof the undoubted Son of God, inspire, Par Reg 1.11

Undoubtedly
Undoubtedly he will relent and turn Par Lost 10.1093

Undrawn
Flashing thick flames, Wheele within Wheele undrawn, Par Lost 6.751

Undreaded
Unnam'd, undreaded, and thy self half starv'd? Par Lost 10.595

Undying
To chains of darkness, and th' undying Worm, Par Lost 6.739

Unearned
Early, and th' hour of Supper comes unearn'd. Par Lost 9.225

Uneasy
He walkt with to support uneasie steps Par Lost 1.295
ms 'vneasy'
From his uneasie station, and upbore Par Reg 4.584

Uneclipsed
To live with him, and sing in endles morn of light. Musick 28
Trinity ms 'endlesse' ←'never-parting' ←'cloudlesse' ←'endlesse' ←'uneclipsed' ←'ever-glorious' ←'ever-endlesse'
Unemployed
Rove idle unimploid, and less need rest; Par Lost 4.617
Inglorious, unimploy'd, with age out-worn. Samson 580
Unenchanted
Of dragon watch with uninchanted eye, Mask 395
Trinity ms 'uninchaunted'
Bridgewater ms 'vninchaunted'
his uninchanted eye, & round the verge Mask Tr. ms 10.10
'uninchanted' ←'never charmed'
Unendeared
Of Harlots, loveless, joyless, unindeard, Par Lost 4.766
Unenjoyed
colouring the pale cheeke of uninjoyd love Lycidas Tr. ms 28.16
Unenvied
Establisht in a safe unenvied Throne Par Lost 2.23
Unequal
For Gods, and too unequal work we find Par Lost 6.453
Against unequal armes to fight in paine, Par Lost 6.454
Himself an Army, now unequal match Samson 346
Unequalled
So faithful Love unequald; but I feel Par Lost 9.983
Unequals
Among unequals what societie Par Lost 8.383
Unespied
Neerer to view his prey, and unespi'd Par Lost 4.399
With silent circumspection unespi'd. Par Lost 6.523
Unessential
Of unessential Night receives him next Par Lost 2.439
Uneven
Belial, in much uneven scale thou weigh'st Par Reg 2.173
Unexampled
For mans offence. O unexampl'd love, Par Lost 3.410
Unexempt
Scorning the unexempt condition Mask 685
line not in Bridgewater ms
Unexpected
First seen, them unexpected joy surpriz'd, Par Lost 6.774
O unexpected stroke, worse then of Death! Par Lost 11.268
Thir unexpected loss and plaints out breath'd. Par Reg 2.29
Unexpectedly
But unexpectedly returns Samson 1750
Unexperienced
With unexperienc't thought, and laid me downe Par Lost 4.457
The wisest, unexperienc't, will be ever Par Reg 3.240
Unexpert
More unexpert, I boast not: them let those Par Lost 2.52
Unexpressive
And hears the unexpressive nuptiall Song, Lycidas 176
With unexpressive notes to Heav'ns new-born Heir. Nativity 116
Unextinguishable
Where pain of unextinguishable fire Par Lost 2.88
Unfaithful
To judge th' unfaithful dead, but to reward Par Lost 12.461
His faithful, left among th' unfaithful herd, Par Lost 12.481
Unfastens
Unfast'ns: on a sudden op'n flie Par Lost 2.879
Unfathomed
& halfe the slow unfadom'd Stygian poole Mask Tr. ms 10.15
Unfeared
Fearless unfeard he slept: in at his Mouth Par Lost 9.187
Unfeigned
Unfained *Halleluiahs* to thee sing, Par Lost 6.744
And sweet compliance, which declare unfeign'd Par Lost 8.603
Of sorrow unfeign'd, and humiliation meek. Par Lost 10.1092
Of sorrow unfeign'd, and humiliation meek. Par Lost 10.1104
Unfelt
Strange horror seise thee, and pangs unfelt before. Par Lost 2.703
Sweetness into my heart, unfelt before, Par Lost 8.475
Unfinished
Were left for hast unfinish't, judgment scant, Samson 1027
Unfit
And for that name unfit. Psalm 88, 16
Unfold
Which I as freely give; Hell shall unfold, Par Lost 4.381
1667 'unfould'
And perfet while they stood; how last unfould Par Lost 5.568
Vanguard, to Right and Left the Front unfould; Par Lost 6.558
Absolv'd, if unforbid thou maist unfould Par Lost 7.94
How comes it thus? unfould, Celestial Guide, Par Lost 11.785
Unfold her Crystal Dores, thence on his head Par Reg 1.82
If cause were to unfold some active Scene Par Reg 2.239
That must be utter'd to unfold the sage Mask 786
line not in Trinity ms
line not in Bridgewater ms
The spirit of *Plato* to unfold Penseroso 89
Whether to settle peace or to unfold Sonnet 17, 5
Thy faithfulness *unfold?* Psalm 88, 48
Unfolding
So spake the Father, and unfoulding bright Par Lost 10.63
Unforbid
Absolv'd, if unforbid thou maist unfould Par Lost 7.94
Unforeknown
Which had no less prov'd certain unforeknown. Par Lost 3.119
Unforeseen
Befalln us unforeseen, unthought of, know Par Lost 2.821
Unforeskinned
From the unforeskinn'd race, of whom thou bear'st Samson 1100
Unforewarned
Surprisal, unadmonisht, unforewarnd. Par Lost 5.245
Unformed
Matter unform'd and void: Darkness profound Par Lost 7.233
Unfortunate
Found so unfortunate; nevertheless, Par Lost 10.970
'Tis true, I am that Spirit unfortunate, Par Reg 1.358
My rash but more unfortunate misdeed. Samson 747
His lot unfortunate in nuptial choice, Samson 1743
Unfound
Once found, which yet unfound most would have thought Par Lost 6.500
Unfounded
Th' unfounded deep, and through the void immense Par Lost 2.829
Unfrequented
Thir living strength, and unfrequented left Par Lost 1.433
ms 'vnfrequented'
This unfrequented place to find some ease, Samson 17
Unfriended
Thou art unknown, unfriended, low of birth, Par Reg 2.413
Unfulfilled
Still unfulfill'd with pain of longing pines; Par Lost 4.511
Unfumed
With Rose and Odours from the shrub unfum'd. Par Lost 5.349
Unfurled
Who forthwith from the glittering Staff unfurld Par Lost 1.535
ms 'vnfurl'd'
Ungodly
Had driven out th' ungodly from his sight Par Lost 7.185
But by ungodly deeds, the contradiction Samson 898
And your ungodly deeds finde me the words. Prose 8, 2
Ungoverned
To serve ungovern'd appetite, and took Par Lost 11.517
Ungraceful
Nor are thy lips ungraceful, Sire of men, Par Lost 8.218
Ungratefully
Ungratefully shall strive to keep him under, Vacation 78
Unguarded
The Throne of God unguarded, and his side Par Lost 6.133
Wide open and unguarded, *Satan* pass'd, Par Lost 10.419
Co. And left your fair side all unguarded Lady? Mask 283
Bridgewater ms 'vnguarded'
Unhallowed
Made common and unhallowd ere our taste; Par Lost 9.931
In this unhallow'd air, but that this Jugler Mask 757
Bridgewater ms 'vnhallowed'
Trinity ms 'unhallowd'
Unhappily
Unhappilie deceav'd; thy suppliant Par Lost 10.917
Unhappy
In this unhappy Mansion, or once more Par Lost 1.268
ms 'vnhappie'
Desire of wandring this unhappie Morn, Par Lost 9.1136
Spir. Ay me unhappy then my fears are true. Mask 511
1637 'unhappie'
Trinity ms 'unhappie'
Bridgewater ms 'vnhappie'
Unharboured
May trace huge Forests, and unharbour'd Heaths, Mask 423
Bridgewater ms 'vnharbour'd'
Unhardy
Irresolute, unhardy, unadventrous: Par Reg 3.243
Unharmonious
No gross, no unharmoneous mixture foule, Par Lost 11.51
Unhazarded
Whole to my self, unhazarded abroad, Samson 809
Unheard
Thir childrens cries unheard, that past through fire Par Lost 1.395
ms 'vnheard'
Nor was his name unheard or unador'd Par Lost 1.738
ms 'vnheard'
He drew not nigh unheard, the Angel bright, Par Lost 3.645
Unheeded
Gave proof unheeded; others on the grass Par Lost 4.350
Unheedy
Pluck't up by som unheedy swain, Winchester 38
Unhidebound
To stuff this Maw, this vast unhide-bound Corps. Par Lost 10.601
Unhoard
Or as a Thief bent to unhoord the cash Par Lost 4.188
Unholy
From hallowd ground th' unholie, and denounce Par Lost 11.106
'Mongst horrid shapes, and shreiks, and sights unholy, Allegro 4
Unhoped
Of this new wondrous Pontifice, unhop't Par Lost 10.348
Unhoused
Unhous'd thy Virgin Soul from her fair biding place. Fair Inf 21
Unhumbled
Unhumbl'd, unrepentant, unreform'd, Par Reg 3.429
Unhurt
Unhurt our mindes, and understanding sound, Par Lost 6.444
Unimaginable
So unimaginable as hate in Heav'n, Par Lost 7.54
Unimmortal
Both to destroy, or unimmortal make Par Lost 10.611

Unimplored
Comes unprevented, unimplor'd, unsought, Par Lost 3.231
Her nightly visitation unimplor'd, Par Lost 9.22
Uninformed
And guided by his voice, nor uninformd Par Lost 8.486
Uninjured
Uninjur'd in this wilde surrounding wast. Mask 403
Bridgewater ms 'vniniur'd'
1637 'Vninjur'd'
Uninterrupted
Uninterrupted joy, unrivald love Par Lost 3.68
Uninvented
Not uninvented that, which thou aright Par Lost 6.470
Union
To union, and firm Faith, and firm accord, Par Lost 2.36
Mee disobeyes, breaks union, and that day Par Lost 5.612
Of Union irresistible, mov'd on Par Lost 6.63
One Kingdom, Joy and Union without end. Par Lost 7.161
Of Union or Communion, deifi'd; Par Lost 8.431
Union of Mind, or in us both one Soule; Par Lost 8.604
Total they mix, Union of Pure with Pure Par Lost 8.627
And gladly of our Union heare thee speak, Par Lost 9.966
Could hold all Heav'n and Earth in happier union. Nativity 108
And in firm union bind. Psalm 83, 20
Unison
Choral or Unison: of incense Clouds Par Lost 7.599
Unite
Her chrystal mirror holds, unite thir streams. Par Lost 4.263
Would utmost vigor raise, and rais'd unite. Par Lost 9.314
Powerful at greatest distance to unite Par Lost 10.247
To his celestial consort us unite, Musick 27
Themselves against thee they unite Psalm 83, 19
To fear thy name my heart unite Psalm 86, 39
United
United thoughts and counsels, equal hope Par Lost 1.88
ms 'Vnited'
Breathing united force with fixed thought Par Lost 1.560
ms 'vnited'
How such united force of Gods, how such Par Lost 1.629
ms 'vnited'
Waterd the Garden; thence united fell Par Lost 4.230
United as one individual Soule Par Lost 5.610
United. But to grant it thee unjust, Par Lost 5.831
United I beheld; no Fair to thine Par Lost 9.608
No wonder, for though in thee be united Par Reg 3.229
Who durst not with thir whole united powers Samson 1110
Unites
Such fatal consequence unites us three: Par Lost 10.364
Of God most High; So God with Man unites. Par Lost 12.382
Unity
In unitie defective, which requires Par Lost 8.425
To sit the midst of Trinal Unity, Nativity 11
Universal
At which the universal Host upsent Par Lost 1.541
ms 'vniversall'
At length a universal hubbub wilde Par Lost 2.951
Presented with a Universal blanc Par Lost 3.48
Anointed universal King; all Power Par Lost 3.317
The Universal Maker we may praise; Par Lost 3.676
The trembling leaves, while Universal *Pan* Par Lost 4.266
Almightie, thine this universal Frame, Par Lost 5.154
Hail universal Lord, be bounteous still Par Lost 5.205
Universal reproach, far worse to beare Par Lost 6.34
In universal ruin last, and now Par Lost 6.797
The hollow Universal Orb they fill'd, Par Lost 7.257
Her Universal Face with pleasant green, Par Lost 7.316
So spake the Universal Lord, and seem'd Par Lost 8.376
Sovran of Creatures, universal Dame. Par Lost 9.612
Thir universal shout and high applause Par Lost 10.505
A dismal universal hiss, the sound Par Lost 10.508
A World devote to universal rack. Par Lost 11.821
Therefore Gods universal Law Samson 1053
Chor. Noise call you it or universal groan Samson 1511
Whom Universal nature did lament, Lycidas 60
1638 'universall'
Trinity ms 'universal'
She strikes a universall Peace through Sea and Land. Nativity 52
1673 'universal'
Universally
Where universally admir'd; but here Par Lost 9.542
Universally crown'd with highest praises. Samson 175
Universe
A Universe of death, which God by curse Par Lost 2.622
The Univers, and to each inward part Par Lost 3.584
The rest in circuit walles this Universe. Par Lost 3.721
This Universe, and all created things: Par Lost 7.227
Adore thee, Author of this Universe, Par Lost 8.360
Queen of this Universe, doe not believe Par Lost 9.684
This Universe we have possest, and rul'd Par Reg 1.49
To mans less universe, and soon are gone; Par Reg 4.459
Unjointed
Dissolves unjointed e're it reach my ear. Samson 177
Unjust
Our strength is equal, nor the Law unjust Par Lost 2.200
Mans mortal crime, and just th' unjust to save, Par Lost 3.215
Confess him rightful King? unjust thou saist Par Lost 5.818
Flatly unjust, to binde with Laws the free, Par Lost 5.819
United. But to grant it thee unjust, Par Lost 5.831

Unjust(*cont*)
Out of thy loyns; th' unjust the just hath slain, Par Lost 11.455
Just for unjust, that in such righteousness Par Lost 12.294
Thy chosen, to what highth thir pow'r unjust Par Reg 2.45
For truths sake suffering death unjust, lives now Par Reg 3.98
Or to the unjust tribunals, under change of times, Samson 695
Just or unjust, alike seem miserable, Samson 703
Surpriz'd by unjust force, but not enthrall'd, Mask 590
Bridgewater ms 'vniust'
If th' unjust will not forbear, Psalm 7, 45
Then an unjust and wicked King Prose 11, 3
Unjustly
Unjustly thou deprav'st it with the name Par Lost 6.174
Thy countrey sought of thee, it sought unjustly, Samson 889
Unkindly
Abortive, monstrous, or unkindly mixt, Par Lost 3.456
Bred of unkindly fumes, with conscious dreams Par Lost 9.1050
Forbidding every bleak unkindly Fog Mask 269
Bridgewater ms 'vnkindly'
Unkindness
As one who loves, and some unkindness meets, Par Lost 9.271
Leans her unpillow'd head fraught with sad fears. Mask 355
Trinity ms 'fraught with sad feares' ←'musing at our unkindnesse'
Unknown
Or unknown Region, what remains him less Par Lost 2.443
Then unknown dangers and as hard escape. Par Lost 2.444
The Paradise of Fools, to few unknown Par Lost 3.496
Not to know mee argues your selves unknown, Par Lost 4.830
Author of evil, unknown till thy revolt, Par Lost 6.262
Unknown, which human knowledg could not reach: Par Lost 7.75
Needless to thee repeated; nor unknown Par Lost 7.494
In Paradise, and various, yet unknown Par Lost 9.619
For good unknown, sure is not had, or had Par Lost 9.756
And yet unknown, is as not had at all. Par Lost 9.757
Of danger tasted, nor to evil unknown Par Lost 9.864
Of Enemie hath beguil'd thee, yet unknown, Par Lost 9.905
To sow a jangling noise of words unknown: Par Lost 12.55
With God, who call'd him, in a land unknown. Par Lost 12.134
Unmarkt, unknown; but him the Baptist soon Par Reg 1.25
Thou art unknown, unfriended, low of birth, Par Reg 2.413
To me is not unknown what hath been done Par Reg 2.444
We come thy friends and neighbours not unknown Samson 180
For grant they be so, while they rest unknown, Mask 361
line not in Trinity ms
line not in Bridgewater ms
1637 'unknowne'
Unknown, and like esteem'd, and the dull swayn Mask 634
1637 'Vnknowne'
Trinity ms 'unknowne'
line not in Bridgewater ms
strange distances to heare & unknowne climes Mask Tr. ms 10.17
Unlaid
Blew meager Hag, or stubborn unlaid ghost, Mask 434
1637 'unlayd'
Bridgewater ms 'vnlayed'
Trinity ms 'unlayd'
Unless
Within Heav'ns bound, unless Heav'ns Lord supream Par Lost 2.236
Unless th' Almighty Maker them ordain Par Lost 2.915
Dye hee or Justice must; unless for him Par Lost 3.210
And not molest us, unless we our selves Par Lost 8.186
That name, unless an age too late, or cold Par Lost 9.44
To dwell, unless by maistring Heav'ns Supreame; Par Lost 9.125
The Serpents head; piteous amends, unless Par Lost 10.1032
By Prophet or by Angel, unless thou Par Reg 3.352
Unless where moral vertue is express't Par Reg 4.351
Unless there be who think not God at all, Samson 295
Unless he feel within Samson 663
Unlesse the Goddes that in rurall shrine Mask 267
Bridgewater ms 'vnless'
1673 'Unless'
1637 'Vnlesse'
Unless the strength of Heav'n, if you mean that? Mask 417
Trinity ms 'unlesse'
1637 'Vnlesse'
'Less *Philomel* will daign a Song, Penseroso 56
Unlettered
Stirs up among the loose unleter'd Hinds, Mask 174
1673 'unletter'd'
Trinity ms 'unletter'd'
Bridgewater ms 'vnlettered'
Unlibidinous
Love unlibidinous reign'd, nor jealousie Par Lost 5.449
Unlicensed
Unlicenc't from his bounds in Hell prescrib'd; Par Lost 4.909
Unlightsome
A mightie Spheare he fram'd, unlightsom first, Par Lost 7.355
Unlike
O how unlike the place from whence they fell! Par Lost 1.75
ms 'vnlike'
Entrails unlike) of Mineral and Stone, Par Lost 6.517
Thir guilt and dreaded shame; O how unlike Par Lost 9.1114
Be not unlike all others, not austere Samson 815
Horribly loud unlike the former shout. Samson 1510
Unlimited
Unlimited of manifold delights: Par Lost 4.435

Unlock
I keep, by him forbidden to unlock — Par Lost 2.852
And, as the old Swain said, she can unlock — Mask 852
1637 'unlocke'
Bridgewater ms 'vnlock'

Unlocked
I yielded, and unlock'd her all my heart, — Samson 407
La. I had not thought to have unlockt my lips — Mask 756
Trinity ms 'unlock'
Bridgewater ms 'vnlockt'

Unlooked
Unlook'd for are we fall'n, our eyes beheld — Par Reg 2.31

Unmake
Abolish thy Creation, and unmake, — Par Lost 3.163

Unmanly
Unmanly, ignominious, infamous, — Samson 417

Unmarked
Of Forrein Worlds: he through the midst unmarkt, — Par Lost 10.441
Unmarkt, unknown; but him the Baptist soon — Par Reg 1.25

Unmeasured
All perfet good unmeasur'd out, descends, — Par Lost 5.399

Unmeditated
Unmeditated, such prompt eloquence — Par Lost 5.149

Unmeet
Whose fellowship therefore unmeet for thee — Par Lost 8.442

Unmerited
Favour unmerited by me, who sought — Par Lost 12.278

Unminded
Hee after *Eve* seduc't, unminded slunk — Par Lost 10.332

Unmindful
Nor stood unmindful *Abdiel* to annoy — Par Lost 6.369
Unmindful of thir Maker, though his Spirit — Par Lost 11.611
Unmindfull of the crown that Vertue gives — Mask 9
Bridgewater ms 'vnmindfull'
1637 'Vnmindfull'
Unmindfull. Hapless they — Horace 12

Unmixed
Then shall thy Saints unmixt, and from th' impure — Par Lost 6.742
The peoples praise, if always praise unmixt? — Par Reg 3.48

Unmoulding
Fixes instead, unmoulding reasons mintage — Mask 529
Bridgewater ms 'vnmouldinge'

Unmoved
Deliberate valour breath'd, firm and unmov'd — Par Lost 1.554
ms 'vnmov'd'
Conscious of highest worth, unmov'd thus spake. — Par Lost 2.429
Into a liquid Plain, then stood unmov'd — Par Lost 4.455
Yet thus, unmovd with fear, accost him soon. — Par Lost 4.822
Among innumerable false, unmov'd, — Par Lost 5.898
Superiour and unmov'd, here onely weake — Par Lost 8.532
Pursuing, not unmov'd to *Eve* thus spake. — Par Lost 11.192
To whom our Saviour answer'd thus unmov'd. — Par Reg 3.386
To whom the Son of God unmov'd reply'd. — Par Reg 4.109

Unmuffle
Eld. Bro. Unmuffle ye faint stars, and thou fair Moon — Mask 331
Bridgewater ms 'Vnmuffle'
1637 'Vnmuffle'

Unnamed
Unnam'd in Heav'n, now plenteous, as thou seest — Par Lost 6.263
Unnam'd, undreaded, and thy self half starv'd? — Par Lost 10.595
(Things by thir names I call, though yet unnam'd) — Par Lost 12.140

Unnumbered
Swarm populous, unnumber'd as the Sands — Par Lost 2.903
Floats, as they pass, fann'd with unnumber'd plumes: — Par Lost 7.432

Unobeyed
Unworshipt, unobey'd the Throne supream — Par Lost 5.670

Unobnoxious
Unwearied, unobnoxious to be pain'd — Par Lost 6.404

Unobscured
Choose to reside, his Glory unobscur'd, — Par Lost 2.265

Unobserved
As he suppos'd, all unobserv'd, unseen. — Par Lost 4.130
Brought on his way with joy; hee unobserv'd — Par Reg 4.638

Unopposed
The highth of thy aspiring unoppos'd, — Par Lost 6.132

Unoriginal
Of unoriginal *Night* and *Chaos* wilde, — Par Lost 10.477

Unowned
Of our unowned sister. *Eld. Bro*. I do not, brother, — Mask 407
Bridgewater ms 'vn owned'

Unpaid
Knee-tribute yet unpaid, prostration vile, — Par Lost 5.782

Unpained
Against unpaind, impassive; from which evil — Par Lost 6.455

Unparalleled
Since man on earth unparallel'd! — Samson 165
A deity so unparalel'd? — Arcades 25

Unpeopled
Long after, now unpeopl'd, and untrod; — Par Lost 3.497

Unperceived
So spake the false dissembler unperceivd; — Par Lost 3.681
Not unperceav'd of *Adam*, who to *Eve*, — Par Lost 11.224

Unpierced
The open field, and where the unpierc't shade — Par Lost 4.245

Unpillowed
Leans her unpillow'd head fraught with sad fears. — Mask 355
Bridgewater ms 'vnpillow'd'
Trinity ms 'unpillow'd' ←'thoughtfull'

Unpitied
Unrespited, unpitied, unrepreevd, — Par Lost 2.185
Though I unpittied: League with you I seek, — Par Lost 4.375
Ejected, emptyed, gaz'd, unpityed, shun'd, — Par Reg 1.414

Unplausible
Baited with reasons not unplausible — Mask 162
Bridgewater ms 'vnplausible'

Unpolluted
Sit unpolluted, and th' Ethereal mould — Par Lost 2.139
The unpolluted temple of the mind, — Mask 461
Bridgewater ms 'vnpolluted'

Unpossessed
For such vast room in Nature unpossest — Par Lost 8.153

Unpractised
Unpractis'd, unprepar'd, and still to seek. — Par Lost 8.197

Unpraised
Unprais'd: for nothing lovelier can be found — Par Lost 9.232
The deed becomes unprais'd, the man at least, — Par Reg 3.103
Th' all-giver would be unthank't, would be unprais'd, — Mask 723
Bridgewater ms 'vnprais'd'

Unpredict
Will unpredict and fail me of the Throne: — Par Reg 3.395

Unpremeditated
Easie my unpremeditated Verse: — Par Lost 9.24

Unprepared
Unpractis'd, unprepar'd, and still to seek. — Par Lost 8.197

Unprevented
Comes unprevented, unimplor'd, unsought, — Par Lost 3.231

Unprincipled
Or so unprincipl'd in vertues book, — Mask 367
Bridgewater ms 'vnprincipl'd'

Unproclaimed
Warr unproclam'd. The Princely Hierarch — Par Lost 11.220

Unpronounced
Half unpronounc't, slide through my infant-lipps, — Vacation 4

Unpropped
With languish't head unpropt, — Samson 119

Unpurged
Whence in her visage round those spots, unpurg'd — Par Lost 5.419
Of human mould with grosse unpurged ear; — Arcades 73

Unpursued
All night the dreadless Angel unpursu'd — Par Lost 6.1

Unquenchable
Unquenchable, the house of woe and paine. — Par Lost 6.877
Impetuous, insolent, unquenchable; — Samson 1422

Unquiet
As through unquiet rest: he on his side — Par Lost 5.11
What thoughts in my unquiet brest are ris'n, — Par Lost 10.975

Unquilt
He with his bare wand can unthred thy joynts, — Mask 614
Trinity ms 'unthred' ←'unquilt'

Unrazored
La. As smooth as *Hebe*'s their unrazor'd lips. — Mask 290
1637 'unrazord'
Bridgewater ms 'vnrazor'd'

Unreal
Voyag'd th' unreal, vast, unbounded deep — Par Lost 10.471

Unrecorded
And unrecorded left through many an Age, — Par Reg 1.16

Unreformed
Unhumbl'd, unrepentant, unreform'd, — Par Reg 3.429

Unreined
Least from this flying Steed unrein'd, (as once — Par Lost 7.17

Unremoved
Like *Teneriff* or *Atlas* unremov'd: — Par Lost 4.987

Unrepentant
Unhumbl'd, unrepentant, unreform'd, — Par Reg 3.429

Unrepented
Shall never, unrepented, find forgiveness. — Samson 1376

Unreprieved
Unrespited, unpitied, unrepreevd, — Par Lost 2.185

Unreproved
Of conjugal attraction unreprov'd, — Par Lost 4.493
In unreproved pleasures free; — Allegro 40

Unrespited
Unrespited, unpitied, unrepreevd, — Par Lost 2.185

Unrest
As from unrest, and each the other viewing, — Par Lost 9.1052
All unconcern'd with our unrest, begins — Par Lost 11.174

Unrevoked
Hear my Decree, which unrevok't shall stand. — Par Lost 5.602

Unrighteous
Thir own both righteous and unrighteous deeds, — Par Lost 3.292

Unrivalled
Uninterrupted joy, unrivald love — Par Lost 3.68

Unsafe
And left large field, unsafe within the wind — Par Lost 6.309

Unsaid
Shall be unsaid for me: against the threats — Mask 586
Bridgewater ms 'vnsaid'

Unsavoury
The Earth to yield; unsavourie food perhaps — Par Lost 5.401
Unsavoury in th' injoyment of it self — Mask 742
1637 'Vnsavourie'
line not in Bridgewater ms

Unsay
Would highth recal high thoughts, how soon unsay — Par Lost 4.95
To say and strait unsay, pretending first — Par Lost 4.947

Unsay(*cont*)
Say and unsay, feign, flatter, or abjure? Par Reg 1.474
Unsearchable
Things else by me unsearchable, now heard Par Lost 8.10
What th' unsearchable dispose Samson 1746
Unsearched
Search through this Garden, leave unsearcht no nook, Par Lost 4.789
Unseasonable
Of somthing not unseasonable to ask Par Lost 8.201
Unseduced
Unshak'n, unseduc'd, unterrifi'd Par Lost 5.899
Unseemliest
To shame obnoxious, and unseemliest seen, Par Lost 9.1094
Unseemly
Unseemly to beare rule, which was thy part Par Lost 10.155
Unseemly falls in human eie, Samson 690
Lest I should see him forc't to things unseemly. Samson 1451
Unseen
Within unseen. Farr less abhorrd than these Par Lost 2.659
Shall dwell at ease, and up and down unseen Par Lost 2.841
With gentle penetration, though unseen, Par Lost 3.585
As he suppos'd, all unobserv'd, unseen. Par Lost 4.130
Unseen, both when we wake, and when we sleep: Par Lost 4.678
Led by her Heav'nly Maker, though unseen, Par Lost 8.485
Entrance unseen. Soon as th' unwelcome news Par Lost 10.21
He sate, and round about him saw unseen: Par Lost 10.448
That all his senses bound; *Eve*, who unseen Par Lost 11.265
Unseen amid the throng: so violence Par Lost 11.671
Unseen, and through thir habitations walks Par Lost 12.49
Unseen before in Heav'n proclaims him com, Par Lost 12.361
Sweet Echo, sweetest Nymph that liv'st unseen Mask 230
Bridgewater ms 'vnseene'
1637 'unseene'
Trinity ms 'unseene'
Som time walking not unseen Allegro 57
And missing thee, I walk unseen Penseroso 65
Or th' unseen Genius of the Wood. Penseroso 154
Unsettled
Uncertain and unsettl'd still remains, Par Reg 4.326
Unshaken
Fell not, but stand unshak'n, from within Par Lost 4.64
Unshak'n, unseduc'd, unterrifi'd Par Lost 5.899
Unshaken; nor yet staid the terror there, Par Reg 4.421
Thy firm unshak'n vertue ever brings Sonnet 15, 5
1694 'unshaken'
Unshared
Tedious, unshar'd with thee, and odious soon. Par Lost 9.880
Unshed
To blood unshed the Rivers must be turnd, Par Lost 12.176
Unshorn
Then thine, while I preserv'd these locks unshorn, Samson 1143
Listening to what unshorn *Apollo* sings Vacation 37
Unshowered
Trampling the unshowr'd Grasse with lowings loud: Nativity 215
Unsightly
That lie bestrowne unsightly and unsmooth, Par Lost 4.631
Desert and bare, unsightly, unadornd, Par Lost 7.314
To such unsightly sufferings be debas't Par Lost 11.510
Amongst the rest a small unsightly root, Mask 629
Bridgewater ms 'vnsightly'
Unskilful
Unskilful with what words to pray, let mee Par Lost 11.32
Unsleeping
All but the unsleeping eyes of God to rest, Par Lost 5.647
Unsmooth
That lie bestrowne unsightly and unsmooth, Par Lost 4.631
Unsought
Comes unprevented, unimplor'd, unsought, Par Lost 3.231
That would be woo'd, and not unsought be won, Par Lost 8.503
Thou sever not: Trial will come unsought. Par Lost 9.366
But if thou think, trial unsought may finde Par Lost 9.370
Where obvious dutie erewhile appear'd unsaught: Par Lost 10.106
To find whom at the first they found unsought: Par Reg 2.59
The Sea o'refraught would swell, & th' unsought diamonds Mask 732
Bridgewater ms 'vnsaught'
Unsound
Unsound and false; nor is it aught but just, Par Lost 6.121
Unspared
The Sithe of Time mowes down, devour unspar'd, Par Lost 10.606
Unsparing
Heaps with unsparing hand; for drink the Grape Par Lost 5.344
Unspeakable
Unspeakable desire to see, and know Par Lost 3.662
Unspeakable, who sitst above these Heavens Par Lost 5.156
Unspeakable; for who, though with the tongue Par Lost 6.297
Unsphere
With thrice great *Hermes*, or unsphear Penseroso 88
Unspied
This Garden, and no corner leave unspi'd; Par Lost 4.529
Unspoiled
Of *Atabalipa*, and yet unspoil'd Par Lost 11.409
Unspotted
His prey, nor suffer my unspotted Soule Par Lost 3.248
And thou unblemish't form of Chastity, Mask 215
Trinity ms 'unblemish't' ←'unspotted'
And from her fair unspotted side Mask 1009
line not in Bridgewater ms
Unstable
For in his faltring mouth unstable Psalm 5, 25
Unstained
Unstain'd with hostile blood, Nativity 57
Who liv'd in both, unstain'd with gold or fee, Sonnet 10, 3
Unsteady
And keep unsteddy Nature to her law, Arcades 70
Trinity ms 'unsteddie'
Unsubstantial
Her shadowy off-spring unsubstantial both, Par Reg 4.399
Unsucceeded
One over all with unsucceeded power. Par Lost 5.821
Unsuccessful
From unsuccessful charge, be not dismaid, Par Lost 10.35
Unsucked
Unsuckt of Lamb or Kid, that tend thir play. Par Lost 9.583
Unsufferable
Hell heard th' unsufferable noise, Hell saw Par Lost 6.867
That glorious Form, that Light unsufferable, Nativity 8
Unsuitable
Hard recompence, unsutable return Par Reg 3.132
Unsummed
You may as well spred out the unsun'd heaps Mask 398
Bridgewater ms 'vnsum'd'
Unsung
In *Sion* also not unsung, where stood Par Lost 1.442
ms 'vnsung'
Half yet remaines unsung, but narrower bound Par Lost 7.21
Nor past uncelebrated, nor unsung Par Lost 7.253
Unsung; or to describe Races and Games, Par Lost 9.33
Worthy t' have not remain'd so long unsung. Par Reg 1.17
Unsunned
You may as well spred out the unsun'd heaps Mask 398
Bridgewater ms 'vnsum'd'
Unsuperfluous
In unsuperfluous eeven proportion, Mask 773
Bridgewater ms 'vnsuperflous'
Unsupported
Her self, though fairest unsupported Flour, Par Lost 9.432
Unsuspect
The good befall'n him, Author unsuspect, Par Lost 9.771
Unsuspected
Found unsuspected way. There was a place, Par Lost 9.69
Unsuspicious
He unsuspitious led him; which when *Samson* Samson 1635
Unsustained
Hung drooping unsustaind, them she upstaies Par Lost 9.430
Untamed
Untam'd reluctance, and revenge though slow, Par Lost 2.337
Untaught
Vain Warr with Heav'n, and by success untaught Par Lost 2.9
Unterrified
Unterrifi'd, and like a Comet burn'd, Par Lost 2.708
Unshak'n, unseduc'd, unterrifi'd Par Lost 5.899
Unthanked
Th' all-giver would be unthank't, would be unprais'd, Mask 723
Bridgewater ms 'vnthank't'
Unthought
Befalln us unforeseen, unthought of, know Par Lost 2.821
Unthread
He with his bare wand can unthred thy joynts, Mask 614
Bridgewater ms 'vnthred'
Trinity ms 'unthred' ←'unquilt'
Unthrone
Our own right lost: him to unthrone we then Par Lost 2.231
Until
Untill their Lord himself bespake, and bid them go. Nativity 76
Untill his revolution was at stay. Another 6
1640 'Vntill'
Unto
Till thou return unto the ground, for thou Par Lost 10.206
Retir'd unto the Desert, but with arms; Par Reg 3.166
And joyn thy voice unto the Angel Quire, Nativity 27
To scorn the sordid world, and unto Heav'n aspire. Fair Inf 63
Small loss it is that thence can come unto thee, Vacation 9
Unto Jehovah, he full soon reply'd Psalm 3, 11
My King and God for unto thee I pray. Psalm 5, 4
Unto my supplication Lord Psalm 86, 17
Unto thy servant give thy strength, Psalm 86, 59
Unto the grave draws nigh. Psalm 88, 12
Untold
What shallow-searching *Fame* hath left untold; Arcades 41
Untouched
As leaves a greater store of Fruit untoucht, Par Lost 9.621
Untractable
Th' untractable Abysse, plung'd in the womb Par Lost 10.476
Untrained
Untraind in Armes, where rashness leads not on. Par Lost 12.222
Untried
Through wayes of danger by himself untri'd, Par Lost 4.934
Mean I to trie, what rash untri'd I sought, Par Lost 9.860
Ventures his filial Vertue, though untri'd, Par Reg 1.177
To whom thou untry'd seem'st fair. Me in my vow'd Horace 13
Untrod
Long after, now unpeopl'd, and untrod; Par Lost 3.497
Was difficult, by humane steps untrod; Par Reg 1.298
Now while the Heav'n by the Suns team untrod, Nativity 19

Untroubled
My droused sense, untroubl'd, though I thought — Par Lost 8.289
Our Saviour meek and with untroubl'd mind — Par Reg 4.401
Untwisting
Untwisting all the chains that ty — Allegro 143
Unused
Har. O *Baal-zebub!* can my ears unus'd — Samson 1231
Unusual
That felt unusual weight, till on dry Land — Par Lost 1.227
ms 'vnusuall'
Till an unusuall stop of sudden silence — Mask 552
1673 'unusual'
Bridgewater ms 'vnvsuall'
Unutterable
Unutterable, which the Spirit of prayer — Par Lost 11.6
Unvalued
Hath from the leaves of thy unvalu'd Book, — Shakespear 11
1632 'unvalued'
1663-4 'unvalued'
Unvanquished
Unvanquisht, easier to transact with mee — Par Lost 6.286
That wise *Minerva* wore, unconquer'd Virgin, — Mask 448
Trinity ms 'unconquer'd' ←'unvanquish't' ←'aeternall'
Unveiled
Apparent Queen unvaild her peerless light, — Par Lost 4.608
Unviolated
The pledge of my unviolated vow. — Samson 1144
Unvisited
Dwell not unvisited of Heav'ns fair Light — Par Lost 2.398
Unvoyageable
Nor this unvoyageable Gulf obscure — Par Lost 10.366
Unwakened
His wonder was to find unwak'nd *Eve* — Par Lost 5.9
Unware
Not wilfully mis-doing, but unware — Par Reg 1.225
Unwares
But all unwares with his cold-kind embrace — Fair Inf 20
Unwary
Bad influence into th' unwarie brest — Par Lost 5.695
Yet more amaz'd unwarie thus reply'd. — Par Lost 9.614
Unwarie, and too desirous, as before, — Par Lost 10.947
Nor think me so unwary or accurst — Samson 930
To inveigle and invite th' unwary sense — Mask 538
Bridgewater ms 'vnwarie'
1637 'unwarie'
Trinity ms 'unwarie'
Unwearied
Unwearied, unobnoxious to be pain'd — Par Lost 6.404
Desisting, though unwearied, up returnd — Par Lost 7.552
Unwedded
Bring the rathe Primrose that forsaken dies. — Lycidas 142
Trinity ms 'forsaken' ←'unwedded'
Unweeting
By *Eve*, though all unweeting, seconded — Par Lost 10.335
I beare thee, and unweeting have offended, — Par Lost 10.916
But contrary unweeting he fulfill'd — Par Reg 1.126
Of them that pass unweeting by the way. — Mask 539
Bridgewater ms 'vnweetinge'
For so *Apollo*, with unweeting hand — Fair Inf 23
Unweetingly
Unweetingly importun'd — Samson 1680
Unwelcome
Entrance unseen. Soon as th' unwelcome news — Par Lost 10.21
Unwholesome
Unwholsom draught: but here I feel amends, — Samson 9
Unwieldy
Gambold before them, th' unwieldy Elephant — Par Lost 4.345
Wallowing unweildie, enormous in thir Gate — Par Lost 7.411
Of wisdom, vast, unwieldy, burdensom, — Samson 54
Unwilling
Is to go hence unwilling; thou to mee — Par Lost 12.617
Unwillingly
Laborious works, unwillingly this rest — Samson 14
Unwise
To serve th' unwise, or him who hath rebelld — Par Lost 6.179
Wise or unwise, no difference, no exemption; — Par Reg 3.115
To interpose them oft, is not unwise. — Sonnet 20, 14
Unwiser
In sad event, when to the unwiser Son — Par Lost 4.716
Unwithdrawing
With such a full and unwithdrawing hand, — Mask 711
Bridgewater ms 'vnwithdraweinge'
Unwonted
Unwonted shall admire: — Horace 8
Unworshipped
Unworshipt, unobey'd the Throne supream — Par Lost 5.670
Unworthier
Th' unworthier they; whence to this day they serve. — Samson 1216
Unworthy
Cloath'd us unworthie, pitying while he judg'd; — Par Lost 10.1059
Within himself unworthie Powers to reign — Par Lost 12.91
Such favour I unworthie am voutsaft, — Par Lost 12.622
Will far be found unworthy to compare — Par Reg 4.346
Nothing dishonourable, impure, unworthy — Samson 1424
Unwounded
Our yet unwounded Enemies, or arme — Par Lost 6.466
Mess. Unwounded of his enemies he fell. — Samson 1582

Up
Stird up with Envy and Revenge, deceiv'd — Par Lost 1.35
Here swallow'd up in endless misery. — Par Lost 1.142
They heard, and were abasht, and up they sprung — Par Lost 1.331
Wav'd round the Coast, up call'd a pitchy cloud — Par Lost 1.340
For which to strive, no strife can grow up there — Par Lost 2.31
Stood up, the strongest and the fiercest Spirit — Par Lost 2.44
Up to our native seat: descent and fall — Par Lost 2.76
To less then Gods. On th' other side up rose — Par Lost 2.108
To perish rather, swallowd up and lost — Par Lost 2.149
Inclines, here to continue; and build up here — Par Lost 2.314
Will once more lift us up, in spight of Fate, — Par Lost 2.393
And hard, that out of Hell leads up to light; — Par Lost 2.433
Rend up both Rocks and Hills, and ride the Air — Par Lost 2.540
Through pain up by the roots *Thessalian* Pines, — Par Lost 2.544
Up to the fiery Concave touring high. — Par Lost 2.635
Shall dwell at ease, and up and down unseen — Par Lost 2.841
Forthwith the huge Porcullis high up drew, — Par Lost 2.874
Lies through your spacious Empire up to light, — Par Lost 2.974
The dark descent, and up to reascend, — Par Lost 3.20
Walk'd up and down alone bent on his prey, — Par Lost 3.441
Up hither like Aereal vapours flew — Par Lost 3.445
Up to the wall of Heaven a Structure high, — Par Lost 3.503
There alwayes, but drawn up to Heav'n somtimes — Par Lost 3.517
Through the calm Firmament; but up or downe — Par Lost 3.574
Volatil *Hermes*, and call up unbound — Par Lost 3.603
And wrought but malice; lifted up so high — Par Lost 4.49
Access deni'd; and over head up grew — Par Lost 4.137
The verdurous wall of paradise up sprung: — Par Lost 4.143
Thence up he flew, and on the Tree of Life — Par Lost 4.194
Of porous Earth with kindly thirst up drawn, — Par Lost 4.228
Of Alablaster, pil'd up to the Clouds, — Par Lost 4.544
Fenc'd up the verdant wall; each beauteous flour, — Par Lost 4.697
Half way up Hill this vast Sublunar Vault, — Par Lost 4.777
Blown up with high conceits ingendring pride. — Par Lost 4.809
Of force to its own likeness: up he starts — Par Lost 4.813
So started up in his own shape the Fiend. — Par Lost 4.819
High up in Heav'n, with songs to hymne his Throne, — Par Lost 4.944
The latter quick up flew, and kickt the beam; — Par Lost 4.1004
To trample thee as mire: for proof look up, — Par Lost 4.1010
If thou resist. The Fiend lookt up and knew — Par Lost 4.1013
Could not but taste. Forthwith up to the Clouds — Par Lost 5.86
Of day-spring, and the Sun, who scarce up risen — Par Lost 5.139
His praise, who out of Darkness call'd up Light. — Par Lost 5.179
That singing up to Heaven Gate ascend, — Par Lost 5.198
Vaild with his gorgeous wings, up springing light — Par Lost 5.250
All things proceed, and up to him return, — Par Lost 5.470
Till body up to spirit work, in bounds — Par Lost 5.478
Stood up, and in a flame of zeale severe — Par Lost 5.807
Ministring Spirits, traind up in Feast and Song; — Par Lost 6.167
Were ready, in a moment up they turnd — Par Lost 6.509
Part hidd'n veins diggd up (nor hath this Earth — Par Lost 6.516
Up rose the Victor Angels, and to Arms — Par Lost 6.525
Up lifting bore them in thir hands: Amaze, — Par Lost 6.646
With thy Celestial Song. Up led by thee — Par Lost 7.12
Up hither, under long obedience tri'd, — Par Lost 7.159
Up from the bottom turn'd by furious windes — Par Lost 7.213
The swelling Gourd, up stood the cornie Reed — Par Lost 7.321
Went up and waterd all the ground, and each — Par Lost 7.334
Limb'd and full grown: out of the ground up rose — Par Lost 7.456
Bore up his branching head: scarse from his mould — Par Lost 7.470
Desisting, though unwearied, up returnd — Par Lost 7.552
Up to the Heav'n of Heav'ns his high abode, — Par Lost 7.553
Answering his great Idea. Up he rode — Par Lost 7.557
Glad we return'd up to the coasts of Light — Par Lost 8.245
By quick instinctive motion up I sprung, — Par Lost 8.259
Smooth sliding without step, last led me up — Par Lost 8.302
Up hither, from among the Trees appeer'd — Par Lost 8.313
But suddenly with flesh fill'd up and heal'd: — Par Lost 8.468
Mean, or in her summd up, in her containd — Par Lost 8.473
Leads up to Heav'n, is both the way and guide; — Par Lost 8.613
So parted they, the Angel up to Heav'n — Par Lost 8.652
Serv'd up in Hall with Sewers, and Seneshals; — Par Lost 9.38
Rose up a Fountain by the Tree of Life; — Par Lost 9.73
Maeotis, up beyond the River *Ob;* — Par Lost 9.78
Of Growth, Sense, Reason, all summ'd up in Man. — Par Lost 9.113
From th' Earths great Altar send up silent praise — Par Lost 9.195
Grow up to thir provision, and more hands — Par Lost 9.623
There swallow'd up and lost, from succour farr. — Par Lost 9.642
And growing up to Godhead; which for thee — Par Lost 9.877
Encumberd, now had left them, up they rose — Par Lost 9.1051
Up into Heav'n from Paradise in haste — Par Lost 10.17
To him with swift ascent he up returnd, — Par Lost 10.224
Tost up and down, together crowded drove — Par Lost 10.287
Offended, worth your laughter, hath giv'n up — Par Lost 10.488
But up and enter now into full bliss. — Par Lost 10.503
A Grove hard by, sprung up with this thir change, — Par Lost 10.548
But on thy rould in heaps, and up the Trees — Par Lost 10.558
At random yielded up to their misrule; — Par Lost 10.628
My Hell-hounds, to lick up the draff and filth — Par Lost 10.630
For ever, and seal up his ravenous Jawes. — Par Lost 10.637
Up to the *Tropic* Crab; thence down amaine — Par Lost 10.675
Flew up, nor missd the way, by envious windes — Par Lost 11.15
Resignes him up with Heav'n and Earth renewd. — Par Lost 11.66
Where entrance up from *Eden* easiest climbes, — Par Lost 11.119
At Eev'n, which I bred up with tender hand — Par Lost 11.276
Of grassie Terfe, and pile up every Stone — Par Lost 11.324
His best of Man, and gave him up to tears — Par Lost 11.497

Up(*cont*)
Of rendring up, and patiently attend Par Lost 11.551
Shall yield up all thir vertue, all thir fame Par Lost 11.623
Sent up amain; and now the thick'nd Skie Par Lost 11.742
Broke up, shall heave the Ocean to usurp Par Lost 11.827
Will he convey up thither to sustain Par Lost 12.75
Bred up in Idol-worship; O that men Par Lost 12.115
Among them to set up his Tabernacle, Par Lost 12.247
Thir natural pravitie, by stirring up Par Lost 12.288
Up to a better Cov'nant, disciplin'd Par Lost 12.302
But say, if our deliverer up to Heav'n Par Lost 12.479
Gave up into my hands *Uzzean Job* Par Reg 1.369
For God hath justly giv'n the Nations up Par Reg 1.442
And for a time caught up to God, as once Par Reg 2.14
Rode up to Heaven, yet once again to come. Par Reg 2.17
And sayings laid up, portending strange events. Par Reg 2.104
Up to the middle Region of thick Air, Par Reg 2.117
As lightly from his grassy Couch up rose Par Reg 2.282
Up to a hill anon his steps he rear'd, Par Reg 2.285
Our Saviour lifting up his eyes beheld Par Reg 2.338
Bred up in poverty and streights at home; Par Reg 2.415
The Son of God up to a Mountain high. Par Reg 3.252
When thou stood'st up his Tempter to the pride Par Reg 3.409
Or torn up sheer: ill wast thou shrouded then, Par Reg 4.419
Clear'd up their choicest notes in bush and spray Par Reg 4.437
So saying he caught him up, and without wing Par Reg 4.541
Then by main force pull'd up, and on his shoulders bore Samson 146
Up to the Hill by *Hebron*, seat of Giants old, Samson 148
Like whom the Gentiles feign to bear up Heav'n. Samson 150
Shut up from outward light Samson 160
How could I once look up, or heave the head, Samson 197
Gave up my fort of silence to a Woman. Samson 236
Abstemious I grew up and thriv'd amain; Samson 637
Grow up and perish, as the summer flie, Samson 676
Quite from his people, and delivered up Samson 1158
Went up with armed powers thee only seeking, Samson 1190
As a league-breaker gave up bound, presum'd Samson 1209
But to thir Masters gave me up for nought, Samson 1215
Fear I incurable; bring up thy van, Samson 1234
And with malitious counsel stir them up Samson 1251
Up to the highth, whether to hold or break; Samson 1349
Rode up in flames after his message told Samson 1433
Chor. Fathers are wont to lay up for thir Sons, Samson 1485
His strength again to grow up with his hair Samson 1496
Strive to keep up a frail, and Feaverish being Mask 8
Bridgewater ms 'vp'
Whom therfore she brought up and *Comus* nam'd, Mask 58
Bridgewater ms 'vp'
Whom thrift keeps up about his Country gear, Mask 167
Bridgewater ms 'vp'
Stirs up among the loose unleter'd Hinds, Mask 174
Bridgewater ms 'vp'
In thy dark lantern thus close up the Stars, Mask 197
line not in Bridgewater ms
Or if your influence be quite damm'd up Mask 336
Bridgewater ms 'vp'
The wonted roar was up amidst the Woods, Mask 549
Bridgewater ms 'vp'
May never this just sword be lifted up, Mask 601
Bridgewater ms 'vp'
I purs't it up, but little reck'ning made, Mask 642
Bridgewater ms 'vp'
Your nervs are all chain'd up in Alablaster, Mask 660
Bridgewater ms 'vp'
Is of such power to stir up joy as this, Mask 677
Bridgewater ms 'vp'
The Sea o'refraught would swell, & th' unsought diamonds Mask 732
Trinity ms 'swell' ← 'heave her waters up above the shoare'
Held up their pearled wrists and took her in, Mask 834
Bridgewater ms 'vp'
Up in the broad fields of the sky: Mask 979
Bridgewater ms 'vp'
1637 'Vp'
Or call up him that left half told Penseroso 109
Hath lockt up mortal sense, then listen I Arcades 62
Trinity ms 'lockt up' ← 'chain'd'
The hungry Sheep look up, and are not fed, Lycidas 125
Make up full consort to th' Angelike symphony. Nativity 132
So mounting up in ycie-pearled carr, Fair Inf 15
Took up, and in fit place did reinstall? Fair Inf 46
The daintest dishes shall be serv'd up last. Vacation 14
Soon swallow'd up in dark and long out-living night. Passion 7
That whirl'd the Prophet up at *Chebar* flood, Passion 37
Take up a weeping on the Mountains wilde, Passion 51
Pluck't up by som unheedy swain, Winchester 38
New shot up from vernall showr; Winchester 40
And that he had tane up his latest Inne, Carrier 13
That labour up the Hill of heav'nly Truth, Sonnet 9, 4
Follow'd thee up to joy and bliss for ever. Sonnet 14, 8
And azure wings, that up they flew so drest, Sonnet 14, 11
Up to the Realm of peace & Joy for ever, Sonnet 14, Tr. ms 41.08
Of heart or hope; but still bear vp and steer Sonnet 22, 8
1694 'up'
Trinity ms 'bear vp and' ← 'attend to'
On us lift up the light Psalm 4, 29
Lift up the favour of thy count'nance bright. Psalm 4, 30
And I here pent up thus. Psalm 88, 36
And *up to thee* my praier *doth hie* Psalm 88, 55

Upbore
Thir march was, and the passive Air upbore Par Lost 6.72
From his uneasie station, and upbore Par Reg 4.584
Upborne
Upborn with indefatigable wings Par Lost 2.408
Or one short sigh of humane breath, up-borne Par Lost 11.147
Upbraid
Yet leudly dar'st our ministring upbraid. Par Lost 6.182
Her own transgressions, to upbraid me mine? Samson 820
Upbraided
Upbraided none; nor was his service hard. Par Lost 4.45
And am I now upbraided, as the cause Par Lost 9.1168
Up-grown
So standing, moving, or to highth upgrown Par Lost 9.677
O're-shadow her: this man born and now up-grown, Par Reg 1.140
Upheave
Emergent, and thir broad bare backs upheave Par Lost 7.286
Upheaved
Behemoth biggest born of Earth upheav'd Par Lost 7.471
Upheld
Whether upheld by strength, or Chance, or Fate, Par Lost 1.133
Sat on his Throne, upheld by old repute, Par Lost 1.639
Upheld by me, yet once more he shall stand Par Lost 3.178
By me upheld, that he may know how frail Par Lost 3.180
Taste after taste upheld with kindliest change, Par Lost 5.336
Then to advise how warr may best, upheld, Sonnet 17, 7
1694 'be upheld'
Uphillward
Right onward. What supports me dost thou ask? Sonnet 22, 9
Trinity ms 'Right onward' ← 'Vphillward'
Uphold
And fainting spirits uphold. Samson 666
Of men conspiring to uphold thir state Samson 892
Uphung
The idle spear and shield were high up hung; Nativity 55
Upland
The up-land Hamlets will invite, Allegro 92
Uplift
With Head up-lift above the wave, and Eyes Par Lost 1.193
ms 'uplift'
They shall up lift thee, lest at any time Par Reg 4.558
Uplifted
Till, as a signal giv'n, th' uplifted Spear Par Lost 1.347
Thus high uplifted beyond hope, aspires Par Lost 2.7
Uplifted spurns the ground, thence many a League Par Lost 2.929
Uplifted imminent one stroke they aim'd Par Lost 6.317
Uplifted, in Paternal Glorie rode Par Lost 7.219
1669 'Up lifted'
Uplifted; and secure with beaked prow Par Lost 11.746
Then with uplifted hands, and eyes devout, Par Lost 11.863
Their loud up-lifted Angel trumpets blow, Musick 11
Trinity ms 'up-lifted' ← 'uplifted' ← 'high lifted'
Trinity ms 'up-lifted' ← 'uplifted' ← 'high lifted' ← 'unsa', ms defective
Up-lock
And here though grief my feeble hands up-lock, Passion 45
1673 'up lock'
Upon
Upon the wing, as when men wont to watch Par Lost 1.332
ms 'Vpon'
One day upon our heads; while we perhaps Par Lost 2.178
Upon the wing, or in swift Race contend, Par Lost 2.529
With ruin upon ruin, rout on rout, Par Lost 2.995
Pursuing. I upon my Frontieres here Par Lost 2.998
Upon his own rebellious head. And now Par Lost 3.86
Much less that durst upon his own head draw Par Lost 3.220
Mean while upon the firm opacous Globe Par Lost 3.418
Upon himself; horror and doubt distract Par Lost 4.18
Upon the rapid current, which through veins Par Lost 4.227
Conferrd upon us, and Dominion giv'n Par Lost 4.430
Upon her Center pois'd, when on a day Par Lost 5.579
Upon confusion rose: and now all Heav'n Par Lost 6.669
Upon his enemies, and to declare Par Lost 6.677
Gird on, and Sword upon thy puissant Thigh; Par Lost 6.714
Whose Seed is in her self upon the Earth. Par Lost 7.312
Upon the Earth, and man to till the ground Par Lost 7.332
But us he sends upon his high behests Par Lost 8.238
Twilight upon the Earth, short Arbiter Par Lost 9.50
And force upon free will hath here no place. Par Lost 9.1174
Upon thy Belly groveling thou shalt goe, Par Lost 10.177
Hovering upon the Waters; what they met Par Lost 10.285
Upon the *Cronian* Sea, together drive Par Lost 10.290
Upon her Husband, saw thir shame that sought Par Lost 10.336
Mine own that bide upon me, all from mee Par Lost 10.738
Instead shall double ours upon our heads. Par Lost 10.1040
Upon thir Tongues a various Spirit to rase Par Lost 12.53
A mightie Nation, and upon him showre Par Lost 12.124
Upon the Temple it self: at last they seise Par Lost 12.356
Working through love, upon thir hearts shall write, Par Lost 12.489
Upon my head, long the decrees of Heav'n Par Reg 1.55
Full weight must be transferr'd upon my head. Par Reg 1.267
To live upon thir tongues and be thir talk, Par Reg 3.55
To sit upon thy Father *David*'s Throne; Par Reg 3.153
So Satan, whom repulse upon repulse Par Reg 4.21
But rush upon me thronging, and present Samson 21
Let us not break in upon him; Samson 116
Are come upon him his deserts? yet why? Samson 205
To set upon them, what advantag'd best; Samson 255

Upon(*cont*)
To gloss upon, and censuring, frown or smile? Samson 948
Of infamy upon my name denounc't? Samson 968
Conferr'd upon me, for the piety Samson 993
Sams. Go baffl'd coward, lest I run upon thee, Samson 1237
Upon thir heads and on his own he pull'd. Samson 1589
Upon the heads of all who sate beneath, Samson 1652
Thir own destruction to come speedy upon them. Samson 1681
This Nymph that gaz'd upon his clustring locks, Mask 54
Bridgewater ms 'vpon'
How sweetly did they float upon the wings Mask 249
Bridgewater ms 'vpon'
Best draw, and stand upon our guard. *Eld. Bro*. Ile hallow, Mask 487
Bridgewater ms 'vpon'
I sate me down to watch upon a bank Mask 543
Bridgewater ms 'vpon'
To meditate my rural minstrelsie, Mask 547
1673 'meditate upon'
And stole upon the Air, that even Silence Mask 557
Bridgewater ms 'vpon'
And first behold this cordial Julep here Mask 672
Trinity ms 'first behold' ←'looke upon'
To gaze upon the Sun with shameless brows. Mask 736
Bridgewater ms 'vpon'
Now heaps upon som few with vast excess, Mask 771
Bridgewater ms 'vpon'
Upon thy streams with wily glance, Mask 884
1637 'Vpon'
Bridgewater ms 'vpon'
Thrice upon thy fingers tip, Mask 914
Bridgewater ms 'vpon'
Thrice upon thy rubied lip, Mask 915
Bridgewater ms 'vpon'
And here and there thy banks upon Mask 936
Bridgewater ms 'vpon'
& may upon any needfull accident Mask Tr. ms 16.55
'upon' ←'on'
& good heaven cast his best regard upon us Mask Tr. ms 21.32
where grows the right-borne gold upon his native tree Mask Tr. ms 27.08
Have sate to wonder at, and gaze upon: Arcades 43
Trinity ms defective here
That sit upon the nine enfolded Sphears, Arcades 64
He must not flote upon his watry bear Lycidas 12
For we were nurst upon the self-same hill, Lycidas 23
See how from far upon the Eastern rode Nativity 22
Should look so neer upon her foul deformities. Nativity 44
His raign of peace upon the earth began: Nativity 63
Pillows his chin upon an Orient wave, Nativity 231
The Faiery Ladies daunc't upon the hearth; Vacation 60
Upon your beds, each one, Psalm 4, 21
Upon me: cause at length to cease Psalm 7, 34
And think'st upon him; or of man begot Psalm 8, 13
Upon the man of thy right hand Psalm 80, 69
Upon the Son of Man, whom thou Psalm 80, 71
Shall call upon thy Name. Psalm 80, 76
As dung upon the plain. Psalm 83, 40
Thou break'st upon me all thy waves, Psalm 88, 31

Upper
'Twixt upper, nether, and surrounding Fires; Par Lost 1.346
Flown to the upper World; the rest were all Par Lost 10.422
Of richest texture spred, at th' upper end Par Lost 10.446

Upraise
In our Confusion, and our Joy upraise Par Lost 2.372

Upraised
And thus with peaceful words uprais'd her soon. Par Lost 10.946
And to our high-rais'd phantasie present, Musick 5
Trinity ms 'high-rays'd' ←'high raysd' ←'up rays'd' ←'high rays'd'

Upreared
Of Trumpets loud and Clarions be upreard Par Lost 1.532
ms 'uprear'd'

Upright
Before all Temples th' upright heart and pure, Par Lost 1.18
Forthwith upright he rears from off the Pool Par Lost 1.221
With upright wing against a higher foe. Par Lost 2.72
As when thou stoodst in Heav'n upright and pure; Par Lost 4.837
Bristl'd with upright beams innumerable Par Lost 6.82
Thy malice into thousands, once upright Par Lost 6.270
They shew us when our foes walk not upright. Par Lost 6.627
His Stature, and upright with Front serene Par Lost 7.509
Thir happiness, and persevere upright. Par Lost 7.632
As thitherward endevoring, and upright Par Lost 8.260
There stand, if thou wilt stand; to stand upright Par Reg 4.551
Whoever tasted, lost his upright shape, Mask 52
Bridgewater ms 'vpright'
For the Lord knows th' upright way of the just, Psalm 1, 15
Jehovah judgeth most upright Psalm 7, 29
Saves th' upright of Heart at last. Psalm 7, 42

Uprightness
In his uprightness answer thus returnd. Par Lost 3.693

Uproar
In whirlwind; Hell scarce holds the wilde uproar. Par Lost 2.541
Confusion heard his voice, and wilde uproar Par Lost 3.710
To this uproar; horrid confusion heapt Par Lost 6.668
My journey strange, with clamorous uproare Par Lost 10.479

Uprolled
Hasted with glad precipitance, uprowld Par Lost 7.291

Uprooted
At his command the uprooted Hills retir'd Par Lost 6.781

Uprose
As lightly from his grassy Couch up rose Par Reg 2.282

Upsent
At which the universal Host upsent Par Lost 1.541

Upsprung
Pasturing at once, and in broad Herds upsprung. Par Lost 7.462

Upstand
muse a vain thing, the Kings of th' earth upstand Psalm 2, 2

Upstart
A race of upstart Creatures, to supply Par Lost 2.834
And upstart Passions catch the Government Par Lost 12.88

Upstayed
His massie Spear upstaid; as if on Earth Par Lost 6.195

Upstays
Hung drooping unsustaind, them she upstaies Par Lost 9.430

Upstood
He sat; and in th' assembly next upstood Par Lost 6.446

Uptore
Betook them, and the neighbouring Hills uptore; Par Lost 6.663

Upturn
And *Thrascias* rend the Woods and Seas upturn; Par Lost 10.700

Upturned
So sented the grim Feature, and upturn'd Par Lost 10.279

Upturns
With adverse blast up-turns them from the South Par Lost 10.701
Up turns it by the roots, Psalm 80, 54

Upward
Dagon his Name, Sea Monster, upward Man Par Lost 1.462
Springs upward like a Pyramid of fire Par Lost 2.1013
Shot upward still direct, whence no way round Par Lost 3.618
Flew upward, spirited with various forms, Par Lost 3.717
The bottom of the Mountains upward turn'd, Par Lost 6.649
And the slope Sun his upward beam Mask 98
Bridgewater ms 'vpward'
And *upward* to that river *wide* Psalm 80, 47

Upwept
Unwept, and welter to the parching wind, Lycidas 13

Upwhirled
The sport of Winds: all these upwhirld aloft Par Lost 3.493

Ur
Ur of *Chaldaea*, passing now the Ford Par Lost 12.130

Urania
Descend from Heav'n *Urania*, by that name Par Lost 7.1
Urania, and fit audience find, though few. Par Lost 7.31

Urchin
Helping all urchin blasts, and ill luck signes Mask 845
Bridgewater ms 'vrchin'

Urge
By Numbers that have name. But this I urge, Par Lost 8.114
Of my foes that urge like fire; Psalm 7, 21

Urged
As not behind in hate; if what was urg'd Par Lost 2.120
Of hard contents, and full of force urg'd home, Par Lost 6.622
Urg'd them behind; headlong themselves they threw Par Lost 6.864
Of that alluring fruit, urg'd me so keene. Par Lost 9.588
At the sad Sentence rigorously urg'd, Par Lost 11.109
And urg'd me hard with doings, which not will Par Reg 1.469
From intimate impulse, and therefore urg'd Samson 223
Her husband, how far urg'd his patience bears, Samson 755
Sollicited, commanded, threatn'd, urg'd, Samson 852
And urg'd them on with mad desire Samson 1677

Urges
Still urges, and a fiery Deluge, fed Par Lost 1.68
And short retirement urges sweet returne. Par Lost 9.250

Uriel
Th' Arch-Angel *Uriel*, one of the seav'n Par Lost 3.648
Uriel, for thou of those seav'n Spirits that stand Par Lost 3.654
Uriel, though Regent of the Sun, and held Par Lost 3.690
Uriel once warnd; whose eye pursu'd him down Par Lost 4.125
Thither came *Uriel*, gliding through the Eeven Par Lost 4.555
Uriel, no wonder if thy perfet sight, Par Lost 4.577
So promis'd hee, and *Uriel* to his charge Par Lost 4.589
Uriel and *Raphael* his vaunting foe, Par Lost 6.363
Since *Uriel* Regent of the Sun descri'd Par Lost 9.60

Urim
Of radiant *Urim*, work divinely wrought, Par Lost 6.761
Urim and *Thummim*, those oraculous gems Par Reg 3.14

Urn
With lucky words favour my destin'd Urn, Lycidas 20
1638 'urn'
Trinity ms 'urne'

Urns
Repairing, in thir gold'n Urns draw Light, Par Lost 7.365
In Urns, and Altars round, Nativity 192

Us
Restore us, and regain the blissful Seat, Par Lost 1.5
Hath lost us Heav'n, and all this mighty Host Par Lost 1.136
Have left us this our spirit and strength intire Par Lost 1.146
Shot after us in storm, oreblown hath laid Par Lost 1.172
Of Heav'n receiv'd us falling, and the Thunder, Par Lost 1.174
Let us not slip th' occasion, whether scorn, Par Lost 1.178
Casts pale and dreadful? Thither let us tend Par Lost 1.183
Here for his envy, will not drive us hence: Par Lost 1.260
And call them not to share with us their part Par Lost 1.267
Th' advantage, and descending tread us down Par Lost 1.327
Transfix us to the bottom of this Gulfe. Par Lost 1.329

Us(*cont*)

At length from us may find, who overcomes	Par Lost 1.648
Could have assur'd us; and by what best way,	Par Lost 2.40
By our delay? no, let us rather choose	Par Lost 2.60
To us is adverse. Who but felt of late	Par Lost 2.77
Insulting, and pursu'd us through the Deep,	Par Lost 2.79
Must exercise us without hope of end	Par Lost 2.89
Calls us to Penance? More destroy'd then thus	Par Lost 2.92
Will either quite consume us, and reduce	Par Lost 2.96
And that must end us, that must be our cure,	Par Lost 2.145
The Deep to shelter us? this Hell then seem'd	Par Lost 2.167
And plunge us in the flames? or from above	Par Lost 2.172
His red right hand to plague us? what if all	Par Lost 2.174
Subdues us, and Omnipotent Decree,	Par Lost 2.198
Not mind us not offending, satisfi'd	Par Lost 2.212
The latter: for what place can be for us	Par Lost 2.235
To whom we hate. Let us not then pursue	Par Lost 2.249
Us here, as with his Golden those in Heav'n.	Par Lost 2.328
Warr hath determin'd us, and foild with loss	Par Lost 2.330
To us enslav'd, but custody severe,	Par Lost 2.333
To be created like to us, though less	Par Lost 2.349
Thither let us bend all our thoughts, to learn	Par Lost 2.354
Hurl'd headlong to partake with us, shall curse	Par Lost 2.374
Will once more lift us up, in spight of Fate,	Par Lost 2.393
Seis'd us, though undismaid: long is the way	Par Lost 2.432
Outrageous to devour, immures us round	Par Lost 2.435
Barr'd over us prohibit all egress.	Par Lost 2.437
Deliverance for us all: this enterprize	Par Lost 2.465
As if (which might induce us to accord)	Par Lost 2.503
Befalln us unforeseen, unthought of, know	Par Lost 2.821
Fell with us from on high: from them I go	Par Lost 2.826
Th' Arch-chimic Sun so farr from us remote	Par Lost 3.609
Of us out-cast, exil'd, his new delight,	Par Lost 4.106
That made us, and for us this ample World	Par Lost 4.413
That rais'd us from the dust and plac't us here	Par Lost 4.416
From us no other service then to keep	Par Lost 4.420
Conferrd upon us, and Dominion giv'n	Par Lost 4.430
Earth, Aire, and Sea. Then let us not think hard	Par Lost 4.432
But let us ever praise him, and extoll	Par Lost 4.436
Mind us of like repose, since God hath set	Par Lost 4.612
Mean while, as Nature wills, Night bids us rest.	Par Lost 4.633
For us too large, where thy abundance wants	Par Lost 4.730
But thou hast promis'd from us two a Race	Par Lost 4.732
To fill the Earth, who shall with us extoll	Par Lost 4.733
To him who sent us, whose charge is to keep	Par Lost 4.842
Will save us trial what the least can doe	Par Lost 4.855
His will who bound us? let him surer barr	Par Lost 4.897
Calls us, we lose the prime, to mark how spring	Par Lost 5.21
By us oft seen; his dewie locks distill'd	Par Lost 5.56
And let us to our fresh imployments rise	Par Lost 5.125
To us invisible or dimly seen	Par Lost 5.157
To give us onely good; and if the night	Par Lost 5.206
To us perhaps he brings, and will voutsafe	Par Lost 5.312
More fruitful, which instructs us not to spare.	Par Lost 5.320
To want, and honour these, voutsafe with us	Par Lost 5.365
To us for food and for delight hath caus'd	Par Lost 5.400
Who formd us from the dust, and plac'd us here	Par Lost 5.516
In us who serve, new Counsels, to debate	Par Lost 5.681
Neerly it now concernes us to be sure	Par Lost 5.721
Let us advise, and to this hazard draw	Par Lost 5.729
All Power, and us eclipst under the name	Par Lost 5.776
Receive him coming to receive from us	Par Lost 5.781
Our minds and teach us to cast off this Yoke?	Par Lost 5.786
Law and Edict on us, who without law	Par Lost 5.798
To make us less, bent rather to exalt	Par Lost 5.829
Know none before us, self-begot, self-rais'd	Par Lost 5.860
Shall teach us highest deeds, by proof to try	Par Lost 5.865
In the mid way: though strange to us it seemd	Par Lost 6.91
Against us from about his Throne, and judg'd	Par Lost 6.426
Sufficient to subdue us to his will,	Par Lost 6.427
May serve to better us, and worse our foes,	Par Lost 6.440
Or equal what between us made the odds,	Par Lost 6.441
Which of us who beholds the bright surface	Par Lost 6.472
Shall yield us pregnant with infernal flame,	Par Lost 6.483
Whom fled we thought, will save us long pursuit	Par Lost 6.538
That all may see who hate us, how we seek	Par Lost 6.559
With hideous orifice gap't on us wide,	Par Lost 6.577
They shew us when our foes walk not upright.	Par Lost 6.627
Us timely of what might else have bin our loss,	Par Lost 7.74
What may no less perhaps availe us known,	Par Lost 7.85
Of Deitie supream, us dispossest,	Par Lost 7.142
Let us make now Man in our image, Man	Par Lost 7.519
And not molest us, unless we our selves	Par Lost 8.186
That which before us lies in daily life,	Par Lost 8.193
And renders us in things that most concerne	Par Lost 8.196
Therefore from this high pitch let us descend	Par Lost 8.198
But us he sends upon his high behests	Par Lost 8.238
Union of Mind, or in us both one Soule;	Par Lost 8.604
Us happie, and without Love no happiness.	Par Lost 8.621
Are his Created, or to spite us more,	Par Lost 9.147
Whom us the more to spite his Maker rais'd	Par Lost 9.177
Aid us, the work under our labour grows,	Par Lost 9.208
Let us divide our labours, thou where choice	Par Lost 9.214
God hath assign'd us, nor of me shalt pass	Par Lost 9.231
Labour, as to debarr us when we need	Par Lost 9.236
He made us, and delight to Reason joyn'd.	Par Lost 9.243
Assist us: But if much converse perhaps	Par Lost 9.247
What hath bin warn'd us, what malicious Foe	Par Lost 9.253

Us(*cont*)

Despairing, seeks to work us woe and shame	Par Lost 9.255
His wish and best advantage, us asunder,	Par Lost 9.258
Hopeless to circumvent us joynd, where each	Par Lost 9.259
Enjoy'd by us excites his envie more;	Par Lost 9.264
From thee alone, which on us both at once	Par Lost 9.303
Tempting affronts us with his foul esteem	Par Lost 9.328
By us? who rather double honour gaine	Par Lost 9.332
Let us not then suspect our happie State	Par Lost 9.337
Us both securer then thus warnd thou seemst,	Par Lost 9.371
May finde us both perhaps farr less prepar'd,	Par Lost 9.381
What hither brought us, hate, not love, nor hope	Par Lost 9.475
To us, in such aboundance lies our choice,	Par Lost 9.620
Conceales not from us, naming thee the Tree	Par Lost 9.751
Forbids us then to taste, but his forbidding	Par Lost 9.753
Forbids us good, forbids us to be wise?	Par Lost 9.759
Bind us with after-bands, what profits then	Par Lost 9.761
Irrational till then. For us alone	Par Lost 9.766
Was death invented? or to us deni'd	Par Lost 9.767
May joyne us, equal Joy, as equal Love;	Par Lost 9.882
Disjoyne us, and I then too late renounce	Par Lost 9.884
To us, as likely tasting to attaine	Par Lost 9.935
Us his prime Creatures, dignifi'd so high,	Par Lost 9.940
For us created, needs with us must faile,	Par Lost 9.942
Us to abolish, least the Adversary	Par Lost 9.947
Shall separate us, linkt in Love so deare,	Par Lost 9.970
In things to us forbidden, it might be wish'd,	Par Lost 9.1025
But come, so well refresh't, now let us play,	Par Lost 9.1027
Which leaves us naked thus, of Honour void,	Par Lost 9.1074
But let us now, as in bad plight, devise	Par Lost 9.1091
There sit not, and reproach us as unclean,	Par Lost 9.1098
No ground of enmitie between us known,	Par Lost 9.1151
For us his ofspring deare? It cannot be	Par Lost 10.238
Impassable, Impervious, let us try	Par Lost 10.254
Such fatal consequence unites us three:	Par Lost 10.364
Hell could no longer hold us in her bounds,	Par Lost 10.365
Within Hell Gates till now, thou us impow'rd	Par Lost 10.369
To Sin and Death a prey, and so to us,	Par Lost 10.490
Between us two let there be peace, both joyning,	Par Lost 10.924
Against a Foe by doom express assign'd us,	Par Lost 10.926
But rise, let us no more contend, nor blame	Par Lost 10.958
If care of our descent perplex us most,	Par Lost 10.979
So Death shall be deceav'd his glut, and with us two	Par Lost 10.990
From what we fear for both, let us make short,	Par Lost 10.1000
Let us seek Death, or he not found, supply	Par Lost 10.1001
So snatcht will not exempt us from the paine	Par Lost 10.1025
To make death in us live: Then let us seek	Par Lost 10.1028
Against us this deceit: to crush his head	Par Lost 10.1035
That cuts us off from hope, and savours onely	Par Lost 10.1043
Or Heat should injure us, his timely care	Par Lost 10.1057
Cloath'd us unworthie, pitying while he judg'd;	Par Lost 10.1059
And teach us further by what means to shun	Par Lost 10.1062
To shew us in this Mountain, while the Winds	Par Lost 10.1065
Of these fair spreading Trees; which bids us seek	Par Lost 10.1067
Hee will instruct us praying, and of Grace	Par Lost 10.1081
Repairing where he judg'd us, prostrate fall	Par Lost 10.1087
But let us call to Synod all the Blest	Par Lost 11.67
O Sons, like one of us Man is become	Par Lost 11.84
But that from us ought should ascend to Heav'n	Par Lost 11.143
To labour calls us now with sweat impos'd,	Par Lost 11.172
Her rosie progress smiling; let us forth,	Par Lost 11.175
Here let us live, though in fall'n state, content.	Par Lost 11.180
O *Eve*, some furder change awaits us nigh,	Par Lost 11.193
Us haply too secure of our discharge	Par Lost 11.196
Of us will soon determin, or impose	Par Lost 11.227
That must be mortal to us both. O flours,	Par Lost 11.273
And in performing end us; what besides	Par Lost 11.300
Nor knowing us nor known: and if by prayer	Par Lost 11.307
To be thus wrested from us? rather why	Par Lost 11.503
Obtruded on us thus? who if we knew	Par Lost 11.504
He gave us onely over Beast, Fish, Fowl	Par Lost 12.67
Let us descend now therefore from this top	Par Lost 12.588
And now too soon for us the circling hours	Par Reg 1.57
When his fierce thunder drove us to the deep;	Par Reg 1.90
What happ'ns new; Fame also finds us out.	Par Reg 1.334
So shalt thou save thy self and us relieve	Par Reg 1.344
Hath rapt him from us? will he now retire	Par Reg 2.40
But let us wait; thus far he hath perform'd,	Par Reg 2.49
Sent his Anointed, and to us reveal'd him,	Par Reg 2.50
Let us be glad of this, and all our fears	Par Reg 2.53
Mock us with his blest sight, then snatch him hence,	Par Reg 2.56
Is ris'n to invade us, who no less	Par Reg 2.127
From us his foes pronounc't glory he exacts.	Par Reg 3.120
That rather *Greece* from us these Arts deriv'd;	Par Reg 4.338
Let us not break in upon him;	Samson 116
Chor. Hee speaks, let us draw nigh. Matchless in might,	Samson 178
Who made our Laws to bind us, not himself,	Samson 309
But God hath set before us, to return thee	Samson 517
Or of him bringing to us some glad news?	Samson 1444
Cho. That hope would much rejoyce us to partake	Samson 1455
The sufferers then will scarce molest us here,	Samson 1525
Man. Tell us the sum, the circumstance defer.	Samson 1557
Are in confusion, give us if thou canst,	Samson 1593
And what may quiet us in a death so noble.	Samson 1724
Let us go find the body where it lies	Samson 1725
(*Gaza* is not in plight to say us nay)	Samson 1729
Com let us our rights begin,	Mask 125
Bridgewater ms 'vs'	

Us(*cont*)
Us thy vow'd Priests, till utmost end Mask 136
Bridgewater ms 'vs'
1637 'Vs'
Of som clay habitation visit us Mask 339
Bridgewater ms 'vs'
Either som one like us night-founder'd here, Mask 483
Bridgewater ms 'vs'
Defence is a good cause, and Heav'n be for us. Mask 489
Bridgewater ms 'vs'
And earths base built on stubble. But com let's on. Mask 599
Bridgewater ms 'lets'
Trinity ms 'lets'
And som good angel bear a sheild before us. Mask 658
Bridgewater ms 'vs'
Listen and appear to us Mask 867
Bridgewater ms 'vs'
Com Lady while Heaven lends us grace, Mask 938
Bridgewater ms 'vs'
Let us fly this cursed place, Mask 939
Bridgewater ms 'vs'
Lest the Sorcerer us intice Mask 940
Bridgewater ms 'vs'
Com let us haste, the Stars grow high, Mask 956
Bridgewater ms 'vs'
& good heaven cast his best regard upon us Mask Tr. ms 21.32
Towred Cities please us then, Allegro 117
Whose lustre leads us, and for her most fit, Arcades 76
Bring your Flocks, and live with us, Arcades 103
And with his Father work us a perpetual peace. Nativity 7
He laid aside; and here with us to be, Nativity 12
And chose with us a darksom House of mortal Clay. Nativity 14
So both himself and us to glorifie: Nativity 154
Let us with a gladsom mind Psalm 136, 1
Let us blaze his Name abroad, Psalm 136, 5
O let us his praises tell, Psalm 136, 9
Beheld us in our misery. Psalm 136, 78
And freed us from the slavery Psalm 136, 81
Let us therfore warble forth Psalm 136, 89
And why from us so quickly thou didst take thy flight. Fair Inf 42
Amongst us here below to hide thy nectar'd head. Fair Inf 49
And cam'st again to visit us once more? Fair Inf 52
To bless us with thy heav'n-lov'd innocence, Fair Inf 65
To stand 'twixt us and our deserved smart Fair Inf 69
Which he for us did freely undergo. Passion 12
And Joy shall overtake us as a flood, On Time 13
Now mourn, and if sad share with us to bear Circum 6
Enter'd the world, now bleeds to give us ease; Circum 11
High thron'd in secret bliss, for us frail dust Circum 19
To his celestial consort us unite, Musick 27
snatch us from earth a while Musick Tr. ms 4.07
us of our selves & native woes beguile Musick Tr. ms 4.08
Dost make us Marble with too much conceaving; Shakespear 14
Rest that gives all men life, gave him his death, Another 11
1640, 1657 'all us'
Cries the stall-reader, bless us! what a word on Sonnet 11, 5
Of Death, call'd Life; which us from Life doth sever. Sonnet 14, 4
Trinity ms 'us' ←'man'
Helpe us to save free Conscience from the paw Sonnet 16, 13
What neat repast shall feast us, light and choice, Sonnet 20, 9
And ride us with a classic Hierarchy Forcers 7
Let us break off, say they, by strength of hand Psalm 2, 6
Their bonds, and cast from us, no more to wear, Psalm 2, 7
Who yet will shew us good? Psalm 4, 26
On us lift up the light Psalm 4, 29
To save us by thy might. Psalm 80, 12
Turn us again, *thy grace divine* Psalm 80, 13
To us O God *vouchsafe;* Psalm 80, 14
Cause thou thy face on us to shine Psalm 80, 15
A strife thou mak'st us *and a prey* Psalm 80, 25
And flouts at us they throw Psalm 80, 28
Return us, *and thy grace divine*, Psalm 80, 29
Cause thou thy face on us to shine, Psalm 80, 31
Behold *us, but without a frown*, Psalm 80, 59
Quick'n us thou, then *gladly* wee Psalm 80, 75
Return us, *and thy grace divine* Psalm 80, 77
Cause thou thy face on us to shine, Psalm 80, 79
Come let us cut them off say they, Psalm 83, 13
Turn us, and us restore, Psalm 85, 14
Toward us, *and chide no more*. Psalm 85, 16
From age to age on us? Psalm 85, 20
And us again revive, Psalm 85, 22
Cause us to see thy goodness Lord, Psalm 85, 25
To us thy mercy shew Psalm 85, 26
Thy saving health to us afford Psalm 85, 27
And life in us renew. Psalm 85, 28

Usage
Sam. Such usage as your honourable Lords Samson 1108
For gentle usage, and soft delicacy? Mask 681
line not in Bridgewater ms

Use
To worst abuse, or to thir meanest use. Par Lost 4.204
All things to mans delightful use; the roofe Par Lost 4.692
All seasons, ripe for use hangs on the stalk; Par Lost 5.323
And God made two great Lights, great for thir use Par Lost 7.346
Greater so manifold to this one use, Par Lost 8.29
From use, obscure and suttle, but to know Par Lost 8.192
The Gods are first, and that advantage use Par Lost 9.718

Use(*cont*)
Thy praise hee also who forbids thy use, Par Lost 9.750
Which might supplie the Sun: such Fire to use, Par Lost 10.1078
And who withholds my pow'r that right to use? Par Reg 2.380
I see thou know'st what is of use to know, Par Reg 3.7
Means I must use thou say'st, prediction else Par Reg 3.394
Chor. O madness, to think use of strongest wines Samson 553
How wouldst thou use me now, blind, and thereby Samson 941
Sam. I know no Spells, use no forbidden Arts; Samson 1139
To use him further yet in some great service, Samson 1499
And bad me keep it as of sovran use Mask 639
Bridgewater ms 'vse'
Were it not better don as others use, Lycidas 67
1638 'others do'
Ye valleys low where the milde whispers use, Lycidas 136
That now I use thee in my latter task: Vacation 8
Thy service in some graver subject use, Vacation 30
All is, if I have grace to use it so, Sonnet 7, 13

Used
Light after light well us'd they shall attain, Par Lost 3.196
Of that life-giving Plant, but only us'd Par Lost 4.199
For prospect, what well us'd had bin the pledge Par Lost 4.200
To make them mirth us'd all his might, and wreathd Par Lost 4.346
Present, or past, as Saints and Patriarchs us'd. Par Lost 4.762
Us'd to the yoak, draw'st his triumphant wheels Par Lost 4.975
Bestowd, the holy salutation us'd Par Lost 5.386
Thus I embold'nd spake, and freedom us'd Par Lost 8.434
As us'd or not, works in the mind no change, Par Lost 8.525
With Man, as with his Friend, familiar us'd Par Lost 9.2
Of rusling Leaves, but minded not, as us'd Par Lost 9.519
Us'd by the Tempter: on that prospect strange Par Lost 10.552
Without means us'd, what it predicts revokes. Par Reg 3.356
Us'd no ambition to commend my deeds, Samson 247
I us'd hostility, and took thir spoil Samson 1203
Crush't the sweet poyson of mis-used Wine Mask 47
Bridgewater ms 'mis-vsed'
Som other means I have which may be us'd, Mask 821
Bridgewater ms 'vsed'
when most were wont which till then us'd to scan Sonnet 13, Tr. ms 40.03

Useful
Useful of hurtful, prosperous of adverse Par Lost 2.259
Useful, whence haply mention may arise Par Lost 8.200
To what can I be useful, wherein serve Samson 564

Useless
Useless and vain, of freedom both despoild, Par Lost 3.109
Useless besides, reasoning I oft admire, Par Lost 8.25
Made Arms ridiculous, useless the forgery Samson 131
Renders them useless, while Samson 1282
Useless, and thence ridiculous about him. Samson 1501
Lodg'd with me useless, though my Soul more bent Sonnet 19, 4

Uses
Ordain'd for uses to his Lord best known. Par Lost 8.106

Usest
Thou usest, and from thence creat'st more good. Par Lost 7.616

Usher
Of Heav'n the Starrs that usher Evening rose: Par Lost 4.355
To fan the Earth now wak'd, and usher in Par Lost 10.94

Ushered
Or usher'd with a shower still, Penseroso 127

Ushering
Co. Could that divide you from neer-ushering guides? Mask 279
1637 'neere-ushering'
Bridgewater ms 'neere vsheringe'
Trinity ms 'neere ushering' ← 'thire ushering'

Usual
Rather accuse him under usual names, Par Reg 4.316

Usurp
Broke up, shall heave the Ocean to usurp Par Lost 11.827
Shall long usurp; ere the third dawning light Par Lost 12.421

Usurpation
All usurpation thence expell'd, reduce Par Lost 2.983
By female usurpation, nor dismay'd. Samson 1060

Usurped
The Realm it self of Satan long usurpt, Par Lost 10.189
Authoritie usurpt, from God not giv'n: Par Lost 12.66
Though Priests, the Crown, and *David*'s Throne usurp'd, Par Reg 3.169
Permitted rather, and by thee usurp't, Par Reg 4.183
Not half so far casts his usurped sway, Nativity 170

Usurper
But this Usurper his encroachment proud Par Lost 12.72

Usurping
So *Jove* usurping reign'd: these first in *Creet* Par Lost 1.514
Usurping over sovran Reason claimd Par Lost 9.1130
With black usurping mists, som gentle taper Mask 337
Bridgewater ms 'vsurpinge'

Utensils
And Waggons fraught with Utensils of war. Par Reg 3.336

Uther
In Fable or *Romance* of *Uthers* Son Par Lost 1.580
ms 'Vthers'

Utmost
As from the Center thrice to th' utmost Pole. Par Lost 1.74
His utmost power with adverse power oppos'd Par Lost 1.103
Of utmost *Arnon*. Nor content with such Par Lost 1.399
And ore the *Celtic* roam'd the utmost Isles. Par Lost 1.521
His utmost ire? which to the highth enrag'd, Par Lost 2.95
The utmost border of his Kingdom, left Par Lost 2.361
From Hell continu'd reaching th' utmost Orbe Par Lost 2.1029

Utmost(*cont*)
Mean while in utmost Longitude, where Heav'n Par Lost 4.539
Full to the utmost measure of what bliss Par Lost 5.517
If not to reign: mean while thy utmost force, Par Lost 6.293
Would utmost vigor raise, and rais'd unite. Par Lost 9.314
Thy utmost reach or *Adams:* Round the Tree Par Lost 9.591
With righteous plea, thir utmost vigilance, Par Lost 10.30
Heav'n-banisht Host, left desert utmost Hell Par Lost 10.437
Or if thou covet death, as utmost end Par Lost 10.1020
Gladly behold though but his utmost skirts Par Lost 11.332
Th' Empire of *Negus* to his utmost Port Par Lost 11.397
Of utmost hope! now clear I understand Par Lost 12.376
Ye see our danger on the utmost edge Par Reg 1.94
His utmost subtilty, because he boasts Par Reg 1.144
With clamour was assur'e qthi qutmost aid Par Reg 2.148
And utmost *Indian* Isle *Taprobane*, Par Reg 4.75
To the utmost of meer man both wise and good, Par Reg 4.535
Have satisfi'd thir utmost of revenge Samson 484
With th' utmost of his Godhead seconded: Samson 1153
Ruin, destruction at the utmost point. Samson 1514
Us thy vow'd Priests, till utmost end Mask 136
Bridgewater ms 'vtmost'
As to make this relation? *Spir*. Care and utmost shifts Mask 617
Bridgewater ms 'vtmost'
Of utmost *Tweed*, or *Oose*, or gulphie *Dun*, Vacation 92
Earths utmost bounds: them shalt thou bring full low Psalm 2, 19
And Tyre with Ethiops *utmost ends*, Psalm 87, 15

Utter
In utter darkness, and thir portion set Par Lost 1.72
Hateful to utter: but what power of mind Par Lost 1.626
In this abhorred deep to utter woe; Par Lost 2.87
And utter dissolution, as the scope Par Lost 2.127
Wide gaping, and with utter loss of being Par Lost 2.440
Through utter and through middle darkness borne Par Lost 3.16
A World from utter loss, and hast been found Par Lost 3.308
Into utter darkness, deep ingulft, his place Par Lost 5.614
To utter is not safe. Assemble thou Par Lost 5.683
From all Heav'ns bounds into the utter Deep: Par Lost 6.716
Or won to what may work his utter loss, Par Lost 9.131
And utter odious Truth, that God would come Par Lost 11.704
Now both abhor, since thou hast dar'd to utter Par Reg 4.172
And sense distract, to know well what I utter. Samson 1556
To utter what will come at last too soon; Samson 1566

Utterance
Beatitude past utterance; on his right Par Lost 3.62
Turnd him all eare to hear new utterance flow. Par Lost 4.410
At length gave utterance to these words constraind. Par Lost 9.1066
To thy large heart give utterance due, thy heart Par Reg 3.10

Uttered
Amidst in Thunder utter'd thus his voice. Par Lost 10.33
To those bright Orders utterd thus his voice. Par Lost 10.615
Perus'd him, then with words thus utt'red spake. Par Reg 1.320
This utter'd, straining all his nerves he bow'd, Samson 1646
That must be utter'd to unfold the sage Mask 786
line not in Bridgewater ms
line not in Trinity ms

Utteredest
And scarce to th' Angel utterdst thus thy plaint. Par Lost 11.762

Uttering
Which uttering thus he to his Father spake. Par Lost 3.143
As from blest voices, uttering joy, Heav'n rung Par Lost 3.347

Uttermost
In circuit to the uttermost convex Par Lost 7.266
Thy counsel in this uttermost distress, Par Lost 10.920

Uxorious
By that uxorious King, whose heart though large, Par Lost 1.444
When I must live uxorious to thy will Samson 945

Uzzean
Gave up into my hands *Uzzean Job* Par Reg 1.369

Uzziel
Uzziel, half these draw off, and coast the South Par Lost 4.782

Vacant
Perhaps our vacant room, though more remov'd, Par Lost 2.835
Into thir vacant room, and thence diffuse Par Lost 7.190
Vacant possession som new trouble raise: Par Lost 11.103
Had left him vacant, and with speed was gon Par Reg 2.116
Hid in her vacant interlunar cave. Samson 89
Be vacant of her plenty, in her own loyns Mask 718
To seise the widdow'd whore Pluralitie Forcers 3
Trinity ms 'widow'd' ←'vacant'
Who alwayes vacant alwayes amiable Horace 10

Vacation
Too long vacation hastned on his term. Another 14
1657 'Vacation'
line not in 1658 text

Vacuity
A vast vacuitie: all unawares Par Lost 2.932

Vacuous
Infinitude, nor vacuous the space. Par Lost 7.169

Vagabond
Blow'n vagabond or frustrate: in they passd Par Lost 11.16

Vagaries
Flew off, and into strange vagaries fell, Par Lost 6.614

Vain
With vain attempt. Him the Almighty Power Par Lost 1.44
ms 'vaine'
Vain Warr with Heav'n, and by success untaught Par Lost 2.9
All these our motions vain, sees and derides; Par Lost 2.191

Vain(*cont*)
The former vain to hope argues as vain Par Lost 2.234
Hatching vain Empires. Thus *Beelzebub* Par Lost 2.378
Vain wisdom all, and false Philosophie: Par Lost 2.565
Fluttring his pennons vain plumb down he drops Par Lost 2.933
Revisit'st not these eyes, that rowle in vain Par Lost 3.23
Useless and vain, of freedom both despoild, Par Lost 3.109
Of all things transitorie and vain, when Sin Par Lost 3.446
Both all things vain, and all who in vain things Par Lost 3.448
Dissolvd on Earth, fleet hither, and in vain, Par Lost 3.457
With many a vain exploit, though then renownd: Par Lost 3.465
Of *Sennaar*, and still with vain designe Par Lost 3.467
Philosophers in vain so long have sought, Par Lost 3.601
In vain, though by thir powerful Art they binde Par Lost 3.602
How dearly I abide that boast so vaine, Par Lost 4.87
Mine eyes till now, and pin'd with vain desire, Par Lost 4.466
Shine not in vain, nor think, though men were none, Par Lost 4.675
Vaine hopes, vaine aimes, inordinate desires Par Lost 4.808
1667 'Vain hopes, vain aimes'
Your message, like to end as much in vain? Par Lost 4.833
He held it vain; awe from above had quelld Par Lost 4.860
Shadowie sets off the face of things; in vain, Par Lost 5.43
Laugh'st at thir vain designes and tumults vain, Par Lost 5.737
Aspirer, but thir thoughts prov'd fond and vain Par Lost 6.90
Or potent tongue; fool, not to think how vain Par Lost 6.135
Vain glorious, and through infamie seeks fame: Par Lost 6.384
Of Spirits apostat and thir Counsels vaine Par Lost 7.610
Seek them with wandring thoughts, and notions vain. Par Lost 8.187
1667 'vaine'
For hee who tempts, though in vain, at least asperses Par Lost 9.296
To gird thir waste, vain Covering if to hide Par Lost 9.1113
And of thir vain contest appeer'd no end. Par Lost 9.1189
Which he presumes already vain and void, Par Lost 10.50
Vain covertures; but when he saw descend Par Lost 10.337
Reluctant, but in vaine, a greater power Par Lost 10.515
Forc't I absolve: all my evasions vain, Par Lost 10.829
His heart I know, how variable and vain Par Lost 11.92
But all in vain: which when he saw, he ceas'd Par Lost 11.726
What oft my steddiest thoughts have searcht in vain, Par Lost 12.377
At least in vain, for they shall find thee mute. Par Reg 1.459
Or in *Perea*, but return'd in vain. Par Reg 2.24
In vain, where no acceptance it can find, Par Reg 2.388
Shall I seek glory then, as vain men seek Par Reg 3.105
Much ostentation vain of fleshly arm, Par Reg 3.387
From Gentils, but by Circumcision vain, Par Reg 3.425
Vain battry, and in froth or bubbles end; Par Reg 4.20
And his vain importunity pursues. Par Reg 4.24
For all his tedious talk is but vain boast, Par Reg 4.307
But shelter'd slept in vain, for at his head Par Reg 4.407
And toil'st in vain, nor me in vain molest. Par Reg 4.498
Down Reason then, at least vain reasonings down, Samson 322
Deceivable and vain! Nay what thing good Samson 350
Vain monument of strength; till length of years Samson 570
In vain thou striv'st to cover shame with shame, Samson 841
To afflict thy self in vain: though sight be lost, Samson 914
Sam. Cam'st thou for this, vain boaster, to survey me, Samson 1227
Chor. Thy hopes are not ill founded nor seem vain Samson 1504
Spir. Ile tell ye, 'tis not vain, or fabulous, Mask 513
Trinity ms 'vaine'
Bridgewater ms 'vayne'
1637 'vaine'
Hence vain deluding joyes, Penseroso 1
Hence with denial vain, and coy excuse, Lycidas 18
Trinity ms 'vaine'
next adde Narcissus that still weeps in vaine Lycidas Tr. ms 28.19
In vain the *Tyrian* Maids their wounded *Thamuz* mourn. Nativity 204
In vain with Cymbals ring, Nativity 208
In vain with Timbrel'd Anthems dark Nativity 219
Which is no more then what is false and vain, On Time 5
Trinity ms 'vaine'
Of Public Fraud. In vain doth Valour bleed Sonnet 15, 13
This thought might lead me through the worlds vain mask Sonnet 22, 13
muse a vain thing, the Kings of th' earth upstand Psalm 2, 2
Things false and vain and nothing else but lies? Psalm 4, 12

Vainly
His deadly arrow; neither vainly hope Par Lost 2.811

Valdarno
Or in *Valdarno*, to descry new Lands, Par Lost 1.290
ms 'Valdarno'

Vale
In billows, leave i' th' midst a horrid Vale. Par Lost 1.224
ms 'vale'
No rest: through many a dark and drearie Vaile Par Lost 2.618
In this infernal Vaile first met thou call'st Par Lost 2.742
Nor streit'ning Vale, nor Wood, nor Stream divides Par Lost 6.70
Ingenderd in the *Pythian* Vale on slime, Par Lost 10.530
Had wasted woods on Mountain or in Vale, Par Lost 11.567
And thou Moon in the vale of *Aialon*, Par Lost 12.266
Sometimes, anon in shady vale, each night Par Reg 1.304
From *Eshtaol* and *Zora*'s fruitful Vale Samson 181
Was in the Vale of *Sorec*, *Dalila*, Samson 229
And in the violet-imbroider'd vale Mask 233
B.M. ms 'thy violet embroiderd Vale'
They pass through Baca's *thirstie* Vale, Psalm 84, 21

Vales
To slumber here, as in the Vales of Heav'n? Par Lost 1.321
ms 'vales'
Fortunate Fields, and Groves and flourie Vales, Par Lost 3.569

Vales(*cont*)
And call the Vales, and bid them hither cast — Lycidas 134
Trinity ms 'vales'
1638 'vales'
The Vales redoubl'd to the Hills, and they — Sonnet 18, 9
Valiant
What wise and valiant man would seek to free — Par Reg 4.143
The highest name for valiant Acts, that honour — Samson 1101
Thither shall all the valiant youth resort, — Samson 1738
Valid
The remedie; perhaps more valid Armes, — Par Lost 6.438
Valley
The pleasant Vally of *Hinnom*, *Tophet* thence — Par Lost 1.404
ms 'vally'
Attest thir joy, that hill and valley rings. — Par Lost 2.495
Retreated in a silent valley, sing — Par Lost 2.547
Of som irriguous Valley spred her store, — Par Lost 4.255
To Hill, or Valley, Fountain, or fresh shade — Par Lost 5.203
And with fresh Flourets Hill and Valley smil'd. — Par Lost 6.784
Of Hill, and Vallie, Rivers, Woods and Plaines, — Par Lost 9.116
Yet doubt not but in Vallie and in plaine — Par Lost 11.349
In Valley or Green Meadow to way-lay — Par Reg 2.185
Then in a flowry valley set him down — Par Reg 4.586
La. To seek i' th vally som cool friendly Spring. — Mask 282
Bridgewater ms 'valley'
Trinity ms 'valley'
And sweeten'd every muskrose of the dale, — Mask 496
Trinity ms 'dale' ← 'valley'
Into a goodly valley, where he sees — Prose 2, 2
Valleys
With tufts the vallies and each fountain side, — Par Lost 7.327
To lay hills plain, fell woods, or valleys fill, — Par Reg 3.332
Ye valleys low where the milde whispers use, — Lycidas 136
Trinity ms 'vallies'
Vallombrosa
In *Vallombrosa*, where th' *Etrurian* shades — Par Lost 1.303
ms 'Vallombrosa'
Valour
Deliberate valour breath'd, firm and unmov'd — Par Lost 1.554
Of dauntless courage, and considerate Pride — Par Lost 1.603
ms 'valour'
For contemplation hee and valour formd, — Par Lost 4.297
Valour or strength, though matchless, quelld with pain — Par Lost 6.457
And Valour and Heroic Vertu call'd; — Par Lost 11.690
While Virtue, Valour, Wisdom sit in want. — Par Reg 2.431
Cho. It is not vertue, wisdom, valour, wit, — Samson 1010
For valour to assail, nor by the sword — Samson 1165
To matchless valour, and adventures high: — Samson 1740
Thy firm unshak'n vertue ever brings — Sonnet 15, 5
1694 'Valour'
Of Public Fraud. In vain doth Valour bleed — Sonnet 15, 13
Value
Any, but God alone, to value right — Par Lost 4.202
Then value: Oft times nothing profits more — Par Lost 8.571
Or value what is best — Samson 1029
Valued
Created thing naught valu'd he nor shun'd; — Par Lost 2.679
1667 'vallu'd'
Valuest
Thou valu'st, because offer'd, and reject'st: — Par Reg 4.156
Van
To Battel in the Clouds, before each Van — Par Lost 2.535
Standards, and Gonfalons twixt Van and Reare — Par Lost 5.589
Of hideous length: before the cloudie Van, — Par Lost 6.107
Fear I incurable; bring up thy van, — Samson 1234
Vane
Vane, young in yeares, but in sage counsell old, — Sonnet 17, 1
1694 '*Vane*'
Vanguard
Vanguard, to Right and Left the Front unfould; — Par Lost 6.558
1667 'Vangard'
Vanish
Will vanish and deliver ye to woe, — Par Lost 4.368
Vanished
Empyreal, from before her vanisht Night, — Par Lost 6.14
Both Table and Provision vanish'd quite — Par Reg 2.402
Vanity
With vanity had filld the works of men: — Par Lost 3.447
And wandring vanitie, when lest was safe, — Par Lost 10.875
Of triumph that insulting vanity; — Par Reg 4.138
And speckl'd vanity — Nativity 136
Still to love vanity, — Psalm 4, 10
He travels big with vanitie, — Psalm 7, 51
Then *in the joyes of Vanity*, — Psalm 84, 35
Vanquish
But to vanquish by wisdom hellish wiles. — Par Reg 1.175
Vanquished
Lay vanquisht, rowling in the fiery Gulfe — Par Lost 1.52
Whom he had vanquisht. After these appear'd — Par Lost 1.476
Lie vanquisht; thou hast givn me to possess — Par Lost 3.243
Vanquish'd *Adramelec*, and *Asmadai*, — Par Lost 6.365
Victor and Vanquisht: on the foughten field — Par Lost 6.410
Who vanquisht with a peal of words (O weakness!) — Samson 235
Of *Madian* and her vanquisht Kings: — Samson 281
Effeminatly vanquish't? by which means, — Samson 562
Vanquisher
My vanquisher, spoild of his vanted spoile; — Par Lost 3.251
1667 'Vanquisher'
Vanquishing
Supplanted *Adam*, and by vanquishing — Par Reg 4.607
Vans
The stedfast Earth. At last his Sail-broad Vannes — Par Lost 2.927
Who on their plumy Vans receiv'd him soft — Par Reg 4.583
Vantbrace
Vant-brass and Greves, and Gauntlet, add thy Spear — Samson 1121
Vapour
Thir noxious vapour, or enur'd not feel, — Par Lost 2.216
Of midnight vapor glide obscure, and prie — Par Lost 9.159
Compact of unctuous vapor, which the Night — Par Lost 9.635
That with exhilerating vapour bland — Par Lost 9.1047
Vapour, and Mist, and Exhalation hot, — Par Lost 10.694
Vapour, and Exhalation dusk and moist, — Par Lost 11.741
And vapour as the *Libyan* Air adust, — Par Lost 12.635
Vapours
Up hither like Aereal vapours flew — Par Lost 3.445
In *Autumn* thwarts the night, when vapors fir'd — Par Lost 4.557
And temperat vapors bland, which th' only sound — Par Lost 5.5
Vapours not yet into her substance turnd. — Par Lost 5.420
With the rank vapours of this Sin-worn mould. — Mask 17
Benighted walks under the mid-day Sun; — Mask 384
Trinity ms 'benighted walks under the midday sun' ← 'walks in black vapours though the noontyde brand'
Bridgewater ms 'walks in black vapours though the noone tyde brand'
Of noisom winds, and blasting vapours chill. — Arcades 49
Variable
His heart I know, how variable and vain — Par Lost 11.92
Variance
Brought him so soon at variance with himself — Samson 1585
Varied
Varied his bounty so with new delights, — Par Lost 5.431
So varied hee, and of his tortuous Traine — Par Lost 9.516
Variety
(For Earth hath this variety from Heav'n — Par Lost 6.640
Varietie without end; but of the Tree — Par Lost 7.542
Various
Then were they known to men by various Names, — Par Lost 1.374
And various Idols through the Heathen World. — Par Lost 1.375
A various mould, and from the boyling cells — Par Lost 1.706
ms defective here
And *Discord* with a thousand various mouths. — Par Lost 2.967
Turn swift thir various motions, or are turnd — Par Lost 3.582
In various shapes old *Proteus* from the Sea, — Par Lost 3.604
Flew upward, spirited with various forms, — Par Lost 3.717
A happy rural seat of various view; — Par Lost 4.247
So various, not to taste that onely Tree — Par Lost 4.423
Of various influence foment and warme, — Par Lost 4.669
And various: wondring at my flight and change — Par Lost 5.89
In various style, for neither various style — Par Lost 5.146
Then with these various fruits the Trees of God — Par Lost 5.390
Indu'd with various forms various degrees — Par Lost 5.473
Various, with boastful Argument portraid, — Par Lost 6.84
That Warr and various; somtimes on firm ground — Par Lost 6.242
Op'ning thir various colours, and made gay — Par Lost 7.318
Incited, dance about him various rounds? — Par Lost 8.125
With various living creatures, and the Aire — Par Lost 8.370
Who meet with various objects, from the sense — Par Lost 8.609
In Paradise, and various, yet unknown — Par Lost 9.619
Sate in thir sad discourse, and various plaint, — Par Lost 10.343
Which now the Skie with various Face begins — Par Lost 10.1064
Were Tents of various hue; by some were herds — Par Lost 11.557
Upon thir Tongues a various Spirit to rase — Par Lost 12.53
So many and so various Laws are giv'n; — Par Lost 12.282
Of various persons each to know his part; — Par Reg 2.240
In various habits on the *Appian* road, — Par Reg 4.68
And all her various objects of delight — Samson 71
That thou towards him with hand so various, — Samson 668
That like to rich, and various gemms inlay — Mask 22
That in the various bussle of resort — Mask 379
He touch'd the tender stops of various Quills, — Lycidas 188
Variously
Variously representing; yet still free — Par Lost 8.610
Various-measured
By voice or hand, and various-measur'd verse, — Par Reg 4.256
Varnish
As varnish on a Harlots cheek, the rest, — Par Reg 4.344
Varnished
Or clos ambition varnisht o're with zeal. — Par Lost 2.485
These false pretexts and varnish'd colours failing, — Samson 901
Vary
Varie to our great Maker still new praise. — Par Lost 5.184
Vassal
Deservedly made vassal, who once just, — Par Reg 4.133
Vassalage
Of splendid vassalage, but rather seek — Par Lost 2.252
Vassals
The Vassals of his anger, when the Scourge — Par Lost 2.90
Vast
Dove-like satst brooding on the vast Abyss — Par Lost 1.21
To bellow through the vast and boundless Deep. — Par Lost 1.177
Live to our selves, though in this vast recess, — Par Lost 2.254
Over the vast abrupt, ere he arrive — Par Lost 2.409
Others with vast *Typhoean* rage more fell — Par Lost 2.539
Voluminous and vast, a Serpent arm'd — Par Lost 2.652
Created vast and round, a place of bliss — Par Lost 2.832
A vast vacuitie: all unawares — Par Lost 2.932

Vast(*cont*)
Stood rul'd, stood vast infinitude confin'd; Par Lost 3.711
Half way up Hill this vast Sublunar Vault, Par Lost 4.777
He speeds, and through the vast Ethereal Skie Par Lost 5.267
Satan with vast and haughtie strides advanc't, Par Lost 6.109
Th' Arch-Angel trumpet; through the vast of Heaven Par Lost 6.203
A vast circumference: At his approach Par Lost 6.256
They view'd the vast immeasurable Abyss Par Lost 7.211
Round through the vast profunditie obscure, Par Lost 7.229
One day and night; in all thir vast survey Par Lost 8.24
For such vast room in Nature unpossest Par Lost 8.153
Voyag'd th' unreal, vast, unbounded deep Par Lost 10.471
To stuff this Maw, this vast unhide-bound Corps. Par Lost 10.601
All his vast force, and drive him back to Hell, Par Reg 1.153
Ecbatana her structure vast there shews, Par Reg 3.286
Of wisdom, vast, unwieldy, burdensom, Samson 54
Though in these chains, bulk without spirit vast, Samson 1238
Uninjur'd in this wilde surrounding wast. Mask 403
Trinity ms 'wide surrounding wast' ←'vast, & hideous wild'
Now heaps upon som few with vast excess, Mask 771
What Worlds, or what vast Regions hold Penseroso 90
With vast increase their corn and wine abounds Psalm 4, 36

Vastness
His vastness: Fleec't the Flocks and bleating rose, Par Lost 7.472

Vault
Hurling defiance toward the Vault of Heav'n. Par Lost 1.669
1667 'vault'
ms 'vault'
Half way up Hill this vast Sublunar Vault, Par Lost 4.777

Vaulted
Smote on him sore besides, vaulted with Fire; Par Lost 1.298
And flying vaulted either Host with fire. Par Lost 6.214
From Hell's deep-vaulted Den to dwell in light, Par Reg 1.116
Half round on two main Pillars vaulted high, Samson 1606
Of silence, through the empty-vaulted night Mask 250
1637 'emptie-vaulted'
Trinity ms 'empty vaulted'
Bridgewater ms 'empty vaulted'

Vaults
Oft seen in Charnell vaults, and Sepulchers Mask 471

Vaunted
My vanquisher, spoild of his vanted spoile; Par Lost 3.251
With that same vaunted name Virginity, Mask 738
line not in Bridgewater ms

Vaunting
Vaunting aloud, but rackt with deep despare: Par Lost 1.126
Uriel and *Raphael* his vaunting foe, Par Lost 6.363
Vaunting my strength in honour to thir *Dagon?* Samson 1360

Vaunts
With other promises and other vaunts Par Lost 4.84
And vaunts of his great cunning to the throng Par Reg 1.145

Veers
Veres oft, as oft so steers, and shifts her Saile; Par Lost 9.515

Vegetable
Of vegetable Gold; and next to Life Par Lost 4.220

Vehemence
With loudest vehemence: thither he plyes, Par Lost 2.954
To such a flame of sacred vehemence, Mask 795
line not in Bridgewater ms
line not in Trinity ms

Vehement
Nor vehement desire, these delicacies Par Lost 8.526
She ended heer, or vehement despaire Par Lost 10.1007

Veil
Approach not, but with both wings veil thir eyes. Par Lost 3.382
Shee as a vail down to the slender waste Par Lost 4.304
Stood to entertain her guest from Heav'n; no vaile Par Lost 5.383
In darker veile) and roseat Dews dispos'd Par Lost 5.646
To veile the Heav'n, though darkness there might well Par Lost 6.11
How dark'nd; innocence, that as a veile Par Lost 9.1054
Wetting the borders of her silk'n veil: Samson 730
Seeming at first all heavenly under virgin veil, Samson 1035
The Saintly Vail of Maiden white to throw, Nativity 42
1673 'Veil'

Veiled
Or dim suffusion veild. Yet not the more Par Lost 3.26
Vaild with his gorgeous wings, up springing light Par Lost 5.250
Nights Hemisphere had veild the Horizon round: Par Lost 9.52
Veild in a Cloud of Fragrance, where she stood, Par Lost 9.425
Dark vaild *Cotytto*, t' whom the secret flame Mask 129
Bridgewater ms 'Darke-vayld'
Trinity ms 'Dark-vaild'
1637 'Dark-vaild'
1673 'vail'd'
Her face was vail'd, yet to my fancied sight, Sonnet 23, 10
Trinity ms 'vaild'

Veils
From yonder blazing Cloud that veils the Hill Par Lost 11.229

Vein
So they among themselves in pleasant veine Par Lost 6.628
Say Heav'nly Muse, shall not thy sacred vein Nativity 15

Veins
That underneath had veins of liquid fire Par Lost 1.701
Upon the rapid current, which through veins Par Lost 4.227
Part hidd'n veins diggd up (nor hath this Earth Par Lost 6.516
Ran through his veins, and all his joynts relax'd; Par Lost 9.891
Down to the veins of Earth, thence gliding hot Par Lost 11.568

Velvet
O're the Cowslips Velvet head, Mask 898
Trinity ms 'velvet'
word not in Bridgewater ms
1637 'velvet'

Venereal
Of fair fallacious looks, venereal trains, Samson 533

Vengeance
His Ministers of vengeance and pursuit Par Lost 1.170
Treble confusion, wrath and vengeance pour'd. Par Lost 1.220
Should intermitted vengeance arm again Par Lost 2.173
To execute fierce vengeance on his foes, Par Lost 3.399
Of *Tobits* Son, and with a vengeance sent Par Lost 4.170
Or som more sudden vengeance wing'd from God Par Lost 6.279
Vengeance is his, or whose he sole appoints; Par Lost 6.808
And vengeance to the wicked, at return Par Lost 12.541
Are but as slavish officers of vengeance, Mask 218
line not in Bridgewater ms

Vengeful
That we may so suffice his vengeful ire, Par Lost 1.148
ms 'vengefull'
Hath wiselier arm'd his vengeful ire then so Par Lost 10.1023
Of vengeful Justice bore for our excess, Circum 24
Trinity ms 'vengefull'

Venial
Venial discourse unblam'd: I now must change Par Lost 9.5

Venom
Or if, inspiring venom, he might taint Par Lost 4.804
Or hurtfull Worm with canker'd venom bites. Arcades 53
Trinity ms 'venome'

Venomed
Next this marble venom'd seat Mask 916

Vent
Put forth, and to a narrow vent appli'd Par Lost 6.583
Without the vent of words, which these he breathd. Par Lost 12.374
By mixing somewhat true to vent more lyes. Par Reg 1.433
Desperate of better course, to vent his rage, Par Reg 4.445

Vented
Vented much policy, and projects deep Par Reg 3.391

Venture
Taught by the heav'nly Muse to venture down Par Lost 3.19
And boldly venture to whatever place Par Lost 4.891
Ile venter, for my new enliv'nd spirits Mask 228
Bridgewater ms 'venture'

Ventured
I fear, hath ventur'd from the deep, to raise Par Lost 4.574

Ventures
Ventures his filial Vertue, though untri'd, Par Reg 1.177

Venturing
Meant mee, by ventring higher then my Lot. Par Lost 9.690
I do it freely; venturing to displease Samson 1373

Venturous
And vent'rous, if that fail them, shrink and fear Par Lost 2.205
This said he paus'd not, but with ventrous Arme Par Lost 5.64
Curs'd as his life. *Spir*. Alas good ventrous youth, Mask 609

Venus
To enamour, as the Zone of *Venus* once Par Reg 2.214
Venus now wakes, and wak'ns Love. Mask 124
Whom lovely *Venus* at a birth Allegro 14

Verbal
And loses, though but verbal, his reward. Par Reg 3.104

Verdant
Fenc'd up the verdant wall; each beauteous flour, Par Lost 4.697
Put forth the verdant Grass, Herb yielding Seed, Par Lost 7.310
Beyond the Earths green Cape and verdant Isles Par Lost 8.631
With burnisht Neck of verdant Gold, erect Par Lost 9.501
Thick overhead with verdant roof imbowr'd Par Lost 9.1038
It was a Mountain at whose verdant feet Par Reg 3.253
That spreds her verdant leaf to th' morning ray, Mask 622

Verdict
That moral verdit quits her of unclean: Samson 324
To descant on my strength, and give thy verdit? Samson 1228

Verdure
Brought forth the tender Grass, whose verdure clad Par Lost 7.315
With all his verdure spoil'd, and Trees adrift Par Lost 11.832

Verdurous
The verdurous wall of paradise up sprung: Par Lost 4.143

Verge
Her fardest verge, and *Chaos* to retire Par Lost 2.1038
Down from the verge of Heav'n, Eternal wrauth Par Lost 6.865
Or serve they as a flourie verge to binde Par Lost 11.881
his uninchanted eye, & round the verge Mask Tr. ms 10.10

Verified
So spake this Oracle, then verifi'd Par Lost 10.182

Verify
To verifie that solemn message late, Par Reg 1.133
So shalt thou best fullfil, best verifie Par Reg 3.177

Vermeil
to write his owne woes on the vermeil graine Lycidas Tr. ms 28.18

Vermeil-tinctured
What need a vermeil-tinctur'd lip for that Mask 752
Trinity ms 'veirmeil tinctur'd'
line not in Bridgewater ms

Vermin
Till vermin or the draff of servil food Samson 574

Vernal
Or sight of vernal bloom, or Summers Rose, Par Lost 3.43
Vernal delight and joy, able to drive Par Lost 4.155

Vernal(*cont*)
The Birds thir quire apply; aires, vernal aires, Par Lost 4.264
Nor breath of Vernal Air from snowy *Alp*. Samson 628
And purple all the ground with vernal flowres. Lycidas 141
1638 'vernall'
New shot up from vernall showr; Winchester 40
1673 'vernal'
Vernant
Perpetual smil'd on Earth with vernant Flours, Par Lost 10.679
Verse
Flowd from thir lips, in Prose or numerous Verse, Par Lost 5.150
Easie my unpremeditated Verse: Par Lost 9.24
By voice or hand, and various-measur'd verse, Par Reg 4.256
Storied of old in high immortal vers Mask 516
1637 'verse'
Bridgewater ms 'verse'
Trinity ms 'verse'
And adde the power of som adjuring verse. Mask 858
Married to immortal verse Allegro 137
Hast thou no vers, no hymn, or solemn strein, Nativity 17
1673 'verse'
These latter scenes confine my roving vers, Passion 22
My plaining vers as lively as before; Passion 47
Sphear-born harmonious Sisters, Voice, and Vers, Musick 2
Trinity ms 'Verse' ←'verse'
Thou honour'st Verse, and Verse must send her wing Sonnet 13, 9
Trinity ms both 'Vers' ←'vers'
Versed
Deep verst in books and shallow in himself, Par Reg 4.327
Vertumnus
Vertumnus, or to *Ceres* in her Prime, Par Lost 9.395
Very
Spoken against, that through my very Soul Par Reg 2.90
To salve his credit, and for very spight Par Reg 4.12
Yea there, where very desolation dwels Mask 428
Enter'd the very lime-twigs of his spells, Mask 646
I must not suffer this, yet 'tis but the lees Mask 809
Trinity ms 'but the lees' ←'the tilted lees' ←'the very lees'
Am very weak and faint; heal and amend me, Psalm 6, 4
Vessel
And like a weather-beaten Vessel holds Par Lost 2.1043
Fit Vessel, fittest Imp of fraud, in whom Par Lost 9.89
Began to build a Vessel of huge bulk, Par Lost 11.729
No more was seen; the floating Vessel swum Par Lost 11.745
Of knowledge, what this Vessel can containe; Par Lost 12.559
1667 'vessel'
My Vessel trusted to me from above, Samson 199
Like to a potters vessel shiver'd so. Psalm 2, 21
Vessels
Wants her fit vessels pure, then strews the ground Par Lost 5.348
Vest
A militarie Vest of purple flowd Par Lost 11.241
Vesta
Thee bright-hair'd *Vesta* long of yore, Penseroso 23
Vested
Sat Sable-vested *Night*, eldest of things, Par Lost 2.962
Before the Altar and the vested Priest, Par Reg 1.257
Came vested all in white, pure as her mind: Sonnet 23, 9
Vesture
Approach, and kiss her sacred vestures hemm. Arcades 83
Vex
A fresh with conscious terrours vex me round, Par Lost 2.801
Vexed
Hath vext the Red-Sea Coast, whose waves orethrew Par Lost 1.306
Vex'd *Scylla* bathing in the Sea that parts Par Lost 2.660
Of glimmering air less vext with tempest loud: Par Lost 3.429
Over the vext Abyss, following the track Par Lost 10.314
On the vext Wilderness, whose tallest Pines, Par Reg 4.416
Co. Why are you vext Lady? why do you frown? Mask 666
Vialed
Which she with pretious viold liquors heals. Mask 847
line not in Bridgewater ms
Viands
And to thir viands fell, nor seemingly Par Lost 5.434
Defends the touching of these viands pure, Par Reg 2.370
Vice
Vice for it self: To him no Temple stood Par Lost 1.492
To vice industrious, but to Nobler deeds Par Lost 2.116
His Image whom they serv'd, a brutish vice, Par Lost 11.518
I hate when vice can bolt her arguments, Mask 760
Vicegerent
Under his great Vice-gerent Reign abide Par Lost 5.609
Vicegerent Son, to thee I have transferr'd Par Lost 10.56
Vices
Rowling in brutish vices, and deform'd, Par Reg 3.86
The vices of thir Deities, and thir own Par Reg 4.340
And by thir vices brought to servitude, Samson 269
Vicious
Servant of Servants, on his vitious Race. Par Lost 12.104
Vicissitude
Grateful vicissitude, like Day and Night; Par Lost 6.8
In thir vicissitude, and rule the Night, Par Lost 7.351
Victor
Nor what the Potent Victor in his rage Par Lost 1.95
ms 'victor'
But see the angry Victor hath recall'd Par Lost 1.169
Th' Almighty Victor to spend all his rage, Par Lost 2.144
The Victors will. To suffer, as to doe, Par Lost 2.199

Victor(*cont*)
Victor; though brutish that contest and foule, Par Lost 6.124
Victor and Vanquisht: on the foughten field Par Lost 6.410
Up rose the Victor Angels, and to Arms Par Lost 6.525
Of Iron Globes, which on the Victor Host Par Lost 6.590
Sole Victor from th' expulsion of his Foes Par Lost 6.880
There didst not; there let him still Victor sway, Par Lost 10.376
Thir fight, what stroke shall bruise the Victors heel. Par Lost 12.385
Then temporal death shall bruise the Victors heel, Par Lost 12.433
A victor people free from servile yoke? Par Reg 4.102
That people victor once, now vile and base, Par Reg 4.132
Fell whence he stood to see his Victor fall. Par Reg 4.571
Sung Victor, and from Heavenly Feast refresht Par Reg 4.637
And Victor over all Samson 1290
Victories
To conquer still; peace hath her victories Sonnet 16, 10
1694 'Victories'
Victorious
Victorious. Thus repuls'd, our final hope Par Lost 2.142
Pourd out by millions her victorious Bands Par Lost 2.997
But I shall rise Victorious, and subdue Par Lost 3.250
Sung Triumph, and him sung Victorious King, Par Lost 6.886
Victorious with his Saints, th' Omnipotent Par Lost 7.136
Of thy victorious Arm, well-pleasing Son, Par Lost 10.634
Into the Desert, his Victorious Field Par Reg 1.9
To which my Spirit aspir'd, victorious deeds Par Reg 1.215
To *Israel*, and now ly'st victorious Samson 1663
To triumph in victorious dance Mask 974
With those just Spirits that wear victorious Palms, Musick 14
Trinity ms 'victorious' ←'blooming' ←'victorious' ←'blooming' ←'fresh greene'
Victors
O Friends, why come not on these Victors proud? Par Lost 6.609
That pleas'd so well our Victors ear, declare Par Reg 4.337
Victory
Which if not Victory is yet Revenge. Par Lost 2.105
Cleer Victory, to our part loss and rout Par Lost 2.770
Presage of Victorie and fierce desire Par Lost 6.201
Of victorie; deeds of eternal fame Par Lost 6.240
All doubt of Victorie, eternal might Par Lost 6.630
Ascended, at his right hand Victorie Par Lost 6.762
With victory, triumphing through the aire Par Lost 12.452
Is fortitude to highest victorie, Par Lost 12.570
Victory and Triumph to the Son of God Par Reg 1.173
Sung Heavenly Anthems of his victory Par Reg 4.594
Broke him, as that dishonest victory Sonnet 10, 6
Victory home, though new rebellions raise Sonnet 15, 6
View
Say first, for Heav'n hides nothing from thy view Par Lost 1.27
Advanc't in view, they stand, a horrid Front Par Lost 1.563
Views all things at one view? he from heav'ns highth Par Lost 2.190
Neerer our ancient Seat; perhaps in view Par Lost 2.394
Before thir eyes in sudden view appear Par Lost 2.890
His own works and their works at once to view: Par Lost 3.59
Looks down with wonder at the sudden view Par Lost 3.542
Sometimes towards *Eden* which now in his view Par Lost 4.27
Of stateliest view. Yet higher then thir tops Par Lost 4.142
A happy rural seat of various view; Par Lost 4.247
Neerer to view his prey, and unespi'd Par Lost 4.399
Reflecting blaze on blaze, first met his view: Par Lost 6.18
In battailous aspect, and neerer view Par Lost 6.81
And to thir foes a laughter; for in view Par Lost 6.603
From Heaven Gate not farr, founded in view Par Lost 7.618
Her Husband, for I view far round, not nigh, Par Lost 9.482
I have in view, calling to minde with heed Par Lost 10.1030
His Children, all in view destroyd at once; Par Lost 11.761
If Cottage were in view, Sheep-cote or Herd; Par Reg 2.287
And just in time thou com'st to have a view Par Reg 3.298
His whispering stream; within the walls then view Par Reg 4.250
Thenceforth I thought thee worth my nearer view Par Reg 4.514
And now at nearer view, no other certain Samson 723
And view him sitting in the house, enobl'd Samson 1491
And therfore to our weaker view, Penseroso 15
To outward view, of blemish or of spot; Sonnet 22, 2
In Ephraims view and Benjamins, Psalm 80, 9
Viewed
View'd first thir lamentable lot, and found Par Lost 2.617
They view'd the vast immeasurable Abyss Par Lost 7.211
View'd, and behold all was entirely good; Par Lost 7.549
Have found him, view'd him, tasted him, but find Par Reg 2.131
He slightly view'd, and slightly over-pass'd; Par Reg 2.198
Of Wood-Gods and Wood-Nymphs; he view'd it round, Par Reg 2.297
At home, scarce view'd the *Gallilean* Towns, Par Reg 3.233
Viewest
Thy Trophies, which thou view'st as not thine own, Par Lost 10.355
Viewing
Thy self in me thy perfect image viewing Par Lost 2.764
As from unrest, and each the other viewing, Par Lost 9.1052
O Son, why sit we here each other viewing Par Lost 10.235
Viewless
Viewless, and underneath a bright Sea flow'd Par Lost 3.518
Of hatefull steps, I must be viewles now. Mask 92
Trinity ms 'veiwlesse'
Or should I thence hurried on viewles wing, Passion 50
Views
At once as far as Angels kenn he views Par Lost 1.59
Through Optic Glass the *Tuscan* Artist views Par Lost 1.288
The whole Battalion views, thir order due, Par Lost 1.569

Views(*cont*)
Views all things at one view? he from heav'ns highth — Par Lost 2.190
He views in bredth, and without longer pause — Par Lost 3.561
Beneath him with new wonder now he views — Par Lost 4.205

Vigilance
The vigilance here plac't, but such as come — Par Lost 4.580
Thir earthy Charge: Of these the vigilance — Par Lost 9.157
With righteous plea, thir utmost vigilance, — Par Lost 10.30

Vigils
So they in Heav'n their Odes and Vigils tun'd: — Par Reg 1.182

Vigorous
Revives, reflourishes, then vigorous most — Samson 1704
Telling their strange and vigorous faculties; — Mask 628

Vigour
Invincible, and vigour soon returns, — Par Lost 1.140
Immortal vigor, though opprest and fall'n, — Par Lost 2.13
Vigour Divine within them, can allow — Par Lost 6.158
Soon closing, and by native vigour heal'd. — Par Lost 6.436
And of thir wonted vigour left them draind, — Par Lost 6.851
His beams, unactive else, thir vigour find. — Par Lost 8.97
1667 'vigor'
With supple joints, and lively vigour led: — Par Lost 8.269
Would utmost vigor raise, and rais'd unite. — Par Lost 9.314
Issuing from mee: on your joynt vigor now — Par Lost 10.405
And celestial vigour arm'd, — Samson 1280

Vile
Shall we then live thus vile, the Race of Heav'n — Par Lost 2.194
Knee-tribute yet unpaid, prostration vile, — Par Lost 5.782
Restor'd by thee, vile as I am, to place — Par Lost 10.971
To thir own vile advantages shall turne — Par Lost 12.510
That people victor once, now vile and base, — Par Reg 4.132
Sole Author I, sole cause: if aught seem vile, — Samson 376
As vile hath been my folly, who have profan'd — Samson 377
Besides, how vile, contemptible, ridiculous, — Samson 1361
Of unblest inchanter vile. — Mask 907

Vilest
Inferiour to the vilest now become — Samson 73
Of man or worm; the vilest here excel me, — Samson 74

Vilified
Forsook them, when themselves they villifi'd — Par Lost 11.516

Village
To Town or Village nigh (nighest is far) — Par Reg 1.332
Or whistle from the Lodge, or village cock — Mask 346
1673 'Village'

Villager
I shall appear som harmles Villager — Mask 166
Trinity ms 'villager'
Bridgewater ms 'villager'
To help you find them. *La*. Gentle villager — Mask 304
Supposing him som neighbour villager; — Mask 576
Bridgewater ms 'neighbour-villager'

Villages
Among the pleasant Villages and Farmes — Par Lost 9.448

Villatic
Of tame villatic Fowl; but as an Eagle — Samson 1695

Vindicate
All fear of thee, arise and vindicate — Par Reg 2.47
To vindicate the glory of his name — Samson 475

Vine
Of coole recess, o're which the mantling vine — Par Lost 4.258
1667 'Vine'
As the Vine curles her tendrils, which impli'd — Par Lost 4.307
Fruitless imbraces: or they led the Vine — Par Lost 5.215
Forth flourish't thick the clustring Vine, forth crept — Par Lost 7.320
I saw them under a green mantling vine — Mask 294
Bridgewater ms 'vyne'
Through the Sweet-Briar, or the Vine, — Allegro 47
With wilde Thyme and the gadding Vine o'regrown, — Lycidas 40
Trinity ms 'vine'
1638 'vine'
A Vine from Aegypt thou hast brought, — Psalm 80, 33
To plant this *lovely* Vine. — Psalm 80, 36
And visit this *thy* Vine. — Psalm 80, 60
Visit this Vine, which thy right hand — Psalm 80, 61

Vines
The flowry Dale of *Sibma* clad with Vines, — Par Lost 1.410
ms 'vines'
Of life ambrosial frutage bear, and vines — Par Lost 5.427
Fruit of delicious Vines, the growth of Heav'n. — Par Lost 5.635

Vintage
Or as a swarm of flies in vintage time, — Par Reg 4.15

Viol
Of Lute, or Viol still, more apt for mournful things. — Passion 28

Violate
Imploi'd it seems to violate sleep, and those — Par Lost 4.883
The strict forbiddance, how to violate — Par Lost 9.903
To violate the sacred trust of silence — Samson 428

Violated
With pitie, violated not thir bliss. — Par Lost 10.25
With temperate sway; oft have they violated — Par Reg 3.160

Violating
By worse then hostile deeds, violating the ends — Samson 893

Violence
With lust and violence the house of God. — Par Lost 1.496
But that implies not violence or harme. — Par Lost 4.901
With violence of this conflict, had not soon — Par Lost 4.995
By violence, no, for that shall be withstood, — Par Lost 5.242
Superior, nor of violence fear'd aught; — Par Lost 5.905

Violence(*cont*)
Then violence: for this was all thy care — Par Lost 6.35
Brooks not the works of violence and Warr. — Par Lost 6.274
Ariel and *Arioc*, and the violence — Par Lost 6.371
By wound, though from thir place by violence mov'd. — Par Lost 6.405
His violence thou fearst not, being such, — Par Lost 9.282
No more be mention'd then of violence — Par Lost 10.1041
Unseen amid the throng: so violence — Par Lost 11.671
When violence was ceas't, and Warr on Earth, — Par Lost 11.780
Or violence, hee of thir wicked wayes — Par Lost 11.812
The whole Earth fill'd with violence, and all flesh — Par Lost 11.888
Brute violence and proud Tyrannick pow'r, — Par Reg 1.219
Never did wrong or violence, by them — Par Reg 1.389
Without ambition, war, or violence; — Par Reg 3.90
Contempts, and scorns, and snares, and violence, — Par Reg 3.191
Violence and stripes, and lastly cruel death, — Par Reg 4.388
To others did no violence nor spoil. — Samson 1191
Mess. By his own hands. *Man*. Self-violence? what cause — Samson 1584
Or do his gray hairs any violence? — Mask 392
And noble grace that dash't brute violence — Mask 451
Where if he be, with dauntless hardihood, — Mask 650
Trinity ms 'dauntless hardyhood' ←'suddaine violence'
Till Truth, and Right from Violence be freed, — Sonnet 15, 11
Of violence will undelay'd — Psalm 7, 59
With rudest violence? — Psalm 80, 52

Violent
Thine own begotten, breaking violent way — Par Lost 2.782
A violent cross wind from either Coast — Par Lost 3.487
Vows made in pain, as violent and void. — Par Lost 4.97
Weapons more violent, when next we meet, — Par Lost 6.439
Suttle or violent, we not endu'd — Par Lost 9.324
Corruption to bring forth more violent deeds. — Par Lost 11.428
Some, as thou saw'st, by violent stroke shall die, — Par Lost 11.471
Exploded and had seiz'd with violent hands, — Par Lost 11.669
Subjects him from without to violent Lords; — Par Lost 12.93
Violent or shameful death thir due reward. — Par Reg 3.87
The brute and boist'rous force of violent men — Samson 1273
And violent men are met — Psalm 86, 50

Violet
Mosaic; underfoot the Violet, — Par Lost 4.700
There on Beds of Violets blew, — Allegro 21
The glowing Violet. — Lycidas 145
1638 'violet'
Trinity ms 'violet'

Violet-embroidered
And in the violet-imbroider'd vale — Mask 233
Bridgewater ms 'violett imbroderd'
B.M. ms 'thy violet embroiderd Vale'
1673 'violet imbroider'd'

Violets
Pansies, and Violets, and Asphodel, — Par Lost 9.1040

Viper
To such a viper his most sacred trust — Samson 1001

Virgin
Made flesh, when time shall be, of Virgin seed, — Par Lost 3.284
Her Virgin Fancies, pouring forth more sweet, — Par Lost 5.296
Yet Innocence and Virgin Modestie, — Par Lost 8.501
To whom the Virgin Majestie of *Eve*, — Par Lost 9.270
Yet Virgin of *Proserpina* from *Jove*. — Par Lost 9.396
If chance with Nymphlike step fair Virgin pass, — Par Lost 9.452
By *Leo* and the *Virgin* and the *Scales*, — Par Lost 10.676
A Virgin is his Mother, but his Sire — Par Lost 12.368
The seed of Woman: Virgin Mother, Haile, — Par Lost 12.379
On which I sent thee to the Virgin pure — Par Reg 1.134
To her a Virgin, that on her should come — Par Reg 1.138
Conceiv'd in me a Virgin, he fore-told — Par Reg 1.239
Perswasive, Virgin majesty with mild — Par Reg 2.159
Seeming at first all heavenly under virgin veil, — Samson 1035
Of hatefull steps, I must be viewles now. — Mask 92
Trinity ms 'hatefull' ←'virgin'
Our number may affright: Som Virgin sure — Mask 148
Bridgewater ms 'virgin'
Trinity ms 'virgin'
But O that haples virgin our lost sister — Mask 350
Trinity ms 'vergin'
Will dare to soyl her Virgin purity, — Mask 427
1637 'virgin'
Bridgewater ms 'virgin'
Trinity ms 'virgin'
That wise *Minerva* wore, unconquer'd Virgin — Mask 448
1637 'virgin'
Bridgewater ms 'virgin'
Trinity ms 'virgin'
But O my Virgin Lady, where is she? — Mask 507
Bridgewater ms 'virgin'
Trinity ms 'virgin'
1637 'virgin'
Against th' unarmed weakness of one Virgin — Mask 582
Bridgewater ms 'virgin'
1637 'virgin'
Trinity ms 'virgin'
And timely rest have wanted, but fair Virgin — Mask 689
1637 'virgin'
Trinity ms 'faire virgin' ←'fairest virgin' ←'sweet Ladie'
Sabrina is her name, a Virgin pure, — Mask 826
1637 'virgin'
Trinity ms 'virgin'
Bridgewater ms 'virgin'

Virgin(*cont*)
To aid a Virgin, such as was her self Mask 856
Trinity ms 'virgin'
1637 'virgin'
Listen where thou art sitting Mask 860
Trinity ms 'Listen' ←'Listen virgin'
Of true Virgin here distrest, Mask 905
Trinity ms 'virgin'
Bridgewater ms 'virgin'
1637 'virgin'
Spir. Virgin, daughter of *Locrine* Mask 922
But, O sad Virgin, that thy power Penseroso 103
Of wedded Maid, and Virgin Mother born, Nativity 3
But see the Virgin blest, Nativity 237
Unhous'd thy Virgin Soul from her fair biding place. Fair Inf 21
The Virgin quire for her request Winchester 17
Hast gain'd thy entrance, Virgin wise and pure. Sonnet 9, 14
For aye, with Temples vow'd, and Virgin quires. Prose 12, 6
Virgin-born
Then hear, O Son of *David*, Virgin-born; Par Reg 4.500
Virginity
Hath hurtfull power o're true virginity. Mask 437
1673 'Virginity'
Bridgewater ms 'virginitie'
With that same vaunted name Virginity, Mask 738
1637 'Virginitie'
line not in Bridgewater ms
Trinity ms 'virginity'
And serious doctrine of Virginity, Mask 787
1637 'Virginitie'
line not in Bridgewater ms
line not in Trinity ms
Virgins
Sidonian Virgins paid thir Vows and Songs, Par Lost 1.441
ms 'virgins'
The Virgins also shall on feastful days Samson 1741
Virtual
Irradiance, virtual or immediate touch? Par Lost 8.617
Fomented by his virtual power and warmd: Par Lost 11.338
Virtue
Your wearied vertue, for the ease you find Par Lost 1.320
Loose all her virtue; least bad men should boast Par Lost 2.483
1667 'vertue'
Free Vertue should enthrall to Force or Chance. Par Lost 2.551
Shoots invisible vertue even to the deep: Par Lost 3.586
To them who liv'd; nor on the vertue thought Par Lost 4.198
Thir stellar vertue on all kinds that grow Par Lost 4.671
Vertue in her shape how lovly, saw, and pin'd Par Lost 4.848
Whom thus th' Angelic Vertue answerd milde. Par Lost 5.371
There fail where Vertue fails, or weakest prove Par Lost 6.117
Can end it. Into thee such Vertue and Grace Par Lost 6.703
And vital vertue infus'd, and vital warmth Par Lost 7.236
Whose vertue on it self workes no effect, Par Lost 8.95
By his attractive vertue and thir own Par Lost 8.124
Her vertue and the conscience of her worth, Par Lost 8.502
Not in themselves, all thir known vertue appeers Par Lost 9.110
Whether such vertue spent of old now faild Par Lost 9.145
Access in every Vertue, in thy sight Par Lost 9.310
With me, best witness of thy Vertue tri'd. Par Lost 9.317
And what is Faith, Love, Vertue unassaid Par Lost 9.335
On what thou hast of vertue, summon all, Par Lost 9.374
The vertue of that Fruit, in thee first prov'd: Par Lost 9.616
The credit of whose vertue rest with thee, Par Lost 9.649
Rather your dauntless vertue, whom the pain Par Lost 9.694
Of vertue to make wise: what hinders then Par Lost 9.778
Whose vertue, for of good still good proceeds, Par Lost 9.973
Of all thir vertue: silent, and in face Par Lost 9.1063
Thine now is all this World, thy vertue hath won Par Lost 10.372
Rather then solid vertu, all but a Rib Par Lost 10.884
Shall yield up all thir vertue, all thir fame Par Lost 11.623
And Valour and Heroic Vertu call'd; Par Lost 11.690
And great exploits, but of true vertu void; Par Lost 11.790
Shall with thir freedom lost all vertu loose Par Lost 11.798
From vertue, which is reason, that no wrong, Par Lost 12.98
Add vertue, Patience, Temperance, add Love, Par Lost 12.583
1667 'Vertue'
All vertue, grace and wisdom to atchieve Par Reg 1.68
From what consummate vertue I have chose Par Reg 1.165
Ventures his filial Vertue, though untri'd, Par Reg 1.177
To what highth sacred vertue and true worth Par Reg 1.231
Vertue, who follow not her lore: permit me Par Reg 1.483
Seated as on the top of Vertues hill, Par Reg 2.217
To Vertue I impute not, or count part Par Reg 2.248
While Virtue, Valour, Wisdom sit in want. Par Reg 2.431
To slacken Virtue, and abate her edge, Par Reg 2.455
His Honour, Vertue, Merit and chief Praise, Par Reg 2.464
Thy Vertue, and not every way secure Par Reg 3.348
Others in vertue plac'd felicity, Par Reg 4.297
But vertue joyn'd with riches and long life, Par Reg 4.298
By him call'd vertue; and his vertuous man, Par Reg 4.301
And in themselves seek vertue, and to themselves Par Reg 4.314
Unless where moral vertue is express't Par Reg 4.351
But thee whose strength, while vertue was her mate, Samson 173
His vertue or weakness which way to assail: Samson 756
Vertue, as I thought, truth, duty so enjoyning. Samson 870
Cho. It is not vertue, wisdom, valour, wit, Samson 1010
A cleaving mischief, in his way to vertue Samson 1039
But vertue which breaks through all opposition, Samson 1050

Virtue(*cont*)
His fierie vertue rouz'd Samson 1690
So vertue giv'n for lost, Samson 1697
Unmindfull of the crown that Vertue gives Mask 9
Bridgewater ms 'vertue'
Trinity ms 'vertue'
Hath met the vertue of this Magick dust, Mask 165
Or so unprincipl'd in vertues book, Mask 367
Vertue could see to do what vertue would Mask 373
Vertue may be assail'd, but never hurt, Mask 589
Bridgewater ms 'virtue'
Trinity ms 'vertue'
And vertue has no tongue to check her pride: Mask 761
In hard besetting need, this will I try Mask 857
Love vertue, she alone is free, Mask 1019
B.M. ms 'Virtue'
Or if Vertue feeble were, Mask 1022
Bridgewater ms 'vertue'
Trinity ms 'vertue'
1637 'vertue'
B.M. ms 'Virtue'
Thy firm unshak'n vertue ever brings Sonnet 15, 5
1694 'Valour'
Virtue-proof
Shee needed, Vertue-proof, no thought infirme Par Lost 5.384
Virtues
Celestial vertues rising, will appear Par Lost 2.15
Ethereal Vertues; or these Titles now Par Lost 2.311
Thrones, Dominations, Princedoms, Vertues, Powers, Par Lost 5.601
Thrones, Dominations, Princedomes, Vertues, Powers, Par Lost 5.772
Thrones, Dominations, Princedoms, Vertues, Powers, Par Lost 5.840
And Vertues, winged Spirits, and Chariots wing'd, Par Lost 7.199
Great are thy Vertues, doubtless, best of Fruits. Par Lost 9.745
Thrones, Dominations, Princedoms, Vertues, Powers, Par Lost 10.460
These God-like Vertues wherefore dost thou hide? Par Reg 3.21
Indu'd with Regal Vertues as thou art, Par Reg 4.98
What shallow-searching *Fame* hath left untold; Arcades 41
Trinity ms 'shallow searching' ←'vertues which dull'
Besides what her vertues fair Winchester 4
And at thy growing vertues fret their spleen, Sonnet 9, 7
Trinity ms 'vertues' ←'vertue' ←'vertues'
So well your words his noble vertues praise, Sonnet 10, 12
Trinity ms 'Vertues'
Virtuous
Potable Gold, when with one vertuous touch Par Lost 3.608
O Sovran, vertuous, precious of all Trees Par Lost 9.795
Then ever, bountie of this vertuous Tree. Par Lost 9.1033
Or vertuous, I should so have lost all sense. Par Reg 1.382
Which every wise and vertuous man attains: Par Reg 2.468
By him call'd vertue; and his vertuous man, Par Reg 4.301
One vertuous rarely found, Samson 1047
The vertuous mind, that ever walks attended Mask 211
line not in Bridgewater ms
In every vertuous plant and healing herb Mask 621
Bridgewater ms 'verteus'
Brightest Lady look on me, Mask 910
Trinity ms 'Brightest' ←'vertuous'
That own'd the vertuous Ring and Glass, Penseroso 113
Devoted to thy vertuous name; Winchester 60
Lawrence of vertuous Father vertuous Son, Sonnet 20, 1
Virtuousest
Seems wisest, vertuousest, discreetest, best; Par Lost 8.550
Visage
With faultring speech and visage incompos'd Par Lost 2.989
Ere he drew nigh, his radiant visage turnd, Par Lost 3.646
Which marrd his borrow'd visage, and betraid Par Lost 4.116
Whence in her visage round those spots, unpurg'd Par Lost 5.419
And visage all enflam'd first thus began. Par Lost 6.261
His Visage drawn he felt to sharp and spare, Par Lost 10.511
Stoop thy pale visage through an amber cloud, Mask 333
Bridgewater ms 'visadge'
The visage quite transforms of him that drinks, Mask 527
Whose Saintly visage is too bright Penseroso 13
His goary visage down the stream was sent, Lycidas 62
Trinity ms 'visage' ←'head' ←'scalpe'
Visaged
His arrows, from the fourfold-visag'd Foure, Par Lost 6.845
Visages
Thir visages and stature as of Gods, Par Lost 1.570
That time Celestial visages, yet mixt Par Lost 10.24
Viscount
A Vicounts daughter, an Earls heir, Winchester 3
Visible
No light, but rather darkness visible Par Lost 1.63
Made visible, th' Almighty Father shines, Par Lost 3.386
To thee not visible, when I alone Par Lost 6.145
Within the visible Diurnal Spheare; Par Lost 7.22
Considerd all things visible in Heav'n, Par Lost 9.604
Stood visible, among these Pines his voice Par Lost 11.321
Visibly
Divine compassion visibly appeerd, Par Lost 3.141
His lustre visibly impar'd; yet seemd Par Lost 4.850
Visibly, what by Deitie I am, Par Lost 6.682
I see ye visibly, and now beleeve Mask 216
line not in Bridgewater ms
Vision
Ezekiel saw, when by the Vision led Par Lost 1.455
ms 'vision'

Vision(*cont*)	
In vision beatific: by him first	Par Lost 1.684
Cast out from God and blessed vision, falls	Par Lost 5.613
And to the Heav'nly vision thus presum'd.	Par Lost 8.356
Thus I presumptuous; and the vision bright,	Par Lost 8.367
Much better seems this Vision, and more hope	Par Lost 11.599
To call by Vision from his Fathers house,	Par Lost 12.121
By Vision, found thee in the Temple, and spake	Par Reg 1.256
Of vision multiplyed through air, or glass	Par Reg 4.41
I took it for a faery vision	Mask 298
And in cleer dream, and solemn vision	Mask 457
Where the great vision of the guarded Mount	Lycidas 161
There doth my soul in holy vision sit	Passion 41
Visions	
In the Visions of God: It was a Hill	Par Lost 11.377
O Visions ill foreseen! better had I	Par Lost 11.763
Visit	
Thee I re-visit now with bolder wing,	Par Lost 3.13
Nightly I visit: nor somtimes forget	Par Lost 3.32
To visit all thy creatures, and to all	Par Lost 3.230
By which, to visit oft those happy Tribes,	Par Lost 3.532
To visit oft this new Creation round;	Par Lost 3.661
To visit thee; lead on then where thy Bowre	Par Lost 5.375
To visit oft the dwellings of just Men	Par Lost 7.570
To visit how they prosper'd, bud and bloom,	Par Lost 8.45
But God who oft descends to visit men	Par Lost 12.48
To visit or bewail thee, or if better,	Samson 182
Visit his Tomb with flowers, only bewailing	Samson 1742
Of som clay habitation visit us	Mask 339
Bridgewater ms 'visite'	
Number my ranks, and visit every sprout	Arcades 59
And cam'st again to visit us once more?	Fair Inf 52
And visit this *thy* Vine.	Psalm 80, 60
Visit this Vine, which thy right hand	Psalm 80, 61
Visitant	
While the great Visitant approachd, thus spake.	Par Lost 11.225
Visitants	
A burdenous drone; to visitants a gaze,	Samson 567
Visitation	
Her nightly visitation unimplor'd,	Par Lost 9.22
My early visitation, and my last	Par Lost 11.275
Visited	
That on my head all might be visited,	Par Lost 10.955
With odours visited and annual flowers.	Samson 987
Visitest	
Visit'st my slumbers Nightly, or when Morn	Par Lost 7.29
Visit'st the bottom of the monstrous world;	Lycidas 158
That him thou visit'st and of him art found;	Psalm 8, 14
Visiting	
Ran Nectar, visiting each plant, and fed	Par Lost 4.240
Visits	
Visits the herds along the twilight meadows,	Mask 844
Bridgewater ms 'visitts'	
Visored	
With visor'd falshood, and base forgery,	Mask 698
line not in Bridgewater ms	
Visual	
No where so cleer, sharp'nd his visual ray	Par Lost 3.620
The visual Nerve, for he had much to see;	Par Lost 11.415
Puts forth no visual beam.	Samson 163
Vital	
And feel thy sovran vital Lamp; but thou	Par Lost 3.22
To vital Spirits aspire, to animal,	Par Lost 5.484
Vital in every part, not as frail man	Par Lost 6.345
And vital vertue infus'd, and vital warmth	Par Lost 7.236
And sing to those that hold the vital shears,	Arcades 65
Vitiated	
As vitiated in Nature: more to know	Par Lost 10.169
Spousal embraces, vitiated with Gold,	Samson 389
Vocal	
Made vocal by my Song, and taught his praise.	Par Lost 5.204
And joind thir vocal Worship to the Quire	Par Lost 9.198
Organic, or impulse of vocal Air,	Par Lost 9.530
And with these raptures moves the vocal air	Mask 247
Bridgewater ms 'vocall'	
Trinity ms 'vocall'	
Smooth-sliding *Mincius*, crown'd with vocall reeds,	Lycidas 86
1673 'vocal'	
Voice	
If once they hear that voyce, thir liveliest pledge	Par Lost 1.274
ms 'voice'	
Yet to thir Generals Voyce they soon obeyd	Par Lost 1.337
ms 'voice'	
My voice disswades; for what can force or guile	Par Lost 2.188
Dreaded not more th' adventure then his voice	Par Lost 2.474
By Haralds voice explain'd: the hollow Abyss	Par Lost 2.518
Before the Heavens thou wert, and at the voice	Par Lost 3.9
No voice exempt, no voice but well could joine	Par Lost 3.370
Confusion heard his voice, and wilde uproar	Par Lost 3.710
O for that warning voice, which he who saw	Par Lost 4.1
But with no friendly voice, and add thy name	Par Lost 4.36
Had not a voice thus warnd me, What thou seest,	Par Lost 4.467
Shot forth peculiar Graces; then with voice	Par Lost 5.15
With gentle voice, I thought it thine; it said,	Par Lost 5.37
The wonted signal, and superior voice	Par Lost 5.705
Before the seat supream; from whence a voice	Par Lost 6.27
So spake the Sovran voice, and Clouds began	Par Lost 6.56
Each to his place, they heard his voice and went	Par Lost 6.782
Voice(*cont*)	
If rightly thou art call'd, whose Voice divine	Par Lost 7.2
More safe I Sing with mortal voice, unchang'd	Par Lost 7.24
Both Harp and Voice; nor could the Muse defend	Par Lost 7.37
Held by thy voice, thy potent voice he heares,	Par Lost 7.100
For *Chaos* heard his voice: him all his Traine	Par Lost 7.221
Descends, thither with heart and voice and eyes	Par Lost 7.513
Temper'd soft Tunings, intermixt with Voice	Par Lost 7.598
So Charming left his voice, that he a while	Par Lost 8.2
line not in 1667 edition	
This answer from the gratious voice Divine.	Par Lost 8.436
And guided by his voice, nor uninformd	Par Lost 8.486
Of Creatures wanting voice, that done, partake	Par Lost 9.199
Though at the voice much marveling; at length	Par Lost 9.551
I knew, but not with human voice endu'd;	Par Lost 9.561
Sole Daughter of his voice; the rest, we live	Par Lost 9.653
Endu'd with human voice and human sense,	Par Lost 9.871
To counterfet Mans voice, true in our Fall,	Par Lost 9.1069
Amidst in Thunder utter'd thus his voice.	Par Lost 10.33
To sentence Man: the voice of God they heard	Par Lost 10.97
I heard thee in the Garden, and of thy voice	Par Lost 10.116
My voice thou oft hast heard, and hast not fear'd,	Par Lost 10.119
Before his voice, or was shee made thy guide,	Par Lost 10.146
Because thou hast heark'nd to the voice of thy Wife,	Par Lost 10.198
To those bright Orders utterd thus his voice.	Par Lost 10.615
Is propagated curse. O voice once heard	Par Lost 10.729
And sleep secure; his dreadful voice no more	Par Lost 10.779
Stood visible, among these Pines his voice	Par Lost 11.321
Mankinds deliverance. But the voice of God	Par Lost 12.235
Mans voice commanding, Sun in *Gibeon* stand,	Par Lost 12.265
Now had the great Proclaimer with a voice	Par Reg 1.18
The Spirit descended, while the Fathers voice	Par Reg 1.31
Would not be last, and with the voice divine	Par Reg 1.35
And out of Heav'n the Sov'raign voice I heard,	Par Reg 1.84
Sung with the voice, and this the argument.	Par Reg 1.172
Strait knew me, and with loudest voice proclaim'd	Par Reg 1.275
And last the sum of all, my Father's voice,	Par Reg 1.283
Praying or vowing, and vouchsaf'd his voice	Par Reg 1.490
Son own'd from Heaven by his Father's voice;	Par Reg 2.85
Twice by a voice inviting him to eat.	Par Reg 2.314
By voice or hand, and various-measur'd verse,	Par Reg 4.256
Though not to be Baptiz'd, by voice from Heav'n	Par Reg 4.512
Worth naming Son of God by voice from Heav'n,	Par Reg 4.539
Shall chase thee with the terror of his voice	Par Reg 4.627
Chor. Look now for no inchanting voice, nor fear	Samson 1065
Spir. What voice is that, my young Lord? speak agen.	Mask 492
Too well I did perceive it was the voice	Mask 563
The melting voice through mazes running;	Allegro 142
If my inferior hand or voice could hit	Arcades 77
Return *Alpheus*, the dread voice is past,	Lycidas 132
And joyn thy voice unto the Angel Quire,	Nativity 27
Divinely-warbled voice	Nativity 96
No voice or hideous humm	Nativity 174
A voice of weeping heard, and loud lament;	Nativity 183
Sphear-born harmonious Sisters, Voice, and Vers,	Musick 2
Trinity ms 'Voice' ←'voice'	
That we on Earth with undiscording voice	Musick 17
Trinity ms 'voice' ←'hart & voice'	
To hear the Lute well toucht, or artfull voice	Sonnet 20, 11
Will hear my voyce what time to him I crie.	Psalm 4, 18
The voyce of my complaining hear	Psalm 5, 3
Jehovah thou my early voyce	Psalm 5, 5
Depart from me, for the voice of my weeping	Psalm 6, 17
Nor hearken to my voice;	Psalm 81, 46
Wilt thou not turn, and *hear our voice*	Psalm 85, 21
I lift my soul *and voice*,	Psalm 86, 12
Voiced	
To the full voic'd Quire below,	Penseroso 162
Voices	
Of Dulcet Symphonies and voices sweet,	Par Lost 1.712
Of stunning sounds and voices all confus'd	Par Lost 2.952
As from blest voices, uttering joy, Heav'n rung	Par Lost 3.347
Celestial voices to the midnight air,	Par Lost 4.682
Joyn voices all ye living Souls, ye Birds,	Par Lost 5.197
So many terrors, voices, prodigies	Par Reg 4.482
Void	
The seat of desolation, voyd of light,	Par Lost 1.181
Familiar the fierce heat, and void of pain;	Par Lost 2.219
These past, if any pass, the void profound	Par Lost 2.438
Th' unfounded deep, and through the void immense	Par Lost 2.829
Won from the void and formless infinite.	Par Lost 3.12
Vows made in pain, as violent and void.	Par Lost 4.97
Far in the dark dislodg'd, and void of rest,	Par Lost 6.415
Matter unform'd and void: Darkness profound	Par Lost 7.233
Which leaves us naked thus, of Honour void,	Par Lost 9.1074
Which he presumes already vain and void,	Par Lost 10.50
And great exploits, but of true vertu void;	Par Lost 11.790
By Faith not void of workes: this God-like act	Par Lost 12.427
Made answer meet, that made void all his wiles.	Par Reg 3.442
Long since. Wert thou so void of fear or shame,	Par Reg 4.189
Though void of corporal sense.	Samson 616
Now void, it fitts thy people; thether bend	Prose 12, 10
Volant	
Thir stops and chords was seen: his volant touch	Par Lost 11.561
Volatile	
Volatil *Hermes*, and call up unbound	Par Lost 3.603
Volley	
His Thunder in mid Volie, for he meant	Par Lost 6.854

Volleyed
Thy blasting volied Thunder made all speed | Par Lost 4.928
Volleys
Of fiery Darts in flaming volies flew, | Par Lost 6.213
Voluble
Diurnal, or this less volubil Earth | Par Lost 4.594
Then voluble and bold, now hid, now seen | Par Lost 9.436
His message will be short and voluble. | Samson 1307
Volumes
Pronounc't and in his volumes taught our Lawes, | Sonnet 21, 3
line not in Trinity ms
Voluminous
Voluminous and vast, a Serpent arm'd | Par Lost 2.652
Voluminous, or single characters, | Par Reg 4.384
Voluntary
Then feed on thoughts, that voluntarie move | Par Lost 3.37
Our voluntarie service he requires, | Par Lost 5.529
Both Ransom and Redeemer voluntarie, | Par Lost 10.61
If of that pow'r I bring thee voluntary | Par Reg 2.394
Voluptuous
At thy right hand voluptuous, as beseems | Par Lost 2.869
Enerve, and with voluptuous hope dissolve, | Par Reg 2.165
Softn'd with pleasure and voluptuous life; | Samson 534
Vomit
Or like the sons of *Vulcan* vomit smoak, | Mask 655
Bridgewater ms 'vomitt'
Votarist
Like a sad Votarist in Palmers weed | Mask 189
Trinity ms 'votarist'
line not in Bridgewater ms
Vote
Princes of Hell? for so the popular vote | Par Lost 2.313
They vote: whereat his speech he thus renews. | Par Lost 2.389
I, as I undertook, and with the vote | Par Reg 2.129
Vouched
At such bold words voucht with a deed so bold: | Par Lost 5.66
Vouchsafe
To us perhaps he brings, and will voutsafe | Par Lost 5.312
To want, and honour these, voutsafe with us | Par Lost 5.365
Nor other strife with them do I voutsafe. | Par Lost 6.823
On whom his leisure will vouchsafe an eye | Par Reg 2.210
To us O God *vouchsafe;* | Psalm 80, 14
O God of Hosts *vouchsafe* | Psalm 80, 30
Lord God of Hosts *voutsafe*, | Psalm 80, 78
Vouchsafed
Voutsaf't or sought; for what peace will be giv'n | Par Lost 2.332
Freely voutsaft; once more I will renew | Par Lost 3.175
Under whose lowly roof thou hast voutsaf't | Par Lost 5.463
Will not be now voutsaf't, other Decrees | Par Lost 5.884
Of what we are. But since thou hast voutsaf't | Par Lost 7.80
1669 'vouchsaf't'
The thirst I had of knowledge, and voutsaf't | Par Lost 8.8
Beyond all other, think the same voutsaf't | Par Lost 8.581
With worship, place by place where he voutsaf'd | Par Lost 11.318
Such favour I unworthie am voutsaft, | Par Lost 12.622
1669 'vouchsaft'
Praying or vowing, and vouchsaf'd his voice | Par Reg 1.490
Vouchsafes
That God voutsafes to raise another World | Par Lost 11.877
For Gods! yet him God the most High voutsafes | Par Lost 12.120
Obedient to his will, that he voutsafes | Par Lost 12.246
Vouchsafest
Who highly thus to entitle me voutsaf'st, | Par Lost 11.170
Vow
Against his vow of strictest purity, | Samson 319
Of vow, and have betray'd it to a woman, | Samson 379
The pledge of my unviolated vow. | Samson 1144
Our Law, or stain my vow of *Nazarite*. | Samson 1386
But vow though the cross Doctors all stood hearers, | Another 19
line not in 1640, 1657, 1658 texts
Vowed
Us thy vow'd Priests, till utmost end | Mask 136
To whom thou untry'd seem'st fair. Me in my vow'd | Horace 13
For aye, with Temples vow'd, and Virgin quires. | Prose 12, 6
Vowing
Praying or vowing, and vouchsaf'd his voice | Par Reg 1.490
Vows
Sidonian Virgins paid thir Vows and Songs, | Par Lost 1.441
ms 'vowes'
Vows made in pain, as violent and void. | Par Lost 4.97
With vows, as thir chief good, and final hope. | Par Lost 11.493
His further ire, with praiers and vows renew'd. | Samson 520
To break all faith, all vows, deceive, betray, | Samson 750
To whom our vows and wishes bend, | Arcades 6
Trinity ms 'vowes'
Or whether thou to our moist vows deny'd, | Lycidas 159
1638 'vowes'
And with stiff Vowes renounc'd his Liturgie | Forcers 2
Trinity ms 'vowes'
Voyage
Alone the dreadful voyage; till at last | Par Lost 2.426
Pondering his Voyage; for no narrow frith | Par Lost 2.919
Her annual Voiage, born on Windes; the Aire | Par Lost 7.431
Bound on a voyage uncouth and obscure, | Par Lost 8.230
Successfully; a calmer voyage now | Par Reg 1.103
Voyaged
Voyag'd th' unreal, vast, unbounded deep | Par Lost 10.471
Vulcan
Or like the sons of *Vulcan* vomit smoak, | Mask 655
Vulgar
Alooff the vulgar Constellations thick, | Par Lost 3.577
Things vulgar, & well weigh'd, scarce worth the praise, | Par Reg 3.51
The vulgar only scap'd who stood without. | Samson 1659
Vulture
As when a Vultur on *Imaus* bred, | Par Lost 3.431
Wades
And swims or sinks, or wades, or creeps, or flyes: | Par Lost 2.950
Waft
Will waft me; and the way found prosperous once | Par Reg 1.104
And, O ye *Dolphins*, waft the haples youth. | Lycidas 164
Wafted
Wafted by Angels, or flew o're the Lake | Par Lost 3.521
Wafting
A gentle wafting to immortal Life. | Par Lost 12.435
Wafts
Wafts on the calmer wave by dubious light | Par Lost 2.1042
Wage
To wage by force or guile eternal Warr | Par Lost 1.121
Waged
Wag'd in the troubl'd Skie, and Armies rush | Par Lost 2.534
Wagons
With Sails and Wind thir canie Waggons light: | Par Lost 3.439
And Waggons fraught with Utensils of war. | Par Reg 3.336
Wail
Would ask a life to wail, but chief of all, | Samson 66
Nothing is here for tears, nothing to wail | Samson 1721
Wailing
Wailing thy absence in my widow'd bed; | Samson 806
Wain
Rose from the hindmost wheels of *Phoebus* wain. | Mask 190
1637 'waine'
Trinity ms 'waine' ← 'chaire'
line not in Bridgewater ms
Yet (strange to think) his wain was his increase: | Another 32
1657 *'waine'*
1640 'waine'
line not in 1658 text
Waist
The one seem'd Woman to the waste, and fair, | Par Lost 2.650
Shee as a vail down to the slender waste | Par Lost 4.304
Girt like a Starrie Zone his waste, and round | Par Lost 5.281
Down clov'n to the waste, with shatterd Armes | Par Lost 6.361
To gird thir waste, vain Covering if to hide | Par Lost 9.1113
Wait
Millions that stand in Arms, and longing wait | Par Lost 2.55
That day and night for his destruction waite. | Par Lost 2.505
To wait them with his Keys, and now at foot | Par Lost 3.485
Why satst thou like an enemie in waite | Par Lost 4.825
Authority and Reason on her waite, | Par Lost 8.554
That lay in wait; beyond this had bin force, | Par Lost 9.1173
But let us wait; thus far he hath perform'd, | Par Reg 2.49
But I to wait with patience am inur'd; | Par Reg 2.102
But on Occasions forelock watchful wait. | Par Reg 3.173
To wait in *Amphitrite*'s bowr. | Mask 921
1637 'waite'
Trinity ms 'waite'
Bridgewater ms 'waite'
Yet *Syrinx* well might wait on her. | Arcades 107
Trinity ms defective here
They also serve who only stand and waite. | Sonnet 19, 14
Waited
A pomp of winning Graces waited still, | Par Lost 8.61
Waited with hellish rancour imminent | Par Lost 9.409
The time prefixt I waited, when behold | Par Reg 1.269
Waiting
Waiting revenge: cruel his eye, but cast | Par Lost 1.604
Worth waiting, since our present lot appeers | Par Lost 2.223
Disturbd not, waiting close th' approach of Morn. | Par Lost 9.191
Waiting desirous her return, had wove | Par Lost 9.839
Waits
More solemn then the tedious pomp that waits | Par Lost 5.354
The tools of death, that waits him near. | Psalm 7, 48
Wake
And oft though wisdom wake, suspicion sleeps | Par Lost 3.686
Unseen, both when we wake, and when we sleep: | Par Lost 4.678
Thy goodness infinite, both when we wake, | Par Lost 4.734
Sam. Not for thy life, lest fierce remembrance wake | Samson 952
Ere morrow wake, or the low roosted lark | Mask 317
Trinity ms 'ere morrow wake' ← 'ere the larke rowse'
And as I wake, sweet musick breath | Penseroso 151
And wake for me, their furi' asswage; | Psalm 7, 22
Waked
When *Adam* wak't, so customd, for his sleep | Par Lost 5.3
Such whispering wak'd her, but with startl'd eye | Par Lost 5.26
And fell asleep; but O how glad I wak'd | Par Lost 5.92
Alternate all night long: but not so wak'd | Par Lost 5.657
Wak't by the circling Hours, with rosie hand | Par Lost 6.3
Then as new wak't thus gratefully repli'd. | Par Lost 8.4
1667 'To whom thus *Adam*'
Induc'd me. As new wak't from soundest sleep | Par Lost 8.253
To pluck and eate; whereat I wak'd, and found | Par Lost 8.309
Shee disappeerd, and left me dark, I wak'd | Par Lost 8.478
Mean while the hour of Noon drew on, and wak'd | Par Lost 9.739
Of *Philistean Dalilah*, and wak'd | Par Lost 9.1061
To fan the Earth now wak'd, and usher in | Par Lost 10.94

Waked(*cont*)
Wak't in the renovation of the just, Par Lost 11.65
Leucothea wak'd, and with fresh dews imbalmd Par Lost 11.135
Lay sleeping ran before, but found her wak't; Par Lost 12.608
Fasting he went to sleep, and fasting wak'd. Par Reg 2.284
I wak'd, she fled, and day brought back my night. Sonnet 23, 14
I lay and slept, I wak'd again, Psalm 3, 13
Wakeful
Against a wakeful Foe, while I abroad Par Lost 2.463
Had from his wakeful custody purloind Par Lost 2.946
Harmonious numbers; as the wakeful Bird Par Lost 3.38
Were slunk, all but the wakeful Nightingale; Par Lost 4.602
Of *Argus*, and more wakeful then to drouze, Par Lost 11.131
The wakefull trump of doom must thunder through the deep, Nativity 156
1673 'wakeful'
Waken
Thir sacred Song, and waken raptures high; Par Lost 3.369
We may no longer stay: go, waken *Eve;* Par Lost 12.594
Wakens
Venus now wakes, and wak'ns Love. Mask 124
Trinity ms 'wakens'
1637 'wakens'
Bridgewater ms 'wakens'
Wakes
By change of place: Now conscience wakes despair Par Lost 4.23
That slumberd, wakes the bitter memorie Par Lost 4.24
If none regard; Heav'n wakes with all his eyes, Par Lost 5.44
Oft in her absence mimic Fansie wakes Par Lost 5.110
Their merry wakes and pastimes keep: Mask 121
Venus now wakes, and wak'ns Love. Mask 124
Wakest
Here sleep below while thou to foresight wak'st, Par Lost 11.368
Waking
And waking cri'd, *This is the Gate of Heav'n* Par Lost 3.515
Beautie, which whether waking or asleep, Par Lost 5.14
Waking thou never wilt consent to do. Par Lost 5.121
Both waking we were one; how then can now Par Lost 5.678
Nor sleeping him nor waking harm'd, his walk Par Reg 1.311
Such sober certainty of waking bliss Mask 263
Bridgewater ms 'wakinge'
Walk
If that way be your walk, you have not farr; Par Lost 2.1007
But first with narrow search I must walk round Par Lost 4.528
Our walk at noon, with branches overgrown, Par Lost 4.627
1667 'walks'
With this her solemn Bird, nor walk by Moon, Par Lost 4.655
Millions of spiritual Creatures walk the Earth Par Lost 4.677
While they keep watch, or nightly rounding walk Par Lost 4.685
Close at mine ear one call'd me forth to walk Par Lost 5.36
To find thee I directed then my walk; Par Lost 5.49
Yee that in Waters glide, and yee that walk Par Lost 5.200
They shew us when our foes walk not upright. Par Lost 6.627
As we need walk, till younger hands ere long Par Lost 9.246
Neerer he drew, and many a walk travers'd Par Lost 9.434
Did, as thou sawst, receave, to walk with God Par Lost 11.707
And love with fear the onely God, to walk Par Lost 12.562
Nor sleeping him nor waking harm'd, his walk Par Reg 1.311
Hard are the ways of truth, and rough to walk, Par Reg 1.478
Set women in his eye and in his walk, Par Reg 2.153
Commun'd in silent walk, then laid him down Par Reg 2.261
If any be, they walk obscure; Samson 296
And over heaps of slaughter'd walk his way? Samson 1530
May trace huge Forests, and unharbour'd Heaths, Mask 423
Trinity ms 'trace' ←'walke through'
And missing thee, I walk unseen Penseroso 65
To walk the studious Cloysters pale, Penseroso 156
From eyes of mortals walk invisible, Vacation 66
Stand spelling fals, while one might walk to Mile- Sonnet 11, 7
Trinity ms 'walke' ←'walk'
To walk my *righteous* waies. Psalm 81, 56
In darkness they walk on Psalm 82, 18
Walked
He walkt with to support uneasie steps Par Lost 1.295
Here walk'd the Fiend at large in spacious field. Par Lost 3.430
Walk'd up and down alone bent on his prey, Par Lost 3.441
Walk'd firm; the crested Cock whose clarion sounds Par Lost 7.443
Among the Trees in Pairs they rose, they walk'd: Par Lost 7.459
By Fowl, Fish, Beast, was flown, was swum, was walkt Par Lost 7.503
Creatures that livd, and movd, and walk'd, or flew, Par Lost 8.264
With what delight could I have walkt thee round, Par Lost 9.114
Long had not walkt, when from the Tents behold Par Lost 11.581
One day forth walk'd alone, the Spirit leading; Par Reg 1.189
Equivalent to Angels walk'd thir streets, Samson 343
I walk'd about admir'd of all and dreaded Samson 530
Hath walk'd about, and each limb to survey, Samson 1089
Through the dear might of him that walk'd the waves; Lycidas 173
Trinity ms 'walkt'
The Subject new: it walk'd the Town a while, Sonnet 11, 3
Trinity ms 'walk'd' ←'It went off well about'
Bless'd is the man who hath not walk'd astray Psalm 1, 1
Walkest
Walk'st on the rowling Sphear, and through the deep, Prose 12, 2
Walking
Now walking in the Garden, by soft windes Par Lost 10.98
Him walking on a Sunny hill he found, Par Reg 4.447
Som time walking not unseen Allegro 57
Walks
Satan alighted walks: a Globe farr off Par Lost 3.422

Walks(*cont*)
Hypocrisie, the onely evil that walks Par Lost 3.683
But if within the circuit of these walks, Par Lost 4.586
Our walk at noon, with branches overgrown, Par Lost 4.627
1667 'walks'
His god-like Guest, walks forth, without more train Par Lost 5.351
Planted, with Walks, and Bowers, that what I saw Par Lost 8.305
Walks, and the melodie of Birds; but here Par Lost 8.528
High overarch't, and echoing Walks between; Par Lost 9.1107
What can be toilsom in these pleasant Walkes? Par Lost 11.179
Thee Native Soile, these happie Walks and Shades, Par Lost 11.270
New reapt, the other part sheep-walks and foulds; Par Lost 11.431
Unseen, and through thir habitations walks Par Lost 12.49
High rooft and walks beneath, and alleys brown Par Reg 2.293
City or Suburban, studious walks and shades; Par Reg 4.243
The vertuous mind, that ever walks attended Mask 211
line not in Bridgewater ms
My daily walks and ancient neighbourhood, Mask 314
Benighted walks under the mid-day Sun; Mask 384
Trinity ms 'benighted walks under the midday sun' ←'walks in black vapours though the noontyde brand'
Bridgewater ms 'walks in black vapours though the noone tyde brand'
Som say no evil thing that walks by night Mask 432
To arched walks of twilight groves, Penseroso 133
Wall
Coasting the wall of Heav'n on this side Night Par Lost 3.71
Save on that side which from the wall of Heav'n Par Lost 3.427
Up to the wall of Heaven a Structure high, Par Lost 3.503
The verdurous wall of paradise up sprung: Par Lost 4.143
And higher then that Wall a circling row Par Lost 4.146
Of Hill or highest Wall, and sheer within Par Lost 4.182
Fenc'd up the verdant wall; each beauteous flour, Par Lost 4.697
And Chrystal wall of Heav'n, which op'ning wide, Par Lost 6.860
Part rise in crystal Wall, or ridge direct, Par Lost 7.293
Thrice Fugitive about *Troy* Wall; or rage Par Lost 9.16
Of length prodigious joyning to the Wall Par Lost 10.302
Assaulting; others from the wall defend Par Lost 11.657
1667 'Wall'
Here *Ninevee*, of length within her wall Par Reg 3.275
Or did of late earths Sonnes besiege the wall Fair Inf 47
Picture the sacred wall declares t' have hung Horace 14
Walled
Machaerus and each Town or City wall'd Par Reg 2.22
Wallowing
Wallowing unweildie, enormous in thir Gate Par Lost 7.411
when the big rowling flakes of pitchie clowds Mask Tr. ms 15.52
'rowling' ←'wallowing'
Walls
Heav'n, whose high walls fear no assault or Siege, Par Lost 2.343
Of light appears, and from the walls of Heav'n Par Lost 2.1035
The rest in circuit walles this Universe. Par Lost 3.721
Farr to the inland retir'd, about the walls Par Lost 10.423
Of mightiest Empire, from the destind Walls Par Lost 11.387
As on drie land between two christal walls, Par Lost 12.197
To that proud Citie, whose high Walls thou saw'st Par Lost 12.342
His whispering stream; within the walls then view Par Reg 4.250
The floods stood still like Walls of Glass, Psalm 136, 49
To save th' *Athenian* Walls from ruine bare. Sonnet 8, 14
Trinity ms 'walls'
Wan
But faded splendor wan; who by his gate Par Lost 4.870
Spreading thir bane; the blasted Starrs lookt wan, Par Lost 10.412
With Cowslips wan that hang the pensive hed, Lycidas 147
With praise enough for Envy to look wan; Sonnet 13, 6
Wand
Of some great Ammiral, were but a wand, Par Lost 1.294
Before his decent steps a Silver wand. Par Lost 3.644
He with his bare wand can unthred thy joynts, Mask 614
But sease his wand, though he and his curst crew Mask 653
Comus. Nay Lady sit; if I but wave this wand, Mask 659
O ye mistook, ye should have snatcht his wand Mask 815
And waving wide her mirtle wand, Nativity 51
Wander
Darkens the Streets, then wander forth the Sons Par Lost 1.501
Those thoughts that wander through Eternity, Par Lost 2.148
Cease I to wander where the Muses haunt Par Lost 3.27
Till final dissolution, wander here, Par Lost 3.458
Erroneous there to wander and forlorne. Par Lost 7.20
Or wander with delight, and love to haunt Par Lost 7.330
How shall I part, and whither wander down Par Lost 11.282
Where may she wander now, whether betake her Mask 351
To all that wander in that perilous flood. Lycidas 185
Wandered
And long he wanderd, till at last a gleame Par Lost 3.499
Through the worlds wilderness long wanderd man Par Lost 12.313
Wandred this barren waste, the same I now: Par Reg 1.354
He wanderd long, till thee he spy'd from farr, Fair Inf 17
Wanderer
Misleads th' amaz'd Night-wanderer from his way Par Lost 9.640
And here to every thirsty wanderer, Mask 524
Wanderers
And airy tongues, that syllable mens names Mask 208
Trinity ms 'syllable mens nams' ←'lure night wanderers' ←'night wandring'
Wandering
Got them new Names, till wandring ore the Earth, Par Lost 1.365
Thir wandring Gods disguis'd in brutish forms Par Lost 1.481

Wandering*(cont)*
Sufficient? who shall tempt with wandring feet Par Lost 2.404
Disband, and wandring, each his several way Par Lost 2.523
And found no end, in wandring mazes lost. Par Lost 2.561
To search with wandring quest a place foretold Par Lost 2.830
Wandring this darksome Desart, as my way, Par Lost 2.973
To find who might direct his wandring flight Par Lost 3.631
Alone thus wandring. Brightest Seraph tell Par Lost 3.667
Runs divers, wandring many a famous Realme Par Lost 4.234
Some wandring Spirit of Heav'n, by Fountain side, Par Lost 4.531
And yee five other wandring Fires that move Par Lost 5.177
Though wandring. He with his consorted *Eve* Par Lost 7.50
With Serpent errour wandring, found thir way, Par Lost 7.302
Thir wandring course now high, now low, then hid, Par Lost 8.126
Seek them with wandring thoughts, and notions vain. Par Lost 8.187
My wandring, had not hee who was my Guide Par Lost 8.312
Bright'ns his Crest, as when a wandring Fire, Par Lost 9.634
Desire of wandring this unhappie Morn, Par Lost 9.1136
Of wandring, as thou call'st it, which who knows Par Lost 9.1146
1667 'wandering'
And wandring vanitie, when lest was safe, Par Lost 10.875
Wandring that watrie Desert: I had hope Par Lost 11.779
Not wandring poor, but trusting all his wealth Par Lost 12.133
Wandring, shall in a glorious Temple enshrine. Par Lost 12.334
They hand in hand with wandring steps and slow, Par Lost 12.648
Wandring this woody maze, and humane food Par Reg 2.246
Native of *Thebez* wandring here was fed Par Reg 2.313
Wandring the Wilderness, whatever place, Par Reg 4.600
Then give the rains to wandring thought, Samson 302
That wandring loose about Samson 675
Threats the forlorn and wandring Passinger. Mask 39
Bridgewater ms 'wandringe'
They had ingag'd their wandring steps too far, Mask 193
Trinity ms 'wandring' ←'youthly'
Bridgewater ms 'wandringe'
And airy tongues, that syllable mens names Mask 208
Trinity ms 'syllable mens nams' ←'lure night wanderers' ←'night wandring'
After her wandring labours long, Mask 1006
line not in Bridgewater ms
To behold the wandring Moon, Penseroso 67
But fie my wandring Muse how thou dost stray! Vacation 53
And to their wandring mind; Psalm 81, 50

Wannish
And letters where my tears have washt a wannish white. Passion 35

Want
With Golden Architrave; nor did there want Par Lost 1.715
Nor want we skill or Art, from whence to raise Par Lost 2.272
Nor will occasion want, nor shall we need Par Lost 2.341
For want of other prey, but that he knows Par Lost 2.806
That heav'n would want spectators, God want praise; Par Lost 4.676
To want, and honour these, voutsafe with us Par Lost 5.365
Obedient? can we want obedience then Par Lost 5.514
By thee communicated, and our want: Par Lost 9.755
But by fulfilling that which thou didst want, Par Lost 12.396
Who dwell this wild, constrain'd by want, come forth Par Reg 1.331
Would scruple that, with want oppest? behold Par Reg 2.331
While Virtue, Valour, Wisdom sit in want. Par Reg 2.431
For want of well pronouncing *Shibboleth*. Samson 289
Sam. For want of words no doubt, or lack of breath, Samson 905
Where other senses want not their delights Samson 916
And quit: not wanting him, I shall want nothing. Samson 1484
As that the single want of light and noise Mask 369
If every just man that now pines with want Mask 768

Wanted
Wanted, nor youthful dalliance as beseems Par Lost 4.338
Sat horror Plum'd; nor wanted in his graspe Par Lost 4.989
Nor holy rapture wanted they to praise Par Lost 5.147
There wanted yet the Master work, the end Par Lost 7.505
I found not what me thought I wanted still; Par Lost 8.355
Wanted not long, though to this shape retain'd. Par Lost 9.601
Nor wanted clouds of foot, nor on each horn, Par Reg 3.327
He would not else who never wanted means, Samson 315
And timely rest have wanted, but fair Virgin Mask 689

Wanting
Nor wanting power to mitigate and swage Par Lost 1.556
Of Creatures wanting voice, that done, partake Par Lost 9.199
Be wanting, but afford thee equal aid, Par Lost 10.271
And what in me seems wanting, but that I Par Reg 2.450
And quit: not wanting him, I shall want nothing. Samson 1484

Wanton
To do him wanton rites, which cost them woe. Par Lost 1.414
Whose wanton passions in the sacred Porch Par Lost 1.454
Dissheveld, but in wanton ringlets wav'd Par Lost 4.306
More hands then ours to lop thir wanton growth: Par Lost 4.629
Mixt Dance, or wanton Mask, or Midnight Bal, Par Lost 4.768
One night or two with wanton growth derides Par Lost 9.211
Curld many a wanton wreath in sight of *Eve*, Par Lost 9.517
In Gems and wanton dress; to the Harp they sung Par Lost 11.583
Cast wanton eyes on the daughters of men, Par Reg 2.180
In wanton dance they praise the bounteous *Pan*, Mask 176
Quips and Cranks, and wanton Wiles, Allegro 27
With wanton heed, and giddy cunning, Allegro 141
With Ringlets quaint, and wanton windings wove. Arcades 47
Of shades and wanton winds, and gushing brooks, Lycidas 137
To wanton with the Sun her lusty Paramour. Nativity 36
Which 'mongst the wanton gods a foul reproach was held. Fair Inf 14

Wantoned
Wantond as in her prime, and plaid at will Par Lost 5.295

Wantonly
As wantonly repaid; in Lust they burne: Par Lost 9.1015

Wantonness
Surfet, and lust, till wantonness and pride Par Lost 11.795

Wants
Wants not her hidden lustre, Gemms and Gold; Par Lost 2.271
For us too large, where thy abundance wants Par Lost 4.730
Wants her fit vessels pure, then strews the ground Par Lost 5.348
And the great Light of Day yet wants to run Par Lost 7.98
And said, thy Mansion wants thee, *Adam*, rise, Par Lost 8.296
Without Copartner? so to add what wants Par Lost 9.821
And hateful; nothing wants, but that thy shape, Par Lost 10.869

War
Rais'd impious War in Heav'n and Battel proud Par Lost 1.43
ms 'warr'
To wage by force or guile eternal Warr Par Lost 1.121
ms 'warr'
That led th' imbattelld Seraphim to Warr Par Lost 1.129
ms 'warr'
By right of Warr, what e're his business be Par Lost 1.150
ms 'warr'
New warr, provok't; our better part remains Par Lost 1.645
For who can think Submission? Warr then, Warr Par Lost 1.661
ms 'warr then, warr'
Clash'd on thir sounding Shields the din of war, Par Lost 1.668
ms 'warr'
Vain Warr with Heav'n, and by success untaught Par Lost 2.9
Whether of open Warr or covert guile, Par Lost 2.41
My sentence is for open Warr: Of Wiles, Par Lost 2.51
I should be much for open Warr, O Peers, Par Lost 2.119
Main reason to perswade immediate Warr, Par Lost 2.121
Say they who counsel Warr, we are decreed, Par Lost 2.160
Designing or exhorting glorious warr, Par Lost 2.179
1667 'Warr'
Warr therefore, open or conceal'd, alike Par Lost 2.187
We warr, if warr be best, or to regain Par Lost 2.230
All thoughts of warr: ye have what I advise. Par Lost 2.283
1667 'Warr'
What sit we then projecting peace and Warr? Par Lost 2.329
Warr hath determin'd us, and foild with loss Par Lost 2.330
As when to warn proud Cities warr appears Par Lost 2.533
Shakes Pestilence and Warr. Each at the Head Par Lost 2.711
A growing burden. Mean while Warr arose, Par Lost 2.767
Against a rumord Warr, the Smuttie graine Par Lost 4.817
Warr he perceav'd, warr in procinct, and found Par Lost 6.19
At first, that Angel should with Angel warr, Par Lost 6.92
The ridges of grim Warr; no thought of flight, Par Lost 6.236
That Warr and various; somtimes on firm ground Par Lost 6.242
Intestine War in Heav'n, the arch foe subdu'd Par Lost 6.259
Brooks not the works of violence and Warr. Par Lost 6.274
Among the Constellations warr were sprung, Par Lost 6.312
From off the files of warr; there they him laid Par Lost 6.339
In might though wondrous and in Acts of Warr, Par Lost 6.377
And silence on the odious dinn of Warr: Par Lost 6.408
For sin, on warr and mutual slaughter bent. Par Lost 6.506
Infernal noise; Warr seem'd a civil Game Par Lost 6.667
Warr wearied hath perform'd what Warr can do, Par Lost 6.695
Of ending this great Warr, since none but Thou Par Lost 6.702
That shake Heav'ns basis, bring forth all my Warr, Par Lost 6.712
The discord which befel, and Warr in Heav'n Par Lost 6.897
And Warr so neer the Peace of God in bliss Par Lost 7.55
With odds what Warr hath lost, and fully aveng'd Par Lost 10.374
Beast now with Beast gan war, and Fowle with Fowle, Par Lost 10.710
One man, Assassin-like had levied Warr, Par Lost 11.219
Warr unproclam'd. The Princely Hierarch Par Lost 11.220
Concours in Arms, fierce Faces threatning Warr, Par Lost 11.641
The brazen Throat of Warr had ceast to roar, Par Lost 11.713
When violence was ceas't, and Warr on Earth, Par Lost 11.780
Peace to corrupt no less then Warr to waste. Par Lost 11.784
The conquerd also, and enslav'd by Warr Par Lost 11.797
With Warr and hostile snare such as refuse Par Lost 12.31
And overwhelm thir Warr: the Race elect Par Lost 12.214
Warr terrifie them inexpert, and feare Par Lost 12.218
That might require th' array of war, thy skill Par Reg 3.17
Without ambition, war, or violence; Par Reg 3.90
And Waggons fraught with Utensils of war. Par Reg 3.336
And fragile arms, much instrument of war Par Reg 3.388
Luggage of war there shewn me, argument Par Reg 3.401
And feats of War defeats Samson 1278
No War, or Battails sound Nativity 53
Devouring war shall never cease to roare: Vacation 86
For what can Warr, but endless warr still breed, Sonnet 15, 10
1694 both 'War'
Not of warr onely, but detractions rude, Sonnet 16, 2
1694 'War'
No less renownd then warr, new foes arise Sonnet 16, 11
1694 'than those of War'
Then to advise how warr may best, upheld, Sonnet 17, 7
1662 'war'
1694 'War'

Warble
Fountains and yee, that warble, as ye flow, Par Lost 5.195
Warble his native Wood-notes wilde, Allegro 134
Let us therfore warble forth Psalm 136, 89
Warble immortal Notes and *Tuskan* Ayre? Sonnet 20, 12

Warbled
With warbl'd Hymns, and to his Godhead sing — Par Lost 2.242
Trills her thick-warbl'd notes the summer long, — Par Reg 4.246
If she be right invok't in warbled Song, — Mask 854
Such notes as warbled to the string, — Penseroso 106
And touch the warbled string. — Arcades 87
Trinity ms 'wav', ms defective
Divinely-warbled voice — Nativity 96
1673 'Divinely-warbl'd'

Warblest
Warbl'st at eeve, when all the Woods are still, — Sonnet 1, 2

Warbling
That wash thy hallowd feet, and warbling flow, — Par Lost 3.31
To the night-warbling Bird, that now awake — Par Lost 5.40
Melodious murmurs, warbling tune his praise. — Par Lost 5.196
Ceas'd warbling, but all night tun'd her soft layes: — Par Lost 7.436
Birds on the branches warbling; all things smil'd, — Par Lost 8.265
Thy fair enchanted cup, and warbling charms — Samson 934
With eager thought warbling his *Dorick* lay: — Lycidas 189

Ward
Of dawning light turnd thither-ward in haste — Par Lost 3.500

Wardrobe
Or Frost to Flowers, that their gay wardrop wear, — Lycidas 47
1638 'wardrobe'
Trinity ms 'wardrope' ←'buttons'
And from thy wardrope bring thy chiefest treasure; — Vacation 18

Wards
Th' intricate wards, and every Bolt and Bar — Par Lost 2.877

Ware
Was took e're she was ware, and wish't she might — Mask 558

Warfare
Faithful hath been your warfare, and of God — Par Lost 6.803
1667 'Warfare'
Of his great warfare, e're I send him forth — Par Reg 1.158

Warlike
Then strait commands that at the warlike sound — Par Lost 1.531
To thir night watches in warlike Parade, — Par Lost 4.780
Thus he in scorn. The warlike Angel mov'd, — Par Lost 4.902
The great Arch-Angel from his warlike toile — Par Lost 6.257
See how in warlike muster they appear, — Par Reg 3.308
In scorn of thir proud arms and warlike tools, — Samson 137

Warm
Of various influence foment and warme, — Par Lost 4.669
Shot down direct his fervid Raies to warme — Par Lost 5.301
Main Ocean flow'd, not idle, but with warme — Par Lost 7.279
From thence a Rib, with cordial spirits warme; — Par Lost 8.466
To warm him wet return'd from field at Eve, — Par Reg 1.318
Mirth and youth, and warm desire, — May Morn 6

Warmed
Warm'd by the Sun, producing every kind, — Par Lost 9.721
Fomented by his virtual power and warmd: — Par Lost 11.338

Warmly
Both where the morning Sun first warmly smote — Par Lost 4.244

Warms
By his Magnetic beam, that gently warms — Par Lost 3.583
What ever clime the Suns bright circle warms. — Sonnet 8, 8
Trinity ms 'warmes'

Warmth
Thir soft Ethereal warmth, and there to pine — Par Lost 2.601
Earths inmost womb, more warmth then *Adam* needs; — Par Lost 5.302
And vital vertue infus'd, and vital warmth — Par Lost 7.236
Of incorporeal speed, her warmth and light; — Par Lost 8.37
Som better shroud, som better warmth to cherish — Par Lost 10.1068
From the bleak air; a Stable was our warmth, — Par Reg 2.74

Warn
As when to warn proud Cities warr appears — Par Lost 2.533
Yet mutable; whence warne him to beware — Par Lost 5.237
But list'n not to his Temptations, warne — Par Lost 6.908
Remember what I warne thee, shun to taste, — Par Lost 8.327
Thy inward fraud, to warn all Creatures from thee — Par Lost 10.871
Forerunners of his purpose, or to warn — Par Lost 11.195
Man is not whom to warne: those few escap't — Par Lost 11.777
May warn thee, as a sure fore-going sign. — Par Reg 4.483

Warned
The rest shall hear me call, and oft be warnd — Par Lost 3.185
While time was, our first-Parents had bin warnd — Par Lost 4.6
Uriel once warnd; whose eye pursu'd him down — Par Lost 4.125
Had not a voice thus warnd me, What thou seest, — Par Lost 4.467
So warnd he them aware themselves, and soon — Par Lost 6.547
Till warn'd, or by experience taught, she learne, — Par Lost 8.190
What hath bin warn'd us, what malicious Foe — Par Lost 9.253
Not keeping strictest watch, as she was warnd. — Par Lost 9.363
Us both securer then thus warnd thou seemst, — Par Lost 9.371
I warn'd thee, I admonish'd thee, foretold — Par Lost 9.1171
Descri'd, divinely warn'd, and witness bore — Par Reg 1.26
Just *Simeon* and Prophetic *Anna*, warn'd — Par Reg 1.255
But warn'd by oft experience: did not she — Samson 382
Or *Lucifer* that often warn'd them thence; — Nativity 74

Warning
O for that warning voice, which he who saw — Par Lost 4.1

Warping
Of *Locusts*, warping on the Eastern Wind, — Par Lost 1.341

Warrant
The last of me or no I cannot warrant. — Samson 1426

Warranted
Less warranted then this, or less secure — Mask 327
Bridgewater ms 'warrented'
Trinity ms 'warrante'd'

Warred
Titanian, or *Earth-born*, that warr'd on *Jove*, — Par Lost 1.198
Warr'd on by Cranes: though all the Giant brood — Par Lost 1.576

Warring
Of those Heav'n-warring Champions could be found — Par Lost 2.424
Levied to side with warring Winds, and poise — Par Lost 2.905
Thou drov'st of warring Angels disarraid. — Par Lost 3.396
Warring in Heav'n against Heav'ns matchless King: — Par Lost 4.41
Of warring Spirits; how without remorse — Par Lost 5.566
Dreadful combustion warring, and disturb, — Par Lost 6.225

Warrior
To whom the winged Warriour thus returnd: — Par Lost 4.576
To whom the warriour Angel, soon repli'd. — Par Lost 4.946
Each Warriour single as in Chief, expert — Par Lost 6.233
Which many a famous Warriour overturns, — Samson 542
Of noble Warriour, so to stain his honour, — Samson 1166

Warriors
Warriers, the Flowr of Heav'n, once yours, now lost, — Par Lost 1.316
Of Warriers old with order'd Spear and Shield, — Par Lost 1.565
ms 'warriors'
Arme, Warriours, Arme for fight, the foe at hand, — Par Lost 6.537
Thy choice of flaming Warriours, least the Fiend — Par Lost 11.101
1667 'warriours' in some copies
Grey-headed men and grave, with Warriours mixt, — Par Lost 11.662
Fled from his Lion ramp, old Warriors turn'd — Samson 139
Ye flaming Powers, and winged Warriours bright, — Circum 1

Wars
Among themselves, and levie cruel warres, — Par Lost 2.501
Of endless Warrs, and by confusion stand. — Par Lost 2.897
1667 'warrs'
Warrs, hitherto the onely Argument — Par Lost 9.28

Wary
Into this wild Abyss the warie fiend — Par Lost 2.917
Exceeded human, and his wary speech — Par Lost 5.459

Was
Th' infernal Serpent; he it was, whose guile — Par Lost 1.34
Was moving toward the shoar; his ponderous shield — Par Lost 1.284
Was fair *Damascus*, on the fertil Banks — Par Lost 1.468
He also against the house of God was bold: — Par Lost 1.470
Was not inglorious, though th' event was dire, — Par Lost 1.624
That in his womb was hid metallic Ore, — Par Lost 1.673
The Roof was fretted Gold. Not *Babilon*, — Par Lost 1.717
And some the Architect: his hand was known — Par Lost 1.732
Nor was his name unheard or unador'd — Par Lost 1.738
By all his Engins, but was headlong sent — Par Lost 1.750
Attended: all access was throng'd, the Gates — Par Lost 1.761
His trust was with th' Eternal to be deem'd — Par Lost 2.46
But all was false and hollow; though his Tongue — Par Lost 2.112
As not behind in hate; if what was urg'd — Par Lost 2.120
Chain'd on the burning Lake? that sure was worse. — Par Lost 2.169
That so ordains: this was at first resolv'd, — Par Lost 2.201
After the Tempest: Such applause was heard — Par Lost 2.290
Of him who rules above; so was his will — Par Lost 2.351
Thir rising all at once was as the sound — Par Lost 2.476
Thir Song was partial, but the harmony — Par Lost 2.552
Satan was now at hand, and from his seat — Par Lost 2.674
For never but once more was either like — Par Lost 2.721
Into my hand was giv'n, with charge to keep — Par Lost 2.775
He had to cross. Nor was his eare less peal'd — Par Lost 2.920
Following his track, such was the will of Heav'n, — Par Lost 2.1025
Beyond compare the Son of God was seen — Par Lost 3.138
O Father, gracious was that word which clos'd — Par Lost 3.144
And silence was in Heav'n: on mans behalf — Par Lost 3.218
Living or liveless to be found was none, — Par Lost 3.443
Each Stair mysteriously was meant, nor stood — Par Lost 3.516
So wondrously was set his Station bright. — Par Lost 3.587
His back was turnd, but not his brightness hid; — Par Lost 3.624
Glad was the Spirit impure as now in hope — Par Lost 3.630
Admonisht by his ear, and strait was known — Par Lost 3.647
While time was, our first-Parents had bin warnd — Par Lost 4.6
Of what he was, what is, and what must be — Par Lost 4.25
From me, whom he created what I was — Par Lost 4.43
Upbraided none; nor was his service hard. — Par Lost 4.45
Artificer of fraud; and was the first — Par Lost 4.121
One Gate there only was, and that look'd East — Par Lost 4.178
Of God the Garden was, by him in the East — Par Lost 4.209
Imbround the noontide Bowrs: Thus was this place, — Par Lost 4.246
Was gatherd, which cost *Ceres* all that pain — Par Lost 4.271
Then was not guiltie shame, dishonest shame — Par Lost 4.313
Declin'd was hasting now with prone carreer — Par Lost 4.353
And from whom I was formd flesh of thy flesh, — Par Lost 4.441
And what I was, whence thither brought, and how. — Par Lost 4.452
Leveld his eevning Rayes: it was a Rock — Par Lost 4.543
The rest was craggie cliff, that overhung — Par Lost 4.547
Silence was pleas'd: now glow'd the Firmament — Par Lost 4.604
On to thir blissful Bower; it was a place — Par Lost 4.690
Of thickest covert was inwoven shade — Par Lost 4.693
Such was thir awe of Man. In shadie Bower — Par Lost 4.705
By thee adulterous lust was driv'n from men — Par Lost 4.753
In that dark durance: thus much what was askt. — Par Lost 4.899
Was this your discipline and faith ingag'd, — Par Lost 4.954
Was Aerie light from pure digestion bred, — Par Lost 5.4
His wonder was to find unwak'nd *Eve* — Par Lost 5.9
My Guide was gon, and I, me thought, sunk down, — Par Lost 5.91
So cheard he his fair Spouse, and she was cheard, — Par Lost 5.129
So all was cleard, and to the Field they haste. — Par Lost 5.136
Perfections, in himself was all his state, — Par Lost 5.353
Thir Table was, and mossie seats had round, — Par Lost 5.392

Was(*cont*)

For know, whatever was created, needs	Par Lost 5.414
Was understood, the injur'd Lovers Hell.	Par Lost 5.450
This was that caution giv'n thee; be advis'd.	Par Lost 5.523
As yet this world was not, and *Chaos* wilde	Par Lost 5.577
Wast wont, I mine to thee was wont to impart;	Par Lost 5.677
Under him Regent, tells, as he was taught,	Par Lost 5.698
The great Hierarchal Standard was to move;	Par Lost 5.701
His name, and high was his degree in Heav'n;	Par Lost 5.707
Far was advanc't on winged speed, an Host	Par Lost 5.744
Messiah was declar'd in sight of Heav'n,	Par Lost 5.765
When this creation was? rememberst thou	Par Lost 5.857
From midst a Golden Cloud thus milde was heard.	Par Lost 6.28
Then violence: for this was all thy care	Par Lost 6.35
Thir march was, and the passive Air upbore	Par Lost 6.72
'Twixt Host and Host but narrow space was left,	Par Lost 6.104
Proud, art thou met? thy hope was to have reacht	Par Lost 6.131
Was never, Arms on Armour clashing bray'd	Par Lost 6.209
Of brazen Chariots rag'd; dire was the noise	Par Lost 6.211
Were don, but infinite: for wide was spred	Par Lost 6.241
Where erst was thickest fight, th' Angelic throng,	Par Lost 6.308
Was giv'n him temperd so, that neither keen	Par Lost 6.322
Forthwith on all sides to his aide was run	Par Lost 6.335
Satan: And thus was heard Commanding loud.	Par Lost 6.557
As likeliest was, when two such Foes met arm'd;	Par Lost 6.688
The storie heard attentive, and was fill'd	Par Lost 7.51
What within *Eden* or without was done	Par Lost 7.65
Great triumph and rejoycing was in Heav'n	Par Lost 7.180
When such was heard declar'd th' Almightie's will;	Par Lost 7.181
Was not; shee in a cloudie Tabernacle	Par Lost 7.248
Sojourn'd the while. God saw the Light was good;	Par Lost 7.249
He nam'd. Thus was the first Day Eev'n and Morn:	Par Lost 7.252
Both when first Eevning was, and when first Morn.	Par Lost 7.260
The Earth was form'd, but in the Womb as yet	Par Lost 7.276
And saw that it was good, and said, Let th' Earth	Par Lost 7.309
None was, but from the Earth a dewie Mist	Par Lost 7.333
Plant of the field, which e're it was in the Earth	Par Lost 7.335
On the green stemm; God saw that it was good.	Par Lost 7.337
To give Light on the Earth; and it was so.	Par Lost 7.345
Surveying his great Work, that it was good:	Par Lost 7.353
First in his East the glorious Lamp was seen,	Par Lost 7.370
But opposite in leveld West was set	Par Lost 7.376
And saw that it was good, and bless'd them, saying,	Par Lost 7.395
By Fowl, Fish, Beast, was flown, was swum, was walkt	Par Lost 7.503
View'd, and behold all was entirely good;	Par Lost 7.549
Was set, and twilight from the East came on,	Par Lost 7.583
With *Halleluiahs:* Thus was Sabbath kept.	Par Lost 7.634
And what before thy memorie was don	Par Lost 7.637
Of what was high: such pleasure she reserv'd,	Par Lost 8.50
Thee I have heard relating what was don	Par Lost 8.203
For I that Day was absent, as befell,	Par Lost 8.229
Or enemie, while God was in his work,	Par Lost 8.234
But who I was, or where, or from what cause,	Par Lost 8.270
I then was passing to my former state	Par Lost 8.290
A woodie Mountain; whose high top was plaine,	Par Lost 8.303
My wandring, had not hee who was my Guide	Par Lost 8.312
Thus farr to try thee, *Adam*, I was pleas'd,	Par Lost 8.437
Good reason was thou freely shouldst dislike,	Par Lost 8.443
And Life-blood streaming fresh; wide was the wound,	Par Lost 8.467
Grace was in all her steps, Heav'n in her Eye,	Par Lost 8.488
I follow'd her, she what was Honour knew,	Par Lost 8.508
Among the Beasts no Mate for thee was found.	Par Lost 8.594
The Sun was sunk, and after him the Starr	Par Lost 9.48
Found unsuspected way. There was a place,	Par Lost 9.69
With second thoughts, reforming what was old!	Par Lost 9.101
For whom all this was made, all this will soon	Par Lost 9.132
Not keeping strictest watch, as she was warnd.	Par Lost 9.363
Meer Serpent in appearance, forth was come,	Par Lost 9.413
Infeebl'd me, to what I was in Heav'n.	Par Lost 9.488
Floted redundant: pleasing was his shape,	Par Lost 9.503
Ammonian Jove, or *Capitoline* was seen,	Par Lost 9.508
I was at first as other Beasts that graze	Par Lost 9.571
As was my food, nor aught but food discern'd	Par Lost 9.573
Why then was this forbid? Why but to awe,	Par Lost 9.703
Was death invented? or to us deni'd	Par Lost 9.767
That all was lost. Back to the Thicket slunk	Par Lost 9.784
Of knowledg, nor was God-head from her thought.	Par Lost 9.790
Made erre, was now exhal'd, and grosser sleep	Par Lost 9.1049
Had shadow'd them from knowing ill, was gon,	Par Lost 9.1055
Was I to have never parted from thy side?	Par Lost 9.1153
Was known in Heav'n; for what can scape the Eye	Par Lost 10.5
Now was the Sun in Western cadence low	Par Lost 10.92
Love was not in thir looks, either to God	Par Lost 10.111
Was shee thy God, that her thou didst obey	Par Lost 10.145
Before his voice, or was shee made thy guide,	Par Lost 10.146
Shee was indeed, and lovely to attract	Par Lost 10.152
Unseemly to beare rule, which was thy part	Par Lost 10.155
Meanwhile ere thus was sin'd and judg'd on Earth,	Par Lost 10.229
Flew divers, and with Power (thir Power was great)	Par Lost 10.284
Great joy was at thir meeting, and at sight	Par Lost 10.350
Was plac't in regal lustre. Down a while	Par Lost 10.447
Was left him, or false glitter: All amaz'd	Par Lost 10.452
Thir mighty Chief returnd: loud was th' acclaime:	Par Lost 10.455
To his bold Riot: dreadful was the din	Par Lost 10.521
As in thir crime. Thus was th' applause they meant,	Par Lost 10.545
And *Ops*, ere yet *Dictaean Jove* was born.	Par Lost 10.584
On what was pure, till cramm'd and gorg'd, nigh burst	Par Lost 10.632
Or down from Heav'n descend. Such was thir song,	Par Lost 10.648

Was(*cont*)

Was bid turn Reines from th' Equinoctial Rode	Par Lost 10.672
Of God, whom to behold was then my highth	Par Lost 10.724
Thy terms too hard, by which I was to hold	Par Lost 10.751
To serve him, thy reward was of his grace,	Par Lost 10.767
Horrid, if true! yet why? it was but breath	Par Lost 10.789
And wandring vanitie, when lest was safe,	Par Lost 10.875
And understood not all was but a shew	Par Lost 10.883
Was meant by Death that day, when lo, to thee	Par Lost 10.1050
Obtain, all thy request was my Decree:	Par Lost 11.47
The Ground whence he was taken, fitter soile.	Par Lost 11.98
That I was heard with favour; peace returnd	Par Lost 11.153
But infinite in pardon was my Judge,	Par Lost 11.167
Direct to th' Eastern Gate was bent thir flight.	Par Lost 11.190
With what to sight or smell was sweet; from thee	Par Lost 11.281
As once thou slepst, while Shee to life was formd.	Par Lost 11.369
In the Visions of God: It was a Hill	Par Lost 11.377
On *Europe* thence, and where *Rome* was to sway	Par Lost 11.405
The others not, for his was not sincere;	Par Lost 11.443
Much at that sight was *Adam* in his heart	Par Lost 11.448
Dire was the tossing, deep the groans, despair	Par Lost 11.489
Was heard, of Harp and Organ; and who moovd	Par Lost 11.560
Thir stops and chords was seen: his volant touch	Par Lost 11.561
From the high neighbouring Hills, which was thir Seat,	Par Lost 11.575
Through all the Plain, and refuge none was found.	Par Lost 11.673
Adam was all in tears, and to his guide	Par Lost 11.674
But who was that Just Man, whom had not Heav'n	Par Lost 11.681
All now was turn'd to jollitie and game,	Par Lost 11.714
No more was seen; the floating Vessel swum	Par Lost 11.745
When violence was ceas't, and Warr on Earth,	Par Lost 11.780
But I was farr deceav'd; for now I see	Par Lost 11.783
As mockt they storm; great laughter was in Heav'n	Par Lost 12.59
And hear the din; thus was the building left	Par Lost 12.61
And therefore was Law given them to evince	Par Lost 12.287
Beyond which was my folly to aspire.	Par Lost 12.560
The World was all before them, where to choose	Par Lost 12.646
To him his Heavenly Office, nor was long	Par Reg 1.28
Such high attest was giv'n, a while survey'd	Par Reg 1.37
And he himself among them was baptiz'd,	Par Reg 1.76
At these sad tidings; but no time was then	Par Reg 1.109
When I was yet a child, no childish play	Par Reg 1.201
To me was pleasing, all my mind was set	Par Reg 1.202
And was admir'd by all, yet this not all	Par Reg 1.214
And told them the Messiah now was born,	Par Reg 1.245
For in the Inn was left no better room:	Par Reg 1.248
The Law and Prophets, searching what was writ	Par Reg 1.260
Not knew by sight) now come, who was to come	Par Reg 1.271
Which I believ'd was from above; but he	Par Reg 1.274
Me him (for it was shew'n him so from Heaven)	Par Reg 1.276
Me him whose Harbinger he was; and first	Par Reg 1.277
As much his greater, and was hardly won;	Par Reg 1.279
He was well pleas'd; by which I knew the time	Par Reg 1.286
Was difficult, by humane steps untrod;	Par Reg 1.298
And he still on was led, but with such thoughts	Par Reg 1.299
Moses was forty days, nor eat nor drank,	Par Reg 1.352
Kept not my happy Station, but was driv'n	Par Reg 1.360
The other service was thy chosen task,	Par Reg 1.427
Moses was in the Mount, and missing long;	Par Reg 2.15
From the bleak air; a Stable was our warmth,	Par Reg 2.74
Had left him vacant, and with speed was gon	Par Reg 2.116
Consenting in full frequence was impowr'd,	Par Reg 2.130
With clamour was assur'd thir utmost aid	Par Reg 2.148
It was the hour of night, when thus the Son	Par Reg 2.260
And by the Angel was bid rise and eat,	Par Reg 2.274
Our Saviour, and found all was but a dream,	Par Reg 2.283
Native of *Thebez* wandring here was fed	Par Reg 2.313
And exquisitest name, for which was drain'd	Par Reg 2.346
Was that crude Apple that diverted *Eve!*	Par Reg 2.349
Such was the Splendour, and the Tempter now	Par Reg 2.366
Famous he was in Heaven, on Earth less known;	Par Reg 3.68
My error was my error, and my crime	Par Reg 3.212
With that (such power was giv'n him then) he took	Par Reg 3.251
It was a Mountain at whose verdant feet	Par Reg 3.253
The Prospect was, that here and there was room	Par Reg 3.263
Or where plain was raise hill, or over-lay	Par Reg 3.333
Such and so numerous was thir Chivalrie;	Par Reg 3.344
But whence to thee this zeal, where was it then	Par Reg 3.407
By three days Pestilence? such was thy zeal	Par Reg 3.412
So little here, nay lost; but *Eve* was *Eve*,	Par Reg 4.6
The strength he was to cope with, or his own:	Par Reg 4.9
For him I was not sent, nor yet to free	Par Reg 4.131
Alone into the Temple; there was found	Par Reg 4.217
Was absent, after all his mischief done,	Par Reg 4.440
Was distant; and these flaws, though mortals fear them	Par Reg 4.454
This Tempest at this Desert most was bent;	Par Reg 4.465
The Son of God I also am, or was,	Par Reg 4.518
And if I was, I am; relation stands;	Par Reg 4.519
Times past, what once I was, and what am now.	Samson 22
O wherefore was my birth from Heaven foretold	Samson 23
Why was my breeding order'd and prescrib'd	Samson 30
Lower then bondslave! Promise was that I	Samson 38
How slight the gift was, hung it in my Hair.	Samson 59
Let there be light, and light was over all;	Samson 84
She all in every part; why was the sight	Samson 93
But thee whose strength, while vertue was her mate,	Samson 173
Yet that which was the worst now least afflicts me,	Samson 195
That what I motion'd was of God; I knew	Samson 222
The work to which I was divinely call'd;	Samson 226

Was(*cont*)
Was in the Vale of *Sorec*, *Dalila*, Samson 229
She was not the prime cause, but I my self, Samson 234
Safe to the rock of *Etham* was retir'd, Samson 253
For of such Doctrine never was there School, Samson 297
Unchaste was subsequent, her stain not his. Samson 325
This well I knew, nor was at all surpris'd, Samson 381
And Rivals? In this other was there found Samson 387
She purpos'd to betray me, and (which was worse Samson 399
As was my former servitude, ignoble, Samson 416
Tacit, was in thy power; true; and thou bear'st Samson 430
Whose drink was only from the liquid brook. Samson 557
Which was expresly giv'n thee to annoy them? Samson 578
I was his nursling once and choice delight, Samson 633
First granting, as I do, it was a weakness Samson 773
Was it not weakness also to make known Samson 778
More strength from me, then in thy self was found. Samson 789
Why then reveal'd? I was assur'd by those Samson 800
Who tempted me, that nothing was design'd Samson 801
I to my self was false e're thou to me, Samson 824
It was not gold, as to my charge thou lay'st, Samson 849
And of Religion, press'd how just it was, Samson 854
Was not behind, but ever at my ear, Samson 858
Parents and countrey; nor was I their subject, Samson 886
Witness when I was worried with thy peals. Samson 906
Dal. I was a fool, too rash, and quite mistaken Samson 907
Which to my countrey I was judg'd to have shewn. Samson 994
Was lavish't on thir Sex, that inward gifts Samson 1026
Or was too much of self-love mixt, Samson 1031
That I was never present on the place Samson 1085
Feigndst at thy birth was giv'n thee in thy hair, Samson 1135
My Nation was subjected to your Lords. Samson 1205
It was the force of Conquest; force with force Samson 1206
I was no private but a person rais'd Samson 1211
I was to do my part from Heav'n assign'd, Samson 1217
Off. My message was impos'd on me with speed, Samson 1343
For never was from Heaven imparted Samson 1438
Was not at present here to find my Son, Samson 1446
But that which mov'd my coming now, was chiefly Samson 1452
The rest was magnanimity to remit, Samson 1470
What noise or shout was that? it tore the Skie. Samson 1472
And since his strength with eye-sight was not lost, Samson 1502
Mercy of Heav'n what hideous noise was that! Samson 1509
Man. The accident was loud, & here before thee Samson 1552
With rueful cry, yet what it was we hear not, Samson 1553
Eye-witness of what first or last was done, Samson 1594
When all abroad was rumour'd that this day Samson 1600
The building was a spacious Theatre Samson 1605
The other side was op'n, where the throng Samson 1609
Was *Samson* as a public servant brought, Samson 1615
Came to the place, and what was set before him Samson 1624
I have perform'd, as reason was, obeying, Samson 1641
With God not parted from him, as was feard, Samson 1719
I was dispatcht for their defence, and guard; Mask 42
What never yet was heard in Tale or Song Mask 44
This way the noise was, if mine ear be true, Mask 170
My best guide now, me thought it was the sound Mask 171
Was rife, and perfet in my list'ning ear, Mask 203
line not in Bridgewater ms
Was I deceiv'd, or did a sable cloud Mask 221
line not in Bridgewater ms
Their port was more then human, as they stood; Mask 297
And play i'th plighted clouds. I was aw-strook, Mask 301
And Courts of Princes, where it first was nam'd, Mask 325
Fear'd her stern frown, and she was queen oth' Woods. Mask 446
What was that snaky-headed *Gorgon* sheild Mask 447
The wonted roar was up amidst the Woods, Mask 549
Was took e're she was ware, and wish't she might Mask 558
Still to be so displac't. I was all eare, Mask 560
Too well I did perceive it was the voice Mask 563
The leaf was darkish, and had prickles on it, Mask 631
And you a statue; or as *Daphne* was Mask 661
Was this the cottage, and the safe abode Mask 693
There was another meaning in these gifts, Mask 754
line not in Bridgewater ms
Whilom she was the daughter of *Locrine*, Mask 827
To aid a Virgin, such as was her self Mask 856
but soft I was not sent to court your wonder Mask Tr. ms 10.16
She was pincht, and pull'd she sed, Allegro 103
Such mixture was not held a stain) Penseroso 26
While yet there was no fear of *Jove*. Penseroso 30
Not trickt and frounc't as she was wont, Penseroso 123
Was never heard the Nymphs to daunt, Penseroso 137
Was all in honour and devotion ment Arcades 35
His goary visage down the stream was sent, Lycidas 62
That strain I heard was of a higher mood: Lycidas 87
That not a blast was from his dungeon stray'd, Lycidas 97
The Ayr was calm, and on the level brine, Lycidas 98
It was that fatall and perfidious Bark Lycidas 100
And now was dropt into the Western bay; Lycidas 191
It was the Winter wilde, Nativity 29
It was no season then for her Nativity 35
Was heard the World around: Nativity 54
As if they surely knew their sovran Lord was by. Nativity 60
But peacefull was the night Nativity 61
Was kindly com to live with them below; Nativity 90
Was all that did their silly thoughts so busie keep. Nativity 92
As never was by mortall finger strook, Nativity 95

Was(*cont*)
Now was almost won Nativity 104
To think her part was don, Nativity 105
Before was never made, Nativity 118
His praise and glory was in *Israel* known. Psalm 114, 6
Of him that ever was, and ay shall last, Psalm 114, 16
Which 'mongst the wanton gods a foul reproach was held. Fair Inf 14
There ended was his quest, there ceast his care. Fair Inf 18
When Beldam Nature in her cradle was; Vacation 46
For once it was my dismal hap to hear Vacation 68
O what a Mask was there, what a disguise! Passion 19
That was the Casket of Heav'ns richest store, Passion 44
Bin as compleat as was her praise, Winchester 12
Was not long a living Tomb. Winchester 34
'Twas such a shifter, that if truth were known, Carrier 5
Death was half glad when he had got him down; Carrier 6
And thinking now his journeys end was come, Carrier 12
Untill his revolution was at stay. Another 6
1658 'made of stay'
'Gainst old truth) motion number'd out his time; Another 8
1640, 1657 ''twas motion'
Ease was his chief disease, and to judge right, Another 21
line not in 1658 text
His leasure told him that his time was com, Another 23
line not in 1658 text
Yet (strange to think) his wain was his increase: Another 32
line not in 1658 text
A Book was writ of late call'd *Tetrachordon;* Sonnet 11, 1
Trinity ms 'was writ' ←'was writt' ←'I writt'
1673 printed 'was was'
Her face was vail'd, yet to my fancied sight, Sonnet 23, 10
Was the Lord. Of many millions Psalm 3, 15
Hast broke the teeth. This help was from the Lord Psalm 3, 23
This was a Statute *giv'n of old* Psalm 81, 13
The Tongue I heard, was strange. Psalm 81, 20
Lo this man there was born: Psalm 87, 16
This and this man was born in her, Psalm 87, 19
That this man there was born. Psalm 87, 24
Ah *Constantine*, of how much ill was cause Prose 1, 1
This was that gift (if you the truth will have) Prose 4, 3

Wash
That wash thy hallowd feet, and warbling flow, Par Lost 3.31
Pretends to wash off sin, and fit them so Par Reg 1.73
With lavers pure and cleansing herbs wash off Samson 1727
Wash far away, where ere thy bones are hurld, Lycidas 155

Washed
As when he wash'd his servants feet so now Par Lost 10.215
To som Caves mouth, or whether washt by stream Par Lost 11.569
Wash'd by the Southern Sea, and on the North Par Reg 4.28
And fresh-blown Roses washt in dew, Allegro 22
And letters where my tears have washt a wannish white. Passion 35
Mine as whom washt from spot of child-bed taint, Sonnet 23, 5

Washing
Of washing them from guilt of sin to Life Par Lost 12.443
And thou hast need much washing to be toucht. Samson 1107

Washy
And on the washie Oose deep Channels wore; Par Lost 7.303

Wassailers
Of such late Wassailers; yet O where els Mask 179
Bridgewater ms 'wassailers'
Trinity ms 'wassailers'

Wast
Wast present, and with mighty wings outspread Par Lost 1.20
That Glorie then, when thou no more wast good, Par Lost 4.838
Wast wont, I mine to thee was wont to impart; Par Lost 5.677
Out of the ground wast taken, know thy Birth, Par Lost 10.207
The ground whence thou wast tak'n, fitter Soile. Par Lost 11.262
Or torn up sheer: ill wast thou shrouded then, Par Reg 4.419
Thou never wast remiss, I bear thee witness: Samson 239
E're I to thee, thou to thy self wast cruel. Samson 784
Being once a wife, for me thou wast to leave Samson 885
The work for which thou wast foretold Samson 1662
Above mortalitie that shew'd thou wast divine. Fair Inf 35

Waste
The dismal Situation waste and wilde, Par Lost 1.60
ms 'wast'
To waste his whole Creation, or possess Par Lost 2.365
To waste Eternal dayes in woe and pain? Par Lost 2.695
Or in the emptier waste, resembling Air, Par Lost 2.1045
Dark, waste, and wild, under the frown of Night Par Lost 3.424
Through wood, through waste, o're hill, o're dale his roam. Par Lost 4.538
Then Both from out Hell Gates into the waste Par Lost 10.282
Of *Turkish* Crescent, leaves all waste beyond Par Lost 10.434
To waste and havoc yonder World, which I Par Lost 10.617
To waste it all my self, and leave ye none! Par Lost 10.820
Peace to corrupt no less then Warr to waste. Par Lost 11.784
Who having spilt much blood, and don much waste Par Lost 11.791
And *Eden* rais'd in the wast Wilderness. Par Reg 1.7
Wandred this barren waste, the same I now: Par Reg 1.354
Led captive, and *Jerusalem* laid waste, Par Reg 3.283
But tedious wast of time to sit and hear Par Reg 4.123
And follow'd thee still on to this wast wild; Par Reg 4.523
Uninjur'd in this wilde surrounding wast. Mask 403
Trinity ms 'wide surrounding wast' ←'vast, & hideous wild'
And strangl'd with her waste fertility; Mask 729
1637 'wast'
Trinity ms 'wast'
Bridgewater ms 'wast'

Waste(*cont*)
Not a waste, or needless sound Mask 942
1637 'wast'
Trinity ms 'wast'
Bridgewater ms 'wast'
halfe his wast flood the wide Atlantique fills Mask Tr. ms 10.14
For all this wast of wealth, and loss of blood. Sonnet 12, 14
Help wast a sullen day; what may be won Sonnet 20, 4
Wasted
Had wasted woods on Mountain or in Vale, Par Lost 11.567
His wasted Country freed from *Punic* rage, Par Reg 3.102
Have wasted *Sogdiana;* to her aid Par Reg 3.302
That wasted all the Coast Psalm 83, 34
Wasteful
Wide on the wasteful Deep; with him Enthron'd Par Lost 2.961
Into the wastful Deep; the monstrous sight Par Lost 6.862
Outrageous as a Sea, dark, wasteful, wilde, Par Lost 7.212
1669 'wastful'
Let in these wastful Furies, who impute Par Lost 10.620
On man, beast, plant, wastful and turbulent, Par Reg 4.461
In the wastfull Wildernes. Psalm 136, 58
Wasting
Wasting the Earth, each other to destroy: Par Lost 2.502
Wide wasting; such destruction to withstand Par Lost 6.253
Marasmus, and wide-wasting Pestilence, Par Lost 11.487
line not in 1667 edition
Without this bodies wasting, I content me, Par Reg 2.256
Watch
Upon the wing, as when men wont to watch Par Lost 1.332
With Armed watch, that render all access Par Lost 2.130
Of this ill Mansion: intermit no watch Par Lost 2.462
His couchant watch, as one who chose his ground. Par Lost 4.406
Charge and strict watch that to this happie Place Par Lost 4.562
While they keep watch, or nightly rounding walk Par Lost 4.685
With strictest watch; these other wheel the North, Par Lost 4.783
Of Angels under watch; and to his state, Par Lost 5.288
Silence, and Sleep listning to thee will watch, Par Lost 7.106
In jointed Armour watch: on smooth the Seale, Par Lost 7.409
That kept thir watch; thence full of anguish driv'n, Par Lost 9.62
From entrance or Cherubic Watch, by stealth Par Lost 9.68
And flaming Ministers to watch and tend Par Lost 9.156
Not keeping strictest watch, as she was warnd. Par Lost 9.363
May have diverted from continual watch Par Lost 9.814
There kept thir Watch the Legions, while the Grand Par Lost 10.427
Many a dark League, reduc't in careful Watch Par Lost 10.438
Then stil at Hels dark threshold to have sate watch, Par Lost 10.594
Cherubic watch, and of a Sword the flame Par Lost 11.120
Darkness defends between till morning Watch; Par Lost 12.207
To simple Shepherds, keeping watch by night; Par Lost 12.365
And in this office of his Mountain watch, Mask 89
Of dragon watch with uninchanted eye, Mask 395
I sate me down to watch upon a bank Mask 543
Where I may oft out-watch the *Bear*, Penseroso 87
And all the spangled host keep watch in squadrons bright? Nativity 21
Passes to bliss at the mid hour of night, Sonnet 9, 13
Trinity ms 'the midd night howr' ←'the midd watch' ←'that hovre of night'
Will rank my Prayers, and watch till thou appear. Psalm 5, 8
Watched
To the bright Minister that watchd, hee blew Par Lost 11.73
The Tempter watch'd, and soon with ugly dreams Par Reg 4.408
Therefore I watch'd thy footsteps from that hour, Par Reg 4.522
To storm me over-watch't, and wearied out, Samson 405
Watches
To thir night watches in warlike Parade, Par Lost 4.780
Encamping, plac'd in Guard thir Watches round, Par Lost 6.412
Watches, no doubt, with greedy hope to find Par Lost 9.257
Count the night watches to his feathery Dames, Mask 347
Watchet
Then her purfl'd scarf can shew, Mask 995
Trinity ms 'purfl'd' ←'watchet'
yellow, watchet, greene, & blew Mask Tr. ms 26.21
yellow, watchett, greene and blew Mask Br. ms 17
Watchful
Which the five watchful Senses represent, Par Lost 5.104
More wise, more watchful, stronger, if need were Par Lost 9.311
Of watchful Cherubim; four faces each Par Lost 11.128
But on Occasions forelock watchful wait. Par Reg 3.173
Who in their nightly watchfull Sphears, Mask 113
the scalie-harnest dragon ever keeps Mask Tr. ms 10.09
'dragon ever keeps' ←'watchfull dragons keep'
Then passing through the Spheres of watchful fire, Vacation 40
First heard by happy watchful Shepherds ear, Circum 3
Trinity ms 'watchfull'
Watching
Of Angels watching round? Here he had need Par Lost 2.413
Watching where Shepherds pen thir Flocks at eeve Par Lost 4.185
Here watching at the head of these that sleep? Par Lost 4.826
To Shepherds watching at their folds by night, Par Reg 1.244
And the same end; still watching to oppress Samson 232
Watch-tower
From his watch-towre in the skies, Allegro 43
Water
The Ford, and of it self the water flies Par Lost 2.612
Consummate lovly smil'd; Aire, Water, Earth, Par Lost 7.502
Your Tribes, and water from th' ambrosial Fount? Par Lost 11.279
Deep under water rould; Sea cover'd Sea, Par Lost 11.749
Out of the water, Heav'n above the Clouds Par Reg 1.81
Water(*cont*)
Powers of Fire, Air, Water, and Earth beneath, Par Reg 2.124
Fierce rain with lightning mixt, water with fire Par Reg 4.412
The water Nymphs that in the bottom plaid, Mask 833
Trinity ms 'waternymphs'
My Bed I water with my tears; mine Eie Psalm 6, 13
I tri'd thee at the water *steep* Psalm 81, 31
Watered
Waterd the Garden; thence united fell Par Lost 4.230
Went up and waterd all the ground, and each Par Lost 7.334
Mellifluous streams that water'd all the schools Par Reg 4.277
Over som wide-water'd shoar, Penseroso 75
Watering
Watering the ground, and with our sighs the Air Par Lost 10.1090
Watering the ground, and with thir sighs the Air Par Lost 10.1102
Waters
The rising world of waters dark and deep, Par Lost 3.11
Luxuriant; mean while murmuring waters fall Par Lost 4.260
Of waters issu'd from a Cave and spread Par Lost 4.454
Yee that in Waters glide, and yee that walk Par Lost 5.200
He said, and as the sound of waters deep Par Lost 5.872
Winds under ground or waters forcing way Par Lost 6.196
Rocks, Waters, Woods, and by the shaggie tops Par Lost 6.645
Amid the Waters, and let it divide Par Lost 7.262
The Waters from the Waters: and God made Par Lost 7.263
The Waters underneath from those above Par Lost 7.268
Built on circumfluous Waters calme, in wide Par Lost 7.270
Of Waters, Embryon immature involv'd, Par Lost 7.277
Be gather'd now ye Waters under Heav'n Par Lost 7.283
Capacious bed of Waters: thither they Par Lost 7.290
Of congregated Waters he call'd Seas: Par Lost 7.308
And God said, let the Waters generate Par Lost 7.387
The waters generated by thir kindes, Par Lost 7.393
And Lakes and running Streams the waters fill; Par Lost 7.397
Of Rainbows and Starrie Eyes. The Waters thus Par Lost 7.446
And over Fields and Waters, as in Aire Par Lost 8.301
Hovering upon the Waters; what they met Par Lost 10.285
By the waters of Life, where ere they sate Par Lost 11.79
As with the force of winds and waters pent, Samson 1647
The Sea o'refraught would swell, & th' unsought diamonds Mask 732
Trinity ms 'swell' ←'heave her waters up above the shoare'
Whilst from off the waters fleet Mask 896
Waters the odorous banks that blow Mask 993
And the Waters murmuring Penseroso 144
Smoothly the waters kist, Nativity 65
Watery
Worshipt in *Rabba* and her watry Plain, Par Lost 1.397
Her watrie Labyrinth, whereof who drinks, Par Lost 2.584
A Shape within the watry gleam appeerd Par Lost 4.461
Then that smooth watry image; back I turnd, Par Lost 4.480
Cover'd th' Abyss: but on the watrie calme Par Lost 7.234
1669 'watery'
Troop to thir Standard, so the watrie throng, Par Lost 7.297
Of Fish within thir watry residence, Par Lost 8.346
Wandring that watrie Desert: I had hope Par Lost 11.779
And the cleer Sun on his wide watrie Glass Par Lost 11.844
The fluid skirts of that same watrie Cloud, Par Lost 11.882
He must not flote upon his watry bear Lycidas 12
Trinity ms 'watrie'
Sunk though he be beneath the watry floar, Lycidas 167
Trinity ms 'watrie'
To rise above the watry plain. Psalm 136, 22
By watry streams, and in his season knows Psalm 1, 8
As through a fruitfull watry Dale Psalm 84, 23
Wattled
The folded flocks pen'd in their watled cotes, Mask 344
Wave
With Head up-lift above the wave, and Eyes Par Lost 1.193
Wafts on the calmer wave by dubious light Par Lost 2.1042
To darkness, such as bound the Ocean wave. Par Lost 3.539
Breathe soft or loud; and wave your tops, ye Pines, Par Lost 5.193
With every Plant, in sign of Worship wave. Par Lost 5.194
And all who under me thir Banners wave, Par Lost 5.687
Wave rowling after Wave, where way they found, Par Lost 7.298
Glide under the green Wave, in Sculles that oft Par Lost 7.402
Address'd his way, not with indented wave, Par Lost 9.496
Gaz'd hot, and of the fresh Wave largely drew, Par Lost 11.845
Comus. Nay Lady sit; if I but wave this wand, Mask 659
Under the glassie, cool, translucent wave, Mask 861
And bridle in thy headlong wave, Mask 887
Wave at his Wings in Airy stream, Penseroso 148
While Birds of Calm sit brooding on the charmed wave. Nativity 68
Pillows his chin upon an Orient wave, Nativity 231
Waved
Wav'd round the Coast, up call'd a pitchy cloud Par Lost 1.340
Dissheveld, but in wanton ringlets wav'd Par Lost 4.306
Now wav'd thir fierie Swords, and in the Aire Par Lost 6.304
Show to the Sun thir wav'd coats dropt with Gold, Par Lost 7.406
Insect or Worme; those wav'd thir limber fans Par Lost 7.476
Wav'd over by that flaming Brand, the Gate Par Lost 12.643
Waver
To waver, or fall off and joyn with Idols; Samson 456
Wavering
Dal. With doubtful feet and wavering resolution Samson 732
Now to the Moon in wavering Morrice move, Mask 116
Bridgewater ms 'waveringe'
Waves
From off the tossing of these fiery waves, Par Lost 1.184

Waves(*cont*)
Hath vext the Red-Sea Coast, whose waves orethrew — Par Lost 1.306
Whose waves of torrent fire inflame with rage. — Par Lost 2.581
His constant Lamp, and waves his purple wings, — Par Lost 4.764
And surging waves, as Mountains to assault — Par Lost 7.214
Silence, ye troubl'd waves, and thou Deep, peace, — Par Lost 7.216
And scourg'd with many a stroak th' indignant waves. — Par Lost 10.311
Rode tilting o're the Waves, all dwellings else — Par Lost 11.747
Of Paradise by might of Waves be moovd — Par Lost 11.830
On thir imbattelld ranks the Waves return, — Par Lost 12.213
In signal of remove, waves fiercely round; — Par Lost 12.593
Or surging waves against a solid rock, — Par Reg 4.18
And chid her barking waves into attention, — Mask 258
May thy brimmed waves for this — Mask 924
He ask'd the Waves, and ask'd the Fellon winds, — Lycidas 91
1638 'waves'
Trinity ms 'waves'
Through the dear might of him that walk'd the waves; — Lycidas 173
And bid the weltring waves their oozy channel keep. — Nativity 124
The ruddy waves he cleft in twain, — Psalm 136, 45
In Heav'ns defiance mustering all his waves; — Vacation 44
Thou break'st upon me all thy waves, — Psalm 88, 31
And all thy waves break me. — Psalm 88, 32
Like waves they me persue. — Psalm 88, 68

Waving
Of thir great Sultan waving to direct — Par Lost 1.348
With Orient Colours waving: with them rose — Par Lost 1.546
Lay waving round; on som great charge imploy'd — Par Lost 3.628
Of *Ceres* ripe for harvest waving bends — Par Lost 4.981
Cherubic waving fires: on th' other part — Par Lost 6.413
Stood waving tipt with fire; while we suspense, — Par Lost 6.580
Wide waving, all approach farr off to fright, — Par Lost 11.121
Sails fill'd, and streamers waving, — Samson 718
And on his shoulders waving down those locks, — Samson 1493
And hush the waving Woods, nor of lesse faith, — Mask 88
Bridgewater ms 'wavinge'
And waving wide her mirtle wand, — Nativity 51

Waxen
Deliciously, and builds her waxen Cells — Par Lost 7.491
Through grief consumes, is waxen old and dark — Psalm 6, 14

Waxing
Gave heed, but waxing more in rage repli'd. — Par Lost 4.969
Waxing well of his deep wound — Mask 1000
line not in Bridgewater ms

Way
Words interwove with sighs found out thir way. — Par Lost 1.621
Could have assur'd us; and by what best way, — Par Lost 2.40
O're Heav'ns high Towrs to force resistless way, — Par Lost 2.62
The way seems difficult and steep to scale — Par Lost 2.71
Our stronger, some worse way his wrath may find — Par Lost 2.83
Scorning surprize. Or could we break our way — Par Lost 2.134
His uncouth way, or spread his aerie flight — Par Lost 2.407
Seis'd us, though undismaid: long is the way — Par Lost 2.432
Disband, and wandring, each his several way — Par Lost 2.523
Thy miscreated Front athwart my way — Par Lost 2.683
Thine own begotten, breaking violent way — Par Lost 2.782
With head, hands, wings or feet pursues his way, — Par Lost 2.949
Which way the neerest coast of darkness lyes — Par Lost 2.958
Wandring this darksome Desart, as my way, — Par Lost 2.973
If that way be your walk, you have not farr; — Par Lost 2.1007
Environ'd wins his way; harder beset — Par Lost 2.1016
Pav'd after him a broad and beat'n way — Par Lost 2.1026
Through all restraint broke loose he wings his way — Par Lost 3.87
And shall grace not find means, that finds her way, — Par Lost 3.228
But in his way lights on the barren Plaines — Par Lost 3.437
Through the pure marble Air his oblique way — Par Lost 3.564
Shot upward still direct, whence no way round — Par Lost 3.618
Thy way thou canst not miss, me mine requires. — Par Lost 3.735
Me miserable! which way shall I flie — Par Lost 4.73
Which way I flie is Hell; my self am Hell; — Par Lost 4.75
The way he went, and on th'*Assyrian* mount — Par Lost 4.126
But further way found none, so thick entwin'd, — Par Lost 4.174
All path of Man or Beast that past that way: — Par Lost 4.177
Gods latest Image: I describ'd his way — Par Lost 4.567
Half way up Hill this vast Sublunar Vault, — Par Lost 4.777
Hasting this way, and now by glimps discerne — Par Lost 4.867
Who would not, finding way, break loose from Hell, — Par Lost 4.889
Her bearded Grove of ears, which way the wind — Par Lost 4.982
On each hand parting, to his speed gave way — Par Lost 5.252
Comes this way moving; seems another Morn — Par Lost 5.310
Well hast thou taught the way that might direct — Par Lost 5.508
Long way through hostile scorn, which he susteind — Par Lost 5.904
Through Heav'ns wide Champain held his way, till Morn, — Par Lost 6.2
In the mid way: though strange to us it seemd — Par Lost 6.91
Forth stepping opposite, half way he met — Par Lost 6.128
Winds under ground or waters forcing way — Par Lost 6.196
Before him Power Divine his way prepar'd; — Par Lost 6.780
They open to themselves at length the way — Par Lost 7.158
Wave rowling after Wave, where way they found, — Par Lost 7.298
With Serpent errour wandring, found thir way, — Par Lost 7.302
In common, rang'd in figure wedge thir way, — Par Lost 7.426
To Gods Eternal house direct the way, — Par Lost 7.576
Seen in the Galaxie, that Milkie way — Par Lost 7.579
The easiest way, nor with perplexing thoughts — Par Lost 8.183
Leads up to Heav'n, is both the way and guide; — Par Lost 8.613
Found unsuspected way. There was a place, — Par Lost 9.69
To intercept thy way, or send thee back — Par Lost 9.410
The way which to her ruin now I tend. — Par Lost 9.493

Way(*cont*)
Address'd his way, not with indented wave, — Par Lost 9.496
To interrupt, side-long he works his way. — Par Lost 9.512
Into the Heart of *Eve* his words made way, — Par Lost 9.550
Empress, the way is readie, and not long, — Par Lost 9.626
Misleads th' amaz'd Night-wanderer from his way — Par Lost 9.640
In ignorance, thou op'nst Wisdoms way, — Par Lost 9.809
And forth to meet her went, the way she took — Par Lost 9.847
Op'ning the way, but of Divine effect — Par Lost 9.865
Nor can I miss the way, so strongly drawn — Par Lost 10.262
The way, thou leading, such a sent I draw — Par Lost 10.267
Mountains of Ice, that stop th' imagin'd way — Par Lost 10.291
Bridging his way, *Europe* with *Asia* joyn'd, — Par Lost 10.310
And now thir way to Earth they had descri'd, — Par Lost 10.325
You two this way, among these numerous Orbs — Par Lost 10.397
Then sufferd. Th' other way *Satan* went down — Par Lost 10.414
By Sin and Death a broad way now is pav'd — Par Lost 10.473
I find no way, from deep to deeper plung'd! — Par Lost 10.844
Or find some other way to generate — Par Lost 10.894
Flew up, nor missd the way, by envious windes — Par Lost 11.15
One way the self-same hour? why in the East — Par Lost 11.203
To find where *Adam* shelterd, took his way, — Par Lost 11.223
But have I now seen Death? Is this the way — Par Lost 11.462
But is there yet no other way, besides — Par Lost 11.527
Paths indirect, or in the mid way faint! — Par Lost 11.631
One way a Band select from forage drives — Par Lost 11.646
Corrupting each thir way; yet those remoov'd, — Par Lost 11.889
Through the wilde Desert, not the readiest way, — Par Lost 12.216
Through *Eden* took thir solitarie way. — Par Lost 12.649
Will waft me; and the way found prosperous once — Par Reg 1.104
Of Saviour to mankind, and which way first — Par Reg 1.187
I am; this chiefly, that my way must lie — Par Reg 1.263
Before Messiah and his way prepare. — Par Reg 1.272
The way he came not having mark'd, return — Par Reg 1.297
What other way I see not, for we here — Par Reg 1.338
Can satisfie that need some other way, — Par Reg 2.254
Thither he bent his way, determin'd there — Par Reg 2.291
Which way or from what hope dost thou aspire — Par Reg 2.417
But to guide Nations in the way of truth — Par Reg 2.473
Thy Vertue, and not every way secure — Par Reg 3.348
Syene, and where the shadow both way falls, — Par Reg 4.70
The tryal hath indamag'd thee no way, — Par Reg 4.206
All to the push of Fate, persue thy way — Par Reg 4.470
Brought on his way with joy; hee unobserv'd — Par Reg 4.638
The tread of many feet stearing this way; — Samson 111
Neglected. I already have made way — Samson 481
Comes this way sailing — Samson 713
No way assur'd. But conjugal affection — Samson 739
His vertue or weakness which way to assail: — Samson 756
To what I did thou shewdst me first the way. — Samson 781
No better way I saw then by importuning — Samson 797
I led the way; bitter reproach, but true, — Samson 823
My love how couldst thou hope, who tookst the way — Samson 838
(Which way soever men refer it) — Samson 1015
A cleaving mischief, in his way to vertue — Samson 1039
Happy that house! his way to peace is smooth: — Samson 1049
The sumptuous *Dalila* floating this way: — Samson 1072
Sam. The way to know were not to see but taste. — Samson 1091
Some way or other yet further to afflict thee. — Samson 1252
For I descry this way — Samson 1301
Return the way thou cam'st, I will not come. — Samson 1332
This day will be remarkable in my life — Samson 1388
And over heaps of slaughter'd walk his way? — Samson 1530
Mess. O whither shall I run, or which way flie — Samson 1541
A dreadful way thou took'st to thy revenge. — Samson 1591
And new-entrusted Scepter, but their way — Mask 36
Bridgewater ms 'waye'
This way the noise was, if mine ear be true, — Mask 170
Bridgewater ms 'waye'
With this long way, resolving here to lodge — Mask 183
Bridgewater ms 'waye'
What readiest way would bring me to that place? — Mask 305
Bridgewater ms 'waye'
Of them that pass unweeting by the way. — Mask 539
Bridgewater ms 'waye'
(As I will give you when we go) you may — Mask 648
Trinity ms 'when we goe' ← 'on the way' ← 'as wee goe'
Som other means I have which may be us'd, — Mask 821
Trinity ms 'some other meanes I have' ← 'there is another way'
Through the Heav'ns wide pathles way; — Penseroso 70
Bending one way their pretious influence, — Nativity 71
Expectance calls thee now another way, — Vacation 54
Wisely hast shun'd the broad way and the green, — Sonnet 9, 2
Love led them on, and Faith who knew them best — Sonnet 14, 9
Trinity ms 'Love led them on' ← 'Faith shew'd the way' ← 'Faith who led on the way'
To peace and truth thy glorious way hast plough'd, — Sonnet 16, 4
A hunder'd-fold, who having learnt thy way — Sonnet 18, 13
Toward solid good what leads the nearest way; — Sonnet 21, 10
In counsel of the wicked, and ith' way — Psalm 1, 2
For the Lord knows th' upright way of the just, — Psalm 1, 15
And the way of bad men to ruine must. — Psalm 1, 16
In anger and ye perish in the way — Psalm 2, 26
They shall return in hast the way they came — Psalm 6, 23
Teach me O Lord thy way *most right*, — Psalm 86, 37

Waylay
In Valley or Green Meadow to way-lay — Par Reg 2.185

Ways

And justifie the wayes of God to men.	Par Lost 1.26
Four ways thir flying March, along the Banks	Par Lost 2.574
Surrounds me, from the chearful wayes of men	Par Lost 3.46
1667 'waies'	
Through dark and desart wayes with peril gone	Par Lost 3.544
To serve him better: wise are all his wayes.	Par Lost 3.680
And the regard of Heav'n on all his waies;	Par Lost 4.620
Through wayes of danger by himself untri'd,	Par Lost 4.934
And on, methought, alone I pass'd through ways	Par Lost 5.50
God to remove his wayes from human sense,	Par Lost 8.119
Gladly into the wayes of God with Man:	Par Lost 8.226
Thir language and thir wayes, they also know,	Par Lost 8.373
The highth and depth of thy Eternal wayes	Par Lost 8.413
From prone, nor in thir wayes complacence find.	Par Lost 8.433
Things in thir Causes, but to trace the wayes	Par Lost 9.682
With long reach interpos'd; three sev'ral wayes	Par Lost 10.323
This said, they both betook them several wayes,	Par Lost 10.610
Through multitude that sung: Just are thy ways,	Par Lost 10.643
Of many ways to die the shortest choosing,	Par Lost 10.1005
1667 'wayes'	
Of Death, and many are the wayes that lead	Par Lost 11.468
And testifi'd against thir wayes; hee oft	Par Lost 11.721
Or violence, hee of thir wicked wayes	Par Lost 11.812
To leave them to thir own polluted wayes;	Par Lost 12.110
Hard are the ways of truth, and rough to walk,	Par Reg 1.478
Chor. Just are the ways of God,	Samson 293
Yet more there be who doubt his ways not just,	Samson 300
(So mutable are all the ways of men)	Samson 1407
Side-ways as on a dying bed,	Winchester 42
For thy Hears to strew the ways,	Winchester 58
Or els the ways being foul, twenty to one,	Carrier 3
1658 'waies'	
Now that the Fields are dank, and ways are mire,	Sonnet 20, 2
Set thy wayes right before, where my step goes.	Psalm 5, 24
To wayes of sin and shame,	Psalm 80, 74
To walk my *righteous* waies.	Psalm 81, 56
And in their hearts thy waies.	Psalm 84, 20
Whose waies are just and right.	Psalm 84, 44
Thy waies, and love the just,	Psalm 86, 6

We

We may with more successful hope resolve	Par Lost 1.120
ms 'Wee'	
That we may so suffice his vengeful ire,	Par Lost 1.148
ms 'wee'	
What can it then avail though yet we feel	Par Lost 1.153
ms 'wee'	
Whom we resist. If then his Providence	Par Lost 1.162
ms 'wee'	
Consult how we may henceforth most offend	Par Lost 1.187
ms 'wee'	
What reinforcement we may gain from Hope,	Par Lost 1.190
ms 'wee'	
That we must change for Heav'n, this mournful gloom	Par Lost 1.244
ms 'wee'	
We shall be free; th' Almighty hath not built	Par Lost 1.259
ms 'Wee'	
Here we may reign secure, and in my choyce	Par Lost 1.261
But wherefore let we then our faithful friends,	Par Lost 1.264
ms 'wee'	
As we erewhile, astounded and amaz'd,	Par Lost 1.281
Henceforth his might we know, and know our own	Par Lost 1.643
More then can be in Heav'n, we now return	Par Lost 2.37
We now debate; who can advise, may speak.	Par Lost 2.42
That in our proper motion we ascend	Par Lost 2.75
We sunk thus low? Th' ascent is easie then;	Par Lost 2.81
Th' event is fear'd; should we again provoke	Par Lost 2.82
We should be quite abolisht and expire.	Par Lost 2.93
What fear we then? what doubt we to incense	Par Lost 2.94
And cannot cease to be, we are at worst	Par Lost 2.100
On this side nothing; and by proof we feel	Par Lost 2.101
Scorning surprize. Or could we break our way	Par Lost 2.134
Is flat despair: we must exasperate	Par Lost 2.143
To punish endless? wherefore cease we then?	Par Lost 2.159
Say they who counsel Warr, we are decreed,	Par Lost 2.160
Whatever doing, what can we suffer more,	Par Lost 2.162
What can we suffer worse? is this then worst,	Par Lost 2.163
What when we fled amain, pursu'd and strook	Par Lost 2.165
A refuge from those wounds: or when we lay	Par Lost 2.168
One day upon our heads; while we perhaps	Par Lost 2.178
Shall we then live thus vile, the Race of Heav'n	Par Lost 2.194
If we were wise, against so great a foe	Par Lost 2.202
Our doom; which if we can sustain and bear,	Par Lost 2.209
If we procure not to our selves more woe.	Par Lost 2.225
We warr, if warr be best, or to regain	Par Lost 2.230
Our own right lost: him to unthrone we then	Par Lost 2.231
We overpower? Suppose he should relent	Par Lost 2.237
Of new Subjection; with what eyes could we	Par Lost 2.239
To whom we hate. Let us not then pursue	Par Lost 2.249
We can create, and in what place so e're	Par Lost 2.260
Of darkness do we dread? How oft amidst	Par Lost 2.263
As he our darkness, cannot we his Light	Par Lost 2.269
Imitate when we please? This Desart soile	Par Lost 2.270
Nor want we skill or Art, from whence to raise	Par Lost 2.272
Of order, how in safety best we may	Par Lost 2.280
Of what we are and were, dismissing quite	Par Lost 2.282
Must we renounce, and changing stile be call'd	Par Lost 2.312
A growing Empire; doubtless; while we dream,	Par Lost 2.315

We(*cont*)

What sit we then projecting peace and Warr?	Par Lost 2.329
Inflicted? and what peace can we return,	Par Lost 2.335
In doing what we most in suffering feel?	Par Lost 2.340
Nor will occasion want, nor shall we need	Par Lost 2.341
Or ambush from the Deep. What if we find	Par Lost 2.344
All as our own, and drive as we were driven,	Par Lost 2.366
And opportune excursion we may chance	Par Lost 2.396
Shall breathe her balme. But first whom shall we send	Par Lost 2.402
In search of this new world, whom shall we find	Par Lost 2.403
All circumspection, and we now no less	Par Lost 2.414
Choice in our suffrage; for on whom we send,	Par Lost 2.415
Say Heav'nly powers, where shall we find such love,	Par Lost 3.213
The Universal Maker we may praise;	Par Lost 3.676
For wee to him indeed all praises owe,	Par Lost 4.444
With first approach of light, we must be ris'n,	Par Lost 4.624
Ask riddance, if we mean to tread with ease;	Par Lost 4.632
Unseen, both when we wake, and when we sleep:	Par Lost 4.678
Of echoing Hill or Thicket have we heard	Par Lost 4.681
Which we in our appointed work imployd	Par Lost 4.726
Thy goodness infinite, both when we wake,	Par Lost 4.734
And when we seek, as now, thy gift of sleep.	Par Lost 4.735
These troublesom disguises which wee wear,	Par Lost 4.740
Calls us, we lose the prime, to mark how spring	Par Lost 5.21
But somtimes in the Air, as wee, somtimes	Par Lost 5.79
All what we affirm or what deny, and call	Par Lost 5.107
Our Heav'nly stranger; well we may afford	Par Lost 5.316
We brush mellifluous Dewes, and find the ground	Par Lost 5.429
Ethereal, as wee, or may at choice	Par Lost 5.499
By steps we may ascend to God. But say,	Par Lost 5.512
Obedient? can we want obedience then	Par Lost 5.514
1667 'wee'	
On other surety none; freely we serve,	Par Lost 5.538
Because wee freely love, as in our will	Par Lost 5.539
To love or not; in this we stand or fall:	Par Lost 5.540
Yet that we never shall forget to love	Par Lost 5.550
And we have yet large day, for scarce the Sun	Par Lost 5.558
(For wee have also our Eevning and our Morn,	Par Lost 5.628
1667 'we'	
Wee ours for change delectable, not need)	Par Lost 5.629
1667 'We'	
Both waking we were one; how then can now	Par Lost 5.678
Of all those Myriads which we lead the chief;	Par Lost 5.684
Homeward with flying march where we possess	Par Lost 5.688
We mean to hold what anciently we claim	Par Lost 5.723
In our defence, lest unawares we lose	Par Lost 5.731
This onely to consult how we may best	Par Lost 5.779
Yet by experience taught we know how good,	Par Lost 5.826
That we were formd then saist thou? and the work	Par Lost 5.853
Doctrin which we would know whence learnt: who saw	Par Lost 5.856
We know no time when we were not as now;	Par Lost 5.859
Whether by supplication we intend	Par Lost 5.867
The strife which thou call'st evil, but wee style	Par Lost 6.289
The strife of Glorie: which we mean to win,	Par Lost 6.290
Too mean pretense, but what we more affect,	Par Lost 6.421
Of future we may deem him, though till now	Par Lost 6.429
Some disadvantage we endur'd and paine,	Par Lost 6.431
Since now we find this our Empyreal form	Par Lost 6.433
Weapons more violent, when next we meet,	Par Lost 6.439
Left them Superiour, while we can preserve	Par Lost 6.443
For Gods, and too unequal work we find	Par Lost 6.453
Of Mightiest. Sense of pleasure we may well	Par Lost 6.459
With what more forcible we may offend	Par Lost 6.465
No less then for deliverance what we owe.	Par Lost 6.468
Of this Ethereous mould whereon we stand,	Par Lost 6.473
Adverse, that they shall fear we have disarmd	Par Lost 6.490
Whom fled we thought, will save us long pursuit	Par Lost 6.538
That all may see who hate us, how we seek	Par Lost 6.559
Heav'n witness thou anon, while we discharge	Par Lost 6.564
What we propound, and loud that all may hear.	Par Lost 6.567
Stood waving tipt with fire; while we suspense,	Par Lost 6.580
Ere while they fierce were coming, and when wee,	Par Lost 6.610
And Brest, (what could we more2) propounded terms	Par Lost 6.612
We should compel them to a quick result.	Par Lost 6.619
Leader, the terms we sent were terms of weight,	Par Lost 6.621
Such as we might perceive amus'd them all,	Par Lost 6.623
Two dayes, as we compute the dayes of Heav'n,	Par Lost 6.685
For which to the infinitly Good we owe	Par Lost 7.76
Of what we are. But since thou hast voutsaf't	Par Lost 7.80
How first began this Heav'n which we behold	Par Lost 7.86
What wee, not to explore the secrets aske	Par Lost 7.95
To magnifie his works, the more we know.	Par Lost 7.97
Or we can bid his absence, till thy Song	Par Lost 7.107
And not molest us, unless we our selves	Par Lost 8.186
Nor less think wee in Heav'n of thee on Earth	Par Lost 8.224
For God we see hath honour'd thee, and set	Par Lost 8.227
Squar'd in full Legion (such command we had)	Par Lost 8.232
Our prompt obedience. Fast we found, fast shut	Par Lost 8.240
Glad we return'd up to the coasts of Light	Par Lost 8.245
Ere Sabbath Eev'ning: so we had in charge.	Par Lost 8.246
(And pure thou wert created) we enjoy	Par Lost 8.623
Adam, well may we labour still to dress	Par Lost 9.205
Luxurious by restraint; what we by day	Par Lost 9.209
Our taske we choose, what wonder if so near	Par Lost 9.221
How we might best fulfill the work which here	Par Lost 9.230
Labour, as to debarr us when we need	Par Lost 9.236
As we need walk, till younger hands ere long	Par Lost 9.246
That such an Enemie we have, who seeks	Par Lost 9.274

We(*cont*)
To God or thee, because we have a foe Par Lost 9.280
As wee, not capable of death or paine, Par Lost 9.283
Suttle or violent, we not endu'd Par Lost 9.324
How are we happie, still in fear of harm? Par Lost 9.326
Firm we subsist, yet possible to swerve, Par Lost 9.359
Serpent, we might have spar'd our coming hither, Par Lost 9.647
But of this Tree we may not taste nor touch; Par Lost 9.651
Sole Daughter of his voice; the rest, we live Par Lost 9.653
Of each Tree in the Garden we may eate, Par Lost 9.660
Our inward freedom? In the day we eate Par Lost 9.762
Of this fair Fruit, our doom is, we shall die. Par Lost 9.763
This Tree is not as we are told, a Tree Par Lost 9.863
Or not restraind as wee, or not obeying, Par Lost 9.868
Not dead, as we are threatn'd, but thenceforth Par Lost 9.870
Our State cannot be severd, we are one, Par Lost 9.958
Since to each meaning savour me apply, Par Lost 9.1019
1667 'we'
Much pleasure we have lost, while we abstain'd Par Lost 9.1022
Op'nd we find indeed, and find we know Par Lost 9.1071
I know not whence possessd thee; we had then Par Lost 9.1137
O Son, why sit we here each other viewing Par Lost 10.235
For this we may thank *Adam;* but his thanks Par Lost 10.736
While yet we live, scarse one short hour perhaps, Par Lost 10.923
In offices of Love, how we may light'n Par Lost 10.960
And torment less then none of what we dread, Par Lost 10.998
From what we fear for both, let us make short, Par Lost 10.1000
Why stand we longer shivering under feares, Par Lost 10.1003
We are by doom to pay; rather such acts Par Lost 10.1026
Shall scape his punishment ordain'd, and wee Par Lost 10.1039
Without wrauth or reviling; wee expected Par Lost 10.1048
Immediate dissolution, which we thought Par Lost 10.1049
How much more, if we pray him, will his ear Par Lost 10.1060
Leave cold the Night, how we his gather'd beams Par Lost 10.1070
Beseeching him, so as we need not fear Par Lost 10.1082
By him with many comforts, till we end Par Lost 10.1084
What better can we do, then to the place Par Lost 10.1086
The good which we enjoy, from Heav'n descends; Par Lost 11.142
Is past, and we shall live. Whence Haile to thee, Par Lost 11.158
Laborious, till day droop; while here we dwell, Par Lost 11.178
Who knows, or more then this, that we are dust, Par Lost 11.199
And wilde, how shall we breath in other Aire Par Lost 11.284
Obtruded on us thus? who if we knew Par Lost 11.504
What we receive, would either not accept Par Lost 11.505
These painful passages, how we may come Par Lost 11.528
Dominion absolute; that right we hold Par Lost 12.68
We may no longer stay: go, waken *Eve;* Par Lost 12.594
This Universe we have possest, and rul'd Par Reg 1.49
This dreaded time have compast, wherein we Par Reg 1.58
At least if so we can, and by the head Par Reg 1.60
His first-begot we know, and sore have felt, Par Reg 1.89
Who this is we must learn, for man he seems Par Reg 1.91
Of God; I saw and heard, for we sometimes Par Reg 1.330
Where ought we hear, and curious are to hear, Par Reg 1.333
What other way I see not, for we here Par Reg 1.338
With Food, whereof we wretched seldom taste. Par Reg 1.345
Unlook'd for are we fall'n, our eyes beheld Par Reg 2.31
Expected of our Fathers; we have heard Par Reg 2.33
Thus we rejoyc'd, but soon our joy is turn'd Par Reg 2.37
In publick, and with him we have convers'd; Par Reg 2.52
Soon we shall see our hope, our joy return. Par Reg 2.57
So may we hold our place and these mild seats Par Reg 2.125
Have we not seen, or by relation heard, Par Reg 2.182
But he whom we attempt is wiser far Par Reg 2.205
Therefore with manlier objects we must try Par Reg 2.225
Well have we speeded, and o're hill and dale, Par Reg 3.267
Look once more e're we leave this specular Mount Par Reg 4.236
We come thy friends and neighbours not unknown Samson 180
Counsel or Consolation we may bring, Samson 183
But had we best retire, I see a storm? Samson 1061
Chor. His fraught we soon shall know, he now arrives. Samson 1075
Of those encounters, where we might have tri'd Samson 1086
Or we shall find such Engines to assail Samson 1396
With thee; say reverend Sire, we thirst to hear. Samson 1456
In both which we, as next participate. Samson 1507
What shall we do, stay here or run and see? Samson 1520
We unawares run into dangers mouth. Samson 1522
From other hands we need not much to fear. Samson 1526
With rueful cry, yet what it was we hear not, Samson 1553
No Preface needs, thou seest we long to know. Samson 1554
More then anough we know; but while things yet Samson 1592
(For so from such as nearer stood we heard) Samson 1631
Chor. All is best, though we oft doubt, Samson 1745
We that are of purer fire Mask 111
Bridgewater ms 'Wee'
Trinity ms 'wee'
Be barr'd that happines, might we but hear Mask 343
Trinity ms 'wee'
Bridgewater ms 'wee'
Or while we speak within the direfull grasp Mask 357
line not in Bridgewater ms
line not in Trinity ms
Wherwith she tam'd the brinded lioness Mask 443
1637 'we tam'd'
Or our neglect, we lost her as we came. Mask 510
Trinity ms both 'wee'
Bridgewater ms both 'wee'
(As I will give you when we go) you may Mask 648

We(*cont*)
Bridgewater ms 'wee'
1637 'wee'
Trinity ms 'when we goe' ←'on the way' ←'as wee goe'
And we should serve him as a grudging master, Mask 725
Bridgewater ms 'wee'
Trinity ms 'wee'
We cannot free the Lady that sits here Mask 818
Trinity ms 'wee'
1637 'Wee'
Bridgewater ms 'wee'
We implore thy powerful hand Mask 903
Trinity ms 'wee'
1637 'Wee'
Bridgewater ms 'Wee'
Till we com to holier ground, Mask 943
Trinity ms 'wee'
Bridgewater ms 'wee'
We shall catch them at their sport, Mask 953
Trinity ms 'wee'
1637 'Wee'
Bridgewater ms 'wee'
Is that which we from hence descry Arcades 3
Trinity ms 'wee'
We may justly now accuse Arcades 10
Trinity ms 'wee may justly now accuse' ←'now seemes guiltie of abuse'
Less then half we find exprest, Arcades 12
Trinity ms 'wee find' ←'she hath'
Inimitable sounds, yet as we go, Arcades 78
Trinity ms 'wee'
For we were nurst upon the self-same hill, Lycidas 23
Trinity ms 'wee'
We drove a field, and both together heard Lycidas 27
Trinity ms 'wee'
But the fair Guerdon when we hope to find, Lycidas 73
Trinity ms 'wee'
Attir'd with Stars, we shall for ever sit, On Time 21
Trinity ms 'wee'
For we by rightfull doom remediles Circum 17
Trinity ms 'wee'
And that great Cov'nant which we still transgress Circum 21
Trinity ms 'wee'
That we on Earth with undiscording voice Musick 17
Trinity ms 'wee'
As once we did, till disproportion'd sin Musick 19
Trinity ms 'we' ←'wee'
O may we soon again renew that Song, Musick 25
Trinity ms 'wee'
Thus we salute thee with our early Song, May Morn 9
But from that mark how far they roave we see Sonnet 12, 13
The bounds of either sword to thee wee ow. Sonnet 17, 12
1662, 1694 'we'
Where shall we sometimes meet, and by the fire Sonnet 20, 3
Of Attick tast, with Wine, whence we may rise Sonnet 20, 10
But we do hope to find out all your tricks, Forcers 13
Trinity ms 'wee'
And then we shall be safe. Psalm 80, 16
And then we shall be safe. Psalm 80, 32
So shall we not go back from thee Psalm 80, 73
Quick'n us thou, then *gladly* wee Psalm 80, 75
And then we shall be safe. Psalm 80, 80
We cry and do not cease. Psalm 83, 4
By right now shall we seize Psalm 83, 46
From thy fierce wrath which we had prov'd Psalm 85, 11
Whom doe we count a good man, whom but he Prose 10, 1

Weak
Fall'n Cherube, to be weak is miserable Par Lost 1.157
Single against thee wicked, and thence weak. Par Lost 4.856
Where thou art weigh'd, and shown how light, how weak, Par Lost 4.1012
Superiour and unmov'd, here onely weake Par Lost 8.532
Shee first his weak indulgence will accuse. Par Lost 9.1186
To witherd weak and gray; thy Senses then Par Lost 11.540
Save by those shadowie expiations weak, Par Lost 12.291
Accomplishing great things, by things deemd weak Par Lost 12.567
In the admiration only of weak minds Par Reg 2.221
Of his weak arguing, and fallacious drift; Par Reg 3.4
(For most do taste through fond intemperate thirst) Mask 67
Trinity ms 'fond' ←'weake'
Hail native Language, that by sinews weak Vacation 1
What need'st thou such weak witnes of thy name? Shakespear 6
1663-4 'dull'
1632 'dull'
1640 'weake'
Am very weak and faint; heal and amend me, Psalm 6, 4
Regard the weak and fatherless Psalm 82, 9
I am a man, but weak alas Psalm 88, 15

Weakening
Weakning the Scepter of old *Night:* first Hell Par Lost 2.1002

Weaker
Thy weaker; let it profit thee to have heard Par Lost 6.909
A Foe so proud will first the weaker seek, Par Lost 9.383
And therfore to our weaker view, Penseroso 15

Weakest
There fail where Vertue fails, or weakest prove Par Lost 6.117
By weakest suttleties, not made to rule, Samson 56

Weakly
But weakly to a woman must reveal it, Samson 50

Weakly(*cont*)
Weakly at least, and shamefully: A sin Samson 499
Weakness
And where thir weakness, how attempted best, Par Lost 2.357
Of weakness, not of Power. Will he, draw out, Par Lost 10.801
His weakness shall o'recome Satanic strength Par Reg 1.161
Of human weakness rather then of strength. Par Reg 3.402
Who vanquisht with a peal of words (O weakness!) Samson 235
His vertue or weakness which way to assail: Samson 756
First granting, as I do, it was a weakness Samson 773
Was it not weakness also to make known Samson 778
Let weakness then with weakness come to parl Samson 785
Confess it feign'd, weakness is thy excuse, Samson 829
And I believe it, weakness to resist Samson 830
Philistian gold: if weakness may excuse, Samson 831
All wickedness is weakness: that plea therefore Samson 834
Dal. Since thou determinst weakness for no plea Samson 843
Or knock the breast, no weakness, no contempt, Samson 1722
Against th' unarmed weakness of one Virgin Mask 582
1637 'weaknesse'
Trinity ms 'weakenesse'
Bridgewater ms 'weaknes'
Weal
The weal or woe in thee is plac't; beware. Par Lost 8.638
Follow, as to him linkt in weal or woe, Par Lost 9.133
Wealth
In wealth and luxurie. Th' ascending pile Par Lost 1.722
Outshon the wealth of *Ormus* and of *Ind*, Par Lost 2.2
In narrow room Natures whole wealth, yea more, Par Lost 4.207
In Triumph and luxurious wealth, are they Par Lost 11.788
Not wandring poor, but trusting all his wealth Par Lost 12.133
And his next Son for Wealth and Wisdom fam'd, Par Lost 12.332
In wealth and multitude, factious they grow; Par Lost 12.352
Of honour, wealth, high fare, aim'd not beyond Par Reg 2.202
Get Riches first, get Wealth, and Treasure heap, Par Reg 2.427
They whom I favour thrive in wealth amain, Par Reg 2.430
Yet Wealth without these three is impotent, Par Reg 2.433
In highth of all thir flowing wealth dissolv'd: Par Reg 2.436
Thou neither dost perswade me to seek wealth Par Reg 3.44
In ample Territory, wealth and power, Par Reg 4.82
Luxurious by thir wealth, and greedier still, Par Reg 4.141
Wealth, pleasure, pain or torment, death and life, Par Reg 4.305
Since neither wealth, nor honour, arms nor arts, Par Reg 4.368
Of pilfering Woolf, not all the fleecy wealth Mask 504
As a penurious niggard of his wealth, Mask 726
For all this wast of wealth, and loss of blood. Sonnet 12, 14
In thy Adulterers, or thy ill got wealth? Prose 3, 4
Wealthy
That the first wealthy *Pope* receiv'd of thee. Prose 1, 3
Weanling
Or Taint-worm to the weanling Herds that graze, Lycidas 46
Weapon
Then with what trivial weapon came to hand, Samson 142
Unarm'd, and with a trivial weapon fell'd Samson 263
Weaponless
And weaponless himself, Samson 130
Weapons
Weapons more violent, when next we meet, Par Lost 6.439
With Mountains as with Weapons arm'd, which makes Par Lost 6.697
All courage; down thir idle weapons drop'd; Par Lost 6.839
Farr other arms, and other weapons must Mask 612
Bridgewater ms 'weopons'
Wear
These troublesom disguises which wee wear, Par Lost 4.740
Are drawn to wear out miserable days, Samson 762
And gives them leave to wear their Saphire crowns, Mask 26
Bridgewater ms 'weare'
Trinity ms 'weare'
1637 'weare'
Drink the clear stream, and nothing wear but Freize, Mask 722
Bridgewater ms 'weare'
1637 'weare'
Trinity ms 'weare'
Or Frost to Flowers, that their gay wardrop wear, Lycidas 47
Trinity ms 'weare' ← 'beare' ← 'weare'
With those just Spirits that wear victorious Palms, Musick 14
Trinity ms 'weare' ← 'beare' ← 'weare'
Their bonds, and cast from us, no more to wear, Psalm 2, 7
Wearers
Cowles, Hoods and Habits with thir wearers tost Par Lost 3.490
Wearied
Your wearied vertue, for the ease you find Par Lost 1.320
To stoop with wearied wings, and willing feet Par Lost 3.73
Orewearied, through the faint Satanic Host Par Lost 6.392
Warr wearied hath perform'd what Warr can do, Par Lost 6.695
Oppress'd them, wearied with thir amorous play. Par Lost 9.1045
Wearied with their iniquities, withdraw Par Lost 12.107
Wearied I fell asleep: but now lead on; Par Lost 12.614
That soon refresh'd him wearied, and repair'd Par Reg 4.591
To storm me over-watch't, and wearied out, Samson 405
Man. Wearied with slaughter then or how? explain. Samson 1583
My Brothers when they saw me wearied out Mask 182
Wearied I am with sighing out my dayes, Psalm 6, 11
Wearing
Th' enameld *Arras* of the Rainbow wearing, Nativity 143
1673 'Orb'd in a Rain-bow and like glories wearing'
Wearisome
In Heav'n this our delight; how wearisom Par Lost 2.247
Wearisome(*cont*)
Wise men have said are wearisom; who reads Par Reg 4.322
Wears
To him who wears the Regal Diadem, Par Reg 2.461
And every flower that sad embroidery wears: Lycidas 148
Trinity ms 'weares' ← 'beares' ← 'weare' ← 'beares' ← 'weares'
And those Pearls of dew she wears, Winchester 43
Weary
To wearie him with my assiduous cries: Par Lost 11.310
Must needs impaire and wearie human sense: Par Lost 12.10
In all her functions weary of her self; Samson 596
Offring to every weary Travailer, Mask 64
1637 'wearie'
Trinity ms 'wearie'
La. They left me weary on a grassie terf. Mask 280
Trinity ms 'wearie' ← 'wearied'
And may at last my weary age Penseroso 167
And wearie of their place do only stay Vacation 25
Weather-beaten
And like a weather-beaten Vessel holds Par Lost 2.1043
Weave
That in their green shops weave the smooth-hair'd silk Mask 716
Weaved
And wov'n close, both matter, form and stile; Sonnet 11, 2
Trinity ms 'wov'n' ← 'weav'd it'
Weaver
A Weavers beam, and seven-times-folded shield, Samson 1122
Webs
These my skie robes spun out of *Iris* Wooff, Mask 83
Bridgewater ms 'skye webs'
Wed
To wed her Elm; she spous'd about him twines Par Lost 5.216
Why thou shouldst wed *Philistian* women rather Samson 216
Mee, not my Parents, that I sought to wed, Samson 220
Wed your divine sounds, and mixt power employ Musick 3
Trinity ms 'Wed' ← 'wed' ← 'Mixe'
Wedded
Haile wedded Love, mysterious Law, true source Par Lost 4.750
His marriage with the seaventimes-wedded Maid. Par Lost 5.223
Harmonie to behold in wedded pair Par Lost 8.605
And *Adam* wedded to another *Eve*, Par Lost 9.828
I saw thee first and wedded thee, adorn'd Par Lost 9.1030
Of wedded Maid, and Virgin Mother born, Nativity 3
If likewise he some fair one wedded not, Fair Inf 11
Wedge
In common, rang'd in figure wedge thir way, Par Lost 7.426
Wedges
In Rhombs and wedges, and half moons, and wings. Par Reg 3.309
Wedlock
In wedlock a reproach; I gain'd a Son, Samson 353
Wedlock-bands
Above the faith of wedlock-bands, my tomb Samson 986
Wedlock-bound
Shall meet, alreadie linkt and Wedlock-bound Par Lost 10.905
Wedlock-treachery
Not wedlock-trechery endangering life. Samson 1009
Weed
Graze the Sea weed thir pasture, and through Groves Par Lost 7.404
Like a sad Votarist in Palmers weed Mask 189
1637 'weeds'
Who having clad thy self in humane weed, Fair Inf 58
Weeds
Dying put on the weeds of *Dominic*, Par Lost 3.479
But now an aged man in Rural weeds, Par Reg 1.314
In slavish habit, ill-fitted weeds Samson 122
I would not soil these pure Ambrosial weeds, Mask 16
Bridgewater ms 'weedes'
And take the Weeds and likenes of a Swain, Mask 84
Trinity ms 'weeds'
Bridgewater ms 'weeds'
1637 'weeds'
For who would rob a Hermit of his Weeds, Mask 390
1637 'weeds'
Trinity ms 'weeds' ← 'beads' ← 'gowne' ← 'beads'
Bridgewater ms 'weeds'
In weeds of Peace high triumphs hold, Allegro 120
My dank and dropping weeds Horace 15
Weekly
Had not his weekly cours of carriage fail'd; Carrier 10
Ween
Strait side by side were laid, nor turnd I weene Par Lost 4.741
Weened
With furious expedition; for they weend Par Lost 6.86
Weening
Weening to prosper, and at length prevaile Par Lost 6.795
Less over-weening, since he fail'd in *Job*, Par Reg 1.147
Weep
Tears such as Angels weep, burst forth: at last Par Lost 1.620
ms 'weepe'
They sate them down to weep, nor onely Teares Par Lost 9.1121
The world erelong a world of tears must weepe. Par Lost 11.627
And lap it in *Elysium*, *Scylla* wept, Mask 257
Trinity ms 'wept' ← 'would weepe'
Weep no more, woful Shepherds weep no more, Lycidas 165
Trinity ms both 'weepe'
Now *Lycidas* the Shepherds weep no more; Lycidas 182
Trinity ms 'weepe'

Weep(*cont*)
And all night long, before thee *weep* Psalm 88, 3
Weeping
She ended weeping, and her lowlie plight, Par Lost 10.937
A voice of weeping heard, and loud lament; Nativity 183
Take up a weeping on the Mountains wilde, Passion 51
Depart from me, for the voice of my weeping Psalm 6, 17
Weeps
Like a fair flower surcharg'd with dew, she weeps Samson 728
next adde Narcissus that still weeps in vaine Lycidas Tr. ms 28.19
Weigh
Not thy subjection: weigh with her thy self; Par Lost 8.570
To weigh thy Spirits down, and last consume Par Lost 11.545
1667 'waigh'
My meditation waigh Psalm 5, 2
Weighed
Wherein all things created first he weighd, Par Lost 4.999
Where thou art weigh'd, and shown how light, how weak, Par Lost 4.1012
Things vulgar, & well weigh'd, scarce worth the praise, Par Reg 3.51
And rash, before-hand had no better weigh'd Par Reg 4.8
But that on th' other side if it be weigh'd Samson 768
Weighest
Belial, in much uneven scale thou weigh'st Par Reg 2.173
Weighs
Weighs his spread wings, at leasure to behold Par Lost 2.1046
And that Crystalline Sphear whose ballance weighs Par Lost 3.482
Weight
That felt unusual weight, till on dry Land Par Lost 1.227
ms 'waight'
The weight of mightiest Monarchies; his look Par Lost 2.307
The weight of all and our last hope relies. Par Lost 2.416
Now falling with soft slumbrous weight inclines Par Lost 4.615
Leader, the terms we sent were terms of weight, Par Lost 6.621
Under the weight of Mountains buried deep, Par Lost 6.652
How little weight my words with thee can finde, Par Lost 10.968
Under her own waight groaning till the day Par Lost 12.539
Full weight must be transferr'd upon my head. Par Reg 1.267
That for the Publick all this weight he bears. Par Reg 2.465
Till time mature thee to a Kingdoms waight; Par Reg 4.282
Who would be quite surcharg'd with her own weight, Mask 728
Trinity ms 'waight'
Bridgewater ms 'waite'
And like an Engin mov'd with wheel and waight, Another 9
1640, 1657, 1658 'weight'
As he were prest to death, he cry'd more waight; Another 26
line not in 1640, 1657, 1658 texts
Weights
Battels and Realms: in these he put two weights Par Lost 4.1002
Welcome
O welcom hour whenever! why delayes Par Lost 10.771
Which thus to *Eve* his welcome words renewd. Par Lost 11.140
To the uncircumcis'd a welcom prey, Samson 260
Hast'n the welcom end of all my pains. Samson 576
Mean while welcom Joy, and Feast, Mask 102
Trinity ms 'welcome'
1637 'welcome'
Bridgewater ms 'welcome'
O welcom pure-ey'd Faith, white-handed Hope, Mask 213
1637 'welcome'
line not in Bridgewater ms
Trinity ms 'welcome'
To welcom him to this his new abode, Nativity 18
1673 'welcome'
There with thee, new welcom Saint, Winchester 71
And welcom thee, and wish thee long. May Morn 10
Welkin
From either end of Heav'n the welkin burns. Par Lost 2.538
Where the bow'd welkin slow doth bend, Mask 1015
B.M. ms 'Welkin'
Well
Too well I see and rue the dire event, Par Lost 1.134
Rouse and bestir themselves ere well awake. Par Lost 1.334
Well have ye judg'd, well ended long debate, Par Lost 2.390
Light after light well us'd they shall attain, Par Lost 3.196
Well pleas'd, on me let Death wreck all his rage; Par Lost 3.241
My sole complacence! well thou know'st how dear, Par Lost 3.276
No voice exempt, no voice but well could joine Par Lost 3.370
Round he surveys, and well might, where he stood Par Lost 3.555
Sutable grace diffus'd, so well he feignd; Par Lost 3.639
Well pleas'd they slack thir course, and many a League Par Lost 4.164
For prospect, what well us'd had bin the pledge Par Lost 4.200
Som dreadful thing no doubt; for well thou knowst Par Lost 4.426
Well known from Heav'n; and since Meridian hour Par Lost 4.581
Insulting Angel, well thou knowst I stood Par Lost 4.926
Our Heav'nly stranger; well we may afford Par Lost 5.316
Tastes, not well joynd, inelegant, but bring Par Lost 5.335
Inhabitant with God, now know I well Par Lost 5.461
Well hast thou taught the way that might direct Par Lost 5.508
All seemd well pleas'd, all seem'd, but were not all Par Lost 5.617
Jarr not with liberty, but well consist. Par Lost 5.793
Thy disobedience. Well thou didst advise, Par Lost 5.888
To veile the Heav'n, though darkness there might well Par Lost 6.11
Servant of God, well done, well hast thou fought Par Lost 6.29
Omnipotence to none. But well thou comst Par Lost 6.159
Of Mightiest. Sense of pleasure we may well Par Lost 6.459
His Adamantine coat gird well, and each Par Lost 6.542
Fit well his Helme, gripe fast his orbed Shield, Par Lost 6.543
Had need from head to foot well understand; Par Lost 6.625

Well(*cont*)
That thou in me well pleas'd, declarst thy will Par Lost 6.728
In measure what the mind may well contain, Par Lost 7.128
And govern well thy appetite, least sin Par Lost 7.546
And all this good to man, for whose well being Par Lost 8.361
Cannot well suite with either, but soon prove Par Lost 8.388
So well converse, nor with the Ox the Ape; Par Lost 8.396
Expressing well the spirit within thee free, Par Lost 8.440
For well I understand in the prime end Par Lost 8.540
And in her self compleat, so well to know Par Lost 8.548
An outside? fair no doubt, and worthy well Par Lost 8.568
Well manag'd; of that skill the more thou know'st, Par Lost 8.573
In loving thou dost well, in passion not, Par Lost 8.588
Let it; I reck not, so it light well aim'd, Par Lost 9.173
His head the midst, well stor'd with suttle wiles: Par Lost 9.184
Adam, well may we labour still to dress Par Lost 9.205
Well hast thou motion'd, well thy thoughts imployd Par Lost 9.229
1667 'wel'
But bid her well beware, and still erect, Par Lost 9.353
Hate stronger, under shew of Love well feign'd, Par Lost 9.492
The guiltie Serpent, and well might, for *Eve* Par Lost 9.785
This may be well: but what if God have seen, Par Lost 9.826
Not well conceav'd of God, who though his Power Par Lost 9.945
Yeild thee, so well this day thou hast purvey'd. Par Lost 9.1021
But come, so well refresh't, now let us play, Par Lost 9.1027
Of amorous intent, well understood Par Lost 9.1035
Mayst ever rest well pleas'd. I go to judge Par Lost 10.71
Were such as under Government well seem'd, Par Lost 10.154
Of happiness: yet well, if here would end Par Lost 10.725
Well if thrown out, as supernumerarie Par Lost 10.887
And one bad act with many deeds well done Par Lost 11.256
Mayst cover: well may then thy Lord appeas'd Par Lost 11.257
To that meek man, who well had sacrific'd; Par Lost 11.451
There is, said *Michael*, if thou well observe Par Lost 11.530
Live well, how long or short permit to Heav'n: Par Lost 11.554
O pittie and shame, that they who to live well Par Lost 11.629
All would have then gon well, peace would have crownd Par Lost 11.781
Thir Ministry perform'd, and race well run, Par Lost 12.505
Well deem in outward Rites and specious formes Par Lost 12.534
1667 'Will'
Well pleas'd, but answer'd not; for now too nigh Par Lost 12.625
Our hated habitation; well ye know Par Reg 1.47
Not force, but well couch't fraud, well woven snares, Par Reg 1.97
At first against mankind so well had thriv'd Par Reg 1.114
He was well pleas'd; by which I knew the time Par Reg 1.286
Lodg'd in his brest, as well might recommend Par Reg 1.301
And not well understood as good not known? Par Reg 1.437
I lost him, but so found, as well I saw Par Reg 2.97
Of all things destitute, and well I know, Par Reg 2.305
Things vulgar, & well weigh'd, scarce worth the praise, Par Reg 3.51
As thou to thy reproach mayst well remember, Par Reg 3.66
Well hath obey'd; just tryal e're I merit Par Reg 3.196
Huge Cities and high towr'd, that well might seem Par Reg 3.261
Well have we speeded, and o're hill and dale, Par Reg 3.267
Houses of Gods (so well I have dispos'd Par Reg 4.56
Frugal, and mild, and temperate, conquer'd well, Par Reg 4.134
Whom well inspir'd the Oracle pronounc'd Par Reg 4.275
That pleas'd so well our Victors ear, declare Par Reg 4.337
In every street, do they not say, how well Samson 204
For want of well pronouncing *Shibboleth*. Samson 289
This well I knew, nor was at all surpris'd, Samson 381
Who with a grain of manhood well resolv'd Samson 408
Rewarded well with servil punishment! Samson 413
About thy ransom: well they may by this Samson 483
And to the bearing well of all calamities, Samson 655
And Love hath oft, well meaning, wrought much wo, Samson 813
My enemies, lov'd thee, as too well thou knew'st, Samson 878
Too well, unbosom'd all my secrets to thee, Samson 879
Is well ejected when the Conquer'd can. Samson 1207
They cannot well impose, nor I sustain; Samson 1258
More Lordly thund'ring then thou well wilt bear. Samson 1353
Sam. I could be well content to try thir Art, Samson 1399
And sense distract, to know well what I utter. Samson 1556
Dispraise, or blame, nothing but well and fair, Samson 1723
Well knows to still the wilde winds when they roar, Mask 87
Be well stock't with as fair a herd as graz'd Mask 152
And well plac't words of glozing courtesie Mask 161
Trinity ms 'well-plac't'
1637 'wel'
This is the place, as well as I may guess, Mask 201
line not in Bridgewater ms
These thoughts may startle well, but not astound Mask 210
line not in Bridgewater ms
Nightly to thee her sad Song mourneth well. Mask 235
You may as well spred out the unsun'd heaps Mask 398
If he be friendly he comes well, if not, Mask 488
Too well I did perceive it was the voice Mask 563
Of small regard to see to, yet well skill'd Mask 620
He lov'd me well, and oft would beg me sing, Mask 623
Natures full blessings would be well dispenc't Mask 772
That hath so well been taught her dazling fence, Mask 791
line not in Trinity ms
line not in Bridgewater ms
Waxing well of his deep wound Mask 1000
line not in Bridgewater ms
But now my task is smoothly don, Mask 1012
Trinity ms 'smoothly' ← 'well is don'
Yet *Syrinx* well might wait on her. Arcades 107

Well(*cont*)
Trinity ms 'w', ms defective
Who would not sing for *Lycidas?* he knew — Lycidas 10
Trinity ms 'he well knew'
Begin then, Sisters of the sacred well, — Lycidas 15
How well could I have spar'd for thee young swain, — Lycidas 113
The Musk-rose, and the well attir'd Woodbine, — Lycidas 146
1638 'well-attired'
Trinity ms 'well-attir'd woodbine' ←'garish columbine'
For sure so well instructed are my tears, — Passion 48
But with a scarce-wel-lighted flame; — Winchester 20
So well your words his noble vertues praise, — Sonnet 10, 12
The Subject new: it walk'd the Town a while, — Sonnet 11, 3
Trinity ms 'walk'd' ←'It went off well about'
Harry whose tuneful and well measur'd Song — Sonnet 13, 1
Trinity ms 'well-measur'd'
What severs each thou 'hast learnt, which few hav don. — Sonnet 17, 11
To hear the Lute well toucht, or artfull voice — Sonnet 20, 11
Hear O my people, *heark'n well*, — Psalm 81, 33

Well
And from the Well of Life three drops instill'd. — Par Lost 11.416

Well-balanced
And the well-ballanc't world on hinges hung, — Nativity 122

Well-feasted
And the well-feasted Priest then soonest fir'd — Samson 1419

Well-governed
To a wel-govern'd and wise appetite. — Mask 705
Trinity ms 'well govern'd'
Bridgewater ms 'well govern'd'
1673 'well-govern'd'

Wellnigh
From servitude inglorious welnigh half — Par Lost 9.141

Well-pleasing
Of thy victorious Arm, well-pleasing Son, — Par Lost 10.634

Well-practised
Without the sure guess of well-practiz'd feet. — Mask 310
Bridgewater ms 'well practiz'd'

Well-trod
Then to the well-trod stage anon, — Allegro 131

Welter
Unwept, and welter to the parching wind, — Lycidas 13

Weltering
He soon discerns, and weltring by his side — Par Lost 1.78
And bid the weltring waves their oozy channel keep. — Nativity 124

Went
There went a fame in Heav'n that he ere long — Par Lost 1.651
Went all his fear: of God, or Hell, or worse — Par Lost 2.49
The way he went, and on th' *Assyrian* mount — Par Lost 4.126
Southward through *Eden* went a River large, — Par Lost 4.223
Pure as th' expanse of Heav'n; I thither went — Par Lost 4.456
Handed they went; and eas'd the putting off — Par Lost 4.739
But like a proud Steed reind, went hautie on, — Par Lost 4.858
Seem twilight here; and now went forth the Morn — Par Lost 6.12
Since *Michael* and his Powers went forth to tame — Par Lost 6.686
Each to his place, they heard his voice and went — Par Lost 6.782
With Jubilie advanc'd; and as they went, — Par Lost 6.884
Went up and waterd all the ground, and each — Par Lost 7.334
With his great Father (for he also went — Par Lost 7.588
Rose, and went forth among her Fruits and Flours, — Par Lost 8.44
Yet went she not, as not with such discourse — Par Lost 8.48
With Goddess-like demeanour forth she went; — Par Lost 8.59
Survey'd, and sometimes went, and sometimes ran — Par Lost 8.268
And forth to meet her went, the way she took — Par Lost 9.847
So counsel'd hee, and both together went — Par Lost 9.1099
Then sufferd. Th' other way *Satan* went down — Par Lost 10.414
I went into the Temple, there to hear — Par Reg 1.211
He could not lose himself; but went about — Par Reg 2.98
Fasting he went to sleep, and fasting wak'd. — Par Reg 2.284
So talk'd he, while the Son of God went on — Par Reg 4.484
Went up with armed powers thee only seeking, — Samson 1190
And Timbrels, on each side went armed guards, — Samson 1617
Next *Camus*, reverend Sire, went footing slow, — Lycidas 103
While the still morn went out with Sandals gray, — Lycidas 187
He di'd for heavines that his Cart went light, — Another 22
1640, 1657 'were'
line not in 1658 text
Went to the ground: And the repeated air — Sonnet 8, 12
The Subject new: it walk'd the Town a while, — Sonnet 11, 3
Trinity ms 'walk'd' ←'It went off well about'
Her other branches *went*. — Psalm 80, 48

Wentest
Whence thou returnst, and whither wentst, I know; — Par Lost 12.610
When slipping from thy Mothers eye thou went'st — Par Reg 4.216

Wept
Groves whose rich Trees wept odorous Gumms and Balme, — Par Lost 4.248
Tenderly wept, much won that he his Love — Par Lost 9.991
Wept at compleating of the mortal Sin — Par Lost 9.1003
Drie-ey'd behold? *Adam* could not, but wept, — Par Lost 11.495
With glory, wept that he had liv'd so long — Par Reg 3.41
And lap it in *Elysium*, *Scylla* wept, — Mask 257
Trinity ms 'wept' ←'would weepe'
Seas wept from our deep sorrow, — Circum 9
Weept for thee in *Helicon*, — Winchester 56

Were
Doubted his Empire, that were low indeed, — Par Lost 1.114
That were an ignominy and shame beneath — Par Lost 1.115
He lights, if it were Land that ever burn'd — Par Lost 1.228
Of some great Ammiral, were but a wand, — Par Lost 1.294

Were(*cont*)
They heard, and were abasht, and up they sprung — Par Lost 1.331
In which they were, or the fierce pains not feel; — Par Lost 1.336
So numberless were those bad Angels seen — Par Lost 1.344
Then were they known to men by various Names, — Par Lost 1.374
The chief were those who from the Pit of Hell — Par Lost 1.381
These were the prime in order and in might; — Par Lost 1.506
The rest were long to tell, though far renown'd, — Par Lost 1.507
All in a moment through the gloom were seen — Par Lost 1.544
Of *Phlegra* with th' Heroic Race were joyn'd — Par Lost 1.577
Were always downward bent, admiring more — Par Lost 1.681
Were set, and Doric pillars overlaid — Par Lost 1.714
Swarm'd and were straitn'd; till the Signal giv'n, — Par Lost 1.776
Reduc'd thir shapes immense, and were at large, — Par Lost 1.790
Maturest Counsels: for his thoughts were low; — Par Lost 2.115
Her stores were open'd, and this Firmament — Par Lost 2.175
If we were wise, against so great a foe — Par Lost 2.202
Of what we are and were, dismissing quite — Par Lost 2.282
1667 'where'
All as our own, and drive as we were driven, — Par Lost 2.366
And thrice threefold the Gates; three folds were Brass, — Par Lost 2.645
And fields were fought in Heav'n; wherein remaind — Par Lost 2.768
Of Heav'n were falling, and these Elements — Par Lost 2.925
So were I equal'd with them in renown, — Par Lost 3.34
So were created, nor can justly accuse — Par Lost 3.112
The Stairs were such as whereon *Jacob* saw — Par Lost 3.510
The Stairs were then let down, whether to dare — Par Lost 3.523
Over Mount *Sion*, and, though that were large, — Par Lost 3.530
So wide the op'ning seemd, where bounds were set — Par Lost 3.538
Grasing the tender herb, were interpos'd, — Par Lost 4.253
Nor those mysterious parts were then conceald, — Par Lost 4.312
Which were it toilsom, yet with thee were sweet. — Par Lost 4.439
Were slunk, all but the wakeful Nightingale; — Par Lost 4.602
Shine not in vain, nor think, though men were none, — Par Lost 4.675
Strait side by side were laid, nor turnd I weene — Par Lost 4.741
Of Father, Son, and Brother first were known. — Par Lost 4.757
Whose easier business were to serve thir Lord — Par Lost 4.943
Soon as they forth were come to open sight — Par Lost 5.138
All seemd well pleas'd, all seem'd, but were not all — Par Lost 5.617
Both waking we were one; how then can now — Par Lost 5.678
Were banded to oppose his high Decree; — Par Lost 5.717
That we were formd then saist thou? and the work — Par Lost 5.853
We know no time when we were not as now; — Par Lost 5.859
Were don, but infinite: for wide was spred — Par Lost 6.241
Among the Constellations warr were sprung, — Par Lost 6.312
Were ready, in a moment up they turnd — Par Lost 6.509
Ere while they fierce were coming, and when wee, — Par Lost 6.610
If our proposals once again were heard — Par Lost 6.618
Leader, the terms we sent were terms of weight, — Par Lost 6.621
Equal in their Creation they were form'd, — Par Lost 6.690
And Wings were set with Eyes, with Eyes the wheels — Par Lost 6.755
Chariots of God, half on each hand were seen: — Par Lost 6.770
About his Chariot numberless were pour'd — Par Lost 7.197
Thir blossoms: with high woods the hills were crownd, — Par Lost 7.326
Fond, were it not in hope of thy reply: — Par Lost 8.209
Therein enjoy'd were worthy to subdue — Par Lost 8.584
More wise, more watchful, stronger, if need were — Par Lost 9.311
And *Eden* were no *Eden* thus expos'd. — Par Lost 9.341
Were better, and most likelie if from mee — Par Lost 9.365
One Flesh; to loose thee were to loose my self. — Par Lost 9.959
Were it I thought Death menac't would ensue — Par Lost 9.977
He led her nothing loath; Flours were the Couch, — Par Lost 9.1039
All were who heard, dim sadness did not spare — Par Lost 10.23
Were such as under Government well seem'd, — Par Lost 10.154
Flown to the upper World; the rest were all — Par Lost 10.422
With peril great achiev'd. Long were to tell — Par Lost 10.469
To forked tongue, for now were all transform'd — Par Lost 10.519
Whom they triumph'd once lapst. Thus were they plagu'd — Par Lost 10.572
Glar'd on him passing: these were from without — Par Lost 10.714
Concurd not to my being, it were but right — Par Lost 10.747
Those terms whatever, when they were propos'd: — Par Lost 10.757
Can he make deathless Death? that were to make — Par Lost 10.798
Satisfi'd never; that were to extend — Par Lost 10.804
That I must leave ye, Sons; O were I able — Par Lost 10.819
Pains onely in Child-bearing were foretold, — Par Lost 10.1051
Part arable and tilth, whereon were Sheaves — Par Lost 11.430
A Lazar-house it seemd, wherein were laid — Par Lost 11.479
Were Tents of various hue; by some were herds — Par Lost 11.557
Those were of hate and death, or pain much worse, — Par Lost 11.601
Those Tents thou sawst so pleasant, were the Tents — Par Lost 11.607
Where good with bad were matcht, who of themselves — Par Lost 11.685
Such were these Giants, men of high renown; — Par Lost 11.688
Anough to beare; those now, that were dispenst — Par Lost 11.766
Which now abated, for the Clouds were fled, — Par Lost 11.841
Were long to tell, how many Battels fought, — Par Lost 12.261
Till truth were freed, and equity restor'd: — Par Reg 1.220
Small consolation then, were Man adjoyn'd: — Par Reg 1.403
The Desert, Fowls in thir clay nests were couch't; — Par Reg 1.501
Were dead, who sought his life, and missing fill'd — Par Reg 2.77
If cause were to unfold some active Scene — Par Reg 2.239
If Cottage were in view, Sheep-cote or Herd; — Par Reg 2.287
Tell me if Food were now before thee set, — Par Reg 2.320
And all the while Harmonious Airs were heard — Par Reg 2.362
Of whom to be disprais'd were no small praise? — Par Reg 3.56
Were better farthest off) is not yet come; — Par Reg 3.397
As for those captive Tribes, themselves were they — Par Reg 3.414
Of Telescope, were curious to enquire: — Par Reg 4.42
The Kingdoms of the world to thee were giv'n, — Par Reg 4.182

Were(*cont*)
Quite at a loss, for all his darts were spent, Par Reg 4.366
Yet with no new device, they all were spent, Par Reg 4.443
Bound with two cords; but cords to me were threds Samson 261
To life obscur'd, which were a fair dismission, Samson 688
Were left for hast unfinish't, judgment scant, Samson 1027
Sam. The way to know were not to see but taste. Samson 1091
Were bristles rang'd like those that ridge the back Samson 1137
If some convenient ransom were propos'd. Samson 1471
Of faithful Souldiery, were not his purpose Samson 1498
Man. That were a joy presumptuous to be thought. Samson 1531
The Edifice where all were met to see him Samson 1588
Semichor. While thir hearts were jocund and sublime, Samson 1669
All other parts remaining as they were, Mask 72
Trinity ms 'they were' ←'before'
Would send a glistring Guardian if need were Mask 219
line not in Bridgewater ms
La. They were but twain, and purpos'd quick return. Mask 284
Co. Were they of manly prime, or youthful bloom? Mask 289
It were a journey like the path to Heav'n, Mask 303
Were in the flat Sea sunk. And Wisdoms self Mask 375
Were all to ruffl'd, and somtimes impair'd. Mask 380
Trinity ms 'were' ←'are'
Of Knot-grass dew-besprent, and were in fold, Mask 542
Ye were the two she mean't, with that I sprung Mask 578
Were it a draft for *Juno* when she banquets, Mask 701
Were shatter'd into heaps o're thy false head. Mask 799
line not in Bridgewater ms
line not in Trinity ms
Or if Vertue feeble were, Mask 1022
to have her by my side, though I were sure Mask Tr. ms 16.41
were they not taken thence Mask Tr. ms 22.07
to have her by my side, though I were suer Mask Br. ms 394
And yet such musick worthiest were to blaze Arcades 74
Though *Syrinx* your *Pans* Mistres were, Arcades 106
Trinity ms defective here
For we were nurst upon the self-same hill, Lycidas 23
Mean while the Rural ditties were not mute, Lycidas 32
Where were ye Nymphs when the remorseless deep Lycidas 50
For neither were ye playing on the steep, Lycidas 52
Were it not better don as others use, Lycidas 67
The idle spear and shield were high up hung; Nativity 55
Jehovah's wonders were in *Israel* shown, Psalm 114, 5
Or in the Elisian fields (if such there were.) Fair Inf 40
Yet I had rather if I were to chuse, Vacation 29
Were lost in death, till he that dwelt above Circum 18
'Twas such a shifter, that if truth were known, Carrier 5
Nor were it contradiction to affirm Another 13
line not in 1658 text
As he were prest to death, he cry'd more waight; Another 26
line not in 1640, 1657, 1658 texts
But had his doings lasted as they were, Another 27
As when those Hinds that were transform'd to Froggs Sonnet 12, 5
when most were wont which till then us'd to scan Sonnet 13, Tr. ms 40.03
Staid not behind, nor in the grave were trod; Sonnet 14, 6
Who were thy Sheep and in their antient Fold Sonnet 18, 6
The Hills were *over-spread* Psalm 80, 42
Deliver'd were *by me*. Psalm 81, 24
I said that ye were Gods, yea all Psalm 82, 21
They were repulst and slain, Psalm 83, 38
Mercy and Truth *that long were miss'd* Psalm 85, 41
Things that on earth were lost, or were abus'd. Prose 2, 4

Wert
Before the Heavens thou wert, and at the voice Par Lost 3.9
(And pure thou wert created) we enjoy Par Lost 8.623
Immutable when thou wert lost, not I, Par Lost 9.1165
Infallible; or wert thou sought to deeds Par Reg 3.16
But say thou wer't possess'd of *David*'s Throne Par Reg 3.357
Long since. Wert thou so void of fear or shame, Par Reg 4.189
Though thou wert firmlier fastn'd then a rock. Samson 1398
Oh say me true if thou wert mortal wight Fair Inf 41
Wert thou some Starr which from the ruin'd roofe Fair Inf 43
Or wert thou that just Maid who once before Fair Inf 50
Or wert thou that sweet smiling Youth! Fair Inf 53
Or wert thou of the golden-winged hoast, Fair Inf 57

West
Our circuit meets full West. As flame they part Par Lost 4.784
In *India* East or West, or middle shoare Par Lost 5.339
But opposite in leveld West was set Par Lost 7.376
Or Shee from West her silent course advance Par Lost 8.163
West from *Orontes* to the Ocean barr'd Par Lost 9.80
Or East or West, which had forbid the Snow Par Lost 10.685
Marching from *Eden* towards the West, shall finde Par Lost 12.40
As far as *Indus* East, *Euphrates* West, Par Reg 3.272
Meroe Nilotic Isle, and more to West, Par Reg 4.71
From *Gallia*, *Gades*, and the *Brittish* West, Par Reg 4.77
Back'd on the North and West by a thick wood, Par Reg 4.448
Co. Due west it rises from this shrubby point. Mask 306
And West winds, with musky wing Mask 989
Trinity ms 'west'
Bridgewater ms 'west'
1637 'west'
Brutus far to the West, in th' Ocean wide Prose 12, 7

Westering
Toward Heav'ns descent had slop'd his westering wheel. Lycidas 31
Trinity ms 'westring' ←'burnisht'
1638 'burnisht wheel'

Western
The Clouds that on his Western Throne attend: Par Lost 4.597
The western Point, where those half-rounding guards Par Lost 4.862
Now was the Sun in Western cadence low Par Lost 10.92
More orient in yon Western Cloud that draws Par Lost 11.205
From *Hermon* East to the great Western Sea, Par Lost 12.141
He brought our Saviour to the western side Par Reg 4.25
And now was dropt into the Western bay; Lycidas 191
1638 'western'
Trinity ms 'wester'n' ←'westren'
Her branches *on the western side* Psalm 80, 45

Westward
Westward, much nearer by Southwest, behold Par Reg 4.237

Wet
Or wet the thirstie Earth with falling showers, Par Lost 5.190
To warm him wet return'd from field at Eve, Par Reg 1.318
Had chear'd the face of Earth, and dry'd the wet Par Reg 4.433
Mee worse then wet thou find'st not; other harm Par Reg 4.486
Nor wet *Octobers* torrent flood Mask 930
Bridgewater ms 'wett'
Fowl of the Heavens, and Fish that through the wet Psalm 8, 21
Wherwith their cheeks are wet. Psalm 80, 24

Wether
Like a tame Weather, all my precious fleece, Samson 538
Or straggling weather the pen't flock forsook? Mask 499
1673 'Weather'

Wetting
Wetting the borders of her silk'n veil: Samson 730

Whales
And God created the great Whales, and each Par Lost 7.391

What
And mad'st it pregnant: What in me is dark Par Lost 1.22
Illumin, what is low raise and support; Par Lost 1.23
Nor the deep Tract of Hell, say first what cause Par Lost 1.28
The Mother of Mankind, what time his Pride Par Lost 1.36
In equal ruin: into what Pit thou seest Par Lost 1.91
From what highth fall'n, so much the stronger prov'd Par Lost 1.92
Nor what the Potent Victor in his rage Par Lost 1.95
And shook his throne. What though the field be lost? Par Lost 1.105
And what is else not to be overcome? Par Lost 1.109
But what if he our Conquerour, (whom I now Par Lost 1.143
What can it then avail though yet we feel Par Lost 1.153
Save what the glimmering of these livid flames Par Lost 1.182
What reinforcement we may gain from Hope, Par Lost 1.190
If not what resolution from despare. *Par Lost 1.191
What shall be right: fardest from him is best Par Lost 1.247
What matter where, if I be still the same, Par Lost 1.256
And what I should be, all but less then he Par Lost 1.257
With rallied Arms to try what may be yet Par Lost 1.269
Regaind in Heav'n, or what more lost in Hell? Par Lost 1.270
Like cumbrous flesh; but in what shape they choose Par Lost 1.428
Awaiting what command thir mighty Chief Par Lost 1.566
Mixt with auxiliar Gods; and what resounds Par Lost 1.579
Hateful to utter: but what power of mind Par Lost 1.626
What force effected not: that he no less Par Lost 1.647
What in an age they with incessant toyle Par Lost 1.698
With what besides, in Counsel or in Fight, Par Lost 2.20
Could have assur'd us; and by what best way, Par Lost 2.40
With what compulsion and laborious flight Par Lost 2.80
Fear to be worse destroy'd: what can be worse Par Lost 2.85
What fear we then? what doubt we to incense Par Lost 2.94
As not behind in hate; if what was urg'd Par Lost 2.120
In what he counsels and in what excels Par Lost 2.125
First, what Revenge? the Towrs of Heav'n are fill'd Par Lost 2.129
Whatever doing, what can we suffer more, Par Lost 2.162
What can we suffer worse? is this then worst, Par Lost 2.163
What when we fled amain, pursu'd and strook Par Lost 2.165
What if the breath that kindl'd those grim fires Par Lost 2.170
His red right hand to plague us? what if all Par Lost 2.174
My voice disswades; for what can force or guile Par Lost 2.188
Contending, and so doubtful what might fall. Par Lost 2.203
What yet they know must follow, to endure Par Lost 2.206
With what is punish't; whence these raging fires Par Lost 2.213
Besides what hope the never-ending flight Par Lost 2.221
Of future dayes may bring, what chance, what change Par Lost 2.222
The latter: for what place can be for us Par Lost 2.235
Of new Subjection; with what eyes could we Par Lost 2.239
We can create, and in what place so e're Par Lost 2.260
Magnificence; and what can Heav'n shew more? Par Lost 2.273
Of what we are and were, dismissing quite Par Lost 2.282
All thoughts of warr: ye have what I advise. Par Lost 2.283
What sit we then projecting peace and Warr? Par Lost 2.329
Voutsaf't or sought; for what peace will be giv'n Par Lost 2.332
Inflicted? and what peace can we return, Par Lost 2.335
In doing what we most in suffering feel? Par Lost 2.340
Or ambush from the Deep. What if we find Par Lost 2.344
What creatures there inhabit, of what mould, Par Lost 2.355
Or substance, how endu'd, and what thir Power, Par Lost 2.356
Synod of Gods, and like to what ye are, Par Lost 2.391
The happy Ile; what strength, what art can then Par Lost 2.410
Suffice, or what evasion bear him safe Par Lost 2.411
Or unknown Region, what remains him less Par Lost 2.443
While here shall be our home, what best may ease Par Lost 2.458
(Certain to be refus'd) what erst they feard; Par Lost 2.470
(What could it less when Spirits immortal sing2) Par Lost 2.553
And shook a dreadful Dart; what seem'd his head Par Lost 2.672
Th' undaunted Fiend what this might be admir'd, Par Lost 2.677
Whence and what art thou, execrable shape, Par Lost 2.681

What(*cont*)

O Father, what intends thy hand, she cry'd,	Par Lost 2.727
Against thy only Son? What fury O Son,	Par Lost 2.728
What it intends; till first I know of thee,	Par Lost 2.740
What thing thou art, thus double-form'd, and why	Par Lost 2.741
(For what could else) to our Almighty Foe	Par Lost 2.769
But what ow I to his commands above	Par Lost 2.856
What readiest path leads where your gloomie bounds	Par Lost 2.976
Onely begotten Son, seest thou what rage	Par Lost 3.80
Not free, what proof could they have givn sincere	Par Lost 3.103
Where onely what they needs must do, appeard,	Par Lost 3.105
Not what they would? what praise could they receive?	Par Lost 3.106
What pleasure I from such obedience paid,	Par Lost 3.107
Both what they judge and what they choose; for so	Par Lost 3.123
For him, what for thy glorie thou hast made?	Par Lost 3.164
What may suffice, and soft'n stonie hearts	Par Lost 3.189
All Heav'n, what this might mean, and whither tend	Par Lost 3.272
So dearly to redeem what Hellish hate	Par Lost 3.300
What wonder then if fields and regions here	Par Lost 3.606
To witness with thine eyes what some perhaps	Par Lost 3.700
But what created mind can comprehend	Par Lost 3.705
Of what he was, what is, and what must be	Par Lost 4.25
That bring to my remembrance from what state	Par Lost 4.38
From me, whom he created what I was	Par Lost 4.43
What could be less then to afford him praise,	Par Lost 4.46
Forgetful what from him I still receivd,	Par Lost 4.54
Indebted and dischargd; what burden then?	Par Lost 4.57
Thou hadst: whom hast thou then or what to accuse,	Par Lost 4.67
Chose freely what it now so justly rues.	Par Lost 4.72
Under what torments inwardly I groane;	Par Lost 4.88
What feign'd submission swore: ease would recant	Par Lost 4.96
For prospect, what well us'd had bin the pledge	Par Lost 4.200
O Hell! what doe mine eyes with grief behold,	Par Lost 4.358
To do what else though damnd I should abhorre.	Par Lost 4.392
To mark what of thir state he more might learn	Par Lost 4.400
And Head, what thou hast said is just and right.	Par Lost 4.443
And what I was, whence thither brought, and how.	Par Lost 4.452
Had not a voice thus warnd me, What thou seest,	Par Lost 4.467
What there thou seest fair Creature is thy self,	Par Lost 4.468
Mother of human Race: what could I doe,	Par Lost 4.475
Yet let me not forget what I have gain'd	Par Lost 4.512
They taste and die: what likelier can ensue?	Par Lost 4.527
What further would be learnt. Live while ye may,	Par Lost 4.533
From what point of his Compass to beware	Par Lost 4.559
My Author and Disposer, what thou bidst	Par Lost 4.635
Laurel and Mirtle, and what higher grew	Par Lost 4.694
What day the genial Angel to our Sire	Par Lost 4.712
Defaming as impure what God declares	Par Lost 4.746
Will save us trial what the least can doe	Par Lost 4.855
How busied, in what form and posture coucht.	Par Lost 4.876
In that dark durance: thus much what was askt.	Par Lost 4.899
Or not, who ask what boldness brought him hither	Par Lost 4.908
Argue thy inexperience what behooves	Par Lost 4.931
What thou and thy gay Legions dare against;	Par Lost 4.942
But mark what I arreede thee now, avant;	Par Lost 4.962
What seemd both Spear and Shield: now dreadful deeds	Par Lost 4.990
Neither our own but giv'n; what follie then	Par Lost 4.1007
To boast what Arms can doe, since thine no more	Par Lost 4.1008
What drops the Myrrhe, and what the balmie Reed,	Par Lost 5.23
Or envie, or what reserve forbids to taste?	Par Lost 5.61
What life the Gods live there, and such live thou.	Par Lost 5.81
All what we affirm or what deny, and call	Par Lost 5.107
That what in sleep thou didst abhorr to dream,	Par Lost 5.120
Raphael, said hee, thou hear'st what stir on Earth	Par Lost 5.224
Converse with *Adam*, in what Bowre or shade	Par Lost 5.230
His danger, and from whom, what enemie	Par Lost 5.239
Eastward among those Trees, what glorious shape	Par Lost 5.309
And what thy stores contain, bring forth and poure	Par Lost 5.314
Save what by frugal storing firmness gains	Par Lost 5.324
What choice to chuse for delicacie best,	Par Lost 5.333
What order, so contriv'd as not to mix	Par Lost 5.334
To rest, and what the Garden choicest bears	Par Lost 5.368
To whom the Angel. Therefore what he gives	Par Lost 5.404
To transubstantiate; what redounds, transpires	Par Lost 5.438
At Heav'ns high feasts to have fed: yet what compare?	Par Lost 5.467
Wonder not then, what God for you saw good	Par Lost 5.491
Your fill what happiness this happie state	Par Lost 5.504
What meant that caution joind, *if ye be found*	Par Lost 5.513
Full to the utmost measure of what bliss	Par Lost 5.517
Willing or no, who will but what they must	Par Lost 5.533
From what high state of bliss into what woe!	Par Lost 5.543
Assur'd me, and still assure: though what thou tellst	Par Lost 5.553
This is dispenc't, and what surmounts the reach	Par Lost 5.571
As may express them best, though what if Earth	Par Lost 5.574
Sleepst thou Companion dear, what sleep can close	Par Lost 5.673
Thy eye-lids? and remembrest what Decree	Par Lost 5.674
What doubtful may ensue, more in this place	Par Lost 5.682
Among the sons of Morn, what multitudes	Par Lost 5.716
Of our Omnipotence, and with what Arms	Par Lost 5.722
We mean to hold what anciently we claim	Par Lost 5.723
In battel, what our Power is, or our right.	Par Lost 5.728
With speed what force is left, and all imploy	Par Lost 5.730
Then what this Garden is to all the Earth,	Par Lost 5.752
With what may be devis'd of honours new	Par Lost 5.780
But what if better counsels might erect	Par Lost 5.785
Thee what thou art, and formd the Pow'rs of Heav'n	Par Lost 5.824
Already known what he for news had thought	Par Lost 6.20
Had to her Center shook. What wonder? when	Par Lost 6.219
Of Angels, can relate, or to what things	Par Lost 6.298
And fierie foaming Steeds; what stood, recoyld	Par Lost 6.391
Too mean pretense, but what we more affect,	Par Lost 6.421
What Heavens Lord had powerfullest to send	Par Lost 6.425
Or equal what between us made the odds,	Par Lost 6.441
Ruin must needs ensue; for what availes	Par Lost 6.456
With what more forcible we may offend	Par Lost 6.465
No less then for deliverance what we owe.	Par Lost 6.468
What we propound, and loud that all may hear.	Par Lost 6.567
What should they do? if on they rusht, repulse	Par Lost 6.600
And Brest, (what could we more2) propounded terms	Par Lost 6.612
Visibly, what by Deitie I am,	Par Lost 6.682
And in whose hand what by Decree I doe,	Par Lost 6.683
Save what sin hath impaird, which yet hath wrought	Par Lost 6.691
Warr wearied hath perform'd what Warr can do,	Par Lost 6.695
But to convince the proud what Signs availe,	Par Lost 6.789
They hard'nd more by what might most reclame,	Par Lost 6.791
By what is past, to thee I have reveal'd	Par Lost 6.895
What might have else to human Race bin hid;	Par Lost 6.896
Say Goddess, what ensu'd when *Raphael*,	Par Lost 7.40
Apostasie, by what befell in Heaven	Par Lost 7.43
What neerer might concern him, how this World	Par Lost 7.62
When, and whereof created, for what cause,	Par Lost 7.64
What within *Eden* or without was done	Par Lost 7.65
Us timely of what might else have bin our loss,	Par Lost 7.74
Of what we are. But since thou hast voutsaf't	Par Lost 7.80
What may no less perhaps availe us known,	Par Lost 7.85
Imbracing round this florid Earth, what cause	Par Lost 7.90
What wee, not to explore the secrets aske	Par Lost 7.95
What words or tongue of Seraph can suffice,	Par Lost 7.113
Yet what thou canst attain, which best may serve	Par Lost 7.115
In measure what the mind may well contain,	Par Lost 7.128
Approach not mee, and what I will is Fate.	Par Lost 7.173
So spake th' Almightie, and to what he spake	Par Lost 7.174
Thy power; what thought can measure thee or tongue	Par Lost 7.603
And what before thy memorie was don	Par Lost 7.637
What thanks sufficient, or what recompence	Par Lost 8.5
Of what was high: such pleasure she reserv'd,	Par Lost 8.50
And no advantage gaine. What if the Sun	Par Lost 8.122
In six thou seest, and what if sev'nth to these	Par Lost 8.128
Still luminous by his ray. What if that light	Par Lost 8.140
In what he gives to thee, this Paradise	Par Lost 8.171
To know what passes there; be lowlie wise:	Par Lost 8.173
Think onely what concernes thee and thy being;	Par Lost 8.174
Dream not of other Worlds, what Creatures there	Par Lost 8.175
Live, in what state, condition or degree,	Par Lost 8.176
Is the prime Wisdom, what is more, is fume,	Par Lost 8.194
Thee I have heard relating what was don	Par Lost 8.203
But who I was, or where, or from what cause,	Par Lost 8.270
Planted, with Walks, and Bowers, that what I saw	Par Lost 8.305
Remember what I warne thee, shun to taste,	Par Lost 8.327
I found not what me thought I wanted still;	Par Lost 8.355
O by what Name, for thou above all these,	Par Lost 8.357
What happiness, who can enjoy alone,	Par Lost 8.365
Or all enjoying, what contentment find?	Par Lost 8.366
What call'st thou solitude, is not the Earth	Par Lost 8.369
Among unequals what societie	Par Lost 8.383
Can sort, what harmonie or true delight?	Par Lost 8.384
What thinkst thou then of mee, and this my State,	Par Lost 8.403
Beneath what other Creatures are to thee?	Par Lost 8.411
Canst raise thy Creature to what highth thou wilt	Par Lost 8.430
What next I bring shall please thee, be assur'd,	Par Lost 8.449
That what seemd fair in all the World, seemd now	Par Lost 8.472
With what all Earth or Heaven could bestow	Par Lost 8.483
I follow'd her, she what was Honour knew,	Par Lost 8.508
Her own, that what she wills to do or say,	Par Lost 8.549
For what admir'st thou, what transports thee so,	Par Lost 8.567
What higher in her societie thou findst	Par Lost 8.586
What inward thence I feel, not therefore foild,	Par Lost 8.608
Approve the best, and follow what I approve.	Par Lost 8.611
Bear with me then, if lawful what I ask;	Par Lost 8.614
On mans destruction, maugre what might hap	Par Lost 9.56
With second thoughts, reforming what was old!	Par Lost 9.101
For what God after better worse would build?	Par Lost 9.102
With what delight could I have walkt thee round,	Par Lost 9.114
By what I seek, but others to make such	Par Lost 9.127
Or won to what may work his utter loss,	Par Lost 9.131
What he *Almightie* styl'd, six Nights and Days	Par Lost 9.137
With Heav'nly spoils, our spoils: What he decreed	Par Lost 9.151
But what will not Ambition and Revenge	Par Lost 9.168
Luxurious by restraint; what we by day	Par Lost 9.209
Or bear what to my minde first thoughts present,	Par Lost 9.213
With Myrtle, find what to redress till Noon:	Par Lost 9.219
Our taske we choose, what wonder if so near	Par Lost 9.221
What hath bin warn'd us, what malicious Foe	Par Lost 9.253
And what is Faith, Love, Vertue unassaid	Par Lost 9.335
But God left free the Will, for what obeyes	Par Lost 9.351
To do what God expresly hath forbid,	Par Lost 9.356
On what thou hast of vertue, summon all,	Par Lost 9.374
Chiefly by what thy own last reasoning words	Par Lost 9.379
Of what so seldom chanc'd, when to his wish,	Par Lost 9.423
What pleasing seemd, for her now pleases more,	Par Lost 9.453
Thoughts, whither have ye led me, with what sweet	Par Lost 9.473
What hither brought us, hate, not love, nor hope	Par Lost 9.475
Save what is in destroying, other joy	Par Lost 9.478
Infeebl'd me, to what I was in Heav'n.	Par Lost 9.488
Half what in thee is fair, one man except,	Par Lost 9.545

What(*cont*)

Who sees thee? (and what is one2) who shouldst be seen	Par Lost 9.546
What may this mean? Language of Man pronounc't	Par Lost 9.553
What thou commandst, and right thou shouldst be obeyd:	Par Lost 9.570
Deterrd not from atchieving what might leade	Par Lost 9.696
Of good, how just? of evil, if what is evil	Par Lost 9.698
And what are Gods that Man may not become	Par Lost 9.716
What can your knowledge hurt him, or this Tree	Par Lost 9.727
In plain then, what forbids he but to know,	Par Lost 9.758
Bind us with after-bands, what profits then	Par Lost 9.761
What fear I then, rather what know to feare	Par Lost 9.773
Of vertue to make wise: what hinders then	Par Lost 9.778
Though others envie what they cannot give;	Par Lost 9.805
About him. But to *Adam* in what sort	Par Lost 9.816
Without Copartner? so to add what wants	Par Lost 9.821
This may be well: but what if God have seen,	Par Lost 9.826
Mean I to trie, what rash untri'd I sought,	Par Lost 9.860
Submitting to what seemd remediless,	Par Lost 9.919
My own in thee, for what thou art is mine;	Par Lost 9.957
Taste so Divine, that what of sweet before	Par Lost 9.986
What best may from the present serve to hide	Par Lost 9.1092
And with what skill they had, together sowd,	Par Lost 9.1112
What words have past thy Lips, *Adam* severe,	Par Lost 9.1144
It seems, in thy restraint: what could I more?	Par Lost 9.1170
What seemd in thee so perfet, that I thought	Par Lost 9.1179
Was known in Heav'n; for what can scape the Eye	Par Lost 10.5
Incurr'd, what could they less, the penaltie,	Par Lost 10.15
Foretold so lately what would come to pass,	Par Lost 10.38
What rests but that the mortal Sentence pass	Par Lost 10.48
Or come I less conspicuous, or what change	Par Lost 10.107
Absents thee, or what chance detains? Come forth.	Par Lost 10.108
Wouldst easily detect what I conceale.	Par Lost 10.136
And what she did, whatever in it self,	Par Lost 10.141
Say Woman, what is this which thou hast done?	Par Lost 10.158
All, though all-knowing, what had past with Man	Par Lost 10.227
Hovering upon the Waters; what they met	Par Lost 10.285
The present, fearing guiltie what his wrauth	Par Lost 10.340
What thy hands builded not, thy Wisdom gain'd	Par Lost 10.373
With odds what Warr hath lost, and fully aveng'd	Par Lost 10.374
In Council sate, sollicitous what chance	Par Lost 10.428
With what permissive glory since his fall	Par Lost 10.451
What I have don, what sufferd, with what paine	Par Lost 10.470
Of my performance: What remains, ye Gods,	Par Lost 10.502
And horrid sympathie; for what they saw,	Par Lost 10.540
What thinkst thou of our Empire now, though earnd	Par Lost 10.592
See with what heat these Dogs of Hell advance	Par Lost 10.616
On what was pure, till cramm'd and gorg'd, nigh burst	Par Lost 10.632
Now death to heare! for what can I encrease	Par Lost 10.731
Made thee without thy leave, what if thy Son	Par Lost 10.760
His hand to execute what his Decree	Par Lost 10.772
Of Life that sinn'd; what dies but what had life	Par Lost 10.790
If guiltless? But from me what can proceed,	Par Lost 10.824
With that bad Woman? Thus what thou desir'st	Par Lost 10.837
And what thou fearst, alike destroyes all hope	Par Lost 10.838
O Conscience, into what Abyss of fears	Par Lost 10.842
What love sincere, and reverence in my heart	Par Lost 10.915
So now of what thou knowst not, who desir'st	Par Lost 10.948
What thoughts in my unquiet brest are ris'n,	Par Lost 10.975
And torment less then none of what we dread,	Par Lost 10.998
From what we fear for both, let us make short,	Par Lost 10.1000
And excellent then what thy minde contemnes;	Par Lost 10.1015
Laid on our Necks. Remember with what mild	Par Lost 10.1046
My bread; what harm? Idleness had bin worse;	Par Lost 10.1055
And teach us further by what means to shun	Par Lost 10.1062
And what may else be remedie or cure	Par Lost 10.1079
What better can we do, then to the place	Par Lost 10.1086
What else but favor, grace, and mercie shon?	Par Lost 10.1096
See Father, what first fruits on Earth are sprung	Par Lost 11.22
Unskilful with what words to pray, let mee	Par Lost 11.32
To *Adam* what shall come in future dayes,	Par Lost 11.114
What can be toilsom in these pleasant Walkes?	Par Lost 11.179
Some days; how long, and what till then our life,	Par Lost 11.198
With what to sight or smell was sweet; from thee	Par Lost 11.281
What justly thou hast lost; nor set thy heart,	Par Lost 11.288
And in performing end us; what besides	Par Lost 11.300
To shew thee what shall come in future dayes	Par Lost 11.357
What miserie th' inabstinence of *Eve*	Par Lost 11.476
Sight so deform what heart of Rock could long	Par Lost 11.494
O miserable Mankind, to what fall	Par Lost 11.500
Degraded, to what wretched state reserv'd!	Par Lost 11.501
What we receive, would either not accept	Par Lost 11.505
In what thou eatst and drinkst, seeking from thence	Par Lost 11.532
To what thou hast, and for the Aire of youth	Par Lost 11.542
Nor love thy Life, nor hate; but what thou livst	Par Lost 11.553
First his own Tooles; then, what might else be wrought	Par Lost 11.572
To whom thus *Michael*. Judg not what is best	Par Lost 11.603
Lamenting turnd full sad; O what are these,	Par Lost 11.675
And what most merits fame in silence hid.	Par Lost 11.699
Exempt from Death; to shew thee what reward	Par Lost 11.709
Awaits the good, the rest what punishment?	Par Lost 11.710
Henceforth to be foretold what shall befall	Par Lost 11.771
Worldlie or dissolute, on what thir Lords	Par Lost 11.803
And now what further shall ensue, behold.	Par Lost 11.839
But say, what mean those colourd streaks in Heavn,	Par Lost 11.879
Henceforth what is to com I will relate,	Par Lost 12.11
With some regard to what is just and right	Par Lost 12.16
Siege and defiance: Wretched man! what food	Par Lost 12.74
Not knowing to what Land, yet firm believes:	Par Lost 12.127

What(*cont*)

I see him, but thou canst not, with what Faith	Par Lost 12.128
What it devours not, Herb, or Fruit, or Graine,	Par Lost 12.184
The Serpent, by what means he shall achieve	Par Lost 12.234
And terror cease; he grants what they besaught	Par Lost 12.238
1667 'them thir desire'	
Erwhile perplext with thoughts what would becom	Par Lost 12.275
What oft my steddiest thoughts have searcht in vain,	Par Lost 12.377
Thir fight, what stroke shall bruise the Victors heel.	Par Lost 12.385
To teach all nations what of him they learn'd	Par Lost 12.440
Must reascend, what will betide the few	Par Lost 12.480
What man can do against them, not affraid,	Par Lost 12.493
Left them inrould, or what the Spirit within	Par Lost 12.523
Shall on the heart engrave. What will they then	Par Lost 12.524
His consort Libertie; what, but unbuild	Par Lost 12.526
Of knowledge, what this Vessel can containe;	Par Lost 12.559
Let her with thee partake what thou hast heard,	Par Lost 12.598
Chiefly what may concern her Faith to know,	Par Lost 12.599
And what will he not do to advance his Son?	Par Reg 1.88
Winning by Conquest what the first man lost	Par Reg 1.154
From what consummate vertue I have chose	Par Reg 1.165
O what a multitude of thoughts at once	Par Reg 1.196
What from within I feel my self, and hear	Par Reg 1.198
What from without comes often to my ears,	Par Reg 1.199
What might be publick good; my self I thought	Par Reg 1.204
What might improve my knowledge or their own;	Par Reg 1.213
To what highth sacred vertue and true worth	Par Reg 1.231
The Law and Prophets, searching what was writ	Par Reg 1.260
Into this Wilderness, to what intent	Par Reg 1.291
For what concerns my knowledge God reveals.	Par Reg 1.293
Sir, what ill chance hath brought thee to this place	Par Reg 1.321
What happ'ns new; Fame also finds us out.	Par Reg 1.334
What other way I see not, for we here	Par Reg 1.338
For what he bids I do; though I have lost	Par Reg 1.377
What I see excellent in good, or fair,	Par Reg 1.381
What can be then less in me then desire	Par Reg 1.383
I lost not what I lost, rather by them	Par Reg 1.390
I gain'd what I have gain'd, and with them dwell	Par Reg 1.391
This wounds me most (what can it less) that Man,	Par Reg 1.404
Wilt thou impute to obedience what thy fear	Par Reg 1.422
What but thy malice mov'd thee to misdeem	Par Reg 1.424
By thee are giv'n, and what confest more true	Par Reg 1.431
But what have been thy answers, what but dark	Par Reg 1.434
To flye or follow what concern'd him most,	Par Reg 1.440
What to the smallest tittle thou shalt say	Par Reg 1.450
What wonder then if I delight to hear	Par Reg 1.481
Alas, from what high hope to what relapse	Par Reg 2.30
For whither is he gone, what accident	Par Reg 2.39
Thy chosen, to what highth thir pow'r unjust	Par Reg 2.45
O what avails me now that honour high	Par Reg 2.66
His Father's business; what he meant I mus'd,	Par Reg 2.99
Recalling what remarkably had pass'd	Par Reg 2.106
Of greatest things; what woman will you find,	Par Reg 2.208
Of what I suffer here; if Nature need not,	Par Reg 2.249
Though needing, what praise is it to endure?	Par Reg 2.251
Nature hath need of what she asks; yet God	Par Reg 2.253
Though ravenous, taught to abstain from what they brought:	Par Reg 2.269
To whom thus Jesus; what conclud'st thou hence?	Par Reg 2.317
What doubts the Son of God to sit and eat?	Par Reg 2.368
What doubt'st thou Son of God? sit down and eat.	Par Reg 2.377
Shall I receive by gift what of my own,	Par Reg 2.381
And with my hunger what hast thou to do?	Par Reg 2.389
What I might have bestow'd on whom I pleas'd,	Par Reg 2.395
What I can do or offer is suspect;	Par Reg 2.399
Which way or from what hope dost thou aspire	Par Reg 2.417
What Followers, what Retinue canst thou gain,	Par Reg 2.419
What rais'd *Antipater* the *Edomite*,	Par Reg 2.423
To me is not unknown what hath been done	Par Reg 2.444
And what in me seems wanting, but that I	Par Reg 2.450
Accomplish what they did, perhaps and more?	Par Reg 2.452
What if with like aversion I reject	Par Reg 2.457
A while as mute confounded what to say,	Par Reg 3.2
What to reply, confuted and convinc't	Par Reg 3.3
I see thou know'st what is of use to know,	Par Reg 3.7
What best to say canst say, to do canst do;	Par Reg 3.8
For what is glory but the blaze of fame,	Par Reg 3.47
And what the people but a herd confus'd,	Par Reg 3.49
They praise and they admire they know not what;	Par Reg 3.52
And what delight to be by such extoll'd,	Par Reg 3.54
Great Cities by assault: what do these Worthies,	Par Reg 3.74
By what he taught and suffer'd for so doing,	Par Reg 3.97
Freely; of whom what could he less expect	Par Reg 3.126
Raign then; what canst thou better do the while?	Par Reg 3.180
What if he hath decreed that I shall first	Par Reg 3.188
What I can suffer, how obey? who best	Par Reg 3.194
But what concerns it thee when I begin	Par Reg 3.198
Sollicitous, what moves thy inquisition?	Par Reg 3.200
Of my reception into grace; what worse?	Par Reg 3.205
Why move thy feet so slow to what is best,	Par Reg 3.224
What of perfection can in man be found,	Par Reg 3.230
Short sojourn; and what thence could'st thou observe?	Par Reg 3.235
His thousands, in what martial equipage	Par Reg 3.304
He look't and saw what numbers numberless	Par Reg 3.310
To what end I have brought thee hither and shewn	Par Reg 3.350
Without means us'd, what it predicts revokes.	Par Reg 3.356
The Tempter stood, nor had what to reply,	Par Reg 4.2
By what strange Parallax or Optic skill	Par Reg 4.40
What conflux issuing forth, or entring in,	Par Reg 4.62

What(*cont*)
Hated of all, and hating; with what ease Par Reg 4.97
On *David*'s Throne, be propheci'd what will. Par Reg 4.108
From Nations far and nigh; what honour that, Par Reg 4.122
A brutish monster: what if I withal Par Reg 4.128
What wise and valiant man would seek to free Par Reg 4.143
Means there shall be to this, but what the means, Par Reg 4.152
On what I offer set as high esteem, Par Reg 4.160
Nor what I part with mean to give for naught; Par Reg 4.161
For what can less so great a gift deserve? Par Reg 4.169
What both from Men and Angels I receive, Par Reg 4.200
Me naught advantag'd, missing what I aim'd. Par Reg 4.208
The *Pentateuch* or what the Prophets wrote, Par Reg 4.226
Thence what the lofty grave Tragoedians taught Par Reg 4.261
Of knowing what I aught: he who receives Par Reg 4.288
Alas what can they teach, and not mislead; Par Reg 4.309
(And what he brings, what needs he elsewhere seek) Par Reg 4.325
What makes a Nation happy, and keeps it so, Par Reg 4.362
What ruins Kingdoms, and lays Cities flat; Par Reg 4.363
What dost thou in this World? the Wilderness Par Reg 4.372
What I foretell thee, soon thou shalt have cause Par Reg 4.375
Or Heav'n write aught of Fate, by what the Stars Par Reg 4.383
A Kingdom they portend thee, but what Kingdom, Par Reg 4.389
Thou shalt be what thou art ordain'd, no doubt; Par Reg 4.473
What I foretold thee, many a hard assay Par Reg 4.478
And threatning nigh; what they can do as signs Par Reg 4.489
In what degree or meaning thou art call'd Par Reg 4.516
And what he is; his wisdom, power, intent, Par Reg 4.528
To win him, or win from him what I can. Par Reg 4.530
Therefore to know what more thou art then man, Par Reg 4.538
What hunger, if aught hunger had impair'd, Par Reg 4.592
Times past, what once I was, and what am now. Samson 22
Divine Prediction; what if all foretold Samson 44
In what part lodg'd, how easily bereft me, Samson 48
But what is strength without a double share Samson 53
Then with what trivial weapon came to hand, Samson 142
That what I motion'd was of God; I knew Samson 222
Israel's oppressours: of what now I suffer Samson 233
Not flying, but fore-casting in what place Samson 254
To set upon them, what advantag'd best; Samson 255
But what more oft in Nations grown corrupt, Samson 268
In mortal strength! and oh what not in man Samson 349
Deceivable and vain! Nay what thing good Samson 350
My capital secret, in what part my strength Samson 394
Lay stor'd, in what part summ'd, that she might know: Samson 395
How openly, and with what impudence Samson 398
Then undissembl'd hate) with what contempt Samson 400
Or *Dagon*. But for thee what shall be done? Samson 478
Reject not then what offerd means, who knows Samson 516
To what end should I seek it? when in strength Samson 522
Sam. But what avail'd this temperance, not compleat Samson 558
What boots it at one gate to make defence, Samson 560
To what can I be useful, wherein serve Samson 564
God of our Fathers, what is man! Samson 667
What do I beg? how hast thou dealt already? Samson 707
But who is this, what thing of Sea or Land? Samson 710
To light'n what thou suffer'st, and appease Samson 744
Thy mind with what amends is in my power, Samson 745
To what I did thou shewdst me first the way. Samson 781
And what if Love, which thou interpret'st hate, Samson 790
Caus'd what I did? I saw thee mutable Samson 793
What Murtherer, what Traytor, Parricide, Samson 832
Hear what assaults I had, what snares besides, Samson 845
What sieges girt me round, e're I consented; Samson 846
Dishonourer of *Dagon:* what had I Samson 861
In what I thought would have succeeded best. Samson 908
Afford me place to shew what recompence Samson 910
Towards thee I intend for what I have misdone, Samson 911
Misguided; only what remains past cure Samson 912
That what by me thou hast lost thou least shalt miss. Samson 927
But what it is, hard is to say, Samson 1013
Or value what is best Samson 1029
What Pilot so expert but needs must wreck Samson 1044
Comes he in peace? what wind hath blown him hither Samson 1070
Sam. Boast not of what thou wouldst have done, but do Samson 1104
What then thou would'st, thou seest it in thy hand. Samson 1105
Again in safety what thou wouldst have done Samson 1128
But come what will, my deadliest foe will prove Samson 1262
Sam. So take it with what speed thy message needs. Samson 1345
Off. I am sorry what this stoutness will produce. Samson 1346
What act more execrably unclean, prophane? Samson 1362
Happ'n what may, of me expect to hear Samson 1423
To what may serve his glory best, & spread his name Samson 1429
To give ye part with me what hope I have Samson 1453
What noise or shout was that? it tore the Skie. Samson 1472
Man. I know your friendly minds and----O what noise! Samson 1508
Mercy of Heav'n what hideous noise was that! Samson 1509
What shall we do, stay here or run and see? Samson 1520
What if his eye-sight (for to *Israels* God Samson 1527
For his people of old; what hinders now? Samson 1533
With rueful cry, yet what it was we hear not, Samson 1553
And sense distract, to know well what I utter. Samson 1556
To utter what will come at last too soon; Samson 1566
What windy joy this day had I conceiv'd Samson 1574
What glorious hand gave *Samson* his deaths wound? Samson 1581
Mess. By his own hands. *Man*. Self-violence? what cause Samson 1584
Eye-witness of what first or last was done, Samson 1594
Came to the place, and what was set before him Samson 1624

What(*cont*)
Hitherto, Lords, what your commands impos'd Samson 1640
And what may quiet us in a death so noble. Samson 1724
The clotted gore. I with what speed the while Samson 1728
What th' unsearchable dispose Samson 1746
What never yet was heard in Tale or Song Mask 44
What hath night to do with sleep? Mask 122
What might this be? A thousand fantasies Mask 205
line not in Bridgewater ms
Co. What chance good Lady hath bereft you thus? Mask 277
Co. Two such I saw, what time the labour'd Oxe Mask 291
What readiest way would bring me to that place? Mask 305
What if in wild amazement, and affright, Mask 356
Bridgewater ms 'or els in wild'
Trinity ms 'what if' ←'or else'
What need a man forestall his date of grief, Mask 362
line not in Trinity ms
line not in Bridgewater ms
And run to meet what he would most avoid? Mask 363
line not in Bridgewater ms
line not in Trinity ms
Vertue could see to do what vertue would Mask 373
Which you remember not. 2. *Bro*. What hidden strength, Mask 416
Trinity ms 'what'
Bridgewater ms 'what'
What was that snaky-headed *Gorgon* sheild Mask 447
2. *Bro*. Me thought so too; what should it be? *Eld*. *Bro*. For certain Mask 482
That hallow I should know, what are you? speak; Mask 490
Spir. What voice is that, my young Lord? speak agen. Mask 492
El. *Bro*. What fears good *Thyrsis?* Prethee briefly shew. Mask 512
What the sage Poets taught by th' heav'nly Muse, Mask 515
Thou told'st me of? What grim aspects are these, Mask 694
1637 'what'
Bridgewater ms 'what'
Trinity ms 'what'
What need a vermeil-tinctur'd lip for that Mask 752
line not in Bridgewater ms
Think what, and be adviz'd, you are but young yet. Mask 755
line not in Bridgewater ms
Fain would I somthing say, yet to what end? Mask 783
line not in Trinity ms
line not in Bridgewater ms
Spir. What, have you let the false enchanter scape? Mask 814
O my simplicity what sights are these? with darke disguises Mask Tr. ms 22.19
What Worlds, or what vast Regions hold Penseroso 90
Or what (though rare) of later age, Penseroso 101
And made Hell grant what Love did seek. Penseroso 108
What sudden blaze of majesty Arcades 2
Mark what radiant state she spreds, Arcades 14
What shallow-searching *Fame* hath left untold; Arcades 41
Or what the cross dire-looking Planet smites, Arcades 52
What time the Gray-fly winds her sultry horn, Lycidas 28
Had ye bin there---for what could that have don? Lycidas 57
What could the Muse her self that *Orpheus* bore, Lycidas 58
Alas! What boots it with uncessant care Lycidas 64
1638 'what'
Trinity ms 'what'
What hard mishap hath doom'd this gentle swain? Lycidas 92
What recks it them? What need they? They are sped; Lycidas 122
Trinity ms 'what need'
1638 'what need'
Besides what the grim Woolf with privy paw Lycidas 128
As if to shew what creatures Heav'n doth breed, Fair Inf 61
Think what a present thou to God hast sent, Fair Inf 74
And render him with patience what he lent; Fair Inf 75
Listening to what unshorn *Apollo* sings Vacation 37
Fore-saw what future dayes should bring to pass, Vacation 72
What power, what force, what mighty spell, if not Vacation 89
O what a Mask was there, what a disguise! Passion 19
And glut thy self with what thy womb devours, On Time 4
Which is no more then what is false and vain, On Time 5
Besides what her vertues fair Winchester 4
What needs my *Shakespear* for his honour'd Bones, Shakespear 1
What need'st thou such weak witnes of thy name? Shakespear 6
Cries the stall-reader, bless us! what a word on Sonnet 11, 5
For what can Warr, but endless warr still breed, Sonnet 15, 10
Both spirituall powre and civill, what each meanes Sonnet 17, 10
What severs each thou 'hast learnt, which few hav don. Sonnet 17, 11
What powre the Church & what the civill meanes Sonnet 17, Tr. ms 45.11
Help wast a sullen day; what may be won Sonnet 20, 4
What neat repast shall feast us, light and choice, Sonnet 20, 9
And what the *Swede* intend, and what the *French*. Sonnet 21, 8
Toward solid good what leads the nearest way; Sonnet 21, 10
Right onward. What supports me dost thou ask? Sonnet 22, 9
By shallow *Edwards* and Scotch what d' ye call: Forcers 12
What slender Youth bedew'd with liquid odours Horace 1
And what he takes in hand shall prosper all. Psalm 1, 10
Will hear my voyce what time to him I crie. Psalm 4, 18
O what is man that thou remembrest yet, Psalm 8, 12
And now what God the Lord will speak Psalm 85, 29
And answer, *what I pray'd*. Psalm 86, 24
What hinders? as some teachers give to Boyes Prose 6, 2
What can be juster in a State then this? Prose 9, 5
What Land, what Seat of rest thou bidst me seek, Prose 12, 4
What certain Seat, where I may worship thee Prose 12, 5

Whatever
By right of Warr, what e're his business be Par Lost 1.150
Whatever doing, what can we suffer more, Par Lost 2.162

Whatever(*cont*)
If thence he scape into whatever world, Par Lost 2.442
1674 'what ever' in some copies
1667 'what ever'
What e're his wrath, which he calls Justice, bids, Par Lost 2.733
Undaunted to meet there what ever power Par Lost 2.955
So neer grows Death to Life, what ere Death is, Par Lost 4.425
Whatever Hypocrites austerely talk Par Lost 4.744
And boldly venture to whatever place Par Lost 4.891
Whatever Earth all-bearing Mother yields Par Lost 5.338
For know, whatever was created, needs Par Lost 5.414
To pieces, and orewhelm whatever stands Par Lost 6.489
At once came forth whatever creeps the ground, Par Lost 7.475
What e're I saw. Thou Sun, said I, faire Light, Par Lost 8.273
Whatever pure thou in the body enjoy'st Par Lost 8.622
Whatever sleights none would suspicious mark, Par Lost 9.92
Of Death denounc't, whatever thing Death be, Par Lost 9.695
Whatever can to sight or thought be formd, Par Lost 9.898
Whatever wiles of Foe or seeming Friend. Par Lost 10.11
And what she did, whatever in it self, Par Lost 10.141
Beyond this Deep; whatever drawes me on, Par Lost 10.245
No homely morsels, and whatever thing Par Lost 10.605
Those terms whatever, when they were propos'd: Par Lost 10.757
A perfect Dove descend, what e're it meant, Par Reg 1.83
Whate're his cruel malice could invent. Par Reg 1.149
Against whate're may tempt, whate're seduce, Par Reg 1.178
My crime; whatever for it self condemn'd, Par Reg 3.213
Wandring the Wilderness, whatever place, Par Reg 4.600
Goes by the worse, whatever be her cause. Samson 904
What e're it be, to wisest men and best Samson 1034
Har. Presume not on thy God, what e're he be, Samson 1156
What ere the skill of lesser gods can show, Arcades 79
What ever clime the Suns bright circle warms. Sonnet 8, 8
Whatever thing is good Psalm 85, 50

Whatsoever
In whatsoever shape he lurk, of whom Par Lost 4.587

Wheat
With flowr of finest wheat, Psalm 81, 66

Wheel
Throws his steep flight in many an Aerie wheele, Par Lost 3.741
With strictest watch; these other wheel the North, Par Lost 4.783
But with swift wheele reverse, deep entring shar'd Par Lost 6.326
Flashing thick flames, Wheele within Wheele undrawn, Par Lost 6.751
Invisible else above all Starrs, the Wheele Par Lost 8.135
And wheel on th' Earth, devouring where it rouls; Par Lost 12.183
Toward Heav'ns descent had slop'd his westering wheel. Lycidas 31
Trinity ms 'weele'
And like an Engin mov'd with wheel and waight, Another 9
1658 'wheeles'
1640, 1657 'wheele'
My God, oh make them as a wheel Psalm 83, 49

Wheeled
First wheeld thir course; Earth in her rich attire Par Lost 7.501
How quick they wheel'd, and flying behind them shot Par Reg 3.323
Guiding the fiery-wheeled throne, Penseroso 53

Wheeling
Half wheeling to the Shield, half to the Spear. Par Lost 4.785
Above the wheeling poles, and at Heav'ns dore Vacation 34

Wheels
And broken Chariot Wheels, so thick bestrown Par Lost 1.311
ms 'wheeles'
Wheels her pale course, they on thir mirth and dance Par Lost 1.786
With rapid wheels, or fronted Brigads form. Par Lost 2.532
Nor stop thy flaming Chariot wheels, that shook Par Lost 3.394
Us'd to the yoak, draw'st his triumphant wheels Par Lost 4.975
With wheels yet hov'ring o're the Ocean brim, Par Lost 5.140
Of Planets and of fixt in all her Wheeles Par Lost 5.621
Horrible discord, and the madding Wheeles Par Lost 6.210
And at his Chariot wheeles to drag him bound Par Lost 6.358
On Wheels (for like to Pillars most they seem'd Par Lost 6.573
Ascend my Chariot, guide the rapid Wheeles Par Lost 6.711
And Wings were set with Eyes, with Eyes the wheels Par Lost 6.755
1667 'Wheels'
Gloomie as Night; under his burning Wheeles Par Lost 6.832
Distinct with eyes, and from the living Wheels Par Lost 6.846
Then staid the fervid Wheeles, and in his hand Par Lost 7.224
1669 'Wheels'
And craze thir Chariot wheels: when by command Par Lost 12.210
And the great *Thisbite* who on fiery wheels Par Reg 2.16
Rose from the hindmost wheels of *Phoebus* wain. Mask 190
line not in Bridgewater ms
Trinity ms 'weeles'
That in the channell strayes, Mask 895
Trinity ms 'in the channell straies' ←'my rich wheeles inlayes'
See see the Chariot, and those rushing wheels, Passion 36

Whelmed
Unaided could have finisht thee, and whelmd Par Lost 6.141
They saw them whelm'd, and all thir confidence Par Lost 6.651
1667 'whelmd'

Whelming
Where thou perhaps under the whelming tide Lycidas 157
Trinity ms 'humming'
1638 'humming'

Whelped
Where luxurie late reign'd, Sea-monsters whelp'd Par Lost 11.751

When
And such appear'd in hue, as when the force Par Lost 1.230

When(*cont*)
Of battel when it rag'd, in all assaults Par Lost 1.277
He scarce had ceas't when the superiour Fiend Par Lost 1.283
Afloat, when with fierce Winds *Orion* arm'd Par Lost 1.305
Upon the wing, as when men wont to watch Par Lost 1.332
Innumerable. As when the potent Rod Par Lost 1.338
Rhene or the *Danaw*, when her barbarous Sons Par Lost 1.353
Peor his other Name, when he entic'd Par Lost 1.412
These Feminine. For Spirits when they please Par Lost 1.423
Ezekiel saw, when by the Vision led Par Lost 1.455
Who mourn'd in earnest, when the Captive Ark Par Lost 1.458
Th' infection when thir borrow'd Gold compos'd Par Lost 1.483
Jehovah, who in one Night when he pass'd Par Lost 1.487
In Temples and at Altars, when the Priest Par Lost 1.494
And injury and outrage: And when Night Par Lost 1.500
In *Gibeah*, when the hospitable door Par Lost 1.504
When *Charlemain* with all his Peerage fell Par Lost 1.586
Of Glory obscur'd: As when the Sun new ris'n Par Lost 1.594
Thir Glory witherd. As when Heavens Fire Par Lost 1.612
A numerous Brigad hasten'd. As when Bands Par Lost 1.675
Thir Kings, when *Aegypt* with *Assyria* strove Par Lost 1.721
In spring time, when the Sun with *Taurus* rides, Par Lost 1.769
Contrive who need, or when they need, not now Par Lost 2.53
Against the Torturer; when to meet the noise Par Lost 2.64
When the fierce Foe hung on our brok'n Rear Par Lost 2.78
The Vassals of his anger, when the Scourge Par Lost 2.90
When he who most excels in fact of Arms, Par Lost 2.124
What when we fled amain, pursu'd and strook Par Lost 2.165
A refuge from those wounds: or when we lay Par Lost 2.168
I laugh, when those who at the Spear are bold Par Lost 2.204
May hope when everlasting Fate shall yeild Par Lost 2.232
Then most conspicuous, when great things of small, Par Lost 2.258
Imitate when we please? This Desart soile Par Lost 2.270
He scarce had finisht, when such murmur filld Par Lost 2.284
Th' Assembly, as when hollow Rocks retain Par Lost 2.285
Which when *Beelzebub* perceiv'd, then whom, Par Lost 2.299
In his disturbance; when his darling Sons Par Lost 2.373
As when from mountain tops the dusky clouds Par Lost 2.488
As when to warn proud Cities warr appears Par Lost 2.533
As when *Alcides* from *Oechalia* Crown'd Par Lost 2.542
(What could it less when Spirits immortal sing2) Par Lost 2.553
As when farr off at Sea a Fleet descri'd Par Lost 2.636
A hideous Peal: yet, when they list, would creep, Par Lost 2.656
Nor uglier follow the Night-Hag, when call'd Par Lost 2.662
Each cast at th' other; as when two black Clouds Par Lost 2.714
In Heav'n, when at th' Assembly, and in sight Par Lost 2.749
To me, for when they list into the womb Par Lost 2.798
Great things with small) then when *Bellona* storms, Par Lost 2.922
As when a Gryfon through the Wilderness Par Lost 2.943
Bordering on light; when strait behold the Throne Par Lost 2.959
And more endanger'd, then when *Argo* pass'd Par Lost 2.1017
Or when *Ulysses* on the Larbord shunnd Par Lost 2.1019
But hee once past, soon after when man fell, Par Lost 2.1023
When Will and Reason (Reason also is choice) Par Lost 3.108
Made flesh, when time shall be, of Virgin seed, Par Lost 3.284
In those who, when they may, accept not grace. Par Lost 3.302
When thou attended gloriously from Heav'n Par Lost 3.323
Thron'd inaccessible, but when thou shad'st Par Lost 3.377
As when a Vultur on *Imaus* bred, Par Lost 3.431
Of all things transitorie and vain, when Sin Par Lost 3.446
Of Heav'ns ascent they lift thir Feet, when loe Par Lost 3.486
Of Guardians bright, when he from *Esau* fled Par Lost 3.512
Of all this World at once. As when a Scout Par Lost 3.543
Potable Gold, when with one vertuous touch Par Lost 3.608
But all Sun-shine, as when his Beams at Noon Par Lost 3.616
I saw when at his Word the formless Mass, Par Lost 3.708
Then when the Dragon, put to second rout, Par Lost 4.3
When God hath showrd the earth; so lovely seemd Par Lost 4.152
Those balmie spoiles. As when to them who saile Par Lost 4.159
On th' other side: which when th' arch-fellon saw Par Lost 4.179
Lights on his feet. As when a prowling Wolfe, Par Lost 4.183
When *Satan* still in gaze, as first he stood, Par Lost 4.356
Your change approaches, when all these delights Par Lost 4.367
Grip't in each paw: When *Adam* first of men Par Lost 4.408
1667 'when'
That day I oft remember, when from sleep Par Lost 4.449
On *Juno* smiles, when he impregns the Clouds Par Lost 4.500
In *Autumn* thwarts the night, when vapors fir'd Par Lost 4.557
When *Adam* thus to *Eve*: Fair Consort, th' hour Par Lost 4.610
When first on this delightful Land he spreads Par Lost 4.643
But neither breath of Morn when she ascends Par Lost 4.650
This glorious sight, when sleep hath shut all eyes? Par Lost 4.658
Unseen, both when we wake, and when we sleep: Par Lost 4.678
Chos'n by the sovran Planter, when he fram'd Par Lost 4.691
In sad event, when to the unwiser Son Par Lost 4.716
Thy goodness infinite, both when we wake, Par Lost 4.734
And when we seek, as now, thy gift of sleep. Par Lost 4.735
When *Gabriel* to his next in power thus spake. Par Lost 4.781
Discoverd and surpriz'd. As when a spark Par Lost 4.814
As when thou stoodst in Heav'n upright and pure; Par Lost 4.837
That Glorie then, when thou no more wast good, Par Lost 4.838
He scarce had ended, when those two approachd Par Lost 4.874
Thy fiercest, when in Battel to thy aide Par Lost 4.927
Then when I am thy captive talk of chaines, Par Lost 4.970
With ported Spears, as thick as when a field Par Lost 4.980
When *Adam* wak't, so customd, for his sleep Par Lost 5.3
Milde, as when *Zephyrus* on *Flora* breathes, Par Lost 5.16
Into her private Cell when Nature rests. Par Lost 5.109

When(*cont*)

Then when fair Morning first smiles on the World,	Par Lost 5.124
In thy eternal course, both when thou climbst,	Par Lost 5.173
And when high Noon hast gaind, and when thou fallst.	Par Lost 5.174
Above all Hills. As when by night the Glass	Par Lost 5.261
When to enshrine his reliques in the Sun's	Par Lost 5.273
On Princes, when thir rich Retinue long	Par Lost 5.355
No fear lest Dinner coole; when thus began	Par Lost 5.396
Thus when with meats and drinks they had suffic'd,	Par Lost 5.451
To proper substance; time may come when men	Par Lost 5.493
Divine instructer, I have heard, then when	Par Lost 5.546
Upon her Center pois'd, when on a day	Par Lost 5.579
Recorded eminent. Thus when in Orbes	Par Lost 5.594
Then most, when most irregular they seem,	Par Lost 5.624
Now when ambrosial Night with Clouds exhal'd	Par Lost 5.642
Illustrates, when they see all Regal Power	Par Lost 5.739
Had audience, when among the Seraphim	Par Lost 5.804
When this creation was? rememberst thou	Par Lost 5.857
We know no time when we were not as now;	Par Lost 5.859
By our own quick'ning power, when fatal course	Par Lost 5.861
When who can uncreate thee thou shalt know.	Par Lost 5.895
Shot through with orient Beams: when all the Plain	Par Lost 6.15
Thir nimble tread, as when the total kind	Par Lost 6.73
When Reason hath to deal with force, yet so	Par Lost 6.125
To thee not visible, when I alone	Par Lost 6.145
How few somtimes may know, when thousands err.	Par Lost 6.148
When he who rules is worthiest, and excells	Par Lost 6.177
Had to her Center shook. What wonder? when	Par Lost 6.219
When to advance, or stand, or turn the sway	Par Lost 6.234
Of Battel, open when, and when to close	Par Lost 6.235
Weapons more violent, when next we meet,	Par Lost 6.439
Now when fair Morn Orient in Heav'n appeerd	Par Lost 6.524
And onward move Embattelld; when behold	Par Lost 6.550
Had ended; when to Right and Left the Front	Par Lost 6.569
Ere while they fierce were coming, and when wee,	Par Lost 6.610
They shew us when our foes walk not upright.	Par Lost 6.627
When coming towards them so dread they saw	Par Lost 6.648
As likeliest was, when two such Foes met arm'd;	Par Lost 6.688
And gladlier shall resign, when in the end	Par Lost 6.731
When the great Ensign of *Messiah* blaz'd	Par Lost 6.775
Or faint retreat; when the great Son of God	Par Lost 6.799
Visit'st my slumbers Nightly, or when Morn	Par Lost 7.29
Say Goddess, what ensu'd when *Raphael*,	Par Lost 7.40
When, and whereof created, for what cause,	Par Lost 7.64
When such was heard declar'd th' Almightie's will;	Par Lost 7.181
By the Celestial Quires, when Orient Light	Par Lost 7.254
Both when first Eevning was, and when first Morn.	Par Lost 7.260
Satiate with genial moisture, when God said	Par Lost 7.282
He scarce had said, when the bare Earth, till then	Par Lost 7.313
With Eevning Harps and Mattin, when God said,	Par Lost 7.450
Forerunning Night; when at the holy mount	Par Lost 7.584
When I behold this goodly Frame, this World	Par Lost 8.15
Not Words alone pleas'd her. O when meet now	Par Lost 8.57
Hereafter, when they come to model Heav'n	Par Lost 8.79
Earth sitting still, when she alone receaves	Par Lost 8.89
This happie Light, when answer none return'd,	Par Lost 8.285
When suddenly stood at my Head a dream,	Par Lost 8.292
When out of hope, behold her, not farr off,	Par Lost 8.481
O're other Creatures; yet when I approach	Par Lost 8.546
Dismiss not her, when most thou needst her nigh,	Par Lost 8.564
Thy mate, who sees when thou art seen least wise.	Par Lost 8.578
When *Satan* who late fled before the threats	Par Lost 9.53
Now when as sacred Light began to dawne	Par Lost 9.192
1667 'whenas'	
Thir morning incense, when all things that breath,	Par Lost 9.194
Labour, as to debarr us when we need	Par Lost 9.236
When I am present, and thy trial choose	Par Lost 9.316
Touchd onely, that our trial, when least sought,	Par Lost 9.380
Likeliest she seemd, *Pomona* when she fled	Par Lost 9.394
Of what so seldom chanc'd, when to his wish,	Par Lost 9.423
As when a Ship by skilful Stearsman wrought	Par Lost 9.513
When from the boughes a savorie odour blow'n,	Par Lost 9.579
Bright'ns his Crest, as when a wandring Fire,	Par Lost 9.634
Which when she saw, thus to her guide she spake.	Par Lost 9.646
She scarse had said, though brief, when now more bold	Par Lost 9.664
As when of old som Orator renound	Par Lost 9.670
That Morn when first they parted; by the Tree	Par Lost 9.848
Deitie for thee, when Fate will not permit.	Par Lost 9.885
With me, as I besought thee, when that strange	Par Lost 9.1135
The Faith they owe; when earnestly they seek	Par Lost 9.1141
Immutable when thou wert lost, not I,	Par Lost 9.1165
And easily approv'd; when the most High	Par Lost 10.31
When first this Tempter cross'd the Gulf from Hell.	Par Lost 10.39
When time shall be, for so I undertook	Par Lost 10.74
The Eevning coole when he from wrauth more coole	Par Lost 10.95
Which when the Lord God heard, without delay	Par Lost 10.163
When *Jesus* son of *Mary* second *Eve*,	Par Lost 10.183
As when he wash'd his servants feet so now	Par Lost 10.215
Of mortal change on Earth. As when a flock	Par Lost 10.273
As when two Polar Winds blowing adverse	Par Lost 10.289
To Paradise first tending, when behold	Par Lost 10.326
Vain covertures; but when he saw descend	Par Lost 10.337
As when the *Tartar* from his *Russian* Foe	Par Lost 10.431
His Seed, when is not set, shall bruise my head:	Par Lost 10.499
To fill his eare, when contrary he hears	Par Lost 10.506
Sublime with expectation when to see	Par Lost 10.536
Of noxious efficacie, and when to joyne	Par Lost 10.660
Thir influence malignant when to showre,	Par Lost 10.662

When(*cont*)

Thir corners, when with bluster to confound	Par Lost 10.665
Sea, Aire, and Shoar, the Thunder when to rowle	Par Lost 10.666
Those terms whatever, when they were propos'd:	Par Lost 10.757
Whom thus afflicted when sad *Eve* beheld,	Par Lost 10.863
And wandring vanitie, when lest was safe,	Par Lost 10.875
Was meant by Death that day, when lo, to thee	Par Lost 10.1050
When angry most he seem'd and most severe,	Par Lost 10.1095
Seem'd thir Petition, then when th' ancient Pair	Par Lost 11.10
When God descended, and perhaps once more	Par Lost 11.75
The Earth, when *Adam* and first Matron *Eve*	Par Lost 11.136
Not that more glorious, when the Angels met	Par Lost 11.213
Then due by sentence when thou didst transgress,	Par Lost 11.253
Thy mortal passage when it comes. Ascend	Par Lost 11.366
Forsook them, when themselves they villifi'd	Par Lost 11.516
Long had not walkt, when from the Tents behold	Par Lost 11.581
But all in vain: which when he saw, he ceas'd	Par Lost 11.726
For Man and Beast: when loe a wonder strange!	Par Lost 11.733
Though comfortless, as when a Father mourns	Par Lost 11.760
When violence was ceas't, and Warr on Earth,	Par Lost 11.780
Griev'd at his heart, when looking down he saw	Par Lost 11.887
With Man therein or Beast; but when he brings	Par Lost 11.895
And craze thir Chariot wheels: when by command	Par Lost 12.210
Save when they journie, and at length they come,	Par Lost 12.258
Sin against Law to fight; that when they see	Par Lost 12.289
Long time shall dwell and prosper, but when sins	Par Lost 12.316
Expect with mortal paine: say where and when	Par Lost 12.384
When this worlds disolution shall be ripe,	Par Lost 12.459
With dread attending when that fatal wound	Par Reg 1.53
When his fierce thunder drove us to the deep;	Par Reg 1.90
I, when no other durst, sole undertook	Par Reg 1.100
When I was yet a child, no childish play	Par Reg 1.201
The time prefixt I waited, when behold	Par Reg 1.269
Against a Winters day when winds blow keen,	Par Reg 1.317
I came among the Sons of God, when he	Par Reg 1.368
And when to all his Angels he propos'd	Par Reg 1.371
So never more in Hell then when in Heaven.	Par Reg 1.420
Idolatrous, but when his purpose is	Par Reg 1.444
To hear thee when I come (since no man comes)	Par Reg 1.484
But to his Mother *Mary*, when she saw	Par Reg 2.60
In such a season born when scarce a Shed	Par Reg 2.72
Conceals him: when twelve years he scarce had seen,	Par Reg 2.96
Then when I dealt with *Adam* first of Men,	Par Reg 2.133
At his command; when from amidst them rose	Par Reg 2.149
Women, when nothing else, beguil'd the heart	Par Reg 2.169
It was the hour of night, when thus the Son	Par Reg 2.260
When suddenly a man before him stood,	Par Reg 2.298
When and where likes me best, I can command?	Par Reg 2.382
When on his shoulders each mans burden lies;	Par Reg 2.462
This is true glory and renown, when God	Par Reg 3.60
When to extend his fame through Heaven and Earth,	Par Reg 3.65
That it shall never end, so when begin	Par Reg 3.185
But what concerns it thee when I begin	Par Reg 3.198
Let that come when it comes; all hope is lost	Par Reg 3.204
When *Agrican* with all his Northern powers	Par Reg 3.338
When that comes think not thou to find me slack	Par Reg 3.398
When thou stood'st up his Tempter to the pride	Par Reg 3.409
When to the promis'd land thir Fathers pass'd;	Par Reg 3.439
So fares it when with truth falshood contends.	Par Reg 3.443
Know therefore when my season comes to sit	Par Reg 4.146
When slipping from thy Mothers eye thou went'st	Par Reg 4.216
Which when he lists, he leaves, or boasts he can,	Par Reg 4.306
When Prophesies of thee are best fullfill'd.	Par Reg 4.381
Nor when, eternal sure, as without end,	Par Reg 4.391
Of gaining *David*'s Throne no man knows when,	Par Reg 4.471
For both the when and how is no where told,	Par Reg 4.472
Not when it must, but when it may be best.	Par Reg 4.476
As when Earths Son *Antaeus* (to compare	Par Reg 4.563
Where they shall dwell secure, when time shall be	Par Reg 4.616
There I am wont to sit, when any chance	Samson 4
God, when he gave me strength, to shew withal	Samson 58
When she deserts the night	Samson 88
When insupportably his foot advanc't,	Samson 136
In that sore battel when so many dy'd	Samson 287
Yet the fourth time, when mustring all her wiles,	Samson 402
At times when men seek most repose and rest,	Samson 406
To what end should I seek it? when in strength	Samson 522
When God with these forbid'n made choice to rear	Samson 555
Take to thy wicked deed: which when thou seest	Samson 826
Witness when I was worried with thy peals.	Samson 906
If in my flower of youth and strength, when all men	Samson 938
When I must live uxorious to thy will	Samson 945
I less conjecture then when first I saw	Samson 1071
Thir Magistrates confest it, when they took thee	Samson 1183
The *Philistines*, when thou hadst broke the league,	Samson 1189
When I perceiv'd all set on enmity,	Samson 1201
Is well ejected when the Conquer'd can.	Samson 1207
When God into the hands of thir deliverer	Samson 1270
When all abroad was rumour'd that this day	Samson 1600
When to thir sports they turn'd. Immediately	Samson 1614
He unsuspitious led him; which when *Samson*	Samson 1635
When Mountains tremble, those two massie Pillars	Samson 1648
When most unactive deem'd,	Samson 1705
Therfore when any favour'd of high *Jove*,	Mask 78
Well knows to still the wilde winds when they roar,	Mask 87
That ne're art call'd, but when the Dragon woom	Mask 131
And hugg him into snares. When once her eye	Mask 164
Bridgewater ms 'when'	

When(*cont*)

1637 'when'	
Trinity ms 'when'	
When for their teeming Flocks, and granges full	Mask 175
Trinity ms 'when' ←'that' ←'when'	
My Brothers when they saw me wearied out	Mask 182
They left me then, when the gray-hooded Eev'n	Mask 188
line not in Bridgewater ms	
Who as they sung, would take the prison'd soul,	Mask 256
Bridgewater ms 'whoe when'	
That when a soul is found sincerely so,	Mask 454
Trinity ms 'when' ←'when it finds'	
Till all be made immortal: but when lust	Mask 463
And mix no more with goodness, when at last	Mask 594
Which when I did, he on the tender grass	Mask 624
(As I will give you when we go) you may	Mask 648
Trinity ms 'when we goe' ←'on the way' ←'as wee goe'	
When the fresh blood grows lively, and returns	Mask 670
Were it a draft for *Juno* when she banquets,	Mask 701
I hate when vice can bolt her arguments,	Mask 760
Dips me all o're, as when the wrath of *Jove*	Mask 803
line not in Trinity ms	
line not in Bridgewater ms	
when the big rowling flakes of pitchie clowds	Mask Tr. ms 15.52
when the bigg rowling flakes of pitchie clouds	Mask Br. ms 345
When the merry Bells ring round,	Allegro 93
When in one night, ere glimps of morn,	Allegro 107
When the gust hath blown his fill,	Penseroso 128
And when the Sun begins to fling	Penseroso 131
When Eev'ning gray doth rise, I fetch my round	Arcades 54
But els in deep of night when drowsines	Arcades 61
When first the White thorn blows;	Lycidas 48
Where were ye Nymphs when the remorseless deep	Lycidas 50
When by the rout that made the hideous roar,	Lycidas 61
But the fair Guerdon when we hope to find,	Lycidas 73
1638 'where we'	
And when they list, their lean and flashy songs	Lycidas 123
when she beheld (the gods farre sighted bee)	Lycidas Tr. ms 29.60
When such musick sweet	Nativity 93
But when of old the sons of morning sung,	Nativity 119
When at the worlds last session,	Nativity 163
So when the Sun in bed,	Nativity 229
When the blest seed of *Terah*'s faithfull Son,	Psalm 114, 1
When Beldam Nature in her cradle was;	Vacation 46
For when as each thing bad thou hast entomb'd,	On Time 9
When every thing that is sincerely good	On Time 14
When once our heav'nly-guided soul shall clime,	On Time 19
Death was half glad when he had got him down;	Carrier 6
1658 'that'	
Warbl'st at eeve, when all the Woods are still,	Sonnet 1, 2
The house of *Pindarus*, when Temple and Towre	Sonnet 8, 11
Thou, when the Bridegroom with his feastfull friends	Sonnet 9, 12
When thou taught'st *Cambridge*, and King *Edward* Greek.	Sonnet 11, 14
When strait a barbarous noise environs me	Sonnet 12, 3
As when those Hinds that were transform'd to Froggs	Sonnet 12, 5
And still revolt when truth would set them free.	Sonnet 12, 10
Trinity ms 'still revolt when Truth would sett them' ←'make them' ←'set them' ←'hate the truth wherby they should be'	
Licence they mean when they cry libertie;	Sonnet 12, 11
when most were wont which till then us'd to scan	Sonnet 13, Tr. ms 40.03
When Faith and Love which parted from thee never,	Sonnet 14, 1
when as they journey'd from this dark abode	Sonnet 14, Tr. ms 41.07
'when as' ←'Still as'	
The helme of Rome, when gownes not armes repelld	Sonnet 17, 3
When all our Fathers worship't Stocks and Stones,	Sonnet 18, 4
When I consider how my light is spent,	Sonnet 19, 1
And when God sends a cheerful hour, refrains.	Sonnet 21, 14
When they shall read this clearly in your charge	Forcers 19
Answer me when I call	Psalm 4, 1
Then when a year of glut	Psalm 4, 33
When I behold thy Heavens, thy Fingers art,	Psalm 8, 9
When as he pass'd through Aegypt land;	Psalm 81, 19
When trouble did thee sore assaile,	Psalm 81, 25
When at the brook of Kishon *old*	Psalm 83, 37
As *when* an *aged* wood takes fire	Psalm 83, 53
When he the Nations doth enrowle	Psalm 87, 23
When I dye, let the earth be roul'd in flames.	Prose 5, 1
This is true Liberty when free born men	Prose 9, 1

Whenas

Now when as sacred Light began to dawne	Par Lost 9.192
1667 'whenas'	
For when as each thing bad thou hast entomb'd,	On Time 9
when as they journey'd from this dark abode	Sonnet 14, Tr. ms 41.07

Whence

O how unlike the place from whence they fell!	Par Lost 1.75
With what is punish't; whence these raging fires	Par Lost 2.213
Covers his Throne; from whence deep thunders roar	Par Lost 2.267
Nor want we skill or Art, from whence to raise	Par Lost 2.272
By *Satan*, and in part propos'd: for whence,	Par Lost 2.380
Of those bright confines, whence with neighbouring Arms	Par Lost 2.395
Of *Ternate* and *Tidore*, whence Merchants bring	Par Lost 2.639
Whence and what art thou, execrable shape,	Par Lost 2.681
To that side Heav'n from whence your Legions fell:	Par Lost 2.1006
Shot upward still direct, whence no way round	Par Lost 3.618
Native perfumes, and whisper whence they stole	Par Lost 4.158
Whence true autoritie in men; though both	Par Lost 4.295
Whence rushing he might surest seize them both	Par Lost 4.407
And what I was, whence thither brought, and how.	Par Lost 4.452

Whence(*cont*)

Flie thither whence thou fledst: if from this houre	Par Lost 4.963
Yet evil whence? in thee can harbour none,	Par Lost 5.99
Yet mutable; whence warne him to beware	Par Lost 5.237
Whence in her visage round those spots, unpurg'd	Par Lost 5.419
Fansie and understanding, whence the Soule	Par Lost 5.486
From that high mount of God, whence light & shade	Par Lost 5.643
Doctrin which we would know whence learnt: who saw	Par Lost 5.856
Before the seat supream; from whence a voice	Par Lost 6.27
These things, as not to mind from whence they grow	Par Lost 6.477
All power on him transferr'd: whence to his Son	Par Lost 6.678
Whence in perpetual fight they needs must last	Par Lost 6.693
Her mural breach, returning whence it rowld.	Par Lost 6.879
With Blessedness. Whence *Adam* soon repeal'd	Par Lost 7.59
But grateful to acknowledge whence his good	Par Lost 7.512
Useful, whence haply mention may arise	Par Lost 8.200
Of foul concupiscence; whence evil store;	Par Lost 9.1078
I know not whence possessd thee; we had then	Par Lost 9.1137
Accompanied to Heaven Gate, from whence	Par Lost 10.88
Whence *Adam* faultring long, thus answer'd brief.	Par Lost 10.115
The Ground whence he was taken, fitter soile.	Par Lost 11.98
Is past, and we shall live. Whence Haile to thee,	Par Lost 11.158
The ground whence thou wast tak'n, fitter Soile.	Par Lost 11.262
Perhaps thy Capital Seate, from whence had spred	Par Lost 11.343
Of Cattel grazing: others, whence the sound	Par Lost 11.558
Too numerous; whence of guests he makes them slaves	Par Lost 12.167
Whence heavie persecution shall arise	Par Lost 12.531
Whence thou returnst, and whither wentst, I know;	Par Lost 12.610
Heaven open'd her eternal doors, from whence	Par Reg 1.281
To thee not known, whence hast thou then thy truth,	Par Reg 1.446
To greatness? whence Authority deriv'st,	Par Reg 2.418
Who sent me, and thereby witness whence I am.	Par Reg 3.107
But whence to thee this zeal, where was it then	Par Reg 3.407
Of that high mountain, whence he might behold	Par Reg 4.26
Fell whence he stood to see his Victor fall.	Par Reg 4.571
Th' unworthier they; whence to this day they serve.	Samson 1216
From whence captivity and loss of eyes.	Samson 1744
Bore witness gloriously; whence *Gaza* mourns	Samson 1752
Whence eev'n now the tumult of loud Mirth	Mask 202
line not in Bridgewater ms	
That brow this bottom glade, whence night by night	Mask 532
Of Attick tast, with Wine, whence we may rise	Sonnet 20, 10
From whence they might not swerve.	Psalm 81, 16

Whenever

When ever that shall be; so Fate pronounc'd.	Par Lost 2.809
O welcom hour whenever! why delayes	Par Lost 10.771

Where

Regions of sorrow, doleful shades, where peace	Par Lost 1.65
Where Joy for ever dwells: Hail horrours, hail	Par Lost 1.250
What matter where, if I be still the same,	Par Lost 1.256
In *Vallombrosa*, where th' *Etrurian* shades	Par Lost 1.303
The Heads and Leaders thither hast where stood	Par Lost 1.357
Came singly where he stood on the bare strand,	Par Lost 1.379
In *Sion* also not unsung, where stood	Par Lost 1.442
Where he fell flat, and sham'd his Worshipers:	Par Lost 1.461
And in luxurious Cities, where the noyse	Par Lost 1.498
Our first eruption, thither or elsewhere:	Par Lost 1.656
ms 'else where'	
Built like a Temple, where *Pilasters* round	Par Lost 1.713
Where Scepter'd Angels held thir residence,	Par Lost 1.734
(Though like a cover'd field, where Champions bold	Par Lost 1.763
Or where the gorgeous East with richest hand	Par Lost 2.3
Of endless pain? where there is then no good	Par Lost 2.30
Where pain of unextinguishable fire	Par Lost 2.88
Of what we are and were, dismissing quite	Par Lost 2.282
1667 'where'	
And where thir weakness, how attempted best,	Par Lost 2.357
Leads him perplext, where he may likeliest find	Par Lost 2.525
Where Armies whole have sunk: the parching Air	Par Lost 2.594
Where all life dies, death lives, and Nature breeds,	Par Lost 2.624
Where I reign King, and to enrage thee more,	Par Lost 2.698
And bring ye to the place where Thou and Death	Par Lost 2.840
The Gods who live at ease, where I shall Reign	Par Lost 2.868
Without dimension, where length, breadth, & highth,	Par Lost 2.893
And time and place are lost; where eldest Night	Par Lost 2.894
What readiest path leads where your gloomie bounds	Par Lost 2.976
Cease I to wander where the Muses haunt	Par Lost 3.27
From the pure Empyrean where he sits	Par Lost 3.57
Where onely what they needs must do, appeard,	Par Lost 3.105
Say Heav'nly powers, where shall we find such love,	Par Lost 3.213
To Heav'n remov'd where first it grew, there grows,	Par Lost 3.356
And where the river of Bliss through midst of Heavn	Par Lost 3.358
Amidst the glorious brightness where thou sit'st	Par Lost 3.376
Love no where to be found less then Divine!	Par Lost 3.411
On Hills where Flocks are fed, flies toward the Springs	Par Lost 3.435
Of *Sericana*, where *Chineses* drive	Par Lost 3.438
To *Beersaba*, where the *Holy Land*	Par Lost 3.536
So wide the op'ning seemd, where bounds were set	Par Lost 3.538
Round he surveys, and well might, where he stood	Par Lost 3.555
Or Longitude, where the great Luminarie	Par Lost 3.576
No where so cleer, sharp'nd his visual ray	Par Lost 3.620
Where all his Sons thy Embassie attend;	Par Lost 3.658
Where no ill seems: Which now for once beguil'd	Par Lost 3.689
Where honour due and reverence none neglects,	Par Lost 3.738
Where wounds of deadly hate have peirc'd so deep:	Par Lost 4.99
Of *Eden*, where delicious Paradise,	Par Lost 4.132
Watching where Shepherds pen thir Flocks at eeve	Par Lost 4.185
Or where the Sons of *Eden* long before	Par Lost 4.213

Where(*cont*)

Both where the morning Sun first warmly smote	Par Lost 4.244
The open field, and where the unpierc't shade	Par Lost 4.245
Of *Enna*, where *Proserpin* gathering flours	Par Lost 4.269
Girt with the River *Triton*, where old *Cham*,	Par Lost 4.276
Nor where *Abassin* Kings thir issue Guard,	Par Lost 4.280
From this *Assyrian* Garden, where the Fiend	Par Lost 4.285
Like consort to thy self canst no where find.	Par Lost 4.448
Under a shade of flours, much wondring where	Par Lost 4.451
And I will bring thee where no shadow staies	Par Lost 4.470
Where neither joy nor love, but fierce desire,	Par Lost 4.509
A chance but chance may lead where I may meet	Par Lost 4.530
Mean while in utmost Longitude, where Heav'n	Par Lost 4.539
Where he first lighted, soon discernd his looks	Par Lost 4.570
Amid the Suns bright circle where thou sitst,	Par Lost 4.578
For us too large, where thy abundance wants	Par Lost 4.730
But chiefly where those two fair Creatures Lodge,	Par Lost 4.790
Such where ye find, seise fast, and hither bring.	Par Lost 4.796
For you, there sitting where ye durst not soare;	Par Lost 4.829
The western Point, where those half-rounding guards	Par Lost 4.862
And brief related whom they brought, where found,	Par Lost 4.875
1667 'wher'	
Farthest from pain, where thou mightst hope to change	Par Lost 4.892
The rest is true, they found me where they say;	Par Lost 4.900
Where thou art weigh'd, and shown how light, how weak,	Par Lost 4.1012
The cool, the silent, save where silence yields	Par Lost 5.39
Among sweet dewes and flours; where any row	Par Lost 5.212
Thousand Celestial Ardors, where he stood	Par Lost 5.249
From large bestowd, where Nature multiplies	Par Lost 5.318
Of God inspir'd, small store will serve, where store,	Par Lost 5.322
In *Pontus* or the *Punic* Coast, or where	Par Lost 5.340
To visit thee; lead on then where thy Bowre	Par Lost 5.375
Reignd where these Heav'ns now rowl, where Earth now rests	Par Lost 5.578
Of surfet where full measure onely bounds	Par Lost 5.639
line not in 1667 edition	
Celestial Tabernacles, where they slept	Par Lost 5.654
Homeward with flying march where we possess	Par Lost 5.688
Where light and darkness in perpetual round	Par Lost 6.6
Abdiel that sight endur'd not, where he stood	Par Lost 6.111
Should yet remain, where faith and realtie	Par Lost 6.115
There fail where Vertue fails, or weakest prove	Par Lost 6.117
Where boldest; though to sight unconquerable?	Par Lost 6.118
Saw where the Sword of *Michael* smote, and fell'd	Par Lost 6.250
Where erst was thickest fight, th' Angelic throng,	Par Lost 6.308
Back to his Chariot; where it stood retir'd	Par Lost 6.338
Memorial, where the might of *Gabriel* fought,	Par Lost 6.355
Where lodg'd, or whither fled, or if for fight,	Par Lost 6.531
Had not th' Almightie Father where he sits	Par Lost 6.671
From the right hand of Glorie where he sate,	Par Lost 6.747
Where now he sits at the right hand of bliss.	Par Lost 6.892
In *Rhodope*, where Woods and Rocks had Eares	Par Lost 7.35
From the Armoury of God, where stand of old	Par Lost 7.200
Wave rowling after Wave, where way they found,	Par Lost 7.298
All but within those banks, where Rivers now	Par Lost 7.305
Seemd like to Heav'n, a seat where Gods might dwell,	Par Lost 7.329
As from his Laire the wilde Beast where he wonns	Par Lost 7.457
Eternal Father (For where is not hee	Par Lost 7.517
Perceaving where she sat retir'd in sight,	Par Lost 8.41
Where God resides, and ere mid-day arriv'd	Par Lost 8.112
But who I was, or where, or from what cause,	Par Lost 8.270
From where I first drew Aire, and first beheld	Par Lost 8.284
Though sleeping, where I lay, and saw the shape	Par Lost 8.463
No more of talk where God or Angel Guest	Par Lost 9.1
Where *Tigris* at the foot of Paradise	Par Lost 9.71
Where to lie hid; Sea he had searcht and Land	Par Lost 9.76
At *Darien*, thence to the Land where flowes	Par Lost 9.81
In every Bush and Brake, where hap may finde	Par Lost 9.160
His midnight search, where soonest he might finde	Par Lost 9.181
Let us divide our labours, thou where choice	Par Lost 9.214
Leads thee, or where most needs, whether to wind	Par Lost 9.215
The clasping Ivie where to climb, while I	Par Lost 9.217
Hopeless to circumvent us joynd, where each	Par Lost 9.259
The Wife, where danger or dishonour lurks,	Par Lost 9.267
And on his Quest, where likeliest he might finde	Par Lost 9.414
In Bowre and Field he sought, where any tuft	Par Lost 9.417
Veild in a Cloud of Fragrance, where she stood,	Par Lost 9.425
Or that, not Mystic, where the Sapient King	Par Lost 9.442
Where Houses thick and Sewers annoy the Aire,	Par Lost 9.446
Nigh Rivers mouth or Foreland, where the Wind	Par Lost 9.514
Where universally admir'd; but here	Par Lost 9.542
Amid the Tree now got, where plenty hung	Par Lost 9.594
But say, where grows the Tree, from hence how far?	Par Lost 9.617
In *Athens* or free *Rome*, where Eloquence	Par Lost 9.671
Obscur'd, where highest Woods impenetrable	Par Lost 9.1086
Hide me, where I may never see them more.	Par Lost 9.1090
Attendance none shall need, nor Train, where none	Par Lost 10.80
Where art thou *Adam*, wont with joy to meet	Par Lost 10.103
Where obvious dutie erewhile appear'd unsaught:	Par Lost 10.106
Where Satan now prevailes, a Monument	Par Lost 10.258
Where Armies lie encampt, come flying, lur'd	Par Lost 10.276
Of *Satan*, to the self same place where hee	Par Lost 10.315
By Night, and listening where the hapless Paire	Par Lost 10.342
Where all yet left of that revolted Rout	Par Lost 10.534
Neer that bituminous Lake where *Sodom* flam'd;	Par Lost 10.562
There best, where most with ravin I may meet;	Par Lost 10.599
Desolate where she sate, approaching nigh,	Par Lost 10.864
Whither shall I betake me, where subsist?	Par Lost 10.922
Repairing where he judg'd us, prostrate fall	Par Lost 10.1087

Where(*cont*)

Repairing where he judg'd them prostrate fell	Par Lost 10.1099
With incense, where the Golden Altar fum'd,	Par Lost 11.18
To better life shall yeeld him, where with mee	Par Lost 11.42
Where entrance up from *Eden* easiest climbes,	Par Lost 11.119
Jacob in *Mahanaim*, where he saw	Par Lost 11.214
To find where *Adam* shelterd, took his way,	Par Lost 11.223
In Manhood where Youth ended; by his side	Par Lost 11.246
Fit haunt of Gods? where I had hope to spend,	Par Lost 11.271
Where he abides, think there thy native soile.	Par Lost 11.292
With worship, place by place where he voutsaf'd	Par Lost 11.318
In yonder nether World where shall I seek	Par Lost 11.328
Down to the golden *Chersonese*, or where	Par Lost 11.392
In *Hispahan*, or where the *Russian Ksar*	Par Lost 11.394
On *Europe* thence, and where *Rome* was to sway	Par Lost 11.405
Had melted (whether found where casual fire	Par Lost 11.566
Where Cattle pastur'd late, now scatterd lies	Par Lost 11.653
Where good with bad were matcht, who of themselves	Par Lost 11.685
Rape or Adulterie, where passing faire	Par Lost 11.717
Where luxurie late reign'd, Sea-monsters whelp'd	Par Lost 11.751
Himself and his rash Armie, where thin Aire	Par Lost 12.76
See where it flows, disgorging at seaven mouthes	Par Lost 12.158
And wheel on th' Earth, devouring where it rouls;	Par Lost 12.183
Untraind in Armes, where rashness leads not on.	Par Lost 12.222
Expect with mortal paine: say where and when	Par Lost 12.384
Descended, *Adam* to the Bowre where *Eve*	Par Lost 12.607
The World was all before them, where to choose	Par Lost 12.646
Where he might likeliest find this new-declar'd,	Par Reg 1.121
Lodg'd in *Bethabara* where *John* baptiz'd,	Par Reg 1.184
Where they might see him, and to thee they came;	Par Reg 1.246
Directed to the Manger where thou lais't,	Par Reg 1.247
Where ought we hear, and curious are to hear,	Par Reg 1.333
Comes to the place where he before had sat	Par Reg 1.412
But misery hath rested from me; where	Par Reg 1.470
Where winds with Reeds, and Osiers whisp'ring play	Par Reg 2.26
But where delays he now? some great intent	Par Reg 2.95
Where all his Potentates in Council sate;	Par Reg 2.118
And now I know he hungers where no food	Par Reg 2.231
Where still from shade to shade the Son of God	Par Reg 2.242
Where will this end? four times ten days I have pass'd	Par Reg 2.245
When and where likes me best, I can command?	Par Reg 2.382
In vain, where no acceptance it can find,	Par Reg 2.388
Where glory is false glory, attributed	Par Reg 3.69
For where no hope is left, is left no fear;	Par Reg 3.206
But I will bring thee where thou soon shalt quit	Par Reg 3.244
Or where plain was raise hill, or over-lay	Par Reg 3.333
But whence to thee this zeal, where was it then	Par Reg 3.407
In cunning, over-reach't where least he thought,	Par Reg 4.11
About the wine-press where sweet moust is powr'd,	Par Reg 4.16
Syene, and where the shadow both way falls,	Par Reg 4.70
Where on the *Aegean* shore a City stands	Par Reg 4.238
Plato's retirement, where the *Attic* Bird	Par Reg 4.245
With Music or with Poem, where so soon	Par Reg 4.332
Where God is prais'd aright, and Godlike men,	Par Reg 4.348
Unless where moral vertue is express't	Par Reg 4.351
Yet as being oft times noxious where they light	Par Reg 4.460
For both the when and how is no where told,	Par Reg 4.472
Where by all best conjectures I collect	Par Reg 4.524
Where they shall dwell secure, when time shall be	Par Reg 4.616
Where I a Prisoner chain'd, scarce freely draw	Samson 7
From off the Altar, where an Off'ring burn'd,	Samson 26
But to subserve where wisdom bears command.	Samson 57
As earst in highest, behold him where he lies.	Samson 339
Where thou mayst bring thy off'rings, to avert	Samson 519
Sam. I thought where all thy circling wiles would end;	Samson 871
Where other senses want not their delights	Samson 916
With me, where my redoubl'd love and care	Samson 923
Where once I have been caught; I know thy trains	Samson 932
But in my countrey where I most desire,	Samson 980
Of those encounters, where we might have tri'd	Samson 1086
Had brought me to the field where thou art fam'd	Samson 1094
Or left thy carkass where the Ass lay thrown:	Samson 1097
Some narrow place enclos'd, where sight may give thee,	Samson 1117
Where strength can least abide, though all thy hairs	Samson 1136
Where I will see thee heartn'd and fresh clad	Samson 1317
Chor. Where the heart joins not, outward acts defile not.	Samson 1368
Sam. Where outward force constrains, the sentence holds	Samson 1369
The Edifice where all were met to see him	Samson 1588
With seats where all the Lords and each degree	Samson 1607
The other side was op'n, where the throng	Samson 1609
He patient but undaunted where they led him,	Samson 1623
Let us go find the body where it lies	Samson 1725
My mansion is, where those immortal shapes	Mask 2
Where his fair off-spring nurs't in Princely lore,	Mask 34
Of such late Wassailers; yet O where els	Mask 179
But where they are, and why they came not back,	Mask 191
Where the love-lorn Nightingale	Mask 234
Tell me but where	Mask 240
But loyal cottage, where you may be safe	Mask 320
And Courts of Princes, where it first was nam'd,	Mask 325
Trinity ms 'where' ←'were'	
Where may she wander now, whether betake her	Mask 351
Where with her best nurse Contemplation	Mask 377
Yet where an equall poise of hope and fear	Mask 410
Where through the sacred rayes of Chastity,	Mask 425
Yea there, where very desolation dwels	Mask 428
Where no crude surfet raigns. *Eld. Bro*. List, list, I hear	Mask 480
But O my Virgin Lady, where is she?	Mask 507

Where(*cont*)	
Where that damn'd wisard hid in sly disguise	Mask 571
Where if he be, with dauntless hardihood,	Mask 650
Where most may wonder at the workmanship;	Mask 747
line not in Bridgewater ms	
Listen where thou art sitting	Mask 860
Where grows the Willow and the Osier dank,	Mask 891
Where this night are met in state	Mask 948
Where day never shuts his eye,	Mask 978
Where young *Adonis* oft reposes,	Mask 999
Where the bow'd welkin slow doth bend,	Mask 1015
amidst the Hesperian gardens, on whose bancks	Mask Tr. ms 10.05
'on whose bancks' ←'where the banks' ←'on whose bancks'	
she might be free from perill where she is	Mask Tr. ms 16.42
& yawning dens where glaring monsters house	Mask Tr. ms 16.63
where grows the right-borne gold upon his native tree	Mask Tr. ms 27.08
she might be free from perill where she is,	Mask Br. ms 395
and yawninge denns, where glaringe monsters house	Mask Br. ms 416
Wher brooding darknes spreads his jealous wings,	Allegro 6
1673 'where'	
Wher the great Sun begins his state,	Allegro 60
1673 'Where'	
Where the nibling flocks do stray,	Allegro 72
Wher perhaps som beauty lies,	Allegro 79
Where *Corydon* and *Thyrsis* met,	Allegro 83
Where throngs of Knights and Barons bold,	Allegro 119
Where glowing Embers through the room	Penseroso 79
Where I may oft out-watch the *Bear*,	Penseroso 87
Where more is meant then meets the ear.	Penseroso 120
Where the rude Ax with heaved stroke,	Penseroso 136
Where no profaner eye may look,	Penseroso 140
Where I may sit and rightly spell,	Penseroso 170
And lead ye where ye may more neer behold	Arcades 40
Where ye may all that are of noble stemm	Arcades 82
Where no print of step hath been,	Arcades 85
I will bring you where she sits,	Arcades 91
Trinity ms 'wher'	
Where were ye Nymphs when the remorseless deep	Lycidas 50
Where your old *Bards*, the famous *Druids* ly,	Lycidas 53
Nor yet where *Deva* spreads her wisard stream:	Lycidas 55
But the fair Guerdon when we hope to find,	Lycidas 73
1638 'where we'	
Ye valleys low where the milde whispers use,	Lycidas 136
To strew the Laureat Herse where *Lycid* lies.	Lycidas 151
Where thou perhaps under the whelming tide	Lycidas 157
Where the great vision of the guarded Mount	Lycidas 161
Where other groves, and other streams along,	Lycidas 174
But thou canst best perform that office where thou art.	Fair Inf 70
Where he had mutely sate two years before:	Vacation 6
Such where the deep transported mind may soare	Vacation 33
Come tripping to the Room where thou didst lie;	Vacation 62
And former sufferings other where are found;	Passion 25
And letters where my tears have washt a wannish white.	Passion 35
To bear me where the Towers of *Salem* stood,	Passion 39
Where the bright Seraphim in burning row	Musick 10
where day dwells without night	Musick Tr. ms 4.29
Shew'd him his room where he must lodge that night,	Carrier 15
O're all th' *Italian* fields where still doth sway	Sonnet 18, 11
Where shall we sometimes meet, and by the fire	Sonnet 20, 3
Set thy wayes right before, where my step goes.	Psalm 5, 24
Where thou do'st dwell so near.	Psalm 84, 4
Where thee they ever praise,	Psalm 84, 18
Where Springs and Showrs abound.	Psalm 84, 24
Hast hid *where none shall know*.	Psalm 85, 8
I mention Egypt, *where proud Kings*	Psalm 87, 11
Where thickest darkness *hovers round*,	Psalm 88, 27
Into a goodly valley, where he sees	Prose 2, 2
Impudent whoore, where hast thou plac'd thy hope?	Prose 3, 3
What certain Seat, where I may worship thee	Prose 12, 5
Sea-girt it lies, where Giants dwelt of old,	Prose 12, 9
Whereat	
To speak; whereat thir doubl'd Ranks they bend	Par Lost 1.616
ms 'where-at'	
They vote: whereat his speech he thus renews.	Par Lost 2.389
Or singular and rash, whereat rejoic'd	Par Lost 5.851
Of Battel: whereat *Michael* bid sound	Par Lost 6.202
To pluck and eate; whereat I wak'd, and found	Par Lost 8.309
Whereat hee inlie rag'd, and as they talk'd,	Par Lost 11.444
Whereat the heart of *Adam* erst so sad	Par Lost 11.868
Began to parch that temperate Clime; whereat	Par Lost 12.636
Whereby	
To objects distant farr, whereby he soon	Par Lost 3.621
Of sense, whereby they hear, see, smell, touch, taste,	Par Lost 5.411
But if the sense of touch whereby mankind	Par Lost 8.579
Whereby they may direct their future life.	Par Reg 1.396
1671 'wherbey' in some copies	
And still revolt when truth would set them free.	Sonnet 12, 10
Trinity ms 'still revolt when Truth would sett them' ←'make them' ←'set them' ←'hate the truth wherby they should be'	
Wherefore	
But wherefore let we then our faithful friends,	Par Lost 1.264
To punish endless? wherefore cease we then?	Par Lost 2.159
Mee from attempting. Wherefore do I assume	Par Lost 2.450
Ah wherefore! he deservd no such return	Par Lost 4.42
But wherfore all night long shine these, for whom	Par Lost 4.657
But wherefore thou alone? wherefore with thee	Par Lost 4.917
Heav'ns awful Monarch? wherefore but in hope	Par Lost 4.960
Remain not; wherfore should not strength and might	Par Lost 6.116

Wherefore(*cont*)	
Foul on himself; then wherefore shund or feard	Par Lost 9.331
1667 'wherfore'	
Wherefore didst thou beget me? I sought it not	Par Lost 10.762
These God-like Vertues wherefore dost thou hide?	Par Reg 3.21
In savage Wilderness, wherefore deprive	Par Reg 3.23
O wherefore was my birth from Heaven foretold	Samson 23
O wherefore did God grant me my request,	Samson 356
But wherefore comes old *Manoa* in such hast	Samson 1441
Wherefore did Nature powre her bounties forth,	Mask 710
Trinity ms 'wherfore'	
Wherein	
Down cast and damp, yet such wherein appear'd	Par Lost 1.523
And fields were fought in Heav'n; wherein remaind	Par Lost 2.768
Wherein past, present, future he beholds,	Par Lost 3.78
Father, to see thy face, wherein no cloud	Par Lost 3.262
New Heav'n and Earth, wherein the just shall dwell,	Par Lost 3.335
Regardless of the Bliss wherein hee sat	Par Lost 3.408
Wherein all things created first he weighd,	Par Lost 4.999
Wherein to read his wondrous Works, and learne	Par Lost 8.68
All rational delight, wherein the brute	Par Lost 8.391
Wherein true Love consists not; love refines	Par Lost 8.589
Wisdom without their leave? and wherein lies	Par Lost 9.725
Wherein God set thee above her made of thee,	Par Lost 10.149
Giv'n thee of Grace, wherein thou may'st repent,	Par Lost 11.255
A Lazar-house it seemd, wherein were laid	Par Lost 11.479
Of wickedness, wherein shall dwell his Race	Par Lost 11.608
Yet empty of all good wherein consists	Par Lost 11.616
Both Heav'n and Earth, wherein the just shall dwell.	Par Lost 11.901
The Plain, wherein a black bituminous gurge	Par Lost 12.41
This dreaded time have compast, wherein we	Par Reg 1.58
To what can I be useful, wherein serve	Samson 564
Wherein consisted all thy strength and safety?	Samson 780
Wherin thou rid'st with *Hecat'*, and befriend	Mask 135
1637 'Wherein'	
Bridgewater ms 'wherein'	
Wherin the Son of Heav'ns eternal King,	Nativity 2
1673 'Wherein'	
Wherin the Prince of light	Nativity 62
1673 'Wherein'	
Wherin your Father flourisht, yet by you	Sonnet 10, 10
Whereof	
Space may produce new Worlds; whereof so rife	Par Lost 1.650
ms 'where of'	
Her watrie Labyrinth, whereof who drinks,	Par Lost 2.584
Had been achiev'd, whereof all Hell had rung,	Par Lost 2.723
At top whereof, but farr more rich appeerd	Par Lost 3.504
Are ever cleer. Whereof hee soon aware,	Par Lost 4.119
And Country whereof here needs no account,	Par Lost 4.235
Aught whereof hee hath need, hee who requires	Par Lost 4.419
This new created World, whereof in Hell	Par Lost 4.937
Whereof to found thir Engins and thir Balls	Par Lost 6.518
When, and whereof created, for what cause,	Par Lost 7.64
In signe whereof each Bird and Beast behold	Par Lost 8.342
One Heart, one Soul in both; whereof good prooff	Par Lost 9.967
Whereof I gave thee charge thou shouldst not eat?	Par Lost 10.123
The Serpents head; whereof to thee anon	Par Lost 12.150
With Food, whereof we wretched seldom taste.	Par Reg 1.345
The strength whereof suffic'd him forty days;	Par Reg 2.276
At sight whereof the Fiend yet more presum'd,	Par Reg 3.345
Whereof this ominous night that clos'd thee round,	Par Reg 4.481
In confidence whereof I once again	Samson 1174
Whereon	
For one of *Syrian* mode, whereon to burn	Par Lost 1.474
ms 'where on'	
The Stairs were such as whereon *Jacob* saw	Par Lost 3.510
Of Jasper, or of liquid Pearle, whereon	Par Lost 3.519
O fair foundation laid whereon to build	Par Lost 4.521
From center to circumference, whereon	Par Lost 5.510
In imitation of that Mount whereon	Par Lost 5.764
Of this Ethereous mould whereon we stand,	Par Lost 6.473
Whereon a Saphir Throne, inlaid with pure	Par Lost 6.758
Fawning, and lick'd the ground whereon she trod.	Par Lost 9.526
Whereon I live, thy gentle looks, thy aid,	Par Lost 10.919
Whereon for different cause the Tempter set	Par Lost 11.382
Part arable and tilth, whereon were Sheaves	Par Lost 11.430
He lookd and saw a spacious Plaine, whereon	Par Lost 11.556
Green Tree or ground whereon his foot may light;	Par Lost 11.858
His triple-colour'd Bow, whereon to look	Par Lost 11.897
Rocks whereon greatest men have oftest wreck'd;	Par Reg 2.228
The leaves should all be black wheron I write,	Passion 34
Th' appointed time, the day wheron	Psalm 81, 11
Whereso	
Frequented thir Assemblies, whereso met,	Par Lost 11.722
Wheresoever	
Nothing but ruin wheresoe're they rove,	Par Reg 3.79
Whereto	
Whereto with speedy words th' Arch-fiend reply'd.	Par Lost 1.156
ms 'Where to'	
Whereto with look compos'd *Satan* repli'd.	Par Lost 6.469
Wherto th' Almighty answer'd, not displeas'd.	Par Lost 8.398
Whereto thus *Adam* fatherly displeas'd.	Par Lost 12.63
Wherever	
Wherever thus created, for no place	Par Lost 7.535
Wherever plac't, let him dispose: joy thou	Par Lost 8.170
Single with like defence, wherever met,	Par Lost 9.325
By the waters of Life, where ere they sate	Par Lost 11.79
Wherere our days work lies, though now enjoind	Par Lost 11.177

Wherever(*cont*)
His Eye might there command wherever stood Par Lost 11.385
Of *Abrahams* Faith wherever through the world; Par Lost 12.449
Wherever, under some concourse of shades Par Reg 4.404
Sam. Where ever fountain or fresh current flow'd Samson 547
As on my enemies, where ever chanc'd, Samson 1202
Wash far away, where ere thy bones are hurld, Lycidas 155
Tell me bright Spirit where e're thou hoverest Fair Inf 38
Me safe where ere I lie Psalm 4, 40
Wherewith
Of Hymns and sacred Songs, wherewith thy Throne Par Lost 3.148
Wherewith to scorne the Earth: but that false Fruit Par Lost 9.1011
High actions; but wherewith to be atchiev'd? Par Reg 2.411
Wherewith to serve him better then thou hast; Samson 585
Wherwith she tam'd the brinded lioness Mask 443
Bridgewater ms 'wherewith'
Wherwith she freez'd her foes to congeal'd stone? Mask 449
1637 'Wherewith'
Trinity ms 'wherwith' ←'freezind wherwith'
Bridgewater ms 'wherewith'
Wherwith she sits on diamond rocks Mask 881
Trinity ms 'wherewith', but line deleted
Bridgewater ms 'wherewith'
Wherwith he wont at Heav'ns high Councel-Table, Nativity 10
1673 'Wherewith'
Wherwith the stage of Ayr and Earth did ring, Passion 2
1673 'Wherewith'
Wherwith their cheeks are wet. Psalm 80, 24
Wherewithal
New *Babels*, had they wherewithall, would build: Par Lost 3.468
Whether
Whether upheld by strength, or Chance, or Fate, Par Lost 1.133
ms 'Whither'
Let us not slip th' occasion, whether scorn, Par Lost 1.178
Whether of open Warr or covert guile, Par Lost 2.41
Let this be good, whether our angry Foe Par Lost 2.152
The Stairs were then let down, whether to dare Par Lost 3.523
Beneath th' *Azores;* whither the prime Orb, Par Lost 4.592
Gravely in doubt whether to hold them wise Par Lost 4.907
Beautie, which whether waking or asleep, Par Lost 5.14
Whether to deck with Clouds the uncolourd skie, Par Lost 5.189
Can hearts, not free, be tri'd whether they serve Par Lost 5.532
Know whether I be dextrous to subdue Par Lost 5.741
Whether by supplication we intend Par Lost 5.867
This to attain, whether Heav'n move or Earth, Par Lost 8.70
But whether thus these things, or whether not, Par Lost 8.159
Whether the Sun predominant in Heav'n Par Lost 8.160
Whether such vertue spent of old now faild Par Lost 9.145
Leads thee, or where most needs, whether to wind Par Lost 9.215
Refreshment, whether food, or talk between, Par Lost 9.237
Whether his first design be to withdraw Par Lost 9.261
In Fruit she never tasted, whether true Par Lost 9.788
All Judgement, whether in Heav'n, or Earth, or Hell. Par Lost 10.57
Celestial, whether among the Thrones, or nam'd Par Lost 11.296
Had melted (whether found where casual fire Par Lost 11.566
To som Caves mouth, or whether washt by stream Par Lost 11.569
And whether here the Race of man will end. Par Lost 11.786
Regardless whether good or evil fame. Par Lost 12.47
Whether in Heav'n or Earth, for then the Earth Par Lost 12.463
Whether I should repent me now of sin Par Lost 12.474
Full forty days he pass'd, whether on hill Par Reg 1.303
And will alike be punish'd; whether thou Par Reg 3.214
If I to try whether in higher sort Par Reg 4.198
True Image of the Father whether thron'd Par Reg 4.596
Endure it, doubtful whether God be Lord, Samson 477
Whether he durst accept the offer or not, Samson 1255
Up to the highth, whether to hold or break; Samson 1349
whether deluded and soothing lies & soothing flatteries. Mask Tr. ms 22.20
Or whether (as som Sager sing) Allegro 17
Whether beyond the stormy *Hebrides*, Lycidas 156
Or whether thou to our moist vows deny'd, Lycidas 159
Whether above that high first-moving Spheare Fair Inf 39
Rivers arise; whether thou be the Son, Vacation 91
But whether by mischance or blame Winchester 27
Whether the Muse, or Love call thee his mate, Sonnet 1, 13
Whether to settle peace or to unfold Sonnet 17, 5
Whets
And the Mower whets his sithe, Allegro 66
His Sword he whets, his Bow hath bended Psalm 7, 46
Which
Which oft times may succeed, so as perhaps Par Lost 1.166
Leviathan, which God of all his works Par Lost 1.201
Which but th' Omnipotent none could have foyld, Par Lost 1.273
His Spear, to equal which the tallest Pine Par Lost 1.292
In which they were, or the fierce pains not feel; Par Lost 1.336
A multitude, like which the populous North Par Lost 1.351
To do him wanton rites, which cost them woe. Par Lost 1.414
To bestial Gods; for which thir heads as low Par Lost 1.435
In loss it self; which on his count'nance cast Par Lost 1.526
Th' Imperial Ensign, which full high advanc't Par Lost 1.536
At which the universal Host upsent Par Lost 1.541
Which tempted our attempt, and wrought our fall. Par Lost 1.642
High on a Throne of Royal State, which far Par Lost 2.1
In Heav'n, which follows dignity, might draw Par Lost 2.25
For which to strive, no strife can grow up there Par Lost 2.31
His utmost ire? which to the highth enrag'd, Par Lost 2.95
Which if not Victory is yet Revenge. Par Lost 2.105
Our doom; which if we can sustain and bear, Par Lost 2.209

Which(*cont*)
Into their temper; which must needs remove Par Lost 2.277
The sound of blustring winds, which all night long Par Lost 2.286
To found this nether Empire, which might rise Par Lost 2.296
Which when *Beelzebub* perceiv'd, then whom, Par Lost 2.299
Great things resolv'd, which from the lowest deep Par Lost 2.392
Which he through hazard huge must earn. But they Par Lost 2.473
Thir specious deeds on earth, which glory excites, Par Lost 2.484
As if (which might induce us to accord) Par Lost 2.503
Of Whirlwind and dire Hail, which on firm land Par Lost 2.589
A Universe of death, which God by curse Par Lost 2.622
Conjur'd against the highest, for which both Thou Par Lost 2.693
What e're his wrath, which he calls Justice, bids, Par Lost 2.733
His wrath which one day will destroy ye both. Par Lost 2.734
I also; at which time this powerful Key Par Lost 2.774
These Gates for ever shut, which none can pass Par Lost 2.776
Which but her self not all the *Stygian* powers Par Lost 2.875
By which he Reigns: next him high Arbiter Par Lost 2.909
Confus'dly, and which thus must ever fight, Par Lost 2.914
Which way the neerest coast of darkness lyes Par Lost 2.958
(Which is my present journey) and once more Par Lost 2.985
That little which is left so to defend, Par Lost 2.1000
Of this frail World; by which the Spirits perverse Par Lost 2.1030
Uncertain which, in Ocean or in Air. Par Lost 3.76
Which had no less prov'd certain unforeknown. Par Lost 3.119
Unchangeable, Eternal, which ordain'd Par Lost 3.127
Which uttering thus he to his Father spake. Par Lost 3.143
O Father, gracious was that word which clos'd Par Lost 3.144
For which both Heav'n and Earth shall high extoll Par Lost 3.146
Which of ye will be mortal to redeem Par Lost 3.214
To mortal men, above which only shon Par Lost 3.268
Immortal Amarant, a Flour which once Par Lost 3.353
Save on that side which from the wall of Heav'n Par Lost 3.427
Direct against which op'nd from beneath, Par Lost 3.526
By which, to visit oft those happy Tribes, Par Lost 3.532
Which to his eye discovers unaware Par Lost 3.547
Which now the Rising Sun guilds with his beams. Par Lost 3.551
There lands the Fiend, a spot like which perhaps Par Lost 3.588
With radiant light, as glowing Iron with fire; Par Lost 3.594
1667 'Which radiant'
That stone, or like to that which here below Par Lost 3.600
Which else might work him danger or delay: Par Lost 3.635
In which of all these shining Orbes hath Man Par Lost 3.668
Where no ill seems: Which now for once beguil'd Par Lost 3.689
Fair Angel, thy desire which tends to know Par Lost 3.694
His day, which else as th' other Hemisphere Par Lost 3.725
That spot to which I point is *Paradise*, Par Lost 3.733
O for that warning voice, which he who saw Par Lost 4.1
Begins his dire attempt, which nigh the birth Par Lost 4.15
Sometimes towards *Eden* which now in his view Par Lost 4.27
Which now sat high in his Meridian Towre: Par Lost 4.30
Me miserable! which way shall I flie Par Lost 4.73
Which way I flie is Hell; my self am Hell; Par Lost 4.75
To which the Hell I suffer seems a Heav'n. Par Lost 4.78
Which would but lead me to a worse relapse Par Lost 4.100
Which marrd his borrow'd visage, and betraid Par Lost 4.116
Which to our general Sire gave prospect large Par Lost 4.144
On which the Sun more glad impress'd his beams Par Lost 4.150
On th' other side: which when th' arch-fellon saw Par Lost 4.179
Upon the rapid current, which through veins Par Lost 4.227
Which from his darksom passage now appeers, Par Lost 4.232
Flours worthy of Paradise which not nice Art Par Lost 4.241
Of coole recess, o're which the mantling vine Par Lost 4.258
Was gatherd, which cost *Ceres* all that pain Par Lost 4.271
As the Vine curles her tendrils, which impli'd Par Lost 4.307
Nectarine Fruits which the compliant boughes Par Lost 4.332
Which I as freely give; Hell shall unfold, Par Lost 4.381
Which were it toilsom, yet with thee were sweet. Par Lost 4.439
And wisdom, which alone is truly fair. Par Lost 4.491
Appointed, which declares his Dignitie, Par Lost 4.619
In Nature and all things, which these soft fires Par Lost 4.667
Which they beheld, the Moons resplendent Globe Par Lost 4.723
Which we in our appointed work imployd Par Lost 4.726
Which God likes best, into thir inmost bowre Par Lost 4.738
These troublesom disguises which we wear, Par Lost 4.740
Or Serenate, which the starv'd Lover sings Par Lost 4.769
Showrd Roses, which the Morn repair'd. Sleep on Par Lost 4.773
Which of those rebell Spirits adjudg'd to Hell Par Lost 4.823
Dole with delight, which in this place I sought; Par Lost 4.894
Which thou incurr'st by flying, meet thy flight Par Lost 4.913
Which taught thee yet no better, that no pain Par Lost 4.915
To which the Fiend thus answerd frowning stern. Par Lost 4.924
Her bearded Grove of ears, which way the wind Par Lost 4.982
Which *Gabriel* spying, thus bespake the Fiend. Par Lost 4.1005
And temperat vapors bland, which th' only sound Par Lost 5.5
Beautie, which whether waking or asleep, Par Lost 5.14
But of offence and trouble, which my mind Par Lost 5.34
Which he had pluckt; the pleasant savourie smell Par Lost 5.84
Which the five watchful Senses represent, Par Lost 5.104
Which Reason joyning or disjoyning, frames Par Lost 5.106
No spot or blame behind: Which gives me hope Par Lost 5.119
More fruitful, which instructs us not to spare. Par Lost 5.320
These bounties which our Nourisher, from whom Par Lost 5.398
The full relation, which must needs be strange, Par Lost 5.556
Hear my Decree, which unrevok't shall stand. Par Lost 5.602
Mystical dance, which yonder starrie Spheare Par Lost 5.620
Of all those Myriads which we lead the chief; Par Lost 5.684
Or Starrs of Morning, Dew-drops, which the Sun Par Lost 5.746

Which(*cont*)

In thir triple Degrees, Regions to which	Par Lost 5.750
Stretcht into Longitude; which having pass'd	Par Lost 5.754
Interpreted) which not long after, he	Par Lost 5.762
Of those Imperial Titles which assert	Par Lost 5.801
Words which no eare ever to hear in Heav'n	Par Lost 5.810
Doctrin which we would know whence learnt: who saw	Par Lost 5.856
That Golden Scepter which thou didst reject	Par Lost 5.886
Long way through hostile scorn, which he susteind	Par Lost 5.904
Lodge and dislodge by turns, which makes through Heav'n	Par Lost 6.7
Of *Tartarus*, which ready opens wide	Par Lost 6.54
At which command the Powers Militant,	Par Lost 6.61
Which hung not, but so swift with tempest fell	Par Lost 6.190
The strife which thou call'st evil, but wee style	Par Lost 6.289
The strife of Glorie: which we mean to win,	Par Lost 6.290
Against unpaind, impassive; from which evil	Par Lost 6.455
Which all subdues, and makes remiss the hands	Par Lost 6.458
But live content, which is the calmest life:	Par Lost 6.461
Not uninvented that, which thou aright	Par Lost 6.470
Which of us who beholds the bright surface	Par Lost 6.472
Which into hallow Engins long and round	Par Lost 6.484
Once found, which yet unfound most would have thought	Par Lost 6.500
Which to our eyes discoverd new and strange,	Par Lost 6.571
Of Iron Globes, which on the Victor Host	Par Lost 6.590
Which God hath in his mighty Angels plac'd)	Par Lost 6.638
Main Promontories flung, which in the Air	Par Lost 6.654
Into thir substance pent, which wrought them pain	Par Lost 6.657
Save what sin hath impaird, which yet hath wrought	Par Lost 6.691
With Mountains as with Weapons arm'd, which makes	Par Lost 6.697
Fulfill'd, which to fulfil is all my bliss.	Par Lost 6.729
In Battel which the stronger proves, they all,	Par Lost 6.819
Grasping ten thousand Thunders, which he sent	Par Lost 6.836
And Chrystal wall of Heav'n, which op'ning wide,	Par Lost 6.860
The discord which befel, and Warr in Heav'n	Par Lost 6.897
Which would be all his solace and revenge,	Par Lost 6.905
Unknown, which human knowledg could not reach:	Par Lost 7.75
For which to the infinitly Good we owe	Par Lost 7.76
Things above Earthly thought, which yet concernd	Par Lost 7.82
How first began this Heav'n which we behold	Par Lost 7.86
Innumerable, and this which yeelds or fills	Par Lost 7.88
Yet what thou canst attain, which best may serve	Par Lost 7.115
Things not reveal'd, which th' invisible King,	Par Lost 7.122
And put not forth my goodness, which is free	Par Lost 7.171
Plant of the field, which e're it was in the Earth	Par Lost 7.335
Soul living, each that crept, which plenteously	Par Lost 7.392
Which tasted works knowledge of Good and Evil,	Par Lost 7.543
Which nightly as a circling Zone thou seest	Par Lost 7.580
Which onely thy solution can resolve.	Par Lost 8.14
Entring on studious thoughts abstruse, which *Eve*	Par Lost 8.40
Invalid that which thee to doubt it mov'd;	Par Lost 8.116
Which else to several Sphears thou must ascribe,	Par Lost 8.131
Of Day and Night; which needs not thy beleefe,	Par Lost 8.136
Which two great Sexes animate the World,	Par Lost 8.151
Down to this habitable, which returnes	Par Lost 8.157
To interrupt the sweet of Life, from which	Par Lost 8.184
That which before us lies in daily life,	Par Lost 8.193
My Storie, which perhaps thou hast not heard;	Par Lost 8.205
In Balmie Sweat, which with his Beames the Sun	Par Lost 8.255
Knowledg of good and ill, which I have set	Par Lost 8.324
The rigid interdiction, which resounds	Par Lost 8.334
Which must be mutual, in proportion due	Par Lost 8.385
Save with the Creatures which I made, and those	Par Lost 8.409
In unitie defective, which requires	Par Lost 8.425
Permissive, and acceptance found, which gain'd	Par Lost 8.435
Which thou hast rightly nam'd, but of thy self,	Par Lost 8.439
Which it had long stood under, streind to the highth	Par Lost 8.454
Of sleep, which instantly fell on me, call'd	Par Lost 8.458
Of Fancie my internal sight, by which	Par Lost 8.461
And in her looks, which from that time infus'd	Par Lost 8.474
Which I enjoy, and must confess to find	Par Lost 8.523
And inward Faculties, which most excell,	Par Lost 8.542
To Cattel and each Beast; which would not be	Par Lost 8.582
By which to heav'nly Love thou maist ascend,	Par Lost 8.592
Not sunk in carnal pleasure, for which cause	Par Lost 8.593
And sweet compliance, which declare unfeign'd	Par Lost 8.603
Thy Judgement to do aught, which else free Will	Par Lost 8.636
Not that which justly gives Heroic name	Par Lost 9.40
Consider'd every Creature, which of all	Par Lost 9.84
Proceeding, which in other Beasts observ'd	Par Lost 9.94
Casual discourse draw on, which intermits	Par Lost 9.223
How we might best fulfill the work which here	Par Lost 9.230
Conjugal Love, then which perhaps no bliss	Par Lost 9.263
His fraud is then thy fear, which plain inferrs	Par Lost 9.285
Thoughts, which how found they harbour in thy brest	Par Lost 9.288
From thee alone, which on us both at once	Par Lost 9.303
Seek not temptation then, which to avoide	Par Lost 9.364
Occasion which now smiles, behold alone	Par Lost 9.480
The way which to her ruin now I tend.	Par Lost 9.493
In *Epidaurus;* nor to which transformd	Par Lost 9.507
Equivalent or second, which compel'd	Par Lost 9.609
Compact of unctuous vapor, which the Night	Par Lost 9.635
Which oft, they say, some evil Spirit attends	Par Lost 9.638
Which when she saw, thus to her guide she spake.	Par Lost 9.646
Shall that be shut to Man, which to the Beast	Par Lost 9.691
Though threat'nd, which no worse then this can bring.	Par Lost 9.715
Fixt on the Fruit she gaz'd, which to behold	Par Lost 9.735
So savorie of that Fruit, which with desire,	Par Lost 9.741
For Beasts it seems: yet that one Beast which first	Par Lost 9.769

Which(*cont*)

Which with bland words at will she thus addrest.	Par Lost 9.855
And growing up to Godhead; which for thee	Par Lost 9.877
Proportional ascent, which cannot be	Par Lost 9.936
Set over all his Works, which in our Fall,	Par Lost 9.941
This happie trial of thy Love, which else	Par Lost 9.975
Which leaves us naked thus, of Honour void,	Par Lost 9.1074
Of wandring, as thou call'st it, which who knows	Par Lost 9.1146
That errour now, which is become my crime,	Par Lost 9.1181
Whoever tempted; which they not obeying,	Par Lost 10.14
Which your sincerest care could not prevent,	Par Lost 10.37
Which he presumes already vain and void,	Par Lost 10.50
Unseemly to beare rule, which was thy part	Par Lost 10.155
Say Woman, what is this which thou hast done?	Par Lost 10.158
Which when the Lord God heard, without delay	Par Lost 10.163
And eaten of the Tree concerning which	Par Lost 10.199
Thence gatherd his own doom, which understood	Par Lost 10.344
Thy Trophies, which thou view'st as not thine own,	Par Lost 10.355
My Heart, which by a secret harmonie	Par Lost 10.358
That thou on Earth hadst prosper'd, which thy looks	Par Lost 10.360
Ascended his high Throne, which under state	Par Lost 10.445
Of horrible confusion, over which	Par Lost 10.472
The new created World, which fame in Heav'n	Par Lost 10.481
Man I deceav'd: that which to mee belongs,	Par Lost 10.496
Is enmity, which he will put between	Par Lost 10.497
Which grew in Paradise, the bait of *Eve*	Par Lost 10.551
The Frutage fair to sight, like that which grew	Par Lost 10.561
Chewd bitter Ashes, which th' offended taste	Par Lost 10.566
Which here, though plenteous, all too little seems	Par Lost 10.600
Sooner or later; which th' Almightie seeing,	Par Lost 10.613
To waste and havoc yonder World, which I	Par Lost 10.617
Which mans polluting Sin with taint hath shed	Par Lost 10.631
Which of them rising with the Sun, or falling,	Par Lost 10.663
Or East or West, which had forbid the Snow	Par Lost 10.685
The growing miseries, which *Adam* saw	Par Lost 10.715
Thy terms too hard, by which I was to hold	Par Lost 10.751
Which God inspir'd, cannot together perish	Par Lost 10.785
Strange contradiction, which to God himself	Par Lost 10.799
By which all Causes else according still	Par Lost 10.806
From this day onward, which I feel begun	Par Lost 10.811
And horrors hast thou driv'n me; out of which	Par Lost 10.843
Which to his evil Conscience represented	Par Lost 10.849
Which infinite calamitie shall cause	Par Lost 10.907
Which must be born to certain woe, devourd	Par Lost 10.980
With like desire, which would be meserie	Par Lost 10.997
Some safer resolution, which methinks	Par Lost 10.1029
Would be revenge indeed; which will be lost	Par Lost 10.1036
Immediate dissolution, which we thought	Par Lost 10.1049
Which now the Skie with various Face begins	Par Lost 10.1064
Of these fair spreading Trees; which bids us seek	Par Lost 10.1067
Which might supplie the Sun: such Fire to use,	Par Lost 10.1078
To evils which our own misdeeds have wrought,	Par Lost 10.1080
Unutterable, which the Spirit of prayer	Par Lost 11.6
And Prayers, which in this Golden Censer, mixt	Par Lost 11.24
Which his own hand manuring all the Trees	Par Lost 11.28
Numberd, though sad, till Death, his doom (which I	Par Lost 11.40
Which thus to *Eve* his welcome words renewd.	Par Lost 11.140
The good which we enjoy, from Heav'n descends;	Par Lost 11.142
Which then not minded in dismay, yet now	Par Lost 11.156
Which Heav'n by these mute signs in Nature shews	Par Lost 11.194
Nor that which on the flaming Mount appeerd	Par Lost 11.216
Eve, now expect great tidings, which perhaps	Par Lost 11.226
At Eev'n, which I bred up with tender hand	Par Lost 11.276
Thus over-fond, on that which is not thine;	Par Lost 11.289
Thy message, which might else in telling wound,	Par Lost 11.299
Which that thou mayst beleeve, and be confirmd	Par Lost 11.355
Which that false Fruit that promis'd clearer sight	Par Lost 11.413
Th' effects which thy original crime hath wrought	Par Lost 11.424
Rowling in dust and gore. To which our Sire.	Par Lost 11.460
In Meats and Drinks, which on the Earth shall bring	Par Lost 11.473
Diseases dire, of which a monstrous crew	Par Lost 11.474
Thy youth, thy strength, thy beauty, which will change	Par Lost 11.539
Which I must keep till my appointed day	Par Lost 11.550
Into fit moulds prepar'd; from which he formd	Par Lost 11.571
From the high neighbouring Hills, which was thir Seat,	Par Lost 11.575
Not hid, nor those things last which might preserve	Par Lost 11.579
The bent of Nature; which he thus express'd.	Par Lost 11.597
(Erelong to swim at large) and laugh; for which	Par Lost 11.626
But call in aide, which makes a bloody Fray;	Par Lost 11.651
Which now direct thine eyes and soon behold.	Par Lost 11.711
But all in vain: which when he saw, he ceas'd	Par Lost 11.726
Which neither his foreknowing can prevent,	Par Lost 11.773
Which now abated, for the Clouds were fled,	Par Lost 11.841
As after thirst, which made thir flowing shrink	Par Lost 11.846
Is lost, which alwayes with right Reason dwells	Par Lost 12.84
From vertue, which is reason, that no wrong,	Par Lost 12.98
Which he will shew him, and from him will raise	Par Lost 12.123
Thou hast reveald, those chiefly which concerne	Par Lost 12.272
Of Conscience, which the Law by Ceremonies	Par Lost 12.297
Without the vent of words, which these he breathd.	Par Lost 12.374
Which hee, who comes thy Saviour, shall recure,	Par Lost 12.393
But by fulfilling that which thou didst want,	Par Lost 12.396
And due to theirs which out of thine will grow:	Par Lost 12.400
Thy ransom paid, which Man from death redeems,	Par Lost 12.424
For death, like that which the redeemer dy'd.	Par Lost 12.445
Then that which by creation first brought forth	Par Lost 12.472
On every conscience; Laws which none shall finde	Par Lost 12.522
Beyond which was my folly to aspire.	Par Lost 12.560

Which(*cont*)

That ye may live, which will be many dayes,	Par Lost 12.602
Which he hath sent propitious, some great good	Par Lost 12.612
Fierce as a Comet; which with torrid heat,	Par Lost 12.634
Of hazard, which admits no long debate,	Par Reg 1.95
On which I sent thee to the Virgin pure	Par Reg 1.134
Of Saviour to mankind, and which way first	Par Reg 1.187
To which my Spirit aspir'd, victorious deeds	Par Reg 1.215
By which they knew thee King of *Israel* born.	Par Reg 1.254
Which I believ'd was from above; but he	Par Reg 1.274
He was well pleas'd; by which I knew the time	Par Reg 1.286
The Authority which I deriv'd from Heaven.	Par Reg 1.289
Or wither'd sticks to gather; which might serve	Par Reg 1.316
Which they who ask'd have seldom understood,	Par Reg 1.436
And urg'd me hard with doings, which not will	Par Reg 1.469
Some troubl'd thoughts, which she in sighs thus clad.	Par Reg 2.65
Or that which only seems to satisfie	Par Reg 2.229
But now I feel I hunger, which declares,	Par Reg 2.252
And exquisitest name, for which was drain'd	Par Reg 2.346
Which way or from what hope dost thou aspire	Par Reg 2.417
Which every wise and vertuous man attains:	Par Reg 2.468
Or lawless passions in him which he serves.	Par Reg 2.472
And oft by force, which to a generous mind	Par Reg 2.479
That which to God alone of right belongs;	Par Reg 3.141
All Horsemen, in which fight they most excel;	Par Reg 3.307
Chuse which thou wilt by conquest or by league.	Par Reg 3.370
That which alone can truly reinstall thee	Par Reg 3.372
Of numbring *Israel*, which cost the lives	Par Reg 3.410
The City which thou seest no other deem	Par Reg 4.44
All these which in a moment thou behold'st,	Par Reg 4.162
But I endure the time, till which expir'd,	Par Reg 4.174
And more blasphemous? which expect to rue.	Par Reg 4.181
Which when he lists, he leaves, or boasts he can,	Par Reg 4.306
Which would have set thee in short time with ease	Par Reg 4.378
And grisly Spectres, which the Fiend had rais'd	Par Reg 4.430
Those terrors which thou speak'st of, did me none;	Par Reg 4.487
The Son of God, which bears no single sence;	Par Reg 4.517
Of highest dispensation, which herein	Samson 61
Annull'd, which might in part my grief have eas'd,	Samson 72
Which shall I first bewail,	Samson 151
(Which Men enjoying sight oft without cause complain)	Samson 157
Yet that which was the worst now least afflicts me,	Samson 195
The work to which I was divinely call'd;	Samson 226
Who seeing those great acts which God had done	Samson 243
She purpos'd to betray me, and (which was worse	Samson 399
The base degree to which I now am fall'n,	Samson 414
Deposited within thee; which to have kept	Samson 429
Which to have come to pass by means of thee,	Samson 444
Which is my chief affliction, shame and sorrow,	Samson 457
Which argues over-just, and self-displeas'd	Samson 514
Which many a famous Warriour overturns,	Samson 542
Effeminatly vanquish't? by which means,	Samson 562
Which was expresly giv'n thee to annoy them?	Samson 578
Man. Believe not these suggestions which proceed	Samson 599
Dire inflammation which no cooling herb	Samson 626
And peoples safety, which in part they effect:	Samson 681
To life obscur'd, which were a fair dismission,	Samson 688
Which to have merited, without excuse,	Samson 734
His vertue or weakness which way to assail:	Samson 756
And what if Love, which thou interpret'st hate,	Samson 790
Take to thy wicked deed: which when thou seest	Samson 826
Which might have aw'd the best resolv'd of men,	Samson 847
For which our countrey is a name so dear;	Samson 894
Exempt from many a care and chance to which	Samson 918
Which to my countrey I was judg'd to have shewn.	Samson 994
(Which way soever men refer it)	Samson 1015
To folly and shameful deeds which ruin ends.	Samson 1043
But vertue which breaks through all opposition,	Samson 1050
Which long shall not with-hold mee from thy head,	Samson 1125
Which greatest Heroes have in battel worn,	Samson 1131
Arm'd thee or charm'd thee strong, which thou from Heaven	Samson 1134
Which I to be the power of *Israel*'s God	Samson 1150
I chose a Wife, which argu'd me no foe;	Samson 1193
That solv'd the riddle which I had propos'd.	Samson 1200
The work of many hands, which earns my keeping	Samson 1260
Set God behind: which in his jealousie	Samson 1375
Some rouzing motions in me which dispose	Samson 1382
Which to no few of them would prove pernicious.	Samson 1400
But that which mov'd my coming now, was chiefly	Samson 1452
Private reward, for which both God and State	Samson 1465
In both which we, as next participate.	Samson 1507
Mess. O whither shall I run, or which way flie	Samson 1541
Which earst my eyes beheld and yet behold;	Samson 1543
Hopeful of his Delivery, which now proves	Samson 1575
Which without help of eye, might be assay'd,	Samson 1625
He unsuspitious led him; which when *Samson*	Samson 1635
The work for which thou wast foretold	Samson 1662
And which is best and happiest yet, all this	Samson 1718
Which men call Earth, and with low-thoughted care	Mask 6
Bridgewater ms 'earth and which'	
Which he to grace his tributary gods	Mask 24
Whom therfore she brought up and *Comus* nam'd,	Mask 58
Bridgewater ms 'which therefore'	
Trinity ms 'which', 'whome' written in margin	
To quench the drouth of *Phoebus*, which as they taste	Mask 66
Which these dun shades will ne're report.	Mask 127
Which must not be, for that's against my course;	Mask 159
Which oft is sooner found in lowly sheds	Mask 323

Which(*cont*)

Which you remember not. 2. *Bro*. What hidden strength,	Mask 416
Which if Heav'n gave it, may be term'd her own:	Mask 419
At which I ceas't, and listen'd them a while,	Mask 551
Which erring men call Chance, this I hold firm,	Mask 588
Yea even that which mischief meant most harm,	Mask 591
Which when I did, he on the tender grass	Mask 624
That *Hermes* once to wise *Ulysses* gave;	Mask 637
Trinity ms 'that' ← 'which' ← 'that'	
Not that *Nepenthes* which the wife of *Thone*,	Mask 675
And to those dainty limms which nature lent	Mask 680
line not in Bridgewater ms	
With that which you receiv'd on other terms,	Mask 684
line not in Bridgewater ms	
By which all mortal frailty must subsist,	Mask 686
line not in Bridgewater ms	
And that which is not good, is not delicious	Mask 704
Of that which lewdly-pamper'd Luxury	Mask 770
Som other means I have which may be us'd,	Mask 821
Trinity ms 'that'	
Bridgewater ms 'that'	
Which once of *Meliboeus* old I learnt	Mask 822
Which she with pretious viold liquors heals.	Mask 847
line not in Bridgewater ms	
For which the Shepherds at their festivals	Mask 848
Which the neat-handed *Phillis* dresses;	Allegro 86
On which the *Tartar* King did ride;	Penseroso 115
Is that which we from hence descry	Arcades 3
What shallow-searching *Fame* hath left untold;	Arcades 41
Trinity ms 'shallow searching' ← 'vertues which dull'	
Which I full oft amidst these shades alone	Arcades 42
On which the fate of gods and men is wound.	Arcades 67
After the heavenly tune, which none can hear	Arcades 72
Which 'mongst the wanton gods a foul reproach was held.	Fair Inf 14
Wert thou some Starr which from the ruin'd roofe	Fair Inf 43
Which carefull *Jove* in natures true behoofe	Fair Inf 45
Which takes our late fantasticks with delight,	Vacation 20
Which deepest Spirits, and choicest Wits desire:	Vacation 22
Which on our dearest Lord did sease er'e long,	Passion 10
Which he for us did freely undergo.	Passion 12
Which is no more then what is false and vain,	On Time 5
And that great Cov'nant which we still transgress	Circum 21
Which the sad morn had let fall	Winchester 45
Toward which Time leads me, and the will of Heav'n;	Sonnet 7, 12
Which after held the Sun and Moon in fee.	Sonnet 12, 7
when most were wont which till then us'd to scan	Sonnet 13, Tr. ms 40.03
When Faith and Love which parted from thee never,	Sonnet 14, 1
Trinity ms 'which' ← 'that'	
Of Death, call'd Life; which us from Life doth sever.	Sonnet 14, 4
And rumors loud, that daunt remotest kings,	Sonnet 15, 4
1694 'which daunt'	
What severs each thou 'hast learnt, which few hav don.	Sonnet 17, 11
Trinity ms 'which' ← 'a praise which few have won'	
And that one Talent which is death to hide,	Sonnet 19, 3
Which others at their Barr so often wrench;	Sonnet 21, 4
line not in Trinity ms	
Of which all Europe talks from side to side.	Sonnet 22, 12
He shall be as a tree which planted grows	Psalm 1, 7
Not so the wicked, but as chaff which fann'd	Psalm 1, 11
And command which I desire.	Psalm 7, 24
And the innocence which is	Psalm 7, 33
The Moon and Starrs which thou so bright hast set,	Psalm 8, 10
Visit this Vine, which thy right hand	Psalm 80, 61
I am the Lord thy God which brought	Psalm 81, 41
Which on a sudden straies,	Psalm 83, 54
From thy fierce wrath which we had prov'd	Psalm 85, 11
Thy wrath *from which no shelter saves*	Psalm 88, 29
Which once smelt sweet, now stinks as odiously;	Prose 4, 2
Which he who can, and will, deserv's high praise,	Prose 9, 3

While

Above th' *Aonian* Mount, while it pursues	Par Lost 1.15
Moors by his side under the Lee, while Night	Par Lost 1.207
Heap on himself damnation, while he sought	Par Lost 1.215
As we erewhile, astounded and amaz'd,	Par Lost 1.281
ms 'ere while'	
While with perfidious hatred they pursu'd	Par Lost 1.308
While the promiscuous croud stood yet aloof?	Par Lost 1.380
While smooth *Adonis* from his native Rock	Par Lost 1.450
Seraphic arms and Trophies: all the while	Par Lost 1.539
Mean while the winged Haralds by command	Par Lost 1.752
Or dreams he sees, while over-head the Moon	Par Lost 1.784
For while they sit contriving, shall the rest,	Par Lost 2.54
One day upon our heads; while we perhaps	Par Lost 2.178
Forc't Halleluiah's; while he Lordly sits	Par Lost 2.243
Or Summers Noon-tide air, while thus he spake.	Par Lost 2.309
A growing Empire; doubtless; while we dream,	Par Lost 2.315
While here shall be our home, what best may ease	Par Lost 2.458
Against a wakeful Foe, while I abroad	Par Lost 2.463
Ascending, while the North wind sleeps, o'respread	Par Lost 2.489
Pain for a while or anguish, and excite	Par Lost 2.567
Mean while the Adversary of God and Man,	Par Lost 2.629
With *Lapland* Witches, while the labouring Moon	Par Lost 2.665
For him who sits above and laughs the while	Par Lost 2.731
In darkness, while thy head flames thick and fast	Par Lost 2.754
A growing burden. Mean while Warr arose,	Par Lost 2.767
Stood on the brink of Hell and look'd a while,	Par Lost 2.918
In that obscure sojourn, while in my flight	Par Lost 3.15
Thus while God spake, ambrosial fragrance fill'd	Par Lost 3.135

While(*cont*)
Th' incensed Deitie, while offerd grace Par Lost 3.187
While by thee rais'd I ruin all my Foes, Par Lost 3.258
By loosing thee a while, the whole Race lost. Par Lost 3.280
Thenceforth shall be for ever shut. Mean while Par Lost 3.333
Heav'ns everlasting Frame, while o're the necks Par Lost 3.395
Mean while upon the firm opacous Globe Par Lost 3.418
Resigns her charge, while goodness thinks no ill Par Lost 3.688
While time was, our first-Parents had bin warnd Par Lost 4.6
While they adore me on the Throne of Hell, Par Lost 4.89
Thus while he spake, each passion dimm'd his face Par Lost 4.114
Luxuriant; mean while murmuring waters fall Par Lost 4.260
The trembling leaves, while Universal *Pan* Par Lost 4.266
Praeeminent by so much odds, while thou Par Lost 4.447
Of bliss on bliss, while I to Hell am thrust, Par Lost 4.508
What further would be learnt. Live while ye may, Par Lost 4.533
Mean while in utmost Longitude, where Heav'n Par Lost 4.539
While other Animals unactive range, Par Lost 4.621
Mean while, as Nature wills, Night bids us rest. Par Lost 4.633
While they keep watch, or nightly rounding walk Par Lost 4.685
While thus he spake, th' Angelic Squadron bright Par Lost 4.977
While day arises, that sweet hour of Prime. Par Lost 5.170
Of his coole Bowre, while now the mounted Sun Par Lost 5.300
Mean while our Primitive great Sire, to meet Par Lost 5.350
Those happie places thou hast deignd a while Par Lost 5.364
Danc'd hand in hand. A while discourse they hold; Par Lost 5.395
As from the Mine. Mean while at Table *Eve* Par Lost 5.443
Whose progenie you are. Mean while enjoy Par Lost 5.503
Hold, as you yours, while our obedience holds; Par Lost 5.537
And perfet while they stood; how last unfould Par Lost 5.568
Mean while th' Eternal eye, whose sight discernes Par Lost 5.711
While Pardon may be found in time besought. Par Lost 5.848
Thy making, while the Maker gave thee being? Par Lost 5.858
Thir Deities to assert, who while they feel Par Lost 6.157
Yet Chains in Hell, not Realms expect: mean while Par Lost 6.186
If not to reign: mean while thy utmost force, Par Lost 6.293
Blaz'd opposite, while expectation stood Par Lost 6.306
And all his Armour staind ere while so bright. Par Lost 6.334
Defence, while others bore him on thir Shields Par Lost 6.337
Mean while in other parts like deeds deservd Par Lost 6.354
Left them Superiour, while we can preserve Par Lost 6.443
Effect shall end our wish. Mean while revive; Par Lost 6.493
A while, but suddenly at head appeerd Par Lost 6.556
Heav'n witness thou anon, while we discharge Par Lost 6.564
Stood waving tipt with fire; while we suspense, Par Lost 6.580
Ere while they fierce were coming, and when wee, Par Lost 6.610
And all his Host derided, while they stood Par Lost 6.633
A while in trouble; but they stood not long, Par Lost 6.634
And solitude; yet not alone, while thou Par Lost 7.28
Mean while inhabit laxe, ye Powers of Heav'n, Par Lost 7.162
So sang the Hierarchies: Mean while the Son Par Lost 7.192
Sojourn'd the while. God saw the Light was good; Par Lost 7.249
Mean while the tepid Caves, and Fens and shoares Par Lost 7.417
While the bright Pomp ascended jubilant. Par Lost 7.564
Thou hast repeld, while impiously they thought Par Lost 7.611
So Charming left his voice, that he a while Par Lost 8.2
line not in 1667 edition
Repeated, while the sedentarie Earth, Par Lost 8.32
On her soft Axle, while she paces Eev'n, Par Lost 8.165
Inviting thee to hear while I relate, Par Lost 8.208
For while I sit with thee, I seem in Heav'n, Par Lost 8.210
Or enemie, while God was in his work, Par Lost 8.234
And gaz'd a while the ample Skie, till rais'd Par Lost 8.258
While thus I call'd, and stray'd I knew not whither, Par Lost 8.283
My Maker, be propitious while I speak. Par Lost 8.380
Rural repast, permitting him the while Par Lost 9.4
The clasping Ivie where to climb, while I Par Lost 9.217
For while so near each other thus all day Par Lost 9.220
Of outward strength; while shame, thou looking on, Par Lost 9.312
Gently with Mirtle band, mindless the while, Par Lost 9.431
Stood in himself collected, while each part, Par Lost 9.673
Mean while the hour of Noon drew on, and wak'd Par Lost 9.739
1667 'Meanwhile'
Pausing a while, thus to her self she mus'd. Par Lost 9.744
Commends thee more, while it inferrs the good Par Lost 9.754
From Nectar, drink of Gods. *Adam* the while Par Lost 9.838
Astonied stood and Blank, while horror chill Par Lost 9.890
Original; while *Adam* took no thought, Par Lost 9.1004
Much pleasure we have lost, while we abstain'd Par Lost 9.1022
Brought to thir Ears, while day declin'd, they heard, Par Lost 10.99
Where obvious dutie erewhile appear'd unsaught: Par Lost 10.106
Whose failing, while her Faith to me remaines, Par Lost 10.129
Idlely, while Satan our great Author thrives Par Lost 10.236
His *Zenith*, while the Sun in *Aries* rose: Par Lost 10.329
Of easie thorough-fare. Therefore while I Par Lost 10.393
There kept thir Watch the Legions, while the Grand Par Lost 10.427
Was plac't in regal lustre. Down a while Par Lost 10.447
So having said, a while he stood, expecting Par Lost 10.504
Mean while in Paradise the hellish pair Par Lost 10.585
While the Creator calling forth by name Par Lost 10.649
Had unbenighted shon, while the low Sun Par Lost 10.682
While yet we live, scarse one short hour perhaps, Par Lost 10.923
Cloath'd us unworthie, pitying while he judg'd; Par Lost 10.1059
To shew us in this Mountain, while the Winds Par Lost 10.1065
Of *Hermes*, or his opiate Rod. Mean while Par Lost 11.133
Laborious, till day droop; while here we dwell, Par Lost 11.178
While the great Visitant approachd, thus spake. Par Lost 11.225
Here sleep below while thou to foresight wak'st, Par Lost 11.368

While(*cont*)
As once thou slepst, while Shee to life was formd. Par Lost 11.369
While they pervert pure Natures healthful rules Par Lost 11.523
This second sours of Men, while yet but few; Par Lost 12.13
And while the dread of judgement past remains Par Lost 12.14
While yet the Patriark liv'd, who scap'd the Flood, Par Lost 12.117
Behinde them, while th' obdurat King pursues: Par Lost 12.205
They first re-edifie, and for a while Par Lost 12.350
I Who e're while the happy Garden sung, Par Reg 1.1
The Spirit descended, while the Fathers voice Par Reg 1.31
Such high attest was giv'n, a while survey'd Par Reg 1.37
Circling the Throne and Singing, while the hand Par Reg 1.171
Mean while the Son of God, who yet some days Par Reg 1.183
Awakn'd in me swarm, while I consider Par Reg 1.197
Flam'd in my heart, heroic acts, one while Par Reg 1.216
Mean while the new-baptiz'd, who yet remain'd Par Reg 2.1
While I to sorrows am no less advanc't, Par Reg 2.69
The while her Son tracing the Desert wild, Par Reg 2.109
And all the while Harmonious Airs were heard Par Reg 2.362
While Virtue, Valour, Wisdom sit in want. Par Reg 2.431
A while as mute confounded what to say, Par Reg 3.2
Raign then; what canst thou better do the while? Par Reg 3.180
While to their native land with joy they hast, Par Reg 3.437
In brief sententious precepts, while they treat Par Reg 4.264
Ill imitated, while they loudest sing Par Reg 4.339
Some bent at thee thir fiery darts, while thou Par Reg 4.424
So talk'd he, while the Son of God went on Par Reg 4.484
Chor. This, this is he; softly a while, Samson 115
But thee whose strength, while vertue was her mate, Samson 173
Mean while the men of *Judah* to prevent Samson 256
Your younger feet, while mine cast back with age Samson 336
Select, and Sacred, Glorious for a while, Samson 363
Thou must not in the mean while here forgot Samson 479
By ransom or how else: mean while be calm, Samson 604
While I at home sate full of cares and fears Samson 805
That in a little time while breath remains thee, Samson 1126
Then thine, while I preserv'd these locks unshorn, Samson 1143
Renders them useless, while Samson 1282
With youthful steps? much livelier then e're while Samson 1442
For evil news rides post, while good news baits. Samson 1538
More then anough we know; but while things yet Samson 1592
As over-tir'd to let him lean a while Samson 1632
Felt in his arms, with head a while enclin'd, Samson 1636
Semichor. While thir hearts were jocund and sublime, Samson 1669
And lay e're while a Holocaust, Samson 1702
The clotted gore. I with what speed the while Samson 1728
Mean while welcom Joy, and Feast, Mask 102
Bridgewater ms 'meane-while'
Trinity ms 'meane while'
1637 'Meane while'
I see ye visibly, and now beleeve Mask 216
Trinity ms '& now beleeve' ←'now I beleeve' ←'& while I see yee'
Or while we speak within the direfull grasp Mask 357
line not in Trinity ms
line not in Bridgewater ms
For grant they be so, while they rest unknown, Mask 361
line not in Bridgewater ms
line not in Trinity ms
At which I ceas't, and listen'd them a while, Mask 551
Trinity ms 'awhile'
Thou haste immanacl'd, while Heav'n sees good. Mask 665
Com Lady while Heaven lends us grace, Mask 938
While the Cock with lively din, Allegro 49
While the Plowman neer at hand, Allegro 63
Of Wit, or Arms, while both contend Allegro 123
While yet there was no fear of *Jove*. Penseroso 30
While *Cynthia* checks her Dragon yoke, Penseroso 59
While rocking Winds are Piping loud, Penseroso 126
While the Bee with Honied thie, Penseroso 142
Mean while the Rural ditties were not mute, Lycidas 32
Trinity ms 'meane while'
While the still morn went out with Sandals gray, Lycidas 187
Now while the Heav'n by the Suns team untrod, Nativity 19
While the Heav'n-born-childe, Nativity 30
While Birds of Calm sit brooding on the charmed wave. Nativity 68
While the Creator Great Nativity 120
While the red fire, and smouldring clouds out brake: Nativity 159
While each peculiar power forgoes his wonted seat. Nativity 196
While the Hebrew Bands did pass. Psalm 136, 50
To th' touch of golden wires, while *Hebe* brings Vacation 38
While sad *Ulisses* soul and all the rest Vacation 50
Ere-while of Musick, and Ethereal mirth, Passion 1
snatch us from earth a while Musick Tr. ms 4.07
while all the starrie rounds & arches blue Musick Tr. ms 4.21
'while all the starrie rounds' ←'starrie frame' ←'whilst then' ←'whilst the whole frame of' ←'while all the' ←'that all'
That he could never die while he could move, Another 2
1640, 1657, 1658 'whilst'
While he might still jogg on, and keep his trot, Another 4
1640, 1657, 1658 'Whilst'
While the jolly hours lead on propitious *May*, Sonnet 1, 4
The Subject new: it walk'd the Town a while, Sonnet 11, 3
Stand spelling fals, while one might walk to Mile- Sonnet 11, 7
Victory home, though new rebellions raise Sonnet 15, 6
1694 'while new'
While Avarice, and Rapine share the land. Sonnet 15, 14

While*(cont)*
While Darwen stream with blood of Scotts imbru'd, Sonnet 16, 7
Their joy, while thou from blame Psalm 5, 34
Thy protection while I crie, Psalm 7, 3
While I thy terrors undergo Psalm 88, 63
Whilere
He who with all Heav'ns heraldry whileare Circum 10
1673 'whilear'
Whilom
Whilom she was the daughter of *Locrine*, Mask 827
Trinity ms 'whilome'
Bridgewater ms 'whilome'
1637 'Whilome'
Whilome did slay his dearly-loved mate Fair Inf 24
Whilst
Whilst from off the waters fleet Mask 896
Whilst the Lantskip round it measures, Allegro 70
Ay me! Whilst thee the shores, and sounding Seas Lycidas 154
1638 'whil'st'
Trinity ms 'whilst'
In perfect Diapason, whilst they stood Musick 23
and as your equall raptures temper'd sweet Musick Tr. ms 4.05
'as' ←'whilst'
while all the starrie rounds & arches blue Musick Tr. ms 4.21
'while all the starrie rounds' ←'starrie frame' ←'whilst then' ←'whilst the whole frame of' ←'while all the' ←'that all'
Whilst thou bright Saint high sit'st in glory, Winchester 61
For whilst to th' shame of slow-endeavouring art, Shakespear 9
1663-4 'whil'st'
1632 'whil'st'
Whip
Least with a whip of Scorpions I pursue Par Lost 2.701
Whirled
That whirl'd the Prophet up at *Chebar* flood, Passion 37
Whirlpool
Charybdis, and by th' other whirlpool steard. Par Lost 2.1020
Whirlwind
In whirlwind; Hell scarce holds the wilde uproar. Par Lost 2.541
Of Whirlwind and dire Hail, which on firm land Par Lost 2.589
Dawning through Heav'n: forth rush'd with whirlwind sound Par Lost 6.749
So with thy whirlwind them pursue, Psalm 83, 57
Whirlwinds
With Floods and Whirlwinds of tempestuous fire, Par Lost 1.77
ms 'whirlwinds'
Of racking whirlwinds, or for ever sunk Par Lost 2.182
Whisper
Native perfumes, and whisper whence they stole Par Lost 4.158
Whispered
Her hand soft touching, whisperd thus. Awake Par Lost 5.17
Whisper'd it to the Woods, and from thir wings Par Lost 8.516
Whispering
Stood whispering soft, by a fresh Fountain side Par Lost 4.326
Such whispering wak'd her, but with startl'd eye Par Lost 5.26
Where winds with Reeds, and Osiers whisp'ring play Par Reg 2.26
His whispering stream; within the walls then view Par Reg 4.250
By whispering Windes soon lull'd asleep. Allegro 116
Whispering new joyes to the milde Ocean, Nativity 66
Whispers
Ye valleys low where the milde whispers use, Lycidas 136
Trinity ms 'wispers'
Whist
The Windes with wonder whist, Nativity 64
Whistle
Or whistle from the Lodge, or village cock Mask 346
Trinity ms 'whistle' ←'wistle'
Whistles
Whistles ore the Furrow'd Land, Allegro 64
Whit
And she no whit encomber'd with her store, Mask 774
White
White, Black and Grey, with all thir trumperie. Par Lost 3.475
Between her white wings mantling proudly, Rowes Par Lost 7.439
O're the blew Firmament a radiant white, Par Lost 11.206
Dusk faces with white silken Turbants wreath'd: Par Reg 4.76
With careful step, Locks white as doune, Samson 327
On both his wings, one black, th' other white, Samson 973
Held up their pearled wrists and took her in, Mask 834
Trinity ms 'pearled' ←'white'
The white Pink, and the Pansie freakt with jeat, Lycidas 144
The Saintly Vail of Maiden white to throw, Nativity 42
And letters where my tears have washt a wannish white. Passion 35
Came vested all in white, pure as her mind: Sonnet 23, 9
Whited
Sees his foule inside through his whited skin. Prose 10, 6
White-handed
O welcom pure-ey'd Faith, white-handed Hope, Mask 213
line not in Bridgewater ms
White-robed
Or that crown'd Matron sage white-robed truth? Fair Inf 54
Whitethorn
When first the White thorn blows; Lycidas 48
Trinity ms 'white thorne'
1673 'White Thorn'
1638 'white-thorn'
Whither
Whether upheld by strength, or Chance, or Fate, Par Lost 1.133
ms 'Whither'

Whither*(cont)*
All Heav'n, what this might mean, and whither tend Par Lost 3.272
Beneath th' *Azores;* whither the prime Orb, Par Lost 4.592
Where lodg'd, or whither fled, or if for fight, Par Lost 6.531
While thus I call'd, and stray'd I knew not whither, Par Lost 8.283
Thoughts, whither have ye led me, with what sweet Par Lost 9.473
Goe whither Fate and inclination strong Par Lost 10.265
Whither shall I betake me, where subsist? Par Lost 10.922
How shall I part, and whither wander down Par Lost 11.282
Whence thou returnst, and whither wentst, I know; Par Lost 12.610
For whither is he gone, what accident Par Reg 2.39
Till at the Ford of *Jordan* whither all Par Reg 4.510
Mess. O whither shall I run, or which way flie Samson 1541
Where may she wander now, whether betake her Mask 351
Who
That Shepherd, who first taught the chosen Seed, Par Lost 1.8
Who first seduc'd them to that foul revolt? Par Lost 1.33
Who durst defie th' Omnipotent to Arms. Par Lost 1.49
From him, who in the happy Realms of Light Par Lost 1.85
He with his Thunder: and till then who knew Par Lost 1.93
Who from the terrour of this Arm so late Par Lost 1.113
Who now triumphs, and in th' excess of joy Par Lost 1.123
Who now is Sovran can dispose and bid Par Lost 1.246
Receive thy new Possessor: One who brings Par Lost 1.252
His Legions, Angel Forms, who lay intrans't Par Lost 1.301
The Sojourners of *Goshen*, who beheld Par Lost 1.309
To adore the Conquerour? who now beholds Par Lost 1.323
Say, Muse, thir Names then known, who first, who last, Par Lost 1.376
The chief were those who from the Pit of Hell Par Lost 1.381
With these came they, who from the bordring flood Par Lost 1.419
Who mourn'd in earnest, when the Captive Ark Par Lost 1.458
A crew who under Names of old Renown, Par Lost 1.477
Jehovah, who in one Night when he pass'd Par Lost 1.487
Or Altar smoak'd; yet who more oft then hee Par Lost 1.493
Turns Atheist, as did *Ely*'s Sons, who fill'd Par Lost 1.495
Of *Doric* Land; or who with *Saturn* old Par Lost 1.519
Who forthwith from the glittering Staff unfurld Par Lost 1.535
And all who since, Baptiz'd or Infidel Par Lost 1.582
For who can yet beleeve, though after loss, Par Lost 1.631
By mee, have lost our hopes. But he who reigns Par Lost 1.637
At length from us may find, who overcomes Par Lost 1.648
For who can think Submission? Warr then, Warr Par Lost 1.661
Who boast in mortal things, and wond'ring tell Par Lost 1.693
Behold a wonder! they but now who seemd Par Lost 1.777
Envy from each inferior; but who here Par Lost 2.26
We now debate; who can advise, may speak. Par Lost 2.42
Contrive who need, or when they need, not now Par Lost 2.53
The Prison of his Tyranny who Reigns Par Lost 2.59
To us is adverse. Who but felt of late Par Lost 2.77
When he who most excels in fact of Arms, Par Lost 2.124
To be no more; sad cure; for who would loose, Par Lost 2.146
Devoid of sense and motion? and who knows, Par Lost 2.151
Say they who counsel Warr, we are decreed, Par Lost 2.160
With him, or who deceive his mind, whose eye Par Lost 2.189
I laugh, when those who at the Spear are bold Par Lost 2.204
Of him who rules above; so was his will Par Lost 2.351
To their defence who hold it: here perhaps Par Lost 2.362
Sufficient? who shall tempt with wandring feet Par Lost 2.404
His look suspence, awaiting who appeer'd Par Lost 2.418
To him who Reigns, and so much to him due Par Lost 2.454
Her watrie Labyrinth, whereof who drinks, Par Lost 2.584
Who first broke peace in Heav'n and Faith, till then Par Lost 2.690
For him who sits above and laughs the while Par Lost 2.731
The most averse, thee chiefly, who full oft Par Lost 2.763
Grim *Death* my Son and foe, who sets them on, Par Lost 2.804
Save he who reigns above, none can resist. Par Lost 2.814
Who hates me, and hath hither thrust me down Par Lost 2.857
The Gods who live at ease, where I shall Reign Par Lost 2.868
Pursues the *Arimaspian*, who by stelth Par Lost 2.945
Answer'd. I know thee, stranger, who thou art, Par Lost 2.990
That mighty leading Angel, who of late Par Lost 2.991
Whose Fountain who shall tell? before the Sun, Par Lost 3.8
And Spirits, both them who stood and them who faild; Par Lost 3.101
Freely they stood who stood, and fell who fell. Par Lost 3.102
That farr be from thee, Father, who art Judg Par Lost 3.154
Son of my bosom, Son who art alone Par Lost 3.169
Man shall not quite be lost, but sav'd who will, Par Lost 3.173
They who neglect and scorn, shall never taste; Par Lost 3.199
Imputed shall absolve them who renounce Par Lost 3.291
In those who, when they may, accept not grace. Par Lost 3.302
Adore him, who to compass all this dies, Par Lost 3.342
Both all things vain, and all who in vain things Par Lost 3.448
All who have thir reward on Earth, the fruits Par Lost 3.451
Others came single; he who to be deemd Par Lost 3.469
Empedocles, and hee who to enjoy Par Lost 3.471
In *Golgotha* him dead, who lives in Heav'n; Par Lost 3.477
And they who to be sure of Paradise Par Lost 3.478
Who after came from Earth, sayling arriv'd, Par Lost 3.520
Thrice happy Iles, but who dwelt happy there Par Lost 3.570
To find who might direct his wandring flight Par Lost 3.631
Who in Gods presence, neerest to his Throne Par Lost 3.649
Who justly hath drivn out his Rebell Foes Par Lost 3.677
Who to the fraudulent Impostor foule Par Lost 3.692
O for that warning voice, which he who saw Par Lost 4.1
Those balmie spoiles. As when to them who saile Par Lost 4.159
Who came thir bane, though with them better pleas'd Par Lost 4.167
To them who liv'd; nor on the vertue thought Par Lost 4.198
Thank him who puts me loath to this revenge Par Lost 4.386

Who(*cont*)

On you who wrong me not for him who wrongd.	Par Lost 4.387
Then as a Tyger, who by chance hath spi'd	Par Lost 4.403
His couchant watch, as one who chose his ground	Par Lost 4.406
In all this happiness, who at his hand	Par Lost 4.417
Aught whereof hee hath need, hee who requires	Par Lost 4.419
One easie prohibition, who enjoy	Par Lost 4.433
And daily thanks, I chiefly who enjoy	Par Lost 4.445
On him who had stole *Joves* authentic fire.	Par Lost 4.719
To fill the Earth, who shall with us extoll	Par Lost 4.733
Our Maker bids increase, who bids abstain	Par Lost 4.748
Who tells of som infernal Spirit seen	Par Lost 4.793
Hitherward bent (who could have thought2) escap'd	Par Lost 4.794
To him who sent us, whose charge is to keep	Par Lost 4.842
But faded splendor wan; who by his gate	Par Lost 4.870
Of others, who approve not to transgress	Par Lost 4.880
Puts me in doubt. Lives ther who loves his pain?	Par Lost 4.888
Who would not, finding way, break loose from Hell,	Par Lost 4.889
To thee no reason; who knowst only good,	Par Lost 4.895
His will who bound us? let him surer barr	Par Lost 4.897
Or not, who ask what boldness brought him hither	Par Lost 4.908
And thou sly hypocrite, who now wouldst seem	Par Lost 4.957
Patron of liberty, who more then thou	Par Lost 4.958
Forbid who will, none shall from me withhold	Par Lost 5.62
Of day-spring, and the Sun, who scarce up risen	Par Lost 5.139
Unspeakable, who sitst above these Heavens	Par Lost 5.156
Speak yee who best can tell, ye Sons of light,	Par Lost 5.160
His praise, who out of Darkness call'd up Light.	Par Lost 5.179
Two onely, who yet by sov'ran gift possess	Par Lost 5.366
Who dwell in Heav'n, whose excellence he saw	Par Lost 5.456
Who formd us from the dust, and plac'd us here	Par Lost 5.516
Willing or no, who will but what they must	Par Lost 5.533
For ever happie: him who disobeyes	Par Lost 5.611
Excess, before th' all bounteous King, who showrd	Par Lost 5.640
Fannd with coole Winds, save those who in thir course	Par Lost 5.655
New Laws from him who reigns, new minds may raise	Par Lost 5.680
In us who serve, new Counsels, to debate	Par Lost 5.681
And all who under me thir Banners wave,	Par Lost 5.687
Who speedily through all the Hierarchies	Par Lost 5.692
Is rising, who intends to erect his Throne	Par Lost 5.725
Who can in reason then or right assume	Par Lost 5.794
Law and Edict on us, who without law	Par Lost 5.798
With him the points of libertie, who made	Par Lost 5.823
Doctrin which we would know whence learnt: who saw	Par Lost 5.856
Who is our equal: then thou shalt behold	Par Lost 5.866
Then who created thee lamenting learne	Par Lost 5.894
When who can uncreate thee thou shalt know.	Par Lost 5.895
Among those friendly Powers, who him receav'd	Par Lost 6.22
The better fight, who single hast maintaind	Par Lost 6.30
By force, who reason for thir Law refuse,	Par Lost 6.41
Messiah, who by right of merit Reigns.	Par Lost 6.43
And in fierce hosting meet, who wont to meet	Par Lost 6.93
That he who in debate of Truth hath won,	Par Lost 6.122
Who out of smallest things could without end	Par Lost 6.137
All are not of thy Train; there be who Faith	Par Lost 6.143
Thir Deities to assert, who while they feel	Par Lost 6.157
When he who rules is worthiest, and excells	Par Lost 6.177
To serve th' unwise, or him who hath rebelld	Par Lost 6.179
The Battel hung; till *Satan*, who that day	Par Lost 6.246
Unspeakable; for who, though with the tongue	Par Lost 6.297
By Angels many and strong, who interpos'd	Par Lost 6.336
Of *Moloc* furious King, who him defi'd,	Par Lost 6.357
Who have sustaind one day in doubtful fight	Par Lost 6.423
All patience. He who therefore can invent	Par Lost 6.464
Which of us who beholds the bright surface	Par Lost 6.472
That all may see who hate us, how we seek	Par Lost 6.559
Freely our part; yee who appointed stand	Par Lost 6.565
And stumbl'd many, who receives them right,	Par Lost 6.624
Not emulous, nor care who them excells;	Par Lost 6.822
To meet him all his Saints, who silent stood	Par Lost 6.882
On high: who into Glorie him receav'd,	Par Lost 6.891
Of those too high aspiring, who rebelld	Par Lost 6.899
With *Satan*, hee who envies now thy state,	Par Lost 6.900
Who now is plotting how he may seduce	Par Lost 6.901
Her Son. So fail not thou, who thee implores:	Par Lost 7.38
At least our envious Foe hath fail'd, who thought	Par Lost 7.139
Boundless the Deep, because I am who fill	Par Lost 7.168
Of all yet don; a Creature who not prone	Par Lost 7.506
And worship God Supream, who made him chief	Par Lost 7.515
Who can impair thee, mighty King, or bound	Par Lost 7.608
The number of thy worshippers. Who seekes	Par Lost 7.613
Hystorian, who thus largely hast allayd	Par Lost 8.7
And Grace that won who saw to wish her stay,	Par Lost 8.43
His secrets to be scann'd by them who ought	Par Lost 8.74
Who art to lead thy ofspring, and supposest	Par Lost 8.86
The Makers high magnificence, who built	Par Lost 8.101
Who since the Morning hour set out from Heav'n	Par Lost 8.111
To thee who hast thy dwelling here on Earth.	Par Lost 8.118
Is hard; for who himself beginning knew?	Par Lost 8.251
But who I was, or where, or from what cause,	Par Lost 8.270
My wandring, had not hee who was my Guide	Par Lost 8.312
I see not who partakes. In solitude	Par Lost 8.364
What happiness, who can enjoy alone,	Par Lost 8.365
Of happiness, or not? who am alone	Par Lost 8.405
Who stooping op'nd my left side, and took	Par Lost 8.465
His Image who made both, and less expressing	Par Lost 8.544
Thy mate, who sees when thou art seen least wise.	Par Lost 8.578
Who meet with various objects, from the sense	Par Lost 8.609

Who(*cont*)

Of my Celestial Patroness, who deignes	Par Lost 9.21
Not Hers who brings it nightly to my Ear.	Par Lost 9.47
When *Satan* who late fled before the threats	Par Lost 9.53
Continu'd making, and who knows how long	Par Lost 9.138
O foul descent! that I who erst contended	Par Lost 9.163
Descend to? who aspires must down as low	Par Lost 9.169
Since higher I fall short, on him who next	Par Lost 9.174
Who guards her, or with her the worst endures.	Par Lost 9.269
As one who loves, and some unkindness meets,	Par Lost 9.271
That such an Enemie we have, who seeks	Par Lost 9.274
For hee who tempts, though in vain, at least asperses	Par Lost 9.296
Suttle he needs must be, who could seduce	Par Lost 9.307
And Matrimonial Love; but *Eve*, who thought	Par Lost 9.319
By us? who rather double honour gaine	Par Lost 9.332
First thy obedience; th' other who can know,	Par Lost 9.368
Not seeing thee attempted, who attest?	Par Lost 9.369
As one who long in populous City pent,	Par Lost 9.445
Hee with *Olympias*, this with her who bore	Par Lost 9.509
At first, as one who sought access, but feard	Par Lost 9.511
Thou canst, who art sole Wonder, much less arm	Par Lost 9.533
Who sees thee? (and what is one2) who shouldst be seen	Par Lost 9.546
Mee who have touch'd and tasted, yet both live,	Par Lost 9.688
Them nothing: If they all things, who enclos'd	Par Lost 9.722
Thy praise hee also who forbids thy use,	Par Lost 9.750
In knowledge, as the Gods who all things know;	Par Lost 9.804
Superior; for inferior who is free?	Par Lost 9.825
To open Eyes, and make them Gods who taste;	Par Lost 9.866
And peril great provok't, who thus hath dar'd	Par Lost 9.922
But past who can recall, or don undoe?	Par Lost 9.926
Not well conceav'd of God, who though his Power	Par Lost 9.945
Most Favors, who can please him long; Mee first	Par Lost 9.949
To sensual Appetite, who from beneathe	Par Lost 9.1129
Of wandring, as thou call'st it, which who knows	Par Lost 9.1146
Who might have liv'd and joyd immortal bliss,	Par Lost 9.1166
Him who to worth in Women overtrusting	Par Lost 9.1183
Omniscient, who in all things wise and just,	Par Lost 10.7
All were who heard, dim sadness did not spare	Par Lost 10.23
So dreadful to thee? that thou art naked, who	Par Lost 10.121
The Guilt on him who made him instrument	Par Lost 10.166
Eevn hee who now foretold his fatal bruise,	Par Lost 10.191
Sin opening, who thus now to Death began.	Par Lost 10.234
Met who to meet him came, his Ofspring dear.	Par Lost 10.349
Congratulant approach'd him, who with hand	Par Lost 10.458
A World who would not purchase with a bruise,	Par Lost 10.500
His will who reigns above, to aggravate	Par Lost 10.549
To mee, who with eternal Famin pine,	Par Lost 10.597
Let in these wastful Furies, who impute	Par Lost 10.620
Who can extenuate thee? Next, to the Son,	Par Lost 10.645
The Glory of that Glory, who now becom	Par Lost 10.722
Who of all Ages to succeed, but feeling	Par Lost 10.733
Or in some other dismal place who knows	Par Lost 10.787
So now of what thou knowst not, who desir'st	Par Lost 10.948
Satan, who in the Serpent hath contriv'd	Par Lost 10.1034
To me transgressour, who for thee ordaind	Par Lost 11.164
That I who first brought Death on all, am grac't	Par Lost 11.168
Who highly thus to entitle me voutsaf'st,	Par Lost 11.170
Who knows, or more then this, that we are dust,	Par Lost 11.199
Against the *Syrian* King, who to surprize	Par Lost 11.218
Not unperceav'd of *Adam*, who to *Eve*,	Par Lost 11.224
That all his senses bound; *Eve*, who unseen	Par Lost 11.265
Who now shall reare ye to the Sun, or ranke	Par Lost 11.278
Of him who all things can, I would not cease	Par Lost 11.309
In some to spring from thee, who never touch'd	Par Lost 11.425
To that meek man, who well had sacrific'd;	Par Lost 11.451
Obtruded on us thus? who if we knew	Par Lost 11.504
Was heard, of Harp and Organ; and who moovd	Par Lost 11.560
In other part stood one who at the Forge	Par Lost 11.564
Who slew his Brother; studious they appere	Par Lost 11.609
O pittie and shame, that they who to live well	Par Lost 11.629
Said th' Angel, who should better hold his place	Par Lost 11.635
Deaths Ministers, not Men, who thus deal Death	Par Lost 11.676
Ten thousandfould the sin of him who slew	Par Lost 11.678
But who was that Just Man, whom had not Heav'n	Par Lost 11.681
Where good with bad were matcht, who of themselves	Par Lost 11.685
Who having spilt much blood, and don much waste	Par Lost 11.791
By Men who there frequent, or therein dwell.	Par Lost 11.838
With soft foot towards the deep, who now had stopt	Par Lost 11.848
O thou who future things canst represent 1667 'that'	Par Lost 11.870
As one who in his journey bates at Noone, line not in 1667 edition	Par Lost 12.1
Of proud ambitious heart, who not content	Par Lost 12.25
But God who oft descends to visit men	Par Lost 12.48
That Son, who on the quiet state of men	Par Lost 12.80
Who oft as undeservedly enthrall	Par Lost 12.94
Of him who built the Ark, who for the shame	Par Lost 12.102
While yet the Patriark liv'd, who scap'd the Flood,	Par Lost 12.117
With God, who call'd him, in a land unknown.	Par Lost 12.134
Is meant thy great deliverer, who shall bruise	Par Lost 12.149
Suspected to a sequent King, who seeks	Par Lost 12.165
But first the lawless Tyrant, who denies	Par Lost 12.173
Though present in his Angel, who shall goe	Par Lost 12.201
His whole descent, who thus shall *Canaan* win.	Par Lost 12.269
Favour unmerited by me, who sought	Par Lost 12.278
His Name and Office bearing, who shall quell	Par Lost 12.311
Men who attend the Altar, and should most	Par Lost 12.354
And guides the Eastern Sages, who enquire	Par Lost 12.362

Who(*cont*)
Which hee, who comes thy Saviour, shall recure, Par Lost 12.393
Proclaiming Life to all who shall believe Par Lost 12.407
Never to hurt them more who rightly trust Par Lost 12.418
To his Disciples, Men who in his Life Par Lost 12.438
And his Salvation, them who shall beleeve Par Lost 12.441
The enemies of truth; who then shall guide Par Lost 12.482
His people, who defend? will they not deale Par Lost 12.483
The promise of the Father, who shall dwell Par Lost 12.487
Who all the sacred mysteries of Heav'n Par Lost 12.509
Who against Faith and Conscience can be heard Par Lost 12.529
On all who in the worship persevere Par Lost 12.532
Who for my wilful crime art banisht hence. Par Lost 12.619
I Who e're while the happy Garden sung, Par Reg 1.1
Thou Spirit who ledst this glorious Eremite Par Reg 1.8
That heard the Adversary, who roving still Par Reg 1.33
His coming, is sent Harbinger, who all Par Reg 1.71
The testimony of Heaven, that who he is Par Reg 1.78
He who obtains the Monarchy of Heav'n, Par Reg 1.87
Who this is we must learn, for man he seems Par Reg 1.91
Of the most High, who in full frequence bright Par Reg 1.128
Mean while the Son of God, who yet some days Par Reg 1.183
Thy Father is the Eternal King, who rules Par Reg 1.236
Not knew by sight) now come, who was to come Par Reg 1.271
He saw approach, who first with curious eye Par Reg 1.319
So far from path or road of men, who pass Par Reg 1.322
Durst ever, who return'd, and dropt not here Par Reg 1.324
Who dwell this wild, constrain'd by want, come forth Par Reg 1.331
To whom the Son of God. Who brought me hither Par Reg 1.335
Proceeding from the mouth of God; who fed Par Reg 1.350
Knowing who I am, as I know who thou art? Par Reg 1.356
Who leagu'd with millions more in rash revolt Par Reg 1.359
Who boast'st release from Hell, and leave to come Par Reg 1.409
Which they who ask'd have seldom understood, Par Reg 1.436
Who ever by consulting at thy shrine Par Reg 1.438
In every Province, who themselves disdaining Par Reg 1.448
Vertue, who follow not her lore: permit me Par Reg 1.483
Thy Father, who is holy, wise and pure, Par Reg 1.486
Mean while the new-baptiz'd, who yet remain'd Par Reg 2.1
And the great *Thisbite* who on fiery wheels Par Reg 2.16
Were dead, who sought his life, and missing fill'd Par Reg 2.77
Is ris'n to invade us, who no less Par Reg 2.127
Or counsel to assist; lest I who erst Par Reg 2.145
Nor proffer'd by an Enemy, though who Par Reg 2.330
Thy gentle Ministers, who come to pay Par Reg 2.375
And who withholds my pow'r that right to use? Par Reg 2.380
Who could do mighty things, and could contemn Par Reg 2.448
To him who wears the Regal Diadem, Par Reg 2.461
Yet he who reigns within himself, and rules Par Reg 2.466
And who attains not, ill aspires to rule Par Reg 2.469
Aetherial, who all pleasures else despise, Par Reg 3.28
A miscellaneous rabble, who extol Par Reg 3.50
His lot who dares be singularly good. Par Reg 3.57
To all his Angels, who with true applause Par Reg 3.63
They err who count it glorious to subdue Par Reg 3.71
Then those thir Conquerours, who leave behind Par Reg 3.78
Who names not now with honour patient *Job?* Par Reg 3.95
Poor *Socrates* (who next more memorable2) Par Reg 3.96
Who sent me, and thereby witness whence I am. Par Reg 3.107
From them who could return him nothing else, Par Reg 3.129
But why should man seek glory? who of his own Par Reg 3.134
Who for so many benefits receiv'd Par Reg 3.137
That who advance his glory, not thir own, Par Reg 3.143
The Prophets old, who sung thy endless raign, Par Reg 3.178
What I can suffer, how obey? who best Par Reg 3.194
Can suffer, best can do; best reign, who first Par Reg 3.195
That thou who worthiest art should'st be thir King? Par Reg 3.226
(As he who seeking Asses found a Kingdom) Par Reg 3.242
As antient, but rebuilt by him who twice Par Reg 3.281
By great *Arsaces* led, who founded first Par Reg 3.295
Who wrought their own captivity, fell off Par Reg 3.415
Who freed, as to thir antient Patrimony, Par Reg 3.428
Thir enemies, who serve Idols with God. Par Reg 3.432
This far his over-match, who self deceiv'd Par Reg 4.7
But as a man who had been matchless held Par Reg 4.10
Still will be tempting him who foyls him still, Par Reg 4.13
And studs of Pearl, to me should'st tell who thirst Par Reg 4.120
Expel a Devil who first made him such? Par Reg 4.129
Deservedly made vassal, who once just, Par Reg 4.133
Who then thou art, whose coming is foretold Par Reg 4.204
The schools of antient Sages; his who bred Par Reg 4.251
And his who gave them breath, but higher sung, Par Reg 4.258
Of knowing what I aught: he who receives Par Reg 4.288
Of mortal things. Who therefore seeks in these Par Reg 4.318
Wise men have said are wearisom; who reads Par Reg 4.322
Who with her radiant finger still'd the roar Par Reg 4.428
Who all things now behold more fresh and green, Par Reg 4.435
Who knowing I shall raign past thy preventing, Par Reg 4.492
To understand my Adversary, who Par Reg 4.527
Her riddle, and him, who solv'd it not, devour'd; Par Reg 4.573
Who durst so proudly tempt the Son of God. Par Reg 4.580
Who on their plumy Vans receiv'd him soft Par Reg 4.583
Twice by an Angel, who at last in sight Samson 24
Who this high gift of strength committed to me, Samson 47
But who are these? for with joint pace I hear Samson 110
Perhaps my enemies who come to stare Samson 112
Who tore the Lion, as the Lion tears the Kid, Samson 128
But safest he who stood aloof, Samson 135

Who(*cont*)
How counterfeit a coin they are who friends Samson 189
Who like a foolish Pilot have shipwrack't, Samson 198
Who hast of sorrow thy full load besides; Samson 214
Who vanquisht with a peal of words (O weakness!) Samson 235
Who seeing those great acts which God had done Samson 243
Enterd *Judea* seeking mee, who then Samson 252
Their choicest youth; they only liv'd who fled. Samson 264
Had dealt with *Jephtha*, who by argument, Samson 283
Unless there be who think not God at all, Samson 295
Yet more there be who doubt his ways not just, Samson 300
Who made our Laws to bind us, not himself, Samson 309
He would not else who never wanted means, Samson 315
The dread of *Israel*'s foes, who with a strength Samson 342
None offering fight; who single combatant Samson 344
Who would be now a Father in my stead? Samson 355
As vile hath been my folly, who have profan'd Samson 377
To them who had corrupted her, my Spies, Samson 386
More Faith? who also in her prime of love, Samson 388
Who with a grain of manhood well resolv'd Samson 408
To *Dagon*, as their God who hath deliver'd Samson 437
Them out of thine, who slew'st them many a slain. Samson 439
On thee, who now no more canst do them harm. Samson 486
Who evermore approves and more accepts Samson 510
Him who imploring mercy sues for life, Samson 512
Then who self-rigorous chooses death as due; Samson 513
Reject not then what offerd means, who knows Samson 516
Of a deceitful Concubine who shore me Samson 537
But God who caus'd a fountain at thy prayer Samson 581
But who is this, what thing of Sea or Land? Samson 710
Who tempted me, that nothing was design'd Samson 801
My love how couldst thou hope, who tookst the way Samson 838
A common enemy, who had destroy'd Samson 856
By thy request, who could deny thee nothing; Samson 881
Living and dead recorded, who to save Samson 984
Jael, who with inhospitable guile Samson 989
And aggravate my folly who committed Samson 1000
Favour'd of Heav'n who finds Samson 1046
Who durst not with thir whole united powers Samson 1110
My trust is in the living God who gave me Samson 1140
At *Askalon*, who never did thee harm, Samson 1187
Who threatning cruel death constrain'd the bride Samson 1198
Who now defies thee thrice to single fight, Samson 1222
Draw thir own ruin who attempt the deed. Samson 1267
His errand on the wicked, who surpris'd Samson 1285
He's gone, and who knows how he may report Samson 1350
Of those who have me in thir civil power. Samson 1367
But who constrains me to the Temple of *Dagon*, Samson 1370
And for a life who will not change his purpose? Samson 1406
Fast by thy side, who from thy Fathers field Samson 1432
More generous far and civil, who confess'd Samson 1467
To free him hence! but death who sets all free Samson 1572
Who had made thir dreadful enemy thir thrall. Samson 1622
And eyes fast fixt he stood, as one who pray'd, Samson 1637
As with amaze shall strike all who behold. Samson 1645
Upon the heads of all who sate beneath, Samson 1652
The vulgar only scap'd who stood without. Samson 1659
Before our living Dread who dwells Samson 1673
Who hurt thir minds, Samson 1676
On *Circes* Iland fell (who knows not *Circe* Mask 50
Bridgewater ms 'whoe'
Who ripe, and frolick of his full grown age, Mask 59
Bridgewater ms 'whoe'
Who with his soft Pipe, and smooth-dittied Song, Mask 86
Bridgewater ms 'whoe'
Who in their nightly watchfull Sphears, Mask 113
Bridgewater ms 'whoe'
Who as they sung, would take the prison'd soul, Mask 256
Bridgewater ms 'whoe when'
For who would rob a Hermit of his Weeds, Mask 390
Bridgewater ms 'whoe'
Who gently ask't if he had seen such two, Mask 575
Bridgewater ms 'whoe'
Who would be quite surcharg'd with her own weight, Mask 728
Bridgewater ms 'whoe'
That had the Scepter from his father *Brute*. Mask 828
Bridgewater ms 'whoe had'
Who piteous of her woes, rear'd her lank head, Mask 836
Bridgewater ms 'whoe'
And who had *Canace* to wife, Penseroso 112
Who had thought this clime had held Arcades 24
Divine *Alpheus*, who by secret sluse, Arcades 30
Who would not sing for *Lycidas?* he knew Lycidas 10
Ah! Who hath reft (quoth he) my dearest pledge? Lycidas 107
1638 'who'
Trinity ms 'who'
Who now hath quite forgot to rave, Nativity 67
That doth the wrathfull tyrants quell. Psalm 136, 10
1673 'Who doth'
That with his miracles doth make Psalm 136, 13
1673 'Who with'
That by his wisdom did create Psalm 136, 17
1673 'Who by'
That did the solid Earth ordain Psalm 136, 21
1673 'Who did'
That by his all-commanding might, Psalm 136, 25
1673 'Who by'
Or wert thou that just Maid who once before Fair Inf 50

Who(*cont*)

Who having clad thy self in humane weed,	Fair Inf 58
Or *Trent*, who like some earth-born Giant spreads	Vacation 93
He who with all Heav'ns heraldry whileare	Circum 10
Who onely thought to crop the flowr	Winchester 39
Who after yeers of barrennes,	Winchester 64
The Flowry *May*, who from her green lap throws	May Morn 3
Here lieth one who did most truly prove,	Another 1
Who liv'd in both, unstain'd with gold or fee,	Sonnet 10, 3
For who loves that, must first be wise and good;	Sonnet 12, 12
Love led them on, and Faith who knew them best	Sonnet 14, 9
Trinity ms 'Love led them on' ←'Faith shew'd the way' ←'Faith who led on the way'	
Before the Judge, who thenceforth bid thee rest	Sonnet 14, 13
Cromwell, our cheif of men, who through a cloud	Sonnet 16, 1
1694 'that'	
Ev'n them who kept thy truth so pure of old	Sonnet 18, 3
Who were thy Sheep and in their antient Fold	Sonnet 18, 6
A hunder'd-fold, who having learnt thy way	Sonnet 18, 13
Either man's work or his own gifts, who best	Sonnet 19, 10
They also serve who only stand and waite.	Sonnet 19, 14
He who of those delights can judge, And spare	Sonnet 20, 13
Who now enjoyes thee credulous, all Gold,	Horace 9
Who alwayes vacant alwayes amiable	Horace 10
Bless'd is the man who hath not walk'd astray	Psalm 1, 1
Their twisted cords: he who in Heaven doth dwell	Psalm 2, 8
Happy all those who have in him their stay.	Psalm 2, 28
Who yet will shew us good?	Psalm 4, 26
Then all who trust in thee shall bring	Psalm 5, 33
And shall triumph in thee, who love thy name.	Psalm 5, 36
Who in the grave can celebrate thy praise?	Psalm 6, 10
In him who both just and wise	Psalm 7, 41
Who leadest like a flock of sheep	Psalm 80, 3
Who hate the Lord should *then be fain*	Psalm 81, 61
Who thence grow bold and strong	Psalm 82, 8
For thou art he who shalt by right	Psalm 82, 27
Happy, who in thy house reside	Psalm 84, 17
Who *only* on thee doth relie,	Psalm 84, 47
Who *still* in thee doth trust.	Psalm 86, 8
Both they who sing, and they who dance	Psalm 87, 25
Or they *who* in perdition *dwell*	Psalm 88, 47
Which he who can, and will, deserv's high praise,	Prose 9, 3
Who neither can nor will, may hold his peace;	Prose 9, 4
Who keepes the lawes and statutes of the Senate,	Prose 10, 2
Who judges in great suits and controversies,	Prose 10, 3
Goddess of Shades, and Huntress, who at will	Prose 12, 1

Whoever

Whoever tempted; which they not obeying,	Par Lost 10.14
Whoever judg'd, the worst on mee must light,	Par Lost 10.73
At this who ever envies or repines	Samson 995
Whoever tasted, lost his upright shape,	Mask 52
Bridgewater ms 'whoe ever'	

Whole

The whole Battalion views, thir order due,	Par Lost 1.569
Ominous conjecture on the whole success:	Par Lost 2.123
That shook Heav'ns whol circumference, confirm'd.	Par Lost 2.353
To waste his whole Creation, or possess	Par Lost 2.365
Where Armies whole have sunk: the parching Air	Par Lost 2.594
Draw after him the whole Race of mankind,	Par Lost 3.161
He with his whole posteritie must dye,	Par Lost 3.209
By loosing thee a while, the whole Race lost.	Par Lost 3.280
In narrow room Natures whole wealth, yea more,	Par Lost 4.207
A whole days journy high, but wide remote	Par Lost 4.284
Came shadowing, and oppress whole Legions arm'd,	Par Lost 6.655
My exaltation, and my whole delight,	Par Lost 6.727
Yawning receavd them whole, and on them clos'd,	Par Lost 6.875
Contiguous might distemper the whole frame:	Par Lost 7.273
The whole included Race, his purposd prey.	Par Lost 9.416
Farr less I now lament for one whole World	Par Lost 11.874
The whole Earth fill'd with violence, and all flesh	Par Lost 11.888
His whole descent, who thus shall *Canaan* win.	Par Lost 12.269
Made it my whole delight, and in it grew	Par Reg 1.208
Toucht with the flame: on thir whole Host I flew	Samson 262
Had *Judah* that day join'd, or one whole Tribe,	Samson 265
Whole to my self, unhazarded abroad,	Samson 809
On his whole life, not sway'd	Samson 1059
Who durst not with thir whole united powers	Samson 1110
Man. His ransom, if my whole inheritance	Samson 1476
As if the whole inhabitation perish'd,	Samson 1512
The whole roof after them, with burst of thunder	Samson 1651
while all the starrie rounds & arches blue	Musick Tr. ms 4.21
'while all the starrie rounds' ←'starrie frame' ←'whilst then' ←'whilst the whole frame of' ←'while all the' ←'that all'	
With my whole heart, and blaze abroad	Psalm 86, 43
But his owne house, and the whole neighbourhood	Prose 10, 5

Wholesome

More easie, wholsom thirst and appetite	Par Lost 4.330
Wholsom and cool, and mild, but with black Air	Par Lost 10.847
And harmless, if not wholsom, as a sneeze	Par Reg 4.458
May with their wholsom and preventive Shears	Forcers 16
Trinity ms 'wholesome'	

Wholly

Intent now wholly on her taste, naught else	Par Lost 9.786
Made and set wholly on the accomplishment	Par Reg 2.207

Whom

Beelzebub. To whom th' Arch-Enemy,	Par Lost 1.81
Myriads though bright: If he whom mutual league,	Par Lost 1.87

Whom(*cont*)

But what if he our Conquerour, (whom I now	Par Lost 1.143
Whom we resist. If then his Providence	Par Lost 1.162
As whom the Fables name of monstrous size,	Par Lost 1.197
Briareos or *Typhon*, whom the Den	Par Lost 1.199
Whom reason hath equald, force hath made supream	Par Lost 1.248
Whom Thunder hath made greater? Here at least	Par Lost 1.258
On duty, sleeping found by whom they dread,	Par Lost 1.333
Came *Astoreth*, whom the *Phoenicians* call'd	Par Lost 1.438
Ahaz his sottish Conquerour, whom he drew	Par Lost 1.472
Whom he had vanquisht. After these appear'd	Par Lost 1.476
Belial came last, then whom a Spirit more lewd	Par Lost 1.490
Or whom *Biserta* sent from *Afric* shore	Par Lost 1.585
A generation, whom his choice regard	Par Lost 1.653
And sat as Princes, whom the supreme King	Par Lost 1.735
Will envy whom the highest place exposes	Par Lost 2.27
Them in his anger, whom his anger saves	Par Lost 2.158
To whom we hate. Let us not then pursue	Par Lost 2.249
Which when *Beelzebub* perceiv'd, then whom,	Par Lost 2.299
Shall breathe her balme. But first whom shall we send	Par Lost 2.402
In search of this new world, whom shall we find	Par Lost 2.403
Choice in our suffrage; for on whom we send,	Par Lost 2.415
Satan, whom now transcendent glory rais'd	Par Lost 2.427
To whom the Goblin full of wrauth reply'd,	Par Lost 2.688
Against thy Fathers head? and know'st for whom;	Par Lost 2.730
T' whom thus the Portress of Hell Gate reply'd;	Par Lost 2.746
At last this odious offspring whom thou seest	Par Lost 2.781
My being gav'st me; whom should I obey	Par Lost 2.865
But thee, whom follow? thou wilt bring me soon	Par Lost 2.866
Thir lighter wings. To whom these most adhere,	Par Lost 2.906
Might in that noise reside, of whom to ask	Par Lost 2.957
T' whom *Satan* turning boldly, thus. Ye Powers	Par Lost 2.968
To tempt or punish mortals, except whom	Par Lost 2.1032
Transports our adversarie, whom no bounds	Par Lost 3.81
To whom the great Creatour thus reply'd.	Par Lost 3.167
O Son, in whom my Soul hath chief delight,	Par Lost 3.168
My Umpire *Conscience*, whom if they will hear,	Par Lost 3.195
In whom the fulness dwels of love divine,	Par Lost 3.225
Thou therefore whom thou only canst redeem,	Par Lost 3.281
Whom else no Creature can behold; on thee	Par Lost 3.387
The same whom *John* saw also in the Sun:	Par Lost 3.623
His chief delight and favour, him for whom	Par Lost 3.664
On whom the great Creator hath bestowd	Par Lost 3.673
Worlds, and on whom hath all these graces powrd;	Par Lost 3.674
From me, whom he created what I was	Par Lost 4.43
Thou hadst: whom hast thou then or what to accuse,	Par Lost 4.67
Among the spirits beneath, whom I seduc'd	Par Lost 4.83
Whom hunger drives to seek new haunt for prey,	Par Lost 4.184
Whom Gentiles *Ammon* call and *Lybian Jove*,	Par Lost 4.277
Little inferior; whom my thoughts pursue	Par Lost 4.362
To you whom I could pittie thus forlorne	Par Lost 4.374
To whom thus *Eve* repli'd. O thou for whom	Par Lost 4.440
And from whom I was formd flesh of thy flesh,	Par Lost 4.441
And without whom am to no end, my Guide	Par Lost 4.442
Whom fli'st thou? whom thou fli'st, of him thou art,	Par Lost 4.482
To keep them low whom knowledge might exalt	Par Lost 4.525
To whom the winged Warriour thus returnd:	Par Lost 4.576
In whatsoever shape he lurk, of whom	Par Lost 4.587
To whom thus *Eve* with perfet beauty adornd.	Par Lost 4.634
But wherfore all night long shine these, for whom	Par Lost 4.657
To whom our general Ancestor repli'd.	Par Lost 4.659
More lovely then *Pandora*, whom the Gods	Par Lost 4.714
In search of whom they sought: him there they found	Par Lost 4.799
To whom thus *Zephon*, answering scorn with scorn.	Par Lost 4.834
Awaiting next command. To whom thir Chief	Par Lost 4.864
And brief related whom they brought, where found,	Par Lost 4.875
To whom with stern regard thus *Gabriel* spake.	Par Lost 4.877
To whom thus *Satan*, with contemptuous brow.	Par Lost 4.885
Since *Satan* fell, whom follie overthrew,	Par Lost 4.905
To whom the warriour Angel, soon repli'd.	Par Lost 4.946
Faithful to whom? to thy rebellious crew?	Par Lost 4.952
On *Adam*, whom imbracing, thus she spake.	Par Lost 5.27
O Sole in whom my thoughts find all repose,	Par Lost 5.28
Whom to behold but thee, Natures desire,	Par Lost 5.45
His danger, and from whom, what enemie	Par Lost 5.239
Berrie or Grape: to whom thus *Adam* call'd.	Par Lost 5.307
To whom thus *Eve*. *Adam*, earths hallowd mould,	Par Lost 5.321
Whom thus th' Angelic Vertue answerd milde.	Par Lost 5.371
Alterd her cheek. On whom the Angel *Haile*	Par Lost 5.385
These bounties which our Nourisher, from whom	Par Lost 5.398
To whom the Angel. Therefore what he gives	Par Lost 5.404
To whom the winged Hierarch repli'd.	Par Lost 5.468
O *Adam*, one Almightie is, from whom	Par Lost 5.469
To whom the Patriarch of mankind repli'd,	Par Lost 5.506
To whom the Angel. Son of Heav'n and Earth,	Par Lost 5.519
To whom our great Progenitor. Thy words	Par Lost 5.544
By whom in bliss imbosom'd sat the Son,	Par Lost 5.597
This day I have begot whom I declare	Par Lost 5.603
Him have anointed, whom ye now behold	Par Lost 5.605
Rebellion rising, saw in whom, how spred	Par Lost 5.715
Son, thou in whom my glory I behold	Par Lost 5.719
To whom the Son with calm aspect and cleer	Par Lost 5.733
Matter to mee of Glory, whom thir hate	Par Lost 5.738
Of King anointed, for whom all this haste	Par Lost 5.777
Abdiel, then whom none with more zeale ador'd	Par Lost 5.805
Equal to him begotten Son, by whom	Par Lost 5.835
Whom the grand foe with scornful eye askance	Par Lost 6.149
To whom in brief thus *Abdiel* stern repli'd.	Par Lost 6.171

Whom(*cont*)

Of *Servitude* to serve whom God ordains,	Par Lost 6.175
Them whom he governs. This is servitude,	Par Lost 6.178
On either side, the least of whom could weild	Par Lost 6.221
So spake the Prince of Angels; to whom thus	Par Lost 6.281
Of airie threats to aw whom yet with deeds	Par Lost 6.283
Whom fled we thought, will save us long pursuit	Par Lost 6.538
That whom they hit, none on thir feet might stand,	Par Lost 6.592
To whom thus *Belial* in like gamesom mood,	Par Lost 6.620
For ever, and in mee all whom thou lov'st:	Par Lost 6.733
But whom thou hat'st, I hate, and can put on	Par Lost 6.734
Whom to obey is happiness entire.	Par Lost 6.741
Because the Father, t' whom in Heav'n supream	Par Lost 6.814
From whom it sprung, impossible to mix	Par Lost 7.58
Drew many, whom thir place knows here no more;	Par Lost 7.144
And sons of men, whom God hath thus advanc't,	Par Lost 7.626
To whom thus *Adam* cleerd of doubt, repli'd.	Par Lost 8.179
To whom thus *Raphael* answer'd heav'nly meek.	Par Lost 8.217
From whom I have that thus I move and live,	Par Lost 8.281
Submiss: he rear'd me, and Whom thou soughtst I am,	Par Lost 8.316
How have I then with whom to hold converse	Par Lost 8.408
Still glorious before whom awake I stood;	Par Lost 8.464
To whom the Angel with contracted brow.	Par Lost 8.560
To whom thus half abash't *Adam* repli'd.	Par Lost 8.595
To whom the Angel with a smile that glow'd	Par Lost 8.618
Him whom to love is to obey, and keep	Par Lost 8.634
So saying, he arose; whom *Adam* thus	Par Lost 8.644
Fit Vessel, fittest Imp of fraud, in whom	Par Lost 9.89
For whom all this was made, all this will soon	Par Lost 9.132
Whom us the more to spite his Maker rais'd	Par Lost 9.177
To whom mild answer *Adam* thus return'd.	Par Lost 9.226
To whom the Virgin Majestie of *Eve*,	Par Lost 9.270
To whom with healing words *Adam* replyd.	Par Lost 9.290
To whom thus *Adam* fervently repli'd.	Par Lost 9.342
To Beasts, whom God on thir Creation-Day	Par Lost 9.556
To whom the guileful Tempter thus reply'd.	Par Lost 9.567
To whom the wilie Adder, blithe and glad.	Par Lost 9.625
To whom the Tempter guilefully repli'd.	Par Lost 9.655
To whom thus *Eve* yet sinless. Of the Fruit	Par Lost 9.659
Rather your dauntless vertue, whom the pain	Par Lost 9.694
Of all Gods works, Creature in whom excell'd	Par Lost 9.897
Triumph and say; Fickle their State whom God	Par Lost 9.948
He ruind, now Mankind; whom will he next?	Par Lost 9.950
To whom soon mov'd with touch of blame thus *Eve*.	Par Lost 9.1143
To whom then first incenst *Adam* repli'd,	Par Lost 9.1162
But whom send I to judge them? whom but thee	Par Lost 10.55
Affraid, being naked, hid my self. To whom	Par Lost 10.117
To whom thus *Adam* sore beset repli'd.	Par Lost 10.124
This Woman whom thou mad'st to be my help,	Par Lost 10.137
To whom the sovran Presence thus repli'd.	Par Lost 10.144
To whom sad *Eve* with shame nigh overwhelm'd,	Par Lost 10.159
Whom he shall tread at last under our feet;	Par Lost 10.190
Whom thus the meager Shadow answerd soon.	Par Lost 10.264
Whom thus the Prince of Darkness answerd glad.	Par Lost 10.383
Bent thir aspect, and whom they wish'd beheld,	Par Lost 10.454
Now Dragon grown, larger then whom the Sun	Par Lost 10.529
Whom they triumph'd once lapst. Thus were they plagu'd	Par Lost 10.572
And Fabl'd how the Serpent, whom they calld	Par Lost 10.580
On his pale Horse: to whom *Sin* thus began.	Par Lost 10.590
Whom thus the Sin-born Monster answerd soon.	Par Lost 10.596
To whom th' incestuous Mother thus repli'd.	Par Lost 10.602
Destin'd restorer of Mankind, by whom	Par Lost 10.646
Of God, whom to behold was then my highth	Par Lost 10.724
Wrath without end on Man whom Death must end?	Par Lost 10.797
Whom thus afflicted when sad *Eve* beheld,	Par Lost 10.863
Or whom he wishes most shall seldom gain	Par Lost 10.901
His counsel whom she had displeas'd, his aide;	Par Lost 10.944
To whom thus *Eve*, recovering heart, repli'd.	Par Lost 10.966
Be meant, whom I conjecture, our grand Foe	Par Lost 10.1033
To whom the Father, without Cloud, serene.	Par Lost 11.45
To whom thus *Eve* with sad demeanour meek.	Par Lost 11.162
But solemn and sublime, whom not to offend,	Par Lost 11.236
Whom thus the Angel interrupted milde.	Par Lost 11.286
To whom thus *Michael* with regard benigne.	Par Lost 11.334
To whom thus *Adam* gratefully repli'd.	Par Lost 11.370
T' whom *Michael* thus, hee also mov'd, repli'd.	Par Lost 11.453
To whom thus *Michael*. Death thou hast seen	Par Lost 11.466
His Image whom they serv'd, a brutish vice,	Par Lost 11.518
The Balme of Life. To whom our Ancestor.	Par Lost 11.546
To whom thus *Michael*. Judg not what is best	Par Lost 11.603
To whom thus *Adam* of short joy bereft.	Par Lost 11.628
His Brother; for of whom such massacher	Par Lost 11.679
But who was that Just Man, whom had not Heav'n	Par Lost 11.681
To whom thus *Michael*. These are the product	Par Lost 11.683
But hee the seventh from thee, whom thou beheldst	Par Lost 11.700
Man is not whom to warne: those few escap't	Par Lost 11.777
To whom thus *Michael*. Those whom last thou sawst	Par Lost 11.787
And fear of God, from whom thir pietie feign'd	Par Lost 11.799
To whom th' Archangel. Dextrously thou aim'st;	Par Lost 11.884
Hee with a crew, whom like Ambition joyns	Par Lost 12.38
To whom thus *Michael*. Justly thou abhorr'st	Par Lost 12.79
From all the rest, of whom to be invok'd,	Par Lost 12.112
Whom *faithful Abraham* due time shall call,	Par Lost 12.152
Pursuing whom he late dismissd, the Sea	Par Lost 12.195
His day, in whom all Nations shall be blest,	Par Lost 12.277
Among whom God will deigne to dwell on Earth	Par Lost 12.281
To whom thus *Michael*. Doubt not but that sin	Par Lost 12.285
But *Joshua* whom the Gentiles *Jesus* call,	Par Lost 12.310

Whom(*cont*)

From whom as oft he saves them penitent	Par Lost 12.319
By Judges first, then under Kings; of whom	Par Lost 12.320
Foretold to *Abraham*, as in whom shall trust	Par Lost 12.328
Thir Lords, whom God dispos'd, the house of God	Par Lost 12.349
To whom thus *Michael*. Dream not of thir fight,	Par Lost 12.386
Or theirs whom he redeems, a death like sleep,	Par Lost 12.434
Powrd first on his Apostles, whom he sends	Par Lost 12.498
Taught this by his example whom I now	Par Lost 12.572
To whom thus also th' Angel last repli'd:	Par Lost 12.574
Nigh Thunder-struck, th' exalted man, to whom	Par Reg 1.36
So to subvert whom he suspected rais'd	Par Reg 1.124
Known partly, and soon found of whom they spake	Par Reg 1.262
Me his beloved Son, in whom alone	Par Reg 1.285
For that to me thou seem'st the man, whom late	Par Reg 1.327
To whom the Son of God. Who brought me hither	Par Reg 1.335
Whom thus answer'd th' Arch Fiend now undisguis'd.	Par Reg 1.357
To see thee and approach thee, whom I know	Par Reg 1.384
To whom our Saviour sternly thus reply'd.	Par Reg 1.406
To whom our Saviour with unalter'd brow.	Par Reg 1.493
Him whom they heard so late expresly call'd	Par Reg 2.3
To find whom at the first they found unsought:	Par Reg 2.59
To whom quick answer Satan thus return'd.	Par Reg 2.172
But he whom we attempt is wiser far	Par Reg 2.205
On whom his leisure will vouchsafe an eye	Par Reg 2.210
To whom thus Jesus; what conclud'st thou hence?	Par Reg 2.317
To whom thus Jesus temperately reply'd:	Par Reg 2.378
To whom thus answer'd Satan malecontent:	Par Reg 2.392
What I might have bestow'd on whom I pleas'd,	Par Reg 2.395
They whom I favour thrive in wealth amain,	Par Reg 2.430
To whom thus Jesus patiently reply'd;	Par Reg 2.432
Great *Julius*, whom now all the world admires	Par Reg 3.39
To whom our Saviour calmly thus reply'd.	Par Reg 3.43
And know not whom, but as one leads the other;	Par Reg 3.53
Of whom to be disprais'd were no small praise?	Par Reg 3.56
Him whom thy wrongs with Saintly patience born,	Par Reg 3.93
To whom the Tempter murmuring thus reply'd.	Par Reg 3.108
To whom our Saviour fervently reply'd.	Par Reg 3.121
Freely; of whom what could he less expect	Par Reg 3.126
Hath nothing, and to whom nothing belongs	Par Reg 3.135
To whom our Saviour answer thus return'd.	Par Reg 3.181
To whom the Tempter inly rackt reply'd.	Par Reg 3.203
To whom our Saviour answer'd thus unmov'd.	Par Reg 3.386
So Satan, whom repulse upon repulse	Par Reg 4.21
To whom the Son of God unmov'd reply'd.	Par Reg 4.109
To whom the Tempter impudent repli'd.	Par Reg 4.154
For giv'n to me, I give to whom I please,	Par Reg 4.164
Whom thus our Saviour answer'd with disdain.	Par Reg 4.170
If given, by whom but by the King of Kings,	Par Reg 4.185
To whom the Fiend with fear abasht reply'd.	Par Reg 4.195
Whom well inspir'd the Oracle pronounc'd	Par Reg 4.275
To whom our Saviour sagely thus repli'd.	Par Reg 4.285
To whom the Fiend now swoln with rage reply'd:	Par Reg 4.499
To whom thus Jesus: also it is written,	Par Reg 4.560
For *Adam* and his chosen Sons, whom thou	Par Reg 4.614
Whom have I to complain of but my self?	Samson 46
Irresistible *Samson?* whom unarm'd	Samson 126
Like whom the Gentiles feign to bear up Heav'n.	Samson 150
Whom long descent of birth	Samson 171
And lorded over them whom now they serve;	Samson 267
Whom God hath of his special favour rais'd	Samson 273
Whom so it pleases him by choice	Samson 311
Alas methinks whom God hath chosen once	Samson 368
Besides whom is no God, compar'd with Idols,	Samson 441
To some *Philistian* Lords, with whom to treat	Samson 482
Whom I by his appointment had provok't,	Samson 643
And now am come to see of whom such noise	Samson 1088
From the unforeskinn'd race, of whom thou bear'st	Samson 1100
Thine or whom I with *Israel*'s Sons adore.	Samson 1177
But I a private person, whom my Countrey	Samson 1208
Whom Patience finally must crown.	Samson 1296
From whom could else a general cry be heard?	Samson 1524
My Countreymen, whom here I knew remaining,	Samson 1549
Man. Relate by whom. *Mess*. By *Samson*. *Man*. That still lessens	Samson 1563
All by him fell thou say'st, by whom fell he,	Samson 1580
Whom therfore she brought up and *Comus* nam'd,	Mask 58
Bridgewater ms 'which'	
Trinity ms 'which', 'whome' written in margin	
Dark vaild *Cotytto*, t' whom the secret flame	Mask 129
Trinity ms 'whome'	
Bridgewater ms 'whome'	
Whom thrift keeps up about his Country gear,	Mask 167
Trinity ms 'whome'	
Bridgewater ms 'whome'	
That he, the Supreme good, t' whom all things ill	Mask 217
Trinity ms 'whome'	
line not in Bridgewater ms	
Whom certain these rough shades did never breed	Mask 266
Trinity ms 'whome'	
Bridgewater ms 'whome'	
Whom lovely *Venus* at a birth	Allegro 14
To win her Grace, whom all commend.	Allegro 124
To whom our vows and wishes bend,	Arcades 6
Trinity ms 'whome'	
Whom with low reverence I adore as mine,	Arcades 37
Trinity ms 'whome'	
Whom Universal nature did lament,	Lycidas 60
Trinity ms 'whome'	

Whom(*cont*)	
To slake his wrath whom sin hath made our foe	Fair Inf 66
Then his *Casella*, whom he woo'd to sing,	Sonnet 13, 13
Then whome a better Senatour nere held	Sonnet 17, 2
1662, 1694 'whom'	
Whom *Joves* great Son to her glad Husband gave,	Sonnet 23, 3
Mine as whom washt from spot of child-bed taint,	Sonnet 23, 5
Pyrrha for whom bindst thou	Horace 3
To whom thou untry'd seem'st fair. Me in my vow'd	Horace 13
(For whom to chuse he knows)	Psalm 4, 16
Upon the Son of Man, whom thou	Psalm 80, 71
And Israel *whom I lov'd so dear*	Psalm 81, 47
Whom thou dost hide and keep.	Psalm 83, 12
The Nations all whom thou hast made	Psalm 86, 29
Whom thou rememberest no more,	Psalm 88, 21
On whom the grave *hath hold*,	Psalm 88, 46
They *fly me now* whom I have lov'd,	Psalm 88, 71
Whom doe we count a good man, whom but he	Prose 10, 1
Whomsoever	
To that false Worm, of whomsoever taught	Par Lost 9.1068
Whore	
To seise the widdow'd whore Pluralitie	Forcers 3
Impudent whoore, where hast thou plac'd thy hope?	Prose 3, 3
Whose	
Of that Forbidden Tree, whose mortal tast	Par Lost 1.2
Th' infernal Serpent; he it was, whose guile	Par Lost 1.34
Of Rebel Angels, by whose aid aspiring	Par Lost 1.38
Of thundring *Aetna*, whose combustible	Par Lost 1.233
Hung on his shoulders like the Moon, whose Orb	Par Lost 1.287
Hath vext the Red-Sea Coast, whose waves orethrew	Par Lost 1.306
To whose bright Image nightly by the Moon	Par Lost 1.440
By that uxorious King, whose heart though large,	Par Lost 1.444
Whose annual wound in *Lebanon* allur'd	Par Lost 1.447
Whose wanton passions in the sacred Porch	Par Lost 1.454
Him follow'd *Rimmon*, whose delightful Seat	Par Lost 1.467
That all these puissant Legions, whose exile	Par Lost 1.632
There stood a Hill not far whose griesly top	Par Lost 1.670
Whose midnight Revels, by a Forrest side	Par Lost 1.782
Precedence, none, whose portion is so small	Par Lost 2.33
With him, or who deceive his mind, whose eye	Par Lost 2.189
Sea-faring men orewatcht, whose Bark by chance	Par Lost 2.288
Heav'n, whose high walls fear no assault or Siege,	Par Lost 2.343
Whose waves of torrent fire inflame with rage.	Par Lost 2.581
Over the dark Abyss, whose boiling Gulf	Par Lost 2.1027
Whose Fountain who shall tell? before the Sun,	Par Lost 3.8
Hee and his faithless Progenie: whose fault?	Par Lost 3.96
Whose but his own? ingrate, he had of mee	Par Lost 3.97
In whose conspicuous count'nance, without cloud	Par Lost 3.385
Of this round World, whose first convex divides	Par Lost 3.419
Whose snowie ridge the roving *Tartar* bounds,	Par Lost 3.432
And that Crystalline Sphear whose ballance weighs	Par Lost 3.482
Look downward on that Globe whose hither side	Par Lost 3.722
Of this new World; at whose sight all the Starrs	Par Lost 4.34
Uriel once warnd; whose eye pursu'd him down	Par Lost 4.125
Of a steep wilderness, whose hairie sides	Par Lost 4.135
Of some rich Burgher, whose substantial dores,	Par Lost 4.189
Groves whose rich Trees wept odorous Gumms and Balme,	Par Lost 4.248
Others whose fruit burnisht with Golden Rinde	Par Lost 4.249
Whose image thou art, him thou shalt enjoy	Par Lost 4.472
Returnd on that bright beam, whose point now raisd	Par Lost 4.590
Whose bed is undefil'd and chaste pronounc't,	Par Lost 4.761
To him who sent us, whose charge is to keep	Par Lost 4.842
Whose dwelling God hath planted here in bliss?	Par Lost 4.884
Whose easier business were to serve thir Lord	Par Lost 4.943
In whose sight all things joy, with ravishment	Par Lost 5.46
Haile Mother of Mankind, whose fruitful Womb	Par Lost 5.388
(Whose praise be ever sung) to man in part	Par Lost 5.405
Who dwell in Heav'n, whose excellence he saw	Par Lost 5.456
Transcend his own so farr, whose radiant forms	Par Lost 5.457
Divine effulgence, whose high Power so far	Par Lost 5.458
Under whose lowly roof thou hast voutsaf't	Par Lost 5.463
Whose progenie you are. Mean while enjoy	Par Lost 5.503
Our maker, and obey him whose command	Par Lost 5.551
Amidst as from a flaming Mount, whose top	Par Lost 5.598
1667 'whoseop', 1668 errata 'whose top'	
Mean while th' Eternal eye, whose sight discernes	Par Lost 5.711
I mean to try, whose Reason I have tri'd	Par Lost 6.120
Whose Eye so superficially surveyes	Par Lost 6.476
From those deep throated Engins belcht, whose roar	Par Lost 6.586
Son in whose face invisible is beheld	Par Lost 6.681
And in whose hand what by Decree I doe,	Par Lost 6.683
Under whose conduct *Michael* soon reduc'd	Par Lost 6.777
Vengeance is his, or whose he sole appoints;	Par Lost 6.808
If rightly thou art call'd, whose Voice divine	Par Lost 7.2
Before his memorie, as one whose drouth	Par Lost 7.66
Whose liquid murmur heard new thirst excites,	Par Lost 7.68
All like himself rebellious, by whose aid	Par Lost 7.140
Glorie to him whose just avenging ire	Par Lost 7.184
Glorie and praise, whose wisdom had ordain'd	Par Lost 7.187
Whose Seed is in her self upon the Earth.	Par Lost 7.312
Brought forth the tender Grass, whose verdure clad	Par Lost 7.315
Walk'd firm; the crested Cock whose clarion sounds	Par Lost 7.443
The silent hours, and th' other whose gay Traine	Par Lost 7.444
A broad and ample rode, whose dust is Gold	Par Lost 7.577
Speed, to describe whose swiftness Number failes.	Par Lost 8.38
Whose vertue on it self workes no effect,	Par Lost 8.95
Whose inward apparition gently mov'd	Par Lost 8.293
A woodie Mountain; whose high top was plaine,	Par Lost 8.303
Whose(*cont*)	
But of the Tree whose operation brings	Par Lost 8.323
And all this good to man, for whose well being	Par Lost 8.361
Whose fellowship therefore unmeet for thee	Par Lost 8.442
Sent from whose sovran goodness I adore.	Par Lost 8.647
Of *Hesperus*, whose Office is to bring	Par Lost 9.49
The Serpent sleeping, in whose mazie foulds	Par Lost 9.161
Each Flour of slender stalk, whose head though gay	Par Lost 9.428
Whose higher intellectual more I shun,	Par Lost 9.483
The credit of whose vertue rest with thee,	Par Lost 9.649
Whose taste, too long forborn, at first assay	Par Lost 9.747
That dwelt within, whose presence had infus'd	Par Lost 9.836
Adam, from whose deare side I boast me sprung,	Par Lost 9.965
Whose vertue, for of good still good proceeds,	Par Lost 9.973
Of *Eve*, whose Eye darted contagious Fire.	Par Lost 9.1036
Some Tree whose broad smooth Leaves together sowd,	Par Lost 9.1095
Whose failing, while her Faith to me remaines,	Par Lost 10.129
And for thee, whose perfection farr excell'd	Par Lost 10.150
Mee not, but the brute Serpent in whose shape	Par Lost 10.495
His full wrauth whose thou feelst as yet lest part,	Par Lost 10.951
Tine the slant Lightning, whose thwart flame driv'n down	Par Lost 10.1075
From his displeasure; in whose look serene,	Par Lost 10.1094
With whose stol'n Fruit Man once more to delude.	Par Lost 11.125
Of Paradise the highest, from whose top	Par Lost 11.378
Guiana, whose great Citie *Geryons* Sons	Par Lost 11.410
To these that sober Race of Men, whose lives	Par Lost 11.621
A Citie and Towre, whose top may reach to Heav'n;	Par Lost 12.44
In time of dearth, a Son whose worthy deeds	Par Lost 12.161
God from the Mount of *Sinai*, whose gray top	Par Lost 12.227
Without Mediator, whose high Office now	Par Lost 12.240
One greater, of whose day he shall foretell,	Par Lost 12.242
Whose foul Idolatries, and other faults	Par Lost 12.337
To that proud Citie, whose high Walls thou saw'st	Par Lost 12.342
Satan, whose fall from Heav'n, a deadlier bruise,	Par Lost 12.391
Eternitie, whose end no eye can reach.	Par Lost 12.556
Thir motion, at whose Front a flaming Sword,	Par Lost 12.592
To him their great Dictator, whose attempt	Par Reg 1.113
Whose constant perseverance overcame	Par Reg 1.148
By whose bright course led on they found the place,	Par Reg 1.252
Or work Redemption for mankind, whose sins	Par Reg 1.266
The Baptist, (of whose birth I oft had heard,	Par Reg 1.270
Me him whose Harbinger he was; and first	Par Reg 1.277
From whose high top to ken the prospect round,	Par Reg 2.286
Whose pains have earn'd the far fet spoil. With that	Par Reg 2.401
Whose off-spring on the Throne of *Juda* sat	Par Reg 2.440
He in whose hand all times and seasons roul.	Par Reg 3.187
(Whose ire I dread more then the fire of Hell)	Par Reg 3.220
It was a Mountain at whose verdant feet	Par Reg 3.253
And seat of *Salmanassar*, whose success	Par Reg 3.278
Against the *Scythian*, whose incursions wild	Par Reg 3.301
Whose off-spring in his Territory yet serve	Par Reg 3.375
Divided by a river, of whose banks	Par Reg 4.32
To *Rome's* great Emperour, whose wide domain	Par Reg 4.81
Who then thou art, whose coming is foretold	Par Reg 4.204
Whose Poem *Phoebus* challeng'd for his own.	Par Reg 4.260
Those antient, whose resistless eloquence	Par Reg 4.268
Wisest of men; from whose mouth issu'd forth	Par Reg 4.276
Whose branching arms thick intertwind might shield	Par Reg 4.405
On the vext Wilderness, whose tallest Pines,	Par Reg 4.416
Over whose heads they rore, and seem to point,	Par Reg 4.463
But thee whose strength, while vertue was her mate,	Samson 173
Whose heads that turbulent liquor fills with fumes.	Samson 552
Whose drink was only from the liquid brook.	Samson 557
To thine whose doors my feet shall never enter.	Samson 950
Soon feel, whose God is strongest, thine or mine.	Samson 1155
Whose ear is ever open; and his eye	Samson 1172
By combat to decide whose god is God,	Samson 1176
Of dire necessity, whose law in death conjoin'd	Samson 1666
But to my task. *Neptune* besides the sway	Mask 18
Trinity ms 'besids' ←'whose'	
The nodding horror of whose shady brows	Mask 38
The daughter of the Sun? Whose charmed Cup	Mask 51
Bridgewater ms 'whoos'	
1637 'whose'	
Trinity ms 'whose'	
El. Bro. Thyrsis? Whose artful strains have oft delaid	Mask 494
Trinity ms 'whose'	
1637 'whose'	
Bridgewater ms 'whose'	
And rifted Rocks whose entrance leads to hell,	Mask 518
With many murmurs mixt, whose pleasing poison	Mask 526
amidst the Hesperian gardens, on whose bancks	Mask Tr. ms 10.05
'on whose bancks' ←'where the banks' ←'on whose bancks'	
& fruits of golden rind, on whose faire tree	Mask Tr. ms 10.08
Mountains on whose barren brest	Allegro 73
With store of Ladies, whose bright eies	Allegro 121
Whose Saintly visage is too bright	Penseroso 13
Whose power hath a true consent	Penseroso 95
Whose lustre leads us, and for her most fit,	Arcades 76
On whose fresh lap the swart Star sparely looks,	Lycidas 138
Whose speed is but the heavy Plummets pace;	On Time 3
Of him, t' whose happy-making sight alone,	On Time 18
To their great Lord, whose love their motion sway'd	Musick 22
Whose chance on these defenceless dores may sease,	Sonnet 8, 2
Harry whose tuneful and well measur'd Song	Sonnet 13, 1
Fairfax, whose name in armes through Europe rings	Sonnet 15, 1
Of hireling wolves whose Gospell is their maw.	Sonnet 16, 14
Avenge O Lord thy slaughter'd Saints, whose bones	Sonnet 18, 1

Whose(*cont*)
Cyriack, whose Grandsire on the Royal Bench — Sonnet 21, 1
line not in Trinity ms
From them whose sin ye envi'd, not abhor'd, — Forcers 4
Men whose Life, Learning, Faith and pure intent — Forcers 9
Whose bounds the Sea doth check. — Psalm 83, 28
Then shall they know that thou whose name — Psalm 83, 65
Happy, whose strength in thee doth bide, — Psalm 84, 19
Whose waies are just and right. — Psalm 84, 44
Whose witnesse and opinion winnes the cause; — Prose 10, 4
And *Kings* be born of thee, whose dredded might — Prose 12, 13
Whoso
That whoso eats thereof, forthwith attains — Par Lost 9.724
Why
What thing thou art, thus double-form'd, and why — Par Lost 2.741
Ambition. Yet why not? som other Power — Par Lost 4.61
Suspicious, reasonless. Why should thir Lord — Par Lost 4.516
Why satst thou like an enemie in waite — Par Lost 4.825
Why ask ye, and superfluous begin — Par Lost 4.832
Why hast thou, *Satan*, broke the bounds prescrib'd — Par Lost 4.878
Why sleepst thou *Eve?* now is the pleasant time, — Par Lost 5.38
Longer thy offerd good, why else set here? — Par Lost 5.63
And why not Gods of Men, since good, the more — Par Lost 5.71
(And if one day, why not Eternal dayes2) — Par Lost 6.424
O Friends, why come not on these Victors proud? — Par Lost 6.609
Why shouldst not thou like sense within thee feel — Par Lost 9.315
Be real, why not known, since easier shunnd? — Par Lost 9.699
Why then was this forbid? Why but to awe, — Par Lost 9.703
Why but to keep ye low and ignorant, — Par Lost 9.704
Why hee should mean me ill, or seek to harme. — Par Lost 9.1152
Being as I am, why didst not thou the Head — Par Lost 9.1155
O Son, why sit we here each other viewing — Par Lost 10.235
Sufficient penaltie, why hast thou added — Par Lost 10.753
O welcom hour whenever! why delayes — Par Lost 10.771
Fixd on this day? why do I overlive, — Par Lost 10.773
Why am I mockt with death, and length'nd out — Par Lost 10.774
Horrid, if true! yet why? it was but breath — Par Lost 10.789
Me now your curse! Ah, why should all mankind — Par Lost 10.822
The day of his offence. Why comes not Death, — Par Lost 10.854
To my just number found. O why did God, — Par Lost 10.888
Why stand we longer shivering under feares, — Par Lost 10.1003
Why else this double object in our sight — Par Lost 11.201
One way the self-same hour? why in the East — Par Lost 11.203
Better end heer unborn. Why is life giv'n — Par Lost 11.502
To be thus wrested from us? rather why — Par Lost 11.503
Under inhuman pains? Why should not Man, — Par Lost 11.511
This yet I apprehend not, why to those — Par Lost 12.280
Why our great expectation should be call'd — Par Lost 12.378
Why dost thou then suggest to me distrust, — Par Reg 1.355
To all mankind: why should I? they to me — Par Reg 1.388
The giver, answer'd Jesus. Why should that — Par Reg 2.322
Why shouldst thou then obtrude this diligence, — Par Reg 2.387
Why shouldst thou not accept it? but I see — Par Reg 2.398
And for thy reason why they should be sought, — Par Reg 2.485
But why should man seek glory? who of his own — Par Reg 3.134
My everlasting Kingdom, why art thou — Par Reg 3.199
Why move thy feet so slow to what is best, — Par Reg 3.224
Why was my breeding order'd and prescrib'd — Samson 30
Why am I thus bereav'd thy prime decree? — Samson 85
She all in every part; why was the sight — Samson 93
Are come upon him his deserts? yet why? — Samson 205
Why thou shouldst wed *Philistian* women rather — Samson 216
Why are his gifts desirable, to tempt — Samson 358
And I perswade me so; why else this strength — Samson 586
Why then reveal'd? I was assur'd by those — Samson 800
Yet now am judg'd an enemy. Why then — Samson 882
Why do I humble thus my self, and suing — Samson 965
And listen why, for I will tell ye now — Mask 43
But where they are, and why they came not back, — Mask 191
Bridgewater ms 'whye'
Why shouldst thou, but for som fellonious end, — Mask 196
line not in Bridgewater ms
Co. By falshood, or discourtesie, or why? — Mask 281
And crumble all thy sinews. *Eld. Bro*. Why prethee Shepherd — Mask 615
Bridgewater ms 'why'
Trinity ms 'why'
Co. Why are you vext Lady? why do you frown? — Mask 666
Bridgewater ms 'Whye'
Why should you be so cruel to your self, — Mask 679
line not in Bridgewater ms
Why fled the Ocean? And why skipt the Mountains? — Psalm 114, 13
Why turned *Jordan* toward his Crystall Fountains? — Psalm 114, 14
And why from us so quickly thou didst take thy flight. — Fair Inf 42
But oh why didst thou not stay here below — Fair Inf 64
For my relief; yet hadst no reason why, — Sonnet 1, 12
End Green. Why is it harder Sirs then Gordon, — Sonnet 11, 8
Why do the Gentiles tumult, and the Nations — Psalm 2, 1
Why hast thou laid her Hedges low — Psalm 80, 49
Why wilt thou Lord my soul forsake, — Psalm 88, 57
Wicked
Single against thee wicked, and thence weak. — Par Lost 4.856
These wicked Tents devoted, least the wrauth — Par Lost 5.890
Thou and thy wicked crew; there mingle broiles, — Par Lost 6.277
Or violence, hee of thir wicked wayes — Par Lost 11.812
Of wicked Sons destroyd, then I rejoyce — Par Lost 11.875
And vengeance to the wicked, at return — Par Lost 12.541
Committing to a wicked Favourite — Par Reg 4.95
Take to thy wicked deed: which when thou seest — Samson 826

Wicked(*cont*)
His errand on the wicked, who surpris'd — Samson 1285
In counsel of the wicked, and ith' way — Psalm 1, 2
Not so the wicked, but as chaff which fann'd — Psalm 1, 11
The wind drives, so the wicked shall not stand — Psalm 1, 12
Favouring the wicked *by your might*. — Psalm 82, 7
Of wicked men the low estate — Psalm 82, 15
This *wicked* earth redress, — Psalm 82, 26
Then an unjust and wicked King — Prose 11, 3
Wickedness
Of wickedness, wherein shall dwell his Race — Par Lost 11.608
All wickedness is weakness: that plea therefore — Samson 834
In wickedness delight — Psalm 5, 10
Or done this, if wickedness — Psalm 7, 8
Of evil men the wickedness — Psalm 7, 35
Wicker
Though a rush Candle from the wicker hole — Mask 338
Wicket
And now Saint *Peter* at Heav'ns Wicket seems — Par Lost 3.484
Wide
Op'ning thir brazen foulds discover wide — Par Lost 1.724
And Porches wide, but chief the spacious Hall — Par Lost 1.762
Scout farr and wide into the Realm of night, — Par Lost 2.133
In the wide womb of uncreated night, — Par Lost 2.150
Wide gaping, and with utter loss of being — Par Lost 2.440
Heard farr and wide, and all the host of Hell — Par Lost 2.519
On bold adventure to discover wide — Par Lost 2.571
Through the wide *Ethiopian* to the Cape — Par Lost 2.641
With wide *Cerberian* mouths full loud, and rung — Par Lost 2.655
Threw forth, till on the left side op'ning wide, — Par Lost 2.755
Excel'd her power; the Gates wide op'n stood, — Par Lost 2.884
So wide they stood, and like a Furnace mouth — Par Lost 2.888
Wide on the wasteful Deep; with him Enthron'd — Par Lost 2.961
Your dungeon stretching far and wide beneath; — Par Lost 2.1003
Farr off th' Empyreal Heav'n, extended wide — Par Lost 2.1047
Wide interrupt can hold; so bent he seems — Par Lost 3.84
A passage down to th' Earth, a passage wide, — Par Lost 3.528
So wide the op'ning seemd, where bounds were set — Par Lost 3.538
Undazl'd, farr and wide his eye commands, — Par Lost 3.614
Still threatning to devour me opens wide, — Par Lost 4.77
A whole days journy high, but wide remote — Par Lost 4.284
See farr and wide: in at this Gate none pass — Par Lost 4.579
The Earth outstretcht immense, a prospect wide — Par Lost 5.88
Discovering in wide Lantskip all the East — Par Lost 5.142
Of Heav'n arriv'd, the gate self-opend wide — Par Lost 5.254
The circuit wide. Strait knew him all the Bands — Par Lost 5.287
Wide over all the Plain, and wider farr — Par Lost 5.648
Through Heav'ns wide Champain held his way, till Morn, — Par Lost 6.2
Of *Tartarus*, which ready opens wide — Par Lost 6.54
Of Heav'n they march'd, and many a Province wide — Par Lost 6.77
Were don, but infinite: for wide was spred — Par Lost 6.241
Wide wasting; such destruction to withstand — Par Lost 6.253
Wide the Celestial soile, and saw beneath — Par Lost 6.510
With hideous orifice gap't on us wide, — Par Lost 6.577
Illustrious farr and wide, but by his own — Par Lost 6.773
And Chrystal wall of Heav'n, which op'ning wide, — Par Lost 6.860
All space, the ambient Aire wide interfus'd — Par Lost 7.89
Though wide, and this high Temple to frequent — Par Lost 7.148
Attendant on thir Lord: Heav'n op'nd wide — Par Lost 7.205
Built on circumfluous Waters calme, in wide — Par Lost 7.270
But they, or under ground, or circuit wide — Par Lost 7.301
That open'd wide her blazing Portals, led — Par Lost 7.575
His laughter at thir quaint Opinions wide — Par Lost 8.78
And for the Heav'ns wide Circuit, let it speak — Par Lost 8.100
Sent from her through the wide transpicuous aire, — Par Lost 8.141
A Circuit wide, enclos'd, with goodliest Trees — Par Lost 8.304
And Life-blood streaming fresh; wide was the wound, — Par Lost 8.467
In wo then; that destruction wide may range: — Par Lost 9.134
The hands dispatch of two Gardning so wide. — Par Lost 9.203
Will keep from Wilderness with ease, as wide — Par Lost 9.245
Stood open wide, belching outrageous flame — Par Lost 10.232
His Nostril wide into the murkie Air, — Par Lost 10.280
Wide Anarchie of *Chaos* damp and dark — Par Lost 10.283
Wide open and unguarded, *Satan* pass'd, — Par Lost 10.419
Through Heav'ns wide bounds; from them I will not hide — Par Lost 11.68
Wide waving, all approach farr off to fright, — Par Lost 11.121
He lookd and saw wide Territorie spred — Par Lost 11.638
Wide hovering, all the Clouds together drove — Par Lost 11.739
And the cleer Sun on his wide watrie Glass — Par Lost 11.844
In the wide Wilderness, there they shall found — Par Lost 12.224
With earths wide bounds, his glory with the Heav'ns. — Par Lost 12.371
O ancient Powers of Air and this wide world, — Par Reg 1.44
Of many a pleasant Realm and Province wide. — Par Reg 1.118
Is to be found, in the wide Wilderness; — Par Reg 2.232
Of Fairy Damsels met in Forest wide — Par Reg 2.359
By Conquest far and wide, to over-run — Par Reg 3.72
A spatious plain out stretch't in circuit wide — Par Reg 3.254
Such forces met not, nor so wide a camp, — Par Reg 3.337
Another plain, long but in bredth not wide; — Par Reg 4.27
To *Rome*'s great Emperour, whose wide domain — Par Reg 4.81
Dingle, or bushy dell of this wilde Wood, — Mask 312
Trinity ms 'wide', 'wild' written in margin
Bridgewater ms 'wide'
Uninjur'd in this wilde surrounding wast. — Mask 403
Bridgewater ms 'wide'
Trinity ms 'wide surrounding wast' ← 'vast, & hideous wild'
Through this gloomy covert wide, — Mask 945
halfe his wast flood the wide Atlantique fills — Mask Tr. ms 10.14

Wide(*cont*)
Shallow Brooks, and Rivers wide. Allegro 76
Through the Heav'ns wide pathles way; Penseroso 70
And waving wide her mirtle wand, Nativity 51
Will open wide the Gates of her high Palace Hall. Nativity 148
And mistie Regions of wide air next under, Vacation 41
E're half my days, in this dark world and wide, Sonnet 19, 2
And *upward* to that river *wide* Psalm 80, 47
Brutus far to the West, in th' Ocean wide Prose 12, 7
Wide-encroaching
Ophion with *Eurynome*, the wide- Par Lost 10.581
Encroaching *Eve* perhaps, had first the rule Par Lost 10.582
Wider
Wider by farr then that of after-times Par Lost 3.529
Wide over all the Plain, and wider farr Par Lost 5.648
Not higher that Hill nor wider looking round, Par Lost 11.381
Widest
To entertain you two, her widest Gates, Par Lost 4.382
Wide-wasting
Marasmus, and wide-wasting Pestilence, Par Lost 11.487
line not in 1667 edition
Wide-watered
Over som wide-water'd shoar, Penseroso 75
Widowed
Wailing thy absence in my widow'd bed; Samson 806
To seise the widdow'd whore Pluralitie Forcers 3
Trinity ms 'widow'd' ←'vacant'
Widowhood
Cherish thy hast'n'd widowhood with the gold Samson 958
Wield
On either side, the least of whom could weild Par Lost 6.221
And calculate the Starrs, how they will weild Par Lost 8.80
Part wield thir Arms, part courb the foaming Steed, Par Lost 11.643
And weild their little tridents, but this Ile Mask 27
Wielded
Wielded at will that fierce Democratie, Par Reg 4.269
Wife
Father and Mother, and to his Wife adhere; Par Lost 8.498
The Wife, where danger or dishonour lurks, Par Lost 9.267
The thickest Trees, both Man and Wife, till God Par Lost 10.101
Because thou hast heark'nd to the voice of thy Wife, Par Lost 10.198
Though *Adam* by his Wives allurement fell, Par Reg 2.134
She proving false, the next I took to Wife Samson 227
Then *Dalila* thy wife. Samson 724
Sam. My Wife, my Traytress, let her not come near me. Samson 725
Being once a wife, for me thou wast to leave Samson 885
I chose a Wife, which argu'd me no foe; Samson 1193
Not that *Nepenthes* which the wife of *Thone*, Mask 675
And who had *Canace* to wife, Penseroso 112
The honour'd Wife of *Winchester*, Winchester 2
Wight
All taste of living wight, as once it fled Par Lost 2.613
Oh say me true if thou wert mortal wight Fair Inf 41
Of labours huge and hard, too hard for human wight. Passion 14
Wild
The dismal Situation waste and wilde, Par Lost 1.60
Seest thou yon dreary Plain, forlorn and wilde, Par Lost 1.180
From *Aroar* to *Nebo*, and the wild Par Lost 1.407
In whirlwind; Hell scarce holds the wilde uproar. Par Lost 2.541
Lies dark and wilde, beat with perpetual storms Par Lost 2.588
Chance governs all. Into this wilde Abyss, Par Lost 2.910
Into this wild Abyss the warie fiend Par Lost 2.917
1667 'wilde'
At length a universal hubbub wilde Par Lost 2.951
Into the wilde expanse, and through the shock Par Lost 2.1014
Dark, waste, and wild, under the frown of Night Par Lost 3.424
Confusion heard his voice, and wilde uproar Par Lost 3.710
With thicket overgrown, grottesque and wilde, Par Lost 4.136
All Beasts of th' Earth, since wilde, and of all chase Par Lost 4.341
Wilde work produces oft, and most in dreams, Par Lost 5.112
Wilde above Rule or Art; enormous bliss. Par Lost 5.297
As yet this world was not, and *Chaos* wilde Par Lost 5.577
Somwhat extravagant and wilde, perhaps Par Lost 6.616
Wild work in Heav'n, and dangerous to the maine. Par Lost 6.698
Through his wilde Anarchie, so huge a rout Par Lost 6.873
Of that wilde Rout that tore the *Thracian* Bard Par Lost 7.34
1669 'wild'
Outrageous as a Sea, dark, wasteful, wilde, Par Lost 7.212
As from his Laire the wilde Beast where he wonns Par Lost 7.457
In Forrest wilde, in Thicket, Brake, or Den; Par Lost 7.458
Tending to wilde. Thou therefore now advise Par Lost 9.212
In this enclosure wild, these Beasts among, Par Lost 9.543
To live again in these wilde Woods forlorn? Par Lost 9.910
With featherd Cincture, naked else and wilde Par Lost 9.1117
Of unoriginal *Night* and *Chaos* wilde, Par Lost 10.477
And wilde, how shall we breath in other Aire Par Lost 11.284
Through the wilde Desert, not the readiest way, Par Lost 12.216
He entred now the bordering Desert wild, Par Reg 1.193
Among wild Beasts: they at his sight grew mild, Par Reg 1.310
Who dwell this wild, constrain'd by want, come forth Par Reg 1.331
And now wild Beasts came forth the woods to roam. Par Reg 1.502
The while her Son tracing the Desert wild, Par Reg 2.109
In this wild solitude so long should bide Par Reg 2.304
Against the *Scythian*, whose incursions wild Par Reg 3.301
And follow'd thee still on to this wast wild; Par Reg 4.523
No strength of man, or fiercest wild beast could withstand; Samson 127
Bears greatest names in his wild aerie flight. Samson 974
Of chaf't wild Boars, or ruffl'd Porcupines. Samson 1138

Wild(*cont*)
Like a wild Beast, I am content to go. Samson 1403
Well knows to still the wilde winds when they roar, Mask 87
Trinity ms 'wild'
1637 'wild'
Bridgewater ms 'wild'
Dingle, or bushy dell of this wilde Wood, Mask 312
1637 'wild'
Trinity ms 'wide', 'wild' written in margin
Bridgewater ms 'wide'
From the chill dew, amongst rude burrs and thistles? Mask 352
Trinity ms 'amoungst rude burrs & thistles' ←'in this surrounding wilde' ←'in this dead solitude'
What if in wild amazement, and affright, Mask 356
Uninjur'd in this wilde surrounding wast. Mask 403
Bridgewater ms 'wide'
Trinity ms 'wide surrounding wast' ←'vast, & hideous wild'
1637 'wild'
Warble his native Wood-notes wilde, Allegro 134
With wilde Thyme and the gadding Vine o'regrown, Lycidas 40
1638 'wild'
Trinity ms 'wild'
It was the Winter wilde, Nativity 29
And wisely learn to curb thy sorrows wild; Fair Inf 73
Take up a weeping on the Mountains wilde, Passion 51
Wild Beasts there brouze, and make their food Psalm 80, 55
Wilderness
As when a Gryfon through the Wilderness Par Lost 2.943
Of a steep wilderness, whose hairie sides Par Lost 4.135
In Wood or Wilderness, Forrest or Den; Par Lost 4.342
A Wilderness of sweets; for Nature here Par Lost 5.294
Will keep from Wilderness with ease, as wide Par Lost 9.245
Our second *Adam* in the Wilderness, Par Lost 11.383
In the wide Wilderness, there they shall found Par Lost 12.224
Through the worlds wilderness long wanderd man Par Lost 12.313
And *Eden* rais'd in the wast Wilderness. Par Reg 1.7
To exercise him in the Wilderness, Par Reg 1.156
Into this Wilderness, to what intent Par Reg 1.291
Is to be found, in the wide Wilderness; Par Reg 2.232
As story tells, have trod this Wilderness; Par Reg 2.307
Command a Table in this Wilderness, Par Reg 2.384
In savage Wilderness, wherefore deprive Par Reg 3.23
What dost thou in this World? the Wilderness Par Reg 4.372
Not yet expir'd) and to the Wilderness Par Reg 4.395
On the vext Wilderness, whose tallest Pines, Par Reg 4.416
Over the Wilderness and o're the Plain; Par Reg 4.543
Wandring the Wilderness, whatever place, Par Reg 4.600
In the wastfull Wildernes. Psalm 136, 58
1673 'Wilderness'
Wildernesses
On Sands, and Shoars, and desert Wildernesses. Mask 209
Trinity ms 'wildernesses'
line not in Bridgewater ms
Wilds
Infamous Hills, and sandy perilous wildes, Mask 424
Trinity ms 'wilds'
1637 'wilds'
Wile
Through the force, and through the wile Mask 906
Wiles
My sentence is for open Warr: Of Wiles, Par Lost 2.51
Then wise to frustrate all our plots and wiles. Par Lost 2.193
Most opportune might serve his Wiles, and found Par Lost 9.85
His head the midst, well stor'd with suttle wiles: Par Lost 9.184
Whatever wiles of Foe or seeming Friend. Par Lost 10.11
In all his wiles, defeated and repuls't, Par Reg 1.6
His easie steps; girded with snaky wiles, Par Reg 1.120
But to vanquish by wisdom hellish wiles. Par Reg 1.175
At length collecting all his Serpent wiles, Par Reg 3.5
Made answer meet, that made void all his wiles. Par Reg 3.442
Yet the fourth time, when mustring all her wiles, Samson 402
Sam. I thought where all thy circling wiles would end; Samson 871
Quips and Cranks, and wanton Wiles, Allegro 27
Wilful
Against our selves, and wilful barrenness, Par Lost 10.1042
Who for my wilful crime art banisht hence. Par Lost 12.619
be it not don in pride or in praesumption Mask Tr. ms 16.56
'or in praesumption' ←'or wilfull tempting'
Wilfully
Least wilfully transgressing he pretend Par Lost 5.244
Not wilfully mis-doing, but unware Par Reg 1.225
Will
To do ought good never will be our task, Par Lost 1.159
Here for his envy, will not drive us hence: Par Lost 1.260
Thir surest signal, they will soon resume Par Lost 1.278
Celestial vertues rising, will appear Par Lost 2.15
Will envy whom the highest place exposes Par Lost 2.27
From Faction; for none sure will claim in Hell Par Lost 2.32
Will covet more. With this advantage then Par Lost 2.35
Will either quite consume us, and reduce Par Lost 2.96
Can give it, or will ever? how he can Par Lost 2.153
Is doubtful; that he never will is sure. Par Lost 2.154
Will he, so wise, let loose at once his ire, Par Lost 2.155
Will slack'n, if his breath stir not thir flames. Par Lost 2.214
Our purer essence then will overcome Par Lost 2.215
In temper and in nature, will receive Par Lost 2.218
This horror will grow milde, this darkness light, Par Lost 2.220
Of servile Pomp. Our greatness will appeer Par Lost 2.257

Will(*cont*)
In heighth or depth, still first and last will Reign Par Lost 2.324
Voutsaf't or sought; for what peace will be giv'n Par Lost 2.332
Nor will occasion want, nor shall we need Par Lost 2.341
Will once more lift us up, in spight of Fate, Par Lost 2.393
His wrath which one day will destroy ye both. Par Lost 2.734
Keep residence; if all I can will serve, Par Lost 2.999
For man will hark'n to his glozing lyes, Par Lost 3.93
Sole pledge of his obedience: So will fall, Par Lost 3.95
Man shall not quite be lost, but sav'd who will, Par Lost 3.173
Freely voutsaft; once more I will renew Par Lost 3.175
Invites; for I will cleer thir senses dark, Par Lost 3.188
And I will place within them as a guide Par Lost 3.194
My Umpire *Conscience*, whom if they will hear, Par Lost 3.195
Which of ye will be mortal to redeem Par Lost 3.214
Account mee man; I for his sake will leave Par Lost 3.238
By thee, and more then half perhaps will reigne; Par Lost 4.112
Will vanish and deliver ye to woe, Par Lost 4.368
And send forth all her Kings; there will be room, Par Lost 4.383
And I will bring thee where no shadow staies Par Lost 4.470
Thir ruine! Hence I will excite thir minds Par Lost 4.522
Or all at once; more glorie will be wonn, Par Lost 4.853
Will save us trial what the least can doe Par Lost 4.855
Forbid who will, none shall from me withhold Par Lost 5.62
To us perhaps he brings, and will voutsafe Par Lost 5.312
Of God inspir'd, small store will serve, where store, Par Lost 5.322
But I will haste and from each bough and break, Par Lost 5.326
Each Plant and juciest Gourd will pluck such choice Par Lost 5.327
Willing or no, who will but what they must Par Lost 5.533
Will ye submit your necks, and chuse to bend Par Lost 5.787
The supple knee? ye will not, if I trust Par Lost 5.788
Will not be now voutsaf't, other Decrees Par Lost 5.884
Due search and consultation will disclose. Par Lost 6.445
Whom fled we thought, will save us long pursuit Par Lost 6.538
Born eevn or high, for this day will pour down, Par Lost 6.544
Endless, and no solution will be found: Par Lost 6.694
And longer will delay to heare thee tell Par Lost 7.101
Haste to thy audience, Night with her will bring Par Lost 7.105
Silence, and Sleep listning to thee will watch, Par Lost 7.106
Self-lost, and in a moment will create Par Lost 7.154
Open, and henceforth oft; for God will deigne Par Lost 7.569
Thither will send his winged Messengers Par Lost 7.572
And calculate the Starrs, how they will weild Par Lost 8.80
The more she will acknowledge thee her Head, Par Lost 8.574
For whom all this was made, all this will soon Par Lost 9.132
But what will not Ambition and Revenge Par Lost 9.168
Will keep from Wilderness with ease, as wide Par Lost 9.245
The Enemie, though bold, will hardly dare, Par Lost 9.304
Thou sever not: Trial will come unsought. Par Lost 9.366
A Foe so proud will first the weaker seek, Par Lost 9.383
Is open? or will God incense his ire Par Lost 9.692
Deitie for thee, when Fate will not permit. Par Lost 9.885
Though threatning, will in earnest so destroy Par Lost 9.939
He ruind, now Mankind; whom will he next? Par Lost 9.950
Will dazle now this earthly, with thir blaze Par Lost 9.1083
Lets her will rule; restraint she will not brook, Par Lost 9.1184
Shee first his weak indulgence will accuse. Par Lost 9.1186
Between Thee and the Woman I will put Par Lost 10.179
Thy sorrow I will greatly multiplie Par Lost 10.193
Is enmity, which he will put between Par Lost 10.497
My own deservings; but this will not serve; Par Lost 10.727
The evil on him brought by me, will curse Par Lost 10.734
Of weakness, not of Power. Will he, draw out, Par Lost 10.801
And to the place of judgment will return, Par Lost 10.932
Will prove no sudden, but a slow-pac't evill, Par Lost 10.963
Living or dying, from thee I will not hide Par Lost 10.974
So snatcht will not exempt us from the paine Par Lost 10.1025
Of contumacie will provoke the highest Par Lost 10.1027
Would be revenge indeed; which will be lost Par Lost 10.1036
My labour will sustain me; and least Cold Par Lost 10.1056
How much more, if we pray him, will his ear Par Lost 10.1060
Hee will instruct us praying, and of Grace Par Lost 10.1081
Undoubtedly he will relent and turn Par Lost 10.1093
Through Heav'ns wide bounds; from them I will not hide Par Lost 11.68
Hard to belief may seem; yet this will Prayer, Par Lost 11.146
Of us will soon determin, or impose Par Lost 11.227
That never will in other Climate grow, Par Lost 11.274
God is as here, and will be found alike Par Lost 11.350
Will be aveng'd, and th' others Faith approv'd Par Lost 11.458
Thy youth, thy strength, thy beauty, which will change Par Lost 11.539
Hopeful and cheerful, in thy blood will reigne Par Lost 11.543
Famin and anguish will at last consume Par Lost 11.778
And whether here the Race of man will end. Par Lost 11.786
Over the Earth a Cloud, will therein set Par Lost 11.896
Henceforth what is to com I will relate, Par Lost 12.11
Will arrogate Dominion undeserv'd Par Lost 12.27
Will he convey up thither to sustain Par Lost 12.75
Above the Clouds will pine his entrails gross, Par Lost 12.77
Yet somtimes Nations will decline so low Par Lost 12.97
Thus will this latter, as the former World, Par Lost 12.105
Which he will shew him, and from him will raise Par Lost 12.123
Such wondrous power God to his Saint will lend, Par Lost 12.200
All night he will pursue, but his approach Par Lost 12.206
God looking forth will trouble all his Host Par Lost 12.209
Shall tremble, he descending, will himself Par Lost 12.228
Among whom God will deigne to dwell on Earth Par Lost 12.281
Will reign among them, as of thee begot; Par Lost 12.286
Heapt to the popular summe, will so incense Par Lost 12.338

Will(*cont*)
And due to theirs which out of thine will grow: Par Lost 12.400
Must reascend, what will betide the few Par Lost 12.480
His people, who defend? will they not deale Par Lost 12.483
Be sure they will, said th' Angel; but from Heav'n Par Lost 12.485
Hee to his own a Comforter will send, Par Lost 12.486
Shall on the heart engrave. What will they then Par Lost 12.524
Infallible? yet many will presume: Par Lost 12.530
Well deem in outward Rites and specious formes Par Lost 12.534
1667 'Will'
That ye may live, which will be many dayes, Par Lost 12.602
In manner at our will th' affairs of Earth, Par Reg 1.50
And what will he not do to advance his Son? Par Reg 1.88
Will waft me; and the way found prosperous once Par Reg 1.104
Will bring me hence, no other Guide I seek. Par Reg 1.336
Into the World, to teach his final will, Par Reg 1.461
Hath rapt him from us? will he now retire Par Reg 2.40
Lay on his Providence; he will not fail Par Reg 2.54
Nor will withdraw him now, nor will recall, Par Reg 2.55
I will not argue that, nor will repine. Par Reg 2.94
At will the manliest, resolutest brest, Par Reg 2.167
Of greatest things; what woman will you find, Par Reg 2.208
On whom his leisure will vouchsafe an eye Par Reg 2.210
Where will this end? four times ten days I have pass'd Par Reg 2.245
Mee hungring more to do my Fathers will. Par Reg 2.259
I can at will, doubt not, as soon as thou, Par Reg 2.383
Of these things others quickly will dispose Par Reg 2.400
Them he himself to glory will advance. Par Reg 3.144
Be now in powerful hands, that will not part Par Reg 3.155
And my promotion will be thy destruction? Par Reg 3.202
And will alike be punish'd; whether thou Par Reg 3.214
The wisest, unexperienc't, will be ever Par Reg 3.240
But I will bring thee where thou soon shalt quit Par Reg 3.244
Will unpredict and fail me of the Throne: Par Reg 3.395
Still will be tempting him who foyls him still, Par Reg 4.13
Will be for thee no sitting, or not long Par Reg 4.107
On *David*'s Throne, be propheci'd what will. Par Reg 4.108
Nothing will please the difficult and nice, Par Reg 4.157
Wielded at will that fierce Democratie, Par Reg 4.269
These rules will render thee a King compleat Par Reg 4.283
Will far be found unworthy to compare Par Reg 4.346
And thither will return thee, yet remember Par Reg 4.374
Mee to thy will; desist, thou art discern'd Par Reg 4.497
Will ask thee skill; I to thy Fathers house Par Reg 4.552
For it is written, He will give command Par Reg 4.556
He never more henceforth will dare set foot Par Reg 4.610
That she might look at will through every pore? Samson 97
Will not connive, or linger, thus provok'd, Samson 466
But will arise and his great name assert: Samson 467
Nothing more certain, will not long defer Samson 474
Against all competition, nor will long Samson 476
God will relent, and quit thee all his debt; Samson 509
With God or Man will gain thee no remission. Samson 835
I to the Lords will intercede, not doubting Samson 920
When I must live uxorious to thy will Samson 945
I only with an Oak'n staff will meet thee, Samson 1123
He will accept thee to defend his cause, Samson 1179
To fight with thee no man of arms will deign. Samson 1226
Chor. He will directly to the Lords, I fear, Samson 1250
Will not dare mention, lest a question rise Samson 1254
But come what will, my deadliest foe will prove Samson 1262
His message will be short and voluble. Samson 1307
Where I will see thee heartn'd and fresh clad Samson 1317
Off. This answer, be assur'd, will not content them. Samson 1322
Return the way thou cam'st, I will not come. Samson 1332
Off. Regard thy self, this will offend them highly. Samson 1333
Will condescend to such absurd commands? Samson 1337
Joyn'd with extream contempt? I will not come. Samson 1342
Off. I am sorry what this stoutness will produce. Samson 1346
I with this Messenger will go along, Samson 1384
This day will be remarkable in my life Samson 1388
And for a life who will not change his purpose? Samson 1406
I will not wish, lest it perhaps offend them Samson 1414
And numbers thither flock, I had no will, Samson 1450
God will restore him eye-sight to his strength. Samson 1503
The sufferers then will scarce molest us here, Samson 1525
Man. He can I know, but doubt to think he will; Samson 1534
A little stay will bring some notice hither, Samson 1536
To utter what will come at last too soon; Samson 1566
Will send for all my kindred, all my friends Samson 1730
Home to his Fathers house: there will I build him Samson 1733
And listen why, for I will tell ye now Mask 43
Which these dun shades will ne're report. Mask 127
Danger will wink on Opportunity, Mask 401
Will dare to soyl her Virgin purity, Mask 427
Trinity ms 'will' ←'shall'
Against th' opposing will and arm of Heav'n Mask 600
(As I will give you when we go) you may Mask 648
Yet will they soon retire, if he but shrink. Mask 656
This will restore all soon. *La*. 'Twill not false traitor, Mask 690
Trinity ms 't'will not' ←'stand back'
Bridgewater ms 't'will'
1637 'T'will'
'Twill not restore the truth and honesty Mask 691
1637 'T'will'
Bridgewater ms 'twill'
Trinity ms 't'will'
And cheeks of sorry grain will serve to ply Mask 750

Will(*cont*)
line not in Bridgewater ms
But this will cure all streight, one sip of this Mask 811
Will bathe the drooping spirits in delight Mask 812
For maid'nhood she loves, and will be swift Mask 855
Bridgewater ms 'wilbe'
In hard besetting need, this will I try Mask 857
Will double all their mirth and chere; Mask 955
The up-land Hamlets will invite, Allegro 92
'Less *Philomel* will daign a Song, Penseroso 56
Or if the Ayr will not permit, Penseroso 77
Som still removed place will fit, Penseroso 78
And I with thee will choose to live. Penseroso 176
And with all helpful service will comply Arcades 38
I will assay, her worth to celebrate, Arcades 80
I will bring you where she sits, Arcades 91
And will not take their flight, Nativity 72
Time will run back, and fetch the age of gold, Nativity 135
Will sicken soon and die, Nativity 137
And leprous sin will melt from earthly mould, Nativity 138
And Hell it self will pass away, Nativity 139
Will down return to men, Nativity 142
And Mercy set between, Nativity 144
1673 'Mercy will sit between'
Will open wide the Gates of her high Palace Hall. Nativity 148
This if thou do he will an off-spring give, Fair Inf 76
Will pierce more neer his heart. Circum 28
Trinity ms 'will' ←'Shall' ←'will'
Portend success in love; O if *Jove*'s will Sonnet 1, 7
Toward which Time leads me, and the will of Heav'n; Sonnet 7, 12
From the hard Season gaining: time will run Sonnet 20, 5
Against heavns hand or will, nor bate a jot Sonnet 22, 7
1694 'Will'
I will declare; the Lord to me hath say'd Psalm 2, 14
Great ones how long will ye Psalm 4, 7
Will hear my voyce what time to him I crie. Psalm 4, 18
Who yet will shew us good? Psalm 4, 26
In peace at once will I Psalm 4, 37
Will rank my Prayers, and watch till thou appear. Psalm 5, 8
But I will in thy mercies dear Psalm 5, 17
Will towards thy holy temple worship low Psalm 5, 20
Him with thy lasting favour and good will. Psalm 5, 40
The Lord will own, and have me in his keeping. Psalm 6, 20
Will surround thee, seeking right, Psalm 7, 26
If th' unjust will not forbear, Psalm 7, 45
Of violence will undelay'd Psalm 7, 59
Then will I Jehovah's praise Psalm 7, 61
Will grant thy full demand. Psalm 81, 44
Then did I leave them to their will Psalm 81, 49
How long will ye pervert the right Psalm 82, 5
They know not nor will understand, Psalm 82, 17
Gods houses, and *will now invade* Psalm 83, 47
And now what God the Lord will speak Psalm 85, 29
I will *go strait and* hear, Psalm 85, 30
To his dear Saints he will speak peace, Psalm 85, 33
The Lord will also then bestow Psalm 85, 49
Then will he come, and not be slow Psalm 85, 55
Will call on thee *for aid;* Psalm 86, 22
I in thy truth will bide, Psalm 86, 38
Thee will I praise O Lord my God Psalm 86, 41
This was that gift (if you the truth will have) Prose 4, 3
Which he who can, and will, deserv's high praise, Prose 9, 3
Who neither can nor will, may hold his peace; Prose 9, 4
Goddess of Shades, and Huntress, who at will Prose 12, 1

Will
From thir Creator, and transgress his Will Par Lost 1.31
ms 'will'
All is not lost; the unconquerable Will, Par Lost 1.106
ms 'will'
As being the contrary to his high will Par Lost 1.161
Had ris'n or heav'd his head, but that the will Par Lost 1.211
Can give it, or will ever? how he can Par Lost 2.153
Is doubtful; that he never will is sure. Par Lost 2.154
The Victors will. To suffer, as to doe, Par Lost 2.199
Of him who rules above; so was his will Par Lost 2.351
Of Providence, Foreknowledge, Will and Fate, Par Lost 2.559
Fixt Fate, free will, foreknowledg absolute, Par Lost 2.560
Following his track, such was the will of Heav'n, Par Lost 2.1025
When Will and Reason (Reason also is choice) Par Lost 3.108
Thir will, dispos'd by absolute Decree Par Lost 3.115
Man shall not quite be lost, but sav'd who will, Par Lost 3.173
Yet not of will in him, but grace in me Par Lost 3.174
Elect above the rest; so is my will: Par Lost 3.184
Glad to be offer'd, he attends the will Par Lost 3.270
The first art wont his great authentic will Par Lost 3.656
By his permissive will, through Heav'n and Earth: Par Lost 3.685
Hadst thou the same free Will and Power to stand? Par Lost 4.66
Nay curs'd be thou; since against his thy will Par Lost 4.71
His will who bound us? let him surer barr Par Lost 4.897
Happiness in his power left free to will, Par Lost 5.235
Left to his own free Will, his Will though free, Par Lost 5.236
Wantond as in her prime, and plaid at will Par Lost 5.295
I have at will. So to the Silvan Lodge Par Lost 5.377
He left it in thy power, ordaind thy will Par Lost 5.526
Willing or no, who will but what they must Par Lost 5.533
Because wee freely love, as in our will Par Lost 5.539
To be both will and deed created free; Par Lost 5.549
Sufficient to subdue us to his will, Par Lost 6.427

Will(*cont*)
That thou in me well pleas'd, declarst thy will Par Lost 6.728
Hath honourd me according to his will. Par Lost 6.816
Immutably his sovran will, the end Par Lost 7.79
Approach not mee, and what I will is Fate. Par Lost 7.173
When such was heard declar'd th' Almightie's will; Par Lost 7.181
Glorie they sung to the most High, good will Par Lost 7.182
Thy Judgement to do aught, which else free Will Par Lost 8.636
O Woman, best are all things as the will Par Lost 9.343
Against his will he can receave no harme. Par Lost 9.350
But God left free the Will, for what obeyes Par Lost 9.351
She dictate false, and missinforme the Will Par Lost 9.355
Impart against his will if all be his? Par Lost 9.728
Which with bland words at will she thus addrest. Par Lost 9.855
For Understanding rul'd not, and the Will Par Lost 9.1127
Imput'st thou that to my default, or will Par Lost 9.1145
And force upon free will hath here no place. Par Lost 9.1174
1667 'Will'
Lets her will rule; restraint she will not brook, Par Lost 9.1184
1667 'her Will'
Of Man, with strength entire, and free will arm'd, Par Lost 10.9
1667 'Will'
His free Will, to her own inclining left Par Lost 10.46
Mine both in Heav'n and Earth to do thy will Par Lost 10.69
In sorrow forth, and to thy Husbands will Par Lost 10.195
His will who reigns above, to aggravate Par Lost 10.549
In this delicious Garden? as my Will Par Lost 10.746
Thy punishment then justly is at his Will. Par Lost 10.768
But all corrupt, both Mind and Will deprav'd, Par Lost 10.825
Not to do onely, but to will the same Par Lost 10.826
Th' Almighty thus pronounc'd his sovran Will. Par Lost 11.83
Of God high-blest, or to incline his will, Par Lost 11.145
Incessant I could hope to change the will Par Lost 11.308
That *Moses* might report to them his will, Par Lost 12.237
Obedient to his will, that he voutsafes Par Lost 12.246
To God more glory, more good will to Men Par Lost 12.477
And urg'd me hard with doings, which not will Par Reg 1.469
But peace, I must not quarrel with the will Samson 60

Willing
To stoop with wearied wings, and willing feet Par Lost 3.73
Som other able, and as willing, pay Par Lost 3.211
Willing or no, who will but what they must Par Lost 5.533
By winning words to conquer willing hearts, Par Reg 1.222
I could be willing though now i' th darke to trie Mask Tr. ms 16.38
'I could be willing' ←'beshrew me but I would' ←'beshew me'
I could be willinge though now i' th darke to trie Mask Br. ms 391
In willing chains and sweet captivitie. Vacation 52

Willinger
The willinger I goe, nor much expect Par Lost 9.382

Willingly
As that more willingly thou couldst not seem Par Lost 5.466
Yet willingly chose rather Death with thee: Par Lost 9.1167
So willingly doth God remit his Ire, Par Lost 11.885
For much more willingly I mention Air, Par Reg 1.45
Willingly I could flye, and hope thy raign, Par Reg 3.216
I willingly on some conditions came Samson 258
May compass it, shall willingly be paid Samson 1477
Not willingly, but tangl'd in the fold, Samson 1665

Willow
Where grows the Willow and the Osier dank, Mask 891
Trinity ms 'willow'
1637 'willow'
Bridgewater ms 'willow'

Willows
The Willows, and the Hazle Copses green, Lycidas 42
1638 'willows'
Trinity ms 'willows'

Wills
Mean while, as Nature wills, Night bids us rest. Par Lost 4.633
Her own, that what she wills to do or say, Par Lost 8.549

Wilt
But thee, whom follow? thou wilt bring me soon Par Lost 2.866
By him corrupted? or wilt thou thy self Par Lost 3.162
Thou wilt not leave me in the loathsom grave Par Lost 3.247
But evil hast not tri'd: and wilt object Par Lost 4.896
Waking thou never wilt consent to do. Par Lost 5.121
Apostat, still thou errst, nor end wilt find Par Lost 6.172
With thir attendant Moons thou wilt descrie Par Lost 8.149
Of thy Associates, *Adam*, and wilt taste Par Lost 8.401
Canst raise thy Creature to what highth thou wilt Par Lost 8.430
Thou didst accept them; wilt thou enjoy the good, Par Lost 10.758
Of all the rest: then wilt thou not be loath Par Lost 12.585
From the beginning, and in lies wilt end; Par Reg 1.408
Wilt thou impute to obedience what thy fear Par Reg 1.422
Of glory as thou wilt, said he, so deem, Par Reg 3.150
Chuse which thou wilt by conquest or by league. Par Reg 3.370
On this condition, if thou wilt fall down, Par Reg 4.166
Without thir learning how wilt thou with them, Par Reg 4.231
How wilt thou reason with them, how refute Par Reg 4.233
To win thy destin'd seat, but wilt prolong Par Reg 4.469
There stand, if thou wilt stand; to stand upright Par Reg 4.551
Man. Wilt thou then serve the *Philistines* with that gift Samson 577
Thy key of strength and safety: thou wilt say, Samson 799
Thou wilt renounce thy seeking, and much rather Samson 828
More Lordly thund'ring then thou well wilt bear. Samson 1353
Chor. How thou wilt here come off surmounts my reach. Samson 1380
By this compliance thou wilt win the Lords Samson 1411

Wilt(*cont*)
Thou wilt destroy that speak a ly Psalm 5, 15
For thou Jehovah wilt be found Psalm 5, 37
As with a shield thou wilt surround Psalm 5, 39
Lord God of Hosts, how long wilt thou, Psalm 80, 17
How long wilt thou declare Psalm 80, 18
If thou wilt list to mee, Psalm 81, 36
Wilt thou be angry without end, Psalm 85, 17
Wilt thou thy frowning ire extend Psalm 85, 19
Wilt thou not turn, and *hear our voice* Psalm 85, 21
For thou wilt *grant* me *free access* Psalm 86, 23
Wilt thou do wonders on the dead, Psalm 88, 41
Why wilt thou Lord my soul forsake, Psalm 88, 57

Wily
From sharpest sight: for in the wilie Snake, Par Lost 9.91
To whom the wilie Adder, blithe and glad. Par Lost 9.625
And to my wily trains, I shall e're long Mask 151
1637 'wilie'
Trinity ms 'wilie' ←'mothers'
Upon thy streams with wily glance, Mask 884
Bridgewater ms 'wilie'
Trinity ms 'wilie'
1637 'wilie'

Win
To win the Mount of God, and on his Throne Par Lost 6.88
Should win in Arms, in both disputes alike Par Lost 6.123
Before thy fellows, ambitious to win Par Lost 6.160
The strife of Glorie: which we mean to win, Par Lost 6.290
His whole descent, who thus shall *Canaan* win. Par Lost 12.269
As did thir Lord before them. Thus they win Par Lost 12.502
Large Countries, and in field great Battels win, Par Reg 3.73
The City of *Gallaphrone*, from thence to win Par Reg 3.340
To win thy destin'd seat, but wilt prolong Par Reg 4.469
To win him, or win from him what I can. Par Reg 4.530
And amorous reproaches to win from me Samson 393
That womans love can win or long inherit; Samson 1012
By this compliance thou wilt win the Lords Samson 1411
To win her Grace, whom all commend. Allegro 124

Winchester
The honour'd Wife of *Winchester*, Winchester 2

Wind
Of subterranean wind transports a Hill Par Lost 1.231
Of *Locusts*, warping on the Eastern Wind, Par Lost 1.341
ms 'wind'
Shon like a Meteor streaming to the Wind Par Lost 1.537
ms 'wind'
As in an Organ from one blast of wind Par Lost 1.708
Ascending, while the North wind sleeps, o'respread Par Lost 2.489
With Sails and Wind thir canie Waggons light: Par Lost 3.439
A violent cross wind from either Coast Par Lost 3.487
Her bearded Grove of ears, which way the wind Par Lost 4.982
The Adversarie. Nor think thou with wind Par Lost 6.282
And left large field, unsafe within the wind Par Lost 6.309
Long strugling underneath, ere they could wind Par Lost 6.659
Wisdom to Folly, as Nourishment to Winde. Par Lost 7.130
Nigh Rivers mouth or Foreland, where the Wind Par Lost 9.514
No more availes then breath against the winde, Par Lost 11.312
Meanwhile the Southwind rose, and with black wings Par Lost 11.738
Drivn by a keen North-winde, that blowing drie Par Lost 11.842
Sam. Fair days have oft contracted wind and rain. Samson 1062
Comes he in peace? what wind hath blown him hither Samson 1070
The frolick Wind that breathes the Spring, Allegro 18
Unwept, and welter to the parching wind, Lycidas 13
But swoln with wind, and the rank mist they draw, Lycidas 126
The wind drives, so the wicked shall not stand Psalm 1, 12
Like stubble from the wind. Psalm 83, 52

Wind
Long strugling underneath, ere they could wind Par Lost 6.659
Leads thee, or where most needs, whether to wind Par Lost 9.215
Wind me into the easie-hearted man, Mask 163

Winding
Conspicuous farr, winding with one ascent Par Lost 4.545
Th' one winding, the other strait and left between Par Reg 3.256
By scaly *Tritons* winding shell, Mask 873
Bridgewater ms 'windinge'
In notes, with many a winding bout Allegro 139

Windings
With Ringlets quaint, and wanton windings wove. Arcades 47

Window
In at the window climbs, or o're the tiles; Par Lost 4.191
And at my window bid good morrow, Allegro 46

Windows
His Sluces, as the Heav'n his windows shut. Par Lost 11.849
And storied Windows richly dight, Penseroso 159

Winds
Sublim'd with Mineral fury, aid the Winds, Par Lost 1.235
ms 'winds'
Afloat, when with fierce Winds *Orion* arm'd Par Lost 1.305
ms 'winds'
The sound of blustring winds, which all night long Par Lost 2.286
Toward the four winds four speedy Cherubim Par Lost 2.516
Hangs in the Clouds, by *Aequinoctial* Winds Par Lost 2.637
Hov'ring a space, till Winds the signal blow Par Lost 2.717
Levied to side with warring Winds, and poise Par Lost 2.905
Thy dread Tribunal: forthwith from all Windes Par Lost 3.326
The sport of Winds: all these upwhirld aloft Par Lost 3.493
His flight precipitant, and windes with ease Par Lost 3.563
Mozambic, off at Sea North-East windes blow Par Lost 4.161

Winds(*cont*)
Impetuous winds: he thus began in haste. Par Lost 4.560
His praise ye Winds, that from four Quarters blow, Par Lost 5.192
Now on the polar windes, then with quick Fann Par Lost 5.269
Fannd with coole Winds, save those who in thir course Par Lost 5.655
Winds under ground or waters forcing way Par Lost 6.196
Up from the bottom turn'd by furious windes Par Lost 7.213
Her annual Voiage, born on Windes; the Aire Par Lost 7.431
And fear of Death deliver to the Windes. Par Lost 9.989
Raind at thir Eyes, but high Winds worse within Par Lost 9.1122
Now walking in the Garden, by soft windes Par Lost 10.98
As when two Polar Winds blowing adverse Par Lost 10.289
Should prove tempestuous: To the Winds they set Par Lost 10.664
Forth rush the *Levant* and the *Ponent* Windes Par Lost 10.704
To shew us in this Mountain, while the Winds Par Lost 10.1065
Justling or pusht with Winds rude in thir shock Par Lost 10.1074
Flew up, nor missd the way, by envious windes Par Lost 11.15
Against a Winters day when winds blow keen, Par Reg 1.317
Where winds with Reeds, and Osiers whisp'ring play Par Reg 2.26
Of chiming strings, or charming pipes and winds Par Reg 2.363
Nations besides from all the quarter'd winds, Par Reg 4.202
In ruine reconcil'd: nor slept the winds Par Reg 4.413
Of thunder, chas'd the clouds, and laid the winds, Par Reg 4.429
Courted by all the winds that hold them play, Samson 719
To prayers, then winds and seas, yet winds to seas Samson 961
As with the force of winds and waters pent, Samson 1647
Coasting the *Tyrrhene* shore, as the winds listed, Mask 49
Well knows to still the wilde winds when they roar, Mask 87
And West winds, with musky wing Mask 989
Bridgewater ms 'wyndes'
By whispering Windes soon lull'd asleep. Allegro 116
1673 'Winds'
While rocking Winds are Piping loud, Penseroso 126
Of noisom winds, and blasting vapours chill. Arcades 49
What time the Gray-fly winds her sultry horn, Lycidas 28
He ask'd the Waves, and ask'd the Fellon winds, Lycidas 91
1673 'Winds'
Of shades and wanton winds, and gushing brooks, Lycidas 137
The Windes with wonder whist, Nativity 64
1673 'Winds'
Rough with black winds and storms Horace 7

Winds
His flight precipitant, and windes with ease Par Lost 3.563
the jealous ocean that old river winds Mask Tr. ms 10.12

Windy
So on this windie Sea of Land, the Fiend Par Lost 3.440
What windy joy this day had I conceiv'd Samson 1574

Wine
Of *Belial*, flown with insolence and wine. Par Lost 1.502
And hight'nd as with Wine, jocond and boon, Par Lost 9.793
As with new Wine intoxicated both Par Lost 9.1008
Corn wine and oyle; and from the herd or flock, Par Lost 12.19
And at a stately side-board by the wine Par Reg 2.350
Fertil of corn the glebe, of oyl and wine, Par Reg 3.259
By th' Idolatrous rout amidst thir wine; Samson 443
Chor. Desire of wine and all delicious drinks, Samson 541
I know not. Lords are Lordliest in thir wine; Samson 1418
Had fill'd thir hearts with mirth, high chear, & wine, Samson 1613
Drunk with Idolatry, drunk with Wine, Samson 1670
Crush't the sweet poyson of mis-used Wine Mask 47
Trinity ms 'wine'
Bridgewater ms 'wyne'
Dropping odours, dropping Wine. Mask 106
Bridgewater ms 'wine'
Trinity ms 'wine'
Of Attick tast, with Wine, whence we may rise Sonnet 20, 10
With vast increase their corn and wine abounds Psalm 4, 36

Wine-offerings
With large Wine-offerings pour'd, and sacred Feast, Par Lost 12.21

Wine-press
About the wine-press where sweet moust is powr'd, Par Reg 4.16

Wines
Their wines of *Setia*, *Cales*, and *Falerne*, Par Reg 4.117
Chor. O madness, to think use of strongest wines Samson 553

Wing
Upon the wing, as when men wont to watch Par Lost 1.332
Hovering on wing under the Cope of Hell Par Lost 1.345
From wing to wing, and half enclose him round Par Lost 1.617
1667 'Wing to Wing'
With upright wing against a higher foe. Par Lost 2.72
Encamp thir Legions, or with obscure wing Par Lost 2.132
Upon the wing, or in swift Race contend, Par Lost 2.529
Now shaves with level wing the Deep, then soares Par Lost 2.634
Wing silently the buxom Air, imbalm'd Par Lost 2.842
Thee I re-visit now with bolder wing, Par Lost 3.13
To wing the desolate Abyss, and spie Par Lost 4.936
Sailes between worlds and worlds, with steddie wing Par Lost 5.268
Of Birds in orderly array on wing Par Lost 6.74
A standing fight, then soaring on main wing Par Lost 6.243
And uncouth paine fled bellowing. On each wing Par Lost 6.362
Zophiel, of Cherubim the swiftest wing, Par Lost 6.535
His Armie, circumfus'd on either Wing, Par Lost 6.778
Above the flight of *Pegasean* wing. Par Lost 7.4
And every Bird of wing after his kinde; Par Lost 7.394
Part loosly wing the Region, part more wise Par Lost 7.425
Flying, and over Lands with mutual wing Par Lost 7.429
With blandishment, each Bird stoop'd on his wing. Par Lost 8.351
Climat, or Years damp my intended wing Par Lost 9.45

Wing(*cont*)
First lighted from his Wing, and landed safe Par Lost 10.316
With prosperous wing full summ'd to tell of deeds Par Reg 1.14
Night with her sullen wing to double-shade Par Reg 1.500
So saying he caught him up, and without wing Par Reg 4.541
Of Angels on full sail of wing flew nigh, Par Reg 4.582
And West winds, with musky wing Mask 989
Bridgewater ms 'winge'
Him that yon soars on golden wing, Penseroso 52
With Turtle wing the amorous clouds dividing, Nativity 50
But headlong joy is ever on the wing, Passion 5
Or should I thence hurried on viewles wing, Passion 50
Stoln on his wing my three and twentith yeer! Sonnet 7, 2
Thou honour'st Verse, and Verse must send her wing Sonnet 13, 9

Winged
Wing'd with red Lightning and impetuous rage, Par Lost 1.175
ms 'Wingd'
The work of Sulphur. Thither wing'd with speed Par Lost 1.674
Mean while the winged Haralds by command Par Lost 1.752
With winged course ore Hill or moarie Dale, Par Lost 2.944
The speediest of thy winged messengers, Par Lost 3.229
To whom the winged Warriour thus returnd: Par Lost 4.576
Ithuriel and *Zephon*, with wingd speed Par Lost 4.788
One shapd and wing'd like one of those from Heav'n Par Lost 5.55
All Justice: nor delaid the winged Saint Par Lost 5.247
A Seraph wingd; six wings he wore, to shade Par Lost 5.277
To whom the winged Hierarch repli'd. Par Lost 5.468
Improv'd by tract of time, and wingd ascend Par Lost 5.498
Far was advanc't on winged speed, an Host Par Lost 5.744
Or som more sudden vengeance wing'd from God Par Lost 6.279
Sate Eagle-wing'd, beside him hung his Bow Par Lost 6.763
And Vertues, winged Spirits, and Chariots wing'd, Par Lost 7.199
Thither will send his winged Messengers Par Lost 7.572
Time counts not, though with swiftest minutes wing'd. Par Lost 10.91
Inspir'd, and wing'd for Heav'n with speedier flight Par Lost 11.7
Rapt in a balmie Cloud with winged Steeds Par Lost 11.706
With winged expedition Samson 1283
Th' earth cumber'd, and the wing'd air dark't with plumes, Mask 730
Or wert thou of the golden-winged hoast, Fair Inf 57
Ye flaming Powers, and winged Warriours bright, Circum 1
And the Cherubick host in thousand quires Musick 12
Trinity ms 'in thousand quires' ← 'sweet-winged squires'

Wings
Wast present, and with mighty wings outspread Par Lost 1.20
Then with expanded wings he stears his flight Par Lost 1.225
Brusht with the hiss of russling wings. As Bees Par Lost 1.768
Upborn with indefatigable wings Par Lost 2.408
Puts on swift wings, and towards the Gates of Hell Par Lost 2.631
False fugitive, and to thy speed add wings, Par Lost 2.700
That with extended wings a Bannerd Host Par Lost 2.885
Thir lighter wings. To whom these most adhere, Par Lost 2.906
With head, hands, wings or feet pursues his way, Par Lost 2.949
Weighs his spread wings, at leasure to behold Par Lost 2.1046
To stoop with wearied wings, and willing feet Par Lost 3.73
Through all restraint broke loose he wings his way Par Lost 3.87
Approach not, but with both wings veil thir eyes. Par Lost 3.382
Illustrious on his Shoulders fledge with wings Par Lost 3.627
In curles on either cheek plaid, wings he wore Par Lost 3.641
Fanning thir odoriferous wings dispense Par Lost 4.157
His constant Lamp, and waves his purple wings, Par Lost 4.764
Ride on thy wings, and thou with thy Compeers, Par Lost 4.974
Bear on your wings and in your notes his praise; Par Lost 5.199
Vaild with his gorgeous wings, up springing light Par Lost 5.250
A Seraph wingd; six wings he wore, to shade Par Lost 5.277
And Wings were set with Eyes, with Eyes the wheels Par Lost 6.755
Hee on the wings of Cherub rode sublime Par Lost 6.771
At once the Four spred out thir Starrie wings Par Lost 6.827
Nor staid, but on the Wings of Cherubim Par Lost 7.218
1669 'wings'
His brooding wings the Spirit of God outspred, Par Lost 7.235
And let Fowle flie above the Earth, with wings Par Lost 7.389
Solac'd the Woods, and spred thir painted wings Par Lost 7.434
Between her white wings mantling proudly, Rowes Par Lost 7.439
For wings, and smallest Lineaments exact Par Lost 7.477
Thir Snakie foulds, and added wings. First crept Par Lost 7.484
Whisper'd it to the Woods, and from thir wings Par Lost 8.516
Subjected to his service Angel wings, Par Lost 9.155
Divinitie within them breeding wings Par Lost 9.1010
Wings growing, and Dominion giv'n me large Par Lost 10.244
Meanwhile the Southwind rose, and with black wings Par Lost 11.738
A Mercie-seat of Gold between the wings Par Lost 12.253
From their soft wings, and *Flora*'s earliest smells. Par Reg 2.365
With sound of Harpies wings, and Talons heard; Par Reg 2.403
In Rhombs and wedges, and half moons, and wings. Par Reg 3.309
Legions and Cohorts, turmes of horse and wings: Par Reg 4.66
On both his wings, one black, th' other white, Samson 973
Thou hovering Angel girt with golden wings, Mask 214
line not in Bridgewater ms
How sweetly did they float upon the wings Mask 249
She plumes her feathers, and lets grow her wings Mask 378
Wher brooding darknes spreads his jealous wings, Allegro 6
Wave at his Wings in Airy stream, Penseroso 148
And question'd every gust of rugged wings Lycidas 93
Are seen in glittering ranks with wings displaid, Nativity 114
And azure wings, that up they flew so drest, Sonnet 14, 11
her brok'n league, to impe their serpent wings, Sonnet 15, 8
1694 'Wings'
Between their wings out-spread, Psalm 80, 6

Wink
Danger will wink on Opportunity, Mask 401
1637 'winke'
Trinity ms 'winke'
Bridgewater ms 'winke'

Winning
His Rivals, winning cheap the high repute Par Lost 2.472
Less winning soft, less amiablie milde, Par Lost 4.479
A pomp of winning Graces waited still, Par Lost 8.61
Winning by Conquest what the first man lost Par Reg 1.154
By winning words to conquer willing hearts, Par Reg 1.222
Descend with all her winning charms begirt Par Reg 2.213

Winnows
Winnows the buxom Air; till within soare Par Lost 5.270

Wins
Environ'd wins his way; harder beset Par Lost 2.1016
Whose witnesse and opinion winnes the cause; Prose 10, 4

Winter
Decrepit Winter, from the South to bring Par Lost 10.655
Against a Winters day when winds blow keen, Par Reg 1.317
Nipt with the lagging rear of winters frost. Samson 1577
It was the Winter wilde, Nativity 29
Bleak winters force that made thy blossome drie; Fair Inf 4
Alack that so to change thee winter had no power. Fair Inf 28
Sav'd with care from Winters nip, Winchester 36

Wintry
In Wintry solstice like the shortn'd light Passion 6

Wipe
And wipe the tears for ever from his eyes. Lycidas 181
Thereby to wipe away th' infamous blot, Fair Inf 12

Wiped
From either eye, and wip'd them with her haire; Par Lost 5.131
Som natural tears they drop'd, but wip'd them soon; Par Lost 12.645

Wire
All sounds on Fret by String or Golden Wire Par Lost 7.597

Wires
To th' touch of golden wires, while *Hebe* brings Vacation 38
Touch their immortal Harps of golden wires, Musick 13

Wisdom
Vain wisdom all, and false Philosophie: Par Lost 2.565
And wisdome at one entrance quite shut out. Par Lost 3.50
My word, my wisdom, and effectual might, Par Lost 3.170
And oft though wisdom wake, suspicion sleeps Par Lost 3.686
At wisdoms Gate, and to simplicitie Par Lost 3.687
Thir number, or the wisdom infinite Par Lost 3.706
Truth, wisdome, Sanctitude severe and pure, Par Lost 4.293
1667 'Wisdome'
And wisdom, which alone is truly fair. Par Lost 4.491
Seavenfold, and scourge that wisdom back to Hell, Par Lost 4.914
Thou with Eternal wisdom didst converse, Par Lost 7.9
Wisdom thy Sister, and with her didst play Par Lost 7.10
Our knowing, as to highest wisdom seemd, Par Lost 7.83
Wisdom to Folly, as Nourishment to Winde. Par Lost 7.130
Glorie and praise, whose wisdom had ordain'd Par Lost 7.187
Is the prime Wisdom, what is more, is fume, Par Lost 8.194
Degraded, Wisdom in discourse with her Par Lost 8.552
Of Wisdom, she deserts thee not, if thou Par Lost 8.563
Wisdom without their leave? and wherein lies Par Lost 9.725
In ignorance, thou op'nst Wisdoms way, Par Lost 9.809
What thy hands builded not, thy Wisdom gain'd Par Lost 10.373
By wisdome, and superiour gifts receav'd. Par Lost 11.636
Like him in faith, in wisdom, and renown; Par Lost 12.154
And his next Son for Wealth and Wisdom fam'd, Par Lost 12.332
Of wisdome; hope no higher, though all the Starrs Par Lost 12.576
1667 'wisdom'
All vertue, grace and wisdom to atchieve Par Reg 1.68
But to vanquish by wisdom hellish wiles. Par Reg 1.175
Thy wisdom, and behold thy God-like deeds? Par Reg 1.386
His words, his wisdom full of grace and truth, Par Reg 2.34
While Virtue, Valour, Wisdom sit in want. Par Reg 2.431
By deeds of peace, by wisdom eminent, Par Reg 3.91
By wisdom; as thy Empire must extend, Par Reg 4.222
True wisdom, finds her not, or by delusion Par Reg 4.319
And what he is; his wisdom, power, intent, Par Reg 4.528
Of wisdom, vast, unwieldy, burdensom, Samson 54
But to subserve where wisdom bears command. Samson 57
In me, of wisdom nothing more then mean; Samson 207
So much of Adders wisdom I have learn't Samson 936
Cho. It is not vertue, wisdom, valour, wit, Samson 1010
Of highest wisdom brings about, Samson 1747
Were in the flat Sea sunk. And Wisdoms self Mask 375
Trinity ms 'wisdom's'
Bridgewater ms 'wisdoms'
Ore laid with black staid Wisdoms hue. Penseroso 16
That by his wisdom did create Psalm 136, 17

Wisdom-giving
O Sacred, Wise, and Wisdom-giving Plant, Par Lost 9.679

Wise
Will he, so wise, let loose at once his ire, Par Lost 2.155
Then wise to frustrate all our plots and wiles. Par Lost 2.193
If we were wise, against so great a foe Par Lost 2.202
To serve him better: wise are all his wayes. Par Lost 3.680
Gabriel, thou hadst in Heav'n th' esteem of wise, Par Lost 4.886
O loss of one in Heav'n to judge of wise, Par Lost 4.904
Gravely in doubt whether to hold them wise Par Lost 4.907
So wise he judges it to fly from pain Par Lost 4.910
Wise to flie pain, professing next the Spie, Par Lost 4.948
Part loosly wing the Region, part more wise Par Lost 7.425

Wise(*cont*)
How Nature wise and frugal could commit Par Lost 8.26
To know what passes there; be lowlie wise: Par Lost 8.173
Thy mate, who sees when thou art seen least wise. Par Lost 8.578
More wise, more watchful, stronger, if need were Par Lost 9.311
Left so imperfet by the Maker wise, Par Lost 9.338
O Sacred, Wise, and Wisdom-giving Plant, Par Lost 9.679
Of highest Agents, deemd however wise. Par Lost 9.683
Forbids us good, forbids us to be wise? Par Lost 9.759
Of vertue to make wise: what hinders then Par Lost 9.778
And hath bin tasted such: the Serpent wise, Par Lost 9.867
Nor can I think that God, Creator wise, Par Lost 9.938
Omniscient, who in all things wise and just, Par Lost 10.7
To trust thee from my side, imagin'd wise, Par Lost 10.881
Creator wise, that peopl'd highest Heav'n Par Lost 10.889
In wise deport, spake much of Right and Wrong, Par Lost 11.666
Subverting worldly strong, and worldly wise Par Lost 12.568
Guided the Wise Men thither from the East, Par Reg 1.250
Thy Father, who is holy, wise and pure, Par Reg 1.486
The wise mans cumbrance if not snare, more apt Par Reg 2.454
Which every wise and vertuous man attains: Par Reg 2.468
Conteins of good, wise, just, the perfect shape. Par Reg 3.11
Th' intelligent among them and the wise Par Reg 3.58
Wise or unwise, no difference, no exemption; Par Reg 3.115
What wise and valiant man would seek to free Par Reg 4.143
Wise, perfect in himself, and all possessing Par Reg 4.302
Wise men have said are wearisom; who reads Par Reg 4.322
To the utmost of meer man both wise and good, Par Reg 4.535
And shall again, pretend they ne're so wise. Samson 212
Chor. Many are the sayings of the wise Samson 652
That wise *Minerva* wore, unconquer'd Virgin, Mask 448
That *Hermes* once to wise *Ulysses* gave; Mask 637
line not in Bridgewater ms
To a wel-govern'd and wise appetite. Mask 705
Beyond the bliss of dreams. Be wise, and taste.---- Mask 813
Might she the wise *Latona* be, Arcades 20
Such as the wise *Demodocus* once told Vacation 48
Hast gain'd thy entrance, Virgin wise and pure. Sonnet 9, 14
For who loves that, must first be wise and good; Sonnet 12, 12
And disapproves that care, though wise in show, Sonnet 21, 12
And now be wise at length ye Kings averse Psalm 2, 22
In him who both just and wise Psalm 7, 41
O that my people would *be wise* Psalm 81, 53
Wiselier
Hath wiselier arm'd his vengeful ire then so Par Lost 10.1023
Wisely
Did wisely to conceal, and not divulge Par Lost 8.73
And wisely learn to curb thy sorrows wild; Fair Inf 73
That far events full wisely could presage, Vacation 70
Wisely hast shun'd the broad way and the green, Sonnet 9, 2
Wiser
Return'd the wiser, or the more instruct Par Reg 1.439
But he whom we attempt is wiser far Par Reg 2.205
Wisest
Audacious neighbourhood, the wisest heart Par Lost 1.400
Seems wisest, vertuousest, discreetest, best; Par Lost 8.550
Of wisest *Solomon*, and made him build, Par Reg 2.170
The wisest, unexperienc't, will be ever Par Reg 3.240
Wisest of men; from whose mouth issu'd forth Par Reg 4.276
The first and wisest of them all profess'd Par Reg 4.293
Chor. Tax not divine disposal, wisest Men Samson 210
That wisest and best men full oft beguil'd Samson 759
Of wisest men; that to the public good Samson 867
What e're it be, to wisest men and best Samson 1034
But wisest Fate sayes no, Nativity 149
Wish
To give his Enemies thir wish, and end Par Lost 2.157
And wish and struggle, as they pass, to reach Par Lost 2.606
Effect shall end our wish. Mean while revive; Par Lost 6.493
That they may have thir wish, to trie with mee Par Lost 6.818
And Grace that won who saw to wish her stay, Par Lost 8.43
Into all Eyes to wish her still in sight. Par Lost 8.63
Thy wish exactly to thy hearts desire. Par Lost 8.451
His wish and best advantage, us asunder, Par Lost 9.258
Of what so seldom chanc'd, when to his wish, Par Lost 9.423
So might the wrauth. Fond wish! couldst thou support Par Lost 10.834
To wish thou never hadst rejected thus Par Reg 4.376
(O that I never had! fond wish too late.) Samson 228
As these perhaps, yet wish it had not been, Samson 1077
Thou oft shalt wish thy self at *Gath* to boast Samson 1127
I will not wish, lest it perhaps offend them Samson 1414
And to our wish I see one hither speeding, Samson 1539
And welcom thee, and wish thee long. May Morn 10
That Kings for such a Tomb would wish to die. Shakespear 16
Wished
Invests the Sea, and wished Morn delayes: Par Lost 1.208
Thus answerd. Ill for thee, but in wisht houre Par Lost 6.150
That wisht the Mountains now might be again Par Lost 6.842
1667 'wish'd'
He sought them both, but wish'd his hap might find Par Lost 9.421
Eve separate, he wish'd, but not with hope Par Lost 9.422
Human, to put on Gods, death to be wisht, Par Lost 9.714
In things to us forbidden, it might be wish'd, Par Lost 9.1025
Bent thir aspect, and whom they wish'd beheld, Par Lost 10.454
So spake, so wish'd much-humbl'd *Eve*, but Fate Par Lost 11.181
Was took e're she was ware, and wish't she might Mask 558
1673 'wisht'
Bridgewater ms 'wisht'

Wished(*cont*)
The aidless innocent Lady his wish't prey, Mask 574
Bridgewater ms 'wisht'
Trinity ms 'wisht'
His wish't presence, and beside Mask 950
Bridgewater ms 'wisht'
Wishes
Or whom he wishes most shall seldom gain Par Lost 10.901
To whom our vows and wishes bend, Arcades 6
Wit
As from his wit and native suttletie Par Lost 9.93
Cho. It is not vertue, wisdom, valour, wit, Samson 1010
Enjoy your deer Wit, and gay Rhetorick Mask 790
line not in Trinity ms
line not in Bridgewater ms
Of Wit, or Arms, while both contend Allegro 123
Thy worth and skill exempts thee from the throng, Sonnet 13, 5
Witcheries
Deep skill'd in all his mothers witcheries, Mask 523
Witches
With *Lapland* Witches, while the labouring Moon Par Lost 2.665
With
Listings of this word are omitted; see the Introduction.
Withal
He swerve not too secure: tell him withall Par Lost 5.238
Rational Libertie; yet know withall, Par Lost 12.82
A brutish monster: what if I withal Par Reg 4.128
God, when he gave me strength, to shew withal Samson 58
Withdraw
Thee to diminish, and from thee withdraw Par Lost 7.612
Whether his first design be to withdraw Par Lost 9.261
Wearied with their iniquities, withdraw Par Lost 12.107
Nor will withdraw him now, nor will recall, Par Reg 2.55
They swarm, but in adverse withdraw their head Samson 192
Withdraws
Her shadowie Cloud withdraws, I am to haste, Par Lost 5.686
Withdrew
Soft she withdrew, and like a Wood-Nymph light Par Lost 9.386
Withered
Thir Glory witherd. As when Heavens Fire Par Lost 1.612
Among th' accurst, that witherd all thir strength, Par Lost 6.850
To witherd weak and gray; thy Senses then Par Lost 11.540
Or wither'd sticks to gather; which might serve Par Reg 1.316
Withers
It withers on the stalk with languish't head. Mask 744
line not in Bridgewater ms
Withheld
Thee also happier, shall not be withheld Par Lost 7.117
By a farr worse, or if she love, withheld Par Lost 10.903
The Sun himself with-held his wonted speed, Nativity 79
No good from them shall be with-held Psalm 84, 43
Withhold
Forbid who will, none shall from me withhold Par Lost 5.62
Which long shall not with-hold mee from thy head, Samson 1125
Withholds
And who withholds my pow'r that right to use? Par Reg 2.380
Sam. No man with-holds thee, nothing from thy hand Samson 1233
Within
Within his Sanctuary it self thir Shrines, Par Lost 1.388
ms 'With in'
A third as soon had form'd within the ground Par Lost 1.705
ms 'with-in'
Within, her ample spaces, o're the smooth Par Lost 1.725
Of that infernal Court. But far within Par Lost 1.792
For since no deep within her gulf can hold Par Lost 2.12
Within Heav'ns bound, unless Heav'ns Lord supream Par Lost 2.236
Wrought still within them; and no less desire Par Lost 2.295
Within unseen. Farr less abhorrd than these Par Lost 2.659
And I will place within them as a guide Par Lost 3.194
Saw within kenn a glorious Angel stand, Par Lost 3.622
The Hell within him, for within him Hell Par Lost 4.20
Fell not, but stand unshak'n, from within Par Lost 4.64
Of Hill or highest Wall, and sheer within Par Lost 4.182
A Shape within the watry gleam appeerd Par Lost 4.461
But if within the circuit of these walks, Par Lost 4.586
Within these hallowd limits thou appeer, Par Lost 4.964
Winnows the buxom Air; till within soare Par Lost 5.270
And *Eve* within, due at her hour prepar'd Par Lost 5.303
Within them every lower facultie Par Lost 5.410
Hath past in Heav'n, som doubt within me move, Par Lost 5.554
Orb within Orb, the Father infinite, Par Lost 5.596
And from within the golden Lamps that burne Par Lost 5.713
Within the Mount of God, fast by his Throne, Par Lost 6.5
Vigour Divine within them, can allow Par Lost 6.158
And left large field, unsafe within the wind Par Lost 6.309
Collected stood within our thoughts amus'd, Par Lost 6.581
Flashing thick flames, Wheele within Wheele undrawn, Par Lost 6.751
Within the visible Diurnal Spheare; Par Lost 7.22
What within *Eden* or without was done Par Lost 7.65
Of knowledge within bounds; beyond abstain Par Lost 7.120
Within appointed bounds be Heav'n and Earth, Par Lost 7.167
Spontaneous, for within them Spirit livd, Par Lost 7.204
All but within those banks, where Rivers now Par Lost 7.305
But long ere our approaching heard within Par Lost 8.242
Of Fish within thir watry residence, Par Lost 8.346
Expressing well the spirit within thee free, Par Lost 8.440
Perfet within, no outward aid require; Par Lost 8.642
Active within beyond the sense of brute. Par Lost 9.96

Within(*cont*)
Torment within me, as from the hateful siege Par Lost 9.121
Why shouldst not thou like sense within thee feel Par Lost 9.315
From his surmise prov'd false, find peace within, Par Lost 9.333
Secure from outward force; within himself Par Lost 9.348
The danger lies, yet lies within his power: Par Lost 9.349
Within me cleere, not onely to discerne Par Lost 9.681
That dwelt within, whose presence had infus'd Par Lost 9.836
So forcible within my heart I feel Par Lost 9.955
Divinitie within them breeding wings Par Lost 9.1010
Raind at thir Eyes, but high Winds worse within Par Lost 9.1122
Within the Gates of Hell sate Sin and Death, Par Lost 10.230
In counterview within the Gates, that now Par Lost 10.231
Methinks I feel new strength within me rise, Par Lost 10.243
Within Hell Gates till now, thou us impow'rd Par Lost 10.369
To sorrow abandond, but worse felt within, Par Lost 10.717
More terrible at th' entrance then within. Par Lost 11.470
Within himself unworthie Powers to reign Par Lost 12.91
His Spirit within them, and the Law of Faith Par Lost 12.488
Left them inrould, or what the Spirit within Par Lost 12.523
A paradise within thee, happier farr. Par Lost 12.587
Within thick Clouds and dark ten-fold involv'd, Par Reg 1.41
What from within I feel my self, and hear Par Reg 1.198
Within her brest, though calm; her brest though pure, Par Reg 2.63
Yet he who reigns within himself, and rules Par Reg 2.466
Subject himself to Anarchy within, Par Reg 2.471
Here *Ninevee*, of length within her wall Par Reg 3.275
His whispering stream; within the walls then view Par Reg 4.250
Within thy self, much more with Empire joyn'd. Par Reg 4.284
Within thir stony caves, but rush'd abroad Par Reg 4.414
Within doors, or without, still as a fool, Samson 77
Prison within Prison Samson 153
Deposited within thee; which to have kept Samson 429
Cause light again within thy eies to spring, Samson 584
My hopes all flat, nature within me seems Samson 595
Unless he feel within Samson 663
Intestin, far within defensive arms Samson 1038
Run to your shrouds, within these Brakes and Trees, Mask 147
Within thy airy shell Mask 231
Or shroud within these limits, I shall know Mask 316
Or while we speak within the direfull grasp Mask 357
 line not in Bridgewater ms
 line not in Trinity ms
He that has light within his own cleer brest Mask 381
Within the navil of this hideous Wood, Mask 520
Within his sacred chest, Nativity 217
Far within the boosom bright Winchester 69
Guard them, and him within protect from harms, Sonnet 8, 4
And be at peace within. Psalm 4, 22
Fools or mad men stand not within thy sight. Psalm 5, 12
To dwell within our Land. Psalm 85, 40
And all within his care. Psalm 87, 8

Without
That comes to all; but torture without end Par Lost 1.67
 ms 'with out'
Though without number still amidst the Hall Par Lost 1.791
Must exercise us without hope of end Par Lost 2.89
That be assur'd, without leave askt of thee: Par Lost 2.685
Without my op'ning. Pensive here I sat Par Lost 2.777
Thy daughter and thy darling, without end. Par Lost 2.870
Illimitable Ocean without bound, Par Lost 2.892
Without dimension, where length, breadth, & highth, Par Lost 2.893
Alone, and without guide, half lost, I seek Par Lost 2.975
Firm land imbosom'd without Firmament, Par Lost 3.75
So without least impulse or shadow of Fate, Par Lost 3.120
Love without end, and without measure Grace, Par Lost 3.142
Be questiond and blaspheam'd without defence. Par Lost 3.166
And now without redemption all mankind Par Lost 3.222
As many as are restor'd, without thee none. Par Lost 3.289
Loud as from numbers without number, sweet Par Lost 3.346
In whose conspicuous count'nance, without cloud Par Lost 3.385
He views in bredth, and without longer pause Par Lost 3.561
Or from without, to all temptations arm'd. Par Lost 4.65
Flours of all hue, and without Thorn the Rose: Par Lost 4.256
And without whom am to no end, my Guide Par Lost 4.442
Or glittering Starr-light without thee is sweet. Par Lost 4.656
Not likely to part hence without contest; Par Lost 4.872
And choral symphonies, Day without Night, Par Lost 5.162
Him first, him last, him midst, and without end. Par Lost 5.165
In mystic Dance not without Song, resound Par Lost 5.178
His god-like Guest, walks forth, without more train Par Lost 5.351
Of warring Spirits; how without remorse Par Lost 5.566
Ordaind without redemption, without end. Par Lost 5.615
Nightly before him, saw without thir light Par Lost 5.714
Law and Edict on us, who without law Par Lost 5.798
Thus farr his bold discourse without controule Par Lost 5.803
Against thee are gon forth without recall; Par Lost 5.885
Who out of smallest things could without end Par Lost 6.137
Instant without disturb they took Allarm, Par Lost 6.549
What within *Eden* or without was done Par Lost 7.65
One Kingdom, Joy and Union without end. Par Lost 7.161
Cannot without process of speech be told, Par Lost 7.178
Varietie without end; but of the Tree Par Lost 7.542
Her end without least motion, and receaves, Par Lost 8.35
Not that they durst without his leave attempt, Par Lost 8.237
Smooth sliding without step, last led me up Par Lost 8.302
Us happie, and without Love no happiness. Par Lost 8.621
Alone, without exterior help sustaind? Par Lost 9.336

Without(*cont*)
Wisdom without their leave? and wherein lies Par Lost 9.725
Greedily she ingorg'd without restraint, Par Lost 9.791
Not without Song, each Morning, and due praise Par Lost 9.800
Without Copartner? so to add what wants Par Lost 9.821
I could endure, without him live no life. Par Lost 9.833
Chiefly I sought, without thee can despise. Par Lost 9.878
How can I live without thee, how forgoe Par Lost 9.908
The gracious Judge without revile repli'd. Par Lost 10.118
Which when the Lord God heard, without delay Par Lost 10.163
Without our hazard, labour, or allarme, Par Lost 10.491
Glar'd on him passing: these were from without Par Lost 10.714
Made thee without thy leave, what if thy Son Par Lost 10.760
Wrath without end on Man whom Death must end? Par Lost 10.797
Both in me, and without me, and so last Par Lost 10.812
With Men as Angels without Feminine, Par Lost 10.893
And with desire to languish without hope, Par Lost 10.995
Without wrauth or reviling; wee expected Par Lost 10.1048
To whom the Father, without Cloud, serene. Par Lost 11.45
Without remorse drive out the sinful Pair, Par Lost 11.105
Rove without rein, till in the amorous Net Par Lost 11.586
Sea without shoar; and in thir Palaces Par Lost 11.750
Subjects him from without to violent Lords; Par Lost 12.93
Without Mediator, whose high Office now Par Lost 12.240
Without the vent of words, which these he breathd. Par Lost 12.374
Is to stay here; without thee here to stay, Par Lost 12.616
What from without comes often to my ears, Par Reg 1.199
And forty days *Eliah* without food Par Reg 1.353
There without sign of boast, or sign of joy, Par Reg 2.119
Without new trouble; such an Enemy Par Reg 2.126
Or God support Nature without repast Par Reg 2.250
Without this bodies wasting, I content me, Par Reg 2.256
Not without hunger. Others of some note, Par Reg 2.306
Yet Wealth without these three is impotent, Par Reg 2.433
That seat, and reign in *Israel* without end. Par Reg 2.442
Without ambition, war, or violence; Par Reg 3.90
Without distrust or doubt, that he may know Par Reg 3.193
My exaltation without change or end. Par Reg 3.197
Without means us'd, what it predicts revokes. Par Reg 3.356
By him thou shalt regain, without him not, Par Reg 3.371
Aim at the highest, without the highest attain'd Par Reg 4.106
Without thir learning how wilt thou with them, Par Reg 4.231
Nor when, eternal sure, as without end, Par Reg 4.391
Without beginning; for no date prefixt Par Reg 4.392
So saying he caught him up, and without wing Par Reg 4.541
Of Tempter and Temptation without fear. Par Reg 4.617
But what is strength without a double share Samson 53
Within doors, or without, still as a fool, Samson 77
Without all hope of day! Samson 82
(Which Men enjoying sight oft without cause complain) Samson 157
Without Reprieve adjudg'd to death, Samson 288
From National obstriction, without taint Samson 312
Heads without name no more rememberd, Samson 677
Which to have merited, without excuse, Samson 734
The constantest to have yielded without blame. Samson 848
Repuls't, without much inward passion felt Samson 1006
Therefore without feign'd shifts let be assign'd Samson 1116
Though in these chains, bulk without spirit vast, Samson 1238
Dispute thy coming? come without delay; Samson 1395
No, I am fixt not to part hence without him. Samson 1481
Which without help of eye, might be assay'd, Samson 1625
Not without wonder or delight beheld. Samson 1642
The vulgar only scap'd who stood without. Samson 1659
Without the sure guess of well-practiz'd feet. Mask 310
Secure without all doubt, or controversie: Mask 409
Eld. Bro. To tell thee sadly Shepherd, without blame, Mask 509
That have been tir'd all day without repast, Mask 688
And bound him fast; without his rod revers't, Mask 816
Here be without duck or nod Mask 960
 Trinity ms 'with out'
The brood of folly without father bred, Penseroso 2
Without the meed of som melodious tear. Lycidas 14
That so they may without suspect or fears Vacation 27
where day dwells without night Musick Tr. ms 4.29
Time numbers motion, yet (without a crime Another 7
And post o're Land and Ocean without rest: Sonnet 19, 13
Full sight of her in Heaven without restraint, Sonnet 23, 8
Behold *us, but without a frown,* Psalm 80, 59
Wilt thou be angry without end, Psalm 85, 17

Withstand
Wide wasting; such destruction to withstand Par Lost 6.253
How best their opposition to withstand. Par Reg 3.250
No strength of man, or fiercest wild beast could withstand; Samson 127
In fight withstand me single and unarm'd, Samson 1111

Withstands
But Fate withstands, and to oppose th' attempt Par Lost 2.610

Withstood
By violence, no, for that shall be withstood, Par Lost 5.242
Soft-ebbing; nor withstood them Rock or Hill, Par Lost 7.300

Witness
Witness the Streets of *Sodom*, and that night Par Lost 1.503
 ms 'Witnesse'
For mee be witness all the Host of Heav'n, Par Lost 1.635
 ms 'witnesse'
To witness with thine eyes what some perhaps Par Lost 3.700
Witness if I be silent, Morn or Eeven, Par Lost 5.202
But that I doubt, however witness Heaven, Par Lost 6.563
Heav'n witness thou anon, while we discharge Par Lost 6.564

Witness*(cont)*
Witness this new-made World, another Heav'n Par Lost 7.617
With me, best witness of thy Vertue tri'd. Par Lost 9.317
Favour from Heav'n, our witness from th' event. Par Lost 9.334
Forsake me not thus, *Adam*, witness Heav'n Par Lost 10.914
Thir inward lost: Witness th' irreverent Son Par Lost 12.101
Descri'd, divinely warn'd, and witness bore Par Reg 1.26
His witness unconfirm'd: on him baptiz'd Par Reg 1.29
Witness those antient Empires of the Earth, Par Reg 2.435
Who sent me, and thereby witness whence I am. Par Reg 3.107
Thou never wast remiss, I bear thee witness: Samson 239
Witness when I was worried with thy peals. Samson 906
Eye-witness of what first or last was done, Samson 1594
Bore witness gloriously; whence *Gaza* mourns Samson 1752
And perfet witnes of all-judging *Jove;* Lycidas 82
1638 'witnesse'
Trinity ms 'witnesse'
What need'st thou such weak witnes of thy name? Shakespear 6
1673 'witness'
1640 'witnesse'
1632 'witnesse'
1663-4 'witnesse'
Whose witnesse and opinion winnes the cause; Prose 10, 4
Witnessed
That witness'd huge affliction and dismay Par Lost 1.57
Witnesses
Eye witnesses of his Almightie Acts, Par Lost 6.883
Wits
And Eloquence, native to famous wits Par Reg 4.241
Which deepest Spirits, and choicest Wits desire: Vacation 22
Numbring good intellects; now seldom por'd on. Sonnet 11, 4
Trinity ms 'intellects' ←'wits'
Wives
With thir four Wives; and God made fast the dore. Par Lost 11.737
And made him bow to the Gods of his Wives. Par Reg 2.171
Among illustrious women, faithful wives: Samson 957
Wizard
Where that damn'd wisard hid in sly disguise Mask 571
Bridgewater ms 'wizard'
And the *Carpathian* wisards hook, Mask 872
Bridgewater ms 'wizards'
Trinity ms 'wizards'
Nor yet where *Deva* spreads her wisard stream: Lycidas 55
Wizards
The Star-led Wisards haste with odours sweet: Nativity 23
Woe
Brought Death into the World, and all our woe, Par Lost 1.3
Serv'd onely to discover sights of woe, Par Lost 1.64
To do him wanton rites, which cost them woe. Par Lost 1.414
In this abhorred deep to utter woe; Par Lost 2.87
Reserv'd and destin'd to Eternal woe; Par Lost 2.161
If we procure not to our selves more woe. Par Lost 2.225
In sweet forgetfulness all pain and woe, Par Lost 2.608
To waste Eternal dayes in woe and pain? Par Lost 2.695
Sad instrument of all our woe, she took; Par Lost 2.872
His journies end and our beginning woe. Par Lost 3.633
Wo to the inhabitants on Earth! that now, Par Lost 4.5
To me alike, it deals eternal woe. Par Lost 4.70
Will vanish and deliver ye to woe, Par Lost 4.368
More woe, the more your taste is now of joy; Par Lost 4.369
From what high state of bliss into what woe! Par Lost 5.543
Unquenchable, the house of woe and paine. Par Lost 6.877
Thee once to gaine Companion of his woe. Par Lost 6.907
Of woe and sorrow. Sternly he pronounc'd Par Lost 8.333
The weal or woe in thee is plac't; beware. Par Lost 8.638
That brought into this World a world of woe, Par Lost 9.11
Follow, as to him linkt in weal or woe, Par Lost 9.133
In wo then; that destruction wide may range: Par Lost 9.134
Despairing, seeks to work us woe and shame Par Lost 9.255
Of prohibition, root of all our woe; Par Lost 9.645
Sighing through all her Works gave signs of woe, Par Lost 9.783
Adam shall share with me in bliss or woe: Par Lost 9.831
Mine never shall be parted, bliss or woe. Par Lost 9.916
Abominable, accurst, the house of woe, Par Lost 10.465
Now ris'n, to work them furder woe or shame; Par Lost 10.555
On me, sole cause to thee of all this woe, Par Lost 10.935
Each others burden in our share of woe; Par Lost 10.961
Which must be born to certain woe, devourd Par Lost 10.980
This other serv'd but to eternize woe; Par Lost 11.60
But still I see the tenor of Mans woe Par Lost 11.632
Companions of my misery and wo. Par Reg 1.398
At first it may be; but long since with wo Par Reg 1.399
Pray'd for, but often proves our woe, our bane? Samson 351
And Love hath oft, well meaning, wrought much wo, Samson 813
Like to that sanguine flower inscrib'd with woe. Lycidas 106
1638 'wo'
And set my Harpe to notes of saddest wo, Passion 9
That Heav'n and Earth are colour'd with my wo; Passion 32
Early may fly the *Babylonian* wo. Sonnet 18, 14
That wrought thy people woe, Psalm 85, 6
Woeful
Into this cursed World a woful Race, Par Lost 10.984
Weep no more, woful Shepherds weep no more, Lycidas 165
1638 'wofull'
Trinity ms 'wofull'
Woes
Short pleasures, for long woes are to succeed. Par Lost 4.535
Of Paradise, deare bought with lasting woes! Par Lost 10.742

Woes*(cont)*
The sense of endless woes? inexplicable Par Lost 10.754
Who piteous of her woes, rear'd her lank head, Mask 836
to write his owne woes on the vermeil graine Lycidas Tr. ms 28.18
us of our selves & native woes beguile Musick Tr. ms 4.08
For cloy'd with woes and trouble store Psalm 88, 9
Wolf
Lights on his feet. As when a prowling Wolfe, Par Lost 4.183
Into som brutish form of Woolf, or Bear, Mask 70
1637 'Wolfe'
Trinity ms 'wolfe'
Bridgewater ms 'Wolfe'
Of pilfering Woolf, not all the fleecy wealth Mask 504
1637 'wolfe'
Trinity ms 'wolfe'
Bridgewater ms 'wolfe'
Besides what the grim Woolf with privy paw Lycidas 128
Trinity ms 'wolfe'
1638 'wolf'
Wolves
Wolves shall succeed for teachers, grievous Wolves, Par Lost 12.508
Like stabl'd wolves, or tigers at their prey, Mask 534
Trinity ms 'wolvs'
Of hireling wolves whose Gospell is their maw. Sonnet 16, 14
1694 'Wolves'
Woman
The one seem'd Woman to the waste, and fair, Par Lost 2.650
Is womans happiest knowledge and her praise. Par Lost 4.638
Before me; Woman is her Name, of Man Par Lost 8.496
In Woman, then to studie houshold good, Par Lost 9.233
1667 'woman'
O Woman, best are all things as the will Par Lost 9.343
The Woman, opportune to all attempts, Par Lost 9.481
This Woman whom thou mad'st to be my help, Par Lost 10.137
Say Woman, what is this which thou hast done? Par Lost 10.158
Between Thee and the Woman I will put Par Lost 10.179
And to the Woman thus his Sentence turn'd. Par Lost 10.192
With that bad Woman? Thus what thou desir'st Par Lost 10.837
My Cov'nant in the womans seed renewd; Par Lost 11.116
1667 'Womans'
Though not of Woman born; compassion quell'd Par Lost 11.496
Womans domestic honour and chief praise; Par Lost 11.617
Holds on the same, from Woman to begin. Par Lost 11.633
A Son, the Womans Seed to thee foretold, Par Lost 12.327
The seed of Woman: Virgin Mother, Haile, Par Lost 12.379
The Womans seed, obscurely then foretold, Par Lost 12.543
(For by the Womans Seed) on all Mankind. Par Lost 12.601
For this ill news I bring, the Womans seed Par Reg 1.64
Destin'd to this, is late of woman born, Par Reg 1.65
Of greatest things; what woman will you find, Par Reg 2.208
The Fugitive Bond-woman with her Son Par Reg 2.308
But weakly to a woman must reveal it, Samson 50
To a deceitful Woman: tell me Friends, Samson 202
Gave up my fort of silence to a Woman. Samson 236
Of vow, and have betray'd it to a woman, Samson 379
And arts of every woman false like thee, Samson 749
Nor shouldst thou have trusted that to womans frailty Samson 783
In man or woman, though to thy own condemning, Samson 844
Dal. In argument with men a woman ever Samson 903
That womans love can win or long inherit; Samson 1012
Till they had hir'd a woman with their gold Samson 1114
Or man or woman. Yet I argue not Sonnet 22, 6
1694 'Woman'
Womankind
Thou thy self doat'st on womankind, admiring Par Reg 2.175
Womb
That in his womb was hid metallic Ore, Par Lost 1.673
ms 'woomb'
In the wide womb of uncreated night, Par Lost 2.150
If aught disturb'd thir noyse, into her woomb, Par Lost 2.657
With me in secret, that my womb conceiv'd Par Lost 2.766
Alone, but long I sat not, till my womb Par Lost 2.778
To me, for when they list into the womb Par Lost 2.798
The Womb of nature and perhaps her Grave, Par Lost 2.911
Of Natures Womb, that in quaternion run Par Lost 5.181
Earths inmost womb, more warmth then *Adam* needs; Par Lost 5.302
Haile Mother of Mankind, whose fruitful Womb Par Lost 5.388
The Earth was form'd, but in the Womb as yet Par Lost 7.276
Op'ning her fertil Woomb teem'd at a Birth Par Lost 7.454
Th' untractable Abysse, plung'd in the womb Par Lost 10.476
Fruit of thy Womb: On mee the Curse aslope Par Lost 10.1053
Thou shalt proceed, and from thy Womb the Son Par Lost 12.381
His destin'd from the womb, Samson 634
From out her ashie womb now teem'd, Samson 1703
That ne're art call'd, but when the Dragon woom Mask 131
Trinity ms 'womb'
1637 'woome'
Bridgewater ms 'woombe'
Or that thy coarse corrupts in earths dark wombe, Fair Inf 30
And glut thy self with what thy womb devours, On Time 4
And the languisht Mothers Womb Winchester 33
As in a womb, and from that mould Psalm 7, 53
Women
To first of women *Eve* thus moving speech, Par Lost 4.409
Him who to worth in Women overtrusting Par Lost 9.1183
A Beavie of fair Women, richly gay Par Lost 11.582
Hale highly favour'd, among women blest; Par Reg 2.68
Of other women, by the birth I bore, Par Reg 2.71

Women(*cont*)
Set women in his eye and in his walk, Par Reg 2.153
Women, when nothing else, beguil'd the heart Par Reg 2.169
Thence to the bait of Women lay expos'd; Par Reg 2.204
Have err'd, and by bad Women been deceiv'd; Samson 211
Why thou shouldst wed *Philistian* women rather Samson 216
Among illustrious women, faithful wives: Samson 957
Of Women, sung at solemn festivals, Samson 983

Won
I pleas'd, and with attractive graces won Par Lost 2.762
From your Dominion won, th' Ethereal King Par Lost 2.978
Won from the void and formless infinite. Par Lost 3.12
Or all at once; more glorie will be wonn, Par Lost 4.853
That he who in debate of Truth hath won, Par Lost 6.122
And Grace that won who saw to wish her stay, Par Lost 8.43
That would be woo'd, and not unsought be won, Par Lost 8.503
Or won to what may work his utter loss, Par Lost 9.131
Motion, each act won audience ere the tongue, Par Lost 9.674
Into her heart too easie entrance won: Par Lost 9.734
Tenderly wept, much won that he his Love Par Lost 9.991
Thine now is all this World, thy vertue hath won Par Lost 10.372
Silence, and with these words attention won. Par Lost 10.459
By suffering, and earne rest from labour won, Par Lost 11.375
How many Kings destroyd, and Kingdoms won, Par Lost 12.262
In this fair Empire won of Earth and Air; Par Reg 1.63
As much his greater, and was hardly won; Par Reg 1.279
With all inflictions, but his patience won? Par Reg 1.426
Won *Asia* and the Throne of *Cyrus* held Par Reg 3.33
Easily from possession won with arms; Par Reg 3.156
From the luxurious Kings of *Antioch* won. Par Reg 3.297
That sleek't his tongue, and won so much on *Eve*, Par Reg 4.5
Of all these boasted Trophies won on me, Samson 470
To *Palestine*, won by a *Philistine* Samson 1099
Certain to have won by mortal duel from thee, Samson 1102
Such streins as would have won the ear Allegro 148
Now was almost won Nativity 104
After long toil their liberty had won, Psalm 114, 2
Then his *Casella*, whom he woo'd to sing, Sonnet 13, 13
  Trinity ms 'woo'd' ←'won'
What severs each thou 'hast learnt, which few hav don. Sonnet 17, 11
Help wast a sullen day; what may be won Sonnet 20, 4

Wonder
No wonder, fall'n such a pernicious highth. Par Lost 1.282
Behold a wonder! they but now who seemd Par Lost 1.777
Looks down with wonder at the sudden view Par Lost 3.542
Such wonder seis'd, though after Heaven seen, Par Lost 3.552
What wonder then if fields and regions here Par Lost 3.606
Beneath him with new wonder now he views Par Lost 4.205
With wonder, and could love, so lively shines Par Lost 4.363
Uriel, no wonder if thy perfet sight, Par Lost 4.577
His wonder was to find unwak'nd *Eve* Par Lost 5.9
Through Spirits with ease; nor wonder; if by fire Par Lost 5.439
Wonder not then, what God for you saw good Par Lost 5.491
Had to her Center shook. What wonder? when Par Lost 6.219
Great things, and full of wonder in our eares, Par Lost 7.70
With wonder, but delight, and, as is due, Par Lost 8.11
Our taske we choose, what wonder if so near Par Lost 9.221
Wonder not, sovran Mistress, if perhaps Par Lost 9.532
Thou canst, who art sole Wonder, much less arm Par Lost 9.533
Say, for such wonder claims attention due. Par Lost 9.566
Your wonder, with an Apple; he thereat Par Lost 10.487
For Man and Beast: when loe a wonder strange! Par Lost 11.733
Replete with joy and wonder thus repli'd. Par Lost 12.468
With wonder, then with envy fraught and rage Par Reg 1.38
What wonder then if I delight to hear Par Reg 1.481
Though of this Age the wonder and the fame, Par Reg 2.209
But much more wonder that the Son of God Par Reg 2.303
All Earth her wonder at thy acts, thy self Par Reg 3.24
No wonder, for though in thee be united Par Reg 3.229
There *Babylon* the wonder of all tongues, Par Reg 3.280
Yet truth to say, I oft have heard men wonder Samson 215
Not without wonder or delight beheld. Samson 1642
And she shall be my Queen. Hail forren wonder Mask 265
Where most may wonder at the workmanship; Mask 747
  line not in Bridgewater ms
but soft I was not sent to court your wonder Mask Tr. ms 10.16
Have sate to wonder at, and gaze upon: Arcades 43
The Windes with wonder whist, Nativity 64
Thou in our wonder and astonishment Shakespear 7
Least as a Lion (and no wonder) Psalm 7, 4

Wondered
Hast thou not wonderd, *Adam*, at my stay? Par Lost 9.856
Of public scorn; he wonderd, but not long Par Lost 10.509

Wonderful
For wonderful indeed are all his works, Par Lost 3.702
Hath bin the cause, and wonderful to heare: Par Lost 9.862
Long had foretold, a Fabrick wonderful Par Lost 10.482
And evil turn to good; more wonderful Par Lost 12.471

Wondering
Who boast in mortal things, and wond'ring tell Par Lost 1.693
  ms 'wondring'
  1667 'wondring'
Wondring; but soon th' Almighty thus reply'd: Par Lost 3.273
Under a shade of flours, much wondring where Par Lost 4.451
And as I wondring lookt, beside it stood Par Lost 5.54
And various: wondring at my flight and change Par Lost 5.89
Strait toward Heav'n my wondring Eyes I turnd, Par Lost 8.257
Much wondring how the suttle Fiend had stoln Par Lost 10.20

Wondering(*cont*)
Had leasure, wondring at himself now more; Par Lost 10.510

Wonders
Or Wonders move th' obdurate to relent? Par Lost 6.790
Creation, and the wonders of his might. Par Lost 7.223
Confess, and promise wonders in her change, Samson 753
To have wrought such wonders with an Asses Jaw; Samson 1095
Jehovah's wonders were in *Israel* shown, Psalm 114, 5
For great thou art, and wonders great Psalm 86, 33
Wilt thou do wonders on the dead, Psalm 88, 41

Wondrous
With wond'rous Art found out the massie Ore, Par Lost 1.703
  ms 'wondrous'
  1667 'wondrous'
Tamely endur'd a Bridge of wondrous length Par Lost 2.1028
By wondrous birth: Be thou in *Adams* room Par Lost 3.285
All these his wondrous works, but chiefly Man, Par Lost 3.663
All these his works so wondrous he ordaind, Par Lost 3.665
Thus wondrous fair; thy self how wondrous then! Par Lost 5.155
In might though wondrous and in Acts of Warr, Par Lost 6.377
Had wondrous, as with Starrs thir bodies all Par Lost 6.754
Wondrous in length and corpulence involv'd Par Lost 7.483
Wherein to read his wondrous Works, and learne Par Lost 8.68
Wondrous indeed, if cause of such effects. Par Lost 9.650
Now had they brought the work by wondrous Art Par Lost 10.312
Of this new wondrous Pontifice, unhop't Par Lost 10.348
Shall build a wondrous Ark, as thou beheldst, Par Lost 11.819
Such wondrous power God to his Saint will lend, Par Lost 12.200
Baptiz'd, shall them with wondrous gifts endue Par Lost 12.500
Remembring *Abraham* by some wond'rous call Par Reg 3.434
By how much from the top of wondrous glory, Samson 167
Nor shall his wondrous gifts be frustrate thus. Samson 589
As in thy wond'rous actions hath been seen. Samson 1440
Some much averse I found and wondrous harsh, Samson 1461
And of the wondrous Hors of Brass, Penseroso 114
O Jehovah our Lord how wondrous great Psalm 8, 1
O Jehovah our Lord how wondrous great Psalm 8, 23
Or wondrous acts be known, Psalm 88, 50

Wondrously
So wondrously was set his Station bright. Par Lost 3.587

Wons
As from his Laire the wilde Beast where he wonns Par Lost 7.457

Wont
Upon the wing, as when men wont to watch Par Lost 1.332
Wont ride in arm'd, and at the Soldans chair Par Lost 1.764
The first art wont his great authentic will Par Lost 3.656
As to superior Spirits is wont in Heaven, Par Lost 3.737
If dream'd, not as I oft am wont, of thee, Par Lost 5.32
That wont to be more chearful and serene Par Lost 5.123
Wast wont, I mine to thee was wont to impart; Par Lost 5.677
And in fierce hosting meet, who wont to meet Par Lost 6.93
As Reapers oft are wont thir Harvest Queen. Par Lost 9.842
Where art thou *Adam*, wont with joy to meet Par Lost 10.103
As thou art wont, my prompted Song else mute, Par Reg 1.12
And dream'd, as appetite is wont to dream, Par Reg 2.264
There I am wont to sit, when any chance Samson 4
Chor. Fathers are wont to lay up for thir Sons, Samson 1485
Sons wont to nurse thir Parents in old age, Samson 1487
Not trickt and frounc't as she was wont, Penseroso 123
Wherwith he wont at Heav'ns high Councel-Table, Nativity 10
when most were wont which till then us'd to scan Sonnet 13, Tr. ms 40.03
Blow, *as is wont*, in the new Moon Psalm 81, 9

Wonted
Like doubtful hue: but he his wonted pride Par Lost 1.527
Firm peace recoverd soon and wonted calm. Par Lost 5.210
The wonted signal, and superior voice Par Lost 5.705
Obsequious, Heav'n his wonted face renewd, Par Lost 6.783
And of thir wonted vigour left them draind, Par Lost 6.851
By sufferance, and thy wonted favour deign'd. Par Lost 8.202
Our wonted Ornaments now soild and staind, Par Lost 9.1076
Out of the wood he starts in wonted shape; Par Reg 4.449
Sam. Out, out *Hyaena;* these are thy wonted arts, Samson 748
The wonted roar was up amidst the Woods, Mask 549
Com, but keep thy wonted state, Penseroso 37
The Sun himself with-held his wonted speed, Nativity 79
While each peculiar power forgoes his wonted seat. Nativity 196

Wontest
That wontst to love the travailers benizon, Mask 332
  Bridgewater ms 'wonst'
  Trinity ms 'wont'st' ←'wond'st'

Woo
I woo to hear thy eeven Song; Penseroso 64

Wood
In Wood or Wilderness, Forrest or Den; Par Lost 4.342
Through wood, through waste, o're hill, o're dale his roam. Par Lost 4.538
Nor streit'ning Vale, nor Wood, nor Stream divides Par Lost 6.70
With branches lopt, in Wood or Mountain fell'd) Par Lost 6.575
Into the thickest Wood, there soon they chose Par Lost 9.1100
Into the Wood fast by, and changing shape Par Lost 10.333
On the cleft Wood, and all due Rites perform'd. Par Lost 11.440
To worship thir own work in Wood and Stone Par Lost 12.119
In Wood or Grove by mossie Fountain side, Par Reg 2.184
Back'd on the North and West by a thick wood, Par Reg 4.448
Out of the wood he starts in wonted shape; Par Reg 4.449
Lies through the perplex't paths of this drear Wood, Mask 37
  Trinity ms 'wood'
  1637 'wood'
  Bridgewater ms 'wood'

Wood(*cont*)
At last betakes him to this ominous Wood, Mask 61
Trinity ms 'wood'
Bridgewater ms 'wood'
1637 'wood'
In the blind mazes of this tangl'd Wood? Mask 181
Bridgewater ms 'wood'
1637 'wood'
Trinity ms 'wood'
To touch the prosperous growth of this tall Wood. Mask 270
Trinity ms 'wood'
Bridgewater ms 'wood'
1637 'wood'
Dingle, or bushy dell of this wilde Wood, Mask 312
1637 'wood'
Trinity ms 'wood'
Within the navil of this hideous Wood, Mask 520
Trinity ms 'wood'
1637 'wood'
Bridgewater ms 'woode'
Through the high wood echoing shrill. Allegro 56
Or th' unseen Genius of the Wood. Penseroso 154
And ye the breathing Roses of the Wood, Arcades 32
Trinity ms 'wood'
Of this fair Wood, and live in Oak'n bowr, Arcades 45
Trinity ms 'w', ms defective
The *tusked* Boar out of the wood Psalm 80, 53
As *when* an *aged* wood takes fire Psalm 83, 53

Woodbine
The Woodbine round this Arbour, or direct Par Lost 9.216
The Musk-rose, and the well attir'd Woodbine, Lycidas 146
1638 'wood-bine'
Trinity ms 'well-attir'd woodbine' ←'garish columbine'

Wood-gods
Of Wood-Gods and Wood-Nymphs; he view'd it round, Par Reg 2.297

Woodman
Or els som neighbour Wood-man, or at worst, Mask 484
1637 'wood man'
Trinity ms 'woodman'
Bridgewater ms 'woodman'

Wood-notes
Warble his native Wood-notes wilde, Allegro 134

Wood-nymph
Then Wood-Nymph, or the fairest Goddess feign'd Par Lost 5.381
Soft she withdrew, and like a Wood-Nymph light Par Lost 9.386

Wood-nymphs
Of Wood-Gods and Wood-Nymphs; he view'd it round, Par Reg 2.297
The Wood-Nymphs deckt with Daisies trim, Mask 120
1637 'Wood-nymphs'
Bridgewater ms 'wood nimphs'
Trinity ms 'wood nimphs'

Woods
Rocks, Waters, Woods, and by the shaggie tops Par Lost 6.645
In *Rhodope*, where Woods and Rocks had Eares Par Lost 7.35
Thir blossoms: with high woods the hills were crownd, Par Lost 7.326
1667 'Woods'
Solac'd the Woods, and spred thir painted wings Par Lost 7.434
Hill, Dale, and shadie Woods, and sunnie Plaines, Par Lost 8.262
Ye Hills and Dales, ye Rivers, Woods, and Plaines, Par Lost 8.275
Whisper'd it to the Woods, and from thir wings Par Lost 8.516
Of Hill, and Vallie, Rivers, Woods and Plaines, Par Lost 9.116
To live again in these wilde Woods forlorn? Par Lost 9.910
Obscur'd, where highest Woods impenetrable Par Lost 9.1086
And *Thrascias* rend the Woods and Seas upturn; Par Lost 10.700
O Woods, O Fountains, Hillocks, Dales and Bowrs, Par Lost 10.860
Down from a Hill the Beast that reigns in Woods, Par Lost 11.187
Had wasted woods on Mountain or in Vale, Par Lost 11.567
And now wild Beasts came forth the woods to roam. Par Reg 1.502
All these are Spirits of Air, and Woods, and Springs, Par Reg 2.374
To lay hills plain, fell woods, or valleys fill, Par Reg 3.332
In the *Arabian* woods embost, Samson 1700
And hush the waving Woods, nor of lesse faith, Mask 88
1637 'woods'
Bridgewater ms 'woods'
Trinity ms 'woods'
Benighted in these Woods. Now to my charms, Mask 150
1637 'woods'
Trinity ms 'woods'
Bridgewater ms 'woods'
As the kind hospitable Woods provide. Mask 187
1637 'woods'
Bridgewater ms 'woods'
Trinity ms 'woods'
Fear'd her stern frown, and she was queen oth' Woods. Mask 446
Bridgewater ms 'woods'
1637 'woods'
Trinity ms 'woods'
The wonted roar was up amidst the Woods, Mask 549
Trinity ms 'woods'
Bridgewater ms 'woods'
1637 'woods'
Thee Chauntress oft the Woods among, Penseroso 63
Thee Shepherd, thee the Woods, and desert Caves, Lycidas 39
1638 'woods'
Trinity ms 'woods'
To morrow to fresh Woods, and Pastures new. Lycidas 193
1638 'woods'
Trinity ms 'woods'

Woods(*cont*)
Woods and Groves, are of thy dressing, May Morn 7
Warbl'st at eeve, when all the Woods are still, Sonnet 1, 2

Woody
Shade above shade, a woodie Theatre Par Lost 4.141
Of Fruit-trees overwoodie reachd too farr Par Lost 5.213
A woodie Mountain; whose high top was plaine, Par Lost 8.303
Among the Trees on Iles and woodie Shores. Par Lost 9.1118
Wandring this woody maze, and humane food Par Reg 2.246
That open'd in the midst a woody Scene, Par Reg 2.294
Of woody *Ida*'s inmost grove, Penseroso 29

Wooed
That would be woo'd, and not unsought be won, Par Lost 8.503
Then his *Casella*, whom he woo'd to sing, Sonnet 13, 13
Trinity ms 'woo'd' ←'won'

Woof
In time of Truce; *Iris* had dipt the wooff; Par Lost 11.244
These my skie robes spun out of *Iris* Wooff, Mask 83
1637 'wooffe'
Trinity ms 'woofe'
Bridgewater ms 'wooffe'

Wool
The sampler, and to teize the huswifes wooll. Mask 751
line not in Bridgewater ms

Woos
She woo's the gentle Air Nativity 38

Worcester
And Dunbarr feild resounds thy praises loud, Sonnet 16, 8
Trinity ms 'Worsters laureat wreath' ←'Dunbarr feild'
And Worsters laureat wreath; yet much remaines Sonnet 16, 9
Trinity ms 'Worsters laureat wreath' ←'twentie battles more'
1694 '*Worcester*'s'

Word
O Father, gracious was that word which clos'd Par Lost 3.144
My word, my wisdom, and effectual might, Par Lost 3.170
Father, thy word is past, man shall find grace; Par Lost 3.227
I saw when at his Word the formless Mass, Par Lost 3.708
None left but by submission; and that word Par Lost 4.81
By word or action markt: about them round Par Lost 4.401
As by his Word the mighty Father made Par Lost 5.836
Of Truth, in word mightier then they in Armes; Par Lost 6.32
And thou my Word, begotten Son, by thee Par Lost 7.163
His Word, the filial Godhead, gave effect. Par Lost 7.175
The King of Glorie in his powerful Word Par Lost 7.208
Said then th' Omnific Word, your discord end: Par Lost 7.217
Attends thee, and each word, each motion formes, Par Lost 8.223
To end me? Shall Truth fail to keep her word, Par Lost 10.856
Man lives not by Bread only, but each Word Par Reg 1.349
And reason; since his word all things produc'd, Par Reg 3.122
O first created Beam, and thou great Word, Samson 83
Gloriously rigg'd; and for a word, a tear, Samson 200
Till further quest'. *La*. Shepherd I take thy word, Mask 321
Cries the stall-reader, bless us! what a word on Sonnet 11, 5
No word is firm or sooth Psalm 5, 26
All Flocks, and Herds, by thy commanding word, Psalm 8, 19

Words
And thence in Heav'n call'd Satan, with bold words Par Lost 1.82
Whereto with speedy words th' Arch-fiend reply'd. Par Lost 1.156
Soon recollecting, with high words, that bore Par Lost 1.528
Words interwove with sighs found out thir way. Par Lost 1.621
He spake: and to confirm his words, out-flew Par Lost 1.663
He reck'd not, and these words thereafter spake. Par Lost 2.50
Thus *Belial* with words cloath'd in reasons garb Par Lost 2.226
She spake, and at her words the hellish Pest Par Lost 2.735
So strange thy outcry, and thy words so strange Par Lost 2.737
His words here ended, but his meek aspect Par Lost 3.266
But still thy words at random, as before, Par Lost 4.930
At such bold words voucht with a deed so bold: Par Lost 5.66
Ill matching words and deeds long past or late. Par Lost 5.113
To whom our great Progenitor. Thy words Par Lost 5.544
So spake th' Omnipotent, and with his words Par Lost 5.616
Ambiguous words and jealousies, to sound Par Lost 5.703
Words which no eare ever to hear in Heav'n Par Lost 5.810
Hoarce murmur echo'd to his words applause Par Lost 5.873
He ended, and his words thir drooping chere Par Lost 6.496
So scoffing in ambiguous words he scarce, Par Lost 6.568
What words or tongue of Seraph can suffice, Par Lost 7.113
Not Words alone pleas'd her. O when meet now Par Lost 8.57
Though pleasant, but thy words with Grace Divine Par Lost 8.215
Pleas'd with thy words no less then thou with mine. Par Lost 8.248
Let not my words offend thee, Heav'nly Power, Par Lost 8.379
Thy words, Creator bounteous and benigne, Par Lost 8.492
From all her words and actions mixt with Love Par Lost 8.602
To whom with healing words *Adam* replyd. Par Lost 9.290
Chiefly by what thy own last reasoning words Par Lost 9.379
Into the Heart of *Eve* his words made way, Par Lost 9.550
He ended, and his words replete with guile Par Lost 9.733
Yet rung of his perswasive words, impregn'd Par Lost 9.737
Which with bland words at will she thus addrest. Par Lost 9.855
Thus in calm mood his Words to *Eve* he turnd. Par Lost 9.920
At length gave utterance to these words constraind. Par Lost 9.1066
Would thou hadst heark'nd to my words, and stai'd Par Lost 9.1134
What words have past thy Lips, *Adam* severe, Par Lost 9.1144
Silence, and with these words attention won. Par Lost 10.459
His thoughts, his looks, words, actions all infect, Par Lost 10.608
Soft words to his fierce passion she assay'd: Par Lost 10.865
And thus with peaceful words uprais'd her soon. Par Lost 10.946

Words(*cont*)
How little weight my words with thee can finde, Par Lost 10.968
1667 'Words' in some copies
Unskilful with what words to pray, let mee Par Lost 11.32
Which thus to *Eve* his welcome words renewd. Par Lost 11.140
To *Michael* thus his humble words addressd. Par Lost 11.295
And scarce recovering words his plaint renew'd. Par Lost 11.499
To sow a jangling noise of words unknown: Par Lost 12.55
Without the vent of words, which these he breathd. Par Lost 12.374
And thus with words not sad she him receav'd. Par Lost 12.609
He ended, and his words impression left Par Reg 1.106
By winning words to conquer willing hearts, Par Reg 1.222
By words at times cast forth inly rejoyc'd, Par Reg 1.228
Perus'd him, then with words thus utt'red spake. Par Reg 1.320
His words, his wisdom full of grace and truth, Par Reg 2.34
And with fair speech these words to him address'd. Par Reg 2.301
He spake no dream, for as his words had end, Par Reg 2.337
And with these words his temptation pursu'd. Par Reg 2.405
With soothing words renew'd, him thus accosts. Par Reg 3.6
Thy actions to thy words accord, thy words Par Reg 3.9
Our Saviour, and new train of words began. Par Reg 3.266
And to our Saviour thus his words renew'd. Par Reg 3.346
Sam. I hear the sound of words, thir sense the air Samson 176
Salve to thy Sores, apt words have power to swage Samson 184
Who vanquisht with a peal of words (O weakness!) Samson 235
Cho. Thy words to my remembrance bring Samson 277
Man. With cause this hope relieves thee, and these words Samson 472
And healing words from these thy friends admit. Samson 605
And words addrest seem into tears dissolv'd, Samson 729
Sam. For want of words no doubt, or lack of breath, Samson 905
Bearing my words and doings to the Lords Samson 947
The bait of honied words; a rougher tongue Samson 1066
Thy words by adding fuel to the flame? Samson 1351
And well plac't words of glozing courtesie Mask 161
Arm his profane tongue with contemptuous words Mask 781
line not in Bridgewater ms
line not in Trinity ms
Her words set off by som superior power; Mask 801
line not in Bridgewater ms
line not in Trinity ms
With puissant words, and murmurs made to bless, Arcades 60
With lucky words favour my destin'd Urn, Lycidas 20
Runs through the arched roof in words deceiving. Nativity 175
And mad'st imperfect words with childish tripps, Vacation 3
So well your words his noble vertues praise, Sonnet 10, 12
Words with just note and accent, not to scan Sonnet 13, 3
Jehovah to my words give ear Psalm 5, 1
And your ungodly deeds finde me the words. Prose 8, 2

Wore
In curles on either cheek plaid, wings he wore Par Lost 3.641
Her unadorned golden tresses wore Par Lost 4.305
A Seraph wingd; six wings he wore, to shade Par Lost 5.277
And on the washie Oose deep Channels wore; Par Lost 7.303
Thus wore out night, and now the Herald Lark Par Reg 2.279
That wise *Minerva* wore, unconquer'd Virgin, Mask 448

Work
Here in the heart of Hell to work in Fire, Par Lost 1.151
To work in close design, by fraud or guile Par Lost 1.646
ms 'worke'
The work of Sulphur. Thither wing'd with speed Par Lost 1.674
Admiring enter'd, and the work some praise Par Lost 1.731
Thrive under evil, and work ease out of pain Par Lost 2.261
The work as of a Kingly Palace Gate Par Lost 3.505
Which else might work him danger or delay: Par Lost 3.635
Accept your Makers work; he gave it me, Par Lost 4.380
Man hath his daily work of body or mind Par Lost 4.618
Which we in our appointed work imployd Par Lost 4.726
Wilde work produces oft, and most in dreams, Par Lost 5.112
On to thir mornings rural work they haste Par Lost 5.211
On golden Hinges turning, as by work Par Lost 5.255
Till body up to spirit work, in bounds Par Lost 5.478
That we were formd then saist thou? and the work Par Lost 5.853
For Gods, and too unequal work we find Par Lost 6.453
Forthwith from Councel to the work they flew, Par Lost 6.507
Wild work in Heav'n, and dangerous to the maine. Par Lost 6.698
Of radiant *Urim*, work divinely wrought, Par Lost 6.761
Number to this dayes work is not ordain'd Par Lost 6.809
In *Chaos*, and the work begun, how soon Par Lost 7.93
Surveying his great Work, that it was good: Par Lost 7.353
There wanted yet the Master work, the end Par Lost 7.505
Yet not till the Creator from his work Par Lost 7.551
The great Creator from his work returnd Par Lost 7.567
Magnificent, his Six days work, a World; Par Lost 7.568
Hath Omnipresence) and the work ordain'd, Par Lost 7.590
Author and end of all things, and from work Par Lost 7.591
As resting on that day from all his work, Par Lost 7.593
Had work and rested not, the solemn Pipe, Par Lost 7.595
Or enemie, while God was in his work, Par Lost 8.234
Or won to what may work his utter loss, Par Lost 9.131
Thir growing work: for much thir work outgrew Par Lost 9.202
Aid us, the work under our labour grows, Par Lost 9.208
Our dayes work brought to little, though begun Par Lost 9.224
How we might best fulfill the work which here Par Lost 9.230
Despairing, seeks to work us woe and shame Par Lost 9.255
Adventrous work, yet to thy power and mine Par Lost 10.255
Nor shall I to the work thou enterprisest Par Lost 10.270
Now had they brought the work by wondrous Art Par Lost 10.312
Mine with this glorious Work, and made one Realm Par Lost 10.391

Work(*cont*)
Now ris'n, to work them furder woe or shame; Par Lost 10.555
Wherere our days work lies, though now enjoind Par Lost 11.177
Ridiculous, and the work Confusion nam'd. Par Lost 12.62
To worship thir own work in Wood and Stone Par Lost 12.119
How best the mighty work he might begin Par Reg 1.186
And make perswasion do the work of fear; Par Reg 1.223
Or work Redemption for mankind, whose sins Par Reg 1.266
All his great work to come before him set; Par Reg 2.112
Natures own work it seem'd (Nature taught Art) Par Reg 2.295
Carv'd work, the hand of fam'd Artificers Par Reg 4.59
Queller of Satan, on thy glorious work Par Reg 4.634
Light the prime work of God to me is extinct, Samson 70
The work to which I was divinely call'd; Samson 226
Into a Dungeon thrust, to work with Slaves? Samson 367
My Nation, and the work from Heav'n impos'd, Samson 565
To some great work, thy glory, Samson 680
The work of many hands, which earns my keeping Samson 1260
With good success to work his liberty. Samson 1454
The work for which thou wast foretold Samson 1662
And set to work millions of spinning Worms, Mask 715
Trinity ms 'worke'
Bridgewater ms 'worke'
That at her flowry work doth sing, Penseroso 143
And with his Father work us a perpetual peace. Nativity 7
And work my flatter'd fancy to belief, Passion 31
Hast reard Gods Trophies and his work pursu'd. Sonnet 16, 6
1694 'Work'
Either man's work or his own gifts, who best Sonnet 19, 10
Depart all ye that work iniquitie. Psalm 6, 16

Workers
All workers of iniquity Psalm 5, 13

Working
Working through love, upon thir hearts shall write, Par Lost 12.489
More then the working day thy hands, Samson 1299

Workmanship
Where most may wonder at the workmanship; Mask 747
line not in Bridgewater ms

Work-master
The great Work-Maister, leads to no excess Par Lost 3.696

Works
Leviathan, which God of all his works Par Lost 1.201
And works of love or enmity fulfill. Par Lost 1.431
Of *Babel*, and the works of *Memphian* Kings Par Lost 1.694
Abolish his own works. This would surpass Par Lost 2.370
As from her outmost works a brok'd foe Par Lost 2.1039
Of Natures works to mee expung'd and ras'd, Par Lost 3.49
His own works and their works at once to view: Par Lost 3.59
To me are all my works, nor Man the least Par Lost 3.277
With vanity had filld the works of men: Par Lost 3.447
All th' unaccomplisht works of Natures hand, Par Lost 3.455
All these his wondrous works, but chiefly Man, Par Lost 3.663
All these his works so wondrous he ordaind, Par Lost 3.665
The works of God, thereby to glorifie Par Lost 3.695
For wonderful indeed are all his works, Par Lost 3.702
Of natures works, honor dishonorable, Par Lost 4.314
More of th' Almighties works, and chiefly Man Par Lost 4.566
All these with ceasless praise his works behold Par Lost 4.679
Works of day pass't, or morrows next designe, Par Lost 5.33
These are thy glorious works, Parent of good, Par Lost 5.153
In these thy lowest works, yet these declare Par Lost 5.158
Brooks not the works of violence and Warr. Par Lost 6.274
To magnifie his works, the more we know. Par Lost 7.97
Obtaine: though to recount Almightie works Par Lost 7.112
God and his works, Creatour him they sung, Par Lost 7.259
Of all his works: therefore the Omnipotent Par Lost 7.516
Which tasted works knowledge of Good and Evil, Par Lost 7.543
Great are thy works, *Jehovah*, infinite Par Lost 7.602
Over his Works, on Earth, in Sea, or Air, Par Lost 7.629
Wherein to read his wondrous Works, and learne Par Lost 8.68
Whose vertue on it self workes no effect, Par Lost 8.95
As us'd or not, works in the mind no change, Par Lost 8.525
And good workes in her Husband to promote. Par Lost 9.234
To interrupt, side-long he works his way. Par Lost 9.512
Sighing through all her Works gave signs of woe, Par Lost 9.783
Of all Gods works, Creature in whom excell'd Par Lost 9.897
1667 'Works'
Set over all his Works, which in our Fall, Par Lost 9.941
Righteous are thy Decrees on all thy Works; Par Lost 10.644
And propitiation, all his works on mee Par Lost 11.34
By Faith and faithful works, to second Life, Par Lost 11.64
To worship God aright, and know his works Par Lost 11.578
Before him, Towns, and rural works between, Par Lost 11.639
To filial, works of Law to works of Faith. Par Lost 12.306
Not by destroying *Satan*, but his works Par Lost 12.394
To save them, not thir own, though legal works. Par Lost 12.410
By Faith not void of workes: this God-like act Par Lost 12.427
Bestuck with slandrous darts, and works of Faith Par Lost 12.536
Mercifull over all his works, with good Par Lost 12.565
All secrets of the deep, all Natures works, Par Lost 12.578
Or works of God in Heav'n, Aire, Earth, or Sea, Par Lost 12.579
Thir taste no knowledge works, at least of evil, Par Reg 2.371
And all the flourishing works of peace destroy, Par Reg 3.80
Laborious works, unwillingly this rest Samson 14
Bewail thy falshood, and the pious works Samson 955
Soon as the Potion works, their human count'nance, Mask 68
Bridgewater ms 'workes'
Thy Works and Alms and all thy good Endeavour Sonnet 14, 5

Works(*cont*)
Trinity ms 'workes' ←'Works'
O're the works of thy hand thou mad'st him Lord, Psalm 8, 17
O Lord, nor any works Psalm 86, 26
Like to thy *glorious* works. Psalm 86, 28

World
Brought Death into the World, and all our woe, Par Lost 1.3
ms 'world'
For one restraint, Lords of the World besides? Par Lost 1.32
ms 'world'
Infernal world, and thou profoundest Hell Par Lost 1.251
And various Idols through the Heathen World. Par Lost 1.375
ms 'world'
Through labour and indurance. This deep world Par Lost 2.262
Err not) another World, the happy seat Par Lost 2.347
In search of this new world, whom shall we find Par Lost 2.403
If thence he scape into whatever world, Par Lost 2.442
That dismal world, if any Clime perhaps Par Lost 2.572
To that new world of light and bliss, among Par Lost 2.867
Now lately Heaven and Earth, another World Par Lost 2.1004
Of this frail World; by which the Spirits perverse Par Lost 2.1030
This pendant world, in bigness as a Starr Par Lost 2.1052
The rising world of waters dark and deep, Par Lost 3.11
On the bare outside of this World, that seem'd Par Lost 3.74
Directly towards the new created World, Par Lost 3.89
A World from utter loss, and hast been found Par Lost 3.308
The World shall burn, and from her ashes spring Par Lost 3.334
Of this round World, whose first convex divides Par Lost 3.419
First from the ancient World those Giants came Par Lost 3.464
Fly o're the backside of the World farr off Par Lost 3.494
Of all this World at once. As when a Scout Par Lost 3.543
At sight of all this World beheld so faire. Par Lost 3.554
Down right into the Worlds first Region throws Par Lost 3.562
This worlds material mould, came to a heap: Par Lost 3.709
Of this new World; at whose sight all the Starrs Par Lost 4.34
Mankind created, and for him this World. Par Lost 4.107
As Man ere long, and this new World shall know. Par Lost 4.113
To seek her through the world; nor that sweet Grove Par Lost 4.272
By conquering this new World, compels me now Par Lost 4.391
That made us, and for us this ample World Par Lost 4.413
This new created World, whereof in Hell Par Lost 4.937
Then when fair Morning first smiles on the World, Par Lost 5.124
Thou Sun, of this great World both Eye and Soule, Par Lost 5.171
In honour to the Worlds great Author rise, Par Lost 5.188
Shall fill the World more numerous with thy Sons Par Lost 5.389
Of things above his World, and of thir being Par Lost 5.455
The secrets of another world, perhaps Par Lost 5.569
As yet this world was not, and *Chaos* wilde Par Lost 5.577
Seemd in thy World erroneous to dissent Par Lost 6.146
What neerer might concern him, how this World Par Lost 7.62
Farr differing from this World, thou hast reveal'd Par Lost 7.71
Another World, out of one man a Race Par Lost 7.155
Farr into *Chaos*, and the World unborn; Par Lost 7.220
This be thy just Circumference, O World. Par Lost 7.231
Dividing: for as Earth, so he the World Par Lost 7.269
Thence to behold this new created World Par Lost 7.554
Magnificent, his Six days work, a World; Par Lost 7.568
Witness this new-made World, another Heav'n Par Lost 7.617
Numerous, and every Starr perhaps a World Par Lost 7.621
How first this World and face of things began, Par Lost 7.636
When I behold this goodly Frame, this World Par Lost 8.15
Be Center to the World, and other Starrs Par Lost 8.123
Which two great Sexes animate the World, Par Lost 8.151
Shalt loose, expell'd from hence into a World Par Lost 8.332
That what seemd fair in all the World, seemd now Par Lost 8.472
That brought into this World a world of woe, Par Lost 9.11
Magnificent this World, and Earth his seat, Par Lost 9.153
Empress of this fair World, resplendent *Eve*, Par Lost 9.568
Over this Maine from Hell to that new World Par Lost 10.257
Immovable of this now fenceless world Par Lost 10.303
Of this round World: with Pinns of Adamant Par Lost 10.318
And of this World, and on the left hand Hell Par Lost 10.322
Thine now is all this World, thy vertue hath won Par Lost 10.372
As Battel hath adjudg'd, from this new World Par Lost 10.377
His Quadrature, from thy Orbicular World, Par Lost 10.381
Hell and this World, one Realm, one Continent Par Lost 10.392
Flown to the upper World; the rest were all Par Lost 10.422
As Lords, a spacious World, to our native Heaven Par Lost 10.467
The new created World, which fame in Heav'n Par Lost 10.481
Both his beloved Man and all his World, Par Lost 10.489
A World who would not purchase with a bruise, Par Lost 10.500
To waste and havoc yonder World, which I Par Lost 10.617
His course intended; else how had the World Par Lost 10.689
Of this new glorious World, and mee so late Par Lost 10.721
Then all the World much heavier, though divided Par Lost 10.836
Of Nature, and not fill the World at once Par Lost 10.892
Into this cursed World a woful Race, Par Lost 10.984
To resalute the World with sacred Light Par Lost 11.134
Into a lower World, to this obscure Par Lost 11.283
In yonder nether World where shall I seek Par Lost 11.328
The World: in Spirit perhaps he also saw Par Lost 11.406
The world erelong a world of tears must weepe. Par Lost 11.627
The onely righteous in a World perverse, Par Lost 11.701
Fame in the World, high titles, and rich prey, Par Lost 11.793
Against allurement, custom, and a World Par Lost 11.810
A World devote to universal rack. Par Lost 11.821
Farr less I now lament for one whole World Par Lost 11.874
That God voutsafes to raise another World Par Lost 11.877

World(*cont*)
Surpass his bounds, nor Rain to drown the World Par Lost 11.894
Betwixt the world destroy'd and world restor'd, Par Lost 12.3
line not in 1667 edition
Thus thou hast seen one World begin and end; Par Lost 12.6
Thus will this latter, as the former World, Par Lost 12.105
Through the worlds wilderness long wanderd man Par Lost 12.313
Of *Abrahams* Faith wherever through the world; Par Lost 12.449
When this worlds disolution shall be ripe, Par Lost 12.459
As at the Worlds great period; and our Sire Par Lost 12.467
Rarely be found: so shall the World goe on, Par Lost 12.537
Satan with his perverted World, then raise Par Lost 12.547
1669 'world'
Measur'd this transient World, the Race of time, Par Lost 12.554
And all the riches of this World enjoydst, Par Lost 12.580
The World was all before them, where to choose Par Lost 12.646
About the world, at that assembly fam'd Par Reg 1.34
O ancient Powers of Air and this wide world, Par Reg 1.44
And all the world, and mass of sinful flesh; Par Reg 1.162
Copartner in these Regions of the World, Par Reg 1.392
Into the World, to teach his final will, Par Reg 1.461
Among the Heathen, (for throughout the World Par Reg 2.443
Of conduct would be such, that all the world Par Reg 3.18
Great *Julius*, whom now all the world admires Par Reg 3.39
Happiest both to thy self and all the world, Par Reg 3.225
The world thou hast not seen, much less her glory, Par Reg 3.236
Plausible to the world, to me worth naught. Par Reg 3.393
The Kingdoms of the world, and all thir glory. Par Reg 4.89
Aim therefore at no less then all the world, Par Reg 4.105
All Monarchies besides throughout the world, Par Reg 4.150
The Kingdoms of the world to thee I give; Par Reg 4.163
The Kingdoms of the world to thee were giv'n, Par Reg 4.182
God of this world invok't and world beneath; Par Reg 4.203
The Kingdoms of this world; I shall no more Par Reg 4.210
So let extend thy mind o're all the world, Par Reg 4.223
Great *Alexander* to subdue the world, Par Reg 4.252
And how the world began, and how man fell Par Reg 4.311
What dost thou in this World? the Wilderness Par Reg 4.372
On *David*'s Throne; or Throne of all the world, Par Reg 4.379
From the four hinges of the world, and fell Par Reg 4.415
To store her children with; if all the world Mask 720
And the low world in measur'd motion draw Arcades 71
Set off to th' world, nor in broad rumour lies, Lycidas 80
Visit'st the bottom of the monstrous world; Lycidas 158
Was heard the World around: Nativity 54
The new-enlightn'd world no more should need; Nativity 82
And the well-ballanc't world on hinges hung, Nativity 122
When at the worlds last session, Nativity 163
Did fill the new-made world with light. Psalm 136, 26
Hid from the world in a low delved tombe; Fair Inf 32
Let down in clowdie throne to do the world some good. Fair Inf 56
To scorn the sordid world, and unto Heav'n aspire. Fair Inf 63
That till the worlds last-end shall make thy name to live. Fair Inf 77
Enter'd the world, now bleeds to give us ease; Circum 11
That to give the world encrease, Winchester 51
E're half my days, in this dark world and wide, Sonnet 19, 2
This thought might lead me through the worlds vain mask Sonnet 22, 13
1694 'this World's'
Talking like this worlds brood; Psalm 4, 27
All people from the worlds foundation. Psalm 7, 30
Shall aw the World, and Conquer Nations bold. Prose 12, 14

Worldly
Worldlie or dissolute, on what thir Lords Par Lost 11.803
Subverting worldly strong, and worldly wise Par Lost 12.568
Then to a worldly Crown, addicted more Par Reg 4.213

Worlds
Space may produce new Worlds; whereof so rife Par Lost 1.650
ms 'worlds'
His dark materials to create more Worlds, Par Lost 2.916
Stars distant, but nigh hand seemd other Worlds, Par Lost 3.566
Or other Worlds they seemd, or happy Iles, Par Lost 3.567
Worlds, and on whom hath all these graces powrd; Par Lost 3.674
Sailes between worlds and worlds, with steddie wing Par Lost 5.268
To stand approv'd in sight of God, though Worlds Par Lost 6.36
His good to Worlds and Ages infinite. Par Lost 7.191
1669 'World'
And Spirit coming to create new Worlds. Par Lost 7.209
Dream not of other Worlds, what Creatures there Par Lost 8.175
In other Worlds, and happier Seat provides Par Lost 10.237
Though distant from thee Worlds between, yet felt Par Lost 10.362
Of Forrein Worlds: he through the midst unmarkt, Par Lost 10.441
Hail Son of the most High, heir of both worlds, Par Reg 4.633
with distant worlds, & strange removed clim Mask Tr. ms 10.17
What Worlds, or what vast Regions hold Penseroso 90

Worm
Beast, Bird, Insect, or Worm durst enter none; Par Lost 4.704
To chains of darkness, and th' undying Worm, Par Lost 6.739
Insect or Worme; those wav'd thir limber fans Par Lost 7.476
To that false Worm, of whomsoever taught Par Lost 9.1068
The fiery Serpent fled, and noxious Worm, Par Reg 1.312
Of man or worm; the vilest here excel me, Samson 74
Or hurtfull Worm with canker'd venom bites. Arcades 53
Trinity ms 'worme'
Or Taint-worm to the weanling Herds that graze, Lycidas 46
1638 'taint-worm'
Trinity ms 'taint-worme'

Worms
And set to work millions of spinning Worms, Mask 715

Worms(*cont*)
Bridgewater ms 'wormes'
Trinity ms 'worms'
1637 'worms'

Wormy
Or that thy beauties lie in wormie bed, Fair Inf 31

Worn
And worn with Famin, long and ceasless hiss, Par Lost 10.573
Of *Sarra*, worn by Kings and Hero's old Par Lost 11.243
O're worn and soild; Samson 123
Inglorious, unimploy'd, with age out-worn. Samson 580
Which greatest Heroes have in battel worn, Samson 1131
With the rank vapours of this Sin-worn mould. Mask 17
Trinity ms 'sin-worne'
1637 'Sin-worne'
Bridgewater ms 'sin-worne'

Worried
Witness when I was worried with thy peals. Samson 906

Worse
In Arms not worse, in foresight much advanc't, Par Lost 1.119
Expos'd a Matron to avoid worse rape. Par Lost 1.505
Went all his fear: of God, or Hell, or worse Par Lost 2.49
Our stronger, some worse way his wrath may find Par Lost 2.83
Fear to be worse destroy'd: what can be worse Par Lost 2.85
Dropt Manna, and could make the worse appear Par Lost 2.113
What can we suffer worse? is this then worst, Par Lost 2.163
Chain'd on the burning Lake? that sure was worse. Par Lost 2.169
Ages of hopeless end; this would be worse. Par Lost 2.186
Chains and these Torments? better these then worse Par Lost 2.196
They dreaded worse then Hell: so much the fear Par Lost 2.293
Abominable, inutterable, and worse Par Lost 2.626
Confusion worse confounded; and Heav'n Gates Par Lost 2.996
If him by force he can destroy, or worse, Par Lost 3.91
Worse; of worse deeds worse sufferings must ensue. Par Lost 4.26
Till Pride and worse Ambition threw me down Par Lost 4.40
Which would but lead me to a worse relapse Par Lost 4.100
Universal reproach, far worse to beare Par Lost 6.34
May serve to better us, and worse our foes, Par Lost 6.440
They worse abhorr'd. *Satan* beheld thir plight, Par Lost 6.607
Strook them with horror backward, but far worse Par Lost 6.863
Wors then can Man with Beast, and least of all. Par Lost 8.397
For what God after better worse would build? Par Lost 9.102
Bane, and in Heav'n much worse would be my state. Par Lost 9.123
As I, though thereby worse to me redound: Par Lost 9.128
Or this, or worse, leave not the faithful side Par Lost 9.265
Though threat'nd, which no worse then this can bring. Par Lost 9.715
Raind at thir Eyes, but high Winds worse within Par Lost 9.1122
To sorrow abandond, but worse felt within, Par Lost 10.717
Would Thunder in my ears, no fear of worse Par Lost 10.780
By a farr worse, or if she love, withheld Par Lost 10.903
My bread; what harm? Idleness had bin worse; Par Lost 10.1055
O unexpected stroke, worse then of Death! Par Lost 11.268
Those were of hate and death, or pain much worse, Par Lost 11.601
Still tend from bad to worse, till God at last Par Lost 12.106
Wors with his followers then with him they dealt? Par Lost 12.484
Of my reception into grace; what worse? Par Reg 3.205
If there be worse, the expectation more Par Reg 3.207
Of worse torments me then the feeling can. Par Reg 3.208
Besides thir other worse then heathenish crimes; Par Reg 3.419
Far worse, her false resemblance only meets, Par Reg 4.320
Mee worse then wet thou find'st not; other harm Par Reg 4.486
Blind among enemies, O worse then chains, Samson 68
Not worse then by his shield and spear Samson 284
She purpos'd to betray me, and (which was worse Samson 399
True slavery, and that blindness worse then this, Samson 418
That rigid score. A worse thing yet remains, Samson 433
By pains and slaveries, worse then death inflicted Samson 485
By worse then hostile deeds, violating the ends Samson 893
Goes by the worse, whatever be her cause. Samson 904
Dangers, and snares, and wrongs, and worse then so, Passion 11
Hated not Learning wors then Toad or Asp; Sonnet 11, 13
Your plots and packing wors then those of *Trent*, Forcers 14
Trinity ms 'worse'
Far worse then fire to burn. Psalm 85, 12

Worship
Eternity so spent in worship paid Par Lost 2.248
With every Plant, in sign of Worship wave. Par Lost 5.194
And worship God Supream, who made him chief Par Lost 7.515
And worship him, and in reward to rule Par Lost 7.628
And joind thir vocal Worship to the Quire Par Lost 9.198
And gaze, and worship thee of right declar'd Par Lost 9.611
With worship, place by place where he voutsaf'd Par Lost 11.318
To worship God aright, and know his works Par Lost 11.578
Bred up in Idol-worship; O that men Par Lost 12.115
To worship thir own work in Wood and Stone Par Lost 12.119
On all who in the worship persevere Par Lost 12.532
To know, and knowing worship God aright, Par Reg 2.475
From God to worship Calves, the Deities Par Reg 3.416
And God with Idols in thir worship joyn'd. Par Reg 3.426
And worship me as thy superior Lord, Par Reg 4.167
The first of all Commandments, Thou shalt worship Par Reg 4.176
To worship thee accurst, now more accurst Par Reg 4.179
That I fall down and worship thee as God? Par Reg 4.192
Sam. Not in thir Idol-worship, but by labour Samson 1365
Will towards thy holy temple worship low Psalm 5, 20
What certain Seat, where I may worship thee Prose 12, 5

Worshipped
Worshipt in *Rabba* and her watry Plain, Par Lost 1.397

Worshipped(*cont*)
Worship't with Temple, Priest and Sacrifice; Par Reg 3.83
And as I past, I worshipt; if those you seek Mask 302
Bridgewater ms 'worship't'
She hutch't th' all-worshipt ore, and precious gems Mask 719
1637 'all worshipt'
Bridgewater ms 'all worshipt'
Trinity ms 'all-worship't'
The sable-stoled Sorcerers bear his worshipt Ark. Nativity 220
When all our Fathers worship't Stocks and Stones, Sonnet 18, 4

Worshippers
Where he fell flat, and sham'd his Worshipers: Par Lost 1.461
ms 'worshippers'
The number of thy worshippers. Who seekes Par Lost 7.613
And multiply a Race of Worshippers Par Lost 7.630
His worshippers; he knows that in the day Par Lost 9.705
And with confusion blank his Worshippers. Samson 471

Worst
In worst extreams, and on the perilous edge Par Lost 1.276
And cannot cease to be, we are at worst Par Lost 2.100
What can we suffer worse? is this then worst, Par Lost 2.163
For happy though but ill, for ill not worst, Par Lost 2.224
To worst abuse, or to thir meanest use. Par Lost 4.204
Thy Rebels, or be found the worst in Heav'n. Par Lost 5.742
But pain is perfet miserie, the worst Par Lost 6.462
Who guards her, or with her the worst endures. Par Lost 9.269
The worst, and not perswade thee rather die Par Lost 9.979
Whoever judg'd, the worst on mee must light, Par Lost 10.73
I would be at the worst; worst is my Port, Par Reg 3.209
If I then to the worst that can be hast, Par Reg 3.223
From worst of other evils, pains and wrongs, Samson 105
Thou art become (O worst imprisonment!) Samson 155
Yet that which was the worst now least afflicts me, Samson 195
The worst that he can give, to me the best. Samson 1264
The worst of all indignities, yet on me Samson 1341
Mess. Then take the worst in brief, *Samson* is dead. Samson 1570
Man. The worst indeed, O all my hope's defeated Samson 1571
Or els som neighbour Wood-man, or at worst, Mask 484
Believe me I have thither packt the worst: Vacation 12

Worth
To reign is worth ambition though in Hell: Par Lost 1.262
At thir great Emperors call, as next in worth Par Lost 1.378
Semblance of worth, not substance, gently rais'd Par Lost 1.529
Worth waiting, since our present lot appeers Par Lost 2.223
Faded so soon. Advise if this be worth Par Lost 2.376
Conscious of highest worth, unmov'd thus spake. Par Lost 2.429
Haste hither *Eve*, and worth thy sight behold Par Lost 5.308
Her vertue and the conscience of her worth, Par Lost 8.502
Him who to worth in Women overtrusting Par Lost 9.1183
Offended, worth your laughter, hath giv'n up Par Lost 10.488
To what highth sacred vertue and true worth Par Reg 1.231
To prove him, and illustrate his high worth; Par Reg 1.370
Of worth, of honour, glory, and popular praise; Par Reg 2.227
Things vulgar, & well weigh'd, scarce worth the praise, Par Reg 3.51
Worth or not worth the seeking, let it pass: Par Reg 3.151
Plausible to the world, to me worth naught. Par Reg 3.393
The rest are barbarous, and scarce worth the sight, Par Reg 4.86
And trifles for choice matters, worth a spunge; Par Reg 4.329
Thenceforth I thought thee worth my nearer view Par Reg 4.514
Worth naming Son of God by voice from Heav'n, Par Reg 4.539
To count them things worth notice, till at length Samson 250
That doth enrich these Downs, is worth a thought Mask 505
Yet should I try, the uncontrouled worth Mask 793
line not in Trinity ms
line not in Bridgewater ms
Fame that her high worth to raise, Arcades 8
I will assay, her worth to celebrate, Arcades 80
His mighty Majesty and worth. Psalm 136, 90
In worth and excellence he shall out-go them, Vacation 79
Thy worth and skill exempts thee from the throng, Sonnet 13, 5
Trinity ms 'worth' ←'wit' ←'worth'

Worthier
Happier thou mayst be, worthier canst not be: Par Lost 5.76
Against his worthier, as thine now serve thee, Par Lost 6.180
More justly, Seat worthier of Gods, as built Par Lost 9.100
As to his worthier, and would have resign'd Par Reg 1.27
All her assaults, on worthier things intent? Par Reg 2.195

Worthies
Great Cities by assault: what do these Worthies, Par Reg 3.74

Worthiest
By place or choice the worthiest; they anon Par Lost 1.759
Found worthiest to be so by being Good, Par Lost 3.310
Pleasant to know, and worthiest to be all Par Lost 3.703
When he who rules is worthiest, and excells Par Lost 6.177
Behests obey, worthiest to be obey'd, Par Lost 6.185
To manifest thee worthiest to be Heir Par Lost 6.707
Worthiest to Reign: he celebrated rode Par Lost 6.888
That thou who worthiest art should'st be thir King? Par Reg 3.226
To heap ingratitude on worthiest deeds? Samson 276
To worthiest deeds, if he through frailty err, Samson 369
And yet such musick worthiest were to blaze Arcades 74

Worthily
To loathsom sickness, worthily, since they Par Lost 11.524

Worthless
Thy Paranymph, worthless to thee compar'd, Samson 1020

Worthy
Flours worthy of Paradise which not nice Art Par Lost 4.241
And worthie seemd, for in thir looks Divine Par Lost 4.291

Worthy(*cont*)
Worthy of Sacred silence to be heard; Par Lost 5.557
Found worthy not of Libertie alone, Par Lost 6.420
An outside? fair no doubt, and worthy well Par Lost 8.568
Therein enjoy'd were worthy to subdue Par Lost 8.584
Though kept from Man, and worthy to be admir'd, Par Lost 9.746
Ill worthie I such title should belong Par Lost 11.163
In time of dearth, a Son whose worthy deeds Par Lost 12.161
Worthy t' have not remain'd so long unsung. Par Reg 1.17
To shew him worthy of his birth divine Par Reg 1.141
Worthy of Memorial) canst thou not remember Par Reg 2.445
To things not glorious, men not worthy of fame. Par Reg 3.70
With those thy boyst'rous locks, no worthy match Samson 1164
And thou art worthy that thou shouldst not know Mask 788
line not in Bridgewater ms
line not in Trinity ms
And shove away the worthy bidden guest. Lycidas 118

Would
All incorruptible would on his Throne Par Lost 2.138
Incapable of stain would soon expel Par Lost 2.140
To be no more; sad cure; for who would loose, Par Lost 2.146
Ages of hopeless end; this would be worse. Par Lost 2.186
Abolish his own works. This would surpass Par Lost 2.370
A hideous Peal: yet, when they list, would creep, Par Lost 2.656
And me his Parent would full soon devour Par Lost 2.805
Not what they would? what praise could they receive? Par Lost 3.106
New *Babels*, had they wherewithall, would build: Par Lost 3.468
Night would invade, but there the neighbouring Moon Par Lost 3.726
Would set me highest, and in a moment quit Par Lost 4.51
Would higth recal high thoughts, how soon unsay Par Lost 4.95
What feign'd submission swore: ease would recant Par Lost 4.96
Which would but lead me to a worse relapse Par Lost 4.100
What further would be learnt. Live while ye may, Par Lost 4.533
That heav'n would want spectators, God want praise; Par Lost 4.676
Who would not, finding way, break loose from Hell, Par Lost 4.889
Doctrin which we would know whence learnt: who saw Par Lost 5.856
Once found, which yet unfound most would have thought Par Lost 6.500
Doubl'd, would render them yet more despis'd, Par Lost 6.602
As they would dance, yet for a dance they seemd Par Lost 6.615
Heav'n ruining from Heav'n and would have fled Par Lost 6.868
Which would be all his solace and revenge, Par Lost 6.905
Chose rather; hee, she knew would intermix Par Lost 8.54
That would be woo'd, and not unsought be won, Par Lost 8.503
To Cattel and each Beast; which would not be Par Lost 8.582
Would not admit; thine and of all thy Sons Par Lost 8.637
Whatever sleights none would suspicious mark, Par Lost 9.92
For what God after better worse would build? Par Lost 9.102
Bane, and in Heav'n much worse would be my state. Par Lost 9.123
Would utmost vigor raise, and rais'd unite. Par Lost 9.314
For high from ground the branches would require Par Lost 9.590
Would never from my heart; no no, I feel Par Lost 9.913
Creation could repeate, yet would be loath Par Lost 9.946
Were it I thought Death menac't would ensue Par Lost 9.977
This my attempt, I would sustain alone Par Lost 9.978
Would thou hadst heark'nd to my words, and stai'd Par Lost 9.1134
Foretold so lately what would come to pass, Par Lost 10.38
A World who would not purchase with a bruise, Par Lost 10.500
According to his doom: he would have spoke, Par Lost 10.517
Of happiness: yet well, if here would end Par Lost 10.725
The miserie, I deserv'd it, and would beare Par Lost 10.726
To deathless pain? how gladly would I meet Par Lost 10.775
Insensible, how glad would lay me down Par Lost 10.777
Would Thunder in my ears, no fear of worse Par Lost 10.780
To mee and to my ofspring would torment me Par Lost 10.781
So disinherited how would ye bless Par Lost 10.821
Would speed before thee, and be louder heard, Par Lost 10.954
With like desire, which would be meserie Par Lost 10.997
Would be revenge indeed; which will be lost Par Lost 10.1036
Of him who all things can, I would not cease Par Lost 11.309
So many grateful Altars I would reare Par Lost 11.323
What we receive, would either not accept Par Lost 11.505
Henceforth I flie not Death, nor would prolong Par Lost 11.547
And utter odious Truth, that God would come Par Lost 11.704
All would have then gon well, peace would have crownd Par Lost 11.781
Erwhile perplext with thoughts what would becom Par Lost 12.275
As to his worthier, and would have resign'd Par Reg 1.27
Would not be last, and with the voice divine Par Reg 1.35
How would one look from his Majestick brow Par Reg 2.216
Would scruple that, with want oppresst? behold Par Reg 2.331
Thy Counsel would be as the Oracle Par Reg 3.13
Of conduct would be such, that all the world Par Reg 3.18
And not returning that would likeliest render Par Reg 3.130
Yet, sacrilegious, to himself would take Par Reg 3.140
I would be at the worst; worst is my Port, Par Reg 3.209
The end I would attain, my final good. Par Reg 3.211
Would stand between me and thy Fathers ire, Par Reg 3.219
Headlong would follow; and to thir Gods perhaps Par Reg 3.430
What wise and valiant man would seek to free Par Reg 4.143
Or if I would delight my private hours Par Reg 4.331
Which would have set thee in short time with ease Par Reg 4.378
The Prince of darkness, glad would also seem Par Reg 4.441
As Earth and Skie would mingle; but my self Par Reg 4.453
Would ask a life to wail, but chief of all, Samson 66
I would be understood) in prosperous days Samson 191
But they persisted deaf, and would not seem Samson 249
As if they would confine th' interminable, Samson 307
He would not else who never wanted means, Samson 315
Who would be now a Father in my stead? Samson 355

Would(*cont*)
Would draw thee forth to perilous enterprises, Samson 804
It would be to ensnare an irreligious Samson 860
Sam. I thought where all thy circling wiles would end; Samson 871
Bin, as it ought, sincere, it would have taught thee Samson 874
In what I thought would have succeeded best. Samson 908
Me their Deliverer sent would not receive, Samson 1214
Which to no few of them would prove pernicious. Samson 1400
Cho. That hope would much rejoyce us to partake Samson 1455
They easily would set to sale, a third Samson 1466
Yet Hope would fain subscribe, and tempts Belief. Samson 1535
Mess. It would burst forth, but I recover breath Samson 1555
I would not soil these pure Ambrosial weeds, Mask 16
Would send a glistring Guardian if need were Mask 219
line not in Bridgewater ms
Who as they sung, would take the prison'd soul, Mask 256
And lap it in *Elysium*, *Scylla* wept, Mask 257
Trinity ms 'wept' ←'would weepe'
What readiest way would bring me to that place? Mask 305
Would overtask the best Land-Pilots art, Mask 309
T'would be som solace yet, som little chearing Mask 348
1673 "Twould'
And run to meet what he would most avoid? Mask 363
line not in Bridgewater ms
line not in Trinity ms
Vertue could see to do what vertue would Mask 373
For who would rob a Hermit of his Weeds, Mask 390
He lov'd me well, and oft would beg me sing, Mask 623
Would sit, and hearken even to extasie, Mask 625
I would not taste thy treasonous offer; none Mask 702
Trinity ms 'would not taste' ←'should reject' ←'hate it from thy hands'
Th' all-giver would be unthank't, would be unprais'd, Mask 723
Who would be quite surcharg'd with her own weight, Mask 728
The herds would over-multitude their Lords, Mask 731
The Sea o'refraught would swell, & th' unsought diamonds Mask 732
Would so emblaze the forhead of the Deep, Mask 733
And so bestudd with Stars, that they below Mask 734
Trinity ms 'and so bestudde with starres' ←'would so be studde the center with thire starre light'
Would grow inur'd to light, and com at last Mask 735
Would think to charm my judgement, as mine eyes Mask 758
As if she would her children should be riotous Mask 763
Trinity ms 'would' ←'ment'
Natures full blessings would be well dispenc't Mask 772
And then the giver would be better thank't, Mask 775
Fain would I somthing say, yet to what end? Mask 783
line not in Trinity ms
line not in Bridgewater ms
Of this pure cause would kindle my rap't spirits Mask 794
line not in Trinity ms
line not in Bridgewater ms
That dumb things would be mov'd to sympathize, Mask 796
line not in Bridgewater ms
line not in Trinity ms
And the brute Earth would lend her nerves, and shake, Mask 797
line not in Trinity ms
line not in Bridgewater ms
Mortals that would follow me, Mask 1018
Heav'n it self would stoop to her. Mask 1023
Such streins as would have won the ear Allegro 148
Who had thought this clime had held Arcades 24
Trinity ms 'had' ←'would have'
Who would not sing for *Lycidas*? he knew Lycidas 10
From the glad sound would not be absent long, Lycidas 35
Yet on the softned Quarry would I score Passion 46
That they would fitly fall in order'd Characters. Passion 49
Would soon unboosom all thir Echoes milde, Passion 53
That Kings for such a Tomb would wish to die. Shakespear 16
Fainted, and died, nor would with Ale be quickn'd; Another 16
line not in 1640, 1657, 1658 texts
That would have made *Quintilian* stare and gasp. Sonnet 11, 11
And still revolt when truth would set them free. Sonnet 12, 10
Trinity ms 'still revolt when Truth would sett them' ←'make them' ←'set them' ←'hate the truth wherby they should be'
Would have been held in high esteem with *Paul* Forcers 10
And yet my people would not *hear*, Psalm 81, 45
O that my people would *be wise* Psalm 81, 53
And O that Israel would *advise* Psalm 81, 55
Then would I soon bring down their foes Psalm 81, 57
And we would feed them *from the shock* Psalm 81, 65

Wouldst
Though thither doomd? Thou wouldst thy self, no doubt, Par Lost 4.890
And thou sly hypocrite, who now wouldst seem Par Lost 4.957
And anger wouldst resent the offer'd wrong, Par Lost 9.300
Wouldst thou approve thy constancie, approve Par Lost 9.367
Wouldst easily detect what I conceale. Par Lost 10.136
Wouldst thou admit for his contempt of thee Par Lost 10.763
Would'st thou not eat? Thereafter as I like Par Reg 2.321
Therefore, if at great things thou wouldst arrive, Par Reg 2.426
Ambitious spirit, and wouldst be thought my God, Par Reg 4.495
Of fancy, feard lest one day thou wouldst leave me Samson 794
How wouldst thou use me now, blind, and thereby Samson 941
And last neglected? How wouldst thou insult Samson 944
Sam. Boast not of what thou wouldst have done, but do Samson 1104
What then thou would'st, thou seest it in thy hand. Samson 1105
Again in safety what thou wouldst have done Samson 1128
And wouldst thou seek again to trap me here Mask 699

Wouldst(*cont*)
line not in Bridgewater ms
1673 'would'st'

Wound
Whose annual wound in *Lebanon* allur'd — Par Lost 1.447
Op'nd into the Hill a spacious wound — Par Lost 1.689
Death his deaths wound shall then receive, and stoop — Par Lost 3.252
The griding sword with discontinuous wound — Par Lost 6.329
Nor in thir liquid texture mortal wound — Par Lost 6.348
By wound, though from thir place by violence mov'd. — Par Lost 6.405
Imperishable, and though peirc'd with wound, — Par Lost 6.435
And Life-blood streaming fresh; wide was the wound, — Par Lost 8.467
Foe not informidable, exempt from wound, — Par Lost 9.486
Earth felt the wound, and Nature from her seat — Par Lost 9.782
Thy message, which might else in telling wound, — Par Lost 11.299
Disabl'd not to give thee thy deaths wound: — Par Lost 12.392
With dread attending when that fatal wound — Par Reg 1.53
Must bide the stroak of that long threatn'd wound, — Par Reg 1.59
Thy wound, yet not thy last and deadliest wound — Par Reg 4.622
What glorious hand gave *Samson* his deaths wound? — Samson 1581
Waxing well of his deep wound — Mask 1000
line not in Bridgewater ms
On which the fate of gods and men is wound. — Arcades 67

Wound
About the mossie Trunk I wound me soon, — Par Lost 9.589
& darknesse wound her in. I Bro. Peace, brother peace — Mask Tr. ms 15.53
'wound' ←'wond'

Wounded
Of *Thammuz* yearly wounded: the Love-tale — Par Lost 1.452
In vain the *Tyrian* Maids their wounded *Thamuz* mourn. — Nativity 204

Wounding
And seals obedience first with wounding smart — Circum 25

Wounds
A refuge from those wounds: or when we lay — Par Lost 2.168
Where wounds of deadly hate have peirc'd so deep: — Par Lost 4.99
Mangl'd with gastly wounds through Plate and Maile, — Par Lost 6.368
Of *Egypt* must lie dead. Thus with ten wounds — Par Lost 12.190
As of a Duel, or the local wounds — Par Lost 12.387
This wounds me most (what can it less) that Man, — Par Reg 1.404
And are as Balm to fester'd wounds. — Samson 186
To the bodies wounds and sores — Samson 607
Nor less then wounds immedicable — Samson 620

Wove
Insinuating, wove with Gordian twine — Par Lost 4.348
Waiting desirous her return, had wove — Par Lost 9.839
With Ringlets quaint, and wanton windings wove. — Arcades 47

Woven
Among thick-wov'n Arborets and Flours — Par Lost 9.437
Not force, but well couch't fraud, well woven snares, — Par Reg 1.97
And wov'n close, both matter, form and stile; — Sonnet 11, 2
Trinity ms 'wov'n' ←'weav'd it'

Wrack
At least had gon to rack, disturbd and torne — Par Lost 4.994
Had gon to wrack, with ruin overspred, — Par Lost 6.670
A World devote to universal rack. — Par Lost 11.821
After a dismal night; I heard the rack — Par Reg 4.452

Wracked
Vaunting aloud, but rackt with deep despare: — Par Lost 1.126
ms 'wrackt'

Wrapped
Under yon boyling Ocean, wrapt in Chains; — Par Lost 2.183
I dread, and to elude, thus wrapt in mist — Par Lost 9.158
Rapt in a balmie Cloud with winged Steeds — Par Lost 11.706
Wrapt in a pleasing fit of melancholy — Mask 546
All meanly wrapt in the rude manger lies; — Nativity 31

Wrath
Reserv'd him to more wrath; for now the thought — Par Lost 1.54
ms 'wrauth'
That Glory never shall his wrath or might — Par Lost 1.110
ms 'wrauth'
Treble confusion, wrath and vengeance pour'd. — Par Lost 1.220
ms 'wrauth'
Our stronger, some worse way his wrath may find — Par Lost 2.83
To whom the Goblin full of wrauth reply'd, — Par Lost 2.688
What e're his wrath, which he calls Justice, bids, — Par Lost 2.733
His wrath which one day will destroy ye both. — Par Lost 2.734
And reconcilement; wrauth shall be no more — Par Lost 3.264
Found out for mankind under wrauth, O thou — Par Lost 3.275
He to appease thy wrauth, and end the strife — Par Lost 3.406
Infinite wrauth, and infinite despaire? — Par Lost 4.74
So judge thou still, presumptuous, till the wrauth, — Par Lost 4.912
These wicked Tents devoted, least the wrauth — Par Lost 5.890
Of wrauth awak't: nor with less dread the loud — Par Lost 6.59
And full of wrauth bent on his Enemies. — Par Lost 6.826
Down from the verge of Heav'n, Eternal wrauth — Par Lost 6.865
Not less but more Heroic then the wrauth — Par Lost 9.14
The Eevning coole when he from wrauth more coole — Par Lost 10.95
The present, fearing guiltie what his wrauth — Par Lost 10.340
Is his wrauth also? be it, man is not so, — Par Lost 10.795
Wrath without end on Man whom Death must end? — Par Lost 10.797
So might the wrauth. Fond wish! couldst thou support — Par Lost 10.834
His full wrauth whose thou feelst as yet lest part, — Par Lost 10.951
Without wrauth or reviling; wee expected — Par Lost 10.1048
And full of peace, denouncing wrauth to come — Par Lost 11.815
From God, and over wrauth grace shall abound. — Par Lost 12.478
Fall'n into wrath divine, — Samson 1683
Dips me all o're, as when the wrath of *Jove* — Mask 803
line not in Bridgewater ms

Wrath(*cont*)
line not in Trinity ms
And wrath to see his Kingdom fail, — Nativity 171
1673 'wroth'
To slake his wrath whom sin hath made our foe — Fair Inf 66
And the full wrath beside — Circum 23
Trinity ms 'wrath' ←'wrauth'
Speak to them in his wrath, and in his fell — Psalm 2, 10
If once his wrath take fire like fuel sere. — Psalm 2, 27
Thy smoaking wrath, *and angry brow* — Psalm 80, 19
From thy fierce wrath which we had prov'd — Psalm 85, 11
Thy wrath *from which no shelter saves* — Psalm 88, 29
Thy fierce wrath over me doth flow — Psalm 88, 65

Wrathful
That doth the wrathfull tyrants quell. — Psalm 136, 10

Wreak
Well pleas'd, on me let Death wreck all his rage; — Par Lost 3.241
To wreck on innocent frail man his loss — Par Lost 4.11

Wreath
Curld many a wanton wreath in sight of *Eve*, — Par Lost 9.517
Golden in shew, is but a wreath of thorns, — Par Reg 2.459
And Dunbarr feild resounds thy praises loud, — Sonnet 16, 8
Trinity ms 'Worsters laureat wreath' ←'Dunbarr feild'
And Worsters laureat wreath; yet much remaines — Sonnet 16, 9
Trinity ms 'Worsters laureat wreath' ←'twentie battles more'
1694 'Wreath'

Wreathed
To make them mirth us'd all his might, and wreathd — Par Lost 4.346
From his slack hand the Garland wreath'd for *Eve* — Par Lost 9.892
Dusk faces with white silken Turbants wreath'd: — Par Reg 4.76
With Ivy berries wreath'd, and his blithe youth, — Mask 55
Nods, and Becks, and Wreathed Smiles, — Allegro 28

Wreaths
In duskie wreathes, reluctant flames, the signe — Par Lost 6.58
And throw sweet garland wreaths into her stream — Mask 850
In wreaths thy golden Hair, — Horace 4

Wreck
Well pleas'd, on me let Death wreck all his rage; — Par Lost 3.241
To wreck on innocent frail man his loss — Par Lost 4.11
What Pilot so expert but needs must wreck — Samson 1044

Wrecked
Rocks whereon greatest men have oftest wreck'd; — Par Reg 2.228

Wrench
Which others at their Barr so often wrench; — Sonnet 21, 4
line not in Trinity ms

Wrested
To be thus wrested from us? rather why — Par Lost 11.503
But misery hath rested from me; where — Par Reg 1.470
The secret wrested from me in her highth — Samson 384

Wrestlers
Of Gymnic Artists, Wrestlers, Riders, Runners, — Samson 1324

Wretched
That after wretched Life must be at last — Par Lost 10.985
Degraded, to what wretched state reserv'd! — Par Lost 11.501
Siege and defiance: Wretched man! what food — Par Lost 12.74
With Food, whereof we wretched seldom taste. — Par Reg 1.345
Grate on their scrannel Pipes of wretched straw, — Lycidas 124

Wring
To wring from me and tell to them my secret, — Samson 1199

Wrinkled
Wrinkl'd the face of Deluge, as decai'd; — Par Lost 11.843
Blew meager Hag, or stubborn unlaid ghost, — Mask 434
Trinity ms 'meager' ←'wrincl'd' ←'wrinckled'
By hoary *Nereus* wrincled look, — Mask 871
Sport that wrincled Care derides, — Allegro 31

Wrists
Held up their pearled wrists and took her in, — Mask 834

Writ
The Law and Prophets, searching what was writ — Par Reg 1.260
With others though in Holy Writ not nam'd, — Par Reg 2.8
If of my raign Prophetic Writ hath told, — Par Reg 3.184
Consolatories writ — Samson 657
A Book was writ of late call'd *Tetrachordon;* — Sonnet 11, 1
Trinity ms 'writ' ←'writt'
To after age thou shalt be writ the man, — Sonnet 13, 7
Trinity ms 'writ' ←'writt'
New Presbyter is but *Old Priest* writ Large. — Forcers 20
Trinity ms 'writt'

Write
Farr be it, that I should write thee sin or blame, — Par Lost 4.758
Working through love, upon thir hearts shall write, — Par Lost 12.489
The *Gentiles* also know, and write, and teach — Par Reg 4.227
Or Heav'n write aught of Fate, by what the Stars — Par Reg 4.383
to write his owne woes on the vermeil graine — Lycidas Tr. ms 28.18
The leaves should all be black wheron I write, — Passion 34
The Lord shall write it in a Scrowle — Psalm 87, 21

Writhed
To make them mirth us'd all his might, and wreathd — Par Lost 4.346
And writh'd him to and fro convolv'd; so sore — Par Lost 6.328
With hatefullest disrelish writh'd thir jaws — Par Lost 10.569

Written
Thir doctrine and thir story written left, — Par Lost 12.506
Left onely in those written Records pure, — Par Lost 12.513
Think'st thou such force in Bread? is it not written — Par Reg 1.347
Thou hast permission on me. It is written — Par Reg 4.175
For it is written, He will give command — Par Reg 4.556
To whom thus Jesus: also it is written, — Par Reg 4.560

Written(*cont*)	
beyond the written date of mortall change	Mask Tr. ms 10.22
Wrong	
On you who wrong me not for him who wrongd.	Par Lost 4.387
And anger wouldst resent the offer'd wrong,	Par Lost 9.300
To Man, and indignation at his wrong,	Par Lost 9.666
In wise deport, spake much of Right and Wrong,	Par Lost 11.666
From vertue, which is reason, that no wrong,	Par Lost 12.98
Never did wrong or violence, by them	Par Reg 1.389
To daily fraud, contempt, abuse and wrong,	Samson 76
In choice, but oftest to affect the wrong?	Samson 1030
With judgment false and wrong	Psalm 82, 6
There ev'n the Sparrow *freed from wrong*	Psalm 84, 9
Wronged	
On you who wrong me not for him who wrongd.	Par Lost 4.387
Wrongs	
Him whom thy wrongs with Saintly patience born,	Par Reg 3.93
From worst of other evils, pains and wrongs,	Samson 105
Dangers, and snares, and wrongs, and worse then so,	Passion 11
Wrote	
The *Pentateuch* or what the Prophets wrote,	Par Reg 4.226
Wroth	
And wrath to see his Kingdom fail,	Nativity 171
1673 'wroth'	
Wrought	
Which tempted our attempt, and wrought our fall.	Par Lost 1.642
Wrought still within them; and no less desire	Par Lost 2.295
And wrought but malice; lifted up so high	Par Lost 4.49
Rear'd high thir flourisht heads between, and wrought	Par Lost 4.699
Nor number, nor example with him wrought	Par Lost 5.901
Into thir substance pent, which wrought them pain	Par Lost 6.657
Save what sin hath impaird, which yet hath wrought	Par Lost 6.691
Of radiant *Urim*, work divinely wrought,	Par Lost 6.761
Wrought in her so, that seeing me, she turn'd;	Par Lost 8.507
Now not, though Sin, not Time, first wraught the change,	Par Lost 9.70
As when a Ship by skilful Stearsman wrought	Par Lost 9.513
They fasten'd, and the Mole immense wraught on	Par Lost 10.300
Acknowledg'd and deplor'd, in *Adam* wraught	Par Lost 10.939
To evils which our own misdeeds have wrought,	Par Lost 10.1080
For dissolution wrought by Sin, that first	Par Lost 11.55
Th' effects which thy original crime hath wrought	Par Lost 11.424
First his own Tooles; then, what might else be wrought	Par Lost 11.572
Wrought that effect on *Jove*, so Fables tell;	Par Reg 2.215
Who wrought their own captivity, fell off	Par Reg 3.415
And Love hath oft, well meaning, wrought much wo,	Samson 813
That wrought with me: thou know'st the Magistrates	Samson 850
To have wrought such wonders with an Asses Jaw;	Samson 1095
Chor. Yet God hath wrought things as incredible	Samson 1532
Be in my hands, if I have wrought	Psalm 7, 9
That wrought thy people woe,	Psalm 85, 6
Xerxes	
Xerxes, the Libertie of *Greece* to yoke,	Par Lost 10.307
Yawning	
Yawning receavd them whole, and on them clos'd,	Par Lost 6.875
Both *Sin*, and *Death*, and yawning *Grave* at last	Par Lost 10.635
& yawning dens where glaring monsters house	Mask Tr. ms 16.63
and yawninge denns, where glaringe monsters house	Mask Br. ms 416
Ychained	
Yet first to those ychain'd in sleep,	Nativity 155
Yclept	
In Heav'n ycleap'd *Euphrosyne*,	Allegro 12
Ye	
Eternal spirits; or have ye chos'n this place	Par Lost 1.318
Or in this abject posture have ye sworn	Par Lost 1.322
ms 'yee'	
All thoughts of warr: ye have what I advise.	Par Lost 2.283
Well have ye judg'd, well ended long debate,	Par Lost 2.390
Synod of Gods, and like to what ye are,	Par Lost 2.391
His wrath which one day will destroy ye both.	Par Lost 2.734
And bring ye to the place where Thou and Death	Par Lost 2.840
With odours; there ye shall be fed and fill'd	Par Lost 2.843
T' whom *Satan* turning boldly, thus. Ye Powers	Par Lost 2.968
Which of ye will be mortal to redeem	Par Lost 3.214
God shall be All in All. But all ye Gods,	Par Lost 3.341
Into the devious Air; then might ye see	Par Lost 3.489
Sin-bred, how have ye troubl'd all mankind	Par Lost 4.315
Ah gentle pair, yee little think how nigh	Par Lost 4.366
Will vanish and deliver ye to woe,	Par Lost 4.368
What further would be learnt. Live while ye may,	Par Lost 4.533
Blest pair; and O yet happiest if ye seek	Par Lost 4.774
Such where ye find, seise fast, and hither bring.	Par Lost 4.796
Know ye not then said *Satan*, fill'd with scorn,	Par Lost 4.827
Know ye not mee? ye knew me once no mate	Par Lost 4.828
For you, there sitting where ye durst not soare;	Par Lost 4.829
The lowest of your throng; or if ye know,	Par Lost 4.831
Why ask ye, and superfluous begin	Par Lost 4.832
Speak yee who best can tell, ye Sons of light,	Par Lost 5.160
1667 'ye who' in some copies	
Angels, for yee behold him, and with songs	Par Lost 5.161
1667 'ye' in some copies	
Circle his Throne rejoycing, yee in Heav'n,	Par Lost 5.163
On Earth joyn all ye Creatures to extoll	Par Lost 5.164
1667 'yee'	
And yee five other wandring Fires that move	Par Lost 5.177
Aire, and ye Elements the eldest birth	Par Lost 5.180
Ye Mists and Exhalations that now rise	Par Lost 5.185
His praise ye Winds, that from four Quarters blow,	Par Lost 5.192
Breathe soft or loud; and wave your tops, ye Pines,	Par Lost 5.193
Ye(*cont*)	
Fountains and yee, that warble, as ye flow,	Par Lost 5.195
Joyn voices all ye living Souls, ye Birds,	Par Lost 5.197
Yee that in Waters glide, and yee that walk	Par Lost 5.200
If ye be found obedient, and retain	Par Lost 5.501
What meant that caution joind, *if ye be found*	Par Lost 5.513
Hear all ye Angels, Progenie of Light,	Par Lost 5.600
Him have anointed, whom ye now behold	Par Lost 5.605
Will ye submit your necks, and chuse to bend	Par Lost 5.787
The supple knee? ye will not, if I trust	Par Lost 5.788
To know ye right, or if ye know your selves	Par Lost 5.789
Freely our part; yee who appointed stand	Par Lost 6.565
Stand still in bright array ye Saints, here stand	Par Lost 6.801
Ye Angels arm'd, this day from Battel rest;	Par Lost 6.802
And as ye have receivd, so have ye don	Par Lost 6.805
Mean while inhabit laxe, ye Powers of Heav'n,	Par Lost 7.162
Silence, ye troubl'd waves, and thou Deep, peace,	Par Lost 7.216
Be gather'd now ye Waters under Heav'n	Par Lost 7.283
Open, ye everlasting Gates, they sung,	Par Lost 7.565
Open, ye Heav'ns, your living dores; let in	Par Lost 7.566
Ye Hills and Dales, ye Rivers, Woods, and Plaines,	Par Lost 8.275
And ye that live and move, fair Creatures, tell,	Par Lost 8.276
Tell, if ye saw, how came I thus, how here?	Par Lost 8.277
Thoughts, whither have ye led me, with what sweet	Par Lost 9.473
Of all these Garden Trees ye shall not eate,	Par Lost 9.657
The Garden, God hath said, Ye shall not eate	Par Lost 9.662
Thereof, nor shall ye touch it, least ye die.	Par Lost 9.663
Those rigid threats of Death; ye shall not Die:	Par Lost 9.685
How should ye? by the Fruit? it gives you Life	Par Lost 9.686
God therefore cannot hurt ye, and be just;	Par Lost 9.700
Why but to keep ye low and ignorant,	Par Lost 9.704
Ye Eate thereof, your Eyes that seem so cleere,	Par Lost 9.706
Op'nd and cleerd, and ye shall be as Gods,	Par Lost 9.708
That ye should be as Gods, since I as Man,	Par Lost 9.710
I of brute human, yee of human Gods.	Par Lost 9.712
So ye shall die perhaps, by putting off	Par Lost 9.713
And brown as Evening: Cover me ye Pines,	Par Lost 9.1088
Ye Cedars, with innumerable boughs	Par Lost 9.1089
Assembl'd Angels, and ye Powers return'd	Par Lost 10.34
I told ye then he should prevail and speed	Par Lost 10.40
High proof ye now have giv'n to be the Race	Par Lost 10.385
My Substitutes I send ye, and Create	Par Lost 10.403
I call ye and declare ye now, returnd	Par Lost 10.462
Successful beyond hope, to lead ye forth	Par Lost 10.463
Or much more grievous pain? Ye have th' account	Par Lost 10.501
Of my performance: What remains, ye Gods,	Par Lost 10.502
That I must leave ye, Sons; O were I able	Par Lost 10.819
To waste it all my self, and leave ye none!	Par Lost 10.820
So disinherited how would ye bless	Par Lost 10.821
From the first op'ning bud, and gave ye Names,	Par Lost 11.277
Who now shall reare ye to the Sun, or ranke	Par Lost 11.278
That ye may live, which will be many dayes,	Par Lost 12.602
Our hated habitation; well ye know	Par Reg 1.47
Ye see our danger on the utmost edge	Par Reg 1.94
Be frustrate all ye stratagems of Hell,	Par Reg 1.180
Deceive ye to perswasion over-sure	Par Reg 2.142
Not to be found, though sought. Yee see, O friends,	Samson 193
Man. Brethren and men of *Dan*, for such ye seem,	Samson 332
To give ye part with me what hope I have	Samson 1453
And listen why, for I will tell ye now	Mask 43
Bridgewater ms 'you'	
Trinity ms 'you'	
I see ye visibly, and now beleeve	Mask 216
line not in Bridgewater ms	
1637 'yee'	
Trinity ms 'yee'	
Eld. Bro. Unmuffle ye faint stars, and thou fair Moon	Mask 331
Bridgewater ms 'yee'	
1637 'yee'	
Do ye beleeve me yet, or shall I call	Mask 438
Bridgewater ms 'you'	
1637 'yee'	
Trinity ms 'yee'	
Spir. Ile tell ye, 'tis not vain, or fabulous,	Mask 513
. Bridgewater ms 'you'	
1637 'you'	
Trinity ms 'you'	
Ye were the two she mean't, with that I sprung	Mask 578
Trinity ms 'yee'	
1637 'Yee'	
Bridgewater ms 'yee'	
How are ye joyn'd with hell in triple knot	Mask 581
1637 'yee'	
Trinity ms 'yee'	
Bridgewater ms 'you'	
Co. Why are you vext Lady? why do you frown?	Mask 666
Trinity ms 'you' ← 'yo' ← 'ye'	
Spir. What, have you let the false enchanter scape?	Mask 814
Bridgewater ms 'have yee'	
O ye mistook, ye should have snatcht his wand	Mask 815
Trinity ms both 'yee'	
Bridgewater ms both 'yee'	
I have brought ye new delight,	Mask 967
B.M. ms 'you'	
Bridgewater ms 'yee'	
1637 'yee'	
Trinity ms 'yee'	
She can teach ye how to clime	Mask 1020

Ye(*cont*)
B.M. ms 'you'
Trinity ms 'yee'
Bridgewater ms 'you'
1637 'yee'
Com, and trip it as ye go Allegro 33
1673 'you'
Of famous *Arcady* ye are, and sprung Arcades 28
Trinity ms 'you'
And ye the breathing Roses of the Wood, Arcades 32
Trinity ms 'yee'
And lead ye where ye may more neer behold Arcades 40
Trinity ms both 'you'
And so attend ye toward her glittering state; Arcades 81
Trinity ms 'you'
Where ye may all that are of noble stemm Arcades 82
Trinity ms 'yee'
I will bring you where she sits, Arcades 91
Trinity ms 'yee'
A better soyl shall give ye thanks. Arcades 101
Trinity ms 'you'
Here ye shall have greater grace, Arcades 104
Trinity ms 'yee'
Yet once more, O ye Laurels, and once more Lycidas 1
Trinity ms 'yee' ←'ye'
Ye Myrtles brown, with Ivy never-sear, Lycidas 2
Trinity ms 'Yee' ←'ye'
Where were ye Nymphs when the remorseless deep Lycidas 50
Trinity ms 'yee'
For neither were ye playing on the steep, Lycidas 52
Trinity ms 'yee'
Had ye bin there---for what could that have don? Lycidas 57
Trinity ms 'yee', but word deleted
Ye valleys low where the milde whispers use, Lycidas 136
Trinity ms 'yee'
And, O ye *Dolphins*, waft the haples youth. Lycidas 164
Trinity ms 'yee'
Ring out ye Crystall sphears, Nativity 125
(If ye have power to touch our senses so) Nativity 127
Ye flaming Powers, and winged Warriours bright, Circum 1
Trinity ms 'yee'
Ye might discern a Cipress bud. Winchester 22
From them whose sin ye envi'd, not abhor'd, Forcers 4
Trinity ms 'yee'
Dare ye for this adjure the Civill Sword Forcers 5
Trinity ms 'yee'
Taught ye by meer *A. S.* and *Rotherford?* Forcers 8
Trinity ms 'yee'
By shallow *Edwards* and Scotch what d' ye call: Forcers 12
Cropp yee as close as marginall P---s eares Forcers Tr. ms 45.17
anointed have my King (though ye rebell) Psalm 2, 12
And now be wise at length ye Kings averse Psalm 2, 22
Be taught ye Judges of the earth; with fear Psalm 2, 23
In anger and ye perish in the way Psalm 2, 26
Great ones how long will ye Psalm 4, 7
Depart all ye that work iniquitie. Psalm 6, 16
How long will ye pervert the right Psalm 82, 5
I said that ye were Gods, yea all Psalm 82, 21
But ye shall die like men, and fall Psalm 82, 23
Yea
Between the Cherubim; yea, often plac'd Par Lost 1.387
In narrow room Natures whole wealth, yea more, Par Lost 4.207
Regents and Potentates, and Kings, yea gods Par Reg 1.117
Yea there, where very desolation dwels Mask 428
Yea even that which mischief meant most harm, Mask 591
Trinity ms 'Yea' ←'and'
Yea Truth, and justice then Nativity 141
Yea it shall be his natural property Vacation 87
Are troubled, yea my soul is troubled sore Psalm 6, 6
I said that ye were Gods, yea all Psalm 82, 21
Yeanling
To gorge the flesh of Lambs or yeanling Kids Par Lost 3.434
Year
Tunes her nocturnal Note. Thus with the Year Par Lost 3.40
1667 'year' in some copies
As Heav'ns great Year brings forth, th' Empyreal Host Par Lost 5.583
And once a year *Jerusalem*, few days Par Reg 3.234
Shatter your leaves before the mellowing year. Lycidas 5
1638 'yeare'
Trinity ms 'yeare'
As thou from yeer to yeer hast sung too late Sonnet 1, 11
1673 both 'year'
Stoln on his wing my three and twentith yeer! Sonnet 7, 2
Trinity ms 'yeere'
Of Sun or Moon or Starre throughout the year, Sonnet 22, 5
1694 'Year'
Then when a year of glut Psalm 4, 33
Yearly
Of *Thammuz* yearly wounded: the Love-tale Par Lost 1.452
Yearly enjoynd, some say, to undergo Par Lost 10.575
Years
Days, months, & years, towards his all-chearing Lamp Par Lost 3.581
For Seasons, and for Dayes, and circling Years, Par Lost 7.342
His Seasons, Hours, or Dayes, or Months, or Yeares: Par Lost 8.69
Climat, or Years damp my intended wing Par Lost 9.45
Till many years over thy head return: Par Lost 11.534
The space of seventie years, then brings them back, Par Lost 12.345
How many Ages, as the years of men, Par Reg 1.48

Years(*cont*)
All righteous things: therefore above my years, Par Reg 1.206
Had measur'd twice six years, at our great Feast Par Reg 1.210
Hath been our dwelling many years, his life Par Reg 2.80
Conceals him: when twelve years he scarce had seen, Par Reg 2.96
Thy years are ripe, and over-ripe, the Son Par Reg 3.31
Yet years, and to ripe years judgment mature, Par Reg 3.37
The more he grew in years, the more inflam'd Par Reg 3.40
Vain monument of strength; till length of years Samson 570
Fully reveng'd, hath left them years of mourning, Samson 1712
Lead in swift round the Months and Years. Mask 114
Trinity ms 'yeares'
Bridgewater ms 'years'
1637 'Yeares'
To nurse the Saplings tall, and curl the grove Arcades 46
Trinity ms 'nurse the saplings tall' ←'live a thousand yeares'
Where he had mutely sate two years before: Vacation 6
Who after yeers of barrennes, Winchester 64
For he had any time this ten yeers full, Carrier 7
1658 'years'
Vane, young in yeares, but in sage counsell old, Sonnet 17, 1
1662, 1694 'years'
Cyriack, this three years day these eys, though clear Sonnet 22, 1
Yelled
Environ'd thee, some howl'd, some yell'd, some shriek'd, Par Reg 4.423
Yelling
These yelling Monsters that with ceasless cry Par Lost 2.795
Thee and thy Legions, yelling they shall flye, Par Reg 4.629
Yellow
First Fruits, the green Eare, and the yellow Sheaf, Par Lost 11.435
And on the Tawny Sands and Shelves, Mask 117
Trinity ms 'tawnie' ←'yellow'
yellow, watchet, greene, & blew Mask Tr. ms 26.21
yellow, watchett, greene and blew Mask Br. ms 17
The yellow Cowslip, and the pale Primrose. May Morn 4
Yellow-skirted
And the yellow-skirted *Fayes*, Nativity 235
Yes
You gave me Brother? *Eld. Bro.* Yes, and keep it still, Mask 584
Bridgewater ms 'yes'
Trinity ms 'yes'
Yesterday
Of yesterday, so late hath past the lips Par Lost 5.675
Yet
Things unattempted yet in Prose or Rhime. Par Lost 1.16
As one great Furnace flam'd, yet from those flames Par Lost 1.62
The force of those dire Arms? yet not for those, Par Lost 1.94
What can it then avail though yet we feel Par Lost 1.153
With rallied Arms to try what may be yet Par Lost 1.269
Yet to thir Generals Voyce they soon obeyd Par Lost 1.337
Nor had they yet among the Sons of *Eve* Par Lost 1.364
While the promiscuous croud stood yet aloof? Par Lost 1.380
Yet thence his lustful Orgies he enlarg'd Par Lost 1.415
And downward Fish: yet had his Temple high Par Lost 1.463
Or Altar smoak'd; yet who more oft then hee Par Lost 1.493
Gods, yet confest later then Heav'n and Earth Par Lost 1.509
Down cast and damp, yet such wherein appear'd Par Lost 1.523
Compare of mortal prowess, yet observ'd Par Lost 1.588
Stood like a Towr; his form had yet not lost Par Lost 1.591
Perplexes Monarchs. Dark'n'd so, yet shon Par Lost 1.599
For his revolt, yet faithfull how they stood, Par Lost 1.611
For who can yet beleeve, though after loss, Par Lost 1.631
Hath bin achievd of merit, yet this loss Par Lost 2.21
Which if not Victory is yet Revenge. Par Lost 2.105
Timorous and slothful: yet he pleas'd the ear, Par Lost 2.117
Heav'ns purest Light, yet our great Enemy Par Lost 2.137
What yet they know must follow, to endure Par Lost 2.206
And Princely counsel in his face yet shon, Par Lost 2.304
Irreparable; tearms of peace yet none Par Lost 2.331
Yet ever plotting how the Conqueror least Par Lost 2.338
Yet live in hatred, enmity, and strife Par Lost 2.500
Yet with a pleasing sorcerie could charm Par Lost 2.566
Than Fables yet have feign'd, or fear conceiv'd, Par Lost 2.627
Yet unconsum'd. Before the Gates there sat Par Lost 2.648
A hideous Peal: yet, when they list, would creep, Par Lost 2.656
And kennel there, yet there still bark'd and howl'd, Par Lost 2.658
Prevented spares to tell thee yet by deeds Par Lost 2.739
Or dim suffusion veild. Yet not the more Par Lost 3.26
Our two first Parents, yet the onely two Par Lost 3.65
Heapt on him there, nor yet the main Abyss Par Lost 3.83
Yet with revenge accomplish't and to Hell Par Lost 3.160
Yet not of will in him, but grace in me Par Lost 3.174
Upheld by me, yet once more he shall stand Par Lost 3.178
But yet all is not don; Man disobeying, Par Lost 3.203
All that of me can die, yet that debt paid, Par Lost 3.246
Silent yet spake, and breath'd immortal love Par Lost 3.267
Yet dazle Heav'n, that brightest Seraphim Par Lost 3.381
None yet, but store hereafter from the earth Par Lost 3.444
Through his glaz'd Optic Tube yet never saw. Par Lost 3.590
Not of the prime, yet such as in his face Par Lost 3.637
Yet not rejoycing in his speed, though bold, Par Lost 4.13
How due! yet all his good prov'd ill in me, Par Lost 4.48
Ambition. Yet why not? som other Power Par Lost 4.61
Yet not anough had practisd to deceive Par Lost 4.124
Of stateliest view. Yet higher then thir tops Par Lost 4.142
Sat like a Cormorant; yet not true Life Par Lost 4.196
Not Spirits, yet to heav'nly Spirits bright Par Lost 4.361
As now is enterd; yet no purpos'd foe Par Lost 4.373

Yet(*cont*)

Like this fair Paradise, your sense, yet such	Par Lost 4.379
Melt, as I doe, yet public reason just,	Par Lost 4.389
Which were it toilsom, yet with thee were sweet.	Par Lost 4.439
Under a Platan, yet methought less faire,	Par Lost 4.478
For envie, yet with jealous leer maligne	Par Lost 4.503
Yet let me not forget what I have gain'd	Par Lost 4.512
Yet happie pair; enjoy, till I return,	Par Lost 4.534
In order, though to Nations yet unborn,	Par Lost 4.663
Blest pair; and O yet happiest if ye seek	Par Lost 4.774
Yet thus, unmovd with fear, accost him soon.	Par Lost 4.822
His lustre visibly impar'd; yet seemd	Par Lost 4.850
Which taught thee yet no better, that no pain	Par Lost 4.915
Hung forth in Heav'n his golden Scales, yet seen	Par Lost 4.997
For God's, yet able to make Gods of Men:	Par Lost 5.70
Yet evil whence? in thee can harbour none,	Par Lost 5.99
But with addition strange; yet be not sad.	Par Lost 5.116
With wheels yet hov'ring o're the Ocean brim,	Par Lost 5.140
In these thy lowest works, yet these declare	Par Lost 5.158
Yet mutable; whence warne him to beware	Par Lost 5.237
Yet with submiss approach and reverence meek,	Par Lost 5.359
Two onely, who yet by sov'ran gift possess	Par Lost 5.366
Vapours not yet into her substance turnd.	Par Lost 5.420
Cover'd with pearly grain: yet God hath here	Par Lost 5.430
Food not of Angels, yet accepted so,	Par Lost 5.465
At Heav'ns high feasts to have fed: yet what compare?	Par Lost 5.467
Yet that we never shall forget to love	Par Lost 5.550
Single, is yet so just, my constant thoughts	Par Lost 5.552
And we have yet large day, for scarce the Sun	Par Lost 5.558
Not lawful to reveal? yet for thy good	Par Lost 5.570
As yet this world was not, and *Chaos* wilde	Par Lost 5.577
Eccentric, intervolv'd, yet regular	Par Lost 5.623
In favour and praeeminence, yet fraught	Par Lost 5.661
Tell them that by command, ere yet dim Night	Par Lost 5.685
If these magnific Titles yet remain	Par Lost 5.773
Knee-tribute yet unpaid, prostration vile,	Par Lost 5.782
By none, and if not equal all, yet free,	Par Lost 5.791
Yet by experience taught we know how good,	Par Lost 5.826
Yet not for thy advise or threats I fly	Par Lost 5.889
That of so many Myriads fall'n, yet one	Par Lost 6.24
Should yet remain, where faith and realtie	Par Lost 6.115
When Reason hath to deal with force, yet so	Par Lost 6.125
Yet leudly dar'st our ministring upbraid.	Par Lost 6.182
Yet Chains in Hell, not Realms expect: mean while	Par Lost 6.186
A Legion; led in fight, yet Leader seemd	Par Lost 6.232
Of airie threats to aw whom yet with deeds	Par Lost 6.283
Yet soon he heal'd; for Spirits that live throughout	Par Lost 6.344
Nor of Renown less eager, yet by doome	Par Lost 6.378
And ignominie, yet to glorie aspires	Par Lost 6.383
Enjoyment of our right as Gods; yet hard	Par Lost 6.452
Our yet unwounded Enemies, or arme	Par Lost 6.466
Nor long shall be our labour, yet ere dawne,	Par Lost 6.492
Once found, which yet unfound most would have thought	Par Lost 6.500
Impossible: yet haply of thy Race	Par Lost 6.501
Doubl'd, would render them yet more despis'd,	Par Lost 6.602
As they would dance, yet for a dance they seemd	Par Lost 6.615
Save what sin hath impaird, which yet hath wrought	Par Lost 6.691
Yet envied; against mee is all thir rage,	Par Lost 6.813
Yet half his strength he put not forth, but check'd	Par Lost 6.853
Yet fell; remember, and fear to transgress.	Par Lost 6.912
Half yet remaines unsung, but narrower bound	Par Lost 7.21
And solitude; yet not alone, while thou	Par Lost 7.28
Led on, yet sinless, with desire to know	Par Lost 7.61
Yet scarce allay'd still eyes the current streame,	Par Lost 7.67
Things above Earthly thought, which yet concernd	Par Lost 7.82
And the great Light of Day yet wants to run	Par Lost 7.98
Yet what thou canst attain, which best may serve	Par Lost 7.115
Yet farr the greater part have kept, I see,	Par Lost 7.145
Thir station, Heav'n yet populous retaines	Par Lost 7.146
Sphear'd in a radiant Cloud, for yet the Sun	Par Lost 7.247
The Earth was form'd, but in the Womb as yet	Par Lost 7.276
Her sacred shades: though God had yet not rain'd	Par Lost 7.331
Her state with Oarie feet: yet oft they quit	Par Lost 7.440
Frequent; and of the Sixt day yet remain'd;	Par Lost 7.504
There wanted yet the Master work, the end	Par Lost 7.505
Of all yet don; a Creature who not prone	Par Lost 7.506
Is yet distinct by name, thence, as thou know'st	Par Lost 7.536
Yet not till the Creator from his work	Par Lost 7.551
Invisible, yet staid (such priviledge	Par Lost 7.589
Creator; something yet of doubt remaines,	Par Lost 8.13
Yet went she not, as not with such discourse	Par Lost 8.48
Yet not to Earth are those bright Luminaries	Par Lost 8.98
Onely to shine, yet scarce to contribute	Par Lost 8.155
And Day is yet not spent; till then thou seest	Par Lost 8.206
My fancy to believe I yet had being,	Par Lost 8.294
Yet dreadful in mine eare, though in my choice	Par Lost 8.335
Social communication, yet so pleas'd,	Par Lost 8.429
Yet Innocence and Virgin Modestie,	Par Lost 8.501
O're other Creatures; yet when I approach	Par Lost 8.546
Yet these subject not; I to thee disclose	Par Lost 8.607
Variously representing; yet still free	Par Lost 8.610
Deaths Harbinger: Sad task, yet argument	Par Lost 9.13
That shine, yet bear thir bright officious Lamps,	Par Lost 9.104
Is Center, yet extends to all, so thou	Par Lost 9.108
Not yet in horrid Shade or dismal Den,	Par Lost 9.185
Nor nocent yet, but on the grassie Herbe	Par Lost 9.186
Yet not so strictly hath our Lord impos'd	Par Lost 9.235
The danger lies, yet lies within his power:	Par Lost 9.349

Yet(*cont*)

Firm we subsist, yet possible to swerve,	Par Lost 9.359
Persisted, yet submiss, though last, repli'd.	Par Lost 9.377
But with such Gardning Tools as Art yet rude,	Par Lost 9.391
Yet Virgin of *Proserpina* from *Jove*.	Par Lost 9.396
Yet more amaz'd unwarie thus reply'd.	Par Lost 9.614
In Paradise, and various, yet unknown	Par Lost 9.619
Yet Lords declar'd of all in Earth or Aire?	Par Lost 9.658
To whom thus *Eve* yet sinless. Of the Fruit	Par Lost 9.659
Fluctuats disturbd, yet comely and in act	Par Lost 9.668
Mee who have touch'd and tasted, yet both live,	Par Lost 9.688
Yet are but dim, shall perfetly be then	Par Lost 9.707
Yet rung of his perswasive words, impregn'd	Par Lost 9.737
Sollicited her longing eye; yet first	Par Lost 9.743
And yet unknown, is as not had at all.	Par Lost 9.757
For Beasts it seems: yet that one Beast which first	Par Lost 9.769
As yet my change, and give him to partake	Par Lost 9.818
Yet oft his heart, divine of somthing ill,	Par Lost 9.845
Of Enemie hath beguil'd thee, yet unknown,	Par Lost 9.905
Another Rib afford, yet loss of thee	Par Lost 9.912
Not God Omnipotent, nor Fate, yet so	Par Lost 9.927
Nor yet on him found deadly, he yet lives,	Par Lost 9.932
Creation could repeate, yet would be loath	Par Lost 9.946
Yet willingly chose rather Death with thee:	Par Lost 9.1167
That time Celestial visages, yet mixt	Par Lost 10.24
Because not yet inflicted, as he fear'd,	Par Lost 10.51
On me deriv'd, yet I shall temper so	Par Lost 10.77
Devolv'd; though should I hold my peace, yet thou	Par Lost 10.135
Confessing soon, yet not before her Judge	Par Lost 10.160
Nor alter'd his offence; yet God at last	Par Lost 10.171
Adventrous work, yet to thy power and mine	Par Lost 10.255
Though distant from thee Worlds between, yet felt	Par Lost 10.362
Where all yet left of that revolted Rout	Par Lost 10.534
Yet parcht with scalding thurst and hunger fierce,	Par Lost 10.556
And *Ops*, ere yet *Dictaean Jove* was born.	Par Lost 10.584
Close following pace for pace, not mounted yet	Par Lost 10.589
Of happiness: yet well, if here would end	Par Lost 10.725
Thy Justice seems; yet to say truth, too late,	Par Lost 10.755
That proud excuse? yet him not thy election,	Par Lost 10.764
With cruel expectation. Yet one doubt	Par Lost 10.782
Horrid, if true! yet why? it was but breath	Par Lost 10.789
While yet we live, scarse one short hour perhaps,	Par Lost 10.923
His full wrauth whose thou feelst as yet lest part,	Par Lost 10.951
Or end, though sharp and sad, yet tolerable,	Par Lost 10.977
It lies, yet ere Conception to prevent	Par Lost 10.987
The Race unblest, to being yet unbegot.	Par Lost 10.988
Then loudest Oratorie: yet thir port	Par Lost 11.8
In Fables old, less ancient yet then these,	Par Lost 11.11
Perpetual banishment. Yet least they faint	Par Lost 11.108
So send them forth, though sorrowing, yet in peace:	Par Lost 11.117
Out of despaire, joy, but with fear yet linkt;	Par Lost 11.139
Hard to belief may seem; yet this will Prayer,	Par Lost 11.146
Which then not minded in dismay, yet now	Par Lost 11.156
Invests him coming? yet not terrible,	Par Lost 11.233
Yet all had heard, with audible lament	Par Lost 11.266
For though I fled him angrie, yet recall'd	Par Lost 11.330
Yet doubt not but in Vallie and in plaine	Par Lost 11.349
Of *Atabalipa*, and yet unspoil'd	Par Lost 11.409
Nor sinn'd thy sin, yet from that derive	Par Lost 11.427
To his grim Cave, all dismal; yet to sense	Par Lost 11.469
But is there yet no other way, besides	Par Lost 11.527
Yet they a beauteous ofspring shall beget;	Par Lost 11.613
Yet empty of all good wherein consists	Par Lost 11.616
Corrupting each thir way; yet those remoov'd,	Par Lost 11.889
Much thou hast yet to see, but I perceave	Par Lost 12.8
This second sours of Men, while yet but few;	Par Lost 12.13
Rational Libertie; yet know withall,	Par Lost 12.82
Yet somtimes Nations will decline so low	Par Lost 12.97
Him on this side *Euphrates* yet residing,	Par Lost 12.114
While yet the Patriark liv'd, who scap'd the Flood,	Par Lost 12.117
For Gods! yet him God the most High voutsafes	Par Lost 12.120
Not knowing to what Land, yet firm believes:	Par Lost 12.127
(Things by thir names I call, though yet unnam'd)	Par Lost 12.140
This yet I apprehend not, why to those	Par Lost 12.280
Barr'd of his right; yet at his Birth a Starr	Par Lost 12.360
High in the love of Heav'n, yet from my Loynes	Par Lost 12.380
Infallible? yet many will presume:	Par Lost 12.530
With cause for evils past, yet much more cheer'd	Par Lost 12.604
This further consolation yet secure	Par Lost 12.620
Mean while the Son of God, who yet some days	Par Reg 1.183
When I was yet a child, no childish play	Par Reg 1.201
To such perfection, that e're yet my age	Par Reg 1.209
And was admir'd by all, yet this not all	Par Reg 1.214
Yet held it more humane, more heavenly first	Par Reg 1.221
Yet neither thus disheartn'd or dismay'd,	Par Reg 1.268
I learn not yet, perhaps I need not know;	Par Reg 1.292
Yet to that hideous place not so confin'd	Par Reg 1.362
Yet thou pretend'st to truth; all Oracles	Par Reg 1.430
To *Balaam* Reprobate, a Prophet yet	Par Reg 1.491
Mean while the new-baptiz'd, who yet remain'd	Par Reg 2.1
Rode up to Heaven, yet once again to come.	Par Reg 2.17
A Manger his, yet soon enforc't to flye	Par Reg 2.75
And sweet allay'd, yet terrible to approach,	Par Reg 2.160
Nature hath need of what she asks; yet God	Par Reg 2.253
Out cast *Nebaioth*, yet found he relief	Par Reg 2.309
Yet Wealth without these three is impotent,	Par Reg 2.433
So many Ages, and shall yet regain	Par Reg 2.441
Riches and Realms; yet not for that a Crown,	Par Reg 2.458

Yet(*cont*)

Yet he who reigns within himself, and rules	Par Reg 2.466
Is yet more Kingly, this attracts the Soul,	Par Reg 2.476
Yet years, and to ripe years judgment mature,	Par Reg 3.37
Inglorious: but thou yet art not too late.	Par Reg 3.42
Made Captive, yet deserving freedom more	Par Reg 3.77
Yet if for fame and glory aught be done,	Par Reg 3.100
Yet, sacrilegious, to himself would take	Par Reg 3.140
Yet so much bounty is in God, such grace,	Par Reg 3.142
Yet of another Plea bethought him soon.	Par Reg 3.149
Thy life hath yet been private, most part spent	Par Reg 3.232
In Mail thir horses clad, yet fleet and strong,	Par Reg 3.313
At sight whereof the Fiend yet more presum'd,	Par Reg 3.345
Whose off-spring in his Territory yet serve	Par Reg 3.375
Were better farthest off) is not yet come;	Par Reg 3.397
Yet he at length, time to himself best known,	Par Reg 3.433
Yet gives not o're though desperate of success,	Par Reg 4.23
All publick cares, and yet of him suspicious,	Par Reg 4.96
For him I was not sent, nor yet to free	Par Reg 4.131
No trifle; yet with this reserve, not else,	Par Reg 4.165
And thither will return thee, yet remember	Par Reg 4.374
Not yet expir'd) and to the Wilderness	Par Reg 4.395
O patient Son of God, yet only stoodst	Par Reg 4.420
Unshaken; nor yet staid the terror there,	Par Reg 4.421
Nor yet amidst this joy and brightest morn	Par Reg 4.439
Yet with no new device, they all were spent,	Par Reg 4.443
Fair morning yet betides thee Son of God,	Par Reg 4.451
Yet as being oft times noxious where they light	Par Reg 4.460
For Son of God to me is yet in doubt,	Par Reg 4.501
Thy manhood last, though yet in private bred;	Par Reg 4.509
All men are Sons of God; yet thee I thought	Par Reg 4.520
And higher yet the glorious Temple rear'd	Par Reg 4.546
Thy wound, yet not thy last and deadliest wound	Par Reg 4.622
Yet stay, let me not rashly call in doubt	Samson 43
Proudly secure, yet liable to fall	Samson 55
They creep, yet see, I dark in light expos'd	Samson 75
As in the land of darkness yet in light,	Samson 99
And buried; but O yet more miserable!	Samson 101
Buried, yet not exempt	Samson 103
Yet that which was the worst now least afflicts me,	Samson 195
Are come upon him his deserts? yet why?	Samson 205
Yet truth to say, I oft have heard men wonder	Samson 215
Yet *Israel* still serves with all his Sons.	Samson 240
Yet more there be who doubt his ways not just,	Samson 300
Yet the fourth time, when mustring all her wiles,	Samson 402
These rags, this grinding, is not yet so base	Samson 415
That rigid score. A worse thing yet remains,	Samson 433
Miraculous yet remaining in those locks?	Samson 587
This one prayer yet remains, might I be heard,	Samson 649
Yet toward these thus dignifi'd, thou oft	Samson 682
Though not disordinate, yet causless suffring	Samson 701
Cho. Yet on she moves, now stands & eies thee fixt,	Samson 726
I cannot but acknowledge; yet if tears	Samson 735
Though late, yet in some part to recompense	Samson 746
Dal. Yet hear me *Samson;* not that I endeavour	Samson 766
Yet always pity or pardon hath obtain'd.	Samson 814
Yet now am judg'd an enemy. Why then	Samson 882
Life yet hath many solaces, enjoy'd	Samson 915
To prayers, then winds and seas, yet winds to seas	Samson 961
Chor. Yet beauty, though injurious, hath strange power,	Samson 1003
As these perhaps, yet wish it had not been,	Samson 1077
Justly, yet despair not of his final pardon	Samson 1171
Some way or other yet further to afflict thee.	Samson 1252
Yet so it may fall out, because thir end	Samson 1265
And yet perhaps more trouble is behind.	Samson 1300
The worst of all indignities, yet on me	Samson 1341
Chor. Yet with this strength thou serv'st the *Philistines*,	Samson 1363
Yet that he may dispense with me or thee	Samson 1377
Yet knowing thir advantages too many,	Samson 1401
Yet this be sure, in nothing to comply	Samson 1408
To use him further yet in some great service,	Samson 1499
Chor. Yet God hath wrought things as incredible	Samson 1532
Yet Hope would fain subscribe, and tempts Belief.	Samson 1535
Which earst my eyes beheld and yet behold;	Samson 1543
With rueful cry, yet what it was we hear not,	Samson 1553
Mess. *Gaza* yet stands, but all her Sons are fall'n,	Samson 1558
Yet e're I give the rains to grief, say first,	Samson 1578
More then anough we know; but while things yet	Samson 1592
I mean to shew you of my strength, yet greater;	Samson 1644
Chor. O dearly-bought revenge, yet glorious!	Samson 1660
And which is best and happiest yet, all this	Samson 1718
Yet som there be that by due steps aspire	Mask 12
What never yet was heard in Tale or Song	Mask 44
Of such late Wassailers; yet O where els	Mask 179
Yet nought but single darknes do I find.	Mask 204
line not in Bridgewater ms	
Yet they in pleasing slumber lull'd the sense,	Mask 260
And if your stray attendance be yet lodg'd,	Mask 315
And yet is most pretended: In a place	Mask 326
T'would be som solace yet, som little chearing	Mask 348
Yet where an equall poise of hope and fear	Mask 410
Bridgewater ms 'but'	
Trinity ms 'but'	
Eld. *Bro*. I mean that too, but yet a hidden strength	Mask 418
Do ye beleeve me yet, or shall I call	Mask 438
2. *Bro*. Heav'n keep my sister, agen agen and neer,	Mask 486
Trinity ms 'agen, agen' ←'yet agen, agen'	
Yet have they many baits, and guilefull spells	Mask 537

Yet(*cont*)

I love thy courage yet, and bold Emprise,	Mask 610
Of small regard to see to, yet well skill'd	Mask 620
And yet more med'cinal is it then that *Moly*	Mask 636
line not in Bridgewater ms	
And yet came off: if you have this about you	Mask 647
Yet will they soon retire, if he but shrink.	Mask 656
Not half his riches known, and yet despis'd,	Mask 724
Think what, and be adviz'd, you are but young yet.	Mask 755
line not in Bridgewater ms	
Fain would I somthing say, yet to what end?	Mask 783
line not in Trinity ms	
line not in Bridgewater ms	
Yet should I try, the uncontrouled worth	Mask 793
line not in Trinity ms	
line not in Bridgewater ms	
And though not mortal, yet a cold shuddring dew	Mask 802
line not in Trinity ms	
line not in Bridgewater ms	
And try her yet more strongly. Com, no more,	Mask 806
word not in Bridgewater ms	
word not in Trinity ms	
I must not suffer this, yet 'tis but the lees	Mask 809
Yet stay, be not disturb'd, now I bethink me,	Mask 820
But night sits monarch yet in the mid sky.	Mask 957
yet thence I come and oft from thence behold	Mask Tr. ms 10.18
Yet thou art higher far descended,	Penseroso 22
While yet there was no fear of *Jove*.	Penseroso 30
And yet such musick worthiest were to blaze	Arcades 74
Inimitable sounds, yet as we go,	Arcades 78
Yet *Syrinx* well might wait on her.	Arcades 107
word deleted in trinity ms	
Yet once more, O ye Laurels, and once more	Lycidas 1
Nor yet where *Deva* spreads her wisard stream:	Lycidas 55
And yet anon repairs his drooping head,	Lycidas 169
This must not yet be so,	Nativity 150
The Babe lies yet in smiling Infancy,	Nativity 151
Yet first to those ychain'd in sleep,	Nativity 155
Yet art thou not inglorious in thy fate;	Fair Inf 22
Yet can I not perswade me thou art dead	Fair Inf 29
Yet I had rather if I were to chuse,	Vacation 29
Yet there is something that doth force my fear,	Vacation 67
Yet every one shall make him underling,	Vacation 76
Yet being above them, he shall be below them;	Vacation 80
Yet on his Brothers shall depend for Cloathing.	Vacation 82
Yet shall he live in strife, and at his dore	Vacation 85
Yet more; the stroke of death he must abide,	Passion 20
Yet on the softned Quarry would I score	Passion 46
Yet had the number of her days	Winchester 11
Had burial, yet not laid in earth,	Winchester 32
Time numbers motion, yet (without a crime	Another 7
Yet (strange to think) his wain was his increase:	Another 32
line not in 1658 text	
For my relief; yet hadst no reason why,	Sonnet 1, 12
Yet be it less or more, or soon or slow,	Sonnet 7, 9
Wherin your Father flourisht, yet by you	Sonnet 10, 10
Madam, me thinks I see him living yet;	Sonnet 10, 11
O yet a nobler task awaites thy hand;	Sonnet 15, 9
And Worsters laureat wreath; yet much remaines	Sonnet 16, 9
Or man or woman. Yet I argue not	Sonnet 22, 6
1694 'yet'	
And such, as yet once more I trust to have	Sonnet 23, 7
Her face was vail'd, yet to my fancied sight,	Sonnet 23, 10
Yet know the Lord hath chose	Psalm 4, 13
Who yet will shew us good?	Psalm 4, 26
O what is man that thou remembrest yet,	Psalm 8, 12
And yet my people would not *hear*,	Psalm 81, 45
E're yet my life be spent,	Psalm 88, 54

Yield

And courage never to submit or yield:	Par Lost 1.108
Or satiate fury yield it from our Foe.	Par Lost 1.179
ms 'yeild'	
May hope when everlasting Fate shall yeild	Par Lost 2.232
Might yield them easier habitation, bend	Par Lost 2.573
1667 'yeild'	
Though now to Death I yield, and am his due	Par Lost 3.245
1667 'yeild'	
The Earth to yield; unsavourie food perhaps	Par Lost 5.401
1667 'yeild'	
Yield Nectar, though from off the boughs each Morn	Par Lost 5.428
1667 'Yeild'	
Shall yield us pregnant with infernal flame,	Par Lost 6.483
1667 'yeild'	
And to realities yield all her shows:	Par Lost 8.575
1667 'yeild'	
Thee satiate, to short absence I could yield.	Par Lost 9.248
1667 'yeild'	
Yeild thee, so well this day thou hast purvey'd.	Par Lost 9.1021
To better life shall yeeld him, where with mee	Par Lost 11.42
I yield it just, said *Adam*, and submit.	Par Lost 11.526
1667 'yeild'	
Shall yield up all thir vertue, all thir fame	Par Lost 11.623
1667 'yeild'	
Into thir hands, and they as gladly yield me	Samson 259
But yield to double darkness nigh at hand:	Samson 593
Private respects must yield; with grave authority	Samson 868
aeternall roses grow & hyacinth	Mask Tr. ms 10.07
'grow' ←'blosme' ←'grow' ←'blow' ←'yeeld' ←'grow'	

Yield(*cont*)
To yield his fruit, and his leaf shall not fall, Psalm 1, 9
And till they yield thee honour due, Psalm 83, 59
Yielded
Expos'd a Matron to avoid worse rape. Par Lost 1.505
1667 'Yielded thir Matrons'
With *Naphtha* and *Asphaltus* yeilded light Par Lost 1.729
ms 'yielded'
Yielded with full consent. The happier state Par Lost 2.24
1667 'Yeilded'
And by her yielded, by him best receivd, Par Lost 4.309
1667 'yeilded'
Yielded with coy submission, modest pride, Par Lost 4.310
1667 'Yeilded'
Yielded them, side-long as they sat recline Par Lost 4.333
1667 'Yeilded'
Seisd mine, I yielded, and from that time see Par Lost 4.489
1667 'yeilded'
Rather how hast thou yeelded to transgress Par Lost 9.902
At random yielded up to their misrule; Par Lost 10.628
1667 'yeilded'
I yielded, and unlock'd her all my heart, Samson 407
The constantest to have yielded without blame. Samson 848
Yielding
Put forth the verdant Grass, Herb yielding Seed, Par Lost 7.310
1667 'yeilding'
And Fruit Tree yielding Fruit after her kind; Par Lost 7.311
1667 'yeilding'
Yields
The cool, the silent, save where silence yields Par Lost 5.39
Whatever Earth all-bearing Mother yields Par Lost 5.338
1667 'yeilds'
Innumerable, and this which yeelds or fills Par Lost 7.88
1669 'yields'
Gave thee, all sorts are here that all th' Earth yields, Par Lost 7.541
1667 'yeelds'
For no allurement yields to appetite, Par Reg 2.409
Thir Superstition yields me; hence with leave Samson 15
Yoke
Hard liberty before the easie yoke Par Lost 2.256
Us'd to the yoak, draw'st his triumphant wheels Par Lost 4.975
Our minds and teach us to cast off this Yoke? Par Lost 5.786
No more be troubl'd how to quit the yoke Par Lost 5.882
Xerxes, the Libertie of *Greece* to yoke, Par Lost 10.307
Reluctance against God and his just yoke Par Lost 10.1045
To rescue *Israel* from the *Roman* yoke, Par Reg 1.217
Thy Glory, free thy people from thir yoke, Par Reg 2.48
Reduc't a Province under Roman yoke, Par Reg 3.158
With bridges rivers proud, as with a yoke; Par Reg 3.334
A victor people free from servile yoke? Par Reg 4.102
But govern ill the Nations under yoke, Par Reg 4.135
Should *Israel* from *Philistian* yoke deliver; Samson 39
Himself in bonds under *Philistian* yoke; Samson 42
While *Cynthia* checks her Dragon yoke, Penseroso 59
Bear his milde yoak, they serve him best, his State Sonnet 19, 11
Did our forefathers yoke, Psalm 87, 12
Yoked
But foul effeminacy held me yok't Samson 410
Yon
Seest thou yon dreary Plain, forlorn and wilde, Par Lost 1.180
Groveling and prostrate on yon Lake of Fire, Par Lost 1.280
Under yon boyling Ocean, wrapt in Chains; Par Lost 2.183
Yon flourie Arbors, yonder Allies green, Par Lost 4.626
And read thy Lot in yon celestial Sign Par Lost 4.1011
More orient in yon Western Cloud that draws Par Lost 11.205
That crawls along the side of yon small hill, Mask 295
Him that yon soars on golden wing, Penseroso 52
To the great Mistres of yon princely shrine, Arcades 36
O Nightingale, that on yon bloomy Spray Sonnet 1, 1
Yonder
To yonder Gates? through them I mean to pass, Par Lost 2.684
Yon flourie Arbors, yonder Allies green, Par Lost 4.626
This spacious ground, in yonder shadie Bowre Par Lost 5.367
Mystical dance, which yonder starrie Spheare Par Lost 5.620
In yonder Spring of Roses intermixt Par Lost 9.218
To waste and havoc yonder World, which I Par Lost 10.617
From yonder blazing Cloud that veils the Hill Par Lost 11.229
In yonder nether World where shall I seek Par Lost 11.328
Mount *Hermon*, yonder Sea, each place behold Par Lost 12.142
By mee encampt on yonder Hill, expect Par Lost 12.591
For yonder bank hath choice of Sun or shade, Samson 3
Yore
Thee bright-hair'd *Vesta* long of yore, Penseroso 23
You
Your wearied vertue, for the ease you find Par Lost 1.320
If that way be your walk, you have not farr; Par Lost 2.1007
To you whom I could pittie thus forlorne Par Lost 4.374
Though I unpittied: League with you I seek, Par Lost 4.375
That I with you must dwell, or you with me Par Lost 4.377
To entertain you two, her widest Gates, Par Lost 4.382
On you who wrong me not for him who wrongd. Par Lost 4.387
For you, there sitting where ye durst not soare; Par Lost 4.829
Wonder not then, what God for you saw good Par Lost 5.491
If I refuse not, but convert, as you, Par Lost 5.492
Whose progenie you are. Mean while enjoy Par Lost 5.503
Hold, as you yours, while our obedience holds; Par Lost 5.537
Do as you have in charge, and briefly touch Par Lost 6.566
By mee, not you but mee they have despis'd, Par Lost 6.812

You(*cont*)
How should ye? by the Fruit? it gives you Life Par Lost 9.686
You two this way, among these numerous Orbs Par Lost 10.397
Of greatest things; what woman will you find, Par Reg 2.208
Man. Peace with you brethren; my inducement hither Samson 1445
Chor. Noise call you it or universal groan Samson 1511
I mean to shew you of my strength, yet greater; Samson 1644
And listen why, for I will tell ye now Mask 43
Trinity ms 'you'
Bridgewater ms 'you'
Co. What chance good Lady hath bereft you thus? Mask 277
Co. Could that divide you from neer-ushering guides? Mask 279
And as I past, I worshipt; if those you seek Mask 302
To help you find them. *La*. Gentle villager Mask 304
I can conduct you Lady to a low Mask 319
But loyal cottage, where you may be safe Mask 320
You may as well spred out the unsun'd heaps Mask 398
As you imagine, she has a hidden strength Mask 415
Which you remember not. 2. *Bro*. What hidden strength, Mask 416
Unless the strength of Heav'n, if you mean that? Mask 417
Do ye beleeve me yet, or shall I call Mask 438
Bridgewater ms 'you'
That hallow I should know, what are you? speak; Mask 490
Com not too neer, you fall on iron stakes else. Mask 491
Spir. Ile tell ye, 'tis not vain, or fabulous, Mask 513
1637 'you'
Bridgewater ms 'you'
Trinity ms 'you'
Into swift flight, till I had found you here, Mask 579
How are ye joyn'd with hell in triple knot Mask 581
Bridgewater ms 'you'
You gave me Brother? *Eld*. *Bro*. Yes, and keep it still, Mask 584
And yet came off: if you have this about you Mask 647
(As I will give you when we go) you may Mask 648
And you a statue; or as *Daphne* was Mask 661
Co. Why are you vext Lady? why do you frown? Mask 666
Trinity ms 'you' ←'yo' ←'ye'
Why should you be so cruel to your self, Mask 679
But you invert the cov'nants of her trust, Mask 682
line not in Bridgewater ms
With that which you receiv'd on other terms, Mask 684
line not in Bridgewater ms
If you let slip time, like a neglected rose Mask 743
line not in Bridgewater ms
Think what, and be adviz'd, you are but young yet. Mask 755
line not in Bridgewater ms
And try her yet more strongly. Com, no more, Mask 806
Trinity ms 'no more' ←'y'are too morall'
Spir. What, have you let the false enchanter scape? Mask 814
Bridgewater ms 'yee'
I have brought ye new delight, Mask 967
B.M. ms 'you'
She can teach ye how to clime Mask 1020
Bridgewater ms 'you'
B.M. ms 'you'
Com, and trip it as ye go Allegro 33
1673 'you'
How little you bested, Penseroso 3
Of famous *Arcady* ye are, and sprung Arcades 28
Trinity ms 'you'
And lead ye where ye may more neer behold Arcades 40
Trinity ms both 'you'
And so attend ye toward her glittering state; Arcades 81
Trinity ms 'you'
I will bring you where she sits, Arcades 91
Trinity ms 'yee'
A better soyl shall give ye thanks. Arcades 101
Trinity ms 'you'
Your Son, said she, (nor can you it prevent) Vacation 73
Wherin your Father flourisht, yet by you Sonnet 10, 10
That all both judge you to relate them true, Sonnet 10, 13
Because you have thrown of your Prelate Lord, Forcers 1
When they shall read this clearly in your charge Forcers 19
Trinity ms 'they' ←'you'
This was that gift (if you the truth will have) Prose 4, 3
Tis you that say it, not I, you do the deeds, Prose 8, 1
Young
Young *Bacchus* from his Stepdame *Rhea*'s eye; Par Lost 4.279
Thir callow young, but featherd soon and fledge Par Lost 7.420
And Judgment from above: him old and young Par Lost 11.668
Therefore as those young Prophets then with care Par Reg 2.18
To Idols, those young *Daniel* could refuse; Par Reg 2.329
At his dispose, young *Scipio* had brought down Par Reg 3.34
The *Carthaginian* pride, young *Pompey* quell'd Par Reg 3.35
Aught suffer'd; if young *African* for fame Par Reg 3.101
Spir. What voice is that, my young Lord? speak agen. Mask 492
1637 'yong'
Trinity ms 'yong'
Slip't from the fold, or young Kid lost his dam, Mask 498
1637 'yong'
Think what, and be adviz'd, you are but young yet. Mask 755
line not in Bridgewater ms
1637 'yong'
Where young *Adonis* oft reposes, Mask 999
Bridgewater ms 'many a Cherub soft'
Trinity ms 'young Adonis oft' ←'many a cherub soft'
B.M. ms 'many'a Cherub soft'
And young and old com forth to play Allegro 97

Young(*cont*)
Shatter your leaves before the mellowing year. Lycidas 5
Trinity ms 'shatter' ←'and crop your young'
For *Lycidas* is dead, dead ere his prime Lycidas 8
Trinity ms 'for' ←'young'
Young *Lycidas*, and hath not left his peer: Lycidas 9
Clos'd o're the head of your lov'd *Lycidas?* Lycidas 51
Trinity ms 'lov'd' ←'youn'
How well could I have spar'd for thee young swain, Lycidas 113
Young *Hyacinth* born on *Eurota*'s strand Fair Inf 25
Young *Hyacinth* the pride of *Spartan* land; Fair Inf 26
Vane, young in yeares, but in sage counsell old, Sonnet 17, 1
1694 'Young'
And the young branch, that for thy self Psalm 80, 63
The Swallow there, to lay her young Psalm 84, 11

Younger
By younger *Saturn*, he from mightier *Jove* Par Lost 1.512
As we need walk, till younger hands ere long Par Lost 9.246
He comes invited by a yonger Son Par Lost 12.160
Your younger feet, while mine cast back with age Samson 336

Youngest
Thy creature late so lov'd, thy youngest Son Par Lost 3.151
Heav'ns youngest teemed Star, Nativity 240

Your
Your wearied vertue, for the ease you find Par Lost 1.320
Did first create your Leader, next free choice, Par Lost 2.19
Your bulwark, and condemns to greatest share Par Lost 2.29
Immeasurably, all things shall be your prey. Par Lost 2.844
The secrets of your Realm, but by constraint Par Lost 2.972
Lies through your spacious Empire up to light, Par Lost 2.974
What readiest path leads where your gloomie bounds Par Lost 2.976
From your Dominion won, th' Ethereal King Par Lost 2.978
To your behoof, if I that Region lost, Par Lost 2.982
To her original darkness and your sway Par Lost 2.984
Your dungeon stretching far and wide beneath; Par Lost 2.1003
To that side Heav'n from whence your Legions fell: Par Lost 2.1006
If that way be your walk, you have not farr; Par Lost 2.1007
Your change approaches, when all these delights Par Lost 4.367
More woe, the more your taste is now of joy; Par Lost 4.369
Long to continue, and this high seat your Heav'n Par Lost 4.371
Like this fair Paradise, your sense, yet such Par Lost 4.379
Accept your Makers work; he gave it me, Par Lost 4.380
Your numerous ofspring; if no better place, Par Lost 4.385
And should I at your harmless innocence Par Lost 4.388
The lowest of your throng; or if ye know, Par Lost 4.831
Your message, like to end as much in vain? Par Lost 4.833
Was this your discipline and faith ingag'd, Par Lost 4.954
Your military obedience, to dissolve Par Lost 4.955
And nourish all things, let your ceasless change Par Lost 5.183
Till the Sun paint your fleecie skirts with Gold, Par Lost 5.187
Breathe soft or loud; and wave your tops, ye Pines, Par Lost 5.193
Bear on your wings and in your notes his praise; Par Lost 5.199
As doth your Rational; and both contain Par Lost 5.409
Your bodies may at last turn all to Spirit, Par Lost 5.497
Your fill what happiness this happie state Par Lost 5.504
At my right hand; your Head I him appoint; Par Lost 5.606
Will ye submit your necks, and chuse to bend Par Lost 5.787
Faithful hath been your warfare, and of God Par Lost 6.803
Said then th' Omnific Word, your discord end: Par Lost 7.217
Open, ye Heav'ns, your living dores; let in Par Lost 7.566
Rather your dauntless vertue, whom the pain Par Lost 9.694
Your feare it self of Death removes the feare. Par Lost 9.702
Ye Eate thereof, your Eyes that seem so cleere, Par Lost 9.706
What can your knowledge hurt him, or this Tree Par Lost 9.727
Causes import your need of this fair Fruit. Par Lost 9.731
Which your sincerest care could not prevent, Par Lost 10.37
Descend through Darkness, on your Rode with ease Par Lost 10.394
Him first make sure your thrall, and lastly kill. Par Lost 10.402
Issuing from mee: on your joynt vigor now Par Lost 10.405
If your joynt power prevailes, th' affaires of Hell Par Lost 10.408
To expedite your glorious march; but I Par Lost 10.474
Your wonder, with an Apple; he thereat Par Lost 10.487
Offended, worth your laughter, hath giv'n up Par Lost 10.488
Me now your curse! Ah, why should all mankind Par Lost 10.822
With other echo late I taught your Shades Par Lost 10.861
Your Tribes, and water from th' ambrosial Fount? Par Lost 11.279
Sam. Your coming, Friends, revives me, for I learn Samson 187
As I suppose, towards your once gloried friend, Samson 334
Your younger feet, while mine cast back with age Samson 336
Sam. Such usage as your honourable Lords Samson 1108
And in your City held my Nuptial Feast: Samson 1194
But your ill-meaning Politician Lords, Samson 1195
My Nation was subjected to your Lords. Samson 1205
Had not disabl'd me, not all your force: Samson 1219
Sam. Brethren farewel, your company along Samson 1413
Man. I know your friendly minds and----O what noise! Samson 1508
Hitherto, Lords, what your commands impos'd Samson 1640
Braid your Locks with rosie Twine Mask 105
Run to your shrouds, within these Brakes and Trees, Mask 147
Co. And left your fair side all unguarded Lady? Mask 283
And if your stray attendance be yet lodg'd, Mask 315
Or if your influence be quite damm'd up Mask 336
How chance she is not in your company? Mask 508
Of my most honour'd Lady, your dear sister. Mask 564
Your nervs are all chain'd up in Alablaster, Mask 660
Enjoy your deer Wit, and gay Rhetorick Mask 790
line not in Bridgewater ms
line not in Trinity ms

Your(*cont*)
This is meer moral babble, and direct Mask 807
Trinity ms 'meere moral bable' ←'your morall stuffe' ←'meere morall stuffe'
I shall be your faithfull guide Mask 944
Is your Fathers residence, Mask 947
Spir. Back Shepherds, back, anough your play, Mask 958
Three fair branches of your own, Mask 969
(List mortals, if your ears be true) Mask 997
line not in Bridgewater ms
but soft I was not sent to court your wonder Mask Tr. ms 10.16
Or fill the fixed mind with all your toyes; Penseroso 4
I see bright honour sparkle through your eyes, Arcades 27
Though *Erymanth* your loss deplore, Arcades 100
Bring your Flocks, and live with us, Arcades 103
Though *Syrinx* your *Pans* Mistres were, Arcades 106
Trinity ms defective here
I com to pluck your Berries harsh and crude, Lycidas 3
Shatter your leaves before the mellowing year. Lycidas 5
Trinity ms 'shatter' ←'and crop your young'
Compels me to disturb your season due: Lycidas 7
Clos'd o're the head of your lov'd *Lycidas?* Lycidas 51
Where your old *Bards*, the famous *Druids* ly, Lycidas 53
1638 'Where the'
Throw hither all your quaint enameld eyes, Lycidas 139
For *Lycidas* your sorrow is not dead, Lycidas 166
And let your silver chime Nativity 128
And with your ninefold harmony Nativity 131
Your Son, said she, (nor can you it prevent) Vacation 73
Your learned hands, can loose this Gordian knot? Vacation 90
So sweetly sung your Joy the Clouds along Circum 4
Your fiery essence can distill no tear, Circum 7
Burn in your sighs, and borrow Circum 8
Wed your divine sounds, and mixt power employ Musick 3
and as your equall raptures temper'd sweet Musick Tr. ms 4.05
Wherin your Father flourisht, yet by you Sonnet 10, 10
So well your words his noble vertues praise, Sonnet 10, 12
Because you have thrown of your Prelate Lord, Forcers 1
But we do hope to find out all your tricks, Forcers 13
Your plots and packing wors then those of *Trent*, Forcers 14
Clip your Phylacteries, though bauk your Ears, Forcers 17
When they shall read this clearly in your charge Forcers 19
Jehovah serve, and let your joy converse Psalm 2, 24
Speak to your hearts alone, Psalm 4, 20
Upon your beds, each one, Psalm 4, 21
Favouring the wicked *by your might*. Psalm 82, 7
And your ungodly deeds finde me the words. Prose 8, 2

Yours
Warriers, the Flowr of Heav'n, once yours, now lost, Par Lost 1.316
Yours be th' advantage all, mine the revenge. Par Lost 2.987
Is oftest yours, the latter most is ours, Par Lost 5.489
Hold, as you yours, while our obedience holds; Par Lost 5.537
All yours, right down to Paradise descend; Par Lost 10.398
I know this quest of yours, and free intent Arcades 34

Yourself
Why should you be so cruel to your self, Mask 679
1637 'your selfe'
line not in Bridgewater ms
Trinity ms 'your selfe'

Yourselves
Not to know mee argues your selves unknown, Par Lost 4.830
To know ye right, or if ye know your selves Par Lost 5.789

Youth
Pour forth thir populous youth about the Hive Par Lost 1.770
Youth smil'd Celestial, and to every Limb Par Lost 3.638
Th' unarmed Youth of Heav'n, but nigh at hand Par Lost 4.552
In Manhood where Youth ended; by his side Par Lost 11.246
Thy youth, thy strength, thy beauty, which will change Par Lost 11.539
To what thou hast, and for the Aire of youth Par Lost 11.542
Of love and youth not lost, Songs, Garlands, Flours, Par Lost 11.594
But his growth now to youths full flowr, displaying Par Reg 1.67
A youth, how all the Beauties of the East Par Reg 2.197
In his prime youth the fair *Iberian* maid. Par Reg 2.200
Thy infancy, thy childhood, and thy youth, Par Reg 4.508
Their choicest youth; they only liv'd who fled. Samson 264
If in my flower of youth and strength, when all men Samson 938
Thither shall all the valiant youth resort, Samson 1738
With Ivy berries wreath'd, and his blithe youth, Mask 55
Curs'd as his life. *Spir*. Alas good ventrous youth, Mask 609
That fancy can beget on youthfull thoughts, Mask 669
Trinity ms 'fancie' ←'youth & fancie'
Heav'n hath timely tri'd their youth, Mask 970
B.M. ms 'Youth'
Youth and Joy; so *Jove* hath sworn. Mask 1011
line not in Bridgewater ms
To many a youth, and many a maid, Allegro 95
And, O ye *Dolphins*, waft the haples youth. Lycidas 164
Or wert thou that sweet smiling Youth! Fair Inf 53
Mirth and youth, and warm desire, May Morn 6
How soon hath Time the suttle theef of youth, Sonnet 7, 1
Trinity ms 'Youth'
Lady that in the prime of earliest youth, Sonnet 9, 1
What slender Youth bedew'd with liquid odours Horace 1

Youthful
Wanted, nor youthful dalliance as beseems Par Lost 4.338
Severe in youthful beautie, added grace Par Lost 4.845
Or as the Snake with youthful Coate repaid; Par Lost 10.218
With youthful courage and magnanimous thoughts Samson 524

Youthful(*cont*)
With youthful steps? much livelier then e're while — Samson 1442
Co. Were they of manly prime, or youthful bloom? — Mask 289
Trinity ms 'youthfull'
Bridgewater ms 'youthfull'
That fancy can beget on youthfull thoughts, — Mask 669
Jest and youthful Jollity, — Allegro 26
Such sights as youthfull Poets dream — Allegro 129
1673 'youthful'
Youthly
They had ingag'd their wandring steps too far, — Mask 193
Trinity ms 'wandring' ←'youthly'
Youths
Tall stripling youths rich clad, of fairer hew — Par Reg 2.352
Ypointing
Under a Star-ypointing *Pyramid?* — Shakespear 4
1632 'starre-ypointed' in some copies, 'starre-ypointing' in others
1663-4 'Starre-ypointing'
1640 'starre-ypointing'
Zalmunna
As Zeba, and Zalmunna *bled* — Psalm 83, 43
Zeal
Or clos ambition varnisht o're with zeal. — Par Lost 2.485
Of painful Superstition and blind Zeal, — Par Lost 3.452
Holy Memorials, acts of Zeale and Love — Par Lost 5.593
Abdiel, then whom none with more zeale ador'd — Par Lost 5.805
Stood up, and in a flame of zeale severe — Par Lost 5.807
So spake the fervent Angel, but his zeale — Par Lost 5.849
His Loyaltie he kept, his Love, his Zeale; — Par Lost 5.900
The Tempter, but with shew of Zeale and Love — Par Lost 9.665
Of Preface brooking through his Zeal of Right. — Par Lost 9.676
Against invaders; therefore coold in zeale — Par Lost 11.801
If Kingdom move thee not, let move thee Zeal, — Par Reg 3.171
And Duty; Zeal and Duty are not slow; — Par Reg 3.172
Zeal of thy Fathers house, Duty to free — Par Reg 3.175
But whence to thee this zeal, where was it then — Par Reg 3.407
By three days Pestilence? such was thy zeal — Par Reg 3.412
Not therefore to be obey'd. But zeal mov'd thee; — Samson 895
With zeal, if aught Religion seem concern'd: — Samson 1420
Zealous
A Spirit, zealous, as he seem'd, to know — Par Lost 4.565
Zealously
Thy care is fixt and zealously attends — Sonnet 9, 9
Zeb
As Zeb and Oreb evil sped — Psalm 83, 41
Zeba
As Zeba, and Zalmunna *bled* — Psalm 83, 43
Zenith
Dropt from the Zenith like a falling Star, — Par Lost 1.745
His *Zenith*, while the Sun in *Aries* rose: — Par Lost 10.329
Zephon
Ithuriel and *Zephon*, with wingd speed — Par Lost 4.788
To whom thus *Zephon*, answering scorn with scorn. — Par Lost 4.834
Or less be lost. Thy fear, said *Zephon* bold, — Par Lost 4.854
Ithuriel and *Zephon* through the shade, — Par Lost 4.868
Zephyr
To recommend coole *Zephyr*, and made ease — Par Lost 4.329
Eurus and *Zephir* with thir lateral noise, — Par Lost 10.705
Zephir with *Aurora* playing, — Allegro 19
Zephyrus
Milde, as when *Zephyrus* on *Flora* breathes, — Par Lost 5.16
Zion
Rose out of *Chaos:* Or if *Sion* Hill — Par Lost 1.10
ms 'Sion'
Jehovah thundring out of *Sion*, thron'd — Par Lost 1.386
ms 'Sion'
In *Sion* also not unsung, where stood — Par Lost 1.442
ms 'Sion'
Infected *Sions* daughters with like heat, — Par Lost 1.453
ms 'Sions'
Thee *Sion* and the flowrie Brooks beneath — Par Lost 3.30
Over Mount *Sion*, and, though that were large, — Par Lost 3.530
Be said of Sion *last* — Psalm 87, 18
Zodiac
As in a glistering *Zodiac* hung the Sword, — Par Lost 11.247
Seaven Lamps as in a Zodiac representing — Par Lost 12.255
Zone
Re-enter Heav'n; or else in some milde Zone — Par Lost 2.397
Girt like a Starrie Zone his waste, and round — Par Lost 5.281
His other half in the great Zone of Heav'n. — Par Lost 5.560
Which nightly as a circling Zone thou seest — Par Lost 7.580
To enamour, as the Zone of *Venus* once — Par Reg 2.214
Zophiel
Zophiel, of Cherubim the swiftest wing, — Par Lost 6.535
Zorah
From *Eshtaol* and *Zora*'s fruitful Vale — Samson 181